The Longman Anthology of British Literature

VOLUME ONE

David Damrosch
HARVARD UNIVERSITY

Kevin J. H. Dettmar
POMONA COLLEGE

Christopher Baswell
BARNARD COLLEGE AND COLUMBIA UNIVERSITY

Clare Carroll
QUEENS COLLEGE, CITY UNIVERSITY OF NEW YORK

Andrew Hadfield
UNIVERSITY OF SUSSEX

Heather Henderson

Peter J. Manning
STATE UNIVERSITY OF NEW YORK, STONY BROOK

Anne Howland Schotter
WAGNER COLLEGE

William Chapman Sharpe
BARNARD COLLEGE

Stuart Sherman
FORDHAM UNIVERSITY

Susan J. Wolfson
PRINCETON UNIVERSITY

The Longman Anthology of British Literature
Fourth Edition

David Damrosch and Kevin J. H. Dettmar
General Editors

VOLUME ONE

THE MIDDLE AGES
Christopher Baswell *and* Anne Howland Schotter

THE EARLY MODERN PERIOD
Clare Carroll *and* Andrew Hadfield

THE RESTORATION AND THE 18TH CENTURY
Stuart Sherman

Longman

New York San Francisco Boston
London Toronto Sydney Tokyo Singapore Madrid
Mexico City Munich Paris Cape Town Hong Kong Montreal

Editor-in-Chief: *Joseph Terry*
Associate Development Editor: *Erin Reilly*
Executive Marketing Manager: *Joyce Nilsen*
Senior Supplements Editor: *Donna Campion*
Production Manager: *Ellen MacElree*
Project Coordination, Text Design, and Page Makeup: GGS Higher Education Resources, a Division of PreMedia Global, Inc.
Cover Design Manager: *Nancy Danahy*
On the Cover: The Pierpont Morgan Library, New York, NY, U.S.A./Art Resource, NY.
Photo Researcher: *Julie Tesser*
Senior Manufacturing Buyer: *Dennis J. Para*
Printer and Binder: *Quebecor-World/Taunton*
Cover Printer: *Lehigh-Phoenix Color/Hagerstown*

For permission to use copyrighted material, grateful acknowledgment is made to the copyright holders on pages 2839–2844, which are hereby made part of this copyright page.

Library of Congress Cataloging-in-Publication Data
The Longman anthology of British literature / David Damrosch and Kevin J.H. Dettmar, general editors.—4th ed.
p. cm.
Includes bibliographical references and index.
ISBN–13: 978–0–205–65524–3 (v. 1 : alk. paper)
ISBN–10: 0–205–65524–6 (v. 1 : alk. paper)
ISBN–13: 978–0–205–65519–9 (v. 2 : alk. paper)
ISBN–10: 0–205–65519–X (v. 2 : alk. paper) 1. English literature. 2. Great Britain—Literary collections. I. Damrosch, David. II. Dettmar, Kevin J. H., 1958–
PR1109.L69 2010
820.8—dc22
2009020241

ISBN-10 Single Volume Edition, Volume 1: 0-205-65524-6
ISBN-13 Single Volume Edition, Volume 1: 978-0-205-65524-3

ISBN-10 Volume 1A, The Middle Ages: 0-205-65530-0
ISBN-13 Volume 1A, The Middle Ages: 978-0-205-65530-4

ISBN-10 Volume 1B, The Early Modern Period: 0-205-65532-7
ISBN-13 Volume 1B, The Early Modern Period: 978-0-205-65532-8

ISBN-10 Volume 1C, The Restoration and the 18th Century: 0-205-65527-0
ISBN-13 Volume 1C, The Restoration and the 18th Century: 978-0-205-65527-4

Longman
is an imprint of

PEARSON

1 2 3 4 5 6 7 8 9 0—QWT—12 11 10 09

www.pearsonhighered.com

CONTENTS

The Early Modern Period

The Restoration and the Eighteenth Century

PERSPECTIVES
Novel Guises 2791

ADDITIONAL RESOURCES

Cultural Editions

Longman Cultural Editions present major texts along with a generous selection of contextual material that reveal the conversations and controversies of its historical moment. Taken together, our new edition and the Longman Cultural Editions offer an unparalleled set of materials for the enjoyment and study of British literary culture from its earliest beginnings to the present. One Longman Cultural Edition is available at no additional cost when packaged with the anthology. Contact your local Pearson Publisher's Representative for packaging details. Some titles of interest for Volume One include the following works:

Beowulf, Anonymous. Translated by Alan Sullivan and Timothy Murphy & ed. Anderson
ISBN-10: 0-321-10720-9 | ISBN-13: 978-0-321-10720-6

Julius Caesar. Shakespeare. ed. Arnold.
ISBN-10: 0-321-20943-5 | ISBN-13: 978-0-321-20943-6

Henry IV, Parts One and Two. Shakespeare. ed. Levao
ISBN-10: 0-321-18274-X | ISBN-13: 978-0-321-18274-6

The Merchant of Venice, Shakespeare. ed. Danson
ISBN-10: 0-321-16419-9 | ISBN-13: 978-0-321-16419-3

Antony and Cleopatra, Shakespeare, ed. Quint
ISBN-10: 0-321-19874-3 | ISBN-13: 978-0-321-19874-7

Hamlet, Shakespeare. ed. Jordan
ISBN-10: 0-321-31729-7 | ISBN-13: 978-0-321-31729-2

King Lear, Shakespeare. ed. McEachern
ISBN-10: 0-321-10722-5 | ISBN-13: 978-0-321-10722-0

Othello and *The Tragedy of Mariam*, Shakespeare and Cary. ed. Carroll and Damrosch
ISBN-10: 0-321-09699-1 | ISBN-13: 978-0-321-09699-9

The History of the Adventures of Joseph Andrews, Fielding. ed. Potkay
ISBN-10: 0-321-20937-0 | ISBN-13: 978-0-321-20937-5

The Castle of Otranto and *The Man of Feeling*, Walpole and MacKenzie. ed. Mandell
ISBN-10: 0-321-39892-0 | ISBN-13: 978-0-321-39892-5

For a complete listing of Longman Cultural Edition titles, please visit www.pearsonhighered.com/literature.

WEB SITE FOR *THE LONGMAN ANTHOLOGY OF BRITISH LITERATURE*

www.myliteraturekit.com

The fourth edition makes connections beyond its covers as well as within them. The Web site we have developed for the course provides a wealth of resources:

Student Resources

- **Discussion Questions for Major Selections and Perspectives Sections.** Designed to prepare students for the kind of deeper-level analysis expected in class discussions, these compelling prompts are available for each period introduction and for major selections and Perspectives groupings.
- **Self-Grading Multiple Choice Practice Questions.** Available for each period introduction and for all major authors and Perspectives groupings, these objective practice quizzes are designed to help students review their basic understanding of the reading.
- **An Interactive Timeline.** Our interactive timeline helps students visualize the key literary, political, and cultural events of an era. Each event is accompanied by a detailed explanation, usually including references to relevant texts that can be found in the anthology, links to helpful sites, and colorful pictures and illustrations.
- **Links to Valuable British Literature Resources.** Our Online Research Guide provides a wealth of annotated links to excellent Web resources on major authors, texts, and related historical and cultural movements and events.
- **An Archive of Additional Texts.** Our new online archive contains a wealth of selections that could not fit within the bounds of the print anthology. A listing of many of these works can be found in context in our table of contents.
- **Additional Reference Materials.** The Web site also features an extensive glossary of literary and cultural terms, useful summaries of British political and religious organizations, and of money, weights, and measures. For further reading, we provide carefully selected, up-to-date bibliographies for each period and author.

Instructor's Section

- **An Online Instructor's Manual (0-205-67976-5).** The online version of our print manual uses a hyperlink format to allow instructors to jump directly to the author or selection they want to access.
- **PowerPoint Presentations.** A visually rich presentation is available for each period.
- **Sample Syllabi.** Our collection of syllabi include samples of a wide variety of approaches to both the survey-level and period-specific courses.

PREFACE

Literature has a double life. Born in one time and place and read in another, literary works are at once products of their age and independent creations, able to live on long after their original world has disappeared. The goal *The Longman Anthology of British Literature* is to present a wealth of poetry, prose, and drama from the full sweep of the literary history of Great Britain and its empire, and to do so in ways that will bring out both the works' original cultural contexts and their lasting aesthetic power. These aspects are in fact closely related: form and content, verbal music and social meanings, go hand in hand. This double life makes literature, as Aristotle said, "the most philosophical" of all the arts, intimately connected to ideas and to realities that the writer transforms into moving patterns of words. The challenge is to show these works in the contexts in which, and for which, they were written, while at the same time not trapping them within those contexts. The warm response this anthology has received from the hundreds of teachers who have adopted it in its first three editions reflects the growing consensus that we are not forced to choose between the literature's aesthetic and cultural dimensions. Our users' responses have now guided us in seeing how we can improve our anthology further, so as to be most pleasurable and stimulating to students, most useful to teachers, and most responsive to ongoing developments in literary studies. This preface can serve as a road map to this book's goals and structure.

New to This Edition

- **Period at a Glance features.** These informative illustrated features open each volume, providing thumbnail sketches of daily life during each period.
- **Enhanced Web site.** A new fourth edition site includes an archive of valuable texts from previous editions, detailed bibliographies, an interactive timeline, discussion questions, and Web resources for major selections and authors.
- **New major, classic texts.** In response to instructors' requests, major additions of important works frequently taught in the British Literature course have been added, including the following selections:
    - A selection from the Irish epic *The Táin Bó Cuailnge*
    - William Baldwin's *Beware the Cat* (sometimes called the first English novel)
    - Edmund Spenser's *The Faerie Queene, Book 6* and *the Cantos of Mutabilitie*
    - William Shakespeare's *Othello* and *King Lear*

- **New selections across the anthology.** We have continued to refine our contents, adding new selections to established units across the anthology, including authors such as John Skelton, Fynes Moryson, Edmund Spenser, and John Donne.
- **Penguin Classics editions of *Beowulf* translated by Michael Alexander and *Sir Gawain and the Green Knight* translated by Brian Stone.** The *Longman Anthology of British Literature* now includes authoritative Penguin Classic translations, trusted throughout the world as editions of classics texts that are both riveting and scholarly.
- **New Perspectives groupings of works in cultural context.** "Perspectives" groupings new to this edition include *The English Sonnet and Sonnet Sequences in the Sixteenth Century*, *Early Modern Books*, and *England, Britain, and the World*.
- **New Response pairings.** A selection from Sir Francis Bacon's *New Atlantis* is paired with Sir Thomas More's *Utopia*.

Literature in Its Time—and in Ours

When we engage with a rich literary history that extends back over a thousand years, we often encounter writers who assume their readers know all sorts of things that are little known today: historical facts, social issues, literary and cultural references. Beyond specific information, these works will have come out of a very different literary culture than our own. Even the contemporary British Isles present a cultural situation—or a mix of cultures—very different from what North American readers encounter at home, and these differences only increase as we go farther back in time. A major emphasis of this anthology is to bring the works' original cultural moment to life: not because the works simply or naively reflect that moment of origin, but because they do refract it in fascinating ways. British literature is both a major heritage for modern North America and, in many ways, a very distinct culture; reading British literature will regularly give an experience both of connection and of difference. Great writers create imaginative worlds that have their own compelling internal logic, and a prime purpose of this anthology is to help readers understand the formal means—whether of genre, rhetoric, or style—with which these writers have created works of haunting beauty. At the same time, as Virginia Woolf says in *A Room of One's Own*, the gossamer threads of the artist's web are joined to reality "with bands of steel."

The Longman Anthology pursues a range of strategies to bring out both the beauty of these webs of words and their points of contact with reality and to bring related authors and works together in several ways:

☞ **Perspectives: Broad groupings that illuminate underlying issues in a variety of the major works of a period.**

☞ **And Its Time: A focused cluster that illuminates a specific cultural moment or a debate to which an author is responding.**

☞ **Responses: One or more texts in which later authors in the tradition respond creatively to the challenging texts of their forebears.**

These groupings provide a range of means of access to the literary culture of each period. The Perspectives sections do much more than record what major writers thought about an issue: they give a variety of views in a range of voices, to illustrate the wider culture within which the literature was being written. Theological reflections by the pioneering scientist Isaac Newton; these and many other vivid readings featured in Volume One give rhetorical as well as social contexts for the poems, plays, and stories around them. Perspectives sections typically relate to several major authors of the period, as with a section on the sixteenth-century sonnet that brings the poetry of Edmund Spenser and Sir Philip Sidney into conversation with less widely read figures like Sir Thomas Wyatt and Henry Howard, Earl of Surrey. Most of the writers included in Perspectives sections are important figures of the period who might be neglected if they were listed on their own with just a few pages each; grouping them together has proved to be useful pedagogically as well as intellectually. Perspectives sections may also include work by a major author whose primary listing appears elsewhere in the period; thus, a Perspective section on the Civil War features a selection from Milton's *Eikonoklastes*, and a section on British perceptions of other lands includes a selection from Spenser's *View of the State of Ireland*, so as to give a rounded presentation of the issue in ways that can inform the reading of those authors in their individual sections.

When we present a major work "And Its Time," we give a cluster of related materials to suggest the context within which the work was written. Thus Sir Philip Sidney's great *Apology for Poetry* is accompanied by readings showing the controversy that was raging at the time concerning the nature and value of poetry. Some of the writers in these groupings and in our Perspectives sections have not traditionally been seen as literary figures, but all have produced lively and intriguing works, from medieval clerics writing about saints and sea monsters, to a polemical seventeenth-century tract giving *The Arraignment of Lewd, Idle, Froward, and Unconstant Women*, to economic writings by William Petty—of the type parodied by Swift in his "Modest Proposal."

We also include "Responses" to significant texts in the British literary tradition, demonstrating the sometimes far-reaching influence these works have had over the decades and centuries, and sometimes across oceans and continents. *Beowulf* and John Gardner's *Grendel* are separated by the Atlantic ocean, perhaps eleven hundred or twelve hundred years—and, most notably, by their attitude toward the poem's monster. The *Morte Darthur* is reinterpreted comically by the 1970s British comedy troupe Monty Python's Flying Circus.

What Is British Literature?

Stepping back from the structure of the book, let us define our basic terms: What is "British" literature? What is literature itself? And just what should an anthology of this material look like at the present time? The term "British" can mean many things, some of them contradictory, some of them even offensive to people on whom the name has been imposed. If the term "British" has no ultimate essence, it does have a history. The first British were Celtic people who inhabited the British Isles and the northern coast of France (still called Brittany) before various Germanic tribes of Angles and Saxons moved onto the islands in the fifth and sixth centuries. Gradually the Angles and Saxons amalgamated into the Anglo-Saxon culture that became dominant in the southern and eastern regions of Britain and then spread outward; the old British people were pushed west, toward what became known as Cornwall,

Wales, and Ireland, which remained independent kingdoms for centuries, as did Celtic Scotland to the north. By an ironic twist of linguistic fate, the Anglo-Saxons began to appropriate the term "British" from the Britons they had displaced, and they took as a national hero the early, semimythic Welsh King Arthur. By the seventeenth century, English monarchs had extended their sway over Wales, Ireland, and Scotland, and they began to refer to their holdings as "Great Britain." Today, Great Britain includes England, Wales, Scotland, and Northern Ireland, but does not include the Republic of Ireland, which has been independent since 1922.

This anthology uses "British" in a broad sense, as a geographical term encompassing the whole of the British Isles. For all its fraught history, it seems a more satisfactory term than to speak simply of "English" literature, for two reasons. First, most speakers of English live in countries that are not the focus of this anthology (for instance, the United States and Canada); second, while the English language and its literature have long been dominant in the British Isles, other cultures in the region have always used other languages and have produced great literature in these languages. Important works by Irish, Welsh, and Scots writers appear regularly in the body of this anthology, some of them written directly in their languages and presented here in translation, and others written in an English inflected by the rhythms, habits of thought, and modes of expression characteristic of these other languages and the people who use them.

We use the term "literature" in a similarly capacious sense, to refer to a range of artistically shaped works written in a charged language, appealing to the imagination at least as much as to discursive reasoning. It is only relatively recently that creative writers have been able to make a living composing poems, plays, and novels, and only in the past hundred years or so has creating "belles lettres" or high literary art been thought of as a sharply separate sphere of activity from other sorts of writing that the same authors would regularly produce. Sometimes, early modern poets wrote sonnets to reflect and honor loves won and lost; at other times, they wrote sonnets to realize courtly ambition and material gain; and always, they wrote their sonnets with an eye to posterity, and with the goal of a poetic form of immortality ("Not marble, nor the gilded monuments / Of princes, shall outlive this pow'rful rhyme"—Shakespeare, *Sonnet* 55).

Varieties of Literary Experience

Above all, we have strived to give as full a presentation as possible to the varieties of great literature produced from the eighth to the eighteenth centuries in the British Isles, by women as well as by men, in outlying regions as well as in the metropolitan center of London, and in prose, drama, and verse alike. For these earlier periods, we include More's entire *Utopia*, Baldwin's *Beware the Cat*, and Milton's *Paradise Lost*, and we give major space to narrative poetry by Chaucer and Spenser, and to Swift's *Gulliver's Travels*, among others. Drama appears throughout the anthology, from the medieval *Second Play of the Shepherds* and *Mankind* to a range of early modern and restoration plays: Marlowe's *The Tragical History of Dr. Faustus*, Shakespeare's *Twelfth Night*, *Othello*, and *King Lear*, Jonson's *The Alchemist*, William Wyncherly's *The Country Wife*, and John Gay's *The Beggar's Opera*. Finally, lyric poetry appears in profusion throughout the anthology, from early lyrics by anonymous Middle English poets and the trenchantly witty Dafydd ap Gwilym to the great flowering of lyric poetry in the early modern period in the writings of Shakespeare, Sidney, and Spenser—to name just the "S's"—to the formal perfection and august rhetoric of Restoration and eighteenth-century poets like Swift, Dryden, Pope, and Johnson. Prose fiction always struggles for space in a literary anthology, but we close this volume with a selection from some of the most vital novelistic writing of the eighteenth century. We hope that this anthology will show that the great works of earlier centuries can speak to us compellingly today, their value only increased by the resistance they offer to our views of ourselves and our world. To read and reread the full sweep of this literature is to be struck anew by the degree to which the most radically new works are rooted in centuries of prior innovation.

Illustrating Visual Culture

Another important context for literary production has been a different kind of culture: the visual. This edition includes a suite of color plates in each volume, along with hundreds of black-and-white illustrations throughout the anthology, chosen to show artistic and cultural images that figured importantly for literary creation. Sometimes, a poem refers to a specific painting, or more generally emulates qualities of a school of visual art. At other times, more popular materials like frontispieces may illuminate scenes in early modern writing. In some cases, visual and literary creation have merged, as in William Hogarth's series *A Rake's Progress*, included in Volume One. Thumbnail portraits of many major authors mark the beginning of author introductions.

Aids to Understanding

We have attempted to contextualize our selections in suggestive rather than exhaustive ways, trying to enhance rather than overwhelm the experience of reading the texts themselves. Thus, when difficult or archaic words need defining in poems, we use glosses in the margins, so as to disrupt the reader's eye as little as possible; footnotes are intended to be concise and informative, rather than massive or interpretive. Important literary and social terms are defined when they are used. For convenience of reference, new Period at a Glance features appear at the beginning of each period, providing a thumbnail sketch of daily life during the period. With these informative, illustrated features readers can begin to connect with the world that the anthology is illuminating. Sums of money, for instance, can be understood better when one knows what a loaf of bread cost at the time; the symbolic values attached to various articles of clothing are sometimes difficult for today's readers to decipher, without some information about contemporary apparel and its class associations. And the gradual shift of the Empire's population from rural regions to urban centers is graphically presented in charts for each period.

Looking—and Listening—Further

Beyond the boundaries of the anthology itself, we have expanded our Web site, available to all readers at www.myliteraturekit.com; this site gives a wealth of information, annotated links to related sites, and an archive of texts for further reading. For reference, there is also an extensive glossary of literary and cultural terms available there, together with useful summaries of British political and religious organization, and of money, weights, and measures. For further reading, carefully selected, up-to-date bibliographies for each period and for each author can be found in on the Web site. A guide to our media resources can be found at the end of the table of contents.

For instructors, we have revised and expanded our popular companion volume, *Teaching British Literature*, written directly by the anthology editors, 600 pages in length, available free to everyone who adopts the anthology.

David Damrosch & Kevin J. H. Dettmar

ACKNOWLEDGMENTS

In planning and preparing the fourth edition of our anthology, the editors have been fortunate to have the support, advice, and assistance of many committed and gifted people. Our editor, Joe Terry, has been unwavering in his enthusiasm for the book and his commitment to it; he and his associates Roth Wilkofsky, Mary Ellen Curley, and Joyce Nilsen have supported us in every possible way throughout the process, ably assisted by Katy Needle, Rosie Ellis, and Annie England. Our developmental editor Erin Reilly guided us and our manuscript from start to finish with unfailing acuity and seemingly unwavering patience. Our copyeditor Stephanie Magean seamlessly integrated the work of a dozen editors. Erin Reilly, Elizabeth Bravo and Stefanie Liebman have devoted enormous energy and creativity to revising our Web site. Karyn Morrison cleared our many permissions, and Julie Tesser tracked down and cleared our many new illustrations. Finally, Nancy Wolitzer and Ellen MacElree oversaw the production with sunny good humor and kept the book successfully on track on a very challenging schedule, working closely with Doug Bell at GGS Higher Education Resources.

Our plans for the new edition have been shaped by comments and suggestions from many faculty who have used the book over the years. We are specifically grateful for the thoughtful advice of our reviewers for this edition, Jesse T. Airaudi (Baylor University), Thomas Crofts (East Tennessee State University), Lois Feuer (California State University, Dominguez Hills), Daniel P. Galvin (Clemson University), S. E. Gontarski (Florida State University), Stephen Harris (University of Massachusetts), Roxanne Kent-Drury (Northern Kentucky University), Carol A. Lowe (McLennan Community College), Darin A Merrill (Brigham Young University—Idaho), David G. Miller (Mississippi College), Crystal L. Mueller (University of Wisconsin Oshkosh), and Gary Schneider (University of Texas—Pan American).

We remain grateful as well for the guidance of the many reviewers who advised us on the creation of the first three editions, the base on which this new edition has been built. In addition to the people named above, we would like to thank Lucien Agosta (California State University, Sacramento), Anne W. Astell (Purdue University), Derek Attridge (Rutgers University), Linda Austin (Oklahoma State University), Arthur D. Barnes (Louisiana State University), Robert Barrett (University of Pennsylvania), Candice Barrington (Central Connecticut State University), Joseph Bartolomeo (University of Massachusetts, Amherst), Mary Been (Clovis Community College), Stephen Behrendt (University of Nebraska), Todd Bender (University of Wisconsin, Madison), Bruce Boehrer (Florida State University), Bruce Brandt (South Dakota State University), Joel J. Brattin (Worcester Polytechnic Institute), James Campbell (University of Central Florida), J. Douglas Canfield (University of Arizona), Paul A. Cantor (University of Virginia), George Allan Cate (University of Maryland, College Park), Philip Collington (Niagra University), Linda McFerrin

Cook (McLellan Community College), Eugene R. Cunnar (New Mexico State University), Earl Dachslager (University of Houston), Elizabeth Davis (University of California, Davis), Andrew Elfenbein (University of Minnesota), Hilary Englert (New Jersey City University), Margaret Ferguson (University of California, Davis), Sandra K. Fisher (State University of New York, Albany), Sandra C. Fowler (The University of Alabama), Allen J. Frantzen (Loyola University, Chicago), Kevin Gardner (Baylor University), Kate Gartner Frost (University of Texas), Leon Gottfried (Purdue University), Leslie Graff (University at Buffalo), Mark L. Greenberg (Drexel University), Peter Greenfield (University of Puget Sound), Natalie Grinnell (Wofford College), James Hala (Drew University), Wayne Hall (University of Cincinnati), Donna Hamilton (University of Maryland), Wendell Harris (Pennsylvania State University), Richard H. Haswell (Washington State University), Susan Sage Heinzelman (University of Texas, Austin), Standish Henning (University of Wisconsin, Madison), Noah Heringman (University of Missouri—Columbia), Jack W. Herring (Baylor University), Carrie Hintz (Queens College), Romana Huk (University of Notre Dame), Maurice Hunt (Baylor University), Mary Anne Hutchison (Utica College), Patricia Clare Ingham (Indiana University), Kim Jacobs (University of Cincinnati Clermont College), Carol Jamison (Armstrong Atlantic State University), Eric Johnson (Dakota State College), Mary Susan Johnston (Minnesota State University), Eileen A. Joy (Southern Illinois University—Edwardsville), Colleen Juarretche (University of California, Los Angeles), George Justice (University of Missouri), Roxanne Kent-Drury (Northern Kentucky University), R. B. Kershner (University of Florida), Lisa Klein (Ohio State University), Adam Komisaruk (West Virginia University), Rita S. Kranidis (Radford University), Leslie M. LaChance (University of Tennessee at Martin), John Laflin (Dakota State University), Lisa Lampert (University of California, San Diego), Dallas Liddle (Augsburg College), Paulino Lim (California State University, Long Beach), Elizabeth B. Loizeaux (University of Maryland), Ed Malone (Missouri Western State College), John J. Manning (University of Connecticut), William W. Matter (Richland College), Evan Matthews (Navarro College), Michael Mays (University of Southern Mississippi), Lawrence McCauley (College of New Jersey), Michael B. McDonald (Iowa State University), James J. McKeown Jr. (McLennan Community College), Kathryn McKinley (Florida International University), Peter E. Medine (University of Arizona), Barry Milligan (Wright State University), Celia Millward (Boston University), Charlotte Morse (Virginia Commonwealth University), Mary Morse (Rider University), Thomas C. Moser, Jr. (University of Maryland), James Najarian (Boston College), Deborah Craig Wester (Worcester State College), Jude V. Nixon (Baylor University), Richard Nordquist (Armstrong Atlantic State University), Daniel Novak (Tulane University), John Ottenhoff (Alma College), Violet O'Valle (Tarrant County Junior College, Texas), Joyce Cornette Palmer (Texas Women's University), Leslie Palmer (University of North Texas), Richard Pearce (Wheaton College), Rebecca Phillips (West Virginia University), Renée Pigeon (California State University, San Bernardino), Tadeusz Pioro (Southern Methodist University), Deborah Preston (Dekalb College), William Rankin (Abilene Christian University), Sherry Rankin (Abilene Christian University), Luke Reinsma (Seattle Pacific University), Elizabeth Robertson (University of Colorado), Deborah Rogers (University of Maine), David Rollison (College of Marin), Brian Rosenberg (Allegheny College), Charles Ross (Purdue University), Kathryn Rummel (California Polytechnic), Harry Rusche (Emory University), Laura E. Rutland (Berry College), Kenneth D. Shields

(Southern Methodist University), R. G. Siemens (Malaspina University-College), Clare A. Simmons (Ohio State University), Sally Slocum (University of Akron), Phillip Snyder (Brigham Young University), Isabel Bonnyman Stanley (East Tennessee University), Brad Sullivan (Florida Gulf Coast University), Margaret Sullivan (University of California, Los Angeles), Herbert Sussmann (Northeastern University), Mary L. Tanter (Tarleton State University), Ronald R. Thomas (Trinity College), Theresa Tinkle (University of Michigan), William A. Ulmer (University of Alabama), Jennifer A. Wagner (University of Memphis), Anne D. Wallace (University of Southern Mississippi), Brett Wallen (Cleveland Community College), Jackie Walsh (McNeese State University, Louisiana), Daniel Watkins (Duquesne University), John Watkins (University of Minnesota), Martin Wechselblatt (University of Cincinnati), Arthur Weitzman (Northeastern University), Bonnie Wheeler (Southern Methodist University), Jan Widmayer (Boise State University), Dennis L. Williams (Central Texas College), William A. Wilson (San Jose State University), Paula Woods (Baylor University), and Julia Wright (University of Waterloo).

Other colleagues brought our developing book into the classroom, teaching from portions of the work-in-progress. Our thanks go to Lisa Abney (Northwestern State University), Charles Lynn Batten (University of California, Los Angeles), Brenda Riffe Brown (College of the Mainland, Texas), John Brugaletta (California State University, Fullerton), Dan Butcher (Southeastern Louisiana University), Lynn Byrd (Southern University at New Orleans), David Cowles (Brigham Young University), Sheila Drain (John Carroll University), Lawrence Frank (University of Oklahoma), Leigh Garrison (Virginia Polytechnic Institute), David Griffin (New York University), Rita Harkness (Virginia Commonwealth University), Linda Kissler (Westmoreland County Community College, Pennsylvania), Brenda Lewis (Motlow State Community College, Tennessee), Paul Lizotte (River College), Wayne Luckman (Green River Community College, Washington), Arnold Markely (Pennsylvania State University, Delaware County), James McKusick (University of Maryland, Baltimore), Eva McManus (Ohio Northern University), Manuel Moyrao (Old Dominion University), Kate Palguta (Shawnee State University, Ohio), Paul Puccio (University of Central Florida), Sarah Polito (Cape Cod Community College), Meredith Poole (Virginia Western Community College), Tracy Seeley (University of San Francisco), Clare Simmons (Ohio State University), and Paul Yoder (University of Arkansas, Little Rock).

As if all this help weren't enough, the editors also drew directly on friends and colleagues in many ways, for advice, for information, sometimes for outright contributions to headnotes and footnotes, even (in a pinch) for aid in proofreading. In particular, we wish to thank David Ackiss, Marshall Brown, James Cain, Cathy Corder, Jeffrey Cox, Michael Coyle, Pat Denison, Tom Farrell, Andrew Fleck, Jane Freilich, Laurie Glover, Lisa Gordis, Joy Hayton, Ryan Hibbet, V. Lauryl Hicks, Nelson Hilton, Jean Howard, David Kastan, Stanislas Kemper, Andrew Krull, Ron Levao, Carol Levin, David Lipscomb, Denise MacNeil, Jackie Maslowski, Richard Matlak, Anne Mellor, James McKusick, Melanie Micir, Michael North, David Paroissien, Stephen M. Parrish, Peter Platt, Cary Plotkin, Desma Polydorou, Gina Renee, Alan Richardson, Esther Schor, Catherine Siemann, Glenn Simshaw, David Tresilian, Shasta Turner, Nicholas Watson, Michael Winckleman, Gillen Wood, and Sarah Zimmerman for all their guidance and assistance.

The pages on the Restoration and the eighteenth century are the work of many collaborators, diligent and generous. Michael F. Suarez, S. J. (Campion Hall,

Oxford) edited the Swift and Pope sections; Mary Bly (Fordham University) edited Sheridan's *School for Scandal;* Michael Caldwell (University of Chicago) edited the portions of "Reading Papers" on *The Craftsman* and the South Sea Bubble. Steven N. Zwicker (Washington University) co-wrote the period introduction, and the headnotes for the Dryden section. Bruce Redford (Boston University) crafted the footnotes for Dryden, Gay, Johnson, and Boswell. Susan Brown, Janice Cable, Christine Coch, Marnie Cox, Tara Czechowski, Susan Greenfield, Mary Nassef, Paige Reynolds, and Andrew Tumminia helped with texts, footnotes, and other matters throughout; William Pritchard gathered texts, wrote notes, and prepared the bibliography. To all, abiding thanks.

It has been a pleasure to work with all of these colleagues in the ongoing collaborative process that has produced this book and brought it to this new stage of its life and use. This book exists for its readers, whose reactions and suggestions we warmly welcome, as these will in turn reshape this book for later users in the years to come.

ABOUT THE EDITORS

David Damrosch is Professor Comparative Literature at Harvard University. He is past President of the American Comparative Literature Association, and has written widely on world literature from antiquity to the present. His books include *What is World Literature?* (2003), *The Buried Book: The Loss and Rediscovery of the Great Epic of Gilgamesh* (2007), and *How to Read World Literature* (2009). He is the founding general editor of the six-volume *The Longman Anthology of World Literature*, 2/e (2009) and the editor of *Teaching World Literature* (2009).

Kevin J. H. Dettmar is W.M. Keck Professor and Chair of the Department of English at Pomona College, and Past President of the Modernist Studies Association. He is the author of *The Illicit Joyce of Postmodernism and Is Rock Dead?*, and the editor of *Rereading the New: A Backward Glance at Modernism; Marketing Modernisms: Self-Promotion, Canonization, and Rereading; Reading Rock & Roll: Authenticity, Appropriation, Aesthetics;* the Barnes & Noble Classics edition of James Joyce's *A Portrait of the Artist as a Young Man and Dubliners;* and *The Blackwell Companion to Modernist Literature and Culture*, of *The Cambridge Companion to Bob Dylan*.

Christopher Baswell is A.W. Olin Chair of English at Barnard College, and Professor of English and Comparative Literature at Columbia University. His interests include classical literature and culture, medieval literature and culture, and contemporary poetry. He is author of *Virgil in Medieval England: Figuring the "Aeneid" from the Twelfth Century to Chaucer*, which won the 1998 Beatrice White Prize of the English Association. He has held fellowships from the NEH, the National Humanities Center, and the Institute for Advanced Study, Princeton.

Clare Carroll is Director of Renaissance Studies at The Graduate Center, City University of New York and Professor of Comparative Literature at Queens College, CUNY. Her research is in Renaissance Studies, with particular interests in early modern colonialism, epic poetry, historiography, and translation. She is the author of *The Orlando Furioso: A Stoic Comedy*, and editor of Richard Beacon's humanist dialogue on the colonization of Ireland, *Solon His Follie*. Her most recent book is *Circe's Cup: Cultural Transformations in Early Modern Ireland*. She has received Fulbright Fellowships for her research and the Queens College President's Award for Excellence in Teaching.

Andrew Hadfield is Professor of English at The University of Sussex. He is the author of a number of books, including *Shakespeare and Republicanism* (2005), which was awarded the 2006 Sixteenth-Century Society Conference Roland H. Bainton Prize for Literature; *Literature, Travel and Colonialism in the English Renaissance, 1540–1625* (1998); and Spenser's *Irish Experience: Wild Fruyt and Salvage Soyl* (1997).

He has also edited a number of texts, most recently, with Matthew Dimmock, *Religions of the Book: Co-existence and Conflict, 1400–1660* (2008), and with Raymond Gillespie, *The Oxford History of the Irish Book, Vol. III: The Irish Book in English, 1550–1800* (2006). He is a regular reviewer for the TLS.

Heather Henderson is a freelance writer and former Associate Professor of English Literature at Mount Holyoke College. A specialist in Victorian literature, she is the recipient of a fellowship from the National Endowment for the Humanities. She is the author of *The Victorian Self: Autobiography and Biblical Narrative*. Her current interests include homeschooling, travel literature, and autobiography.

Peter J. Manning is Professor at Stony Brook University. He is the author of *Byron and His Fictions* and *Reading Romantics*, and of numerous essays on the British Romantic poets and prose writers. With Susan J. Wolfson, he has co-edited *Selected Poems of Byron*, and *Selected Poems of Beddoes, Hood, and Praed*. He has received fellowships from the National Endowment for the Humanities and the John Simon Guggenheim Memorial Foundation, and the Distinguished Scholar Award of the Keats-Shelley Association.

Anne Schotter is Professor of English at Wagner College. She is the co-editor of *Ineffability: Naming the Unnamable from Dante to Beckett* and author of articles on Middle English poetry, Dante, and medieval Latin poetry. Her current interests include the medieval reception of classical literature, particularly the work of Ovid. She has held fellowships from the Woodrow Wilson and Andrew W. Mellon foundations.

William Sharpe is Professor of English Literature at Barnard College. A specialist in Victorian poetry and the literature of the city, he is the author of *Unreal Cities: Urban Figuration in Wordsworth, Baudelaire, Whitman, Eliot, and Williams*. He is also co-editor of *The Passing of Arthur* and *Visions of the Modern City*. He is the recipient of Guggenheim, National Endowment of the Humanities, Fulbright, and Mellon fellowships, and recently published *New York Nocturne: The City After Dark in Literature, Painting, and Photography*.

Stuart Sherman is Associate Professor of English at Fordham University. He received the Gottschalk Prize from the American Society for Eighteenth-Century Studies for his book *Telling Time: Clocks, Diaries, and English Diurnal Form, 1660–1775*, and is currently at work on a study called "News and Plays: Evanescences of Page and Stage, 1620–1779." He has received the Quantrell Award for Undergraduate Teaching, as well as fellowships from the American Council of Learned Societies and the Chicago Humanities Institute.

Susan J. Wolfson teaches at Princeton University and is general editor of Longman Cultural Editions. She has also produced editions of Felicia Hemans, Lord Byron, Thomas L. Beddoes, William M. Praed, and Thomas Hood. She is the editor of the innovative Longman Cultural Editions of John Keats, and of Mary Shelley's *Frankenstein*, and coeditor (with Barry V. Qualls) of *Three Tales of Doubles*, and (with Claudia Johnson) of Jane Austen's *Pride and Prejudice*. She is author of *The Questioning Presence* (1986), *Formal Charges: The Shaping of Poetry in British Romanticism* (1997), and *Borderlines: The Shiftings of Gender* (2007).

The Longman Anthology of British Literature

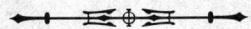

VOLUME ONE

Laurence, Prior of Durham, depicted as a scribe, from a 12th-century manuscript.

The Middle Ages

Population[1]

National Population (in millions)[2]

	England	Scotland	Ireland
1100	around 2	—	—
1300	4.5 to 5.5[3]	0.5 to 1.0	c. 0.9
1377	2.5 to 3.0[4]	—	c. 0.5
Late Middle Ages	4.0[5]	—	—

Urban Population[6]

	London	Edinburgh	Dublin
	London is already a major city during the Roman occupation. After a population collapse in the early 5th century, its population grows again in the 9th century. By 1200, it is a populous city, with more than 100 parish churches.	Edinburgh is a royal burgh by 1127.	Dublin is a Viking trading center by the mid-9th century. It is conquered by the Anglo-Angevins in 1170 and became their colonial administrative center.
1300	60,000–80,000	10,000	11,000
1340s	Near 90,000	—	—
1377	50,000 at the most[7]	—	—

Life Expectancy

In the years after the Black Death, life expectancy at birth is 25–30 years. As many as 50% of babies die in their first year.

Daily Life

Wages

1300s	A master mason makes 5 pounds per year. A laborer makes 2 pounds per year at the maximum.
1316	A common knight, working as a mercenary, might make 30 pounds per year for his services; knightly income from land varies enormously.
1350s	Laborers' wages rise after the population decline caused by the Black Death. A thatcher makes 3 pence per day; his assistant makes 1 penny.
1379	A chantry priest earns about 5 pounds per year.
1380s	A thatcher make 4 pence per day; his assistant, a little over 2 pence.

Coin from the reign of Alfred the Great

1. Population estimates for the Middle Ages are highly speculative.
2. The population of today's United Kingdom is 60,943,912 (July 2008 est.).
3. England's medieval population peaked in the late 12th and 13th centuries.
4. After peaking, population then declined in 1315–1317 perhaps 10% after poor crops and famine. The Black Death first struck in the summer of 1348, then again in 1361, 1368, and 1375, causing a massive decline in population.
5. The population rose only slowly after the Black Death. For much of the Middle Ages, the population was densest in East Anglia. The Black Death had its greatest impact there.
6. The population of today's London is over 7.6 million (October 2008 est.).
7. The Black Death of 1348 and the years that followed cut London's population by more than a third. It did not rise to more than 60,000 until around 1500.

Cost of Goods

1374	A knight's two horses costs 10 pounds. (A fine war horse could cost 80 pounds.) One knight's total armor is worth 16 pounds.
14th century	A cow costs 10 shillings (120 pence). A sheep costs between 1 and 1½ shillings; a pig 2 or 3 shillings; two chickens or a dozen eggs cost a penny. Good wine costs 4–8 pence per gallon. Average ale costs 1 penny per gallon. A wealthy peasant's shoes might cost 6 pence; his tunic, 3 shillings. Fine wool fabric is 5 shillings a yard.

Food and Drink

Most trade in food is local. It includes grains, dairy, fish, poultry, and meat. Wheat is the preferred grain for bread, but the more easily grown rye and barley are used. The cheapest bread is made from a meal of peas and beans. Oats are used for gruel and for brewing. Ale is a major part of daily nutrition. Because it is perishable, it is locally produced, most often by women until the mid-14th century. At that point guilds increasingly organize production and women's roles decline.[8]

As the population grows between 1200 and 1348, most people depend on grains for their nutrition. Population pushes the edges of agricultural production, and protein deficiency may have been widespread by the 1300s. In the smaller population that followed the Black Death, consumption of wheat bread, barley ale, and meat rises fast.

Apparel

Most British clothing during the middle ages is made of wool, although linen is also used for underclothing. Wool and cloth are the main sources of England's wealth, and high taxes on their export are key sources of royal income. In the 1270s, almost 27,000 sacks (each containing the wool of 240 sheep) are exported each year; by the mid-14th century, the number rises to 40,000 sacks per year. English cloth appears as an export by the early 14th century. By the later 15th century, England is the largest maker of woolen cloth in Europe.

In military apparel, chain mail is a knight's major protection until about 1200. Plate armor appears before 1214, and the breast plate by 1250. In 1314, at the Battle of Bannockburn, the Earl of Gloucester dies from the weight of his plate armor.

Rulers

Before the Norman Conquest (1066)
Alfred the Great (871–899)
Edmund I (940–946)
Ethelred the Unready (948–1016)
Edward the Confessor (1042–1066)
Harold II (1066)
House of Normandy
William I, the Conqueror (1066–1087)

William the Conqueror

8. Guilds were important organizers of urban life by the late 13th century. They controlled production (leather, jewelry, etc.) and trade (especially in food). But the craft guilds overlapped with guilds mostly devoted to social and religious activities. Religious guilds provided burial if a member died in poverty, and hired priests to pray for the souls of deceased members. In many cities, guilds were involved in forms of civic display, like plays and processions.

Rulers

William II, Rufus (1087–1100)

Henry I (1100–1135)

House of Blois

Stephen (1135–1154)

House of Plantagenet

Henry II (1154–1189)

Richard I "Coeur de Lion" (1189–1199)

John (1199–1216)

Henry III (1216–1272)

Edward I (1272–1307)

Edward II (1307–1327)

Edward III (1327–1377)

Richard II (1377–1399)

House of Lancaster

Henry IV (1399–1413)

Henry V (1413–1422)

Henry VI (1422–1471)

House of York

Edward IV (1461–1483)

Edward V (1483)

Richard III (1483–1485)

(Clockwise from upper left) Henry II, Richard I, John, and Henry III

Timeline

410 Roman occupation of England ends.

597 St. Augustine of Canterbury's mission begins the conversion of England.

c. 600 King Arthur is first mentioned.

c. 650 Ruthwell Cross (page 149)

680 Abbess Hilda dies.

c. 700 *Book of Kells*

731 Bede's *Ecclesiastical History* (page 154)

c. 844–899 King Alfred is noted for learning to read in his middle years. Many of his clergy are illiterate in Latin, one reason he sponsors translation of key texts into Old English.

899 King Alfred dies.

c. 1000 The *Beowulf* manuscript appears, although the story itself is probably 200 years older (page 32).

1066 William the Conqueror crosses the English Channel and defeats King Harold to begin the Norman Conquest. Between 7,000 and 10,000 men fight on each side of the Battle of Hastings.

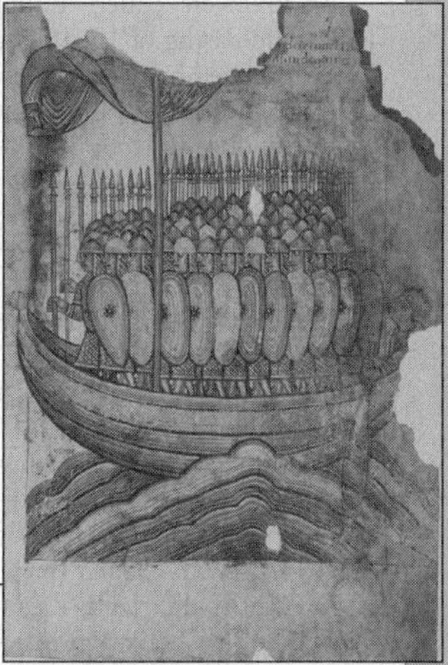

1075 The Investiture Controversy, a debate concerning who has the authority to "invest" or appoint bishops to their positions, results when the papacy claims sole authority to appoint bishops and to depose secular rulers who oppose this right.

1086 The Domesday Book is the first—and still astonishing—systematic public record in English history.

1086 Water mills are the main source of power during the Middle Ages. While there were fewer than 100 in the 900s, the Domesday Book records 5,624.

1095 Pope Urban II calls for the First Crusade.
12th century *The Táin* "Recension II" (page 111)
c. 1136 Geoffrey of Monmouth's *The History of the Kings of Britain* (page 183)
1154 The last entries in *The Peterborough Chronicle*, a series of (usually) yearly descriptions of important events throughout England that began in the late 9th century
1170 Thomas Becket is murdered in Canterbury Cathedral after quarrelling with Henry II over the right of the church or the state to try priests for criminal acts.
1170–1180 Marie de France's *Lais* (page 201)
1200 An increasingly diverse but still limited population is able to read.
1215 *The Magna Carta*, the founding document of British constitutional history, is signed by King John.

1215 The Fourth Lateran Council promulgates the doctrine of transubstantiation, an educational program based upon preaching, a set of disciplinary codes for wayward clerics, and the call for yearly confession at Easter.
1258 The Provisions of Oxford (a declaration of baronial rights) is distributed to sheriffs across England in Latin, French, and English.
1286 Mechanical clocks appear; their spread leads to the standardization of the hour.
14th century Dafydd ap Gwilym (page 566)
14th century Windmills become numerous.
1327 Edward II is deposed.
1337 The Hundred Years' War between France and England begins.
1346–1347 The largest known English army, totaling over 36,000, is assembled at the Siege of Calais.
1347 The Black Death, also known as the Bubonic Plague because of the swollen lymph nodes or "buboes" of its victims, strikes Europe. According to many authorities, up to 50% of the population of Europe and Asia is killed by the wave of infection.
1351 The Statute of Laborers sets wages to pre-Plague levels and prevents the working classes from leaving their feudal domains to seek better work and pay.
1375–1400 London literary culture flourishes—home to Geoffrey Chaucer, John Gower, and William Langland.
1378 The Great Schism begins, during which there were two lines of popes (and even a third line for a time), one in France and one in Rome.
1380 John Wyclif, often seen as a predecessor to the Protestant Reformation, is condemned as a heretic, and his followers, called "Lollards," are persecuted.
1381 The Rising of 1381 occurs. Led by Wat Tyler and encouraged by the preaching of John Ball, rebels from throughout the countryside converge upon London in response to the punitive poll tax of that year (page 468).

1399 Richard II is deposed.
1400 Roughly 30% of the population can read English; some know French and Latin. Literacy is increasingly taken for granted in the upper classes.
1400 Chaucer dies (page 312).
1415 At the Battle of Agincourt, a pivotal battle of the Hundred Years' War, Henry V of England defeats a much larger French army.
c.1420 Julian of Norwich dies (page 481).
c. 1438 Margery Kempe dies (page 529).
1453 The Hundred Years' War ends.
c. 1464–1479 *Mankind* (page 587)
1465 Charles d'Orléans dies (page 584).
1474 The first book is printed in English by William Caxton.
1485 At the Battle of Bosworth Field, Henry Tudor kills Richard III and ascends the throne as Henry VII, beginning the Tudor reign in England.
1485 William Caxton publishes *Morte Darthur* (page 279).
1492 Columbus sails.
Late 15th century Scotland enjoys a brief flowering of poetry centered in a sophisticated court society (page 573).
1517 To protest the disingenuous sale of indulgences (forgiveness of sins after death), Martin Luther posts his 95 Theses on a door at the University of Wittenberg, starting the Reformation in Germany.

The Middle Ages

> At the present time, there are five languages in Britain, just as the divine law is written in five books, all devoted to seeking out and setting forth one and the same kind of wisdom, namely the knowledge of sublime truth and of true sublimity. These are the English, British, Irish, Pictish, as well as the Latin languages; through the study of the scriptures, Latin is in general use among them all.
>
> —*Bede, Ecclesiastical History of the English People*

The Venerable Bede's famous and enormously influential *Ecclesiastical History of the English People*, written in the early 700s, reflects a double triumph. First, its very title acknowledges the dominance by Bede's day of the Anglo-Saxons, who, centuries earlier, had established themselves on an island already inhabited by Celtic Britons and by Picts. Second, the Latin of Bede's text and his own life as a monk point to the presence of ancient Mediterranean influences in the British Isles, earlier through Rome's military colonization of ancient Britain and later through the conversion of Bede's people to Roman Christianity.

In this first chapter of his first book, Bede shows a complex awareness of the several populations still active in Britain and often resisting or encroaching on Anglo-Saxon rule, and much of his *History* narrates the successive waves of invaders and missionaries who had brought their languages, governments, cultures, and beliefs to his island. This initial emphasis on peoples and languages should not be taken as early medieval multiculturalism, however: Bede's brief comparison to the single truth embodied in the five books of divine law also shows us his eagerness to draw his fragmented world into a coherent and transcendent system of Latin-based Christianity.

It is useful today, however, to think about medieval Britain, before and long after Bede, as a multilingual and multicultural setting, densely layered with influences and communities that divide, in quite different ways, along lines of geography, language, and ethnicity, as well as religion, gender, and class. These elements produced extraordinary cultures and artistic works, whose richness and diversity challenge the modern imagination. The medieval British Isles were a meeting place, but also a point of resistance, for wave after wave of cultural and political influences. Awareness of these multiple origins, moreover, persisted. In the mid-thirteenth century, Matthew Paris's map of England (Color Plate 4) reflects an alertness to the complex geography of history and settlement on his island. Six hundred years after Bede we encounter a historian like Sir Thomas Gray complaining that recent disorders were "characteristic of a medley of different races. Wherefore some people are of the opinion that the diversity of spirit among the English is the cause of their revolutions" (*Scalacronica*, c. 1363).

This complex mixture sometimes resulted from systematic conquest, as with the Romans and, three centuries after Bede, the famous Norman Conquest of 1066; sometimes it was from slower, less unified movements of ethnic groups, such as the Celts, Anglo-Saxons, the Irish in Scotland, and the Vikings. Other important influences arrived more subtly: various forms of Christianity, classical Latin literature and learning, continental French culture in the thirteenth century, and an imported Italian humanism toward the close of the British Middle Ages.

Our understanding of this long period and our very name for it also reflect a long history of multiple influences and cultural and political orders. The term "medieval" began as a condescending and monolithic label, first applied by Renaissance humanists who were eager to distinguish their revived classical scholarship from what they interpreted as a "barbarous" past. They and later readers often dismissed the Middle Ages as rigidly hierarchical, feudal, and Church-dominated. Others embraced the period for equally tendentious reasons, rosily picturing "feudal" England and Europe as a harmonious society of contented peasants, chivalrous nobles, and holy clerics. It is true that those who exercised political and religious control during the Middle Ages—the Roman church and the Anglo-Norman and then the English monarchy—sought to impose hierarchy on their world and created explicit ideologies to justify doing so. They were not unopposed, however; those who had been pushed aside continued to resist—and to contribute to Britain's multiple and dynamic literatures.

The term "medieval" began as a condescending and monolithic label . . .

The period that we call "the Middle Ages" is vast and ungainly, spanning eight hundred years by some accounts. Scholars traditionally divide medieval English literature into the Old English period, from about 700 to 1066 (the date of the Norman Conquest), and the Middle English period, from 1066 to about 1500. Given the very different state of the English language during the two periods and given the huge impact of the Norman Conquest, this division is reasonable and is reflected in this collection under the headings "Before the Norman Conquest" and "After the Norman Conquest." There were substantial continuities, nevertheless, before and after the Conquest, especially in the Celtic areas beyond the Normans' immediate control.

The Celts

It is with the Celts, in fact, that the recorded history of Britain begins, and their literatures continue to the present day in Ireland and Wales. The Celts first migrated to Britain about 400 B.C.E., after spreading over most of Europe in the two preceding centuries. In England these "Brittonic" Celts absorbed some elements of Roman culture and social order during Rome's partial occupation of the island from the first to the fifth centuries C.E. After the conversion of the Roman emperor Constantine in the fourth century and the establishment of Christianity as the official imperial religion, many British Celts adopted Christianity. The language of these "British" to whom Bede refers gave rise to Welsh. The Celts maintained contact with their people on the Continent, who were already being squeezed toward what is now Brittany, in the west of France. The culture of the Brittonic Celts was thus not exclusively insular, and their myths and legends came to incorporate these cross-Channel memories, especially in the stories of King Arthur.

Celts also arrived in Ireland; and as one group, the "Goidelic" Celts, achieved linguistic and social dominance there, their language split off from that of the Britons. Some of these Irish Celts later established themselves in Argyll and the western isles of Scotland, "either by friendly treaty or by the sword," says Bede, and from them the Scottish branch of the Celtic languages developed. Bede mentions this language as the "Irish" that is spoken in Britain. The Irish converted to Christianity early but slowly, without the pressure of a Christianized colonizer. When the great Irish monasteries flourished in the sixth century, their extraordinary Latin scholarship seems to have developed alongside the traditional learning preserved by the rigorous schools of vernacular poetry, as we see in the section "Early Irish Verse" (pages 133–42). If anything, Irish monastic study was stimulated by these surviving institutions of a more poetic and priestly class. The Irish monasteries in turn became the impetus behind Irish and Anglo-Saxon missionaries who carried Christianity to the northern and eastern reaches of Europe. Both as missionaries and as scholars, insular Christians had great impact on continental Europe, especially in the eighth and ninth centuries.

By 597 when Pope Gregory the Great sent Augustine (later "of Canterbury") to expand the Christian presence in England, there was already a flourishing Christian Celtic society, especially in Ireland. Ensuing disagreements over Celtic versus Roman ways of worship were ultimately resolved in favor of the Roman liturgy and calendar, but the cultural impact of Celts on British Christianity remained enormous. The Irish *Book of Kells* (page 14), and the Lindisfarne Gospels (Color Plate 1), produced in England, are enlivened by the swirls, interlace, and stylized animals long evident in the work of pagan Celtic craftsmen on the continent. The monks who illuminated such magnificent gospel books also copied classical Latin texts, notably Virgil's *Aeneid* and works by Cicero and Seneca, thereby helping keep ancient Roman literature alive when much of continental Europe fell into near chaos during the Germanic invasions that led to the fall of Rome.

Included in this anthology are examples from the two great literatures written in Celtic languages, Irish and Welsh. Passages from the eighth-century Irish *Táin Bó Cuailnge* reveal a heroic spirit and an acceptance of the magical which can be compared with aspects of *Beowulf*. Like much Irish heroic narrative, though, the *Táin* also reveals a far more prominent and assertive role for women, some of whom retain resemblances to the goddess figures of Ireland's pagan era. Welsh literature is represented first by lyrics attributed to the early, shadowy poet Taliesin and later by the sophisticated lyrics of fourteenth-century Dafydd ap Gwilym, who draws on Latin and European traditions as well as on the rich poetic techniques of Wales.

The Germanic Migrations

While Celtic culture flourished in Ireland, the British Celts and their faith suffered a series of disastrous reversals after the withdrawal of the Romans and the aggressive incursions of the pagan Angles, Saxons, and Jutes from the continent. The Picts and Scots in the north, never Romanized, had begun to harass the Britons, who responded by inviting allies from among the Germanic tribes on the continent in the mid-fifth century. These protectors soon became predators, demanding land and establishing small kingdoms of their own in roughly the eastern half of modern-day England. Uneasy and temporary treaties followed. The Britons retained a presence in the northwest, in the kingdoms of Rheged and of the Strathclyde Welsh; others were slowly pressed toward present-day Wales in the southwest.

The Angles, Saxons, and Jutes were not themselves a monolithic force, though. Divided into often warring states, they faced resistance, however diminishing, from the Britons and still had to battle the aggressive Picts and Scots, who were the original reason for their arrival. Their own culture was further changed as they converted to Christianity. The piecemeal Anglo-Saxon colonization of England in the sixth and seventh centuries and the island's conversion and later reconversion to Christianity present a complex picture, then—one that could be retold very differently depending on the perspectives of later historians. As the Angles and Saxons settled in and extended their control, the emerging "English" culture drew on new interpretations of the region's history. The most influential account of all was Bede's *Ecclesiastical History*, completed in 731. Our most reliable and eloquent source for early British history, Bede nonetheless wrote as an Anglo-Saxon. He presented his people's history from a providential perspective, seeing their role in Britain and their conversion to Christianity as a crucial part of a divine plan. King Alfred extended this world view when, in the late ninth century, he wrote of his people's struggle against the invading pagan Vikings.

Bede thus adopts an approach to history that reflects his own devout Christian faith and the disciplined religious practices of his monastic brethren in Northumberland. Nevertheless, Bede lived in a wider culture still deeply imbued with the tribal values of its Germanic and pagan past, a culture that maintained at least a nostalgic regard for the kind of individual heroic glory that rarely looks beyond this world. Even in Bede's day, most kings died young and on the battlefield. And natural disasters such as those in 664 (a plague, and the deaths of a king and an archbishop occurring on the day of an eclipse) could send the Anglo-Saxons back to pagan worship. The two worlds, one with its roots in Mediterranean Christianity and the other in Germanic paganism, overlapped and interpenetrated for generations.

The two worlds, one with its roots in Mediterranean Christianity and the other in Germanic paganism, overlapped and interpenetrated for generations.

The pagan culture that is the setting for the epic *Beowulf* still strongly resembled that of the Germanic "barbarians" described by the Roman historian Tacitus in the first century. The heroic code of the Germanic warrior bands—what Tacitus called the "*comitatus*"—valued courage in battle above all, followed by loyalty to the tribal leader and the warband. These formed the core of heroic identity. A warrior whose leader fell in battle was obliged to seek vengeance at any cost; it was an indelible shame to survive an unavenged leader. Family links were also profound, however, and a persistent tragic theme in Germanic and Anglo-Saxon heroic narrative pits the claims of vengeance against those of family loyalty.

Early warrior culture in the British Isles, as elsewhere, was fraught with violence, as fragile truces between warring tribes and clans were continually broken.

The tone of Old English poetry (as of much of Old Irish heroic narrative) is consequently somber, often suffused with a sense of doom. Even moments of high festivity are darkened by allusions to later disasters. Humor often occurs through a kind of ironic understatement: a poet may state that a warrior strode less swiftly into battle, for example, when the warrior in fact is dead. Similarly Cet, an Irish warrior, claims that if his brother were in the house, he would overcome his opponent, Conall. Conall replies, "But he is in the house," and almost casually flings the brother's head at Cet. A lighter tone is found mostly in shorter forms, such as the playful Anglo-Saxon riddles and in some Old Irish poetry.

The Angles and Saxons had come to England as military opportunists, and they in turn faced attacks and settlement from across the Channel. Their increasingly ordered political world and their thriving monastic establishments, such as Bede's monastery of Jarrow, were plundered by Vikings in swift attacks by boat as early as the end of the eighth century. Irish monastic culture faced similar depradations. This continued for a hundred years, and eventually resulted in widespread Scandinavian settlements north of the Thames, in areas called the Danelaw, and around modern-day Dublin. By the 890s Christian Viking kings reigned at York and in East Anglia, extending a history of independence from the southern kingdoms. The period of raids and looting was largely over by 900, but even King Alfred (d. 899) faced Viking incursions in Wessex and consciously depicted himself as a Christian hero holding the line against pagan invaders. Only his kingdom, in fact, resisted their attacks with complete success. Vikings also intermarried with Anglo-Saxons and expanded their influence by political means. Profiting from English dynastic disorder around the turn of the eleventh century, aristocrats in the Danelaw became brokers of royal power. From 1016 to 1035 the Danish Cnut (Canute) was king of both England and Denmark, briefly uniting the two in a maritime empire. The Scandinavian presence was not exclusively combative, however. They sent peaceful traders to the British Isles—among them Ohthere, whose tale of his voyages is included here. They also left their mark on literature and language, as in the early Middle English romance *Havelock the Dane*, which contains many words borrowed from Old Norse.

PAGAN AND CHRISTIAN: TENSION AND CONVERGENCE

Given that writing in the Roman alphabet was introduced to pre-Conquest England by churchmen, it is not surprising that most texts from the period are written in Latin on Christian subjects. Most writing even in the Old English language was also religious. In Anglo-Saxon England and in the Celtic cultures, vernacular literature tended at first to be orally composed and performed. The body of written vernacular Anglo-Saxon poetry that survives is thus very small indeed, although there are plenty of prose religious works. It is something of a miracle that *Beowulf*, which celebrates the exploits of a pagan hero, was deemed worthy of being copied by scribes who were almost certainly clerics. (In fact, almost all the

It is something of a miracle that Beowulf, *which celebrates the exploits of a pagan hero, was deemed worthy of being copied by scribes who were almost certainly clerics.*

greatest Anglo-Saxon poetry survives in only a single copy—so tenuous is our link to that past.) Yet the copying of *Beowulf* also hints at the complex interaction of the pagan and Christian traditions in Anglo-Saxon culture.

The conflict between the two traditions was characterized (and perhaps exaggerated) by Christian writers and readers as a struggle between pagan violence and Christian values of forgiveness. The old, deep-seated respect for treasure as a sign of power and achievement seemed to conflict with Christian contempt for worldly goods. In fact, however, pagan Germanic and Christian values were alike in many respects and coexisted with various degrees of mutual influence.

Old English poets explored the tensions as well as the overlap between the two sets of values in two primary poetic modes—the heroic and the elegiac. The heroic mode, of which *Beowulf* is the supreme example, celebrates the values of bravery, loyalty, vengeance, and desire for treasure. The great buckle from the Sutton Hoo ship-burial (Color Plate 2) is a surviving artifact of such treasure. The elegiac mode, by contrast, calls the value of these things into question, as at best transient and at worst a worldly distraction from spiritual life. The elegiac speaker, usually an exile, laments the loss of earthly goods—his lord, his comrades, the joys of the mead hall—and, in the case of the short poem known as *The Wanderer*, turns his thoughts to heaven. *Beowulf*, composed most likely by a Christian poet looking back at the deeds of his pagan Scandinavian ancestors, uses elements of both the heroic and the elegiac to focus on the overlap of pagan and Christian virtues. A similar, though less adversarial, interaction of a heroic code and the new religion is also encountered in medieval Irish literature, such as the examples of early Irish verse offered here.

The goals of earthly glory and heavenly salvation that concern Old English poetry are presented primarily as they affect men. Recent scholarship, however, reveals the active roles played in society by Anglo-Saxon women, particularly aristocratic ones. One of these is Aethelflaed, daughter of King Alfred, who co-ruled the kingdom of Mercia with her brother Edward at the turn of the tenth century, taking an active military role in fighting off the Danes. Better known today is Abbess Hilda, who founded and ran the great monastery at Whitby from 657 until her death in 680; five Whitby monks became bishops across England during her rule. Nevertheless, women generally take a marginal role in Old English poetry. In secular works marriages are portrayed as being arranged to strengthen military alliances, in efforts (often doomed) to heal bloody rifts between clans. Women thus function primarily as "peace weavers," a term referring occasionally to their active diplomacy in settling disputes but more often to their passive role in marriage exchanges. This latter role was fraught with danger, for if a truce were broken between the warring groups, the woman would face tragically conflicting loyalties to husband and male kin.

In secular works marriages are portrayed as being arranged to strengthen military alliances, in efforts (often doomed) to heal bloody rifts between clans.

The effect of the Germanic heroic code on women is explored in two tantalizingly short poems that invest the elegiac mode with women's voices: *Wulf and Eadwacer* and *The Wife's Lament*. In both, a woman speaker laments her separation from her lord, whether husband or lover, through some shadowy events of heroic warfare. More indicative of the actual power of aristocratic and religious women in Anglo-Saxon society, perhaps, is the Old English poem *Judith,* a biblical narrative which uses heroic diction reminiscent of that in *Beowulf* to celebrate the heroine's military triumph over the pagan Holofernes.

Oral Poetry, Written Manuscripts

For all their deep linguistic differences and territorial conflicts, the Celts and Anglo-Saxons had affinities in the heroic themes and oral settings of their greatest surviving narratives and in the echoes of a pre-Christian culture that endure there. Indeed, these can be compared to conditions of authorship in oral cultures worldwide, from Homer's Greece to parts of contemporary Africa. In a culture with little or no writing, the singer of tales has an enormously important role as the conservator of the past. In *Beowulf,* for instance, the traditional content and verbal formulas of the poetry of praise are swiftly reworked to celebrate the hero's killing of the monster Grendel:

> a fellow of the king's,
> whose head was a storehouse of the storied verse,
> whose tongue gave gold to the language
> of the treasured repertory, wrought a new lay
> made in the measure.

A poet of this kind (in Anglo-Saxon, a *scop* or "shaper") does not just enhance the great warrior's prestige by praising his hero's ancestors and accomplishments. He also recalls and performs the shared history and beliefs of the entire people, in great feats of memory that make the poet virtually the encyclopedia of his culture. A poet from the oral tradition might also become a singer of the new Christian cosmology, like the illiterate herdsman Caedmon, whom Bede describes as having been called to monastic vows by the Abbess Hilda, in honor of his Christian poems composed in the vernacular oral mode.

In Celtic areas, oral poets had even greater status. The ancient class of learned Irish poets were honored servants of noblemen and kings; they remained as a powerful if reduced presence after the establishment of Christianity. The legal status of such a poet (a *fili*) was similar to that of a bishop, and indeed the *fili* carried out some functions of spells and divination inherited from the pagan priestly class, the druids. The ongoing influence of these poets in Irish politics and culture is reflected in the body of surviving secular literature from medieval Ireland, which is considerably larger than that from Anglo-Saxon England. A comparable situation prevailed in Wales. Even in the quite late Welsh *Tale of Taliesin,* the poet Taliesin appears as a public performer before the king as well as a possessor of arcane wisdom, magic, and prophecy.

This attitude of awe toward the word as used by the oral poet was only enhanced by the arrival of Christianity, a faith that attributes creation itself to an act of divine speech. Throughout the Middle Ages and long after orally composed poetry had retreated from many centers of high culture, the power of the word also inhered in its written form, as encountered in certain prized books. Chief among these were the Bible and other books of religious story, especially by such church

Saint John, from *The Book of Kells*. Late 8th century.

fathers as Saints Augustine and Jerome, and books of the liturgy. Since these texts bore the authority of divine revelation, the manuscripts that contained them shared in their charisma.

The power of these manuscripts was both reflected and aided by their visual grandeur. Among the highest expressions of the fervor and discipline of early insular monasticism is its production of beautifully copied and exquisitely decorated books of the Bible. The extreme elaboration of their production and the great labor and expense lavished on them suggest their almost holy status. Figures depicted holding a book in the late eighth-century *Book of Kells*, or writing in the Lindisfarne Gospels, indicate this importance; a fascination with the new technology is suggested by Old English riddles whose answers are "a hand writing," "a book worm," or "a bookcase."

The cost and effort of making manuscript books and their very scarcity contributed to their aura. Parchment was produced from animal skins, stretched and scraped. The training and discipline involved in copying texts, especially sacred texts, were great. The decoration of the most ambitious manuscripts involved rare colors, gold leaf, and often supreme artistry. Thus these magnificent manuscripts could become almost magical icons: Bede, for example, tells of scrapings from Irish manuscripts which mixed with water cured the bites of poisonous snakes.

Manuscripts slowly became more widely available. By the twelfth century we hear more of manuscripts in private hands and the beginning of production outside ecclesiastical settings. By the fourteenth century merchants and private scholars were buying books from shops that resembled modern booksellers. The glamour and prestige of beautiful manuscripts remained, though, even if the sense of their magic faded to a degree. Great families would donate psalters and gospels to religious foundations, with the donor carefully represented in the decoration presenting the book to the Virgin Mary or the Christ child. Spectacular books of private devotion were at once a medium for spiritual meditation and proof of great wealth (see Color Plate 10). Stories of epic conquest like the *Aeneid* would sometimes feature their aristocratic owners' coat of arms.

The Norman Conquest

By the time of these developments in book production, though, a gigantic change had occurred. In a single year, 1066, England witnessed the death of the Anglo-Saxon King Edward and the coronation of his disputed successor King Harold, the invasion and triumph of the foreigner William of Normandy, and his own coronation as King William. These events are recorded, from very different perspectives, in *The Anglo-Saxon Chronicle* and the Bayeux Tapestry (page 166). The Normans conquered, with relative ease, an Anglo-Saxon kingdom disordered by civil strife. The monastic movement had lost much of its earlier fervor and discipline, despite reform in the tenth century. Baronial interests had weakened severely the reign of the late King Edward "the Confessor." On an island that already perceived itself as repeatedly colonized, 1066 nonetheless represented a climactic change, experienced and registered at virtually all levels of social, religious, and cultural experience.

One sign of how great a breach had been opened in England, paradoxically, is the multifaceted effort put forth by conquerors and conquered to maintain—or invent—continuity with the pre-Conquest past. In religious institutions, in dynastic genealogies, in the intersection of history and racial myth, in the forms and records of social institutions, the generations after 1066 sought to absorb a radically changed world yet to ground their world in an increasingly mythicized Anglo-Saxon or Briton antiquity. The Normans and their dynastic successors the Angevins eagerly took up and adapted to their own preoccupations ancient Briton political myths such as that of King Arthur and his court, and the stories of such saintly Anglo-Saxon kings as Oswald and Edward the Confessor.

They promoted narratives of their ancestors, like Wace's *Roman de Rou,* the story of the Normans' founder Rollo, commissioned by Henry II. Geoffrey of Monmouth dedicated his *History of the Kings of England* partly to Henry II's uncle, Robert Duke of Gloucester. In that work Geoffrey links the Celtic myths of King Arthur and his followers to an equally ancient myth that England was founded by descendants of the survivors of Troy; he makes his combined, largely fictive but enormously appealing work available to a Norman audience by writing it in Latin. Geoffrey's story was soon retold in "romance," the French from which vernacular

The Three Living and the Three Dead, from *The De Lisle Psalter*. The transience of life, especially of worldly glory, was never far from the medieval imagination. In this image from a Psalter made in the early 14th century for Baron Robert de Lisle, three kings in elegant courtly array face three rotting corpses. While most of the Psalter is in French and Latin, this scene has a "caption" in rhymed Middle English at the top. The kings say in turn (in modernized form), "I am afeared. Lo, what I see! I think that here are devils three." The corpses reply, "I was well fair. Such shall thou be. For God's love beware by me."

texts took their name. The Angevin court also supported the "romances of antiquity," poems in French that narrate the story of Troy (the *Roman de Troie*), its background (*Roman de Thèbes*), and its aftermath (*Roman d'Eneas*), thus creating a model in the antique past for the Normans and their westward conquest of England. And the *Song of Roland,* the great crusading narrative celebrating the heroic death of Charlemagne's nephew as he protected Christendom from the Spanish Moslems, was probably written in the milieu of Henry II's court.

The Normans brought with them a new system of government, a freshly renovated Latin culture, and most important a new language. Anglo-Saxon sank into relative insignificance at the level of high culture and central government. Norman French became the language of the courts of law, of literature, and of most of the nobility. By the time English rose again to widespread cultural significance, about 250 years later, it was a hybrid that combined Romance and Germanic elements.

Latin offered a lifeline of communication at some social levels of this initially fractured society. The European clerics who arrived under the immigrant archbishops Lanfranc and Anselm brought a new and different learning, and often new and deeply unwelcome religious practices: a celibate priesthood, skepticism about local saints, and newly disciplined monasticism. Yet despite these differences and the tensions that accompanied them, clerics of European or British origin were linked by a common liturgy, a considerable body of shared reading, and most of all

Latin offered a lifeline of communication at some social levels of this initially fractured society.

a common learned language. Secular as well as religious society were coming to be based more and more on the practical use of the written word: the letter, the charter, the documentary record, and the written book. Whereas Anglo-Saxon England had been governed by the word enacted and performed—a law of oral witness and a culture of oral poets—Norman England increasingly became a land of documents and books.

Social and Religious Order

The famed Domesday Book is a first instance of many of these developments. The Domesday survey was a gigantic undertaking, carried out with a speed that still astonishes between Christmas 1085 and William the Conqueror's death in September 1087. A county-by-county survey of the lands of King William and those held by his tenants-in-chief and subtenants, Domesday also records the obligations of landholders and thus reflects a new feudal system by which, increasingly, land was held in post-Conquest England.

Under the Normans, a nobleman held land from the king as a fief, in exchange for which he owed the king certain military and judicial services, including the provision of armed knights. These knights in turn held land from their lord, to whom they also owed military service and other duties. Some of this land they might keep for their own farming and profit, and the rest they divided among serfs (who were obliged, in theory, to stay on the land to which they were born) and free peasantry. Both groups owed their knight or lord labor and either a portion of their agricultural produce or rents in cash. This system of land tenure was surely more complex and irregular in practice than in the theoretical model called feudalism. For instance, services at all levels were sometimes (and increasingly) commuted to cash payment, and while fiefs were theoretically held only by an individual for a lifetime, increasingly there were expectations that they would be inherited. Royal power gradually grew during the thirteenth and fourteenth centuries, yet the local basis of landholding and social order always acted as a counterbalance, even a block, to royal ambition.

The Domesday Book was only one piece of the multifaceted effort by which the Norman and later kings sought to extend and centralize royal power in their territories. William and his successors established a system of royal justices who traveled throughout the realm and reported ultimately to the king, and an organized royal bureaucracy began to appear. The most powerful and learned of these Anglo-Norman kings was William the Conqueror's great-grandson, Henry II, who ruled from 1154 to 1189. Under Henry, royal justice, bureaucracy, and record-keeping made great advances; the production of documents was centralized and took on more standardized forms, and copies of these documents (called "pipe rolls") began to be produced for later reference and proof.

Along with a stronger royal government, the Normans brought a clergy invigorated both by new learning and by the spirituality of recent monastic reforms. Saint Anselm, the second of the Norman archbishops of Canterbury, was a great prelate and the writer of beautiful and widely influential texts and prayers of private devotion. The Victorines and the Cistercians (inspired in part by Saint Bernard of Clairvaux) also brought a strong mystical streak to English monasticism. All these would bear fruit once again in the fourteenth century in a group of mystics writing in Latin and in English.

On the other hand, the Norman prelates, like their kings, brought an urge toward centralized order in the church and a belief that the church and its public justice (the "canon law") should be independent of secular power. This created frequent conflict with kings and aristocrats, who wanted to extend their judicial power and expected to wield considerable influence in the appointment of church officials.

The most explosive moment in this ongoing controversy occurred in the disagreements between Henry II and Thomas Becket, who was Henry's Chancellor and then Archbishop of Canterbury. Becket's increasingly public refusal to accommodate the king, either in the judicial sphere or the matter of clerical appointments, finally led to his murder by Henry's henchmen in 1170 at the altar of Canterbury Cathedral and his canonization very soon thereafter. A large body of hagiography (narratives of his martyrdom and posthumous miracles) swiftly developed, adding to an already rich tradition of writing about the lives of English saints. As Saint Thomas, Becket became a powerful focus for ecclesiastical ambition, popular devotion and pilgrimage, and religious and secular narrative. In fact, the characters of Chaucer's *Canterbury Tales* tell their stories while making a pilgrimage to his shrine.

At least in theory, feudal tenure involved an obligation of personal loyalty between lord and vassal that was symbolically enacted in the rituals of enfeoffment, in which the lord would bestow a fief on his vassal. This belief was elaborated in a large body of secular literature in the twelfth century and after. Yet feudal loyalty was always fragile and ideologically charged. Vassals regularly resisted the wills of their lord or king when their interests collided, sometimes to the extent of officially withdrawing from the feudal bond. Connected to feudal relations was the notion of a chivalric code among the knightly class (those who fought on horses, *chevaliers*), which involved not just loyalty to the lord but also honorable behavior within the class, even among enemies. Chivalric literature is thus full of stories of captured opponents being treated with the utmost politeness, as indeed happened when Henry II's son Richard was held hostage for years in Germany, awaiting ransom.

Connected to feudal relations was the notion of a chivalric code among the knightly class . . .

Similarly, although medieval theories of social order had some basis in fact, they exercised shifting influence within a much more complex social reality. For instance, medieval society was often analyzed by the model of the "three estates"—those who fought (secular aristocrats), those who prayed (the clergy), and those who worked the land (the free and servile peasantry). This model appears more or less explicitly in the poetry of William Langland and Chaucer. Such a system, though, did not allow for the gradual increase in manufacturing (weaving, pottery, metalwork, even the copying of books) or for the urban merchants who traded in such products. As society became more complex, a model of the "mystical social body" gained popularity, especially in the fourteenth century. Here a wider range of classes and jobs was compared to limbs and other body parts. Even this more flexible image was strictly hierarchical, though. Peasants and laborers were the feet, knights (on

The Murder of Thomas Becket, from Matthew Paris's *Historia Major*, mid-13th century.

the right) and merchants (on the left) were hands, and townspeople were the heart, but the head was made up of kings, princes, and prelates of the church.

Continental and Insular Cultures

The arrival of the Normans, and especially the learned clerics who came then and after, opened England to influences from a great intellectual current that was stirring on the continent, the "renaissance of the twelfth century," which was to have a significant impact in the centuries that followed. A period of comparative political stability and economic growth made travel easier, and students and teachers were on the move, seeking new learning in Paris and the Loire valley, in northern Italy, and in Toledo with its Arab and Jewish cultures. Schools were expanding beyond the monasteries and into the precincts of urban cathedrals and other religious foundations. Along with offering traditional biblical and theological study, these schools sparked a revived interest in elegant Latin writing, Neoplatonic philosophy, and science deriving from Aristotle.

Because the Normans and Angevins ruled large territories on the Continent, movement across the Channel was frequent; by the mid-twelfth century learned English culture was urbane and international. English clerics like John of Salisbury studied at Chartres and Paris, and texts by eminent speculative and scientific writers like William of Conches and Bernard Silvestris came to England. As these foreign works entered England, education became more ambitious and widely available, and its products show growing contact with the works of classical Latin writers such as Horace, Virgil, Terence, Cicero, Seneca, and Ovid in his erotic as much as in his mythological poetry.

The renewed attention to these works went along with a revival of interest in the *trivium*, the traditional division of the arts of eloquence: grammar, rhetoric, and dialectic. The most aggressive of these was dialectic, a form of logic developed by the Greeks and then rediscovered by Christian Europe from Arab scholars who had preserved and pursued Greek learning. John of Salisbury, who promoted dialectic in his *Metalogicon*, described dialectic with metaphors of military prowess, as though it were an extension of knightly jousting. "Since dialectic is carried on between two persons," he writes, Aristotle's *Topics* "teaches the matched contestants whom it trains and provides with reasons and topics, to handle their proper weapons and engage in verbal, rather than physical conflict." Rhetoric was elaborately codified in technical manuals of poetry. Though in one sense it was merely ornamental, teaching how to flesh out a description or incident with figures of speech, rhetoric could be as coercive as dialectic, though, since it specified strategies of persuasion in a tradition deriving from ancient oratory. Rhetorical texts also instructed the student in letter-writing, increasingly important as an administrative skill and as a form of elevated composition.

John of Salisbury, who promoted dialectic in his Metalogicon, *described dialectic with metaphors of military prowess, as though it were an extension of knightly jousting.*

The study of the *trivium* generated many Latin school texts and helped foster a high level of Latinity and a self-consciously sophisticated, classicizing literature in the second half of the twelfth century. Some school texts had great influence on vernacular literature, such as the *Poetria Nova* by Geoffrey of Vinsauf, a rhetorical handbook filled with vivid poetic examples. More intriguing is *Pamphilus*, a short Ovidian poem about a seduction, aided by Venus, which turns into a rape. It is thought to have been an exercise in *disputatio*, the oral form that dialectic assumed in the classroom. The poem was immensely popular in the next few centuries and was translated into many vernacular languages. *Pamphilus* was a conduit at once for Ovidian eroticism and for the language of debate on love. Chaucer mentions it as a model of passionate love and seems to have adapted some of its plot devices in his *Troilus and Criseyde*.

While classical Latin literature was often read with a frank interest in pagan ideas and practices, commentators also offered allegorical interpretations that drew pagan stories into the spiritual and cosmological preoccupations of medieval Christianity. Ovid's *Metamorphoses* were thus interpreted in a French poem, the *Ovide Moralisé*, that was clearly known to Chaucer, and in Latin commentaries such as the *Ovidius moralizatus* of Pierre Bersuire. For instance, Ovid describes Jupiter, in the form of a bull, carrying the Tyrian princess Europa into the sea to rape her. Bersuire interprets this as Christ taking on human flesh in order to take up the human soul he loves. Alternatively, he offers an explicitly misogynist allegory, casting Europa as young women who like to see handsome young men—bulls: "They are drawn through the stormy sea of evil temptations and are raped." Neither text is often very subtle in the extraction of Christian or moral analogies from Ovid's stories, yet both were popular and influential, if only because they also tell Ovid's tales before allegorizing them.

Allegory became a complex and fruitful area of the medieval imagination, with profound implications not only for reading, but for artistic production as well. In its simplest sense, an allegorical text takes a metaphor and extends it into narrative, often personifying a quality as a character. For instance, the enormously popular dream vision the *Roman de la Rose* by Guillaume de Lorris and Jean de Meun (which Chaucer translated into English) presents a lady's ambivalence toward courtship as the conflict between such personifications as "Reserve" and "Fair Welcome," both aspects of her own mind. When Christine de Pizan came to challenge the misogynist texts of Western tradition—the *Roman de la Rose* among them—she too chose the allegorical mode. In the *Book of the City of Ladies*, it is three virtues personified as ladies—Reason, Rectitude, and Justice—who refute the slanders of men and who encourage the poet to build a city celebrating female achievements. (The continuing influence of this text is reflected by the English translation printed in 1521.) The English morality play *Mankind* uses allegory to portray external forces, presenting its hero as tempted by the vices of the modern age, "New-Guise" (trendy behavior), "Nowadays," and "Nought." Medieval writers also employed an allegorical method known as typology, derived from biblical interpretation, in which Old Testament events are seen as literally true but also symbolically predictive of, and fulfilled by, events in the New Testament. An example of this occurs in *Piers Plowman*, which, among all its other allegorical devices, presents Abraham both as an Old Testament Patriarch, and, in his willingness to sacrifice his son, a type of Faith.

The Continent, particularly France, provided a variety of vernacular influences. French was the international language of aristocratic culture and an important literary language in England; continental French literature was crucial in the rise of courtly literature in Middle English. Many English Arthurian works, including *Sir Gawain and the Green Knight* and Sir Thomas Malory's *Morte Darthur*, are less indebted to English sources than to French romances, whether written on the Continent or in England by authors such as Marie de France and Thomas of Britain. Chaucer borrowed the conventions and imagery of the love poetry of Guillaume de Machaut and Eustache Deschamps, and even the meter of his earlier poetry derives from their French octosyllabic couplets. To a lesser extent, influences from Italy can be seen in Chaucer's use of Dante's *Divine Comedy*, and his extensive borrowing from Petrarch and Boccaccio. Such continental vernacular literatures infiltrated even the Celtic cultures, as we see in the witty mix of Welsh and European traditions in the poems of Dafydd ap Gwilym.

French literature was critical in the rise of courtly literature in Middle English. Many English Arthurian works . . . are less indebted to English sources than to French romances . . .

If such writers and records reflect the higher achievements of education in England of the twelfth century and later, literacy was also diffusing in wider circles and new venues. In a society like England's that continued to produce considerable oral and public literature, indeed, the divide between literacy and illiteracy was always unstable and permeable. A secular aristocrat might have a clerk read to him or her; an urbanite could attend and absorb parts of public rituals that involved poems and orations; even a peasant would be able to pick up Latin tags from sermons or the liturgy. Thus a fourteenth-century writer like William Langland could expect his wide and mixed audience to recognize at least some of the Latin phrases he used along with English; and Chaucer could imagine a character like the Wife of

Bath who, at best semiliterate, could still quote bits of the Latin liturgy. Access to texts and the self-awareness fostered by private reading may have helped promote the social ambitions and disruptions within the mercantile and even peasant classes during the later Middle Ages.

Women, Courtliness, and Courtly Love

Access to books also increased the self-awareness of women. Possession of books that encouraged prayer and private devotion, such as psalters and Books of Hours, appears to have facilitated early language training in the home. The many images in manuscripts of women reading—especially the Virgin Mary and her mother, Saint Anne—have interesting implications for our understanding of women's literacy and cultural roles. (See for instance the illumination from the *Bedford Hours*, Color Plate 10.) A number of aristocratic Norman and Angevin women received good educations at convents. Women in the holy life possessed at least some literacy, though this often may have been minimal indeed. Even well-educated women were more likely to read English or French than Latin, with the exception of liturgical books.

The roles of women in the society and cultural imagination of post-Conquest England are complex and contradictory. No Anglo-Norman woman held ecclesiastical prestige like the Anglo-Saxon abbess Hilda or other Anglo-Saxon holy women. Women's power seems to have declined in the long term, both in worldly affairs and in the church, as the Normans consolidated their hold on England and imposed their order on society. Nevertheless, ambitious women could have great influence, especially when they siezed upon moments of disruption. In civil strife over the succession to King Henry I, the Empress Matilda organized an army, issued royal writs, and in the end guaranteed the accession of her son Henry II. If Henry II's wife, Eleanor of Aquitaine, spent the latter decades of her husband's reign under virtual house arrest, it was largely because she had conspired with her sons to raise an army against her own husband.

Despite the limitations of their actual power, women were the focus, often the worshiped focus, of much of the best imaginative literature of the twelfth and thirteenth centuries; and women were central to the social rituals we associate with courtliness and the idea of courtly love. Despite her later imprisonment, Eleanor of Aquitaine was a crucial influence in the diffusion of courtly ideas from the continent, especially the south of France; and among the great writers of the century was Marie de France, who was probably related to Henry II. Scholars continue to debate whether the observances of "courtly love" were in fact widely practiced and whether its worship of women was empowering or restrictive: the image of the distant, adored lady implies immobility and even silence on her part. Certainly lyrics and narratives that embody courtly values are widespread, even if they often question what they celebrate; and the ideals of courtliness may have had as great an impact through these imaginative channels as through actual enactment.

Despite the limitations of their actual power, women were the focus, often the worshiped focus, of much of the best imaginative literature . . .

Grotesques and a Courtly Scene, from the *Ormesby Psalter*, c. 1310–1325.

The ideas and rituals of courtliness reach back to Greek and Roman models of controlled and stylized behavior in the presence of great power. In the Middle Ages, values of discretion and modesty also may have filtered into the secular world from the rigidly disciplined setting of the monasteries. As the society of western Europe took on a certain degree of order in the eleventh and twelfth centuries, courtly attainments began to converge and even compete with simple martial prowess in the achievement of worldly power. The presence of large numbers of armed and ambitious men at the great courts provided at once an opportunity for courtly behavior and the threat of its disruption.

Whatever its historical reality, courtly love as a literary concept had an immense influence. In this it adopted the vocabulary of two distinct traditions: the veneration of the Virgin Mary and the love poetry of Ovid and his heirs. Mariolatry, which has a particularly rich tradition in England, celebrates the perfection of Mary as a woman and mother, who undid the sins of Eve and now intercedes for fallen mankind. Ovid, with his celebration of sensuality and cynical instructions for achieving the lover's desire, provided medieval Europe with a whole catalog of love psychology and erotic persuasion.

Whatever its historical reality, courtly love as a literary concept had an immense influence.

The self-conscious command of fine manners, whether the proper way of hunting, dressing, addressing a superior, or wooing a lady, became a key mark of an aristocrat. Great reputations grew around courtly attainment, as in the legends that circulated about Richard I. Centuries later, the hero of *Sir Gawain and the Green Knight* is tested as much through his courtly behavior as through his martial bravery. A literature of etiquette emerged as early as the reign of Henry I in England and continued through the thirteenth century. In the court of Henry II, Daniel of Beccles wrote *Urbanus Magnus*, a verse treatise in Latin on courtesy. In this poem he offers detailed advice in many arenas of specific behavior at court: avoiding frivolity, giving brief counsel, and especially comporting oneself among the wealthy:

> Eating at the table of the rich, speak little
> Lest you be called a chatterbox among the diners.
> Be modest, make reverence your companion.

In a mildly misogynist passage, Daniel especially warns against becoming involved with the lord's wife, even if she makes an overture, as occurs in Marie de France's *Lanval*. Should this happen, Daniel offers polite evasive strategies, skills we see demonstrated in *Sir Gawain and the Green Knight*.

A Knight, early 14th century. This rubbing from a funerary brass depicts a knight as he presented himself to eternity, sheathed in chain mail and fully armed but with his hands joined in prayer. The dog at his feet is a symbol of fidelity.

Romance

Courtliness was expressed both in lyric poetry and in a wide range of vernacular narratives that we now loosely call "romances"—referring both to their genre and to the romance language in which they were first written. The Arthurian tradition, featured in this anthology, is only one of many romance traditions; others include the legends of Tristan and Isolde, Alexander, and Havelock the Dane. In romances that focus on courtly love, the hero's devotion to an unapproachable lady tends to elevate his character. Although many courtly romances conclude in a happy and acceptable marriage of hero and heroine, others such as Marie's *Lanval* warn of the dangers of transgressive love to the hero and his society. To the extent that they portray women as disruptive agents of erotic desire, some romances take on elements of the misogynist tradition that persisted in clerical thought alongside the adoration of the Virgin. Near the end of *Sir Gawain and the Green Knight*, even the courtly Gawain explodes in a virulent diatribe against women.

Love was not the only subject of romance, however. Stories of love and war typically lead the protagonists into encounters with the uncanny, the marvelous, the taboo. This is not so surprising when we recall the practices of medieval Christianity that brought the believer into daily contact with such miracles as the Eucharist; even chronicles of saints' lives regularly showed the divine will breaking miraculously into everyday life. We may say today that romance looses the hero and heroine onto the landscape of the private or social subconscious; a medieval writer might have stressed that nature itself is imbued with mystery both by God and by other, more shadowy, spiritual forces.

In romances, the line between the mundane and the extraordinary is often highly permeable: an episode may move swiftly from a simple ride to a meeting with a magical lady or malevolent dwarf, as often occurs in Thomas Malory. Romance also seems to be a form of imaginative literature in which medieval society could acknowledge the transgressions of its own ordering principles: adultery, incest, unmotivated martial violence. And it often revisits areas of belief and imagination that official culture long had put aside: *Sir Gawain and the Green Knight*, for instance, features a magical knight who can survive having his head cut off and a powerful aged woman who is called a goddess. Both characters reach back, however indirectly, to pre-Christian figures encountered in early Irish and Welsh stories.

The Return of English

The romances are another of the dense points of contact among the many languages and ethnicities of the medieval British Isles. These powerful and evocative narratives often feature figures of Celtic origin like the British King Arthur and his court who came to French- and English-language culture through the Latin *History* of Geoffrey of Monmouth. Such transmission is typical of the linguistic mix in post-Conquest England. The language of the aristocracy was French, used in government and law as well as in the nascent vernacular literature. A few conservative monasteries continued the famed *Anglo-Saxon Chronicle* in its original language after the Conquest. But increasingly English or an evolving form of Anglo-Saxon was the working language of the peasantry. Mixed-language households must have appeared as provincial Anglo-Saxon gentry began, quite quickly, to intermarry with the Normans and their descendants. The twelfth-century satirist Nigel of Canterbury (or "Wireker"), author of the *Mirror of Fools*, came from just such a mixed family.

Few writings in Middle English survive from the late twelfth century, and very little of value besides the extraordinary *Brut* of Layamon, which retranslates much of Geoffrey of Monmouth's *History* from a French version. A manuscript containing the earliest English lyric in this collection, the thirteenth-century *Cuckoo Song*, can suggest the linguistic complexity of the era: it contains lyrics in English and French, and instructions for performance in Latin.

English began to reenter the world of official discourse in the thirteenth century. Communications between the church and the laity took place increasingly in English, and by the late 1250s, Archbishop Sewal of York tended to reject papal candidates for bishoprics if they did not have good English. In 1258 King Henry III issued a proclamation in Latin, French, and English, though the circumstances were unusual. Teaching glossaries include a growing number of English words, as well as the French traditionally used to explain difficult Latin.

The fourteenth century inaugurated a distinct change in the status of English, however, as it became the language of parliament and a growing number of governmental activities. We hear of Latin being taught in the 1340s through English rather than French. In 1362 a statute tried (but failed) to switch the language of law courts from French to English, and in 1363 Parliament was opened in English. The period also witnesses tremendous activity in translating a wide range of works into English, including Chaucer's version of Boethius' *Consolation of Philosophy* and the Wycliffite translations of the Bible, completed by 1396. Finally, at the close of the century, the Rolls of Parliament record in Latin the overthrow of Richard II, but they feature Henry IV (in what was probably a self-consciously symbolic gesture) claiming the throne in a brief, grave speech in English and promising to uphold "the gude lawes and custumes of the Rewme."

The reemergence of English allowed an extraordinary flowering of vernacular literature, most notably the achievements of Chaucer, Langland, and the anonymous genius who wrote *Sir Gawain and the Green Knight*. It would be more accurate, nevertheless, to speak of the reemergence of "Englishes" in the second half of the fourteenth century. The language scholars now call Middle English divides into four quite distinct major dialects in different regions of the island. These dialects were in many ways mutually unintelligible, so that Chaucer, who was from London in the Southeast Midlands, might have been hard-pressed to understand *Sir Gawain and the Green Knight*, written in the West Midlands near Lancashire. (Certainly Chaucer was aware of dialects and mimics some northern vocabulary in his *Canterbury Tales*.) London was the center of government and commerce in this era and later the place of early book printing, which served to stabilize the language. Thus Chaucer's dialect ultimately dominated and developed into modern English. Therefore English-speaking students today can read Chaucer in the original without much difficulty, whereas Langland's *Piers Plowman* is very challenging and *Sir Gawain* may seem virtually a foreign tongue. As a result, the latter two works are offered in translation in this anthology. (For a practical guide to Chaucer's Middle English, also helpful in reading some of the lyrics and plays in this section, see pages 315–17.)

Color Plate 1 Stylized Beasts and Sacred Words. First page of the Gospel of Matthew, from the *Lindisfarne Gospels*, c. 698. This illustrated gospel book was made on the "holy island" of Lindisfarne off the coast of Northumberland, partly in honor of St. Cuthbert, who had died there 11 years earlier and whose cult was fast developing at the time. The manuscript reflects an extraordinary flowering of artistic production during these years, the meeting of world cultures that occurred in Northumbrian monastic life: Mediterranean Latin language and imagery, Celtic interlace, and Germanic animal motifs. In the 10th century an Anglo-Saxon translation was added in the margins and between the lines.

Color Plate 2 A Prince's Burial Horde. Gold buckle, from the Sutton Hoo ship-burial, c. 625–630. Fragments of a remarkably preserved ship-burial, probably for an Anglo-Saxon king, were discovered among other burial mounds at Sutton Hoo, in Suffolk, England, in 1939. The burial mound contained numerous coins and 41 objects in gold, among them this magnificent buckle. Stylized animal heads (including two dragons in the circle at bottom) invite comparison with the powerful animal imagery in *Beowulf*. Other objects in the ship include two silver spoons inscribed "Saul" and "Paul," signs of the mixing of pagan practices and Christian influences in this era. *(Copyright © The Trustees of the British Museum.)*

Color Plate 3 Celtic Arts and Christian Ceremony. The Ardagh Chalice, c. 9th century. This greatest surviving piece of medieval Celtic metalwork was found near the site of an ancient fort at Ardagh, in County Limerick in the southwest of Ireland. Measuring 9.5 inches across and 7 inches tall, the chalice was probably used for wine on great holidays like Easter, when laypeople took Communion. In the 7th century, the learned Irish monk Adamnan had described the chalice of the Last Supper as a silver cup with two opposite handles. The Ardagh Chalice is very similar. It is made of silver alloy, magnificently decorated with gilt and enamel. Its elaborate interlace decoration uses a wide range of Celtic motifs, including fearsomely toothed animal heads. In a band running around the entire bowl are the names of the 12 apostles, further linking its liturgical role to the Last Supper. *(National Museum of Ireland.)*

Color Plate 4 A Map of Multi-Ethnic Britain. Map of England, from Matthew Paris's *Historia Major*, mid-13th century. A monk of St. Albans, Matthew Paris wrote a monumental *History of England*, of which two illustrated copies in his own hand survive. Matthew's richly detailed map of England, including counties and major towns, illustrates the geographical knowledge of his day. It further suggests how alert he was to the ethnic divisions that still crossed his island and to the settlements and invasions, both mythic and actual, that had given rise to them. His inscription near the depiction of Hadrian's Wall, for example, informs us that the wall "once divided the English and the Picts." Recalling the claim that the original Britons were Trojan refugees, he writes about Wales (left center): "The people of this region are descended from the followers of Brutus." The story of Arthur's conception may have led Paris to identify Tintagel ("Tintaiol," lower left). Matthew also links geography and racial character, as in his comment on northern Scotland (top center): "A mountainous, woody region producing an uncivilized people." *(Copyright © British Library Board. All Rights Reserved.)*

Color Plate 5 Ethnic Hostilities and the Sufferings of Christ. *Passion Scenes*, from the *Winchester Psalter*, 1150–1160. A series of full-page miniatures of crucial scenes from the Bible precedes the Psalter texts of this manuscript. The page reproduced here depicts scenes of the betrayal and flagellation of Christ. The vividly drawn images show the clinging drapery and exaggerated expressions typical of the manuscript; equally exaggerated are the African and Semitic features of some of the tormentors, associating them with peoples who were exotic or reviled in 12th-century England. Some of the original richness of color of this manuscript has been lost through damp, but also because blue pigment has been scraped off, presumably for reuse—a sign of how costly was the making of such manuscripts. *(Copyright © British Library Board. All Rights Reserved.)*

Color Plate 6 The Storytellers of the Round Table. *King Arthur and His Knights*, from a manuscript of the *Prose Lancelot*, late 13th century. This miniature appears in a manuscript of French prose Arthurian romances, which were also widely known in England. Here, King Arthur asks his knights to tell about their adventures on the quest for the Holy Grail. *(Beinecke Rare Book and Manuscript Library, Yale University.)*

Color Plate 7 Language Miracles at the Birth of Christ. *Annunciation to the Shepherds* (top) and *Nativity Scene* (bottom), from *The Holkham Bible Picture Book*, c. 1325–1330. This vividly illustrated manuscript depicts episodes from the Bible, adding events from later Christian legends. Crowded scenes are vigorous and full of gesture; they may reflect contact with liturgical drama and look forward to vernacular enactments such as the *Second Play of the Shepherds*. Short rhyming narratives above each picture mix up the major languages of early 14th-century England. At first the shepherds cannot understand the angel's Latin "*Gloria in excelsis*"; in Anglo-French they say "Glum? Glo? That means nothing. Let's go there, we'll understand better." At the scene of the Nativity, below, Middle English breaks in and "Songen alle with one stevene [voice]," though the shepherds can now sing famous Latin hymns: "*Gloria in excelsis deo*" and "*Te deum laudamus*." Both the images and French and Middle English text mediate between the learned clerical class and the wealthy laypeople who were the manuscript's intended audience. *(Copyright © British Library Board. All Rights Reserved.)*

Color Plate 8 Symbols of Royal Power. *Richard II with His Regalia*, 1394–1395. Richard himself commissioned this splendid life-size and unusually lifelike portrait soon after the death of his beloved first wife, Anne of Bohemia. It was probably mounted at the back of the King's private pew at Westminster Abbey in London, but it also may suggest his wish to be perpetually near Anne, who was entombed nearby. At the same time, the throne, crown, orb, and scepter are all signs of Richard's sense of kingship and secular authority. *(Copyright © The Dean and Chapter of Westminster.)*

Color Plate 9 The Wife of Bath Begins Her Tale. From the Ellesmere manuscript of Chaucer's *Canterbury Tales*, 1405–1410. One of the two earliest surviving manuscripts of the *Tales*, it was owned for centuries by the Egerton family, who became Earls of Ellesmere in the nineteenth-century. The Ellesmere Chaucer was probably made in London, by then the center of book production in England. Its elaborate decoration and illustration are all the more striking, given how few Middle English texts received such treatment. The portrait of the Wife of Bath is positioned to highlight the beginning of her tale. Her red clothing, whip, and large hat follow details of her description in the *General Prologue* of the *Tales*, and her own words in the prologue to her tale. The grandeur of the treatment of text and decoration in this manuscript—clearly meant both for display and reading—reflect the speed with which Chaucer became a "canonical" author in the years after his death in 1400, and perhaps the wish of wealthy patrons to associate themselves and their interests with work. It is partly the same wish that ultimately led the American railroad tycoon Henry E. Huntington to buy the manuscript in 1917 and leave it to his library in San Marino, California. *(Copyright © The Huntington Library Art Collection & Botanical Gardens, San Marino California/Superstock, Inc.)*

Color Plate 10 The Virgin Mary Learns to Read. *Anne, Duchess of Bedford, Kneeling Before the Virgin Mary and Saint Anne*, from the *Bedford Hours*, early 15th century. A book of hours was a prayerbook used by laypeople for private devotion. The *Bedford Hours* was produced in a Paris workshop for the Duke of Bedford, a brother of Henry V, and his wife, Anne of Burgundy. Here, Saint Anne is shown teaching her daughter, the Virgin Mary, to read; another book lies open on a lectern in front of the kneeling Anne of Burgundy. *(Copyright © British Library Board. All Rights Reserved.)*

Not only are *Piers Plowman* and *Sir Gawain* written in dialects different from that of Chaucer's London, they also employ a quite distinct poetic style which descends from the alliterative meter of Old English poetry, based on repetitions of key consonants and on general patterns of stress. By contrast, the rhymed syllabic style used by poets like Chaucer developed under the influence of medieval French poetry and its many lyric forms. Fourteenth-century alliterative poetry was part of a revival that occurred in the North and West of the country, at a time when the form would have seemed old fashioned to many readers in the South. In the next two centuries, in a region even more distant from London, alliterative poetry or its echoes persisted in the Middle Scots poetry of William Dunbar, Robert Henryson, and Gavin Douglas.

Politics and Society in the Fourteenth Century

The fourteenth-century authors wrote in a time of enormous ferment, culturally and politically as well as linguistically. During the second half of the fourteenth century, new social and theological movements shook past certainties about the divine right of kings, the division of society among three estates, the authority of the church, and the role of women. An optimistic backward view can see in that time the struggle of the peasantry for greater freedom, the growing power of the Commons in Parliament, and the rise of a mercantile middle class. These changes often appeared far darker at the time, though, with threatening, even apocalyptic implications, as can be seen in *Piers Plowman*.

The forces of nature also cast a shadow across the century. In a time that never produced large agricultural surpluses, poor harvests led to famine in the second and third decades of the century, and an accompanying deflation drove people off the land. In 1348 the Black Death arrived in England, killing at least thirty-five percent of the population by 1350. Plague struck violently three more times before 1375, emptying whole villages. Overall, as much as half the population may have died.

In 1348 the Black Death arrived in England, killing at least thirty-five percent of the population by 1350.

The kingship was already in trouble. After the consolidation of royal power under Henry II and the Angevins in the twelfth century, the regional barons began to reassert their power. In a climactic confrontation in 1215, they forced King John to sign the Magna Carta, guaranteeing (in theory at least) their traditional rights and privileges as well as due process in law and judgment by peers. In the fourteenth century the monarchy came under considerable new pressures. Edward II (1307–1327) was deposed by one of his barons, Roger de Mortimer, and with the connivance of his own queen, Isabella. His son Edward III had a long and initially brilliant reign, marked by great military triumphs in a war against France, but the conflict dragged on so long that it became known as the Hundred Years' War. Edward III's reign was marked at home by famine, deflation, and then, most horribly, plague. His later years were marked by premature senility and control by a court circle. These years were further darkened by the death of that paragon of chivalry, Edward's son and heir-apparent, Edward "The Black Prince." Edward's successor, the Black Prince's son Richard II, launched a major peace initiative in the Hundred

Years' War and became a great patron of the arts, but he was also capable of great tyranny. In 1399 like his great-grandfather, he was deposed. An ancient and largely creaky royal bureaucracy had difficulty running a growing mercantile economy, and when royal justice failed to control crime in the provinces, it was increasingly replaced by local powers.

The aristocracy too experienced pressures from the increased economic power of the urban merchants and from the peasants' efforts to exploit labor shortages and win better control over their land. The aristocrats responded with fierce, though only partly successful, efforts to limit wages and with stricter and more articulate divisions within society, even between the peerage and gentry. It is not clear, however, that fourteenth-century aristocrats perceived themselves as a threatened order. If anything, events may have pressed them toward a greater class cohesion, a more self-conscious pursuit of chivalric culture and values. The reign of Edward III saw the foundation of the royal Order of the Garter, a select group of nobles honored for their chivalric accomplishments as much as their power (the order is almost certainly evoked at the close of *Sir Gawain and the Green Knight*). Edward further exploited the Arthurian myth in public rituals such as tournaments and Round Tables. The ancient basis of the feudal tie, land tenure, began to give way to contract and payment in the growing, hierarchicalized retinues of the period. These were still lifelong relationships between lord and retainer, nevertheless, and contemporary historians of aristocratic sympathies like Jean Froissart idealize an ongoing community of chivalric conduct that could reach even across combating nations.

The second estate, the church, was also troubled—in part, paradoxically, because of the growing and active piety of the laity. Encouraged by the annual confession that had been required since the Fourth Lateran Council of 1215, laymen increasingly took control of their own spiritual lives. But the new emphasis on confession also led to clerical corruption. Mendicant (begging) friars, armed with manuals of penance, spread across the countryside to confess penitents in their own homes and sometimes accepted money for absolving them. Whether or not these abuses were truly widespread, they inspired much anticlerical satire—as is reflected in the works of Chaucer and Langland—and the Church's authority diminished in the process. The traditional priesthood, if better educated, was also more worldly than in the past, increasingly pulled from parish service into governmental bureaucracy; it too faced widespread literary satire. Well aware of clerical venality, the church nevertheless fearfully resisted the criticisms and innovations of "reforming clerics" like John Wyclif and his supporters among the gentry, the "Lollard knights." The church's control over religious experience was further complicated and perhaps undermined by the rise of popular mysticism, among both the clergy and the laity, which was difficult to contain within the traditional ecclesiastical hierarchy. Mystical writing by people as varied as Richard Rolle, Julian of Norwich, the anonymous author of *The Cloud of Unknowing*, and the emotive Margery Kempe all promulgate the notion of an individual's direct experience of the divine. Finally, and on a much broader scale, all of Christian Europe was rocked by the Great Schism of 1378, when believers faced the disconcerting spectacle of two popes ruling simultaneously.

The third estate, the commoners, was the most problematic and rapidly evolving of the three in the fourteenth century. The traditional division of medieval society into three estates had no place for the rising mercantile bourgeoisie and grouped them with the peasants who worked the land. In fact the new urban wealthy formed a class quite of their own. Patrons and consumers of culture, they also served in the royal bureaucracy under Edward III, as is illustrated by the career of Geoffrey Chaucer who came from just such a background. Yet only the wealthiest married into the landed gentry, and poor health conditions in the cities made long mercantile dynasties uncommon. Cities in anything like a modern sense were few and retained rural features. Houses often had gardens, even orchards, and pigs (and pig dung) filled the narrow, muddy streets. Only magnates built in stone; only they and ecclesiastical institutions had the luxury of space and privacy. Otherwise, cities were crowded and dirty—the suburbs especially disreputable—and venues for communicable disease.

The peasants too had a new sense of class cohesion. Events had already loosened the traditional bond of serfs to the land on which they were born, and the plagues further shifted the relative economic power of landowning and labor. As peasants found they could demand better pay, fiercely repressive laws were passed to stop them. These and other discontents, like the arrival of foreign labor and technologies, led to the Rising of 1381 (also known as the Peasants' Revolt). Led by literate peasants and renegade priests, the rebels attacked aristocrats, foreigners, and some priests. They were swiftly and violently put down, but the event was nevertheless a watershed and haunted the minds of the English.

Led by literate peasants and renegade priests, the rebels attacked aristocrats, foreigners, and some priests.

When one leader of the revolt, the priest John Ball, cited Langland's fictional character Piers Plowman with approval, Langland reacted with dismay and revised his poem to emphasize the proper place of peasants. Even more conservative, Chaucer's friend John Gower wrote a horrified Latin allegory on the revolt, *Vox Clamantis* (*The Voice of One Crying*), where he compared the rebels to beasts. By contrast, Chaucer virtually ignored the revolt, aside from a brief comic reference in *The Nun's Priest's Tale*; it remains unclear, though, whether Chaucer's silence reflects comfortable bourgeois indifference or stems from deep anxiety and discomfort. At the same time, these disruptions introduced a period of cultural ferment, and the mercantile middle class also provided a creative force, appearing (though not without some nervous condescension) in some of Chaucer's most enduring characters like *The Canterbury Tales*' Merchant, the Wife of Bath, and the Miller.

It is both from this new middle class and from the established upper class that wider choices in the lives of women emerged in the later Middle Ages. Their social and political power had been curtailed both by clerical antifeminism and by the increasingly centralized government during the twelfth and thirteenth centuries. Starting in the fourteenth century, however, women began to regain an increased voice and presence. Among the aristocracy, Edward II's wife Isabella was an important player in events that brought about the king's deposition. And at the end of the century, Edward III's mistress Alice Perrers was widely criticized for her avarice and her influence on the aging king (for instance by William Langland who refers to her in the allegorical figure Lady Meed).

Women were also important in the spread of lay literacy among the middle class. In France, Christine de Pizan reexamined whole areas of her culture, especially ancient and biblical narrative, from a feminist perspective; her work was known and translated in England. Important autobiographical works were composed in Middle English by Julian of Norwich and Margery Kempe. Julian was an anchoress, living a cloistered religious life but able to speak to visitors such as Margery herself; Margery was an illiterate but prosperous townswoman, daughter of a mayor, who dictated to scribes her experiences of wifehood and rebellion against it, of travel to holy places, and of spiritual growth. Still, for the representation of women's voices in this period we are largely dependent on the fictional creations of men. Chaucer's famous Wife of Bath, for instance, strikes many modern readers as an articulate voice opposing women's repression and expressing their ambitions, but for all her critique of the antifeminist stereotypes of the church, she is in many ways their supreme embodiment. And in a number of Middle English lyrics, probably by men, the woman's voice may evoke scorn rather than pity as she laments her seduction and abandonment by a smooth-talking man, usually a cleric.

The Spread of Book Culture in the Fifteenth Century

Geoffrey Chaucer died in 1400, a convenient date for those who like their eras to end with round numbers. Certainly literary historians have often closed off the English Middle Ages with Chaucer and left the fifteenth century as a sort of drab and undefined waiting period before the dawn of the Renaissance. Yet parts of fifteenth-century England are sites of vital and burgeoning literary culture. Book ownership spread more and more widely. Already in the late fourteenth century, Chaucer had imagined a fictional Clerk of Oxford with a solid collection of university texts despite his relative poverty. More of the urban bourgeoisie bought books and even had appealing collections assembled for them. When printing came to England in the later fifteenth century, books became even more available, though still not cheap.

Whether in manuscript or print, a swiftly growing proportion of these books was in English. The campaigns of Henry V in the second decade of the fifteenth century and his death in 1422 mark England's last great effort to reclaim the old Norman and Angevin territories on the continent. With the loss of all but a scrap of this land and the decline of French as a language of influence, these decades consolidate a notion of cultural and nationalistic Englishness. The Lancastrian kings, Henry the Fourth, Fifth, and Sixth, seem to have adopted English as the medium for official culture and patronized translators like Lydgate. Later in the period William Caxton made a great body of French and English texts available to aristocratic and middle-class readers, both by translating and by diffusing them in the new medium of print.

Whether in manuscript or print, a swiftly growing proportion of these books was in English.

Ancient aristocratic narratives continued to evolve, as in Thomas Malory's retelling of the Arthurian story in his *Morte Darthur*, one of the books printed by Caxton. Malory works mostly from French prose versions but trims back much of the exploration of love and the uncanny; the result is a recharged tale of chivalric battle and familial and political intrigue. Other continental and local traditions are revived in another courtly setting by a group of Scots poets including William Dunbar and Robert Henryson.

As more and more commoners had educational and financial access to books, they also participated in a lively public literary culture in towns and cities. The fifteenth century sees the flowering of the great dramatic "mystery cycles," sets of plays on religious themes produced and in part performed by craft guilds of larger towns in the Midlands and North. Included here are two brilliant samples, the play of the *Crucifixion* from York and *The Second Play of the Shepherds* from Wakefield. Probably written by clerics, these plays are nonetheless dense with the preoccupations of contemporary working people and enriched by implicit analogies between the lives of their actors and the biblical events they portray. Lyrics and political poems continue to flourish. Sermons remain a popular and widespread form of religious instruction and literary production. And highly literary public rituals, such as Henry V's triumphal civic entries as he returned from his French campaigns, are part of Lancastrian royal propaganda.

By the time Caxton was editing and printing Malory in 1485 with an eye to sales and profit, over eight hundred years had passed since Caedmon is said to have composed his first Christian hymn under angelic direction. The idea of the poet had moved from a version of magician and priest to something more like a modern author; and the dominant model of literary transmission was shifting from listening to an oral performance to reading a book privately. Chaucer, that most bookish of poets, is a case in point. Many of his early poems refer to the pleasures of reading, not only for instruction but even as a mere pastime, often to avoid insomnia. He opens the dream vision *The Parliament of Fowls* with the poet reading a classical Latin text, Cicero's *Dream of Scipio*. Chaucer, of course, read his books and disseminated his own work in handwritten manuscript; in his humorous lyric *To His Scribe Adam* he expresses his frustration with copyists who might mistranscribe his words.

Despite such private bookishness, however, a more public and oral literary culture never disappeared from medieval Britain. Considerable interdependence between oral and literate modes of communication remained; poetry was both silently read and orally performed. In *The Canterbury Tales*, for instance, when the pilgrim Chaucer apologizes for the bawdiness of *The Miller's Tale*, he suggests that if the listener/reader does not like what he *hears*, he should simply turn the *page* and choose another tale. At the same time, literate clerics practiced what we might call learned orality, through lectures or disputations at Oxford and Cambridge or from the pulpit in a more popular setting. Langland imitates such sophisticated oral practice in the theological debates in *Piers Plowman*, and Chaucer uses the sermon form in *The Wife of Bath's Prologue*, *The Pardoner's Tale*, and *The Parson's Tale*. The popular orality of minstrel performance, harking back however distantly to the world of the Anglo-Saxon *scop* and the Irish *fili*, was also exploited with great self-consciousness by literate poets. Langland expresses harsh disapproval of those minstrels who were mere entertainers, undercutting the serious work of preachers. *Sir Gawain and the Green Knight* presents itself as an oral performance, based on a tale that the narrator has heard recited. By contrast, Chaucer gently twits minstrels in his marvelous parody of popular romance, *Sir Thopas*. Chaucer remains a learned poet whose greatest achievement, paradoxically, was the presentation of fictional oral performances—the tale-telling of the Canterbury pilgrims.

The speed with which communication technologies are changing in our own era has heightened our awareness of such changes in the past. We are now closing the era of the book and moving into the era of the endlessly malleable electronic text. In many ways the means by which we have come to receive and transmit information—television, radio, CD-ROM, Internet—mix orality and literacy in a fashion wholly new yet also intriguingly reminiscent of the later Middle Ages. In contrast to the seeming fixity of texts in the intervening centuries, contemporary literary culture may be recovering the sense of textual and cultural fluidity that brought such dynamism to literary creation in the Middle Ages.

. . . the means by which we have come to receive and transmit information . . . mix orality and literacy in a fashion wholly new yet also intriguingly reminiscent of the later Middle Ages.

For additional resources on the Middle Ages, including an interactive timeline of the period, go to *The Longman Anthology of British Literature* Web site at www.myliteraturekit .com.

BEFORE THE NORMAN CONQUEST

Beowulf

Beowulf has come down to us as if by chance, for it is preserved only in a single manuscript now in the British Library, Cotton Vitellius A.xv, which almost perished in a fire in 1731. An anonymous poem in the West Saxon dialect of Old English, it may stretch back as early as the late eighth century, although recent scholars think the version we now have was composed within one hundred years of its transcription in the late tenth century. If the later date is correct, this first "English epic" could have appealed to one of the Viking kings who ruled in northern and eastern England. This would help explain a king's burial at sea, a Viking practice, that occurs early in the poem (page 37), and the setting of most of the poem's action in Scandinavia (see map, page 33). Although it was studied by a few antiquarians during the early modern period, *Beowulf* remained virtually unknown until its first printing in 1815, and it was only in the twentieth century that it achieved a place in the canon, not just as a cultural artifact or a good adventure story but as a philosophical epic of great complexity and power.

Several features of *Beowulf* make its genre problematic: the vivid accounts of battles with monsters link it to the folktale, and the sense of sorrow for the passing of worldly things mark it as elegiac. Nevertheless, it is generally agreed to be the first postclassical European epic. Like the *Iliad* and the *Odyssey*, it is a primary epic, originating in oral tradition and recounting the legendary wars and exploits of its audience's tribal ancestors from the heroic age.

The values of Germanic tribal society are indeed central to *Beowulf*. The tribal lord was held to ideals of extraordinary martial valor. More practically, he rewarded his successful followers with treasure that symbolized their mutual obligations. A member of the lord's *comitatus*—his band of warriors—was expected to follow a rigid code of heroic behavior stressing

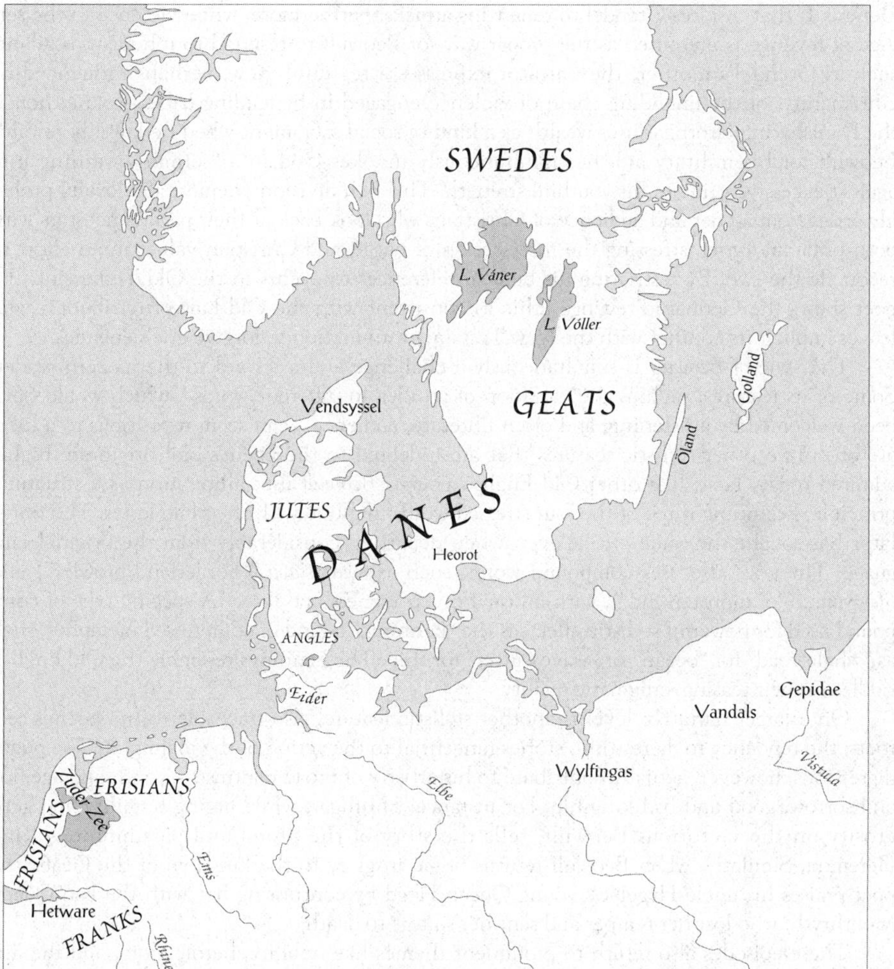

Peoples and places in *Beowulf*, after F. Klaeber.

bravery, loyalty, and willingness to avenge lord and comrades at any cost. He would suffer the shame of exile if he should survive his lord in battle; the speaker of *The Wanderer* (pages 172–75) may be such a man. Such values are explicitly invoked at the end of *Beowulf*, when Wiglaf, the hero's only loyal retainer, upbraids his comrades for having abandoned Beowulf to the dragon: he says that their prince wasted his war gear on them, and predicts the demise of their people, the Geats, once their ancient enemies, the Swedes, hear that Beowulf is dead.

Beowulf offers an extraordinary double perspective, however. First, for all its acceptance of the values of the pagan heroic code, it also refers to Christian concepts that in many cases conflict with them. Although all characters in the poem—Danes, Swedes, and Geats, as well as the monsters—are pagan, the monster Grendel is described as descended from Cain and destined for hell. It is the joyous song of creation at Hrothgar's banquet, reminiscent of

Genesis 1, that inspires Grendel to renew his attacks. Furthermore, while violence in the service of revenge is presented as the proper way for Beowulf to respond to inhuman assailants such as Grendel's mother, the narrator expresses a regretful view, perhaps influenced by Christianity, of the unending chain of violence engaged in by feuding tribes. And although the Danish king Hrothgar uses wealth as a kind of social sacrament when he lavishly rewards Beowulf for his military aid, he simultaneously invokes God in a "sermon" warning him against excessive pride in his youthful strength. This rich division of emotional loyalty probably arises from a poet and audience of Christians who look back at their pagan ancestors with both pride and grief, stressing the intersection of pagan and Christian values in an effort to reconcile the two. By restricting his biblical references to events in the Old Testament, the poet shows the Germanic revenge ethic as consistent with the Old Law of retribution, and leaves implicit its conflict with the New Testament injunction to forgive one's enemies.

The style *of Beowulf* is simultaneously a challenge and a reward to the modern reader. Some of its features, such as the variation of an idea in different words—which would have been welcomed by a listening, and often illiterate, audience—can seem repetitious to a literate one. Two other stylistic features that are indebted to the poem's oral origin are highly admired today. First, like other Old English poems, *Beowulf* uses alliteration as a structural principle, beginning three of the four stressed words in a line with the same letter. The translator has sought the same effect, even when departing considerably from the original language. The poet also uses compound words, such as *mearcstapa* ("borderland-prowler") and *fifelcynnes* ("of monsterkind"), with unusual inventiveness and force. A specific type of compound used for powerful stylistic effects is the "kenning," a kind of compressed metaphor, such as "whale-road" for "ocean" or "wave-cutter" for ship. The kennings resemble the Old English riddles in their teasing, enigmatic quality.

On a larger narrative level is another stylistic feature, also traceable to the poem's oral roots: the tendency to digress into stories tangential to the action of the main plot. The poet's digressions, however, actually contribute to his artistry of broad contrasts—youth and age, joy and sorrow, good and bad kingship. For instance, Hrothgar, while urging humility and generosity on the victorious Beowulf, tells the story of the proud and parsimonious King Heremod. Similarly, when Beowulf returns home in glory to the kingdom of the Geats, the poet praises his uncle Hygelac's young Queen Hygd by contrasting her with the bad Queen Modthryth, who lost her temper and sent her suitors to death.

These episodes also return to prominent themes like nobility, heroic glory, and the distribution of treasure. Such return to key themes, as well as the poem's formulaic repetition and stylistic variation, all bear comparison to insular art of its time. As seen in the page from the *Book of Kells* illustrated on page 14, the dense repetition of lines and intertwined curves, even zoomorphic shapes (often called interlace) competes for attention with the central image of Saint John. This intricately crafted biblical image, like the royal treasure from the Sutton Hoo ship-burial (Color Plate 2), help remind us that the extraordinary artistic accomplishments of Anglo-Saxon culture went hand-in-hand with its nostalgia for heroic violence.

The poet uses digression and repetition in an especially subtle way to foreshadow dark events to come. To celebrate Beowulf's victory over Grendel, the bard at Hrothgar's hall sings of events of generations earlier, in which a feud caused the deaths of a Danish princess's brother and son. Although this story has nothing to do with the main plot of the poem, there is an implied parallel a few lines later, when, ominously, Hrothgar's queen Wealtheow hints that her husband's nephew Hrothulf should treat her young sons honorably, remembering the favors Hrothgar has shown him, and soon after, urges Beowulf also to be kind them. The original audience would have known that after Hrothgar's death, his queen will suffer a disaster like that of the princess in the song. The poet thus applies his broad principle of comparison and contrast to complex narrative situations as well as to simpler concepts such as good and

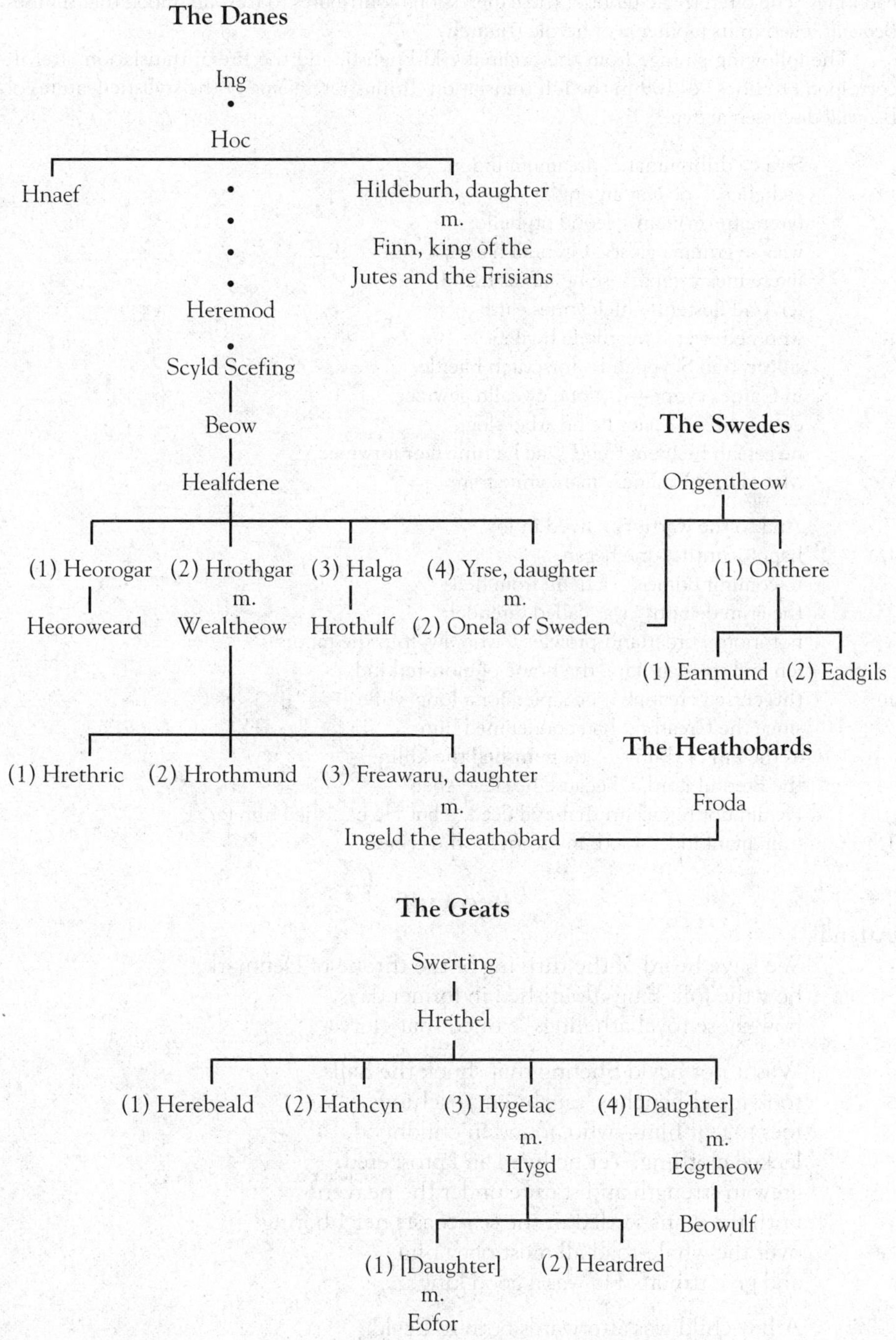

Royal genealogies of the Northern European tribes according to the *Beowulf* text.

bad kings. The often tragic tenor of these digressions contributes to the dark mood that suffuses *Beowulf*, even in its moments of heroic triumph.

The following passage from the original Old English, and the literal translation after it, correspond to lines 98–109 in the full translation. It illustrates some of the stylistic features of *Beowulf* discussed above.*

Swā ðā drihtguman drēamum lifdon,
ēadiglice, oð ðæt ān ongan
fyrene fre(m)man fēond on helle;
wæs se grimma gǣst Grendel hāten,
mǣre mearcstapa, sē þe mōras hēold,
fen ond fæsten; fifẹlcynnes eard
wonsāeli wer weardode hwile,
siþðan him Scyppend forscrifen haefde
in Cāines cynne— þone cwealm gewraec
ēce Drihten, þaes þe hē Ābel slōg;
ne gefeah hē þǣre fǣðe, ac hē hine feor forwraec,
Metod for þȳ māne mancynne fram.

And so the warriors lived in joy
happily until one began
to commit crimes, a fiend from hell
the grim demon was called Grendel,
notorious borderland-prowler who dwelt in the moors
fen and stronghold; the home of monsterkind
this cursed creature occupied for a long while
since the Creator had condemned him
as the kin of Cain— he punished the killing,
the Eternal Lord, because he slew Abel;
He did not rejoice in that evil deed, but He banished him far
from mankind, God, in return for the crime.

Beowulf[1]

Attend!

We have heard of the thriving of the throne of Denmark,
how the folk-kings flourished in former days,
how those royal athelings[2] earned that glory.

Was it not Scyld Shefing that shook the halls,
took mead-benches, taught encroaching
foes to fear him—who, found in childhood,
lacked clothing? Yet he lived and prospered,
grew in strength and stature under the heavens
until the clans settled in the sea-coasts neighboring
over the whale-road all must obey him
and give tribute. He was a good king!

A boy child was afterwards born to Scyld,
a young child in hall-yard, a hope for the people,

*The passage is taken from *Beowulf and the Fight at Finnsburg*, 3rd ed., ed. Frederick Klaeber (Boston: D. C. Heath, 1950). The translation is by Anne Schotter.

1. This translation, which captures the alliteration of the original Old English, is by Michael Alexander.

2. Noblemen.

sent them by God; the griefs long endured
were not unknown to Him, the harshness of years
without a lord. Therefore the life-bestowing
Wielder of Glory granted them this blessing.
Through the northern lands the name of Beow,
the son of Scyld, sprang widely.
For in youth an atheling should so use his virtue,
give with a free hand while in his father's house,
that in old age, when enemies gather,
established friends shall stand by him
and serve him gladly. It is by glorious action
that a man comes by honor in any people.

At the hour shaped for him Scyld departed,
the hero crossed into the keeping of his Lord.
They carried him out to the edge of the sea,
his sworn arms-fellows, as he had himself desired them
while he wielded his words, Warden of the Scyldings,
beloved folk-founder; long had he ruled.

A boat with a ringed neck rode in the haven,
icy, out-eager, the atheling's vessel,
and there they laid out their lord and master,
dealer of wound gold, in the waist of the ship,
in majesty by the mast. A mound of treasures
from far countries was fetched aboard her,
and it is said that no boat was ever more bravely fitted out
with the weapons of a warrior, war accoutrement,
swords and body-armor; on his breast were set
treasures and trappings to travel with him
on his far faring into the flood's sway.

This hoard was not less great than the gifts he had had
from those who at the outset had adventured him
over seas, alone, a small child.

High over head they hoisted and fixed
a gold *signum*,[3] gave him to the flood,
let the seas take him, with sour hearts
and mourning mood. Men under heaven's
shifting skies, though skilled in counsel,
cannot say surely who unshipped that cargo.

Then for a long space there lodged in the stronghold
Beowulf the Dane,[4] dear king of his people,
famed among nations—his father had taken
leave of the land—when late was born to him
the lord Healfdene, lifelong the ruler

3. Banner.

4. Not to be confused with Beowulf the Geat, the hero of the poem.

and war-feared patriarch of the proud Scyldings.
He next fathered four children
that leapt into the world, this leader of armies,
Heorogar and Hrothgar and Halga the Good;
and Ursula,[5] I have heard, who was Onela's queen,
knew the bed's embrace of the Battle-Scylfing.

Then to Hrothgar was granted glory in battle,
mastery of the field; so friends and kinsmen
gladly obeyed him, and his band increased
to a great company. It came into his mind
that he would command the construction
of a huge mead-hall, a house greater
than men on earth ever had heard of,
and share the gifts God had bestowed on him
upon its floor with folk young and old—
apart from public land and the persons of slaves.
Far and wide (as I heard) the work was given out
in many a tribe over middle earth,
the making of the mead-hall. And, as men reckon,
the day of readiness dawned very soon
for this greatest of houses. Heorot he named it
whose word ruled a wide empire.
He made good his boast, gave out rings,
arm-bands at the banquet. Boldly the hall reared
its arched gables; unkindled the torch-flame
that turned it to ashes. The time was not yet
when the blood-feud should bring out again
sword-hatred in sworn kindred.

It was with pain that the powerful spirit
dwelling in darkness endured that time,
hearing daily the hall filled
with loud amusement; there was the music of the harp,
the clear song of the poet, perfect in his telling
of the remote first making of man's race.
He told how, long ago, the Lord formed Earth,
a plain bright to look on, locked in ocean,
exulting established the sun and the moon
as lights to illumine the land-dwellers
and furnished forth the face of Earth
with limbs and leaves. Life He then granted
to each kind of creature that creeps and moves.

So the company of men led a careless life,
all was well with them: until One began
to encompass evil, an enemy from hell.
Grendel they called this cruel spirit,

5. The manuscript is defective at this point. "Ursula" is a name reconstructed from Scandinavian tradition.

the fell and fen his fastness was,
the march his haunt. This unhappy being
had long lived in the land of monsters
since the Creator cast them out
as kindred of Cain. For that killing of Abel
the eternal Lord took vengeance.
There was no joy of that feud: far from mankind
God drove him out for his deed of shame!
From Cain came down all kinds misbegotten
—ogres and elves and evil shades—
as also the Giants, who joined in long
wars with God. He gave them their reward.

With the coming of night came Grendel also,
sought the great house and how the Ring-Danes
held their hall when the horn had gone round.
He found in Heorot the force of nobles
slept after supper, sorrow forgotten,
the condition of men. Maddening with rage,
he struck quickly, creature of evil:
grim and greedy, he grasped on their pallets
thirty warriors, and away he was out of there,
thrilled with his catch: he carried off homeward
his glut of slaughter, sought his own halls.
As the day broke, with the dawn's light
Grendel's outrage was openly to be seen:
night's table-laughter turned to morning's
lamentation. Lord Hrothgar
sat silent then, the strong man mourned,
glorious king, he grieved for his thanes
as they read the traces of a terrible foe,
a cursed fiend. That was too cruel a feud,
too long, too hard!
                                        Nor did he let them rest
but the next night brought new horrors,
did more murder, manslaughter and outrage
and shrank not from it: he was too set on these things.

It was not remarked then if a man looked
for sleeping-quarters quieter, less central,
among the outer buildings; now openly shown,
the new hall-thane's hatred was manifest
and unmistakable. Each survivor
then kept himself at safer distance.

So Grendel became ruler; against right he fought,
one against all. Empty then stood
the best of houses, and for no brief space;
for twelve long winters torment sat
on the Friend of the Scyldings, fierce sorrows

and woes of every kind; which was not hidden
from the sons of men, but was made known
in grieving songs, how Grendel warred
long on Hrothgar, the harms he did him
through wretched years of wrong, outrage
and persecution. Peace was not in his mind
towards any companion of the court of Hrothgar,
the feud was not abated, the blood-price was unpaid.
Nor did any counselor have cause to look for
a bright man-price[6] at the murderer's hand:
the dark death-shadow drove always against them,
old and young; abominable
he watched and waited for them, walked nightlong
the misty moorland. Men know not
where hell's familiars fleet on their errands!

Again and again the enemy of men
stalking unseen, struck terrible
and bitter blows. In the black nights
he camped in the hall, under Heorot's gold roof;
yet he could not touch the treasure-throne
against the Lord's will, whose love was unknown to him.
A great grief was it for the Guardian of the Scyldings,
crushing to his spirit. The council lords
sat there daily to devise some plan,
what might be best for brave-hearted
Danes to contrive against these terror-raids.
They prayed aloud, promising sometimes
on the altars of their idols unholy sacrifices
if the Slayer of souls would send relief
to the suffering people.
Such was their practice,
a heathen hope; Hell possessed
their hearts and minds: the Maker was unknown to them,
the Judge of all actions, the Almighty was unheard of,
they knew not how to praise the Prince of Heaven,
the Wielder of Glory.
Woe to him who must
in terrible trial entrust his soul
to the embrace of the burning, banished from thought
of change or comfort! Cheerful the man
able to look to the Lord at his death-day,
to find peace in the Father's embrace!
This season rocked the son of Healfdene[7]

6. *Wergild*, a cash payment to the family in compensation for a person's death in Anglo-Saxon culture. Since it was considered an advance over violent revenge, Grendel is marked as uncivilized for refusing to acknowledge the practice.

7. Hrothgar. An example of the poet's frequent reference to a male character by the name of his father.

with swingeing sorrows; nor could the splendid man
put his cares from him. Too cruel the feud,
too strong and long-lasting, that struck that people,
a wicked affliction, the worst of nightmares!

This was heard of at his home by one of Hygelac's followers,
a good man among the Geats,[8] Grendel's raidings;
he was for main strength of all men foremost
that trod the earth at that time of day;
build and blood matched.
He bade a seaworthy
wave-cutter be fitted out for him; the warrior king
he would seek, he said, over swan's riding,
that lord of great name, needing men.
The wiser sought to dissuade him from voyaging
hardly or not at all, thought they held him dear;
they whetted his quest-thirst, watched omens.
The prince had already picked his men
from the folk's flower, the fiercest among them
that might be found. With fourteen men
he sought sound-wood; sea-wise Beowulf
led them right down to the land's edge.

Time running on, she rode the waves now,
hard in by headland. Harnessed warriors
stepped on her stem; setting tide churned
sea with sand, soldiers carried
bright mail-coats to the mast's foot,
war-gear well-wrought; willingly they shoved her out,
thorough-braced craft, on the craved voyage.

Away she went over a wavy ocean,
boat like a bird, breaking seas,
wind-whetted, white-throated,
till the curved prow had ploughed so far
—the sun standing right on the second day—
that they might see land loom on the skyline,
then the shimmer of cliffs, sheer fells behind,
reaching capes.
The crossing was at an end;
closed the wake. Weather-Geats
stood on strand, stepped briskly up;
a rope going ashore, ring-mail clashed,
battle-girdings. God they thanked
for the smooth going over the salt trails.

8. A Germanic tribe that lived along the southwestern coast of what is now Sweden.

The watchman saw them. From the wall where he stood,
posted by the Scyldings to patrol the cliffs,
he saw the polished lindens[9] pass along the gangway
and the clean equipment. Curiosity
moved him to know who these men might be.

Hrothgar's thane, when his horse had picked
its way down to the shore, shook his spear
fiercely at arm's length, framed the challenge:
"Strangers, you have steered this steep craft
through the sea-ways, sought our coast.
I see you are warriors; you wear that dress now.
I must ask who you are.
In all the years
I have lived as look-out at land's end here
—so that no foreigners with a fleet-army
might land in Denmark and do us harm—
shield-carriers have never come ashore
more openly. You had no assurance
of welcome here, word of leave
from Hrothgar and Hrothulf!
I have not in my life
set eyes on a man with more might in his frame
than this helmed lord. He's no hall-fellow
dressed in fine armor, or his face belies him;
he has the head of a hero.
I'll have your names now
and the names of your fathers; or further you shall not go
as undeclared spies in the Danish land.
Stay where you are, strangers, hear
what I have to say! Seas crossed,
it is best and simplest straightaway to acknowledge
where you are from, why you have come."

The captain gave him a clear answer,
leader of the troop, unlocked his word-hoard:
"We here are come from the country of the Geats
and are King Hygelac's hearth-companions.
My noble father was known as Edgetheow,
a front-fighter famous among nations,
who had seen many seasons when he set out at last
an old man from the halls; all the wiser men
in the world readily remember him.

It is with loyal and true intention that we come
to seek your lord the son of Healfdene,
guardian of the people: guide us well therefore!
We have a great errand to the glorious hero,

9. Lindenwood shields.

the Shepherd of the Danes; the drift of it
shall not be kept from you. You must know if indeed
there is truth in what is told in Geatland,
that among the Scyldings some enemy,
an obscure assailant in the opaque night-times,
makes spectacles of spoil and slaughter
in hideous feud. To Hrothgar I would
openheartedly unfold a plan
how the old commander may overcome his foe;
if indeed an easing is ever to slacken
these besetting sorrows, a settlement
when chafing cares shall cool at last.
Otherwise he must miserably live out
this lamentable time, for as long as Heorot,
best of houses, bulks to the sky."

The mounted coastguard made reply,
unshrinking officer: "A sharp-witted man,
clear in his mind, must be skilled
to discriminate deeds and words.
I accept what I am told, that this troop is loyal
to the Scyldings' Protector. Pass forward with your
weapons and war-dress! I am willing to guide you,
commanding meanwhile the men under me
to guard with care this craft of yours,
this new-tarred boat at its berth by our strand
against every enemy until again it bear
its beloved captain over the current sea,
curve-necked keel, to the coasts of the Geat;
such a warrior shall be accorded
unscathed passage through the shocks of battle."

The vessel was still as they set forward,
the deep-chested ship, stayed at its mooring,
fast at its anchor. Over the cheek-pieces
boar-figures[1] shone, bristling with gold,
blazing and fire-hard, fierce guards
of their bearers' lives. Briskly the men went
marching together, making out at last
the ample eaves adorned with gold:
to earth's men the most glorious
of houses under heaven, the home of the king;
its radiance lighted the lands of the world.
The coastguard showed them the shining palace,
the resort of heroes, and how they might
rightly come to it; this captain in the wars
then brought his horse about, and broke silence:
"Here I must leave you. May the Lord Almighty

1. Boars were often depicted on Anglo-Saxon weapons and helmets.

Boar, from a bas-relief carving on Saint Nicholas Church, Ipswich, England. Although this large and vigorous boar dates from the 12th century, it retains stylistic elements of earlier Anglo-Saxon and Viking art. An ancient totem of power, boars were often depicted on early medieval weapons and helmets.

afford His grace in your undertakings
and bring you to safety. Back at the sea-shore
I resume the watch against sea-raiders."

There was stone paving on the path that brought
the war-band on its way. The war-coats shone
and the links of hard hand-locked iron
sang in their harness as they stepped along
in their gear of grim aspect, going to the hall.
Sea-wearied, they then set against the wall
their broad shields of special temper,
and bowed to bench, battle-shirts clinking,
the war-dress of warriors. The weapons of the seamen
stood in the spear-rack, stacked together,
an ash-wood gray-tipped. These iron-shirted men
were handsomely armed.
A high-mannered chieftain
then inquired after the ancestry of the warriors.
"From whence do you bring these embellished shields,
gray mail-shirts, masked helmets,
this stack of spears? I am spokesman here,
herald to Hrothgar; I have not seen
a body of strangers bear themselves more proudly.
It is not exile but adventure, I am thinking,
boldness of spirit, that brings you to Hrothgar."
The gallant Geat gave answer then,
valor-renowned, and vaunting spoke,
hard under helmet: "At Hygelac's table
we are sharers in the banquet; Beowulf is my name.

I shall gladly set out to the son of Healfdene,
most famous of kings, the cause of my journey,
lay it before your lord, if he will allow us kindly
to greet in person his most gracious self."

Then Wulfgar spoke; the warlike spirit
of this Wendel prince, his wisdom in judgement,
were known to many. "The Master of the Danes,
Lord of the Scyldings, shall learn of your request.
I shall gladly ask my honored chief,
giver of arm-bands, about your undertaking,
and soon bear the answer back again to you
that my gracious lord shall think good to make."

He strode rapidly to the seat of Hrothgar,
old and gray-haired among the guard of earls,
stepped forward briskly, stood before the shoulders
of the King of the Danes; a court's ways were known to him.
Then Wulfgar addressed his dear master:
"Men have come here from the country of the Geats,
borne from afar over the back of the sea;
these battle-companions call the man
who leads them, Beowulf. The boon they ask
is, my lord, that they may hold
converse with you. Do not, kind Hrothgar,
refuse them audience in the answer you vouchsafe;
accoutrement would clearly bespeak them
of earls' rank. Indeed the leader
who guided them here seems of great account."

The Guardian of the Scyldings gave his answer:
"I knew him when he was a child!
It was to his old father, Edgetheow, that
Hrethel the Geat gave in marriage
his one daughter. Well does the son
now pay this call on a proven ally!

The seafarers used to say, I remember,
who took our gifts to the Geat people
in token of friendship—that this fighting man
in his hand's grasp had the strength
of thirty other men. I am thinking that
the Holy God, as a grace to us
Danes in the West, has directed him here
against Grendel's oppression. This good man shall be
offered treasures in return for his courage.

Waste no time now but tell them to come in
that they may see this company seated together.
Make sure to say that they are most welcome
to the people of the Danes."
Promptly Wulfgar

turned to the doors and told his message:
"The Master of Battles bids me announce,
the Lord of the North Danes, that he knows your ancestry;
I am to tell you all, determined venturers
over the seas, that you are sure of welcome.
You may go in now in your gear of battle,
set eyes on Hrothgar, helmed as you are.
But battle-shafts and shields of linden wood
may here await you words' outcome."

The prince arose, around him warriors
in dense escort; detailed by the chief,
a group remained to guard the weapons.
The Geats swung in behind their stout leader
over Heorot's floor. The hero led on,
hard under helmet, to the hearth, where he stopped.
Then Beowulf spoke; bent by smith's skill
the meshed rings of his mail-shirt glittered.
"Health to Hrothgar! I am Hygelac's kinsman
and serve in his fellowship. Fame-winning deeds
have come early to my hands. The affair of Grendel
has been made known to me on my native turf.
The sailors speak of this splendid hall,
this most stately building, standing idle
and silent of voices, as soon as the evening light
has hidden below the heaven's bright edge.
Whereupon it was urged by the ablest men
among our people, men proved in counsel,
that I should seek you out, most sovereign Hrothgar.
These men knew well the weight of my hands.
Had they not seen me come home from fights
where I had bound five Giants—their blood was upon me—
cleaned out a nest of them? Had I not crushed on the wave
sea-serpents by night in narrow struggle,
broken the beasts? (The bane of the Geats,
they had asked for their trouble.) And shall I not try
a single match with this monster Grendel,
a trial against this troll?
To you I now
put one request, Royal Scylding,
Shield of the South Danes, one sole favor
that you'll not deny me, dear lord of your people,
now that I have come thus far, Fastness of Warriors;
that I alone may be allowed, with my loyal and determined
crew of companions, to cleanse your hall Heorot.

As I am informed that this unlovely one
is careless enough to carry no weapon,
so that my lord Hygelac, my leader in war,
may take joy in me, I abjure utterly

the bearing of sword or shielding yellow
board in this battle! With bare hands shall I
grapple with the fiend, fight to the death here,
hater and hated! He who is chosen
shall deliver himself to the Lord's judgement.

If he can contrive it, we may count upon Grendel
to eat quite fearlessly the flesh of Geats
here in this war-hall; has he not chewed
on the strength of this nation? There will be no need, Sir,
for you to bury my head; he will have me gladly,
if death should take me, though darkened with blood.
He will bear my bloody corpse away, bent on eating it,
make his meal alone, without misgiving,
bespatter his moor-lair. The disposing of my body
need occupy you no further then.
But if the fight should take me, you would forward to Hygelac
this best of battle-shirts, that my breast now wears.
The queen of war-coats, it is the bequest of Hrethel
and from the forge of Wayland.[2] Fate will take its course!"

Then Hrothgar spoke, the Helmet of the Scyldings:
"So it is to fight in our defence, my friend Beowulf,
and as an office of kindness that you have come to us here!
Great was the feud that your father set off
when his hand struck down Heatholaf in death
among the Wylfings. The Weather-Geats
did not dare to keep him then, for dread of war,
and he left them to seek out the South-Danish folk,
the glorious Scyldings, across the shock of waters.
I had assumed sway over the Scylding nation
and in my youth ruled this rich kingdom,
storehouse of heroes. Heorogar was then dead,
the son of Healfdene had hastened from us,
my elder brother; a better man than I!
I then settled the feud with fitting payment,
sent to the Wylfings over the water's back
old things of beauty; against which I'd the oath of your father.

It is a sorrow in spirit for me to say to any man
—a grief in my heart—what the hatred of Grendel
has brought me to in Heorot, what humiliation,
what harrowing pain. My hall-companions,
my war-band, are dwindled; Weird[3] has swept them
into the power of Grendel. Yet God could easily
check the ravages of this reckless fiend!
They often boasted, when the beer was drunk,
and called out over the ale-cup, my captains in battle,

2. Legendary blacksmith of the Norse gods. 3. Fate.

that they would here await, in this wassailing-place,
with deadliness of iron edges, the onset of Grendel.
When morning brought the bright daylight
this mead-hall was seen all stained with blood:
blood had soaked its shining floor,
it was a house of slaughter. More slender grew my
strength of dear warriors; death took them off . . .
Yet sit now to the banquet, where you may soon attend,
should the mood so take you, some tale of victory."

A bench was then cleared for the company of Geats
there in the beer-hall, for the whole band together.
The stout-hearted warriors went to their places,
bore their strength proudly. Prompt in his office,
the man who held the horn of bright mead
poured out its sweetness. The song of the poet
again rang in Heorot. The heroes laughed loud
in the great gathering of the Geats and the Danes.

Then Unferth[4] spoke, the son of Edgelaf,
sitting at the feet of the Father of the Scyldings,
unbound a battle-rune[5] Beowulf's undertaking,
the seaman's bold venture, vexed him much.
He could not allow that another man
should hold under heaven a higher care
for wonders in the world than went with his own name.
"Is this the Beowulf of Breca's swimming-match,
who strove against him on the stretched ocean,
when for pride the pair of you proved the seas
and for a trite boast entrusted your lives
to the deep waters, undissuadable
by effort of friend or foe whatsoever
from that swimming on the sea? A sorry contest!
Your arms embraced the ocean's streams,
you beat the wave-way, wove your hand-movements,
and danced on the Spear-Man. The sea boiled with whelming
waves of winter; in the water's power
you labored seven nights: and then you lost your swimming-match,
his might was the greater; morning found him
cast by the sea on the coast of the Battle-Reams.
He made his way back to the marches of the Brondings,
to his father-land, friend to his people,
and to the city-fastness where he had subjects, treasure
and his own stronghold. The son of Beanstan
performed to the letter what he had promised to you.
I see little hope then of a happier outcome
—though in other conflicts elsewhere in the world

4. Hrothgar's spokesman or court jester. His rude behavior to Beowulf resembles that of other epic and romance figures who taunt the hero before he undertakes his exploits.
5. Unleashed his hostile thought.

you may indeed have prospered—if you propose awaiting
Grendel all night, on his own ground, unarmed."

Then spoke Beowulf, son of Edgetheow:
"I thank my friend Unferth, who unlocks us this tale
of Breca's bragged exploit; the beer lends
eloquence to his tongue. But the truth is as I've said:
I had more sea-strength, outstaying Breca's,
and endured underwater a much worse struggle.

It was in early manhood that we undertook
with a pubic boast—both of us still
very young men—to venture our lives
on the open ocean; which we accordingly did.
Hard in our right hands we held each a sword
as we went through the sea, so to keep off
the whales from us. If he whitened the ocean,
no wider appeared the water between us.
He could not away from me; nor would I from him.
Thus stroke for stroke we stitched the ocean
five nights and days, drawn apart then
by cold storm on the cauldron or waters;
under lowering night the northern wind
fell on us in warspite: the waves were rough!

The unfriendliness was then aroused of the fishes of the deep.
Against sea-beasts my body-armor,
hand-linked and hammered, helped me then,
this forge-knit battleshirt bright with gold,
decking my breast. Down to the bottom
I was plucked in range by this reptile-fish,
pinned in his grip. But I got the chance
to thrust once at the ugly creature
with my weapon's point: war took off then
the mighty monster; mine was the hand did it.
Then loathsome snouts snickered by me,
swarmed at my throat. I served them out
with my good sword, gave them what they asked for:
those scaly flesh-eaters sat not down
to dine on Beowulf, they browsed not on me
in that picnic they'd designed in the dingles[6] of the sea.
Daylight found them dispersed instead
up along the beaches where my blade had laid them
soundly asleep; since then they have never
troubled the passage of travellers over
that deep water-way. Day in the east grew,
God's bright beacon, and the billows sank
so that I then could see the headlands,

6. Valleys.

the windy cliffs. 'Weird saves oft
the man undoomed if he undaunted be!'—
and it was my part then to put to the sword
nine sea-monsters, the severest fight
by night I have heard of under heaven's vault;
a man more sorely pressed the seas never held.
I came with my life from the compass of my foes,
but tired from the struggle. The tide bore me
away on its currents to the coasts of Norway,
whelms of water.
No whisper has yet reached me
of sword-ambushes survived, nor such scathing perils
in connection with your name! Never has Breca,
nor you Unferth either, in open battle-pay
framed such a deed of daring with your
shining swords—small as my action was.
You have killed only kindred, kept your blade
for those closest in blood; you're a clever man, Unferth,
but you'll endure hell's damnation for that.

It speaks for itself, my son of Edgelaf,[7]
that Grendel had never grown such a terror,
this demon had never dealt your lord
such havoc in Heorot, had your heart's intention
been so grim for battle as you give us to believe.
He's learnt there's in fact not the least need
excessively to respect the spite of this people,
the scathing steel-thresh of the Scylding nation.
He spares not a single sprig of your Danes
in extorting his tribute, but treats himself proud,
butchering and dispatching, and expects no resistance
from the spear-wielding Scyldings.
I'll show him Geatish
strength and stubbornness shortly enough now,
a lesson in war. He who wishes shall go then
blithe to the banquet when the breaking light
of another day shall dawn for men
and the sun shine glorious in the southern sky."

Great then was the hope of the gray-locked Hrothgar,
warrior, giver of rings. Great was the trust
of the Shield of the Danes, shepherd of the people,
attending to Beowulf's determined resolve.

There was laughter of heroes, harp-music ran,
words were warm-hearted. Wealhtheow[8] moved,
mindful of courtesies, the queen of Hrothgar,

7. Unferth.
8. Wealhtheow is the ideal Anglo-Saxon queen. She is a gracious hostess to her husband's guests, and later uses her diplomacy to try to safeguard the future of her sons.

glittering to greet the Geats in the hall,
peerless lady; but to the land's guardian
she offered first the flowing cup,
bade him be blithe at the beer-drinking,
gracious to his people; gladly the conqueror
partook of the banquet, tasted the hall-cup.
The Helming princess then passed about among
the old and the young men in each part of the hall,
bringing the treasure-cup, until the time came
when the flashing-armed queen, complete in all virtues,
carried out to Beowulf the brimming vessel;
she greeted the Geat, and gave thanks to the Lord
in words wisely chosen, her wish being granted
to meet with a man who might be counted on
for aid against these troubles. He took then the cup,
a man violent in war, at Wealhtheow's hand,
and framed his utterance, eager for the conflict.

Thus spoke Beowulf son of Edgetheow:
"This was my determination in taking to the ocean,
benched in the ship among my band of fellows,
that I should once and for all accomplish the wishes
of your adopted people, or pass to the slaughter,
viced in my foe's grip. This vow I shall accomplish,
a deed worthy of an earl; decided otherwise
here in this mead-hall to meet my ending-day!"

This speech sounded sweet to the lady,
the vaunt of the Geat; glittering she moved
to her lord's side, splendid folk-queen.

Then at last Heorot heard once more
words of courage, the carousing of a people
singing their victories, till the son of Healfdene
desired at length to leave the feast,
be away to his night's rest; aware of the monster
brooding his attack on the tall-gabled hall
from the time they had seen the sun's lightness
to the time when darkness drowns everything
and under its shadow-cover shapes do glide
dark beneath the clouds. The company came to its feet.

Then did the heroes, Hrothgar and Beowulf,
salute each other; success he wished him,
control of the wine-hall, and with this word left him:
"Never since I took up targe and sword
have I at any instance to any man beside,
thus handed over Heorot, as I here do to you.
Have and hold now the house of the Danes!
Bend your mind and your body to this task
and wake against the foe! There'll be no want of liberality

if you come out alive from this ordeal of courage."
Then Hrothgar departed, the Protector of the Danes
passed from the hall at the head of his troop.
The war-leader sought Wealhtheow his queen,
the companion of his bed.
Thus did the King of Glory,
to oppose this Grendel, appoint a hall-guard
—so the tale went abroad—who took on a special
task at the court—to cope with the monster.
The Geat prince placed all his trust
in his mighty strength, his Maker's favor.

He now uncased himself of his coat of mail,
unhelmed his head, handed his attendant
his embellished sword, best of weapons,
and bade him take care of these trappings of war.
Beowulf then made a boasting speech,
the Geat man, before mounting his bed:
"I fancy my fighting-strength, my performance in combat,
at least as greatly as Grendel does his;
and therefore I shall not cut short his life
with a slashing sword—too simple a business.
He has not the art to answer me in kind,
hew at my shield, shrewd though he be
at his nasty catches. No, we'll at night play
without any weapons—if unweaponed he dare
to face me in fight. The Father in His wisdom
shall apportion the honors then, the All-holy Lord,
to whichever side shall seem to Him fit."

Then the hero lay down, leant his head
on the bolster there; about him many
brave sea-warriors bowed to their hall-rest.
Not one of them thought he would thence be departing
ever to set eyes on his own country,
the home that nourished him, or its noble people;
for they had heard how many men of the Danes
death had dragged from that drinking-hall.
But God was to grant to the Geat people
the clue to war-success in the web of fate—
His help and support; so that they did
overcome the foe—through the force of one
unweaponed man. The Almighty Lord
has ruled the affairs of the race of men
thus from the beginning.
Gliding through the shadows came
the walker in the night; the warriors slept
whose task was to hold the horned building,
all except one. It was well-known to men
that the demon could not drag them to the shades

without God's willing it; yet the one man kept
unblinking watch. He awaited, heart swelling
with anger against his foe, the ordeal of battle.
Down off the moorlands' misting fells came
Grendel stalking; God's brand was on him.
The spoiler meant to snatch away
from the high hall some of human race.
He came on under the clouds, clearly saw at last
the gold-hall of men, the mead-drinking place
nailed with gold plates. That was not the first visit
he had paid to the hall of Hrothgar the Dane:
he never before and never after
harder luck nor hall-guards found.

Walking to the hall came this warlike creature
condemned to agony. The door gave way,
toughened with iron, at the touch of those hands.
Rage-inflamed, wreckage-bent, he ripped open
the jaws of the hall. Hastening on,
the foe then stepped onto the unstained floor,
angrily advanced: out of his eyes stood
an unlovely light like that of fire.
He saw then in the hall a host of young soldiers,
a company of kinsmen caught away in sleep,
a whole warrior-band. In his heart he laughed then,
horrible monster, his hopes swelling
to a gluttonous meal. He meant to wrench
the life from each body that lay in the place
before night was done. It was not to be;
he was no longer to feast on the flesh of mankind
after that night.
Narrowly the powerful
kinsman of Hygelac kept watch how the ravager
set to work with his sudden catches;
not did the monster mean to hang back.
As a first step he set his hands on
a sleeping soldier, savagely tore at him,
gnashed at his bone-joints, bolted huge gobbets,
sucked at his veins, and had soon eaten
all of the dead man, even down to his
hands and feet.
Forward he stepped,
stretched out his hands to seize the warrior
calmly at rest there, reached out for him with his
unfriendly fingers: but the faster man
forestalling, sat up, sent back his arm.
The upholder of evils at once knew
he had not met, on middle earth's
extremest acres, with any man

of harder hand-grip: his heart panicked.
He was quit of the place no more quickly for that.

Eager to be away, he ailed for his darkness
and the company of devils; the dealings he had there
were like nothing he had come across in his lifetime.
Then Hygelac's brave kinsman called to mind
that evening's utterance, upright he stood,
fastened his hold till fingers were bursting.
The monster strained away: the man stepped closer.
The monster's desire was for darkness between them,
direction regardless, to get out and run
for his fen-bordered lair; he felt his grip's strength
crushed by his enemy. It was an ill journey
the rough marauder had made to Heorot.

The crash in the banqueting-hall came to the Danes,
the men of the guard that remained in the buildings,
with the taste of death. The deepening rage
of the claimants to Heorot caused it to resound.
It was indeed wonderful that the wine-supper-hall
withstood the wrestling pair, that the world's palace
fell not to the ground. But it was girt firmly,
both inside and out, by iron braces
of skilled manufacture. Many a figured
gold-worked wine-bench, as we heard it,
started from the floor at the struggles of that pair.
The men of the Danes had not imagined that
any of mankind by what method soever
might undo that intricate, antlered hall,
sunder it by strength—unless it were swallowed up in
the embraces of fire.
Fear entered into
the listening North Danes, as that noise rose up again
strange and strident. It shrilled terror
to the ears that heard it through the hall's side-wall,
the grisly plaint of God's enemy,
his song of ill-success, the sobs of the damned one
bewailing his pain. He was pinioned there
by the man of all mankind living
in this world's estate the strongest of his hands.

Not for anything would the earls' guardian
let his deadly guest go living:
he did not count his continued existence
of the least use to anyone. The earls ran
to defend the person of their famous prince;
they drew their ancestral swords to bring
what aid they could to their captain, Beowulf.
They were ignorant of this, when they entered the fight,

boldly-intentioned battle-friends,
to hew at Grendel, hunt his life
on every side—that no sword on earth,
not the truest steel, could touch their assailant;
for by a spell he had dispossessed all
blades of their bite on him.
A bitter parting
from life was that day destined for him;
the eldritch[9] spirit was sent off on his
far faring into the fiends' domain.

It was then that this monster, who, moved by spite
against human kind, had caused so much harm
—so feuding with God—found at last
that flesh and bone were to fail him in the end;
for Hygelac's great-hearted kinsman
had him by the hand; and hateful to each
was the breath of the other.
A breach in the giant
flesh-frame showed then, shoulder-muscles
sprang apart, there was a snapping of tendons,
bone-locks burst. To Beowulf the glory
of this fight was granted; Grendel's lot
to flee the slopes fen-ward with flagging heart,
to a den where he knew there could be no relief,
no refuge for a life at its very last stage,
whose surrender-day had dawned. The Danish hopes
in this fatal fight had found their answer.

He had cleansed Heorot. He who had come from afar,
deep-minded, strong-hearted, had saved the hall
from persecution. He was pleased with this night's work,
the deed he had done. Before the Danish people
the Geat captain had made good his boast,
had taken away all their unhappiness,
the evil menace under which they had lived,
enduring it by dire constraint,
no slight affliction. As a signal to all
the hero hung up the hand, the arm
and torn-off shoulder, the entire limb,
Grendel's whole grip, below the gable of the roof.

There was, as I heard it, at hall next morning
a great gathering in the gift-hall yard
to see the wonder. Along the wide highroads
the chiefs of the clans came from near and far
to see the foe's footprints. It may fairly be said
that his parting from life aroused no pity in any

9. Eerie, spooky.

who tracked the spoor-blood of his blind flight
for the monsters' mere-pool; with mood flagging
and strength crushed, he had staggered onwards;
each step evidenced his ebbing life's blood.
The tarn[1] was troubled; a terrible wave-thrash
brimmed it, bubbling; black-mingled,
the warm wound-blood welled upwards.
He had dived to his doom, he had died miserably;
here in his fen-lair he had laid aside
his heathen soul. Hell welcomed it.

Then the older retainers turned back on the way
journeyed with much joy; joined by the young men,
the warriors on white horses wheeled away from the Mere
in bold mood. Beowulf's feat
was much spoken of, and many said,
that between the seas, south or north,
over earth's stretch no other man
beneath the sky's shifting excelled Beowulf,
of all who wielded the sword he was worthiest to rule.
In saying this they did not slight in the least
the gracious Hrothgar, for he was a good king.
Where, as they went, their way broadened
they would match their mounts, making them leap
along the best stretches, the strife-eager
on their fallow horses. Or a fellow of the king's
whose head was a storehouse of the storied verse,
whose tongue gave gold to the language
of the treasured repertory, wrought a new lay
made in the measure. The man struck up,
found the phrase, framed rightly
the deed of Beowulf, drove the tale,
rang word-changes.
Of Wæls's great son,
Sigemund,[2] he spoke then, spelling out to them
all he had heard of that hero's strife,
his fights, strange feats, far wanderings,
the feuds and the blood spilt. Fitela alone heard
these things not well nor widely known to men,
when Sigemund chose to speak in this vein
to his sister's son. They were inseparable
in every fight, the firmest of allies;
their swords had between them scythed to the ground
a whole race of monsters. The reputation
that spread at his death was no slight one:
Sigemund it was who had slain the dragon,

1. A small lake.
2. The story of Sigemund is also told in the Old Norse *Volsunga Saga* and with major variations in the Middle High German *Niebelungenlied*. The poet's comparison of Siegmund with Beowulf is ironic in that the order and the outcome of Beowulf's later encounter with a dragon will be reversed.

the keeper of the hoard; the king's son walked
under the gray rock, he risked alone
that fearful conflict; Fitela was not there.
Yet it turned out well for him, his weapon transfixed
the marvelous snake, struck in the cave-wall,
best of swords; the serpent was dead.
Sigemund's valor had so prevailed
that the whole ring-hoard was his to enjoy,
dispose of as he wished. Wæls's great son
loaded his ship with shining trophies,
stacking them by the mast; the monster shriveled away.
He was by far the most famous of adventurers
among the peoples, this protector of warriors,
for the deeds by which he had distinguished himself.

Heremod's[3] stature and strength had decayed then,
his daring diminished. Deeply betrayed
into the fiends' power, far among the Giants
he was done to death. Dark sorrows
drove him mad at last. A deadly grief
he had become to his people and the princes of his land.
Wise men among the leaders had lamented that career,
their fierce one's fall, who in former days
had looked to him for relief of their ills,
hoping that their lord's son would live and in ripeness
assume the kingdom, the care of his people,
the hoard and the stronghold, the storehouse of heroes,
the Scylding homeland. Whereas Hygelac's kinsman
endeared himself ever more deeply to friends
and to all mankind, evil seized Heremod.

The riders returning came racing their horses
along dusty-pale roads. The dawn had grown
into broadest day, and, drawn by their eagerness
to see the strange sight, there had assembled at the hall
many keen warriors. The king himself,
esteemed for excellence, stepped glorious
from his wife's chambers, the warden of ring-hoards,
with much company; and his queen walked
the mead-path by him, her maidens following.
Taking his stand on the steps of the hall,
Hrothgar beheld the hand of Grendel
below the gold gable-end; and gave speech:
"Let swift thanks be given to the Governor of All,
seeing this sight! I have suffered a thousand
spites from Grendel: but God works ever
miracle upon miracle, the Master of Heaven.

3. Heremod, an earlier Danish king, was used as an illustration of the unjust and unwise ruler. Hrothgar mentions him again below, in line 1708.

Until yesterday I doubted whether
our afflictions would find a remedy
in my lifetime, since this loveliest of halls
stood slaughter-painted, spattered with blood.
For all my counselors this was a cruel sorrow,
for none of them imagined they could mount a defence
of the Scylding stronghold against such enemies—
warlocks, demons!
But one man has,
by the Lord's power, performed the thing
that all our thought and arts to this day
had failed to do. She may indeed say,
whoever she be that brought into the world
this young man here—if yet she lives—
that the God of Old was gracious to her
in her child-bearing. Beowulf, I now take you
to my bosom as a son, O best of men,
and cherish you in my heart. Hold yourself well
in this new relation! You will lack for nothing
that lies in my gift of the goods of this world:
lesser offices have elicited reward,
we have honored from our hoard less heroic men,
far weaker in war. But you have well ensured
by the deeds of your hands an undying honor
for your name for ever. May the Almighty Father
yield you always the success that you yesternight enjoyed!"

Beowulf spoke, son of Edgetheow:
"We willingly undertook this test of courage,
risked a match with the might of the stranger,
and performed it all. I would prefer, though,
that you had rather seen the rest of him here,
the whole length of him, lying here dead.
I had meant to catch him, clamp him down
with a cruel lock to his last resting-place;
with may hands upon him, I would have him soon
in the throes of death—unless he disappeared!
But I had not a good enough grip to prevent
his getting away, when God did not wish it;
the fiend in his flight was far too violent,
my life's enemy. But he left his hand
behind him here, so as to have his life,
and his arm and shoulder. And all for nothing:
it bought him no respite, wretched creature.
He lives no longer, laden with sins,
to plague mankind: pain has set
heavy hands on him, and hasped about him
fatal fetters. He is forced to await now,
like a guilty criminal, a greater judgement,
where the Lord in His splendor shall pass sentence upon him."

The son of Edgelaf was more silent then
in boasting of his own battle-deeds:
the athelings gazed at what the earl's strength
had hung there—the hand, high up under the roof,
and the fingers of their foe. From the front, each one
of the socketed nails seemed steel to the eye,
each spur on the hand of that heathen warrior
a terrible talon. They told each other
nothing could be hard enough to harm it at all,
not the most ancient of iron swords
would bite on that bloody battle-hand.

Other hands were pressed then to prepare the inside
of the banqueting-hall, and briskly too.
Many were ready, both men and women,
to adorn the guest-hall. Gold-embroidered tapestries
glowed from the walls, with wonderful sights
for every creature that cared to look at them.
The bright building had badly started
in all its inner parts, despite its iron bands,
and the hinges were ripped off. Only the roof survived
unmarred and in one piece when the monstrous one,
flecked with his crimes, had fled the place
in despair of his life.
But to elude death
is not easy: attempt it who will,
he shall go to the place prepared for each
of the sons of men, the soul-bearers
dwelling on earth, ordained them by fate:
laid fast in that bed, the body shall sleep
when the feast is done.
In due season
the king himself came to the hall;
Healfdene's son would sit at the banquet.
No people has gathered in greater retinue,
borne themselves better about their ring-giver.
Men known for their courage came to the benches,
rejoiced in the feast; they refreshed themselves kindly
with many a mead-cup; in their midst the brave kinsmen,
father's brother and brother's son,
Hrothgar and Hrothulf. Heorot's floor was
filled with friends: falsity in those days
had no place in the dealings of the Danish people.

Then as a sign of victory the son of Healfdene
bestowed on Beowulf a standard worked in gold,
a figured battle-banner, breast and head-armor;
and many admired the marvelous sword
that was borne before the hero. Beowulf drank with
the company in the hall. He had no cause to be ashamed of

gifts so fine before the fighting-men!
I have not heard that many men at arms
have given four such gifts of treasure
more openly to another at the mead.
At the crown of the helmet, the head-protector,
was a rim, with wire wound round it, to stop
the file-hardened blade that fights have tempered
from shattering it, when the shield-warrior
must go out against grim enemies.

The king then ordered eight war-horses
with glancing bridles to be brought within walls
and onto the floor. Fretted with gold
and studded with stones was one saddle there!
This was the battle-seat of the Bulwark of the Danes,
when in the sword-play the son of Healfdene
would take his part; the prowess of the king
had never failed at the front where the fighting was mortal.
The Protector of the Sons of Scyld then gave
both to Beowulf, bidding him take care
to use them well, both weapons and horses.
Thus did the glorious prince, guardian of the treasure,
reward these deeds, with both war-horses and armor;
of such open-handedness no honest man
could ever speak in disparagement.

Then the lord of men also made a gift
of treasure to each who had adventure with Beowulf
over the sea's paths, seated now at the benches—
an old thing of beauty. He bade compensation
to be made too, in gold, for the man whom Grendel
had horribly murdered; more would have gone
had not the God overseeing us, and the resolve of a man,
stood against that weird. The Wielder guided then
the dealings of mankind, as He does even now.
A mind that seeks to understand and grasp this
is therefore best. Both bad and good,
and much of both, must be borne in a lifetime
spent on this earth in these anxious days.
Then string and song sounded together
before Healfdene's Helper-in-battle:
the lute was taken up and tales recited
when Hrothgar's bard was bidden to sing
a hall-song for the men on the mead-benches.[4]
It was how disaster came to the sons of Finn:

4. The following episode is one of the most obscure in *Beowulf*. Apparently Hnaef and Hildeburh are the children of Hoc, an earlier Danish king. Hildeburh has been sent as a "peace-weaver" to marry Finn, son of Folcwalda and king of the Jutes and the Frisians, in order to make an alliance between the two feuding tribes. Upon visiting his sister and her husband, Hnaef is ambushed and killed by Finn's men, and Hildeburh's son by Finn is also killed. Hildeburh's tragic fate foreshadows that of Hrothgar's own daughter Freawaru in her marriage to Ingeld.

first the Half-Dane champion, Hnæf of the Scyldings,
was fated to fall in the Frisian ambush.
Hildeburh their lady had little cause to speak
of the good faith of the Jutes; guiltless she had suffered
in that linden-wood clash the loss of her closest ones,
her son and her brother, both born to die there,
struck down by the spear. Sorrowful princess!
This decree of fate the daughter of Hoc
mourned with good reason; for when morning came
the clearness of heaven disclosed to her
the murder of those kindred who were the cause of all
her earthly bliss.
Battle had also claimed
all but a few of Finn's retainers
in that place of assembly; he was unable therefore
to bring to a finish the fight with Hengest,
force out and crush the few survivors
of Hnæf's troop. The truce-terms they put to him
were that he should make over a mead-hall to the Danes,
with high-seat and floor; half of it
to be held by them, half by the Jutes.
In sharing out goods, that the son of Folcwalda
should every day give honor to the Danes
of Hengest's party, providing rings
and prizes from the hoard, plated with gold,
treating them identically in the drinking-hall
as when he chose to cheer his own Frisians.
On both sides they then bound themselves fast
in a pact of friendship. Finn then swore
strong unexceptioned oaths to Hengest
to hold in honor, as advised by his counselors,
the battle-survivors; similarly no man
by word or deed to undo the pact,
as by mischievous cunning to make complaint of it,
despite that they were serving the slayer of their prince,
since their lordless state so constrained them to do;
but that if any Frisian should fetch the feud to mind
and by taunting words awaken the bad blood,
it should be for the sword's edge to settle it then.

The pyre was erected, the ruddy gold
brought from the hoard, and the best warrior
of Scylding race was ready for the burning.
Displayed on his pyre, plain to see
were the bloody mail-shirt, the boars on the helmets,
iron-hard, gold-clad; and gallant men about him
all marred by their wounds; mighty men had fallen there.
Hildeburgh then ordered her own son
to be given to the funeral fire of Hnæf
for the burning of his bones; bade him be laid

at his uncle's side. She sang the dirges,
bewailed her grief. The warrior went up;
the greatest of corpse-fires coiled to the sky,
roared before the mounds. There were melting heads
and bursting wounds, as the blood sprang out
from weapon-bitten bodies. Blazing fire,
most insatiable of spirits, swallowed the remains
of the victims of both nations. Their valor was no more.

The warriors then scattered and went to their homes.
Missing their comrades, they made for Friesland,
the home and high stronghold. But Hengest still,
as he was constrained to do, stayed with Finn
a death-darkened winter in dreams of his homeland.
He was prevented from passage of the sea
in his ring-beaked boat: the boiling ocean
fought with the wind; winter locked the seas
in his icy binding; until another year
came at last to the dwellings, as it does still,
continually keeping its season,
the weather of rainbows.
Now winter had fled
and earth's breast was fair, the exile strained
to leave these lodgings; yet it was less the voyage
that exercised his mind than the means of his vengeance,
the bringing about of the bitter conflict
that he meditated for the men of the Jutes.
So he did not decline the accustomed remedy,
when the son of Hunlaf set across his knees
that best of blades, his battle-gleaming sword;
the Jutes were acquainted with the edges of that steel.

And so, in his hall, at the hands of his enemies,
Finn received the fatal sword-thrust;
Guthlaf and Oslaf, after the sea-crossing,
proclaimed their tribulations, their treacherous entertainment,
and named the author of them; anger in the breast
rose irresistible. Red was the hall then
with the lives of foemen. Finn was slain there,
the king among his troop, and the queen taken.
The Scylding crewmen carried to the ship
the hall-furnishings of Friesland's king,
all they could find at Finnsburh
in gemstones and jewelwork. Journeying back,
they returned to the Danes their true-born lady,
restored her to her people.
Thus the story was sung,
the gleeman's[5] lay. Gladness mounted,

5. Bard, oral poet.

bench-mirth rang out, the bearers gave
wine from wonderful vessels. Then came Wealhtheow forward,
going with golden crown to where the great heroes
were sitting, uncle and nephew; their bond was sound at that time,[6]
each was true to the other. Likewise Unferth the spokesman
sat at the footstool of Hrothgar. All had faith in his spirit,
accounted his courage great—though toward his kinsmen he had not been
kind at the clash of swords.
The Scylding queen then spoke:
"Accept this cup, my king and lord,
giver of treasure. Let your gaiety be shown,
gold-friend of warriors, and to the Geats speak
in words of friendship, for this well becomes a man.
Be gracious to these Geats, and let the gifts you have had
from near and far, not be forgotten now.

I hear it is your wish to hold this warrior
henceforward as your son. Heorot is cleansed,
the ring-hall bright again: therefore bestow while you may
these blessings liberally, and leave to your kinsmen
the land and its people when your passing is decreed,
your meeting with fate. For may I not count
on my gracious Hrothulf to guard honorably
our young ones here, if you, my lord,
should give over this world earlier than he?
I am sure that he will show to our children
answerable kindness, if he keeps in remembrance
all that we have done to indulge and advance him,
the honors we bestowed on him when he was still a child."

Then she turned to the bench where her boys were sitting,
Hrethric and Hrothmund, among the heroes' sons,
young men together; where the good man sat also
between the two brothers, Beowulf the Geat.
Then the cup was taken to him and he was entreated kindly
to honor their feast; ornate gold
was presented in trophy: two arm-wreaths,
with robes and rings also, and the richest collar
I have ever heard of in all the world.[7]

Never under heaven have I heard of a finer
prize among heroes—since Hama carried off
the Brising necklace to his bright city,
that gold-cased jewel; he gave the slip
to the machinations of Eormenric, and made his name forever.

6. Likely an allusion to the later usurpation of the Danish throne by Hrothgar's nephew Hrothulf.
7. The narrative here jumps ahead beyond Beowulf's return home to the Geats. His uncle, King Hygelac, will not only receive the collar from Beowulf but will die with it in battle among the Frisians. The collar thus connects different events at different times.

This gold was to be on the neck of the grandson of Swerting
on the last of his harryings, Hygelac the Geat,
as he stood before the standard astride his plunder,
defending his war-haul: Weird struck him down;
in his superb pride he provoked disaster
in the Frisian feud. This fabled collar
the great war-king wore when he crossed
the foaming waters; he fell beneath his shield.
The king's person passed into Frankish hands,
together with his corselet, and this collar also.
They were lesser men that looted the slain;
for when the carnage was over, the corpse-field was littered
with the people of the Geats.
Applause filled the hall;
then Wealhtheow spoke, and her words were attended.

"Take pride in this jewel, have joy of this mantle
drawn from our treasuries, most dear Beowulf!
May fortune come with them and may you flourish in your youth!
Proclaim your strength; but in counsel to these boys
be a gentle guardian, and my gratitude will be seen.
Already you have so managed that men everywhere
will hold you in honor for all time,
even to the cliffs at the world's end, washed by Ocean,
the wind's range. All the rest of your life
must be happy, prince; and prosperity I wish you too,
abundance of treasure! But be to my son
a friend in deed, most favored of men.
You see how open is each earl here with his neighbor,
temperate of heart, and true to his lord.
The nobles are loyal, the lesser people dutiful;
wine mellows the men to move to my bidding."

She walked back to her place. What a banquet that was!
The men drank their wine: the weird they did not know,
destined from of old, the doom that was to fall
on many of the earls there. When evening came
Hrothgar departed to his private bower,[8]
the king to his couch; countless were the men
who watched over the hall, as they had often done before.
They cleared away the benches and covered the floor
with beds and bolsters: the best at the feast
bent to his hall-rest, hurried to his doom.
Each by his head placed his polished shield,
the lindens of battle. On the benches aloft,
above each atheling, easily to be seen,
were the ring-stitched mail-coat, the mighty helmet

8. Bed chamber.

steepling above the fray, and the stout spear-shaft.
It was their habit always, at home or on campaign,
to be ready for war, in whichever case,
whatsoever the hour might be
that the need came on their lord: what a nation they were!

Then they sank into sleep. A savage penalty
one paid for his night's rest! It was no new thing for that people
since Grendel had occupied the gold-giving hall,
working his evil, until the end came,
death for his misdeeds. It was declared then to men,
and received by every ear, that for all this time
a survivor had been living, an avenger for their foe
and his grim life's-leaving: Grendel's Mother herself,
a monstrous ogress, was ailing for her loss.
She had been doomed to dwell in the dread waters,
in the chilling currents, because of that blow
whereby Cain became the killer of his brother,
his own father's son. He stole away, branded,
marked for his murder, from all that men delight in,
to inhabit the wastelands.
Hosts of the ill ones
sprang from his begetting; as Grendel, that hateful
accursed outcast, who encountered at Heorot
a watchful man waiting for the fight.
The grim one fastened his grip upon him there,
but he remembered his mighty strength,
the gift that the Lord had so largely bestowed on him,
and, putting his faith in the favor of the Almighty
and His aid and comfort, he overcame the foe,
put down the hell-fiend. How humbling was that flight
when the miserable outcast crept to his dying-place!
Thus mankind's enemy. But his Mother now purposed
to set out at last—savage in her grief—
on that wrath-bearing visit of vengeance for her son.

She came down to Heorot, where the heroes of the Danes
slept about the hall. A sudden change
was that for the men there when the Mother of Grendel
found her way in among them—though the fury of her onslaught
was less frightful than his; as the force of a woman,
her onset in a fight, is less feared by men,
where the bound blade, beaten out by hammers,
cuts, with its sharp edges shining with blood,
through the boars that bristle above the foes' helmets!

Many a hard sword was snatched up in the hall
from its rack above the benches; the broad shield was raised,
held in the hand firm; helmet and corselet

lay there unheeded when the horror was on them.
She was all eager to be out of the place
now that she was discovered, and escape with her life.
She caught a man quickly, clutched him to herself,
one of the athelings, and was away to the fen.
This was the hero that Hrothgar loved better
than any on earth among his retinue,
destroyed thus as he slept; he was a strong warrior,
noted in battle. (Beowulf was not there:
separate lodging had been assigned that night,
after the treasure-giving, to the Geat champion.)
Heorot was in uproar; the hand had gone with her,
blood-stained, familiar.
And so a fresh sorrow
came again to those dwellings. It was an evil bargain,
with both parties compelled to batter
the lives of their dearest. What disturbance of spirit
for the wise king, the white-haired soldier,
hearing the news that the nearest of his thanes
was dead and gone, his dearest man!

Beowulf was soon summoned to the chamber,
victory-blest man. And that valiant warrior
came with his following—it was at first light—
captain of his company, to where the king waited
to see if by some means the Swayer of All
would work a turning into this tale of sorrow.
The man excellent in warfare walked across the hall
flanked by his escort—the floor-timbers boomed—
to make his addresses to the Danish lord,
the Guide of the Ingwine. He inquired of him whether
the night had been quiet, after a call so urgent.

Hrothgar spoke, the Helmet of the Scyldings:
"Do not ask about our welfare! Woe has returned
to the Danish people with the death of Ashhere,
the elder brother of Yrmenlaf.
He was my closest counselor, he was keeper of my thoughts,
he stood at my shoulder when we struck for our lives
at the crashing together of companies of foot,
when blows rained on boar-crests. Men of birth and merit
all should be as Ashhere was!
A bloodthirsty monster has murdered him in Heorot,
a wandering demon; whither this terrible one,
glorying in her prey, glad of her meal,
has returned to, I know not. She has taken vengeance
for the previous night, when you put an end to Grendel
with forceful finger-grasp, and in a fierce manner,
because he had diminished and destroyed my people
for far too long. He fell in that struggle

and forfeited his life; but now is followed by another
most powerful ravager. Revenge is her motive,
and in furthering her son's feud she has gone far enough,
—or thanes may be found who will think it so;
in their breasts they will grieve for their giver of rings,
bitter at heart. For the hand is stilled
that would openly have granted your every desire.

I have heard it said by subjects of mine
who live in the country, counselors in this hall,
that they have seen such a pair
of huge wayfarers haunting the moors,
otherworldly ones; and one of them,
so far as they might make it out,
was in woman's shape; but the shape of a man,
though twisted, trod also the tracks of exile
—save that he was more huge than any human being.
The country people have called him from of old
by the name of Grendel; they know of no father for him,
nor whether there have been such beings before
among the monster-race.
Mysterious is the region
they live in—of wolf-fells, wind-picked moors
and treacherous fen-paths: a torrent of water
pours down dark cliffs and plunges into the earth,
an underground flood. It is not far from here,
in terms of miles, that the Mere[9] lies,
overcast with dark, crag-rooted trees
that hang in groves horary with frost.
An uncanny sight may be seen at night there
—the fire in the water! The wit of living men
is not enough to know its bottom.
The hart that roams the heath, when hounds have pressed him
long and hard, may hide in the forest
his antlered head; but the hart will die there
sooner than swim and save his life;
he will sell it on the brink there, for it is not a safe place.
And the wind can stir up wicked storms there,
whipping the swirling waters up
till they climb the clouds and clog the air,
making the skies weep.
Our sole remedy
is to turn again to you. The treacherous country
where that creature of sin is to be sought out
is strange to you as yet: seek then if you dare!
I shall reward the deed, as I did before,
with wealthy gifts of wreathèd ore,

9. A small lake.

treasures from the hoard, if you return once more."
Beowulf spoke, son of Edgetheow:
"Bear your grief, wise one! It is better for a man
to avenge his friend than to refresh his sorrow.
As we must all expect to leave
our life on this earth, we must earn some renown,
if we can, before death; daring is the thing
for a fighting man to be remembered by.

Let Denmark's lord arise, and we shall rapidly see then
where this kinswoman of Grendel's has gone away to!
I can promise you this, that she'll not protect herself by hiding
in any fold of the field, in any forest of the mountain,
in any dingle of the sea, dive where she will!
For this day, therefore, endure all your woes
with the patience that I may expect of you."

The ancient arose and offered thanks to God,
to the Lord Almighty, for what this man had spoken.
A steed with braided mane was bridled then,
a horse for Hrothgar; the hero-patriarch
rode out shining; shieldbearers marched
in troop beside him. The trace of her going
on the woodland paths was plainly to be seen,
stepping onwards; straight across
the fog-bound moor she had fetched away there
the lifeless body of the best man
of all who kept the courts of Hrothgar.
The sons of men then made their way
up steep screes, by scant tracks
where only one might walk, by wall-faced cliffs,
through haunted fens—uninhabitable country.
Going on ahead with a handful of the
keener men to reconnoitre,
Beowulf suddenly saw where some ash-trees
hung above a hoary rock
—a cheerless wood! And the water beneath it
was turbid with blood; bitter distress
was to be endured by the Danes who were there,
a grief for the earls, for every thane
of the Friends of the Scyldings, when they found there
the head of Ashhere by the edge of the cliff.

The men beheld the blood on the water,
its warm upwellings. The war-horn sang
an eager battle-cry. The band of foot-soldiers,
sitting by the water, could see multitudes
of strange sea-drakes swerving through the depths,
and water-snakes lay on the ledges of the cliffs,
such serpents and wild beasts as will sally out

in middle morning to make havoc
in the seas where ships sail.
Slithering away
at the bright phrases of the battle-horn,
they were swollen with anger. An arrow from the
bow of Beowulf broke the life's thread
of one wave-thrasher; wedged in his throat
the iron dart; with difficulty then
did he swim through the deep, until death took him.
They struck him as he swam, and straightaway,
with their boar-spears barbed and tanged;
gaffed and battered, he was brought to the cliff-top,
strange lurker of the waves. They looked with wonder
at their grisly guest!
The Geat put on
the armor of a hero, unanixious for his life:
the manufacture of the mailed shirt,
figured and vast, that must venture in the deep,
made it such a bulwark to his bone-framed chest
that the savage attack of an incensed enemy
could do no harm to the heart within it.
His head was encircled by a silver helmet
that was to strike down through the swirl of water,
disturb the depths. Adorned with treasure,
clasped with royal bands, it was right as at first
when the weapon-smith had wonderfully made it,
so that no sword should afterward be able to cut through
the defending wild boars that faced about it.
Not least among these mighty aids
was the hilted sword that Hrothgar's spokesman,
Unferth, lent him in his hour of trial.
Hrunting was its name; unique and ancient,
its edge was iron, annealed in venom
and tempered in blood; in battle it never
failed any hero whose hand took it up
at his setting out on a stern adventure
for the house of foes. This was not the first time
that it had to do heroic work.

It would seem that the strapping son of Edgelaf
had forgotten the speech he had spoken earlier,
eloquent with wine, for he offered the weapon now
to the better swordsman; himself he would not go
beneath the spume to display his valor
and risk his life; he lost his reputation there
for nerve and action. With the other man
it was otherwise once he had armed himself for battle.

Beowulf spoke, son of Edgetheow:
"I am eager to begin, great son of Healfdene.

Remember well, then, my wise lord,
provider of gold, what we agreed once before,
that if in your service it should so happen
that I am sundered from life, that you would assume the place
of a father towards me when I was gone.
Now extend your protection to the troop of my companions,
my young fellows, if the fight should take me;
convey also the gifts that you have granted to me,
beloved Hrothgar, to my lord Hygelac.
For on seeing this gold, the Geat chieftain,
Hrethel's son, will perceive from its value
that I had met with magnificent patronage
from a giver of jewels, and that I had joy of him.
Let Unferth have the blade that I inherited
—he is a widely-known man—this wave-patterned sword
of rare hardness. With Hrunting shall I
achieve this deed—or death shall take me!'

After these words the Weather-Geat prince
dived into the Mere—he did not care
to wait for an answer—and the waves closed over
the daring man. It was a day's space almost
before he could glimpse ground at the bottom.
The grim and greedy guardian of the flood,
keeping her hungry hundred-season watch,
discovered at once that one from above,
a human, had sounded the home of the monsters.
She felt for the man and fastened upon him
her terrible hooks; but no harm came thereby
to the hale body within—the harness so ringed him
that she could not drive her dire fingers
through the mesh of the mail-shirt masking his limbs.

When she came to the bottom she bore him to her lair,
the mere-wolf, pinioning the mail-clad prince.
Not all his courage could enable him
to draw his sword; but swarming through the water,
throngs of sea-beasts threw themselves upon him
with ripping tusks to tear his battle-coat,
tormenting monsters. Then the man found
that he was in some enemy hall
where there was no water to weigh upon him
and the power of the flood could not pluck him away,
sheltered by its roof: a shining light he saw,
a bright fire blazing clearly.

It was then that he saw the size of this water-hag,
damned thing of the deep. He dashed out his weapon,
not stinting the stroke, and with such strength and violence
that the circled sword screamed on her head

a strident battle-song. But the stranger saw
his battle-flame refuse to bite
or hurt her at all; the edge failed
its lord in his need. It had lived through many
hand-to-hand conflicts, and carved through the helmets
of fated men. This was the first time
that this rare treasure had betrayed its name.
Determined still, intent on fame,
the nephew of Hygelac renewed his courage.
Furious, the warrior flung it to the ground,
spiral-patterned, precious in its clasps,
stiff and steel-edged; his own strength would suffice him,
the might of his hands. A man must act so
when he means in a fight to frame himself
a long-lasting glory; it is not life he thinks of.

The Geat prince went for Grendel's mother,
seized her by the shoulder—he was not sorry to be fighting—
his mortal foe, and with mounting anger
the man hard in battle hurled her to the ground.
She promptly repaid this present of his
as her ruthless hands reached out for him;
and the strongest of fighting-men stumbled in his weariness,
the firmest of foot-warriors fell to the earth.
She was down on this guest of hers and had drawn her knife,
broad, burnished of edge; for her boy was to be avenged,
her only son. Overspreading his back,
the shirt of mail shielded his life then,
barred the entry to edge and point.
Edgetheow's son would have ended his venture
deep under ground there, the Geat fighter,
had not the battle-shirt then brought him aid,
his war-shirt of steel. And the wise Lord,
the holy God, gave out the victory;
the Ruler of the Heavens rightly settled it
as soon as the Geat regained his feet.

He saw among the armor there the sword to bring him victory,
a Giant-sword from former days: formidable were its edges,
a warrior's admiration. This wonder of its kind
was yet so enormous that no other man
would be equal to bearing it in battle-play
—it was a Giant's forge that had fashioned it so well.
The Scylding champion, shaking with war-rage,
caught it by its rich hilt, and, careless of his life,
brandished its circles, and brought it down in fury
to take her full and fairly across the neck,
breaking the bones; the blade sheared
through the death-doomed flesh. She fell to the ground;
the sword was gory; he was glad at the deed.

Light glowed out and illumined the chamber
with a clearness such as the candle of heaven
sheds in the sky. He scoured the dwelling
in single-minded anger, the servant of Hygelac;
with his weapon high, and, holding to it firmly,
he stalked by the wall. Nor was the steel useless yet
to that man of battle, for he meant soon enough
to settle with Grendel for those stealthy raids
—there had been many of them—he had made on the West-Danes;
far more often than on that first occasion
when he had killed Hrothgar's hearth-companions,
slew them as they slept, and in their sleep ate up
of the folk of Denmark fifteen good men,
carrying off another of them
in foul robbery. The fierce champion
now settled this up with him: he saw where Grendel
lay at rest, limp from the fight;
his life had wasted through the wound he had got
in the battle at Heorot. The body gaped open
as it now suffered the stroke after death
from the hard-swung sword; he had severed the neck.

And above, the wise men who watched with Hrothgar
the depths of the pool descried soon enough
blood rising in the broken water
and marbling the surface. Seasoned warriors,
gray-headed, experienced, they spoke together,
said it seemed unlikely that they would see once more
the prince returning triumphant to seek out
their famous master. Many were persuaded
the she-wolf of the deep had done away with him.
The ninth hour had come; the keen-hearted Scyldings
abandoned the cliff-head; the kindly gold-giver
turned his face homeward. But the foreigners sat on,
staring at the pool with sickness at heart,
hoping they would look again on their beloved captain,
believing they would not.
The blood it had shed
made the sword dwindle into deadly icicles;
the war-tool wasted away. It was wonderful indeed
how it melted away entirely, as the ice does in the spring
when the Father unfastens the frost's grip,
unwinds the water's ropes—He who watches over
the times and the seasons; He is the true God.
The Great champion did not choose to take
any treasures from that hall, from the heaps he saw there,
other than that richly ornamented hilt,
and the head of Grendel. The engraved blade
had melted and burnt away: the blood was too hot,

the fiend that had died there too deadly by far.
The survivor of his enemies' onslaught in battle
now set to swimming, and struck up through the water;
both the deep reaches and the rough wave-swirl
were thoroughly cleansed, now the creature from the otherworld
drew breath no longer in this brief world's space.

Then the seamen's Helm came swimming up
strongly to land, delighting in his sea-trove,
those mighty burdens that he bore along with him.
They went to meet him, a manly company,
thanking God, glad of their lord,
seeing him safe and sound once more.
Quickly the champion's corselet and helmet
were loosened from him. The lake's waters,
sullied with blood, slept beneath the sky.

Then they turned away from there and retraced their steps,
pacing the familiar paths back again
as bold as kings, carefree at heart.
The carrying of the head from the cliff by the Mere
was no easy task for any of them,
brave as they were. They bore it up,
four of them, on a spear, and transported back
Grendel's head to the gold-giving hall.
Warrior-like they went, and it was not long
before they came, the fourteen bold Geats,
marching to the hall, and, among the company
walking across the land, their lord the tallest.
The earl of those thanes then entered boldly
—a man who had dared deeds and was adorned with their glory,
a man of prowess—to present himself to Hrothgar.
Then was the head of Grendel, held up by its locks,
manhandled in where men were drinking;
it was an ugly thing for the earls and their queen,
an awesome sight; they eyed it well.

Beowulf spoke, son of Edgetheow:
"Behold! What you see here, O son of Healfdene,
prince of the Scyldings, was pleasant freight for us:
—these trophies from the lake betoken victory!

Not easily did I survive
the fight under water; I performed this deed
not without a struggle. Our strife had ended
at its very beginning if God had not saved me.
Nothing could I perform in that fight with Hrunting,
it had no effect, fine weapon though it be.
But the Guide of mankind granted me the sight
—He often brings aid to the friendless—

of a huge Giant-sword hanging on the wall,
ancient and shining—and I snatched up the weapon.
When the hour afforded, in that fight I slew
the keepers of the hall. The coiling-patterned
blade burnt all away, as the blood sprang forth,
the hottest ever shed; the hilt I took from them.
So I avenged the violent slaughter
and outrages against the Danes; indeed it was fitting.
Now, I say, you may sleep in Heorot
free from care—your company of warriors
and every man of your entire people,
both the young men and the guard. Gone is the need
to fear those fell attacks of former times
on the lives of your earls, my lord of the Scyldings."

Then the golden hilt was given into the hand
of the older warrior, the white-haired leader.
A Giant had forged it. With the fall of the demons
it passed into the possession of the prince of the Danes,
this work of wonder-smiths. The world was rid
of that invidious enemy of God
and his mother also, with their murders upon them;
and the hilt now belonged to the best of the kings
who ruled the earth in all the North
and distributed treasure between the seas.
Hrothgar looked on that long-treasured hilt
before he spoke. The spring was cut on it
of the primal strife, with the destruction at last
of the race of Giants by the rushing Flood,
a terrible end. Estranged was that race
from the Lord of Eternity: the tide of water
was the final reward that the Ruler sent them.
On clear gold labels let into the cross-piece
it was rightly told in runic letters,
set down and sealed, for whose sake it was
that the sword was first forged, that finest of iron,
spiral-hilted, serpent-bladed.
At the speaking of the wise
son of Healfdene the hall was silent:
"One who has tendered justice and truth to his people,
their shepherd from of old, surely may say this,
remembering all that's gone—that this man was born
to be the best of men. Beowulf, my friend,
your name shall resound in the nations of the earth
that are furthest away.

How wise you are to bear
your great strength so peaceably! I shall perform my vows
agreed in our forewords. It is granted to your people

that you shall live to be a long-standing comfort
and bulwark to the heroes.
Heremod was not so
for the honored Scyldings, the sons of Edgewela:
his manhood brought not pleasure but a plague upon us,
death and destruction to the Danish tribes.
In his fits he would cut down his comrade in war
and his table-companion—until he turned away
from the feastings of men, that famous prince.
This though the Almighty had exalted him in the bliss
of strength and vigor, advancing him far
above all other men. Yet inwardly his heart-hoard
grew raw and blood-thirsty; no rings did he give
to the Danes for his honor. And he dwelt an outcast,
paid the penalty for his persecution of them
by a life of sorrow. Learn from this, Beowulf:
study openhandedness! It is for your ears that I relate this,
and I am old in winters.
It is wonderful to recount
how in his magnanimity the Almighty God
deals out wisdom, dominion and lordship
among mankind. The Master of all things
will sometimes allow to the soul of a man
of well-known kindred to wander in delight:
He will grant him earth's bliss in his own homeland,
the sway of the fortress-city of his people,
and will give him to rule regions of the world,
wide kingdoms: he cannot imagine,
in his unwisdom, that an end will come.
His life of bounty is not blighted by hint
of age or ailment; no evil care
darkens his mind, malice nowhere
bares the sword-edge, but sweetly the world
swings to his will; worse is not looked for.
At last his part of pride within him
waxes and climbs, the watchman of the soul
slumbering the while. That sleep is too deep,
tangled in its cares! Too close is the slayer
who shoots the wicked shaft from his bow!
For all his armor he is unable to protect himself:
the insidious bolt buries in his chest,
the crooked counsels of the accursed one.
What he has so long enjoyed he rejects as too little;
in niggardly anger renounces his lordly
gifts of gilt torques, forgets and misprises
his fore-ordained part, endowed thus by God,
the Master of Glory, with these great bounties.
And ultimately the end must come,

the frail house of flesh must crumble
and fall at its hour. Another then takes
the earl's inheritance; open-handedly
he gives out its treasure, regardless of fear.

Beloved Beowulf, best of warriors,
resist this deadly taint, take what is better,
your lasting profit. Put away arrogance,
noble fighter! The noon of your strength
shall last for a while now, but in a little time
sickness or a sword will strip it from you:
either enfolding flame or a flood's billow
or a knife-stab or the stoop of a spear
or the ugliness of age; or your eyes' brightness
lessens and grows dim. Death shall soon
have beaten you then, O brave warrior!

So it is with myself. I swayed the Ring-Danes
for fifty years here, defending them in war
with ash and with edge over the earth's breadth
against many nations; until I numbered at last
not a single adversary beneath the skies' expanse:
But what change of fortune befell me at my hearth
with the coming of Grendel; grief sprang from joy
when the old enemy entered our hall!
Great was the pain that persecution
thrust upon me. Thanks be to God,
the Lord everlasting, that I have lived until this day,
seen out this age of ancient strife
and set my gaze upon this gory head!
But join those who are seated, and rejoice in the feast,
O man clad in victory! We shall divide between us
many treasures when morning comes."
The Geat went most gladly to take
his seat at the bench, at the bidding of the wise one.
Quite as before, the famous men,
guests of the hall, were handsomely feasted
on this new occasion. Then night's darkness
grew on the company. The guard arose,
for their wise leader wished to rest,
the gray-haired Scylding. The Geat was ready enough
to go to his bed too, brave shieldsman.

The bower-thane soon brought on his way
this fight-wearied and far-born man.
His courteous office was to care for all
a guest's necessities, such as at that day
the wants of a seafaring warrior might be.
The hero took his rest; the hall towered up
gilded, wide-gabled, its guest within sleeping

until the black raven blithe-hearted greeted
the heaven's gladness. Hastening, the sunlight
shook out above the shadows. Sharp were the bold ones,
each atheling eager to set off,
back to his homeland: the high-mettled stranger
wished to be forging far in his ship.
That hardy man ordered Hrunting to be carried
back to the son of Edgelaf, bade him accept again
his well-loved sword; said that he accounted it
formidable in the fight, a good friend in war,
thanked him for the loan of it, without the least finding fault
with the edge of that blade; ample was his spirit!

By then the fighting-men were fairly armed-up
and ready for the journey; the Joy of the Danes went,
a prince, to the high seat where Hrothgar was,
one hero brave in battle hailed the other.

Beowulf then spoke, son of Edgetheow.
"We now wish to say, seafarers who
are come from far, how keenly we desire
to return again to Hygelac. Here we were rightly,
royally, treated; you have entertained us well.
If I can ever on this earth earn of you,
O lord of men, more of your love
than I have so far done, by deeds of war,
I shall at once be ready. If ever I hear
that the neighboring tribes intend your harm,
as those who hate you have done in the past,
I'll bring a thousand thanes and heroes
here to help you. As for Hygelac, I know
that the Lord of the Geats, Guide of his flock,
young though he is, will yield his support
both in words and deeds so I may do you honor
and bring you a grove of gray-tipped spears
and my strength in aid when you are short of men.
Further, when Hrethric shall have it in mind
to come, as a king's son, to the courts of the Geats
he shall find many friends there. Far countries are seen
by a man of mark to much advantage."

Hrothgar spoke to him in answer:
"These words you have delivered, the Lord in His wisdom
put in your heart. I have heard no man
of the age that you are utter such wisdom.
You are rich in strength and ripe of mind,
you are wise in your utterance. If ever it should happen
that spear or other spike of battle,
sword or sickness, should sweep away
the son of Hrethel; your sovereign lord,

shepherd of his people, my opinion is clear,
that the Sea-Geats will not be seeking for a better
man to be their king and keep their war-hoard,
if you still have life and would like to rule
the kingdom of your kinsmen. As I come to know
your temper, dear Beowulf, the better it pleases me.
You have brought it about that both the peoples,
the Sea-Geats and the Spear-Danes,
shall share out peace; the shock of war,
the old sourness, shall cease between us.
So long as I shall rule the reaches of this kingdom
we shall exchange wealth; a chief shall greet
his fellow with gifts over the gannet's bath
as the ship with curved prow crosses the seas
with presents and pledges. Your people, I know,
always open-natured in the old manner,
are fast to friends and firm toward enemies."

Then the Shield of the Heroes, Healfdene's son,
presented him with twelve new treasures in the hall,
bade him with these tokens betake himself
safe to his people; and soon return again.
Then that king of noble race, ruler of the Scyldings,
embraced and kissed that best of thanes,
taking him by the neck; tears fell from
the gray-haired one. With the wisdom of age
he foresaw two things, the second more likely,
that they would never again greet one another,
meet thus as heroes. The man was so dear to him
that he could not stop the surging in his breast;
but hidden in the heart, held fast in its strings,
a deep longing for this dearly loved man
burned against the blood.
Beowulf went from him,
trod the green earth, a gold-resplendent warrior
rejoicing in his rings. Riding at anchor
the strayer of ocean stayed for her master.
Chiefly the talk returned as they walked
to Hrothgar's giving. He was a king
blameless in all things, until old age at last,
that brings down so many, removed his proud strength.

They came then to the sea-flood, the spirited band
of warrior youth, wearing the ring-meshed
coat of mail. The coastguard saw
the heroes approaching, as he had done before.
Nor was it ungraciously that he greeted the strangers
from his ridge by the cliff; but rode down to meet them:
how welcome they would be to the Weather-Geats, he said
to those shipward-bound men in their shining armor.

The wide sea-boat with its soaring prow
was loaded at the beach there with battle-raiment,
with horses and arms. High rose the mast
above the lord Hrothgar's hoard of gifts.
To the boat-guard Beowulf gave
a gold-cleated sword; it gained the man
much honor on the mead-benches,
that treasured heirloom. Out moved the boat then
to divide the deep water, left Denmark behind.
A special sea-dress, a sail, was hoisted
and belayed to the mast. The beams spoke.
The wind did not hinder the wave-skimming ship
as it ran through the seas, but the sea-going craft
with foam at its throat, furled back the waves,
her ring-bound prow planning the waters
till they caught sight of the cliffs of the Geats
and headlands they knew. The hull drove ahead,
urged by the breeze, and beached on the shore.

The harbor-guard was waiting at the water's edge;
his eye had been scouring the stretches of the flood
in a long look-out for these loved men.
Now he moored the broad-ribbed boat in the sand,
held fast with hawsers, so no heft of the waves
should drive away again those darling timbers.
He had the heroes' hoard brought ashore,
their gold-plated armor. To go to their lord
was now but a step, to see again Hygelac
the son of Hrethel, at his home where he dwells
himself with his hero-band, hard by the sea-wall.

That was a handsome hall there. And high within it sat
a king of great courage. His consort was young,
but wise and discreet for one who has lived
so few years at court; the queen's name was Hygd,
Hareth's daughter. When she dealt out treasure
to the Geat nation, the gifts were generous,
there was nothing narrowly done.
It was not so with Modthryth,[1]
imperious queen, cruel to her people.
There was no one so rash among the retainers of the house
as to risk a look at her—except her lord himself—
turn his eyes on her, even by day;
or fatal bonds were fettled for him,
twisted by hand: and when hands had been laid on him
he could be sure that the sword would be present,

1. The rash and arrogant queen Modthryth (or Thryth) is described in order to contrast her to the wise queen Hygd. The principle of broad contrast was similarly used in the earlier comparison between the unwise king Heremod and Beowulf.

and settle it quickly, its spreading inlays
proclaim its killing-power. Unqueenly ways
for a woman to follow, that one who weaves peace,
though of matchless looks, should demand the life
of a well-loved man for an imagined wrong!
Hemming's son Offa put an end to that.
And the ale-drinkers then told a tale quite different:
little was the hurt or harm that she brought
on her subjects then, as soon as she was given,
gold-decked, in marriage, to the mighty young champion
of valiant lineage, when she voyaged out
on the pale flood at her father's bidding
to the hall of Offa. All that followed
of a life destined to adorn a throne
she employed well, and was well-loved for it,
strong in her love for that leader of heroes,
the outstanding man, as I have heard tell,
of all mankind's mighty race
from sea to sea. So it was that Offa,
brave with the spear, was spoken of abroad
for his wars and his gifts; he governed with wisdom
the land of his birth. To him was born Eomer,
helper of the heroes, Hemming's kinsman,
Garmund's grandson, great in combat.

The war-man himself came walking along
by the broad foreshores with his band of picked men,
trod the sea-beach. From the south blazed
the sun, the world's candle. They carried themselves forward,
stepping on eagerly to the stronghold where
Ongentheow's conqueror, the earls' defender,
the warlike young king, was well-known for his
giving of neck-rings. The news of Beowulf's
return was rapidly told to Hygelac
—that the shield of warriors, his own shoulder-companion,
had walked alive within the gates,
unscathed from the combat, and was coming to the hall.
The floor was quickly cleared of men
for the incoming guests, by order of the king.

When he had offered greetings in grave words,
as usage obliged him, to his lord of men,
the survivor of the fight sat facing the king,
kinsman and kinsman. Carrying the mead-cup
about the hall was Hareth's daughter,
lover of the people, presenting the wine-bowl
to the hand of each Geat. Hygelac then made
of his near companion in that noble hall
courteous inquiry. Curiosity burned in him
to hear the adventures of this voyage of the Geats.

"What luck did you meet with, beloved Beowulf,
on your suddenly resolved seeking out
of distant strife over salt water,
battle at Heorot? Did you bring to that famous
leader Hrothgar some alleviation
of those woes so widely known? Overwhelming doubts
troubled my mind, mistrusting this voyage
of my dear liegeman. Long did I beg you
never to meet with this murderous creature
but to let the South Danes themselves bring an end
to their feud with Grendel. God be thanked
that safe and sound I see you here today!"

Thus spoke Beowulf, son of Edgetheow:
"It has been told aloud, my lord Hygelac,
and to many men by now, the meeting that there was
between myself and Grendel, the great time
we fought in that place where he had inflicted so much
grief and outrage, age-long disgrace
on the Victor-Scyldings. I avenged all.
No kinsman of Grendel shall have cause to take pride
in the sound that arose in the stretches of the night
—not the last of that alien and evil brood
on the face of the earth.
First I went in
to greet Hrothgar in the hall of the ring-giving.
As soon as the glorious son of Healfdene
knew my mind, he immediately
offered me a seat at his sons' bench.
What hall-joys were there! A happier company
seated over mead I've not met with in my time
beneath the heavens. A noble princess
fit to be the pledge of peace between nations
would move through the young men in the hall,
stirring their spirits; bestowing a torque
often upon a warrior before she went to her seat.
Or the heroes would look on as Hrothgar's daughter
bore the ale-flagon to each earl in turn.
I heard those who sat in the hall calling her
by the name of Freawaru[2] as she fetched each warrior
the nailed treasure-cup.
She is betrothed to Ingeld,
this girl attired in gold, to the gracious son of Froda.
The Protector of the Danes has determined this
and accounts it wisdom, the keeper of the land,
thus to end all the feud and their fatal wars

2. Freawaru's tragic fate as a "peace-weaver" married off to cement an alliance between warring tribes recalls that of Hildeburh in the earlier song of Finn.

by means of the lady. Yet when a lord is dead
it is seldom the slaying-spear sleeps for long—
seldom indeed—dear though the bride may be.

The lord of the Heathobards may not like it well
at the bringing home of his bride to the hall:
nor may it please every earl in that nation
to have the pride and daring of Denmark at table
—their guests resplendent in the spoil of their ancestors!
Heathobards had treasured these trenchant, ring-patterned
weapons until they could wield them no longer,
having taken part in that play of the shields
where they lost their lives and the lives of their friends.

An old spear-fighter shall speak at the feast,
eyeing the hilt-ring—his heart grows fierce
as he remembers all the slaying of the man by the spear.
In his dark mood he deliberately
tries out the mettle of a man who is younger,
awakens his war-taste in words such as these:
'My friend, is that not a familiar sword?
Your father carried it forth to battle,
—excellent metal—masked as for war
on his last expedition. There the Danes slew him,
the keen Scyldings, and kept the field
when Withergyld was dead, when the warriors had fallen.
The son of one of his slayers now
sports the weapon here, and, spurning our hall-floor,
boasts of the killing: he carries at his side
the prize that you should possess by right.'

With such biting words of rebuke and reminder
he taunts him at every turn; until the time comes
when one sleeps blood-stained from the blow of a sword:
the follower of the lady forfeits with his life
for the actions of his father; the other contrives
to lose himself, and lives; the land is familiar to him.
Both sides then will break the pact
sworn by the earls; and Ingeld's vengefulness
will well up in him, overwhelming gall
shall cause his wife-love to cool thereafter.
So I do not believe that this liking of the Heathobards
for alliance with the Danes is all what it seems,
or that their friendship is sound.

I shall speak further
of Grendel again, O giver of treasure,
that you may rightly know the result of the champions'
hand-to-hand meeting. When heaven's jewel
had glided from the world, the wrathful creature,
dire dusk-fiend, came down to seek us out

where, still whole, we held the building.
The weight of the fight fell on Handscio,
the doomed blow came down on him; he died the first,
a warrior in his harness; the hero, my fellow,
was ground to death between Grendel's jaws,
our friend's body was bolted down whole.
But the bloody-toothed slayer, bent on destruction,
was not going to go from that gold-giving hall
any the sooner: not empty-handed!
Proud of his might, he made proof of me,
groped out his greedy palm. A glove hung from it,
uncouth and huge, clasped strangely,
and curiously contrived; it was cobbled together
all of dragons' skins, and with devilish skill.
It was inside this bag that the bold marauder
was going to put me, guiltless as I was,
as the first of his catch; but he could not manage it
once I had stood up in anger against him.
Too long to repeat here how I paid back
the enemy of the people for his every crime;
but to your people, O my prince, my performance there
will bring honor. He broke away,
tasted life's joys for a little while,
but his strong right hand stayed behind
in the hall of Heorot; humbled he went thence
and sank despairing in the depths of the Mere.

For this deadly fight the Friend of the Scyldings
recompensed me with plated gold,
a mort of treasure, when the morrow came
and we had benched ourselves as the banqueting table.
There was music and laughter, lays were sung:
the veteran of the Scyldings, versed in saga,
would himself fetch back far-off times to us;
the daring-in-battle would address the harp,
the joy-wood, delighting; or deliver a reckoning
both true and sad; or he would tell us the story
of some wonderful adventure, valiant-hearted king.
Or the seasoned warrior, wrapped in age,
would again fall to fabling of his youth
and the days of his battle-strength; his breast was troubled
as his mind filled with the memories of those years.

And thus we spent the space of a day there
seeking delight, until the ensuing dusk
came to mankind. Quick on its heels
the mother of Grendel moved to her revenge,
spurred on by sorrow; her son was death-taken
by Geat warspite. That gruesome she

avenged her son, struck down a warrior,
and boldly enough! The breath was taken
from the ancient counselor, Ashhere, there.
Nor could the Danish people, when day came,
give their death-wearied dear one to be burned,
escort him to the pyre: she had carried the body
to the mountain-torrent's depth in her monstrous embrace.
This was for Hrothgar the harshest of the blows
that since so long had fallen on the leader of the people.
Distraught with care, the king then asked of me
a noble action—and in your name, Hygelac—
that I should risk my life among the rush of waters
and perform a great deed; he promised me reward.

Far and wide it is told how I found in the surges
the grim and terrible guardian of the deep.
After a hard hand-to-hand struggle
the whirlpool boiled with the blood of the mother;
I had hewn off her head in that hall underground
with a sword of huge size. I survived that fight
not without difficulty; but my doom was not yet.

The protector of warriors rewarded me
with a heap of treasure, Healfdene's son.
The ways of that king accorded to usage:
I was not to forgo the guerdon he had offered,
the meed of my strength; he bestowed upon me
the treasures I would have desired, the son of Healfdene;
now, brave king, I bring them to you.
I rejoice to present them. Joy, for me, always
lies in your gift. Little family
do I have in the world, Hygelac, besides yourself."

Then he bade them bring in the boar's head standard,
the battle-dwarfing helmet, the hoar war-shirt
and the lambent sword; and delivered this speech:
"Hrothgar gave me all this garb of war
with one word—the wisest of princes—
that I should first relate to you whose legacy it is.
His brother Heorogar had it, he told me,
for a long while, as Lord of the Scyldings,
yet chose not to give this guardian of his breast
to his own son, the spirited Heoroweard,
friend though he was to him.
Flourish in the use if it!"

I heard that four fast-stepping horses
followed these treasures, a team of bays
matching as apples. All these he gave him,
both horses and armor—the act of a kinsman!
A kinsman knits no nets of malice

darkly for his fellow. Does he devise the end
of the man that is next to him? The nephew of Hygelac
held fast to that man hardy in battle;
each thought only of the other's welfare.

Beowulf, I heard, gave Hygd the neck-ring,
the wonderful treasure work Wealhtheow had given him
—high was her breeding—and three horses also,
graceful in their gait, and with gay saddles.
Her breast was made more beautiful by the jewel.

Such was the showing of the son of Edgetheow,
known for his combats and his courage in action.
His dealings were honorable: in drink he did not strike
at the slaves of his hearth; his heart was not savage.
The hero guarded well the great endowment
God had bestowed on him, a strength unequalled
among mankind. He had been misprised for long,
the sons of the Geats seeing little in him
and the lord of the Weather-Geats not willing to pay him
much in the way of honor on the mead-benches.
They firmly believed in his laziness
—"the atheling was idle"! But for all such humblings
time brought reversal, invested him with glory.

Then the king bold in war, keeper of the warriors,
required them to bring in the bequest of Hrethel,
elaborate in gold; the Geats at that day
had no more royal treasure of the rank of sword.
This he then laid in the lap of Beowulf
and bestowed on him an estate of seven thousand hides,
a chief's stool and a hall. Inherited land,
a domain by birthright, had come down to them both
in the Geat nation; the greater region
to the better-born of them—the broad kingdom.

But it fell out after, in other days,
among the hurl of battle—when Hygelac lay dead
and the bills of battle had dealt death to his Heardred,
despite the shield's shelter, when the Scylfings found him
amid his conquering people, and those keen war-wolves
grimly hemmed in Hereric's nephew—
that the broad kingdom came by this turn
into Beowulf's hands.
Half a century
he ruled it, well: until One began
—the king had grown gray in the guardianship of the land—
to put forth his power in the pitch-black night-times
—the hoard-guarding Dragon of a high barrow
raised above the moor.
Men did not know

of the way underground to it; but one man did enter,
went right inside, reached the treasure,
the heathen hoard, and his hand fell
on a golden goblet. The guardian, however,
if he had been caught sleeping by the cunning of the thief,
did not conceal this loss. It was not long till the near-
dwelling people discovered that the dragon was angry.

The causer of his pain had not purposed this;
it was without relish that he had robbed the hoard;
necessity drove him. The nameless slave
of one of the warriors, wanting shelter,
on the run from a flogging, had felt his way inside,
a sin-tormented soul. When he saw what was there
the intruder was seized with sudden terror;
but for all his fear, the unfortunate wretch
still took the golden treasure-cup . . .
There were heaps of hoard-things in this hall underground
which once in gone days gleamed and rang;
the treasure of a race rusting derelict.

In another age an unknown man,
brows bent, had brought and hid here
the beloved hoard. The whole race
death-rapt, and of the ring of earls
one left alive; living on in that place
heavy with friend-loss, the hoard-guard
waited the same weird. His wit acknowledged
that the treasures gathered and guarded over the years
were his for the briefest while.
The barrow stood ready
on flat ground where breakers beat at the headland,
new, near at hand, made narrow of access.
The keeper of rings carried into it
the earls' holdings, the hoard-worthy part
fraught with gold, and few words he spoke:[3]
"Hold, ground, the gold of the earls!
Men could not. Cowards they were not
who took it from thee once, but war-death took them,
that stops life, struck them, spared not one
man of my people, passed on now.
They have had their hall-joys. I have not with me
a man able to unsheathe this . . .
Who shall polish this plated vessel,
this treasured cup? The company is elsewhere.
This hardened helmet healed with gold

3. The speech of the "last survivor" that follows resembles Old English elegies such as *The Wanderer* in its lament for the transience of the joys of heroic society.

shall lose its shell. They sleep now
whose work was to burnish the battle-masks;
so with the cuirass that in the crash took
bite of iron among breaking shields:
it moulders with the man. This mail-shirt travelled far,
hung from a shoulder that shouldered warriors:
it shall not jingle again.
There's no joy from harp-play,
glee-wood's gladness, no good hawk
swings through hall now, no swift horse
tramps at the threshold. Terrible slaughter
has carried into darkness many kindreds of mankind."

So the sole survivor, in sorrowful mood,
bewailed his grief; he wandered cheerless
through days and nights until death's flood
reached to his heart.
The Ravager of the night,
the burner who has sought out barrows from of old,
then found this hoard of undefended joy.
The smooth evil dragon swims through the gloom
enfolded in flame; the folk of that country
hold him in dread. He is doomed to seek out
hoards in the ground, and guard for an age there
the heathen gold: much good does it do him!

Thus for three hundred winters this waster of peoples
guarded underground the great hoard-hall
with his enormous might; until a man awoke
the anger in his breast by bearing to his master
the plated goblet as a peace-offering,
a token of new fealty. Thus the treasure was lightened
and the treasure-house was breached; the boon was granted
to the luckless slave, and his lord beheld
for the first time that work of a former race of men.

The waking of the worm awoke a new feud:
he glided along the rock, glared at the sight
of a foeman's footprint: far too near his head
the intruder had stepped as he stole by him!
(An undoomed man may endure affliction
and even exile lightly, for as long as the Ruler
continues to protect him.) The treasure-guard eagerly
quartered the ground to discover the man
who had done him wrong during his sleep.
Seething with rage, he circled the barrow's
whole outer wall, but no hint of a man
showed in the wilderness. Yet war's prospect pleased him,
the thought of battle-action! He went back into the mound

to search for the goblet, and soon saw that one
of the tribe of men had tampered with the gold
of the glorious hoard.
The hoard's guardian
waited until evening only with difficulty.
The barrow-keeper was bursting with rage:
his fire would cruelly requite the loss
of the dear drinking-vessel.
At last day was gone,
to the worm's delight; he delayed no further
inside his walls, but issued forth flaming,
armed with fire.
That was a fearful beginning
for the people of that country; uncomfortable and swift
was the end to be likewise for their lord and treasure-giver!

So the visitant began to vomit flames
and burn the bright dwellings; the blazing rose skyward
and men were afraid: the flying scourge
did not mean to leave one living thing.
On every side the serpent's ravages,
the spite of the foe, sprang to the eye—
how this hostile assailant hated and injured
the men of the Geats. Before morning's light
he flew back to the hoard in its hidden chamber.
He had poured out fire and flame on the people,
he had put them to the torch; he trusted now to the barrow's walls
and to his fighting strength. His faith misled him.

Beowulf was acquainted quickly enough
with the truth of the horror, for his own hall had itself
been swallowed in flame, the finest of buildings,
and the gift-stool of the Geats. Grief then struck
into his ample heart with anguished keenness.
The chieftain supposed he had sorely angered
the Ruler of all, the eternal Lord,
by breach of ancient law. His breast was thronged
with dark unaccustomed care-filled thoughts.
The fiery dragon's flames had blasted
all the land by the sea, and its safe stronghold,
the fortress of the people. The formidable king
of the Geats now planned to punish him for this.
The champion of the fighting-men, chief of the earls,
gave orders for the making of a marvelous shield
worked all in iron; well he knew
that a linden shield would be of little service
—wood against fire. For the foremost of athelings
the term of his days in this transitory world
was soon to be endured; it was the end, too, for the dragon's
long watch over the wealth of the hoard.

The distributor of rings disdained to go
with a troop of men or a mighty host
to seek the far-flier. He had no fear for himself
and discounted the worm's courage and strength,
its prowess in battle. Battles in plenty
he had survived; valiant in all dangers,
he had come though many clashes since his cleansing of Heorot
and his extirpation of the tribe of Grendel,
hated race.
That was hardly the least
of hand-to-hand combats when Hygelac was slain,
when that kindly lord of peoples, the king of the Geats,
the son of Hrethel, among the hurl of battle
slaked the sword's thirst on the soil of Friesland
and the blows beat down on him!
Beowulf came away
by the use of his force in a feat of swimming;
alone into the ocean he leapt, holding
thirty men's mail-coats on his arm.

There was little cause for crowing among the Hetware
about their conduct of the foot-fight: they carried their lindens
forward against him; but few came back
from the wolf in war, walked home again.
Solitary and wretched was the son of Edgetheow[4]
on the sweep of waters as he swam back to his people.
There Hygd offered him the hoard and the kingdom,[5]
the gift-stool and its treasure; not trusting that her son
would be able to hold the inherited seats
against foreign peoples now his father was dead.
But the bereaved people could arrive at no conditions
under which the atheling[6] would accept the kingdom
or allow himself to be lord over Heardred.
Rather he fostered him among the people with friendly counsel,
with kindliness and respect, until he came of age
and ruled the Geats.
Guests sought out Heardred,
outcasts from oversea: Ohthere's sons.

They had risen against Onela, ruler of the Scylfings,
highest of the princes who provided treasure
in all the sea-coasts of the Swedish realms,
a famous lord. This led to the end
of Hygelac's son;[7] his hospitality
cost him a weapon-thrust and a wound to the life.

4. Beowulf.
5. Beowulf refuses the throne when Hygd offers it to him after Hygelac's death. Instead, he serves as her son Heardred's adviser until he is old enough to rule. Only after Heardred is killed in battle by the Swedish king Onela does Beowulf finally agree to be king of the Geats.
6. I.e., Beowulf.
7. Heardred.

Ongentheow's son, Onela, turned
to seek his home again once Heardred was dead;
the gift-stool and the ruling of the Geat people
he left to Beowulf; who was a brave king,
and kept it before his mind to requite his lord's death.
In after-days he was Eadgils' friend
when Eadgils was deserted, supporting his cause
across the wide water with weapons and an army,
Ohthere's son; who took his own revenge
by terror-campaigns that at last trapped Onela.

So the son of Edgetheow survived unscathed
each of these combats, calamitous onslaughts,
works of prowess: until this one day
when he must wage war on the serpent.
The Lord of the Geats went with eleven companions
to set eyes on the dragon; his anger rose in him.
He had by then discovered the cause of the attack
that had ravaged his people; the precious drinking-cup
had come into his hands from the hands of the informer.
He who had brought about the beginning of the feud
now made the thirteenth man in their company,
a miserable captive; cowed, he must show them
the way to the place, an unwilling guide.
For he alone knew the knoll and its earth-hall,
hard by the strand and the strife of the waves,
the underground hollow heaped to the roof
with intricate treasures. Attendant on the gold
was that underground ancient, eager as a wolf,
an awesome guardian; it was no easy bargain
for any mortal man to make himself its owner.

The stern war-king sat on the headland,
spoke encouragement to the companions of his hearth,
the gold-friend of the Geats. Gloomy was his spirit though,
death-eager, wandering; the weird was at hand
that was to overcome the old man there,
seek his soul's hoard, and separate
the life from the body; not for long now
would the atheling's life be lapped in flesh.
Beowulf spoke, son of Edgetheow:
"Many were the struggles I survived in youth
in times of danger; I do not forget them.
When that open-handed lord beloved by the people
received me from my father I was seven years old:
King Hrethel kept and fostered me,
gave me treasure and table-room, true to our kinship.
All his life he had as little hatred for me,
a warrior in hall, as he had for a son,
Herebeald, or Hathkin, or Hygelac my own lord.

A murderous bed was made for the eldest
by the act of a kinsman, contrary to right:
a shaft from Hathkin's horn-tipped bow
shot down the man that should have become his lord;
mistaking his aim, he struck his kinsman,
his own brother, with the blood-stained arrow-head.
A sin-fraught conflict that could not be settled,
unthinkable in the heart; yet thus it was,
and the atheling lost his life unavenged.

Grief such as this a gray-headed man
might feel if he saw his son in youth
riding the gallows. Let him raise the lament then,
a song of sorrow, while his son hangs there,
a sport for the raven. Remedy is there none
that an age-stricken man may afford him then.
Every morning reminds him again
that his son has gone elsewhere; another son,
an heir in his courts, he cares not to wait for,
now that the first has found his deeds
have come to an end in the constriction of death.
He sorrows to see among his son's dwellings
the wasted wine-hall, the wind's home now,
bereft of all joy. The riders are sleeping,
the heroes in the grave. The harp does not sound,
there is no laughter in the yard as there used to be of old.
He goes then to his couch, keens the lament
for his one son alone there; too large now seem to him
his houses and fields.
The Helm of the Geats
sustained a like sorrow for Herebeald
surging in his heart. Hardly could he settle
the feud by imposing a price on the slayer;
no more could he offer actions to that warrior
manifesting hatred; though he held him not dear.

Hard did this affliction fall upon him:
he renounced men's cheer, chose God's light.
But he left to sons his land and stronghold
at his life's faring-forth—as the fortunate man does.

On Hrethel's death the hatred and strife
of the Swedes and the Geats, the grievances between them,
broke into bitter war across the broad water.
The sons of Ongentheow were strong fighters,
active in war; they would not keep
peace on the lakes, but plotted many
a treacherous ambush about Hreosnabeorgh.

It has come to be known that my kinsmen and friends
revenged both the feud and the violent attack,

though the price that one of them paid was his life,
a hard bargain. That battle proved
mortal for Hathkin, Master of the Geats.
But came the morrow, and a kinsman, as I heard,
avenged him on his slayer with the sword's edge:
in his attack on Eofor, Ongentheow's
war-mask shattered, and the Scylfing patriarch
fell pale from the wound; the wielding hand
forgot not the feud, flinched not from the death-blow.

I had the fortune in that battle, by my bright sword,
to make return to Hygelac for the treasures he had given me.
He had granted me land, land to enjoy
and leave to my heirs. Little need was there
that Hygelac should go to the Gifthas or the Spear-Danes
or seek out ever in the Swedish kingdom
a weaker champion, and chaffer for his services.
I was always before him in the footing host,
by myself in the front.
So, while I live,
I shall always do battle, while this blade lasts
that early and late has often served me
since, with my bare hands, I broke Dayraven,
the champion of the Franks, before the flower of the host.
He was not to be permitted to present his Frisian lord
with the breast-armor that had adorned Hygelac,
for he was slain in the struggle, the standard-bearer,
noble in his prowess. It was not my sword
that broke his bone-cage and the beatings of his heart
but my warlike hand-grasp.
Now shall hard edge,
hand and blade, do battle for the hoard!"
Beowulf made speech, spoke a last time
a word of boasting: "Battles in plenty
I ventured in youth; and I shall venture this feud
and again achieve glory, the guardian of my people,
old though I am, if this evil destroyer
dares to come out of his earthen hall."

Then he addressed each of the men there
on this last occasion, courageous helm-bearers,
cherished companions: "I would choose not to take
any weapon to this worm, if I well knew
of some other fashion fitting to my boast
of grappling with this monster, as with Grendel before.
But as I must expect here the hot war-breath
of venom and fire, for this reason I have
my board and corselet. From the keeper of the barrow
I shall not flee one foot; but further than that
shall be worked out at the wall as our weird is given us

by the Creator of men. My mood is strong;
I forgo further words against the winged fighter.

Men in armor! Your mail-shirts protect you:
await on the barrow the one of us two
who shall be better able to bear his wounds
after this onslaught. This affair is not for you,
nor is it measured to any man but myself alone
to match strength with this monstrous being,
attempt this deed. By daring will I
win this gold; war otherwise
shall take your king, terrible life's-bane!"
The strong champion stood up beside his shield,
brave beneath helmet, he bore his mail-shirt
to the rocky cliff's foot, confident in his strength,
a single man; such is not the coward's way!
Then did the survivor of a score of conflicts,
the battle-clashes of encountering armies,
excelling in manhood, see in the wall
a stone archway, and out of the barrow broke
a stream surging through it, a stream of fire
with waves of deadly flame; the dragon's breath
meant he could not venture into the vault near the hoard
for any time at all without being burnt.

Passion filled the prince of the Geats:
he allowed a cry to utter from his breast,
roared from his stout heart: as the horn clear in battle
his voice re-echoed through the vault of gray stone.
The hoard-guard recognized a human voice,
and there was no more time for talk of friendship:
hatred stirred. Straightaway
the breath of the dragon billowed from the rock
in a hissing gust; the ground boomed.

He swung up his shield, overshadowed by the mound,
the lord of the Geats against this grisly stranger.
The temper of the twisted tangle-thing was fired
to close now in battle. The brave warrior-king
shook out his sword so sharp of edge,
an ancient heirloom. Each of the pair,
intending destruction, felt terror at the other:
intransigent beside his towering shield
the lord of friends, while the fleetness of the serpent
wound itself together; he waited in his armor.
It came flowing forward, flaming and coiling,
rushing on its fate.

For the famous prince
the protection lent to his life and person
by the shield was shorter than he had shaped it to be.

He must now dispute this space of time,
the first in his life when fate had not assigned him
the glory of the battle. The Geat chieftain
raised his hand, and reached down such a stroke
with his huge ancestral sword on the horribly-patterned snake
that, meeting the bone, its bright edge turned
and it bit less strongly than its sorely-straitened lord
required of it then. The keeper of the barrow
after this stroke grew savage in mood,
spat death-fire; the sparks of their battle
blazed into the distance.
He boasted of no triumphs then,
the gold-friend of the Geats, for his good old sword
bared in the battle, his blade, had failed him,
as such iron should not do.
That was no easy adventure,
when the celebrated son of Edgetheow
had to pass from that place on earth
and against his will take up his dwelling
in another place; as every man must give up
the days that are lent him.
It was not long again
to the next meeting of those merciless ones.
The barrow-guard took heart: his breast heaved
with fresh out-breath: fire enclosed
the former folk-king; he felt bitter pain.

The band of picked companions did not come
to stand about him, as battle-usage asks
offspring of athelings; they escaped to the wood,
saved their lives.
Sorrow filled
the breast of one man. The bonds of kinship
nothing may remove for a man who thinks rightly.
This was Wiglaf, Weoxstan's son,
well-loved shieldsman, a Scylfing prince
of the stock of Alfhere; he could see his lord
tormented by the heat through his mask of battle.
He remembered then the favors he had formerly bestowed on him,
the wealthy dwelling-place of the Waymundings,
confirming him in the landrights his father had held.
He could not then hold back: hand gripped the yellow
linden-wood shield, shook out that ancient
sword that Eanmund, Ohthere's son,
had left among men.
He met his end in battle,
a friendless exile, felled by the sword
wielded by Weoxstan: who went back to his kinsmen
with the shining helm, the shirt of ring-mail
and the ancient giant-sword. All this war-harness,

eager for use, Onela then gave to him,
though it had been his nephew's; nor did he speak
of the blood-feud to the killer of his brother's son.
Weoxstan kept this war-gear many years,
sword and breast-armor, till his son was able
to perform manly deeds as his father had of old.
He gave him among the Geats these garments of battle
of incalculable worth; then went his life's journey
wise and full of years.
For the youthful warrior
this was the first occasion when he was called on to stand
at his dear lord's shoulder in the shock of battle.
His courage did not crumble, nor did his kinsman's heirloom
weaken at the war-play: as the worm found
when they had got to grips with one another.

Wiglaf then spoke many words that were fitting,
addressed his companions; dark was his mood.
"I remember the time, as we were taking mead
in the banqueting hall, when we bound ourselves
to the gracious lord who granted us arms,
that we would make return for these trappings of war,
these helms and hard swords, if an hour such as this
should ever chance for him. He chose us himself
out of all his host for this adventure here,
expecting action; he armed me with you
because he accounted us keen under helmet,
men able with the spear—even though our lord
intended to take on this task of courage
as his own share, as shepherd of the people,
and champion of mankind in the achieving of glory
and deeds of daring.
That day has now come
when he stands in need of the strength of good fighters,
our lord and liege. Let us go to him,
help our leader for as long as it requires,
the fearsome fire-blast. I had far rather
that the flame should enfold my flesh-frame there
alongside my gold-giver—as God knows of me.
To bear our shields back to our homes
would seem unfitting to me, unless first we have been able
to kill the foe and defend the life
of the prince of the Weather-Geats. I well know
that former deeds deserve not that, alone
of the flower of the Geats, he should feel the pain,
sink in the struggle; sword and helmet,
corselet and mail-shirt, shall be our common gear."

He strode through the blood-smoke, bore his war-helmet
to the aid of his lord, uttered few words:

"Beloved Beowulf, bear all things well!
You gave it out long ago in your youth
that, living, you would not allow your glory
ever to abate. Bold-tempered chieftain,
famed for your deeds, you must defend your life now
with all your strength. I shall help you."

When these words had been spoken, the worm came on wrathful,
attacked a second time, terrible visitant,
sought out his foes in a surge of flame,
the hated men.
Mail-shirt did not serve
the young spear-man; and shield was withered
back to the boss by the billow of fire;
but when the blazing had burnt up his own,
the youngster stepped smartly to take
the cover of his kinsman's. Then did that kingly warrior
remember his deeds again and dealt out a sword-blow
with his full strength: it struck into the head
with annihilating weight. But Nailing snapped,
failed in the battle, Beowulf's sword
of ancient gray steel. It was not granted to him
that an iron edge could ever lend him
help in a battle; his hand was too strong.
I have heard that any sword, however hardened by wounds,
that he bore into battle, his blow would overtax
—any weapon whatever; it was the worse for him.

A third time the terrible fire-drake
remembered the feud. The foe of the people
rushed in on the champion when a chance offered:
seething with warspite, he seized his whole neck
between bitter fangs: blood covered him,
Beowulf's life-blood, let in streams.
Then I heard how the earl alongside the king
in the hour of need made known the valor,
boldness and strength that were bred in him.
His hand burned as he helped his kinsman,
but the brave soldier in his splendid armor
ignored the head and hit the attacker
somewhat below it, so that the sword went in,
flashing-hilted; and the fire began
to slacken in consequence.
The king once more
took command of his wits, caught up a stabbing-knife
of the keenest battle-sharpness, that he carried in his harness:
and the Geats' Helm struck through the serpent's body.
So daring drove out life: they had downed their foe
by common action, the atheling pair,

and had made an end of him. So in the hour of need
a warrior must live! For the lord this was
the last victory in the list of his deeds
and works in the world. The wound that the earth-drake
had first succeeded in inflicting on him
began to burn and swell; he swiftly felt
the bane beginning to boil in his chest,
the poison within him. The prince walked across
to the side of the barrow, considering deeply;
he sat down on a ledge, looked at the giant-work,
saw how the age-old earth-hall contained
stone arches anchored on pillars.
Then that excellent thane with his own hands washed
his battle-bloodied prince, bathed with water
the famous leader, his friend and lord,
sated with fighting; he unfastened his helmet.

Beowulf spoke; he spoke through the pain
of his fatal wound. He well knew
that he had come to the end of his allotted days,
his earthly happiness; all the number
of his days had disappeared: death was very near.
"I would now wish to give my garments in battle
to my own son, if any such
after-inheritor, an heir of my body,
had been granted to me. I have guarded this people
for half a century; not a single ruler
of all the nations neighboring about
has dared to affront me with his friends in war,
or threaten terrors. What the times had in store for me
I awaited in my homeland; I held my own,
sought no secret feud, swore very rarely
a wrongful oath.
In all of these things,
sick with my life's wound, I may still rejoice:
for when my life shall leave my body
the Ruler of Men may not charge me
with the slaughter of kinsmen.
Quickly go now,
beloved Wiglaf, and look upon the hoard
under the gray stone, now the serpent lies dead,
sleeps rawly wounded, bereft of his treasure.
Make haste, that I may gaze upon that golden inheritance,
that ancient wealth; that my eyes may behold
the clear skilful jewels: more calmly then may I
on the treasure's account take my departure
of life and of the lordship I have long held."

Straightaway, as I have heard, the son of Weoxstan

obeyed his wounded lord, weak from the struggle.
Following these words, he went in his ring-coat,
his broidered battle-tunic, under the barrow's roof.
Traversing the ledge to the treasure-house of jewels,
the brave young thane was thrilled by the sight
of the gold gleaming on the ground where it lay,
the devices by the wall and the den of the serpent,
winger of the darkness. Drinking-cups stood there,
the unburnished vessels of a vanished race,
their ornaments awry. Old and tarnished
were the rows of helmets and the heaps of arm-rings,
twisted with cunning. Treasure can easily,
gold in the ground, get the better of
one of human race, hide it who will!
High above the hoard there hung, as he also saw,
a standard all woven wonderfully in gold,
the finest of finger-linkages: the effulgence it gave
allowed him to see the surface of the ground
and examine the treasures. No trace of the worm
was to be seen there, for the sword had finished him.
I heard of the plundering of the hoard in the knoll,
that ancient Giant-work, by that one man;
he filled his bosom with such flagons and vessels
as he himself chose; the standard he took also,
best of banners.
Old Beowulf's sword,
iron of edge, had already struck
the creature who had been keeper of the treasures
for so long an age, employing his fire-blast
in the hoard's defence, flinging out its heat
in the depth of the nights; he died at last, violently.

The envoy made haste in his eagerness to return,
urged on by his prizes. He was pressed by anxiety
as to whether he would find his fearless man,
the lord of the Geats, alive in the open
where he had left him, lacking in strength.
Carrying the treasures, he came upon his prince,
the famous king, covered in blood
and at his life's end; again he began
to sprinkle him with water, until this word's point
broke through the breast-hoard.
The battle-king spoke,
an aged man in sorrow; he eyed the gold.
"I wish to put in words my thanks
to the King of Glory, the Giver of All,
the Lord of Eternity, for these treasures that I gaze upon,
that I should have been able to acquire for my people
before my death-day an endowment such as this.

My life's full portion I have paid out now
for this hoard of treasure; you must attend the people's
needs henceforward; no further may I stay.
Bid men of battle build me a tomb
fair after fire, on the foreland by the sea
that shall stand as a reminder of me to my people,
towering high above Hronesness
so that ocean travelers shall afterwards name it
Beowulf's barrow, bending in the distance
their masted ships through the mists upon the sea."

He unclasped the golden collar from his neck,
staunch-hearted prince, and passed it to the thane,
with the gold-plated helmet, harness and arm-ring;
he bade the young spear-man use them well:
"You are the last man left of our kindred,
the house of the Waymundings! Weird has lured
each of my family to his fated end,
each earl through his valor; I must follow them."

This was the aged man's uttermost word
from the thoughts of his breast; he embraced the pyre's
seething surges; soul left its case,
going its way to the glory of the righteous.

How wretchedly it went with the warrior then,
the younger soldier, when he saw on the ground
his best-beloved at his life's end
suffering miserably! The slayer lay also
bereft of life, beaten down in ruin,
terrible earth-drake. He was unable any longer
to rule the ring-hoard, the writhing serpent,
since the hammers' legacy, hard and battle-scarred,
the iron edges, had utterly destroyed him;
the far-flier lay felled along the ground
beside his store-house, still from his wounds.
He did not mount the midnight air,
gliding and coiling, glorying in his hoard,
flaunting his aspect; he fell to the earth
at the powerful hand of that prince in war.
Not one of the men of might in that land,
however daring in deeds of every kind,
had ever succeeded, from all I have heard,
in braving the venomous breath of that foe
or putting rude hands on the rings in that hall
if his fortune was to find the defender of the barrow
waiting and on his guard. The gaining of the hoard
of beautiful treasure was Beowulf's death;
so it was that each of them attained the end
of his life's lease.

It was not long then
till they budged from the wood, the battle-shirkers,
ten of them together, those traitors and weaklings
who had not dared deploy their spears
in their own lord's extreme need.
They bore their shields ashamedly,
their armor of war, to where the old man lay.
They regarded Wiglaf. Wearily he sat,
a foot-soldier, at the shoulder of his lord,
trying to wake him with water; but without success.
For all his desiring it, he was unable to hold
his battle-leader's life in this world
or affect anything of the All-Wielder's;
for every man's action was under the sway
of God's judgement, just as it is now.

There was a rough and a ready answer
on the young man's lips for those who had lost their nerve.
Wiglaf spoke, Weoxstan's offspring,
looked at the unloved ones with little joy at heart:
"A man who would speak the truth may say with justice
that a lord of men who allowed you those treasures,
who bestowed on you the trappings that you stand there in
—as, at the ale-bench, he would often give
to those who sat in hall both helmet and mail-shirt
as a lord to his thanes, and things of the most worth
that he was able to find anywhere in the world—
that he had quite thrown away and wasted cruelly
all that battle-harness when the battle came upon him.
The king of our people had no cause to boast
of his companions of the guard. Yet God vouchsafed him,
the Master of Victories, that he should avenge himself
when courage was wanted, by his weapon alone.
I was little equipped to act as body-guard
for him in the battle, but, above my own strength,
I began all the same to support my kinsman.
Our deadly enemy grew ever the weaker—
when I had struck him with my sword—less strongly welled
the fire from his head. Too few supporters
flocked to our prince when affliction came.
Now there shall cease for your race the receiving of treasure,
the bestowal of swords, all satisfaction of ownership,
all comfort of home. Your kinsmen every one,
shall become wanderers without land-rights
as soon as athelings over the world
shall hear the report of how you fled,
a deed of ill fame. Death is better
for any earl than an existence of disgrace!"

He bade that the combat's result be proclaimed in the city

over the brow of the headland; there the band of earls
had sat all morning beside their shields
in heavy spirits, half expecting
that it would be the last day of their beloved man,
half hoping for his return. The rider from the headland
in no way held back the news he had to tell;
as his commission was, he called out over all:
"The Lord of the Geats lies now on his slaughter-bed,
the leader of the Weathers, our loving provider,
dwells in his death-rest through the dragon's power.
Stretched out beside him, stricken with the knife,
lies his deadly adversary. With the edge of the sword
he could not contrive, try as he might,
to wound the monster. Weoxstan's son
Wiglaf abides with Beowulf there,
one earl waits on the other one lifeless;
in weariness of heart he watches by the heads
of friend and foe.
The fall of the king,
when it spreads abroad and is spoken of
among the Frisians and the Franks, forebodes a time
of wars for our people. The war against the Hugas
had a hard beginning when Hygelac[8] sailed
into the land of the Frisians with his fleet-army:
there it was that the Hetware hurled themselves upon him
and with their greater strength stoutly compelled
that battle-clad warrior to bow before them;
he fell among the troop, distributed no arms
as lord to the guard. It has not been granted to us since
to receive mercy from the Merovingian king.

Nor can I expect peace or fair dealing
from the Swedish nation; it is no secret
that it was Ongentheow who put an end to the life
of Hrethel's son, Hathkin, by Hrefnawudu
when in their pride the people of the Geats
first made attack upon the fighting Scylfings.
Quickly did the formidable father of Ohthere,
terrible veteran, return that blow,
he cut down the sea-king, recaptured his wife,
the mother of Onela and Ohthere in her youth,
now an aged woman, her ornaments stripped from her.
He then drove after his deadly foes
so that they hid themselves, hard-pressed,
in the Ravenswood, and without a lord.

With his host he besieged those whom swords had left
ailing from their wounds. All through the night

8. One of the only historical events in the poem, Hygelac's disastrous raid is mentioned by the Latin historian Gregory of Tours as occurring in 521.

he promised horrors to that unhappy band,
saying that on the morrow he would mutilate them
with the edges of the sword, and set some on the gallows
as sport for the birds. With break of day
what comfort came to those care-oppressed men
when they heard Hygelac's horn and trumpet
giving voice, as that valiant one came up
with the flower of his host, following on their tracks!

The bloody swathe of the Swedes and the Geats
in their slaughterous pursuit could be seen from afar
—how the peoples had stirred up the strife between them.
The earl Ongentheow took the upper ground;
the wise champion went up to his stronghold
in the van of his kinsmen; the veteran grieved,
but he knew the power of the superb Hygelac,
his strength in war; he was not confident
of his resistance, that he could stand against the vikings,
defend his hoard against the fighters from the sea,
his children and his queen. He chose to draw back,
old behind his earth-wall.
Then was the offering of the chase
to the people of the Swedes; sweeping forward,
the standards of Hygelac surged over the camp
as Hrethel's brood broke through the rampart.
Then was Ongentheow the ashen-haired
brought to bay by the brightness of swords
and the king of a nation must kneel as Eofor
singly disposed. It was a desperate blow
that Wulf Wonreding's weapon fetched him,
and at the stroke streams of blood
sprang forth beneath his hair. The hoary-headed Scylfing,
undismayed by this deadly blow,
gave in exchange a graver stroke
as he came round to face him, king of the people.
Wonred's brave son was incapable
of the answer-blow upon the older man,
for the king had cut through the casque[9] on his head,
forced him to bend; he bowed to the earth
marked with blood. Yet he was not marked for death;
it was a keen wound, but he recovered from it.
Then as his brother lay there, the brave Eofor,
Hygelac's follower, fetched his broad sword,
an ancient giant-blade, to the giant-helm of Ongentheow
above his shield, and split it; then the shepherd of the people,
the king, fell down, fatally wounded.

There were many to bind up the brother's wounds;

9. Helmet.

they raised him at once, now the way was open
and the battlefield had fallen to them.
One sturdy warrior then stripped the other,
took from Ongentheow his iron war-shirt,
his hilted sword and his helmet also,
the old man's accoutrement, and carried it to Hygelac.
He accepted the harness with a handsome promise
of rewards among the people; a promise he kept.
For at his homecoming Hrethel's offspring
rewarded Eofor and Wulf for their assault
with copious treasures. The king of the Geats
handed to each of them a hundred thousand
in lands and linked rings; there was little cause for any
on middle earth to begrudge them these glories earned in battle.
He also gave to Eofor his only daughter,
a grace to his home and a guarantee of favor.

It is this feud, this fierce hostility,
this murder-lust between men, I am moved to think,
that the Swedish people will prosecute against us
when once they learn that life has fled
from the lord of the Geats, guardian for so long
of hoard and kingdom, of keen shield-warriors
against every foe. Since the fall of the princes
he has taken care of our welfare, and accomplished yet more
heroic deeds.
Haste is best now,
that we should go to look on the lord of the people,
then bring our ring-bestower on his road,
escort him to the pyre. More than one portion of wealth
shall melt with the hero, for there's a hoard of treasure
and gold uncounted; a grim purchase,
for in the end it was with his own life
that he bought these rings: which the burning shall devour,
the fire enfold. No fellow shall wear
an arm-ring in his memory; no maiden's neck
shall be enhanced in beauty by the bearing of these rings.
Bereft of gold, rather, and in wretchedness of mind
she shall tread continually the tracks of exile
now that the leader of armies has laid aside his mirth,
his sport and glad laughter. Many spears shall therefore
feel cold in the mornings to the clasping fingers
and the hands that raise them. Nor shall the harper's melody
arouse them for battle; and yet the black raven,
quick on the marked men, shall have much to speak of
when he tells the eagle of his takings at the feast
where he and the wolf bared the bodies of the slain."

Such was the rehearsal of the hateful tidings
by that bold messenger; amiss in neither

words nor facts. The war-band arose;
they went unhappily under Earna-ness
to look on the wonder with welling tears.
They found him on the sand, his soul fled,
keeping his resting-place: rings he had given them
in former times! But the final day
had come for the champion; and the chief of the Geats,
the warrior-king, had met his wondrous death.

Stranger the creature they encountered first
in the level place—the loathsome worm
stretched out opposite. Scorched by its own flames
lay the fire-drake in its fatal markings,
and it measured fifty feet as it lay.
He had once been master of the midnight air,
held sweet sway there, and swooped down again
to seek his den; now death held him fast,
he had made his last use of lairs in the earth.

Standing by him there were bowls and flagons,
there were platters lying there, and precious swords,
quite rusted through, as they had rested there
a thousand winters in the womb of earth.

And this gold of former men was full of power,
the huge inheritance, hedged about with a spell:
no one among men was permitted to touch
that golden store of rings unless God Himself,
the true King of Victories, the Protector of mankind,
enabled one He chose to open the hoard,
whichever among men should seem meet to Him.
It was plain to see then that this plan had failed
the creature who had kept these curious things hidden
wrongfully within the wall; the warden had slain
a man like few others; but the feud was straightaway
avenged and wrathfully. It is a wonder to know
where the most courageous of men may come to the end
of his allotted life, and no longer dwell
a man in the mead-hall among companions!

So it was for Beowulf when he embarked on that quarrel,
sought out the barrow-guard; he himself did not know
in what way his parting from the world was to come.
The great princes who had placed the treasure there
had laid on it a curse to last until Doomsday,
that the man who should plunder the place would thereby
commit a crime, and be confined with devils,
tortured grievously in the trammels of hell.
But Beowulf had not looked on the legacy of these men
with too eager an eye, for all its gold.

Wiglaf spoke, Weoxstan's son:
"Many must often endure distress
for the sake of one; so it is with us.
We could not urge any reason
on our beloved king, the keeper of the land,
why he should not approach the protector of the gold
but let him lie where he had long been already
and abide in his den until the end of the world.
He held to his high destiny.
The hoard has been seen
that was acquired at such a cost; too cruel the fate
that impelled the king of the people towards it!
I myself was inside there, and saw all
the wealth of the chamber once my way was open
—little courtesy was shown in allowing me to pass
beneath the earth-wall. I urgently filled
my hands with a huge heap of the treasures
stored in the cave, carried them out
to my lord here. He was alive still
and commanded his wits. Much did he say
in his grief, the old man; he asked me to speak to you,
ordered that on the place of the pyre you should raise
a barrow fitting your friend's achievements;
conspicuous, magnificent, as among men he was
while he could wield the wealth of his stronghold
the most honored of warriors on the wide earth.

Let us now hasten to behold again,
and approach once more that mass of treasures,
awesome under the walls; I shall guide you,
so that from near at hand you may behold sufficiently
the thick gold and the bracelets. Let a bier be made ready,
contrive it quickly, so that when we come out again
we may take up our king, carry the man
beloved by us to his long abode
where he must rest in the Ruler's keeping."

Then the son of Weoxstan, worthy in battle,
had orders given to owners of homesteads
and a great many warriors, that the governors of the people
from far and wide should fetch in wood
for the hero's funeral pyre.
"Now the flames shall grow dark
and the fire destroy the sustainer of the warriors
who often endured the iron shower
when, string-driven, the storm of arrows
sang over shield-wall, and the shaft did its work,
sped by its feathers, furthered the arrow-head."

Then in his wisdom Weoxstan's son
called out from the company of the king's own thanes
seven men in all, who excelled among them,
and, himself the eighth warrior, entered in beneath
that unfriendly roof. The front-stepping man
bore in his hand a blazing torch.

When the men perceived a piece of the hoard
that remained unguarded, mouldering there
on the floor of the chamber, they did not choose by lot
who should remove it; undemurring,
as quickly as they could, they carried outside
the precious treasures; and they pushed the dragon,
the worm, over the cliff, let the waves take him
and the flood engulf the guardian of the treasures.
Untold profusion of twisted gold
was loaded onto a wagon, and the warrior prince
borne hoary-headed to Hronesness.

The Great race then reared up for him
a funeral pyre. It was not a petty mound,
but shining mail-coats and shields of war
and helmets hung upon it, as he had desired.
Then the heroes, lamenting, laid out in the middle
their great chief, their cherished lord.
On top of the mound the men then kindled
the biggest of funeral-fires. Black wood-smoke
arose from the blaze, and the roaring of flames
mingled with weeping. The winds lay still
as the heat at the fire's heart consumed
the house of bone. And in heavy mood
they uttered their sorrow at the slaughter of their lord.

A woman of the Geats in grief sang out
the lament for his death. Loudly she sang,
her hair bound up, the burden of her fear
that evil days were destined her
—troops cut down, terror of armies,
bondage, humiliation. Heaven swallowed the smoke.

Then the Storm-Geat nation constructed for him
a stronghold on the headland, so high and broad
that seafarers might see it from afar.
The beacon to that battle-reckless man
they made in ten days. What remained from the fire
they cast a wall around, of workmanship
as fine as their wisest men could frame for it.
They placed in the tomb both the torques[1] and the jewels,
all the magnificence that the men had earlier
taken from the hoard in hostile mood.

1. Collars or necklaces with twisted bands.

They left the earls' wealth in the earth's keeping,
the gold in the dirt. It dwells there yet,
of no more use to men than in ages before.

Then the warriors rode around the barrow,
twelve of them in all, athelings' sons.
They recited a dirge to declare their grief,
spoke of the man, mourned their king.
They praised his manhood and the prowess of his hands,
they raised his name; it is right a man
should be lavish in honoring his lord and friend,
should love him in his heart when the leading-forth
from the house of flesh befalls him at last.
This was the manner of the mourning of the men of the Geats,
sharers in the feast, at the fall of their lord:
they said that he was of all the world's kings
the gentlest of men, and the most gracious,
the kindest to his people, the keenest for fame.

RESPONSE

John Gardner: from *Grendel*[1]

CHAPTER ONE

The old ram stands looking down over rockslides, stupidly triumphant. I blink. I stare in horror. "Scat!" I hiss. "Go back to your cave, go back to your cowshed—whatever." He cocks his head like an elderly, slow-witted king, considers the angles, decides to ignore me. I stamp. I hammer the ground with my fists. I hurl a skull-size stone at him. He will not budge. I shake my two hairy fists at the sky and I let out a howl so unspeakable that the water at my feet turns sudden ice and even I myself am left uneasy. But the ram stays; the season is upon us. And so begins the twelfth year of my idiotic war.

The pain of it! The stupidity!

"Ah, well," I sigh, and shrug, trudge back to the trees.

Do not think my brains are squeezed shut, like the ram's, by the roots of horns. Flanks atremble, eyes like stones, he stares at as much of the world as he can see and feels it surging in him, filling his chest as the melting snow fills dried-out creekbeds, tickling his gross, lopsided balls and charging his brains with the same unrest that made him suffer last year at this time, and the year before, and the year before that. (He's forgotten them all.) His hindparts shiver with the usual joyful, mindless ache

1. John Gardner was a best-selling American novelist and professor of medieval literature who died in a motorcycle accident in 1982 at the age of 49. His first popular success came with the 1971 publication of *Grendel*, a rewriting of *Beowulf* from the monster's point of view. Alienated from traditional morality and the comforts of the beer hall, Grendel gorges himself gleefully on the bodies he has carried off from Hrothgar's hall, and fondly recalls the places where he "tore off sly old Athelgard's head" or ate an old woman who "tasted of urine and spleen." Though Gardner does not portray him entirely sympathetically, Grendel can be seen in the romantic tradition of the outsider hero, like the monster in Mary Shelley's *Frankenstein* or Satan in Blake's rereading of Milton's *Paradise Lost*.

While Gardner's interpretation of the monster is distinctly modern, the style of the novel reveals his background as a medievalist: he imitates the Old English of *Beowulf* in his use of alliteration and of Germanic compound words such as "falconswift," "whalecocks," and "earth-rim-rover."

to mount whatever happens near—the storm piling up black towers to the west, some rotting, docile stump, some spraddle-legged ewe. I cannot bear to look. "Why can't these creatures discover a little dignity?" I ask the sky. The sky says nothing, predictably. I make a face, uplift a defiant middle finger, and give an obscene little kick. The sky ignores me, forever unimpressed. Him too I hate, the same as I hate these brainless budding trees, these brattling birds.

Not, of course, that I fool myself with thoughts that I'm more noble. Pointless, ridiculous monster crouched in the shadows, stinking of dead men, murdered children, martyred cows. (I am neither proud nor ashamed, understand. One more dull victim, leering at seasons that never were meant to be observed.) "Ah, sad one, poor old freak!" I cry, and hug myself, and laugh, letting out salt tears, he he! till I fall down gasping and sobbing. (It's mostly fake.) The sun spins mindlessly overhead, the shadows lengthen and shorten as if by plan. Small birds, with a high-pitched yelp, lay eggs. The tender grasses peek up, innocent yellow, through the ground: the children of the dead. (It was just here, this shocking green, that once when the moon was tombed in clouds, I tore off sly old Athelgard's head. Here, where the startling tiny jaws of crocuses snap at the late-winter sun like the heads of baby watersnakes, here I killed the old woman with the irongray hair. She tasted of urine and spleen, which made me spit. Sweet mulch for yellow blooms. Such are the tiresome memories of a shadow-shooter, earth-rim-roamer, walker of the world's weird wall.) "Waaah!" I cry, with another quick, nasty face at the sky, mournfully observing the way it is, bitterly remembering the way it was, and idiotically casting tomorrow's nets. "Aargh! Yaww!" I reel, smash trees. Disfigured son of lunatics. The big-boled oaks gaze down at me yellow with morning, beneath complexity. "No offense," I say, with a terrible, sycophantish smile, and tip an imaginary hat.

It was not always like this, of course. On occasion it's been worse.

No matter, no matter.

The doe in the clearing goes stiff at sight of my horridness, then remembers her legs and is gone. It makes me cross. "Blind prejudice!" I bawl at the splintered sunlight where half a second ago she stood. I wring my fingers, put on a long face. "Ah, the unfairness of everything," I say, and shake my head. It is a matter of fact that I have never killed a deer in all my life, and never will. Cows have more meat and, locked up in pens, are easier to catch. It is true, perhaps, that I feel some trifling dislike of deer, but no more dislike than I feel for other natural things—discounting men. But deer, like rabbits and bears and even men, can make, concerning my race, no delicate distinctions. That is their happiness: they see all life without observing it. They're buried in it like crabs in mud. Except men, of course. I am not in a mood, just yet, to talk of men.

So it goes with me day by day and age by age, I tell myself. Locked in the deadly progression of moon and stars. I shake my head, muttering darkly on shaded paths, holding conversation with the only friend and comfort this world affords, my shadow. Wild pigs clatter away through brush. A baby bird falls feet-up in my path, squeaking. With a crabby laugh, I let him lie, kind heaven's merciful bounty to some sick fox. So it goes with me, age by age. (Talking, talking. Spinning a web of words, pale walls of dreams, between myself and all I see.)

The first grim stirrings of springtime come (as I knew they must, having seen the ram), and even under the ground where I live, where no light breaks but the red of my fires and nothing stirs but the flickering shadows on my wet rock walls, or scampering rats on my piles of bones, or my mother's fat, foul bulk rolling over, restless again—molested by nightmares, old memories—I am aware in my chest of tuberstirrings in the blacksweet duff of the forest overhead. I feel my anger coming back, building up like invisible fire, and at last, when my soul can no longer resist, I go up—as mechanical as anything else—fists clenched against my lack of will, my belly growling, mindless as wind, for blood. I swim up through the firesnakes, hot dark whalecocks prowling the luminous green of the mere, and I surface with a gulp among churning waves and smoke. I crawl up onto the bank and catch my breath.

It's good at first to be out in the night, naked to the cold mechanics of the stars. Space hurls outward, falconswift, mounting like an irreversible injustice, a final disease. The cold night air is reality at last: indifferent to me as a stone face carved on a high cliff wall to show that the world is abandoned. So childhood too feels good at first, before one happens to notice the terrible sameness, age after age. I lie there resting in the steaming grass, the old lake hissing and gurgling behind me, whispering patterns of words my sanity resists. At last, heavy as an ice-capped mountain, I rise and work my way to the inner wall, beginning of wolfslopes, the edge of my realm. I stand in the high wind balanced, blackening the night with my stench, gazing down to cliffs that fall away to cliffs, and once again I am aware of my potential: I could die. I cackle with rage and suck in breath.

"Dark chasms!" I scream from the cliff-edge, "seize me! Seize me to your foul black bowels and crush my bones!" I am terrified at the sound of my own huge voice in the darkness. I stand there shaking from head to foot, moved to the deep-sea depths of my being, like a creature thrown into audience with thunder.

At the same time, I am secretly unfooled. The uproar is only my own shriek, and chasms are, like all things vast, inanimate. They will not snatch me in a thousand years, unless, in a lunatic fit of religion, I jump.

I sigh, depressed, and grind my teeth. I toy with shouting some tidbit more—some terrifying, unthinkable threat, some blackly fuliginous riddling hex—but my heart's not in it. "Missed me!" I say with a coy little jerk and a leer, to keep my spirits up. Then, with a sigh, a kind of moan, I start very carefully down the cliffs that lead to the fens and moors and Hrothgar's hall. Owls cross my path as silently as raiding ships, and at the sound of my foot, lean wolves rise, glance at me awkwardly, and, neat of step as lizards, sneak away. I used to take some pride in that—the caution of owls when my shape looms in, the alarm I stir in these giant northern wolves. I was younger then. Still playing cat and mouse with the universe.

I move down through the darkness, burning with murderous lust, my brains raging at the sickness I can observe in myself as objectively as might a mind ten centuries away. Stars, spattered out through lifeless night from end to end, like jewels scattered in a dead king's grave, tease, torment my wits toward meaningful patterns that do not exist. I can see for miles from these rock walls: thick forest suddenly still at my coming—cowering stags, wolves, hedgehogs, boars, submerged in their stifling, unmemorable fear; mute birds, pulsating, thoughtless clay in hushed old trees, thick limbs interlocked to seal drab secrets in.

I sigh, sink into the silence, and cross it like wind. Behind my back, at the world's end, my pale slightly glowing fat mother sleeps on, old, sick at heart, in our dingy underground room. Life-bloated, baffled, long-suffering hag. Guilty, she imagines, of some unremembered, perhaps ancestral crime. (She must have some human in her.) Not that she thinks. Not that she dissects and ponders the dusty mechanical bits of her miserable life's curse. She clutches at me in her sleep as if to crush me. I break away. "Why are we here?" I used to ask her. "Why do we stand this putrid, stinking hole?" She trembles at my words. Her fat lips shake. "Don't ask!" her wiggling claws implore. (She never speaks.) "Don't ask!" It must be some terrible secret, I used to think. I'd give her a crafty squint. She'll tell me, in time, I thought. But she told me nothing. I waited on. That was before the old dragon, calm as winter, unveiled the truth. He was not a friend.

And so I come through trees and towns to the lights of Hrothgar's meadhall. I am no stranger here. A respected guest. Eleven years now and going on twelve I have come up this clean-mown central hill, dark shadow out of the woods below, and have knocked politely on the high oak door, bursting its hinges and sending the shock of my greeting inward like a cold blast out of a cave. "Grendel!" they squeak, and I smile like exploding spring. The old Shaper, a man I cannot help but admire, goes out the back window with his harp at a single bound, though blind as a bat. The drunkest of Hrothgar's thanes come reeling and clanking down from their wall-hung beds, all shouting their meady, outrageous boasts, their heavy swords aswirl like eagles' wings. "Woe, woe, woe!" cries Hrothgar, hoary with winters, peeking in, wide-eyed, from his bedroom in back. His wife, looking in behind him, makes a scene. The thanes in the meadhall blow out the lights and cover the wide stone fireplace with shields. I laugh, crumple over; I can't help myself. In the darkness, I alone see clear as day. While they squeal and screech and bump into each other, I silently sack up my dead and withdraw to the woods. I eat and laugh and eat until I can barely walk, my chest-hair matted with dribbled blood, and then the roosters on the hill crow, and dawn comes over the roofs of the houses, and all at once I am filled with gloom again.

"This is some punishment sent us," I hear them bawling from the hill.

My head aches. Morning nails my eyes.

"Some god is angry," I hear a woman keen. "The people of Scyld and Herogar and Hrothgar are mired in sin!"

My belly rumbles, sick on their sour meat. I crawl through bloodstained leaves to the eaves of the forest, and there peek out. The dogs fall silent at the edge of my spell, and where the king's hall surmounts the town, the blind old Shaper, harp clutched tight to his fragile chest, stares futilely down, straight at me. Otherwise nothing. Pigs root dully at the posts of a wooden fence. A rumple-horned ox lies chewing in dew and shade. A few men, lean, wearing animal skins, look up at the gables of the king's hall, or at the vultures circling casually beyond. Hrothgar says nothing, hoarfrost-bearded, his features cracked and crazed. Inside, I hear the people praying—whimpering, whining, mumbling, pleading—to their numerous sticks and stones. He doesn't go in. The king has lofty theories of his own.

"Theories," I whisper to the bloodstained ground. So the dragon once spoke. ("They'd map out roads through Hell with their crackpot theories!" I recall his laugh.)

Then the groaning and praying stop, and on the side of the hill the dirge-slow shoveling begins. They throw up a mound for the funeral pyre, for whatever arms or legs or heads my haste has left behind. Meanwhile, up in the shattered hall, the builders are hammering, replacing the door for (it must be) the fiftieth or sixtieth time, industrious and witless as worker ants—except that they make small, foolish changes, adding a few more iron pegs, more iron bands, with tireless dogmatism.

Now fire. A few little lizard tongues, then healthy flames reaching up through the tangled nest of sticks. (A feeble-minded crow could have fashioned a neater nest.) A severed leg swells up and bursts, then an arm, then another, and the red fire turns on the blackening flesh and makes it sizzle, and it reaches higher, up and up into greasy smoke, turning, turning like falcons at warplay, rushing like circling wolves up into the swallowing, indifferent sky. And now, by some lunatic theory, they throw on golden rings, old swords, and braided helmets. They wail, the whole crowd, women and men, a kind of song, like a single quavering voice. The song rings up like the greasy smoke and their faces shine with sweat and something that looks like joy. The song swells, pushes through woods and sky, and they're singing now as if by some lunatic theory they had won. I shake with rage. The red sun blinds me, churns up my belly to nausea, and the heat thrown out of the bone-fire burns my skin. I cringe, clawing my flesh, and flee for home.

The Táin Bó Cuailnge

The Táin Bó Cuailnge (The Cattle Raid of Cooley), the chief work in the "Ulster Cycle" of Irish heroic narratives, was already a famed and ancient story by the twelfth century, when an expanded version was copied into the manuscript now called the Book of Leinster. That manuscript also contains a legend about the recovery of the whole *Táin* by the poets of Ireland, who knew it only in fragments. Followers of the chief poet set out for Brittany, the story reports, where a complete copy had been carried. In the course of their journey, though, they pass the grave of Fergus mac Roich, an earlier poet and a hero in the events of the *Táin*. Alone at the grave, the chief poet's son calls up the spirit of Fergus, who recites to him the tale in its entirety.

This legend offers a window on Irish literary culture and its sense of the past at the time. The legend comes from a world of written books that could be sought out and copied; yet it also recalls the prestige and priority of an oral tradition. Further, the story evokes the aura of magic surrounding poets in medieval Ireland and the poets' own sense of themselves as spiritual and even genealogical heirs of an ancient calling which stretched back into the mythic past. Ireland had developed a deeply Christian culture yet celebrated its native secular stories and did so with a vigor that has little of the elegiac nostalgia and biblical echoes seen in *Beowulf*. The highest class of poets, the *filid* (singular *fili)*, also inherited practices like divination which had been the work of other learned classes, such as the druids, in the pagan era.

If the Book of Leinster thus displays a lively but complicated connection to a rich literary past, the *Táin* itself looks backward to a still more ancient world of warring heroes, magical weapons, shape-shifters, and wondrous beasts, in which the line between mortals and gods was blurry and often crossed. The earliest version of the *Táin* stems from an oral tradition perhaps as early as the fourth century, but the society it depicts—with warriors riding in battle chariots, fighting naked, and taking the heads of conquered enemies—mirrors what we know of Celtic peoples on the Continent as early as the second century B.C.E. The Roman geographer Strabo called the "whole race . . . madly fond of war, high-spirited and quick to battle." Some of their habits persisted in Ireland but were long over by the sixth century C.E. Other social practices—such as clientship, rigid standards of hospitality, and the obligation to safeguard anyone taken under protection—continued late into the medieval period.

Four great stories converge in the *Táin*. It draws, first, on the history of the bulls Finnbennach the White Horned and Donn Cuailnge the Brown Bull of Cooley, who originated as two pig-keepers and passed through a series of animal forms before the moment of the main narrative. Second, the immediate occasion of the cattle raid emerges from a debate between Ailill, king of Connacht, and his wife, Medb.

Medb's quest to match the wealth of Ailill leads her into an armed attempt to take Donn Cuailnge from its owner on the borderlands of Ulster. To achieve this end, third, Medb and Ailill gather an army to march against Ulster. Finally, the hero Cú Chulainn single-handedly protects Ulster's borders until the men of Ulster can recover from a seasonal debility with which they have been long cursed.

The debate of Ailill and Medb introduces one of the most powerful women in medieval Irish literature, stemming partly from a pagan goddess of sovereignty. Medb and similar women reflect a persistent aspect of mythic and literary imagination in the Irish heroic narratives, although in medieval Irish law women actually had fewer rights than their Anglo-Saxon counterparts. The story acknowledges Medb's power as a wealthy woman, leader of armies, and queen, but constantly places that power in question. Indeed, several important men are openly hostile to Medb's strong will; even the bull Finnbennach is in Ailill's herds because he refused to be owned by a woman. Medb's power is explicity sexual. Far from the passive object of desire that we often meet elsewhere in the period, she uses her sexuality as an active force, often for political gain. Yet Medb is much more than a cunning body; she exploits her wealth and is willing to debate and even to battle with her own ally and husband over issues of military strategy.

The armies that gather against the Ulstermen are replete with heroic fighters and complex allegiances, and much of the *Táin*'s emotional weight lies in the passionate devotion and divided loyalties of its warriors. There is particular sadness in the plight of a group of Ulstermen, among them Fergus mac Roich, whose own king Conchobar had killed men taken under their protection; they have fled his court and placed themselves in the service of Ailill. Even more personal is the repeated clash between political fidelity and the quasi-familial link of fosterage in the story.

These issues press hard on the *Táin*'s heroic center, Cú Chulainn, the preeminent hero of the Ulster Cycle. The line between the heroic, the superhuman, and the monstrous can be fluid in the *Táin*, as it is in the curious links between Beowulf and Grendel. Cú Chulainn is of divine birth, and has performed a series of wondrous boyhood exploits, before the events of this story. Even within the *Táin*, he is persistently boyish in appearance and often distracted by activities that approach play. We witness Cú Chulainn coming into his maturity as he fights an exhausting series of border combats single-handedly and unwaveringly, and as he finally must face and defeat his foster-brother Ferdia. Despite this poignant humanity, Cú Chulainn possesses godlike strength and skill with weapons; yet his heroic rage works a physical distortion on him that is almost monstrous, eliciting comparisons with a giant or "a man from the sea-kingdom."

Geography is as important as heroism in the *Táin*. Battles, wonders, and other events repeatedly lead to the naming of a locale, so that the story virtually maps the mythic significance of place in the northern parts of Ireland. It also enfolds much of the genealogy of its legendary heroes. In style and theme, too, the *Táin* counterbalances the wonders of superhuman force by the works of human skill, with elaborate descriptions of clothing, ornament, and decorated weaponry. It narrates the physical beauty of men and women alike with an exquisite attention not found in *Beowulf*. Like much narrative that derives closely from its oral background, the *Táin* is as much the encyclopedia of a people's beliefs and values—or a commemoration of its past beliefs and their impact on current values—as it is a single story of heroic action.

These indications are imprecise but give a rough sense of how key names in the *Táin* sounded in Old Irish. The spelling *-ch* is slightly guttural, as in *loch* or *Bach*.

Ailill *AL-ill*	Finnbennach *finn-VEN-ach*
Bricriu *BRIK-roo*	Láeg *loig*
Cet *ket*	Medb *maive*
Conchobar *CON-cho-wer*	Morrígu *MO-ree-ga*
Cú Chulainn *coo-CHULL-in*	Nemain *NE-van*
Dubthach Dáel Ulad *DUV-thach doil u-lad*	Ráth Crúachain *rawth CROO-a-chan*
Emain Macha *EV-in MA-cha*	Samain *SA-win*
Fedelm *FETH-elm*	Sid *sheethe*
Ferdia *fer-DEE-a*	Táin Bó Cuailnge *toin bow COO-ling-e*
Findabair *FIN-a-wer*	

from The Táin[1]

The Pillow Talk

One night when the royal bed had been prepared for Ailill and Medb in Crúachan Fort[2] in Connacht, they engaged in pillow-talk:

"It's true what they say, girl," said Ailill. "Well-off woman, wealthy man's wife."

"True enough," said the woman. "What makes you say it?"

"Just this," said Ailill, "that you're better off now than the day I took you."

"I was well-off before it," said Medb.

"If you were, I never heard tell of it," said Ailill, "apart from your woman's assets that your neighbor enemies kept plundering and raiding."

"Not so," said Medb, "for my father was High King of Ireland[3]—namely, Eochu Feidlech son of Finn son of Finnoman son of Finnen son of Fingall son of Roth son of Rigéon son of Blathacht son of Beothacht son of Enna Agnech son of Angus Turbech. He had six daughters: Derbriu, Ethne, Éle, Clothru, Muguin, Medb. I was the noblest and most celebrated of them all. The most generous in bestowing gifts and favors. The best at warfare, strife and combat.[4] I had fifteen hundred royal mercenaries, the sons of exiles, and as many more the sons of freeborn native men, and for every soldier of them I had ten, and for every ten I had nine more, and eight, and seven, and six, and five, and four, and three, and two, and one. And that was just my household guard.

"Then my father gave me a province of Ireland, Connacht that is ruled from Crúachan. That is why I am called Medb of Crúachan. Envoys came from Finn the King of Leinster, the son of Ross Ruad, to woo me, and from Cairbre the son of Niafer King of Tara—another son of Ross Ruad—and from Conchobar King of Ulster, son of Fachtna, and from Eochaid Bec. I turned them all down. I asked a more exacting wedding-gift than any woman ever before me—a man without meanness, jealousy and fear.

1. Translated by Ciaran Carson. Carson's translation uses the early, perhaps eighth century "Recension I" of the *Táin*; for some passages (such as the opening section here), absent from that recension, Carson uses "Recension II," copied in the 12th-century Book of Leinster.

2. Ráth Crúachan, the royal fortress of Connacht. Like many fortress towns in Irish legend, it was founded by a woman (Cruacha) and retained traces of its ancient role as a sacred place.

3. Early Ireland was ruled by a shifting company of petty kings, some of whom entered into dependence and service (clientship) with "high kings." The idea of a high king of all Ireland was pure legend until long after the era of the *Táin*.

4. Medb's wealth and military resources probably derive from her namesake, the goddess of sovereignty on whose assent (and sometimes sexual favors) the kingship depended.

"If he were mean, we'd be ill-matched, because I am generous in bestowing gifts and favors. And it would be a disgrace if I were more generous than him, but no disgrace if we are equal, both bestowing freely. If he were cowardly, we'd be ill-matched, for I am powerful in warfare, fight and fray. It would be a disgrace if I were more forcible than him, but no disgrace if both of us are forcible. Nor would it do for my husband to be jealous: I never had one man without another waiting in his shadow. I got the right man—yourself, Ailill, the other son of Ross Ruad of Leinster. You are not mean, you are not jealous, you are not cowardly. When we made the contract, I gave you a bride-price that befits a woman: outfits for a dozen men, a chariot worth thrice seven bondmaids, the breadth of your face in red gold, the weight of your left arm in white bronze. Whoever brings you shame or strife or trouble, you've no claim to compensation or redress, beyond what I claim, for you're a man dependent on a woman's wealth."

"Not so," said Ailill, "for I have two brothers, Cairbre who rules Tara, and Finn the King of Leinster. And I let them rule because of seniority, not because they were more generous with their largesse. I never heard of a province of Ireland that depended on a woman's assets except this one, which is why I came and assumed the throne in succession to my mother, for she is Máta Muiresc, Mágach's daughter. And what better queen for me, than the daughter of the High King of Ireland?"

"All the same," said Medb, "my wealth is greater than yours."

"You astonish me," said Ailill. "No one has more wealth, more goods and jewels than myself. I know this for a fact."

So the least valuable of their assets were brought out, to see who had more wealth and goods and jewels: their cauldrons and buckets and pots, their porringers and tubs and basins. Then their gold artefacts, their rings and their bracelets and their thumb-rings were brought out, and their outfits of purple and blue and black and green and yellow, whether plain or multi-colored, plaid, checked or striped. Their flocks of sheep were brought in from the fields and the meadows and the green lawns. They were counted and compared, and found to be equal in number and size. Among Medb's sheep was a prize ram worth one bondmaid, and among Ailill's was one to match.

From pasture and paddock and stable their horses and steeds were brought in. Among Medb's horses was a prize stallion worth one bondmaid, and Ailill had one to match. Their great herds of swine were brought in from the woods and the glens and the wastelands. They were reckoned and counted and claimed, and found to be equal in size and number. Medb had a prize boar, and Ailill had another.

Then their herds of cows and droves of cattle were brought in from the woods and the wastes of the province. They were reckoned and counted and claimed, and found to be equal in size and number. But among Ailill's cattle was a prize bull, that had been a calf of one of Medb's cows—Finnbennach his name, the White-horned.[5] Not wanting to be reckoned as a woman's asset, he had gone over to the king's herd. And to Medb it was as if she hadn't a single penny, for there was no bull to equal Finnbennach among her cattle.

Mac Roth the Messenger[6] was summoned by Medb, and Medb told Mac Roth to go and see if the match of the bull might be found in any of the provinces of Ireland.

5. A gigantic, blood-red bull with white head and feet. He and Donn Cúailnge, the Brown Bull of Cooley, are the final incarnations of two pig-keepers who fought over their supernatural powers in a series of animal and human shapes.

6. The name means "son of wheel," apt for a messenger.

"I know where to find such a bull and better," said Mac Roth, "in the province of Ulster in the district of Cúailnge, in the house of Dáire Mac Fiachna. His name is the Donn Cúailnge, the Brown Bull of Cúailnge."[7]

"Take yourself there, Mac Roth," said Medb, "and ask Dáire for a year's loan of the Donn Cúailnge, and when the year is up I'll give him back the Brown Bull and fifty heifers to boot. And you can make him another offer, Mac Roth. If the people of those borderlands begrudge the loan of the Pride of the Herd, the Donn Cúailnge, let Dáire himself bring me the bull and I'll grant him a piece of the smooth plain of Aí as big as all his lands, and a chariot worth thrice seven bondmaids, as well as the friendship of my own thighs."

Messengers set out for Dáire Mac Fiachna's house. There were nine of them in Mac Roth's band. Mac Roth was made welcome in Dáire's house, as was right and proper for a Head Messenger. Dáire asked him what had brought him on his journey, and why he had come. The Messenger told him why he had come, and of the dispute between Medb and Ailill.

"So I've come to ask for the loan of the Donn Cúailnge," he said, "to match the White-horned Bull. And when the loan is up, you'll get back the Brown Bull and fifty heifers into the bargain. And there's more on offer: if you bring the bull yourself, you'll get a piece of the smooth plain of Aí as big as all your lands, and a chariot worth thrice seven bondmaids, as well as the friendship of Medb's thighs."

Dáire was well pleased by this. He leaped up and down on his couch and the seams of the flock mattress burst beneath him.

"'Pon my soul!" he cried. "Let the Ulstermen say what they will, I'll take the Pride of the Herd, the Donn Cúailnge, to Ailill and Medb in the land of Connacht."

Mac Roth was well pleased by Dáire's response.

The messengers were attended to, and straw and fresh rushes strewn for them. They were given a feed of meat and drink, until they were well full. Two of the messengers' tongues got loose.

"It's true what they say," said one, "that the man of this house is a great man."

"Very true," said the other.

"Is there a better man in Ulster?" said the first messenger.

"There is indeed," said the second messenger. "Dáire's master, Conchobar,[8] is a better man, for if every man in Ulster bowed to him, there'd be no shame on them. Mind you, it was very great of Dáire to give us nine foot-soldiers what would have been a job for the four strong provinces of Ireland, that is, to bring the Donn Cúailnge out of Ulster."

A third messenger joined the conversation.

"What's all the talk about?" he said.

"Your man here was saying that the man of this house is a great man. Very true, says your other man. Is there a better man in Ulster? says your man here. There is indeed, says your other man. Dáire's master, Conchobar, is a better man, for if every man in Ulster bowed to him there'd be no shame on them. Mind you, it was very great of Dáire to give us nine foot-soldiers what would been for a job for the four strong provinces of Ireland, that is, to bring the Donn Cúailnge out of Ulster."

"I'd like to see the mouth that said that spout blood, for if he hadn't given willingly, we would have taken the bull anyway."

7. An outlying district on the east coast of Ireland, on the borders of Ulster.

8. High king of Ulster and, in some stories, Mebd's lover before her marriage to Ailill.

Just then Dáire Mac Fiachna's head butler came into their quarters with a man carrying drink and another food, and he heard what they were saying. In a fit of rage he put down the food and drink. And he didn't say, "Help yourselves," and he didn't say, "Don't help yourselves." He went straight to Dáire Mac Fiachna's quarters, and said:

"Are you the man who gave the messengers the Pride of the Herd, the Donn Cúailnge?"

"I am indeed," said Dáire.

"That's not the gesture of a king, for what they say is true, that if you hadn't given him willingly, he would have been taken anyway by the forces of Ailill and Medb, and the craftiness of Fergus Mac Róich."[9]

"By the gods I worship, nothing will leave here without my leave!"

They waited until morning. The messengers were up early and they went to Dáire's quarters.

"Tell us, your lordship, where we might find the Donn Cúailnge."

"Indeed I will not," said Dáire, "and if I were the sort of man to give foul play to any messenger or traveler or guest that comes this way, none of you would leave here alive."

"Why's that?" said Mac Roth.

"There's a very good reason why," said Dáire, "You said that whatever I didn't give willingly, it would be taken from me anyway by the forces of Ailill and Medb, and craftiness of Fergus Mac Róich."

"Come now," said Mac Roth, "you shouldn't heed what messengers say when they've a feed of your meat and drink in them. It's not as if it was Ailill's and Medb's fault."

"All the same, Mac Roth, I won't be giving up my bull."

The messengers returned to Crúachan Fort in Connacht. Medb asked them for their news, and Mac Roth broke the news—that they had not brought back the bull from Dáire.

"Why not?" said Medb.

Mac Roth told her why not.

"There's no need to iron out the knots in this one, Mac Roth," said Medb, "for it was known that if the bull were not given willingly, he would be taken by force. And taken he shall be."

The Táin Begins

A great army was mustered in Connacht by Ailill and Medb, and a call to arms went out to the other three provinces. Ailill sent messengers to his six brothers, namely, Cet, Anlúan, Maccorb, Bascall, Én and Dóche, all sons of Mágach. Each brought three thousand men. And Ailill sent word to Cormac Conn Longas the Exile,[1] who was billeted in Connacht with his three thousand men.

Cormac's men marched to Crúachan in three divisions. The first division wore dappled cloaks. Their heads were shaved. They wore knee-length tunics. Each man was equipped with a long shield, a silver-handled sword and a broad bright spear on a slender shaft.

9. Warrior, poet, and prophet, he had been king of Ulster before Conchobar took the throne from him. Conchobar had further violated Fergus's honor by arranging the murder of men who were under his protection, after which Fergus and Ulstermen loyal to him fled into Connacht. He became an advisor to Ailill and one of Medb's many lovers.

1. Cormac, "Leader of the Exiles," is a son of Conchobar who had fled with Fergus and entered the service of Ailill and Medb.

"Is that Cormac?" said they all.

"Not yet," said Medb.

The second division wore dun-gray cloaks and calf-length tunics with red embroidery. Their long hair hung down their backs. Each man was equipped with a bright shield, swords with guards of gold and a five-pronged spear.

"Is that Cormac?" said they all.

"Not yet," said Medb.

The third division arrived. They wore purple cloaks and hooded, ankle-length tunics with red embroidery. Their hair was cut shoulder-length. Each man was equipped with a curved, scallop-edged shield and a "palace-turret" spear. Together they lifted their feet, and together they put them down again.

"Is that Cormac?" said they all.

"That's Cormac," said Medb.

That night they pitched camp and thick smoke rose from their fires between the four fords of Aí—Moga, Bercna, Slissen and Coltna. They stayed there for a fortnight, drinking and feasting and reveling to ease the hardship of the imminent campaign. Then Medb asked her charioteer to hitch up the horses for her to go and consult her druid.[2] She arrived at the druid's place and asked him to look into the future.

"There are those today who leave behind lovers, friends and relations. And if they do not come back safe and sound, they all will curse me, because I made the call to arms. Yet I too have to go, and count myself as much as them. Find out for me if I will come back or not."

And the druid said: "Whoever comes back or not, you will come back."

The driver turned the chariot round. As they made to go back to camp a young woman appeared before them. She had yellow hair. She wore a dappled cloak with a gold pin, a hooded tunic with red embroidery and shoes with gold buckles. Her face was broad above and slender beneath, her eyebrows dark, and her black eyelashes cast a shadow halfway down her cheek. Her lips were of a Parthian red, inset with teeth like pearls. Her hair was done up in three plaits, two wound round her head and the third hanging down her back to her calf. In her hand was a weaver's beam of white bronze inlaid with gold. Her eyes had triple irises. The young woman was armed. Her chariot was drawn by two black horses.

"What is your name?" said Medb to the young woman.

"My name is Fedelm, one of the women poets of Connacht."

"Where have you come from?" said Medb.

"From learning poetry in Alba," said the young woman.

"Have you the Second Sight?" said Medb.

"I have that too," said the young woman.

"Look for us, then, and see how our expedition will fare."

The girl looked.

And Medb said: "For our army, Fedelm, what lies ahead?"

Fedelm replied: "I see it crimson, I see it red."

"That can't be right," said Medb, "for Conchobar is in Emain, laid low by the Curse, together with the rest of the Ulster warriors.[3] My spies have told me so."

2. Another archaizing touch. The Druids had been a pagan priestly class, expert in prophecy.

3. Macha, a goddess of war, had come among the Ultstermen in human guise. Conchobar forced her to race with his horses even though she was pregnant. She won but gave birth just over the finish line. She cursed the Ulstermen, in times of danger, to suffer a period of weakness like that of a woman in labor. Only women, children, and Cú Chulainn were exempt. Emain is Conchobar's capital.

And Medb said: "For our army, Fedelm, what lies ahead?"

Fedelm replied: "I see it crimson, I see it red."

"That can't be right," said Medb, "for Conchobar Mac Uthidir is in Dún Lethglaise with a third of Ulster's forces, and Fergus son of Róich Mac Echdach and his force of three thousand are here with us in exile."

And Medb said: "For our army, Fedelm, what lies ahead?"

Fedelm replied: "I see it crimson, I see it red."

"That's neither here nor there," said Medb. "Whenever a great army musters, there is bound to be trouble and strife and bloody wounds. Soldiers will boast and soldiers will quarrel before the onset of any expedition. I want the truth."

And Medb said: "For our army, Fedelm, what lies ahead?"

Fedelm replied: "I see it crimson, I see it red."

Then the young woman chanted this verse:

I see a forceful blond man,
on whom victories are built.
A fierce light springs from his head,
wounds hang on him like a belt.

Seven jewels play about
the stark pupil of each eye.
His sharp teeth are unsheathed.
He wears a shirt of crimson dye.

His features are beautiful,
his form pleasing to women—
deadly handsome and youthful,
in battle like a dragon.

That same courage can be found
in the famous Blacksmith's Hound—
Cú Chulainn of Muirthemne.[4]
Who this is I do not know,
but this I know for certain—
he stains red his every foe.

I see him loom on the plain,
a whole army to withstand,
wielding four short, sharp, smart swords
in each of his two deft hands.

He attacks in battle-gear
with his fierce barbed *gae bolga*,[5]
his bone-hilted sword, his spear,
each picked for a special use.

Red-cloaked he drives through the field,
uttering a battle-hymn.

4. The "hound of Culann," so named for a boyhood feat in which he killed the savage dog of Culann the Smith, then offered to guard his house in the dog's place. Muirthemne is a plain on the coast of County Louth.

5. The "belly spear" is one of Cú Chulainn's magical weapons, the gift of the woman warrior who trained him in arms. Once it enters the body, it opens into 30 barbs.

From his chariot he deals
death across the left wheel-rim,
the Torqued Man[6] changed terribly
from when his form first struck me.

He's taken the war-path now.
Havoc unless you pay heed
to Sualdam's son, the Hound.
He pursues you with all speed.

Acres will be dense with dead,
as he mows the battlefield,
leaving a thousand lopped heads:
these things I do not conceal.

Blood spurts from soldiers' bodies,
released by this hero's hand.
He kills on sight, scattering
Dada's followers and clan.[7]
Women wail at the corpse-mound
because of him—the Forge-Hound.

They set out the Monday after Samhain. This was their route, south-east from Crúachan Aí:[8]

through Mag Cruinn, the Round Plain,
through Tuaim Móna, the Mound of Turf,
through Turloch Teóra Crích, the Vanishing
    Lake of the Borderlands,
through Cúl Sílinne, the Dripping Backwater,
through Dubloch, the Black Lake,
through Fid Dubh, the Black Wood,
through Badbna,
through Coltain, the Feast,
across the Shannon,
through Glúine Gabur, the Goat's Knees,
through Mag Trega, the Plain of Spears,
through North Tethba,
through South Tethba,
through Cúl, the Backwater,
through Ochaín,
northwards through Uata,
southwards through Tiarthechta,
through Ord, the Hammer,
thorugh Slaiss, the Blows,
through Indeoin, the Anvil . . .

* * *

Such was the route they took.

6. In his battle frenzy, Cú Chulainn undergoes a monstrous distortion, one eye swelling over his cheek, a beam of light leaping from his forehead, and blood erupting from his skull.

7. One of the three warrior races of Ireland.

8. This catalog of place-names, along with genealogies elsewhere, reflects the encyclopedic impulse in the *Táin*.

On the first stage of their march they went from Crúachan to Cúl Sílinne, the site of Loch Carrcín today. Medb told her driver to hitch up her nine chariots for her to make a circuit of the camp, to see who was keen to be on the march, and who was not so keen.

Meanwhile Ailill's tent had been pitched, and fitted with beds and blankets. Next to Ailill was Fergus Mac Róich in his tent; next to Fergus, Cormac Conn Longas; next to him, Conall Cernach; and next to him, Fiacha Mac Fir Febe, the son of Conchobar's daughter. Medb, daughter of Eochaid Fedlech, was on Aillil's other side; next to her, their daughter Finnabair; next to her was Flidais. Not to mention underlings and servants.

Medb came back from inspecting the army and said it wouldn't do for them to proceed further if the three-thousand-strong division of the Gailéoin[9] were to go as well.

"Why do you disrespect them?" said Ailill.

"I don't disrespect them," said Medb. "They are excellent soldiers. While the others were just getting round to building their huts, they had thatched theirs, and were busy cooking. While the others were beginning to eat, they had finished, and their harpers were playing for them. So it won't do for them to come. They'd take all the credit for our army's triumph."

"But they're on our side," said Ailill.

"They can't come," said Medb.

"Let them stay, then," said Ailill.

THE GATHERING OF THE ULSTERMEN[1]

While these events were taking place, Sualdam of Ráith Sualdaim in Muirthemne Plain heard how his son Cú Chulainn had been under constant attack. And he said:

"Are the heavens rent? Does the sea leave its bed? Does the earth open up? Or is this the cry of my son as he fights against the odds?"

He went to his son. But the son was not pleased to see him. True, he was badly wounded, but he knew his father would not be strong enough to fight on anyone's account.

"Go to the men of Ulster," said Cú Chulainn, "and get them to do battle with the army. If they do not, we will never be avenged."

Then his father saw that on Cú Chulainn's body there was not so much as a spot that the tip of a rush couldn't cover that wasn't pierced. Even the left hand, which was protected by his shield, had fifty wounds in it. Sualdam went to Emain Macha and cried out to the men of Ulster:

"Men murdered, women raped, cattle plundered!"

His first cry was from the side of the fort, his next from the royal rampart, and his third from the Mound of Hostages inside Emain itself.

9. A tribe from North Leinster.

1. In the intervening episodes the men of Ireland do succeed in seizing the Brown Bull of Cooley. The armies of Medb and Ailill also move around a large part of central and northern Ireland, trying to penetrate the borders of Ulster. Cú Chulainn repeatedly prevents this, despite the continuing debility of the Ulstermen. He first places impassable taboo signs along their route, then stages night raids on the armies, and finally conducts an exhausting series of single combats, mostly at fords, which climax in a three-day battle with his foster-brother Ferdia. In the face of his onslaught and the gathering army of the Ulstermen as they begin to recover, the men of Ireland retreat southward into Meath, toward Connacht.

No one answered, for among the Ulster people it was not permissible to speak until Conchobar had spoken, and Conchobar would not speak until his druids had spoken. Then a druid said:

"Who rapes? Who plunders? Who murders?"

"Ailill Mac Máta murders and rapes and plunders," said Sualdam, "aided and abetted by Fergus Mac Róich. Your people have been harassed as far as Dún Sobairche. Their cattle, their women and their herds have been carried off. Cú Chulainn has kept them out of Muirthemne and Crích Rois for the three months of winter. He's held together with bent hoops of wood, and dry wisps plug his wounds. Wounds that almost finished him off."[2]

"It would be appropriate" said the druid, "for a man who so provokes the king to die."

"It would serve him right," said Conchobar.

"And serve him right," said the men of Ulster.

"What Sualdam says is true," said Conchobar. "Since the last Monday of summer to the first Monday of spring we've been raped and pillaged."

Sualdam stormed out, dissatisfied with this response. He fell on to his shield and his head was cut off by the scalloped rim. His horse brought his head on the shield back to his house in Emain, and the head kept repeating the same warning.

"Truly, that is too powerful a cry," said Conchobar, "and I swear by the sea before them and the sky above them and the earth beneath them that I will restore every cow to its byre and every woman and child to their homes after victory in battle."

Then Conchobar laid his hand on his son Finnchad Ferr Benn the Horned Man, so called because he wore silver horns. And he said:

"Arise, Finnchad! Go to Dedad in his inlet, to Leamain, to Fallach, to Illann Mac Fergusa, to Gabar, to Dorlunsa, to Imchlár, to Feidlimid Cilair Cétaig, to Fáeladán, to Rochaid Mac Faithemain at Rigdonn, to Lugaid, to Lugda, to Cathbath in his inlet, to the three Cairpres . . .[3]

* * *

It was not difficult for Finnchad to deliver that summons, for all the chieftains in Conchobar's province had been waiting for the word from Conchobar. From east and north and west of Emain they came, and entered Emain to hear the news that Conchobar had risen from his sick-bed. Then they struck out southwards from Emain in search of the enemy. The first stage of their march brought them to Iraird Cuillenn.

"Why are you waiting here?" said Conchobar.

"We're waiting for your sons," said the Ulster army. "They've gone to Tara with three thousand men to contact Erc, the Freckled Calf, son of Coirpre Nia Fer and Fedelm Noíchride. We won't leave this spot until they return to join us."

"Well, I'll not wait," said Conchobar, "for the men of Ireland to find out that I've risen from my sick-bed, recovered from the Curse."

So Conchobar and Celtchar set off with three fifties of chariots, and brought back eight score enemy heads from the ford of Airthir Mide in East Meath. Hence its name now, Áth Féne, Warrior Ford. These were the heads of men who had been watching there for Conchobar's army. They also brought back eight score women

2. Near collapse, Cú Chulainn is tied down with wooden hoops lest he return to battle and injure himself mortally.

3. A catalog of Ulster warriors follows.

who had been held captive. When Conchobar and Celtchar brought the heads to the camp Celtchar said to Conchobar:

ramparts awash with blood the king
of slaughter beyond compare sundered
body parts the ground surrendered
to a hundred streams thirty four-horsed chariots
steeds harnessed to a hundred cruelties
no want of leaders two hundred druids
a steadfast man at Conchobar's back prepare
for battle warriors arise
the battle will erupt at Gáirech and Ilgáirech

The same night Dubthach the Beetle of Ulster had a vision where he saw the army assembled at Gáirech and Ilgáirech. He spoke these words in his sleep:

bewildering morning bewildering times
disordered armies kings cast down
necks broken in the bloody sand
three armies wiped out by the Ulster army
Conchobar at the heart their women huddled
herds driven dawn after morning
heroes cut down hounds torn apart
horses mangled in the bloody mire
as tribe tramples tribe

This disturbed their sleep. The Nemain[4] deranged the army. A hundred men fell dead. When everything was silent they heard Cormac Con Longes—or it might have been Ailill Mac Máta—chanting to the west of the camp:

great the truce the truce at Cuillenn
great the plot the plot at Delind
great the cavalcade the cavalcade at Assal
great the torment the torment at Tuath Bressi

While these visions were happening the men of Connacht, advised by Ailill and Medb and Fergus, decided to send scouts to see if the men of Ulster had reached the plain.

"Go, Mac Roth," said Ailill, "and find out if their men have arrived on the plain of Meath. As it is, I've taken all their goods and cattle. If they want a fight, they can have one. But if they haven't reached the plain, we'll be off."

Mac Roth went out to scan the plain. He returned to Ailill and Medb and reported that when he first looked into the distance from Sliab Fúait he had seen all the beasts of the forest leaving their home and pouring out on to the plain.

"Then I took a second look," said Mac Roth, "and saw a thick mist filling the glens and valleys, so that the hills appeared like islands in a lake. I saw sparks of fire coming through the mist, sparks of every shade and color in the world. Then there was a flash of lightning, and a great rumble of thunder, and a wind that nearly took the hair from my head and threw me on my back, though there's hardly a breeze today."

"What is this, Fergus?" said Ailill. "What can it mean?"

4. Panic, one of a group of war goddesses and wife of the war god, Net.

"I can tell you exactly what it means," said Fergus. "It's the men of Ulster, risen from their sick-beds. It was they who entered the forest. The vast number of their warriors and the violence of their passage shook the forest and caused the beasts of the forest to flee before them on to the plain. The thick mist that you saw was the breath of those powerful men filling the low ground so that the high ground appeared like islands in a lake. The lightning and the sparks of fire and the many colors that you saw, Mac Roth," said Fergus, "those were the eyes of the warriors flashing in their heads like sparks of fire. The thunder and the rumble and the clamor that you heard, that was the whirring of their swords and their ivory-hilted blades, their weapons rattling, chariots clattering, hoof-beats hammering, the shouts and roars and cries of chariot-fighters, warriors and soldiers, the ferocious rage and fury of heroes as they storm towards the battle. They're so fired up, they think they'll never get there."

"We'll be waiting for them," said Ailill. "We have warriors to take them on."

"You'll need them," said Fergus, "for no one—not in Ireland, nor the western world from Greece and Scythia westwards to the Orkney Islands and the Pillars of Hercules, as far as Breogan's Tower and the Isles of Gades—can withstand the men of Ulster in their battle-fury."

Mac Roth set off again to gauge the advance of the Ulstermen and went as far as their camp at Slane in Meath. He reported back to Ailill and Medb and Fergus, giving them a detailed account of what he had seen.

"A great company came to the hill at Slane in Meath," said Mac Roth, "proud and powerful and battle-hungry. I'd put their numbers at about three thousand. Without further ado they stripped down and dug a mound of sods as a throne for their leader. He was a most impressive, regal figure as he led that company, slim, tall and handsome, with finely cut blond hair falling down in waves and curls between his shoulder-blades. He wore a pleated shirt of royal purple and a red-embroidered white hooded tunic. A dazzling brooch of red gold was pinned to the breast of his mantle. His gray eyes had a calm gaze. His face was ruddy-cheeked, with a broad brow and a fine jaw. He had a forked beard of golden curls. Slung across his shoulders was a sword with a gold pommel and a bright shield inlaid with animal designs. He held a slender-shafted spear with a blued steel head. His retinue was the finest of any prince on earth, a fearsome and formidable body of men, magnificently equipped, whose bearing spoke of triumph, rage, implacable resolve and dignity.

"Another company came up," said Mac Roth, "almost as impressive as the first in terms of numbers, bearing, dress and fierce resolve. A handsome young hero led that company. He wore a bordered knee-length tunic and a green cloak fastened at the shoulder with a gold brooch. He had a head of curly yellow hair. An ivory-hilted sword hung at his left side, and he carried a deadly scallop-edged shield. In his hand was a spear like a palace torch-standard, with three silver rings around it that ran freely up and down the shaft from grip to tip and back again. The company took up a position to the left of the first company, with knee to ground and shield-rim held to chin. I detected a stammer in the speech of the great stern warrior who led that company.

"Another company came up," said Mac Roth. "I'd put their numbers at above three thousand. A brave, handsome, broad-faced man was at their head. He had wavy brown hair and a long, forked, wispy beard. He wore a white knee-length hooded tunic and dark-gray fringed cloak pinned at the breast with a leaf-shaped brooch of white bronze. He carried a shield inlaid with animal designs in many colors. At his waist hung a sword with a domed silver pommel, and he held a five-pronged spear in his hand. He sat down facing the leader of the first company."

"Who were they, Fergus?" said Ailill.

"I know them well," said Fergus. "Conchobar, king of a province of Ireland, is the one who was seated on the mound of sods. Seancha Mac Ailill, the most eloquent man in Ulster, is the one who sat facing him. And Cúscraid Menn Macha the Stammerer, Conchobar's son, is the one who sat by his father's side. As for those three rings around his spear, they only run up and down like that before a victory. And as for the companies assembled there, these are men you can count on to do great damage in any battle, said Fergus.

"They'll find men to answer them here," said Medb.

"I swear by the gods my people swear by," said Fergus, "that the army has not been raised in Ireland that could withstand the men of Ulster."

"Another company came up," said Mac Roth, "more than three thousand of them, led by a big strong warrior, swarthy, fiery-faced and fearsome, with a glib of brown hair plastered to his forehead. He carried a curved scallop-edged shield. He held a five-pronged spear and a forked javelin besides. A bloodstained sword was slung on his back. He wore a white knee-length tunic, and a purple cloak pinned at the shoulder with a gold brooch."

"Who was that, Fergus?" said Ailill.

"A man built for battle," said Fergus, "first to the fray, the doom of enemies: Eoghan Mac Durthacht, King of Fernmag."

"Another powerful and imperious company came to the hill at Slane in Meath," said Mac Roth, "harbingers of dread and terror, their cloaks thrown back behind them, marching resolutely towards the hill with a fearsome clattering of arms. Their leader was a grim-looking fellow with a thick-set, grizzled head and big yellow eyes. He was wrapped in a yellow cloak with a white border. A deadly scalloped-edged shield hung by his side. In one hand he held a long, broad-bladed spear; in the other he held its match, the blade stained with the blood of his enemies. A long, lethal sword was slung across his shoulders."

"Who was that, Fergus?" said Ailill.

"A warrior who never turns his back on battle: Láegaire Buadach the Victorious, son of Connad son of Ilech from Impail in the north," said Fergus.

"Another great company came to the hill at Slane in Meath," said Mac Roth, "headed by a fine-looking, barrel-chested, thick-necked warrior. He had ruddy cheeks, a shock of black curls and flashing gray eyes. He wore a cloak of brown shaggy wool pinned with a bright silver brooch. He carried a black shield with a bronze boss. A spear with a needle's-eye head glittered in his hand. The ivory pommel of his sword sat proud against his red-embroidered braided tunic."

"Who was that, Fergus?" said Ailill.

"The instigator of many battles. A tidal wave that overwhelms little streams. A man of three cries. The vicious doom of enemies," said Fergus. "Munremar Mac Gerrcinn the Thick-Necked, from Moduirn in the north."

"Another great company came to the hill at Slane in Meath," said Mac Roth, "a most impressive company, their cohorts well drilled and splendidly kitted out. They marched imperiously up to the hill. The clatter of their arms as they advanced shook everyone. They were led by a majestic warrior, superlative among men for his hair and eyes and grim demeanor, for dress and build and clarity of voice, for dignity and grandeur and gracefulness, for range and style of fighting skills, for equipment, application and discernment, for honor and nobility of lineage."

"You have him in a nutshell," said Fergus. "That brilliant figure is Feidlimid the Handsome, the raging warrior, the overwhelming wave, the irresistible force, who comes home in triumph after slaughtering his enemies abroad: Feidlimid Cilair Cétaig."

"Another company came to the hill at Slane in Meath," said Mac Roth, "at least three thousand strong, led by a big, stalwart warrior, sallow-complexioned, with a head of black curls and a haughty stare in his gray eyes. A great, rugged bull of a man. He wore a white hooded tunic and a gray cloak with a silver pin at the shoulder. A sword hung at his hip, and he carried a red shield with a hammered silver boss. The spear in his hand had a broad blade and triple rivets."

"Who was that, Fergus?" said Ailill.

"A furious flame, bold in battle, a man who wins wars: Connad Mac Morna from Callann," said Fergus.

"Another company came to the hill at Slane in Meath," said Mac Roth, "a veritable army of them. As for the leader of that vast force, seldom will you find a warrior so poised and stylishly equipped. His auburn hair was neatly trimmed, his handsome, well-proportioned face aglow. Finely shaped red lips, pearl-white teeth, a firm, clear voice: every aspect of him was superlative. Draped over his red-embroidered hooded tunic was a purple cloak with an inlaid gold brooch. At his left side hung a silver-bossed shield inlaid with animal designs in many colors. In one hand he held a spear with a head of blued steel: in the other hand he held a deadly sharp dagger. A gold-hilted golden sword was slung on his back."

"Who was that, Fergus?" said Ailill.

"Someone well known to us," said Fergus. "A men equal to an army, tenacious as a bloodhound, a deciding factor in any combat: Rochad Mac Faithemain from Brig Dumae, your son-in-law, who took your daughter Finnabair."

"Another company came to the hill at Slane in Meath," said Mac Roth, "led by a feisty-looking, dark-haired warrior with brawny lags and bulging thighs. Each of his four limbs was as thick as a man. He was every inch a man, and more," said Mac Roth. "He had a scarred, purple face and haughty, bloodshot eyes: a formidable, bustling man, alert and dangerous, his entourage equipped and kitted out in admirable fashion; a proud, aggressive man, whose scorn and anger drives him into battle against overwhelming odds to beat his enemies, who ventures unprotected into hostile territory—no wonder his company marched so boldly to the hill at Slane in Meath."

"A brave warlike man indeed," said Fergus, "hot-blooded, tough, vehement and dignified, a force to be reckoned with in any army: my own foster-brother, Fergus Mac Leiti, King of Líne, battle-spearhead of the north of Ireland."

"Another great imposing company came to the hill at Slane in Meath," said Mac Roth. "They were wonderfully equipped. At their head was a fine, tall figure of a man with brilliant hair and eyes and skin, magnificently proportioned. He held himself with immense aplomb. He wore five gold chains, a green cloak pinned at the shoulder with a gold brooch, and a white hooded tunic. In his hand was a spear like the turret of a palace. A gold-hilted sword was slung on his back."

"Fearsome and formidable indeed the same conquering hero," said Fergus. "That was Amargin son of Eiccet Salach the smith, from Buais in the north."[5]

* * *

5. Mac Roth goes on to describe eight further companies and their leaders, and Fergus identifies each in turn as heroic Ulstermen.

"Another company came to the hill at Slane in Meath," said Mac Roth, "countless numbers of heroes wearing strange outfits, very different to the other companies. With all their gear and weapons and equipment they made a marvelous spectacle as they advanced. They were an army in themselves. At their head was a bright-faced, freckled, perfectly formed little boy. He held a gold-studded, gold-rimmed shield with a white boss and a shimmering, keen-bladed light javelin. He wore a red-embroidered white hooded tunic and a purple fringed cloak held at the breast with a silver pin. A gold-hilted sword sat proud against his garments."

Fergus paused before he spoke.

"I don't know," said Fergus, "of any boy among the Ulster people who would fit that description. These must be the men of Tara, and this must be the fine and noble Erc, son of Coirpre Niad Fer and Conchobar's daughter. There's no love lost between Coirpre and Conchobar, and the boy must have come to his grandfather's aid without the permission of his father. Because of that young lad," said Fergus, "you will lose the battle. He will plunge fearlessly into the heart of the fray, and the warriors of Ulster will raise a great shout as they rush forward, cutting down your army before them to rescue their beloved little calf. They will all feel the ties that bind them when they see the boy under attack. Then will be heard the whirr of Conchobar's sword, like the growl of a bloodhound, as he comes to save the boy. Conchobar will cast up three ramparts of dead men around the battlefield in the search for his grandson. And, moved by the ties that bind them, the warriors of Ulster will descend on your vast army."

"I have been overlong," said Mac Roth, "in describing everything I saw. But I thought I should let you know what was going on."

"You have certainly done that," said Fergus.

"However," said Mac Roth, "Conall Cernach did not come with his great company. Nor did Conchobar's three sons, with their three divisions. Nor did Cú Chulainn come, for he was wounded fighting against the odds. But many hundreds and thousands converged on the Ulster camp. Many heroes, champions and warriors came racing on their horses to that great meeting. And many more companies were still arriving as I left. Wherever I cast my eye," said Mac Roth, "on any hill or height from Fer Diad's Ford to Slane in Meath, all I could see was men and horses."

"What you saw was a people coming together," said Fergus.

* * *

The Final Battle

Conchobar came with his forces and camped beside the others. He asked Ailill for a truce until sunrise. Ailill consented on behalf of the men of Ireland and the Ulster exiles, and Conchobar consented on behalf of the men of Ulster. The men of Ireland pitched their tents, and before the sun had set there was hardly a bare piece of ground between them and the Ulstermen. In the twilight between the two camps the Morrígan[6] spoke:

ravens gnaw   men's necks   blood gushes
fierce fray   hacked flesh   battle-drunk
men's sides   blade-struck   war-torn
raking fingers   battle-brave   men of Crúachan

6. Great Queen or Queen of Demons, the major goddess of war, a shape-shifter and sower of discord.

ruination bodies crushed underfoot
long live Ulster woe to Ireland
woe to Ulster long live Ireland

These last words—"woe to Ulster"—she conveyed to the ears of the men of Ireland,[7] to make them think the war was as good as won. That night Nét's consorts, Nemain and the Badb, began howling at the men of Ireland, and a hundred warriors dropped dead of fright. It was not the most peaceful of nights for them.

On the eve of the battle Ailill Mac Mata chanted:

"Rise up, Traighthrén, powerful of foot. Summon for me the three Conaires from Sliab Mis, the three Lussens from Lúachair, the three Niad Chorb from Tilach Loiscthe, the three Dóelfers from Dell, the three Dámaltachs from Dergderc, the three Bodars from the Buas, the three Baeths from the river Buaidnech, the three Búageltachs from Mag mBreg, the three Suibnes from the river Suir, the three Eochaids from Ane, the three Malleths from Loch Erne, the three Abatruads from Loch Ríb, the three Mac Amras from Ess Rúaid, the three Fiachas from Fid Nemain, the three Maines from Mureisc, the three Muredachs from Mairg, the three Loegaires from Lecc Derg, the three Brodonns from the river Barrow, the three Brúchnechs from Cenn Abrat, the three Descertachs from Druim Fornacht, the three Finns from Finnabair, the three Conalls from Collamair, the three Carbres from Cliu, the three Maines from Mossa, the three Scáthglans from Scaire, the three Echtaths from Erce, the three Trénfers from Taite, the three Fintans from Femen, the three Rótanachs from Raigne, the three Sárchorachs from Suide Lagen, the three Etarscéls from Étarbán, the three Aeds from Aidne, the three Guaires from Gabal."

These Triads, as they were known, had survived Cú Chulainn's attacks on the Irish army.

Meanwhile Cú Chulainn was close by at Fedain Collna. His supporters would bring him food by night, and talk things over with him by day. He killed no one north of Fer Diad's Ford.

"Some cattle have strayed from the western camp to the eastern camp," his charioteer said to Cú Chulainn, "and look, a party of young fellows have gone out to round them up. What's more, a party of our own young fellows have gone after the cattle too."[8]

"The two lots of young fellows will clash," said Cú Chulainn, "and they'll be joined by others who will give no quarter. The cattle will stray all the more."

It happened as Cú Chulainn said it would.

"How are the Ulster boys fighting?" said Cú Chulainn.

"Like men," said the charioteer.

"The same boys would be proud to die for their herd," said Cú Chulainn. "And now?"

"The beardless youngsters have joined them now," said the charioteer.

"Is there any ray of sunlight yet?" said Cú Chulainn.

"Not a glimmer," said the charioteer.

"If only I was fit to go and help them," said Cú Chulainn.

"Now the real fighting begins," said the charioteer as the sun came up. "The higher echelons are going into battle, except the kings, for they are asleep."

7. The allies of Mebd and Ailill from outside Connacht, who now begin to withdraw their allegiance.

8. Probably the boy troops who train in mock battles around Conchobar's capital. Cú Chulainn, when still a boy and untutored in the ways of the court, had first challenged and then joined them. Because of their age they are untouched by the debility of the Ulstermen and rush into battle before their elders.

As the sun came up, Fachtna spoke (or maybe it was Conchobar, chanting in his sleep):

Arise brave kings of Macha generous people
sharpen swords wage war dig in
strike shields arms weary bellowing herds
of men in rightful strife battle ranks
their reign brought down by fighting men
as enemies ambush killing all day
imbibing deep draughts of blood
the hearts of queens swelling
with grief and blood soaks
the trampled grass whereon they stand
and fall arise kings of Macha

"Who chanted that?" said they all.

"Conchobar Mac Nessa," said some.

"Fachtna," said others.

"Sleep on, sleep on, but still keep watch!"

And Láegaire Buadach the Victorious said:

Beware kings of Macha
ready swords to guard what cattle
you have plundered drive the Connachtmen
from Uisnech Hill body torque-twisted
sinews blazing he will strike the world
on the plain of Gáirech

"Who chanted that?" said they all.

"Láegaire Buadach, son of Connad Buide son of Illiach. Sleep on, sleep on, but still keep watch!"

"Wait a little longer," said Conchobar, "till the sun has risen well above the hills and glens of Ireland."

When Cú Chulainn saw the western kings putting on their crowns and rallying their troops, he told his charioteer to rouse up the men of Ulster.

The charioteer spoke—or maybe it was the poet Amargin Mac Eicit:

Arise brave kings of Macha
generous people the Badb lusts after
Impail cattle heart's blood pouring forth
as men pour in to battle brave deeds
heads skewed in flight bogged down
in blood and battle-weariness for there is
no one like Cú Chulainn to enforce
the will of Macha all for Cúailnge cattle
arise kings of Macha

"I've roused them up," said the charioteer. "They've charged into battle stark naked, wearing nothing but their weapons. Any man whose tent door was facing east, he's gone westward through his tent for a shortcut."

"Speedy help in time of need," said Cú Chulainn.

After a while, he said:

"Take a look for us, comrade Láeg, and tell us how the men of Ulster are fighting."

"Bravely," said the charioteer. "If Conall Cernach's charioteer En and myself were to drive from one wing of the battle to the other, not a wheel nor a hoof would touch ground, so closely do they fight."

"This has the makings of a great encounter," said Cú Chulainn. "Whatever happens in the battle, be sure to let me know about it."

"I'll do my level best," said the charioteer.

"Right now the western warriors have broken through the eastern battle-line," he said.

"And now the eastern warriors have broken through the western battle-line."

"If only I were fit," said Cú Chulainn, "you'd see me breaking through along with the rest."

The Irish Triads began to advance towards the battle at Gáirech and Ilgáirech. Accompanying them were the nine chariot-fighters from Iruath, each preceded by three foot-soldiers keeping pace with the chariots. Medb was keeping them in reserve to take Ailill out of harm's way if they were beaten, or to kill Chochobar if they won.

Then the charioteer told Cú Chulainn that Ailill and Medb were pressurizing Fergus to go into battle, saying that it was only right that he should do so, after all that they had done for him during his exile.

"If only I had my own sword," said Fergus, "the soldiers' heads I'd cut off would bounce off their shields like hailstones into the mud churned up by the king's horses as they plough through the battlefield."[9]

And he swore his oath:

"I swear by the god my people swear by, that I'd strike jaws from necks, necks from shoulders, shoulders from elbows, elbows from forearms, forearms from fists, fists from fingers, fingers from nails; crowns from skulls, skulls from trunks, trunks from thighs, thighs from calves, calves from feet, feet from toes, and toes from nails. Heads would fly from necks like bees buzzing to and fro on a fine day."

Then Ailill said to his charioteer:

"Bring me the sword that violates flesh. I swear the oath of my people that if it has lost any of its bloom since the day I gave it to you on that wet hill-slope in Ulster, all of Ireland will not save you from me.

The sword was brought to Fergus and Ailill said:

> take your sword   though once   you struck out
> at Ireland   one of her sons   a mighty hero
> will fight at Gáirech   if this be   the truth
> for the sake of   your honor   wreak not
> your wrath   on us but on   Ulster's chariot-warriors
> at dawn   at Gáirech   the field sodden
> with the deep   red morning

Fergus said:

> well met   Harshblade   Léte's sword[1]
> the Badb's swift messenger   of doom
> and horror   no longer concealed   come
> avenge   and sever   sinews

9. Ailill's charioteer had taken the sword when he spotted Fergus having sex with Medb, and Fergus was reduced to carrying a wooden sword.

1. Léte was Fergus's father.

topple heads this sword no longer
in a king's keeping the story to be told
again I take my kingly stance
before the men of Ireland

"A pity indeed, were you to fall in the thick of battle," said Fergus to Ailill.

Fergus seized his weapons and went towards the fighting. Wielding his sword in both hands, he took out a hundred men. Medb also seized her weapons and plunged into the fray. Three times she cleared all before her until she was repelled by a thicket of spears.

"I'd like to know," said Conchobar to his companions, "who it is that's taking the battle to us in the north. Hold the line here and I'll go and seek him out."

"We'll stick to this spot," said the warriors, "and unless the ground opens up under us, or the heavens fall on us, we'll not give an inch."

Then Conchobar went to meet Fergus. He raised his shield against him—the shield Óchaín, the Dazzling Ear, with its four gold spikes and four gold plates. Fergus dealt it three blows, but the rim of the shield did not even touch Conchobar's head.

"Who is the Ulsterman that holds this shield?" said Fergus.

"A better man than you," said Conchobar. "One who drove you into exile to dwell among the wolves and foxes; one who by dint of his deeds will repel you before all the men of Ireland."

With that, Fergus raised his sword in a two-handed grip, intending to deal Conchobar a vengeful blow. As the point of his sword touched the ground on the backswing, Cormac Mac Loinges gripped his arm with his two hands and said:

reckless careful
comrade Fergus too considered
ill considered comrade Fergus
friend becoming foe
behold your enemies
the friends you forsook
as you prepare to strike
these wicked blows comrade Fergus

"What then should I do?" said Fergus.

"Strike out at those three hills yonder. Turn your hand. Strike anywhere. Be as reckless as you like. But remember that the honor of Ulster has never been compromised, and never will be, unless by you today."

"Come away from here, Conchobar," said Cormac to his father. "This man will no longer vent his rage on Ulstermen."

Fergus turned round and in a single onslaught cut down a hundred Ulstermen with his sword. He came up against Conall Cernach.

"You're very fierce," said Conall, "against your own kith and kin, and all for the sake of a whore's backside."

"What then should I do?" said Fergus.

"Strike out at those hills yonder, and anything on top of them," said Conall.

Fergus struck the hills and with three blows sheared off the tops of the Máela Midi, the Flat-topped Hills of Meath.

Cú Chulainn, heard the blows which Fergus dealt the hills, just as he heard those struck on Conchobar's shield.

"Who strikes those tremendous blows in the distance?" said Cú Chulainn,

the heart swells with blood
rage sunders the world
quick, undo the hoops

Láeg answered:

"Those blows were struck by the bold and dauntless Fergus Mac Róich. A man who is a byword for much blood and slaughter. His sword was hidden in the chariot-shaft in the event of Conchobar's horse-soldiers joining the war."

And Cú Chulainn said:

quick, undo the hoops
men covered in blood
swords to be wielded
lives to be cut short

Then the dry wisps which had plugged his wounds soared up into the air like skylarks and the hoops around him sprang asunder and bits of them landed as far away as Mag Tuag—the Plain of the Hoops—in Connacht. They flew away from him in all directions. The blood in his wounds began to boil. He knocked together the heads of the two women who had been watching over him so that each was spattered with gray from the other's brains. These were two handmaidens sent by Medb to make a show of sorrow over him, so that his wounds would open afresh, and to tell him that Ulster had been beaten and Fergus killed in battle because Cú Chulainn was not fit to join the fight. Then the Torque seized him. The twenty-seven leather corsets he would wear going into battle, lashed to his body with ropes and thongs, were now brought to him. He took up his chariot on his back—frame, wheels and all—and walked the battle-field in search of Fergus.

"Over here, comrade Fergus," said Cú Chulainn.

Three times he called him. Three times there was no answer.

"I swear by the god of the Ulstermen," said Cú Chulainn, "that I'll thrash you like flax in a pond! I'll rear up on you like a tail over a cat! I'll spank you the way a fond mother spanks her wee boy!"

"Who's the Irishman who speaks to me like that?" said Fergus.

"Cú Chulainn, son of Sualdam and Conchobar's sister," said Cú Chulainn, "Now yield to me."

"I did promise that once," said Fergus.

"Then give what's due," said Cú Chulainn.

"All right, so," said Fergus. "You yielded to me once, and now look at you, all full of holes."

So Fergus left the field and took his three thousand men with him. The Gailéoin and the men of Munster left too. Nine divisions of three thousand—those of Medb and Ailill and their seven sons—were left in the battle. It was noon when Cú Chulainn joined the fray. By the time the sun had brushed the tops of the trees, he had scattered the last of their companies, and all that remained of his chariot was a handful of ribs from the frame and handful of spokes from the wheels.

Medb covered the retreat of the men of Ireland. She sent the Donn Cúailnge on to Crúachan along with fifty of his heifers and eight of her messengers, so that the Bull would arrive there, as she had sworn.

Then Medb got her gush of blood.

"Fergus," she said, "cover the retreat of the men of Ireland, for I must relieve myself."

"By god," said Fergus, "you picked a bad time to go."

"I can't help it," said Medb. "I'll die if I don't go."

So Fergus covered the retreat. Medb relieved herself, and it made three great trenches, each big enough for a cavalcade. Hence the place is known as Fúal Medba, Medb's Piss-pot.

Cú Chulainn came upon Medb as she was doing what she had to.

"I'm at your mercy," said Medb.

"If I were to strike, and kill you," said Cú Chulainn, "I'd be within my rights."

But he spared her, because usually he did not kill women. He escorted them west until they crossed the ford of Áth Luain.[2] He struck three blows with his sword at the nearby hills, which are now known as Máelana Átha Luain, the Flat-topped Hills of Athlone: this was his response to the Flat-topped Hills of Meath.

Now that they had lost the battle, Medb said to Fergus:

"The pot was stirred, Fergus, and today a mess was made."

"That's usually what happens," said Fergus, "when a mare leads a herd of horses—all their energy gets pissed away, following the rump of a skittish female."

The Donn Cúailnge was brought to Connacht. When he saw this strange and beautiful new land he let three great bellows out of him. Finnbennach, the White-horned Bull, heard him. On account of Finnbennach no male beast on the Plain of Aí dared raise a sound louder than a moo. He threw up his head and proceeded to Crúachan to seek out the Brown Bull. Everyone who had escaped the battle now had nothing better to do than to watch the two bulls fighting.

The men of Ireland debated as to who should referee the contest of the two bulls. They agreed it should be Bricriu Mac Carbada the Venom-tongued. A year before the events narrated in the Táin, Bricriu had gone from one province to the other to negotiate some deal or other with Fergus. Fergus took him into his employ until such times as his possessions would arrive. They were playing chess when they had a difference of opinion, and Bricriu insulted Fergus rather badly. Fergus struck him on the head with the chessman he had been holding and broke a bone in his skull. So Bricriu had lain recuperating while the men of Ireland went forth on the Táin. The day they returned, he got up from his sick-bed. They chose Bricriu because he did not discriminate between friend and foe. They brought him to the gap between the bulls to referee the contest.

When the two bulls saw each other they pawed the ground and hurled the earth over their shoulders. Their eyes blazed in their heads like great fiery orbs and their cheeks and their nostrils swelled like forge bellows. They charged towards each other and Bricriu got caught in between. He was flattened, trampled and killed. Such was the death of Bricriu.

The Brown Bull got his hoof stuck on his opponent's horn. For a day and a night he made no attempt to withdraw the hoof, until Fergus gave off to him and took a stick to his hide.

"It would be a poor show," said Fergus, "for this feisty old calf to be brought all this way only to disgrace his fine breeding. Especially since so many died on his account."

2. Modern Athlone, on the river Shannon at the border of Connacht.

When the Brown Bull heard this he pulled away his hoof and broke his leg. The other bull's horn flew off and stuck in the side of a nearby mountain. Hence the name Sliab nAdarca, Horn Mountain.

The bulls fought for a long time. Night fell upon the men of Ireland and they could do nothing but listen to the bulls roaring and bellowing in the darkness. All next day the Donn Cúailnge drove Finnbennach before him and at nightfall they plunged into the lake at Crúachan. He emerged with Finnbennach's loins and shoulderblade and liver on his horns. The army went to kill him but Fergus stopped them, saying he should be let roam. So the Bull headed for his homeland. He stopped on the way to drink at Finnleithe, where he left Finnbennach's shoulderblade. Hence the name Finnleithe, White Shoulder. He drank again at Áth Luain, and left Finnbennach's loins there. Hence the name Áth Luain, the Ford of the Loins. At Iraird Cuillenn he let a great bellow out of him that was heard all over the province. He drank again at Tromma, where Finnbennach's liver fell from his horns. Hence the name Tromma, Liver. He went then to Éten Tairb, where he rested his brow against the hill. Hence the name Éten Tairb, the Bull's Brow, in Muirthemne Plain. Then he went by the Midluachair Road to Cuib, where he used to dwell with the dry cows of Dáire, and he tore up the ground there. Hence the name Gort mBúraig, Trench Field. Then he went on and fell dead at the ridge between Ulster and Uí Echach. That place is now called Druim Tairb, Bull Ridge.

Ailill and Medb made a peace with the Ulstermen and Cú Chulainn. For seven years after that no one was killed in battle between them. The men of Connacht went back to their own country, and the men of Ulster returned in triumph to Emain Macha.

Early Irish Verse

Although copied by clerics in a world of written manuscripts, *The Táin Bó Cuailnge* looks backward to an age of oral tales about legendary heroes and heroines, many of them still closely linked to the native gods and goddesses of pre-Christian Ireland. The following samples of Irish verse from the ninth and tenth centuries suggest some of the complex but enormously fruitful interactions of those native Irish traditions and the new Christian culture.

Ireland began to be Christianized from the mid-fifth century, but Christianity came to Ireland more by genuine and gradual conversion than by the point of a sword. The learned monks and hermits, well established by the ninth and tenth centuries, encountered far more disruption from the raids of Vikings, beginning in 795 B.C.E., than from surviving Irish pre-Christian cultures. Instead, the ancient native dynasties of learned poets, genealogists, and diviners interacted with the new learning of Latin Christianity. Indeed, Saint Columba (c. 521–597) was partly educated by the *fili* Gemmán, the chief poet of Leinster. (*Fili*, plural *filid*, was the highest class of poet in medieval Ireland.) One of Columba's few returns to Ireland after founding his monastery on the isle of Iona was to defend the native poets from clerical forces that wanted them suppressed. In fact we know that many monks were also vernacular poets; and conversely, secular *filid* wrote praise poems to clerics, most famously to Saint Columba himself. Their cultural prestige and preservation of ancient learning continued, even as their religious and quasi-magical activity dwindled. All this led to a rich and persistent convergence (not without competition) of native and Christian elements in medieval Irish culture.

The figure addressed in *To Crinog*, for instance, is at once a wise crone—a traditional figure of initiation—and a book of Christian wisdom, perhaps a Latin primer. Irish myths report instruction in craft or battle by a wise woman, with whom the apprentice also enjoys physical intimacy (as a youthful Cú Chulainn had with the woman warrior Scáthach), although in this poem Crinog's teaching is explicitly chaste. Monks also began using the resources of Irish poetry to record religious study—the Word, to which their faith was so attached—and the making of written books. *Pangur the Cat* explores the solitary pleasures of the monk or hermit, and the challenge of textual interpretation, in contrast with the more heroic mold of many saints' lives or contemporary heroic tales: "Fame comes second to the peace/Of study. . . ." *Writing in the Wood* is a poem of labor, but undertaken in a holiday spirit, away from the monastic scriptorium where books were usually copied.

Other voices look to the legendary past with open regret. *A Grave Marked with Ogam* evokes a disastrous battle in which the speaker, now quite alone, fought on the losing side. *Findabair Remembers Fróech* is a yearning lament for a lost lover. It is quite unconnected to monasticism, but a similar history of passions that efface the present also informs the powerful monologue *The Old Woman of Beare*; there the contrast also involves the shift from a lost world of secular heroes to declining mortality in a convent. Her name, and the memories she has of past generations and eras, may link the Old Woman of Beare to a mythic figure of sovereignty, rejuvenated by each man to whom she gives her body and her powers. At the same time, she is a voice of wise lament on the passing of greater times (not unlike many moments in *Beowulf*); she is a rich concubine who has lost her beauty and become a nun; and—in a land where women's powers were usually quite limited—she is a woman who has gone her own way and made choices that now leave her poor, unprotected, and rueful, but not regretful. *The Old Woman of Beare* records the unresolved dialogue between the era of heroic legend and the era of Christ, between joys mortal and immortal: "for Mary's Son / too soon redeems."

The Voyage of Máel Dúin shows us, perhaps most clearly of all, how native secular genres and attitudes persisted, but were revised, under the influence of Christianity. Both in structure and detail, the *Voyage* echoes the *immrana*, native tales of wondrous voyages to otherworldly islands, places both of terror and sybaritic pleasures. Máel Dúin and his companions visit many such islands, but they also pause at the island homes of four Christian hermits, themselves not without magical qualities. Máel Dúin's own genealogy mirrors this meeting of traditions; he is the illegitimate child of a nun and a great warrior. His father has been killed by raiders, he learns, and his voyage is a quest to find them and take obligatory vengeance in the heroic style. The fourth hermit he meets, though, convinces Máel Dúin to forgive his father's murderers and return home in peace. At the levels of genre, genealogy, and narrative, then, the *Voyage* enacts at once a preservation and revision of native traditions under Christian influence.

To Crinog[1]

Crinog, melodious is your song.
Though young no more you are still bashful.
We two grew up together in Niall's[2] northern land,
When we used to sleep together in tranquil slumber.

1. Translated by Kuno Meyer.

2. Legendary Irish king, whose dynasty ruled Ulster and other areas.

That was my age when you slept with me.
O peerless lady of pleasant wisdom:
A pure-hearted youth, lovely without a flaw,
A gentle boy of seven sweet years.

We lived in the great world of Banva[3]
Without sullying soul or body,
My flashing eyes full of love for you,
Like a poor innocent untempted by evil.

Your just counsel is ever ready,
Wherever we are to seek it:
To love your penetrating wisdom is better
Than glib discourse with a king.

Since then you have slept with four men after me,
Without folly or falling away:
I know, I hear it on all sides,
You are pure, without sin from man.

At last, after weary wanderings,
You have come to me again,
Darkness of age has settled on your face:
Sinless your life draws near its end.

You are still dear to me, faultless one,
You shall have welcome from me without stint:
You will not let us be drowned in torment;
We will earnestly practice devotion with you.

The lasting world is full of your fame.
Far and wide you have wandered on every track:
If every day we followed your ways,
We should come safe into the presence of dread God.

You leave an example and a bequest
To every one in this world,
You have taught us by your life:
Earnest prayer to God is no fallacy.

Then may God grant us peace and happiness!
May the countenance of the King
Shine brightly on us
When we leave behind us our withered bodies.

Pangur the Cat[1]

Myself and Pangur, cat and sage
Go each about our business;
I harass my beloved page,
He his mouse.

3. An early name for Ireland

1. Translated by Eavan Boland.

Fame comes second to the peace
Of study, a still day.
Unenvious, Pangur's choice
Is child's play.

Neither bored, both hone
At home a separate skill,
Moving, after hours alone,
To the kill.

On my cell wall here,
His sight fixes. Burning.
Searching. My old eyes peer
At new learning.

His delight when his claws
Close on his prey
Equals mine, when sudden clues
Light my way.

So we find by degrees
Peace in solitude,
Both of us—solitaries—
Have each the trade

He loves. Pangur, never idle
Day or night
Hunts mice. I hunt each riddle
From dark to light.

Writing in the Wood[1]

Overwatched by woodland wall
merles make melody full well;
above my book—lined, lettered—
birds twittered a soothing spell.

Cuckoos call clear—fairest phrase—
cloaked in grays, from leafy leas.
Lord's love, what blessings show' ring!
Good to write 'neath tow' ring trees.

The Viking Terror[1]

Bitter is the wind to-night,
It tosses the ocean's white hair:
To-night I fear not the fierce warriors of Norway
Coursing on the Irish Sea.

1. Translated by Ruth P. M. Lehmann. This translation aims to reproduce much of the complex internal rhyme and end-rhyme, assonance, and alliteration of the original; it takes minor liberties with the literal sense.

1. Translated by Kuno Meyer.

The Old Woman of Beare[1]

The ebbing that has come on me
is not the ebbing of the sea.
What knows the sea of grief or pain?—
Happy tide will flood again.

I am the hag of Bui and Beare[2]—
the richest cloth I used to wear.
Now with meanness and with thrift
I even lack a change of shift.

It is wealth
and not men that you love.
In the time that we lived
it was men that we loved.

Those whom we loved, the plains
we ride today bear their names;
gaily they feasted with laughter
nor boasted thereafter.

To-day they gather in the tax
but, come to handing out, are lax;
the very little they bestow
be sure that everyone will know.

Chariots there were, and we
had horses bred for victory.
Such things came in a great wave;
pray for the dead kings who gave.

Bitterly does my body race
seeking its destined place;
now let God's Son come and take
that which he gave of his grace.

These arms, these scrawny things you see,
    scarce merit now their little joy
when lifted up in blessing
    over sweet student boy.

These arms you see,
    these bony scrawny things,
had once more loving craft
    embracing kings.

When Maytime comes
    the girls out there are glad,

1. Translated by James Carney. The speaker's name, "caillech," "veiled one," can mean old woman, hag, widow, and nun. The hag figure has resonance with teachers of crafts and wisdom, as well as early mythic female figures of sovereignty and initiation, rejuvenated when they are embraced by a chosen hero.

2. A peninsula in Munster, in the far southwest of Ireland, or a tiny island off its coast. "Bui" may be the small nearby island of Dursey.

and I, old hag, old bones,
    alone am sad.

No wedding wether killed for me,
an end to all coquetry;
a pitiful veil I wear
on thin and faded hair.

Well do I wear
plain veil on faded hair;
many colors I wore
and we feasting before.

Were it not for Feven's plain[3]
    I'd envy nothing old;
I have a shroud of aged skin,
    Feven's crop is gold.

Ronan's city there in Bregon[4]
    and in Feven the royal standing stone,
why are their cheeks not weathered,
    only mine alone?

Winter comes and the sea will rise
    crying out with welcoming wave;
but no welcome for me from nobleman's son
    or from son of a slave.

What they do now, I know, I know:
    to and fro they row and race;
but they who once sailed Alma's ford[5]
    rest in a cold place.

It's more than a day
    since I sailed youth's sea,
beauty's years not devoured
    and sap flowing free.

It's more than a day, God's truth,
that I'm lacking in youth;
I wrap myself up in the sun—
I know Old Age, I see him come.

There was a summer of youth
    nor was autumn the worst of the year,
but winter is doom
    and its first days are here.

God be thanked, I had joy in my youth.
    I swear that it's true,

3. In inland Munster; connected with power and wealth.
4. Probably an 8th-century king who ruled in the area of Feven.
5. An unidentified site.

if I hadn't leapt the wall
    this old cloak still were not new.

The Lord on the world's broad back
    threw a lovely cloak of green;
first fleecy, then it's bare,
    and again the fleece is seen.

All beauty is doomed.
    God! Can it be right
to kneel in a dark prayer-house
    after feasting by candlelight?

I sat with kings drinking wine and mead
    for many a day,
and now, a crew of shriveled hags,
    we toast in whey.

Be this my feast, these cups of whey;
    and let me always count as good
the vexing things that come of Christ
    who stayed God's ire with flesh and blood.

The mind is not so clear,
    there's mottling of age on my cloak,
gray hairs sprouting through skin,
    I am like a stricken oak.

For deposit on heaven
    of right eye bereft,
I conclude the purchase
    with loss of the left.

Great wave of flood
    and wave of ebb and lack!
What flooding tide brings in
    the ebbing tide takes back.

Great wave of flood
    and wave of ebbing sea,
the two of them I know
    for both have washed on me.

Great wave of flood
    brings no step to silent cellar floor;
a hand fell on all the company
    that feasted there before.

The Son of Mary knew right well
    he'd walk that floor one day;
grasping I was, but never sent
    man hungry on his way.

Pity Man!—
    If only like the elements he could

come out of ebbing in the very way
that he comes out of flood.

Christ left with me on loan
flood tide of youth, and now it seems
there's ebb and misery, for Mary's Son
too soon redeems.

Blessed the island in the great sea
with happy ebb and happy flood.
For me, for me alone, no hope:
the ebbing is for good.

Findabair Remembers Fróech[1]

This, thereafter, is what Findabair used to say,
seeing anything beautiful:
it would be more beautiful for her
to see Fróech crossing the dark water,
body for shining whiteness,
hair for loveliness,
face for shapeliness,
eye for blue-grayness,
a well-born youth
without fault or blemish,
face broad above, narrow below,
and he straight and perfect,
the red branch with its berries
between throat and white face.
This is what Findabair used to say:
She had never seen
anything a half
or a third as beautiful as he.

A Grave Marked with Ogam[1]

Ogam in stone on grave stead,
where men sometimes tread on course;
king's son of Ireland cut low,
hit by spear's throw hurled from horse.

Cairpre let a quick cast fly
from high on horseback, stout steed;

1. Translated by James Carney. Findabair (*FIN-a-wer*) was a daughter of Medb and Ailill (central characters in the *Táin*). She falls in love with the famously handsome warrior Fróech (Froich, guttural -ch) but her parents resist their marriage. When Fróech is killed by Cú Chulainn, Findabair ultimately dies of heartbreak.

1. Translated by Ruth P. M. Lehmann. This translation again aims to reproduce much of the rhyme, assonance, and alliteration of the original; it takes minor liberties with the literal sense. Ogam is the earliest Irish alphabet, used before the Latin alphabet was applied to Irish. It is a system of long lines marked with short dashes, crosshatches, and small figures. Most often found in inscriptions or associated with secret messages and divination, it is too awkward an alphabet for writing longer texts.

ere he wearied his hand struck,
 cut down Oscar, cruel deed.[2]

Oscar hurled a hard throw, crude,
 like a lion, rude his rage;
killed Con's kin, Cairpre proud,
 ere they bowed on battle stage.

Tall, keen, cruel were the lads
 who found their death in the strife,
just before their weapons met;
 more were left in death than life.

I myself was in the fight
 on right, south of Gabair green;
twice fifty warriors I killed,
 my skilled hand slew them, clear, clean.

I'd play for pirates in bale,
 the while the trail I must tread,
in holy holt boar I'd fell,
 or would snatch the snell bird's egg.

That ogam there in the stone,
 around which the slain fall prone,
if Finn the fighter could come,
 long would he think on ogam.

from The Voyage of Máel Dúin[1]

They went to an island with a high enclosure of the color of a swan
In which they found a noble pavilion, a dwelling of brightness.
Silver brooches, gold-hilted swords, large necklets,
Beautiful beds, excellent food, golden rows.
Strengthening delicate food in the midst of the house, sound savory liquor;
With fierce greediness upon a high pillar a seemly very quick cat.
It leapt then over the pillars, a speedy feat;
Not very big was the guardian of the meat, it was not repulsive.
One of the three foster brothers of the powerful chief, it was a
 courageous action,
Takes with him—it was a proud ounce-weight—a golden necklet.[2]
The fiery claw of the mysterious cat rent his body,
The guilty body of the unfortunate man was burnt ash.
The large necklet was brought back, it created friendship again,
The ashes of the unfortunate man were cast into the ocean.

* * *

2. Characters from the "Finn Cycle," a group of tales even more popular than the Ulster Cycle and its central epic the *Táin*. Oscar is Finn's grandson and the cycle's greatest warrior. He and Cairpre, high king of Ireland, kill one another at the Battle of Gabair (*GAV-ar*), which ends the power of Finn's people.

1. Verse redaction of chs. 11, 19, and 34, translated by H. P. A. Oskamp. Máel Dúin (*Moil Doon*), the illegitimate son of a nun and a warrior, is brought up by a queen. Learning at the same time of his father's death, he sets out on a sea journey to find and take vengeance on his father's killers. Máel Dúin and his companions came upon a series of islands, each with its marvel or danger.

2. Máel Dúin's foster brothers had swum to his boat as it departed, violating a druid's prohibition; none return from the journey.

Then they saw in a small island a psalm-singing old man;
Excellent was his dignified noble appearance, holy were his words.
Hair of his noble head—delightful the bright covering—a garment
with whiteness,
A brilliant large mantle; bright-covered coloring covering was around him.
The excellent chief said to him: "Whence were you sent?"
"I shall not hide from you what you ask: from Ireland.
My pilgrimage brought me without any penance
In the body of a boat over the swift sea; I did not regret it.
My prowed boat came apart under me on the very violent sea;
A bitter, twisting, active, big-waved course put me ashore.
I cut a sod from the gray-green surface of my fatherland;
To the place in which I am a breeze brought me: small is the fame.
The star-strong King established under me out of the miraculous sod
A delightful island with the color of a seagull over the dark sea.
A foot was added to the island every year—
It is a victorious achievement—and a tree above the sea's crest.
A clear well came to me—everlasting food—
By the grace of angels, sound beautiful food—a holy gathering.
You will all reach your countries, a fruitful company along the ocean's track,
Though it will be a long journey; all except one man."[3]
By the grace of the angels to each single man of them
Came a complete half-loaf and a noble morsel of fish as provision.

* * *

Then they went to an island full of flocks, a famed halting-place,
A victorious achievement; they found there an Irish falcon.
Then they rowed after it, swift to encounter,
Over the crest of the waves to an island in which was their enemy.
They made peace there with the swift Máel Dúin, in the presence of
every swift man;
After true pledging they went to their country, a prosperous journey.
Many remarkable things, many marvels, many mysteries
Was their pleasant story, as swift Máel Dúin told.
A long life and peace while I am in the famous world,
May I have cheerful company with virtue from my King of Kings.
When I die may I then reach heaven past the fierce, violent host of demons
In the Kingdom of angels, a famous affair, a very high dwelling.

Judith

The Old English poem *Judith*, concerning the legendary beheader of the Assyrian general Holofernes, has been seen most often as a heroic poem, like *Beowulf*, which it immediately follows in the same unique manuscript. It expresses the same fierce love of battle, and uses the same heroic poetic conventions—archaic diction, formulas, and themes. *Judith* achieves ironic

3. One of the three foster brothers still remains with the voyagers at this point. A later hermit prophesies, "though you will meet your enemies, you will not slay them."

effects, however, by placing these conventions in unexpected contexts—for instance, calling Holofernes a "brave man" as he hides behind a net to spy on his retainers. Similarly, it presents his raucous feast as an antifeast—a symbol of misrule rather than of social harmony—and his henchmen as a parody of the traditional band of loyal retainers, as they flee in terror to save their lives.

In addition to *Beowulf*, *Judith* has affinities with Old English poems based on the Old Testament, like *Exodus* and *Daniel*, whose heroes devote their military zeal to the glory of God. Like them, it assumes the timeless perspective of Christian salvation history, so that the apparent anachronisms of Judith's praying to the Trinity or Christ's abhorring Holofernes are entirely appropriate. Based on the Book of Judith in the Latin Bible, which the Anglo-Saxons considered canonical, this poem, like many others in Old English, exists only in fragmentary form. The original audience would have known that Holofernes had entered Judea to besiege the Hebrew city of Bethulia. At the point where the Old English poem begins, the "wickedly promiscuous" general, after his drunken feast, orders the beautiful Hebrew maiden Judith to be brought to his bed. Finding him stretched out in a drunken stupor, she first prays for help and then decapitates him. She thereupon returns to her camp, brandishing the head and exhorting the Hebrews to battle with a stirring speech, which inspires them to victory over the leaderless Assyrians.

The poem does not simply express the timeless Christian theme of the struggle of God's people against the pagans, but also comments on the immediate social and historical context of its time. It seems to reflect the resistance of the Christian Anglo-Saxons against the pagan Danes during the ninth-century invasions, perhaps exaggerating the Assyrians' drunkenness in order to comment on the notorious Danish drinking habits. Furthermore, Holofernes' plan to rape Judith may evoke the rape of Anglo-Saxon women by Danish soldiers in the presence of their husbands and fathers.

Judith's identity as a woman warrior also puts the poem in the social context of the time. The poem's emphasis on her power, in contrast to the biblical source's emphasis on God's power to operate through the hand of a mere woman, reflects the relatively strong role of aristocratic women in England before the Norman Conquest. (Other Old English poems that reflect this strength include *Juliana*, a typical saint's legend whose heroine is martyred while resisting a Roman general's advances, and *Elene*, whose heroine—Constantine's mother Saint Helen—was believed to have discovered the true cross.) Finally, Judith's heroic action has been seen as an inversion of the rape which Holofernes himself intends to commit upon her, as, seeing him unconscious on his bed, she "took the heathen man by the hair, dragged him ignominiously towards her with her hands, and carefully laid out the debauched and odious man."

Judith[1]

. . . She was suspicious of gifts in this wide world. So she readily met with a helping hand from the glorious Prince when she had most need of the supreme Judge's support and that he, the Prime Mover, should protect her against this supreme danger. The illustrious Father in the skies granted her request in this because she always had firm faith in the Almighty.

I have heard, then, that Holofernes cordially issued invitations to a banquet and had dishes splendidly prepared with all sorts of wonderful things, and to it this lord over men summoned all the most senior functionaries. With great alacrity those shield-wielders complied and came wending to the puissant prince, the nation's chief

1. Prose translation by S. A. J. Bradley.

person. That was on the fourth day after Judith, shrewd of purpose, the woman of elfin beauty first visited him.

So they went and settled down to the feasting, insolent men to the wine-drinking, all those brash armored warriors, his confederates in evil. Deep bowls were borne continually along the benches there and brimming goblets and pitchers as well to the hall-guests. They drank it down as doomed men, those celebrated shield-wielders—though the great man, the awesome lord over evils, did not foresee it. Then Holofernes, the bountiful lord of his men, grew merry with tippling. He laughed and bawled and roared and made a racket so that the children of men could hear from far away how the stern-minded man bellowed and yelled, insolent and flown with mead, and frequently exhorted the guests on the benches to enjoy themselves well. So the whole day long the villain, the stern-minded dispenser of treasure, plied his retainers with wine until they lay unconscious, the whole of his retinue drunk as though they had been struck dead, drained of every faculty.

Thus the men's elder commanded the hall-guests to be ministered to until the dark night closed in on the children of men. Then, being wickedly promiscuous, he commanded the blessed virgin, decked with bracelets and adorned with rings, to be fetched in a hurry to his bed. The attendants promptly did as their master, the ruler of armored warriors, required them. They went upon the instant to the guest-hall where they found the astute Judith, and then the shield-wielding warriors speedily conducted the noble virgin to the lofty pavilion where the great man always rested of a night, Holofernes, abhorrent to the Savior.

There was an elegant all-golden fly-net there, hung about the commandant's bed so that the debauched hero of his soldiers could spy through on every one of the sons of men who came in there, but no one of humankind on him, unless, brave man, he summoned one of his evilly renowned soldiers to go nearer to him for a confidential talk.

Hastily, then, they brought the shrewd lady to bed. Then they went, stout-hearted heroes, to inform their master that the holy woman had been brought to his pavilion. The man of mark, lord over cities, then grew jovial of mood: he meant to defile the noble lady with filth and with pollution. To that heaven's Judge, Shepherd of the celestial multitude, would not consent but rather he, the Lord, Ruler of the hosts, prevented him from the act.

So this species of fiend, licentious, debauched, went with a crowd of his men to seek his bed—where he was to lose his life, swiftly, within the one night: he had then come to his violent end upon earth, such as he had previously deserved, the stern-minded prince over men, while he lived in this world under the roof of the skies.

Then the great man collapsed in the midst of his bed, so drunk with wine that he was oblivious in mind of any of his designs. The soldiers stepped out of his quarters with great alacrity, wine-glutted men who had put the perjurer, the odious persecutor, to bed for the last time.

Then the glorious handmaid of the Savior was sorely preoccupied as to how she might most easily deprive the monster of his life before the sordid fellow, full of corruption, awoke. Then the ringletted girl, the Maker's maiden, grasped a sharp sword, hardy in the storms of battle, and drew it from its sheath with her right hand. Then she called by name upon the Guardian of heaven, the Savior of all the world's inhabitants, and spoke these words:

"God of beginnings, Spirit of comfort, Son of the universal Ruler, I desire to entreat you for your grace upon me in my need, Majesty of the Trinity. My heart is now sorely anguished and my mind troubled and much afflicted with anxieties. Give me, Lord of heaven, victory and true faith so that with this sword I may hew down this dispenser of violent death. Grant me my safe deliverance, stern-minded Prince over men. Never have I had greater need of your grace. Avenge now, mighty Lord, illustrious Dispenser of glory, that which is so bitter to my mind, so burning in my breast."

Then the supreme Judge at once inspired her with courage—as he does every single man dwelling here who looks to him for help with resolve and with true faith. So hope was abundantly renewed in the holy woman's heart. She then took the heathen man firmly by his hair, dragged him ignominiously towards her with her hands and carefully laid out the debauched and odious man so as she could most easily manage the wretch efficiently. Then the ringletted woman struck the malignant-minded enemy with the gleaming sword so that she sliced through half his neck, so that he lay unconscious, drunk and mutilated.

He was not then yet dead, not quite lifeless. In earnest then the courageous woman struck the heathen dog a second time so that his head flew off on to the floor. His foul carcass lay behind, dead; his spirit departed elsewhere beneath the deep ground and was there prostrated and chained in torment ever after, coiled about by snakes, trussed up in tortures and cruelly prisoned in hellfire after his going hence. Never would he have cause to hope, engulfed in darkness, that he might get out of that snake-infested prison, but there he shall remain forever to eternity henceforth without end in that murky abode, deprived of the joys of hope.

Judith then had won outstanding glory in the struggle according as God the Lord of heaven, who gave her the victory, granted her. Then the clever woman swiftly put the harrier's head, all bloody, into the bag in which her attendant, a pale-cheeked woman, one proved excellent in her ways, had brought food there for them both; and then Judith put it, all gory, into her hands for her discreet servant to carry home. From there the two women then proceeded onwards, emboldened by courage, until they had escaped, brave, triumphant virgins, from among the army, so that they could clearly see the walls of the beautiful city, Bethulia, shining. Then the ring-adorned women hurried forward on their way until, cheered at heart, they had reached the rampart gate.

There were soldiers, vigilant men, sitting and keeping watch in the fortress just as Judith the artful-minded virgin had enjoined the despondent folk when she set out on her mission, courageous lady. Now she had returned, their darling, to her people, and quickly then the shrewd woman summoned one of the men to come out from the spacious city to meet her and speedily to let them in through the gate of the rampart; and to the victorious people she spoke these words:

"I can tell you something worthy of thanksgiving: that you need no longer grieve in spirit. The ordaining Lord, the Glory of kings, is gracious to you. It has been revealed abroad through the world that dazzling and glorious success is impending for you and triumph is granted you over those injuries which you long have suffered."

Then the citizens were merry when they heard how the saintly woman spoke across the high rampart. The army was in ecstasies and the people rushed towards the fortress gate, men and women together, in flocks and droves; in throngs and troops they surged forward and ran towards the handmaid of the Lord, both old and young in their thousands. The heart of each person in that city of mead-halls was exhilarated when they realized that Judith had returned home; and then with humility they hastily let her in.

Then the clever woman ornamented with gold directed her attentive servant-girl to unwrap the harrier's head and to display the bloody object to the citizens as proof of how she had fared in the struggle. The noble lady then spoke to the whole populace:

"Victorious heroes, leaders of the people; here you may openly gaze upon the head of that most odious heathen warrior, the dead Holofernes, who perpetrated upon us the utmost number of violent killings of men and painful miseries, and who intended to add to it even further, but God did not grant him longer life so that he might plague us with afflictions. I took his life, with God's help. Now I want to urge each man among these citizens, each shield-wielding soldier, that you immediately get yourselves ready for battle. Once the God of beginnings, the steadfastly gracious King, has sent the radiant light from the east, go forth bearing shields, bucklers in front of your breasts and mail-coats and shining helmets into the ravagers' midst; cut down the commanders, the doomed leaders, with gleaming swords. Your enemies are sentenced to death and you shall have honor and glory in the fight according as the mighty Lord has signified to you by my hand."

Then an army of brave and keen men was quickly got ready for the battle. Renowned nobles and their companions advanced; they carried victory-banners; beneath their helms the heroes issued forth straight into battle from out of the holy city upon the very dawning of the day. Shields clattered, loudly resonated. At that, the lean wolf in the wood rejoiced, and that bird greedy for carrion, the black raven. Both knew that the men of that nation meant to procure them their fill among those doomed to die; but in their wake flew the eagle, eager for food, speckled-winged; the dark-feathered, hook-beaked bird sang a battle-chant.

On marched the soldiers, warriors to the warfare, protected by their shields, hollowed linden bucklers, they who a while previously had been suffering the abuse of aliens, the blasphemy of heathens. This was strictly repaid to all the Assyrians in the spear-fight once the Israelites under their battle-ensigns had reached the camp. Firmly entrenched, they vigorously let fly from the curved bow showers of darts, arrows, the serpents of battle. Loudly the fierce fighting-men roared and sent spears into their cruel enemies' midst. The heroes, the in-dwellers of the land, were enraged against the odious race. Stern of mood they advanced; hardened of heart they roughly roused their drink-stupefied enemies of old. With their hands, retainers unsheathed from scabbards bright-ornamented swords, proved of edge, and set about the Assyrian warriors in earnest, intending to smite them. Of that army they spared not one of the men alive, neither the lowly nor the mighty, whom they could overpower.

Thus in the hour of morn those comrades in arms the whole time harried the aliens until those who were their adversaries, the chief sentries of the army, acknowledged that the Hebrew people were showing them very intensive swordplay. They went to inform the most senior officers of this by word of mouth and they roused those warriors and fearfully announced to them in their drunken stupor the dreadful news, the terror of the morning, the frightful sword-encounter.

Then, I have heard, those death-doomed heroes quickly shook off their sleep and thronged in flocks, demoralized men, to the pavilion of the debauched Holofernes. They meant to give their lord warning of battle at once, before the terror and the force of the Hebrews descended upon him; all supposed that the men's leader and that beautiful woman were together in the handsome tent, the noble Judith and the lecher, fearsome and ferocious. Yet there was not one of the nobles who dared awaken the warrior to inquire how it had turned out for the soldier with the holy virgin, the woman of the Lord.

The might of the Hebrews, their army, was drawing closer; vehemently they fought with tough and bloody weapons and violently they indemnified with gleaming swords their former quarrels and old insults: in that day's work the Assyrians' repute was withered, their arrogance abased. The men stood around their lord's tent, extremely agitated and growing gloomier in spirit. Then all together they began to cough and loudly make noises and, having no success, to chew the grist with their teeth, suffering agonies. The time of their glory, good fortune and valorous doings was at an end. The nobles thought to awaken their lord and friend; they succeeded not at all.

Then one of the soldiers belatedly and tardily grew so bold that he ventured pluckily into the pavilion as necessity compelled him. Then he found his lord lying pallid on the bed, deprived of his spirit, dispossessed of life. Straightway then he fell chilled to the ground, and distraught in mind he began to tear his hair and his clothing alike and he uttered these words to the soldiers who were waiting there miserably outside:

"Here is made manifest our own perdition, and here it is imminently signalled that the time is drawn near, along with its tribulations, when we must perish and be destroyed together in the strife. Here, hacked by the sword, decapitated, lies our lord."

Then distraught in mind they threw down their weapons; demoralized they went scurrying away in flight. The nation magnified in strength attacked them in the rear until the greatest part of the army lay on the field of victory levelled by battle, hacked by swords, as a treat for the wolves and a joy to the carrion-greedy birds. Those who survived fled from the linden spears of their foes. In their wake advanced the troop of Hebrews, honored with the victory and glorified in the judgment: the Lord God, the almighty Lord, had come handsomely to their aid. Swiftly then with their gleaming swords those valiant heroes made an inroad through the thick of their foes; they hacked at targes and sheared through the shield-wall. The Hebrew spear-throwers were wrought up to the fray; the soldiers lusted mightily after a spear-contest on that occasion. There in the dust fell the main part of the muster-roll of the Assyrian nobility, of that odious race. Few survivors reached their native land.

The soldiers of royal renown turned back in retirement amidst carnage and reeking corpses. That was the opportunity for the land's in-dwellers to seize from those most odious foes, their old dead enemies, bloodied booty, resplendent accoutrements, shield and broad sword, burnished helmets, costly treasures. The guardians of their homeland had honorably conquered their enemies on the battlefield and destroyed with swords their old persecutors. In their trail lay dead those who of living peoples had been most inimical to their existence.

Then the whole nation, most famous of races, proud, curled-locked, for the duration of one month were carrying and conveying into the beautiful city, Bethulia, helmets and hip-swords, gray mail-coats, and men's battle-dress ornamented with gold, more glorious treasures than any man among ingenious men can tell. All that the people splendidly gained, brave beneath their banners in the fray, through the shrewd advice of Judith, the courageous woman. As a reward the celebrated spearmen brought back for her from the expedition the sword and the bloodied helmet of Holofernes as well as his huge mail-coat adorned with red gold; and everything the ruthless lord of the warriors owned of riches or personal wealth, of rings and of beautiful treasures, they gave it to that beautiful and resourceful lady.

For all this Judith gave glory to the Lord of hosts who granted her esteem and renown in the realm of earth and likewise too a reward in heaven, the prize of victory in the glory of the sky because she always had true faith in the Almighty. Certainly at the end she did not doubt the reward for which she long had yearned.

For this be glory into eternity to the dear Lord who created the wind and the clouds, the skies and the spacious plains and likewise the cruel seas and the joys of heaven, through his peculiar mercy.

The Dream of the Rood

The Dream of the Rood is a remarkable tenth-century poem, a mystical dream vision whose narrator tells of his dream that the rood—Christ's cross—appeared to him and told the story of its unwilling role in the crucifixion. The poem is an excellent illustration of how the conventions of Old English heroic poems like *Beowulf* were adapted to the doctrines of Christianity. Christ's Passion is converted into a heroic sacrifice as the cross reports that it watched him—the young hero—strip himself naked, as if preparing for battle, and bravely ascend it. In the same vein, the cross presents itself as a thane (retainer) forced into disloyalty, as it watches—and participates in—the crucifixion, unable to avenge its beloved Lord.

In addition to heroic poetry, *The Dream of the Rood* recalls Old English genres such as the riddle and the elegy. In riddle fashion, the cross asks, "What am I?"—that started as a tree, became an instrument of torture, and am now a beacon of victory, resplendent with jewels. In the manner of elegies like *The Wanderer*, the speaker, stained with sin, presents himself as a lonely exile whose companions have left him and gone to heaven. After his vision, he resolves to seek the fellowship of his heavenly Lord and his former companions, which he pictures as taking place in a celestial mead hall: "the home of joy and happiness, / where the people of God are seated at the feast / in eternal bliss."

One of the most striking poetic effects of *The Dream of the Rood* is its focus on the Incarnation, God's taking on human flesh. The poet often juxtaposes references to Christ's humanity and divinity in the same line, thereby achieving a powerful effect of paradox, as when he tells of the approach of "the young warrior, God Almighty." It is noteworthy that the aspect of Christ's humanity which the poet stresses is the heroism rather than the pathos which was to become so prominent in later medieval poetry and art. This heroism provides a context for a cryptic passage at the end of the poem, where the dreamer refers to Christ's "journey" to bring "those who before suffered burning" victoriously to heaven. In *The Harrowing of Hell* (based on the apocryphal Gospel of Nicodemus), Christ heroically freed the virtuous Old Testament patriarchs from damnation and led them to eternal bliss.

The fame of *The Dream of the Rood* appears to have been widespread in its own time. Our knowledge of it comes from three sources: the huge stone Ruthwell Cross in southern Scotland built in the eighth century (on which a short version is inscribed in runic letters); the silver Brussels Cross, made in England in the tenth century; and the manuscript found in Vercelli in northern Italy, also written in the tenth century—the only complete version of the poem. These varied locations are a testament to the wide influence of Anglo-Saxon scholars, not only in the British Isles but on the Continent as well.

The Dream of the Rood[1]

Listen! I will describe the best of dreams
which I dreamed in the middle of the night
when, far and wide, all men slept.
It seemed that I saw a wondrous tree
soaring into the air, surrounded by light,
the brightest of crosses; that emblem was entirely
cased in gold; beautiful jewels
were strewn around its foot, just as five
studded the cross-beam. All the angels of God,

1. Translated by Kevin Crossley-Holland.

The Ruthwell Cross, north side, top section, 7th–8th century. Preserved in a church in southern Scotland, this 18-foot stone cross is carved with many Christian scenes, including this depiction of Saint John the Baptist, bearded and holding the Lamb of God. The Latin inscription beneath the saint is written in runes—the traditional Germanic alphabet, used for ritualistic purposes. Runic inscriptions elsewhere on the cross reproduce portions of *The Dream of the Rood* in Old English. Still other inscriptions are in Latin and employ the Roman alphabet. Thus, like *The Dream of the Rood* itself, whose Christlike hero resembles a Germanic warrior, the Ruthwell Cross illustrates the fusion of Mediterranean and Germanic traditions in Anglo-Saxon Christian culture.

fair creations, guarded it. That was no cross
of a criminal, but holy spirits and men on earth
watched over it there—the whole glorious universe.

Wondrous was the tree of victory, and I was stained
by sin, stricken by guilt. I saw this glorious tree
joyfully gleaming, adorned with garments,
decked in gold; the tree of the Ruler
was rightly adorned with rich stones;
yet through that gold I could see the agony
once suffered by wretches, for it had bled
down the right hand side. Then I was afflicted,
frightened at this sight; I saw that sign often change
its clothing and hue, at times dewy with moisture,
stained by flowing blood, at times adorned with treasure.
Yet I lay there for a long while

and gazed sadly at the Savior's cross
until I heard it utter words;
the finest of trees began to speak:
"I remember the morning a long time ago
that I was felled at the edge of the forest
and severed from my roots. Strong enemies seized me,
bade me hold up their felons on high,
made me a spectacle. Men shifted me
on their shoulders and set me on a hill.
Many enemies fastened me there. I saw the Lord of Mankind
hasten with such courage to climb upon me.
I dared not bow or break there
against my Lord's wish, when I saw the surface
of the earth tremble. I could have felled
all my foes, yet I stood firm.
Then the young warrior, God Almighty,
stripped Himself, firm and unflinching. He climbed
upon the cross, brave before many, to redeem mankind.
I quivered when the hero clasped me,
yet I dared not bow to the ground,
fall to the earth. I had to stand firm.
A rood was I raised up; I bore aloft the mighty King,
the Lord of Heaven. I dared not stoop.
They drove dark nails into me; dire wounds are there to see,
the gaping gashes of malice; I dared not injure them.
They insulted us both together; I was drenched in the blood
that streamed from the Man's side after He set His spirit free.

"On that hill I endured many grievous trials;
I saw the God of Hosts stretched
on the rack; darkness covered the corpse
of the Ruler with clouds, His shining radiance.
Shadows swept across the land, dark shapes
under the clouds. All creation wept,
wailed for the death of the King; Christ was on the cross.
Yet men hurried eagerly to the Prince
from afar; I witnessed all that too.
I was oppressed with sorrow, yet humbly bowed to the hands of men,
and willingly. There they lifted Him from His heavy torment,
they took Almighty God away. The warriors left me standing there,
stained with blood; sorely was I wounded by the sharpness of spear-shafts.
They laid Him down, limb-weary; they stood at the corpse's head,
they beheld there the Lord of Heaven; and there He rested for a while,
worn-out after battle. And then they began to build a sepulchre;
under his slayers' eyes, they carved it from the gleaming stone,
and laid therein the Lord of Victories. Then, sorrowful at dusk,
they sang a dirge before they went, weary,
from their glorious Prince; He rested in the grave alone.
But we still stood there, weeping blood,

long after the song of the warriors
had soared to heaven; the corpse grew cold,
the fair human house of the soul. Then our enemies
began to fell us; that was a terrible fate.
They buried us in a deep pit; but friends
and followers of the Lord found me there
and girded me with gold and shimmering silver.

"Now, my loved man, you have heard
how I endured bitter anguish
at the hands of evil men. Now the time is come
when men far and wide in this world,
and all this bright creation, bow before me;
they pray to this sign. On me the Son of God
suffered for a time; wherefore I now stand on high,
glorious under heaven; and I can heal
all those who stand in awe of me.
Long ago I became the worst of tortures,
hated by men, until I opened
to them the true way of life.
Lo! The Lord of Heaven, the Prince of Glory,
honored me over any other tree
just as He, Almighty God, for the sake of mankind
honored Mary, His own mother,
before all other women in the world.
Now I command you, my loved man,
to describe your vision to all men;
tell them with words this is the tree of glory
on which the Son of God suffered once
for the many sins committed by mankind,
and for Adam's wickedness long ago.
He sipped the drink of death. Yet the Lord rose
with His great strength to deliver man.
Then He ascended into heaven. The Lord Himself,
Almighty God, with His host of angels,
will come to the middle-world again
on Domesday to reckon with each man.
Then He who has the power of judgment
will judge each man just as he deserves
for the way in which he lived this fleeting life.
No-one then will be unafraid
as to what words the Lord will utter.
Before the assembly, He will ask where that man is
who, in God's name, would undergo the pangs of death,
just as He did formerly upon the cross.
Then men will be fearful and give
scant thought to what they say to Christ.
But no-one need be numbed by fear
who has carried the best of all signs in his breast;

each soul that has longings to live with the Lord
must search for a kingdom far beyond the frontiers of this world."

Then I prayed to the cross, eager
and light-hearted, although I was alone
with my own poor company. My soul
longed for a journey, great yearnings
always tugged at me. Now my hope in this life
is that I can turn to that tree of victory
alone and more often than any other man
and honor it fully. These longings master
my heart and mind, and my help comes
from holy cross itself. I have not many friends
of influence on earth; they have journeyed on
from the joys of this world to find the King of Glory,
they live in heaven with the High Father,
dwell in splendor. Now I look day by day
for that time when the cross of the Lord,
which once I saw in a dream here on earth,
will fetch me away from this fleeting life
and lift me to the home of joy and happiness
where the people of God are seated at the feast
in eternal bliss, and set me down
where I may live in glory unending and share
the joy of the saints. May the Lord be a friend to me,
He who suffered once for the sins of men
here on earth on the gallows-tree.
He has redeemed us; He has given life to us,
and a home in heaven.
Hope was renewed,
blessed and blissful, for those who before suffered burning.
On that journey the Son was victorious,
strong and successful. When He, Almighty Ruler,
returned with a thronging host of spirits
to God's kingdom, to joy among the angels
and all the saints who lived already
in heaven in glory, then their King,
Almighty God, entered His own country.

PERSPECTIVES
Ethnic and Religious Encounters

In the centuries of their insurgency and the consolidation of their influence in Britain, the Angles and Saxons negotiated a series of encounters that left them, and England, profoundly transformed. They arrived from the distant coasts of northwest continental Europe as self-conscious foreigners, divided into large tribal groups and often warring among themselves. They were pagans and masters of a great but essentially oral culture. By the end of their dominance, in 1066, they were long-Christianized and increasingly had come to perceive themselves as a single people. Moreover, their conversion involved a new commitment to the practical uses of writing and the talismanic power of the written book, as well as a heightened sense of the conflicting claims and uses of their ancient vernacular and of Latin. They now experienced England as their native place and registered their ancestral geography on the Continent as an area of nostalgic exploration or, equally, the source of hostile invasion.

All this was the work of centuries. It was not an unconscious or "natural" development, however. The passages in this section, in their different ways, offer key moments in the lengthy and complex process by which the Germanic newcomers encountered other peoples, religions, textual cultures, and geographies.

The initial contact between the Germanic invaders and the prior inhabitants of England—Britons, the "Irish" of the northwest, and the Picts—was based on military service which turned into military aggression. Relatively soon, though, and even as their territorial ambitions continued, the Angles and Saxons developed other contacts, especially with the Britons. The British were already Christian, and the Angles and Saxons first came to Christianity through British models if not by British hands. Later, the Anglo-Saxons themselves would face invasion by Vikings, who ultimately settled north of the Humber in the "Danelaw." Much of Asser's *Life of King Alfred* documents Alfred's struggle against Viking raiders.

Though he celebrated Alfred's West Saxon kingship and culture, Asser was himself a Welshman. His presence at Alfred's court is a sign of how Latin learning had declined in the disordered era of Viking incursions; Alfred was obliged to turn to other peoples to restore education in his own realm. The Norwegian trader Ohthere, too, came to Alfred's court even while the King was fending off Viking raiders. Ohthere seems to have sparked lively interest in his own people and their social order, as well as in his visits to what the Anglo-Saxons knew was their ancestral home.

Christianization was also a slow, complex, and incomplete process of acculturation. Bede recounts a number of moments when the differing responses to a single event register the encounters of pagan and Christian, literate and illiterate, and Latin and Germanic traditions. The conversion of King Edwin, for instance, involved not just the King fulfilling a promise made in a vision but also his nobles learning to imagine a new spiritual geography which went far beyond the brief joys of their warrior cohort. In the story of Imma, the magical loosing of a prisoner's chains is seen by some as the effect of an ancient pagan "loosing spell," but by Imma (and Bede's Christian readers) as the effect of masses said for his soul.

Language and literacy equally figure in the conversion of the Angles and Saxons and in the slow emergence of the idea of an "English" people. Imma is freed by the uncanny (and somewhat misdirected) power of the Latin mass. The high level of Bede's own Latin suggests how that language was becoming a cohesive force, at least among clerics. Yet in one of his tenderest stories, Bede tells about the illiterate Caedmon who learned, by divine intervention, to tell biblical stories in vernacular poetry. Bede admits that his Latin version of *Caedmon's Hymn* is inadequte, which suggests that Anglo-Saxon could assume its own place in the operations of the sacred. And Asser celebrates Alfred's childhood love of Saxon poems, laments Alfred's illiteracy, yet tells how the illiterate prince competed for the gift of a book he valued almost as a talisman. Alfred's acquisition of literacy and of Latin is part of his rise to successful kingship, and he caps his own reign with the series of translations that bring crucial texts of Latin Christianity into an Anglo-Saxon that Alfred now seems to see as a unifying national tongue.

Finally, even as some Anglo-Saxons aspire to nationhood, they do so by nostalgic memories of their foreign past, as seen in the information they draw from the Norwegian visitor Ohthere. At the same time, though, they mark themselves off from this geography and see themselves as the sinning victims of invasions that will end their power, just as their own successful invasions had punished and subdued the earlier Britons. This is repeatedly made explicit in *The Anglo-Saxon Chronicle*'s report of the twin battles fought by King Harold against Norwegian aggressors in the North and then against the triumphant Normans in the South. Their sense of nationhood and of being folded into processes of Christian history is clearest as the Chronicler witnesses the close of Anglo-Saxon dominance.

For additional resources on medieval ethnic and religious encounters, go to *The Longman Anthology of British Literature* Web site at www.myliteraturekit.com.

Bede
672–735

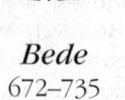

Bede was born on lands belonging to the abbey of Wearmouth-Jarrow. He entered that monastery at the age of seven and never traveled more than seventy-five miles away. Bede is the most enduring product of the golden age of Northumbrian monasticism. In the generations just preceding his, a series of learned abbots had brought Roman liturgical practices and monastic habits to Wearmouth-Jarrow, as well as establishing there the best library in England. Out of this settled life and disciplined religious culture Bede created a diverse body of writings that are learned both in scholarly research and in the purity of their Latin. They include biblical commentaries, school texts from spelling to metrics, treatises on the liturgical calendar, hymns, and lives of saints.

Bede's *An Ecclesiastical History of the English People*, completed in 731, marks the apex of his achievement. Given the localism of his life, Bede's grasp of English history is extraordinary, not just in terms of his eager pursuit of information, but equally in his balanced and complex sense of the broad movement of history. Bede registers a persistent concern about his sources and their reliability. He prefers written and especially documentary evidence, but he will use oral reports if they come from several sources and are close enough to the original event.

The *Ecclesiastical History* suggests the contours of a national history, even a providential history, in the arrival of the Angles and Saxons, and in the island's uneven conversion to Christianity. Despite his frequent stories of battles among the Germanic peoples in Britain, Bede speaks of the English people emphatically in the singular. Nevertheless, Bede is delicately aware of the historical layering brought about by colonization and the ongoing resistance of earlier inhabitants. Further, he is always alert to profoundly transformative influences, aside from ethnicity, that color his time: the process of conversion to Christianity, and the variable coexistence of Christian and pagan instincts in individual minds; the interplay of oral and written culture; the status in religious and official life of Latin and the Anglo-Saxon vernaculars.

from An Ecclesiastical History of the English People[1]

[The Conversion of King Edwin][2]

King Edwin hesitated to accept the word of God which Paulinus[3] preached but, as we have said, used to sit alone for hours at a time, earnestly debating within himself what he ought to do and what religion he should follow. One day Paulinus came to him and, placing his right hand on the king's head, asked him if he recognized this sign. The king began to tremble and would have thrown himself at the bishop's feet but Paulinus raised him up and said in a voice that seemed familiar, "First you have escaped with God's help from the hands of the foes you feared; secondly you have acquired by His gift the kingdom you desired; now, in the third place, remember your own promise; do not delay in fulfilling it but receive the faith and keep the commandments of Him who rescued you from your earthly foes and raised you to the honor of an earthly kingdom. If from henceforth you are willing to follow His will which is made known to you through me, He will also rescue you from the everlasting torments of the wicked and make you a partaker with Him of His eternal kingdom in heaven."

When the king had heard his words, he answered that he was both willing and bound to accept the faith which Paulinus taught. He said, however, that he would confer about this with his loyal chief men and his counselors so that, if they agreed with him, they might all be consecrated together in the waters of life. Paulinus agreed and the king did as he had said. A meeting of his council was held and each one was asked in turn what he thought of this doctrine hitherto unknown to them and this new worship of God which was being proclaimed.

Coifi, the chief of the priests, answered at once, "Notice carefully, King, this doctrine which is now being expounded to us. I frankly admit that, for my part, I have found that the religion which we have hitherto held has no virtue nor profit in it. None of your followers has devoted himself more earnestly than I have to the worship of our gods, but nevertheless there are many who receive greater benefits and greater honor from you than I do and are more successful in all their undertakings. If the gods had any power they would have helped me more readily, seeing that I have always served them with greater zeal. So it follows that if, on examination, these new doctrines which have now been explained to us are found to be better and more effectual, let us accept them at once without any delay."

Another of the king's chief men agreed with this advice and with these wise words and then added, "This is how the present life of man on earth, King, appears to me in comparison with that time which is unknown to us. You are sitting feasting with your ealdormen and thegns[4] in winter time; the fire is burning on the hearth in the middle of the hall and all inside is warm, while outside the wintry storms of rain and snow are raging; and a sparrow flies swiftly through the hall. It enters in at one door and quickly flies out through the other. For the few moments it is inside, the storm and wintry tempest cannot touch it, but after the briefest moment of calm, it

1. Edited and translated by Bertram Colgrave and R. A. B. Mynors.

2. From bk. 2, chs. 12–14. Edwin became king of Northumbria in 616, aided by Raedwald, king of the East Angles. Exiled at Raedwald's court, Edwin had a vision wherein he promised a shadowy visitor he would convert if he achieved the crown. The visitor laid his right hand on Edwin's head as a sign to remember that promise when the gesture was repeated.

3. Later archbishop of York, Paulinus had been sent to Northumbria from Kent with Edwin's Christian wife after Edwin had promised tolerance of Christian worship.

4. Ealdorman: the highest Anglo-Saxon rank below king; thegn: a noble warrior still serving within the king's household.

flits from your sight, out of the wintry storm and into it again. So this life of man appears but for a moment; what follows or indeed what went before, we know not at all. If this new doctrine brings us more certain information, it seems right that we should accept it."[5] Other elders and counselors of the king continued in the same manner, being divinely prompted to do so.

Coifi added that he would like to listen still more carefully to what Paulinus himself had to say about God. The king ordered Paulinus to speak, and when he had said his say, Coifi exclaimed, "For a long time now I have realized that our religion is worthless; for the more diligently I sought the truth in our cult, the less I found it. Now I confess openly that the truth shines out clearly in this teaching which can bestow on us the gift of life, salvation, and eternal happiness. Therefore I advise your Majesty that we should promptly abandon and commit to the flames the temples and the altars which we have held sacred without reaping any benefit." Why need I say more? The king publicly accepted the gospel which Paulinus preached, renounced idolatry, and confessed his faith in Christ. When he asked the high priest of their religion which of them should be the first to profane the altars and the shrines of the idols, together with their precincts, Coifi answered, "I will; for through the wisdom the true God has given me no one can more suitably destroy those things which I once foolishly worshiped, and so set an example to all." And at once, casting aside his vain superstitions, he asked the king to provide him with arms and a stallion; and mounting it he set out to destroy the idols. Now a high priest of their religion was not allowed to carry arms or to ride except on a mare. So, girded with a sword, he took a spear in his hand and mounting the king's stallion he set off to where the idols were. The common people who saw him thought he was mad. But as soon as he approached the shrine, without any hesitation he profaned it by casting the spear which he held into it; and greatly rejoicing in the knowledge of the worship of the true God, he ordered his companions to destroy and set fire to the shrine and all the enclosures. The place where the idols once stood is still shown, not far from York, to the east, over the river Derwent. Today it is called Goodmanham, the place where the high priest, through the inspiration of the true God, profaned and destroyed the altars which he himself had consecrated.[6]

So King Edwin, with all the nobles of his race and a vast number of the common people, received the faith and regeneration by holy baptism in the eleventh year of his reign, that is in the year of our Lord 627 and about 180 years after the coming of the English to Britain. He was baptized at York on Easter Day, 12 April, in the church of Saint Peter the Apostle, which he had hastily built of wood while he was a catechumen and under instruction before he received baptism. He established an episcopal see for Paulinus, his instructor and bishop, in the same city.

[THE STORY OF IMMA][7]

In this battle in which King Aelfwine[8] was killed, a remarkable incident is known to have happened which in my opinion should certainly not be passed over in silence, since the story may lead to the salvation of many. During the battle one of the king's retainers, a young man named Imma was struck down among others; he lay all that

5. This famous simile is put in the mouth of a lay nobleman, not the pagan priest Coifi whose argument for conversion was based on disappointed self-interest.

6. This detail is typical of Bede's liking for textual or archaeological authentication.

7. Bk. 4, ch. 22.

8. A battle in 679, between King Ecgfrith of Northumbria and Aethelred king of the Mercians caused the death of this under-king and brother of Ecgfrith.

day and the following night as though dead, among the bodies of the slain, but at last he recovered consciousness, sat up, and bandaged his wounds as best he could; then, having rested for a short time, he rose and set out to find friends to take care of him. But as he was doing so, he was found and captured by men of the enemy army and taken to their lord, who was a *gesith*[9] of King Aethelred. On being asked who he was, he was afraid to admit that he was a thegn; but he answered instead that he was a poor peasant and married; and he declared that he had come to the army in company with other peasants to bring food to the soldiers. The *gesith* took him and had his wounds attended to. But when Imma began to get better, he ordered him to be bound at night to prevent his escape. However, it proved impossible to bind him, for no sooner had those who chained him gone, than his fetters were loosed.

Now he had a brother whose name was Tunna, a priest and abbot of a monastery in a city which is still called *Tunnacaestir* after him. When Tunna heard that his brother had perished in the fight, he went to see if he could find his body; having found another very like him in all respects, he concluded that it must be his brother's body. So he carried it to the monastery, buried it with honor, and took care to offer many masses for the absolution of his soul. It was on account of these celebrations that, as I have said, no one could bind Imma because his fetters were at once loosed. Meanwhile the *gesith* who kept him captive grew amazed and asked him why he could not be bound and whether he had about him any loosing spells such as are described in stories. But Imma answered that he knew nothing of such arts. "However," said he, "I have a brother in my country who is a priest and I know he believes me to be dead and offers frequent masses on my behalf; so if I had now been in another world, my soul would have been loosed from its punishment by his intercessions." When he had been a prisoner with the *gesith* for some time, those who watched him closely realized by his appearance, his bearing, and his speech that he was not of common stock as he had said, but of noble family. Then the *gesith* called him aside and asked him very earnestly to declare his origin, promising that no harm should come to him, provided that he told him plainly who he was. The prisoner did so, revealing that he had been one of the king's thegns. The *gesith* answered, "I realized by every one of your answers that you were not a peasant, and now you ought to die because all my brothers and kinsmen were killed in the battle: but I will not kill you for I do not intend to break my promise."

As soon as Imma had recovered, the *gesith* sold him to a Frisian in London; but he could neither be bound on his way there nor by the Frisian. So after his enemies had put every kind of bond on him and as his new master realized that he could not be bound, he gave him leave to ransom himself if he could. Now the bonds were most frequently loosed from about nine in the morning, the time when masses were usually said. So having sworn that he would either return or send his master the money for his ransom, he went to King Hlothhere of Kent, who was the son of Queen Aethelthryth's sister already mentioned, because he had once been one of Aethelthryth's thegns; he asked for and received the money from him for his ransom and sent it to his master as he had promised.[1]

He afterwards returned to his own country, where he met his brother and gave him a full account of all his troubles and the comfort that had come to him in those

9. A nobleman, serving a king but having his own household of retainers and servants.
1. Imma had been thegn to Aethelthryth, wife of King Ecgfrith, before he entered Aelfwine's service. He now turns to her nephew, implicitly invoking obligations of kinship, for help with his ransom.

adversities; and from what his brother told him, he realized that his bonds had generally been loosed at the time when masses were being celebrated on his behalf; so he perceived that the other comforts and blessings which he had experienced during his time of danger had been bestowed by heaven, through the intercession of his brother and the offering up of the saving Victim. Many who heard about this from Imma were inspired to greater faith and devotion, to prayer and almsgiving and to the offering up of sacrifices to God in the holy oblation, for the deliverance of their kinsfolk who had departed from the world; for they realized that the saving sacrifice availed for the everlasting redemption of both body and soul.

This story was told me by some of those who heard it from the very man to whom these things happened; therefore since I had so clear an account of the incident, I thought that it should undoubtedly be inserted into this *History*.

[CAEDMON'S HYMN][2]

In the monastery of this abbess[3] there was a certain brother who was specially marked out by the grace of God, so that he used to compose godly and religious songs; thus, whatever he learned from the holy Scriptures by means of interpreters, he quickly turned into extremely delightful and moving poetry, in English, which was his own tongue. By his songs the minds of many were often inspired to despise the world and to long for the heavenly life. It is true that after him other Englishmen attempted to compose religious poems, but none could compare with him. For he did not learn the art of poetry from men nor through a man but he received the gift of song freely by the grace of God. Hence he could never compose any foolish or trivial poem but only those which were concerned with devotion and so were fitting for his devout tongue to utter. He had lived in the secular habit until he was well advanced in years and had never learned any songs.[4] Hence sometimes at a feast, when for the sake of providing entertainment, it had been decided that they should all sing in turn, when he saw the harp approaching him, he would rise up in the middle of the feasting, go out, and return home.

On one such occasion when he did so, he left the place of feasting and went to the cattle byre, as it was his turn to take charge of them that night. In due time he stretched himself out and went to sleep, whereupon he dreamed that someone stood by him, saluted him, and called him by name: "Caedmon," he said, "sing me something." Caedmon answered, "I cannot sing; that is why I left the feast and came here because I could not sing." Once again the speaker said, "Nevertheless you must sing to me." "What must I sing?" said Caedmon. "Sing," he said, "about the beginning of created things." Thereupon Caedmon began to sing verses which he had never heard before in praise of God the Creator, of which this is the general sense: "Now we must praise the Maker of the heavenly kingdom, the power of the Creator and his counsel, the deeds of the Father of glory and how He, since he is the eternal God, was the Author of all marvels and first created the heavens as a roof for the children of men and then, the almighty Guardian of the human race, created the earth." This is the sense but not the order of the words which he sang as he slept. For it is not possible to translate verse, however well composed, literally from one

2. Bk. 4, ch. 24.
3. Hild, an aristocratic woman famed for her piety, who had founded and ruled the abbey of Whitby.
4. Monks, who devoted their lives to prayer and the celebration of the liturgy, needed to be literate in Latin. Caedmon was one of the lay brothers, who performed menial tasks and were often uneducated.

language to another without some loss of beauty and dignity. When he awoke, he remembered all that he had sung while asleep and soon added more verses in the same manner, praising God in fitting style.

In the morning he went to the reeve[5] who was his master, telling him of the gift he had received, and the reeve took him to the abbess. He was then bidden to describe his dream in the presence of a number of the more learned men and also to recite his song so that they might all examine him and decide upon the nature and origin of the gift of which he spoke; and it seemed clear to all of them that the Lord had granted him heavenly grace. They then read to him a passage of sacred history or doctrine, bidding him make a song out of it, if he could, in metrical form. He undertook the task and went away; on returning next morning he repeated the passage he had been given, which he had put into excellent verse. The abbess, who recognized the grace of God which the man had received, instructed him to renounce his secular habit and to take monastic vows. She and all her people received him into the community of the brothers and ordered that he should be instructed in the whole course of sacred history. He learned all he could by listening to them and then, memorizing it and ruminating over it, like some clean animal chewing the cud, he turned it into the most melodious verse: and it sounded so sweet as he recited it that his teachers became in turn his audience. He sang about the creation of the world, the origin of the human race, and the whole history of Genesis, of the departure of Israel from Egypt and the entry into the promised land and of many other of the stories taken from the sacred Scriptures: of the incarnation, passion, and resurrection of the Lord, of His ascension into heaven, of the coming of the Holy Spirit and the teaching of the apostles. He also made songs about the terrors of future judgment, the horrors of the pains of hell, and the joys of the heavenly kingdom. In addition he composed many other songs about the divine mercies and judgments, in all of which he sought to turn his hearers away from delight in sin and arouse in them the love and practice of good works. He was a most religious man, humbly submitting himself to the discipline of the Rule; and he opposed all those who wished to act otherwise with a flaming and fervent zeal. It was for this reason that his life had a beautiful ending.

When the hour of his departure drew near he was afflicted, fourteen days before, by bodily weakness, yet so slight that he was able to walk about and talk the whole time. There was close by a building to which they used to take those who were infirm or who seemed to be at the point of death. On the night on which he was to die, as evening fell, he asked his attendant to prepare a place in this building where he could rest. The attendant did as Caedmon said though he wondered why he asked, for he did not seem to be by any means at the point of death. They had settled down in the house and were talking and joking cheerfully with each of those who were already there and it was past midnight, when he asked whether they had the Eucharist in the house. They answered, "What need have you of the Eucharist? You are not likely to die, since you are talking as cheerfully with us as if you were in perfect health." "Nevertheless," he repeated, "bring me the Eucharist." When he had taken it in his hand he asked if they were all charitably disposed towards him and had no complaint nor any quarrel nor grudge against him. They answered that they were all in charity with him and without the slightest feeling of anger; then they asked him in turn whether he was charitably disposed towards them. He

5. Person responsible for running the monastery's estates.

answered at once, "My sons, I am in charity with all the servants of God." So, fortifying himself with the heavenly viaticum, he prepared for his entrance into the next life. Thereupon he asked them how near it was to the time when the brothers had to awake to sing their nightly praises to God. They answered, "It will not be long." And he answered, "Good, let us wait until then." And so, signing himself with the sign of the holy cross, he laid his head on the pillow, fell asleep for a little while, and so ended his life quietly. Thus it came about that, as he had served the Lord with a simple and pure mind and with quiet devotion, so he departed into His presence and left the world by a quiet death; and his tongue which had uttered so many good words in praise of the Creator also uttered its last words in His praise, as he signed himself with the sign of the cross and commended his spirit into God's hands; and from what has been said, it would seem that he had foreknowledge of his death.

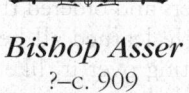

Bishop Asser

?–c. 909

When Bede died in 735, he left an island that was very unstable in its political geography but apparently ever more stable and accomplished in its religion and learning. By the end of the century, that world was shattered. In 793 Vikings sacked the monastery of Lindisfarne, not far from Wearmouth-Jarrow. Waves of raiders and then settlers followed. Monastic communities fled inland, and some shifted for generations before resettling finally. However sporadic and temporary may have been the worldly impact of these Viking raiders, however quickly they became peaceful settlers, they had a disastrous effect on the kind of disciplined learning witnessed by the life of Bede. By the time of Asser, Latin learning in most of England was fragmented and in decline, though not so bad as it suits Alfred to claim. Asser, a Welsh monk and later bishop of Sherborne, was summoned to Wessex by King Alfred as part of a project to revive learning and extend its audience beyond those who read Latin. Alfred accomplished this, in part, by looking to men like Asser, from areas such as Wales which had preserved some traditions of classical learning.

Asser's worshipful and disorganized but lively *Life of King Alfred* was written in Latin during the king's life, about 893. It depicts the origins of the king's scholarly ambitions, interwoven with the struggles by which Alfred established and extended his rule and resisted renewed Viking incursions. Asser thus offers a double narrative of texts and conquests which make one another possible and worthy. The diffusion of learning and revival of religious discipline become enmeshed in a logic that also includes Alfred's ambitions to rule all the Anglo-Saxons.

from The Life of King Alfred[1]

[ALFRED'S BOYHOOD]

Now he was greatly cherished above all his brothers by the united and ardent love of his father and mother, and indeed of all people; and he was ever brought up entirely at the royal court. As he passed through his infancy and boyhood he surpassed all his brothers in beauty, and was more pleasing in his appearance, in his speech, and in his manners. From his earliest childhood the noble character of his mind gave him a desire for all things useful in this present life, and, above all, a longing for wisdom; but, alas! the culpable negligence of his relations, and of those who had care of him,

1. Translated by L. C. Jane.

allowed him to remain ignorant of letters until his twelfth year, or even to a later age. Albeit, day and night did he listen attentively to the Saxon poems, which he often heard others repeating, and his retentive mind enabled him to remember them.

An ardent hunter, he toiled persistently at every form of that art, and not in vain. For in his skill and success at this pursuit he surpassed all, as in all other gifts of God. And this skill we have ourselves seen on many occasions.

Now it chanced on a certain day that his mother showed to him and to his brothers a book of Saxon poetry, which she had in her hand, and said, "I will give this book to that one among you who shall the most quickly learn it." Then, moved at these words, or rather by the inspiration of God, and being carried away by the beauty of the initial letter in that book, anticipating his brothers who surpassed him in years but not in grace, he answered his mother, and said, "Will you of a truth give that book to one of us? To him who shall soonest understand it and repeat it to you?" And at this she smiled and was pleased, and affirmed it, saying, "I will give it to him." Then forthwith he took the book from her hand and went to his master, and read it; and when he had read it he brought it back to his mother and repeated it to her.

After this he learnt the Daily Course, that is, the services for each hour, and then some psalms and many prayers. These were collected in one book, which, as we have ourselves seen, he constantly carried about with him everywhere in the fold of his cloak, for the sake of prayer amid all the passing events of this present life. But, alas! the art of reading which he most earnestly desired he did not acquire in accordance with his wish, because, as he was wont himself to say, in those days there were no men really skilled in reading in the whole realm of the West Saxons.

With many complaints, and with heartfelt regrets, he used to declare that among all the difficulties and trials of this life this was the greatest. For at the time when he was of an age to learn, and had leisure and ability for it, he had no masters; but when he was older, and indeed to a certain extent had anxious masters and writers, he could not read. For he was occupied day and night without ceasing both with illnesses unknown to all the physicians of that island, and with the cares of the royal office both at home and abroad, and with the assaults of the heathen by land and sea.[2] None the less, amid the difficulties of this life, from his infancy to the present day, he has not in the past faltered in his earnest pursuit of knowledge, nor does he even now cease to long for it, nor, as I think, will he ever do so until the end of his life.

[Alfred's Kingship]

Yet amid the wars and many hindrances of this present life, and amid the assaults of the pagans, and his daily illness, the king ceased not from the governance of the kingdom and from the pursuit of every form of hunting. Nor did he omit to instruct also his goldsmiths and all his artificers, his falconers and his huntsmen and the keepers of his dogs; nor to make according to new designs of his own articles of goldsmiths' work, more venerable and more precious than had been the wont of all his predecessors. He was constant in the reading of books in the Saxon tongue, and more especially in committing to memory the Saxon poems, and in commanding others to do so. And he by himself labored most zealously with all his might.

2. Alfred's patient suffering in illness is one of several patterns by which Asser implies analogies with the lives of saints.

Moreover he heard the divine offices daily, the Mass, and certain psalms and prayers. He observed the services of the hours by day and by night, and oftentimes was he wont, as we have said, without the knowledge of his men, to go in the night-time to the churches for the sake of prayer. He was zealous in the giving of alms, and generous towards his own people and to those who came from all nations. He was especially and wonderfully kindly towards all men, and merry. And to the searching out of things not known did he apply himself with all his heart.

Moreover many Franks, Frisians and Gauls, pagans, Britons, Scots and Armoricans, of their own free will, submitted them to his rule, both nobles and persons of low degree. All these he ruled, according to his excellent goodness, as he did his own people, and loved them and honored them, and enriched them with money and with power.

He was eager and anxious to hear the Holy Scripture read to him by his own folk, but he would also as readily pray with strangers, if by any chance one had come from any place. Moreover he loved with wonderful affection his bishops and all the clergy, his ealdormen and nobles, his servants and all his household. And cherishing their sons, who were brought up in the royal household, with no less love than he bore towards his own children, he ceased not day and night, among other things, himself to teach them all virtue and to make them well acquainted with letters.

But it was as though he found no comfort in all these things. For, as if he suffered no other care from within or without, in anxious sorrow, day and night, he would make complaint to the Lord and to all who were joined to him in close affection, lamenting with many sighs for that Almighty God had not made him skilled in divine wisdom and in the liberal arts.

King Alfred

849–899

Alfred, king of the West Saxons, had ambitions to be king of all England, at least south of the Humber. He spent much of his reign in a series of campaigns against Viking raiders. After a decisive victory at the battle of Edington in 878, Alfred negotiated a peace that included the departure of the Danes from Wessex and the baptism of their king Guthrum. In the later years of his reign, starting about 890, he embarked on a quite different, but ultimately more influential, campaign of conquest and Christian conversion, through the series of Anglo-Saxon translations from Latin produced by his own hand and under his patronage. Pope Gregory the Great's *Pastoral Care* (c. 591), a handbook for bishops, was the first. This effort assuredly had charitable and scholarly motivations, but it also takes on interesting national overtones when it assumes that Anglo-Saxon is one language and known by all, and even more when it is linked to earlier translations and the westward movement of ancient power.

Preface to Saint Gregory's *Pastoral Care*[1]

King Alfred bids greet Bishop Waerferth[2] with his words lovingly and with friendship; and I let it be known to thee that it has very often come into my mind what wise men there formerly were throughout England, both of sacred and secular orders;

1. Translated by Kevin Crossley-Holland.
2. Waerferth, bishop of Worcester, had earlier translated Gregory's *Dialogues* for Alfred and perhaps inspired the king's more ambitious program.

and what happy times there were then throughout England; and how the kings who had power over the nation in those days obeyed God and His ministers; how they preserved peace, morality, and order at home, and at the same time enlarged their territory abroad; and how they prospered both with war and with wisdom; and also how zealous the sacred orders were both in teaching and learning, and in all the services they owed to God; and how foreigners came to this land in search of wisdom and instruction, and how we should now have to get them from abroad if we were to have them. So general was its decay in England that there were very few on this side of the Humber who could understand their rituals in English, or translate a letter from Latin into English; and I believe that there were not many beyond the Humber. There were so few of them that I cannot remember a single one south of the Thames when I came to the throne. Thanks be to Almighty God that we have any teachers among us now. And therefore I command thee to do as I believe thou art willing, to disengage thyself from worldly matters as often as thou canst, that thou mayest apply the wisdom which God has given thee wherever thou canst. Consider what punishments would come upon us on account of this world, if we neither loved it [wisdom] ourselves nor suffered other men to obtain it: we should love the name only of Christian, and very few the virtues. When I considered all this, I remembered also that I saw, before it had been all ravaged and burned, how the churches throughout the whole of England stood filled with treasures and books; and there was also a great multitude of God's servants, but they had very little knowledge of the books, for they could not understand anything of them, because they were not written in their own language. As if they had said: "Our forefathers, who formerly held these places, loved wisdom, and through it they obtained wealth and bequeathed it to us. In this we can still see their tracks, but we cannot follow them, and therefore we have lost both the wealth and the wisdom, because we would not incline our hearts after their example." When I remembered all this, I wondered extremely that the good and wise men who were formerly all over England, and had perfectly learned all the books, had not wished to translate them into their own language. But again I soon answered myself and said: "They did not think that men would ever be so careless, and that learning would so decay; through that desire they abstained from it, since they wished that the wisdom in this land might increase with our knowledge of languages." Then I remembered how the law was first known in Hebrew, and again, when the Greeks had learned it, they translated the whole of it into their own language, and all other books besides. And again the Romans, when they had learned them, translated the whole of them by learned interpreters into their own language. And also all other Christian nations translated a part of them into their own language.[3] Therefore it seems better to me, if you think so, for us also to translate some books which are most needful for all men to know into the language which we can all understand, and for you to do as we very easily can if we have tranquility enough, that is, that all the youth now in England of free men, who are rich enough to be able to devote themselves to it, be set to learn as long as they are not fit for any other occupation, until they are able to read English writing well: and let those be afterwards taught more in the Latin language who are to continue in learning, and be promoted to a higher rank. When I remembered how the knowledge

3. An early statement of the widespread medieval idea of the persistent westward movement of learning, *translatio studii*, in parallel with the westward movement of power, *translatio imperii*. If Alfred will now revive learning in England, he may imply, should he not also consolidate power?

of Latin had formerly decayed throughout England, and yet many could read English writing, I began, among other various and manifold troubles of this kingdom, to translate into English the book which is called in Latin *Pastoralis*, and in English *Shepherd's Book*, sometimes word by word, and sometimes according to the sense, as I had learned it from Plegmund my archbishop, and Asser my bishop, and Grimbald my mass-priest, and John my mass-priest. And when I had learned it as I could best understand it, and as I could most clearly interpret it, I translated it into English; and I will send a copy to every bishopric in my kingdom; and in each there is a book-mark worth fifty mancuses.[4] And I command in God's name that no man take the book-mark from the book, or the book from the monastery. It is uncertain how long there may be such learned bishops as now, thanks be to God, there are nearly everywhere; therefore I wish them always to remain in their places unless the bishop wish to take them with him, or they be lent out anywhere, or any one be making a copy from them.

Ohthere's Journeys

Along with religious and speculative works like *Pastoral Care* and Boethius's *Consolation of Philosophy*, Alfred also sponsored the translation of histories, both Bede's *Ecclesiastical History of the English People* and the early fifth-century *Seven Books of History against the Pagans*, of Paulus Orosius. In the latter, Orosius's opening survey of geography is expanded to include lands north of the Alps, and the translator inserts the following account of two northern voyages by the Norwegian trader Ohthere, who later came to Alfred's court.

Ohthere describes two journeys, one made largely for curiosity (but also for walrus tusks) and the other mostly for trade. In the first, he heads north along the west coast of Norway, around the north edge of modern Sweden and Finland, and into the White Sea—a little-known area, inhabited only by hunters and fishermen. In the second he goes to the main trading town of his nation, Sciringes-heal (on the south coast of modern Norway), and then to a large town and trading center, Hedeby (modern Schleswig in northern Germany). Along with keen details of fauna and almost anthropological observation of local tribes, Ohthere notes the great exports of his area: furs, amber, and ivory—some of which he has brought to King Alfred. Throughout the passage, an implicit, curious interlocutor mediates between the interests (and ignorance) of the English audience and the foreign traveler.

Ohthere's Journeys[1]

Ohthere told his lord, King Alfred,[2] that he lived the furthest north of all Norwegians. He said that he lived in the north of Norway on the coast of the Atlantic. He also said that the land extends very far north beyond that point, but it is all uninhabited, except for a few places here and there where the *Finnas*[3] have their camps, hunting in winter, and in summer fishing in the sea.

He told how he once wished to find out how far the land extended due north, or whether anyone lived to the north of the unpopulated area. He went due north along the coast, keeping the uninhabited land to starboard and the open sea to port

4. Gold coins.

1. Translated by Christine E. Fell.

2. As a foreign visitor, Ohthere would need the official protection of the king, who is thus "his lord."

3. The *Finnas* (modern Lapps) are a nomadic people who give tribute to the Norwegians. They herd deer, hunt, and fish. They are not the peoples we now call Finns, whom Ohthere called *Beormas* and *Cwenas*.

continuously for three days. He was then as far north as the whale hunters go at their furthest. He then continued due north as far as he could reach in the second three days. There the land turned due east, or the sea penetrated the land he did not know which—but he knew that he waited there for a west-northwest wind, and then sailed east along the coast as far as he could sail in four days. There he had to wait for a due northern wind, because there the land turned due south, or the sea penetrated the land he did not know which. Then from there he sailed due south along the coast as far as he could sail in five days. A great river went up into the land there. They turned up into the river, not daring to sail beyond it without permission, since the land on the far side of the river was fully settled. He had not previously come across any settled district since he left his own home, but had, the whole way, land to starboard that was uninhabited apart from fishers and bird-catchers and hunters, and they were all *Finnas*. To port he always had the open sea. The *Beormas* had extensive settlements in their country but the Norwegians did not dare to venture there. But the land of the *Terfinnas* was totally uninhabited except where hunters made camp, or fishermen or bird-catchers.

The *Beormas* told him many stories both about their own country and about the lands which surrounded them, but he did not know how much of it was true because he had not seen it for himself. It seemed to him that the *Finnas* and the *Beormas* spoke almost the same language. His main reason for going there, apart from exploring the land, was for the walruses, because they have very fine ivory in their tusks—they brought some of these tusks to the king—and their hide is very good for ship-ropes. This whale [i.e., walrus] is much smaller than other whales; it is no more than seven ells long. The best whale-hunting is in his own country; those are forty-eight ells long, the biggest fifty ells long; of these he said that he, one of six, killed sixty in two days.

He was a very rich man in those possessions which their riches consist of, that is in wild deer. He had still, when he came to see the king, six hundred unsold tame deer. These deer they call "reindeer." Six of these were decoy-reindeer. These are very valuable among the *Finnas* because they use them to catch the wild reindeer. He was among the chief men in that country, but he had not more than twenty cattle, twenty sheep and twenty pigs, and the little that he plowed he plowed with horses. Their wealth, however, is mostly in the tribute which the *Finnas* pay them. That tribute consists of the skins of beasts, the feathers of birds, whale-bone, and ship-ropes made from whale-hide and sealskin. Each pays according to his rank. The highest in rank has to pay fifteen marten skins, five reindeer skins, one bear skin and ten measures of feathers, and a jacket of bearskin or otterskin and two ship-ropes. Each of these must be sixty ells long, one made from whale-hide the other from seal.

He said that the land of the Norwegians is very long and narrow. All of it that can be used for grazing or plowing lies along the coast and even that is in some places very rocky. Wild mountains lie to the east, above and alongside the cultivated land. In these mountains live the *Finnas*. The cultivated land is broadest in the south, and the further north it goes the narrower it becomes. In the south it is perhaps sixty miles broad or a little broader; and in the middle, thirty or broader; and to the north, he said, where it is narrowest, it might be three miles across to the mountains. The mountains beyond are in some places of a width that takes two weeks to cross, in others of a width that can be crossed in six days.

Beyond the mountains Sweden borders the southern part of the land as far as the north, and the country of the *Cwenas* borders the land in the north. Sometimes

The Death of Harold, from *The Bayeux Tapestry*, c. 1073–1088. This narrative tapestry was made within living memory of the Conquest, and the scenes depicted on it overlap much of the story as told in the *Anglo-Saxon Chronicle*. The tapestry is an extraordinary production: a roll about 20 inches high and some 230 feet long thought to have been embroidered by English women, whose needlework had international fame. In this climactic scene, at left King Harold is cut down by a mounted Norman knight; at center, Anglo-Saxon foot soldiers parry spears thrown by mounted Normans. In the marginal decoration at top, birds of prey and lions face off, emblems perhaps of the noble combatants; at the bottom, in a very different tone, lie the corpses and arms of fallen soldiers.

the *Cwenas* make raids on the Norwegians across the mountains, and sometimes the Norwegians make raids on them. There are very large fresh-water lakes throughout these mountains, and the *Cwenas* carry their boats overland onto the lakes and from there make raids on the Norwegians. They have very small, very light boats.

Ohthere said that the district where he lived is called *Halgoland*.[4] He said no-one lived to the north of him. In the south part of Norway there is a trading-town which is called *Sciringes heal*. He said that a man could scarcely sail there in a month, assuming he made camp at night, and each day had a favorable wind. He would sail by the coast the whole way. To starboard is first of all *Iraland*[5] and then those islands which are between *Iraland* and this land, and then this land until he comes to *Sciringes heal*, and Norway is on the port side the whole way. To the south of *Sciringes heal* a great sea penetrates the land; it is too wide to see across. Jutland is on the far side and after that *Sillende*.[6] This sea flows into the land for many hundred miles.

From *Sciringes heal* he said that he sailed in five days to the trading-town called Hedeby, which is situated among Wends, Saxons and Angles and belongs to the Danes. When he sailed there from *Sciringes heal* he had Denmark to port and the open sea to starboard for three days. Then two days before he arrived at Hedeby he had Jutland and *Sillende* and many islands to starboard. The Angles lived in these districts before they came to this land. On the port side he had, for two days, those islands which belong to Denmark.

4. The northernmost province of Norway, much of it within the polar circle.

5. Possibly a corruption of Iceland.

6. Probably southern Jutland, modern North Schleswig.

The Anglo-Saxon Chronicle

The Anglo-Saxon Chronicle began to be assembled in the 890s at Winchester, in the heart of King Alfred's Wessex and at the high point of his reign. The decision to use Anglo-Saxon in this originally monastic product reflects the influence of Alfred's translation projects. The original version of the *Chronicle* was distributed to a number of monasteries, which made their own additions sometimes as late as the mid-twelfth century. If the various *Chronicles* began as a gesture of common language and shared history, though, their later entries—like the one below—increasingly record dynastic struggle and civil strife. And the *Chronicles* themselves, in their extensions after the Conquest, emblematize the fate of the Anglo-Saxon vernacular and culture: increasingly isolated, fragmentary, and recorded in a disappearing tongue.

from The Anglo-Saxon Chronicle[1]

STAMFORD BRIDGE AND HASTINGS

1066 In this year King Harold came from York to Westminster at the Easter following the Christmas that the king died,[2] and Easter was then on 16 April. Then over all England there was seen a sign in the skies such as had never been seen before. Some said it was the star "comet" which some call the long-haired star; and it first appeared on the eve of the Greater Litany, that is 24 April, and so shone all the week. And soon after this Earl Tosti came from overseas into the Isle of Wight with as large a fleet as he could muster and both money and provisions were given him.[3] And King Harold his brother assembled a naval force and a land force larger than any king had assembled before in this country, because he had been told that William the Bastard[4] meant to come here and conquer this country. This was exactly what happened afterwards. Meanwhile Earl Tosti came into the Humber with sixty ships and Earl Edwin came with a land force and drove him out, and the sailors deserted him. And he went to Scotland with twelve small vessels, and there Harold, king of Norway, met him with three hundred ships, and Tosti submitted to him and became his vassal; and they both went up the Humber until they reached York. And there Earl Edwin and Morcar his brother fought against them; but the Norwegians had the victory. Harold, king of the English, was informed that things had gone thus; and the fight was on the Vigil of Saint Matthew. Then Harold our king came upon the Norwegians by surprise and met them beyond York at Stamford Bridge with a large force of the English people; and that day there was a very fierce fight on both sides. There was killed Harold Fairhair and Earl Tosti, and the Norwegians who survived took to flight; and the English attacked them fiercely as they pursued them until some got to the ships. Some were drowned, and some burned, and some destroyed in various ways so that few survived and the English remained in command of the field. The king gave quarter to Olaf, son of the Norse king, and their bishop and the earl of Orkney and all those who survived on the ships, and they went up to our king and swore oaths that they would always keep peace and friendship with this country; and the king let them go home with twenty-four ships. These two pitched battles were fought within five nights.

1. Translated by Kevin Crossley-Holland.
2. Edward "the Confessor" ruled 1042–1066. Harold claims the throne through his sister Edith, Edward's widow.
3. Tosti was Harold's estranged brother, and now supported the rival claim of Harold Fairhair, king of Norway.
4. William of Normandy, "the Conqueror."

Then Count William came from Normandy to Pevensey on Michaelmas Eve, and as soon as they were able to move on they built a castle at Hastings. King Harold was informed of this and he assembled a large army and came against him at the hoary apple-tree. And William came against him by surprise before his army was drawn up in battle array. But the king nevertheless fought hard against him, with the men who were willing to support him, and there were heavy casualties on both sides. There King Harold was killed and Earl Leofwine his brother, and Earl Gyrth his brother, and many good men, and the French remained masters of the field, even as God granted it to them because of the sins of the people. Archbishop Aldred and the citizens of London wanted to have Edgar *Cild*[5] as king, as was his proper due; and Edwin and Morcar promised him that they would fight on his side; but always the more it ought to have been forward the more it got behind, and the worse it grew from day to day, exactly as everything came to be at the end. The battle took place on the festival of Calixtus the pope. And Count William went back to Hastings, and waited there to see whether submission would be made to him. But when he understood that no one meant to come to him, he went inland with all his army that was left to him, and that came to him afterwards from overseas, and ravaged all the region that he overran until he reached Berkhamstead. There he was met by Archbishop Aldred and Edgar *Cild*, and Earl Edwin and Earl Morcar, and all the chief men from London. And they submitted out of necessity after most damage had been done—and it was a great piece of folly that they had not done it earlier, since God would not make things better, because of our sins. And they gave hostages and swore oaths to him, and he promised them that he would be a gracious liege lord, and yet in the meantime they ravaged all that they overran. Then on Christmas Day, Archbishop Aldred consecrated him king at Westminster. And he promised Aldred on Christ's book and swore moreover (before Aldred would place the crown on his head) that he would rule all this people as well as the best of the kings before him, if they would be loyal to him. All the same he laid taxes on people very severely, and then went in spring overseas to Normandy, and took with him Archbishop Stigand, and Aethelnoth, abbot of Glastonbury, and Edgar *Cild* and Earl Edwin and Earl Morcar, and Earl Waltheof, and many other good men from England. And Bishop Odo and Earl William stayed behind and built castles far and wide throughout this country, and distressed the wretched folk, and always after that it grew much worse. May the end be good when God wills!

END OF PERSPECTIVES: ETHNIC AND RELIGIOUS ENCOUNTERS

Taliesin

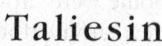

The name of Taliesin resonated through Welsh literary imagination for more than a millennium, from the late sixth century until the end of the Middle Ages. Only a small cluster of about a dozen poems can be securely identified with him, all of them praise poems and elegies for contemporary kings. These must have circulated for generations in oral form. They appear in their earliest surviving manuscript, the late thirteenth-century Book of Taliesin, already

5. Son of Edgar the Exile, grandson and great-grandson of kings; his great-uncle King Edward had titled him "Aetheling," or "throne-worthy." He was still a minor in 1066 and would have had to rule through a regent.

embedded within a nimbus of intriguing legends and falsely attributed works that had been attached to the prestige of his name across the centuries.

Despite this central role, Taliesin was not a poet of "Wales" in anything like its modern geography. In the later sixth century when he was active, Welsh-speaking kingdoms survived in the north and west of Britain and into modern Scotland. They were embattled, pressured by the expanding Anglo-Saxon kingdoms to the east and south, by Picts in the north, and by Irish Celts in the kingdom of Dalriada to the far northwest. Among these unstable Welsh kingdoms, especially Rheged around the Solway Firth, Taliesin became an important court poet.

The warrior kings in the Welsh north, such as Taliesin's chief patrons Urien king of Rheged and his son Owain, were extolled in a poetic culture that celebrated treasure and heroic violence, yet did so in forms of considerable intricacy and language of dramatic spareness. Taliesin's poems use ambitious meters and stanzas involving internal rhyme, end rhyme, and alliteration. They do not merely glory in armed bloodshed but also explore the boasts and emotions leading up to battle; they often display a haunting visual sense of its grisly aftermath. Taliesin further celebrates the generosity and gaiety of the triumphant court: in ways reminiscent of the Anglo-Saxon *Wanderer*, one poem here registers the poet's terror at the thought of losing his patron and protector. In an elegy for Owain ap Urien, Taliesin combines all these elements, yet brackets them with a suddenly broadened and suggestively discordant perspective, a Christian plea for the needs of Owain's soul.

Urien Yrechwydd[1]

Urien of Yrechwydd   most generous of Christian men,
much do you give   to the people of your land;
as you gather   so also you scatter,
the poets of Christendom   rejoice while you stand.
More is the gaiety   and more is the glory
that Urien and his heirs   are for riches renowned,
and he is the chieftain,   the paramount ruler,
the far-flung refuge,   first of fighters found.
The Lloegrians[2] know it   when they count their numbers,
death have they suffered   and many a shame,
their homesteads a-burning,   stripped their bedding,
and many a loss   and many a blame,
and never a respite   from Urien of Rheged.
Rheged's defender,   famed lord, your land's anchor,
all that is told of you   has my acclaim.
Intense is your spear-play   when you hear ploy of battle,
when to battle you come   'tis a killing you can,
fire in their houses ere day   in the lord of Yrechwydd's way,
Yrechwydd the beautiful   and its generous clan.
The Angles are succorless.   Around the fierce king
are his fierce offspring.   Of those dead, of those living,
of those yet to come,   you head the column.
To gaze upon him   is a widespread fear;

1. "I-*rech*-ooeed" (guttural "ch"), or Rheged. Like many Anglo-Saxon poems, this poem uses a break (caesura) in midline. Translated by Saunders Lewis.
2. The Angles and Saxons.

Gaiety clothes him, the ribald ruler,
gaiety clothes him and riches abounding,
gold king of the Northland and of kings king.

The Battle of Argoed Llwyfain[1]

There was a great battle Saturday morning
From when the sun rose until it grew dark.
The fourfold hosts of Fflamddwyn[2] invaded,
Goddau and Rheged gathered in arms,
Summoned from Argoed as far as Arfynydd[3]—
They might not delay by as much as a day.
With a great blustering din, Fflamddwyn shouted,
"Have these the hostages come? Are they ready?"[4]
To him then Owain, scourge of the eastlands,
"They've not come, no! they're not, nor shall they be ready."
And a whelp of Coel would indeed be afflicted
Did he have to give any man as a hostage!

And Urien, lord of Erechwydd, shouted,
"If they would meet us now for a treaty,
High on the hilltop let's raise our ramparts,
Carry our faces over the shield rims,
Raise up our spears, men, over our heads
And set upon Fflamddwyn in the midst of his hosts
And slaughter him, ay, and all that go with him!"

There was many a corpse beside Argoed Llwyfain;
From warriors ravens grew red
And with their leader a host attacked.
For a whole year I shall sing to their triumph.

The War-Band's Return[1]

Through a single year
This man has poured out
Wine, bragget, and mead,
Reward for valor.
A host of singers,
A swarm about spits,
Their torques round their heads,
Their places splendid.
Each went on campaign,

1. "Ar-goid Lloo-ee-vine," the Welsh "ll" rather like "tl" pronounced quickly as a single sound. Translated by Anthony Conran.
2. "Flom-thoo-een," the Flame-bearer, identity uncertain.
3. Goddau ("Go-thy") and Arfynydd ("Ar-vi-nith"), British territories.
4. Fflamddwyn arrogantly demands hostages, guarantees of submission, before the battle. The use of direct quotation is unique among Taliesin's poems.
1. Translated by Joseph P. Clancy.

Eager in combat,
His steed beneath him,
Set to raid Manaw
For the sake of wealth,
Profit in plenty,
Eight herds alike
Of calves and cattle,
Milch cows and oxen,
And each one worthy.

I could have no joy
Should Urien be slain,
So loved before he left,
Brandishing his lance,
And his white hair soaked,
And a bier his fate,
And gory his cheek
With the stain of blood,
A strong, steadfast man,
His wife made a widow,
My faithful king,
My faithful trust,
My bulwark, my chief,
Before savage pain.

Go, lad, to the door:
What is that clamor?
Is the earth shaking?
Is the sea in flood?
The chant grows stronger
From marching men!

Were a foe in hill,
Urien will stab him;
Were a foe in dale,
Urien has pierced him;
Were foe in mountain,
Urien conquers him;
Were foe on hillside,
Urien will wound him;
Were foe on rampart,
Urien will smite him:
Foe on path, foe on peak,
Foe at every bend,
Not one sneeze or two
He permits before death.
No famine can come,
Plunder about him.
Like death his spear
Piercing a foeman.

And until I die, old,
By death's strict demand,
I shall not be joyful
Unless I praise Urien.

Lament for Owain Son of Urien[1]

God, consider the soul's need
Of Owain son of Urien!
Rheged's prince, secret in loam:
No shallow work to praise him.

A straight° grave, a man much praised, *narrow*
His whetted spear the wings of dawn:
That lord of bright Llwyfenydd,
Where is his peer?

Reaper of enemies; strong of grip;
One kind with his fathers;
Owain, to slay Fflamddwyn,
Thought it no more than sleep.

Sleepeth the wide host of England
With light in their eyes,
And those that had not fled
Were braver than were wise.

Owain dealt them doom
As the wolves devour sheep;
That warrior, bright of harness,
Gave stallions for the bard.

Though he hoarded wealth like a miser
For his soul's sake he gave it.
God, consider the soul's need
Of Owain son of Urien!

The Wanderer

In the Exeter Book, a manuscript copied about 975 and donated to the Bishop of Exeter, are preserved some of the greatest short poems in Old English, including a number of poems referred to as elegies—laments that contrast past happiness with present sorrow and remark on how fleeting is the former. Along with *The Wanderer*, the elegies include its companion piece *The Seafarer*; *The Ruin*; *The Husband's Message*; *The Wife's Lament*; and *Wulf and Eadwacer*. While the last two are exceptional in dealing with female experience, elegies for the most part focus on male bonds and companionship, particularly the joys of the mead hall.

1. Translated by Saunders Lewis.

Old English poetry as a whole is almost entirely devoid of interest in romantic love between men and women and focuses instead on the bond between lord and retainer; elegiac poems such as *The Wanderer* have in fact been called "the love poetry of a heroic society."

The Wanderer opens with an appeal to a Christian concept, as the third-person narrator speaks of the wanderer's request for God's mercy. The body of the poem, however—primarily a first-person account in the wanderer's voice—reflects more pagan values in its regret for the loss of earthly joys. Though the poem's structure is somewhat confusing, one can discern two major parts. In the first, the wanderer laments his personal situation: he was once a member of a warrior band, but his lord—his beloved "gold-friend"—has died, leaving him a homeless exile. He dreams that he "clasps and kisses" his lord, but he then wakes to see only the dark waves, the snow, and the sea birds.

The second part of the poem turns from personal narrative to a more general statement of the transitoriness of all earthly things. The speaker (possibly someone other than the wanderer at this point), looking at the ruin of ancient buildings, is moved to express the ancient Roman motif known as "*ubi sunt*" (Latin for "where are"): "Where has the horse gone? Where the man? Where the giver of gold? / Where is the feasting place? And where the pleasures of the hall?" In the concluding five lines, the reader is urged to seek comfort in heaven.

There has been much debate about the degrees of Christianity and paganism in this tenth-century poem. The positions range from the view that the Christian opening and closing are totally extraneous to the poem and have been tacked on by a monkish copyist, to the view that the poem is a Christian allegory about a soul exiled from his heavenly home, longing for his lord Jesus Christ. It is now generally held that the poem is authentically Christian, in a literal rather than an allegorical way, but that the values of pagan society still exert a powerful pull in it.

The Wanderer[1]

Often the wanderer pleads for pity
and mercy from the Lord; but for a long time,
sad in mind, he must dip his oars
into icy waters, the lanes of the sea;
he must follow the paths of exile: fate is inflexible.

Mindful of hardships, grievous slaughter,
the ruin of kinsmen, the wanderer said:
"Time and again at the day's dawning
I must mourn all my afflictions alone.
There is no one still living to whom I dare open
the doors of my heart. I have no doubt
that it is a noble habit for a man
to bind fast all his heart's feelings,
guard his thoughts, whatever he is thinking.
The weary in spirit cannot withstand fate,
a troubled mind finds no relief:
wherefore those eager for glory often
hold some ache imprisoned in their hearts.
Thus I had to bind my feelings in fetters,

1. Translated by Kevin Crossley-Holland.

often sad at heart, cut off from my country,
far from my kinsmen, after, long ago,
dark clods of earth covered my gold-friend;
I left that place in wretchedness,
plowed the icy waves with winter in my heart;
in sadness I sought far and wide
for a treasure-giver, for a man
who would welcome me into his mead-hall,
give me good cheer (for I boasted no friends),
entertain me with delights. He who has experienced it
knows how cruel a comrade sorrow can be
to any man who has few loyal friends:
for him are the ways of exile, in no wise twisted gold;
for him is a frozen body, in no wise the fruits of the earth.
He remembers hall-retainers and treasure
and how, in his youth, his gold-friend
entertained him. Those joys have all vanished.
A man who lacks advice for a long while
from his loved lord understands this,
that when sorrow and sleep together
hold the wretched wanderer in their grip,
it seems that he clasps and kisses
his lord, and lays hands and head
upon his lord's knee as he had sometimes done
when he enjoyed the gift-throne in earlier days.
Then the friendless man wakes again
and sees the dark waves surging around him,
the sea-birds bathing, spreading their feathers,
frost and snow falling mingled with hail.
"Then his wounds lie more heavy in his heart,
aching for his lord. His sorrow is renewed;
the memory of kinsmen sweeps through his mind;
joyfully he welcomes them, eagerly scans
his comrade warriors. Then they swim away again.
Their drifting spirits do not bring many old songs
to his lips. Sorrow upon sorrow attend
the man who must send time and again
his weary heart over the frozen waves.
"And thus I cannot think why in the world
my mind does not darken when I brood on the fate
of brave warriors, how they have suddenly
had to leave the mead-hall, the bold followers.
So this world dwindles day by day,
and passes away; for a man will not be wise
before he has weathered his share of winters
in the world. A wise man must be patient,
neither too passionate nor too hasty of speech,
neither too irresolute nor too rash in battle;

not too anxious, too content, nor too grasping,
and never too eager to boast before he knows himself.
When he boasts a man must bide his time
until he has no doubt in his brave heart
that he has fully made up his mind.
A wise man must fathom how eerie it will be
when all the riches of the world stand waste,
as now in diverse places in this middle-earth
old walls stand, tugged at by winds
and hung with hoar-frost, buildings in decay.
The wine-halls crumble, lords lie dead,
deprived of joy, all the proud followers
have fallen by the wall: battle carried off some,
led them on journeys; the bird carried one
over the welling waters; one the gray wolf
devoured; a warrior with downcast face
hid one in an earth-cave.
Thus the Maker of Men laid this world waste
until the ancient works of the giants stood idle,
hushed without the hubbub of inhabitants.
Then he who has brooded over these noble ruins,
and who deeply ponders this dark life,
wise in his mind, often remembers
the many slaughters of the past and speaks these words:
Where has the horse gone? Where the man? Where the giver of gold?
Where is the feasting-place? And where the pleasures of the hall?
I mourn the gleaming cup, the warrior in his corselet,
the glory of the prince. How that time has passed away,
darkened under the shadow of night as if it had never been.
Where the loved warriors were, there now stands a wall
of wondrous height, carved with serpent forms.
The savage ash-spears, avid for slaughter,
have claimed all the warriors—a glorious fate!
Storms crash against these rocky slopes,
sleet and snow fall and fetter the world,
winter howls, then darkness draws on,
the night-shadow casts gloom and brings
fierce hailstorms from the north to frighten men.
Nothing is ever easy in the kingdom of earth,
the world beneath the heavens is in the hands of fate.
Here possessions are fleeting, here friends are fleeting,
here man is fleeting, here kinsman is fleeting,
the whole world becomes a wilderness."
So spoke the wise man in his heart as he sat apart in thought.
Brave is the man who holds to his beliefs; nor shall he ever
show the sorrow in his heart before he knows how he
can hope to heal it. It is best for a man to seek
mercy and comfort from the Father in heaven, the safe home that awaits us all.

Wulf and Eadwacer *and* The Wife's Lament

Old English literature focuses largely on masculine and military concerns and lacks a concept of romantic love—what the twelfth-century French would later call "*fine amour*." Against this backdrop *Wulf and Eadwacer* and *The Wife's Lament* stand out, first, by their use of woman's voice and second, by their treatment of the sorrows of love.

Though the exact genre of these poems is problematic, some scholars classifying them as riddles and others as religious allegories, most group them with a class of Old English poems known as elegies, with which they are preserved in the same manuscript, the Exeter Book. The elegies lament the loss of earthly goods, comradeship, and the "hall joys," often, as in *The Wanderer* and *The Seafarer*, by a speaker in exile. *The Wife's Lament* and *Wulf and Eadwacer* differ from the other elegies in that the speakers, as women, had no experience of comradeship to lose, as their main function was to be exchanged in marriage to cement relationships between feuding tribes. They are in a sense twice exiled, first from the noble brotherhood by their gender, and second from their beloved by their personal history. Furthermore, unlike the speakers in *The Wanderer* and *The Seafarer*, they do not look forward to the consolation of a heavenly kingdom imagined as a warlord with his group of retainers.

Although the two elegies in woman's voice are unique in the Old English corpus, they have analogues within the larger tradition of continental woman's song, which flourished in medieval Latin and the vernaculars from the eleventh century on. Their composition was so early—990 at the latest—that this tradition could not have influenced them, although the Roman poet Ovid's *Heroides* (verse letters of abandoned heroines to their faithless lovers) could have done so. One critic has raised the question of female authorship, on the grounds that continental nuns in the eighth century were criticized for writing romantic songs. As the critic Marilynn Desmond has suggested, perhaps Virginia Woolf's speculation that "anonymous was a woman" is true of these poems.

Though scholars agree that *Wulf and Eadwacer* is "heartrending" and "haunting," they cannot agree on the dramatic situation—each translation is an act of interpretation. The present translator, Kevin Crossley-Holland, sees the poem as involving the female speaker; her husband (Eadwacer); her lover (Wulf), from whom she is separated; and her child (a "cub"). Although what transpired before is unclear, she wistfully concludes, "men easily savage what was never secure, our song together." The dramatic setting of *The Wife's Lament* is similarly ambiguous; it is not clear whether the woman's anger is directed toward her husband or to a third person who plotted to separate them.

Wulf and Eadwacer[1]

Prey, it's as if my people have been handed prey.
They'll tear him to pieces if he comes with a troop.

O, we are apart.

Wulf is on one island, I on another,
a fastness that island, a fen-prison.
Fierce men roam there, on that island;
they'll tear him to pieces if he comes with a troop.

O, we are apart.

1. Translated by Kevin Crossley-Holland.

How I have grieved for my Wulf's wide wanderings.
When rain slapped the earth and I sat apart weeping,
when the bold warrior wrapped his arms about me,
I seethed with desire and yet with such hatred.
Wulf, my Wulf, my yearning for you
and your seldom coming have caused my sickness,
my mourning heart, not mere starvation.
Can you hear, Eadwacer? Wulf will spirit
our pitiful whelp to the woods.
Men easily savage what was never secure,
our song together.

The Wife's Lament[1]

I draw these words from my deep sadness,
my sorrowful lot. I can say that,
since I grew up, I have not suffered
such hardships as now, old or new.

I am tortured by the anguish of exile.
First my lord forsook his family
for the tossing waves; I fretted at dawn
as to where in the world my lord might be.
In my sorrow I set out then,
a friendless wanderer, to search for my man.
But that man's kinsmen laid secret plans
to part us, so that we should live
most wretchedly, far from each other
in this wide world; I was seized with longings.

My lord asked me to live with him here;
I had few loved ones, loyal friends
in this country; that is reason for grief.
Then I found my own husband was ill-starred,
sad at heart, pretending, plotting
murder behind a smiling face. How often
we swore that nothing but death should ever
divide us; that is all changed now;
our friendship is as if it had never been.
Early and late, I must undergo hardship
because of the feud of my own dearest loved one.
Men forced me to live in a forest grove,
under an oak tree in the earth-cave.
This cavern is age-old; I am choked with longings.
Gloomy are the valleys, too high the hills,
harsh strongholds overgrown with briars:
a joyless abode. The journey of my lord so often
cruelly seizes me. There are lovers on earth,

1. Translated by Kevin Crossley-Holland.

lovers alive who lie in bed,
when I pass through this earth-cave alone
and out under the oak tree at dawn;
there I must sit through the long summer's day
and there I mourn my miseries,
my many hardships; for I am never able
to quiet the cares of my sorrowful mind,
all the longings that are my life's lot.

Young men must always be serious in mind
and stout-hearted; they must hide
their heartaches, that host of constant sorrows,
behind a smiling face.
Whether he is master
of his own fate or is exiled in a far-off land—
sitting under rocky storm-cliffs, chilled
with hoar-frost, weary in mind,
surrounded by the sea in some sad place—
my husband is caught in the clutches of anguish;
over and again he recalls a happier home.
Grief goes side by side with those
who suffer longing for a loved one.

Riddles

Riddles were a popular genre in Anglo-Saxon England, appealing to a taste for intellectual puzzles, which we also see in *Beowulf*, with its kennings; *The Dream of the Rood*, with its speaking cross; and *Wulf and Eadwacer*, with its cryptic dramatic situation. In the Exeter Book, one of the four major manuscripts containing Anglo-Saxon poetry (including *The Wanderer*, *The Wife's Lament*, and *Wulf and Eadwacer*) there are nearly a hundred riddles in Old English, dating from the seventh to the tenth centuries. They were in some cases modeled on collections of a hundred Latin riddles by the seventh-century Anglo-Saxon scholar Aldhelm, but they also derive in large part from indigenous folk tradition. In fact, they mark an important point of intersection between literate and oral culture in Anglo-Saxon England: though designed to be recited, they are written and sometimes focus on the technology of writing.

The three Anglo-Latin riddles of Aldhelm included here reveal an attitude of awe toward writing, conceived as an almost magical act, partly because of its novelty in a recently oral culture, but more because of its ownership by a priestly class in control of Christianity, the religion of "the Book." Aldhelm gives a sense of the tremendous effort that went into book-making—scratching treated animal skins with a quill pen or cutting into tablets made of wax, wood, and leather—and the resultant splendid object, adorned with "artful windings," cut into a "fair design." In the *Alphabet*, he makes the personified letters express their pride in the paradox of writing as voiceless speech: "We / in silence quickly bring out hoarded words." The pen in the riddle of that name speaks of its origin as a bird's feather and of its ability, despite its present earthbound state, to help lead the virtuous to heaven.

Of the Old English riddles included here, four also have to do with writing, an activity important in the daily life of priests. Old English Riddle 2 traces the making of a book by speaking as a sheep slain for its skin to make parchment, describing the "bird's feather" leaving tracks on its surface, and concluding in the person of the Bible itself, decorated with "the wondrous work of smiths," sacred and useful at the same time. Old English Riddle 5 similarly traces a tool from its origin in nature to its status as a manufactured thing. The narrator speaks of its life growing by the water (as a plant), the paradox that, though "mouthless," it should "sing / to men sitting at the mead-bench" (as a flute), and the "miracle" by which it can send a private message (as a pen).

In contrast to those Old English riddles concerned with writing, the majority deal with aspects of Anglo-Saxon secular life, with answers such as a shield, a storm, an iceberg, or a ship. The poem of this sort included here, Old English Riddle 1, explores areas of experience usually ignored by Old English epic, elegiac, and religious poetry. Beginning traditionally, "I'm a strange creature," it treats domestic activity—the storage and preparation of food—by a lower-class woman, a churl's daughter. One of several sexual riddles in the Exeter Book, it is a finely sustained *double entendre,* showing that there was indeed humor in Old English poetry.

(Following the manuscripts, Aldhelm's riddles are printed with the titles that state their solutions, while those from the Exeter Book—which offers no solutions—are followed by solutions given by modern editors).

Three Anglo-Latin Riddles by Aldhelm[1]

Alphabet

We seventeen sisters, voiceless all, declare
Six others bastards are, and not of us.
Of iron we are born, and find our death
Again by iron; or at times we come
From pinion of a lofty-flying bird.
Three brothers got us of an unknown mother.
To him who thirsts for instant counsel, we
In silence quickly bring out hoarded words.

Writing Tablets

Of honey-laden bees I first was born,
But in the forest grew my outer coat;
My tough backs came from shoes. An iron point
In artful windings cuts a fair design,
And leaves long, twisted furrows, like a plow.
From heaven unto that field is borne the seed
Or nourishment, which brings forth generous sheaves
A thousandfold. Alas, that such a crop,
A holy harvest, falls before grim war.

Pen

The shining pelican, whose yawning throat
Gulps down the waters of the sea, long since
Produced me, white as he. Through snowy fields
I keep a straight road, leaving deep-blue tracks

1. Translated by James Hall Pitman.

Upon the gleaming way, and darkening
The fair champaign with black and tortuous paths;
Yet one way through the plain suffices not,
For with a thousand bypaths runs the road,
And them who stray not from it, leads to heaven.

Five Old English Riddles[1]

1

I'm a strange creature, for I satisfy women,
a service to the neighbors! No one suffers
at my hands except for my slayer.
I grow very tall, erect in a bed,
I'm hairy underneath. From time to time
a good-looking girl, the doughty daughter
of some churl dares to hold me,
grips my russet skin, robs me of my head
and puts me in the pantry. At once that girl
with plaited hair who has confined me
remembers our meeting. Her eye moistens.

2

An enemy ended my life, took away
of my bodily strength; then he dipped me
in water and drew me out again,
and put me in the sun where I soon shed
all my hair. The knife's sharp edge
bit into me once my blemishes had been scraped away;
fingers folded me and the bird's feather
often moved across my brown surface,
sprinkling useful drops; it swallowed the wood-dye
(part of the stream) and again traveled over me
leaving black tracks. Then a man bound me,
he stretched skin over me and adorned me
with gold; thus I am enriched by the wondrous work
of smiths, wound about with shining metal.
Now my clasp and my red dye
and these glorious adornments bring fame far and wide
to the Protector of Men, and not to the pains of hell.
If the sons of men would make use of me
they would be the safer and more sure of victory,
their hearts would be bolder, their minds more at ease,
their thoughts wiser, they would have more friends,
companions and kinsmen (true and honorable,
brave and kind) who would gladly increase
their honor and prosperity, and heap

1. Translated by Kevin Crossley-Holland.

benefits upon them, holding them fast
in love's embraces. Ask what I am called,
of such use to men. My name is famous,
of service to men and sacred in itself.

3

A moth devoured words. When I heard
of that wonder it struck me as a strange event
that a worm should swallow the song of some man,
a thief gorge in the darkness on fine phrases
and their firm foundation. The thievish stranger
was not a whit the wiser for swallowing words.

4

I watched four curious creatures
traveling together; their tracks were swart,
each imprint very black. The birds' support
moved swiftly; it flew in the air,
dived under the wave. The toiling warrior
worked without pause, pointing the paths
to all four over the beaten gold.

5

I sank roots first of all, stood
near the shore, close by the dyke
and dash of waves; few men
saw my home in that wilderness,
but each dawn, each dusk,
the tawny waves surged and swirled
around me. Little did I think
that I, mouthless, should ever sing
to men sitting at the mead-bench,
varying my pitch. It is rather puzzling,
a miracle to men ignorant of such arts,
how a knife's point and a right hand
(mind and implement moving as one)
could cut and carve me—so that I
can send you a message without fear,
and no one else can overhear
or noise abroad the words we share.

Solutions: 1. Penis or onion; 2. Bible; 3. Book worm; 4. Pen and fingers; 5. Reed.

AFTER THE NORMAN CONQUEST

PERSPECTIVES
Arthurian Myth in the History of Britain

Almost since it first appeared, the story of King Arthur has occupied a contested zone between myth and history. Far from diminishing the Arthurian tradition, though, this ambiguity has lent it a tremendous and protean impact on the political and cultural imagination of Europe, from the Middle Ages to the present. Probably no other body of medieval legend remains today as widely known and as often revisited as the Arthurian story.

One measure of Arthur's undiminished importance is the eager debate, eight centuries old and going strong, about his historical status. Whether or not a specific "Arthur" ever existed, legends and attributes gathered around his name from a very early date, mostly in texts of Welsh background. Around 600 a Welsh poem refers briefly to Arthur's armed might, and by about 1000, the story *Culhwch and Olwen*, from the Mabinogion, assumes knowledge of Arthur as a royal warlord. Other early Welsh texts begin to give him more-than-mortal attributes, associating Arthur with such marvels as an underworld quest and a mysterious tomb. In the ninth century, the Latin *History of the Britons* by the Welshman Nennius confidently speaks of Arthur as a great leader and lists his twelve victories ending with that at Mount Badon.

Some of this at least fits with better-documented history and with less-shadowy commanders who might have been models for an Arthurian figure, even if they were not "Arthur." When the Romans withdrew in 410, the romanized Britons soon faced territorial aggression from the Saxons and Picts. In the decades after midcentury, the Britons mounted a successful defense, led in part by Aurelius Ambrosius and culminating, it appears, with the battle of Badon in roughly 500, after which Saxon incursions paused for a time. In those same years of territorial threat, some Britons had emigrated to what is now Brittany, and in the 460s or 470s a warlord named Riothamus led an army, probably from Britain, and fought successfully in Gaul in alliance with local rulers sympathetic to Rome. His name was latinized from a British title meaning "supreme king." Both Riothamus and Aurelius Ambrosius correspond to parts of the later narratives of Arthur: his role as high king, his triumphs against the Saxons, his links to Rome (both friendly and hostile), and his campaigns on the continent.

Whether the origins of Arthur's story lie in fact or in an urge among the Welsh to imagine a great leader who once restored their power against the ever-expanding Anglo-Saxons, he was clearly an established figure in Welsh oral and written literature by the ninth century. Arthur, however, also held a broader appeal for other peoples of England. The British Isles were felt to lie at the outer edge of world geography, but the story of Arthur and his ancestor Brutus served to create a Britain with other kinds of centrality. The legend of Brutus made Britain the end point of an inexorable westward movement of Trojan imperial power, the *translatio imperii*, and Arthur's forebears became linked to Roman imperial dynasties. Finally, the general movement of Arthur's continental campaigns neatly reversed the patterns of Roman and then Norman colonization.

In the later Middle Ages and after, Arthur and his court are most often encountered in works that lay little claim to historical accuracy. Rather, they exploit the very uncertainty of Arthurian narrative to explore the highest (if sometimes self-deceiving) yearnings of private emotion and social order. These Arthurian romances also probe, often in tragic terms, the limits and taboos that both define and subvert such ideals, including the mutual threats posed by private emotion and social order.

Nevertheless, the Arthurian tradition has also been pulled persistently into the realm of the real. It was presented as serious historical writing from the twelfth century through the end of the Middle Ages. Political agents have used Arthur's kingship as a model or precedent for their own aspirations, as seen in the Kennedy administration's portrayal as a version of Camelot. Even elements of the Christian church wrote their doctrines into Arthurian narrative or claimed Arthur as a patron.

The texts in this section present three illuminating moments of Arthur's emergence into history and politics. Geoffrey of Monmouth's *History of the Kings of Britain*, finished around 1138, was the fullest version yet of Arthur's origin and career. Geoffrey was the first to make Arthur such a central figure in British history, and it was largely through Geoffrey's Latin "history" that Arthur became so widespread a feature of cultural imagination in the Middle Ages and beyond. Writing at the close of the twelfth century, Gerald of Wales narrates an occasion, possibly orchestrated by Henry II, in which Arthurian tradition was slightly altered and folded into emergent Norman versions of British antiquity. The section ends with two politically charged versions of national origin, English and Scottish, proposed in 1301 as part of Edward I's efforts to influence royal succession in Scotland.

Geoffrey of Monmouth

c. 1100–1155

From the perspective of surviving British peoples in Wales and Cornwall, the Norman Conquest of 1066 was only the last among successive waves of invasion by Romans, Picts, Anglo-Saxons, and Vikings. The Celtic Britons had long been pushed into the far southwest by the time the Normans arrived, where they continued to resist colonization. The Welsh maintained a vital language, culture, and ethnic mythology, including a memory of their fellow Celts in Brittany and a divided nostalgia for the long-departed Romans. Thus a whole Celtic linguistic and political world offered an alternative to the languages and legends of the Normans, much of which derived ultimately from Mediterranean antiquity. Arthur, king of the Britons, emerged as a key figure as these peoples and cultures began to articulate the complex new forms of political and private identity precipitated by the Conquest.

No one was more important in this process than Geoffrey of Monmouth. He was prior of the Abbey of Monmouth in Wales and later was named bishop of Saint Asaph, though civil disorder prevented his taking the post. Yet he was also active in the emerging schools of Oxford, he was patronized by Norman nobles and bishops, and he wrote in Latin. Geoffrey's learning reflects this double allegiance. Well schooled in the Latin curriculum that embraced ancient Roman and Christian literature, he was also deeply versed in the oral and written culture of Wales. As a creative negotiater between Welsh and Anglo-Norman legends and languages, his influence was without parallel.

Both of Geoffrey's surviving prose works, the *Prophecies of Merlin* (finished around 1135) and the *History of the Kings of Britain* (about 1138) present themselves as translations of ancient texts from Wales or Brittany. Geoffrey also wrote a *Life of Merlin* in Latin verse. He probably synthesized a number of sources and added material of his own in his "translations." It was a pointed gesture, nevertheless, to posit a Celtic text whose authority rivaled the Latin culture and legends that had underwritten later Anglo-Saxon and then Norman power in England. Geoffrey daringly inverted the general hierarchy of Latin and vernaculars in his time; instead, he offered "British" as the ancient tongue that he wanted to make more broadly accessible for Latin-reading newcomers.

Geoffrey's central heroes are Brutus, the exiled Trojan descendant who colonized and named Britain, and Arthur, who reunified England after Saxon and Pictish attacks, and repulsed Roman efforts to re-establish power there. Geoffrey's own purposes in the *History* were complex but he was responding in part to contemporary events. The 1130s were a decade of civil strife in England, as nobles shifted their allegiances between King Stephen and the other claimant to the throne, the future Henry II. Welsh nobles took advantage of this disorder to rebel and set up their own principalities. Scholars remain divided as to whether Geoffrey was more interested in a return to strong and unified rule in Norman England, or wanted rather to encourage the Welsh princes with the story of a great predecessor who might one day return.

Geoffrey's narrative carefully presents itself as history, in a century of great historical writing. He uses the typical armature of documentary and other written records, archaeological evidence, and claims to well-founded witness. Casting the story of Arthur into this respected form allows Geoffrey to employ but also to counter the dominant master-narrative of Christian history in England, which was Bede's. Rather than a story of Anglo-Saxon arrival and conversion, Geoffrey offers a story of an earlier foundation and a prior conversion; he thus creates imaginative space for a convergence between Norman power and the culture and ambitions of people and languages at its edges. Moreover, the *History* generates an exterior (if now conveniently absent) common enemy in the imperial Romans. Geoffrey pulls in yet more ancient models by frequently echoing Virgil's *Aeneid* and its story of exile and refoundation, and by placing his story within biblical, Trojan, and Roman chronologies. And he points forward to his own time by inserting the earlier *Prophecies of Merlin* in the midst of the *History*.

The continued influence of Geoffrey's *History* on later literature is testimony to the powerful themes he folded into his story. Much that is developed in later romance explorations of the Arthurian world is already here: the tragedy of a people bravely battling its own decline; the danger and overwhelming attraction of illicit sexual desire; the ambivalent position of Mordred as cousin or nephew; the Arthurian realm brought down, ultimately, by the treachery of the king's own kin and by a transgression of the marriage bed that echoes Arthur's own conception.

The following selections from Geoffrey's *History* feature the Trojan background of Britain and the birth and early kingship of Arthur. Other texts in this section and following trace later episodes in his evolving legend: the development of Arthur's court, the celebration and tragedy of romantic desire, and the death of the king.

from History of the Kings of Britain[1]

Dedication

Whenever I have chanced to think about the history of the kings of Britain, on those occasions when I have been turning over a great many such matters in my mind, it has seemed a remarkable thing to me that, apart from such mention of them as Gildas and Bede had each made in a brilliant book on the subject, I have not been able to discover anything at all on the kings who lived here before the Incarnation of Christ, or indeed about Arthur and all the others who followed on after the Incarnation. Yet the deeds of these men were such that they deserve to be praised for all time. What is more, these deeds were handed joyfully down in oral tradition, just as if they had been committed to writing, by many peoples who had only their memory to rely on.

At a time when I was giving a good deal of attention to such matters, Walter, Archdeacon of Oxford, a man skilled in the art of public speaking and well-informed about the history of foreign countries, presented me with a certain very ancient book written in the British language.[2] This book, attractively composed to

1. Translated by Lewis Thorpe (1966).
2. Walter and Geoffrey were both associated with an early Oxford college, and their names appear together on several legal documents. In two of these, Geoffrey calls himself a *magister*, a teacher at an advanced level.

form a consecutive and orderly narrative, set out all the deeds of these men, from Brutus, the first King of the Britons, down to Cadwallader, the son of Cadwallo.[3] At Walter's request I have taken the trouble to translate the book into Latin, although, indeed, I have been content with my own expressions and my own homely style and I have gathered no gaudy flowers of speech in other men's gardens. If I had adorned my page with high-flown rhetorical figures, I should have bored my readers, for they would have been forced to spend more time in discovering the meaning of my words than in following the story.

I ask you, Robert, Earl of Gloucester,[4] to do my little book this favor. Let it be so emended by your knowledge and your advice that it must no longer be considered as the product of Geoffrey of Monmouth's small talent. Rather, with the support of your wit and wisdom, let it be accepted as the work of one descended from Henry, the famous King of the English; of one whom learning has nurtured in the liberal arts and whom his innate talent in military affairs has put in charge of our soldiers, with the result that now, in our own lifetime, our island of Britain hails you with heartfelt affection, as if it had been granted a second Henry.

You too, Waleran, Count of Mellent, second pillar of our kingdom, give me your support, so that, with the guidance provided by the two of you, my work may appear all the more attractive when it is offered to its public.[5] For indeed, sprung as you are from the race of the most renowned King Charles, Mother Philosophy has taken you to her bosom, and to you she has taught the subtlety of her sciences. What is more, so that you might become famous in the military affairs of our army, she has led you to the camp of kings, and there, having surpassed your fellow-warriors in bravery, you have learned, under your father's guidance, to be a terror to your enemies and a protection to your own folk. Faithful defender as you are of those dependent on you, accept under your patronage this book which is published for your pleasure. Accept me, too, as your writer, so that, reclining in the shade of a tree which spreads so wide, and sheltered from envious and malicious enemies, I may be able in peaceful harmony to make music on the reed-pipe of a muse who really belongs to you.

[Troy, Aeneas, Brutus' Exile][6]

After the Trojan war, Aeneas fled from the ruined city with his son Ascanius and came by boat to Italy. He was honorably received there by King Latinus, but Turnus, King of the Rutuli, became jealous of him and attacked him. In the battle between them Aeneas was victorious. Turnus was killed and Aeneas seized both the kingdom of Italy and the person of Lavinia, who was the daughter of Latinus.[7]

When Aeneas' last day came, Ascanius was elected King. He founded the town of Alba on the bank of the Tiber and became the father of a son called Silvius. This Silvius was involved in a secret love-affair with a certain niece of Lavinia's; he married her and made her pregnant. When this came to the knowledge of his father

3. Bede's *Ecclesiastical History of the English People* was the source most used by 12th-century historians, but it has little to say about England before the coming of the Angles and Saxons. Geoffrey offers a (perhaps fictive) source for a more ancient history of the people who preceded the Saxons.

4. An illegitimate son of King Henry I. He had a hand in the education of the future Henry II, his nephew.

5. Waleran de Beaumont, Count of Meulan (1104–1166) moved in the same circles as the Earl of Gloucester, and was patron of the Norman Abbey of Bec, a great center of learning. Geoffrey's fulsome tone is typical of dedications to great magnates in the period.

6. From bk. 1, ch. 3.

7. This summarizes the political narrative of Virgil's *Aeneid*, a text Geoffrey knew well and echoed frequently throughout his *History*.

Ascanius, the latter ordered his soothsayers to discover the sex of the child which the girl had conceived. As soon as they had made sure of the truth of the matter, the soothsayers said that she would give birth to a boy, who would cause the death of both his father and his mother; and that after he had wandered in exile through many lands this boy would eventually rise to the highest honor.

The soothsayers were not wrong in their forecast. When the day came for her to have her child, the mother bore a son and died in childbirth. The boy was handed over to the midwife and was given the name Brutus. At last, when fifteen years had passed, the young man killed his father by an unlucky shot with an arrow, when they were out hunting together. Their beaters drove some stags into their path and Brutus, who was under the impression that he was aiming his weapon at these stags, hit his own father below the breast. As the result of this death Brutus was expelled from Italy by his relations, who were angry with him for having committed such a crime. He went in exile to certain parts of Greece; and there he discovered the descendants of Helenus, Priam's son, who were held captive in the power of Pandrasus, King of the Greeks. After the fall of Troy, Pyrrhus, the son of Achilles, had dragged this man Helenus off with him in chains, and a number of other Trojans, too. He had ordered them to be kept in slavery, so that he might take vengeance on them for the death of his father.

When Brutus realized that these people were of the same race as his ancestors, he stayed some time with them. However, he soon gained such fame for his military skill and prowess that he was esteemed by the kings and princes more than any young man in the country.

[THE NAMING OF BRITAIN][8]

[Brutus conquers the Greek king (reversing the Greek conquest of his ancestral Troy), marries the king's daughter Ignoge, and leads the Trojan descendants off to seek a new land. They pass through continental Europe, where they do battle with the Gauls.]

In their pursuit the Trojans continued to slaughter the Gauls, and they did not abandon the bloodshed until they had gained victory.

Although this signal triumph brought him great joy, Brutus was nevertheless filled with anxiety, for the number of his men became smaller every day, while that of the Gauls was constantly increasing. Brutus was in doubt as to whether he could oppose the Gauls any longer; and he finally chose to return to his ships in the full glory of his victory while the greater part of his comrades were still safe, and then to seek out the island which divine prophecy had promised would be his. Nothing else was done. With the approval of his men Brutus returned to his fleet. He loaded his ships with all the riches which he had acquired and then went on board. So, with the winds behind him, he sought the promised island, and came ashore at Totnes.

At this time the island of Britain was called Albion. It was uninhabited except for a few giants. It was, however, most attractive, because of the delightful situation of its various regions, its forests and the great number of its rivers, which teemed with fish; and it filled Brutus and his comrades with a great desire to live there. When they had explored the different districts, they drove the giants whom they had discovered

8. From bk. 1, chs. 15–18 and bk. 2, ch. 1.

into the caves in the mountains. With the approval of their leader they divided the land among themselves. They began to cultivate the fields and to build houses, so that in a short time you would have thought that the land had always been inhabited.

Brutus then called the island Britain from his own name, and his companions he called Britons. His intention was that his memory should be perpetuated by the derivation of the name. A little later the language of the people, which had up to then been known as Trojan or Crooked Greek, was called British, for the same reason.[9]

[BRUTUS BUILDS NEW TROY]

Once he had divided up his kingdom, Brutus decided to build a capital. In pursuit of this plan, he visited every part of the land in search of a suitable spot. He came at length to the River Thames, walked up and down its banks and so chose a site suited to his purpose. There then he built his city and called it Troia Nova. It was known by this name for long ages after, but finally by a corruption of the word it came to be called Trinovantum. * * *

When the above-named leader Brutus had built the city about which I have told you, he presented it to the citizens by right of inheritance, and gave them a code of laws by which they might live peacefully together. At that time the priest Eli was ruling in Judea and the Ark of the Covenant was captured by the Philistines. The sons of Hector reigned in Troy, for the descendants of Antenor had been driven out. In Italy reigned Aeneas Silvius, son of Aeneas and uncle of Brutus, the third of the Latin Kings.[1] * * *

In the meantime Brutus had consummated his marriage with his wife Ignoge. By her he had three sons called Locrinus, Kamber and Albanactus, all of whom were to become famous. When their father finally died, in the twenty-third year after his landing, these three sons buried him inside the walls of the town which he had founded. They divided the kingdom of Britain between them in such a way that each succeeded to Brutus in one particular district. Locrinus, who was the first-born, inherited the part of the island which was afterwards called Loegria after him. Kamber received the region which is on the further bank of the River Severn, the part which is now known as Wales but which was for a long time after his death called Kambria from his name. As a result the people of that country still call themselves Kambri today in the Welsh tongue. Albanactus, the youngest, took the region which is nowadays called Scotland in our language. He called it Albany, after his own name.

[MERLIN AND THE FIRST CONQUEST OF IRELAND][2]

[*The descendants of Brutus' three sons include Leir (Shakespeare's King Lear), the brothers Brennius and Belinus who conquer Rome, and Lud who rebuilds New Troy and names it Kaerlud after himself (whence "London"). In the reign of Lud's brother, Julius Caesar invades England; generations of Britons resist, until King Coel makes peace with the Roman legate Constantius. The latter succeeds Coel, marries Coel's daughter, and sires Constantine who becomes emperor of Rome. The Romans tire of defending Britain against invaders and withdraw from the island. Vortigern usurps the throne from the Briton line,*

9. With this detail, Geoffrey creates a linguistic history in which early Welsh is as ancient as classical Latin, and more purely "Trojan."

1. Medieval historians often made such parallels between biblical and secular chronologies.

2. From bk. 8, chs. 10–13.

then holds it in alliance with the Saxons Hengist and Horsa. The Saxons become aggressors, and Vortigern flees them but is overcome by the brothers Aurelius Ambrosius and Utherpendragon, who restore the Briton royal line and drive the Saxons into the north. Aurelius reigns, restoring churches and the rule of law; he wants to commemorate the Britons who died fighting off the Saxons.]

Aurelius collected carpenters and stone-masons together from every region and ordered them to use their skill to contrive some novel building which would stand forever in memory of such distinguished men. The whole band racked their brains and then confessed themselves beaten. Then Tremorinus, Archbishop of the City of the Legions,[3] went to the King and said: "If there is anyone anywhere who has the ability to execute your plan, then Merlin, the prophet of Vortigern, is the man to do it.[4] In my opinion, there is no one else in your kingdom who has greater skill, either in the foretelling of the future or in mechanical contrivances. Order Merlin to come and use his ability, so that the monument for which you are asking can be put up."

Aurelius asked many questions about Merlin; then he sent a number of messengers through the various regions of the country to find him and fetch him. They traveled through the provinces and finally located Merlin in the territory of the Gewissei, at the Galabes Springs, where he often went. They explained to him what they wanted of him and then conducted him to the King. The King received Merlin gaily and ordered him to prophesy the future, for he wanted to hear some marvels from him. "Mysteries of that sort cannot be revealed," answered Merlin, "except where there is the most urgent need for them. If I were to utter them as an entertainment, or where there was no need at all, then the spirit which controls me would forsake me in the moment of need."

He gave the same refusal to everyone present. The King had no wish to press him about the future, but he spoke to him about the monument which he was planning. "If you want to grace the burial-place of these men with some lasting monument," replied Merlin, "send for the Giants' Ring which is on Mount Killaraus in Ireland. In that place there is a stone construction which no man of this period could ever erect, unless he combined great skill and artistry. The stones are enormous and there is no one alive strong enough to move them. If they are placed in position round this site, in the way in which they are erected over there, they will stand forever."

At these words of Merlin's Aurelius burst out laughing. "How can such large stones be moved from so far-distant a country?" he asked. "It is hardly as if Britain itself is lacking in stones big enough for the job!" "Try not to laugh in a foolish way, your Majesty," answered Merlin. "What I am suggesting has nothing ludicrous about it. These stones are connected with certain secret religious rites and they have various properties which are medicinally important. Many years ago the Giants transported them from the remotest confines of Africa and set them up in Ireland at a time when they inhabited that country. Their plan was that, whenever they felt ill, baths should be prepared at the foot of the stones; for they used to pour water over

3. Also called Caerusk or Caerleon; Geoffrey mentions it often and may have had some connection with it.

4. Merlin, son of a Briton princess and a demonic spirit, has already appeared; he triumphed over Vortigern's magicians and uttered a series of prophecies. Merlin's roles as a royal advisor, a prophet, and even a shape-shifter can be compared to those of poets in early Celtic cultures.

them and to run this water into baths in which their sick were cured. What is more, they mixed the water with herbal concoctions and so healed their wounds. There is not a single stone among them which hasn't some medicinal virtue."

When the Britons heard all this, they made up their minds to send for the stones and to make war on the people of Ireland if they tried to hold them back. In the end the King's brother, Utherpendragon, and fifteen thousand men, were chosen to carry out the task. Merlin, too, was co-opted, so that all the problems which had to be met could have the benefit of his knowledge and advice. They made ready their ships and they put to sea. The winds were favorable and they arrived in Ireland.

At that time there reigned in Ireland a young man of remarkable valor called Gillomanius. As soon as he heard that the Britons had landed in the country, he collected a huge army together and hurried to meet them. When he learned the reason of their coming, Gillomanius laughed out loud at those standing round him. "I am not surprised that a race of cowards has been able to devastate the island of the Britons," said he, "for the Britons are dolts and fools. Who ever heard of such folly? Surely the stones of Ireland aren't so much better than those of Britain that our realm has to be invaded for their sake! Arm yourselves, men, and defend your fatherland, for as long as life remains in my body they shall not steal from us the minutest fragment of the Ring."

When he saw that the Irish were spoiling for a fight, Uther hurriedly drew up his own line of battle and charged at them. The Britons were successful almost immediately. The Irish were either mangled or killed outright, and Gillomanius was forced to flee. Having won the day, the Britons made their way to Mount Killaraus. When they came to the stone structure, they were filled with joy and wonder. Merlin came up to them as they stood round in a group. "Try your strength, young men," said he, "and see whether skill can do more than brute strength, or strength more than skill, when it comes to dismantling these stones!"

At his bidding they all set to with every conceivable kind of mechanism and strove their hardest to take the Ring down. They rigged up hawsers and ropes and they propped up scaling-ladders, each preparing what he thought most useful, but none of these things advanced them an inch. When he saw what a mess they were making of it, Merlin burst out laughing. He placed in position all the gear which he considered necessary and dismantled the stones more easily than you could ever believe. Once he had pulled them down, he had them carried to the ships and stored on board, and they all set sail once more for Britain with joy in their hearts.

The winds were fair. They came to the shore and then set off with the stones for the spot where the heroes had been buried. The moment that this was reported to him, Aurelius dispatched messengers to all the different regions of Britain, ordering the clergy and the people to assemble and, as they gathered, to converge on Mount Ambrius, where they were with due ceremony and rejoicing to re-dedicate the burial-place which I have described. At the summons from Aurelius the bishops and abbots duly assembled with men from every rank and file under the King's command. All came together on the appointed day. Aurelius placed the crown on his head and celebrated the feast of Whitsun in right royal fashion, devoting the next three days to one long festival. * * *

Once he had settled these matters, and others of a similar nature, Aurelius ordered Merlin to erect round the burial-place the stones which he had brought from Ireland. Merlin obeyed the King's orders and put the stones up in a circle round the sepulchre, in exactly the same way as they had been arranged on Mount Killaraus in Ireland, thus proving that his artistry was worth more than any brute strength.

[UTHERPENDRAGON SIRES ARTHUR][5]

[*Vortigern's son attacks Aurelius Ambrosius and Utherpendragon. They drive him off, though Aurelius is poisoned through Saxon treachery. A miraculous star appears, which Merlin interprets as a sign of Uther's destined kingship, the coming of Arthur, and the rule of Uther's dynasty. At the same time, however, Merlin prophesies the decline of the Britons. As king, Uther fights off more Saxon incursions.*]

The next Eastertide Uther told the nobles of his kingdom to assemble in that same town of London, so that he could wear his crown and celebrate so important a feast-day with proper ceremony. They all obeyed, traveling in from their various cities and assembling on the eve of the feast. The King was thus able to celebrate the feast as he had intended and to enjoy himself in the company of his leaders. They, too, were all happy, seeing that he had received them with such affability. A great many nobles had gathered there, men worthy of taking part in such a gay festivity, together with their wives and daughters.

Among the others there was present Gorlois, Duke of Cornwall, with his wife Ygerna, who was the most beautiful woman in Britain. When the King saw her there among the other women, he was immediately filled with desire for her, with the result that he took no notice of anything else, but devoted all his attention to her. To her and to no one else he kept ordering plates of food to be passed and to her, too, he kept sending his own personal attendants with golden goblets of wine. He kept smiling at her and engaging her in sprightly conversation. When Ygerna's husband saw what was happening, he was so annoyed that he withdrew from the court without taking leave. No one present could persuade him to return, for he was afraid of losing the one object that he loved better than anything else. Uther lost his temper and ordered Gorlois to come back to court, so that he, the King, could seek satisfaction for the way in which he had been insulted. Gorlois refused to obey. The King was furious and swore an oath that he would ravage Gorlois' lands, unless the latter gave him immediate satisfaction.

Without more ado, while the bad blood remained between the two of them, the King collected a huge army together and hurried off to the Duchy of Cornwall, where he set fire to towns and castles. Gorlois' army was the smaller of the two and he did not dare to meet the King in battle. He preferred instead to garrison his castles and to bide his time until he could receive help from Ireland. As he was more worried about his wife than he was about himself, he left her in the castle of Tintagel,[6] on the seacoast, which he thought was the safest place under his control. He himself took refuge in a fortified camp called Dimilioc,[7] so that, if disaster overtook them, they should not both be endangered together. When the King heard of this, he went to the encampment where Gorlois was, besieged it and cut off every line of approach.

Finally, after a week had gone by, the King's passion for Ygerna became more than he could bear. He called to him Ulfin of Ridcaradoch, one of his soldiers and a

5. From bk. 8, chs. 19–24.
6. Tin-*ta*-jel, on the rocky northwestern coast of Cornwall.
7. Di-*mi*-li-oc, perhaps a site roughly five miles from Tintagel.

familiar friend, and told him what was on his mind. "I am desperately in love with Ygerna," said Uther, "and if I cannot have her I am convinced that I shall suffer a physical breakdown. You must tell me how I can satisfy my desire for her, for otherwise I shall die of the passion which is consuming me." "Who can possibly give you useful advice," answered Ulfin, "when no power on earth can enable us to come to her where she is inside the fortress of Tintagel? The castle is built high above the sea, which surrounds it on all sides, and there is no other way in except that offered by a narrow isthmus of rock. Three armed soldiers could hold it against you, even if you stood there with the whole kingdom of Britain at your side. If only the prophet Merlin would give his mind to the problem, then with his help I think you might be able to obtain what you want." The King believed Ulfin and ordered Merlin to be sent for, for he, too, had come to the siege.

Merlin was summoned immediately. When he appeared in the King's presence, he was ordered to suggest how the King could have his way with Ygerna. When Merlin saw the torment which the King was suffering because of this woman, he was amazed at the strength of his passion. "If you are to have your wish," he said, "you must make use of methods which are quite new and until now unheard-of in your day. By my drugs I know how to give you the precise appearance of Gorlois, so that you will resemble him in every respect. If you do what I say, I will make you exactly like him, and Ulfin exactly like Gorlois' companion, Jordan of Tintagel. I will change my own appearance, too, and come with you. In this way you will be able to go safely to Ygerna in her castle and be admitted."

The King agreed and listened carefully to what he had to do. In the end he handed the siege over to his subordinates, took Merlin's drugs, and was changed into the likeness of Gorlois. Ulfin was changed into Jordan and Merlin into a man called Britaelis, so that no one could tell what they had previously looked like. They then set off for Tintagel and came to the Castle in the twilight. The moment the guard was told that his leader was approaching, he opened the gates and the men were let in. Who, indeed, could possibly have suspected anything, once it was thought that Gorlois himself had come? The King spent that night with Ygerna and satisfied his desire by making love with her. He had deceived her by the disguise which he had taken. He had deceived her, too, by the lying things that he said to her, things which he planned with great skill. He said that he had come out secretly from his besieged encampment so that he might make sure that all was well with her, whom he loved so dearly, and with his castle, too. She naturally believed all that he said and refused him nothing that he asked. That night she conceived Arthur, the most famous of men, who subsequently won great renown by his outstanding bravery.

Meanwhile, when it was discovered at the siege of Dimilioc that the King was no longer present, his army, acting without his instructions, tried to breach the walls and challenge the beleaguered Duke to battle. The Duke, equally ill-advisedly, sallied forth with his men, imagining apparently that he could resist such a host of armed men with his own tiny band. As the struggle between them swayed this way and that, Gorlois was among the first to be killed. His men were scattered and the besieged camp was captured. The treasure which had been deposited there was shared out in the most inequitable way, for each man seized in his greedy fist whatever good luck and his own brute strength threw in his way.[8]

8. Geoffrey emphasizes the destructive potential of private greed, private ambition, and brute force, even in the rule of a strong king like Uther. This becomes a dominant theme in Geoffrey and later Arthurian narratives.

Not until the outrages which followed this daring act had finally subsided did messengers come to Ygerna to announce the death of the Duke and the end of the siege. When they saw the King sitting beside Ygerna in the likeness of their leader, they blushed red with astonishment to see that the man whom they had left behind dead in the siege had in effect arrived there safely before them. Of course, they did not know of the drugs prepared by Merlin. The King put his arms round the Duchess and laughed aloud to hear these reports. "I am not dead," he said. "Indeed, as you see, I am very much alive! However, the destruction of my camp saddens me very much and so does the slaughter of my comrades. What is more, there is great danger that the King may come this way and capture us in this castle. I will go out to meet him and make peace with him, lest even worse should befall us."

The King set out and made his way towards his own army, abandoning his disguise as Gorlois and becoming Utherpendragon once more. When he learned all that had happened, he mourned for the death of Gorlois; but he was happy, all the same, that Ygerna was freed from her marital obligations. He returned to Tintagel Castle, captured it and seized Ygerna at the same time, she being what he really wanted. From that day on they lived together as equals, united by their great love for each other; and they had a son and a daughter. The boy was called Arthur and the girl Anna.

[ANGLO-SAXON INVASION]

As the days passed and lengthened into years, the King fell ill with a malady which affected him for a long time. Meanwhile the prison warders who guarded Octa and Eosa,[9] as I have explained above, led a weary life. In the end they escaped with their prisoners to Germany and in doing so terrified the kingdom: for rumor had it that they had already stirred up Germany, and had fitted out a huge fleet in order to return to the island and destroy it. This, indeed, actually happened. They came back with an immense fleet and more men than could ever be counted. They invaded certain parts of Albany[1] and busied themselves in burning the cities there and the citizens inside them. The British army was put under the command of Loth of Lodonesia, with orders that he should keep the enemy at a distance. This man was one of the leaders, a valiant soldier, mature both in wisdom and age. As a reward for his prowess, the King had given him his daughter Anna and put him in charge of the kingdom while he himself was ill. When Loth moved forward against the enemy he was frequently driven back again by them, so that he had to take refuge inside the cities. On other occasions he routed and dispersed them, forcing them to fly either into the forests or to their ships. Between the two sides the outcome of each battle was always in doubt, it being hard to tell which of them was victorious. Their own arrogance was a handicap to the Britons, for they were unwilling to obey the orders of their leaders. This undermined their strength and they were unable to beat the enemy in the field.

Almost all the island was laid waste. When this was made known to the King, he fell into a greater rage than he could really bear in his weakened state. He told all his leaders to appear before him, so that he could rebuke them for their overweening pride and their feebleness. As soon as he saw them all assembled in his presence, he

9. A son and a kinsman of the Saxon Hengist; Uther had imprisoned them in London. Geoffrey closely connects the resurgence of the Saxon invaders with Uther's adultery and the disorder within his own army.

1. That is, Scotland, named for Brutus's son Albanactus.

reproached them bitterly and swore that he himself would lead them against the enemy. He ordered a litter to be built, so that he could be carried in it; for his weakness made any other form of progress impossible. Then he instructed them all to be in a state of preparedness, so that they could advance against the enemy as soon as the opportunity offered. The litter was constructed immediately, the men were made ready to start and the opportunity duly came.

They put the King in his litter and set out for Saint Albans, where the Saxons I have told you about were maltreating all the local population * * *

[*Despite his illness, Uther prevails. Octa and Eosa are killed.*]

Once the Saxons had been defeated, as I have explained above, they did not for that reason abandon their evil behavior. On the contrary, they went off to the northern provinces and preyed relentlessly upon the people there. King Uther was keen to pursue them, as he had proposed, but his princes dissuaded him from it, for after his victory his illness had taken an even more serious turn. As a result the enemy became bolder still in their enterprises, striving by every means in their power to take complete control of the realm. Having recourse, as usual, to treachery, they plotted to see how they could destroy the King by cunning. When every other approach failed, they made up their minds to kill him with poison. This they did: for while Uther lay ill in the town of St. Albans, they sent spies disguised as beggars, who were to discover how things stood at court. When the spies had obtained all the information that they wanted, they discovered one additional fact which they chose to use as a means of betraying Uther. Near the royal residence there was a spring of very limpid water which the King used to drink when he could not keep down any other liquids because of his illness. These evil traitors went to the spring and polluted it completely with poison, so that all the water which welled up was infected. When the King drank some of it, he died immediately. Some hundred men died after him, until the villainy was finally discovered. Then they filled the well in with earth. As soon as the death of the King was made known, the bishops of the land came with their clergy and bore his body to the monastery of Ambrius and buried it with royal honors at the side of Aurelius Ambrosius, inside the Giants' Ring.

[ARTHUR OF BRITAIN][2]

After the death of Utherpendragon, the leaders of the Britons assembled from their various provinces in the town of Silchester and there suggested to Dubricius, the Archbishop of the City of the Legions, that as their King he should crown Arthur, the son of Uther. Necessity urged them on, for as soon as the Saxons heard of the death of King Uther, they invited their own countrymen over from Germany, appointed Colgrin as their leader and began to do their utmost to exterminate the Britons. They had already over-run all that section of the island which stretches from the River Humber to the sea named Caithness.[3]

Dubricius lamented the sad state of his country. He called the other bishops to him and bestowed the crown of the kingdom upon Arthur. Arthur was a young man only fifteen years old; but he was of outstanding courage and generosity, and his

2. From bk. 9, chs. 1–11.

3. That is, Northumberland and Scotland.

inborn goodness gave him such grace that he was loved by almost all the people. Once he had been invested with the royal insignia, he observed the normal custom of giving gifts freely to everyone. Such a great crown of soldiers flocked to him that he came to an end of what he had to distribute. However, the man to whom open-handedness and bravery both come naturally may indeed find himself momentarily in need, but poverty will never harass him for long. In Arthur courage was closely linked with generosity, and he made up his mind to harry the Saxons, so that with their wealth he might reward the retainers who served his own household. The justness of his cause encouraged him, for he had a claim by rightful inheritance to the kingship of the whole island. He therefore called together all the young men whom I have just mentioned and marched on York.[4] * * *

[*Arthur and his followers attack Colgrin and ultimately subdue the Saxons; then they repel armies of Scots, Picts, and Irish. Arthur restores Briton dynasties throughout England, marries Guinevere, and establishes a stable peace.*]

Arthur then began to increase his personal entourage by inviting very distinguished men from far-distant kingdoms to join it. In this way he developed such a code of courtliness in his household that he inspired peoples living far away to imitate him. The result was that even the man of noblest birth, once he was roused to rivalry, thought nothing at all of himself unless he wore his arms and dressed in the same way as Arthur's knights. At last the fame of Arthur's generosity and bravery spread to the very ends of the earth; and the kings of countries far across the sea trembled at the thought that they might be attacked and invaded by him, and so lose control of the lands under their dominion. They were so harassed by these tormenting anxieties that they rebuilt their towns and the towers in their towns, and then went so far as to construct castles on carefully chosen sites, so that, if invasion should bring Arthur against them, they might have a refuge in their time of need.

All this was reported to Arthur. The fact that he was dreaded by all encouraged him to conceive the idea of conquering the whole of Europe.

Gerald of Wales

c. 1146–1222

Geoffrey of Monmouth's *History of the Kings of Britain* was soon retold in French, early Middle English, and Welsh, and it reappears in other languages for centuries. Contemporary historians, especially those interested in pre-Saxon history, were enthusiastic about this new story. Others were skeptical. Nevertheless, Geoffrey's narrative was soon accepted widely as fact, adopted, and revised to serve the interests of the Angevin dynasty.

The discovery of Arthur's bones at Glastonbury Abbey in 1191, as reported by the prolific writer Gerald of Wales, is a particularly rich instance of this habit, benefiting both the status of Henry II and the prestige of the abbey. Glastonbury faced a crisis common among Anglo-Saxon monastic foundations after the Norman Conquest. It was, in fact, probably the earliest Christian community in Britain; nonetheless, the oral tradition of its antiquity was

4. Geoffrey links the ancient practice of a king's largesse to his warrior band together with the claim of dynastic genealogy. Arthur will again use the latter claim when he decides to invade Gaul and then march toward Rome.

weakened as the Normans took power, bringing with them a new insistence on written documentation. Glastonbury had little proof of its claims to ancient privilege, either by way of charters (and those mostly spurious) or the related prestige of holy relics. At the same time, Henry II was interested in ancient narratives that might legitimize his imperial aims.

Gerald's version of events both suggests Henry's almost wondrous wisdom in identifying the very spot of Arthur's burial and implies the existence of early written records at Glastonbury. To have Arthur as a patron, authenticated by King Henry himself, greatly substantiated the abbey's other claims. At the same time, Henry's knowledge mysteriously linked him to Arthur, and the corpse itself neatly altered Arthurian tradition, certifying Arthur's actual death and perhaps damping Welsh hopes for a messianic return.

from The Instruction of Princes[1]

The memory of Arthur, that most renowned King of the Britons, will endure forever. In his own day he was a munificent patron of the famous Abbey at Glastonbury, giving many donations to the monks and always supporting them strongly, and he is highly praised in their records. More than any other place of worship in his kingdom he loved the church of the Blessed Mary, Mother of God, in Glastonbury, and he fostered its interests with much greater loving care than that of any of the others. When he went out to fight, he had a full-length portrait of the Blessed Virgin painted on the front of his shield, so that in the heat of battle he could always gaze upon her; and whenever he was about to make contact with the enemy he would kiss her feet with great devoutness.

In our lifetime Arthur's body was discovered at Glastonbury, although the legends had always encouraged us to believe that there was something otherworldly about his ending, that he had resisted death and had been spirited away to some far-distant spot.[2] The body was hidden deep in the earth in a hollowed-out oak-bole and between two stone pyramids which had been set up long ago in the churchyard there. They carried it into the church with every mark of honor and buried it decently there in a marble tomb. It had been provided with most unusual indications which were, indeed, little short of miraculous, for beneath it—and not on top, as would be the custom nowadays—there was a stone slab, with a leaden cross attached to its underside. I have seen this cross myself and I have traced the lettering which was cut into it on the side turned towards the stone, instead of being on the outer side and immediately visible. The inscription read as follows: HERE IN THE ISLE OF AVALON LIES BURIED THE RENOWNED KING ARTHUR, WITH GUINEVERE, HIS SECOND WIFE.

There are many remarkable deductions to be made from this discovery. Arthur obviously had two wives, and the second one was buried with him. Her bones were found with those of her husband, but they were separate from his. Two-thirds of the coffin, the part towards the top end, held the husband's bones, and the other section, at his feet, contained those of his wife. A tress of woman's hair, blond, and still fresh and bright in color, was found in the coffin. One of the monks snatched it up and it immediately disintegrated into dust. There had been some indications in the Abbey records that the body would be discovered on this spot, and another clue was provided by lettering carved on the pyramids, but this had been almost completely erased by the

1. Translated by Lewis Thorpe. Gerald reports the same events again in a later text, the *Speculum Ecclesiae*.

2. In his other version (the *Speculum Ecclesiae*) Gerald is more nervously dismissive: "In their stupidity the British people maintain that he is still alive. . . . According to them, once he has recovered from his wounds this strong and all-powerful King will return to rule over the Britons in the normal way."

passage of the years. The holy monks and other religious had seen visions and revelations. However, it was Henry II, King of England, who had told the monks that, according to a story which he had heard from some old British soothsayer,[3] they would find Arthur's body buried at least sixteen feet in the ground, not in a stone coffin but in a hollowed-out oak-bole. It had been sunk as deep as that, and carefully concealed, so that it could never be discovered by the Saxons, whom Arthur had attacked relentlessly as long as he lived and whom, indeed, he had almost wiped out, but who occupied the island [of Britain] after his death. That was why the inscription, which was eventually to reveal the truth, had been cut into the inside of the cross and turned inwards towards the stone. For many a long year this inscription was to keep the secret of what the coffin contained, but eventually, when time and circumstance were both opportune, the lettering revealed what it had so long concealed.

What is now known as Glastonbury used in ancient times to be called the Isle of Avalon. It is virtually an island, for it is completely surrounded by marshlands. In Welsh it is called "Ynys Avallon," which means the Island of Apples. "Aval" is the Welsh word for apple, and this fruit used to grow there in great abundance.[4] After the Battle of Camlann,[5] a noblewoman called Morgan, who was the ruler and patroness of these parts as well as being a close blood-relation of King Arthur, carried him off to the island now known as Glastonbury, so that his wounds could be cared for. Years ago the district had also been called "Ynys Gutrin" in Welsh, that is the Island of Glass, and from these words the invading Saxons later coined the place-name "Glastingebury." The word "glass" in their language means "vitrum" in Latin, and "bury" means "castrum" [camp] or "civitas" [city].

You must know that the bones of Arthur's body which were discovered there were so big that in them the poet's words seem to be fulfilled:

> All men will exclaim at the size of the bones they've exhumed.[6]

The Abbot showed me one of the shin-bones. He held it upright on the ground against the foot of the tallest man he could find, and it stretched a good three inches above the man's knee. The skull was so large and capacious that it seemed a veritable prodigy of nature, for the space between the eyebrows and the eye-sockets was as broad as the palm of a man's hand. Ten or more wounds could clearly be seen, but they had all mended except one. This was larger than the others and it had made an immense gash. Apparently it was this wound which had caused Arthur's death.

Edward I

1239–1307

Beginning in 1291, King Edward I of England revived an ancient claim to be feudal overlord of Scotland and thereby sought to control a disputed succession to its throne. By 1293 the Scottish king John Balliol had become Edward's vassal, but rebelled and was forced to abdicate in 1296. The military and diplomatic struggle (later called the "Great Cause") stretched

3. In the *Speculum Ecclesiae*, Gerald says that Henry learned this "from the historical accounts of the Britons and from their bards."

4. Citing and explaining words from the various British vernaculars is a widespread habit in Latin historical writing as early as Bede.

5. Arthur's last battle, fought against the rebel army of his kinsman Mordred. Arthur kills Mordred but is himself mortally wounded.

6. Virgil, *Georgics*, 1.497.

across the decade. By the turn of the fourteenth century, in an extraordinary move, both the English and Scots had turned to the court of Pope Boniface VIII for a legal decision. In pursuing Edward's claim, his agents ransacked chronicles—including Geoffrey of Monmouth's *History*—as well as ancient charters, to compile a dossier of historical and legal precedents. Despite his own bureaucratic reforms requiring documentary proof for most legal claims, Edward was ready to invoke common memory and ancient legends to support his position regarding Scotland. Knowing that such chronicle material would have no status in court, in May of 1301 Edward resorted to the letter below before Pope Boniface ruled in the matter.

The written letter was a highly developed and self-conscious genre during the Middle Ages. Letters were often meant to be public and could carry the force of law. Indeed, the form of many legal documents had developed from royal letters. Letter writing became an area for textbooks and school study, the *ars dictaminis*. Elaborate formulas of salutation and closing, and other rhetorical figures, were taught and used for important correspondence as a way of establishing the sender's learning and prestige. The papal curia employed a particularly challenging system of prose rhythm called the *cursus*, which was imitated in some royal chanceries and is found in the Latin of Edward's letter.

Letter sent to the Papal Court of Rome
Concerning the king's rights in the realm of Scotland[1]

To the most Holy Father in Christ lord Boniface, by divine providence the supreme pontiff of the Holy Roman and Universal Church, Edward, by grace of the same providence king of England, lord of Ireland, and duke of Aquitaine offers his humblest devotion to the blessed saints.[2] What follows we send to you not to be treated in the form or manner of a legal plea, but altogether extrajudicially, in order to set the mind of your Holiness at rest. The All-Highest, to whom all hearts are open, will testify how it is graven upon the tablets of our memory with an indelible mark, that our predecessors and progenitors, the kings of England, by right of lordship and dominion, possessed, from the most ancient times, the suzerainty of the realm of Scotland and its kings in temporal matters, and the things annexed thereto, and that they received from the self-same kings, and from such magnates of the realm as they so desired, liege homage and oaths of fealty. We, continuing in the possession of that very right and dominion, have received the same acknowledgments in our time, both from the king of Scotland, and from the magnates of that realm; and indeed such prerogatives of right and dominion did the kings of England enjoy over the realm of Scotland and its kings, that they have even granted to their faithful folk the realm itself, removed its kings for just causes, and constituted others to rule in their place under themselves. Beyond doubt these matters have been familiar from times long past and still are, though perchance it has been suggested otherwise to your Holiness' ears by foes of peace and sons of rebellion, whose elaborate and empty fabrications your wisdom, we trust, will treat with contempt.

Thus, in the days of Eli and of Samuel the prophet, after the destruction of the city of Troy, a certain valiant and illustrious man of the Trojan race called Brutus, landed with many noble Trojans, upon a certain island called, at that time, Albion.[3] It was

1. Translated by E. L. G. Stones (1965). Although sent in the name of the King, a Latin letter of such formality would have been written by notaries in his chancery. A French draft also survives, which might have been used by Edward himself.
2. A flowery opening formula was typical of formal letters between persons of power; it also provided a place for Edward to make ambitious (and in the case of Aquitaine, highly optimistic) territorial claims.
3. Here the letter borrows closely from Geoffrey of Monmouth's foundation narrative; see page 186.

then inhabited by giants, and after he had defeated and slain them, by his might and that of his followers, he called it, after his own name, Britain, and his people Britons, and built a city which he called Trinovant, now known as London. Afterwards he divided his realm among his three sons, that is he gave to his first born, Locrine, that part of Britain now called England, to the second, Albanact, that part then known as Albany, after the name of Albanact, but now as Scotland, and to Camber, his youngest son, the part then known by his son's name as Cambria and now called Wales, the royal dignity being reserved for Locrine, the eldest. Two years after the death of Brutus there landed in Albany a certain king of the Huns, called Humber, and he slew Albanact, the brother of Locrine. Hearing this, Locrine, the king of the Britons, pursued him, and he fled and was drowned in the river which from his name is called Humber, and thus Albany reverted to Locrine. * * * Again, Arthur, king of the Britons, a prince most renowned, subjected to himself a rebellious Scotland, destroyed almost the whole nation, and afterwards installed as king of Scotland one Angusel by name. Afterwards, when King Arthur held a most famous feast at Caerleon, there were present there all the kings subject to him, and among them Angusel, king of Scotland, who manifested the service due for the realm of Scotland by bearing the sword of King Arthur before him; and in succession all the kings of Scotland have been subject to all the kings of the Britons. Succeeding kings of England enjoyed both monarchy and dominion in the island, and subsequently Edward, known as the elder, son of Alfred, king of England, had subject and subordinate to him, as lord superior, the kings of the Scots, the Cumbrians, and the Strathclyde Welsh. * * *

Since, indeed, from what has been said already, and from other evidence, it is perfectly clear and well-known that the realm of Scotland belongs to us of full right, by reason of property and of possession, and that we have not done and have not dared to do anything, as indeed we could not do, in writing or in action, by which any prejudice may be implied to our right or possession, we humbly beseech your Holiness to weigh all this with careful meditation, and to condescend to keep it all in mind when making your decision, setting no store, if you please, by the adverse assertions which come to you on this subject from our enemies, but, on the contrary, retaining our welfare and our royal rights, if it so please you, in your fatherly regard. May the Most High preserve you, to rule his Holy Church through many years of prosperity.

Kempsey, 7 May 1301, the twenty-ninth year of our reign.

RESPONSE

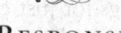

A Report to Edward I[1]

Sir, seeing that you have lately sent a statement to the pope concerning your right to Scotland, the Scots are making efforts to nullify that statement by certain objections which are given below. * * * They say that in that letter you ground your right on old

1. The Scots learned about Edward's letter and made their own response to the pope; this report to Edward, written in the French he would actually have used with his counselors, specifies the Scots' rebuttal. The Scots carefully assert the superior force of later charters and other legal instruments, and dismiss Edward's reliance on unauthenticated legends. In case Edward's story should carry weight with Boniface, however, they also provide a counternarrative of their own national foundation by Scota, daughter of the Pharaoh, and how she expelled British influence from her land. The English and Scots diplomats thus tell opposing prehistories that underwrite their current claims. Just as important, though, they are negotiating around an unusually articulate moment in the contest between different forms of textuality—legendary and chronicle tradition versus legal documents—in the creation of contemporary political power.

chronicles, which contain various falsehoods and lies, and are abrogated and made void by the subsequent contrary actions of your predecessors and of yourself, which vitiate all the remaining part of your letter, and therefore one should give no credence to such a document. And they say further, that with only this unworthy and feeble case to rely upon, you are striving to evade the cognizance of your true judge, and to suppress the truth, and unlawfully, by force of arms, to repel your weaker neighbors, and to prevent the pope from pursuing the examination of this case. * * *

Again, they say that the old chronicles that you use as evidence of your right could not assist you, even if they were authenticated, as is not the case, they say, because it is notorious that these same old chronicles are utterly made naught and of no avail by other subsequent documents of greater significance, by contrary agreements and actions, and by papal privileges. * * * Then, sir, in order that credence be not given to the documents, histories, and deeds described in your statement, they say that allegations like those recounted in your narrative are put out of court by the true facts, and they endeavor to demonstrate their assertion by chronicles and narratives of a contrary purport. Brutus divided between his three sons the island once called Britain, and now England, and gave to one son Loegria, to another Wales, and to the third what is now called Scotland, and made them peers, so that none of them was subject to another. Afterwards came a woman named Scota, daughter of Pharaoh of Egypt, who came via Spain and occupied Ireland, and afterwards conquered the land of Albany, which she had called, after her name, *Scotland*,[2] and one place in that land she had called after the names of her son Erk and her husband Gayl, wherefore that district was called *Ergaill* [Argyll], and they drove out the Britons, and from that time the Scots, as a new race and possessing a new name, had nothing to do with the Britons, but pursued them daily as their enemies, and were distinguished from them by different ranks and customs, and by a different language. Afterwards they joined company with the Picts, by whose strength they destroyed the Britons, and the land which is now called England, and for this reason the Britons gave tribute to the Romans, to obtain the help of the Roman emperor, whose name was Severus, against the Scots, and by his help the Britons made a wall between themselves and the Scots, having a length of 130 leagues in length from one sea to the other, and they say that by this it appears that Scotland was not at any time under the lordship of the Britons.[3] But they do not deny that King Arthur by his prowess conquered Denmark, France, Norway and also Scotland, and held them until he and Mordred were slain in battle, and from that time the realm of Scotland returned to its free status. They say that the Britons were then expelled by the Saxons, and then the Saxons by the Danes, and then the Danes by the Saxons, and that in the whole period of the Saxon kings the Scots remained free without being subject to them, and at that time, by the relics of Saint Andrew which came from Greece, they were converted to the faith five hundred years before the English became Christians, and from that time the realm of Scotland, with the king and the realm [*sic*], were under the lordship of the Roman church without any intermediary, and by it were they defended against all their enemies. * * *

END OF PERSPECTIVES: ARTHURIAN MYTH IN THE HISTORY OF BRITAIN

2. This neatly replicates Brutus's trajectory from the eastern Mediterranean, across part of continental Europe, and thence to the British Isles.

3. The Scots artfully shift the emphasis found in Geoffrey of Monmouth. Roman colonization and Hadrian's wall become evidence of an ancient ethnic division and Scots independence both from the Britons and from the Britons' later invaders.

ARTHURIAN ROMANCE

Marie de France

fl. 2nd half of the 12th century

In a famous line from the prologue to her *Lais*, Marie de France suggested that serious readers could approach an obscure old book and "supply its significance from their own wisdom." The original French text, "*de lur sen le surplus mettre*," implies that such readers add on something that is missing. In part a gesture of respect toward the study of pagan Latin literature in a Christian setting, this statement also seems to permit Marie herself a dramatically new perspective when she encounters long-established Arthurian stories such as *Lanval*, and the related tale of Tristan and Isolt in *Chevrefoil*. Starting with a scene of war that readers of Geoffrey of Monmouth might recognize, Marie swiftly brings into play elements that had been largely absent in the historicizing stories of Arthur: bodily desire and its dangers, romantic longing, the realm of the uncanny, the power of women, the force of wealth and influence in even the noblest courts. Similarly, in *Chevrefoil* the lovers' brief, ecstatic meeting occurs as a crowd of courtiers awaits her.

Marie's specific identity remains obscure, but it is clear that she was a woman of French background writing in England in the later decades of the twelfth century, widely educated, and in touch with the royal court. She dedicates her book of *Lais* to a "noble King" who was probably Henry II, and she may have been his kinswoman. Marie's works draw into that courtly culture the languages and traditions of the English and Celtic past. She rewrote a Latin narrative about the origin of "Saint Patrick's Purgatory" and the adventure of an Irish knight there; and she retold the fables of Aesop using an English translation that she attributed to King Alfred. The *Lais*, she says, came to her through oral transmission, and she connects them with the Bretons. Indeed, the best early copy of the *Lais*, Harley manuscript 978 in the British Library, is itself a multilingual compilation that includes the early Middle English poem *The Cuckoo Song* ("Sumer is icumen in"; see page 551).

Writing a generation after Geoffrey of Monmouth and not long before Gerald of Wales, Marie brings a quite different and rather critical set of preoccupations to her Arthurian stories. She opens her tale with a realistic and admirable occasion of male power and strong kingship: Arthur's battle for territory and his reward of faithful vassals. A bleaker side of that courtly world, and perhaps of Marie's own, is also implicit, however. With a terseness and indirection typical of her *lais*, Marie shows women as property in the king's gift, knights forgotten when their wealth runs out, and the perversion of judicial process. In *Chevrefoil*, again, Isolt has only the title she gained by marriage, "the queen," never her own name.

Marvels and erotic desire dominate her tales, though, and women's power, for good or ill, is their primary motivating force. Guinevere, in a hostile portrait of adulterous aggression and vengeful dishonesty, nonetheless manages to manipulate Arthur and his legal codes when Lanval rejects her advances. The queen is countered by Lanval's supernatural mistress, who commands luxurious riches that dwarf Arthur's; she rescues Lanval by being an unimpeachable legal witness in his defense. Indeed, she arrives on her white palfrey as the moment of judgment nears, almost like a knightly champion in a trial by battle. Lanval vanishes into a timeless world of fulfilled desire and limitless wealth that has analogies in much older Celtic tradition—for instance, in *The Voyage of Máel Dúin* (page 141). This closing scene defies the reintegration of male courtly order that is typical even in the erotic romances of Marie's contemporary Chrétien de Troyes.

The realm of eroticism and women's power in *Lanval,* though, is not automatically any more virtuous or stable than the ostentatious wealth and corruptible law of the world of Arthurian men. If Lanval's mysterious lady is beautiful and generous, she also takes his knightliness from him. Lanval is last seen riding behind the lady, and not on a warhorse but on a palfrey. Guinevere swiftly reduces Arthur to a weak and temporizing king. And in her initial explosion after Lanval rejects her, Guinevere accuses him of homosexuality. For all its absurdity, the moment articulates unnerving implications of the profound bonds among men in the Arthurian world, implications that could interrupt genealogical transmission of wealth and power. Marie's Guinevere again voices fears the tradition has left unsaid.

Chevrefoil ("The Honeysuckle") involves romantic desires far more elevated than those in *Lanval,* but equally dangerous to the social order, and ultimately disastrous to the lovers. Even in this brief episode, the lovers' one intimate moment is hedged about by an anxious sense of a public and hostile world nearby, as well as a more distant royal power that crushes private love. Marie can assume her readers know the story of Tristan and Isolt and their tragic love. Tristan is sent to Ireland to fetch Isolt, the fiancée of his uncle, King Mark. On a boat returning to Cornwall, Tristan and Isolt share a love potion that had been meant to seal her marriage with Mark. The adulterous (and, from a medieval Catholic perspective, incestuous) affair that follows entangles all three in a web of desire, dependency, and family loyalty. The intense joy of the lovers' brief encounter in this episode, then, is complicated and darkened by the many echoes of other famous moments in their affair: a meeting under a tree, joint exile in a forest, and the intertwining vine and rose that later grow from their adjacent graves. And Marie's readers would have known that the reconciliation Isolt promises never, in fact, takes place. This tone of superabundant meaning—perhaps another version of the "*surplus*" mentioned above—is mirrored in the *lai* by the long message Isolt can interpret from a single word, Tristan's name carved on a piece of wood.

Marie de France may be trying less to propound a critique of the received stories of Arthur and Tristan than to recall her readers' attention to elements that tradition has left aside, as she suggests in her prologue. Some of this is no more troubling than a delightful fantasy of wealth and pleasure, outside time and without consequences. Other elements imply, with startling economy, forces that (in the hands of later romancers) tear the Arthurian world to pieces.

For additional resources on Marie de France, go to *The Longman Anthology of British Literature* Web site at www.myliteraturekit.com.

from LAIS[1]

Prologue

Whoever has received knowledge
and eloquence in speech from God
should not be silent or secretive
but demonstrate it willingly.
When a great good is widely heard of,
then, and only then, does it bloom,
and when that good is praised by many,
it has spread its blossoms.
The custom among the ancients—
as Priscian[2] testifies—
was to speak quite obscurely

1. Translated by Robert Hanning and Joan Ferrante.
2. A famed grammarian of the late Roman empire, Priscian remained widely influential in the study of Latin language and literature in the 12th century.

Marie de France Writing, from an illuminated manuscript of her works. While most images of writing feature men, women were also writers and copyists as well as readers (see Color Plate 10). Here, in a late-13th-century manuscript of her poems, Marie de France is shown at her writing desk, strikingly similar in posture and detail (and in authority) to Laurence of Durham more than a century earlier (see page 2).

in the books they wrote,
so that those who were to come after
and study them
might gloss the letter
and supply its significance from their own wisdom.[3]
Philosophers knew this,
they understood among themselves
that the more time they spent,
the more subtle their minds would become
and the better they would know how to keep themselves
from whatever was to be avoided.
He who would guard himself from vice
should study and understand
and begin a weighty work
by which he might keep vice at a distance,
and free himself from great sorrow.
That's why I began to think
about composing some good stories
and translating from Latin to Romance;[4]
but that was not to bring me fame:
too many others have done it.
Then I thought of the *lais* I'd heard.[5]
I did not doubt, indeed I knew well,

3. Marie refers to the practice of supplying glosses—explanatory notes such as this one—to school texts; she also implies that later readers bring their own perspective to earlier works, a point relevant to her own free adaptation of earlier Arthurian stories.

4. That is, to French.

5. A *lai* was typically a short verse narrative, meant for oral performance with music. A particular group of these, often including Arthurian tales, was especially connected with Brittany.

that those who first began them
and sent them forth
composed them in order to preserve
adventures they had heard.
I have heard many told;
and I don't want to neglect or forget them.
To put them into word and rhyme
I've often stayed awake.

In your honor, noble King,[6]
who are so brave and courteous,
repository of all joys
in whose heart all goodness takes root,
I undertook to assemble these *lais*
to compose and recount them in rhyme.
In my heart I thought and determined,
sire, that I would present them to you.
If it pleases you to receive them,
you will give me great joy;
I shall be happy forever.
Do not think me presumptuous
if I dare present them to you.
Now hear how they begin.

Lanval

I shall tell you the adventure of another *lai*,
just as it happened:
it was composed about a very noble vassal;
in Breton, they call him Lanval.[1]

Arthur, the brave and the courtly king,
was staying at Cardoel,[2]
because the Scots and the Picts
were destroying the land.[3]
They invaded Logres° *England*
and laid it waste.
At Pentecost, in summer,[4]
the king stayed there.
He gave out many rich gifts:
to counts and barons,
members of the Round Table—
such a company had no equal in all the world—
he distributed wives and lands,

6. Probably Henry II.
1. Marie seems to imply knowledge of Breton, a Celtic language related to Welsh. In other works, she shows knowledge of English as well, and excellent Latin.
2. Carlisle, in the north of England.
3. Scots and Picts were Arthur's traditional enemies.
4. "Summer" here refers to late spring. The feast of Pentecost commemorates the descent of the Holy Spirit among Christ's apostles; it is often the occasion of Arthurian stories, especially those that involve marvels.

to all but one who had served him.
That was Lanval; Arthur forgot him,
and none of his men favored him either.
For his valor, for his generosity,
his beauty and his bravery,
most men envied him;
some feigned the appearance of love
who, if something unpleasant happened to him,
would not have been at all disturbed.
He was the son of a king of high degree
but he was far from his heritage.
He was of the king's household
but he had spent all his wealth,
for the king gave him nothing
nor did Lanval ask.
Now Lanval was in difficulty,
depressed and very worried.
My lords, don't be surprised:
a strange man, without friends,
is very sad in another land,
when he doesn't know where to look for help.
The knight of whom I speak,
who had served the king so long,
one day mounted his horse
and went off to amuse himself.
He left the city
and came, all alone, to a field;
he dismounted by a running stream
but his horse trembled badly.
He removed the saddle and went off,
leaving the horse to roll around in the meadow.
He folded his cloak beneath his head
and lay down.
He worried about his difficulty,
he could see nothing that pleased him.
As he lay there
he looked down along the bank
and saw two girls approaching;
he had never seen any lovelier.
They were richly dressed,
tightly laced,
in tunics of dark purple;
their faces were very lovely.
The older one carried basins,
golden, well made, and fine;
I shall tell you the truth about it, without fail.
The other carried a towel.
They went straight
to where the knight was lying.

Lanval, who was very well bred,
got up to meet them.
They greeted him first
and gave him their message:
"Sir Lanval, my lady,
who is worthy and wise and beautiful,
sent us for you.
Come with us now.
We shall guide you there safely.
See, her pavilion is nearby!"
The knight went with them;
giving no thought to his horse
who was feeding before him in the meadow.
They led him up to the tent,[5]
which was quite beautiful and well placed.
Queen Semiramis,
however much more wealth,
power, or knowledge she had,
or the emperor Octavian[6]
could not have paid for one of the flaps.
There was a golden eagle on top of it,
whose value I could not tell,
nor could I judge the value of the cords or the poles
that held up the sides of the tent;
there is no king on earth who could buy it,
no matter what wealth he offered.
The girl was inside the tent:
the lily and the young rose
when they appear in the summer
are surpassed by her beauty.
She lay on a beautiful bed—
the bedclothes were worth a castle—
dressed only in her shift.
Her body was well shaped and elegant;
for the heat, she had thrown over herself,
a precious cloak of white ermine,
covered with purple alexandrine,° *embroidery*
but her whole side was uncovered,
her face, her neck and her bosom;
she was whiter than the hawthorn flower.
The knight went forward
and the girl addressed him.
He sat before the bed.
"Lanval," she said, "sweet love,

5. Elaborate tents are often found in contemporary narratives of kings going out to battle.
6. Semiramis, legendary queen of Assyria and builder of Babylon, led armies of conquest; she is also a conventional figure of uncontrolled sexual desire. She is interestingly placed here as a female counterpart to Octavian (Augustus Caesar), the first Roman emperor.

because of you I have come from my land;
I came to seek you from far away.
If you are brave and courtly,
no emperor or count or king
will ever have known such joy or good;
for I love you more than anything."
He looked at her and saw that she was beautiful;
Love stung him with a spark
that burned and set fire to his heart.
He answered her in a suitable way.
"Lovely one," he said, "if it pleased you,
if such joy might be mine
that you would love me,
there is nothing you might command,
within my power, that I would not do,
whether foolish or wise.
I shall obey your command;
for you, I shall abandon everyone.
I want never to leave you.
That is what I most desire."
When the girl heard the words
of the man who could love her so,
she granted him her love and her body.
Now Lanval was on the right road!
Afterward, she gave him a gift:
he would never again want anything,
he would receive as he desired;
however generously he might give and spend,
she would provide what he needed.
Now Lanval is well cared for.
The more lavishly he spends,
the more gold and silver he will have.
"Love," she said, "I admonish you now,
I command and beg you,
do not let any man know about this.
I shall tell you why:
you would lose me for good
if this love were known;
you would never see me again
or possess my body."
He answered that he would do
exactly as she commanded.
He lay beside her on the bed;
now Lanval is well cared for.
He remained with her
that afternoon, until evening
and would have stayed longer, if he could,
and if his love had consented.
"Love," she said, "get up.

You cannot stay any longer.
Go away now; I shall remain
but I will tell you one thing:
when you want to talk to me
there is no place you can think of
where a man might have his mistress
without reproach or shame,
that I shall not be there with you
to satisfy all your desires.
No man but you will see me
or hear my words."
When he heard her, he was very happy,
he kissed her, and then got up.
The girls who had brought him to the tent
dressed him in rich clothes;
when he was dressed anew,
there wasn't a more handsome youth in all the world;
he was no fool, no boor.
They gave him water for his hands
and a towel to dry them,
and they brought him food.
He took supper with his love;
it was not to be refused.
He was served with great courtesy,
he received it with great joy.
There was an entremet° *side dish*
that vastly pleased the knight
for he kissed his lady often
and held her close.
When they finished dinner,
his horse was brought to him.
The horse had been well saddled;
Lanval was very richly served.
The knight took his leave, mounted,
and rode toward the city,
often looking behind him.
Lanval was very disturbed;
he wondered about his adventure
and was doubtful in his heart;
he was amazed, not knowing what to believe;
he didn't expect ever to see her again.
He came to his lodging
and found his men well dressed.
That night, his accommodations were rich
but no one knew where it came from.
There was no knight in the city
who really needed a place to stay
whom he didn't invite to join him
to be well and richly served.

Lanval gave rich gifts,
Lanval released prisoners,
Lanval dressed jongleurs,° *performers*
Lanval offered great honors.
There was no stranger or friend
to whom Lanval didn't give.
Lanval's joy and pleasure were intense;
in the daytime or at night,
he could see his love often;
she was completely at his command.
In that same year, it seems to me,
after the feast of Saint John,
about thirty knights
were amusing themselves
in an orchard beneath the tower
where the queen was staying.
Gawain was with them
and his cousin, the handsome Yvain;[7]
Gawain, the noble, the brave,
who was so loved by all, said:
"By God, my lords, we wronged
our companion Lanval,
who is so generous and courtly,
and whose father is a rich king,
when we didn't bring him with us."
They immediately turned back,
went to his lodging
and prevailed on Lanval to come along with them.
At a sculpted window
the queen was looking out;
she had three ladies with her.
She saw the king's retinue,
recognized Lanval and looked at him.
Then she told one of her ladies
to send for her maidens,
the loveliest and the most refined;
together they went to amuse themselves
in the orchard where the others were.
She brought thirty or more with her;
they descended the steps.
The knights came to meet them,
because they were delighted to see them.
The knights took them by the hand;
their conversation was in no way vulgar.
Lanval went off to one side,

7. Gawain and Yvain serve to place Marie's hero in the context of more famous Arthurian episodes. Gawain, nephew of Arthur and distinguished both for bravery and courtesy, increasingly acts as Lanval's sponsor in the rest of the *lai*.

far from the others; he was impatient
to hold his love,
to kiss and embrace and touch her;
he thought little of others' joys
if he could not have his pleasure.
When the queen saw him alone,
she went straight to the knight.
She sat beside him and spoke,
revealing her whole heart:
"Lanval, I have shown you much honor,
I have cherished you, and loved you.
You may have all my love;
just tell me your desire.
I promise you my affection.
You should be very happy with me."
"My lady," he said, "let me be!
I have no desire to love you.
I've served the king a long time;
I don't want to betray my faith to him.
Never, for you or for your love,
will I do anything to harm my lord."
The queen got angry;
in her wrath, she insulted him:
"Lanval," she said, "I am sure
you don't care for such pleasure;
people have often told me
that you have no interest in women.
You have fine-looking boys
with whom you enjoy yourself.
Base coward, lousy cripple,
my lord made a bad mistake
when he let you stay with him.
For all I know, he'll lose God because of it."
When Lanval heard her, he was quite disturbed;
he was not slow to answer.
He said something out of spite
that he would later regret.
"Lady," he said, "of that activity
I know nothing,
but I love and I am loved
by one who should have the prize
over all the women I know.
And I shall tell you one thing;
you might as well know all:
any one of those who serve her,
the poorest girl of all,
is better than you, my lady queen,
in body, face, and beauty,
in breeding and in goodness."

The queen left him
and went, weeping, to her chamber.
She was upset and angry
because he had insulted her.
She went to bed sick;
never, she said, would she get up
unless the king gave her satisfaction
for the offense against her.
The king returned from the woods,
he'd had a very good day.
He entered the queen's chambers.
When she saw him, she began to complain.
She fell at his feet, asked his mercy,
saying that Lanval had dishonored her;
he had asked for her love,
and because she refused him
he insulted and offended her:
he boasted of a love
who was so refined and noble and proud
that her chambermaid,
the poorest one who served her,
was better than the queen.
The king got very angry;
he swore an oath:
if Lanval could not defend himself in court
he would have him burned or hanged.
The king left her chamber
and called for three of his barons;
he sent them for Lanval
who was feeling great sorrow and distress.
He had come back to his dwelling,
knowing very well
that he'd lost his love,
he had betrayed their affair.
He was all alone in a room,
disturbed and troubled;
he called on his love, again and again,
but it did him no good.
He complained and sighed,
from time to time he fainted;
then he cried a hundred times for her to have mercy
and speak to her love.
He cursed his heart and his mouth;
it's a wonder he didn't kill himself.
No matter how much he cried and shouted,
ranted and raged,
she would not have mercy on him,
not even let him see her.
How will he ever contain himself?

The men the king sent
arrived and told him
to appear in court without delay:
the king had summoned him
because the queen had accused him.
Lanval went with his great sorrow;
they could have killed him, for all he cared.
He came before the king;
he was very sad, thoughtful, silent;
his face revealed great suffering.
In anger the king told him:
"Vassal, you have done me a great wrong!
This was a base undertaking,
to shame and disgrace me
and to insult the queen.
You have made a foolish boast:
your love is much too noble
if her maid is more beautiful,
more worthy, than the queen."
Lanval denied that he'd dishonored
or shamed his lord,
word for word, as the king spoke:
he had not made advances to the queen;
but of what he had said,
he acknowledged the truth,
about the love he had boasted of,
that now made him sad because he'd lost her.
About that he said he would do
whatever the court decided.
The king was very angry with him;
he sent for all his men
to determine exactly what he ought to do
so that no one could find fault with his decision.
They did as he commanded,
whether they liked it or not.
They assembled,
judged, and decided,
that Lanval should have his day;
but he must find pledges for his lord
to guarantee that he would await the judgment,
return, and be present at it.[8]
Then the court would be increased,
for now there were none but the king's household.
The barons came back to the king
and announced their decision.
The king demanded pledges.

8. Marie introduces judicial procedures that may have recalled those in Henry's reign: summons and accusation, setting a day for judgment, the rise of royal jurisdiction, the possibility of a champion, and trial by battle.

Lanval was alone and forlorn,
he had no relative, no friend.
Gawain went and pledged himself for him,
and all his companions followed.
The king addressed them: "I release him to you
on forfeit of whatever you hold from me,
lands and fiefs, each one for himself."
When Lanval was pledged, there was nothing else to do.
He returned to his lodging.
The knights accompanied him,
they reproached and admonished him
that he give up his great sorrow;
they cursed his foolish love.
Each day they went to see him,
because they wanted to know
whether he was drinking and eating;
they were afraid that he'd kill himself.
On the day that they had named,
the barons assembled.
The king and the queen were there
and the pledges brought Lanval back.
They were all very sad for him:
I think there were a hundred
who would have done all they could
to set him free without a trial
where he would be wrongly accused.
The king demanded a verdict
according to the charge and rebuttal.
Now it all fell to the barons.
They went to the judgment,
worried and distressed
for the noble man from another land
who'd gotten into such trouble in their midst.
Many wanted to condemn him
in order to satisfy their lord.
The Duke of Cornwall said:
"No one can blame us;
whether it makes you weep or sing
justice must be carried out.
The king spoke against his vassal
whom I have heard named Lanval;
he accused him of felony,
charged him with a misdeed—
a love that he had boasted of,
which made the queen angry.
No one but the king accused him:
by the faith I owe you,
if one were to speak the truth,
there should have been no need for defense,

except that a man owes his lord honor
in every circumstance.
He will be bound by his oath,
and the king will forgive us our pledges
if he can produce proof;
if his love would come forward,
if what he said,
what upset the queen, is true,
then he will be acquitted,
because he did not say it out of malice.
But if he cannot get his proof,
we must make it clear to him
that he will forfeit his service to the king;
he must take his leave."
They sent to the knight,
told and announced to him
that he should have his love come
to defend and stand surety for him.
He told them that he could not do it:
he would never receive help from her.
They went back to the judges,
not expecting any help from Lanval.
The king pressed them hard
because of the queen who was waiting.
When they were ready to give their verdict
they saw two girls approaching,
riding handsome palfreys.
They were very attractive,
dressed in purple taffeta,
over their bare skin.
The men looked at them with pleasure.
Gawain, taking three knights with him,
went to Lanval and told him;
he pointed out the two girls.
Gawain was extremely happy, and begged him
to tell if his love were one of them.
Lanval said he didn't know who they were,
where they came from or where they were going.
The girls proceeded
still on horseback;
they dismounted before the high table
at which Arthur, the king, sat.
They were of great beauty,
and spoke in a courtly manner:
"King, clear your chambers,
have them hung with silk
where my lady may dismount;
she wishes to take shelter with you."
He promised it willingly

and called two knights
to guide them up to the chambers.
On that subject no more was said.
The king asked his barons
for their judgment and decision;
he said they had angered him very much
with their long delay.
"Sire," they said, "we have decided.
Because of the ladies we have just seen
we have made no judgment.
Let us reconvene the trial."
Then they assembled, everyone was worried;
there was much noise and strife.
While they were in that confusion,
two girls in noble array,
dressed in Phrygian silks
and riding Spanish mules,
were seen coming down the street.
This gave the vassals great joy;
to each other they said that now
Lanval, the brave and bold, was saved.
Gawain went up to him,
bringing his companions along.
"Sire," he said, "take heart.
For the love of God, speak to us.
Here come two maidens,
well adorned and very beautiful;
one must certainly be your love."
Lanval answered quickly
that he did not recognize them,
he didn't know them or love them.
Meanwhile they'd arrived,
and dismounted before the king.
Most of those who saw them praised them
for their bodies, their faces, their coloring;
each was more impressive
than the queen had ever been.
The older one was courtly and wise,
she spoke her message fittingly:
"King, have chambers prepared for us
to lodge my lady according to her need;
she is coming here to speak with you."
He ordered them to be taken
to the others who had preceded them.
There was no problem with the mules.
When he had seen to the girls,
he summoned all his barons
to render their judgment;

it had already dragged out too much.
The queen was getting angry
because she had fasted so long.
They were about to give their judgment
when through the city came riding
a girl on horseback:
there was none more beautiful in the world.
She rode a white palfrey,
who carried her handsomely and smoothly:
he was well apportioned in the neck and head,
no finer beast in the world.
The palfrey's trappings were rich;
under heaven there was no count or king
who could have afforded them all
without selling or mortgaging lands.
She was dressed in this fashion:
in a white linen shift
that revealed both her sides
since the lacing was along the side.
Her body was elegant, her hips slim,
her neck whiter than snow on a branch,
her eyes bright, her face white,
a beautiful mouth, a well-set nose,
dark eyebrows and an elegant forehead,
her hair curly and rather blond;
golden wire does not shine
like her hair in the light.
Her cloak, which she had wrapped around her,
was dark purple.
On her wrist she held a sparrow hawk,
a greyhound followed her.
In the town, no one, small or big,
old man or child,
failed to come look.
As they watched her pass,
there was no joking about her beauty.
She proceeded at a slow pace.
The judges who saw her
marveled at the sight;
no one who looked at her
was not warmed with joy.
Those who loved the knight
came to him and told him
of the girl who was approaching,
if God pleased, to rescue him.
"Sir companion, here comes one
neither tawny nor dark;
this is, of all who exist,

the most beautiful woman in the world."
Lanval heard them and lifted his head;
he recognized her and sighed.
The blood rose to his face;
he was quick to speak.
"By my faith," he said, "that is my love.
Now I don't care if I am killed,
if only she forgives me.
For I am restored, now that I see her."
The lady entered the palace;
no one so beautiful had ever been there.
She dismounted before the king
so that she was well seen by all.
And she let her cloak fall
so they could see her better.
The king, who was well bred,
rose and went to meet her;
all the others honored her
and offered to serve her.
When they had looked at her well,
when they had greatly praised her beauty,
she spoke in this way,
she didn't want to wait:
"I have loved one of your vassals:
you see him before you—Lanval.
He has been accused in your court—
I don't want him to suffer
for what he said; you should know
that the queen was in the wrong.
He never made advances to her.
And for the boast that he made,
if he can be acquitted through me,
let him be set free by your barons."
Whatever the barons judged by law
the king promised would prevail.
To the last man they agreed
that Lanval had successfully answered the charge.
He was set free by their decision
and the girl departed.
The king could not detain her,
though there were enough people to serve her.
Outside the hall stood
a great stone of dark marble
where heavy men mounted
when they left the king's court;
Lanval climbed on it.
When the girl came through the gate
Lanval leapt, in one bound,
onto the palfrey, behind her.

With her he went to Avalun,[9]
so the Bretons tell us,
to a very beautiful island;
there the youth was carried off.
No man heard of him again,
and I have no more to tell.

Chevrefoil (The Honeysuckle)

I should like very much
to tell you the truth
about the *lai* men call *Chevrefoil*—
why it was composed and where it came from.
Many have told and recited it to me
and I have found it in writing,
about Tristan and the queen
and their love that was so true,
that brought them much suffering
and caused them to die the same day.
King Mark was annoyed,
angry at his nephew Tristan;
he exiled Tristan from his land
because of the queen whom he loved.
Tristan returned to his own country,
South Wales, where he was born,
he stayed a whole year;
he couldn't come back.
Afterward he began to expose himself
to death and destruction.
Don't be surprised at this:
for one who loves very faithfully
is sad and troubled
when he cannot satisfy his desires.
Tristan was sad and worried,
so he set out from his land.
He traveled straight to Cornwall,
where the queen lived,
and entered the forest all alone—
he didn't want anyone to see him;
he came out only in the evening
when it was time to find shelter.
He took lodging that night,
with peasants, poor people.
He asked them for news
of the king—what he was doing.

9. Avalon is the mysterious island to which Arthur is also carried, mortally wounded, after his final battle. Marie's contemporary Gerald of Wales expresses far older associations of Avalon with powerful women (see pages 195–96).

They told him they had heard
that the barons had been summoned by ban.[1]
They were to come to Tintagel[2]
where the king wanted to hold his court,
at Pentecost they would all be there,
there'd be much joy and pleasure,
and the queen would be there too.
Tristan heard and was very happy;
she would not be able to go there
without his seeing her pass.
The day the king set out,
Tristan also came to the woods
by the road he knew
their assembly must take.
He cut a hazel tree in half,
then he squared it.
When he had prepared the wood,
he wrote his name on it with his knife.
If the queen noticed it—
and she should be on the watch for it,
for it had happened before
and she had noticed it then—
she'd know when she saw it,
that the piece of wood had come from her love.
This was the message of the writing[3]
that he had sent to her:
he had been there a long time,
had waited and remained
to find out and to discover
how he could see her,
for he could not live without her.
With the two of them it was just
as it is with the honeysuckle
that attaches itself to the hazel tree:
when it has wound and attached
and worked itself around the trunk,
the two can survive together;
but if someone tries to separate them,
the hazel dies quickly
and the honeysuckle with it.
"Sweet love, so it is with us:
You cannot live without me, nor I without you."
The queen rode along;
she looked at the hillside
and saw the piece of wood; she knew what it was,

1. A royal summons to feudal service.
2. One of Mark's castles, on the north coast of Cornwall. In Arthurian legend, it is the site of Arthur's conception.
3. From Tristan's name alone, or possibly a few words in code or runic letters, Isolt can elicit the entire message that follows.

she recognized all the letters.
The knights who were accompanying her,
who were riding with her,
she ordered to stop:
she wanted to dismount and rest.
They obeyed her command.
She went far away from her people
and called her girl
Brenguein,[4] who was loyal to her.
She went a short distance from the road;
and in the woods she found him
whom she loved more than any living thing.
They took great joy in each other.
He spoke to her as much as he desired,
she told him whatever she liked.
Then she assured him
that he would be reconciled with the king—
for it weighed on him
that he had sent Tristan away;
he'd done it because of the accusation.[5]
Then she departed, she left her love,
but when it came to the separation,
they began to weep.
Tristan went to Wales,
to wait until his uncle sent for him.
For the joy that he'd felt
from his love when he saw her,
by means of the stick he inscribed
as the queen had instructed,
and in order to remember the words,
Tristan, who played the harp well,
composed a new *lai* about it.
I shall name it briefly:
in English they call it *Goat's Leaf*
the French call it *Chevrefoil*.
I have given you the truth
about the *lai* that I have told here.

Sir Gawain and the Green Knight

As a subject of literary romance, Arthurian tradition never had the centrality in later medieval England it had gained in France. It was only one of a wide range of popular topics like Havelok the Dane, King Horn, and the Troy story. Nevertheless Arthur and his court played

4. Isolt's maid, who earlier substituted herself for Isolt in the marriage bed with King Mark.

5. Envious courtiers had plotted to expose the lovers' affair to the king.

an ongoing role in English society, written into histories and emulated by aristocrats and kings. And in the later fourteenth or early fifteenth century, several very distinguished Arthurian poems appeared, such as the alliterative *Morte Arthure* and the *Awntyrs* (Adventures) *off Arthure*.

Sir Gawain and the Green Knight is the greatest of the Arthurian romances produced in England. The poem embraces the highest aspirations of the late medieval aristocratic world, both courtly and religious, even while it eloquently admits the human failings that threaten those values. A knight's troth and word, a Christian's election and covenant, the breaking point of a person's or a society's virtues, all come in for celebration and painful scrutiny during Gawain's adventure.

Like *Beowulf*, *Sir Gawain and the Green Knight* comes down to us by the thread of a single copy. Its manuscript contains a group of poems (*Sir Gawain*, *Pearl*, *Purity*, and *Patience*) that mark their anonymous author as a poet whose range approaches that of his contemporary Chaucer, and whose formal craft is in some ways more ambitious than Chaucer's.

Gawain is the work of a highly sophisticated provincial court poet (likely in the northwest Midlands), working in a form and narrative tradition that is conservative in comparison with Chaucer's. The poet uses the alliterative long line, a meter with its roots in Anglo-Saxon poetry; the unrhymed alliterative stanzas, of irregular length, each end with five shorter rhymed lines often called a "bob-and-wheel" stanza. (For a further discussion of the alliterative style, see the introduction to William Langland, page 444.) Within these traditional constraints, however, the poem achieves an apex of medieval courtly literature, as a superlatively crafted and stylized version of quest romance.

The romance never aims to detach itself from society or history, though. It opens and closes by referring to Troy, the ancient, fallen empire whose survivors were legendary founders of Britain, a connection well known through Geoffrey of Monmouth. Arthur, their ultimate heir, went on later in his myth to pursue imperial ambitions that, like those of Troy, were foiled by adulterous desire and political infidelity. *Sir Gawain* also echoes its contemporary world in the technical language of architecture, crafts, and arms. This helps draw in the kind of conservative, aristocratic court for which the poem seems to have been written, probably in Cheshire or Lancashire, a somewhat backward region whose nobles remained loyal to Richard II. Along with the pleasure it takes in fine armor and courtly ritual, the poem seems to enfold anxieties about the economic pressures of maintaining chivalric display in a period of costly new technology, inflation, and declining income from land.

By the time this poem was written, toward the close of the fourteenth century, Gawain was a famous Arthurian hero. His reputation was ambiguous, though; he was both Arthur's faithful retainer and nephew, but also a suave seducer. Which side of Gawain would dominate in this particular poem? Would he stand for a civilization of Christian chivalry or one of cynical sophistication?

The test that begins to answer this question occurs during Arthur's ritual celebrations of Christmas and the New Year, and within the civilized practices of Eucharist and secular feast. A gigantic green knight interrupts Arthur's banquet to offer a deadly game of exchanged ax-blows, to be resolved in one year's time. Although the Green Knight, with his ball of holly leaves, seems at first to come from the tradition of the Wild Man—a giant force of nature itself—he is also a sophisticated knight, gorgeously attired. He knows, too, just how to taunt a young king without quite overstepping the bounds of courtly behavior. Gawain takes up the challenge, but a still greater marvel ensues.

As the term of the agreement approaches, Gawain rides off, elaborately armed, to find the Green Knight and fulfill his obligation, even if that means his death. What Gawain encounters first, though, are temptations of character and sexuality even trickier and more crucial than they at first seem.

Sir Gawain and the Green Knight is remarkable not only for the intricacy of its plot but also for the virtuosity of its descriptions, such as the almost elegiac review of the passing seasons ("So the year in passing yields its many yesterdays"). The poem rejoices in the masterful exercise of skill as the mark of civilization. Beautifully crafted knots appear everywhere, and we encounter artisanal craft as well in narrative elements like the Green Knight's dress (a dazzling mixture of leafy green and jeweler's gold), Gawain's decorated shield and arms, and the expertise of the master of the hunt who carves up the prey of Gawain's host with ritual precision. Even Gawain's exquisite courtly manners appear as a civilizing artifice.

The ambition of the poem's own craft is equally evident in its extraordinary range of formal devices. Preeminent among these is the symbolic register of number. The poem can be seen as a single unit, circling back to the Trojan scene with which it begins. It has a double structure, too, as it shifts between the courts of Arthur and Gawain's mysterious host. In the manuscript it is divided into four parts ("fits") that respond to the seasonal description at the opening of Part 2. In the original text, the narrative proper ends by echoing the very start of the poem, at line 2525 (in the original Middle English), itself a multiple of fives that recalls the pentangle on Gawain's shield symbolizing his virtues. The final rhyming stanza, with its formula of grace and salvation, brings the line total to 2530, whose individual digits add up to ten, a number associated with the divine in medieval numerology.

This symbolic structure can seem sometimes overdetermined. A range of elements, however, invites the reader to come at the poem from other perspectives. The poem's very circularity, narrative and formal, allows it to be viewed from beginning or ending. From the front it is a poem of male accomplishment, largely celebrating *men's* courts and *men's* virtues (even men's horses). At the other end, however, it focuses on a court presided over by an old woman (later called a goddess), a court whose irruption into the Arthurian world is explained as the playing out of an old and mysterious rivalry between two queens. Male, even patriarchal from one direction, the poem seems matriarchal, almost pagan, from the other. For all its formal cohesion and celebration of craft, the poem also pulls the reader back and keeps its mysteries intact by leaving many narrative loose ends and unanswered questions.

Unresolvable ambiguities reside most clearly in the pentangle on Gawain's shield and in the "green girdle" whose true owner remains uncertain. For all their differences, both are figures that insist on repetition, end where they begin, and possess a geometry that can be traced forward or backward. Yet the static perfection of the pentangle is subtly set against the protean green girdle, which passes through so many hands, alters its shape (being untied and retied repeatedly), and connects with so many issues in the poem: mortality, women's power, Gawain's fault and the acceptance of that fault by the whole Arthurian court. The girdle becomes an image both of flaw and triumph and of all the loose ends in this early episode of the Arthurian myth.

The girdle also serves to link *Sir Gawain* to political and social issues of the poet's own time, particularly efforts to revalidate a declining system of chivalry. After the last line in the manuscript, a later medieval hand has added "Hony Soyt Qui Mal Pence" ("shamed be he who thinks ill thereof"), the motto of the royal Order of the Garter, founded by Edward III in 1349 to promote a revival of knighthood. The Arthurian myth had already been redeployed to buttress royal power when Edward III refounded a Round Table in 1344. King Arthur's wisdom at the close of Gawain's adventure lies in transforming Gawain's shame, rage, and humiliated sense of sin into an emblem at once of mortal humanity and aristocratic cohesion. This is the place—back with the king and ritually connected with the Order of the Garter—where the closed circle of the poem opens to the social, historical world of empire, court, and kingship.

Sir Gawain and the Green Knight[1]

Part 1

The siege and the assault being ceased at Troy,
The battlements broken down and burnt to brands and ashes,
The treacherous trickster whose treasons there flourished
Was famed for his falsehood, the foulest on earth.
Aeneas[2] the noble and his knightly kin
Then conquered kingdoms, and kept in their hand
Wellnigh all the wealth of the western lands.[3]
Royal Romulus to Rome first turned,
Set up the city in splendid pomp,
Then named her with his own name, which now she still has:
Ticius[4] founded Tuscany, townships raising,
Longbeard[5] in Lombardy lifted up homes,
And far over the French flood Felix Brutus
On many spacious slopes set Britain with joy
    And grace;
  Where war and feud and wonder
  Have ruled the realm a space,
  And after, bliss and blunder
  By turns have run their race.

And when this Britain was built by this brave noble,[6]
Here bold men bred, in battle exulting,
Stirrers of trouble in turbulent times.
Here many a marvel, more than in other lands,
Has befallen by fortune since that far time.
But of all who abode here of Britain's kings,
Arthur was highest in honor, as I have heard;
So I intend to tell you of a true wonder,
Which many folk mention as a manifest marvel,
A happening eminent among Arthur's adventures.
Listen to my lay but a little while:
Straightway shall I speak it, in city as I heard it,
    With tongue;
  As scribes have set it duly
  In the lore of the land so long,
  With letters linking truly
  In story bold and strong.

This king lay at Camelot[7] one Christmastide
With many mighty lords, manly liegemen,

1. This translation, remarkably faithful to the original alliterative meter and stanza form, is by Brian Stone.
2. Aeneas led the survivors of Troy to Italy, after a series of ambiguous omens and misadventures. In medieval tradition, he was also said to have plotted to betray his own city. The "treacherous trickster" in line 3, though, may refer to the Trojan Antenor, also said to have betrayed Troy.
3. Perhaps Europe, or just the British Isles. Many royal houses traced their ancestry to Rome and Troy.
4. Possibly Titus Tatius, ancient king of the Sabines.
5. Ancestor of the Lombards, and a nephew of Brutus.
6. According to Geoffrey of Monmouth and others, a great-grandson of Aeneas, exiled after accidentally killing his father, then, later founder of Britain.
7. Arthur's capital, probably in Wales, perhaps at Caerleon-on-Usk where Arthur had been crowned. Knights were expected to gather at his court, in celebration and homage, on the five liturgical holidays on which Arthur wore his crown: Easter, Ascension, Pentecost, All Saints' Day, and Christmas.

Members rightly reckoned of the Round Table,[8]
In splendid celebration, seemly and carefree.
There tussling in tournament time and again
Jousted in jollity these gentle knights,
Then in court carnival sang catches and danced;
For fifteen days the feasting there was full in like measure
With all the meat and merry-making men could devise,
Gladly ringing glee, glorious to hear,
A noble din by day, dancing at night!
All was happiness in the height in halls and chambers
For lords and their ladies, delectable joy.
With all delights on earth they housed there together,
Saving Christ's self, the most celebrated knights,
The loveliest ladies to live in all time,
And the comeliest king ever to keep court.
For this fine fellowship was in its fair prime[9]
Far famed,
Stood well in heaven's will,
Its high-souled king acclaimed:
So hardy a host on hill
Could not with ease be named.

The year being so young that yester-even saw its birth,
That day double on the dais were the diners served.
Mass sung and service ended, straight from the chapel
The King and his company came into hall.
Called on with cries from clergy and laity,
Noël was newly announced, named time and again.
Then lords and ladies leaped forth, largesse distributing,
Offered New Year gifts in high voices, handed them out,
Bustling and bantering about these offerings.
Ladies laughed full loudly, though losing their wealth,
And he that won was not woeful, you may well believe.[1]
All this merriment they made until meal time.
Then in progress to their places they passed after washing,
In authorized order, the high-ranking first;
With glorious Guinevere, gay in the midst,
On the princely platform[2] with its precious hangings
Of splendid silk at the sides, a state over her
Of rich tapestry of Toulouse and Turkestan
Brilliantly embroidered with the best gems
Of warranted worth that wealth at any time
Could buy.
Fairest of form was this queen,

8. Its shape symbolized the unity of Arthur's knights but also avoided disputes over precedence.
9. Arthur is emphatically a young king here. The phrase may also recall the Golden Age, an era of uncorrupted happiness.
1. The distribution of gifts on New Year's Day displayed the king's wealth and power; it was also the occasion here of some courtly game of exchange, in which the loser perhaps gave up a kiss.
2. A medieval nobleman's hall typically had a raised dais at one end, on which the "high table" stood.

Glinting and gray of eye;
No man could say he had seen
A lovelier, but with a lie.

But Arthur would not eat until all were served.
He was charming and cheerful, child-like and gay,
And loving active life, little did he favor
Lying down for long or lolling on a seat,
So robust his young blood and his beating brain.
Still, he was stirred now by something else:
His noble announcement that he never would eat
On such a fair feast-day till informed in full
Of some unusual adventure, as yet untold,
Of some momentous marvel that he might believe,
About ancestors, or arms, or other high theme;
Or till a stranger should seek out a strong knight of his,
To join with him in jousting, in jeopardy to lay
Life against life, each allowing the other
The favor of Fortune, the fairer lot.
Such was the King's custom when he kept court,
At every fine feast among his free retinue
In hall.
So he throve amid the throng,
A ruler royal and tall,
Still standing staunch and strong,
And young like the year withal.

Erect stood the strong King, stately of mien,
Trifling time with talk before the topmost table.
Good Gawain was placed at Guinevere's side,
And Agravain of the Hard Hand sat on the other side,
Both the King's sister's sons, staunchest of knights.
Above, Bishop Baldwin began the board,
And Ywain,[3] Urien's son ate next to him.
These were disposed on the dais and with dignity served,
And many mighty men next, marshaled at side tables.
Then the first course came in with such cracking of trumpets,
(Whence bright bedecked blazons in banners hung)
Such din of drumming and a deal of fine piping,
Such wild warbles whelming and echoing
That hearts were uplifted high at the strains.[4]
Then delicacies and dainties were delivered to the guests,
Fresh food in foison, such freight of full dishes
That space was scarce at the social tables
For the several soups set before them in silver

3. Another nephew of Arthur. The relationship of uncle and nephew is close in many Arthurian romances, and noble youths were often sent to be raised by an uncle on the mother's side.

4. Holiday banquets were formalized, almost theatrical.

On the cloth.
Each feaster made free with the fare,
Took lightly and nothing loth;
Twelve plates were for every pair,
Good beer and bright wine both.

Of their meal I shall mention no more just now,
For it is evident to all that ample was served;
Now another noise, quite new, neared suddenly,
Likely to allow the liege lord to eat;
For barely had the blast of trump abated one minute
And the first course in the court been courteously served,
When there heaved in at the hall door an awesome fellow
Who in height outstripped all earthly men.
From throat to thigh he was so thickset and square,
His loins and limbs were so long and so great,
That he was half a giant on earth, I believe;
Yet mainly and most of all a man he seemed,
And the handsomest of horsemen, though huge, at that;
For though at back and at breast his body was broad,
His hips and haunches were elegant and small,
And perfectly proportioned were all parts of the man,
As seen.
Men gaped at the hue of him
Ingrained in garb and mien,
A fellow fiercely grim,
And all a glittering green.

And garments of green girt the fellow about—
A two-third length tunic, tight at the waist,
A comely cloak on top, accomplished with lining
Of the finest fur to be found, made of one piece,
Marvelous fur-trimmed material, with matching hood
Lying back from his locks and laid on his shoulders;
Fitly held-up hose, in hue the same green,
That was caught at the calf, with clinking spurs beneath
Of bright gold on bases of embroidered silk,
But no iron shoe armored that horseman's feet.
And verily his vesture was all vivid green,
So were the bars on his belt and the brilliants set
In ravishing array on the rich accoutrements
About himself and his saddle on silken work.
It would be tedious to tell a tithe of the trifles
Embossed and embroidered, such as birds and flies,
In gay green gauds, with gold everywhere.
The breast-hangings of the horse, its haughty crupper,
The enameled knobs and nails on its bridle,
And the stirrups that he stood on, were all stained with the same;
So were the splendid saddle-skirts and bows
That ever glimmered and glinted with their green stones.

The steed that he spurred on was similar in hue
    To the sight,
  Green and huge of grain,
  Mettlesome in might
  And brusque with bit and rein—
  A steed to serve that knight!

Yes, garbed all in green was the gallant rider,
And the hair of his head was the same hue as his horse,
And floated finely like a fan round his shoulders;
And a great bushy beard on his breast flowing down,
With the heavy hair hanging from his head,
Was shorn below the shoulder, sheared right round,
So that half his arms were under the encircling hair,
Covered as by a king's cape, that closes at the neck.
The mane of that mighty horse, much like the beard,
Well crisped and combed, was copiously plaited
With twists of twining gold, twinkling in the green,
First a green gossamer, a golden one next.
His flowing tail and forelock followed suit,
And both were bound with bands of bright green,
Ornamented to the end with exquisite stones,
While a thong running through them threaded on high
Many bright golden bells, burnished and ringing.
Such a horse, such a horseman, in the whole wide world
Was never seen or observed by those assembled before,
    Not one.
  Lightning-like he seemed
  And swift to strike and stun.
  His dreadful blows, men deemed,
  Once dealt, meant death was done.

Yet hauberk[5] and helmet had he none,
Nor plastron[6] nor plate-armor proper to combat,
Nor shield for shoving, nor sharp spear for lunging;
But he held a holly cluster in one hand, holly
That is greenest when groves are gaunt and bare,
And an axe in his other hand, huge and monstrous,
A hideous helmet-smasher for anyone to tell of;
The head of that axe was an ell-rod long.
Of green hammered gold and steel was the socket,
And the blade was burnished bright, with a broad edge,
Acutely honed for cutting, as keenest razors are.
The grim man gripped it by its great strong handle,
Which was wound with iron all the way to the end,
And graven in green with graceful designs.
A cord curved round it, was caught at the head,

5. A tunic of chain mail.

6. A piece of armor to protect the upper part of the chest and neck.

Then hitched to the haft at intervals in loops,
With costly tassels attached thereto in plenty
On bosses of bright green embroidered richly.
In he rode, and up the hall, this man,
Driving towards the high dais, dreading no danger.
He gave no one a greeting, but glared over all.
His opening utterance was, "Who and where
Is the governor of this gathering? Gladly would I
Behold him with my eyes and have speech with him."
He frowned;
Took note of every knight
As he ramped and rode around;
Then stopped to study who might
Be the noble most renowned.

The assembled folk stared, long scanning the fellow,
For all men marveled what it might mean
That a horseman and his horse should have such a color
As to grow green as grass, and greener yet, it seemed,
More gaudily glowing than green enamel on gold.
Those standing studied him and sidled towards him
With all the world's wonder as to what he would do.
For astonishing sights they had seen, but such a one never;
Therefore a phantom from Fairyland the folk there deemed him.
So even the doughty were daunted and dared not reply,
All sitting stock-still, astounded by his voice.
Throughout the high hall was a hush like death;
Suddenly as if all had slipped into sleep, their voices were
At rest;
Hushed not wholly for fear,
But some at honor's behest;
But let him whom all revere
Greet that gruesome guest.

For Arthur sensed an exploit before the high dais,
And accorded him courteous greeting, no craven he,
Saying to him, "Sir knight, you are certainly welcome.
I am head of this house: Arthur is my name.
Please deign to dismount and dwell with us
Till you impart your purpose, at a proper time."
"May he that sits in heaven help me," said the knight,
"But my intention was not to tarry in this turreted hall.
But as your reputation, royal sir, is raised up so high,
And your castle and cavaliers are accounted the best,
The mightiest of mail-clad men in mounted fighting,
The most warlike, the worthiest the world has bred,
Most valiant to vie with in virile contests,
And as chivalry is shown here, so I am assured,
At this time, I tell you, that has attracted me here.
By this branch that I bear, you may be certain

That I proceed in peace, no peril seeking;[7]
For had I fared forth in fighting gear,
My hauberk and helmet, both at home now,
My shield and sharp spear, all shining bright,
And other weapons to wield, I would have brought;
However, as I wish for no war here, I wear soft clothes.
But if you are as bold as brave men affirm,
You will gladly grant me the good sport I demand
By right."
Then Arthur answer gave:
"If you, most noble knight,
Unarmored combat crave,
We'll fail you not in fight."

"No, it is not combat I crave, for come to that,
On this bench only beardless boys are sitting.
If I were hasped in armor on a high steed,
No man among you could match me, your might being meager.
So I crave in this court a Christmas game,
For it is Yuletide and New Year, and young men abound here.
If any in this household is so hardy in spirit,
Of such mettlesome mind and so madly rash
As to strike a strong blow in return for another,
I shall offer to him this fine axe freely;
This axe, which is heavy enough, to handle as he please.
And I shall bide the first blow, as bare as I sit here.
If some intrepid man is tempted to try what I suggest,
Let him leap towards me and lay hold of this weapon,
Acquiring clear possession of it, no claim from me ensuing.
Then shall I stand up to his stroke, quite still on this floor—
So long as I shall have leave to launch a return blow
Unchecked.
Yet he shall have a year
And a day's reprieve, I direct.
Now hasten and let me hear
Who answers, to what effect."

If he had astonished them at the start, yet stiller now
Were the henchmen in hall, both high and low.
The rider wrenched himself round in his saddle
And rolled his red eyes about roughly and strangely,
Bending his brows, bristling and bright, on all,
His beard swaying as he strained to see who would rise.
When none came to accord with him, he coughed aloud,
Then pulled himself up proudly, and spoke as follows:
"What, is this Arthur's house, the honor of which
Is bruited abroad so abundantly?

7. A holly branch could symbolize peace and was used in games of the Christmas season.

Has your pride disappeared? Your prowess gone?
Your victories, your valor, your vaunts, where are they?
The revel and renown of the Round Table
Is now overwhelmed by a word from one man's voice,
For all flinch for fear from a fight not begun!"
Upon this, he laughed so loudly that the lord grieved.
His fair features filled with blood
 For shame.
 He raged as roaring gale;
 His followers felt the same.
 The King, not one to quail,
 To that cavalier then came.

"By heaven," then said Arthur, "What you ask is foolish,
But as you firmly seek folly, find it you shall.
No good man here is aghast at your great words.
Hand me your axe now, for heaven's sake,
And I shall bestow the boon you bid us give."
He sprang towards him swiftly, seized it from his hand,
And fiercely the other fellow footed the floor.
Now Arthur had his axe, and holding it by the haft
Swung it about sternly, as if to strike with it.
The strong man stood before him, stretched to his full height,
Higher than any in the hall by a head and more.
Stern of face he stood there, stroking his beard,
Turning down his tunic in a tranquil manner,
Less unmanned and dismayed by the mighty strokes,
Than if a banqueter at the bench had brought him a drink
 Of wine.
 Then Gawain at Guinevere's side
 Bowed and spoke his design:
 "Before all, King, confide
 This fight to me. May it be mine."

"If you would, worthy lord," said Gawain to the King,
"Bid me stir from this seat and stand beside you,
Allowing me without lese-majesty to leave the table,
And if my liege lady were not displeased thereby,
I should come there to counsel you before this court of nobles.
For it appears unmeet to me, as manners go,
When your hall hears uttered such a haughty request,
Though you gladly agree, for you to grant it yourself,
When on the benches about you many such bold men sit,
Under heaven, I hold, the highest-mettled,
There being no braver knights when battle is joined.
I am the weakest, the most wanting in wisdom, I know,
And my life, if lost, would be least missed, truly.
Only through your being my uncle, am I to be valued;
No bounty but your blood in my body do I know.
And since this affair is too foolish to fall to you,

And I first asked it of you, make it over to me;
And if I fail to speak fittingly, let this full court judge
    Without blame."
  Then wisely they whispered of it,
  And after, all said the same:
  That the crowned King should be quit,
  And Gawain given the game.

Then the King commanded the courtly knight to rise.
He directly uprose, approached courteously,
Knelt low to his liege lord, laid hold of the weapon;
And he graciously let him have it, lifted up his hand
And gave him God's blessing, gladly urging him
To be strong in spirit and stout of sinew.
"Cousin, take care," said the King, "To chop once,
And if you strike with success, certainly I think
You will take the return blow without trouble in time."
Gripping the great axe, Gawain goes to the man
Who awaits him unwavering, not quailing at all.
Then said to Sir Gawain the stout knight in green,
"Let us affirm our pact freshly, before going farther.
I beg you, bold sir, to be so good
As to tell me your true name, as I trust you to."
"In good faith," said the good knight, "Gawain is my name,
And whatever happens after, I offer you this blow,
And in twelve months' time I shall take the return blow
With whatever weapon you wish, and with no one else
    Shall I strive."
  The other with pledge replied,
  "I'm the merriest man alive
  It's a blow from you I must bide,
  Sir Gawain, so may I thrive."

"By God," said the Green Knight, "Sir Gawain, I rejoice
That I shall have from your hand what I have asked for here.
And you have gladly gone over, in good discourse,
The covenant I requested of the King in full,
Except that you shall assent, swearing in truth,
To seek me yourself, in such place as you think
To find me under the firmament, and fetch your payment
For what you deal me today before this dignified gathering."
"How shall I hunt for you? How find your home?"
Said Gawain, "By God that made me, I go in ignorance;
Nor, knight, do I know your name or your court.
But instruct me truly thereof, and tell me your name,
And I shall wear out my wits to find my way there;
Here is my oath on it, in absolute honor!"
"That is enough this New Year, no more is needed,"
Said the gallant in green to Gawain the courteous,

"To tell you the truth, when I have taken the blow
After you have duly dealt it, I shall directly inform you
About my house and my home and my own name.
Then you may keep your covenant, and call on me,
And if I waft you no words, then well may you prosper,
Stay long in your own land and look for no further
Trial.
Now grip your weapon grim;
Let us see your fighting style."
"Gladly," said Gawain to him,
Stroking the steel the while.

On the ground the Green Knight graciously stood,
With head slightly slanting to expose the flesh.
His long and lovely locks he laid over his crown,
Baring the naked neck for the business now due.
Gawain gripped his axe and gathered it on high,
Advanced the left foot before him on the ground,
And slashed swiftly down on the exposed part,
So that the sharp blade sheared through, shattering the bones,
Sank deep in the sleek flesh, split it in two,
And the scintillating steel struck the ground.
The fair head fell from the neck, struck the floor,
And people spurned it as it rolled around.
Blood spurted from the body, bright against the green.
Yet the fellow did not fall, nor falter one whit,
But stoutly sprang forward on legs still sturdy,
Roughly reached out among the ranks of nobles,
Seized his splendid head and straightway lifted it.
Then he strode to his steed, snatched the bridle,
Stepped into the stirrup and swung aloft,
Holding his head in his hand by the hair.
He settled himself in the saddle as steadily
As if nothing had happened to him, though he had
No head.
He twisted his trunk about,
That gruesome body that bled;
He caused much dread and doubt
By the time his say was said.

For he held the head in his hand upright,
Pointed the face at the fairest in fame on the dais;
And it lifted its eyelids and looked glaringly,
And menacingly said with its mouth as you may now hear:
"Be prepared to perform what you promised, Gawain;
Seek faithfully till you find me, my fine fellow,
According to your oath in this hall in these knights' hearing.
Go to the Green Chapel without gainsaying to get
Such a stroke as you have struck. Strictly you deserve

That due redemption on the day of New Year.
As the Knight of the Green Chapel I am known to many;
Therefore if you ask for me, I shall be found.
So come, or else be called coward accordingly!"
Then he savagely swerved, sawing at the reins,
Rushed out at the hall door, his head in his hand,
And the flint-struck fire flew up from the hooves.
What place he departed to no person there knew,
Nor could any account be given of the country he had come from.
        What then?
    At the Green Knight Gawain and King
    Grinned and laughed again;
    But plainly approved the thing
    As a marvel in the world of men.

Though honored King Arthur was at heart astounded,
He let no sign of it be seen, but said clearly
To the comely queen in courtly speech,
"Do not be dismayed, dear lady, today:
Such cleverness comes well at Christmastide,
Like the playing of interludes,[8] laughter and song,
As lords and ladies delight in courtly carols.
However, I am now able to eat the repast,
Having seen, I must say, a sight to wonder at."
He glanced at Sir Gawain, and gracefully said,
"Now sir, hang up your axe:[9] you have hewn enough."
And on the backcloth above the dais it was boldly hung
Where all men might mark it and marvel at it
And with truthful testimony tell the wonder of it.
Then to the table the two went together,
The King and the constant knight, and keen men served them
Double portions of each dainty with all due dignity,
All manner of meat, and minstrelsy too.
Daylong they delighted till darkness came
        To their shores.
    Now Gawain give a thought,
    Lest peril make you pause
    In seeking out the sport
    That you have claimed as yours.

Part 2

Such earnest of noble action had Arthur at New Year,
For he was avid to hear exploits vaunted.
Though starved of such speeches when seated at first,
Now had they high matter indeed, their hands full of it.

8. Brief performances between the courses of the banquet.

9. A literal suggestion, but also an invitation to put the matter aside.

Gawain was glad to begin the games in hall,
But though the end be heavy, have no wonder,
For if men are spritely in spirit after strong drink,
Soon the year slides past, never the same twice;
There is no foretelling its fulfilment from the start.
Yes, this Yuletide passed and the year following;
Season after season in succession went by.[1]
After Christmas comes the crabbed Lenten time,
Which forces on the flesh fish and food yet plainer.
Then weather more vernal wars with the wintry world,
The cold ebbs and declines, the clouds lift,
In shining showers the rain sheds warmth
And falls upon the fair plain, where flowers appear;
The grassy lawns and groves alike are garbed in green;
Birds prepare to build, and brightly sing
The solace of the ensuing summer that soothes hill
And dell.
By hedgerows rank and rich
The blossoms bloom and swell,
And sounds of sweetest pitch
From lovely woodlands well.

Then comes the season of summer with soft winds,
When Zephyrus himself breathes on seeds and herbs.
In paradise is the plant that springs in the open
When the dripping dew drops from its leaves,
And it bears the blissful gleam of the bright sun.
Then Harvest comes hurrying, urging it on,
Warning it because of winter to wax ripe soon;
He drives the dust to rise with the drought he brings,
Forcing it to fly up from the face of the earth.
Wrathful winds in raging skies wrestle with the sun;
Leaves are lashed loose from the trees and lie on the ground
And the grass becomes gray which was green before.
What rose from root at first now ripens and rots;
So the year in passing yields its many yesterdays,
And winter returns, as the way of the world is,
I swear;
So came the Michaelmas moon;[2]
With winter threatening there,
And Gawain considered soon
The fell way he must fare.

Yet he stayed in hall with Arthur till All Saints' Day,[3]
When Arthur provided plentifully, especially for Gawain,
A rich feast and high revelry at the Round Table.

1. This famous passage on the cycle of seasons draws both on Germanic conventions of the battle of Winter and Summer, and on Romance spring-time lyrics, the reverdies.

2. The harvest moon at Michaelmas, on September 29.

3. On November 1, another holiday on which Arthur presided, crowned, over his court.

The gallant lords and gay ladies grieved for Gawain,
Anxious on his account; but all the same
They mentioned only matters of mirthful import,
Joylessly joking for that gentle knight's sake.
For after dinner with drooping heart he addressed his uncle
And spoke plainly of his departure, putting it thus:
"Now, liege lord of my life, I beg my leave of you.
You know the kind of covenant it is: I care little
To tell over the trials of it, trifling as they are,
But I am bound to bear the blow and must be gone tomorrow
To seek the gallant in green, as God sees fit to guide me."
Then the most courtly in that company came together,[4]
Ywain and Eric and others in troops,
Sir Dodinal the Fierce, The Duke of Clarence,
Lancelot and Lionel and Lucan the Good,
Sir Bors and Sir Bedivere, both strong men,
And many admired knights, with Mador of the Gate.
All the company of the court came near to the King
With carking care in their hearts, to counsel the knight.
Much searing sorrow was suffered in the hall
That such a gallant man as Gawain should go in quest
To suffer a savage blow, and his sword no more
Should bear.
Said Gawain, gay of cheer,
"Whether fate be foul or fair,
Why falter I or fear?
What should man do but dare?"

He dwelt there all that day, and at dawn on the morrow
Asked for his armor. Every item was brought.
First a crimson carpet was cast over the floor
And the great pile of gilded war-gear glittered upon it.
The strong man stepped on it, took the steel in hand.
The doublet he dressed in was dear Turkestan stuff;
Then came the courtly cape, cut with skill,
Finely lined with fur, and fastened close.
Then they set the steel shoes on the strong man's feet,
Lapped his legs in steel with lovely greaves,
Complete with knee-pieces, polished bright
And connecting at the knee with gold-knobbed hinges.
Then came the cuisses, which cunningly enclosed
His thighs thick of thew, and which thongs secured.
Next the hauberk, interlinked with argent steel rings
Which rested on rich material, wrapped the warrior round.
He had polished armor on arms and elbows,
Glinting and gay, and gloves of metal,

4. The list that follows would have recalled, especially to readers of French romances, other great quests and challenges encountered by Arthur's knights. The list's order may also suggest later and more tragic episodes in the Arthurian narrative, ending with Bedivere who throws Excalibur into a mere after Arthur is mortally wounded.

And all the goodly gear to give help whatever
Betide;
With surcoat richly wrought,
Gold spurs attached in pride,
A silken sword-belt athwart,
And steadfast blade at his side.

When he was hasped in armor his harness was noble;
The least lace or loop was lustrous with gold.
So, harnessed as he was, he heard his mass
As it was offered at the high altar in worship.
Then he came to the King and his court-fellows,
Took leave with loving courtesy of lord and lady,
Who commended him to Christ and kissed him farewell.
By now Gringolet had been got ready, and girt with a saddle
That gleamed most gaily with many golden fringes,
Everywhere nailed newly for this noble occasion.
The bridle was embossed and bound with bright gold;
So were the furnishings of the fore-harness and the fine skirts.
The crupper and the caparison[5] accorded with the saddle-bows,
And all was arrayed on red with nails of richest gold,
Which glittered and glanced like gleams of the sun.
Then his casque, equipped with clasps of great strength
And padded inside, he seized and swiftly kissed;
It towered high on his head and was hasped at the back,
With a brilliant silk band over the burnished neck-guard,
Embroidered[6] and bossed with the best gems
On broad silken borders, with birds about the seams,
Such as parrots painted with periwinkles between,
And turtles and true-love-knots traced as thickly
As if many beauties in a bower had been busy seven winters
Thereabout.
The circlet on his head
Was prized more precious no doubt,
And perfectly diamonded,
Threw a gleaming luster out.

Then they showed him the shield of shining gules,
With the Pentangle[7] in pure gold depicted thereon.
He brandished it by the baldric, and about his neck
He slung it in a seemly way, and it suited him well.
And I intend to tell you, though I tarry therefore,
Why the Pentangle is proper to this prince of knights.
It is a symbol which Solomon conceived once
To betoken holy truth, by its intrinsic right,

5. A cloth or covering spread over the saddle or harness of a horse, often ornamented.
6. The technical language of armor is now joined by an equally technical description of needlework, for which English women were famous.
7. A five-pointed star and symbol of perfection and eternity, since it can be drawn with an uninterrupted line ending at the point of the star where it begins. Inscribed within a circle, it was called Solomon's seal.

For it is a figure which has five points,
And each line overlaps and is locked with another;
And it is endless everywhere, and the English call it,
In all the land, I hear, the Endless Knot.
Therefore it goes with Sir Gawain and his gleaming armor,
For, ever faithful in five things, each in fivefold manner,
Gawain was reputed good and, like gold well refined,
He was devoid of all villainy, every virtue displaying
In the field.
Thus this Pentangle new
He carried on coat and shield,
As a man of troth most true
And knightly name annealed.

First he was found faultless in his five wits.
Next, his five fingers never failed the knight,
And all his trust on earth was in the five wounds
Which came to Christ on the Cross, as the Creed tells.
And whenever the bold man was busy on the battlefield,
Through all other things he thought on this,
That his prowess all depended on the five pure Joys
That the holy Queen of Heaven had of her Child.[8]
Accordingly the courteous knight had that queen's image
Etched on the inside of his armored shield,
So that when he beheld her, his heart did not fail.
The fifth five I find the famous man practised
Were—Liberality and Lovingkindness leading the rest;
Then his Continence and Courtesy, which were never corrupted;
And Piety, the surpassing virtue. These pure five
Were more firmly fixed on that fine man
Than on any other, and every multiple,
Each interlocking with another, had no end,
Being fixed to five points which never failed,
Never assembling on one side, nor sundering either,
With no end at any angle; nor can I find
Where the design started or proceeded to its end.
Thus on his shining shield this knot was shaped
Royally in red gold upon red gules.
That is the pure Pentangle, so people who are wise
Are taught.
Now Gawain was ready and gay;
His spear he promptly caught
And gave them all good day
For ever, as he thought.

He struck the steed with his spurs and sprang on his way
So forcefully that the fire flew up from the flinty stones.

8. Poems and meditations on the Virgin's joys and sorrow were widespread. Her five joys were the Annunciation, Nativity, Resurrection, Ascension, and Assumption.

All who saw that seemly sight were sick at heart,
And all said to each other softly, in the same breath,
In care for that comely knight, "By Christ, it is evil
That yon lord should be lost, who lives so nobly!
To find his fellow on earth in faith is not easy.
It would have been wiser to have worked more warily,
And to have dubbed the dear man a duke of the realm.
A magnificent master of men he might have been,
And so had a happier fate than to be utterly destroyed,
Beheaded by an unearthly being out of arrogance.
Who supposed the Prince would approve such counsel
As is giddily given in Christmas games by knights?"
Many were the watery tears that whelmed from weeping eyes,
When on quest that worthy knight went from the court
    That day.
  He faltered not nor feared,
  But quickly went his way;
  His road was rough and weird,
  Or so the stories say.

Now the gallant Sir Gawain in God's name goes
Riding through the realm of Britain,[9] no rapture in his mind.
Often the long night he lay alone and companionless,
And did not find in front of him food of his choice;
He had no comrade but his courser in the country woods and hills,
No traveler to talk to on the track but God,
Till he was nearly nigh to Northern Wales.
The isles of Anglesey he kept always on his left,
And fared across the fords by the foreshore
Over at Holy Head to the other side
Into the wilderness of Wirral, where few dwelled
To whom God or good-hearted man gave his love.
And always as he went, he asked whomever he met
If they knew or had knowledge of a knight in green,
Or could guide him to the ground where a green chapel stood.
And there was none but said him nay, for never in their lives
Had they set eyes on someone of such a hue
    As green.
  His way was wild and strange
  By dreary hill and dean.
  His mood would many times change
  Before that fane was seen.

He rode far from his friends, a forsaken man,
Scaling many cliffs in country unknown.
At every bank or beach where the brave man crossed water,
He found a foe in front of him, except by a freak of chance,

9. "Logres," identified with England in Geoffrey of Monmouth, elsewhere a vaguer term for Arthur's kingdom. Here, Gawain is heading northward through Wales, then along the coast of the Irish Sea and into the forest of Wirral in Cheshire—a wild area and resort of outlaws in the 14th century.

And so foul and fierce a one that he was forced to fight.
So many marvels did the man meet in the mountains,
It would be too tedious to tell a tenth of them.
He had death-struggles with dragons, did battle with wolves,
Warred with wild men who dwelt among the crags;
Battled with bulls and bears and boars at other times,
And ogres that panted after him on the high fells.
Had he not been doughty in endurance and dutiful to God,
Doubtless he would have been done to death time and again.
Yet the warring little worried him; worse was the winter,
When the cold clear water cascaded from the clouds
And froze before it could fall to the fallow earth.
Half-slain by the sleet, he slept in his armor
Night after night among the naked rocks,
Where the cold streams splashed from the steep crests
Or hung high over his head in hard icicles.
So in peril and pain, in parlous plight,
This knight covered the country till Christmas Eve
Alone;
And he that eventide
To Mary made his moan,
And begged her be his guide
Till some shelter should be shown.

Merrily in the morning by a mountain he rode
Into a wondrously wild wooded cleft,
With high hills on each side overpeering a forest
Of huge hoary oaks, a hundred together.
The hazel and the hawthorn were intertwined
With rough ragged moss trailing everywhere,
And on the bleak branches birds in misery
Piteously piped away, pinched with cold.
The gallant knight on Gringolet galloped under them
Through many a swamp and marsh, a man all alone,
Fearing lest he should fail, through adverse fortune,
To see the service of him who that same night
Was born of a bright maiden to banish our strife.
And so sighing he said, "I beseech thee Lord,
And thee Mary, mildest mother so dear,
That in some haven with due honor I may hear Mass
And Matins[1] tomorrow morning: meekly I ask it,
And promptly thereto I pray my Pater and Ave
And Creed."[2]
He crossed himself and cried
For his sins, and said, "Christ speed
My cause, his cross my guide!"
So prayed he, spurring his steed.

1. First of the canonical hours of prayer and praise in monastic tradition, observed between midnight and dawn.

2. The Paternoster ("Our Father . . ."), Ave Maria ("Hail Mary . . ."), and Creed (the articles of the Catholic faith).

Thrice the sign of the Savior on himself he had made,
When in the wood he was aware of a dwelling with a moat
On a promontory above a plateau, penned in by the boughs
And tremendous trunks of trees, and trenched about;
The comeliest castle that ever a knight owned,
It was pitched on a plain, with a park all round,
Impregnably palisaded with pointed stakes,
And containing many trees in its two-mile circumference.
The courteous knight contemplated the castle from one side
As it shimmered and shone through the shining oaks.
Then humbly he took off his helmet and offered thanks
To Jesus and Saint Julian,[3] gentle patrons both,
Who had given him grace and gratified his wish.
"Now grant it be good lodging!" the gallant knight said.
Then he goaded Gringolet with his golden heels,
And mostly by chance emerged on the main highway,
Which brought the brave man to the bridge's end
With one cast.
The drawbridge vertical,
The gates shut firm and fast,
The well-provided wall—
It blenched at never a blast.

The knight, still on his steed, stayed on the bank
Of the deep double ditch that drove round the place.
The wall went into the water wonderfully deep,
And then to a huge height upwards it reared
In hard hewn stone, up to the cornice;
Built under the battlements in the best style, courses jutted
And turrets protruded between, constructed
With loopholes in plenty with locking shutters.
No better barbican had ever been beheld by that knight.[4]
And inside he could see a splendid high hall
With towers and turrets on top, all tipped with crenellations,
And pretty pinnacles placed along its length,
With carved copes, cunningly worked.
Many chalk-white chimneys the chevalier saw
On the tops of towers twinkling whitely,
So many painted pinnacles sprinkled everywhere,
Congregated in clusters among the crenellations,
That it appeared like a prospect of paper patterning.[5]
To the gallant knight on Gringolet it seemed good enough
If he could ever gain entrance to the inner court,
And harbor in that house while Holy Day lasted,
Well cheered.
He hailed, and at a height

3. Patron saint of hospitality.

4. The poet again revels in technical vocabulary, here architectural; this is a fashionable (if exaggerated) building of the 14th century.

5. Models in cut paper sometimes decorated elaborate feasts such as that at the beginning of the poem.

A civil porter appeared,
Who welcomed the wandering knight,
And his inquiry heard.

"Good sir," said Gawain, "Will you give my message
To the high lord of this house, that I ask for lodging."
"Yes, by Saint Peter,"[6] replied the porter, "and I think
You may lodge here as long as you like, sir knight."
Then away he went eagerly, and swiftly returned
With a host of well-wishers to welcome the knight.
They let down the drawbridge and in a dignified way
Came out and did honor to him, kneeling
Courteously on the cold ground to accord him worthy welcome.
They prayed him to pass the portcullis, now pulled up high,
And he readily bid them rise and rode over the bridge.
Servants held his saddle while he stepped down,
And his steed was stabled by sturdy men in plenty.
Strong knights and squires descended then
To bring the bold warrier blithely into hall.
When he took off his helmet, many hurried forward
To receive it and to serve this stately man,
And his bright sword and buckler were both taken as well.
Then graciously he greeted each gallant knight,
And many proud men pressed forward to pay their respects.
Garbed in his fine garments, he was guided to the hall,
Where a fine fire was burning fiercely on the hearth.
Then the prince of those people appeared from his chamber
To meet in mannerly style the man in his hall.
"You are welcome to dwell here as you wish," he said,
"Treat everything as your own, and have what you please
In this place."
"I yield my best thanks yet:
May Christ make good your grace!"
Said Gawain and, gladly met,
They clasped in close embrace.

Gawain gazed at the gallant who had greeted him well
And it seemed to him the stronghold possessed a brave lord,
A powerful man in his prime, of stupendous size.
Broad and bright was his beard, all beaver-hued;
Strong and sturdy he stood on his stalwart legs;
His face was fierce as fire, free was his speech,
And he seemed in good sooth a suitable man
To be prince of a people with companions of mettle.
This prince led him to an apartment and expressly commanded
That a man be commissioned to minister to Gawain;
And at his bidding a band of men bent to serve

6. Swearing by St. Peter, keeper of the keys to heaven.

Brought him to a beautiful room where the bedding was noble.
The bed-curtains, of brilliant silk with bright gold hems,
Had skilfully-sewn coverlets with comely facings,
And the fairest fur on the fringes was worked.
With ruddy gold rings on the cords ran the curtains;
Toulouse and Turkestan tapestries on the wall
And fine carpets underfoot, on the floor, were fittingly matched.
There amid merry talk the man was disrobed,
And stripped of his battle-sark and his splendid clothes.
Retainers readily brought him rich robes
Of the choicest kind to choose from and change into.
In a trice when he took one, and was attired in it,
And it sat on him in style, with spreading skirts,
It certainly seemed to those assembled as if spring
In all its hues were evident before them;
His lithe limbs below the garment were gleaming with beauty.
Jesus never made, so men judged, more gentle and handsome
A knight:
From wherever in the world he were,
At sight it seemed he might
Be a prince without a peer
In field where fell men fight.

At the chimneyed hearth where charcoal burned, a chair was placed
For Sir Gawain in gracious style, gorgeously decked
With cushions on quilted work, both cunningly wrought;
And then on that man a magnificent mantle was thrown,
A gleaming garment gorgeously embroidered,
Fairly lined with fur, the finest skins
Of ermine on earth, and his hood of the same.
In that splendid seat he sat in dignity,
And warmth came to him at once, bringing well-being.
In a trice on fine trestles a table was put up,[7]
Then covered with a cloth shining clean and white,
And set with silver spoons, salt-cellars and overlays.
The worthy knight washed willingly, and went to his meat.
In seemly enough style servants brought him
Several fine soups, seasoned lavishly
Twice-fold, as is fitting, and fish of all kinds—
Some baked in bread, some browned on coals,
Some seethed, some stewed and savored with spice,
But always subtly sauced, and so the man liked it.
The gentle knight generously judged it a feast,
And often said so, while the servers spurred him on thus
As he ate:
"This present penance do;

7. A castle's great hall had many uses; tables were set up for dining and then put aside or hung.

It soon shall be offset."[8]
The knight rejoiced anew,
For the wine his spirits whet.

Then in seemly style they searchingly inquired,
Putting to the prince private questions,
So that he courteously conceded he came of that court
Where high-souled Arthur held sway alone,
Ruler most royal of the Round Table;
And that Sir Gawain himself now sat in the house,
Having come that Christmas, by course of fortune.
Loudly laughed the lord when he learned what knight
He had in his house; such happiness it brought
That all the men within the moat made merry,
And promptly appeared in the presence of Gawain,
To whose person are proper all prowess and worth,
And pure and perfect manners, and praises unceasing.
His reputation rates first in the ranks of men.
Each knight neared his neighbor and softly said,
"Now we shall see displayed the seemliest manners
And the faultless figures of virtuous discourse.
Without asking we may hear how to hold conversation
Since we have seized upon this scion of good breeding.
God has given us of his grace good measure
In granting us such a guest as Gawain is,
When, contented at Christ's birth, the courtiers shall sit
And sing.
This noble knight will prove
What manners the mighty bring;
His converse of courtly love
Shall spur our studying."[9]

When the fine man had finished his food and risen,
It was nigh and near to the night's mid-hour.
Priests to their prayers paced their way
And rang the bells royally, as rightly they should,
To honor that high feast with evensong.
The lord inclines to prayer, the lady too;
Into her private pew she prettily walks;
Gawain advances gaily and goes there quickly,
But the lord gripped his gown and guided him to his seat,
Acknowledged him by name and benevolently said
In the whole world he was the most welcome of men.
Gawain spoke his gratitude, they gravely embraced,
And sat in serious mood the whole service through.
Then the lady had a longing to look on the knight;

8. An exchange courtesies. Gawain has politely praised the many fish dishes; his hosts demur, remind him that Christmas Eve is a day of fasting, and promise him better meals later.

9. Though Gawain is engaged on a serious quest, his reputation as a graceful courtier and master in the arts of love has preceded him.

With her bevy of beauties she abandoned her pew.
Most beautiful of body and bright of complexion,
Most winsome in ways of all women alive,
She seemed to Sir Gawain, excelling Guinevere.
To squire that splendid dame, he strode through the chancel.
Another lady led her by the left hand,
A matron, much older, past middle age,
Who was highly honored by an escort of squires.
Most unlike to look on those ladies were,
For if the one was winsome, then withered was the other.
Hues rich and rubious were arrayed on the one,
Rough wrinkles on the other rutted the cheeks.
Kerchiefed with clear pearls clustering was the one,
Her breast and bright throat bare to the sight,
Shining like sheen of snow shed on the hills;
The other was swathed with a wimple wound to the throat
And choking her swarthy chin in chalk-white veils.
On her forehead were folded enveloping silks,
Trellised about with trefoils and tiny rings.
Nothing was bare on that beldame but the black brows,
The two eyes, protruding nose and stark lips,
And those were a sorry sight and exceedingly bleary:
A grand lady, God knows, of greatness in the world
        Well tried!
    Her body was stumpy and squat,
    Her buttocks bulging and wide;
    More pleasure a man could plot
    With the sweet one at her side.

When Gawain had gazed on that gracious-looking creature
He gained leave of the lord to go along with the ladies.
He saluted the senior, sweeping a low bow,
But briefly embraced the beautiful one,
Kissing her in courtly style and complimenting her.
They craved his acquaintance and he quickly requested
To be their faithful follower, if they would so favor him.
They took him between them, and talking, they led him
To a high room. By the hearth they asked first
For spices, which unstintingly men sped to bring,
And always with heart-warming, heady wine.
In lovingkindness the lord leaped up repeatedly
And many times reminded them that mirth should flow;
Elaborately lifted up his hood, looped it on a spear,
And offered it as a mark of honor to whoever should prove able
To make the most mirth that merry Yuletide.
"And I shall essay, I swear, to strive with the best
Before this garment goes from me, by my good friends' help."
So with his mirth the mighty lord made things merry
To gladden Sir Gawain with games in hall

Courtly Women Hunting, from the *Taymouth Hours*, 14th century. Women in courtly dress dismember a stag, usually the work of aristocratic men.

That night;
Until, the time being spent,
The lord demanded light.
Gawain took his leave and went
To rest in rare delight.

On that morning when men call to mind the birth
Of our dear Lord born to die for our destiny,
Joy waxes in dwellings the world over for his sake:
And so it befell there on the feast day with fine fare.
Both at main meals and minor repasts strong men served
Rare dishes with fine dressings to the dais company.
Highest, in the place of honor, the ancient crone sat,
And the lord, so I believe, politely next.
Together sat Gawain and the gay lady
In mid-table, where the meal was mannerly served first;
And after throughout the hall, as was held best,
Each gallant by degree was graciously served.
There was meat and merry-making and much delight,
To such an extent that it would try me to tell of it,
Even if perhaps I made the effort to describe it.
But yet I know the knight and the nobly pretty one

Found such solace and satisfaction seated together,
In the discreet confidences of their courtly dalliance,
Their irreproachably pure and polished repartee,
That with princes' sport their play of wit surpassingly
Compares.
Pipes and side-drums sound,
Trumpets entune their airs;
Each soul its solace found,
And the two were enthralled with theirs.

That day they made much merriment, and on the morrow again,
And thickly the joys thronged on the third day after;
But gentle was the jubilation on St John's Day,[1]
The final one for feasting, so the folk there thought.
As there were guests geared to go in the gray dawn
They watched the night out with wine in wonderful style,
Leaping night-long in their lordly dances.
At last when it was late those who lived far off,
Each one, bid farewell before wending their ways.
Gawain also said goodbye, but the good host grasped him,
Led him to the hearth of his own chamber,
And held him back hard, heartily thanking him
For the fine favor he had manifested to him
In honoring his house that high feast-tide,
Brightening his abode with his brilliant company:
"As long as I live, sir, I believe I shall thrive
Now Gawain has been my guest at God's own feast."
"Great thanks, sir," said Gawain. "In good faith, yours,
All yours is the honor, may the High King requite it!
I stand at your service, knight, to satisfy your will
As good use engages me, in great things and small,
By right."
The lord then bid his best
Longer to delay the knight,
But Gawain, replying, pressed
His departure in all despite.

Then with courteous inquiry the castellan asked
What fierce exploit had sent him forth, at that festive season,
From the King's court at Camelot, so quickly and alone,
Before the holy time was over in the homes of men.
"You may in truth well demand," admitted the knight.
"A high and urgent errand hastened me from thence,
For I myself am summoned to seek out a place
To find which I know not where in the world to look.
For all the land in Logres—may our Lord help me!
I would not fail to find it on the feast of New Year.

1. December 27, traditionally given over to drinking and celebration.

So this is my suit, sir, which I beseech of you here,
That you tell me in truth if tale ever reached you
Of the Green Chapel, or what ground or glebe it stands on,
Or of the knight who holds it, whose hue is green.
For at that place I am pledged, by the pact between us,
To meet that man, if I remain alive.
From now until the New Year is not a great time,
And if God will grant it me, more gladly would I see him
Than gain any good possession, by God's son!
I must wend my way, with your good will, therefore;
I am reduced to three days in which to do my business,
And I think it fitter to fall dead than fail in my errand."
Then the lord said laughingly, "You may linger a while,
For I shall tell you where your tryst is by your term's end.
Give yourself no more grief for the Green Chapel's whereabouts.
For you may lie back in your bed, brave man, at ease
Till full morning on the First, and then fare forth
To the meeting place at mid-morning to manage how you may
Out there.
Leave not till New Year's Day,
Then get up and go with cheer;
You shall be shown the way;
It is hardly two miles from here."

Then Gawain was glad and gleefully exclaimed,
"Now above all, most heartily do I offer you thanks!
For my goal is now gained, and by grace of yours
I shall dwell here and do what you deem good for me."
So the lord seized Sir Gawain, seated him beside himself,
And to enliven their delight, he had the ladies fetched,
And much gentle merriment they long made together.
The lord, as one like to take leave of his senses
And not aware of what he was doing, spoke warmly and merrily.
Then he spoke to Sir Gawain, saying out loud,
"You have determined to do the deed I ask:
Will you hold to your undertaking here and now?"
"Yes, sir, in good sooth," said the true knight,
"While I stay in your stronghold, I shall stand at your command."
"Since you have spurred," the lord said, "from afar,
Then watched awake with me, you are not well supplied
With either sustenance or sleep, for certain, I know;
So you shall lie long in your room, late and at ease
Tomorrow till the time of mass, and then take your meal
When you will, with my wife beside you
To comfort you with her company till I come back to court.
You stay,
And I shall get up at dawn.
I will to the hunt away."

When Gawain's agreement was sworn
He bowed, as brave knights may.

"Moreover," said the man, "Let us make a bargain
That whatever I win in the woods be yours,
And any achievement you chance on here, you exchange for it.
Sweet sir, truly swear to such a bartering,
Whether fair fortune or foul befall from it."
"By God," said the good Gawain, "I agree to that,
And I am happy that you have an eye to sport."
Then the prince of that people said, "What pledge of wine
Is brought to seal the bargain?" And they burst out laughing.
They took drink and toyed in trifling talk,
These lords and ladies, as long as they liked,
And then with French refinement and many fair words
They stood, softly speaking, to say goodnight,
Kissing as they parted company in courtly style.
With lithe liege servants in plenty and lambent torches,
Each brave man was brought to his bed at last,
Full soft.
Before they fared to bed
They rehearsed their bargain oft.
That people's prince, men said,
Could fly his wit aloft.

PART 3

In the faint light before dawn folk were stirring;
Guests who had to go gave orders to their grooms,
Who busied themselves briskly with the beasts, saddling,
Trimming their tackle and tying on their luggage.
Arrayed for riding in the richest style,
Guests leaped on their mounts lightly, laid hold of their bridles,
And each rider rode out on his own chosen way.
The beloved lord of the land was not the last up,
Being arrayed for riding with his retinue in force.
He ate a sop hastily when he had heard mass,
And hurried with horn to the hunting field;
Before the sun's first rays fell on the earth,
On their high steeds were he and his knights.[2]
Then these cunning hunters came to couple their hounds,
Cast open the kennel doors and called them out,
And blew on their bugles three bold notes.
The hounds broke out barking, baying fiercely,
And when they went chasing, they were whipped back.

2. The hunts that follow, for all their violent energy, are as ritualized in their procedure as the earlier feasts and games. The poet delights in describing still another quite technical area of knightly lore. A number of contemporary treatises on the hunt survive.

There were a hundred choice huntsmen there, whose fame
    Resounds.
  To their stations keepers strode;
  Huntsmen unleashed hounds:
  The forest overflowed
  With the strident bugle sounds.

At the first cry wild creatures quivered with dread.
The deer in distraction darted down to the dales
Or up to the high ground, but eagerly they were
Driven back by the beaters, who bellowed lustily.
They let the harts with high-branching heads have their freedom,
And the brave bucks, too, with their broad antlers,
For the noble prince had expressly prohibited
Meddling with male deer in the months of close season.
But the hinds were held back with a "Hey" and a "Whoa!"
And does driven with much din to the deep valleys.
Lo! the arrows' slanting flight as they were loosed!
A shaft flew forth at every forest turning,
The broad head biting on the brown flank.
They screamed as the blood streamed out, sank dead on the sward,
Always harried by hounds hard on their heels,
And the hurrying hunters' high horn notes.
Like the rending of ramped hills roared the din.
If one of the wild beasts slipped away from the archers
It was dragged down and met death at the dog-bases
After being hunted from the high ground and harried to the water,
So skilled were the hunt-servants at stations lower down,
So gigantic the greyhounds that grabbed them in a flash,
Seizing them savagely, as swift, I swear,
    As sight.
  The lord, in humor high
  Would spur, then stop and alight.
  In bliss the day went by
  Till dark drew on, and night.

Thus by the forest borders the brave lord sported,
And the good man Gawain, on his gay bed lying,
Lay hidden till the light of day gleamed on the walls,
Covered with fair canopy, the curtains closed,
And as in slumber he slept on, there slipped into his mind
A slight, suspicious sound, and the door stealthily opened.
He raised up his head out of the bedclothes,
Caught up the corner of the curtain a little
And watched warily towards it, to see what it was.
It was the lady, loveliest to look upon,
Who secretly and silently secured the door,
Then bore towards his bed: the brave knight, embarrassed,
Lay flat with fine adroitness and feigned sleep.
Silently she stepped on, stole to his bed,

Caught up the curtain, crept within,
And seated herself softly on the side of the bed.
There she watched a long while, waiting for him to wake.
Slyly close this long while lay the knight,
Considering in his soul this circumstance,
Its sense and likely sequel, for it seemed marvelous.
"Still, it would be more circumspect," he said to himself,
"To speak and discover her desire in due course."
So he stirred and stretched himself, twisting towards her,
Opened his eyes and acted as if astounded;
And, to seem the safer by such service, crossed himself
In dread.
With chin and cheek so fair,
White ranged with rosy red,
With laughing lips, and air
Of love, she lightly said:

"Good morning, Sir Gawain," the gay one murmured,
"How unsafely you sleep, that one may slip in here!
Now you are taken in a trice. Unless a truce come between us,
I shall bind you to your bed—of that be sure."
The lady uttered laughingly those playful words.
"Good morning, gay lady," Gawain blithely greeted her.
"Do with me as you will: that well pleases me.
For I surrender speedily and sue for grace,
Which, to my mind, since I must, is much the best course."
And thus he repaid her with repartee and ready laughter.
"But if, lovely lady, your leave were forthcoming,
And you were pleased to free your prisoner and pray him to rise,
I would abandon my bed for a better habiliment,
And have more happiness in our honey talk."
"Nay, verily, fine sir," urged the voice of that sweet one,
"You shall not budge from your bed. I have a better idea.
I shall hold you fast here on this other side as well
And so chat on with the chevalier my chains have caught.
For I know well, my knight, that your name is Sir Gawain,
Whom all the world worships, wherever he ride;
For lords and their ladies, and all living folk,
Hold your honor in high esteem, and your courtesy.
And now—here you are truly, and we are utterly alone;
My lord and his liegemen are a long way off;
Others still bide in their beds, my bower-maidens too;
Shut fast and firmly with a fine hasp is the door;
And since I have in this house him who pleases all,
As long as my time lasts I shall lingering in talk take
My fill.
My young body is yours,
Do with it what you will;
My strong necessities force
Me to be your servant still."

"In good truth," said Gawain, "that is a gain indeed,
Though I am hardly the hero of whom you speak.
To be held in such honor as you here suggest,
I am altogether unworthy, I own it freely.
By God, I should be glad, if you granted it right
For me to essay by speech or some other service,
To pleasure such a perfect lady—pure joy it would be."
"In good truth, Sir Gawain," the gay lady replied,
"If I slighted or set at naught your spotless fame
And your all-pleasing prowess, it would show poor breeding.
But there is no lack of ladies who would love, noble one,
To hold you in their arms, as I have you here,
And linger in the luxury of your delightful discourse,
Which would perfectly pleasure them and appease their woes—
Rather than have riches or the red gold they own.
But as I love that Lord, the Celestial Ruler,
I have wholly in my hand what all desire
Through his grace."
Not loth was she to allure,
This lady fair of face;
But the knight with speeches pure
Answered in each case.

"Madam," said the merry man, "May Mary requite you!
For in good faith I have found in you free-hearted generosity.
Certain men for their deeds receive esteem from others,
But for myself, I do not deserve the respect they show me;
Your honorable mind makes you utter only what is good.
"Now by Mary," said the noble lady, "Not so it seems to me,
For were I worth the whole of womankind,
And all the wealth in the world were in my hand,
And if bargaining I were to bid to bring myself a lord—
With your noble qualities, knight, made known to me now,
Your good looks, gracious manner and great courtesy,
All of which I have heard of before, but here prove true—
No lord that is living could be allowed to excel you."
"Indeed, dear lady, you did better," said the knight,
"But I am proud of the precious price you put on me,
And solemnly as your servant say you are my sovereign.
May Christ requite it you: I have become your knight."
Then of many matters they talked till mid-morning and after,
And all the time she behaved as if she adored him;
But Sir Gawain was on guard in a gracious manner.
Though she was the winsomest woman the warrior had known,
He was less love-laden because of the loss he must
Now face—
His destruction by the stroke,
For come it must was the case.
The lady of leaving then spoke;
He assented with speedy grace.

Then she gave him goodbye, glinting with laughter,
And standing up, astounded him with these strong words:
"May He who prospers every speech for this pleasure reward you!
I cannot bring myself to believe that you could be Gawain."
"How so?" said the knight, speaking urgently,
For he feared he had failed to observe the forms of courtesy.
But the beauteous one blessed him and brought out this argument:
"Such a great man as Gawain is granted to be,
The very vessel of virtue and fine courtesy,
Could scarcely have stayed such a sojourn with a lady
Without craving a kiss out of courtesy,
Touched by some trifling hint at the tail-end of a speech."
"So be it, as you say," then said Gawain,
"I shall kiss at your command, as becomes a knight
Who fears to offend you; no further plea is needed."
Whereupon she approached him, and penned him in her arms,
Leaned over him lovingly and gave the lord a kiss.
Then they commended each other to Christ in comely style,
And without more words she went out by the door.
He made ready to rise with rapid haste,
Summoned his servant, selected his garb,
And walked down, when he was dressed, debonairly to mass.
Then he went to the well-served meal which awaited him,
And made merry sport till the moon rose
At night.
Never was baron bold
So taken by ladies bright,
That young one and the old:
They throve all three in delight.

And still at his sport spurred the castellan,
Hunting the barren hinds in holt and on heath.
So many had he slain, by the setting of the sun,
Of does and other deer, that it was downright wonderful.
Then at the finish the folk flocked in eagerly,
And quickly collected the killed deer in a heap.
Those highest in rank came up with hosts of attendants,
Picked out what appeared to be the plumpest beasts
And, according to custom, had them cut open with finesse.
Some who ceremoniously assessed them there
Found two fingers' breadth of fat on the worst.
Then they slit open the slot, seized the first stomach,
Scraped it with a keen knife and tied up the tripes.
Next they hacked off all the legs, the hide was stripped,
The belly broken open and the bowels removed
Carefully, lest they loosen the ligature of the knot.
Then they gripped the gullet, disengaged deftly
The wezand[3] from the windpipe and whipped out the guts.

3. The esophagus.

Then their sharp knives shore through the shoulder-bones,
Which they slid out of a small hole, leaving the sides intact.
Then they cleft the chest clean through, cutting it in two.
Then again at the gullet a man began to work
And straight away rived it, right to the fork,
Flicked out the shoulder-fillets, and faithfully then
He rapidly ripped free the rib-fillets.
Similarly, as is seemly, the spine was cleared
All the way to the haunch, which hung from it;
And they heaved up the whole haunch and hewed it off;
And that is called, according to its kind, the numbles,[4]
I find.
At the thigh-forks then they strain
And free the folds behind,
Hurrying to hack all in twain,
The backbone to unbind.

Then they hewed off the head and also the neck,
And after sundered the sides swiftly from the chine,
And into the foliage they flung the fee of the raven.[5]
Then each fellow, for his fee, as it fell to him to have,
Skewered through the stout flanks beside the ribs,
And then by the hocks of the haunches they hung up their booty.
On one of the finest fells they fed their hounds,
And let them have the lights,[6] the liver and the tripes,
With bread well imbrued with blood mixed with them.
Boldly they blew the kill amid the baying of hounds.
Then off they went homewards, holding their meat,
Stalwartly sounding many stout horn-calls.
As dark was descending, they were drawing near
To the comely castle where quietly our knight stayed.
Fires roared,
And blithely hearts were beating
As into hall came the lord.
When Gawain gave him greeting,
Joy abounded at the board.

Then the master commanded everyone to meet in the hall,
Called the ladies to come down with their company of maidens.
Before all the folk on the floor, he bid men
Fetch the venison and place it before him.
Then gaily and in good humor to Gawain he called,
Told over the tally of the sturdy beasts,
And showed him the fine fat flesh flayed from the ribs.
"How does the sport please you? Do you praise me for it?
Am I thoroughly thanked for thriving as a huntsman?"
"Certainly," said the other, "Such splendid spoils

4. Internal organs such as the heart, liver, lungs.
5. The gristle at the end of the breastbone was left for the ravens, still another of the prescribed rituals of the hunt.
6. Lungs.

Have I not seen for seven years in the season of winter."
"And I give you all, Gawain," said the good man then,
"For according to our covenant you may claim it as your own."
"Certes, that is so, and I say the same to you,"
Said Gawain, "For my true gains in this great house,
I am not loth to allow, must belong to you."
And he put his arms round his handsome neck, hugging him,
And kissed him in the comeliest way he could think of.
"Accept my takings, sir, for I received no more;
Gladly would I grant them, however great they were."
"And therefore I thank you," the thane said, "Good!
Yours may be the better gift, if you would break it to me
Where your wisdom won you wealth of that kind."
"No such clause in our contract! Request nothing else!"
Said the other, "You have your due: ask more,
None should."
They laughed in blithe assent
With worthy words and good;
Then to supper they swiftly went,
To fresh delicious food.

And sitting afterwards by the hearth of an audience chamber,
Where retainers repeatedly brought them rare wines,
In their jolly jesting they jointly agreed
On a settlement similar to the preceding one;
To exchange the chance achievements of the morrow,
No matter how novel they were, at night when they met.
They accorded on this compact, the whole court observing,
And the bumper was brought forth in banter to seal it.
And at last they lovingly took leave of each other,
Each man hastening thereafter to his bed.
The cock having crowed and called only thrice,
The lord leaped from bed, and his liegemen too,
So that mass and a meal were meetly dealt with,
And by first light the folk to the forest were bound
For the chase.
Proudly the hunt with horns
Soon drove through a desert place:
Uncoupled through the thorns
The great hounds pressed apace.

By a quagmire they quickly scented quarry and gave tongue,
And the chief huntsman urged on the first hounds up,
Spurring them on with a splendid spate of words.
The hounds, hearing it, hurried there at once,
Fell on the trial furiously, forty together,
And made such echoing uproar, all howling at once,
That the rocky banks round about rang with the din.
Hunters inspirited them with sound of speech and horn.
Then together in a group, across the ground they surged

At speed between a pool and a spiteful crag.
On a stony knoll by a steep cliff at the side of a bog,
Where rugged rocks had roughly tumbled down,
They careered on the quest, the cry following,
Then surrounded the crag and the rocky knoll as well,
Certain their prey skulked inside their ring,
For the baying of the bloodhounds meant the beast was there.
Then they beat upon the bushes and bade him come out,
And he swung out savagely aslant the line of men,
A baneful boar of unbelievable size,
A solitary long since sundered from the herd,
Being old and brawny, the biggest of them all,
And grim and ghastly when he grunted: great was the grief
When he thrust through the hounds, hurling three to earth,
And sped on scot-free, swift and unscathed.
They hallooed, yelled, "Look out!" cried, "Hey, we have him!"
And blew horns boldly, to bring the bloodhounds together;
Many were the merry cries from men and dogs
As they hurried clamoring after their quarry to kill him on
        The track.
    Many times he turns at bay
    And tears the dogs which attack.
    He hurts the hounds, and they
    Moan in a piteous pack.

Then men shoved forward, shaped to shoot at him,
Loosed arrows at him, hitting him often,
But the points, for all their power, could not pierce his flanks,
Nor would the barbs bite on his bristling brow.
Though the smooth-shaven shaft shattered in pieces,
Wherever it hit, the head rebounded.
But when the boar was battered by blows unceasing,
Goaded and driven demented, he dashed at the men,
Striking them savagely as he assailed them in rushes,
So that some lacking stomach stood back in fear.
But the lord on a lithe horse lunged after him,
Blew on his bugle like a bold knight in battle,
Rallied the hounds as he rode through the rank thickets,
Pursuing this savage boar till the sun set.
And so they disported themselves this day
While our lovable lord lay in his bed.
At home the gracious Gawain in gorgeous clothes
        Reclined:
    The gay one did not forget
    To come with welcome kind,
    And early him beset
    To make him change his mind.

She came to the curtain and cast her eye
On Sir Gawain, who at once gave her gracious welcome,

And she answered him eagerly, with ardent words,
Sat at his side softly, and with a spurt of laughter
And a loving look, delivered these words:
"It seems to me strange, if, sir, you are Gawain,
A person so powerfully disposed to good,
Yet nevertheless know nothing of noble conventions,
And when made aware of them, wave them away!
Quickly you have cast off what I schooled you in yesterday
By the truest of all tokens of talk I know of."
"What?" said the wondering knight, "I am not aware of one.
But if it be true what you tell, I am entirely to blame."
"I counseled you then about kissing," the comely one said;
"When a favor is conferred, it must be forthwith accepted:
That is becoming for a courtly knight who keeps the rules."
"Sweet one, unsay that speech," said the brave man,
"For I dared not do that lest I be denied.
If I were forward and were refused, the fault would be mine."
"But none," said the noblewoman, "could deny you, by my faith!
You are strong enough to constrain with your strength if you wish,
If any were so ill-bred as to offer you resistance."
"Yes, good guidance you give me, by God," replied Gawain,
"But threateners are ill thought of and do not thrive in my country,
Nor do gifts thrive when given without good will.
I am here at your behest, to offer a kiss to when you like;
You may do it whenever you deem fit, or desist,
        In this place."
    The beautiful lady bent
    And fairly kissed his face;
    Much speech the two then spent
    On love, its grief and grace.

"I would know of you, knight," the noble lady said,
"If it did not anger you, what argument you use,
Being so hale and hearty as you are at this time,
So generous a gentleman as you are justly famed to be;
Since the choicest thing in Chivalry, the chief thing praised,
Is the loyal sport of love, the very lore of arms?[7]
For the tale of the contentions of true knights
Is told by the title and text of their feats,
How lords for their true loves put their lives at hazard,
Endured dreadful trials for their dear loves' sakes,
And with valor avenged and made void their woes,
Bringing home abundant bliss by their virtues.
You are the gentlest and most just of your generation;
Everywhere your honor and high fame are known;
Yet I have sat at your side two separate times here
Without hearing you utter in any way

7. The lady compares Gawain's behavior to descriptions of courtly love in romances; the poem is mirrored within itself.

A single syllable of the saga of love.
Being so polished and punctilious a pledge-fulfiller,
You ought to be eager to lay open to a young thing
Your discoveries in the craft of courtly love.
What! Are you ignorant, with all your renown?
Or do you deem me too dull to drink in your dalliance?
For shame!
I sit here unchaperoned, and stay
To acquire some courtly game;
So while my lord is away,
Teach me your true wit's fame."

"In good faith," said Gawain, "may God requite you!
It gives me great happiness, and is good sport to me,
That so fine a fair one as you should find her way here
And take pains with so poor a man, make pastime with her knight,
With any kind of clemency—it comforts me greatly.
But for me to take on the travail of interpreting true love
And construing the subjects of the stories of arms
To you who, I hold, have more skill
In that art, by half, than a hundred of such
As I am or ever shall be on the earth I inhabit,
Would in faith be a manifold folly, noble lady.
To please you I would press with all the power in my soul,
For I am highly beholden to you, and evermore shall be
True servant to your bounteous self, so save me God!"
So that stately lady tempted him and tried him with questions
To win him to wickedness, whatever else she thought.
But he defended himself so firmly that no fault appeared,
Nor was there any evil apparent on either side,
But bliss;
For long they laughed and played
Till she gave him a gracious kiss.
A fond farewell she bade,
And went her way on this.

Sir Gawain bestirred himself and went to mass:
Then dinner was dressed and with due honor served.
All day long the lord and the ladies disported,
But the castellan coursed across the country time and again,
Hunted his hapless boar as it hurtled over the hills,
Then bit the backs of his best hounds asunder
Standing at bay, till the bowmen obliged him to break free
Out into the open for all he could do,
So fast the arrows flew when the folk there concentrated.
Even the strongest he sometimes made start back,
But in time he became so tired he could tear away no more,
And with the speed he still possessed, he spurted to a hole
On a rise by a rock with a running stream beside.
He got the bank at his back, and began to abrade the ground.

The froth was foaming foully at his mouth,
And he whetted his white tusks; a weary time it was
For the bold men about, who were bound to harass him
From a distance, for none dared to draw near him
For dread.
He had hurt so many men
That it entered no one's head
To be torn by his tusks again,
And he raging and seeing red.

Till the castellan came himself, encouraging his horse,
And saw the boar at bay with his band of men around.
He alighted in lively fashion, left his courser,
Drew and brandished his bright sword and boldly strode forward,
Striding at speed through the stream to where the savage beast was.
The wild thing was aware of the weapon and its wielder,
And so bridled with its bristles in a burst of fierce snorts
That all were anxious for the lord, lest he have the worst of it.
Straight away the savage brute sprang at the man,
And baron and boar were both in a heap
In the swirling water: the worst went to the beast,
For the man had marked him well at the moment of impact,
Had put the point precisely at the pit of his chest,
And drove it in to the hilt, so that the heart was shattered,
And the spent beast sank snarling and was swept downstream,
Teeth bare.
A hundred hounds and more
Attack and seize and tear;
Men tug him to the shore
And the dogs destroy him there.

Bugles blew the triumph, horns blared loud.
There was hallooing in high pride by all present;
Braches bayed at the beast, as bidden by their masters,
The chief huntsmen in charge of that chase so hard.
Then one who was wise in wood-crafts
Started in style to slash open the boar.
First he hewed off the head and hoisted it on high,
Then rent him roughly along the ridge of his back,
Brought out the bowels and broiled them on coals
For blending with bread as the braches' reward.
Then he broke out the brawn from the bright broad flanks,
Took out the offal, as is fit,
Attached the two halves entirely together,
And on a strong stake stoutly hung them.
Then home they hurried with the huge beast,
With the boar's head borne before the baron himself,
Who had destroyed him in the stream by the strength of his arm,
Above all:
It seemed to him an age

Till he greeted Gawain in hall.
To reap his rightful wage
The latter came at his call.

The lord exclaimed loudly, laughing merrily
When he saw Sir Gawain, and spoke joyously.
The sweet ladies were sent for, and the servants assembled.
Then he showed them the shields, and surely described
The large size and length, and the malignity
Of the fierce boar's fighting when he fled in the woods;
So that Gawain congratulated him on his great deed,
Commended it as a merit he had manifested well,
For a beast with so much brawn, the bold man said,
A boar of such breadth, he had not before seen.
When they handled the huge head the upright man praised it,
Expressed horror thereat for the ear of the lord.
"Now Gawain," said the good man, "this game is your own
By our contracted treaty, in truth, you know."
"It is so," said the knight, "and as certainly
I shall give you all my gains as guerdon, in faith."
He clasped the castellan's neck and kissed him kindly,
And then served him a second time in the same style.
"In all our transactions since I came to sojourn," asserted Gawain,
"Up to tonight, as of now, there's nothing that
I owe."
"By Saint Giles,"[8] the castellan quipped,
"You're the finest fellow I know:
Your wealth will have us whipped
If your trade continues so!"

Then the trestles and tables were trimly set out,
Complete with cloths, and clearly flaming cressets
And waxen torches were placed in the wall-brackets
By retainers, who then tended the entire hall-gathering.
Much gladness and glee then gushed forth there
By the fire on the floor: and in multifarious ways
They sang noble songs at supper and afterwards,
A concert of Christmas carols and new dance songs,
With the most mannerly mirth a man could tell of,
And our courteous knight kept constant company with the lady.
In a bewitchingly well-mannered way she made up to him,
Secretly soliciting the stalwart knight
So that he was astounded, and upset in himself.
But his upbringing forbade him to rebuff her utterly,
So he behaved towards her honorably, whatever aspersions might
Be cast.
They reveled in the hall
As long as their pleasure might last

8. St. Giles, a hermit and patron saint of woodlands.

And then at the castellan's call
To the chamber hearth they passed.

There they drank and discoursed and decided to enjoy
Similar solace and sport on New Year's Eve.
But the princely knight asked permission to depart in the morning,
For his appointed time was approaching, and perforce he must go.
But the lord would not let him and implored him to linger,
Saying, "I swear to you, as a staunch true knight,
You shall gain the Green Chapel to give your dues,
My lord, in the light of New Year, long before sunrise.
Therefore remain in your room and rest in comfort,
While I fare hunting in the forest; in fulfilment of our oath
Exchanging what we achieve when the chase is over.
For twice I have tested you, and twice found you true.
Now 'Third time, throw best!' Think of that tomorrow!
Let us make merry while we may, set our minds on joy,
For hard fate can hit man whenever it likes."
This was graciously granted and Gawain stayed.
Blithely drink was brought, then to bed with lights
They pressed.
All night Sir Gawain sleeps
Softly and still at rest;
But the lord his custom keeps
And is early up and dressed.

After mass, he and his men made a small meal.
Merry was the morning; he demanded his horse.
The men were ready mounted before the main gate,
A host of knightly horsemen to follow after him.
Wonderfully fair was the forest-land, for the frost remained,
And the rising sun shone ruddily on the ragged clouds,
In its beauty brushing their blackness off the heavens.
The huntsmen unleashed the hounds by a holt-side,
And the rocks and surrounding bushes rang with their horn-calls.
Some found and followed the fox's tracks,
And wove various ways in their wily fashion.
A small hound cried the scent, the senior huntsman called
His fellow foxhounds to him and, feverishly sniffing,
The rout of dogs rushed forward on the right path.
The fox hurried fast, for they found him soon
And, seeing him distinctly, pursued him at speed,
Unmistakably giving tongue with tumultuous din.
Deviously in difficult country he doubled on his tracks,
Swerved and wheeled away, often waited listening,
Till at last by a little ditch he leaped a quickset hedge,
And stole out stealthily at the side of a valley,
Considering his stratagem had given the slip to the hounds.
But he stumbled on a tracking-dogs' tryst-place unawares,
And there in a cleft three hounds threatened him at once,

All gray.
He swiftly started back,
And, full of deep dismay,
He dashed on a different track;
To the woods he went away.

Then came the lively delight of listening to hounds
When they had all met in a muster, mingling together,
For, catching sight of him, they cried such curses on him
That the clustering cliffs seemed to be crashing down.
Here he was hallooed when the hunters met him,
There savagely snarled at by intercepting hounds;
Then he was called thief and threatened often;
With the tracking dogs on his tail, no tarrying was possible.
When out in the open he was often run at,
So he often swerved in again, that artful Reynard.
Yes, he led the lord and his liegemen a dance
In this manner among the mountains till mid-afternoon,
While harmoniously at home the honored knight slept
Between the comely curtains in the cold morning.
But the lady's longing to woo would not let her sleep,
Nor would she impair the purpose pitched in her heart,
But rose up rapidly and ran to him
In a ravishing robe that reached to the ground,
Trimmed with finest fur from pure pelts;
Not coifed as to custom, but with costly jewels
Strung in scores on her splendid hairnet.
Her fine-featured face and fair throat were unveiled,
Her breast was bare and her back as well.
She came in by the chamber door and closed it after her,
Cast open a casement and called on the knight,
And briskly thus rebuked him with bountiful words
Of good cheer.
"Ah sir! What, sound asleep?
The morning's crisp and clear,"
He had been drowsing deep,
But now he had to hear.

The noble sighed ceaselessly in unsettled slumber
As threatening thoughts thronged in the dawn light
About destiny, which the day after would deal him his fate
At the Green Chapel where Gawain was to greet his man,
And be bound to bear his buffet unresisting.
But having recovered consciousness in comely fashion,
He heaved himself out of dreams and answered hurriedly.
The lovely lady advanced, laughing adorably,
Swooped over his splendid face and sweetly kissed him.
He welcomed her worthily with noble cheer
And, gazing on her gay and glorious attire,
Her features so faultless and fine of complexion,

He felt a flush of rapture suffuse his heart.
Sweet and genial smiling slid them into joy
Till bliss burst forth between them, beaming gay
And bright;
With joy the two contended
In talk of true delight,
And peril would have impended
Had Mary not minded her knight.

For that peerless princess pressed him so hotly,
So invited him to the very verge, that he felt forced
Either to allow her love or blackguardly rebuff her.
He was concerned for his courtesy, lest he be called caitiff,
But more especially for his evil plight if he should plunge into sin,
And dishonor the owner of the house treacherously.
"God shield me! That shall not happen, for sure," said the knight.
So with laughing love-talk he deflected gently
The downright declarations that dropped from her lips.
Said the beauty to the bold man, "Blame will be yours
If you love not the living body lying close to you
More than all wooers in the world who are wounded in heart;
Unless you have a lover more beloved, who delights you more,
A maiden to whom you are committed, so immutably bound
That you do not seek to sever from her—which I see is so.
Tell me the truth of it, I entreat you now;
By all the loves there are, do not hide the truth
With guile."
Then gently, "By Saint John,"
Said the knight with a smile,
"I owe my oath to none,
Nor wish to yet a while."

"Those words," said the fair woman, "are the worst there could be,
But I am truly answered, to my utter anguish.
Give me now a gracious kiss, and I shall go from here
As a maid that loves much, mourning on this earth."
Then, sighing, she stooped, and seemlily kissed him,
And, severing herself from him, stood up and said,
"At this adieu, my dear one, do me this pleasure:
Give me something as gift, your glove if no more,
To mitigate my mourning when I remember you."
"Now certainly, for your sake," said the knight,
"I wish I had here the handsomest thing I own,
For you have deserved, forsooth, superabundantly
And rightfully, a richer reward than I could give.
But as tokens of true love, trifles mean little.
It is not to your honor to have at this time
A mere glove as Gawain's gift to treasure.
For I am here on an errand in unknown regions,
And have no bondsmen, no baggages with dear-bought things in them.

This afflicts me now, fair lady, for your sake.
Man must do as he must; neither lament it
Nor repine."
"No, highly honored one,"
Replied that lady fine,
"Though gift you give me none,
You must have something of mine."

She proffered him a rich ring wrought in red gold,
With a sparkling stone set conspicuously in it,
Which beamed as brilliantly as the bright sun;
You may well believe its worth was wonderfully great.
But the courteous man declined it and quickly said,
"Before God, gracious lady, no giving just now!
Not having anything to offer, I shall accept nothing."
She offered it him urgently and he refused again,
Fast affirming his refusal on his faith as a knight.
Put out by this repulse, she presently said,
"If you reject my ring as too rich in value,
Doubtless you would be less deeply indebted to me
If I gave you my girdle, a less gainful gift."
She swiftly slipped off the cincture of her gown
Which went round her waist under the wonderful mantle,
A girdle of green silk with a golden hem,
Embroidered only at the edges, with hand-stitched ornament.
And she pleaded with the prince in a pleasant manner
To take it notwithstanding its trifling worth;
But he told her that he could touch no treasure at all,
Not gold nor any gift, till God gave him grace
To pursue to success the search he was bound on.
"And therefore I beg you not to be displeased:
Press no more your purpose, for I promise it never
Can be.
I owe you a hundredfold
For grace you have granted me;
And ever through hot and cold
I shall stay your devotee."

"Do you say no to this silk?" then said the beauty,
"Because it is simple in itself? And so it seems.
Lo! It is little indeed, and so less worth your esteem.
But one who was aware of the worth twined in it
Would appraise its properties as more precious perhaps,
For the man that binds his body with this belt of green,
As long as he laps it closely about him,
No hero under heaven can hack him to pieces,
For he cannot be killed by any cunning on earth."
Then the prince pondered, and it appeared to him
A precious gem to protect him in the peril appointed him
When he gained the Green Chapel to be given checkmate:

It would be a splendid stratagem to escape being slain.
Then he allowed her to solicit him and let her speak.
She pressed the belt upon him with potent words
And having got his agreement, she gave it him gladly,
Beseeching him for her sake to conceal it always,
And hide it from her husband with all diligence.
That never should another know of it, the noble swore
Outright.
Then often his thanks gave he
With all his heart and might,
And thrice by then had she
Kissed the constant knight.

Then with a word of farewell she went away,
For she could not force further satisfaction from him.
Directly she withdrew, Sir Gawain dressed himself,
Rose and arrayed himself in rich garments,
But laid aside the love-lace the lady had given him,
Secreted it carefully where he could discover it later.
Then he went his way at once to the chapel,
Privily approached a priest and prayed him there
To listen to his life's sins and enlighten him
On how he might have salvation in the hereafter.
Then, confessing his faults, he fairly shrove himself,
Begging mercy for both major and minor sins.
He asked the holy man for absolution
And was absolved with certainty and sent out so pure
That Doomsday could have been declared the day after.
Then he made merrier among the noble ladies,
With comely caroling and all kinds of pleasure,
Than ever he had done, with ecstasy, till came
Dark night.
Such honor he did to all,
They said, "Never has this knight
Since coming into hall
Expressed such pure delight,"

Now long may he linger there, love sheltering him!
The prince was still on the plain, pleasuring in the chase,
Having finished off the fox he had followed so far.
As he leaped over a hedge looking out for the quarry,
Where he heard the hounds that were harrying the fox,
Reynard came running through a rough thicket
With the pack all pell-mell, panting at his heels.
The lord, aware of the wild beast, waited craftily,
Then drew his dazzling sword and drove at the fox.
The beast baulked at the blade to break sideways,
But a dog bounded at him before he could,
And right in front of the horse's feet they fell on him,
All worrying their wily prey with a wild uproar.

The lord quickly alighted and lifted him up,
Wrenched him beyond reach of the ravening fangs,
Held him high over his head and hallooed lustily,
While the angry hounds in hordes bayed at him.
Thither hurried the huntsmen with horns in plenty,
Sounding the rally splendidly till they saw their lord.
When the company of his court had come up to the kill,
All who bore bugles blew at once,
And the others without horns hallooed loudly.
The requiem that was raised for Reynard's soul
And the commotion made it the merriest meet ever,
        Men said.
    The hounds must have their fee:
    They pat them on the head,
    Then hold the fox; and he
    Is reft of his skin of red.

Then they set off for home, it being almost night,
Blowing their big horns bravely as they went.
At last the lord alighted at his beloved castle
And found upon the floor a fire, and beside it
The good Sir Gawain in a glad humor
By reason of the rich friendship he had reaped from the ladies.
He wore a turquoise tunic extending to the ground;
His softly-furred surcoat suited him well,
And his hood of the same hue hung from his shoulder.
All trimmed with ermine were hood and surcoat.
Meeting the master in the middle of the floor,
Gawain went forward gladly and greeted him thus:
"Forthwith, I shall be the first to fulfil the contract
We settled so suitably without sparing the wine."
Then he clasped the castellan and kissed him thrice
As sweetly and steadily as a strong knight could.
"By Christ!" quoth the other, "You will carve yourself a fortune
By traffic in this trade when the terms suit you!"
"Do not chop logic about the exchange," chipped in Gawain,
"As I have properly paid over the profit I made."
"Marry," said the other man, "Mine is inferior,
For I have hunted all day and have only taken
This ill-favored fox's skin, may the Fiend take it!
And that is a poor price to pay for such precious things
As you have pressed upon me here, three pure kisses
        So good."
    "Enough!" acknowledged Gawain,
    "I thank you, by the Rood."
    And how the fox was slain
    The lord told him as they stood.

With mirth and minstrelsy, and meals when they liked,

They made as merry then as ever men could;
With the laughter of ladies and delightful jesting,
Gawain and his good host were very gay together,
Save when excess or sottishness seemed likely.
Master and men made many a witty sally,
Until presently, at the appointed parting-time,
The brave men were bidden to bed at last.
Then of his host the hero humbly took leave,
The first to bid farewell, fairly thanking him:[9]
"May the High King requite you for your courtesy at this feast,
And the wonderful week of my dwelling here!
I would offer to be one of your own men if you liked,
But that I must move on tomorrow, as you know,
If you will give me the guide you granted me.
To show me the Green Chapel where my share of doom
Will be dealt on New Year's Day, as God deems for me."
"With all my heart !" said the host. "In good faith,
All that I ever promised you, I shall perform."
He assigned him a servant to set him on his way,
And lead him in the hills without any delay,
Faring through forest and thicket by the most straightforward route
They might.
With every honor due
Gawain then thanked the knight,
And having bid him adieu,
Took leave of the ladies bright.

So he spoke to them sadly, sorrowing as he kissed,
And urged on them heartily his endless thanks,
And they gave to Sir Gawain words of grace in return,
Commending him to Christ with cries of chill sadness.
Then from the whole household he honorably took his leave,
Making all the men that he met amends
For their several services and solicitous care,
For they had been busily attendant, bustling about him;
And every soul was as sad to say farewell
As if they had always had the hero in their house.
Then the lords led him with lights to his chamber,
And blithely brought him to bed to rest.
If he slept—I dare not assert it—less soundly than usual,
There was much on his mind for the morrow, if he meant to give
It thought.
Let him lie there still,
He almost has what he sought;
So tarry a while until
The process I report.

9. Gawain's highly stylized leave-taking is typical of courtly romance and again emphasizes his command of fine manners.

Part 4

Now the New Year neared, the night passed,
Daylight fought darkness as the Deity ordained.
But wild was the weather the world awoke to;
Bitterly the clouds cast down cold on the earth,
Inflicting on the flesh flails from the north.
Bleakly the snow blustered, and beasts were frozen;
The whistling wind wailed from the heights,
Driving great drifts deep in the dales.
Keenly the lord listened as he lay in his bed;
Though his lids were closed, he was sleeping little.
Every cock that crew recalled to him his tryst.
Before the day had dawned, he had dressed himself,
For the light from a lamp illuminated his chamber.
He summoned his servant, who swiftly answered,
Commanded that his mail-coat and mount's saddle he brought.
The man fared forth and fetched him his armor,
And set Sir Gawain's array in splendid style.
First he clad him in his clothes to counter the cold,
Then in his other armor which had been well kept;
His breast- and belly-armor had been burnished bright,
And the rusty rings of his rich mail-coat rolled clean,
And all being as fresh as at first, he was fain to give thanks
        Indeed.
    Each wiped and polished piece
    He donned with due heed.
    The gayest from here to Greece,
    The strong man sent for his steed.

While he was putting on apparel of the most princely kind—
His surcoat, with its symbol of spotless deeds
Environed on velvet with virtuous gems,
Was embellished and bound with embroidered seams,
And finely fur-lined with the fairest skins—
He did not leave the lace belt, the lady's gift:
For his own good, Gawain did not forget that!
When he had strapped the sword on his swelling hips,
The knight lapped his loins with his love-token twice,
Quickly wrapped it with relish round his waist.
The green silken girdle suited the gallant well,
Backed by the royal red cloth that richly showed.
But Gawain wore the girdle not for its great value,
Nor through pride in the pendants, in spite of their polish,
Nor for the gleaming gold which glinted on the ends,
But to save himself when of necessity he must
Stand an evil stroke, not resisting it with knife
        Or sword.
    When ready and robed aright,

Out came the comely lord;
To the men of name and might
His thanks in plenty poured.

Then was Gringolet got ready, that great huge horse.
Having been assiduously stabled in seemly quarters,
The fiery steed was fit and fretting for a gallop.
Sir Gawain stepped to him and, inspecting his coat,
Said earnestly to himself, asserting with truth,
"Here in this castle is a company whose conduct is honorable.
The man who maintains them, may he have joy!
The delightful lady, love befall her while she lives!
Thus for charity they cherish a chance guest
Honorably and open-handedly; may He on high,
The King of Heaven, requite you and your company too!
And if I could live any longer in lands on earth,
Some rich recompense, if I could, I should readily give you."
Then he stepped into the stirrup and swung aloft.
His man showed him his shield; on his shoulder he put it,
And gave the spur to Gringolet with his gold-spiked heels.
The horse sprang forward from the paving, pausing no more
To prance.
His man was mounted and fit,
Laden with spear and lance.
"This castle to Christ I commit:
May He its fortune enhance!"

The drawbridge was let down and the broad double gates
Were unbarred and borne open on both sides.
Passing over the planks, the prince blessed himself
And praised the kneeling porter, who proffered him "Good day,"
Praying God to grant that Gawain would be saved.
And Gawain went on his way with the one man
To put him on the right path for that perilous place
Where the sad assault must be received by him.
By bluffs where boughs were bare they passed,
Climbed by cliffs where the cold clung:
Under the high clouds, ugly mists
Merged damply with the moors and melted on the mountains;
Each hill had a hat, a huge mantle of mist.
Brooks burst forth above them, boiling over their banks
And showering down sharply in shimmering cascades.
Wonderfully wild was their way through the woods;
Till soon the sun in the sway of that season
Brought day.
They were on a lofty hill
Where snow beside them lay,
When the servant stopped still
And told his master to stay.

"For I have guided you to this ground, Sir Gawain, at this time,
And now you are not far from the noted place
Which you have searched for and sought with such special zeal.
But I must say to you, forsooth, since I know you,
And you are a lord whom I love with no little regard:
Take my governance as guide, and it shall go better for you,
For the place is perilous that you are pressing towards.
In that wilderness dwells the worst man in the world,
For he is valiant and fierce and fond of fighting,
And mightier than any man that may be on earth,
And his body is bigger than the best four
In Arthur's house, or Hector,[1] or any other.
At the Green Chapel he gains his great adventures.
No man passes that place, however proud in arms,
Without being dealt a death-blow by his dreadful hand.
For he is an immoderate man, to mercy a stranger;
For whether churl or chaplain by the chapel rides,
Monk or mass-priest or man of other kind,
He thinks it as convenient to kill him as keep alive himself.
Therefore I say, as certainly as you sit in your saddle,
If you come there you'll be killed, I caution you, knight,
Take my troth for it, though you had twenty lives
And more.
He has lived here since long ago
And filled the field with gore.
You cannot counter his blow,
It strikes so sudden and sore.

"Therefore, good Sir Gawain, leave the grim man alone!
Ride by another route, to some region remote!
Go in the name of God, and Christ grace your fortune!
And I shall go home again and undertake
To swear solemnly by God and his saints as well
(By my halidom,[2] so help me God, and every other oath)
Stoutly to keep your secret, not saying to a soul
That ever you tried to turn tail from any man I knew."
"Great thanks," replied Gawain, somewhat galled, and said,
"It is worthy of you to wish for my well-being, man,
And I believe you would loyally lock it in your heart.
But however quiet you kept it, if I quit this place,
Fled from the fellow in the fashion you propose,
I should become a cowardly knight with no excuse whatever,
For I will go to the Green Chapel, to get what Fate sends,
And have whatever words I wish with that worthy,
Whether weal or woe is what Fate
Demands.
Fierce though that fellow be,

1. Chief hero among the defenders of Troy and, like Arthur, one of the "Nine Worthies" celebrated for their heroic valor; or perhaps Arthur's knight Hector de Maris.
2. By my holy relics.

Clutching his club where he stands,
Our Lord can certainly see
That his own are in safe hands."

"By Mary!" said the other man, "If you mean what you say,
You are determined to take all your trouble on yourself.
If you wish to lose your life, I'll no longer hinder you.
Here's your lance for your hand, your helmet for your head.
Ride down this rough track round yonder cliff
Till you arrive in a rugged ravine at the bottom,
Then look about on the flat, on your left hand,
And you will view there in the vale that very chapel,
And the grim gallant who guards it always.
Now, noble Gawain, good-bye in God's name.
For all the gold on God's earth I would not go with you,
Nor foot it an inch further through this forest as your fellow."
Whereupon he wrenched at his reins, that rider in the woods,
Hit the horse with his heels as hard as he could,
Sent him leaping along, and left the knight there
Alone.
"By God!" said Gawain, "I swear
I will not weep or groan:
Being given to God's good care,
My trust in Him shall be shown."

Then he gave the spur to Gringolet and galloped down the path,
Thrust through a thicket there by a bank,
And rode down the rough slope right into the ravine.
Then he searched about, but it seemed savage and wild,
And no sign did he see of any sort of building;
But on both sides banks, beetling and steep,
And great crooked crags, cruelly jagged;
The bristling barbs of rock seemed to brush the sky.
Then he held in his horse, halted there,
Scanned on every side in search of the chapel.
He saw no such thing anywhere, which seemed remarkable,
Save, hard by in the open, a hillock of sorts,
A smooth-surfaced barrow[3] on a slope beside a stream
Which flowed forth fast there in its course,
Foaming and frothing as if feverishly boiling.
The knight, urging his horse, pressed onwards to the mound,
Dismounted manfully and made fast to a lime-tree
The reins, hooking them round a rough branch;
Then he went to the barrow, which he walked round, inspecting,
Wondering what in the world it might be.
It had a hole in each end and on either side,
And was overgrown with grass in great patches.

3. Perhaps a burial mound, which seems to link the moment to ancient, probably pagan inhabitants.

All hollow it was within, only an old cavern
Or the crevice of an ancient crag: he could not explain it
Aright.
"O God, is the Chapel Green
This mound?" said the noble knight.
"At such might Satan be seen
Saying matins at midnight."

"Now certainly the place is deserted," said Gawain,
"It is a hideous oratory, all overgrown,
And well graced for the gallant garbed in green
To deal out his devotions in the Devil's fashion.
Now I feel in my five wits, it is the Fiend himself
That has tricked me into this tryst, to destroy me here.
This is a chapel of mischance—checkmate to it!
It is the most evil holy place I ever entered."
With his high helmet on his head, and holding his lance,
He roamed up to the roof of that rough dwelling.
Then from that height he heard, from a hard rock
On the bank beyond the brook, a barbarous noise.
What! It clattered amid the cliffs fit to cleave them apart,
As if a great scythe were being ground on a grindstone there.
What! It whirred and it whetted like water in a mill.
What! It made a rushing, ringing din, rueful to hear.
"By God!" then said Gawain, "that is going on,
I suppose, as a salute to myself, to greet me
Hard by.
God's will be warranted:
'Alas!' is a craven cry.
No din shall make me dread
Although today I die."

Then the courteous knight called out clamorously,
"Who holds sway here and has an assignation with me?
For the good knight Gawain is on the ground here.
If anyone there wants anything, wend your way hither fast,
And further your needs either now, or not at all."
"Bide there!" said one on the bank above his head,
"And you shall swiftly receive what I once swore to give you."
Yet for a time he continued his tumult of scraping,
Turning away as he whetted, before he would descend.
Then he thrust himself round a thick crag through a hole,
Whirling round a wedge of rock with a frightful weapon,
A Danish axe[4] duly honed for dealing the blow,
With a broad biting edge, bow-bent along the handle,
Ground on a grindstone, a great four-foot blade—
No less, by that love-lace gleaming so brightly!
And the gallant in green was garbed as at first,

4. A long-bladed ax, associated with Viking raiders.

His looks and limbs the same, his locks and beard;
Save that steadily on his feet he strode on the ground,
Setting the handle to the stony earth and stalking beside it.
He would not wade through the water when he came to it,
But vaulted over on his axe, then with huge strides
Advanced violently and fiercely along the field's width
    On the snow.
  Sir Gawain went to greet
  The knight, not bowing low.
  The man said, "Sir so sweet,
  You honor the trysts you owe."

"Gawain," said the green knight, "may God guard you!
You are welcome to my dwelling, I warrant you,
And you have timed your travel here as a true man ought.
You know plainly the pact we pledged between us:
This time a twelvemonth ago you took your portion,
And now at this New Year I should nimbly requite you.
And we are on our own here in this valley
With no seconds to sunder us, spar as we will.
Take your helmet off your head, and have your payment here.
And offer no more argument or action than I did
When you whipped off my head with one stroke."
"No," said Gawain,"by God who gave me a soul,
The grievous gash to come I grudge you not at all;
Strike but the one stroke and I shall stand still
And offer you no hindrance; you may act freely,
    I swear."
  Head bent, Sir Gawain bowed,
  And showed the bright flesh bare.
  He behaved as if uncowed,
  Being loth to display his care.

Then the gallant in green quickly got ready,
Heaved his horrid weapon on high to hit Gawain,
With all the brute force in his body bearing it aloft,
Swinging savagely enough to strike him dead.
Had it driven down as direly as he aimed,
The daring dauntless man would have died from the blow.
But Gawain glanced up at the grim axe beside him
As it came shooting through the shivering air to shatter him,
And his shoulders shrank slightly from the sharp edge.
The other suddenly stayed the descending axe,
And then reproved the prince with many proud words:
"You are not Gawain," said the gallant, "whose greatness is such
That by hill or hollow no army ever frightened him;
For now you flinch for fear before you feel harm.
I never did know that knight to be a coward.
I neither flinched nor fled when you let fly your blow,
Nor offered any quibble in the house of King Arthur.

My head flew to my feet, but flee I did not.
Yet you quail cravenly though unscathed so far.
So I am bound to be called the better man
Therefore."
Said Gawain, "Not again
Shall I flinch as I did before;
But if my head pitch to the plain,
It's off for evermore.

"But be brisk, man, by your faith, and bring me to the point;
Deal me my destiny and do it out of hand,
For I shall stand your stroke, not starting at all
Till your axe has hit me. Here is my oath on it."
"Have at you then!" said the other, heaving up his axe,
Behaving as angrily as if he were mad.
He menaced him mightily, but made no contact,
Smartly withholding his hand without hurting him.
Gawain waited unswerving, with not a wavering limb,
But stood still as a stone or the stump of a tree
Gripping the rocky ground with a hundred grappling roots.
Then again the green knight began to gird:
"So now you have a whole heart I must hit you.
May the high knighthood which Arthur conferred
Preserve you and save your neck, if so it avail you!"
Then said Gawain, storming with sudden rage,
"Thrash on, you thrustful fellow, you threaten too much.
It seems your spirit is struck with self-dread."
"Forsooth," the other said, "You speak so fiercely
I will no longer lengthen matters by delaying your business,
I vow."
He stood astride to smite,
Lips pouting, puckered brow.
No wonder he lacked delight
Who expected no help now.

Up went the axe at once and hurtled down straight
At the naked neck with its knife-like edge.
Though it swung down savagely, slight was the wound,
A mere snick on the side, so that the skin was broken.
Through the fair fat to the flesh fell the blade,
And over his shoulders the shimmering blood shot to the ground.
When Sir Gawain saw his gore glinting on the snow,
He leapt feet close together a spear's length away,
Hurriedly heaved his helmet on to his head,
And shrugging his shoulders, shot his shield to the front,[5]
Swung out his bright sword and said fiercely,
(For never had the knight since being nursed by his mother

5. Gawain, who has displayed so much courtly refinement and religious emotion, now shows himself a practiced fighter, swiftly pulling his armor into place.

Been so buoyantly happy, so blithe in this world)
"Cease your blows, sir, strike me no more.
I have sustained a stroke here unresistingly,
And if you offer any more I shall earnestly reply.
Resisting, rest assured, with the most rancorous
Despite.
The single stroke is wrought
To which we pledged our plight
In high King Arthur's court:
Enough now, therefore, knight!"

The bold man stood back and bent over his axe,
Putting the haft to earth, and leaning on the head.
He gazed at Sir Gawain on the ground before him,
Considering the spirited and stout way he stood,
Audacious in arms; his heart warmed to him.
Then he gave utterance gladly in his great voice,
With resounding speech saying to the knight,
"Bold man, do not be so bloodily resolute.
No one here has offered you evil discourteously,
Contrary to the covenant made at the King's court.
I promised a stroke, which you received: consider yourself paid.
I cancel all other obligations of whatever kind.
If I had been more active, perhaps I could
Have made you suffer by striking a savager stroke.
First in foolery I made a feint at striking,
Not rending you with a riving cut—and right I was,
On account of the first night's covenant we accorded;
For you truthfully kept your trust in troth with me,
Giving me your gains, as a good man should.
The further feinted blow was for the following day,
When you kissed my comely wife, and the kisses came to me:
For those two things, harmlessly I thrust twice at you
Feinted blows.
Truth for truth's the word;
No need for dread, God knows.
From your failure at the third
The tap you took arose.

"For that braided belt you wear belongs to me.
I am well aware that my own wife gave it you.
Your conduct and your kissings are completely known to me,
And the wooing by my wife—my work set it on.
I instructed her to try you, and you truly seem
To be the most perfect paladin ever to pace the earth.
As the pearl to the white pea in precious worth,
So in good faith is Gawain to other gay knights.
But here your faith failed you, you flagged somewhat, sir,
Yet it was not for a well-wrought thing, nor for wooing either,
But for love of your life, which is less blameworthy."

The other strong man stood considering this a while,
So filled with fury that his flesh trembled,
And the blood from his breast burst forth in his face
As he shrank for shame at what the chevalier spoke of.
The first words the fair knight could frame were:
"Curses on both cowardice and covetousness!
Their vice and villainy are virtue's undoing."
Then he took the knot, with a twist twitched it loose,
And fiercely flung the fair girdle to the knight.
"Lo! There is the false thing, foul fortune befall it!
I was craven about our encounter, and cowardice taught me
To accord with covetousness and corrupt my nature
And the liberality and loyalty belonging to chivalry.
Now I am faulty and false and found fearful always.
In the train of treachery and untruth go woe
 And shame.
I acknowledge, knight, how ill
I behaved, and take the blame.
Award what penance you will:
Henceforth I'll shun ill-fame."

Then the other lord laughed and politely said,
"In my view you have made amends for your misdemeanor;
You have confessed your faults fully with fair acknowledgement,
And plainly done penance at the point of my axe.
You are absolved of your sin and as stainless now
As if you had never fallen in fault since first you were born.
As for the gold-hemmed girdle, I give it you, sir,
Seeing it is as green as my gown. Sir Gawain, you may
Think about this trial when you throng in company
With paragons of princes, for it is a perfect token,
At knightly gatherings, of the great adventure at the Green Chapel.
You shall come back to my castle this cold New Year,
And we shall revel away the rest of this rich feast;
 Let us go."
Thus urging him, the lord
Said, "You and my wife, I know
We shall bring to clear accord,
Though she was your fierce foe."

"No, forsooth," said the knight, seizing his helmet,
And doffing it with dignity as he delivered this thanks,
"My stay has sufficed me. Still, luck go with you!
May He who bestows all good, honor you with it!
And commend me to the courteous lady, your comely wife;
Indeed, my due regards to both dear ladies,
Who with their wanton wiles have thus waylaid their knight.
But it is no marvel for a foolish man to be maddened thus
And saddled with sorrow by the sleights of women.
For here on earth was Adam taken in by one,

And Solomon by many such, and Samson likewise;
Delilah dealt him his doom; and David, later still,
Was blinded by Bathsheba, and badly suffered for it.[6]
Since these were troubled by their tricks, it would be true joy
To love them but not believe them, if a lord could,
For these were the finest of former times, most favored by fortune
Of all under the heavenly kingdom whose hearts were
        Abused;
    These four all fell to schemes
    Of women whom they used.
    If I am snared, it seems
    I ought to be excused.

"But your girdle," said Gawain, "God requite you for it!
Not for the glorious gold shall I gladly wear it,
Nor for the stuff nor the silk nor the swaying pendants,
Nor for its worth, fine workmanship or wonderful honor;
But as a sign of my sin I shall see it often,
Remembering with remorse, when I am mounted in glory,
The fault and faintheartedness of the perverse flesh,
How it tends to attract tarnishing sin.
So when pride shall prick me for my prowess in arms,
One look at this love-lace will make lowly my heart.
But one demand I make of you, may it not incommode you:
Since you are master of the demesne I have remained in a while,
Make known, by your knighthood—and now may He above,
Who sits on high and holds up heaven, requite you!—
How you pronounce your true name; and no more requests."
"Truly," the other told him, "I shall tell you my title.
Bertilak of the High Desert I am called here in this land.
Through the might of Morgan the Fay,[7] who remains in my house,
Through the wiles of her witchcraft, a lore well learned—
Many of the magical arts of Merlin she acquired,
For she lavished fervent love long ago
On that susceptible sage: certainly your knights know
        Of their fame.
    So 'Morgan the Goddess'
    She accordingly became;
    The proudest she can oppress
    And to her purpose tame—

"She sent me forth in this form to your famous hall
To put to the proof the great pride of the house,
The reputation for high renown of the Round Table;

6. Gawain suddenly erupts in a brief but fierce diatribe, including this list of treacherous Biblical women, often mentioned in contemporary antifeminist texts.
7. Morgan is Arthur's half-sister and ruler of the mysterious Avalon; she learned magical arts from Merlin. Her presence can bode good or ill. In some stories she holds a deep grudge against Guinevere, yet she carries off the wounded Arthur after his final battle, perhaps to heal him. The earlier Celtic Morrigan, possibly related, is queen of demons, sower of discord, and goddess of war.

She bewitched me in this weird way to bewilder your wits,
And to grieve Guinevere and goad her to death
With ghastly fear of that ghost's ghoulish speaking
With his head in his hand before the high table.
That is the aged beldame who is at home:
She is indeed your own aunt, Arthur's half-sister,
Daughter of the Duchess of Tintagel who in due course,
By Uther, was mother of Arthur, who now holds sway.[8]
Therefore I beg you, bold sir, come back to your aunt,
Make merry in my house, for my men love you,
And by my faith, brave sir, I bear you as much good will
As I grant any man under God, for your great honesty."
But Gawain firmly refused with a final negative.
They clasped and kissed, commending each other
To the Prince of Paradise, and parted on the cold ground
        Right there.
    Gawain on steed serene
    Spurred to court with courage fair,
    And the gallant garbed in green
    To wherever he would elsewhere.

Now Gawain goes riding on Gringolet
In lonely lands, his life saved by grace.
Often he stayed at a house, and often in the open,
And often overcame hazards in the valleys,
Which at this time I do not intend to tell you about.
The hurt he had had in his neck was healed,
And the glittering girdle that girt him round
Obliquely, like a baldric,[9] was bound by his side
And laced under the left arm with a lasting knot,
In token that he was taken in a tarnishing sin;
And so he came to court, quite unscathed.
When the great became aware of Gawain's arrival
There was general jubilation at the joyful news.
The King kissed the knight, and the Queen likewise,
And so did many a staunch noble who sought to salute him.
They all asked him about his expedition,
And he truthfully told them of his tribulations—
What chanced at the chapel, the good cheer of the knight,
The lady's love-making, and lastly, the girdle.
He displayed the scar of the snick on his neck
Where the bold man's blow had hit, his bad faith to
        Proclaim;
    He groaned at his disgrace,
    Unfolding his ill-fame,

8. The poem now recalls an earlier transgression of guest-host obligations, when Uther began to lust for Ygerne while her husband, Gorlois, was at his court; he later killed Gorlois and married Ygerne.

9. A belt for a sword or bugle, worn over one shoulder and across the chest.

And blood suffused his face
When he showed his mark of shame.
"Look, my lord," said Gawain, the lace in his hand.
"This belt confirms the blame I bear on my neck,
My bane and debasement, the burden I bear
For being caught by cowardice and covetousness.
This is the figure of the faithlessness found in me,
Which I must needs wear while I live.
For man can conceal sin but not dissever from it,
So when it is once fixed, it will never be worked loose."
First the King, then all the court, comforted the knight,
And all the lords and ladies belonging to the Table
Laughed at it loudly, and concluded amiably
That each brave man of the brotherhood should bear a baldric,
A band, obliquely about him, of bright green,
Of the same hue as Sir Gawain's and for his sake wear it.
So it ranked as renown to the Round Table,
And an everlasting honor to him who had it,
As is rendered in Romance's rarest book.
Thus in the days of Arthur this exploit was achieved,
To which the books of Brutus bear witness;
After the bold baron, Brutus, came here,
The siege and the assault being ceased at Troy
Before.
Such exploits, I'll be sworn,
Have happened here of yore.
Now Christ with his crown of thorn
Bring us his bliss evermore! AMEN

HONY SOYT QUI MAL PENCE[1]

Sir Thomas Malory

c. 1410–1471

The full identity of Sir Thomas Malory shimmers just beyond our grasp. In several of his colophons—those closing formulas to texts—the author of the *Morte Darthur* says he is "a knyght presoner, sir Thomas Malleorré," and prays that "God sende hym good delyveraunce sone and hastely." Scholars have traced a number of such names in the era, among whom two seem particularly likely: Sir Thomas Malory of Newbold Revell, and Thomas Malory of Papworth. The former Thomas Malory had a scabrous criminal record and was long kept prisoner awaiting trial, while the latter had links to a rich collection of Arthurian books.

1. "Shamed be he who thinks ill thereof," the motto of the Order of the Garter, a chivalric order founded by Edward III about 1350. While the green girdle does not resemble the blue garter, this motto at the end of the poem serves to connect it with contemporary efforts to celebrate traditional knighthood.

Another colophon provides the more useful information that "the hoole book of kyng Arthur and of his noble knyghtes of the Rounde Table" was completed in the ninth year of King Edward IV, that is 1469 or 1470. So whichever Malory wrote the *Morte Darthur*, he was certainly working in the unsettled years of the Wars of the Roses, in which the great ducal families of York and Lancaster battled for control of the English throne. As one family gained dominance, adherents of the other were often jailed on flimsy charges. The spectacle of a nation threatening to crumble into clan warfare provides much of the thematic weight of the *Morte Darthur*, while the declining chivalric order of the later fifteenth century underlies Malory's increasingly elegiac tone.

Whether he gained his remarkable knowledge of French and English Arthurian tradition in or out of jail, Malory infused his version of these stories with a darkening perspective very much his own. Malory sensed the high aspirations, especially the bonds of honor and fellowship in battle, that held together Arthur's realm. Yet he was also bleakly aware of how tenuous those bonds were and how easily undone by tragically competing pressures. These include the centuries-old Arthurian preoccupation with transgressive love, but Malory is more concerned with the conflicting claims of loyalty to clan or king, the urge to avenge the death of a fellow knight, and the resulting alienation even among the best of knights. Still more unnerving, agents of a virtually unmotivated or unexplained malice have ever more impact as the *Morte Darthur* progresses.

For all his initial energy and control, Malory's Arthur is increasingly a king forced to suppress knightly grievances, to deplore religious quest, even to overlook the adultery of his wife and his greatest knight, all in the interest of his fading hopes for chivalric honor and unity. Arthur's commitment to courtesy finally undoes his honor in the eyes of his own knights. As the Round Table is broken (an image Malory uses repeatedly) Arthur is put in the agonizing position of acting as judge in his wife's trial, making war on his early companion Lancelot, and finally engaging in single combat with his own treacherous son Mordred.

Malory would have found many of these themes in his sources. Twelfth-century Arthurian romances in French verse had explored the elevation and danger of courtly eroticism, and the theme was extended in the enormous French prose versions of the thirteenth century that Malory had read in great detail. In these prose romances, too, religious and chivalric themes converged around the story of the Grail. Malory also knew the *Morte Arthur* poems of fourteenth-century England, with their emphases on conquest, treachery, and the military details of Arthur's final battles.

Malory regularly acknowledges these sources, but his powers of synthesis and the stamp of his style make his *Morte Darthur* unique. While he occasionally writes a complex, reflective sentence, Malory's prose is typically composed of simple, idiomatic narrative statements, and speeches so brief as to be almost gnomic. On hearing of his brother's death, Gawain faints, then rises and says only "Alas!" Yet the grief of his cry resonates across the closing episodes of the work. Malory's imagery is similarly resonant. He tends to strip it of the explanations that had become frequent in the French prose works, and he concentrates its impact by an almost obsessive repetition. The later episodes of the work become almost an incantation of breakage and dispersal, blood and wounds, each image cluster reaching alternately toward religious experience or secular destruction.

These versions of chivalric ambition, sacred or secular, do not divide easily in the *Morte Darthur*. The saintly Galahad and the scheming Mordred may represent extremes of contrary ambition, but Malory is more preoccupied by the sadly mixed motives of Lancelot or Arthur himself. In three late episodes offered below, the reader is drawn into the perspective of lesser knights like Bors and Bedivere, who witness great moments while affecting them only marginally. They bring back to the world of lesser men stories of uncanny experience and oversee their conversion from verbal rumor to written form, whether in books or on tombs. Much of Malory's power and his continuing appeal come from his unresolved doubleness of perspective. Whether by way of his characters or his style, resonant and mysterious elements emerge from a narrative of gritty realism.

For additional resources on Malory, go to *The Longman Anthology of British Literature* Web site at www.myliteraturekit.com.

from Morte Darthur

from Caxton's Prologue[1]

After that I had accomplysshed and fynysshed dyuers hystoryes as
wel of° contemplacyon as of other hystoryal and worldly actes of *both about*
grete conquerours and prynces, and also certeyn bookes of en-
saumples° and doctryne, many noble and dyuers gentylmen of thys *moral tales*
royame° of Englond camen and demaunded me many and oftymes, *realm*
wherefore that I haue not do made and enprynte the noble hystorye
of the Sayntgreal° and of the moost renomed° Crysten kyng, fyrst *Holy Grail / famed*
and chyef of the thre best Crysten[2] and worthy, Kyng Arthur,
whyche ought moost to be remembred emonge vs Englysshemen
tofore° al other Crysten kynges. * * * *before*

To whome I answerd that dyuers men holde oppynyon that
there was no suche Arthur, and that alle suche bookes as been maad
of hym ben° but fayned and fables, bycause that somme cronycles *are*
make of hym no mencyon ne° remembre hym noothynge ne of his *nor*
knyghtes.

Wherto they answerd, and one in specyal sayd, that in hym
that shold say or thynke that there was neuer suche a kyng callyd
Arthur myght wel be aretted° grete folye and blyndenesse; for he *presumed*
sayd that there were many euydences of the contrarye. Fyrst ye
may see his sepulture° in the monasterye of Glastyngburye. And *tomb*
also in Polycronycon,[3] * * * where his body was buryed and after
founden and translated into the sayd monasterye. Ye shal se also
in th'ystory of Bochas, in his book De Casu Principum,[4] parte of
his noble actes and also of his falle; also Galfrydus in his Brutysshe
book[5] recounteth his lyf. And in dyuers places of Englond many
remembraunces ben yet of hym and shall remayne perpetuelly, and
also of his knyghtes. Fyrst in the Abbey of Westmestre at Saynt
Edwardes Shryne remayneth the prynte of his seal in reed waxe

1. The first English printer, William Caxton exerted a major literary influence through his translations of French works and his pioneering editions of English writers, including Chaucer and Gower. In 1485 he published a version of *Le Morte Darthur*, probably based on a revision by Malory himself but different from the text edited by Eugene Vinaver (1947, 1975) and used here. Caxton's *Prologue* is interesting in its own right as an early response to Malory, even as Caxton takes the opportunity to promote interest in his book. To give a sense of early printed English, the passages from Caxton's *Prologue* are presented in unaltered spelling.

2. Arthur appears in the traditional list of "nine worthies," three heroes each from pagan, Jewish, and Christian narratives.

3. The *Polychronicon*, a universal history by the monk Ranulph Higden (d. 1364).

4. Boccaccio's *On the Fall of Princes*.

5. Geoffrey of Monmouth, *History of the Kings of Britain*, whose later versions were often called simply *Brut*.

closed in beryll, in which is wryton, PATRICIUS ARTHURUS BRITANNIE GALLIE GERMANIE DACIE IMPERATOR.[6] Item° *also* in the Castel of Douer ye may see Gauwayns skulle and Cradoks mantel; at Wynchester, the Round Table; in other places, Launcelottes swerde, and many other thynges.

Thenne, al these thynges consydered, there can no man resonably gaynsaye but there was a kyng of thys lande named Arthur. * * *

Thenne al these thynges forsayd aledged, I coude not wel denye but that there was suche a noble kynge named Arthur, and reputed one of the ix worthy, and fyrst and chyef of the Cristen men. And many noble volumes be made of hym and of his noble knyghtes in Frensshe, which I haue seen and redde beyonde the see, which been not had in our maternal tongue. But in Walsshe ben many, and also in Frensshe, and somme in Englysshe, but nowher nygh alle. Wherfore suche as haue late ben drawen oute bryefly° *abridged* into Englysshe, I haue, after the symple connyng° *wit* that God hath sente to me, vnder the fauour and correctyon of al noble lordes and gentylmen, enprysed° *undertaken* to enprynte a book of the noble hystoryes of the sayd Kynge Arthur and of certeyn of his knyghtes, after a copye vnto me delyuerd, whyche copye Syr Thomas Malorye dyd take oute of certeyn bookes of Frensshe and reduced it into Englysshe. And I, accordyng to my copye, haue doon sette it in enprynte, to the entente° *with the aim* that noble men may see and lerne the noble actes of chyualrye, the ientyl° *noble* and vertuous dedes that somme knyghtes used in tho° *those* dayes, by whyche they came to honour, and how they that were vycious were punysshed and ofte put to shame and rebuke. Humbly bysechyng al noble lordes and ladyes, wyth al other estates° *ranks* of what estate or degree they been of, that shal see and rede in this sayd book and werke, that they take the good and honest actes in their remembraunce and to folowe the same, wherin they shalle fynde many ioyous and playsaunt hystoryes and noble and renomed actes of humanyte, gentylness, and chyualryes. For herein may be seen noble chyualrye, curtosye, humanyte, frendlynesse, hardynesse, loue, frendshyp, cowardyse, murdre, hate, vertue, and synne. Doo after the good and leue the euyl, and it shal brynge you to good fame and renommee.° *renown*

And for to passe the tyme thys book shal be plesaunte to rede in, but for to gyue fayth and byleue that al is trewe that is conteyned herin, ye be at your lyberte. But al is wryton for our doctryne and for to beware that we falle not to vyce ne synne, but t'excersyse° *to practice* and folowe vertu, by whyche we may come and atteyne to good fame and renomme in thys lyf, and after thys shorte and transytorye lyf to come vnto euerlastyng blysse in heuen, the whyche He graunte vs that reygneth in heuen, the Blessyd Trynyte. Amen.

6. The Noble Arthur, Emperor of Britain, Gaul, Germany, Dacia.

The Miracle of Galahad[1]

Now saith the tale that Sir Galahad rode many journeys in vain, and at last he came to the abbey where King Mordrains was. And when he heard that, he thought he would abide to see him.

And so upon the morn, when he had heard mass, Sir Galahad came unto King Mordrains. And anon the king saw him, which had lain blind of long time, and then he dressed him against° *(rose to meet)* him and said,

"Sir Galahad, the servant of Jesu Christ and very° *(true)* knight, whose coming I have abiden° *(awaited)* long, now embrace me and let me rest on thy breast, so that I may rest° *(die)* between thine arms! For thou art a clean virgin above all knights, as the flower of the lily in whom virginity is signified. And thou art the rose which is the flower of all good virtue, and in colour of fire.[2] For the fire of the Holy Ghost is taken so in thee that my flesh, which was all dead of oldness, is become again young."

When Galahad heard these words, then he embraced him and all his body. Then said he,° *(Mordrains)*

"Fair Lord Jesu Christ, now I have my will! Now I require Thee, in this point° *(state)* that I am in, that Thou come and visit me."

And anon Our Lord heard his prayer, and therewith the soul departed from the body. And then Sir Galahad put him in the earth as a king ought to be, and so departed and came into a perilous forest where he found the well which boiled with great waves, as the tale telleth tofore.° *(earlier)*

And as soon as Sir Galahad set his hand thereto it ceased, so that it brent° *(burned)* no more, and anon the heat departed away. And cause why it brent, it was a sign of lechery that was that time much used. But that heat might not abide his pure virginity. And so this was taken in the country for a miracle, and so ever after was it called Galahad's Well.

So by adventure he came unto the country of Gore, and into the abbey where Sir Lancelot had been toforehand and found the tomb of King Bagdemagus; but he was founder thereof.[3] For there was the tomb of Joseph of Arimathea's son and the tomb of Simeon, where Lancelot had failed.[4] Then he looked into a croft° *(crypt)* under the minster,° *(church)* and there he saw a tomb which brent full marvellously. Then asked he the brethren what it was.

"Sir," said they, "a marvellous adventure that may not be brought to an end but by him that passeth of bounty and of knighthood all them of the Round Table."

1. From *The Holy Grail*, in *King Arthur and His Knights*, ed. Eugène Vinaver (1975). Earlier in the text, Lancelot's saintly son Galahad had come to the Round Table and precipitated a brief apparition of the Holy Grail (the cup or dish with which Christ had celebrated the Last Supper). One hundred fifty of Arthur's knights then took a vow to seek a fuller vision of the Grail, but in the mysterious adventures that followed, many died or despaired. Malory's attention now narrows to Lancelot and his partial vision of the Grail, and the continuing quest of Galahad, Perceval, and Bors. The blind King Mordrains is one of several maimed or aged kings cured by Galahad's presence.

2. Galahad's physical and spiritual purity are shown in a number of earlier episodes.

3. Gore, the mysterious realm of Bagdemagus, who had been gravely wounded when he presumed to take a shield intended for Galahad. Words may be missing from the final phrase.

4. In Arthurian tradition, Joseph of Arimathea was keeper of the Grail and used it to catch Christ's blood at the Crucifixion. His son Joseph was the first Christian bishop and carried both the faith and the Grail to England. Galahad is the last of their lineage. Lancelot's failure refers to an episode in the French source that Malory never tells, either inadvertently or because he assumed that many readers would know the story.

"I would," said Sir Galahad, "that ye would bring me thereto."

"Gladly," said they, and so led him till° a cave. And he went down upon greses° and came unto the tomb. And so the flaming failed, and the fire staunched° which many a day had been great. *to* *steps* *was quenched*

Then came there a voice which said,

"Much are ye beholden to thank God which hath given you a good hour,° that ye may draw out the souls of earthly pain and to put them into the joys of Paradise. Sir, I am of your kindred, which hath dwelled in this heat this three hundred winter and four-and-fifty to be purged of the sin that I did against Arimathea Joseph." *good luck*

Then Sir Galahad took the body in his arms and bare it into the minster. And that night lay Sir Galahad in the abbey; and on the morn he gave him his service and put him in the earth before the high altar.

So departed he from thence, and commended the brethren to God, and so he rode five days till that he came to the Maimed King. And ever followed Perceval the five days asking where he had been, and so one told him how the adventures of Logres were achieved.[5] So on a day it befell that he came out of a great forest, and there they met at traverse with Sir Bors[6] which rode alone. It is no need to ask if they were glad! And so he salewed them, and they yielded to him° honour and good adventure, and everych told other how they had sped. Then said Sir Bors, *wished him*

"It is more than a year and a half that I ne lay° ten times where men dwelled, but in wild forests and in mountains. But God was ever my comfort." *have not slept*

Then rode they a great while till they came to the castle of Corbenic. And when they were entered within, King Pelles knew them. So there was great joy, for he wist well by their coming that they had fulfilled the Sankgreall.[7]

Then Eliazar, King Pelles' son, brought tofore them the broken sword wherewith Joseph was stricken through the thigh.[8] Then Bors set his hand thereto to essay if he might have sowded° it again; but it would not be. Then he took it to Perceval, but he had no more power thereto than he. *joined*

"Now have ye it again," said Sir Perceval unto Sir Galahad, "for an° it be ever achieved by any bodily man, ye must do it." *if*

And then he took the pieces and set them together, and seemed to them as it had never be broken, and as well as it was first forged. And when they within espied that the adventure of the sword was achieved, then they gave the sword to Sir Bors, for it might no better be set,° for he was so good a knight and a worthy man. *used*

And a little before even the sword[9] arose, great and marvellous, and was full of great heat, that many men fell for dread. And anon alight a voice among them and said, "They that ought not to sit at

5. Perceval has followed Galahad's movements. Malory reduces a five-year period in his source to five days and omits the two knights' meeting.
6. Sir Bors has also been wandering in search of the Grail.
7. Pelles is the maimed king and keeper of Corbenic, the Grail Castle. The past tense looks forward to events not yet achieved.
8. This sword had wounded Joseph of Arimathea; joining its broken halves is part of the Grail quest.
9. Malory misconstrues a phrase meaning "a wind."

the table of Our Lord Jesu Christ, avoid° hence! For now there shall *withdraw*
very° knights be fed." *true*

So they went thence, all save King Pelles and Eliazar, his son, which were holy men, and a maid which was his niece. And so there abode these three knights and these three; else were no more. And anon they saw knights all armed come in at the hall door, and did off their helms and their arms, and said unto Sir Galahad,

"Sir, we have hied° right much for to be with you at this table *hastened*
where the holy meat shall be departed."° *distributed*

Then said he, "Ye be welcome! But of whence be ye?"

So three of them said they were of Gaul, and other three said they were of Ireland, and other three said they were of Denmark.

And so as they sat thus, there came out a bed of tree° *wood*
of° a chamber, which four gentlewomen brought; and in the bed *from*
lay a good man sick, and had a crown of gold upon his head. And there, in the midst of the palace, they set him down and went again. Then he lift up his head and said,

"Sir Galahad, good knight, ye be right welcome, for much have I desired your coming! For in such pain and in such anguish as I
have no man else° might have suffered long. But now I trust to God *no other man*
the term is come that my pain shall be allayed, and so I shall pass out of this world, so as it was promised me long ago."

And therewith a voice said, "There be two among you that be not in the quest of the Sankgreall, and therefore departeth!"

Then King Pelles and his son departed. And therewithal be-
seemed them° that there came an old man and four angels from *it seemed*
heaven, clothed in likeness of a bishop, and had a cross in his hand. And these four angels bare him up in a chair and set him down before the table of silver whereupon the Sankgreall was. And it seemed that he had in midst of his forehead letters which said: "See ye here Joseph, the first bishop of Christendom, the same which Our Lord succoured[1] in the city of Sarras in the spiritual palace." Then the knights marvelled, for that bishop was dead more than three hundred year tofore.

"Ah, knights," said he, "marvel not, for I was sometime an earthly man."

So with that they heard the chamber door open, and there they saw angels; and two bare candles of wax, and the third bare a towel,[2] and the fourth a spear which bled marvellously, that the drops fell within a box which he held with his other hand. And anon they set the candles upon the table, and the third the towel upon the vessel,
and the fourth the holy spear even° upright upon the vessel. *straight*

And then the bishop made semblaunt as though he would
have gone to the sacring° of a mass, and then he took an *consecration*
ubblie° which was made in likeness of bread. And at the lifting *wafer*
up there came a figure in likeness of a child, and the visage was as
red and as bright as any fire, and smote himself° into the bread, *impressed itself*
that all they saw it that the bread was formed of a fleshly man.

1. Joseph of Arimathea was blessed by Christ.
2. In the French source, a veil of samite.

And then he put it into the holy vessel again, and then he did that longed° to a priest to do mass. *what was right*

And then he went to Sir Galahad and kissed him and bade him go and kiss his fellows. And so he did anon.

"Now," said he, "the servants of Jesu Christ, ye shall be fed afore this table with sweet meats that never knights yet tasted."

And when he had said he vanished away. And they set them at the table in great dread and made their prayers. Then looked they and saw a Man come out of the holy vessel that had all the signs of the Passion of Jesu Christ, bleeding all openly, and said,

"My knights and my servants and my true children which be come out of deadly life into the spiritual life, I will no longer cover me from you, but ye shall see now a part of my secrets and of my hid things. Now holdeth and receiveth the high order and meat which ye have so much desired."

Then took He himself the holy vessel and came to Sir Galahad. And he kneeled down and received his Saviour. And after him so received all his fellows, and they thought it so sweet that it was marvellous to tell. Then said He to Sir Galahad,

"Son, wotest thou what I hold betwixt my hands?"

"Nay," said he, "but if ye tell me."

"This is," said He, "the holy dish wherein I ate the lamb on Easter Day, and now hast thou seen that thou most desired to see. But yet hast thou not seen it so openly as thou shalt see it in the city of Sarras, in the spiritual palace. Therefore thou must go hence and bear with thee this holy vessel, for this night it shall depart from the realm of Logres, and it shall nevermore be seen here. And knowest thou wherefore? For he° is not served nother worshipped to his right° by them of this land, for they be turned to evil living, and therefore I shall disinherit them of the honour which I have done them. And therefore go ye three to-morn unto the sea, where ye shall find your ship ready, and with you take the sword with the strange girdles,° and no more with you but Sir Perceval and Sir Bors. Also I will that ye take with you of this blood of this spear for to anoint the Maimed King, both his legs and his body, and he shall have his heal." *it / properly* *belts*

"Sir," said Galahad, "why shall not these other fellows go with us?"

"For this cause: for right as I depart° my apostles one here and another there, so I will that ye depart. And two of you shall die in my service, and one of you shall come again and tell tidings." *separate*

Then gave He them His blessing and vanished away.

And Sir Galahad went anon to the spear which lay upon the table and touched the blood with his fingers, and came after to the maimed knight and anointed his legs and his body. And therwith he clothed him anon, and start upon his feet out of his bed as an whole man, and thanked God that He had healed him. And anon he left the world and yielded himself to a place of religion of white monks,[3] and was a full holy man.

3. The white monks were Cistercians, whose spirituality had some role in Malory's French sources.

And that same night, about midnight, came a voice among them which said,

"My sons, and not my chief sons,[4] my friends, and not mine enemies, go ye hence where ye hope best to do, and as I bade you do."

"Ah, thanked be Thou, Lord, that Thou wilt whightsauf° to call us Thy sons! Now may we well prove that we have not lost our pains." *vouchsafe*

And anon in all haste they took their harness and departed; but the three knights of Gaul (one of them hight Claudine, King Claudas' son, and the other two were great gentlemen) then prayed° Sir Galahad to everych of them, that an° they come to King Arthur's court, "to salew my lord Sir Lancelot, my father and them all of the Round Table"; and prayed them, an they came on that party,° not to forget it. *asked* *if* *to that region*

Right so departed Sir Galahad, and Sir Perceval and Sir Bors with him, and so they rode three days. And then they came to a rivage° and found the ship whereof the tale speaketh of tofore. And when they came to the board° they found in the midst of the bed the table of silver which they had left with the Maimed King, and the Sankgreall which was covered with red samite.° Then were they glad to have such things in their fellowship; and so they entered and made great reverence thereto, and Sir Galahad fell on his knees and prayed long time to Our Lord, that at what time he asked he might pass out of this world. And so long he prayed till a voice said, *shore* *on board* *silk*

"Sir Galahad, thou shalt have thy request, and when thou asketh the death of thy body thou shalt have it, and then shalt thou have the life of thy soul."

Then Sir Perceval heard him a little, and prayed him of° fellowship that was between them wherefore he asked such things. *for the sake of*

"Sir, that shall I tell you," said Sir Galahad. "This other day, when we saw a part of the adventures of the Sankgreall, I was in such a joy of heart that I trow° never man was that was earthly. And therefore I wot° well, when my body is dead, my soul shall be in great joy to see the Blessed Trinity every day, and the majesty of Our Lord, Jesu Christ." *believe* *know*

And so long were they in the ship that they said to Galahad,

"Sir, in this bed ye ought to lie, for so saith the letters."° *writings*

And so he laid him down, and slept a great while. And when he awaked he looked tofore him and saw the city of Sarras. And as they would have landed they saw the ship wherein Sir Perceval had put his sister in.

"Truly," said Sir Perceval, "in the name of God, well hath my sister holden us covenant."[5]

Then they took out of the ship the table of silver, and he took it to Sir Perceval and to Sir Bors to go tofore, and Sir Galahad came behind, and right so they went into the city. And at the gate of the

4. A confusing phrase, perhaps in error for "stepsons."

5. Kept her promise to us. In an earlier episode Perceval's sister died after giving a basin of her blood to heal a leper woman.

city they saw an old man crooked, and anon Sir Galahad called him and bade him help "to bear this heavy thing."

"Truly," said the old man, "it is ten year ago that I might not go but with crutches."

"Care thou not," said Galahad, "and arise up and show thy good will!"

And so he essayed, and found himself as whole as ever he was. Then ran he to the table and took one part against° Galahad. *beside*

Anon arose there a great noise in the city that a cripple was made whole by knights marvellous that entered into the city. Then anon after the three knights went to the water and brought up into the palace Sir Perceval's sister, and buried her as richly as them ought a king's daughter.

And when the king of that country knew that and saw that fellowship (whose name was Estorause), he asked them of whence they were, and what thing it was that they had brought upon the table of silver. And they told him the truth of the Sankgreall, and the power which God hath set there.

Then this king was a tyrant, and was come of the line of paynims,° and took them and put them in prison in a deep hole. But as soon as they were there Our Lord sent them the Sankgreall, through whose grace they were alway fulfilled° while that they were in prison. *pagans* *fed*

So at the year's end it befell that this king lay sick and felt that he should die. Then he sent for the three knights, and they came afore him, and he cried them mercy of that he had done to them, and they forgave it him goodly, and he died anon.

When the king was dead all the city stood dismayed and wist° not who might be their king. Right so as they were in council there came a voice among them, and made them choose the youngest knight of three to be their king, "for he shall well maintain you and all yours." *knew*

So they made Sir Galahad king by all the assent of the whole city, and else they would have slain him. And when he was come to behold his land he let make° above the table of silver a chest of gold and of precious stones that covered the holy vessel, and every day early the three knights would come before it and make their prayers. *had made*

Now at the year's end, and the self Sunday after that Sir Galahad had borne the crown of gold, he arose up early and his fellows, and came to the palace, and saw tofore them the holy vessel and a man kneeling on his knees in likeness of a bishop that had about him a great fellowship of angels, as it had been Jesu Christ himself. And then he arose and began a mass of Our Lady. And so he came to the sacring, and anon made an end. He called Sir Galahad unto him and said,

"Come forth, the servant of Jesu Christ, and thou shalt see that thou hast much desired to see."

And then he began to tremble right hard when the deadly° flesh began to behold the spiritual things. Then he held up his hands toward heaven and said, *mortal*

"Lord, I thank Thee, for now I see that that hath been my desire many a day. Now, my Blessed Lord, I would not live in this wretched world no longer, if it might please Thee, Lord."

And therewith the good man took Our Lord's Body[6] betwixt his hands, proffered it to Sir Galahad, and he received it right gladly and meekly.

"Now wotest thou what I am?" said the good man.

"Nay, Sir," said Sir Galahad.

"I am Joseph, the son of Joseph of Arimathea, which Our Lord hath sent to thee to bear thee fellowship. And wotest thou wherefore He hath sent me more than any other? For thou hast resembled me in two things: that thou hast seen, that is the marvels of the Sankgreall, and for thou hast been a clean maiden° as I have been and am."

chaste virgin

And when he had said these words Sir Galahad went to Sir Perceval and kissed him and commended him to God. And so he went to Sir Bors and kissed him and commended him to God, and said,

"My fair lord, salew me° unto my lord Sir Lancelot, my father, and as soon as ye see him bid him remember of this world unstable."

give my greeting

And therewith he kneeled down tofore the table and made his prayers. And so suddenly departed his soul to Jesu Christ, and a great multitude of angels bare it up to heaven, even in the sight of his two fellows.

Also these two knights saw come from heaven an hand, but they saw not the body, and so it came right to the vessel, and took it, and the spear, and so bare it up to heaven. And sithen° was there never man so hardy to say that he had seen the Sankgreall.

since then

So when Sir Perceval and Sir Bors saw Sir Galahad dead they made as much sorrow as ever did men. And if they had not been good men they might lightly° have fallen in despair. And so people of the country and city, they were right heavy. But so he was buried, and soon as he was buried Sir Perceval yielded him to an hermitage out of the city and took religious clothing. And Sir Bors was alway with him, but he changed never his secular clothing, for that he purposed him to go again into the realm of Logres.

easily

Thus a year and two months lived Sir Perceval in the hermitage a full holy life, and then passed out of the world. Then Sir Bors let bury him by[7] his sister and by Sir Galahad in the spiritualities.°

consecrated ground

So when Bors saw that he was in so far° countries as in the parts of Babylon, he departed from the city of Sarras and armed him and came to the sea, and entered into a ship. And so it befell him, by good adventure, he came unto the realm of Logres, and so he rode a pace° till he came to Camelot where the king was.

remote

swiftly

And then was there made great joy of him in all the court, for they weened all he had been lost forasmuch as he had been so long out of the country. And when they had eaten, the king made great clerks to come before him, for cause they should chronicle of° the high adventures of the good knights. So when Sir Bors had told him

record

6. The wafer of the Eucharist.

7. Had him buried next to.

of the high adventures of the Sankgreall such as had befallen him and his three fellows, which were Sir Lancelot, Perceval, Sir Galahad and himself, then Sir Lancelot told the adventures of the Sankgreall that he had seen. All this was made in great books and put up in almeries° at Salisbury. *libraries*

And anon Sir Bors said to Sir Lancelot,

"Sir Galahad, your own son, salewed you by me, and after you my lord King Arthur and all the whole court, and so did Sir Perceval. For I buried them with both mine own hands in the city of Sarras. Also, Sir Lancelot, Sir Galahad prayed you to remember of this unsiker° world, *uncertain* as ye behight him° when ye were together more than half a year." *promised*

"This is true," said Sir Lancelot; "now I trust to God his prayer shall avail me."

Then Sir Lancelot took Sir Bors in his arms and said,

"Cousin, ye are right welcome to me! For all that ever I may do for you and for yours, ye shall find my poor body ready at all times while the spirit is in it, and that I promise you faithfully, and never to fail. And wit ye well, gentle cousin Sir Bors, ye and I shall never depart in sunder while our lives may last."

"Sir," said he, "as ye will, so will I."

THUS ENDETH THE TALE OF THE SANKGREAL THAT WAS BRIEFLY DRAWN OUT OF FRENCH, WHICH IS A TALE CHRONICLED FOR ONE OF THE TRUEST AND OF THE HOLIEST THAT IS IN THIS WORLD, BY SIR THOMAS MALEORRÉ, KNIGHT.

O BLESSED JESU HELP HIM THROUGH HIS MIGHT! AMEN.

The Poisoned Apple[1]

So after the quest of the Sankgreall was fulfilled, and all knights that were left on live were come home again unto the Table Round, as *The Book of the Sankgreall* maketh mention, then was there great joy in the court, and in especial King Arthur and Queen Guinevere made great joy of the remnant that were come home. And passing glad was the king and the queen of Sir Lancelot and of Sir Bors, for they had been passing long away in the quest of the Sankgreall.

Then, as the book saith, Sir Lancelot began to resort unto Queen Guinevere again and forgat the promise and the perfection° that he *of perfection* made in the quest; for, as the book saith, had not Sir Lancelot been in his privy° thoughts and in his mind so set inwardly to the queen as he *secret* was in seeming outward to God, there had no knight passed him in the quest of the Sankgreall. But ever his thoughts privily were on the queen, and so they loved together more hotter than they did to forehand, and had many such privy draughts° together that many in the *meetings* court spake of it, and in especial Sir Agravain, Sir Gawain's brother, for he was ever open-mouthed.

So it befell that Sir Lancelot had many resorts of° ladies and *entreaties from* damsels which daily resorted unto him, that besought him to be

1. From the section titled *The Book of Sir Launcelot and Queen Guinevere*, in *King Arthur and His Knights*, ed. Eugène Vinaver (1975).

their champion. In all such matters of right Sir Lancelot applied him daily to do for the pleasure of Our Lord Jesu Christ, and ever as much as he might he withdrew him from the company of Queen Guinevere for to eschew the slander and noise.° Wherefore the queen waxed wroth with Sir Lancelot. *rumor*

So on a day she called him unto her chamber and said thus:

"Sir Lancelot, I see and feel daily that your love beginneth to slake,° for ye have no joy to be in my presence, but ever ye are out of this court, and quarrels and matters ye have nowadays for ladies, maidens and gentlewomen, more than ever ye were wont to have beforehand." *cool*

"Ah, madam," said Sir Lancelot, "in this ye must hold me excused for divers causes. One is, I was but late in the quest of the Sankgreall, and I thank God of His great mercy, and never of my deserving, that I saw in that my quest as much as ever saw any sinful man living, and so was it told me. And if that I had not had my privy thoughts to return to your love again as I do, I had° seen as great mysteries as ever saw my son, Sir Galahad, Perceval, other Sir Bors. And therefore, madam, I was but late in that quest, and wit you well, madam, it may not be yet lightly forgotten, the high service in whom I did my diligent labour. *should have*

"Also, madam, wit you well that there be many men speaketh of our love in this court, and have you and me greatly in await,° as this Sir Agravain and Sir Mordred.[2] And, madam, wit you well I dread them more for your sake than for any fear I have of them myself, for I may happen to escape and rid myself in a great need where, madam, ye must abide all that will be said unto you. And then, if that ye fall in any distress throughout° wilful folly, then is there none other help but by me and my blood.° *suspicion* *through* *kinsmen*

"And wit you well, madam, the boldness of you and me will bring us to shame and slander; and that were me loath to see you dishonoured. And that is the cause I take upon me more for to do for damsels and maidens than ever I did toforn:° that men should understand my joy and my delight is my pleasure to have ado for damsels and maidens." *before*

All this while the queen stood still and let Sir Lancelot say what he would; and when he had all said she brast out of weeping, and so she sobbed and wept a great while. And when she might speak she said,

"Sir Lancelot, now I well understand that thou art a false, recreant° knight and a common lecher, and lovest and holdest other ladies, and of me thou hast disdain and scorn. For wit thou well, now I understand thy falsehood I shall never love thee more, and look thou be never so hardy° to come in my sight. And right here I discharge thee this court, that thou never come within it, and I forfend° thee my fellowship, and upon pain° of thy head that thou see me nevermore!" *cowardly* *bold* *forbid / at the risk*

2. Mordred was Arthur's illegitimate son, by an incestuous encounter with his half-sister Morgause (or in some versions, Morgan le Fay).

Right so Sir Lancelot departed with great heaviness that unneth° he might sustain himself for great dole-making. *scarcely*

Then he called Sir Bors, Ector de Maris and Sir Lionel, and told them how the queen had forfended him the court, and so he was in will to depart into his own country.

"Fair sir," said Bors de Ganis, "ye shall not depart out of this land by mine advice, for ye must remember you what ye are, and renowned the most noblest knight of the world, and many great matters ye have in hand. And women in their hastiness will do oftentimes that after them sore repenteth. And therefore, by mine advice, ye shall take your horse and ride to the good hermit here beside Windsor, that sometime was a good knight; his name is Sir Brastias. And there shall ye abide till that I send you word of better tidings."

"Brother," said Sir Lancelot, "wit you well I am full loath to depart out of this realm, but the queen hath defended° me so highly,° *dismissed / angrily* that meseemeth she will never be my good lady as she hath been."

"Say ye never so," said Sir Bors, "for many times or° this time *before* she hath been wroth with you, and after that she was the first that repented it."

"Ye say well," said Sir Lancelot, "for now will I do by your counsel and take mine horse and mine harness and ride to the hermit Sir Brastias, and there will I repose me till I hear some manner of tidings from you. But, fair brother, in that° ye can get me the love *so far as* of my lady, Queen Guinevere."

"Sir," said Sir Bors, "ye need not to move° me of such matters, *persuade* for well ye wot I will do what I may to please you."

And then Sir Lancelot departed suddenly, and no creature wist where he was become° but Sir Bors. So when Sir Lancelot was de- *had gone* parted the queen outward made no manner of sorrow in showing to none of his blood nor to none other, but wit ye well, inwardly, as the book saith, she took great thought;° but she bare it out with a *grief* proud countenance, as though she felt no thought nother danger.° *fear*

So the queen let make° a privy dinner in London unto the *had made* knights of the Round Table, and all was for to show outward that she had as great joy in all other knights of the Round Table as she had in Sir Lancelot. So there was all only at that dinner Sir Gawain and his brethren, that is for to say Sir Agravain, Sir Gaheris, Sir Gareth and Sir Mordred, also there was Sir Bors de Ganis, Sir Blamore de Ganis, Sir Bleoberis de Ganis, Sir Galihad, Sir Eliodin, Sir Ector de Maris, Sir Lionel, Sir Palomides, Sir Safir, his brother, Sir La Cote Male Tayle, Sir Persaunt, Sir Ironside, Sir Braundiles, Sir Kay le Seneschal, Sir Mador de la Porte, Sir Patrise, a knight of Ireland, Sir Aliduke, Sir Ascamore, and Sir Pinel le Savage, which was cousin to Sir Lamorak de Galis, the good knight that Sir Gawain and his brethren slew by treason.[3]

And so these four-and-twenty knights should dine with the queen in a privy place by themselves, and there was made a great

3. This catalog draws together most of the Round Table knights who survived the Grail quest.

feast of all manner of dainties. But Sir Gawain had a custom that he used daily at meat and at supper, that he loved well all manner of fruit, and in especial apples and pears. And therefore whosomever dined other° feasted Sir Gawain would commonly purvey for° good *or / provide* fruit for him. And so did the queen; for to please Sir Gawain she let purvey for him all manner of fruit. For Sir Gawain was a passing hot° knight of nature, and this Sir Pinel hated Sir Gawain because *hot-tempered* of his kinsman Sir Lamorak's death, and therefore, for pure envy and hate, Sir Pinel enpoisoned certain apples for to enpoison Sir Gawain.

So this was well yet unto° the end of meat, and so it befell by *toward* misfortune a good knight Sir Patrise, which was cousin unto Sir Mador de la Porte, took an apple, for he was enchafed° with heat of *inflamed* wine. And it mishapped him to take a poisoned apple. And when he had eaten it he swall° sore till he brast,° and there Sir Patrise fell *swelled / burst* down suddenly° dead among them. *instantly*

Then every knight leap from the board ashamed, and araged for° wrath out of their wits, for they wist not what to say; consider- *enraged with* ing Queen Guinevere made the feast and dinner they had all suspicion unto her.

"My lady the queen!" said Sir Gawain. "Madam, wit you that this dinner was made for me and my fellows, for all folks that knoweth my condition understand that I love well fruit. And now I see well I had near been slain. Therefore, madam, I dread me lest ye will be shamed."

Then the queen stood still and was so sore abashed that she wist not what to say.

"This shall not so be ended," said Sir Mador de la Porte, "for here have I lost a full noble knight of my blood, and therefore upon this shame and despite° I will be revenged to the utterance!"° *wrong / utmost*

And there openly Sir Mador appealed° the queen of the death *accused* of his cousin Sir Patrise.

Then stood they all still, that° none would speak a word against *for* him, for they all had great suspicion unto the queen because she let make that dinner. And the queen was so abashed that she could none otherways do but wept so heartily that she fell on a swough. So with this noise and cry came to them King Arthur, and when he wist of the trouble he was a passing heavy° man. And ever Sir *sad* Mador stood still before the king, and appealed the queen of treason. (For the custom was such at that time that all manner of shameful death was called treason.)

"Fair lords," said King Arthur, "me repenteth of this trouble, but the case is so I may not have ado° in this matter, for I must be a *intervene* rightful judge. And that repenteth me that I may not do battle[4] for my wife, for, as I deem, this deed came never by her.° And therefore *by her doing* I suppose she shall not be all disdained° but that some good knight *dishonored* shall put his body in jeopardy for my queen rather than she should

4. Malory refers to a procedure in law, archaic in his day, wherein an armed champion could vindicate a person's innocence in a "trial by battle."

be brent° [*burned*] in a wrong quarrel.° [*unjustly*] And therefore, Sir Mador, be not so hasty; for, perdy,° [*by God*] it may happen she shall not be all friendless. And therefore desire thou thy day of battle, and she shall purvey her of° [*find herself*] some good knight that shall answer you, other else it were to me great shame and to all my court."

"My gracious lord," said Sir Mador, "ye must hold me excused, for though ye be our king, in that degree° [*rank*] ye are but a knight as we are, and ye are sworn unto knighthood as well as we be. And therefore I beseech you that ye be not displeased, for there is none of all these four-and-twenty knights that were bidden to this dinner but all they have great suspicion unto the queen. What say ye all, my lords?" said Sir Mador.

Then they answered by and by and said they could not excuse the queen for why she made the dinner, and other it must come by her other by her servants.

"Alas," said the queen, "I made this dinner for a good intent and never for none evil, so Almighty Jesu help me in my right,° [*just cause*] as I was never purposed to do such evil deeds, and that I report me unto God."[5]

"My lord the king," said Sir Mador, "I require you as ye be a righteous king, give me my day that I may have justice."

"Well," said the king, "this day fifteen days look thou be ready armed on horseback in the meadow beside Winchester. And if it so fall° [*happens*] that there be any knight to encounter against you, there may you do your best, and God speed the right. And if so befall that there be no knight ready at that day, then must my queen be brent, and there she shall be ready to have her judgment."

"I am answered," said Sir Mador.

And every knight yode° [*went*] where him liked.

So when the king and the queen were together the king asked the queen how this case° [*misfortune*] befell. Then the queen said,

"Sir, as Jesu be my help!" She wist not how nother° [*nor*] in what manner.

"Where is Sir Lancelot?" said King Arthur. "An° [*if*] he were here he would not grudge to do battle for you."

"Sir," said the queen, "I wot not where he is, but his brother and his kinsmen deem that he be not within this realm."

"That me repenteth," said King Arthur, "for an he were here he would soon stint° [*stop*] this strife. Well, then I will counsel you," said the king, "that ye go unto Sir Bors, and pray him for to do battle for you for Sir Lancelot's sake, and upon my life he will not refuse you. For well I see," said the king, "that none of the four-and-twenty knights that were at your dinner where Sir Patrise was slain that will do battle for you, nother none of them will say well of you, and that shall be great slander to you in this court."

"Alas," said the queen, "an I may not do withall,[6] but now I miss Sir Lancelot, for an he were here he would soon put me in my heart's ease."

5. I appeal to God to confirm.

6. If I cannot help it.

"What aileth you," said the king, "that ye cannot keep Sir Lancelot upon your side? For wit you well," said the king, "who hath Sir Lancelot upon his party° hath the most man of worship in this world upon his side. Now go your way," said the king unto the queen, "and require Sir Bors to do battle for you for Sir Lancelot's sake." *faction*

So the queen departed from the king and sent for Sir Bors into the chamber. And when he came she besought him of succour.

"Madam," said he, "what would ye that I did? For I may not with my worship° have ado in this matter, because I was at the same dinner, for dread of any of those knights would have you in suspicion. Also Madam," said Sir Bors, "now miss ye Sir Lancelot, for he would not a failed you in your right nother in your wrong, for when ye have been in right great dangers he hath succoured you. And now ye have driven him out of this country, by whom ye and all we were daily worshipped° by. Therefore, madam, I marvel how ye dare for shame to require me to do anything for you, insomuch ye have enchased out of your court by whom° we were upborne and honoured." *with honor* *honored* *the man by whom*

"Alas, fair knight," said the queen, "I put me wholly in your grace, and all that is amiss I will amend as ye will counsel me." And therewith she kneeled down upon both her knees, and besought Sir Bors to have mercy upon her, "other else I shall have a shameful death, and thereto I never offended."° *did wrong*

Right so came King Arthur and found the queen kneeling. And then Sir Bors took her up, and said,

"Madam, ye do me great dishonour."

"Ah, gentle knight," said the king, "have mercy upon my queen, courteous knight, for I am now in certain she is untruly defamed! And therefore, courteous knight," the king said, "promise her to do battle for her, I require you for the love ye owe unto Sir Lancelot."

"My lord," said Sir Bors, "ye require me the greatest thing that any man may require me. And wit you well, if I grant to do battle for the queen I shall wrath° many of my fellowship of the Table Round. But as for that," said Sir Bors, "I will grant° for my lord Sir Lancelot's sake, and for your sake: I will at that day be the queen's champion unless that there come by adventures a better knight than I am to do battle for her." *enrage* *consent*

"Will ye promise me this," said the king, "by your faith?"

"Yea sir," said Sir Bors, "of that I shall not fail you, nother her; but if there come a better knight than I am, then shall he have the battle."

Then was the king and the queen passing glad, and so departed, and thanked him heartily.

Then Sir Bors departed secretly upon a day, and rode unto Sir Lancelot thereas he was with Sir Brastias, and told him of all this adventure.

"Ah Jesu," Sir Lancelot said, "this is come happily as I would have it. And therefore I pray you make you ready to do battle, but look that ye tarry till ye see me come as long as ye may. For I am sure Sir Mador is an hot knight when he is enchafed for the more ye suffer him the hastier will he be to battle."

"Sir," said Sir Bors, "let me deal with him. Doubt ye not ye
shall have all your will."

So departed Sir Bors from him and came to the court again.
Then it was noised° in all the court that Sir Bors should do battle *rumored*
for the queen, wherefore many knights were displeased with him
that he would take upon him to do battle in the queen's quarrel; for
there were but few knights in all the court but they deemed the
queen was in the wrong and that she had done that treason. So Sir
Bors answered thus to his fellows of the Table Round.

"Wit you well, my fair lords, it were shame to us all an we suffered to see the most noble queen of the world to be shamed openly,
considering her lord and our lord is the man of most worship christened, and he hath ever worshipped° us all in all places." *honored*

Many answered him again: "As for our most noble King Arthur,
we love him and honour him as well as ye do, but as for Queen
Guinevere we love her not, because she is a destroyer of good knights."

"Fair lords," said Sir Bors, "meseemeth ye say not as ye should
say, for never yet in my days knew I never ne° heard say that ever *nor*
she was a destroyer of good knights, but at all times as far as ever I
could know, she was a maintainer of good knights; and ever she
hath been large° and free of her goods to all good knights, and the *generous*
most bounteous lady of her gifts and her good grace that ever I saw
other heard speak of. And therefore it were shame to us all and to
our most noble king's wife whom we serve an we suffered her to be
shamefully slain. And wit ye well," said Sir Bors, "I will not suffer it,
for I dare say so much, for the queen is not guilty of Sir Patrise's
death: for she owed° him never none evil will nother none of the *felt towards*
four-and-twenty knights that were at that dinner, for I dare say for
good love she bade us to dinner, and not for no mal engine.° And *evil intent*
that, I doubt not, shall be proved hereafter, for howsomever the
game goeth, there was treason among us."

Then some said to Bors, "We may well believe your words."
And so some were well pleased and some were not.

So the day came on fast until the even that° the battle should be. *evening before*
Then the queen sent for Sir Bors and asked him how he was disposed.° *resolved*

"Truly, madam," said he, "I am disposed in like wise as I
promised you, that is to say I shall not fail you unless there by adventure come a better knight than I am to do battle for you. Then,
madam, I am of° you discharged° of my promise." *by / released*

"Will ye," said the queen, "that I tell my lord the king thus?"

"Do as it pleaseth you, madam."

Then the queen yode° unto the king and told the answer of Sir *went*
Bors.

"Well, have ye no doubt," said the king, "of Sir Bors, for I call
him now that is living° one of the noblest knights of the world, and *of those now alive*
most perfectest man."

And thus it passed on till the morn, and so the king and the
queen and all manner of knights that were there at that time drew° *gathered*
them unto the meadow beside Winchester where the battle should

be. And so when the king was come with the queen and many knights of the Table Round, so the queen was then put in the constable's award,° *custody* and a great fire made about an iron stake, that an Sir Mador de le Porte had the better, she should there be brent; for such custom was used in those days: for favour, love, nother affinity° *kinship* there should be none other but righteous judgment, as well upon a king as upon a knight, and as well upon a queen as upon another° *any* poor lady.

So this meanwhile came in Sir Mador de la Porte, and took his oath before the king, how that the queen did this treason until° *toward* his cousin Sir Patrise, "and unto mine oath I will prove it with my body, hand for hand, who that will say the contrary."

Right so came in Sir Bors de Ganis and said that as for Queen Guinevere, "she is in the right, and that will I make good that she is not culpable of this treason that is put upon her."

"Then make thee ready," said Sir Mador, "and we shall prove whether thou be in the right or I."

"Sir Mador," said Sir Bors, "wit you well, I know you for a good knight. Notforthen° *nevertheless* I shall not fear you so greatly but I trust to God I shall be able to withstand your malice. But thus much have I promised my lord Arthur and my lady the queen, that I shall do battle for her in this cause to the utterest, unless that there come a better knight than I am and discharge° *release* me."

"Is that all?" said Sir Mador. "Other come thou off and do battle with me, other else say nay!"

"Take your horse," said Sir Bors, "and, as I suppose, I shall not tarry long but ye shall be answered."

Then either departed to their tents and made them ready to horseback° *to mount* as they thought best. And anon Sir Mador came into the field with his shield on his shoulder and his spear in his hand, and so rode about the place crying unto King Arthur,

"Bid your champion come forth an he dare!"

Then was Sir Bors ashamed, and took his horse and came to the lists'° *jousting field's* end. And then was he ware° *noticed* where came from a wood there fast by a knight all armed upon a white horse with a strange shield of strange arms, and he came driving all that° *as fast as* his horse might run. And so he came to Sir Bors and said thus:

"Fair knight, I pray you be not displeased, for here must a better knight than ye are have this battle. Therefore I pray you withdraw you, for wit you well I have had this day a right great journey and this battle ought to be mine. And so I promised you when I spake with you last, and with all my heart I thank you of your good will."

Then Sir Bors rode unto King Arthur and told him how there was a knight come that would have the battle to fight for the queen.

"What knight is he?" said the king.

"I wot not," said Sir Bors, "but such covenant he made with me to be here this day. Now, my lord," said Sir Bors, "here I am discharged."

Then the king called to that knight, and asked him if he would fight for the queen. Then he answered and said,

"Sir, therefore come I hither. And therefore, sir king, tarry° me no longer, for anon as I have finished this battle I must depart hence, for I have to do many battles elsewhere. For wit you well," said the knight, "this is dishonour to you and to all knights of the Round Table to see and know so noble a lady and so courteous as Queen Guinevere is, thus to be rebuked and shamed amongst you." *delay*

Then they all marvelled what knight that might be that so took the battle upon him, for there was not one that knew him but if it were Sir Bors. Then said Sir Mador de la Porte unto the king:

"Now let me wit with whom I shall have ado."

And then they rode to the lists' end, and there they couched° their spears and ran together with all their mights. And anon Sir Mador's spear brake all to pieces, but the other's spear held and bare Sir Mador's horse and all backwards to the earth a great fall. But mightily and deliverly he avoided his horse from him and put his shield before him and drew his sword and bade the other knight alight and do battle with him on foot. *lowered*

Then that knight descended down from his horse and put his shield before him and drew his sword. And so they came eagerly unto battle, and either gave other many sad° strokes, tracing and traversing and foining° together with their swords as it were wild boars, thus fighting nigh an hour; for this Sir Mador was a strong knight, and mightily proved in many strong battles. But at the last this knight smote Sir Mador grovelling upon the earth, and the knight stepped near him to have pulled Sir Mador flatling° upon the ground; and therewith Sir Mador arose, and in his rising he smote that knight through the thick of the thighs, that the blood brast out fiercely. *grievous* *thrusting* *at full length*

And when he felt himself so wounded and saw his blood, he let him arise upon his feet, and then he gave him such a buffet upon the helm that he fell to the earth flatling. And therewith he strode to him to have pulled off his helm off his head. And so Sir Mador prayed that knight to save his life. And so he yielded him as overcome, and released the queen of his quarrel.° *accusation*

"I will not grant thee thy life," said the knight, "only that° thou freely release the queen forever, and that no mention be made upon Sir Patrise's tomb that ever Queen Guinevere consented to that treason." *unless*

"All this shall be done," said Sir Mador, "I clearly discharge my quarrel forever."

Then the knights parters° of the lists took up Sir Mador and led him till his tent. And the other knight went straight to the stairfoot where sat King Arthur. And by that time was the queen came to the king, and either kissed other heartily. *stewards*

And when the king saw that knight he stooped down to him and thanked him, and in like wise did the queen. And the king prayed him put off his helmet and to repose him and to take a sop of wine.

And then he put off his helm to drink, and then every knight knew him that it was Sir Lancelot. And anon as the king wist that, he took the queen in his hand and yode unto Sir Lancelot and said,

"Sir, gramercy of your great travail° that ye have had this day for me and for my queen." *labor*

"My lord," said Sir Lancelot, "wit you well I ought of right ever to be in your quarrel,° and my lady the queen's quarrel, to do battle; for ye are the man that gave me the high Order of Knighthood, and that day my lady, your queen, did me worship.° And else I had been shamed, for that same day that ye made me knight through my hastiness I lost my sword, and my lady, your queen, found it, and lapped° it in her train, and gave me my sword when I had need thereto; and else had I been shamed among all knights. And therefore, my lord Arthur, I promised her at that day ever to be her knight in right other in wrong." *on your side* *honor* *wrapped*

"Gramercy," said the king, "for this journey. And wit you well," said the king, "I shall acquit° your goodness." *reward*

And evermore the queen beheld Sir Lancelot and wept so tenderly that she sank almost to the ground for sorrow, that he had done to her so great kindness where she showed him great unkindness. Then the knights of his blood drew unto him, and there either of them made great joy of other. And so came all the knights of the Table Round that were there at that time and welcomed him.

And then Sir Mador was healed of his leechcraft,° and Sir Lancelot was healed of his play.° And so there was made great joy and many mirths there was made in that court. *by surgery* *wound*

And so it befell that the Damsel of the Lake that hight Ninive, which wedded the good knight Sir Pelleas, and so she came to the court, for ever she did great goodness unto King Arthur and to all his knights through her sorcery and enchantments. And so when she heard how the queen was grieved° for the death of Sir Patrise, then she told it openly that she was never guilty, and there she disclosed by whom it was done, and named him Sir Pinel, and for what cause he did it. There it was openly known and disclosed, and so the queen was excused. And this knight Sir Pinel fled into his country, and was openly known that he enpoisoned the apples at that feast to that intent to have destroyed Sir Gawain, because Sir Gawain and his breathren destroyed Sir Lamorak de Galis which Sir Pinel was cousin unto. *blamed*

Then was Sir Patrise buried in the church of Westminster in a tomb, and thereupon was written: "Here lieth Sir Patrise of Ireland, slain by Sir Pinel le Savage, that enpoisoned apples to have slain Sir Gawain, and by misfortune Sir Patrise ate one of the apples, and then suddenly he brast." Also there was written upon the tomb that Queen Guinevere was appealed° of treason of° the death of Sir Patrise by Sir Mador de la Porte, and there was made the mention how Sir Lancelot fought with him for Queen Guinevere and overcame him in plain battle. All this was written upon the tomb of Sir Patrise in excusing of the queen. *accused / for*

And then Sir Mador sued daily and long to have the queen's good grace, and so by the means of Sir Lancelot he caused him to stand in the queen's good grace, and all was forgiven.

[In intervening episodes, Agravain and Mordred, nursing long-held grudges, connive to expose the adultery of Lancelot and Guinevere. Their brother, Gawain, reluctantly joins their plot. Mordred traps Lancelot at night in Guinevere's chamber, and in escaping Lancelot kills Agravain. Rescuing Guinevere as she is about to be burned at the stake, Lancelot kills another of Gawain's brothers, Gareth, thereby earning Gawain's implacable enmity. Arthur must now make war on Lancelot and, pressed by Gawain, repeats his siege even after Guinevere is returned to him. Arthur thus besieges Lancelot in his French domain, leaving Mordred as regent.]

The Day of Destiny[1]

As Sir Mordred was ruler of all England, he let make° letters as though that they had come from beyond the sea, and the letters specified that King Arthur was slain in battle with Sir Lancelot. Wherefore Sir Mordred made a parliament, and called the lords together, and there he made them to choose him king. And so was he crowned at Canterbury, and held a feast there fifteen days. *commissioned*

And afterward he drew him unto Winchester, and there he took Queen Guinevere, and said plainly that he would wed her (which was his uncle's wife and his father's wife). And so he made ready for the feast, and a day prefixed that they should be wedded; wherefore Queen Guinevere was passing heavy,° but spake fair, and agreed to Sir Mordred's will. *sad*

And anon she desired of Sir Mordred to go to London to buy all manner things that longed to the bridal. And because of her fair speech Sir Mordred trusted her and gave her leave; and so when she came to London she took the Tower of London and suddenly in all haste possible she stuffed it with all manner of victual, and well garnished° it with men, and so kept it. *garrisoned*

And when Sir Mordred wist this he was passing wroth out of measure. And short tale to make, he laid a mighty siege about the Tower and made many assaults, and threw engines° unto them, and shot great guns. But all might not prevail, for Queen Guinevere would never, for fair speech neither for foul, never to trust unto Sir Mordred to come in his hands again. *siege machines*

Then came the Bishop of Canterbury, which was a noble clerk and an holy man, and thus he said unto Sir Mordred:

"Sir, what will ye do? Will you first displease God and sithen° shame yourself and all knighthood? For is not King Arthur your uncle, and no farther but your mother's brother, and upon her he himself begat you, upon his own sister? Therefore how may you wed your own father's wife? And therefore, sir," said the Bishop, "leave this opinion,° other else I shall curse you with book, bell and candle." *then* *intention*

"Do thou thy worst," said Sir Mordred, "and I defy thee!"

1. From the section titled *The Most Piteous Tale of the Morte Arthur Saunz Guerdon*, in *King Arthur and His Knights*, ed. Eugène Vinaver (1975).

"Sir," said the Bishop, "and wit you well I shall not fear me to do that me ought to do. And also ye noise° that my lord Arthur is slain, and that is not so, and therefore ye will make a foul work in this land!" *spread rumors*

"Peace, thou false priest!" said Sir Mordred, "for an thou chafe° me any more, I shall strike off thy head." *anger*

So the Bishop departed, and did the cursing in the most orgulust° wise that might be done. And then Sir Mordred sought the Bishop of Canterbury for to have slain him. Then the Bishop fled, and took part of his goods with him, and went nigh unto Glastonbury. And there he was a priest-hermit in a chapel, and lived in poverty and in holy prayers; for well he understood that mischievous war was at hand. *defiant*

Then Sir Mordred sought upon Queen Guinevere by letters and sonds,° and by fair means and foul means, to have her to come out of the Tower of London; but all this availed nought, for she answered him shortly, openly and privily,[2] that she had liefer° slay herself than be married with him. *messengers* *rather*

Then came there word unto Sir Mordred that King Arthur had araised the siege from Sir Lancelot and was coming homeward with a great host to be avenged upon Sir Mordred; wherefore Sir Mordred made write writs° unto all the barony of this land, and much people drew unto him. For then was the common voice among them that with King Arthur was never other life but war and strife, and with Sir Mordred was great joy and bliss. Thus was King Arthur depraved° and evil said of; and many there were that King Arthur had brought up of nought, and given them lands, that might not then say him a good word. *summonses* *disparaged*

Lo ye Englishmen, see ye not what a mischief° here was? For he that was the most kind and noblest knight of the world, and most loved the fellowship of noble knights, and by him they all were upholden, and yet might not these Englishmen hold them content with him. Lo thus was the old custom and the usages of this land, and men say that we of this land have not yet lost that custom. Alas! this is a great default of us Englishmen, for there may no thing us please no term.° *evil* *length of time*

And so fared the people at that time: they were better pleased with Sir Mordred than they were with the noble King Arthur, and much people drew unto Sir Mordred and said they would abide with him for better and for worse. And so Sir Mordred drew with a great host to Dover, for there he heard say that King Arthur would arrive, and so he thought to beat his own father from his own lands. And the most party of all England held with Sir Mordred, for the people were so new-fangle.° *fond of new things*

And so as Sir Mordred was at Dover with his host, so came King Arthur with a great navy of ships and galleys and carracks, and there was Sir Mordred ready awaiting upon his landing, to let° his own father to land° upon the land that he was king over. *stop* *from landing*

2. At once, publicly and privately.

Then there was launching of great boats and small, and full of noble men of arms; and there was much slaughter of gentle knights, and many a full bold baron was laid full low, on both parties. But King Arthur was so courageous that there might no manner of knight let him to land, and his knights fiercely followed him. And so they landed maugre° Sir Mordred's head° and all his power, and put Sir Mordred aback, that he fled and all his people. *against / will*

So when this battle was done King Arthur let search his people[3] that were hurt and dead. And then was noble Sir Gawain found in a great boat, lying more than half dead. When King Arthur knew that he was laid so low he went unto him and so found him. And there the king made great sorrow out of measure, and took Sir Gawain in his arms, and thrice he there swooned. And then when he was waked, King Arthur said,

"Alas! Sir Gawain, my sister son, here now thou liest, the man in the world that I loved most. And now is my joy gone! For now, my nephew, Sir Gawain, I will discover me unto° you, that in your person and in Sir Lancelot I most had my joy and my affiance.° And now have I lost my joy of you both, wherefore all mine earthly joy is gone from me!" *disclose* *trust*

"Ah, mine uncle," said Sir Gawain, "now I will that ye wit that my death-days be come! And all I may wite° mine own hastiness° and my wilfulness, for through my wilfulness I was causer of mine own death; for I was this day hurt and smitten upon mine old wound that Sir Lancelot gave me, and I feel myself that I must needs be dead by the hour of noon. And through me and my pride ye have all this shame and disease,° for had that noble knight, Sir Lancelot, been with you, as he was and would have been, this unhappy war had never been begun; for he, through his noble knighthood and his noble blood, held all your cankered° enemies in subjection and danger.° And now," said Sir Gawain, "ye shall miss Sir Lancelot. But alas that I would not accord° with him! And therefore, fair uncle, I pray you that I may have paper, pen and ink, that I may write unto Sir Lancelot a letter written with mine own hand." *blame / rashness* *sorrow* *malignant* *control* *make peace*

So when paper, pen and ink was brought, then Sir Gawain was set up weakly° by King Arthur, for he was shriven a little afore. And then he took his pen and wrote thus, as the French book maketh mention: *gently*

"Unto thee, Sir Lancelot, flower of all noble knights that ever I heard of or saw by my days, I, Sir Gawain, King Lot's son of Orkney, and sister's son unto the noble King Arthur, send thee greeting, letting thee to have knowledge that the tenth day of May I was smitten upon the old wound that thou gave me afore the city of Benwick, and through that wound I am come to my death-day. And I will that all the world wit that I, Sir Gawain, knight of the Table Round, sought my death, and not through thy deserving, but mine own seeking. Wherefore I beseech thee, Sir Lancelot, to return again unto this realm and see my tomb and pray some prayer more

3. Had his people searched for.

other less for my soul. And this same day that I wrote the same cedle° I was hurt to the death, which wound was first given of thine hand, Sir Lancelot; for of a more nobler man might I not be slain. *letter*

"Also, Sir Lancelot, for all the love that ever was betwixt us, make no tarrying, but come over the sea in all the goodly haste that ye may, with your noble knights, and rescue that noble king that made thee knight, for he is full straitly bestead with° a false traitor which is my half-brother, Sir Mordred. For he hath crowned himself king and would have wedded my lady, Queen Guinevere; and so had he done, had she not kept the Tower of London with strong hand. And so the tenth day of May last past my lord King Arthur and we all landed upon them at Dover, and there he put that false traitor, Sir Mordred, to flight. And so it misfortuned me to be smitten upon the stroke that ye gave me of old. *hard-pressed by*

"And the date of this letter was written but two hours and a half before my death, written with mine own hand and subscribed with part of my heart blood. And therefore I require thee, most famous knight of the world, that thou wilt see my tomb."

And then he wept and King Arthur both, and swooned. And when they were awaked both, the king made Sir Gawain to receive his sacrament, and then Sir Gawain prayed the king for to send for Sir Lancelot and to cherish him above all other knights.

And so at the hour of noon Sir Gawain yielded up the ghost. And then the king let inter him° in a chapel within Dover Castle. And there yet all men may see the skull of him, and the same wound is seen that Sir Lancelot gave in battle. *had him buried*

Then was it told the king that Sir Mordred had pight a new field upon Barham Down.[4] And so upon the morn King Arthur rode thither to him, and there was a great battle betwixt them, and much people were slain on both parties. But at the last King Arthur's party stood best, and Sir Mordred and his party fled unto Canterbury.

And there the king let search all the downs for his knights that were slain and interred them; and salved them with soft salves° that full sore were wounded. Then much people drew unto King Arthur, and then they said that Sir Mordred warred upon King Arthur with wrong. *ointments*

And anon King Arthur drew him with his host down by the seaside westward, toward Salisbury. And there was a day assigned betwixt King Arthur and Sir Mordred, that they should meet upon a down beside Salisbury, and not far from the seaside. And this day was assigned on Monday after Trinity Sunday, whereof King Arthur was passing glad that he might be avenged upon Sir Mordred.

Then Sir Mordred araised much people about London, for they of Kent, Sussex and Surrey, Essex, Suffolk and Norfolk held the most party with Sir Mordred. And many a full noble knight drew unto him and also to the king; but they that loved Sir Lancelot drew unto Sir Mordred.

4. Set up a new battleground at Barham Down (southeast of Canterbury).

So upon Trinity Sunday at night King Arthur dreamed a wonderful dream, and in his dream him seemed that he saw upon a chafflet° a chair, and the chair was fast to a wheel, and thereupon sat King Arthur in the richest cloth of gold that might be made. And the king thought there was under him, far from him, an hideous deep black water, and therein was all manner of serpents and worms° and wild beasts, foul and horrible. And suddenly the king thought that the wheel turned up-so-down, and he fell among the serpents, and every beast took him by a limb. And then the king cried as he lay in his bed, "Help! help!"

platform

dragons

And then knights, squires and yeomen awaked the king, and then he was so amazed that he wist not where he was. And then so he awaked until it was nigh day, and then he fell on slumbering again, not sleeping nor thoroughly waking. So° the king seemed verily that there came Sir Gawain unto him with a number of fair ladies with him. So when King Arthur saw him he said,

to

"Welcome, my sister's son, I weened° ye had been dead. And now I see thee on live, much am I beholden unto Almighty Jesu. Ah, fair nephew, what been these ladies that hither be come with you?"

thought

"Sir," said Sir Gawain, "all these be ladies for whom I have foughten for, when I was man living. And all these are those that I did battle for in righteous quarrels, and God hath given them that grace at their great prayer, because I did battle for them for their right, that they should bring me hither unto you. Thus much hath given me leave God for to warn you of your death: for an ye fight as to-morn with Sir Mordred, as ye both have assigned, doubt ye not ye shall be slain, and the most party of your people on both parties. And for the great grace and goodness that Almighty Jesu hath unto you, and for pity of you and many more other good men there shall be slain, God hath sent me to you of His especial grace to give you warning that in no wise ye do battle as to-morn, but that ye take a treatise for a month-day.[5] And proffer you largely,° so that to-morn ye put in a delay. For within a month shall come Sir Lancelot with all his noble knights, and rescue you worshipfully, and slay Sir Mordred and all that ever will hold with him."

generously

Then Sir Gawain and all the ladies vanished, and anon the king called upon his knights, squires, and yeomen, and charged° them mightly to fetch his noble lords and wise bishops unto him. And when they were come the king told them of his avision: that Sir Gawain had told him and warned him that an he fought on the morn he should be slain. Then the king commanded Sir Lucan the Butler and his brother Sir Bedivere the Bold, with two bishops with them, and charged them in any wise to take a treatise for a month-day with Sir Mordred:

ordered

"And spare not, proffer him lands and goods as much as you think reasonable."

So then they departed and came to Sir Mordred where he had a grim° host of an hundred thousand. And there they entreated

fierce

5. Make a compact for a month from today.

Sir Mordred long time, and at the last Sir Mordred was agreed for to have Cornwall and Kent by° King Arthur's days;° *[during / lifetime]* and after that all England, after the days of King Arthur. Then were they condescended° *[agreed]* that King Arthur and Sir Mordred should meet betwixt both their hosts, and every each of them should bring fourteen persons. And so they came with this word unto Arthur. Then said he,

"I am glad that this is done," and so he went into the field.

And when King Arthur should depart he warned all his host that an they see any sword drawn, "look ye come on fiercely and slay that traitor, Sir Mordred, for I in no wise trust him." In like wise Sir Mordred warned his host that "an ye see any manner of sword drawn look that ye come on fiercely and so slay all that ever before you standeth, for in no wise I will not trust for this treatise." And in the same wise said Sir Mordred unto his host: "for I know well my father will be avenged upon me."

And so they met as their pointment was, and were agreed and accorded thoroughly. And wine was fette,° *[fetched]* and they drank together. Right so came out an adder of a little heath-bush, and it stang a knight in the foot. And so when the knight felt him so stung, he looked down and saw the adder; and anon he drew his sword to slay the adder, and thought none other harm. And when the host on both parties saw that sword drawn, then they blew beams,° *[bugles]* trumpets, and horns, and shouted grimly, and so both hosts dressed them together.° *[confronted each other]* And King Arthur took his horse and said, "Alas, this unhappy day!" And so rode to his party, and Sir Mordred in like wise.

And never since was there seen a more dolefuller battle in no Christian land, for there was but rushing and riding, foining° *[thrusting]* and striking, and many a grim word was there spoken of either to other, and many a deadly stroke. But ever King Arthur rode throughout the battle° *[battle formation]* of Sir Mordred many times and did full nobly, as a noble king should do, and at all times he fainted never. And Sir Mordred did his devour° *[utmost effort]* that day and put himself in great peril.

And thus they fought all the long day, and never stinted° *[ceased]* till the noble knights were laid to the cold earth. And ever they fought still till it was near night, and by then was there an hundred thousand laid dead upon the earth. Then was King Arthur wood wroth° *[wild with rage]* out of measure, when he saw his people so slain from him.

And so he looked about him and could see no mo° *[more]* of all his host, and good knights left no mo on live but two knights: the tone° *[one]* was Sir Lucan de Butler and his brother, Sir Bedivere; and yet they were full sore wounded.

"Jesu mercy!" said the king, "where are all my noble knights become? Alas, that ever I should see this doleful day! For now," said King Arthur, "I am come to mine end. But would to God," said he, "that I wist now where were that traitor Sir Mordred that hath caused all this mischief."° *[evil]*

Then King Arthur looked about and was ware where stood Sir Mordred leaning upon his sword among a great heap of dead men.

"Now, give me my spear," said King Arthur unto Sir Lucan, "for yonder I have espied the traitor that all this woe hath wrought."

"Sir, let him be," said Sir Lucan, "for he is unhappy.° And if ye *unlucky*
pass this unhappy day ye shall be right well revenged. And, good lord, remember ye of your night's dream and what the spirit of Sir Gawain told you to-night, and yet God of His great goodness hath preserved you hitherto. And for God's sake, my lord, leave off this, for, blessed be God, ye have won the field: for yet we been here three on live, and with Sir Mordred is not one of live. And therefore if ye leave off now, this wicked day of Destiny is past!"

"Now tide° me death, tide me life," said the king, "now I see *befall*
him yonder alone, he shall never escape mine hands! For at a better
avail° shall I never have him." *advantage*

"God speed you well!" said Sir Bedivere.

Then the king gat his spear in both his hands, and ran toward Sir Mordred, crying and saying,

"Traitor, now is thy death-day come!"

And when Sir Mordred saw King Arthur he ran until° him with *toward*
his sword drawn in his hand, and there King Arthur smote Sir
Mordred under the shield with a foin° of his spear throughout the *thrust*
body more than a fathom. And when Sir Mordred felt that he had his death wound he thrust himself with the might that he had up to the
burr° of King Arthur's spear, and right so he smote his father, King *hand guard*
Arthur, with his sword holding in both his hands, upon the side of
the head, that the sword pierced the helmet and the tay° of the brain. *lining*
And therewith Mordred dashed down stark dead to the earth.

And noble King Arthur fell in a swough to the earth, and there he swooned oftentimes, and Sir Lucan and Sir Bedivere oftentimes
hove° him up. And so weakly° betwixt them they led him to a little *lifted / gently*
chapel not far from the sea, and when the king was there, him thought him reasonably eased.

Then heard they people cry in the field.

"Now go thou, Sir Lucan," said the king, "and do me to wit° *let me know*
what betokens that noise in the field."

So Sir Lucan departed, for he was grievously wounded in many places; and so as he rode he saw and harkened by the moonlight
how that pillers° and robbers were come into the field to pille and *plunderers*
to rob many a full noble knight of brooches and bees° and of many a *bracelets*
good ring and many a rich jewel. And who that were not dead all
out, there they slew them for their harness° and their riches. *armor*

When Sir Lucan understood his work he came to the king as soon as he might, and told him all what he had heard and seen.

"Therefore by my rede,"° said Sir Lucan, "it is best that we *advice*
bring you to some town."

"I would it were so," said the king, "but I may not stand, my
head works° so. . . . Ah, Sir Lancelot!" said King Arthur, "this day *aches*
have I sore missed thee! And alas, that ever I was against thee! For now have I my death, whereof Sir Gawain me warned in my dream."

Then Sir Lucan took up the king the tone party° and Sir Bedivere the other party, and in the lifting up the king swooned, and in the lifting Sir Lucan fell in a swoon, that part of his guts fell out of his body; and therewith the noble knight his heart brast. And when the king awoke he beheld Sir Lucan, how he lay foaming at the mouth and part of his guts lay at his feet. *on one side*

"Alas," said the king, "this is to me a full heavy sight, to see this noble duke so die for my sake, for he would have holpen° me that had more need of help than I! Alas, that he would not complain him, for his heart was so set to help me. Now Jesu have mercy upon his soul!" *helped*

Then Sir Bedivere wept for the death of his brother.

"Now leave this mourning and weeping, gentle knight," said the king, "for all this will not avail° me. For wit thou well an I might live myself, the death of Sir Lucan would grieve me evermore. But my time passeth on fast," said the king. "Therefore," said King Arthur unto Sir Bedivere, "take thou here Excalibur, my good sword, and go with it to yonder water's side; and when thou comest there, I charge thee throw my sword in that water, and come again and tell me what thou seest there." *aid*

"My lord," said Sir Bedivere, "your commandment shall be done, and lightly° bring you word again." *I will quickly*

So Sir Bedivere departed. And by the way he beheld that noble sword, and the pomell° and the haft° was all precious stones. And then he said to himself, "If I throw this rich sword in the water, thereof shall never come good, but harm and loss." And then Sir Bedivere hid Excalibur under a tree, and so soon as he might he came again unto the king and said he had been at the water and thrown the sword into the water. *hand guard / handle*

"What saw thou there?" said the king.

"Sir," he said, "I saw nothing but waves and winds."

"That is untruly said of thee," said the king. "And therefore go thou lightly again, and do my commandment as thou art to me lief° and dear: spare not but throw it in." *beloved*

Then Sir Bedivere returned again and took the sword in his hand; and yet him thought sin and shame to throw away that noble sword. And so eft° he hid the sword and returned again and told the king that he had been at the water and done his commandment. *again*

"What sawest thou there?" said the king.

"Sir," he said, "I saw nothing but waters wap° and waves wan."° *dark / lapping*

"Ah, traitor unto me and untrue," said King Arthur, "now hast thou betrayed me twice! Who would ween° that thou who has been to me so lief and dear, and also named so noble a knight, that thou would betray me for the riches of this sword? But now go again lightly; for thy long tarrying putteth me in great jeopardy of my life, for I have taken cold. And but if° thou do now as I bid thee, if ever I may see thee, I shall slay thee mine own hands, for thou wouldest for my rich sword see me dead." *believe* *unless*

Then Sir Bedivere departed and went to the sword and lightly took it up, and so he went unto the water's side. And there he bound the girdle about the hilt, and threw the sword as far into the water as he might. And there came an arm and an hand above the water, and took it and cleight° it, and shook it thrice and brandished, and then vanished with the sword into the water. *clutched*

So Sir Bedivere came again to the king and told him what he saw.

"Alas!" said the king, "help me hence, for I dread me I have tarried over long."

Then Sir Bedivere took the king upon his back and so went with him to the water's side. And when they were there, even fast by° the bank hoved° a little barge with many fair ladies in it, and among them all was a queen, and all they had black hoods. And all they wept and shrieked when they saw King Arthur. *next to / floated*

"Now put me into that barge," said the king.

And so he did softly, and there received him three ladies with great mourning. And so they set him down, and in one of their laps King Arthur laid his head. And then the queen said,

"Ah, my dear brother![6] Why have you tarried so long from me? Alas, this wound on your head hath caught overmuch cold!"

And anon they rowed fromward° the land, and Sir Bedivere beheld all those ladies go fromward him. Then Sir Bedivere cried and said, *away from*

"Ah, my lord Arthur, what shall become of me, now ye go from me and leave me here alone among mine enemies?"

"Comfort thyself," said the king, "and do as well as thou mayst, for in me is no trust for to trust in. For I must into the vale of Avalon to heal me of my grievous wound. And if thou hear nevermore of me, pray for my soul!"

But ever the queen and ladies wept and shrieked, that it was pity to hear. And as soon as Sir Bedivere had lost sight of the barge he wept and wailed, and so took° the forest and went all that night. *went into*

And in the morning he was ware, betwixt two holts hoar,° of a chapel and an hermitage. Then was Sir Bedivere fain,° and thither he went, and when he came into the chapel he saw where lay an hermit grovelling° on all fours, fast thereby a tomb was new graven.° When the hermit saw Sir Bedivere he knew him well, for he was but little tofore Bishop of Canterbury, that Sir Mordred fleamed.° *gray woods* *glad* *face down / freshly dug* *put to flight*

"Sir," said Sir Bedivere, "what man is there here interred that you pray so fast° for?" *intently*

"Fair son," said the hermit, "I wot not verily but by deeming.° But this same night, at midnight, here came a number of ladies and brought here a dead corse and prayed me to inter him. And here they offered an hundred tapers, and gave me a thousand besants."° *guessing* *gold coins*

6. The queen is thus revealed as Morgan le Fay, in whose story magical healing powers mixed with inveterate hostility to Guinevere and sometimes to Arthur himself.

"Alas," said Sir Bedivere, "that was my lord King Arthur, which lieth here graven° in this chapel." *buried*

Then Sir Bedivere swooned, and when he awoke he prayed the hermit that he might abide with him still, there to live with fasting and prayers:

"For from hence will I never go," said Sir Bedivere, "by my will, but all the days of my life here to pray for my lord Arthur."

"Sir, ye are welcome to me," said the hermit, "for I know you better than ye ween that I do: for ye are Sir Bedivere the Bold, and the full noble duke Sir Lucan de Butler was your brother."

Then Sir Bedivere told the hermit all as you have heard tofore, and so he beleft° with the hermit that was beforehand Bishop of *remained* Canterbury. And there Sir Bedivere put upon him poor clothes, and served the hermit full lowly in fasting and in prayers.

Thus of Arthur I find no more written in books that been authorised, neither more of the very certainty of his death heard I never read, but thus was he led away in a ship wherein were three queens; that one was King Arthur's sister, Queen Morgan le Fay, the tother was the Queen of North Galis, and the third was the Queen of the Waste Lands.

Now more of the death of King Arthur could I never find, but that these ladies brought him to his grave, and such one was interred there which the hermit bare witness that sometime° Bishop *was once* of Canterbury. But yet the hermit knew not in certain that he was verily the body of King Arthur; for this tale Sir Bedivere, a knight of the Table Round, made it to be written.

Yet some men say in many parts of England that King Arthur is not dead, but had° by the will of our Lord Jesu into another place; *was carried* and men say that he shall come again, and he shall win the Holy Cross. Yet I will not say that it shall be so, but rather I would say: here in this world he changed his life. And many men say that there is written upon the tomb this:

HIC IACET ARTHURUS REX QUONDAM REXQUE FUTURUS[7]

And thus leave I here Sir Bedivere with the hermit that dwelled that time in a chapel beside Glastonbury, and there was his hermitage. And so they lived in prayers and fastings and great abstinence.

And when Queen Guinevere understood that King Arthur was dead and all the noble knights, Sir Mordred and all the remnant, then she stole away with five ladies with her, and so she went to Amesbury. And there she let make herself° a nun, and *became* weared white clothes and black, and great penance she took upon her, as ever did sinful woman in this land. And never creature could make her merry, but ever she lived in fasting, prayers and alms-deeds, that all manner of people marvelled how virtuously she was changed.

7. Here lies Arthur, once and future king.

RESPONSES

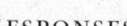

Marion Zimmer Bradley: from *The Mists of Avalon*

PROLOGUE[1]

MORGAINE SPEAKS . . .

In my time I have been called many things: sister, lover, priestess, wise-woman, queen. Now in truth I have come to be wise-woman, and a time may come when these things may need to be known. But in sober truth, I think it is the Christians who will tell the last tale. For ever the world of Fairy drifts further from the world in which the Christ holds sway. I have no quarrel with the Christ, only with his priests, who call the Great Goddess a demon and deny that she ever held power in this world. At best, they say that her power was of Satan. Or else they clothe her in the blue robe of the Lady of Nazareth—who indeed had power in her way, too—and say that she was ever virgin. But what can a virgin know of the sorrows and travail of mankind?

And now, when the world has changed, and Arthur—my brother, my lover, king who was and king who shall be—lies dead (the common folk say sleeping) in the Holy Isle of Avalon, the tale should be told as it was before the priests of the White Christ came to cover it all with their saints and legends.

For, as I say, the world itself has changed. There was a time when a traveller, if he had the will and knew only a few of the secrets, could send his barge out into the Summer Sea and arrive not at Glastonbury of the monks, but at the Holy Isle of Avalon; for at that time the gates between the worlds drifted within the mists, and were open, one to another, as the traveller thought and willed. For this is the great secret, which was known to all educated men in our day: that by what men think, we create the world around us, daily new.

And now the priests, thinking that this infringes upon the power of their God, who created the world once and for all to be unchanging, have closed those doors (which were never doors, except in the minds of men), and the pathway leads only to the priests' Isle, which they have safeguarded with the sound of their church bells, driving away all thoughts of another world lying in the darkness. Indeed, they say that *world, if it indeed exists, is the property of Satan, and the doorway to Hell, if not Hell itself.*

I do not know what their God may or may not have created. In spite of the tales that are told, I never knew much about their priests and never wore the black of one of their slave-nuns. If those at Arthur's court at Camelot chose to think me so when I came there (since I always wore the dark robes of the Great Mother in her guise as wise-woman), I did not undeceive them. And indeed, toward the end of Arthur's reign it would have been dangerous to do so, and I bowed my head to expediency as my great mistress would never have done: Viviane, Lady of the Lake, once Arthur's greatest friend, save for myself, and then his darkest enemy—again, save for myself.

But the strife is over; I could greet Arthur at last, when he lay dying, not as my enemy and the enemy of my Goddess, but only as my brother, and as a dying man in need of the

1. The continuing appeal of the Arthurian tradition is reflected in its many retellings since the Middle Ages, and especially its revival in the nineteenth and twentieth centuries. Each era has been able to find a setting for its own fears and aspirations in the ambitions, accomplishments, and final tragedies of Arthur's court. Working in the first wave of the women's movement, Marion Zimmer Bradley (1930–1999) was a hugely productive writer of science fiction and fantasy literature. She created her most popular work, *The Mists of Avalon* (1982), by returning to these ancient legends, and reimagining the great events of Arthur's career in the perspectives and voices of Arthurian women, especially Morgan le Fay and Guinevere. Medieval Arthurian legends often include bonds among men that verge on the erotic, an idea Bradley makes explicit in her version of Lancelot; she also imagines lesbian attraction among the legends' women. What she shares with her predecessors, as in the Prologue included here, is a strongly elegiac tone for worlds inevitably passing. The world Bradley's Morgaine most laments is a somewhat vaguely imagined Celtic matriarchy, perhaps as laden with fantasy as were the medieval regrets for a lost, idealized chivalry.

Mother's aid, where all men come at last. Even the priests know this, with their ever-virgin Mary in her blue robe; for she too becomes the World Mother in the hour of death.

And so Arthur lay at last with his head in my lap, seeing in me neither sister nor lover nor foe, but only wise-woman, priestess, Lady of the Lake; and so rested upon the breast of the Great Mother from whom he came to birth and to whom at last, as all men, he must go. And perhaps, as I guided the barge which bore him away, not this time to the Isle of the Priests, but to the true Holy Isle in the dark world behind our own, that Island of Avalon where, now, few but I could go, he repented the enmity that had come between us.

AS I TELL THIS TALE *I will speak at times of things which befell when I was too young to understand them, or of things which befell when I was not by; and my hearer will draw away, perhaps, and say:* This is her magic. *But I have always held the gift of the Sight, and of looking within the minds of men and women; and in all this time I have been close to all of them. And so, at times, all that they thought was known to me in one way or another. And so I will tell this tale.*

For one day the priests too will tell it, as it was known to them. Perhaps between the two, some glimmering of the truth may be seen.

For this is the thing the priests do not know, with their One God and One Truth: that there is no such thing as a true tale. Truth has many faces and the truth is like to the old road to Avalon; it depends on your own will, and your own thoughts, whither the road will take you, and whether, at the end, you arrive in the Holy Isle of Eternity or among the priests with their bells and their death and their Satan and Hell and damnation . . . but perhaps I am unjust even to them. Even the Lady of the Lake, who hated a priest's robe as she would have hated a poisonous viper, and with good cause too, chid me once for speaking evil of their God.

"For all the Gods are one God," she said to me then, as she had said many times before, and as I have said to my own novices many times, and as every priestess who comes after me will say again, "and all the Goddesses are one Goddess, and there is only one Initiator. And to every man his own truth, and the God within."

And so, perhaps, the truth winds somewhere between the road to Glastonbury, Isle of the Priests, and the road to Avalon, lost forever in the mists of the Summer Sea.

But this is my truth; I who am Morgaine tell you these things, Morgaine who was in later days called Morgan le Fay.

Graham Chapman, John Cleese, Terry Gilliam, Eric Idle, Terry Jones, and Michael Palin: scene from *Monty Python and the Holy Grail*[1]

ARTHUR AND THE PEASANTS

[*Exterior. Day.*]

ARTHUR *and* PATSY *riding. They stop and look. We see a castle in the distance, and before it a* PEASANT *is working away on his knees trying to dig the earth with his bare hands and a twig.* ARTHUR *and* PATSY *ride up, and stop before the* PEASANT.

1. If Marion Zimmer Bradley honors a lost Arthurian past of powerful women, the Pythons hilariously skewer every sentimental Arthurian piety they can put their hands on. First released in 1975, their film *Monty Python and the Holy Grail* elaborates the skit comedy they had developed in the Monty Python's Flying Circus series on the BBC. In a loosely strung series of episodes, many recognizable from Malory and Tennyson, the movie deflates notions of the divine right of kings, chivalric bravery (the knights don't even have horses, only the sound effect of coconut halves), elevated love, and Camelot itself ("it is a silly place"). In the brilliant episode here, King Arthur's airy rhetoric of his elevation to the throne meets up with a band of dismissive Marxists whose own self-importance is equally parodied. All the Pythons are credited for the screenplay and all appear in the film, some in multiple roles: John Cleese, Graham Chapman, Terry Gilliam, Eric Idle, Terry Jones, and Michael Palin.

ARTHUR: Old woman!
DENNIS [*turning*]: Man.
ARTHUR: Man. I'm sorry. Old man, what knight lives in that castle?
DENNIS: I'm thirty-seven.
ARTHUR: What?
DENNIS: I'm only thirty-seven . . . I'm not *old*.
ARTHUR: Well—I can't just say: "Hey, Man!"
DENNIS: You could say: "Dennis."
ARTHUR: I didn't know you were called Dennis.
DENNIS: You didn't bother to find out, did you?
ARTHUR: I've said I'm sorry about the old woman, but from behind you looked . . .
DENNIS: What I object to is that you automatically treat me as an inferior . . .
ARTHUR: Well . . . I *am* King.
DENNIS: Oh, very nice. King, eh! I expect you've got a palace and fine clothes and courtiers and plenty of food. And how d'you get that? By exploiting the workers! By hanging on to outdated imperialistic dogma, which perpetuates the social and economic differences in our society! If there's *ever* going to be any progress . . .

[*An* OLD WOMAN *appears*.]

OLD WOMAN: Dennis! There's some lovely filth down here . . . Oh! How d'you do?
ARTHUR: How d'you do, good lady . . . I am Arthur, King of the Britons . . . can you tell me who lives in that castle?
OLD WOMAN: King of the *who?*
ARTHUR: The Britons.
OLD WOMAN: Who are the Britons?
ARTHUR: All of us . . . we are all Britons.

[DENNIS *winks at the* OLD WOMAN.]

ARTHUR: . . . And I am your King . . .
OLD WOMAN: Ooooh! I didn't know we had a king. I thought we were an autonomous collective . . .
DENNIS: You're fooling yourself. We're living in a dictatorship, a self-perpetuating autocracy in which the working classes . . .
OLD WOMAN: There you are, bringing class into it again . . .
DENNIS: That's what it's all about . . . If only—
ARTHUR: Please, please, good people, I am in haste. What knight lives in that castle?
OLD WOMAN: No one lives there.
ARTHUR: Well, who is your lord?
OLD WOMAN: We don't have a lord.
ARTHUR: What?
DENNIS: I told you, we're an anarcho-syndicalist commune, we take it in turns to act as a sort of executive officer for the week.
ARTHUR: Yes . . .
DENNIS: . . . But all the decisions of that officer . . .
ARTHUR: Yes, I see.
DENNIS: . . . must be approved at a bi-weekly meeting by a simple majority in the case of purely internal affairs.
ARTHUR: Be quiet.
DENNIS: . . . But a two-thirds majority . . .
ARTHUR: Be quiet! I order you to shut up.
OLD WOMAN: Order, eh? Who does he think he is?

Still of Arthur and his servant Patsy from *Monty Python and the Holy Grail*, the 1975 film directed by Terry Gilliam and Terry Jones and written and performed by the British comic troupe Monty Python's Flying Circus.

ARTHUR: I am your King.

OLD WOMAN: Well, I didn't vote for you.

ARTHUR: You don't vote for kings.

OLD WOMAN: Well, how did you become King, then?

ARTHUR: The Lady of the Lake, her arm clad in purest shimmering samite, held Excalibur aloft from the bosom of the waters to signify that by Divine Providence . . . I, Arthur, was to carry Excalibur . . . that is why I am your King.

DENNIS: Look, strange women lying on their backs in ponds handing over swords . . . that's no basis for a system of government. Supreme executive power derives from a mandate from the masses not from some farcical aquatic ceremony.

ARTHUR: Be quiet!

DENNIS: You can't expect to wield supreme executive power just because some watery tart threw a sword at you.

ARTHUR: Shut up!

DENNIS: I mean, if I went round saying I was an emperor because some moistened bint[2] had lobbed a scimitar at *me*, people would put me away.

ARTHUR [*grabbing him by the collar*]: Shut up, will you. Shut up!

DENNIS: Ah! *Now* ... we see the violence inherent in the system.

ARTHUR: Shut up!

[*PEOPLE (i.e. other PEASANTS) are appearing and watching.*]

DENNIS [*calling*]: Come and see the violence inherent in the system. Help, help, I'm being repressed!

2. Derogatory slang for a woman.

ARTHUR [*aware that people are now coming out and watching*]: Bloody peasant! [*Pushes* DENNIS *over into the mud and prepares to ride off*.]

DENNIS: Oooooh! Did you hear that! What a give-away.

ARTHUR: Come on, Patsy.

[*They ride off*.]

DENNIS [*in background as we pull out*]: Did you see him repressing me, then? That's what I've been on about . . .

Geoffrey Chaucer

c. 1340–1400

On Easter weekend 1300, the Italian poet Dante Alighieri had a vision in which he descended to hell, climbed painfully through purgatory, and then attained a transcendent experience of paradise. He tells his tale in his visionary, passionately judgmental *Divine Comedy*. One hundred years later, on 25 October 1400, Geoffrey Chaucer—the least judgmental of poets—died quietly in his house at the outskirts of London. By a nice accident of history, these two great writers bracket the last great century of the Middle Ages.

Of Chaucer's own life our information is abundant but often frustrating. Many documents record the important and sensitive posts he held in government, but there are only faint hints of his career as a poet. During his lifetime, he was frequently in France and made at least two trips to Italy, which proved crucial for his own growth as a writer and indeed for the history of English literature. He also served under three kings: the aging Edward III, his brilliant and sometimes tyrannical grandson Richard II, and—at the very end of his life—Richard's usurper Henry IV.

Chaucer was born into a rising mercantile family, part of the growing bourgeois class that brought so much wealth to England even while it disrupted medieval theories of social order. Chaucer's family fit nowhere easily in the old model of the three estates: those who pray (the clergy), those who fight (the aristocracy), and those who work the land (the peasants). Yet like many of their class, they aspired to a role among the aristocracy, and in fact Chaucer's parents succeeded in holding minor court positions. Chaucer himself became a major player in the cultural and bureaucratic life of the court, and Thomas Chaucer (who was very probably his son) was ultimately knighted.

Geoffrey was superbly but typically educated. He probably went to one of London's fine grammar schools, and as a young man he very likely followed a gentlemanly study of law at one of the Inns of Court. He shows signs of knowing and appreciating the topics debated in the university life of his time. His poems reflect a vast reading in classical Latin, French, and Italian (of which he was among the earliest English readers). *The Parliament of Fowls*, for instance, reveals the influence not only of French court poetry but also of Dante's *Divine Comedy*; and the frame-story structure of *The Canterbury Tales* may have been inspired by Boccaccio's *Decameron*.

By 1366 Chaucer had married Philippa de Roet, a minor Flemish noblewoman, and a considerable step up the social hierarchy. Her sister later became the mistress and ultimately the wife of Chaucer's great patron, John of Gaunt. Thus, when Gaunt's son Henry Bolingbroke seized the throne from Richard II, the elderly Geoffrey Chaucer found himself a distant in-law of his king. Chaucer had been associated with Richard II and suffered reverses when Richard's power was restricted by the magnates. But he was enough of a cultural figure that Henry IV continued (perhaps with some prompting) the old man's royal annuities. Whatever Western literature owes to Chaucer (and its debts are profound), in his own life his writing made a place in the world for him and his heirs.

Despite his lifelong productivity as a writer, and despite the slightly obtuse narrative voice he consistently uses, Geoffrey Chaucer was a canny and ambitious player in the world of his time. He was a soldier, courtier, diplomat, and government official in a wide range of jobs. These included controller of the customs on wool and other animal products, a lucrative post, and later controller of the Petty Custom that taxed wine and other goods. Chaucer's frequent work overseas extended his contacts with French and Italian literature. He was ward of estates for several minors, a job that also benefited the guardian. Chaucer began to accumulate property in Kent, where he served as justice of the peace (an important judicial post) and then Member of Parliament in the mid-1380s.

Despite the comfortable worldly progress suggested by such activities, these were troubled years in the nation and in Chaucer's private life. Chaucer's personal fortunes were affected by the frequent struggles between King Richard and his magnates over control of the government. From another direction there exploded the Rising of 1381 (see pages 468–80), rocking all of English society. The year before that, Chaucer had been accused of *raptus* by Cecilia Chaumpaigne, daughter of a baker in London. A great deal of nervous scholarship has been exercised over this case, but it becomes increasingly clear that in legal language *raptus* meant some form of rape. The case was settled, and there are signs of efforts to hush it up at quite high levels of government. The somewhat bland and bumbling quality of Chaucer's narrative persona would probably have seemed more artificially constructed and more ironic to Chaucer's contemporaries than it does at first glance today.

Chaucer was a Janus-faced poet, truly innovative at the levels of language and theme yet deeply involved with literary and intellectual styles that stretched back to Latin antiquity and twelfth- and thirteenth-century France. His early poems—the dream visions such as *The Parliament of Fowls* and the tragic romance *Troilus and Criseyde*—derive from essentially medieval genres and continental traditions: the French poets Deschamps and Machaut and the Italians Dante, Boccaccio, and Petrarch. Yet in his reliance on the English vernacular, Chaucer was in a vanguard generation along with the *Gawain* poet and William Langland. English was indeed gaining importance in other parts of this world, such as in Parliament, some areas of education, and in the "Wycliffite" translations of the Bible. Chaucer's own exclusive use of English was particularly ambitious, though, for a poet whose patronage came from the court of the francophile Richard II.

The major work of Chaucer's maturity, *The Canterbury Tales*, founds an indisputably English tradition. While he still uses the craft and allusions he learned from his continental masters, he also experiments with the subject matter of everyday English life and the vocabularies of the newly valorized English vernacular. Moreover, starting with traditional forms and largely traditional models of society and the cosmos, Chaucer found spaces for new and sometimes disruptive perspectives, especially those of women and the rising mercantile class into which he had been born. Though always a court poet, Chaucer increasingly wrote in ways that reflected both the richness and the uncertainties of his entire social world. The *Tales* include a Knight who could have stepped from a twelfth-century heroic poem; yet they also offer the spectacle of the Knight's caste being aped, almost parodied, and virtually shouted down by a sword-carrying peasant, the Miller. And the entire notion of old writings as sources of authoritative wisdom is powerfully challenged by the illiterate or only minimally literate Wife of Bath.

The Canterbury Tales also differ from the work of many of Chaucer's continental predecessors in their deep hesitation to cast straightforward judgment, either socially or spiritually. Here we may return to Chaucer's connection with Dante. His *Divine Comedy* presented mortal life as a pilgrimage and an overt test in stable dogma, a journey along a dangerous road toward certain damnation or the reward of the heavenly Jerusalem. *The Canterbury Tales* are literally about a pilgrimage, and Chaucer presents the road as beautiful and fascinating in its own right. The greatness of the poem lies in its exploration of the variousness of the journey and that journey's reflection of a world pressured by spiritual and moral fractures. In depicting a mixed company of English men and women traveling England's most famous pilgrimage route and telling one

Portrait of Geoffrey the Canterbury Pilgrim, from the Ellesmere manuscript of *The Canterbury Tales*, early 15th century. This carefully produced and beautifully decorated manuscript reflects the speed with which Chaucer's works took on wide cultural prestige and were enshrined in luxury books for a wealthy, probably aristocratic audience.

another stories, Chaucer suggests not only the spiritual meaning of humankind's earthly pilgrimage, but also its overflowing beauties and attractions as well as the evils and temptations that lie along the way. The vision of the serious future, the day of judgment, is constantly attended in *The Canterbury Tales* by the troubling yet hilarious and distracting present.

Unlike Dante, however, Chaucer almost never takes it upon himself to judge, at least not openly. He records his characters with dizzying immediacy, but he never tells his reader quite what to think of them, leaving the gaps for us as readers to fill. He does end the *Tales* with a kind of sermon, the Parson's long prose treatise on the Christian vices and virtues. That coda by no means erases the humor and seriousness, sentiment and ribaldry, high spiritual love and unmasked carnal desire, profound religious belief and squalid clerical corruption that have been encountered along the way. Indeed, Chaucer's genius is to transmute the disorder of his world almost into an aesthetic of plenitude: "foyson" in Middle English. His poem overflows constantly with rich detail, from exquisite visions to squabbling pilgrims. His language overflows with its multiple vocabularies, Anglo-Saxon, Latin, and French. And finally, the tales themselves are notable for the range of genres used by the pilgrims: the Miller's bawdy fabliau, the Wife of Bath's romance, the Franklin's story of courtly love and clerkly magic, the Nun's Priest's beast fable, the Pardoner's hypocritical cautionary tale, as well as the Parson's sermon. *The Canterbury Tales* are an anthology embracing almost every important literary type of Chaucer's day.

None of this celebratory richness, however, fully masks the unresolved social and spiritual tensions that underlie the *Tales*. The notion of spiritual pilgrimage is deeply challenged by the very density of characterization and worldly detail that so enlivens the work. And the model of a competitive game, which provides the fictional pretext for the tales themselves, is only one version of what the critic Peggy Knapp has called Chaucer's "social contest" in the work as a whole. The traditional estates such as knight and peasant openly clash during the pilgrimage, and the estate of the clergy is more widely represented by its corrupt than by its virtuous members. Women, merchants, common landowners, and others from outside the traditional three estates bulk large in the tales. And their stories cast doubt upon such fundamental religious institutions as penance and such social institutions as marriage. For all their pleasures, *The Canterbury Tales* have survived, in part, because they are so riven by challenge and doubt.

For additional resources on Chaucer, including the *Parliament of Fowles* and the *The Franklin's Tale*, go to *The Longman Anthology of British Literature* Web site at www.myliteraturekit.com.

Chaucer's Middle English

Grammar

The English of Chaucer's London, and particularly the English of government bureaucracy, became the source for the more standardized vernacular that emerged in the era of print at the close of the Middle Ages. As a result, Chaucer's English is easier to understand today than the dialect of many of his great contemporaries such as the *Gawain* poet, who worked far to the north. The text that follows preserves Chaucer's language, with some spellings slightly modernized and regularized by its editor, E. Talbot Donaldson. To help beginners, we include David Wright's fine translation of the General Prologue on facing pages with the original text.

The marginal glosses in the readings are intended to help the nonspecialist reader through Chaucer's language without elaborate prior study. It will be helpful, though, to explain a few key differences from Modern English.

Nouns: The possessive is sometimes formed without a final *-s*.

Pronouns: Readers will recognize the archaic *thou, thine, thee* of second-person singular, and *ye* of the plural. Occasional confusion can arise from the form *hir*, which can mean "her" or "their." *Hem* is Chaucer's spelling for "them," and *tho* for "those." Chaucer uses *who* to mean "whoever."

Adverbs: Formed, as today, with *-ly*, but also with *-liche*. Sometimes an adverb is unchanged from its adjective form: *fairly, fairliche, faire* can all be adverbs.

Verbs: Second-person singular is formed with *-est* (*thou lovest*, past tense *thou lovedest*); third-person singular often with *-eth* (*he loveth*); plurals often with *-n* (*we loven*); and infinitive with *-n* (*loven*).

Strong verbs/impersonal verbs: Middle English has many "strong verbs," which form the past and perfect by changing a vowel in their stem; these are usually recognizable by analogy with surviving forms in Modern English (*go, went, gone; sing, sang, sung*; etc.). Middle English also often uses "impersonal verbs" (*liketh*, "it pleases"; *as me thinketh*, "as I think"), in which case sometimes no obvious subject noun or pronoun occurs.

Pronunciation

A few guidelines will help approximate the sound of Chaucer's English and the richness of his versification. For fuller discussion, consult sources listed in the bibliography.

Pronounce all consonants: *knight* is "k/neecht" with a guttural *ch*, not "nite"; *gnaw* is "g/naw." Middle English consonants preserve many of the sounds of the language's Germanic roots: guttural *gh*; sounded *l* and *w* in words like *folk* or *write*. (Exceptions occur in some words that derive from French, like *honour* whose *h* is silent.)

Final *-e* was sounded in early Middle English. Such pronunciation was becoming archaic by Chaucer's time, but was available to aid meter in the stylized context of poetry.

The distinction between short and long vowels was greater in Middle English than today. Middle English short vowels have mostly remained short in Modern English, with some shift in pronunciation: short *a* sounds like the *o* in *hot*, short *o* like a quick version of the *aw* in *law*, short *u* like the *u* in *full*.

Long vowels in Middle English (here usually indicated by doubling, when vowel length is unclear by analogy to modern spelling) are close to long vowels in modern Romance languages. The chart shows some differences in Middle English long vowels.

Middle English	**pronounced as in**	**Modern English**
a (as in *name*)		*father*
open *e* (*deel*)		*swear*, *bread*
close *e* (*sweet*)		*fame*
i (*whit*)		*feet*
open *o* (*holy*)		*law*
close *o* (*roote*)		*note*
u (as in *town*, *aboute*)		*root*
u (*vertu*)		*few*

Open and close long vowels are a challenge for modern readers. Generally, open long *e* in Middle English (*deel*) has become Modern English spelling with *ea* (*deal*); close long *e* (*sweet*) has become Modern English spelling with *ee* (*sweet*). Open long *o* in Middle English has come to be pronounced as in *note*; close long *o* in Middle English has come to be pronounced *root*. This latter case illustrates the idea of "vowel shift" across the centuries, in which some long vowels have moved forward in the throat and palate.

Versification

All of Chaucer's poetry presented here is in a loosely iambic pentameter line, which Chaucer was greatly responsible for bringing into prominence in England. He is a fluid versifier, though, and often shifts stress, producing metrical effects that have come to be called trochees and spondees. Final *-e* is often pronounced within lines to provide an unstressed syllable and is typically pronounced at the end of each line. Yet final *-e* may also elide with a following word that begins with a vowel. The following lines from *The Nun's Priest's Tale* have a proposed scansion, but the reader will see that alternate scansions are possible at several places.

"Ăvoi," quod she, "fy on you, hertelees!
Ăllas," quod she, "for by that God above,
Now han ye lost myn herte and al my love!
I can nat love a coward, by my faith.
For certes, what so any womman saith,
We alle desiren, if it mighte be,
To han housbondes hardy, wise, and free,
Ănd secree, and no nigard, ne no fool,
Ne him that is agast of every tool,
Ne noon avauntour. By that God above,
How dorste ye sayn for shame unto youre love
That any thing mighte make you aferd?
Have ye no mannes herte and han a beerd?

from THE CANTERBURY TALES

The General Prologue The twenty-nine "sondry folke" of the Canterbury company gather at the Tabard Inn, ostensibly with the pious intent of making a pilgrimage to England's holiest shrine, the tomb of Saint Thomas Becket at

Canterbury. From the start in the raffish and worldly London suburb of Southwark, though, the pilgrims' attentions and energy veer wildly between the sacred and the profane. The mild story-telling competition proposed by the Host also slides swiftly into a contest among social classes. Set in Chaucer's own time and place, *The Canterbury Tales* reflect both the dynamism and the uncertainties of a society still nostalgic for archaic models of church and state, yet riven by such crises as plague, economic disruption, and the new claims of peasants and mercantile bourgeoisie—claims expressed and repressed most violently in the recent Rising, or "Peasants' Revolt," of 1381.

Chaucer's *Prologue* has roots in the genre known as "estates satire." Such writings criticized the failure of the members of the three traditional "estates" of medieval society—the aristocracy, the clergy, and the peasants—to fulfill their ordained function of fighting, praying, and working the land, respectively. From the beginning the pilgrims' portraits are couched in language fraught with class connotations. The Knight, the idealized (if archaic) representative of the aristocracy, is called *gentil* (that is, "noble, aristocratic") and is said never to have uttered any *vileynye*—speech characteristic of peasants or *villeyns*. Many of the pilgrims in the other two estates display aristocratic manners, among the clergy notably the Prioress, with her "cheere of court," and the Monk, who lives like a country gentleman, hunting with greyhounds and a stable full of fine horses. Both pilgrims contrast with the ideal of their estate, the Parson, who, though "*povre*" is "rich" in holy works.

The commons are traditionally the last of the "three estates," yet they bulk largest in the Canterbury company and fit least well in that model of social order. There are old-fashioned laborers on the pilgrimage, but many more characters from the emerging and disruptive world of small industry and commerce. They are commoners, but have ambitions that lead them both to envy and to mock the powers held by their aristocratic and clerical companions.

Among the group that traditionally comprised the commons, the peasants, Chaucer singles out one ideal, the Plowman, who is, significantly, the Parson's brother. He is characterized as a diligent *swynkere* (worker), in implicit contrast to the lazy peasants castigated in estates satire. Most of the rest of the commons, however, such as the Miller and the Cook, are presented as "churlish," and their tales have a coarse vigor that Chaucer clearly relishes even as he disassociates himself from their vulgarity.

In theory, women were treated as a separate category, defined by their sexual nature and marital role rather than by their class. Nevertheless, the Prioress and the Wife of Bath are both satirized as much for their social ambition as for the failings of their gender. The Prioress prides herself on her courtesy, and the commoner Wife of Bath aspires to the same social recognition as the guildsmen's upwardly mobile wives. Her portrait is complex, however, for she is simultaneously satirized and admired for challenging the expected roles of women at the time, with her economic independence (as a rich widow and a cloth-maker) and her resultant freedom to travel. The narrator's suggestion that she goes on many pilgrimages in order to find a sixth husband bears out the stereotype of unbridled female sexuality familiar from estates satire, as her fondness of talking and laughing bears out the stereotype of female garrulousness.

Chaucer's satire is pointed but also exceptionally subtle, largely because of the irony achieved through his use of the narrator, seemingly naive and a little dense. His deadpan narration leaves the readers themselves to supply the judgment.

from THE CANTERBURY TALES

The General Prologue[1]

Whan that April with his showres soote° — *sweet*
The droughte of March hath perced to the roote,
And bathed every veine in swich licour,° — *such liquid*
Of which vertu° engendred is the flowr; — *by whose strength*
Whan Zephyrus[2] eek° with his sweete breeth — *also*
Inspired hath in every holt and heeth° — *wood and field*
The tendre croppes, and the yonge sonne
Hath in the Ram° his halve cours yronne, — *the zodiac sign Aries*
And smale fowles maken melodye
That sleepen al the night with open yë°— — *eye*
So priketh hem Nature in hir corages°— — *hearts, spirits*
Thanne longen folk to goon on pilgrimages,
And palmeres[3] for to seeken straunge strondes° — *shores*
To ferne halwes,° couthe° in sondry londes; — *far-off shrines / known*
And specially from every shires ende
Of Engelond to Canterbury they wende,° — *go*
The holy blisful martyr[4] for to seeke
That hem hath holpen° whan that they were seke.° — *helped / sick*
  Bifel that in that seson on a day,
In Southwerk[5] at the Tabard as I lay,
Redy to wenden on my pilgrimage
To Canterbury with ful devout corage,
At night was come into that hostelrye
Wel nine and twenty in a compaignye
Of sondry folk, by aventure yfalle
In felaweshipe, and pilgrimes were they alle
That toward Canterbury wolden ride.
The chambres° and the stables weren wide, — *guestrooms*
And wel we weren esed° at the beste. — *accommodated*
And shortly, whan the sonne was to reste,
So hadde I spoken with hem everichoon
That I was of hir felaweshipe anoon,
And made forward° erly for to rise, — *agreed*
To take oure way ther as I you devise.° — *relate*
  But nathelees, whil I have time and space,° — *opportunity*

1. Each page of The General Prologue in Middle English is followed by its modern English translation by David Wright on the facing page. Because the number of verse lines in the modern translation does not always match the Middle English precisely—for example, Wright translates Chaucer's first 36 lines of The General Prologue in 35 lines—no line numbers have been included in Wright's translation.

2. In Roman mythology Zephyrus was the demigod of the west wind, herald of warmer weather.

3. Pilgrims who had traveled to the Holy Land.

4. St. Thomas Becket, murdered in Canterbury Cathedral in 1170.

5. Southwark, a suburb of London south of the Thames and the traditional starting point for the pilgrimage to Canterbury in Kent, was notorious as a center of gambling and prostitution. The Tabard Inn was an actual public house at the time, named for the shape of its sign which resembled the coarse, sleeveless outer garment worn by members of the lower classes, monks, and foot soldiers alike.

The General Prologue

When the sweet showers of April have pierced
The drought of March, and pierced it to the root,
And every vein is bathed in that moisture
Whose quickening force will engender the flower;
And when the west wind too with its sweet breath
Has given life in every wood and field
To tender shoots, and when the stripling sun
Has run his half-course in Aries, the Ram,
And when small birds are making melodies,
That sleep all the night long with open eyes,
(Nature so prompts them, and encourages);
Then people long to go on pilgrimages.
And palmers to take ship for foreign shores,
And distant shrines, famous in different lands;
And most especially, from all the shires
Of England, to Canterbury they come,
The holy blessed martyr there to seek,
Who gave his help to them when they were sick.
  It happened at this season, that one day
In Southwark at the Tabard where I stayed
Ready to set out on my pilgrimage
To Canterbury, and pay devout homage,
There came at nightfall to the hostelry
Some nine-and-twenty in a company,
Folk of all kinds, met in accidental
Companionship, for they were pilgrims all;
It was to Canterbury that they rode.
The bedrooms and the stables were good-sized,
The comforts offered us were of the best.
And by the time the sun had gone to rest
I'd talked with everyone, and soon became
One of their company, and promised them
To rise at dawn next day to take the road
For the journey I am telling you about.
  But, before I go further with this tale,

Er that I ferther in this tale pace,° *proceed*
Me thinketh it accordant to resoun
To telle you al the condicioun° *circumstances*
Of eech of hem, so as it seemed me,
And whiche they were, and of what degree,° *social status*
And eek in what array that they were inne:
And at a knight thanne wol I first biginne.
  A Knight ther was, and that a worthy man,
That fro the time that he first bigan
To riden out, he loved chivalrye,
Trouthe and honour, freedom and curteisye.[6]
Ful worthy was he in his lordes werre,° *war*
And therto hadde he riden, no man ferre,° *farther*
As wel in Cristendom as hethenesse,° *heathen lands*
And evere honoured for his worthinesse.
  At Alisandre[7] he was whan it was wonne;
Ful ofte time he hadde the boord bigonne[8]
Aboven alle nacions in Pruce;
In Lettou had he reised,° and in Ruce, *campaigned*
No Cristen man so ofte of his degree;
In Gernade at the sege eek hadde he be
Of Algezir, and riden in Belmarye;
At Lyeis was he, and at Satalye,
Whan they were wonne; and in the Grete See
At many a noble arivee° hadde he be. *military landing*
  At mortal batailes[9] hadde he been fifteene,
And foughten for oure faith at Tramissene
In listes° thries, and ay° slain his fo. *duels / always*
  This ilke° worthy Knight hadde been also *same*
Somtime with the lord of Palatye
Again° another hethen in Turkye; *against*
And everemore he hadde a soverein pris.° *reputation*
And though that he were worthy, he was wis,
And of his port° as meeke as is a maide. *bearing*
He nevere yit no vilainye° ne saide *rudeness*
In al his lif unto no manere wight:° *no kind of man*
He was a verray,° parfit,° gentil° knight. *true / perfect / noble*
But for to tellen you of his array,° *equipment*
His hors were goode, but he was nat gay.° *gaily attired*
Of fustian° he wered a gipoun° *coarse cloth / tunic*
Al bismotered with his haubergeoun,[1]

6. Fidelity and good reputation, generosity and courtliness.
7. The place-names Chaucer lists over the next 15 lines were primarily associated with 14th-century Crusades against both Muslims and Eastern Orthodox Christians. Alisandre: Alexandria in Egypt; Pruce: Prussia; Lettou: Lithuania; Ruce: Russia; Gernade and Algezir: Granada and Algeciras in Spain; Belmarye: Ben-Marin near Morocco; Lyeis: Ayash in Turkey; Satalye: Atalia in Turkey; Grete See: Mediterranean; Tramissene: Tlemcen near Morocco; Palatye: Balat in Turkey.
8. Held the place of honor at feasts.
9. Tournaments waged to the death.
1. Rust-stained from his coat of mail.

And while I can, it seems reasonable
That I should let you have a full description
Of each of them, their sort and condition,
At any rate as they appeared to me;
Tell who they were, their status and profession,
What they looked like, what kind of clothes they dressed in;
And with a knight, then, I shall first begin.
  There was a knight, a reputable man,
Who from the moment that he first began
Campaigning, had cherished the profession
Of arms; he also prized trustworthiness,
Liberality, fame, and courteousness.
In the king's service he'd fought valiantly,
And travelled far; no man as far as he
In Christian and in heathen lands as well,
And ever honoured for his ability.
  He was at Alexandria when it fell,
Often he took the highest place at table
Over the other foreign knights in Prussia;
He'd raided in Lithuania and Russia,
No Christian of his rank fought there more often.
Also he'd been in Granada, at the siege
Of Algeciras; forayed in Benmarin;
At Ayas and Adalia he had been
When they were taken; and with the great hosts
Freebooting on the Mediterranean coasts;
  Fought fifteen mortal combats; thrice as champion
In tournaments, he at Tramassene
Fought for our faith, and each time killed his man.
  This worthy knight had also, for a time,
Taken service in Palatia for the Bey,
Against another heathen in Turkey;
And almost beyond price was his prestige.
Though eminent, he was prudent and sage,
And in his bearing mild as any maid.
He'd never been foul-spoken in his life
To any kind of man; he was indeed
The very pattern of a noble knight.
But as for his appearance and outfit,
He had good horses, yet was far from smart.
He wore a tunic made of coarse thick stuff,
Marked by his chainmail, all begrimed with rust,

For he was late come from his viage,° *expedition*
And wente for to doon his pilgrimage.
With him ther was his sone, a yong Squier,
A lovere and a lusty bacheler,[2]
With lokkes crulle° as they were laid in presse. *curled*
Of twenty yeer of age he was, I gesse.
Of his stature he was of evene° lengthe, *average*
And wonderly delivere,° and of greet strengthe. *agile*
And he hadde been som time in chivachye° *cavalry expedition*
In Flandres, in Artois, and Picardye,[3]
And born him wel as of so litel space,° *time*
In hope to stonden in his lady grace.° *lady's favor*
Embrouded° was he as it were a mede,° *embroidered / meadow*
Al ful of fresshe flowres, white and rede;
Singing he was, or floiting,° al the day: *playing the flute*
He was as fressh as is the month of May.
Short was his gowne, with sleeves longe and wide.
Wel coude he sitte on hors, and faire ride;
He coude songes make, and wel endite,° *compose*
Juste° and eek daunce, and wel portraye° and write. *joust / draw*
So hote he loved that by nightertale° *nighttime*
He slepte namore than dooth a nightingale.
Curteis he was, lowely,° and servisable,° *humble /attentive*
And carf° biforn his fader° at the table *carved / father*
A Yeman[4] hadde he° and servants namo *i.e., the Knight*
At that time, for him liste° ride so; *he liked*
And he was clad in cote and hood of greene.
A sheef of pecok arwes,° bright and keene, *peacock arrows*
Under his belt he bar ful thriftily;
Wel coude he dresse° his takel° yemanly: *arrange / gear*
His arwes drouped nought with fetheres lowe.
And in his hand he bar a mighty bowe.
A not-heed° hadde he with a brown visage.° *short haircut / face*
Of wodecraft° wel coude he al the usage. *forestry*
Upon his arm he bar a gay bracer,° *archer's armguard*
And by his side a swerd and a bokeler,° *small shield*
And on that other side a gay daggere,
Harneised wel and sharp as point of spere;
A Cristophre[5] on his brest of silver sheene;
An horn he bar, the baudrik° was of greene. *shoulder strap*
A forster° was he soothly,° as I gesse. *gamekeeper / truly*
Ther was also a Nonne, a Prioresse,
That of hir smiling was ful simple and coy.° *quiet, shy*

2. An unmarried and unpropertied younger knight.
3. Regions in the north of France and in what is now Belgium, where the English and the French were fighting out the Hundred Years' War.
4. A yeoman was a freeborn servant (not a peasant), who looked after the affairs of the gentry. This particular yeoman was a forester and gamekeeper for the Knight.
5. Medal of St. Christopher, patron saint of travelers.

Having just returned from an expedition,
And on his pilgrimage of thanksgiving.
With him there was his son, a young squire,
A lively knight-apprentice, and a lover,
With hair as curly as if newly waved;
I took him to be twenty years of age.
In stature he was of an average length,
Wonderfully athletic, and of great strength.
He'd taken part in cavalry forays
In Flanders, in Artois, and Picardy,
With credit, though no more than a novice,
Hoping to stand well in his lady's eyes.
His clothes were all embroidered like a field
Full of the freshest flowers, white and red.
He sang, or played the flute, the livelong day,
And he was fresher than the month of May.
Short was his gown, with sleeves cut long and wide.
He'd a good seat on horseback, and could ride,
Make music too, and songs to go with it;
Could joust and dance, and also draw and write.
So burningly he loved, that come nightfall
He'd sleep no more than any nightingale.
Polite, modest, willing to serve, and able,
He carved before his father at their table.
The knight had just one servant, a yeoman,
For so he wished to ride, on this occasion.
The man was clad in coat and hood of green.
He carried under his belt, handily,
For he looked to his gear in yeoman fashion,
A sheaf of peacock arrows, sharp and shining,
Not liable to fall short from poor feathering;
And in his hand he bore a mighty bow.
He had a cropped head, and his face was brown;
Of woodcraft he knew all there was to know.
He wore a fancy leather guard, a bracer,
And by his side a sword and a rough buckler,
And on the other side a fancy dagger,
Well-mounted, sharper than the point of spear,
And on his breast a medal: St Christopher,
The woodman's patron saint, in polished silver.
He bore a horn slung from a cord of green,
And my guess is, he was a forester.
There was also a nun, a prioress,
Whose smile was unaffected and demure;

Hir gretteste ooth was but by Sainte Loy![6]
And she was cleped° Madame Eglantine.° *called / Brier-rose*
Ful wel she soong the service divine,
Entuned in hir nose ful semely;° *becomingly*
And Frenssh she spak ful faire and fetisly,° *elegantly*
After the scole of Stratford at the Bowe[7]
For Frenssh of Paris was to hire unknowe.
At mete° wel ytaught was she withalle: *meals*
She leet no morsel from hir lippes falle,
Ne wette hir fingres in hir sauce deepe;
Wel coude she carye a morsel, and wel keepe° *safeguard*
That no drope ne fille upon hir brest.
In curteisye was set ful muchel hir lest.° *her great pleasure*
Hir over-lippe° wiped she so clene *upper lip*
That in hir coppe ther was no ferthing[8] seene
Of grece,° whan she dronken hadde hir draughte; *grease*
Ful semely after hir mete she raughte.° *reached for her food*
And sikerly° she was of greet disport,° *certainly / good cheer*
And ful plesant, and amiable of port,
And pained hire to countrefete cheere° *appearance*
Of court, and to been estatlich° of manere, *stately*
And to been holden digne° of reverence. *worthy*
But, for to speken of hir conscience,
She was so charitable and so pitous
She wolde weepe if that she saw a mous
Caught in a trappe, if it were deed or bledde.
Of smale houndes hadde she that she fedde
With rosted flessh,° or milk and wastelbreed;[9] *meat*
But sore wepte she if oon of hem were deed,
Or if men smoot° it with a yerde° smerte;° *hit / rod / painfully*
And al was conscience and tendre herte.
Ful semely hir wimpe[1] pinched was,
Hir nose tretis,° hir yën greye as glas, *shapely*
Hir mouth ful smal, and therto softe and reed—
But sikerly she hadde a fair forheed:
It was almost a spanne[2] brood, I trowe,° *believe*
For hardily,° she was nat undergrowe.° *assuredly / short*
Ful fetis° was hir cloke, as I was war; *elegant*
Of smal coral aboute hir arm she bar
A paire of bedes, gauded al with greene,[3]
And theron heeng a brooch of gold ful sheene,

6. St. Eligius, patron saint of metalworkers, believed never to have sworn an oath in his life.
7. From the school (i.e., after the manner) of Stratford, a suburb of London where the prosperous convent of St. Leonard's was located; her French is Anglo-Norman as opposed to the French spoken on the Continent.
8. Spot the size of a farthing.
9. Bread of the finest quality.
1. A pleated headdress covering all but the face, such as nuns and married women wore.
2. A hand's width, 7 to 9 inches.
3. A set of rosary beads, marked off by larger beads (gauds) to indicate where the Paternosters should be said.

Her greatest oath was just, "By St Eloi!"
And she was known as Madame Eglantine.
She sang the divine service prettily,
And through the nose, becomingly intoned;
And she spoke French well and elegantly
As she'd been taught it at Stratford-at-Bow,
For French of Paris was to her unknown.
Good table manners she had learnt as well:
She never let a crumb from her mouth fall;
She never soiled her fingers, dipping deep
Into the sauce; when lifting to her lips
Some morsel, she was careful not to spill
So much as one small drop upon her breast.
Her greatest pleasure was in etiquette.
She used to wipe her upper lip so clean,
No print of grease inside her cup was seen,
Not the least speck, when she had drunk from it.
Most daintily she'd reach for what she ate.
No question, she possessed the greatest charm,
Her demeanour was so pleasant, and so warm;
Though at pains to ape the manners of the court,
And be dignified, in order to be thought
A person well deserving of esteem.
But, speaking of her sensibility,
She was so full of charity and pity
That if she saw a mouse caught in a trap,
And it was dead or bleeding, she would weep.
She kept some little dogs, and these she fed
On roast meat, or on milk and fine white bread.
But how she'd weep if one of them were dead,
Or if somebody took a stick to it!
She was all sensitivity and tender heart.
Her veil was pleated most becomingly;
Her nose well-shaped; eyes blue-grey, of great beauty;
And her mouth tender, very small, and red.
And there's no doubt she had a fine forehead,
Almost a span in breadth, I'd swear it was,
For certainly she was not undersized.
Her cloak, I noticed, was most elegant.
A coral rosary with gauds of green
She carried on her arm; and from it hung
A brooch of shining gold; inscribed thereon

On which ther was first writen a crowned A.[4]
And after, *Amor vincit omnia*.[5]
  Another Nonne with hire hadde she
That was hir chapelaine,° and preestes three. *secretary*
  A Monk ther was, a fair for the maistrye,° *very good-looking*
An outridere[6] that loved venerye,° *hunting*
A manly° man, to been an abbot able. *courageous*
Ful many a daintee° hors hadde he in stable, *fine*
And whan he rood, men mighte his bridel heere
Ginglen° in a whistling wind as clere *jingling*
And eek as loude as dooth the chapel belle
Ther as this lord was kepere of the celle.[7]
The rule of Saint Maure or of Saint Beneit,[8]
By cause that it was old and somdeel strait°— *somewhat strict*
This ilke Monk leet olde thinges pace,
And heeld after the newe world the space.° *the times (customs)*
He yaf nought of that text° a pulled° hen *regulation / plucked*
That saith that hunteres been nought holy men,
Ne that a monk, whan he is recchelees,° *careless*
Is likned til a fissh that is waterlees—
This is to sayn, a monk out of his cloistre;
But thilke° text heeld he nat worth an oystre. *that same*
And I saide his opinion was good:
What sholde he studye and make himselven wood° *crazy*
Upon a book in cloistre alway to poure,
Or swinke° with his handes and laboure, *work*
As Austin[9] bit?° How shal the world be served? *orders*
Lat Austin have his swink° to him reserved! *toil*
Therfore he was a prikasour° aright. *hunter on horseback*
Grehoundes he hadde as swift as fowl in flight.
Of priking and of hunting for the hare
Was al his lust,° for no cost wolde he spare. *pleasure*
I sawgh his sleeves purfiled° at the hand *fur-lined*
With gris,° and that the fineste of a land; *gray fur*
And for to festne his hood under his chin
He hadde of gold wrought a ful curious° pin: *elaborate*
A love-knotte[1] in the grettere° ende ther was. *larger*
His heed was balled,° that shoon as any glas, *bald*
And eek his face, as he hadde been anoint:
He was a lord ful fat and in good point;° *in good shape*
His yën steepe,° and rolling in his heed, *bright*

4. The letter "A" with a crown on top.
5. Love conquers all (Virgil, *Eclogues*, 10.69). Though pagan and secular in origin, the phrase was often used to refer to divine love as well.
6. A monk who worked outside the confines of the monastery.
7. Supervisor of the outlying cell of the monastery.
8. St. Benedict (Beneit) was the founder of Western monasticism, and his Rule prohibited monks from leaving the grounds of the monastery without special permission. St. Maurus introduced the Benedictine order into France.
9. St. Augustine recommended that monks perform manual labor.
1. An elaborate knot.

Was, first of all, a crowned "A,"
And under, *Amor vincit omnia.*
  With her were three priests, and another nun,
Who was her chaplain and companion.
  There was a monk; a nonpareil was he,
Who rode, as steward of his monastery,
The country round; a lover of good sport,
A manly man, and fit to be an abbot.
He'd plenty of good horses in his stable,
And when he went out riding, you could hear
His bridle jingle in the wind, as clear
And loud as the monastery chapel-bell.
Inasmuch as he was keeper of the cell,
The rule of St Maurus or St Benedict
Being out of date, and also somewhat strict,
This monk I speak of let old precepts slide,
And took the modern practice as his guide.
He didn't give so much as a plucked hen
For the maxim, "Hunters are not pious men,"
Or "A monk who's heedless of his regimen
Is much the same as a fish out of water,"
In other words, a monk out of his cloister.
But that's a text he thought not worth an oyster;
And I remarked his opinion was sound.
What use to study, why go round the bend
With poring over some book in a cloister,
Or drudging with his hands, to toil and labour
As Augustine bids? How shall the world go on?
You can go keep your labour, Augustine!
So he rode hard—no question about that—
Kept greyhounds swifter than a bird in flight.
Hard riding, and the hunting of the hare,
Were what he loved, and opened his purse for.
I noticed that his sleeves were edged and trimmed
With squirrel fur, the finest in the land.
For fastening his hood beneath his chin,
He wore an elaborate golden pin,
Twined with a love-knot at the larger end.
His head was bald and glistening like glass
As if anointed; and likewise his face.
A fine fat patrician, in prime condition,
His bright and restless eyes danced in his head,

That stemed as a furnais of a leed;[2]
His bootes souple,° his hors in greet estat[3]— *supple*
Now certainly he was a fair prelat.[4]
He was nat pale as a forpined° gost: *tormented*
A fat swan loved he best of any rost.
His palfrey° was as brown as is a berye. *saddle horse*
  A Frere° ther was, a wantoune[5] and a merye, *Friar*
A limitour,[6] a ful solempne man.
In alle the ordres foure[7] is noon that can° *knows*
So muche of daliaunce° and fair langage: *flirtation*
He hadde maad ful many a mariage
Of yonge wommen at his owene cost;
Unto his ordre he was a noble post.° *pillar*
Ful wel biloved and familier was he
With frankelains[8] over al in his contree,
And with worthy wommen of the town—
For he hadde power of confessioun,
As saide himself, more than a curat,° *parish priest*
For of his ordre he was licenciat.[9]
Ful swetely herde he confessioun,
And plesant was his absolucioun.
He was an esy man to yive penaunce
Ther as he wiste to have a good pitaunce;[1]
For unto a poore ordre for to yive
Is signe that a man is wel yshrive;° *absolved*
For if he yaf, he dorste make avaunt° *boast*
He wiste that a man was repentaunt;
For many a man so hard is of his herte
He may nat weepe though him sore smerte:° *hurts*
Therfore, in stede of weeping and prayeres,
Men mote yive silver to the poore freres.
  His tipet° was ay farsed° ful of knives *scarf / packed*
And pinnes, for to yiven faire wives;
And certainly he hadde a merye note;
Wel coude he singe and playen on a rote;° *fiddle*
Of yeddinges° he bar outrely the pris.[2] *singing ballads*
His nekke whit was as the flowr-de-lis;[3]
Therto he strong was as a champioun.
He knew the tavernes wel in every town,
And every hostiler and tappestere,° *innkeeper and barmaid*
Bet than a lazar or a beggestere.° *a leper or a beggar*
For unto swich a worthy man as he

2. Glowed like a furnace under a cauldron.
3. Excellent condition.
4. Prelate, important churchman.
5. Jovial, pleasure-seeking.
6. Friar licensed by his order to beg for alms within a given district.
7. The four orders of friars were the Carmelites, Augustinians, Dominicans, and Franciscans.
8. Franklins, important property holders.
9. Licensed by the Church to hear confessions.
1. Where he knew he would get a good donation.
2. Utterly took the prize.
3. Lily, emblem of the royal house of France.

And sparkled like the fire beneath a pot;
Boots of soft leather, horse in perfect trim:
No question but he was a fine prelate!
Not pale and wan like some tormented spirit.
A fat roast swan was what he loved the best.
His saddle-horse was brown as any berry.
  There was a begging friar, a genial merry
Limiter and a most imposing person.
In all of the four Orders there was none
So versed in small talk and in flattery:
And many was the marriage in a hurry
He'd had to improvise and even pay for.
He was a noble pillar of his Order,
And was well in and intimate with every
Well-to-do freeman farmer of his area,
And with the well-off women in the town;
For he was qualified to hear confession,
And absolve graver sins than a curate,
Or so he said; he was a licentiate.
How sweetly he would hear confession!
How pleasant was his absolution!
He was an easy man in giving shrift,
When sure of getting a substantial gift:
For, as he used to say, generous giving
To a poor Order is a sign you're shriven;
For if you gave, then he could vouch for it
That you were conscience-stricken and contrite;
For many are so hardened in their hearts
They cannot weep, though burning with remorse.
Therefore, instead of weeping and prayers,
They should give money to the needy friars.
The pockets of his hood were stuffed with knives
And pins to give away to pretty wives.
He had a pleasant singing voice, for sure,
Could sing and play the fiddle beautifully;
He took the biscuit as a ballad-singer,
And though his neck was whiter than a lily,
Yet he was brawny as a prize-fighter.
He knew the taverns well in every town,
And all the barmaids and the innkeepers,
Better than lepers or the street-beggars;
It wouldn't do, for one in his position,

Accorded nat, as by his facultee,°[4] *official position*
To have with sike° lazars aquaintaunce: *such*
It is nat honeste,° it may nought avaunce,° *dignified / profit*
For to delen with no swich poraile,° *poor people*
But al with riche, and selleres of vitaile;° *food*
And over al ther as profit sholde arise,
Curteis he was, and lowely° of servise. *humble*
Ther was no man nowher so vertuous:° *capable*
He was the beste beggere in his hous.
And yaf a certain ferme for the graunt:[5]
Noon of his bretheren cam ther in his haunt.° *territory*
For though a widwe hadde nought a sho,
So plesant was his *In principio*[6]
Yit wolde he have a ferthing er he wente;
His purchas° was wel bettre than his rente.° *income / expense*
And rage° he coude as it were right a whelpe;° *flirt / puppy*
In love-dayes[7] ther coude he muchel helpe,
For ther he was nat lik a cloisterer,
With a thredbare cope, as is a poore scoler,
But he was lik a maister° or a pope. *professor*
Of double worstede was his semicope,°[8] *short cloak*
And rounded as a belle out of the presse.° *bell-mold*
Somwhat he lipsed for his wantounesse
To make his Englissh sweete upon his tonge;
And in his harping, whan that he hadde songe,
His yën twinkled in his heed aright
As doon the sterres in the frosty night.
This worthy limitour was cleped° Huberd. *called*
 A Marchant was ther with a forked beerd,
In motlee,° and hye on hors he sat, *multicolored fabric*
Upon his heed a Flandrissh° bevere hat, *Flemish*
His bootes clasped faire and fetisly.° *elegantly*
His resons° he spak ful solempnely, *opinions*
Souning° alway th'encrees of his winning. *announcing*
He wolde the see were kept for any thing° *protected at all costs*
Bitwixen Middelburgh and Orewelle.[9]
Wel coude he in eschaunge sheeldes[1] selle.
This worthy man ful wel his wit bisette:° *employed*
Ther wiste° no wight° that he was in dette, *knew / person*
So estatly° was he of his governaunce,° *dignified / management*
With his bargaines, and with his chevissaunce.° *borrowing*
Forsoothe° he was a worthy man withalle; *in truth*
But, sooth to sayn, I noot° how men him calle. *do not know*

4. It was unbecoming to his official post.
5. And gave a certain fee for the license to beg.
6. "In the beginning," the opening line in Genesis and the Gospel of John, popular for devotions.
7. Holidays for settling disputes out of court.
8. His short cloak was made of thick woolen cloth.
9. Middleburgh in the Netherlands and Orwell in Suffolk were major ports for the wool trade.
1. Unit of exchange, a credit instrument for foreign merchants.

One of his ability and distinction,
To hold acquaintance with diseased lepers.
It isn't seemly, and it gets you nowhere,
To have any dealings with that sort of trash,
Stick to provision-merchants and the rich!
And anywhere where profit might arise
He'd crawl with courteous offers of service.
You'd nowhere find an abler man than he,
Or a better beggar in his friary;
He paid a yearly fee for his district,
No brother friar trespassed on his beat.
A widow might not even own a shoe,
But so pleasant was his *In principio*
He'd win her farthing in the end, then go.
He made his biggest profits on the side.
He'd frolic like a puppy. He'd give aid
As arbitrator upon settling-days,
For there he was not like some cloisterer
With threadbare cape, like any poor scholar,
But like a Master of Arts, or the Pope!
Of the best double-worsted was his cloak,
And bulging like a bell that's newly cast.
He lisped a little, from affectation,
To make his English sweet upon his tongue;
And when he harped, as closing to a song,
His eyes would twinkle in his head just like
The stars upon a sharp and frosty night.
This worthy limiter was called Hubert.
  A merchant was there, on a high-saddled horse:
He'd a forked beard, a many-coloured dress,
And on his head a Flanders beaver hat,
Boots with expensive clasps, and buckled neatly.
He gave out his opinions pompously,
Kept talking of the profits that he'd made,
How, at all costs, the sea should be policed
From Middleburg in Holland to Harwich.
At money-changing he was an expert;
He dealt in French gold florins on the quiet.
This worthy citizen could use his head:
No one could tell whether he was in debt,
So impressive and dignified his bearing
As he went about his loans and bargaining.
He was a really estimable man,
But the fact is I never learnt his name.

A Clerk ther was of Oxenforde also
That unto logik hadde longe ygo.° *gone (studied)*
As lene was his hors as is a rake,
And he was nought right fat, I undertake,
But looked holwe,° and therto sobrely. *emaciated*
Ful thredbare was his overeste courtepy,° *outer cloak*
For he hadde geten him yit no benefice,° *church income*
Ne was so worldly for to have office.° *secular employment*
For him was levere° have at his beddes heed *he preferred*
Twenty bookes, clad in blak or reed,
Of Aristotle and his philosophye,
Than robes riche, or fithele,° or gay sautrye.° *fiddle / harp*
But al be that he was a philosophre[2]
Yit hadde he but litel gold in cofre;
But al that he mighte of his freendes hente,° *get*
On bookes and on lerning he it spente,
And bisily gan for the soules praye
Of hem that yaf him wherwith to scoleye.° *study*
Of studye took he most cure° and most heede. *care*
Nought oo° word spak he more than was neede, *one*
And that was said in forme° and reverence, *formally*
And short and quik, and ful of height sentence:° *lofty meaning*
Souning in° moral vertu was his speeche, *consonant with*
And gladly wolde he lerne, and gladly teche.
A Sergeant of the Lawe,[3] war and wis,
That often hadde been at the Parvis[4]
Ther was also, ful riche of excellence.
Discreet he was, and of greet reverence—
He seemed swich, his wordes weren so wise.
Justice he was ful often in assise[5]
By patente and by plein commissioun.[6]
For his science° and for his heigh renown *knowledge*
Of fees and robes hadde he many oon.
So greet a purchasour° was nowher noon; *buyer of land*
Al was fee simple[7] to him in effect—
His purchasing mighte nat been infect.° *invalidated*
Nowher so bisy a man as he ther nas;
And yit he seemed bisier than he was.
In termes hadde he caas and doomes° alle *lawsuits and judgments*
That from the time of King William[8] were falle.
Therto he coude endite and make a thing,[9]
Ther coude no wight° pinchen° at his writing; *person / find fault with*
And every statut coude he plein by rote.[1]

2. A philosopher could be a scientist or alchemist.
3. A lawyer of the highest rank.
4. The porch of St. Paul's Cathedral, a meeting place for lawyers.
5. He was often judge in the court of assizes (civil court).
6. By letter of appointment from the king and by full jurisdiction.
7. Owned outright with no legal impediments.
8. Since the introduction of Norman law in England under William the Conqueror.
9. Compose and draw up a deed.
1. He knew entirely from memory.

There was a scholar from Oxford as well,
Not yet an MA, reading Logic still;
The horse he rode was leaner than a rake,
And he himself, believe me, none too fat,
But hollow-cheeked, and grave and serious.
Threadbare indeed was his short overcoat:
A man too unworldly for lay office,
Yet he'd not got himself a benefice.
For he'd much rather have at his bedside
A library, bound in black calf or red,
Of Aristotle and his philosophy,
Than rich apparel, fiddle, or fine psaltery.
And though he was a man of science, yet
He had but little gold in his strongbox;
But upon books and learning he would spend
All he was able to obtain from friends;
He'd pray assiduously for their souls,
Who gave him wherewith to attend the schools.
Learning was all he cared for or would heed.
He never spoke a word more than was need,
And that was said in form and decorum,
And brief and terse, and full of deepest meaning.
Moral virtue was reflected in his speech,
And gladly would he learn, and gladly teach.
There was a wise and wary sergeant-at-law,
A well-known figure in the portico
Where lawyers meet; one of great excellence,
Judicious, worthy of reverence,
Or so he seemed, his sayings were so wise.
He'd often acted as Judge of Assize
By the king's letters patent, authorized
To hear all cases. And his great renown
And skill had won him many a fee, or gown
Given in lieu of money. There was none
To touch him as a property-buyer; all
He bought was fee-simple, without entail;
You'd never find a flaw in the conveyance.
And nowhere would you find a busier man;
And yet he seemed much busier than he was.
From yearbooks he could quote, chapter and verse,
Each case and judgement since William the First.
And he knew how to draw up and compose
A deed; you couldn't fault a thing he wrote;
And he'd reel all the statutes off by rote.

He rood but hoomly° in a medlee° cote, *simply / multicolored*
Girt with a ceint° of silk, with barres° smale. *belt / stripes*
Of his array telle I no lenger tale.
A Frankelain[2] was in his compaignye:
Whit was his beerd as is the dayesye;° *daisy*
Of his complexion he was sanguin.[3]
Wel loved he by the morwe a sop in win.[4]
To liven in delit° was evere his wone,° *pleasure / custom*
For he was Epicurus owene sone,
That heeld opinion that plein° delit *complete*
Was verray felicitee parfit.[5]
An housholdere and that a greet was he:
Saint Julian[6] he was in his contree.
His breed, his ale, was always after oon;° *just as good*
A bettre envined° man was nevere noon. *stocked with wine*
Withouten bake mete was nevere his hous,
Of fissh and flessh, and that so plentevous° *plentiful*
It snewed° in his hous of mete and drinke, *snowed*
Of alle daintees that men coude thinke.
After the sondry sesons of the yeer
So chaunged he his mete and his soper.[7]
Ful many a fat partrich° hadde he in mewe,° *partridge / cage*
And many a breem,° and many a luce° in stewe.° *carp / pike / pond*
Wo was his cook but if his sauce were
Poinant° and sharp, and redy al his gere. *pungent*
His table dormant[8] in his halle alway
Stood redy covered al the longe day.
At sessions[9] ther was he lord and sire.
Ful ofte time he was Knight of the Shire.[1]
An anlaas° and a gipser° al of silk *dagger / purse*
Heeng at his girdel, whit as morne milk.
A shirreve hadde he been, and countour.[2]
Was nowher swich a worthy vavasour.[3]
An Haberdasshere° and a Carpenter, *hat-maker*
A Webbe, a Dyere, and a Tapicer[4]—
And they were clothed alle in oo liveree° *in the same uniform*
Of a solempne and a greet fraternitee.° *parish guild*
Ful fresshe and newe hir gere apiked was;[5]
Hir knives were chaped° nought with bras, *mounted*
But al with silver; wrought ful clene° and weel *quite nicely made*
Hir girdles and hir pouches everydeel.° *entirely*

2. A large landholder, freeborn but not belonging to the nobility.
3. In temperament he was sanguine (optimistic, governed by blood as his chief humor).
4. In the morning a sop of bread soaked in wine.
5. True and perfect happiness.
6. Patron saint of hospitality.
7. For health he changed his diet according to the different seasons.
8. Left standing rather than dismantled between meals.
9. Meetings of the justices of the peace.
1. A representative of the district at Parliament.
2. He had been sheriff and auditor of the county finances.
3. Lower member of the feudal elite.
4. A weaver, dyer, and tapestry-maker, all members of the same commercial guild.
5. Their gear was decorated.

He was dressed simply, in a coloured coat,
Girt by a silk belt with thin metal bands.
I have no more to tell of his appearance.
  A franklin—that's a country gentleman
And freeman landowner—was his companion.
White was his beard, as white as any daisy;
Sanguine his temperament; his face ruddy.
He loved his morning draught of sops-in-wine,
Since living well was ever his custom,
For he was Epicurus' own true son
And held with him that sensuality
Is where the only happiness is found.
And he kept open house so lavishly
He was St Julian to the country round,
The patron saint of hospitality.
His bread and ale were always of the best,
Like his wine-cellar, which was unsurpassed.
Cooked food was never lacking in his house,
Both meat and fish, and that so plenteous
That in his home it snowed with food and drink,
And all the delicacies you could think.
According to the season of the year,
He changed the dishes that were served at dinner.
He'd plenty of fat partridges in coop,
And kept his fishpond full of pike and carp.
His cook would catch it if his sauces weren't
Piquant and sharp, and all his equipment
To hand. And all day in his hall there stood
The great fixed table, with the places laid.
When the justices met, he'd take the chair;
He often served as MP for the shire.
A dagger, and a small purse made of silk,
Hung at his girdle, white as morning milk.
He'd been sheriff, and county auditor:
A model squireen, no man worthier.
  A haberdasher and a carpenter,
A weaver, dyer, tapestry-maker—
And they were in the uniform livery
Of a dignified and rich fraternity,
A parish-guild: their gear all trim and fresh,
Knives silver-mounted, none of your cheap brass;
Their belts and purses neatly stitched as well,
All finely finished to the last detail.

Wel seemed eech of hem a fair burgeis° *townsperson*
To sitten in a yeldehalle° on a dais. *guildhall*
Everich, for the wisdom that he can,° *knows*
Was shaply° for to been an alderman.° *fit / mayor*
For catel° hadde they ynough and rente,° *property / income*
And eek hir wives wolde it wel assente—
And elles certain were they to blame:
It is ful fair to been ycleped° "Madame," *called*
And goon to vigilies[6] al bifore,
And have a mantel royalliche ybore.
A Cook they hadde with hem for the nones,° *for the occasion*
To boile the chiknes with the marybones,° *marrowbones*
And powdre-marchant tart and galingale.° *aromatic spices*
Wel coude he knowe a draughte of London ale.
He coude roste, and seethe,° and broile, and frye, *boil*
Maken mortreux,° and wel bake a pie. *stews*
But greet harm was it, as it thoughte me,
That on his shine a mormal° hadde he. *ulcer*
For blankmanger,° that made he with the beste. *thick stew*
A Shipman was ther, woning° fer by weste— *dwelling*
For ought I woot,° he was of Dertemouthe.[7] *know*
He rood upon a rouncy° as he couthe, *nag*
In a gowne of falding° to the knee. *coarse brown cloth*
A daggere hanging on a laas° hadde he *strap*
Aboute his nekke, under his arm adown.
The hote somer hadde maad his hewe al brown;
And certainly he was a good felawe.
Ful many a draughte of win hadde he drawe
Fro Burdeuxward, whil that the chapman° sleep:[8] *merchant*
Of nice° conscience took he no keep;° *scrupulous / care*
If that he faught and hadde the hyer hand,
By water he sente hem hoom to every land.
But of his craft, to rekene wel his tides,
His stremes° and his daungers° him bisides, *currents / hazards*
His herberwe° and his moone, his lodemenage,° *harboring / navigation*
Ther was noon swich from Hulle to Cartage.[9]
Hardy he was and wis to undertake;
With many a tempest hadde his beerd been shake;
He knew alle the havenes as they were
Fro Gotlond to the Cape of Finistere,[1]
And every crike° in Britaine° and in Spaine. *inlet / Brittany*
His barge ycleped was the Maudelaine.
With us ther was a Doctour of Physik:° *Medicine*

6. Feasts held the night before a holy day.
7. Dartmouth, a port on the southwestern coast.
8. On the trip back from Bordeaux while the merchant slept.
9. Hull, on the northeastern coast in Yorkshire; Cartage: Carthage in North Africa or Cartagena on the Mediterranean coast of Spain.
1. Gotland in the Baltic Sea; Finistere: Land's End in western Spain.

Each of them looked indeed like a burgess,
And fit to sit on any guildhall dais.
Each was, in knowledge and ability,
Eligible to be an alderman;
For they'd income enough and property.
What's more, their wives would certainly agree,
Or otherwise they'd surely be to blame
It's very pleasant to be called "Madam"
And to take precedence at church processions,
And have one's mantle carried like a queen's.
They had a cook with them for the occasion,
To boil the chickens up with marrowbones,
Tart powdered flavouring, spiced with galingale.
No better judge than he of London ale.
And he could roast, and seethe, and boil, and fry,
Make a thick soup, and bake a proper pie;
But to my mind it was the greatest shame
He'd got an open sore upon his shin;
For he made chicken-pudding with the best.
A sea-captain, whose home was in the west,
Was there—a Dartmouth man, for all I know
He rode a cob as well as he knew how,
And was dressed in a knee-length woollen gown.
From a lanyard round his neck, a dagger hung
Under his arm. Summer had tanned him brown.
As rough a diamond as you'd hope to find,
He'd tapped and lifted many a stoup of wine
From Bordeaux, when the merchant wasn't looking.
He hadn't time for scruples or fine feeling,
For if he fought, and got the upper hand,
He'd send his captives home by sea, not land.
But as for seamanship, and calculation
Of moon, tides, currents, all hazards at sea,
For harbour-lore, and skill in navigation,
From Hull to Carthage there was none to touch him.
He was shrewd adventurer, tough and hardy.
By many a tempest had his beard been shaken.
And he knew all the harbours that there were
Between the Baltic and Cape Finisterre,
And each inlet of Britanny and Spain.
The ship he sailed was called "The Magdalen."
With us there was a doctor, a physician;

In al this world ne was ther noon him lik
To speken of physik and of surgerye.
For he was grounded in astronomye,° *astrology*
He kepte his pacient a ful greet deel
In houres° by his magik naturel. *astronomical hours*
Wel coude he fortunen the ascendent[2]
Of his images° for his pacient. *talismans*
He knew the cause of every maladye,
Were it of hoot or cold or moiste or drye,[3]
And where engendred° and of what humour:[4] *originated*
He was a verray parfit praktisour.° *practitioner*
The cause yknowe, and of his harm the roote,
Anoon he yaf the sike man his boote.° *remedy*
Ful redy hadde he his apothecaries
To senden him drogges and his letuaries,° *medicines*
For eech of hem made other for to winne:
Hir frendshipe was nought newe to biginne.
Wel knew he the olde Esculapius,[5]
And Deiscorides and eek Rufus,
Olde Ipocras, Hali, and Galien,
Serapion, Razis, and Avicen,
Averrois, Damascien, and Constantin,
Bernard, and Gatesden, and Gilbertin.
Of his diete mesurable° was he, *moderate*
For it was of no superfluitee,
But of greet norissing and digestible.
His studye was but litel on the Bible.
In sanguin° and in pers° he clad was al, *red / Persian blue*
Lined with taffata and with sendal;° *silks*
And yit he was but esy of dispence;° *thrifty*
He kepte that he wan in pestilence.
For gold in physik is a cordial,° *tonic*
Therfore he loved gold in special.
A good Wif was ther of biside Bathe,
But she was somdeel deef,° and that was scathe.° *somewhat deaf / a pity*
Of cloth-making she hadde swich an haunt,° *practice*
She passed hem of Ypres and of Gaunt.[6]
In al the parissh wif ne was ther noon
That to the offring[7] bifore hire sholde goon,
And if ther dide, certain so wroth° was she *angry*
That she was out of alle charitee.

2. Calculate the ascendent (propitious moment).
3. The qualities of the four natural elements, corresponding to the humors of the body and the composition of the universe, needed to be kept in perfect balance.
4. Bodily fluids, or "humors," thought to govern moods (blood, phlegm, black bile, yellow bile).
5. The Physician is acquainted with a full range of medical authorities from among the ancient Greeks (Aesculapius, Dioscorides, Rufus, Hippocrates, Galen, and Serapion), the Persians (Hali and Rhazes), the Arabs (Avicenna and Averroes), the Mediterranean transmitters of Eastern science to the West (John of Damascus, Constantine the African), and later medical school professors (Bernard of Gordon, who taught at Montpellier; John of Gaddesden, who taught at Merton College; and Gilbertus Anglicus, an early contemporary of Chaucer's).
6. Centers of Flemish cloth-making.
7. The collection of gifts at the consecration of the Mass.

Nowhere in all the world was one to match him
Where medicine was concerned, or surgery;
Being well grounded in astrology
He'd watch his patient with the utmost care
Until he'd found a favourable hour,
By means of astrology, to give treatment.
Skilled to pick out the astrologic moment
For charms and talismans to aid the patient,
He knew the cause of every malady,
If it were "hot" or "cold" or "moist" or "dry,"
And where it came from, and from which humour.
He was a really fine practitioner.
Knowing the cause, and having found its root,
He'd soon give the sick man an antidote.
Ever at hand he had apothecaries
To send him syrups, drugs, and remedies,
For each put money in the other's pocket—
Theirs was no newly founded partnership.
Well-read was he in Aesculapius,
In Dioscorides, and in Rufus,
Ancient Hippocrates, Hali, and Galen,
Avicenna, Rhazes, and Serapion,
Averroës, Damascenus, Constantine,
Bernard, and Gilbertus, and Gaddesden.
In his own diet he was temperate,
For it was nothing if not moderate,
Though most nutritious and digestible.
He didn't do much reading in the Bible.
He was dressed all in Persian blue and scarlet
Lined with taffeta and fine sarsenet,
And yet was very chary of expense.
He put by all he earned from pestilence;
In medicine gold is the best cordial.
So it was gold that he loved best of all.
  There was a business woman, from near Bath,
But, more's the pity, she was a bit deaf;
So skilled a clothmaker, that she outdistanced
Even the weavers of Ypres and Ghent.
In the whole parish there was not a woman
Who dared precede her at the almsgiving,
And if there did, so furious was she,
That she was put out of all charity.

Hir coverchiefs ful fine were of ground[8]—
I dorste swere they weyeden° ten pound *weighed*
That on a Sonday weren upon hir heed.
Hir hosen° weren of fin scarlet reed, *stockings*
Ful straite yteyd,° and shoes ful moiste° and newe. *tightly laced / supple*
Bold was hir face and fair and reed of hewe.
She was a worthy womman al hir live:
Housbondes at chirche dore she hadde five,
Withouten other compaignye in youthe—
But therof needeth nought to speke as nouthe.° *for now*
And thries hadde she been at Jerusalem;
She hadde passed many a straunge streem;
At Rome she hadde been, and at Boloigne,[9]
In Galice at Saint Jame, and at Coloigne:
She coude° muchel of wandring by the waye. *knew*
Gat-toothed° was she, soothly for to saye. *gap-toothed*
Upon an amblere[1] esily she sat,
Ywimpled[2] wel, and on hir heed an hat
As brood as is a bokeler or a targe,° *small shields*
A foot-mantel° aboute hir hipes large, *riding skirt*
And on hir feet a paire of spores° sharpe. *spurs*
In felaweshipe wel coude she laughe and carpe:
Of remedies of love she knew parchaunce,[3]
For she coude of that art the olde daunce.° *tricks*
  A good man was ther of religioun,
And was a poore Person° of a town, *parson*
But riche he was of holy thought and werk.
He was also a lerned man, a clerk,
That Cristes gospel trewely wolde preche;
His parisshens° devoutly wolde he teche. *parishioners*
Benigne he was, and wonder diligent,
And in adversitee ful pacient,
And swich he was preved ofte sithes.
Ful loth were him to cursen for his tithes,[4]
But rather wolde he yiven, out of doute,
Unto his poore parisshens aboute
Of his offring and eek of his substaunce:° *possessions*
He coude in litel thing have suffisaunce.
Wid was his parissh, and houses fer asonder,
But he ne lafte nought for rain ne thonder,
In siknesse nor in meschief, to visite
The ferreste in his parissh, muche and lite,[5]
Upon his feet, and in his hand a staf.

8. Her linen kerchiefs were fine in texture.
9. Rome, Boulogne, Santiago Compostela, and Cologne were major European pilgrimage sites.
1. A horse with a gentle pace.
2. Wearing a large headdress that covers all but the face.
3. She knew cures for lovesickness, as it happened.
4. And so was he shown to be many times. / He was most unwilling to curse parishioners (with excommunication) if they failed to pay his tithes (a tenth of their income due to the Church).
5. The furthest away in his parish, great and small.

Her headkerchiefs were of the finest weave,
Ten pounds and more they weighed, I do believe,
Those that she wore on Sundays on her head.
Her stockings were of finest scarlet red,
Very tightly laced; shoes pliable and new.
Bold was her face, and handsome; florid too.
She had been respectable all her life,
And five times married, that's to say in church,
Not counting other loves she'd had in youth,
Of whom, just now, there is no need to speak.
And she had thrice been to Jerusalem;
Had wandered over many a foreign stream;
And she had been at Rome, and at Boulogne,
St James of Compostella, and Cologne;
She knew all about wandering—and straying:
For she was gap-toothed, if you take my meaning.
Comfortably on an ambling horse she sat,
Well-wimpled, wearing on her head a hat
That might have been a shield in size and shape;
A riding-skirt round her enormous hips,
Also a pair of sharp spurs on her feet.
In company, how she could laugh and joke!
No doubt she knew of all the cures for love,
For at that game she was a past mistress.
    And there was a good man, a religious.
He was the needy priest of a village,
But rich enough in saintly thought and work.
And educated, too, for he could read;
Would truly preach the word of Jesus Christ,
Devoutly teach the folk in his parish.
Kind was he, wonderfully diligent;
And in adversity most patient,
As many a time had been put to the test.
For unpaid tithes he'd not excommunicate,
For he would rather give, you may be sure,
From his own pocket to the parish poor;
Few were his needs, so frugally he lived.
Wide was his parish, with houses far asunder,
But he would not neglect, come rain or thunder,
Come sickness or adversity, to call
On the furthest of his parish, great or small;
Going on foot, and in his hand a staff.

This noble ensample° to his sheep he yaf *example*
That first he wroughte,° and afterward he taughte. *did*
Out of the Gospel he tho° wordes caughte, *those*
And this figure° he added eek therto: *saying*
That if gold ruste, what shal iren do?
For if a preest be foul, on whom we truste,
No wonder is a lewed° man to ruste. *uneducated*
And shame it is, if a preest take keep,° *is concerned*
A shiten° shepherde and a clene sheep. *shit-covered*
Wel oughte a preest ensample for to yive
By his clennesse how that his sheep sholde live.
He sette nought his benefice to hire[6]
And leet his sheep encombred in the mire
And ran to London, unto Sainte Poules,
To seeken him a chaunterye for soules,
Or with a bretherhede to been withholde,
But dwelte at hoom and kepte wel his folde,
So that the wolf ne made it nought miscarye:
He was a shepherde and nought a mercenarye.
And though he holy were and vertuous,
He was to sinful men nought despitous,° *scornful*
Ne of his speeche daungerous ne digne,° *haughty*
But in his teching discreet and benigne,
To drawen folk to hevene by fairnesse
By good ensample—this was his bisinesse.
But it were any persone obstinat,
What so he were, of heigh or lowe estat,
Him wolde he snibben° sharply for the nones:° *rebuke / on the spot*
A bettre preest I trowe° ther nowher noon is. *believe*
He waited after° no pompe and reverence, *expected*
Ne maked him a spiced° conscience, *overly critical*
But Cristes lore° and his Apostles twelve *teaching*
He taughte, but first he folwed° it himselve. *followed*
  With him ther was a Plowman, was his brother,
That hadde ylad of dong ful many a fother.[7]
A trewe swinkere° and a good was he, *worker*
Living in pees° and parfit° charitee. *peace / perfect*
God loved he best with al his hoole herte
At alle times, though him gamed or smerte,[8]
And thanne his neighebor right as himselve.
He wolde thresshe, and therto dike and delve,° *make ditches and dig*
For Cristes sake, for every poore wight,° *person*
Withouten hire,° if it laye in his might. *pay*
His tithes payed he ful faire and wel,

6. The priest did not rent out his parish to another in order to take a more profitable position saying masses for the dead at the chantries of St. Paul's in London or to serve as chaplain to a wealthy guild (bretherhede).
7. That had carried many a cartload of manure.
8. Enjoyed himself or suffered pain.

This was the good example that he set:
He practised first what later he would teach.
Out of the gospel he took that precept;
And what's more, he would cite this saying too:
"If gold can rust, then what will iron do?"
For if a priest be rotten, whom we trust,
No wonder if a layman comes to rust.
It's shame to see (let every priest take note)
A shitten shepherd and a cleanly sheep.
It's the plain duty of a priest to give
Example to his sheep; how they should live.
He never let his benefice for hire
And left his sheep to flounder in the mire
While he ran off to London, to St Paul's
To seek some chantry and sing mass for souls,
Or to be kept as chaplain by a guild;
But stayed at home, and took care of his fold,
So that no wolf might do it injury.
He was a shepherd, not a mercenary.
And although he was saintly and virtuous,
He wasn't haughty or contemptuous
To sinners, speaking to them with disdain,
But in his teaching tactful and humane.
To draw up folk to heaven by goodness
And good example, was his sole business.
But if a person turned out obstinate,
Whoever he was, of high or low estate,
He'd earn a stinging rebuke then and there.
You'll never find a better priest, I'll swear.
He never looked for pomp or deference,
Nor affected an over-nice conscience.
But taught the gospel of Christ and His twelve
Apostles; but first followed it himself.
With him there was his brother, a ploughman,
Who'd fetched and carried many a load of dung;
A good and faithful labourer was he,
Living in peace and perfect charity.
God he loved best, and that with all his heart,
At all times, good and bad, no matter what;
And next he loved his neighbour as himself.
He'd thresh, and ditch, and also dig and delve,
And for Christ's love would do as much again
If he could manage it, for all poor men,
And ask no hire. He paid his tithes in full,

Bothe of his propre swink[9] and his catel.° *possessions*
In a tabard° rood upon a mere.° *smock / mare*
Ther was also a Reeve° and a Millere, *estate manager*
A Somnour, and a Pardoner[1] also,
A Manciple,° and myself—ther were namo. *Steward*
The Millere was a stout carl° for the nones. *fellow*
Ful big he was of brawn and eek of bones—
That preved wel, for overal ther he cam
At wrastling he wolde have alway the ram.[2]
He was short-shuldred, brood, a thikke knarre.° *bully*
Ther was no dore that he nolde heve of harre,° *push off its hinges*
Or breke it at a renning with his heed.
His beerd as any sowe or fox was reed,
And therto brood, as though it were a spade;
Upon the cop° right of his nose he hade *tip*
A werte, and theron stood a tuft of heres,
Rede as the bristles of a sowes eres;
His nosethirles° blake were and wide. *nostrils*
A swerd and a bokeler° bar° he by his side. *small shield / carried*
His mouth as greet was as a greet furnais.
He was a janglere and a Goliardais,[3]
And that was most of sinne and harlotries.° *obscenities*
Wel coude he stelen corn and tollen thries[4]—
And yit he hadde a thombe of gold,[5] pardee.° *by God*
A whit cote and a blew hood wered he.
A baggepipe wel coude he blowe and soune,
And therwithal he broughte us out of towne.
A gentil Manciple was ther of a temple,° *law school*
Of which achatours° mighte take exemple *buyers*
For to been wise in bying of vitaile;° *food*
For wheither that he paide or took by taile,° *on credit*
Algate he waited so in his achat[6]
That he was ay biforn° and in good stat.° *always ahead / well off*
Now is nat that of God a ful fair grace° *blessing*
That swich a lewed° mannes wit shal pace° *uneducated / surpass*
The wisdom of an heep of lerned men?
Of maistres° hadde he mo than thries ten *scholars*
That weren of lawe expert and curious,° *skillful*
Of whiche ther were a dozeine in that house
Worthy to been stiwardes of rente° and lond *managers of revenues*
Of any lord that is in Engelond,
To make him live by his propre good° *own wealth*

9. Money earned from his own work.
1. A Summoner, a server of summonses for the ecclesiastical courts; Pardoner: a seller of indulgences.
2. Awarded as a prize for wrestling.
3. He was a teller of dirty stories and a reveller.
4. Collect three times as much tax as was due.
5. It was proverbial that millers were dishonest and that an honest miller was as rare as one who had a golden thumb. The statement is meant ironically.
6. He was always so watchful for his opportunities to purchase.

On what he earned and on his goods as well.
He wore a smock, and rode upon a mare.
There was a reeve as well, also a miller,
A pardon-seller and a summoner,
A manciple, and myself—there were no more.
The miller was a burly fellow—brawn
And muscle, big of bones as well as strong,
As was well seen—he always won the ram
At wrestling-matches up and down the land.
He was barrel-chested, rugged and thickset,
And would heave off its hinges any door
Or break it, running at it with his head.
His beard was red as any fox or sow,
And wide at that, as though it were a spade.
And on his nose, right on its tip, he had
A wart, upon which stood a tuft of hairs
Red as the bristles are in a sow's ears.
Black were his nostrils; black and squat and wide.
He bore a sword and buckler by his side.
His big mouth was as big as a furnace.
A loudmouth and a teller of blue stories
(Most of them vicious or scurrilous),
Well versed in stealing corn and trebling dues,
He had a golden thumb—by God he had!
A white coat he had on, and a blue hood.
He played the bagpipes well, and blew a tune,
And to its music brought us out of town.
A worthy manciple of the Middle Temple
Was there; he might have served as an example
To all provision-buyers for his thrift
In making purchase, whether on credit
Or for cash down: he kept an eye on prices,
So always got in first and did good business.
Now isn't it an instance of God's grace,
Such an unlettered man should so outpace
The wisdom of a pack of learned men?
He'd more than thirty masters over him,
All of them proficient experts in law,
More than a dozen of them with the power
To manage rents and land for any peer
So that—unless the man were off his head—

In honour dettelees but if he were wood,° *unless he were crazy*
Or live as scarsly° as him list° desire, *thriftily / pleases*
And able for to helpen al a shire
In any caas° that mighte falle° or happe, *event / befall*
And yit this Manciple sette hir aller cappe!° *made fools of them all*
The Reeve was a sclendre° colerik° man; *lean / ill-tempered*
His beerd was shave as neigh° as evere he can; *close*
His heer was by his eres ful round yshorn;
His top was dokked° lik a preest biforn;° *clipped / in front*
Ful longe were his legges and ful lene,
Ylik° a staf, ther was no calf yseene.° *like / visible*
Wel coude he keepe a gerner° a binne— *granary*
Ther was noon auditour coude on him winne.[7]
Wel wiste he by the droughte and by the rain
The yeelding of his seed and of his grain.
His lordes sheep, his neet,° his dayerye,° *cattle / dairy cattle*
His swim, his hors, his stoor,° and his pultrye *livestock*
Was hoolly in this Reeves governinge,
And by his covenant° yaf the rekeninge,° *contract / gave account*
Sin that his lord was twenty yeer of age.
Ther coude no man bringe him in arrerage.° *financial arrears*
Ther nas baillif, hierde, nor other hine,[8]
That he ne knew his sleighte° and his covine°— *tricks / plotting*
They were adrad of him as of the deeth.
His woning° was ful faire upon an heeth;° *dwelling / meadow*
With greene trees shadwed was his place.
He coude bettre than his lord purchace.° *buy property*
Ful riche he was astored prively.° *stocked in secret*
His lord wel coude he plesen subtilly,
To yive and lene° him of his owene good,° *lend / possessions*
And have a thank,° and yit a cote and hood. *gratitude*
In youthe he hadde lerned a good mister:° *profession*
He was a wel good wrighte, a carpenter.
This Reeve sat upon a ful good stot° *stallion*
That was a pomely° grey and highte° Scot. *dappled / named*
A long surcote° of pers° upon he hade, *overcoat / blue*
And by his side he bar a rusty blade.
Of Northfolk[9] was this Reeve of which I telle,
Biside a town men clepen° Baldeswelle. *call*
Tukked[1] he was as is a frere aboute,
And evere he rood the hindreste° of oure route.° *hindmost / group*
A Somnour was ther with us in that place
That hadde a fir-reed° cherubinnes° face, *fire-red / cherub's*
For saucefleem° he was, with yën narwe, *pimply*
And hoot he was, and lecherous as a sparwe,° *sparrow*

7. Gain anything (by catching him out).
8. There was no foreman, herdsman, or other farmhand.
9. Norfolk in the north of England. The Reeve is notable for his northern dialect and regionalisms.
1. He wore his clothes tucked up with a cinch as friars did.

He could live honourably, free of debt,
Or sparingly, if that were his desire;
And able to look after a whole shire
In whatever emergency might befall;
And yet this manciple could hoodwink them all.
There was a reeve, a thin and bilious man;
His beard he shaved as close as a man can;
Around his ears he kept his hair cropped short,
Just like a priest's, docked in front and on top.
His legs were very long, and very lean,
And like a stick; no calf was to be seen.
His granary and bins were ably kept;
There was no auditor could trip him up.
He could foretell, by noting drought and rain,
The likely harvest from his seed and grain.
His master's cattle, dairy, cows, and sheep,
His pigs and horses, poultry and livestock,
Were wholly under this reeve's governance.
And, as was laid down in his covenant,
Of these he'd always rendered an account
Ever since his master reached his twentieth year.
No man could ever catch him in arrears.
He was up to every fiddle, every dodge
Of every herdsman, bailiff, or farm-lad.
All of them feared him as they feared the plague.
His dwelling was well placed upon a heath,
Set with green trees that overshadowed it.
At business he was better than his lord:
He'd got his nest well-feathered, on the side,
For he was cunning enough to get round
His lord by lending him what was his own,
And so earn thanks, besides a coat and hood.
As a young man he'd learned a useful trade
As a skilled artisan, a carpenter.
The reeve rode on a sturdy farmer's cob
That was called Scot: it was a dapple grey.
He had on a long blue-grey overcoat,
And carried by his side a rusty sword.
A Norfolk man was he of whom I tell,
From near a place that they call Bawdeswell.
Tucked round him like a friar's was his coat;
He always rode the hindmost of our troop.
A summoner was among us at the inn,
Whose face was fire-red, like the cherubim;
All covered with carbuncles; his eyes narrow;
He was as hot and randy as a sparrow.

With scaled° browes blake and piled[2] beerd: *scabby*
Of his visage children were aferd.° *frightened*
Ther nas quiksilver, litarge, ne brimstoon,
Boras, ceruce, ne oile of tartre noon,[3]
Ne oinement that wolde clense and bite,
That him mighte helpen of his whelkes° white, *blotches*
Nor of the knobbes° sitting on his cheekes. *lumps*
Wel loved he garlek, oinons, and eek leekes,
And for to drinke strong win reed as blood.
Thanne wolde he speke and crye as he were wood;° *crazy*
And whan that he wel dronken hadde the win,
Thanne wolde he speke no word but Latin:
A fewe termes hadde he, two or three,
That he hadde lerned out of som decree;
No wonder is—he herde it al the day,
And eek ye knowe wel how that a jay° *parrot*
Can clepen "Watte°" as wel as can the Pope— *call "Walter"*
But whoso coude in other thing him grope,° *examine*
Thanne hadde he spent all his philosophye;
Ay *Questio quid juris*[4] wolde he crye.
He was a gentil harlot° and a kinde; *rascal*
A bettre felawe sholde men nought finde:
He wolde suffre,° for a quart of win, *allow*
A good felawe to have his concubin° *mistress*
A twelfmonth, and excusen him at the fulle;
Ful prively a finch eek coude he pulle.[5]
And if he foond owher° a good felawe *anywhere*
He wolde techen him to have noon awe
In swich caas of the Ercedekenes curs,[6]
But if a mannes soule were in his purs,° *wallet*
For in his purs he sholde ypunisshed be.
"Purs is the Ercedekenes helle," saide he.
But wel I woot° he lied right in deede: *know*
Of cursing° oughte eech gilty man him drede,° *excommunication / fear*
For curs wol slee° right as assoiling° savith— *will kill / absolving*
And also war him of a *significavit*.[7]
In daunger hadde he at his owene gise[8]
The yonge girles of the diocise,
And knew hir conseil,° and was al hir reed.° *secrets / advice*
A gerland hadde he set upon his heed
As greet as it were for an ale-stake;° *tavern sign*
A bokeler hadde he maad him of a cake.° *loaf of bread*
With him ther rood a gentil Pardoner
Of Rouncival,[9] his freend and his compeer,° *companion*

2. With hair falling out.
3. There was not mercury, lead ointment, or sulphur, / Borax, white lead, nor any oil of tartar that could clean him.
4. "The question as to what point of law (applies)"; often used in ecclesiastical courts.
5. And secretly he also knew how to fool around.
6. In case of excommunication by the archdeacon.
7. Order of transfer from ecclesiastical to secular courts.
8. Under his control he had at his disposal.
9. A hospital at Charing Cross in London.

He'd scabbed black eyebrows, and a scraggy beard,
No wonder if the children were afraid!
There was no mercury, white lead, or sulphur,
No borax, no ceruse, no cream of tartar,
Nor any other salves that cleanse and burn,
Could help with the white pustules on his skin,
Or with the knobbed carbuncles on his cheeks.
He'd a great love of garlic, onions, leeks,
Also for drinking strong wine, red as blood,
When he would roar and gabble as if mad.
And once he had got really drunk on wine,
Then he would speak no language but Latin.
He'd picked up a few tags, some two or three,
Which he'd learned from some edict or decree—
No wonder, for he heard them every day.
Also, as everybody knows, a jay
Can call out "Wat" as well as the Pope can.
But if you tried him further with a question,
You'd find his well of learning had run dry;
"*Questio quid juris*" was all he'd ever say.
  A most engaging rascal, and a kind,
As good a fellow as you'd hope to find:
For he'd allow—given a quart of wine—
A scallywag to keep his concubine
A twelvemonth, and excuse him altogether.
He'd dip his wick, too, very much sub rosa.
And if he found some fellow with a woman,
He'd tell him not to fear excommunication
If he were caught, or the archdeacon's curse,
Unless the fellow's soul was in his purse,
For it's his purse must pay the penalty.
"Your purse is the archdeacon's Hell," said he.
  Take it from me, the man lied in his teeth:
Let sinners fear, for that curse is damnation,
Just as their souls are saved by absolution.
Let them beware, too, of a "*Significavit*."
  Under his thumb, to deal with as he pleased,
Were the young people of his diocese;
He was their sole adviser and confidant.
Upon his head he sported a garland
As big as any hung outside a pub,
And, for a shield, he'd a round loaf of bread.
  With him there was a peerless pardon-seller
Of Charing Cross, his friend and his confrère,

That straight was comen fro the Court of Rome.
Ful loude he soong, "Com hider, love, to me."[1]
This Somnour bar to him a stif burdoun:° *a strong baritone*
Was nevere trompe° of half so greet a soun. *trumpet*
  This Pardoner hadde heer as yelow as wex,
But smoothe it heeng as dooth a strike of flex;° *clump of flax*
By ounces° heenge his lokkes that he hadde, *thin strands*
And therwith he his shuldres overspradde,
But thinne it lay, by colpons,° oon by oon; *strands*
But hood for jolitee° wered he noon, *fanciness*
For it was trussed up in his walet:° *pack*
Him thoughte he rood al of the newe jet.° *fashion*
Dischevelee° save his cappe he rood al bare. *loose-haired*
Swiche glaring yën hadde he as an hare.
A vernicle[2] hadde he sowed upon his cappe,
His walet biforn him in his lappe,
Bretful of pardon,[3] comen from Rome al hoot.
A vois he hadde as smal° as hath a goot;° *high-pitched / goat*
No beerd hadde he, ne nevere sholde have;
As smoothe it was as it were late yshave:
I trowe he were a gelding or a mare.[4]
But of his craft,° fro Berwik into Ware,[5] *skill*
Ne was ther swich another pardoner;
For in his male° he hadde a pilwe-beer° *bag / pillowcase*
Which that he saide was Oure Lady veil;
He saide he hadde a gobet° of the sail *chunk*
That Sainte Peter hadde whan that he wente
Upon the see, til Jesu Crist him hente.° *grabbed*
He hadde a crois of laton,° ful of stones, *brass cross*
And in a glas he hadde pigges bones,
But with thise relikes whan that he foond
A poore person° dwelling upon lond, *parson*
Upon a day he gat him more moneye
Than that the person gat in monthes twaye;° *two*
And thus with feined flaterye and japes° *tricks*
He made the person and the peple his apes.° *dupes*
But trewely to tellen at the laste,
He was in chirche a noble ecclesiaste;
Wel coude he rede a lesson and a storye,° *liturgical texts*
But alderbest° he soong an offertorye, *best of all*
For wel he wiste whan that song was songe,
He moste preche and wel affile° his tonge *sharpen*
To winne silver, as he ful wel coude—
Therfore he soong the merierly and loude.
  Now have I told you soothly° in a clause° *truly / briefly*
Th'estaat, th'array, the nombre, and eek the cause

1. A popular ballad.
2. A pilgrim badge, reproducing St. Veronica's veil bearing the imprint of Christ's face.
3. Full to the brim with indulgences.
4. I believe he was a gelding (eunuch) or a mare (perhaps a passive homosexual).
5. Towns north and south of London.

Who'd come straight from the Vatican in Rome.
Loudly he sang, "Come to me, love, come hither!"
The summoner sang the bass, a loud refrain;
No trumpet ever made one half the din.
  This pardon-seller's hair was yellow as wax,
And sleekly hanging, like a hank of flax.
In meagre clusters hung what hair he had;
Over his shoulders a few strands were spread,
But they lay thin, in rat's tails, one by one.
As for a hood, for comfort he wore none,
For it was stowed away in his knapsack.
Save for a cap, he rode with head all bare,
Hair loose; he thought it was the *dernier cri*.
He had big bulging eyes, just like a hare.
He'd sewn a veronica on his cap.
His knapsack lay before him, on his lap,
Chockful of pardons, all come hot from Rome.
His voice was like a goat's, plaintive and thin.
He had no beard, nor was he like to have;
Smooth was his face, as if he had just shaved.
I took him for a gelding or a mare.
As for his trade, from Berwick down to Ware
You'd not find such another pardon-seller.
For in his bag he had a pillowcase
Which had been, so he said, Our Lady's veil;
He said he had a snippet of the sail
St Peter had, that time he walked upon
The sea, and Jesus Christ caught hold of him.
And he'd a brass cross, set with pebble-stones,
And a glass reliquary of pigs' bones.
But with these relics, when he came upon
Some poor up-country priest or backwoods parson,
In just one day he'd pick up far more money
Than any parish priest was like to see
In two whole months. With double-talk and tricks
He made the people and the priest his dupes.
But to speak truth and do the fellow justice,
In church he made a splendid ecclesiastic.
He'd read a lesson, or saint's history,
But best of all he sang the offertory:
For, knowing well that when that hymn was sung.
He'd have to preach and polish smooth his tongue
To raise—as only he knew how—the wind,
The louder and the merrier he would sing.
  And now I've told you truly and concisely
The rank, and dress, and number of us all,

Why that assembled was this compaignye
In Southwerk at this gentil hostelrye
That highte the Tabard, faste by the Belle;[6]
But now is time to you for to telle
How that we baren us that like° night *same*
Whan we were in that hostelrye alight;
And after wol I telle of oure viage,° *trip*
And al the remenant of oure pilgrimage.
 But first I praye you of youre curteisye
That ye n'arette° it nought my vilainye° *consider / rudeness*
Though that I plainly speke in this matere
To telle you hir wordes and hir cheere,° *comportment*
Ne though I speke hir wordes proprely;° *accurately*
For this ye knowen also wel as I:
Who so shal telle a tale after a man
He moot reherce,° as neigh as evere he can, *must repeat*
Everich a word, if it be in his charge,
Al speke he nevere so rudeliche° and large,° *crudely / freely*
Or elles he moot telle his tale untrewe,
Or feine° thing, or finde wordes newe; *invent, falsify*
He may nought spare although he were his brother:
He moot as wel saye oo word as another.
Crist spak himself ful brode° in Holy Writ, *plainly*
And wel ye woot° no vilainye is it; *know*
Eek Plato saith, who so can him rede,
The wordes mote be cosin° to the deede. *closely related*
 Also I praye you to foryive it me
Al° have I nat set folk in hir degree° *although / rank*
Here in this tale as that they sholde stonde:
My wit is short, ye may wel understonde.
 Greet cheere made oure Host us everichoon,
And to the soper sette he us anoon.
He served us with vitaile at the beste.
Strong was the win, and wel to drinke us leste.° *it pleased*
A semely° man oure Hoste was withalle *apt*
For to been a marchal° in an halle; *master of ceremonies*
A large man he was, with yën steepe;° *glaring eyes*
A fairer burgeis was ther noon in Chepe°— *Cheapside (in London)*
Bold of his speeche, and wis, and wel ytaught,
And of manhood him lakkede° right naught. *he lacked*
Eek therto he was right a merye man,
And after soper playen he bigan,
And spak of mirthe amonges othere thinges—
Whan that we hadde maad oure rekeninges°— *paid the bill*
And saide thus, "Now, lordinges, trewely,
Ye been to me right welcome, hertely.
For by my trouthe, if that I shal nat lie,

6. Another tavern in Southwark.

And why we gathered in a company
In Southwark, at that noble hostelry
Known as the Tabard, that's hard by the Bell.
But now the time has come for me to tell
What passed among us, what was said and done
The night of our arrival at the inn;
And afterwards I'll tell you how we journeyed,
And all the remainder of our pilgrimage.
  But first I beg you, not to put it down
To my ill-breeding if my speech be plain
When telling what they looked like, what they said,
Or if I use the exact words they used.
For, as you all must know as well as I,
To tell a tale told by another man
You must repeat as nearly as you can
Each word, if that's the task you've undertaken,
However coarse or broad his language is;
Or, in the telling, you'll have to distort it
Or make things up, or find new words for it.
You can't hold back, even if he's your brother:
Whatever word is used, you must use also.
Christ Himself spoke out plain in Holy Writ,
And well you know there's nothing wrong with that.
Plato, as those who read him know, has said,
"The word must be related to the deed."
  Also I beg you to forgive it me
If I overlooked all standing and degree
As regards the order in which people come
Here in this tally, as I set them down:
My wits are none too bright, as you can see.
  Our host gave each and all a warm welcome,
And set us down to supper there and then.
The eatables he served were of the best;
Strong was the wine; we matched it with our thirst.
A handsome man our host, handsome indeed,
And a fit master of ceremonies.
He was a big man with protruding eyes
—You'll find no better burgess in Cheapside—
Racy in talk, well-schooled and shrewd was he;
Also a proper man in every way.
And moreover he was a right good sort,
And after supper he began to joke,
And, when we had all paid our reckonings,
He spoke of pleasure, among other things:
"Truly," said he, ladies and gentlemen,
Here you are all most heartily welcome.
Upon my word—I'm telling you no lie—

I sawgh nat this yeer so merye a compaignye
At ones in this herberwe° as is now. *inn*
Fain wolde I doon you mirthe, wiste I how.
And of a mirthe I am right now bithought,
To doon you ese, and it shal coste nought.
  Ye goon to Canterbury—God you speede;
The blisful martyr quite° you youre meede.° *repay / reward*
And wel I woot° as ye goon by the waye *know*
Ye shapen° you to talen° and to playe, *intend / tell tales*
For trewely, confort ne mirthe is noon
To ride by the waye domb as stoon;
And therfore wol I maken you disport
As I saide erst,° and doon you som confort; *before*
And if you liketh alle, by oon assent,
For to stonden at my juggement,
And for to werken as I shal you saye,
Tomorwe whan ye riden by the waye—
Now by my fader soule that is deed,
But° ye be merye I wol yive you myn heed! *unless*
Holde up youre handes withouten more speeche."
  Oure conseil was nat longe for to seeche;° *seek*
Us thoughte it was nat worth to make it wis,° *deliberate*
And graunted him withouten more avis,° *opinions*
And bade him saye his voirdit° as him leste. *verdict*
  "Lordinges," quod he, "now herkneth for the beste;
But taketh it nought, I praye you, in desdain.
This is the point, to speken short and plain,
That eech of you, to shorte with oure waye
In this viage, shal tellen tales twaye°— *two*
To Canterburyward, I mene it so,
And hoomward he shal tellen othere two,
Of aventures that whilom° have bifalle; *long ago*
And which of you that bereth him best of alle—
That is to sayn, that telleth in this cas
Tales of best sentence° and most solas°— *substance / pleasure*
Shal have a soper at oure aller cost,
Here in this place, sitting by this post,
Whan that we come again fro Canterbury.
And for to make you the more mury
I wol myself goodly° with you ride— *gladly*
Right at myn owene cost—and be youre gide.
And who so wol my juggement withsaye° *contradict*
Shal paye al that we spende by the waye.
And if ye vouche sauf° that it be so, *grant*
Telle me anoon, withouten wordes mo,
And I wol erly shape° me therfore." *prepare*
  This thing was graunted and oure othes swore
With ful glad herte, and prayden him also

All year I've seen no jollier company
At one time in this inn, than I have now.
I'd make some fun for you, if I knew how.
And, as it happens, I have just now thought
Of something that will please you, at no cost.
"You're off to Canterbury—so Godspeed!
The blessed martyr give you your reward!
And I'll be bound, that while you're on your way,
You'll be telling tales, and making holiday;
It makes no sense, and really it's no fun
To ride along the road dumb as a stone.
And therefore I'll devise a game for you,
To give you pleasure, as I said I'd do.
And if with one accord you all consent
To abide by my decision and judgement,
And if you'll do exactly as I say,
Tomorrow, when you're riding on your way,
Then, by my father's soul—for he is dead—
If you don't find it fun, why, here's my head!
Now not another word! Hold up your hands!"
We were not long in making up our minds.
It seemed not worth deliberating, so
We gave our consent without more ado,
Told him to give us what commands he wished,
"Ladies and gentlemen," began our host,
"Do yourselves a good turn, and hear me out:
But please don't turn your noses up at it.
I'll put it in a nutshell: here's the nub:
It's that you each, to shorten the long journey,
Shall tell two tales *en route* to Canterbury,
And, coming homeward, tell another two,
Stories of things that happened long ago.
Whoever best acquits himself, and tells
The most amusing and instructive tale,
Shall have a dinner, paid for by us all,
Here in this inn, and under this roof-tree,
When we come back again from Canterbury.
To make it the more fun, I'll gladly ride
With you at my own cost, and be your guide.
And anyone who disputes what I say
Must pay all our expenses on the way!
And if this plan appeals to all of you,
Tell me at once, and with no more ado,
And I'll make my arrangements here and now."
To this we all agreed, and gladly swore
To keep our promises; and furthermore
We asked him if he would consent to do

That he wolde vouche sauf for to do so,
And that he wolde been oure governour,
And of oure tales juge° and reportour,° *judge / recordkeeper*
And sette a soper at a certain pris,° *price*
And we wol ruled been at his devis,° *plan*
In heigh and lowe; and thus by oon assent
We been accorded to his juggement.
And therupon the win was fet° anoon; *fetched*
We dronken and to reste wente eechoon° *everyone*
Withouten any lenger taryinge.
Amorwe° whan that day bigan to springe *next morning*
Up roos oure Host and was oure aller cok,° *cock, wake-up call*
And gadred us togidres in a flok,
And forth we riden, a litel more than pas,° *slow walk*
Unto the watering of Saint Thomas;[7]
And ther oure Host bigan his hors arreste,° *stop*
And saide, "Lordes, herkneth if you leste:° *it please*
"Ye woot youre forward° and it you recorde:° *agreement / remember*
If evensong and morwesong accorde,
Lat see now who shal telle the firste tale.
As evere mote I drinken win or ale,
Who so be rebel to my juggement
Shal paye for al that by the way is spent.
Now draweth cut° er that we ferrer twinne:° *lots / separate further*
He which that hath the shorteste shal biginne.
"Sire Knight," quod he, "my maister and my lord,
Now draweth cut, for that is myn accord.° *wish*
Cometh neer," quod he, "my lady Prioresse,
And ye, sire Clerk, lat be youre shamefastnesse°— *modesty*
Ne studieth nought. Lay hand to, every man!"
Anoon to drawen every wight° bigan, *person*
And shortly for to tellen as it was,
Were it by aventure, or sort, or cas,° *luck, fate or chance*
The soothe° is this, the cut fil° to the Knight; *truth / fell*
Of which ful blithe° and glad was every wight, *happy*
And telle he moste his tale, as was resoun,
By forward and by composicioun,° *agreement*
As ye han herd. What needeth wordes mo?
And whan this goode man sawgh that it was so,
As he that wis was and obedient
To keepe his forward by his free assent,
He saide, "Sin I shal biginne the game,
What, welcome be the cut, in Goddes name!
Now lat us ride, and herkneth what I saye."
And with that word we riden forth oure waye,
And he bigan with right a merye cheere° *expression*
His tale anoon, and saide as ye may heere.

7. A brook two miles from London.

As he had said, and come and be our leader,
And judge our tales, and act as arbiter,
Set up our dinner too, at a fixed price;
And we'd obey whatever he might decide
In everything. And so, with one consent,
We bound ourselves to bow to his judgement.
And thereupon wine was at once brought in.
We drank; and not long after, everyone
Went off to bed, and that without delay.
    Next morning our host rose at break of day:
He was our cockcrow; so we all awoke.
He gathered us together in a flock,
And we rode, at little more than walking-pace
Till we had reached St Thomas' watering-place,
Where our host began reining in his horse.
"Ladies and gentlemen, attention please!"
Said he. "All of you know what we agreed,
And I'm reminding you. If evensong
And matins are in harmony—that's to say,
If you are still of the same mind today—
Let's see who'll tell the first tale, and begin.
And whosoever baulks at my decision
Must pay for all we spend upon the way,
Or may I never touch a drop again!
And now let's draw lots before going on.
The one who draws the short straw must begin.
    Sir Knight, my lord and master," said our host,
"Now let's draw lots, for such is my request.
Come near," said he, "my lady Prioress,
And, Mister Scholar, lay by bashfulness,
Stop dreaming! Hands to drawing, everyone!"
    To cut the story short, the draw began,
And, whether it was luck, or chance, or fate,
The truth is this: the lot fell to the knight,
Much to the content of the company.
Now, as was only right and proper, he
Must tell his tale, according to the bargain
Which, as you know, he'd made. What more to say?
And when the good man saw it must be so,
Being sensible, and accustomed to obey
And keep a promise he had freely given,
He said, "Well, since I must begin the game,
Then welcome to the short straw, in God's name!
Now let's ride on, and listen to what I say."
And at these words we rode off on our way,
And he at once began, with cheerful face,
His tale. The way he told it was like this.

The Miller's Tale *The Miller's Tale* both answers and parodies *The Knight's Tale*, a long aristocratic romance about two knights in rivalry for the hand of a lady. While the Miller tells a nearly analogous story of erotic competition, his tale is radically shorter and explicitly sexual. Such brevity and physicality fit his tale's genre—a fabliau, or short comic tale, usually bawdy and often involving a clerk, a wife, and a cuckolded husband. Following the convention (if not the reality) that romances were written by and for the nobility and fabliaux by and for the commons, Chaucer suits *The Miller's Tale* to its teller as aptly as he does the Knight's. Slyly disclaiming responsibility for the tale, he explains its bawdiness by the Miller's class status: "the Millere is a cherle" and like his peer the Reeve who follows and "requites" him, tells "harlotrye."

The drunken Miller's insistence on telling his tale to requite the Knight's tale has been called a "literary peasants' revolt." Although the Miller, a free man, was not actually a peasant, yeomen of his status were active in the Rising of 1381, and millers in particular played a symbolic role in it (see the letters of John Ball, page 475). In fact, this tale is highly literate, with its echoes of the Song of Songs and its parody of the language of courtly love: an actual miller would have had neither the education nor the social sophistication to tell it. Yet a parody implies some degree of attachment to the very model being ridiculed, and *The Miller's Tale* is as much a claim upon the Knight's world as a repudiation of it. The Miller wants to "quiten" the Knight's tale, he says, using a word that can mean to repay or avenge, but also to fulfill. The tale's several plots converge brilliantly upon a single cry: "Water!" The tale's impact derives as well from its plenitude of pleasures (sexual, comic, even religious) after the austere and rigid desires of *The Knight's Tale*.

The Miller's Tale
The Introduction

Whan that the Knight hadde thus his tale ytold,
In al the route° nas ther yong ne old *group*
That he ne saide it was a noble storye,
And worthy for to drawen° to memorye, *recall*
And namely the gentils° everichoon. *upper class*
Oure Hoste lough° and swoor, "So mote I goon,[1] *laughed*
This gooth aright: unbokeled is the male.[2]
Lat see now who shal telle another tale.
For trewely the game is wel bigonne.
Now telleth ye, sire Monk, if that ye conne,° *know*
Somwhat to quite° with the Knightes tale." *repay*
The Millere, that for dronken was al pale,
So that unnethe° upon his hors he sat, *barely*
He nolde avalen° neither hood ne hat, *would not remove*
Ne abiden no man for his curteisye,
But in Pilates[3] vois he gan to crye,
And swoor, "By armes and by blood and bones,° *(of Christ)*
I can° a noble tale for the nones, *know*
With which I wol now quite the Knightes tale."
Oure Hoste sawgh that he was dronke of ale,
And saide, "Abide,° Robin, leve° brother, *wait / dear*

1. Thus I may proceed.
2. The bag is opened (i.e., the games are begun).
3. The role of Pilate was traditionally played in a loud and raucous voice in the mystery plays.

Som bettre man shal telle us first another.
Abide, and lat us werken thriftily."° *properly*
"By Goddes soule," quod he, "that wol nat I,
For I wol speke or elles go my way."
Oure Host answerde, "Tel on, a devele way!° *in the devil's name*
Thou art a fool; thy wit is overcome."
"Now herkneth," quod the Millere, "alle and some.° *one and all*
But first I make a protestacioun
That I am dronke: I knowe it by my soun.° *sound*
And therfore if that I mis speke or saye,
Wite it° the ale of Southwerk, I you praye; *blame it on*
For I wol telle a legende and a lif[4]
Bothe of a carpenter and of his wif,
How that a clerk hath set the wrightes cappe."[5]
The Reeve answerde and saide, "Stint thy clappe!° *hold your tongue*
Lat be thy lewed° dronken harlotrye.° *unlearned / obscenity*
It is a sinne and eek a greet folye
To apairen° any man or him defame, *injure*
And eek to bringen wives in swich fame.
Thou maist ynough of othere thinges sayn."
This dronken Millere spak ful soone again,
And saide, "Leve brother Osewold,
Who hath no wif, he is no cokewold.° *cuckold*
But I saye nat therfore that thou art oon.
Ther ben ful goode wives many oon,
And evere a thousand goode ayains oon badde.° *against one bad*
That knowestou wel thyself but if thou madde.° *go insane*
Why artou angry with my tale now?
I have a wif, pardee,° as wel as thou, *by God*
Yet nolde I, for the oxen in my plough,[6]
Take upon me more than ynough
As deemen° of myself that I were oon:° *judge / one (a cuckold)*
I wol bileve wel that I am noon.
An housbonde shal nought been inquisitif
Of Goddes privetee,° nor of his wif. *secrets*
So he may finde Goddes foison° there, *plenty*
Of the remenant needeth nought enquere."
What sholde I more sayn but this Millere
He nolde° his wordes for no man forbere, *would not*
But tolde his cherles° tale in his manere. *commoner's*
M'athinketh° that I shal reherce° it here, *I regret / repeat*
And therfore every gentil wight° I praye, *person*
Deemeth nought, for Goddes love, that I saye
Of yvel entente, but for° I moot° reherse *because / must*
Hir tales alle, be they bet or werse,
Or elles falsen som of my matere.

4. The story of a saint's life.
5. Made a fool of the carpenter.
6. Yet I wouldn't, not even (in wager) for the oxen in my plough.

And therfore, whoso list it nought yheere
Turne over the leef,° and chese° another tale, *page / choose*
For he shal finde ynowe,° grete and smale, *enough*
Of storial° thing that toucheth gentilesse,° *historical / nobility*
And eek moralitee and holinesse:
Blameth nought me if that ye chese amis.
The Millere is a cherl, ye knowe wel this,
So was the Reeve eek, and othere mo,
And harlotrye they tolden bothe two.
Aviseth you,° and putte me out of blame: *be warned*
And eek men shal nought maken ernest of game.° *treat jokes seriously*

The Tale

Whilom° ther was dwelling at Oxenforde *long ago*
A riche gnof° that gestes heeld to boorde,° *fool / took in boarders*
And of his craft he was a carpenter.
With him ther was dwelling a poore scoler,
Hadde lerned art,[7] but al his fantasye° *fancy*
Was turned for to lere° astrologye, *learn*
And coude a certain of conclusiouns,° *predictions*
To deemen by interrogaciouns,[8]
If that men axed° him in certain houres *asked*
Whan that men sholde have droughte or elles showres,
Or if men axed him what shal bifalle
Of every thing—I may nat rekene° hem alle. *count*
This clerk was cleped° hende[9] Nicholas. *called*
Of derne° love he coude, and of solas,[1] *secret*
And therto he was sly and ful privee,° *secretive*
And lik a maide meeke for to see.
A chambre hadde he in that hostelrye° *inn*
Allone, withouten any compaignye,
Ful fetisly ydight with herbes swoote,[2]
And he himself as sweete as is the roote
Of licoris or any setewale.[3]
His Almageste[4] and bookes grete and smale,
His astrelabye,[5] longing for° his art, *belonging to*
His augrim stones,° layen faire apart *abacus beads*
On shelves couched° at his beddes heed; *arranged*
His presse° ycovered with a falding° reed; *dresser / coarse cloth*
And al above ther lay a gay sautrye,° *harp*
On which he made a-nightes melodye
So swetely that al the chambre roong,
And *Angelus ad Virginem*[6] he soong,

7. The arts curriculum (trivium).
8. To estimate by consulting (the stars).
9. Handsome, courteous, handy.
1. Pleasure, (sexual) comforts.
2. Elegantly decked out with sweet herbs.
3. Setwall, a gingerlike spice used as a stimulant.
4. An astrological treatise by Ptolemy.
5. Astrolabe, an astrological instrument.
6. A prayer commemorating the Annunciation.

And after that he soong the *Kinges Note*:[7]
Ful often blessed was his merye throte.
And thus this sweete clerk his time spente
After his freendes finding and his rente.[8]
  This carpenter hadde wedded newe a wif
Which that he loved more than his lif.
Of eighteteene yeer she was of age;
Jalous he was, and heeld hire narwe in cage,
For she was wilde and yong, and he was old,
And deemed° himself been lik a cokewold. *supposed*
He knew nat Caton,[9] for his wit was rude,
That bad men sholde wedde his similitude:° *equal in age*
Men sholde wedden after hir estat,° *station in life*
For youthe and elde is often at debat.
But sith that he was fallen in the snare,
He moste endure, as other folk, his care.
  Fair was this yonge wif, and therwithal
As any wesele hir body gent and smal.[1]
A ceint° she wered, barred° al of silk; *belt / striped*
A barmcloth° as whit as morne milk *apron*
Upon hir lendes,° ful of many a gore;° *loins / flounce*
Whit was hir smok,° and broiden° al bifore *slip / embroidered*
And eek bihinde, on hir coler aboute,° *around her collar*
Of col-blak silk, withinne and eek withoute;
The tapes° of hir white voluper° *ribbons / cap*
Were of the same suite° of hir coler; *pattern*
Hir filet° brood° of silk and set ful hye; *headband / broad*
And sikerly she hadde a likerous yë;[2]
Ful smale ypulled° were hir browes two, *plucked*
And tho° were bent, and blake as any slo.° *they / plum*
She was ful more blisful on to see
Than is the newe perejonette° tree, *pear*
And softer than the wolle is of a wether;° *ram*
And by hir girdel° heeng a purs of lether, *belt*
Tasseled with silk and perled° with latoun.° *decorated / brass*
In al this world, to seeken up and down,
Ther nis no man so wis that coude thenche° *imagine*
So gay a popelote° or swich a wenche.[3] *doll*
Ful brighter was the shining of hir hewe
Than in the Towr the noble° yforged newe.[4] *gold coin*
But of hir song, it was as loud and yerne° *lively*
As any swalwe sitting on a berne.
Therto she coude skippe and make game

7. A popular song.
8. According to what his friends gave him and his income.
9. Cato, Latin author of a book of maxims used in elementary education.
1. Her body as delicate and slender as any weasel.
2. And certainly she had a wanton eye.
3. Woman of the working class.
4. Than the new-forged gold coin in the Tower (of London, the royal mint).

As any kide or calf folwing his dame.° *mother*
Hir mouth was sweete as bragot or the meeth,° *honey drinks*
Or hoord of apples laid in hay or heeth.° *heather*
Winsing° she was as is a joly° colt, *skittish / spirited*
Long as a mast, and upright° as a bolt.° *strait / arrow*
A brooch she bar upon hir lowe coler
As brood as is the boos° of a bokeler; *boss / shield*
Hir shoes were laced on hir legges hye.
She was a primerole,° a piggesnye,[5] *primrose*
For any lord to leggen in his bedde,
Or yet for any good yeman to wedde.
  Now sire, and eft° sire, so bifel the cas *again*
That on a day this hende Nicholas
Fil with this yonge wif to rage° and playe, *sport*
Whil that hir housbonde was at Oseneye° *Osney, near Oxford*
(As clerkes been ful subtil and ful quainte°), *clever*
And prively he caughte hire by the queinte,[6]
And saide, "Ywis,° but if ich have my wille, *certainly*
For derne° love of thee, lemman,° I spille,"° *secret / sweetheart / die*
And heeld hire harde by the haunche-bones,
And saide, "Lemman, love me al atones,° *at once*
Or I wol dien, also° God me save." *so*
And she sproong as a colt dooth in a trave,[7]
And with hir heed she wried° faste away; *twisted*
She saide, "I wol nat kisse thee, by my fay.° *faith*
Why, lat be," quod she, "lat be, Nicholas!
Or I wol crye 'Out, harrow, and allas!'
Do way youre handes, for your curteisye!"
  This Nicholas gan mercy for to crye,
And spak so faire, and profred him° so faste, *pressed his case*
That she hir love him graunted atte laste,
And swoor hir ooth by Saint Thomas of Kent
That she wolde been at his comandement,
Whan that she may hir leiser° wel espye. *opportunity*
"Myn housbonde is so ful of jalousye
That but ye waite wel and been privee,[8]
I woot° right wel I nam but deed,"° quod she. *know / am no more than*
"Ye moste been ful derne° as in this cas." *secret*
  "Nay, therof care thee nought," quod Nicholas.
"A clerk hadde litherly biset his while,° *wasted his time*
But if he coude a carpenter bigile."
And thus they been accorded and ysworn
To waite a time, as I have told biforn.
Whan Nicholas hadde doon this everydeel,
And thakked° hire upon the lendes° weel, *patted / loins*
He kiste hire sweete, and taketh his sautrye,

5. Pig's eye, a flower.
6. Literally "dainty part," slang for the female genitals.
7. A restraint for horses when they are being shod.
8. That unless you're very cautious and discreet.

And playeth faste, and maketh melodye.
 Thanne fil it thus, that to the parissh chirche,
Cristes owene werkes for to wirche,
This goode wif wente on an haliday:° *holy day*
Hir forheed shoon as bright as any day,
So was it wasshen whan she leet° hir werk. *left off*
 Now was ther of that chirche a parissh clerk,
The which that was ycleped° Absolon: *called*
Crul° was his heer, and as the gold it shoon, *curly*
And strouted as a fanne[9] large and brode;
Ful straight and evene lay his joly shode.° *part in his hair*
His rode° was reed, his y'n greye as goos. *complexion*
With Poules window[1] corven° on his shoos, *carved*
In hoses rede he wente fetisly.° *elegantly*
Yclad he was ful smale° and proprely, *fine*
Al in a kirtel° of a light waget°— *tunic / blue*
Ful faire and thikke been the pointes° set— *laces*
And therupon he hadde a gay surplis,° *clerical robe*
As whit as is the blosme upon the ris.° *twig*
A merye child° he was, so God me save. *lad*
Wel coude he laten blood,[2] and clippe,° and shave, *cut hair*
And maken a chartre of land, or acquitaunce;° *legal release*
In twenty manere coude he trippe and daunce
After the scole of Oxenforde tho,
And with his legges casten° to and fro, *fling*
And playen songes on a smal rubible;° *fiddle*
Therto he soong somtime a loud quinible,° *high treble*
And as wel coude he playe on a giterne:° *guitar*
In al the town nas brewhous ne taverne
That he ne visited with his solas,[3]
Ther any gailard tappestere° was. *saucy barmaid*
But sooth to sayn, he was somdeel squaimous° *somewhat squeamish*
Of farting, and of speeche daungerous.° *haughty*
 This Absolon, that joly was and gay,
Gooth with a cencer° on the haliday, *incense bowl*
Cencing the wives of the parissh faste,
And many a lovely look on hem he caste,
And namely on this carpenteres wif:
To looke on hire him thoughte a merye lif.
She was so propre and sweete and likerous,° *sexy*
I dar wel sayn, if she hadde been a mous,
And he a cat, he wolde hire hente° anoon. *catch*
This parissh clerk, this joly Absolon,
Hath in his herte swich a love-longinge
That of no wif ne took he noon offringe—

9. And spread out like a winnowing fan (for separating wheat from chaff).
1. The windows of St. Paul's Chapel were intricately patterned.
2. Let blood (a medical treatment performed by barbers).
3. Entertainment (also with sexual connotations).

For curteisye he saide he wolde noon.
The moone, whan it was night, ful brighte shoon,
And Absolon his giterne hath ytake—
For paramours he thoughte for to wake[4]—
And forth he gooth, jolif° and amorous, *pretty*
Til he cam to the carpenteres hous,
A litel after cokkes hadde ycrowe,
And dressed° him up by a shot-windowe° *placed / hinged window*
That was upon the carpenteres wal.
He singeth in his vois gentil and smal,° *high*
"Now dere lady, if thy wille be,
I praye you that ye wol rewe° on me," *take pity*
Ful wel accordant° to his giterninge. *harmonizing*
This carpenter awook and herde him singe,
And spak unto his wif, and saide anoon,
"What, Alison, heerestou nought Absolon
That chaunteth thus under oure bowres° wal?" *bedroom's*
And she answerde hir housbonde therwithal,
"Yis, God woot,° John, I heere it everydeel."° *knows / every bit*
  This passeth forth. What wol ye bet than weel?[5]
Fro day to day this joly Absolon
So woweth° hire that him is wo-bigoon: *woos*
He waketh al the night and al the day;
He kembed° his lokkes brode° and made him gay; *combed / wide-spreading*
He woweth hire by menes and brocage,[6]
And swoor he wolde been hir owene page;° *attendant*
He singeth, brokking° as a nightingale; *trilling*
He sente hire piment,° meeth,° and spiced ale, *spiced wine / mead*
And wafres° piping hoot out of the gleede;° *pastries / coals*
And for she was of towne, he profred meede°— *bribes*
For som folk wol be wonnen for richesse,
And som for strokes,° and som for gentilesse. *by force*
Somtime to shewe his lightnesse° and maistrye,° *agility / skill*
He playeth Herodes[7] upon a scaffold° hye. *platform*
But what availeth him as in this cas?
She loveth so this hende Nicholas
That Absolon may blowe the bukkes horn;[8]
He ne hadde for his labour but a scorn.
And thus she maketh Absolon hir ape,° *fool*
And al his ernest turneth til a jape.° *joke*
Ful sooth° is this proverbe, it is no lie; *true*
Men saith right thus: "Alway the nye slye° *sly one nearby*
Maketh the ferre leve to be loth."[9]
For though that Absolon be wood° or wroth,° *crazy / angry*

4. For the sake of love he thought to keep a vigil.
5. What more would you want?
6. He woos her with go-betweens and mediation.
7. In the English mystery plays, Herod was often portrayed as a bully.
8. Undertake a useless endeavor.
9. Makes the distant beloved seem hateful.

By cause that he fer was from hir sighte,
This nye Nicholas stood in his lighte.° *in the way*
  Now beer thee wel, thou hende Nicholas,
For Absolon may waile and singe allas.
  And so bifel it on a Saterday
This carpenter was goon til Oseney,
And hende Nicholas and Alisoun
Accorded been to this conclusioun,
That Nicholas shal shapen hem a wile° *devise them a trick*
This sely° jalous housbonde to bigile, *innocent*
And if so be this game wente aright,
She sholden sleepen in his arm al night—
For this was his desir and hire also.
And right anoon, withouten wordes mo,
This Nicholas no lenger wolde tarye,
But dooth ful softe unto his chambre carye
Bothe mete and drinke for a day or twaye,
And to hir housbonde bad hire for to saye,
If that he axed after Nicholas,
She sholde saye she niste° wher he was— *did not know*
Of al that day she sawgh him nought with yë:
She trowed° that he was in maladye, *believed*
For for no cry hir maide coude him calle,
He nolde° answere for no thing that mighte falle.° *would not / happen*
  This passeth forth al thilke° Saterday *that same*
That Nicholas stille in his chambre lay,
And eet, and sleep, or dide what him leste,° *he liked*
Til Sonday that the sonne gooth to reste.
  This sely carpenter hath greet mervaile° *wonder*
Of Nicholas, or what thing mighte him aile,
And saide, "I am adrad,° by Saint Thomas, *afraid*
It stondeth nat aright with Nicholas.
God shilde° that he deide sodeinly! *forbid*
This world is now ful tikel,° sikerly:° *changeable / surely*
I sawgh today a corps yborn to chirche
That now a Monday last I sawgh him wirche.° *working*
Go up," quod he unto his knave° anoon, *manservant*
"Clepe° at his dore or knokke with a stoon. *call*
Looke how it is and tel me boldely."
  This knave gooth him up ful sturdily,
And at the chambre dore whil that he stood
He cride and knokked as that he were wood,
"What? How? What do ye, maister Nicholay?
How may ye sleepen al the longe day?".
But al for nought: he herde nat a word.
An hole he foond ful lowe upon a boord,
Ther as the cat was wont in for to creepe,
And at that hole he looked in ful deepe,
And atte laste he hadde of him a sighte.

This Nicholas sat evere caping° uprighte — *staring*
As he hadde kiked° on the newe moone. — *gazed*
A down he gooth and tolde his maister soone
In what array° he saw this ilke° man. — *condition / same*
This carpenter to blessen him[1] bigan.
And saide, "Help us, Sainte Frideswide![2]
A man woot litel what him shal bitide.
This man is falle, with his astromye,
In som woodnesse° or in som agonye.° — *madness / fit*
I thoughte ay° wel how that it sholde be: — *always*
Men sholde nought knowe of Goddes privetee.
Ye, blessed be alway a lewed° man — *unlearned*
That nought but only his bileve can.° — *knows his creed*
So ferde° another clerk with astromye: — *fared*
He walked in the feeldes for to prye° — *gaze*
Upon the sterres, what ther sholde bifalle,
Til he was in a marle-pit° yfalle— — *clay-pit*
He saw nat that. But yet, by Saint Thomas,
Me reweth sore° for hende Nicholas. — *feel sorry*
He shal be rated° of his studying, — *scolded*
If that I may, by Jesus, hevene king!
Get me a staf that I may underspore,° — *pry upward*
Whil that thou, Robin, hevest up the dore.
He shal out of his studying, as I gesse."
And to the chambre dore he gan him dresse.° — *placed himself*
His knave was a strong carl° for the nones,° — *fellow / purpose*
And by the haspe° he haaf° it up atones: — *hinge / heaved*
Into the floor the dore fil anoon.
This Nicholas sat ay as stille as stoon,
And evere caped up into the air.
This carpenter wende° he were in despair, — *thought*
And hente° him by the shuldres mightily, — *grabbed*
And shook him harde, and cride spitously,° — *vigorously*
"What, Nicholay, what, how! What! Looke adown!
Awaak and thenk on Cristes passioun![3]
I crouche° thee from elves and fro wightes."° — *bless / evil spirits*
Therwith the nightspel° saide he anoonrightes — *charm*
On foure halves° of the hous aboute, — *sides*
And on the thresshfold on the dore withoute:
"Jesu Crist and Sainte Benedight,[4]
Blesse this hous from every wikked wight!
For nightes nerye° the White Pater Noster.[5] — *protect*
Where wentestou, thou Sainte Petres soster?"° — *sister*
And at the laste this hende Nicholas
Gan for to sike° sore, and saide, "Allas, — *sigh*

1. Bless himself (with the sign of the cross).
2. A saint venerated for her healing powers.
3. Thinking about Christ's death and resurrection was supposed to ward off evil spells.
4. St. Benedict, founder of Western monasticism.
5. The Lord's Prayer, used as a charm.

Shal al the world be lost eftsoones° now"? *immediately*
This carpenter answerde, "What saistou?
What, thenk on God as we doon, men that swinke."° *work*
This Nicholas answerde, "Fecche me drinke,
And after wol I speke in privetee
Of certain thing that toucheth me and thee.
I wol telle it noon other man, certain."
This carpenter gooth down and comth again,
And broughte of mighty ale a large quart,
And whan that eech of hem hadde dronke his part,
This Nicholas his dore faste shette,° *shut*
And down the carpenter by him he sette,
And saide, "John, myn hoste lief° and dere, *beloved*
Thou shalt upon thy trouthe° swere me here *word of honor*
That to no wight thou shalt this conseil° wraye;° *advice / disclose*
For it is Cristes conseil that I saye,
And if thou telle it man, thou art forlore,° *lost*
For this vengeance thou shalt have therfore,
That if thou wraye° me, thou shalt be wood."° *reveal / mad*
"Nay, Crist forbede it, for his holy blood,"
Quod tho this sely man. "I nam no labbe,° *am no blabbermouth*
And though I saye, I nam nat lief° to gabbe. *do not like*
Say what thou wilt, I shal it nevere telle
To child ne wif, by him that harwed helle."[6]
"Now John," quod Nicholas, "I wol nought lie.
I have yfounde in myn astrologye,
As I have looked in the moone bright,
That now a Monday next, at quarter night,° *near dawn*
Shal falle a rain, and that so wilde and wood,° *furious*
That half so greet was nevere Noees° flood. *Noah's*
This world," he saide, "in lasse than an hour
Shal al be dreint,° so hidous is the showr. *drowned*
Thus shal mankinde drenche° and lese hir lif."° *drown / lose their lives*
This carpenter answerde, "Allas, my wif!
And shal she drenche? Allas, myn Alisoun!"
For sorwe of this he fil almost adown,
And saide, "Is there no remedye in this cas?"
"Why yis, for Gode," quod hende Nicholas,
"If thou wolt werken° after lore° and reed°— *act / learning / advice*
Thou maist nought werken after thyn owene heed;
For thus saith Salomon that was ful trewe,
'Werk al by conseil and thou shalt nought rewe.'° *regret*
And if thou werken wolt by good conseil,
I undertake, withouten mast or sail,
Yet shal I save hire and thee and me.
Hastou nat herd how saved was Noee

6. Christ, who harrowed hell upon his resurrection, releasing captive souls.

Whan that Oure Lord hadde warned him biforn
That al the world with water sholde be lorn?"° — *lost*
"Yis," quod this carpenter, "ful yore° ago." — *long*
"Hastou nat herd," quod Nicholas, "also
The sorwe° of Noee with his felaweshipe?° — *sorrow / companions*
Er that he mighte gete his wif to shipe,
Him hadde levere,° I dar wel undertake, — *would have preferred*
At thilke° time than alle his wetheres blake° — *that / black rams*
That she hadde had a ship hirself allone.[7]
And therfore woostou° what is best to doone? — *do you know*
This axeth haste, and of an hastif° thing — *urgent*
Men may nought preche or maken tarying.
Anoon go gete us faste into this in° — *inn*
A kneeding trough or elles a kimelin° — *brewing trough*
For eech of us, but looke that they be large,
In whiche we mowen swimme as in a barge,
And han therinne vitaile suffisaunt° — *enough food*
But for a day—fy on the remenaunt!
The water shal aslake° and goon away — *recede*
Aboute prime° upon the nexte day. — 6 A.M.
But Robin may nat wite° of this, thy knave, — *know*
Ne eek thy maide Gille I may nat save.
Axe nought why, for though thou axe me,
I wol nought tellen Goddes privetee.
Suffiseth thee, but if thy wittes madde,° — *go mad*
To han° as greet a grace as Noee hadde. — *have*
Thy wif shal I wel saven, out of doute.
Go now thy way, and speed thee heraboute.
But whan thou hast for hire and thee and me
Ygeten° us thise kneeding-tubbes three, — *gotten*
Thanne shaltou hangen hem in the roof ful hye,
That no man of oure purveyance° espye. — *preparations*
And whan thou thus hast doon as I have said,
And hast oure vitaile faire in hem ylaid,
And eek° an ax to smite° the corde atwo, — *also / cut*
Whan that the water comth that we may go,
And broke an hole an heigh° upon the gable — *on high*
Unto the gardinward,° over the stable, — *toward the garden*
That we may freely passen forth oure way,
Whan that the grete showr is goon away,
Thanne shaltou swimme as merye, I undertake,
As dooth the white doke° after hir drake. — *female duck*
Thanne wol I clepe,° 'How, Alison? How, John? — *call out*
Be merye, for the flood wol passe anoon.'
And thou wolt sayn, 'Hail, maister Nicholay!
Good morwe, I see thee wel, for it is day!'

7. Noah's wife was traditionally portrayed in the mystery plays as a complaining wife who resisted boarding the ark.

And thanne shal we be lordes al oure lif
Of al the world, as Noee and his wif.
But of oo thing I warne thee ful right:
Be wel avised on that ilke night
That we been entred into shippes boord
That noon of us ne speke nought a word,
Ne clepe,° ne crye, but been in his prayere, *call out*
For it is Goddes owene heeste° dete. *commandment*
Thy wif and thou mote° hange fer atwinne,° *must / apart*
For that bitwixe you shal be no sinne—
Namore in looking than ther shal in deede.
This ordinance is said: go, God thee speede.
Tomorwe at night whan men been alle asleepe,
Into oure kneeding-tubbes wol we creepe,
And sitten there, abiding Goddes grace.
Go now thy way, I have no lenger space° *time*
To make of this no lenger sermoning.
Men sayn thus: 'Send the wise and say no thing.'
Thou art so wis it needeth thee nat teche:
Go save oure lif, and that I thee biseeche."
This sely° carpenter gooth forth his way: *hapless*
Ful ofte he saide allas and wailaway,
And to his wif he tolde his privetee,
And she was war,° and knew it bet° than he, *aware / better*
What al this quainte cast° was for to saye.° *clever trick / mean*
But nathelees she ferde° as she wolde deye, *acted*
And saide, "Allas, go forth thy way anoon.
Help us to scape,° or we been dede eechoon. *escape*
I am thy trewe verray wedded wif:
Go, dere spouse, and help to save oure lif."
Lo, which a greet thing is affeccioun!° *emotion*
Men may dien,° of imaginacioun,° *die / fantasy*
So deepe may impression be take.
This sely carpenter biginneth quake;
Him thinketh verrailiche° that he may see *truly*
Noees flood come walwing° as the see *rolling in*
To drenchen Alison, his hony dere.
He weepeth, waileth, maketh sory cheere;° *expression*
He siketh° with ful many a sory swough,° *sighs / breath*
And gooth and geteth him a kneeding-trough,
And after a tubbe and a kimelin,
And prively he sente hem to his in,
And heeng hem in the roof in privetee;
His owene hand he made laddres three,
To climben by the ronges and the stalkes° *uprights*
Unto the tubbes hanging in the balkes,° *rafters*
And hem vitailed, bothe trough and tubbe,
With breed and cheese and good ale in a jubbe,° *jug*
Suffising right ynough as for a day.

But er that he hadde maad al this array,
He sente his knave, and eek his wenche also,
Upon his neede° to London for to go. *errand*
And on the Monday whan it drow to nighte,
He shette his dore withouten candel-lighte,
And dressed° alle thing as it sholde be, *arranged*
And shortly up they clomben alle three.
They seten stille wel a furlong way.[8]
"Now, Pater Noster, clum,"[9] saide Nicholay,
And "Clum" quod John, and "Clum" saide Alisoun.
This carpenter saide his devocioun,
And stille he sit and biddeth his prayere,
Awaiting on the rain, if he it heere.
The dede sleep, for wery bisinesse,
Fil on this carpenter right as I gesse
Aboute corfew time,° or litel more. *dusk*
For travailing of his gost° he groneth sore, *spirit*
And eft he routeth,° for his heed mislay. *snores*
Down of the laddre stalketh Nicholay,
And Alison ful softe adown she spedde:
Withouten wordes mo they goon to bedde
Ther as the carpenter is wont to lie.
Ther was the revel and the melodye,
And thus lith Alison and Nicholas
In bisinesse of mirthe and of solas,
Til that the belle of Laudes[1] gan to ringe,
And freres° in the chauncel° gonne singe. *friars / chapel*
This parissh clerk, this amorous Absolon,
That is for love alway so wo-bigoon,
Upon the Monday was at Oseneye,
With compaignye him to disporte and playe,
And axed upon caas° a cloisterer[2] *by chance*
Ful prively after John the carpenter;
And he drow him apart out of the chirche,
And saide, "I noot:° I sawgh him here nought wirche° *don't know / working*
Sith Saterday. I trowe that he be went
For timber ther oure abbot hath him sent.
For he is wont for timber for to go,
And dwellen atte grange° a day or two. *outlying farm*
Or elles he is at his hous, certain.
Where that he be I can nought soothly° sayn." *truly*
This Absolon ful jolif was and light,° *amorous and happy*
And thoughte, "Now is time to wake al night,
For sikerly,° I sawgh him nought stiringe *surely*
Aboute his dore sin° day bigan to springe.° *since / break*
So mote I thrive,° I shal at cokkes crowe *may I prosper*

8. The length of time to travel a furlong.
9. Say the Lord's Prayer and hush.
1. Lauds, daily church service before sunrise.
2. Member of the monastery.

Ful prively knokken at his windowe
That stant ful lowe upon his bowres° wal. *bedroom's*
To Alison now wol I tellen al
My love-longing, for yet I shal nat misse
That at the leeste way I shal hire kisse.
Som manere confort shal I have, parfay.° *indeed*
My mouth hath icched° al this longe day: *itched*
That is a signe of kissing at the leeste.
Al night me mette° eek I was at a feeste. *dreamed*
Therfore I wol go sleepe an hour or twaye,
And al the night thanne wol I wake and playe."
  Whan that the firste cok hath crowe, anoon
Up rist this joly lovere Absolon,
And him arrayeth gay at point devis.° *fastidiously*
But first he cheweth grain[3] and licoris,
To smellen sweete, er he hadde kembd his heer.
Under his tonge a trewe-love[4] he beer.
For therby wende° he to be gracious.° *supposed / attractive*
He rometh to the carpenteres hous,
And stille he stant under the shot-windowe—
Unto his brest it raughte,° it was so lowe— *reached*
And ofte he cougheth with a semisoun.° *soft noise*
"What do ye, hony-comb, sweete Alisoun,
My faire brid,° my sweete cinamome? *bird or bride*
Awaketh, lemman° myn, and speketh to me. *sweetheart*
Wel litel thinken ye upon my wo
That for your love I swete° ther I go. *dissolve*
No wonder is though that I swelte° and swete: *swelter*
I moorne as dooth a lamb after the tete.
Ywis,° lemman, I have swich love-longinge, *certainly*
That lik a turtle° trewe is my moorninge: *turtle-dove*
I may nat ete namore than a maide."
  "Go fro the windowe, Jakke fool," she saide.
"As help me God, it wol nat be com-pa-me.° *come kiss me*
I love another, and elles I were to blame,
Wel bet than thee, by Jesu, Absolon.
Go forth thy way or I wol caste a stoon,
And lat me sleepe, a twenty devele way."[5]
  "Allas," quod Absolon, "and wailaway,
That trewe love was evere so yvele biset.° *badly done to*
Thanne kis me, sin that it may be no bet,
For Jesus love and for the love of me."
  "Woltou thanne go thy way therwith?" quod she.
  "Ye, certes, lemman," quod this Absolon.
  "Thanne maak thee redy," quod she. "I come anoon."
And unto Nicholas she said stille,

3. Grain of paradise, an aromatic spice.
4. Four-leafed herb in the shape of a love knot.
5. In the name of 20 devils.

"Now hust,° and thou shalt laughen al thy fille." *hush*
This Absolon down sette him on his knees,
And saide, "I am a lord at alle degrees,° *in every way*
For after this I hope ther cometh more.
Lemman, thy grace, and sweete brid, thyn ore!"° *mercy*
The windowe she undooth, and that in haste.
"Have do," quod she, "com of and speed thee faste,
Lest that oure neighebores thee espye."
This Absolon gan wipe his mouth ful drye:
Derk was the night as pich or as the cole,
And at the windowe out she putte hir hole.
And Absolon, him fil no bet ne wers,
But with his mouth he kiste hir naked ers,
Ful savourly,° er he were war of this. *enthusiastically*
Abak he sterte, and thoughte it was amis,
For wel he wiste a womman hath no beerd.
He felte a thing al rough and longe yherd,° *haired*
And saide, "Fy, allas, what have I do?"
"Teehee," quod she, and clapte the windowe to.
And Absolon gooth forth a sory pas.° *with downcast step*
"A beerd, a beerd!" quod hende Nicholas,
"By Goddes corpus,° this gooth faire and weel." *body*
This sely Absolon herde everydeel,
And on his lippe he gan for anger bite,
And to himself he saide, "I shal thee quite."° *repay*
Who rubbeth now, who froteth now his lippes
With dust, with sond, with straw, with cloth, with chippes,
But Absolon, that saith ful ofte allas?
"My soule bitake° I unto Satanas, *hand over*
But me were levere than[6] all this town," quod he,
"Of this despit° awroken° for to be. *insult / avenged*
Allas," quod he, "allas I ne hadde ybleint!"° *turned aside*
His hote love was cold and al yqueint,° *quenched*
For fro that time that he hadde kist hir ers
Of paramours he sette nought a kers,[7]
For he was heled of his maladye.
Ful ofte paramours he gan defye,° *renounce*
And weep as dooth a child that is ybete.° *beaten*
A softe paas he wente over the streete
Until a smith men clepen daun Gervais,° *call Sir*
That in his forge smithed plough harneis:° *equipment*
He sharpeth shaar° and cultour° bisily. *plowshare / plough-blade*
This Absolon knokketh al esily,° *softly*
And saide, "Undo,° Gervais, and that anoon." *open up*
"What, who artou?" "It am I, Absolon."
"What, Absolon? What, Cristes sweete tree!

6. I would rather than (have).

7. Did not value as much as a piece of cress.

Why rise ye so rathe?° Ey, benedicite,° *early / bless me*
What aileth you? Som gay girl, God it woot,
Hath brought you thus upon the viritoot.° *on the prowl*
By Sainte Note,[8] ye woot wel what I mene."
This Absolon ne roughte nat a bene° *did not care a bean*
Of al his play. No word again he yaf:° *gave*
He hadde more tow on his distaf[9]
Than Gervais knew, and saide, "Freend so dere,
This hote cultour in the chimenee° here, *fireplace*
As lene it me:[1] I have therwith to doone.
I wol bringe it thee again ful soone."
Gervais answerde, "Certes, were it gold,
Or in a poke nobles alle untold,[2]
Thou sholdest have, as I am trewe smith.
Ey, Cristes fo,[3] what wol ye do therwith?"
"Therof," quod Absolon, "be as be may.
I shal wel telle it thee another day,"
And caughte the cultour by the colde stele.° *handle*
Ful softe out at the dore he gan to stele,
And wente unto the carpenteres wal:
He cougheth first and knokketh therwithal
Upon the windowe, right as he dide er.° *before*
This Alison answerde, "Who is ther
That knokketh so? I warante° it a thief." *bet*
"Why, nay," quod he, "God woot, my sweete lief,° *dear*
I am thyn Absolon, my dereling.
Of gold," quod he, "I have thee brought a ring—
My moder yaf it me, so God me save;
Ful fin it is and therto wel ygrave:° *engraved*
This wol I yiven thee if thou me kisse."
This Nicholas was risen for to pisse,
And thoughte he wolde amenden al the jape:[4]
He sholde kisse his ers er that he scape.
And up the windowe dide he hastily,
And out his ers he putteth prively,
Over the buttok to the haunche-boon.° *thigh*
And therwith spak this clerk, this Absolon,
"Speek, sweete brid, I noot nought wher thou art."
This Nicholas anoon leet flee° a fart *let fly*
As greet as it hadde been a thonder-dent° *thunderbolt*
That with the strook he was almost yblent,° *blinded*
And he was redy with his iren hoot,
And Nicholas amiddle the ers he smoot:
Of gooth the skin an hande-brede° aboute; *hand's width*

8. St. Noet, a ninth-century saint, with possible pun on Noah.
9. Flax on his distaff (i.e., cares on his mind).
1. Be so good as to lend it to me.
2. Or in a pouch of uncounted gold coins.
3. By Christ's foe (i.e., the Devil).
4. Make the joke even better.

The hote cultour brende so his toute° *backside*
That for the smert° he wende° for to die; *pain / thought*
As he were wood for wo he gan to crye,
"Help! Water! Water! Help, for Goddes herte!"
This carpenter out of his slomber sterte,
And herde oon cryen "Water!" as he were wood,
And thoughte, "Allas, now cometh Noweles° flood!" *Noah's*
He sette him up withoute wordes mo,
And with his ax he smooth the corde atwo,
And down gooth al: he foond neither to selle
Ne breed ne ale til he cam to the celle,[5]
Upon the floor, and ther aswoune° he lay. *stunned*
Up sterte° hire Alison and Nicholay, *leaped*
And criden "Out" and "Harrow" in the streete.
The neighebores, bothe smale and grete,[6]
In ronnen for to gauren° on this man *stare*
That aswoune lay bothe pale and wan,
For with the fal he brosten° hadde his arm; *broken*
But stonde he moste unto his owene harm,
For whan he spak he was anoon bore down° *restrained*
With° hende Nicholas and Alisoun: *by*
They tolden every man that he was wood°— *crazy*
He was agast° so of Noweles flood, *afraid*
Thurgh fantasye, that of his vanitee° *folly*
He hadde ybought him kneeding-tubbes three,
And hadde hem hanged in the roof above,
And that he prayed hem, for Goddes love,
To sitten in the roof, *par compaignye*.° *for fellowship*
The folk gan laughen at his fantasye.
Into the roof they kiken° and they cape,° *peer / gape*
And turned al his harm unto a jape,
For what so that this carpenter answerde,
It was for nought: no man his reson herde;
With othes grete he was so sworn adown,° *refuted by oaths*
That he was holden wood in al the town,
For every clerk anoonright heeld with other:
They saide, "The man was wood, my leve brother,"
And every wight° gan laughen at this strif. *person*
Thus swived° was the carpenteres wif *screwed*
For al his keeping and his jalousye,
And Absolon hath kist hir nether° yë, *lower*
And Nicholas is scalded in the toute:
This tale is doon, and God save al the route!

5. He found no time to sell either bread or ale until he reached the floor (i.e., he fell to the ground too quickly to be aware of what was happening).
6. Lower- and upper-class people alike.

The Wife of Bath's Prologue and Tale Dame Alison, the Wife of Bath, is Chaucer's greatest contribution to the stock characters of Western culture. She has a long literary ancestry, most immediately in the Duenna of the thirteenth-century French poem, *The Romance of the Rose,* and stretching back to the Roman poet Ovid. Dame Alison stands out in bold relief, even among the vivid Canterbury pilgrims, partly because Chaucer gives her so rebellious and explicitly self-created a biography. She has outlived five husbands, accumulated wealth from the first three, and made herself rich in the growing textile industry of her time. At once a great companion and greatly unnerving, Alison lives in constant battle with a secular and religious world mostly controlled by men and yet has a keen appetite both for the men and for the battle.

The Wife of Bath's *Prologue* and *Tale* seem only the current installments of a multifaceted struggle in which Dame Alison has long been engaged, at first through her body and social role and now, in the face of advancing years, through the remaining agency of retrospective storytelling. She battles a society in which many young women are almost chattels in a marital market, as was the twelve-year-old version of herself who first was married off to a wealthier, much older man. She battles him and later husbands for power within the marriage, and her ambition to social dominance, as the *General Prologue* reports, extends to life in her urban parish.

By the moment of the Canterbury pilgrimage, though, the Wife's adversaries are more daunting, less easily conquered. The *Wife's Prologue,* for all its autobiographical energy, is primarily a debate with the clergy and with "auctoritee"—the whole armature of learning and literacy by which the clergy (like her clerically educated fifth husband, Jankyn) seeks to silence her.

The Wife's *Tale,* too, can be seen as an angry riposte to the secular fantasies of Arthurian chivalry and genetic nobility. The Wife's well-born Arthurian knight is a common rapist, who finds himself at the mercy of a queen and then in the arms of a crone. The tale turns Arthurian conventions on their head, lays sexual violence in the open, and puts legal and magical power in the hands of women. It is explicitly a fantasy, but a powerful one.

Alison's final enemy, mortality itself, is what makes her both most desperate and most sympathetic. The husbands are gone. Even the fondly recalled Jankyn slips into a rosy glow and the past tense; so does her own best friend and "gossip," the odd mirror-double "Alisoun." The Wife of Bath keeps addressing other "wives" in her *Prologue,* but there are no others on the pilgrimage. Her very argument with the institutionalized church distances her from its comforts, and she is deeply aware that time is stealing her beauty as it has taken away the companions who made up her earlier life. If Alison's *Tale* closes with a delicious fantasy of restored youth, it is only a pendant to the much longer *Prologue* and its cheerful yet poignant acceptance of age.

The Wife of Bath's Prologue

Experience, though noon auctoritee[1]
Were in this world, is right ynough for me
To speke of wo that is in mariage:
For lordinges,° sith I twelf yeer was of age— *gentlemen*
Thanked be God that is eterne on live—
Housbondes at chirche dore I have had five
(If I so ofte mighte han wedded be),
And alle were worthy men in hir° degree. *their*
But me was told, certain, nat longe agoon is,
That sith that Crist ne wente nevere but ones° *once*

1. Even if no authority, textual precedent.

To wedding in the Cane of Galilee,[2]
That by the same ensample taughte he me
That I ne sholde wedded be but ones.
Herke eek, lo, which a sharp word for the nones,° *for the purpose*
Biside a welle, Jesus, God and man,
Spak in repreve° of the Samaritan:[3] *reproof*
"Thou hast yhad five housbondes," quod he,
"And that ilke° man that now hath thee *same*
Is nat thyn housbonde." Thus saide he certain.
What that he mente therby I can nat sayn,
But that I axe why that the fifthe man
Was noon housbonde to the Samaritan?
How manye mighte she han in mariage?
Yit herde I nevere tellen in myn age
Upon this nombre diffinicioun.
Men may divine° and glosen° up and down, *guess / interpret*
But wel I woot,° expres,° withouten lie, *know / manifestly*
God bad us for to wexe° and multiplye: *increase*
That gentil text can I wel understonde.
 Eek wel I woot he saide that myn housbonde
Sholde lete° fader and moder and take to me, *leave*
But of no nombre mencion made he—
Of bigamye or of octogamye:
Why sholde men thanne speke of it vilainye?° *as churlish*
 Lo, here the wise king daun° Salomon: *Lord*
I trowe° he hadde wives many oon, *believe*
As wolde God it leveful° were to me *lawful*
To be refresshed half so ofte as he.
Which yifte° of God hadde he for alle his wives! *what a gift*
No man hath swich that in this world alive is.
God woot° this noble king, as to my wit,° *knows / understanding*
The firste night hadde many a merye fit
With eech of hem, so wel was him on live.
Blessed be God that I have wedded five,
Of whiche I have piked° out the beste, *picked*
Bothe of hir nether purs and of hir cheste.[4]
Diverse° scoles maken parfit° clerkes, *different / accomplished*
And diverse practikes in sondry werkes
Maken the werkman° parfit sikerly:° *craftsman / surely*
Of five housbondes scoleying° am I. *studying*
Welcome the sixte whan that evere he shal!
For sith I wol nat keepe me chast in al,
Whan myn housbonde is fro the world agoon,
Som Cristen man shal wedde me anoon.
For thanne th'Apostle[5] saith that I am free

2. Cana, where Jesus performed his first miracle at a wedding feast (John 2.1).
3. The story of Jesus and the Samaritan woman is related in John 4.6 ff.
4. Money chest, with a pun on body parts.
5. St. Paul, in Romans 7.2.

To wedde, a Goddes half,[6] where it liketh° me. *please*
He said that to be wedded is no sinne:
Bet° is to be wedded than to brinne.° *better / burn (in hell)*
What rekketh° me though folk saye vilainye *do I care*
Of shrewed° Lamech[7] and his bigamye? *cursed*
I woot wel Abraham was an holy man,
And Jacob eek, as fer as evere I can,° *know*
And eech of hem hadde wives mo than two,
And many another holy man also.
Where can ye saye in any manere age
That hye God defended° mariage *prohibited*
By expres word? I praye you, telleth me.
Or where comanded he virginitee?
I woot as wel as ye, it is no drede,° *doubt*
Th'Apostle, whan he speketh of maidenhede,° *virginity*
He saide that precept° therof hadde he noon: *command*
Men may conseile a womman to be oon,° *single*
But conseiling nis no comandement.
He putte it in oure owene juggement.
For hadde God comanded maidenhede,
Thanne hadde he dampned° wedding with the deede; *condemned*
And certes, if ther were no seed ysowe,
Virginitee, thanne wherof sholde it growe?
Paul dorste nat comanden at the leeste
A thing of which his maister yaf no heeste.° *commandment*
The dart° is set up for virginitee: *prize*
Cacche whoso may, who renneth° best lat see. *runs*
But this word is nought take° of every wight,° *required / person*
But ther as God list° yive it of his might. *pleases*
I woot wel that th'Apostle was a maide,° *virgin*
But nathelees, though that he wroot or saide
He wolde that every wight were swich as he,
Al nis but° conseil to virginitee; *it is only*
And for to been a wif he yaf me leve
Of indulgence; so nis it no repreve
To wedde me if that my make° die, *mate*
Withouten excepcion° of bigamye— *legal objection*
Al were it good no womman for to touche
(He mente as in his bed or in his couche,
For peril is bothe fir and tow t'assemble[8]—
Ye knowe what this ensample may resemble).
This al and som,° he heeld virginitee *all told*
More parfit than wedding in freletee.° *due to weakness*
(Freletee clepe° I but if° that he and she *call / except*
Wolde leden al hir lif in chastitee).
I graunte it wel, I have noon envye

6. From God's perspective.
7. The earliest bigamist in the Bible (Genesis 4.19).
8. To bring together fire and flax.

Though maidenhede preferre° bigamye: *surpasses*
It liketh hem to be clene in body and gost.° *soul*
Of myn estaat° ne wol I make no boost; *condition*
For wel ye knowe, a lord in his houshold
Ne hath nat every vessel al of gold:
Some been of tree,° and doon hir lord servise. *wood*
God clepeth° folk to him in sondry wise, *calls*
And everich hath of God a propre yifte,
Som this, som that, as him liketh shifte.[9]
Virginitee is greet perfeccioun,
And continence eek with devocioun,
But Crist, that of perfeccion is welle,° *source*
Bad nat every wight° he sholde go selle *person*
Al that he hadde and yive it to the poore,
And in swich wise folwe° him and his fore:° *follow / footsteps*
He spak to hem that wolde live parfitly°— *perfectly*
And lordinges, by youre leve, that am nat I.
I wol bistowe the flour of al myn age
In th'actes and in fruit of mariage.
  Telle me also, to what conclusioun° *end*
Were membres maad of generacioun
And of so parfit wis a wrighte ywrought?[1]
Trusteth right wel, they were nat maad for nought.
Glose whoso wol, and saye bothe up and down
That they were maked for purgacioun
Of urine, and oure bothe thinges smale
Was eek to knowe a femele from a male,
And for noon other cause—saye ye no?
Th'experience woot wel it is nought so.
So that the clerkes be nat with me wrothe,° *angry*
I saye this, that they maked been for bothe—
That is to sayn, for office° and for ese° *use / pleasure*
Of engendrure,° ther we nat God displese. *procreation*
Why sholde men elles in hir bookes sette
That man shal yeelde° to his wif hir dette?° *pay / marriage debt*
Now wherwith sholde he make his payement
If he ne used his sely° instrument? *innocent*
Thanne were they maad upon a creature
To purge urine, and eek for engendrure.
  But I saye nought that every wight is holde,° *bound*
That hath swich harneis° as I to you tolde, *equipment*
To goon and usen hem in engendrure:
Thanne sholde men take of chastitee no cure.° *heed*
Crist was a maide and shapen as a man,
And many a saint sith that the world bigan,
Yit lived they evere in parfit° chastitee. *perfect*

9. As it pleases him to provide.

1. And created by so perfectly wise a Creator?

I nil envye no virginitee:
Lat hem be breed° of pured° whete seed, *bread / refined*
And lat us wives hote° barly breed— *be called*
And yit with barly breed, Mark telle can,
Oure Lord Jesu refresshed many a man.
In swich estaat as God hath cleped° us *called*
I wol persevere: I nam nat precious.° *am not fussy*
In wifhood wol I use myn instrument
As freely° as my Makere hath it sent. *generously*
If I be daungerous,° God yive me sorwe:° *withholding / sorrow*
Myn housbonde shal it han both eve and morwe,° *morning*
Whan that him list come forth and paye his dette.
An housbonde wol I have, I wol nat lette,° *forgo*
Which shal be bothe my dettour and my thral,° *slave*
And have his tribulacion withal
Upon his flessh whil that I am his wif.
I have the power during al my lif
Upon his propre° body, and nat he: *own*
Right thus th'Apostle tolde it unto me,
And bad oure housbondes for to love us weel.
Al this sentence° me liketh everydeel. *interpretation*

An Interlude

Up sterte° the Pardoner and that anoon: *started*
"Now dame," quod he, "by God and by Saint John,
Ye been a noble prechour° in this cas. *preacher*
I was aboute to wedde a wif: allas,
What° sholde I bye° it on my flessh so dere? *why / buy*
Yit hadde I levere° wedde no wif toyere."° *rather / this year*
"Abid," quod she, "my tale is nat bigonne.
Nay, thou shalt drinken of another tonne,° *barrel*
Er that I go, shal savoure wors than ale.
And whan that I have told thee forth my tale
Of tribulacion in mariage,
Of which I am expert in al myn age—
This is to saye, myself hath been the whippe—
Thanne maistou chese° wheither thou wolt sippe *may you choose*
Of thilke° tonne that I shal abroche:° *that same / open*
Be war of it, er thou too neigh approche,
For I shal telle ensamples mo than ten.
'Whoso that nile° be war by othere men, *will not*
By him shal othere men corrected be.'
Thise same wordes writeth Ptolomee:[2]
Rede in his Almageste and take it there."
"Dame, I wolde praye you if youre wil it were,"
Saide this Pardoner, "as ye bigan,

2. Ptolemy, ancient Greek astronomer and author of the *Almageste*.

Telle forth youre tale; spareth for no man,
And teche us yonge men of youre practike."
"Gladly," quod she, "sith it may you like;
But that I praye to al this compaignye,
If that I speke after my fantasye,° *fancy*
As taketh nat agrief° of that I saye, *amiss*
For myn entente nis but° for to playe." *intent is only*

The Wife Continues

Now sire, thanne wol I telle you forth my tale.
As evere mote I drinke win or ale,
I shal saye sooth:° tho° housbondes that I hadde, *truth / those*
As three of hem were goode, and two were badde.
The three men were goode, and riche, and olde;
Unnethe° mighte they the statut holde *scarcely*
In which they were bounden unto me—
Ye woot wel what I mene of this, pardee.° *by God*
As help me God, I laughe whan I thinke
How pitously anight I made hem swinke;° *work*
And by my fay,° I tolde of it no stoor:° *faith / gave it no heed*
They hadde me yiven hir land and hir tresor;° *wealth*
Me needed nat do lenger diligence
To winne hir love or doon hem reverence.
They loved me so wel, by God above,
That I ne tolde no daintee° of hir love. *set no value on*
A wis womman wol bisye hire evere in oon° *constantly*
To gete hire love, ye, ther as she hath noon.
But sith I hadde hem hoolly in myn hand,
And sith that they hadde yiven me al hir land,
What sholde I take keep° hem for to plese, *care*
But it were for my profit and myn ese?
I sette hem so awerke, by my fay,° *faith*
That many a night they songen wailaway.
The bacon was nat fet° for hem, I trowe, *collected*
That some men han in Essexe at Dunmowe.[3]
I governed hem so wel after my lawe
That eech of hem ful blisful was and fawe° *glad*
To bringe me gaye thinges fro the faire;
They were ful glade whan I spak to hem faire,
For God it woot, I chidde° hem spitously.° *scolded / cruelly*
Now herkneth how I bar me proprely:
Ye wise wives, that conne understonde,
Thus sholde ye speke and bere him wrong on honde°— *wrongly accuse*
For half so boldely can ther no man
Swere and lie as a woman can.
I saye nat this by wives that been wise,

3. At Dunmowe, spouses who had spent a year without quarrelling were awarded a side of bacon.

But if it be whan they hem misavise.° *err*
A wis wif, if that she can hir good,[4]
Shal bere him on hande the cow is wood,[5]
And take witnesse of hir owene maide
Of hir assent.° But herkneth how I saide: *as her accomplice*
"Sire olde cainard,° is this thyn array? *dotard*
Why is my neighebores wif so gay?
She is honoured overal ther she gooth:
I sitte at hoom; I have no thrifty° cloth. *decent*
What doostou at my neighebores hous?
Is she so fair? Artou so amorous?
What roune° ye with oure maide, benedicite?° *whisper / bless us*
Sire olde lechour, lat thy japes° be. *tricks*
And if I have a gossib° or a freend, *confidante*
Withouten gilt ye chiden as a feend,
If that I walke or playe unto his hous.
Thou comest hoom as dronken as a mous,
And prechest on thy bench, with yvel preef.° *bad luck to you*
Thou saist to me, it is a greet meschief
To wedde a poore womman for costage.° *expense*
And if that she be riche, of heigh parage,° *breeding*
Thanne saistou that it is a tormentrye
To suffre hir pride and hir malencolye.
And if that she be fair, thou verray knave,
Thou saist that every holour° wol hire have: *whoremonger*
She may no while in chastitee abide
That is assailed upon eech a side.
"Thou saist som folk desiren us for richesse,
Som for oure shap, and som for oure fairnesse,
And som for she can outher° singe or daunce, *either*
And som for gentilesse and daliaunce,° *conversation*
Som for hir handes and hir armes smale—
Thus gooth al to the devel by thy tale![6]
Thou saist men may nat keepe a castel wal,
It may so longe assailed been overal.
And if that she be foul, thou saist that she
Coveiteth° every man that she may see; *desires*
For as a spaniel she wol on him lepe,
Til that she finde som man hire to chepe.° *take*
Ne noon so grey goos gooth ther in the lake,
As, saistou, wol be withoute make;° *mate*
And saist it is an hard thing for to weelde° *control*
A thing that no man wol, his thankes,° heelde.° *willingly / hold*
Thus saistou, lorel,° whan thou goost to bedde, *scoundrel*
And that no wis man needeth for to wedde,
Ne no man that entendeth° unto hevene— *expects (to go)*

4. Knows what's good for her.
5. Shall convince him the chough is mad. The chough, a crow-like bird, was fabled to reveal wives' infidelities.
6. According to what you say.

With wilde thonder-dint° and firy levene° *thunderclap / lightning*
Mote° thy welked° nekke be tobroke!° *may / withered / broken*
Thou saist that dropping° houses and eek smoke *leaking*
And chiding wives maken men to flee
Out of hir owene houses: a, benedicite,
What aileth swich an old man for to chide?
Thou saist we wives wil oure vices hide
Til we be fast,° and thanne we wol hem shewe— *bound (in marriage)*
Wel may that be a proverbe of a shrewe!° *scoundrel*
Thou saist that oxen, asses, hors, and houndes,
They been assayed° at diverse stoundes;° *tested / times*
Bacins,° lavours,° er that men hem bye, *basins / wash bowls*
Spoones, stooles, and al swich housbondrye,
And so be pottes, clothes, and array—
But folk of wives maken noon assay° *trial*
Til they be wedded—olde dotard shrewe!
And thanne, saistou, we wil oure vices shewe.
Thou saist also that it displeseth me
But if° that thou wolt praise my beautee, *unless*
And but thou poure alway upon my face,
And clepe° me 'Faire Dame' in every place, *call*
And but thou make a feeste on thilke° day *that*
That I was born, and make me fressh and gay,
And but thou do to my norice° honour, *nurse*
And to my chamberere° within my bowr,° *chambermaid / bedroom*
And to my fadres folk, and his allies°— *kinsmen*
Thus saistou, olde barel-ful of lies.
And yit of our apprentice Janekin,
For his crispe heer,° shining as gold so fin, *curly hair*
And for he squiereth° me bothe up and down, *chaperones*
Yit hastou caught a fals suspecioun;
I wil° him nat though thou were deed tomorwe. *desire*
"But tel me this, why hidestou with sorwe
The keyes of thy cheste away fro me?
It is my good as wel as thyn, pardee.° *by God*
What, weenestou° make an idiot of oure dame? *do you suppose*
Now by that lord that called is Saint Jame,[7]
Thou shalt nought bothe, though that thou were wood,° *enraged*
Be maister of my body and of my good:
That oon thou shalt forgo, maugree thine yën.[8]
"What helpeth it of me enquere and spyen?
I trowe thou woldest loke° me in thy cheste. *lock*
Thou sholdest saye, 'Wif, go wher thee leste.° *it pleases*
Taak youre disport.° I nil leve° no tales: *amusement / believe*
I knowe you for a trewe wif, dame Alis.'
We love no man that taketh keep° or charge *notice*

7. Santiago de Compostela, whose shrine in Spain the Wife of Bath has already made a pilgrimage to visit.

8. In spite of your eyes (an oath).

Wher that we goon: we wol been at oure large.° *liberty*
Of alle men yblessed mote he be
The wise astrologen daun Ptolomee,
That saith this proverbe in his Almageste:
'Of alle men his wisdom is the hyeste
That rekketh° nat who hath the world in honde.' *cares*
By this proverbe thou shalt understonde,
Have thou ynough, what thar° thee rekke° or care *need / be concerned*
How merily that othere folkes fare?° *go about*
For certes, olde dotard, by youre leve,
Ye shal han queinte° right ynough at eve: *sex*
He is too greet a nigard that wil werne° *refuse*
A man to lighte a candle at his lanterne;
He shal han nevere the lasse lighte, pardee.° *by God*
Have thou ynough, thee thar nat plaine thee.° *complain*
"Thou saist also that if we make us gay
With clothing and with precious array,
That it is peril of oure chastitee,
And yit with sorwe thou moste enforce thee,[9]
And saye thise wordes in th'Apostles name:
'In habit° maad with chastitee and shame *clothing*
Ye wommen shal apparaile you,' quod he,
'And nat in tressed heer° and gay perree,° *styled hair / jewels*
As perles ne with gold ne clothes riche.'
After thy text, ne after thy rubriche,[1]
I wol nat werke as muchel as a gnat.
Thou saidest this, that I was lik a cat:
For whoso wolde senge° a cattes skin, *singe*
Thanne wolde the cat wel dwellen in his in;° *inn*
And if the cattes skin be slik° and gay, *sleek*
She wol nat dwelle in house half a day,
But forth she wol, er any day be dawed,° *dawned*
To shewe her skin and goon a-caterwawed.° *caterwauling*
This is to saye, if I be gay, sire shrewe,
I wol renne out, my borel° for to shewe. *coarse cloth*
Sire olde fool, what helpeth thee t'espyen?
Though thou praye Argus[2] with his hundred yën
To be my wardecors,° as he can best, *bodyguard*
In faith, he shal nat keepe me but me lest:
Yit coude I make his beerd,[3] so mote I thee.° *so may I prosper*
"Thou saidest eek that ther been thinges three,
The whiche thinges troublen al this erthe,
And that no wight° may endure the ferthe.° *person / fourth*
O leve sire shrewe, Jesu shorte thy lif!
Yit prechestou and saist an hateful wif

9. Reinforce (your position).
1. Rubric, interpretive heading on a text.
2. Mythical hundred-eyed monster employed by Juno to guard over Io, one of Jove's many lovers, whom the goddess turned into a cow.
3. Deceive him.

Yrekened° is for oon of thise meschaunces. *accounted*
Been ther nat none othere resemblaunces
That ye may likne youre parables to,
But if a sely° wif be oon of tho? *innocent*
"Thou liknest eek wommanes love to helle,
To bareine land ther water may nat dwelle;
Thou liknest it also to wilde fir—
The more it brenneth,° the more it hath desir *burns*
To consumen every thing that brent wol be;
Thou saist right as wormes shende° a tree, *destroy*
Right so a wif destroyeth hir housbonde—
This knowen they that been to wives bonde."
Lordinges, right thus, as ye han understonde,
Bar I stifly° mine olde housbondes on honde° *firmly / swore*
That thus they saiden in hir dronkenesse—
And al was fals, but that I took witnesse
On Janekin and on my nece° also. *kinswoman*
O Lord, the paine I dide hem and the wo,
Ful giltelees, by Goddes sweete pine!° *suffering*
For as an hors I coude bite and whine;
I coude plaine and° I was in the gilt,° *when / wrong*
Or elles often time I hadde been spilt.° *ruined*
Whoso that first to mille comth first grint.° *grinds*
I plained first: so was oure werre° stint.° *war / stopped*
They were ful glad to excusen hem ful blive° *quickly*
Of thing of which they nevere agilte° hir live. *offended (in)*
Of wenches wolde I beren hem on honde,
Whan that for sik they mighte unnethe° stonde, *barely*
Yit tikled I his herte for that he
Wende° I hadde had of him so greet cheertee.° *supposed / fondness*
I swoor that al my walking out by nighte
Was for to espye wenches that he dighte.° *had sex with*
Under that colour° hadde I many a mirthe. *pretense*
For al swich wit is yiven us in oure birthe:
Deceite, weeping, spinning God hath yive
To wommen kindely° whil they may live. *by nature*
And thus of oo thing I avaunte° me: *boast*
At ende I hadde the bet in eech degree,
By sleighte° or force, or by som manere thing, *deception*
As by continuel murmur° or grucching;° *complaining / grumbling*
Namely abedde° hadden they meschaunce:° *in bed / misfortune*
Ther wolde I chide and do hem no plesaunce;
I wolde no lenger in the bed abide
If that I felte his arm over my side,
Til he hadde maad his raunson° unto me; *amends*
Thanne wolde I suffre him do his nicetee.° *lust*
And therfore every man this tale I telle:
Winne whoso may, for al is for to selle;
With empty hand men may no hawkes lure.

For winning° wolde I al his lust endure, *profit*
And make me a feined appetit—
And yit in bacon° hadde I nevere delit. *old meat*
That made me that evere I wolde hem chide;
For though the Pope hadde seten° hem biside, *sat*
I wolde nought spare hem at hir owene boord.° *table*
For by my trouthe, I quitte° hem word for word. *repaid*
As help me verray God omnipotent,
Though I right now sholde make my testament,
I ne owe hem nat a word that it nis quit.° *is not repaid*
I broughte it so aboute by my wit
That they moste yive it up as for the beste,
Or elles hadde we nevere been in reste;
For though he looked as a wood leoun,° *crazed lion*
Yit sholde he faile of his conclusion.° *purpose*
  Thanne wolde I saye, "Goodelief,° taak keep, *Sweetheart*
How mekely looketh Wilekin, oure sheep!
Com neer my spouse, lat me ba° thy cheeke— *kiss*
Ye sholden be al pacient and meeke,
And han a sweete-spiced conscience,
Sith ye so preche of Jobes[4] pacience;
Suffreth alway, sin ye so wel can preche;
And but ye do, certain, we shal you teche
That it is fair to han a wif in pees.
Oon of us two moste bowen, doutelees,
And sith a man is more resonable
Than womman is, ye mosten been suffrable.° *patient*
What aileth you to grucche thus and grone?
Is it for ye wolde have my queinte allone?
Why, taak it al—lo, have it everydeel.
Peter,° I shrewe° you but ye love it weel. *by St. Peter / curse*
For if I wolde selle my bele chose,[5]
I coude walke as fressh as is a rose;
But I wol keepe it for youre owene tooth.° *taste*
Ye be to blame. By God, I saye you sooth!"
Swiche manere wordes hadde we on honde.
Now wol I speke of my ferthe housbonde.
  My ferthe housbonde was a revelour—
This is to sayn, he hadde a paramour°— *lover*
And I was yong and ful of ragerye,° *wantonness*
Stibourne° and strong and joly as a pie:° *stubborn / magpie*
How coude I daunce to an harpe smale,° *gracefully*
And singe, ywis,° as any nightingale, *certainly*
Whan I hadde dronke a draughte of sweete win.
Metellius,[6] the foule cherl,° the swin, *ruffian*

4. The biblical Job, who suffers patiently the trials imposed by God.
5. "Beautiful thing," a euphemism for female genitals.
6. Egnatius Metellius, whose actions are described in Valerius Maximus's *Facta et dicta memorabilia*, 6.3.

That with a staf birafte his wif hir lif
For she drank win, though I hadde been his wif,
Ne sholde nat han daunted me fro drinke;
And after win on Venus moste I thinke,
For also siker° as cold engendreth hail, *certainly*
A likerous° mouth moste han a likerous° tail: *gluttonous / lecherous*
In womman vinolent° is no defence— *drunken*
This knowen lechours by experience.
    But Lord Crist, whan that it remembreth me
Upon my youthe and on my jolitee,
It tikleth me aboute myn herte roote°— *bottom of my heart*
Unto this day it dooth myn herte boote° *good*
That I have had my world as in my time.
But age, allas, that al wol envenime,° *poison*
Hath me biraft my beautee and my pith°— *vigor*
Lat go, farewel, the devel go therwith!
The flour is goon, ther is namore to telle:
The bren° as I best can now moste I selle; *bran*
But yit to be right merye wol I fonde.° *try*
Now wol I tellen of my ferthe housbonde.
    I saye I hadde in herte greet despit
That he of any other hadde delit,
But he was quit,° by God and by Saint Joce:° *repaid / St. Judocus*
I made him of the same wode a croce°— *cross*
Nat of my body in no foul manere—
But, certainly, I made folk swich cheere
That in his owene grece° I made him frye, *grease*
For angre and for verray jalousye.
By God, in erthe I was his purgatorye,
For which I hope his soule be in glorye.
For God it woot, he sat ful ofte and soong
Whan that his sho° ful bitterly him wroong.° *shoe / pinched*
Ther was no wight° save God and he that wiste *person*
In many wise how sore I him twiste.
He deide whan I cam fro Jerusalem,
And lith ygrave° under the roode-beem,° *buried / crossbeam*
Al is his tombe nought so curious° *carefully made*
As was the sepulcre of him Darius,[7]
Which that Appelles wroughte subtilly:
It nis but wast to burye him preciously.° *expensively*
Lat him fare wel, God yive his soule reste;
He is now in his grave and in his cheste.
    Now of my fifthe housbonde wol I telle—
God lete his soule nevere come in helle—
And yit he was to me the moste shrewe:
That feele I on my ribbes al by rewe,° *in a row*

7. Persian Emperor defeated by Alexander the Great, whose tomb was elaborately designed by the Jewish craftsman Apelles.

And evere shal unto myn ending day.
But in oure bed he was so fressh and gay,
And therwithal so wel coude he me glose° *flatter*
Whan that he wolde han my bele chose,° *pretty thing*
That though he hadde me bet° on every boon,° *beaten / bone*
He coude winne again my love anoon.
I trowe I loved him best for that he
Was of his love daungerous° to me. *hard to get*
We wommen han, if that I shal nat lie,
In this matere a quainte fantasye:
Waite° what thing we may nat lightly° have, *note that / easily*
Therafter wol we crye al day and crave;
Forbede us thing, and that desiren we;
Presse on us faste, and thanne wol we flee.
With daunger oute we al oure chaffare:[8]
Greet prees° at market maketh dere ware,° *crowd / costly goods*
And too greet chepe° is holden at litel pris. *bargain*
This knoweth every womman that is wis.
  My fifthe housbonde—God his soule blesse!—
Which that I took for love and no richesse,
He somtime was a clerk of Oxenforde,
And hadde laft scole° and wente at hoom to boorde *left school*
With my gossib,° dwelling in oure town— *close friend*
God have hir soule!—hir name was Alisoun;
She knew myn herte and eek my privetee° *secrets*
Bet than oure parissh preest, as mote I thee.
To hire biwrayed° I my conseil° al, *revealed / thoughts*
For hadde myn housbonde pissed on a wal,
Or doon a thing that sholde han cost his lif,
To hire, and to another worthy wif,
And to my nece which that I loved weel,
I wolde han told his conseil everydeel;
And so I dide ful often, God it woot,
That made his face often reed° and hoot° *red / hot*
For verray shame, and blamed himself for he
Hadde told to me so greet a privetee.
  And so bifel that ones in a Lente—
So often times I to my gossib wente,
For evere yit I loved to be gay,
And for to walke in March, Averil, and May,
From hous to hous, to heere sondry tales—
That Janekin clerk and my gossib dame Alis
And I myself into the feeldes wente.
Myn housbonde was at London al that Lente:
I hadde the better leiser° for to playe, *opportunity*
And for to see, and eek for to be seye° *seen*

8. With coyness we spread out all our merchandise.

Of lusty° folk—what wiste I wher my grace° *merry / luck*
Was shapen° for to be, or in what place? *destined*
Therfore I made my visitaciouns
To vigilies[9] and to processiouns,
To preching eek, and to thise pilgrimages,
To playes of miracles and to mariages,
And wered upon my gaye scarlet gites°— *robes*
Thise wormes ne thise motthes ne thise mites,
Upon my peril, frete° hem neveradeel: *devoured*
And woostou why? For they were used weel.
Now wol I tellen forth what happed me.
I saye that in the feeldes walked we,
Til trewely we hadde swich daliaunce,° *flirtation*
This clerk and I, that of my purveyaunce° *providence*
I spak to him and saide him how that he,
If I were widwe, sholde wedde me.
For certainly, I saye for no bobaunce° *boast*
Yit was I nevere withouten purveyaunce
Of mariage n'of othere thinges eek:
I holde a mouses herte nought worth a leek
That hath but oon hole for to sterte° to, *flee*
And if that faile thanne is al ydo.
I bar him on hand he hadde enchaunted me
(My dame taughte me that subtiltee);
And eek I saide I mette° of him al night: *dreamed*
He wolde han slain me as I lay upright,° *facing up*
And al my bed was ful of verray blood—
"But yit I hope that ye shul do me good;
For blood bitokeneth gold, as me was taught."
And al was fals, I dremed of it right naught,
But as I folwed ay° my dames lore° *always / teaching*
As wel of that as of othere thinges more.
But now sire—lat me see, what shal I sayn?
Aha, by God, I have my tale again.
Whan that my ferthe housbonde was on beere,° *funeral bier*
I weep algate,° and made sory cheere, *constantly*
As wives moten, for it is usage,° *custom*
And with my coverchief covered my visage;
But for that I was purveyed° of a make,° *provided / mate*
I wepte but smale, and that I undertake.° *vouch*
To chirche was myn housbonde born amorwe° *next morning*
With neighebores that for him maden sorwe,
And Janekin oure clerk was oon of tho.
As help me God, whan that I saw him go
After the beere, me thoughte he hadde a paire
Of legges and of feet so clene and faire,

9. Services on the eve of holy days.

That al myn herte I yaf unto his hold.° *possession*
He was, I trowe, twenty winter old,
And I was fourty, if I shal saye sooth°— *truth*
But yit I hadde alway a coltes tooth:° *youthful tastes*
Gat-toothed° was I, and that bicam me weel; *gap-toothed*
I hadde the prente° of Sainte Venus seel.° *imprint / beauty mark*
As help me God, I was a lusty oon,
And fair and riche and yong and wel-bigoon,° *well situated*
And trewely, as mine housbondes tolde me,
I hadde the beste quoniam° mighte be. *you-know-what*
For certes I am al Venerien[1]
In feeling, and myn herte is Marcien:° *governed by Mars*
Venus me yaf my lust, my likerousnesse,
And Mars yaf me my sturdy hardinesse.
Myn ascendent° was Taur° and Mars therinne— *zodiac sign / Taurus*
Allas, allas, that evere love was sinne!
I folwed ay my inclinacioun
By vertu of my constellacioun;
That made me I coude nought withdrawe° *withhold*
My chambre of Venus from a good felawe.
Yit have I Martes° merk upon my face, *Mars's*
And also in another privee place.
For God so wis° be my savacioun,° *surely / salvation*
I loved nevere by no discrecioun,
But evere folwede° myn appetit, *followed*
Al were he short or long or blak or whit;
I took no keep, so that he liked° me, *pleased*
How poore he was, ne eek of what degree.
  What sholde I saye but at the monthes ende
This joly clerk Janekin that was so hende° *courteous*
Hath wedded me with greet solempnitee,
And to him yaf I al the land and fee° *property*
That evere was me yiven therbifore—
But afterward repented me ful sore:
He nolde suffre° no thing of my list.° *would allow / pleasure*
By God, he smoot° me ones on the list° *struck / ear*
For that I rente° out of his book a leef,° *tore / page*
That of the strook myn ere weex° al deef. *grew, became*
Stibourne I was as is a leonesse,
And of my tonge a verray jangleresse,° *chatterbox*
And walke I wolde, as I hadde doon biforn,
From hous to hous, although he hadde it sworn;° *prohibited*
For which he often times wolde preche,
And me of olde Romain geestes° teche, *Latin stories*
How he Simplicius Gallus[2] lafte his wif,
And hire forsook for terme of al his lif,

1. Governed by Venus, the planet.

2. Narrated in Valerius Maximus, *Facta et dicta memorabilia* 6.3.

Nought but for open-heveded° he hire sey° *bareheaded / saw*
Looking out at his dore upon a day.
  Another Romain[3] tolde he me by name
That, for his wif was at a someres° game *summer's*
Withouten his witing,° he forsook hire eke; *knowledge*
And thanne wolde he upon his Bible seeke
That ilke proverbe of Ecclesiaste[4]
Where he comandeth and forbedeth faste
Man shal nat suffre his wif go roule° aboute; *roam*
Thanne wolde he saye right thus withouten doute:
"Whoso that buildeth his hous al of salwes,° *willow branches*
And priketh° his blinde hors over the falwes,° *rides / open fields*
And suffreth his wif to go seeken halwes,° *shrines*
Is worthy to be hanged on the galwes."
But al for nought—I sette nought an hawe[5]
Of his proverbes n'of his olde sawe;
N'I wolde nat of him corrected be:
I hate him that my vices telleth me,
And so doon mo, God woot, of us than I.
This made him with me wood al outrely:° *utterly*
I nolde nought forbere° him in no cas. *would not submit*
  Now wol I saye you sooth, by Saint Thomas,
Why that I rente out of his book a leef,
For which he smoot me so that I was deef.
He hadde a book that gladly night and day
For his disport° he wolde rede alway. *amusement*
He cleped° it Valerie and Theofraste,[6] *called*
At which book he lough° alway ful faste; *laughed*
And eek ther was somtime a clerk at Rome,
A cardinal, that highte Saint Jerome,
That made a book again Jovinian;
In which book eek ther was Tertulan,
Crysippus, Trotula, and Helouis,
That was abbesse nat fer fro Paris;
And eek the Parables of Salomon,
Ovides Art, and bookes many oon—
And alle thise were bounden in oo volume.
And every night and day was his custume,° *custom*
Whan he hadde leiser and vacacioun
From other worldly occupacioun,
To reden in this book of wikked wives.

3. P. Sempronius Sophus, as related in Valerius Maximus, *Facta* 6.3.
4. Ecclesiasticus 25.25.
5. Hawthorn berry (i.e., little value).
6. Janekin's book is a collection of different works, nearly all of which are directed against women: Walter Map's fictitious letter entitled *Valerius's Dissuasion of Rufinus from Marrying* (Valerius); Theophrastus's *Golden Book on Marriage* (Theofraste); Saint Jerome's *Against Jovinian;* Tertullian's misogynist tracts on sexual continence (Tertulan); Crysippus's writings, mentioned by Jerome but otherwise unknown; *The Sufferings of Women*, an 11th-century book on gynecology by Trotula di Ruggiero, a female physician from Sicily (Trotula); the letters of the abbess Heloise to her lover Abelard (Helouis); the biblical Book of Proverbs (Parables of Salomon), and Ovid's *Art of Love*.

He knew of hem mo legendes and lives
Than been of goode wives in the Bible.
For trusteth wel, it is an impossible° *impossibility*
That any clerk wol speke good of wives,
But if it be of holy saintes lives,
N'of noon other womman nevere the mo—
Who painted the leon, tel me who?[7]
By God, if wommen hadden writen stories,
As clerkes han within hir oratories,
They wolde han writen of men more wikkednesse
Than al the merk of° Adam may redresse. *mark, sex*
The children of Mercurye and Venus[8]
Been in hir werking° ful contrarious:° *deeds / contradictory*
Mercurye loveth wisdom and science,
And Venus loveth riot° and dispence;° *celebration / expense*
And for hir diverse disposicioun
Each falleth in otheres exaltacioun,[9]
And thus, God woot, Mercurye is desolat° *powerless*
In Pisces wher Venus is exaltat,
And Venus falleth ther Mercurye is raised:
Therfore no womman of no clerk is praised.
The clerk, whan he is old and may nought do
Of Venus werkes worth his olde sho,° *shoe*
Thanne sit he down and writ in his dotage
That wommen can nat keepe hir mariage.
  But now to purpos why I tolde thee
That I was beten for a book, pardee:° *by God*
Upon a night Janekin, that was oure sire,° *master of our house*
Redde on his book as he sat by the fire
Of Eva[1] first, that for hir wikkednesse
Was al mankinde brought to wrecchednesse,
For which that Jesu Crist himself was slain
That boughte° us with his herte blood again— *redeemed*
Lo, heer expres of wommen may ye finde
That womman was the los° of al mankinde. *ruin*
  Tho° redde he me how Sampson loste his heres:° *then / hair*
Sleeping his lemman° kitte° it with hir sheres, *lover / cut*
Thurgh which treson loste he both his yën.
  Tho redde he me, if that I shal nat lien,
Of Ercules and of his Dianire,[2]
That caused him to sette himself afire.
No thing forgat he the sorwe and wo

7. In one of Aesop's fables, a lion asked this question when confronted by a painting of a man killing a lion, indicating that if a lion had painted the picture, the scene would have been very different.
8. Followers of Mercury, the god of rhetoric (scholars, poets, orators); followers of Venus (lovers).
9. Astrologically, one planet diminishes in influence as the other ascends.
1. Eve's temptation by the serpent was blamed for humanity's fall from grace and thus required Christ's incarnation to redeem the world.
2. Deianira gave her husband, Hercules, a robe which she believed was charmed with a love potion, but once he put it on, it burned his flesh so badly that he died.

That Socrates hadde with his wives two—
How Xantippa[3] caste pisse upon his heed:
This sely man sat stille as he were deed;
He wiped his heed, namore dorste he sayn
But "Er° that thonder stinte,° comth a rain." *before / stops*
Of Phasipha[4] that was the queene of Crete—
For shrewednesse° him thoughte the tale sweete— *wickedness*
Fy, speek namore, it is a grisly thing
Of hir horrible lust and hir liking.
Of Clytermistra[5] for hir lecherye
That falsly made hir housbonde for to die,
He redde it with ful good devocioun.
He tolde me eek for what occasioun
Amphiorax[6] at Thebes loste his lif:
Myn housbonde hadde a legende of his wif
Eriphylem, that for an ouche° of gold *trinket*
Hath prively unto the Greekes told
Wher that hir housbonde hidde him in a place,
For which he hadde at Thebes sory grace.
Of Livia[7] tolde he me and of Lucie:
They bothe made hir housbondes for to die,
That oon for love, that other was for hate;
Livia hir housbonde on an even late
Empoisoned hath for that she was his fo;
Lucia likerous loved hir housbonde so
That for he sholde alway upon hire thinke,
She yaf him swich a manere love-drinke
That he was deed er it were by the morwe.
And thus algates° housbondes han sorwe. *continually*
Thanne tolde he me how oon Latumius
Complained unto his felawe Arrius
That in his gardin growed swich a tree,
On which he saide how that his wives three
Hanged hemself for herte despitous.° *cruel*
"O leve brother," quod this Arrius,
"Yif° me a plante of thilke° blessed tree, *give / that same*
And in my gardin planted shal it be."
Of latter date of wives hath he red
That some han slain hir housbondes in hir bed
And lete hir lechour dighte° hire al the night, *screw*
Whan that the cors° lay in the floor upright;° *corpse / face up*
And some han driven nailes in hir brain
Whil that they sleepe, and thus they han hem slain;

3. Xanthippe was famous for nagging her husband, the philosopher Socrates.
4. Pasiphae, wife of Minos, became enamored of a bull, engendering the Minotaur.
5. Clytemnestra, queen of Mycenae, slew her husband Agamemnon when he returned from the Trojan War.
6. Amphiaraus died at the Siege of Thebes after listening to the advice of his wife, Eriphyle.
7. Livia poisoned her husband, Drusus, to satisfy her lover Sejanus; Lucia unwittingly poisoned her husband, the poet Lucretius, with a potion meant to keep him faithful.

Some han hem yiven poison in hir drinke.
He spak more harm than herte may bithinke,
And therwithal he knew of mo proverbes
Than in this world ther growen gras or herbes:
"Bet is," quod he, "thyn habitacioun
Be with a leon or a foul dragoun
Than with a wommman using° for to chide." *accustomed*
"Bet is," quod he, "hye in the roof abide
Than with an angry wif down in the hous:
They been so wikked and contrarious,
They haten that hir housbondes loveth ay."° *always*
He saide, "A womman cast hir shame away
Whan she cast of hir smok,"° and ferthermo, *slip*
"A fair womman, but she be chast also,
Is lik a gold ring in a sowes nose."
Who wolde weene, or who wolde suppose
The wo that in myn herte was and pine?
  And whan I sawgh he wolde nevere fine° *end*
To reden on this cursed book al night,
Al sodeinly three leves have I plight° *plucked*
Out of his book right as he redde, and eke
I with my fist so took° him on the cheeke *struck*
That in oure fir he fil bakward adown.
And up he sterte as dooth a wood° leoun, *enraged*
And with his fist he smoot me on the heed
That in the floor I lay as I were deed.
And whan he sawgh how stille that I lay,
He was agast,° and wolde have fled his way, *afraid*
Til atte laste out of my swough° I braide: *faint / arose*
"O hastou slain me, false thief?" I saide,
"And for my land thus hastou mordred me?
Er I be deed yit wol I kisse thee."
  And neer he cam and kneeled faire adown,
And saide, "Dere suster Alisoun,
As help me God, I shal thee nevere smite.
That I have doon, it is thyself to wite.° *blame*
Foryif it me, and that I thee biseeke."
And yit eftsoones° I hitte him on the cheeke, *immediately*
And saide, "Thief, thus muchel am I wreke.° *avenged*
Now wol I die: I may no lenger speke."
  But at the laste with muchel care and wo
We fille accorded by us selven two.
He yaf me al the bridel° in myn hand, *bridle, control*
To han the governance of hous and land,
And of his tonge and his hand also;
And made him brenne his book anoonright tho.
And whan that I hadde geten unto me
By maistrye° al the sovereinetee,° *skill / dominance*
And that he saide, "Myn owene trewe wif,

Do as thee lust° the terme of al thy lif, *please*
Keep thyn honour, and keep eek myn estat,"
After that day we hadde nevere debat.
God help me so, I was to him as kinde
As any wif from Denmark unto Inde,
And also trewe, and so was he to me.
I praye to God that sit in majestee,
So blesse his soule for his mercy dere.
Now wol I saye my tale if ye wol heere.

Another Interruption

The Frere lough whan he hadde herd al this:
"Now dame," quod he, "so have I joye or blis,
This is a long preamble of a tale."
And whan the Somnour herde the Frere gale,° *exclaim*
"Lo," quod the Somnour, "Goddes armes two,
A frere wol entremette him° everemo! *interfere*
Lo, goode men, a flye and eek a frere
Wol falle in every dissh and eek matere.
What spekestou of preambulacioun?
What, amble or trotte or pisse or go sitte down!
Thou lettest° oure disport in this manere." *hinder*
"Ye, woltou so, sire Somnour?" quod the Frere.
"Now by my faith, I shal er that I go
Telle of a somnour swich a tale or two
That al the folk shal laughen in this place."
"Now elles, Frere, I wol bishrewe thy face,"
Quod this Somnour, "and I bishrewe me,
But if I telle tales two or three
Of freres, er I come to Sidingborne,[8]
That I shal make thyn herte for to moorne—
For wel I woot thy pacience is goon."
Oure Hoste cride, "Pees, and that anoon!"
And saide, "Lat the womman telle hir tale:
Ye fare° as folk that dronken been of ale. *behave*
Do, dame, tel forth youre tale, and that is best."
"Al redy, sire," quod she, "right as you lest°— *it pleases*
If I have licence of this worthy Frere."
"Yis, dame," quod he, "tel forth and I wol heere."

The Wife of Bath's Tale

In th'olde dayes of the King Arthour,
Of which that Britouns° speken greet honour, *Bretons*
Al was this land fulfild° of faïrye: *filled*
The elf-queene° with hir joly compaignye *fairy queen*

8. Sittingbourne, a town about 40 miles from London.

Daunced ful ofte in many a greene mede°— *meadow*
This was the olde opinion as I rede;
I speke of many hundred yeres ago.
But now can no man see none elves mo,
For now the grete charitee and prayeres
Of limitours,[1] and othere holy freres,
That serchen every land and every streem,
As thikke as motes° in the sonne-beem, *dust particles*
Blessing halles, chambres, kichenes, bowres,° *bedrooms*
Citees, burghes,° castels, hye towres, *boroughs*
Thropes,° bernes,° shipnes,° dayeries— *villages / barns / stables*
This maketh that ther been no faïries.
For ther as wont° to walken was an elf *where there used*
Ther walketh now the limitour himself,
In undermeles° and in morweninges,° *afternoons / mornings*
And saith his Matins° and his holy thinges, *morning prayers*
As he gooth in his limitacioun.° *prescribed district*
Wommen may go saufly° up and down: *safely*
In every bussh or under every tree
Ther is noon other incubus[2] but he,
And he ne wol doon hem but dishonour.
  And so bifel it that this King Arthour
Hadde in his hous a lusty bacheler,° *young knight*
That on a day cam riding fro river,° *hunting waterfowl*
And happed that, allone as he was born,
He sawgh a maide walking him biforn;
Of which maide anoon, maugree hir heed,° *against her will*
By verray force he rafte° hir maidenheed; *stole*
For which oppression was swich clamour,
And swich pursuite° unto the King Arthour, *petitioning*
That dampned° was this knight for to be deed *condemned*
By cours of lawe, and sholde han lost his heed—
Paraventure° swich was the statut tho°— *as it happens / then*
But that the queene and othere ladies mo
So longe prayeden the king of grace,
Til he his lif him graunted in the place,
And yaf him to the queene, al at hir wille,
To chese° wheither she wolde him save or spille.° *decide / destroy*
The queene thanked the king with al hir might,
And after this thus spak she to the knight,
Whan that she saw hir time upon a day:
"Thou standest yit," quod she, "in swich array° *situation*
That of thy lif yit hastou no suretee.° *guarantee*
I graunte thee lif if thou canst tellen me
What thing it is that wommen most desiren:
Be war and keep thy nekke boon° from iren.° *bone / iron*

1. Friars licensed to beg within set districts.
2. Demon who fornicates with women.

And if thou canst nat tellen me anoon,
Yit wol I yive thee leve for to goon
A twelfmonth and a day to seeche° and lere° *seek out / learn*
An answere suffisant° in this matere, *satisfactory*
And suretee° wol I han er that thou pace,° *pledge / pass*
Thy body for to yeelden° in this place." *surrender*
Wo was this knight, and sorwefully he siketh.° *sighs*
But what, he may nat doon al as him liketh,
And atte laste he chees him° for to wende, *decided / travel*
And come again right at the yeres ende,
With swich answere as God wolde him purveye,° *provide*
And taketh his leve and wendeth forth his waye.
He seeketh every hous and every place
Wher as he hopeth for to finde grace,
To lerne what thing wommen love most.
But he ne coude arriven in no coost° *country*
Wher as he mighte finde in this matere
Two creatures according in fere.° *agreeing together*
Some saiden wommen loven best richesse;
Some saide honour, some saide jolinesse;° *pleasure*
Some riche array, some saiden lust abedde,
And ofte time to be widwe and wedde.
Some saide that oure herte is most esed
Whan that we been yflatered and yplesed—
He gooth ful neigh the soothe,° I wol nat lie: *near the truth*
A man shal winne us best with flaterye,
And with attendance and with bisinesse° *attentive service*
Been we ylimed,° bothe more and lesse. *ensnared*
And some sayen that we loven best
For to be free, and do right as us lest,° *pleases*
And that no man repreve° us of oure vice, *scold*
But saye that we be wise and no thing nice.° *foolish*
For trewely, ther is noon of us alle,
If any wight wol clawe us on the galle,° *rub a sore spot*
That we nil kike° for he saith us sooth:° *kick / the truth*
Assaye° and he shal finde it that so dooth. *try*
For be we nevere so vicious withinne,
We wol be holden° wise and clene of sinne. *considered*
And some sayn that greet delit han we
For to be holden stable° and eek secree,° *constant / discreet*
And in oo purpos stedefastly to dwelle,
And nat biwraye° thing that men us telle— *reveal*
But that tale is nat worth a rake-stele.° *rake handle*
Pardee,° we wommen conne no thing hele:° *by God / conceal*
Witnesse on Mida.[3] Wol ye heere the tale?
Ovide, amonges othere thinges smale,

3. Midas's story is recounted in Ovid's *Metamorphoses* 9.

Saide Mida hadde under his longe heres,
Growing upon his heed, two asses eres,
The whiche vice° he hidde as he best mighte *fault*
Ful subtilly from every mannes sighte,
That save his wif ther wiste of it namo.° *no one else know*
He loved hire most and trusted hire also.
He prayed hire that to no creature
She sholde tellen of his disfigure.° *deformity*
  She swoor him nay, for al this world to winne,
She nolde° do that vilainye or sinne *would not*
To make hir housbonde han so foul a name:
She nolde nat telle it for hir owene shame.
But nathelees, hir thoughte that she dyde° *would die*
That she so longe sholde a conseil° hide; *secret*
Hire thoughte it swal so sore aboute hir herte
That nedely° som word hire moste asterte,° *surely / come out*
And sith she dorste nat telle it to no man,
Down to a mareis° faste° by she ran— *marsh / close*
Til she cam there hir herte was afire—
And as a bitore° bombleth° in the mire, *heron / squawks*
She laide hir mouth unto the water down:
"Biwray° me nat, thou water, with thy soun,"° *betray / sound*
Quod she. "To thee I telle it and namo:
Myn housbonde hath longe asses eres two.
Now is myn herte al hool, now is it oute.
I mighte no lenger keepe it, out of doute."
Here may ye see, though we a time abide,
Yit oute it moot:° we can no conseil hide. *must*
The remenant of the tale if ye wol heere,
Redeth Ovide, and ther ye may it lere.° *learn*
  This knight of which my tale is specially,
Whan that he sawgh he mighte nat come therby—
This is to saye what wommen loven most—
Within his brest ful sorweful was his gost,° *spirit*
But hoom he gooth, he mighte nat sojurne:° *linger*
The day was come that hoomward moste he turne.
And in his way it happed him to ride
In al this care under a forest side,
Wher as he sawgh upon a daunce go
Of ladies foure and twenty and yit mo;
Toward the whiche daunce he drow° ful yerne,° *drew / gladly*
In hope that som wisdom sholde he lerne.
But certainly, er he cam fully there,
Vanisshed was this daunce, he niste° where. *did not know*
No creature sawgh he that bar lif,
Save on the greene he sawgh sitting a wif—
A fouler wight° ther may no man devise.° *creature / imagine*
Again the knight this olde wif gan rise,
And saide, "Sire knight, heer forth lith no way.° *road*

Telle me what ye seeken, by youre fay.° *faith*
Paraventure it may the better be:
Thise olde folk conne° muchel thing," quod she. *know*
"My leve moder,"° quod this knight, "certain, *dear mother*
I nam but° deed but if that I can sayn *am no more than*
What thing it is that wommen most desire.
Coude ye me wisse,° I wolde wel quite youre hire."° *inform / repay you*
"Plight° me thy trouthe° here in myn hand," quod she, *pledge / promise*
"The nexte thing that I requere thee,
Thou shalt it do, if it lie in thy might,
And I wol telle it you er it be night."
"Have heer my trouthe," quod the knight. "I graunte."
"Thanne," quod she, "I dar me wel avaunte° *brag*
Thy lif is sauf, for I wol stande therby.
Upon my lif the queene wol saye as I.
Lat see which is the pruddeste° of hem alle *proudest*
That wereth on a coverchief or a calle° *headdress*
That dar saye nay of that I shal thee teche.
Lat us go forth withouten lenger speeche."
Tho rouned° she a pistel° in his ere, *whispered / message*
And bad him to be glad and have no fere.
When they be comen to the court, this knight
Saide he hadde holde his day as he hadde hight,° *promised*
And redy was his answere, as he saide.
Ful many a noble wif, and many a maide,
And many a widwe—for that they been wise—
The queene hirself sitting as justise,° *judge*
Assembled been this answere for to heere,
And afterward this knight was bode appere.
To every wight comanded was silence,
And that the knight sholde telle in audience
What thing that worldly wommen loven best.
This knight ne stood nat stille° as dooth a best,° *silent / beast*
But to his question anoon answerde
With manly vois that al the court it herde.
"My lige° lady, generally," quod he, *liege*
"Wommen desire to have sovereinetee
As wel over hir housbonde as hir love,
And for to been in maistrye him above.
This is youre moste desir though ye me kille.
Dooth as you list: I am here at youre wille."
In al the court ne was ther wif ne maide
Ne widwe that contraried that he saide,
But saiden he was worthy han his lif.
And with that word up sterte that olde wif,
Which that the knight sawgh sitting on the greene;
"Mercy," quod she, "my soverein lady queene,
Er that youre court departe, do me right.
I taughte this answere unto the knight,

For which he plighte me his trouthe there
The firste thing I wolde him requere
He wolde it do, if it laye in his might.
Bifore the court thanne praye I thee, sire knight,"
Quod she, "that thou me take unto thy wif,
For wel thou woost° that I have kept° thy lif. *know / saved*
If I saye fals, say nay, upon thy fay."
This knight answerde, "Allas and wailaway,
I woot° right wel that swich was my biheeste.° *know / promise*
For Goddes love, as chees° a newe requeste: *choose*
Taak al my good and lat my body go."
"Nay thanne," quod she, "I shrewe° us bothe two. *curse*
For though that I be foul and old and poore,
I nolde° for al the metal ne for ore *would not wish*
That under erthe is grave° or lith above, *buried*
But if thy wif I were and eek thy love."
"My love," quod he. "Nay, my dampnacioun!
Allas, that any of my nacioun° *lineage*
Sholde evere so foule disparaged° be." *degraded*
But al for nought, th'ende is this, that he
Constrained was: he needes moste hire wedde,
And taketh his olde wif and gooth to bedde.
Now wolden some men saye, paraventure,
That for my necligence I do no cure
To tellen you the joy and al th'array
That at the feeste was that ilke day.
To which thing shortly answere I shal:
I saye ther nas no joye ne feeste at al;
Ther nas but hevinesse and muche sorwe.
For prively he wedded hire on morwe,° *in the morning*
And al day after hidde him as an owle,
So wo was him, his wif looked so foule.
Greet was the wo the knight hadde in his thought:
Whan he was with his wif abedde brought,
He walweth° and he turneth to and fro. *rolls over*
His olde wif lay smiling everemo,
And saide, "O dere housbonde, benedicite,° *bless us*
Fareth° every knight thus with his wif as ye? *behaves*
Is this the lawe of King Arthures hous?
Is every knight of his thus daungerous?° *reserved*
I am youre owene love and youre wif;
I am she which that saved hath youre lif;
And certes yit ne dide I you nevere unright.° *injustice*
Why fare° ye thus with me this firste night? *behave*
Ye faren like a man hadde lost his wit.
What is my gilt? For Goddes love, telle it,
And it shal been amended if I may."
"Amended!" quod this knight. "Allas, nay, nay,
It wol nat been amended neveremo.

Thou art so lothly° and so old also, *loathsome*
And therto comen of so lowe a kinde,° *breeding*
That litel wonder is though I walwe and winde.° *turn*
So wolde God myn herte wolde breste!"° *burst*
"Is this," quod she, "the cause of youre unreste?"
"Ye, certainly," quod he. "No wonder is."
"Now sire," quod she, "I coude amende al this,
If that me liste,° er it were dayes three, *it pleased me*
So° wel ye mighte bere you° unto me. *provided that / behave*
"But for ye speken of swich gentilesse° *nobility*
As is descended out of old richesse—
That therfore sholden ye be gentilmen—
Swich arrogance is nat worth an hen.
Looke who that is most vertuous alway,
Privee and apert,° and most entendeth ay *privately and publicly*
To do the gentil deedes that he can,
Taak him for the gretteste gentilman.
Crist wol° we claime of him oure gentilesse, *wishes*
Nat of oure eldres for hir 'old richesse.'
For though they yive us al hir heritage,
For which we claime to been of heigh parage,° *noble lineage*
Yit may they nat biquethe for no thing
To noon of us hir vertuous living,
That made hem gentilmen ycalled be,
And bad us folwen° hem in swich degree. *to follow*
"Wel can the wise poete of Florence,
That highte° Dant,[4] speken in this sentence;° *was called / opinion*
Lo, in swich manere rym is Dantes tale:
'Ful selde° up riseth by his braunches[5] smale *seldom*
Prowesse° of man, for God of his prowesse *excellence*
Wol that of him we claime oure gentilesse.'
For of oure eldres may we no thing claime
But temporel thing that man may hurte and maime.
Eek every wight woot° this as wel as I, *person knows*
If gentilesse were planted natureelly
Unto a certain linage down the line,
Privee and apert, thanne wolde they nevere fine° *end*
To doon of gentilesse the faire office°— *duty*
They mighte do no vilainye or vice.
"Taak fir and beer° it in the derkeste hous *bring*
Bitwixe this and the Mount of Caucasus,
And lat men shette° the dores and go thenne,° *shut / thence*
Yit wol the fir as faire lie and brenne
As twenty thousand men mighte it biholde:
His° office natureel ay° wol it holde, *its / always*
Up peril of my lif, til that it die.

4. Dante Alighieri, the 13th-century Italian poet, expressed similar views in his *Convivio*.

5. Branches (of his family tree).

Heer may ye see wel how that genterye° *gentility*
Is nat annexed° to possessioun, *connected*
Sith° folk ne doon hir operacioun° *since / their work*
Alway, as dooth the fir, lo, in his kinde.° *nature*
For God it woot, men may wel often finde
A lordes sone do shame and vilainye;
And he that wol han pris° of his gentrye,° *esteem / noble birth*
For he was boren of a gentil hous,
And hadde his eldres noble and vertuous,
And nil° himselven do no gentil deedes, *will not*
Ne folwen his gentil auncestre that deed is,
He nis nat gentil, be he duc or erl—
For vilaines sinful deedes maken a cherl.° *ruffian*
Thy gentilesse nis but renomee° *reputation*
Of thine auncestres for hir heigh bountee,° *generosity*
Which is a straunge° thing for thy persone. *foreign*
For gentilesse cometh fro God allone.
Thanne comth oure verray gentilesse of grace:
It was no thing biquethe us with oure place.
Thenketh how noble, as saith Valerius,[6]
Was thilke° Tullius Hostilius[7] *that*
That out of poverte roos to heigh noblesse.
Redeth Senek,[8] and redeth eek Boece:
Ther shul ye seen expres that no drede° is *doubt*
That he is gentil that dooth gentil deedes.
And therfore, leve housbonde, I thus conclude:
Al were it that mine auncestres weren rude,° *lowborn*
Yit may the hye God—and so hope I—
Graunte me grace to liven vertuously.
Thanne am I gentil whan that I biginne
To liven vertuously and waive° sinne. *avoid*
"And ther as ye of poverte me repreve,
The hye God, on whom that we bileve,
In wilful poverte chees to live his lif;
And certes every man, maiden, or wif
May understonde that Jesus, hevene king,
Ne wolde nat chese a vicious living.
Glad poverte is an honeste° thing, certain; *honorable*
This wol Senek and othere clerkes sayn.
Whoso that halt him paid of his poverte,[9]
I holde him riche al° hadde he nat a sherte.° *although / shirt*
He that coveiteth is a poore wight,
For he wolde han that is nat in his might;
But he that nought hath, ne coveiteth have,
Is riche, although we holde him but a knave.° *servant*

6. The Roman historian Valerius Maximus, in his *Facta et dicta memorabilia* 3.4.

7. The legendary third king of Rome who started as a shepherd.

8. Seneca, the Stoic author, in his *Epistle* 44; Boece: Boethius in his *Consolation of Philosophy*.

9. Whoever is satisfied with poverty.

Verray poverte it singeth proprely.
Juvenal[1] saith of poverte, 'Merily
The poore man, whan he gooth by the waye,
Biforn the theves he may singe and playe.'
Poverte is hateful good, and as I gesse,
A ful greet bringere out of bisinesse;° *worldly cares*
A greet amendere eek of sapience° *wisdom*
To him that taketh it in pacience;
Poverte is thing, although it seeme elenge,° *miserable*
Possession that no wight wol chalenge;
Poverte ful often, whan a man is lowe,
Maketh his God and eek himself to knowe;
Poverte a spectacle° is, as thinketh me, *eyeglass*
Thurgh which he may his verray freendes see.
And therfore, sire, sin that I nought you greve,
Of my poverte namore ye me repreve.
"Now sire, of elde° ye repreve me: *old age*
And certes sire, though noon auctoritee
Were in no book, ye gentils of honour
Sayn that men sholde an old wight° doon favour, *person*
And clepe° him fader for youre gentilesse— *call*
And auctours° shal I finden, as I gesse. *authorities*
"Now ther ye saye that I am foul and old:
Thanne drede you nought to been a cokewold,° *cuckold*
For filthe and elde, also mote I thee,
Been grete wardeins° upon chastitee. *guardians*
But nathelees, sin I knowe your delit,
I shal fulfille youre worldly appetit.
"Chees° now," quod she, "oon of thise thinges twaye: *choose*
To han me foul and old til that I deye
And be to you a trewe humble wif,
And nevere you displese in al my lif,
Or elles ye wol han me yong and fair,
And take youre aventure° of the repair° *chances / visits*
That shal be to youre hous by cause of me—
Or in som other place, wel may be.
Now chees youreselven wheither° that you liketh." *whichever*
This knight aviseth him° and sore siketh;° *considers / sighs*
But atte laste he saide in this manere:
"My lady and my love, and wif so dere,
I putte me in youre wise governaunce:
Cheseth youreself which may be most plesaunce
And most honour to you and me also.
I do no fors° the wheither of the two, *do not care*
For as you liketh it suffiseth° me." *satisfies*
"Thanne have I gete of you° maistrye," quod she, *won from you*
"Sin I may chese and governe as me lest?"° *it pleases*

1. The misogynist Roman poet in his *Satires* 10.21, 22.

"Ye, certes, wif," quod he. "I holde it best."
"Kisse me," quod she. "We be no lenger wrothe.° *opposed*
For by my trouthe, I wol be to you bothe—
This is to sayn, ye, bothe fair and good.
I praye to God that I mote sterven wood,° *die mad*
But I to you be al so good and trewe
As evere was wif sin that the world was newe.
And but I be tomorn° as fair to seene *in the morning*
As any lady, emperisse, or queene,
That is bitwixe the eest and eek the west,
Do with my lif and deeth right as you lest:
Caste up the curtin, looke how that it is."
And whan the knight sawgh verraily al this,
That she so fair was and so yong therto,
For joye he hente° hire in his armes two; *seized*
His herte bathed in a bath of blisse;
A thousand time arewe° he gan hire kisse, *in a row*
And she obeyed him in every thing
That mighte do him plesance or liking.
And thus they live unto hir lives ende
In parfit° joye. And Jesu Crist us sende *perfect*
Housbondes meeke, yonge, and fresshe abedde—
And grace t'overbide° hem that we wedde. *outlive*
And eek I praye Jesu shorte hir lives
That nought wol be governed by hir wives,
And olde and angry nigardes of dispence°— *misers in spending*
God sende hem soone a verray pestilence!

The Pardoner's Prologue and Tale There is something in Chaucer's Pardoner to unnerve practically everyone. The Pardoner's physiology blurs gender itself, his apparent homosexuality challenges the dominant heterosexual ordering of medieval society, his *Prologue* subverts the notion that the intent and effect of words are connected, and his willingness to convert religious discourse into cash undermines the very bases of faith. He initiates a sequence of moments in the later tales that threaten to puncture or tear the social fabric of the Canterbury company.

The Pardoner and "his freend and his compeer," the Summoner, are the last two pilgrims described in *The General Prologue*, reflecting the distaste with which such marginal clergy were often regarded in the period. Summoners were the policing branch of the ecclesiastical courts, paid to bring in transgressors against the canon law. Pardoners had the job, criticized even within the church, of exchanging indulgences for cash. The sufferings of Christ and saintly martyrs, it was thought, had left the church with a legacy of goodness. This could be transferred to sinners, freeing them from a period in Purgatory, if they proved their penitence (among other ways) by gifts to support good works such as the hospital for which the Pardoner worked.

The Pardoner has turned this part of the structure of penitence into a profit center. In his own *Prologue*, the Pardoner is boastfully explicit about this:

> For myn entente is nat but for to winne,
> And no thing for correccion of sinne . . .

This merciless equation of his verbal power with cash profit deeply subverts the logic of Christian language and the priestly role in salvation. These are replaced by language working in a strange self-consuming circle: the Pardoner brilliantly achieves the very sin his sermon most vituperates.

The Pardoner's physiology—he has either lost his testicles or never had them—may emblematize this exploitation of language emptied of spiritual intention. His uncertain or incomplete gender, though, also challenges the fundamental distinctions of the body within the medieval social economy, as does his apparent homosexuality. The Pardoner's theatrical self-presentation, abetted by rhetorical techniques he lovingly describes, draws the fascinated if queasy attention of his audience and seems to provide him a monstrous though (as it turns out) fragile power.

The Pardoner's tale of three rioters and their encounter with death is actually folded into his Prologue as an exemplum, an illustrative story, in the sermon against cupidity he proposes to offer as a sample of his skills. Yet the Pardoner's obsession with bodies in extremity, seeking or denying death, skeletal or gorged, pulls against his tale as a parable of greed. The tale draws toward its close in a scene of rage, exposure, and angry silence, which threatens to undo the pilgrim society, rather as the Pardoner and his discourse have threatened so much of the broader social contract. The Knight steps in, though, and almost bullies the Host and the Pardoner into a kiss of peace. This ritual gesture, nearly as empty of real goodwill as any of the Pardoner's most cynical words, does allow the shaken group to continue on their way, even as it hints at the emptiness that may hide in other, less openly challenged systems of value in the tales and their world.

The Pardoner's Prologue

The Introduction

Oure Hoste gan to swere as he were wood;° *mad*
"Harrow," quod he, "by nailes[1] and by blood,
This was a fals cherl° and a fals justice.°[2] *villain / judge*
As shameful deeth as herte may devise
Come to thise juges and hir advocats.° *lawyers*
Algate° this sely° maide is slain, allas! *anyway / innocent*
Allas, too dere boughte she beautee!
Wherfore I saye alday° that men may see *always*
The yiftes of Fortune and of Nature
Been cause of deeth to many a creature.
As bothe yiftes° that I speke of now, *gifts*
Men han ful ofte more for harm than prow.° *profit*
"But trewely, myn owene maister dere,
This is a pitous tale for to heere.
But nathelees, passe over, is no fors:° *concern*
I praye to God so save thy gentil° cors,° *noble / body*
And eek thine urinals[3] and thy jurdones,° *chamber pots*
Thyn ipocras and eek thy galiones,[4]
And every boiste° ful of thy letuarye°— *box / medicine*
God blesse hem, and oure lady Sainte Marye.
So mote I theen,° thou art a propre man, *so may I prosper*

1. Nails (of Christ's cross).
2. Harry Bailey, the host, is responding to *The Physician's Tale* and the story of a young woman named Virginia whose father kills her rather than surrender her to a wicked judge and his accomplice.
3. Physician's vessels for analyzing urine samples.
4. Medicines named after the ancient Greek physicians Hippocrates and Galen.

And lik a prelat,° by Saint Ronian![5] *Church officer*
Saide I nat wel? I can nat speke in terme.° *jargon*
But wel I woot,° thou doost myn herte to erme° *know / grieve*
That I almost have caught a cardinacle.° *heart condition*
By corpus bones,[6] but if I have triacle,° *medicine*
Or elles a draughte of moiste° and corny° ale, *fresh / malted*
Or but I heere anoon a merye tale,
Myn herte is lost for pitee of this maide.
"Thou bel ami,[7] thou Pardoner," he saide,
"Tel us som mirthe or japes° right anoon." *joke*
"It shal be doon," quod he, "by Saint Ronian.
But first," quod he, "here at this ale-stake° *tavern marker*
I wol bothe drinke and eten of a cake."° *loaf of bread*
And right anoon thise gentils gan to crye,
"Nay, lat him telle us of no ribaudye.° *obscenity*
Tel us som moral thing that we may lere,° *learn*
Som wit, and thanne wol we gladly heere."
"I graunte, ywis,"° quod he, "but I moot° thinke *certainly / must*
Upon som honeste° thing whil that I drinke." *honorable*

The Prologue

Lordinges—quod he—in chirches whan I preche,
I paine me to han an hautein° speeche, *loud*
And ringe it out as round as gooth a belle,
For I can al by rote° that I telle. *know it all by heart*
My theme is alway oon,° and evere was: *the same*
Radix malorum est cupiditas.[8]
First I pronounce whennes that I come,
And thanne my bulles° shewe I alle and some: *indulgences*
Oure lige lordes seel[9] on my patente,° *license*
That shewe I first, my body to warente,° *safeguard*
That no man be so bold, ne preest ne clerk,
Me to destourbe of Cristes holy werk.
And after that thanne telle I forth my tales—
Bulles of popes and of cardinales,
Of patriarkes and bisshopes I shewe,
And in Latin I speke a wordes fewe,
To saffron° with my predicacioun,° *season / preaching*
And for to stire hem to devocioun.
Thanne shewe I forth my longe crystal stones,° *jars*
Ycrammed ful of cloutes° and of bones— *rags*
Relikes been they, as weenen they eechoon.° *they all suppose*
Thanne have I in laton° a shulder-boon *brazened*
Which that was of an holy Jewes sheep.

5. St. Ronan, a Scottish saint, with a possible pun on "runnions," the male sexual organs.
6. A confused oath mixing God's body and God's bones.
7. Fair friend (French, affected).
8. Greed is the root of all evil.
9. Seal of our liege lord (i.e., the Pope).

"Goode men," I saye, "take of my wordes keep:° *notice*
If that this boon be wasshe in any welle,
If cow, or calf, or sheep, or oxe swelle,
That any worm° hath ete or worm ystonge, *snake*
Take water of that welle and wassh his tonge,
And it is hool° anoon. And ferthermoor, *healthy*
Of pokkes° and of scabbe and every soor *pox*
Shal every sheep be hool that of this welle
Drinketh a draughte. Take keep eek that I telle:
If that the goode man that the beestes oweth° *owns*
Wol every wike,° er that the cok him croweth, *week*
Fasting drinken of this welle a draughte—
As thilke° holy Jew oure eldres taughte— *that*
His beestes and his stoor° shal multiplye. *stock*
"And sire, also it heleth jalousye:
For though a man be falle in jalous rage
Lat maken with this water his potage,° *soup*
And nevere shal he more his wif mistriste,
Though he the soothe° of hir defaute wiste,° *truth / offense knows*
Al hadde she taken preestes two or three.
"Here is a mitein° eek that ye may see: *mitten*
He that his hand wol putte in this mitein
He shal have multiplying of his grain,
Whan he hath sowen, be it whete or otes—
So that he offre pens° or elles grotes.° *pennies / silver coins*
"Goode men and wommen, oo thing warne I you:
If any wight° be in this chirche now *person*
That hath doon sinne horrible, that he
Dar nat for shame of it yshriven° be, *confessed*
Or any womman, be she yong or old,
That hath ymaked hir housbonde cokewold,° *cuckold*
Swich folk shal have no power ne no grace
To offren to my relikes in this place;
And whoso findeth him out of swich blame,
He wol come up and offre in Goddes name,
And I assoile° him by the auctoritee *absolve*
Which that by bulle ygraunted was to me."
By this gaude° have I wonne, yeer by yeer, *trick*
An hundred mark[1] sith I was pardoner.
I stonde lik a clerk in my pulpet,
And whan the lewed° peple is down yset, *ignorant*
I preche so as ye han herd bifore,
And telle an hundred false japes° more. *tricks*
Thanne paine I me to strecche forth the nekke,
And eest and west upon the peple I bekke° *nod*
As dooth a douve,° sitting on a berne;° *dove / barn*

1. About 66 pounds.

Mine handes and my tonge goon so yerne° *fast*
That it is joye to see my bisinesse.
Of avarice and of swich cursednesse
Is al my preching, for to make hem free° *generous*
To yiven hir pens, and namely unto me,
For myn entente is nat but for to winne,° *profit*
And no thing for correccion of sinne:
I rekke° nevere whan that they been beried° *care / buried*
Though that hir soules goon a-blakeberied.[2]
For certes, many a predicacioun
Comth ofte time of yvel entencioun:
Som for plesance of folk and flaterye,
To been avaunced by ypocrisye,
And som for vaine glorye, and som for hate;
For whan I dar noon otherways debate,
Thanne wol I stinge him with my tonge smerte° *hurting*
In preching, so that he shal nat asterte° *escape*
To been defamed falsly, if that he
Hath trespassed to my bretheren or to me.
For though I telle nought his propre name,
Men shal wel knowe that it is the same
By signes and by othere circumstaunces.
Thus quite° I folk that doon us displesaunces;° *repay / trouble*
Thus spete I out my venim under hewe° *color*
Of holinesse, to seeme holy and trewe.
But shortly myn entente I wol devise:° *describe*
I preche of no thing but for coveitise;° *greed*
Therfore my theme is yit and evere was
Radix malorum est cupiditas.
Thus can I preche again that same vice
Which that I use, and that is avarice.
But though myself be gilty in that sinne,
Yit can I make other folk to twinne° *separate*
From avarice, and sore to repente—
But that is nat my principal entente:
I preche no thing but for coveitise.
Of this matere it oughte ynough suffise.
Thanne telle I hem ensamples° many oon *exemplary tales*
Of olde stories longe time agoon,
For lewed peple loven tales olde—
Swiche thinges can they wel reporte° and holde.° *repeat / remember*
What, trowe° ye that whiles I may preche, *believe*
And winne gold and silver for I teche,
That I wol live in poverte wilfully?
Nay, nay, I thoughte it nevere, trewely,
For I wol preche and begge in sondry landes;

2. Looking for blackberries.

I wol nat do no labour with mine handes,
Ne make baskettes and live therby,
By cause I wol nat beggen idelly.° *in vain*
I wol none of the Apostles countrefete:° *imitate*
I wol have moneye, wolle,° cheese, and whete, *wool*
Al were it yiven of the pooreste page,° *servant*
Or of the pooreste widwe in a village—
Al sholde hir children sterve° for famine. *die*
Nay, I wol drinke licour of the vine
And have a joly wenche in every town.
But herkneth, lordinges, in conclusioun,
Youre liking is that I shal telle a tale:
Now have I dronke a draughte of corny ale,
By God, I hope I shal you telle a thing
That shal by reson been at youre liking;
For though myself be a ful vicious man,
A moral tale yit I you telle can,
Which I am wont to preche for to winne.
Now holde youre pees, my tale I wol biginne.

The Pardoner's Tale

In Flandres whilom° was a compaignye *once*
Of yonge folk that haunteden° folye— *practiced*
As riot, hasard, stewes,[1] and tavernes,
Wher as with harpes, lutes, and gвисernes° *guitars*
They daunce and playen at dees° bothe day and night, *dice*
And ete also and drinke over hir might,
Thurgh which they doon the devel sacrifise
Withinne that develes temple in cursed wise
By superfluitee° abhominable. *overindulgence*
Hir othes been so grete and so dampnable
That it is grisly for to heere hem swere:
Oure blessed Lordes body they totere°— *rip apart*
Hem thoughte that Jewes rente° him nought ynough. *tore*
And eech of hem at otheres sinne lough.° *laughed*
And right anoon thanne comen tombesteres,° *dancing girls*
Fetis° and smale,° and yonge frutesteres,[2] *elegant / slender*
Singeres with harpes, bawdes,° wafereres°— *pimps / cake sellers*
Whiche been the verray develes officeres,
To kindle and blowe the fir of lecherye
That is annexed° unto glotonye:° *connected / gluttony*
The Holy Writ take I to my witnesse
That luxure° is in win and dronkenesse. *lechery*
Lo, how that dronken Lot[3] unkindely° *against nature*
Lay by his doughtres two unwitingly:

1. Such as carousing, gambling, brothels.
2. Girls selling fruit.
3. Lot, the nephew of Abraham, whose story is told in Genesis 19.30–38.

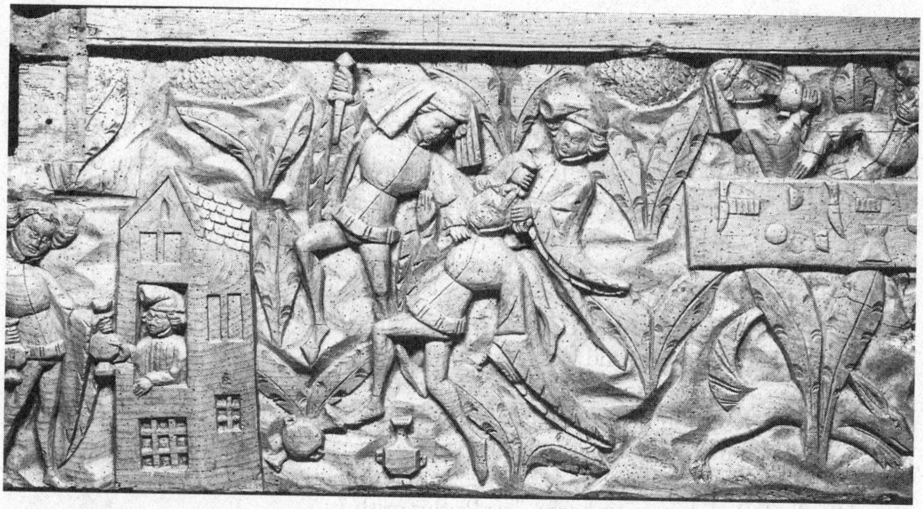

Detail from a carved chest, c. 1410. This large wooden panel is the surviving half of the front of a massive chest. It presents scenes from *The Pardoner's Tale:* at left, the youngest rioter buys wine; in the center, his two companions stab him to death; at right, they die from the wine their companion had poisoned. The composition and carving have much of the energy and economical narrative style of the tale itself. Produced about a decade after Chaucer's death, the panel reflects the impact of his tales in settings very different from those that supported such grand aristocratic productions as the Ellesmere manuscript, created around the same time (see Color Plate 9 and page 314).

So dronke he was he niste what he wroughte.° *knew not what he did*
Herodes,[4] who so wel the stories soughte,
Whan he of win was repleet at his feeste,
Right at his owene table he yaf his heeste° *command*
To sleen° the Baptist John, ful giltelees. *slay*
　Senek[5] saith a good word doutelees:
He saith he can no difference finde
Bitwixe a man that is out of his minde
And a man which that is dronkelewe,° *drunk*
But that woodnesse, yfallen in a shrewe,[6]
Persevereth lenger than dooth dronkenesse.
O glotonye, ful of cursednesse!
O cause first of oure confusioun!° *ruin*
O original of oure dampnacioun,
Til Crist hadde bought° us with his blood again! *redeemed*
Lo, how dere, shortly for to sayn,
Abought was thilke° cursed vilainye; *that*
Corrupt was al this world for glotonye:
Adam oure fader and his wif also
Fro Paradis to labour and to wo

4. King Herod, who was enticed by Salome into bringing her the head of John the Baptist (Mark 6.17–29, Matthew 14.1–12).

5. The stoic author Seneca in his *Epistle* 83.18.493–97.

6. Madness, occurring in a wicked person.

Were driven for that vice, it is no drede.° *doubt*
For whil that Adam fasted, as I rede,
He was in Paradis; and whan that he
Eet of the fruit defended° on a tree, *forbidden*
Anoon he was out cast to wo and paine.
O glotonye, on thee wel oughte us plaine!° *lament*
O, wiste a man how manye maladies
Folwen of° excesse and of glotonies, *result from*
He wolde been the more mesurable° *moderate*
Of his diete, sitting at his table.
Allas, the shorte throte, the tendre mouth,
Maketh that eest and west and north and south,
In erthe, in air, in water, men to swinke,° *labor*
To gete a gloton daintee mete and drinke.
Of this matere, O Paul, wel canstou trete:° *discuss*
"Mete unto wombe, and wombe° eek unto mete, *belly*
Shal God destroyen bothe," as Paulus saith.[7]
Allas, a foul thing is it, by my faith,
To saye this word, and fouler is the deede
Whan man so drinketh of the white and rede° *white and red wines*
That of his throte he maketh his privee° *toilet*
Thurgh thilke cursed superfluitee.
The Apostle[8] weeping saith ful pitously,
"Ther walken manye of which you told have I—
saye it now weeping with pitous vois—
They been enemies of Cristes crois,° *cross*
Of whiche the ende is deeth—wombe is hir god!"
O wombe, O bely, O stinking cod,° *bag*
Fulfilled of dong° and of corrupcioun! *dung*
At either ende of thee foul is the soun.° *sound*
How greet labour and cost is thee to finde!° *provide for*
Thise cookes, how they stampe and straine and grinde,
And turnen substance into accident[9]
To fulfillen al thy likerous talent!° *greedy desire*
Out of the harde bones knokke they
The mary,° for they caste nought away *marrow*
That may go thurgh the golet° softe and soote.° *gullet / sweet*
Of spicerye of leef and bark and roote
Shal been his sauce ymaked by delit,
To make him yit a newer appetit.
But certes, he that haunteth swiche delices° *delicacies*
Is deed whil that he liveth in tho° vices. *those*
A lecherous thing is win, and dronkenesse
Is ful of striving° and of wrecchednesse. *quarreling*
O dronke man, disfigured is thy face!

7. St. Paul in 1 Corinthians 6.13.
8. St. Paul, in Philippians 3.18–19.
9. A learned joke about the Eucharist where, in Catholic doctrine, the essence ("substance") of bread and wine is transformed into the body and blood of Christ, though their form ("accident") remains unchanged.

Sour is thy breeth, foul artou to embrace!
And thurgh thy dronke nose seemeth the soun
As though thou saidest ay° "Sampsoun, Sampsoun." *always*
And yit, God woot,° Sampson drank nevere win. *knows*
Thou fallest as it were a stiked swin;° *stuck pig*
Thy tonge is lost, and al thyn honeste cure,° *care for honor*
For dronkenesse is verray sepulture° *grave*
Of mannes wit and his discrecioun.
In whom that drinke hath dominacioun
He can no conseil keepe, it is no drede.
Now keepe you fro the white and fro the rede—
And namely fro the white win of Lepe[1]
That is to selle in Fisshstreete or in Chepe:[2]
The win of Spaine creepeth subtilly[3]
In othere wines growing faste° by, *close*
Of which ther riseth swich fumositee° *vapors*
That whan a man hath dronken draughtes three
And weeneth that he be at hoom in Chepe,
He is in Spaine, right at the town of Lepe,
Nat at The Rochele ne at Burdeux town;
And thanne wol he sayn "Sampsoun, Sampsoun."
But herkneth, lordinges, oo word I you praye,
That alle the soverein actes,° dar I saye, *excellent deeds*
Of victories in the Olde Testament,
Thurgh verray God that is omnipotent,
Were doon in abstinence and in prayere:
Looketh the Bible and ther ye may it lere.° *learn*
Looke Attilla, the grete conquerour,[4]
Deide in his sleep with shame and dishonour,
Bleeding at his nose in dronkenesse:
A capitain sholde live in sobrenesse.
And overal this, aviseth you right wel
What was comanded unto Lamuel[5]—
Nat Samuel, but Lamuel, saye I—
Redeth the Bible and finde it expresly,
Of win-yiving° to hem that han° justise: *wine-serving / dispense*
Namore of this, for it may wel suffise.
And now that I have spoken of glotonye,
Now wol I you defende hasardrye:° *gambling*
Hasard is verray moder of lesinges,° *lies*
And of deceite and cursed forsweringes,
Blaspheme of Crist, manslaughtre, and wast° also *waste*
Of catel° and of time; and ferthermo, *property*

1. Wine-growing region in Spain.
2. Commercial districts in London.
3. Chaucer is referring to the illegal practice of using cheap wine (here, Spanish wine from Lepe) to dilute more expensive wines (from the neighboring French provinces of La Rochelle and Bordeaux).
4. Attila the Hun died on his wedding night from excessive drinking.
5. Biblical king of Massa, warned against drinking in Proverbs 31.4.

It is repreve° and contrarye of honour *reprobate*
For to been holden a commune hasardour,
And evere the hyer he is of estat
The more is he holden desolat.° *dissolute*
If that a prince useth hasardrye,
In alle governance and policye
He is, as by commune opinioun,
Yholde the lasse in reputacioun.
   Stilbon,[6] that was a wis embassadour,
Was sent to Corinthe in ful greet honour
Fro Lacedomye° to make hir alliaunce, *Sparta*
And whan he cam him happede parchaunce
That alle the gretteste that were of that lond
Playing at the hasard he hem foond,
For which as soone as it mighte be
He stal him hoom again to his contree,
And saide, "Ther wol I nat lese° my name, *lose*
N'I wol nat take on me so greet defame
You to allye unto none hasardours:
Sendeth othere wise embassadours,
For by my trouthe, me were levere° die *I would rather*
Than I you sholde to hasardours allye.
For ye that been so glorious in honours
Shal nat allye you with hasardours
As by my wil, ne as by my tretee."
This wise philosophre, thus saide he.
   Looke eek that to the king Demetrius
The King of Parthes,[7] as the book saith us,
Sente him a paire of dees of gold in scorn,
For he hadde used hasard therbiforn,
For which he heeld his glorye or his renown
At no value or reputacioun.
Lordes may finden other manere play
Honeste ynough to drive the day away.
   Now wol I speke of othes false and grete
A word or two, as olde bookes trete:
   Greet swering is a thing abhominable,
And fals swering is yit more reprevable.° *reprehensible*
The hye God forbad swering at al—
Witnesse on Mathew. But in special
Of swering saith the holy Jeremie,[8]
"Thou shalt swere sooth° thine othes and nat lie, *truly*
And swere in doom° and eek in rightwisnesse, *judgment*
But idel swering is a cursednesse."
   Biholde and see that in the firste Table° *tablet*
Of hye Goddes heestes° honorable *commandments*

6. Possibly referring to the Greek philosopher Stilbo or Chilon.

7. Parthia in northern Persia.

8. The prophet Jeremiah (4.2).

How that the seconde heeste of him is this:
"Take nat my name in idel or amis."
Lo, rather° he forbedeth swich swering *sooner*
Than homicide, or many a cursed thing.
I saye that as by ordre thus it stondeth—
This knoweth that° his heestes understondeth *he who*
How that the seconde heeste of God is that.
And fertherover, I wol thee telle al plat° *flatly*
That vengeance shal nat parten from his hous
That of his othes is too outrageous.
"By Goddes precious herte!" and "By his nailes!"
And "By the blood of Crist that is in Hailes,[9]
Sevene is my chaunce, and thyn is cink and traye!"° *five and three*
"By Goddes armes, if thou falsly playe
This daggere shal thurghout thyn herte go!"
This fruit cometh of the bicche bones° two— *cursed dice*
Forswering, ire, falsnesse, homicide.
Now for the love of Crist that for us dyde,
Lete° youre othes bothe grete and smale. *leave off*
But sires, now wol I telle forth my tale.
  Thise riotoures° three of whiche I telle, *revelers*
Longe erst er° prime° ronge of any belle, *before / 6 A.M.*
Were set hem in a taverne to drinke,
And as they sat they herde a belle clinke
Biforn a cors° was caried to his grave. *corpse*
That oon of hem gan callen to his knave:° *servant*
"Go bet,"° quod he, "and axe redily *quickly*
What cors is this that passeth heer forby,
And looke that thou reporte his name weel."
  "Sire," quod this boy, "it needeth neveradeel:[1]
It was me told er ye cam heer two houres.
He was, pardee,° an old felawe of youres, *by God*
And sodeinly he was yslain tonight,
Fordronke° as he sat on his bench upright; *very drunk*
Ther cam a privee° thief men clepeth° Deeth, *stealthy / call*
That in this contree al the peple sleeth,° *slays*
And with his spere he smoot his herte atwo,
And wente his way withouten wordes mo.
He hath a thousand slain this pestilence.° *during this plague*
And maister, er ye come in his presence,
Me thinketh that it were necessarye
For to be war of swich an adversarye;
Beeth redy for to meete him everemore:
Thus taughte me my dame.° I saye namore." *mother*
  "By Sainte Marye," saide this taverner,
"The child saith sooth,° for he hath slain this yeer, *truth*

9. Hales Abbey in Gloucestershire owned a relic of Christ's blood.

1. Is not necessary in the least.

Henne° over a mile, within a greet village, *from here*
Bothe man and womman, child and hine° and page.° *farmhand / servant*
I trowe his habitacion be there.
To been avised° greet wisdom it were *warned*
Er that he dide a man a dishonour."
"Ye, Goddes armes," quod this riotour,
"Is it swich peril with him for to meete?
I shal him seeke by way and eek by streete,
I make avow to Goddes digne° bones. *worthy*
Herkneth, felawes, we three been alle ones:
Lat eech of us holde up his hand to other
And eech of us bicome otheres brother,
And we wol sleen this false traitour Deeth.
He shal be slain, he that so manye sleeth,
By Goddess dignitee, er it be night."
Togidres han thise three hir trouthes° plight° *words of honor / pledged*
To live and dien eech of hem with other,
As though he were his owene ybore° brother. *born*
And up they sterte, al dronken in this rage,
And forth they goon towardes that village
Of which the taverner hadde spoke biforn.
And many a grisly ooth thanne han they sworn,
And Cristes blessed body they torente:° *tore apart*
Deeth shal be deed if that they may him hente.° *capture*
Whan they han goon nat fully, half a mile,
Right as they wolde han treden° over a stile, *stepped*
An old man and a poore with hem mette;
This olde man ful mekely hem grette,° *greeted*
And saide thus, "Now lordes, God you see."° *look after*
The pruddeste° of thise riotoures three *proudest*
Answerde again, "What, carl with sory grace,° *unlucky fellow*
Why artou al forwrapped° save thy face? *bundled up*
Why livestou so longe in so greet age?"
This olde man gan looke in his visage,
And saide thus, "For I ne can nat finde
A man, though that I walked into Inde,
Neither in citee ne in no village,
That wolde chaunge his youthe for myn age;
And therfore moot I han° myn age stille, *I must have*
As longe time as it is Goddes wille.
"Ne Deeth, allas, ne wol nat have my lif.
Thus walke I lik a restelees caitif,° *wretch*
And on the ground which is my modres° gate *mother's*
I knokke with my staf bothe erly and late,
And saye, 'Leve° moder, leet me in: *dear*
Lo, how I vanisshe, flessh and blood and skin.
Allas, whan shal my bones been at reste?
Moder, with you wolde I chaunge° my cheste° *exchange / strongbox*
That in my chambre longe time hath be,

Ye, for an haire-clout° to wrappe me.' *winding sheet*
But yit to me she wol nat do that grace,
For which ful pale and welked° is my face. *withered*
But sires, to you it is no curteisye
To speken to an old man vilainye,° *discourtesy*
But he trespasse in word or elles in deede.
In Holy Writ ye may yourself wel rede,
'Agains an old man, hoor° upon his heed, *grey*
Ye shal arise.' Wherfore I yive you reed,° *advice*
Ne dooth unto an old man noon harm now,
Namore than that ye wolde men dide to you
In age, if that ye so longe abide.
And God be with you wher ye go or ride:
I moot go thider as I have to go."
"Nay, olde cherl, by God thou shalt nat so,"
Saide this other hasardour anoon.
"Thou partest nat so lightly,° by Saint John! *easily*
Thou speke right now of thilke traitour Deeth,
That in this contree alle oure freendes sleeth:
Have here my trouthe, as thou art his espye,
Tel wher he is, or thou shalt it abye,° *pay for*
By God and by the holy sacrament!
For soothly thou art oon of his assent° *in league with him*
To sleen us yonge folk, thou false thief."
"Now sires," quod he, "if that ye be so lief° *eager*
To finde Deeth, turne up this crooked way,
For in that grove I lafte him, by my fay,
Under a tree, and ther he wol abide:
Nat for youre boost he wol him no thing hide.
See ye that ook?° Right ther ye shal him finde. *oak*
God save you, that boughte again° mankinde, *redeemed*
And you amende." Thus saide this olde man.
And everich of thise riotoures ran
Til he cam to that tree, and ther they founde
Of florins° fine of gold ycoined rounde *gold coins*
Wel neigh an eighte busshels as hem thoughte—
Ne lenger thanne after Deeth they soughte,
But eech of hem so glad was of the sighte,
For that the florins been so faire and brighte,
That down they sette hem by this precious hoord.
The worste of hem he spak the firste word:
"Bretheren," quod he, "take keep what that I saye:
My wit is greet though that I bourde° and playe. *joke*
This tresor hath Fortune unto us yiven
In mirthe and jolitee oure lif to liven,
And lightly as it cometh so wol we spende.
Ey, Goddes precious dignitee, who wende° *would suppose*
Today that we sholde han so fair a grace?
But mighte this gold be caried fro this place

Hoom to myn hous—or elles unto youres—
For wel ye woot that al this gold is oures—
Thanne were we in heigh felicitee.° *happiness*
But trewely, by daye it mighte nat be:
Men wolde sayn that we were theves stronge,° *flagrant*
And for oure owene tresor doon us honge.° *have us hanged*
This tresor moste ycaried be by nighte,
As wisely and as slyly as it mighte.
Therfore I rede° that cut° amonges us alle *advise / lots*
Be drawe, and lat see wher the cut wol falle;
And he that hath the cut with herte blithe° *happy*
Shal renne to the town, and that ful swithe,° *swiftly*
And bringe us breed and win ful prively;
And two of us shal keepen subtilly
This tresor wel, and if he wol nat tarye,
Whan it is night we wol this tresor carye
By oon assent wher as us thinketh best."
That oon of hem the cut broughte in his fest° *fist*
And bad hem drawe and looke wher it wol falle;
And it fil on the yongeste of hem alle,
And forth toward the town he wente anoon.
And also soone as that he was agoon,
That oon of hem spak thus unto that other:
"Thou knowest wel thou art my sworen brother;
Thy profit wol I telle thee anoon:
Thou woost wel that oure felawe is agoon,
And here is gold, and that ful greet plentee,
That shal departed° been among us three. *divided*
But nathelelees, if I can shape° it so *arrange*
That it departed were among us two,
Hadde I nat doon a freendes turn to thee?"
That other answerde, "I noot° how that may be: *do not know*
He woot° that the gold is with us twaye. *knows*
What shal we doon? What shal we to him saye?"
"Shal it be conseil°?" saide the firste shrewe.° *secret / villain*
"And I shal telle in a wordes fewe
What we shul doon, and bringe it wel aboute."
"I graunte," quod that other, "out of doute,
That by my trouthe I wol thee nat biwraye."° *betray*
"Now," quod the firste, "thou woost wel we be twaye,
And two of us shal strenger be than oon:
Looke whan that he is set that right anoon
Aris as though thou woldest with him playe,
And I shal rive° him thurgh the sides twaye, *stab*
Whil that thou strugelest with him as in game,
And with thy daggere looke thou do the same;
And thanne shal al this gold departed be,
My dere freend, bitwixe thee and me.
Thanne we may bothe oure lustes° al fulfille, *desires*

And playe at dees right at oure owene wille."
And thus accorded been thise shrewes twaye
To sleen the thridde, as ye han herd me saye.
This yongeste, which that wente to the town,
Ful ofte in herte he rolleth up and down
The beautee of thise florins newe and brighte.
"O Lord," quod he, "if so were that I mighte
Have al this tresor to myself allone,
Ther is no man that liveth under the trone° *throne*
Of God that sholde live so merye as I."
And at the laste the feend oure enemy
Putte in his thought that he sholde poison beye,° *buy*
With which he mighte sleen his felawes twaye—
Forwhy° the feend foond him in swich livinge *wherefore*
That he hadde leve° him to sorwe° bringe: *permission / sorrow*
For this was outrely his fulle entente,
To sleen hem bothe, and nevere to repente.
And forth he gooth—no lenger wolde he tarye—
Into the town unto a pothecarye,° *druggist*
And prayed him that he him wolde selle
Som poison that he mighte his rattes quelle,° *kill*
And eek ther was a polcat° in his hawe° *weasel / yard*
That, as he saide, his capons° hadde yslawe,° *chickens / slain*
And fain° he wolde wreke° him if he mighte *gladly / avenge*
On vermin that destroyed him by nighte.
The pothecarye answerde, "And thou shalt have
A thing that, also° God my soule save, *so*
In al this world ther is no creature
That ete or dronke hath of this confiture°— *concoction*
Nat but the mountance° of a corn° of whete— *amount / grain*
That he ne shal his lif anoon forlete.° *lose*
Ye, sterve° he shal, and that in lasse while *die*
Than thou wolt goon a paas° nat but a mile, *walking*
The poison is so strong and violent."
This cursed man hath in his hand yhent° *taken*
This poison in a box and sith he ran
Into the nexte streete unto a man
And borwed of him large botels three,
And in the two his poison poured he—
The thridde he kepte clene for his drinke,
For al the night he shoop° him for to swinke° *prepared / work*
In carying of the gold out of that place.
And whan this riotour with sory grace
Hadde filled with win his grete botels three,
To his felawes again repaireth he.
What needeth it to sermone of it more?
For right as they had cast° his deeth bifore, *planned*
Right so they han him slain, and that anoon.
And whan that this was doon, thus spak that oon:

"Now lat us sitte and drinke and make us merye,
And afterward we wol his body berye."
And with that word it happed him par cas° *by chance*
To take the botel ther the poison was,
And drank, and yaf his felawe drinke also,
For which anoon they storven bothe two.
But certes I suppose that Avicen[2]
Wroot nevere in no canon ne in no *fen*
Mo wonder signes of empoisoning
Than hadde thise wrecches two er hir ending:
Thus ended been thise homicides two,
And eek the false empoisonere also.
O cursed sinne of alle cursednesse!
O traitours homicide, O wikkednesse!
O glotonye, luxure,° and hasardrye! *lechery*
Thou balsphemour of Crist with vilainye
And othes grete of usage° and of pride! *habit*
Allas, mankinde, how may it bitide
That to thy Creatour which that thee wroughte,
And with his precious herte blood thee boughte,
Thou art so fals and so unkinde,° allas? *unnatural*
Now goode men, God foryive you youre trespas,
And ware° you fro the sinne of avarice: *guard*
Myn holy pardon may you alle warice°— *save*
So that ye offre nobles or sterlinges,° *gold or silver coins*
Or elles silver brooches, spoones, ringes.
Boweth your heed under this holy bulle!
Cometh up, ye wives, offreth of youre wolle!° *wool*
Youre name I entre here in my rolle: anoon
Into the blisse of hevene shul ye goon.
I you assoile° by myn heigh power— *absolve*
Ye that wol offre—as clene and eek as cleer° *pure*
As ye were born.—And lo, sires, thus I preche.
And Jesu Crist that is oure soules leeche° *physician*
So graunte you his pardon to receive,
For that is best—I wol you nat deceive.

The Epilogue

"But sires, oo word forgat I in my tale:
I have relikes and pardon in my male° *bag*
As faire as any man in Engelond,
Whiche were me yiven by the Popes hond.
If any of you wol of devocioun
Offren and han myn absolucioun,

2. The 12th-century Arab philosopher Avicenna composed a *Canon of Medicine*, divided into sections called "fens."

Come forth anoon, and kneeleth here adown,
And mekely receiveth my pardoun,
Or elles taketh pardon as ye wende,° — *travel*
Al newe and fressh at every miles ende—
So that ye offre alway newe and newe° — *over and over*
Nobles or pens whiche that be goode and trewe.
It is an honour to everich that is heer
That ye mowe have a suffisant° pardoner — *competent*
T'assoile you in contrees as ye ride,
For aventures whiche that may bitide:
Paraventure ther may falle oon or two
Down of his hors and breke his nekke atwo;
Looke which a suretee° is it to you alle — *safeguard*
That I am in youre felaweshipe yfalle
That may assoile you, bothe more and lasse,
Whan that the soule shal fro the body passe.
I rede° that oure Hoste shal biginne, — *advise*
For he is most envoluped in sinne.
Com forth, sire Host, and offre first anoon,
And thou shalt kisse the relikes everichoon,
Ye, for a grote:° unbokele anoon thy purs." — *fourpence coin*
"Nay, nay," quod he, "thanne have I Cristes curs!
Lat be," quod he, "it shal nat be, so theech!° — *may I prosper*
Thou woldest make me kisse thyn olde breech
And swere it were a relik of a saint,
Though it were with thy fundament° depeint.° — *bowels / stained*
But, by the crois° which that Sainte Elaine[3] foond, — *cross*
I wolde I hadde thy coilons° in myn hond, — *testicles*
In stede of relikes or of saintuarye.° — *container of relics*
Lat cutte hem of: I wol thee helpe hem carye.
They shal be shrined in an hogges tord."° — *turd*
This Pardoner answerde nat a word:
So wroth° he was no word ne wolde he saye. — *angry*
"Now," quod oure Host, "I wol no lenger playe
With thee, ne with noon other angry man."
But right anoon the worthy Knight bigan,
Whan that he sawgh that al the peple lough,
"Namore of this, for it is right ynough.
Sire Pardoner, be glad and merye of cheere,
And ye, sire Host that been to me so dere,
I praye you that ye kisse the Pardoner,
And Pardoner, I praye thee, draw thee neer,
And as we diden lat us laughe and playe."
Anoon they kiste and riden forth hir waye.

3. St. Helen, who was said to have found the True Cross on which Jesus was crucified.

The Nun's Priest's Tale Of all his varied and ambitious output, *The Nun's Priest's Tale* may be Chaucer's most impressive tour de force. At its core is a wonderful animal fable, free of the conventionality and sometimes easy moralities this ancient form had taken on by the fourteenth century. The fable of Chauntecleer and Pertelote achieves quite extraordinary density, further, because of the multiple frames—structural and thematic—that surround it.

As part of the Canterbury tale-telling competition, the priest's fable plays a role in that broadest contest of classes and literary genres. More locally, it is one of many moments in which the Host, Harry Bailey, demands a tale from a male pilgrim in a style that also suggests a sexual challenge, and then adjusts his estimate of the teller's virility (even his social position) to suit. The fable itself is surrounded by an intimate portrait of Chauntecleer's peasant owner and her simple life, content with "hertes suffisaunce," a marked contrast to courtly values.

The central story of Chauntecleer's dream, danger, and escape works within a subtle and funny exploration of relations between the sexes. This is conditioned by courtly love conventions, literacy and education, and even the vocabulary of Pertelote's mostly Anglo-Saxon diction and Chauntecleer's love of French. This linguistic competition has its high point when Chauntecleer condescendingly mistranslates a misogynist Latin tag. Linguistic vanity, though, is exactly what puts Chauntecleer most in jeopardy. It is not the destiny Chauntecleer thinks he glimpses in his dream that almost costs his life, but rather another verbal competition, and an almost Oedipal challenge to his father.

Much of the story's energy, however, derives not from its frames but from the explosion of those frames—literary, spatial, even social—enacted and recalled at the heart of the tale. The chickens are simultaneously, and hilariously, both courtly lovers and very realistic fowl. When Chauntecleer is carried off, the whole world of the tale—widow, daughters, dogs, even bees—bursts outward in pursuit. In the midst of mock-epic and mock-romance comparisons to this joyful disorder, Chaucer even inserts one of his very few direct references to the greatest disorder of his time, the Rising of 1381 (see page 468).

The Nun's Priest's Tale is a comedy as well as a fable, reversing a lugubrious series of tragedies in the preceding *Monk's Tale*. In the end, it is a story of canniness, acquired self-knowledge, and self-salvation. Woven into the priest's humor are a gentle satire and a quiet assertion that free will is the final resource of any agent, avian or human.

The Nun's Priest's Tale

The Introduction

"Ho!" quod the Knight, "good sire, namore of this:
That ye han said is right ynough, ywis,° *indeed*
And muchel more, for litel hevinesse
Is right ynough to muche folk° I gesse:[1] *for most folks*
I saye for me it is a greet disese,
Wher as men han been in greet welthe and ese,
To heeren of hir sodein° fal, allas; *sudden*
And the contrarye is joye and greet solas,° *comfort*
As whan a man hath been in poore estat,
And climbeth up and wexeth° fortunat, *becomes*
And there abideth in prosperitee:
Swich thing is gladsom, as it thinketh° me, *seems to*
And of swich thing were goodly for to telle."
"Ye," quod oure Host, "by Sainte Poules° belle, *Paul's*
Ye saye right sooth:° this Monk he clappeth° loude. *truly / chatters*

1. The Monk has just told a series of stark and repetitive "tragedies"—the falls of men both ancient and modern.

He spak how Fortune covered with a cloude—
I noot nevere what.° And als of a tragedye *I don't know what*
Right now ye herde, and pardee,° no remedye *by God*
It is for to biwaile ne complaine
That that is doon, and als° it is a paine, *also*
As ye han said, to heere of hevinesse.
"Sire Monk, namore of this, so God you blesse:
Youre tale anoyeth al this compaignye;
Swich talking is nat worth a boterflye,
For therinne is ther no disport ne game.
Wherfore, sire Monk, or daun° Piers by youre name, *Master*
I praye you hertely telle us somwhat elles:
For sikerly, nere clinking of youre belles,[2]
That on youre bridel hange on every side,
By hevene king that for us alle dyde,
I sholde er this have fallen down for sleep,
Although the slough° hadde nevere been so deep. *mud*
Thanne hadde youre tale al be told in vain;
For certainly, as that thise clerkes sayn,
Wher as a man may have noon audience,
Nought helpeth it to tellen his sentence;° *statement*
And wel I woot° the substance is in me, *know*
If any thing shal wel reported be.
Sire, saye somwhat of hunting, I you praye."
"Nay," quod this Monk, "I have no lust° to playe. *wish*
Now lat another telle, as I have told."
Thanne spak oure Host with rude speeche and bold,
And saide unto the Nonnes Preest anoon,
"Com neer, thou Preest,[3] com hider, thou sire John:
Tel us swich thing as may oure hertes glade.° *gladden our hearts*
Be blithe,° though thou ride upon a jade!° *happy / nag*
What though thyn hors be bothe foul and lene?° *thin*
If he wol serve thee, rekke nat a bene.° *don't care a bean*
Looke that thyn herte be merye everemo."
"Yis, sire," quod he, "yis, Host, so mote I go,
But I be merye, ywis, I wol be blamed."
And right anoon his tale he hath attamed,° *begun*
And thus he saide unto us everichoon,
This sweete Preest, this goodly man sire John.

The Tale

A poore widwe somdeel stape° in age *well along*
Was whilom° dwelling in a narwe cotage, *once upon a time*
Biside a grove, stonding in a dale:
This widwe of which I telle you my tale,
Sin° thilke° day that she was last a wif, *since / that*

2. For truly, were it not for the jingling of your bells.

3. The Host uses the familiar, somewhat condescending "thou," then contemptuously calls the priest "Sir John."

In pacience ladde a ful simple lif.
For litel was hir catel° and hir rente,° *property / income*
By housbondrye° of swich as God hire sente *management*
She foond° hirself and eek hir doughtren two. *provided for*
Three large sowes hadde she and namo,
Three kin,° and eek a sheep that highte° Malle. *cows / was named*
Ful sooty was hir bowr° and eek hir halle, *bedroom*
In which she eet ful many a sclendre meel;
Of poinant° sauce hire needed neveradeel: *pungent*
No daintee morsel passed thurgh hir throte—
Hir diete was accordant to hir cote.° *cottage*
Replecciou n° ne made hire nevere sik: *gluttony*
Attempre° diete was al hir physik, *moderate*
And exercise and hertes suffisaunce.
The goute lette hire nothing for to daunce,[4]
N'apoplexye shente° nat hir heed. *hurt*
No win ne drank she, neither whit ne reed:
Hir boord° was served most with whit and blak, *table*
Milk and brown breed, in which she foond no lak;° *fault*
Seind° bacon, and somtime an ey° or twaye,° *singed / egg / two*
For she was as it were a manere daye.° *dairy maid*
A yeerd° she hadde, enclosed al withoute *yard*
With stikkes, and a drye dich aboute,
In which she hadde a cok heet° Chauntecleer: *called*
In al the land of crowing nas his peer.
His vois was merier than the merye orgon
On massedayes that in the chirche goon;° *is played*
Wel sikerer° was his crowing in his logge° *surer / dwelling*
Than is a clok or an abbeye orlogge;° *timepiece*
By nature he knew eech ascensioun
Of th'equinoxial[5] in thilke town:
For whan degrees fifteene were ascended,
Thanne crew he that it mighte nat been amended.° *surpassed*
His comb was redder than the fin coral,
And batailed° as it were a castel wal; *crenellated*
His bile° was blak, and as the jeet° it shoon; *beak / jet*
Like asure° were his legges and his toon;° *azure / toes*
His nailes whitter than the lilye flowr,
And lik the burned° gold was his colour. *burnished*
This gentil cok hadde in his governaunce
Sevene hennes for to doon al his plesaunce,
Whiche were his sustres and his paramours,° *lovers*
And wonder like to him as of colours;
Of whiche the faireste hewed° on hir throte *colored*
Was cleped° faire damoisele Pertelote: *called*
Curteis she was, discreet, and debonaire,° *gracious*

4. Did not keep her from dancing.

5. The points marking the celestial hours.

And compaignable,° and bar hirself so faire, *sociable*
Sin thilke° day that she was seven night old, *that*
That trewely she hath the herte in hold
Of Chauntecleer, loken in every lith.[6]
He loved hire so that wel was him therwith.
But swich a joye was it to heere hem singe,
Whan that the brighte sonne gan to springe,
In sweete accord "My Lief is Faren in Londe"[7]—
For thilke time, as I have understonde,
Beestes and briddes° couden speke and singe. *birds*
  And so bifel that in a daweninge,
As Chauntecleer among his wives alle
Sat on his perche that was in the halle,
And next him sat this faire Pertelote,
This Chauntecleer gan gronen in his throte,
As man that in his dreem is drecched° sore. *disturbed*
  And whan that Pertelote thus herde him rore,
She was agast, and saide, "Herte dere,
What aileth you to grone in this manere?
Ye been a verray° slepere, fy, for shame!" *true*
  And he answerde and saide thus, "Madame,
I praye you that ye take it nat agrief.° *amiss*
By God, me mette° I was in swich meschief *I dreamed*
Right now, that yit myn herte is sore afright.
Now God," quod he, "my swevene recche aright,[8]
And keepe my body out of foul prisoun!
Me mette how that I romed up and down
Within oure yeerd, wher as I sawgh a beest,
Was lik an hound and wolde han maad arrest° *taken captive*
Upon my body, and han had me deed.
His colour was bitwixe yelow and reed,
And tipped was his tail and bothe his eres
With blak, unlik the remenant of his heres;° *the rest of his hair*
His snoute smal, with glowing yën twaye.
Yit of his look for fere almost I deye:
This caused me my groning, doutelees."
  "Avoi,"° quod she, "fy on you, hertelees!° *Have done! / coward*
Allas," quod she, "for by that God above,
Now han ye lost myn herte and al my love!
I can nat love a coward, by my faith.
For certes, what so any womman saith,
We alle desiren, if it mighte be,
To han housbondes hardy, wise, and free,° *generous*
And secree,° and no nigard, ne no fool, *discreet*
Ne him that is agast° of every tool,° *afraid / weapon*
Ne noon avauntour.° By that God above, *braggart*

6. Locked in every limb (i.e., thoroughly).
7. A popular ballad, "My Lefe Is Faren in a Lond" (see page 554).
8. Intepret my dream correctly.

How dorste ye sayn for shame unto youre love
That any thing mighte make you aferd?
Have ye no mannes herte and han a beerd?
Allas, and conne ye been agast of swevenes?
No thing, God woot,° but vanitee° in swevene is! *knows / illusion*
Swevenes engendren of replexiouns,° *surfeits*
And ofte of fume° and of complexiouns,° *gas / bodily humors*
Whan humours been too habundant in a wight.° *creature*
Certes, this dreem which ye han met tonight
Comth of the grete superfluitee
Of youre rede colera,[9] pardee,° *by God*
Which causeth folk to dreden in hir dremes
Of arwes,° and of fir with rede lemes,° *arrows / flames*
Of rede beestes, that they wol hem bite,
Of contek,° and of whelpes° grete and lite— *strife / dogs*
Right as the humour of malencolye[1]
Causeth ful many a man in sleep to crye
For fere of blake beres or boles° blake, *bulls*
Or elles blake develes wol hem take.
Of othere humours coude I telle also
That werken many a man in sleep ful wo,
But I wol passe as lightly as I can.
Lo, Caton,[2] which that was so wis a man,
Saide he nat thus? 'Ne do no fors° of dremes.' *pay no attention to*
Now, sire," quod she, "whan we flee° fro the bemes,° *fly / rafters*
For Goddes love, as take som laxatif.
Up° peril of my soule and of my lif, *upon*
I conseile you the beste, I wol nat lie,
That bothe of colere and of malencolye
Ye purge you; and for ye shal nat tarye,
Though in this town is noon apothecarye,
I shal myself to herbes techen you,
That shal been for youre hele° and for youre prow,° *health / profit*
And in oure yeerd tho° herbes shal I finde, *then*
The whiche han of hir propretee by kinde° *nature*
To purge you binethe and eek above.
Foryet nat this, for Goddes owene love.
Ye been ful colerik of complexioun;
Ware° the sonne in his ascencioun *beware lest*
Ne finde you nat repleet° of humours hote; *full / hot*
And if it do, I dar wel laye[3] a grote° *fourpence*
That ye shul have a fevere terciane,[4]
Or an agu° that may be youre bane.° *fever / death*
A day or two ye shul han digestives
Of wormes, er ye take youre laxatives

9. Choleric bile, thought to overheat the body.
1. Black bile, thought to produce dark thoughts.
2. Marcus Porcius Cato, ancient author of a book of proverbs used by schoolchildren.
3. Bet (with a pun on egg-laying).
4. Recurring fever.

Of lauriol, centaure, and fumetere,[5]
Or elles of ellebor that groweth there,
Of catapuce, or of gaitres beries,
Of herbe-ive growing in oure yeerd ther merye is.° *where it is pleasant*
Pekke hem right up as they growe and ete hem in.
Be merye, housbonde, for youre fader kin!
Dredeth no dreem: I can saye you namore."
"Madame," quod he, "graunt mercy of youre lore.° *learning*
But nathelees, as touching daun Catoun,
That hath of wisdom swich a greet renown,
Though that he bad no dremes for to drede,
By God, men may in olde bookes rede
Of many a man more of auctoritee
Than evere Caton was, so mote I thee,° *so may I prosper*
That al the revers sayn of his sentence,° *opinion*
And han wel founden by experience
That dremes been significaciouns
As wel of joye as tribulaciouns
That folk enduren in this lif present.
Ther needeth make of this noon argument:
The verray preve° sheweth it in deede. *proof*
"Oon of the gretteste auctour that men rede
Saith thus, that whilom two felawes wente
On pilgrimage in a ful good entente,
And happed so they comen in a town,
Wher as ther was swich congregacioun
Of peple, and eek so strait of herbergage,° *short of lodging*
That they ne founde as muche as oo° cotage *one*
In which they bothe mighte ylogged be;
Wherfore they mosten of necessitee
As for that night departe compaignye.
And eech of hem gooth to his hostelrye,
And took his logging as it wolde falle.
That oon of hem was logged in a stalle,
Fer in a yeerd, with oxen of the plough;
That other man was logged wel ynough,
As was his aventure or his fortune,
That us governeth alle as in commune.
And so bifel that longe er it were day,
This man mette in his bed, ther as he lay,
How that his felawe gan upon him calle,
And saide, 'Allas, for in an oxes stalle
This night I shal be mordred° ther I lie! *murdered*
Now help me, dere brother, or I die!
In alle haste com to me,' he saide.
"This man out of his sleep for fere abraide,° *bolted up*

5. These and the following are bitter herbs that produce hot and dry sensations and lead to purging.

But whan that he was wakened of his sleep,
He turned him and took of this no keep:° *heed*
Him thoughte his dreem nas° but a vanitee. *was not*
Thus twies in his sleeping dremed he,
And atte thridde time yit his felawe
Cam, as him thoughte, and saide, 'I am now slawe:° *slain*
Bihold my bloody woundes deepe and wide.
Aris up erly in the morwe tide° *morning time*
And atte west gate of the town,' quod he,
A carte ful of dong° ther shaltou see, *dung*
In which my body is hid ful prively:
Do thilke° carte arresten° boldely. *that / have seized*
My gold caused my mordre, sooth° to sayn'— *truth*
And tolde him every point how he was slain,
With a ful pitous face, pale of hewe.
And truste wel, his dreem he foond ful trewe,
For on the morwe as soone as it was day,
To his felawes in he took the way,
And whan that he cam to this oxes stalle,
After his felawe he bigan to calle.
"The hostiler° answerde him anoon, *innkeeper*
And saide, 'Sire, youre felawe is agoon:
As soone as day he wente out of the town.'
"This man gan fallen in suspecioun,
Remembring on his dremes that he mette;
And forth he gooth, no lenger wolde he lette,° *delay*
Unto the west gate of the town, and foond
A dong carte, wente as it were to donge° lond, *spread manure on*
That was arrayed in that same wise
As ye han herd the dede man devise;
And with an hardy herte he gan to crye,
'Vengeance and justice of this felonye!
My felawe mordred is this same night,
And in this carte he lith gaping upright!° *facing up*
I crye out on the ministres,"° quod he, *magistrates*
'That sholde keepe and rulen this citee.
Harrow, allas, here lith my felawe slain!'
What sholde I more unto this tale sayn?
The peple up sterte and caste the carte to grounde,
And in the middel of the dong they founde
The dede man that mordred was al newe.° *just recently*
"O blisful God that art so just and trewe,
Lo, how that thou biwrayest° mordre alway! *reveal*
Mordre wol out, that see we day by day:
Mordre is so wlatsom° and abhominable *loathsome*
To God that is so just and resonable,
That he ne wol nat suffre it heled° be, *concealed*
Though it abide a yeer or two or three.
Mordre wol out: this my conclusioun.

And right anoon ministres of that town
Han hent° the cartere and so sore him pined,° *seized / tortured*
And eek the hostiler so sore engined,
That they biknewe° hir wikkednesse anoon, *confessed*
And were anhanged by the nekke boon.
Here may men seen that dremes been to drede.
"And certes, in the same book I rede—
Right in the nexte chapitre after this—
I gabbe° nat, so have I joye or blis— *lie*
Two men that wolde han passed over see
For certain cause into a fer contree,
If that the wind ne hadde been contrarye
That made hem in a citee for to tarye,
That stood ful merye upon an haven° side— *harbor*
But on a day again° the even tide *toward*
The wind gan chaunge, and blewe right as hem leste:° *they wanted*
Jolif° and glad they wenten unto reste, *merry*
And casten hem° ful erly for to saile. *decided*
"But to that oo man fil a greet mervaile;
That oon of hem, in sleeping as he lay,
Him mette a wonder dreem again the day:
Him thoughte a man stood by his beddes side,
And him comanded that he sholde abide,
And saide him thus, 'If thou tomorwe wende,° *travel*
Thou shalt be dreint:° my tale is at an ende.' *drowned*
"He wook and tolde his felawe what he mette,
And prayed him his viage to lette;° *put off his journey*
As for that day he prayed him to bide.
His felawe that lay by his beddes side
Gan for to laughe, and scorned him ful faste.
'No dreem,' quod he, 'may so myn herte agaste
That I wol lette for to do my thinges.° *business*
I sette nat a straw by thy dreminges,
For swevenes been but vanitees and japes:° *tricks*
Men dreme alday° of owles or of apes, *constantly*
And of many a maze° therwithal— *delusion*
Men dreme of thing that nevere was ne shal.
But sith° I see that thou wolt here abide, *since*
And thus forsleuthen° wilfully thy tide, *waste due to sloth*
Good woot, it reweth me; and have good day.'
And thus he took his leve and wente his way.
But er that he hadde half his cours ysailed—
Noot° I nat why ne what meschaunce it ailed°— *know / went wrong*
But casuelly° the shippes botme rente,° *by accident / split apart*
And ship and man under the water wente,
In sighte of othere shippes it biside,
That with hem sailed at the same tide.
And therfore, faire Pertelote so dere,
By swiche ensamples olde maistou lere° *may you learn*

That no man sholde been too recchelees° *careless*
Of dremes, for I saye thee doutelees
That many a dreem ful sore is for to drede.
"Lo, in the lif of Saint Kenelm[6] I rede—
That was Kenulphus sone, the noble king
Of Mercenrike—how Kenelm mette a thing
A lite° er he was mordred on a day. *little while*
His mordre in his avision° he sey.° *dream / saw*
His norice° him expounded everydeel *nurse*
His swevene, and bad him for to keepe him° weel *guard against*
For traison, but he nas but seven yeer old,
And therfore litel tale hath he told° *he cared little for*
Of any dreem, so holy was his herte.
By God, I hadde levere than my sherte° *would give my shirt*
That ye hadde rad his legende as have I.
"Dame Pertelote, I saye you trewely,
Macrobeus,[7] that writ the Avisioun
In Affrike of the worthy Scipioun,
Affermeth° dremes, and saith that they been *confirms*
Warning of thinges that men after seen.
"And ferthermore, I praye you looketh wel
In the Olde Testament of Daniel,
If he heeld dremes any vanitee.[8]
"Rede eek of Joseph and ther shul ye see
Wher° dremes be somtime—I saye nat alle— *whether*
Warning of thinges that shul after falle.
"Looke of Egypte the king daun Pharao,
His bakere and his botelere° also, *butler*
Wher they ne felte noon effect in dremes.[9]
Whoso wol seeke actes of sondry remes° *various kingdoms*
May rede of dremes many a wonder thing.
"Lo Cresus, which that was of Lyde° king, *Lydia*
Mette he nat that he sat upon a tree,
Which signified he sholde anhanged be?
"Lo here Andromacha, Ectores° wif, *Hector of Troy*
That day that Ector sholde lese° his lif, *lose*
She dremed on the same night biforn
How that the lif of Ector sholde be lorn,
If thilke day he wente into bataile;
She warned him, but it mighte nat availe:
He wente for to fighte nathelees,
But he was slain anoon of Achilles.
But thilke tale is al too long to telle,
And eek it is neigh day, I may nat dwelle.

6. St. Cenhelm, son of Cenwulf, a 9th-century child-king in Mercia who was murdered at his sister's orders.

7. Macrobius, a 4th-century author, wrote an extensive commentary on Cicero's *Dream of Scipio*.

8. Daniel interprets the pagan King Nebuchadnezzar's dream, which foretells his downfall (Daniel 4).

9. Joseph interpreted dreams for the pharaoh's chief baker and butler (Genesis 40–41).

Shortly I saye, as for conclusioun,
That I shal han of this avisioun
Adversitee, and I saye ferthermoor
That I ne telle of laxatives no stoor,° *hold no regard for*
For they been venimes,° I woot° it weel: *poisons / know*
I hem defye, I love hem neveradeel.
"Now lat us speke of mirthe and stinte° al this. *stop*
Madame Pertelote, so have I blis,
Of oo thing God hath sente me large grace:
For whan I see the beautee of youre face—
Ye been so scarlet reed aboute youre yën—
It maketh al my drede for to dien.
For also siker° as *In principio*,[1] *certain*
Mulier est hominis confusio.[2]
Madame, the sentence° of this Latin is, *meaning*
'Womman is mannes joye and al his blis.'
For whan I feele anight youre softe side—
Al be it that I may nat on you ride,
For that oure perche is maad so narwe, allas—
I am so ful of joye and of solas° *delight*
That I defye bothe swevene and dreem."
And with that word he fleigh down fro the beem,
For it was day, and eek° his hennes alle, *also*
And with a "chuk" he gan hem for to calle,
For he hadde founde a corn lay in the yeerd.
Real° he was, he was namore aferd:° *regal / afraid*
He fethered Pertelote twenty time,
And trad° hire as ofte er it was prime.[3] *mounted*
He looketh as it were a grim leoun,° *lion*
And on his toes he rometh up and down:
Him deined nat to sette his foot to grounde.
He chukketh whan he hath a corn yfounde,
And to him rennen thanne his wives alle.
Thus royal, as a prince is in his halle,
Leve I this Chauntecleer in his pasture,
And after wol I telle his aventure.
Whan that the month in which the world bigan,
That highte March, whan God first maked man,
Was compleet, and passed were also,
Sin March biran,° thritty days and two,[4] *finished*
Bifel that Chauntecleer in al his pride,
His sevene wives walking him biside,
Caste up his yën to the brighte sonne,
That in the signe of Taurus hadde yronne
Twenty degrees and oon and somwhat more,

1. "In the beginning," the opening verse of the Book of Genesis and the Gospel of John.
2. "Woman is the ruination of mankind."
3. First hour of the day.
4. The date is thus May 3.

And knew by kinde,° and by noon other lore, *nature*
That it was prime, and crew with blisful stevene.° *voice*
"The sonne," he saide, "is clomben up on hevene
Fourty degrees and oon and more, ywis.° *indeed*
Madame Pertelote, my worldes blis,
Herkneth thise blisful briddes° how they singe, *birds*
And see the fresshe flowres how they springe:
Ful is myn herte of revel and solas."
But sodeinly him fil a sorweful cas,° *event*
For evere the latter ende of joye is wo—
God woot that worldly joye is soone ago,
And if a rethor° coude faire endite,° *rhetorician / compose*
He in a cronicle saufly° mighte it write, *safely*
As for a soverein notabilitee.
Now every wis man lat him herkne me:
This storye is also° trewe, I undertake, *as*
As is the book of Launcelot de Lake,[5]
That wommen holde in ful greet reverence.
Now wol I turne again to my sentence.° *topic*
A colfox° ful of sly iniquitee, *black fox*
That in the grove° hadde woned° yeres three, *woods / lived*
By heigh imaginacion forncast,[6]
The same night thurghout the hegges brast° *burst*
Into the yeerd ther Chauntecleer the faire
Was wont, and eek his wives, to repaire;
And in a bed of wortes° stille he lay *cabbages*
Til it was passed undren° of the day, *midmorning*
Waiting his time on Chauntecleer to falle,
As gladly doon thise homicides alle,
That in await liggen to mordre men.
O false mordrour, lurking in thy den!
O newe Scariot! Newe Geniloun![7]
False dissimilour!° O Greek Sinoun,[8] *dissembler*
That broughtest Troye al outrely° to sorwe! *entirely*
O Chauntecleer, accursed be that morwe
That thou into the yeerd flaugh fro the bemes!
Thou were ful wel ywarned by thy dremes
That thilke day was perilous to thee;
But what that God forwoot moot° needes be, *foreknew must*
After the opinion of certain clerkes:
Witnesse on him that any parfit° clerk is *accomplished*
That in scole is greet altercacioun
In this matere, and greet disputisoun,
And hath been of an hundred thousand men.

5. The adventures of the Arthurian knight.
6. Predicted (in Chauntecleer's dream).
7. Judas Iscariot, who handed Jesus over to the Roman authorities for execution; Ganelon, a medieval traitor who betrayed the hero Roland to his Saracen enemies.
8. The Greek who tricked the Trojans into accepting the Trojan horse behind the city walls.

But I ne can nat bulte it to the bren,[9]
As can the holy doctour Augustin,
Or Boece, or the bisshop Bradwardin[1]—
Wheither that Goddes worthy forwiting° *foreknowledge*
Straineth° me nedely for to doon a thing *compels*
("Nedely" clepe I simple necessitee),
Or elles if free chois be graunted me
To do that same thing or do it nought,
Though God forwoot it er that I was wrought;° *made*
Or if his witing straineth neveradeel,
But by necessitee condicionel[2]—
I wol nat han to do of swich matere:
My tale is of a cok, as ye may heere,
That took his conseil of his wif with sorwe,
To walken in the yeerd upon that morwe
That he hadde met the dreem that I you tolde.
Wommenes conseils been ful ofte colde,° *disastrous*
Wommanes conseil broughte us first to wo,
And made Adam fro Paradis to go,
Ther as he was ful merye and wel at ese.
But for I noot° to whom it mighte displese *do not know*
If I conseil of wommen wolde blame,
Passe over, for I saide it in my game—
Rede auctours° where they trete of swich matere, *authors*
And what they sayn of wommen ye may heere—
Thise been the cokkes wordes and nat mine:
I can noon harm of no womman divine.° *guess at*
    Faire in the sond° to bathe hire merily *sand*
Lith° Pertelote, and alle hir sustres by, *lies*
Again the sonne, and Chauntecleer so free
Soong merier than the mermaide in the see—
For Physiologus[3] saith sikerly
How that they singen wel and merily.
    And so bifel that as he caste his yë
Among the wortes on a boterflye,° *butterfly*
He was war of this fox that lay ful lowe.
No thing ne liste him° thanne for to crowe, *he wanted*
But cride anoon "Cok cok!" and up he sterte,
As man that was affrayed in his herte—
For naturelly a beest desireth flee
Fro his contrarye° if he may it see, *natural enemy*
Though he nevere erst° hadde seen it with his yë. *before*
This Chauntecleer, whan he gan him espye,
He wolde han fled, but that the fox anoon

9. Sift it from the husks (i.e., discriminate).
1. St. Augustine, the ancient writer Boethius, and the 14th-century Archbishop of Canterbury Thomas Bradwardine attempted to explain how God's predestination of events still allowed for humans to have free will.
2. Boethius argued only for conditional necessity, which still permitted for much exercise of free will.
3. Said to have written a bestiary.

Saide, "Gentil sire, allas, wher wol ye goon?
Be ye afraid of me that am youre freend?
Now certes, I were worse than a feend° *devil*
If I to you wolde harm or vilainye.
I am nat come youre conseil for t'espye,
But trewely the cause of my cominge
Was only for to herkne how that ye singe:
For trewely, ye han as merye a stevene° *voice*
As any angel hath that is in hevene.
Therwith ye han in musik more feelinge
Than hadde Boece,[4] or any that can singe.
My lord your fader—God his soule blesse!—
And eek youre moder, of hir gentilesse,° *gentility*
Han in myn hous ybeen, to my grete ese.
And certes sire, ful fain° wolde I you plese. *gladly*
  But for men speke of singing, I wol saye,
So mote I brouke° wel mine yën twaye, *use*
Save ye, I herde nevere man so singe
As dide youre fader in the morweninge.
Certes, it was of herte° al that he soong. *heartfelt*
And for to make his vois the more strong,
He wolde so paine him that with bothe his yën
He moste winke,° so loude wolde he cryen; *shut his eyes*
And stonden on his tiptoon therwithal,
And strecche forth his nekke long and smal;
And eek he was of swich discrecioun
That ther nas no man in no regioun
That him in song or wisdom mighte passe.° *surpass*
I have wel rad in Daun Burnel the Asse.[5]
Among his vers how that ther was a cok,
For° a preestes sone yaf him a knok *because*
Upon his leg whil he was yong and nice,° *foolish*
He made him for to lese his benefice.[6]
But certain, ther nis no comparisoun
Bitwixe the wisdom and discrecioun
Of youre fader and of his subtiltee.
Now singeth, sire, for sainte° charitee! *holy*
Lat see, conne ye youre fader countrefete?"° *imitate*
  This Chauntecleer his winges gan to bete,
As man that coude his traison nat espye,
So was he ravisshed with his flaterye.
  Allas, ye lordes, many a fals flatour
Is in youre court, and many a losengeour,° *deceiver*
That plesen you wel more, by my faith,
Than he that soothfastnesse° unto you saith! *truth*

4. In addition to theology, Boethius also wrote a music textbook.
5. The hero of a 12th-century satirical poem, *Speculum Stultorum*, by Nigel Wirecker, Brunellus was a donkey who traveled around Europe trying to educate himself.
6. Lose his commission (because he overslept).

Redeth Ecclesiaste[7] of flaterye.
Beeth war, ye lordes, of hir trecherye.
This Chauntecleer stood hye upon his toos,
Strecching his nekke, and heeld his yën cloos,
And gan to crowe loude for the nones;° *for the purpose*
And daun Russel the fox sterte up atones,° *at once*
And by the gargat° hente° Chauntecleer, *throat / seized*
And on his bak toward the wode him beer,
For yit ne was ther no man that him sued.
O destinee that maist nat been eschued!° *avoided*
Allas that Chauntecleer fleigh fro the bemes!
Allas his wif ne roughte° nat of dremes! *cared*
And on a Friday[8] fil al this meschaunce!
O Venus that art goddesse of plesaunce,
Sin that thy servant was this Chauntecleer,
And in thy service dide al his power—
More for delit than world° to multiplye— *population*
Why woldestou suffre him on thy day to die?
O Gaufred,[9] dere maister soverein,
That, whan thy worthy king Richard was slain
With shot,° complainedest his deeth so sore, *(of an arrow)*
Why ne hadde I now thy sentence and thy lore,
The Friday for to chide as diden ye?
For on a Friday soothly° slain was he. *truly*
Thanne wolde I shewe you how that I coude plaine° *lament*
For Chauntecleres drede and for his paine.
Certes, swich cry ne lamentacioun
Was nevere of ladies maad whan Ilioun° *Troy*
Was wonne, and Pyrrus[1] with his straite° swerd, *drawn*
Whan he hadde hent King Priam by the beerd
And slain him, as saith us Eneidos,° *Virgil's* Aeneid
As maden alle the hennes in the cloos,° *yard*
Whan they hadde seen of Chauntecleer the sighte.
But sovereinly Dame Pertelote shrighte° *shrieked*
Ful louder than dide Hasdrubales wif[2]
Whan that hir housbonde hadde lost his lif,
And that the Romains hadden brend Cartage:
She was so ful of torment and of rage
That wilfully unto the fir she sterte,
And brende hirselven with a stedefast herte.
O woful hennes, right so criden ye
As, whan that Nero[3] brende the citee
Of Rome, criden senatoures wives

7. The Book of Ecclesiasticus.

8. Venus's day, but also an ominous day of the week.

9. Geoffrey of Vinsauf, who wrote a poem when King Richard the Lion-Hearted died, cursing the day of the week on which he died, a Friday.

1. Pyrrhus, the son of Achilles, who slew Troy's King Priam.

2. Hasdrubal was King of Carthage when it was defeated by the Romans during the Punic Wars.

3. The Emperor Nero set fire to Rome, killing many of his senators.

For that hir housbondes losten alle hir lives:
Withouten gilt this Nero hath hem slain.
Now wol I turne to my tale again.
The sely° widwe and eek hir doughtres two *innocent*
Herden thise hennes crye and maken wo,
And out at dores sterten they anoon,
And sien° the fox toward the grove goon, *saw*
And bar upon his bak the cok away,
And criden, "Out, harrow, and wailaway,
Ha, ha, the fox," and after him they ran,
And eek with staves many another man;
Ran Colle oure dogge, and Talbot and Gerland,[4]
And Malkin with a distaf in hir hand,
Ran cow and calf, and eek the verray hogges,
Sore aferd for berking of the dogges
And shouting of the men and wommen eke.
They ronne so hem thoughte hir herte breke;
They yelleden as feendes doon in helle;
The dokes° criden as men wolde hem quelle;° *ducks / kill*
The gees for fere flowen over the trees;
Out of the hive cam the swarm of bees;
So hidous was the noise a, benedicite,
Certes, he Jakke Straw[5] and his meinee
Ne made nevere shoutes half so shrille
Whan that they wolden any Fleming kille,
As thilke day was maad upon the fox:
Of bras they broughten bemes° and of box,° *trumpets / boxwood*
Of horn, of boon, in whiche they blewe and pouped,° *puffed*
And therwithal they skriked and they houped—
It seemed as that hevene sholde falle.
Now goode men, I praye you herkneth alle:
Lo, how Fortune turneth sodeinly
The hope and pride eek of hir enemy.
This cok that lay upon the foxes bak,
In al his drede unto the fox he spak,
And saide, "Sire, if that I were as ye,
Yit sholde I sayn, as wis° God helpe me, *certainly*
'Turneth ayain, ye proude cherles° alle! *ruffians*
A verray pestilence upon you falle!
Now am I come unto this wodes side,
Maugree° your heed,° the cok shal here abide. *despite / planning*
I wol him ete, in faith, and that anoon.'"
The fox answerde, "In faith, it shal be doon."
And as he spak that word, al sodeinly
The cok brak from his mouth deliverly,° *nimbly*
And hye upon a tree he fleigh anoon.

4. Common names for dogs.

5. Jack Straw was one of the leaders of the Peasants' Revolt of 1381, which was directed in part against the Flemish traders in London.

And whan the fox sawgh that he was agoon,
"Allas," quod he, "O Chauntecleer, allas!
I have to you," quod he, "ydoon trespas,
In as muche as I maked you aferd
Whan I you hente and broughte out of the yeerd.
But sire, I dide it in no wikke° entente: *wicked*
Come down, and I shal telle you what I mente.
I shal saye sooth to you, God help me so."
"Nay thanne," quod he, "I shrewe° us bothe two: *curse*
But first I shrewe myself, bothe blood and bones,
If thou bigile me ofter than ones;
Thou shalt namore thurgh thy flaterye
Do° me to singe and winken with myn yë.° *make*
For he that winketh whan he sholde see,
Al wilfully, God lat him nevere thee."° *prosper*
"Nay," quod the fox, "but God yive him meschaunce
That is so undiscreet of governaunce
That jangleth° whan he sholde holde his pees." *chatters*
Lo, swich it is for to be recchelees° *careless*
And necligent and truste on flaterye.
But ye that holden this tale a folye
As of a fox, or of a cok and hen,
Taketh the moralitee, goode men.
For Saint Paul saith that al that writen is
To oure doctrine° it is ywrit, ywis:° *instruction / indeed*
Taketh the fruit, and lat the chaf be stille.
Now goode God, if that it be thy wille,
As saith my lord, so make us alle goode men,
And bringe us to his hye blisse. Amen.

The Epilogue

"Sire Nonnes Preest," oure Hoste saide anoon,
"Yblessed be thy breech° and every stoon:° *buttocks / testicle*
This was a merye tale of Chauntecleer.
But by my trouthe, if thou were seculer° *a layman*
Thou woldest been a tredefowl° aright: *a cock*
For if thou have corage° as thou hast might *desire*
Thee were neede of hennes, as I weene,° *suppose*
Ye, mo than sevene times seventeene.
See whiche brawnes° hath this gentil preest— *muscles*
So greet a nekke and swich a large breest.
He looketh as a sperhawk° with his yën; *sparrowhawk*
Him needeth nat his colour for to dyen
With brasil ne with grain of Portingale.[6]
Now sire, faire falle you for youre tale."
And after that he with ful merye cheere
Saide unto another as ye shul heere.

6. Two types of red dye, the latter from Portugal.

THE PARSON'S TALE Although *The Canterbury Tales* remain unfinished and even the order of the tales is unclear, we know that Chaucer's plan was to end them with *The Parson's Tale*, just as it was to begin them with the pilgrimage to Canterbury in *The General Prologue*. Thus, when the Parson responds to the Host's request for a final tale by praying Jesus to show the way to the "glorious pilgrimage" called "Jerusalem celestial," there is a sense of closure in his return to an idea that has been obscured during the tale-telling. His shift of the destination from Canterbury to the heavenly city, however, gives us pause. The view that life on earth is a pilgrimage to heaven was a Christian commonplace, but was it Chaucer's view? The three parts of *The Parson's Tale* included here raise questions about how Chaucer's religious beliefs relate to his art. What is his final judgment of the artful, but often sinful, tales he has been telling?

In the introduction, the Parson rejects the idea of poetry entirely, scornfully refusing to tell a "fable" or to adorn his tale with alliteration or rhyme; instead, he will tell what he refers to as a "merye tale in prose," which turns out to be a forty-page treatise on penitence. Thus Chaucer specifically attributes to him an ascetic view of art which is hard to reconcile with his own extraordinary poetry. Does the Parson speak for Chaucer? Although he has a measure of authority as the only exemplary member of the clergy on the pilgrimage, he is nevertheless a fictional character. Since, however, Chaucer is thought to have written the introduction to this tale as well as the *Retraction* at the same time at the end of his life, perhaps he could have come to share the Parson's aesthetic views.

The Parson begins his tale proper with a second reference to celestial Jerusalem, stating that the route to it is through penitence. The tale, which Chaucer had translated at an earlier period, belongs to a common type of manual of confession for either clergy or laity. Included in it is an analysis of the seven deadly sins—pride, envy, anger, sloth, avarice, gluttony, and lechery—in an order that suggests that Chaucer, like Dante, considered the last to be the least serious, although still worthy of damnation. The passage on lechery excerpted here offers an opportunity to measure *The Parson's Tale* against the tales that have gone before, particularly such "sinful" works as *The Miller's Tale* and *The Wife of Bath's Prologue*.

Whatever conclusion we draw about the relevance of *The Parson's Tale* to the tales preceding, the *Retraction* appended to it is troubling yet intriguing. In it Chaucer repudiates much of the work for which he is most loved and admired, such "worldly vanitees" as *Troilus and Criseyde*, *The Parliament of Fowls*, and those of the *Canterbury Tales* that "sounen [lead] into sinne." On the other hand, he thanks God for his works of "moralitee," including his translation of Boethius and his saints' legends, works that are seldom read today. He himself is engaged in penance—repentance, confession, and satisfaction—thus connecting his own spiritual experience with the manual he has translated. However disappointing it is to read this rejection of his most artistically satisfying tales, we must remember that a concept of art for art's sake would have been historically unavailable to him. Perhaps his last tale was indeed his last word.

from The Parson's Tale
The Introduction

By that° the Manciple hadde his tale al ended, *by that time*
The sonne fro the south line[1] was descended
So lowe, that he nas nat to my sighte
Degrees nine and twenty as in highte.
Four of the clokke it was, so as I gesse,
For elevene foot,° or litel more or lesse, *feet*

1. Astronomical marking parallel to the celestial equator.

My shadwe was at thilke° time as there, *that*
Of swich feet as my lengthe parted were
In sixe feet equal of proporcioun.
  Therwith the moones exaltacioun°— *dominant influence*
I mene Libra[2]—alway gan ascende,
As we were entring at a thropes ende.° *village boundary*
For which oure Host, as he was wont to gie° *lead*
As in this caas oure joly compaignye,
Saide in this wise, "Lordinges everichoon,
Now lakketh us no tales mo than oon:
Fulfild is my sentence° and my decree; *design*
I trowe° that we han herd of eech degree; *believe*
Almost fulfild is al myn ordinaunce.
I praye to God, so yive him right good chaunce
That telleth this tale to us lustily.
Sire preest," quod he, "artou a vicary,° *vicar*
Or arte a Person?° Say sooth, by thy fay.° *parish priest / faith*
Be what thou be, ne breek thou nat oure play,
For every man save thou hath told his tale.
Unbokele and shew us what is in thy male!° *bag*
For trewely, me thinketh by thy cheere° *expression*
Thou sholdest knitte up wel a greet matere.
Tel us a fable anoon, for cokkes bones!"[3]
  This Person answerde al atones,
"Thou getest fable noon ytold for me,
For Paul, that writeth unto Timothee,[4]
Repreveth hem that waiven soothfastnesse,° *truth*
And tellen fables and swich wrecchednesse.
Why sholde I sowen draf° out of my fest,° *chaff / fist*
Whan I may sowen whete if that me lest?° *it pleases*
For which I saye that if you list to heere
Moralitee and vertuous matere,
And thanne that ye wol yive me audience,
I wol ful fain,° at Cristes reverence, *gladly*
Do you plesance leveful° as I can. *lawfully*
But trusteth wel, I am a southren man:[5]
I can nat geeste° Rum-Ram-Ruf by lettre— *tell stories*
Ne, God woot,° rym holde° I but litel bettre. *knows / appreciate*
And therfore, if you list, I wol nat glose;° *adorn my speech*
I wol you telle a merye tale in prose,
To knitte up al this feeste and make an ende.
And Jesu for his grace wit me sende
To shewe you the way in this viage° *journey*
Of thilke parfit° glorious pilgrimage *that perfect*

2. Seventh sign in the Zodiac, the Scales.
3. Cock's bones, a euphemism for God's bones.
4. St. Paul's Epistle to Timothy.
5. The parson, like Chaucer himself, comes from the south of England and so is not accustomed to telling stories in the alliterative meter used traditionally in the north. Rum-Ram-Ruf is an example of alliteration.

That highte Jerusalem celestial.
And if ye vouche-sauf,° anoon I shal (*agree*)
Biginne upon my tale, for which I praye
Telle youre avis:° I can no bettre saye. (*opinion*)
But nathelees, this meditacioun
I putte it ay° under correccioun (*always*)
Of clerkes, for I am nat textuel:° (*a literalist*)
I take but the sentence,° trusteth wel. (*sense*)
Therfore I make protestacioun
That I wol stonde to correccioun."
Upon this word we han assented soone,
For, as it seemed, it was for to doone
To enden in som vertuous sentence,° (*topic*)
And for to yive him space° and audience; (*time*)
And bede oure Host he sholde to him saye
That alle we to telle his tale him praye.
Oure Hoste hadde the wordes for us alle:
"Sire preest," quod he, "now faire you bifalle:
Telleth," quod he, "youre meditacioun.
But hasteth you, the sonne wol adown.
Beeth fructuous, and that in litel space,
And to do wel God sende you his grace.
Saye what you list, and we wol gladly heere."
And with that word he saide in this manere.

from *The Tale*

Oure sweete Lord God of Hevene, that no man wol perisse[1] but wol that we comen alle to the knowliche of him and to the blisful lif that is perdurable,° amonesteth° us by the prophete Jeremie[2] that saith in this wise: "Stondeth upon the wayes and seeth and axeth of olde pathes (that is to sayn, of olde sentences°) which is the goode way, and walketh in that way, and ye shul finde refresshing for youre soules." (*enduring / warns*; *opinions*)

Manye been the wayes espirituels that leden folk to oure Lord Jesu Crist and to the regne of glorye: of whiche wayes ther is a ful noble way and a ful covenable° which may nat faile to man ne to womman that thurgh sinne hath misgoon fro the righte way of Jerusalem celestial; and this way is cleped° Penitence. * * * (*suitable*; *called*)

The Remedy for the Sin of Lechery

Now cometh the remedye agains Lecherye, and that is generally Chastitee and Continence that restraineth alle the desordainee mevinges° that comen of flesshly talents.° And evere the gretter merite shal he han that most restraineth the wikkede eschaufinges° of the ardure of this sinne. And this is in two maneres: that is to sayn, chastitee in mariage and chastitee of widwehood. (*impulses / desires*; *inflammations*)

1. Who wishes no man to perish.

2. Jeremiah 6.16.

Now shaltou understonde that matrimoine is leeful° assembling of man and of womman that receiven by vertu of the sacrement the bond thurgh which they may nat be departed in al hir life—that is to sayn, whil that they liven bothe. This, as saith the book, is a ful greet sacrement: God maked it, as I have said, in Paradis, and wolde himself be born in mariage. And for to halwen° mariage, he was at a wedding where as he turned water into win, which was the firste miracle that he wroughte in erthe biforn his disciples. Trewe effect of mariage clenseth fornicacion and replenisseth Holy Chirche of good linage° (for that is the ende of mariage), and it chaungeth deedly sinne[3] into venial sinne bitwixe hem that been ywedded, and maketh the hertes al oon° of hem that been ywedded, as wel as the bodies.

lawful / *bless* / *offspring* / *united*

This is verray mariage that was establissed by God er that sinne bigan, whan naturel lawe was in his right point° in Paradis; and it was ordained that oo man sholde have but oo womman, and oo womman but oo man (as saith Saint Augustine) by manye resons: First, for mariage is figured° bitwixe Crist and Holy Chirche; and that other is for a man is heved° of a womman—algate,° by ordinance it sholde be so. For if a womman hadde mo men than oon, thanne sholde she have mo hevedes than oon, and that were an horrible thing biforn God; and eek a womman ne mighte nat plese to many folk at ones. And also ther ne sholde nevere be pees ne reste amonges hem, for everich wolde axen his owene thing. And fortherover, no man sholde knowe his owene engendrure,° ne who sholde have his heritage, and the womman sholde been the lesse biloved fro the time that she were conjoint to manye men.

order / *represented* / *head / at least* / *offspring*

Now cometh how that a man sholde bere him with his wif, and namely in two thinges, that is to sayn, in suffrance° and in reverence, as shewed Crist whan he made first womman. For he ne made hire nat of the heved of Adam for she sholde nat claime too greet lorshipe: for ther as womman hath the maistrye she maketh too greet desray° (ther needen none ensamples of this: the experience of day by day oughte suffise). Also, certes, God ne made nat womman of the foot of Adam, for she ne sholde nat be holden too lowe, for she can nat paciently suffre. But God made womman of the rib of Adam for womman sholde be felawe unto man. Man sholde bere him to his wif in faith, in trouthe, and in love, as saith Sainte Paul, that a man sholde loven his wif as Crist loved Holy Chirche, that loved it so wel that he deide for it. So sholde a man for his wif, if it were neede.

obedience / *disorder*

Now how that a womman sholde be subjet to hir housbonde, that telleth Sainte Peter: First, in obedience. And eek, as saith the decree, a womman that is a wif, as longe as she is a wif, she hath noon auctoritee° to swere ne to bere witnesse withoute leve of hir housbonde that is hir lord—algate, he sholde be so by reson. She sholde eek serven him in alle honestee, and been attempree° of hir array; I woot wel that they sholde setten hir entente° to plesen hir

power / *moderate* / *purpose*

3. Sex remains a minor sin even within marriage, but it is a more serious sin outside of marriage.

housbondes, but nat by hir quaintise of array:° Saint Jerome saith that wives that been apparailed in silk and in precious purpre ne mowe nat clothen hem in Jesu Crist. What saith Saint John eek in this matere? Saint Gregorye eek saith that no wight° seeketh precious array but only for vaine glorye to been honoured the more biforn the peple. It is a greet folye a womman to have a fair array outward and in hireself be foul inward. A wif sholde eek be mesurable° in looking and in bering and in laughing, and discreet in alle hir wordes and hir deedes. And aboven alle worldly thinges she sholde loven hir housbonde with al hir herte, and to him be trewe of hir body (so sholde an housbonde eek be to his wif): for sith that° al the body is the housbondes, so sholde hir herte been, or elles ther is bitwixe hem two as in that no parfit mariage.

flamboyant attire / *person* / *modest* / *since*

Thanne shul men understonde that for three thinges a man and his wif flesshly mowen° assemble. The firste is in entente of engendrure of children to the service of God: for certes, that is the cause final of matrimoine. Another cause is to yeelden everich° of hem to other the dette of hir bodies, for neither of hem hath power of his owene body. The thridde is for to eschewe lecherye and vilainye. The ferthe is, for soothe, deedly sinne. As to the firste, it is meritorye; the seconde also, for, as saith the decree, that she hath merite of chastitee that yeeldeth to hir housbonde the dette of hir body, ye, though it be again hir liking and the lust of hir herte. The thridde manere is venial sinne—and, trewely, scarsly may any of thise be withoute venial sinne, for the corrupcion and for the delit. The ferthe manere is for to understonde if they assemble only for amorous love and for noon of the forsaide causes, but for to accomplice thilke brenning delit—they rekke° nevere how ofte—soothly, it is deedly sinne. And yit with sorwe some folk wol painen hem° more to doon than to hir appetit suffiseth. * * *

may / *each* / *care* / *trouble themselves*

Another remedye agains lecherye is specially to withdrawen swiche thinges as yive occasion to thilke vilainye, as ese,° eting, and drinking: for certes, whan the pot boileth strongly, the beste remedye is to withdrawe the fir. Sleeping longe in greet quiete is eek a greet norice° to lecherye. Another remedye agains lecherye is that a man or a womman eschewe the compaignye of hem by whiche he douteth° to be tempted: for al be it so that the deede be withstonden, yit is ther greet temptacion. Soothly, a whit wal,° although it ne brenne nought fully by stiking of a candele, yit is the wal blak of the leit.° Ful ofte time I rede that no man truste in his owene perfeccion but he be stronger than Sampson, holier than David, and wiser than Salomon.

leisure / *nurse* / *suspects* / *wall* / *from the flame*

Chaucer's Retraction

Here Taketh the Makere of This Book His Leve

Now praye I to hem alle that herkne this litel tretis° or rede,° that if ther be any thing in it that liketh° hem, that therof they thanken oure Lord Jesu Crist, of whom proceedeth al wit and al goodnesse.

treatise / advice / *pleases*

And if ther be any thing that displese hem, I praye hem also that
they arrette° it to the defaute of myn unconning,° and nat to my wil, *attribute / inability*
that wolde ful fain° have said bettre if I hadde had conning. For oure *gladly*
book saith, "Al that is writen is writen for oure doctrine," and that is
myn entente. Wherfore I biseeke you mekely, for the mercy of God,
that ye praye for me that Crist have mercy on me and foryive me my
giltes,° and namely of my translacions and enditinges° of worldly *sins / writings*
vanitees, the whiche I revoke in my retraccions:[4] as is the book of
Troilus; the book also of Fame; the book of the five and twenty
Ladies; the book of the Duchesse; the book of Saint Valentines Day
of the Parlement of Briddes; the tales of Canterbury, thilke that
sounen° into sinne; the book of the Leon; and many another book, if *lead*
they were in my remembrance, and many a song and many a lecch-
erous lay: that Crist for his grete mercy foryive me the sinne. But of
the translacion of Boece *de Consolatione*, and othere bookes of legendes of saintes, and omelies, and moralitee, and devocion, that
thanke I oure Lord Jesu Crist and his blisful Moder and alle the
saintes of hevene, biseeking hem that they from hennes forth unto
my lives ende sende me grace to biwaile° my giltes and to studye to *repent*
the salvacion of my soule, and graunte me grace of verray penitence,
confession, and satisfaccion to doon in this present lif, thurgh the
benigne grace of him that is king of kinges and preest over alle
preestes, that boughte° us with the precious blood of his herte, so *redeemed*
that I may been oon of hem at the day of doom° that shulle be saved. *judgment*
*Qui cum patre et Spiritu Sancto vivis et regnas Deus per omnia saecula.
Amen.*[5]

To His Scribe Adam[1]

Adam scrivain,° if evere it thee bifalle *copyist*
Boece[2] or Troilus for to writen newe,
Under thy longe lokkes thou moste have° the scalle,° *may you get / mange*
But after my making thou write more trewe,[3]
So ofte a day I moot° thy werk renewe, *must*
It to correcte, and eek to rubbe and scrape:
And al is thurgh thy necligence and rape.° *haste*

4. Here Chaucer repents having written most of his major works: *Troilus and Criseyde*, *The Book* (or *House*) *of Fame*, *The Legend of Good Women*, *The Book of the Duchess*, *The Parliament of Fowls*, and various of *The Canterbury Tales*. *The Book of the Lion* has not been preserved. Chaucer's translation of Boethius's *Consolation of Philosophy* is excepted.

5. You who live with the Father and the Holy Spirit and reign as God through all the centuries. Amen.

1. Given his position at court, Chaucer was asked to write many lyrics and occasional poems, such as this poem and the one that follows. In both, he wittily bemoans the conditions of authorship under which he was forced to work, depending on scribes to reproduce his poetry and on patrons to support it. In *To His Scribe Adam*, he strikes a pose of affectionate raillery toward his scribe, whose occupation writers widely scorned. Perhaps he sees it as fitting to curse Adam with a skin disease which will make him scratch his scalp, just as Chaucer has had to scratch out the errors from his manuscripts. However, the poem has a serious undertone too. In fearing that Adam will miscopy his great romance, *Troilus and Criseyde*, he echoes a concern for the accurate reproduction of his work, which he voiced at the end of *Troilus* itself: he prays God that, in view of the great dialectal "diversitee / in Englissh, and in writing of oure tonge," no one "miswrite" his book (5.1793–94).

2. Chaucer's translation of Boethius's *Consolation of Philosophy*.

3. Unless you make a more reliable copy of what I have composed.

Complaint to His Purse[1]

To you, my purs, and to noon other wight,° *creature*
Complaine I, for ye be my lady dere
I am so sory, now that ye be light,° *empty, wanton*
For certes, but if° ye make me hevy cheere,[2] *unless*
Me were as lief° be laid upon my beere;° *I would prefer / bier*
For which unto youre mercy thus I crye:
Beeth hevy again, or elles moot° I die. *must*

Now voucheth sauf° this day er it be night *grant*
That I of you the blisful soun may heere,
Or see youre colour, lik the sonne bright,
That of yelownesse hadde nevere peere.
Ye be my lif, ye be myn hertes steere,° *guide*
Queene of confort and of good compaignye:
Beeth hevy again, or elles moot I die.

Ye purs, that been to me my lives light
And saviour, as in this world down here,
Out of this tonne° helpe me thurgh your might, *dark situation*
Sith that ye wol nat be my tresorere;
For I am shave as neigh° as any frere.[3] *close*
But yit I praye unto youre curteisye:
Beeth hevy again, or elles moot I die.

Envoy to Henry IV[4]

O conquerour of Brutus Albioun,[5]
Which that by line° and free eleccioun *inheritance*
Been verray king, this song to you I sende:
And ye, that mowen° alle oure harmes amende, *may*
Have minde upon my supplicacioun.

William Langland

c. 1330–1387

Little is known of William Langland. On the basis of internal evidence in *Piers Plowman*, he is thought to have been a clerk in minor orders whose career in the church was curtailed by his marriage. He may have come from the Malvern Hills in the west of England, but he spent

1. This is a traditional "begging" poem, based on French models. The request for money is presented humorously, as a parody of a courtly love complaint to a cruel mistress. The parallel takes on ironic force when one recalls Chaucer's presentation of himself, in such early poems as *The Parliament of Fowls*, as a failed lover. This is one of Chaucer's last poems, written a year before his death. It was addressed to Henry IV when he took the throne in 1399, to request a renewal of the annuity Chaucer had received from the deposed Richard II. The flattering "envoy" to Henry at the end alludes to the tradition dating from Geoffrey of Monmouth that Britain was founded by Brutus, the grandson of Aeneas, the exiled prince of Troy and founder of Rome.
2. Serious expression (in a person); full weight (in a purse).
3. Friar (with a bald tonsure).
4. The "envoy" is the traditional close of a ballad, usually directed to its addressee.
5. According to legend, Brutus conquered the kingdom of Albion and renamed it "Britain," after himself.

much of his professional life in London. He was clearly learned, using many Latin quotations from the Bible (given below primarily in English translation, designated by italics and unnumbered), and the style of his poem in many ways resembles sermon rhetoric.

Piers Plowman is an ambitious and multilayered allegory, an attempt to combine Christian history, social satire, and an account of the individual soul's quest for salvation. It is presented as a dream vision whose hero is a humble plowman, and whose narrator, the naive dreamer named Will, may be only a convenient fiction. Even its first audience sometimes reacted to this mysterious poem in surprising ways. *Piers Plowman* was so inspiring to the leaders of the Rising of 1381 that they saw Piers not as a fictional character but as an actual seditious person, as can be seen in the letter of radical priest John Ball in the readings following this poem (pages 475–77). This interpretation of the poem is remarkable given Langland's profound conservatism; despite his scathing social satire, he offers no program for social change. In fact, he supports the traditional model of the three estates, whereby the king and knights protect the body politic, the clergy prays for it, and the commons provide its food. Although he was sympathetic toward the poor and scornful of the rich and powerful, he felt that what ailed society was that *none* of the three estates was performing its proper role.

Piers Plowman survives in many manuscripts, a fact that suggests a large audience, which most likely included secular readers in the government and law as well as the clergy. Most of John Ball's followers would have been unable to read it. The poem exists in three versions—known as the A-, B-, and C-texts—and their history throws light on the poem's role in the Rising of 1381. The short A-text was expanded into the B-text some time between 1377 and 1381, when John Ball and other rebel leaders referred to it, while the C-text (which is translated in the excerpts below) is generally agreed to reflect Langland's attempt to distance himself from the radical beliefs of the rebels. Nevertheless, the poem remained popular for the next two centuries as a document of social protest and was ultimately regarded as a prophecy of the English Reformation. Langland's social criticism, however, is only part of his project, for he considered individual salvation to be equally important. A strictly political reading of *Piers Plowman*—whether in the fourteenth century or the twenty-first—misses a great deal of its originality and its power.

Piers Plowman is a challenge to read: it is almost surrealistic in its rapid and unexplained transitions, its many dreams, and its complex use of allegory. It is as confusing to people reading it in its entirety as to those reading it in excerpts, as here. Nevertheless, the poem does have a kind of unity, of a thematic rather than a narrative sort. It is held together by the dreamer's vision of the corruption of society and his personal quest to save his own soul. This quest is loosely structured by the metaphor of the journey, which is reflected in the poem's subdivision into parts called *passūs*—Latin for "steps." The poem is further unified by the allegorical character of Piers the plowman: a literal fourteenth-century English farmer when we first meet him, in the course of the poem he becomes a figural representation of Saint Peter, the first pope and founder of the church, and of Christ himself.

The five passages included here suggest the connection between the social and spiritual aspects of the poem. In the *Prologue,* the dreamer has a vision of a tower on a hill (later explained as the seat of Truth, i.e., God), a hellish dungeon beneath, and between them, a "field full of folk," representing various professions from the three estates, who are later said to be more concerned with their material than their spiritual welfare.

Passus 2 is the first of three on the marriage of Lady Meed, an ambiguous allegorical figure whose name can mean "just reward," "bribery," or the profit motive generally, the last being a cause for anxiety as England moved from a barter economy to one based on money. The dreamer is invited by Lady Holy Church to Meed's marriage to "False Fickle Tongue." Members of all three estates attend this event, a sign of corruption on every social level.

Langland sees greed as a sin of the poor as well as the rich, and in a comic passage of personification allegory represents the seven deadly sins as members of the commons. Included here from *Passus* 6 is the vividly realized portrait of Glutton, who revels in his sin as he confesses it. Langland discusses the issues of poverty and work most directly in *Passus 8*, where Piers Plowman insists that the assembled people help him plow his half-acre before he will agree to lead them on a pilgrimage to Truth. Piers supports the traditional division of labor, explicitly exempting the knight from producing food, as long as he protects the commons and clergy from "wasters"—lazy shirkers. He insists, however, that the knight treat peasants well—in part because roles may be reversed in heaven, and earthly underlings can become heavenly masters. Yet Langland is not simply taking the workers' side. The knight turns out to be too courteous to control wasters, and Hunger must be called in to offer an incentive to work. When Piers takes pity on the poor and sends Hunger away, Waster refuses to work and the laborers demand more money, cursing the king for the statutes that have instituted wage freezes.

The spiritual climax of the poem takes place in *Passus 20*, which depicts Christ's crucifixion, harrowing of hell (release of the souls of Adam and other Old Testament figures), and resurrection. After many *passūs* of theological debate about his own salvation, the dreamer falls asleep on Palm Sunday and dreams of a man entering Jerusalem on a donkey. The dreamer thinks the man looks like Piers the Plowman, until he recognizes him as Jesus. This man is presented as a young knight going to be dubbed: he will joust against the devil in Piers's armor ("human nature") for the "fruit of Piers the Plowman" (human souls).

Before Christ can release the souls from hell, a lively debate takes place among the "four daughters of God"—Mercy and Truth, Righteousness and Peace—homely "wenches" who embody the words of Psalm 84.11: "Mercy and Truth have met together, Righteousness and Peace have kissed each other." They concede that forgiveness can take precedence over retribution, whereupon Jesus, having "jousted well," leads out the patriarchs and prophets in victory. As church bells ring to signal the resurrection, the dreamer awakes and calls his wife and daughter to church to celebrate Easter with him, thus connecting the grand scheme of salvation history to his personal experience.

The remainder of the poem, *Passūs* 21–22, which are not included here, recount the foundation of the church (by Piers as Saint Peter), and offer an apocalyptic vision of its subsequent corruption by the friars and its attack by Antichrist. There are no answers: the poem ends inconclusively with the allegorical figure of Conscience setting out on a pilgrimage in search of Piers Plowman.

Langland did not write French-inspired rhymed poetry, which was fashionable in London and used by Chaucer, but rather he composed old-fashioned alliterative poetry, which survived from Old English. The so-called Alliterative Revival was divided into two traditions, one based in the north of England and featuring romances in the alliterative "high" style, such as *Sir Gawain and the Green Knight*, and the other based in the south and west, and tending to social protest poems in a plain style. Langland's subject matter and style link him to the latter tradition, which includes satirical poems such as *Richard the Redeless*, *Mum and the Sothsegger*, and *Jack Upland*. In Middle English alliterative poetry, each line contains at least four major stressed syllables, with the first three usually beginning with the same sound. The translations of alliterative poems in this anthology—including *Beowulf* and *Sir Gawain*, as well as *Piers Plowman*—all sufficiently retain the alliteration to convey its flavor in modern English. The following passage from *Piers Plowman* in Middle English, the description of Lady Meed in her gaudy clothes, makes the point more clearly. The dreamer, with naive admiration, reports that he

> . . . was *w*ar of a *w*omman *w*onderliche yclothed,
> *P*urfiled with *P*elure, the *p*ureste on erthe,
> Ycorouned in a coroune, the *k*yng hath noon bettre.
> Fetisliche hire *f*yngres were *f*retted with gold wyr
> And theron *r*iche *R*ubyes as *r*ede as any gleede,
> And *D*iamaundes of *d*errest pris and *d*ouble manere saphires,
> Orientals and *E*wages *e*nuenymes to destroye.

Hire *R*obe ful *r*iche, of *r*eed scarlet engreyned,
With *R*ibanes of *r*eed gold and of *r*iche stones.
Hire *arr*ay me *r*auysshed; swich *r*ichesse saugh I neuere.

Although Langland generally uses the plainer alliterative style of southern protest poetry, here he uses the high style of northern alliterative romances, for satirical purposes. Meed's dress recalls that of Bercilak's lady in *Sir Gawain,* in "rich red rayled" (line 952), as well as the elegant clothing of the Green Knight, "with pelure pured apert, the pane ful clene" (154). In contrast to the clothing of Lady Holy Church, whom Langland introduces in *Passus* 1 simply as "a lady lovely of look, clothed in linen," the robes of lady Meed seem dangerously seductive, thus underscoring a sexual metaphor for bribery which Langland consistently develops. Thus, in a more subtle fashion than some of his followers, such as the Wycliffite author of *Pierce the Ploughman's Crede,* Langland was able to use the specialized language of alliterative poetry in the service of social criticism.

from Piers Plowman[1]

Prologue

In a summer season when the sun shone softly
I wrapped myself in woolens as if I were a sheep;
In a hermit's habit, unholy in his works,
I went out into the world to hear wonders
And to see many strange and seldom-known things.
But on a May morning in the Malvern Hills[2]
I happened to fall asleep, worn out from walking;
And in a meadow as I lay sleeping,
I dreamed most marvelously, as I recall.
All the world's wealth and all of its woe,
Dozing though I was, I certainly saw;
Truth and treachery, treason and guile,
Sleeping I saw them all, as I shall record.
I looked to the East toward the rising sun
And saw a tower—I took it Truth was inside.
To the West then I looked after a while
And saw a deep dale—Death, as I believe,
Dwelled in that place, along with wicked spirits.
Between them I found a fair field full of folk
Of all manner men, the common and the poor,
Working and wandering as this world asks us.
Some put themselves to the plow, and seldom played,
To work hard as they can at planting and sowing
And won what these wasters through gluttony destroy.
And some put themselves in pride's ways and apparel
Themselves accordingly in clothes of all kinds.
Many put themselves to prayers and penances,
All for love of our lord they live so severely
In hope of good ending and heaven-kingdom's bliss;

1. Translated by George Economou.

2. These hills in the west of England were probably Langland's original home.

As anchorites and hermits[3] that keep to their cells,
With no great desire to cruise the countryside
Seeking carnal pleasures and luxurious lives.
And some turned to trade—they made out better,
As it always seems to us that such men thrive;
And some know as minstrels how to make mirth,
Will neither work nor sweat, but swear out loud,
Invent sleazy stories and make fools of themselves
Though it's in their power to work if they want.
What Paul preached about them I surely can prove;
Qui turpiloquium loquitur[4] is Lucifer's man.
Beggars and moochers moved about quickly
Till their bags and their bellies were crammed to the top,
Faking it for food and fighting over ale.
In gluttony those freeloaders go off to bed
And rise to rob and run off at the mouth.
Sleep and sloth are their steady companions.
Pilgrims and palmers[5] pledged to travel together
To seek Saint James[6] and the saints of Rome,
Went on their way with many wise tales
And took leave to lie about it for a lifetime.
A heap of hermits with their hooked staves
Went to Our Lady of Walsingham,[7] with wenches in tow;
Great deadbeats that hated a good day's work
Clothed themselves in hooded cloaks to stand apart
And proclaimed themselves hermits, for the easy life.
I found there friars from all four orders,[8]
Preaching to people to profit their gut,
And glossing the gospel to their own good liking;
Coveting fine copes,° some of these doctors° contradicted authorities. *monk's capes / of divinity*
Many of these masterful mendicant° friars *begging*
Bind their love of money to their proper business.
And since charity's become a broker and chief agent for lords' confessions[9]
Many strange things have happened these last years;
Unless Holy Church and charity clear away such confessors
The world's worst misfortune mounts up fast.
A pardoner[1] preached there as if he were a priest
And brought forth a bull° with the bishops' seals, *papal license*
Said that he himself could absolve them all

3. Both were vowed to a religious life of solitude, hermits in the wilderness and anchorites walled in a tiny dwelling.
4. Who speaks filthy language; not Paul, though (cf. Ephesians 5.3–4).
5. "Professional" pilgrims who took advantage of the hospitality offered them in order to travel.
6. That is, his shrine at Compostela, in Spain.
7. English town, site of a famous shrine to the Virgin Mary.
8. The four orders of friars—Franciscans, Dominicans, Carmelites, and Augustinians. In 14th-century England they were much satirized for their corruption (cf. the friar in the *General Prologue* to Chaucer's *Canterbury Tales*).
9. Confession and the remission of sins is cynically sold by the friars.
1. An official empowered to pass on from the Pope absolution for the sins of people who had given money to charity.

Of phony fasts and of broken vows.
Illiterates believed him and liked what they heard
And came up and kneeled to kiss his pardons;
He bonked them with his bulls and bleared their eyes
And with this rigmarole raked in their brooches and rings.
Thus you give your gold to help out gluttons
And lose it for good to full-time lechers.
If the bishop were true and kept his ear to the ground
He'd not consign his seal to deceit of the people.
But it's not through the bishop that this guy preaches,
For the parish priest and pardoner split the silver
That, if not for them, the parishoners would have.

* * *

Still I kept dreaming about poor and rich,
Like barons and burgesses and village bondmen,[2]
All I saw sleeping as you shall hear next:
Bakers and brewers, butchers and others,
Weavers and websters, men that work with their hands,
Like tailors and tanners and tillers of earth,
Like dike and ditch diggers that do their work badly
And drive out their days with "*Dew vous saue, dame Emme*."[3]
Cooks and their helpers cried, "Get your hot pies!
Good geese and pig meat! Come on up and eat!"
And taverners touted in much the same way:
"White wine of Alsace and wine from Gascony,
Wash down your roast with La Reole and La Rochelle!"
All this, and seven times more, I saw in my sleep.

Passus 2

[THE MARRIAGE OF LADY MEAD]

And then I kneeled before her[1] and cried to her for grace,
"Mercy, madame, for the love of Mary in heaven
That bore the blessed child that bought us on the cross,
Teach me the way to recognize Falsehood."
"Look to your left and see where he stands.
Falsehood and Fave[2] and fickle-tongued Liar
And many more men and women like them."
I looked to my left as the lady said
And saw a woman wonderfully clothed.
She was trimmed all in fur, the world's finest,
And crowned with a coronet as good as the king's;
On all five fingers were the richest rings
Set with red rubies and other precious gems.

2. Barons were members of the higher aristocracy; burgesses were town-dwellers with full rights as citizens; and bondmen were peasants who held their land from a lord in return for services or rent.

3. Presumably a popular song.

1. Lady Holy Church.

2. "Lying"; the name of characters representing deceit in Old French literature.

Her robes were richer than I can describe,
To talk of her attire I don't have time;
Her raiment and riches ravished my heart.
Whose wife she was and her name I wanted to know,
"Dear lady," I then asked, "conceal nothing from me."
"That is the maid Meed[3] who has hurt me many times
And lied against my beloved who is called Loyalty
And slanders him to the lords that keep all our laws,
In the king's court and the commons' she contradicts my teaching,
In the pope's palace is privy as I,
But Truth would she weren't for she's a bastard.
Favel was her father who has a fickle tongue
And seldom speaks truth unless it's a trick,
And Meed takes after him, as men remark on kin:
Like father, like daughter.
For never shall a briar put forth berries
Nor on a rough, crooked thorn a real fig grow:
A good tree bringeth forth good fruit.[4]
I should be higher, for I come from better stock;
He that fathered me *filius dei*° is named, son of God
Who never lied or laughed in his entire life,
And I am his dear daughter, duchess of heaven,
The man that loves me and follows my will
Shall have grace a-plenty and a good end,
And the man that loves Meed, I'll bet my life,
Will lose for her love a morsel of charity.
What is man's most help to heaven Meed will most hinder—
I base this on King David, whose book[5] does not lie:
Lord, who shall dwell in thy tabernacle.[6]
And David himself explains, as his mute book shows:
And not taken bribes against the innocent.[7]
Tomorrow Meed marries a miserable wretch,
One False Faithless of the Fiend's lineage.
With flattery Favel's fouly enchanted Meed
And Liar's made all the arrangements for the match.
Be patient and you will see those that are pleased
By Meed's marriage, tomorrow you'll view it.
Get to know them if you can and avoid all those
Who love her lordship, both the high and the low.
Don't fault them but let them be till Loyalty's judge
And has power to punish them, then do your pleading.
Now I commend you to Christ and his pure mother,
And never load your conscience with coveting meed."
Thus the lady left me lying asleep

3. A richly ambiguous word referring to a wide variety of "reward," both positive and negative, including just reward, heavenly salvation, recompense, the profit motive, graft, and bribery.

4. Matthew 7.17.

5. The book of Psalms.

6. Psalms 14.1.

7. Psalms 14.5.

And still dreaming I saw Meed's marriage.
All the rich retinue rooted in false living
Were bid to the bridal from the entire country,
All kinds of men that were Meed's kin,
Knights, clerics, and other common people,
Like jurors, summoners, sheriffs and their clerks,
Beadles, bailiffs, businessmen, and agents,
Purveyors, victualers, advocates of the Arches,[8]
I can't keep count of the crowd that ran with Meed.
But Simony and Civil[9] and his jurymen
Were tightest with Meed it seemed of all men.
But Favel was first to fetch her out of chamber
And like a broker brought her to be joined with False.

from *Passus 6*
[The Confession of Glutton]

Now Glutton heads for confession
And moves towards the Church, his *mea culpa*[1] to say.
Fasting on a Friday he made forth his way
By the house of Betty Brewer, who bid him good morning
And where was he going that brew-wife asked.
"To Holy Church," he said, "to hear mass,
And then sit and be shriven and sin no more."
"I have good ale, Glutton, old buddy, want to give it a try?"
"Do you have," he asked, "any hot spices?"
"I have pepper, peony, and a pound of garlic,
A farthing-worth of fennel seed[2] for fasting days I bought it."
Then in goes Glutton and great oaths after.
Cissy the shoemaker sat on the bench,
Wat the game warden and his drunken wife,
Tim the tinker and two of his workmen,
Hick the hackney-man and Hugh the needler,
Clarice of Cock's Lane[3] and the clerk of the church,
Sir Piers of Pridie and Purnel of Flanders,
A hayward, a hermit, the hangman of Tyburn,
Daw the ditchdigger and a dozen rascals
In the form of porters and pickpockets and bald tooth-pullers,
A fiddler, a rat-catcher, a street-sweeper and his helper,
A rope-maker, a road-runner, and Rose the dish-seller,
Godfrey the garlic-man and Griffith the Welshman,
And a heap of secondhand salesmen, early in the morning
Stood Glutton with glad cheers to his first round of ale.

8. The officials in this and the two preceding lines had jobs that made them particularly open to bribery.
9. Simony is the buying and selling of church offices or spiritual functions; Civil is civil as opposed to criminal law (especially noted for its bribery and corruption).

1. By my own fault; formula used in Christian prayers and confession.
2. An herb thought to be good for someone drinking on an empty stomach.
3. Clarice and Purnel (of the next line) are prostitutes.

Clement the cobbler took off his cloak
And put it up for a game of New Fair[4]
Hick the hackney-man saw with his hood
And asked Bart the butcher to be on his side.
Tradesmen were chosen to appraise this bargain,
That whoso had the hood should not have the cloak,
And that the better thing, according to the arbiters, compensate the worse.
They got up quickly and whispered together
And appraised these items apart in private,
And there was a load of swearing, for one had to get the worse.
They could not in conscience truthfully accord
Till Robin the rope-maker they asked to arise
And named him umpire so that all arguing would stop.
Hick the hostler got the cloak
On condition that Clement should fill the cup
And have Hick the hostler's hood and rest content;
And whoever took it back first had to get right up
And greet Sir Glutton with a gallon of ale.
There was laughing and louring and "please pass the cup!"
Bargaining and drinking they kept starting up
And sat so till evensong[5] and sang from time to time,
Until Glutton had gobbled down a gallon and a gill° *1/4 pint*
His guts began to rumble like two greedy sows;
He pissed half a gallon in the time of a *pater noster*,[6]
He blew his round bugle at his backbone's bottom,
So that all who heard that horn had to hold their noses
And wished it had been well plugged with a wisp of briars.
He could neither step nor stand unless he held a staff,
And then he moved like a minstrel's performing dog,
Sometimes sideways and sometimes backwards,
Like some one laying lines in order to trap birds.
And when he reached the door, then his eyes dimmed,
And he stumbled on the threshold and fell to the ground,
And Clement the cobbler grabbed him by the waist
And in order to lift him up set him on his knees.
But Glutton was a huge boor and troubled in the lifting
And barfed up a mess into Clement's lap;
There is no hound so hungry in Hertfordshire
That he'd dare lap up that leaving, so unlovely it smacked.° *tasted*
With all the woe in this world his wife and his daughter
Bore him to his bed and put him in it,
And after all this excess he had a bout of sloth;
He slept through Saturday and Sunday till sundown.
Then he awoke pale and wan and wanted a drink;

4. An elaborate game involving the exchange of clothing.
5. Vespers, the evening prayer service said just before sunset.
6. The time it takes to say the Paternoster, the Lord's Prayer.

The first thing he said was "Who's got the bowl?"
His wife and his conscience reproached him for his sin;
He became ashamed, that scoundrel, and made quick confession
To Repentance like this: "Have pity on me," he said,
"Lord who are aloft and shape all that lives!
   To you God, I, Glutton, acknowledge my guilt
Of how I've trespassed with tongue, how often I can't tell,
Sworn 'God's soul and his sides!' and 'So help me God, Almighty!'
There was no need for it so many times falsely;
And overate at supper and sometime at noon
More than my system could naturally handle,
And like a dog that eats grass I began to throw up
And wasted what I might have saved—I can't speak for my shame
Of the depravity of my foul mouth and maw—
And on fasting days before noon I fed myself ale
Beyond all reason, among dirty jokesters, their dirty jokes to hear.
   For this, good God, grant me forgiveness
For my worthless living during my entire lifetime.
For I swear by the true God, despite any hunger or thirst,
Never shall on Friday a piece of fish digest in my stomach
Till my aunt Abstinence has given me leave—
And yet I've hated her all my lifetime."

from *Passus 8*
[PIERS PLOWING THE HALF-ACRE]

Perkin[1] the plowman said, "By Saint Peter of Rome!
I have a half-acre to plow by the highway;
Had I plowed this half-acre and afterwards sown it
I'd go along with you and teach you the way."
   "That would be a long delay," said a lady in a veil,
"What should we women work on meanwhile?"
   "I appeal to you for your profit," said Piers to the ladies,
"That some sew the sack to keep the wheat from spilling,
And you worthy women with your long fingers
That you have silk and sandal[2] to sew when you've time
Chasubles° for chaplains to the church's honor. *robes*
Wives and widows spin wool and flax;
Conscience counsels you to make cloth
To benefit the poor and for your own pleasure.
For I shall see to their sustenance, unless the land fail,
As long as I live, for love of the Lord of heaven.
And all manner of men who live off the land
Help him work well who obtains your food."
   "By Christ," said a knight then, "he teaches us the best;
But truly on the plow theme I was never taught.
I wish I knew how," said the knight, "by Christ and his mother;

1. A nickname for Piers, or Peter.
2. A thin, rich form of silk.

Plowmen, from the *Luttrell Psalter*, early 14th century.

I'd try it sometime for fun as it were."
    Certainly, sir knight," said Piers then,
"I shall toil and sweat and sow for us both
And labor for those you love all my lifetime,
On condition you protect Holy Church and me
From wasters and wicked men who spoil the world,
And go hunt hardily for hares and foxes,
Boars and bucks that break down my hedges,
And train your falcons to kill the wild birds
Because they come to my croft° and defile my corn."° *field / grain*
    Courteously the knight then commenced with these words:
"By my power, Piers, I pledge you my truth
To defend you faithfully, though I should fight."
    "And still one point," said Piers, "I ask of you further:
Try not to trouble any tenant unless Truth agrees
And when you fine any man let Mercy be assessor
And Meekness your master, despite Meed's moves.
And though poor men offer you presents and gifts
Don't take them on the chance you're not deserving,
For it may be you'll have to return them or pay for them dearly.
Don't hurt your bondman, you'll be better off;
Though he's your underling here, it may happen in heaven
He'll be sooner received and more honorably seated.
    Friend, go up higher[3]
At church in the charnel[4] it's hard to discern churls
Or between knight and knave or a queen on a corner[5] and one on the
    throne.
It becomes you, knight, to be courteous and gracious,
True of tongue and loth to hear tales
Unless they're about goodness, battles, or good faith.

3. Luke 14.10.
4. Crypt for dead bodies.
5. I.e., "queen," a prostitute.

Don't keep company with crude-mouths or listen to their stories,
And especially at your meals avoid such men
For they are the Devil's entertainers and draw men to sin.
And do not oppose Conscience or the rights of Holy Church."
"I assent, by Saint Giles," said the knight then,
"To work by your wisdom and my wife, too."
"And I shall dress myself," said Perkin, "in pilgrims' fashion
And go with all those who wish to live in Truth."

* * *

Now Perkin and these pilgrims go to their plowing;
Many helped him to turn over the half-acre.
Ditchers and diggers dug up the strip-ridges;
All this pleased Perkin and he paid them good wages.
Other workmen were there who worked very hard,
Each man in his way made himself useful
And some to please Perkin picked weeds in the field.
At high prime, about nine[6] Piers let the plow stand
And oversaw them himself; whoever worked best
Would later be hired when harvest time comes.
And then, some sat down and sang at ale
And helped plow this half-acre with a "hey trolliloly![7]
Said Piers the plowman in a pure anger:
"If you don't get up quickly and rush back to work
No grain that grows here will cheer you in need,
And though you die of grief, the devil take him who cares."
Then the phonies were frightened and pretended to be blind
And twisted their legs backwards as such losers know how
And moaned to Piers about how they couldn't work:
"And we pray for you Piers and for your plow, too,
That God for his grace multiply your grain
And reward you for the alms you give us here.
We may neither sweat nor strain, such sickness ails us,
Nor have we limbs to labor with, the Lord God we thank."
"Your prayers," said Piers, "if you were upright,
Might help, as I hope, but high Truth would
That no fakery were found in people that go begging.
You're wasters, I know well, and waste and devour
What true land-tilling men loyally work for.
But Truth shall teach you to drive his team
Or you'll eat barley bread and drink from the brook,
Unless he's blind or broken-legged or braced with iron—
Such poor," said Piers, "shall share in my goods,
Both of my corn and my cloth to keep them from want.
But anchorites and hermits who eat only at noon
And friars who don't flatter and poor sick people,
Hey! I and mine will provide for their needs."

6. Nine in the morning, after a substantial amount of work has been done.

7. Probably the refrain of a popular song.

Then Waster got angry and wanted to fight
And pressed Piers the plowman to "put 'em up!"
And told him to go piss with his plow, pigheaded creep!
A Breton came bragging and threatened Piers also:
"Whether you like it or not," he said, "we'll have our way,
And take your flour and meat whenever we like
And make merry with it, despite any grumbling."
Piers the plowman then complained to the knight
To keep him and his property as they had agreed:
"Avenge me on these wasters who bring harm to the world;
Excommunication they take no account of nor fear Holy Church.
There will be no plenty," said Piers, "if the plow stands still."
Then the knight, as was his nature, courteously
Warned Waster and advised him to improve:
"Or I'll beat you according to the law and put you in the stocks."
"I'm not used to working," said Waster, "and I won't start now!"
And made light of the law and less of the knight
And sized up Piers as a pea to complain wherever he would.
"Now by Christ," said Piers the plowman, "I'll punish you all,"
And whooped after Hunger who heard right away.
"I pray you," Piers said then, "Sir Hunger, *pour charite*[8]
Avenge me on these wasters, for the knight will not."
Hunger in haste then grabbed Waster around the belly
And hugged him so tight that his eyes watered.
He battered the Breton about the cheeks
So that he looked like a lantern the rest of his life,
And he so beat both of them up he nearly busted their guts
Had not Piers with a peas-load[9] called him off.
"Have mercy on them, Hunger," said Piers, "and let me give them beans,
And what was baked for Bayard[1] may come to their relief."
Then the fakers were frightened and flew into Piers' barns.
And flapped with flails from morning till evening,
So that Hunger was less intent on looking upon them.
For a potful of pottage that Piers' wife had made
A heap of hermits took up spades,
Dug and spread dung to despite Hunger.
They cut up their capes and made them short coats
And went as workmen to weeding and mowing
All for fear of death, so hard did Hunger hit.
The blind and broken-legged he bettered by the thousand
And lame men he healed with animal entrails.
Priests and other people drew towards Piers
And friars from all five orders,[2] all for fear of Hunger.
For what was baked for Bayard relieved many hungry,

8. For charity's sake.
9. Cheapest kind of bread, standard fare for the poor.
1. A generic name for a horse; a bread made of beans and bran was fed to horses.
2. See Prologue, n.8 (line 56) on the four orders. The fifth order referred to here may be the Crutched Friars, a minor order.

Dross and dregs were drink for many beggars.
There was no lad living that wouldn't bow to Piers
To be his faithful servant though he had no more
Than food for his labor and his gift at noon.
  Then Piers was proud and put them all to work
At daubing and digging, at dung bearing afield,
At threshing, at thatching, at whittling pins,
At every kind of true craft that man can devise.
There was no beggar so bold, unless he were blind,
Dared oppose what Piers said for fear of Sir Hunger.
And Piers was proud of that and put them all to work
And gave them food and money according to their deserts.
  Then Piers had pity for all poor people
And bade Hunger hurry up out of the country
Back home to his own yard and stay there forever.

* * *

  "I promise you," said Hunger, "I won't go away
Before I have this day both dined and drunk."
  "I've no penny," said Piers, "with which to buy pullets,
Nor goose or pork but two green cheeses
And a few curds and cream and an oat cake
And bean and pea bread for my kids.
And still I say, by my soul, I've no salt bacon
Nor any egg, by Christ, to fry up together.
But I have leeks, parsley and scallions,
Chives and chervil and half-ripe cherries,
And a cow with a calf and a cart-mare
To draw my dung afield during dry spells.
And we must live by this means of life till Lammas time[3]
And by then I hope to have harvest in my fields;
Then may I make dinner just as I like."
  All the poor people then fetched peascods;
Beans and baked apples they brought by the lapful,
And offered Piers this present with which to please Hunger.
Hunger ate it all in haste and asked for more.
For fear then poor folk fed Hunger quickly
With cream and curds, with cress and other herbs.
By then harvest drew near and new corn came to market
And people were happy and fed Hunger deliciously,
And then Glutton with good ale put Hunger to sleep.
  And then Waster refused to work and wandered around,
Nor'd any beggar eat bread in which there were beans,
But the finest white breads and of pure wheat,
Nor no way would they drink half-penny ale
But the best and brownest that brewsters sell.
Laborers with no land to live on but their own hands

3. The harvest festival, August 1, when a loaf made from the first wheat of the season was offered at mass.

Wouldn't deign to dine today on last night's veggies;
No penny-ale or piece of bacon pleased them
But it had to be fresh meat or fish, fried or baked,
And that *chaud* or *plus chaud*[4] against a chilled stomach.
And unless he's hired for high pay he'll otherwise argue
And curse the time he was made a workman.
He begins to grumble against Cato's counsel:
Paupertatis onus pacienter ferre memento.[5]
And then he curses the king and all his justices
For teaching such laws that grieve workingmen[6]
But as long as Hunger was master none of them would bitch,
Nor strive against his statute, he looked so stern.
  I warn you workmen, get ahead while you can,
For Hunger's hurrying this way fast as he can.
He shall awake through water, wasters to punish,
And before a few years finish famine shall arise,
And so says Saturn[7] and sends us warning.
Through floods and foul weather fruits shall fail;
Pride and pestilence shall take out many people.
Three ships and a sheaf with an 8 following
Shall bring bane and battle under both halves of the moon.
And then death shall withdraw and dearth be the judge
And Dave the ditcher° die of hunger *ditch-digger*
Unless God of his goodness grant us a truce.

Passus 20

[The Crucifixion and the Harrowing of Hell]

Wool-shirted and wet-shoed I went forth after
Like a careless man who takes no care of sorrow,
And tramped forth like a vagrant all my lifetime
Till I grew weary of the world and wanted to sleep again
And lay down till Lent and slept a long time.
  I dreamed a great deal of children and of *gloria laus*[1]
And how to instruments elder folks sang osanna.° *Hosanna*
One who resembled the Samaritan and Piers the plowman
  somewhat
Barefoot came riding bootless on an ass's back
Without spurs or spear—sprightly he looked,
As is natural for a knight who came to be dubbed,
To get his gilt spurs and cut-away shoes.
And then Faith was in a window and cried, "A, *filii Dauid*"[2]

4. Hot or very hot.
5. Remember to bear your burden of poverty patiently. From Cato's *Distichs*, a collection of phrases used to teach Latin to beginning students.
6. A reference to the Statutes of Laborers, passed after 1351, when the Black Death depopulated the countryside and a labor shortage ensued. They were intended to control the mobility and the wages of laborers.
7. Planet thought to influence the weather, generally perceived to be hostile.
1. "Glory, praise [and honor]": the first words of an anthem sung by children on Palm Sunday. This part of the poem reflects the biblical account of Christ's entry into Jerusalem.
2. On the first Palm Sunday, crowds greeted Christ crying "Hosanna [line 7] to the son of David."

As a herald of arms does when adventurous knights come to jousts.
Old Jews of Jerusalem sang for joy,
  Blessed is he that cometh in the name of the Lord.[3]
  Then I asked Faith what all this activity meant,
And who should joust in Jerusalem? "Jesus," he said,
"And fetch what the Fiend claims, the fruit of Piers the plowman."
"Is Piers in this place?" I said, and he looked at me knowingly:
"*Liberum-dei-arbitrium*"[4] has for love undertaken
That this Jesus for his gentility will joust in Piers' armor,
In his helmet and in his mail, *humana natura;*[5]
So that Christ not be known as *consummatus deus*,[6]
In the plate-armor of Piers the plowman this cavalier will ride,
For no dent will damage him as *in deitate patris*."[7]
  "Who will joust with Jesus," I said, "Jews or scribes?"[8]
  "No," Faith said, "but the Fiend and False-doom-to-die.
Death says he will undo and bring down
All that live or look on land or in water.
Life says he lies and lays his life as pledge,
That for all Death can do, within three days, he'll walk
And fetch from the Fiend the fruit of Piers the plowman,
And lay it wherever he likes and Lucifer bind
And beat down death and bring death to death forever.
  O death, I will be thy death, thy bite!"[9]
  Then came Pilate with many people, *sedens pro tribunali*,[1]
To see how doughtily Death would do and to judge both their
  rights.
The Jews and the justices were against Jesus,
And all the court cried "*Crucifige*"[2] loud.
Then a prosecutor appeared before Pilate and said.
"This Jesus made jokes and despised our Jewish Temple,
To demolish it in one day, and in three days after
Rebuild it anew—here he stands who said it—
And still make it as sizable in all ways,
Both as long and as large, aloft and on ground,
And as broad as it was ever; this we all heard."
"*Crucifige*" said a court officer, "he practices witchcraft."
"*Tolle, Tolle!*"[3] said another, and took sharp thorns
And began to make of green thorns a garland
And set it roughly on his head, and then hatefully said,
"*Aue, raby*,[4] that scoundrel said, and poked reeds at his eyes;
And they nailed him with three nails naked upon a cross

3. Matthew 21.9.
4. The Free Will of God.
5. In the Incarnation Christ assumed human nature, to redeem humankind.
6. The perfect (triune) God.
7. In the godhead of the Father: as God Christ could not suffer, but as man he could.
8. Scribes were persons who made a strict literal interpretation of the Old Law and hence rejected Christ's teaching of the New.
9. Hosea 13.14.
1. Sitting as a judge (Matthew 27.19).
2. Crucify! (John 19.6).
3. "Away with him! Away with him!" (John 19.15).
4. "Hail, Rabbi [i.e., Master]" (Matthew 26.49): the words Judas spoke when he kissed Christ to identify him to the arresting officers.

And with a pole put poison up to his lips
And bade him drink, to delay his death and lengthen his days,
And said, "If he's subtle, he'll help himself now;"
And "If you're Christ—and Christ, God's Son—
Come down from this cross and then we'll believe!
That Life loves you and won't let you die."
"*Consummatum est*,"[5] said Christ and started to swoon.
Piteously and pale, like a dying prisoner,
The Lord of Life and Light then laid his eyes together.
For dread the day withdrew and dark became the sun;
The wall of the Temple split apart all to pieces,
The hard rock completely riven, and darkest night it seemed.
The earth shivered and shook as if it were alive
And dead men for that din came out of deep graves
And told why the storm had lasted so long:
"For a bitter battle," the dead body said;
"Life and Death in this darkness destroy one another,
And no man will know for sure who shall have the mastery
Before Sunday, around sunrise," and sank with that to earth.
Some said he was God's Son who died so fairly,
Indeed this was the Son of God,[6]
And some said, "He's a sorcerer; good that we test
Whether he's dead or not dead before he's taken down."
At that time two thieves suffered death
Upon crosses beside Christ, such was the common law.
A court officer came and cracked their legs in two
And the arms after of each of those thieves.
But there was no punk so bold as to touch God's body;
Because he was a knight and a king's son, Kind[7] fully granted that time
That no punk had nerve enough to touch him in dying.
But a blind knight with a sharply honed spear came forth,
Named Longinus,[8] as the record shows, and he had long lost his sight;
Before Pilate and the other people in the place he waited in readiness.
Over his protests he was forced at that time
To joust with Jesus, this blind Jew Longinus;
For they were all gutless who hovered or stood there
To touch him or contact him or take him down and bury him,
Except this blind bachelor, who pierced him through the heart.
The blood sprang down the spear and spread open the knight's eyes.
Then the knight fell straight on his knees and cried Jesus mercy—
"It was against my will," he said, "that I was made to wound you."
And sighed and said, "Sorely I repent it,
For the deed that I've done I put myself in your grace.
Both my land and my body take at your pleasure,
And have mercy on me, rightful Jesus!" and right with that he wept.

5. "It is finished" (John 19.30).
6. Matthew 27.54.
7. Nature (an aspect of God).
8. Longinus appears in the apocryphal Gospel of Nicodemus, which was the principal source of this account of Christ's harrowing of hell.

Then Faith began fiercely to upbraid the false Jews[9]
Called them low-down no-goods, accursed forever:
"For this was a vile villainy; may vengeance befall you
Who made the blind beat the dead—this was a punk's doing!
Cursed low-downs! It was never knighthood
To beat a bound body with any bright weapon.
Yet he's taken the prize for all his great wounds,
For your champion rider, chief knight of you all,
Surrendered crying out defeat, right at the will of Jesus.
When this darkness passes, Death shall be vanquished,
And you clowns have lost, for Life shall have mastery,
And your unstinted freedom fall into servitude,
And all your children, churls, will never achieve prosperity,
Nor have lordship over land or any land to till,
And as barren be, and live by usury,
Which is a life that our Lord forbids in all laws.
Now your good times are over, as Daniel told you,
When Christ through the cross overcame, your kingdom will fall apart.
When the holy of holies comes, it ceases, etc."[1]
What for fear of wonder and of the false Jews
I withdrew in that darkness to *descendit ad inferna*,[2]
And there I surely saw, *secundum scripturas*,[3]
Out of the west, as it were, a young woman, as I thought,
Came walking on the way, hellward she looked.
Mercy that maid was named, a mild thing as well
And a very good-willed maiden and modest of speech.
Her sister, as it seemed, came walking softly
Squarely out of the east, and westward she was headed,
A comely and pure creature, Truth was her name.
Because of the virtue that followed her, she was never afraid.
When these maidens met, Mercy and Truth,
They asked each other about this great wonder,
About the din and the darkness and how the day dawned,
And what a light and a shining lay before hell.
"I'm astonished by this business, in faith," said Truth,
"And I'm coming to discover what this wonder means."
"Don't marvel at it," said Mercy, "joy is its meaning.
A maid called Mary, and mother without contact
With any kind of creature, conceived through speech
And grace of the Holy Ghost, grew great with child,
Without womanly spot brought him into this world;
And that my tale is true I take God to witness.
Since this baby was born thirty winters have passed,
Died and suffered death this day about midday;
And that is the cause of this eclipse that now shuts out the sun,

9. This and the next 18 lines are an example of late medieval antisemitism.
1. Compare with Daniel 9.24.
2. He descended into hell (from the Apostles' Creed)
3. According to the Scriptures.

In meaning that man shall be drawn out of murkiness
While this light and this beam will blind Lucifer.
For patriarchs and prophets have preached of this often,
That what was lost through a tree, a tree shall win back,[4]
And what death brought down, death shall raise up."
"What you're saying," said Truth, "Is nothing but hot air!
For Adam and Eve and Abraham with other
Patriarchs and prophets who lie in pain,
Never believe that yonder light will lift them up
Or have them out of hell—hold your tongue, Mercy!
What you're saying is just a trifle; I, Truth, know the truth,
That a thing that's once in hell never comes out.
Job the perfect patriarch discredits your sayings:
Because there is no redemption in hell."[5]
Then Mercy most mildly mouthed these words:
"From experience," she said, "I hope they'll be saved;
For venom undoes venom, from which I fetch proof
That Adam and Eve shall have remedy.
Of all devouring venoms the vilest is the scorpion's;
No medicine may amend the place where it stings
Until it's dead and applied thereto, and then it destroys
The first poisoning through its own virtue.
And so this death shall undo, I'll bet my life,
All that Death and the Devil first did to Eve.
And just as the deceiver through deceit deceived men first,
So shall grace, which began all, make a good end
And deceive the deceiver, and that's a good deception:
It takes a trick to undo a trick."[6]
"Now let's just hold it," said Truth; "it seems to me I see
Out of the nip° of the north, not very far from here, *chill*
Righteousness come running. Let's take it easy,
For she knows more than we—she was before we both were."
"That's true," said Mercy, "and I see here to the south
Where Peace, clothed in patience, comes ready to play;
Love has desired her long—I believe none other
But Love has sent her some letter about what this light means
That hovers over hell thus; she'll tell us."
When Peace, clothed in patience, approached them both,
Righteousness reverenced Peace in her rich clothing
And prayed Peace tell her to what place she was going
And whom she meant to gladden in her gay garments.
"My wish is to go," said Peace, "and welcome them all
Who for many a day I could not see for murkiness of sin,
Adam and Eve and many others in hell.
Moses and many more will sing merrily

4. The first tree bore the fruit that Adam and Eve ate, thereby damaging humankind; the second tree is the cross on which Christ was crucified, thereby redeeming humankind.
5. Compare with Job 7.9.
6. From a hymn sung on Palm Sunday.

And I'll dance to their tune—do the same, sister!
For Jesus jousted well, joy begins to dawn.
In the evening weeping shall have place, and in the morning gladness.[7]
Love, who is my lover, sent me such letters
That my sister Mercy and I shall save mankind,
And that God has forgiven and granted to all mankind
Mercy, my sister, and me to bail them all out;
And that Christ has converted the nature of righteousness
Into peace and pity out of his pure grace.
Look, here's the letter patent![8] said Peace, "*in pace in idipsum*—
And that this deed shall endure—*dormiam et requiescam*."[9]
"Do you rave?" said Righteousness, "or are you just drunk!
Do you believe that yonder light might unlock hell
And save man's soul? Sister, never believe it!
At the world's beginning, God gave the judgment himself
That Adam and Eve and all their issue
Should downright die and dwell in pain forever
If they touched that tree and ate of its fruit.
Afterwards Adam against his prohibition
Ate of the fruit and forsook, as it were,
The love of our Lord and his teachings, too,
And followed what the Fiend taught and his flesh's will,
Against reason; I, Righteousness, record this with Truth
That their pain is perpetual—no prayer can help them.
Therefore let them chew as they chose and let's not fight about it, sisters,
For it is care past cure, the bite that they ate."
"And I shall prove," said Peace, "their pain must end,
And finally their woe must turn into well-being.
For had they known no woe, they'd not know well-being;
For no one knows well-being who never suffered woe,
Nor what hot hunger is who never was famished.
Who could naturally describe with color
If all the world were white or all things swan-white?
If there were no night, I believe no man
Should really know what day means;
Or had God suffered at the hands of some one other than himself,
He'd never have known for sure whether death is sour or sweet.
For never would a very rich man, who lives in rest and health,
Know what woe is if there were no natural death.
So God, who began all, of his good will
Became man of a maiden, to save mankind,
And suffered to be sold to see the sorrow of dying,
Which unknits all care and is the beginning of rest.
For until plague meets with us, I give you assurance,
Nobody knows, as I see it, the meaning of enough.

7. Psalms 29.6.
8. Document conferring authority.
9. In peace in the self-same: . . . I will find rest (Psalms 4.9).

Therefore, God of his goodness the first man Adam
Set up in first solace and in sovereign joy;
And then suffered him to sin, in order to feel sorrow,
To know thereby what well-being was, to understand it naturally.
And afterward, God ventured himself and took Adam's nature
To know what he had suffered in three different places,
Both in heaven and on earth—and now to hell he heads,
To know what all woe is, he who knew all joy.
But prove all things; hold fast that which is good.[1]
So it shall go for these folk: their folly and their sin
Shall teach them what love is and bliss without end.
For nobody knows what war is where peace rules
Nor what is real well-being till he's taught by woe-is-me."
Then there was a person with two broad eyes;[2]
Book that good father was named, a bold man of speech.
"By God's body," said this Book, "I will bear witness,
That when this baby was born a star blazed
So that all the wise men in the world fully agreed
That such a baby was born in Bethlehem city
Who should save man's soul and destroy sin.
And all the elements," said the Book, "bear witness of this.
That he was God that made everything the sky showed first:
Those in heaven took *stella comata*[3]
And tended it like a torch to reverence his birth;
The light followed the Lord into the low earth.
The water witnessed that he was God, for he walked on it dry:
Peter the Apostle perceived his passage
And as he went on the water knew him well, and said,
'*Lord, bid me come to thee.*'[4]
And oh, how the sun locked up her light in herself
When she saw him suffer, who made the sun and sea!
Oh, how the earth for heaviness that he would suffer
Quaked as if alive and the rocks cracked also!
Oh no, hell might not hold, but opened when God suffered
And let out Simeon's sons[5] to see him hang on cross.
He should not see death.[6]
And now shall Lucifer believe it, loath though he be;
For Jesus comes yonder as a giant with an engine[7]
To break and beat down all that oppose him
And to have out of hell all those he pleases.
And yet I, Book, will be burnt if he not arise to life
And comfort all his kin and bring them out of care
And all joy of the Jews dissolve and despise,

1. 1 Thessalonians 5.21.
2. Book's two broad eyes suggest the Old and New Testaments.
3. Hairy star (i.e., comet).
4. Matthew 14.28.
5. According to the apocryphal Gospel of Nicodemus, Simeon's sons were raised from the dead at the time of Christ's crucifixion.
6. Luke 2.26, which continues, "before he had seen the Christ the Lord."
7. A military device, perhaps like a giant slingshot.

And unless they revere this resurrection and honor the cross
And believe in a new law, be lost body and soul."
"Quiet," said Truth: "I both hear and see
A spirit speaks to hell and bids the gates be opened."
Lift up your gates.[8]
A loud voice within that light said to Lucifer:
"*Princepes*° of this place, quickly undo these gates, Princes
For he comes here with crown, the king of all glory!"
Then Satan[9] sighed and said to Hell,
"Such a light against our leave fetched away Lazarus;[1]
Care and encumbrance is come to us all.
If this king comes in, he'll fetch mankind
And lead it where Lazarus is and bind me easily.
Patriarchs and prophets have long talked of this
That such a lord and light shall lead them all hence.
But rise up, Ragamuffin, and hand over all the bars
That Belial your grandfather beat with your mother,
And I shall block this lord and stop his light.
Before we're blinded by this brightness, let's go bar the gates.
Let's check and chain and stop every chink
So that no light leaps in through louver or loophole.
Ashtaroth, call out, and have out our boys,
Colting and his kin to save the castle.
Boiling brimstone pour it out burning
All hot on their heads who come near the walls.
Set high tension cross bows and brazen guns
And shoot out enough shot to blind his squadron.
Set Mahmet[2] at the siege-engine and throw out millstones
And with hooks and caltrops[3] let's block them all!"
"Listen," said Lucifer, "for I know this lord;
Both this lord and this light, I knew him long ago.
No death may hurt this lord, nor devil's cunning,
And where he wills is his way—but let him beware the dangers:
If he deprives me of my rights, he robs me by a power play.
For by right and reason the crowd that is here
Belongs to me body and soul, both good and evil.
For he himself said it, who is Sire of heaven,
That Adam and Eve and all their issue
Should grievously die and dwell here forever
If they touched a tree or took an apple from it.
Thus this lord of light made such a law,
And since he is a loyal lord I can't believe
He'll deprive us of our rights, since reason damned them.
And since we've possessed them seven thousand winters

8. The first words from Psalms 23.9, which reads in the Latin Bible, "Lift up your gates, O princes, and be ye lifted up, ye everlasting doors, and the King of Glory shall come in."

9. Langland pictures hell as populated by a number of devils: Satan, Lucifer, Goblin, Belial, and Ashtaroth.

1. Compare with John 11.

2. Mohammed.

3. Iron balls with spikes meant to impede the progress of enemy cavalry.

Without any objections, and if now he begins,
Then his word is deceitful, who is truth's witness."
    "That's true," said Satan, "but I sorely fear,
For you got them with guile and broke into his garden;
Against his love and his leave went into his land,
Not in a fiend's form but in form of an adder
And enticed Eve to eat on her own—
    Woe to him that is alone![4]—
And promised her and him then to know
As two gods, with God, both good and evil.
Thus with treason and treachery you bewitched them both
And made them break their obedience through false promises,
And so you had them out and in here at the end."
    "It's not duly got where guile is the root,
And God will not be duped," said Goblin, "or taken in.
We have no true title to them, for your treason caused it.
I'm afraid, therefore," the Devil said, "lest Truth fetch them out.
For as you beguiled God's image by going as an adder,
So has God beguiled us all by going as a man.
For God has gone," said Goblin, "in man's likeness
These thirty winters, I believe, and went around preaching.
I've assailed him with sin, and sometimes asked
Whether he was God or God's son? His answer was short.
Thus he's rolled on like a proper man these thirty-two winters;
And when I saw it was so, I contrived how I might
Slow down those who loved him not, lest they martyr him.
I would have lengthened his life, for I believed, if he died,
That if his soul came here it would destroy us all.
For the body, while its bones walked, was ever about
To teach men to be loyal and to love one another;
Which life and law, should it be long in use,
It will undo us devils and bring us all down."
    "And now I see where his soul comes sailing this way
With glory and great light—it's God, I know it.
I advise we flee," said the Fiend, "straightaway from here,
For it were better not to be than to abide in his sight.
Because of your lies, Lucifer, we first lost our joy,
And your pride made us fall here out of heaven;
Because we believed in your lies, we had to lose our bliss.
And now, for a later lie you told Eve,
We've lost our lordship on land and in hell.
    Now shall the prince of this world, etc."[5]
    After Satan so rudely berated
Lucifer for his lying, I believe none other
But our Lord in the end rebuked liars here
And blamed on them all the misery that is made here on earth.

4. Ecclesiastes 4.10.

5. John 12.31, continues "be cast out"; "prince of this world" is a title of the devil.

Take note, you wise clerks and you smart lawyers,
That you not mislead unlettered men, for David in the end
Witnesses in his writing what is the reward of liars:
Thou hatest all workers of iniquity: thou wilt destroy all that speak a lie.[6]
(I've digressed a bit for the sake of lies,
To call them as I saw them, pursuing my theme!)
For again that light commanded them unlock, and Lucifer answered.
"What lord are you?" asked Lucifer. A voice said aloud:
"The lord of might and main, that made all things.
Dukes of this dim place, undo these gates now
That Christ may come in, the son of heaven's king."
And with that breath hell with all of Belial's bars broke;
Despite all prevention, the gates were wide open.
Patriarchs and prophets, *populus in tenebris*,[7]
Sang with Saint John, "*Ecce agnus dei!*"[8]
Lucifer could not look, so blinded him had the light,
And those whom our Lord loved with that light flowed forth.
"Now hear this," said our Lord, "both body and soul,
To live up to both our rights to all sinful souls.
Mine they were and of me; I may the better claim them.
Though reason recorded, and right of myself,
That if they ate the apple all should die,
I consigned them not here to hell forever.
For the deadly sin they did was caused by your deceit;
You got them with guile against all reason.
For in my palace, paradise, in an adder's person
You falsely fetched there those I happened to watch over,
Sweet-talked and deceived them and broke into my garden
Against my love and my leave. The Old Law teaches
That deceivers be deceived and fall in their guile,
And whoever knocks out a man's eye or else his front teeth
Or any manner member maims or hurts,
The same injury he'll have who strikes another so.
Tooth for tooth and eye for eye.[9]
So a life shall lose life where a life has life destroyed,
So that life pays for life—the Old Law demands it;
Ergo,[1] soul shall pay for soul and sin counter sin,
And all that men did wrong, I became man to amend;
And that death my death destroys to relieve
And both revive and requite what was quenched through sin,
And guile be beguiled through grace in the end.
It takes a trick to undo a trick.
So do not believe it, Lucifer, that against the law I fetch
From here any sinful soul by a pure power play,

6. Psalms 5.7.
7. People in darkness (Matthew 4.16, citing Isaiah 9.2).
8. Behold the Lamb of God (John 1.36).
9. Matthew 5.38, citing Exodus 21.14.
1. "Therefore," a central term in scholastic argument, used to introduce the logical conclusion to an argument.

But through right and reason ransom here my servants.
I am not come to destroy the law, but to fulfill it.[2]
So what was gotten with guile, is now through grace won back.
And as Adam and all through a tree died
Adam and all through a tree shall return to life.
And now your guile begins to turn back on you
And my grace to grow wider and wider.
The bitterness you've brewed, enjoy it now yourself;
You who are doctor of death, drink what you've mixed!
For I who am Lord of life, love is my drink,
And for that drink I died today, as it seemed.
But I will drink from no deep dish of learning
But from the common cups of all Christian souls;
But your drink becomes death and deep hell your bowl.
I fought so, I thirst even more for the sake of man's soul.
I thirst.[3]
May no sweet wine or cider or precious drink
Fully wet my whistle or my thirst slake
Till grape harvest time fall in the vale of Jehosaphat,[4]
And I drink fully ripe new wine, *resureccio mortuorum.*[5]
And then I shall come as king, with crown and with angels,
And have out of hell all men's souls.
Fiends and fiendkins shall stand before me
And be at my bidding, of bliss or of pain.
But to be merciful to man then my nature demands,
For we are brothers of one blood, but not all in baptism.
But all that are my full brothers in blood and in baptism
Shall never come to hell again, once they are out.
To thee only have I sinned, and have done evil before thee[6]
It's not the practice on earth to hang any felons
More often than once, though they were traitors.
And if the king of the kingdom come in the time
When a thief should suffer death or other sentence,
The law requires he grant him a reprieve if he sees him.
And I who am King of Kings shall come at such time
When doom damns to death all the wicked,
And if law wills I look on them it lies within my grace
Whether they die or die not, did they never so ill.
Be it to any extent paid for, the boldness of their sin,
I may do mercy out of my righteousness and all my true words.
For holy writ wills that I take satisfaction from those who did ill,
As *nullum malum impunitum, et nullum bonum irremuneratum.*[7]
And so on all the wicked I will take vengeance here.
And yet my kind nature in my keen anger shall constrain my will—

2. Matthew 5.17.
3. John 19.28.
4. On the evidence of Joel 3.2, 12, the Last Judgment was to take place at the Vale of Jehosaphat.
5. The resurrection of the dead (from the Nicene Creed).
6. Psalms 50.6.
7. [He is a just judge who leaves] no evil unpunished [and no good unrewarded] (from Pope Innocent III's tract *Of Contempt for the World*; see 4.143–44).

Rebuke me not, O Lord, in thy indignation[8]—
To be merciful to many of my half-brothers.
For blood may see blood both thirsty and cold
But blood may not see blood bleed without taking pity.
I heard secret words, which it is not granted to man to utter.[9]
But my righteousness and right shall reign in hell,
And mercy over all mankind before me in heaven.
For I'd be an unkind king unless I help my kin,
And namely in such need that needs to ask for help.
Enter not into judgment with thy servant.[1]
Thus by law," said our Lord, "I will lead out of here
The people I love and who believe in my coming.
But for the lies that you lied, Lucifer, to Eve
You shall bitterly abide," God said, and bound him with chains.
Ashtoreth and company hid in nooks and crannies,
They dared not look on our Lord, the least of them all,
But let him lead forth those he liked and leave behind whomever he pleased.
Many hundreds of angels then harped and sang,
Flesh sins, flesh clears, flesh of God reigns as God.[2]
Then Peace piped a note of poetry:
After darkest clouds, the sun will shine bright;
And love shine brighter after every fight.[3]
"After sharpest showers," said Peace, "brightest is the sun;
There is no warmer weather than after watery clouds,
Nor any love dearer, nor dearer friends,
Than after war and wreckage when love and peace are masters.
There was never a war in this world nor wickeder envy
That Love, if he wanted to, could not turn it to laughter,
And Peace through patience stop all perils."
"Truce," said Truth, "You tell us the truth, by Jesus!
Let us kiss each other and clutch in covenant!"
"And let no people," said Peace, "perceive that we squabbled,
For nothing's impossible to him who is almighty."
"That's the truth," said Righteousness and kissed Peace reverently,
And Peace her, *per secula seculorum.*[4]
Mercy and truth have met each other; justice and peace have kissed.[5]
Truth trumpeted then and sang *Te deum laudamus*,[6]
And then Love strummed a loud note on the lute,
Behold how good and how pleasant it is, etc.[7]
Till dawn the next day these damoiselles caroled
On which men rang bells for the resurrection, and right with that I awoke

8. Psalms 37.2.
9. In 2 Corinthians 12.4, St. Paul tells of how in a mystical vision he was caught up to heaven, where he saw things that cannot be repeated.
1. Psalms 142.2.
2. From a medieval Latin hymn.
3. From Alain de Lille, a 12th-century poet and philosopher.
4. Forever and ever (the liturgical formula).
5. Psalms 84.11.
6. We praise thee, God (a celebrated Latin hymn).
7. Psalms 132.1.

And called Kit my wife and my daughter Calote:
"Arise, and go reverence God's resurrection,
And creep on your knees to the cross and kiss it as a jewel
And most rightfully as a relic, none richer on earth.
For it bore God's blessed body for our good,
And it terrified the Fiend, for such is its might
No grisly ghost may glide in its shadow!"

"PIERS PLOWMAN" AND ITS TIME

The Rising of 1381

The event previously known as the "Peasants' Revolt" is generally referred to by today's historians as the "Rising of 1381," since it is now recognized that it included many members of the commons who were not peasants but rather middle-class landholders, artisans, and so forth. William Langland had a rather ambiguous relation to the rising, for while deploring the conditions that caused it, he refused to endorse its radical social program. When the rebels invoked his character Piers as a cultural hero, he revised *Piers Plowman* for a second time (the so-called C-text), thus disassociating himself from them. This section brings together a number of documents that record the events of the rising, and more importantly, reveal the subjective responses of contemporary writers to it.

The causes of the rising were varied. Among them was the "Statute of Laborers" enacted by Parliament in 1351 to freeze wages and restrict laborers' mobility, both of which had been increasing as a result of the depopulation caused by the Black Death. The more immediate catalyst, however, was a flat poll tax enacted in 1380, which hurt the poor disproportionately and which the government collected in a particularly ruthless way.

The rising itself was astonishingly brief, beginning at the end of May 1381 and collapsing by the end of July. From the prosperous southern counties of Essex and Kent the rebels marched to London, swearing loyalty to one another and to Richard II. Their hostility was directed against the church hierarchy and the feudal lords rather than against the monarchy. In London they burned the Savoy Palace, the local residence of the powerful John of Gaunt, Duke of Lancaster and uncle of King Richard. The king, then only fourteen years old, found his advisers ineffectual, and so retreated with them to the Tower of London.

Having agreed to meet the Essex contingent outside the city, at Mile End, the king acceded to their demands of an end to villeinage (serfdom), and ordered his office of chancery to make multiple copies of charters to that effect. During this meeting, some rebels broke into the Tower of London and beheaded two of the most hated men in the kingdom, Simon Sudbury (the king's chancellor and Archbishop of Canterbury) and Robert Hales (his treasurer). Afterward, they displayed their heads on London Bridge, as a sign that they were traitors to the commons.

The next day the king met with the Kentish rebels, again outside the city, at Smithfield. Here their captain Wat Tyler demanded not only the abolition of villeinage but fixed rents, partial disendowment of the church and dispersal of its goods to the poor, and punishment of all "traitors" held to be responsible for the poll tax. In the course of a scuffle, the Lord Mayor of London, William Walworth, stabbed Tyler and mortally wounded him; thereupon, the king rode before the rebels and declared himself their new captain, successfully leading them off the field.

Adam and Eve, detail of a misericord, c. 1379. Misericords were shallow seats in the choir stalls of medieval churches, on which worshipers could rest, still standing, during the long celebrations of the Mass and Daily Office. Their undersides were often carved with animal grotesques and scenes of common life, both seen in this depiction of Adam and Eve from a misericord in Worcester Cathedral. Eve spins and Adam digs, in a moment reminiscent of the couplet from John Ball's sermon: "Whan Adam dalf and Eve span, / who was thanne a gentilman?"

Tyler's death broke the will of the rebels, and the king promptly revoked the charters freeing the serfs. In a series of trials, he prosecuted the instigators, among them John Ball, the priest who had shortly before preached to the rebels at Blackheath the famous sermon challenging the division of society into three estates: "Whan Adam dalf and Eve span, / who was thanne a gentilman?" Ball was found guilty of treason, and drawn, hanged, and quartered. Aside from such punishments, there were few apparent effects of the rising, although the nobles and the clergy relented in their treatment of the commons, and in the long run, the institution of villeinage declined. For the ruling class itself, the rising caused intense anxiety. John Gower, in his allegorized account, *The Voice of One Crying*, reports hiding in the woods to escape the peasants. Like him, the monastic chroniclers like Thomas of Walsingham generally present the rebels as mad beasts.

What is perhaps most significant about the written reception of the rising is the languages—Latin, French, and English—in which it occurs. Like Gower's *Voice of One Crying*, the chronicles are generally written in Latin, although the *Anonimalle Chronicle*, from which a passage is included here, is in French. Langland and Chaucer wrote in English, while the short poem below, *The Course of Revolt*, is macaronic, alternating English lines with Latin ones. Although there is little written evidence in the voice of the rebels themselves (who were generally illiterate), there are two tantalizing scraps identified as John Ball's letters, written in English although embedded in hostile Latin chronicle accounts of Ball's trial and execution. It has been suggested recently that the most important fact about the rebel speeches and writings is their "vernacularity"—the fact that they appear in a language that the common people could understand.

from *The Anonimalle Chronicle*[1]

[*Wat Tyler's Demands to Richard II, and His Death*]

At this time a great body of the commons[2] went to the Tower of London to speak with the king. As they could not get a hearing from him, they laid siege to the Tower from the side of Saint Katherine's, towards the south. Another group of the commons, who were within the city, went to the Hospital of Saint John, Clerkenwell, and on their way they burned the place and houses of Roger Legett, questmonger,[3] who had been beheaded in Cheapside, as well as all the rented property and tenements of the Hospital of Saint John they could find. Afterwards they came to the beautiful priory of the said hospital, and set on fire several fine and pleasant buildings within it—a great and horrible piece of damage to the priory for all time to come. They then returned to London to rest or to do more mischief.

At this time the king was in a turret of the great Tower of London, and saw the manor of the Savoy[4] and the Hospital of Clerkenwell, and the houses of Simon Hosteler near Newgate, and John Butterwick's place, all in flames. He called all the lords about him into a chamber, and asked their counsel as to what should be done in such a crisis. But none of them could or would give him any counsel; and so the young king said that he would order the mayor of the city to command the sheriffs and aldermen to have it cried within their wards that everyone between the age of fifteen and sixty, on pain of life and limb, should go next morning (which was Friday) to Mile End, and meet him there at seven of the bell. He did this in order that all the commons who were stationed around the Tower would be persuaded to abandon the siege, and come to Mile End to see him and hear him, so that those who were in the Tower could leave safely at their will and save themselves as they wished. But it came to nothing, for some of them did not have the good fortune to be saved.

Later that Thursday, the said feast of Corpus Christi, the king, remaining anxiously and sadly in the Tower, climbed on to a little turret facing Saint Katherine's, where a large number of the commons were lying. He had it proclaimed to them that they should all go peaceably to their homes, and he would pardon them all their different offenses. But all cried with one voice that they would not go before they had captured the traitors within the Tower, and obtained charters to free them from all manner of serfdom, and certain other points which they wished to demand. The king benevolently granted their requests and made a clerk write a bill in their presence in these terms: "Richard, king of England and France, gives great thanks to his good commons, for that they have so great a desire to see and maintain their king; and he grants them pardon for all manner of trespasses and misprisions and felonies done up to this hour, and wills and commands that every one should now quickly return to his own home: He wills and commands that everyone should put his grievances in writing, and have them sent to him; and he will provide, with the aid of his loyal lords and his good council, such remedy as shall be profitable both to him and to them, and to the kingdom." He put his signet seal to this document in their presence and then sent the said bill by the hands of two of his knights to the

1. This gripping account describes the rebel Wat (Walter) Tyler's confrontation with the King. Written in French rather than Latin, *The Anonimalle Chronicle* is considered to be more contemporary and more balanced than judgmental Latin accounts like that of Thomas of Walsingham. Translated by R. B. Dobson.

2. The common people as opposed to the nobility or the clergy; the third estate.

3. One who made a business of conducting inquests.

4. The beautiful palace of John of Gaunt, the King's powerful uncle.

people around Saint Katherine's. And he caused it to be read to them, the man who read it standing up on an old chair above the others so that all could hear. All this time the king remained in the Tower in great distress of mind. And when the commons had heard the bill, they said that it was nothing but a trifle and mockery. Therefore they returned to London and had it cried around the city that all lawyers, all the men of the Chancery and the Exchequer and everyone who could write a writ or a letter should be beheaded,[5] wherever they could be found. At this time they burnt several more houses within the city. The king himself ascended to a high garret of the Tower to watch the fires; then he came down again, and sent for the lords to have their counsel. But they did not know how to advise him, and were surprisingly abashed.

On the next day, Friday, the commons of the country and the commons of London assembled in fearful strength, to the number of a hundred thousand or more, besides some four score who remained on Tower Hill to watch those who were within the Tower. Some went to Mile End, on the way to Brentwood, to wait for the king's arrival, because of the proclamation that he had made. But others came to Tower Hill, and when the king knew that they were there, he sent them orders by a messenger to join their companions at Mile End, saying that he would come to them very soon. And at this time of the morning he advised the archbishop of Canterbury and the others who were in the Tower, to go down to the little water-gate, and take a boat and save themselves. And the archbishop proceeded to do this; but a wicked woman raised a cry against him, and he had to turn back to the Tower, to his own confusion.

And by seven of the bell the king himself came to Mile End, and with him his mother in a carriage, and also the earls of Buckingham, Kent, Warwick and Oxford, as well as Sir Thomas Percy, Sir Robert Knolles, the mayor of London and many knights and squires; and Sir Aubrey de Vere carried the royal sword. And when the king arrived and the commons saw him, they knelt down to him, saying "Welcome our Lord King Richard, if it pleases you, and we will not have any other king but you." And Wat Tyghler, their master and leader, prayed on behalf of the commons that the king would suffer them to take and deal with all the traitors against him and the law. The king granted that they should freely seize all who were traitors and could be proved to be such by process of law. The said Walter and the commons were carrying two banners as well as pennons and pennoncels[6] while they made their petition to the king. And they required that henceforward no man should be a serf nor make homage or any type of service to any lord, but should give four pence for an acre of land. They asked also that no one should serve any man except at his own will and by means of regular covenant. And at this time the king had the commons arrayed in two lines, and had it proclaimed before them that he would confirm and grant that they should be free, and generally should have their will; and that they could go through all the realm of England and catch all traitors and bring them to him in safety, and then he would deal with them as the law demanded.

Because of this grant Wat Tyghler and the commons took their way to the Tower, to seize the archbishop and the others while the king remained at Mile End. Meanwhile the archbishop had sung his mass devoutly in the Tower, and confessed

5. Chancery held the archives of public record and the Exchequer dealt with the collection of revenue. The Latin chroniclers saw the rising as a threat to writing itself; Thomas of Walsingham, for example, reports that the rebels gleefully burned records they saw as guaranteeing the lords' legal power over them.

6. Small flags and streamers borne on a lance.

the prior of the Hospital of Clerkenwell and others; and then he heard two or three masses and chanted the *Commendatio*, and the *Placebo* and *Dirige*, and the Seven Psalms, and the Litany; and when he was at the words "*Omnes sancti orate pro nobis*" [All saints pray for us], the commons entered and dragged him out of the chapel of the Tower, and struck and hustled him roughly, as they did also the others who were with him, and led them to Tower Hill. There they cut off the heads of Master Simon of Sudbury, archbishop of Canterbury, of Sir Robert Hales,[7] High Prior of the Hospital of Saint John's of Clerkenwell, Treasurer of England, of Brother William of Appleton, a great physician and surgeon, and one who had much influence with the king and the duke of Lancaster. And some time after they beheaded John Legge, the king's serjeant-at-arms, and with him a certain juror. At the same time the commons had it proclaimed that whoever could catch any Fleming[8] or other aliens of any nation, might cut off their heads; and so they did accordingly. Then they took the heads of the archbishop and of the others and put them on wooden poles, and carried them before them in procession through all the city as far as the shrine of Westminster Abbey, to the contempt of themselves, of God and of Holy Church: for which reason vengeance descended on them shortly afterwards. Then they returned to London Bridge and set the head of the archbishop above the gate, with the heads of eight others they had executed, so that all who passed over the bridge could see them. This done, they went to the church of Saint Martin's in the Vintry, and found therein thirty-five Flemings, whom they dragged outside and beheaded in the street. On that day there were beheaded 140 or 160 persons. Then they took their way to the places of Lombards and other aliens, and broke into their houses, and robbed them of all their goods that they could discover. So it went on for all that day and the night following with hideous cries and horrible tumult.

At this time, because the Chancellor had been beheaded, the king made the earl of Arundel Chancellor for the day, and entrusted him with the Great Seal; and all that day he caused various clerks to write out charters, patents, and letters of protection, granted to the commons in consequence of the matters before mentioned, without taking any fines for the sealing or transcription.

On the next day, Saturday, great numbers of the commons came into Westminster Abbey at the hour of Tierce,[9] and there they found John Imworth, Marshal of the Marshalsea and warden of the prisoners, a tormentor without pity; he was near the shrine of Saint Edward, embracing a marble pillar, hoping for aid and succor from the saint to preserve him from his enemies. But the commons wrenched his arms away from the pillar of the shrine, and dragged him into Cheap, and there beheaded him. And at the same time they took from Bread Street a valet named John of Greenfield, merely because he had spoken well of Brother William Appleton and the other murdered persons; and they brought him into Cheap and beheaded him. All this time the king was having it cried through the city that every one should go peaceably to his own country and his own house, without doing more mischief; but to this the commons would not agree.

And on this same day, at three hours after noon, the king came to Westminster Abbey and about two hundred persons with him. The abbot and convent of the said

7. Sudbury and Hales were especially hated by the rebels—the former, as chancellor of England, for instituting the poll tax, and the latter, as treasurer, for collecting it.

8. Immigrants from Flanders, who had become wealthy in the London wool trade; they were particular targets of the rebels (see Chaucer, *The Nun's Priest's Tale*, line 576).

9. The third of seven canonical "hours" around which clerics organized their day; usually, the third hour after sunrise.

abbey, and the canons and vicars of Saint Stephen's Chapel, came to meet him in procession, clothed in their copes and their feet bare, halfway to Charing Cross; and they brought him to the abbey, and then to the high altar of the church. The king made his prayers devoutly, and left an offering for the altar and the relics. Afterwards he spoke with the anchorite,[1] and confessed to him, and remained with him some time. Then the king caused a proclamation to be made that all the commons of the country who were still within the city should come to Smithfield[2] to meet him there; and so they did.

And when the king with his retinue arrived there, he turned to the east, in a place before Saint Bartholomew's a house of canons: and the commons arrayed themselves in bands of great size on the west side. At this moment the mayor of London, William of Walworth, came up, and the king ordered him to approach the commons, and make their chieftain come to him. And when he was called by the mayor, this chieftain, Wat Tyghler of Maidstone by name, approached the king with great confidence, mounted on a little horse so that the commons might see him. And he dismounted, holding in his hand a dagger which he had taken from another man; and when he had dismounted he half bent his knee and took the king by the hand, shaking his arm forcefully and roughly, saying to him, "Brother, be of good comfort and joyful, for you shall have, in the fortnight that is to come, forty thousand more commons than you have at present, and we shall be good companions." And the king said to Walter, "Why will you not go back to your own country?" But the other answered, with a great oath, that neither he nor his fellows would leave until they had got their charter as they wished to have it with the inclusion of certain points which they wished to demand. Tyghler threatened that the lords of the realm would rue it bitterly if these points were not settled at the commons' will. Then the king asked him what were the points which he wished to have considered, and he should have them freely and without contradiction, written out and sealed. Thereupon the said Wat rehearsed the points which were to be demanded; and he asked that there should be no law except for the law of Winchester[3] and that henceforward there should be no outlawry[4] in any process of law, and that no lord should have lordship in future, but it should be divided among all men, except for the king's own lordship. He also asked that the goods of Holy Church should not remain in the hands of the religious, nor of parsons and vicars, and other churchmen; but that clergy already in possession should have a sufficient sustenance and the rest of their goods should be divided among the people of the parish. And he demanded that there should be only one bishop in England and only one prelate, and all the lands and tenements of the possessioners should be taken from them and divided among the commons, only reserving for them a reasonable sustenance. And he demanded that there should be no more villeins[5] in England, and no serfdom nor villeinage but that all men should be free and of one condition. To this the king gave an easy answer, and said that Wat should have all that he could fairly grant, reserving only for himself the regality of his crown. And then he ordered him to go back to his own home, without causing further delay.

During all the time that the king was speaking, no lord or counselor dared or wished to give answer to the commons in any place except for the king himself. Presently Wat Tyghler, in the presence of the king, sent for a jug of water to rinse his mouth, because of the great heat that he felt; and as soon as the water was

1. A religious recluse who lived enclosed in a tiny dwelling.
2. An area outside the walls of the city of London.
3. The reference is unclear; it may refer to a claim by the rebels to the rights of tenants on royal lands.
4. Condition of being outside traditional legal protection.
5. Serfs tied to the land; bondmen.

brought he rinsed out his mouth in a very rude and villainous manner before the king. And then he made them bring him a jug of ale, and drank a great draught, and then, in the presence of the king, climbed on his horse again. At that time a certain valet from Kent, who was among the king's retinue, asked to see the said Wat, chieftain of the commons. And when he saw him, he said aloud that he was the greatest thief and robber in all Kent. Wat heard these words, and commanded the valet to come out to him, shaking his head at him as a sign of malice; but Wat himself refused to go to him for fear that he had of the others there. But at last the lords made the valet go out to Wat, to see what the latter would do before the king. And when Wat saw him he ordered one of his followers, who was mounted on horseback and carrying a banner displayed, to dismount and behead the said valet. But the valet answered that he had done nothing worthy of death, for what he had said was true, and he would not deny it, although he could not lawfully debate the issue in the presence of his liege lord, without leave, except in his own defense: but that he could do without reproof, for whoever struck him would be struck in return. For these words Wat wanted to strike the valet with his dagger, and would have slain him in the king's presence; but because he tried to do so, the mayor of London, William of Walworth, reasoned with the said Wat for his violent behavior and contempt, done in the king's presence, and arrested him. And because he arrested him, the said Wat stabbed the mayor with his dagger in the body in great anger. But, as it pleased God, the mayor was wearing armor and took no harm, but like a hardy and vigorous man drew his dagger and struck back at the said Wat, giving him a deep cut in the neck, and then a great blow on the head. And during this scuffle a valet of the king's household drew his sword, and ran Wat two or three times through the body, mortally wounding him. Wat spurred his horse, crying to the commons to avenge him, and the horse carried him some four score paces, and then he fell to the ground half dead. And when the commons saw him fall, and did not know for certain how it happened, they began to bend their bows and to shoot. Therefore the king himself spurred his horse, and rode out to them, commanding them that they should all come to him at the field of Saint John of Clerkenwell.

Meanwhile the mayor of London rode as hastily as he could back to the city, and commanded those who were in charge of the twenty-four wards to have it cried round their wards, that every man should arm himself as quickly as he could, and come to the king's aid in Saint John's Fields, where the commons were, for he was in great trouble and necessity. But at this time almost all of the knights and squires of the king's household, and many others, were so frightened of the affray that they left their liege lord and went each his own way.

Afterwards, when the king had reached the open fields, he made the commons array themselves on the west side. And presently the aldermen came to him in a body, bringing with them the keepers of the wards arrayed in several bands, a fine company of well-armed men in great strength. And they enveloped the commons like sheep within a pen. Meanwhile, after the mayor had sent the keepers of the town on their way to the king, he returned with a good company of lances to Smithfield in order to make an end of the captain of the commons. And when he came to Smithfield he failed to find there the said captain Wat Tyghler, at which he marveled much, and asked what had become of the traitor. And he was told that Wat had been carried by a group of the commons to the hospital for the poor near Saint Bartholomew's, and put to bed in the chamber of the master of the hospital. The mayor went there and found him, and had him carried out to the middle of Smithfield, in the presence of his companions, and had him beheaded. And so ended his wretched life. But the mayor had his head set on a pole and carried before him to the king, who still remained in the field. And when the king saw the head he had it brought near him to subdue the commons, and thanked the mayor greatly for what he had done. And when the commons saw that their chieftain, Wat Tyghler, was dead in such a manner, they fell to the ground there among the corn, like beaten men, imploring the king for mercy for their misdeeds. And the king benevolently granted them mercy, and most of them took to flight.

Three Poems on the Rising of 1381

John Ball's First Letter[1]

John Ball Saint Mary Priest, greeteth well all manner of men, and biddeth them in name of the Trinitie, Father, Sonne, & holy Ghost, stand manlike together in truth, & helpe truth, and truth shall helpe you:

now raygneth pride in price,
couetise° is holden° wise *greed / held*
lechery without shame,
gluttonie without blame,
enuye raygneth° with reason, *reigns*
and sloath is taken in great season,
God doe boote° for nowe is time. Amen. *make amends*

John Ball's Second Letter[2]

LITTERA IOHANNIS BALLE MISSA COMMUNIBUS ESTSEXIE
[THE LETTER OF JOHN BALL TO THE ESSEX COMMONS]

Iohan schep, som-tyme seynte marie prest of york, and now of colchestre, Greteth wel Iohan nameles & Iohn the mullere and Iohon cartere, and biddeth hem thei bee war of gyle [treachery] in borugh, and stondeth to-gidere in godes name, and biddeth Pers ploughman / go to his werk and chastise wel hobbe the robbere; and taketh with yow Iohan Trewman and alle hijs felawes and no mo, and loke schappe you to on heued[3] and no mo.

Iohan the mullere hath y-grounde smal, smal, smal.
The kynges sone of heuene schal paye for al.
be war or the be wo.° *beware or be sorry*
knoweth your freend fro your foo.

1. This and the piece following can only provisionally be called "poems," despite their rhymed couplets and sporadic alliteration. The court that tried and convicted Ball regarded them as actual directions to his followers, and modern scholarship has tended to concur. If so they are directions in code, for they are, in the words of one chronicler, "full of enigmas." In this poem the complaint about the seven deadly sins running rampant is conventional, but the conclusion, "God do bote for now is time" (God make amends, for now is the time) is highly unusual in its call to action. Significantly, the sin of anger is absent from the list.

2. According to the chronicle from which this "letter" was taken, Ball sent it to "the leaders of the commons in Essex . . . in order to urge them to finish what they had begun," and it was "afterwards found in the sleeve of a man about to be hanged for disturbing the peace." It appears in Thomas Walsingham's Latin *Historia Anglicana,* where it is included as evidence of the treason for which Ball was hanged. In the prose introduction to the poem, John the "shep," priest of Colchester, is the assumed name of John Ball (as "pastor"), while John Carter and John the Miller are both generic occupational names often ascribed to the leaders of the rebels. The reference to "Pers Ploughman" in the poem's introduction indicates that the rebels interpreted Langland's conservative poem for their own purposes. It presents Piers not as Langland's patient laborer, but as one who should get to his "work" of punishing "robbers," perhaps "Hobbe" (Robert) Hales, the treasurer of the king, beheaded by the rebels for his role in collecting the poll tax.

3. Take one head for yourself; possibly a reference to the rebels' loyalty to Richard II as opposed to the nobles.

haueth y-now & seith hoo!
and do wel and bettre and fleth° synne, *flee*
and seketh pees and hold yow ther-inne.
and so biddeth Iohan trewaman and alle his felawes.

Hanc litteram Idem Iohannes balle confessus est scripisse, et communibus transmisisse, et plura alia fatebatur et fecit; propter-que, ut diximus, traitus, suspensus, et decollatus apud sanctum albanum Idibus Iulij, presente rege, et cadauer eius quadripertitum quatuor regni cuntatibus missum est. [John Ball confessed that he wrote this letter and sent it to the commons, and said and did many other things. For which reason, as we have said, he was drawn, hanged, and beheaded before the king at Saint Albans, on the ides of July; and his body was quartered and sent to four cities in the kingdom.]

The Course of Revolt[4]

The taxe hath tened° vs alle, *harmed*
probat hoc mors tot validorum;° *this death tests so many of the strong[?]*
The Kyng therof had small,
ffuit in manibus cupidorum°[5] *it was in the hands of the greedy ones*
yt had ful hard hansell,° *bad omen*
dans causam fine dolorum;° *giving cause to an end of sorrows*
vengeaunce nedes most° fall, *must*
propter peccata malorum.° *on account of the sins of the wicked*

In Kent care° be-gan,[6] *troubles*
mox infestando potentes;° *soon attacking the rulers*
On rowtes° tho Rebawdes° they ran, *crowds / rascals*
Sua turpida arma ferentes.° *bearing their shameful weapons*
ffoles° they dred no man, *fools*
Regni Regem, neque gentes;° *neither king of the realm, nor the people*
laddes° they were there Cheveteyns,° *churls / captains*
Sine iure fere superantes.° *lawlessly rising above their station*

laddes° lowde they lowght,° *churls / laughed*
Clamantes voce sonora,° *shouting in a loud voice*
The bischop[7] wan they slowght,° *slew*
Et corpora plura decora.° *and many handsome people*
Maners down they drowght,° *they threw down manor houses*
In regno non meliora;° *there were none better in the kingdom*
Harmes they dyde y-nowght;° *enough*
habuerunt libera lora.° *they had free rein*
Iak strawe[8] made yt stowte° *swaggered*
Cum profusa comitiua,° *with a captain's munificence*
And seyd al schuld hem lowte,° *bow down to them*

4. Unlike the two preceding letters, there is no doubt that this piece is a poem: it is written in six- or eight-line stanzas of English alternating with Latin, with a rhyme scheme *ababab (ab)*. The masculine rhymes of the English (*alle, small,* etc.) contrast with the feminine rhymes of the Latin (*validorum, cupidorum,* etc.) to give it a lilting quality. The poem laments the violence of the rising, although it opens with a recognition of the rebels' grievances: the poll tax of 1377, 1379, and 1380–1381 "hath tened [harmed] vs alle."
5. Much of the tax revenue was diverted to collectors rather than returned to the king.
6. The rising actually began in Essex and spread to Kent.
7. Simon Sudbury, Archbishop of Canterbury.
8. Jack Straw was a fictional character believed to have been a leader of the rising; see Chaucer, *Nun's Priest's Tale,* lines 628–31.

Anglorum corpora viua.° — *the living community of Englishmen*
Sadly° can they schowte,° — *vigorously / shouted*
pulsant pietatis oliua,° — *they beat the olive branch of pity*
The wycche were wont to lowte,° — *those who used to skulk*
aratrum traducere stiua.° — *disgrace the plough and plough handle*

Hales,[9] that dowghty° knyght, — *brave*
quo splenduit Anglia tota,° — *in whom all England shone*
dolefully° he was dyght,° — *pitiably / cut down*
Cum stultis pace remota.° — *when removed from peace by fools*
There he myght not fyght,
nec Christo soluere vota.° — *nor say his prayers to Christ*

Savoy[1] semely set° — *beautifully built*
heu! funditus igne cadebat.° — *alas, it was given over to the fire*
Arcan don there they bett,[2]
Et eos virtute premebat.° — *and threatened them with force*
deth was ther dewe dett,
qui captum quisque ferebat.° — *whoever carried off stolen goods*
Oure kyng myght have no rest,
Alii latuere cauerna;° — *others hid in caves*
To ride he was ful prest,
recolendo gesta paterna.° — *remembering his father's deeds*
Iak straw dovn they cast[3]
Smethefeld virtute superna.° — *at Smithfield with superior strength*
god, as thou may best,
Regem defende, guberna.° — *defend the kingdom and govern it*

John Gower

from *The Voice of One Crying*[1]

from Prologue

In the beginning of this work, the author intends to describe how the lowly peasants violently revolted against the freemen and nobles of the realm. And since an event of this kind was as loathsome and horrible as a monster, he reports that in a dream

9. Sir Robert Hales, treasurer of England and therefore closely associated with the collection of the poll tax. He was beheaded at the Tower of London during the rising.

1. John of Gaunt's London residence.

2. A reference to Achan (Joshua 7), who transgressed the law of God by stealing valuables from Jericho. Several chronicles mention the rebels' restraint in not looting the houses of the nobles.

3. It was not (the fictional) Jack Straw, but Wat Tyler who was mortally wounded at Smithfield.

1. Gower grew up in Kent (one of the counties where the Rising of 1381 started), in a well-connected family, and both Richard II and Henry IV were his patrons. He was a friend of Chaucer, who refers to him as "moral Gower." The immorality of contemporary society, particularly the refusal of the three estates to work together, is in fact the unifying theme of Gower's work. Of his three long poems (written in the three languages of the period, English, Anglo-Norman, and Latin), the Middle English *Lover's Confession* (*Confessio amantis*), though primarily a dream vision exploring the frustrations and folly of human divine love, is set a framing complaint about the three estates, and the Anglo-Norman *Mirror of Man* (*Mirour de l'Omme*) is based on such a complaint.

Gower's Latin *Voice of One Crying* (*Vox Clamantis*) laments the failure of the three estates in a more prophetic way: the speaker identifies himself with John the Baptist, crying in the wilderness of 14th-century England. Like *Piers Plowman*, the poem rakes the form of an allegorical dream vision. Like Langland, Gower revised his work in response to the revolt. He had written Books 2-7 by 1378 as a general complaint about the three estates, though he blamed the peasants in particular. Their refusal to produce food "by the sweat of their brow" as God decreed shows their laziness, and their demand of higher wages shows their wickedness and greed (bk. 5.9). After the Rising of 1381 occurred, he composed what is now Book 1 to decry the violence, which he saw as led by the devil; in it, he casts the peasants as beasts lacking reason, and their leader, Wat Tyler, as a rabble-rousing jackdaw, or jay (bk. 1.9). Translated by Eric W. Stockton.

he saw different throngs of the rabble transformed into different kinds of domestic animals. He says, moreover, that those domestic animals deviated from their true nature and took on the barbarousness of wild beasts. In accordance with the separate divisions of this book, which is divided into seven parts (as will appear more clearly below in its headings), he treats furthermore of the causes for such outrages taking place among men. * * *

[Wat Tyler as a Jackdaw Inciting the Peasants to Riot][2]

> Here he says that in his dream he saw that when all the aforementioned madmen stood herded together, a certain Jackdaw (in English a Jay, which is commonly called Wat) assumed the rank of command over the others. And to tell the truth of the matter, this Wat was their leader.

When this great multitude of monsters like wild beasts stood united, a multitude like the sands of the sea, there appeared a Jackdaw, well instructed in the art of speaking, which no cage could keep at home. While all were looking on, this bird spread his wings and claimed to have top rank, although he was unworthy. Just as the Devil was placed in command over the army of the lower world, so this scoundrel was in charge of the wicked mob. A harsh voice, a fierce expression, a very faithful likeness to a death's head—these things gave token of his appearance. He checked the murmuring and all kept silent so that the sound from his mouth might be better heard. He ascended to the top of a tree, and with the voice from his open mouth he uttered such words as these to his compeers:

"O you low sort of wretches, which the world has subjugated for a long time by its law, look, now the day has come when the peasantry will triumph and will force the freemen to get off their lands. Let all honor come to an end, let justice perish, and let no virtue that once existed endure further in the world. Let the law give over which used to hold us in check with its justice, and from here on let our court rule."

The whole mob was silent and took note of the speaker's words, and they liked every command he delivered from his mouth. The rabble lent a deluded ear to his fickle talk, and it saw none of the future things that would result. For when he had been honored in this way by the people, he quickly grabbed all the land for himself. Indeed, when the people had unadvisedly given themselves into servitude, he called the populace together and gave orders. Just as a billow usually grows calm after a stiff breeze, and just as a wave swells by the blast of a whirlwind, so the Jackdaw stirred up all the others with his outrageous shouting, and he drew the people's minds toward war. The stupid portion of the people did not know what its "court" might be, but he ordered them to adopt the laws of force. He said, "Strike," and one man struck. He said, "Kill," and another killed. He said, "Commit crime"; everyone committed it, and did not oppose his will. Everyone he called to in his madness listened with ears pricked up, and once aroused to his voice, pursued the [prescribed] course. Thus many an unfortunate man, driven by his persuasive raving, stuck his hand into the fire again and again. All proclaimed in a loud voice, "So be it," so that the sound was like the din of the sea. Stunned by the great noise of their voice, I now could scarcely lift my trembling feet. Yet from a distance I

2. From Book 1.

observed how they made their mutual arrangements by clasping their hands. For they said this, that the mob from the country would destroy whatever was left of the noble class in the world.

With these words, they all marched together in the same fashion, and the wicked ruler of hell led the way. A black cloud mingled with the furies of hell approached, and every wickedness poured into their hearts rained down. The earth was so thoroughly soaked with the dew of hell that no virtue could flourish from that time forth. But every vice that a worthy man abhors flourished and filled men's hearts from that time on. Then at midday the Devil attacked and his hard-shot arrow flew during that painful day. Satan himself was freed and on hand, together with all the sinful band of servile hell. Behold, the untutored heart's sense of shame was lost, and it no longer feared the terrors of crime or punishment. And so when I saw the leaders of hell ruling the world, the rights of heaven were worth nothing. The more I saw them, the more I judged I ought to be afraid of them, not knowing what sort of end would be bound to come.

[The Laziness and Greed of Ploughmen][3]

> Now that he has spoken of those of knightly rank who ought to keep the state unharmed, it is necessary to speak of those who are under obligation to enter into the labors of agriculture, which are necessary for obtaining food and drink for the sustenance of the human race.

Now you have heard what knighthood is, and I shall speak in addition of what the guiding principle for other men ought to be. For after knighthood there remains only the peasant rank; the rustics in it cultivate the grains and vineyards. They are the men who seek food for us by the sweat of their heavy toil, as God Himself has decreed. The guiding principle of our first father Adam, which he received from the mouth of God on high, is rightly theirs. For God said to him, when he fell from the glories of Paradise, "O sinner, the sweat and toil of the world be thine; in them shalt thou eat thy bread."[4] So if God's peasant pays attention to the plowshare as it goes along, and if he thus carries on the work of cultivation with his hand, then the fruit which in due course the fertile field will bear and the grape will stand abundant in their due seasons. Now, however, scarcely a farmer wishes to do such work; instead, he wickedly loafs everywhere.

An evil disposition is widespread among the common people, and I suspect that the servants of the plow are often responsible for it. For they are sluggish, they are scarce, and they are grasping. For the very little they do they demand the highest pay. Now that this practice has come about, see how one peasant insists upon more than two demanded in days gone by. Yet a short time ago one performed more service than three do now, as those maintain who are well acquainted with the facts. For just as the fox seeks his hole and enters it while the woods are echoing on every side of the hole, so does the servant of the plow, contrary to the law of the land, seek to make a fool of the land. They desire the leisures of great men, but they have nothing to feed themselves with, nor will they be servants. God and Nature have ordained that they shall serve, but neither knows how to keep them within bounds. Everyone owning land complains in his turn about these people;

3. From Book 5.

4. Genesis 3.19.

each stands in need of them and none has control over them. The peasants of old did not scorn God with impunity or usurp a noble worldly rank. Rather, God imposed servile work upon them, so that the peasantry might subdue its proud feelings; and liberty, which remained secure for freemen, ruled over the serfs and subjected them to its law.

The experience of yesterday makes us better informed as to what perfidy the unruly serf possesses. As the teasel[5] harmfully thins out the standing crops if it is not thinned out itself, so does the unruly peasant weigh heavily upon the well-behaved ones. The peasant strikes at the subservient and soothes the troublesome, yet the principle which the old order of things teaches is not wrong: let the law accordingly cut down the harmful teasels of rabble, lest they uproot the nobler grain with their stinging. Unless it is struck down first, the peasant race strikes against freemen, no matter what nobility or worth they possess. Its actions outwardly show that the peasantry is base, and it esteems the nobles the less because of their very virtues. Just as lopsided ships begin to sink without the right load, so does the wild peasantry, unless it is held in check.

God and our toil confer and bestow everything upon us. Without toil, man's advantages are nothing. The peasant should therefore put his limbs to work, as is proper for him to do. Just as a barren field cultivated by the plowshare fails the granaries and brings home no crop in autumn, so does the worthless churl, the more he is cherished by your love, fail you and bring on your ruin. The serfs perform none of their servile duties voluntarily and have no respect for the law. Whatever the serf's body suffers patiently under compulsion, inwardly his mind ever turns toward utter wickedness. Miracles happen only contrary to nature; only the divinity of nature can go against its own powers. It is not for man's estate that anyone from the class of serfs should try to set things right.

END OF "PIERS PLOWMAN" AND ITS TIME

MYSTICAL WRITINGS

Throughout the Middle Ages, religious belief was communally expressed in the great public liturgies: the mass and the Divine Office—those prayers, hymns, and readings performed, especially by monastic communities, at the eight liturgical "hours" from dawn until dark. Private devotion, however, also had a continuous place in medieval Christianity. The British Isles enjoyed a particularly rich and ancient tradition of lives led in holy solitude and of texts and collections intended for private devotion by both clergy and laity. Such early works were enriched in the late eleventh century by the influential *Prayers or Meditations* of Anselm, Archbishop of Canterbury.

Anselm's prayers and related works were collected into portable books. Beginning in the thirteenth century, England also produced distinguished, sometimes elaborately decorated psalters—collections of psalms and other prayers—that were often privately owned. Toward the middle of the thirteenth century, an Oxford workshop produced the earliest of the decorated

5. A bristly plant like a thistle.

Books of Hours, a form that was to prove enormously popular across Europe for the rest of the Middle Ages.

Books of Hours typically contained the "Little Hours of the Virgin," an abbreviated version of the Divine Office that allowed for private commemoration of the holy hours, as well as other prayers, extracts from the gospels, and the "seven penitential psalms." Psalters and Books of Hours both featured texts devoted to the Virgin Mary, only one manifestation of a widespread English tradition. Many were explicitly intended for use by women, both lay and clerical, and emphasize female readership in their illustrations, as in the scene of women reading from the Bedford Hours (see Color Plate 10). Psalters and especially Books of Hours played a key role in the growth of lay literacy during the later Middle Ages.

By the fourteenth century, then, England had an ancient tradition of private religious devotion and varied books created especially for that purpose as well as a growing readership, lay and clerical. Two further, related elements added to the growth in that century of works that have been grouped, largely retrospectively, as "mystical." First, across Europe there was a renewed expression of "affective spirituality," the emotionally, even physically empathetic contemplation of the crises of salvation, especially the crucifixion of Christ and the sufferings of the Virgin Mary. This is reflected in the vision of the crucifixion in *Passus* 18 of Langland's *Piers Plowman*, and in many lyrics, as well as in sculpture and drawings like that on page 530. Second, widespread dissatisfaction with the established church—or a more diffuse sense of spiritual needs left unfulfilled there—led a growing number of Christians to explore more immediate and often private avenues of religious experience. The quest for a mystical union with Christ or God the Father is a particularly ambitious aspect of such exploration.

This search was often exercised, particularly in the lay community and among religious women, in the recently invigorated vernacular, which (whether French or English) had long had a place along with Latin in Books of Hours. Among these expressions were the "Wycliffite" translations of the Bible into Middle English, as well as texts intended for religious recluses and for people seeking mystical experience even as they remained active in the mundane world. These emergent religious aspirations, as well as some of their accompanying fears and tensions, are expressed below in Julian of Norwich's *Book of Showings* and the Companion Readings that follow it.*

Julian of Norwich

1342–c. 1420

Dame Julian of Norwich was an anchoress, a woman dedicated to prayer and contemplation who lived separate from the world, literally enclosed in a modest residence and symbolically "dead" to the secular world. Yet Julian also lived in the midst of the world. Her anchorhold at the church of Saint Julian—hence her name—was in a busy market neighborhood of Norwich. Dame Julian's lifelong stability as an anchoress, and her persistent rhetoric of humility (she most often speaks of herself only as a "creature"), may have masked or softened the daring of her theology. This she developed from decades of meditation on a sequence of sixteen visions of the Crucifixion—"showings"—that she received in extreme illness at age thirty.

The urban space and domestic arrangements of Julian's anchorhold serve as an emblem for her theology and her place in the spiritual world. She had a maidservant, and received and

*The editors express their gratitude to Professor Nicholas Watson for his advice on this section.

spoke to guests. Some of those encounters were reported, as for example by Margery Kempe from nearby Lynn, whose own work appears later in this anthology (page 529). Julian brought eminence to the churches of Norwich without threatening their hierarchy; she lived under the direction of a priestly confessor, made no claim to worldly power, and insisted upon her orthodoxy. Yet a visitor like Margery Kempe could use Julian's approval as a defense for her own more mobile and subversive quest for holiness.

Dame Julian used her own background of household and family as images to create a complex and subtle domestic theology of the trinity and especially of the sacrifice of Christ. Julian's metaphors for the divine are not exclusively intimate or domestic, however. She repeatedly speaks of God in socially conservative terms, as a great secular lord whose grace is a form of public "courtesy." Her revelation of the soul as a great citadel (ch. 68) features Jesus as its bishop, king, and lord.

Julian probably dictated the two versions of her *Book of Showings*, although it is clear that she was deeply versed in the Bible and liturgy, and in the writings of English and Continental mystics. The earlier version is largely focused on the visions themselves, while the very much longer version (selections from which follow) reflects the ensuing decades of theological speculations to which Julian's visions led her. She will often expound a statement by Christ in one of her visions with all the nuance that contemporary theologians would apply to a line from the Bible. In an extraordinary series of reflections, Julian at once meditates upon key moments in her initial visions, and explores the role of Christ in mankind and in the Trinity through the multifaceted image of the Lord as mother. Julian exploits all the moments of motherhood—conception, labor, breast-feeding, nurture, and upbringing—to articulate the place of Christ in the scheme of salvation and the necessity of sin. At the same time, other aspects of motherhood also serve Julian to explore the other persons of the Trinity, God the Father and the Holy Spirit, as well as the sufferings and joys of the Virgin Mary.

Even more than Richard Rolle or the *Cloud of Unknowing* (selections from which follow in the Companion Readings), Julian is explicitly concerned with the love and salvation of all the faithful, not just private communion with the divine. She addresses herself, more broadly than her predecessors, to the entire community of the faithful. She explicitly does not privilege herself above those of simple belief, and again uses the imagery of a nurturing mother to urge the sinful soul's recourse to the Holy Church.

from A Book of Showings[1]

[THREE GRACES. ILLNESS. THE FIRST REVELATION]

CHAPTER 2

This revelation was made to a simple, unlettered creature, living in this mortal flesh, the year of our Lord one thousand, three hundred and seventy-three, on the thirteenth day of May;[2] and before this the creature had desired three graces by the gift of God. The first was recollection of the Passion. The second was bodily sickness. The third was to have, of God's gift, three wounds. As to the first, it seemed to me that I had some feeling for the Passion of Christ, but still I desired to have more by the grace of God. I thought that I wished that I had been at that time with Magdalen and with the others who were Christ's lovers, so that I might have seen with my own eyes the Passion which our Lord suffered for me, so that I might have suffered with him as others did who loved him. Therefore I desired a bodily sight, in which I might have more knowledge of our savior's bodily pains, and of the compassion of our Lady and of all his true lovers who were living at that time and saw his pains, for I would have been one of them and have

1. Translated by Edmund Colledge and James Walsh.

2. Julian provides the biographical setting of her visions in this chapter. By "unlettered" she may mean that she was not formally schooled; it is clear she was literate.

suffered with them. I never desired any other sight of God or revelation, until my soul would be separated from the body, for I believed that I should be saved by the mercy of God. This was my intention, because I wished afterwards, because of that revelation, to have truer recollection of Christ's Passion. As to the second grace, there came into my mind with contrition—a free gift which I did not seek—a desire of my will to have by God's gift a bodily sickness. I wished that sickness to be so severe that it might seem mortal, so that I might in it receive all the rites which Holy Church has to give me, whilst I myself should think that I was dying, and everyone who saw me would think the same; for I wanted no comfort from any human, earthly life in that sickness. I wanted to have every kind of pain, bodily and spiritual, which I should have if I had died, every fear and temptation from devils, and every other kind of pain except the departure of the spirit. I intended this because I wanted to be purged by God's mercy, and afterwards live more to his glory because of that sickness; because I hoped that this would be to my reward when I should die, because I desired soon to be with my God and my Creator.

These two desires about the Passion and the sickness which I desired from him were with a condition, for it seemed to me that this was not the ordinary practice of prayer; therefore I said: Lord, you know what I want, if it be your will that I have it, and if it be not your will, good Lord, do not be displeased, for I want nothing which you do not want. When I was young I desired to have this sickness when I would be thirty years old. As to the third, by the grace of God and the teaching of Holy Church I conceived a great desire to receive three wounds in my life, that is, the wound of true contrition, the wound of loving compassion, and the wound of longing with my will for God. Just as I asked for the other two conditionally, so I asked urgently for this third without any condition. The two desires which I mentioned first passed from my mind, and the third remained there continually.

Chapter 3

And when I was thirty and a half years old, God sent me a bodily sickness in which I lay for three days and three nights, and on the third night I received all the rites of Holy Church, and did not expect to live until day. And after this I lay for two days and two nights, and on the third night I often thought that I was on the point of death, and those who were with me often thought so. And yet in this I felt a great reluctance to die, not that there was anything on earth which it pleased me to live for, or any pain of which I was afraid, for I trusted in the mercy of God. But it was because I wanted to live to love God better and longer, so that I might through the grace of that living have more knowledge and love of God in the bliss of heaven. Because it seemed to me that all the time that I had lived here was very little and short in comparison with the bliss which is everlasting, I thought: Good Lord, can my living no longer be to your glory? And I understood by my reason and the sensation of my pains that I should die; and with all the will of my heart I assented to be wholly as was God's will.

So I lasted until day, and by then my body was dead from the middle downwards, as it felt to me. Then I was helped to sit upright and supported, so that my heart might be more free to be at God's will, and so that I could think of him whilst my life would last. My curate was sent for to be present at my end; and before he came my eyes were fixed upwards, and I could not speak. He set the cross before my face, and said: I have brought the image of your savior; look at it and take comfort from it. It seemed to me that I was well, for my eyes were set upwards towards heaven, where I trusted that I by God's mercy was going; but nevertheless I agreed to fix my eyes on the face of the crucifix if I could, and so I did, for it seemed to me that I would hold out longer with my eyes set in front of me rather than upwards. After this my sight began to fail. It grew as dark around me in the room as if it had been night, except that there was ordinary light trained upon the image of the cross, I did not know how. Everything around the cross was ugly and terrifying to me, as if it were occupied by a great crowd of devils.

After this the upper part of my body began to die, until I could scarcely feel anything. My greatest pain was my shortness of breath and the ebbing of my life. Then truly I believed that I was at the point of death. And suddenly at that moment all my pain was taken from me, and I was as sound, particularly in the upper part of my body, as ever I was before. I was astonished by this sudden change, for it seemed to me that it was by God's secret doing and not natural; and even so, in this ease which I felt, I had no more confidence that I should live, nor was the ease I felt complete for me, for I thought that I would rather have been delivered of this world, because that was what my heart longed for.

Then suddenly it came into my mind that I ought to wish for the second wound as a gift and a grace from our Lord, that my body might be filled full of recollection and feeling of his blessed Passion, as I had prayed before, for I wished that his pains might be my pains, with compassion which would lead to longing for God. So it seemed to me that I might with his grace have the wounds which I had before desired; but in this I never wanted any bodily vision or any kind of revelation from God, but the compassion which I thought a loving soul could have for our Lord Jesus, who for love was willing to become a mortal man. I desired to suffer with him, living in my mortal body, as God would give me grace.

Chapter 4

And at this, suddenly I saw the red blood running down from under the crown, hot and flowing freely and copiously, a living stream, just as it was at the time when the crown of thorns was pressed on his blessed head.[3] I perceived, truly and powerfully, that it was he who just so, both God and man, himself suffered for me, who showed it to me without any intermediary.

And in the same revelation, suddenly the Trinity filled my heart full of the greatest joy, and I understood that it will be so in heaven without end to all who will come there. For the Trinity is God, God is the Trinity. The Trinity is our maker, the Trinity is our protector, the Trinity is our everlasting lover, the Trinity is our endless joy and our bliss, by our Lord Jesus Christ and in our Lord Jesus Christ. And this was revealed in the first vision and in them all, for where Jesus appears the blessed Trinity is understood, as I see it. And I said: Blessed be the Lord! This I said with a reverent intention and in a loud voice, and I was greatly astonished by this wonder and marvel, that he who is so to be revered and feared would be so familiar with a sinful creature living in this wretched flesh.

I accepted it that at that time our Lord Jesus wanted, out of his courteous love, to show me comfort before my temptations began; for it seemed to me that I might well be tempted by devils, by God's permission and with his protection, before I would die. With this sight of his blessed Passion, with the divinity which I saw in my understanding, I knew well that this was strength enough for me, yes, and for all living creatures who were to be saved, against all the devils of hell and against all their spiritual enemies.

3. This begins the first of Julian's 16 revelations.

In this he brought our Lady Saint Mary to my understanding. I saw her spiritually in her bodily likeness, a simple, humble maiden, young in years, grown a little taller than a child, of the stature which she had when she conceived.[4] Also God showed me part of the wisdom and the truth of her soul, and in this I understood the reverent contemplation with which she beheld her God, who is her Creator, marveling with great reverence that he was willing to be born of her who was a simple creature created by him. And this wisdom and truth, this knowledge of her Creator's greatness and of her own created littleness, made her say very meekly to Gabriel: Behold me here, God's handmaiden. In this sight I understood truly that she is greater, more worthy and more fulfilled, than everything else which God has created, and which is inferior to her. Above her is no created thing, except the blessed humanity of Christ, as I saw.

Chapter 5

At the same time as I saw this sight of the head bleeding, our good Lord showed a spiritual sight of his familiar love. I saw that he is to us everything which is good and comforting for our help. He is our clothing, who wraps and enfolds us for love, embraces us and shelters us, surrounds us for his love, which is so tender that he may never desert us. And so in this sight I saw that he is everything which is good, as I understand.

And in this he showed me something small, no bigger than a hazelnut, lying in the palm of my hand, as it seemed to me, and it was as round as a ball. I looked at it with the eye of my understanding and thought: What can this be? I was amazed that it could last, for I thought that because of its littleness it would suddenly have fallen into nothing. And I was answered in my understanding: It lasts and always will, because God loves it; and thus everything has being through the love of God.

In this little thing I saw three properties. The first is that God made it, the second is that God loves it, the third is that God preserves it. But what did I see in it? It is that God is the Creator and the protector and the lover. For until I am substantially united to him, I can never have perfect rest or true happiness, until, that is, I am so attached to him that there can be no created thing between my God and me.

This little thing which is created seemed to me as if it could have fallen into nothing because of its littleness. We need to have knowledge of this, so that we may delight in despising as nothing everything created, so as to love and have uncreated God. For this is the reason why our hearts and souls are not in perfect ease, because here we seek rest in this thing which is so little, in which there is no rest, and we do not know our God who is almighty, all wise and all good, for he is true rest. God wishes to be known, and it pleases him that we should rest in him; for everything which is beneath him is not sufficient for us. And this is the reason why no soul is at rest until it has despised as nothing all things which are created. When it by its will has become nothing for love, to have him who is everything, then is it able to receive spiritual rest.

And also our good Lord revealed that it is very greatly pleasing to him that a simple soul should come naked, openly and familiarly. For this is the loving yearning of the soul through the touch of the Holy Spirit, from the understanding which I have in this revelation: God, of your goodness give me yourself, for you are enough for me, and I can ask for nothing which is less which can pay you full

4. Julian will have two further visions of the Virgin Mary in different manifestations: as mother mourning at the Crucifixion and as ascended saint.

worship. And if I ask anything which is less, always I am in want; but only in you do I have everything.

And these words of the goodness of God are very dear to the soul, and very close to touching our Lord's will, for his goodness fills all his creatures and all his blessed works full, and endlessly overflows in them. For he is everlastingness, and he made us only for himself, and restored us by his precious Passion and always preserves us in his blessed love; and all this is of his goodness.

Chapter 9

I am not good because of the revelations, but only if I love God better; and inasmuch as you love God better, it is more to you than to me. I do not say this to those who are wise, because they know it well. But I say it to you who are simple, to give you comfort and strength; for we are all one in love, for truly it was not revealed to me that God loves me better than the humblest soul who is in a state of grace. For I am sure that there are many who never had revelations or visions, but only the common teaching of Holy Church, who love God better than I. If I pay special attention to myself, I am nothing at all; but in general I am, I hope, in the unity of love with all my fellow Christians. For it is in this unity that the life of all men consists who will be saved. For God is everything that is good, as I see; and God has made everything that is made, and God loves everything that he has made. And he who has general love for all his fellow Christians in God has love towards everything that is. For in mankind which will be saved is comprehended all, that is to say all that is made and the maker of all. For God is in man and in God is all. And he who loves thus loves all. And I hope by the grace of God that he who may see it so will be taught the truth and greatly comforted, if he has need of comfort.

I speak of those who will be saved, for at this time God showed me no one else. But in everything I believe as Holy Church preaches and teaches. For the faith of Holy Church, which I had before I had understanding, and which, as I hope by the grace of God, I intend to preserve whole and to practice, was always in my sight, and I wished and intended never to accept anything which might be contrary to it. And to this end and with this intention I contemplated the revelation with all diligence, for throughout this blessed revelation I contemplated it as God intended.

All this was shown in three parts,[5] that is to say, by bodily vision and by words formed in my understanding and by spiritual vision. But I may not and cannot show the spiritual visions as plainly and fully as I should wish. But I trust in our Lord God almighty that he will, out of his goodness and for love of you, make you accept it more spiritually and more sweetly than I can or may tell it.

[Laughing at the Devil]

Chapter 13[6]

And after this, before God revealed any words, he allowed me to contemplate him for a fitting length of time, and all that I had seen, and all the significance that was contained in it, as well as my soul's simplicity could accept it. And then he, without voice and without opening of lips, formed in my soul this saying: With this the fiend is overcome. Our Lord said this to me with reference to his blessed Passion, as he had shown it before. In this he showed a part of the fiend's malice, and all of his impotence,

5. Or three ways of perception.

6. The fifth revelation.

because he showed that his Passion is the overcoming of the fiend. God showed me that the fiend has now the same malice as he had before the Incarnation, and he works as hard, and he sees as constantly as he did before that all souls who will be saved escape him to God's glory by the power of our Lord's precious Passion. And that is the devil's sorrow, and he is put to terrible shame, for everything which God permits him to do turns to joy for us and to pain and shame for him. And he has as much sorrow when God permits him to work as when he is not working. And that is because he can never do as much evil as he would wish, for his power is all locked in God's hands. But in God there can be no anger, as I see it, and it is with power and justice, to the profit of all who will be saved, that he opposes the damned, who in malice and malignity work to frustrate and oppose God's will.

Also I saw our Lord scorn his malice and despise him as nothing, and he wants us to do so. Because of this sight I laughed greatly, and that made those around me to laugh as well; and their laughter was pleasing to me. I thought that I wished that all my fellow Christians had seen what I saw. Then they would all have laughed with me; but I did not see Christ laughing, but I know well that it was the vision he showed me which made me laugh, for I understood that we may laugh, to comfort ourselves and rejoice in God, because the devil is overcome. And when I saw our Lord scorn his malice, that was through the fixing of my understanding on him, that is, that this was an interior revelation of his truth, in which his demeanour did not change. For as I see it, this is an attribute of God which must be honoured, and which lasts forever.

And after this I became serious again, and said: I see three things: sport and scorn and seriousness. I see sport, that the devil is overcome; and I see scorn, that God scorns him and he will be scorned; and I see seriousness, that he is overcome by the blessed Passion and death of our Lord Jesus Christ, which was accomplished in great earnest and with heavy labour. And when I said that he is scorned, I meant that God scorns him, that is, because he sees him now as he will forever. For in this God revealed that the devil is damned. And I meant this when I said that he ought to be scorned; for I saw that on Judgment Day he will be generally scorned by all who will be saved, of whose salvation he has had great envy. For then he will see that all the woe and tribulation which he has caused them will be changed into the increase of their eternal joy. And all the pain and the sorrow that he wanted to bring them into will go forever with him to hell.

[Christ Draws Julian in through His Wound]

Chapter 24[7]

With a kindly countenance our good Lord looked into his side, and he gazed with joy, and with his sweet regard he drew his creature's understanding into his side by the same wound;[8] and there he revealed a fair and delectable place, large enough for all mankind that will be saved and will rest in peace and in love. And with that he brought to mind the dear and precious blood and water which he suffered to be shed for love. And in this sweet sight he showed his blessed heart split in two, and as he rejoiced he showed to my understanding a part of his blessed divinity, as much as was his will at that time, strengthening my poor soul to understand what can be said, that is the endless love which was without beginning and is and always shall be.

7. This chapter recounts Julian's tenth revelation.

8. The spear wound in Christ's side.

And with this our good Lord said most joyfully: See how I love you, as if he had said, my darling, behold and see your Lord, your God, who is your Creator and your endless joy; see your own brother, your savior; my child, behold and see what delight and bliss I have in your salvation, and for my love rejoice with me.

And for my greater understanding, these blessed words were said: See how I love you, as if he had said, behold and see that I loved you so much, before I died for you, that I wanted to die for you. And now I have died for you, and willingly suffered what I could. And now all my bitter pain and my hard labor is turned into everlasting joy and bliss for me and for you. How could it now be that you would pray to me for anything pleasing to me which I would not very gladly grant to you? For my delight is in your holiness and in your endless joy and bliss in me.

This is the understanding, as simply as I can say it, of these blessed words: See how I loved you. Our Lord revealed this to make us glad and joyful.

Chapter 25[9]

And with this same appearance of mirth and joy our good Lord looked down on his right, and brought to my mind where our Lady stood at the time of his Passion, and he said: Do you wish to see her? And these sweet words were as if he had said, I know well that you wish to see my blessed mother, for after myself she is the greatest joy that I could show you, and the greatest delight and honor to me, and she is what all my blessed creatures most desire to see. And because of the wonderful, exalted and singular love that he has for this sweet maiden, his blessed mother, our Lady Saint Mary, he reveals her bliss and joy through the sense of these sweet words, as if he said, do you wish to see how I love her, so that you could rejoice with me in the love which I have in her and she has in me?

And for greater understanding of these sweet words our good Lord speaks in love to all mankind who will be saved, addressing them all as one person, as if he said, do you wish to see in her how you are loved? It is for love of you that I have made her so exalted, so noble, so honorable; and this delights me. And I wish it to delight you. For next to him, she is the most blissful to be seen. But in this matter I was not taught to long to see her bodily presence whilst I am here, but the virtues of her blessed soul, her truth, her wisdom, her love, through which I am taught to know myself and reverently to fear my God.

And when our good Lord had revealed this, and said these words: Do you wish to see her? I answered and said: Yes, good Lord, great thanks, yes, good Lord, if it be your will. Often times I had prayed for this, and I had expected to see her in a bodily likeness; but I did not see her so. And Jesus, saying this, showed me a spiritual vision of her. Just as before I had seen her small and simple, now he showed her high and noble and glorious and more pleasing to him than all creatures. And so he wishes it to be known that all who take delight in him should take delight in her, and in the delight that he has in her and she in him.

And for greater understanding he showed this example, as if, when a man loves some creature particularly, more than all other creatures, he will make all other creatures to love and delight in that creature whom he loves so much. And in these words which Jesus said: Do you wish to see her? it seemed to me that these were the most delectable words which he could give me in this spiritual vision of her which he gave me. For our Lord showed me no particular person except our Lady Saint

9. The eleventh revelation.

Mary, and he showed her on three occasions. The first was as she conceived, the second was as she had been under the Cross, and the third was as she is now, in delight, honor and joy.

CHAPTER 26[1]

And after this our Lord showed himself to me, and he appeared to me more glorified than I had seen him before, in which I was taught that our soul will never have rest till it comes into him, acknowledging that he is full of joy, familiar and courteous and blissful and true life. Again and again our Lord said: I am he, I am he, I am he who is highest. I am he whom you love. I am he in whom you delight. I am he whom you serve. I am he for whom you long. I am he whom you desire. I am he whom you intend. I am he who is all. I am he whom Holy Church preaches and teaches to you. I am he who showed himself before to you. The number of the words surpasses my intelligence and my understanding and all my powers, for they were the most exalted, as I see it, for in them is comprehended I cannot tell what; but the joy which I saw when they were revealed surpasses all that the heart can think or the soul may desire. And therefore these words are not explained here, but let every man accept them as our Lord intended them, according to the grace God gives him in understanding and love.

[THE NECESSITY OF SIN, AND OF HATING SIN]

CHAPTER 27[2]

And after this our Lord brought to my mind the longing that I had for him before, and I saw that nothing hindered me but sin, and I saw that this is true of us all in general, and it seemed to me that if there had been no sin, we should all have been pure and as like our Lord as he created us. And so in my folly before this time I often wondered why, through the great prescient wisdom of God, the beginning of sin was not prevented. For then it seemed to me that all would have been well.

The impulse to think this was greatly to be shunned; and nevertheless I mourned and sorrowed on this account, unreasonably, lacking discretion. But Jesus, who in this vision informed me about everything needful to me, answered with these words and said: Sin is necessary, but all will be well, and all will be well, and every kind of thing will be well. In this naked word "sin," our Lord brought generally to my mind all which is not good, and the shameful contempt and the direst tribulation which he endured for us in this life, and his death and all his pains, and the passions, spiritual and bodily, of all his creatures. For we are all in part troubled, and we shall be troubled, following our master Jesus until we are fully purged of our mortal flesh and all our inward affections which are not very good.

And with the beholding of this, with all the pains that ever were or ever will be, I understood Christ's Passion for the greatest and surpassing pain. And yet this was shown to me in an instant, and it quickly turned into consolation. For our good Lord would not have the soul frightened by this ugly sight. But I did not see sin, for I believe that it has no kind of substance, no share in being, nor can it be recognized except by the pain caused by it. And it seems to me that this pain is something for a time, for it purges and makes us know ourselves and ask for mercy; for the Passion of our Lord is comfort to us against all this, and that is his blessed will. And because of the tender love which our good Lord has for all who will be saved, he comforts readily

1. The twelfth revelation.

2. The thirteenth revelation.

and sweetly, meaning this: It is true that sin is the cause of all this pain, but all will be well, and every kind of thing will be well.

These works were revealed most tenderly, showing no kind of blame to me or to anyone who will be saved. So it would be most unkind of me to blame God or marvel at him on account of my sins, since he does not blame me for sin.

And in these same words I saw hidden in God an exalted and wonderful mystery, which he will make plain and we shall know in heaven. In this knowledge we shall truly see the cause why he allowed sin to come, and in this sight we shall rejoice forever.

Chapter 40

And this is a supreme friendship of our courteous Lord, that he protects us so tenderly whilst we are in our sins; and furthermore he touches us most secretly, and shows us our sins by the sweet light of mercy and grace. But when we see ourselves so foul, then we believe that God may be angry with us because of our sins. Then we are moved by the Holy Spirit through contrition to prayer, and we desire with all our might an amendment of ourselves to appease God's anger, until the time that we find rest of soul and ease of conscience. And then we hope that God has forgiven us our sin; and this is true. And then our courteous Lord shows himself to the soul, happily and with the gladdest countenance, welcoming it as a friend, as if it had been in pain and in prison, saying: My dear darling, I am glad that you have come to me in all your woe. I have always been with you, and now you see me loving, and we are made one in bliss.

So sins are forgiven by grace and mercy, and our soul is honorably received in joy, as it will be when it comes into heaven, as often as it comes by the operation of grace of the Holy Spirit and the power of Christ's Passion.

Here I truly understood that every kind of thing is made available to us by God's great goodness, so much so that when we ourselves are at peace and in charity we are truly safe. But because we cannot have this completely whilst we are here, therefore it is fitting for us to live always in sweet prayer and in loving longing with our Lord Jesus. For he always longs to bring us to the fullness of joy, as has been said before, where he reveals his spiritual thirst. But now, because of all this spiritual consolation which has been described, if any man or woman be moved by folly to say or to think "If this be true, then it would be well to sin so as to have the greater reward, or else to think sin less important," beware of this impulse, for truly, should it come, it is untrue and from the fiend.

For the same true love which touches us all by its blessed strength, that same blessed love teaches us that we must hate sin only because of love. And I am sure by what I feel that the more that each loving soul sees this in the courteous love of our Lord God, the greater is his hatred of sinning and the more he is ashamed. For if it were laid in front of us, all the pain there is in hell and in purgatory and on earth, death and all the rest, we should choose all that pain rather than sin. For sin is so vile and so much to be hated that it can be compared with no pain which is not itself sin. And no more cruel hell than sin was revealed to me, for a loving soul hates no pain but sin; for everything is good except sin, and nothing is evil except sin. And when by the operation of mercy and grace we set our intention on mercy and grace, we are made all fair and spotless.

And God is as willing as he is powerful and wise to save man. And Christ himself is the foundation of all the laws of Christian men, and he taught us to do good in return for evil. Here we may see that he is himself this love, and does to us as he teaches us to do; for he wishes us to be like him in undiminished, everlasting love towards ourselves and our fellow Christians. No more than his love towards us is withdrawn because of our sin does he wish our love to be withdrawn from ourselves or from our fellow Christians; but we must unreservedly hate sin and endlessly love the soul as God loves it. Then we should hate sin just as God hates it, and love the soul as God loves it. For these words which God said are an endless strength: I protect you most truly.

[God as Father, Mother, Husband]

Chapter 58

God the blessed Trinity, who is everlasting being, just as he is eternal from without beginning, just so was it in his eternal purpose to create human nature, which fair nature was first prepared for his own Son, the second person; and when he wished, by full agreement of the whole Trinity he created us all once. And in our creating he joined and united us to himself, and through this union we are kept as pure and as noble as we were created. By the power of that same precious union we love our Creator and delight in him, praise him and thank him and endlessly rejoice in him. And this is the work which is constantly performed in every soul which will be saved, and this is the godly will mentioned before.

And so in our making, God almighty is our loving Father, and God all wisdom is our loving Mother,[3] with the love and the goodness of the Holy Spirit, which is all one God, one Lord. And in the joining and the union he is our very true spouse and we his beloved wife and his fair maiden, with which wife he was never displeased; for he says: I love you and you love me, and our love will never divide in two.

I contemplated the work of all the blessed Trinity, in which contemplation I saw and understood these three properties: the property of the fatherhood, and the property of the motherhood, and the property of the lordship in one God. In our almighty Father we have our protection and our bliss, as regards our natural substance, which is ours by our creation from without beginning; and in the second person, in knowledge and wisdom we have our perfection, as regards our sensuality, our restoration and our salvation, for he is our Mother, brother and savior; and in our good Lord the Holy Spirit we have our reward and our gift for our living and our labor, endlessly surpassing all that we desire in his marvelous courtesy, out of his great plentiful grace. For all our life consists of three: In the first we have our being, and in the second we have our increasing, and in the third we have our fulfillment. The first is nature, the second is mercy, the third is grace.

As to the first, I saw and understood that the high might of the Trinity is our Father, and the deep wisdom of the Trinity is our Mother, and the great love of the Trinity is our Lord; and all these we have in nature and in our substantial creation. And furthermore I saw that the second person, who is our Mother, substantially the same beloved person, has now become our mother sensually, because we are double by God's creating, that is to say substantial and sensual. Our substance is the higher part, which we have in our Father, God almighty; and the second person of the Trinity is our Mother in nature in our substantial creation, in whom we are founded

3. The image of God as a wise woman draws from an ancient tradition of the female Sophia, Holy Wisdom, who figures in the apocryphal book of Ecclesiasticus (ch. 24).

and rooted, and he is our Mother of mercy in taking our sensuality. And so our Mother is working on us in various ways, in whom our parts are kept undivided; for in our Mother Christ we profit and increase, and in mercy he reforms and restores us, and by the power of his Passion, his death and his Resurrection, he unites us to our substance. So our Mother works in mercy on all his beloved children who are docile and obedient to him, and grace works with mercy, and especially in two properties, as it was shown, which working belongs to the third person, the Holy Spirit. He works, rewarding and giving. Rewarding is a gift for our confidence which the Lord makes to those who have labored; and giving is a courteous act which he does freely, by grace, fulfilling and surpassing all that creatures deserve.

Thus in our Father, God almighty, we have our being, and in our Mother of mercy we have our reforming and our restoring, in whom our parts are united and all made perfect man, and through the rewards and the gifts of grace of the Holy Spirit we are fulfilled. And our substance is in our Father, God almighty, and our substance is in our Mother, God all wisdom, and our substance is in our Lord God, the Holy Spirit, all goodness, for our substance is whole in each person of the Trinity, who is one God. And our sensuality is only in the second person, Christ Jesus, in whom is the Father and the Holy Spirit; and in him and by him we are powerfully taken out of hell and out of the wretchedness on earth, and gloriously brought up into heaven, and blessedly united to our substance, increased in riches and nobility by all the power of Christ and by the grace and operation of the Holy Spirit.

Chapter 59

And we have all this bliss by mercy and grace, and this kind of bliss we never could have had and known, unless that property of goodness which is in God had been opposed, through which we have this bliss. For wickedness has been suffered to rise in opposition to that goodness; and the goodness of mercy and grace opposed that wickedness, and turned everything to goodness and honor for all who will be saved. For this is that property in God which opposes good to evil. So Jesus Christ, who opposes good to evil, is our true Mother. We have our being from him, where the foundation of motherhood begins, with all the sweet protection of love which endlessly follows.

As truly as God is our Father, so truly is God our Mother, and he revealed that in everything, and especially in these sweet words where he says: I am he; that is to say: I am he, the power and goodness of fatherhood; I am he, the wisdom and the lovingness of motherhood; I am he, the light and the grace which is all blessed love; I am he, the Trinity; I am he, the unity; I am he, the great supreme goodness of every kind of thing; I am he who makes you to love; I am he who makes you to long; I am he, the endless fulfilling of all true desires. For where the soul is highest, noblest, most honorable, still it is lowest, meekest and mildest.

And from this foundation in substance we have all the powers of our sensuality by the gift of nature, and by the help and the furthering of mercy and grace, without which we cannot profit. Our great Father, almighty God, who is being, knows us and loved us before time began. Out of this knowledge, in his most wonderful deep love, by the prescient eternal counsel of all the blessed Trinity, he wanted the second person to become our Mother, our brother and our savior. From this it follows that as truly as God is our Father, so truly is God our Mother. Our Father wills, our Mother works, our good Lord the Holy Spirit confirms. And therefore it is our part to love our God in whom we have our being, reverently thanking and praising him for our creation, mightily praying to our Mother for mercy and pity, and to our Lord the Holy Spirit for help and grace. For in these three is all our life: nature, mercy and grace, of which we have mildness, patience and pity, and hatred of sin and wickedness; for the virtues must of themselves hate sin and wickedness.

And so Jesus is our true Mother in nature by our first creation, and he is our true Mother in grace by his taking our created nature. All the lovely works and all the sweet loving offices of beloved motherhood are appropriated to the second person, for in him we have this godly will, whole and safe forever, both in nature and in grace, from his own goodness proper to him.

I understand three ways of contemplating motherhood in God. The first is the foundation of our nature's creation; the second is his taking of our nature, where the motherhood of grace begins; the third is the motherhood at work. And in that, by the same grace, everything is penetrated, in length and in breadth, in height and in depth without end; and it is all one love.

CHAPTER 60

But now I should say a little more about this penetration, as I understood our Lord to mean: How we are brought back by the motherhood of mercy and grace into our natural place, in which we were created by the motherhood of love, a mother's love which never leaves us.

Our Mother in nature, our Mother in grace, because he wanted altogether to become our Mother in all things, made the foundation of his work most humbly and most mildly in the maiden's womb. And he revealed that in the first revelation, when he brought that meek maiden before the eye of my understanding in the simple stature which she had when she conceived; that is to say that our great God, the supreme wisdom of all things, arrayed and prepared himself in this humble place, all ready in our poor flesh, himself to do the service and the office of motherhood in everything. The mother's service is nearest, readiest and surest: nearest because it is most natural, readiest because it is most loving, and surest because it is truest. No one ever might or could perform this office fully, except only him. We know that all our mothers bear us for pain and for death. O, what is that? But our true Mother Jesus, he alone bears us for joy and for endless life, blessed may he be. So he carries us within him in love and travail, until the full time when he wanted to suffer the sharpest thorns and cruel pains that ever were or will be, and at the last he died. And when he had finished, and had borne us so for bliss, still all this could not satisfy his wonderful love. And he revealed this in these great surpassing words of love: If I could suffer more, I would suffer more. He could not die any more, but he did not want to cease working; therefore he must needs nourish us, for the precious love of motherhood has made him our debtor.

The mother can give her child to suck of her milk, but our precious Mother Jesus can feed us with himself, and does, most courteously and most tenderly, with the blessed sacrament, which is the precious food of true life; and with all the sweet sacraments he sustains us most mercifully and graciously, and so he meant in these blessed words, where he said: I am he whom Holy Church preaches and teaches to you. That is to say: All the health and the life of the sacraments, all the power and the grace of my word, all the goodness which is ordained in Holy Church for you, I am he.

The mother can lay her child tenderly to her breast, but our tender Mother Jesus can lead us easily into his blessed breast through his sweet open side, and show us there a part of the godhead and of the joys of heaven, with inner certainty of endless bliss. And that he revealed in the tenth revelation, giving us the same understanding in these sweet words which he says: See, how I love you, looking into his blessed side, rejoicing.

This fair lovely word "mother" is so sweet and so kind in itself that it cannot truly be said of anyone or to anyone except of him and to him who is the true Mother of life and of all things. To the property of motherhood belong nature, love, wisdom and knowledge, and this is God. For though it may be so that our bodily bringing to birth is only little, humble and simple in comparison with our spiritual bringing to birth, still it is he who does it in the creatures by whom it is done. The kind, loving mother who knows and sees the need of her child guards it very tenderly, as the nature and condition of motherhood will have. And always as the child grows in age and in stature, she acts differently, but she does not change her love. And when it is even older, she allows it to be chastised to destroy its faults, so as to make the child receive virtues and grace. This work, with everything which is lovely and good, our Lord performs in those by whom it is done. So he is our Mother in nature by the operation of grace in the lower part, for love of the higher part. And he wants us to know it, for he wants to have all our love attached to him; and in this I saw that every debt which we owe by God's command to fatherhood and motherhood is fulfilled in truly loving God, which blessed love Christ works in us. And this was revealed in everything, and especially in the great bounteous words when he says: I am he whom you love.

Chapter 61

And in our spiritual bringing to birth he uses more tenderness, without any comparison, in protecting us. By so much as our soul is more precious in his sight, he kindles our understanding, he prepares our ways, he eases our conscience, he comforts our soul, he illumines our heart and gives us partial knowledge and love of his blessed divinity, with gracious memory of his sweet humanity and his blessed Passion, with courteous wonder over his great surpassing goodness, and makes us to love everything which he loves for love of him, and to be well satisfied with him and with all his works. And when we fall, quickly he raises us up with his loving embrace and his gracious touch. And when we are strengthened by his sweet working, then we willingly choose him by his grace, that we shall be his servants and his lovers, constantly and forever.

And yet after this he allows some of us to fall more heavily and more grievously than ever we did before, as it seems to us. And then we who are not all wise think that everything which we have undertaken was all nothing. But it is not so, for we need to fall, and we need to see it; for if we did not fall, we should not know how feeble and how wretched we are in ourselves, nor, too, should we know so completely the wonderful love of our Creator.

For we shall truly see in heaven without end that we have sinned grievously in this life; and notwithstanding this, we shall truly see that we were never hurt in his love, nor were we ever of less value in his sight. And by the experience of this falling we shall have a great and marvelous knowledge of love in God without end; for enduring and marvelous is that love which cannot and will not be broken because of offenses.

And this was one profitable understanding; another is the humility and meekness which we shall obtain by the sight of our fall, for by that we shall be raised high in heaven, to which raising we might never have come without that meekness. And therefore we need to see it; and if we do not see it, though we fell, that would not profit us. And commonly we first fall and then see it; and both are from the mercy of God.

The mother may sometimes suffer the child to fall and to be distressed in various ways, for its own benefit, but she can never suffer any kind of peril to come to her child, because of her love. And though our earthly mother may suffer her child to perish, our heavenly Mother Jesus may never suffer us who are his children to perish, for he is almighty, all wisdom and all love, and so is none but he, blessed may he be.

But often when our falling and our wretchedness are shown to us, we are so much afraid and so greatly ashamed of ourselves that we scarcely know where we can put ourselves. But then our courteous Mother does not wish us to flee away, for nothing would be less pleasing to him; but he then wants us to behave like a child. For when it is distressed and frightened, it runs quickly to its mother; and if it can do no more, it calls to the mother for help with all its might. So he wants us to act as a meek child, saying: My kind Mother, my gracious Mother, my beloved Mother, have mercy on me. I have made myself filthy and unlike you, and I may not and cannot make it right except with your help and grace.

And if we do not then feel ourselves eased, let us at once be sure that he is behaving as a wise Mother. For if he sees that it is profitable to us to mourn and to weep, with compassion and pity he suffers that until the right time has come, out of his love. And then he wants us to show a child's characteristics, which always naturally trusts in its mother's love in well-being and in woe. And he wants us to commit ourselves fervently to the faith of Holy Church, and find there our beloved Mother in consolation and true understanding, with all the company of the blessed. For one single person may often be broken, as it seems to him, but the entire body of Holy Church was never broken, nor ever will be without end. And therefore it is a certain thing, and good and gracious to will, meekly and fervently, to be fastened and united to our mother Holy Church, who is Christ Jesus. For the flood of mercy which is his dear blood and precious water is plentiful to make us fair and clean. The blessed wounds of our savior are open and rejoice to heal us. The sweet gracious hands of our Mother are ready and diligent about us; for he in all this work exercises the true office of a kind nurse, who has nothing else to do but attend to the safety of her child.

It is his office to save us, it is his glory to do it, and it is his will that we know it; for he wants us to love him sweetly and trust in him meekly and greatly. And he revealed this in these gracious words: I protect you very safely.

[The Soul as Christ's Citadel]

Chapter 68

And then our good Lord opened my spiritual eye, and showed me my soul in the midst of my heart. I saw the soul as wide as if it were an endless citadel, and also as if it were a blessed kingdom, and from the state which I saw in it, I understood that it is a fine city. In the midst of that city sits our Lord Jesus, true God and true man, a handsome person and tall, highest bishop, most awesome king, most honourable lord. And I saw him splendidly clad in honours. He sits erect there in the soul, in peace and rest, and he rules and guards heaven and earth and everything that is. The humanity and the divinity sit at rest, the divinity rules and guards, without instrument or effort. And the soul is wholly occupied by the blessed divinity, sovereign power, sovereign wisdom and sovereign goodness.

The place which Jesus takes in our soul he will nevermore vacate, for in us is his home of homes and his everlasting dwelling. And in this he revealed the delight that he has in the creation of man's soul; for as well as the Father could create a creature and as well as the Son could create a creature, so well did the Holy Spirit want man's spirit to be created, and so it was done. And therefore the blessed Trinity rejoices without end in the creation of man's soul, for it saw without beginning what would delight it without end.

Everything which God has made shows his dominion, as understanding was given at the same time by the example of a creature who is led to see the great nobility and the rulership which is fitting to a lord, and when it had seen all the nobility beneath, then in wonder it was moved to seek up above for that high place where the lord dwells, knowing by reason that his dwelling is in the most honourable place. And thus I understood truly that our soul may never have rest in anything which is beneath itself. And when it comes above all creatures into itself, still it cannot remain contemplating itself; but all its contemplation is blessedly set in God, who is the Creator, dwelling there, for in man's soul is his true dwelling.

And the greatest light and the brightest shining in the city is the glorious love of our Lord God, as I see it. And what can make us to rejoice more in God than to see in him that in us, of all his greatest works, he has joy? For I saw in the same revelation that if the blessed Trinity could have created man's soul any better, any fairer, any nobler than it was created, the Trinity would not have been fully pleased with the creation of man's soul. But because it made man's soul as beautiful, as good, as precious a creature as it could make, therefore the blessed Trinity is fully pleased without end in the creation of man's soul. And it wants our hearts to be powerfully lifted above the depths of the earth and all empty sorrows, and to rejoice in it.

This was a delectable sight and a restful showing, which is without end, and to contemplate it while we are here is most pleasing to God and very great profit to us. And this makes the soul which so contemplates like to him who is contemplated, and unites it in rest and peace. And it was a singular joy and bliss to me that I saw him sitting, for the truth of sitting revealed to me endless dwelling; and he gave me true knowledge that it was he who had revealed everything to me before. And when I had contemplated this with attention, our Lord very humbly revealed words to me, without voice and without opening of lips, just as he had done before, and said very sweetly: Know it well, it was no hallucination which you saw today, but accept and believe it and hold firmly to it, and comfort yourself with it and trust in it, and you will not be overcome.

These last words were said to me to teach me perfect certainty that it is our Lord Jesus who revealed everything to me; and just as in the first words which our good Lord revealed, alluding to his blessed Passion: With this the fiend is overcome, just so he said in the last words, with perfect fidelity, alluding to us all: You will not be overcome. And all this teaching and this true strengthening apply generally to all my fellow Christians, as is said before, and so is the will of God.

And these words: You will not be overcome, were said very insistently and strongly, for certainty and strength against every tribulation which may come. He did not say: You will not be troubled, you will not be belaboured, you will not be disquieted; but he said: You will not be overcome. God wants us to pay attention to these words, and always to be strong in faithful trust, in well-being and in woe, for he loves us and delights in us, and so he wishes us to love him and delight in him and trust greatly in him, and all will be well.

And soon all was hidden, and I saw no more after this.

[The Meaning of the Visions is Love]

Chapter 86

This book is begun by God's gift and his grace, but it is not yet performed, as I see it. For charity, let us all join with God's working in prayer, thanking, trusting, rejoicing, for so will our good Lord be entreated, by the understanding which I took in all his own intention, and in the sweet words where he says most happily: I am the foundation of your beseeching. For truly I saw and understood in our Lord's meaning that he revealed it because he wants to have it better known than it is. In which knowledge he wants to give us grace to love him and to cleave to him, for he beholds his heavenly treasure with so great love on earth that he will give us more light and solace in heavenly joy, by drawing our hearts from the sorrow and the darkness which we are in.

And from the time that it was revealed, I desired many times to know in what was our Lord's meaning. And fifteen years after and more, I was answered in spiritual understanding, and it was said: What, do you wish to know your Lord's meaning in this thing? Know it well, love was his meaning. Who reveals it to you? Love. What did he reveal to you? Love. Why does he reveal it to you? For love. Remain in this, and you will know more of the same. But you will never know different, without end.

So I was taught that love is our Lord's meaning. And I saw very certainly in this and in everything that before God made us he loved us, which love was never abated and never will be. And in this love he has done all his works, and in this love he has made all things profitable to us, and in this love our life is everlasting. In our creation we had beginning, but the love in which he created us was in him from without beginning. In this love we have our beginning, and all this shall we see in God without end.

Thanks be to God. Here ends the book of revelations of Julian the anchorite of Norwich, on whose soul may God have mercy.[4]

May Jesus grant us this. Amen. So ends the revelation of love of the blessed Trinity, shown by our savior Jesus Christ for our endless comfort and solace, and also that we may rejoice in him in the passing journey of this life. Amen. Jesus. Amen. I pray almighty God that this book may not come except into the hands of those who wish to be his faithful lovers, and those who will submit themselves to the faith of Holy Church and obey the wholesome understanding and teaching of men who are of virtuous life, settled age and profound learning; for this revelation is exalted divinity and wisdom, and therefore it cannot remain with him who is a slave to sin and to the devil. And beware that you do not accept one thing which is according to your pleasure and liking, and reject another, for that is the disposition of heretics. But accept it all together, and understand it truly; it all agrees with Holy Scripture, and is founded upon it, and Jesus, our true love and light and truth, will show this to all pure souls who meekly and perseveringly ask this wisdom from him. And you to whom this book will come, give our savior Christ Jesus great and hearty thanks that he made these showings and revelations for you and to you out of his endless love, mercy and goodness, for a safe guide and conduct for you and us to everlasting bliss, which may Jesus grant us. Amen. Here end the sublime and wonderful revelations of the unutterable love of God, in Jesus Christ vouchsafed to a dear lover of his, and in her to all his dear friends and lovers whose hearts like hers do flame in the love of our dearest Jesus.

4. What follows is a lengthy version of the traditional "colophon" in which the author takes leave of the work and its audience; expressions of inadequacy and appeals to God are common elements.

COMPANION READINGS

Richard Rolle: from *The Fire of Love*[1]

It is obvious to those who are in love that no one attains the heights of devotion at once, or is ravished with contemplative sweetness. In fact it is only very occasionally—and then only momentarily—that they are allowed to experience heavenly things; their progress to spiritual strength is a gradual one. When they have attained the gravity of behavior so necessary and have achieved a certain stability of mind—as much as changing circumstances permit—a certain perfection is acquired after great labor. It is then that they can feel some joy in loving God.

Notwithstanding, it appears that all those who are mighty performers in virtue immediately and genuinely experience the warmth of uncreated or created charity, melt in the immense fire of love, and sing within their hearts the song of divine praise. For this mystery is hidden from the many, and is revealed to the few, and those the most special. So the more sublime such a level is, the fewer—in this world—are those who find it. Rarely in fact have we found a man who is so holy or even perfect in this earthly life endowed with love so great as to be raised up to contemplation to the level of jubilant song. This would mean that he would receive within himself the sound that is sung in heaven, and that he would echo back the praises of God as it were in harmony, pouring forth sweet notes of music and composing spiritual songs as he offers his heavenly praises, and that he would truly experience in his heart the genuine fire of the love of God. It would be surprising if anyone without such experience should claim the name of contemplative when the psalmist, speaking in character as the typical contemplative, exclaims, *I will go into the house of the Lord, with the voice of praise and thanksgiving*.[2] The praise, of course, is the praise offered by the banqueter, one who is feeding on heavenly sweetness.

Further, perfect souls who have been caught up into this friendship—surpassing, abundant, and eternal!—discover that life is suffused with imperishable sweetness from the glittering chalice of sweet charity. In holy happy wisdom they inhale joyful heat into their souls, and as a result are much cheered by the indescribable comfort of God's healing medicine. Here at all events is refreshment for those who love their high and eternal heritage, even though in their earthly exile distress befell them. However they think it not unfitting to endure a few years' hardship in order to be raised to heavenly thrones, and never leave them. They have been selected out of all mankind to be the beloved of their Maker and to be crowned with glory, since, like the seraphim in highest heaven, they have been inflamed with the same love. Physically they may have sat in solitary state, but in mind they have companied with angels, and have yearned for their Beloved. Now they sing most sweetly a prayer of love everlasting as they rejoice in Jesus:

1. Richard Rolle (c. 1300–1349) studied at Oxford and then spent part of his life as a hermit, but he also acted as spiritual director for women engaged in solitary contemplation. In seeking to express and draw his readers toward the ineffable experience of the divine, Rolle made particularly intensive use of the imagery of bodily sensation and action—warmth, sweetness, and song. Well-known biblical texts such as the Song of Songs provided both a precedent and a language for Rolle's explorations. Unlike more rigorous mystics, he presents at least the earlier stages of the mystical ascent as an almost spontaneous, if also conflict-ridden, rising of the soul like a spark toward God. Rolle wrote a number of English lyrics and meditations; *The Fire of Love* is his most famous treatise in Latin. The passage here, taken from ch. 2, is translated by Clifton Wolters.

2. Psalms 42.4.

O honeyed flame, sweeter than all sweet, delightful beyond all creation!
My God, my Love, surge over me, pierce me by your love, wound me with
your beauty.
Surge over me, I say, who am longing for your comfort.
Reveal your healing medicine to your poor lover.
See, my one desire is for you; it is you my heart is seeking.
My soul pants for you; my whole being is athirst for you.
Yet you will not show yourself to me; you look away;
you bar the door, shun me, pass me over;
You even laugh at my innocent sufferings.
And yet you snatch your lovers away from all earthly things.
You lift them above every desire for worldly matters.
You make them capable of loving you—
and love you they do indeed.
So they offer you their praise in spiritual song
which bursts out from that inner fire;
they know in truth the sweetness of the dart of love.
Ah, eternal and most lovable of all joys,
you raise us from the very depths,
and entrance us with the sight of divine majesty so often!
Come into me, Beloved!
All ever I had I have given up for you;
I have spurned all that was to be mine,
that you might make your home in my heart,
and I your comfort.
Do not forsake me now, smitten with such great longing,
whose consuming desire is to be amongst those who love you.
Grant me to love you, to rest in you, that in your kingdom I may be worthy
to appear before you world without end.

from *The Cloud of Unknowing*[1]

CHAPTER 3

Lift up your heart to God with humble love: and mean God himself, and not what you get out of him. Indeed, hate to think of anything but God himself, so that nothing occupies your mind or will but only God. Try to forget all created things that he ever made, and the purpose behind them, so that your thought and longing do not turn or reach out to them either in general or in particular. Let them go, and pay no attention to them. It is the work of the soul that pleases God most. All saints and angels rejoice over it, and hasten to help it on with all their might. All the fiends, however, are furious at what you are doing, and try to defeat it in every conceivable

1. Written toward the end of the 14th century, *The Cloud of Unknowing* draws upon an influential tradition of Neoplatonic Christianity. One strand of this tradition extolled the *via negativa:* the approach to union with God by emptying the mind of worldly consciousness, and entering instead a dark place of uncertainty, a "cloud of unknowing." Though informed by a very private notion of disciplined spiritual quest, the *Cloud* nevertheless insists that the mystic's work serves the salvation of all the faithful. At the same time, the text also betrays considerable anxiety about, even hostility to, the spread of an undirected and body-oriented spirituality in its time. It particularly warns against the danger of demonic influence in those seeking too eagerly some bodily sign of the divine. It mentions the sensation of heat and other enthusiastic bodily manifestations, which may recall the affective imagery of Rolle. The translation here is by Clifton Wolters.

way. Moreover, the whole of mankind is wonderfully helped by what you are doing, in ways you do not understand. Yes, the very souls in purgatory find their pain eased by virtue of your work. And in no better way can you yourself be made clean or virtuous than by attending to this. Yet it is the easiest work of all when the soul is helped by grace and has a conscious longing. And it can be achieved very quickly. Otherwise it is hard and beyond your powers.

Do not give up then, but work away at it till you have this longing. When you first begin, you find only darkness, and as it were a cloud of unknowing. You don't know what this means except that in your will you feel a simple steadfast intention reaching out towards God. Do what you will, this darkness and this cloud remain between you and God, and stop you both from seeing him in the clear light of rational understanding, and from experiencing his loving sweetness in your affection. Reconcile yourself to wait in this darkness as long as is necessary, but still go on longing after him whom you love. For if you are to feel him or to see him in this life, it must always be in this cloud, in this darkness. And if you will work hard at what I tell you, I believe that through God's mercy you will achieve this very thing.

from CHAPTER 4

So that you may make no mistake, or go wrong in this matter, let me tell you a little more about it as I see it. This work does not need a long time for its completion. Indeed, it is the shortest work that can be imagined! It is no longer, no shorter, than one atom, which as a philosopher of astronomy will tell you is the smallest division of time. It is so small that it cannot be analyzed: it is almost beyond our grasp. Yet it is as long as the time of which it has been written, "All the time that is given to thee, it shall be asked of thee how thou hast spent it." And it is quite right that you should have to give account of it. It is neither shorter nor longer than a single impulse of your will, the chief part of your soul. * * *

So pay great attention to this marvelous work of grace within your soul. It is always a sudden impulse and comes without warning, springing up to God like some spark from the fire. An incredible number of such impulses arise in one brief hour in the soul who has a will to this work! In one such flash the soul may completely forget the created world outside. Yet almost as quickly it may relapse back to thoughts and memories of things done and undone—all because of our fallen nature. And as fast again it may rekindle.

This then, in brief, is how it works. It is obviously not make-believe, nor wrong thinking, nor fanciful opinion. These would not be the product of a devout and humble love, but the outcome of the pride and inventiveness of the imagination. If this work of grace is to be truly and genuinely understood, all such proud imaginings must ruthlessly be stamped out!

For whoever hears or reads about all this, and thinks that it is fundamentally an activity of the mind, and proceeds then to work it all out along these lines, is on quite the wrong track. He manufactures an experience that is neither spiritual nor physical. He is dangerously misled and in real peril. So much so, that unless God in his great goodness intervenes with a miracle of mercy and makes him stop and submit to the advice of those who really know, he will go mad, or suffer some other dreadful form of spiritual mischief and devilish deceit. Indeed, almost casually as it were, he may be lost eternally, body and soul. So for the love of God be careful, and do not attempt to achieve this experience intellectually. I tell you truly it cannot come this way. So leave it alone.

Do not think that because I call it a "darkness" or a "cloud" it is the sort of cloud you see in the sky, or the kind of darkness you know at home when the light is out. That kind of darkness or cloud you can picture in your mind's eye in the height of summer, just as in the depth of a winter's night you can picture a clear and shining light. I do not mean this at all. By "darkness" I mean "a lack of knowing"—just as anything that you do not know or may have forgotten may be said to be "dark" to you, for you cannot see it with your inward eye. For this reason it is called "a cloud," not of the sky, of course, but "of unknowing," a cloud of unknowing between you and your God.

Chapter 52

The madness I speak of is effected like this: they read and hear it said that they should stop the "exterior" working with their mind, and work interiorly. And because they do not know what this "interior" work means, they do it wrong. For they turn their actual physical minds inwards to their bodies, which is an unnatural thing, and they strain as if to see spiritually with their physical eyes, and to hear within with their outward ears, and to smell and taste and feel and so on inwardly in the same way. So they pervert the natural order, and with this false ingenuity they put their minds to such unnecessary strains that ultimately their brains are turned. And at once the devil is able to deceive them with false lights and sounds, sweet odors and wonderful tastes, glowing and burning in their hearts or stomachs, backs or loins or limbs.

In all this make-believe they imagine they are peacefully contemplating their God, unhindered by vain thoughts. So they are, in a fashion, for they are so stuffed with falsehood that a little extra vanity cannot disturb them. Why? Because it is the same devil that is working on them now as would be tempting them if they were on the right road. You know very well that he will not get in his own way. He does not remove all thought of God from them, lest they should become suspicious.

[END OF MYSTICAL WRITINGS]

MEDIEVAL BIBLICAL DRAMA

Medieval biblical drama entertains with both comedy and pathos, but it was meant to instruct as well. It developed not from classical drama, which was little imitated in the Middle Ages, but from church liturgies, especially those associated with Easter and the feast of Corpus Christi, a holiday celebrating Christ's presence among the faithful through the Eucharist. Although biblical dramas originated on the Continent, in Latin and then the vernacular languages, they also had a great flowering in England from the late fourteenth to the late sixteenth centuries. Two surviving play collections, from Chester and York, were conceived as complete cycles of sacred history from Creation to the Last Judgment, including such events as the fall of Lucifer, Noah's flood, the nativity of Christ, and Christ's crucifixion and resurrection. The York plays were performed, across a single vastly ambitious day, around the feast of Corpus Christi in midsummer. The huge arc of biblical narrative gains coherence in these plays (as in other medieval treatments) by a pattern of typology whereby Old Testament events are understood to be fulfilled in the New Testament. Hence Satan's deception and Adam's fall are redeemed by Christ's sacrifice. At a level of analogy, Old Testament events and characters predict and are fulfilled by New Testament ones—Isaac and Moses, for instance, are seen as "types" of Christ, while Cain and Pharaoh are types of Satan.

Other surviving groups of plays, some individually much longer and more ambitious than those from York and Chester, may have been collected together in play-books without being conceived or performed as a cycle. These include the plays now known only as "N-Town" and the Townley plays. Some of the Townley plays are linked to the town of Wakefield, not far from York. These Middle English biblical plays represent a wide range of styles, staging techniques, and sponsors. The York plays were financed by craft guilds (also called "mysteries," which led to the cycles being called mystery plays); the Townley plays may have been produced individually under parish sponsorship. The York plays were enacted on large carts that rolled from one public space to another, each play performed repeatedly; some Townley plays (like the *Second Play of the Shepherds*) require a central acting area surrounded by several more specific scenes, perhaps on scaffolds. What the plays have in common is their largely outdoor production, their association with prosperous towns and cities, many (not all) in the north, and their connection with a newly prosperous mercantile class. Often guilds sponsored plays specifically linked to their craft; at York, the Shipwrights produced the play of Noah's Ark, and the Fishers and Mariners the play of the Flood.

The popularity of these dramas—as well as their function as a surrogate Bible for the poor—can be seen in Chaucer's *Miller's Tale*. The Miller himself insists on telling his tale out of order, and does so in "Pilate's voice," the ranting manner of Pontius Pilate in the Passion plays, and in the tale, the foppish Absolon woos his beloved Alison by playing the role of the tyrant Herod on a scaffold. Indeed, Chaucer's tale may be our first solid reference to Middle English biblical drama, and the locales both of the Miller's performance (between London and Canterbury) and of Absolon's (Oxford, where the tale is set) suggest the geographical range of these plays, many of which must have been lost when they were discouraged during the Reformation.

The Second Play of the Shepherds

Nowhere are the sacred and the profane paired as brilliantly as in the Nativity play known as the *Second Play of the Shepherds*, one of the Townley collection of plays probably performed at the prosperous Yorkshire town of Wakefield. The play was written or revised by an artist of dramatic imagination and poetic skill, often called the Wakefield Master. His great achievement is his ability to make biblical stories relevant to fifteenth-century England in such a way that daily life takes on typological significance. The key example of this, at once moving and funny, is the parallel between Mak's stolen sheep, hidden in swaddling clothes in a cradle, and the newborn Christ child whom the shepherds visit at the end of the play. The mercy that the shepherds show to Mak by tossing him in a blanket rather than delivering him to be hanged prefigures the mercy that Christ will bring into the world.

No matter how neatly the typological scheme works, however, the author does not present the birth of Christ as nullifying the complaints of the play's characters. With his guileful assault on the sheepfold and his concealment of the "horned lad" swaddled in a cradle, Mak may be a type of the devil, but his complaints of poverty are real: he steals the sheep to feed a hungry family. Just as real are the complaints of the shepherds, to which the first 180 lines of the play are devoted. The shepherds grumble about taxes, lords and their condescending servants, and their own nagging, prolific wives.

The plight of the shepherds reflects the impact of the wool and cloth trade; it enriched England in the fourteenth and fifteenth centuries, but it also impoverished peasant farmers when landlords enclosed tracts of land for conversion to lucrative sheep farming. These complaints cannot simply be dismissed as the "moan" of fallen men who fail to understand their need for divine grace. Nor can the complaints of Mak's wife Gill against women's work be seen as simply setting her up as a contrast with the patient Virgin Mary at the end of the play. Nonetheless, the social and musical harmony exhibited as the play closes does suggest the transformation these shepherds undergo, and into which the play invites its believing audience.

The Second Play of the Shepherds

[*Scene: Field near Bethlehem.*]

I PASTOR: Lord, what these weathers are cold! And I am ill happed.[1]
I am near hand dold,° so long have I napped; *almost numb*
My legs they fold, my fingers are chapped.
It is not as I would, for I am all lapped° *tied up*
In sorrow.
In storms and tempest,
Now in the east, now in the west,
Woe is him has never rest
Mid-day nor morrow!

But we sely° shepherds that walks on the moor, *poor*
In faith we are near hands out of the door.
No wonder, as it stands, if we be poor,
For the tilthe of our lands lies fallow as the floor,
As ye ken.° *know*
We are so hamed,° *hamstrung*
For-taxed° and ramed,° *overburdened / oppressed*
We are made hand tamed
With these gentlery men.° *gentry, aristocrats*

Thus they reave° us our rest, our Lady them wary!° *rob / curse*
These men that are lord-fest,[2] they cause the plow tarry.
That men say is for the best, we find it contrary.
Thus are husbandys° oppress, in point to miscarry *farmhands*
On live.
Thus hold they us hunder;° *under*
Thus they bring us in blonder;° *trouble*
It were great wonder
And ever should we thrive.

For may he get a paint slefe° or a broche now on days, *painted sleeve*
Woe is him that him grefe° or once again says! *troubles*
Dare noman him reprefe,° what mastry° he mays, *reprove / power*
And yet may noman lefe° one word that he says, *believe*
No letter.
He can make purveance° *provision*
With boast and bragance,
And all is through maintenance
Of men that are greater.

1. Clothed.

2. Bound to their lords.

There shall come a swane as proud as a po,[3]
He must borrow my wane,° my plow also, *wagon*
Then I am full fane° to grant or he go. *pleased*
Thus live we in pain, anger, and woe,
By night and day.
He must have if he langed,° *desired*
If I should forgang° it; *forgo*
I were better be hanged
Then once say him nay.

It does me good, as I walk thus by mine one,
Of this world for to talk in manner of moan.
To my sheep will I stalk, and hearken anone,° *awhile*
There abide on a balk,° or sit on a stone, *ridge*
Full soon.
For I trowe,° perde,° *believe / by God*
True men if they be,
We get more company
Or° it be noon. *before*

[*The Second Shepherd enters without noticing the First*.]

II PASTOR: Benste and Dominus![4] What may this bemean?
Why fares this world thus? Oft have we not seen?
Lord, these weathers are spytus,° and the winds full keen, *spiteful*
And the frosts so hideous they water my eyes—
No lie.
Now in dry, now in wete,
Now in snow, now in sleet;
When my shoen° freeze to my feet, *shoes*
It is not all easy.

But as far as I ken, or yet as I go,
We sely wedmen dre mekyll woe;[5]
We have sorrow then and then: it falls oft so.
Sely Copple,[6] our hen, both to and fro
She cackles;
But begin she to croak,
To groan or to cluck,
Woe is him is of our cock,
For he is in the shackels.

These men that are wed have not all their will;
When they are full hard sted,° they sigh full still; *placed*
God wayte° they are led full hard and full ill; *knows*
In bower° nor in bed they say nought there till,° *bedroom / thereto*
This tide.° *time*
My part have I fun;° *found*

3. A servant as proud as a peacock.
4. Corruption of a Latin blessing, *Benedicite ad Dominum*.
5. We poor, innocent married men suffer much.
6. A copple is the crest on a bird's head.

I know my lesson.
Woe is him that is bun,° *bound in marriage*
For he must abide.
But now late in our lives a marvel to me,
That I think my heart rives° such wonders to see. *breaks*
What that destiny drives it should so be;
Some men will have two wives and some men three,
In store;
Some are woe that has any,
But so far can I,
Woe is him that has many,
For he felys° sore. *suffers*

But young men of a-wooing, for God that you bought,° *redeemed*
Be well ware of wedding, and think in your thought,
"Had I wist"° is a thing it serves of nought; *known*
Mekyll° still° mourning has wedding home brought, *much / constant*
And griefs,
With many a sharp shower;
For thou may catch in an hour
That shall savour fulle sour
As long as thou lives.

For, as ever read I pistill[7] I have one to my fere,° *mate*
As sharp as a thistle, as rough as a brere;
She is browed like a bristle with a sour-loten cheer;[8]
Had she once wet her whistle she could sing full clear
Her *Paternoster*.° *Lord's Prayer*
She is as great as a whale;
She has a gallon of gall.
By him that died for us all,
I would I had run to° I had lost her. *until*

I PASTOR: God look over the raw![9] Full deafly ye stand.
II PASTOR: Yea, the devil in thy maw,° so tariand.° *mouth / slow*
Saw thou awre° of Daw?[1] *anywhere*
I PASTOR: Yea, on a ley land° *fallow ground*
Hard I him blaw.[2] He comes here at hand,
Not far.
Stand still.
II PASTOR: Why?
I PASTOR: For he comes, hope I.
II PASTOR: He will make us both a lie
But if° we beware. *unless*

7. [St. Paul's] Epistle.
8. Sour-looking face.
9. Let God pay attention to his audience (row), i.e., God attend me.
1. The Third Shepherd.
2. I just blew by him.

[*Enter Third Shepherd.*]
III PASTOR: Christ's cross me speed, and Saint Nicholas!
There of had I need; it is worse than it was.
Whoso could take heed and let the world pass,
It is ever in dread and brekill° as glass, *brittle*
And slithes.° *slides away*
This world fowre° never so, *fared*
With marvels mo and mo,
Now in weal, now in woe,
And all thing writhes.° *turns about*

Was never sin° Noah's flood such floods seen; *since*
Winds and rains so rude, and storms so keen;
Some stammerd, some stood in doubt,° as I ween; *fear*
Now God turn all to good! I say as I mean,
For° ponder. *to*
These floods so they drown,
Both fields and in town,
And bears all down,
And that is a wonder.

We that walk on the nights, our cattle to keep,
We see sudden sights when other men sleep.
Yet me think my heart lights; I see shrews peep;[3]
Ye are two ill wights. I will give my sheep
A turn.
But full ill have I meant;
As I walk on this bent,
I may lightly repent,
My toes if I spurn.

Ah, sir, God you save, and master mine!
A drink fain would I have, and somewhat to dine
I PASTOR: Christ's curse, my knave, thou art a leder hine!° *lazy servant*
II PASTOR: What, the boy list rave! Abide unto sine;[4]
We have made it.[5]
Ill thrift on thy pate!
Though the shrew came late,
Yet is he in state
To dine, if he had it.

III PASTOR: Such servants as I, that sweats and swinks,° *works*
Eats our bread full dry, and that me forthinks;° *upsets*
We are oft wet and weary when master-men winks;° *sleeps*
Yet comes full lately both diners and drinks,
But nately.° *thoroughly*
Both our dame and our sire,
When we have run in the mire,
They can nip° at our hire,° *trim / wages*

3. I see villains peeping out.
4. The boy is crazy; wait a while.
5. We have already eaten.

And pay us full lately.

But here my troth, master: for the fare that ye make,
I shall do therafter, work as I take;
I shall do a little, sir, and emang ever lake,[6]
For yet lay my supper never on my stomach
In fields.
Whereto should I threpe?° *wrangle*
With my staff can I leap,
And men say "Light cheap° *little cost*
Letherly for-yields."° *poorly yields*

I PASTOR: Thou were an ill lad to ride a-wooing
With a man that had but little of spending.
II PASTOR: Peace, boy, I bade. No more jangling,° *chattering*
Or I shall make there full rad,° by the heavens king! *quickly*
With thy gauds°— *tricks*
Where are our sheep, boy?—we scorn.° *despise*
III PASTOR: Sir, this same day at morn
I them left in the corn,
When they rang lauds.[7]

They have pasture good, they cannot go wrong.
I PASTOR: That is right, by the roode![8] these nights are long,
Yet I would, or we yode,° one gave us a song. *went*
II PASTOR: So I thought as I stood, to mirth us among.
III PASTOR: I grant.
I PASTOR: Let me sing the tenory.
II PASTOR: And I treble so hee.
III PASTOR: Then the meyne° falls to me: *middle*
Let see how ye chant.
[*They sing.*]
Tunc intrat Mak in clamide se super togam vestitus.[9]

MAK: Now, Lord, for thy names vii,[1] that made both moon and starns° *stars*
Well mo then can I neven° thy will, Lord, of me tharns;[2] *say*
I am all uneven, that moves oft my harness.
Now would God I were in heaven, for there weep no barnes° *babies*
So still.
I PASTOR: Who is that pipes so poor?
MAK: Would God ye wist how I foor!° *fared*
Lo, a man that walks on the moor,
And has not all his will!

II PASTOR: Mak, where has thou gone? Tell us tiding.
III PASTOR: Is he comme? Then ylkon° take heed to his thing. *everyone*

6. Keep playing besides.
7. The first church service of the day.
8. Cross; the humor here, as with the other oaths, is based on the anachronism that Jesus has not yet been born, much less crucified.
9. Then Mak enters, wearing a cloak over his garment.
1. Seven (written by the copyist as the roman numeral).
2. Is lacking.

Et accipit clamidem ab ipso.[3]

MAK: What! Ich be a yoman,[4] I tell you, of the king;
The self and the same, sond° from a great lording, *messenger*
And sich.° *such like*
Fy on you! Goeth hence
Out of my presence!
I must have reverence;
Why, who be ich?

I PASTOR: Why make ye it so quaint?[5] Mak, ye do wrang.
II PASTOR: But, Mak, list ye saint? I trow that ye lang.[6]
III PASTOR: I trow the shrew can paint, the devill might him hang!
MAK: Ich shall make complaint, and make you all to thwang[7]
At a word,
And tell even how ye doth.
I PASTOR: But, Mak, is that sooth?
Now take out that southren tooth,° *accent*
And set in a turd!

II PASTOR: Mak, the devil in your eye! A stroke would I lean° you. *lend*
III PASTOR: Mak, know ye not me? By God, I could teen° you. *rage at*
MAK: God look you all three! Me thought I had seen you;
Ye are a fair company.
I PASTOR: Can ye now mean you?
II PASTOR: Shrew, pepe![8]
Thus late as thou goes,
What will men suppose?
And thou has an ill nose° *reputation*
Of steeling of sheep.

MAK: And I am true as steel, all men waytt,° *know*
But a sickness I feel that holds me full haytt;° *hot*
My belly fares not weel; it is out of estate.
III PASTOR: Seldom lies the devil dead by the gate.[9]
MAK: Therfore
Full sore am I and ill,
If I stand stone still;
I eat not an nedill° *scrap*
This month and more.

I PASTOR: How fares thy wife? By my hood, how fares sho?° *she*
MAK: Lies waltering,° by the rood, by the fire, lo! *collapsed*
And a house full of brood.° She drinks well, too; *children*
Ill spede° other good that she will do! *success*
But sho
Eats as fast as she can,

3. And he takes his cloak from him.
4. Freeborn property-holder.
5. Why act so elegant?
6. Do you want to be a saint? I think you long to be.
7. Be beaten.
8. Villain, look around!
9. Proverbial: The devil seldom lies dead by the wayside; i.e., the devil is not often an innocent victim.

And ilk° year that comes to man *each*
She brings forth a lakan,° *baby*
And some years two.
But were I not more gracious and richer by far;
I were eaten out of house and of harbar;° *home*
Yet is she a foul dowse,° if ye come nar; *wench*
There is none that trowse° nor knows a war° *imagines / worse*
Than ken I.
Now will ye see what I proffer,
To give all in my coffer
To morn at next to offer
Her hed mas-penny.[1]

II PASTOR: I wote so forwaked° is none in this shire: *sleepless*
I would sleep if I taked less to my hire.
III PASTOR: I am cold and naked, and would have a fire.
I PASTOR: I am weary, for-rakyd,° and run in the mire. *exhausted*
Wake thou!
II PASTOR: Nay, I will lyg° down by, *lie*
For I must sleep truly.
III PASTOR: As good a man's son was I
As any of you.

But, Mak, come hither! Between shall thou lyg down.
[*Mak lies down with the Shepherds.*]
MAK: Then might I let you bedene of that ye would rowne,[2]
No drede.
From my top to my toe,
Manus was commendo,
Poncio Pilato,[3]
Christ cross me speed!
Tunc surgit, pastoribus dormientibus, et dicit[4]

Now were time for a man that lacks what he would
To stalk privily than unto a fold,
And nimbly to work than, and be not too bold,
For he might aby the bargain, if it were told
At the ending.
Now were time for to reyll;° *revel*
But he needs good counsel
That fain would fare well,
And has but little spending.

But about you a circle, as round as a moon,
Too I have done that I will, till° that it be noon,[5] *until*

1. Penny offering for a mass for the dead.
2. That way I can readily prevent you from whispering together.
3. An amusing corruption of two Bible verses: "Into your hands I commend my soul" and "I wash my hands of this man."
4. Then Mak arises, while the shepherds are sleeping, and speaks.
5. Mak is casting a spell on the shepherds in the form of a fairy circle to keep them from waking.

That ye lyg stone still to that I have done,
And I shall say theretill of good words a foyne.° *a few*
"On hight
Over your heads my hand I lift;
Out go your eyes! Fordo° your sight!" *ruin*
But yet I must make better shift,
And it be right.

Lord, what they sleep hard! That may ye all here;
Was I never a shepherd, but now will I lere.° *learn*
If the flock be scared, yet shall I nip near.
How, drawes° hitherward! Now mends our cheer *come*
From sorrow:
A fat sheep, I dare say,
A good fleece, dare I lay,
Eft-whyte when I may,[6]
But this will I borrow.
[*Mak goes home to his wife.*]

How, Gill, art thou in? Get us some light.
UXOR EIUS:[7] Who makes such din this time of the night?
I am set for to spin; I hope not[8] I might
Rise a penny to win,° I shrew° them on height! *gain / curse*
So fares
A housewife that has been
To be raised° thus between: *disturbed*
Here may no note° be seen *scrap*
For such small chares.° *chores*

MAK: Good wife, open the hek!° Sees thou not what I bring? *inner door*
UXOR: I may thole the dray the snek.[9] Ah, come in, my sweeting!
MAK: Yea, thou thar not rek° of my long standing. *care*
UXOR: By the naked neck art thou like for to hing.
MAK: Do way:
I am worthy my meat,° *supper*
For in a strait° can I get *tight spot*
More than they that swink° and sweat *work*
All the long day.

Thus it fell to my lot, Gill, I had such grace.
UXOR: It were a foul blot to be hanged for the case.
MAK: I have skaped, Jelot,[1] oft as hard a glase.° *blow*
UXOR: But so long goes the pot to the water, men says,
At last
Comes it home broken.
MAK: Well know I the token,

6. I will pay it back when I can.
7. His wife.
8. I don't expect that.
9. I will let you draw the latch.
1. Affectionate nickname for "Gill."

But let it never be spoken;
But come and help fast.
I would he were flayn;° I lyst° well eat: *skinned / wish*
This twelvemonth was I not so fain of one sheep mete.
UXOR: Come they or° he be slain, and hear the sheep bleat— *before*
MAK: Then might I be tane.° That were a cold sweat! *taken*
Go spar° *lock*
The gate-door.
UXOR: Yes, Mak,
For and° they come at thy back— *if*
MAK: Then might I buy, for all the pack,[2]
The devil of the war.

UXOR: A good bowrde° have I spied, sin thou can none. *trick*
Here shall we him hide to° they be gone; *until*
In my cradle abide. Let me alone,
And I shall lyg beside in childbed, and groan.
MAK: Thou red;° *get ready*
And I shall say thou was light° *delivered*
Of a knave child this night.
UXOR: Now well is me day bright,
That ever was I bred.

This is a good gise° and a far cast; *way*
Yet a woman avise helps at the last.
I wote° never who spies, agane° go thou fast. *know / back*
MAK: But I come or they rise, else blows a cold blast!
I will go sleep.
[*Mak returns to the Shepherds and lies down.*]
Yet sleeps all this meneye,° *household*
And I shall go stalk privily
As it had never been I
That carried there sheep.

I PASTOR: *Resurrex a mortruis!*[3] Have hold my hand.
Iudas carnas dominus![4] I may not well stand:
My foot sleeps, by Jesus, and I water fastand.[5]
I thought that we had laid us full near England.
II PASTOR: Ah ye!
Lord, what I have slept well;
As fresh as an eel,
As light I me feel
As leaf on a tree.

III PASTOR: Benste° be here in! So my heart quakes, *a blessing*
My heart is out of skin,° what so it makes. *(body)*

2. Then I may have the worse, for there are such a pack of them.
3. Corruption from the Latin Bible of "He rose from the dead."
4. A corruption into Latin gibberish, "Judas lord of the flesh."
5. Stagger from lack of food.

Who makes all this din? So my brows blakes° — *darkens*
To the door will I win. Hark, fellows, wakes!
We were four:
See ye awre° of Mak now? — *anywhere*

I PASTOR: We were up or thou.

II PASTOR: Man, I give God a vow,
Yet yede° he nawre.° — *went / nowhere*

III PASTOR: Me thought he was lapt,° in a wolf skin. — *clothed*

I PASTOR: So are many hapt° now namely within. — *covered*

II PASTOR: When we had long napped, me thought with a gyn° — *trap*
A fat sheep he trapped, but he made no din.

III PASTOR: Be still:
Thy dream makes thee woode:° — *mad*
It is but phantom, by the roode.° — *cross*

I PASTOR: Now God turn all to good,
If it be his will.

II PASTOR: Rise, Mak, for shame! Thou lies right long.

MAK: Now Christ's holy name be us among!
What is this? For Saint Jame, I may not well gang!
I trow I be the same. Ah, my neck has lain wrong
Enough.
Mekill,° thanks syn° yister even, — *many / since*
Now, by Saint Steven,
I was flayd° with a sweven,° — *frightened / dream*
My heart out of slough.° — *skin*

I thought Gill began to croak and travail° full sad, — *struggle*
Welner° at the first cock, of a young lad — *nearly*
For to mend our flock. Then be I never glad;
I have tow° on my rock° more then ever I had. — *flax / distaff*
Ah, my head!
A house full of young tharms;° — *children*
The devil knock out their harns!° — *brains*
Woe is him has many barns,
And thereto little bread!

I must go home, by your leave, to Gill, as I thought.
I pray you looke,° my sleeve that I steal nought: — *inspect*
I am loath you to grieve, or from you take ought.

III PASTOR: Go forth, ill might thou chefe!° Now would I we sought, — *fare*
This morn,
That we had all our store.

I PASTOR: But I will go before;
Let us meet.

II PASTOR: Whore?

III PASTOR: At the crooked thorn.

[*The Shepherds leave. Mak knocks at his door.*]

MAK: Undo this door! Who is here? How long shall I stand?

UXOR EIUS: Who makes such a bere?° Now walk in the wenyand.[6] *noise*
MAK: Ah Gill, what cheer? It is I, Mak, your husband.
UXOR: Then may we be here the devil in a band,
Sir Gyle:[7]
Lo, he comes with a lote° *noise*
As he were holden° in the throat. *held*
I may not sit at my note,° *work*
A hand-lang° while. *little*

MAK: Will ye hear what fare she makes to get her a glose?[8]
And does nought but lakes° and claws her toes. *plays*
UXOR: Why, who wanders, who wakes? Who commes, who goes?
Who brews, who bakes? What makes me thus hose?° *hoarse*
And than,
It is rewthe° to behold, *pitiful*
Now in hot, now in cold,
Full woeful is the household
That wants a woman.

But what end has thou made with the herds, Mak?
MAK: The last word that thay said when I turned my back,
They would look that they had their sheep, all the pack.
I hope[9] they will not be well paid when they their sheep lack,
Perde!
But how so the game goes,
To me they will suppose,
And make a foul noise,
And cry out upon me.

But thou must do as thou hight.° *said*
UXOR: I accord me there till.
I shall swaddle him right in my cradle;
If it were a greater sleight,° yet could I help till. *trick*
I will lyg down straight. Come hap me.
MAK: I will.
UXOR: Behind!
Come Coll[1] and his maroo,° *mate*
They will nyp° us full naroo.° *pinch / hard*
MAK: But I may cry out "Haroo!"
The sheep if they find.

UXOR: Harken ay when they call; they will come onone.° *soon*
Come and make ready all and sing by thine one;
Sing "lullay" thou shall, for I must groan,
And cry out by the wall on Mary and John,
For sore.

6. Waning hour, unlucky time.
7. Mister Deceiver (the Devil).
8. Make up an excuse.
9. Expect.
1. The First Shepherd.

Sing "lullay" on fast
When thou hears at the last;
And but I play a false cast,° *trick*
Trust me no more.

[*At the crooked thorn.*]

III PASTOR: Ah, Coll, good morn. Why sleeps thou not?
I PASTOR: Alas, that ever was I born! We have a foul blot.
A fat wether° have we lorne.° *ram / lost*
III PASTOR: Mary, God's forbot!
II PASTOR: Who should do us that scorn?° That were a foul spot. *harm*
I PASTOR: Some shrewe.° *villain*
I have sought with my dogs
All Horbury[2] shrogs,° *hedges*
And of xv° hogs *fifteen*
Found I but one ewe.

III PASTOR: Now trow me, if ye will, by Saint Thomas of Kent,
Either Mak or Gill was at that assent.° *affair*
I PASTOR: Peace, man, be still! I saw when he went;
Thou slanders him ill; thou ought to repent,
Good speed.
II PASTOR: Now as ever might I the,° *thrive*
If I should even here die,
I would say it were he,
That did that same deed.

III PASTOR: Go we thither, I read, and run on our feet.
Shall I never eat bread the sothe to I wytt.[3]
I PASTOR: Nor drink in my head with him till I meet.
II PASTOR: I will rest in no stead till that I him greet,
My brother.
One I will hight:° *promise*
Till I see him in sight
Shall I never sleep one night
There I do another.

[*They approach Mak's house.*]

III PASTOR: Will ye hear how they hack?[4] Our sire list croon.
I PASTOR: Heard I never none crack so clear out of toon;
Call on him.
II PASTOR: Mak, undo your door soon.
MAK: Who is that spake, as it were noon
On loft?
Who is that, I say?

2. A town south of Wakefield.
3. Until I know the truth.
4. Sing (badly).

III PASTOR: Good felows, were it day.
MAK: As far as ye may,
Good, speaks soft,
Over a sick woman's head that is at malaise;
I had lever° be dead or she had any disease. *rather*
UXOR: Go to another stead! I may not well qweasse.° *breathe*
Each foot that ye tread goes through my nese,° *nose*
So hee!° *loudly*
I PASTOR: Tell us, Mak, if ye may,
How fare ye, I say?
MAK: But are ye in this town to-day?
Now how fare ye?

Ye have run in the mire, and are wet yit:
I shall make you a fire, if you will sit.
A nurse would I hire. Think ye on yit,
Well quit is my hire[5]— my dream this is it—
A season.
I have barns, if ye knew,
Well mo then enewe,
But we must drink as we brew,
And that is but reason.

I would ye dined or ye yode.[6] Me think that ye sweat.
II PASTOR: Nay, neither mends our mood drink nor meat.
MAK: Why, sir, ails you ought but good?
III PASTOR: Yea, our sheep that we get,
Are stolen as they yode. Our loss is great.
MAK: Sirs, drinks!
Had I been there,
Some should have bought it full sore.
I PASTOR: Mary, some men trowes° that ye wore, *believes*
And that us forthinks.° *disturbs*

II PASTOR: Mak, some men trowys that it should be ye.
III PASTOR: Either ye or your spouse, so say we.
MAK: Now if ye have suspowse° to Gill or to me, *suspicion*
Come and ripe° our house, and then may ye see *search*
Who had her;
If I any sheep fot,° *took*
Either cow or stot;° *heifer*
And Gill, my wife, rose not
Here sin she laid her.

As I am true and leal,° to God here I pray, *loyal*
That this be the first meal that I shall eat this day.
I PASTOR: Mak, as have I ceyll,° advise thee, I say; *heaven*

5. My wages are paid; i.e., his dream has been fulfilled.
6. I would like you to eat before you go.

He learned timely to steal that could not say nay.
UXOR: I swelt!° *die*
Out, thieves, from my wonys!° *home*
Ye come to rob us for the nonys.° *for the purpose*
MAK: Here ye not how she groans?
Your hearts should melt.

UXOR: Out, thieves, from my barn! Nigh him not thor!° *there*
MAK: Wist ye how she had farn,° your hearts would be sore. *fared*
Ye do wrong, I you warn, that thus comes before
To a woman that has farn— but I say no more.
UXOR: Ah, my medill!° *middle*
I pray to God so mild,
If ever I you beguiled,
That I eat this child
That lies in this cradle.

MAK: Peace, woman, for God's pain, and cry not so:
Thou spills thy brain, and makes me full woe.
II PASTOR: I trow our sheep be slain. What find ye two?
III PASTOR: All work we in vain; as well may we go.
But hatters,° *(an oath)*
I can find no flesh,
Hard nor nesh,° *soft*
Salt nor fresh,
But two tome° platters. *empty*

Whik° cattle but this, tame nor wild, *living*
None, as have I bliss, as loud as he smiled.° *smelled*
UXOR: No, so God me bliss, and give me joy of my child!
I PASTOR: We have marked amiss; I hold us beguiled.
II PASTOR: Sir, don,° *it is done*
Sir, our Lady him save,
Is your child a knave?[7]
MAK: Any lord might him have
This child to his son.

When he wakens he kips,° that joy is to see. *snatches*
III PASTOR: In good time to his hips, and in cele.° *heaven*
But who was his gossips,° so soon rede?° *godparents / ready*
MAK: So fair fall their lips!
I PASTOR: Hark now, a le.° *lie*
MAK: So God them thank,
Parkin, and Gibon Waller I say,
And gentle John Horne,[8] in good fay,
He made all the garray,° *noise*

7. Boy-child (of the serving-class).
8. Parkin, Gibon Waller, and John Horne are the names of the shepherds in the First Play of the Shepherds, possibly referring to actual townspeople.

With the great shank.° *leg*
II PASTOR: Mak, friends will we be, for we are all one.
MAK: We? Now I hold for me, for mends° get I none. *profit*
Farewell all three! All glad were ye gone.
[*The Shepherds depart.*]
III PASTOR: Fair words may there be, but love is there none
This year.
I PASTOR: Gave ye the child anything?
II PASTOR: I trow not one farthing.
III PASTOR: Fast again will I fling,° *hurry*
Abide ye me there.
[*Returns to the house.*]

Mak, take it to no grief if I come to thy barn.° *baby*
MAK: Nay, thou does me great reproof, and foul has thou farn.° *done*
III PASTOR: The child will it not grief, that little daystarn.[9]
Mak, with your leaf, let me give your barn
But vi° pence. *six*
MAK: Nay, do way: he sleeps.
III PASTOR: Me think he peeps.
MAK: When he wakens he weeps.
I pray you go hence.
[*The other Shepherds return.*]

III PASTOR: Give me leave him to kiss, and lift up the clout.° *cloth*
What the devil is this? He has a long snout.
I PASTOR: He is marked amiss. We wat° ill about. *watch*
II PASTOR: Ill-spun weft, iwys, ay comes foul out.[1]
Aye, so!
He is like to our sheep!
III PASTOR: How, Gyb,° may I peep? *the Second Shepherd*
I PASTOR: I trow kind° will creep *Nature*
Where it may not go.° *walk*

II PASTOR: This was a quaint gawde,° and a far cast. *clever trick*
It was a high fraud.

III PASTOR: Yea, sirs, was't.
Let bren° this bawd, and bind her fast. *burn*
A false skawd° hang at the last; *scold*
So shall thou.
Will ye see how they swaddle
His four feet in the middle?
Saw I never in a cradle
A horned lad[2] or° now. *before*

MAK: Peace bid I. What, let be youre fare;

9. Little day star; a term also used for the Christ child later in the play, indicating a parallel with Mak's baby.

1. Badly spun thread always makes poor cloth.

2. A horned child (devil).

I am he that him gat,° and yond woman him bare. *begat*
I PASTOR: What devil shall he hat,° Mak? Lo, God, Mak's heir. *be called*
II PASTOR: Let be all that. Now God give him care,
I sagh.° *saw*
UXOR: A pretty child is he
As sits on a woman's knee;
A dillydown,° perde, *darling*
To gar° a man laugh. *make*

III PASTOR: I know him by the earn mark: that is a good token.
MAK: I tell you, sirs, hark!— his nose was broken.
Sithen° told me a clerk that he was forspoken.° *since / bewitched*
I PASTOR: This is a false work; I would fain be wroken.° *avenged*
Get wepyn.
UXOR: He was taken with° an elf; *by*
I saw it myself.
When the clock struck twelve
Was he forshapen.° *changed*

II PASTOR: Ye two are well feft° sam° in a stead. *endowed / together*
III PASTOR: Sin they maintain their theft, let do them to dead.
MAK: If I trespass eft,° gird° off my head. *again / cut*
With you will I be left.
I PASTOR: Sirs, do my read.° *advice*
For this trespass,
We will neither ban ne flite,° *curse nor quarrel*
Fight nor chite,° *chide*
But have done as tite,° *quickly*
And cast him in canvas.
[*They toss Mak in a sheet.*]

Lord, what I am sore, in point for to brist.
In faith I may no more; therefore will I rist.
II PASTOR: As a sheep of vii score[3] he weighed in my fist.
For to sleep ay-whore° me think that I list. *anywhere*
III PASTOR: Now I pray you,
Lyg down on this green.
I PASTOR: On these thieves yet I mene.° *speak*
III PASTOR: Whereto should ye tene?° *be angry*
Do as I say you.
[*The Shepherds sleep.*]
Angelus cantat "Gloria in excelsis"; postea dicat[4]

ANGELUS: Rise, herd-men heynd!° For now is he born *virtuous*
That shall take fro the fiend that Adam had lorn;° *lost*
That warloo° to shend,° this night is he born. *devil / destroy*
God is made your friend now at this morn.

3. Seven score pounds (140 lbs).

4. The Angel sings "Glory to God in the highest," and afterward says.

He behestys° *orders*
At Bedlem° go see: *Bethlehem*
There lies that fre° *lord*
In a crib full poorly,
Betwyx two bestys.

I PASTOR: This was a quaint steven° that ever yet I heard. *voice*
It is a marvel to neven,° thus to be scared. *mention*
II PASTOR: Of God's son of heaven he spake upward.° *on high*
All the wood on a leven me thought that he gard
Appear.[5]
III PASTOR: He spake of a barn
In Bedlem, I you warn.
I PASTOR: That betokens yond starn.° *star*
Let us seek him there.

II PASTOR: Say, what was his song? Heard ye not how he cracked° it? *roared*
Three breves to a long.[6]
III PASTOR: Yea, marry, he hakt° it. *sang*
Was no crochett° wrong, nor nothing that lacked it. *note*
I PASTOR: For to sing us among right as he knacked° it, *sang*
I can.
II PASTOR: Let se how ye croon.
Can ye bark at the moon?
III PASTOR: Hold your tongues, have done!
I PASTOR: Hark after than.
[*Sings*.]

II PASTOR: To Bedlem he bade that we should gang:
I am full fard° that we tarry too lang. *afraid*
III PASTOR: Be merry and not sad; of mirth is our sang;
Ever-lasting glad to mede° may we fang,° *reward / get*
Without noise.
I PASTOR: Hie we thither for-thy;° *therefore*
If we be wet and weary,
To that child and that lady,
We have it not to lose.

II PASTOR: We find by the prophecy— let be your din—
Of David and Isay,[7] and mo than I min,
They prophesied by clergy that in a virgin
Should he light and lie, to sloken° our sin *remove*
And slake it,
Our kynd° from woe; *humankind*
For Isay said so,
Ecce virgo

5. I thought he lit up the woods like lightning.
6. Three short notes to one long.
7. The prophet Isaiah.

Concipiet[8] a child that is naked.

III PASTOR: Full glad may we be, and abide that day
That lovely to see, that all mights may.
Lord, well were me, for once and for ay,
Might I kneel on my knee, some word for to say
To that child.
But the angel said
In a crib was he laid;
He was poorly arrayed,
Both mener° and milde. *poor*

I PASTOR: Patriarchs that has been, and prophets beforn,
They desired to have seen this child that is born.
They are gone full clean,° that have they lorn.° *entirely / lost*
We shall see him, I ween, or it be morn,
To token.° *as proof*
When I see him and feel,
Then wot I full weel
It is true as steel
That prophets have spoken:

To so poore as we are that he would appear,
First find, and declare by his messenger.
II PASTOR: Go we now, let us fare; the place is us near.
III PASTOR: I am ready and yare;° go we in fere° *prepared / together*
To that bright.
Lord, if thy wills be,
We are lewde° all three, *unschooled*
Thou grant us somkyns glee° *some kind of joy*
To comfort thy wight.° *creature*
[*They enter the stable*.]

I PASTOR: Hail, comely and clean! Hail, young child!
Hail, maker, as I mean, of a maiden so mild!
Thou has waryd,° I ween, the warlo° so wild; *cursed / devil*
The false gyler° of teen° now goes he beguiled. *deceiver / anger*
Lo, he merries!
Lo, he laughs, my sweeting!
A well fair meeting!
I have holden my heting;° *kept my promise*
Have a bob° of cherries. *bunch*

II PASTOR: Hail, sovereign saviour, for thou has us sought!
Hail, freely food and flour,[9] that all thing has wrought!
Hail, full of favour, that made all of nought!
Hail! I kneel and I cower. A bird have I brought
To my barn.

8. Behold, a virgin conceives (Isaiah 7.14).
9. Noble child and flower.

Hail, little tyne mop!° *tiny baby*
Of our creed thou art crop:° *fruit, fulfillment*
I would drink on thy cop,° *cup*
Little day starn.° *star*

III PASTOR: Hail, darling dear, full of Godhede!
I pray thee be near when that I have need.
Hail, sweet is thy cheer! My heart would bleed
To see thee sit here in so poor weed,° *clothing*
With no pennies.
Hail, put forth thy dall!° *hand*
I bring thee but a ball:
Have and play thee with all,
And go to the tenys.° *tennis*

MARIA: The Father of heaven, God omnipotent,
That set all on seven,[1] his son has he sent.
My name could he neven,° and light or he went. *name*
I conceived him full even through might, as he ment,° *intended*
And now is he born.
He keep you from woe!
I shall pray him so.
Tell forth as ye go,
And myn° on this morn. *remember*

I PASTOR: Farewell, lady, so fair to behold,
With thy child on thy knee.
II PASTOR: But he lies full cold.
Lord, well is me! Now we go, thou behold.
III PASTOR: Forsooth already it seems to be told
Full oft.
I PASTOR: What grace we have fun!° *found*
II PASTOR: Come forth: now are we won.
III PASTOR: To sing are we bun:° *bound*
Let take on loft![2]
[*They go out singing.*]

Explicit pagina Pastorum.[3]

The York Play of the Crucifixion

The York *Crucifixion* serves as a counterpoint to the *Second Play of the Shepherds*, focusing not on the beginning of Christ's earthly life but on its end. Like the Towneley play, it was shaped by an anonymous playwright of great literary skill, a master of concrete detail, colloquial speech,

1. Made everything in seven days.
2. Let us sing on high.
3. The play of the Shepherds is finished.

and sometimes grotesque humor. This writer is often called the "York Realist" by historians of drama, but such a title raises more issues than it answers. Why do we need a name for an unknown reviser (or series of revisers)? What kind of "realism" characterizes a moment so fraught with uncanny implications as is the Crucifixion?

Like many of the cycle plays, the York *Crucifixion* was produced by a guild whose business bore some relation to the subject at hand. In this case, it is the pinners—the makers of wooden pegs—whose craft provides a certain grim irony. The soldiers carrying out the Crucifixion joke about their task, at once boasting about their skills yet repeatedly unable to accomplish them. Their frustrated patter provides a powerful counter-rhythm and counter-tone to the overwhelming moment they help enact.

In striking contrast to the busy buffoonery of the soldiers is the dignified demeanor and physical stability of Christ. He speaks only twice, first to accept the sacrifice of his life, and second to beg God's forgiveness for his torturers. His portrayal reflects a balance of two conflicting images: the heroic Christ who defeats Satan and the human Christ who suffers. The former, militant image can be seen in poems as early as the Old English *Dream of the Rood* and as late as Passus 18 of *Piers Plowman*. The latter, "gothic" image is widespread in religious lyrics and mystical writings of the later Middle Ages, whose purpose was to inspire the laity to meditation by focusing on Christ's wounds. Both in the agitated shouting of the soldiers and the silent agony of Christ, theatrical enactment of grim realities serves a profound and symbolic purpose.

The York Play of the Crucifixion

SOLDIER 1: Sir knights, take heed hither in hie,° *in haste*
This deed on dreigh we may not draw.[1]
Ye wot° yourselves as well as I *know*
How lords and leaders of our law
Have given doom° that this dote° shall die. *judgment / fool*
SOLDIER 2: Sir, all their counsel well we know.
Since we are come to Calvary
Let ilk° man help now as him owe.° *each / ought*
SOLDIER 3: We are all ready, lo,
That foreward° to fulfil. *undertaking*
SOLDIER 4: Let hear how we shall do,
And go we tite theretill.° *quickly thereto*

SOLDIER 1: It may not help here for to hone° *delay*
If we shall any worship° win. *honor*
SOLDIER 2: He must be dead needlings° by noon. *necessarily*
SOLDIER 3: Then is good time that we begin.
SOLDIER 4: Let ding° him down, then is he done— *knock*
He shall not dere° us with his din. *harm*
SOLDIER 1: He shall be set and learned soon,[2]
With care° to him and all his kin. *sorrow*
SOLDIER 2: The foulest death of all
Shall he die for his deeds.
SOLDIER 3: That means cross° him we shall. *crucify*
SOLDIER 4: Behold, so right he redes.° *he advises well*

1. We may not draw this task out too long.

2. He shall be put in his place and taught a lesson.

SOLDIER 1: Then to this work us must take heed,
So that our working be not wrong.
SOLDIER 2: None other note° to neven° is need, *matter / mention*
But let us haste him for to hang.° *crucify*
SOLDIER 3: And I have gone for gear good speed,° *with haste*
Both hammers and nails large and long.
SOLDIER 4: Then may we boldly do this deed.
Come on, let kill this traitor strong.
SOLDIER 1: Fair might ye fall in fere[3]
That has wrought on this wise.
SOLDIER 2: Us needs not for to lere[4]
Such faitours° to chastise. *traitors*

SOLDIER 3: Since ilka° thing is right arrayed,° *every / prepared*
The wiselier° now work may we. *more wisely*
SOLDIER 4: The cross on ground is goodly graid° *prepared*
And bored° even as it ought to be. *drilled*
SOLDIER 1: Look° that the lad on length be laid *see to it*
And made me° then unto this tree.° *fastened / cross*
SOLDIER 2: For all his fare° he shall be flayed,° *deeds / tortured*
That on assay° soon shall ye see. *by trial*
SOLDIER 3: Come forth, thou cursed knave,
Thy comfort soon shall keel.° *turn cold*
SOLDIER 4: Thine hire° here shall thou have. *reward*
SOLDIER 1: Walk on—now work we well.

JESUS: Almighty God, my Father free,° *gracious*
Let these matters be made in mind:
Thou bade° that I should buxom° be, *commanded / willing*
For Adam's plight for to be pined.° *tormented*
Here to death I oblige me,° *pledge myself*
For that sin for to save mankind,
And sovereignly beseech I thee
That they for me may favour find.
And from the fiend° them fend,° *devil / defend*
So that their souls be safe
In wealth° without end— *joy*
I keep° nought else to crave.° *care / ask for*

SOLDIER 1: We, hark sir knights, for Mahound's° blood, *Muhammad's*
Of Adam's kind° is all his thought. *offspring*
SOLDIER 2: The warlock waxes war than wood;[5]
This doleful° death ne dreadeth° he nought. *terrible / fears*
SOLDIER 3: Thou should have mind,° with main° and mood, *recall / might*
Of wicked works that thou hast wrought.
SOLDIER 4: I hope° that he had been as good *think*
Have ceased of saws° that he upsought.° *sayings / thought up*
SOLDIER 1: Tho saws shall rue him° sore, *words he will regret*

3. Good fortune to all of you.
4. We do not need to be taught.
5. The sorcerer grows worse than mad.

For all his sauntering,° soon. *babbling*
SOLDIER 2: Ill speed them° that him spare *bad luck (to) them*
Till he to death be done.

SOLDIER 3: Have done belive, boy, and make thee boun,[6]
And bend thy back unto this tree.
SOLDIER 4: Behold, himself has laid him down
In length and breadth as he should be.
SOLDIER 1: This traitor here tainted° of treason, *convicted*
Go fast and fetter him then ye three;
And since he claimeth kingdom with crown,
Even as a king here hang shall he.
SOLDIER 2: Now, certes,° I shall not fine° *indeed / stop*
Ere° his right hand be fast.° *before / tightly tied*
SOLDIER 3: The left hand then is mine—
Let see who bears him best.

SOLDIER 4: His limbs on length then shall I lead,° *stretch*
And even unto the bore° them bring. *bored holes*
SOLDIER 1: Unto his head I shall take heed,
And with mine hand help him to hang.
SOLDIER 2: Now since we four shall do this deed
And meddle with this unthrifty° thing, *unprofitable*
Let no man spare for° special speed *refrain from (using)*
Till that we have made ending.
SOLDIER 3: This foreward° may not fail; *deed*
Now are we right arrayed.° *prepared*
SOLDIER 4: This boy° here in our bail° *rascal / custody*
Shall bide° full bitter braid.° *suffer / torment*

SOLDIER 1: Sir knights, say, how work we now?
SOLDIER 2: Yes, certes,° I hope° I hold this hand, *indeed / think*
And to the bore° I have it brought *bored holes*
Full buxomly° without band.° *obediently / ropes*
SOLDIER 1: Strike on then hard, for him thee bought.° *redeemed*
SOLDIER 2: Yes, here is a stub° will stiffly stand, *thick nail*
Through bones and sinews it shall be sought°— *found*
This work is well, I will warrand.° *warrant*
SOLDIER 1: Say sir, how do we there?
This bargain° may not blin.° *business / cease*
SOLDIER 3: It fails a foot and more,° *i.e., is too short*
The sinews are so gone in.° *shrunken*

SOLDIER 4: I hope that mark amiss° be bored.° *wrongly / drilled*
SOLDIER 2: Then must he bide° in bitter bale.° *suffer / torment*
SOLDIER 3: In faith, it was over-scantily scored,° *marked too short*
That makes it foully° for to fail. *badly*
SOLDIER 1: Why carp° ye so? Fast on° a cord *speak / fasten*

6. Be done quickly, wretch, and make yourself ready.

And tug° him to, by top and tail.° *stretch / head and feet*
SOLDIER 3: Yah, thou commands lightly° as a lord; *effortlessly*
Come help to haul, with ill hail.° *bad luck to you*
SOLDIER 1: Now certes that shall I do—
Full snelly° as a snail. *quickly*
SOLDIER 3: And I shall tache° him to,° *attach / to (the cross)*
Full nimbly with a nail.

This work will hold, that dare I hete,° *promise*
For now are fest° fast both his hend.° *fastened / hands*
SOLDIER 4: Go we all four then to his feet,
So shall our space° be speedily spend.° *time / usefully spent*
SOLDIER 2: Let see what bourd his bale might beet,[7]
Thereto my back now would I bend.
SOLDIER 4: Oh, this work is all unmeet°— *out of place*
This boring must all be amend.° *corrected*
SOLDIER 1: Ah, peace man, for Mahound,° *by Muhammad*
Let no man wot° that wonder,° *know about / miracle*
A rope shall rug° him down *yank*
If° all his sinews go asunder. *even if*

SOLDIER 2: That cord full kindly° can I knit,° *fittingly / fasten*
The comfort of this carl° to keel.° *churl / cool, lessen*
SOLDIER 1: Fast° on then fast, that all be fit,° *fasten / ready*
It is no force° how fell° he feel. *matter / terrible*
SOLDIER 2: Lug° on ye both a little yet. *pull*
SOLDIER 3: I shall not cease, as I have sele.° *joy*
SOLDIER 4: And I shall fond° him for to hit. *try*
SOLDIER 2: Oh, hale!° *haul*
SOLDIER 4: Whoa, now, I hold it well.
SOLDIER 1: Have done, drive in that nail,
So that no fault be found.
SOLDIER 4: This working would not fail
If four bulls here were bound.

SOLDIER 1: These cords have evil° increased his pains, *sorely*
Ere he were to the borings° brought. *bored holes*
SOLDIER 2: Yea, asunder are both sinews and veins
On ilka° side, so have we° sought. *each / as we have*
SOLDIER 3: Now all his gauds nothing him gains,[8]
His sauntering shall with bale be bought.[9]
SOLDIER 4: I will go say to our sovereigns
Of all these works how we have wrought.
SOLDIER 1: Nay sirs, another thing
Falls first to you and me,
They bade we should him hang
On high, that men might see.

7. Let us see what joke might lighten his sorrow.
8. Now all his tricks gain him nothing.
9. His babbling shall be paid for with pain.

SOLDIER 2: We wot° well so° their words were, *know / what*
But sir, that deed will do us dere.° *harm*
SOLDIER 1: It may not mend° for to moot° more, *help / argue*
This harlot° must be hanged here. *rascal*
SOLDIER 2: The mortice° is made fit° therefore. *slot / ready*
SOLDIER 3: Fast° on your fingers then, in fere.° *fasten / together*
SOLDIER 4: I ween° it will never come° there— *believe / rise*
We four raise° it not right to-year.° *will raise / this year*
SOLDIER 1: Say man, why carps° thou so? *talk*
Thy lifting was but light.° *weak*
SOLDIER 2: He means there must be more
To heave him up on height.

SOLDIER 3: Now certes, I hope it shall not need° *be necessary*
To call to us more company.° *help*
Methink we four should do this deed
And bear him to yon hill on high.
SOLDIER 1: It must be done, without dread.° *doubt*
No more, but look ye be ready,
And this part° shall I lift and lead; *(the head)*
On length he shall no longer lie.
Therefore now make you boun,° *ready*
Let bear him to yon hill.
SOLDIER 4: Then will I bear here down,
And tent his toes until.° *attend to his toes*

SOLDIER 2: We two shall see to either side,
For else this work will wry° all wrong. *go awry*
SOLDIER 3: We are ready.
SOLDIER 4: Good sirs, abide,
And let me first his feet up fang.° *take up*
SOLDIER 2: Why tent ye so to tales this tide?[1]
SOLDIER 1: Lift up!
SOLDIER 4: Let see!
SOLDIER 2: Oh, lift along.
SOLDIER 3: From all this harm he should him hide° *protect himself*
And° he were God. *if*
SOLDIER 4: The devil him hang!
SOLDIER 1: For-great harm have I hent,° *received*
My shoulder is in sunder.° *asunder*
SOLDIER 2: And certes, I am near shent,° *ruined*
So long have I borne under.° *lifted up*

SOLDIER 3: This cross and I in two must twin,° *separate*
Else breaks my back in sunder° soon. *asunder*
SOLDIER 4: Lay down again and leave° your din,° *stop / noise*
This deed for us will never be done.
SOLDIER 1: Assay,° sirs, let see if any gin° *try / device*
May help him up without hone,° *delay*
For here should wight men worship win,

1. Why are you paying so much attention to talk at this time (i.e., instead of working)?

And not with gauds° all day to gone.° *tricks / spend*
SOLDIER 2: More wighter° men than we *stronger*
Full few I hope° ye find. *expect*
SOLDIER 3: This bargain° will not be,° *job / (ever) be done*
For certes, me wants wind.° *I am winded*

SOLDIER 4: So will° of work never we were— *bewildered*
I hope this carl some cautels cast.[2]
SOLDIER 2: My burden sat° me wonder sore, *distressed*
Unto the hill I might not last.
SOLDIER 1: Lift up, and soon he shall be there,
Therefore fast on° your fingers fast. *fasten*
SOLDIER 3: Oh, lift!
SOLDIER 1: We, lo!
SOLDIER 4: A little more.
SOLDIER 2: Hold then!
SOLDIER 1: How now?
SOLDIER 2: The worst is past.
SOLDIER 3: He weighs a wicked weight.
SOLDIER 2: So may we all four say,
Ere he was heaved on height° *aloft*
And raised in this array.° *fashion*

SOLDIER 4: He made us stand as° any stones, *as (still) as*
So boistous° was he for to bear. *awkward*
SOLDIER 1: Now raise him nimbly for the nonce
And set him by this mortice° here, *slot*
And let him fall in all at once,
For certes, that pain shall have no peer.
SOLDIER 3: Heave up!
SOLDIER 4: Let down, so all his bones
Are asunder now on sides sere.° *in many places*
SOLDIER 1: This falling was more fell° *cruel*
Than all the harms he had.
Now may a man well tell° *easily count*
The least lith° of this lad. *smallest limbs*

SOLDIER 3: Methinketh this cross will not abide° *hold firm*
Ne stand still in this mortice° yet. *slot*
SOLDIER 4: At the first time was it made over-wide;
That makes it wave,° thou may well wit.° *wobble / know*
SOLDIER 1: It shall be set on ilka° side *each*
So that it shall no further flit.° *move*
Good wedges shall we take this tide° *time*
And fast the foot,° then is all fit. *fasten the base*
SOLDIER 2: Here are wedges arrayed° *ready*
For that, both great and small.
SOLDIER 3: Where are our hammers laid
That we should work withal?° *with*

2. I think this churl has cast some spells.

SOLDIER 4: We have them even here at our hand.
SOLDIER 2: Give me this wedge, I shall it in drive.
SOLDIER 4: Here is another yet ordained.° *ready*
SOLDIER 3: Do take it me hither belive.° *to me quickly*
SOLDIER 1: Lay on then fast.
SOLDIER 2: Yes, I warrand.° *warrant*
I thring them sam, so mote I thrive.[3]
Now will this cross full stably° stand, *firmly*
All if° he rave they will not rive.° *even if / split*
SOLDIER 1: Say sir, how likes you now,
This work that we have wrought?
SOLDIER 4: We pray you say° us how *tell*
Ye feel, or faint ye aught.° *if you feel faint at all*

JESUS: All men that walk by way or street,
Take tent ye shall no travail tine.[4]
Behold mine head, mine hands, and my feet,
And fully feel now, ere ye fine,° *before you finish*
If any mourning may be meet,° *matched with*
Or mischief measured° unto mine. *misfortune compared*
My father, that all bales° may beet,° *sorrows / remedy*
Forgive these men that do me pine.° *pain*
What they work,° wot° they not; *do / know*
Therefore, my father, I crave,
Let never their sins be sought,° *examined*
But see° their souls to save. *see that*

SOLDIER 1: We, hark, he jangles° like a jay. *chatters*
SOLDIER 2: Methink he patters like a pie.° *magpie*
SOLDIER 3: He has been doing all this day,
And made great moving of° mercy. *reference to*
SOLDIER 4: Is this the same that gan us say° *is said to us*
That he was God's son almighty?
SOLDIER 1: Therefore he feels full fell affray,° *cruel assault*
And deemed° this day for to die. *was judged*
SOLDIER 2: *Vath, qui destruis templum!*[5]
SOLDIER 3: His saws° were so, certain. *words*
SOLDIER 4: And sirs, he said to some
He might raise it again.

SOLDIER 1: To muster° that he had no might, *manifest*
For all the cautels° that he could cast. *spells*
All if he were in word so wight,[6]
For all his force now is he fast.° *bound*
As Pilate deemed is done and dight,° *dealt with*
Therefore I rede° that we go rest. *advise*
SOLDIER 2: This race° mun be rehearsed° right, *action / reported*

3. I'll thrust them together, so I may prosper.
4. Take heed that you miss none of my suffering.
5. Ah! thou who destroyeth the temple! (Mark 14:58, John 2:19).
6. Even though his words were so bold.

Through the world both east and west.
SOLDIER 3: Yea, let him hang there still
And make mows on° the moon. — *faces at*
SOLDIER 4: Then may we wend at will.° — *go when we please*
SOLDIER 1: Nay, good sirs, not so soon.

For certes us needs another note:° — *we have other business*
This kirtle° would I of you crave. — *garment*
SOLDIER 2: Nay, nay, sir, we will look by lot° — *draw lots*
Which of us four falls it to° have. — *it falls to*
SOLDIER 3: I rede° we draw cut° for this coat— — *advise / straws*
Lo, see how soon—all sides to save.° — *to satisfy all parties*
SOLDIER 4: The short cut shall win, that well ye wot,° — *know*
Whether it fall to knight or knave.
SOLDIER 1: Fellows, ye tharf° not flite,° — *need / quarrel*
For this mantle is mine.
SOLDIER 2: Go we then hence tite,° — *quickly*
This travail° here we tine.° — *effort / waste*

[END OF MEDIEVAL BIBLICAL DRAMA]

Margery Kempe

c. 1373–after 1439

Margery Kempe's religious life—its temptations, visions, ecstasies, and pilgrimages—was unusual in intensity, but not in kind, for her time. She was very much in the mainstream of later medieval affective piety. What gained Margery both admiration and contempt, to the extent of endangering her life, was her drive to express these experiences publicly and have them acknowledged within an official hierarchy that had very little place for her. *The Book of Margery Kempe* is only one aspect of a lifetime of religious performance—from "holy conversation" and the vexed dictation of her book, through the kinds of bodily gestures, weeping, and roaring that Margery knew to be almost theatrical in their impact.

The daughter of a mayor in the prosperous market town of Lynn, Margery began her adult life quite traditionally, married to the burger John Kempe. The mental and religious crisis following the birth of her first child inspired her to pursue a holier form of life. To create this mixed life of secular marriage and sacred quest, Margery Kempe had to struggle and negotiate with a hierarchy of male authority. By canon law, her husband could demand the rights of the marriage bed, and did so for many years. She approached her local confessors for permission to undertake pilgrimages. Only a bishop could allow the weekly Eucharist for which Margery yearned, or officially approve her wearing white clothes. Hostile officials and clerics at all levels repeatedly attempted to misrepresent or silence her. She depended on male readers for her knowledge of other mystics, and on a sequence of recalcitrant male amanuenses for the very writing of her book.

Kempe's activities enraged political and ecclesiastical authorities, alienated her fellow pilgrims, and angered people at home. Yet those same activities gained her many admirers, increasingly among common laypeople. Her weeping and noisy mourning for the sufferings of Christ intruded upon daily life and often interrupted religious ceremonies. Just as daringly in the anxious and repressive religious climate of her day, Kempe spoke about her experiences

Crucifixion Scene, from a manuscript of Michael de Massa's *On the Passion of Our Lord*, 1405. This illumination is found at the beginning of a narrative of the Passion written in Latin and Middle English. Delicate yet emotive, it evokes much of the "affective spirituality" of its era. The drawing is in pale brown ink and wash, which only renders more emphatic and disturbing the bright red of Christ's elaborately detailed wounds. The weeping Virgin Mary sways, nearly fainting, while Mary Magdalene kneels and clutches Christ's legs. Even the angels look down in sorrow, though the men at right are more restrained. Late-medieval worshipers were encouraged to imagine themselves as if present at such scenes of high pathos. Here, the author of the text, Michael de Massa, is depicted among the witnesses of Christ's suffering; the scroll hanging from his desk contains the first words of his book: *Angeli pacis*. . . .

without clerical mediation, and defended herself effectively before the highest clerics in England, including the Archbishop of York. She did not even hesitate to criticize them. She was repeatedly accused and taken into custody as a Lollard heretic, although she was doctrinally quite conservative (almost radically orthodox), as she ably and repeatedly proved under hostile examination.

Along with this pattern of negotiation and striving with a largely male ecclesiastical establishment, Kempe engaged more quietly with a network of female religious. She knew she had predecessors among married women who experienced visions and moved into a holy life while still living in the secular world. She specifically mentions "Saint Bride"—Bridget of Sweden (c. 1303–1373), who like Margery had many children and took up the holy life (once widowed), traveled to Rome and Jerusalem, and engaged in prophecy. Margery may also have known about the Blessed Angela of Foligno (1248–1309), whose temptations, weeping, and conversations with Christ are similar to Margery's own. She records a visit and long conversation with the mystic and anchoress Julian of Norwich. During her arrest by agents of the Duke of Bedford, local women sympathize with Margery, bring her wine, and listen to her religious discourse. Indeed, it seems that the Duke had Margery arrested because he suspected her of having encouraged a woman cousin to leave her own husband and pursue a religious life.

It is possible, though, to exaggerate Kempe's struggle with male power, secular and ecclesiastical. She was warmly supported by a number of holy men including the bishop of Lincoln. She met the Archbishop of Canterbury and gained at least his qualified approval. For all the conflicts within her marriage, Margery often expressed a wry and affectionate sense of John Kempe's indulgence, and sympathy for his weakness. Indeed, when John became ill and senile in later years, Margery suspended her life of prayer and returned to their home to care for him. Much of the domestic imagery of the *Book* derives from this fractious but loving relationship with her husband.

Perhaps the most appealing aspects of Kempe's religious imagery derive in fact from urban and domestic life. Money is a constant hindrance to her ambitions, and figures in her conversations with Christ. Her understanding of mystical language is often highly literal. If Jesus becomes her mystic lover, he does so very much as a husband, inviting her embraces; and when Kempe has a vision of Christ's birth she bustles about like a midwife. Her concentration on the Eucharist is continuous with her experience of meals (and fasting) within the family and in society. Indeed, a long negotiation with her husband, crucial to Margery's pursuit of chastity, centers upon the heat and thirst of travel, a cake and a bottle of beer. The humble meal that caps their agreement has clear eucharistic implications. Whatever the spectacle of her religious expression, and the struggle to maintain and record it, Margery Kempe's religion and sense of her own limits are grounded in the very life she was eager to abjure.

from The Book of Margery Kempe[1]

The Preface

A short treatise of a creature set in great pomp and pride of the world, who later was drawn to our Lord by great poverty, sickness, shame, and great reproofs in many diverse countries and places, of which tribulations some shall be shown hereafter, not in the order in which they befell, but as the creature could remember them when they were written.

For it was twenty years and more from the time when this creature had forsaken the world and busily cleaved to our Lord before this book was written, notwithstanding that this creature had much advice to have her tribulations and her feelings

1. Translated by B. A. Windeatt.

written down, and a White Friar[2] freely offered to write for her if she wished. And she was warned in her spirit that she should not write so soon. And many years later she was bidden in her spirit to write.

And then it was written first by a man who could neither write English nor German well, so that it could not be read except by special grace alone, for there was so much obloquy and slander of this creature that few men would believe her.

And so at last a priest was greatly moved to write this treatise, and he could not read it for four years together. And afterwards, at the request of this creature, and compelled by his own conscience, he tried again to read it, and it was much easier than it was before. And so he began to write in the year of our Lord 1436, on the next day after Mary Magdalene,[3] after the information of this creature.

[Early Life and Temptations, Revelation, Desire for Foreign Pilgrimage]

Chapter 1

When this creature was twenty years of age, or somewhat more, she was married to a worshipful burgess and was with child within a short time, as nature would have it. And after she had conceived, she was troubled with severe attacks of sickness until the child was born. And then, what with the labor-pains she had in childbirth and the sickness that had gone before, she despaired of her life, believing she might not live. Then she sent for her confessor, for she had a thing on her conscience which she had never revealed before that time in all her life. For she was continually hindered by her enemy—the devil—always saying to her while she was in good health that she didn't need to confess but to do penance by herself alone, and all should be forgiven, for God is merciful enough. And therefore this creature often did great penance in fasting on bread and water, and performed other acts of charity with devout prayers, but she would not reveal that one thing in confession.

And when she was at any time sick or troubled, the devil said in her mind that she should be damned, for she was not shriven of that fault.[4] Therefore, after her child was born, and not believing she would live, she sent for her confessor, as said before, fully wishing to be shriven of her whole lifetime, as near as she could. And when she came to the point of saying that thing which she had so long concealed, her confessor was a little too hasty and began sharply to reprove her before she had fully said what she meant, and so she would say no more in spite of anything he might do. And soon after, because of the dread she had of damnation on the one hand, and his sharp reproving of her on the other, this creature went out of her mind and was amazingly disturbed and tormented with spirits for half a year, eight weeks and odd days.

And in this time she saw, as she thought, devils opening their mouths all alight with burning flames of fire, as if they would have swallowed her in, sometimes pawing at her, sometimes threatening her, sometimes pulling her and hauling her about both night and day during the said time. And also the devils called out to her with great threats, and bade her that she should forsake her Christian faith and belief, and deny her God, his mother, and all the saints in heaven, her good works and all good virtues, her father, her mother, and all her friends. And so she did. She slandered her husband, her friends, and her own self. She spoke many sharp and reproving words; she recognized no virtue nor goodness; she desired all wickedness; just as

2. Alan of Lynne, a Carmelite.
3. July 23.
4. Margery had not completed the stages of penance: contrition, confession, restitution (or other act of repentance), absolution. She never says openly what her unconfessed sin was.

the spirits tempted her to say and do, so she said and did. She would have killed herself many a time as they stirred her to, and would have been damned with them in hell,[5] and in witness of this she bit her own hand so violently that the mark could be seen for the rest of her life. And also she pitilessly tore the skin on her body near her heart with her nails, for she had no other implement, and she would have done something worse, except that she was tied up and forcibly restrained both day and night so that she could not do as she wanted.

And when she had long been troubled by these and many other temptations, so that people thought she should never have escaped from them alive, then one time as she lay by herself and her keepers were not with her, our merciful Lord Christ Jesus—ever to be trusted, worshiped be his name, never forsaking his servant in time of need—appeared to his creature who had forsaken him, in the likeness of a man, the most seemly, most beauteous, and most amiable that ever might be seen with man's eye, clad in a mantle of purple silk, sitting upon her bedside, looking upon her with so blessed a countenance that she was strengthened in all her spirits, and he said to her these words: "Daughter, why have you forsaken me, and I never forsook you?"

And as soon as he had said these words, she saw truly how the air opened as bright as any lightning, and he ascended up into the air, not hastily and quickly, but beautifully and gradually, so that she could clearly behold him in the air until it closed up again.

And presently the creature grew as calm in her wits and her reason as she ever was before, and asked her husband, as soon as he came to her, if she could have the keys of the buttery to get her food and drink as she had done before. Her maids and her keepers advised him that he should not deliver up any keys to her, for they said she would only give away such goods as there were, because she did not know what she was saying, as they believed.

Nevertheless, her husband, who always had tenderness and compassion for her, ordered that they should give her the keys. And she took food and drink as her bodily strength would allow her, and she once again recognized her friends and her household, and everybody else who came to her in order to see how our Lord Jesus Christ had worked his grace in her—blessed may he be, who is ever near in tribulation. When people think he is far away from them he is very near through his grace. Afterwards this creature performed all her responsibilities wisely and soberly enough, except that she did not truly know our Lord's power to draw us to him.

Chapter 2

And when this creature had thus through grace come again to her right mind, she thought she was bound to God and that she would be his servant. Nevertheless, she would not leave her pride or her showy manner of dressing, which she had previously been used to, either for her husband, or for any other person's advice. And yet she knew full well that people made many adverse comments about her, because she wore gold pipes on her head,[6] and her hoods with the tippets were fashionably slashed. Her cloaks were also modishly slashed and underlaid with various colors between the slashes, so that she would be all the more stared at, and all the more esteemed.

5. Suicide was considered a mortal sin.

6. Margery wore the fashionable *crespine*, a horned headdress of wire, often in gold or silver.

And when her husband used to try and speak to her, to urge her to leave her proud ways, she answered sharply and shortly, and said that she was come of worthy kindred—he should never have married her—for her father was sometime mayor of the town of N., and afterwards he was alderman of the High Guild of the Trinity in N.[7] And therefore she would keep up the honor of her kindred, whatever anyone said.

She was enormously envious of her neighbors if they were dressed as well as she was. Her whole desire was to be respected by people. She would not learn her lesson from a single chastening experience, nor be content with the worldly goods that God had sent her—as her husband was—but always craved more and more.

And then, out of pure covetousness, and in order to maintain her pride, she took up brewing, and was one of the greatest brewers in the town of N. for three or four years until she lost a great deal of money, for she had never had any experience in that business. For however good her servants were and however knowledgeable in brewing, things would never go successfully for them. For when the ale had as fine a head of froth on it as anyone might see, suddenly the froth would go flat, and all the ale was lost in one brewing after another, so that her servants were ashamed and would not stay with her. Then this creature thought how God had punished her before—and she could not take heed—and now again by the loss of her goods; and then she left off and did no more brewing.

And then she asked her husband's pardon because she would not follow his advice previously, and she said that her pride and sin were the cause of all her punishing, and that she would willingly put right all her wrongdoing. But yet she did not entirely give up the world, for she now thought up a new enterprise for herself. She had a horse-mill. She got herself two good horses and a man to grind people's corn, and thus she was confident of making her living. This business venture did not last long, for shortly afterwards, on the eve of Corpus Christi,[8] the following marvel happened. The man was in good health, and his two horses were strong and in good condition and had drawn well in the mill previously, but now, when he took one of those horses and put him in the mill as he had done before, this horse would not pull in the mill in spite of anything the man might do. The man was sorry, and tried everything he could think of to make his horse pull. Sometimes he led him by the head, sometimes he beat him, and sometimes he made a fuss of him, but nothing did any good, for the horse would rather go backwards than forwards. Then this man set a pair of sharp spurs on his heels and rode on the horse's back to make him pull, but it was no better. When this man saw it was no use, he put the horse back in his stable, and gave him food, and the horse ate well and freshly. And afterwards he took the other horse and put him in the mill. And just as his fellow had done so did he, for he would not pull for anything the man might do. And then this man gave up his job and would not stay any longer with the said creature.[9]

Then it was noised about in the town of N. that neither man nor beast would serve the said creature, and some said she was accursed; some said God openly took vengeance on her; some said one thing and some said another. And some wise men, whose minds were more grounded in the love of our Lord, said it was the high mercy of our Lord Jesus Christ that called her from the pride and vanity of this wretched world.

7. Margery here uses an initial for her town; later she openly calls it Lynn.

8. A feast day toward midsummer commemorating the Eucharist; marked by the performance of mystery plays in major mercantile towns such as York.

9. Popular superstition can be glimpsed behind the failure in brewing and milling, and the servants' refusal to stay with Margery thereafter.

And then this creature, seeing all these adversities coming on every side, thought they were the scourges of our Lord that would chastise her for her sin. Then she asked God for mercy, and forsook her pride, her covetousness, and the desire that she had for worldly dignity, and did great bodily penance, and began to enter the way of everlasting life as shall be told hereafter.

Chapter 3

One night, as this creature lay in bed with her husband, she heard a melodious sound so sweet and delectable that she thought she had been in paradise.[1] And immediately she jumped out of bed and said, "Alas that ever I sinned! It is full merry in heaven." This melody was so sweet that it surpassed all the melody that might be heard in this world, without any comparison, and it caused this creature when she afterwards heard any mirth or melody to shed very plentiful and abundant tears of high devotion, with great sobbings and sighings for the bliss of heaven, not fearing the shames and contempt of this wretched world. And ever after her being drawn towards God in this way, she kept in mind the joy and the melody that there was in heaven, so much so that she could not very well restrain herself from speaking of it. For when she was in company with any people she would often say, "It is full merry in heaven!"

And those who knew of her behavior previously and now heard her talk so much of the bliss of heaven said to her, "Why do you talk so of the joy that is in heaven? You don't know it, and you haven't been there any more than we have." And they were angry with her because she would not hear or talk of worldly things as they did, and as she did previously.

And after this time she never had any desire to have sexual intercourse with her husband, for paying the debt of matrimony was so abominable to her that she would rather, she thought, have eaten and drunk the ooze and muck in the gutter than consent to intercourse, except out of obedience.

And so she said to her husband, "I may not deny you my body, but all the love and affection of my heart is withdrawn from all earthly creatures and set on God alone." But he would have his will with her, and she obeyed with much weeping and sorrowing because she could not live in chastity. And often this creature advised her husband to live chaste and said that they had often (she well knew) displeased God by their inordinate love, and the great delight that each of them had in using the other's body, and now it would be a good thing if by mutual consent they punished and chastised themselves by abstaining from the lust of their bodies. Her husband said it was good to do so, but he might not yet—he would do so when God willed. And so he used her as he had done before, he would not desist. And all the time she prayed to God that she might live chaste, and three or four years afterwards, when it pleased our Lord, her husband made a vow of chastity, as shall be written afterwards, by Jesus's leave.

And also, after this creature heard this heavenly melody, she did great bodily penance. She was sometimes shriven two or three times on the same day, especially of that sin which she had so long concealed and covered up, as is written at the beginning of this book. She gave herself up to much fasting and keeping of vigils; she rose at two or three of the clock and went to church, and was there at her prayers until midday and also the whole afternoon. And then she was slandered and reproved by many people because she led so strict a life. She got herself a hair-cloth from a kiln—the sort that malt is dried on—and put it inside her gown as discreetly

1. Compare Richard Rolle's discussion of heavenly music, pages 498–99.

and secretly as she could, so that her husband should not notice it. And nor did he, although she lay beside him every night in bed and wore the hair-shirt every day, and bore him children during that time.

Then she had three years of great difficulty with temptations, which she bore as meekly as she could, thanking our Lord for all his gifts, and she was as merry when she was reproved, scorned or ridiculed for our Lord's love, and much more merry than she was before amongst the dignities of this world. For she knew very well that she had sinned greatly against God and that she deserved far more shame and sorrow than any man could cause her, and contempt in this world was the right way heavenwards, for Christ himself chose that way. All his apostles, martyrs, confessors and virgins, and all those who ever came to heaven, passed by the way of tribulation, and she desired nothing as much as heaven. Then she was glad in her conscience when she believed that she was entering upon the way which would lead her to the place that she most desired.

And this creature had contrition and great compunction, with plentiful tears and much loud and violent sobbing, for her sins and for her unkindness towards her maker. She reflected on her unkindness since her childhood, as our Lord would put it into her mind, very many times. And then when she contemplated her own wickedness, she could only sorrow and weep and ever pray for mercy and forgiveness. Her weeping was so plentiful and so continual that many people thought that she could weep and leave off when she wanted, and therefore many people said she was a false hypocrite, and wept when in company for advantage and profit. And then very many people who loved her before while she was in the world abandoned her and would not know her, and all the while she thanked God for everything, desiring nothing but mercy and forgiveness of sin.

Chapter 5

Then on a Friday before Christmas Day, as this creature was kneeling in a chapel of Saint John, within a church of Saint Margaret in N., weeping a very great deal and asking mercy and forgiveness for her sins and her trespasses, our merciful Lord Christ Jesus—blessed may he be—ravished her spirit and said to her, "Daughter, why are you weeping so sorely? I have come to you, Jesus Christ, who died on the cross suffering bitter pains and passion for you. I, the same God, forgive you your sins to the uttermost point. And you shall never come into hell nor into purgatory, but when you pass out of this world, within the twinkling of an eye, you shall have the bliss of heaven, for I am the same God who has brought your sins to your mind and caused you to be shriven of them. And I grant you contrition until your life's end.

"Therefore, I command you, boldly call me Jesus, your love, for I am your love and shall be your love without end. And, daughter, you have a hair-shirt on your back. I want you to leave off wearing it, and I shall give you a hair-shirt in your heart which shall please me much more than all the hair-shirts in the world. But also, my beloved daughter, you must give up that which you love best in this world, and that is the eating of meat. And instead of meat you shall eat my flesh and my blood, that is the true body of Christ in the sacrament of the altar. This is my will, daughter, that you receive my body every Sunday, and I shall cause so much grace to flow into you that everyone shall marvel at it.[2]

2. Weekly communion was uncommon, and required special ecclesiastical permission. Margery may have known that an admired predecessor, St. Bridget of Sweden, took weekly communion.

"You shall be eaten and gnawed by the people of the world just as any rat gnaws the stockfish.[3] Don't be afraid, daughter, for you shall be victorious over all your enemies. I shall give you grace enough to answer every cleric in the love of God. I swear to you by my majesty that I shall never forsake you whether in happiness or in sorrow. I shall help you and protect you, so that no devil in hell shall ever part you from me, nor angel in heaven, nor man on earth—for devils in hell may not, nor angels in heaven will not, nor man on earth shall not.

"And daughter, I want you to give up your praying of many beads, and think such thoughts as I shall put into your mind. I shall give you leave to pray until six o'clock to say what you wish. Then you shall lie still and speak to me in thought, and I shall give you high meditation and true contemplation.[4] And I command you to go to the anchorite at the Preaching Friars and tell him my confidences and counsels which I reveal to you, and do as he advises, for my spirit shall speak in him to you."

Then this creature went off to see the anchorite as she was commanded, and revealed to him the revelations that had been shown to her. Then the anchorite, with great reverence and weeping, thanking God, said, "Daughter, you are sucking even at Christ's breast, and you have received a pledge of paradise.[5] I charge you to receive such thoughts—when God will give them—as meekly and devoutly as you can, and then come and tell me what they are, and I shall, by the leave of our Lord Jesus Christ, tell you whether they are from the Holy Ghost or else from your enemy the devil."

Chapter 11

It happened one Friday, Midsummer Eve,[6] in very hot weather—as this creature was coming from York carrying a bottle of beer in her hand, and her husband a cake tucked inside his clothes against his chest—that her husband asked his wife this question: "Margery, if there came a man with a sword who would strike off my head unless I made love with you as I used to do before, tell me on your conscience—for you say you will not lie—whether you would allow my head to be cut off, or else allow me to make love with you again, as I did at one time?"

"Alas, sir," she said, "why are you raising this matter, when we have been chaste for these past eight weeks?"

"Because I want to know the truth of your heart."

And then she said with great sorrow, "Truly, I would rather see you being killed, than that we should turn back to our uncleanness."

And he replied, "You are no good wife."

And then she asked her husband what was the reason that he had not made love to her for the last eight weeks, since she lay with him every night in his bed. And he said that he was made so afraid when he would have touched her, that he dared do no more.

"Now, good sir, mend your ways and ask God's mercy, for I told you nearly three years ago that your desire would suddenly be slain—and this is now the third year, and I hope yet that I shall have my wish. Good sir, I pray you to grant what I shall ask, and I shall pray for you to be saved through the mercy of our Lord Jesus Christ, and you shall have more reward in heaven than if you wore a hair-shirt or wore a coat of

3. Dried cod.
4. Christ thus promises Margery the mystic way, without the ecclesiastical mediation of set prayers.
5. The image of Christ as mother particularly recalls Julian of Norwich, whom Margery later visits.
6. Probably 23 June 1413. The feast of Corpus Christi fell on the previous day, and it is likely that Margery and her husband had seen the great cycle of biblical plays traditionally performed in York on that day.

mail as a penance. I pray you, allow me to make a vow of chastity at whichever bishop's hand that God wills."

"No," he said, "I won't allow you to do that, because now I can make love to you without mortal sin, and then I wouldn't be able to."

Then she replied, "If it be the will of the Holy Ghost to fulfill what I have said, I pray God that you may consent to this; and if it be not the will of the Holy Ghost, I pray God that you never consent."

Then they went on towards Bridlington[7] and the weather was extremely hot, this creature all the time having great sorrow and great fear for her chastity. And as they came by a cross her husband sat down under the cross, calling his wife to him and saying these words to her: "Margery, grant me my desire, and I shall grant you your desire. My first desire is that we shall still lie together in one bed as we have done before; the second, that you shall pay my debts before you go to Jerusalem; and the third, that you shall eat and drink with me on Fridays as you used to do."

"No, sir," she said, "I will never agree to break my Friday fast as long as I live."

"Well," he said, "then I'm going to have sex with you again."

She begged him to allow her to say her prayers, and he kindly allowed it. Then she knelt down beside a cross in the field and prayed in this way, with a great abundance of tears: "Lord God, you know all things. You know what sorrow I have had to be chaste for you in my body all these three years, and now I might have my will and I dare not, for love of you. For if I were to break that custom of fasting from meat and drink on Fridays which you commanded me, I should now have my desire. But, blessed Lord, you know I will not go against your will, and great is my sorrow now unless I find comfort in you. Now, blessed Jesus, make your will known to my unworthy self, so that I may afterwards follow and fulfill it with all my might."

And then our Lord Jesus Christ with great sweetness spoke to this creature, commanding her to go again to her husband and pray him to grant her what she desired: "And he shall have what he desires. For, my beloved daughter, this was the reason why I ordered you to fast, so that you should the sooner obtain your desire, and now it is granted to you. I no longer wish you to fast, and therefore I command you in the name of Jesus to eat and drink as your husband does."

Then this creature thanked our Lord Jesus Christ for his grace and his goodness, and afterwards got up and went to her husband, saying to him, "Sir, if you please, you shall grant me my desire, and you shall have your desire. Grant me that you will not come into my bed, and I grant you that I will pay your debts before I go to Jerusalem. And make my body free to God, so that you never make any claim on me requesting any conjugal debt after this day as long as you live—and I shall eat and drink on Fridays at your bidding."[8]

Then her husband replied to her, "May your body be as freely available to God as it has been to me."

This creature thanked God greatly, rejoicing that she had her desire, praying her husband that they should say three paternosters in worship of the Trinity for the great grace that had been granted them. And so they did, kneeling under a cross, and afterwards they ate and drank together in great gladness of spirit. This was on a Friday, on Midsummer's Eve.

Then they went on to Bridlington and also to many other places, and spoke with God's servants, both anchorites and recluses, and many other of our Lord's

7. On the coast, east of York.

8. Margery may have received an inheritance from her father by now, giving her the financial leverage to strike a deal, in effect, for her chastity.

lovers, with many worthy clerics, doctors and bachelors of divinity as well, in many different places. And to various people amongst them this creature revealed her feelings and her contemplations, as she was commanded to do, to find out if there were any deception in her feelings.

[Meeting with Bishop of Lincoln and Archbishop of Canterbury]

Chapter 15

This creature, when our Lord had forgiven her her sin (as has been written before), had a desire to see those places where he was born, and where he suffered his Passion and where he died, together with other holy places where he was during his life, and also after his resurrection.

While she was feeling these desires, our Lord commanded her in her mind—two years before she went[9]—that she should go to Rome, to Jerusalem, and to Santiago de Compostela, and she would gladly have gone, but she had no money to go with.

And then she said to our Lord, "Where shall I get the money to go to these holy places with?"

Our Lord replied to her, "I shall send you enough friends in different parts of England to help you. And, daughter, I shall go with you in every country and provide for you. I shall lead you there and bring you back again in safety, and no Englishman shall die in the ship that you are in. I shall keep you from all wicked men's power. And, daughter, I say to you that I want you to wear white clothes and no other color, for you shall dress according to my will."[1]

"Ah, dear Lord, if I go around dressed differently from how other chaste women dress, I fear people will slander me. They will say I am a hypocrite and ridicule me."

"Yes, daughter, the more ridicule that you have for love of me, the more you please me."

Then this creature dared not do otherwise than as she was commanded in her soul. And so she set off on her travels with her husband, for he was always a good and easygoing man with her. Although he sometimes—out of groundless fear—left her on her own for a while, yet he always came back to her again, and felt sorry for her, and spoke up for her as much as he dared for fear of other people. But all others that went along with her forsook her, and they most falsely accused her—through temptation of the devil—of things that she was never guilty of.

And so did one man in whom she greatly trusted, and who offered to travel with her, at which she was very pleased, believing he would give her support and help her when she needed it, for he had been staying a long time with an anchorite, a doctor of divinity and a holy man, and that anchorite was this woman's confessor.

And so his servant—at his own inward stirring—took his leave to travel with this creature; and her own maidservant went with her too, for as long as things went well with them and nobody said anything against them.

But as soon as people—through the enticing of our spiritual enemy, and by permission of our Lord—spoke against this creature because she wept so grievously, and said she was a false hypocrite and deceived people, and threatened her with burning, then this man, who was held to be so holy, and in whom she trusted so much, rebuked her with the utmost force and scorned her most foully, and would not go any further with her. Her maidservant, seeing discomfort on every side, grew obstreperous

9. Probably 1411.

1. White dress implied special holiness or virginity.

with her mistress. She would not do as she was told, or follow her mistress's advice. She let her mistress go alone into many fine towns and would not go with her.

And always, her husband was ready when everybody else let her down, and he went with her where our Lord would send her, always believing that all was for the best, and would end well when God willed.

And at this time, he took her to speak with the Bishop of Lincoln, who was called Philip,[2] and they stayed for three weeks before they could speak to him, for he was not at home at his palace. When the Bishop came home, and heard tell of how such a woman had waited so long to speak to him, he then sent for her in great haste to find out what she wanted. And then she came into his presence and greeted him, and he warmly welcomed her and said he had long wanted to speak with her, and he was very glad she had come. And so she asked him if she might speak with him in private and confide in him the secrets of her soul, and he appointed a convenient time for this.

When the time came, she told him all about her meditations and high contemplations, and other secret things, both of the living and the dead, as our Lord revealed to her soul.[3] He was very glad to hear them, and graciously allowed her to say what she pleased, and greatly commended her feelings and her contemplations, saying they were high matters and most devout matters, and inspired by the Holy Ghost, advising her seriously that her feelings should be written down.

And she said that it was not God's will that they should be written so soon, nor were they written for twenty years afterwards and more.

And then she said furthermore, "My Lord, if it please you, I am commanded in my soul that you shall give me the mantle and the ring, and clothe me all in white clothes. And if you clothe me on earth, our Lord Jesus Christ shall clothe you in heaven, as I understand through revelation."[4]

Then the Bishop said to her, "I will fulfill your desire if your husband will consent to it."

Then she said to the Bishop, "I pray you, let my husband come into your presence, and you shall hear what he will say."

And so her husband came before the Bishop, and the Bishop asked him, "John, is it your will that your wife shall take the mantle and the ring and that you live chaste, the two of you?"

"Yes, my lord," he said, "and in token that we both vow to live chaste I here offer my hands into yours," and he put his hands between the Bishop's hands.

And the Bishop did no more with us on that day, except that he treated us very warmly and said we were most welcome.[5] * * *

Chapter 16

Then this creature went on to London with her husband, to Lambeth,[6] where the Archbishop was in residence at that time. And as they came into the hall in the afternoon, there were many of the Archbishop's clerks about and other heedless men, both squires and yeomen, who swore many great oaths and spoke many

2. Philip Repyngdon, Bishop of Lincoln 1405–1419. This journey occurred after their private agreement of chastity in June 1413.

3. Margery had some prophetic visions, though on a smaller scale than those of her predecessor St. Bridget of Sweden.

4. By clothing her, the bishop would acknowledge Margery and John's vow of chastity. In the Book of Revelation, the saints in heaven are clothed in white robes.

5. The Bishop instructs Margery to approach the Archbishop of Canterbury, England's highest prelate, and obtain his permission to receive the mantle and ring. She agrees to go but says she will not ask the archbishop for that particular gift.

6. Lambeth Palace was (and is) the Archbishop's home nearest London.

thoughtless words, and this creature boldly rebuked them, and said they would be damned unless they left off their swearing and the other sins they practised.[7]

And with that there came forward a woman of that town dressed in a pilch[8] who reviled this creature, cursed her, and said very maliciously to her in this way: "I wish you were in Smithfield,[9] and I would bring a bundle of sticks to burn you with—it is a pity that you are alive."

This creature stood still and did not answer, and her husband endured it with great pain and was very sorry to hear his wife so rebuked.

Then the Archbishop sent for this creature to come to him in his garden.[1] When she came into his presence she made her obeisances to him as best she could, praying him, out of his gracious lordship, to grant her authority to choose her confessor and to receive communion every Sunday—if God would dispose her to this—under his letter and his seal throughout all his province. And he granted her with great kindness her whole desire without any silver or gold, nor would he let his clerks take anything for the writing or sealing of the letter.

When this creature found this grace in his sight, she was much comforted and strengthened in her soul, and so she told this worshipful lord about her manner of life, and such grace as God wrought in her mind and in her soul, in order to discover what he would say about it, and if he found any fault with either her contemplation or her weeping.

And she also told him the cause of her weeping, and the manner in which our Lord conversed with her soul. And he did not find fault at all, but approved her manner of life, and was very glad that our merciful Lord Christ Jesus showed such grace in our times—blessed may he be.

Then this creature spoke to him boldly about the correction of his household, saying with reverence, "My lord, our Lord of all, Almighty God, has not given you your benefice and great worldly wealth in order to maintain those who are traitors to him, and those who slay him every day by the swearing of great oaths. You shall answer for them, unless you correct them or else put them out of your service."

In the most meek and kindly way he allowed her to say what was on her mind and gave her a handsome answer, she supposing that things would then be better. And so their conversation continued until stars appeared in the sky. Then she took her leave, and her husband too.

Afterwards they went back to London, and many worthy men wanted to hear her converse, for her conversation was so much to do with the love of God that those who heard it were often moved to weep very sadly.

And so she had a very warm welcome there—and her husband because of her—for as long as they wished to stay in the city. Afterwards they returned to Lynn, and then this creature went to the anchorite at the Preaching Friars in Lynn and told him how she had been received, and how she had got on while she was travelling round the country. And he was very pleased at her homecoming and held it to be a great miracle, her coming and going to and fro.

And he said to her: "I have heard much evil talk of you since you went away, and I have been strongly advised to leave you and not to associate with you any more, and great friendships are promised me on condition that I give you up. And I

7. Margery frequently reproaches people for swearing.

8. A garment of animal skin with the hair still on it.

9. This is not an idle threat. Lollard heretics were put to death in Margery's lifetime, beginning in 1401 when William Sawtry (formerly a priest at Lynn) was burned at Smithfield outside London.

1. Thomas Arundel (Archbishop of Canterbury 1396–1414) was a vigorous opponent of Lollards.

answered for you in this way: 'If you were still the same as you were when we parted, I certainly dared say you were a good woman, a lover of God, and highly inspired with the Holy Ghost. I will not forsake her for any lady in this realm, if speaking with the lady means leaving her, for I would rather leave the lady and speak with Margery, if I might not do both, than do the contrary.'" (Read first the twenty-first chapter and then this chapter after that.)

[VISIT WITH JULIAN OF NORWICH]

CHAPTER 17

One day long before this time, while this creature was bearing children and was newly delivered of a child, our Lord Christ Jesus said to her that she should bear no more children, and therefore he commanded her to go to Norwich. * * *

CHAPTER 18

This creature was charged and commanded in her soul that she should go to a White Friar in the same city of Norwich, who was called William Southfield, a good man who lived a holy life, to reveal to him the grace that God had wrought in her, as she had done to the good Vicar before. She did as she was commanded and came to the friar one morning, and was with him in a chapel for a long time, and told him her meditations and what God had wrought in her soul, in order to know if she were deceived by any delusions or not.[2]

This good man, the White Friar, all the time that she told him of her feelings, held up his hands and said, "Jesus, mercy, and thanks be to Jesus."

"Sister," he said, "have no fear about your manner of life, for it is the Holy Ghost plentifully working his grace in your soul. Thank him highly of his goodness, for we are all bound to thank him for you, who now in our times inspires you with his grace, to the help and comfort of all of us who are supported by your prayers and by others such as you. And we are preserved from many misfortunes and troubles which we should deservedly suffer for our trespasses, were there not such good creatures among us. Blessed be Almighty God for his goodness.

"And therefore, sister, I advise you to dispose yourself to receive the gifts of God as lowly and meekly as you can, and put up no obstacle or objections against the goodness of the Holy Ghost, for he may give his gifts where he will, and the unworthy he makes worthy, the sinful he makes righteous. His mercy is always ready for us unless the fault be in ourselves, for he does not dwell in a body subject to sin. He flies from all false pretense and falsehood; he asks of us a low, a meek, and a contrite heart, with a good will.[3] Our Lord says himself, 'My spirit shall rest upon a meek man, a contrite man, and one who fears my words.'[4]

"Sister, I trust to our Lord that you have these conditions either in your will or in your affections or else in both, and I do not consider that our Lord allows to be endlessly deceived those who place their trust in him, and seek and desire nothing but him only, as I hope you do. And therefore believe fully that our Lord loves you and is working his grace in you. I pray God increase it and continue it to his everlasting worship, for his mercy."

2. Southfield was a Carmelite friar who received visions of the Virgin Mary. Many mystical texts warn against the possibility that visions may be of demonic origin; see selections from *The Cloud of Unknowing*, pages 499–501.
3. Psalm 51.17.
4. Isaiah 66.2.

The said creature was much comforted both in body and in soul by this good man's words, and greatly strengthened in her faith.

And then she was commanded by our Lord to go to an anchoress in the same city who was called Dame Julian.[5] And so she did, and told her about the grace, that God had put into her soul, of compunction, contrition, sweetness and devotion, compassion with holy meditation and high contemplation, and very many holy speeches and converse that our Lord spoke to her soul, and also many wonderful revelations, which she described to the anchoress to find out if there were any deception in them, for the anchoress was expert in such things and could give good advice.

The anchoress, hearing the marvelous goodness of our Lord, highly thanked God with all her heart for his visitation, advising this creature to be obedient to the will of our Lord and fulfill with all her might whatever he put into her soul, if it were not against the worship of God and the profit of her fellow Christians.[6] For if it were, then it were not the influence of a good spirit, but rather of an evil spirit. "The Holy Ghost never urges a thing against charity, and if he did, he would be contrary to his own self, for he is all charity. Also he moves a soul to all chasteness, for chaste livers are called the temple of the Holy Ghost,[7] and the Holy Ghost makes a soul stable and steadfast in the right faith and the right belief.

"And a double man in soul is always unstable and unsteadfast in all his ways.[8] He that is forever doubting is like the wave of the sea which is moved and borne about with the wind, and that man is not likely to receive the gifts of God.[9]

"Any creature that has these tokens may steadfastly believe that the Holy Ghost dwells in his soul. And much more, when God visits a creature with tears of contrition, devotion or compassion, he may and ought to believe that the Holy Ghost is in his soul. Saint Paul says that the Holy Ghost asks for us with mourning and weeping unspeakable;[1] that is to say, he causes us to ask and pray with mourning and weeping so plentifully that the tears may not be numbered. No evil spirit may give these tokens, for Saint Jerome says that tears torment the devil more than do the pains of hell. God and the devil are always at odds, and they shall never dwell together in one place, and the devil has no power in a man's soul.

"Holy Writ says that the soul of a righteous man is the seat of God,[2] and so I trust, sister, that you are. I pray God grant you perseverance. Set all your trust in God and do not fear the talk of the world, for the more contempt, shame and reproof that you have in this world, the more is your merit in the sight of God.[3] Patience is necessary for you, for in that shall you keep your soul."[4]

Great was the holy conversation that the anchoress and this creature had through talking of the love of our Lord Jesus Christ for the many days that they were together.

This creature revealed her manner of life to many a worthy clerk, to honored doctors of divinity, both religious men and others of secular habit, and they said that God wrought great grace in her and bade her not to be afraid—there was no delusion

5. Julian of Norwich; see selections from her *Book of Showings*, pages 481–97.

6. This concern with the whole community of the faithful, a new note in Kempe's book, is highly characteristic of Julian's spirituality.

7. 1 Corinthians 6.19. The density of biblical reference in this passage suggests not only Dame Julian's learning but also Kempe's powerful memory for Scripture and theology. It is important that such biblical justification comes to Kempe through another holy woman.

8. James 1.8.

9. James 1.6–7.

1. Romans 8.26.

2. 2 Corinthians 6.16, Revelation 21.3.

3. Luke 6.22–23.

4. Luke 21.19.

in her manner of living. They counseled her to be persevering, for their greatest fear was that she would turn aside and not keep her perfection. She had so many enemies and so much slander, that it seemed to them that she might not bear it without great grace and a mighty faith. * * *

[Pilgrimage to Jerusalem]

Chapter 28[5]

* * * And so they went on into the Holy Land until they could see Jerusalem. And when this creature saw Jerusalem—she was riding on an ass—she thanked God with all her heart, praying him for his mercy that, just as he had brought her to see this earthly city of Jerusalem, he would grant her grace to see the blissful city of Jerusalem above, the city of heaven. Our Lord Jesus Christ, answering her thought, granted her her desire.

Then for the joy that she had and the sweetness that she felt in the conversation of our Lord, she was on the point of falling off her ass, for she could not bear the sweetness and grace that God wrought in her soul. Then two German pilgrims went up to her and kept her from falling—one of them was a priest, and he put spices in her mouth to comfort her, thinking she was ill. And so they helped her onwards to Jerusalem, and when she arrived there she said, "Sirs, I beg you, don't be annoyed though I weep bitterly in this holy place where our Lord Jesus Christ lived and died."

Then they went to the Church of the Holy Sepulchre in Jerusalem, and they were let in on the one day at evensong time, and remained until evensong time on the next day. Then the friars lifted up a cross and led the pilgrims about from one place to another where our Lord had suffered his pains and his Passion, every man and woman carrying a wax candle in one hand.[6] And the friars always, as they went about, told them what our Lord suffered in every place. And this creature wept and sobbed as plenteously as though she had seen our Lord with her bodily eyes suffering his Passion at that time. Before her in her soul she saw him in truth by contemplation, and that caused her to have compassion. And when they came up on to the Mount of Calvary, she fell down because she could not stand or kneel, but writhed and wrestled with her body, spreading her arms out wide, and cried with a loud voice as though her heart would have burst apart, for in the city of her soul she saw truly and freshly how our Lord was crucified. Before her face she heard and saw in her spiritual sight the mourning of our Lady, of Saint John and Mary Magdalene, and of many others that loved our Lord.

And she had such great compassion and such great pain to see our Lord's pain, that she could not keep herself from crying and roaring though she should have died for it. And this was the first crying that she ever cried in any contemplation. And this kind of crying lasted for many years after this time, despite anything that anyone might do, and she suffered much contempt and much reproof for it. The crying was so loud and so amazing that it astounded people, unless they had heard it before, or else knew the reason for the cryings. And she had them so often that they made her very weak in her bodily strength, and specially if she heard of our Lord's Passion.

5. In autumn 1413, Margery sets out to the Holy Land. Her party of pilgrims repudiates Margery, and she is helped by the Papal legate at Constance, an English friar. She continues her travel toward Italy with an elderly Englishman. She rejoins the English pilgrims at Bologna, but continues to suffer their hostility because of her austere diet and dramatic displays of religious emotion.

6. Although Jerusalem was under Islamic control, Franciscan friars had negotiated permission to keep a convent next to the Church of the Holy Sepulchre and to guide pilgrims around a number of holy sites.

And sometimes, when she saw the crucifix, or if she saw a man had a wound, or a beast, whichever it were, or if a man beat a child before her or hit a horse or other beast with a whip, if she saw or heard it, she thought she saw our Lord being beaten or wounded, just as she saw it in the man or in the beast, either in the fields or in the town, and alone by herself as well as among people.

When she first had her cryings at Jerusalem, she had them often, and in Rome also. And when she first came home to England her cryings came but seldom, perhaps once a month, then once a week, afterwards daily, and once she had fourteen in one day, and another day she had seven, just as God would visit her with them, sometimes in church, sometimes in the street, sometimes in her chamber, sometimes in the fields, when God would send them, for she never knew the time nor hour when they would come. And they never came without surpassingly great sweetness of devotion and high contemplation.

And as soon as she perceived that she was going to cry, she would hold it in as much as she could, so that people would not hear it and get annoyed. For some said it was a wicked spirit tormented her; some said it was an illness; some said she had drunk too much wine; some cursed her; some wished she was in the harbor; some wished she was on the sea in a bottomless boat; and so each man as he thought. Other, spiritually inclined men loved her and esteemed her all the more. Some great clerks said our Lady never cried so, nor any saint in heaven, but they knew very little what she felt, nor would they believe that she could not stop herself from crying if she wanted.

And therefore, when she knew that she was going to cry, she held it in as long as she could, and did all that she could to withstand it or else to suppress it, until she turned the color of lead, and all the time it would be seething more and more in her mind until such time as it burst out. And when the body might no longer endure the spiritual effort, but was overcome with the unspeakable love that worked so fervently in her soul, then she fell down and cried astonishingly loud. And the more that she labored to keep it in or to suppress it, so much the more would she cry, and the louder.

And thus she did on the Mount of Calvary, as it is written before: she had as true contemplation in the sight of her soul as if Christ had hung before her bodily eye in his manhood.[7] And when through dispensation of the high mercy of our sovereign savior, Christ Jesus, it was granted to this creature to behold so truly his precious tender body, all rent and torn with scourges, more full of wounds than a dovecote ever was of holes, hanging upon the cross with the crown of thorns upon his head, his blessed hands, his tender feet nailed to the hard wood, the rivers of blood flowing out plenteously from every limb, the grisly and grievous wound in his precious side shedding out blood and water for her love and her salvation, then she fell down and cried with a loud voice, twisting and turning her body amazingly on every side, spreading her arms out wide as if she would have died, and could not keep herself from crying and these physical movements, because of the fire of love that burned so fervently in her soul with pure pity and compassion.[8]

7. The detailed rendering of Christ's suffering corresponds to Julian of Norwich's visions and to depictions of the Crucifixion in later medieval art. Margery's gestures reinforce the pattern of imitation of Christ seen throughout her book.

8. Margery's images of the dovecote and the fire of love echo Richard Rolle.

[Arrest by Duke of Bedford's Men; Meeting with Archbishop of York]

Chapter 53[9]

Afterwards that good man who was her escort brought her out of the town, and they went on to Bridlington to her confessor, who was called Sleytham, and spoke with him and with many other good men who had encouraged her previously and done much for her. Then she would not stay there, but took her leave to walk on upon her journey. And then her confessor asked her if she dared not stay because of the Archbishop of York, and she said, "No, truly."

Then the good man gave her silver, begging her to pray for him. And so she went on to Hull. And there, on one occasion, as they went in procession, a great woman treated her with utter contempt, and she said not a word in reply. Many other people said that she ought to be put in prison and made great threats. And notwithstanding all their malice, a good man still came and asked her to a meal, and made her very welcome. Then the malicious people who had despised her before came to this good man, and told him that he ought not do her any kindness, for they considered that she was not a good woman. On the next day, in the morning, her host escorted her out to the edge of town, for he dared not keep her with him any longer.

And so she went to Hessle and would have crossed over the Humber.[1] Then she happened to find there two Preaching Friars, and two yeomen of the Duke of Bedford's.[2] The friars told the yeomen which woman she was, and the yeomen arrested her as she was about to board her boat, and also arrested a man who travelled with her.

"For our lord," they said, "the Duke of Bedford, has sent for you, and you are held to be the greatest Lollard in all this part of the country, or around London either. We have sought you in many a part of the land, and we shall have a hundred pounds for bringing you before our lord."

She said to them, "With a good will, sirs, I shall go with you wherever you will lead me."

Then they brought her back to Hessle, and there men called her Lollard, and women came running out of their houses with their distaffs, crying to the people, "Burn this false heretic."

So as she went on towards Beverley with the said yeomen and friars, they many times met with men of that district who said to her, "Woman, give up this life that you lead, and go and spin, and card wool, as other women do, and do not suffer so much shame and so much unhappiness. We would not suffer so much for any money on earth."

Then she said to them, "I do not suffer as much sorrow as I would do for our Lord's love, for I only suffer cutting words, and our merciful Lord Christ Jesus—worshipped be his name—suffered hard strokes, bitter scourgings, and shameful death at the last, for me and for all mankind, blessed may he be. And therefore, it is truly nothing that I suffer, in comparison to what he suffered."

And so, as she went along with the said men, she told them good stories, until one of the Duke's men who had arrested her said to her, "I rather regret that I met with you, for it seems to me that you speak very good words."

9. Margery returns from pilgrimage to Santiago de Compostela. Traveling from Bristol to York, she has twice been detained by civil and clerical authorities, and questioned as a suspected Lollard. Each time she establishes her orthodoxy, most recently to the Archbishop of York, who nevertheless has her escorted from his archdiocese.

1. By crossing the Humber, Margery would have passed beyond the authority of the Archbishop of York, and closer to the Bishop of Lincoln, who had been sympathetic to her.

2. John, third son of King Henry IV, first Duke of Bedford, 1389–1435; at this time he was Lieutenant of the kingdom. (See the Book of Hours made for him, Color Plate 10.)

Then she said to him, "Sir, do not regret nor repent that you met with me. Do your lord's will, and I trust that all shall be for the best, for I am very well pleased that you met with me."

He replied, "If ever you're a saint in heaven, lady, pray for me."

She answered, saying to him, "Sir, I hope you will be a saint yourself, and every man that shall come to heaven."

So they went on till they came into Beverley, where lived the wife of one of the men who had arrested her. And they escorted her there and took away from her her purse and her ring. They provided her with a nice room and a decent bed in it, with all the necessaries, locking the door with a key, and bearing the key away with them. * * *

* * * Then she stood looking out at a window, telling many edifying tales to those who would hear her, so much so that women wept bitterly, and said with great heaviness of heart, "Alas, woman, why should you be burned?"

Then she begged the good wife of the house to give her a drink, for she was terribly thirsty. And the good wife said her husband had taken away the key, because of which she could not come in to her, nor give her a drink. And then the women took a ladder and set it up against the window, and gave her a pint of wine in a pot, and also a cup, begging her to conceal the pot and cup, so that when the good man came back he might not notice it.

Chapter 54

The said creature, lying in her bed on the following night, heard with her bodily ears a loud voice calling, "Margery." With that voice she awoke, greatly frightened, and, lying still in silence, she said her prayers as devoutly as she could at that time. And soon our merciful Lord, everywhere present, comforting his unworthy servant, said to her, "Daughter, it is more pleasing to me that you suffer scorn and humiliation, shame and rebukes, wrongs and distress, than if your head were struck off three times a day every day for seven years. And therefore, daughter, do not fear what any man can say to you. But in my goodness, and in your sorrows that you have suffered, you have great cause to rejoice, for when you come home to heaven, then shall every sorrow be turned into joy for you."

On the next day she was brought into the Chapterhouse of Beverley,[3] and there was the Archbishop of York, and many great clerics with him, priests, canons, and secular men. Then the Archbishop said to this creature, "What, woman, have you come back again? I would gladly be rid of you."

And then a priest brought her before him, and the Archbishop said, in the hearing of all present, "Sirs, I had this woman before me at Cawood, and there I with my clerics examined her in her faith and found no fault in her. Furthermore, sirs, I have since that time spoken with good men who hold her to be a perfect woman and a good woman. Notwithstanding all this, I gave one of my men five shillings to lead her out of this part of the country, in order to quieten the people down. And as they were going on their journey they were taken and arrested, my man put in prison because of her; also her gold and her silver was taken away from her, together with her beads and her ring, and she is brought before me again here. Is there any man here who can say anything against her?"

3. Just north of the Humber.

Then other men said, "Here is a friar who knows many things against her."

The friar came forward and said that she disparaged all men of Holy Church—and he uttered much evil talk about her that time. He also said that she would have been burnt at Lynn, had his order—that was the Preaching Friars—not been there. "And, sir, she says that she may weep and have contrition when she will."

Then came the two men who had arrested her, saying with the friar that she was Cobham's daughter, and was sent to carry letters about the country.[4] And they said she had not been to Jerusalem, nor in the Holy Land, nor on other pilgrimage, as she had been in truth. They denied all truth, and maintained what was wrong, as many others had done before. When they had said enough for a long while, they held their peace.

Then the Archbishop said to her, "Woman, what do you say to all this?"

She said, "My lord, saving your reverence, all the words that they say are lies."

Then the Archbishop said to the friar, "Friar, the words are not heresy; they are slanderous words and erroneous."

"My lord," said the friar, "she knows her faith well enough. Nevertheless, my lord of Bedford is angry with her, and he will have her."[5] * * *

A short time afterwards the Archbishop sent for her, and she was led into his chamber, and even up to his bedside. Then she, bowing, thanked him for his gracious favour that he had shown her before.

"Yes, yes," said the Archbishop, "I am told worse things of you than I ever was before."

She said, "My lord, if you care to examine me, I shall avow the truth, and if I be found guilty, I will be obedient to your correction."

Then a Preaching Friar came forward, who was Suffragan[6] to the Archbishop, to whom the Archbishop said, "Now, sir, as you said to me when she was not present, say now while she is present."

"Shall I do so?" said the Suffragan.

"Yes," said the Archbishop.

Then the Suffragan said to this creature, "Woman, you were at my Lady Westmorland's."[7]

"When, sir?" said she.

"At Easter," said the Suffragan.

She, not replying, said, "Well, sir?"

Then he said, "My Lady herself was well pleased with you and liked your talk, but you advised my Lady Greystoke to leave her husband,[8] and she is a baron's wife, and daughter to my Lady of Westmorland. And now you have said enough to be burned for." And so he multiplied many sharp words in front of the Archbishop—it is not fitting to repeat them.

At last she said to the Archbishop, "My lord, if it be your will, I have not seen my Lady Westmorland these two years and more. Sir, she sent for me before I went to Jerusalem[9] and, if you like, I will go to her again for a testimonial that I prompted no such matter."

4. Sir John Oldcastle, Lord Cobham, a leading Lollard, had mounted an unsuccessful rising against Henry V. He was executed, in the presence of the Duke of Bedford, 14 December 1417.

5. Margery becomes part of a potential dispute over jurisdiction between clergy and laity.

6. A subsidiary bishop, usually assisting a bishop or archbishop in local matters.

7. Joan de Beaufort (d. 1440), daughter of John of Gaunt and at this time wife of Ralph Neville, first Earl of Westmorland. She was the Duke of Bedford's aunt.

8. Elizabeth, Lady Greystoke, daughter of Joan de Beaufort, hence a relative of the Duke of Bedford. Margery had already been accused of encouraging the wives of urban commoners to leave their husbands.

9. At least four years earlier.

"No," said those who stood round about, "let her be put in prison, and we will send a letter to the noble lady, and, if it be the truth that she is saying, let her go free, without any grudging."

And she said she was quite satisfied that it should be so.

Then a great cleric who stood a little to one side of the Archbishop said, "Put her in prison forty days, and she will love God the better for the rest of her life."

The Archbishop asked her what tale it was that she told the Lady of Westmorland when she spoke with her.

She said, "I told her a good tale of a lady who was damned because she would not love her enemies, and of a bailiff who was saved because he loved his enemies and forgave them their trespasses against him, and yet he was held to be an evil man."

The Archbishop said it was a good tale. Then his steward said, and many others with him, crying with a loud voice to the Archbishop, "My lord, we pray you, let her go from here this time, and if she ever comes back again, we will burn her ourselves."

The Archbishop said, "I believe there was never woman in England so treated as she is, and has been."

Then he said to this creature, "I do not know what I shall do with you."

She said, "My lord, I pray you, let me have your letter and your seal as a record that I have vindicated myself against my enemies, and that nothing admissible is charged against me, neither error nor heresy that may be proved against me, our Lord be thanked. And let me have John, your man, again to bring me over the water."

And the Archbishop very kindly granted her all she desired—our Lord grant him his reward—and delivered to her her purse with her ring and beads, which the Duke of Bedford's men had taken from her before. The Archbishop was amazed at where she got the money to travel about the country with, and she said good men gave it her so that she would pray for them.

Then she, kneeling down, received his blessing and took her leave with a very glad heart, going out of his chamber. And the Archbishop's household asked her to pray for them, but the Steward was angry because she laughed and was so cheerful, saying to her, "Holy folk should not laugh."

She said, "Sir, I have great cause to laugh, for the more shame and scorn I suffer, the merrier I may be in our Lord Jesus Christ."

Then she came down into the hall, and there stood the Preaching Friar who had caused her all that unhappiness. And so she passed on with a man of the Archbishop's, bearing the letter which the Archbishop had granted her for a record, and he brought her to the River Humber, and there he took his leave of her, returning to his lord and bearing the said letter with him again, and so she was left alone, without any knowledge of the people.[1]

All the aforesaid trouble befell her on a Friday, God be thanked for everything.[2]

Chapter 55

When she had crossed the River Humber, she was immediately arrested as a Lollard and led towards prison. There happened to be a person there who had seen her before the Archbishop of York, and he got her leave to go where she wanted, and excused her to the bailiff, and undertook for her that she was no Lollard. And so she escaped away in the name of Jesus. * * *

1. At the southern edge of the archbishop's territory, Margery is again left alone and without the document that would guarantee her orthodoxy.

2. Margery's greatest trials often occur on a Friday, connecting her sufferings to events of the Crucifixion.

Middle English Lyrics

Although many Middle English lyrics have a beguilingly fresh and unselfconscious tone, they owe much to learned and sophisticated continental sources—the medieval Latin lyrics of the "Goliard poets" and the Provençal and French lyrics of the Troubadours and Trouvères. Most authors were clerics, aware of the similarities between earthly and divine love, and fond of punning in Latin or English.

The anonymity of the Middle English lyrics prevents us from seeing them as part of a single poet's *oeuvre*, as we can, for instance, with the poems of Chaucer, Dunbar, and Dafydd ap Gwilym. Rather, we must rely on more general contexts, such as genre, to establish relationships among poems. One of the most popular genres among the secular lyrics was the *reverdie*, a poem celebrating the return of spring. The early thirteenth-century *Cuckoo Song* ("Sumer is icumen in") joyfully invokes the bird's song, and revels in the blossoming of the countryside and the calls of the animals to their young. More typical examples of the *reverdie* are *Alisoun* and *Spring*, whose male speakers ruefully contrast the burgeoning of nature with the stinginess of their beloveds; in *Spring*, flowers bloom, birds sing, animals mate—but one woman remains unmoved. In the genre of the love complaint, *My Lefe Is Faren in a Lond* and *Fowls in the Frith* express erotic loss and frustration with great succinctness.

Frustration was not the only attitude in Middle English love lyrics, however. A stance more boasting than adoring or despairing is taken in the witty lyric *I Have a Noble Cock*. Furthermore, clerical misogyny is expressed in *Abuse of Women*, which ostensibly praises women by absolving them of the vices—gossip, infidelity, shrewishness—typically attributed to them in satires against women; yet the refrain first praises women as the best of creatures but then undercuts this claim in Latin, which few women would have been able to understand.

Although most of the Middle English lyrics are in the male voice, there are a few "women's songs"—most likely written by men—which convey female experience. Occasionally these songs are invitations (for instance, the enigmatic *Irish Dancer*), but more often they are laments by an abandoned, and often pregnant, woman. *A Forsaken Maiden's Lament* is punctuated by the regretful refrain: "Were it undo that is ido, / I wolde bewar." Two of the women's songs, while concluding with laments about pregnancy, stress the cleverness and charm of the clerical seducers, perhaps suggesting that churchmen were their audience as well as their authors. *The Wily Clerk* attributes a young man's skill at deception to his scholarly training, as does *Jolly Jankin*, whose clerk engages in multilingual wordplay, turning the "Kyrie Eleison" into a request for mercy from the woman herself, "Alison."

The majority of Middle English lyrics were not secular but religious. Songs in praise of the Virgin Mary or Christ, however, employ the same erotic language as the secular lyrics, often in conjunction with typological figures linking events in the Old Testament to those in the New. In *Adam Lay Ibounden*, for instance, the poet follows a statement of the "fortunate Fall"—that Adam's sin was necessary to permit Christ's redemption—with a courtly compliment to the Virgin Mary. Similarly, *I Sing of a Maiden* draws on the typological significance of Gideon's fleece in Judges 6 (the soaking of the fleece by dew figuring Mary's impregnation by the Holy Spirit) while also employing the courtly imagery of a poet "singing of a maiden" who "chooses" Christ as her son, as if he were a lover. In a much longer poem in praise of the Virgin, the poet—casting himself as Mary's "knight" caught in the bonds of love—begs her mercy and also compliments her by contrasting her with her antitype, Eve.

Occasionally the Middle English religious lyric uses secular motifs and genres in a way that approaches parody. For instance, the second stanza of the Nativity poem *Mary Is with Child* resembles a pregnancy lament by a young girl. Mary, however, explains that her condition will be a source of joy rather than shame, when she will sing a lullaby to her "darling."

This Middle English poet, far from blaspheming, was trying to humanize the mystery of the Nativity and relate it to daily life.

Other religious poems either celebrate Christ or reject the world. The poems to Christ, in their tenderness and immediacy, resemble those to Mary. In only four lines, *Now Goeth Sun Under Wood* evokes nature's oneness with Christ (the setting sun figuring the crucifixion) and the poet's empathy with the Virgin mother. Poets used erotic language in poems to Christ as well as those to Mary, as in *Sweet Jesus, King of Bliss* and *Jesus, My Sweet Lover*. Finally, in a different vein, the *Contempt of the World* questions the values of courtly life, with the "*ubi sunt*" ("where are") motif. "Where beth they biforen us weren?" it asks, evoking the lovely women who enjoyed their paradise on earth and now suffer the eternal fires of hell.

The Cuckoo Song

Sumer is icumen in,° *spring has come in*
Lhude° sing, cuccu!° *loudly / cuckoo*
Groweth sed° and bloweth° med° *seed / blooms / meadow*
And springth° the wude° nu.° *grows / forest / now*
Sing, cuccu!

Awe° bleteth after lomb, *ewe*
Lhouth° after calve° cu,° *lows / calf / cow*
Bulluc sterteth,° bucke ferteth.° *leaps / farts*
Murie° sing, cuccu! *merrily*
Cuccu, cuccu,
Wel singes thu, cuccu.
Ne swik° thu naver° nu! *cease / never*

Sing cuccu nu, sing cuccu!
Sing cuccu, sing cuccu nu!

Spring

Lenten° is come with love to toune,° *spring / town*
With blosmen° and with briddes° roune,° *flowers / birds' / song*
That all this blisse bringeth.
Dayeseyes° in this° dales, *daisies / these*
Notes swete of nightegales—
Uch° foul° song singeth. *each / bird*
The threstelcok him threteth o;[1]
Away is here° winter wo *their*
When woderove° springeth.° *woodruff / grows*
This foules° singeth ferly fele,° *birds / wonderfully much*
And wliteth on here winne wele,[2]
That all the wode ringeth.

The rose raileth hire rode,° *puts on her rosy hue*
The leves on the lighte° wode *bright*
Waxen° all with wille.° *grow / pleasure*
The mone mandeth hire bleo,[3]

1. The song thrush contends always.
2. And chirp their wealth of joys.
3. The moon sends forth her light.

This page contains the words and music to one of the earliest and best loved of Middle English lyrics, *The Cuckoo Song* ("Sumer is icumen in"). The lyric is a *reverdie*, or spring song, but its joyful description of nature's rebirth is given a more sober allegorical interpretation by the interlinear Latin gloss, apparently to be sung to the same tune. The gloss parallels the lyric's celebration of the reawakening landscape with an account of the "heavenly farmer" *(celicus agricola)* whom "rot on the vine" *(vitis vicio)* leads to sacrifice his Son. The fact that the manuscript was copied at a monastery reminds us that this song, like much other early English secular poetry, survives only because it was seen to have religious relevance.

The lilie is lossom° to seo,° — *lovely / see*
    The fenil° and the fille.° — *fennel / chervil*
Wowes° this° wilde drakes; — *woo / these*
Miles murgeth here makes,[4]
    Ase strem that striketh° stille.° — *flows / softly*
Mody meneth, so doth mo;[5]
Ichot° ich° am one of tho,° — *I know / I / those*
    For love that likes° ille. — *pleases*

The mone mandeth hire light;
So doth the semly° sonne bright, — *lovely*
    When briddes singeth breme.° — *loudly*
Deawes donketh the dounes;[6]
Deores with here derne rounes,[7]
    Domes for to deme;[8]
Wormes woweth under cloude,° — *the soil*
Wimmen waxeth° wounder° proude, — *become / wondrously*

4. Beasts gladden their mates.
5. The high-spirited man mourns, so do others.
6. Dew moistens the downs (hills).
7. Animals with their secret whispers.
8. Speak their opinions.

So well it wol hem° seme.° *to them / appear*
If me shall wonte wille of on,[9]
This wunne weole° I wole forgon *wealth of joys*
And wight° in wode be fleme.° *quickly / exile*

Alisoun

Bitwene Mersh° and Averil° *March / April*
When spray° biginneth to springe,° *twig / grow*
The lutel° fowl° hath hire° will *little / bird / her*
On° hire lud° to singe. *in / language*
Ich° libbe° in love-longinge *I / live*
For semlokest° of alle thinge: *fairest*
He° may me blisse bringe; *she*
Ich° am in hire baundoun.° *I / power*
An hendy hap ich habbe ihent![1]
Ichot°from hevene it is me sent; *I know*
From alle wimmen my love is lent,° *taken away*
And light°on Alisoun.[2] *settled*

On hew° hire her° is fair inogh, *color / hair*
Hire browe browne, hire eye blake;
With lossum chere he on me logh,[3]
With middel° small and well imake.° *waist / made*
Bote° he me wolle° to hire take *unless / will*
For to ben hire° owen° make,° *her / own / mate*
Longe to liven ichulle° forsake,° *I will / refuse*
And feye° fallen adoun. *doomed*
An hendy hap ich habbe ihent!
Ichot from hevene it is me sent;
From alle wimmen my love is lent,
And light on Alisoun.

Nightes° when I wende° and wake— *at night / turn*
Forthy min wonges waxeth won[4]—
Levedy,° all for thine sake *lady*
Longinge is ilent° me on. *come*
In world nis non so witer° mon *wise*
That all hire° bounte° telle con: *her / excellence*
Hire swire° is whittore° then the swon, *neck / whiter*
And feirest may° in toune. *maiden*
An hendy hap ich habbe ihent!
Ichot from hevene it is me sent;

9. If I shall lack the pleasure of one.
1. A fair destiny I have received.
2. Alison is a stock name for a country woman, shared by the wife in Chaucer's *Miller's Tale* and by his Wife of Bath.
3. With lovely manner she laughed at me.
4. Therefore my cheeks become pale.

From alle wimmen my love is lent,
And light on Alisoun.

Ich am for wowing all forwake,[5]
Wery so water in wore[6]
Lest eny reve° me my make° — *steal / mate*
Ich habbe iyerned yore.[7]
Betere is tholien while sore[8]
Then mournen evermore.
Geynest° under gore,° — *kindest / petticoat*
Herkne to my roun!° — *song*
An hendy hap ich habbe ihent!
Ichot from hevene it is me sent;
From alle wimmen my love is lent,
And light on Alisoun.

I Have a Noble Cock

I have a gentil° cok, — *noble*
Croweth° me day; — *who crows*
He doth° me risen erly, — *makes*
My matins for to say.

I have a gentil cok,
Comen he is of gret;° — *a great family*
His comb is of red corel,
His tayel is of jet.

I have a gentil cok,
Comen he is of kinde;° — *good lineage*
His comb is of red corel,
His tail is of inde.° — *indigo*

His legges ben of asor,° — *azure*
So gentil and so smale;
His spores° arn of silver white, — *spurs*
Into the worte-wale.° — *root of cock's spur*

His eynen° arn of cristal, — *eyes*
Loken° all in aumber; — *set*
And every night he percheth him
In min ladyes chaumber.

My Lefe Is Faren in a Lond[1]

My lefe is faren in a lond[2]—
Alas! why is she so?
And I am so sore bound

5. I am for wooing all sleepless.
6. Weary as water in a troubled pool.
7. (For whom) I have long yearned.
8. It is better to suffer sorely for a time.

1. Chaucer alludes to this poem in *The Nun's Priest's Tale*, line 113.
2. My beloved has gone away.

I may nat com her to.
She hath my hert in hold,° *imprisoned*
Where-ever she ride or go,
With trew love a thousandfold.

Fowls in the Frith

Foweles° in the frith,° *birds / wood*
The fisses° in the flod,° *fishes / river*
And I mon° waxe° wod.° *must / become / mad*
Mulch° sorw° I walke with *much / sorrow*
For beste[1] of bon° and blod.° *bone / blood*

Abuse of Women

Of all creatures women be best:
Cuius contrarium verum est.[1]

In every place ye may well see
That women be trewe as tirtil° on tree, *turtledove*
Not liberal° in langage, but ever in secree,° *licentious / secrecy*
And gret joye amonge them is for to be.

Of all creatures women be best:
Cuius contrarium verum est.

The stedfastnes of women will never be don,
So jentil, so curtes they be everychon,[2]
Meke as a lambe, still as a stone,
Croked° nor crabbed find ye none! *perverse*

Of all creatures women be best:
Cuius contrarium verum est.

Men be more cumbers° a thousand fold, *troublesome*
And I mervail how they dare be so bold
Against women for to hold,
Seeing them so pacient, softe, and cold.

Of all creatures women be best:
Cuius contrarium verum est.

For tell a woman all your counsaile,
And she can kepe it wonderly well;
She had lever go quik° to hell, *alive*
Than to her neighbour she wold it tell!

Of all creatures women be best:
Cuius contrarium verum est.

1. Either "beast" or "best."
1. Latin for "The opposite of this is true."
2. So well-bred, so courteous is each one.

For by women men be reconsiled,
For by women was never man begiled,
For they be of the condicion of curtes Grisell,[3]
For they be so meke and milde.

Of all creatures women be best:
Cuius contrarium verum est.

Now say well by° women or elles be still, *about*
For they never displesed man by ther will;
To be angry or wroth they can° no skill, *have*
For I dare say they think non ill.

Of all creatures women be best:
Cuius contrarium verum est.

Trow° ye that women list° to smater,° *think / like / chatter*
Or against ther husbondes for to clater?
Nay, they had lever° fast bred and water, *rather*
Then for to dele in suche a mater.

Of all creatures women be best:
Cuius contrarium verum est.

Though all the paciens in the world were drownd,
And non were lefte here on the ground,
Again in a woman it might be found,
Suche vertu in them dothe abound!

Of all creatures women be best:
Cuius contrarium verum est.

To the tavern they will not go,
Nor to the alehous never the mo,° *more*
For, God wot,° ther hartes wold be wo, knows *knows*
To spende ther husbondes money so.

Of all creatures women be best:
Cuius contrarium verum est.

If here were a woman or a maid,
That list for to go freshely arayed,
Or with fine kirchers° to go displayed, *kerchiefs*
Ye wold say, "They be proude": it is ill said.

Of all creatures women be best:
Cuius contrarium verum est.

The Irish Dancer

Ich° am of Irlaunde, *I*
And of the holy londe
Of Irlande.
Gode° sire, pray ich thee, *good*

3. Griselda, the long-suffering wife of Chaucer's *Clerk's Tale*; the tale ends with the observation that there are no more Griseldas left.

For of sainte° charitee,° *holy / charity*
Come and daunce wit me
In Irlaunde.

A Forsaken Maiden's Lament

Were it undo° that is ido,° *undone / done*
I wolde bewar.

I lovede a child° of this cuntree, *young man*
And so I wende° he had do me; *thought*
Now myself the sothe° I see, *truth*
That he is far.

Were it undo that is ido,
I wolde bewar.

He seide to me he wolde be trewe,
And change me for non other newe;
Now I sikke° and am pale of hewe, *sigh*
For he is far.

Were it undo that is ido,
I wolde bewar.

He seide his sawes° he wolde fulfille: *promises*
Therfore I lat him have all his wille;
Now I sikke and morne stille,° *quietly*
For he is far.

Were it undo that is ido,
I wolde bewar.

The Wily Clerk

A, *dere God, what I am fayn,*
For I am madyn now gane![1]

This enther° day I mete a clerke,° *other / cleric*
And he was wily in his werke;
He prayd me with° him to herke,° *to / listen*
And his counsel all for to layne.° *conceal*

A, *dere God, what I am fayn,*
For I am madyn now gane!

I trow° he coud° of gramery;[2] *believe / knew*
I shall now telle a good skill° why: *reason*
For what I hade siccurly,° *certainly*
To warne° his will had I no mayn.° *resist / strength*

1. Ah, dear God, how worthless I am, / For I am no longer a virgin.

2. Latin learning, or magic—indicates the magical power which the speaker attributes to the clergy, who could read Latin.

A, dere God, what I am fayn,
For I am madyn now gane!

Whan he and me brout° un° us the schete,° — *brought / on / sheet*
Of all his will I him lete;° — *permitted*
Now will not my girdil met°— — *meet*
A, dere God, what shall I sayn?

A, dere God, what I am fayn,
For I am madyn now gane!

I shall sey to man and page° — *youth*
That I have bene of pilgrimage.
Now will I not lete° for no rage° — *permit / lust*
With me a clerk for to pleyn.° — *play*

A, dere God, what I am fayn,
For I am madyn now gane!

Jolly Jankin[1]

"Kyrie,"°so "Kyrie," — *Lord*
Jankin singeth merie,° — *merrily*
With "aleison."[2]

As I went on Yol° Day in our procession, — *Yule (Christmas)*
Knew I joly Jankin be° his mery ton.° — *by / tone*
Kyrieleison.

"Kyrie," so "Kyrie,"
Jankin singeth merie,
With "aleison."

Jankin began the offis° on the Yol Day, — *church service*
And yet me thinketh[3] it dos me good, so merie gan he say
Kyrieleison.

"Kyrie," so "Kyrie,"
Jankin singeth merie,
With "aleison."

Jankin red the pistil° full fair and full well, — *Epistle*
And yet me thinketh it dos me good, as evere have I sell.° — *luck*
Kyrieleison.

"Kyrie," so "Kyrie,"
Jankin singeth merie,
With "aleison."

Jankin at the *Sanctus* craked° a merie note, — *uttered*
And yet me thinketh it dos me good—I payed for his cote.
Kyrieleison.

1. "Johnny," a stock name. Also the name of Chaucer's Wife of Bath's fifth husband, who was a clerk.
2. "*Kyrie eleison,*" Greek for "Lord have mercy upon us" (an early part of the Mass). The poem puns on "Alison," supposedly the speaker's name (a stock female name).
3. It seems to me.

"Kyrie," so "Kyrie,"
Jankin singeth merie,
With "aleison."

Jankin craked notes an hundered on a knot,° *at once*
And yet he hakked hem smaller than wortes[4] to the pot.
Kyrieleison.

"Kyrie," so "Kyrie,"
Jankin singeth merie,
With "aleison."

Jankin at the *Angnus* bered the *pax-brede;*[5]
He twinkeled, but said nout, and on min fot he trede.[6]
Kyrieleison.

"Kyrie," so "Kyrie,"
Jankin singeth merie,
With "aleison."

Benedicamus Domino,[7] Crist fro° schame me schilde.° *from / shield*
Deo gracias,[8] therto—alas, I go with childe!
Kyrieleison.

"Kyrie," so "Kyrie,"
Jankin singeth merie,
With "aleison."

Adam Lay Ibounden

Adam lay ibounden,° *bound*
Bounden in a bond;
Foure thousand winter
Thowt° he not too long. *thought*
And all was for an appil,
An appil that he took,
As clerkes finden wreten
In here° book. *their*
Ne hadde° the appil take° ben, *had not / taken*
The appil taken ben,
Ne° hadde never our lady *not*
A ben hevene quen.[1]
Blissed be the time
That appil take was!
Therfore we moun° singen *may*
"Deo gracias!"° *Thanks be to God!*

4. Vegetables.
5. At the *Agnus Dei* (at the later part of the Mass), Jankin carried the *pax-brede*, an article signalling the exchanging of the kiss of peace.
6. He winked, but said nothing, and on my foot he stepped.
7. Let us bless the Lord.
8. Thanks be to God.
1. Have been heaven's queen.

I Sing of a Maiden

I sing of a maiden
That is makeles,[1]
King of alle kinges
To° here° sone she ches.° *for / her / chose*

He cam also° stille° *as / quietly*
Ther° his moder was *where*
As dew in Aprille
That falleth on the gras.

He cam also stille
To his moderes bowr
As dew in Aprille
That falleth on the flour.

He cam also stille
Ther his moder lay
As dew in Aprille
That falleth on the spray.° *twigs*

Moder and maiden
Was never non but she:
Well may swich° a lady *such*
Godes moder be.

In Praise of Mary

Edi° be thu, Hevene Quene, *blessed*
Folkes froure° and engles° blis, *comfort / angels'*
Moder unwemmed° and maiden clene, *unspotted*
Swich° in world non other nis.° *such / is*
On thee it is well eth° sene° *easily / seen*
Of alle wimmen thu havest that pris.° *prize*
My swete Levedy,° her my bene,° *Lady / prayer*
And rew° of me yif° thy wille is. *take pity / if*

Thu asteye° so° the dais-rewe° *climb / as / dawn's ray*
The° deleth° from the derke night; *that / separates*
Of thee sprong a leme° newe *light*
That all this world haveth ilight.° *illuminated*
Nis non maide of thine hewe
So fair, so shene,° so rudy, so bright. *beautiful*
Swete Levedy, of me thu rewe,
And have mercy of thine knight.

Spronge° blostme° of one rote,° *sprung / blossom / root*
The Holy Ghost thee reste upon;
That wes for monkunnes° bote,° *mankind's / healing*

1. Spotless, matchless, and mateless.

And here° soule to alesen° for on. [*their / deliver*]
Levedy milde, softe and swote,° [*sweet*]
Ic° crye thee mercy: ic am thy mon,° [*I / man*]
Bothe to honde and to fote,
On alle wise° that ic con.° [*way / can*]

Thu ert° erthe° to° gode sede; [*art / earth / for*]
On thee lighte° the Hevene° dews; [*came down / of heaven*]
Of thee sprong the edi° blede°— [*blessed / fruit*]
The Holy Ghost hire on thee sews.° [*sowed it*]
Thu bring us ut of care, of drede,° [*fear*]
That Eve bitterliche us brews.
Thu shalt us into Hevene lede—
Welle° swete is the ilke° dews. [*most / same*]

Moder, full of thewes° hende,° [*virtues / gracious*]
Maide, dreigh° and well itaught,° [*patient / taught*]
Ic em in thine lovebende,° [*bonds of love*]
And to thee is all my draught.° [*leaning*]
Thu me shilde° from the Fende,° [*shield / Fiend*]
Ase thu ert fre,° and wilt° and maught:° [*noble / will / can*]
Help me to my lives ende,
And make me with thine sone isaught.° [*reconciled*]

Thu ert icumen° of heghe° cunne,° [*come / high / lineage*]
Of David the riche king.
Nis non maiden under sunne
The° mey be thine evening,° [*that / equal*]
Ne that so derne° loviye cunne,° [*secretly / can*]
Ne non so trewe of alle thing.
Thy love us broughte eche° wunne:° [*eternal / bliss*]
Ihered° ibe° thu, swete thing! [*praised / be*]

Selcudliche ure Louerd it dighte[1]
That thu, maide, withute were,° [*mate*]
That all this world bicluppe ne mighte,° [*could not encompass*]
Thu sholdest of thine boseme° bere.° [*womb / bear*]
Thee ne stighte,° ne thee ne prighte,° [*stabbed / pricked*]
In side, in lende° ne elleswhere:° [*loins / elsewhere*]
That wes° with full muchel° righte, [*was / much*]
For thu bere° thine Helere.° [*bore / Savior*]

Tho° Godes sune alighte wolde° [*when / wished*]
On erthe, all for ure° sake, [*our*]
Herre° teyen° he him nolde [*higher / servant*]
Thene° that maide to ben° his make:° [*than / be / mate*]
Betere ne mighte he, thaigh° he wolde, [*though*]
Ne swetture thing on erthe take.

1. Marvellously our Lord arranged it.

Levedy,° bring us to thine bolde° *Lady / abode*
And shild° us from helle wrake.° *shield / vengeance*
Amen.

Mary Is with Child

Nowel! nowel! nowel!
Sing we with mirth!
Christ is come well
With us to dwell,
By his most noble birth.
Under a tree
In sporting me,
Alone by a wod-side,° *side of a wood*
I hard° a maid[1] *heard*
That swetly said,
"I am with child this tide.° *time*

"Graciously
Conceived have I
The Son of God so swete:
His gracious will
I put me till,
As moder° him to kepe. *mother*

"Both night and day
I will him pray,
And her° his lawes taught, *hear*
And every dell° *in every way*
His trewe gospell
In his apostles fraught.° *carried*

"This ghostly° case° *spiritual / act*
Doth me embrace,
Without despite or mock;
With my derling,
'Lullay,'° to sing, *lullabye*
And lovely him to rock.

"Without distress
In grete lightness
I am both night and day.
This hevenly fod° *child*
In his childhod
Shall daily with me play.

"Soone must I sing
With rejoicing,
For the time is all ronne° *run out*

1. A poem that opens with the speaker in the countryside overhearing a woman's lament raises expectations that we will hear a *chanson d'aventure*, with erotic connotations.

That I shall child,° *give birth to*
All undefil'd,
The King of Heven's Sonne."

Sweet Jesus, King of Bliss

Swete Jesu, king of blisse,
Min herte° love, min herte lisse,° *heart's / joy*
Thou art swete mid iwisse.° *certainly*
Wo is him that thee shall misse!

Swete Jesu, min herte light,
Thou art day withoute night,
Thou geve° me streinthe and eke° might *may you give / also*
For to lovien thee aright.

Swete Jesu, min herte bote,° *remedy*
In min herte thou sete° a rote° *may you set / root*
Of thy love, that is so swote,° *sweet*
And leve° that it springe mote.° *grant / may grow*

Swete Jesu, min herte gleem,° *light*
Brightore then the sonnebeem,
Ibore° thou were in Bedleheem; *born*
Thou make me here thy swete dreem.[1]

Swete Jesu, thy love is swete;
Wo is him that thee shall lete!° *abandon*
Gif me grace for to grete° *cry*
For my sinnes teres° wete.° *with tears / wet*

Swete Jesu, king of londe,
Thou make me fer° understonde *to*
That min herte mote° fonde° *may / experience*
How swete beth° thy love-bonde. *is*

Swete Jesu, Louerd° min, *Lord*
My lif, min herte, all is thin;° *yours*
Undo° min herte and light° therin, *open / alight*
And wite° me from fendes° engin.° *guard / the Devil's / trick*

Swete Jesu, my soule° fode, *soul's*
Thin werkes beth° bo° swete and gode; *are / both*
Thou boghtest° me upon the rode;° *redeemed / cross*
For me thou sheddest thy blode.

Swete Jesu, me reoweth° sore *I regret*
Gultes that I ha wroght yore;[2]
Tharefore I bidde° thin milse° and ore;° *beg / mercy / grace*
Mercy, Lord, I nul° namore. *will not*

1. May thou make me hear thy sweet melody.

2. The sins that I have committed in the past.

Swete Jesu, Louerd God,
Thou me boghtest with thy blod;
Out of thin herte orn° the flod; *ran*
Thy moder° it segh° that thee by stod. *mother / saw*

Swete Jesu, bright and shene,° *beautiful*
I preye thee thou here my bene° *prayer*
Thourgh ernding° of the hevene quene, *intercession*
That thy love on me be sene.° *seen*

Swete Jesu, berne° best, *of men*
With thee ich hope habbe° rest; *to have*
Whether I be south other° west, *or*
The help of thee be me nest.° *nearest*

Swete Jesu, well may him be
That thee may in blisse see.
With love-cordes drawe thou me
That I may comen and wone° with thee. *dwell*

Swete Jesu, hevene king,
Feir and best of alle thing,
Thou bring me of° this longing *out of*
To come to thee at min ending.

Swete Jesu, all folkes reed,° *counsel*
Graunte us er we buen° ded *are*
Thee underfonge° in fourme of bred, *to receive*
And sethe° to heovene thou us led.° *later / may lead*

Now Goeth Sun under Wood

Now goth° sonne under wod: *goes / forest*
Me reweth,[1] Marye, thy faire rode.° *face*
Now goth sonne under tree:
Me reweth, Marye, thy sone and thee.

Jesus, My Sweet Lover

Jesu Christ, my lemmon° swete, *lover*
That diyedest on the Rode Tree,° *Cross*
With all my might I thee beseche,
For thy woundes two and three,
That also° faste mot° thy love *as / may*
Into mine herte fitched° be *fixed*
As was the spere into thine herte,
Whon thou soffredest deth for me.

1. I feel pity for.

Contempt of the World

Where beth° they biforen us weren? *are*
Houndes ladden° and hawkes beren,° *led / bore*
And hadden feld and wode;
The riche levedies° in here° bour,° *ladies / their / bower*
That wereden° gold in here tressour,° *wore / head-dress*
With here° brighte rode:° *their / face*

Eten and drounken and maden hem° glad; *themselves*
Here lif was all with gamen° ilad.° *sport / spent*
Men keneleden° hem° biforen; *kneeled / them*
They beren hem well swithe° heye°— *very / high*
And in a twinkling of an eye
Here soules weren forloren.° *lost*

Where is that laughing and that song,
That trailing[1] and that proude gong,° *gait*
Tho° hawkes and tho houndes? *those*
All that joye is went away,
That wele° is comen to weylaway,° *prosperity / woe*
To manye harde stoundes.° *times*

Here° paradis hy° nomen° here, *their / they / took*
And now they lien° in helle ifere;° *lie / together*
The fuir° it brennes° evere. *fire / burns*
Long is "ah!" and long is "oh!"
Long is "wy!" and long is "wo!"
Thennes° ne cometh they nevere. *thence*

Drey° here, man, thenne, if thou wilt, *suffer*
A litel pine that me thee bit;[2]
Withdraw thine eyses° ofte. *comforts*
They° thy pine° be unrede,° *though / pain / severe*
And° thou thenke° on thy mede,° *if / think / reward*
It shall thee thinken° softe. *seem*

If that fend,° that foule thing, *the Devil*
Thorou wikke roun, thorou fals egging,° *counsel*
Nethere° thee haveth icast, *down*
Up and be good chaunpioun!
Stond, ne fall namore adoun
For a litel blast.

Thou tak the rode° to° thy staf, *cross / as*
And thenk on him that thereonne gaf° *gave*
His lif that wes so lef.° *dear*
He it gaf for thee; thou yelde° it him; *give back*
Agein° his of that staf thou nim° *against / take*
And wrek° him of that thef.° *avenge / thief*

1. Walking with trailing garments.

2. A little pain that one enjoins.

Of righte bileve° thou nim that sheld, *belief*
The whiles that thou best° in that feld, *are*
Thin hond to strengthen fonde;° *try*
And kep thy of with° staves° ord,° *at / staff's / point*
And do° that traitre seyen that word. *make*
Biget° that murie° londe. *win/ happy*

Thereinne is day withouten night,
Withouten ende strengthe and might,
And wreche° of everich fo; *punishment*
Mid° God himselven eche° lif, *with / eternal*
And pes° and rest withoute strif, *peace*
Wele° withouten wo. *happiness*

Maiden moder,° hevene° quene, *mother / heaven's*
Thou might and const and owest to bene[3]
Oure sheld agein the fende;° *Devil*
Help us sunne° for to flen,° *sin / flee*
That we moten° thy sone° iseen° *may / Son / see*
In joye withouten ende.

Dafydd ap Gwilym

Widely regarded as the greatest Welsh poet, Dafydd ap Gwilym flourished in the fourteenth century, during a period of relative peace between two failed rebellions—that of Llywelyn, the last native prince of Wales, in 1282, and that of Owain Glyn Dwr (Owen Glendower), in 1400. A member of an upper-class family whose ancestors had served the English king, he wrote for a sophisticated audience of poets and patrons.

Dafydd drew inspiration from both continental and Welsh poetry but not, significantly, from English. (Influence, if any, went the other way, for the Middle English Harley lyrics, composed near the Welsh border, may owe their intricate rhyme scheme and ornamental alliteration to Welsh poetry; see *Spring* and *Alisoun*, pages 551–54). Among continental poets, the Roman Ovid is the greatest influence, whether directly or through twelfth-century Latin adaptations. He is the only foreign poet whom Dafydd mentions by name (*One Saving Place*, line 39). Dafydd is also indebted to medieval French and Provençal lyric genres—the *aubade* (dawn song), and the *reverdie* (spring song)—as well as to the *fabliau*.

Much of Dafydd's charm comes from his undercutting and transforming inherited poetic conventions through his personal revelations. His most endearing device, the self-deprecating persona, has been compared to that of his younger contemporary, Geoffrey Chaucer. There is an important difference, however, for while Chaucer in early love poems like *The Parliament of Fowls* presents himself as a failed lover, Dafydd often boasts of his success. Although he gives comic accounts of romantic failures in such anecdotal poems as the *Tale of a Wayside Inn* (in which a tryst ends in disaster when he goes to the wrong room), these are as often due to external obstacles as to his own inadequacy. In fact, Dafydd's persona is much more akin to Ovid's than to Chaucer's. In *The Ruin*, Dafydd gives an erotic twist to the ascetic Christian motif of the impermanence of worldly pleasures (as in the Old English *Wanderer*, page 172,

3. You may and can and ought to be.

and the Middle English *Contempt of the World*, page 565) by recalling that he once made love in a cottage that is now abandoned. He concludes his complaint *The Winter* with the observation that he would not venture out in such snowy weather for the sake of any girl.

Dafydd's poetry owes an equal debt to the rich poetic tradition of Wales. He shows familiarity with characters from the Arthurian tradition, which was originally Celtic although transformed by French adaptations by the time it reached him. In the poems included here, he often emphasizes the local Welsh setting. In *One Saving Place*, for instance, he lists all the locales where he sought his beloved Morvith, or she refused him—places with names like Meirch, Eleirch, Rhiw, and Cwcwll hollow. In *The Winter*, it is specifically in north Wales that he is assailed by snow. Finally, part of the humor in the *Tale of a Wayside Inn* derives from Dafydd's self-presentation as a "Welshman" whose accidental presence in their bedroom is discovered by three coarse Englishmen.

Dafydd's work is also distinguished by the poetic techniques of Welsh poetry, which are extraordinarily complex. His *cywyddau* (lyric poems) are written in the traditional lines of seven syllables, which rhyme in couplets, with the rhyming syllables alternately stressed and unstressed. He applies further ornamentation with a technique called *cynghanned*—internal alliteration or rhyme, which he sometimes extends over many lines. Although such an intricate style is impossible to capture in English, Rolfe Humphries has tried to approximate it in the translations given here. Easier to reproduce are Daffyd's *dyfalu*—strings of fanciful comparisons, such as the metaphors for snow used in *The Winter:*

The snowflakes wander,
A swarm of white bees.
Over the woods
A cold veil lies.
A load of chalk
Bows down the trees.

* * *

Will someone tell me
What angels lift
Planks in the flour-loft
Floor of heaven
Shaking down dust?
An angel's cloak
Is cold quicksilver.

In extending the virtuoso techniques of the native tradition, Dafydd set the standard for Welsh poets for the next two centuries.

Aubade[1]

It seemed as if we did not sleep
One wink that night; I was sighing deep.
The cruellest judge in the costliest court
Could not condemn a night so short.
We had the light out, but I know,
Each time I turned, a radiant glow
Suffused the room, and shining snow

1. The *aubade* or dawn song is a genre of love lyric with a long European tradition, in which two lovers lament the necessity of parting at dawn. Chaucer uses the aubade, as later do Shakespeare (in *Romeo and Juliet*) and John Donne in *The Sun Rising*.

Alit from Heaven's candle-fires
Illuminated our desires.

But the last time I held her, strong,
Excited, closest, very long,
Something started going wrong.
The edge of dawn's despotic veil
Showed at the eastern window-pale
And there it was,—the morning light!
Gwen[2] was seized with a fearful fright,
Became an apparition, cried,
"Get up, go now with God, go hide!

"Love is a salt, a gall, a rue,
A vinegar-vintage. *Dos y Ddw,*
Vaya con Dios,[3] quickly, too!"
"Ah, not yet, never yet, my love;
The stars and moon still shine above."
"Then why do the raucous ravens talk
With such a loud insistent squawk?"
"Crows always cry like that, when fleas
Nibble their ankles, nip their knees."

"And why do the dogs yip, yammer, yell?"
"They think they've caught a fox's smell."
"Poet, the wisdom of a fool
Offers poor counsel as a rule.
Open the door, open it wide
As fast as you can, and leap outside.
The dogs are fierce when they get untied."
"The woods are only a bound from here,
And I can outjump a deer, my dear!"

"But tell me, best beloved of men,
Will you come again? Will you come again?"
"Gwen, you know I'm your nightingale,
And I'll be with you, without fail,
When the cloud is cloak, and the dark is sky,
And when the night comes, so will I."

One Saving Place

What wooer ever walked through frost and snow,
Through rain and wind, as I in sorrow?
My two feet took me to a tryst in Meirch[1]
No luck; I swam and waded the Eleirch,
No golden loveliness, no glimpse of her;

2. Along with Morvith and Dovekie, a woman's name which recurs in many of Dafydd's love poems.
3. "Go with God"; this Spanish phrase represents license, on the part of the translator, in the spirit of Dafydd's playfulness.
1. This and other Welsh place names are listed by Dafydd in his account of his search for his beloved, Morvith.

Night or day, I came no nearer
Except in Bleddyn's arbors, where I sighed
When she refused me, as she did beside
Maesalga's murmuring water-tide.
I crossed the river, Bergul, and went on
Beyond its threatening voices; I have gone
Through the mountain-pass of Meibion,
Came to Camallt, dark in my despair,
For one vision of her golden hair.
All for nothing. I've looked down from Rhiw,
All for nothing but a valley view,
Kept on going, on my journey through
Cyfylfaen's gorge, with rock and boulder,
Where I had thought to ermine-cloak her shoulder.
Never; not here, there, thither, thence,
Could I ever find her presence.
Eagerly on summer days I'd go
Brushing my way through Cwcwll hollow,
Never stopped, continued, skirting
Gastell Gwrgan and its ring
Where the red-winged blackbirds sing,
Tramped across fields where goslings feed
Below the cat-tail and the reed.
I have limped my way, a weary hound,
In shadow of the walls that bound
Adail Heilyn's broken ground.
I have hidden, like a friar,
In Ifor's Court, among the choir,
Sought to seek my sweet one there,
But there was no sign of her.
On both sides of Nant-y-glo
There's no vale, no valley, no
Stick or stump where I failed to go,
Only Gwynn of the Mist for guide,
Without Ovid[2] at my side.

Gwenn-y-Talwrn!—there I found
My hand close on hers, on ground
Where no grass was ever green,
Where not even a shrub was seen,
There at last I made the bed
For my Morvith,[3] my moon-maid,
Underneath the dark leaf-cloak
Woven by saplings of an oak.
Bitter, if a man must move
On his journeys without love.

2. See introduction to Dafydd for Dafydd's indebtedness to the Roman love poet.

3. The lady most frequently mentioned in Dafydd's love poems, apparently married.

Bitter, if soul's pilgrimage
Must be like the body's rage,
Must go down the desolate road
Midway through the darkling wood.

Tale of a Wayside Inn

With one servant, I went down
To a sportive sort of town
Where a Welshman might secure
Comely welcome, and pleasure.
There we found the book to sign
In the inn, and ordered wine.

But whatever did I see
But the loveliest lady
Blooming beautiful and bright,
Blossom stemming from sunlight,
Graceful as the gossamer.
I said, "Let me banquet her!"
Feasting's a fine way, it seems,
For fulfilling young men's dreams.

So, unshy, she took her seat
At my side, and we did eat,
Sipped our wine, and smiled and dallied
Like a man and maid, new-married.
Bold I was, but whispering,
And the others heard nothing.

Troth and tryst we pledged, to keep
When the others were asleep.
I should find my way, and come
Through the darkness to her room.
Love would haul my steps aright
Down the hallways of the night;
Love would steer my steps,—alas,

This was not what came to pass.
For, by some outrageous miss,
What I got was not a kiss,
But a stubble-whiskered cheek
And a triple whiskey-reek,
Not one Englishman, but three,
(What a Holy Trinity!)
Diccon, 'Enry, Jerk-off Jack,
Each one pillowed on his pack.

One of them let out a yell,
"What's that thing I think I smell?
There's a Welshman must have hid

In the closet or under t' bed,
Come to cut our throats with knives,
Guard your wallets and your lives,
They're all thieves, beyond all doubt,
Throw the bloody bugger out!"

None too nimble for my need,
First I found how shins will bleed
When you bark them in your haste
On a stool that's been misplaced
By some ostler-stupid fool,
Then the sawney of a stool
Squealed its pig-stuck tattle-tale
After my departing trail.

By good luck, I never got
Wet-foot from the chamber-pot.
That was all I saved myself,
Knocked my noggin on a shelf,
Overturned the table-trestles,
Down came all the pans and kettles.
As I dove to outer dark,
All the dogs began to bark.

Asses bray, and scullions rouse
Every sleeper in the house.
I could hear the hunt come round me,
Scowl-faced scoundrels, till they found me.
I could feel their stones and sticks,
So I clasped my crucifix,
Jesu, Jesu, Jesu dear,
Don't let people catch me here!

Since my prayer was strong, I came
Through the mercy of His name
Safely to my room at last,
All my perils over-passed.
No girl's love to ease my plight,
Only God's that dreadful night,
To the saints be brought the praise,
And the Good Lord mend my wicked ways.

The Winter

Across North Wales
The snowflakes wander,
A swarm of white bees.
Over the woods
A cold veil lies.
A load of chalk
Bows down the trees.

No undergrowth
Without its wool,
No field unsheeted;
No path is left
Through any field;
On every stump
White flour is milled.

Will someone tell me
What angels lift
Planks in the flour-loft
Floor of heaven
Shaking down dust?
An angel's cloak
Is cold quicksilver.

And here below
The big drifts blow,
Blow and billow
Across the heather
Like swollen bellies.
The frozen foam
Falls in fleeces.

Out of my house
I will not stir
For any girl
To have my coat
Look like a miller's
Or stuck with feathers
Of eider down.
What a great fall
Lies on my country!
A wide wall, stretching
One sea to the other,
Greater and graver
Than the sea's graveyard.
When will rain come?

The Ruin

Nothing but a hovel now
Between moorland and meadow,
Once the owners saw in you
A comely cottage, bright, new,
Now roof, rafters, ridge-pole, all
Broken down by a broken wall.

A day of delight was once there
For me, long ago, no care
When I had a glimpse of her

Fair in an ingle-corner.
Beside each other we lay
In the delight of that day.

Her forearm, snowflake-lovely,
Softly white, pillowing me,
proferred a pleasant pattern
For me to give in my turn,
And that was our blessing for
The new-cut lintel and door.

"Now the wild wind, wailing by,
Crashes with curse and with cry
Against my stones, a tempest
Born and bred in the East,
Or south ram-batterers break
The shelter that folk forsake."

Life is illusion and grief;
A tile whirls off, as a leaf
Or a lath goes sailing, high
In the keening of kite-kill cry.
Could it be, our couch once stood
Sturdily under that wood?

"Pillar and post, it would seem
Now you are less than a dream.
Are you that, or only the lost
Wreck of a riddle, rune-ghost?"

"Dafydd, the cross on their graves
Marks what little it saves,
Says, *They did well in their lives*."

MIDDLE SCOTS POETS

In the late fifteenth and early sixteenth centuries, Scotland enjoyed a brief flowering of poetry centered in a sophisticated court society. Relations with England were fraught with irony, marked, on the one hand, by royal alliance (James IV married Margaret Tudor, daughter of England's Henry VII in 1503) and on the other by disastrous warfare (James IV also, in alliance with France, invaded England and perished with most of the Scottish nobility at the Battle of Flodden in 1513). The poets of this period have been variously known as the "Scottish Chaucerians," the "Middle Scots Poets," and the "Makars"—each term privileging a significant, though only partial, aspect of their work. The first conveys the debt that William Dunbar, Robert Henryson, and Gavin Douglas (to name the three most famous) owed to Chaucer's subject matter, rhetorical style, and techniques of parody. The second suggests their equal debt to a native Scottish tradition, which includes such overtly nationalist works as Barbour's *Bruce* and Blind Harry's *Wallace*. The best term to describe these poets is perhaps the one used by Dunbar himself—"Makars" (makers)—for it suggests their powerful and self-conscious artistry.

William Dunbar

Of all the Makars, Dunbar is the greatest virtuoso, intoxicated with language, whether it be the elevated vocabulary borrowed from Latin, or the Germanic diction of alliterative poetry, whose tradition was kept alive in Scotland a century after it had died out in England. He was versatile in his choice of genres, writing occasional poems (such as an allegory in celebration of the marriage of James IV and Princess Margaret), divine poems, and parodies such as *The Treatise of the Two Married Women and the Widow*, a bawdy satire on the morals of court ladies written in the traditional alliterative long line. Included here are a meditation on death (*Lament for the Makars*), an Easter hymn (*Done Is a Battell*) and a parody of the courtly genre of the *chanson d'aventure* (*In Secreit Place This Hyndir Nycht*).

Lament for the Makars[1]

I that in heill° wes° and gladnes — *health / was*
Am trublit now with gret seiknes
And feblit with infermite:
Timor mortis conturbat me.[2]

Our plesance heir is all vane glory,
This fals warld is bot transitory,
The flesche is brukle,° the Fend° is sle:° — *frail / Devil / sly*
Timor mortis conturbat me.

The stait of man dois change and vary,
Now sound, now seik, now blith, now sary,
Now dansand mery, now like to dee:° — *die*
Timor mortis conturbat me.

No stait in erd° heir standis sickir;° — *on earth / secure*
As with the wynd wavis the wickir,
Wavis this warldis vanite:
Timor mortis conturbat me.

On to the ded gois all estatis,
Princis, prelotis,° and potestatis,° — *prelates / rulers*
Baith riche and pur of al degre:
Timor mortis conturbat me.

He takis the knychtis° in to feild,° — *knights / the field*
Anarmit° under helme and scheild; armed — *armed*
Victour he is at all mellie:° — *battles*
Timor mortis conturbat me.

1. This poem reflects the late medieval fascination with death. The speaker wistfully observes that beautiful ladies, brave knights, and wise clerks have had their lives cut short but gives most of his attention to poets. He lists 23 of these—three English (Chaucer, Gower, and Lydgate) and 20 Scots, only half of whom modern scholars can identify. Since Death has taken all his "brothers," he regards himself as next and resolves to prepare himself for the next world. The poem was printed in 1508 by Walter Chepman and Andrew Myllar, who introduced the printing press to Scotland.

2. Fear of death shakes me (from the liturgical Office of the Dead).

That strang unmercifull tyrand
Takis, on the moderis° breist sowkand,° *mother's / sucking*
The bab full of benignite:
Timor mortis conturbat me.

He takis the campion° in the stour,° *champion / conflict*
The capitane closit in the tour,
The lady in bour° full of bewte: *bower*
Timor mortis conturbat me.

He sparis no lord for his piscence,° *power*
Na clerk for his intelligence;
His awfull strak° may no man fle: *stroke*
Timor mortis conturbat me.

Art magicianis and astrologgis,
Rethoris,° logicianis and theologgis, *rhetoricians*
Thame helpis no conclusionis sle:° *clever*
Timor mortis conturbat me.

In medicyne the most practicianis,
Lechis,° surrigianis,° and phisicianis, *doctors / surgeons*
Thame self fra ded° may not supple:° *death / deliver*
Timor mortis conturbat me.

I se that makaris° amang the laif° *poets / remainder*
Playis heir ther pageant, syne gois to graif;° *grave*
Sparit° is nocht ther faculte: *spared*
Timor mortis conturbat me.

He hes done petuously devour
The noble Chaucer of makaris flour,° *flower of poets*
The Monk of Bery,[3] and Gower, all thre:
Timor mortis conturbat me.

The gude Syr Hew of Eglintoun,[4]
And eik Heryot, and Wyntoun,[5]
He hes tane out of this cuntre:
Timor mortis conturbat me.

That scorpion fell° hes done infek° *fierce / infect*
Maister Johne Clerk and James Afflek[6]
Fra ballat making and tragidie:
Timor mortis conturbat me.

Holland and Barbour[7] he hes berevit;
Allace,° that he nocht with us levit *alas*

3. John Lydgate, monk of Bury St. Edmunds, a minor poet who was an imitator of Chaucer. He also used the "*timor mortis*" refrain in a poem on the same subject.
4. Brother-in-law of Robert II and not otherwise known as a poet.
5. Andrew of Wyntoun, author of the *Oryginale Chronykil of Scotland*.
6. These two are unknown, as are the other poets in this list not identified.
7. Sir Richard Holland, author of the allegorical *Buke of the Howlat* (c. 1450), and John Barbour, author of the patriotic *Actes and Life . . . of Robert Bruce* (1376).

Schir Mungo Lokert of the Le:[8]
Timor mortis conturbat me.

Clerk of Tranent eik he hes tane,
That maid the Anteris° of Gawane; *adventures*
Schir Gilbert Hay endit hes he:[9]
Timor mortis conturbat me.

He hes Blind Hary and Sandy Traill
Slaine with his schour° of mortall haill, *shower*
Quhilk Patrik Johnestoun[1] myght nocht fle:
Timor mortis conturbat me.

He hes reft° Merseir his endite° *taken from / talent*
That did in luf so lifly° write, *in a lively manner*
So schort, so quyk, of sentence hie:
Timor mortis conturbat me.

He hes tane Roull of Aberdene
And gentill Roull of Corstorphin;
Two bettir fallowis did no man se:
Timor mortis conturbat me.

In Dunfermelyne he hes done roune° *held conversation*
With Maister Robert Henrisoun.[2]
Schir Johne the Ros enbrast° hes he: *embraced*
Timor mortis conturbat me.

And he hes now tane last of aw
Gud gentill Stobo and Quintyne Schaw,[3]
Of quham all wichtis hes pete:[4]
Timor mortis conturbat me.

Gud Maister Walter Kennedy[5]
In° poynt of dede° lyis veraly;° *on / death / truly*
Gret reuth° it wer that so suld be: *pity*
Timor mortis conturbat me.

Sen he hes all my brether tane
He will nocht lat me lif alane;
On forse° I man his nyxt pray be: *of necessity*
Timor mortis conturbat me.

Sen for the deid remeid° is none, *remedy*
Best is that we for dede dispone° *prepare*
Eftir our deid that lif may we:
Timor mortis conturbat me.

8. This Scotsman (d. 1489?) is not otherwise known as a poet.
9. The "clerk of Tranent" is unknown, but Arthurian romances focusing on Gawain were popular in Scotland; Sir Gilbert Hay (d. 1456) translated the poem *The Buik of Alexander* from French.
1. Blind Harry is credited with writing the Scots epic *Wallace* (c. 1475); Patrick Johnstoune was a producer of stage entertainments at court in the late 1400s.
2. Henryson was a major Middle Scots poet; see his *Robene and Makyne*, page 580.
3. John Reid, known as Stobo, was priest and secretary to James II, James III, and James IV; Schaw was a minor Scots poet.
4. On whom all people have pity.
5. Known for his *Flyting* (poem of ritual insult) with Dunbar.

Done Is a Battell[1]

Done is a battell on° the dragon blak, *with*
Our campioun° Chryst confountet hes his force; *champion*
The yettis° of hell ar brokin with a crak, *gates*
The signe triumphall rasit is of the croce,° *cross*
The divillis trymmillis° with hiddous voce, *trembles*
The saulis° ar borrowit° and to the blis can go, *souls / redeemed*
Chryst with his blud our ransonis dois indoce:° *endorse*
Surrexit dominus de sepulchro.[2]

Dungin° is the deidly dragon Lucifer, *beaten*
The crewall° serpent with the mortall stang,° *cruel / sting*
The auld kene tegir with his teith on char° *ajar*
Quhilk° in a wait hes lyne° for us so lang, *which / lain*
Thinking to grip us in his clowis strang:
The mercifull lord wald° nocht that it wer so, *would*
He maid him for to felye° of that fang:° *fail / booty*
Surrexit dominus de sepulchro.

He for our saik that sufferit to be slane
And lyk a lamb in sacrifice wes dicht,° *prepared*
Is lyk a lyone° rissin up agane, *lion*
And as a gyane raxit him on hicht.[3]
Sprungin° is Aurora radius° and bricht, *arisen / radiant*
On loft° is gone the glorius Appollo,[4] *aloft*
The blisfull day depairtit° fro the nycht: *separated*
Surrexit dominus de sepulchro.

The grit victour agane is rissin on hicht
That for our querrell to the deth wes woundit;
The sone that wox° all paill now schynis bricht, *became*
And, dirknes clerit, our fayth is now refoundit:° *reestablished*
The knell of mercy fra the hevin is soundit,[5]
The Cristin ar deliverit of thair wo,
The Jowis° and thair errour ar confoundit: *Jews*
Surrexit dominus de sepulchro.

The fo is chasit, the battell is done ceis,° *ceased*
The presone brokin, the jevellouris fleit and flemit,[6]
The weir° is gon, confermit is the peis,° *war / peace*
The fetteris lowsit° and the dungeoun temit,° *loosed / emptied*
The ransoun maid, the presoneris° redemit,° *prisoners / redeemed*

1. This Easter hymn heroically portrays Christ's Resurrection as a battle with the devil, drawing on the account of the harrowing of hell in the apocryphal Gospel of Nicodemus, in which Christ journeys to hell to release worthy souls who had been born before his coming. It gains much of its power from the juxtaposition of alliterative diction from the Scots tradition with Latinate vocabulary. As in the *Lament for the Makars*, the Latin refrain fits within the overall English rhyme scheme.
2. The Lord is risen from the tomb. From the opening of the service for matins on Easter Sunday.
3. And like a giant stretched himself on high. A reference to Samson, who in bearing off the gates of Gaza was seen as a type of Christ breaking the gates of hell.
4. Christ, the sun (and Son) of righteousness, is identified with Apollo, the sun god, which explains the reference to Aurora, goddess of the dawn.
5. An allusion to the ringing of the bells on Easter morning.
6. The prison broken, the jailers fled and banished.

The feild is win°, ourcummin° is the fo, — *won / overcome*
Dispulit° of the tresur that he yemit:° — *despoiled / kept*
Surrexit dominus de sepulchro.

In Secreit Place This Hyndir Nycht[1]

In secreit place this hyndir° nycht — *last*
I hard ane beyrne° say till ane bricht,° — *man / fair lady*
"My huny, my hart, my hoip, my heill,[2]
I have bene lang° your luifar° leill° — *long / lover / loyal*
And can of yow get confort nane:° — *none*
How lang will ye with danger deill?[3]
Ye brek my hart, my bony ane."° — *pretty one*

His bony beird was kemmit and croppit,[4]
Bot all with cale° it was bedroppit,° — *soup / smeared*
And he wes townysche, peirt and gukit.[5]
He clappit fast, he kist and chukkit[6]
As with the glaikis° he wer ouirgane;° — *lust / overcome*
Yit be his feirris° he wald have fukkit: — *manner*
"Ye brek my hart, my bony ane."

Quod he, "My hairt, sweit° as the hunye, — *sweet*
Sen that I borne wes of my mynnye° — *mother*
I never wowit° weycht° bot yow; — *wooed / creature*
My wambe° is of your luif sa fow° — *belly / full*
That as ane gaist° I glour° and grane,° — *ghost / glower / groan*
I trymble° sa, ye will not trow:° — *tremble / believe*
Ye brek my hart, my bony ane."

"Tehe,"° quod scho, and gaif ane gawfe;° — *Teehee / guffaw*
"Be still my tuchan[7] and my calfe,
My new spanit howffing fra the sowk,[8]
And all the blythnes° of my bowk;° — *joy / body*
My sweit swanking,° saif yow allane — *fine fellow*
Na leid° I luiffit° all this owk:° — *no man / loved / week*
Full leifis° me° your graceles gane."° — *dear / to me / face*

Quod he, "My claver° and my curldodie,° — *clover / a plant*
My huny soppis, my sweit possodie,° — *sheep's head broth*
Be not oure bosteous° to your billie,° — *rough / sweetheart*
Be warme hairtit° and not evill willie;° — *hearted / ill-willed*
Your heylis quhyt as quhalis bane,[9]

1. This comic account of the wooing of a kitchen maid by a boorish man parodies the *chanson d'aventure*, a genre in which the speaker overhears a dialogue between two lovers. Dunbar undercuts the poem's courtly language, which he has used seriously elsewhere, with overtly sexual references. In addition to words familiar to modern readers, the poem features terms of endearment from colloquial Scots which have long since been lost.
2. My honey, my heart, my hope, my salvation.
3. Ladies were expected to be "dangerous" (reluctant) in a courtship situation.
4. His handsome beard was combed and trimmed.
5. And he was townish (uncourtly), pert, and foolish.
6. He fondled fast, kissed, and chucked her under the chin.
7. Calf skin stuffed with straw, to encourage a cow to give milk.
8. My clumsy fellow newly weaned from nursing.
9. Your neck white as whale's bone; a common alliterative phrase in the conventional love poetry.

Garris ryis° on loft my quhillelillie:° *makes rise / penis*
Ye brek my hart, my bony ane."
Quod scho, "My clype, my unspaynit gyane[1]
With moderis° mylk yit in your mychane,° *mother's / mouth*
My belly huddrun,° my swete hurle bawsy,[2] *big-bellied glutton*
My huny gukkis,° my slawsy gawsy, *sweet fool*
Your musing waild perse° ane hart of stane: *would pierce*
Tak gud confort, my grit heidit° slawsy, *great-headed*
Full leifis me your graceles gane."

Quod he, "My kid, my capirculyoun,° *woodgrouse*
My bony baib° with the ruch° brylyoun, *babe / rough*
My tendir gyrle, my wallie gowdye,° *pretty goldfinch*
My tyrlie myrlie, my crowdie mowdie,° *milky porridge*
Quhone° that oure mouthis dois meit° at ane *when / do meet*
My stang dois storkyn with your towdie:[3]
Ye brek my hairt, my bony ane."

Quod scho, "Now tak me be the hand,
Welcum, my golk° of Marie° land, *cuckoo / fairy*
My chirrie and my maikles munyoun,[4]
My sowklar° sweit as ony unyoun,° *suckling / any onion*
My strumill stirk yit new to spane,[5]
I am applyit° to your opunyoun:° *inclined / opinion*
I luif rycht weill° your graceles gane." *love right well*

He gaiff to hir ane apill rubye;° *apple red*
Quod scho, "Gramercye,° my sweit cowhubye."° *thanks / fool*
And thai tway to ane play began
Quhilk° men dois call the dery dan,[6] *which*
Quhill° that thair myrthis° met baythe in ane: *while / pleasure*
"Wo is me," quod scho, "Quhair will ye,° man? *where will you go*
Best now I luif° that graceles gane." *love*

Robert Henryson

We know little about Robert Henryson, although he is said to have been a schoolmaster at the town of Dumferline, and Dunbar implies that he was dead by 1506, when he mentions him in the *Lament for the Makars*. Unlike Dunbar, he wrote not for the Scottish court but for the literate middle class, which gives his poetry a more moralistic and less witty tone. Henryson is a "Scottish Chaucerian" with a somber cast, for his major work, the *Testament of Crisseid*, picks up where Chaucer's great romance, *Troilus and Criseide*, leaves off, depicting the faithless heroine as punished with leprosy, achieving a kind of redemption, and writing her will. *Robene and Makyne*, however, is a much more lighthearted poem. Like Dunbar's *In*

1. Said she, "My big soft fellow, my unweaned giant."
2. An obscure term of endearment, as are several other phrases in the following lines.
3. My pole does stiffen by your thing.
4. My cherry and my matchless darling.
5. My stumbling bullock still newly weaned.
6. A dance (i.e., copulation).

Secreit Place, it is a *chanson d'aventure* which parodies the language of courtly love, though its shepherd and shepherdess are far more appealing than Dunbar's grimy lovers. The roles are comically reversed, with the shepherdess Makyne, offering to instruct the shepherd Robene in the "ABCs" of love's lore, while he, in his ignorance, resists. After Robene dutifully departs with his sheep, he has regrets and returns, only to have Makyne tell him that he has delayed too long. She states the poem's moral, *carpe diem:*

> The man that will nocht quhen he may
> Sall haif nocht quhen he wald.

Robyn is thus left to repeat in vain courtly love sentiments that he learned from her.

Robene and Makyne[1]

Robene sat on gud grene hill
Kepand° a flok of fe;° *keeping / sheep*
Mirry Makyne said him till:° *to*
"Robene, thow rew° on me! *have pity*
I haif the luvit lowd and still[2]
Thir yeiris° two or thre; *these years*
My dule in dern bot gif thow dill,[3]
Dowtless but dreid° I de." *surely*
Robene ansuerit: "Be the Rude,° *by the Cross*
Nathing of lufe I knaw,
Bot keipis my scheip under yone° wude— *yonder*
Lo quhair thay raik on raw![4]
Quhat° hes marrit° the in thy mude,° *what / harmed / mind*
Makyne, to me thow schaw:° *declare*
Or quhat is lufe, or to be lude?° *loved*
Fane° wald I leir° that law." *gladly / learn*

"At luvis lair gife thow will leir,[5]
Tak thair ane ABC:
Be heynd, courtas and fair of feir,[6]
Wyse, hardy° and fre;° *brave / generous*
So that no denger° do the deir,° *disdain / do harm*
Quhat dule in dern thow dre,[7]
Preiss° the with pane at all poweir°— *strive / effort*
Be patient and previe."° *discreet*

Robene anserit hir agane:
"I wait° nocht quhat is luve, *know*
Bot I haif mervell° in certane *wonder*
Quhat makis the this wanrufe;° *restless*
The weddir is fair and I am fane,° *happy*

1. In Scots, as in Middle English poetry, Makyn (or Malkin) was a conventional name for a rustic girl, as Robin was for a boy.
2. I have loved thee openly and secretly.
3. Unless you relieve my secret pain.
4. See how they wander afield!
5. Of love's learning if you would learn.
6. Be gentle, courteous, and fair of manners (these and the qualities that follow are conventional attributes of the courtly lover; cf. Chaucer's *Nun's Priest's Tale*, page 420).
7. What sorrow in secret you suffer.

My scheip gois haill aboif;[8]
And we wald play° us in this plane° *disport / valley*
Thay wald us bayth reproif."

"Robene, tak tent° unto my taill,° *heed / advice*
And wirk° all as I reid°, *do / advise*
And thow sall haif my hairt all haill,° *entirely*
Eik° and my madinheid: *also*
Sen God sendis bute° for baill° *cure / pain*
And for murnyng° remeid,° *sorrow / remedy*
I dern with the bot gif I daill,[9]
Dowtles I am bot deid.[1]

"Makyne, tomorne this ilka° tyde,° *same / time*
And° ye will meit me heir, *if*
Peraventure my scheip ma gang besyd° *fend for themselves*
Quhill we haif liggit full neir[2]—
Bot mawgre haif I and I byd,[3]
Fra° thay begin to steir;° *when / stray*
Quhat lyis on hairt° I will nocht hyd;° *lies in my heart / not*
Makyn, than mak gud cheir."
"Robene, thow reivis° me roif° and rest— *rob / tranquility*
I luve bot the allone."
"Makyne, adew; the sone gois west,
The day is neir-hand gone."
"Robene, in dule° I am so drest° *to pain / resigned*
That lufe wil be my bone."° *bane*
"Ga lufe, Makyne, quhairever thow list,[4]
For lemman° I lue° none." *lover / love*

"Robene, I stand in sic a styll;° *such a plight*
I sicht°—and that full sair."° *sigh / painfully*
"Makyne, I haif bene heir this quhyle;° *while*
At hame God gif I wair![5]
"My huny Robene, talk ane quhill,° *a while*
Gif thow will do na mair."
"Makyne, sum uthir man begyle,[6]
For hamewart° I will fair."° *homeward / go*

Robene on his wayis went
Als licht as leif of tre;[7]
Mawkin murnit° in hir intent *mourned*
And trowd° him nevir to se;° *expected / see*
Robene brayd attour the bent;[8]

8. Are all around me on this hill.
9. Unless in secret I deal (i.e., have sex) with you.
1. Conventionally, the courtly lover threatens to die unless his lady takes pity on him.
2. While we have lain nearby.
3. But yet I am uneasy if I wait.
4. Go love, Makyn, wherever you wish.
5. I wish to God I were at home!
6. Seduce some other man.
7. As light as a leaf on a tree.
8. Bounded across the field.

Than Mawkyne cryit on hie:° *loudly*
"Now ma thow sing, for I am schent!° *ruined*
Quhat alis° lufe at me?" *ails*

Mawkyne went hame withowttin faill;
Full wery eftir cowth weip:[9]
Than Robene in a ful fair daill° *very neat order*
Assemblit all his scheip.
Be that, sum pairte of Mawkynis aill° *pain*
Outthrow his hairt cowd creip;[1]
He fallowit fast thair till assaill,[2]
And till hir tuke gude keip.° *paid good heed*

"Abyd, abyd, thow fair Makyne!
A word for ony thing!
For all my luve it sal be thyne,
Withowttin depairting.° *wholly*
All haill° thy harte for till haif myne *whole*
Is all my cuvating;
My scheip tomorne quhill houris nyne° *until nine o'clock*
Will neid of no keiping."

"Robene, thow hes hard° soung and say *hast heard*
In gestis° and storeis auld, *legends*
The man that will nocht quhen° he may *when*
Sall haif nocht quhen he wald.° *would*
I pray to Jesu every day
Mot eik thair cairis cauld[3]
That first preiss° with the to play *strives*
Be firth,° forrest or fawld."° *wood / sheepfold*

"Makyne, the nicht° is soft and dry, *night*
The wedder° is warme and fair, *weather*
And the grene woid° rycht° neir us by *wood / right*
To walk attour° allquhair;° *across / everywhere*
Thair ma na janglour[4] us espy,
That is to lufe contrair;
Thairin, Makyne, bath ye and I
Unsene we ma repair."

"Robene, that warld is all away
And quyt° brocht° till ane end, *entirely / brought*
And nevir agane thairto perfay,° *by my faith*
Sall it be as thow wend:° *think*
For of my pane thow maid it play,[5]
And all in vane I spend:° *made an effort*
As thow hes done, sa sall I say:
Murne° on! I think to mend." *grieve*

9. Wearily afterward wept.
1. Entered his heart.
2. He went back to accost her there.
3. That he might make them too suffer.
4. Gossip; "janglours" were a stock threat to courtly lovers.
5. For you made fun of my pain.

"Mawkyne, the howp° of all my heill,°[6] — *hope / salvation*
My hairt on the° is sett, — *thee*
And evirmair to the be leill,° — *loyal*
Quhill I may leif but lett;[7]
Nevir to faill—as utheris feill—
Quhat grace° that evir I gett." — *favor*
"Robene, with the I will nocht deill;[8]
Adew!° For thus we mett." — *adieu*
Malkyne went hame blyth annewche° — *blithe enough*
Attour the holttis hair,°[9]
Robene murnit, and Malkyne lewche,° — *laughed*
Scho sang,° he sichit sair°— — *sang / sighed sorely*
And so left him bayth wo° and wrewche,° — *sad / troubled*
In dolour° and in cair, — *sorrow*
Kepand his hird under a huche,° — *hovel*
Amangis° the holtis hair. — *among*

[END OF MIDDLE SCOTS POETS]

LATE MEDIEVAL ALLEGORY

The end of the Middle Ages saw an extraordinary flowering of allegory, a literary mode that at its simplest is a narrative in which a symbolic meaning runs parallel to a literal one, but remains distinct from it. Gone, for the most part, was the elaborate multileved allegory based on biblical exegesis that had held sway in earlier centuries, to be replaced by the more transparent personification allegory, which embodies an abstract quality in a person or a thing, often used to convey an erotic or spiritual quest, or a psychological crisis.

This volume includes passages from the greatest English allegory of the fourteenth century, William Langland's *Piers Plowman,* which uses personification as well as other types of allegory to convey the quest of its hero and its critique of society. The poem's dreamer/narrator "Will" stands for the errant human will, as well as the author's nickname, and the flamboyant Lady Meed stands for monetary reward, whether just or unjust. Borrowing techniques from contemporary sermons, Langland makes many of his personifications grotesquely realistic. When Gluttony goes to confess his sin to Repentance, for instance, he is portrayed as a fourteenth-century churl who is lured into a tavern, then eats and drinks so much that he vomits, and has to be carried home to bed.

By the fifteenth century, when the examples of allegory included in this section were written, personification allegory was even more prominent. Charles d'Orléans imagines himself as a lover in conflict with Fortune and Disdain. The hero of *Mankind* finds himself caught between Mercy and three personifications of novelty—Nowadays, Newguise, and Nought—until he chooses the path of redemption. Christine de Pizan's protagonist, dismayed by the force of misogynist tradition, receives comfort from three allegorical ladies: Reason, Rectitude, and Justice. Two of these writers use the common allegorical image of the building to clarify their points, Charles d'Orléans portraying his own heart as a castle under siege, and Christine constructing a fortified city to honor women.

6. Robene uses the religious metaphors of courtly love.
7. Unceasingly, while I live.
8. Robene, I will not have dealings (i.e., sex) with you.
9. Across the woods gray (a traditional alliterative phrase).

Allegory, with its tendency to abstraction, has often been seen as supporting the status quo. Christine's *City of Ladies* and *Mankind,* however, use allegory in more complex and sometimes subversive ways, as had *Piers Plowman* when criticizing the corruption of the clergy. Christine's protagonist learns to take pride in the achievements of women; her city offers a systematic reinterpretation of women's stories. And while Mankind finally rejects the temptations of Nowadays, Newguise, and Nought, these exuberant figures threaten to steal the show. However one chooses to read these particular texts, personification allegory as a mode proved flexible enough to respond to the social changes of the later Middle Ages and to persist into the Renaissance and Reformation. Its influence can be seen in Butler's *Pilgrim's Progress*, Spenser's *Faerie Queene*, and Shakespeare's plays—most memorably in his villains.

Charles d'Orléans

1394–1465

No other writer of medieval England even approaches the glamour, wealth, and culture that Charles, Duke of Orléans experienced for much of his life. A prince of the French royal house, Charles d'Orléans was superbly educated but also trained in the chivalric arts of battle. Practicing these, Charles was captured at the Battle of Agincourt in 1415 and spent the next twenty-five years of his life as both an aristocratic guest and an enemy prisoner of a series of English nobles, as his ransom and release were painfully negotiated. In these years, he acquired very good but never fully colloquial English; and he certainly read works by Chaucer and other English writers, in addition to his wide reading in Latin, French, and Italian. He finally returned home in 1440, remarried, and rebuilt his fortunes.

In his long exile, Charles cast himself as a prisoner of Fortune, an allegorical figure he inherited from Boethius's late-classical *Consolation of Philosophy*. He adapted the figure of Fortune in lyrics that sometimes hint at his own life, yet equally play on conventions of courtly love, such as the allegorical conceit of the heart as a besieged fortress assailed by the fire of love, or the idea of losing his lady in a game of chess. Charles wrote his fine poems both in English and French, using traditional set forms, especially the ballade and roundel. They circle around love, but reach in many further directions. His frequent theme of separation from a beloved but unidentified lady resonates with other kinds of isolation—political, national, economic, even linguistic—that also affected Charles's life. And like much poetry in established forms, Charles's lyrics invite the reader to delight in their playful wit and technical mastery as well as their message.

Ballade 26[1]

Brennyng Desire to see my fayre maystres° *mistress*
Hath newe assaylid the nakid, pore loggyng° *lodging*
Of my faynt hert, which drepith° in distres, *languishes*
That in eche where within his fyre brennyng
Hath he so sett that in a gret feryng
Stande y,[2] God wot, lest hit woll not ben queynt° *quenched*
Without thi grace. "O God of Love," y cry,

1. The medieval ballade is a variable form. Here, typically, it repeats a rhyme scheme across its three main stanzas. A fourth, shorter stanza, often called an "envoy," repeats the final rhymes of the earlier stanzas, and marks a turn from earlier themes, or sends the poem off to its addressee. All the stanzas are linked by a common refrain line.
2. So that everywhere inside [my heart] He has so set his fire burning that I stand in great fear.

"Helpe now myn hert, that many helpe hast sent!"
—Thus calle y for yowre socoure° pitously. *aid*

I have asayd with Teeris of Larges° *plentiful tears*
This forto quenche, but all to my felyng,
The werse is hit! This fyre, hit will not cesse
Without elliswhere y have sum relevyng.[3]
I brenne, y brenne! O frendis, come rennyng
And helpe! Alas, this fyre were fro me rent!° *removed from me*
For if thorugh fawt in slouthe of yow y dey,[4]
Ye are in synne and blame, to myn entent!° *opinion*
Thus calle y for yowre socoure pitously.

But what if so y spille° thorugh yowre lacches?° *die / negligence*
I yow biseche but this unsely° thyng: *serious*
That eche of yow do synge for me a messe,° *mass*
And sone in Paradice have y trustyng
Among lovers to se myn hert sittyng
As a gret seynt and martir, for turment
Hath he evene for his trouth and al onewhi,[5]
For which as now in this grevous talent° *state of mind*
Thus calle y for yowre socoure pitously.

What nede y spende more enke° or parchement, *ink*
That fele the crampe of deth myn hert so nyghe° *near*
As thorugh this rageous° fyre which hath me hent?° *fierce / seized*
Thus calle y for yowre socoure pitously.

Ballade 61[1]

Toforne Love[2] have y pleyd at the chesse
To passe the tyme with cursid false Daungere° *disdain*
And kepte eche poynt bi good avysynes[3]
Withouten losse, to that° (as wol ye here) *until*
That Fortune came to strengthyn his matere.
O woo worthe she° that my game[4] ovyrthrew! *a curse on her*
For tane° she hath my lady, welaway! *taken*
That y am matt,[5] this may y se and say,
Without° so be y make[6] a lady newe. *unless*

In my lady lay all my sikirnes,° *security*
For ay at nede hir socoure was me nere[7]
To helpe me in eche trobill or distres,

3. Unless I have help from somewhere else.
4. For if I die through your sin of sloth.
5. For he suffers torment for his loyalty and that entirely unjustly.

1. This ballade, full of dense wordplay, exploits both the figure of Fortune and an allegorical game of chess. The game is played against "Daungere," a courtly-love personification of the lady's distance or disdain. But the game is undone, the board perhaps literally overthrown, when Fortune takes away the Queen piece: the beloved lady herself. The identity of the lady is unknown, and perhaps irrelevant. Charles's first wife died before he turned 15; his second wife died some years before his return to France; and he seems to have had at least ritual love affairs during his English imprisonment.
2. In the presence of (the god of) Love.
3. And held on to each piece with great skill.
4. "Game" here may be both the game of chess and the alternate sense of joy or pleasure.
5. Checkmated, or destroyed.
6. A pawn is made queen if it reaches the far end of the board. "Make" can also mean to choose as a mate.
7. For always in time of need her help was near me.

For all my warde that kepte my lady dere[8]
More then knyght, that is of more powere,
Or Afyn,° pown, or rook (this fynde y trewe) *bishop*
For all my game y lost it have and pley
And all my good, god wot, that on it lay,° *was wagered*
Without so be y make a lady newe.

Not kan y skyfte me° from the sotilnes *escape*
Of seytfull° Fortune, with hir dowbil chere,[9] *deceitful*
That doth eche game so torne and ovyrdresse
That where to drawe not wot y,[1] there or here.
She cometh on me in a so sodeyne gere° *caprice*
That y may not myn harmes lo eschewe.
Mi game is all forcast in suche aray[2]
That in no wise y hit amenden° may, *rectify*
Without so be y make a lady newe.
Fare wel, princesse! yowre losse sore doth me rewe
And evir shall unto myn endyng day,
For shulde y thenke rekewre[3] me now? Nay, nay,
Without so be y make a lady newe!

Roundel 94[1]

Sum tyme y was a poore serviture° *servant*
In Lovys court and had a governaunce,
To crewel Fortune, ful of disseyvaunce,
Dischargid me of my good aventure,[2]

And the ricches that y had undir cure° *in my custody*
Bitook it hoole° to Dethis ordinaunce,°— *wholly / juddment*
Sum tyme y was a poore serviture
In Loveys court and had a governaunce.—

And bad me walke, an ofcast° creature, *outcast*
On the wilde desert of Desperaunce,° *despair*
Where now y dwelle in turment and penaunce
And must unto y dey,° this am y sewre. *until I die*

Svm tyme y was a poore serviture
In Loueys court and had a governaunce,
To crewel Fortune, ful of disseyvaunce,
Dischargid me of my good aventure.

8. For my dear lady (i.e., the queen) kept up my primary defense.
9. Fortune is often depicted smiling on one side of her face, and scowling on the other.
1. Who so twists and reverses each game / That I don't know where to make my move.
2. Put in such utter disarray.
3. To recover myself, to win back the game.
1. The roundel (or rondel) can vary in length, but typically uses only two rhyme sounds, features at least two lines used as a refrain within the poem (see lines 7–8 here), and usually an entire stanza of four lines as a refrain at the end (lines 13–16). The repetition of lines and sounds resists much development of ideas, but helps intensity of expression and, as here, pathos.
2. Was under (Love's) control, / Until cruel Fortune, full of deceit, / Deprived me of my good luck.

Mankind

c. 1464–1479

Mankind is an allegorical drama about the temptation and salvation of a generalized man—at once a laborer with a shovel and a writer with pen and ink. This double figure, named "Mankind," wavers between attachment to a beneficent Mercy and an inclination to figures of vice like Mischief and three personifications of novelty—Nowadays, Newguise (trendy behavior), and Nought. It has been called a "morality play," and grouped with other late-medieval and Tudor dramas like *Everyman* and *The Castle of Perseverance*. While each is quite different, these works do create allegories that explore the inner conflict of one life at a moment of crisis.

Far from the abstract work we might expect from the play's personified characters, *Mankind* is raucous, funny, and often obscene. The play moves between measured descriptions of divine grace, mostly by Mercy, and the blasphemy and disorder of Mischief and his henchmen. Shifting from harmony to carnival and back, *Mankind* mocks a whole range of ideas and institutions (like the church and its message of redemption), yet finally affirms them. Other aspects of the established social order—pomposity, empty learning, legal ritual—are left hilariously shredded. The play works as well as it does exactly because the vices are so funny and attractive, even if Mercy, and Mankind's faith, ultimately triumph over them.

Quite specific local references in *Mankind* suggest that the play, surviving in only one manuscript, was performed between 1464 and 1479, for an audience that would recognize names from around Cambridge and King's Lynn, in the district called East Anglia. References to local

Mankynde: A Postmodern Medieval Musical was adapted by Julie Crosby for the Off-Off-Broadway New York International Fringe Festival, the largest multi-arts festival in North America, in 2004. Here Mischief (Christine Rea) tries to subdue Mercy (Andy Paris), as part of a broadly comic staging of the struggle for the soul of Mankind.

characters, ranging from a Member of Parliament to a tradesman, also contribute a kind of intimacy, and perhaps specific comedy, that would have further engaged the original audience. The ambitious pacing, long speeches, and sometimes swift comic patter of *Mankind* probably required professional players of some sort, though it is unclear whether they were an organized troupe or who paid them. (One moment in the play does involve the collection of money; see lines 457–72.)

Even if he is an allegorical figure, Mankind shows complexity and conflict. He moves from an easy piety to petulance, anger, a frivolity that merges swiftly into despair, and finally contrition. Mercy is more complicated still. Always dignified, in the play's opening scenes, he can also seem long-winded, a bit of a stiff. Mercy's complicated syntax and Latin-derived "aureate" diction invite parody by Newguise and his friends, and presumably aroused complicit laughter by the audience. But we can laugh at things that we still ultimately respect. As a pedantic, sometimes awkward man, Mercy can be funny; as an allegory of one aspect of a Christian God, he can be simultaneously very serious indeed. Mercy's grave dignity is finally what saves Mankind. Some of his speeches have real rhetorical impact, and toward the end of the play they take on the added authority of repeated biblical quotations. Mankind himself moves in and out of such diction (he even writes down a bit of Latin), partly as a measure of whether he's under the influence of Mercy or the vices.

Mankind's faith and agricultural labor are closely linked in the play. This draws on traditional connections of religious virtue and hard work, seen for instance in the episode of Piers sowing his half-acre in *Piers Plowman* (page 451), yet it also recalls the hard work Adam drew on all men as a result of the fall. At the same time, Mankind's easy adoption of urban dress and more urban pleasures reflects the attraction of the cities for common people facing a life of harsh rural labor, especially in areas like East Anglia, where some cities were growing rich from the cloth industry and other trade.

Unlike the biblical plays, allegorical dramas continued to flourish into the Early Modern period. *Mankind* in particular can be seen as part of the background to Early Modern drama, as the play's characters combine allegorical elements with psychological complexity, and its plot veers between low humor and great gravity. A character like the demon Titivillus, and the mortal temptations he offers, echo (though not directly) in Shakespearean villains like Iago in *Othello*, while the more benign personifications of novelty suggest the exuberant and unrepentant Falstaff in *Henry IV, Part I*. The continuing appeal of the play, too, is suggested by a recent New York City production from which we offer an illustration.

The text used here is an "acting edition" by Peter Meredith. It modernizes spellings but retains the original vocabulary.

Mankind

Dramatis Personae

Mercy	Mischief
Newguise	Nowadays
Nought	Mankind
Titivillus	

MERCY The very founder and beginner of our first creation,
Among us sinful wretches he oweth° to be magnified,° *ought / praised*
That for our disobedience he had none indignation
To send his own son to be torn and crucified.
Our obsequious service to him should be applied;
Where° he, was° Lord of all and made all thing of nought, *since / (who) was*
For the sinful sinner to had° him revived, *have*
And for his redemption, set his own son at nought.

It may be said and verified, mankind was dear bought.
By the piteous death of Jesu he had his remedy.
He was purged of his default, that wretchedly had wrought,
By his glorious passion, that blessed lavatory.° *cleansing*
O sovereigns, I beseech you your conditions to rectify,
And with humility and reverence to have a remotion° *turn*
To this blessed prince that our nature doth glorify,
That ye may be participable of his retribution.[1]

I have be° the very mean for your restitution. *been*
Mercy is my name that mourneth for your offence.
Divert not yourself in time of temptation,
That ye may be acceptable to God at your going hence.
The great mercy of God, that is of most pre-eminence,
By [mediation] of our Lady, that is ever abundant
To the sinful creature that will repent his negligence.
I pray God, at your most need, that mercy be your defendant.[2]

In good works I advise you, sovereigns, to be perseverant,° *persevering*
To purify your souls that they be not corrupt,
For your ghostly° enemy will make his avaunt,° *spiritual / boast*
Your good conditions° if he may interrupt. *habits*

O ye sovereigns that sit and ye brethren that stand right up,[3]
Prick° not your felicities in things transitory! *place*
Behold not the earth, but lift your eye up!
See how the head the members daily do magnify.
Who is the head? Forsooth, I shall you certify;
I mean our Saviour, that was likened to a lamb.
And his saints be the members° that daily he doth satisfy *limbs*
With the precious river that runneth from his womb.° *side*

There is none such food, by water nor by land,
So precious, so glorious, so needful to our intent;
For it hath dissolved mankind from the bitter bond
Of the mortal enemy, that venomous serpent—
From the which God preserve you all at the Last Judgment!
For, sickerly,° there shall be a strait° examination *truly / strict*
The corn shall be saved, the chaff shall be brent;°[4] *burnt*
I beseech you heartily, have this premeditation.° *bear this in mind*

MISCHIEF I beseech you heartily, leave your calcination,° *burning*
Leave your chaff, leave your corn, leave your dalliation;° *idle talk*
Your wit is little, your head is mickle;° ye are full of *big*
predication.° *preaching*

But, sir, I pray, this question to clarify:
Mish-mash, driff-draff;[5]

1. That you may share in his reward (i.e., salvation).
2. That mercy will protect you.
3. I.e., the audience. *Sovereigns that sit* are rich masters with seats, while *brethren that stand* are those of lower status who are standing.
4. A common agricultural metaphor, drawn from the Book of Isaiah in the Bible, for the separation of the saved from the damned on the Day of Judgment.
5. Nonsense verse.

Some was corn and some was chaff;
My dame said my name was Raff,
Unshut your lock and take an ha'penny!

MERCY Why come ye hither, brother? Ye were not desired.
MISCHIEF For a winter corn-thresher, sir, I have hired.
And ye said the corn should be saved and the chaff
should be fired,
And he proveth nay, as it sheweth by this verse:

"Corn *servit bredibus*, chaff *horsibus*, straw *firibusque*."[6]

This is as much to say to your lewd° understanding *ignorant*
As: the corn shall serve to° bread at the next baking. *to make*
"Chaff *horsibus, et reliqua*:"[7]
The chaff to horse shall be good provent;° *food*
When a man is for cold° the straw may be brent;° *very cold / burnt*
And so forth, *et cetera*.

MERCY Avoid,° good brother; ye ben culpable *be gone*
To interrupt thus my talking delectable.
MISCHIEF Sir, I have neither horse nor saddle;
Therefore I may not ride.
MERCY Hie you forth° on foot, brother, in God's name! *go away*
MISCHIEF I say, sir, I am come hither to make you game.° *sport*
Yet bade ye me not to go out in the devil's name,
And I will abide.
MERCY

[*At this point, an entire leaf has disappeared from the manuscript. When the text resumes, Mischief has gone, leaving Newguise, Nowadays, and Nought to harass Mercy. Musicians are also present. Newguise and Nowadays are urging Nought to dance.*]

NOWADAYS And how, minstrels, play the common trace!° *dance*
Lay on with thy baleis° till his belly brest!° *stick / burst*

NOUGHT I put case° I break my neck; how then? *suppose*
NEWGUISE I give no force, by St Anne![8]
NOWADAYS Leap about lively! Thou art a wight° man. *nimble*
Let us be merry while we be here.
NOUGHT Shall I break my neck to show you sport?
NOWADAYS Therefore ever beware of thy report.[9]
NOUGHT I beshrew° ye all! Here is a shrewd sort.[1] *curse*
Have thereat, then, with a merry cheer!

Here they dance. MERCY *saith:*

MERCY Do way!° Do way this rule,° sirs, do way! *give up / behavior*
NOWADAYS Do way, good Adam, do way?
This is no part of thy play.
NOUGHT Yes, marry,° I pray you, for I love not this revelling! *indeed*
Come forth, good father, I you pray;

6. Corn serves for bread; chaff serves for horses; straw serves for fires.
7. Chaff for horses, and the rest.
8. Mother of the Virgin Mary.
9. Be careful of your reputation (or, Be careful of what you say).
1. Rascally company.

By a little ye may assay.° *try it*
Anon, off with your clothes, if ye will, pray!
Go to, for I have had a pretty scuttling!° *prancing about*

MERCY Nay, brother, I will not dance.
NEWGUISE If ye will, sir, my brother will make you to prance.
NOWADAYS With all my heart, sir, if I may you advance!
Ye may assay by a little trace.° *dance*
NOUGHT Yea, sir, will ye do well?
Trace not with them, by my counsel,
For I have traced somewhat too fell.° *violently*

I tell it is a narrow space!

But, sir, I trow° of us three I heard you speak. *think*
NEWGUISE Christ's curse had° therefore, for I was in sleep. *(you) had*
NOWADAYS And I had the cup ready in my hand, ready to go to meat;° *dinner*
Therefore, sir, curtly, greet you well.
MERCY Few words, few and well set!
NEWGUISE Sir, it is the new guise and the new jet:° *fashion*
Many words, and shortly set;
This is the new guise, every dell.° *bit*

MERCY Lady,[2] help! How wretches delight in their simple ways!
NOWADAYS Say nought again the new guise nowadays;
Thou shall find us shrews° at all assays *rascals*
Beware, ye may soon lick a buffet!° *take a knock*
MERCY He was well occupied that brought you, brether!° *brothers*
NOUGHT I heard you call Newguise, Nowadays, Nought—all these three together.
If ye say that I lie, I shall make you to slither.
Lo, take you here a trippet!° *trip*

MERCY Say me your names. I know you not.
NEWGUISE Newguise, I.
NOWADAYS I, Nowadays.
NOUGHT I, Nought.
MERCY By Jesu Christ, that me dear bought,[3]
Ye betray many men!
NEWGUISE Betray? Nay, nay, sir, nay, nay!
We make them both fresh and gay.
But of your name, sir I you pray,
That we may you ken.° *know*

MERCY Mercy is my name and my denomination.° *title*
I conceive ye have but a little favour in my communication.

NEWGUISE Ey, ey, your body is full of English Latin,[4]
I am afeard it will brest.° *burst*
"*Pravo te*"[5] quod° the butcher unto me *said*

2. The Virgin Mary.
3. Redeemed me (a reference to Christ's death on the cross to redeem mankind's sins).
4. Newguise makes fun of Mercy's use of "aureate" terms coined from Latin, such as "denomination."
5. I curse you.

When I stole a leg o'mutton.
Ye are a strong cunning clerk.[6]

NOWADAYS I pray you heartily, worshipful clerk,
To have this English made in Latin:
"I have eaten a dishful of curds,
And I have shitten your mouth full of turds."
Now, open your satchel with Latin words,
And say me this in clerical manner.
Also, I have a wife (her name is Rachel)
Betwix her and me was a great battle,
And fain° of you I would hear tell — *gladly*
Who was the most master.

NOUGHT Thy wife Rachel, I dare lay twenty lice!
NOWADAYS Who spake to thee, fool? Thou art not wise!
Go and do that longeth° to thine office: — *belongs*
Osculare fundamentum![7]
NOUGHT Lo, master, lo, here is a pardon belly-met,[8]
It is granted of Pope Pocket:
If ye will put your nose in his wife's socket[9]
Ye shall have forty days of pardon.

MERCY This idle language ye shall repent.
Out of this place I would ye went.
NEWGUISE Go we hence all three, with one assent.
My father is irk° of our eloquence! — *annoyed by*
Therefore, I will no longer tarry.° — *delay*
God bring you, master, and blessed Mary,
To the number of the demonical friary![1]

NOWADAYS Come wind, come rain,
Though I come never again,
The devil put out both your een!° — *eyes*
Fellows, go we hence tite.° — *quickly*
NOUGHT Go we hence, a devil way!
Here is the door, here is the way.
Farewell, gentle Geoffrey,
I pray God give you good night!

Exeant simul. Cantent[2]

MERCY Thanked be God we have a fair deliverance
Of these three unthrifty° guests! — *profligate*
They know full little what is their ordinance.° — *proper place*
I prove by reason they be worse than beasts:
A beast doth after his natural institution.[3]

6. You are a very clever scholar.
7. Kiss my ass.
8. Here is a gut-sized (i.e., very full) pardon. Pardons were official documents of the church, sanctioned by the Pope, granting "indulgences" for sins committed in return for cash payment.
9. Hole, with a pun on vagina.
1. I.e., to hell.
2. Let them go out together. Let them sing.
3. Instinctive nature.

Ye may conceive by their disport° and behaviour, *conduct*
Their joy and delight is in derision
Of their own Christ, to his dishonour.

This condition of living, it is prejudicial,
Beware thereof! It is worse than any felony or treason.
How may it be excused before the Justice of all,
When for every idle word we must yield a reason?

They have great ease, therefore they will take no thought.
But, how then, when the angel of heaven shall blow the trump° *trumpet*
And say to the transgressors that wickedly hath wrought:
"Come forth unto your judge, and yield your account?"

Then shall I, Mercy, begin sore to weep.
Neither comfort nor counsel there shall none be had,
But such as they have sown, such shall they reap.[4]
They be wanton° now, but then shall they be sad. *carefree*

The good new guise nowadays I will not disallow,
I discommend the vicious guise. I pray have me excused;
I need not to speak of it; your reason will tell it you.
Take that is to be taken, and leave that is to be refused.

MANKIND Of the earth and of the clay we have our propagation,
By the providence of God thus be we derivate;° *derived*
To whose mercy I recommend this whole congregation.
I hope unto his bliss ye be all predestinate.° *predestined*
Every man, for his degree, I trust shall be participate,[5]
If we will mortify° our carnal condition *suppress*
And our voluntary desires that ever be perversionate,° *perverted*
To renounce them and yield us under God's provision.

My name is Mankind. I have my composition
Of a body and of a soul, of condition contrary.
Betwix them twain° is a great division; *two*
He[6] that should be subject, now he hath the victory.
This is to me a lamentable story,
To see my flesh of my soul to have governance.
Where the good-wife° is master the good-man may be sorry. *woman*
I may both sigh and sob; this is a piteous remembrance!

O thou, my soul, so subtle° in thy substance, *pure*
Alas! what was thy fortune and thy chance
To be associate with my flesh, that stinking dunghill?

Lady,° help! Sovereigns, it doth my soul much ill *Virgin Mary*
To see the flesh prosperous and the soul trodden under foot.
I shall go to yonder man and assay° him I will; *test*
I trust of ghostly° solace he will be my boot.° *spiritual / help*

4. See Job 4.8 and Galatians 6.8.
5. Every man, according to his place, I believe will partake.
6. I.e., the body.

All hail, seemly° father! Ye be welcome to this house. *worthy*
Of the very° wisdom ye have participation.° *true / access*
My body with my soul is ever quarrellous;
I pray you, for saint° charity, of your supportation.° *holy / support*

I beseech you heartily of your ghostly comfort.
I am unsteadfast in living, my name is Mankind.
My ghostly enemy, the devil, will have a great disport,° *delight*
In simple guiding if he may see me end.[7]

MERCY Christ send you good comfort! Ye be welcome, my friend.
Stand up on your feet, I pray you, arise!
My name is Mercy; ye be to me full hend.° *very dear*
To eschew vice I will you advise.

MANKIND O Mercy, of all grace and virtue ye are the well!
I have heard tell, of right worshipful clerks,
Ye be approximate to° God and near of his counsel. *next to*
He hath institute° you above all his works. *established*

O your lovely words to my soul are sweeter than honey!

MERCY The temptation of the flesh ye must resist like a man,
For there is ever a battle betwix the soul and the body:
Vita hominis est militia super terram.[8]

Oppress your ghostly enemy, and be Christ's own knight;
Be never a coward again° your adversary. *against*
If ye will be crowned, ye must needs fight.
Intend well, and God will be you adjutory.[9]

Remember, my friend, the time of continuance,
So help me God, it is but a cherry-time;[1]
Spend it well! Serve God with heart's affiance.° *loyalty*
Distemper° not your brain with good ale nor with wine; *sicken*

"Measure is treasure." I forbid you not the use.
Measure yourself ever, beware of excess.
The superfluous guise I will that ye refuse;
When nature is sufficed, anon that ye cease.

If a man have an horse, and keep him not too high,
He may then rule him at his own desire.
If he be fed over-well, he will disobey,
And, in hap,° cast his master in the mire. *perhaps*

NEWGUISE Ye say true, sir, ye are no faitour.° *liar*
I have fed my wife so well till she is my master.
I have a great wound on my head, lo, and thereon lieth a
plaster° *poultice*
And another there° I piss, my peson.° *where / penis*

7. If he may see me end (i.e., die) in foolish living.
8. The life of man is warfare upon the earth (Job 7.1).
9. And God will help you.
1. I.e., brief (like the short period of time when cherries may be harvested).

An my wife were your horse, she would you all to-ban.° *curse*
Ye feed your horse in measure, ye are a wise man;
I trow an° ye were the king's palfreyman,° *think if / groom*
A good horse should be geason.° *rare*

MANKIND Where speaks this fellow? Will he not come near?
MERCY All too soon, my brother, I fear me, for you.
He was here right now (by him that bought me dear)[2]
With other of his fellows—they can much sorrow![3]
They will be here right soon if I out depart.
Think on my doctrine; it shall be your defence.
Learn while I am here, set my words in heart,
Within a short space I must needs° hence. *must go*

NOWADAYS The sooner the liefer, an° it be even anon! *better, if*
I trow your name is Do-little, ye be so long fro home.
If ye would go hence, we shall come everychone,° *every one*
Mo° than a good sort.° *more / company*
Ye have leave,° I dare well say; *permission*
When ye will, go forth your way.
Men have little dainty° of your play, *pleasure in*
Because ye make no sport.

NOUGHT Your pottage° shall be for-cold, sir, when will ye go dine? *porridge*
I have seen a man lost twenty nobles[4] in as little time—
Yet it was not I, by St Quentin!
For I was never worth a potful of worts° sithen I was born. *cabbages*
My name is Nought; I love well to make merry.
I have be sithen° with the common tapster of Bury; *been just now*
A° played so long the fool that I am even very weary. *He (or She)*
Yet shall I be there again tomorn.° *tomorrow*

MERCY I have much care for you, my own friend,
Your enemies will be here anon; they make their avaunt.° *boast*
Think well in your heart: your name is Mankind,
Be not unkind° to God, I pray you, be his servant. *unnatural*
Be steadfast in condition, see ye be not variant.
Lose not through folly that is bought so dear.[5]
God will prove° you soon, and, if that ye be constant, *test*
Of his bliss perpetual ye shall be partner.
Ye may not have your intent at your first desire.
See the great patience of Job[6] in tribulation;
Like as the smith trieth° iron in the fire, *tests*
So was he tried by God's visitation.

2. I.e., Christ.
3. Know much sorrow / are acquainted with causing trouble.
4. Coins worth 80 pence, or one-third of a pound. Twenty nobles would have been an enormous sum.
5. That which is bought at such cost (i.e., salvation).
6. The biblical Job, who suffers patiently the trials imposed by God.

He was of your nature and of your fragility.
Follow the steps of him, my own sweet son,
And say, as he said, in your trouble and adversity:
Dominus dedit, Dominus abstulit; sicut sibi placuit, ita
factum est. Sit nomen Domini benedictum.[7]

Moreover, in special, I give you in charge,
Beware of Newguise, Nowadays, and Nought.
Nice° in their array, in language they be large; *fashionable*
To pervert your conditions° all their means shall be sought. *behavior*

Good son, intromit° not yourself in their company. *mix*
They heard not a mass this twelvemonth, I dare well say.
Give them none audience; they will tell you many a lie.
Do truly your labour, and keep your holy day.
Beware of Titivillus,[8] for he loseth no way,
That goeth invisible and will not be seen.
He will roun° in your ear, and cast a net before your eye. *whisper*
He is worst of them all, God let him never theen!° *prosper*

If ye displease God, ask mercy anon,
Else Mischief will be ready to brace° you in his bridle. *fasten*
Kiss me now, my dear darling. God shield you from your fon!° *foes*
Do truly your labour, and be never idle.

The blessing of God be with you, and with all these worshipful men![9]

MANKIND Amen, for saint° charity, amen! *holy*

Now blessed be Jesu, my soul is well satiate° *satisfied*
With the mellifluous° doctrine of this worshipful man. *sweet*
The rebellion of my flesh now it is superate.° *overcome*
Thanking be God of the cunning that I can.[1]

Here will I sit, and title° in this paper *write*
The incomparable estate of my promition.° *promised place*
Worshipful sovereigns, I have written here
The glorious remembrance of my noble condition

To° have remorse and memory of myself. Thus written it is *in order to*
To defend me from all supersititious charms:
"Memento, homo, quod cinis es et in cinerem reverteris."[2]
Lo, I bear on my breast the badge of mine arms.[3]

NEWGUISE The weather is cold; God send us good fires!
Cum sancto sanctus eris, et cum perverso perverteris.
"Ecce quam bonum et quam jocundum," quod the devil to the friars,

7. The Lord gave and the Lord has taken away; as it has pleased him, so it is done. Blessed be the name of the Lord (Job 1.21).
8. A demon. Literally, "all vile things."
9. I.e., the audience.
1. What wisdom I have.
2. Remember, man, you are dust and to dust you will return. (Genesis 3.19; see also Job 34.15.) This verse is strongly associated with Christian burial services.
3. Behold, I carry on my breast the sign of my nature. (Also a play on heraldic devices, such as coats-of-arms, associated with the aristocracy.)

"Habitare fratres in unum."[4]

MANKIND I hear a fellow speak. With him I will not mell.° *meddle*
This earth with my spade I shall assay to delve.
To eschew idleness, I do it mine own self.
I pray God send it his foison!° *plenty*

NOWADAYS Make room, sirs, for we have be° long! *been*
We will come give you a Christmas song.

NOUGHT Now I pray all the yeomanry[5] that is here,
To sing with us with a merry cheer.

It is written with a coal, it is written with a coal
NEWGUISE & NOWADAYS It is written with a coal, it is written *cetera*
NOUGHT He that shitteth with his hole, he that shitteth with his hole.
NEWGUISE & NOWADAYS He that shitteth with his hole, *cetera*.

NOUGHT But he wipe his arse clean, but he *cetera*
NEWGUISE & NOWADAYS But he wipe his arse clean, but he *cetera*

NOUGHT On his breech it shall be seen, on his breech *cetera*
NEWGUISE & NOWADAYS On his breech it shall be seen, on his *cetera*

Cantant omnes.[6]
Holyke, holyke, holyke, holyke, holyke, holyke.[7]

NEWGUISE Ey, Mankind, God speed you with your spade!
I shall tell you of a marriage:
I would your mouth and his arse, that this made,[8]
Were married junctly° together! *jointly*
MANKIND Hie you hence, fellows, with braiding!° *scolding*
Leave your derision and your japing!° *horseplay*
I must needs labour; it is my living.
NOWADAYS What, sir, we came but late hither!

Shall all this corn° grow here *grain*
That ye shall have the next year?
If it be so, corn had need be dear,[9]
Else ye shall have a poor life.
NOUGHT Alas, good father, this labour fretteth° you to the bone. *wears*
But for your crop I take great moan;[1]
Ye shall never spend it alone,
I shall assay to get you a wife.

How many acres suppose ye here by estimation?
NEWGUISE Ey, how ye turn the earth up and down!
I have be in my days in many good town,
Yet saw I never such another tilling!
MANKIND Why stand ye idle? It is pity that ye were born!

4. With the holy you will be holy, and with the perverse perverted. (Psalms 18.26.) Behold how good and how pleasant it is for brothers to dwell together in unity. (Psalms 133.1.)
5. A class of small freeholders who cultivated their own land.
6. Let them all sing.
7. A play on "holy" and "hole lick."
8. Meaning unclear, perhaps "that made this song" or "that made this stain."
9. Will have to be expensive.
1. I am very sad.

NOWADAYS We shall bargain with you, and neither mock nor scorn:
Take a good cart in harvest, and load it with your corn
And what shall we give you for the leaving?° *what is left*

NOUGHT He is a good stark° labourer, he would fain° do well. *strong / wants to*
He hath met with the good-man Mercy, in a shrewd sell.[2]
For all this he may have many a hungry meal.
Yet, will ye see, he is politic?° *prudent*
Here shall be good corn, he may not miss it;
If he will have rain, he may over-piss it.

And if he will have compost, he may over-bless it
A little with his arse, like . . .

MANKIND Go and do your labour! God let you never thee!° *prosper*
Or with my spade I shall you ding, by the holy Trinity.
Have ye none other man to mock, but ever me?
Ye would have me of your set.° *gang*
Hie you forth lively, for hence I will you drive!
NEWGUISE Alas, my jewels!° I shall be shent of my wife![3] *testicles*
NOWADAYS Alas, and I am like never for to thrive,
I have such a buffet!° *blow*

MANKIND Hence, I say, Newguise, Nowadays, and Nought!
It was said beforn, all the means shall be sought
To pervert my conditions and bring me to nought.
Hence, thieves! Ye have made many a leasing!° *lie*
NOUGHT Marred° I was for cold, but now am I warm! *troubled*
Ye are evil-avised, sir, for ye have done harm.
By Cock's body sackered,[4] I have such a pain in my arm
I may not change a man a farthing![5]

MANKIND Now I thank God kneeling on my knee;
Blessed be his name! He is of high degree.
By the subsidy° of his grace that he hath sent me, *help*
Three of mine enemies I have put to flight.

Yet this instrument, sovereigns, is not made to defend;

David saith: "*Nec in hasta, nec in gladio, salvat Dominus*."[6]
NOUGHT No, marry, I beshrew you, it is *in* spad*ibus*![7]
Therefore Christ's curse come on your head*ibus*
To send you less might!

Exeant.[8]

MANKIND I promit° you these fellows will no more come here. *promise*
For some of them, certainly, were somewhat too near!

2. At a bad time.
3. I will be in disgrace with my wife (because I'm impotent).
4. God's sacred body.
5. I can't buy or sell from men worth a farthing (quarter-penny); i.e., I'm incapacitated.
6. Neither with spear, nor with sword, does the Lord save (Kings 17.47).
7. With spades.
8. Let them go out.

My father, Mercy, advised me to be of a good cheer,
And again° my enemies manly for to fight. *against*
I shall convict° them, I hope, everychone. *overcome*
Yet I say amiss; I do it not alone.
With the help of the grace of God I resist my fon° *foes*
And their malicious heart.
With my spade I will depart, my worshipful sovereigns,
And live ever with labour, to correct my insolence.
I shall go fetch corn for my land. I pray you of patience;
Right soon I shall revert.° *return*

MISCHIEF Alas, alas, that ever I was wrought!° *made*
Alas the while, I am worse than nought!° *nothing*
Sithen° I was here, by him that me bought, *since*
I am utterly undone!
I, Mischief, was here at the beginning of the game,
And argued with Mercy, God give him shame!
He hath taught Mankind, while I have be wane,[9]
To fight manly again his fon.° *foes*

For, with his spade that was his weapon,
Newguise, Nowadays, Nought he hath all to-beaten.
I have great pity to see them weepen.
Will ye list?° I hear them cry. *listen*

Clamant.[1]

Alas, alas, come hither! I shall be your borrow.° *protection*
Alack, alack, *ven, ven*![2] Come hither, with sorrow!
Peace, fair babes! Ye shall have an apple, tomorrow.
Why greet° ye so, why? *cry*

NEWGUISE Alas, master, alas! My privity!° *private parts*
MISCHIEF Ah, where? Alack, fair babe, ba me!° *kiss me*
Abide! Too soon I shall it see.
NOWADAYS Here, here, see my head, good master!
MISCHIEF Lady, help! Seely° darling, *ven, ven*! *poor*
I shall help thee of thy pain;
I shall smite off thy head and set it on again!
NOUGHT By our Lady, sir, a fair plaster![3]

Will ye off with his head? It is a shrewd charm![4]
As for me, I have none harm.
I were loath to forbear° mine arm! *do without*
Ye play: *In nomine patris*,[5] chop!
NEWGUISE Ye shall not chop my jewels,° an I may![6] *testicles*
NOWADAYS Yea, Christ's cross! Will ye smite my head away?

9. While I have been away.
1. They cry out.
2. Come, come.
3. Fine poultice.
4. Dangerous cure.
5. In the name of the father. The opening words of the Catholic mass and the first words spoken when making the sign of the cross.
6. If I can help it.

There. Where? One and° one. Out, ye shall not assay!° *by / try it*
I might well be called a fop.° *fool*

MISCHIEF I can chop it off and make it again.
NEWGUISE I had a shrewd *recumbentibus*,[7] but I feel no pain.
NOWADAYS And my head is all safe and whole again.
Now, touching° the matter of Mankind, *regarding*
Let us have an interlection° sithen ye be come hither. *conference*
It were good to have an end.[8]
MISCHIEF How, how, a minstrel! Know ye any ought?° *at all*
NOUGHT I can pipe in a Walsingham whistle,[9] I, Nought, Nought.
MISCHIEF Blow apace!° and thou shall bring him in with a flute. *quickly*
TITIVILLUS I come with my legs under me!
MISCHIEF How Newguise, Nowadays! hark, ere I go;
When our heads were together I spake of *si dedero*.[1]
NEWGUISE Yea, go thy way! We shall gather money unto,° *for it*
Else there shall no man him[2] see.

Now ghostly to our purpose, worshipful sovereigns,
We intend to gather money, if it please your negligence,[3]
For a man with a head that is of great omnipotence.
NOWADAYS Keep your tale,[4] in goodness I pray you, good brother!
He is a worshipful man, sirs, saving your reverence,[5]
He loveth no groats, nor pence of tuppence.
Give us red royals,[6] if ye will see his abominable presence.
NEWGUISE Not so! Ye that mow° not pay the ton,° pay the tother. *may / the one*

At the good-man° of this house first we will assay. *master*
God bless you, master! Ye say as ill,[7] yet ye will not say nay.
Let us go by and by, and do them pay.[8]
Ye pay all alike, well mote ye fare![9]
NOUGHT I say, Newguise, Nowadays, *estis vos pecuniatus?*[1]
I have cried a fair while, I beshrew° your pates!° *curse / heads*
NOWADAYS *Ita vere, magister*, come forth now your gates.[2]
He is a goodly man, sirs. Make space, and beware!

TITIVILLUS *Ego sum dominantium dominus*,[3] and my name is Titivillus.
Ye that have good horse, to you I say *caveatis*![4]
Here is an able fellowship to trice° 'em out at your gates! *trick*

7. A rough knock-down.
8. I.e., it were good to bring the matter of Mankind's temptation to completion.
9. Whistle associated with pilgrimage to Walsingham, where there was a shrine commemorating the Virgin Mary's appearance to Lady Richeldis of the manor of Walsingham. This might suggest disruptive behavior, as there are records of complaints about pilgrims' whistling.
1. Lit., "if I shall have given." They are collecting money from the audience in order to bring Titivillus into the play.
2. I.e., Titivillus.
3. Play on "your reverence."
4. Both "stick to your story" and "keep your tally (of money collected)."
5. He (Titivillus) is a worshipful man, sirs, begging your pardon.
6. Groats were four-penny pieces, pence of tuppence were two-penny pieces, and red royals were gold coins worth ten shillings each (each shilling is worth 12 pence).
7. You can say disparaging things.
8. Get them to pay.
9. May you have good luck.
1. Are you monied?
2. Yes indeed, master, now make your entrance.
3. I am lord of lords. "Lord of lords" is one of the titles for God in the Bible; Titivillus's use of it is therefore blasphemous.
4. Beware.

Ego probo sic:[5]
Loquitur ad NEWGUISE[6]
Sir Newguise, lend me a penny.
NEWGUISE I have a great purse, sir, but I have no money.
By the mass, I fail two farthings of an ha'penny.
Yet had I ten pound this night that was.[7]
Loquitur ad NOWADAYS
TITIVILLUS What is in thy purse? Thou art a stout felon.° *great rogue*
NOWADAYS The devil a whit! I am a clean gentleman![8]
I pray God I be never worse stored° than I am. *provided*
It shall be otherwise, I hope, ere this night pass.

Loquitur ad NOUGHT
TITIVILLUS Hark now, I say thou hast many a penny!
NOUGHT *Non nobis, Domine, non nobis,*[9] by St Denny![1]
The devil may dance in my purse for any penny—
It is as clean as a bird's arse!

TITIVILLUS Now I say yet again, *caveatis*![2]
Here is an able fellowship to trice° 'em out of your gates! *trick*

Now I say, Newguise, Nowadays, and Nought,
Go and search the country—anon it be sought—
Some here, some there, what if ye may catch ought.[3]

If ye fail of horse, take what ye may else.
NEWGUISE Then speak to Mankind for the *recumbentibus* of my jewels![4]
NOWADAYS Remember my broken head, in the worship of the five vowels![5]
NOUGHT Yea, good sir, and the sciatica in my arm!
TITIVILLUS I know full well what Mankind did to you.
Mischief hath informed of all the matter through.
I shall venge your quarrel, I make God avow!° *vow to god*
Forth, and espy where ye may do harm!

Take William Fide,[6] if ye will have any mo.° *more*
I say, Newguise, whither art thou avised° to go? *intending*

NEWGUISE First I shall begin at Master Huntington of Sawston.
Fro thence I shall go to William Thurlay of Hauxton,
And so forth to Pichard of Trumpington;
I will keep me to these three.
NOWADAYS I shall go to William Baker of Walton,
To Richard Bollman of Gayton.
I shall spare Master Wood of Fulbourn,
He is a *noli me tangere!*[7]

5. I prove (their cleverness) thus.
6. He speaks to Newguise.
7. Last night.
8. The devil a bit! I am a pure gentleman (i.e., I lack money).
9. Not unto us, O Lord, not unto us (Psalms 115.1).
1. Saint Denis, patron saint of Paris.
2. Beware.
3. If you can steal anything.
4. For the hitting of my testicles.
5. A play on the five wounds of Christ.
6. This and the following names almost certainly made topical references to the play's original audience in Cambridgeshire and Norfolk, near Cambridge and Lynn, where all the towns mentioned are located.
7. Touch me not (John 20.17). Jesus's words to Mary Magdalene after the resurrection.

NOUGHT I shall go to William Patrick of Massingham;
I shall spare Master Allington of Bottisham
And Hammond of Swaffham
For dread of *In manus tuas*,[8] queck![9]
Fellows, come forth, and go we hence together.
NEWGUISE Sith we shall go, let us be well ware and wither.[1]
If we may be take,° we come no more hither. *taken*
Let us con well our neck-verse that we have not a check.[2]

TITIVILLUS Go your way, a devil way, go your way all!
I bless you with my left hand; foul you befall![3]
Come again, I warn, as soon as I you call,
And bring your advantage° into this place. *profits*
To speak with Mankind I will tarry here this tide,° *while*
And assay his good purpose for to set aside.
The good-man Mercy shall no longer be his guide;
I shall make him to dance another trace!° *step*

Ever I go invisible, it is my jet;° *fashion*
And before his eye thus I will hang my net,
To blench° his sight. I hope to have his foot met.° *confuse / measure*
To irk him of his labour I shall make a frame.° *plan*
This board shall be hid under the earth, privily.° *secretly*
His spade shall enter, I hope, unreadily!
By then° he hath assayed, he shall be very angry, *by the time*
And lose his patience, pain° of shame. *on penalty*
I shall meng his corn with drawk and with darnel;[4]
It shall not be like° to sow nor to sell. *fit*
Yonder he cometh! I pray of counsel.[5]
He shall ween° grace were wane.° *think / lacking*

MANKIND Now God of his mercy send us of his sand!° *grace*
I have brought seed here to sow with my land.
While I over-delve it,° here it shall stand. *dig it over*
In nomine Patris, et Filii, et Spiritus Sancti,[6] now I will begin.
This land is so hard it maketh me unlusty° and irk!° *tired / annoyed*
I shall sow my corn at venture,° and let God work. *randomly*
Alas, my corn is lost! Here is a foul work.
I see well by tilling little shall I win.

Here I give up my spade for now and for ever!

8. Into your hands (I commend my spirit) (Luke 23.46). The last words Jesus speaks before dying, and therefore commonly spoken by those on their deathbed.
9. A choking sound.
1. Let us be very watchful and bold.
2. Let us learn our neck-verse well so that we don't have a disaster. The neck-verse was the first verse of the fifty-first psalm, the recitation of which in court allowed a defendant to claim benefit of clergy and so avoid the death penalty.
3. May ill fortune befall you.
4. I will mix his grain with weeds.
5. I ask you (i.e., the audience) to say nothing.
6. "In the name of the Father, and of the Son, and of the Holy Spirit." Opening words of the mass and the words spoken when making the sign of the cross.

Here Titivillus goeth out with the spade.

To occupy my body I will not put me in dever.° *make the effort*
I will hear my evensong[7] here, ere I dissever.° *depart*
This place I assign as for my kirk.° *church*
Here in my kirk I kneel on my knees.
Pater noster, qui es in celis . . .[8]

TITIVILLUS I promise you I have no lead on my heels![9]
I am here again to make this fellow irk.
Whist!° Peace! I shall go to his ear and tittle° therein: *hush / whisper*
A short prayer thirleth° heaven. Of thy prayer blin.° *pierces / cease*
Thou art holier than ever was any of thy kin.
Arise and avent thee!° Nature compels. *relieve yourself*

MANKIND I will° into the yard, sovereigns, and come again soon. *will go*
For dread of the colic and eek° of the stone, *also*
I will go do that needs must be done.
My beads° shall be here for whosomever will else. *prayer beads*

Exeat.[1]

TITIVILLUS Mankind was busy in his prayer, yet I did° him arise. *made*
He is conveyed,° by Christ, from his divine service. *removed*
Whither is he, trow° ye? Iwis° I am wonder wise, *think / indeed*
I have sent him forth to shit leasings.° *lies*
If ye have any silver, in hap° pure brass, *perhaps*
Take a little powder-of-Paris,[2] and cast over his° face, *its (the coin's)*
And even in the owl-flight[3] let him° pass. *it*
Titivillus can learn° you many pretty things. *teach*

I trow Mankind will come again soon,
Or else, I fear me, evensong will be done.
His beads shall be triced aside,° and that anon. *removed*
Ye shall° a good sport if ye will abide. *will have*
Mankind cometh again. Well fare he!
I shall answer him *ad omnia "quare?"*.[4]
There shall be set abroach° a clerical matter; *started*
I hope of his purpose to set him aside.

MANKIND Evensong hath be in the saying, I trow, a fair while.
I am irk° of it; it is too long by one mile. *tired*
Do way![5] I will no more so oft over the church stile;
Be as be may, I shall do another.° *something else*
Of labour and prayer, I am near irk of both.
I will no more of it, though Mercy be wrath.° *angry*
My head is very heavy, I tell you, forsooth.° *truly*
I shall sleep full my belly an° he were my brother. *even if*

7. Also called Vespers, the sixth of the seven canonical hours into which the Catholic church divided each day.
8. "Our Father, who art in heaven. . . ." The opening words of the Lord's Prayer.
9. I.e., I'm not slow.
1. Let him go out.
2. Exact meaning uncertain, probably a white powder.
3. I.e., twilight or night.
4. At every "why" (i.e., on every point).
5. Enough! I will no longer go so often over the steps in the churchyard wall.

TITIVILLUS An ever ye did,[6] for me keep now your silence!
Not a word, I charge you, pain° of forty pence! *on penalty*
A pretty game shall be showed you, ere ye go hence.
  Ye may hear him snore. He is sad° asleep. *deeply*

Whist!° Peace! The devil is dead. I shall go roun° in his ear. *hush / whisper*
Alas, Mankind, alas! Mercy hath stolen a mare.
He is run away fro his master, there wot° no man where. *knows*
  Moreover he stole both a horse and a neat.° *cow*

But yet I heard say he brake° his neck as he rode in France. *broke*
But I think he rideth on the gallows to learn for to dance.[7]
Because of his theft, that is his governance.
  Trust no more on him, he is a marred° man. *ruined*

Mickle° sorrow with thy spade beforn° thou hast wrought. *much / before*
Arise, and ask mercy of Newguise, Nowadays, and Nought.
They can advise thee for the best; let their good will be sought.
  And thy own wife brethel,° and take thee a lemman.° *deceive / lover*

Farewell, everychone, for I have done my game,
For I have brought Mankind to mischief and to shame!

MANKIND Whoop ho! Mercy hath broken his neckercher, a vows;° *neck, they say*
Or he hangeth by the neck high upon the gallows.
Adieu,[8] fair masters! I will haste me to the ale-house,
  And speak with Newguise, Nowadays, and Nought,
And get me a lemman with a smattering face![9]

NEWGUISE Make space, for Cock's body sackered,[1] make space!
Aha, well over-run! God give him[2] evil grace!
  We were near St Patrick's way,[3] by him that me bought.

I was twitched by the neck; the game was begun;
And grace was the halter brast° asunder—*Ecce signum*![4] *burst*
The half is about my neck. We had a near run.
  "Beware," quod the good-wife, when she smote off her
    husband's head, "Beware!"
Mischief is a convict, for he could° his neck-verse.[5] *knew*
My body gave a swing when I hung upon the cross.[6]
Alas, he will hang such a likely° man and a fierce *promising*
  For stealing of an horse! I pray God give him care!

Do way this halter! What devil doth Mankind here, with sorrow?[7]
Alas, how my neck is sore, I make avow!° *I swear*

MANKIND Ye be welcome, Newguise, sir. What cheer with you?
NEWGUISE Well, sir; I have no cause to mourn.
MANKIND What was that about your neck, so God you amend?

6. If ever you did.
7. I.e., to swing at the end of a noose.
8. Good-bye (French).
9. Meaning unclear, perhaps "kissable" or "wanton."
1. God's sacred body.
2. The hangman.
3. St. Patrick is the patron saint of Ireland.
4. Behold the sign.
5. See note at line 520.
6. Gallows, with a play on Christ's cross.
7. I curse it.

NEWGUISE In faith, St Audrey's holy band.[8]
I have a little disease, as it please God to send,
With a running ringworm.

NOWADAYS Stand a-room,° I pray thee, brother mine, *make way*
I have laboured all this night. When shall we go dine?
A church herebeside° shall pay for ale, bread, and wine— *near here*
Lo, here is stuff will serve!
NEWGUISE Now, by the holy Mary, thou art better merchant than I!
NOUGHT Avaunt,° knaves, let me go by! *out of the way*
I cannot get an° I should starve! *even if*

MISCHIEF Here cometh a man of arms! Why stand ye so still?
Of murder and manslaughter I have my belly-fill!
NOWADAYS What, Mischief, have ye been in prison, an it be your will?[9]
Meseemeth ye have scoured° a pair of fetters! *rubbed clean*
MISCHIEF I was chained by the arms. Lo! I have them here.
The chains I brast° asunder and killed the jailer. *burst*
Yea, and his fair wife halsed° in a corner. *embraced*
Ah, how sweetly I kissed the sweet mouth of hers.

When I had do,° I was mine own butler; *finished*
I brought away with me both dish and doubler.° *platter*
Here is enow° for me! Be of good cheer. *enough*
Yet well fare the new chesance![1]
MANKIND I ask mercy of Newguise, Nowadays, and Nought.
Once with my spade I remember that I fought.
I will make you amends if I hurt you ought° *at all*
Or did any grievance.

NEWGUISE What a° devil liketh thee to be of this disposition? *the*
MANKIND I dreamt Mercy was hang, this was my vision,
And that to you three I should have recourse and remotion.° *inclination*
Now I pray you heartily of your good will;
I cry° you mercy of all that I did amiss. *ask*
NOWADAYS I say, Newguise, Nought; Titivillus made all this;
As sicker° as God is in heaven, so it is. *surely*
NOUGHT Stand up on your feet. Why stand ye so still?

NEWGUISE Master Mischief, we will you exhort
Mankind's name in your book for to report.
MISCHIEF I will not so: I will set a court,
And do it *sub forma juris*,[2] dastard!° *fool*

Nowadays, make proclamation!

NOWADAYS Oyez, oyez, oyez!° All manner of men and common women *hear ye*
To the court of Mischief either come or send.
Mankind shall return; he is one of our men.

8. A neckband blessed at the shrine of the Anglo-Saxon St. Audrey, in Ely, a town in eastern England.
9. If you don't mind my asking.
1. Good luck to our new venture.
2. "In a legal manner." Mischief has decided that the apprenticeship needs the legal and ritual sanction of a manor-court session.

MISCHIEF Nought, come forth, thou shall be steward.[3]

NEWGUISE Master Mischief, his side-gown° may be sold. *long coat*
He may have a jacket thereof, and money told.[4]
MANKIND I will do for the best, so I have no cold.
Hold, I pray you, and take it with you,
And let me have it again in any wise.

NOUGHT *scribit*.[5]

NEWGUISE I promit you a fresh jacket after the new guise.
MANKIND Go and do that longeth° to your office, *what belongs*
And spare that ye mow.° *what you can*

NOUGHT Hold, Master Mischief, and read this.
MISCHIEF Here is '*Blottibus in blottis*
Blottorum blottibus istis'.[6]
I beshrew° your ears, a fair hand! *curse*
NOWADAYS Yea, it is a good running fist;° *cursive hand*
Such an hand may not be missed.
NOUGHT I should have done better, had I wist.° *known how*
MISCHIEF Take heed, sirs, it stand you on hand.[7]

"*Curia tenta generalis*,
In a place there good ale is,
Anno regni regitalis
Edwardi nullateni.[8]
On yestern day in February"—the year passeth fully,
As Nought hath written (here is our Tully!)[9]—
"*Anno regni regis nulli*."[1]

NOWADAYS What, ho, Newguise, thou makest much tarrying° *delay*
That jacket shall not be worth a farthing.
NEWGUISE Out of my way, sirs, for dread of fighting!
Lo, here is a feat tail, light to leap about.[2]
NOUGHT It is not shapen worth a morsel of bread;
There is too much cloth; it weighs as any lead!
I shall go and mend it, else I will lose my head.
Make space, sirs, let me go out!

MISCHIEF Mankind, come hither, God send you the gout!
Ye shall go to all the good fellows in the country about,
Unto the good-wife when the good-man is out;
"I will," say ye.
MANKIND I will, sir.
NEWGUISE There arn° but six deadly sins, lechery is none; *are*

3. The man who presided over a manor-court session.
4. Money left over.
5. Nought writes.
6. Nonsense Latin; literally, "To the blots in blots / With these blots of blots."
7. It affects you.
8. "A general court having been held . . . / In the year of the reign of kingly / Edward the Nothing." This is a play on the usual heading for a record of manor-court proceedings.
9. Marcus Tullius Cicero, a Roman orator and statesman, renowned in the Middle Ages as a Latin prose stylist.
1. In the regnal year of no king.
2. Look, here is a becoming style, easy to move about in.

As it may be verified by us brethels° everychone. *rogues*
Ye shall go rob, steal, and kill, as fast as ye may gone;
"I will," say ye.

MANKIND I will, sir.

NOWADAYS On Sundays, on the morrow early betime,° *very early*
Ye shall with us to the ale-house early to go dine,
And forbear mass and matins, hours and prime;[3]
"I will," say ye.

MANKIND I will, sir.

MISCHIEF Ye must have by your side a long *da-pacem*,[4]
As true men ride by the way for to unbrace them,° *carve them up*
Take their money, cut their throats, thus over-face them;
"I will," say ye.

MANKIND I will, sir.

NOUGHT Here is a jolly jacket! How say ye?

NEWGUISE It is a good jack-of-fence° for a man's body. *protective jacket*
Hey, dog, hey! Whoop ho! Go your way lightly!
Ye are well made for to run.

MISCHIEF Tidings, tidings! I have espied one!° *someone*
Hence with your stuff! Fast we were° gone! *let us be*
I beshrew the last shall come to his home!

Dicant omnes.[5]
Amen!

MERCY What ho, Mankind, flee that fellowship, I you pray!

MANKIND I shall speak with thee another time, tomorn or the next day.
We shall go forth together, to keep my father's year-day.° *death anniversary*
A tapster,° a tapster! Stow, stot,° stow! *barmaid / where, slut*

MISCHIEF A mischief go with thee, here I have a foul fall!
Hence, away fro me, or I shall beshit you all!

NEWGUISE What ho! Ostler,° ostler, lend us a football! *innkeeper*
Whoop, ho! Anow, anow, anow, anow!

MERCY My mind is dispersed, my body trembleth as the aspen leaf.
The tears should trickle down by my cheeks, were not your reverence.[6]
It were to me solace, the cruel visitation of death.
Without rude behaviour I can not express this inconvenience.° *misfortune*
Weeping, sighing, and sobbing were my sufficience;° *sustenance*
All natural nutriment to me as carrion is odible.° *hateful*
My inward affliction yieldeth° me tedious unto your presence. *makes*
I cannot bear it evenly that Mankind is so flexible.

Man, unkind wherever thou be, for all this world was not apprehensible° *sufficient*
To discharge thine original offence, thraldom, and captivity,
Till God's own well-beloved son was obedient and passible.° *willing to suffer*

3. I.e., all church services. Matins and prime are two of the seven canonical hours into which the Catholic church divides each day.
4. Lit. "give peace," i.e., a dagger.
5. Let them all say.
6. Were you revered people (i.e., the audience) not here.

Every drop of his blood was shed to purge thine iniquity.
I discommend and disallow this often mutability.
To every creature thou art dispectuous° and odible. *contemptible*
Why art thou so uncourteous, so inconsiderate? Alas, woe is me,
As the vane° that turneth with the wind, so thou art convertible. *weather vane*
In trust is treason; thy promise is not credible.
This perversious° ingratitude I cannot rehearse. *perverse*
To God and to all the holy court of heaven thou art despectible,° *despicable*
As a noble versifier maketh mention in this verse:

"Lex et natura, Cristus et omnia jura
Damnant ingratum; lugent eum fore natum."[7]

O good Lady and Mother of Mercy, have pity and compassion
Of the wretchedness of mankind, that is so wanton and so frail!
Let mercy exceed justice! Dear Mother, admit this supplication:
Equity to be laid on party,° and mercy to prevail. *aside*

Too sensual living is reprovable that is nowadays,
As by the comprehence° of this matter it may be specified. *understanding*
Newguise, Nowadays, Nought, with their allectuous° ways, *alluring*
They have perverted Mankind, my sweet son, I have well espied.

Ah, with these cursed caitiffs, an° I may, he shall not long endure! *wretches, if*
I, Mercy, his father ghostly, will proceed forth and do my property.° *task*
Lady, help! This manner of living is a detestable pleasure.
Vanitas vanitatum[8] all is but a vanity!

Mercy shall never be convict° of his uncourteous condition. *conquered by*
With weeping tears, by night and by day, I will go and never cease.
Shall I not find him? Yes, I hope. Now God be my protection!
My predilect° son, where be ye? Mankind, *ubi es?*°[9] *dearest*

MISCHIEF My prepotent father, when ye sup, sup out your mess!
Ye are all to-gloried in your terms; ye make many a lease.
Will ye hear? He crieth ever: 'Mankind, *ubi es?*'.

NEWGUISE *Hic, hic, hic, hic, hic, hic, hic, hic!*[1]
That is to say: 'Here, here, here', nigh dead in the creek!
If ye will have him, go and seek, seek, seek!
Seek not overlong, for losing of your mind.

7. Law and nature, Christ and all justice condemn the ingrate; they lament that he was born. (The source is unidentified.)
8. Vanity of vanities (Ecclesiastes 1.2).
9. Where are you?
1. Here.

NOWADAYS If ye will have Mankind, ho, *Domine*, *Domine*, *Dominus*![2]
Ye must speak to the shrive° for a *cape corpus*,[3] *sheriff*
Else ye must be fain to return with *non est inventus*.[4]
How say ye, sir? My bolt° is shot. *arrow*

NOUGHT I am doing of my needings.[5] Beware how ye shoot!
Fie, fie, fie! I have foul arrayed° my foot! *foully soiled*
Be wise for shooting with your tackles,° for, God wot,° *weapons / knows*
My foot is foully overshot!

MISCHIEF A parliament, a parliament! Come forth, Nought, behind!
A council, belive.° I am afeard Mercy will him find. *quickly*
How say ye? And what say ye? How shall we do with Mankind?

NEWGUISE Tish, a fly's wing![6] Will ye do well?
He weeneth° Mercy were hung for stealing of a mare; *thinks*
Mischief, go say to him that Mercy seeketh everywhere;
He will hang himself, I undertake, for fear.

MISCHIEF I assent thereto; it is wittily said and well.

NOWADAYS Whip° it in thy coat, anon it were done! *put*
Now, St Gabriel's mother[7] save the clouts° of thy shoon!° *patches / shoes*
All the books in the world, if they had be undone,° *been opened*
Could not a° counselled us bet. *have*

Hic exit Mischief.[8]

MISCHIEF How, Mankind, come and speak with Mercy. He is here fast by.

MANKIND A rope, a rope, a rope, I am not worthy!

MISCHIEF Anon, anon, anon, I have it here ready!
With a tree also, that I have get.

Hold the tree, Nowadays! Nought, take heed, and be wise!

NEWGUISE Lo, Mankind, do as I do. This is thy new guise.
Give the rope just to [thy] neck. This is mine advice.

MISCHIEF Help thyself, Nought! Lo, Mercy is here!
He scareth us with a baleis;° we may no longer tarry! *rod*

NEWGUISE Queck![9] queck! queck! Alas, my throat! I beshrew you, marry!
Ah, Mercy, Christ's copped° curse go with you, and St Davy![1] *greatest*
Alas, my weasand!° Ye were somewhat too near! *windpipe*

Exeant.[2]

MERCY Arise, my precious redempt° son, ye be to me full dear. *saved*
He is so timorous, meseemeth his vital spirit doth expire.

MANKIND Alas! I have be so bestially disposed I dare not appear;
To see your solacious° face I am not worthy to desire. *comforting*

2. O Lord, O Lord, Lord.
3. Lit., "take the body," a writ of arrest.
4. Lit., "he is not found," a sheriff's certificate that a prisoner cannot be found.
5. I am moving my bowels.
6. I.e., no problem.
7. A hyperbolic oath, since St. Gabriel is, typically, the archangel Gabriel, who has no mother.
8. Here Mischief goes out.
9. A choking sound.
1. St. David, patron saint of Wales.
2. Let them go out.

MERCY Your criminous complaint° woundeth my heart as a lance. *guilty lament*
Dispose yourself meekly to ask mercy, and I will assent.
Yield me neither gold nor treasure, but your humble obeisance,° *obedience*
The voluntary subjection of your heart, and I am content.

MANKIND What? Ask mercy yet once again? Alas, it were a vile petition!
Ever to offend and ever to ask mercy, it is a puerility.° *childish act*
It is so abominable to rehearse my iterate° transgression; *repeated*
I am not worthy to have mercy, by no possibility.

MERCY O Mankind, my singular solace, this is a lamentable excuse!
The dolorous tears of my heart, how they begin to amount!° *build up*
O pierced Jesu, help thou this sinful sinner to reduce!° *lead back*
Nam haec est mutatio dexterae Excelsi; vertit impios, et non sunt.[3]

Arise, and ask mercy, Mankind, and be associate to° me. *linked with*
Thy death shall be my heaviness. Alas, 'tis pity it should be thus!

Thy obstinacy will exclude thee fro the glorious perpetuity.
Yet, for my love, ope° thy lips, and say: "*Miserere mei, Deus*!"[4] *open*

MANKIND The egal° justice of God will not permit such a sinful wretch *impartial*
To be revived and restored again. It were impossible.

MERCY The justice of God will as I will, as himself doth preach:
Nolo mortem peccatoris, inquit[5] if he will be reducible.° *repentant*

MANKIND Then, Mercy, good Mercy, what is a man without mercy?
Little is our part of paradise where mercy ne were.[6]
Good Mercy, excuse the inevitable objection of my ghostly enemy.
The proverb saith: "The truth trieth the self." Alas, I have much care!

MERCY God will not make you privy unto[7] his Last judgment.
Justice and equity shall be fortified, I will not deny.
But Truth may not so cruelly proceed in his strait° argument *strict*
But that Mercy shall rule the matter without controversy.

Arise now, and go with me in this deambulatory.° *walking area*
Incline your capacity;[8] my doctrine is convenient.° *appropriate*
Sin not in hope of mercy,[9] that is a crime notary;° *notorious*
To trust overmuch in a prince, it is not expedient.

In hope, when ye sin, ye think to have mercy, beware of that adventure.
The good Lord said to the lecherous woman of Canaané

3. For this is the change of the right hand of the Most High: he overthrows the wicked, and they are no more. (A mixture of Psalms 77.10 and Proverbs 12.7.)
4. "Have mercy on me, O God!" (Psalms 51.1). Also called the Miserere, it is the most famous of the penitential psalms.
5. I do not want the death of a sinner, he said (see Ezekiel 33.11).
6. If mercy were lacking.
7. Share with you the secrets of.
8. Submit your understanding.
9. See Ecclesiastes 5.4–7.

The holy Gospel is the authority, as we read in scripture:
"*Vade, et iam amplius noli peccare!*"[1]

Christ preserved this sinful woman taken in adultery.
He said to her these words: 'Go, and sin no more!'
So to you: 'Go, and sin no more!'. Beware of vain confidence of mercy.
Offend not a prince on trust of his favour, as I said before.

If ye feel yourself trapped in the snare of your ghostly enemy,
Ask mercy anon. Beware of the continuance.
While a wound is fresh, it is proved curable by surgery,
That, if it proceed overlong, it is cause of great grievance.

MANKIND To ask mercy and to have, this is a liberal° possession. — *generous*
Shall this expeditious° petition ever be allowed, as ye have insight? — *urgent*

MERCY In this present life mercy is plenty, till death maketh his division.
But when ye be go,° *usque ad minimum quadrantem*[2] ye shall reckon your right. — *are gone (dead)*

Ask mercy and have, while the body with the soul hath his annexion;° — *is joined*
If ye tarry till your decease, ye may hap° of your desire to miss. — *chance*
Be repentant here; trust not the hour of death. Think on this lesson:
"*Ecce nunc tempus acceptabile, ecce nunc dies salutis.*"[3]
All the virtue in the world if ye might comprehend,° — *contain*
Your merits were not premiable to° the bliss above, — *worthy to (gain)*
Not to the least joy of heaven of your proper effort to ascend.
With mercy ye may; I tell you no fable, scripture doth prove.

MANKIND O Mercy, my suavious° solace and singular recreatory,° — *sweet / comfort*
My predilect° special, ye are worthy to have my love! — *dearest*
For, without desert and means supplicatory,[4]
Ye be compatient to my inexcusable reprove.° — *shame*

Ah, it sweameth° my heart to think how unwisely I have wrought! — *grieves*
Titivillus, that goeth invisible, hung his net before my eye,
And by his fantastical visions, seditiously sought,
To Newguise, Nowadays, Nought caused me to obey.

MERCY Mankind, ye were oblivious of my doctrine monitory.° — *warning*
I said before, Titivillus would assay you a brunt.[5]
Beware fro henceforth of his fables delusory.° — *deceitful*
The proverb saith: *Jacula praestita minus laedunt*.[6]

1. "Go and sin no more" (John 8.11). In the gospel story, Jesus stops people from stoning to death a woman taken in adultery by suggesting that someone who was without sin should cast the first stone. Since no one was without sin, the woman was spared. He then sends her away with this phrase.

2. To the uttermost farthing. (See Matthew 5.26.)

3. Behold now is the acceptable time, behold now is the day of salvation (2 Corinthians 6.2).

4. Undeserving and unable to plead.

5. Have a go at you.

6. Prepared-for darts wound less.

Ye have three adversaries, and he is master of them all,
That is to say, the Devil, the World, the Flesh and the fell.° *skin*
The Newguise, Nowadays, Nought, the World we may them call,
And properly Titivillus signifieth the Fiend of hell;
The Flesh, that is the unclean concupiscence of your body.
These be your three ghostly enemies, in whom ye have put your confidence.
They brought you to mischief, to conclude° your temporal° glory, *end / earthly*
As it hath be showed before this worshipful audience.

Remember how ready I was to help you? Fro such I was not dangerous.
Wherefore, good son, abstain fro sin evermore after this.
Ye may both save and spill° your soul, that is so precious. *destroy*
Libere velle, libere nolle,[7] God may not deny, iwis.° *indeed*

Beware of Titivillus with his net, and of all envious will,
Of your sinful delectation° that grieveth your ghostly substance.[8] *pleasure*
Your body is your enemy; let him° not have his° will. *it / its*
Take your leave when ye will. God send you good perseverance!

MANKIND Sith° I shall depart, bless me, father, ere then I go. *since*
God send us all plenty of his great mercy!

MERCY *Dominus custodit te ab omni malo*[9]
In nomine Patris, et Filii, et Spiritus Sancti.[1]
Amen.

Hic exit Mankind.[2]

Worshipful sovereigns, I have do my property:° *done my part*
Mankind is delivered by my favoural patrociny.° *kind protection*
God preserve him fro all wicked captivity,
And send him grace his sensual conditions to mortify!

Now for his love that for us received his humanity,[3]
Search your conditions with due examination.
Think and remember the world is but a vanity,
As it is proved daily by diverse transmutation.° *changes*

Mankind is wretched; he hath sufficient proof;
Therefore God grant you all, *per suam misericordiam,*[4]
That ye may be play-feres° with the angels above, *play-fellows*
And have to your portion *vitam aeternam.*[5]
Amen!

Finis[6]

7. "Freely accept, freely reject." A reference to man's free will.
8. I.e., the soul.
9. (May) the Lord preserve you from all evil (Psalms 121.7).
1. In the name of the Father, and of the Son, and of the Holy Spirit (see note at line 544).
2. Here Mankind goes out.
3. I.e., Christ.
4. Through his mercy.
5. Eternal life.
6. The end.

Christine de Pizan

c. 1364–c. 1430

Christine de Pizan is an epochal figure in the history of European literature, not only for the quality and influence of her many works, but equally because she was Europe's first professional woman of letters. There were many important women writers in the Middles Ages, several of them represented in this anthology, but Christine—widowed in 1389 with three children and no family money—was the first to make writing the sole source of her income. She was well aware of this and wove her unique perspective, as a woman engaged with a largely male (and often misogynist) intellectual tradition, into much of her writing.

Like many late medieval writers, Christine de Pizan spent a good part of her energies translating, adapting, and consolidating earlier works on a wide range of topics. She wrote love poetry in traditional forms such as the ballade, but innovated by writing lyrics on widowhood as well. Like other writers of her time, too, Christine frames many of her books as dream-visions populated by allegorical figures, especially teachers or guides, such as the three ladies (Reason, Rectitude, and Justice) whom she encounters in the *Book of the City of Ladies*. Also like her contemporaries, Christine had to seek patronage in the noble and royal courts of France (where she spent most of her life) and Burgundy, as well as England. She was an innovator here as well, though, carefully supervising the scribes and painters who produced splendid manuscripts of her works for presentation to her patrons.

Christine innovated most of all, however, by persistently reacting to her cultural inheritance from the perspective of women. At the turn of the fifteenth century, she was a major voice in the debate surrounding the famous but often misogynist *Romance of the Rose*. Classical and medieval Latin had an even greater store of works hostile to women. With the *Book of the City of Ladies*, though, Christine offers a systematic response to the depiction of women in biblical and classical texts. The three allegorical ladies who appear to her as the book opens instruct Christine to build a walled city of and for the virtuous women of her cultural past. In doing so, Christine radically reinterprets women's histories as they have been recorded by men, and imagines a symbolic space from which a female literary tradition might emanate.

The works of Christine de Pizan were widely known in England in her own lifetime and well into the early modern period. Splendid manuscripts of her French works came into the hands of English kings and nobles. Her elder son was raised for three years in the household of the Duke of Salisbury, an influential member of the court of Richard II. Christine's *Letter of Othea* was translated three times in the fifteenth century; and Thomas Hoccleve, a late contemporary of Chaucer, adapted her *Letter of the God of Love*—a feminist response to courtly love—as the *Letter of Cupid*. England's first printer, William Caxton, translated and published yet other of her works (some by royal commission) in the 1480s, as did early sixteenth-century printers like Henry Pepwell, who published Brian Anslay's 1521 translation of the *Book of the City of Ladies*.

Her role in England places Christine de Pizan within several key transitions there. The ongoing translations of her works reflect the importation of Continental texts into an increasingly English-language literary and political culture under the Lancastrian and Yorkist kings. The numerous early printings of these translations is part of a massive dissemination of late medieval texts made possible by the rise of print. And in turn, this widespread access to later medieval literary modes carried their influences—not least, that of allegory—into early modern culture in England. Works like the *Book of the City of Ladies* lie behind the allegorized, often female-controlled cities and castles of early modern works like Spenser's *Faerie Queene*. The translation used here is by Earl Jeffrey Richards.

Woodblock from Brian Anslay's English translation of *Book of the City of Ladies*, 1521.

from *Book of the City of Ladies*

[*In the first chapter Christine presents herself surrounded by books in her study, and is dismayed to read philosophers and poets all claiming that women are full of vice. While such a view is contrary to her perception of herself and of other women she has known, she concludes that so many famous men cannot be wrong. She is so over-whelmed by sorrow that she asks God why he created women, if they are so vile, and why he did not make her a man, so that she might serve him better.*]

[PART I, CHAPTER 2]

[*Here Christine Describes how three ladies appeared to her and how the one who was in front spoke first and comforted her in her pain.*]

So occupied with these painful thoughts, my head bowed in shame, my eyes filled with tears, leaning on the pommel of my chair's armrest, I suddenly saw a ray of light fall on my lap, as though it were the sun. I shuddered then, as if wakened from sleep, for I was sitting in a shadow where the sun could not have shone at that hour. And as I lifted my head to see where this light was coming from, I saw three crowned ladies standing before me, and the splendor of their bright faces shone on me and throughout the entire room. Now no one would ask whether I was surprised, for my doors were shut and they had still entered. Fearing that some phantom had come to tempt me and filled with great fright, I made the Sign of the Cross on my forehead.

Then she who was the first of the three smiled and began to speak, "Dear daughter, do not be afraid, for we have not come here to harm or trouble you but to console you, for we have taken pity on your distress, and we have come to bring you out of the ignorance which so blinds your own intellect that you shun what you know for a certainty and believe what you do not know or see or recognize except by virtue of many strange opinions. You resemble the fool in the prank who was dressed in women's clothes while he slept; because those who were making fun of him repeatedly told him he was a woman, he believed their false testimony more readily than the certainty of his own identity. Fair daughter, have you lost all sense? Have you forgotten that when fine gold is tested in the furnace, it does not change or vary in strength but becomes purer the more it is hammered and handled in different ways? Do you not know that the best things are the most debated and the most discussed? If you wish to consider the question of the highest form of reality, which consists in ideas or celestial substances, consider whether the greatest philosophers who have lived and whom you support against your own sex have ever resolved whether ideas are false and contrary to the truth. Notice how these same philosophers contradict and criticize one another, just as you have seen in the *Metaphysics* where Aristotle takes their opinions to task and speaks similarly of Plato and other philosophers. And note, moreover, how even Saint Augustine and the Doctors of the Church have criticized Aristotle in certain passages, although he is known as the prince of philosophers in whom both natural and moral philosophy attained their highest level. It also seems that you think that all the words of the philosophers are articles of faith, that they could never be wrong. As far as the poets of whom you speak are concerned, do you not know that they spoke on many subjects in a fictional way and that often they mean the contrary of what their words openly say? One can interpret them according to the grammatical figure of *antiphrasis*, which means, as you know, that if you call something bad, in fact, it is good, and also vice versa. Thus I advise you to profit from their works and to interpret them in the manner in which they are intended in those passages where they attack women. Perhaps this man, who called himself Mathéolus in his own book, intended it in such a way, for there are many things which, if taken literally, would be pure heresy.[1] As for the attack against the estate of marriage—which is a holy estate, worthy and ordained by God—made not only by Mathéolus but also by others and even by the *Romance of the Rose* where greater credibility is averred because of the authority of its author, it is evident and proven by experience that the contrary of the evil which they posit and claim to be found in this estate through the obligation and fault of women is true. For where has the husband ever been found who would allow his wife to have authority to abuse and insult him as a matter of course, as these authorities maintain? I believe that, regardless of what you might have read, you will never see such a husband with your own eyes, so badly colored are these lies. Thus, in conclusion, I tell you, dear friend, that simplemindedness has prompted you to hold such an opinion. Come back to yourself, recover your senses, and do not trouble yourself anymore over such absurdities. For you know that any evil spoken of women so generally only hurts those who say it, not women themselves."

1. *The Book of the Lamentations of Matheolus*, the misogynist work that most troubled Christine in her study.

[PART I, CHAPTER 3]

[Here Christine tells how the lady who had said this showed her who she was and what her character and function were and told her how she would construct a city with the help of these same three ladies.]

The famous lady spoke these words to me, in whose presence I do not know which one of my senses was more overwhelmed: my hearing from having listened to such worthy words or my sight from having seen her radiant beauty, her attire, her reverent comportment, and her most honored countenance. The same was true of the others, so that I did not know which one to look at, for the three ladies resembled each other so much that they could be told apart only with difficulty, except for the last one, for although she was of no less authority than the others, she had so fierce a visage that whoever, no matter how daring, looked in her eyes would be afraid to commit a crime; for it seemed that she threatened criminals unceasingly. Having stood up out of respect, I looked at them without saying a word, like someone too overwhelmed to utter a syllable. Reflecting on who these beings could be, I felt much admiration in my heart and, if I could have dared, I would have immediately asked their names and identities and what was the meaning of the different scepters which each one carried in her right hand, which were of fabulous richness, and why they had come here. But since I considered myself unworthy to address these questions to such high ladies as they appeared to me, I did not dare to, but continued to keep my gaze fixed on them, half-afraid and half-reassured by the words which I had heard, which had made me reject my first impression. But the most wise lady who had spoken to me and who knew in her mind what I was thinking, as one who has insight into everything, addressed my reflections, saying:

"Dear daughter, know that God's providence, which leaves nothing void or empty, has ordained that we, though celestial beings, remain and circulate among the people of the world here below, in order to bring order and maintain in balance those institutions we created according to the will of God in the fulfillment of various offices, that God whose daughters we three all are and from whom we were born. Thus it is my duty to straighten out men and women when they go astray and to put them back on the right path. And when they stray, if they have enough understanding to see me, I come to them quietly in spirit and preach to them, showing them their error and how they have failed, I assign them the causes, and then I teach them what to do and what to avoid. Since I serve to demonstrate clearly and to show both in thought and deed to each man and woman his or her own special qualities and faults, you see me holding this shiny mirror which I carry in my right hand in place of a scepter. I would thus have you know truly that no one can look into this mirror, no matter what kind of creature, without achieving clear self-knowledge. My mirror has such great dignity that not without reason is it surrounded by rich and precious gems, so that you see, thanks to this mirror, the essences, qualities, proportions, and measures of all things are known, nor can anything be done well without it. And because, similarly, you wish to know what are the offices of my other sisters whom you see here, each will reply in her own person about her name and character, and this way our testimony will be all the more certain to you. But now I myself will declare the reason for our coming. I must assure you, as we do nothing without good cause, that our appearance here is not at all in vain. For, although we are not common to many places and our knowledge does not come to all people, nevertheless you, for your great love of investigating the truth through long and continual study, for which you come here, solitary and separated from the world, you have deserved and deserve, our devoted friend, to be visited and consoled by us in your agitation and sadness, so that you might also see clearly, in the midst of the darkness of your thoughts, those things which taint and trouble your heart.

"There is another greater and even more special reason for our coming which you will learn from our speeches: in fact we have come to vanquish from the world the same error into which you had fallen, so that from now on, ladies and all valiant women may have a refuge and defense against the various assailants, those ladies who have been abandoned for so long, exposed like a field without a surrounding hedge, without finding a champion to afford them an adequate defense, notwithstanding those noble men who are required by order of law to protect them, who by negligence and apathy have allowed them to be mistreated. It is no wonder then that their jealous enemies, those outrageous villains who have assailed them with various weapons, have been victorious in a war in which women have had no defense. Where is there a city so strong which could not be taken immediately if no resistance were forthcoming, or the law case, no matter how unjust, which was not won through the obstinance of someone pleading without opposition? And the simple, noble ladies, following the example of suffering which God commands, have cheerfully suffered the great attacks which, both in the spoken and the written word, have been wrongfully and sinfully perpetrated against women by men who all the while appealed to God for the right to do so. Now it is time for their just cause to be taken from Pharaoh's hands, and for this reason, we three ladies whom you see here, moved by pity, have come to you to announce a particular edifice built like a city wall, strongly constructed and well founded, which has been predestined and established by our aid and counsel for you to build, where no one will reside except all ladies of fame and women worthy of praise, for the walls of the city will be closed to those women who lack virtue."

[Part I, Chapter 4]

[*Here the lady explains to Christine the city which she has been commissioned to build and how she was charged to help Christine build the wall and enclosure, and then gives her name.*]

"Thus, fair daughter, the prerogative among women has been bestowed on you to establish and build the City of Ladies. For the foundation and completion of this City you will draw fresh waters from us as from clear fountains, and we will bring you sufficient building stone, stronger and more durable than any marble with cement could be. Thus your City will be extremely beautiful, without equal, and of perpetual duration in the world.

"Have you not read that King Tros founded the great city of Troy with the aid of Apollo, Minerva, and Neptune, whom the people of that time considered gods, and also how Cadmus founded the city of Thebes with the admonition of the gods? And yet over time these cities fell and have fallen into ruin. But I prophesy to you, as a true sybil, that this City, which you will found with our help, will never be destroyed, nor will it ever fall, but will remain prosperous forever, regardless of all its jealous enemies. Although it will be stormed by numerous assaults, it will never be taken or conquered.

"Long ago the Amazon kingdom was begun through the arrangement and enterprise of several ladies of great courage who despised servitude, just as history books have testified. For a long time afterward they maintained it under the rule of several queens, very noble ladies whom they elected themselves, who governed them well and maintained their dominion with great strength. Yet, although they were strong and powerful and had conquered a large part of the entire Orient in the course of their rule and terrified all the neighboring lands (even the Greeks, who were then the flower of all countries in the world, feared them), nevertheless, after a time, the power of this kingdom declined, so that as with all earthly kingdoms, nothing but its name has survived to the present. But the edifice erected by you in this City which you must construct will be far stronger, and for its founding I was commissioned, in the course of our common deliberation, to supply you with durable and pure mortar to lay the sturdy foundations and to raise the lofty walls all around, high and thick, with mighty towers and strong bastions, surrounded by moats with firm blockhouses, just as is fitting for a city with a strong and lasting defense. Following our plan, you will set the foundations deep to last all the longer, and then you will raise the walls so high that they will not fear anyone. Daughter, now that I have told you the reason for our coming and so that you will more certainly believe my words, I want you to learn my name, by whose sound alone you will be able to learn and know that, if you wish to follow my commands, you have in me an administrator so that you may do your work flawlessly. I am called Lady Reason; you see that you are in good hands. For the time being then, I will say no more."

[*In the following chapters, the other two ladies identify themselves as Rectitude and Justice. Just as Lady Reason had carried a mirror signifying self-knowledge, Rectitude carries a ruler signifying the distinction of right from wrong, and offers to help Christine measure her City of Ladies with it. Lady Justice carries a gold flask from which she portions out justice to all, and promises to help Christine populate her city. The remainder of the book describes Christine's questions to the three ladies about the achievements of women. Countering charges of physical weakness and cowardice, Lady Reason cites the bravery of the Amazons Hippolyta and Penthesilea. As examples of women's intelligence and learning, she offers the wisdom of Sappho and (more problematically) the cleverness of Medea and Circe. Lady Rectitude absolves women of the charge of lustfulness with the biblical examples of Susannah, Sarah, and Rebecca, and the Greek example of Penelope. After praising Christine's construction work, Lady Justice welcomes the Virgin Mary into the City of Ladies, to rule as queen. In the final chapter, Christine offers advice to women of all marital conditions and social stations on how to bear their lot.*]

[Part 3, Chapter 19]

The End of the Book: Christine Addresses the Ladies.

My most honored ladies, may God be praised, for now our City is entirely finished and completed, where all of you who love glory, virtue, and praise may be lodged in great honor, ladies from the past as well as from the present and future, for it has been built and established for every honorable lady. And my most dear ladies, it is natural for the human heart to rejoice when it finds itself victorious in any enterprise and its enemies confounded. Therefore you are right, my ladies, to rejoice greatly in God and in honest mores upon seeing this new City completed, which can be not only the refuge for you all, that is, for virtuous women, but also the defense and guard against your enemies and assailants, if you guard it well. For you can see that the substance with which it is made is entirely of virtue, so resplendent that you may see yourselves mirrored in it, especially in the roofs built in the last part as well as in the other parts which concern you. And my dear ladies, do not misuse this new inheritance like the arrogant who turn proud when their prosperity grows and their wealth multiplies, but rather follow the example of your Queen, the sovereign Virgin, who, after the extraordinary honor of being chosen Mother of the Son of God was announced to her humbled herself all the more by calling herself the handmaiden of God. Thus, my ladies, just as it is true that a creature's humility and kindness wax with the increase of its virtues, may this City be an occasion for you to conduct yourselves honestly and with integrity and to be all the more virtuous and humble.

And you ladies who are married, do not scorn being subject to your husbands, for sometimes it is not the best thing for a creature to be independent. This is attested by what the angel said to Ezra: Those, he said, who take advantage of their free will can fall into sin and despise our Lord and deceive the just, and for this they perish. Those women with peaceful, good, and discreet husbands who are devoted to them, praise God for this boon, which is not inconsiderable, for a greater boon in the world could not be given them. And may they be diligent in serving, loving, and cherishing their husbands in the loyalty of their heart, as they should, keeping their peace and praying to God to uphold and save them. And those women who have husbands neither completely good nor completely bad should still praise God for not having the worst and should strive to moderate their vices and pacify them, according to their conditions. And those women who have husbands who are cruel, mean, and savage should strive to endure them while trying to overcome their vices and lead them back, if they can, to a reasonable and seemly life. And if they are so obstinate that their wives are unable to do anything, at least they will acquire great merit for their souls through the virtue of patience. And everyone will bless them and support them.

So, my ladies, be humble and patient, and God's grace will grow in you, and praise will be given to you as well as the Kingdom of Heaven. For Saint Gregory has said that patience is the entrance to Paradise and the way of Jesus Christ. And may none of you be forced into holding frivolous opinions nor be hardened in them, lacking all basis in reason, nor be jealous or disturbed in mind, nor haughty in speech, nor outrageous in your acts, for these things disturb the mind and lead to madness. Such behavior is unbecoming and unfitting for women.

And you, virgin maidens, be pure, simple, and serene, without vagueness, for the snares of evil men are set for you. Keep your eyes lowered, with few words in your mouths, and act respectfully. Be armed with the strength of virtue against the tricks of the deceptive and avoid their company.

And widows, may there be integrity in your dress, conduct, and speech; piety in your deeds and way of life; prudence in your bearing; patience (so necessary!), strength, and resistance in tribulations and difficult affairs; humility in your heart, countenance, and speech; and charity in your works.

In brief, all women—whether noble, bourgeois, or lower-class—be well-informed in all things and cautious in defending your honor and chastity against your enemies! My ladies, see how these men accuse you of so many vices in everything. Make liars of them all by showing forth your virtue, and prove their attacks false by acting well, so that you can say with the Psalmist, "the vices of the evil will fall on their heads." Repel the deceptive flatterers who, using different charms, seek with various tricks to steal that which you must consummately guard, that is, your honor and the beauty of your praise. Oh my ladies, flee, flee the foolish love they urge on you! Flee it, for God's sake, flee! For no good can come to you from it.

Rather, rest assured that however deceptive their lures, their end is always to your detriment. And do not believe the contrary, for it cannot be otherwise. Remember, dear ladies, how these men call you frail, unserious, and easily influenced but yet try hard, using all kinds of strange and deceptive tricks, to catch you, just as one lays traps for wild animals. Flee, flee, my ladies, and avoid their company—under these smiles are hidden deadly and painful poisons. And so may it please you, my most respected ladies, to cultivate virtue, to flee vice, to increase and multiply our City, and to rejoice and act well. And may I, your servant, commend myself to you, praying to God who by His grace has granted me to live in this world and to persevere in His holy service. May He in the end have mercy on my great sins and grant to me the joy which lasts forever, which I may, by His grace, afford to you. Amen.

HERE ENDS THE THIRD AND LAST PART OF THE BOOK OF THE CITY OF LADIES.

[END OF LATE MEDIEVAL ALLEGORY]

Frontispiece from Saxton's *Atlas*, 1579.

The Early Modern Period

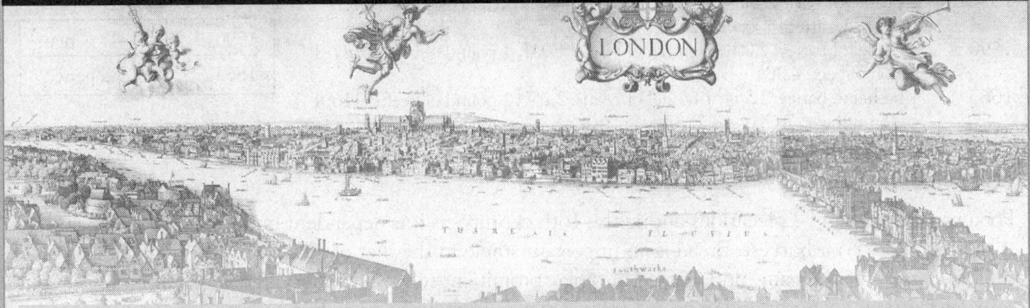

Population[1]

National Populations (in millions)[2]

	England	Scotland	Ireland
1500	3.3[3]	0.5	0.5–0.8
1700	5.6[4]	1.23	1.8–2.0

Urban Populations[5]

	London	Edinburgh	Dublin
1500	40,000–50,000[6]	12,000	5,000–7,000
1600	200,000[7]	30,000	15,000
1700	575,000[8]	40,000	60,000

Life Expectancy

Life expectancy at birth is about 48 years in Elizabethan England, lower in cities where poor sanitation and crowded conditions cause the plague and other diseases—such as typhus, small pox, consumption (tuberculosis), syphilis, scurvy—to spread more easily. The plague is half as severe in the rich parishes in the city center as it had been in 1563 and 83.3% of all deaths are in the poorer areas at the periphery of the city.

1563 17,404 Londoners die of the plague.
1603 25,045 Londoners die of the plague.
1625 26,350 Londoners die of the plague.
1665 55,797 Londoners die of the plague.

Daily Life

Currency[9]

4 farthings	1d. (1 penny)	One silver penny would be worth approximately $1.23 today.
12d.	1s. (1 shilling)	One shilling would be worth approximately $12.06 today.
5s.	1 crown	One crown would be worth approximately $60.30 today.
20s.	1£ (1 pound)	One pound would be worth approximately $241.20 today.
21s.	1 guinea	One guinea would be worth approximately $253.26 today.

Wages

	1590s	1663–1683
Craftsmen	18 pence/day	30 pence/day
Laborers	12 pence/day	18 pence/day

1. Any population figures before 1801, when the first official census was taken, are only hypothetical.
2. The population of today's United Kingdom is 60,943,912 (July 2008 est.).
3. 1.5% of England's population lived in London.
4. 11.5% of England's population lived in London.
5. The population of today's London is over 7.6 million (a figure reported in October 2008).
6. Ten European cities had more inhabitants; six had a similar number.
7. Only Naples and Paris had more people than London; Constantinople had twice as many people as London.
8. London became the largest city in Europe, and by 1750 it had 600,000, as many people as Constantinople.
9. Historical equivalences for the purchasing power of a given sum are very approximate. Different types of calculation provide quite different results. A calculation based on wages, for instance, yields a different figure from a calculation based on the prices of basic consumer goods; and those consumer goods thought essential to daily life change drastically over time. These conversions, then, are meant only to be suggestive.

Cost of Goods

1532 1 bushel of barley: £0.490; 1 bushel of beans: £0.361: 1 pound of beef: £0.865; 1 gallon of beer: £2.651

1590 1 bushel of barley: 2.001; 1 bushel of beans: 1.947; 1 pound of beef: 2.127; 1 gallon of beer: 4.304

1663 1 bushel of barley: 2.554; 1 bushel of beans: 2.251; 1 pound of beef: 3.116; 1 gallon of beer: 7.651

Cost of 4-pound loaf of bread (in London)

1590	4.1 pence
1663	5.8 pence

Food and Drink

Food production can be precarious during the 16th century, as it is dependent on local agriculture, which is susceptible to poor harvest. Bread is an important staple in the diet of all classes. In the upper and middle classes, roasted game and seafood also play prominent roles. The poor often get their protein from milk, eggs, and nuts. Sugar and imported spices are cost-prohibitive and often used to demonstrate social position, but even the lower classes grow some spices in their gardens. Because of unsanitary water supplies, ale is the main beverage for people of all ages. The average adult man consumes about a gallon a day; however, the alcohol content is much less than we know today.

Apparel

Men of the upper and middle classes typically wear a ruff (a separate ruffled collar worn at the neck), codpiece (a pouch that attached to the crotch area of a man's breeches), breeches (pants that stopped just below the knee, each leg was separate), stockings (long socks that covered the entire calf), a doublet (close-fitting, buttoned jacket), and a jerkin (sleeveless jacket worn over the doublet).

Women of the upper and middle classes typically wear a ruff (a separate ruffled collar worn at the neck), bodice (covered from the neck to waist, usually laced closed), sleeves (separate garments), skirt, and farthingale (wheel-shaped stiffening below the waist to which the skirt was pinned).

Most Elizabethan clothing is made from wool or linen, with some items of leather or, for the formal wear of the upper classes, silk. Fashions of the lower classes largely follow those of the upper classes except they rely on cheaper, durable fabrics and styles that allow greater freedom of motion.

Rulers

Oliver Cromwell

Charles II

Rulers
The Tudors
Henry VII, King of England, Lord of Ireland (1485–1509)
Henry VIII, King of England, Lord of Ireland (1509–1547), King of Ireland (1541–1547). His six wives were Catherine of Aragon, Anne Boleyn, Jane Seymour, Anne of Cleves, Catherine Howard, and Catherine Parr.
Edward VI, King of England and Ireland (1547–1553), son of Henry VIII and Jane Seymour
Mary I, Queen of England and Ireland (1553–1558), daughter of Henry VIII and Catherine of Aragon
Elizabeth I, Queen of England and Ireland (1558–1603), daughter of Henry VIII and Anne Boleyn
The Stuarts
James I, James VI, King of Scotland (1567–1615), King of England and Ireland (1603–1625), son of Mary Queen of Scots and Henry Stuart, Lord Darnley
Charles I, King of England, Scotland, and Ireland (1625–1649), son of James I and Anne of Denmark

Rulers

Rulers
Commonwealth of England
Oliver Cromwell, Lord Protector of England, Scotland, and Ireland (1653–1658)
Richard Cromwell, Second Lord Protector of England, Scotland, and Ireland (1658–1659)
Restoration of the Stuart Monarchy
Charles II (Charles Stuart) King of Scotland (1649–1685) and King of England and Ireland (1660–1685), son of Charles I and Henrietta Maria of France

Timeline

1500 10% of men and 1% of women in England can sign their names.
1509 Henry VIII becomes King of England, Lord of Ireland.
1516 Sir Thomas More's *Utopia* (page 716)
1517 Luther protests the Roman Catholic Church's sale of indulgences.
1534 The Act of Supremacy declares Henry VIII to be the "only supreme head on earth of the Church of England," and thus, he severs allegiance to the Pope and Roman Catholicism.
1538 Henry VIII is excommunicated by the Roman Catholic Church.
1547 Henry VIII dies; Edward VI (son of Henry VIII and Jane Seymour) becomes King of England and Ireland.
1553 Edward VI dies of tuberculosis. Edward attempts to exclude Mary (daughter of Henry VIII and Catherine of Aragon) from the throne for fear that she would restore Catholicism. With the support of Edward's advisors, his cousin Lady Jane Grey assumes the throne briefly. The attempt quickly fails and Mary I becomes Queen of England and Ireland.
1558 Mary I dies; Elizabeth I (daughter of Henry VIII and Anne Boleyn) becomes Queen of England and Ireland.
1563 John Foxe publishes his *Acts and Monuments of These Latter and Perilous Days*—later widely known as the *Book of Martyrs* (page 1063).

1565 The Royal Exchange is built by Thomas Gresham as a commercial headquarters for London merchants.
1570 William Baldwin's prose fiction, the *Marvelous History Entitled Beware the Cat, Concerning Diverse Wonderful and Incredible Matters*, is written in 1552 but not published until 1570 (page 790).
1576 Blackfriars, once a Dominican monastery, opens as a theater.
1587 The Catholic Mary Queen of Scots is beheaded having been found guilty of complicity in a plot to murder Queen Elizabeth I.
1587 The Rose Theatre opens.
1588 English naval forces defeat the Spanish Armada.

1590–1596 Edmund Spenser's *The Faerie Queene* (page 824)
1591 Sir Philip Sidney's *Astrophil and Stella* (composed in 1582) is published posthumously (page 680).
1592 Shakespeare begins career in London.
1595 The Swan Theatre opens.
1598 Christopher Marlowe's *Hero and Leander* is published posthumously (page 1092).
1599 The Globe Theatre opens.
1601 Robert Devereux, Earl of Essex, once Queen Elizabeth's favorite, is executed for his rebellion.

1602 William Shakespeare's *Twelfth Night* is first performed (page 1215).
1603 Queen Elizabeth dies; James I (James VI, King of Scotland; son of Mary Queen of Scots and Henry Stuart, Lord Darnley), becomes King of England and Ireland.
1603 Unaware of Elizabeth's death, Hugh O'Neill surrenders after nine years of leading his Irish forces in armed conflict against the crown.
1604 The short version of Christopher Marlowe's *The Tragical History of Dr. Faustus* is published (page 1111).

1604 William Shakespeare's *Othello* is performed for King James I and his guests at Whitehall Palace (page 1272).
1605 Guy Fawkes is captured in the act of attempting to blow up the Houses of Parliament with gunpowder.

1607 Jamestown is established as the first English settlement in North America.
1608 John Smith returns to England (page 1194).
1610 Ben Jonson's *The Alchemist* is first performed (page 1468).
1611 *The King James Bible* is published.
1618 The Thirty Years' War begins.
1619 The banqueting house, Whitehall, is designed by Inigo Jones.

1620 Hic Mulier and Haec-Vir, two pamphlets published within a week of each other, explore issues of gender and apparel (page 1458).
1621 Lady Mary Wroth publishes the first Petrarchan sonnet sequence in English by a woman, *Pamphilia to Amphilanthus* (page 1609).
1625 James I dies; Charles I (son of James I and Anne of Denmark) becomes King of England, Scotland, and Ireland.
1631 John Donne dies (page 1586).
1637 Rioting breaks out in St. Giles Cathedral, Edinburgh, when Charles I imposes the *Book of Common Prayer* on Scots Presbyterians.
1640 "The Short Parliament," the first called by Charles I in 11 years, discusses the king's abuses of power.
1641 Treaty of London is signed granting concessions from Charles I to the Scots Covenanters who had rebelled in the Bishops' War of 1639–1640.
1641 Catholics rebel in Ireland.
1641 The House of Commons passes the Grand Remonstrance, a list of grievances against actions by ministers of Charles I.
1642 30% of men and 10% of women in all of England are literate.
1642 All theaters are shut down in London.
1643 Parliament is purged of those hostile to trying Charles I for treason, and the Rump Parliament is formed.
1643 The Solemn League and Convent, both a military league and a religious covenant, is formed by the Scottish Covenanters and the English Parliamentarians against Charles I and the Royalists.
1644 The Globe Theater is demolished by Puritans, and Sir Matthew Brend builds tenement houses on the site.
1648 The Thirty Years' War ends with the Treaty of Westphalia.
1649 Charles I is beheaded, and Parliament abolishes the monarchy, the Privy Council, and the House of Lords.
1649 The Rump Parliament declares England to be a Commonwealth.
1651 Thomas Hobbes' *Leviathan*
1652 Act for the Settlement of Ireland sentences the rebels of the Confederacy (1641–1652) to be executed and have their lands confiscated.
1653 Oliver Cromwell dismisses the Rump Parliament.

1653 The Barebone's Parliament forms, every member nominated by Oliver Cromwell.
1654–1655 Lord Protector Oliver Cromwell summons the First Protectorate Parliament.
1656–1658 Second Protectorate Parliament.
1659 The Rump Parliament is reinstated by Cromwell's son.
1659 John Lambert and Charles Fleetwood set up a Committee of Safety to rule the Parliament instead of the Rump.
1660 The Royal Society is founded.
1660 General George Monck, commanding the English army in Scotland, reopens the Long Parliament by restoring those Presbyterians purged in 1648.
1660 The Long Parliament is dissolved after creating the Convention Parliament, which invites Charles II to become the English monarch.
1660 Charles II issues the Declaration of Breda, in which he makes known the terms of his acceptance of the crown of England.
1666 Great Fire of London
1667 John Milton's *Paradise Lost* (page 1726)

The Early Modern Period

An Experimental Age

John Milton claimed that in *Paradise Lost* his aim was to produce a work that "things unattempted yet in prose or rhyme." Milton's ambitious boast provides us with a useful key to one of the principal goals of writers in the English Early Modern period—namely, their desire and need to produce work that was new and different from what had gone before, however carefully they acknowledged the past and reused and rethought what had already been written. Virtually every writer included in this section of the anthology can be read as an experimental figure, pushing the boundaries of what was possible in a literary text, more akin perhaps to James Joyce or Virginia Woolf than a writer of realist fiction or a poet following well-trodden paths of lyric style. At the start of this period, in the early sixteenth century, John Skelton invented his own style of English poetry, "Skeltonics," based on short lines of six syllables, enabling him to produce work of great satirical force; Thomas Wyatt and Henry Howard, the Earl of Surrey, concerned that the English lyric lacked the sophistication of the Italian tradition, translated and adapted the sonnets of Petrarch, inventing new English rhyme schemes and styles in the process, as well as complex love poems that often told the reader more about the fears and anxieties of the courtier than they did about the lady in question. In the middle of the century William Baldwin composed a new form of prose fiction that could be regarded as the first novel in English. Toward the end, in one of the most creative periods of English literary history, major writers such as Sir Philip Sidney and Edmund Spenser experimented with new types of poetry, Sidney writing the first sonnet sequence in English, as well as a loosely constructed prose romance, the *Arcadia*, while Spenser, perhaps the most original and innovative poet who had ever written in English, tried out a whole variety of new verse forms, from the populist *Shepheardes Calendar* to the elitist *Fowre Hymns*, producing his own stanza form in his epic-romance, *The Faerie Queene*. John Donne created a distinctive literary voice in his forceful and unsettling erotic and divine poetry, as, in a different way, did George Herbert in his exploration of the meaning of the church and Christian faith in *The Temple*. Women writers also worked hard to forge a literary identity, Isabella Whitney and Lady Mary Wroth writing often angry and despairing lyrics representing the woman's powerlessness in courtship rituals; Aemilia Lanyer producing the first "country house," a poem that represented the sadness at the dissolution of an ideal female community; and other women producing a particularly female approach to the Christian faith.

Virtually every writer included in this section of the anthology can be read as an experimental figure, pushing the boundaries of what was possible in literary text . . .

If anything, English drama was even more willing to push the boundaries of what was possible. The professional stage dates only from the 1560s and became a mass phenomenon in the 1580s, a development few could have predicted.

If anything, English drama was even more willing to push the boundaries of what was possible.

Drama was not taken seriously as a literary form until Ben Jonson produced a folio of his works in 1616, the same year that King James published a similar collection of his political and religious writings. Nevertheless plays did reach a wide audience and, with large theaters such as the Globe, accommodated an audience of 2,000 to 3,000, a significant section of the London population regularly went to see plays before the theaters were closed on the orders of Oliver Cromwell in 1642. Plays had to grab an audience's attention or they risked being trumped by rival companies and fierce "Wars of the Theatres" broke out as companies sought to lure audiences in. Drama thrived in such conditions, especially given the lack of precedents, playwrights being forced to live on their wits and "make it new." The first great star of the new age of commercial theater was Christopher Marlowe, who transformed what it was possible to achieve on stage with the production of *Tamburlaine* in 1587, probably the most influential play of that period, which spawned a host of imitations and helped to characterize a particular, bombastic style of relentless tragedy, based on powerful, overbearing protagonists speaking mighty, rolling lines of blank verse. *Dr. Faustus*, another major play, rethought and adapted the miracle and morality plays that had characterized English drama before the commercial age, and it is a sign of this controversial work's enduring success that generations of readers have not been able to agree whether the play is a subversive or fundamentally conservative work.

The range and variety of Shakespeare's work is stunning, from his early Roman comedy, *The Comedy of Errors*, and historical epic sequence of three plays chronicling the reign of Henry VI (one of the great successes of the early 1590s, even if now it has been relegated to a minor position in his canon), through the major tragedies (written between 1599 and 1607), to the romances, Shakespeare did not stand still. There had been plays about powerful and impressive Moorish and Turkish tyrants, such as Marlowe's Tamburlaine and Robert Greene's *Selimus* (1594); no one, however, raised such a figure to tragic status as Shakespeare did when he wrote *Othello*. Ben Jonson, one of his major rivals, created works that were clearly designed to compete with Shakespeare's in the marketplace. While Shakespeare's company produced romantic comedies based on confusion of identities and genders, most notably, *As You Like It* and *Twelfth Night*, Jonson wrote comedies of humors, city satires that exposed human greed and folly, such as *Everyman in His Humour*, *The Alchemist*, and *The Devil Is an Ass*.

Historical Perspectives

We see the past through lenses that show us something of the world we are living in. How we mark periods in history depends less on an objective evaluation of evidence than on our sense of its relation to our own present. The centuries between 1500 and 1700 have been termed the "Renaissance," and, more recently, "the early modern period." They were also centuries in which Europe and England saw a massive change in Christian religious thought and practice; this has been called the "Reformation." What do these names mean, and what do they tell us about our understanding of this single and continuous stretch of time?

However we describe these centuries, they encompassed events that altered the ways people lived and thought. In 1500 England, and the rest of the nations of Europe, were Catholic. Apart from its few communities of Jews, Christendom was united by a universal church whose head was the Pope in Rome, and its faithful prayed according to a common liturgy in Latin. The shape of the cosmos was determined by Aristotelian physics and what could be deduced from the scriptural story of creation. It was believed that the earth was the center of the universe and composed of four elements—earth, air, fire, and water; that the human body was a balance of these elements; and that nature, read as if it were a book, revealed a divinely sanctioned moral order. Christian subjects generally respected their national or positive law, which they saw as a mirror of God's law of nature and providentially guaranteed; they assumed it would protect them from tyranny as well as anarchy. A person's place in society tended to be fixed at birth; the majority of folk lived in country villages, worked the land, and traded in regional markets.

By the end of the seventeenth century, much—though not all—of this way of life had vanished. Certain of its features would remain in place for the next hundred years, as historians who study *la longue durée* ("the long term" from the seventeenth to the nineteenth century) during which social, political and economic structures change very slowly, remind us: land continued to be farmed by methods followed "time out of mind"; manufacture was still largely done by individuals on small, handmade machines. Religion continued to determine every aspect of life; science and art, politics and economics were discussed in terms supplied by religious thought and institutions. But Christianity was no longer of one piece. Europe had become divided by the establishment of Protestantism in the Low Countries, Scandinavia, and most of Germany. England and Scotland were also Protestant, but with a difference: the first conformed to the doctrine and practices of the Church of England, the second to the requirements of Presbyterianism. Ireland, speaking its Celtic language and retaining many of its ancient customs, remained Catholic despite English attempts at conquest and conversion. Catholics in England, always suspected of subversive intentions, were barely tolerated. Sects proliferated: among them were Anabaptists, Puritans, and Quakers; commonly, their religious doctrines called for massive social change. Cosmic order, too, had changed; it was no longer thought of as geocentric, nor did its elements consist of four primary materials. A natural philosophy based on experimental methods had begun to reshape the disciplines of physics, medicine, and biology; such ancient authorities as Aristotle, Galen, and Pliny were no longer unquestioned. Though sketched in principle by Sir Francis Bacon in his treatise on scientific inquiry, *Novum Organum* ("the new instrument"), published in 1620, a systematic investigation of nature was not underway before the Restoration of the Stuart monarchy in 1660, when scientists in England consolidated their status as intellectuals by forming the Royal Society of London for the Improvement of Natural Knowledge—an organization vigorously supported by the new Stuart king, Charles II. But the worldview that this investigation would help to confirm was already evident early in the seventeenth century. The work of the Italian physicist Galileo Galilei on gravitational force had demonstrated that the most elementary laws of nature were mathematical; the German astronomer Johannes Kepler had confirmed that the universe was heliocentric; the English physician William Harvey had

Religion continued to determine every aspect of life . . .

established that the body was energized not by the eccentric flow of "humors" but by a circulation of blood to and from the heart; and the Dutch cosmographer Gerhardus Mercator had discovered the means to navigate the globe safely by accurately mapping latitude and longitude. An international trade, now hugely stimulated by the development of colonies in the Americas, promised wealth to investors willing to take risks and prosperity to the towns and cities in which they lived.

In England, social and political life had been transformed by the activities of city-dwellers . . .

In England, social and political life had been transformed by the activities of city-dwellers, or "burgesses," many of whom were merchants, and also by a civil war. Involving English, Scots, and Irish subjects and parties, it had been fought over religious and social issues but also on a matter of principle. British subjects were to be governed by a monarch whose authority and power were not absolute but limited by law and the actions of Parliament, a legislative assembly representing the monarch's subjects. As a whole, the nation was conceived of as a "mystical body politic"; as the radical Bishop of Winchester John Ponet had declared, the monarch's office—not his person—was sacred. Towns and cities became crowded even as they expanded with new streets, marketplaces, and buildings for private as well as public use. Country folk, flocking to these burgeoning urban centers, succumbed to diseases created by filth and overcrowding and died younger than did their rural relatives. But England was becoming a nation of city dwellers, and everyone knew of "citizens" who had gained wealth and station in these exciting, if also terrifying, cities.

The Humanist Renaissance and Early Modern Society

The period from 1500 to 1700 has been understood as a "Renaissance"—literally a "rebirth." Many of its features had already been registered in that earlier renaissance of the twelfth century, particularly an interest in classical authors and their modes of expression in logic and rhetoric. By 1400, however, Italian scholars had begun to reread with fresh eyes the works of Greek and Roman authors such as Plato, Aristotle, Virgil, Ovid, and Horace. What was "reborn" as a result was a sense of the meanings to be discovered in the here and now, in the social, political, and economic everyday world. Writing about the intellectual vitality of the age, the French humanist François Rabelais had his amiable character, the giant Gargantua, confess that his own education had been "darksome, obscured with clouds of ignorance." Gargantua knows, however, that his son will be taught differently:

> Good literature has been restored unto its former light and dignity, and with such amendment and increase of knowledge, that now hardly should I be admitted unto the first form of the little grammar-school boys . . . I see robbers, hangmen, freebooters, tapsters, ostlers, and such like, of the very rubbish of the people, more learned now than the doctors and preachers were in my time.

These comically overstated remarks nevertheless convey the spirit of the Renaissance: learning was no longer to be devoted only to securing salvation but should address the conditions of ordinary life as well. More important, it should be disseminated through all ranks of society.

IMAGO·ERASMI·ROTERODA·
MI·AB·ALBERTO·DVRERO·AD
VIVAM·EFFIGIEM·DELINIATA·
THN·KPEITTΩ·TA·ΣΥΓΓPAM
MATA·ΔΕΙΞΕΙ
·MDXXVI·

Albrecht Dürer, *Erasmus of Rotterdam,* 1521.

The writers and scholars responsible for the rebirth of a secular culture, derived in large measure from the pre-Christian cultures of the ancient Mediterranean, have been known as "humanists," because they read "humane" as well as "sacred" letters; their intellectual and artistic practices have been termed "humanism." They cultivated certain habits of thought that became widely adopted by early modern thinkers of all kinds: skill in using language analytically, attentiveness to public and political affairs as well as private and moral ones, and an acute appreciation for differences between peoples, regions, and times. It was, after all, the humanists who began to realize that the classical past required *understanding.* They recognized it as unfamiliar, neither Christian nor European, and they knew, therefore, that it had to be studied, interpreted, and, in a sense, reborn. From its inception in Italy, the work of the humanists traveled north and west, to France, the Low Countries, Germany, the Iberian peninsula, and eventually the British Isles.

. . . learning was no longer to be devoted only to securing salvation but should address the conditions of ordinary life as well.

At the same time, the cultures of these regions were changing in unprecedented ways. As much as an older world was being reborn, a modern world was being born, and it is in this sense that we can speak of these centuries not only as the Renaissance but also as the "early modern period." Its modernity was registered in various ways, many of them having to do with systems of quantification. Instruments for measuring time and space provided a knowledge of physical nature and its control. Sailing to the new world in 1585, Sir Walter Raleigh made use of Mercator's projection, published in 1568. Means were designed to compute the wealth that was being created by manufacture and trade. Money was used in new and complex ways, its flow managed through such innovations as double-entry bookkeeping and letters of exchange that registered debt and credit in inter-regional markets. The capital that accumulated as a result of these kinds of transactions fueled merchant banks, joint-stock companies, and—notably in England—trading companies that sponsored colonies abroad. Heralded with enthusiasm by William Drayton in 1606, the Virginia colony was reflected in a more muted fashion five years later in Shakespeare's *The Tempest.* In England especially, wealth was increasingly based not on land but on money, and the change encouraged a social mobility that reflected but also exploited the old hierarchy. The effort to ascend the social ladder could prove ruinous, as George Gascoigne's career confirmed. But riches could also make it possible for an artisan's son to purchase a coat of arms and become a gentleman, as Shakespeare did. More important, moneyed wealth supported the artistic and scholarly institutions that allowed the stepson of a bricklayer to attend the best school in London, to profit from the business of the theater, and to compose literary works of sufficient brilliance to make him Poet Laureate—as Ben Jonson did. "Ambition is like choler," warned Francis Bacon; it makes men "active, earnest, full of alacrity and stirring." But if ambition "be stopped and cannot have his way, it becommeth adust, and thereby maligne and venomous." Early modern society was certainly both active and stirring, but the very energy that gave it momentum could also lead to hardship, distress, and personal tragedy.

Writing for a New Age

The sixteenth-century was a time of discontinuities and lost possibilities as well as spectacular advances and transformations.

The sixteenth-century was a time of discontinuities and lost possibilities as well as spectacular advances and transformations. Henry VIII was known throughout Europe as a monarch sympathetic to humanist ideas and educational programs in the first half of his reign. Many writers were enthusiastic about his reign and his desire to transform England into a modern European nation after the austere and straightened reign of his father Henry VII. However, after his divorce from Catherine of Aragon and the break with Rome in 1532, Henry became increasingly despotic and unpredictable, becoming notorious as a tyrant among many of his more enlightened subjects. It would have been hard to predict the end of the reign from its promising beginnings.

English history and literary history is characterized by such breaks and unforeseen changes. The English adaptation of the European sonnet, for example, was hardly a smooth process. Chaucer adapted sonnet forms in his longer narrative poems in the late fourteenth century; Wyatt and Surrey adapted Italian sonnets at Henry's court that were republished in the first major anthology of English lyric poetry Tottel's *Miscellany* (1557); and after Sir Phillip Sidney's *Astrophil and Stella* (composed 1582, published posthumously 1591) there was a vogue for sonnet sequences in the 1590s, which appeared to have died out until it was revived by the publication of William Shakespeare's *Sonnets* in 1609 (some of which may have been written in the 1590s). This does not tell the whole story of the complicated nature of English literary history. Sonnets came in and out of vogue, and other verse forms dominated the literary scene at different points in the century. At the court of Edward VI, more obviously Protestant types of literary verse were promoted by significant intellectual figures, some of them like John Bale returning from exile in the last years of Henry's reign. Allegorical and political poetry experienced a resurgence; and there was an attempt to establish a native English Protestant tradition that looked back to the figure of the plowman (represented most famously in the works of William Langland), intimately connected to the soil and the land, and so able to tell the truth about the corruption of the court. One of the most important writers in Edward's reign was William Baldwin who wrote what many consider to be the first English novel, *Beware the Cat* (page 790) and was the leading light behind the collaborative project *A Mirror Magistrates*, one of Shakespeare's favorite works. *A Mirror* was begun in the reign of Edward VI, but it was not published until 1559, because it fell afoul of the censors in 1555. *A Mirror* is very much a product of a militant Protestant literary culture, but after the death of the young king from tuberculosis in 1553, the work was not received sympathetically at the Catholic court of Edward's half-sister Mary.

A Mirror was one of the most important literary texts of the second half of the sixteenth century and went through a number of different editions and versions well into the seventeenth century. The work consists of a series of verse laments by ghosts of dead political figures who usually lament their own failings and ask the assembled group of writers to learn from their mistakes. The team of writers led by Baldwin comment on the particular tragedy and point a moral for the readers to learn from. The work revises the well established genre of advice literature, the mirror for princes (showing monarchs how to rule through a series of negative and positive examples of government), refocusing attention on the individual magistrates as a governing class. Had Edward VI not died so young, it is likely that similar forms of literature would have proliferated in subsequent years and changed the shape and nature of English literary history.

But this is not the only way to look at English literature and history in the sixteenth century. It used to be an orthodox judgment to see the reign of Mary Tudor (1553–1558) as an attempt to artificially revive a long-gone Catholic sensibility and impose it on the English people from above. Recent research, proposed by Eamon Duffy, sees the map of English religious history in a very different way. For Duffy, it is Henry VIII, Edward VI, and Protestant revolutionaries who sought to impose their vision on a reluctant English people. Rather than translators of the Bible and advocates of a break with Rome being those who correctly read the religious desires of the nation, it was, in fact, adherence to the traditional idea of the late medieval church. Whereas Protestants wanted people to read the Bible and determine their own understanding of the word of God, Marian Catholics placed much greater importance on the institution of the church itself and its ability to interpret God's word for an obedient people, concentrating more on liturgy and ritual than sermons and exegesis. Hence, the widespread Catholic taunt, "Where was your church before Luther?"

In Mary's reign many Protestants went into exile in Switzerland, France and the Low Countries, developing their own ideas and their own version of English history, especially in Basel and Geneva, which became centers of resistance to Mary's regime. One of the main achievements of the exiles was the Geneva Bible, often popularly known as the "Breeches Bible," because the translator claimed that Adam and Eve made trousers ("breeches") out of leaves to cover their nakedness. The

Geneva Bible was first published in 1563 and went through several editions, becoming the most popular English Bible in the sixteenth and seventeenth centuries, principally because it was the most widely available and the cheapest. The Bible had an extensive commentary which directed readers to see the history of the church as a battle between the good Protestant forces and the evil Catholic Church of Rome. It had a crucial influence on later English writing. For example, Edmund Spenser cast the duplicitous Duessa as the Whore of Babylon from the Book of Revelation, the seductive and diabolical figure of the Catholic Church in the last days of the world, a reading that could only have been derived from the Geneva Bible.

The other major achievement of the exiles was John Foxe's *Acts and Monuments of the Christian Church*, first published in 1563, a work deemed so important by the Elizabethan authorities that a copy had to be kept in every cathedral church (the principal church connected with a bishop) in the country (see page 1063). Foxe's purpose was to explain that the Protestant church did have a history and was not merely the brainchild of a few disgruntled clergymen. Foxe saw the medieval church as a divided institution, a battleground between those good men who wished to spread the word of God as widely as possible and those evil and deluded priests who wished to suppress the truth and control the people for their own purposes. Like the Geneva Bible, Foxe's history also had a significant impact on the course of English literary history, providing Protestants with a story that they could call their own.

. . . religious history was complex and conflicted in the sixteenth century.

The point to be made is that religious history was complex and conflicted in the sixteenth century. Battle lines were drawn between Catholic and Protestant interpretations and contingent events often determined the course of English history and its literature. However, we must not imagine that divisions were always clear-cut. As the work of Alison Shell has demonstrated, Protestant and Catholic writers borrowed liberally from each other's work, often sharing a common religious and literary language. It is not always easy to tell apart the work of writers such as George Herbert, an Anglican priest, and Robert Southwell, a Catholic martyr. To take another important example, John Donne uses both Catholic and Protestant ideas and vocabulary in his work, perhaps the product of his upbringing as a Catholic and his later conversion to Protestantism, perhaps simply a sign of complicated religious times that tolerated significant overlap between varieties of the same faith.

One of the great surprises for people living at the end of the sixteenth century was that Elizabeth lived so long. The longest reigning monarch since Henry I (1087–1135), the fourth son of William the Conqueror, Elizabeth had been seriously ill at various points in her reign and had not been expected to survive. Historians often make a distinction between the first half of her reign from about 1558 to 1585—when Elizabeth was undoubtedly a shrewd, popular, and successful monarch who united the disparate factions of her kingdoms—and the second half of her reign, when, whatever her merits, many of her leading subjects tired of her style of government and were looking forward to the reign of her successor, whoever that might be. Elizabeth, the Virgin Queen, encouraged a particular style of obeisance in which courtiers paid homage to her as if she were a love object, and she was notorious for encouraging young male favorites, most notably in her later years Robert Devereux, first Earl of Essex, who was eventually

Jan van der Straet, called Stradanus, Impressio Librorum (Book Printing): Plate 4 of the *Nova Reperta* (New Discoveries), late 16th century.

executed after he led a desperate and suicidal rebellion against her in 1601. One of the great ironies of English literary history is that the literature that we often think of as the golden age of Elizabethan writing was produced in the late 1580s and 1590s, a disastrous decade characterized by desperate uncertainty, famine, and political disasters (not least the protracted and terrifying war in Ireland, which nearly bankrupted the crown). The work of Marlowe, Sidney, Shakespeare, Spenser, and Donne was all the product of turbulent times. Moreover, had Elizabeth died earlier, much of it would either never have been written or would have appeared in a very different form.

Many features of Renaissance and early modern culture are again in transition today . . .

Many features of Renaissance and early modern culture are again in transition today: the printed book, which once superseded the manuscript, is now challenged by computer-generated hypertext; the nation state, which once eclipsed the feudal domain and divided "Christendom," is now qualified by an international economy; and the belief in human progress, which was once applauded as an advance over the medieval faith in divine providence, is now subject to criticism, in large part because of such kinds of injustice and inequity as slavery, colonialism, and the exploitation of wage labor—all factors in the growth of early modern England and other states in Europe. As modern and postmodern readers, we have a special affinity with our early modern counterparts. Like them, we study change.

HISTORY AND EPIC

The political life of the sixteenth century was dominated by the genius of a single dynasty: the Tudors. Its founder was Owen Tudor, a squire of an ancient Welsh family. Employed at the court of Henry V, he eventually married Henry's widow, Catherine of Valois. The first Tudor monarch was their grandson, Henry, Earl of Richmond, who defeated Richard III at Bosworth Field in 1485 to become Henry VII. He married Elizabeth, daughter of Edward IV, whom Richard III had succeeded—a fortunate event for the people of England, as it united the two parties by whom the crown had been disputed for many decades. Once Henry, who represented the House of Lancaster (whose emblem was a red rose) was joined to Elizabeth, a member of the House of York (signified by a white rose), the so-called "Wars of the Roses" were at an end. Henry VII's bureaucratic skills then settled the kingdom in ways that allowed it to grow and become identified as a single nation, however much it also comprised different peoples: the midlands and the north were distinguished from the more populous south by dialectal forms of speech; and to the west, in Cornwall and Wales, many English subjects still spoke Cornish and Welsh. Ireland, across the sea to the west, and the Scottish highlands to the north were still largely Gaelic speaking. While the Anglo-Normans had invaded Ireland in the twelfth century, it was not until the reign of Elizabeth that the English pursued the subjugation of Ireland by colonizing plantations and conducting a brutal military campaign that produced famine, massacres, and the forced relocation of people. But this supposed English fiefdom remained rebellious and effectively unconquered for Elizabeth's entire reign. Its resistance to English rule was crushed only in 1603, an event that marked the end of an independent Ireland for three hundred years. Oliver Cromwell's account of the massacre of the city of Drogheda in 1649, related in his *Letters from Ireland,* illustrates a later instance of the brutality typical of the English conquest of Ireland. Scotland, to the far north, was a separate and generally unfriendly kingdom with strong ties to France until James VI of Scotland became James I of England. His accession to the English throne in 1603 began a process that would end with the complete union of the two kingdoms in 1707. And there were even more remote regions to consider: England's colonization of the Americas began under Elizabeth I, progressed under James I, and allowed the English to think of themselves as an imperial power.

Writing history offered a way to reinforce the developing sense of nationhood, a project all the more appealing after the creation of an English church and the beginnings of what was thought to be a British empire. Medieval historians had concentrated on the actions of ambitious men and women whose lives reflected their good or bad qualities; early modern historians wrote about events and their manifold causes. William Camden's *Britannia* and Raphael Holinshed's *Chronicles of England, Scotland, and Ireland* (the source for many of Shakespeare's plays) celebrate the deeds and the character of the early peoples of the British Isles. The land itself became the subject of comment: William Harrison wrote a description of the English counties (included in Holinshed); John Stow surveyed the neighborhoods of London; and Michael Drayton, a Stuart poet, wrote a mythopoetic account of England's towns and countryside entitled *Poly-Olbion.* As a history, however, it is Richard Hakluyt's collection of travel stories, *The Principal Navigations, Voyages and Discoveries of the English Nation*, that has proved most memorable over time. It reports in magnificent detail the exploration of the Americas in the latter half of the sixteenth century. Accounts of this wild and fruitful land fired the imaginations of English readers, who, it was hoped, would decide to promote and even participate in the laborious task of colonization. Describing landfall on the coast of Virginia in 1585, Arthur Barlow evoked the image of a paradise, "where we smelled so sweet and so strong a smell as if we had been in the midst of some delicate garden abounding with all kind of odoriferous flowers. . . . I think in all the world the like abundance is not to be found." Attempts to occupy this land of incredible natural wealth were determined by two principal objectives: securing profitable trade with the Indians, and possessing land from which to extract such resources as timber, furs, fish, and eventually, tobacco. The hope of finding gold was on everyone's mind. The Chesapeake Bay and its environs were settled by men interested in commerce, often at great personal expense. The Massachusetts coast attracted Puritan divines and their flocks, and while these colonists also profited from trade, matters of faith were supposed to be their principal concern. By celebrating a national identity, these and other contemporary narratives reveal their thematic connections with the epic, a genre of poetic fiction. But they do not conform to that genre as contemporary poetry represented it—expressing heroic grandeur not only in action but also in the musical verse form and elevated language of the epic tradition.

The masterpieces of early modern English epic are represented by Edmund Spenser's *The Faerie Queene* and John Milton's *Paradise Lost*. Spenser imitated continental models to create an English Protestant epic-romance, an optimistic projection of Elizabethan culture. The realities of Elizabeth I's reign were indeed far from the poet's vision of things, but they were nonetheless very impressive. England's cities had grown to be centers of world commerce, and the bold explorations of such men as Sir Francis Drake testified to the nation's seafaring power. In the figures of his poem, Spenser embodied the energies producing this expansive growth. His virtuous knights overcome monstrous threats to order, peace, and tranquillity. Aspects of the queen's own genius are reflected in his heroines. Like the warrior maiden Britomart, Elizabeth I assumed a martial character when England was in danger from abroad; like his Queen Mercilla, she was supposed to be gracious to her enemies—a trait somewhat belied by her speeches to Parliament agreeing to the execution of Mary Queen of Scots. Like the virgin Una, she stood for what the poet and most of his readers believed was the one true faith: Protestantism. And like Spenser's enigmatic and distant Queen Gloriana, the Faerie Queene of the title, she exercised her authority and power in unpredictable ways: secrecy and dissimulation were her stock in trade. To her subjects, her majesty was awful and sometimes terrifying. But she was also mortal, and at her death, few could have foreseen the new and divided nation that would come into being with the accession of James I.

England's cities had grown to be centers of world commerce . . .

The new king was greeted with mixed feelings. On the one hand, his claim to the throne was not disputed; on the other hand, he came from Scotland, long an enemy of England and always a source of anxiety to those who sought dominion over the British Isles as a whole. Although educated by the humanist George Buchanan, whose treatises praising republican government were widely known and read, James, as his own treatise *The True Law of Free Monarchy* shows, favored absolute rule and believed that a monarch should be *lex loquens*, the living spirit of the law, and therefore not bound by the terms of national or positive law. His personal conduct appeared to be dubious. His critics represented him as frequently unkempt and claimed that he preferred to hunt deer rather than to take charge of matters of state. Disputes with the House of Commons over money to support the Crown's activities were frequent. Reports of intrigue with Catholic Spain shattered the nation's sense of security; an attempt in 1605 to blow up the Houses of Parliament, revealed as the Gunpowder Plot, caused a near panic. These and other kinds of unrest grew more intense when James's heir, Charles I, proved to be even more autocratic than his father. Charles's queen, Henrietta Maria, the daughter of Henry IV of France, was a Catholic, and it was rumored that she was treacherous. Religious controversy raged throughout the British Isles, and the struggle over the authority and power of the monarch culminated in a bloody civil war. Across England and Scotland, forces loyal to the king fought the army of Parliament, led by Oliver Cromwell, a Puritan Member of the Commons. The war, which lasted from 1642 to 1651, ended with the defeat of the royalists.

. . . the struggle over the authority and power of the monarch culminated in a bloody civil war.

In 1649 Charles I was captured and executed by order of Parliament, and England began to be governed as a republic. She was no longer a kingdom but a Commonwealth, and this period in her history is known as the Interregnum, the period between kingdoms. The long-advocated change, now a reality, could hardly have begun in a more shocking way. The monarchy had always been regarded as a sacred office and institution, as Shakespeare's Richard II had said:

> Not all the water in the rough rude sea
> Can wash the balm off from an anointed king;
> The breath of worldly men cannot depose
> The deputy elected by the Lord.

But in the course of half a century, the people had proved themselves to be a sovereign power, and it was politically irrelevant that Charles, on the block, exemplified a regal self-control. As the Parliamentarian poet Andrew Marvell later wrote of the King's admirable courage at his execution: "He nothing common did or mean / Upon that memorable scene . . . Nor called the gods with vulgar spite / To vindicate his helpless right."

The conflict itself, its causes and its outcome, have been variously interpreted. As a religious and cultural struggle, the Civil War, also known as the Wars of Three Kingdoms, expressed the resistance of Scots Presbyterians and Irish Catholics to the centralizing control of the English church and government. As a revolution in government, the conflict was defined by common lawyers, energized by Puritan enthusiasm, and marked the nation's transition to a society in which the absolute rule by a monarch was no longer a possibility. The people themselves had acquired a voice. To some extent this was a religious voice. Puritans who professed a belief in congregational church government were generally proponents of republican rule. Their dedication to the ideal of a society of equals under the law was shared by men and women of other sects: the Levellers, led

The people themselves had acquired a voice.

by John Lilburne, who argued for a written constitution, universal manhood suffrage, and religious toleration (for God, Lilburne wrote, "doth not choose many rich, nor many wise"); the Diggers, led by Gerrard Winstanley, who proposed to institute a communistic society in the wastelands they were ploughing and cultivating; the Quakers, led by George Fox, who rejected all forms of church order in deference to the inner light of an individual conscience and, insisting on social equality, refused to take off their hats before gentry or nobility; and the Ranters, who denied the authority of Scripture and saw God everywhere in nature. Without widespread acceptance of the egalitarian concept that had initiated the Protestant reformation—all believers are members of a real though invisible priesthood—it is hard to see how the move from a monarchy to a representative and republican government could have taken place.

The most comprehensive contemporary history of the war, *The True Historical Narrative of the Rebellion and Civil Wars in England,* by Edward Hyde, Earl of Clarendon, was not published before 1704, but the troubled period found an oblique commentary in what is arguably England's greatest and certainly most humanistic epic poem: Milton's *Paradise Lost,* in print by 1667. Milton's career was inextricably bound up with the fate of the Commonwealth. Educated at Cambridge and with his reputation as a poet well established, Milton had begun by 1649 to contribute to a defense of Puritanism and the creation of a republican government. Despite worsening eyesight, he published *The Tenure of Kings and Magistrates,* a sustained and eloquent apology for tyrannicide, after the execution of Charles I; and in his *Eikonoklastes* ("image-breaker"), written after he was made Latin secretary to the new executive, the Council of State, he derided attempts by royalists to celebrate Charles I in John Gauden's pamphlet *Eikon Basilike* ("image of a king"). In 1660, disturbed by the proposed restoration of Charles Stuart, soon to be Charles II, Milton—now completely blind—published his last political treatise, *The Ready and Easy Way to Establish a Commonwealth.* It presented the case for a republicanism that had already lost most of its popularity: the government of the Commonwealth had adopted measures that resembled the autocratic rule of the monarchy it had overthrown. Meanwhile, the composition of *Paradise Lost* was underway. Indebted to many of Spenser's themes in *The Faerie Queene,* Milton infused his subject—the fall of the rebellious angels and the exile from paradise of the disobedient Adam and Eve—with the spirit of the account in Genesis. His poem is the product of a doubly dark vision of life. Sightless and suffering again what he felt were the constraints of a monarchy, Milton's story of exile from paradise spoke to his own and England's loss of innocence and painful acquisition of the knowledge of good and evil during the period of the war and its aftermath. His *Paradise Lost* and its sequel, *Paradise Regained,* express the most provocative ambiguities of contemporary English culture; they were—and still are—praised as rivalling the epics of Homer, Virgil, and Dante in their power and scope.

DRAMA

Drama provided another perspective on English life. While epics depicted the grander aspirations of the nation, its human character was expressed in stage plays, masques or speaking pageants, and dramatic processions. These forms exploited the material of chronicle to illustrate not only the virtues of heroes but also their foibles and limitations; history's villains warned viewers that evil would be punished, if not by civil

While epics depicted the grander aspirations of the nation, its human character was expressed in stage plays . . .

authority then by providence. Writing tragedy based on history and legend, Marlowe and Shakespeare complicated the direct moralism of medieval drama. Rather than portraying characters who became victims of their own misdoings, rising to power only to fall in disgrace, the early modern stage showed virtue and vice as intertwined—a hero's tragic error could also be at the heart of his greatness. The origins of evil were seen as mysterious, even obscure. Some sense of this moral ambiguity can be traced to the tragedies of the Roman philosopher Seneca, which were translated into English and published in 1581. English drama reproduced many of their features: the five-act structure, rapid-fire dialogue punctuated by pithy maxims, and images of tyranny, revenge, and fate illustrated by haunting dreams and echoing curses.

If tragedy turned away from straightforward piety, so did comedy. The medieval drama of Christian salvation, in which the hero's struggle against sin was ended by his acknowledgment of grace, was replaced with plays about the wars between the sexes and between parents and children. Much of this material was modeled on the comedies of Plautus, a Roman playwright, and on the tales or *novellas* of contemporary Italian writers. Playwrights like Ben Jonson also found a wealth of material in the improvisatory Italian *commedia dell'arte*, with its stock characters of the old dotard, the cuckolded husband, the damsel in distress, and the mountebank or quack. *The Alchemist*, chiefly a satire on confidence men and their credulous victims, those tradesmen and entrepreneurs seeking a quick and easy return on investments (especially in the Americas), concludes somewhat ironically by giving the prize to the burgess Lovewit, who disdains censorious critique in favor of a genial wit. An even more topical form of comedy combined some of these continental traditions with themes and figures specifically drawn from London life.

The stage was generally regarded as responsible for both illustrating social failings and stirring up discontent. Although some, like the playwright Thomas Heywood, praised plays as a form of instruction for the unschooled, others, like the Puritan pamphleteer Philip Stubbes, asserted that plays "maintain bawdry, insinuate foolery, and revive the remembrance of heathen idolatry." As Stephen Gosson wrote in *Plays Confuted in Five Actions:*

The stage was generally regarded as responsible for both illustrating social failings and stirring up discontent.

> If private men be suffered to forsake their calling because they desire to talk gentlemen-like in satin & velvet, with a buckler at their heels, proportion is so broken, unity dissolved, harmony confounded, that the whole body must be dismembered, and the prince or head cannot choose but sicken.

The fear was not only that the tricksters of drama would be the objects of emulation rather than scorn, but also that the actors' masquerade of identities would spur social instability in the public theater's audience, ranging from the groundlings in the pit to the gentry in the higher-priced seats. Parliament had tried to maintain social order by regulating, through sumptuary laws, what style and fabrics persons of a particular rank could wear. A subject's experience of the

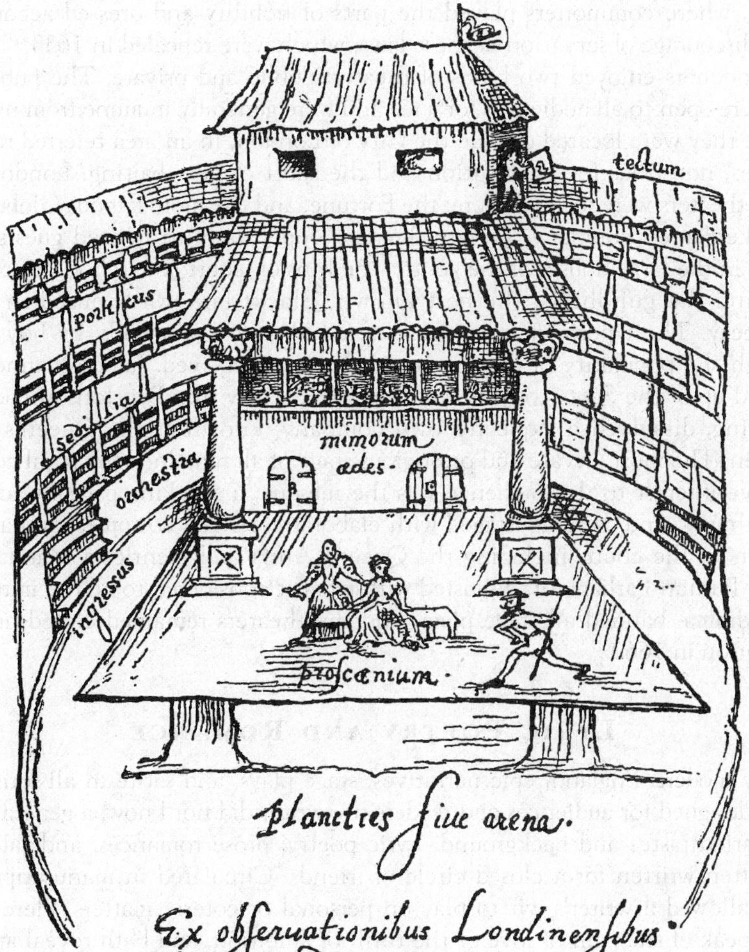

Arend von Buchell, *The Swan Theatre*, after Johannes de Witt, c. 1596. The only extant drawing of a public theater in 1590s London, this sketch shows what Shakespeare's Globe must have looked like. The round playhouse centered on the curtainless platform of the stage (*proscenium*), which projected into the yard (*planities sive arena*). Raised above the stage by two pillars, the roof (*tectum*) stored machinery. At the back of the stage, the tiring house (*mimorum aedes*), where the actors dressed, contained two doors for entrances and exits. There were no stage sets and only movable props such as thrones, tables, beds, and benches, like the one shown here. Other documents on the early modern stage are the contract of the Fortune Theatre, where *The Roaring Girl* was performed, and stage directions in the plays themselves. Modeled on the Globe, although square in shape, the Fortune featured a stage forty-three feet broad and twenty-seven and a half feet deep. Stage directions include further clues: sometimes a curtained booth made "discovery" scenes possible; trapdoors allowed descents; and a space "aloft," such as the gallery above the stage doors, represented a room above the street. Eyewitness accounts fill out the picture. In the yard stood the groundlings who paid a penny for standing room, exposed to the sky, which provided natural lighting. For those willing to pay a penny or two more, three galleries (*orchestra, sedilia,* and *porticulus*) provided seats—the most expensive of which were cushioned. Spectators could buy food and drink during the performance. The early modern theater held an audience of roughly eight hundred standing in the yard, and fifteen hundred more seated in the galleries. According to Thomas Platter, who had seen Shakespeare's *Julius Caesar* in 1599, "everyone has a good view."

theater, where commoners played the parts of nobility and dressed accordingly, might discourage observation of these laws, which were repealed in 1633.

Londoners enjoyed two kinds of theater: public and private. The public theaters were open to all audiences for a fee and were generally immune from oversight because they were located outside the City of London, in an area referred to as the Liberties, notorious for prostitution and the sport of bear-baiting. London's two biggest theaters were located there: the Fortune, and the more famous Globe, home to Shakespeare's company. Private theaters—open only to invited guests—were located in the large houses of the gentry, the Inns of Court (the schools of common law), and the guildhalls; the best known, Blackfriars, was housed in an old monastery. Their performances were acted almost exclusively by boy actors, although the popularity of these companies was short-lived. James I, annoyed by the send-up of the Scots court in *Eastward Ho!*, a play that Ben Jonson had a part in writing, dissolved his queen's own company, known as the Queen's Revels Children. The most private and prestigious stage of all remained the royal court. Of exclusive interest to this audience was the masque, a speaking pageant accompanied by music and dancing, staged with elaborate sets and costumes, and acted by members of the court, including the Queens Anna and Henrietta Maria. But in 1649, a Puritan Parliament, disgusted with what it considered to be the immorality of the drama, banned all stage plays, and the theaters remained closed until the Restoration in 1660.

Lyric Poetry and Romance

In early modern England, epic narratives, stage plays, and satire in all forms were genres designed for audiences and readers the writer did not know, a general public with varied tastes and background. Lyric poetry, prose romances, and tales were more often written for a closed circle of friends. Circulated in manuscript, these genres allowed a writer's wit to play on personal or coterie matters. Here writers could speak of the pain of love or the thrill of ambition, and both reveal and, in a sense, create their own identities in and through language. By imitating and at the same time changing the conventions of the lyric, particularly as they were illustrated by the Italian poet Francesco Petrarch, English poets were able to represent a persona, or fictive self, that became in turn a model for others. Unlike Petrarch, who saw his lady as imbued with numinous power before which he could only submit, Sir Thomas Wyatt and Sir Philip Sidney imagined love in social and very human terms. In the struggle to gain affection and power, their subjectivity took strength from their conquests as well as their resistance to defeat. The origins of the lyric in song are attested in the verse of Thomas Campion, much of which was actually set to music. Its uses in pastoral (whether erotic or spiritual) are illustrated by poets as different as Robert Herrick, John Donne, and Andrew Marvell. At times, its objects of adoration could be divine or mystical, as in the verse of George Herbert and Henry Vaughan. Women poets, such as Lady Mary Wroth and Katherine Philips, reworked the conventions of the love lyric to encompass a feminine perspective on passion and, equally important, on friendship. Sonnet sequences were popular and, reflecting a taste for narrative romance, often dramatized a conflict between lovers. Shakespeare wrote the best-known sonnets of

Color Plate 11 Surviving the Reformation. Rowland Lockey, *Sir Thomas More, 1478–1535, His Family and Descendants*, 1593. Commissioned by Thomas More II, grandson of Sir Thomas More, this painting portrays five generations of this Roman Catholic family. The first seven figures from left to right are modeled on a lost painting by Hans Holbein. Sir Thomas More himself is shown seated at the left, wearing a brown robe. His father, in red, sits next to him, while behind him to either side stand his wife, Anne, and his son, John. His daughters Cecily, Elizabeth, and Margaret are grouped at the center. *(Copyright © National Portrait Gallery, London.)*

Color Plate 12 Faithfully Portraying Nature. Hans Holbein, The Younger, *Lady with a Squirrel and a Starling,* c. 1526–8. This painting shows Holbein's almost obsessive concern with representing detail. Artists who represented naturalistic detail played a role in developing the new sense of nature that emerged in the sixteenth century. Nature was now something that could be empirically observed as well as magically divined. If only indirectly, this new representation of nature had its impact upon the new sense of how science might record nature. Thus, the *way* Holbein's technique portrays his subject bears comparison with a whole range of discussions about nature that can be seen in texts as diverse as Shakespeare's *The Tempest* and Bacon's *Advancement of Learning*. The subject, a London lady, is said to be the nurse to Edward VI, the son of Henry VIII. An innovation in early Renaissance interior decoration, such portraits reveal a new sense of the individual subject. *(The Bridgeman Art Library International.)*

Color Plate 13 "Come live with me and be my love." Nicholas Hilliard, *The Young Man Amongst Roses*, c. 1597. Hilliard, the greatest miniaturist of the Elizabethan age, here represents an exquisite aristocratic young man in the pose of melancholic lover. *(V&A Images/Victoria and Albert Museum.)*

Color Plate 14 Something Rich and Strange. Inigo Jones, *Fiery Spirit*, costume design for a torchbearer in *The Lord's Masque*, performed 14 February 1613. Jones designed this masque as part of the celebrations for the marriage of James I's daughter Elizabeth to Frederick V, the Elector Palatine. The elaborate costume designs were modeled on those created for Florentine court theater. *(Copyright © Devonshire Collection, Chatsworth. Reproduced by permission of Chatsworth Settlement Trustees.)*

Color Plate 15 English or Irish? Marcus Gheeraerts the Younger, *Captain Thomas Lee*, 1594. Thomas Lee served as an army officer during the Elizabethan colonization of Ireland. This painting portrays him as part barefoot Irish foot soldier and part elaborately accoutered English gentleman. On the tree behind him appears a Latin quotation from Livy, "both to act and to suffer with fortitude is a Roman's part," which is what the Roman patriot Scaevola is supposed to have said when he was captured by rebel Etruscans as he entered their camp disguised in their garb. The painting is thus an elaborate allegory protesting Lee's English loyalty despite his friendship with such Irish chiefs as Hugh O'Neill. On 13 February 1601, Lee died a traitor's death as punishment for his role in the Earl of Essex's rebellion. *(Tate Gallery, London. Art Resource, New York.)*

Color Plate 16 A Passion for Collecting. Daniel Mytens, *Thomas Howard, second Earl of Arundel and Surrey*, c. 1618. One of the greatest collectors of art in seventeenth-century England, the Earl of Arundel points to the long gallery of marble statues. Henry Peacham, author of *The Compleat Gentleman*, writes that these Classical statues give the viewer "the pleasure of seeing and conversing with these old heroes." Arundel House was full of learned inscriptions. So, the collector's goal was not just to acquire art but to preserve the past, and to provide a visual humanist education in the Classics of ancient Greece and Rome. *(Copyright © National Portrait Gallery, London.)*

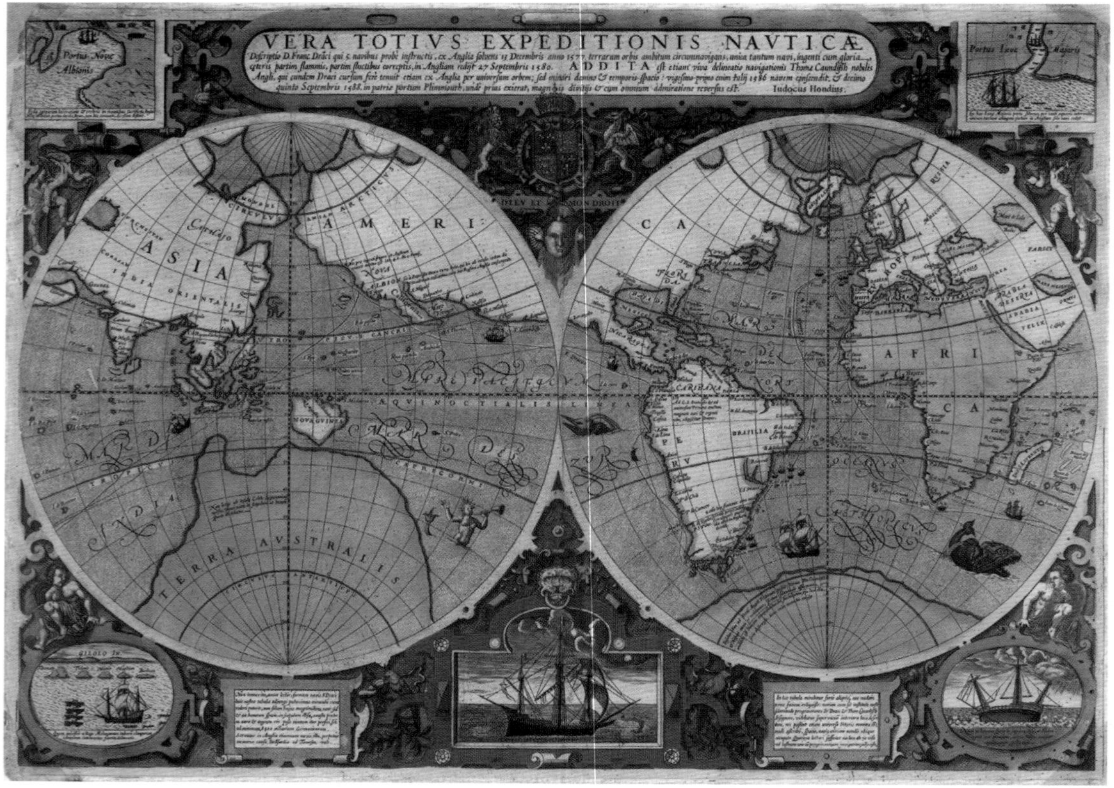

Color Plate 17 **Sailing West to Discover the East.** The title of this magnificent map, executed by cartographer Jodocus Hondius, claims it is "The true description of the whole voyage of Francis Drake, who with five well furnished ships left England on the 13th of December, 1577, and returned to England on Sept 27th 1580, with great glory; circumnavigating the circuit of the lands of the earth, one of his ships returned to England on Sept 27th, 1580; of the rest, some were destroyed by fire, some by flood. . . ." Topographical inserts around the frame depict Drake's landing in California, his entry to the port of Java, his wreck on rocks near Celebes, his ship the Golden Hind, and his welcome at the Moluccas. *(Courtesy of the Library of Congress.)*

Color Plate 18 Staging the Monarchy. Anthony Van Dyck, *Charles I of England*, c. 1637. Charles I, reputedly a retiring personality, is here transformed into a martial hero, modeled on the great equestrian figures of Ancient Rome. This painting by the great court painter Van Dyck helped create the iconography of the Stuart monarchy. For the representation of Charles I in print, see his *Eikon Basilike* (ghostwritten by John Gauden) and Milton's *Eikonoklastes* in *Perspectives: The Civil War, or The Wars of Three Kingdoms*. *(Art Resource, New York.)*

Color Plate 19 Order on the Eve of the Civil War. Cornelius Johnson, *Arthur Capel, 1st Baron Capel, 1604–1649, and His Family*, c. 1640. This painting in the style of Van Dyck portrays the royalist Arthur Capel, who was executed the same year as Charles I. In the background appear gardens, perhaps those of his home at Little Hadham. *(Copyright © National Portrait Gallery, London.)*

the period. His cast of characters—including the poet as principal speaker, his beloved male friend, a rival poet, and a fickle lady—appear as protagonists in a drama of love, betrayal, devotion, and despair. Some poets embedded their love poetry in prose narratives that told a story, as the Italian poet Dante Alighieri had in his sequence of songs and sonnets to the lady Beatrice entitled *The New Life*. A brilliant tale of seduction frames George Gascoigne's lyrics in his *Adventures of Master F. J.*, and Sidney's eclogues (pastoral poems) punctuate the long and complicated narrative of his prose romance, *Arcadia*.

Prose romances also provided images of new kinds of identity. Stories of marvels surrounded the lives of the powerful and exotic, such as Robert Greene's *Pandosto* (the source for Shakespeare's *The Winter's Tale*) and Thomas Lodge's *Rosalind*, while tales of lower-class artisan-adventurers illustrate the enthusiasm with which early modern writers and readers embraced a freedom to reinvent themselves. The romantic notion of the "marvelous" gained a new meaning in tales of tricksters and of sturdy entrepreneurs who survived against all odds—they represented the creative energies possessed by plain folk. The short fiction of Thomas Nashe, Thomas Deloney, and the hilarious (and anonymous) *Life and Pranks of Long Meg of Westminster* conclusively break with the delicate sentimentality of pure romance and, appealing to a taste for the ordinarily wonderful, point the way for such later novelists as Daniel Defoe, Henry Fielding, and Charles Dickens.

. . . tales of tricksters and of sturdy entrepreneurs who survived against all odds—represented the creative energies possessed by plain folk.

The spirit of romance infused narratives of travel as well, many of which made little distinction between fact and fantasy. Sir John Mandeville's fifteenth-century *Travels*, in print throughout the sixteenth century, responded to the growing curiosity of Europeans about the wonders of nature in distant lands, which harbored whole peoples who were pictured as utterly different from anything known at home. The wonders reported in popular collections of travel narratives like Samuel Purchas's immensely popular *Purchas His Pilgrimage, or Relations of the World and the Religions Observed in All Ages* (1613) were designed to attract, not repel, readers, but a horror of the "other" was nevertheless implied in many of these accounts. Shakespeare's Othello holds the Venetian senate spellbound when he reports that parts of the world are inhabited by "Cannibals that each other eat, / The Anthropophagi," as well as "men whose heads / Do grow beneath their shoulders." In *The Tempest*, such claims are parodied in the figure of Caliban: despite Prospero's accusations, Caliban bears a very human aspect and is no monster. The lure of distant lands could also attract the social critic who sought to devise images of an ideal world in order to better the real world. Sir Thomas More's *Utopia* projects a fantasy of a communal state that does double duty by pointing both to the inequities of English society *and* to the absurdities of reforms that assume men and women can be consistently reasonable. Literally describing a utopia, a "nowhere," his treatise is also effectively a dystopia, a work describing a "bad place." Neither Sir Francis Bacon's *New Atlantis* (1627) nor James Harrington's *Commonwealth of Oceans* (1656)—each a true utopia suggesting a radical reform of political and intellectual life—emulate More's embrace of both utopian and dystopian perspectives. But the dystopias of later writers, such as

Jonathan Swift's *Gulliver's Travels* (1726), Samuel Butler's *Erewhon* (an anagram for "nowhere," 1872) and George Orwell's *1984* (1949), impressively illustrate the hazards of idealistic and visionary social thought.

Changing Social, Political and Personal Roles

The imaginative work of "self-fashioning" in early modern lyric and romance kept pace, to a degree, with actual social change. During this period, a person was born into a place—defined by locale, family, and work—but did not necessarily remain there. The social ladder was traveled in both directions. An impecunious member of the gentry, a second son of a poor squire, or a widow whose noble husband had left her without a suitable jointure or estate could sink below the rank to which they had been born and effectively become a "commoner." In turn, a prosperous artisan, a thrifty yoeman, or an enterprising merchant could eventually become a member of the gentry—folk who were entitled to signal their identity by a coat of arms and were not supposed to do manual work. The new rich were sometimes mocked for seeking advice in conduct books regarding the proper behavior for gentlefolk, but no one could overlook the change in their status. More important, representatives of the "middling sort" were gaining political power. They generally had the right to vote for a member of the House of Commons, and they regularly held local office as bailiffs, magistrates, or sheriffs, and served on juries in towns and villages throughout the kingdom. They administered property, engaged in business, and traded on international markets. Creating much of the wealth of early modern England, they defined the concept of an economic class independent of social rank or family background: "What is Gentry if wealth be wanting, but base servile beggery?" asked Robert Greene. The idea that a person inherited a way of life was undercut by evidence of continuous shifts in both urban and rural society.

The idea that a person inherited a way of life was undercut by evidence of continuous shifts in both urban and rural society.

The situation for women in particular exhibited a certain ideological ambivalence. Ancient philosophy and medieval theology had insisted that *woman*kind was essentially and naturally different from *man*kind, characterized by physical weakness, intellectual passivity, and an aptitude for housework, childcare, and the minor decorative arts. That some women had distinguished themselves in occupations traditionally reserved for men was understood to signal an exception; in general, social doctrine imposed rigid codes of behavior on men and women. This thinking was countered by the text of Scripture—but also and increasingly by evidence from history, which revealed that ordinary women had undertaken all kinds of activity and therefore that a woman had the same range of talents as a man. Literary representation and authorship reflected some of this argument.

Departing from medieval social norms, humanists had stressed that men should be educated in the arts as well as arms, and writers like Sir Philip Sidney, illustrating the sensitivity of men to emotional life, devised characters whose masculinity was amplified by attributes that were conventionally associated with women: passion, sympathy, and a certain self-indulgence. The frustrated lover of his sonnet sequence

Astrophil and Stella is both resourceful and humorously pitiable. Flexibility with respect to categories of gender is also a feature of much lyric poetry; the male poet's beloved is sometimes another man. Shakespeare's sonnets are the chief example of homosexual verse in this period, but homoerotic innuendo, often suggested as a feature of a love triangle, is common in all genres of writing. In Marlowe's poem *Hero and Leander*, the youth Leander loves the girl Hero and attracts the sexual attentions of the sea-god Neptune.

Ideas as well as social forms and practices were also changing. The repeated shifts in religious practice—from medieval Catholicism to Henrician Protestantism, then back to the Catholicism dictated by Queen Mary I, and then on to the Anglican Church of Queen Elizabeth I—revealed that divine worship could alter its form without bringing on the apocalypse. More subtly, the emerging capitalist economy produced a conceptual model for cultural exchange. Just as material goods flowed through regional and national markets, entering a particular locale only to move elsewhere, sometimes over great distances, so might ideas, styles, and artistic sensibilities. Drama especially conveyed how fluid were the customs, codes, and practices that gave society its sense of identity. The enthusiasm for stage plays was motivated in part by an interest in role-playing: if an actor who in real life might have been born a servant could perform the part of a king in a play, then might he not also perform the part of a king indeed? Was there more to being than performing? This mutability was both liberating and dangerous, as Shakespeare showed by dramatizing the protean powers of Othello's false friend, Iago, who chillingly boasts, "I am not what I am."

. . . the emerging capitalist economy produced a conceptual model for cultural exchange.

The Business of Literature

Writers throughout this period often had to depend on patrons for support in order to produce their work. Patrons often employed writers as secretaries, carrying out important administrative tasks, and employed skilful writers who were adept at producing text to order. Or, they admired the work of writers and wanted to encourage literary endeavour. The Sidney family supported a number of writers, including Ben Jonson, who writes about his relationship to them in his country house poem, *To Penshurst*, not without a series of barbs which hint at the uncomfortable position of a writer for hire who has to see himself as little better than the workers on the family estate. The advent of print opened up new possibilities for writers, who were able to disseminate their work to a wider audience without having to deal with a patron. This was, however, a hazardous route as publishing did not generally provide a substantial living for a writer. Michael Drayton, a poet who appears to have had a fraught and complicated relationship with his patrons, insulting a number in printed works when they failed to value his work as highly as he did, lived a comfortable enough life but died leaving only a few pounds in his estate.

The advent of print opened up new possibilities for writers . . .

The relationships between writers and patrons often helps to explain a number of issues that are not apparent if we read a work without a knowledge of the conditions under which it was probably written. John Donne's poem, "Twickenham Gardens" seems on first reading like a jilted lover's misogynist tirade against a cruel mistress. However, if we bear in mind that Lucy, Countess of Bedford, one of Donne's most important patrons, owned the estate, then the chances are that the poem is a shared joke that was read by both men and women. It is hard to imagine that the countess did not know of this work or that Donne, who was grateful for her help, wrote this work as a sly attack on a generous supporter. Knowing about the conditions of writing often opens up new possibilities for the reader and different ways of reading works that might seem to have an obvious significance but are actually more nuanced and complex pieces of literature than they appear to be.

Virtually nothing written by Donne was published in his lifetime and he preferred to circulate his work in manuscript. Other writers were much keener to reach a wider audience by having their work printed and published. Inevitably, this led to conflict with the authorities who were not always keen to let anything appear in print. A rudimentary system of licensing texts was established so that anything submitted for publication was supposed to be vetted and approved by the censors headed by the Archbishop of Canterbury. It is clear that, while the desires of the state may well have been draconian, the system did not operate very effectively and most cases of censorship were reactions to a work that caused offense once it was printed. John Stubbs wrote a pamphlet, *The Discoverie of a gaping Gulf whereunto England is like to be swallowed* (1579), which attacked the queen's projected marriage to François, Duke of Alençon, and he had his right hand severed as a result (this punishment did not prevent him from having a successful career as a Member of Parliament, loyal to the crown, afterward). Thomas Middleton wrote a scandalous play, *A Game at Chess* (1624), which openly attacked the Spanish ambassador and caused a diplomatic incident. But it ran for nine consecutive nights before it was banned. Nevertheless, many writers resented the fact that their work was subject to the state control and the possibility of censorship, a factor that influenced the ways in which writers produced their work.

The most eloquent attack on a state-controlled press was by Milton, whose *Areopagitica* protested the practice of licensing books before their publication—that is, before readers had a chance to make up their minds about what these books contained. He drew on ideas of democracy that were current in ancient Athens and on the Puritan notion that good emerges only in contact with evil. "I cannot praise a fugitive and cloistered virtue," he announced, because no true virtue is untested, unchallenged, unexamined; it is valid only when it has deliberately and consciously rejected what is false. The journalistic enterprise of this period fostered the right to free speech and a free press that is now the bedrock of modern democracies.

Nature and Change

Language and style were changing notions of the world and of God's design in creating it. Habits of thought that had prevailed during the medieval period now seemed to be incompatible with knowledge derived from the experience of nature. Europeans had inherited from classical philosophy an idea of creation as a vast aggregate of layered systems, or "spheres." Supposedly centered on the densest matter at the earth's core, they emanated outward and upward, ending finally in the sphere of pure spirit, or the ethereal presence of divinity. The entities in these layered spheres had assigned places that determined their natures both within their particular sphere and in relation to other spheres. Thus gold, the most precious metal, was superior to silver, but it was at the same time analogous to a lion, a king, and the sun, each also representing the peak of perfection within its particular class of beings. Human nature was also systematized, with the body and personality alike regulated by a balanced set of "humors," each of which consisted of a primary element. The earth, water, air, and fire that made up the great world, or macrocosm, of nature also composed the small universe, or microcosm, of the individual man or woman, whose personality was ideally balanced between impulses that were melancholic (caused by a kind of bile), phlegmatic (brought on by a watery substance), sanguine (bloody), and choleric (hot tempered). Excessive learning, the contemplation of death, the darkness of night, and isolation were all associated with melancholia, a diseased condition that in more or less severe form is represented in such disparate texts as Marlowe's *Dr. Faustus* and Milton's *Il Penseroso*.

Habits of thought that had prevailed during the medieval period now seemed to be incompatible with knowledge derived from the experience of nature.

This view of creation was important for artists and writers because it gave them a symbolic language of correspondences by which they could refer to creatures in widely differing settings and conditions. In a sense, it made nature hospitable to poetry by seeing creation as a divine work of art, designed to inspire not only awe but also a kind of familiarity. Things were the likenesses of other things. Particularly in so-called "metaphysical" poetry, whose chief exponent is John Donne, human emotional experience is compared to the realms of astronomy, geography, medicine, Neoplatonic philosophy, and Christian theology. These correspondences are created through strikingly unusual metaphors, which some have called metaphysical conceits, from the Italian *concetto* ("concept"). The result is a pervasive sense of a universal harmony in all human experience.

Such analogies were not always respected, however. Increasingly, they were questioned by proponents of a kind of vision that depended on a quantitative or denotative sense of identity or difference. Poetic metaphor might not be able to account for creation in all its complexity; instead, nature had to be understood through the abstractions of science. By the seventeenth century, it was becoming difficult to regard creation as a single and comprehensive whole; natural philosophers and scientists in the making wanted to analyze it piece by individual piece. As John Donne wrote of the phenomenon of uniqueness in his elegy for Elizabeth Drury, *The Anniversary:*

> The element of fire is quite put out;
> The Sun is lost, and th' earth, and no man's wit
> Can well direct him, where to look for it.
> And freely men confess, that this world's spent,
> When in the Planets, and the Firmament
> They seek so many new; they see that this
> Is crumbled out again to his Atoms.
> 'Tis all in pieces, all coherence gone;
> All just supply, and all Relation:
> Prince, Subject, Father, Son, are things forgot,

The Souldiers in their passage to York turn unto reformers pull down Popish pictures, break down rayles, turn altars into Tables

Wenceslaus Hollar, *Parliamentarian soldiers in Yorkshire destroying "Popish" paintings, etc*. Illustration to *Sight of the Transactions of these latter yeares*, by John Vicars, 1646.

For every man alone thinks he has got
To be a Phoenix, and that there can be
None of that kind, of which he is but he.

The earth had been decentered by the insights of the astronomer Nicholas Copernicus, who in the 1520s deduced that the earth orbits the sun. This "Copernican revolution" was confirmed by the calculations of Tycho Brahe and Johannes Kepler, and our solar system itself was revealed as but one among many. With traditional understandings of the natural order profoundly shaken, many thinkers feared for the survival of the human capacity to order and understand society as well. Ironically, Donne complains of radical individualism by invoking the emblem of the Phoenix, the very sort of traditional metaphor that constituted the coherence he claims has "gone." But whereas the symbol in an emblem book carried with it the myth of the bird's Christ-like death and rebirth, the image of the rare bird takes on a newly skeptical and even satirical meaning in *The Anniversary:* it becomes the sign of a dangerous fragmentation within nature's order. Donne's audience would have been familiar with such symbols from emblem books, poems, and coats of arms, as well as in interior decoration, clothing, and the printers' marks on title pages of books. They were also featured on the standards or flags carried in the Civil War—antique signs in a decidedly modern conflict.

With traditional understandings of the natural order profoundly shaken, many thinkers feared for the survival of the human capacity to order and understand society as well.

The War and the Modern Order of Things

The Wars of Three Kingdoms ended with the restoration of the Stuart monarchy, but the society that Charles II was heir to was very different from the one his grandfather, James I, had come from Scotland to rule. The terms of modern life were formulated during this period, even though they were only partially and inconsistently realized. They helped to shape these essentially modern institutions: a representative government under law, a market economy fueled by concentrations of capital, and a class system determined by wealth and the power it conferred. They supported a culture in which extreme and opposing points of view were usual. Milton's republican *Tenure of Kings and Magistrates* was followed by Thomas Hobbes's defense of absolute rule, *The Leviathan, or the Matter, Form, and Power of a Commonwealth, Ecclesiastical and Civil* (1651). Hobbes rejected the assumption that had determined all previous political thought—Aristotle's idea that man was naturally sociable—by characterizing the natural condition of human life as "solitary, poor, nasty, brutish and short." A civil state, said Hobbes, depended on the willingness of each and every citizen to relinquish all his or her rights to the sovereign, which is the Commonwealth. The vigorous language of Puritan sermons, preached and published during the 1640s and 1650s, was replicated in the corantos and diurnals of the period. These new forms would eventually lead to the sophisticated commentary of eighteenth-century journalism. Nationalism, however problematic, was registered in history and epic, as well as in attempts to colonize the Americas and to subdue the Gaelic peoples to the west and the north. Irish poems supporting the Stuarts and lamenting the losses of the Cromwellian wars would become rallying cries during the late seventeenth- and eighteenth-century nationalist risings against English control, eventually to result in Ireland's inclusion in the 1801 Union of Great Britain.

Intellectual thought, mental attitudes, religious practices, and the customs of the people fostered new relations to the past and a new sense of self. While Milton was perhaps the greatest humanist of his time, able to read and write Hebrew, Greek, Latin, Italian, and French, his contemporaries witnessed the disappearance of the culture of Petrarch, Erasmus, and More—humanists who had fashioned the disciplines of humanism. As more particularized portraits of individual life emerged, new philosophical trends promoted denotative descriptions and quantitative figurations of the world. Shortly after the Restoration of Charles II, the Royal Academy of Science would form a "committee for improving the English language," an attempt to design a universal grammar and an ideal philosophical language. This project, inspired by the intellectual reforms of Francis Bacon, would have been uncongenial to the skeptical casts of mind exhibited by Erasmus and More. The abstract rationalism of the new science, the growth of an empire overseas, a burgeoning industry and commerce at home, and a print culture spreading news throughout Europe and across the Atlantic, would continue to be features of life in the British Isles through the eighteenth century.

Intellectual thought, mental attitudes, religious practices, and the customs of the people fostered new relations to the past and a new sense of self.

For additional resources on the early modern period, including an interactive timeline of the period, go to *The Longman Anthology of British Literature* Web site at www.myliteraturekit.com.

John Skelton

1460?–1529

The first great Tudor satirist, John Skelton illustrates the appeal of the unorthodox. Taking orders at the age of thirty-eight, Skelton already enjoyed an impressive reputation as a writer of satire and love lyrics. His poems must have appealed to Henry VII, who made him responsible for the education of his second son, the future Henry VIII, and they would eventually prompt Erasmus to call Skelton "a light and ornament of British literature." In 1502, following the death of Henry's older brother Arthur, Skelton lost his employment as royal tutor. Henry, now heir apparent to the English throne, was obliged to trade Skelton's gentle instruction in humane and sacred letters for practical training in statecraft and the art of war. At forty-two and already an old man (by contemporary reckoning), Skelton undertook pastoral duties, although he lived away from his rectory for much of the rest of his life. His satires of the clergy in *Colin Clout* and of Cardinal Wolsey in *Why Come Ye Not to Court* may have placed him in some jeopardy; it is said that a threat from the Cardinal forced Skelton to take refuge on the grounds of Westminster Abbey in London. Skelton never got the satisfaction of witnessing Wolsey's disgrace; he died just a few months before Wolsey lost the office of Lord Chancellor for failing to procure a divorce for the king.

Skelton's poetry is as unusual as was his career. His favorite verse form has become known as "skeltonics"; it consists of a series of lines of two or three stresses whose end rhyme repeats itself for an unspecified number of lines. The lines themselves show alliteration and move at a headlong pace. Skelton excused his practice in *Colin Clout* by noting the "pith" or substance it conveys:

> For though my rhyme be ragged,
> Tattered and jagged,
> Rudely rain-beaten,
> Rusty and moth-eaten,
> If ye take well therewith,
> It hath in it some pith.

Skelton's satires poke fun at the pretensions that characterize all forms of public life, including the ways of courtiers and vagabonds. His dream poem, *The Bowge of Court,* and his morality play about wealth and power, *Magnificence,* provide a witty view of court corruption. His verse includes tender tributes to ladies he loves or has loved as well as anticourtly lyrics accusing women of bad behavior and sexual indiscretion. His verse can even be conversational, as when he appears to be addressing a particular person or representing two or more people speaking to each other.

The Bowge of Court is an early satirical poem, probably written in 1498. Its title derives from the *bouche de court,* the free board and lodging to which the king's courtiers and servants were entitled. Skelton represents a cross-section of English society as a "ship of fools," knaves and charlatans out for what they can get and held together by nothing more than their own self-interest. Any society based on such flimsy principles is in serious trouble. The narrator concludes that he cannot join in the free-for-all, and needs instead to write down what is going on, setting him aside as a truth-telling, honest man, a persona frequently adopted by Skelton, most famously in his Colin Clout poems.

For more on John Skelton, including his poem "Philip Sparrow," go to *The Longman Anthology of British Literature* Web site at www.myliteraturekit.com.

The Bowge of Courte
[from *The Poetical Works* (1856)]

THE PROLOGUE TO THE BOWGE OF COURTE.

In autumpne, whan the sonne *in Virgine*° *Virgo*
By radyante hete enryped hath our corne;
Whan Luna, full of mutabylyte,
As emperes the dyademe hath worne
Of our pole artyke, smylynge halfe in scorne
At our foly and our unstedfastnesse;
The tyme whan Mars to werre hym dyde dres;

I, callynge to mynde the greate auctoryte
Of poetes olde, whyche full craftely,
Under as coverte termes as coude be,
Can touche a trouth° and cloke it subtylly *truth*
Wyth fresshe utteraunce full sentencyously;
Dyverse in style, some spared not vyce to wryte,
Some of moralyte nobly dyde endyte;° *write*

Wherby I rede theyr renome and theyr fame
Maye never dye, bute evermore endure:
I was sore moved to aforce° the same, *attempt*
But Ignoraunce full soone dyde me dyscure,° *betray*
And shewed that in this arte I was not sure;
For to illumyne, she sayde, I was to dulle,
Avysynge me my penne alwaye to pulle,

And not wryte; for he so° wyll atteyne *whoever*
Excedynge ferther than his connynge is,
His hede maye be harde, but feble is his brayne,
Yet have I knowen suche er this;
But of reproche surely he maye not mys,
That clymmeth hyer than he may fotynge have;
What and° he slyde downe, who shall hym save? *if*

Thus up and down my mynde was drawen and cast,
That I ne wyste° what to do was beste; *did not know*
So sore enwered,° that I was at the laste *tired, weary*
Enforsed to slepe and for to take some reste;
And to lye downe as soone as I me dreste,° *was ready*
At Harwyche Porte slumbrynge as I laye,
In myne hostes house, called Powers Keye,

Methoughte I sawe a shyppe, goodly of sayle,
Come saylynge forth into that haven brood,
Her takelynge ryche and of hye apparayle:° *rigging*
She kyste an anker, and there she laye at rode.° *anchor*
Marchauntes her borded to see what she had lode:
Therein they founde royall marchaundyse,
Fraghted with plesure of what ye coude devyse.

But than I thoughte I woulde not dwell behynde;
Amonge all other I put myselfe in prece.° *among the crowd*
Than there coude I none aquentaunce fynde:
There was moche noyse; anone one cryed, Cese!
Sharpely commaundynge eche man holde hys pece:
Maysters, he sayde, the shyp that ye here see,
The Bowge of Courte it hyghte° for certeynte: *called*

The owner therof is lady of estate,
Whoos name to tell is dame Saunce-pere;° *without equal*
Her marchaundyse is ryche and fortunate,° *valuable*
But who wyll have it muste paye therfore dere;
This royall chaffre° that is shypped here *merchandise*
Is called Favore, to stonde in her good grace.
Than sholde ye see there pressynge in a pace

Of one and other that wolde this lady see;
Whiche sat behynde a traves° of sylke fyne, *screen*
Of golde of tessew° the fynest that myghte be, *cloth*
In a trone° whiche fer clerer dyde shyne *train*
Than Phebus in his spere celestyne;
Whoos beaute, honoure, goodly porte,° *bearing*
I have to lytyll connynge° to reporte. *skill*

But, of eche thynge there as I toke hede,
Amonge all other was wrytten in her trone,
In golde letters, this worde, whiche I dyde rede,
Garder le fortune, que est mauelz et bone!° *beware fortune,*
And, as I stode redynge this verse myselfe allone, *which is bad and good*
Her chyef gentylwoman, Daunger by her name,
Gaue me a taunte, and sayde I was to blame

To be so perte° to prese so proudly uppe: *forward*
She sayde she trowed that I had eten sause;° *been too bold*
She asked yf ever I dranke of saucys cuppe.
And I than softly answered to that clause,° *those words*
That, so to saye, I had gyven her no cause.
Than asked she me, Syr, so God thé spede,° *prosper*
What is thy name? and I sayde, it was Drede.

What movyd thé, quod she, hydder to come?
Forsoth, quod I, to bye some of youre ware.° *goods*
And with that worde on me she gave a glome° *sullen look*
With browes bente, and gan on me to stare
Full daynnously,° and fro me she dyde fare, *disdainfully*
Levynge me stondynge as a mased° man: *bewildered*
To whome there came an other gentylwoman;

Desyre her name was, and so she me tolde,
Sayenge to me, Broder, be of good chere,
Abasshe you not, but hardely be bolde,

Avaunce yourselfe to aproche and come nere:
What though our chaffer° be never so dere, *merchandise*
Yet I avyse you to speke, for ony drede:° *despite any fear*
Who spareth to speke, in fayth he spareth to spede.° *succeed*

Maystres, quod I, I have none aquentaunce,
That wyll for me be medyatoure and mene;
And this an other, I have but smale substaunce.
Pece, quod Desyre, ye speke not worth a bene:
Yf ye have not, in fayth I wyll you lene° *lend*
A precyous jewell, no rycher in this londe;
Bone Aventure° have here now in your honde. *good luck*

Shyfte now therwith, let see, as ye can,
In Bowge of Courte chevysaunce° to make; *profit*
For I dare saye that there nys erthly man
But, an he can Bone Aventure take,
There can no favour nor frendshyp hym forsake;
Bone Aventure may brynge you in suche case
That ye shall stonde in favoure and in grace.

But of one thynge I werne you er I goo,
She that styreth the shyp, make her your frende.
Maystres, quod I, I praye you tell me why soo,
And how I maye that waye and meanes fynde.
Forsothe, quod she, how ever blowe the wynde
Fortune gydeth and ruleth all oure shyppe:
Whome she hateth shall over the see boorde skyp;

Whome she loveth, of all plesyre is ryche,
Whyles she laugheth and hath luste for to playe;
Whome she hateth, she casteth in the dyche,
For whan she frouneth, she thynketh to make a fray;° *conflict*
She cheryssheth him, and hym she casseth awaye.
Alas, quod I, how myghte I have her sure?
In fayth, quod she, by Bone Aventure.

Thus, in a rowe, of martchauntes a grete route° *group*
Suwed to Fortune that she wold be theyre frynde:
They thronge in fast, and flocked her aboute;
And I with them prayed her to have in mynde.
She promysed to us all she wolde be kynde:
Of Bowge of Court she asketh what we wold have;
And we asked Favoure, and Favour she us gave.

Thus endeth the Prologue; and begynneth the Bowge of Courte brevely compyled.

DREDE

The sayle is up, Fortune ruleth our helme,
We wante no wynd to passe now over all;
Favoure we have tougher than ony elme,

That wyll abyde and never from us fall:
But under hony ofte tyme lyeth bytter gall;
For, as me thoughte, in our shyppe I dyde see
Full subtyll persones, in nombre foure and thre.

The fyrste was Favell,° full of flatery, *duplicity*
Wyth fables false that well coude fayne a tale;
The seconde was Suspecte, whiche that dayly
Mysdempte° eche man, with face deedly and pale; *misjudged*
And Haruy Hafter,° that well coude picke a male;° *deceiver / purse*
With other foure of theyr affynyte,
Dysdayne, Ryotte, Dyssymuler, Subtylte.

Fortune theyr frende, with whome oft she dyde daunce;
They coude not faile, thei thought, they were so sure;
And oftentymes I wolde myselfe avaunce
With them to make solace and pleasure;
But my dysporte they coude not well endure;
They sayde they hated for to dele with Drede.
Than Favell gan wyth fayre speche me to fede.

FAVELL

Noo thynge erthely that I wonder so sore
As of your connynge, that it is so excellent;
Deynte° to have with us suche one in store, *pleasure*
So vertuously that hath his dayes spente:
Fortune to you gyftes of grace hath lente:
Loo, what it is a man to have connynge!° *learning*
All erthly tresoure it is surmountynge.

Ye be an apte man, as ony can be founde,
To dwell with us, and serve my ladyes grace;
Ye be to her yea worth a thousande pounde;
I herde her speke of you within shorte space,
Whan there were dyverse that sore dyde you manace;
And, though I say it, I was myselfe your frende,
For here be dyverse to you that be unkynde.

But this one thynge ye maye be sure of me;
For, by that Lorde that bought dere all mankynde,
I can not flater, I muste be playne to thé;
And ye nede ought, man, shewe to me your mynde,
For ye have me whome faythfull ye shall fynde;
Whyles I have ought, by God, thou shalt not lacke,
And yf nede be, a bolde worde I dare cracke.° *boast*

Nay, naye, be sure, whyles I am on your syde,
Ye maye not fall, truste me, ye maye not fayle;
Ye stonde in favoure, and Fortune is your gyde,
And, as she wyll, so shall our grete shyppe sayle:
Thyse lewde cok wattes° shall nevermore prevayle *fools*

Ageynste you hardely, therfore be not afrayde:
Farewell tyll soone; but no worde that I sayde.

DREDE

Than thanked I hym for his grete gentylnes:
But, as me thoughte, he ware on hym a cloke,
That lyned was with doubtfull doublenes;
Me thoughte, of wordes that he had full a poke;° *bag*
His stomak stuffed ofte tymes dyde reboke:° *belch*
Suspycyon, me thoughte, mette hym at a brayde,° *suddenly*
And I drewe nere to herke what they two sayde.

In faythe, quod Suspecte, spake Drede no worde of me?
Why, what than? wylte thou lete° men to speke? *stop*
He sayth, he can not well accorde with thé.
Twyst, quod Suspecte, goo playe, hym I ne reke.° *care*
By Cryste, quod Favell, Drede is soleyne freke:° *unsociable person*
What lete us holde him up, man, for a whyle?
Ye soo, quod Suspecte, he maye us bothe begyle.

And whan he came walkynge soberly,
Wyth whom and ha, and with a croked loke,
Me thoughte, his hede was full of gelousy,
His eyne rollynge, his hondes faste they quoke;
And to me warde the strayte waye he toke:
God spede, broder! to me quod he than;
And thus to talke with me he began.

SUSPYCYON

Ye remembre the gentylman ryghte nowe
That commaunde° with you, me thought, a party space?° *talked / long time*
Beware of him, for, I make God avowe,
He wyll begyle you and speke fayre to your face;
Ye never dwelte in suche an other place,
For here is none that dare well other truste;
But I wolde telle you a thynge, and I durste.

Spake he a faith° no worde to you of me? *in truth*
I wote, and° he dyde, ye wolde me telle. *wonder if*
I have a favoure to you, wherof it be
That I muste shewe you moche of my counselle:
But I wonder what the devyll of helle
He sayde of me, whan he with you dyde talke:
By myne avyse use not with him to walke.

The soveraynst° thynge that ony man maye have, *most valuable*
Is lytyll to saye, and moche to here and see;
For, but I trusted you, so God me save,
I wolde noo thynge so playne be;
To you oonly, me thynke, I durste shryve° me; *confess*

For now am I plenarely° disposed *fully*
To shewe you thynges that may not be disclosed.

DREDE

Than I assured hym my fydelyte,
His counseyle secrete never to dyscure,° *disclose*
Yf he coude fynde in herte to truste me;
Els I prayed hym, with all my besy cure,° *careful attention*
To kepe it hymselfe, for than he myghte be sure
That noo man erthly coude hym bewreye,° *betray*
Whyles of hys mynde it were lockte with the keye.

By God, quod he, this and thus it is;
And of his mynde he shewed me all and some.
Farewell, quod he, we wyll talke more of this:
Soo he departed there he wolde be come.
I dare not speke, I promysed to be dome:
But, as I stode musynge in my mynde,
Harvy Hafter came lepynge, lyghte as lynde.° *nimbly*

Upon his breste he bare a versynge boxe;° *dice*
His throte was clere, and lustely coude fayne;° *sing, invent*
Me thoughte, his gowne was all furred wyth foxe;
And ever he sange, Sythe I am no thynge playne.
To kepe him frome pykyng° it was a grete payne: *stealing*
He gased on me with his gotyshe berde;
Whan I loked on hym, my purse was half aferde.

HARVY HAFTER

Syr, God you save! why loke ye so sadde?
What thynge is that I maye do for you?
A wonder thynge that ye waxe not madde!
For, and I studye sholde as ye doo nowe,
My wytte wolde waste, I make God avowe.
Tell me your mynde: me thynke, ye make a verse;
I coude it skan, and ye wolde it reherse.

But to the poynte shortely to procede,
Where hathe your dwellynge ben, er ye cam here?
For, as I trowe, I have sene you indede
Er this, whan that ye made me royall chere.
Holde up the helme, loke up, and lete God stere:
I wolde be mery, what wynde that ever blowe,
Heve and how rombelow, row the bote, Norman, rowe!

Prynces of yougthe can ye synge by rote?° *by heart*
Or shall I sayle wyth you a felashyp assaye;° *together*
For on the booke° I can not synge a note. *i.e., with sheet music*
Wolde to God, it wolde please you some daye

A balade boke before me for to laye,
And lerne me to synge, Re, my, fa, sol!
And, whan I fayle, bobbe me on the noll.° *hit me on the head*

Loo, what is to you a pleasure grete,
To have that connynge and wayes that ye have!
By Goddis soule, I wonder how ye gete
Soo greate pleasyre, or who to you it gave:
Syr, pardone me, I am an homely knave,
To be with you thus perte and thus bolde;
But ye be welcome to our housholde.

And, I dare saye, there is no man here inne
But wolde be glad of your company:
I wyste° never man that so soone coude wynne *knew*
The favoure that ye have with my lady;
I praye to God that it maye never dy:
It is your fortune for to have that grace;
As I be saved, it is a wonder case.

For, as for me, I served here many a daye,
And yet unneth° I can have my lyvynge: *scarcely*
But I requyre you no worde that I saye;
For, and I knowe ony erthly thynge
That is agayne you, ye shall have wetynge:° *knowledge*
And ye be welcome, syr, so God me save:
I hope here after a frende of you to have.

DREDE

Wyth that, as he departed soo fro me,
Anone ther mette with him, as me thoughte,
A man, but wonderly besene° was he; *attractive*
He loked hawte,° he sette eche man at noughte; *proud*
His gawdy garment with scornnys° was all wrought; *scorn, taunts*
With indygnacyon lyned was his hode;
He frowned, as he wolde swere by Cockes° blode; *God's*

He bote° the lyppe, he loked passynge coye; *bit*
His face was belymmed,° as byes had him stounge: *disfigured*
It was no tyme with him to jape nor toye;
Envye hathe wasted his lyver and his lounge,
Hatred by the herte so had hym wrounge,
That he loked pale as asshes to my syghte:
Dysdayne, I wene, this comerous carkes° hyghte. *difficult person*

To Hervy Hafter than he spake of me,
And I drewe nere to harke what they two sayde.
Now, quod Dysdayne, as I shall saved be,
I have grete scorne, and am ryghte evyll apayed.
Than quod Hervy, why arte thou so dysmayde?

By Cryste, quod he, for it is shame to saye;
To see Johan Dawes, that came but yester daye,

How he is now taken in conceyte,
  This doctour Dawcocke, Drede, I wene, he hyghte:
By Goddis bones, but yf we have som sleyte,° *strategy*
  It is lyke he wyll stonde in our lyghte.
  By God, quod Hervy, and it so happen myghte;
Lete us therfore shortely at a worde
Fynde some mene to caste him over the borde.

By Him that me boughte,° than quod Dysdayne, *i.e., Christ*
  I wonder sore he is in suche conceyte.
Turde, quod Hafter, I wyll thé no thynge layne,° *hide*
  There muste for hym be layde some prety beyte;
  We tweyne, I trowe, be not withoute dysceyte:
Fyrste pycke a quarell, and fall oute with hym then,
And soo outface hym with a carde of ten.° *i.e., a bluff*

Forthwith he made on me a prowde assawte,
  With scornfull loke mevyd° all in moode; *angry*
He wente aboute to take me in a fawte;
  He frounde, he stared, he stampped where he stoode.
  I lokyd on hym, I wende he had be woode.° *thought he was mad*
He sent the arme proudly under the syde,
And in this wyse he gan with me to chyde.

DISDAYNE

Remembrest thou what thou sayd yester nyght?
  Wylt thou abyde by the wordes agayne?
By God, I have of thé now grete dyspyte;
  I shall thé angre ones in every vayne:
  It is greate scorne to see suche an hayne° *wretch*
As thou arte, one that cam but yesterdaye,
With us olde servauntes suche maysters to playe.

I tell thé, I am of countenaunce:° *i.e., important*
  What weneste I were? I trowe, thou knowe not me.
By Goddis woundes, but for dysplesaunce,
  Of my querell soone wolde I venged be:
  But no force, I shall ones mete with thé;
Come whan it wyll, oppose thé I shall,
What somever aventure therof fall.

Trowest thou, drevyll,° I saye, thou gawdy knave, *drudge*
  That I have deynte° to see thé cherysshed thus? *pleasure*
By Goddis syd, my sworde thy berde shall shave;
  Well, ones thou shalte be chermed, I wus:° *think, know*
  Naye, strawe for tales, thou shalte not rule us;
We be thy betters, and so thou shalte us take,
Or we shall thé oute of thy clothes shake.

Drede

Wyth that came Ryotte, russhynge all at ones,
A rusty gallande, to-ragged and to-rente;
And on the borde he whyrled a payre of bones,
Quater treye dews° he clatered as he wente; *four, three, deuce*
Now have at all, by saynte Thomas of Kente!
And ever he threwe and kyst° I wote nere what: *cast*
His here was growen thorowe oute his hat.

Thenne I behelde how he dysgysed was:
His hede was hevy for watchynge over nyghte,
His eyen blereed, his face shone lyke a glas;
His gowne so shorte that it ne cover myghte
His rumpe, he wente so all for somer lyghte;° *dressed for summer*
His hose was garded wyth a lyste° of grene, *strip*
Yet at the knee they were broken, I wene.

His cote was checked with patches rede and blewe;
Of Kyrkeby Kendall° was his shorte demye;° *cheap wool / jacket*
And ay he sange, In fayth, decon thou crewe;
His elbowe bare, he ware his gere so nye;° *worn*
His nose a droppynge, his lyppes were full drye;
And by his syde his whynarde° and his pouche, *dagger*
The devyll myghte daunce therin for ony crowche.° *coin*

Counter° he coude O *lux* upon a potte; *accompany*
An eestryche° fedder of a capons tayle *ostrich*
He set up fresshely upon his hat alofte:
What, revell route! quod he, and gan to rayle
How oft he hadde hit Jenet on the tayle,
Of Felyce fetewse,° and lytell prety Cate, *handsome*
How ofte he knocked at her klycked gate.

What sholde I tell more of his rebaudrye?° *roguery*
I was ashamed so to here hym prate:
He had no pleasure but in harlotrye.
Ay, quod he, in the devylles date,° *name*
What art thou? I sawe thé nowe but late.
Forsothe, quod I, in this courte I dwell nowe.
Welcome, quod Ryote, I make God avowe.

Ryote

And, syr, in fayth why comste not us amonge,
To make thé mery, as other felowes done?
Thou muste swere and stare, man, al daye longe,
And wake all nyghte, and slepe tyll it be none;° *noon*
Thou mayste not studye, or muse on the mone;
This worlde is nothynge but ete, drynke, and slepe,
And thus with us good company to kepe.

Plucke up thyne herte upon a mery pyne,° *note?*
And lete us laugh a placke° or tweyne at nale:° *draught / alehouse*
What the devyll, man, myrthe was never one!° *alone*
What, loo, man, see here of dyce a bale!° *set*
A brydelynge° caste for that is in thy male!° *final / bag*
Now have at all that lyeth upon the burde!° *board, table?*
Fye on this dyce, they be not worth a turde!

Have at the hasarde,° or at the dosen browne,° *game / full dozen?*
Or els I pas° a peny to a pounde! *Give you odds*
Now, wolde to God, thou wolde leye money downe!
Lorde, how that I wolde caste it full rounde!
Ay, in my pouche a buckell I have founde!
The armes of Calyce,° I have no coyne nor crosse! *Calais (a low value coin)*
I am not happy, I renne ay on the losse.

Now renne muste I to the stewys° syde, *brothel*
To wete° yf Malkyn, my lemman,° have gete oughte: *find out / sweetheart*
I lete her to hyre, that men maye on her ryde,
Her armes easy ferre and nere is soughte:
By Goddis sydes, syns I her thyder broughte,
She hath gote me more money with her tayle
Than hath some shyppe that into Bordews sayle.

Had I as good an hors as she is a mare,
I durst aventure to journey through Fraunce;
Who rydeth on her, he nedeth not to care,
For she is trussed for to breke a launce;
It is a curtel° that well can wynche and praunce: *horse*
To her wyll I nowe all my poverte lege;° *i.e., trust her to get rid of my poverty*
And, tyll I come, have here is myne hat to plege.

DREDE

Gone is this knave, this rybaude° foule and leude; *rogue*
He ran as fast as ever that he myghte:
Unthryftynes° in hym may well be shewed, *prodigality*
For whome Tyborne° groneth both daye and nyghte. *i.e., the gallows*
And, as I stode and kyste asyde my syghte,
Dysdayne I sawe with Dyssymulacyon
Standynge in sadde° communicacion. *serious*

But there was poyntynge and noddynge with the hede,
And many wordes sayde in secrete wyse;
They wandred ay, and stode styll in no stede:° *place*
Me thoughte, alwaye Dyscymular dyde devyse;
Me passynge sore myne herte than gan agryse,
I dempte and drede theyr talkynge was not good.
Anone Dyscymular came where I stode.

Than in his hode I sawe there faces tweyne;
That one was lene and lyke a pyned goost,

That other loked as he wolde me have slayne;
And to me warde as he gan for to coost,° *approach*
Whan that he was even at me almoost,
I sawe a knyfe hyd in his one sleve,
Wheron was wryten this worde, *Myscheve*.

And in his other sleve, me thought, I sawe
A spone of golde, full of hony swete,
To fede a fole, and for to preve a dawe;° *confirm a simpleton*
And on that sleve these wordes were wrete,° *written*
A false abstracte cometh from a fals concrete:
His hode was syde,° his cope° was roset graye: *long / hood*
Thyse were the wordes that he to me dyde saye.

DYSSYMULATION

How do ye, mayster? ye loke so soberly:
As I be saved at the dredefull daye,° *Judgment Day*
It is a perylous vyce, this envy:
Alas, a connynge man ne dwelle maye
In no place well, but foles with hym fraye!° *fight*
But as for that, connynge hath no foo° *foe*
Save hym that nought can, Scrypture sayth soo.

I knowe your vertu and your lytterature° *learning*
By that lytel connynge that I have:
Ye be malygned sore, I you ensure;
But ye have crafte your selfe alwaye to save:
It is grete scorne to se a mysproude° knave *arrogant*
With a clerke that connynge is to prate:° *prattle*
Lete theym go lowse theym, in the devylles date!

For all be it that this longe not to me,° *does not concern me*
Yet on my backe I bere suche lewde delynge:
Ryghte now I spake with one, I trowe,° I see; *know*
But, what, a strawe! I maye not tell all thynge.
By God, I saye there is grete herte brennynge° *burning*
Betwene the persone ye wote° of, you; *know*
Alas, I coude not dele so with a Jew!

I wolde eche man were as playne as I;
It is a worlde, I saye, to here of some;
I hate this faynynge, fye upon it, fye!
A man can not wote where to be come:
I wys I coude tell,—but humlery, home;
I dare not speke, we be so layde awayte,° *spied on*
For all our courte is full of dysceyte.

Now, by saynte Fraunceys, that holy man and frere,
I hate these wayes agayne you that they take:
Were I as you, I wolde ryde them full nere;° *press them (to give an answer)*

And, by my trouthe, but yf an ende they make,
Yet wyll I saye some wordes for your sake,
That shall them angre, I holde thereon a grote;
For some shall wene be hanged by the throte.

I have a stoppynge° oyster in my poke,° — *blocking (i.e., silencing) / bag*
Truste me, and yf it come to a nede:
But I am lothe for to reyse a smoke,
Yf ye coude be otherwyse agrede;
And so I wolde it were, so God me spede,
For this maye brede to a confusyon,
Withoute God make a good conclusyon.

Naye, see where yonder stondeth the teder° man! — *other*
A flaterynge knave and false he is, God wote;
The drevyll° stondeth to herken, and he can: — *drudge*
It were more thryft, he boughte him a newe cote;
It will not be, his purse is not on flote:° — *full of money*
All that he wereth, it is borowed ware;
His wytte is thynne, his hode is threde bare.

More coude I saye, but what this is ynowe:° — *enough*
Adewe tyll soone, we shall speke more of this:
Ye muste be ruled as I shall tell you howe;
Amendis maye be of that is now amys;
And I am your, syr, so have I blys,
In every poynte that I can do or saye;
Gyve me your honde, farewell, and have good daye.

DREDE

Sodaynly, as he departed me fro,
Came pressynge in one in a wonder araye:° — *strange clothes*
Er I was ware, behynde me he sayde, Bo!
Thenne I, astonyed of that sodeyne fraye,° — *attack*
Sterte all at ones, I lyked no thynge his playe;
For, yf I had not quyckely fledde the touche,
He had plucte oute the nobles° of my pouche. — *gold coins*

He was trussed° in a garmente strayte:° — *dressed / tight*
I have not sene suche an others page;
For he coude well upon a casket wayte;
His hode all pounsed° and garded° lyke a cage; — *perforated / trimmed*
Lyghte lyme fynger,° he toke none other wage. — *sticky fingers, i.e., thieving*
Harken, quod he, loo here myne honde in thyne;
To us welcome thou arte, by saynte Quyntyne.

DISCEYTE

But, by that Lorde that is one, two, and thre,
I have an errande to rounde in your ere:
He tolde me so, by God, ye maye truste me,

Parte remembre whan ye were there,
There I wynked on you,—wote ye not where?
In A *loco*,° I mene *juxta* B:° *location / near*
Woo is hym that is blynde and maye not see!

But to here the subtylte and the crafte,
As I shall tell you, yf ye wyll harke agayne;
And, whan I sawe the horsons wolde you hafte,° *deceive, rob*
To holde myne honde, by God, I had grete payne;
For forthwyth there I had him slayne,
But that I drede mordre wolde come oute:
Who deleth with shrewes hath nede to loke aboute.

DREDE

And as he rounded thus in myne ere
Of false collusyon confetryd° by assente, *joined*
Me thoughte, I see lewde felawes here and there
Came for to slee me of mortall entente;
And, as they came, the shypborde faste I hente,° *grasped*
And thoughte to lepe; and even with that woke,
Caughte penne and ynke, and wrote thys lytyll boke.

I wolde therwith no man were myscontente;
Besechynge you that shall it see or rede,
In every poynte to be indyfferente,
Syth all in substaunce of slumbrynge doth procede:
I wyll not saye it is mater in dede,° *fact*
But yet oftyme suche dremes be founde trewe:
Now constrewe ye what is the resydewe.

Thus endeth the Bowge of Courte.

PERSPECTIVES

The English Sonnet and Sonnet Sequences in the Sixteenth Century

No lyric form was more important than the sonnet in sixteenth-century England and most poets with courtly ambitions felt the need to write sonnets as a sign of their mastery of the form, especially toward the end of the century. Writing a successful sonnet demanded a good ear for verse, rhyme, and rhythm, as well as an ability to make a telling, memorable argument in a short space, often one that surprises or startles the reader. Accordingly, sonnets are not always quite what they seem to be and often play tricks on the reader. The most famous English sonnet, Shakespeare's Sonnet 18 ("Shall I compare thee to a summer's day?") is often taken to be an especially beautiful love poem. But its wit depends to a large part on the ironies and uncertainties that surround it: the poem is actually addressed to a young man, who may or may not have a sexual relationship with the speaker who may or may not be the author of the poem, and it does not actually compare the young man to a summer's day at all, as we learn nothing about his beauty from the poem itself. Rather, the last lines of the sonnet assert that beauty cannot fade if it is captured in verse, "So long as men can breathe or eyes can see, / So long lives this, and this gives life to thee," something the poem has—very wittily and self-consciously—not done. Given the long-recognized genre of ekphrastic poetry—a verbal description of a picture or work of art—the poem's witty refusal to carry out what it claims it will do is striking.

The sonnet was usually—but not always—a poem of fourteen lines with a complicated, interlaced rhyme scheme that could vary and so alter the structure and balance of the poem. Sonnets were divided into shorter units. Often the first eight lines would describe something or a situation, making up an octave. The concluding six lines, the sestet, would comment on them, drawing a moral or making a point. Sonnets could also be divided further into three units of four lines, quatrains, concluding with a couplet that commented on what had gone before, a preferred form for English writers, especially Shakespeare.

The sonnet was principally an Italian form and was regarded as especially sophisticated and accorded high cultural status in England, a country that was painfully aware of its relatively humble artistic and cultural achievements at the start of the sixteenth century, a situation the king, Henry VIII, was determined to change. The most famous sonneteer was Francesco Petrarca (1304–1374), known as Petrarch in the English-speaking world, the first poet laureate of the modern world. Petrarch composed a long series of poems to Laura, a woman he loved but who married someone else and then died relatively young, in his *Canzoniere* many of which were sonnets. Petrarch gave his name to the most widely used sonnet form, the Petrarchan sonnet. The octave (the first eight lines) was rhymed *abab, abab* or *abba, abba*, and the sestet (the last six lines), *cdecde, cdccdc* or *cdcdcd*, all forms that predated Petrarch in Italian sonnet writing but spread throughout Europe after the popularity of his verse. Such a demanding poetic form was possible in Italian and French, which had a large variety of similar endings that enabled writers to produce poems with a narrow range of rhyme schemes. The sonnet flourished in France as well as in Italy, and major collections of poetry were produced by Pierre de Ronsard (1524–1585) and Joachim Du Bellay (1522–1560), poets who also enjoyed a pan-European reputation.

The situation was very different for English writers. While the first English sonneteers, Sir Thomas Wyatt and Henry Howard, Earl of Surrey, produced translations and adaptations of Petrarch that remained faithful to the original rhyme schemes of the Italian, it soon become obvious that a language such as English, which did not rely on inflected word endings but specific grammatical forms, could not easily imitate Italian poetry owing to the lack of possible rhyming words. The result was the development of the English sonnet, which employed far more rhyme words, and so made it possible for poets to use their wit and imagination more easily and freely when composing such a straightened form. The usual rhyme scheme for the English sonnet is *abab cdcd efef gg*, giving the poet at least two more words to use than the Italian version. Whereas the Italian sonnet invariably divided up into an octave and a sestet, the English often contained three quatrains that described the substance of the poem and a couplet that commented on its significance. Sometimes, poets employed both structures and made them overlap, providing a further layer of interpretation for the reader to confront.

The sonnet first appeared in English at the court of Henry VIII, as part of a concerted plan to make English culture more sophisticated. This did not mean, however, that the sonnet can be read as a patriotic form supporting the monarchy and celebrating court life. In fact, the opposite is generally the case, and sonnets often comment obliquely on the unstable situation of the courtier-poet, close to the center of power but also subject to the dangers of life near the mighty. Wyatt's famous sonnet, *Whoso List to Hunt*, undoubtedly refers to his relationship with Anne Boleyn and the danger in which he was placed when she became Henry's second wife in 1533. Wyatt adapts Petrarch's Sonnet 190 to comment on the perils of earthly love at the court of a powerful and vindictive monarch. Petrarch describes the vision of the dead Laura leading him away from earthly vices so that when we see that her necklace has inscribed on it Christ's words to Mary Magdalene before the tomb, *Noli me tangere* (Do not touch me), we realize that this shows the author being led away from his false faith in earthly delights. When Wyatt sees the same necklace, the words mean that he needs to avoid his former lover because she now belongs to the king. A religious poem has become a secular one in which, as Arthur Marotti has pointed out, "love is not love".

Such skillful twists and transformations characterize the English sonnet throughout the sixteenth century, although it would be a mistake to assume that it enjoyed a smooth and straightforward path into English cultural life. The mid-Tudor years when Edward VI and Mary reigned (1547–1558) saw little in the way of sonnet production, although *Tottel's Miscellany*, a collection of English verse that included many poems by Wyatt, Surrey, and others, was published in 1557. Perhaps this lacuna is not surprising given the interest in experiments based on native English writing in Edward's reign, and the relative lack of literary production during Mary's reign. Sonnets were produced throughout Elizabeth's reign, although not always in vast numbers until Sir Philip Sidney produced the first sonnet sequence in English, *Astrophil and Stella*, written in the 1580s and published in the 1590s. Later, sonnet sequences enjoyed a considerable literary vogue, with major authors such as Samuel Daniel (1562–1619), Michael Drayton (1563–1631), Edmund Spenser (1552?–1599), Fulke Greville (1554–1628), all writing their own sequences. The vogue appeared to have died out by the end of Elizabeth's reign and Shakespeare's sonnets (1609) mark a return back to the past as well as a break in their deliberate transgression of its loosely established conventions. As Margaretta De Grazia has argued, the real scandal of Shakespeare's sonnets is probably the representation of the lascivious and transgressive "dark lady," not the fair young man.

The selection of sonnets here charts the poem's progress throughout the century from Wyatt's pioneering adaptations to extracts from Spenser's and Barnfield's sequences published in the 1590s. While Sidney charts the frustrated and unhappy passion of Astrophil for Stella, who is married to another man, Spenser adapts the genre to celebrate his own courtship of and marriage to Elizabeth Boyle, and Barnfield represents homosexual desire. Also included are other variations on the sonnet's subject matter, such as George Gascoigne's sonnets to Alexander Neville, which reflect on his own life and its troubled course.

Sir Thomas Wyatt

1503?–1542

Sir Thomas Wyatt, courtier and poet, was the most important and accomplished lyric poet at the court of Henry VIII. Wyatt had a career that combined success with danger, holding a number of important diplomatic positions but also falling foul of his royal master, not least because he had been involved with Henry's second wife, Anne Boleyn. Wyatt had more than one spell in prison. None of his poetry was published in his lifetime as it circulated solely in manuscript. After his death it became clear that his experiments with the sonnet and other lyric forms were of major importance. Many were published in *Tottel's Miscellany* (1557) alongside Surrey's, which helped influence later generations of poets and establish a dominant strain of English writing.

For more on Wyatt, see his principal listing on page 701.

The Long Love, That in My Thought Doth Harbor

The long love, that in my thought doth harbor
And in mine heart doth keep his residence,
Into my face presseth with bold pretence,
And therein campeth, spreading his banner.
She that me learneth° to love and suffer, *teaches*
And will that my trust and lust's negligence
Be reined by reason, shame and reverence,
With his hardiness° taketh displeasure. *boldness*
Wherewithal, unto the heart's forest he fleeth,
Leaving his enterprise with pain and cry,
And there him hideth and not appeareth.
What may I do when my master feareth
But in the field with him to live and die?
For good is the life, ending faithfully.

Companion Reading

Petrarch, Sonnet 140[1]

Amor, che nel penser mio vive et regna
e 'l suo seggio maggior nel mio cor tene,
talor armato ne la fronte vene;
ivi si loca et ivi pon sua insegna.
Quella ch' amare et sofferir ne 'nsegna
e vol che 'l gran desio, l'accesa spene

1. Petrarch (1304–1374), known to his fellow Italians as Francesco Petrarca, was the virtual inventor of modern lyric poetry. Comprising sonnets, songs (*canzone*), and odes, his *Rimé sparse* or "various poems"—widely circulated during and after his lifetime—were translated and imitated by poets throughout Europe. Petrarch's verse demonstrated to his early modern readers that a lyric poet could invest subjects with a spirituality and a seriousness previously attributed to the epic, the ode, and to philosophical poems. Petrarch's *Sonnet 140* is a good example of what English poets like Wyatt were responding to as they worked to bring the sonnet form into the repertory of English poetry. Translations by Robert M. Durling.

ragion, vergogna, et reverenza affrene,
di nostro ardir fra se stessa si sdegna.
Onde Amor paventoso fugge al core,
lasciando ogni sua impresa, et piange et trema;
ivi s'asconde et non appar più fore.
Che poss' io far, temendo il mio signore,
se non star seco infin a l'ora estrema?
ché bel fin fa chi ben amando more.

Petrarch, Sonnet 140: A Translation

Love, who lives and reigns in my thought and keeps his principal seat in my heart, sometimes comes forth all in armor into my forehead, there camps, and there sets up his banner.

She who teaches us to love and to be patient, and wishes my great desire, my kindled hope, to be reined in by reason, shame, and reverence, at our boldness is angry within herself.

Wherefore Love flees terrified to my heart, abandoning his every enterprise, and weeps and trembles; there he hides and no more appears outside.

What can I do, when my lord is afraid, except stay with him until the last hour? For he makes a good end who dies loving well.

Whoso List to Hunt

Who so list° to hunt, I know where is an hind,° *wishes / doe*
But as for me, helas, I may no more:
The vain travail° hath wearied me so sore. *idle labor*
I am of them that farthest cometh behind.
Yet may I by no means my wearied mind
Draw from° the deer: but as she fleeth afore, *forget*
Fainting I follow. I leave off therefore,
Since in a net I seek to hold the wind.
Who list her hunt I put him out of doubt,
As well as I may spend his time in vain:
And, graven° with diamonds, in letters plain *engraved*
There is written her fair neck round about:
Noli me tangere,[1] for Caesar's I am,
And wild for to hold though I seem tame.

COMPANION READING
Petrarch, Sonnet 190

Una candida cerva sopra l'erba
verde m'apparve con duo corna d'oro,
fra due riviere all' ombra d'un alloro,

1. "Touch me not," the words the resurrected but not yet risen Christ spoke to Mary Magdalene before his tomb (John 20.17). The "deer" of the poem has often been identified with Anne Boleyn and "Caesar" with Henry VIII.

Levando 'l sole a la stagione acerba.
Era sua vista sì dolce superba
ch' i'lasciai per seguirla ogni lavoro,
come l'avaro che 'n cercar tesoro
con diletto l'affanno disacerba.
"Nessun mi tocchi," al bel collo d'intorno
scritto avea di diamanti et di topazi.
"Libera farmi al mio Cesare parve."
Et era 'l sol già vòlto al mezzo giorno,
gli occhi miei stanchi di mirar, non sazi,
quand' io caddi ne l'acqua et ella sparve.

Petrarch, Sonnet 190: A Translation

A white doe on the green grass appeared to me, with two golden horns, between two rivers, in the shade of a laurel, when the sun was rising in the unripe season.

Her look was so sweet and proud that to follow her I left every task, like the miser who as he seeks treasure sweetens his trouble with delight.

"Let no one touch me," she bore written with diamonds and topazes around her lovely neck. "It has pleased my Caesar to make me free."

And the sun had already turned at midday; my eyes were tired by looking but not sated, when I fell into the water, and she disappeared.

My Galley

My galley charged° with forgetfulness *loaded*
Through sharp seas in winter nights doth pass
'Tween rock and rock; and eke° mine enemy, alas, *also*
That is my lord, steereth with cruelness;
And every oar a thought in readiness,
As though that death were light° in such a case. *easy*
An endless wind doth tear the sail apace.
Of forced sighs and trusty fearfulness.
A rain of tears, a cloud of dark disdain
Hath done the wearied cords° great hindrance, *worn rigging*
Wreathed with error and eke with ignorance.
The stars be hid that led me to this pain,
Drowned is reason that should me comfort,
And I remain despairing of the port.

Some Time I Fled the Fire[1]

Some time I fled the fire that me brent° *burned*
By sea, by land, by water and by wind;
And now I follow the coals that be quent° *quenched*
From Dover to Calais against my mind.
Lo! how desire is both sprung and spent!

1. This poem appears to record Wyatt's attitude as he attended Anne Boleyn on her way to Calais in October 1532. Having been burned by her "fire" (a possible reference to a love affair), he now follows the dead coals of that fire against his will.

And he may see that whilom° was so blind; *formerly*
And all his labor now he laugh° to scorn, *may laugh*
Mashed in the breers° that erst° was all to torn.° *briars / once / torn up*

Henry Howard, Earl of Surrey

1517?–1547

Henry Howard, Earl of Surrey, was the heir to the earldom of Norfolk, one of the most powerful positions in England, when he was executed for treason in the last years of Henry VIII's reign for displaying the royal insignia on his shield, taken as a sign that he had inappropriate ambition. The Norfolks were the most significant Catholic family and so often regarded with suspicion after the Reformation. Surrey was a major poet whose career was cut tragically short. He was one of the first imitators—along with Thomas Wyatt—of Italian Petrarchan verse, helping to introduce the sonnet form into English. His blank verse translation of Virgil was also a major literary landmark. His poetry was published in the landmark collection, *Tottel's Miscellany* (1557) and he was singled out by Sir Philip Sidney as one of the few English writers worth reading.

For more on Sidney, see his principal listing on page 709.

Love That Doth Reign and Live within My Thought

Love that doth reign and live within my thought,
And built his seat within my captive breast,
Clad in the arms wherein with me he fought
Oft in my face he doth his banner rest.
But she that taught me love and suffer pain,
My doubtful hope and eke° my hot desire *also*
With shamefast° cloak to shadow and refrain, *ashamed*
Her smiling grace converteth straight to ire.
And coward love then to the heart apace
Taketh his flight, where he doth lurk and plain° *complain*
His purpose lost, and dare not show his face.
For my lord's guilt thus faultless bide° I pain; *suffer*
Yet from my lord shall not foot remove:
Sweet is the death that taketh end by love.

Th'Assyrians' King, in Peace with Foul Desire

Th'Assyrians' king,[1] in peace with foul desire
And filthy lusts that stained his regal heart,
In war that should set princely hearts afire
Vanquished did yield for want of martial art.
The dent of swords from kisses seemed strange,[2]
And harder than his lady's side his targe;° *shield*

1. The king was Sardanapalus, often regarded as dissolute. He committed suicide by self-immolation.

2. I.e., the dent of swords seemed distasteful compared to kisses.

From glutton feasts to soldiers' fare a change,
His helmet, far above a garland's charge.[3]
Who scarce the name of manhood did retain,
Drenched in sloth and womanish delight;
Feeble of sprite,° unpatient of pain, *spirit*
When he had lost his honor and his right—
Proud time of wealth, in storms appalled with dread—
Murdered himself to show some manful deed.

Set Me Whereas the Sun Doth Parch the Green

Set me whereas the sun doth parch the green,
Or where his beams may not dissolve the ice,
In temperate heat where he is felt and seen;
With proud people, in presence sad and wise;
Set me in base, or yet in high degree,
In the long night or in the shortest day,
In clear weather or where mists thickest be,
In lusty youth, or when my hairs be grey;
Set me in earth, in heaven, or yet in hell,
In hill, in dale, or in the foaming flood;
Thrall,° or at large, alive whereso I dwell, *captive*
Sick, or in health, in ill fame or in good:
Yours will I be, and with that only thought
Comfort myself when that my hap° is nought. *fortune*

The Soote Season

The soote° season, that bud and bloom forth brings, *sweet*
With green hath clad the hill and eke the vale:
The nightingale with feathers new she sings:
The turtle to her make° hath told her tale: *mate*
Summer is come, for every spray now springs,
The hart° hath hung his old head° on the pale:° *stag / horns / stake*
The buck in brake° his winter coat he flings: *thicket*
The fishes float with new repaired scale:
The adder all her slough away she slings:
The swift swallow pursueth the flies small:
The busy bee her honey now she minges:° *remembers*
Winter is worn° that was the flowers' bale:° *passed / evil*
And thus I see among these pleasant things
Each care decays, and yet my sorrow springs.

Alas, So All Things Now Do Hold Their Peace

Alas, so all things now do hold their peace.
Heaven and earth disturbed in nothing:
The beasts, the air, the birds their song do cease:

3. I.e., his helmet was a greater burden than a garland.

The night's chair° the stars about doth bring: *Ursa Major*
Calm is the sea, the waves work less and less:
So am not I, whom love alas doth wring,
Bringing before my face the great increase
Of my desires, whereat I weep and sing
In joy and woe as in a doubtful ease.
For my sweet thoughts sometime do pleasure bring:
But by and by the cause of my disease
Gives me a pang, that inwardly doth sting,
When that I think what grief it is again,
To live and lack the thing should rid my pain.

COMPANION READING
Petrarch, Sonnet 164[1]

Or che 'l ciel et la terra e 'l vento tace
et le fere e gli augelli il sonno affrena,
notte il carro stellato in giro mena
et nel suo letto il mar senz' onda giace,

vegghio, penso, ardo, piango; et chi mi sface
sempre m'è inanzi per mia dolce pena:
guerra è 'l mio stato, d'ira e di duol piena,
et sol di lei pensando ò qualche pace.

Così sol d'una chiara fonte viva
move 'l dolce et l'amaro ond' io mi pasco,
una man sola mi risana et punge;
et perché 'l mio martir non giunga a riva,
mille volte il dì moro et mille nasco,
tanto da la salute mia son lunge.

Petrarch, Sonnet 164: A Translation

Now that the heavens and the earth and the wind are silent, and sleep reins in the beasts and the birds, Night drives her starry car about, and in its bed the sea lies without a wave,

I am awake, I think, I burn, I weep; and she who destroys me is always before me, to my sweet pain: war is my state, full of sorrow and suffering, and only thinking of her do I have any peace.

Thus from one clear living fountain alone spring the sweet and the bitter on which I feed; one hand alone heals me and pierces me.

And that my suffering may not reach an end, a thousand times a day I die and a thousand am born, so distant am I from health.

1. For Petrarch, see the introductory footnote to the Wyatt response, page 667. This translation is also by Robert M. Durling.

George Gascoigne

c. 1534–1577

Satire may produce ambiguous results, particularly when it is directed at the author's own life and work. To judge from his candidly witty self-portraits in *Alexander Neville's Theme* and *Woodmanship*, Gascoigne saw a good subject in his own career. The events of his life indicate that whatever ventures he attempted, he failed "to hit the whites [bulls-eyes] which live with all good luck." Educated at Cambridge and trained as a lawyer at Gray's Inn, Gascoigne went into debt trying to keep up with fashionable life in London. His election to Parliament was voided by the claims of his creditors, and in 1561 he compounded his legal difficulties by a bigamous marriage to Elizabeth Boyes, the widow of Willam Breton and the estranged wife of Edward Boyes. His service in the Low Countries was no more successful. He commanded English troops against the Spanish but, after several miscalculated maneuvers, surrendered to the Spanish at Leiden and spent four months as a prisoner of Spain. Upon returning to England he found himself under yet another kind of attack, this time for poetry that was supposed to report the scandalous behavior of certain figures at court. It had been published in 1573 in his absence (and perhaps without his knowledge) in a volume entitled *A Hundreth Sundrie Flowres*. After augmenting the collection—and reworking much of its material so that it conformed to more conventional standards of propriety, he reissued the volume as *The Posies of George Gascoigne* (1575), the version used here. The same volume also contains a prose romance, *The Adventures of Master F.J.*, a racy account of seduction and betrayal, opportunistic lovers, and resourceful ladies.

As Sir Thomas Wyatt had shown, the conventions that had dictated modes of self-expression in lyric poetry were capable of great transformation. Professions of virtuous love and devotion to patriotic ideals in the manner of Petrarch and his followers were no longer the only topics a poet was supposed to address, and Gascoigne, like Wyatt and such later poets as Sir Philip Sidney and John Donne, retuned the lyric voice so that it became capable of illustrating a sense of self charged not only with desire, but also with chagrin, dismay, bitterness, and even revulsion. At the same time, Gascoigne's vision of society remained essentially humorous; throughout his verse he is more committed to castigating himself than those who may have exploited him. Rarely has an author plagued by so many reversals represented as mellow a vision of society. As a rule, satire flattens its subjects to achieve pointed and deliberate effects; Gascoigne's satire gives his subjects a complexity that makes them seem less outrageous than familiar.

Seven Sonnets to Alexander Neville

Alexander Neville delivered him this theme, *Sat cito, si sat bene*, whereupon he compiled these seven sonnets in sequence, therein bewraying his own *Nimis cito*, and therewith his *Vix bene*, as followeth.[1]

1

In haste, post haste, when first my wand'ring mind,
Beheld the glist'ring court with gazing eye,
Such deep delights I seemed therein to find,
As might beguile a graver guest than I.

1. Gascoigne states that he composed these sonnets at the request of Alexander Neville (a poet, translator of Seneca, and secretary to Archbishop Matthew Parker). He was given a theme, *sat cito, si sat bene*, "if it be [done] well, let it be quickly," which he developed to satirize his own fault of acting too quickly: *nimis cito, vix bene*, or "if it be [done] very quickly, it is hardly well."

The stately pomp of princes and their peers,
Did seem to swim in floods of beaten gold,
The wanton world of young delightful years,
Was not unlike a heaven for to behold.
Wherin did swarm (for every saint) a dame,
So fair of hue, so fresh of their attire,
As might excel dame Cynthia[2] for fame,
Or conquer Cupid with his own desire.
These and such like were baits that blazed still
Before mine eye to feed my greedy will.

2

Before mine eye to feed my greedy will,
'Gan° muster eke° mine old acquainted mates, *began to / also*
Who helped the dish (of vain delight) to fill
My empty mouth with dainty delicates:
And foolish boldness took the whip in hand,
To lash my life into this trustless trace,° *harness*
Till all in haste I leaped aloof° from land, *aloft*
And hoist° up sail to catch a courtly grace: *hoisted*
Each ling'ring day did seem a world of woe,
Till in that hapless haven my head was brought:
Waves of wanhope° so tossed me to and fro, *discouragement*
In deep despair to drown my dreadful thought:
Each hour a day, each day a year did seem,
And every year a world my will did deem.

3

And every year a world my will did deem,
Till lo, at last, to court now am I come,
A seemly swaine, that might the place beseem,
A gladsome guest embraced of all and some:
Not there content with common dignity,
My wand'ring eye in haste, (yea post post haste)
Beheld the blazing badge of bravery,
For want whereof, I thought myself disgraced:
Then peevish pride puffed up my swelling heart,
To further forth so hot an enterprise:
And comely cost began to play his part,
In praising patterns of mine own devise.° *devising*
Thus all was good that might be got in haste,
To prink° me up, and make me higher placed. *dress*

4

To prink me up and make me higher placed,
All came too late that taried any time,
Pill of provision[3] pleased not my taste,

2. The goddess of the moon, an aspect of the goddess Diana, the goddess of chastity.

3. The property his family had provided him as his inheritance. Requiring greater wealth, he began to cut the trees on his estate.

They made my heels too heavy for to climb:
Me thought it best that boughs of boist'rous oak,
Should first be shred to make my feathers gay.
Till at the last a deadly dinting stroke,
Brought down the bulk with edgetools of decay:
Of every farm I then let fly a lease,
To feed the purse that paid for peevishness,
Till rent and all were fall'n in such disease,
As scarce could serve to maintain cleanliness:
They bought the body, fine,° farm, lease, and land, *recorded grant*
All were too little for the merchant's hand.[4]

5

All were too little for the merchant's hand,
And yet my bravery bigger than his book:
But when this hot accompt° was coldly scanned, *account*
I thought high time about me for to look:
With heavy cheer I cast my head aback,
To see the fountain of my furious race.
Compared my loss, my living, and my lack,
In equal balance with my jolly grace.
And saw expenses grating on the ground
Like lumps of lead to press my purse full oft,
When light reward and recompense were found,
Fleeting like feathers in the wind aloft:
These thus compared, I left the court at large,
For why? the gains doth seldom quit° the charge. *compensate for*

6

For why? the gains doth seldom quit the charge,
And so say I, by proof too dearly bought,
My haste made waste, my brave and brainsick barge,
Did float too fast, to catch a thing of naught:
With leisure, measure, mean, and many mo,° *more*
I mought° have kept a chair of quiet state, *might*
But hasty heads cannot be settled so,
Till crooked Fortune give a crabbed mate:[5]
As busy brains must beat on tickle° toys, *fickle*
As rash invention breeds a raw device,
So sudden falls do hinder hasty joys,
And as swift baits do fleetest fish entice.
So haste makes waste, and therefore now I say,
No haste but good, where wisdom makes the way.

7

No haste but good, where wisdom makes the way,
For proof whereof, behold the simple snail,

4. Having leased his farms, he could no longer sell what they produced; in all, none of the financial arrangements he made to acquire more money proved adequate to meet what the merchant charged for his apparel and upkeep.
5. Fortune will give those who act in haste an outcome that is unsatisfactory.

(Who sees the soldier's carcass cast away,
With hot assault the castle to assail,)
By line and leisure climbs the lofty wall,
And wins the turret's top more cunningly,
Than doughty Dick, who lost his life and all,
With hoisting up his head too hastily.
The swiftest bitch brings forth the blindest whelps,
The hottest fevers coldest cramps ensue,
The naked'st need hath over latest helps:[6]
With Neville then I find this proverb true,
That haste makes waste, and therefore still I say,
No haste but good, where wisdom makes the way.

Sic tuli[7]

Edmund Spenser

1552?–1599

Edmund Spenser apparently wrote the sequence entitled *Amoretti* for Elizabeth Boyle, whom he married in 1594, although some of its eighty-nine sonnets may be of an earlier date and intended for another woman. The sequence was published in 1595 together with *Epithalamion*, Spenser's marriage hymn in celebration of his wedding. The two works are linked thematically by their allusions to the passage of time. The *Amoretti* refers to seasons of the year, the *Epithalamion* to the twenty-four hours of a day that begins at one in the morning and ends at 12 midnight. Epithalamia, a feature of the literature of ancient Greece, were usually written by a professional for a family with whom the poet had no personal connection. Spenser's hymn is unusual in that its poet is also the husband it honors.

For more about Spenser, see his principal listing, on page 822.

from Amoretti[1]

1

Happy ye leaves° when as those lilly hands, *of the book*
Which hold my life in their dead doing° might, *death-dealing*
Shall handle you and hold in loves soft bands,° *bonds*
Lyke captives trembling at the victors sight.
And happy lines, on which with starry light,
Those lamping° eyes will deigne sometimes to look *flashing*
And reade the sorrowes of my dying spright,° *spirit*
Written with teares in harts close bleeding book.
And happy rymes bath'd in the sacred brooke,[2]
Of Helicon whence she derived is,
When ye behold that Angels blessed looke,

6. Gascoigne alludes to the ironies of Fortune; in sum, the most dire need is met with help, but that help comes too late.
7. Thus I have persevered.

1. "Little loves."
2. Aganippe, which rises (or is "derived") from Helicon, a mountain that is home to the Muses, goddesses of all the arts but known especially for their inspiration of poets.

My soules long lacked foode, my heavens blis.
Leaves, lines, and rymes, seeke her to please alone,
Whom if ye please, I care for other none.

4

New yeare forth looking out of Janus[3] gate,
Doth seeme to promise hope of new delight:
And bidding th'old Adieu, his passed date
Bids all old thoughts to die in dumpish spright° *low spirits*
And calling forth out of sad Winters night,
Fresh love, that long hath slept in cheerlesse bower:
Wils him awake, and soone about him dight
His wanton wings and darts of deadly power.
For lusty spring now in his timely howre,
Is ready to come forth him to receive:
And warnes the Earth with divers colord flowre,
To decke hir selfe, and her faire mantle weave.
Then you faire flowre, in whom fresh youth doth raine,° *reign*
Prepare your selfe new love to entertaine.

13

In that proud port,° which her so goodly graceth,[4] *bearing*
Whiles her faire face she reares up to the skie:
And to the ground her eie lids low embaseth° *casts down*
Most goodly temperature° ye may descry,° *temperament / perceive*
Myld humblesse° mixt with awfull° majesty, *humility / awesome*
For looking on the earth whence she was borne:
Her minde remembreth her mortalitie,
What so is fayrest shall to earth returne.
But that same lofty countenance seemes to scorne
Base thing, and thinke how she to heaven may clime:
Treading downe earth as lothsome and forlorne,
That hinders heavenly thoughts with drossy° slime. *heavy*
Yet lowly still vouchsafe° to looke on me, *condescend*
Such lowlinesse shall make you lofty be.

22

This holy season fit to fast and pray,[5]
Men to devotion ought to be inclynd:
Therefore, I lykewise on so holy day,

3. A Roman god of the new year who has two faces; one looks back at December, the other ahead to January. For Christians the liturgical new year began on March 25, the Feast of the Annunciation, when the Angel Gabriel was thought to have announced the coming of Jesus Christ to the Virgin Mary. Throughout the sequence, Spenser plays with these two concepts of the year, juxtaposing the time dictated by nature, figured by the Roman calendar, with time according to Christian history and celebrated by the fasts and feasts of the church.

4. Spenser describes the lady to whom the sonnet is addressed.

5. The holy season is Lent; the holy day is Ash Wednesday. The sonnet celebrates the poet's admission that his love has a spiritual dimension; complimenting his heart's desire is the worship he gives to his lady's image in the temple of his mind.

For my sweet Saynt some service fit will find.
Her temple fayre is built within my mind,
In which her glorious ymage placed is,
On which my thoughts doo day and night attend
Lyke sacred priests that never thinke amisse.
There I to her as th'author of my blisse,
Will builde an altar to appease her yre:° *anger*
And on the same my hart will sacrifise,
Burning in flames of pure and chast desyre:
The which vouchsafe O goddesse to accept,
Amongst thy deerest relicks to be kept.

62

The weary yeare his race now having run,
The new[6] begins his compast° course anew: *encompassed*
With shew of morning mylde he hath begun,
Betokening peace and plenty to ensew.
So let us, which this chaunge of weather vew,
Chaunge eeke° our mynds and former lives amend, *also*
The old yeares sinnes forepast° let us eschew,° *gone by / avoid*
And fly the faults with which we did offend.
Then shall the new yeares joy forth freshly send,
Into the glooming° world his gladsome ray: *gloomy*
And all these stormes which now his beauty blend,° *dim*
Shall turne to caulmes and tymely cleare away.
So likewise love cheare you your heavy spright,
And chaunge old yeares annoy° to new delight. *grief*

65

The doubt° which ye misdeeme,° fayre love, is vaine, *fear / misconceive*
That fondly° feare to loose° your liberty, *foolishly / lose*
When loosing one, two liberties ye gayne,
And make him bond that bondage earst dyd fly.
Sweet be the bands, the which true love doth tye,
Without constraynt or dread of any ill:
The gentle birde feeles no captivity
Within her cage, but singes and feeds her fill.
There pride dare not approch, nor discord spill
The league twixt them, that loyal love hath bound:
But simple truth and mutuall good will,
Seekes with sweet peace to salve° each others wound: *heal*
There fayth doth fearlesse dwell in brasen towre,
And spotlesse pleasure builds her sacred bowre.

6. The Christian new year, the Feast of the Annunciation.

66

To all those happy blessings which ye have,
With plenteous hand by heaven upon you thrown:
This one disparagement they to you gave,
That ye your love lent to so meane a one.[7]
Yee whose high worths surpassing paragon,
Could not on earth have found one fit for mate,
Ne but in heaven matchable to none,
Why did ye stoup unto so lowly state.
But ye thereby much greater glory gate,° *got*
Then° had ye sorted° with a princes pere:° *than / consorted / peer*
For now your light doth more it selfe dilate,° *spread*
And in my darknesse greater doth appeare.
Yet since your light hath once enlumind° me, *illuminated*
With my reflex° yours shall encreased be. *reflected light*

68

Most glorious Lord of lyfe that on this day,[8]
Didst make thy triumph over death and sin:
And having harrowd hell, didst bring away
Captivity thence captive us to win.[9]
This joyous day, deare Lord, with joy begin,
And grant that we for whom thou diddest dye
Being with thy deare blood clene washt from sin,
May live for ever in felicity.
And that thy love we weighing worthily,
May likewise love thee for the same againe:
And for thy sake that all lyke deare° didst buy, *at the same cost*
With love may one another entertayne.
So let us love, deare love, lyke as we ought,
Love is the lesson which the Lord us taught.

75

One day I wrote her name upon the strand,° *beach*
But came the waves and washed it away:
Agayne I wrote it with a second hand,
But came the tyde, and made my paynes his pray.
Vayne man, sayd she, that doest in vaine assay,° *attempt*
A mortall thing so to immortalize.
For I my selve shall lyke to this decay,

7. Working forward from Sonnet 62 and counting each sonnet as representing a day of love and devotion, Sonnet 66 corresponds to Good Friday. Spenser exploits the idea of humility, consistent with the passion of Christ, to express his own sense of devotion to his lady's virtue.
8. The sonnet addresses the "dear Lord" of the Passion on Easter Day to harmonize the poet's love for his lady and his obligation to follow the lesson of Christ.
9. Christians believed that after his Resurrection, Christ descended into hell to rescue Adam and Eve and the patriarchs and prophets of the Hebrew Bible. The event is often described as the harrowing of hell.

And eek my name bee wyped out lykewize.
Not so, (quod I) let baser things devize,° *consent*
To dy in dust, but you shall live by fame:
My verse your vertues rare shall eternize,° *make eternal*
And in the hevens wryte your glorious name:
Where whenas death shall all the world subdew,
Our love shall live, and later life renew.

Sir Philip Sidney

1554–1586

Courtier, poet and author of prose romances, Sir Philip Sidney stands as the most important writer and literary theorist of the first half of Elizabeth's reign who showed what it was possible to achieve in English. However, Sidney's own sense of himself suggests that he valued his political interventions more highly than his literary work. Sidney witnessed the Massacre of Saint Bartholomew's Day (1572) when Protestants were slaughtered in a sudden Catholic uprising, one of the key events that formed Protestant opinion in Europe. Sidney became well-known for advocating a more "forward" policy in Europe that would help the Dutch rebels against the Spanish but he died of his wounds in the battle of Zutphen. He was granted a state funeral, which was used to support his political ideals. His works were principally edited by his sister, Mary (1561–1621), one of the first women to obtain a major reputation as a poet in English.

For more on Sidney, see his principal listing on page 998.

from Astrophil and Stella[1]

1

Loving in truth, and fain° in verse my love to show, *wishing*
That she (dear she) might take some pleasure of my pain:
Pleasure might cause her read, reading might make her know,
Knowledge might pity win, and pity grace obtain,
I sought fit words to paint the blackest face of woe,
Studying inventions[2] fine, her wits to entertain:
Oft turning others' leaves, to see if thence would flow
Some fresh and fruitfull showers upon my sun-burned brain.
But words came halting forth, wanting Invention's stay,° *support*
Invention Nature's child, fled step-dame Study's blows,
And others' feet still seemed but strangers in my way.
Thus great with child to speak, and helpless in my throes,° *agonies*
Biting my trewand° pen, beating my self for spite, *truant*
Fool, said my Muse to me, look in thy heart and write.

1. This sonnet sequence was composed in 1582 and published in 1591.

2. "Invention" was the term early modern rhetoricians used to designate the choice of a literary subject and its development as an argument, in contrast to the forms of expression, figures of thought and speech, and imagery by which that subject was conveyed. As Sidney suggests, "invention" depended on the writer's imaginative intelligence, not on his literary education.

3

Let dainty wits cry on the sisters nine,[3]
That bravely masked, their fancies may be told;
Or, Pindar's apes[4] flaunt they in phrases fine,
Enam'ling with pied flowers their thoughts of gold;
Or else let them in statelier glory shine,
Ennobling new-found tropes° with problems° old; *figures of speech / subjects*
Or with strange similes enrich each line,
Of herbs or beasts which Ind or Afric hold.
For me, in sooth, no Muse but one I know;
Phrases and problems from my reach do grow,
And strange things cost too dear for my poor sprites.
How then? Even thus—in Stella's face I read
What love and beauty be; then all my deed
But copying is, what, in her, Nature writes.

7

When Nature made her chief work, Stella's eyes,
In color black, why wrapt° she beams so bright? *enwrapped*
Would she in beamy° black, like painter wise, *glowing*
Frame daintiest° luster, mixed of shades and light? *subtlest*
Or did she else that sober hue devise,
In object best to knit and strength° our sight, *strengthen*
Least if no veil these brave gleams did disguise,
They sun-like should more dazzle then delight?[5]
Or would she her miraculous power show,
That whereas black seems beáuty's contrary,
She even in black doth make all beauties flow?
Both so and thus, she minding Love should be
Placed ever there, gave him this mourning weed,
To honor all their deaths, who for her bleed.[6]

9

Queen Virtue's court, which some call Stella's face,[7]
Prepared by Nature's choicest furniture,
Hath his front° built of Alabaster pure; *forehead*
Gold is the covering° of that stately place. *her hair*
The door° by which sometimes comes forth her Grace, *her mouth*
Red porphir is, which lock of pearl° makes sure:° *her teeth / secure*
Whose porches rich (which name of cheeks endure°) *allow*
Marble mixt red and white do interlace.

3. The nine Muses, sponsors of the arts, music, and poetry.
4. Poets who slavishly imitated the literary works of the Greek poet Pindar, 522–442. C.E.
5. Did Nature make Stella's eyes black so that their bright beams might be softened to a mixed hue or not blind us with their brilliance?
6. Love is conventionally conveyed by the lady's glance, from her eyes, to the lover's heart, through his eyes; Stella's eyes are dark and in mourning because her glance is lethal.
7. The poet compares Stella's appearance to that of a building, the site of Virtue's court.

The windows° now through which this heavenly guest — *her eyes*
Looks over the world, and can find nothing such,
Which dare claim from those lights the name of best.[8]
Of touch° they are that without touch doth touch,° — *touchstone / attain*
Which° Cupid's self from Beauty's mind did draw: — *that which*
Of touch° they are, and poor I am their straw.[9] — *touchwood, tinder*

10

Reason, in faith thou art well served, that still
Wouldst brabbling° be with sense and love in me; — *babbling*
I rather wished thee climb the Muses' hill;° — *Mt. Helicon*
Or reach the fruit of Nature's choicest tree;[1]
Or seek heaven's course or heaven's inside to see.
Why shouldst thou toil our thorny soil to till?
Leave sense and those which sense's objects be;
Deal thou with powers of thoughts; leave love to will.
But thou wouldst needs fight both with love and sense,
With sword of wit giving wounds of dispraise,
Till downright blows did foil thy cunning fence;° — *swordsmanship*
For, soon as they[2] strake thee with Stella's rays,
Reason, though kneel'dst, and offer'dst straight to prove,
By reason good, good reason her to love.

14

Alas, have I not pain enough, my friend,
Upon whose breast a fiercer grip doth tire[3]
Than did on him who first stole down the fire,[4]
While Love on me doth all his quiver spend—
But with your rhubarb° words ye must contend, — *bitter*
To grieve me worse, in saying that desire
Doth plunge my well-formed soul even in the mire
Of sinful thoughts, which do in ruin end?
If that be sin which doth the manners° frame, — *decent behavior*
Well stayed with truth in word[5] and faith of deed,
Ready of wit, and fearing naught but shame;
If that be sin, which in fixed hearts doth breed
A loathing of all loose unchastity,
Then love is sin, and let me sinful be.

8. Stella's eyes reveal to her that nothing in the world is better than they are; they are uniquely the best.

9. The last three lines of the poem play on the meanings of "touch": Stella's eyes are touchstone, the mineral that reveals whether an ore contains gold; they make contact with their object without touching it; they attain the form that Cupid drew from Beauty; and they act as tinder does to the straw that is the poet: they set him on fire.

1. The tree of knowledge in the Garden of Eden.

2. Love and sense.

3. Grasp does hold.

4. Prometheus, the mythical hero who stole fire from heaven to give to mankind, an act for which the gods ordered his liver torn out by an eagle.

5. Firmly rooted in truthful language.

15

You that do search for every purling spring
Which from the ribs of old Parnassus[6] flows,
And every flower, not sweet perhaps, which grows
Near thereabouts, into your poesy wring;
You that do dictionary's method bring
Into your rhymes, running in rattling rows;[7]
You that poor Petrarch's long deceased woes
With newborn sighs and denizened wit do sing:[8]
You take wrong ways; those far-fet° helps be such *far-fetched*
As do bewray° a want of inward touch, *reveal*
And sure at length stolen goods do come to light;
But if, both for your love and skill, your name
You seek to nurse at fullest breasts of fame,
Stella behold, and then begin to indite.° *write*

23

The curious wits, seeing dull pensiveness
Bewray itself in my long-settled eyes,
Whence those same fumes of melancholy rise,
With idle pains and missing aim do guess.
Some, that know how my spring° I did address, *youth*
Deem that my Muse some fruit of knowledge plies;
Others, because the prince my service tries,
Think that I think state errors to redress.
But harder judges judge ambition's rage,
Scourge of itself, still climbing slippery place,
Holds my young brain captived° in golden cage. *captivated*
O fools, or over-wise: alas, the race
Of all my thoughts hath neither stop nor start
But only Stella's eyes and Stella's heart.

24

Rich fools there be whose base and filthy heart
Lies hatching still the goods wherein they flow,
And damning their own selves to Tantal's[9] smart,
Wealth breeding want, more blissed,° more wretched grow. *blessed*
Yet to those fools heaven such wit doth impart
As what their hands do hold, their heads do know,
And knowing, love, and loving, lay apart
As sacred things, far from all danger's show.
But that rich fool who by blind Fortune's lot

6. A mountain in Greece sacred to Apollo and the Muses.
7. I.e., exhibiting alliteration, repeating the same sound within a few lines.
8. I.e., represent the themes and motifs of the 14th-century Italian poet Petrarch.
9. The mythical sinner, condemned forever in Hades to reach for food and drink which were always already out of reach.

The richest gem of love and life enjoys,
And can with foul abuse such beauties blot,
Let him, deprived of sweet but unfelt joys,
Exiled for aye from those high treasures which
He knows not, grow in only folly rich![1]

31

With how sad steps, O Moon, thou climb'st the skies,
How silently, and with how wan° a face, *pale*
What may it be, that even in heavenly place
That busy archer° his sharp arrows tries? *Cupid*
Sure if° that long with Love acquainted eyes *surely if those*
Can judge of Love, thou feel'st a lover's case;
I read it in thy looks, thy languished grace
To me that feel the like, thy state descries.° *reveals*
Then even of fellowship, O Moon, tell me
Is constant Love deemed there but want of wit?
Are beauties there as proud as here they be?
Do they above love to be loved, and yet
Those lovers scorn whom that Love doth possess?
Do they call Virtue there ungratefulness?

37

My mouth doth water, and my breast doth swell,
My tongue doth itch, my thoughts in labor be.
Listen then, lordings, with good ear to me,
For, of my life, I must a riddle tell.
Toward Aurora's[2] court a nymph doth dwell,
Rich in all beauties which man's eye can see
(Beauties so far from reach of words, that we
Abase her praise saying she doth excel),
Rich in the treasure of deserved renown,
Rich in the riches of a royal heart,
Rich in those gifts which give the eternal crown,
Who (though most rich in these and every part
Which make the patents° of true worldly bliss) *royal grants*
Hath no misfortune but that Rich she is.

39

Come sleep, O sleep, the certain knot of peace,
The baiting° place of wit, the balm of woe, *resting*
The poor man's wealth, the prisoner's release,
Th'indifferent judge between the high and low;
With shield of proof° shield me from out the prease° *proven shield / throng*

1. The sonnet mocks Lord Rich, the husband of Penelope Devereux, the model for Sidney's Stella.

2. Goddess of the dawn.

Of those fierce darts, despair at me doth throw:
O make in me those civil wars to cease;
I will good tribute pay if thou do so.
Take thou of me smooth pillows, sweetest bed,
A chamber deaf to noise, and blind to light:
A rosy garland, and a weary head:
And if these things, as being thine by right,
Move not thy heavy grace, thou shalt in me
Livelier then elsewhere Stella's image see.

45

Stella oft sees the very face of woe
Painted in my beclouded stormy face:
But cannot skill° to pity my disgrace, *does not know how*
Not though thereof the cause herself she know:
Yet hearing late a fable, which did show
Of lovers never known, a grievous case,° *situation*
Pity thereof gate° in her breast such place, *got*
That from that sea derived tears' spring did flow.[3]
Alas, if Fancy drawn by imaged things,
Though false, yet with free scope more grace doth breed
Than servants' wrack, where new doubts honor brings;[4]
Then think my dear, that you in me do read
Of lovers' ruin some sad tragedy:
I am not I, pity the tale of me.

47

What, have I thus betrayed my liberty?
Can those black beams such burning marks engrave
In my free side; or am I born a slave,
Whose neck becomes° such yoke of tyranny? *suits*
Or want I sense to feel my misery,
Or sprite,° disdain of such disdain to have, *spirit*
Who for long faith, though daily help I crave,
May get no alms, but scorn of beggary?
Virtue, awake! Beauty but beauty is;
I may, I must, I can, I will, I do
Leave following that which it is gain to miss.
Let her go! Soft, but here she comes! Go to;
Unkind, I love you not. Oh me, that eye
Doth make my heart give to my tongue the lie!

52

A strife is grown between Virtue and Love,
While each pretends that Stella must be his.

3. I.e., derived from that sea [of pity], a spring of tears did flow.
4. I.e., Fancy with free scope breeds more grace or sympathy than the actual destruction of a servant, a situation in which a sense of honor provokes new doubts about that person's worth.

Her eyes, her lips, her all, saith Love, do this,
Since they do wear his badge, most firmly prove.
But Virtue thus that title does disprove
That Stella (oh dear name!), that Stella is
That virtuous soul, sure heir of heavenly bliss,
Not this fair outside which our hearts doth move;
And therefore, though her beauty and her grace
Be Love's indeed, in Stella's self he may
By no pretense claim any manner place.
Well, Love, since this demur° our suit doth stay, *objection*
Let Virtue have that Stella's self; yet thus,
That Virtue but that body grant to us.

60

When my good Angel guides me to the place,
Where all my good I do in Stella see,
That heaven of joys throws only down on me
Thundered disdains and lightnings of disgrace:
But when the ruggedst step of Fortune's race° *course*
Makes me fall from her sight, then sweetly she
With words, wherein the Muses' treasures be,
Shows love and pity to my absent case.[5]
Now I wit-beaten long by hardest Fate,
So dull am, that I cannot look into
The ground of this fierce love and lovely hate:
Then some good body tell me how I do,
Whose presence, absence, absence presence is;[6]
Blissed° in my curse, and cursed in my bliss. *blessed*

63

O grammar-rules, O now your virtues show,
So children still read you with awful° eyes, *respectful*
As my young dove may, in your precepts wise,
Her grant to me by her own virtue know;
For late, with heart most high, with eyes most low,
I craved the thing which ever she denies;
She, lightning love, displaying Venus' skies,
Lest once should not be heard, twice said, "No, no!"
Sing then, my muse, now Io Paean sing;[7]
Heavens envy not at my high triumphing,
But grammar's force with sweet success confirm,
For grammar says,—oh this, dear Stella, weigh,—
For grammar says,—to grammar who says nay?—
That in one speech two negatives affirm!

5. I.e., when a good angel or good fortune guides the poet to Stella, heaven throws at him only the "joys" of disdain and disgrace. On the other hand, when he is away from her, she shows him love and pity.
6. This paradox is repeated in sonnets 106 and 108.
7. Hymn of thanksgiving.

64

No more, my dear, no more these counsels try;
O give my passions leave to run their race;
Let Fortune lay on me her worst disgrace;
Let folk o'ercharged with brain against me cry;
Let clouds bedim my face, break in mine eye;
Let me no steps but of lost labor trace;
Let all the earth with scorn recount my case;
But do not will me from my love to fly.
I do not envy Aristotle's wit,
Nor do aspire to Caesar's bleeding fame,
Nor aught do care though some above me sit,
Nor hope nor wish another course to frame
But that which once may win thy cruel heart.
Thou art my wit, and thou my virtue art.

68

Stella, the only planet of my light,
Light of my life, and life of my desire,
Chief good whereto my hope doth only aspire,
World of my wealth, and heaven of my delight,
Why dost thou spend the treasures of thy sprite° *spirit*
With voice more fit to wed Amphion's[8] lyre,
Seeking to quench in me the noble fire
Fed by thy worth and blinded by thy sight?
And all in vain; for while they breath most sweet
With choicest words, thy words with reasons rare,
Thy reasons firmly set on Virtue's feet,
Labor to kill in me this killing care;
O think I then, what paradise of joy
It is, so fair a virtue to enjoy!

71

Who will in fairest book of Nature[9] know,
How Virtue may best lodged in beauty be,
Let him but learn of Love to read in thee,
Stella, those fair lines, which true goodness show.
There shall he find all vices overthrow,° *overthrown*
Not by rude force, but sweetest sovereignty
Of reason, from whose light those night-birds fly;
That inward sun in thine eyes shineth so.
And not content to be Perfection's heir

8. The legendary lyre-player whose music moved the stones that built the walls of Thebes.

9. All of creation, in effect the second "book" of God and a supplement to the Bible. It was a philosophical commonplace that Nature was the repository of natural law, which all human beings could discover through reason, just as the Bible held divine law, which was revealed to the faithful through grace.

Thyself, doest strive all minds that way to move:
Who mark in thee what is in thee most fair.
So while thy beauty draws the heart to love,
As fast thy virtue bends that love to good:
But ah, Desire still cries, give me some food.

Second song

Have I caught my heavenly jewel
Teaching sleep most fair to be?
Now will I teach her that she,
When she wakes, is too too cruel.

Since sweet sleep her eyes hath charmed
The two only darts of Love,
Now will I with that boy prove
Some play while he is disarmed.[1]

Her tongue, waking, still refuseth,
Giving frankly niggard no;
Now will I attempt to know
What no her tongue, sleeping, useth.

See the hand which, waking, guardeth,
Sleeping, grants a free resort.
Now will I invade the fort.
Cowards love with loss rewardeth.

But, O fool, think of the danger
Of her just and high disdain!
Now will I, alas, refrain.
Love fears nothing else but anger.

Yet those lips, so sweetly swelling,
Do invite a stealing kiss.
Now will I but venture this.
Who will read must first learn spelling.

O, sweet kiss! But ah, she's waking!
Louring° beauty chastens me. *scowling*
Now will I away hence flee:
Fool, more fool, for no more taking!

74

I never drank of Aganippe well,[2]
Nor ever did in shade of Tempe[3] sit,
And Muses scorn with vulgar brains to dwell,
Poor layman I, for sacred rites unfit.

1. Stella's eyes have charmed and disarmed Cupid, leaving him open to the poet's play or contest of wills.

2. Spring on Mt. Helicon, sacred to the Muses.

3. A valley in Arcadia.

Some do I hear of poets' fury[4] tell,
But, God wot, wot not what they mean by it;
And this I swear by blackest brook of hell,
I am no pick-purse of another's wit.
How falls it then that with so smooth an ease
My thoughts I speak; and what I speak doth flow
In verse, and that my verse best wits doth please?
Guess we the cause. "What, is it thus?" Fie, no.
"Or so?" Much less. "How then?" Sure thus it is:
My lips are sweet, inspired with Stella's kiss.

Fourth song

Only joy, now here you° are, *Stella*
Fit to hear and ease my care:
Let my whispering voice obtain,
Sweet reward for sharpest pain:
Take me to thee, and thee to me.
No, no, no, no, my dear, let be.[5]

Night hath closed all in her cloak,
Twinkling stars love-thoughts provoke:
Danger hence good care doth keep,[6]
Jealousy itself doth sleep:
Take me to thee, and thee to me.
No, no, no, no, my dear, let be.

Better place no wit can find,
Cupid's yoke to loose or bind:
These sweet flowers on fine bed too,
Us in their best language woo:
Take me to thee, and thee to me.
No, no, no, no, my dear, let be.

This small light the moon bestows,
Serves thy beams but to disclose,
So to raise my hap more high;[7]
Fear not else, none can us spy:
Take me to thee, and thee to me.
No, no, no, no, my dear, let be.

That you heard was but a mouse,
Dumb sleep holdeth all the house:
Yet asleep, me thinks they say,

4. Divine frenzy; Sidney identifies it as the poets' inspiration in *The Apology for Poetry*.
5. The last line of each stanza is Stella's reply to Astrophil's entreaties in the preceding five lines. An earlier sonnet has suggested that logically two negatives are the same as a positive; thus it is possible to read a certain ambiguity into Stella's rejection of Astrophil here.
6. I.e., good care keeps danger away.
7. Astrophil states that the moon reveals Stella's beauty and thus raises his fortune. Writers and artists in this period imagined fortune as a goddess or a kind of fatal force that turned a wheel to which a person's prosperity was tied; when one was at the top of Fortune's wheel, pleasure and power were within one's grasp. In the last stanza, Astrophil declares that Stella's hate will signal his fall and foresees his death. The images of rising and dying also have a sexual meaning.

Young folks, take time while you may:
Take me to thee, and thee to me.
No, no, no, no, my dear, let be.

Niggard° Time threats, if we miss *miserly*
This large offer of our bliss:
Long stay ere[8] he grant the same:
Sweet then, while each thing doth frame:° *suit*
Take me to thee, and thee to me.
No, no, no, no, my dear, let be.

Your fair mother is abed,
Candles out, and curtains spread:
She thinks you do letters write:
Write, but let me first indite:° *speak*
Take me to thee, and thee to me.
No, no, no, no, my dear, let be.

Sweet alas, why strive you thus?
Concord better fitteth us:
Leave to Mars the force of hands,
Your power in your beauty stands:
Take thee to me, and me to thee.
No, no, no, no, my dear, let be.

Woe to me, and do you swear
Me to hate, but I forbear,
Cursed be my destines° all, *destinies*
That brought me so high to fall:
Soon with my death I will please thee.
No, no, no, no, my dear, let be.

86

Alas, whence came this change of looks? If I
Have changed desert let mine own conscience be
A still-felt plague to self-condemning me,
Let woe grip on my heart, shame load mine eye;
But if all faith like spotless ermine[9] lie
Safe in my soul, which only doth to thee
As his sole object of felicity
With wings of Love in air of wonder fly,
O ease your hand, treat not so hard your slave:
In justice pains come not till faults do call.
Or if I needs, sweet judge, must torments have,
Use something else to chasten me withal
Than those blessed eyes where all my hopes do dwell:
No doom° should make one's heaven become his hell. *judgment*

8. I.e., it will be long before Time will give us another chance.

9. A kind of weasel whose fur is brown in summer and white in winter.

Eighth song

In a grove most rich of shade,
Where birds wanton music made,
May then young his pied weeds showing,[1]
New perfumed with flowers fresh growing,

Astrophil with Stella sweet,
Did for mutual comfort meet,
Both within themselves oppressed,
But each in the other blessed.

Him great harms had taught much care,
Her fair neck a foul yoke[2] bare,
But her sight his cares did banish,
In his sight her yoke did vanish.

Wept they had, alas the while,
But now tears themselves did smile,
While their eyes by love directed,
Interchangeably reflected.

Sigh they did, but now betwixt° *between*
Sighs of woes were glad sighs mixed,
With arms crossed, yet testifying
Restless rest, and living dying.

Their ears hungry of each word,
Which the dear tongue would afford,
But their tongues restrained from walking,
Till their hearts had ended talking.
But when their tongues could not speak,
Love itself did silence break;
Love did set his lips asunder,
Thus to speak in love and wonder:

Stella, sovereign of my joy,
Fair triumpher of° annoy,° *over / despair*
Stella, star of heavenly fire,
Stella, loadstar° of desire. *magnet*

Stella, in whose shining eyes,
Are the lights of Cupid's skies,
Whose beams where they once are darted,
Love therewith is straight imparted.

Stella, whose voice when it speaks,
Senses all asunder breaks;
Stella, whose voice when it singeth,
Angels to acquaintance bringeth.

1. I.e., May, young then, showed his many-colored garments.
2. The "yoke" Stella wears is her marriage to Lord Rich; it is "foul" to Astrophil because it means that he can no longer court her, at least openly.

Stella, in whose body is
Writ° each character of bliss, *written*
Whose face all, all beauty passeth,
Save thy mind which yet surpasseth.

Grant, O grant, but speech alas,
Fails me fearing on to pass,
Grant, O me, what am I saying?
But no fault there is in praying.

Grant, O dear, on knees I pray,
(Knees on ground he then did stay)
That not I but since I love you,
Time and place for me may move you.

Never season was more fit,
Never room more apt for it;
Smiling air allows my reason,
These birds sing; now use the season.

This small wind which so sweet is,
See how it the leaves doth kiss,
Each tree in his best attiring,
Sense of love to love inspiring.

Love makes earth the water drink,
Love to earth makes water sink;
And if dumb things be so witty,
Shall a heavenly grace want pity?

There his hands in their speech fain
Would have made tongue's language plain;[3]
But her hands his hands repelling,
Gave repulse all grace excelling.[4]

Then she spake; her speech was such,
As not ears but heart did touch:
While such wise she love denied,
As yet love she signified.

Astrophil said she, my love
Cease in these effects to prove:
Now be still, yet still believe me,
Thy grief more than death would grieve me.

If that any thought in me,
Can taste comfort but of thee,° *except from you*
Let me feed with hellish anguish,
Joyless, hopeless, endless languish.

3. I.e., he would have had the language of his hands make plain what he had spoken.
4. I.e., she rejected him in a way that excelled all the grace that would have accompanied her acceptance of him.

If those eyes you praised, be
Half so dear as you to me,
Let me home return, stark blinded
Of those eyes, and blinder minded.[5]

If to secret° of my heart, *the secrets*
I do any wish impart,
Where thou art not foremost placed,
Be both wish and I defaced.

If more may be said, I say,
All my bliss in thee I lay;
If thou love, my love content thee,
For all love, all faith is meant thee,

Trust me while I thee deny,
In myself the smart° I try,° *pain / feel*
Tyran honor doth thus use thee,
Stella's self might not refuse thee.

Therefore, dear, this no more move,
Lest, though I leave not thy love,
Which too deep in me is framed,
I should blush when thou art named.

Therewithal away she went,
Leaving him so passion rent,
With what she had done and spoken,
That therewith my song is broken.

Ninth song

Go, my flock, go get you hence,
Seek a better place of feeding,
Where you may have some defense
From the storms in my breast breeding,
And showers from mine eyes proceeding.

Leave a wretch in whom all woe
Can abide to keep no measure;
Merry flock, such one forgo,
Unto whom mirth is displeasure,
Only rich in mischief's treasure.

Yet, alas, before you go,
Hear your woeful master's story,
Which to stones I else would show:
Sorrow only then hath glory
When 'tis excellently° sorry. *exceedingly*

5. I.e., even blinder in my mind.

Stella, fiercest shepherdess,
Fiercest but yet fairest ever,
Stella whom, O heavens, do bless,
Though against me she persever,
Though I bliss inherit never,

Stella hath refused me;
Stella who more love hath proved
In this caitiff° heart to be
Than can in good ewes be moved
Toward lambkins best beloved.

°*wretched*

Stella hath refused me,
Astrophel, that so well served,
In this pleasant spring must see,
While in pride flowers be preserved,
Himself only winter-starved.

Why, alas, doth she then swear
That she loveth me so dearly,
Seeing me so long to bear
Coals of love that burn so clearly,
And yet leave me helpless merely?

Is that love? forsooth I trow
If I saw my good dog grieved,
And a help for him did know,
My love should not be believed
But he were by me relieved.

No, she hates me (wellaway!)
Feigning love somewhat to please me,
For she knows if she display
All her hate, death soon would seize me
And of hideous torments ease me.

Then adieu, dear flock, adieu!
But, alas, if in your straying
Heavenly Stella meet with you,
Tell her, in your piteous blaying,
Her poor slave's unjust decaying.

89

Now that, of absence, the most irksome night
With darkest shade doth overcome my day,
(Since Stella's eyes, wont to give me my day,
Leaving my hemisphere, leave me in night)
Each day seems long and longs for long-stayed night;
The night, as tedious, woos the approach of day
Tired with the dusty toils of busy day,
Languished with horrors of the silent night,

Suffering the evils both of the day and night,
(While no night is more dark than is my day,
Nor no day hath less quiet than my night)
With such bad-mixture of my night and day
That living thus in blackest winter night,
I feel the flames of hottest summer day.

90

Stella, think not that I by verse seek fame—
Who seek, who hope, who love, who live—but thee,
Thine eyes my pride, thy lips mine history.
If thou praise not, all other praise is shame.
Nor so ambitious am I as to frame
A nest for my young praise in laurel tree.[6]
In truth, I swear I wish not there should be
Graved in mine epitaph a poet's name.
Nay, if I would, I could just title make
That any laud° to me thereof should grow *praise*
Without my plumes from others' wings I take,[7]
For nothing from my wit or will doth flow
Since all my words thy beauty doth indite,° *record*
And Love doth hold my hand, and makes me write.

91

Stella, while now by honor's cruel might
I am from you (light of my life) misled,
And that fair you, my sun, thus overspread
With absence' veil,[8] I live in sorrow's night,
If this dark place yet show like candle-light,
Some beauty's piece (as amber-colored head,
Milk hands, rose cheeks, or lips more sweet, more red,
Or seeing gets, black,[9] but in blackness bright)
They please, I do confess, they please mine eyes.
But why? Because of you they models be,
Models such be wood-globes of glistering skies.[1]
Dear, therefore be not jealous over me,
If you hear that they seem my heart to move;
Not them, O no, but you in them I love.

97

Dian,[2] that fain would cheer her friend the Night,
Shows her oft, at the full, her fairest face,
Bringing with her those starry nymphs, whose chase

6. The laurel tree was identified with Apollo and excellence in poetry.
7. I.e., I do not copy the work of other poets.
8. The veil of absence, obscuring presence.
9. Bright jet-black eyes.
1. Presumably, wooden globes on which are illustrated the stars and planets of the night sky.
2. Diana, the goddess of chastity, hunting, and the moon.

From heavenly standing° hits each mortal wight. *ambush*
But ah, poor Night, in love with Phoebus'[3] light
And endlessly despairing of his grace,
Herself, to show no other joy hath place,
Silent and sad, in mourning weeds doth dight.
Even so, alas, a lady, Dian's peer,
With choice delights and rarest company
Would fain drive clouds from out my heavy cheer.
But, woe is me, though joy itself were she,
She could not show my blind brain ways of joy,
While I despair my sun's sight to enjoy.

104

Envious wits,[4] what hath been mine offense,
That with such poisonous care my looks you mark,
That to each word, nay sigh of mine, you hark,
As grudging me my sorrow's eloquence?
Ah, is it not enough that I am thence,
Thence, so far thence, that scarcely any spark
Of comfort dare come to this dungeon dark,
Where rigorous exile locks up all my sense?
But if I by a happy° window pass, *lucky*
If I but stars upon mine armor bear[5]—
Sick, thirsty, glad (though but of empty glass),
Your moral notes straight my hid meaning tear
From out my ribs, and, puffing, prove that I
Do Stella love; fools, who doth it deny?

106

O absent presence, Stella is not here;
False flattering hope, that with so fair a face,
Bare° me in hand, that in this orphan place, *took*
Stella, I say my Stella, should appear.
What sayest thou now, where is that dainty cheer,° *food*
Thou toldst mine eyes should help their famished case?
But thou art gone now that self-felt disgrace
Doth make me most to wish thy comfort near.[6]
But here I do store of fair ladies meet,
Who may with charm of conversation sweet,
Make in my heavy mold new thoughts to grow:
Sure they prevail as much with me, as he
That bad his friend but then new maimed,° to be *wounded*
Merry with him, and not think of his woe.

3. Apollo, the god of poetry, music, and medicine, often identified with the sun.
4. Poets who identified Sidney as Stella's lover.
5. I.e., Astrophil wears armor decorated with stars in Stella's honor.
6. I.e., you are gone now that that self (my own self) has felt the disgrace of rejection; this makes me wish you here.

107

Stella, since thou so right° a princess art *true*
Of all the powers which life bestows on me,
That ere by them aught undertaken be
They first resort unto the sovereign part;
Sweet, for a while give respite to my heart,
Which pants as though it still should leap to thee,
And on my thoughts give thy lieutenancy[7]
To this great cause, which needs both use and art.
And as a queen, who from her presence sends
Whom she employs, dismiss from thee my wit
Till it have wrought what thy own will attends.
On servants' shame oft master's blame doth sit.
O let not fools in me thy works reprove,
And scorning say, "See what it is to love!"

108

When sorrow (using mine own fire's might)
Melts down his lead into my boiling breast,
Through that dark furnace to heart oppressed,
There shines a joy from thee my only light;
But soon as thought of thee breeds my delight,
And my young soul flutters to thee his nest,
Most rude despair, my daily unbidden guest,
Clips straight my wings, straight wraps me in his night,
And makes me then bow down my head, and say,
Ah what doth Phoebus' gold that wretch avail,
Whom iron doors do keep from use of day?
So strangely (alas) thy works[8] in me prevail,
That in my woes for thee thou art my joy,
And in my joys for thee my only annoy.

Richard Barnfield

1577–1627

Richard Barnfield, a precocious yet only briefly productive poet, published four books of verse before his twenty-fifth birthday but then nothing else; we know merely that he lived to the age of fifty-two, comfortably settled on his Staffordshire estate, a husband and the father of a son, Robert. As a poet, he chose to follow the conventions of the amorous pastoral, fashionable for the ease with which they allowed the representation of lovers' intrigues. His frankly homoerotic verses express the love of a shepherd, Daphnis, for a boy called Ganimede or

7. Dominate my thoughts.
8. I.e., "your works," what you have done and meant, affect me strangely.

Ganymede, the mythological cup-bearer to Jupiter, the king of the gods. *The Tears of an Affectionate Shepherd* describes two phases to Daphnis's love; in *The Complaint* he offers Ganimede gifts from the pastoral world; in *The Lamentation*, claiming that what is fair is not necessarily good, he specifies steps to moral virtue. Complicating his narrative is the story of Ganimede's love for a woman, Queen Guendolen, whom Daphnis accuses of promiscuity. This rival threesome can be compared with the central figures of Shakespeare's (virtually contemporaneous) sonnet sequence: the poet, the young man, and the so-called dark lady. Finally, however, Barnfield creates his own poetic character, playing with occasional irony on the semantic and biblical association between shepherds and pastors. Barnfield's second collection of poems, published as *Cynthia*, continues to describe the competition for Ganimede's affection.

Slight as his total output was, Barnfield got the attention of readers. Francis Meres, his fellow student at Oxford and later critic of contemporary literature, placed him with Spenser, Sidney, and Abraham Fraunce as "best for pastoral." Barnfield's style is more vividly sensuous than theirs, however; his poems are best compared with the erotic pastoral verse of Theocritus, a Greek poet of the third century B.C.E., the first of its kind in Europe and a model for all subsequent examples of that genre.

Sonnets from *Cynthia*

1

Sporting at fancy, setting light by love,
    There came a thief and stole away my heart,
    (And therefore robbed me of my chiefest part)
Yet cannot reason him a felon prove.
For why his beauty (my heart's thief) affirmeth,
    Piercing no skin (the body's fensive° wall) *defensive*
    And having leave, and free consent withal,
Himself not guilty, from love guilty termeth,[1]
Conscience the judge, twelve reasons are the jury,
    They find mine eyes the beauty t'have let in,
    And on this verdict given, agreed they been,
Wherefore, because his beauty did allure ye,[2]
    Your doom is this: in tears still to be drowned,
    When his fair forehead with disdain is frowned.

5

It is reported of fair Thetis'[3] son,
    (Achilles, famous for his chivalry,
    His noble mind and magnanimity),
That when the Trojan wars were new begun,
Whos'ever was deep-wounded with his spear,
    Could never be recurred° of his maim,° *cured / wound*
    Nor ever after be made whole again;
Except with that spear's rust he holpen were.° *could be helped*
Even so it fareth with my fortune now,

1. The thief, beauty, having been given leave to steal the speaker's heart, declares himself not guilty; rather, it is love that is guilty.

2. You, i.e., the speaker addresses himself.

3. The mother of Achilles, the great Greek hero of the Trojan War.

Who being wounded with his piercing eye,
Must either thereby find a remedy,
Or else to be relieved, I know not how,
Then if thou hast a mind still to annoy me,
Kill me with kisses, if thou wilt destroy me.

9

Diana° (on a time) walking the wood, *goddess of the hunt*
To sport herself, of her fair train forlorn,
Chancest for to prick her foot against a thorn,
And from thence issued out a stream of blood.
No sooner she was vanished out of sight,
But love's fair Queen° came there by chance, *Venus*
And having of this hap a glimmering glance,
She put the blood into a crystal bright,
When being now come unto Mount Rhodope,
With her fair hands she forms a shape of snow,
And blends it with this blood; from whence doth grow
A lovely creature, brighter than the day.
And being christened in fair Paphos'[4] shrine,
She called him Ganimede: as all divine.

11

Sighing, and sadly sitting by my love,
He asked the cause of my heart's sorrowing,
Conjuring me by heaven's eternal king
To tell the cause which me so much did move.
Compelled (quoth I) to thee will I confess,
Love is the cause; and only love it is
That doth deprive me of my heavenly bliss.
Love is the pain that doth my heart oppress.
And what is she (quoth he) whom thou dost love?
Look in this glass (quoth I) there shalt thou see
The perfect form of my felicity.
When, thinking that it would strange magic prove,
He opened it; and taking off the cover,
He straight perceived himself to be my lover.

13

Speak, Echo, tell; how may I call my love? Love[5]
But how his lamps that are so crystalline? Eyne° *eyes*
Oh, happy stars that make your heavens divine:
And happy gems that admiration move.
How term'st his golden tresses waved with air? Hair

4. Cyprus, sacred to Venus.

5. This poem exploits a rhetorical figure called *paronomasia*, in which sounds are repeated; in this case, the repetition is of the last syllable of a line, which produces the effect of an echo.

Oh, lovely hair of your more lovely master,
Image of love, fair shape of alabaster,
Why dost thou drive thy lover to despair?
How dost thou call the bed where beauty grows? Rose
Fair virgin rose, whose maiden blossoms cover
The milk-white lily, thy embracing lover:
Whose kisses makes thee oft thy red to love.
And blushing oft for shame, when he hath kissed thee,
He vades° away, and thou rangest° where it list thee. *fades / wander*

19

Ah no; nor I myself: though my pure love
(Sweet Ganimede) to thee hath still been pure,
And even till my last gasp shall aye endure,
Could ever thy obdurate beauty move:
Then cease, oh goddess' son (for sure thou are,
A goddess' son that canst resist desire)
Cease thy hard heart, and entertain love's fire,
Within thy sacred breast: by nature's art.
And as I love thee more than any creature,
(Love thee, because thy beauty is divine;
Love thee because thyself, my soul, is thine:
Wholly devoted to thy lovely feature)
Even so of all the vowels, I and U,
Are dearest unto me, as doth ensue.

1595

Michael Drayton

1563–1631

Michael Drayton was considered a major poet in his lifetime. The recently verified portrait in the National Portrait Gallery, London, shows him with a laurel crown, making him the unofficial poet laureate. Given its date, 1599, the painting suggests that Drayton saw himself as the heir of his most important precursor, Spenser, who died early in the same year. Like Spenser, Drayton wrote a major sonnet sequence, *Ideas Mirrour*, first published in 1594, and revised four times, most importantly in 1599 and 1619, the work proving a commercial success long after the sonnet sequence had ceased to be a popular form for aspiring poets. Most critics agree on the formal subtlety and innovation in *Ideas Mirrour*, but are less united about the tone and purpose of the work. Some read Drayton's overturning of Petrarchan convention as comic parody; others see the sequence characterized by deeply felt erotic anguish.

Sonnet 12

To nothing fitter can I thee compare,
Than to the son of some rich penny-father,° *miser*
Who having now brought on his end with care,
Leaves to his son all he had heap'd together.
This new rich novice, lavish of his chest,

To one man gives, and on another spends,
Then here he riots, yet amongst the rest,
Haps to lend some to one true honest friend.
Thy gifts thou in obscurity do waste,
False friends thy kindness, born but to deceive thee,
Thy love, that is on the unworthy plac'd,
Time hath thy beauty, which with age will leave thee;
Only that little which to me was lent,
I give thee back, when all the rest is spent.

Sonnet 61

Since there's no help, come let us kiss and part.
Nay, I have done: you get no more of me,
And I am glad, yea glad with all my heart,
That thus so cleanly I myself can free,
Shake hands forever, cancel all our vows,
And when we meet at any time again,
Be it not seen in either of our brows
That we one jot of former love retain.
Now at the last gasp of Love's latest breath,
When his pulse failing, Passion speechless lies,
When Faith is kneeling by his bed of death,
And Innocence is closing up his eyes,
Now if thou would'st, when all have given him over,
From death to life, thou might'st him yet recover.

END OF PERSPECTIVES: THE ENGLISH SONNET AND SONNET SEQUENCES IN THE SIXTEENTH CENTURY

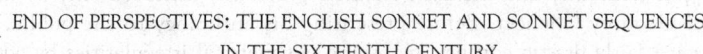

Sir Thomas Wyatt

1503–1542

A gifted poet and diplomat, Sir Thomas Wyatt exemplified the ambitious mixture of social and artistic skills that later ages would see as the ideal of the "Renaissance man." Having entered the household of King Henry VIII immediately after his education at Cambridge, Wyatt promoted English interests on missions to France, Venice, Rome, Spain, and the Low Countries. His career was to prove more precarious at home, where he became involved in court politics. He was deeply attached to the Lady Anne Boleyn, who, by 1527, was the object of Henry's affections and a probable pretext for the King's divorce from Catherine of Aragon and England's break from the Roman Catholic Church. Made Henry's queen in 1533, but out of favor by 1536, Anne implicated by association those who were supposed to have been her lovers. Wyatt, who according to several contemporary accounts, admitted to the King that the Queen had been his mistress, was lucky to suffer no more than imprisonment; the Queen's other favorites were executed. Wyatt subsequently regained political status both at home and abroad, although not without periods of disappointment: His verse letter *Mine Own John Poyns* praises the security of a country life away from London and its intrigues. Wyatt's most protracted mission was from 1537 to 1539, as the King's ambassador to the court of the Holy Roman Emperor in Spain: he tells of his anticipated return to England in the hauntingly brief lyric *Tagus, Farewell*. Despite the execution of his powerful patron, Sir Thomas Cromwell, and a second prison term in 1541 for suspected treason, Wyatt obtained Henry's goodwill at the end of his short life. He died from a fever at the age of thirty-nine while on a diplomatic mission for the king.

By any poetic reckoning, Wyatt is to be valued as a pioneer of English verse. Although many of his poems exhibit irregular meters, they have been praised for their remarkable texture and sense of surprise. His translations of Francesco Petrarch's sonnets established the principal forms of English lyric, the rhyming sonnet with its pentameter line and the more loosely configured song derived from the Italian *canzone*. Wyatt's own poems change the spirit of their Petrarchan themes by giving erotic subjects a satirical and even bitter twist and political topics an inward and personal reference. In one of his best-known sonnets, *Whoso List to Hunt,* he writes of vainly pursuing a "hind" or "deer" (a dear or beloved lady) belonging to "Caesar" (King Henry VIII). Long understood to be a reference to Anne Boleyn, Wyatt's "deer" is quite a different figure than the "deer" in his source, Petrarch's sonnet to a "white doe," who represents his lady, Laura, whom he met in 1327 and loved from a distance until her death in 1350. While Petrarch's lady is imagined as chastely devoted to a heavenly Caesar or God, and therefore as inspiring a religious awe, Wyatt's beloved is the possession of an earthly Caesar, King Henry VIII, and is thus the cause of his immediate frustration.

Wyatt's verse was circulated in manuscript during his lifetime and probably read only by his friends and his acquaintances at court. A few poems were published in 1540, in a collection entitled *The Court of Venus,* but the majority—ninety-seven poems in all—appeared in 1557, in a massive anthology called *Songs and Sonnets,* published by the printer Richard Tottel. This volume, which includes poems by Henry Howard, Earl of Surrey and others, was a milestone in the history of literature. Unlike the earlier sixteenth-century poetry of the British Isles, which remained relatively simple in its genres and diction, *Tottel's Miscellany* (as it has come to be known) exhibited a range of new forms and meters: the sonnet, the song (or *canzone*), the epigram, and rhyming and blank verse. Familiar to writers and readers of Italian and French, these forms allowed poets (now writing a recognizably modern English) to develop a stylistic flexibility and thematic richness previously achieved only by the Middle English poet Geoffrey Chaucer. Before presenting his anthology to the public, however, Tottel did some fairly drastic editing: smoothing out metrical irregularities by adding, subtracting, or changing words, he obviously sought to impress readers with what he judged to be the elegant and up-to-date styles represented by the works in his collection. The poems reprinted here are based not on the *Songs and Sonnets* but on Wyatt's original texts.

They Flee from Me

They flee from me that sometime did me seek
With naked foot stalking in my chamber.
I have seen them gentle tame and meek
That now are wild and do not remember
That sometime they put themself in danger
To take bread at my hand; and now they range
Busily seeking with a continual change.
Thanked be fortune, it hath been otherwise
Twenty times better; but once in special,
In thine array after a pleasant guise,° *manner, disguise*
When her loose gown from her shoulders did fall,
And she me caught in her arms long and small;
Therewithal sweetly did me kiss,
And softly said, "dear heart, how like you this?"

It was no dream: I lay broad waking.
But all is turned through my gentleness
Into a strange fashion of forsaking;
And I have leave to go of her goodness,
And she also to use new fangledness.
But since that I so kindly am served,
I would fain° know what she hath deserved. *wish to*

My Lute, Awake!

My lute, awake! perform the last
Labor that thou and I shall waste
  And end that I have now begun,
For when this song is sung and past,
  My lute be still, for I have done.

As to be heard where ere is none,° *there is no one*
As lead to grave in marble stone,
  My song may pierce her heart as sone;° *soon*
Should we then sigh, or sing, or moan?
  No, no, my lute, for I have done.

The rocks do not so cruelly
Repulse the waves continually,
  As she my suit and affection,
So that I am past remedy,
  Whereby my lute and I have done.

Proud of the spoil that thou hast got
Of simple hearts through love's shot,
  By whom, unkind, thou has them won,
Think not he hath his bow forgot,
  Although my lute and I have done.

Vengeance shall fall on thy disdain,
That makest but game on earnest pain;
  Think not alone under the sun
Unquit° to cause thy lover's plain,° *freely / lament*
  Although my lute and I have done.

Perchance thee lie weathered and old,
The winter nights that are so cold,
  Plaining in vain unto the mone;° *moon*
Thy wishes then dare not be told,
  Care then who list,° for I have done. *wishes*

And then may chance thee to repent
The time that thou hast lost and spent
  To cause thy lover's sigh and swoon;
Then shalt thou know beauty but lent
  And wish and want as I have done.

Now cease, my lute, this is the last
Labor that thou and I shall wast,° *waste*
And ended is that we begun;
Now is this song both sung and past,
My lute be still, for I have done.

Tagus, Farewell

Tagus,[1] farewell, that westward with thy streams
Turns up the grains of gold already tried:
With spur and sail for I go seek the Thames,
Gainward° the sun that showeth her wealthy pride; *toward*
And to the town which Brutus[2] sought by dreams
Like bended moon doth lend her lusty side.
My King,° my country, alone for whom I live, *Henry VIII*
Of mighty love the wings for this me give.

Forget Not Yet

Forget not yet the tried° intent *proven*
Of such a truth as I have meant,
My great travail° so gladly spent *effort*
Forget not yet.

Forget not yet when first began
The weary life ye know since whan,° *when*
The suit, the service none tell can,
Forget not yet.

Forget not yet the great assays,° *trials*
The cruel wrong, the scornful ways,
The painful patience in denays,° *denials*
Forget not yet.

Forget not yet, forget not this,
How long ago hath been and is
The mind that never meant amiss,
Forget not yet.

Forget not then thine own aprovyd,[1]
The which so long hath thee so lovyd,
Whose steadfast faith yet never movyd,
Forget not this.

Blame Not My Lute

Blame not my lute for he must sound
Of this or that as liketh me,
For lack of wit the lute is bound

1. The Tagus, or Tajo, River is the longest on the Iberian peninsula and empties into the Atlantic at Portugal. Wyatt was sent to Spain as a diplomat but returned to England in 1539.

2. The legendary Trojan hero Brutus was supposed to have settled the British Isles and founded London, to which he was led by a series of dreams sent to him by the goddess Diana.

1. The poet himself, her "approved" lover.

To give such tunes as pleaseth me:
Though my songs be somewhat strange,
And speaks such words as touch thy change,[1]
Blame not my lute.

My lute, alas, doth not offend,
Though that perforce he must agree
To sound such tunes as I intend
To sing to them that heareth me;
Then though my songs be somewhat plain,
And toucheth some that used to fain,[2]
Blame not my lute.

My lute and strings may not deny,
But as I strike they must obey;
Break not them then so wrongfully,
But wreak° thyself some wiser way: *revenge*
And though the songs which I endite° *write*
Do quit° thy change with rightful spite, *discharge, answer*
Blame not my lute.

Spite asketh spite and changing change,
And falsed° faith must needs be known; *betrayed*
The fault so great, the case so strange,
Of right it must abroad be blown:
Then since that by thine own desart° *desert*
My songs do tell how true thou art,
Blame not my lute.

Blame but thyself that hast misdone
And well deserved to have blame;
Change thou thy way, so evil begun,
And then my lute shall sound that same:
But if till then my fingers play
By thy desart their wonted way,
Blame not my lute.

Farewell, unknown, for though thou break
My strings in spite with great disdain,
Yet have I found out for thy sake
Strings for to string my lute again;
And if perchance this folys° rhyme *foolish*
Do make thee blush at any time,
Blame not my lute.

Lucks, My Fair Falcon, and Your Fellows All

Lucks, my fair falcon, and your fellows all,
How well pleasant it were your liberty!
Ye not forsake me that fair might ye befall.[1]

1. I.e., the lady's change of heart, probably also to be signified by a change of tone in the music to which this lyric was supposedly set.
2. Who used to be desirous or who used to feign desire.

1. I.e., "You do not forsake me so that good luck may come your way." Wyatt states that despite the falcon's name, which suggests that he seeks good fortune, Lucks is loyal to his master.

But they that sometime liked my company,
Like lice away from dead bodies they crawl:
Lo, what a proof in light adversity![2]
But ye my birds I swear by all your bells,
Ye be my friends, and so be but few else.

Stand Whoso List

Stand whoso list° upon the slipper° top — *wishes / slippery*
Of courts' estates, and let me here rejoice;
And use me° quiet without let° or stop, — *my / hindrance*
Unknown in court, that hath such brackish joys:
In hidden place, so let my days forth pass,
That when my years be done, withouten noise,
I may die aged after the common trace.[1]
For him death greep' the° right hard by the crop° — *grips / throat*
That is much known of other; and of himself alas,
Doth die unknown, dazed with dreadful face.

Mine Own John Poyns

Mine own John Poyns,[1] since ye delight to know
The cause why that homeward I me draw,
And flee the press of courts[2] where so they° go, — *courtiers*
Rather then to live thrall° under the awe — *enslaved*
Of lordly looks, wrapped within my cloak,
To will and lust learning to set a law;
It is not for because I scorn or mock
The power of them to whom fortune hath lent
Charge over us, of right, to strike the stroke.
But true it is that I have always meant
Less to esteem them than the common sort
Of outward things that judge in their intent
Without regard what doth inward resort.
I grant sometime that of glory the fire
Doth touch my heart: me list° not to report — *I wish*
Blame by honor and honor to desire.
But how may I this honor now attain
That cannot dye the color black a liar?[3]
My Poyns, I cannot frame my tongue to feign,
To cloak the truth for praise, without desert,
Of them that list all vice for to retain.[4]

2. Wyatt may have written this poem during one of his imprisonments; in any event, he complains here that in prison only his falcons visit and befriend him. Falcons wore bells on their legs to let their masters know where they were.

1. In the common or usual manner; from age and sickness rather than murder. Wyatt alludes to the perilous existence of a man in public life.

1. John Poyns, or Poynz, a friend of Wyatt, spent time at court in the 1520s.

2. Here Wyatt's posing as a retired courtier critical of the court may illustrate his attitude during one of the periods in which he was out of favor with Henry VIII. He had extensive holdings in Kent, to which he could retire and from which he was elected to Parliament shortly before his death.

3. I.e., who cannot change (dye) black another color and hence call black a liar.

I cannot honor them that sets their part
With Venus and Bacchus[5] all their life long;
Nor hold my piece of them although I smart.
I cannot crouch nor kneel nor do so great a wrong,
To worship them like God on earth alone,
That are as wolves these sely° lambs among. *innocent*
I cannot with my words complain and moan
And suffer nought, nor smart without complaint,
Nor turn the word that from my mouth is gone.
I cannot speak and look like a saint,
Use wiles for wit and make deceit a pleasure,
And call craft counsel, for profit still to paint.[6]
I cannot wrest the law to fill the coffer,
With innocent blood to feed myself fat,
And do most hurt where most help I offer.
I am not he that can allow the state
Of high Caesar and damn Cato to die,[7]
That with his death did scape out of the gate
From Caesar's hands, if Livy do not lie,
And would not live where liberty was lost:
So did his heart the common weal° apply.° *state / value*
I am not he such eloquence to boast,
To make the crow singing as the swan,
Nor call the lion of coward beasts the most
That cannot take a mouse as the cat can:
And he that dieth for hunger of the gold
Call him Alessaundre;[8] and say that Pan
Passeth Apollo in music manifold;° *many times*
Praise Sir Thopas[9] for a noble tale,
And scorn the story that the knight told.
Praise him for counsel that is drunk of ale;
Grin when he laugheth that beareth all the sway,
Frown when he frowneth and groan when he is pale;
On others lust to hang both night and day:
None of these points would ever frame in me;
My wit is nought, I cannot learn the way.
And much the less of things that greater be,
That asken help of colors of device° *kinds of deception*
To join the mean with each extremity,

4. I.e., to lie by praising those who wish to retain vicious ways and therefore do not deserve praise.
5. Venus: the goddess of love; Bacchus: the god of wine (also known as Dionysius). Together they represented lust and excess.
6. I.e., to represent a falsehood as the truth for profit.
7. I.e., I cannot condone the rule of Caesar and damn Cato. Livy: a Roman historian of the republican period; he records the story of Cato of Utica, who opposed the tyrannical impulses of Julius Caesar and committed suicide rather than live under tyranny.
8. I.e., flatter as Alexander the Great a man so greedy for gold that he dies of hunger. Wyatt continues to list the flattery he cannot give: Pan—half-man, half-goat—was god of shepherds and famous for his music on his reed pipe, but the undisputed god of music was Apollo.
9. *The Tale of Sir Thopas,* one of Chaucer's *Canterbury Tales,* was composed to illustrate how not to tell a story; *The Knight's Tale,* by contrast, exemplified the high style of poetic narrative.

With the nearest virtue to cloak alway the vice:
And as to purpose likewise it shall fall,[1]
To press° the virtue that it may not rise; *suppress*
As drunkenness good fellowship to call;
The friendly foe with his double face
Say he is gentle and courteous therewithal;
And say that Favel° hath a goodly grace *Flattery, a character*
In eloquence, and cruelty to name
Zeal of justice and change in time and place;
And he that suffereth offence without blame
Call him pitiful; and him true and plain
That raileth reckless° to every man's shame. *carelessly criticizes*
Say he is rude that cannot lie and feign,
The lecher a lover, and tyranny
To be the right of a prince's reign.
I cannot, I. No, no, it will not be.
This is the cause that I could never yet
Hang on their sleeves that weigh as thou mayst see
A chip of chance more than a pound of wit.[2]
This maketh me at home to hunt and to hawk
And in foul weather at my book to sit.
In frost and snow then with my bow to stalk;
No man doth mark whereso I ride or go;
In lusty lees° at liberty I walk, *meadows*
And of these news I feel nor weal° nor woe, *happiness*
Sauf° that a clog doth hang yet at my heel: *except*
No force for that, for it is ordered so
That I may leap both hedge and dike full well.
I am not now in France to judge the wine,
With saffry° sauce the delicates to feel; *saffron*
Nor yet in Spain where one must him incline
Rather than to be, outwardly to seem.
I meddle not with wits that be so fine,
Nor Flanders' cheer[3] letteth° not my sight to deem° *hinders / judge*
Of black and white, nor taketh my wit away
With beastliness, they beasts do so esteem;[4]
Nor I am not where Christ is given in prey° *in exchange*
For money, poison and treason at Rome,
A common practice used night and day:
But here I am in Kent and Christendom
Among the muses where I read and rhyme;
Where if thou list, my Poyns, for to come,
Thou shalt be judge how I do spend my time.

1. Also, when occasion permits.
2. I.e., follow those who value a little good fortune more than a lot of intelligence.
3. The Flemish were reputed to love drinking.
4. The Flemish esteem beasts, i.e., drunks.

Henry Howard, Earl of Surrey

1517?–1547

To belong to a rich and powerful family was no guarantee of a secure and prosperous life. Henry Howard, son of the Duke of Norfolk, was one of the most gifted young men in the court of King Henry VIII, yet he was embroiled in factionalism from a very early age. As a boy, he was the companion of Henry Fitzroy, Duke of Richmond, the king's illegitimate son. They spent a year together as guests of the King of France and, after their return to England, continued their friendship at Windsor Castle. After Richmond's death in 1536, Surrey apparently ran afoul of the law and found himself again at Windsor Castle, this time as the king's prisoner. Playing up the irony of his situation in *So Cruel Prison,* he memorializes Windsor, formerly a "place of bliss" but now the site of his sorrow at the loss of his freedom and the greater loss of his friend. Surrey was imprisoned again five years later in London, ostensibly for breaking windows. This punishment occasioned a satire, *London, Thou Hast Accused Me,* on the real corruption in the city. At twenty-seven, Surrey took part in the war against the French, was wounded, and a year later, was made commander of Boulogne. But he fell from favor when he opposed his sister's marriage to the brother of his rival, Edward Seymour, Lord Hertford, and denounced Seymour as guardian of Prince Edward, Henry's heir. Angered beyond all reconciliation, Henry had Surrey tried and executed for treason in 1547.

As a poet, Surrey is often coupled with Wyatt, who was actually a generation older. Many of his poems (like Wyatt's) emulated Petrarchan forms, themes, and imagery and were published initially by Richard Tottel in 1557 in a volume entitled *Songs and Sonnets.* But Surrey's own accomplishments were unique. He perfected English blank or unrhymed verse, characterized by the pentameter or five-stress line, and he was the likely inventor of the form that became the standard for the English sonnet: three quatrains followed by a couplet, rhyming *ababcdcdefefgg.* Some of his poems on social subjects adopt a satirical tone and convey his vigorous rejection of contemporary manners and morals.

So Cruel Prison

So cruel prison, how could betide,° alas, *it happen*
As proud Windsor,[1] where I in lust and joy
With a king's son my childish years did pass,
In greater feast than Priam's sons of Troy;[2]

Where° each sweet place returns a taste full sour. *that*
The large green courts, where we were wont to hove,° *accustomed to linger*
With eyes cast up unto the maidens' tower,
And easy sighs, such as folk draw in love.

The stately sales,° the ladies bright of hue, *halls*
The dances short, long tales of great delight,
With words and looks that tigers could but rue,
Where each of us did plead the other's right.

1. Surrey was imprisoned in Windsor Castle in 1537. In this poem, his distress at his imprisonment is augmented by his memories of Henry Fitzroy, the Earl of Richmond and bastard son of Henry VIII, with whom he spent time at Windsor when they were young. Richmond married Surrey's sister in 1533; he died in 1536.

2. Priam, King of Troy, was defeated by the Greeks in the Trojan War.

The palm play,[3] where, despoiled for the game,
With dazed eyes oft we by gleams of love
Have missed the ball and got sight of our dame
To bait her eyes which kept the leads° above. *roofs*

The graveled ground,° with sleeves tied on the helm,[4] *jousting arena*
On foaming horse, with swords and friendly hearts,
With cheer,° as° though the one should overwhelm, *joyfully / even*
Where we have fought and chased oft with darts.

With silver drops the meads yet spread for ruth,° *pity*
In active games of nimbleness and strength
Where we did strain, trailed by swarms of youth,
Our tender limbs, that yet shot up in length.

The secret groves, which oft we made resound
Of pleasant plaint° and of our ladies' praise, *complaint*
Recording soft what grace each one had found,
What hope of speed, what dread of long delays.

The wild forest, the clothed holts° with green, *woods*
With reins avaled° and swift ybreathed° horse, *slackened / panting*
With cry of hounds and merry blasts between,
Where we did chase the fearful hart a force.° *ran it down*

The void° walls eke, that harbored us each night; *empty*
Wherewith, alas, revive within my breast
The sweet accord, such sleeps as yet delight,
The pleasant dreams, the quiet bed of rest,

The secret thoughts imparted with such trust,
The wanton talk, the divers change of play,
The friendship sworn, each promise kept so just,
Wherewith we passed the winter nights away.

And with this thought the blood forsakes my face,
The tears berain my cheeks of deadly hue;
The which, as soon as sobbing sighs, alas,
Upsupped° have, thus I my plaint renew: *absorbed*

O place of bliss! renewer of my woes!
Give me accompt where is my noble fere,° *companion*
Whom in thy walls thou didst each night enclose,
To other lief,° but unto me most dear. *dear*

Each wall, alas, that doth my sorrow rue,
Returns thereto a hollow sound of plaint.
Thus I, alone, where all my freedom grew,
In prison pine with bondage and restraint,

3. Surrey refers to court tennis, a game resembling modern tennis but played against the walls of a court; he remembers that as players, he and Fitzroy watched the ladies who followed the game from the "leads," sheets of metal used to cover roofs.

4. When jousting, a man would tie the sleeve of a lady's garment to his helmet as a sign of her favor.

And with remembrance of the greater grief,
To banish the less, I find my chief relief.

London, Hast Thou Accused Me

London, hast thou accused me
Of breach of laws, the root of strife?[1]
Within whose breast did boil to see,
(So fervent hot) thy dissolute life,
That even the hate of sins, that grow
Within thy wicked walls so rife,
For to break forth did convert° so *convert me*
That terror could it not repress.
The which, by words, since preachers know
What hope is left for to redress,
By unknown means it liked me
My hidden burden to express,
Whereby it might appear to thee
That secret sin hath secret spite;
From Justice° rod no fault is free; *Justice's*
But that all such as works unright
In most quiet are next ill rest.[2]
In secret silence of the night
This made me, with a reckless breast,
To wake thy sluggards with my bow;
A figure of the Lord's behest,[3]
Whose scourge for sin the scriptures show.
That, as the fearful thunder clap
By sudden flame at hand we know,
Of pebble stones the soundless rap,
The dreadful plage° might make thee see *shore*
Of God's wrath, that doth thee enwrap;[4]
That pride might know, from conscience free,
How lofty works may her defend;[5]
And envy find, as he hath sought,
How other seek him to offend;
And wrath taste of each cruel thought
The just shapp hire in the end;[6]
And idle sloth, that never wrought,
To heaven his spirit lift° may begin; *to lift*
And greedy lucre live in dread

1. Surrey was accused of breaking windows with his bow in the city of London in 1543. He states that he was moved to this action by his hatred of the dissolute life within the city (line 4) and that he was responding to an idea of Justice (line 15).
2. I.e., all those who act wrongly, if they are resting quietly, are nearest to being disturbed.
3. Surrey imagines that he is like a prophet who does the Lord's command (cf. Isaiah 47.11).
4. The phrase is obscure: "just as we know lightening by thunder, so the soundless rap of pebble stones might make you see the dreadful shore of God's wrath that surrounds you."
5. Surrey becomes ironic: "Pride, free from conscience, might know how lofty works may defend her"—i.e., important or prodigious works do not defend from punishment the proud, who are (by definition) without a conscience.
6. I.e., wrath receives, for each of its cruel thoughts, the justly shaped or appointed hire or payment in the end.

To see what hate ill-got goods win;
The lechers, ye that lusts do feed,
Perceive what secrecy is in sin;
And gluttons' hearts for sorrow bleed,
Awaked when their fault they find.
In loathsome vice, each drunken wight° *man*
To stir to God, this was my mind.
Thy windows had done me no spite;
But proud people that dread no fall,
Clothed with falsehed° and unright *falsehood*
Bred in the closures of thy wall,
But wrested to wrath in fervent zeal
Thou hast to strife my secret call.[7]
Endured° hearts no warning feel. *hardened*
Oh shameless whore! is dread then gone
By such thy foes as meant thy weal?[8]
Oh member of false Babylon!
The shop of craft! the den of ire!
Thy dreadful dome° draws fast upon; *judgment*
Thy martyrs' blood, by sword and fire,
In heaven and earth for Justice call.
The Lord shall hear their just desire;
The flame of wrath shall on thee fall;
With famine and pest lamentably
Stricken shall be thy lechers all;
Thy proud towers and turrets high,
Enemies to God, beat° stone from stone; *beaten*
Thine idols burnt that wrought iniquity.
When none thy ruin shall bemoan,
But render unto the right wise Lord,
That so hath judged Babylon,
Immortal praise with one accord.

Wyatt Resteth Here

Wyatt resteth here, that quick° could never rest;[1] *alive*
Whose heavenly gifts increased by disdain
And virtue sank the deeper in his breast:
Such profit he of envy could obtain.

A head, where wisdom mysteries did frame;
Whose hammers beat still in that lively brain
As on a stith,° where some work of fame *anvil*
Was daily wrought, to turn to Britain's gain.

A visage, stern and mild; where both did grow,
Vice to condemn, in virtues to rejoice;

7. I.e., you have heard my secret call to strife or struggle.
8. Surrey addresses London as the whore of Babylon, the epitome of iniquity, and asks ironically, "Do you no longer fear those enemies that intend your happiness?"
1. This elegy for the poet Thomas Wyatt was published in 1542, shortly after his death.

Amid great storms whom grace assured so
To live upright and smile at fortune's choice.

A hand that taught what might be said in rhyme;
That reft° Chaucer the glory of his wit; *took from*
A mark the which (unperfited, for time)[2]—
Some may approach, but never none shall hit.

A tongue that served in foreign realms his king;
Whose courteous talk to virtue did enflame
Each noble heart, a worthy guide to bring
Our English youth, by travail[3] unto fame.

An eye whose judgment no affect° could blind, *feeling*
Friends to allure, and foes to reconcile;
Whose piercing look did represent a mind
With virtue fraught, reposed, void of guile.

A heart where dread yet never so impressed
To hide the thought that might the truth avaunce;° *advance*
In neither fortune lift, nor so repressed,[4]
To swell in wealth, or yield unto mischance.

A valiant corps,° where force and beauty met, *body*
Happy, alas! too happy, but for foes,
Lived, and ran the race that nature set;
Of manhood's shape, where she the mold did lose.

But to the heavens that simple soul is fled;
Which left with such, as covet° Christ to know *desire*
Witness to faith that never shall be dead:
Sent for our wealth, but not received so.

Thus, for our guilt, this jewel have we lost;
The earth his bones, the heavens possess his ghost.
Amen.

My Radcliffe, When Thy Reckless Youth Offends

My Radcliffe,[1] when thy reckless youth offends:
Receive thy scourge by others' chastisement.
For such calling, when it works none° amends: *no*
Then plagues are sent without advertisement.
Yet Salomon[2] said, the wronged shall recure:° *recover*
But Wyatt said true, the scar doth aye endure.

2. I.e., was left unperfected for lack of time.
3. Work, but also travel, in that Surrey describes Wyatt as a "guide."
4. I.e., neither raised up by fortune to get rich, nor so depressed (by ill fortune) as to yield to a temptation that will lead to misfortune.

1. This epigram is probably addressed to Thomas Radcliffe, third Earl of Essex.
2. Surrey concludes by contrasting an optimistic sentence of King Solomon, which he probably associated with the book of Ecclesiasticus, with the dour reflection of Wyatt.

Sir Thomas More
1477?–1535

Sir Thomas More.

After fifteen years of loyal and distinguished service as a government minister and, finally, Lord Chancellor, Sir Thomas More refused to do the King's bidding. He declined to take the Oath of Allegiance that Henry VIII required of all his subjects, a token of their repudiation of the Pope and recognition of the king as "Defender of the Faith" in England. More's stubborn fidelity to the only church he had ever known drove Henry to extreme measures. He ordered More to the Tower of London and, a year later, had him executed for treason. More may not have been surprised by the decision; he once observed that "If my head should win [Henry] a castle in France, it should not fail to go." It is reported that More's parboiled severed head was fastened to a pole on London Bridge for all to see. By displaying this pathetic remnant of the most conspicuously brilliant man in England, Henry signaled his iron determination to control not only the religious destiny of his kingdom but also its intellectual life.

More's beginnings were auspicious. The son of Agnes and John More, a barrister, he was sent to be a page in the household of Thomas Morton, Archbishop of Canterbury and Lord Chancellor, and then to Oxford, where he met John Colet (1467?–1519), who became, in More's words, "the director of my life." Colet was in many respects a paradoxical source of inspiration for More. A schoolmaster and later a university don, Colet was identified with the scholarship of a Christian humanism that had as its purpose a return to the practices of the primitive and apostolic church. More would end his life professing the authority of the Pope and affirming the Catholic faith as the only true way to salvation.

More was called to the bar and, in 1504, was elected to Parliament. Married that year to Jane Colte and soon the father of four, More organized his household in Chelsea as a center of intellectual activity; there his guests included Desiderius Erasmus and even the King himself. In 1526 the painter Holbein began the first of several visits; his portrait of Thomas More surrounded by numerous family members, including More's gifted daughter Margaret, testifies to the highly conscientious civility that More cultivated in domestic life.

Busy with state and diplomatic affairs from 1504 on, More was knighted and made subtreasurer to the king in 1521. As Lord Chancellor from 1529 to 1532, More was known for his wit, his judicial acumen, and his deft treatment of parties to a case. A popular jingle suggests how swiftly he saw justice done:

When More some time had Chancellor been,
  No more suits did remain;
The like will never more be seen,
  Till More be there again.

Perhaps More's dispatch in matters of law gave him some leisure for literature. In any case, his talent as a writer was obvious in his first works: Latin translations of Lucian's dialogues, the *Life of Johan Picus*, *Earl of Mirandula*, *Utopia* (in Latin), and the *History of Richard III*. Later works reflect the passion for religious orthodoxy that drove him to oppose reforms proposed by Luther, Calvin, and their followers. In 1528 he published *A Dialogue of Sir Thomas More* against the opinions of the English reformer William Tyndale, whose "Englishing" of the

Bible had resolved many of its readers to espouse the new faith. *Supplication of Souls* and *The Confutation of Tyndale's Answer*—similarly directed against the reformation—appeared in 1529 and 1532. More's religious enthusiasm was also expressed in punitive action against those he decided were enemies of the church. John Foxe, whose *Acts and Monuments of These Latter Perilous Days* chronicles the persecution of Christians from the earliest days of the church to his present moment, described More as "blinded in the zeal of popery to all humane considerations." Blinded More was not, however, when he cast an eye to the future. Foreseeing the consequences of Henry's divorce from Catherine of Aragon and his intention to marry again, More resigned his chancellorship in 1532, the year that Parliament published the *Supplication Against the Ordinaries*, a list of grievances against the Catholic Church, and the English church accepted the king as its head. More wrote two more works, the first while still a free (although suspect) man and the second as the King's prisoner: *The Apology of Sir Thomas More* (1533) denounces the reformation, and *A Dialogue of Comfort Against Tribulation* (1533) testifies to the courage that faith could instill in a man who, once possessed of great authority and power, finally found himself in desperate circumstances.

UTOPIA When More published his account of a hitherto unknown island republic in 1516, Europeans were still largely ignorant of the world beyond their continent. The exploration that would open up so much of the globe was just getting underway, and accounts of voyages to places hardly dreamed of were yet to constitute a literary genre. What travel writing there was catered to readers who loved reports of "marvels" and had no clear appreciation for what later centuries would call a "fact." Sir John Mandeville, whose still-popular account of his travels was first circulated in 1356, described the peoples, customs, and wild life of lands in the East in utterly fantastic terms. But when More called his newly discovered land *Utopia*, literally "nowhere" in Greek, he did so only half in fun. Although his island republic was clearly a figment of More's imagination, the political order that he gave it challenged many of the ideals and practices of contemporary monarchies in Europe, especially in England. His *Utopia* is therefore deceptive: apparently a report of a new people and their society, it was also a critique of the habits of thought and the government that had sustained European and English society for centuries. More composed this work, in Latin, between late September 1515 and September 3, 1516, when he sent it to Erasmus, who helped arrange for the book's first publication in Holland; the first English translation, by Ralph Robinson, appeared in 1551. *Utopia*'s text reflects the international scope of its own production. In fact, More the author did, like "More" the character, visit Peter Giles in Antwerp while on a diplomatic mission; and John Clement was More's "pupil-servant"—a tutor to his children and eventually one of the king's physicians.

The second book of *Utopia*, written before the first, describes a government in which administrative and legal authority rotates among the elders of the society, a society in which all property is common, and a culture supported by citizens who have identical tastes, aspirations, and outlooks on life. In the words of the aged philosopher and world traveler, a character More names Hythlodaeus (literally "learned in nonsense"), Utopian society is populated entirely by rational beings. Each citizen is trained in a trade, is guaranteed employment, and will get what he or she needs from cradle to grave. The economy is one in which exchange is by barter, not money; clothing is uniform; education and medical care are free to everyone; and defense is conducted by foreigners whom the Utopians hire to protect them. Utopians who protest or rebel against these policies and practices are seen as unreasonable. The first book, evidently an afterthought, establishes a perspective by which to view the extraordinary claims of the second; it shows why Hythlodaeus can be considered an idealistic dreamer as well as an acute critic. Here More prefaces the praise he will have Hythlodaeus give Utopian society by having the philosopher point out the social ills of contemporary England. Refusing to compromise the ideals he says were practiced in Utopia, Hythlodaeus maintains that he must withdraw from societies like those in England and Europe because he can do them no good. His critique of governments is supported by his denunciation of enclosures and capital punishment for minor felonies, and of kings and magistrates who are driven by greed and a lust for power.

More's account of Utopia, as reported by his character Hythlodaeus, has convinced some readers that he meant his treatise to be taken as a model for the future. Others have given more weight to its elaborate framing as a report from "nowhere" and have seen it rather as a satire on the idea of a wholly rational society. Whatever balance the reader finds in More's brilliant distinctions, his images of an ideal and imaginary society find analogues in those later represented by Jonathan Swift in *Gulliver's Travels*, Samuel Butler in *Erewhon*, and William Morris in *News from Nowhere*. By contrast, George Orwell's *1984* represents the dark side of the "Utopian" state: its absolute repression of individualism.

Presented in the Response section that follows *Utopia* is a selection from Sir Francis Bacon's *The New Atlantis* (c. 1623, published 1626), a witty response to *Utopia*, which shows a scientific community working on a remote island. Bacon shows an open-minded and egalitarian society at work, establishing control over nature and exploiting the world's resources in a useful way.

Utopia[1]

The Best State of a Commonwealth and the New Island Of Utopia A Truly Golden Handbook, No Less Beneficial Than Entertaining, by the Distinguished and Eloquent Author THOMAS MORE Citizen and Sheriff of the Famous City of London

Thomas More to Peter Giles,[2] Greetings.

I am almost ashamed, my dear Peter Giles, to send you this little book about the state of Utopia after almost a year, when I am sure you looked for it within a month and a half. Certainly you know that I was relieved of all the labor of gathering materials for the work and that I had to give no thought at all to their arrangement. I had only to repeat what in your company I heard Raphael[3] relate. Hence there was no reason for me to take trouble about the style of the narrative, seeing that his language could not be polished. It was, first of all, hurried and impromptu and, secondly, the product of a person who, as you know, was not so well acquainted with Latin as with Greek. Therefore the nearer my style came to his careless simplicity the closer it would be to the truth, for which alone I am bound to care under the circumstances and actually do care.

I confess, my dear Peter, that all these preparations relieved me of so much trouble that scarcely anything remained for me to do. Otherwise the gathering or the arrangement of the materials could have required a good deal of both time and application even from a talent neither the meanest nor the most ignorant. If it had been required that the matter be written down not only accurately but eloquently, I could not have performed the task with any amount of time or application. But, as it was, those cares over which I should have had to perspire so hard had been removed. Since it remained for me only to write out simply what I had heard, there was no difficulty about it.

1. Translated by C. G. Richards, rev. Edward Surtz, S.J.
2. More was made undersheriff of London in 1510, sitting as judge and representing the sheriff's cases in the city court. His friend Peter Giles (c. 1486–1533) was a classical scholar, a member of Erasmus's circle, and city clerk of Antwerp, where he oversaw commercial business.
3. Raphael Hythlodaeus, the fictional traveler who tells the character Sir Thomas More about Utopia.

Yet even to carry through this trifling task, my other tasks left me practically no leisure at all. I am constantly engaged in legal business, either pleading or hearing, either giving an award as arbiter or deciding a case as judge. I pay a visit of courtesy to one man and go on business to another. I devote almost the whole day in public to other men's affairs and the remainder to my own. I leave to myself, that is to learning, nothing at all.

When I have returned home, I must talk with my wife, chat with my children, and confer with my servants. All this activity I count as business when it must be done—and it must be unless you want to be a stranger in your own home. Besides, one must take care to be as agreeable as possible to those whom nature has supplied, or chance has made, or you yourself have chosen, to be the companions of your life, provided you do not spoil them by kindness, or through indulgence make masters out of your servants.

Amid these occupations that I have named, the day, the month, the year slip away. When, then, can we find time to write? Nor have I spoken a word about sleep, nor even of food, which for many people takes up as much time as sleep—and sleep takes up almost half a man's life! So I get for myself only the time I filch from sleep and food. Slowly, therefore, because this time is but little, yet finally, because this time *is* something, I have finished *Utopia* and sent it to you, my dear Peter, to read—and to remind me of anything that has escaped me.

In this respect I do not entirely distrust myself. (I only wish I were as good in intelligence and learning as I am not altogether deficient in memory!) Nevertheless, I am not so confident as to believe that I have forgotten nothing. As you know, John Clement,[4] my pupil-servant, was also present at the conversation. Indeed I do not allow him to absent himself from any talk which can be somewhat profitable, for from this young plant, seeing that it has begun to put forth green shoots in Greek and Latin literature, I expect no mean harvest some day. He has caused me to feel very doubtful on one point.

According to my own recollection, Hythlodaeus[5] declared that the bridge which spans the river Anydrus at Amaurotum is five hundred paces in length. But my John says that two hundred must be taken off, for the river there is not more than three hundred paces in breadth. Please recall the matter to mind. If you agree with him, I shall adopt the same view and think myself mistaken. If you do not remember, I shall put down, as I have actually done, what I myself seem to remember. Just as I shall take great pains to have nothing incorrect in the book, so, if there is doubt about anything, I shall rather tell an objective falsehood than an intentional lie—or I would rather be honest than wise.

Nevertheless, it would be easy for you to remedy this defect if you ask Raphael himself by word of mouth or by letter. You must do so on account of another doubt which has cropped up, whether more through my fault or through yours or Raphael's I do not know. We forgot to ask, and he forgot to say, in what part of the new world Utopia lies. I am sorry that point was omitted, and I would be willing to pay a considerable sum to purchase that information, partly because I am rather ashamed to be ignorant in what sea lies the island of which I am saying so much, partly because there are several among us, and one in particular, a devout man and a theologian by profession, burning with an extraordinary desire to visit Utopia. He does so not from an

4. John Clement (d. 1572), who tutored More's children, was also a distinguished humanist: a Reader at Oxford; coeditor of the first Greek edition of Galen (c. 130–200), a celebrated physician whose works on medicine remained authoritative through the early modern period; and physician to Henry VIII.

5. This reference introduces the play on Greek words that will characterize the description of Utopia in Book 2. Hythlodaeus means "learned in nonsense"; the river Anydrus and the city Amaurotum mean "waterless" and "made dark or dim," respectively.

idle and curious lust for sight-seeing in new places but for the purpose of fostering and promoting our religion, begun there so felicitously.

To carry out his plan properly, he has made up his mind to arrange to be sent by the pope and, what is more, to be named bishop for the Utopians. He is in no way deterred by any scruple that he must sue for this prelacy, for he considers it a holy suit which proceeds not from any consideration of honor or gain but from motives of piety.

Therefore I beg you, my dear Peter, either by word of mouth if you conveniently can or by letter if he has gone, to reach Hythlodaeus and to make sure that my work includes nothing false and omits nothing true. I am inclined to think that it would be better to show him the book itself. No one else is so well able to correct any mistake, nor can he do this favor at all unless he reads through what I have written. In addition, in this way you will find out whether he accepts with pleasure or suffers with annoyance the fact that I have composed this work. If he himself has decided to put down in writing his own adventures, perhaps he may not want me to do so. By making known the commonwealth of Utopia, I should certainly dislike to forestall him and to rob his narrative of the flower and charm of novelty.

Nevertheless, to tell the truth, I myself have not yet made up my mind whether I shall publish it at all. So varied are the tastes of mortals, so peevish the characters of some, so ungrateful their dispositions, so wrongheaded their judgments, that those persons who pleasantly and blithely indulge their inclinations seem to be very much better off than those who torment themselves with anxiety in order to publish something that may bring profit or pleasure to others, who nevertheless receive it with disdain or ingratitude.

Very many men are ignorant of learning; many despise it. The barbarian rejects as harsh whatever is not positively barbarian. The smatterers despise as trite whatever is not packed with obsolete expressions. Some persons approve only of what is old; very many admire only their own work. This fellow is so grim that he will not hear of a joke; that fellow is so insipid that he cannot endure wit. Some are so dull-minded that they fear all satire as much as a man bitten by a mad dog fears water. Others are so fickle that sitting they praise one thing and standing another thing.

These persons sit in taverns, and over their cups criticize the talents of authors. With much pontificating, just as they please, they condemn each author by his writings, plucking each one, as it were, by the hair. They themselves remain under cover and, as the proverb goes, out of shot. They are so smooth and shaven that they present not even a hair of an honest man by which they might be caught.

Besides, others are so ungrateful that, though extremely delighted with the work, they do not love the author any the more. They are not unlike discourteous guests who, after they have been freely entertained at a rich banquet, finally go home well filled without thanking the host who invited them. Go now and provide a feast at your own expense for men of such dainty palate, of such varied taste, and of such unforgetful and grateful natures!

At any rate, my dear Peter, conduct with Hythlodaeus the business which I mentioned. Afterwards I shall be fully free to take fresh counsel on the subject. However, since I have gone through the labor of writing, it is too late for me to be wise now. Therefore, provided it be done with the consent of Hythlodaeus, in the matter of publishing which remains I shall follow my friends' advice, and yours first and foremost. Good-by, my sweetest friend, with your excellent wife. Love me as you have ever done, for I love you even more than I have ever done.

The Best State of a Commonwealth,
The Discourse of the Extraordinary
Character, Raphael Hythlodaeus, as
Reported by the Renowned Figure,
THOMAS MORE,
Citizen and Sheriff
of the Famous City of
Great Britain,
London

Book 1

The most invincible King of England, Henry, the eighth of that name, who is distinguished by all the accomplishments of a model monarch, had certain weighty matters[6] recently in dispute with His Serene Highness, Charles, Prince of Castile.[7] With a view to their discussion and settlement, he sent me as a commissioner to Flanders—as a companion and associate of the peerless Cuthbert Tunstal, whom he has just created Master of the Rolls[8] to everyone's immense satisfaction. Of the latter's praises I shall say nothing, not because I fear that the testimony of a friend should be given little credit but because his integrity and learning are too great for it to be possible, and too well-known for it to be necessary, for me to extol them—less I should wish to give the impression, as the proverb goes, of displaying the sun with a lamp!

We were met at Bruges, according to previous arrangement, by those men put in charge of the affair by the Prince—all outstanding persons. Their leader and head was the Burgomaster[9] of Bruges, a figure of magnificence, but their chief speaker and guiding spirit was Georges de Themsecke,[1] Provost of Cassel, a man not only trained in eloquence but a natural orator—most learned, too, in the law and consummately skillful in diplomacy by native ability as well as by long experience. When after one or two meetings there were certain points on which we could not agree sufficiently, they bade farewell to us for some days and left for Brussels to seek an official pronouncement from the Prince.

Meanwhile, as my business led me, I made my way to Antwerp. While I stayed there, among my other visitors, but of all of them the most welcome, was Peter Giles, a native of Antwerp, an honorable man of high position in his home town yet worthy of the very highest position, being a young man distinguished equally by learning and character; for he is most virtuous and most cultured, to all most courteous, but to his friends so open-hearted, affectionate, loyal, and sincere that you can hardly find one or two anywhere to compare with him as the perfect friend on every score. His modesty is uncommon; no one is less given to deceit, and none has a wiser simplicity of nature. Besides, in conversation he is so polished and so witty without offense that his delightful society and charming discourse largely took away my nostalgia and made me less conscious than before of the separation from my home, wife, and children to whom I was exceedingly anxious to get back, for I had then been more than four months away.

6. The "weighty matters" that took More to Flanders concerned the payment of tolls to Flemish ports by the English merchant fleet.
7. The future Charles I of Spain and Charles V, Holy Roman emperor; he ruled the Spanish kingdoms, Spanish America, Naples, Sicily, the Low Countries, and parts of Austria.
8. The principal clerk of the Chancery Court, a court of appeals from decisions by the common-law courts.
9. Mayor.
1. A Flemish diplomat, employed on numerous missions, who died in 1536.

One day I had been at divine service in Notre Dame, the finest church in the city and the most crowded with worshippers. Mass being over, I was about to return to my lodging when I happened to see him in conversation with a stranger, a man of advanced years, with sunburnt countenance and long beard and cloak hanging carelessly from his shoulder, while his appearance and dress seemed to me to be those of a ship's captain.

When Peter had espied me, he came up and greeted me. As I tried to return his salutation, he drew me a little aside and, pointing to the man I had seen him talking with, said:

"Do you see this fellow? I was on the point of taking him straight to you."

"He would have been very welcome," said I, "for your sake."

"No," said he, "for his own, if you knew him. There is no mortal alive today who can give you such an account of unknown peoples and lands, a subject about which I know you are always most greedy to hear."

"Well, then," said I, "my guess was not a bad one. The moment I saw him, I was sure he was a ship's captain."

"But you are quite mistaken," said he, "for his sailing has not been like that of Palinurus but that of Ulysses or, rather, of Plato.[2] Now this Raphael—for such is his personal name, with Hythlodaeus as his family name—is no bad Latin scholar, and most learned in Greek. He had studied that language more than Latin because he had devoted himself unreservedly to philosophy, and in that subject he found that there is nothing valuable in Latin except certain treatises of Seneca and Cicero.[3] He left his patrimony at home—he is a Portuguese—to his brothers, and, being eager to see the world, joined Amerigo Vespucci[4] and was his constant companion in the last three of those four voyages which are now universally read of, but on the final voyage he did not return with him. He importuned and even wrested from Amerigo permission to be one of the twenty-four who at the farthest point of the last voyage were left behind in the fort. And so he was left behind that he might have his way, being more anxious for travel than about the grave. These two sayings are constantly on his lips: 'He who has no grave is covered by the sky,' and 'From all places it is the same distance to heaven.' This attitude of his, but for the favor of God, would have cost him dear.[5] However, when after Vespucci's departure he had traveled through many countries with five companions from the fort, by strange chance he was carried to Ceylon, whence he reached Calicut.[6] There he conveniently found some Portuguese ships, and at length arrived home again, beyond all expectation."

When Peter had rendered this account, I thanked him for his kindness in taking such pains that I might have a talk with one whose conversation he hoped would give me pleasure; then I turned to Raphael. After we had greeted each other and exchanged the civilities which commonly pass at the first meeting of strangers, we went off to my house. There in the garden, on a bench covered with turfs of grass, we sat down to talk together.

2. Palinurus: the pilot of the ship sailed by Aeneas from Troy to Italy in Virgil's *Aeneid;* he fell overboard while sleeping at the helm. Ulysses: the Latin name for Odysseus, the hero of Homer's epic poem, the *Odyssey*, who returns to his kingdom, Ithaka, after years of wandering. Plato: the Greek philosopher who is said to have traveled throughout the Mediterranean world.

3. Two Roman writers who composed works on moral and political philosophy.

4. Florentine merchant adventurer (1451–1512), whose accounts of his voyages to the New World were reprinted in many editions; the Americas are named for him.

5. More's paraphrases of two classical authors indicate his humanist training. From Lucan's epic *Pharsalia* he takes: "Mother Earth has room for all her children, and he who lacks an urn has the sky to cover him" (8.819); and from Cicero's *Tusculan Disputations* he takes: "There is a fine remark of Anaxagoras. He was dying at Lampasacus, and his friends asked if he wanted to be taken home. . . . 'There's no need,' he said, 'it's the same distance from anywhere to the underworld'" (1.43.104).

6. Seaport on the west coast of India.

He recounted how, after the departure of Vespucci, he and his friends who had stayed behind in the fort began by degrees through continued meetings and civilities to ingratiate themselves with the natives till they not only stood in no danger from them but were actually on friendly terms and, moreover, were in good repute and favor with a ruler (whose name and country I have forgotten). Through the latter's generosity, he and his five companions were supplied with ample provision and travel resources and, moreover, with a trusty guide on their journey (which was partly by water on rafts and partly over land by wagon) to take them to other rulers with careful recommendations to their favor. For, after traveling many days, he said, they found towns and cities and very populous commonwealths with excellent institutions.

To be sure, under the equator and on both sides of the line nearly as far as the sun's orbit extends, there lie waste deserts scorched with continual heat. A gloomy and dismal region looms in all directions without cultivation or attractiveness, inhabited by wild beasts and snakes or, indeed, men no less savage and harmful than are the beasts. But when you have gone a little farther, the country gradually assumes a milder aspect, the climate is less fierce, the ground is covered with a pleasant green herbage, and the nature of living creatures becomes less wild. At length you reach peoples, cities, and towns which maintain a continual traffic by sea and land not only with each other and their neighbors but also with far-off countries.

Then they had opportunity of visiting many countries in all directions, for every ship which was got ready for any voyage made him and his companions welcome as passengers. The ships they saw in the parts first traveled were flat-bottomed and moved under sails made of papyrus or osiers[7] stitched together and sometimes under sails made of leather. Afterwards they found ships with pointed keels and canvas sails, in fact, like our own in all respects.

Their mariners were skilled in adapting themselves to sea and weather. But he reported that he won their extraordinary favor by showing them the use of the magnetic needle[8] of which they had hitherto been quite ignorant so that they had hesitated to trust themselves to the sea and had boldly done so in the summer only. Now, trusting to the magnet, they do not fear wintry weather, being dangerously confident. Thus, there is a risk that what was thought likely to be a great benefit to them may, through their imprudence, cause them great mischief.

What he said he saw in each place would be a long tale to unfold and is not the purpose of this work. Perhaps on another occasion we shall tell his story, particularly whatever facts would be useful to readers, above all, those wise and prudent provisions which he noticed anywhere among nations living together in a civilized way. For on these subjects we eagerly inquired of him, and he no less readily discoursed; but about stale travelers' wonders we were not curious. Scyllas and greedy Celaenos and folk-devouring Laestrygones[9] and similar frightful monsters are common enough, but well and wisely trained citizens are not everywhere to be found.

To be sure, just as he called attention to many ill-advised customs among these new nations, so he rehearsed not a few points from which our own cities, nations, races, and kingdoms may take example for the correction of their errors. These instances, as I said, I must mention on another occasion. Now I intend to relate merely what he told us of the manners and customs of the Utopians, first, however, giving the talk which drew and led him on to mention that commonwealth.

7. Papyrus: reed paper. Osiers: willow twigs.
8. Compass.
9. Fabulous monsters from the *Odyssey* and the *Aeneid:* Scylla is a six-headed sea monster; Celaeno, a harpy, is a bird with a woman's face; the Lestrygonians were gigantic cannibals.

Raphael had touched with much wisdom on faults in this hemisphere and that, of which he found very many in both, and had compared the wiser measures which had been taken among us as well as among them; for he remembered the manners and customs of each nation as if he had lived all his life in places which he had only visited. Peter expressed his surprise at the man as follows:

"Why, my dear Raphael, I wonder that you do not attach yourself to some king. I am sure there is none of them to whom you would not be very welcome because you are capable not only of entertaining a king with this learning and experience of men and places but also of furnishing him with examples and of assisting him with counsel. Thus, you would not only serve your own interests excellently but be of great assistance in the advancement of all your relatives and friends."

"As for my relatives and friends," he replied, "I am not greatly troubled about them, for I think I have fairly well performed my duty to them already. The possessions, which other men do not resign unless they are old and sick and even then resign unwillingly when incapable of retention, I divided among my relatives and friends when I was not merely hale and hearty but actually young. I think they ought to be satisfied with this generosity from me and not to require or expect additionally that I should, for their sakes, enter into servitude to kings."

"Fine words!" declared Peter. "I meant not that you should be in servitude but in service to kings."

"The one is only one syllable less than the other," he observed.

"But my conviction is," continued Peter, "whatever name you give to this mode of life, that it is the very way by which you can not only profit people both as private individuals and as members of the commonwealth but also render your own condition more prosperous."

"Should I," said Raphael, "make it more prosperous by a way which my soul abhors? As it is, I now live as I please, which I surely fancy is very seldom the case with your grand courtiers. Nay, there are plenty of persons who court the friendship of the great, and so you need not think it a great loss if they have to do without me and one or two others like me."

"Well," I then said, "it is plain that you, my dear Raphael, are desirous neither of riches nor of power. Assuredly, I reverence and look up to a man of your mind no whit less than to any of those who are most high and mighty. But it seems to me you will do what is worthy of you and of this generous and truly philosophic spirit of yours if you so order your life as to apply your talent and industry to the public interest, even if it involves some personal disadvantages to yourself. This you can never do with as great profit as if you are councilor to some great monarch and make him follow, as I am sure you will, straightforward and honorable courses. From the monarch, as from a never-failing spring, flows a stream of all that is good or evil over the whole nation. You possess such complete learning that, even had you no great experience of affairs, and such great experience of affairs that, even had you no learning, you would make an excellent member of any king's council."

"You are twice mistaken, my dear More," said he, "first in me and then in the matter in question. I have no such ability as you ascribe to me and, if I had ever so much, still, in disturbing my own peace and quiet, I should not promote the public interest. In the first place almost all monarchs prefer to occupy themselves in the pursuits of war—with which I neither have nor desire any acquaintance—rather than in the honorable activities of peace, and they care much more how, by hook or by crook, they may win fresh kingdoms than how they may administer well what they have got.

"In the second place, among royal councilors everyone is actually so wise as to have no need of profiting by another's counsel, or everyone seems so wise in his own eyes as not to condescend to profit by it, save that they agree with the most absurd sayings of, and play the parasite to, the chief royal favorites whose friendliness they strive to win by flattery. To be sure, it is but human nature that each man favor his own discoveries most—just as the crow and the monkey like their own offspring best.

"If anyone, when in the company of people who are jealous of others' discoveries or prefer their own, should propose something which he either has read of as done in other times or has seen done in other places, the listeners behave as if their whole reputation for wisdom were jeopardized and as if afterwards they would deserve to be thought plain blockheads unless they could lay hold of something to find fault with in the discoveries of others. When all other attempts fail, their last resource is a remark such as this: 'Our forefathers were happy with that sort of thing, and would to heaven we had their wisdom.' And then, as if that comment were a brilliant conclusion to the whole business, they take their seats—implying, of course, that it would be a dangerous thing to be found with more wisdom on any point than our forefathers. And yet, no matter what excellent ideas our forefathers may have had, we very serenely bid them a curt farewell. But if in any situation they failed to take the wiser course, that defect gives us a handle which we greedily grab and never let go. Such proud, ridiculous, and obstinate prejudices I have encountered often in other places and once in England too."

"What," I asked, "were you ever in our country?"

"Yes," he answered, "I spent several months there, not long after the disastrous end of the insurrection of western Englishmen against the king, which was put down with their pitiful slaughter.[1] During that time I was much indebted to the Right Reverend Father, John Cardinal Morton, Archbishop of Canterbury, and then also Lord Chancellor of England.[2] He was a man, my dear Peter (for More knows about him and needs no information from me), who deserved respect as much for his prudence and virtue as for his authority. He was of middle stature and showed no sign of his advanced age. His countenance inspired respect rather than fear. In conversation he was agreeable, though serious and dignified. Of those who made suit to him he enjoyed making trial by rough address, but in a harmless way, to see what mettle and what presence of mind a person would manifest. Provided it did not amount to impudence, such behavior gave him pleasure as being akin to his own disposition and excited his admiration as being suited to those holding public office. His speech was polished and pointed. His knowledge of law was profound, his ability incomparable, and his memory astonishingly retentive, for he had improved his extraordinary natural qualities by learning and practice.

"The king placed the greatest confidence in his advice, and the commonwealth seemed much to depend upon him when I was there. As one might expect, almost in earliest youth he had been taken straight from school to court, had spent his whole life in important public affairs, and had sustained numerous and varied vicissitudes

1. In 1497 the people of Cornwall rebelled against taxation by the crown; they were defeated by the king's army outside London, in the Battle of Blackheath.

2. More served for two years as a page in the household of Cardinal Morton (1420–1500).

of fortune, so that by many and great dangers he had acquired a statesman's sagacity which, when thus learned, is not easily forgotten.

"It happened one day that I was at his table when a layman, learned in the laws of your country, was present. Availing himself of some opportunity or other, he began to speak punctiliously of the strict justice which was then dealt out to thieves. They were everywhere executed, he reported, as many as twenty at a time being hanged on one gallows, and added that he wondered all the more, though so few escaped execution, by what bad luck the whole country was still infested with them. I dared be free in expressing my opinions without reserve at the Cardinal's table, so I said to him:

"'You need not wonder, for this manner of punishing thieves goes beyond justice and is not for the public good. It is too harsh a penalty for theft and yet is not a sufficient deterrent. Theft alone is not a grave offense that ought to be punished with death, and no penalty that can be devised is sufficient to restrain from acts of robbery those who have no other means of getting a livelihood. In this respect not your country alone but a great part of our world resembles bad schoolmasters, who would rather beat than teach their scholars. You ordain grievous and terrible punishments for a thief when it would have been much better to provide some means of getting a living, that no one should be under this terrible necessity first of stealing and then of dying for it.'

"'We have,' said the fellow, 'made sufficient provision for this situation. There are manual crafts. There is farming. They might maintain themselves by these pursuits if they did not voluntarily prefer to be rascals.'

"'No,' I countered, 'you shall not escape so easily. We shall say nothing of those who often come home crippled from foreign or civil wars, as recently with you Englishmen from the battle with the Cornishmen and not long ago from the war in France.[3] They lose their limbs in the service of the commonwealth or of the king, and their disability prevents them from exercising their own crafts, and their age from learning a new one. Of these men, I say, we shall take no account because wars come sporadically, but let us consider what happens every day.

"'Now there is the great number of noblemen who not only live idle themselves like drones on the labors of others, as for instance the tenants of their estates whom they fleece to the utmost by increasing the returns[4] (for that is the only economy they know of, being otherwise so extravagant as to bring themselves to beggary!) but who also carry about with them a huge crowd of idle attendants who have never learned a trade for a livelihood. As soon as their master dies or they themselves fall sick, these men are turned out at once, for the idle are maintained more readily than the sick, and often the heir is not able to support as large a household as his father did, at any rate at first.

"'In the meantime the fellows devote all their energies to starving, if they do not to robbing. Indeed what can they do? When by a wandering life they have worn out their clothes a little, and their health to boot, sickly and ragged as they are, no gentleman deigns to engage them and the farmers dare not do so either. The latter know full well that a man who has been softly brought up in idleness and luxury and has been wont[5] in sword and buckler to look down with a swaggering face on the whole neighborhood and to think himself far above everybody will hardly be fit to

3. Hythlodaeus refers to actual battles at Dixmude in 1489 and in Boulogne in 1492.

4. Rents.

5. Accustomed.

render honest service to a poor man with spade and hoe, for a scanty wage, and on frugal fare.'

"'But this,' the fellow retorted, 'is just the sort of man we ought to encourage most. On them, being men of a loftier and nobler spirit than craftsmen and farmers, depend the strength and sinews of our army when we have to wage war.'

"'Of course,' said I, 'you might as well say that for the sake of war we must foster thieves. As long as you have these men, you will certainly never be without thieves. Nay, robbers do not make the least active soldiers, nor do soldiers make the most listless robbers, so well do these two pursuits agree. But this defect, though frequent with you, is not peculiar to you, for it is common to almost all peoples.

"'France in particular is troubled with another more grievous plague. Even in peacetime (if you can call it peacetime) the whole country is crowded and beset with mercenaries hired because the French follow the train of thought you Englishmen take in judging it a good thing to keep idle retainers. These wiseacres think that the public safety depends on having always in readiness a strong and reliable garrison, chiefly of veterans, for they have not the least confidence in tyros.[6] This attitude obliges them always to be seeking for a pretext for war just so they may not have soldiers without experience, and men's throats must be cut without cause lest, to use Sallust's witty saying, "the hand or the mind through lack of practice become dulled." Yet how dangerous it is to rear such wild beasts France has learned to its cost, and the examples of Rome, Carthage, Syria, and many other nations show.[7] Not only the supreme authority of the latter countries but their land and even their cities have been more than once destroyed by their own standing armies.

"'Now, how unnecessary it is to maintain them is clearly proved by this consideration: not even the French soldiers, assiduously trained in arms from infancy, can boast that they have very often got the better of it face to face with your draftees.[8] Let me say no more for fear of seeming to flatter you barefacedly. At any rate, your town-bred craftsmen or your rough and clodhopper farmers are not supposed to be much afraid of those idle attendants on gentlemen, except those of the former whose build of body is unfitted for strength and bravery or those whose stalwart spirit is broken by lack of support for their family. Consequently there is no danger that those attendants whose bodies, once strong and vigorous (for it is only the picked men that gentlemen deign to corrupt), are now either weakened by idleness or softened by almost womanish occupations, should become unmanned if trained to earn their living in honest trades and exercised in virile labors!

"'However the case may be, it seems to me by no means profitable to the common weal to keep for the emergency of a war a vast multitude of such people as trouble and disturb the peace. You never have war unless you choose it, and you ought to take far more account of peace than of war. Yet this is not the only situation that makes thieving necessary. There is another which, as I believe, is more special to you Englishmen.'

"'What is that?' asked the Cardinal.

"'Your sheep,' I answered, 'which are usually so tame and so cheaply fed, begin now, according to report, to be so greedy and wild that they devour human beings

6. Raw recruits.

7. The Romans, Carthaginians, and Syrians used mercenary armies but suffered mutinies as a result.

8. Hythlodaeus refers to English soldiers who won victories over French forces in such battles as Crecy (1346), Poitiers (1356), and Agincourt (1415).

themselves and devastate and depopulate fields, houses, and towns.[9] In all those parts of the realm where the finest and therefore costliest wool is produced, there are noblemen, gentlemen, and even some abbots, though otherwise holy men, who are not satisfied with the annual revenues and profits which their predecessors used to derive from their estates. They are not content, by leading an idle and sumptuous life, to do no good to their country; they must also do it positive harm. They leave no ground to be tilled; they enclose every bit of land for pasture; they pull down houses and destroy towns, leaving only the church to pen the sheep in. And, as if enough of your land were not wasted on ranges and preserves of game, those good fellows turn all human habitations and all cultivated land into a wilderness.

"'Consequently, in order that one insatiable glutton and accursed plague of his native land may join field to field and surround many thousand acres with one fence, tenants are evicted. Some of them, either circumvented by fraud or overwhelmed by violence, are stripped even of their own property, or else, wearied by unjust acts, are driven to sell. By hook or by crook the poor wretches are compelled to leave their homes—men and women, husbands and wives, orphans and widows, parents with little children and a household not rich but numerous, since farm work requires many hands. Away they must go, I say, from the only homes familiar and known to them, and they find no shelter to go to. All their household goods which would not fetch a great price if they could wait for a purchaser, since they must be thrust out, they sell for a trifle.

"'After they have soon spent that trifle in wandering from place to place, what remains for them but to steal and be hanged—justly, you may say!—or to wander and beg. And yet even in the latter case they are cast into prison as vagrants for going about idle when, though they most eagerly offer their labor, there is no one to hire them. For there is no farm work, to which they have been trained, to be had, when there is no land for plowing left. A single shepherd or herdsman is sufficient for grazing livestock on that land for whose cultivation many hands were once required to make it raise crops.

"'A result of this situation is that the price of food has risen steeply in many localities. Indeed, the price of raw wools has climbed so high that your poor people who used to make cloth cannot possibly buy them, and so great numbers are driven from work into idleness. One reason is that, after the great increase in pasture land, a plague carried off a vast multitude of sheep as though God were punishing greed by sending upon the sheep a murrain[1]—which should have fallen on the owners' heads more justly! But, however much the number of sheep increases, their price does not decrease a farthing because, though you cannot brand that a monopoly which is a sale by more than one person, yet their sale is certainly an oligopoly,[2] for all sheep have come into the hands of a few men, and those already rich, who are not obligated to sell before they wish and who do not wish until they get the price they ask.

"'By this time all other kinds of livestock are equally high-priced on the same account and still more so, for the reason that, with the pulling down of farmsteads and the lessening of farming, none are left to devote themselves to the breeding of

9. Hythlodaeus criticizes the management of the English wool trade. The potential for profit from sheep's wool led landlords to fence off or enclose vast open spaces that had previously been shared in common and farmed by peasants. Many of these displaced people sought work in the cities or became migrant day-laborers throughout the country.

1. A disease of livestock.

2. Control of a commercial market by a small number of companies or merchants.

stock. These rich men will not rear young cattle as they do lambs, but they buy them lean and cheap abroad and then, after they are fattened in their pastures, sell them again at a high price. In my estimation, the whole mischief of this system has not yet been felt. Thus far, the dealers raise the prices only where the cattle are sold, but when, for some time, they have been removing them from other localities faster than they can be bred there, then, as the supply gradually diminishes in the markets where they are purchased, great scarcity must needs be here.

"'Thus, the unscrupulous greed of a few is ruining the very thing by virtue of which your island was once counted fortunate in the extreme. For the high price of food is causing everyone to get rid of as many of his household as possible, and what, I ask, have they to do but to beg, or—a course more readily embraced by men of mettle—to become robbers?

"'In addition, alongside this wretched need and poverty you find wanton luxury. Not only the servants of noblemen but the craftsmen and almost the clodhoppers themselves, in fact all classes alike, are given to much ostentatious sumptuousness of dress and to excessive indulgence at table. Do not dives, brothels, and those other places as bad as brothels, to wit, taverns, wine shops and ale-houses—do not all those crooked games of chance, dice, cards, backgammon, ball, bowling, and quoits, soon drain the purses of their votaries[3] and send them off to rob someone?

"'Cast out these ruinous plagues. Make laws that the destroyers of farmsteads and country villages should either restore them or hand them over to people who will restore them and who are ready to build. Restrict this right of rich individuals to buy up everything and this license to exercise a kind of monopoly for themselves. Let fewer be brought up in idleness. Let farming be resumed and let cloth-working be restored once more that there may be honest jobs to employ usefully that idle throng, whether those whom hitherto pauperism has made thieves or those who, now being vagrants or lazy servants, in either case are likely to turn out thieves. Assuredly, unless you remedy these evils, it is useless for you to boast of the justice you execute in the punishment of theft. Such justice is more showy than really just or beneficial. When you allow your youths to be badly brought up and their characters, even from early years, to become more and more corrupt, to be punished, of course, when, as grown-up men, they commit the crimes which from boyhood they have shown every prospect of committing, what else, I ask, do you do but first create thieves and then become the very agents of their punishment?'

"Even while I was saying these things, the lawyer had been busily preparing himself to reply and had determined to adopt the usual method of disputants who are more careful to repeat what has been said than to answer it, so highly do they regard their memory.

"'Certainly, sir,' he began, 'you have spoken well, considering that you are but a stranger who could hear something of these matters rather than get exact knowledge of them—a statement which I shall make plain in a few words. First, I shall repeat, in order, what you have said; then I shall show in what respects ignorance of our conditions has deceived you; finally I shall demolish and destroy all your arguments. So, to begin with what I promised first, on four points you seemed to me—'

"'Hold your peace,' interrupted the Cardinal, 'for you hardly seem about to reply in a few words if you begin thus. So we shall relieve you of the trouble of making your answer now, but we shall reserve your right unimpaired till your next meeting,

3. Devotees.

which I should like to set for tomorrow, provided neither you nor Raphael here is hindered by other business.

"'But now I am eager to have you tell me, my dear Raphael, why you think that theft ought not to be punished with the extreme penalty, or what other penalty you yourself would fix, which would be more beneficial to the public. I am sure that not even you think it ought to go unpunished. Even as it is, with death as the penalty, men still rush into stealing. What force and what fear, if they once were sure of their lives, could deter the criminals? They would regard themselves as much invited to crime by the mitigation of the penalty as if a reward were offered.'

"'Certainly,' I answered, 'most reverend and kind Father, I think it altogether unjust that a man should suffer the loss of his life for the loss of someone's money. In my opinion, not all the goods that fortune can bestow on us can be set in the scale against a man's life. If they say that this penalty is attached to the offense against justice and the breaking of the laws, hardly to the money stolen, one may well characterize this extreme justice as extreme wrong. For we ought not to approve such stern Manlian rules of law[4] as would justify the immediate drawing of the sword when they are disobeyed in trifles nor such Stoical[5] ordinances as count all offenses equal so that there is no difference between killing a man and robbing him of a coin when, if equity has any meaning, there is no similarity or connection between the two cases.[6]

"'God has said, "Thou shalt not kill," and shall we so lightly kill a man for taking a bit of small change? But if the divine command against killing be held not to apply where human law justifies killing, what prevents men equally from arranging with one another how far rape, adultery, and perjury are admissible? God has withdrawn from man the right to take not only another's life but his own. Now, men by mutual consent agree on definite cases where they may take the life of one another. But if this agreement among men is to have such force as to exempt their henchmen from the obligation of the commandment, although without any precedent set by God they take the life of those who have been ordered by human enactment to be put to death, will not the law of God then be valid only so far as the law of man permits? The result will be that in the same way men will determine in everything how far it suits them that God's commandments should be obeyed.

"'Finally, the law of Moses,[7] though severe and harsh—being intended for slaves, and those a stubborn breed—nevertheless punished theft by fine and not by death. Let us not suppose that God, in the new law of mercy in which He gives commands as a father to his sons, has allowed us greater license to be cruel to one another.

"'These are the reasons why I think this punishment unlawful. Besides, surely everyone knows how absurd and even dangerous to the commonwealth it is that a thief and a murderer should receive the same punishment. Since the robber sees that he is in as great danger if merely condemned for theft as if he were convicted of murder as well, this single consideration impels him to murder the man whom otherwise he would only have robbed. In addition to the fact that he is in no greater danger if

4. Manlius Torquatus, a Roman general of the 4th century B.C.E., who, having made a law against single encounters, executed his own son for fighting and defeating an enemy warrior.
5. Austere.
6. Hythlodaeus alludes to an important feature of the law: Cases in which the law invoked to cover them is too general to do justice to their complexity are decided by addressing the circumstances in which the alleged violation was committed, the condition of the disputants, and the remedies apart from the law that might serve to settle the case. Such a mitigated justice was known as equity.
7. The Decalogue or Ten Commandments, one of which is "Thou shalt not kill" (Exodus 20.13).

caught, there is greater safety in putting the man out of the way and greater hope of covering up the crime if he leaves no one left to tell the tale. Thus, while we endeavor to terrify thieves with excessive cruelty, we urge them on to the destruction of honest citizens.

"'As to the repeated question about a more advisable form of punishment, in my judgment it is much easier to find a better than a worse. Why should we doubt that a good way of punishing crimes is the one which we know long found favor of old with the Romans, the greatest experts in managing the commonwealth? When men were convicted of atrocious crimes they condemned them for life to stone quarries and to digging in metal mines, and kept them constantly in chains.

"'Yet, as concerns this matter, I can find no better system in any country than that which, in the course of my travels, I observed in Persia among the people commonly called the Polylerites,[8] a nation that is large and well-governed and, except that it pays an annual tribute to the Persian padishah [emperor], otherwise free and autonomous in its laws. They are far from the sea, almost ringed round by mountains, and satisfied with the products of their own land, which is in no way infertile. In consequence they rarely pay visits to other countries or receive them. In accordance with their long-standing national policy, they do not try to enlarge their territory and easily protect what they have from all aggression by their mountains and by the tribute paid to their overlord. Being completely free from militarism, they live a life more comfortable than splendid and more happy than renowned or famous, for even their name, I think, is hardly known except to their immediate neighbors.

"'Now, in their land, persons who are convicted of theft repay to the owner what they have taken from him, not, as is usual elsewhere, to the prince, who, they consider, has as little right to the thing stolen as the thief himself. But if the object is lost, the value is made up out of the thieves' goods, and the balance is then paid intact to their wives and children. They themselves are condemned to hard labor. Unless the theft is outrageous, they neither are confined to prison nor wear shackles about their feet but, without any bonds or restraints, are set to public works. Convicts who refuse to labor or are slack are not put in chains but urged on by the lash. If they do a good day's work, they need fear no insult or injury. The only check is that every night, after their names are called over, they are locked in their sleeping quarters.

"'Except for the constant toil, their life has no hardship. For example, as serviceable to the common weal, they are fed well at the public's expense, the mode varying from place to place. In some parts, what is spent on them is raised by almsgiving. Though this method is precarious, the Polylerite people are so kindhearted that no other is found to supply the need more plentifully. In other parts, fixed public revenues are set aside to defray the cost. Elsewhere, all pay a specified personal tax for these purposes. Yes, and in some localities the convicts do no work for the community, but, whenever a private person needs a hired laborer, he secures in the market place a convict's service for that day at a fixed wage, a bit lower than what he would have paid for free labor. Moreover, the employer is permitted to chastise with stripes a hired man if he be lazy. The result is that they are never out of work and that each one, besides earning his own living, brings in something every day to the public treasury.

"'All of them wear clothes of a color not worn by anyone else. Their hair is not shaved but cropped a little above the ears, from one of which the tip is cut off. Food

8. "People of Much Nonsense."

and drink and clothes of the proper color may be given them by their friends. The gift of money is a capital offense, both for the donor and the receiver. It is no less dangerous for a free man to receive a penny for any reason from a condemned person, or for slaves (which is the name borne by the convicts) to touch weapons. The slaves of each district are distinguished by a special badge, which it is a capital offense to throw away, as it is to appear beyond their own bounds or to talk to a slave from another district. Further, it is no safer to plot escape than actually to run away. Yes, and the punishment for connivance in such a plan is death for the slave and slavery for the free man. On the other hand, rewards are appointed for an informer: money for a free man, liberty for a slave, and pardon and immunity for both for their complicity. The purpose is never to make it safer to follow out an evil plan than to repent of it.

"'This is the law and this the procedure in the matter, as I have described it to you. You can easily see how humane and advantageous it is. The object of public anger is to destroy the vices but to save the persons and so to treat them that they necessarily become good and that, for the rest of their lives, they repair all the damage done before.

"'Further, so little is it to be feared that they may sink back into their old evil ways, even travelers who have to go on a journey think themselves most safe if they secure as guides these slaves, who are changed with each new district. For the latter have nothing suitable with which to commit robbery. They bear no arms; money would merely insure the detection of the crime; punishment awaits the man who is caught; and there is absolutely no hope of escaping to a safe place. How could a man so cover his flight as to elude observation when he resembles ordinary people in no part of his attire—unless he were to run away naked? Even then his ear would betray him in his flight!

"'But, of course, would there not at least be risk of their taking counsel together and conspiring against the commonwealth? As if any district could conceive a hope of success without having first sounded and seduced the slave gangs of many other districts! The latter are so little able to conspire together that they may not even meet and converse or greet one another. Much less will they boldly divulge to their own fellow slaves the plot, which they know is dangerous to those concealing it and very profitable to those betraying it. On the other hand, no one is quite without hope of gaining his freedom eventually if he accepts his punishment in a spirit of obedience and resignation and gives evidence of reforming his future life; indeed, every year a number of them are granted their liberty which they have merited by their submissive behavior.'

"When I had finished this speech, I added that I saw no reason why this method might not be adopted even in England and be far more beneficial in its working than the justice which my legal opponent had praised so highly. The lawyer replied: 'Never could that system be established in England without involving the commonwealth in a very serious crisis.' In the act of making this statement, he shook his head and made a wry face and so fell silent. And all who were present gave him their assent.

"Then the Cardinal remarked: 'It is not easy to guess whether it would turn out well or ill inasmuch as absolutely no experiment has been made. If, after pronouncement of the sentence of death, the king were to order the postponement of its execution and, after limitation of the privileges of sanctuary,[9] were to try this system,

9. From the 7th century until the Reformation, English churches and sometimes their surrounding precincts provided limited asylum for fugitives from judicial authority.

then, if success proved its usefulness, it would be right to make the system law. In case of failure, then and there to put to death those previously condemned would be no less for the public good and no more unjust than if execution were done here and now. In the meantime no danger can come of the experiment. Furthermore, I am sure that vagrants might very well be treated in the same way for, in spite of repeated legislation against them, we have made no progress.'

"When the Cardinal had finished speaking, they all vied in praising what they all had received with contempt when suggested by me, but especially the part relating to vagrants because this was the Cardinal's addition.

"I am at a loss as to whether it were better to suppress what followed next, for it was quite absurd. But I shall relate it since it was not evil in itself and had some bearing on the matter in question.

"There happened to be present a hanger-on, who wanted to give the impression of imitating a jester but whose imitation was too close to the real thing. His ill-timed witticisms were meant to raise a laugh, but he himself was more often the object of laughter than his jests. The fellow, however, sometimes let fall observations which were to the point, thus proving the proverb true, that if a man throws the dice often he will sooner or later make a lucky throw. One of the guests happened to say:

"'Raphael's proposal has made good provision for thieves. The Cardinal has taken precautions also for vagrants. It only remains now that public measures be devised for persons whom sickness or old age has brought to want and made unable to work for their living.'

"'Give me leave,' volunteered the hanger-on. 'I shall see that this situation, too, be set right. I am exceedingly anxious to get this sort of person out of my sight. They have often harassed me with their pitiful whinings in begging for money—though they never could pitch a tune which would get a coin out of my pocket. For one of two things always happens: either I do not want to give or I cannot, since I have nothing to give. Now they have begun to be wise. When they see me pass by, they say nothing and spare their pains. They no longer expect anything from me—no more, by heaven, than if I were a secular priest! As for me, I should have a law passed that all those beggars be distributed and divided among the Benedictine monasteries and that the men be made so-called lay brothers.[1] The women I should order to become nuns.'

"The Cardinal smiled and passed it off in jest, but the rest took it in earnest. Now a certain theologian who was a friar[2] was so delighted by this jest at the expense of secular priests and of monks that he also began to make merry, though generally he was serious almost to the point of being dour.

"'Nay,' said he, 'not even so will you be rid of mendicants unless you make provision for us friars too.'

"'But this has been taken care of already,' retorted the hanger-on. 'His Eminence made excellent provision for you when he determined that tramps should be confined and made to work, for you are the worst tramps of all.'

"When the company, looking at the Cardinal, saw that he did not think this jest any more amiss than the other, they all proceeded to take it up with vigor—but not the friar. He—and I do not wonder—deluged by these taunts, began to be so

1. Members of the regular religious orders who performed manual labor and sometimes administrative or temporal functions within the monastery. They were distinct from those men who had taken monastic vows and devoted their lives entirely to following the word of God.

2. Friars were members of the mendicant orders who lived solely off alms in return for their prayers and preaching.

furious and enraged that he could not hold back even from abusing the joker. He called him a rascal, a slanderer, and a 'son of perdition,' quoting the while terrible denunciations out of Holy Scripture. Now the scoffer began to scoff in earnest and was quite in his element:

"'Be not angry, good friar. It is written: "In your patience shall you possess your souls."'[3]

"Then the friar rejoined—I shall repeat his very words: 'I am not angry, you gallows bird, or at least I do not sin, for the psalmist says: "Be angry, and sin not."'[4]

"At this point the Cardinal gently admonished the friar to calm his emotions, but he replied:

"'No, my lord, I speak motivated only by a good zeal—as I should. For holy men have had a good zeal; wherefore Scripture says, "The zeal of Thy house has eaten me up,"[5] and churches resound with the hymn: "The mockers of Eliseus[6] as he went up to the house of God felt the zeal of the baldhead"—just as this mocking, scorning, ribald fellow will perhaps feel it.'

"'Maybe,' said the Cardinal, 'you behave with proper feeling, but I think that you would act, if not more holily, at any rate more wisely, if you would not set your wits against those of a silly fellow and provoke a foolish duel with a fool.'

"'No, my lord,' he replied, 'I should not do more wisely. Solomon himself, the wisest of men, says: "Answer a fool according to his folly"[7]—as I do now. I am showing him the pit into which he will fall if he does not take good heed, for, if many scorners of Eliseus, who numbered only one baldhead, felt the zeal of the baldhead, how much more will one scorner of many friars, among whom are numbered many baldheads! And, besides, we have a papal bull[8] by which all who scoff at us are excommunicated!'

"When the Cardinal realized there was no making an end, he sent away the hanger-on by a motion of his head and tactfully turned the conversation to another subject. Soon afterwards he rose from the table and, going to hear the petitions of his suitors, dismissed us.

"Look, my dear More, with how lengthy a tale I have burdened you. I should have been quite ashamed to protract it if you had not eagerly called for it and seemed to listen as if you did not want any part of the conversation to be left out. Though I ought to have related this conversation more concisely, still I felt bound to tell it to exhibit the attitude of those who had rejected what I had said first yet who, immediately afterward, when the Cardinal did not disapprove of it, also gave their approval, flattering him so much that they even smiled on and almost allowed in earnest the fancies of the hanger-on, which his master in jest did not reject. From this reaction you may judge what little regard courtiers would pay to me and my advice."

"To be sure, my dear Raphael," I commented, "you have given me great pleasure, for everything you have said has been both wise and witty. Besides, while listening to you, I felt not only as if I were at home in my native land but as if I were become a boy again, by being pleasantly reminded of the very Cardinal in whose

3. Luke 21.19.
4. Psalms 4.4.
5. Psalms 69.9.
6. Elisha, the heir of the prophet Elijah. Hythlodaeus refers to a hymn ascribed to the medieval writer Adam of St. Victor. It alludes to the story of Elisha, who, when mocked by children for his baldness, curses them "in the name of the Lord"; this causes two bears to emerge from the woods and rip 42 of the children to pieces (2 Kings 2.23–24).
7. Proverbs 26.5.
8. Edict.

court I was brought up as a lad. Since you are strongly devoted to his memory, you cannot believe how much more attached I feel to you on that account, attached exceedingly as I have been to you already. Even now, nevertheless, I cannot change my mind but must needs think that, if you could persuade yourself not to shun the courts of kings, you could do the greatest good to the common weal by your advice. The latter is the most important part of your duty as it is the duty of every good man. Your favorite author, Plato, is of opinion that commonwealths will finally be happy only if either philosophers become kings or kings turn to philosophy.[9] What a distant prospect of happiness there will be if philosophers will not condescend even to impart their counsel to kings!"

"They are not so ungracious," he rejoined, "that they would not gladly do it—in fact, many have already done it in published books—if the rulers would be ready to take good advice. But, doubtless, Plato was right in foreseeing that if kings themselves did not turn to philosophy, they would never approve of the advice of real philosophers because they have been from their youth saturated and infected with wrong ideas. This truth he found from his own experience with Dionysius.[1] If I proposed beneficial measures to some king and tried to uproot from his soul the seeds of evil and corruption, do you not suppose that I should be forthwith banished or treated with ridicule?

"Come now, suppose I were at the court of the French king and sitting in his privy council. In a most secret meeting, a circle of his most astute councilors over which he personally presides is setting its wits to work to consider by what crafty machinations he may keep his hold on Milan and bring back into his power the Naples which has been eluding his grasp; then overwhelm Venice and subjugate the whole of Italy; next bring under his sway Flanders, Brabant, and finally, the whole of Burgundy—and other nations, too, whose territory he has already conceived the idea of usurping.

"At this meeting, one advises that a treaty should be made with the Venetians to last just as long as the king will find it convenient, that he should communicate his intentions to them, and that he should even deposit in their keeping part of the booty, which, when all has gone according to his mind, he may reclaim. Another recommends the hiring of German *Landsknechte* [infantry], and another the mollification of the Swiss with money, and another the propitiation of the offended majesty of the emperor with gold as an acceptable offering. Another thinks that a settlement should be made with the King of Aragon and that, as a guarantee of peace, someone else's kingdom of Navarre should be ceded him! Another proposes that the Prince of Castile be caught by the prospect of a marriage alliance and that some nobles of his court be drawn to the French side by a fixed pension.

"Meanwhile the most perplexing question of all comes up: what is to be done with England? They agree that negotiations for peace should be undertaken, that an alliance always weak at best should be strengthened with the strongest bonds, and that the English should be called friends but suspected as enemies. The Scots therefore must be posted in readiness, prepared for any opportunity to be let loose on the

9. *Republic*, 5.473d.
1. Having tried to instruct Dionysius II, King of Syracuse, in the art of ruling as a philosopher, Plato became a virtual prisoner of the court.

English if they make the slightest movement. Moreover, some exiled noble must be fostered secretly—for treaties prevent it being done openly—to maintain a claim to the throne, that by this handle France may keep in check a king in whom it has no confidence.

"In such a meeting, I say, when such efforts are being made, when so many distinguished persons are vying with each other in proposals of a warlike nature, what if an insignificant fellow like myself were to get up and advise going on another tack? Suppose I expressed the opinion that Italy should be left alone. Suppose I argued that we should stay at home because the single kingdom of France by itself was almost too large to be governed well by a single man so that the king should not dream of adding other dominions under his sway. Suppose, then, I put before them the decisions made by the people called the Achorians[2] who live on the mainland to the south-southeast of the island of Utopia.

"Once upon a time they had gone to war to win for their king another kingdom to which he claimed to be the rightful heir by virtue of an old tie by marriage. After they had secured it, they saw they would have no less trouble in keeping it than they had suffered in obtaining it. The seeds of rebellion from within or of invasion from without were always springing up in the people thus acquired. They realized they would have to fight constantly for them or against them and to keep an army in continual readiness. In the meantime they were being plundered, their money was being taken out of the country, they were shedding their blood for the little glory of someone else, peace was no more secure than before, their morals at home were being corrupted by war, the lust for robbery was becoming second nature, criminal recklessness was emboldened by killings in war, and the laws were held in contempt—all because the king, being distracted with the charge of two kingdoms, could not properly attend to either.

"At length, seeing that in no other way would there be any end to all this mischief, they took counsel together and most courteously offered their king his choice of retaining whichever of the two kingdoms he preferred. He could not keep both because there were too many of them to be ruled by half a king, just as no one would care to engage even a muleteer whom he had to share with someone else. The worthy king was obliged to be content with his own realm and to turn over the new one to one of his friends, who was driven out soon afterwards.

"Furthermore, suppose I proved that all this war-mongering, by which so many nations were kept in a turmoil on the French king's account, would, after draining his resources and destroying his people, at length by some mischance end in naught and that therefore he had better look after his ancestral kingdom and make it as prosperous and flourishing as possible, love his subjects and be loved by them, live with them and rule them gently, and have no designs upon other kingdoms since what he already possessed was more than enough for him. What reception from my listeners, my dear More, do you think this speech of mine would find?"

"To be sure, not a very favorable one," I granted.

"Well, then, let us proceed," he continued. "Picture the councilors of some king or other debating with him and devising by what schemes they may heap up treasure for him. One advises crying up the value of money when he has to pay any and crying down its value below the just rate when he has to receive any—with the double result that he may discharge a large debt with a small sum and, when only a small

2. A people "without place, region, or district."

sum is due to him, may receive a large one. Another suggests a make-believe war under pretext of which he would raise money and then, when he saw fit, make peace with solemn ceremonies to throw dust in his simple people's eyes because their loving monarch in compassion would fain avoid human bloodshed.

"Another councilor reminds him of certain old and moth-eaten laws, annulled by long non-enforcement, which no one remembers being made and therefore everyone has transgressed. The king should exact fines for their transgression, there being no richer source of profit nor any more honorable than such as has an outward mask of justice! Another recommends that under heavy penalties he prohibit many things and especially such as it is to the people's advantage not to allow. Afterwards for money he should give a dispensation to those with whose interests the prohibition has interfered. Thus favor is won with the people and a double profit is made: first, by exacting fines from those whose greed of gain has entangled them in the snare and, second, by selling privileges to others—and, to be sure, the higher the price the better the king, since he hates to give any private citizen a privilege which is contrary to the public welfare and will not do so except at a great price!

"Another persuades him that he must bind to himself the judges, who will in every case decide in favor of the king's side. In addition, he must summon them to the palace and invite them to debate his affairs in his presence. There will be no cause of his so patently unjust in which one of them will not, either from a desire to contradict or from shame at repeating another's view or to curry favor, find some loophole whereby the law can be perverted. When through the opposite opinions of the judges a thing in itself as clear as daylight has been made a subject of debate, and when truth has become a matter of doubt, the king is opportunely furnished a handle to interpret the law in his own interest. Everyone else will acquiesce from shame or from fear. Afterwards the decision is boldly pronounced from the Bench. Then, too, a pretext can never be wanting for deciding on the king's side. For such a judge it is enough that either equity be on his side or the letter of the law or the twisted meaning of the written word or, what finally outweighs all law with conscientious judges, the indisputable royal prerogative![3]

"All the councilors agree and consent to the famous statement of Crassus:[4] no amount of gold is enough for the ruler who has to keep an army. Further, the king, however much he wishes, can do no wrong; for all that all men possess is his, as they themselves are, and so much is a man's own as the king's kindness has not taken away from him. It is much to the king's interest that the latter be as little as possible, seeing that his safeguard lies in the fact that the people do not grow insolent with wealth and freedom. These things make them less patient to endure harsh and unjust commands, while, on the other hand, poverty and need blunt their spirits, make them patient, and take away from the oppressed the lofty spirit of rebellion.

"At this point, suppose I were again to rise and maintain that these counsels are both dishonorable and dangerous for the king, whose very safety, not merely his

3. Conditions in which the principle of equity is subverted: The law, rather than being applied in such a way as to respect the conditions and circumstances of a particular case, is bent or twisted to suit the interest of a particular party. In England the courts of equity were often devoted to matters of state and were susceptible to corruption in the interest of promoting royal business. The prerogative was the absolute power of the monarch only in special categories of activity (e.g., the import and export trade), and it was exempt from any legal restrictions.

4. Marcus Licinius Crassus (d. 53 B.C.E.), a man of great wealth who, together with Julius Caesar and Pompey, formed a coalition known as the first triumvirate.

honor, rests on the people's resources rather than his own. Suppose I should show that they choose a king for their own sake and not for his—to be plain, that by his labor and effort they may live well and safe from injustice and wrong. For this very reason, it belongs to the king to take more care for the welfare of his people than for his own, just as it is the duty of a shepherd, insofar as he is a shepherd, to feed his sheep rather than himself.[5]

"The blunt facts reveal that they are completely wrong in thinking that the poverty of the people is the safeguard of peace. Where will you find more quarreling than among beggars? Who is more eager for revolution than he who is discontented with his present state of life? Who is more reckless in the endeavor to upset everything, in the hope of getting profit from some source or other, than he who has nothing to lose? Now if there were any king who was either so despicable or so hateful to his subjects that he could not keep them in subjection otherwise than by ill usage, plundering, and confiscation and by reducing them to beggary, it would surely be better for him to resign his throne than to keep it by such means—means by which, though he retain the name of authority, he loses its majesty. It is not consistent with the dignity of a king to exercise authority over beggars but over prosperous and happy subjects. This was certainly the sentiment of that noble and lofty spirit, Fabricius,[6] who replied that he would rather be a ruler of rich people than be rich himself.

"To be sure, to have a single person enjoy a life of pleasure and self-indulgence amid the groans and lamentations of all around him is to be the keeper, not of a kingdom, but of a jail. In fine, as he is an incompetent physician who cannot cure one disease except by creating another, so he who cannot reform the lives of citizens in any other way than by depriving them of the good things of life must admit that he does not know how to rule free men.

"Yea, the king had better amend his own indolence or arrogance, for these two vices generally cause his people either to despise him or to hate him. Let him live harmlessly on what is his own. Let him adjust his expenses to his revenues. Let him check mischief and crime, and, by training his subjects rightly, let him prevent rather than allow the spread of activities which he will have to punish afterwards. Let him not be hasty in enforcing laws fallen into disuse, especially those which, long given up, have never been missed. Let him never take in compensation for violation anything that a private person would be forbidden in court to appropriate for the reason that such would be an act of crooked craftiness.

"What if then I were to put before them the law of the Macarians,[7] a people not very far distant from Utopia? Their king, on the day he first enters into office, is bound by an oath at solemn sacrifices that he will never have at one time in his coffer more than a thousand pounds of gold or its equivalent in silver. They report that this law was instituted by a very good king, who cared more for his country's interest than his own wealth, to be a barrier against hoarding so much money as would cause a lack of it among his people. He saw that this treasure would be sufficient for the

5. A king who did not care for the welfare of his people was usually identified as a tyrant. As Aristotle stated, a tyranny is a perversion of a monarchy and it is characterized by "irresponsible rule over subjects . . . with a view to its own private interest and not in the interest of the persons ruled" (*Politics*, 4.8.3).

6. Roman commander of the republican period; whether he actually made the statement attributed to him is unclear. In any case, it outlines a critique of monarchy common in antityrannical literature of the early modern period.

7. "Happy Ones."

king to put down rebellion and for his kingdom to meet hostile invasions. It was not large enough, however, to tempt him to encroach on the possessions of others. The prevention of the latter was the primary purpose of his legislation. His secondary consideration was that provision was thus made to forestall any shortage of the money needed in the daily business transactions of the citizens. He felt, too, that since the king had to pay out whatever came into his treasury beyond the limit prescribed by law, he would not seek occasion to commit injustice. Such a king will be both a terror to the evil and beloved by the good. To sum it all up, if I tried to obtrude these and like ideas on men strongly inclined to the opposite way of thinking, to what deaf ears should I tell the tale!"

"Deaf indeed, without doubt," I agreed, "and, by heaven, I am not surprised. Neither, to tell the truth, do I think that such ideas should be thrust on people, or such advice given, as you are positive will never be listened to. What good could such novel ideas do, or how could they enter the minds of individuals who are already taken up and possessed by the opposite conviction? In the private conversation of close friends this academic philosophy is not without its charm, but in the councils of kings, where great matters are debated with great authority, there is no room for these notions."

"That is just what I meant," he rejoined, "by saying there is no room for philosophy with rulers."

"Right," I declared, "that is true—not for this academic philosophy which thinks that everything is suitable to every place. But there is another philosophy, more practical for statesmen, which knows its stage, adapts itself to the play in hand, and performs its role neatly and appropriately. This is the philosophy which you must employ. Otherwise we have the situation in which a comedy of Plautus is being performed and the household slaves are making trivial jokes at one another and then you come on the stage in a philosopher's attire and recite the passage from the *Octavia* where Seneca is disputing with Nero.[8] Would it not have been preferable to take a part without words than by reciting something inappropriate to make a hodgepodge of comedy and tragedy? You would have spoiled and upset the actual play by bringing in irrelevant matter—even if your contribution would have been superior in itself. Whatever play is being performed, perform it as best you can, and do not upset it all simply because you think of another which has more interest.

"So it is in the commonwealth. So it is in the deliberations of monarchs. If you cannot pluck up wrongheaded opinions by the root, if you cannot cure according to your heart's desire vices of long standing, yet you must not on that account desert the commonwealth. You must not abandon the ship in a storm because you cannot control the winds.

"On the other hand, you must not force upon people new and strange ideas which you realize will carry no weight with persons of opposite conviction.

8. More's character "More" illustrates the poor social skills of the philosopher by imagining a situation in which the philosopher quotes lines from Seneca's tragedy while everyone else is enjoying a comedy by Plautus. "More" asks not only that the philosopher observe conditions of time and place, but also that—in political situations in which the philosopher might like to instruct his people in moral action but finds that they do not want to listen to him—he not give up his civic obligations and go into retirement. The predicament was one that More and many of his contemporary humanist statesmen actually confronted when they attempted to give advice to their political superiors.

On the contrary, by the indirect approach you must seek and strive to the best of your power to handle matters tactfully. What you cannot turn to good you must at least make as little bad as you can. For it is impossible that all should be well unless all men were good, a situation which I do not expect for a great many years to come!"

"By this approach," he commented, "I should accomplish nothing else than to share the madness of others as I tried to cure their lunacy. If I would stick to the truth, I must needs speak in the manner I have described. To speak falsehoods, for all I know, may be the part of a philosopher, but it is certainly not for me. Although that speech of mine might perhaps be unwelcome and disagreeable to those councilors, yet I cannot see why it should seem odd even to the point of folly. What if I told them the kind of things which Plato creates in his republic or which the Utopians actually put in practice in theirs? Though such institutions were superior (as, to be sure, they are), yet they might appear odd because here individuals have the right of private property, there all things are common.

"To persons who had made up their minds to go headlong by the opposite road, the man who beckons them back and points out dangers ahead can hardly be welcome. But, apart from this aspect, what did my speech contain that would not be appropriate or obligatory to have propounded everywhere? Truly, if all the things which by the perverse morals of men have come to seem odd are to be dropped as unusual and absurd, we must dissemble among Christians almost all the doctrines of Christ. Yet He forbade us to dissemble them to the extent that what He had whispered in the ears of His disciples He commanded to be preached openly from the housetops.[9] The greater part of His teaching is far more different from the morals of mankind than was my discourse. But preachers, crafty men that they are, finding that men grievously disliked to have their morals adjusted to the rule of Christ and following I suppose your advice, accommodated His teaching to men's morals as if it were a rule of soft lead that at least in some way or other the two might be made to correspond.[1] By this method I cannot see what they have gained, except that men may be bad in greater comfort.

"And certainly I should make as little progress in the councils of princes. For I should hold either a different opinion, which would amount to having none at all, or else the same, and then I should, as Mitio says in Terence, help their madness.[2] As to that indirect approach of yours, I cannot see its relevancy; I mean your advice to use my endeavors, if all things cannot be made good, at least to handle them tactfully and, as far as one may, to make them as little bad as possible. At court there is no room for dissembling, nor may one shut one's eyes to things. One must openly approve the worst counsels and subscribe to the most ruinous decrees.

9. Hythlodaeus paraphrases Matthew 10.27 and Luke 12.3; he proposes that the practical and accommodating flexibility that "More" advocates finds its limits in the absolute moral doctrine preached by Jesus Christ and therefore to be followed by Christians.

1. The "rule of soft lead," or the Lesbian rule (after the leaden measure used in architecture on the island of Lesbos in the Aegean), is the figure Aristotle uses to illustrate the concept of equity. The measure, supposedly a rule or an absolute, corresponds to the idea of a written law; but because it is flexible, it is also a written law that is always interpreted in such a way as to fit the particulars of a case.

2. Hythlodaeus insists that for a philosopher to cross a person in authority and with power will only make the philosopher appear nonsensical and therefore render the ruler less reasonable than he was at first; that is, both philosopher and ruler will appear to be madmen. He instances Mitio, a character in Terence's play *The Brothers*, who declares: "Still, if I inflamed or even fell in with his passionate temper, I should surely give him another madman for company" (1.145–147).

He would be counted a spy and almost a traitor, who gives only faint praise to evil counsels.

"Moreover, there is no chance for you to do any good because you are brought among colleagues who would easily corrupt even the best of men before being reformed themselves. By their evil companionship, either you will be seduced yourself or, keeping your own integrity and innocence, you will be made a screen for the wickedness and folly of others. Thus you are far from being able to make anything better by that indirect approach of yours.

"For this reason, Plato by a very fine comparison shows why philosophers are right in abstaining from administration of the commonwealth. They observe the people rushing out into the streets and being soaked by constant showers and cannot induce them to go indoors and escape the rain. They know that, if they go out, they can do no good but will only get wet with the rest. Therefore, being content if they themselves at least are safe, they keep at home, since they cannot remedy the folly of others.[3]

"Yet surely, my dear More, to tell you candidly my heart's sentiments, it appears to me that wherever you have private property and all men measure all things by cash values, there it is scarcely possible for a commonwealth to have justice or prosperity—unless you think justice exists where all the best things flow into the hands of the worst citizens or prosperity prevails where all is divided among very few—and even they are not altogether well off, while the rest are downright wretched.

"As a result, when in my heart I ponder on the extremely wise and holy institutions of the Utopians, among whom, with very few laws, affairs are ordered so aptly that virtue has its reward, and yet, with equality of distribution, all men have abundance of all things, and then when I contrast with their policies the many nations elsewhere ever making ordinances and yet never one of them achieving good order—nations where whatever a man has acquired he calls his own private property, but where all these laws daily framed are not enough for a man to secure or to defend or even to distinguish from someone else's the goods which each in turn calls his own, a predicament readily attested by the numberless and ever new and interminable lawsuits—when I consider, I repeat, all these facts, I become more partial to Plato and less surprised at his refusal to make laws for those who rejected that legislation which gave to all an equal share in all goods.

"This wise sage, to be sure, easily foresaw that the one and only road to the general welfare lies in the maintenance of equality in all respects. I have my doubts that the latter could ever be preserved where the individual's possessions are his private property. When every man aims at absolute ownership of all the property he can get, be there never so great abundance of goods, it is all shared by a handful who leave the rest in poverty. It generally happens that the one class preeminently deserves the lot of the other, for the rich are greedy, unscrupulous, and useless, while the poor are well-behaved, simple, and by their daily industry more beneficial to the commonwealth than to themselves. I am fully persuaded that no just and even distribution of goods can be made and that no happiness can be found in human affairs

3. Cf. *Republic* 6.496d: "he keeps quiet and minds his own business—as a man in a storm . . . stands aside under a little wall. Seeing others filled with lawlessness, he is content if somehow he himself can live his life here pure of injustice and unholy deeds."

unless private property is utterly abolished.[4] While it lasts, there will always remain a heavy and inescapable burden of poverty and misfortunes for by far the greatest and by far the best part of mankind.

"I admit that this burden can be lightened to some extent, but I contend that it cannot be removed entirely. A statute might be made that no person should hold more than a certain amount of land and that no person should have a monetary income beyond that permitted by law. Special legislation might be passed to prevent the monarch from being overmighty and the people overweening; likewise, that public offices should not be solicited with gifts, nor be put up for sale, nor require lavish personal expenditures. Otherwise, there arise, first, the temptation to recoup one's expenses by acts of fraud and plunder and, secondly, the necessity of appointing rich men to offices which ought rather to have been administered by wise men. By this type of legislation, I maintain, as sick bodies which are past cure can be kept up by repeated medical treatments, so these evils, too, can be alleviated and made less acute. There is no hope, however, of a cure and a return to a healthy condition as long as each individual is master of his own property. Nay, while you are intent upon the cure of one part, you make worse the malady of the other parts. Thus, the healing of the one member reciprocally breeds the disease of the other as long as nothing can so be added to one as not to be taken away from another."[5]

"But," I ventured, "I am of the contrary opinion. Life cannot be satisfactory where all things are common. How can there be a sufficient supply of goods when each withdraws himself from the labor of production? For the individual does not have the motive of personal gain and he is rendered slothful by trusting to the industry of others. Moreover, when people are goaded by want and yet the individual cannot legally keep as his own what he has gained, must there not be trouble from continual bloodshed and riot? This holds true especially since the authority of magistrates and respect for their office have been eliminated, for how there can be any place for these among men who are all on the same level I cannot even conceive."

"I do not wonder," he rejoined, "that it looks this way to you, being a person who has no picture at all, or else a false one, of the situation I mean. But you should have been with me in Utopia and personally seen their manners and customs as I did, for I lived there more than five years and would never have wished to leave except to make known that new world. In that case you unabashedly would admit that you had never seen a well-ordered people anywhere but there."

"Yet surely," objected Peter Giles, "it would be hard for you to convince me that a better-ordered people is to be found in that new world than in the one known to us. In the latter I imagine there are equally excellent minds, as well as commonwealths which are older than those in the new world. In these commonwealths long experience has

4. It was thought that primordial humans did not understand that property could be private and belong to one party only. With the congregation of men and women into tribes, however, private property was established by markers: boundary lines, signs and emblems, and distinctive styles of manufacture. This moment also saw the institution of a civil society characterized by religion and law. By advocating a state in which there is no private property, Hythlodaeus posits a political and economic situation that his contemporaries would have recognized in such limited societies as those under monastic or some other kind of religious rule.

5. The trope of the body politic is ubiquitous in early modern political thought. In *The Education of a Christian Prince*, Erasmus argues: "[A monarch] should consider his kingdom as a great body of which he is the most outstanding member and remember that they who have entrusted all their fortunes and their very safety to the good faith of one man are deserving of consideration. He should keep constantly in mind the example of those rulers to whom the welfare of their people was dearer than their own lives; for it is obviously impossible for a prince to do violence to the state without injuring himself." See also Plato's *Republic*, 5.462.

come upon very many advantages for human life—not to mention also the chance discoveries made among us, which no human mind could have devised."

"As for the antiquity of commonwealths," he countered, "you could give a sounder opinion if you had read the historical accounts of that world. If we must believe them, there were cities among them before there were men among us. Furthermore, whatever either brains have invented or chance has discovered hitherto could have happened equally in both places. But I hold for certain that, even though we may surpass them in brains, we are far inferior to them in application and industry.

"According to their chronicles, up to the time of our landing they had never heard anything about our activities (they call us the Ultra-equinoctials) except that twelve hundred years ago a ship driven by a tempest was wrecked on the island of Utopia. Some Romans and Egyptians were cast on shore and remained on the island without ever leaving it. Now mark what good advantage their industry took of this one opportunity. The Roman empire possessed no art capable of any use which they did not either learn from the shipwrecked strangers or discover for themselves after receiving the hints for investigation—so great a gain was it to them that on a single occasion some persons were carried to their shores from ours.

"But if any like fortune has ever driven anyone from their shores to ours, the event is as completely forgotten as future generations will perhaps forget that I had once been there. And, just as they immediately at one meeting appropriated to themselves every good discovery of ours, so I suppose it will be long before we adopt anything that is better arranged with them than with us. This trait, I judge, is the chief reason why, though we are inferior to them neither in brains nor in resources, their commonwealth is more wisely governed and more happily flourishing than ours."

"If so, my dear Raphael," said I, "I beg and beseech you, give us a description of the island. Do not be brief, but set forth in order the terrain, the rivers, the cities, the inhabitants, the traditions, the customs, the laws, and, in fact, everything which you think we should like to know. And you must think we wish to know everything of which we are still ignorant."

"There is nothing," he declared, "I shall be more pleased to do, for I have the facts ready to hand. But the description will take time."

"In that case," I suggested, "let us go in to dine. Afterwards we shall take up as much time as we like."

"Agreed," he replied.

So we went in and dined. We then returned to the same place, sat down on the same bench, and gave orders to the servants that we should not be interrupted. Peter Giles and I urged Raphael to fulfill his promise. As for him, when he saw us intent and eager to listen, after sitting in silent thought for a time, he began his tale as follows.

THE END OF BOOK ONE

BOOK 2

The island of the Utopians extends in the center (where it is broadest) for two hundred miles and is not much narrower for the greater part of the island, but toward both ends it begins gradually to taper. These ends form a circle five hundred miles in circumference and so make the island look like a new moon, the horns of which are divided by straits about eleven miles across. The straits then unfold into a wide expanse. As the winds are kept off by the land which everywhere surrounds it, the bay is like a huge lake, smooth rather than rough, and thus converts almost the whole center of the country into a harbor which lets ships cross in every direction to the great convenience of the inhabitants.

The mouth of this bay is rendered perilous here by shallows and there by reefs. Almost in the center of the gap stands one great crag which, being visible, is not dangerous. A tower built on it is occupied by a garrison. The other rocks are hidden and therefore treacherous. The channels are known only to the natives, and so it does not easily happen that any foreigner enters the bay except with a Utopian pilot. In fact, the entrance is hardly safe even for themselves, unless they guide themselves by landmarks on the shore. If these were removed to other positions, they could easily lure an enemy's fleet, however numerous, to destruction.

On the outer side of the island, harbors are many. Everywhere, however, the landing is so well defended by nature or by engineering that a few defenders can prevent strong forces from coming ashore.

As the report goes and as the appearance of the ground shows, the island once was not surrounded by sea. But Utopus,[6] who as conqueror gave the island its name (up to then it had been called Abraxa[7]) and who brought the rude and rustic people to such a perfection of culture and humanity as makes them now superior to almost all other mortals, gained a victory at his very first landing. He then ordered the excavation of fifteen miles on the side where the land was connected with the continent and caused the sea to flow around the land. He set to the task not only the natives but, to prevent them from thinking the labor a disgrace, his own soldiers also. With the work divided among so many hands, the enterprise was finished with incredible speed and struck the neighboring peoples, who at first had derided the project as vain, with wonder and terror at its success.

The island contains fifty-four city-states,[8] all spacious and magnificent, identical in language, traditions, customs, and laws. They are similar also in layout and everywhere, as far as the nature of the ground permits, similar even in appearance. None of them is separated by less than twenty-four miles from the nearest, but none is so isolated that a person cannot go from it to another in a day's journey on foot. From each city three old and experienced citizens meet to discuss the affairs of common interest to the island once a year at Amaurotum, for this city, being in the very center of the country, is situated most conveniently for the representatives of all sections. It is considered the chief as well as the capital city.

The lands are so well assigned to the cities that each has at least twelve miles of country on every side, and on some sides even much more, to wit, the side on which the cities are farther apart. No city has any desire to extend its territory, for they consider themselves the tenants rather than the masters of what they hold.

Everywhere in the rural districts they have, at suitable distances from one another, farmhouses well equipped with agricultural implements. They are inhabited by citizens who come in succession to live there. No rural household numbers less

6. Ruler over no place.
7. The name for the highest of 365 heavens, according to the Gnostic philosopher Basilides.
8. When More wrote *Utopia*, England consisted of 53 counties and the City of London, its principal urban center. This allusion to England establishes a connection between Books 1 and 2 and suggests that More intended aspects of Utopia to be understood in relation to life in England.

than forty men and women, besides two serfs attached to the soil.[9] Over them are set a master and a mistress, serious in mind and ripe in years. Over every group of thirty households rules a phylarch.[1]

Twenty from each household return every year to the city, namely, those having completed two years in the country. As substitutes in their place, the same number are sent from the city. They are to be trained by those who have been there a year and who therefore are more expert in farming; they themselves will teach others in the following years. There is thus no danger of anything going wrong with the annual food supply through want of skill, as might happen if all at one time were newcomers and novices at farming. Though this system of changing farmers is the rule, to prevent any individual's being forced against his will to continue too long in a life of rather hard work, yet many men who take a natural pleasure in agricultural pursuits obtain leave to stay several years.

The occupation of the farmers is to cultivate the soil, to feed the animals, and to get wood and convey it to the city either by land or by water, whichever way is more convenient. They breed a vast quantity of poultry by a wonderful contrivance. The hens do not brood over the eggs, but the farmers, by keeping a great number of them at a uniform heat, bring them to life and hatch them. As soon as they come out of the shell, the chicks follow and acknowledge humans as their mothers!

They rear very few horses, and these only high-spirited ones, which they use for no other purpose than for exercising their young men in horsemanship. All the labor of cultivation and transportation is performed by oxen, which they admit are inferior to horses in a sudden spurt but which are far superior to them in staying power and endurance and not liable to as many diseases. Moreover, it requires less trouble and expense to feed them. When they are past work, they finally are of use for food.

They sow grain only for bread. Their drink is wine or cider or perry,[2] or it is even water. The latter is sometimes plain and often that in which they have boiled honey or licorice, whereof they have a great abundance.

Though they are more than sure how much food the city with its adjacent territory consumes, they produce far more grain and cattle than they require for their own use: they distribute the surplus among their neighbors. Whenever they need things not found in the country, they send for all the materials from the city and, having to give nothing in exchange, obtain it from the municipal officials without the bother of bargaining. For very many go there every single month to observe the holyday.

When the time of harvest is at hand, the agricultural phylarchs inform the municipal officials what number of citizens they require to be sent. The crowd of harvesters, coming promptly at the appointed time, dispatch the whole task of harvesting almost in a single day of fine weather.

The Cities, Especially Amaurotum

The person who knows one of the cities will know them all, since they are exactly alike insofar as the terrain permits. I shall therefore picture one or other (nor does it matter which), but which should I describe rather than Amaurotum? First, none is

9. According to feudal practice in medieval Europe, a serf was a person who was in servitude for life and could not leave the land whose lord he served. Unlike most slaves, however, who were generally men or women taken captive in the course of a war and who could buy their freedom, a serf was never freed from his connection to an estate. Hythlodaeus refers to other kinds of Utopian slaves later in his account of how Utopians organize their society.

1. Chief.

2. Pear liqueur.

worthier, the rest deferring to it as the meeting place of the national senate; and, secondly, none is better known to me, as being one in which I had lived for five whole years.

To proceed. Amaurotum is situated on the gentle slope of a hill and is almost four-square in outline. Its breadth is about two miles starting just below the crest of the hill and running down to the river Anydrus; its length along the river is somewhat more than its breadth.

The Anydrus rises eighty miles above Amaurotum from a spring not very large; but, being increased in size by several tributaries, two of which are of fair size, it is half a mile broad in front of the city. After soon becoming still broader and after running farther for sixty miles, it falls into the ocean. Through the whole distance between the city and the sea, and even above the city for some miles, the tide alternately flows in for six whole hours and then ebbs with an equally speedy current. When the sea comes in, it fills the whole bed of the Anydrus with its water for a distance of thirty miles, driving the river back. At such times it turns the water salt for some distance farther, but above that point the river grows gradually fresh and passes the city uncontaminated. When the ebb comes, the fresh and pure water extends down almost to the mouth of the river.[3]

The city is joined to the opposite bank of the river not by a bridge built on wooden pillars or piles but by one magnificently arched with stonework. It is situated in the quarter which is farthest from the sea so that ships may pass along the whole of that side of the city without hindrance.

They have also another river, not very large, but very gentle and pleasant, which rises out of the same hill whereon the city is built and runs down through its middle into the river Anydrus. The head and source of this river just outside the city has been connected with it by outworks, lest in case of hostile attack the water might be cut off and diverted or polluted. From this point the water is distributed by conduits made of baked clay into various parts of the lower town. Where the ground makes that course impossible, the rain water collected in capacious cisterns is just as useful.

The city is surrounded by a high and broad wall with towers and ravelins at frequent intervals. A moat, dry but deep and wide and made impassable by thorn hedges, surrounds the fortifications on three sides; on the fourth the river itself takes the place of the moat.

The streets are well laid out both for traffic and for protection against the winds. The buildings, which are far from mean, are set together in a long row, continuous through the block and faced by a corresponding one. The house fronts of the respective blocks are divided by an avenue twenty feet broad. On the rear of the houses, through the whole length of the block, lies a broad garden enclosed on all sides by the backs of the blocks. Every home has not only a door into the street but a back door into the garden. What is more, folding doors, easily opened by hand and then closing of themselves, give admission to anyone. As a result, nothing is private property anywhere. Every ten years they actually exchange their very homes by lot.

The Utopians are very fond of their gardens. In them they have vines, fruits, herbs, flowers, so well kept and flourishing that I never saw anything more fruitful and more tasteful anywhere. Their zest in keeping them is increased not merely by the pleasure afforded them but by the keen competition between blocks as to which

3. These features of the Anydrus resemble those of London's Thames River.

will have the best kept garden. Certainly you cannot readily find anything in the whole city more productive of profit and pleasure to the citizens. Therefore it would seem their founder attached the greatest importance to these gardens.

In fact, they report that the whole plan of the city had been sketched at the very beginning by Utopus himself. He left to posterity, however, to add the adornment and other improvements for which he saw one lifetime would hardly suffice. Their annals, embracing the history of 1760 years, are preserved carefully and conscientiously in writing. Here they find stated that at first the houses were low, mere cabins and huts, haphazardly made with any wood to hand, with mud-plastered walls. They had thatched the ridged roofs with straw.

But now all the homes are of handsome appearance with three stories. The exposed faces of the walls are made of stone or cement or brick, rubble being used as filling for the empty space between the walls. The roofs are flat and covered with a kind of cement which is cheap but so well mixed that it is impervious to fire and superior to lead in defying the damage caused by storms. They keep the winds out of their windows by glass (which is in very common use in Utopia) or sometimes by thin linen smeared with translucent oil or amber. The advantage is twofold: the device results in letting more light in and keeping more wind out.

The Officials

Every thirty families choose annually an official whom in their ancient language they call a syphogrant[4] but in their newer a phylarch. Over ten syphogrants with their families is set a person once called a tranibor but now a protophylarch.[5] The whole body of syphogrants, in number two hundred, having sworn to choose the man whom they judge most useful, by secret balloting appoint a governor, specifically one of the four candidates named to them by the people, for one is selected out of each of the four quarter of the city to be commended to the senate.

The governor holds office for life, unless ousted on suspicion of aiming at a tyranny. The tranibors are elected annually but are not changed without good reason. The other officials all hold their posts for one year.

The tranibors enter into consultation with the governor every other day and sometimes, if need arises, oftener. They take counsel about the commonwealth. If there are any disputes between private persons—there are very few—they settle them without loss of time. They always admit to the senate chamber two syphogrants, and different ones every day. It is provided that nothing concerning the commonwealth be ratified if it has not been discussed in the senate three days before the passing of the decree. To take counsel on matters of common interest outside the senate or the popular assembly is considered a capital offense. The object of these measures, they say, is to prevent it from being easy, by a conspiracy between the governor and the tranibors and by tyrannous oppression of the people, to change the order of the commonwealth. Therefore whatever is considered important is laid before the assembly of the syphogrants who, after informing their groups of families, take counsel together and report their decision to the senate. Sometimes the matter is laid before the council of the whole island.

In addition, the senate has the custom of debating nothing on the same day on which it is first proposed but of putting it off till the next meeting. This is their rule

4. Wise old man.

5. Tranibor: glutton; protophylarch: principal chief.

lest anyone, after hastily blurting out the first thought that popped into his head, should afterwards give more thought to defending his opinion than to supporting what is for the good of the commonwealth, and should prefer to jeopardize the public welfare rather than to risk his reputation through a wrongheaded and misplaced shame, fearing he might be thought to have shown too little foresight at the first—though he should have been enough foresighted at the first to speak with prudence rather than with haste!

Occupations

Agriculture is the one pursuit which is common to all, both men and women, without exception. They are all instructed in it from childhood, partly by principles taught in school, partly by field trips to the farms closer to the city as if for recreation. Here they do not merely look on, but, as opportunity arises for bodily exercise, they do the actual work.

Besides agriculture (which is, as I said, common to all), each is taught one particular craft as his own. This is generally either wool-working or linen-making or masonry or metal-working or carpentry. There is no other pursuit which occupies any number worth mentioning. As for clothes, these are of one and the same pattern throughout the island and down the centuries, though there is a distinction between the sexes and between the single and married. The garments are comely to the eye, convenient for bodily movement, and fit for wear in heat and cold. Each family, I say, does its own tailoring.

Of the other crafts, one is learned by each person, and not the men only, but the women too. The latter as the weaker sex have the lighter occupations and generally work wool and flax. To the men are committed the remaining more laborious crafts. For the most part, each is brought up in his father's craft, for which most have a natural inclination. But if anyone is attracted to another occupation, he is transferred by adoption to a family pursuing that craft for which he has a liking. Care is taken not only by his father but by the authorities, too, that he will be assigned to a grave and honorable householder. Moreover, if anyone after being thoroughly taught one craft desires another also, the same permission is given. Having acquired both, he practices his choice unless the city has more need of the one than of the other.

The chief and almost the only function of the syphogrants is to manage and provide that no one sit idle, but that each apply himself industriously to his trade, and yet that he be not wearied like a beast of burden with constant toil from early morning till late at night. Such wretchedness is worse than the lot of slaves, and yet it is almost everywhere the life of workingmen—except for the Utopians. The latter divide the day and night into twenty-four equal hours and assign only six to work. There are three before noon, after which they go to dinner. After dinner, when they have rested for two hours in the afternoon, they again give three to work and finish up with supper. Counting one o'clock as the first hour after noon, they go to bed about eight o'clock, and sleep claims eight hours.

The intervals between the hours of work, sleep, and food are left to every man's discretion, not to waste in revelry or idleness, but to devote the time free from work to some other occupation according to taste. These periods are commonly devoted to intellectual pursuits. For it is their custom that public lectures are daily delivered in the hours before daybreak. Attendance is compulsory only for those who have been specially chosen to devote themselves to learning. A great number of all classes, however, both males and females, flock to hear the lectures, some to one and some to another, according to their natural inclination. But if anyone should prefer to devote this time to his trade, as is the case with many minds which do not reach the level for any of the higher intellectual disciplines, he is not hindered; in fact, he is even praised as useful to the commonwealth.

After supper they spend one hour in recreation, in summer in the gardens, in winter in the common halls in which they have their meals. There they either play music or entertain themselves with conversation. Dice and that kind of foolish and ruinous game they are not acquainted with. They do play two games not unlike chess. The first is a battle of numbers in which one number plunders another. The second is a game in which the vices fight a pitched battle with the virtues. In the latter is exhibited very cleverly, to begin with, both the strife of the vices with one another and their concerted opposition to the virtues; then, what vices are opposed to what virtues, by what forces they assail them openly, by what stratagems they attack them indirectly, by what safeguards the virtues check the power of the vices, by what arts they frustrate their designs; and, finally, by what means the one side gains the victory.

But here, lest you be mistaken, there is one point you must examine more closely. Since they devote but six hours to work, you might possibly think the consequence to be some scarcity of necessities. But so far is this from being the case that the aforesaid time is not only enough but more than enough for a supply of all that is requisite for either the necessity or the convenience of living. This phenomenon you too will understand if you consider how large a part of the population in other countries exists without working. First, there are almost all the women, who constitute half the whole; or, where the women are busy, there as a rule the men are snoring in their stead. Besides, how great and how lazy is the crowd of priests and so-called religious! Add to them all the rich, especially the masters of estates, who are commonly termed gentlemen and noblemen. Reckon with them their retainers—I mean, that whole rabble of good-for-nothing swashbucklers. Finally, join in the lusty and sturdy beggars who make some disease an excuse for idleness. You will certainly find far less numerous than you had supposed those whose labor produces all the articles that mortals require for daily use.

Now estimate how few of those who do work are occupied in essential trades. For, in a society where we make money the standard of everything, it is necessary to practice many crafts which are quite vain and superfluous, ministering only to luxury and licentiousness. Suppose the host of those who now toil were distributed over only as few crafts as natural needs and conveniences require. In the great abundance of commodities which must then arise, the prices set on them would be too low for the craftsmen to earn their livelihood by their work. But suppose all those fellows who are now busied with unprofitable crafts, as well as all the lazy and idle throng, any one of whom now consumes as much of the fruits of other men's labors as any two of the workingmen, were all set to work and indeed to useful work. You can easily see how small an allowance of time would be enough and to spare for the production of all that is required by necessity or comfort (or even pleasure, provided it be genuine and natural).

The very experience of Utopia makes the latter clear. In the whole city and its neighborhood, exemption from work is granted to hardly five hundred of the total of men and women whose age and strength make them fit for work. Among them the syphogrants, though legally exempted from work, yet take no advantage of this privilege so that by their example they may the more readily attract the others to work.

The same exemption is enjoyed by those whom the people, persuaded by the recommendation of the priests, have given perpetual freedom from labor through the secret vote of the syphogrants so that they may learn thoroughly the various branches of knowledge. But if any of these scholars falsifies the hopes entertained of him, he is reduced to the rank of workingman. On the other hand, not seldom does it happen that a craftsman so industriously employs his spare hours on learning and makes such progress by his diligence that he is relieved of his manual labor and advanced into the class of men of learning. It is out of this company of scholars that they choose ambassadors, priests, tranibors, and finally the governor himself, whom they call in their ancient tongue Barzanes but in their more modern language Ademus.[6]

Nearly all the remaining populace being neither idle nor busied with useless occupations, it is easy to calculate how much good work can be produced in a very few hours. Besides the points mentioned, there is this further convenience that in most of the necessary crafts they do not require as much work as other nations. In the first place the erection or repair of buildings requires the constant labor of so many men elsewhere because what a father has built, his extravagant heir allows gradually to fall into ruin. As a result, what might have been kept up at small cost, his successor is obliged to erect anew at great expense. Further, often even when a house has cost one man a large sum, another is so fastidious that he thinks little of it. When it is neglected and therefore soon becomes dilapidated, he builds a second elsewhere at no less cost. But in the land of the Utopians, now that everything has been settled and the commonwealth established, a new home on a new site is a rare event, for not only do they promptly repair any damage, but they even take care to prevent damage. What is the result? With the minimum of labor, buildings last very long, and masons and carpenters sometimes have scarcely anything to do, except that they are set to hew out timber at home and to square and prepare stone meantime so that, if any work be required, a building may the sooner be erected.

In the matter of clothing, too, see how little toil and labor is needed. First, while at work, they are dressed unpretentiously in leather or hide, which lasts for seven years. When they go out in public, they put on a cape to hide their comparatively rough working clothes. This garment is of one color throughout the island and that the natural color. Consequently not only is much less woolen cloth needed than elsewhere, but what they have is much less expensive. On the other hand, since linen cloth is made with less labor, it is more used. In linen cloth only whiteness, in woolen cloth only cleanliness, is considered. No value is set on fineness of thread. So it comes about that, whereas elsewhere one man is not satisfied with four or five woolen coats of different colors and as many silk shirts, and the more fastidious not even with ten, in Utopia a man is content with a single cape, lasting generally for two years. There is no reason, of course, why he should desire more, for if he had them he would not be better fortified against the cold nor appear better dressed in the least.

Wherefore, seeing that they are all busied with useful trades and are satisfied with fewer products from them, it even happens that when there is an abundance of all commodities, they sometimes take out a countless number of people to repair whatever public roads are in bad order. Often, too, when there is nothing even of

6. Barzanes: "son of Zeus"; Ademus, "peopleless." These names indicate that the governor of Utopia, although considered a divinity in the primitive period of the state, is so impartial in his efforts to rule that he seems to belong to no family, region, or people.

this kind of work to be done, they announce publicly that there will be fewer hours of work. For the authorities do not keep the citizens against their will at superfluous labor since the constitution of their commonwealth looks in the first place to this sole object: that for all the citizens, as far as the public needs permit, as much time as possible should be withdrawn from the service of the body and devoted to the freedom and culture of the mind. It is in the latter that they deem the happiness of life to consist.

Social Relations

But now, it seems, I must explain the behavior of the citizens toward one another, the nature of their social relations, and the method of distribution of goods. Since the city consists of households, households as a rule are made up of those related by blood. Girls, upon reaching womanhood and upon being settled in marriage, go to their husbands' domiciles. On the other hand, male children and then grandchildren remain in the family and are subject to the oldest parent, unless he has become a dotard with old age. In the latter case the next oldest is put in his place.

But that the city neither be depopulated nor grow beyond measure, provision is made that no household shall have fewer than ten or more than sixteen adults; there are six thousand such households in each city, apart from its surrounding territory. Of children under age, of course, no number can be fixed.[7] This limit is easily observed by transferring those who exceed the number in larger families into those that are under the prescribed number. Whenever all the families of a city reach their full quota, the extra persons help to make up the deficient population of other cities.

And if the population throughout the island should happen to swell above the fixed quotas, they enroll citizens out of every city and, on the mainland nearest them, wherever the natives have much unoccupied and uncultivated land, they found a colony under their own laws. They join with themselves the natives if they are willing to dwell with them. When such a union takes place, the two parties gradually and easily merge and together absorb the same way of life and the same customs, much to the great advantage of both peoples. By their procedures they make the land sufficient for both, which previously seemed poor and barren to the natives. The inhabitants who refuse to live according to their laws, they drive from the territory which they carve out for themselves. If they resist, they wage war against them. They consider it a most just cause for war when a people which does not use its soil but keeps it idle and waste nevertheless forbids the use and possession of it to others who by the rule of nature ought to be maintained by it.

If ever any misfortune so diminishes the number in any of their cities that it cannot be made up out of other parts of the island without bringing other cities below their proper strength (this has happened, they say, only twice in all the ages on account of the raging of a fierce pestilence), they are filled up by citizens returning from colonial territory. They would rather that the colonies should perish than that any of the cities of the island should be enfeebled.

But to return to the dealings of the citizens. The oldest, as I have said, rules the household. Wives wait on their husbands, children on their parents, and generally the younger on their elders.

7. In England, women came of age at 18, men at 22.

Every city is divided into four equal districts. In the middle of each quarter is a market of all kinds of commodities. To designated market buildings the products of each family are conveyed. Each kind of goods is arranged separately in storehouses. From the latter any head of a household seeks what he and his require and, without money or any kind of compensation, carries off what he seeks. Why should anything be refused? First, there is a plentiful supply of all things and, secondly, there is no underlying fear that anyone will demand more than he needs. Why should there be any suspicion that someone may demand an excessive amount when he is certain of never being in want? No doubt about it, avarice and greed are aroused in every kind of living creature by the fear of want, but only in man are they motivated by pride alone—pride which counts it a personal glory to excel others by superfluous display of possessions. The latter vice can have no place at all in the Utopian scheme of things.

Next to the market place that I have mentioned are the food markets. Here are brought not only different kinds of vegetables, fruit, and bread but also fish and whatever is edible of bird and four-footed beast. Outside the city are designated places where all gore and offal may be washed away in running water. From these places they transport the carcasses of the animals slaughtered and cleaned by the hands of slaves. They do not allow their citizens to accustom themselves to the butchering of animals, by the practice of which they think that mercy, the finest feeling of our human nature, is gradually killed off. In addition, they do not permit to be brought inside the city anything filthy or unclean for fear that the air, tainted by putrefaction, should engender disease.

To continue, each street has spacious halls, located at equal distance from one another, each being known by a special name of its own. In these halls live the syphogrants. To each hall are assigned thirty families, fifteen on either side, to take their meals in common. The managers of each hall meet at a fixed time in the market and get food according to the number of person in their individual charge.

Special care is first taken of the sick who are looked after in public hospitals. They have four at the city limits, a little outside the walls. These are so roomy as to be comparable to as many small towns. The purpose is twofold: first, that the sick, however numerous, should not be packed too close together in consequent discomfort and, second, that those who have a contagious disease likely to pass from one to another may be isolated as much as possible from the rest.[8] These hospitals are very well furnished and equipped with everything conducive to health. Besides, such tender and careful treatment and such constant attendance of expert physicians are provided that, though no one is sent to them against his will, there is hardly anybody in the whole city who, when suffering from illness, does not prefer to be nursed there rather than at home.

After the supervisor for the sick has received food as prescribed by the physicians, then the finest of everything is distributed equally among the halls according to the number in each, except that special regard is paid to the governor, the high priest, and the tranibors, as well as to ambassadors and all foreigners (if there are any, but they are few and far between). Yet the latter, too, when they are in Utopia, have definite homes got ready for them.

8. The germ theory of disease dates from the 19th century and the work of Louis Pasteur. Here More seems to be basing his idea of contagion on the experience of the bubonic plague, or Black Death, a major 14th-century European epidemic that killed roughly three-quarters of the population in 20 years.

To these halls, at the hours fixed for dinner and supper, the entire syphograncy assembles, summoned by the blast of a brazen trumpet, excepting persons who are taking their meals either in the hospitals or at home. No one is forbidden, after the halls have been served, to fetch food from the market to his home: they realize that no one would do it without good reason. For, though nobody is forbidden to dine at home, yet no one does it willingly since the practice is considered not decent and since it is foolish to take the trouble of preparing an inferior dinner when an excellent and sumptuous one is ready at hand in the hall nearby.

In this hall all menial offices which to some degree involve heavy labor or soil the hands are performed by slaves. But the duty of cooking and preparing the food and, in fine, of arranging the whole meal is carried out by the women alone, taking turns for each family. Persons sit down at three or more tables according to the number of the company. The men sit with their backs to the wall, the women on the outside, so that if they have any sudden pain or sickness, such as sometimes happens to women with child, they may rise without disturbing the arrangements and go to the nurses.

The nurses sit separately with the infants in a dining room assigned for the purpose, never without a fire and a supply of clean water nor without cradles. Thus they can both lay the infants down and, when they wish, undo their wrappings and let them play freely by the fire. Each woman nurses her own offspring, unless prevented by either death or disease. When that happens, the wives of the syphogrants quickly provide a nurse and find no difficulty in doing so. The reason is that women who can do the service offer themselves with the greatest readiness since everybody praises this kind of pity and since the child who is thus fostered looks on his nurse as his natural mother. In the nurses' quarters are all children up to five years of age. All other minors, among whom they include all of both sexes below the age of marriage, either wait at table on the diners or, if they are not old and strong enough, stand by—and that in absolute silence. Both groups eat what is handed them from the table and have no other separate time for dining.

The syphogrant and his wife sit in the middle of the first table, which is the highest place and which allows them to have the whole company in view, for it stands crosswise at the farthest end of the dining room. Alongside them are two of the eldest, for they always sit four by four at all tables. But if there is a temple in the syphograncy, the priest and his wife so sit with the syphogrant as to preside. On both sides of them sit younger people, and next to them old people again, and so through the house those of the same age sit together and yet mingle with those of a different age. The reason for this practice, they say, is that the grave and reverend behavior of the old may restrain the younger people from mischievous freedom in word and gesture, since nothing can be done or said at table which escapes the notice of the old present on every side.

The trays of food are not served in order from the first place and so on, but all the old men, who are seated in conspicuous places, are served first with the best food, and then equal portions are given to the rest. The old men at their discretion give a share of their delicacies to their neighbors when there is not enough to go around to everybody in the house. Thus, due respect is paid to seniority, and yet all have an equal advantage.

They begin every dinner and supper with some reading which is conducive to morality but which is brief so as not to be tiresome. Taking their cue from the reading, the elders introduce approved subjects of conversation, neither somber nor dull. But they do not monopolize the whole dinner with long speeches: they are ready to hear the young men too, and indeed deliberately draw them out that they may test each one's ability and character, which are revealed in the relaxed atmosphere of a feast.

Their dinners are somewhat short, their suppers more prolonged, because the former are followed by labor, the latter by sleep and a night's rest. They think the night's rest to be more efficacious to wholesome digestion. No supper passes without music, nor does the dessert course lack delicacies. They burn spices and scatter perfumes and omit nothing that may cheer the company. For they are somewhat more inclined to this attitude of mind: that no kind of pleasure is forbidden, provided no harm comes of it.

This is the common life they live in the city. In the country, however, since they are rather far removed from their neighbors, all take their meals in their own homes. No family lacks any kind of edible inasmuch as all the food eaten by the city dwellers comes from those who live in the country.

Utopian Travel, [Etc.]

Now if any citizens conceive a desire either to visit their friends who reside in another city or to see the place itself, they easily obtain leave from their syphogrants and tranibors, unless some good reason prevents them. Accordingly a party is made up and dispatched carrying a letter from the governor which bears witness to the granting of leave to travel and fixes the day of their return. A wagon is granted them with a public slave to conduct and see to the oxen, but, unless they have women in their company, they dispense with the wagon, regarding it as a burden and hindrance. Throughout their journey, though they carry nothing with them, yet nothing is lacking, for they are at home everywhere. If they stay longer than a day in any place, each practices his trade there and is entertained very courteously by workers in the same trade.

If any person gives himself leave to stray out of his territorial limits and is caught without the governor's certificate, he is treated with contempt, brought back as a runaway, and severely punished. If he dares to repeat the offense, he is punished with slavery.

If anyone is seized with the desire of exploring the country belonging to his own city, he is not forbidden to do so, provided he obtain his father's leave and his wife's consent. In any district of the country to which he comes, he receives no food until he has finished the morning share of the day's work or the labor that is usually performed there before supper. If he keep to this condition, he may go where he pleases within the territory belonging to his city. In this way he will be just as useful to the city as if he were in it.

Now you can see how nowhere is there any license to waste time, nowhere any pretext to evade work—no wine shop, no alehouse, no brothel anywhere, no opportunity for corruption, no lurking hole, no secret meeting place. On the contrary, being under the eyes of all, people are bound either to be performing the usual labor or to be enjoying their leisure in a fashion not without decency. This universal behavior must of necessity lead to an abundance of all commodities. Since the latter are distributed evenly among all, it follows, of course, that no one can be reduced to poverty or beggary.

In the senate at Amaurotum (to which, as I said before, three are sent annually from every city), they first determine what commodity is in plenty in each particular place and again where on the island the crops have been meager. They at once fill up the scarcity of one place by the surplus of another. This service they perform without payment, receiving nothing in return from those to whom they give. Those who have given out of their stock to any particular city without requiring any return from it receive what they lack from another to which they have given nothing. Thus, the whole island is like a single family.

But when they have made sufficient provision for themselves (which they do not consider complete until they have provided for two years to come, on account of the next year's uncertain crop), then they export into other countries, out of their surplus, a great quantity of grain, honey, wool, linen, timber, scarlet and purple dyestuffs, hides, wax, tallow, leather, as well as livestock. Of all these commodities they bestow the seventh part on the poor of the district and sell the rest at a moderate price.

By this trade they bring into their country not only such articles as they lack themselves—and practically the only thing lacking is iron—but also a great quantity of silver and gold. This exchange has gone on day by day so long that now they have everywhere an abundance of these metals, more than would be believed. In consequence, they now care little whether they sell for ready cash or appoint a future day for payment, and in fact have by far the greatest amount out on credit. In all transactions on credit, however, they never trust private citizens but the municipal government, the legal documents being drawn up as usual. When the day for payment comes, the city collects the money due from private debtors and puts it into the treasury and enjoys the use of it until the Utopians claim payment.

The Utopians never claim payment of most of the money. They think it hardly fair to take away a thing useful to other people when it is useless to themselves. But if circumstances require that they should lend some part of it to another nation, then they call in their debts—or when they must wage war. It is for that single purpose that they keep all the treasure they possess at home: to be their bulwark in extreme peril or in sudden emergency. They use it above all to hire at sky-high rates of pay foreign mercenaries (whom they would jeopardize rather than their own citizens), being well aware that by large sums of money even their enemies themselves may be bought and set to fight one another either by treachery or by open warfare.

For these military reasons they keep a vast treasure, but not as a treasure. They keep it in a way which I am really quite ashamed to reveal for fear that my words will not be believed. My fears are all the more justified because I am conscious that, had I not been there and witnessed the phenomenon, I myself should have been with difficulty induced to believe it from another's account. It needs must be almost always the rule that, as far as a thing is unlike the ways of the hearers, so far is it from obtaining their credence. An impartial judge of things, however, seeing that the rest of their institutions are so unlike ours, will perhaps wonder less that their use of silver and gold should be adapted to their way of life rather than to ours. As stated, they do not use money themselves but keep it only for an emergency, which may actually occur, yet possibly may never happen.

Meanwhile, gold and silver, of which money is made, are so treated by them that no one values them more highly than their true nature deserves. Who does not see that they are far inferior to iron in usefulness since without iron mortals cannot live any more than without fire and water? To gold and silver, however, nature has given no use that we cannot dispense with, if the folly of men had not made them valuable because they are rare. On the other hand, like a most kind and indulgent mother, she has exposed to view all that is best, like air and water and earth itself, but has removed as far as possible from us all vain and unprofitable things.

If in Utopia these metals were kept locked up in a tower, it might be suspected that the governor and the senate—for such is the foolish imagination of the common folk—were deceiving the people by the scheme and they themselves were deriving some benefit therefrom. Moreover, if they made them into drinking vessels and other such skillful handiwork, then if occasion arose for them all to be melted down again and applied to the pay of soldiers, they realize that people would be unwilling to be deprived of what they had once begun to treasure.

To avoid these dangers, they have devised a means which, as it is consonant with the rest of their institutions, so it is extremely unlike our own—seeing that we value gold so much and are so careful in safeguarding it—and therefore incredible except to those who have experience of it. While they eat and drink from earthenware and glassware of fine workmanship but of little value, from gold and silver they make chamber pots and all the humblest vessels for use everywhere, not only in the common halls but in private homes also. Moreover, they employ the same metals to make the chains and solid fetters which they put on their slaves. Finally, as for those who bear the stigma of disgrace on account of some crime, they have gold ornaments hanging from their ears, gold rings encircling their fingers, gold chains thrown around their necks, and, as a last touch, a gold crown binding their temples. Thus by every means in their power they make gold and silver a mark of ill fame. In this way, too, it happens that, while all other nations bear the loss of these metals with as great grief as if they were losing their very vitals, if circumstances in Utopia ever required the removal of all gold and silver, no one would feel that he were losing as much as a penny.[9]

They also gather pearls by the seashore and diamonds and rubies on certain cliffs. They do not look for them purposely, but they polish them when found by chance. With them they adorn little children, who in their earliest years are proud and delighted with such decorations. When they have grown somewhat older and perceive that only children use such toys, they lay them aside, not by any order of their parents, but through their own feeling of shame, just as our own children, when they grow up, throw away their marbles, rattles, and dolls.

What opposite ideas and feelings are created by customs so different from those of other people came home to me never more clearly than in the case of the Anemolian ambassadors. They arrived in Amaurotum during my stay there. Because they came to treat of important matters, the three representatives of each city had assembled before their appearance. Now all the ambassadors of neighboring nations, who had previously visited the land, were well acquainted with the manners of the Utopians and knew that they paid no respect to costly clothes but looked with contempt on silk and regarded gold as a badge of disgrace. These persons usually came in the simplest possible dress. But the Anemolians, living farther off and having had fewer dealings with them, since they heard that in Utopia all were dressed alike, and in a homespun fashion at that, felt sure that they did not possess what they made no use of. Being more proud than wise, they determined by the grandeur of their apparel to represent the gods themselves and by their splendid adornment to dazzle the eyes of the poor Utopians.

Consequently the three ambassadors made a grand entry with a suite of a hundred followers, all in parti-colored clothes and most in silk. The ambassadors themselves, being noblemen at home, were arrayed in cloth of gold, with heavy gold

9. Hythlodaeus distinguishes first between the use value and the exchange value of an object: Gold, a soft metal, is useless except as decoration; but as a scarce commodity, it can be exchanged for other objects that do have a use value. He then places a moral construction on precious (or scarce) metals because they are used to indicate wealth and promote ostentation.

necklaces and earrings, with gold rings on their fingers, and with strings of gleaming pearls and gems upon their caps; in fact, they were decked out with all those articles which in Utopia are used to punish slaves, to stigmatize evil-doers, or to amuse children. It was a sight worth seeing to behold their cockiness when they compared their grand clothing with that of the Utopians, who had poured out into the street to see them pass. On the other hand, it was no less delightful to notice how much they were mistaken in their sanguine[1] expectations and how far they were from obtaining the consideration which they had hoped to get. To the eyes of all the Utopians, with the exception of the very few who for a good reason had visited foreign countries, all this gay show appeared disgraceful. They therefore bowed to the lowest of the party as to the masters but took the ambassadors themselves to be slaves because they were wearing gold chains, and passed them over without any deference whatever.

Why, you might have seen also the children who had themselves discarded gems and pearls, when they saw them attached to the caps of the ambassadors, poke and nudge their mothers and say to them:

"Look, mother, that big rascal is still wearing pearls and jewels as if he were yet a little boy!"

But the mother, also in earnest, would say:

"Hush, son, I think it is one of the ambassadors' fools."

Others found fault with the golden chains as useless, being so slender that a slave could easily break them or, again, so loose that at his pleasure he could throw them off and escape anywhere scot-free.

After spending one or more days there, the ambassadors saw an immense quantity of gold held as cheaply and in as great contempt there as in honor among themselves. They saw, too, that more gold and silver were amassed to make the chains and fetters of one runaway slave than had made up the whole array of the three of them. They then were crestfallen and for shame put away all the finery with which they had made themselves haughtily conspicuous, especially when, after familiar talk with the Utopians, they had learned their ways and opinions.

The Utopians wonder that any mortal takes pleasure in the uncertain sparkle of a tiny jewel or precious stone when he can look at a star or even the sun itself. They wonder that anyone can be so mad as to think himself more noble on account of the texture of a finer wool, since, however fine the texture is, a sheep once wore the wool and yet all the time was nothing more than a sheep.

They wonder, too, that gold, which by its very nature is so useless, is now everywhere in the world valued so highly that man himself, through whose agency and for whose use it got this value, is priced much cheaper than gold itself. This is true to such an extent that a blockhead who has no more intelligence than a log and who is as dishonest as he is foolish keeps in bondage many wise men and good men merely for the reason that a great heap of gold coins happens to be his. Yet if some chance or some legal trick (which is as apt as chance to confound high and low) transfers it from this master to the lowest rascal in his entire household, he will surely very soon pass into the service of his former servant—as if he were a mere appendage of and addition to the coins! But much more do they wonder at and abominate the madness of persons who pay almost divine honors to the rich, to whom they neither owe anything nor are obligated in any other respect than that they are rich. Yet they know

1. Optimistic.

them to be so mean and miserly that they are more than sure that of all that great pile of cash, as long as the rich men live, not a single penny will ever come their way.

These and similar opinions they have conceived partly from their upbringing, being reared in a commonwealth whose institutions are far removed from follies of the kind mentioned, and partly from instruction and reading good books. Though there are not many in each city who are relieved from all other tasks and assigned to scholarship alone, that is to say, the individuals in whom they have detected from childhood an outstanding personality, a first-rate intelligence, and an inclination of mind toward learning, yet all children are introduced to good literature. A large part of the people, too, men and women alike, throughout their lives, devote to learning the hours which, as we said, are free from manual labor.

They learn the various branches of knowledge in their native tongue. The latter is copious in vocabulary and pleasant to the ear and a very faithful exponent of thought. It is almost the same as that current in a great part of that side of the world, only that everywhere else its form is more corrupt, to different degrees in different regions.

Of all those philosophers whose names are famous in the part of the world known to us, the reputation of not even a single one had reached them before our arrival. Yet in music, dialectic, arithmetic, and geometry they have made almost the same discoveries as those predecessors of ours in the classical world. But while they measure up to the ancients in almost all other subjects, still they are far from being a match for the inventions of our modern logicians. In fact, they have discovered not even a single one of those very ingeniously devised rules about restrictions, amplifications, and suppositions which our own children everywhere learn in the *Small Logicals*. In addition, so far are they from ability to speculate on second intentions that not one of them could see even man himself as a so-called universal—though he was, as you know, colossal and greater than any giant, as well as pointed out by us with our finger.[2]

They are most expert, however, in the courses of the stars and the movements of the celestial bodies. Moreover, they have ingeniously devised instruments in different shapes, by which they have most exactly comprehended the movements and positions of the sun and moon and all the other stars which are visible in their horizon. But of the agreements and discords of the planets and, in sum, of all that infamous and deceitful divination by the stars, they do not even dream.

They forecast rains, winds, and all the other changes in weather by definite signs which they have ascertained by long practice. But as to the causes of all these phenomena, and of the flow of the sea and its saltiness, and, in fine, of the origin and nature of the heavens and the universe, they partly treat of them in the same way as our ancient philosophers and partly, as the latter differ from one another, they, too, in introducing new theories disagree with them all and yet do not in all respects agree with fellow Utopians.

In that part of philosophy which deals with morals, they carry on the same debates as we do. They inquire into the good: of the soul and of the body and of external gifts. They ask also whether the name of good may be applied to all three or

2. In logic, a first intention is the conception gained from the apprehension of an object as a whole; a second intention is the abstracted conception gained by generalizing upon a first intention and as such, exists only in the mind. The Utopians cannot conceive of second intentions, because they are themselves second intentions; they are the product of More's reflection upon the particular European governments he has studied.

simply belongs to the endowments of the soul. They discuss virtue and pleasure, but their principal and chief debate is in what thing or things, one or more, they are to hold that happiness consists. In this matter they seem to lean more than they should to the school that espouses pleasure as the object by which to define either the whole or the chief part of human happiness.

What is more astonishing is that they seek a defense for this soft doctrine from their religion, which is serious and strict, almost solemn and hard. They never have a discussion of happiness without uniting certain principles taken from religion as well as from philosophy, which uses rational arguments. Without these principles they think reason insufficient and weak by itself for the investigation of true happiness. The following are examples of these principles. The soul is immortal and by the goodness of God born for happiness. After this life rewards are appointed for our virtues and good deeds, punishment for our crimes. Though these principles belong to religion, yet they hold that reason leads men to believe and to admit them.[3]

Once the principles are eliminated, the Utopians have no hesitation in maintaining that a person would be stupid not to realize that he ought to seek pleasure by fair means or foul, but that he should only take care not to let a lesser pleasure interfere with a greater nor to follow after a pleasure which would bring pain in retaliation. To pursue hard and painful virtue and not only to banish the sweetness of life but even voluntarily to suffer pain from which you expect no profit (for what profit can there be if after death you gain nothing for having passed the whole present life unpleasantly, that is, wretchedly?)—this policy they declare to be the extreme of madness.

As it is, they hold happiness rests not in every kind of pleasure but only in good and decent pleasure. To such, as to the supreme good, our nature is drawn by virtue itself, to which the opposite school alone attributes happiness. The Utopians define virtue as living according to nature since to this end we were created by God. That individual, they say, is following the guidance of nature who, in desiring one thing and avoiding another, obeys the dictates of reason.[4]

Now reason first of all inflames men to a love and veneration of the divine majesty, to whom we owe both our existence and our capacity for happiness. Secondly, it admonishes and urges us to lead a life as free from care and as full of joy as possible and, because of our natural fellowship, to help all other men, too, to attain that end. No one was ever so solemn and severe a follower of virtue and hater of pleasure that he, while imposing on you labors, watchings, and discomforts, would not at the same time bid you do your best to relieve the poverty and misfortunes of others. He would bid you regard as praiseworthy in humanity's name that one man should provide for another man's welfare and comfort—if it is especially humane (and humanity is the virtue most peculiar to man) to relieve the misery of others and, by taking away all sadness from their life, restore them to enjoyment, that is, to pleasure. If so, why should not nature urge everyone to do the same for himself also?

3. By believing in the immortality of the soul, an afterlife of rewards or punishments, and the goodness of God, the Utopians show that they are aware of "natural law," held to be apprehensible by reason.

4. The Utopians represent a people for whom religion is manifest in nature, as it was for the Greeks and the Romans, rather than revealed by God, as it was for the ancient Israelites and, after them, the disciples of Christ. The Utopian is typically reasonable, follows the dictates of reason, and is guided by a beneficent nature that has not been revealed as fallen from an Edenic state of purity and excellence. Hence in Utopia there is no harm in seeking and enjoying pleasure. Nothing in this conception of human nature admits that humankind is inherently corrupted by original sin, a point of doctrine for Christians.

For either a joyous life, that is, a pleasurable life, is evil, in which case not only ought you to help no one to it but, as far as you can, should take it away from everyone as being harmful and deadly, or else, if you not only are permitted but are obliged to win it for others as being good, why should you not do so first of all for yourself, to whom you should show no less favor than to others? When nature bids you to be good to others, she does not command you conversely to be cruel and merciless to yourself. So nature herself, they maintain, prescribes to us a joyous life or, in other words, pleasure, as the end of all our operations. Living according to her prescription they define as virtue.

To pursue this line. Nature calls all men to help one another to a merrier life. (This she certainly does with good reason, for no one is raised so far above the common lot of mankind as to have his sole person the object of nature's care, seeing that she equally favors all whom she endows with the same form.) Consequently nature surely bids you take constant care not so to further your own advantages as to cause disadvantages to your fellows.[5]

Therefore they hold that not only ought contracts between private persons to be observed but also public laws for the distribution of vital commodities, that is to say, the matter of pleasure, provided they have been justly promulgated by a good king or ratified by the common consent of a people neither oppressed by tyranny nor deceived by fraud. As long as such laws are not broken, it is prudence to look after your own interests, and to look after those of the public in addition is a mark of devotion. But to deprive others of their pleasure to secure your own, this is surely an injustice. On the contrary, to take away something from yourself and to give it to others is a duty of humanity and kindness which never takes away as much advantage as it brings back. It is compensated by the return of benefits as well as by the actual consciousness of the good deed. Remembrance of the love and good will of those whom you have benefited gives the mind a greater amount of pleasure than the bodily pleasure which you have forgone would have afforded. Finally—and religion easily brings this home to a mind which readily assents—God repays, in place of a brief and tiny pleasure, immense and never-ending gladness. And so they maintain, having carefully considered and weighed the matter, that all our actions, and even the very virtues exercised in them, look at last to pleasure as their end and happiness.

By pleasure they understand every movement and state of body or mind in which, under the guidance of nature, man delights to dwell. They are right in including man's natural inclinations. For just as the senses as well as right reason aim at whatever is pleasant by nature—whatever is not striven after through wrong-doing, nor involves the loss of something more pleasant, nor is followed by pain—so they hold that whatever things mortals imagine by a futile consensus to be sweet to them in spite of being against nature (as though they had the power to change the nature of things as they do their names) are all so far from making for happiness that they are even a great hindrance to it. The reason is that they possess the minds of persons in whom they have once become deep-seated with a false idea of pleasure so that no room is left anywhere for true and genuine delights. In fact, very many are the things which, though of their own nature they contain no sweetness, nay, a good part of

5. Hythlodaeus describes the classical notion of a benefit, an action that furthers the welfare of a community of persons rather than that of a particular person. The logic of a benefit dictates that an individual can act to confer an advantage not only to himself but also to the community of which he is a part; correspondingly, an action that is to the disadvantage of another individual or his community may not be beneficial to him, however profitable it may seem in the short run.

them very much bitterness, still are, through the perverse attraction of evil desires, not only regarded as the highest pleasures but also counted among the chief reasons that make life worth living.

In the class that follow this spurious pleasure, they put those whom I mentioned before, who think themselves the better men, the better the coat they wear. In this one thing they make a twofold mistake: they are no less deceived in thinking their coat better than in thinking themselves better. If you consider the use of the garment, why is wool of finer thread superior to that of thicker? Yet, as if it were by nature and not by their own mistake that they had the advantage, they hold their heads high and believe some extra worth attaches to themselves thereby. Thus, the honor which, if ill-clad, they would not have ventured to hope for, they require as if of right for a smarter coat. If passed by with some neglect, they are indignant.

Again, does it not show the same stupidity to think so much of empty and unprofitable honors? What natural and true pleasure can another's bared head or bent knees afford you? Will this behavior cure the pain in your own knees or relieve the lunacy in your own head? In this conception of counterfeit pleasure, a strange and sweet madness is displayed by men who imagine themselves to be noble and plume themselves on it and applaud themselves because their fortune has been to be born of certain ancestors of whom the long succession has been counted rich—for that is now the only nobility—and especially rich in landed estates. They consider themselves not a whit less noble even if their ancestors have not left them a square foot or if they themselves have consumed in extravagant living what was left them.

With these persons they class those who, as I said, dote on jewels and gems and who think they become a species of god if ever they secure a fine specimen, especially of the sort which at the period is regarded as of the highest value in their country. It is not everywhere or always that one kind of stone is prized. They will not purchase it unless taken out of its gold setting and exposed to view, and not even then unless the seller takes an oath and gives security that it is a true gem and a true stone, so anxious are they lest a spurious stone in place of a genuine one deceive their eyes. But why should a counterfeited one give less pleasure to your sight when your eye cannot distinguish it from the true article? Both should be of equal value to you, even as they would be, by heaven, to a blind man!

What can be said of those who keep superfluous wealth to please themselves, not with putting the heap to any use but merely with looking at it?[6] Do they feel true pleasure, or are they not rather cheated by false pleasure? Or, what of those who have the opposite failing and hide the gold, which they will never use and perhaps never see again, and who, in their anxiety not to lose it, thereby do lose it? What else but loss is it to deprive yourself of its use, and perhaps all other men too, and to put it back in the ground? And yet you joyfully exult over your hidden treasure as though your mind were now free from all anxiety. Suppose that someone removed it by stealing it and that you died ten years afterwards knowing nothing of the theft. During the whole decade which you lived after the money was stolen, what did it matter to you whether it was stolen or safe? In either case it was of just as little use to you.

Among those who indulge such senseless delights they reckon dicers (whose madness they know not by experience but by hearsay only), as well as hunters and hawkers. What pleasure is there, they ask, in shooting dice upon a table? You have

6. Hythlodaeus implies that money is useful because it can be exchanged for goods in a market. Money exchange is more efficient than barter, as it can always find a commensurable value.

shot them so often that, even if some pleasure had been in it, weariness by now could have arisen from the habitual practice. Or what sweetness can there be, and not rather disgust, in hearing the barking and howling of dogs? Or what greater sensation of pleasure is there when a dog chases a hare than when a dog chases a dog? The same thing happens in both cases: there is racing in both if speed gives you delight.

But if you are attracted by the hope of slaughter and the expectation of a creature being mangled under your eyes, it ought rather to inspire pity when you behold a weak, fugitive, timid, and innocent little hare torn to pieces by a strong, fierce, and cruel dog. In consequence the Utopians have imposed the whole activity of hunting, as unworthy of free men, upon their butchers—a craft, as I explained before, they exercise through their slaves. They regard hunting as the meanest part of the butcher's trade and its other functions as more useful and more honorable, seeing that they do much more positive good and kill animals only from necessity, whereas the hunter seeks nothing but pleasure from the killing and mangling of a poor animal. Even in the case of brute beasts, this desire of looking on bloodshed, in their estimation, either arises from a cruel disposition or degenerates finally into cruelty through the constant practice of such brutal pleasure.

Although the mob of mortals regards these and all similar pursuits—and they are countless—as pleasures, yet the Utopians positively hold them to have nothing to do with true pleasure since there is nothing sweet in them by nature. The fact that for the mob they inspire in the senses a feeling of enjoyment—which seems to be the function of pleasure—does not make them alter their opinion. The enjoyment does not arise from the nature of the thing itself but from their own perverse habit. The latter failing makes them take what is bitter for sweet, just as pregnant women by their vitiated taste suppose pitch and tallow sweeter than honey. Yet it is impossible for any man's judgment, depraved either by disease or by habit, to change the nature of pleasure any more than that of anything else.

The pleasures which they admit as genuine they divide into various classes, some pleasures being attributed to the soul and others to the body. To the soul they ascribe intelligence and the sweetness which is bred of contemplation of truth. To these two are joined the pleasant recollection of a well-spent life and the sure hope of happiness to come.

Bodily pleasure they divide into two kinds. The first is that which fills the sense with clearly perceptible sweetness. Sometimes it comes from the renewal of those organs which have been weakened by our natural heat. These organs are then restored by food and drink. Sometimes it comes from the elimination of things which overload the body. This agreeable sensation occurs when we discharge feces from our bowels or perform the activity generative of children or relieve the itching of some part by rubbing or scratching. Now and then, however, pleasure arises, not in process of restoring anything that our members lack, nor in process of eliminating anything that causes distress, but from something that tickles and affects our senses with a secret but remarkable moving force and so draws them to itself. Such is that pleasure which is engendered by music.

The second kind of bodily pleasure they claim to be that which consists in a calm and harmonious state of the body. This is nothing else than each man's health undisturbed by any disorder. Health, if assailed by no pain, gives delight of itself, though there be no motion arising from pleasure applied from without. Even though it is less obvious and less perceptible by the sense than that overblown craving for eating and drinking, yet none the less many hold it to be the greatest of pleasures.

Almost all the Utopians regard it as great and as practically the foundation and basis of all pleasures. Even by itself it can make the state of life peaceful and desirable, whereas without it absolutely no place is left for any pleasure. The absence of pain without the presence of health they regard as insensibility rather than pleasure.

They long ago rejected the position of those who held that a state of stable and tranquil health (for this question, too, had been actively discussed among them) was not to be counted as a pleasure because its presence, they said, could not be felt except through some motion from without. But on the other hand now they almost all agree that health is above all things conducive to pleasure. Since in disease, they query, there is pain, which is the bitter enemy of pleasure no less than disease is of health, why should not pleasure in turn be found in the tranquillity of health? They think that it is of no importance in the discussion whether you say that disease is pain or that disease is accompanied with pain, for it comes to the same thing either way. To be sure, if you hold that health is either a pleasure or the necessary cause of pleasure, as fire is of heat, in both ways the conclusion is that those who have permanent health cannot be without pleasure.

Besides, while we eat, say they, what is that but health, which has begun to be impaired, fighting against hunger, with food as its comrade in arms? While it gradually gains strength, the very progress to the usual vigor supplies the pleasure by which we are thus restored. Shall the health which delights in conflict not rejoice when it has gained the victory? When at length it has successfully acquired its former strength, which was its sole object through the conflict, shall it immediately become insensible and not recognize and embrace its own good? The assertion that health cannot be felt they think to be far wide of the truth. Who in a waking state, ask they, does not feel that he is in good health—except the man who is not? Who is bound fast by such insensibility or lethargy that he does not confess that health is agreeable and delightful to him? And what is delightful except pleasure under another name?

To sum up, they cling above all to mental pleasures, which they value as the first and foremost of all pleasures. Of these the principal part they hold to arise from the practice of the virtues and the consciousness of a good life. Of these pleasures which the body supplies, they give the palm to health. The delight of eating and drinking, and anything that gives the same sort of enjoyment, they think desirable, but only for the sake of health. Such things are not pleasant in themselves but only in so far as they resist the secret encroachment of ill health. Just as a wise man should pray that he may escape disease rather than crave a remedy for it and that he may drive pain off rather than seek relief from it, so it would be better not to need this kind of pleasure rather than to be soothed by it.

If a person thinks that his felicity consists in this kind of pleasure, he must admit that he will be in the greatest happiness if his lot happens to be a life which is spent in perpetual hunger, thirst, itching, eating, drinking, scratching, and rubbing. Who does not see that such a life is not only disgusting but wretched? These pleasures are surely the lowest of all as being most adulterated, for they never occur unless they are coupled with the pains which are their opposites. For example, with the pleasure of eating is united hunger—and on no fair terms, for the pain is the stronger and lasts the longer. It comes into existence before the pleasure and does not end until the pleasure dies with it. Such pleasures they hold should not be highly valued and only insofar as they are necessary. Yet they enjoy even these pleasures and gratefully acknowledge the kindness of mother nature who, with alluring sweetness, coaxes her offspring to that which of necessity they must constantly do.

In what discomfort should we have to live if, like all other sicknesses which less frequently assail us, so also these daily diseases of hunger and thirst had to be expelled by bitter poisons and drugs?

Beauty, strength, and nimbleness—these as special and pleasant gifts of nature they gladly cherish. Nay, even those pleasures entering by the ears, eyes, or nostrils, which nature intended to be peculiarly characteristic of man (for no other species of living creature either takes in the form and fairness of the world or is affected by the pleasantness of smell, except in choice of food, or distinguishes harmonious and dissonant intervals of sound)—these, too, I say, they follow after as pleasant seasonings of life.[7] But in all they make this limitation: that the lesser is not to interfere with the greater and that pleasure is not to produce pain in aftermath. Pain they think a necessary consequence if the pleasure is base.

But to despise the beauty of form, to impair the strength of the body, to turn nimbleness into sluggishness, to exhaust the body by fasts, to injure one's health, and to reject all the other favors of nature, unless a man neglects these advantages to himself in providing more zealously for the pleasure of other persons or of the public, in return for which sacrifice he expects a greater pleasure from God—but otherwise to deal harshly with oneself for a vain and shadowy reputation of virtue to no man's profit or for preparing oneself more easily to bear adversities which may never come—this attitude they think is extreme madness and the sign of a mind which is both cruel to itself and ungrateful to nature, to whom it disdains to be indebted and therefore renounces all her benefits.

This is their view of virtue and pleasure. They believe that human reason can attain to no truer view, unless a heaven-sent religion inspire man with something more holy. Whether in this stand they are right or wrong, time does not permit us to examine—nor is it necessary. We have taken upon ourselves only to describe their principles, and not also to defend them. But of this I am sure, that whatever you think of their ideas, there is nowhere in the world a more excellent people nor a happier commonwealth. They are nimble and active of body, and stronger than you would expect from their stature. The latter, however, is not dwarfish. Though they have not a very fertile soil or a very wholesome climate, they protect themselves against the atmosphere by temperate living and make up for the defects of the land by diligent labor. Consequently, nowhere in the world is there a more plentiful supply of grain and cattle, nowhere are men's bodies more vigorous and subject to fewer diseases. Not only may you behold the usual agricultural tasks carefully administered there, whereby the naturally barren soil is improved by art and industry, but you may also see how a whole forest has been uprooted in one place by the hands of the people and planted in another. Herein they were thinking not so much of abundance as of transport, that they might have wood closer to the sea or the rivers or the cities themselves. For it takes less labor to convey grain than timber to a distance by land.

The people in general are easygoing, good-tempered, ingenious, and leisure-loving. They patiently do their share of manual labor when occasion demands, though otherwise they are by no means fond of it. In their devotion to mental study they are unwearied. When they had heard from us about the literature and learning of the Greeks (for in Latin there was nothing, apart from history and poetry, which

7. Just as the Utopians imagine humankind without original sin, so they cannot imagine any point in ascetic discipline of the body for the sake of curbing or controlling its inherent tendency to sin.

seemed likely to gain their great approval), it was wonderful to see their extreme desire for permission to master them through our instruction.

We began, therefore, to give them public lessons, more at first that we should not seem to refuse the trouble than that we expected any success. But after a little progress, their diligence made us at once feel sure that our own diligence would not be bestowed in vain. They began so easily to imitate the shapes of the letters, so readily to pronounce the words, so quickly to learn by heart, and so faithfully to reproduce what they had learned that it was a perfect wonder to us. The explanation was that most of them were scholars picked for their ability and mature in years, who undertook to learn their tasks not only fired by their own free will but acting under orders of the senate. In less than three years they were perfect in the language and able to peruse good authors without any difficulty unless the text had faulty readings. According to my conjecture, they got hold of Greek literature more easily because it was somewhat related to their own. I suspect that their race was derived from the Greek because their language, which in almost all other respects resembles the Persian, retains some traces of Greek in the names of their cities and officials.

When about to go on the fourth voyage, I put on board, in place of wares to sell, a fairly large package of books,[8] having made up my mind never to return rather than to come back soon. They received from me most of Plato's works, several of Aristotle's, as well as Theophrastus on plants, which I regret to say was mutilated in parts. During the voyage an ape found the book, left lying carelessly about, and in wanton sport tore out and destroyed several pages in various sections. Of grammarians they have only Lascaris, for I did not take Theodore with me. They have no dictionaries except those of Hesychius and Dioscorides. They are very fond of the works of Plutarch and captivated by the wit and pleasantry of Lucian. Of the poets they have Aristophanes, Homer, and Euripides, together with Sophocles in the small Aldine type. Of the historians they possess Thucydides and Herodotus, as well as Herodian.

In medicine, moreover, my companion Tricius Apinatus had carried with him some small treatises of Hippocrates and the *Ars medica* of Galen, to which books they attribute great value. Even though there is scarcely a nation in the whole world that needs medicine less, yet nowhere is it held in greater honor—and this for the reason that they regard the knowledge of it as one of the finest and most useful branches of philosophy. When by the help of this philosophy they explore the secrets of nature, they appear to themselves not only to get great pleasure in doing so but also to win the highest approbation of the Author and Maker of nature. They presume that, like

8. Hythlodaeus has given the Utopians only works in Greek, even though they cover topics in the history of Rome. By this, More clearly intended to emphasize what he thought was the intellectual superiority of Greek over Roman culture. Beyond the works of Plato and Aristotle, Hythlodaeus's library contains the works of Theophrastus (3rd century B.C.E.), who wrote a history of plants; Constantine Lascaris and Theodore of Gaza, both grammarians of the 15th century; Hesychius, a Greek lexicographer of the 4th century B.C.E.; Dioscurides, a Greek physician of the 1st century, who wrote a medical textbook, known and used through the early modern period; Plutarch, a Greek biographer and moralist of the 2nd century; Lucian, a Greek rhetorician of the 2nd century, who wrote satirical dialogues; Aristophanes, a Greek dramatist of the 4th century B.C.E., who wrote comic drama; Homer, the name given the author or authors of the Greek epics, the *Iliad* and the *Odyssey*, committed to writing about 800 B.C.E.; and Euripides and Sophocles, both Greek tragedians of the 5th century B.C.E. Herodotus and Thucydides lived during the 5th century B.C.E.; Herodotus wrote of the wars between the kingdoms of the near east and the Greek states in his *Histories*, Thucydides of the tragic fall of the Athenian state in his *Peloponnesian Wars*. Herodian, a Syrian historian, wrote, in Greek, of the Roman emperors from the death of Marcus Aurelius in 180 to 238 C.E. "Tricius Apinatus" is a fictitious author, but Hippocrates and Galen were Greek physicians of the 5th century B.C.E. and the 2nd century, respectively, whose medical treatises were popular until the end of the 17th century. "Aldine type" was the particular typeface used by the early 16-century Venetian printer Aldus Manutius, who was famous for his publication of fine editions of Greek authors.

all other artificers, He has set forth the visible mechanism of the world as a spectacle for man, whom alone He has made capable of appreciating such a wonderful thing. Therefore He prefers a careful and diligent beholder and admirer of His work to one who like an unreasoning brute beast passes by so great and so wonderful a spectacle stupidly and stolidly.

Thus, trained in all learning, the minds of the Utopians are exceedingly apt in the invention of the arts which promote the advantage and convenience of life. Two, however, they owe to us, the art of printing and the manufacture of paper—though not entirely to us but to a great extent also to themselves. When we showed them the Aldine printing in paper books, we talked about the material of which paper is made and the art of printing without giving a detailed explanation, for none of us was expert in either art. With the greatest acuteness they promptly guessed how it was done. Though previously they wrote only on parchment, bark, and papyrus, from this time they tried to manufacture paper and print letters. Their first attempts were not very successful, but by frequent experiment they soon mastered both. So great was their success that if they had copies of Greek authors, they would have no lack of books. But at present they have no more than I have mentioned, but by printing books they have increased their stock by many thousands of copies.

Whoever, coming to their land on a sight-seeing tour, is recommended by any special intellectual endowment or is acquainted with many countries through long travel, is sure of a hearty welcome, for they delight in hearing what is happening in the whole world. On this score our own landing was pleasing to them. Few persons, however, come to them in the way of trade. What could they bring except iron, or what everybody would rather take back home with him—gold and silver! And as to articles of export, the Utopians think it wiser to carry them out of the country themselves than to let strangers come to fetch them. By this policy they get more information about foreign nations and do not forget by disuse their skill in navigation.

Slavery, [Etc.]

Prisoners of war are not enslaved unless captured in wars fought by the Utopians themselves; nor are the sons of slaves,[9] nor anyone who was in slavery when acquired of slaves, nor anyone whom they could acquire from slavery in other countries. Their slaves are either such or such as have been condemned to death elsewhere for some offense. The greater number are of this latter kind. They carry away many of them; sometimes they buy them cheaply; but often they ask for them and get them for nothing. These classes of slaves they keep not only continually at work but also in chains. Their own countrymen are dealt with more harshly, since their conduct is regarded as all the more regrettable and deserving a more severe punishment as an object lesson because, having had an excellent rearing to a virtuous life, they still could not be restrained from crime.

There is yet another class of slaves, for sometimes a hard-working and poverty-stricken drudge of another country voluntarily chooses slavery in Utopia. These individuals are well treated and, except that they have a little more work assigned to them as being used to it, are dealt with almost as leniently as citizens. If anyone

9. More uses the Latin word *servus*, which means servant, slave, and serf. Most commonly captives in war, slaves were also persons punished for crime, as in Utopia. Voluntary slavery, aside from indentured servitude (for a term), was rare except in theory; presumably such persons chose to work as slaves in exchange for a subsistence living.

wishes to depart, which seldom happens, they do not detain him against his will nor send him away empty-handed.

The sick, as I said, are very lovingly cared for, nothing being omitted which may restore them to health, whether in the way of medicine or diet. They console the incurable diseased by sitting and conversing with them and by applying all possible alleviations. But if a disease is not only incurable but also distressing and agonizing without any cessation, then the priests and the public officials exhort the man, since he is now unequal to all life's duties, a burden to himself, and a trouble to others, and is living beyond the time of his death, to make up his mind not to foster the pest and plague any longer nor to hesitate to die now that life is torture to him but, relying on good hope, to free himself from this bitter life as from prison and the rack, or else voluntarily to permit others to free him.[1] In this course he will act wisely, since by death he will put an end not to enjoyment but to torture. Because in doing so he will be obeying the counsels of the priests, who are God's interpreters, it will be a pious and holy action.

Those who have been persuaded by these arguments either starve themselves to death or, being put to sleep, are set free without the sensation of dying. But they do not make away with anyone against his will, nor in such a case do they relax in the least their attendance upon him. They do believe that death counseled by authority is honorific. But if anyone commits suicide without having obtained the approval of priests and senate, they deem him unworthy of either fire or earth and cast his body ignominiously into a marsh without proper burial.

Women do not marry till eighteen, men not till they are four years older. If before marriage a man or woman is convicted of secret intercourse, he or she is severely punished, and they are forbidden to marry altogether unless the governor's pardon remits their guilt. In addition, both father and mother of the family in whose house the offense was committed incur great disgrace as having been neglectful in doing their duties. The reason why they punish this offence so severely is their foreknowledge that, unless persons are carefully restrained from promiscuous intercourse, few will contract the tie of marriage, in which a whole life must be spent with one companion and all the troubles incidental to it must be patiently borne.

In choosing mates, they seriously and strictly espouse a custom which seemed to us very foolish and extremely ridiculous. The woman, whether maiden or widow, is shown naked to the suitor by a worthy and respectable matron, and similarly the suitor is presented naked before the maiden by a discreet man. We laughed at this custom and condemned it as foolish. They, on the other hand, marvelled at the remarkable folly of all other nations. In buying a colt, where there is question of only a little money, persons are so cautious that though it is almost bare they will not buy until they have taken off the saddle and removed all the trappings for fear some sore lies concealed under these coverings. Yet in the choice of a wife, an action which will cause either pleasure or disgust to follow them the rest of their lives, they are so careless that, while the rest of her body is covered with clothes, they estimate the value of the whole woman from hardly a single handbreadth of her, only the face being visible, and clasp her to themselves not without great danger of their agreeing ill together if something afterwards gives them offense.

1. Neither suicide nor euthanasia was considered immoral in Greek and Roman society.

All are not so wise as to regard only the character of the spouse, and even in the marriages of the wise, bodily attractions also are no small enhancement to the virtues of the mind. Certainly such foul deformity may be hidden beneath these coverings that it may quite alienate a man's mind from his wife when bodily separation is no longer lawful. If such a deformity arises by chance after the marriage has been contracted, each person must bear his own fate, but beforehand the laws ought to protect him from being entrapped by guile.

This provision was the more necessary because the Utopians are the only people in those parts of the world who are satisfied with one spouse and because matrimony there is seldom broken except by death, unless it be for adultery or for intolerable offensiveness of character. When husband or wife is thus offended, leave is granted by the senate to take another mate.[2] The other party perpetually lives a life of disgrace as well as of celibacy. But they cannot endure the repudiation of an unwilling wife, who is in no way to blame, because some bodily calamity has befallen her. They judge it cruel that a person should be abandoned when most in need of comfort and that old age, since it both entails disease and is a disease itself, should have only an unreliable and weak fidelity.

It sometimes happens, however, that when a married couple agree insufficiently in their dispositions and both find others with whom they hope to live more agreeably, they separate by mutual consent and contract fresh unions, but not without the sanction of the senate. The latter allows of no divorce until its members and their wives have carefully gone into the case. Even then they do not readily give consent because they know that it is a very great drawback to cementing the affection between husband and wife if they have before them the easy hope of a fresh union.

Violators of the conjugal tie are punished by the strictest form of slavery. If both parties are married, the injured parties, provided they consent, are divorced from their adulterous mates and couple together, or else are allowed to marry whom they like. But if one of the injured parties continues to feel affection for so undeserving a mate, it is not forbidden to have the marriage continue in force on condition that the party is willing to accompany and share the labor of the other who has been condemned to slavery. Now and then it happens that the penance of the one and the dutiful assiduity of the other move the compassion of the governor and win back their liberty. Relapse into the same offense, however, involves the penalty of death.

For all other crimes there is no law prescribing any fixed penalty, but the punishment is assigned by the senate according to the atrocity, or veniality, of the individual crime. Husbands correct their wives, and parents their children, unless the offense is so serious that it is to the advantage of public morality to have it punished openly. Generally the worst offenses are punished by the sentence of slavery since this prospect, they think, is no less formidable to the criminal and more advantageous to the state than if they make haste to put the offenders to death and get them out of the way at once. Their labor is more profitable than their death, and their example lasts longer to deter others from like crimes. But if they rebel and kick against this treatment, they are thereupon put to death like untameable beasts that cannot be restrained by prison or chain. If they are patient, however, they are not entirely deprived of all hope. When tamed by long and hard punishment, if they show such

2. In England, divorce was granted only on the grounds of adultery. By contrast, the Utopians grant divorce for incompatibility and extend the privilege to the wife as well as the husband. Adultery, however, is punished with slavery.

repentance as testifies that they are more sorry for their sin than for their punishment, then sometimes by the prerogative of the governor and sometimes by the vote of the people their slavery is either lightened or remitted altogether.

To tempt another to an impure act is no less punishable than the commission of that impure act. In every crime the deliberate and avowed attempt is counted equal to the deed, for they think that failure ought not to benefit one who did everything in his power not to fail.

They are very fond of fools.[3] It is a great disgrace to treat them with insult, but there is no prohibition against deriving pleasure from their foolery. The latter, they think, is of the greatest benefit to the fools themselves. If anyone is so stern and morose that he is not amused with anything they either do or say, they do not entrust him with the care of a fool. They fear that he may not treat him with sufficient indulgence since he would find in him neither use nor even amusement, which is his sole faculty.

To deride a man for a disfigurement or the loss of a limb is counted as base and disfiguring, not to the man who is laughed at but to him who laughs, for foolishly upbraiding a man with something as if it were a fault which he was powerless to avoid. While they consider it a sign of a sluggish and feeble mind not to preserve natural beauty, it is, in their judgment, disgraceful affectation to help it out by cosmetics. Experience itself shows them how no elegance of outward form recommends wives to husbands as much as probity and reverence. Some men are attracted only by a handsome shape, but no man's love is kept permanently except by virtue and obedience.

Not merely do they discourage crime by punishment but they offer honors to invite men to virtue. Hence, to great men who have done conspicuous service to their country they set up in the market place statues to stand as a record of noble exploits and, at the same time, to have the glory of forefathers serve their descendants as a spur and stimulus to virtue.

The man who solicits votes to obtain any office is deprived completely of the hope of holding any office at all. They live together in affection and good will. No official is haughty or formidable. They are called fathers and show that character. Honor is paid them willingly, as it should be, and is not exacted from the reluctant. The governor himself is distinguished from citizens not by a robe or a crown but by the carrying of a handful of grain, just as the mark of the high priest is a wax candle borne before him.

They have very few laws because very few are needed for persons so educated. The chief fault they find with other peoples is that almost innumerable books of laws and commentaries are not sufficient. They themselves think it most unfair that any group of men should be bound by laws which are either too numerous to be read through or too obscure to be understood by anyone.

Moreover, they absolutely banish from their country all lawyers, who cleverly manipulate cases and cunningly argue legal points. They consider it a good thing that every man should plead his own cause and say the same to the judge as he would tell his counsel. Thus there is less ambiguity and the truth is more easily elicited when a man, uncoached in deception by a lawyer, conducts his own case and the judge skillfully weighs each statement and helps untutored minds to defeat the false accusations of the crafty. To secure these advantages in other countries is difficult, owing to the

3. In early modern Europe, a "fool" could be a professional jester; usually, he was employed at a royal or noble court and had special license to amuse and even criticize his master.

immense mass of extremely complicated laws. But with the Utopians each man is expert in law. First, they have, as I said, very few laws and, secondly, they regard the most obvious interpretation of the law as the most fair interpretation.

This policy follows from their reasoning that, since all laws are promulgated to remind every man of his duty, the more recondite interpretation reminds only very few (for there are few who can arrive at it) whereas the more simple and obvious sense of the laws is open to all. Otherwise, what difference would it make for the common people, who are the most numerous and also most in need of instruction, whether you framed no law at all or whether the interpretation of the law you framed was such that no one could elicit it except by great ingenuity and long argument? Now, the untrained judgment of the common people cannot attain to the meaning of such an interpretation nor can their lives be long enough, seeing that they are wholly taken up with getting a living.

These virtues of the Utopians have spurred their neighbors (who are free and independent since many of them were long ago delivered from tyrants by the Utopians) to obtain officials from them, some for one year and others for five years. On the expiration of their office they escort them home with honor and praise and bring back successors with them to their own country. Certainly these peoples make very good and wholesome provision for the commonwealth. Seeing that the latter's prosperity or ruin depends on the character of officials, of whom could they have made a wiser choice than of those who cannot be drawn from the path of honor by any bribe since it is no good to them as they will shortly return home, nor influenced by crooked partiality or animosity toward any since they are strangers to the citizens? These two evils, favoritism and avarice, wherever they have settled in men's judgments, instantly destroy all justice, the strongest sinew of the commonwealth. The nations who seek their administrators from Utopia are called allies by them; the name of friend is reserved for all the others whom they have benefited.

Treaties which all other nations so often conclude among themselves, break, and renew, they never make with any nation. "What is the use of a treaty," they ask, "as though nature of herself did not sufficiently bind one man to another? If a person does not regard nature, do you suppose he will care anything about words?"

They are led to this opinion chiefly because in those parts of the world treaties and alliances between kings are not observed with much good faith. In Europe, however, and especially in those parts where the faith and religion of Christ prevails, the majesty of treaties is everywhere holy and inviolable, partly through the justice and goodness of kings, partly through the reverence and fear of the Sovereign Pontiffs. Just as the latter themselves undertake nothing which they do not most conscientiously perform, so they command all other rulers to abide by their promises in every way and compel the recalcitrant by pastoral censure and severe reproof.[4] Popes are perfectly right, of course, in thinking it a most disgraceful thing that those who are specially called the faithful should not faithfully adhere to their commitments.

But in that new world, which is almost as far removed from ours by the equator as their life and character are different from ours, there is no trust in treaties. The more numerous and holy the ceremonies with which a treaty is struck the more quickly is it broken. They find some defect in the wording, which sometimes they cunningly devise of set purpose, so that they can never be held by such strong bonds

4. More is being ironic in extolling the faithful observance of treaties by the papacy. Pope Julius II, who died a few years before the publication of More's treatise, was notorious for breaking his word.

as not somehow to escape from them and break both the treaty and their faith. If this cunning, nay fraud and deceit, were found to have occurred in the contracts of private persons, the treaty-makers with great disdain would exclaim against it as sacrilegious and meriting the gallows—though the very same men plume themselves on being the authors of such advice when given to kings.

In consequence men think either that all justice is only a plebeian and low virtue which is far below the majesty of kings or that there are at least two forms of it: the one which goes on foot and creeps on the ground, fit only for the common sort and bound by many chains so that it can never overstep its barriers; the other a virtue of kings, which, as it is more august than that of ordinary folk, is also far freer so that everything is permissible to it—except what it finds disagreeable.

This behavior, as I said, of rulers there who keep their treaties so badly is, I suppose, the reason why the Utopians make none; if they lived here, they would perhaps change their minds. Nevertheless they believe that, though treaties are faithfully observed, it is a pity that the custom of making them at all had grown up. The result (as though peoples which are divided by the slight interval of a hill or a river were joined by no bond of nature) is men's persuasion that they are born one another's adversaries and enemies and that they are right in aiming at one another's destruction except in so far as treaties prevent it. What is more, even when treaties are made, friendship does not grow up but the license of freebooting continues to the extent that, for lack of skill in drawing up the treaty, no sufficient precaution to prevent this activity has been included in the articles. But the Utopians, on the contrary, think that nobody who has done you no harm should be accounted an enemy, that the fellowship created by nature takes the place of a treaty, and that men are better and more firmly joined together by good will than by pacts, by spirit than by words.

Military Affairs

War, as an activity fit only for beasts and yet practiced by no kind of beast so constantly as by man, they regard with utter loathing. Against the usage of almost all nations they count nothing so inglorious as glory sought in war. Nevertheless men and women alike assiduously exercise themselves in military training on fixed days lest they should be unfit for war when need requires. Yet they do not lightly go to war. They do so only to protect their own territory or to drive an invading enemy out of their friends' lands or, in pity for a people oppressed by tyranny, to deliver them by force of arms from the yoke and slavery of the tyrant, a course prompted by human sympathy.

They oblige their friends with help, not always indeed to defend them merely but sometimes also to requite and avenge injuries previously done to them. They act, however, only if they themselves are consulted before any step is taken and if they themselves initiate the war after they have approved the cause and demanded restitution in vain. They take the final step of war not only when a hostile inroad has carried off booty but also much more fiercely when the merchants among their friends undergo unjust persecution under the color of justice in any other country, either on the pretext of laws in themselves unjust or by the distortion of laws in themselves good.

Such was the origin of the war which the Utopians had waged a little before our time on behalf of the Nephelogetes[5] against the Alaopolitans. The Nephelogetic

5. "Cloud born" (insubstantial) people; the Alaopolitans are "citizens without a people or a country"—that is, stateless.

traders suffered a wrong, as they thought, under pretence of law, but whether right or wrong, it was avenged by a fierce war. Into this war the neighboring nations brought their energies and resources to assist the power and to intensify the rancor of both sides. Most flourishing nations were either shaken to their foundations or grievously afflicted. The troubles upon troubles that arose were ended only by the enslavement and surrender of the Alaopolitans. Since the Utopians were not fighting in their own interest, they yielded them into the power of the Nephelogetes, a people who, when the Alaopolitans were prosperous, were not in the least comparable to them.

So severely do the Utopians punish wrong done to their friends, even in money matters—but not wrongs done to themselves. When they lose their goods anywhere through fraud, but without personal violence, their anger goes no further than abstention from trade with that nation until satisfaction is made. The reason is not that they care less for their citizens than their allies. They are more grieved at their allies' pecuniary loss than their own because their friends' merchants suffer severely by the loss as it falls on their private property, but their own citizens lose nothing but what comes from the common stock and what was plentiful and, as it were, superfluous at home—or else it would not have been exported. As a result, the loss is not felt by any individual. They consider it excessively cruel to avenge such a loss by the death of many when the disadvantage of the loss affects neither the life nor the subsistence of any of their own people.

If a Utopian citizen, however, is wrongfully disabled or killed anywhere, whether the plot is due to the government or to a private citizen, they first ascertain the facts by an embassy and then, if the guilty persons are not surrendered, they cannot be appeased but forthwith declare war. If the guilty persons are surrendered, they are punished either with death or with enslavement.

They not only regret but blush at a victory that has cost much bloodshed, thinking it folly to purchase wares, however precious, too dear. If they overcome and crush the enemy by stratagem and cunning, they feel great pride and celebrate a public triumph over the victory and put up a trophy as for a strenuous exploit. They boast themselves as having acted with valor and heroism whenever their victory is such as no animal except man could have won, that is, by strength of intellect; for, by strength of body, say they, bears, lions, boars, wolves, dogs, and other wild beasts are wont to fight. Most of them are superior to us in brawn and fierceness, but they are all inferior in cleverness and calculation.

Their one and only object in war is to secure that which, had it been obtained beforehand, would have prevented the declaration of war. If that is out of the question, they require such severe punishment of those on whom they lay the blame that for the future they may be afraid to attempt anything of the same sort. These are their chief interests in the enterprise, which they set about promptly to secure, yet taking more care to avoid danger than to win praise or fame.

The moment war is declared, they arrange that simultaneously a great number of placards, made more effective by bearing their public seal, should be set up secretly in the most prominent spots of enemy territory. Herein they promise huge rewards to anyone who will kill the enemy king. Further, they offer smaller sums, but those considerable, for the heads of the individuals whose names they specify in the same proclamations. These are the men whom, next to the king himself, they regard as responsible for the hostile measures taken against them. Whatever reward they fix for an assassin, they double for the man who brings any of the denounced parties alive to them. They actually offer the same rewards, with a guarantee of personal safety, to the persons proscribed, if they will turn against their fellows.

So it swiftly comes about that their enemies suspect all outsiders and, in addition, neither trust nor are loyal to one another. They are in a state of utter panic and no less peril. It is well known that it has often happened that many of them, and especially the king himself, have been betrayed by those in whom they had placed the greatest trust, so easily do bribes incite men to commit every kind of crime. They are boundless in their offers of reward. Remembering, however, what a risk they invite the man to run, they take care that the greatness of the peril is balanced by the extent of the rewards. In consequence they promise and faithfully pay down not only an immense amount of gold but also landed property with high income in very secure places in the territory of friends.

This habit of bidding for and purchasing an enemy, which is elsewhere condemned as the cruel deed of a degenerate nature, they think reflects great credit, first on their wisdom because they thus bring to a conclusion great wars without any battle at all, and secondly on their humanity and mercy because by the death of a few guilty people they purchase the lives of many harmless persons who would have fallen in battle, both on their own side and that of the enemy. They are almost as sorry for the throng and mass of the enemy as for their own citizens. They know that the common folk do not go to war of their own accord but are driven to it by the madness of kings.

If this plan does not succeed, they sow the seeds of dissension broadcast and foster strife by leading a brother of the king or one of the noblemen to hope that he may obtain the throne. If internal strife dies down, then they stir up and involve the neighbors of their enemies by reviving some forgotten claims to dominion such as kings have always at their disposal. Promising their own assistance for the war, they supply money liberally but are very chary of sending their own citizens. They hold them so singularly dear and regard one another of such value that they would not care to exchange any of their own people for the king of the opposite party. As to gold and silver, since they keep it all for this one use, they pay it out without any reluctance, for they would live just as well if they spent it all. Moreover, in addition to the riches which they keep at home, they have also a vast treasure abroad in that many nations, as I said before, are in their debt.

With the riches, they hire and send to war soldiers from all parts, but especially from among the Zapoletans.[6] These people live five hundred miles to the east of Utopia and are fearsome, rough, and wild. They prefer their own rugged woods and mountains among which they are bred. They are a hard race, capable of enduring heat, cold, and toil, lacking all refinements, engaging in no farming, careless about the houses they live in and the clothes they wear, and occupied only with their flocks and herds. To a great extent they live by hunting and plundering. They are born for warfare and zealously seek an opportunity for fighting. When they find it, they eagerly embrace it. Leaving the country in great force, they offer themselves at a cheap rate to anyone who needs fighting men. The only trade they know in life is that by which they seek their death.

6. "Busy sellers," that is, of their services.

They fight with ardor and incorruptible loyalty for those from whom they receive their pay. Yet they bind themselves for no fixed period but take sides on such terms that the next day when higher pay is offered them, even by the enemy, they take his side, and then the day after, if a trifle more is offered to tempt them back, return to the side they took at first.

In almost every war that breaks out there are many of them in both armies. It is a daily occurrence that men connected by ties of blood, who were hired on the same side and so became intimate with one another, soon afterward are separated into two hostile forces and meet in battle. Forgetting both kinship and friendship, they run one another through with the utmost ferocity. They are driven to mutual destruction for no other reason than that they are hired by opposing kings for a tiny sum of which they take such careful account that they are readily induced to change sides by the addition of a penny to their daily rate of pay. So have they speedily acquired a habit of avarice which nevertheless profits them not one whit. What they get by exposing their lives they spend instantly in debauchery and that of a dreary sort.

This people will battle for the Utopians against any mortals whatsoever because their service is hired at a rate higher than they could get anywhere else. The Utopians, just as they seek good men to use them, so enlist these villains to abuse them. When need requires, they thrust them under the tempting bait of great promises into greatest perils. Generally a large proportion never returns to claim payment, but the survivors are honestly paid what has been promised them to incite them again to like deeds of daring. The Utopians do not care in the least how many Zapoletans they lose, thinking that they would be the greatest benefactors to the human race if they could relieve the world of all the dregs of this abominable and impious people.

Next to them they employ the forces of the people for whom they are fighting and then auxiliary squadrons of all their other friends. Last of all they add a contingent of their own citizens out of which they appoint some man of tried valor to command the whole army. For him they have two substitutes who hold no rank as long as he is safe. But if he is captured or killed, the first of the two becomes as it were his heir and successor, and he, if events require, is succeeded by the third. They thus avoid the disorganization of the whole army through the endangering of the commander, the fortunes of war being always incalculable.

In each city a choice is made among those who volunteer. No one is driven to fight abroad against his will because they are convinced that if anyone is somewhat timorous by nature, he not only will not acquit himself manfully but will throw fear into his companions. Should any war, however, assail their own country, they put the fainthearted, if physically fit, on shipboard mixed among the braver sort or put them here and there to man the walls where they cannot run away. Thus, shame at being seen to flinch by their own side, the close quarters with the enemy, and the withdrawal of hope of escape combine to overpower their timidity, and often they make a virtue of extreme necessity.

Just as no one of the men is made to go to a foreign war against his will, so if the women are anxious to accompany their husbands on military service, not only do they not forbid them but actually encourage them and incite them by expressions of praise. When they have gone out, they are placed alongside their husbands on the battle front. Each man is surrounded by his own children and relations by marriage and blood so that those may be closest and lend one another mutual assistance whom nature most impels to help one another. It is the greatest reproach for one spouse to return without the other or for a son to come back having lost his parent.

The result is that, when it comes to hand-to-hand fighting, if the enemy stands his ground, the battle is long and anguished and ends with mutual extermination.

As I have said, they take every care not to be obliged to fight in person as long as they can finish the war by the assistance of hired substitutes. When personal service is inevitable, they are as courageous in fighting as they were ingenious in avoiding it as long as they might. They are not fierce in the first onslaught, but their strength increases by degrees through their slow and hard resistance. Their spirit is so stubborn that they would rather be cut to pieces than give way. The absence of anxiety about livelihood at home, as well as the removal of that worry which troubles men about the future of their families (for such solicitude everywhere breaks the highest courage), makes their spirit exalted and disdainful of defeat.

Moreover, their expert training in military discipline gives them confidence. Finally, their good and sound opinions, in which they have been trained from childhood both by teaching and by the good institutions of their country, give them additional courage. So they do not hold their life so cheap as recklessly to throw it away and not so immoderately dear as greedily and shamefully to hold fast to it when honor bids them give it up.

While the battle is everywhere most hot, a band of picked youths who have taken an oath to devote themselves to the task hunt out the opposing general. They openly attack him; they secretly ambush him. They assail him both from far and from near. A long and continuous wedge of men, fresh comers constantly taking the place of those exhausted, keeps up the attack. It seldom happens, unless he look to his safety by running away, that he is not killed or does not fall alive into the enemy's hands.

If the victory rests with them, there is no indiscriminate carnage, for they would rather take the routed as prisoners than kill them. They never pursue the fleeing enemy without keeping one division all the time drawn up ready for engagement under their banners. To such an extent is this the case that if, after the rest of the army has been beaten, they win the victory by this last reserve force, they prefer to let all their enemies escape rather than get into the habit of pursuing them with their own ranks in disorder. They remember that more than once it has happened to themselves that, when the great bulk of their army has been beaten and routed and when the enemy, flushed with victory, has been chasing the fugitives in all directions, a few of their number, held in reserve and ready for emergencies, have suddenly attacked the scattered and straying enemy who, feeling themselves quite safe, were off their guard. Thereby they have changed the whole fortune of the battle and, wresting out of the enemy's hands a certain and undoubted victory, have, though conquered, conquered their conquerors in turn.

It is not easy to say whether they are more cunning in laying ambushes or more cautious in avoiding them. You would think they contemplated flight when that is the very last thing intended; but, on the other hand, when they do determine to flee, you would imagine that they were thinking of anything but that. If they feel themselves to be inferior in number or in position, either by night they noiselessly march and move their camp or evade the enemy by some stratagem, or else by day they retire so imperceptibly and in such regular order that it is as dangerous to attack them in retreat as it would be in advance. They protect their camp most carefully by a deep and broad ditch, the earth taken out of it being thrown inside. They do not utilize the labor of the lowest workmen for the purpose, but the soldiers do it with their own hands. The whole army is set at work, except those who watch under arms in front of the rampart in case of emergencies. Thus, through the efforts of so many, they complete great fortifications, enclosing a large space, with incredible speed.

They wear armor strong enough to turn blows but easily adapted to all motions and gestures of the body. They do not feel any awkwardness even in swimming, for they practice swimming under arms as part of their apprenticeship in military discipline. The weapons they use at a distance are arrows, which they shoot with great strength and sureness of aim not only on foot but also on horseback. At close quarters they use not swords but battle-axes which, because of their sharp point and great weight, are deadly weapons, whether employed for thrusting or hacking. They are very clever in inventing war machines. They hide them, when made, with the greatest care lest, if made known before required by circumstances, they be rather a laughingstock than an instrument of war. In making them, their first object is to have them easy to carry and handy to pivot.

If a truce is made with the enemy, they keep it so religiously as not to break it even under provocation. They do not ravage the enemy's territory nor burn his crops. Rather, they do not even allow them to be trodden down by the feet of men or horses, as far as can be, thinking that they grow for their own benefit. They injure no noncombatant unless he is a spy. When cities are surrendered to them, they keep them intact. They do not plunder even those which they have stormed but put to death the men who prevented surrender and make slaves of the rest of the defenders. They leave unharmed the crowd of noncombatants. If they find out that any persons recommended the surrender of the town, they give them a share of the property of the condemned. They present their auxiliaries with the rest of the confiscated goods, but not a single one of their own men gets any of the booty.

When the war is over, they do not charge the expense against their friends, for whom they have borne the cost, but against the conquered. Under this head they make them not only pay money, which they lay aside for similar warlike purposes, but also surrender estates, from which they may enjoy forever a large annual income. In many countries they have such revenues which, coming little by little from various sources, have grown to the sum of over seven hundred thousand ducats a year.[7] To these estates they dispatch some of their own citizens under the title of Financial Agents to live there in great style and to play the part of magnates. Yet much is left over to put into the public treasury, unless they prefer to give the conquered nation credit. They often do the latter until they need to use the money, and even then it scarcely ever happens that they call in the whole sum. From these estates they confer a share on those who at their request undertake the dangerous mission which I have previously described.

If any king takes up arms against them and prepares to invade their territory, they at once meet him in great strength beyond their borders. They never lightly make war in their own country nor is any emergency so pressing as to compel them to admit foreign auxiliaries into their island.

Utopian Religions

There are different kinds of religion not only on the island as a whole but also in each city. Some worship as god the sun, others the moon, others one of the planets. There are some who reverence a man conspicuous for either virtue or glory in

7. A vast sum of money; by today's reckoning, the amount would equal several million dollars.

the past not only as god but even as the supreme god. But by far the majority, and those by far the wiser, believe in nothing of the kind but in a certain single being, unknown, eternal, immense, inexplicable, far above the reach of the human mind, diffused throughout the universe not in mass but in power. Him they call father. To him alone they attribute the beginnings, the growth, the increase, the changes, and the ends of all things as they have perceived them. To no other do they give divine honors.

In addition, all the other Utopians too, though varying in their beliefs, agree with them in this respect that they hold there is one supreme being, to whom are due both the creation and the providential government of the whole world. All alike call him Mithras[8] in their native language, but in this respect they disagree, that he is looked on differently by different persons. Each professes that whatever that is which he regards as supreme is that very same nature to whose unique power and majesty the sum of all things is attributed by the common consent of all nations. But gradually they are all beginning to depart from this medley of superstitions and are coming to unite in that one religion which seems to surpass the rest in reasonableness. Nor is there any doubt that the other beliefs would all have disappeared long ago had not whatever untoward event, that happened to anyone when he was deliberating on a change of religion, been construed by fear as not having happened by chance but as having been sent from heaven as if the deity whose worship he was forsaking were thus avenging an intention so impious against himself.

But after they had heard from us the name of Christ, His teaching, His character, His miracles, and the no less wonderful constancy of the many martyrs whose blood freely shed had drawn so many nations far and wide into their fellowship, you would not believe how readily disposed they, too, were to join it, whether through the rather mysterious inspiration of God or because they thought it nearest to that belief which has the widest prevalence among them. But I think that this factor, too, was of no small weight, that they had heard that His disciples' common way of life had been pleasing to Christ and that it is still in use among the truest societies of Christians. But whatever it was that influenced them, not a few joined our religion and were cleansed by the holy water of baptism.

But because among us four (for that was all that was left, two of our group having succumbed to fate) there was, I am sorry to say, no priest, they were initiated in all other matters, but so far they lack those sacraments which with us only priests administer. They understand, however, what they are, and desire them with the greatest eagerness. Moreover, they are even debating earnestly among themselves whether, without the dispatch of a Christian bishop, one chosen out of their own number might receive the sacerdotal character. It seemed that they would choose a candidate, but by the time of my departure they had not yet done so.

Even those who do not agree with the religion of Christ do not try to deter others from it. They do not attack any who have made their profession. Only one of our company, while I was there, was interfered with. As soon as he was baptized, in spite of our advice to the contrary, he spoke publicly of Christ's religion with more zeal than discretion. He began to grow so warm in his preaching that not only did he prefer our worship to any other but he condemned all the rest outright. He proclaimed them to be profane in themselves and their followers to be impious and sacrilegious

8. Persian sun god.

and worthy of everlasting fire. When he had long been preaching in this style, they arrested him, tried him, and convicted him not for despising their religion but for stirring up a riot among the people. His sentence after the verdict of guilty was exile. Actually, they count this principle among their most ancient institutions, that no one should suffer for his religion.

Utopus had heard that before his arrival the inhabitants had been continually quarreling among themselves about religion. He had observed that the universal dissensions between the individual sects who were fighting for their country had given him the opportunity of overcoming them all. From the very beginning, therefore, after he had gained the victory, he especially ordained that it should be lawful for every man to follow the religion of his choice, that each might strive to bring others over to his own, provided that he quietly and modestly supported his own by reasons nor bitterly demolished all others if his persuasions were not successful nor used any violence and refrained from abuse. If a person contends too vehemently in expressing his views, he is punished with exile or enslavement.

Utopus laid down these regulations not merely from regard for peace, which he saw to be utterly destroyed by constant wrangling and implacable hatred, but because he thought that this method of settlement was in the interest of religion itself. On religion he did not venture rashly to dogmatize. He was uncertain whether God did not desire a varied and manifold worship and therefore did not inspire different people with different views. But he was certain in thinking it both insolence and folly to demand by violence and threats that all should think to be true what you believe to be true. Moreover, even if it should be the case that one single religion is true and all the rest are false, he readily foresaw that, provided the matter was handled reasonably and moderately, truth by its own natural force would finally emerge sooner or later and stand forth conspicuously. But if the struggle were decided by arms and riots, since the worst men are always the most unyielding, the best and holiest religion would be overwhelmed because of the conflicting false religions, like grain choked by thorns and underbrush.

So he made the whole matter of religion an open question and left each one free to choose what he should believe. By way of exception, he conscientiously and strictly gave injunction that no one should fall so far below the dignity of human nature as to believe that souls likewise perish with the body or that the world is the mere sport of chance and not governed by any divine providence. After this life, accordingly, vices are ordained to be punished and virtue rewarded. Such is their belief, and if anyone thinks otherwise, they do not regard him even as a member of mankind, seeing that he has lowered the lofty nature of his soul to the level of a beast's miserable body—so far are they from classing him among their citizens whose laws and customs he would treat as worthless if it were not for fear. Who can doubt that he will strive either to evade by craft the public laws of his country or to break them by violence in order to serve his own private desires when he has nothing to fear but laws and no hope beyond the body?

Therefore an individual of this mind is tendered no honor, is entrusted with no office, and is put in charge of no function. He is universally regarded as of a sluggish and low disposition. But they do not punish him in any way, being convinced that it is in no man's power to believe what he chooses, nor do they compel him by threats to disguise his views, nor do they allow in the matter any deceptions or lies which they hate exceedingly as being next door to calculated malice. They forbid him to argue in support of his opinion in the presence of the common people, but in private before the priests and important personages they not only permit but also encourage it, being sure that such madness will in the end give way to reason.

There are others, too, and these not a few, who are not interfered with because they do not altogether lack reason for their view and because they are not evil men. By a much different error, these believe that brute animals also have immortal souls, but not comparable to ours in dignity or destined to equal felicity. Almost all Utopians are absolutely certain and convinced that human bliss will be so immense that, while they lament every man's illness, they regret the death of no one but him whom they see torn from life anxiously and unwillingly. This behavior they take to be a very bad omen as though the soul, being without hope and having a guilty conscience, dreaded its departure through a secret premonition of impending punishment. Besides, they suppose that God will not be pleased with the coming of one who, when summoned, does not gladly hasten to obey but is reluctantly drawn against his will. Persons who behold this kind of death are filled with horror and therefore carry the dead out to burial in melancholy silence. Then, after praying God to be merciful to their shades and graciously to pardon their infirmities, they cover the corpse with earth.

On the other hand, when men have died cheerfully and full of good hope, no one mourns for them, but they accompany their funerals with song, with great affection commending their souls to God. Then, with reverence rather than with sorrow, they cremate the bodies. On the spot they erect a pillar on which are inscribed the good points of the deceased. On returning home they recount his character and his deeds. No part of his life is more frequently or more gladly spoken of than his cheerful death.

They judge that this remembrance of uprightness is not only a most efficacious means of stimulating the living to good deeds but also a most acceptable form of attention to the dead. The latter they think are present when they are talked about, though invisible to the dull sight of mortals. It would be inconsistent with the lot of the blessed not to be able to travel freely where they please, and it would be ungrateful of them to reject absolutely all desire of revisiting their friends to whom they were bound during their lives by mutual love and charity. Charity, like all other good things, they conjecture to be increased after death rather than diminished in all good men. Consequently they believe that the dead move about among the living and are witnesses of their words and actions. Hence they go about their business with more confidence because of reliance on such protection. The belief, moreover, in the personal presence of their forefathers keeps men from any secret dishonorable deed.

They utterly despise and deride auguries and all other divinations of vain superstition, to which great attention is paid in other countries. But miracles, which occur without the assistance of nature, they venerate as operations and witnesses of the divine power at work.[9] In their country, too, they say, miracles often occur. Sometimes in great and critical affairs they pray publicly for a miracle, which they very confidently look for and obtain.

They think that the investigation of nature, with the praise arising from it, is an act of worship acceptable to God. There are persons, however, and these not so very few, who for religious motives eschew learning and scientific pursuit and yet allow themselves no leisure. It is only by keeping busy and by all good offices that they are

9. Christian doctrine held that a miracle was an intervention by God into the natural order of things. God can perform miracles among non-Christians as well as among Christians.

determined to merit the happiness coming after death. Some tend the sick. Others repair roads, clean out ditches, rebuild bridges, dig turf and sand and stone, fell and cut up trees, and transport wood, grain, and other things into the cities in carts. Not only for the public but also for private persons they behave as servants and as more than slaves.

If anywhere there is a task so rough, hard, and filthy that most are deterred from it by the toil, disgust, and despair involved, they gladly and cheerfully claim it all for themselves. While perpetually engaged in hard work themselves, they secure leisure for the others and yet claim no credit for it. They neither belittle insultingly the life of others nor extol their own. The more that these men put themselves in the position of slaves the more are they honored by all.

Of these persons there are two schools. The one is composed of celibates who not only eschew all sexual activity but also abstain from eating flesh meat and in some cases from eating all animal food. They entirely reject the pleasures of this life as harmful. They long only for the future life by means of their watching and sweat. Hoping to obtain it very soon, they are cheerful and active in the meantime.

The other school is just as fond of hard labor, but regards matrimony as preferable, not despising the comfort which it brings and thinking that their duty to nature requires them to perform the marital act and their duty to the country to beget children. They avoid no pleasure unless it interferes with their labor. They like flesh meat just because they think that this fare makes them stronger for any work whatsoever. The Utopians regard these men as the saner but the first-named as the holier. If the latter based upon arguments from reason their preference of celibacy to matrimony and of a hard life to a comfortable one, they would laugh them to scorn. Now, however, since they say they are prompted by religion, they look up to and reverence them. For there is nothing about which they are more careful than not lightly to dogmatize on any point of religion. Such, then, are the men whom in their language they call by a special name of their own, Buthrescae, a word which may be translated as "religious par excellence."

They have priests of extraordinary holiness, and therefore very few. They have no more than thirteen in each city—with a like number of churches—except when they go to war. In that case, seven go forth with the army, and the same number of substitutes is appointed for the interval. When the regular priests come back, everyone returns to his former duties. Then those who are above the number of thirteen, until they succeed to the places of those who die, attend upon the high priest in the meantime. One, you see, is appointed to preside over the rest.They are elected by the people, just as all the other officials are, by secret ballot to avoid party spirit. When elected, they are ordained by their own group.

They preside over divine worship, order religious rites, and are censors of morals. It is counted a great disgrace for a man to be summoned or rebuked by them as not being of upright life. It is their function to give advice and admonition, but to check and punish offenders belongs to the governor and the other civil officials. The priests, however, do exclude from divine services persons whom they find to be unusually bad. There is almost no punishment which is more dreaded: they incur very great disgrace and are tortured by a secret fear of religion. Even their bodies will not long go scot-free. If they do not demonstrate to the priests their speedy repentance, they are seized and punished by the senate for their impiety.

To the priests is entrusted the education of children and youths. They regard concern for their morals and virtue as no less important than for their advancement in learning. They take the greatest pains from the very first to instill into children's minds, while still tender and pliable, good opinions, which are also useful for the preservation of their commonwealth. When once they are firmly implanted in children, they accompany them all through their adult lives and are of great help in watching over the condition of the commonwealth. The latter never decays except through vices which arise from wrong attitudes.

The feminine sex[1] is not debarred from the priesthood, but only a widow advanced in years is ever chosen, and that rather rarely. Unless they are women, the priests have for their wives the very finest women of the country.

To no other office in Utopia is more honor given, so much so that, even if they have committed any crime, they are subjected to no tribunal, but left only to God and to themselves. They judge it wrong to lay human hands upon one, however guilty, who has been consecrated to God in a singular manner as a holy offering. It is easier for them to observe this custom because their priests are very few and very carefully chosen.

Besides, it does not easily happen that one who is elevated to such dignity for being the very best among the good, nothing but virtue being taken into account, should fall into corruption and wickedness. Even if it does happen, human nature being ever prone to change, yet since they are but few and are invested with no power except the influence of honor, it need not be feared that they will cause any great harm to the state. In fact, the reason for having but few and exceptional priests is to prevent the dignity of the order, which they now reverence very highly, from being cheapened by communicating the honor to many. This is especially true since they think it hard to find many men so good as to be fit for so honorable a position for the filling of which it is not enough to be endowed with ordinary virtues.

They are not more esteemed among their own people than among foreign nations. This can easily be seen from a fact which, I think, is its cause. When the armies are fighting in battle, the priests are to be found separate but not very far off, settled on their knees, dressed in their sacred vestments. With hands outstretched to heaven, they pray first of all for peace, next for a victory to their own side—but without much bloodshed on either side. When their side is winning, they run among the combatants, and restrain the fury of their own men against the routed enemy. Merely to see and to appeal to them suffices to save one's life; to touch their flowing garments protects one's remaining goods from every harm arising from war.

This conduct has brought them such veneration among all nations everywhere and has given them so real a majesty that they have saved their own citizens from the enemy as often as they have protected the enemy from their own men. The following is well known. Sometimes their own side had given way, their case had been desperate, they were taking to flight, and the enemy was rushing on to kill and to plunder. But the carnage was then averted by the intervention of the priests. After the armies were parted from each other, peace was concluded and settled on just terms. Never was there any nation so savage, cruel, and barbarous that it did not regard their persons as sacred and inviolable.

They celebrate as holydays the first and the last day of each month and likewise of each year. The latter they divide into months, measured by the orbit of the moon

1. In Greek and Roman religious practice, women could perform priestly functions. As these were the peoples whom More identified as understanding natural law, he must have thought that natural law did not limit a woman's role in religion.

just as the course of the sun rounds out the year. In their language they call the first days Cynemerni and the last days Trapemerni. These names have the same meaning as if they were rendered "First-Feasts" and "Final-Feasts."

Their temples are fine sights, not only elaborate in workmanship but also capable of holding a vast throng, and necessarily so, since there are so few of them. The temples are all rather dark. This feature, they report, is due not to an ignorance of architecture but to the deliberate intention of the priests. They think that excessive light makes the thoughts wander, whereas scantier and uncertain light concentrates the mind and conduces to devotion.

In Utopia, as has been seen, the religion of all is not the same, and yet all its manifestations, though varied and manifold, by different roads as it were, tend to the same end, the worship of the divine nature. Therefore nothing is seen or heard in the temples which does not seem to agree with all in common. If any sect has a rite of its own, it is performed within the walls of each man's home. Public worship is conducted according to a ritual which does not at all detract from any of the private devotions. Therefore no image of the gods is seen in the temple so that the individual may be free to conceive of God with the most ardent devotion in any form he pleases. They invoke God by no special name except that of Mithras. By this word they agree to represent the one nature of the divine majesty whatever it be. The prayers formulated are such as every man may utter without offense to his own belief.

On the evening of the Final-Feasts, they gather in the temple, still fasting. They thank God for the prosperity they have enjoyed in the month or year of which that holyday is the last day. Next day, which is the First-Feast, they flock to the temples in the morning. They pray for good luck and prosperity in the ensuing year or month, of which this holyday is the auspicious beginning.

On the Final-Feasts, before they go to the temple, wives fall down at the feet of their husbands, children at the feet of their parents. They confess that they have erred, either by committing some fault or by performing some duty carelessly, and beg pardon for their offense. Hence, if any cloud of quarrel in the family has arisen, it is dispelled by this satisfaction so that with pure and clear minds they may be present at the sacrifices, for they are too scrupulous to attend with a troubled conscience. If they are aware of hatred or anger against anyone they do not assist at the sacrifices until they have been reconciled and have cleansed their hearts, for fear of swift and great punishment.

When they reach the temple, they part, the men going to the right side and the women to the left. Then they arrange their places so that the males in each home sit in front of the head of the household and the womenfolk are in front of the mother of the family. They thus take care that every gesture of everyone abroad is observed by those whose authority and discipline govern them at home. They also carefully see to it that everywhere the younger are placed in the company of the elder. If children were trusted to children, they might spend in childish foolery the time in which they ought to be conceiving a religious fear toward the gods, the greatest and almost the only stimulus to the practice of virtues.

They slay no animal in their sacrifices. They do not believe that the divine clemency delights in bloodshed and slaughter, seeing that it has imparted life to animate creatures that they might enjoy life. They burn incense and other fragrant substances and also offer a great number of candles. They are not unaware that these things add nothing to the divine nature, any more than do human prayers, but they like this harmless kind of worship. Men feel that, by these sweet smells and lights, as well as the other ceremonies, they somehow are uplifted and rise with livelier devotion to the worship of God.

The people are clothed in white garments in the temple. The priest wears vestments of various colors, of wonderful design and shape, but not of material as costly as one would expect. They are not interwoven with gold or set with precious stones but wrought with the different feathers of birds so cleverly and artistically that no costly material could equal the value of the handiwork. Moreover, in these birds' feathers and plumes and the definite order and plan by which they are set off on the priest's vestment, they say certain hidden mysteries are contained. By knowing the meaning as it is carefully handed down by the priests, they are reminded of God's benefits toward them and, in turn, of their own piety toward God and their duty toward one another.

As soon as the priest thus arrayed appears from the vestibule, all immediately fall on the ground in reverence. The silence all around is so deep that the very appearance of the congregation strikes one with awe as if some divine power were really present. After remaining a while on the ground, at a signal from the priest they rise.

At this point they sing praises to God, which they diversify with musical instruments, largely different in shape from those seen in our part of the world. Very many of them surpass in sweetness those in use with us, but some are not even comparable with ours. But in one respect undoubtedly they are far ahead of us. All their music, whether played on instruments or sung by the human voice, so renders and expresses the natural feelings, so suits the sound to the matter (whether the words be supplicatory, or joyful, or propitiatory, or troubled, or mournful, or angry), and so represents the meaning by the form of the melody that it wonderfully affects, penetrates, and inflames the souls of the hearers.

At the end, the priest and the people together repeat solemn prayers fixed in form, so drawn up that each individual may apply to himself personally what all recite together. In these prayers every man recognizes God to be the author of creation and governance and all other blessings besides. He thanks Him for all the benefits received, particularly that by the divine favor he has chanced on that commonwealth which is the happiest and has received that religion which he hopes to be the truest. If he errs in these matters or if there is anything better and more approved by God than that commonwealth or that religion, he prays that He will, of His goodness, bring him to the knowledge of it, for he is ready to follow in whatever path He may lead him. But if this form of a commonwealth be the best and his religion the truest, he prays that then He may give him steadfastness and bring all other mortals to the same way of living and the same opinion of God—unless there be something in this variety of religions which delights His inscrutable will.

Finally, he prays that God will take him to Himself by an easy death, how soon or late he does not venture to determine. However, if it might be without offense to His Majesty, it would be much more welcome to him to die a very hard death and go to God than to be kept longer away from Him even by a very prosperous career in life.[2]

After this prayer has been said, they prostrate themselves on the ground again. Then shortly they rise and go away to dinner. The rest of the day they pass in games and in exercises of military training.

2. The Utopians do not pray for forgiveness of the sins they have committed in the past, although they do pray for divine guidance in avoiding the errors they may commit in the future.

Now I have described to you, as exactly as I could, the structure of that commonwealth which I judge not merely the best but the only one which can rightly claim the name of a commonwealth. Outside Utopia, to be sure, men talk freely of the public welfare—but look after their private interests only. In Utopia, where nothing is private, they seriously concern themselves with public affairs. Assuredly in both cases they act reasonably. For, outside Utopia, how many are there who do not realize that, unless they make some separate provision for themselves, however flourishing the commonwealth, they will themselves starve? For this reason, necessity compels them to hold that they must take account of themselves rather than of the people, that is, of others.

On the other hand, in Utopia, where everything belongs to everybody, no one doubts, provided only that the public granaries are well filled, that the individual will lack nothing for his private use. The reason is that the distribution of goods is not niggardly. In Utopia there is no poor man and no beggar. Though no man has anything, yet all are rich.

For what can be greater riches for a man than to live with a joyful and peaceful mind, free of all worries—not troubled about his food or harassed by the querulous demands of his wife or fearing poverty for his son or worrying about his daughter's dowry, but feeling secure about the livelihood and happiness of himself and his family: wife, sons, grandsons, great-grandsons, great-great-grandsons, and all the long line of their descendants that gentlefolk anticipate? Then take into account the fact that there is no less provision for those who are now helpless but once worked than for those who are still working.

At this point I should like anyone to be so bold as to compare this fairness with the so-called justice prevalent in other nations, among which, upon my soul, I cannot discover the slightest trace of justice and fairness. What brand of justice is it that any nobleman whatsoever or goldsmith-banker or moneylender or, in fact, anyone else from among those who either do no work at all or whose work is of a kind not very essential to the commonwealth, should attain a life of luxury and grandeur on the basis of his idleness or his nonessential work? In the meantime, the common laborer, the carter, the carpenter, and the farmer perform work so hard and continuous that beasts of burden could scarcely endure it and work so essential that no commonwealth could last even one year without it. Yet they earn such scanty fare and lead such a miserable life that the condition of beasts of burden might seem far preferable. The latter do not have to work so incessantly nor is their food much worse (in fact, sweeter to their taste) nor do they entertain any fear for the future. The workmen, on the other hand, not only have to toil and suffer without return or profit in the present but agonize over the thought of an indigent old age. Their daily wage is too scanty to suffice even for the day: much less is there an excess and surplus that daily can be laid by for their needs in old age.

Now is not this an unjust and ungrateful commonwealth? It lavishes great rewards on so-called gentlefolk and banking goldsmiths and the rest of that kind, who are either idle or mere parasites and purveyors of empty pleasures. On the contrary, it makes no benevolent provision for farmers, colliers, common laborers, carters, and carpenters without whom there would be no commonwealth at all. After it has misused the labor of their prime and after they are weighed down with age and disease and are in utter want, it forgets all their sleepless nights and all the great benefits received at their hands and most ungratefully requites them with a most miserable death.

What is worse, the rich every day extort a part of their daily allowance from the poor not only by private fraud but by public law. Even before they did so it seemed unjust that persons deserving best of the commonwealth should have the worst return. Now they have further distorted and debased the right and, finally, by making laws, have palmed it off as justice. Consequently, when I consider and turn over in my mind the state of all commonwealths flourishing anywhere today, so help me God, I can see nothing else than a kind of conspiracy of the rich, who are aiming at their own interests under the name and title of the commonwealth.[3] They invent and devise all ways and means by which, first, they may keep without fear of loss all that they have amassed by evil practices and, secondly, they may then purchase as cheaply as possible and abuse the toil and labor of all the poor. These devices become law as soon as the rich have once decreed their observance in the name of the public—that is, of the poor also!

Yet when these evil men with insatiable greed have divided up among themselves all the goods which would have been enough for all the people, how far they are from the happiness of the Utopian commonwealth! In Utopia all greed for money was entirely removed with the use of money. What a mass of troubles was then cut away! What a crop of crimes was then pulled up by the roots! Who does not know that fraud, theft, rapine, quarrels, disorders, brawls, seditions, murders, treasons, poisonings, which are avenged rather than restrained by daily executions, die out with the destruction of money? Who does not know that fear, anxiety, worries, toils, and sleepless nights will also perish at the same time as money? What is more, poverty, which alone money seemed to make poor, forthwith would itself dwindle and disappear if money were entirely done away with everywhere.

To make this assertion clearer, consider in your thoughts some barren and unfruitful year in which many thousands of men have been carried off by famine. I emphatically contend that at the end of that scarcity, if rich men's granaries had been searched, as much grain could have been found as, if it had been divided among the people killed off by starvation and disease, would have prevented anyone from feeling that meager return from soil and climate. So easily might men get the necessities of life if that blessed money, supposedly a grand invention to ease access to those necessities, was not in fact the only barrier to our getting what we need.

Even the rich, I doubt not, have such feelings. They are not unaware that it would be a much better state of affairs to lack no necessity than to have abundance of superfluities—to be snatched from such numerous troubles rather than to be hemmed in by great riches. Nor does it occur to me to doubt that a man's regard for his own interests or the authority of Christ our Savior—who in His wisdom could not fail to know what was best and who in His goodness would not fail to counsel what He knew to be best—would long ago have brought the whole world to adopt the laws of

3. Hythlodaeus condemns practices associated with the accumulation of wealth as capital and the corresponding exploitation of workers in the interest of increasing capital. This goal is promoted by various legal "devices," particularly involving estates, that preserve capital within the upper ranks of society. But capital cannot be accumulated in a barter economy, where goods are exchanged for goods rather than for money. Hence Hythlodaeus eliminates money as a way of preventing the formation of capital.

the Utopian commonwealth, had not one single monster, the chief and progenitor of all plagues, striven against it—I mean, Pride.

Pride measures prosperity not by her own advantages but by others' disadvantages.[4] Pride would not consent to be made even a goddess if no poor wretches were left for her to domineer over and scoff at, if her good fortune might not dazzle by comparison with their miseries, if the display of her riches did not torment and intensify their poverty. This serpent from hell entwines itself around the hearts of men and acts like the suckfish in preventing and hindering them from entering on a better way of life.

Pride is too deeply fixed in men to be easily plucked out. For this reason, the fact that this form of a commonwealth—which I should gladly desire for all—has been the good fortune of the Utopians at least, fills me with joy. They have adopted such institutions of life as have laid the foundations of the commonwealth not only most happily, but also to last forever, as far as human prescience can forecast. At home they have extirpated the roots of ambition and factionalism, along with all the other vices. Hence there is no danger of trouble from domestic discord, which has been the only cause of ruin to the well-established prosperity of many cities. As long as harmony is preserved at home and its institutions are in a healthy state, not all the envy of neighboring rulers, though it has rather often attempted it and has always been repelled, can avail to shatter or to shake that nation.

When Raphael had finished his story, many things came to my mind which seemed very absurdly established in the customs and laws of the people described—not only in their method of waging war, their ceremonies and religion, as well as their other institutions, but most of all in that feature which is the principal foundation of their whole structure. I mean their common life and subsistence—without any exchange of money. This latter alone utterly overthrows all the nobility, magnificence, splendor, and majesty which are, in the estimation of the common people, the true glories and ornaments of the commonwealth.

I knew, however, that he was wearied with his tale, and I was not quite certain that he could brook any opposition to his views, particularly when I recalled his censure of others on account of their fear that they might not appear to be wise enough, unless they found some fault to criticize in other men's discoveries. I therefore praised their way of life and his speech and, taking him by the hand, led him in to supper. I first said, nevertheless, that there would be another chance to think about these matters more deeply and to talk them over with him more fully. If only this were some day possible!

Meanwhile, though in other respects he is a man of the most undoubted learning as well as of the greatest knowledge of human affairs, I cannot agree with all that he said. But I readily admit that there are very many features in the Utopian commonwealth which it is easier for me to wish for in our countries than to have any hope of seeing realized.

4. Pride therefore prevents a society based on benefits, which typically redound to the welfare of a community rather than to that of particular individuals.

END OF BOOK TWO
THE END OF THE AFTERNOON DISCOURSE OF
RAPHAEL HYTHLODAEUS ON THE LAWS
AND CUSTOMS OF THE ISLAND OF
UTOPIA, HITHERTO KNOWN BUT
TO FEW, AS REPORTED BY THE
MOST DISTINGUISHED AND
MOST LEARNED MAN,
MR. THOMAS MORE,
CITIZEN AND SHERIFF OF LONDON
FINIS

RESPONSE

Francis Bacon[1] from *The New Atlantis*

[The Jew who shows the travellers around the island speaks to the narrator] "God bless thee, my son; I will give thee the greatest jewel I have. For I will impart unto thee, for the love of God and men, a relation of the true state of Salomon's House. Son, to make you know the true state of Salomon's House, I will keep this order. First, I will set forth unto you the end of our foundation. Secondly, the preparations and instruments we have for our works. Thirdly, the several employments and functions whereto our fellows are assigned. And fourthly, the ordinances and rites which we observe.

The end of our foundation is the knowledge of causes, and secret motions of things; and the enlarging of the bounds of human empire, to the effecting of all things possible.

The Preparations and Instruments are these. We have large and deep caves of several depths: the deepest are sunk six hundred fathom: and some of them are digged and made under great hills and mountains: so that if you reckon together the depth of the hill and the depth of the cave, they are (some of them) above three miles deep. For we find, that the depth of a hill, and the depth of a cave from the flat, is the same thing; both remote alike, from the sun and heaven's beams, and from the open air. These caves we call the Lower Region; and we use them for all coagulations, indurations, refrigerations, and conservations of bodies. We use them likewise for the imitation of natural mines; and the producing also of new artificial metals, by compositions and materials which we use, and lay there for many years. We use them also sometimes, (which may seem strange,) for curing of some diseases, and for prolongation of life in some hermits that choose to live

1. Francis Bacon (1561–1626), philosopher, lawyer, essayist, scientist and politician. Bacon was a prolific author of tremendous energy who combined a varied writing career with an interest in scientific experimentation (he died from a chill caught making experiments in the snow), and a checkered political career (he was notoriously corrupt). *The New Atlantis* (1626) is an imaginative response to More's *Utopia*, which makes use of Bacon's scientific knowledge allied to his predictions of what might happen in the future. It can be looked upon as an early forerunner of science fiction and read alongside Bacon's work on scientific reasoning such as *The Advancement of Learning* (1605) and the Latin treatise *Novum Orgum* (1620).

there, well accommodated of all things necessary, and indeed live very long; by whom also we learn many things.

We have burials in several earths, where we put diverse cements, as the Chineses do their porcellain. But we have them in greater variety, and some of them more fine. We have also great variety of composts and soils, for the making of the earth fruitful.

We have high towers; the highest about half a mile in height; and some of them likewise set upon high mountains; so that the vantage of the hill with the tower is in the highest of them three miles at least. And these places we call the Upper Region; accounting the air between the high places and the low, as a Middle Region. We use these towers, according to their several heights, and situations, for insolation, refrigeration, conservation; and for the view of divers meteors; as winds, rain, snow, hail; and some of the fiery meteors also. And upon them, in some places, are dwellings of hermits, whom we visit sometimes, and instruct what to observe.

We have great lakes, both salt, and fresh; whereof we have use for the fish and fowl. We use them also for burials of some natural bodies: for we find a difference in things buried in earth or in air below the earth, and things buried in water. We have also pools, of which some do strain fresh water out of salt; and others by art do turn fresh water into salt. We have also some rocks in the midst of the sea, and some bays upon the shore for some works, wherein is required the air and vapor of the sea. We have likewise violent streams and cataracts, which serve us for many motions: and likewise engines for multiplying and enforcing of winds, to set also on going diverse motions.

We have also a number of artificial wells and fountains, made in imitation of the natural sources and baths; as tincted upon vitriol, sulphur, steel, brass, lead, nitre, and other minerals. And again we have little wells for infusions of many things, where the waters take the virtue quicker and better, than in vessels or basins. And amongst them we have a water which we call Water of Paradise, being, by that we do to it made very sovereign for health, and prolongation of life.

We have also great and spacious houses where we imitate and demonstrate meteors; as snow, hail, rain, some artificial rains of bodies and not of water, thunders, lightnings; also generations of bodies in air; as frogs, flies, and divers others.

We have also certain chambers, which we call Chambers of Health, where we qualify the air as we think good and proper for the cure of divers diseases, and preservation of health.

We have also fair and large baths, of several mixtures, for the cure of diseases, and the restoring of man's body from arefaction: and others for the confirming of it in strength of sinewes, vital parts, and the very juice and substance of the body.

We have also large and various orchards and gardens; wherein we do not so much respect beauty, as variety of ground and soil, proper for divers trees and herbs: and some very spacious, where trees and berries are set whereof we make divers kinds of drinks, besides the vineyards. In these we practise likewise all conclusions of grafting, and inoculating as well of wild-trees as fruit-trees, which produceth many effects. And we make (by art) in the same orchards and gardens, trees and flowers to come earlier or later than their seasons; and to come up and bear more speedily than by their natural course they do. We make them also by art greater much than their nature; and their fruit greater and sweeter and of differing taste, smell, colour, and figure, from their nature. And many of them we so order, as they become of medicinal use.

We have also means to make divers plants rise by mixtures of earths without seeds; and likewise to make divers new plants, differing from the vulgar; and to make one tree or plant turn into another.

We have also parks and enclosures of all sorts of beasts and birds which we use not only for view or rareness, but likewise for dissections and trials; that thereby we may take light what may be wrought upon the body of man. Wherein we find many strange effects; as continuing life in them, though divers parts, which you account vital, be perished and taken forth; resuscitating of some that seem dead in appearance; and the like. We try also all poisons and other medicines upon them, as well of chirurgery,[1] as physic. By art likewise, we make them greater or taller than their kind is; and contrariwise dwarf them, and stay their growth: we make them more fruitful and bearing than their kind is; and contrariwise barren and not generative. Also we make them differ in colour, shape, activity, many ways. We find means to make commixtures and copulations of different kinds; which have produced many new kinds, and them not barren, as the general opinion is. We make a number of kinds of serpents, worms, flies, fishes, of putrefaction; whereof some are advanced (in effect) to be perfect creatures, like bests or birds; and have sexes, and do propagate. Neither do we this by chance, but we know beforehand, of what matter and commixture what kind of those creatures will arise.

We have also particular pools, where we make trials upon fishes, as we have said before of beasts and birds.

We have also places for breed and generation of those kinds of worms and flies which are of special use; such as are with you your silk-worms and bees.

I will not hold you long with recounting of our brewhouses, bake-houses, and kitchens, where are made divers drinks, breads, and meats, rare and of special effects. Wines we have of grapes; and drinks of other juice of fruits, of grains, and of roots; and of mixtures with honey, sugar, manna, and fruits dried, and decocted; Also of the tears or woundings of trees; and of the pulp of canes. And these drinks are of several ages, some to the age or last of forty years. We have drinks also brewed with several herbs, and roots, and spices; yea with several fleshes, and white-meats; whereof some of the drinks are such, as they are in effect meat and drink both: so that divers, especially in age, do desire to live with them, with little or no meat or bread. And above all, we strive to have drink of extreme thin parts, to insinuate into the body, and yet without all biting, sharpness, or fretting; insomuch as some of them put upon the back of your hand will, with a little stay, pass through to the palm, and yet taste mild to the mouth. We have also waters which we ripen in that fashion, as they become nourishing; so that they are indeed excellent drink; and many will use no other. Breads we have of several grains, roots, and kernels; yea and some of flesh and fish dried; with divers kinds of leavenings and seasonings: so that some do extremely move appetites; some do nourish so, as divers do live of them, without any other meat; who live very long. So for meats, we have some of them so beaten and made tender and mortified, "yet without all corrupting, as a weak heat of the stomach will turn them into good chylus;[2] as well as a strong heat would meat otherwise prepared. We have some meats also and breads and drinks, which taken by men enable them to fast long after; and some other, that used make the very flesh of

1. Surgery.

2. Digestion.

men's bodies sensibly" more hard and tough and their strength far greater than otherwise it would be.

We have dispensatories, or shops of medicines. Wherein you may easily think, if we have such variety of plants and living creatures more than you have in Europe, (for we know what you have,) the simples,[3] drugs, and ingredients of medicines, must likewise be in so much the greater variety. We have them likewise of divers ages, and long fermentations. And for their preparations, we have not only all manner of exquisite distillations and separations, and especially by gentle heats and percolations through divers strainers, yea and substances; but also exact forms of composition, whereby they incorporate almost, as they were natural simples.

We have also divers mechanical arts, which you have not; and stuffs made by them; as papers, linen, silks, tissues; dainty works of feathers of wonderful lustre; excellent dies, and, many others; and shops likewise, as well for such as are not brought into vulgar use amongst us as for those that are. For you must know that of the things before recited, many of them are grown into use throughout the kingdom; but yet, if they did flow from our invention, we have of them also for patterns and principals.

We have also furnaces of great diversities, and that keep great diversity of heats; fierce and quick; strong and constant; soft and mild; blown, quiet; dry, moist; and the like. But above all, we have heats, in imitation of the Sun's and heavenly bodies' heats, that pass divers inequalities, and (as it were) orbs, progresses, and returns, whereby we produce admirable effects. Besides, we have heats of dungs; and of bellies and maws of living creatures, and of their bloods and bodies; and of hays and herbs laid up moist; of lime unquenched; and such like. Instruments also which generate heat only by motion. And farther, places for strong insulations; and again, places under the earth, which by nature, or art, yield heat. These divers heats we use, as the nature of the operation, which we intend, requireth.

We have also perspective-houses, where we make demonstrations of all lights and radiations; and of all colours: and out of things uncoloured and transparent, we can represent unto you all several colours; not in rain-bows, (as it is in gems, and prisms,) but of themselves single. We represent also all multiplications of light, which we carry to great distance, and make so sharp as to discern small points and lines. Also all colourations of light; all delusions and deceits of the sight, in figures, magnitudes, motions, colours all demonstrations of shadows. We find also divers means, yet unknown to you, of producing of light originally from divers bodies. We procure means of seeing objects afar off; as in the heaven and remote places; and represent things near as afar off; and things afar off as near; making feigned distances. We have also helps for the sight, far above spectacles and glasses in use. We have also glasses and means to see small and minute bodies perfectly and distinctly; as the shapes and colours of small flies and worms, grains and flaws in gems, which cannot otherwise be seen, observations in urine and blood not otherwise to be seen. We make artificial rain-bows, halo's, and circles about light. We represent also all manner of reflexions, refractions, and multiplications of visual beams of objects.

We have also precious stones of all kinds, many of them of great beauty, and to you unknown; crystals likewise; and glasses of divers kinds; and amongst them some of metals vitrificated, and other materials besides those of which you make glass. Also a number of fossils, and imperfect minerals, which you have not.

3. Medications made of one ingredient, such as an herb.

Likewise loadstones of prodigious virtue; and other rare stones, both natural and artificial.

We have also sound-houses, where we practise and demonstrate all sounds, and their generation. We have harmonies which you have not, of quarter-sounds, and lesser slides of sounds. Divers instruments of music likewise to you unknown, some sweeter than any you have, together with bells and rings that are dainty and sweet. We represent small sounds as great and deep; likewise great sounds extenuate and sharp; we make divers tremblings and warblings of sounds, which in their original are entire. We represent and imitate all articulate sounds and letters, and the voices and notes of beasts and birds. We have certain helps which set to the ear do further the hearing greatly. We have also divers strange and artificial echoes, reflecting the voice many times, and as it were tossing it: and some that give back the voice louder than it came, some shriller, and some deeper; yea, some rendering the voice differing in the letters or articulate sound from that they receive. We have also means to convey sounds in trunks and pipes, in strange lines and distances.

We have also perfume-houses; wherewith we join also practices of taste. We multiply smells, which may seem strange. We imitate smells, making all smells to breathe outs of other mixtures than those that give them. We make divers imitations of taste likewise, so that they will deceive any man's taste. And in this house we contain also a confiture-house; where we make all sweet-meats, dry and moist; and divers pleasant wines, milks, broths, and sallets;[4] in far greater variety than you have.

We have also engine-houses, where are prepared engines and instruments for all sorts of motions. There we imitate and practise to make swifter motions than any you have, either out of your muskets or any engine that you have: and to make them and multiply them more easily, and with small force, by wheels and other means: and to make them stronger and more violent than yours are; exceeding your greatest cannons and basilisks. We represent also ordnance and instruments of war, and engines of all kinds: and likewise new mixtures and compositions of gun-powder, wild-fires burning in water, and unquenchable. Also fireworks of all variety both for pleasure and use. We imitate also flights of birds; we have some degrees of flying in the air. We have ships and boats for going under water, and brooking of seas; also swimming-girdles and supporters. We have divers curious clocks, and other like motions of return: and some perpetual motions. We imitate also motions of living creatures, by images, of men, beasts, birds, fishes, and serpents. We have also a great number of other various motions, strange for equality, fineness, and subtilty.

We have also a mathematical house, where are represented all instruments, as well of geometry as astronomy, exquisitely made.

We have also houses of deceits of the senses; where we represent all manner of feats of juggling, false apparitions, impostures, and illusions; and their fallacies. And surely you will easily believe that we that have so many things truly natural which induce admiration, could in a world of particulars deceive the senses, if we would disguise those things and labour to make them seem more miraculous. But we do hate all impostures, and lies; insomuch as we have severely forbidden it to all our fellows, under pain of ignominy and fines, that they do not show any natural work or thing, adorned or swelling; but only pure as it is, and without all affectation of strangeness.

These are (my son) the riches of Salomon's[5] House.

4. Salads.

5. Solomon.

William Baldwin

d.1563?

William Baldwin is not as well known as he might be or might have been had the course of English history run in a slightly different direction. Baldwin was the principal editor behind one of the most successful literary projects of the sixteenth century, *A Mirror for Magistrates*, published around 1554, but suppressed and then re-published in 1559. Baldwin published other works, including a treatise of moral philosophy and was one of the key literary figures at the court of Edward VI. Sadly, with Edward's premature death in 1553 and the accession of the Protestant Edward's Catholic half-sister, Mary, Baldwin appears to have lapsed into relative obscurity and ended his days as a minor cleric.

Baldwin's prose fiction, the *Marvelous History Entitled Beware the Cat, Concerning Diverse Wonderful and Incredible Matters*, was written in 1552 but not published until 1570. The work is notable as the first sustained piece of prose fiction in English, but it is much more than simply a fact of literary history. The work contains a series of "orations" by the narrator, Streamer, who has discovered how he can understand the speech of cats and so infiltrate their dark and subversive world. Baldwin's brilliant text works as a satire of human folly and stupidity. But it is also a disturbing analysis of the fine lines between obedience and subversion, a pressing issue for all Englishmen and women in times of religious change and conflicting loyalties. The cats are, on one level, Catholics, but they cannot be classified simply in terms of their religious affiliation, which is one of the key points of the book. People are far too complex to be labeled in this way, as many recent histories of the religious identities of the period have demonstrated. Like the cats in Baldwin's fiction, they have their own idiosyncrasies, belong to communities, exist in a different world if they are excluded from the one that everyone else inhabits. Baldwin is not suggesting that cats are rational and have their own world, but he is enough of a philosopher to force his readers to think about the boundaries they draw up between the human and the nonhuman as well as different groups of people. The cats certainly have some more sensible practices and customs than their human counterparts, including many of their laws.

Beware the Cat

T.K. to the Reader

This little book, *Beware the Cat*,
  most pleasantly compiled,
In time obscured was, and so
  since that hath been exiled.

Exiled because, perchance at first,
  it showed the toys[1] and drifts
Of such as then, by wiles and wills,
  maintained Popish shifts.

Shifts[2] such as those, in such a time,
  delighted for to use,
Whereby full many simple souls
  they did full sore abuse.

1. Whims.

2. Devices, plans.

Abuse? Yea sure, and that with spight,
whenas the Cat gan tell
Of many pranks of Popish priests
both foolish, mad, and fell.[3]

Fell? Sure, and vain, if judgment right
appear to be in place,
And so as fell in pleasant wise
this fiction shows their grace.

Grace? Nay sure, ungraciousness
of such and many mo,
Which may be told in these our days
to make us laugh also.

Also to laugh? Nay, rather weep
to see such shifts now used,
And that in every sort of men
true virtue is abused.

Abused? Yea, and quite down cast,
let us be sure of that;
And therefore now, as hath been said,
I say, "Beware the Cat."

The Cat full pleasantly will show
some sleights that now are wrought,
And make some laugh which unto mirth
to be constrained are loath.

Loath? Yea, for over-passing grief
that much bereaves their mind,
For such disorder as in states
of every sort they find.

Find? Yea, who can now boast but that
the Cat will him disclose?
Therefore, in midst of mirth I say,
"Beware the Cat" to those.

Vale.

THE EPISTLE DEDICATORY

Love and Live.
To the Right Worshipful Esquire
Master John Young,[4]
Grace and Health.

I have penned for your mastership's pleasure one of the stories which Master Streamer told the last Christmas, and which you so fain would have heard reported by Master Ferrers[5] himself. And although I be unable to pen or speak it so pleasantly

3. Fierce, savage.
4. Probably the courtier, John Young.
5. George Ferrers (c. 1510–1579), a soldier, courtier and writer, who worked with Baldwin in writing *A Mirror for Magistrates*. This might suggest that Master Streamer is also a real person, although it is more likely that Baldwin has mixed up factual and fictional characters in the fiction. Master Willot is also probably an invention.

as he could, yet have I so nearly used both the order and words of him that spake them (which is not the least virtue of a reporter) that I doubt not but that he and Master Willot shall in the reading think they hear Master Streamer speak, and he himself in the like action shall doubt whether he speaketh or readeth. I have divided his oration into three parts, and set the argument before them and an instruction after them, with such notes as might be gathered thereof, so making it book-like, and entitled *Beware the Cat*.

But because I doubt whether Master Streamer will be contented that other men plow with his oxen (I mean pen such things as he speaketh, which perhaps he would rather do himself to have, as he deserveth, the glory of both), therefore I beseech you to learn his mind herein, and if he agree it pass in such sort, yet that he peruse it before the printing and amend it if in any point I have mistaken him. I pray you likewise to ask Master Ferrers his judgement herein, and show him that the *Cure of the Great Plague*,[6] of Master Streamer's translation out of the Arabic which he sent me from Margate,[7] shall be imprinted as soon as I may conveniently.

And if I shall perceive by your trial that Master Streamer allow my endeavors in this kind, I will hereafter, as Plato did by Socrates,[8] pen out such things of the rest of our Christmas communications as shall be to his great glory, and no less pleasure to all them that desire such kinds of knowledge. In the meanwhile I beseech you to accept my good will, and learn to Beware the Cat. So shall you not only perform that I seek, but also please the Almighty, who always preserve you. Amen.

Yours to his power,
G[ulielmus] B[aldwin].

The Argument

It chanced that at Christmas last I was at Court with Master Ferrers, then master of the King's Majesty's pastimes, about setting forth of certain interludes,[9] which for the King's recreation we had devised and were in learning. In which time, among many other exercises among ourselves, we used nightly at our lodging to talk of sundry things for the furtherance of such offices wherein each man as then served. For which purpose it pleased Master Ferrers to make me his bedfellow,[1] and upon a pallet cast upon the rushes in his own chamber to lodge Master Willot and Master Streamer, the one his Astronomer, the other his Divine.[2] And among many other things too long to rehearse, it happened on a night (which I think was the twenty-eight of December), after that Master Ferrers was come from the Court and in bed, there fell a controversy between Master Streamer, who with Master Willot had already slept his first sleep, and me, that was newly come unto bed, the effect whereof was whether birds and beasts had reason.

The occasion thereof was this: I had heard that the King's players were learning a play of Aesop's Crow[3] wherein the most part of the actors were birds, the device whereof I discommended, saying it was not comical to make either speechless things

6. Probably an invented work, like the Arabic translation.
7. A small town in Kent. Later known for its vulgarity (unlike nearby Folkestone, where the annotator grew up, which was more classy but rather boring).
8. Plato wrote down what Socrates said in his dialogues with other philosophers.
9. Short stage plays, often performed at court.

1. Men and women often shared beds owing to lack of space in cities and the cold in winter.
2. Priest.
3. No such play exists. The fable tells the story of a foolish bird who is ridiculed for wearing feathers from other birds to make himself look more attractive.

to speak or brutish[4] things to common[5] reasonably; and although in a tale it were sufferable to imagine and tell of something by them spoken or reasonably done (which kind Aesop laudably used), yet it was uncomely, said I, and without example of any author, to bring them in lively personages to speak, do, reason, and allege authorities out of authors. Master Streamer, my lord's Divine, being more divine in this point than I was ware of, held the contrary part, affirming that beasts and fowls had reason, and that as much as men, yea, and in some points more.

Master Ferrers himself and his Astronomer wakened with our talk and harkened to us, but would take part on neither side. And when Master Streamer had for proof of his assertion declared many things (of elephants that walked upon cords, hedgehogs that knew always what weather would come, foxes and dogs that after they had been all night abroad killing geese and sheep would come home in the morning and put their necks into their collars, parrots that bewailed their keepers' deaths, swallows that with celandine[6] open their young ones' eyes, and an hundred things more), which I denied to come of reason, and to be but natural kindly actions, alleging for my proof authority of most grave and learned philosophers.

"Well," quoth Master Streamer, "I know what I know, and I speak not only what by hearsay of some philosophers I know, but what I myself have proved."

"Why," quoth I then, "have you proof of beasts' and fowls' reason?"

"Yea," quoth he, "I have heard them and understand them both speak and reason as well as I hear and understand you."

At this Master Ferrers laughed. But I, remembering what I had read in Albertus' works,[7] thought there might be somewhat more than I did know; wherefore I asked him what beasts or fowls he had heard, and where and when. At this he paused awhile, and at last said: "If that I thought you could be content to hear me, and without any interruption till I have done mark what I say, I would tell you such a story of one piece of mine own experimenting as should both make you wonder and put you out of doubt concerning this matter; but this I promise you afore, if I do tell it, that as soon as any man curiously interrupteth me, I will leave off and not speak one word more." When we had promised quietly to hear, he, turning himself so in his bed as we might best hear him, said as followeth.

The First Part of Master Streamer's Oration

Being lodged (as, I thank him, I have been often) at a friend's house of mine,[8] which, more roomish within than garish without, standeth at Saint Martin's Lane end and hangeth partly upon the town wall that is called Aldersgate (either of one Aldrich, or else of Elders, that is to say ancient men of the city which among them builded it—as bishops did Bishopsgate; or else of eldern trees, which perchance as they do in the gardens now thereabout, so while the common there was vacant grew abundantly in the same place where the gate was after builded, and called thereof Elderngate—as Moorgate took the name of the field without it, which hath been a very moor; or else, because it is the most ancient gate of the City, was thereof in respect of the other, as Newgate, called the Eldergate; or else, as

Why Aldersgate was so named.

Bishops builded Bishopsgate.

Why Moorgate.

Why Newgate.

4. Of beasts.
5. Talk together.
6. A yellow flower that was thought to cure sight.
7. Albertus Magnus, a compiler of marvels.
8. The Protestant printer, John Day, a friend of Baldwin.

Ludgate taketh the name of Lud who builded it—so most part of heralds, I know, will soonest assent that Aluredus builded this; but they are deceived, for he and his wife Algay builded Aldgate, which thereof taketh the name as Cripplegate doth of a cripple, who begged so much in his life, as put to the silver weather cock which he stole from Paul's steeple, after his death builded it).[9] But whereofsoever this gate Aldersgate took the name (which longeth chiefly to historiers to know), at my friend's house, which, as I said standeth so near that it is over it, I lay oftentimes, and that for sundry causes, sometime for lack of other lodging, and sometime as while my Greek alphabets were in printing to see that it might truly be corrected. And sure it is a shame for all young men that they be no more studious in the tongues; but the world is now come to that pass, that if he can prate[1] a little Latin and handle a racquet and a pair of six-square bowls,[2] he shall sooner obtain any living than the best learned in a whole city; which is the cause that learning is so despised and baggagical[3] things so much advanced.

Why Ludgate.

Why Aldgate.

Why Cripplegate.

Paul's weathercock was silver.

Against young men's negligence.

Against unlawful games.

While I lay at the foresaid house for the causes aforesaid, I was lodged in a chamber hard by the Printing House, which had a fair bay window opening into the garden, the earth whereof is almost as high as Saint Anne's Church top, which standeth thereby. At the other end of the Printing House, as you enter in, is a side door and three or four steps which go up to the leads of the Gate, whereas sometime quarters of men,[4] which is a loathely and abhominable sight, do stand up upon poles. I call it abhominable because it is not only against nature but against Scripture; for God commanded by Moses that, after the sun went down, all such as were hanged or otherwise put to death should be buried, lest if the sun saw them the next day His wrath should come upon them and plague them, as He hath done this and many other realms for the like transgression. And I marvel where men have learned it or for what cause they do it, except it be to feed and please the devils. For sure I believe that some spirits, Misanthropi or Molochitus, who lived by the savor of man's blood, did, after their sacrifices failed (in which men were slain and offered unto them), put into butcherly heathen tyrants' heads to mangle and boil Christian transgressors and to set up their quarters for them to feed upon. And therefore I would counsel all men to bury or burn all executed bodies, and refrain from making such abhominable sacrifice as I have often seen, with ravens or rather devils feeding upon them, in this foresaid leads[5]—in the which every night many cats assembled, and there made such a noise that I could not sleep for them.

God plagueth abhomination.

Evil spirits live by the savor of man's blood.

Good ghostly counsel of Master Streamer.

Wherefore, on a time as I was sitting by the fire with certain of the house, I told them what a noise and what a wawling the cats

9. Streamer's description of the names of London districts is fanciful and often wrong.
1. Speak (derogatory).
2. Dice.
3. Worthless.
4. Those executed for treason would be hanged, cut down while still alive, disembowelled, and then quartered, with heads and body parts placed on the city gates. Rebellions in 1549 and 1550 had seen various men suffer this fate in London.
5. Roofs.

had made there the night before from ten o'clock till one, so that neither I could sleep nor study for them; and by means of this introduction we fell in communication of cats. And some affirming, as I do now (but I was against it then), that they had understanding, for confirmation whereof one of the servants told this story.

A wise man may in some things change his opinion.

"There was in my country," quod he, "a man" (the fellow was born in Staffordshire) "that had a young cat which he had brought up of a kitling,[6] and would nightly dally and play with it; and on a time as he rode through Kankwood[7] about certain business, a cat, as he thought, leaped out of a bush before him and called him twice or thrice by his name. But because he made none answer nor spake (for he was so afraid that he could not), she spake to him plainly twice or thrice these words following: 'Commend me unto Titton Tatton and to Puss thy Catton, and tell her that Grimalkin is dead.' This done she went her way, and the man went forward about his business. And after that he was returned home, in an evening sitting by the fire with his wife and his household, he told of his adventure in the wood. And when he had told them all the cat's message, his cat, which had harkened unto the tale, looked upon him sadly, and at the last said, 'And is Grimalkin dead? Then farewell dame,' and therewith went her way and was never seen after."

A cat spake to a man in Kankwood.

A wonderful wit of a cat.

When this tale was done, another of the company, which had been in Ireland, asked this fellow when this thing which he had told happened. He answered that he could not tell well, howbeit, as he conjectured, not passing forty years, for his mother knew both the man and the woman which ought[8] the cat that the message was sent unto. "Sure," quod the other, "then it may well be; for about that same time, as I heard, a like thing happened in Ireland where, if I conjecture not amiss, Grimalkin of whom you spake was slain."

Grimalkin was slain in Ireland.

"Yea sir," quod I, "I pray you how so?"

"I will tell you, Master Streamer," quod he, "that which was told me in Ireland, and which I have till now so little credited, that I was ashamed to report it. But hearing that I hear now, and calling to mind my own experience when it was, I do so little misdoubt it that I think I never told, nor you ever heard, a more likely tale. While I was in Ireland, in the time that Mac Murrough and all the rest of the wild lords were the King's enemies, what time also mortal war was between the Fitz Harrises and the Prior and Convent of the Abbey of Tintern, who counted them the King's friends and subjects, whose neighbor was Cahir Mac Art, a wild Irishman then the King's enemy and one which daily made inroads into the county of Wexford and burned such towns and carried away all such cattle as he might come by, by means whereof all the country from Clonmines to Ross became a waste wilderness and is scarce recovered until this day. In this time, I say, as I was on a night at coshery[9]

Experience is an infallible persuader.

Civil war between the King's subjects.

The fashion of the Irish wars.

6. Kitten.
7. Cannock Wood, a royal forest in Staffordshire.
8. Owned.
9. A feast.

with one of Fitz Harris' churls, we fell in talk (as we have done now) of strange adventures, and of cats. And there, among other things, the churl (for so they call all farmers and husbandmen) told me as you shall hear.

A churl's tale.

"There was, not seven years past, a kern[1] of John Butler's dwelling in the fassock[2] of Bantry called Patrick Apore, who minding to make a prey in the night upon Cahir Mac Art, his master's enemy, got him with his boy (for so they call their horse-keepers be they never so old knaves) into his country, and in the night time entered into a town of two houses, and brake in and slew the people, and then took such cattle as they found, which was a cow and a sheep, and departed therewith homeward. But doubting they should be pursued (the cur dogs made such a shrill barking), he got him into a church, thinking to lurk there till midnight was past, for there he was sure that no man would suspect or seek him—for the wild Irishmen have had churches in such reverence (till our men taught them the contrary) that they neither would, nor durst, either rob ought thence or hurt any man that took the churchyard for sanctuary, no, though he had killed his father.

This was an Irish town.

Irish curs bark sore.

The wild Irishmen were better than we in reverencing their religion.

"And while this kern was in the church he thought it best to dine, for he had eaten little that day. Wherefore he made his boy go gather sticks, and strake fire with his feres,[3] and made a fire in the church, and killed the sheep, and after the Irish fashion laid it thereupon and roasted it. But when it was ready, and that he thought to eat it, there came in a cat and set her by him, and said in Irish, 'Shane foel,' which is, 'give me some meat.' He, amazed at this, gave her the quarter that was in his hand, which immediately she did eat up, and asked more till she had consumed all the sheep; and, like a cormorant not satisfied therewith, asked still for more. Wherefore they supposed it were the Devil, and therefore thinking it wisdom to please him, killed the cow which they had stolen, and when they had flayed it gave the cat a quarter, which she immediately devoured. Then they gave her two other quarters; and in the meanwhile, after their country fashion, they did cut a piece of the hide and pricked it upon four stakes which they set about the fire, and therein they sod[4] a piece of the cow for themselves, and with the rest of the hide they made each of them laps[5] to wear about their feet like brogues, both to keep their feet from hurt all the next day, and also to serve for meat the next night, if they could get none other, by broiling them upon coals.

The old Irish diet was to dine at night.

A malapert guest that cometh unbidden.

A cat eat a sheep.

The woodkern's cookery.

Kerns for lack of meat eat their shoes roasted.

"By this time the cat had eaten three quarters and called for more. Wherefore they gave her that which was a-seething; and doubting lest, when she had eaten that, she would eat them too because they had no more for her, they got them out of the church and the kern took his horse and away he rode as fast as he could hie.

1. Soldier.
2. Wilderness.
3. Means for firelighting.
4. Boiled.
5. Wrappings, i.e., shoes.

When he was a mile or two from the church the moon began to shine, and his boy espied the cat upon his master's horse behind him and told him. Whereupon the kern took his dart, and turning his face toward her, flang it and struck her through with it. But immediately there came to her such a sight of cats that, after long fight with them, his boy was killed and eaten up, and he himself, as good and as swift as his horse was, had much to do to scape.

A kern killed Grimalkin. Cats did kill and eat a man.

"When he was come home and had put off his harness (which was a corslet of mail made like a shirt, and his skull covered over with gilt leather and crested with otter skin), all weary and hungry he set him down by his wife and told her his adventure, which, when a kitling which his wife kept, scarce half a year old, had heard, up she started and said, 'Hast thou killed Grimalkin!' And therewith she plunged in his face, and with her teeth took him by the throat, and ere that she could be plucked away, she had strangled him. This the churl told me now about thirty-three winters past; and it was done, as he and divers other creditable men informed me, not seven years before. Whereupon I gather that this Grimalkin was it which the cat in Kankwood sent news of unto the cat which we heard of even now."

The kern's armor.

A kitling killeth the kern that slew Grimalkin. A very strange conjecture.

"Tush," quod another that sat by, "your conjecture is too unreasonable; for to admit that cats have reason and that they do in their own language understand one another, yet how should a cat in Kankwood know what is done in Ireland?"

"How?" quod he, "even as we know what is done in the realms of France, Flanders, and Spain, yea, and almost in all the world beside. There be few ships but have cats belonging unto them, which bring news unto their fellows out of all quarters."

Each realm knoweth what is done in all other. Cats carry news.

"Yea," quod the other, "but why should all cats love to hear of Grimalkin, or how should Grimalkin eat so much meat as you speak of, or why should all cats so labor to revenge her death?"

"Nay, that passeth my cunning," quod he, "to show in all; howbeit in part conjectures may be made, as thus. It may be that Grimalkin and her line is as much esteemed and hath the same dignity among cats, as either the humble or master bee hath among the whole hive, at whose commandment all bees are obedient, whose succor and safeguard they seek, whose wrongs they all revenge; or as the Pope hath had ere this over all Christendom, in whose cause all his clergy would not only scratch and bite, but kill and burn to powder (though they knew not why) whomsoever they thought to think but once against him—which Pope, all things considered, devoureth more at every meal than Grimalkin did at her last supper."

Bees love and obey their governor. The Pope's clergy are crueller than cats. The Pope a great waster.

"Nay," said I then, "although the Pope, by exactions and other baggagical trumpery, have spoiled all people of mighty spoils, yet (as touching his own person) he eateth and weareth as little as any other man, though peradventure more sumptuous and costly, and in greater abundance provided. And I heard a very proper saying in this behalf of King Henry VII: When a servant of his told him what abundance of meat he had seen at an abbot's table, he reported him

A little sufficeth him that hath enough.

to be a great glutton; he asked if the abbot eat up all, and when he answered no, but his guests did eat the most part, 'Ah,' quod the king, 'thou callest him glutton for his liberality to feed thee and such other unthankful churls.' Like to this fellow are all ruffians, for let honest, worshipful men of the city make them good cheer or lend them money as they commonly do, and what have they for their labor? Either foul, reproachful names (as 'dunghill churls,' 'cuckold knaves'), or else spiteful and slanderous reports, as to be usurers and decayers of the common weal. And although that some of them be such indeed, yet I abhor to hear other of whom they deserve well, so lewdly to report them. But now, to return to your communication, I marvel how Grimalkin (as you term her), if she were no bigger, could eat so much meat at once."

Such jests a man may have enough.

The wisdom of King Henry the Seventh.

The unthankful are to be abhorred.

"I do not think," quod he that told the tale, "that she did eat all (although she asked all), but took her choice and laid the rest by, as we see in the feeding of many things. For a wolf, although a cony[6] be more than he can eat, yet will he kill a cow or twain for his breakfast—likewise all other ravenous beasts. Now, that love and fellowship and a desire to save their kind is among cats, I know by experience. For there was one that hired a friend of mine, in pastime, to roast a cat alive,[7] and promised him for his labor twenty shillings. My friend, to be sure, caused a cooper to fasten him into a hogshead, in which he turned a spit, whereupon was a quick[8] cat. But ere he had turned a while, whether it was the smell of the cat's wool that singed, or else her cry that called them, I cannot tell, but there came such a sort of cats that if I and other hardy men (which were well scrat for our labor) had not behaved us the better, the hogshead, as fast as it was hooped, could not have kept my cousin from them."

Ravenours spoil more than they occupy.

Like loveth the like.

A quick cat roasted.

Cat will to kind.

"Indeed," quod a well-learned man and one of excellent judgment that was then in the company, "it doth appear that there is in cats, as in all other kinds of beasts, a certain reason and language whereby they understand one another. But, as touching this, Grimalkin I take rather to be an hagat[9] or a witch than a cat. For witches have gone often in that likeness—and thereof hath come the proverb, as true as common, that a cat hath nine lives (that is to say, a witch may take on her a cat's body nine times)."

Some think this was Master Sherry.

Witches may take upon them the likeness of other things.

"By my faith, sir, this is strange," quod I myself, "that a witch should take on her a cat's body. I have read that the Pythonesses could cause their spirits to take upon them dead men's bodies, and the airy spirits which we call demons (of which kind are incubus and succubus, Robin Goodfellow the fairy, and goblins, which the miners call telchines) could at their pleasure take upon them any other sorts. But that a woman, being so large a body, should strain her into the body of a cat (or into that form either), I have not much heard of, nor can well perceive how it may be, which maketh me (I promise you) believe it the less."

Airy spirits take on them dead men's bodies.

6. Rabbit.
7. A common pastime, especially in France.
8. Live.
9. Witch.

"Well, Master Streamer," quod he, "I know you are not so ignorant herein as you make yourself; but this is your accustomed fashion, always to make men believe that you be not so well learned as you be. *Sapiens enim celat scientism,*[1] which appeared well by Socrates. For I know, being skilled as you be in the tongues (chiefly the Calde, Arabic, and Egyptian) and having read so many authors therein, you must needs be skillful in these matters; but where you spake of instrusion of a woman's body into a cat's, you either play Nichodem[2] or the stubborn Popish conjurer: whereof one would creep into his mother's belly again, the other would bring Christ out of Heaven to thrust him into a piece of bread (but as the one of them is gross and the other perverse, so in this point I must place you with one of them). For although witches may take upon them cats' bodies, or alter the shape of their or other bodies, yet this is not done by putting their own bodies thereinto, but either by bringing their souls for the time out of their bodies and putting them in the other, or by deluding the sight and fantasies of the seers. As when I make a candle with the brain of a horse and brimstone, the light of the candle maketh all kinds of heads appear horseheads, but yet it altereth the form of no head, but deceiveth the right conception of the eye (which, through the false light, receiveth a like form)."

Wise men dissemble their cunning.

Master Streamer is well seen in tongues.

Transubstantiationers destroy Christ's manhood.

How witches transform their shape.

One kind of magic consisteth in deceiving the senses.

Then quod he that had been in Ireland, "I cannot tell, sir, by what means witches do change their own likeness and the shapes of other things, but I have heard of so many and seen so much myself, that I am sure they do it. For in Ireland, as they have been ere this in England, witches are for fear had in high reverence. They be so cunning that they can change the shapes of things as they list at their pleasure and so deceive the people thereby that an act was made in Ireland that no man should buy any red swine. The cause whereof was this: The witches used to send to the markets many red swine, fair and fat to see unto as any might be, and would in that form continue long; but if it chanced the buyers of them to bring them to any water, immediately they found them returned either into wisps of hay, straw, old rotten boards, or such like trumpery, by means whereof they lost their money or such other cattle as they gave in exchange for them.

Witches are reverenced for fear.

An act forbidding to buy red swine.

Sorcerers make swine of hay and other baggage.

"There is also, in Ireland, one nation whereof some one man and woman are at every seven years' end turned into wolves, and so continue in the woods the space of seven years. And if they hap to live out the time, they return to their own form again, and other twain are turned for the like time into the same shape—which is a penance (as they say) enjoined that stock by Saint Patrick for some wickedness of their ancestors. And that this is true witnessed a man whom I left alive in Ireland who had performed this seven years' penance, whose wife was slain while she was a wolf in her last year. This man told to many men, whose cattle he had worried and whose bodies he had assailed while he was a wolf, so plain and

Men turned into wolves.

Saint Patrick's plague.

A man proved himself to have been a wolf seven years.

1. The wise hide their knowledge.

2. Nicodemus.

evident tokens and showed such scars of wounds which other men had given him, both in his man's shape before he was a wolf and in his wolf's shape since, which all appeared upon his skin, that it was evident to all men (yea, and to the bishop, too, upon whose grant it was recorded and registered) that the matter was undoubtedly past all peradventure.

A Bishop confirmeth Saint Partick's plague.

"And I am sure you are not ignorant of the hermit whom, as St. Augustine writeth, a witch would in an ass's form ride upon to market. But now how these witches made their swine, and how these folk were turned from shape to shape, whether by some ointment whose clearness deceived men's sights till either the water washed away the ointment, or else that the clearness of the water excelled the clearness of the ointment (and so betrayed the operation of it), I am as uncertain as I am sure that it were the spirits called demons, forced by enchantments, which moved those bodies till shame of their shape discovered caused them to leave them. But as for the transformation of the wolves, [it] is either miraculous as Naaman's leprosy in the stock of Gehesie, or else [due] to shameful, crafty, malicious sorcery. And as the one way is unsearchable, so I think there might means be found to guess how it is done the other way. For witches are by nature exceeding malicious, and if it chance that some witch, for displeasure taken with this wolvish nation, gave her daughter charge in her death bed when she taught her the science (for till that time witches never teach it, nor then but to their eldest and best-beloved daughter) that she should, at every seven years' end, confect some ointment which seven years' space might be in force against all other clearness to represent unto men's eyes the shape of a wolf; and in the night season to go herself in likeness either of the mare or some other night form and anoint therewith the bodies of some couple of that kindred which she hated; and that after her time she should charge her daughter to observe the same, and to charge her daughter after her to do the like forever, so that this charge is given always by tradition with the science, and so is continued and observed by this witch's offspring, by whom two of this kindred (as it may be supposed) are every seven years' space turned into wolves."

How sorcerers may make swine.

Demons are the souls of counterfeit bodies.

Witches are by nature malicious.

When and to whom witches teach their science.

How men are changed into wolves.

Witchcraft is kin to unwritten verities, for both go by traditions.

When I had heard these tales and the reason of the doing showed by the teller, "Ah, Thomas," quod I (for that was his name; he died afterwards of a disease which he took in Newgate, where he lay long for suspicion of magic because he had desired a prisoner to promise him his soul after he was hanged), "I perceive now the old proverb is true: 'The still sow eateth up all the draff.' You go and behave yourself so simply that a man would think you were but a fool, but you have uttered such proof of natural knowledge in this your brief talk, as I think (except myself and few more the best-learned alive) none could have done the like."

Many shrewd diseases do breed in Newgate.

The best learned are not the greatest boasters.

"You say your pleasure, Master Streamer," quod he. "As for me, I have said nothing but that I have seen, and whereof any man might conjecture as I do."

That a man seeth, he may boldly say.

"You have spoken full well," quod he that gave occasion of this tale, "and your conjectures are right reasonable. For like as by ointments (as you suppose) the Irish witches do make the form of swine and wolves appear to all men's sight, so think I that by the like power English witches and Irish witches may and do turn themselves into cats. For I heard it told while I was in the university, by a credible clerk of Oxford, how that in the days when he was a child an old woman was brought before the official and accused for a witch, which (in the likeness of a cat) would go into her neighbors' houses and steal thence what she listed. Which complaint was proved true by a place of the woman's skin, which her accusers (with a firebrand that they hurled at her) had singed while she went a-thieving in her cat's likeness. So that, to conclude as I began, I think that the cat which you call Grimalkin, whose name carrieth in it matter to confirm my conjecture (for Malkin is a woman's name, as witnesseth the proverb 'there be more maids than Malkin'), I think, I say, that it was a witch in a cat's likeness; and that for the wit and craft of her, other natural cats that were not so wise have had her and her race in reverence among them, thinking her to be but a mere cat as they themselves were—like as we silly fools long time, for his sly and crafty juggling, reverenced the Pope, thinking him to have been but a man (though much holier than we ourselves were), whereas indeed he was a very incarnated devil, like as this Grimalkin was an incarnate witch."

A woman was found in a cat's likeness and punished.

Witches never use their art but to evil.

It is to be thought that Grimalkin was a witch.

Cats may be deceived as well as Christian folk.

"Why then, sir," said I, "do you think that natural cats have wit and that they understand one another?" "What else, Master Streamer?" quod he. "There is no kind of sensible creatures but have reason and understanding; whereby, in their kind, each understandeth other and do therein in some points so excel that the consideration thereof moved Pythagoras (as you know) to believe and affirm that after death men's souls went into beasts and beasts' souls into men, and every one according to his desert in his former body. And although his opinion be fond and false, yet that which drew him thereto is evident and true—and that is the wit and reason of diverse beasts, and again the dull, beastly, brutish ignorance of diverse men.

All sensible creatures have reason and understanding.

Pythagoras' opinion concerning souls.

Some beasts are wiser than men.

"But that beasts understand one another, and fowls likewise, beside that we see by daily experience in marking them, the story of the Bishop of Alexandria by record doth prove. For he found the means, either through diligence so to mark them, or else through magic natural so to subtiliate his sensible powers, either by purging his brain by dry drinks and fumes, or else to augment the brains of his power perceptible by other natural medicines, that he understood all kind of creatures by their voices. For being on a time sitting at dinner in a house among his friends, he harkened diligently to a sparrow that came fleeing and chirping to other that were about the house, and smiled to himself to hear her. And when one of the company desired to know why he smiled, he said 'At the sparrow's tale. For she telleth them,' quod he, 'that in the highway, not a quarter of

A Bishop understood all kind of creatures' voices.

The brain is the organ of understanding.

A sparrow called her fellows to a banquet.

a mile hence, a sack of wheat is even now fallen off a horseback and broken, and all the wheat run out, and therefore biddeth them come thither to dinner.' And when the guests, musing hereat, sent to prove the truth, they found it even so as he had told them."

When this tale was ended, the clock struck nine; whereupon old Thomas, because he had far to his lodging, took his leave and departed. The rest of the company got them also either to their business or to their beds. And I went straight to my chamber (before remembered) and took a book in my hand to have studied, but the remembrance of this former talk so troubled me that I could think of nothing else, but mused still and, as it were, examined more narrowly what every man had spoken.

Master Streamer is always given much to study.

The Second Part of Master Streamer's Oration

Ere I had been long in this contemplation, the cats, whose crying the night before had been occasion of all that which I have told you, were assembled again in the leads which I spake of, where the dead men's quarters were set up; and after the same sort as they did the night before, one sang in one tune, another in another, even such another service as my Lord's chapel upon the scaffold[3] sang before the King. They observed no musical chords, neither diatesseron, diapente, nor diapason;[4] and yet I ween I lie, for one cat, groaning as a bear[5] doth when dogs be let slip to him, trolled out so low and so loud a bass that, in comparison of another cat which, crying like a young child, squealed out the shrieking treble, it might be well counted a double diapason. Wherefore, to the intent I might perceive the better the cause of their assembly, and by their gestures perceive part of their meaning, I went softly and fair into a chamber which hath a window into the same leads, and in the dark standing closely,[6] I viewed through the trellis, as well as I could, all their gestures and behavior.

Cats assembled in the leads.

Cats have sundry voices.

The diligence of the author to understand all things.

And I promise you it was a thing worth the marking to see what countenances, what becks,[7] yea and what order was among them. For one cat, which was a mighty big one, grey-haired, bristle-bearded, and having broad eyes which shone and sparkled like two stars, sat in the midst, and on either side of her sat another. And before her stood three more, whereof one mewed continually, save when the great cat groaned. And ever when the great cat had done, this mewing cat began again, first stretching out her neck and, as it were, making 'beisance to them which sat. And oftentimes, in the midst of this cat's mewing, all the rest would suddenly each one in his tune bray forth and incontinently[8] hush again, as it were laughing at somewhat which they heard the other cat declare. And after this sort I beheld them from ten till it was twelve o'clock, at which

Cats keep order among themselves.

Cats make courtesy with their necks and tails.

3. Stage.
4. Musical terms.
5. I.e., bear-bating.
6. Secretly.
7. Gestures.
8. Immediately.

time, whether it were some vessel in the kitchen under or some board in the printing house hard by I cannot tell, but somewhat fell with such a noise that all the cats got them up upon the house; and I, fearing lest any arose to see what was fallen they would charge me with the hurling down of it if they found me there, I whipped into my chamber quickly and, finding my lamp still burning, I set me down upon my bed and devised upon the doings of these cats, casting all manner of ways what might be conjectured thereof to know what they meant.

Note here the painfulness of the author.

The good housewife's candle never goeth out.

And by and by I deemed that the grey cat which sat in the midst was the chief and sat as judge among the rest, and that the cat which continually mewed declared some matter or made account to her of somewhat. By means whereof I was straight caught with such a desire to know what she had said that I could not sleep of all that night, but lay devising by what means I might learn to understand them. And calling to mind that I had read in Albertus Magnus' works a way how to be able to understand birds' voices, I made no more to do, but sought in my library for the little book entitled *De Virtutibus Animalium,*[9] *etc.*, and greedily read it over. And when I came to "Si vis voces avium intelligere, etc.," Lord how glad I was. And when I had thoroughly marked the description of the medicine, and considered with myself the nature and power of everything therein and how and upon what it wrought, I devised thereby how, with part of those things and additions of other of like virtue and operation, to make a philter for to serve my purpose.

Earnest desire banisheth sleep.

Albertus Magnus teacheth many wonders.

A philosopher searcheth the nature of all things.

And as soon as restless Phoebus was come up out of the smoking sea and, with shaking his golden-colored beams which were all the night long in Thetis' moist bosom, had dropped off his silver sweat into Hera's dry lap, and kissing fair Aurora with glowing mouth had driven from her the advouterer[1] Lucifer, and was mounted so high to look upon Europa that, for all the height of Mile-End steeple, he spied me through the glass window lying upon my bed, up I arose and got me abroad to seek for such things as might serve for the earnest business which I went about.

A description of the resurrection of the sun.

And because you be all my friends that are here I will hide nothing from you, but declare from point to point how I behaved myself both in making and taking my philter. "If thou wilt understand," saith Albert, "the voices of birds or of beasts, take two in thy company, and upon Simon and Jude's day early in the morning, get thee with hounds into a certain wood, and the first beast that thou meetest take, and prepare with the heart of a fox, and thou shalt have thy purpose; and whosoever thou kissest shall understand them as well as thyself."

Nothing may be hid from friends.

How to understand birds.

Because his writing here is doubtful, because he saith "quoddam nemus," a certain wood, and because I knew three men not many years past which, while they went about this hunting were so 'fraid, whether with an evil spirit or with their own imagination

Men and dogs 'fraid out of their wits in proving an experiment.

9. *Of The Virtues of Animals* . . . 'if you want to understand the voices of the birds'.

1. Adulterer.

I cannot tell, but home they came with their hair standing on end, and some of them have been the worse ever since, and their hounds likewise; and seeing it was so long to St. Jude's Day, therefore I determined not to hunt at all. But conjecturing that the beast which they should take was an hedgehog (which at that time of the year goeth most abroad), and knowing by reason that the flesh thereof was by nature full of natural heat—and therefore, the principal parts being eaten, must needs expulse gross matters and subtile the brain (as by the like power it engendreth fine blood and helpeth much both against the gout and the cramp)—I got me forth towards St. John's Wood, whereas not two days before I had seen one. And see the lucky and unlucky chance! By the way as I went I met with hunters who had that morning killed a fox and three hares, who (I thank them) gave me an hare and the fox's whole body (except the case[2]) and six smart lashes with a slip,[3] because (wherein I did mean no harm) I asked them if they had seen anywhere an hedgehog that morning.

An hedgehog is one of the planetical beasts, and therefore good in magic.

Medicine for the gout.

The liberality of hunters.

And here, save that my tale is otherwise long, I would show you my mind of these wicked, superstitious observations of foolish hunters, for they be like (as me seemeth) to the papists, which for speaking of good and true words punish good and honest men. Are not apes, owls, cuckoos, bears, and urchins God's good creatures? Why, then, is it not lawful to name them? If they say it bringeth ill luck in the game, then are they unlucky, idolatrical, miscreant infidels and have no true belief in God's providence. I beshrew their superstitious hearts, for my buttocks did bear the burden of their misbelief.

Superstitious hunters are kin to the papists.

All creatures are good.

To observe times, days, or words argueth infidelity.

And yet I thank them again for the fox and the hare which they gave me; for with the two hounds at my girdle I went a-hunting, till indeed under an hedge in a hole of the earth by the root of an hollow tree I found an hedgehog with a bushel of crabs[4] about him, whom I killed straight with my knife, saying "Shavol swashmeth, gorgona Iiscud," and with the other beasts, hung him at my girdle, and came homeward as fast as I could hie. But when I came in the close besides Islington, commonly called St. John's Field, a kite, belike very hungry, spied at my back the skinless fox, and thinking to have a morsel strake at it, and that so eagerly that one of his claws was entered so deep that, before he could loose it, I drew out my knife and killed him, saying "Javol sheleg hutotheca Iiscud," and to make up the mess brought him home with the rest.

He that seeketh findeth.

Albertus saith if a man when he prepareth any medicine tell aloud why he maketh it, it will be of more force.

And ere I had laid them out of my hand, came Thomas (whom you heard of before) and brought me a cat, which for doing evil turns they had that morning caught in a snare set for her two days before, which for the skin's sake being flain, was so exceeding fat that, after I had taken some of the grease, the inwards, and the head, to make (as I made him believe) a medicine for the gout, they parboiled the rest,

One good hap followeth another.

Cat's grease is good for the gout.

2. The hide.
3. Whip.
4. Crab apples.

and at night, roasted and farced[5] with good herbs, did eat it up every morsel, and was as good meat as was or could be eaten.

A cat was roasted and eaten.

But now mark! For when Thomas was departed with his cat, I shut my chamber door to me and flayed mine urchin,[6] wishing oft for Doctor Nicholas, or some other expert physician, to make the dissection for the better knowledge of the anatomy. The flesh I washed clean and put it in a pot, and with white wine, Mellisophillos or Melissa (commonly called balm), rosemary, neat's tongue,[7] four parts of the first and two of the second, I made a broth and set it on a fire and boiled it, setting on a limbec,[8] with a glass at the end over the mouth of the pot to receive the water that distilled from it, in the seething whereof I had a pint of a pottle of wine which I put in the pot. Then, because it was about the *solstitium estivale*,[9] and that in confections the hours of the planets must for the better operation be observed, I tarried till ten o'clock before dinner, what time Mercury began his lucky reign.

A solitary man is either a god or a beast.

Par prior numerus, impar posterior est. gib.

Omne opus fiat in sua planeta. Zoroast.

And then I took a piece of the cat's liver and a piece of the kidney, a piece of the milt[1] and the whole heart, the fox's heart and the lights,[2] the hare's brain, the kite's maw,[3] and the urchin's kidneys. All these I beat in a mortar together until it were small, and then made a cake of it, and baked it upon a hot stone till it was dry like bread. And while this was a-baking I took seven parts of the cat's grease, as much of her brain, with five hairs of her beard (three black and two grey), three parts of the fox's grease, as much of the brain, with the hoofs of his left feet, the like portion of the urchin's grease and brain with his stones,[4] all the kite's brain, with all the marrow of her bones, the juice of her heart, her upper beak and the middle claw of her left foot, the fat of the hare's kidneys and the juice of his right shoulder bone. All these things I pounded together in a mortar by the space of an hour, and then I put it in a cloth and hung it over a basin in the sun, out of which dropped within four hours after about half a pint of oil very fair and clear.

Omne totum totaliter malum. Trismeg.

Deus impari numero gaudet.

Dextra bona bonis sinistra vero sinistris.

Calor solis est ignis alichimistice distillationis.

Then took I the galls of all these beasts, and the kite's toe, and served them likewise, keeping the liquor that dropped from them. At twelve of the clock, what time the sun began his planetical dominion, I went to dinner. But meat I ate none, save the boiled urchin; my bread was the cake mentioned before; my drink was the distillation of the urchin's broth, which was exceeding strong and pleasant both in taste and savor.

Master Streamer varieth from the astronomers in his planet hours.

After that I had dined well, my head waxed so heavy that I could not choose but sleep. And after that I waked again, which was within an hour. My mouth and my nose purged exceedingly such yellow, white, and tawny matters as I never saw before, nor thought that any such had been in man's body. When a pint of this gear was come

The intelligible diet.

5. Stuffed.
6. Hedgehog.
7. Cow's tongue.
8. A stand for scientific experiments.
9. Summer solstice.

1. Spleen.
2. Lungs.
3. Stomach.
4. Testicles.

forth my rheum ceased, and my head and all my body was in exceeding good temper, and a thousand things which I had not thought of in twenty years before came so freshly to my mind as if they had been then presently done, heard, or seen. *There be many strange humors in many men's heads.* Whereby I perceived that my brain (chiefly the nuke memorative)[5] was marvelously well purged. *The remembrance lieth in the noodle of the head.* My imagination also was so fresh that by and by I could show a probable reason what, and in what sort, and upon what matter, everything which I had taken wrought, and the cause why. *A good philosopher.*

Then, to be occupied after my sleep, I cast away the carcass of the fox and of the kite, with all the garbage both of them and of the rest, saving the tongues and the ears which were very necessary for my purpose. *Exercise is good after sleep.* And thus I prepared them: I took all the ears and scalded off the hair; then stamped I them in a mortar; and when they were all a dry jelly, I put to them rue, fennel, lowache,[6] and leek blades, of each an handful, and pounded them afresh. *Hot things purge the head.* Then divided I all the matter into two equal parts, and made two little pillows and stuffed them therewith. And when Saturn's dry hour of dominion approached, I fried these pillows in good oil olive and laid them hot to mine ears, to each ear one, and kept them thereto till nine o'clock at night, which holp exceedingly to comfort my understanding power. *A good medicine for aching ears.* But, because as I perceived the cell perceptible of my brain intelligible was yet too gross, by means that the filmy pannicle[7] coming from *dura mater*[8] made too strait oppilations[9] by ingrossing the pores and conduits imaginative, I devised to help that with this gargaristical fume, whose subtle ascension is wonderful. *What hindreth the imaginative power.* I took the cat's, the fox's, and the kite's tongue and sod them in wine well near to jelly. Then I took them out of the wine and put them in a mortar and added to them of new cat's dung an ounce; of mustard seed, garlic, and pepper as much; and when they were with beating incorpored, I made lozenges and trochisks[1] thereof. *The wholesome things are not always most toothsome.*

And at six o'clock at night, what time the sun's dominion began again, I supped with the rest of the meat which I left at dinner. And when Mercury's reign approached, which was within two hours after, I drank a great draught of my stilled water, and anointed all my head over with the wine and oil before described, and with the water which came out of the galls I washed mine eyes. *Mercury furthereth all fine and subtle practices.* And because no humors should ascend into my head by evaporation of my reins[2] through the chine bone,[3] I took an ounce of Alkakengi[4] in powder, which I had for a like purpose not two days afore bought at the 'pothecaries, and therewith rubbed and chafed my back from the neck down to the middle, and heated in a frying pan my pillows afresh, and laid them to mine ears, and tied a kercher about my head, and with my lozenges and trochisks in a box, I went out among the servants, among whom was a shrewd boy, a very crack-rope,[5] *The chiefest point of wisdom is to prevent inconveniences. Heat augmenteth the virtue of outward plasters.*

5. I.e., the memory.
6. Lovage.
7. Membrane.
8. Membrane covering the brain.
9. Obstructions.

1. Lozenges.
2. Kidneys.
3. Jaw bone.
4. Winter cherry.
5. I.e., a person who is destined to be hanged.

that needs would know what was in my box. And I, to sauce him after his sauciness, called them "presciencial[6] pills," affirming that whoso might eat one of them should not only understand wonders, but also prophesy after them. Whereupon the boy was exceeding earnest in entreating me to give him one; and when at last very loathly, as it seemed, I granted his request, he took a lozenge, and put it in his mouth, and chewed it apace, by means whereof when the fume ascended he began to spattle and spit, saying, "By God's bones, it is a cat's turd." At this the company laughed apace; and so did I too, verifying it to be as he said, and that he was a prophet.

The ungracious should be ungraciously served.

Strange things are delectable.

We laugh gladly at shrewd turns.

But that he might not spew too much by imagination, I took a lozenge in my mouth and kept it under my tongue, showing thereby that it was not evil. While this pastime endured, methought I heard one cry with a loud voice, "What Isegrim,[7] what Isegrim"; and therefore I asked whose name was Isegrim, saying that one did call him. But they said that they knew none of that name, nor heard any that did call. "No," quod I (for it called still), "Hear you nobody? Who is that called so loud?"

"We hear nothing but a cat," quod they, "which meweth above in the leads."

When I saw it was so indeed, and that I understood what the cat said, glad was I as any man alive. And taking my leave of them as though I would to bed straight, I went into my chamber (for it was past nine of the clock). And because the hour of Saturnus' cold dominion approached, I put on my gown and got me privily to the place in the which I had viewed the cats the night before. And when I had settled myself where I might conveniently hear and see all things done in the leads where this cat cried still for Isegrim, I put into my two nostrils two trochisks and into my mouth two lozenges, one above my tongue the other under; and put off my left shoe, because of Jupiter's appropinquation;[8] and laid the fox tail under my foot. And to hear the better, I took off my pillows which stopped mine ears; and then listened and viewed as attentively as I could.

Good success of things maketh men joyous.

Saturn is a cold, old planet.

There is great cunning in due applying of medicines.

But I warrant you the pellicle, or filmy rime, that lyeth within the bottom of mine ear hole, from whence little veins carry the sounds to the senses, was with this medicine in my pillows so purged and parched, or at least dried, that the least moving of the air, whether struck with breath of living creatures, which we call voices, or with the moving of dead (as winds, waters, trees, carts, falling of stones, etc.), which are named noises, sounded so shrill in my head by reverberation of my 'fined films, that the sound of them altogether was so disordered and monstrous that I could discern no one from other, save only the harmony of the moving of the spheres, which noise excelled all other as much both in pleasance and shrill highness of sound as the Zodiac itself surmounteth all other

The cause of hearing.

The difference between voices and noises.

The harmony of heaven excelleth all other.

6. I.e, able to predict the future.
7. A name for a wolf.
8. Approach.

creatures in altitude of place. For in comparison of the basest of this noise, which is the moving of Saturn by means of his large compass, the highest voices of birds and the straitest whistling of the wind, or any other organ pipes whose sounds I heard confused together, appeared but a low bass. And yet was those an high treble to the voice of beasts, to which as a mean the running of rivers was a tenor; and the boiling of the sea and the cataracts[9] or gulfs thereof a goodly bass; and the rushing, brising, and falling of the clouds a deep diapason.[1]

The harmony of elemental mixtures.

While I harkened to this broil, laboring to discern both voices and noises asunder, I heard such a mixture as I think was never in Chaucer's House of Fame; for there was nothing within an hundred mile of me done on any side (for from so far, but no farther, the air may come because of obliquation[2]) but I heard it as well as if I had been by it, and could discern all voices, but by means of noises understand none. Lord what ado women made in their beds—some scolding; some laughing; some weeping; some singing to their sucking children, which made a woeful noise with their continual crying. And one shrewd wife a great way off (I think at St. Albans) called her husband "cuckold" so loud and shrilly that I heard that plain; and would fain have heard the rest, but could not by no means for barking of dogs, grunting of hogs, wawling of cats, rumbling of rats, gaggling of geese, humming of bees, rousing of bucks, gaggling of ducks, singing of swans, ringing of pans, crowing of cocks, sewing of socks, cackling of hens, scrabbling of pens, peeping of mice, trulling of dice, curling of frogs, and toads in the bogs, chirking of crickets, shutting of wickets, shriking of owls, flittering of fowls, routing of knaves, snorting of slaves, farting of churls, fizzling of girls, with many things else—as ringing of bells, counting of coins, mounting of groins, whispering of lovers, springling of plovers, groaning and spewing, baking and brewing, scratching and rubbing, watching and shrugging—with such a sort of commixed noises as would a-deaf anybody to have heard; much more me, seeing that the pannicles of mine ears were with my medicine made so fine and stiff, and that by the temperate heat of the things therein, that like a tabor dried before the fire or else a lute string by heat shrunk nearer, they were incomparably amended in receiving and yielding the shrillness of any touching sounds.

Chaucer's House of Fame.

At every hundred mile the air reflecteth by means of the roundness of the world.

The cart and cucking stool groveth for such.

Here the poetical fury came upon him.

Many noises in the night which all men hear not.

Over much noise maketh one deaf.

Heat shrilleth all moist instruments.

While I was earnestly harkening, as I said, to hear the woman, minding nothing else, the greatest bell in St. Botolph's steeple, which is hard by, was tolled for some rich body that then lay in passing, the sound whereof came with such a rumble into mine ear that I thought all the devils in Hell had broken loose and were come about me, and was so afraid therewith that, when I felt the foxtail under my foot (which through fear I had forgot), I deemed it had been the Devil indeed. And therefore I cried out as loud as ever I could, "The Devil, the Devil, the Devil!" But when some of the folks, raised with my noise, had sought me in my chamber and

All sudden things astonish us.

9. Water spouts.
1. Harmony.
2. Changing course.

found me not there, they went seeking about, calling one to another, "Where is he? Where is he? I cannot find Master Streamer." Which noise and stir of them was so great in mine ears and passing man's common sound, that I thought they had been devils indeed which sought and asked for me.

Fertilitas sibi ipsi nocus.[3]

Wherefore I crept close into a corner in the chimney and hid me, saying many good prayers to save me from them. And because their noise was so terrible that I could not abide it, I thought best to stop mine ears, thinking thereby I should be the less afraid. And as I was thereabout, a crow, which belike was nodding asleep on the chimney top, fell down into the chimney over my head, whose flittering in the fall made such a noise that, when I felt his feet upon my head, I thought that the Devil had been come indeed and seized upon me. And when I cast up my hand to save me, and therewith touched him, he called me "knave" in his language, after such a sort that I swooned for fear. And by that I was come to myself again, he was flowen from me into the chamber roof, and there he sat all night.

Danger maketh men devout.

How evil haps run together.

A man may die only by imagination of harm.

Then took I my pillows to stop mine ears; for the rumble that the servants made I took for the devils, it was so great and shrill. And I had no sooner put them on, but by and by I heard it was the servants which sought for me, and that I was deceived through my clearness of hearing, for the bell which put me in all this fear (for which I never loved bells since) tolled still, and I perceived well enough what it was. And seeing that the servants would not leave calling and seeking till they found me, I went down to them and feigned that a cat had been in my chamber and 'fraid me. Whereupon they went to bed again, and I to mine old place.

We hate forever whatsoever hath harmed us.

The Third Part of Master Streamer's Oration

By this time waning Cynthia, which the day before had filled her growing horns, was come upon our hemisphere and freshly yielded forth her brother's light, which the reverberation[4] of Thetis' trembling face, now full by means of spring, had fully cast upon her, whereof she must needs lose every day more and more, by means the neap abasing Thetis' swollen face would make her to cast beyond her those rades,[5] which before the full the spring had caused her to throw short—like as, with a crystal glass a man may, by the placing of it either high or low, so cast the sun or a candlelight upon any round glass of water that it shall make the light thereof both in waxing and waning to counterfeit the moon. For you shall understand—chiefly you, Master Willot, that are my lord's astronomer—that all our ancestors have failed in knowledge of natural causes; for it is not the moon that causeth the sea to ebb and flow, neither to neap and spring, but the neaping and springing of the sea is the cause of the moon's both waxing and waning. For the moonlight is nothing save

The description of the moon at full.

How to counterfeit the moon.

Astronomers are deceived.

The spring and neaping of the sea causeth the moon to wax and wane.

3. Fertility is harmful to itself.
4. Reflection.
5. Rays.

the shining of the sun cast into the element by opposition of the sea; as also the stars are nothing else but the sunlight reflected upon the face of rivers and cast upon the crystalline heaven, which because rivers alway keep like course, therefore are the stars alway of one bigness. As for the course of the stars, from east to west is natural by means of the sun's like moving; but in that they ascend and descend (that is, sometime come northward and sometime go southward), that is caused also by the sun's being either on this side or on the other side his line like-nightical. The like reason followeth for the poles not moving, and that is the situation of those rivers or dead seas which cast them and the roundness and egg-form of the firmament. But to let this pass, which in my *Book of Heaven and Hell* shall be plainly not only declared but both by reason and experience proved, I will come again to my matter.

What the moon and stars be.

The sun's moving is cause of divers moving of the stars.

Why the poles do not move.

I take this book to be it that is entitled Of the Great Egg.

When Cynthia, I say, as following her brother's steps, had looked in at my chamber window and saw me neither in my bed nor at my book, she hied her apace into the south, and at a little hole in the house roof peeped in and saw me where I was set to harken to the cats. And by this time all the cats which were there the night before were assembled with many other, only the great grey one excepted. Unto whom, as soon as he was come, all the rest did their 'beisance as they did the night before. And when he was set, thus he began in his language (which I understood as well as if he had spoken English).

The man is studious.

Light searcheth all things.

Good manners among cats.

"Ah my dear friends and fellows, you may say I have been a lingerer this night and that I have tarried long; but you must pardon me for I could come no sooner. For when this evening I went into an ambry[6] where was much good meat to steal my supper, there came a wench not thinking I had been there and clapped the lid down, by means whereof I have had much to do to get forth. Also, in the way as I came hither over the housetops, in a gutter were thieves breaking in at the window, who 'fraid me so that I lost my way and fell down into the street and had much to do to escape the dogs. But seeing that by the grace of Hagat and Heg I am now come, although I perceive by the tail of the Great Bear and by Alhabor,[7] which are now somewhat southward, that the fifth hour of our night approacheth; yet, seeing this is the last night of my charge and that tomorrow I must again to my lord Cammoloch (at this all the cats spread along their tails and cried, 'Hagat and Heg save him'), go to now good Mouse-slayer," quod he, "and that time which my misfortune hath lost, recover again by the briefness of thy talk."

The strange hap of Grisard.

Sweet meat must have sour sauce.

Cats are afraid of thieves.

Hagat and Heg are witches which the cats do worship.

Cats are skilled in astronomy.

Cammoloch is chief prince among cats.

Gentleness becometh officers.

"I will my lord," quod Mouse-slayer, which is the cat which as I told you stood before the great cat the night before continually mewing; who in her language, after that with her tail she had made courtesy, shrunk in her neck and said, "Whereas by virtue of your commission from my lord Cammoloch (whose life Hagat and Heg defend), who by inheritance and our free election enjoyeth the

Mouse-slayer telleth on her story.

6. Storehouse.

7. Sirius, the dog star.

empire of his traitorously murdered mother the goddess Grimolochin, you his greffier[8] and chief counselor, my lord Grisard, with Isegrim and Pol-noir your assistants, upon a complaint put up in your high dais[9] by that false accuser Catch-rat, who beareth me malice because I refused his lecherously offered delights, have caused me, in purging of myself before this honorable company, to declare my whole life since the blind days of my kitlinghood. You remember, I trust, how in the two nights passed I have declared my life for four years' space, wherein you perceive how I behaved me all that time.

Grimolochin is the same that was late called Grimalkin.

She purgeth herself by declaring her life.

"Wherefore, to begin where I left last, ye shall understand that my lord and lady, whose lives I declared unto you last yesternight, left the city and went to dwell in the country, and carried me with them. And being there strange I lost their house, and with Bird-hunt my mate, the gentlest in honest venery that ever I met with, went to a town where he dwelt called Stratford—either Stony, upon Tine, or upon Avon, I do not well remember which—where I dwelled half a year—and this was in the time when preachers had leave to speak against the Mass, but it was not forbidden till half a year after. In this time I saw nothing worthy to certify my lord of, save this.

Mouse-slayer was by her mistress carried into the country.

Bird-hunt was Mouse-slayer's mate.

"My dame, with whom I dwelt, and her husband were both old, and therefore hard to be turned from their rooted belief which they had in the Mass, which caused divers young folk, chiefly their sons and a learned kinsman of theirs, to be the more earnest to teach and persuade them. And when they had almost brought the matter to a good point, I cannot tell how it chanced, but my dame's sight failed her, and she was so sick that she kept her bed two days. Wherefore she sent for the parish priest, her old ghostly father; and when all were voided the chamber save I and they two, she told him how sick she was and how blind, so that she could see nothing, and desired him to pray for her and give her good counsel. To whom he said thus, 'It is no marvel though you be sick and blind in body which suffer your soul willingly to be blinded. You send for me now, but why send you not for me when these new heretics teach you to leave the Catholic belief of Christ's flesh in the sacrament?' 'Why sir,' quod she, 'I did send for you once, and when you came they posed you so with Holy Writ and saints' writings that you could say nothing but call them "heretics," and that they had made the New Testament themselves.'

Old errors are hard to be removed.

A sudden disease.

Cats are admitted to all secrets.

A jolly, persuading knave.

Railing and slandering are the Papists' Scriptures.

"'Yea,' quod he, 'but did I not bid you take heed then, and told you how God would plague you?' 'Yes, good sir,' quod she, 'you did, and now to my pain I find you too true a prophet. But I beseech you forgive me and pray to God for me, and whatsoever you will teach me, that will I believe unto the death.' 'Well,' quod he, 'God refuseth no sinners that will repent, and therefore in any case believe that Christ's flesh, body, soul, and bone is as it was born of our Blessed Lady in the consecrated Host, and see that therefore you worship it, pray, and offer to it. For by it any of your friends' souls

A true coal prophet.

Ghostly counsel of a Popish confessor.

8. Clerk.

9. Raised platform.

may be brought out of Purgatory (which these new heretics say is no place at all—but when their souls fry in it, they shall tell me another tale). And that you may know that all I say is true, and that the Mass can deliver such as trust in it from all manner of sins, I will by and by say you a Mass that shall restore your sight and health.'

No such persuasion as miracles chiefly in helping one from grief.

"Then took he out of his bosom a wafer cake and called for wine. And then, shutting the door unto him, revised[2] himself in a surplice, and upon a table set before the bed he laid his porteous,[3] and thereout he said Mass. And when he came to the elevation, he lifted up the cake and said to my dame (which in two days afore saw nothing), 'Wipe thine eyes thou sinful woman and look upon thy Maker.' With that she lifted up herself and saw the cake, and had her sight and her health as well as ever she had before. When Mass was done she thanked God and him exceedingly, and he gave charge that she should tell to no young folks how she was holp, for his bishop had throughout the diocese forbidden them to say or sing any Mass, but commanded her that secretly unto old honest men and women she should at all times most devoutly rehearse it. And by reason of this miracle, many are so confirmed in that belief that, although by a common law all Masses upon penalty were since forbidden, divers have them privily and nightly said in their chambers until this day.

Veritas quaerit angulos.[1]

A young knave made an old woman's maker.

Old folk are lighter of credit than young.

Cats hear many privy night Masses.

"'Marry sir,' quod Pol-noir, 'this was either a mighty miracle or else a mischievous subtlety of a magistical minister. But sure if the priest by magical art blinded her not afore, and so by like magical sorcery cured her again, it were as good for us to hire him or other priests at our delivery to sing a Mass before our kitlings, that they might in their birth be delivered of their blindness. And sure, if I knew the priest, it should scape me hard but I would have one litter of kitlings in some chamber where he useth now to say his privy night Masses.' 'What need that?' quod Mouse-slayer, 'it would do them no good. For I myself, upon like consideration, kittened since in another mistress's chamber of mine where a priest every day said Mass; but my kitlings saw naught the better, but rather the worse.'

Sorcerers may make folk blind.

Why Masses may serve well.

Devout kitlings that heard Mass so young.

"But when I heard that the Lord with whom I went into the country would to London to dwell again, I kept the house so well for a month before that my Lady when she went carried me with her. And when I was come to London again, I went in visitation to mine old acquaintance. And when I was great with kitling, because I would not be unpurveyed of a place to kitten in, I got in favor and household with an old gentlewoman, a widow, with whom I passed out this whole year.

Flatterers are diligent when they spy a profit.

"This woman got her living by boarding young gentlemen, for whom she kept always fair wenches in store, for whose sake she had the more resort. And to tell you the truth of her trade, it was fine and crafty, and not so dangerous as deceitful. For when she had

The trade of an old gentlewoman.

1. Truth seeks corner.
2. Dressed.
3. Portas, a portable breviary (the Catholic book containing instructions for religious services each day).

soaked from young gentlemen all that they had, then would she cast them off, except they fell to cheating. Wherefore many of them in the nighttime would go abroad and bring the next morning home with them sometimes money, sometime jewels (as rings or chains), sometime apparel; and sometime they would come again cursing their ill fortune, with nothing save peradventure dry blows or wet wounds. But whatsoever they brought, my dame would take it and find the means either so to gage[4] it that she would never fetch it again, or else melt it and sell it to the goldsmiths.

Whores, gaming, and good hostesses make many gentlemen make shameful shifts.

All is fish that cometh to the net.

"And notwithstanding that she used these wicked practices, yet was she very holy and religious. And therefore, although that all images were forbidden, yet kept she one of Our Lady in her coffer. And every night, when everybody were gone to bed and none in her chamber but she and I, then would she fetch Her out, and set Her upon her cupboard, and light up two or three wax candles afore Her, and then kneel down to Her, sometime an whole hour, saying over her beads and praying Her to be good unto her and to save her and all her guests both from danger and shame, and promising that then she would honor and serve Her during all her life.

A Catholic queen.

Images cannot see to hear, except they have much light.

Our Lady is hired to play the bawd.

"While I was with this woman I was alway much cherished and made of, for on nights while she was a-praying, I would be playing with her beads and alway catch them as she let them fall, and would sometime put my head in the compass of them and run away with them about my neck, whereat many times she took great pleasure, yea and so did Our Lady too. For my dame would say sometimes to Her, 'Yea, Blessed Lady, I know thou hearest me by thy smiling at my cat.'

Old women love their cats well.

The image laughed to see the cat play with her dame's beads.

"And never did my dame do me any hurt save once, and that I was even with her for; and that was thus. There was a gentleman, one of her boarders, much enamored in the beauty of a merchantman's wife in the city, whom he could by no means persuade to satisfy his lust. Yea, when he made her great banquets, offered her rich apparel and all kind of jewels precious which commonly women delight in, yea and large sums of money which corrupt even the gods themselves, yet could he by no means alter her mind, so much she esteemed her good name and honesty. Wherefore, forced through desire of that which he could not but long for, and so much the more because it was most earnestly denied him, he brake his mind to my dame, and entreated her to aid him to win this young woman's favor, and promised her for her labor whatsoever she would require.

Love is loiterers' occupation.

An honest wife.

Quid non mortalia pectora cogis, auri sacra fames?

"Whereupon my dame, which was taken for as honest as any in the city, found the means to desire this young woman to a dinner. And against she should come, my dame gave me a piece of pudding which she had filled full of mustard, which as soon as I had eaten wrought so in my head that it made mine eyes run all the day after; and to mend this she blew pepper in my nose to make me neese. And when the young wife was come, after that my dame had

All is not gold that glistereth.

Mustard purgeth the head and pepper maketh one neese.

4. Pawn.

showed her all the commodities of her house (for women delight much to show forth what they have), they set them down together at the table, none save only they two. And while they were in gossips'[5] talk about the behaviors of this woman and that, I came as I was accustomed and sat by my dame. And when the young woman, hearing me cough and seeing me weep continually, asked what I ailed, my dame, who had tears at her commandment, sighed and, fallen as it were into a sudden dump, brast forth a-weeping and said: 'In faith, mistress, I think I am the infortunatest woman alive, upon whom God hath at once poured forth all his plagues. For my husband, the honestest man that lived, He hath taken from me; and with him mine heir and only son, the most towardly young man that was alive; and yet, not satisfied herewith, lo here my only daughter, which (though I say it) was as fair a woman and as fortunately married as any in this city, He hath, for her honesty or cruelty I cannot tell whether, turned into this likeness, wherein she hath been above this two months, continually weeping as you see and lamenting her miserable wretchedness.'

Women are glorious.

Gossips' common chat.

Women can weep when they will.

There is no deceit to the cheat of an old bawd.

A shameful lie shamefully set forth.

"The young woman, astonished at this tale, and crediting it by means of my dame's lachrymable protestion and deep dissimulation, asked her the more earnestly how and by what chance, and for what cause as she thought, she was so altered. 'Ah,' quod my dame, 'as I said before, I cannot tell what I should think; whether excuse my daughter and accuse God, or else blame her and acquit Him. For this my daughter, being as I said fortunately married, and so beloved of her husband and loving again to him as now we both too late do and forever I think shall rue, was loved exceedingly of another young man, who made great suit and labor unto her. But she, as I think all women should, esteeming her honesty and promise made to her husband the day of their marriage, refused still his desire. But because he was importunate, she came at last and told me it. And I, thinking that I did well, charged her in any case (which full oft since I have repented) that she should not consent unto him, but to shake him off with shrewd words and threatening answers. She did so; alas, alas the while. And the young man, seeing none other boot,[6] went home and fell sick; and loving so honestly and secretly that he would make none other of his counsel, forpined and languished upon his bed the space of three days, receiving neither meat nor drink. And then, perceiving his death to approach, he wrote a letter, which I have in my purse, and sent it by his boy to my daughter. If you can read you shall see it; I cannot, but my daughter here could very well, and write too.' Herewith my dame wept apace, and took the letter out of her purse and gave it this young woman, who read it in form following.

Tears move young minds lightly.

Women are orators by nature.

All women ought above all things to esteem their honesty.

Sharp words and threatening answers will soon cool adulterers.

It is as much pity to see a woman weep as to see a goose go barefoot.

The Nameless Lover to the Nameless Beloved, in whose love, sith he may not live, he only desireth license to die.

5. Friends.

6. Cure.

Cursed be the woeful time wherein mutual love first mixed the mass of my miserable carcass. Cursed be the hour that ever the fatal destinies have ought for me purveyed. Yea, cursed be the unhappy hour, may I say, in which I first saw those piercing eyes which, by insensible and unquenchable power inflaming my heart to desire, are so blind of all mercy as will rather with rigor consume my life than rue my grief with one drop of pity. I sue not to you, my dear unloving love, for any kind of grace, the doubtful hope whereof despair hath long since with the pouring showers of cruel words utterly quenched. But thus much I desire, which also by right me thinketh my faithful love hath well deserved, that sith your fidelity in wedlock (which I can and must needs praise, as would to God I could not) will suffer my pined corse no longer to retain the breath through cold cares wholly consumed, yet at the least, which is also an office of friendship before the gods meritorious, come visit him, who if ought might quench love should not love, whose mouth these three days hath taken no food, whose eyes the like time have taken no rest, whose heart this three weeks was never merry, whose mind these three months was never quiet, whose bed this seven nights was never made, and who (to be brief) is in all parts so enfeebled that living he dieth and dead awhile he liveth. And when this silly ghost shall leave this cruel and miserable prison, in recompense of his love, life, and death, let those white and tender hands of yours close up those open windows through which the uncomfortable light of your beauty shone first into his heart. If you refuse this to do, I beseech the gods immortal, to whom immediately I go, that as without any kind of either love or kindness you have caused me to die, so that none other caught with your beauty do likewise perish; I beseech (I say) the just gods that either they change that honest stony heart, or else disfigure that fair merciless favor.[7] Thus, for want of force either to endite or write any more, I take my leave, desiring you either to come and see me die, or if I be dead before, to see me honestly buried.
Yours unregarded alive. G.S.

A tender heart is easily pierced.

"When the young woman had read this letter, she took it again to my dame, and with much to do to withhold her swelling tears, she said, 'I am sorry for your heaviness, much more for this poor man's, but most of all for your daughter's. But what did she after she saw this letter?' 'Ah,' quod my dame, 'she esteemed it as she did his suits before. She sent him a rough answer in writing; but or ever the boy came home with it, his master was dead. Within two days after, my son-in-law (her husband) died suddenly. And within two days after, as she sat here with me lamenting his death, a voice cried aloud, "Ah, flinty heart, repent thy cruelty." And immediately (oh extreme rigor) she was changed as you now see her. Whereupon I gather that though God would have us keep our faith to our

Women's answers are never to seek.

7. Face.

husbands, yet rather than any other should die for our sakes, we should not make any conscience to save their lives. For it fareth in this point as it doth in all other; for as all extremities are vices, so is it a vice, as appeareth plainly by the punishment of my daughter, to be too extreme in honesty, chastity, or any other kind of virtue.'

Note the craft of a bawd.

All extremities are to be forsaken.

"This, with other talk of my dame in the dinner time, so sank into the young woman's mind that the same afternoon she sent for the gentleman whom she had erst so constantly refused and promised him that, if he would appoint her an unsuspected place, she would be glad to meet him to fulfill all his lust, which he appointed to be the next day at my dame's house. Where, when they were all assembled, I, minding to acquit my dame for giving me mustard, caught a quick mouse, whereof my dame always was exceedingly afraid, and came with it under her clothes and there let it go, which immediately crope up upon her leg. But Lord, how she bestirred her then; how she cried out; and how pale she looked. And I, to amend the matter, making as though I leaped at the mouse, all to-bescrat her thighs and her belly, so that I dare say she was not whole again in two months after. And when the young woman, to whom she showed her pounced[8] thighs, said I was an unnatural daughter to deal so with my mother, 'Nay, nay,' quod she, 'I cannot blame her, for it was through my counsel that she suffered all this sorrow. And yet I dare say she did it against her will, thinking to have caught the mouse, which else I dare say would have crept into my belly.' By this means was this innocent woman, otherwise invincible, brought to consent to commit whoredom.

Evil communication confoundeth good virtues.

Cats are malicious.

Women are afraid of their own shadows.

The cat payeth her dame for her mustard.

It is an unnatural child that will hurt the mother.

Let young women take heed of old bawds.

"Shortly after, this young woman begged me of my dame; and to her I went, and dwelled with her all that year. In which year, as all the cats in the parish can tell, I never disobeyed or transgressed our holy law in refusing the concupiscential company of any cat nor the act of generation, although sometimes it were more painful to me than pleasant, if it were offered in due and convenient time. Indeed, I confess I refused Catch-rat, and bit him and scrat him, which our law forbiddeth. For on a time this year when I was great with kitlings, which he of a proud stomach refused to help to get, although I earnestly wooed him thereto; what time he loved so much his own daughter Slick-skin that all other seemed vile in his sight, which also esteemed him as much as he did the rest—that is, never a whit. In this time (I say) when I was great with kitling, I found him in a gutter eating a bat which he had caught that evening; and as you know not only we, but also women in our case, do oft long for many things, so I then longed for a piece of the reremouse,[9] and desired him, for saving of my kitten, to give me a morsel, though it were but of the leather-like wing. But he, like an unnatural, ravenous churl, eat it all up and would give me none. And as men do nowadays to their wives, he gave me bitter words,

Cats have laws among them which they keep better than we do ours.

He that despiseth those that love him shall be despised of them that he loveth.

Cats do long while they be with kitten.

There be churls among cats as well as among Christian folk.

8. Scratched.

9. Bat.

saying we longed for wantonness and not for any need. This grieved me so sore, chiefly for the lack of that I longed for, that I was sick two days after, and had not it been for good dame Isegrim, who brought me a piece of a mouse and made me believe it was of a back, I had lost by burden by kittening ten days before my time.

It is the conceit of a thing and not the thing itself that is longed for.

"When I was recovered and went abroad again, about three days, this cruel churl met me and needs would have been doing with me. To whom, when I had made answer according to his deserts, and told him withall, which he might see too by my belly what case I was in, tush, there was no remedy (I think he had eaten savory), but for all that I could say, he would have his will. I, seeing that, and that he would ravish me perforce, I cried out for help as loud as ever I could squawl, and to defend myself till succor came I scrat and bit as hard as ever I could. And this notwithstanding, had not Isegrim and her son Lightfoot come the sooner (who both are here and can witness), he would have marred me quite. Now, whether I might in this case refuse him, and do as I did without breach of our holy law, which forbiddeth us females to refuse any males not exceeding the number of ten in a night, judge you, my lords, to whom the interpretation of the laws belongeth.

Churls must be churlishly served.

Savory is an hot herb provoking lust in cats.

A law for adultery among cats.

"'Yes, surely,' quod Grisard, 'for in the third year of the reign of Glascalon, at a court holden in Cat-wood, as appeareth in the records, they decreed upon that exception, forbidding any male in this case to force any female, and that upon great penalties. But to let this pass, whereof we were satisfied in your purgation the first night, tell us how you behaved you with your new mistress, and that as briefly as you can; for lo where Corleonis is almost plain west, whereby ye know the goblins' hour approacheth.'

Glascalon was chief prince of the cats after Grimolochin.

After one a clock at midnight the goblins go abroad, and as soon as any cock croweth, which is their hour, that is at three, they return homeward.

"After I was come to my young mistress," quod Mouse-slayer, "she made much of me, thinking that I had been my old dame's daughter, and many tales she told thereof to her gossips. My master also made much of me, because I would take meat in my foot and therewith put it in my mouth and feed. In this house dwelt an ungracious fellow who, delighting much in unhappy turns, on a time took four walnut shells and filled them full of soft pitch, and put them upon my feet, and then put my feet into cold water till the pitch was hardened, and then he let me go. But Lord, how strange it was to me to go in shoes, and how they vexed me, for when I ran upon any steep thing they made me slide and fall down. Wherefore all that afternoon, for anger that I could not get off my shoes, I hid me in a corner of the garret which was boarded, under which my master and mistress lay. And at night when they were all in bed, I spied a mouse playing in the floor; and when I ran at her to catch her, my shoes made such a noise upon the boards that it waked my master, who was a man very fearful of spirits. And when he with his servants harkened well to the noise, which went pit-pat, pit-pat, as it had been the trampling of an horse, they waxed all afraid and said surely it was the Devil.

Divers men delight in divers fond things.

A cat was shoed.

Natural delight expelleth melancholy.

The fearful are always suspicious.

"And as one of them, an hardy fellow (even he that had shoed me), came upstairs to see what it was, I went downward to meet him and made such a rattling that, when he saw my glistering eyes, he fell down backward and brake his head, crying out, 'The Devil, the Devil, the Devil.' Which his master and all the rest hearing, ran naked as they were into the street and cried the same cry.

Wickedness is a scourge itself to such as invent it.

"Whereupon the neighbors arose and called up, among other, an old priest, who lamented much the lack of holy water which they were forbidden to make. Howbeit, he went to church and took out of the font some of the christening water, and took his chalice, and therein a wafer unconsecrate, and put on a surplice, and his stole about his neck, and fet out of his chamber a piece of holy candle which he had kept two year. And herewith he came to the house, and with his candle-light in the one hand and a holy-water sprinkle in the other hand, and his chalice and wafer in sight of his bosom, and a pot of font-water at his girdle, up he came praying towards the garret, and all the people after him.

Holy water was good for conjurers.

This fellow thought to beguile the Devil.

A conjurer can have no better apparel.

"And when I saw this, and thinking I should have seen some Mass that night, as many nights before in other places I had, I ran towards them thinking to meet them. But when the priest heard me come, and by a glimpsing had seen me, down he fell upon them that were behind him, and with his chalice hurt one, with his water pot another, and his holy candle fell into another priest's breech beneath (who, while the rest were hawsoning[1] me, was conjuring our maid at the stair foot) and all to-besinged him, for he was so afraid with the noise of the rest which fell that he had not the power to put it out. When I saw all this business, down I ran among them where they lay on heaps. But such a fear as they were all in then I think was never seen afore; for the old priest, which was so tumbled among them that his face lay upon a boy's bare arse, which belike was fallen headlong under him, was so astonished that, when the boy, which for fear had beshit himself, had all to-rayed his face, he neither felt nor smelt it, nor removed from him.

Cats hear mo Masses than all men hear of.

Priests have been good conjurers of such kind of spirits.

Fear taketh away the senses.

"Then went I to my dame, which lay among the rest God knoweth very madly, and so mewed and curled about her that at last she said, 'I ween it be my cat.' That hearing the knave that had shoed me, and calling to mind that erst he had forgot, said it was so indeed and nothing else. That hearing the priest, in whose holy breech the holy candle all this while lay burning, he took heart a grace, and before he was spied rose up and took the candle in his hand, and looked upon me and all the company, and fell a-laughing at the handsome lying of his fellow's face. The rest, hearing him, came every man to himself and arose and looked upon me, and cursed the knave which had shoed me, who would in no case be a-known of it. This done, they got hot water and dissolved the pitch and plucked off my shoes. And then every man (after they desired each other not to be a-known of this night's work) for shame departed to their lodgings, and all our household went to bed again."

A liar and a doer of shrewd turns ought to have a good memory.

One hardy man encourageth many cowards.

Silence is the best friend that shame hath. The author laughed in a cat's voice.

1. Exorcizing.

When all the cats, and I too for company, had laughed at this space, Mouse-slayer proceeded and said, "After this about three-quarters of a year, which was at Whitsuntide last, I played another prank, and that was this. The gentleman, who by mine old dame's lying and my weeping was accepted and retained of my mistress, came often home to our house, and always in my master's absence was doing with my dame. Wherefore, desirous that my master might know it (for they spent his goods so lavishly between them that, notwithstanding his great trade of merchandise, they had, unweeting to him, almost undone him already), I sought how I might bewray them. Which as hap would, at the time remembered afore, came to pass thus. While this gentleman was doing with my dame, my master came in—so suddenly that he had no leisure to pluck up his hose, but with them about his legs ran into a corner behind the painted cloth, and there stood (I warrant you) as still as a mouse. As soon as my master came in, his wife, according to her old wont, caught him about his neck and kissed him, and devised many means to have got him forth again. But he, being weary, sat down and called for his dinner. And when she saw there was none other remedy, she brought it him, which was a mess of potage and a piece of beef, whereas she and her franion[2] had broke their fast with capons, hot venison, marrow bones, and all other kind of dainties.

Adulterers are diligent in waiting their times.

A wanton wife and a back door will soon make a rich man poor.

Chance oftentimes betrayeth evil.

None seem outwardly so loving as whores.

Sine Baccho et cetera friget Venus.[3]

"I, seeing this, and minding to show my master how he was ordered, got behind the cloth, and to make the man speak I all to-pawed him with my claws upon his bare legs and buttocks. And for all this, he stood still and never moved. But my master heard me and, thinking I was catching a mouse, bade my dame go help me. Who, knowing what beast was there, came to the cloth and called me away, saying, 'Come puss, come puss,' and cast me meat into the floor. But I, minding another thing, and seeing that scratching could not move him, suddenly I leaped up and caught him by the genitals with my teeth, and bote so hard that, when he had restrained more than I thought any man could, at last he cried out, and caught me by the neck thinking to strangle me. My master, not smelling but hearing such a rat as was not wont to be about such walls, came to the cloth and lift it up, and there found this bare-arst gentleman strangling me who had his stones in my mouth. And when I saw my master I let go my hold, and the gentleman his. And away I ran immediately to the place where I now dwell, and never came there since. So that how they agreed among them I cannot tell, nor never durst go see for fear of my life.

Fear overcometh smart.

All are not mice that are behind painted cloths.

It is justice to punsh those parts that offend.

Whoredom will be known be it never so warily hid.

"Thus have I told you, my good lords, all things that have been done and happened through me, wherein you perceive my loyalty and obedience to all good laws, and how shamelessly and falsely I am accused for a transgressor. And I pray you, as you have perceived, so certify my liege great Cammoloch (whose life both Hagat and Heg preserve) of my behavior."

There be false accusers among all kind of creatures.

2. Darling.

3. Without Bacchus and Ceres, Venus is frigid.

When Grisard, Isegrim, and Pol-noir, the commissioners, had heard this declaration and request of Mouse-slayer, they praised her much. And after that they had commanded her, with all the cats there, to be on St. Catherine's day next ensuing at Caithness where, as they said, Cammoloch would hold his court, they departed. And I, glad to have heard that I heard, and sorry that I had not understood what was said the other two nights before, got me to my bed and slept a-good.

Justices should cherish the innocents accused.

Travail and watching maketh sound sleeping.

And the next morning, when I went out into the garden, I heard a strange cat ask of our cat what Mouse-slayer had done before the commissioners those three nights. To whom our cat answered, that she had purged herself of a crime that was laid to her charge by Catch-rat, and declared her whole life for six years' space. Whereof in the first two years as she said, said she, she had five masters: a priest, a baker, a lawyer, a broker, and a butcher; all whose privy deceits which she had seen she declared the first night. In the next two years she had seven masters: a bishop, a knight, a pothecary, a goldsmith, an usurer, an alchemist, and a lord; whose cruelty, study, craft, cunning, niggishness,[4] folly, waste, and oppression she declared the second night, wherein this doing was notable. Because the knight, having a fair lady to his wife, gave his mind so much to his book that he seldom lay with her, this cat, pitying her mistress and minding to fray him from lying alone, on a night when her master lay from her, got to his mouth and drew so his breath that she almost stifled him. A like part she played with the usurer, who, being rich and yet living miserably and feigning him poor, she got one day, while his treasure chest stood open, and hid her therein; whereof he not knowing locked her in it. And when at night he came thither again and heard one stirring there, and thinking it had been the Devil, he called the priest and many other persons to come and help him to conjure. And when in their sight he opened his chest, out leaped she and they saw what riches he had and cessed[5] him thereafter. As for what was done and said yesternight, both of my lord Grisard's hard adventure and of Mouse-slayer's bestowing her other two last years, which is nothing in comparison of any of the other two years before, I need not tell you for you were present and heard it yourself."

Mouse-slayer was six year old.

Cats change their dwellings often.

Men ought to lie with their wives.

A niggard is neither good to his self nor to any other.

The Devil delighteth to dwell among money.

All in this book is nothing in comparison of that the cat told before.

This talk, lo, I heard between these two cats. And then I got me in, and brake my fast with bread and butter, and dined at noon with common meat, which so repleted my head again and my other powers in the first digestion, that by nighttime they were as gross as ever they were before. For when I harkened at night to other two cats, which as I perceived by their gestures spake of the same matter, I understood never a word.

Gross meats make gross wits.

Lo, here have I told you all (chiefly you, my lord) a wonderful matter, and yet as incredible as it is wonderful. Notwithstanding,

Wonders are incredible.

4. Meanness.

5. Taxed.

when I may have convenient time, I will tell you other things which these eyes of mine have seen and these ears of mine have heard, and that of mysteries so far passing this, that all which I have said now shall in comparison thereof be nothing at all to be believed. In the meanwhile, I will pray you to help to get me some money to convey me on my journey to Caithness, for I have been going thither these five years and never was able to perform my journey.

In comparison of a diamond, crystal hath no color. Poverty hindreth many excellent attempts.

When Master Ferrers had promised that he would, every man shut up his shop windows,[6] which the foresaid talk kept open two hours longer than they should have been.

An Exhortation

I know these things will seem marvelous to many men, that cats should understand and speak, have a governor among themselves, and be obedient to their laws. And were it not for the approved authority of the ecstatical author of whom I heard it, I should myself be as doubtful as they. But seeing I know the place and the persons with whom he talked of these matters before he experimented his wonderful and strange confections, I am the less doubtful of any truth therein. Wherefore, seeing he hath in his oration proved that cats do understand us and mark our secret doings, and so declare them among themselves; that through help of the medicines by him described any man may, as he did, understand them; I would counsel all men to take heed of wickedness, and eschew secret sins and privy mischievous counsels, lest, to their shame, all the world at length do know thereof. But if any man, for doubt hereof, do put away his cat, then shall his so doing testify his secret naughty living, which he is more ashamed his cat should see than God and His angels, which see, mark, and behold all men's closest doings.

And that we may take profit by this declaration of Master Streamer, let us so live, both openly and privily that neither our own cat, admitted to all secrets, be able to declare aught of us to the world save what is laudable and honest; nor the Devil's cat, which will we or nill we seeth and writeth all our ill doings, have ought to lay against us afore the face of God, who not only with shame but with everlasting torment will punish all sin and wickedness. And ever when thou goest about anything, call to mind this proverb, *Beware the Cat*; not to tie up thy cat till thou have done, but to see that neither thine own nor the Devil's cat (which cannot be tied up) find anything therein whereof to accuse thee to thy shame.

Thus doing, thou canst not do amiss; but shalt have such good report through the cat's declaration, that thou shalt, in recompence of Master Streamer's labor who giveth thee this warning, sing unto God this hymn of his making.

The Hymn

Who givest wit to whales, to apes, to owls;
And kindly speech to fish, to flesh, to fowls;
And spirit to men in soul and body clean,
To mark and know what other creatures mean;

6. I.e., eyes.

Which hast given grace to Gregory, no Pope,
No King, no Lord; whose treasures are their hope;
But silly priest, which like a streamer waves
In ghostly good, despised of foolish knaves.

Which hast, I say, given grace to him to know
The course of things above and here below,
With skill so great in languages and tongues
As never breathed from Mithridates' lungs.

To whom the hunter of birds, of mice and rats,
Did speak as plain as Kate that thrummeth[7] hats;
By mean of whom is openly bewrayed
Such things as closely were both done and said.

To him grant, Lord, with healthy wealth and rest,
Long life to unload to us his learned breast;
With fame so great to overlive his grave,
As none had erst, nor any after have.

FINIS

Edmund Spenser

1552?–1599

H. W. Smith, *Edmund Spenser*.

A man whose poetry has come to be known as a monument to Queen Elizabeth's England began life modestly enough. Attending Cambridge as a "sizar," or "poor scholar," he worked as a servant to pay for his fees. Allegiance to the English church was expected of all subjects, and Spenser showed his support of the faith while still a student by contributing anti-Catholic verses to the first emblem book published in England. The genre, consisting of emblems or symbolic scenes explained by clever captions, acquainted the aspiring poet with elements of the mode he was later to master: allegory. Literally a writing that conveys "other" (from the Greek *allos*, "other") than literal meanings, the allegory that Spenser would eventually perfect for his epic poem *The Faerie Queene* produced narrative verse of great flexibility and verve. Building on powerful images, his verse allegories of education in a "virtuous" chivalry convey the challenges he saw attending the creation of a civil society in early modern England.

Shortly after leaving Cambridge in 1576, Spenser found employment as a secretary in the London household of the rich and influential Earl of Leicester, a favorite courtier of Queen Elizabeth and an ardent defender of international Protestantism. There he met Leicester's already famous nephew, Sir Philip Sidney, to whom Spenser dedicated his first work, the deliberately archaic, neo-Chaucerian *The Shepheardes Calender*, a sequence of

7. Make fringes for.

twelve eclogues or poems on pastoral subjects, one for each month of the year. A work of a paradoxically innovative style, *The Shepheardes Calender* demonstrated a range of metrical forms that had yet to be seen in English poetry; probably more compelling to the general reader was Spenser's use of pastoral motifs and settings to represent opinions on love, poetry, and social order. Sidney's response to the poem was, nevertheless, somewhat ambivalent. While recognizing that Spenser's eclogues had "much poetry" in them, he stated that he disliked verse composed in an "old rustic language"; among earlier and model poets of pastoral, "neither Theocritus in Greek, Virgil in Latin, nor Sannazaro in Italian did affect it." But precisely because this "old rustic language" could be recognized as purely English and independent of European traditions, Spenser would use a modified form of it in *The Faerie Queene;* in this way he hoped to demonstrate that English literature had as rich a past as any in Europe. He probably began the poem while in Leicester's service; the seventeenth-century biographer John Aubrey reported the discovery of "an abundance of cards, with stanzas of the *Faerie Queene* written on them" in the wainscoting of Spenser's London lodging.

From 1580 to the end of his life, Spenser lived in Ireland, serving as secretary to the Lord Deputy of Ireland, Arthur Grey. At such a distance from Queen Elizabeth's court, Spenser could not have secured royal favor. He was rescued from obscurity in 1589 by Sir Walter Raleigh, who, impressed with the first three books of *The Faerie Queene,* invited Spenser to present his poem to the queen. Beside the gallant and charismatic Raleigh, the poet—said to have been a "little man, who wore short hair, little bands (collars) and little cuffs"—must have cut a poor figure. But the queen liked the poem that illustrated her majesty in so many ways, "desired at timely hours to hear" it, and rewarded Spenser with a life pension of £50 a year. When Spenser returned to Ireland in 1590, he met and fell in love with Elizabeth Boyle, a woman much his junior. They were married in 1594, and Spenser celebrated their courtship and wedding in the *Amoretti* (page 676), a sonnet sequence describing the poet's quest for his "deer" or dear, and *Epithalamion,* a hymn to each of the twenty-four hours of their wedding day. The second three books of *The Faerie Queene,* published in 1596, proved as popular with readers as the first three, although James VI of Scotland (later James I of England) thought slanderous its portrait of the evil queen Duessa, whom he identified as his mother, Mary Queen of Scots. He demanded that Spenser be "duly tried and punished." Fortunately, however, Spenser's friends at court intervened, and nothing came of the king's displeasure.

The last years of the poet's life were full of grief and bitter disappointment. In 1598 the Irish in the province of Munster, rebelling against the English colonial authorities, burned the castle in which Spenser lived. The poet and his wife fled; their newborn child was reported to have perished in the flames. In December of that year, Spenser went to London to deliver letters to the queen from the Governor of Ireland concerning the uprising. He included a note describing his own assessment of the situation—a note that may have included material in a treatise entitled *A View of the Present State of Ireland,* supporting a militaristic policy to colonize the people of Ireland, which he is supposed to have written. He died a month after arriving in London in January of 1599 and was buried in Westminster Abbey near Geoffrey Chaucer, whose poetry had meant so much to him. The monument placed on his grave is inscribed with these words: "Prince of poets in his time, whose Divine Spirit needs no other witness than the works which he left behind."

Consciously aspiring both to Chaucer's humane dignity and to his vividly colloquial style, Spenser saw himself as fashioning and refashioning a tradition of English and possibly British poetry. As he made a point of using older terms and spelling, his poems are presented here unmodernized. Spenser's choice of language parallels his use of the motifs of knightly romance: turning to the past, he sought a vital perspective on the present. John Milton would later describe him as a "sage and serious" poet, who, in *The Faerie Queene,* wrote of the struggle of good against evil and the triumph of faith over falsehood. The subject, treated by weaving different story lines together to form a vast tapestry, interested not only Milton, who was clearly inspired by Spenser's complex understanding of human psychology, but also the next generation of poets in England, especially Ben Jonson, John Donne, and George Herbert, who turned to Spenser for a poetry of satirical vigor and spiritual insight. Yet other readers have been moved by Spenser's lyrics. His shorter poems and occasional verse show his skillful use of repetitive sounds or verbal echoes and reveal his unerring sense of language as a musical medium.

***The Faerie Queene*, Books 6 and 7** It is hard to place Spenser's great poem, as there had been nothing like it before. Spenser invented his own rhyme scheme and stanza form, and he wrote in an archaic way that no one could place easily. Ben Jonson famously remarked that "Spenser, in affecting the ancients, writ no language." Perhaps the best way of thinking of the poem is as an epic-romance, one that follows the history of a nation (an epic path), but also meanders away from its main subject in following stories that may or may not be of consequence (a romance path). Spenser joins these two forms in *The Faerie Queene* and so creates a new, flexible type of poetry that can take the reader in different directions. The "letter to Raleigh" appended to the first edition of the poem, tells the reader that Spenser's plan was to write a work of twelve books following the cardinal virtues as defined by Aristotle. Whether this was ever a serious plan is open to conjecture. The poem as we have it consists of six complete books, and a fragment of a seventh. The first edition contained the first three books of Holiness, Temperance, and Chastity; the second, the next three books of Friendship, Justice, and Courtesy. After Spenser's death, the work was republished with the addition of part of the seventh book, "The Two Cantos of Mutability," part of a book of Constancy.

Book Six follows the adventures of Calidore, the Knight of Courtesy. While the other knights in the poem had at least some idea of the purpose of their quests, Calidore is confronted with complex and contradictory definitions of courtesy and has no clear idea of what he is doing. His stated aim is to capture the Blatant Beast, a fearsome figure who has a multitude of tongues and whose allegorical role appears to be the abuse of language itself. But Calidore spends his time on a series of apparently aimless and disconnected tasks and disappears altogether from the narrative for the middle section of the book. He also tries to turn himself into a shepherd and so avoid the hard work of being a knight. Spenser's pastoral book is not what it seems to be and is a warning of the dark forces that threaten a society when good men are unable and unwilling to act. The poem shows besieged and unprotected shepherds always at the mercy of those who wish to undermine and overthrow their fragile society. In some ways Spenser would appear to have been thinking of his own situation in Ireland; in others, he was imagining the dire fate that could befall an unprotected England at the mercy of hostile neighbors.

The book contains a series of images of courtesy and its opposite, discourtesy, forcing the reader to think about the true nature of this civilizing value and how it could be followed. It also contains a key debate on the nature of the good life, one of the fundamental philosophical questions, when Calidore and Meliobee have their debate in Canto 9. The book also contains a number of incidents that have distinctly humorous elements, most notably when Calidore, the Knight of Courtesy, is told by Colin Clout that he has made the Graces—a form of courtesy—disappear. The knight himself is the problem, at odds with a confused, topsy-turvy society that has confused and confusing values. Whether Calidore is to blame is another question, one that the reader has to consider.

"Two Cantos of Mutability" are, arguably, Spenser's finest poem. The cantos stand as an etiological myth (a myth of origins) that underlies the poem and that explain the meaning, location, and purpose of Spenser's Faerie Land. Mutability challenges Cynthia, the goddess chosen by Jove to rule the universe he has conquered, claiming that she has the real right to be queen, as things change endlessly according to her desire. It is agreed that Jove and Mutability will present their cases before Nature on Arlo Hill, the small mountain nearest to Spenser's house in Ireland. Ireland used to be the fairest of the British Isles which attracted the attention of Diana who spent a great deal of her time there bathing and hunting with her nymphs and satyrs. The foolish god Faunus had an uncontrollable desire to see the goddess naked and so persuaded her nymph, Molanna, to let him know where Diana bathed. Hiding in the bushes, he was so overwhelmed with emotion, that he burst out laughing, inspiring the wrath of the goddess, who cursed the island and never returned, condemning it to its current miserable state. In Canto 7 the protagonists meet on Arlo Hill and make their respective cases. Jove argues that he has conquered the universe and established order so he rules by right; Mutability counters that she should rule as her powers actually control it, whatever Jove might claim. Nature takes little time to decide to award victory to Jove, before she vanishes. The fragment concludes with two stanzas of the "unperfect" Canto 8 which seem to suggest that constancy is the principle that underlies the universe not perpetual change. In reading them we witness Spenser's understanding of the powers that hold sway in the universe and the fragile hold that men and women have on life.

For additional resources on Spenser, including *"The Faerie Queene, A Letter of the Authors," Booke One of the Faerie Queene*, The Second Booke of *the Faerie Queene*, Canto 12, and "Epithalamion," go to *The Longman Anthology of British Literature* Web site at www.myliteraturekit.com.

The Sixte Booke of the Faerie Queene

Contayning the Legend of S. Calidore or of Courtesie.

1

The waies, through which my weary steps I guyde,
In this delightfull land of Faery,
Are so exceeding spacious and wyde,
And sprinckled with such sweet variety,
Of all that pleasant is to eare or eye,
That I nigh ravisht with rare thoughts delight,
My tedious travell doe forget thereby;
And when I gin to feele decay of might,
It strength to me supplies, & chears my dulled spright.

2

Such secret comfort, and such heavenly pleasures,
Ye sacred imps,[1] that on *Parnasso* dwell,
And there the keeping have of learnings threasures,
Which doe all worldly riches farre excell,
Into the mindes of mortall men doe well,[2]
And goodly fury into them infuse;
Guyde ye my footing, and conduct me well
In these strange waies, where never foote did use,
Ne none can find, but who was taught them by the Muse.[3]

1. The Muses, whose home was Mount Parnassus.
2. Flow.
3. Spenser is following Ariosto's boast that he is attempting something that no other poet has attempted (Ariosto, *Orlando Furioso* 1.2). Milton imitates both poets in claiming that his poem "pursues Things unattempted yet in Prose or Rhyme" (Milton's *Paradise Lost*).

3

Revele to me the sacred noursery
Of vertue, which with you doth there remaine,
Where it in silver bowre does hidden ly
From view of men, and wicked worlds disdaine.
Since it at first was by the Gods with paine
Planted in earth, being deriv'd at furst
From heavenly seedes of bounty soveraine,
And by them long with carefull labour nurst,
Till it to ripenesse grew, and forth to honour burst.

4

Amongst them all growes not a fayrer flowre,
Then is the bloosme of comely courtesie,
Which though it on a lowly stalke doe bowre,
Yet brancheth forth in brave nobilitie,
And spreds it selfe through all civilitie:
Of which though present age doe plenteous seeme,
Yet being matcht with plaine Antiquitie,[4]
Ye will them all but fayned showes esteeme,
Which carry colours faire, that feeble eies misdeeme.

5

But in the triall of true curtesie,
Its now so farre from that, which then it was,
That it indeed is nought but forgerie,
Fashion'd to please the eies of them, that pas,
Which see not perfect things but in a glas:[5]
Yet is that glasse so gay, that it can blynd
The wisest sight, to thinke gold that is bras.
But vertues seat is deepe within the mynd,
And not in outward shows, but inward thoughts defynd.[6]

6

But where shall I in all Antiquity
So faire a patterne finde, where may be seene
The goodly praise of Princely curtesie,
As in your selfe, O soveraine Lady Queene,
In whose pure minde, as in a mirrour sheene,
It showes, and with her brightnesse doth inflame
The eyes of all, which thereon fixed beene;
But meriteth indeede an higher name:
Yet so from low to high uplifted is your name.

4. The lament for the lost simplicity of ancient times recalls the proem to Book V.

5. See 1 Corinthians 13.12: "For now we see through a glass darkly."

6. The idea that virtue is not simply a form of social activity but a state of mind or condition of the soul is very important throughout Book 6.

7

Then pardon me, most dreaded Soveraine,
That from your selfe I doe this vertue bring,
And to your selfe doe it returne againe:
So from the Ocean all rivers spring,
And tribute backe repay as to their King.[7]
Right so from you all goodly vertues well
Into the rest, which round about you ring,
Faire Lords and Ladies, which about you dwell,
And doe adorne your Court, where courtesies excell.

Canto I

Calidore saves from Maleffort,° *French: evil attempt*
A Damzell used vylde:
Doth vanquish Crudor, and doth make
Briana wexe more mylde.

1

Of Court it seemes, men Courtesie doe call,
For that it there most useth to abound;
And well beseemeth° that in Princes hall *it is appropriate*
That vertue should be plentifully found,
Which of all goodly manners is the ground,
And roote of civill conversation.[8]
Right so in Faery court it did redound,° *abound, overflow*
Where curteous Knights and Ladies most did won
Of all on earth, and made a matchlesse paragon.° *example or model of excellence*

2

But mongst them all was none more courteous Knight,
Then *Calidore*,[9] beloved over all,
In whom it seemes, that gentlenesse of spright
And manners mylde were planted naturall;
To which he adding comely guize° withall, *appearance*
And gracious speach, did steale mens hearts away.
Nathlesse thereto he was full stout and tall,
And well approv'd in batteilous affray,° *attack*
That him did much renowme, and far his feme display.

7. See Ecclesiastes 1.7: "All the rivers go into the sea, yet the sea is not full: for the rivers go unto the place whence they return, and go."

8. Civilized relationships. The phrase means more than the modern meanings of these words imply. Perhaps an allusion to Stefano Guazzo's *La civile conversatione* (1574), a courtesy book of enormous popularity.

9. Greek: "beauty, gift." The hero of this book has been identified with Sir Philip Sidney and with Robert Devereux, Earl of Essex. See *The Works of Edmund Spenser: A Variorum Edition*, ed. Edwin Greenlaw, G. G. Osgood, F. M. Padelford, et al. 2 vols., Baltimore, 1932–1957, Henceforth abbreviated *Var*.

3

Ne was there Knight, ne was there Lady found[1]
In Faery court, but him did deare embrace,
For his faire vsage and conditions sound,
The which in all mens liking gayned place,
And with the greatest purchast greatest grace:
Which he could wisely use, and well apply,
To please the best, and th'evill to embase.° *humble*
For he loathd leasing,° and base flattery, *falsehood*
And loved simple truth and stedfast honesty.

4

And now he was in travell on his way,
Uppon an hard adventure sore bestad,° *beset by difficulty*
Whenas by chaunce he met uppon a day
With *Artegall*,[2] returning yet halfe sad
From his late conquest, which he gotten had.
Who whenas each of other had a sight,
They knew themselves, and both their persons rad:° *knew, recognized*
When *Calidore* thus first; Haile noblest Knight
Of all this day on ground, that breathen living spright.[3]

5

Now tell, if please you, of the good successe,
Which ye have had in your late enterprize.
To whom Sir *Artegall* gan to expresse
His whole exploite, and valorous emprize,
In order as it did to him arize.
Now happy man (sayd then Sir *Calidore*)
Which have so goodly, as ye can devize,
Atchiev'd so hard a quest, as few before;
That shall you most renowmed make for evermore.

6

But where ye ended have, now I begin
To tread an endlesse trace,° withouten guyde, *track, path*
Or good direction, how to enter in,
Or how to issue forth in waies untryde,
In perils strange, in labours long and wide,
In which although good Fortune me befall,
Yet shall it not by none be testifyde.

1. The courtesy books placed great emphasis on attaining public recognition of one's virtues.
2. Arthegall, the hero of Book 5, had just returned from freeing Irena from the power of Grantorto.
3. I.e., of all knights living. "Breathen" is an obsolete third person plural form of "breathe"; its implied subject is "all knights."

What is that quest (quoth then Sir *Artegall*)
That you into such perils presently doth call?

7

The Blattant Beast (quoth he) I doe pursew,
And through the world incessantly doe chase,
Till I him overtake, or else subdew:
Yet know I not or how, or in what place
To find him out, yet still I forward trace.
What is that Blattant Beast?[4] (then he replide)
It is a Monster bred of hellishe race,
(Then answerd he) which often hath annoyd
Good Knights and Ladies true, and many else destroyd.

8

Of *Cerberus* whilome he was begot,
And fell *Chimœra* in her darkesome den,
Through fowle commixture of his filthy blot;
Where he was fostred long in *Stygian*[5] fen,
Till he to perfect ripenesse grew, and then
Into this wicked world he forth was sent,
To be the plague and scourge of wretched men:
Whom with vile tongue and venemous intent
He sore doth wound, and bite, and cruelly torment.

9

Then since the salvage Island I did leave
Sayd *Artegall*, I such a Beast did see,[6]
The which did seeme a thousand tongues to have,
That all in spight and malice did agree,
With which he bayd and loudly barkt at mee,
As if that he attonce would me devoure.
But I that knew my selfe from perill free,
Did nought regard his malice nor his powre,
But he the more his wicked poyson forth did poure.

10

That surely is that Beast (saide *Calidore*)
Which I pursue, of whom I am right glad

4. Latin: *blatire*, "to babble." The Blatant Beast is generally interpreted as slander or detraction, although Ben Jonson reported that Spenser in a letter to Ralegh (also spelled Raleigh) had identified the Beast with the Puritans (*Var*., p. 382). Obviously the Blatant Beast does not refer only to Puritans, or to all Puritans. The pursuit of the beast by the knight represents the efforts of courtesy to overcome slander. Since the impulse behind slander or detraction is malice (wishing evil to another person), courtesy must try to grapple with malice, the sin opposed to Christian charity.

5. The Styx was a river flowing through Hades.

6. Arthegall's encounter with the Blatant Beast is generally understood as a reference to the accusations made against Lord Grey de Wilton for his handling of the Irish situation.

To heare these tidings, which of none afore
Through all my weary travell I have had:
Yet now some hope your words unto me add.
Now God you speed (quoth then Sir *Artegall*)
And keepe your body from the daunger drad:
For ye have much adoe to deale withall;
So both tooke goodly leave, and parted severall.° *in different directions*

11

Sir *Calidore* thence travelled not long,[7]
When as by chaunce a comely Squire he found,
That thorough some more mighty enemies wrong,
Both hand and foote unto a tree was bound:
Who seeing him from farre, with piteous sound
Of his shrill cries him called to his aide.
To whom approching, in that painefull stound
When he him saw, for no demaunds he staide,° *waited, delayed*
But first him losde,° and afterwards thus to him saide. *loosed*

12

Unhappy Squire, what hard mishap thee brought
Into this bay[8] of perill and disgrace?
What cruell hand thy wretched thraldome wrought,
And thee captyued in this shamefull place?
To whom he answerd thus; My haplesse case
Is not occasiond through my misdesert,
But through misfortune, which did me abase
Unto this shame, and my young hope subvert,
Ere that I in her guilefull traines was well expert.

13

Not farre from hence, uppon yond rocky hill,[9]
Hard by a streight there stands a castle strong,
Which doth observe a custome lewd and ill,
And it hath long mayntaind with mighty wrong:
For may no Knight nor Lady passe along
That way, (and yet they needs must passe that way,)
By reason of the streight,[1] and rocks among,
But they that Ladies lockes doe shave away,
And that knights berd for toll, which they for passage pay.

7. Upton (*Var.*, p. 189) points out that Calidore's first adventure is like the first adventure of Cervantes's Don Quixote.
8. Situation of a hunted animal (e.g., "at bay").
9. Spenser was probably most influenced by the French romance *Perlesvaus*, Malory 1.24 and Ariosto, *Orlando Furioso*, 37, 42.
1. Narrow or confined place, such as a mountain pass or a narrow pathway.

14

A shamefull use as ever I did heare,
Sayd *Calidore*, and to be overthrowne.
But by what meanes did they at first it reare,
And for what cause, tell if thou have it knowne.
Sayd then that Squire: The Lady which doth owne
This Castle, is by name *Briana*[2] hight.
Then which a prouder Lady liveth none:
She long time hath deare lov'd a doughty Knight,
And sought to win his love by all the meanes she might.

15

His name is *Crudor*,[3] who through high disdaine
And proud despight of his selfe pleasing mynd,
Refused hath to yeeld her love againe,
Untill a Mantle she for him doe fynd,
With beards of Knights and locks of Ladies lynd.
Which to provide, she hath this Castle dight,
And therein hath a Seneschall° assynd, *steward*
Cald *Maleffort*,[4] a man of mickle might,
Who executes her wicked will, with worse despight.

16

He this same day, as I that way did come
With a faire Damzell, my beloved deare,
In execution of her lawlesse doome,
Did set uppon us flying both for feare:
For little bootes against him hand to reare.
Me first he tooke, unhable to withstond;
And whiles he her pursued every where,
Till his returne unto this tree he bond:
Ne wote I surely, whether her he yet have fond.

17

Thus whiles they spake, they heard a ruefull shrieke
Of one loud crying, which they streight way ghest,
That it was she, the which for helpe did seeke.
Tho looking up unto the cry to lest,° *listen*
They saw that Carle from farre, with hand unblest
Hayling° that mayden by the yellow heare, *dragging, pulling*
That all her garments from her snowy brest,

2. Possibly Greek: "strong."
3. Latin: *crudus*, "cruel."
4. French: "evil attempt."

And from her head her lockes he nigh did teare,
Ne would he spare for pitty, nor refraine for feare.

18

Which haynous sight when *Calidore* beheld,
Eftsoones he loosd that Squire, and so him left,
With hearts dismay and inward dolour queld,
For to pursue that villaine, which had reft° *stolen*
That piteous spoile by so injurious theft.
Whom overtaking, loude to him he cryde;
Leave faytor quickely that misgotten weft° *stolen prize*
To him, that hath it better justifyde,
And turne thee soone to him, of whom thou art defyde.

19

Who hearkning to that voice, him selfe upreard,
And seeing him so fiercely towardes make,° *move in his direction*
Against him stoutly ran, as nought afeard,
But rather more enrag'd for those words sake;
And with sterne count'naunce thus unto him spake.
Art thou the caytive, that defyest me,
And for this Mayd, whose party thou doest take,
Wilt give thy beard, though it but little bee?
Yet shall it not her lockes for raunsome fro me free.

20

With that he fiercely at him flew, and layd
On hideous strokes with most importune° might, *severe, persistent*
That oft he made him stagger as unstayd,
And oft recuile° to shunne his sharpe despight. *recoil*
But *Calidore*, that was well skild in fight,
Him long forbore,° and still his spirite spar'd, *endured, stood up to*
Lying in waite, how him he damadge might.
But when he felt him shrinke, and come to ward,[5]
He greater grew, and gan to drive at him more hard.

21

Like as a water streame, whose swelling sourse
Shall drive a Mill, within strong bancks is pent,
And long restrayned of his ready course;
So soone as passage is unto him lent,
Breakes forth, and makes his way more violent.
Such was the fury of Sir *Calidore*,
When once he felt his foeman to relent;

5. Begin to shield himself, take the defensive.

He fiercely him pursu'd, and pressed sore,
Who as he still decayd, so he encreased more.

22

The heavy burden of whose dreadfull might
When as the Carle no longer could sustaine,
His heart gan faint, and streight he tooke his flight
Toward the Castle, where if need constraine,
His hope of refuge used to remaine.
Whom *Calidore* perceiving fast to flie,
He him pursu'd and chaced through the plaine,
That he for dread of death gan loude to crie
Unto the ward,° to open to him hastilie. *guard*

23

They from the wall him seeing so aghast,
The gate soone opened to receive him in,
But *Calidore* did follow him so fast,
That even in the Porch[6] he him did win,
And cleft his head asunder to his chin.
The carcasse tumbling downe within the dore,
Did choke the entraunce with a lumpe of sin,
That it could not be shut, whilest *Calidore*
Did enter in, and slew the Porter on the flore.

24

With that the rest, the which the Castle kept,
About him flockt, and hard at him did lay;
But he them all from him full lightly swept,
As doth a Steare, in heat of sommers day,
With his long taile the bryzes° brush away. *gadflies*
Thence passing forth, into the hall he came,
Where of the Lady selfe in sad dismay
He was ymett, who with uncomely shame
Gan him salute, and fowle upbrayd with faulty blame.

25

False traytor Knight, (sayd she) no Knight at all,
But scorne of armes that hast with guilty hand
Murdred my men, and slaine my Seneschall;
Now comest thou to rob my house unmand,° *unprotected*
And spoile° my selfe, that can not thee withstand? *rob, despoil, ravish*
Yet doubt thou not, but that some better Knight
Then thou, that shall thy treason understand,

6. I.e., just as he reached the porch.

Will it avenge, and pay thee with thy right:° *i.e., what you deserve*
And if none do, yet shame shal thee with shame requight.

26

Much was the Knight abashed at that word;
Yet answerd thus; Not unto me the shame,
But to the shamefull doer it afford.° *grant, attribute*
Bloud is no blemish; for it is no blame
To punish those, that doe deserve the same;
But they that breake bands of civilitie,
And wicked customes make, those doe defame
Both noble armes and gentle curtesie.
No greater shame to man then inhumanitie.

27

Then doe your selfe, for dread of shame, forgoe
This evill manner, which ye here maintaine,
And doe in stead thereof mild curt'sie showe
To all, that passe. That shall you glory gaine
More then his love, which thus ye seeke t'obtaine.
Wherewith all full of wrath, she thus replyde;
Vile recreant, know that I doe much disdaine
Thy courteous lore, that doest my love deride,
Who scornes thy ydle scoffe, and bids thee be defyde.

28

To take defiaunce at a Ladies word
(Quoth he) I hold it no indignity;
But were he here, that would it with his sword
Abett,° perhaps he mote it deare aby.° *support / pay for*
Cowherd° (quoth she) were not, that thou wouldst fly, *coward*
Ere he doe come, he should be soone in place.
If I doe so, (sayd he) then liberty
I leave to you, for aye me to disgrace
With all those shames, that erst ye spake me to deface.

29

With that a Dwarfe she cald to her in hast,
And taking from her hand a ring of gould,
A privy token, which betweene them past,
Bad him to flie with all the speed he could,
To *Crudor*, and desire him that he would
Vouchsafe to reskue her against a Knight,
Who through strong powre had now her self in hould,
Having late slaine her Seneschall in fight,
And all her people murdred with outragious might.

30

The Dwarfe his way did hast, and went all night;
But *Calidore* did with her there abyde
The comming of that so much threatned[7] Knight,
Where that discourteous Dame with scornfull pryde,
And fowle entreaty him indignifyde,° *dishonored*
That yron heart it hardly could sustaine:
Yet he, that could his wrath full wisely guyde,
Did well endure her womanish disdaine,
And did him selfe from fraile impatience refraine.

31

The morrow next, before the lampe of light,
Above the earth upreard his flaming head,
The Dwarfe, which bore that message to her knight,
Brought aunswere backe, that ere he tasted bread,
He would her succour, and alive or dead
Her foe deliver up into her hand:
Therefore he wild her doe away all dread;
And that of him she mote assured stand,
He sent to her his basenet,° as a faithfull band. *steel head piece*

32

Thereof full blyth the Lady streight became,
And gan t'augment her bitternesse much more:
Yet no whit more appalled for the same,
Ne ought dismayed was Sir *Calidore*,
But rather did more chearefull seeme therefore.
And having soone his armes about him dight,
Did issue forth, to meete his foe afore;° *in front*
Where long he stayed not, when as a Knight
He spide come pricking on with al his powre and might.

33

Well weend he streight, that he should be the same,
Which tooke in hand her quarrell to maintaine;
Ne stayd to aske if it were he by name,
But coucht his speare, and ran at him amaine.
They bene ymett in middest of the plaine,
With so fell fury, and dispiteous forse,
That neither could the others stroke sustaine,
But rudely rowld to ground both man and horse,
Neither of other taking pitty nor remorse.

7. I.e., threatening to Calidore.

34

But *Calidore* uprose againe full light,
Whiles yet his foe lay fast in sencelesse sound,° *swoon*
Yet would he not him hurt, although he might:
For shame he weend a sleeping° wight to wound. *unconscious*
But when *Briana* saw that drery stound,
There where she stood uppon the Castle wall,
She deem'd him sure to have bene dead on ground,
And made such piteous mourning therewithall,
That from the battlements she ready seem'd to fall.

35

Nathlesse at length him selfe he did upreare
In lustlesse wise,° as if against his will, *i.e., listlessly, wearily*
Ere he had slept his fill, he wakened were,
And gan to stretch his limbs; which feeling ill
Of his late fall, a while he rested still:
But when he saw his foe before in vew,
He shooke off luskishnesse,° and courage chill *sluggishness*
Kindling a fresh, gan battell to renew,
To prove if better foote then horsebacke would ensew.

36

There then began a fearefull cruell fray
Betwixt them two, for maystery of might.
For both were wondrous practicke° in that play, *experienced*
And passing well° expert in single fight, *extremely*
And both inflam'd with furious despight:
Which as it still encreast, so still increast
Their cruell strokes and terrible affright;
Ne once for ruth their rigour they releast,
Ne once to breath a while their angers tempest ceast.

37

Thus long they trac'd and traverst to and fro,
And tryde all waies, how each mote entrance make
Into the life of his malignant foe;
They hew'd their helmes, and plates asunder brake,
As they had potshares[8] bene; for nought mote slake
Their greedy vengeaunces, but goary blood,
That at the last like to a purple lake
Of bloudy gore congeal'd about them stood,
Which from their riven° sides forth gushed like a flood. *cut*

8. Broken pieces of earthenware, potsherds.

38

At length it chaunst, that both their hands on hie,
At once did heave, with all their powre and might,
Thinking the utmost of their force to trie,
And prove the finall fortune of the fight:
But *Calidore*, that was more quicke of sight,
And nimbler handed, then his enemie,
Prevented him before his stroke could light,
And on the helmet smote him formerlie,[9]
That made him stoupe to ground with meeke humilitie.

39

And ere he could recover foot againe,
He following that faire advantage fast,
His stroke redoubled with such might and maine,
That him upon the ground he groveling cast;
And leaping to him light, would have unlast
His Helme, to make unto his vengeance way.
Who seeing, in what daunger he was plast,
Cryde out, Ah mercie Sir, doe me not slay,
But save my life, which lot° before your foot doth lay. (*destiny*)

40

With that his mortall hand a while he stayd,
And having somewhat calm'd his wrathfull heat
With goodly patience, thus he to him sayd;
And is the boast of that proud Ladies threat,
That menaced me from the field to beat,
Now brought to this? By this now may ye learne,
Strangers no more so rudely to intreat,
But put away proud looke, and vsage sterne,
The which shal nought to you but foule dishonor yearne.° (*earn*)

41

For nothing is more blamefull to a knight,
That court'sie doth as well as armes professe,
How ever strong and fortunate in fight,
Then the reproch of pride and cruelnesse.
In vaine he seeketh others to suppresse,
Who hath not learnd him selfe first to subdew:
All flesh is frayle, and full of ficklenesse,
Subiect to fortunes chance, still chaunging new;° (*always changing anew*)
What haps to day to me, to morrow may to you.

9. First (i.e., before Crudor could strike).

42

Who will not mercie unto others shew,
How can he mercy ever hope to have?[1]
To pay each with his owne is right and dew.
Yet since ye mercie now doe need to crave,
I will it graunt, your hopelesse life to save;
With these conditions, which I will propound:
First, that ye better shall your selfe behave
Unto all errant knights, whereso on ground;
Next that ye Ladies ayde in every stead and stound.

43

The wretched man, that all this while did dwell
In dread of death, his heasts° did gladly heare, *orders*
And promist to performe his precept well,
And whatsoever else he would requere.
So suffring him to rise, he made him sweare
By his owne sword, and by the crosse thereon,
To take *Briana* for his loving fere,° *companion, partner*
Withouten dowre or composition;[2]
But to release° his former foule condition. *withdraw*

44

All which accepting, and with faithfull oth
Bynding himselfe most firmely to obay,
He up arose, how ever liefe or loth,
And swore to him true fealtie for aye.
Then forth he cald from sorrowfull dismay
The sad *Briana*, which all this beheld:
Who comming forth yet full of late affray,
Sir *Calidore* upcheard, and to her teld
All this accord, to which he *Crudor* had compeld.

45

Whereof she now more glad, then sory earst,
All overcome with infinite affect,° *feeling, emotion*
For his exceeding courtesie, that pearst
Her stubborne hart with inward deepe effect,
Before his feet her selfe she did project,
And him adoring as her lives deare Lord,
With all due thankes, and dutifull respect,
Her selfe acknowledg'd bound for that accord,
By which he had to her both life and love restord.

1. See James 2.13 and Matthew 5.7.
2. Sum of money paid in settlement.

46

So all returning to the Castle glad,
Most joyfully she them did entertaine,
Where goodly glee and feast to them she made,
To shew her thankefull mind and meaning faine,
By all the meanes she mote it best explaine:
And after all, unto Sir *Calidore*
She freely gave that Castle for his paine,
And her selfe bound to him for evermore;
So wondrously now chaung'd, from that she was afore.

47

But *Calidore* himselfe would not retaine
Nor land nor fee, for hyre° of his good deede, *payment*
But gave them straight unto that Squire againe,
Whom from her Seneschall he lately freed,
And to his damzell as their rightfull meed,
For recompence of all their former wrong:
There he remaind with them right well agreed,
Till of his wounds he wexed hole and strong,
And then to his first quest he passed forth along.

Canto II

Calidore sees young Tristram slay
A proud discourteous knight,
He makes him Squire, and of him learnes
his state and present plight.

1

What vertue is so fitting for a knight,
Or for a Ladie, whom a knight should love,
As Curtesie, to beare themselves aright
To all of each degree, as doth behove?
For whether they be placed high above,
Or low beneath, yet ought they well to know
Their good, that none them rightly may reprove° *accuse*
Of rudenesse, for not yeelding what they owe:
Great skill it is such duties timely to bestow.

2

Thereto great helpe dame Nature selfe doth lend:
For some so goodly gracious are by kind,
That every action doth them much commend,
And in the eyes of men great liking find;
Which others, that have greater skill in mind,
Though they enforce themselves, cannot attaine.

For everie thing, to which one is inclin'd,
Doth best become, and greatest grace doth gaine:
Yet praise likewise deserve good thewes,° enforst with paine. *manners, customs*

3

That well in courteous *Calidore* appeares,
Whose every act and deed, that he did say,
Was like enchantment, that through both the eyes,[1]
And both the eares did steale the hart away.
He now againe is on his former way,
To follow his first quest, when as he spyde
A tall young man from thence not farre away,
Fighting on foot, as well he him descryde,
Against an armed knight, that did on horsebacke ryde.

4

And them beside a Ladie faire he saw,
Standing alone on foot, in foule array:
To whom himselfe he hastily did draw,
To weet the cause of so uncomely fray,
And to depart them, if so be he may.
But ere he came in place, that youth had kild
That armed knight, that low on ground he lay;
Which when he saw, his hart was inly child
With great amazement, & his thought with wonder fild.

5

Him stedfastly he markt, and saw to bee
A goodly youth of amiable grace,
Yet but a slender slip, that scarse did see
Yet seventeene yeares, but tall and faire of face
That sure he deem'd him borne of noble race.
All in a woodmans iacket he was clad
Of Lincolne greene,[2] belayd° with silver lace; *decorated*
And on his head an hood with aglets[3] sprad,
And by his side his hunters horne he hanging had.

6

Buskins he wore of costliest cordwayne,[4]
Pinckt[5] upon gold, and paled[6] part per part,
As then the guize° was for each gentle swayne; *fashion*

1. Some editors emend to *ears* for sake of the rhyme.
2. Lincolne greene: bright green cloth made at Lincoln.
3. Metallic tips of cords or laces.
4. Cordovan, Spanish leather.
5. Ornamented with figures cut in such a way that the gold lining showed through.
6. Marked with vertical stripes.

In his right hand he held a trembling dart,
Whose fellow he before had sent apart;
And in his left he held a sharpe borespeare,
With which he wont to launch the salvage hart
Of many a Lyon, and of many a Beare
That first unto his hand in chase did happen neare.

7

Whom *Calidore* a while well having vewed,[7]
At length bespake; what meanes this, gentle swaine?
Why hath thy hand too bold it selfe embrewed° *stained*
In blood of knight, the which by thee is slaine,
By thee no knight; which armes impugneth plaine?
Certes (said he) loth were I to have broken
The law of armes; yet breake it should againe,
Rather then let my selfe of wight be stroken,
So long as these two armes were able to be wroken.° *avenged*

8

For not I him as this his Ladie here
May witnesse well, did offer first to wrong,
Ne surely thus unarm'd I likely were;
But he me first, through pride and puissance strong
Assayld, not knowing what to armes doth long.° *belong*
Perdie great blame, (then said Sir *Calidore*)
For armed knight a wight unarm'd to wrong.
But then aread, thou gentle chyld, wherefore
Betwixt you two began this strife and sterne uprore.

9

That shall I sooth (said he) to you declare.
I whose unryper yeares are yet unfit
For thing of weight, or worke of greater care,
Doe spend my dayes, and bend my carelesse wit
To salvage chace, where I thereon may hit
In all this forrest, and wyld wooddie raine:° *domain*
Where, as this day I was enraunging° it, *rambling in*
I chaunst to meete this knight, who there lyes slaine,
Together with his Ladie, passing on the plaine.

10

The knight, as ye did see, on horsebacke was,
And this his Ladie, (that him ill became,)
On her faire feet by his horse side did pas
Through thicke and thin, unfit for any Dame.

7. The problem is that a woodsman should not attack a knight, and vice versa.

Yet not content, more to increase his shame,
When so she lagged, as she needs mote so,[8]
He with his speare, that was to him great blame,
Would thumpe her forward, and inforce to goe,
Weeping to him in vaine, and making piteous woe.

11

Which when I saw, as they me passed by,
Much was I moved in indignant mind,
And gan to blame him for such cruelty
Towards a Ladie, whom with vsage kind
He rather should have taken up behind.
Wherewith he wroth, and full of proud disdaine,
Tooke in foule scorne, that I such fault did find,
And me in lieu thereof revil'd againe,
Threatning to chastize me, as doth t'a chyld pertaine.[9]

12

Which I no lesse disdayning, backe returned
His scornefull taunts unto his teeth againe,
That he streight way with haughtie choler burned,
And with his speare strooke me one stroke or twaine;
Which I enforst to beare though to my paine,
Cast to requite,° and with a slender dart, *avenge*
Fellow of this I beare, throwne not in vaine,
Strooke him, as seemeth, underneath the hart,
That through the wound his spirit shortly did depart.

13

Much did Sir *Calidore* admyre his speach
Tempred so well, but more admyr'd the stroke
That through the mayles had made so strong a breach
Into his hart, and had so sternely wroke° *inflicted*
His wrath on him, that first occasion broke.
Yet rested not, but further gan inquire
Of that same Ladie, whether what he spoke,
Were soothly so, and that th'unrighteous ire
Of her owne knight, had given him his owne due hire.° *reward*

14

Of all which, when as she could nought deny,
But cleard that stripling of th'imputed blame,
Sayd then Sir *Calidore*; neither will I
Him charge with guilt, but rather doe quite clame:° *acquit, declare free*

8. I.e., as she necessarily did.

9. I.e., treating me like a child.

For what he spake, for you he spake it, Dame,
And what he did, he did him selfe to save:
Against both which that knight wrought knightlesse shame.
For knights and all men this by nature have,
Towards all womenkind them kindly to behave.

15

But sith that he is gone irrevocable,
Please it you Ladie, to us to aread,
What cause could make him so dishonourable,
To drive you so on foot unfit to tread,
And lackey by him, gainst all womanhead?
Certes Sir knight (sayd she) full loth I were
To rayse a lyving blame against the dead:
But since it me concernes, my selfe to clere,
I will the truth discover,° as it chaunst whylere. *reveal*

16

This day, as he and I together roade
Upon our way, to which we weren bent,
We chaunst to come foreby° a covert glade *near*
Within a wood, whereas a Ladie gent
Sate with a knight in joyous jolliment,
Of their franke loves, free from all gealous spyes:
Faire was the Ladie sure, that mote content
An hart, not carried with too curious eyes,
And unto him did shew all lovely courtesyes.

17

Whom when my knight did see so lovely faire,
He inly gan her lover to envy,
And wish, that he part of his spoyle might share.
Whereto when as my presence he did spy
To be a let,° he bad me by and by *hindrance*
For to alight: but when as I was loth,
My loves owne part to leave so suddenly,
He with strong hand down from his steed me throw'th,
And with presumpteous powre against that knight streight [go'th.

18

Unarm'd all was the knight, as then more meete
For Ladies service, and for loves delight,
Then fearing any foeman there to meete:
Whereof he taking oddes, streight bids him dight
Himselfe to yeeld his love, or else to fight.

Whereat the other starting up dismayd,
Yet boldly answer'd, as he rightly might;
To leave his love he should be ill apayd,° *ill pleased*
In which he had good right gaynst all, that it gainesayd.

19

Yet since he was not presently in plight
Her to defend, or his to justifie,
He him requested, as he was a knight,
To lend him day his better right to trie,
Or stay till he his armes, which were thereby,
Might lightly fetch. But he was fierce and whot,
Ne time would give, nor any termes aby,° *abide, submit to*
But at him flew, and with his speare him smot;
From which to thinke to save himselfe, it booted not.

20

Meanewhile his Ladie, which this outrage saw,
Whilest they together for the quarrey° strove, *prey*
Into the covert did her selfe withdraw,
And closely hid her selfe within the grove.
My knight hers soone, as seemes, to daunger drove
And left sore wounded: but when her he mist,
He woxe halfe mad, and in that rage gan rove
And range through all the wood, where so he wist
She hidden was, and sought her so long, as him list.

21

But when as her he by no meanes could find,
After long search and chauff,° he turned backe *rage*
Unto the place, where me he left behind:
There gan he me to curse and ban,° for lacke *curse*
Of that faire bootie, and with bitter wracke° *vengeance*
To wreake on me the guilt of his owne wrong.
Of all which I yet glad to beare the packe,
Strove to appease him, and perswaded long:
But still his passion grew more violent and strong.

22

Then as it were t'avenge his wrath on mee,
When forward we should fare, he flat refused
To take me up (as this young man did see)
Upon his steed, for no iust cause accused,
But forst to trot on foot, and foule misused,
Pounching me with the butt end of his speare,
In vaine complayning, to be so abused.

For he regarded neither playnt nor teare,
But more enforst my paine, the more my plaints to heare.

23

So passed we, till this young man us met,
And being moov'd with pittie of my plight,
Spake, as was meet, for ease of my regret:
Whereof befell, what now is in your sight.
Now sure (then said Sir *Calidore*) and right
Me seemes, that him befell by his owne fault:
Who ever thinkes through confidence of might,
Or through support of count'nance proud and hault° *haughty*
To wrong the weaker, oft falles in his owne assault.

24

Then turning backe unto that gentle boy,
Which had himselfe so stoutly well acquit;
Seeing his face so lovely sterne and coy,° *shy, modest*
And hearing th'answeres of his pregnant wit,
He praysd it much, and much admyred it;
That sure he weend him borne of noble blood,
With whom those graces did so goodly fit:
And when he long had him beholding stood,
He burst into these words, as to him seemed good.

25

Faire gentle swayne, and yet as stout° as fayre, *brave*
That in these woods amongst the Nymphs dost wonne,
Which daily may to thy sweete lookes repayre,
As they are wont unto *Latonaes* sonne,[1]
After his chace on woodie *Cynthus*[2] donne:
Well may I certes such an one thee read,
As by thy worth thou worthily hast wonne,
Or surely borne of some Heroicke sead,
That in thy face appeares and gratious goodly head.

26

But should it not displease thee it to tell;
(Unlesse thou in these woods thy selfe conceale,
For love amongst the woodie Gods to dwell;)
I would thy selfe require thee to reveale,
For deare affection and unfayned zeale,
Which to thy noble personage I beare,
And wish thee grow in worship and great weale.° *wealth, prosperity*

1. Apollo.

2. A hill on Delos. Apollo is supposed to have enjoyed chasing nymphs on Delos.

For since the day that armes I first did reare,
I never saw in any greater hope appeare.

27

To whom then thus the noble youth; may be
Sir knight, that by discovering my estate,
Harme may arise unweeting unto me;
Nathelesse, sith ye so courteous seemed late,
To you I will not feare it to relate.
Then wote ye that I am a Briton borne,
Sonne of a King, how ever thorough fate
Or fortune I my countrie have forlorne,
And lost the crowne, which should my head by right adorne.

28

And *Tristram* is my name, the onely heire[3]
Of good king *Meliogras* which did rayne
In Cornewale, till that he through lives despeire
Untimely dyde, before I did attaine
Ripe yeares of reason, my right to maintaine.
After whose death, his brother seeing mee
An infant, weake a kingdome to sustaine,
Upon him tooke the roiall high degree,
And sent me, where him list, instructed for to bee.

29

The widow Queene my mother, which then hight
Faire *Emiline*, conceiving then great feare
Of my fraile safetie, resting in the might
Of him, that did the kingly Scepter beare,
Whose gealous dread° induring not a peare, *fear*
Is wont to cut off all, that doubt may breed,
Thought best away me to remove somewhere
Into some forrein land, where as no need
Of dreaded daunger might his doubtfull humor° feed. *i.e., suspicion*

30

So taking counsell of a wise man red,° *learned*
She was by him adviz'd, to send me quight
Out of the countrie, wherein I was bred,
The which the fertile *Lionesse* is hight,
Into the land of *Faerie*, where no wight
Should weet of me, nor worke me any wrong.
To whose wise read° she hearkning, sent me streight *counsel*

3. Spenser's version of the early life of Sir Tristram follows closely Malory, 8.I, but Spenser changes the mother's name from Elizabeth to Emiline.

Into this land, where I have wond thus long,
Since I was ten yeares old, now growen to stature strong.

31

All which my daies I have not lewdly spent,
Nor spilt the blossome of my tender yeares
In ydlesse, but as was convenient,
Have trayned bene with many noble feres° *companions*
In gentle thewes,° and such like seemely leres.° *customs / lessons*
Mongst which my most delight hath alwaies been,
To hunt the salvage chace amongst my peres,
Of all that raungeth in the forrest greene;
Of which none is to me unknowne, that ev'r was seene.

32

Ne is there hauke, which mantleth° her on pearch, *stretches wings*
Whether high towring, or accoasting° low, *skimming along the ground*
But I the measure of her flight doe search,
And all her pray, and all her diet know.
Such be our joyes, which in these forrests grow:
Onely the use of armes, which most I joy,
And fitteth most for noble swayne to know,
I have not tasted yet, yet past a boy,
And being now high time these strong joynts to imploy.

33

Therefore, good Sir, sith now occasion fit
Doth fall, whose like hereafter seldome may,
Let me this crave, unworthy though of it,
That ye will make me Squire without delay,
That from henceforth in batteilous array
I may beare armes, and learne to use them right;
The rather since that fortune hath this day
Given to me the spoile of this dead knight,
These goodly gilden armes, which I have won in fight.

34

All which when well Sir *Calidore* had heard,
Him much more now, then earst he gan admire,
For the rare hope which in his yeares appear'd,
And thus replide; faire chyld, the high desire
To love of armes, which in you doth aspire,
I may not certes without blame denie;
But rather wish, that some more noble hire,
(Though none more noble then is chevalrie,)
I had, you to reward with greater dignitie.

35

There him he causd to kneele, and made to sweare
Faith to his knight, and truth to Ladies all,
And never to be recreant, for feare
Of perill, or of ought that might befall:
So he him dubbed,° and his Squire did call. *made a knight*
Full glad and joyous then young *Tristram* grew,
Like as a flowre, whose silken leaves small,
Long shut up in the bud from heavens vew,
At length breakes forth, and brode displayes his smyling hew.

36

Thus when they long had treated to and fro,[4]
And *Calidore* betooke him to depart,
Chyld° *Tristram* prayd, that he with him might goe *knight*
On his adventure, vowing not to start,
But wayt on him in every place and part.
Whereat Sir *Calidore* did much delight,
And greatly joy'd at his so noble hart,
In hope he sure would prove a doughtie knight:
Yet for the time this answere he to him behight.

37

Glad would I surely be, thou courteous Squire,
To have thy presence in my present quest,
That mote thy kindled courage set on fire,
And flame forth honour in thy noble brest:
But I am bound by vow, which I profest
To my dread Soveraine, when I it assayd,
That in atchievement of her high behest,
I should no creature joyne unto mine ayde,
For thy I may not graunt, that ye so greatly prayde.

38

But since this Ladie is all desolate,
And needeth safegard now upon her way,
Ye may doe well in this her needfull state
To succour her, from daunger of dismay;
That thankfull guerdon may to you repay.
The noble ympe of such new service fayne,
It gladly did accept, as he did say.
So taking courteous leave, they parted twayne,
And *Calidore* forth passed to his former payne.° *labor, quest*

4. I.e., conversed about various subjects.

39

But *Tristram* then despoyling that dead knight
Of all those goodly implements of prayse,
Long fed his greedie eyes with the faire sight
Of the bright mettall, shyning like Sunne rayes;
Handling and turning them a thousand wayes.
And after having them upon him dight,
He tooke that Ladie, and her up did rayse
Upon the steed of her owne late dead knight,
So with her marched forth, as she did him behight.

40

There to their fortune leave we them awhile,
And turne we backe to good Sir *Calidore*;
Who ere he thence had traveild many a mile,
Came to the place, whereas ye heard afore
This knight, whom *Tristram* slew, had wounded sore
Another knight in his despiteous pryde;
There he that knight found lying on the flore,
With many wounds full perilous and wyde,
That all his garments, and the grasse in vermeill° dyde. *red*

41

And there beside him sate upon the ground
His wofull Ladie, piteously complayning
With loud laments that most unluckie stound,
And her sad selfe with carefull hand constrayning
To wype his wounds, and ease their bitter payning.
Which sorie sight when *Calidore* did vew
With heavie eyne, from teares uneath refrayning,
His mightie hart their mournefull case can rew,
And for their better comfort to them nigher drew.

42

Then speaking to the Ladie, thus he sayd:
Ye dolefull Dame, let not your griefe empeach° *hinder, prevent*
To tell, what cruell hand hath thus arayd° *afflicted*
This knight unarm'd, with so unknightly breach
Of armes, that if I yet him nigh may reach,
I may avenge him of so foule despight.
The Ladie hearing his so courteous speach,
Gan reare her eyes as to the chearefull light,
And from her sory hart few heavie words forth sight.° *sighed*

43

In which she shew'd, how that discourteous knight
(Whom *Tristram* slew) them in that shadow found,

Joying together in unblam'd delight,
And him unarm'd, as now he lay on ground,
Charg'd with his speare and mortally did wound,
Withouten cause, but onely her to reaue° *steal*
From him, to whom she was for ever bound:
Yet when she fled into that covert greave,° *grove, thicket*
He her not finding, both them thus nigh dead did leave.

44

When *Calidore* this ruefull storie had
Well understood, he gan of her demand,
What manner wight he was, and how yclad,
Which had this outrage wrought with wicked hand.
She then, like as she best could understand,
Him thus describ'd, to be of stature large,
Clad all in gilden armes, with azure band
Quartred athwart,° and bearing in his targe° *transversely / shield*
A Ladie on rough waves, row'd in a sommer barge.

45

Then gan Sir *Calidore* to ghesse streight way
By many signes, which she described had,
That this was he, whom *Tristram* earst did slay,
And to her said; Dame be no longer sad:
For he, that hath your Knight so ill bestad,° *beset*
Is now him selfe in much more wretched plight;
These eyes him saw upon the cold earth sprad,
The meede of his desert for that despight,
Which to your selfe he wrought, & to your loved knight.

46

Therefore faire Lady lay aside this griefe,
Which ye have gathered to your gentle hart,
For that displeasure; and thinke what reliefe
Were best devise for this your lovers smart,
And how ye may him hence, and to what part
Convay to be recur'd.° She thankt him deare, *recovered*
Both for that newes he did to her impart,
And for the courteous care, which he did beare
Both to her love; and to her selfe in that sad dreare.

47

Yet could she not devise by any wit,
How thence she might convay him to some place.
For him to trouble she it thought unfit,
That was a straunger to her wretched case;

And him to beare, she thought it thing too base.
Which when as he perceiv'd, he thus bespake;
Faire Lady let it not you seeme disgrace,
To beare this burden on your dainty backe;
My selfe will beare a part, coportion of your packe.

48

So off he did his shield, and downeward layd
Upon the ground, like to an hollow beare;[5]
And powring balme, which he had long purvayd,
Into his wounds, him up thereon did reare,
And twixt them both with parted° paines did beare, *divided in parts, shared*
Twixt life and death, not knowing what was donne.
Thence they him carried to a Castle neare,
In which a worthy auncient Knight did wonne:
Where what ensu'd, shall in next Canto be begonne.

Canto III

Calidore brings Priscilla home,
Pursues the Blatant Beast:
Saves Serena whitest Calepine
By Turpine is opprest.

1

True is, that whilome that good Poet[1] sayd,
The gentle minde by gentle deeds is knowne.
For a man by nothing is so well bewrayd,
As by his manners, in which plaine is showne
Of what degree and what race he is growne.
For seldome seene, a trotting Stalion get
An ambling Colt, that is his proper owne:
So seldome seene, that one in basenesse set
Doth noble courage shew, with curteous manners met.[2]

2

But evermore contrary hath bene tryde,
That gentle bloud will gentle manners breed;
As well may be in *Calidore* descryde,
By late ensample of that courteous deed,
Done to that wounded Knight in his great need,
Whom on his backe he bore, till he him brought
Unto the Castle where they had decreed.
There of the Knight, the which that Castle ought,
To make abode that night he greatly was besought.

5. I.e., bier, a stretcher. Calidore is using his shield to carry off a wounded man.

1. Chaucer.

2. Bhattacherje (*Var.*, p. 330) cites Castiglione as source.

3

He was to weete a man of full ripe yeares,
That in his youth had beene of mickle might,
And borne great sway in armes amongst bis peares:
But now weake age had dimd his candle light.
Yet was he courteous still to every wight,
And loved all that did to armes incline.
And was the father of that wounded Knight,
Whom *Calidore* thus carried on his chine,° *back*
And *Aldus* was his name, and his sonnes *Aladine*.[3]

4

Who when he saw his sonne so ill bedight,
With bleeding wounds, brought home upon a Beare,° *bier*
By a faire Lady, and a straunger Knight,
Was inly touched with compassion deare,
And deare affection of so dolefull dreare,
That he these words burst forth; Ah sory boy,
Is this the hope that to my hoary heare
Thou brings? aie me, is this the timely joy,
Which I expected long, now turnd to sad annoy?

5

Such is the weakenesse of all mortall hope;
So tickle° is the state of earthly things, *unreliable, changeable*
That ere they come unto their aymed° scope, *intended*
They fall too short of our fraile reckonings,
And bring us bale and bitter sorrowings,
In stead of comfort, which we should embrace:
This is the state of Keasars° and of Kings. *emperors*
Let none therefore, that is in meaner place,
Too greatly grieve at any his unlucky case.

6

So well and wisely did that good old Knight
Temper his griefe, and turned it to cheare,
To cheare his guests, whom he had stayd that night,
And make their welcome to them well appeare:
That to Sir *Calidore* was easie geare;° *matter*
But that faire Lady would be cheard for nought,
But sigh'd and sorrow'd for her lover deare,
And inly did afflict her pensive thought,
With thinking to what case her name should now be brought.

3. The meaning of these names has not been established.

7

For she was daughter to a noble Lord,
Which dwelt thereby, who sought her to affy° *betroth*
To a great pere; but she did disaccord,
Ne could her liking to his love apply,
But lov'd this fresh young Knight, who dwelt her ny,
The lusty *Aladine*, though meaner borne,
And of lesse livelood° and liability, *livelihood, prosperity*
Yet full of valour, the which did adorne
His meanesse much, & make her th'others riches scorne.[4]

8

So having both found fit occasion,
They met together in that luckelesse glade;
Where that proud Knight in his presumption
The gentle *Aladine* did earst invade,
Being unarm'd, and set in secret shade.
Whereof she now bethinking, gan t'advize,
How great a hazard she at earst had made
Of her good feme, and further gan devize,
How she the blame might salve with coloured disguize.

9

But *Calidore* with all good courtesie
Fain'd her to frolicke, and to put away
The pensive fit of her melancholie;
And that old Knight by all meanes did assay,
To make them both as merry as he may.
So they the evening past, till time of rest,
When *Calidore* in seemly good array
Unto his bowre was brought, and there undrest,
Did sleepe all night through weary travell of his quest.

10

But faire *Priscilla* (so that Lady hight)
Would to no bed, nor take no kindely sleepe,
But by her wounded love did watch all night,
And all the night for bitter anguish weepe,
And with her teares his wounds did wash and steepe.° *soak*
So well she washt them, and so well she wacht him,
That of the deadly swound, in which full deepe

4. Spenser is not claiming that Aladine is of mean or humble birth, merely that he is not a "great pere" as is Priscilla's father. Aladine is, nevertheless, of gentle origin.

He drenched was, she at the length dispacht him,
And drove away the stound, which mortally attacht him.

11

The morrow next, when day gan to uplooke,
He also gan uplooke with drery eye,
Like one that out of deadly dreame awooke:
Where when he saw his faire *Priscilla* by,
He deepely sigh'd, and groaned inwardly,
To thinke of this ill state, in which she stood,
To which she for his sake had weetingly
Now brought her selfe, and blam'd° her noble blood: *dishonored*
For first, next after life, he tendered° her good. *cherished, cared for*

12

Which she perceiving, did with plenteous teares
His care more then her owne compassionate,
Forgetfull of her owne, to minde his feares:
So both conspiring, gan to intimate
Each others griefe with zeale affectionate,
And twixt them twaine with equall care to cast,
How to save whole her hazarded estate;
For which the onely helpe now left them last
Seem'd to be *Calidore:* all other helpes were past.

13

Him they did deeme, as sure to them he seemed,
A courteous Knight, and full of faithfull trust:
Therefore to him their cause they best esteemed
Whole to commit, and to his dealing just.
Earely, so soone as *Titans*° beames forth brust *the sun's*
Through the thicke clouds, in which they steeped lay
All night in darkenesse, duld with yron rust,
Calidore rising up as fresh as day,
Gan freshly him addresse unto his former way.

14

But first him seemed fit, that wounded Knight
To visite, after this nights perillous passe,° *passage*
And to salute him, if he were in plight,
And eke that Lady his faire lovely lasse.
There he him found much better then he was,
And moved speach to him of things of course,° *i.e., ordinary, usual*
The anguish of his paine to overpasse:
Mongst which he namely did to him discourse,
Of former daies mishap, his sorrowes wicked sourse.

15

Of which occasion *Aldine* taking hold,
Gan breake to him the fortunes of his love,
And all his disadventures to unfold;
That *Calidore* it dearly deepe did move.
In th'end his kyndly courtesie to prove,
He him by all the bands of love besought,
And as it mote a faithfull friend behove,
To safeconduct his love, and not for ought
To leave, till to her fathers house he had her brought.

16

Sir *Calidore* his faith thereto did plight,
It to performe: so after little stay,
That she her selfe had to the journey dight,
He passed forth with her in faire array,
Fearelesse, who ought did thinke, or ought did say,
Sith his own thought he knew most cleare from wite.° *blame*
So as they past together on their way,
He can devize this counter-cast° of slight, *trick*
To give faire colour to that Ladies cause in sight.

17

Streight to the carkasse of that Knight he went,
The cause of all this evill, who was slaine
The day before by just avengement
Of noble *Tristram*, where it did remaine:
There he the necke thereof did cut in twaine,
And tooke with him the head, the signe of shame.
So forth he passed thorough that daies paine,
Till to that Ladies fathers house he came,
Most pensive man, through feare, what of his childe became.

18

There he arriving boldly, did present
The fearefull Lady to her father deare,
Most perfect pure, and guiltlesse innocent
Of blame, as he did on his Knighthood sweare,
Since first he saw her, and did free from feare
Of a discourteous Knight, who her had reft,
And by outragious force away did beare:
Witnesse thereof he shew'd his head there left,
And wretched life forlorne for vengement of his theft.[5]

5. Calidore's "white lie" has been the occasion of much tongue-clacking among the critics, but Judson (*Var.*, p. 341) cites Guazzo: "I denie not, but that it is commendable to coyne a lye at some time, and in some place, so that it tende to some honest ende."

19

Most joyfull man her sire was her to see,
And heare th'adventure of her late mischaunce;
And thousand thankes to *Calidore* for fee
Of his large paines in her deliveraunce
Did yeeld; Ne lesse the Lady did advaunce.
Thus having her restored trustily,
As he had vow'd, some small continuaunce
He there did make, and then most carefully
Unto his first exploite he did him selfe apply.

20

So as he was pursuing of his quest
He chaunst to come whereas a jolly Knight,
In covert shade him selfe did safely rest,
To solace with his Lady in delight:
His warlike armes he had from him undight;
For that him selfe he thought from daunger free,
And far from envious eyes that mote him spight
And eke the Lady was full faire to see,
And courteous withall, becomming her degree.[6]

21

To whom Sir *Calidore* approaching nye,
Ere they were well aware of living wight,
Them much abasht, but more him selfe thereby,
That he so rudely did uppon them light,
And troubled had their quiet loves delight.
Yet since it was his fortune, not his fault,
Him selfe thereof he labour'd to acquite,
And pardon crav'd for his so rash default,
That he gainst courtesie so fowly did default.

22

With which his gentle words and goodly wit
He soone allayd that Knights conceiv'd displeasure,
That he besought him downe by him to sit,
That they mote treat of things abrode at leasure;
And of adventures, which had in his measure
Of so long waies to him befallen late.
So downe he sate, and with delightfull pleasure
His long adventures gan to him relate,
Which he endured had through daungerous debate.° *contest*

6. Spenser now places Calidore in a situation that parallels the Aladine-Priscilla episode. The purpose is to contrast courtesy with rudeness.

23

Of which whilest they discoursed both together,
The faire *Serena* (so his Lady hight)
Allur'd with myldnesse of the gentle wether,
And pleasaunce of the place, the which was dight
With divers flowres distinct° with rare delight; *marked*
Wandred about the fields, as liking led
Her wavering lust° after her wandring sight, *pleasure*
To make a garland to adorne her hed,
Without suspect of ill or daungers hidden dred.

24

All sodainely out of the forrest nere
The *Blatant Beast* forth rushing unaware,
Caught her thus loosely wandring here and there,
And in his wide great mouth away her bare.
Crying aloud in vaine, to shew her sad misfare° *misfortune*
Unto the Knights, and calling oft for ayde,
Who with the horrour of her haplesse care
Hastily starting up, like men dismayde,
Ran after fast to reskue the distressed mayde.

25

The Beast with their pursuit incited more,
Into the wood was bearing her apace
For to have spoyled her, when *Calidore*
Who was more light of foote and swift in chace,
Him overtooke in middest of his race:
And fiercely charging him with all his might,
Forst to forgoe his pray there in the place,
And to betake him selfe to fearefull flight;
For he durst not abide with *Calidore* to fight.

26

Who nathelesse, when he the Lady saw
There left on ground, though in full evill plight,
Yet knowing that her Knight now neare did draw,
Staide not to succour her in that affright,
But follow'd fast the Monster in his flight:
Through woods and hils he follow'd him so fast,
That he nould let him breath nor gather spright,
But forst him gape and gaspe, with dread aghast,
As if his lungs and lites° were nigh a sunder brast.[7] *lungs*

7. Calidore does not appear again until Canto 9.

27

And now by this Sir *Calepine*[8] (so hight)
Came to the place, where he his Lady found
In dolorous dismay and deadly plight,
All in gore bloud there tumbled on the ground,
Having both sides through grypt with griesly wound.
His weapons soone from him he threw away,
And stouping downe to her in drery swound,
Uprear'd her from the ground, whereon she lay,
And in his tender armes her forced up to stay.

28

So well he did his busie paines apply,
That the faint sprite he did revoke° againe, *call back*
To her fraile mansion of mortality.
Then up he tooke her twixt his armes twaine,
And setting on his steede, her did sustaine
With carefull hands soft footing° her beside, *walking*
Till to some place of rest they mote attaine,
Where she in safe assuraunce mote abide,
Till she recured were of those her woundes wide.

29

Now when as *Phœbus* with his fiery waine° *wagon*
Unto his Inne° began to draw apace; *house of the zodiac*
Tho wexing weary of that toylesome paine,
In travelling on foote so long a space,
Not wont on foote with heavy armes to trace,° *walk*
Downe in a dale forby a rivers syde,
He chaunst to spie a faire and stately place,
To which he meant his weary steps to guyde,
In hope there for his love some succour to provyde.

30

But comming to the rivers side, he found
That hardly passable on foote it was:
Therefore there still he stood as in a stound,
Ne wist which way he through the foord mote pas.
Thus whilest he was in this distressed case,
Devising what to doe, he nigh espyde
An armed Knight approaching to the place,
With a faire Lady lincked by his syde,
The which themselves prepard through the foord to ride.[9]

8. Calepine, whose adventures make up the action of this book until Calidore returns in Canto 9, seems to be related by his name to Calidore: Greek: *kale*, "beautiful."

9. The Turpine episode is modeled on the Pinabello episode in Aristo, *Orlando Furioso* 22.104 ff.

31

Whom *Calepine* saluting (as became)
Besought of courtesie in that his neede,
For safe conducting of his sickely Dame,
Through that same perillous foord with better heede,
To take him up behinde upon his steed,
To whom that other did this taunt returne.
Perdy thou peasant Knight, mightst rightly reed
Me then to be full base and evill borne,
If I would beare behinde a burden of such scorne.

32

But as thou hast thy steed forlorne with shame,
So fare on foote till thou another gayne,
And let thy Lady likewise doe the same,
Or beare her on thy backe with pleasing payne,
And prove thy manhood on the billowes vayne.
With which rude speach his Lady much displeased,
Did him reprove, yet could him not restrayne,
And would on her owne Palfrey him have eased,
For pitty of his Dame, whom she saw so diseased.° *ill and uncomfortable*

33

Sir *Calepine* her thanckt, yet inly wroth
Against her Knight, her gentlenesse refused,
And carelesly into the river goth,
As in despight to be so fowle abused
Of a rude churle, whom often he accused
Of fowle discourtesie, unfit for Knight
And strongly wading through the waves unused,° *unaccustomed*
With speare in th'one hand, stayd him selfe upright,
With th'other staide his Lady up with steddy might.

34

And all the while, that same discourteous Knight,
Stood on the further bancke beholding him,
At whose calamity, for more despight
He laught, and mockt to see him like to swim.
But when as *Calepine* came to the brim,
And saw his carriage past that perill well,
Looking at that same Carle with count'nance grim,
His heart with vengeaunce inwardly did swell,
And forth at last did breake in speaches sharpe and fell.

35

Unknightly Knight, the blemish of that name,
  And blot of all that armes uppon them take,
  Which is the badge of honour and of fame,
  Loe I defie thee, and here challenge make,
  That thou for ever doe those armes forsake;
  And be for ever held a recreant Knight,
  Unlesse thou dare for thy deare Ladies sake,
  And for thine owne defence on foote alight,
To justifie thy fault gainst me in equall fight.

36

The dastard, that did heare him selfe defyde,
  Seem'd not to weigh his threatfull words at all,
  But laught them out, as if his greater pryde,
  Did scorne the challenge of so base a thrall:
  Or had no courage, or else had no gall.
  So much the more was *Calepine* offended,
  That him to no revenge he forth could call,
  But both his challenge and him selfe contemned,
Ne cared as a coward so to be condemned.

37

But he nought weighing what he sayd or did,
  Turned his steede about another way,
  And with his Lady to the Castle rid,
  Where was his won; ne did the other stay,
  But after went directly as he may,
  For his sicke charge some harbour there to seeke;
  Where he arriving with the fall of day,
  Drew to the gate, and there with prayers meeke,
And myld entreaty lodging did for her beseeke.

38

But the rude Porter that no manners had,
  Did shut the gate against him in his face,
  And entraunce boldly unto him forbad.
  Nathelesse the Knight now in so needy case,
  Gan him entreat even with submission base,
  And humbly praid to let them in that night:
  Who to him aunswer'd, that there was no place
  Of lodging fit for any errant Knight,
Unlesse that with his Lord he formerly° did fight. *first*

39

Full loth am I (quoth he) as now at earst,
  When day is spent, and rest us needeth most,

And that this Lady, both whose sides are pearst
With wounds, is ready to forgo the ghost:
Ne would I gladly combate with mine host,
That should to me such curtesie afford,
Unlesse that I were thereunto enforst.
But yet aread to me, how hight thy Lord,
That doth thus strongly ward the Castle of the ford.

40

His name (quoth he) if that thou list to learne,
Is hight Sir *Turpine*,[1] one of mickle might,
And manhood rare, but terrible and stearne
In all assaies to every errant Knight,
Because of one, that wrought him fowle despight.
Ill seemes (sayd he) if he so valiaunt be,
That he should be so sterne to stranger wight:
For seldome yet did living creature see,
That curtesie and manhood ever disagree.

41

But go thy waies to him, and fro me say,
That here is at his gate an errant Knight,
That house-rome craves, yet would be loth t'assay
The proofe of battell, now in doubtfull night,
Or curtesie with rudenesse to requite:
Yet if he needes will fight, crave leave till morne,
And tell withall, the lamentable plight,
In which this Lady languisheth forlorne,
That pitty craves, as he of woman was yborne.

42

The groome went streight way in, and to his Lord
Declar'd the message, which that Knight did move;
Who sitting with his Lady then at bord,° *table*
Not onely did not his demaund approve,
But both himselfe revil'd, and eke his love;
Albe his Lady, that *Blandina*[2] hight,
Him of ungentle vsage did reprove
And earnestly entreated that they might
Finde favour to be lodged there for that same night.

43

Yet would he not perswaded be for ought,
Ne from his currish will awhit reclame.° *recant*
Which answer when the groome returning, brought

1. Latin: *turpis*, "base."

2. Latin: *blandus*, "tempting."

To *Calepine*, his heart did inly flame
With wrathfull fury for so foule a shame,
That he could not thereof avenged bee:
But most for pitty of his dearest Dame,
Whom now in deadly daunger he did see;
Yet had no meanes to comfort, nor procure her glee.

44

But all in vaine; for why,° no remedy *because*
He saw, the present mischiefe to redresse,
But th'utmost end perforce for to aby,° *endure*
Which that nights fortune would for him addresse.
So downe he tooke his Lady in distresse,
And layd her underneath a bush to sleepe,
Cover'd with cold, and wrapt in wretchednesse,
Whiles he him selfe all night did nought but weepe,
And wary watch about her for her safegard keepe.

45

The morrow next, so soone as joyous day
Did shew it selfe in sunny beames bedight,
Serena full of dolorous dismay,
Twixt darkenesse dread, and hope of living light,
Uprear'd her head to see that chearefull sight.
Then *Calepine*, how ever inly wroth,
And greedy to avenge that vile despight,
Yet for the feeble Ladies sake, full loth
To make there lenger stay, forth on his journey goth.

46

He goth on foote all armed by her side,
Upstaying still her selfe uppon her steede,
Being unhable else alone to ride;
So sore her sides, so much her wounds did bleede:
Till that at length, in his extreamest neede,
He chaunst far off an armed Knight to spy,
Pursuing him apace with greedy speede,
Whom well he wist to be some enemy,
That meant to make advantage of his misery.

47

Wherefore he stayd, till that he nearer drew,
To weet what issue would thereof betyde,
Tho whenas he approched nigh in vew,
By certaine signes he plainely him descryde,
To be the man, that with such scornefull pryde

Had him abusde, and shamed yesterday;
Therefore misdoubting, least he should misguyde
His former malice to some new assay,
He cast to keepe him selfe so safely as he may.

48

By this the other came in place likewise,
And couching close his speare and all his powre,
As bent to some malicious enterprise,
He bad him stand, t'abide the bitter stoure
Of his sore vengeaunce, or to make avoure° *answer*
Of the lewd words and deedes, which he had done:
With that ran at him, as he would devoure
His life attonce; who nought could do, but shun
The perill of his pride, or else be overrun.

49

Yet he him still pursew'd from place to place,
With full intent him cruelly to kill,
And like a wilde goate round about did chace,
Flying the fury of his bloudy will.
But his best succour and refuge was still
Behinde his Ladies backe, who to him cryde,
And called oft with prayers loud and shrill,
As ever he to Lady was affyde,
To spare her Knight, and rest with reason pacifyde.

50

But he the more thereby enraged was,
And with more eager felnesse him pursew'd,
So that at length, after long weary chace,
Having by chaunce a close advantage vew'd,
He over raught him, having long eschew'd
His violence in vaine, and with his spere
Strooke through his shoulder, that the blood ensew'd
In great aboundance, as a well it were,
That forth out of an hill fresh gushing did appere.

51

Yet ceast he not for all that cruell wound,
But chaste him still, for all his Ladies cry,
Not satisfyde till on the fatall ground
He saw his life powrd forth dispiteously:
The which was certes in great jeopardy,
Had not a wondrous chaunce his reskue wrought,
And saved from his cruell villany.

Such chaunces oft exceed all humaine thought:
That in another Canto shall to end be brought.

Canto IV

Calepine by a salvage man
from Turpine reskewed is,
And whylest an Infant from a Beare
he saves, his love doth misse.

1

Like as a ship with dreadfull storme long tost,
Having spent all her mastes and her ground-hold,° *anchor*
Now farre from harbour likely to be lost,
At last some fisher barke° doth neare behold, *fishing boat*
That giveth comfort to her courage cold.
Such was the state of this most courteous knight
Being oppressed by that faytour bold,
That he remayned in most perilous plight,
And his sad Ladie left in pitifull affright.

2

Till that by fortune, passing all foresight,
A salvage man,[1] which in those woods did wonne,
Drawne with that Ladies loud and piteous shright,° *shriek*
Toward the same incessantly did ronne,
To understand what there was to be donne.
There he this most discourteous craven found,
As fiercely yet, as when he first begonne,
Chasing the gentle *Calepine* around,
Ne sparing him the more for all his grievous wound.

3

The salvage man, that never till this houre
Did taste of pittie, neither gentlesse knew,
Seeing his sharpe assault and cruell stoure
Was much emmoved at his perils vew,
That even his ruder hart began to rew,
And feele compassion of his evill plight,
Against his foe that did him so pursew:
From whom he meant to free him, if he might,
And him avenge of that so villenous despight.

1. Such savage men are common in 16th-century literature. See Richard Bernheimer, *Wild Men in the Middle Ages*, Cambridge, Mass., 1952.

4

Yet armes or weapon had he none to fight,
Ne knew the use of warlike instruments,
Save such as sudden rage him lent to smite,
But naked without needfull vestiments,
To clad his corpse with meete habiliments,
He cared not for dint of sword nor speere,
No more then for the strokes of strawes or bents:° *reeds*
For from his mothers wombe, which him did beare
He was invulnerable made by Magicke leare.° *learning*

5

He stayed not to advize, which way were best
His foe t'assayle, or how himselfe to gard,
But with fierce fury and with force infest° *hostile*
Upon him ran; who being well prepard,
His first assault full warily did ward,
And with the push of his sharp-pointed speare
Full on the breast him strooke, so strong and hard,
That forst him backe recoyle, and reele areare;° *backward*
Yet in his bodie made no wound nor bloud appeare.

6

With that the wyld man more enraged grew,
Like to a Tygre that hath mist his pray,
And with mad mood againe upon him flew,
Regarding neither speare, that mote him slay,
Nor his fierce steed, that mote him much dismay.
The salvage nation doth all dread despize:
Tho on his shield he griple° hold did lay, *tenacious, obstinate*
And held the same so hard, that by no wize
He could him force to loose, or leave his enterprize.

7

Long did he wrest and wring it to and fro,
And every way did try, but all in vaine:
For he would not his greedie grype forgoe,
But hayld and puld with all his might and maine,
That from his steed him nigh he drew againe.
Who having now no use of his long speare,
So nigh at hand, nor force his shield to straine,
Both speare and shield, as things that needlesse were,
He quite forsooke, and fled himselfe away for feare.

8

But after him the wyld man ran apace,
And him pursewed with importune speed,

(For he was swift as any Bucke in chace)
And had he not in his extreamest need,
Bene helped through the swiftnesse of his steed,
He had him overtaken in his flight.
Who ever, as he saw him nigh succeed,
Gan cry aloud with horrible affright,
And shrieked out, a thing uncomely for a knight.

9

But when the Salvage saw his labour vaine,
In following of him, that fled so fast,
He wearie woxe, and backe return'd againe
With speede unto the place, whereas he last
Had left that couple, nere their utmost cast.° *extreme situation*
There he that knight full sorely bleeding found,
And eke the Ladie fearefully aghast,
Both for the perill of the present stound,
And also for the sharpnesse of her rankling° wound. *festering*

10

For though she were right glad, so rid to bee
From that vile lozell,° which her late offended, *scoundrel*
Yet now no lesse encombrance she did see,
And perill by this salvage man pretended;° *presented, intended*
Gainst whom she saw no meanes to be defended,
By reason that her knight was wounded sore.
Therefore her selfe she wholy recommended
To Gods sole grace, whom she did oft implore,
To send her succour, being of all hope forlore.

11

But the wyld man, contrarie to her feare,
Came to her creeping like a fawning hound,
And by rude° tokens made to her appeare *uncivilized, primitive*
His deepe compassion of her dolefull stound,
Kissing his hands, and crouching to the ground;
For other language had he none nor speach,
But a soft murmure, and confused sound
Of senselesse words, which nature did him teach,
T'expresse his passions, which his reason did empeach.° *hinder*

12

And comming likewise to the wounded knight,
When he beheld the streames of purple blood
Yet flowing fresh, as moved with the sight,
He made great mone after° his salvage mood, *according to*

And running streight into the thickest wood,
A certaine herbe from thence unto him brought,
Whose vertue he by use well understood:
The ivyce whereof into his wound he wrought,
And stopt the bleeding straight, ere he it staunched° thought. *stopped up, blocked*

13

Then taking up that Recreants shield and speare,
Which earst he left, he signes unto them made,
With him to wend unto his worming neare:
To which he easily did them perswade.
Farre in the forrest by a hollow glade,
Covered with mossie shrubs, which spredding brode
Did underneath them make a gloomy shade;
There foot of living creature never trode,
Ne scarse wyld beasts durst come, there was this wights abode.

14

Thether he brought these unacquainted guests;
To whom faire semblance, as he could, he shewed
By signes, by lookes, and all his other gests.° *gestures, behavior*
But the bare ground, with hoarie mosse bestrowed,
Must be their bed, their pillow was unsowed,° *unsewn*
And the frutes of the forrest was their feast:
For their bad[2] Stuard neither plough'd nor sowed,
Ne fed on flesh, ne ever of wyld beast
Did taste the bloud, obaying natures first beheast.

15

Yet howsoever base and meane it were,
They tooke it well, and thanked God for all,
Which had them freed from that deadly feare,
And sav'd from being to that caytive thrall.
Here they of force (as fortune now did fall)
Compelled were themselves a while to rest,
Glad of that easement, though it were hut small;
That having there their wounds awhile redrest,
They mote the abler be to passe unto the rest.

16

During which time, that wyld man did apply
His best endevour, and his daily paine,
In seeking all the woods both farre and nye

2. Probably used here in the sense of "inadequate," because he did not provide them with meat or cultivated food.

For herbes to dresse their wounds; still seeming faine,
When ought he did, that did their lyking gaine.
So as ere long he had that knightes wound
Recured well, and made him whole againe:
But that same Ladies hurts no herbe he found,
Which could redresse, for it was inwardly unsound.[3]

17

Now when as *Calepine* was woxen strong,
Upon a day he cast abrode to wend,
To take the ayre, and heare the thrushes song,
Unarm'd, as fearing neither foe nor frend,
And without sword his person to defend,
There him befell, unlooked for before,
An hard adventure with unhappie end,
A cruell Beare, the which an infant bore
Betwixt his bloodie jawes, besprinckled all with gore.

18

The litle babe did loudly scrike° and squall, *shriek*
And all the woods with piteous plaints did fill,
As if his cry did meane for helpe to call
To *Calepine*, whose eares those shrieches shrill
Percing his hart with pities point did thrill;
That after him, he ran with zealous haste,
To rescue th'infant, ere he did him kill:
Whom though he saw now somewhat overpast,° *gone beyond*
Yet by the cry he follow'd, and pursewed fast.

19

Well then him chaunst his heavy armes to want,[4]
Whose burden mote empeach° his needfull speed, *hinder*
And hinder him from libertie to pant:
For having long time, as his daily weed,
Them wont to weare, and wend on foot for need,
Now wanting them he felt himselfe so light,
That like an Hauke, which feeling her selfe freed
From bels and jesses,[5] which did let° her flight, *prevent*
Him seem'd his feet did fly, and in their speed delight.

3. The nature of Serena's wound, inflicted by the Blatant Beast, becomes clearer in VI.5. 28 and 6.8–9.
4. I.e., it was fortunate that he lacked his armor and weapons.
5. Leather straps bound to the feet of falcons, to which the leash was attached. When falcons were released, they ordinarily flew with the bells and jesses on their legs.

20

So well he sped him, that the wearie Beare
Ere long he overtooke, and forst to stay,
And without weapon him assayling neare,
Compeld him soone the spoyle adowne to lay.
Wherewith the beast enrag'd to lose his pray,
Upon him turned, and with greedie force
And furie, to be crossed in his way,
Gaping full wyde, did thinke without remorse
To be aveng'd on him, and to devoure his corse.

21

But the bold knight no whit thereat dismayd,
But catching up in hand a ragged stone,
Which lay thereby (so fortune him did ayde)
Upon him ran, and thrust it all attone
Into his gaping throte, that made him grone
And gaspe for breath, that he nigh choked was,
Being unable to digest that bone;
Ne could it upward come, nor downward passe,
Ne could he brooke the coldnesse of the stony masse.

22

Whom when as he thus combred did behold,
Stryving in vaine that nigh his bowels brast,
He with him closd,° and laying mightie hold *came together*
Upon his throte, did gripe his gorge so fast,
That wanting breath, him downe to ground he cast;
And then oppressing him with urgent paine,
Ere long enforst to breath his utmost blast,
Gnashing his cruell teeth at him in vaine,
And threatning his sharpe clawes, now wanting powre to
[straine.

23

Then tooke he up betwixt his armes twaine
The litle babe, sweet relickes of his pray;
Whom pitying to heare so sore complaine,
From his soft eyes the teares he wypt away,
And from his face the filth that did it ray,° *soil*
And every litle limbe he searcht around,
And every part, that under sweathbands° lay, *swaddling clothes*
Least that the beasts sharpe teeth had any wound
Made in his tender flesh, but whole them all he found.

24

So having all his bands againe uptyde,
He with him thought backe to returne againe:
But when he lookt about on every syde,
To weet which way were best to entertaine,° *take*
To bring him to the place, where he would faine,
He could no path nor tract of foot descry,
Ne by inquirie learne, nor ghesse by ayme.
For nought but woods and forrests farre and nye,
That all about did close the compasse of his eye.

25

Much was he then encombred, ne could tell
Which way to take: now West he went a while,
Then Norm; then neither, but as fortune fell.
So up and downe he wandred many a mile,
With wearie travell and uncertaine toile,
Yet nought the nearer to his journeys end;
And evermore his lovely litle spoile
Crying for food, did greatly him offend.° *bother*
So all that day in wandring vainely he did spend.

26

At last about the setting of the Sunne,
Him selfe out of the forest he did wynd,
And by good fortune the plaine champion° wonne: *open plain*
Where looking all about, where he mote fynd
Some place of succour to content his mynd,
At length he heard under the forrests syde
A voice, that seemed of some woman kynd,
Which to her selfe lamenting loudly cryde,
And oft complayn'd of fate, and fortune oft defyde.

27

To whom approching, when as she perceived
A stranger wight in place, her plaint she stayd,
As if she doubted to have bene deceived,
Or loth to let her sorrowes be bewrayd.
Whom when as *Calepine* saw so dismayd,
He to her drew, and with faire blandishment
Her chearing up, thus gently to her sayd;
What be you wofull Dame, which thus lament,
And for what cause declare, so mote ye not repent.° *be sad*

28

To whom she thus, what need me Sir to tell,
That which your selfe have earst ared so right?

A wofull dame ye have me termed well;
So much more wofull, as my wofull plight
Cannot redressed be by living wight.
Nathlesse (quoth he) if need doe not you bynd,
Doe it disclose, to ease your grieved spright:
Oftimes it haps, that sorrowes of the mynd
Find remedie unsought, which seeking cannot fynd.

29

Then thus began the lamentable Dame;
Sith then ye needs will know the griefe I hoord,
I am th'unfortunate *Matilde*[6] by name,
The wife of bold Sir *Bruin*,[7] who is Lord
Of all this land, late conquer'd by his sword
From a great Gyant, called *Cormoraunt*;[8]
Whom he did overthrow by yonder foord,
And in three battailes did so deadly daunt,
That he dare not returne for all his daily vaunt.

30

So is my Lord now seiz'd° of all the land, *in possession of*
As in his fee,[9] with peaceable estate,
And quietly doth hold it in his hand,
Ne any dares with him for it debate.
But to these happie fortunes, cruell fate
Hath joyn'd one evill, which doth overthrow
All these our joyes, and all our blisse abate;
And like in time to further ill to grow,
And all this land with endlesse losse to overflow.

31

For th'heavens envying our prosperitie,
Have not vouchsaft to graunt unto us twaine
The gladfull blessing of posteritie,
Which we might see after our selves remaine
In th'heritage of our unhappie paine:
So that for want of heires it to defend,
All is in time like to returne againe
To that foule feend, who dayly doth attend
To leape into the same after our lives end.

6. Matilda is the nurse and teacher of Rinaldo (Tasso, *Gerusalemme libratu*. 55). Matilda is also the name of the woman who replaces Virgil as Dante's guide (*Purgatorio* 28–33).
7. A common name for the brown bear. Sir Bruin receives as heir the baby stolen by a bear.
8. A cormorant is a large sea-bird, notorious for its appetite, whence the name was used to describe greedy or rapacious people.
9. According to his right of possession as conqueror.

32

But most my Lord is grieved herewithall,
And makes exceeding mone, when he does thinke
That all this land unto his foe shall fall,
For which he long in vaine did sweat and swinke,° *work*
That now the same he greatly doth forthinke.° *plan ahead*
Yet was it sayd, there should to him a sonne
Be gotten, not begotten, which should drinke
And dry up all the water, which doth ronne
In the next brooke, by whom that feend shold be fordonne.

33

Well hop't he then, when this was propheside,
That from his sides some noble chyld should rize,
The which through fame should farre be magnifide,
And this proud gyant should with brave emprize
Quite overthrow, who now ginnes to despize
The good Sir *Bruin*, growing farre in yeares;
Who thinkes from me his sorrow all doth rize.
Lo this my cause of griefe to you appeares;
For which I thus doe mourne, and poure forth ceaselesse teares.

34

Which when he heard, he inly touched was
With tender ruth for her unworthy griefe,
And when he had devized of her case,
He gan in mind conceive a fit reliefe
For all her paine, if please her make the priefe.° *trial, test*
And having cheared her, thus said; faire Dame,
In evils counsell is the comfort chiefe,
Which though I be not wise enough to frame,
Yet as I well it meane, vouchsafe it without blame.[1]

35

If that the cause of this your languishment
Be lacke of children, to supply your place,
Low how good fortune doth to you present
This litle babe, of sweete and lovely face,
And spotlesse spirit, in which ye may enchace° *engrave*
What ever formes ye list thereto apply,
Being now soft and fit them to embrace;
Whether ye list him traine in chevalry,
Or noursle up in lore of learn'd Philosophy.

1. I.e., in troubled times the best remedy is good advice, which I cannot well put into words; yet as I mean well, take no offense.

36

And certes it hath oftentimes bene seene,
  That of the like, whose linage was unknowne,
  More brave and noble knights have raysed beene,
  As their victorious deedes have often showen,
  Being with fame through many Nations blowen,
  Then those, which have bene dandled in the lap.
  Therefore some thought, that those brave imps were sowen
  Here by the Gods, and fed with heavenly sap,
That made them grow so high t'all honorable hap.

37

The Ladie hearkning to his sensefull speach,
  Found nothing that he said, unmeet nor geason,° *extraordinary*
  Having oft seene it tryde,° as he did teach. *proven*
  Therefore inclyning to his goodly reason,
  Agreeing well both with the place and season,
  She gladly did of that same babe accept,
  As of her owne by liverey and seisin,[2]
  And having over it a litle wept,
She bore it thence, and ever as her owne it kept.

38

Right glad was *Calepine* to be so rid
  Of his young charge, whereof he skilled nought:
  Ne she lesse glad; for she so wisely did,
  And with her husband under hand so wrought,
  That when that infant unto him she brought,
  She made him thinke it surely was his owne,
  And it in goodly thewes° so well upbrought, *manners*
  That it became a famous knight well knowne
And did right noble deedes, the which elswhere are showne.[3]

39

But *Calepine*, now being left alone
  Under the greenewoods side in sorie plight,
  Withouten armes or steede to ride upon,
  Or house to hide his head from heavens spight,
  Albe that Dame by all the meanes she might,
  Him oft desired home with her to wend,
  And offred him, his courtesie to requite,

2. Legal phrase indicating that a sign of possession (some kind of token) has been received.
3. Spenser apparently intended to include the "famous knight" in some unwritten book of *The Faerie Queene*. The fact that Matilda was the person who raised the hero Rinaldo in Tasso, *Gerusalemme liberatu* suggests that this foundling-knight was to have been a major figure.

Both horse and armes, and what so else to lend,
Yet he them all refusd, though thankt her as a frend.

40

And for exceeding griefe which inly grew,
That he his love so lucklesse now had lost,
On the cold ground, maugre himselfe he threw,
For fell despight, to be so sorely crost;
And there all night himselfe in anguish tost,
Vowing, that never he in bed againe
His limbes would rest, ne lig° in ease embost,° *lie / wrapped*
Till that his Ladies sight he mote attaine,
Or understand, that she in safetie did remaine.

Canto V

The salvage serves Serena well
till she Prince Arthure fynd,
Who her together with his Squyre
with th'Hermit leaves behynd.

1

O what an easie thing is to descry
The gentle bloud, how ever it be wrapt
In sad misfortunes foule deformity,
And wretched sorrowes, which have often hapt?
For howsoever it may grow mis-shapt,
Like this wyld man, being undisciplynd,
That to all vertue it may seeme unapt,
Yet will it shew some sparkes of gentle mynd,
And at the last breake forth in his owne proper kynd.

2

That plainely may in this wyld man be red,
Who though he were still in his desert wood,
Mongst salvage beasts, both rudely borne and bred,
Ne ever saw faire guize, ne learned good,
Yet shewd some token of his gentle blood,
By gentle usage of that wretched Dame.
For certes he was borne of noble blood,
How ever by hard hap he hether came;
As ye may know, when time shall be to tell the same.[1]

3

Who when as now long time he lacked had
The good Sir *Calepine*, that farre was strayd,

1. The parentage of the savage man is never revealed.

Did wexe exceeding sorrowfull and sad,
As he of some misfortune were afrayd:
And leaving there this Ladie all dismayd,
Went forth streightway into the forrest wyde,
To seeke, if he perchance a sleepe were layd,
Or what so else were unto him betyde:
He sought him farre & neare, yet him no where he spyde.

4

Tho backe returning to that sorie Dame,
He shewed semblant of exceeding mone,
By speaking signes, as he them best could frame;
Now wringing both his wretched hands in one,
Now beating his hard head upon a stone,
That ruth it was to see him so lament.
By which she well perceiving, what was done,
Gan teare her hayre, and all her garments rent,
And beat her breast, and piteously her selfe torment.

5

Upon the ground her selfe she fiercely threw,
Regardlesse of her wounds, yet bleeding rife,
That with their bloud did all the flore imbrew,° *stain*
As if her breast new launcht with murdrous knife,
Would streight dislodge the wretched wearie life.
There she long groveling, and deepe groning lay,
As if her vitall powers were at strife
With stronger death, and feared their decay,
Such were this Ladies pangs and dolorous assay.

6

Whom when the Salvage saw so sore distrest,
He reared her up from the bloudie ground,
And sought by all the meanes, that he could best
Her to recure out of that stony swound,
And staunch the bleeding of her dreary wound.
Yet nould she be recomforted for nought,
Ne cease her sorrow and impatient stound,
But day and night did vexe her carefull thought,
And ever more and more her owne affliction wrought.

7

At length, when as no hope of his retourne
She saw now left, she cast to leave the place,
And wend abrode, though feeble and forlorne,
To seeke some comfort in that sorie case.

His steede now strong through rest so long a space,
Well as she could, she got, and did bedight,
And being thereon mounted, forth did pace,
Withouten guide, her to conduct aright,
Or gard her to defend from bold oppressors might.

8

Whom when her Host saw readie to depart,
He would not suffer her alone to fare,
But gan himselfe addresse to take her part.
Those warlike armes, which *Calepine* whyleare
Had left behind, he gan efisoones prepare,
And put them all about himselfe unfit,
His shield, his helmet, and his curats[2] bare.
But without sword upon his thigh to sit:
Sir *Calepine* himselfe away had hidden it.

9

So forth they traveld an uneven payre,
That mote to all men seeme an uncouth sight;
A salvage man matcht with a Ladie fayre,
That rather seem'd the conquest of his might,
Gotten by spoyle, then purchaced aright.
But he did her attend most carefully,
And faithfully did serve both day and night,
Withouten thought of shame or villeny,
Ne ever shewed signe of foule disloyalty.

10

Upon a day as on their way they went,
It chaunst some furniture° about her steed *equipment*
To be disordred by some accident:
Which to redresse, she did th'assistance need
Of this her groome, which he by signes did reede,
And streight his combrous armes aside did lay
Upon the ground, withouten doubt or dreed,
And in his homely wize began to assay
T'amend what was amisse, and put in right aray.

11

Bout which whilest he was busied thus hard,
Lo where a knight together with his squire,
All arm'd to point came ryding thetherward,
Which seemed by their portance and attire,
To be two errant knights, that did inquire

2. Curats, armor for the top part of the body.

After adventures, where they mote them get.
Those were to weet (if that ye it require)
Prince *Arthur* and young *Timias*, which met
By straunge occasion, that here needs forth be set.

12

After that *Timias* had againe recured
The favour of *Belphebe*, (as ye heard)
And of her grace did stand againe assured,
To happie blisse he was full high uprear'd,
Nether of envy, nor of chaunge afeard,
Though many foes did him maligne therefore,
And with unjust detraction him did beard;° *affront*
Yet he himselfe so well and wisely bore,
That in her soveraine lyking he dwelt evermore.[3]

13

But of them all, which did his ruine seeke
Three mightie enemies did him most despight,
Three mightie ones, and cruell minded eeke,
That him not onely sought by open might
To overthrow, but to supplant by slight.
The first of them by name was cald *Despetto*,
Exceeding all the rest in powre and hight;
The second not so strong but wise, *Decetto;*
The third nor strong nor wise, but spightfullest *Defetto*.[4]

14

Oftimes their sundry powres they did employ,
And severall deceipts, but all in vaine:
For neither they by force could him destroy,
Ne yet entrap in treasons subtill traine.
Therefore conspiring all together plaine,
They did their counsels now in one compound;
Where singled forces faile, conjoynd may gaine.
The *Blatant Beast* the fittest meanes they found,
To worke his utter shame, and throughly him confound.

15

Upon a day as they the time did waite,
When he did ravnge the wood for salvage game,
They sent that *Blatant Beast* to be a baite,
To draw him from his deare beloved dame,
Unwares into the daunger of defame.° *disgrace, defamation*
For well they wist, that Squire to be so bold,

3. Timias and Arthur part in Book IV.7.47 of the *Faerie Queene*. Timias regains the favor of Belphoebe in IV.8.1–18.

4. Despetto, Decetto and Defetto are Spenser's invented Italianate names for despite, deceit, and defect.

That no one beast in forrest wylde or tame,
Met him in chase, but he it challenge would,
And plucke the pray oftimes out of their greedy hould.

16

The hardy boy, as they devised had,
Seeing the ugly Monster passing by,
Upon him set, of perill nought adrad,
Ne skilfull of the uncouth jeopardy;
And charged him so fierce and furiously,
That his great force unable to endure,
He forced was to turne from him and fly:
Yet ere he fled, he with his tooth impure
Him heedlesse bit, the whiles he was thereof secure.

17

Securely he did after him pursew,
Thinking by speed to overtake his flight;
Who through thicke woods and brakes & briers him drew,
To weary him the more, and waste his spight,
So that he now has almost spent his spright.
Till that at length unto a woody glade
He came, whose covert stopt his further sight,
There his three foes shrowded in guilefull shade,
Out of their ambush broke, and gan him to invade.

18

Sharpely they all attonce did him assaile,
Burning with inward rancour and despight,
And heaped strokes did round about him haile
With so huge force, that seemed nothing might
Beare off their blowes, from percing thorough quite.
Yet he them all so warily did ward,
That none of them in his soft flesh did bite,
And all the while his backe for best safegard,
He lent against a tree, that backeward onset bard.

19

Like a wylde Bull, that being at a bay,
Is bayted° of a mastiffe, and a hound, *harassed*
And a curre-dog; that doe him sharpe assay
On every side, and beat about him round;
But most that curre barking with bitter sownd,
And creeping still behinde, doth him incomber,
That in his chauffe° he digs the trampled ground, *rage*
And threats his horns, and bellowes like the thonder,
So did that Squire his foes disperse, and drive asonder.

20

Him well behoved so; for his three foes
  Sought to encompasse him on every side,
  And dangerously did round about enclose.
  But most of all *Defetto* him annoyde,
  Creeping behinde him still to have destroyde:
  So did *Decetto* eke him circumvent,
  But stout *Despetto* in his greater pryde,
  Did front him face to face against him bent,
Yet he them all withstood, and often made relent.

21

Till that at length nigh tyrd with former chace,
  And weary now with carefull keeping ward,
  He gan to shrinke, and somewhat to give place,
  Full like ere long to have escaped hard;
  When as unwares he in the forrest heard
  A trampling steede, that with his neighing fast
  Did warne his rider be uppon his gard;
  With noise whereof the Squire now nigh aghast,
Revived was, and sad dispaire away did cast.

22

Eftsoones he spide a Knight approching nye,
  Who seeing one in so great daunger set
  Mongst many foes, him selfe did faster hye;° *hasten*
  To reskue him, and his weake part abet,
  For pitty so to see him overset.° *oppressed*
  Whom soone as his three enemies did vew,
  They fled, and fast into the wood did get:
  Him booted not to thinke them to pursew,
The covert was so thicke, that did no passage shew.

23

Then turning to that swaine, him well he knew
  To be his *Timias*, his owne true Squire,
  Whereof exceeding glad, he to him drew,
  And him embracing twixt his armes entire,
  Him thus bespake; My liefe, my lifes desire,
  Why have ye me alone thus long yleft?
  Tell me what worlds despight, or heavens yre
  Hath you thus long away from me bereft?
Where have ye all this while bin wandring, where bene weft?° *wafted, carried*

24

With that he sighed deepe for inward tyne:° *sorrow*
To whom the Squire nought aunswered againe,
But shedding few soft teares from tender eyne,
His deare affect° with silence did restraine, *affection*
And shut up all his plaint in privy paine.
There they awhile some gracious speaches spent,
As to them seemed fit time to entertaine.
After all which up to their steedes they went,
And forth together rode a comely couplement.

25

So now they be arrived both in sight
Of this wyld man, whom they full busie found
About the sad *Serena* things to dight,
With those brave armours lying on the ground,
That seem'd the spoile of some right well renownd.
Which when that Squire beheld, he to them stept,
Thinking to take them from that hylding° hound: *base, worthless*
But he it seeing, lightly to him lept,
And sternely with strong hand it from his handling kept.

26

Gnashing his grinded teeth with griesly looke,
And sparkling fire out of his furious eyne,
Him with his fist unwares on th'head he strooke,
That made him downe unto the earth encline;
Whence soone upstarting much he gan repine,
And laying hand upon his wrathfull blade,
Thought therewithall forthwith him to have slaine,
Who it perceiving, hand upon him layd,
And greedily him griping, his avengement stayd.

27

With that aloude the faire *Serena* cryde
Unto the Knight, them to dispart in twaine:
Who to them stepping did them soone divide,
And did from further violence restraine,
Albe the wyld-man hardly would refraine.
Then gan the Prince, of her for to demand,
What and from whence she was, and by what traine° *snare*
She fell into that salvage villaines hand,
And whether free with him she now were, or in band.° *in bondage*

28

To whom she thus; I am, as now ye see,
The wretchedst Dame, that live this day on ground,
Who both in minde, the which most grieveth me,
And body have receiv'd a mortall wound,
That hath me driven to this drery stound.
I was erewhile, the love of *Calepine*,
Who whether he alive be to be found,
Or by some deadly chaunce be done to pine,° *made to suffer*
Since I him lately lost, uneath is to define.

29

In salvage forrest I him lost of late,
Where I had surely long ere this bene dead,
Or else remained in most wretched state,
Had not this wylde man in that wofull stead
Kept, and delivered me from deadly dread.
In such a salvage wight, of brutish kynd,
Amongst wilde beastes in desert forrests bred,
It is most straunge and wonderfull to fynd
So milde humanity, and perfect gentle mynd.

30

Let me therefore this favour for him finde,
That ye will not your wrath upon him wreake,
Sith he cannot expresse his simple minde,
Ne yours conceive, ne but by tokens speake:
Small praise to prove your powre on wight so weake.
With such faire words she did their heate asswage,
And the strong course of their displeasure breake,
That they to pitty turnd their former rage,
And each sought to supply the office of her page.

31

So having all things well about her dight,
She on her way cast forward to proceede,
And they her forth conducted, where they might
Finde harbour fit to comfort her great neede.
For now her wounds corruption gan to breed;
And eke this Squire, who likewise wounded was
Of that same Monster late, for lacke of heed,
Now gan to faint, and further could not pas
Through feeblenesse, which all his limbes oppressed has.

32

So forth they rode together all in troupe,
To seeke some place, the which mote yeeld some ease
To these sicke twaine, that now began to droupe,
And all the way the Prince sought to appease
The bitter anguish of their sharpe disease,
By all the courteous meanes he could invent,
Somewhile with merry purpose° fit to please, *conversation*
And otherwhile with good encouragement,
To make them to endure the pains, did them torment.[5]

33

Mongst which, *Serena* did to him relate
The foule discourt'sies and unknightly parts,
Which *Turpine* had unto her shewed late,
Without compassion of her cruell smarts,
Although *Blandina* did with all her arts
Him otherwise perswade, all that she might;
Yet he of malice, without her desarts,
Not onely her excluded late at night,
But also trayterously did wound her weary Knight.

34

Wherewith the Prince sore moved, there avoud,
That soone as he returned backe againe,
He would avenge th'abuses of that proud
And shamefull Knight, of whom she did complaine.
This wize did they each other entertaine,
To passe the tedious travell of the way;
Till towards night they came unto a plaine,
By which a little Hermitage there lay,
Far from all neighbourhood, the which annoy it may.

35

And nigh thereto a little Chappell stoode,
Which being all with Yuy overspred,
Deckt all the roofe, and shadowing the roode,° *crucifix*
Seem'd like a grove faire braunched over hed:
Therein the Hermite, which his life here led
In streight° observaunce of religious vow, *strict*
Was wont his howres[6] and holy things to bed;° *bid, offer*
And therein he likewise was praying now,
Whenas these Knights arriv'd, they wist not where nor how.

5. I.e., that did them torment.

6. The prayers, or offices, assigned to be read at the canonical hours.

36

They stayd not there, but streight way in did pas.
  Whom when the Hermite present saw in place,
  From his devotion streight he troubled was;
  Which breaking off he toward them did pace,
  With stayed steps, and grave beseeming grace:
  For well it seem'd, that whilome he had beene
  Some goodly person, and of gentle race,
  That could his good to all, and well did weene,
How each to entertaine with curt'sie well beseene.

37

And soothly it was sayd by common fame,[7]
  So long as age enabled him thereto,
  That he had bene a man of mickle name,
  Renowmed much in armes and derring doe:
  But being aged now and weary to
  Of warres delight, and worlds contentious toyle,
  The name of knighthood he did disavow,
  And hanging up his armes and warlike spoyle,
From all this worlds incombraunce did himselfe assoyle.[8]

38

He thence them led into his Hermitage,
  Letting their steedes to graze upon the greene:
  Small was his house, and like a little cage,
  For his owne turne,° yet inly neate and clene, *service, use*
  Deckt with greene boughes, and flowers gay beseene.
  Therein he them full faire did entertaine
  Not with such forged showes, as fitter beene
  For courting fooles, that curtesies would faine,
But with entire affection and appearaunce plaine.

39

Yet was their fare but homely, such as hee
  Did use, his feeble body to sustaine;
  The which full gladly they did take in glee,
  Such as it was, ne did of want complaine,
  But being well suffiz'd, them rested faine.
  But faire *Serene* all night could take no rest,
  Ne yet that gentle Squire for grievous paine
  Of their late woundes, the which the *Blatant Beast*
Had given them, whose griefe through suffraunce sore increast.

7. Report (Latin: *fama*).
8. Absolve, release. It was not uncommon for old knights in romances to turn from martial heroism to seclusion and prayer.

40

So all that night they past in great disease,
Till that the morning, bringing earely light
To guide mens labours, brought them also ease,
And some asswagement of their painefull plight.
Then up they rose, and gan them selves to dight
Unto their journey; but that Squire and Dame
So faint and feeble were, that they ne might
Endure to travell, nor one foote to frame:° *direct, move*
Their hearts were sicke, their sides were sore, their feete were [lame.

41

Therefore the Prince, whom great affaires in mynd
Would not permit, to make there lenger stay,
Was forced there to leave them both behynd,
In that good Hermits charge, whom he did pray
To tend them well. So forth he went his way,
And with him eke the salvage, that whyleare
Seeing his royall vsage and array,
Was greatly growne in love of that brave pere,
Would needes depart, as shall declared be elsewhere.

Canto VI

The Hermite heales both Squire and dame
Of their sore maladies:
He° Turpine doth defeate, and shame *Arthur*
For his late villanies.

1

No wound, which warlike hand of enemy
Inflicts with dint of sword, so sore doth light,
As doth the poysnous sting, which infamy
Infixeth in the name of noble wight:
For by no art, nor any leaches° might *physician's*
It ever can recured be againe;
Ne all the skill, which that immortall spright
Of *Podalyrius*[1] did in it retaine,
Can remedy such hurts; such hurts are hellish paine.

2

Such were the wounds, the which that *Blatant Beast*
Made in the bodies of that Squire and Dame;
And being such, were now much more increast,

1. Son of Aesculapius, the son of Apollo, famed for his healing powers.

For want of taking heede unto the same,
That now corrupt and curelesse they became.
Howbe° that carefull Hermite did his best, *howbeit*
With many kindes of medicines meete, to tame
The poysnous humour, which did most infest
Their ranckling wounds, & every day them duely drest.

3

For he right well in Leaches craft was seene,° *versed, practiced*
And through the long experience of his dayes,
Which had in many fortunes tossed beene,
And past through many perillous assayes,
He knew the diverse went° of mortall wayes, *course, passage*
And in the mindes of men had great insight;
Which with sage counsell, when they went astray,
He could enforme, and them reduce aright,
And al the passions heale, which wound the weaker spright.

4

For whylome he had bene a doughty Knight,
As any one, that lived in his daies,
And proved oft in many perillous fight,
Of which he grace and glory wonne alwaies,
And in all battels bore away the baies.[2]
But being now attacht with timely age,
And weary of this worlds unquiet waies,
He tooke him selfe unto this Hermitage,
In which he liv'd alone, like carelesse bird in cage.[3]

5

One day, as he was searching of their wounds,
He found that they had festred privily,
And ranckling inward with unruly stounds,
The inner parts now gan to putrify,
That quite they seem'd past helpe of surgery,
And rather needed to be disciplinde[4]
With holesome reede[5] of sad sobriety,
To rule the stubborne rage of passion blinde:
Give salves to every sore, but counsell to the minde.

6

So taking them apart into his cell,
He to that point fit speaches gan to frame,

2. I.e., a garland of bay leaves traditionally given to the winner of a contest.
3. cf. *King Lear* 5.3.9.
4. Controlled, restrained, but also subjected to the discipline of rod or whip to bring the flesh under the control of the reason.
5. Advice, counsel, but also the physical instrument of discipline (see preceeding note).

As he the art of words knew wondrous well,
And eke could doe, as well as say the same,
And thus he to them sayd; faire daughter Dame,
And you faire sonne, which here thus long now lie
In piteous languor, since ye hither came,
In vaine of me ye hope for remedie,
And I likewise in vaine doe salves to you applie.

7

For in your selfe your onely helpe doth lie,
To heale your selves, and must proceed alone
From your owne will, to cure your maladie.
Who can him cure, that will be cur'd of none?
If therefore health ye seeke, observe this one.
First learne your outward sences to refraine
From things, that stirre up fraile affection;
Your eies, your eares, your tongue, your talke restraine[6]
From that they most affect, and in due termes containe.

8

For from those outward sences ill affected,
The seede of all this evill first doth spring,
Which at the first before it had infected,
Mote easie be supprest with little thing:
But being growen strong, it forth doth bring
Sorrow, and anguish, and impatient paine
In th'inner parts, and lastly scattering
Contagious poyson close through every vaine,
It never rests, till it have wrought his finall bane.° *destruction*

9

For that beastes teeth, which wounded you tofore,
Are so exceeding venemous and keene,
Made all of rusty yron, rankling sore,
That where they bite, it booteth not to weene
With salve, or antidote, or other mene
It ever to amend: ne marvaile ought;
For that same beast was bred of hellish strene,° *strain, race*
And long in darksome *Stygian* den[7] upbrought,
Begot of foule *Echidna*,[8] as in bookes[9] is taught.

6. The hermit advises Serena and Timias to restrain their passions since one can do little more than avoid the occasions that lead malice and slander to flourish. See stanza 14.

7. The underworld, region of the river Styx.

8. A monster, half woman, half snake, the mother of Cerberus.

9. I.e., Hesiod's *Theogony*.

10

Echidna is a Monster direfull dred,
Whom Gods doe hate, and heavens abhor to see;
So hideous is her shape, so huge her hed,
That even the hellish fiends affrighted bee
At sight thereof, and from her presence flee:
Yet did her face and former parts professe
A faire young Mayden, full of comely glee;
But all her hinder parts did plaine expresse
A monstrous Dragon, full of fearefull uglinesse.

11

To her the Gods, for her so dreadfull face,
In fearefull darkenesse, furthest from the skie,
And from the earth, appointed have her place,
Mongst rocks and caves, where she enrold doth lie
In hideous horrour and obscurity,° *darkness*
Wasting the strength of her immortall age.
There did *Typhaon* with her company,[1]
Cruell *Typhaon*, whose tempestuous rage
Make th'heavens tremble oft, & him with vowes asswage.

12

Of that commixtion they did then beget
This hellish Dog, that hight the *Blatant Beast;*
A wicked Monster, that his tongue doth whet
Gainst all, both good and bad, both most and least;
And poures his poysnous gall forth to infest
The noblest wights with notable defame:
Ne ever Knight, that bore so lofty creast,
Ne ever Lady of so honest name,
But he them spotted with reproch, or secrete shame.

13

In vaine therefore it were, with medicine
To goe about to salve such kynd of sore,
That rather needes wise read and discipline,
Then outward salves, that may augment it more.
Aye me (sayd then *Serena* signing sore)
What hope of helpe doth then for us remaine,
If that no salves may us to health restore?
But sith we need good counsell (sayd the swaine)
Aread good sire, some counsell, that may us sustaine.

1. According to Hesiod, Echidna and Typhaon were the parents of a number of beasts, including Geryon's dog Orthrus and his dragon.

14

The best (sayd he) that I can you advize,
Is to avoide the occasion of the ill:
For when the cause, whence evill doth arize,
Removed is, th'effect surceaseth still.
Abstaine from pleasure, and restraine your will,
Subdue desire, and bridle loose delight,
Use scanted diet, and forbeare your fill,
Shun secresie, and talke in open sight:
So shall you soone repaire your present evill plight.

15

Thus having sayd, his sickely patients
Did gladly hearken to his grave beheast,
And kept so well his wise commaundements,
That in short space their malady was ceast,
And eke the biting of that harmefull Beast
Was throughly heal'd. Tho when they did perceave
Their wounds recur'd, and forces reincreast,
Of that good Hermite both they tooke their leave,
And went both on their way, ne ech would other leave.

16

But each the other vow'd t'accompany,
The Lady, for that she was much in dred,
Now left alone in great extremity,
The Squire, for that he courteous was indeed,
Would not her leave alone in her great need.
So both together traveld, till they met
With a faire Mayden clad in mourning weed,
Upon a mangy jade° unmeetely set, *inferior horse*
And a lewd foole her leading thorough dry and wet.

17

But by what meanes that shame to her befell,
And how thereof her selfe she did acquite,
I must a while forbeare to you to tell;
Till that, as comes by course, I doe recite,[2]
What fortune to the Briton Prince did lite,° *befall*
Pursuing that proud Knight, the which whileare
Wrought to Sir *Calepine* so foule despight;
And eke his Lady, though she sickely were,
So lewdly had abusde, as ye did lately heare.[3]

2. The story of Mirabella and Disdain is told in Canto 7.27 ff.

3. See Canto 3.27 ff.

18

The Prince according to the former token,
Which faire *Serene* to him delivered had,
Pursu'd him streight, in mynd to bene ywroken° *avenged*
Of all the vile demeane,° and usage bad, *treatment*
With which he had those two so ill bestad:
Ne wight with him on that adventure went,
But that wylde man, whom though he oft forbad,
Yet for no bidding, nor for being shent,
Would he restrayned be from his attendement.

19

Arriving there, as did by chaunce befall,
He found the gate wyde ope, and in he rode,
Ne stayd, till that he came into the hall:
Where soft dismounting like a weary lode,
Upon the ground with feeble feete he trode,
As he unable were for very neede
To move one foote, but there must make abode;
The whiles the salvage man did take his steede,
And in some stable neare did set him up to feede.

20

Ere long to him a homely groome there came,
That in rude wise him asked, what he was,
That durst so boldly, without let° or shame, *permission, hesitation*
Into his Lords forbidden hall to passe.
To whom the Prince, him fayning to embase,[4]
Mylde answer made; he was an errant Knight,
The which was fall'n into this feeble case,
Through many wounds, which lately he in fight,
Received had, and prayd to pitty his ill plight.

21

But he, the more outrageous and bold,
Sternely did bid him quickely thence avaunt,° *depart*
Or deare aby,° for why his Lord of old *suffer severely*
Did hate all errant Knights, which there did haunt,
Ne lodging would to any of them graunt,
And therefore lightly bad him packe away,
Not sparing him with bitter words to taunt;
And therewithall rude hand on him did lay,
To thrust him out of dore, doing his worst assay.

4. I.e., pretending to be much less imposing than he actually was.

22

Which when the Salvage comming now in place,
Beheld, eftsoones he all enraged grew,
And running streight upon that villaine base,
Like a fell Lion at him fiercely flew,
And with his teeth and nailes, in present vew,
Him rudely rent, and all to peeces tore:
So miserably him all helpelesse slew,
That with the noise, whilest he did loudly rore,
The people of the house rose forth in great uprore.

23

Who when on ground they saw their fellow slaine,
And that same Knight and Salvage standing by,
Upon them two they fell with might and maine,
And on them layd so huge and horribly,
As if they would have slaine them presently.
But the bold Prince defended him so well,
And their assault withstood so mightily,
That maugre all their might, he did repell,
And beat them back, whilest many undemeath him fell.

24

Yet he them still so sharpely did pursew,
That few of them he left alive, which fled,
Those evill tidings to their Lord to shew.
Who hearing how his people badly sped,° *fared*
Came forth in hast: where when as with the dead
He saw the ground all strow'd, and that same Knight
And salvage with their bloud fresh steeming red,
He woxe nigh mad with wrath and fell despight,
And with reprochfull words him thus bespake on hight.

25

Art thou he, traytor, that with treason vile,
Hast slaine my men in this unmanly maner,
And now triumphest in the piteous spoile
Of these poore folk, whose soules with black dishonor
And foule defame doe decke thy bloudy baner?
The meede whereof shall shortly be thy shame,
And wretched end, which still attendeth on her.
With that him selfe to battell he did frame;
So did his forty yeomen,° which there with him came. *servants*

26

With dreadfull force they all did him assaile,
And round about with boystrous strokes oppresse,
That on his shield did rattle like to haile,
In a great tempest; that in such distresse,
He wist not to which side him to addresse.
And evermore that craven cowherd Knight,
Was at his backe with heardesse heedinesse,° *attention*
Wayting if he unwares him murther might:
For cowardize doth still in villany delight.

27

Whereof whenas the Prince was well aware,
He to him turnd with furious intent,
And him against his powre gan to prepare;
Like a fierce Bull, that being busie bent
To fight with many foes about him ment,
Feeling some curre behinde his heeles to bite,
Turnes him about with fell avengement;
So likewise turnde the Prince upon the Knight,
And layd at him amaine with all his will and might.

28

Who when he once his dreadfull strokes had tasted,
Durst not the furie of his force abyde,
But turn'd abacke, and to retyre him hasted
Through the thick prease,° there thinking him to hyde. *crowd*
But when the Prince had once him plainely eyde,
He foot by foot him followed alway,
Ne would him suffer once to shrinke asyde
But joyning close, huge lode at him did lay:
Who flying still did ward, and warding fly away.

29

But when his foe he still so eger saw,
Unto his heeles himselfe he did betake,
Hoping unto some refuge to withdraw:
Ne would the Prince him ever foot forsake,
Where so he went, but after him did make.
He fled from roome to roome, from place to place,
Whylest every joynt for dread of death did quake,
Still looking after him, that did him chace;
That made him evermore increase his speedie pace.

30

At last he up into the chamber came,
Whereas his love was sitting all alone,
Wayting what tydings of her folke became.
There did the Prince him overtake anone,
Crying in vaine to her, him to bemone;
And with his sword him on the head did smyte,
That to the ground he fell in senselesse swone:
Yet whether thwart° or flatly it did lyte, *transversely, sideways*
The tempred Steele did not into his braynepan° byte. *head*

31

Which when the Ladie saw, with great affright
She starting up, began to shrieke aloud,
And with her garment covering him from sight,
Seem'd under her protection him to shroud;
And falling lowly at his feet, her bowd
Upon her knee, intreating him for grace,
And often him besought, and prayd, and vowd;
That with the ruth of her so wretched case,
He stayd his second strooke, and did his hand abase.

32

Her weed she then withdrawing, did him discover,
Who now come to himselfe, yet would not rize,
But still did lie as dead, and quake, and quiver,
That even the Prince his basenesse did despize,
And eke his Dame him seeing in such guize,
Gan him recomfort, and from ground to reare.
Who rising up at last in ghastly wize,
Like troubled ghost did dreadfully appeare,
As one that had no life him left through former feare.

33

Whom when the Prince so deadly saw dismayd,
He for such basenesse shamefully him shent,
And with sharpe words did bitterly upbrayd;
Vile cowheard dogge, now doe I much repent,
That ever I this life unto thee lent,
Whereof thou caytive so unworthie art;
That both thy love, for lacke of hardiment,
And eke thy selfe, for want of manly hart,
And eke all knights hast shamed with this knightlesse part.

34

Yet further hast thou heaped shame to shame,
And crime to crime, by this thy cowheard feare.

For first it was to thee reprochfull blame,
To erect this wicked custome, which I heare,
Gainst errant Knights and Ladies thou dost reare;
Whom when thou mayst, thou dost of arms despoile
Or of their upper garment, which they weare:
Yet doest thou not with manhood, but with guile
Maintaine this evill use, thy foes thereby to foile.

35

And lastly in approvance of thy wrong,
To shew such faintnesse and foule cowardize,
Is greatest shame: for oft it falles, that strong
And valiant knights doe rashly enterprize,
Either for fame, or else for exercize,
A wrongfull quarrell to maintaine by fight;
Yet have, through prowesse and their brave emprize,
Gotten great worship in this worldes sight.
For greater force there needs to maintaine wrong, then right.

36

Yet since thy life unto this Ladie fayre
I given have, live in reproch and scorne;
Ne ever armes, ne ever knighthood dare
Hence to professe: for shame is to adorne
With so brave badges one so basely borne;
But onely breath sith that° I did forgive. *because*
So having from his craven bodie torne
Those goodly armes, he them away did give
And onely suffred him this wretched life to live.

37

There whilest he thus was setling things above,
Atwene that Ladie myld and recreant knight,
To whom his life he graunted for her love,
He gan bethinke him, in what perilous plight
He had behynd him left that salvage wight,
Amongst so many foes, whom sure he thought
By this quite slaine in so unequall fight:
Therefore descending backe in haste, he sought
If yet he were alive, or to destruction brought.

38

There he him found environed about
With slaughtred bodies, which his hand had slaine,
And laying yet a fresh with courage stout
Upon the rest, that did alive remaine;
Whom he likewise right sorely did constraine,

Like scattred sheepe, to seeke for safetie,
After he gotten had with busie paine
Some of their weapons, which thereby did lie,
With which he layd about,° and made them fast to flie. *struck vigorously*

39

Whom when the Prince so felly saw to rage,
Approching to him neare, his hand he stayd,
And sought, by making signes, him to asswage:
Who them perceiving, streight to him obayd,
As to his Lord, and downe his weapons layd,
As if he long had to his heasts bene trayned.
Thence he him brought away, and up convayd
Into the chamber, where that Dame remayned
With her unworthy knight, who ill him entertayned.

40

Whom when the Salvage saw from daunger free,
Sitting beside his Ladie there at ease,
He well remembred, that the same was hee,
Which lately sought his Lord for to displease:
Tho all in rage, he on him streight did seaze,
As if he would in peeces him have rent;
And were not, that the Prince did him appeaze,
He had not left one limbe of him unrent:
But streight he held his hand at his commaundement.

41

Thus having all things well in peace ordayned,
The Prince himselfe there all that night did rest,
Where him *Blandina* fayrely entertayned,
With all the courteous glee and goodly feast,
The which for him she could imagine best.
For well she knew the wayes to win good will
Of every wight, that were not too infest,° *hostile*
And how to please the minds of good and ill,
Through tempering of her words & lookes by wondrous skill.

42

Yet were her words and lookes but false and fayned,
To some hid end to make more easie way,
Or to allure such fondlings, whom she trayned° *snared*
Into her trap unto their owne decay:
Thereto, when needed, she could weepe and pray,
And when her listed, she could fawne and flatter;
Now smyling smoothly, like to sommers day,
Now glooming sadly, so to cloke her matter;
Yet were her words but wynd, & all her teares but water.

43

Whether such grace were given her by kynd,
As women wont their guilefull wits to guyde;
Or learn'd the art to please, I doe not fynd.
This well I wote, that she so well applyde
Her pleasing tongue, that soone she pacifyde
The wrathfull Prince, & wrought her husbands peace.
Who nathelesse not therewith satisfyde,
His rancorous despight did not releasse,
Ne secretly from thought of fell revenge surceasse.

44

For all that night, the whyles the Prince did rest
In carelesse couch, not weeting what was ment,
He watcht in close awayt with weapons prest,
Willing to worke his villenous intent
On him, that had so shamefully him stent:
Yet durst he not for very cowardize
Effect the same, whylest all the night was spent.
The morrow next the Prince did early rize,
And passed forth, to follow his first enterprize.

Canto VII

Turpine is baffuld,[1] *his two knights*
doe gaine their treasons meed,
Fayre Mirabellaes punishment
for loves disdaine decreed.

1

Like as the gentle hart it selfe bewrayes,
In doing gentle deedes with franke delight,
Even so the baser mind it selfe displayes,
In cancred malice and revengefull spight.
For to maligne, t'envie, t'use shifting slight,
Be arguments of a vile donghill mind,
Which what it dare not doe by open might,
To worke by wicked treason wayes doth find,
By such discourteous deeds discovering his base kind.

2

That well appeares in this discourteous knight,
The coward *Turpine*, whereof now I treat;
Who notwithstanding that in former fight
He of the Prince his life received late,
Yet in his mind malitious and ingrate

1. Disgraced as a perjured knight.

He gan devize, to be aveng'd anew
For all that shame, which kindled inward hate.
Therefore so soone as he was out of vew,
Himselfe in hast he arm'd, and did him fast pursew.

3

Well did he tract° his steps, as he did ryde, *traced, followed*
Yet would not neare approch in daungers eye,
But kept aloofe for dread to be descryde,
Untill fit time and place he mote espy,
Where he mote worke him scath and villeny.
At last he met two knights to him unknowne,
The which were armed both agreeably,
And both combynd, what ever chaunce were blowne,
Betwixt them to divide, and each to make his owne.

4

To whom false *Turpine* comming courteously,
To cloke the mischiefe, which he inly ment,
Gan to complaine of great discourtesie,
Which a straunge knight, that neare afore him went,
Had doen to him, and his deare Ladie shent:
Which if they would afford him ayde at need
For to avenge, in time convenient,
They should accomplish both a knightly deed,
And for their paines obtaine of him a goodly meed.

5

The knights beleev'd, that all he sayd, was trew,
And being fresh and full of youthly spright,
Were glad to heare of that adventure new,
In which they mote make triall of their might,
Which never yet they had approv'd in fight;
And eke desirous of the offred meed,[2]
Said then the one of them; where is that wight,
The which hath doen to thee this wrongfull deed,
That we may it avenge, and punish him with speed?

6

He rides (said *Turpine*) there not farre afore,
With a wyld man soft footing by his syde,
That if ye list to haste a litle more,
Ye may him overtake in timely tyde:° *period of time*
Eftsoones they pricked forth with forward pryde,

2. Sir Enias (named in VI.8.4.3) and his nameless companion are not only breaking the rules of chivalry (which required assistance without payment; cf. VI.1.46–7); they are debasing themselves to the status of hired assassins.

And ere that litle while they ridden had,
The gentle Prince not farre away they spyde,
Ryding a softly pace with portance° sad, *bearing*
Devizing of his love more, then of daunger drad.

7

Then one of them aloud unto him cryde,
Bidding him turne againe, false traytour knight,
Foule womanwronger, for he him defyde.
With that they both at once with equall spight
Did bend their speares, and both with equall might
Against him ran; but th'one did misse his marke,
And being carried with his force forthright,
Glaunst swiftly by; like to that heavenly sparke,
Which glyding through the ayre lights all the heavens darke.[3]

8

But th'other ayming better, did him smite
Full in the shield, with so impetuous powre,
That all his launce in peeces shivered quite,
And scattered all about, fell on the flowre.
But the stout Prince, with much more steddy stowre
Full on his bever° did him strike so sore, *faceguard of helmet*
That the cold steele through piercing, did devowre
His vitall[4] breath, and to the ground him bore,
Where still he bathed lay in his owne bloody gore.

9

As when a cast° of Faulcons make their flight *couple*
At an Herneshaw,° that lyes aloft on wing, *young heron*
The whyles they strike at him with heedlesse might,
The warie foule his bill doth backward wring;
On which the first, whose force her first doth bring,
Her selfe quite through the bodie doth engore,
And falleth downe to ground like senselesse thing,
But th'other not so swift, as she before,
Fayles of her souse,[5] and passing by doth hurt no more.

10

By this the other, which was passed by,
Himselfe recovering, was return'd to fight;
Where when he saw his fellow lifelessely,
He much was daunted with so dismall sight;
Yet nought abating of his former spight,

3. The reference is either to a meteor or to lightning.
4. Necessary for life, life–sustaining.
5. Swooping down at a bird in flight.

Let drive at him with so malitious mynd,
As if he would have passed through him quight:
But the steele-head no stedfast hold could fynd,
But glauncing by, deceiv'd him of that he desynd.

11

Not so the Prince: for his well learned speare
Tooke surer hould, and from his horses backe
Above a launces length him forth did beare,
And gainst the cold hard earth so sore him strake,
That all his bones in peeces nigh he brake.
Where seeing him so lie, he left his steed,
And to him leaping, vengeance thought to take
Of him, for all his former follies meed,
With flaming sword in hand his terror more to breed.

12

The fearefull swayne beholding death so nie,
Cryde out aloud for mercie him to save;
In lieu whereof he would to him descrie,
Great treason to him meant, his life to reave.
The Prince soone hearkned, and his life forgave.
Then thus said he, There is a straunger knight,
The which for promise of great meed, us drave
To this attempt, to wreake his hid despight,
For that himselfe thereto did want sufficient might.

13

The Prince much mused at such villenie,
And sayd; Now sure ye well have earn'd your meed,
For th'one is dead, and th'other soone shall die,
Unlesse to me thou hether bring with speed
The wretch, that hyr'd you to this wicked deed,
He glad of life, and willing eke to wreake
The guilt on him, which did this mischiefe breed,
Swore by his sword, that neither day nor weeke
He would surceasse, but him, where so he were, would seeke.

14

So up he rose, and forth straight way he went
Backe to the place, where *Turpine* late he lore;° *left*
There he him found in great astonishment,
To see him so bedight with bloodie gore,
And griesly wounds that him appalled sore.
Yet thus at length he said, how now Sir knight?
What meaneth this, which here I see before?

How fortuneth this foule uncomely plight,
So different from that, which earst ye seem'd in sight?

15

Perdie (said he) in evill houre it fell,
That ever I for meed did undertake
So hard a taske, as life for hyre to sell;
The which I earst adventur'd for your sake.
Witnesse the wounds, and this wyde bloudie lake,
Which ye may see yet all about me steeme.
Therefore now yeeld, as ye did promise make,
My due reward, the which right well I deeme
I yearned have, that life so dearely did redeeme.

16

But where then is (quoth he halfe wrothfully)
Where is the bootie,[6] which therefore I bought,
That cursed caytive, my strong enemy,
That recreant knight, whose hated life I sought?
And where is eke your friend, which halfe it ought?[7]
He lyes (said he) upon the cold bare ground,
Slayne of that errant knight, with whom he fought;
Whom afterwards my selfe with many a wound
Did slay againe, as ye may see there in the stound.

17

Thereof false *Turpin* was full glad and faine,
And needs with him streight to the place would ryde,
Where he himselfe might see his foeman slaine;
For else his feare could not be satisfyde.
So as they rode, he saw the way all dyde
With streames of bloud; which tracting° by the traile, *following*
Ere long they came, whereas in evill tyde
That other swayne, like ashes deadly pale,
Lay in the lap of death, rewing his wretched bale.

18

Much did the Craven seeme to mone his case,
That for his sake his deare life had forgone;
And him bewayling with affection base,
Did counterfeit kind pittie, where was none:
For wheres no courage, theres no ruth nor mone.
Thence passing forth, not farre away he found,
Whereas the Prince himselfe lay all alone,

6. I.e., Arthur's corpse.
7. I.e., which owed half of it to me.

Loosely displayd upon the grassie ground,
Possessed of sweete sleepe, that luld him soft in swound.

19

Wearie of travell in his former fight,
He there in shade himselfe had layd to rest,
Having his armes and warlike things undight,
Fearelesse of foes that mote his peace molest;
The whyles his salvage page, that wont be prest,
Was wandred in the wood another way,
To doe some thing, that seemed to him best,
The whyles his Lord in silver slomber lay,
Like to the Evening starre adorn'd with deawy ray.

20

Whom when as *Turpin* saw so loosely layd,
He weened well, that he in deed was dead,
Like as that other knight to him had sayd:
But when he nigh approcht, he mote aread
Plaine signes in him of life and livelihead.
Whereat much griev'd against that straunger knight,
That him too light of credence did mislead,
He would have backe retyred from that sight,
That was to him on earth the deadliest despight.

21

But that same knight would not once let him start,
But plainely gan to him declare the case
Of all his mischiefe, and late lucklesse smart;
How both he and his fellow there in place
Were vanquished, and put to foule disgrace,
And how that he in lieu of life him lent,
Had vow'd unto the victor, him to trace
And follow through the world, where so he went,
Till that he him delivered to his punishment.

22

He therewith much abashed and affrayd,
Began to tremble every limbe and vaine;
And softly whispering him, entyrely prayd,
T'advize him better, then by such a traine
Him to betray unto a straunger swaine:
Yet rather counseld him contrarywize,
Sith he likewise did wrong by him sustaine,
To joyne with him and vengeance to devize,
Whylest time did offer meanes him sleeping to surprize.

23

Nathelesse for all his speach, the gentle knight
Would not be tempted to such villenie,
Regarding more his faith, which he did plight,
All were[8] it to his mortall enemie,
Then to entrap him by false treacherie:
Great shame in lieges blood to be embrew'd.
Thus whylest they were debating diverslie,
The Salvage forth out of the wood issew'd
Backe to the place, whereas his Lord he sleeping vew'd.

24

There when he saw those two so neare him stand,
He doubted much what mote their meaning bee,
And throwing downe his load out of his hand,
To weet great store of forrest firute, which hee
Had for his food late gathered from the tree,
Himselfe unto his weapon he betooke,
That was an oaken plant, which lately hee
Rent by the roof, which he so sternely shooke,
That like an hazell wand, it quivered and quooke.

25

Whereat the Prince awaking, when he spyde
The traytour *Turpin* with that other knight,
He started up, and snatching neare his syde
His trustie sword, the servant of his might,
Like a fell Lyon leaped to him light,
And his left hand upon his collar layd.
Therewith the cowheard deaded° with affright, *stupefied*
Fell flat to ground, ne word unto him sayd,
But holding up his hands, with silence mercie prayd.

26

But he so full of indignation was,
That to his prayer nought he would incline,
But as he lay upon the humbled gras,
His foot he set on his vile necke, in signe
Of servile yoke, that nobler harts repine.
Then letting him arise like abject thrall,
He gan to him obiect his haynous crime,
And to revile, and rate, and recreant call,
And lastly to despoyle of knightly bannerall.[9]

8. Even if it were.

9. Banderole, small pennant or ornamental banner.

27

And after all, for greater infamie,
He by the heeles him hung upon a tree,
And baffuld° so, that all which passed by, *disgraced*
The picture of his punishment might see,
And by the like ensample warned bee,
How ever they through treason doe trespasse.
But turne we now backe to that Ladie free,[1]
Whom late we left ryding upon an Asse,
Led by a Carle and foole, which by her side did passe.

28

She was a Ladie of great dignitie,
And lifted up to honorable place,
Famous through all the land of Faerie,
Though of meane parentage and kindred base,
Yet deckt with wondrous giftes of natures grace,
That all men did her person much admire,
And praise the feature of her goodly face,
The beames whereof did kindle lovely fire
In th'harts of many a knight, and many a gentle squire.

29

But she thereof grew proud and insolent,
That none she worthie thought to be her fere,° *companion*
But scornd them all, that love unto her ment;° *intended*
Yet was she lov'd of many a worthy pere,
Unworthy she to be belov'd so dere,
That could not weigh of worthinesse aright.
For beautie is more glorious bright and clere,
The more it is admir'd of many a wight,
And noblest she, that served is of noblest knight.

30

But this coy Damzell thought contrariwize,
That such proud looks would make her praysed more;
And that the more she did all love despize,
The more would wretched lovers her adore.
What cared she, who sighed for her sore,
Or who did wayle or watch the wearie night?
Let them that list, their lucklesse lot deplore;
She was borne free, not bound to any wight,
And so would ever live, and love her owne delight.

1. The noble or gentle Mirabella, who first appeared in VI.6.16–17. It has been suggested that Mirabella (Italian: *mirabile*, "admirable, marvellous"; *mirari*, "to gaze at," *bella* "beautiful") represents the haughty pride of the sonnet lady who scorns the lover's pains.

31

Through such her stubborne stifnesse, and hard hart,
Many a wretch, for want of remedie,
Did languish long in lifeconsuming smart,
And at the last through dreary dolour die:
Whylest she, the Ladie of her libertie,
Did boast her beautie had such soveraine might,
That with the onely twinckle of her eye,
She could or save, or spill, whom she would hight.
What could the Gods doe more, but doe it more aright?

32

But loe the Gods, that mortall follies vew,
Did worthily revenge this maydens pride;
And nought regarding her so goodly hew,
Did laugh at her, that many did deride,
Whilest she did weepe, of no man mercifide.
For on a day, when *Cupid* kept his court,
As he is wont at each Saint Valentide,[2]
Unto the which all lovers doe resort,
That of their loves successe they there may make report.

33

It fortun'd then, that when the roules were red,
In which the names of all loves folke were fyled,
That many there were missing, which were ded,
Or kept in bands, or from their loves exyled,
Or by some other violence despoyled.
Which when as *Cupid* heard, he wexed wroth,
And doubting° to be wronged, or beguyled, *fearing*
He bad his eyes to be unblindfold both,
That he might see his men, and muster them by oth.

34

Then found he many missing of his crew,
Which wont doe suit and service to his might;
Of whom what was becomen, no man knew.
Therefore a Jurie was impaneld streight,
T'enquire of them, whether by force, or sleight,
Or their owne guilt, they were away convayd.
To whom foule *Infamie*, and fell *Despight*
Gave evidence, that they were all betrayd,
And murdred cruelly by a rebellious Mayd.

2. As in Chaucer's *Parliament of Fowls*, the God of Love holds court on St. Valentine's Day.

35

Fayre *Mirabella* was her name, whereby
Of all those crymes she there indited was:
All which when *Cupid* heard, he by and by
In great displeasure, wild a *Capias*[3]
Should issue forth, t'attach that scornefull lasse.
The warrant straight was made, and therewithall
A Baylieffe errant forth in post did passe,
Whom they by name there *Portamore*[4] did call;
He which doth summon lovers to loves judgement hall.

36

The damzell was attacht,° and shortly brought *seized*
Unto the barre, whereas she was arrayned:
But she thereto nould plead, nor answere ought
Even for stubborne pride, which her restrayned.
So judgement past, as is by law ordayned
In cases like, which when at last she saw,
Her stubborne hart, which love before disdayned,
Gan stoupe, and falling downe with humble awe,
Cryde mercie, to abate the extremitie of law.

37

The sonne of *Venus* who is myld by kynd,
But where he is provokt with peevishnesse,
Unto her prayers piteously enclynd,
And did the rigour of his doome represse;
Yet not so freely, but that nathelesse
He unto her a penance did impose,
Which was, that through this worlds wyde wildernesse
She wander should in companie of those,
Till she had sav'd so many loves, as she did lose.

38

So now she had bene wandring two whole yeares
Throughout the world, in this uncomely case,
Wasting her goodly hew in heavie teares,
And her good dayes in dolorous disgrace:
Yet had she not in all these two yeares space,
Saved but two, yet in two yeares before,
Throgh her dispiteous pride, whilest love lackt place,
She had destroyed two and twenty more.
Aie me, how could her love make half amends therefore.

3. Latin: "you may take"; a written authorization to make an arrest.

4. Italian: *portare*, "to carry," *amore*, "love."

39

And now she was uppon the weary way,
When as the gentle Squire, with faire *Serene*,
Met her in such misseeming foule array;
The whiles that mighty man did her demeane
With all the evill termes and cruell meane,
That he could make; And eeke that angry foole
Which follow'd her, with cursed hands uncleane
Whipping her horse, did with his smarting toole
Oft whip her dainty selfe, and much augment her doole.° *grief*

40

Ne ought it mote availe her to entreat
The one or th'other, better her to use:
For both so wilfull were and obstinate,
That all her piteous plaint they did refuse,
And rather did the more her beate and bruse.
But most the former villaine, which did lead
Her tyreling° jade, was bent her to abuse; *weary*
Who though she were with wearinesse nigh dead,
Yet would not let her lite, nor rest a little stead.° *period of time*

41

For he was sterne, and terrible by nature,
And eeke of person huge and hideous,
Exceeding much the measure of mans stature,
And rather like a Gyant monstruous.
For sooth he was descended of the hous
Of those old Gyants,° which did warres darraine *Titans*
Against the heaven in order battailous,
And sib to great *Orgolio*, which was slaine
By *Arthure*, when as *Unas* Knight he did maintaine.

42

His lookes were dreadfull, and his fiery eies
Like two great Beacons, glared bright and wyde,
Glauncing askew, as if his enemies
He scorned in his overweening pryde;
And stalking stately like a Crane, did stryde
At every step uppon the tiptoes hie,
And all the way he went, on every syde
He gaz'd about, and stared horriblie,
As if he with his lookes would all men terrifie.

43

He wore no armour, ne for none did care,
As no whit dreading any living wight;

But in a Jacket quilted richly rare,
Upon checklaton[5] he was straungely dight,
And on his head a roll of linnen plight,
Like to the Mores of Malaber[6] he wore;
With which his locks, as blacke as pitchy night,
Were bound about, and voyded from before,
And in his hand a mighty yron club he bore.

44

This was *Disdaine*, who led that Ladies horse
Through thick & thin, through mountains & through plains,
Compelling her, wher she would not by force
Haling her palfrey by the hempen raines.
But that same foole, which most increast her paines,
Was *Scorne*, who having in his hand a whip,
Her therewith yirks, and still when she complaines,
The more he laughes, and does her closely quip,
To see her sore lament, and bite her tender lip.

45

Whose cruell handling when that Squire beheld,
And saw those villaines her so vildely use,
His gentle heart with indignation sweld,
And could no lenger beare so great abuse,
As such a Lady so to beate and bruse;
But to him stepping, such a stroke him lent,
That forst him th'halter from his hand to loose,
And maugre all his might, backe to relent:
Else had he surely there bene slaine, or fowly shent.

46

The villaine wroth for greeting him so sore,
Gathered him selfe together soone againe,
And with his yron batton, which he bore,
Let drive at him so dreadfully amaine,
That for his safety he did him constraine
To give him ground, and shift to every side,
Rather then once his burden to sustaine:
For bootelesse thing him seemed, to abide,
So mighty blowes, or prove the puissaunce of his pride.

5. Ciclaton, defined by Spenser, *View of the Present State of Ireland* (*Var*., p. 225): "The quilted leather jack[et] is old english: For it was the proper weed of the horseman, as you may read in Chaucer, when he describeth Sir Thopas's apparel, and armour, as he went to fight against the gyant, in his robe of checklaton, which is that kind of gilded leather with which they use to embroider their irish jackets" ("Tale of Sir Thopas," 734).

6. Malabar is in India. The word *Moors* was sometimes used to refer to all non-Christian nations.

47

Like as a Mastiffe having at a bay
A salvage Bull, whose cruell homes doe threat
Desperate daunger, if he them assay,
Traceth his ground, and round about doth beat,
To spy where he may some advauntage get;
The whiles the beast doth rage and loudly rore,
So did the Squire, the whiles the Carle did fret,
And fume in his disdainefull mynd the more,
And oftentimes by Turmagant and Mahound swore.[7]

48

Nathelesse so sharpely still he him pursewd,
That at advantage him at last he tooke,
When his foote slipt (that slip he dearely rewd,)
And with his yron club to ground him strooke;
Where still he lay, ne out of swoune awooke,
Till heavy hand the Carle upon him layd,
And bound him fast: Tho when he up did looke,
And saw him selfe captiv'd, he was dismayd,
Ne powre had to withstand, ne hope of any ayd.

49

Then up he made him rise, and forward fare,
Led in a rope, which both his hands did bynd;
Ne ought that foole for pitty did him spare,
But with his whip him following behynd,
Him often scourg'd, and forst his feete to fynd:
And other whiles with bitter mockes and mowes
He would him scorne, that to his gentle mynd
Was much more grievous, then the others blowes:
Words sharpely wound, but greatest griefe of scorning growes.

50

The faire *Serena*, when she saw him fall
Under that villaines club, then surely thought
That slaine he was, or made a wretched thrall,
And fled away with all the speede she mought,
To seeke for safety, which long time she sought:
And past through many perils by the way,
Ere she againe to *Calepine* was brought;
The which discourse as now I must delay,
Till *Mirabettaes* fortunes I doe further say.

7. Oaths used by infidel warriors.

Canto VIII

Prince Arthure overcomes Disdaine,
Quites Mirabell from dreed:
Serena found of Salvages,
By Calepine is freed.

1

Ye gentle Ladies, in whose soveraine powre
Love hath the glory of his kingdome left,
And th'hearts of men, as your eternall dowre,
In yron chaines, of liberty bereft,
Delivered hath into your hands by gift;
Be well aware, how ye the same doe use,
That pride doe not to tyranny you lift;
Least if men you of cruelty accuse,
He from you take that chiefedome, which ye doe abuse.

2

And as ye soft and tender are by kynde,
Adornd with goodly gifts of beauties grace,
So be ye soft and tender eeke in mynde;
But cruelty and hardnesse from you chace,
That all your other praises will deface,
And from you turne the love of men to hate.
Ensample take of *Mirabellaes* case,
Who from the high degree of happy state,
Fell into wretched woes, which she repented late.

3

Who after thraldome of the gentle Squire,° *Timias*
Which she beheld with lamentable eye,
Was touched with compassion entire,
And much lamented his calamity,
That for her sake fell into misery:
Which booted nought for prayers, nor for threat
To hope for to release or mollify;
For aye the more, that she did them entreat
The more they him misust, and cruelly did beat.

4

So as they forward on their way did pas,
Him still reviling and afflicting sore,
They met Prince *Arthure* with Sir *Enias*,
(That was that courteous Knight, whom he before
Having subdew'd, yet did to life restore,)
To whom as they approcht, they gan augment

Their cruelty, and him to punish more,
Scourging and haling him more vehement;
As if it them should grieve to see his punishment.

5

The Squire him selfe when as he saw his Lord,
The witnesse of his wretchednesse, in place,
Was much asham'd, that with an hempen cord
He like a dog was led in captive case,
And did his head for bashfulnesse abase,
As loth to see, or to be seene at all:
Shame would be bid. But whenas *Enias*
Beheld two such, of two such villaines thrall,
His manly mynde was much emmoved therewithall.

6

And to the Prince thus sayd; See you Sir Knight
The greatest shame that ever eye yet saw?
Yond Lady and her Squire with foule despight
Abusde, against all reason and all law,
Without regard of pitty or of awe.
See how they doe that Squire beat and revile;
See how they doe the Lady hale and draw.
But if ye please to lend me leave a while,
I will them soone acquite,° and both of blame assoile.° *free / absolve*

7

The Prince assented, and then he streight way
Dismounting light, his shield about him threw,
With which approching, thus he gan to say;
Abide ye caytive treachetours untrew,
That have with treason thralled unto you
These two, unworthy of your wretched bands;
And now your crime with cruelty pursew.
Abide, and from them lay your loathly hands;
Or else abide the death, that hard before you stands.

8

The villaine stayd not aunswer to invent,
But with his yron club preparing way,
His mindes sad message backe unto him sent;
The which descended with such dreadfull sway,
That seemed nought the course thereof could stay:
No more then lightening from the lofty sky.
Ne list the Knight the powre thereof assay,
Whose doome was death, but lightly slipping by,
Unwares defrauded his intended destiny.

9

And to requite him with the like againe,
With his sharpe sword he fiercely at him flew,
And strooke so strongly, that the Carle with paine
Saved him selfe, but that he there him slew:
Yet sav'd not so, but that the bloud it drew,
And gave his foe good hope of victory.
Who therewith flesht, upon him set anew,
And with the second stroke, thought certainely
To have supplyde° the first, and paide the usury.[1] *supplemented*

10

But Fortune aunswerd not unto his call;
For as his hand was heaved up on hight,
The villaine met him in the middle fall,° *in mid-stroke*
And with his club bet backe his brondyron° bright *sword*
So forcibly, that with his owne hands might
Rebeaten backe upon him selfe againe,
He driven was to ground in selfe despight;
From whence ere he recovery could gaine,
He in his necke had set his foote with fell disdaine.

11

With that the foole, which did that end awayte,
Came running in, and whilest on ground he lay,
Laide heavy hands on him, and held so strayte,
That downe he kept him with his scornefull sway,
So as he could not weld him any way.
The whiles that other villaine went about
Him to have bound, and thrald without delay;
The whiles the foole did him revile and flout,
Threatning to yoke them two & tame their corage stout.

12

As when a sturdy ploughman with his hynde° *laborer, servant*
By strength have overthrowne a stubborne steare,
They downe him hold, and fast with cords do bynde,
Till they him force the buxome° yoke to beare: *yielding, obedient*
So did these two this Knight oft tug and teare.
Which when the Prince beheld, there standing by,
He left his lofty steede to aide him neare,
And buckling soone him selfe, gan fiercely fly
Uppon that Carle, to save his friend from jeopardy.

1. I.e., struck extra hard.

13

The villaine leaving him unto his mate
To be captiv'd, and handled as he list,
Himselfe addrest unto this new debate,
And with his club him all about so blist,° *brandished*
That he which way to turne him scarcely wist:
Sometimes aloft he layd, sometimes alow;
Now here, now there, and oft him neare° he mist; *nearly*
So doubtfully, that hardly one could know
Whether more wary were to give or ward the blow.

14

But yet the Prince so well enured° was *accustomed familiar*
With such huge strokes, approved oft in fight,
That way to them he gave forth right to pas.
Ne would endure the daunger of their might,
But wayt advantage, when they downe did light.
At last the caytive after long discourse,
When all his strokes he saw avoyded quite,
Resolved in one t'assemble all his force,
And make one end of him without ruth or remorse.

15

His dreadfull hand he heaved up aloft,
And with his dreadfull instrument of yre,
Thought sure have pownded him to powder soft,
Or deepe emboweld in the earth entyre:
But Fortune did not with his will conspire.
For ere his stroke attayned his intent,
The noble childe preventing his desire,
Under his club with wary boldnesse went,
And smote him on the knee, that never yet was bent.

16

It never yet was bent, ne bent it now,
Albe the stroke so strong and puissant were,
That seem'd a marble pillour it could bow,
But all that leg, which did his body beare,
It crackt throughout, yet did no bloud appeare;
So as it was unable to support
So huge a burden on such broken geare,° *apparatus (i.e., his knee)*
But fell to ground, like to a lumpe of durt,
Whence he assayd to rise, but could not for his hurt.

17

Eftsoones the Prince to him full nimbly stept,
And least he should recover foote againe,

His head meant from his shoulders to have swept.
Which when the Lady saw, she cryde amaine;
Stay stay, Sir Knight, for love of God abstaine,
From that unwares ye weetlesse doe intend;
Slay not that Carle, though worthy to be slaine:
For more on him doth then him selfe depend;
My life will by his death have lamentable end.

18

He staide his hand according her desire,
Yet nathemore him suffred to arize;
But still suppressing gan of her inquire,
What meaning mote those uncouth words comprize,
That in that villaines health her safety lies:
That, were no might in man, nor heart in Knights,
Which durst her dreaded reskue enterprize,
Yet heavens them selves, that favour feeble rights,
Would for it selfe redresse, and punish such despights.

19

Then bursting forth in teares, which gushed fast
Like many water streames, a while she stayd;° *hesitated*
Till the sharpe passion being overpast,
Her tongue to her restord, then thus she sayd;
Nor heavens, nor men can me most wretched mayd
Deliver from the doome of my desart,
The which the God of love hath on me layd,
And damned to endure this direfull smart,
For penaunce of my proud and hard rebellious hart.

20

In prime of youthly yeares, when first the flowre
Of beauty gan to bud, and bloosme delight,
And nature me endu'd with plenteous dowre,
Of all her gifts, that pleasde each living sight,
I was belov'd of many a gentle Knight,
And sude° and sought with all the service dew: *pursued*
Full many a one for me deepe groand and sight,
And to the dore of death for sorrow drew,
Complayning out on me, that would not on them rew.

21

But let them love that list, or live or die;
Me list not die for any lovers doole:
Ne list me leave my loved libertie,
To pitty him that list to play the foole:
To love my selfe I learned had in schoole.

Thus I triumphed long in lovers paine,
And sitting carelesse on the scorners stoole,
Did laugh at those that did lament and plaine:
But all is now repayd with interest againe.

22

For loe the winged God,° that woundeth harts, *Cupid*
Causde me be called to accompt therefore,
And for revengement of those wrongfull smarts,
Which I to others did inflict afore,
Addeem'd me to endure this penaunce sore;
That in this wize, and this unmeete array,° *unsuitable clothing*
With these two lewd companions, and no more,
Disdaine and *Scorne*, I through the world should stray,
Till I have sav'd so many, as I earst did slay.

23

Certes (sayd then the Prince) the God is just,
That taketh vengeaunce of his peoples spoile.
For were no law in love, but all that lust,
Might them oppresse, and painefully turmoile,
His kingdome would continue but a while.
But tell me Lady, wherefore doe you beare
This bottle thus before you with such toile,
And eeke this wallet at your backe arreare,
That for these Carles to carry much more comely were?

24

Here in this bottle (sayd the sory Mayd)
I put the teares of my contrition,
Till to the brim I have it full defrayd:
And in this bag which I behinde me don,
I put repentaunce for things past and gon.
Yet is the bottle leake, and bag so torne,
That all which I put in, fals out anon;
And is behinde me trodden downe of *Scorne*,
Who mocketh all my paine, & laughs the more I mourn.

25

The Infant° hearkned wisely to her tale, *Arthur*
And wondred much at *Cupids* judg'ment wise,
That could so meekly make proud hearts avale,[2]
And wreake him selfe on them, that him despise.
Then suffred he *Disdaine* up to arise,

2. Go down (i.e., be humbled).

Who was not able up him selfe to reare,
By meanes his leg through his late luckelesse prise,
Was crackt in twaine, but by his foolish feare° *partner*
Was holpen up, who him supported standing neare.

26

But being up, he lookt againe aloft,
As if he never had received fall;
And with sterne eye-browes stared at him oft,
As if he would have daunted him with all:
And standing on his tiptoes, to seeme tall,
Downe on his golden feete he often gazed,
As if such pride the other could apall;
Who was so far from being ought amazed,
That he his lookes despised, and his boast dispraized.

27

Then turning backe unto that captive thrall,
Who all this while stood there beside them bound,
Unwilling to be knowne, or seene at all,
He from those bands weend him to have unwound.
But when approching neare, he plainely found,
It was his owne true groome, the gentle Squire,° *Timias*
He thereat wext exceedingly astound,
And him did oft embrace, and oft admire,° *marveled, wondered*
Ne could with seeing satisfie his great desire.

28

Meane while the Salvage man, when he beheld
That huge great foole oppressing th'other Knight,[3]
Whom with his weight unweldy downe he held,
He flew upon him, like a greedy kight° *bird of prey*
Unto some carrion offered to his sight,
And downe him plucking, with his nayles and teeth
Gan him to hale, and teare, and scratch, and bite;
And from him taking his owne whip, therewith
So sore him scourgeth, that the bloud downe followeth.

29

And sure I weene, had not the Ladies cry
Procur'd the Prince his cruell hand to stay,
He would with whipping, him have done to dye:° *killed*
But being checkt, he did abstains streight way,
And let him rise. Then thus the Prince gan say;
Now Lady sith your fortunes thus dispose,

3. Sir Enias.

That if ye list have liberty, ye may,
Unto your selfe I freely leave to chose,
Whether I shall you leave, or from these villaines lose.° *loose, i.e., free*

30

Ah nay Sir Knight (sayd she) it may not be,
But that I needes must by all meanes fulfill
This penaunce, which enjoyned is to me,
Least unto me betide a greater ill;
Yet no lesse thankes to you for your good will.
So humbly taking leave, she turnd aside,
But *Arthure*[4] with the rest, went onward still
On his first quest, in which did him betide
A great adventure, which did him from them devide.

31

But first it falleth me by course to tell
Of faire *Serena*,[5] who as earst you heard,
When first the gentle Squire at variaunce fell
With those two Carles, fled fast away, afeard
Of villany to be to her inferd:° *brought upon*
So fresh the image of her former dread,
Yet dwelling in her eye, to her appeard,
That every foote did tremble, which did tread,
And every body two, and two she foure did read.

32

Through hils & dales, through bushes & through breres
Long thus she fled, till that at last she thought
Her selfe now past the perill of her feares.
Then looking round about, and seeing nought,
Which doubt° of daunger to her offer mought, *fear*
She from her palfrey lighted on the plaine,
And sitting downe, her selfe a while bethought
Of her long travell and turmoyling paine;
And often did of love, and oft of lucke complaine.

33

And evermore she blamed *Calepine*,[6]
The good Sir *Calepine*, her owne true Knight,
As th'onely author of her wofull tine:° *unhappiness*
For being of his love to her so light,
As her to leave in such a piteous plight.

4. This is Arthur's last appearance in the poem.
5. Serena flees when Timias is captured by Disdain and Scorn, 7.50.
6. Calepine was separated from Serena when he pursued the bear carrying off the baby, 4.17 ff.

Yet never Turtle° truer to his make, *turtledove*
Then he was tride° unto his Lady bright: *united, joined*
Who all this while endured for her sake,
Great perill of his life, and restlesse paines did take.

34

Tho when as all her plaints, she had displayd,
And well disburdened her engrieved brest,
Upon the grasse her selfe adowne she layd;
Where being tyrde with travell, and opprest
With sorrow, she betooke her selfe to rest.
There whitest in *Morpheus*[7] bosome safe she lay,
Fearelesse of ought, that mote her peace molest,
False Fortune did her safety betray,
Unto a straunge mischaunce, that menac'd her decay.

35

In these wylde deserts, where she now abode,[8]
There dwelt a salvage nation, which did live
Of stealth and spoile, and making nightly rode° *raid*
Into their neighbours borders; ne did give
Them selves to any trade, as for to drive
The painefull plough, or cattell for to breed,
Or by adventrous marchandize to thrive;
But on the labours of poore men to feed,
And serve their owne necessities with others need.

36

Thereto they usde one most accursed order,° *custom*
To eate the flesh of men, whom they mote fynde,
And straungers to devoure, which on their border
Were brought by errour, or by wreckfull wynde.
A monstrous cruelty gainst course of kynde.° *Laws of nature*
They towards evening wandring every way,
To seeke for booty, came by fortune blynde,
Whereas this Lady, like a sheepe astray,
Now drowned in the depth of sleepe all fearelesse lay.

37

Soone as they spide her, Lord what gladfull glee
They made amongst them selves; but when her face
Like the faire yvory shining they did see,
Each gan his fellow solace and embrace,
For joy of such good hap by heavenly grace.

7. God of sleep.

8. See VI.10.39.

Then gan they to devize what course to take:
Whether to slay her there upon the place,
Or suffer her out of her sleepe to wake,
And then her eate attonce; or many meales to make.

38

The best advizement was of bad,[9] to let her
Sleepe out her fill, without encomberment:
For sleepe they sayd would make her battill° better. *grow fat*
Then when she wakt, they all gave one consent,
That since by grace of God she there was sent,
Unto their God they would her sacrifize,
Whose share, her guiltlesse bloud they would present,
But of her dainty flesh they did devize
To make a common feast, & feed with gurmandize.

39

So round about her they them selves did place[1]
Upon the grasse, and diversely dispose,
As each thought best to spend the lingring space.
Some with their eyes the daintest morsels chose;
Some praise her paps, some praise her lips and nose;
Some whet their knives, and strip their elboes bare:
The Priest him selfe a garland doth compose
Of finest flowres, and with full busie care
His bloudy vessels wash; and holy fire prepare.

40

The Damzell wakes, then all attonce upstart,
And round about her flocke, like many flies,
Whooping, and hallowing on every part,
As if they would have rent the brasen skies.
Which when she sees with ghastly griefful eies,
Her heart does quake, and deadly pallid hew
Benumbes her cheekes: Then out aloud she cries,
Where none is nigh to heare, that will her rew,
And rends her golden locks, and snowy brests embrew.° *stain*

41

But all bootes not: they hands upon her lay;
And first they spoile her of her jewls deare,
And afterwards of all her rich array;
The which amongst them they in peeces teare,

9. I.e., the best advice was bad.

1. This stanza parodies the blazon, or poetic catalog of a lady's particular physical beauties.

And of the pray each one a part doth beare.
Now being naked, to their sordid eyes
The goodly threasures of nature appeare:
Which as they view with lustfull fantasyes,
Each wisheth to him selfe, and to the rest envyes.

42

Her yvorie necke, her alablaster brest,
Her paps, which like white silken pillowes were,
For love in soft delight thereon to rest;[2]
Her tender sides, her bellie white and clere,
Which like an Altar did it selfe uprere,
To offer sacrifice divine thereon;
Her goodly thighes, whose glorie did appeare
Like a triumphall Arch, and thereupon
The spoiles of Princes hang'd, which were in battel won.

43

Those daintie parts, the dearlings of delight,
Which mote not be prophan'd of common eyes,
Those villeins vew'd with loose lascivious sight,
And closely tempted with their craftie spyes;
And some of them gan mongst themselves devize,
Thereof by force to take their beastly pleasure.
But them the Priest rebuking, did advize
To dare not to pollute so sacred threasure,
Vow'd to the gods: religion held even theeves in measure.

44

So being stayd, they her from thence directed
Unto a litle grove not farre asyde,
In which an altar shortly they erected,
To slay her on. And now the Eventyde
His brode black wings had through the heavens wyde
By this dispred, that was the tyme ordayned
For such a dismall deed, their guilt to hyde:
Of few greene turfes an altar soone they fayned,° *fashioned*
And deckt it all with flowres, which they nigh hand obtayned.

45

Tho when as all things readie were aright,
The Damzell was before the altar set,
Being alreadie dead with fearefull fright.
To whom the Priest with naked armes full net° *clean*

2. In these stanzas, with their echoes of the Song of Songs, Spenser continues the blazon begun in stanza 39.

Approching nigh, and murdrous knife well whet,° sharpened
Gan mutter close a certaine secret charme,
With other divelish ceremonies met:
Which doen he gan aloft t'advance his arme,
Whereat they shouted all, and made a loud alarme.

46

Then gan the bagpypes and the homes to shrill,
And shrieke aloud, that with the peoples voyce
Confused, did the ayre with terror fill,
And made the wood to tremble at the noyce:
The whyles she wayld, the more they did rejoyce.
Now mote ye understand that to this grove
Sir *Calepine* by chaunce, more then by choyce,
The selfe same evening fortune hether drove,
As he to seeke *Serena* through the woods did rove.

47

Long had he sought her, and through many a soyle
Had traveld still on foot in heavie armes,
Ne ought was tyred with his endlesse toyle,
Ne ought was feared of his certaine harmes:
And now all weetlesse of the wretched stormes,
In which his love was lost, he slept full fast,
Till being waked with these loud alarmes,
He lightly started up like one aghast,
And catching up his arms streight to the noise forth past.

48

There by th'uncertaine glims of starry night,
And by the twinkling of their sacred fire,
He mote perceive a litle dawning sight
Of all, which there was doing in that quire:
Mongst whom a woman spoyld of all attire
He spyde, lamenting her unluckie strife,
And groning sore from grieved hart entire;
Eftsoones he saw one with a naked knife
Readie to launch° her brest, and let out loved life. pierce, cut

49

With that he thrusts into the thickest throng,
And even as his right hand adowne descends,
He him preventing, layes on earth along,
And sacrifizeth to th'infernall feends.
Then to the rest his wrathfull hand he bends,
Of whom he makes such havocke and such hew,° slaughter

That swarmes of damned soules to hell he sends:
The rest that scape his sword and death eschew,
Fly like a flocke of doves before a Faulcons vew.

50

From them returning to that Ladie backe,
Whom by the Altar he doth sitting find,
Yet fearing death, and next to death the lacke
Of clothes to cover, what they ought by kind,
He first her hands beginneth to unbind;
And then to question of her present woe;
And afterwards to cheare with speaches kind.
But she for nought that he could say or doe,
One word durst speake, or answere him awhit thereto.

51

So inward shame of her uncomely case
She did conceive, through care of womanhood,
That though the night did cover her disgrace,
Yet she in so unwomanly a mood,
Would not bewray the state in which she stood.
So all that night to him unknowen she past.
But day, that doth discover bad and good,
Ensewing, made her knowen to him at last:[3]
The end whereof Ile keepe untill another cast.

Canto IX

Calidore hostes with Melibœ
and loves fayre Pastorell;
Coridon envies him, yet he
for ill rewards him well.

1

Now turne againe my teme thou jolly swayne,° *farm laborer or shepherd*
Backe to the furrow which I lately left;
I lately left a furrow, one or twayne
Unplough'd, the which my coulter° hath not cleft: *blade of a plow*
Yet seem'd the soyle both fayre and frutefull eft,
As I it past, that were too great a shame,
That so rich frute should be from us bereft;
Besides the great dishonour and defame,
Which should befall to *Calidores*[1] immortall name.

3. At this point Calepine and Serena leave the narrative. Spenser's promise to finish their tale is in the manner of Ariosto, but, unlike Ariosto, Spenser never provides the promised conclusion.

1. Calidore has not been mentioned since 3.26. He was then in pursuit of the Blatant Beast.

2

Great travell hath the gentle *Calidore*
And toyle endured, sith I left him last
Sewing° the *Blatant beast*, which I forbore *pursuing*
To finish then, for other present hast.
Full many pathes and perils he hath past,
Through hils, through dales, throgh forests, & throgh plaines
In that same quest which fortune on him cast,
Which he atchieved to his owne great gaines,
Reaping eternall glorie of his restlesse paines.

3

So sharply he the Monster did pursew,
That day nor night he suffred him to rest,
Ne rested he himselfe but natures dew,
For dread of daunger, not to be redrest,
If he for slouth forslackt° so famous quest. *neglected*
Him first from court he to the citties coursed,° *followed*
And from the citties to the townes him prest,
And from the townes into the countrie forsed,
And from the country back to private farmes he scorsed.° *chased*

4

From thence into the open fields he fled,
Whereas the Heardes° were keeping of their neat,° *shepherds / cattle*
And shepheards singing to their flockes, that fed,
Layes° of sweete love and youthes delightfull heat: *lays, songs*
Him thether eke for all his fearefull threat
He followed fast, and chaced him so nie,
That to the folds, where sheepe at night doe seat,
And to the litle cots,° where shepherds lie *little cottages*
In winters wrathfull time, he forced him to flie.

5

There on a day as he pursew'd the chace,
He chaunst to spy a sort° of shepheard groomes, *group*
Playing on pypes, and caroling apace,
The whyles their beasts there in the budded broomes° *shrubs, the broom plant*
Beside them fed, and nipt the tender bloomes:
For other worldly wealth they cared nought.
To whom Sir *Calidore* yet sweating comes,
And them to tell him courteously besought,
If such a beast they saw, which he had thether brought.

6

They answer'd him, that no such beast they saw,
Nor any wicked feend, that mote offend

Their happie flockes, nor daunger to them draw:
But if that such there were (as none they kend)
They prayd high God him farre from them to send.
Then one of them him seeing so to sweat,
After his rusticke wise,[2] that well he weend,
Offred him drinke, to quench his thirstie heat,
And if he hungry were, him offred eke to eat.

7

The knight was nothing nice,° where was no need, *not fastidious*
And tooke their gentle offer: so adowne
They prayd him sit, and gave him for to feed
Such homely what,° as serves the simple clowne,° *simple food / rustic*
That doth despise the dainties of the towne.
Tho having fed his fill, he there besyde
Saw a faire damzell, which did weare a crowne
Of sundry flowres, with silken ribbands tyde,
Yclad in home-made greene that her owne hands had dyde.

8

Upon a litle hillocke she was placed
Higher then all the rest, and round about
Environ'd with a girland, goodly graced,
Of lovely lasses, and them all without
The lustie shepheard swaynes sate in a rout,° *crowd*
The which did pype and sing her prayses dew,
And oft rejoyce, and oft for wonder shout,
As if some miracle of heavenly hew
Were downe to them descended in that earthly vew.

9

And soothly sure she was full fayre of face,
And perfectly well shapt in every lim,
Which she did more augment with modest grace,
And comely carriage of her count'nance trim,
That all the rest like lesser lamps did dim:
Who her admiring as some heavenly wight,
Did for their soveraine goddesse her esteeme,
And caroling her name both day and night,
The fayrest *Pastorella*[3] her by name did hight.

10

Ne was there heard, ne was there shepheards swayne
But her did honour, and eke many a one

2. I.e., in his rustic, or country, way.

3. Her name means shepherdess (Latin: *pastor*, "shepherd"); she is revealed to be of noble birth (VI.12.14–22).

Burnt in her love, and with sweet pleasing payne
Full many a night for her did sigh and grone:
But most of all the shepheard *Coridon*[4]
For her did languish, and his deare life spend;
Yet neither she for him, nor other none
Did care a whit, ne any liking lend:
Though meane her lot, yet higher did her mind ascend.

11

Her whyles Sir *Calidore* there vewed well,
And markt her rare demeanure, which him seemed
So farre die meane° of shepheards to excell, *demeanor, bearing*
As that he in his mind her worthy deemed,
To be a Princes Paragone° esteemed, *a prince's equal*
He was unwares surprisd in subtile bands
Of the blynd boy,° ne thence could be redeemed *Cupid*
By any skill out of his cruell hands,
Caught like the bird, which gazing still on others stands.[5]

12

So stood he still long gazing thereupon,
Ne any will had thence to move away,
Although his quest were farre afore him gon;
But after he had fed, yet did he stay,
And sate there still, untill the flying day
Was farre forth spent, discoursing diversly
Of sundry things, as fell° to worke delay; *befell*
And evermore his speach he did apply
To th'heards, but meant them to the damzels fantazy.

13

By this the moystie night approching fast,
Her deawy humour gan on th'earth to shed,
That warn'd the shepheards to their homes to hast
Their tender flocks, now being fully fed,
For feare of wetting them before their bed;
Then came to them a good old aged syre,
Whose silver lockes bedeckt his beard and hed,
With shepheards hooke in hand, and fit attyre,
That wild the damzell rise; the day did now expyre.

14

He was to weet by common voice esteemed
The father of the fayrest *Pastorell*,

4. A conventional shepherd name in the pastoral tradition.

5. Maclean suggests the lark caught in a net while staring in fascination at the hawk held by the fowler.

And of her selfe in very deede so deemed;
Yet was not so, but as old stories tell
Found her by fortune, which to him befell,
In th'open fields an Infant left alone,
And taking up brought home, and noursed well
As his owne chyld; for other he had none,
That she in tract of time accompted° was his owne. *accounted, considered*

15

She at his bidding meekely did arise,
And streight unto her litle flocke did fare:
Then all the rest about her rose likewise,
And each his sundrie sheepe with severall° care *separate*
Gathered together, and them homeward bare:
Whylest everie one with helping hands did strive
Amongst themselves, and did their labours share,
To helpe faire *Pastorella*, home to drive
Her fleecie flocke; but *Coridon* most helpe did give.

16

But *Melibœe*[6] (so hight that good old man)
Now seeing *Calidore* left all alone,
And night arrived hard at hand, began
Him to invite unto his simple home;
Which though it were a cottage clad with lome,
And all things therein meane, yet better so
To lodge, then in the salvage fields to rome.
The knight full gladly soone agreed thereto,
Being his harts owne wish, and home with him did go.

17

There he was welcom'd of that honest syre,
And of his aged Beldame° homely well; *wife*
Who him besought himselfe to disattyre,
And rest himselfe, till supper time befell.
By which home came the fayrest *Pastorell*,
After her flocke she in their fold had tyde,
And supper readie dight, they to it fell
With small adoe, and nature satisfyde,
The which doth litle crave contented to abyde.

18

Tho when they had their hunger slaked well,
And the fayre mayd the table ta'ne away,

6. Greek: "honey-toned." This is a conventional pastoral name.

The gentle knight, as he that did excell
In courtesie, and well could doe and say,
For so great kindnesse as he found that day,
Gan greatly thanke his host and his good wife;
And drawing thence his speach another way,
Gan highly to commend the happie life,
Which Shepheards lead, without debate or bitter strife.

19

How much (sayd he) more happie is the state,[7]
In which ye father here doe dwell at ease,
Leading a life so free and fortunate,
From all the tempests of these worldly seas,
Which tosse the rest in daungerous disease?
Where warres, and wreckes, and wicked enmitie
Doe them afflict, which no man can appease,
That certes I your happinesse envie,
And wish my lot were plast in such felicitie.

20

Surely my sonne (then answer'd he againe)
If happie, then it is in this intent,
That having small, yet doe I not complaine
Of want, ne wish for more it to augment,
But doe my selfe, with that I have, content;
So taught of nature, which doth litle need
Of forreine helpes to lifes due nourishment:
The fields my food, my flocke my rayment breed;
No better doe I weare, no better doe I feed.

21

Therefore I doe not any one envy,
Nor am envyde of any one therefore;
They that have much, feare much to lose thereby,
And store of cares doth follow riches store.
The litle that I have, growes dayly more
Without my care, but onely to attend it;
My lambes doe every yeare increase their score,
And my flockes father daily doth amend it.
What have I, but to praise th'Almighty, that doth send it?

22

To them, that list, the worlds gay showes I leave,
And to great ones such follies doe forgive,° *give up*

7. The contrast of courtly and country life described in these stanzas is a convention of pastoral literature. Spenser is imitating specifically Tasso, *Gerusalemme liberata* 7.8–13.

Which oft through pride do their owne perill weave,
And through ambition downe themselves doe drive
To sad decay, that might contented live.
Me no such cares nor combrous thoughts offend,
Ne once my minds unmoved quiet grieve,
But all the night in silver sleepe I spend,
And all the day, to what I list, I doe attend.

23

Sometimes I hunt the Fox, the vowed foe
Unto my Lambes, and him dislodge away;
Sometime the fawne I practise° from the Doe, *scheme, devise strategems*
Or from the Goat her kidde how to convay;° *steal*
Another while I baytes and nets display,
The birds to catch, or fishes to beguyle:
And when I wearie am, I downe doe lay
My limbes in every shade, to rest from toyle,
And drinke of every brooke, when thirst my throte doth boyle.

24

The time was once, in my first prime of yeares,
When pride of youth forth pricked my desire,
That I disdain'd amongst mine equall peares
To follow sheepe, and shepheards base attire:
For further fortune then I would inquire.
And leaving home, to roiall court I sought;
Where I did sell my selfe for yearely hire,
And in the Princes gardin daily wrought:
There I beheld such vainenesse, as I never thought.

25

With sight whereof soone cloyd, and long deluded
With idle hopes, which them doe entertaine,
After I had ten yeares my selfe excluded
From native home, and spent my youth in vaine,
I gan my follies to my selfe to plaine,
And this sweet peace, whose lacke did then appeare.
Tho backe returning to my sheepe againe,
I from thenceforth have learn'd to love more deare
This lowly quiet life, which I inherite here.

26

Whylest thus he talkt, the knight with greedy eare
Hong still upon his melting mouth attent;° *attentive*
Whose sensefull words empierst his hart so neare,
That he was rapt with double ravishment,
Both of his speach that wrought him great content,

And also of the object of his vew,
On which his hungry eye was alwayes bent;
That twixt his pleasing tongue, and her faire hew,
He lost himselfe, and like one halfe entraunced grew.

27

Yet to occasion meanes, to worke his mind,
And to insinuate his harts desire,
He thus replyde; Now surely syre, I find,
That all this worlds gay showes, which we admire,
Be but vaine shadowes to this safe retyre° *retirement*
Of life, which here in lowlinesse ye lead,
Fearelesse of foes, or fortunes wrackfull yre,
Which tosseth states, and under foot doth tread
The mightie ones, affrayd of every chaunges dread.

28

That even I which daily doe behold
The glorie of the great, mongst whom I won,
And now have prov'd, what happinesse ye hold
In this small plot of your dominion,
Now loath great Lordship and ambition;
And wish th'heavens so much had graced mee,
As graunt me live in like condition;
Or that my fortunes might transposed bee
From pitch° of higher place, unto this low degree. *height*

29

In vaine (said then old *Melibœ*) doe men[8]
The heavens of their fortunes fault accuse,
Sith they know best, what is the best for them:
For they to each such fortune doe diffuse,° *disperse*
As they doe know each can most aptly use.
For not that, which men covet most, is best,
Nor that thing worst, which men do most refuse;
But fittest is, that all contented rest
With that they hold: each hath his fortune in his brest.

30

It is the mynd, that maketh good or ill,
That maketh wretch or happie, rich or poore:
For some, that hath abundance at his will,
Hath not enough, but wants in greatest store;

8. Meliboe's advice is the traditional Christian precept about earthly fortune: one must use what God has given us and not look for more. Man's content of mind rests in his acceptance of this principle, which was defined crucially for the Middle Ages and Renaissance by St. Augustine in his distinction between the use and *enjoyment* of the goods of this world.

And other, that hath litle, askes no more,
But in that litle is both rich and wise.
For wisedome is most riches; fooles therefore
They are, which fortunes doe by vowes devize,
Sith each unto himselfe his life may fortunize.° *make fortunate*

31

Since then in each mans self (said *Calidore*)
It is, to fashion his owne lyfes estate,
Give leave awhyle, good father, in this shore
To rest my barcke[9] which hath bene beaten late
With stormes of fortune and tempestuous fate,
In seas of troubles and of toylesome paine,
That whether quite from them for to retrate
I shall resolve, or backe to turne againe,
I may here with your selfe some small repose obtaine.

32

Not that the burden of so bold a guest
Shall chargefull° be, or chaunge[1] to you at all; *burdensome*
For your meane food shall be my daily feast,
And this your cabin both my bowre and hall.
Besides for recompence hereof, I shall[2]
You well reward, and golden guerdon give,
That may perhaps you better much withall,
And in this quiet make you safer live.
So forth he drew much gold, and toward him it drive.° *thrust*

33

But the good man, nought tempted with the offer
Of his rich mould,° did thrust it farre away, *dross*
And thus bespake; Sir knight, your bounteous proffer
Be farre fro me, to whom ye ill display
That mucky masse, the cause of mens decay,
That mote empaire my peace with daungers dread.
But if ye algates covet to assay
This simple sort of life, that shepheards lead,
Be it your owne: our rudenesse° to your selfe aread. *rusticity and simplicity*

34

So there that night Sir *Calidore* did dwell,
And long while after, whilest him list remaine,
Dayly beholding the faire *Pastorell*,

9. Boat, i.e., myself. The image of man as a storm-besieged boat was common in classical and later literature and especially favored by Augustine and Boethius.

1. I.e., change in your mode of life.

2. Calidore's offer of money to Meliboe shows that he has not understood the "courtesy" of the pastoral world in which he now finds himself.

And feeding on the bayt of his owne bane.° *destruction*
During which time he did her entertaine
With all kind courtesies, he could invent;
And every day, her companie to gaine,
When to the field she went, he with her went:
So for to quench his fire, he did it more augment.

35

But she that never had acquainted beene
With such queint usage, fit for Queenes and Kings,[3]
Ne ever had such knightly service seene,
But being bred under base shepheards wings,
Had ever learn'd to love the lowly things,
Did litle whit regard his courteous guize,
But cared more for *Colins*[4] carolings
Then all that he could doe, or ever devize:
His layes, his loves, his lookes she did them all despize.

36

Which *Calidore* perceiving, thought it best
To chaunge the manner of his loftie looke;
And doffing his bright armes, himselfe addrest
In shepheards weed, and in his hand he tooke,
In stead of steelehead speare, a shepheards hooke,
That who had seene him then, would have bethought
On *Phrygian Paris* by *Plexippus* brooke,
When he the love of fayre *Oenone* sought,
What time the golden apple was unto him brought.[5]

37

So being clad, unto the fields he went
With the faire *Pastorella* every day,
And kept her sheepe with diligent attent,
Watching to drive the ravenous Wolfe away,
The whylest at pleasure she mote sport and play;
And every evening helping them to fold:
And otherwhiles for need, he did assay
In his strong hand their rugged teats to hold,
And out of them to presse the milke: love so much could.

3. Cf. Chaucer, "The Knight's Tale."

4. Colin Clout, Spenser's pseudonym throughout his work. Cf. *Shepheardes Calender*, *Colin Clouts Come Home Again* and VI10. The name was used earlier by John Skelton, *Colin Clout* (1523?) and Clement Marot, *Complaincte de ma Dame Loyse de Savoye* (1531).

5. The Phrygian Paris is Paris, son of Priam of Troy, who precipitated the destruction of Troy by his error in choosing Venus as the recipient of the golden apple of discord. Paris abandoned Oenone to accept Helen, the wife of Menelaus. No brook Plexippus (Greek: "driver of horses") has been identified in ancient or later literature.

38

Which seeing *Coridon*, who her likewise
Long time had lov'd, and hop'd her love to gaine,
He much was troubled at that straungers guize,
And many gealous thoughts conceiv'd in vaine,
That this of all his labour and long paine
Should reap the harvest, ere it ripened were,
That made him scoule, and pout, and oft complaine
Of *Pastorell* to all the shepheards there,
That she did love a stranger swayne then him more dere.

39

And ever when he came in companie,
Where *Calidore* was present, he would lovre,
And byte his lip, and even for gealousie
Was readie oft his owne hart to devoure,
Impatient of any paramoure:
Who on the other side did seeme so farre
From malicing, or grudging his good houre,[6]
That all he could, he graced him with her,
Ne ever shewed signe of rancour or of jarre.° *contention*

40

And oft, when *Coridon* unto her brought
Or litle sparrowes, stolen from their nest,
Or wanton squirrels, in the woods farre sought,
Or other daintie thing for her addrest,
He would commend his guift, and make the best.
Yet she no whit his presents did regard,
Ne him could find to fancie in her brest:
This newcome shepheard had his market mard.
Old love is litle worth when new is more prefard.

41

One day when as the shepheard swaynes together
Were met, to make their sports and merrie glee,
As they are wont in faire sunshynie weather,
The whiles their flockes in shadowes shrouded bee,
They fell to daunce: then did they all agree,
That *Colin Clout* should pipe as one most fit;
And *Calidore* should lead the ring, as hee
That most in *Pastorellaes* grace did sit.
Thereat frown'd *Coridon*, and his lip closely bit.

6. I.e., fortune.

42

But *Calidore* of courteous inclination
Tooke *Coridon*, and set him in his place,
That he should lead the daunce, as was his fashion;
For *Coridon* could daunce, and trimly trace.° *dance gracefully*
And when as *Pastorella*, him to grace,
Her flowry garlond tooke from her owne head,
And plast on his, he did it soone displace,
And did it put on *Coridons* in stead:
Then *Coridon* woxe frollicke, that earst seemed dead.

43

Another time, when as they did dispose
To practise games, and majsteries to try,
They for their judge did *Pastorella* chose;
A garland was the meed of victory.
There *Coridon* forth stepping openly,
Did chalenge *Calidore* to wrestling game:
For he through long and perfect industry,
Therein well practisd was, and in the same
Thought sure t'avenge his grudge, & worke his foe great shame.

44

But *Calidore* he greatly did mistake;
For he was strong and mightily stifle pight,° *sturdily built*
That with one fall his necke he almost brake,
And had he not upon him fallen light,
His dearest joynt he sure had broken quight.
Then was the oaken crowne by *Pastorell*
Given to *Calidore*, as his due right;
But he, that did in courtesie excell,
Gave it to *Coridon*, and said he wonne it well.

45

Thus did the gentle knight himselfe abeare
Amongst that rusticke rout in all his deeds,
That even they, the which his rivals were,
Could not maligne him, but commend him needs:
For courtesie amongst the rudest breeds
Good will and favour. So it surely wrought
With this faire Mayd, and in her mynde the seeds
Of perfect love did sow, that last forth brought
The fruite of joy and blisse, though long time dearely bought.

46

Thus *Calidore* continu'd there long time,
To winne the love of the faire *Pastorell*;

Which having got, he used without crime
Or blamefull blot, but menaged so well,
That he of all the rest, which there did dwell,
Was favoured, and to her grace commended.
But what straunge fortunes unto him befell,
Ere he attain'd the point by him intended,
Shall more conveniently in other place be ended.

Canto X

Calidore sees the Graces daunce,
To Colins melody:
The whiles his Pastorell is led,
Into captivity.

1

Who now does follow the foule *Blatant Beast*,
Whilest *Calidore* does follow that faire Mayd,
Unmyndfull of his vow and high beheast,[1]
Which by the Faery Queene was on him layd,
That he should never leave, nor be delayd
From chacing him, till he had it attchieved?
But now entrapt of love, which him betrayd,
He mindeth more, how he may be relieved
With grace from her, whose love his heart hath sore engrieved.

2

That from henceforth he meanes no more to sew° *pursue*
His former quest, so full of toile and paine;
Another quest, another game in vew
He hath, the guerdon of his love to gaine:
With whom he myndes for ever to remaine,
And set his rest amongst the rusticke sort,
Rather then hunt still after shadowes vaine
Of courtly favour, fed with light report,
Of every blaste, and sayling alwaies on the port.[2]

3

Ne certes mote he greatly blamed be,
From so high step to stoupe unto so low.

1. Spenser seems to be saying that Calidore's sojourn in the pastoral world recalls Odysseus's stay with Circe (*Odyssey* 10), Aeneas' with Dido (*Aeneid* 4), Ruggiero's with Alcina (Ariosto, *Orlando furioso* 6–8), and Rinaldo's with Armida (*Tasso, Gerusalemme liberata* 16); cf. Calypso (*Odyssey* 5). Calidore's predecessors were entrapped by lust and temporarily drawn into realms of sensual enjoyment and diverted from their quests. While Calidore puts aside for a time his promise to capture the Blatant Beast, he is not mired in a world of lust and spiritual torpor. Calidore's stay in the pastoral world may seem a "truancy," but one should keep in mind both the philosophy expressed in the discussion between Meliboe and Calidore in the preceding canto and Spenser's characteristic irony in beginning his cantos.

2. I.e., never resuming his quest.

For who had tasted once (as oft did he)
The happy peace, which there doth overflow,
And prov'd the perfect pleasures, which doe grow
Amongst poore hyndes, in hils, in woods, in dales,
Would never more delight in painted show
Of such false blisse, as there is set for stales,° *lures*
T'entrap unwary fooles in their eternall bales.

4

For what hath all that goodly glorious gaze
Like to one sight, which *Calidore* did vew?
The glaunce whereof their dimmed eies would daze,
That never more they should endure the shew
Of that sunne-shine, that makes them looke askew.
Ne ought in all that world of beauties rare,
(Save onely *Glorianaes* heavenly hew
To which what can compare?) can it compare;
The which as commeth now, by course[3] I will declare.

5

One day as he did raunge the fields abroad,
Whilest his faire *Pastorella* was elsewhere,
He chaunst to come, far from all peoples troad,° *tread, path*
Unto a place, whose pleasaunce did appere
To passe all others, on the earth which were:
For all that ever was by natures skill
Devized to worke delight, was gathered there,
And there by her were poured forth at fill,
As if this to adorne, she all the rest did pill.° *plunder, pillage*

6

It was an hill plaste in an open plaine,
That round about was bordered with a wood
Of matchlesse hight, that seem'd th'earth to disdaine,
In which all trees of honour stately stood,
And did all winter as in sommer bud,
Spredding pavilions for the birds to bowre,
Which in their lower braunches sung aloud;
And in their tops the soring hauke did towre,° *perch*
Sitting like King of fowles in majesty and powre.

7

And at the foote thereof, a gentle flud
His silver waves did softly tumble downe,

3. I.e., in the progress of the narrative.

Unmard with ragged mosse or filthy mud,
Ne mote wylde beastes, ne mote the ruder clowne
Thereto approch, ne filth mote therein drowne:° *drench*
But Nymphes and Faeries by the bancks did sit,
In the woods shade, which did the waters crowne,
Keeping all noysome° things away from it, *harmful*
And to the waters fall tuning their accents fit.

8

And on the top thereof a spacious plaine
Did spred it selfe, to serve to all delight,
Either to daunce, when they to daunce would faine,
Or else to course about their bases light;[4]
Ne ought there wanted, which for pleasure might
Desired be, or thence to banish bale:
So pleasauntly the hill with equall hight,
Did seeme to overlooke the lowly vale;
Therefore it rightly cleeped was mount *Acidale*.[5]

9

They say that *Venus*, when she did dispose
Her selfe to pleasaunce, used to resort
Unto this place, and therein to repose
And rest her selfe, as in a gladsome port,
Or with the Graces there to play and sport;
That even her owne Cytheron, though in it
She used most to keepe her royall court,
And in her soveraine Majesty to sit,
She in regard hereof refusde and thought unfit.

10

Unto this place when as the Elfin Knight
Approcht, him seemed that the merry sound
Of a shrill pipe he playing heard on hight,° *aloud*
And many feete fast thumping th'hollow ground,
That through the woods their Eccho did rebound.[6]
He nigher drew, to weete what mote it be;
There he a troupe of Ladies dauncing found
Full merrily, and making gladfull glee,
And in the midst a Shepheard piping he did see.

4. Play at game of prisoner's base.
5. Mount Acidale, *Acidalia* being an epithet for Venus (Greek: "without care"), is contrasted with Cytheron, the mountain where Venus showed herself in royal splendor. Spenser confused the name *Cytheron* with *Cythera* (see III.6.29). The distinction between Acidale and Cytheron-Cythera was probably meant to figure the distinction between Calidore's "truancy" in the pastoral world and his royally appointed task of catching the Blatant Beast.
6. Cf. refrain in *Epithalamion:* "That all the woods shall answer and theyr eccho ring," etc.

11

He durst not enter into th'open greene,
For dread of them unwares to be descryde,
For breaking of their daunce, if he were seene;
But in the covert of the wood did byde,
Beholding all, yet of them unespyde.
There he did see, that pleased much his sight,
That even he him selfe his eyes envyde,
An hundred naked maidens lilly white,
All raunged in a ring, and dauncing in delight.

12

All they without were raunged in a ring,
And daunced round; but in the midst of them
Three other Ladies did both daunce and sing,
The whilest the rest them round about did hemme,
And like a girlond did in compasse stemme:° *encircled*
And in the middest of those same three, was placed
Another Damzell, as a precious gemme,
Amidst a ring most richly well enchaced,
That with her goodly presence all the rest much graced.

13

Looke how the Crowne, which *Ariadne* wore[7] [8]
Upon her yvory forehead that same day,
That *Theseus* her unto his bridale bore,
When the bold *Centaures* made that bloudy fray
With the fierce *Lapithes*, which did them dismay;
Being now placed in the firmament,
Through the bright heaven doth her beams display,
And is unto the starres an ornament,
Which round about her move in order excellent.

14

Such was the beauty of this goodly band,
Whose sundry parts were here too long to tell:
But she that in the midst of them did stand,
Seem'd all the rest in beauty to excell,
Crownd with a rosie girlond, that right well
Did her beseeme. And ever, as the crew
About her daunst, sweet flowres, that far did smell,
And fragrant odours they uppon her threw;
But most of all, those three did her with gifts endew.

7. Spenser conflates two myths: (1) Ariadne, who helped Theseus escape the labyrinth of Minos, was deserted by Theseus, and received her wedding crown from Bacchus, who later transformed it into the constellation. (2) The battle between the Centaurs and the Lapiths took place at the marriage of Pirithous and Hippodamia.

8. Like; commonly used to introduce a simile: see Samuel Daniel, *Complaint of Rosamond*, 113, 582.

15

Those were the Graces, daughters of delight,[9]
Handmaides of *Venus*, which are wont to haunt
Uppon this hill, and daunce there day and night:
Those three to men all gifts of grace do graunt,
And all, that *Venus* in her selfe doth vaunt,
Is borrowed of them. But that faire one,
That in the midst was placed parauaunt,° *most prominently*
Was she to whom that shepheard pypt alone,
That made him pipe so merrily, as never none.

16

She was to weete that jolly Shepheards lasse,[1]
Which piped there unto that merry rout,
That jolly shepheard, which there piped, was
Poore *Colin Clout* (who knowes not *Colin Clout?*)
He pypt apace, whitest they him daunst about.
Pype jolly shepheard, pype thou now apace
Unto thy love, that made thee low to lout;
Thy love is present there with thee in place,
Thy love is there advaunst to be another Grace.

17

Much wondred *Calidore* at this straunge sight,
Whose like before his eye had never seene,
And standing long astonished in spright,
And rapt with pleasaunce, wist not what to weene;
Whether it were the traine of beauties Queene,
Or Nymphes, or Faeries, or enchaunted show,
With which his eyes mote have deluded beene.
Therefore resolving, what it was, to know,
Out of the wood he rose, and toward them did go.

18

But soone as he appeared to their vew,
They vanisht all away out of his sight,
And cleane were gone, which way he never knew;

9. See stanza 22.

1. The woman at the center of the 100 dancing maidens and the three Graces is Colin Clout's love. Some critics identify her as the Rosalind of the *Shepheardes Calender*, in which Spenser first identified himself as Colin Clout. Other critics identify her as Elizabeth I, an identification that Colin himself refutes by his apology to Elizabeth in stanza 28. These critics generally cite *Shepheardes Calender*, "Aprill", in which Elizabeth is advanced to be a fourth Grace. Still others identify her as Elizabeth Boyle, whom Spenser married in 1594 and for whom he wrote the *Amoretti* and *Epithalamion* (page 676). The difficulty of trying to specify one historical identification for this "lass" is resolved by referring to *Amoretti* 74, in which Spenser gives praise in one figure to the three Elizabeths who were important to him: his mother, his wife, and his Queen. The "lass" is love, wife, Queen, and source of inspiration.

All save the shepheard, who for fell despight[2]
Of that displeasure, broke his bag-pipe quight,
And made great mone for that unhappy turne.
But *Calidore*, though no lesse sory wight,
For that mishap, yet seeing him to mourne,
Drew neare, that he the truth of all by him mote learne.

19

And first him greeting, thus unto him spake,
Haile jolly shepheard, which thy joyous dayes
Here leadest in this goodly merry make,° *making*
Frequented of these gentle Nymphes alwayes,
Which to thee flocke, to heare thy lovely layes;
Tell me, what mote these dainty Damzels be,
Which here with thee doe make their pleasant playes?
Right happy thou, that mayst them freely see:
But why when I them saw, fled they away from me?

20

Not I so happy answerd then that swaine,[3]
As thou unhappy, which them thence didst chace,
Whom by no meanes thou canst recall againe,
For being gone, none can them bring in place,
But whom they of them selves list so to grace.
Right sory I, (saide then Sir *Calidore*,)
That my ill fortune did them hence displace.
But since things passed none may now restore,
Tell me, what were they all, whose lacke thee grieves so sore.

21

Tho gan that shepheard thus for to dilate;
Then wote thou shepheard, whatsoever thou bee,
That all those Ladies, which thou sawest late,
Are *Venus* Damzels, all within her fee,
But differing in honour and degree:
They all are Graces, which on her depend,
Besides a thousand more, which ready bee
Her to adorne, when so she forth doth wend:
But those three in the midst, doe chiefe on her attend.

2. Colin's breaking of his pipe is an allusion to his similar gesture in *Shepheardes Calender*, "Januarye." It may also be a suggestion that he is breaking off his poem before his grand scheme, outlined in the Letter to Ralegh, is finished.

3. Colin's explanation of the vision of the dance is the most self-conscious artistic act in Renaissance poetry. Critics have often noted that Prospero's speech "Our revels now are ended" (*Tempest* 4.1.148 ff) is in reality Shakespeare's farewell to the stage, but Spenser, under his mask of Colin Clout, not only cuts off his vision because of the intrusion of Calidore but also explains its meaning, relating the vision to the source of civilization, "Civility."

22

They are the daughters of sky-ruling Jove,[4]
By him begot of faire *Eurynome*,
The Oceans daughter, in this pleasant grove,
As he this way comming from feastfull glee,
Of *Thetis* wedding with *Æacidee*,
In sommers shade him selfe here rested weary.
The first of them hight mylde *Euphrosyne*,
Next faire *Aglaia*, last *Thalia* merry:
Sweete Goddesses all three which me in mirth do cherry.° *make cheerful*

23

These three on men all gracious gifts bestow,
Which decke the body or adorne the mynde,
To make them lovely or well favoured show,
As comely carriage, entertainement kynde,
Sweete semblaunt, friendly offices that bynde,
And all the complements of curtesie:
They teach us, how to each degree and kynde
We should our selves demeane, to low, to hie;
To friends, to foes, which skill men call Civility.[5]

24

Therefore they alwaies smoothly seeme to smile,
That we likewise should mylde and gentle be,
And also naked are, that without guile
Or false dissemblaunce all them plaine may see,
Simple and true from covert malice free:
And eeke them selves so in their daunce they bore,
That two of them still forward seem'd to bee,
But one still towards shew'd her selfe afore;° *frontally*
That good should from us goe, then come in greater store.[6]

4. Spenser follows Hesiod, *Theogony*, in making Jove and Eurynome (Greek: "wide rule") parents of the Graces. Spenser is responsible for making the occasion of this mating the return of Jove from the marriage of Thetis and Peleus (*Æacidee*), thus combining the conception of the Graces with the occasion that precipitated the Trojan War.

5. Social order, and the kind of behavior that perpetuates social order.

6. The problem of these lines is whether two Graces are facing toward or away from the viewer; this apparently simple problem, however, lies at the heart of Spenser's courtesy and any possible interpretation of the poem, because of the iconographic traditions of depicting the Graces. The pertinent critics are DeWitt T. Starnes and E. W. Talbert, *Classical Myth and Legend in Renaissance Dictionaries* (Chapel Hill, 1955) and Starnes's two earlier articles, *PQ* 21, 1942, 268–82 and *SP* 39, 1942, 143–59; Edgar Wind, *Pagan Mysteries in the Renaissance*, second edition (Harmondsworth, 1967), pp. 28 ff; Tonkin, *Spenser's Courteous Pastoral*, pp. 248 ff. Seneca, *De beneficiis*, 1.3, states that the circling dance of the Graces symbolizes the three phases of liberality: offering, accepting, and returning benefits. Servius, in his commentary on *Aen.* 1.720, says that one Grace is pictured from the back while two are shown facing front because for one benefit issuing from us two are supposed to return. E. K. in his gloss on *Shepheardes Calender*, "Aprill" 109 ff, reproduces much of the Senecan and Servian iconography:

> The Graces be three sisters, the daughters of Jupiter, (whose names are Aglaia, Thalia, Euphrosyne, and Homer onely addeth a fourth, s. Pasithea) otherwise called Charites, that is thanks, whom the Poetes feyned to be the Goddesses of al bountie and comelines, which therefore (as sayth Theodontius) they make three, to wete, that men first ought to be gracious and bountiful to other freely, then to receiue

25

Such were those Goddesses, which ye did see;
But that fourth Mayd, which there amidst them traced,° *danced*
Who can aread, what creature mote she bee,
Whether a creature, or a goddesse graced
With heavenly gifts from heven first enraced?° *implanted*
But what so sure she was, she worthy was,
To be the fourth with those three other placed:
Yet was she certes but a countrey lasse,
Yet she all other countrey lasses farre did passe.

26

So farre as doth the daughter of the day,
All other lesser lights in light excell,
So farre doth she in beautyfull array,
Above all other lasses beare the bell,° *win the prize, lead the crowd*
Ne lesse in vertue that beseemes her well,
Doth she exceede the rest of all her race,
For which the Graces that here wont to dwell,
Have for more honor brought her to this place,
And graced her so much to be another Grace.

27

Another Grace she well deserves to be,
In whom so many Graces gathered are,
Excelling much the meane° of her degree; *norm, median*
Divine resemblaunce, beauty soveraine rare,
Firme Chastity, that spight ne blemish dare;
All which she with such courtesie doth grace,
That all her peres cannot with her compare,
But quite are dimmed, when she is in place.
She made me often pipe and now to pipe apace.

---

benefits at other mens hands curteously, and thirdly to requite them thankfully: which are three sundry Actions in liberalitye. [Seneca] And Boccace saith, that they be painted naked, (as they were indeede on the tombe of C. Julius Cæsar) the one hauing her backe toward vs, and her face fromwarde, as proceeding from vs: the other two toward vs, noting double thanke to be due to vs for the benefit, we have done [Servius].

In addition to this late classical iconography, which continued into the Renaissance as E. K.'s gloss shows, there was another specifically Christian tradition, which allegorized the Graces as the three theological virtues: faith, hope, and charity, because of the etymology of their Greek name *Charites*. This etymological allegory is reinforced in English by the coincidence of the name *Graces* and the theological meaning of the word *grace*, which produced another visual image of two Graces pictured from the back and one facing forward. Since faith and hope are virtues related to the afterlife, they are pictured facing away from the viewer; charity as a virtue directed to action in this life is pictured as facing toward the viewer. This double iconographic tradition is the basis for interpreting Spenser's lines. Most editors emend "forward" as printed in 1596 and 1609 to "froward" to conform with the late classical iconography. But Spenser always uses "froward" in its negative sense of "evilly disposed, perverse, adverse." Line 8, in which the third Grace is described as "afore" (viewed frontally), is another reason given for emendation. If, however, one interprets the "forward" of line 7 as meaning that two Graces are nearer the viewer without specifying that they are dorsally or frontally displayed, this difficulty is solved. Spenser is trying to accommodate both iconographic traditions verbally; his language insists that we read the lines both ways; he is being genuinely ambiguous. The "then" of line 9 can be read in both ways: either as the late classical view that good should from us go, then come in greater store, or in the spirit of Christian charity: greater good should from us go *than* come in greater store.

28

Sunne of the world, great glory of the sky,
That all the earth doest lighten with thy rayes,
Great *Gloriana*, greatest Majesty,
Pardon thy shepheard, mongst so many layes,
As he hath sung of thee in all his dayes,
To make one minime° of thy poore handmayd, *short musical note*
And underneath thy feete to place her prayse,
That when thy glory shall be farre displayd
To future age of her this mention may be made.

29

When thus that shepherd ended had his speach,
Sayd *Calidore;* Now sure it yrketh mee,
That to thy blisse I made this luckelesse breach,
As now the author of thy bale to be,
Thus to bereave thy loves deare sight from thee:
But gentle Shepheard pardon thou my shame,
Who rashly sought that, which I mote not see.
Thus did the courteous Knight excuse his blame,
And to recomfort him, all comely meanes did frame.

30

In such discourses they together spent
Long time, as fit occasion forth them led;
With which the Knight him selfe did much content,
And with delight his greedy fancy fed,
Both of his words, which he with reason red;
And also of the place, whose pleasures rare
With such regard° his sences ravished, *observation*
That thence, he had no will away to fare,
But wisht, that with that shepheard he mote dwelling share.

31

But that envenimd sting,[7] the which of yore,
His poysnous point deepe fixed in his hart
Had left, now gan afresh to rancle sore,
And to renue the rigour of his smart:
Which to recure, no skill of Leaches° art *doctor's*
Mote him availe, but to returne againe
To his wounds worker, that with lovely dart
Dinting° his brest, had bred his restlesse paine, *striking*
Like as the wounded Whale to shore flies from the maine.° *deep sea*

7. I.e., the wound of Cupid's arrow (VI.9.11).

32

So taking leave of that same gentle swaine,
He backe returned to his rusticke wonne,
Where his faire *Pastorella* did remaine:
To whome in sort, as he at first begonne,
He daily did apply him selfe to donne,
All dewfull service voide of thoughts impure
Ne any paines ne perill did he shonne,
By which he might her to his love allure,
And liking in her yet untamed heart procure.

33

And evermore the shepheard *Coridon*,
What ever thing he did her to aggrate,° *please*
Did strive to match with strong contention,
And all his paines did closely emulate;
Whether it were to caroll, as they sate
Keeping their sheepe, or games to exercize,
Or to present her with their labours late;
Through which if any grace chaunst to arize
To him, the Shepheard streight with jealousie did frize.

34

One day as they all three together went
To the greene wood, to gather strawberies,
There chaunst to them a dangerous accident;
A Tigre forth out of the wood did rise,
That with fell clawes full of fierce gourmandize,° *gluttony*
And greedy mouth, wide gaping like hell gate,
Did runne at *Pastorell* her to surprize:
Whom she beholding, now all desolate
Gan cry to them aloud, to helpe her all too late.

35

Which *Coridon* first hearing, ran in hast
To reskue her, but when he saw the feend,
Through cowherd feare he fled away as fast,
Ne durst abide the daunger of the end;
His life he steemed° dearer then his frend. *esteemed, valued*
But *Calidore* soone comming to her ayde,
When he the beast saw ready now to rend
His loves deare spoile, in which his heart was prayde,° *captured as booty*
He ran at him enraged in stead of being frayde.

36

He had no weapon, but his shepheards hooke,
To serve the vengeaunce of his wrathfull will,

With which so sternely he the monster stroke,
That to the ground astonished he fell;
Whence ere he could recov'r, he did him quell,
And hewing off his head, it presented
Before the feete of the faire *Pastorell;*
Who scarcely yet from former feare exempted,
A thousand times him thankt, that had her death prevented.

37

From that day forth she gan him to affect,° *have a preference for*
And daily more her favour to augment;
But *Coridon* for cowherdize reject,
Fit to keepe sheepe, unfit for loves content:
The gentle heart scornes base disparagement.
Yet *Calidore* did not despise him quight,
But usde him friendly for further intent,
That by his fellowship, he colour° might *disguise*
Both his estate, and love from skill° of any wight. *knowledge*

38

So well he woo'd her, and so well he wrought her,
With humble service, and with daily sute,
That at the last unto his will he brought her;
Which he so wisely well did prosecute,
That of his love he reapt the timely finite,
And joyed long in close felicity:
Till fortune fraught with malice, blinde, and brute,
That envies lovers long prosperity,
Blew up a bitter storme of foule adversity.

39

It fortuned one day, when *Calidore*[8]
Was hunting in the woods (as was his trade)
A lawlesse people, *Brigants* hight of yore,
That never usde to live by plough nor spade,
But fed on spoile and booty, which they made
Upon their neighbours, which did nigh them border,
The dwelling of these shepheards did invade,
And spoyld their houses, and them selves did murder;
And drove away their flocks, with other much disorder.

40

Amongst the rest, the which they then did pray,
They spoyld old *Melibee* of all he had,
And all his people captive led away,

8. See VI.8.35.

Mongst which this lucklesse mayd away was lad,
Faire *Pastorella*, sorrowfull and sad,
Most sorrowfull, most sad, that ever sight,
Now made the spoile of theeves and *Brigants* bad,
Which was the conquest of the gentlest Knight,
That ever liv'd, and th'onely glory of his might.

41

With them also was taken *Coridon*,
And carried captive by those theeves away;
Who in the covert of the night, that none
Mote them descry, nor reskue from their pray,
Unto their dwelling did them close convay.
Their dwelling in a little Island was,
Covered with shrubby woods, in which no way
Appeard for people in nor out to pas,
Nor any footing fynde for overgrowen gras.

42

For underneath the ground their way was made,
Through hollow caves, that no man mote discover
For the thicke shrubs, which did them alwaies shade
From view of living wight, and covered over:
But darkenesse dred and daily night did hover
Through all the inner parts, wherein they dwelt.
Ne lightned was with window, nor with louer,[9]
But with continuall candlelight, which delt
A doubtfull sense of things, not so well seene, as felt.

43

Hither those *Brigants* brought their present pray,
And kept them with continuall watch and ward,° *guard*
Meaning so soone, as they convenient may,
For slaves to sell them, for no small reward,
To merchants, which them kept in bondage hard,
Or sold againe. Now when faire *Pastorell*
Into this place was brought, and kept with gard
Of griesly theeves, she thought her self in hell,
Where with such damned fiends she should in darknesse dwell.

44

But for to tell the dolefull dreriment,
And pittifull complaints, which there she made,
Where day and night she nought did but lament

9. Louvre, an opening in the roof.

Her wretched life, shut up in deadly shade,
And waste her goodly beauty, which did fade
Like to a flowre, that feeles no heate of sunne,
Which may her feeble leaves with comfort glade.° *make cheerful or glad*
But what befell her in that theevish wonne,
Will in an other Canto better be begonne.

Canto XI

The theeves fall out for Pastorell,
Whilest Melibee is slaine:
Her Calidore from them redeemes,
And bringeth backe againe.

1

The joyes of love, if they should ever last,
Without affliction or disquietnesse,
That worldly chaunces doe amongst them cast,
Would be on earth too great a blessednesse,
Liker to heaven, then mortall wretchednesse.
Therefore the winged God, to let men weet,
That here on earth is no sure happinesse,
A thousand sowres hath tempred with one sweet,
To make it seeme more deare and dainty, as is meet.

2

Like as is now befalne to this faire Mayd,
Faire *Pastorell*, of whom is now my song,
Who being now in dreadfull darknesse layd,
Amongst those theeves, which her in bondage strong
Detaynd, yet Fortune not with all this wrong
Contented, greater mischiefe on her threw,
And sorrowes heapt on her in greater throng;
That who so heares her heavinesse, would rew[1]
And pitty her sad plight, so chang'd from pleasaunt hew.

3

Whylest thus she in these hellish dens remayned,
Wrapped in wretched cares and hearts unrest,
It so befell (as Fortune had ordayned)
That he, which was their Capitaine profest,
And had the chiefe commaund of all the rest,
One day as he did all his prisoners vew,
With lustfull eyes, beheld that lovely guest,
Faire *Pastorella*, whose sad mournefull hew
Like the faire Morning clad in misty fog did shew.

1. Spenser bases this episode on the story of Isabel in *Orlando furioso* 12.91 ff.

4

At sight whereof his barbarous heart was fired,
And inly burnt with flames most raging whot,
That her alone he for his part desired
Of all the other pray, which they had got,
And her in mynde did to him selfe allot.
From that day forth he kyndnesse to her showed,
And sought her love, by all the meanes he mote;
With looks, with words, with gifts he oft her wowed:° *wooed*
And mixed threats among, and much unto her vowed.

5

But all that ever he could doe or say,
Her constant mynd could not a whit remove,
Nor draw unto the lure of his lewd lay,° *song*
To graunt him favour, or afford him love.
Yet ceast he not to sew and all waies prove,
By which he mote accomplish his request,
Saying and doing all that mote behove;
Ne day nor night he suffred her to rest,
But her all night did watch, and all the day molest.

6

At last when him she so importune saw,
Fearing least he at length the raines would lend
Unto his lust, and make his will[2] his law,
Sith in his powre she was to foe or frend,[3]
She thought it best, for shadow° to pretend *pretense*
Some shew of favour, by him gracing small,
That she thereby mote either freely wend,
Or at more ease continue there his thrall:
A little well is lent, that gaineth more withall.

7

So from thenceforth, when love he to her made,
With better tearmes she did him entertaine,
Which gave him hope, and did him halfe perswade,
That he in time her joyaunce should obtaine.
But when she saw, through that small favours gaine,
That further, then she willing was, he prest,
She found no meanes to barre him, but to faine
A sodaine sickenesse, which her sore opprest,
And made unfit to serve his lawlesse mindes behest.

2. Passion, particularly sexual passion. See Shakespeare, *Sonnets* 135 and 136.

3. I.e., she was to be either foe or friend.

8

By meanes whereof she would not him permit
Once to approch to her in privity,
But onely mongst the rest by her to sit,
Mourning the rigour of her malady,
And seeking all things meete for remedy.
But she resolv'd no remedy to fynde,
Nor better cheare to shew in misery,
Till Fortune would her captive bonds unbynde,
Her sickenesse was not of the body but the mynde.

9

During which space that she thus sicke did lie,
It chaunst a sort° of merchants, which were wount — *group*
To skim those coastes, for bondmen° there to buy, — *slaves*
And by such trafficke after gaines to hunt,
Arrived in this Isle though bare and blunt,
T'inquire for slaves; where being readie met
By some of these same theeves at the instant brunt,° — *suddenly*
Were brought unto their Captaine, who was set
By his faire patients side with sorrowfull regret.

10

To whom they shewed, how those marchants were
Arriv'd in place, their bondslaves for to buy,
And therefore prayd, that those same captives there
Mote to them for their most commodity° — *profit*
Be sold, and mongst them shared equally.
This their request the Captaine much appalled;
Yet could he not their just demaund deny,
And willed streight the slaves should forth be called,
And sold for most advantage not to be forstalled.

11

Then forth the good old *Melibœ* was brought,
And *Coridon*, with many other moe,
Whom they before in diverse spoyles had caught:
All which he to the marchants sale did showe.
Till some, which did the sundry prisoners knowe,
Gan to inquire for that faire shepherdesse,
Which with the rest they tooke not long agoe,
And gan her forme and feature to expresse,
The more t'augment her price, through praise of comlinesse.

12

To whom the Captaine in full angry wize
Made answere, that the Mayd of whom they spake,

Was his owne purchase and his onely prize,
With which none had to doe, ne ought partake,
But he himselfe, which did that conquest make;
Litle for him to have one silly° lasse: *weak, helpless*
Besides through sicknesse now so wan and weake,
That nothing meet in marchandise to passe.
So shew'd them her, to prove how pale & weake she was.

13

The sight of whom, though now decayd and mard,
And eke hut hardly seene by candle-light,
Yet like a Diamond of rich regard,° *appearance*
In doubtfull shadow of the darkesome night,
With starrie beames about her shining bright,
These marchants fixed eyes did so amaze,
That what through wonder, & what through delight,
A while on her they greedily did gaze,
And did her greatly like, and did her greatly praize.

14

At last when all the rest them offred were,
And prises to them placed at their pleasure,
They all refused in regard of her,
Ne ought would buy, how ever prisd with measure,
Withouten her, whose worth above all threasure
They did esteeme, and offred store of gold.
But then the Captaine fraught with more displeasure,
Bad them be still, his love should not be sold:
The rest take if they would, he her to him would hold.

15

Therewith some other of the chiefest theeves
Boldly him bad such injurie forbeare;
For that same mayd, how ever it him greeves,
Should with the rest be sold before him theare,
To make the prises of the rest more deare.
That with great rage he stoutly doth denay;
And fiercely drawing forth his blade, doth sweare,
That who so hardie hand on her doth lay,
It dearely shall aby,° and death for handsell° pay. *pay / reward*

16

Thus as they words amongst them multiply,
They fall to strokes, the frute of too much talke,
And the mad steele about doth fiercely fly,

Not sparing wight, ne leaving any balke,[4]
But making way for death at large to walke:
Who in the horror of the griesly night,
In thousand dreadful shapes doth mongst them stalke,
And makes huge havocke, whiles the candlelight
Out quenched, leaves no skill nor difference of wight.[5]

17

Like as a sort° of hungry dogs ymet *group*
About some carcase by the common way,
Doe fall together, stryving each to get
The greatest portion of the greedie pray;
All on confused heapes themselves assay,
And snatch, and byte, and rend, and tug, and teare;
That who them sees, would wonder at their fray,
And who sees not, would be affrayd to heare.
Such was the conflict of those cruell *Brigants* there.

18

But first of all, their captives they doe kill,
Least they should joyne against the weaker side,
Or rise against the remnant at their will;
Old *Melibœ* is slain, and him beside
His aged wife, with many others wide,° *round about*
But *Coridon* escaping craftily,
Creepes forth of dores, whilst darknes him doth hide,
And flyes away as fast as he can hye,
Ne stayeth leave to take, before his friends doe dye.

19

But *Pastorella*, wofull wretched Elfe,
Was by the Captaine all this while defended,
Who minding more her safety then himselfe,
His target° alwayes over her pretended;[6] *shield*
By meanes whereof, that mote not be amended,
He at the length was slaine, and layd on ground,
Yet holding fast twixt both his armes extended
Fayre *Pastorell*, who with the selfe same wound [swound.
Launcht through the arme, fell down with him in drerie.

20

There lay she covered with confused preasse° *crowd*
Of carcases, which dying on her fell.

4. An unploughed ridge of land.
5. I.e., makes it impossible to distinguish between merchants and pirates.
6. Covered (Latin: *prætendere*).

Tho when as he was dead, the fray gan ceasse,
And each to other calling, did compell
To stay their cruell hands from slaughter fell,
Sith they that were the cause of all, were gone.
Thereto they all attonce agreed well,
And lighting candles new, gan search anone,
How many of their friends were slaine, how many fone.

21

Their Captaine there they cruelly found kild,
And in his armes the dreary dying mayd,
Like a sweet Angell twixt two clouds uphild:
Her lovely light was dimmed and decayd,
With cloud of death upon her eyes displayd;
Yet did the cloud make even that dimmed light
Seeme much more lovely in that darknesse layd,
And twixt the twinckling of her eye-lids bright,
To sparke out litle beames, like starres in foggie night.

22

But when they mov'd the carcases aside,
They found that life did yet in her remaine:
Then all their helpes they busily applyde,
To call the soule backe to her home againe;
And wrought so well with labour and long paine,
That they to life recovered her at last.
Who sighing sore, as if her hart in twaine
Had riven bene, and all her hart strings brast,
With drearie drouping eyne lookt up like one aghast.

23

There she beheld, that sore her griev'd to see,
Her father and her friends about her lying,
Her selfe sole left, a second spoyle to bee
Of those, that having saved her from dying,
Renew'd her death by timely death denying:
What now is left her, but to wayle and weepe,
Wringing her hands, and ruefully loud crying?
Ne cared she her wound in teares to steepe,° *bathe, wet*
Albe with all dieir might those *Brigants* her did keepe.

24

But when they saw her now reliv'd againe,
They left her so, in charge of one the best

Of many worst, who with unkind disdaine
And cruell rigour her did much molest;
Scarse yeelding her due food, or timely rest,
And scarsely suffring her infestred wound,
That sore her payn'd, by any to be drest.
So leave we her in wretched thraldome bound,
And turne we backe to *Calidore*, where we him found.

25

Who when he backe returned from the wood,
And saw his shepheards cottage spoyled quight,
And his love reft away, he wexed wood,
And halfe enraged at that ruefull sight,
That even his hart for very fell despight,
And his owne flesh he readie was to teare,
He chauft, he griev'd, he fretted, and he sight,
And fared like a furious wyld Beare,
Whose whelpes are stolne away, she being otherwhere.

26

Ne wight he found, to whom he might complaine,
Ne wight he found, of whom he might inquire;
That more increast the anguish of his paine.
He sought the woods; but no man could see there,
He sought the plaines; but could no tydings heare.
The woods did nought but ecchoes vaine rebound;[7]
The playnes all waste and emptie did appeare:
Where wont the shepheards oft their pypes resound,
And feed an hundred flocks, there now not one he found.

27

At last as there he romed up and downe,
He chaunst one comming towards him to spy,
That seem'd to be some sorie simple clowne,
With ragged weedes, and lockes upstaring hye,
As if he did from some late daunger fly,
And yet his feare did follow him behynd:
Who as he unto him approched nye,
He mote perceive by signes, which he did fynd,
That *Coridon* it was, the silly shepherds hynd.° *rustic*

7. Spenser again echoes the refrain from *Epithalamion* as he did in VI.10.10.5.

28

Tho to him running fast, he did not stay
To greet him first, but askt where were the rest;
Where *Pastorell?* who full of fresh dismay,
And gushing forth in teares, was so opprest,
That he no word could speake, but smit his brest,
And up to heaven his eyes fast streming threw.
Whereat the knight amaz'd, yet did not rest,
But askt againe, what ment that rufull hew:
Where was his *Pastorell*? where all the other crew?

29

Ah well away (sayd he then sighing sore)
That ever I did live, this day to see,
This dismall day, and was not dead before,
Before I saw faire *Pastorella* dye.
Die? out alas then *Calidore* did cry:
How could the death dare ever her to quell?
But read thou shepheard, read what destiny,
Or other dyrefull hap from heaven or hell
Hath wrought this wicked deed, doe feare° away, and tell. *expel fear*

30

Tho when the shepheard breathed had a whyle,
He thus began: where shall I then commence
This wofull tale? or how those *Brigants* vyle,
With cruell rage and dreadfull violence
Spoyld all our cots, and caried us from hence?
Or how faire *Pastorell* should have bene sold
To marchants, but was sav'd with strong defence?
Or how those theeves, whilest one sought her to hold,
Fell all at ods, and fought through fury fierce and bold.

31

In that same conflict (woe is me) befell
This fatall chaunce, this dolefull accident,
Whose heavy tydings now I have to tell.
First all the captives, which they here had hent,° *seized*
Were by them slaine by generall consent;
Old *Meliboe* and his good wife withall
These eyes saw die, and dearely did lament:
But when the lot to *Pastorell* did fall,
Their Captaine long withstood, & did her deam forstall.

32

But what could he gainst all them doe alone:
It could not boot; needs mote she die at last:
I onely scapt through great confusione
Of cryes and clamors, which amongst them past,
In dreadfull darknesse dreadfully aghast;
That better were with them to have bene dead,
Then here to see all desolate and wast,
Despoyled of those joyes and jolly head,
Which with those gentle shepherds here I wont to lead.

33

When *Calidore* these ruefull newes had raught,
His hart quite deaded was with anguish great,
And all his wits with doole were nigh distraught,
That he his face, his head, his brest did beat,
And death it selfe unto himselfe did threat;
Oft cursing th'heavens, that so cruell were
To her, whose name he often did repeat;
And wishing oft, that he were present there,
When she was slaine, or had bene to her succour nere.

34

But after griefe awhile had had his course,
And spent it selfe in mourning, he at last
Began to mitigate his swelling sourse,[8]
And in his mind with better reason cast,
How he might save her life, if life did last;
Or if that dead, how he her death might wreake,
Sith otherwise he could not mend thing past;
Or if it to revenge he were too weake,
Then for to die with her, and his lives threed[9] to breake.

35

Tho *Coridon* he prayd, sith he well knew
The readie way unto that theevish wonne,
To wend with him, and be his conduct trew
Unto the place, to see what should be donne.
But he, whose hart through feare was late fordonne,
Would not for ought be drawne to former drede,
But by all meanes the daunger knowne did shonne:
Yet *Calidore* so well him wrought with meed,[1]
And faire bespoke with words, that he at last agreed.

8. Fountain-head (i.e., he stopped crying).
9. The thread of life spun out by the Fates.
1. I.e., worked with promise of reward.

36

So forth they goe together (God before)
Both clad in shepheards weeds agreeably,
And both with shepheards hookes: But *Calidore*
Had underneath, him armed privily.
Tho to the place when they approched nye,
They chaunst, upon an hill not farre away,
Some flockes of sheepe and shepheards to espy;
To whom they both agreed to take their way,
In hope there newes to learne, how they mote best assay.

37

There did they find, that which they did not feare,
The selfe same flocks, the which those theeves had reft
From *Melibœ* and from themselves whyleare,
And certaine of the theeves there by them left,
The which for want of heards themselves then kept.
Right well knew *Coridon* his owne late sheepe,
And seeing them, for tender pittie wept:
But when he saw the theeves, which did them keepe
His hart gan fayle, albe he saw them all asleepe.

38

But *Calidore* recomforting his griefe,
Though not his feare: for nought may feare disswade;
Him hardly forward drew, whereas the thiefe
Lay sleeping soundly in the bushes shade,
Whom *Coridon* him counseld to invade
Now all unwares, and take the spoyle away;
But he, that in his mind had closely made
A further purpose, would not so them slay,
But gently waking them, gave them the time of day.

39

Tho sitting downe by them upon the greene,
Of sundrie things he purpose gan to faine;[2]
That he by them might certaine tydings weene
Of *Pastorell*, were she alive or slaine.
Mongst which the theeves them questioned againe,
What mister men,° and eke from whence they were. *kind of men*
To whom they answer'd, as did appertaine,
That they were poore heardgroomes, the which whylere
Had from their maisters fled, & now sought hyre elswhere.

2. I.e., began to invent conversation.

40

Whereof right glad they seem'd, and offer made
To hyre them well, if they their flockes would keepe:
For they themselves were evill groomes, they sayd,
Unwont with heards to watch, or pasture sheepe,
But to forray the land, or scoure the deepe.
Thereto they soone agreed, and earnest tooke,[3]
To keepe their flockes for litle hyre and chepe:
For they for better hyre did shortly looke,
So there all day they bode, till light the sky forsooke.

41

Tho when as towards darksome night it drew,
Unto their hellish dens those theeves them brought,
Where shortly they in great acquaintance grew,
And all the secrets of their entrayles° sought. *minds*
There did they find, contrarie to their thought,
That *Postorell* yet liv'd, but all the rest
Were dead, right so as *Coridon* had taught:
Whereof they both full glad and blyth did rest,
But chiefly *Calidore*, whom griefe had most possest.

42

At length when they occasion fittest found,
In dead of night, when all the theeves did rest
After a late forray, and slept full sound,
Sir *Calidore* him arm'd, as he thought best,
Having of late by diligent inquest,
Provided him a sword of meanest sort:
With which he streight went to the Captaines nest.
But *Coridon* durst not with him consort,
Ne durst abide behind, for dread of worse effort.

43

When to the Cave they came, they found it fast:° *securely closed*
But *Calidore* with huge resistlesse might,
The dores assayled, and the locks upbrast.
With noyse whereof the theefe awaking light,
Unto the entrance ran: where the bold knight
Encountring him with small resistance slew;
The whiles faire *Pastorell* through great affright
Was almost dead, misdoubting least of new
Some uprore were like that, which lately she did vew.

3. I.e., received an initial payment for their services.

44

But when as *Calidore* was comen in,
And gan aloud for *Pastorell* to call,
Knowing his voice although not heard long sin,
She sudden was revived therewithall,
And wondrous joy felt in her spirits thrall:
Like him that being long in tempest tost,
Looking each houre into deathes mouth to fall,
At length espyes at hand the happie cost,
On which he safety hopes, that earst feard to be lost.

45

Her gentle hart, that now long season past
Had never joyance felt, nor chearefull thought,
Began some smacke of comfort new to tast,
Like lyfull heat to nummed senses brought,
And life to feele, that long for death had sought;
Ne lesse in hart rejoyced *Calidore*,
When he her found, but like to one distraught
And robd of reason, towards her him bore,
A thousand times embrast, and kist a thousand more.

46

But now by this, with noyse of late uprore,
The hue and cry was raysed all about;
And all the *Brigants* flocking in great store,
Unto the cave gan preasse, nought having dout
Of that was doen, and entred in a rout.
But *Calidore* in th'entry close did stand,
And entertayning them with courage stout,
Still slew the formost, that came first to hand,
So long till all the entry was with bodies mand.

47

Tho when no more could nigh to him approch,
He breath'd° his sword, and rested him till day: *rested*
Which when he spyde upon the earth t'encroch,
Through the dead carcases he made his way,
Mongst which he found a sword of better say,° *assay, temper*
With which he forth went into th'open light:
Where all the rest for him did readie stay,
And fierce assayling him, with all their might
Gan all upon him lay: there gan a dreadfull fight.

Canto XII

Fayre Pastorella by great hap
her parents understands,
Calidore doth the Blatant beast
subdew, and bynd in bands.

1

Like as a ship, that through the Ocean wyde
Directs her course unto one certaine cost,
Is met of many a counter winde and tyde,
With which her winged speed is let° and crost, *hindered*
And she her selfe in stormie surges tost;
Yet making many a borde, and many a bay,
Still winneth way, ne hath her compasse lost:
Right so it fares with me in this long way,
Whose course is often stayd, yet never is astray.

2

For all that hetherto hath long delayd
This gentle knight, from sewing his first quest,
Though out of course, yet hath not bene mis-sayd,
To shew the courtesie by him profest,
Even unto the lowest and the least.
But now I come into my course againe,
To his atchievement of the *Blatant beast;*
Who all this while at will did range and raine,
Whilst none was him to stop, nor none him to restraine.

3

Sir *Calidore* when thus he now had raught[1]
Faire *Pastorella* from those *Brigants* powre,
Unto the Castle of *Belgard*[2] her brought,
Whereof was Lord the good Sir *Bellamoure;*[3]
Who whylome was in his youthes freshest flowre
A lustie knight, as ever wielded speare,
And had endured many a dreadfull stoure
In bloudy battell for a Ladie deare,
The fayrest Ladie then of all that living were.

4

Her name was *Claribell,*[4] whose father hight
The Lord of *Many Ilands*, farre renound
For his great riches and his greater might.
He through the wealth, wherein he did abound,

1. The recognition of Pastorella by her parents through the agency of Melissa uses a common motif in romance: a lost child found.
2. French: "good protection" or "loving look."
3. French: "beautiful love."
4. French: "bright beauty."

This daughter thought in wedlocke to have bound
Unto the Prince of *Picteland*° bordering nere, *Scotland*
But she whose sides before with secret wound
Of love to *Bellamoure* empierced were,
By all meanes shund to match with any forrein fere.° *companion, mate*

5

And *Bellamour* againe so well her pleased,
With dayly service and attendance dew,
That of her love he was entyrely seized,
And closely did her wed, but knowne to few.
Which when her father understood, he grew
In so great rage, that them in dongeon deepe
Without compassion cruelly he threw;
Yet did so streightly them a sunder keepe,
That neither could to company of th'other creepe.

6

Nathlesse Sir *Bellamour*, whether through grace
Or secret guifts so with his keepers wrought,
That to his love sometimes he came in place,
Whereof her wombe unwist to wight was fraught,
And in dew time a mayden child forth brought.
Which she streight way for dread least, if her syre
Should know thereof, to slay he would have sought,
Delivered to her handmayd, that for hyre° *payment*
She should it cause be fostred under straunge attyre.

7

The trustie damzell bearing it abrode
Into the emptie fields, where living wight
Mote not bewray the secret of her lode,
She forth gan lay unto the open light
The litle babe, to take thereof a sight.
Whom whylest she did with watrie eyne behold,
Upon the litle brest like christall bright,
She mote perceive a litle purple mold,° *mole*
That like a rose her silken leaves did faire unfold.

8

Well she it markt, and pittied the more,
Yet could not remedie her wretched case,
But closing it againe like as before,
Bedeaw'd with teares there left it in the place:
Yet left not quite, but drew a litle space
Behind the bushes, where she her did hyde,
To weet what mortall hand, or heavens grace

Would for the wretched infants helpe provyde,
For which it loudly cald, and pittifully cryde.

9

At length a Shepheard, which there by did keepe
His fleecie flocke upon the playnes around,
Led with the infants cry, that loud did weepe,
Came to the place, where when he wrapped found
Th'abandond spoyle, he softly it unbound,
And seeing there, that did him pittie sore,
He tooke it up, and in his mantle wound;
So home unto his honest wife it bore,
Who as her owne it nurst, and named evermore.

10

Thus long continu'd *Claribell* a thrall,
And *Bellamour* in bands, till that her syre
Departed life, and left unto them all.
Then all the stormes of fortunes former yre
Were turnd, and they to freedome did retyre.
Thenceforth they joy'd in happinesse together,
And lived long in peace and love entyre,
Without disquiet or dislike of ether,
Till time that *Calidore* brought *Pastorella* thether.

11

Both whom they goodly well did entertaine;
For *Bellamour* knew *Calidore* right well,
And loved for his prowesse, sith they twaine
Long since had fought in field. Als *Claribell*
No lesse did tender the faire *Pastorell*,
Seeing her weake and wan, through durance° long. *suffering*
There they a while together thus did dwell
In much delight, and many joyes among,
Untill the damzell gan to wex more sound and strong.

12

Tho gan Sir *Calidore* him to advize
Of his first quest, which he had long forlore,° *forsaken*
Asham'd to thinke, how he that enterprize,
The which the Faery Queene had long afore
Bequeath'd to him, forslacked had so sore;
That much he feared, least reprochfull blame
With foule dishonour him mote blot therefore;
Besides the losse of so much loos[5] and fame,
As through the world thereby should glorifie his name.

5. A variant spelling of "lose," fame, reputation.

13

Therefore resolving to returne in hast
Unto so great atchievement, he bethought
To leave his love, now perill being past,
With *Claribell*, whylest he that monster sought
Throughout the world, and to destruction brought.
So taking leave of his faire *Pastorell*,
Whom to recomfort, all the meanes he wrought,
With thanks to *Bellamour* and *Claribell*,
He went forth on his quest, and did, that him befell.

14

But first, ere I doe his adventures tell,
In this exploite, me needeth to declare,
What did betide to the faire *Pastorell*,
During his absence left in heavy care,
Through daily mourning, and nightly misfare:
Yet did that auncient matrone all she might,
To cherish her with all things choice and rare;
And her owne handmayd, that *Melissa*[6] hight,
Appointed to attend her dewly day and night.

15

Who in a morning, when this Mayden faire
Was dighting her, having her snowy brest
As yet not laced, nor her golden haire
Into their comely tresses dewly drest,
Chaunst to espy upon her yvory chest
The rosie marke, which she remembred well
That litle Infant had, which forth she kest,° *cast*
The daughter of her Lady *Claribell*,
The which she bore, the whiles in prison she did dwell.

16

Which well avizing, streight she gan to cast
In her conceiptfull° mynd, that this faire Mayd *clever, imaginative*
Was that same infant, which so long sith past
She in the open fields had loosely layd
To fortunes spoile, unable it to ayd.
So full of joy, streight forth she ran in hast
Unto her mistresse, being halfe dismayd,
To tell her, how the heavens had her graste,
To save her chylde, which in misfortunes mouth was plaste.

6. Greek: "bee." Melissa is also a prophet in Aristo, *Orlando furioso* 3 and 7.

17

The sober mother seeing such her mood,
Yet knowing not, what meant that sodaine thro,
Askt her, how mote her words be understood,
And what the matter was, that mov'd her so.
My liefe (sayd she) ye know, that long ygo,
Whilest ye in durance dwelt, ye to me gave
A little mayde, the which ye chylded tho;
The same againe if now ye list to have,
The same is yonder Lady, whom high God did save.

18

Much was the Lady troubled at that speach,
And gan to question streight how she it knew.
Most certaine markes, (sayd she) do me it teach,
For on her brest I with these eyes did vew
The litle purple rose, which thereon grew,
Whereof her name ye then to her did give.
Besides her countenaunce, and her likely hew,
Matched with equall yeares, do surely prieve° *prove*
That yond same is your daughter sure, which yet doth live.

19

The matrone stayd no lenger to enquire,
But forth in hast ran to the straunger Mayd;
Whom catching greedily for great desire,
Rent up her brest, and bosome open layd,
In which that rose she plainely saw displayd.
Then her embracing twixt her armes twaine,
She long so held, and softly weeping sayd;
And livest thou my daughter now againe?
And art thou yet alive, whom dead I long did faine?° *imagine*

20

Tho further asking her of sundry things,
And times comparing with their accidents,
She found at last by very certaine signes,
And speaking markes of passed monuments,
That this young Mayd, whom chance to her presents
Is her owne daughter, her owne infant deare.
Tho wondring long at those so straunge events,
A thousand times she her embraced nere,
With many a joyfull kisse, and many a melting teare.

21

Who ever is the mother of one chylde,
Which having thought long dead, she fyndes alive,

Let her by proofe of that, which she hath fylde
In her owne breast, this mothers joy descrive:° *describe*
For other none such passion can contrive
In perfect forme, as this good Lady felt,
When she so faire a daughter saw survive,
As *Pastorella* was, that nigh she swelt
For passing joy, which did all into pitty melt.

22

Thence running forth unto her loved Lord,
She unto him recounted, all that fell:
Who joyning joy with her in one accord,
Acknowledg'd for his own faire *Pastorell*.
There leave we them in joy, and let us tell
Of *Calidore*, who seeking all this while
That monstrous Beast by finall force to quell,
Through every place, with restlesse paine and toile
Him follow'd, by the tract° of his outragious spoile. *trail*

23

Through all estates he found that he had past,[7]
In which he many massacres had left,
And to the Clergy now was come at last;
In which such spoile, such havocke, and such theft
He wrought, that thence all goodnesse he bereft,
That endlesse were to tell. The Elfin Knight,
Who now no place besides unsought had left,
At length into a Monastere did light,
Where he him found despoyling all with maine & might.

24

Into their cloysters now he broken had,
Through which the Monckes he chaced here & there,
And them pursu'd into their dortours° sad, *sleeping rooms*
And searched all their cels and secrets neare;
In which what filth and ordure did appeare,
Were yrkesome to report; yet that foule Beast
Nought sparing them, the more did tosse and teare,
And ransacke all their dennes from most to least,
Regarding nought religion, nor their holy heast.° *vow*

25

From thence into the sacred Church he broke,
And robd the Chancell, and the deskes downe threw,

7. Spenser is making a distinction between the secular clergy, those who were pastors to the people, and monks, those who had retired from the world. The fact that Henry VIII had dissolved the monasteries in England does not alter the point Spenser is making: no one escapes the Blatant Beast.

And Altars fouled, and blasphemy spoke,
And th'Images for all their goodly hew,
Did cast to ground, whilest none was them to rew;
So all confounded and disordered there.
But seeing *Calidore*, away he flew,
Knowing his fatall hand by former feare;
But he him fast pursuing, soone approched neare.

26

Him in a narrow place he overtooke,
And fierce assailing forst him turne againe:
Sternely he turnd againe, when he him strooke
With his sharpe steele, and ran at him amaine
With open mouth, that seemed to containe
A full good pecke° within the utmost brim, *a great number (of teeth)*
All set with yron teeth in raunges twaine,
That terrifide his foes, and armed him,
Appearing like the mouth of *Orcus*° griesly grim. *Hell*

27

And therein were a thousand tongs empight,° *implanted*
Of sundry kindes, and sundry quality,
Some were of dogs, that barked day and night,
And some of cats, that wrawling° still did cry: *mewing*
And some of Beares, that groynd continually,
And some of Tygres, that did seeme to gren,
And snar at all, that ever passed by:
But most of them were tongues of mortall men,
Which spake reprochfully, not caring when.

28

And them amongst were mingled here and there,
The tongues of Serpents with three forked stings,
That spat out poyson and gore bloudy gere[8]
At all, that came within his ravenings,
And spake licentious words, and hatefull things
Of good and bad alike, of low and hie;
Ne Kesars° spared he a whit, nor Kings, *rulers*
But either blotted them with infamie,
Or bit them with his banefull teeth of injury.

29

But *Calidore* thereof no whit afrayd,
Rencountred him with so impetuous might,
That th'outrage of his violence he stayd,

Corrupt, foul matter, pus.

And bet abacke, threatning in vaine to bite,
And spitting forth the poyson of his spight,
That fomed all about his bloody jawes.
Tho rearing up his former° feete on hight, *situated more forward*
He rampt° upon him with his ravenous pawes, *seized*
As if he would have rent him with his cruell clawes.

30

But he right well aware, his rage to ward,
Did cast his shield atweene, and therewithall
Putting his puissaunce forth, pursu'd so hard,
That backeward he enforced him to fall,
And being downe, ere he new helpe could call,
His shield he on him threw, and fast downe held,
Like as a bullocke, that in bloudy stall
Of butchers balefull hand to ground is feld,
Is forcibly kept downe, till he be throughly queld.

31

Full cruelly the Beast did rage and rore,
To be downe held, and maystred so with might,
That he gan fret and fome out bloudy gore,
Striving in vaine to rere him selfe upright.
For still the more he strove, the more the Knight
Did him suppresse, and forcibly subdew;
That made him almost mad for fell despight.
He grind, hee bit, he scratcht, he venim threw,
And fared like a feend, right horrible in hew.

32

Or like the hell-borne *Hydra*, which they faine
That great *Alcides* whilome overthrew,[9]
After that he had labourd long in vaine,
To crop his thousand heads, the which still new
Forth budded, and in greater number grew.
Such was the fury of this hellish Beast,
Whilest *Calidore* him under him downe threw;
Who nathemore his heavy load releast,
But aye the more he rag'd, the more his powre increast.

33

Tho when the Beast saw, he mote nought availe,
By force, he gan his hundred tongues apply,
And sharpely at him to revile and raile,

9. The many-headed monster whom Hercules (Alcides) slew as one of his twelve labors.

With bitter termes of shamefull infamy;
Oft interlacing many a forged lie,
Whose like he never once did speake, nor heare,
Nor ever thought thing so unworthily:
Yet did he nought for all that him forbeare,
But strained him so streightly, that he chokt him neare.

34

At last when as he found his force to shrincke,
And rage to quaile, he tooke a muzzell strong
Of surest yron, made with many a lincke;
Therewith he mured[1] up his mouth along,
And therein shut up his blasphemous tong,
For never more defaming gentle Knight,
Or unto lovely Lady doing wrong:
And thereunto a great long chaine he tight,
With which he drew him forth, even in his own despight.

35

Like as whylome that strong *Tirynthian* swaine,[2]
Brought forth with him the dreadfull dog of hell,
Against his will fast bound in yron chaine,
And roring horribly, did him compell
To see the hatefull sunne, that he might tell
To griesly *Pluto*,[3] what on earth was donne,
And to the other damned ghosts, which dwell
For aye in darkenesse, which day light doth shonne.
So led this Knight his captyve with like conquest wonne.

36

Yet greatly did the Beast repine° at those *show discontent*
Straunge bands, whose like till then he never bore,
Ne ever any durst till then impose,
And chauffed inly, seeing now no more
Him liberty was left aloud to rore;
Yet durst he not draw backe; nor once withstand
The proved powre of noble *Calidore*,
But trembled underneath his mighty hand,
And like a fearefull dog him followed through the land.

37

Him through all Faery land he follow'd so,
As if he learned had obedience long,
That all the people where so he did go,

1. Closed (Latin: *murus*, "wall").
2. Hercules, who was born in Tiryns, brought Cerberus out of hell (Ovid, *Metamorphoses* 7.408–15).
3. God of the underworld.

Out of their townes did round about him throng,
To see him leade that Beast in bondage strong,
And seeing it, much wondred at the sight;
And all such persons, as he earst did wrong,
Rejoyced much to see his captive plight,
And much admyr'd the Beast, but more admyr'd the Knight.

38

Thus was this Monster by the maystring might
Of doughty *Calidore*, supprest and tamed,
That never more he mote endammadge wight
With his vile tongue, which many had defamed,
And many causelesse caused to be blamed:
So did he eeke long after this remaine,
Untill that, whether wicked fate so framed,
Or fault of men, he broke his yron chaine,
And got into the world at liberty againe.

39

Thenceforth more mischiefe and more scath he wrought
To mortall men, then he had done before;
Ne ever could by any more be brought
Into like bands, ne maystred any more:
Albe that long time after *Calidore*,
The good Sir *Pelleas him* tooke in hand,
And after him Sir *Lamoracke*[4] of yore,
And all his brethren borne in Britaine land;
Yet none of them could ever bring him into band.

40

So now he raungeth through the world againe,
And rageth sore in each degree and state;
Ne any is, that may him now restraine,
He growen is so great and strong of late,
Barking and biting all that him doe bate,
Albe they worthy blame, or cleare of crime:
Ne spareth he most learned wits to rate,° *scold, assault verbally*
Ne spareth he the gentle Poets rime,
But rends without regard of person or of time.

41

Ne may this homely verse, of many meanest,
Hope to escape his venemous despite,
More then my former writs, all° were they clearest[5] *although*

4. Both characters in Malory, but neither of them pursues the beast in that work.

5. Most free. Some editors emend to *cleanest* for the sake of the rhyme.

From blamefull blot, and free from all that wite,° *blame*
With which some wicked tongues did it backebite,
And bring into a mighty Peres displeasure,
That never so deserved to endite.° *censure*
Therfore do you my rimes keep better measure,
And seeke to please, that now is counted wisemens threasure.

Two Cantos of Mutabilitie:

Which, Both for Forme and Matter, Appeare to be Parcell of Some Following Booke of the Faerie Queene Under the Legend of Constancie.

Canto VI

Proud Change *(not pleasd, in mortall things,*
beneath the Moone*, to raigne)*
Pretends, as well of Gods*, as* Men*,*
to be the Soveraine.

1

What man that sees the ever-whirling wheele
Of *Change*, the which all mortall dungs doth sway,° *have power over*
But that therby doth find, & plainly feele,
How MUTABILITY in them doth play
Her cruell sports, to many mens decay?
Which that to all[1] may better yet appeare,
I will rehearse that whylome I heard say,
How she at first her selfe began to reare,
Gainst all the Gods, and th'empire sought from them to beare.

2

But first, here falleth fittest to unfold
Her antique race and linage ancient,
As I have found it registred of old,
In *Faery* Land mongst records permanent:
She was, to weet, a daughter by descent
Of those old *Titans*,[2] that did whylome strive

1. I.e., so that it may appear more clearly to all.

2. The Titans were the offspring of Heaven (Uranus) and Earth (Gaea) and constitute a generation of gods older than the reigning Olympians (Jupiter, etc.). The most important of them was Saturn, who had dethroned his father Uranus. Because Earth prophesied that Saturn would be dethroned in turn by one of his sons, he devoured each of his children immediately after birth. His wife managed to preserve one, Jupiter, by sending him off to Crete. Jupiter lived to fulfill the prophecy and not only dethroned but also emasculated Saturn. Thus began the reign of the Olympian gods. Saturn's brothers and sisters, offended at Jupiter's presumptions, contended with him for supremacy. The victorious Jupiter thrust the Titans into the pit of Tartarus. Mutability is a descendant of the Titans and bases her claim on the legal right derived from her lineage.

With *Saturnes* sonne for heavens regiment.° *rule*
Whom, though high *Jove* of kingdome did deprive,
Yet many of their stemme long after did survive.

3

And many of them, afterwards obtain'd
Great power of *Jove*, and high authority;
As *Hecaté*,[3] in whose almighty hand,
He plac't all rule and principality,
To be by her disposed diversly,
To Gods, and men, as she them list divide:
And drad *Bellona*,[4] that doth sound on hie
Warres and allarums unto Nations wide,
That makes both heaven & earth to tremble at her pride.

4

So likewise did this *Titanesse* aspire,
Rule and dominion to her selfe to gaine;
That as a Goddesse, men might her admire,° *wonder at*
And heavenly honours yield, as to them twaine.[4]
And first, on earth she sought it to obtaine;
Where she such proofe and sad examples shewed
Of her great power, to many ones great paine,
That not men onely (whom she soone subdewed)
But eke all other creatures, her bad dooings rewed.

5

For, she the face of earthly things so changed,
That all which Nature had establisht first
In good estate, and in meet order ranged,
She did pervert, and all their statutes burst:
And all the worlds faire frame (which none yet durst
Of Gods or men to alter or misguide)
She alter'd quite, and made them all accurst
That God had blest; and did at first provide[5]
In that still° happy state for ever to abide. *continuously*

6

Ne shee the lawes of Nature onely brake,
But eke of Justice, and of Policie;° *good government*
And wrong of right, and bad of good did make.
And death for life exchanged foolishlie:
Since which, all living wights have learn'd to die,
And all this world is woxen daily worse.

3. A Titaness, the infernal aspect of the triple goddess Hecate-Diana-Cynthia. A Titaness, goddess of war.

4. I.e., Hecate and Bellona.

5. Prepare, with overtones of Providential ordering.

O pittious worke of MUTABILITIE!
By which, we all are subiect to that curse,° *the fall of man*
And death in stead of life have sucked from our Nurse.[6]

7

And now, when all the earth she thus had brought
To her behest, and thralled to her might,
She gan to cast in her ambitious thought,
T'attempt[7] th'empire of the heavens hight,
And *Jove* himselfe to shoulder from his right.
And first, she past the region of the ayre,° *the atmosphere*
And of the fire,[8] whose substance thin and slight,
Made no resistance, ne could her contraire,° *oppose, thwart*
But ready passage to her pleasure did prepaire.° *provide, furnish*

8

Thence, to the Circle of the Moone she clambe,
Where *Cynthia*[9] raignes in everlasting glory,
To whose bright shining palace straight she came,
All fairely deckt with heavens goodly story;
Whose silver gates (by which there sate an hory
Old aged Sire, with hower-glasse in hand,
Hight *Tyme*) she entred, were he liefe or sory:° *willing or not*
Ne staide till she the highest stage° had scand,° *level / climbed*
Where *Cynthia* did sit, that never still did stand.

9

Her sitting on an Ivory throne shee found,
Drawne of two steeds, th'one black, the other white,
Environd with tenne thousand starres around,
That duly her attended day and night;
And by her side, there ran her Page, that hight
Vesper, whom we the Evening-starre intend:° *call*
That with his Torche, still twinkling like twylight;
Her lightened all the way where she should wend,
And joy to weary wandring travailers did lend:

10

That when the hardy *Titanesse* beheld
The goodly building of her Palace bright,
Made of the heavens substance, and up-held
With thousand Crystall pillors of huge hight,

6. Nature, or earthly life.
7. To take by force.
8. It was believed that a sphere of fire enclosed the atmosphere.
9. The moon, also called Phoebe.

Shee gan to burne in her ambitious spright,
And t'envie her that in such glorie raigned.
Eftsoones she cast by force and tortious° might, *wrongful, illegal*
Her to displace, and to her selfe to have gained
The kingdome of the Night, and waters by her wained.[1]

11

Boldly she bid the Goddesse downe descend,
And let her selfe into that Ivory throne;
For, shee her selfe more worthy thereof wend,
And better able it to guide alone:
Whether to men, whose fall she did bemone,
Or unto Gods, whose state she did maligne,
Or to th'infernall Powers, her need give lone
Of her faire light, and bounty most benigne,
Her selfe of all that rule shee deemed most condigne.° *worthy, deserving*

12

But shee that had to her that soveraigne seat
By highest *Jove* assign'd, therein to beare
Nights burning lamp, regarded not her threat,
Ne yielded ought for favour or for feare;
But with sterne countenaunce and disdainfull cheare,
Bending her horned browes,[2] did put her back:
And boldly blaming her for comming there,
Bade her attonce from heavens coast to pack,
Or at her perill bide the wrathfull Thunders wrack.

13

Yet nathemore the *Giantesse* forbare:
But boldly preacing-on, raught forth her hand
To pluck her downe perforce from off her chaire;
And there-with lifting up her golden wand,
Threatned to strike her if she did with-stand.
Where-at the starres, which round about her blazed,
And eke the Moones bright wagon,[3] still did stand,
All beeing with so bold attempt amazed,
And on her uncouth habit and sterne looke still gazed.

14

Meane-while, the lower World, which nothing knew
Of all that chaunced here, was darkned quite;
And eke the heavens, and all the heavenly crew
Of happy wights, now unpurvaide of light,

1. Suggests "drawn" as in "moved by a wain"; but it may also mean "waned, diminished."

2. The crescent moon is often an attribute of Cynthia.

3. See VII.6.9.

Were much afraid, and wondred at that sight;
Fearing least *Chaos*[4] broken had his chaine,
And brought againe on them eternall night:
But chiefely *Mercury*,[5] that next doth raigne,
Ran forth in haste, unto the king of Gods to plaine.

15

All ran together with a great out-cry,
To *Joves* faire Palace, fixt in heavens hight;
And beating at his gates full earnestly,
Gan call to him aloud with all their might,
To know what meant that suddaine lack of light.
The father of the Gods when this he heard,
Was troubled much at their so strange affright,
Doubting least *Typhon*[6] were againe uprear'd,
Or other his old foes, that once him sorely fear'd.[7]

16

Eftsoones the sonne of *Maia*[8] forth he sent
Downe to the Circle of the Moone, to knowe
The cause of this so strange astonishment,
And why shee did her wonted course forslowe;[9]
And if that any were on earth belowe
That did with charmes or Magick her molest,
Him to attache,[1] and downe to hell to throwe:
But, if from heaven it were, then to arrest
The Author, and him bring before his presence prest.° *quickly*

17

The wingd-foot God,[2] so fast his plumes did beat,
That soone he came where-as the *Titanesse*
Was striving with faire *Cynthia* for her seat:
At whose strange sight, and haughty hardinesse,° *boldness*
He wondred much, and feared her no lesse.
Yet laying feare aside to doe his charge,[3]
At last, he bade her (with bold stedfastnesse)
Ceasse to molest the Moone to walke at large,
Or come before high *Jove*, her dooings to discharge.

4. The undifferentiated mass of warring elements before the imposition of form by Love often identified with the "void" of Genesis 1.
5. Nearest planet to the moon. Mercury is also the traditional messenger of the gods.
6. A giant imprisoned by Jupiter under Mount Aetna for joining with the Titans in their war against him.
7. I.e., frightened Jupiter.
8. Mercury, son of Jupiter and Maia.
9. Make go more slowly, delay.
1. To seize him.
2. Winged sandals are an attribute of Mercury.
3. To carry out Jupiter's command.

18

And there-with-all, he on her shoulder laid
His snaky-wreathed Mace,[4] whose awfull power
Doth make both Gods and hellish fiends affraid:
Where-at the *Titanesse* did sternely lower,
And stoutly answer'd, that in evill hower
He from his *Jove* such message to her brought,
To bid her leave faire *Cynthias* silver bower;
Sith shee his *Jove* and him esteemed nought,
No more then *Cynthias* selfe; but all their kingdoms sought.

19

The Heavens Herald[5] staid not to reply,
But past away, his doings to relate
Unto his Lord; who now in th'highest sky,
Was placed in his principall Estate,
With all the Gods about him congregate:° *gathered*
To whom when *Hermes*° had his message told, *Mercury*
It did them all exceedingly amate,
Save *Jove*; who, changing nought his count'nance bold,
Did unto them at length these speeches wise unfold;

20

Harken to mee awhile yee heavenly Powers;
Ye may remember since th'Earths° cursed seed° *when / the Titans*
Sought to assaile the heavens eternal towers,
And to us all exceeding feare did breed:
But how we then defeated all their deed,° *acts*
Yee all doe knowe, and them destroied quite;
Yet not so quite, but that there did succeed
An off-spring of their bloud, which did alite
Upon the fruitfull earth, which doth us yet despite.

21

Of that bad seed is this bold woman bred,
That now with bold presumption doth aspire
To thrust faire *Phoebe* from her silver bed,
And eke our selves from heavens high Empire,
If that° her might were match to her desire: *if only*
Wherefore, it now behoves us to advise
What way is best to drive her to retire;
Whether by open force, or counsell wise,
Areed ye sonnes of God, as best ye can devise.° *contrive*

4. The caduceus, the wand of peace and attribute of Mercury.

5. Mercury as messenger of the gods.

22

So having said, he ceast; and with his brow
(His black eye-brow, whose doomefull dreaded beck° *nod*
Is wont to wield the world unto his vow,° *will*
And even the highest Powers of heaven to check)
Made signe to them in their degrees° to speake: *hierarchical order*
Who straight gan cast their counsell grave and wise.
Meane-while, th'Earths daughter, thogh she nought° did reck *did not care about*
Of *Hermes* message; yet gan now advise,
What course were best to take in this hot bold emprize.

23

Eftsoones she thus resolv'd; that whil'st the Gods
(After returne of *Hermes* Embassie)
Were troubled, and amongst themselves at ods,
Before they could new counsels re-allie,
To set upon them in that extasie;° *bewildered state*
And take what fortune time and place would lend:
So, forth she rose, and through the purest sky
To *Joves* high Palace straight cast to ascend,
To prosecute her plot: Good on-set boads good end.

24

Shee there arriving, boldly in did pass;
Where all the Gods she found in counsell close,
All quite unarm'd, as then their manner was.
At sight of her they suddaine all arose,
In great amaze, ne wist what way to chose.
But *Jove*, all fearelesse, forc't them to aby;° *to remain*
And in bis soveraine throne, gan straight dispose
Himselfe more full of grace and Majestie,
That mote encheare° his friends, & foes mote terrific. *give cheer to*

25

That, when the haughty *Titanesse* beheld,
All were she fraught with pride and impudence,
Yet with the sight thereof was almost queld;
And inly quaking, seem'd as reft of sense,
And voyd of speech in that drad audience,
Untill that *Jove* himselfe, her selfe bespake:
Speake thou fraile woman, speake with confidence,
Whence art thou, and what doost thou here now make?° *now do*
What idle errand hast thou, earths mansion to forsake?

26

Shee, halfe confused with his great commaund,
Yet gathering spirit of her natures pride,
Him boldly answer'd thus to his demaund:
I am a daughter, by the mothers side,[6]
Of her that is Grand-mother magnifide
Of all the Gods, great *Earth*, great *Chaos* child:
But by the fathers (be it not envide)
I greater am in bloud (whereon I build)
Then all the Gods, though wrongfully from heaven exil'd.

27

For, *Titan* (as ye all acknowledge must)
Was *Saturnes* elder brother by birth-right;
Both, sonnes of *Uranus:* but by unjust
And guilefull meaties, through *Corybantes* slight,[7]
The younger thrust the elder from his right:
Since which, thou *Jove*, injuriously hast held
The Heavens rule from *Titans* sonnes by might;
And them to hellish dungeons downe hast feld:
Witnesse ye Heavens the truth of all that I have teld.

28

Whilst she thus spake, the Gods that gave good eare
To her bold words, and marked well her grace,
Beeing of stature tall as any there
Of all the Gods, and beautifull of face,
As any of the Goddesses in place,
Stood all astonied, like a sort of Steeres;° *herd of steers*
Mongst whom, some beast of strange & forraine race,
Unwares is chaunc't, far straying from his peeres:
So did their ghastly gaze bewray their hidden feares.

29

Till having pauz'd awhile, *Jove* thus bespake;
Will never mortall thoughts ceasse to aspire,
In this bold sort,° to Heaven claime to make, *way*

6. Mutability is the daughter of Earth and Titan, Saturn's elder brother.

7. At the birth of Jupiter his mother Cybele urged the Corybantes, a group of fanatically wild women devoted to her, to make a great uproar to drown the cries of the newborn child. She then presented Saturn with a stone, which he duly ate, thinking it to be Jupiter. This whole passage seems to refer to an alternate version of the war between Jupiter and the Titans. According to this version, Titan, the elder brother of Saturn, was persuaded to abdicate the throne on condition that Saturn should kill all his children so that he might have no descendants to succeed him. As a result of this original compact between Titan and Saturn and Mutability's relation to Titan, Jupiter might be considered a usurper and Mutability the legal heir, as a result of the Corybantes' trick.

And touch celestiall seates with earthly mire?
I would have thought, that bold *Procrustes* hire,[8]
Or *Typhons* fall, or proud *Ixions* paine,
Or great *Prometheus*, tasting of our ire,[9]
Would have suffiz'd, the rest for to restraine;
And warn'd all men by their example to refraine:

30

But now, this off-scum of that cursed fry,[1]
Dare to renew the like hold enterprize,
And chalenge th'heritage of this our skie;
Whom what should hinder,[2] but that we likewise
Should handle as the rest of her allies,
And thunder-drive to hell? With that, he shooke
His Nectar-deawed locks, with which the skyes
And all the world beneath for terror quooke,
And eft his burning levin-brond° in hand he tooke. *lightning bolt*

31

But, when he looked on her lovely face,
In which, faire beames of beauty did appeare,
That could the greatest wrath soone turne to grace
(Such sway° doth beauty even in Heaven beare) *power*
He staide bis hand: and having chang'd his cheare,
He thus againe in milder wise began;
But ah! if Gods should strive with flesh yfere,
Then shortly should the progeny of Man
Be rooted out, if *Jove* should doe still what he can:

32

But thee faire *Titans* child, I rather weene,
Through some vaine errour or inducement light,
To see that° mortall eyes have never seene; *that which*
Or through ensample of thy sisters might,
Bellona;[3] whose great glory thou doost spight,° *envy*
Since thou hast seene her dreadfull power belowe,
Mongst wretched men (dismaide with her affright)° *fright of her*
To bandie Crownes, and Kingdomes to bestowe:
And sure thy worth,[4] no lesse then hers doth seem to showe.

8. The "reward" of Procrustes, who made his guests fit his bed either by chopping them off if they were too large or by stretching them if they were too small. His "reward" was similar treatment by Theseus. He is included here as an example of what happens to those people who do not observe distinctions either in persons or in hierarchies.
9. Examples of those already punished by Jupiter for opposing his supremacy. For Typhon see VII.6.15.8. Ixion was bound to a burning wheel for trying to seduce Juno. For stealing fire from heaven and giving it to man Prometheus was bound on the Caucasuses where each day a vulture devoured his liver, which grew again each night.
1. Brood, i.e., the Titans.
2. I.e., what should hinder us from handling her (whom).
3. A Titaness, goddess of war.
4. I.e., and surely thy worth does seem to appear no less than hers.

33

But wote thou this, thou hardy *Titanesse*,
That not the worth of any living wight
May challenge ought in Heavens interesse;° *legal interest*
Much lesse the Title of old *Titans*[5] Right:
For, we by Conquest of our soveraine might,
And by eternall doome of Fates decree,[6]
Have wonne the Empire of the Heavens bright;
Which to our selves we hold, and to whom wee
Shall worthy deeme partakers of our blisse to bee.

34

Then ceasse thy idle claime thou foolish gerle,
And seeke by grace and goodnesse to obtaine
That place from which by folly *Titan* fell;
There-to thou maist[7] perhaps, if so thou faine
Have *Jove* thy gratious Lord and Soveraigne.
So, having said, she thus to him replide;
Ceasse *Saturnes* sonne,[8] to seeke by proffers vaine
Of idle hopes t'allure mee to thy side,
For to betray my Right, before I have it tride.° *decided by trial*

35

But thee, ô *Jove*, no equall Judge I deeme
Of my desert, or of my dewfull Right;
That in thine owne behalfe maist partiall seeme:
But to the highest him, that is behight
Father of Gods and men by equall might;° *equally*
To weet, the God of Nature,[9] I appeale.
There-at *Jove* wexed wroth, and in his spright
Did inly grudge,° yet did it well concede; *complain within*
And bade *Dan Phæbus* Scribe[1] her Appellation° seale. *appeal*

36

Eftsoones the time and place appointed were,
Where all, both heavenly Powers, & earthly wights,
Before great Natures presence should appeare,
For triall of their Titles and best Rights:
That was, to weet, upon the highest hights

5. Mutability is the daughter of Earth and Titan, because of this relationship Jupiter might be considered a usurper and Mutability a legal heir.
6. Divine order of Providence.
7. To that place you may get.
8. Mutability's patronymic epithet is intended as an insult in that it deprives Jupiter of his sovereignty and presses home her claim.
9. Nature's changed sex is explained by lines 5–7 and is part of literal tradition.
1. Apollo as secretary of this encounter is a humorous touch.

Of *Arlo-hill*[2] (Who knowes not *Arlo-hill?*)[3]
That is the highest head° (in all mens sights) *peak*
Of my old father *Mole*,[4] whom Shepheards quill
Renowmed hath with hymnes fit for a rurall skill.

37

And, were it not ill fitting for this file,[5]
To sing of hilles & woods, mongst warres & Knights,
I would abate° the sternenesse of my stile, *diminish*
Mongst these sterne stounds to mingle soft delights;
And tell how *Arlo* through *Dianaes* spights[6]
(Beeing of old the best and fairest Hill
That was in all this holy-Islands hights)
Was made the most unpleasant, and most ill.
Meane while, ô *Clio*, lend *Calliope* thy quill.[7]

38

Whylome, when IRELAND florished in fame[8]
Of wealths and goodnesse, far above the rest
Of all that beare the *British* Islands name,
The Gods then us'd (for pleasure and for rest)
Oft to resort there-to, when seem'd them best:
But none of all there-in more pleasure found,
Then *Cynthia;* that is soveraine Queene protest
Of woods and forrests, which therein abound,
Sprinkled with wholsom waters, more then most on ground.° *on earth*

39

But mongst them all, as fittest for her game,
Either for chace of beasts with hound or boawe,
Or for to shroude in shade from *Phœbus* flame,
Or bathe in fountaines that doe freshly flowe,
Or from high hilles, or from the dales belowe,
She chose this *Arlo;* where shee did resort
With all her Nymphes enranged on a rowe,° *arranged in a row*
With whom the woody Gods did oft consort:° *mingle*
For, with the Nymphes, the Satyres love to play & sport.

2. Galtymore, highest peak in the mountain range near Spenser's home Kilcolman in County Cork, so called because it overlooks the Vale of Aherlow in County Tipperary.
3. Aside from the impertinence of answering Spenser's question with an annotation, one might compare the similar self-awareness in VI.10.16.4: "Poore *Colin Clout* (who knowes not *Colin Clout?*)."
4. Spenser's name for the mountain range near his home, which his "shepherd's quill" had already described in *Colin Clouts Come Home Again* (1595).
5. And if it were not inappropriate in this recital . . .
6. Injuries of Cynthia. Diana is the more common name for Cynthia when she is associated with the forest and hunting, as here.
7. Spenser invokes the aid of Clio, Muse of history, to help Calliope, the Muse of epic poetry, as he always does when he treats of real historical events or geographical places.
8. Between the sixth and ninth centuries Ireland was a famous center of learning and art.

40

Amongst the which, there was a Nymph that hight
Molanna;[9] daughter of old father *Mole*,
And sister unto *Mulla*,[1] faire and bright:
Unto whose bed false *Bregog*[2] whylome stole,
That Shepheard *Colin*[3] dearely did condole,
And made her lucklesse loves well knowne to be.
But this *Molanna*, were she not so shole,° *shallow*
Were no lesse faire and beautifull then shee:
Yet as she is, a fairer flood° may no man see. *flowing river*

41

For, first, she springs out of two marble Rocks,
On which, a grove of Oakes high mounted growes,
That as a girlond seemes to deck the locks
Of som faire Bride, brought forth with pompous[4] showes
Out of her bowre, that many flowers strowes:
So, through the flowry Dales she tumbling downe,
Through many woods, and shady coverts° flowes *glades*
(That on each side her silver channell crowne)
Till to the Plaine she come, whose Valleyes shee doth drowne.

42

In her sweet streames, *Diana* used oft
(After her sweatie chace and toilesome play)
To bathe her selfe; and after, on the soft
And downy grasse, her dainty limbes to lay
In covert shade, where none behold her may:
For, much she hated sight of living eye.
Foolish God *Faunus*,° though full many a day *a faun*
He saw her clad, yet longed foolishly
To see her naked mongst her Nymphes in privity.[5]

43

No way he found to compasse[6] his desire,
But to corrupt *Molanna*, this her maid,
Her° to discover° for some secret hire: *Diana / to reveal*
So, her with flattering words he first assaid;
And after, pleasing gifts for her purvaid,

9. The river Behanagh near Spenser's home. Her name suggests her genealogy: Mol-, "old father *Mole*," -anna, Beh*anna*.
1. The river Awbeg, renamed by Spenser from Kilnemullah, the ancient name for Buttevant, a city on its banks. Spenser annotates the name himself in *Colin Clouts Come Home Again*.
2. Another river, the story of whose marriage with Mulla Spenser tells in *Colin Clouts Come Home Again*.
3. Spenser's name for himself from *The Shepheardes Calender* through VI.10. He is referring here to his *Colin Clouts Come Home Again*.
4. Full of pomp, no pejorative sense intended.
5. In secret, but the rhyme word is meant to expose more of his prurient interests.
6. To achieve, with overtones of "to embrace."

Queene-apples, and red Cherries[7] from the tree,
With which he her allured and betraid,
To tell what time he might her Lady see
When she her selfe did bathe, that he might secret bee.

44

There-to hee promist, if shee would him pleasure° *please*
With this small boone, to quit her with a better;
To weet, that where-as shee had out of measure
Long lov'd the *Fanchin*,[8] who by nought did set her,
That he would undertake, for this to get her
To be his Love, and of him liked well:
Besides all which, he vow'd to be her debter
For many moe good turnes then he would tell;
The least of which, this litte pleasure should excell.

45

The simple maid did yield to him anone;
And eft him placed where he close might view
That never any saw, save onely one;[9]
Who, for his hire to so foole-hardy dew,[1]
Was of his hounds devour'd in Hunters hew.° *slaughter*
Tho, as her manner was on sunny day,
Diana, with her Nymphes about her, drew
To this sweet spring; where, doffing her array,° *clothes*
She bath'd her lovely limbes, for *Jove* a likely pray.

46

There *Faunus* saw that pleased much his eye,
And made his hart to tickle in his brest,
That for great joy of some-what° he did spy, *something*
He could him not containe in silent rest;
But breaking forth in laughter, loud profest
His foolish thought. A foolish *Faune* indeed,
That couldst not hold thy selfe so hidden blest,
But wouldest needs thine owne conceit° areed. *thought*
Babblers unworthy been of so divine a meed.

7. These are typical pastoral gifts, but here they carry overtones of the temptation of Eve.
8. The river Funsheon into which die Behanagh flows.
9. Actaeon; a reference to the myth of Diana and Actaeon, a hunter who in chase came upon Diana naked. In fury she turned him into a stag, and his own dogs devoured him. See Ovid's *Metamorphoses*. 3.173–252, although some of Spenser's details may derive from other Ovidian myths: Callisto, 2.409 ff; Arethusa, 5.572 ff. The whole episode of Faunus and Diana closely parallels the structure of the Actaeon story. The parallelism of characters (Cynthia: Diana; Mutability: Faunus; Molanna: reader), the similarity in theme: an act of presumptuous rebellion, echoing the Christian myth of the Fall, the numerous verbal parallels, all suggest that Spenser wanted his retelling of the Actaeon myth to be an analog of and commentary on the main narrative of the poem.
1. Due to one so foolhardy.

47

The Goddesse, all abashed with that noise,
In haste forth started from the guilty brooke;
And running straight where-as she heard his voice,
Enclos'd the bush about, and there him tooke,
Like darred[2] Larke; not daring up to looke
On her whose sight before so much he sought.
Thence, forth they drew him by the homes, & shooke
Nigh all to peeces, that they left him nought;
And then into the open light they forth him brought.

48

Like as an huswife, that with busie care
Thinks of her Dairie to make wondrous gaine,
Finding where-as some wicked beast unware
That breakes into her Dayr'house, there doth draine
Her creaming pannes, and frustrate all her paine;
Hath in some snare or gin set close behind,
Entrapped him, and caught into her traine,
Then thinkes what punishment were best assign'd,
And thousand deathes deviseth in her vengefull mind:

49

So did *Diana* and her maydens all
Use silly *Faunus*, now within their baile:° *custody*
They mocke and scorne him, and him foule miscall;
Some by the nose him pluckt, some by the taile,
And by his goatish beard some did him haile:° *pull*
Yet he (poore soule) with patience all did beare;
For, nought against their wils might countervaile:° *resist*
Ne ought he said what ever he did heare;
But hanging downe his head, did like a Mome appeare.[3]

50

At length, when they had flouted° him their fill, *derided*
They gan to cast what penaunce him to give.
Some would have gelt him, but that same would spill° *destroy*
The Wood-gods breed, which must for ever live:
Others would through the river him have drive,° *driven*
And ducked deepe: but that seem'd penaunce light;
But most agreed and did this sentence give,
Him in Deares skin to clad; & in that plight,
To hunt him with their hounds, him selfe save how hee might.

2. Dazzled, with a pun on "daring." Larks were dazzled by mirrors or bits of glass so they could be caught.

3. Fool, blockhead, unknowing comic butt.

51

But *Cynthia's* selfe, more angry then the rest,
Thought not enough, to punish him in sport,
And of her shame to make a gamesome° jest; *sportive*
But gan examine him in straighter sort,° *in stricter manner*
Which of her Nymphes, or other close consort,
Him thither brought, and her to him betraid?
He, much affeard, to her confessed short,
That't was *Molanna* which her so bewraid.
Then all attonce their hands upon *Molanna* laid.

52

But him (according as they had decreed)
With a Deeres-skin they covered, and then chast
With all their hounds that after him did speed;
But he more speedy, from them fled more fast
Then any Deere: so sore him dread aghast.[4]
They after follow'd all with shrill out-cry,
Shouting as they the heavens would have brast:
That all the woods and dales where he did flie,
Did ring againe, and loud reeccho to the skie.[5]

53

So they him follow'd till they weary were;
When, back returning to *Molann'* againe,
They, by commaund'ment of *Diana*, there
Her whelm'd° with stones. Yet *Faunus* (for her paine) *overwhelmed*
Of her beloved *Fanchin* did obtaine,
That her he would receive unto his bed.
So now her waves passe through a pleasant Plaine,
Till with the *Fanchin* she her selfe doe wed,
And (both combin'd) themselves in one faire river spred.[6]

54

Nath'lesse, *Diana*, full of indignation,
Thence-forth abandond her delicious brooke;
In whose sweet streame, before that bad occasion,
So much delight to bathe her limbes she tooke:
Ne onely her, but also quite forsooke
All those faire forrests about *Arlo* hid,
And all that Mountaine, which doth over-looke
The richest champian° that may else be rid,[7] *plain*
And the faire *Shure*,[8] in which are thousand Salmons bred.

4. I.e., so sorely did his dread terrify him.
5. Compare the refrains of *Epithalamion*: "The woods shall to me answer, and my eccho ring," etc.
6. This is another Spenserian river marriage in which Spenser symbolizes the triumph of love over mutability in a fallen world through the merging of rivers.
7. Past participle of "to read," seen.
8. The river Suir that flows through rich country.

55

Them all, and all that she so deare did way,°[9] *consider*
Thence-forth she left; and parting from the place,
There-on an heavy haplesse curse did lay,
To weet, that Wolves, where she was wont to space,° *roam*
Should harbour'd be, and all those Woods deface,
And Thieves should rob and spoile that Coast around.
Since which, those Woods, and all that goodly Chase,° *hunting ground*
Doth to this day with Wolves and Thieves abound:
Which too-too true that lands in-dwellers since have found.

Canto VII

Pealing,° from Jove, *to* Natur's *Bar,°* *appealing / court*
bold Alteration[1] *pleades*
Large° Evidence: but Nature *soone* *extensive*
her righteous Doome areads.

1

Ah! whither doost thou now thou greater Muse° *Calliope*
Me from these woods & pleasing forrests bring?
And my fraile spirit (that dooth oft refuse
This too high flight, unfit for her weake wing)
Lift up aloft, to tell of heavens King[2]
(Thy soveraine Sire)[3] his fortunate successe,
And victory, in bigger noates to sing,
Which he obtain'd against that *Titanesse*,
That him of heavens Empire sought to dispossesse.

2

Yet sith I needs must follow thy behest,
Doe thou my weaker wit with skill inspire,
Fit for this turne;[4] and in my sable brest
Kindle fresh sparks of that immortall fire,
Which learned minds inflameth with desire
Of heavenly things: for, who but thou alone,
That art yborne of heaven and heavenly Sire,
Can tell things doen in heaven so long ygone;
So farre past memory of man that may be knowne.

9. Spenser intends Diana's curse to explain the present state of Ireland, harassed and torn by faction, an etiological myth.
1. Another name for Mutability.
2. Spenser invokes the Muse to lift his firail spirit, whose wing, too weak, may refuse to undertake such a high poetic flight.
3. Spenser makes Jupiter the father of the Muses. The more traditional father is Apollo.
4. Change of direction, in returning to his original narrative. sable: the 1609 reading. Some editors emend to "feeble." Milton, for one, was not bothered by the original reading, which he imitates in *Pardise Lost* 1.22–3: "What in me is dark Illumine."

3

Now, at the time that was before agreed,
The Gods assembled all on *Arlo* hill;
As well those that are sprung of heavenly seed,
As those that all the other world doe fill,
And rule both sea and land unto their will:
Onely th'infernall Powers might not appeare;
Aswell for horror of their count'naunce ill,
As for th'unruly fiends which they did feare;
Yet *Pluto* and *Proserpina*[5] were present there.

4

And thither also came all other creatures,
What-ever life or motion doe retaine,
According to their sundry kinds of features;
That *Arlo* scarsly could them all containe;
So full they filled every hill and Plaine:
And had not *Natures* Sergeant (that is *Order*)
Them well disposed by his busie paine,
And raunged farre abroad in every border,
They would have caused much confusion and disorder.

5

Then forth issewed (great goddesse) great dame *Nature*,[6]
With goodly port° and gracious Majesty; *bearing*
Being far greater and more tall[7] of stature
Then any of the gods or Powers on hie:
Yet certes by her face and physnomy.° *countenance*
Whether she man or woman inly were,
That could not any creature well descry:° *discover*
For, with a veile that wimpled° every where, *lay in folds*
Her head and face was hid, that mote to none appeare.

6

That some doe say was so by skill devized,
To hide the terror of her uncouth hew,
From mortall eyes that should be sore agrized;° *horrified*
For that her face did like a Lion shew,
That eye of wight could not indure to view:
But others tell that it so beautious was,

5. The king and queen of the underworld. Their presence at this trial is essential because their power is derived from Nature, whose laws reach to and regulate even the anomalies of the underworld.

6. This is the same "god of Nature" referred to in VII.6.3 5.6. Her apparently changed sex is explained by lines 5–7 and by the literary tradition of which she is a part. She is God's vice-regent of the Providential order of nature and can be identified with the Wisdom or Sapience that Spenser describes in *Hymn of Heavenly Beauty*, 183 ff. The ambiguity of her description is part of the tradition beginning with Boethius, *De consolatione philosophiae* and extending through Jean de Meun, *Roman de la Rose*, Alanus de Insulis, *De planctu naturae* and Chaucer, *Parliament of Fowls*.

7. To show her greater importance.

And round about such beames of splendor threw,
That it the Sunne a thousand times did pass,
Ne could be seene, but like an image in a glass.

7

That well may seemen true: for, well I weene
That this same day, when she on *Arlo* sat,
Her garment was so bright and wondrous sheene,° *bright, beautiful*
That my fraile wit cannot devize to what
It to compare, nor finde like stuffe to that,
As those three sacred *Saints*,[8] though else most wise,
Yet on mount *Thabor* quite their wits forgat,
When they their glorious Lord in strange disguise
Transfigur'd sawe; his garments so did daze their eyes.

8

In a fayre Plaine upon an equall Hill,
She placed was in a pavilion;
Not such as Craftes-men by their idle° skill *vain*
Are wont for Princes states to fashion:
But th'earth her self of her owne motion,
Out of her fruitfull bosome made to growe
Most dainty trees; that, shooting up anon,
Did seeme to bow their bloosming heads full lowe,
For homage unto her, and like a throne did shew.

9

So heard° it is for any living wight, *hard*
All her array and vestiments to tell,
That old *Dan Geffrey*[9] (in whose gentle spright
The pure well head[1] of Poesie did dwell)
In his *Foules*[2] *parley* durst not with it mel,
But it transferd to *Alane*, who he thought
Had in his *Plaint of kindes* describ'd it well:
Which who will read set forth so as it ought,° *as it should be*
Go seek he out that *Alane* where he may be sought.

10

And all the earth far underneath her feete
Was dight with flowres, that voluntary grew

8. Peter, James, and John, who saw Christ transfigured on Mount Tabor. See Matthew 17.1–8; Mark 9.2–3. The Transfiguration was the first time that Christ's divinity shone through his humanity and became apparent to his disciples.

9. Master Geoffrey Chaucer, whose *Parliament of Fowls*, describes Nature, as does Alanus de Insulis in *De planctu naturae (Pleynt of Kynde)*. Spenser is placing himself squarely in the tradition of regarding Nature as a Wisdom figure.

1. Source; Spenser, like most sixteenth-century poets, considered Chaucer the father of English poetry and imitated many of his poems. Spenser's *Daphnaida* is based on Chaucer's *Book of the Duchess*, and is a continuation of Chaucer's "The Squire's Tale."

2. Chaucer's *Parliament of Fowls*.

Out of the ground, and sent forth odours sweet;
Tenne thousand mores° of sundry sent and hew, *roots, plants*
That might delight the smell, or please the view:
The which, the Nymphes, from all the brooks thereby
Had gathered, which they at her foot-stoole threw;
That richer seem'd then any tapestry,
That Princes bowres adorne with painted imagery.

11

And *Mole*[3] himselfe, to honour her the more,
Did deck himself in freshest faire attire,
And his high head, that seemeth alwaies hore
With hardned frosts of former winters ire,
He with an Oaken girlond now did tire,
As if the love of some new Nymph late seene,
Had in him kindled youthfull fresh desire,
And made him change his gray attire to greene;
Ah gentle *Mole!* such joyance hath thee well beseene.

12

Was never so great joyance since the day,
That all the gods whylome assembled were,
On *Hæmus* hill[4] in their divine array,
To celebrate the solemne bridall cheare,
Twixt *Peleus*,[5] and dame *Thetis* pointed° there; *appointed*
Where *Phæbus* self, that god of Poets hight,
They say did sing the spousall hymne full cleere,
That all the gods were ravisht with delight
Of his celestiall song, & Musicks wondrous might.

13

This great Grandmother of all creatures bred
Great *Nature*, ever young yet full of eld,
Still mooving, yet unmoved from her sted;
Unseene of any, yet of all beheld;
Thus sitting in her throne as I have teld,
Before her came dame *Mutabilitie*;
And being lowe before her presence feld,° *prostrate*
With meek obaysance° and humilitie, *obedience*
Thus gan her plaintif Plea, with words to amplifie;[6]

3. See VII.6.36.8.
4. The marriage of Peleus and Thetis did not take place on Haemus Hill. Spenser transfers the location because of Ovid's description of Haemus (*Metamorcphoses*. 6.87–9), who was changed into a mountain for daring to assume the names of the gods.
5. Jupiter insisted that the goddess Thetis be married to the mortal Peleus when he learned that any son of hers would be more powerful than his father. Thetis objected and resisted Peleus by changing into a number of shapes, but Peleus' persistence was successful. Their son was Achilles, the hero of Homer's *Iliad*. Spenser stresses their wedding day, when Eris threw the apple of discord at the feet of Juno, Minerva, and Venus, the event that led to the Trojan war.
6. Speak with rhetorical figures.

14

To thee ô greatest goddesse, onely great,[7]
An humble suppliant loe, I lowely fly
Seeking for Right, which I of thee entreat;
Who Right to all dost deale indifferently,° *impartially*
Damning all Wrong and tortious° Injurie, *wrongful*
Which any of thy creatures doe to other
(Oppressing them with power, unequally)
Sith of them all thou art the equall mother,
And knittest each to'each, as brother unto brother.

15

To thee therefore of this same *Jove* I plaine,
And of his fellow gods that faine to be,
That challenge° to themselves the whole worlds raign; *claim*
Of which, the greatest part is due to me,
And heaven it selfe by heritage[8] in Fee:
For, heaven and earth I both alike do deeme,
Sith heaven and earth are both alike to thee;[9]
And, gods no more then men thou doest esteeme:
For, even the gods to thee, as men to gods do seeme.

16

Then weigh, ô soveraigne goddesse, by what right
These gods do claime the worlds whole soverainty;
And that° is onely dew unto thy might *and that which*
Arrogate to themselves ambitiously:
As for the gods owne principality,
Which *Jove* usurpes unjustly; that to be
My heritage, *Jove's* self cannot deny,
From my great Grandsire *Titan*, unto mee,
Deriv'd by dew descent;[1] as is well knowen to thee.

17

Yet mauger *Jove*, and all his gods beside,
I doe possesse the worlds most regiment;° *most power*
As, if ye please it into parts divide,
And every parts inholders° to convent,° *tenants / to assemble*
Shall to your eyes appeare incontinent.° *immediately*
And first, the Earth (great mother of us all)
That only seems unmov'd and permanent,

7. Mutability's case is orderly in the extreme and may be divided in two parts: her plea (14–26) and her presentation of witnesses (27–47).
8. I.e., hold as one's absolute and rightful possession.
9. Mutability's presumption is evident here in her lapse of logic: I consider heaven and earth alike because you consider them alike, but she is forgetting about the principle of hierarchy.
1. See radiance.

And unto *Mutability* not thrall;
Yet is she chang'd in part, and eeke in generall.

18

For, all that from her springs, and is ybredde,
How-ever feyre it flourish for a time,
Yet see we soone decay; and, being dead,
To turne again unto their earthly slime:° *material source of being*
Yet, out of their decay and mortall° crime, *deadly*
We daily see new creatures to arize;
And of their Winter spring another Prime,° *spring*
Unlike in forme, and chang'd by strange disguise:
So turne they still about, and change in restlesse wise.

19

As for her tenants; that is, man and beasts,
The beasts we daily see massacred dy,
As thralls and vassalls unto mens beheasts:
And men themselves doe change continually,
From youth to eld, from wealth to poverty,
From good to bad, from bad to worst of all.
Ne doe their bodies only flit and fly:
But eeke their minds (which they immortall call)
Still° change and vary thoughts, as new occasions fall. *continually*

20

Ne is the water in more constant case;° *condition*
Whether those same on high, or these belowe.
For, th'Ocean moveth stil, from place to place;
And every River still doth ebbe and flowe:
Ne any Lake, that seems most still and slowe,
Ne Poole so small, that can his smoothnesse holde,
When any winde doth under heaven blowe;
With which, the clouds are also tost and roll'd;
Now like great Hills; &, streight, like sluces, them unfold.° *open themselves*

21

So likewise are all watry living wights
Still tost, and turned, with continuall change,
Never abyding in their stedfast plights.° *condition*
The fish, still floting, doe at randon range,
And never rest; but evermore exchange
Their dwelling places, as the streames them carrie:
Ne have the watry foules a certaine grange,° *fixed dwelling*
Wherein to rest, ne in one stead do tarry;
But flitting still doe flie, and still their places vary.

22

Next is the Ayre: which who feeles not by sense
(For, of all sense it is the middle meane)[2]
To flit still? and, with subtill influence[3]
Of his thin spirit,[4] all creatures to maintaine,
In state of life? O weake life! that does leane
On thing so tickle° as th'unsteady ayre; *unstable*
Which every howre is chang'd, and altred cleane
With every blast that bloweth fowle or faire:
The faire doth it prolong; the fowle doth it impaire.

23

Therein the changes infinite beholde,
Which to her creatures every minute chaunce;
Now, boyling hot: streight, friezing deadly cold:
Now, faire sun-shine, that makes all skip and daunce:
Streight,° bitter storms and balefull countenance, *immediately*
That makes them all to shiver and to shake:
Rayne, hayle, and snowe do pay them sad penance,
And dreadfull thunder-claps (that make them quake)
With flames & flashing lights that thousand changes make.

24

Last is the fire: which, though it live for ever,
Ne can be quenched quite; yet, every day,
Wee see his parts, so soone as they do sever,° *separate*
To lose their heat, and shortly to decay;
So, makes himself his owne consuming pray.
Ne any living creatures doth he breed:
But all, that are of others bredd, doth slay;
And, with their death, his cruell life dooth feed;
Nought leaving, but their barren ashes, without seede.

25

Thus, all these fower (the which the ground-work[5] bee
Of all the world, and of all living wights)
To thousand sorts of *Change* we subject see:
Yet are they chang'd (by other wondrous slights)
Into themselves, and lose their native mights;[6]
The Fire to Aire, and th'Ayre to Water sheere,° *bright, crystal clear*
And Water into Earth: yet Water fights

2. I.e., air is the medium by which sense perceptions are transmitted.
3. Air maintains life in creatures by flowing into them (influencing them) because it is a less material element than either earth or water, hence subtle.
4. Thin substance, less, that is, than earth or water.
5. The four elements are the basis of all creation.
6. Natural powers. It was believed that elements could be transmuted into one another.

With Fire, and Aire with Earth approaching neere:
Yet all are in one body, and as one appeare.

26

So, in them all raignes *Mutabilitie;*
How-ever these, that Gods themselves do'call,
Of them doe claime the rule and soveraintry:
As, *Vesta*,[7] of the fire æthereall;° *heavenly*
Vulcan,[8] of this, with us so usuall;
Ops,[9] of the earth; and *Juno* of the Ayre;[1]
Neptune,[2] of Seas; and Nymphes,[3] of Rivers all.
For, all those Rivers to me subject are:
And all the rest, which they usurp, be all my share.

27

Which to approven true, as I have told,
Vouchsafe, ô goddesse, to thy presence call
The rest which doe the world in being hold:[4]
As, times and seasons of the yeare that fall:
Of all the which, demand in generall,
Or judge thy selfe, by verdit of thine eye,
Whether to me they are not subject all.
Nature did yeeld thereto; and by-and-by,
Bade *Order*[5] call them all, before her Majesty.

28

So, forth issew'd° the Seasons of the yeare;[6] *came forth*
First, lusty *Spring*, all dight in leaves of flowres
That freshly budded and new bloosmes did beare
(In which a thousand birds had built their bowres
That sweetly sung, to call forth Paramours):
And in his hand a javelin he did beare,
And on his head (as fit for warlike stoures)
A guilt engraven morion° he did weare; *helmet*
That as some did him love, so others did him feare.

29

Then came the jolly *Sommer*, being dight
In a thin silken cassock coloured greene,

7. Roman goddess of heavenly fire.
8. Vulcan, as opposed to Vesta, is god of earthly fire, a more common phenomenon to us.
9. Goddess of the earth.
1. Juno's special province was the air.
2. God of the seas.
3. Guardian spirits of rivers.
4. Mutability has in mind the participants in the procession about to start, by which man maintains order in his temporal existence.
5. As in VII.7.4.6 Order as sergeant is an important part of the reason that Nature can finally decide against Mutability.
6. Spenser uses only two rhymes in this stanza, as in VII.7.44.

That was unlyned all, to be more light:
And on his head a girlond well beseene° *well adorned*
He wore, from which as he had chauffed[7] been
The sweat did drop; and in his hand he bore
A boawe and shaftes, as he in forrest greene
Had hunted late the Libbard° or the Bore, *leopard*
And now would bathe his limbes, with labor heated sore.

30

Then came the *Autumne* all in yellow clad,
As though he joyed in his plentious store,
Laden with fruits that made him laugh, full glad
That he had banisht hunger, which to-fore° *before*
Had by the belly oft him pinched sore.
Upon his head a wreath that was enrold
With eares of corne, of every sort he bore:
And in his hand a sickle he did holde,
To reape the ripened fruits the which the earth had yold.

31

Lastly, came *Winter* cloathed all in frize,[8]
Chattering his teeth for cold that did him chill,
Whil'st on his hoary beard his breath did freese;
And the dull drops that from his purpled bill° *nose*
As from a limbeck[9] did adown distill.
In his right hand a tipped staffe he held,
With which his feeble steps he stayed still:
For, he was faint with cold, and weak with eld;
That scarse his loosed[1] limbes he hable was to weld.° *wield, manage*

32

These, marching softly,° thus in order went,[2] *slowly*
And after them, the Monthes all riding came;

7. Chauffed: heated (French: *chauffer*).
8. Frieze is a coarse woollen cloth.
9. Alembic, a vessel for distilling; a retort.
1. Out of joint.
2. The stanzas describing the months have certain common features. In each the sign of the zodiac appropriate to it is included, and very often this sign is associated with a well-known classical myth. The procession begins with March because March was the first month of the legal year according to the old calendar, and the first month of the rebirth of nature. New Year's Day was still celebrated on 1 January, a form of the calendar Spenser uses by beginning his *Shepheardes Calender* with January. Below is a brief chart of the months, their zodiacal signs, and the myths associated with them.

March	Aries (ram)	Helle and Phrixus
April	Taurus (bull)	Europa and Jove as bull
May	Gemini (twins)	Castor and Pollux
June	Cancer (crab)	
July	Leo (lion)	Hercules and the Nemean lion
August	Virgo (maid)	Astraea, goddess of justice
September	Libra (scales)	
October	Scorpio (scorpion)	Diana and Orion
November	Sagittarius (centaur)	Chiron
December	Capricorn (goat)	Jupiter and Amalthea
January	Aquarius (urn)	Saturn (?)
February	Pisces (fish)	

Spenser also incorporates the labors of the months, an ancient theme in Christian art, which makes of the farming cycle of the year a symbol of man's finding his way to salvation through the proper use of the curse on Adam that man must work (Genesis 3.17).

First, sturdy *March* with brows full sternly bent,
And armed strongly, rode upon a Ram,
The same which over *Hellespontus*[3] swam:
Yet in his hand a spade he also hent,° *held*
And in a bag all sorts of seeds ysame,° *together*
Which on the earth he strowed as he went,
And fild her womb with fruitfull hope of nourishment.

33

Next came fresh *Aprill* full of lustyhed,° *lustiness*
And wanton as a Kid whose horne new buds:
Upon a Bull he rode, the same which led
Europa[4] floting through *th'Argolick* fluds:[5]
His hornes were gilden all with golden studs
And garnished with garlonds goodly dight
Of all the fairest flowres and freshest buds
Which th'earth brings forth, and wet he seem'd in sight
With waves, through which he waded for his loves delight.

34

Then came faire *May*, the fayrest mayd[6] on ground,
Deckt all with dainties of her seasons pryde,
And throwing flowres out of her lap around:
Upon two brethrens shoulders she did ride,
The twinnes of *Leda;* which on eyther side[7]
Supported her like to their soveraine Queene.
Lord! how all creatures laught, when her they spide,
And leapt and daunc't as they had ravisht beene!
And *Cupid* selfe about her fluttred all in greene.[8]

35

And after her, came jolly *June*, arrayd
All in greene leaves, as he a Player were;[9]
Yet in his time, he wrought° as well as playd, *worked*
That by his plough-yrons° mote right well appeare: *ploughshare*
Upon a Crab he rode, that him did beare
With crooked crawling steps an uncouth pase,
And backward yode, as Bargemen wont to fare

3. *Hellespontus:* Ovid, *Fasti* 3.851–76, tells the story of Helle and Phrixus, who escaped the wrath of Ino through the aid of a ram with golden fleece, which carried them across the body of water now called the Hellespont, whose name came from the fact that Helle slipped off the ram's back and drowned. This ram has been associated with the zodiacal sign Aries and is identified with Jupiter by Boccaccio.

4. Jupiter in the form of a white bull enticed Europa onto his back and then fled into the sea in order to capture her love.

5. The gulf of Argolis in the Aegean.

6. With a pun on the name of the month.

7. Castor and Pollux. There are many versions of this myth, but basically, when Jupiter in the form of a swan seduced Leda she bore him not only Helen of Troy but also these twins.

8. No source has been found for Cupid's being in green. The association of Cupid with spring is a natural but insufficient explanation.

9. Probably a reference to the savage man, or Woodwose, a common figure in Elizabethan pageantry.

Bending their force contrary to their face,
Like that ungracious crew which faines demurest grace.[1]

36

Then came hot *July* boyling like to fire,
That all his garments he had cast away:
Upon a Lyon raging yet with ire
He boldly rode and made him to obay:
It was the beast that whylome did forray° *ravage*
The Nemæan forrest,[2] till th'*Amphytrionide*
Him slew, and with his hide did him array;
Behinde his back a sithe, and by his side
Under his belt he bore a sickle circling wide.

37

The sixt was *August*, being rich arrayd
In garment all of gold downe to the ground:
Yet rode he not, but led a lovely Mayd[3]
Forth by the lilly hand, the which was cround
With eares of corne, and full her hand was found;
That was the righteous Virgin, which of old
Liv'd here on earth, and plenty made abound;
But, after Wrong was lov'd and Justice solde,
She left th'unrighteous world and was to heaven extold.° *raised, stellified*

38

Next him, *September* marched eeke on foote;
Yet was he heavy laden with the spoyle
Of harvests riches, which he made his boot,
And him enricht with bounty of the soyle:
In his one hand, as fit for harvests toyle,
He held a knife-hook; and in th'other hand
A paire of waights,[4] with which he did assoyle° *determine*
Both more and lesse, where it in doubt did stand,
And equall gave to each as Justice duly scann'd.° *measured*

39

Then came *October* full of merry glee:
For, yet his noule was totty of the must,[5]
Which he was treading in the wine-fats see,° *sea of the wine vats*
And of the joyous oyle, whose gentle gust° *taste*
Made him so frollick° and so full of lust: *joyful*

1. Probably a reference to deferential courtiers who back out of the presence of the monarch.
2. A reference to the Nemean lion, killed by Hercules (*Amphytrionide*, son of Amphitryon) as the first of his twelve labors.
3. Astraea, goddess of justice, who fled from the earth because of its wickedness; often associated with Ceres.
4. The scales of Libra.
5. I.e., head was dizzy from the new wine.

Upon a dreadfull Scorpion he did ride,
The same which by *Dianaes* doom unjust
Slew great *Orion:*[6] and eeke by his side
He had his ploughing share, and coulter ready tyde.

40

Next was *November*, he full grosse and fat,
As fed with lard, and that right well might seeme;
For, he had been a fatting hogs[7] of late,
That yet his browes with sweat, did reek and steem,
And yet the season was full sharp and breem;° *cold, chill, rough, harsh*
In planting eeke he took no small delight:
Whereon he rode, not easie was to deeme;[8]
For it a dreadfull *Centaure* was in sight,
The seed *of Saturne*, and faire *Nais*, *Chiron* hight.[9]

41

And after him, came next the chill *December*:
Yet he through merry feasting which he made,
And great bonfires, did not the cold remember;
His Saviours birth his mind so much did glad:
Upon a shaggy-bearded Goat he rode,[1]
The same wherewith *Dan Jove* in tender yeares,
They say, was nourisht by th'*Idæan* mayd;[2]
And in his hand a broad deepe boawle he beares;
Of which, he freely drinks an health° to all his peeres. *toast*

42

Then came old *January*, wrapped well
In many weeds to keep the cold away;
Yet did he quake and quiver like to quell,° *as if he might die*
And blowe his nayles to warme them if he may:
For, they were numbd with holding all the day
An hatchet keene, with which he felled wood,
And from the trees did lop the needlesse spray:
Upon an huge great Earth-pot steane° he stood; *earthen pottery urn*
From whose wide mouth, there flowed forth the Romane[3] [floud.

6. In anger at Orion's boasts of his skill as a hunter Diana sent a scorpion to kill him. In remorse she had both Orion and the scorpion stellified.

7. Fattening or butchering hogs.

8. I.e., it was not easy to think about.

9. Spenser's description of Chiron the centaur has not been satisfactorily explained. He is more usually the son of Saturn and Philyra, but he also was called the son of Magnes and Nais (Greek: "water nymph").

1. 1609 reads "rode," although some editors emend to "rade."

2. Jupiter was sent to Amalthea, "th'Idæan mayd," who nursed him. She is sometimes represented as a goat nursing Jupiter, who later stellified her as the goat Capricorn.

3. The Tiber? The details are unclear, but Spenser probably has in mind the common picture of an ancient man holding or lying near an urn that pours forth a flood of water. The image is appropriate for the water-carrier Aquarius.

43

And lastly, came cold *February*, sitting
In an old wagon, for he could not ride;
Drawne of two fishes[4] for the season fitting,[5]
Which through the flood before did softly slyde
And swim away: yet had he by his side
His plough and harnesse fit to till the ground,
And tooles to prune the trees, before the pride
Of hasting Prime° did make them burgein° round: *hastening spring / to bud*
So past the twelve Months forth, & their dew places found.

44

And after these, there came the *Day*, and *Night*,[6]
Riding together both with equall pase,° *abreast*
Th'one on a Palfrey[7] blacke, the other white;
But *Night* had covered her uncomely° face *unattractive*
With a blacke veile, and held in hand a mace,
On top whereof the moon and stars were pight,
And sleep and darknesse round about did trace:° *dance*
But *Day* did beare, upon his scepters hight,
The goodly Sun, encompast all with beames bright.

45

Then came the *Howres*, faire daughters of high *Jove*,[8]
And timely *Night*, the which were all endewed
With wondrous beauty fit to kindle love;
But they were Virgins all, and love eschewed,
That might forslack the charge to them fore-shewed
By mighty *Jove*;[9] who did them Porters make
Of heavens gate (whence all the gods issued)
Which they did dayly watch, and nightly wake
By even turnes,° ne ever did their charge forsake. *equal turns*

46

And after all came *Life*, and lastly *Death*;
Death with most grim and griesly visage seene,
Yet is he nought but parting of the breath;
Ne ought to see, but like a shade to weene,[1]
Unbodied, unsoul'd, unheard, unseene.
But *Life* was like a faire young lusty boy,

4. The sign of Pisces.
5. Fit for the season of Lent, when meat was prohibited.
6. Spenser uses only two rhymes in this stanza as in VII.7.28.
7. A small saddle horse.
8. The Hours, whose parentage may be a Spenserian invention, for they are more commonly the daughters of Jupiter and Themis (law). Their guarding Heaven's gate is derived from Iliad 5.748–50.
9. I.e., that might cause them to neglect the charge ordained for them by mighty Jupiter.
1. I.e., and nothing to see but one would think him a mere shade.

Such as they faine *Dan Cupid* to have beene,
Full of delightfull health and lively joy,
Deckt all with flowres, and wings of gold fit to employ.

47

When these were past, thus gan the *Titanesse*;
Lo, mighty mother, now be judge and say,
Whether in all thy creatures more or lesse
CHANGE doth not raign & beare the greatest sway:
For, who sees not, that *Time* on all doth pray?
But *Times* do change and move continually.
So nothing here long standeth in one stay:° *in one place*
Wherefore, this lower world who can deny
But to be subject still to *Mutabilitie?*

48

Then thus gan *Jove*; Right true it is, that these
And all things else that under heaven dwell
Are chaung'd of° *Time*, who doth them all disseise° *by / deprive*
Of being: But, who is it (to me tell)
That *Time* himselfe doth move and still compell
To keepe his course? Is not that namely wee
Which poure that vertue from our heavenly cell,
That moves them all, and makes them changed be?
So them we gods doe rule, and in them also thee.

49

To whom, thus *Mutability:* The things
Which we see not how they are mov'd and swayd,
Ye may attribute to your selves as Kings,
And say they by your secret powre are made:
But what we see not, who shall us perswade?
But were they so, as ye them faine to be,
Mov'd by your might, and ordred by your ayde;
Yet what if I can prove, that even yee
Your selves are likewise chang'd, and subject unto mee?

50

And first, concerning her that is the first,
Even you faire *Cynthia*, whom so much ye make[2]
Joves dearest darling, she was bred and nurst
On *Cynthus* hill,[3] whence she her name did take:
Then is she mortall borne, how-so ye crake;° *however you brag*
Besides, her face and countenance every day

2. I.e., whom the rest of you gods make.

3. A hill on Delos, the birthplace of Diana and Apollo.

We changed see, and sundry forms partake,
Now hornd, now round, now bright, now brown & gray:
So that *as changefull as the Moone* men use to° say. *are accustomed*

51

Next, *Mercury*, who though he lesse appeare
To change his hew, and alwayes seeme as one;
Yet, he his course doth altar every yeare,
And is of late far out of order gone:
So *Venus* eeke, that goodly Paragone,[4]
Though faire all night, yet is she darke all day;
And *Phœbus* self, who lightsome° is alone, *radiant*
Yet is he oft eclipsed by the way,
And fills the darkned world with terror and dismay.

52

Now *Mars* that valiant man is changed most:
For, he some times so far runs out of square,
That he his way doth seem quite to have lost,
And cleane without his usuall sphere to fare;
That even these Star-gazers stonisht are
At sight thereof, and damne their lying bookes:
So likewise, grim Sir *Satume*[5] oft doth spare
His sterne aspect,[6] and calme his crabbed lookes:
So many turning cranks these have, so many crookes.

53

But you *Dan Jove*,[7] that only constant are,
And King of all the rest, as ye do clame,
Are you not subject eeke to this misfare?° *mishap*
Then let me aske you this withouten blame,
Where were ye borne? some say in *Crete* by name,
Others in *Thebes*, and others other-where;[8]
But wheresoever they comment the same,
They all consent that ye begotten were,
And borne here in this world, ne other can appeare.[9]

54

Then are ye mortall borne, and thrall to me,
Unlesse the kingdome of the sky yee make
Immortall, and unchangeable to be;
Besides, that power and vertue[1] which ye spake,

4. Model of excellence, with a sneer at her loves.
5. "Sir" used contemptuously here.
6. Saturn was a malevolent planetary influence.
7. "Master," used contemptuously here.
8. There are many versions of Jupiter's birthplace. Mutability's point is that Jupiter is earth–bred.
9. Nor can it appear otherwise.
1. See VII.7.48.7 and VII.7.49.4.

That ye here worke, doth many changes take,
And your owne natures change: for, each of you
That vertue have, or this, or that to make,
Is checkt and changed from his nature trew,
By others opposition or obliquid° view. *directed obliquely*

55

Besides, the sundry motions of your Spheares,
So sundry waies and fashions as clerkes° faine, *learned men*
Some in short space, and some in longer yeares;
What is the same but alteration plaine?
Onely the starrie skie[2] doth still remaine:
Yet do the Starres and Signes therein still move,
And even itself is mov'd, as wizards saine.[3]
But all that moveth, doth mutation love:
Therefore both you and them to me I subject prove.[4]

56

Then since within this wide great *Universe*
Nothing doth firme and permanent appeare,
But all things tost and turned by transverse:° *in a haphazard way*
What then should let,° but I aloft should reare *prevent*
My Trophee,° and from all, the triumph beare? *sign of victory*
Now judge then (ô thou greatest goddesse trew!)
According as thy selfe doest see and heare,
And unto me addoom° that is my dew; *give a judgement*
That is the rule of all, all being rul'd by you.

57

So having ended, silence long ensewed,
Ne *Nature* to or fro° spake for a space, *to one side or the other*
But with firme eyes affixt, the ground still viewed.
Meanewhile, all creatures, looking in her face,
Expecting th'end of this so doubtfull case,
Did hang in long suspence what would ensew,
To whether side should fall the soveraigne place:
At length, she looking up with chearefull view,
The silence brake, and gave her doome in speeches° few. *words*

58

I well consider all that ye have sayd,
And find that all things stedfastnes doe hate
And changed be: yet being rightly wayd
They are not changed from their first estate;° *original nature*

2. The sphere of the fixed stars above the planets.
3. Movement initiated by the primum mobile.
4. This is Latinate word order: therefore I prove both you and them subject to me.

But by their change their being doe dilate:° — *expand, extend, perfect*
And turning to themselves at length againe,
Doe worke their owne perfection so by fate:
Then over them Change doth not rule and raigne;
But they raigne over change, and doe their states maintaine.

59

Cease therefore daughter further to aspire,
And thee content thus to be rul'd by me:
For thy decay thou seekst by thy desire;
But time shall come that all shall changed bee,
And from thenceforth, none no more change shall see.
So was the *Titaness* put downe and whist,° — *silenced*
And *Jove* confirm'd in his imperiall see.° — *seat, throne*
Then was that whole assembly quite dismist,
And *Natur's* selfe did vanish, whither no man wist.

1

When I bethinke me on that speech whyleare,[5]
Of *Mutability*, and well it way:
Me seemes, that though she all unworthy were
Of the Heav'ns Rule; yet very sooth to say,
In all things else she beares the greatest sway.
Which makes me loath this state of life so tickle,° — *unstable, inconstant*
And love of things so vaine to cast away;
Whose flowring pride, so fading and so fickle,
Short *Time* shall soon cut down with his consuming sickle.

2

Then gin I thinke on that which Nature sayd,
Of that same time when no more *Change* shall be,
But stedfast rest of all things firmely stayd
Upon the pillours of Eternity,
That is contrayr° to *Mutabilitie:* — *contrary to*
For, all that moveth, doth in *Change* delight:
But thence-forth all shall rest eternally
With Him that is the God of Sabbaoth[6] hight:
O that great Sabbaoth God, graunt me that Sabaoths sight.[7]

FINIS

5. There have been so many attempts to read these last two stanzas either as a pessimistic renunciation of life or as a too easy acceptance of Christian consolation that their superb appropriateness as conclusion has been obscured. Spenser is not trying to escape the vagaries of this "life so tickle"; he is praying to be able to use them properly so that this changing life will have earned him the right to that unchanging life to come.

6. Hebrew: "armies," "hosts," retained untranslated in the English New Testament (as in the original Greek and Vulgate) and the *Te Deum*, in the designation "The Lord of Sabaoth"; in translating Old Testament passages the English versions have the rendering "The Lord of Hosts."

7. Much scholarly effort has been expended on the two spellings of Sabbaoth in this line. Some critics think that Spenser meant to write Sabbath sight—that is, day of rest or eternal rest, and so emend the second occurrence of the word. The point is that Spenser is calling upon the God of the universe, the Lord of Hosts, both heavenly and earthly, to grant him that seventh-day rest not merely as the cessation of earthly labors but the perfection of them in the full knowledge of the beatific vision.

Sir Philip Sidney

1554–1586

Reality is often stranger but hardly ever more perfect than fiction. As Sir Philip Sidney tells us, the poets bring forth a "golden world." Exempt from judgments about its truth or falsehood, "poetry" (by which Sidney meant fiction) should construct forms of the ideal to mitigate our suffering and move us to good action. Sidney's own work comments brilliantly on contemporary moral and political issues: his sonnet sequence *Astrophil and Stella* (page 680) illustrates the lover's paradox (love may require chastity); his prose romance *The Arcadia* describes the politics of love and sexuality; and his *Apology for Poetry* defends poetic and dramatic art from critics who would dismiss it in favor of philosophy and history. Yet to his countrymen, Sidney's most important achievement may have been a life dedicated to a public heroism and shaped by a sense of personal honor.

History has portrayed him as a prodigy. As his friend Fulke Greville wrote, "though I knew him from a child, yet I never knew him other than a man, . . . his very play tending to enrich his mind, so that even his teachers found something in him to observe and learn above that which they had usually read or taught." Play—understood in the Renaissance manner as "serious play"—took up much of Sidney's early career. Leaving Oxford at the age of seventeen but without a degree, Sidney embarked on what in later centuries was known as the Grand Tour. He visited Europe's major cities, seeking men and women who were fashioning the political goals and aesthetic sensibilities of the age. They included the philosopher Hubert Languet, whose Protestantism was linked to a fiercely antityrannical politics; the artists Tintoretto and Paolo Veronese, whose luminous realism was to determine painterly style for more than a generation; and, finally, Henry of Navarre (later King Henry IV of France) and his wife, Margaret of Valois, whose reign would see the worst of the religious wars in Europe. Back in England by 1575, Sidney espoused a politics that challenged authority. Siding with his father, Henry Sidney, Queen Elizabeth's Lord Deputy Governor of Ireland, he argued for imposing a land tax on the Anglo-Irish nobility, citing their "unreasonable and arrogant pretensions" as a cause of civil unrest. And in 1580, seeking to protect the monarchy from foreign influences, he wrote to the Queen cautioning her against a match with Francis, Duke of Alençon and brother to the French king, Henry III. She was furious at his temerity and ordered him to the country, where he was to remain out of touch with court affairs. By 1584 she had relented, sending Sidney to the Netherlands to assess the Protestant resistance to Spanish rule. There, in 1586, fighting for the Queen's interest and the Protestant cause she championed, he died of an abscessed bullet wound in his thigh.

Sidney's first literary work was a brief pastoral masque entitled *The Lady of May*, composed in honor of the Queen in 1578. His subsequent exile from court provided him with extensive time to write. He was often at Wilton, the estate of his sister, Mary Herbert, Countess of Pembroke; it was there that he wrote the first two of his major works, in all likelihood with his sister and her circle as his first readers and critics. *The Apology for Poetry*, a work defending what Sidney called his "unelected vocation," answers attacks on art, poetry, and the theater by such censorious writers as Stephen Gosson. But its argument exceeds the limits of antitheatrical debate to embrace questions about the uses of history and the effectiveness of philosophy—a subject that bears comparison with the poetics of Aristotle and Horace. Readers have remembered most its insistence that "poetry" goes beyond nature to fashion an ideal; it works "not only to make a Cyrus, which had been but a particular excellency as nature might have done, but to bestow a Cyrus upon the world to make many

Cyruses." Poetry's creatures—whether heroes, heroines, or villains—cannot misrepresent fact because they exist only in the imagination of readers and listeners: "for the poet," Sidney declared, "he nothing affirms, and therefore never lieth."

Sidney's second work from his period at Wilton, the pastoral prose romance known as *The Arcadia*, was finished in 1581 and circulated in manuscript thereafter (and in print in 1973), depicts the willfulness of a superstitious and lazy duke, Basilius, who sequesters his marriageable daughters, Pamela and Philoclea, in the country where no suitor can meet them. His plans are foiled by two foreign princes, Pyrocles and Musidorus, who, disguised as a woman and a shepherd, manage to court and win the love of these ladies. Interspersed throughout the prose narrative of these events are poems, termed *eclogues*, expressing the joys and sorrows of pastoral life, one of which, *As I my little flock on Ister bank*, has persuaded many readers that Sidney was arguing for a radical, essentially republican politics.

A second version of the *Arcadia*, apparently written two or three years later, very explicitly introduces politics to the plot: Sidney sketches the characters of several rulers, magnificent and tyrannical; includes arguments for resistance and rebellion; and illustrates the nature of justice and equity. This version, revised after Sidney's death by his sister, Mary Herbert, Countess of Pembroke, and published in 1593, contains splendid portraits of queens both good and bad. Especially memorable is the wicked Cecropia, who plots to capture and kill the Arcadian princesses. The mother of Amphialus, who is a kind of moving target for misfortune's arrows, Cecropia has sometimes been understood to figure Catherine de'Medici, the powerful French queen, who many maintained had helped plan the massacre of hundreds of Protestants on Saint Bartholomew's Day, 1572.

For additional resources on Sidney, including Book1 of *Arcadia*, go to *The Longman Anthology of British Literature* Web site at www.myliteraturekit.com.

The Apology for Poetry

When the right virtuous Edward Wotton[1] and I were at the Emperor's court together, we gave ourselves to learn horsemanship of John Pietro Pugliano, one that with great commendation had the place of an esquire in his stable. And he, according to the fertileness of the Italian wit, did not only afford us the demonstration of his practice, but sought to enrich our minds with the contemplations therein, which he thought most precious. But with none I remember mine ears were at that time more laden, than when (either angered with slow payment, or moved with our learner-like admiration) he exercised his speech in the praise of his faculty. He said soldiers were the noblest estate of mankind, and horsemen the noblest of soldiers. He said they were the masters of war and ornaments of peace, speedy goers and strong abiders, triumphers both in camps and courts. Nay, to so unbelieved a point he proceeded as that no earthly thing bred such wonder to a prince as to be a good horseman—skill of government was but a *pedanteria* [pedantry] in comparison. Then would he add certain praises, by telling what a peerless beast the horse was, the only serviceable courtier without flattery, the beast of most beauty, faithfulness, courage, and such more, that if I had not been a piece of a logician before I came to him, I think he would have persuaded me to have wished myself a horse. But thus much at least with his no few words he drave

1. Edward Wotton (1548–1626), half-brother of Henry Wotton who saw diplomatic service under James I. Edward Wotton and Sidney undertook a mission to the court of the Emperor Maximilian at Vienna in 1574–1575.

into me, that self-love is better than any gilding to make that seem gorgeous wherein ourselves be parties. Wherein, if Pugliano's strong affection and weak arguments will not satisfy you, I will give you a nearer example of myself, who (I know not by what mischance) in these my not old years and idlest times having slipped into the title of a poet, am provoked to say something unto you in the defense of that my unelected vocation,[2] which if I handle with more good will than good reasons, bear with me, since the scholar is to be pardoned that followeth the steps of his master. And yet I must say that, as I have more just cause to make a pitiful defense of poor poetry, which from almost the highest estimation of learning is fallen to be the laughingstock of children, so have I need to bring some more available proofs: since the former is by no man barred of his deserved credit, the silly latter hath had even the names of philosophers used to the defacing of it, with great danger of civil war among the Muses.[3]

And first, truly, to all them that, professing learning, inveigh against poetry may justly be objected that they go very near to ungratefulness, to seek to deface that which, in the noblest nations and languages that are known, hath been the first light-giver to ignorance, and first nurse, whose milk by little and little enabled them to feed afterwards of tougher knowledges. And will they now play the hedgehog that, being received into the den, drive out his host? Or rather the vipers, that with their birth kill their parents?

Let learned Greece in any of his manifold sciences be able to show me one book before Musaeus, Homer, and Hesiod, all three nothing else but poets.[4] Nay, let any history be brought that can say any writers were there before them, if they were not men of the same skill, as Orpheus, Linus,[5] and some other are named, who, having been the first of that country that made pens deliverers of their knowledge to the posterity, may justly challenge to be called their fathers in learning: for not only in time they had this priority (although in itself antiquity be venerable) but went before them, as causes to draw with their charming sweetness the wild untamed wits to an admiration of knowledge. So, as Amphion[6] was said to move stones with his poetry to build Thebes, and Orpheus to be listened to by beasts—indeed stony and beastly people—so among the Romans were Livius Andronicus and Ennius. So in the Italian language the first that made it aspire to be a treasure-house of science were the poets Dante, Boccaccio, and Petrarch. So in our English were Gower and Chaucer, after whom, encouraged and delighted with their excellent fore-going,[7] others have followed, to beautify our mother tongue, as well in the same kind as in other arts.

2. Sidney refers to writing poetry as his "unelected vocation" because he would have readers believe that he undertook it only after Elizabeth I had exiled him from court.

3. Mythological figures who were thought to inspire the liberal arts.

4. Musaeus was in fact a poet of the 5th century C.E., reported to be a pupil of the mythical Orpheus, the first musician. Homer was the legendary author of the *Iliad*, an epic poem telling of the seige of Troy by the army of the Greeks led by the hero, Achilles; and of the *Odyssey*, recounting the return of the hero, Odysseus, from Troy to his homeland in Ithaka. Hesiod is known as the poet of the *Theogony*, which tells the story of the gods in Greece; and of *Works and Days*, which describes the rituals and practices of the agricultural year. Both Homer and Hesiod lived in the 8th century B.C.E.

5. Supposed to have been the teacher of Orpheus.

6. Sidney lists historical and legendary poets to illustrate his claim that they were the founders of civilization and culture. Amphion was supposed to have moved stones by playing his music and thus to have built the walls of Troy; Livius Andronicus (c. 284–204 B.C.E.) was believed to have been the first Latin poet; Ennius (c. 239–169 B.C.E.) was traditionally regarded as the greatest of the early Latin poets. Dante, Boccaccio, and Petrarch were the first of the great Italian poets of the early Renaissance; Chaucer and Gower were the most important of the late medieval poets who wrote in English.

7. Example.

This did so notably show itself, that the philosophers of Greece durst not a long time appear to the world but under the masks of poets. So Thales, Empedocles, and Parmenides[8] sang their natural philosophy in verses; so did Pythagoras and Phocylides their moral counsels; so did Tyrtaeus in war matters, and Solon in matters of policy: or rather they, being poets, did exercise their delightful vein in those points of highest knowledge, which before them lay hid to the world. For that wise Solon was directly a poet it is manifest, having written in verse the notable fable of the Atlantic Island, which was continued by Plato. And truly even Plato[9] whosoever well considereth shall find that in the body of his work, though the inside and strength were philosophy, the skin, as it were, and beauty depended most of[1] poetry: for all standeth upon dialogues, wherein he feigneth many honest burgesses of Athens to speak of such matters, that, if they had been set on the rack, they would never have confessed them, besides his poetical describing the circumstances of their meetings, as the well ordering of a banquet,[2] the delicacy of a walk, with interlacing mere tales, as Gyges' ring and others, which who knoweth not to be flowers of poetry did never walk into Apollo's garden.[3]

And even historiographers (although their lips sound of things done, and verity[4] be written in their foreheads) have been glad to borrow both fashion and, perchance, weight of the poets. So Herodotus entitled his History by the name of the nine Muses;[5] and both he and all the rest that followed him either stale[6] or usurped of poetry their passionate describing of passions, the many particularities of battles, which no man could affirm; or, if that be denied me, long orations put in the mouths of great kings and captains, which it is certain they never pronounced.

So that truly neither philosopher nor historiographer could at the first have entered into the gates of popular judgments, if they had not taken a great passport of poetry, which in all nations at this day where learning flourisheth not, is plain to be seen; in all which they have some feeling of poetry.

In Turkey, besides their law-giving divines, they have no other writers but poets. In our neighbor country Ireland, where truly learning goeth very bare, yet are their poets held in a devout reverence. Even among the most barbarous and simple Indians where no writing is, yet have they their poets who make and sing songs, which they call *areytos*,[7] both of their ancestors' deeds and praises of their gods: a sufficient probability that, if ever learning come among them, it must be by having their hard dull wits softened and sharpened with the sweet delights of poetry—for until they find a pleasure in the exercises of the mind, great promises of much

8. Sidney lists the best-known of the Greek philosophers before Plato: Thales, a geometrician; Empedocles, who studied the concepts of change and permanence; Parmeneides, who investigated the nature of being; Pythagoras, a mathematician and astronomer; Phocylides, a moralist; and Tyrtaeus, a poet. Solon (c. 640–558 B.C.E.) was an Athenian statesman, poet, and constitutional reformer. No trace remains of a poem by Solon telling of Atlantis, an island beyond the pillars of Hercules that vanishes beneath the sea; Sidney recalls Plato's dialogue (*Timaeus*, 21–24), in which Critias tells Socrates that the story of Atlantis originates in an unfinished poem of Solon.

9. Author of many works of philosophy in dialogue form, notably *The Republic*, on the construction of an ideal state, and *The Symposium*, on the nature of love and its association with beauty and truth. He was a key influence on Renaissance thinkers.

1. On.

2. A banquet is the setting of *The Symposium*; speakers take a walk in the *The Phaedrus*; and the story of Gyges' ring is told in *The Republic*.

3. Apollo was the god of poetry.

4. Truth.

5. Herodotus, a Greek historian (480–425 B.C.E.), wrote about the struggle between Asia and Greece; later classical editors divided his work, which he entitled simply *History*, into nine books named after the nine Muses: Calliope, Clio, Euterpe, Melpomene, Terpsichore, Erato, Polyhymnia, Urania, and Thalia.

6. Stole.

7. A West Indian dance, recorded by José de Acosta in his *Natural and Moral History of the West Indies* (translated into English in 1604).

knowledge will little persuade them that know not the fruits of knowledge. In Wales, the true remnant of the ancient Britons, as there are good authorities to show the long time they had poets, which they called bards, so through all the conquests of Romans, Saxons, Danes, and Normans, some of whom did seek to ruin all memory of learning from among them, yet do their poets even to this day last; so as it is not more notable in soon beginning than in long continuing.

But since the authors of most of our sciences[8] were the Romans, and before them the Greeks, let us a little stand upon their authorities, but even so far as to see what names they have given unto this now scorned skill.

Among the Romans a poet was called *vates*, which is as much as a diviner, foreseer, or prophet, as by his conjoined words *vaticinium* [prediction] and *vaticinari* [to foretell] is manifest: so heavenly a title did that excellent people bestow upon this heart-ravishing knowledge. And so far were they carried into the admiration thereof, that they thought in the chanceable hitting upon any such verses great foretokens of their following fortunes were placed. Whereupon grew the word of *Sortes Virgilianae*,[9] when by sudden opening Virgil's book they lighted upon any verse of his making, whereof the histories of the emperors' lives are full: as of Albinus, the governor of our island, who in his childhood met with this verse

Arma amens capio nec sat rationis in armis[1]

and in his age performed it. Which, although it were a very vain and godless superstition, as also it was to think spirits were commanded by such verses—whereupon this word charms, derived of *carmina* [songs], cometh—so yet serveth it to show the great reverence those wits were held in; and altogether not without ground, since both the oracles of Delphos and Sibylla's prophecies were wholly delivered in verses.[2] For that same exquisite observing of number and measure[3] in the words, and that high flying liberty of conceit proper to the poet, did seem to have some divine force in it.

And may not I presume a little further, to show the reasonableness of this word *vates*, and say that the holy David's Psalms are a divine poem? If I do, I shall not do it without the testimony of great learned men, both ancient and modern. But even the name of Psalms will speak for me, which being interpreted, is nothing but songs; then that it is fully written in meter, as all learned Hebricians agree, although the rules be not yet fully found; lastly and principally, his handling his prophecy, which is merely poetical: for what else is the awaking his musical instruments, the often and free changing of persons, his notable *prosopopoeias* [personifications], when he maketh you, as it were, see God coming in His majesty, his telling of the beasts' joyfulness and hills leaping,[4] but a heavenly poesy, wherein almost he showeth himself a passionate lover of that unspeakable and everlasting beauty to be seen by the eyes of the mind, only cleared by faith? But truly now having named him, I fear me I seem to profane that holy name, applying it to poetry, which is among us thrown down to so ridiculous an estimation. But they that with quiet judgments will look a

8. Any body of knowledge, typically natural philosophy and also including ethics and politics.
9. The Virgilian lots, or fortune as it is implied in lines from the *Aeneid*, which the reader chose at random and then subjects to interpretation.
1. "I seize arms madly, nor is there reason in arming" (2.314).
2. The shrine of Apollo at Delphi was presided over by a priestess who was believed to know the god's thoughts about the future; the Sibyls were supposed to be ancient prophetesses whose words were collected in the *Sibylline Books*.
3. Meter and rhythm.
4. Psalm 29.

little deeper into it, shall find the end and working of it such as, being rightly applied, deserveth not to be scourged out of the Church of God.

But now let us see how the Greeks named it, and how they deemed of it. The Greeks called him a "poet," which name hath, as the most excellent, gone through other languages. It cometh of this word ποιεῖν, which is, to make: wherein, I know not whether by luck or wisdom, we Englishmen have met with the Greeks in calling him a maker: which name, how high and incomparable a title it is, I had rather were known by marking the scope of other sciences than by any partial allegation.

There is no art delivered to mankind that hath not the works of nature for his principal object, without which they could not consist, and on which they so depend, as they become actors and players, as it were, of what nature will have set forth. So doth the astronomer look upon the stars, and, by that he seeth, set down what order nature hath taken therein. So doth the geometrician and arithmetician in their diverse sorts of quantities. So doth the musicians in time tell you which by nature agree, which not. The natural philosopher thereon hath his name, and the moral philosopher standeth upon the natural virtues, vices, or passions of man; and follow nature (saith he) therein, and thou shalt not err. The lawyer saith what men have determined; the historian what men have done. The grammarian speaketh only of the rules of speech; and the rhetorician and logician, considering what in nature will soonest prove and persuade, thereon give artificial rules, which still are compassed within the circle of a question according to the proposed matter. The physician weigheth the nature of man's body, and the nature of things helpful or hurtful unto it. And the metaphysic,[5] though it be in the second and abstract notions, and therefore be counted supernatural, yet doth he indeed build upon the depth of nature. Only the poet, disdaining to be tied to any such subjection, lifted up with the vigor of his own invention, doth grow in effect another nature, in making things either better than nature bringeth forth, or, quite anew, forms such as never were in nature, as the Heroes, Demigods, Cyclops, Chimeras, Furies,[6] and such like: so as he goeth hand in hand with nature, not enclosed within the narrow warrant[7] of her gifts, but freely ranging only within the zodiac of his own wit. Nature never set forth the earth in so rich tapestry as divers poets have done; neither with so pleasant rivers, fruitful trees, sweet-smelling flowers, nor whatsoever else may make the too much loved earth more lovely. Her world is brazen, the poets only deliver a golden.

But let those things alone, and go to man—for whom as the other things are, so it seemeth in him her uttermost cunning is employed—and know whether she have brought forth so true a lover as Theagenes, so constant a friend as Pylades, so valiant a man as Orlando, so right a prince as Xenophon's Cyrus, so excellent a man every way as Virgil's Aeneas.[8] Neither let this be jestingly conceived, because the works of

5. A philosopher who considered abstractions and aspects of mental and spiritual life entertained in a state of contemplation rather than of action.

6. Furies: supernatural forces figured as mad goddesses pursuing revenge; demigods: male offspring of a god and a mortal, having some divine powers; cyclops: a one-eyed giant; chimeras: imaginary monsters made up of grotesquely disparate parts.

7. Authority.

8. Sidney cites men recognized for their virtues. Theagenes exemplifies the true lover in Heliodorus's romance, the *Aethiopica;* Pylades, who helped Orestes avenge his father Agamemnon's murder, was cited by Renaissance commentators as a perfect friend; Orlando (modeled on Roland, the knight who fought for Charlemagne against the Basques at the battle of Roncesvalles, 778 C.E.) was the hero of Ariosto's *Orlando Furioso* and illustrated the Renaissance idea of valor. The *Anabasis* of Xenophon (himself a general in Cyrus's army) relates how Cyrus the Younger, a Persian prince, helped the Peloponnesians resist the army of Athens and then died in an attempt to take the Persian throne from his brother Artaxerxes in the 5th century B.C.E. Aeneas, the hero of Virgil's *Aeneid* and the mythical founder of the Roman Empire, was generally considered to be the epitome of the statesman.

the one be essential, the other in imitation or fiction; for any understanding knoweth the skill of each artificer standeth in that *idea* or fore-conceit[9] of the work, and not in the work itself. And that the poet hath that *idea* is manifest, by delivering them forth in such excellency as he had imagined them. Which delivering forth also is not wholly imaginative, as we are wont to say by them that build castles in the air; but so far substantially it worketh, not only to make a Cyrus, which had been but a particular excellency as nature might have done, but to bestow a Cyrus upon the world to make many Cyruses, if they will learn aright why and how that maker made him.

Neither let it be deemed too saucy a comparison to balance the highest point of man's wit with the efficacy of nature; but rather give right honor to the heavenly Maker of that maker, who having made man to His own likeness, set him beyond and over all the works of that second nature: which in nothing he showeth so much as in poetry, when with the force of a divine breath he bringeth things forth surpassing her doings—with no small arguments to the credulous of that first accursed fall of Adam, since our erected wit maketh us know what perfection is, and yet our infected will keepeth us from reaching unto it. But these arguments will by few be understood, and by fewer granted. This much (I hope) will be given me, that the Greeks with some probability of reason gave him the name above all names of learning.

Now let us go to a more ordinary opening of him, that the truth may be the more palpable: and so I hope, though we get not so unmatched a praise as the etymology of his names will grant, yet his very description, which no man will deny, shall not justly be barred from a principal commendation.

Poesy therefore is an art of imitation,[1] for so Aristotle termeth it in the word μίμησις—that is to say, a representing, counterfeiting, or figuring forth—to speak metaphorically, a speaking picture—with this end, to teach and delight.

Of this have been three general kinds. The chief, both in antiquity and excellency, were they that did imitate the unconceivable excellencies of God. Such were David in his Psalms; Solomon in his Song of Songs, in his Ecclesiastes, and Proverbs; Moses and Deborah in their Hymns; and the writer of Job: which, beside other, the learned Emanuel Tremellius and Franciscus Junius[2] do entitle the poetical part of the Scripture. Against these none will speak that hath the Holy Ghost in due holy reverence. (In this kind, though in a full wrong divinity, were Orpheus, Amphion, Homer in his Hymns, and many other, both Greeks and Romans.)[3] And this poesy must be used by whosoever will follow St. James's counsel in singing psalms when they are merry, and I know is used with the fruit of comfort by some, when, in sorrowful pangs of their death-bringing sins, they find the consolation of the never-leaving goodness.

9. The element of the literary work that determines how and to what end its subject is conveyed. Sidney later states that an *Idea* works "substantially" because it makes readers want to imitate the virtuous characters represented in a literary work.

1. Aristotle stated that poetry was a mimetic (from *mimesis*) or imitative art; Sidney (following Horace, who sees that poetry is like painting) adds that this imitation is (in some sense) pictorial.

2. Sixteenth-century translators of the Hebrew and Greek Bible into Latin who considered the books here mentioned (all in the Hebrew Bible) to be poetry.

3. Sidney distinguishes the mystical works of Hellenic antiquity as erroneous in their depiction and understanding of divinity.

The second kind is of them that deal with matters philosophical, either moral, as Tyrtaeus,[4] Phocylides, Cato, or natural, as Lucretius and Virgil's *Georgics;* or astronomical, as Manilius and Pontanus; or historical, as Lucan: which who mislike, the fault is in their judgment quite out of taste, and not in the sweet food of sweetly uttered knowledge.

But because this second sort is wrapped within the fold of the proposed subject, and takes not the course of his own invention, whether they properly be poets or no let grammarians dispute, and go to the third, indeed right poets, of whom chiefly this question ariseth: betwixt whom and these second is such a kind of difference as betwixt the meaner sort of painters, who counterfeit only such faces as are set before them, and the more excellent, who having no law but wit, bestow that in colors upon you which is fittest for the eye to see: as the constant though lamenting look of Lucretia,[5] when she punished in herself another's fault, wherein he painteth not Lucretia whom he never saw, but painteth the outward beauty of such a virtue. For these third be they which most properly do imitate to teach and delight, and to imitate borrow nothing of what is, hath been, or shall be; but range, only reined with learned discretion, into the divine consideration of what may be and should be. These be they that, as the first and most noble sort may justly be termed *vates,* so these are waited on in the excellentest languages and best understandings with the fore-described name of poets. For these indeed do merely make to imitate, and imitate both to delight and teach; and delight, to move men to take that goodness in hand, which without delight they would fly as from a stranger; and teach, to make them know that goodness whereunto they are moved—which being the noblest scope to which ever any learning was directed, yet want there not idle tongues to bark at them.

These be subdivided into sundry more special denominations. The most notable be the heroic, lyric, tragic, comic, satiric, iambic, elegiac, pastoral,[6] and certain others, some of these being termed according to the matter they deal with, some by the sorts of verses they liked best to write in; for indeed the greatest part of poets have apparelled their poetical inventions in that numbrous kind of writing which is called verse—indeed but apparelled, verse being but an ornament and no cause to poetry, since there have been many most excellent poets that never versified, and now swarm many versifiers that need never answer to the name of poets. For Xenophon, who did imitate so excellently as to give us *effigiem iusti imperii,* the portraiture of a just empire, under the name of Cyrus (as Cicero saith of him), made therein an absolute heroical poem.[7] So did Heliodorus in his sugared invention of that picture of

4. Sidney lists poets who he considers wrote some kind of philosophy and are not altogether "right," that is, pure poets. Tyrtaeus: mid-7th century B.C.E. Greek poet known for his praise of valor; Phocylides: a moralist of the 6th century B.C.E. Cato: Dionysius Cato (c. 300 C.E.), a moralist of whom little is known, who wrote a collection of moral sayings in verse couplets, published by Erasmus for use in schools; Lucretius: the Roman poet of the 1st century B.C.E. who wrote about the creation of the physical world; Virgil: the poet who stated the principles of farming in his *Georgics;* Manilius: the poet of the 1st century C.E. who wrote a versified treatise on astronomy; Pontanus: Joannes Jovius Pontanus, a late 15th-century poet who wrote a work on astronomy; and Lucan: the Roman poet of the 1st century C.E. who wrote the epic *Pharsalia,* which describes the events in the civil war between Caesar and Pompey up to Caesar's seduction of the Egyptian queen, Cleopatra.

5. Legendary heroine of the ancient Roman republic who committed suicide rather than live in shame after being raped by the tyrant Sextus Tarquinius. Her story was told in versions by Ovid, Livy, Chaucer, Christine de Pisan, Shakespeare, and others.

6. Sidney lists the eight genres of poetry; "iambic" was a kind of satiric verse written in iambics, a meter made up of units or feet, each of which consists of a lightly stressed syllable followed by a heavily stressed syllable.

7. Sidney refers to Xenophon's *Cyropaedia,* his history of Cyrus, the emperor of Persia, a work that he thinks has a heroic quality because it deals with the fate of an empire.

love in Theagenes and Chariclea;[8] and yet both these wrote in prose: which I speak to show that it is not rhyming and versing that maketh a poet—no more than a long gown maketh an advocate, who though he pleaded in armor should be an advocate and no soldier. But it is that feigning notable images of virtues, vices, or what else, with that delightful teaching, which must be the right describing note to know a poet by; although indeed the senate of poets hath chosen verse as their fittest raiment, meaning, as in matter they passed all in all, so in manner to go beyond them: not speaking (table-talk fashion or like men in a dream) words as they chanceably fall from the mouth, but peising[9] each syllable of each word by just proportion according to the dignity of the subject.

Now therefore it shall not be amiss first to weigh this latter sort of poetry by his works, and then by his parts; and if in neither of these anatomies he be condemnable, I hope we shall obtain a more favorable sentence.

This purifying of wit—this enriching of memory, enabling of judgment, and enlarging of conceit—which commonly we call learning, under what name soever it come forth, or to what immediate end soever it be directed, the final end is to lead and draw us to as high a perfection as our degenerate souls, made worse by their clayey lodgings, can be capable of.

This, according to the inclination of the man, bred many-formed impressions. For some that thought this felicity principally to be gotten by knowledge, and no knowledge to be so high or heavenly as acquaintance with the stars, gave themselves to astronomy; others, persuading themselves to be demigods if they knew the causes of things, became natural and supernatural philosophers; some an admirable delight drew to music; and some the certainty of demonstration to the mathematics. But all, one and other, having this scope: to know, and by knowledge to lift up the mind from the dungeon of the body to the enjoying his own divine essence.

But when by the balance of experience it was found that the astronomer, looking to the stars, might fall in a ditch, that the inquiring philosopher might be blind in himself, and the mathematician might draw forth a straight line with a crooked heart, then lo, did proof, the overruler of opinions, make manifest that all these are but serving sciences, which, as they have each a private end in themselves, so yet are they all directed to the highest end of the mistress-knowledge, by the Greeks called ἀρχιτεκτονικη, which stands (as I think) in the knowledge of a man's self, in the ethic and politic consideration, with the end of well-doing and not of well-knowing only—even as the saddler's next end is to make a good saddle, but his further end to serve a nobler faculty, which is horsemanship, so the horseman's to soldiery, and the soldier not only to have the skill, but to perform the practice of a soldier. So that, the ending end of all earthly learning being virtuous action, those skills that most serve to bring forth that have a most just title to be princes over all the rest.

Wherein, if we can, show we the poet's nobleness, by setting him before his other competitors. Among whom as principal challengers step forth the moral philosophers, whom, me thinketh, I see coming towards me with a sullen gravity, as though they could not abide vice by daylight, rudely clothed for to witness outwardly their contempt of outward things, with books in their hands against glory, whereto they set their names, sophistically speaking against subtlety, and angry

8. Characters in Heliodorus's romance, *Aethiopica*.

9. Weighing.

with any man in whom they see the foul fault of anger. These men casting largess as they go, of definitions, divisions, and distinctions, with a scornful interrogative do soberly ask whether it be possible to find any path so ready to lead a man to virtue as that which teacheth what virtue is; and teach it not only by delivering forth his very being, his causes and effects, but also by making known his enemy, vice, which must be destroyed, and his cumbersome servant, passion, which must be mastered; by showing the generalities that containeth it, and the specialities that are derived from it; lastly, by plain setting down how it extendeth itself out of the limits of a man's own little world to the government of families and maintaining of public societies.

The historian scarcely giveth leisure to the moralist to say so much, but that he, laden with old mouse-eaten records, authorizing himself (for the most part) upon other histories, whose greatest authorities are built upon the notable foundation of hearsay; having much ado to accord differing writers and to pick truth out of their partiality; better acquainted with a thousand years ago than with the present age, and yet better knowing how this world goeth than how his own wit runneth; curious for antiquities and inquisitive of novelties; a wonder to young folks and a tyrant in table talk, denieth, in a great chafe,[1] that any man for teaching of virtue, and virtuous actions is comparable to him. "I am *testis temporum, lux veritatis, vita memoriae, magistra vitae, nuntia vetustatis*.[2] The philosopher," saith he, "teacheth a disputative virtue, but I do an active. His virtue is excellent in the dangerless Academy of Plato,[3] but mine showeth forth her honorable face in the battles of Marathon, Pharsalia, Poitiers, and Agincourt.[4] He teacheth virtue by certain abstract considerations, but I only bid you follow the footing of them that have gone before you. Old-aged experience goeth beyond the fine-witted philosopher, but I give the experience of many ages. Lastly, if he make the songbook, I put the learner's hand to the lute; and if he be the guide, I am the light." Then would he allege you innumerable examples, confirming story by stories, how much the wisest senators and princes have been directed by the credit of history, as Brutus, Alphonsus of Aragon,[5] and who not, if need be? At length the long line of their disputation maketh a point in this, that the one giveth the precept, and the other the example.

Now whom shall we find (since the question standeth for the highest form in the school of learning) to be moderator? Truly, as me seemeth, the poet; and if not a moderator, even the man that ought to carry the title from them both, and much more from all other serving sciences. Therefore compare we the poet with the historian and with the moral philosopher; and if he go beyond them both, no other human skill can match him. For as for the divine, with all reverence it is ever to be excepted, not only for having his scope as far beyond any of these as eternity exceedeth a moment, but even for passing each of these in themselves.

1. Heat, fury.
2. Sidney quotes Cicero in his *De Oratore* (*Concerning the Orator*): "I am the witness of time, the light of truth, the life of memory, the governess of life, the herald of antiquity."
3. The olive grove near Athens, where Plato and his successors taught philosophy.
4. Sidney mentions some memorable battles: The Athenians defeated the invading Persians at Marathon in 490 B.C.E.; Caesar defeated Pompey at Pharsalus in 48 B.C.E.; the Franks, under Charles Martel, defeated the Moors, led by Spanish emir Abd al-Rahman Ghafiqi in 732; the English, under Edward, the Black Prince, overcame the French army and captured their king, John II in 1356, each time at Poitiers; finally, Henry V defeated the French in 1415 at Agincourt.
5. Brutus: Roman statesman, one of Caesar's assassins, who is said to have spent the night before the battle of Pharsalus reading history; Alphonsus: King of Aragon and Sicily who encouraged his soldiers to seize the libraries of those they conquered and to bring their books to him.

And for the lawyer, though *Ius* [Right] be the daughter of Justice, and justice the chief of virtues, yet because he seeketh to make men good rather *formidine poenae* than *virtutis amore;*[6] or, to say righter, doth not endeavor to make men good, but that their evil hurt not others; having no care, so he be a good citizen, how bad a man he be: therefore as our wickedness maketh him necessary, and necessity maketh him honorable, so is he not in the deepest truth to stand in rank with these who all endeavor to take naughtiness away and plant goodness even in the secretest cabinet of our souls. And these four are all that any way deal in that consideration of men's manners, which being the supreme knowledge, they that best breed it deserve the best commendation.

The philosopher, therefore, and the historian are they which would win the goal, the one by precept, the other by example. But both, not having both, do both halt.[7] For the philosopher, setting down with thorny arguments the bare rule, is so hard of utterance and so misty to be conceived, that one that hath no other guide but him shall wade in him till he be old before he shall find sufficient cause to be honest. For his knowledge standeth so upon the abstract and general, that happy is that man who may understand him, and more happy that can apply what he doth understand. On the other side, the historian, wanting the precept, is so tied, not to what should be but to what is, to the particular truth of things and not to the general reason of things, that his example draweth no necessary consequence, and therefore a less fruitful doctrine.

Now doth the peerless poet perform both: for whatsoever the philosopher saith should be done, he giveth a perfect picture of it in someone by whom he presupposeth it was done, so as he coupleth the general notion with the particular example. A perfect picture I say, for he yieldeth to the powers of the mind an image of that whereof the philosopher bestoweth but a wordish description, which doth neither strike, pierce, nor possess the sight of the soul so much as that other doth. For as in outward things, to a man that had never seen an elephant or a rhinoceros, who should tell him most exquisitely all their shapes, color, bigness, and particular marks, or of a gorgeous palace, an *architector* [architect], with declaring the full beauties, might well make the hearer able to repeat, as it were by rote, all he had heard, yet should never satisfy his inward conceit[8] with being witness to itself of a true lively knowledge; but the same man, as soon as he might see those beasts well painted, or the house well in model, should straightways grow, without need of any description, to a judicial comprehending of them: so no doubt the philosopher with his learned definitions—be it of virtue, vices, matters of public policy or private government—replenisheth the memory with many infallible grounds of wisdom, which, notwithstanding, lie dark before the imaginative and judging power, if they be not illuminated or figured forth by the speaking picture of poesy.

Tully[9] taketh much pains, and many times not without poetical helps, to make us know the force love of our country hath in us. Let us but hear old Anchises speaking in the midst of Troy's flames,[1] or see Ulysses in the fullness of all Calypso's delights bewail his absence from barren and beggarly Ithaca. Anger, the Stoics said,

6. I.e., rather "from fear of punishment" than "from love of virtue" (Horace, *Epistles* 1.2.62). Sidney distinguishes between staying within the law and moral behavior.
7. Limp.
8. The listener's mental picture or image.
9. Cicero.
1. In the remainder of this paragraph, Sidney refers to exemplary moments in the lives of mythical figures as illustrated in the literature of antiquity, especially the works of Virgil, Homer, and the Greek and Roman dramatists.

was a short madness: let but Sophocles bring you Ajax on a stage, killing or whipping sheep and oxen, thinking them the army of Greeks, with their chieftains Agamemnon and Menelaus, and tell me if you have not a more familiar insight into anger than finding in the schoolmen his *genus* [race] and difference.[2] See whether wisdom and temperance in Ulysses and Diomedes, valor in Achilles, friendship in Nisus and Euryalus, even to an ignorant man carry not an apparent shining; and, contrarily, the remorse of conscience in Oedipus, the soon repenting pride in Agamemnon, the self-devouring cruelty in his father Atreus, the violence of ambition in the two Theban brothers, the sour-sweetness of revenge in Medea; and, to fall lower, the Terentian Gnatho and our Chaucer's Pandar so expressed that we now use their names to signify their trades:[3] and finally, all virtues, vices, and passions so in their own natural seats laid to the view, that we seem not to hear of them, but clearly to see through them.

But even in the most excellent determination of goodness, what philosopher's counsel can so readily direct a prince, as the feigned Cyrus in Xenophon; or a virtuous man in all fortunes, as Aeneas in Virgil; or a whole commonwealth, as the way of Sir Thomas More's *Utopia?* I say the way, because where Sir Thomas More erred, it was the fault of the man and not of the poet, for that way of patterning a commonwealth was most absolute, though he perchance hath not so absolutely performed it. For the question is, whether the feigned image of poetry or the regular instruction of philosophy hath the more force in teaching: wherein if the philosophers have more rightly showed themselves philosophers than the poets have attained to the high top of their profession, as in truth

Mediocribus esse poetis,
Non dii, non homines, non concessere columnae;[4]

it is, I say again, not the fault of the art, but that by few men that art can be accomplished.

Certainly, even our Savior Christ could as well have given the moral commonplaces of uncharitableness and humbleness as the divine narration of Dives and Lazarus;[5] or of disobedience and mercy, as that heavenly discourse of the lost child and the gracious father; but that His through-searching wisdom knew the estate of Dives burning in hell, and of Lazarus in Abraham's bosom, would more constantly (as it were) inhabit both the memory and judgment. Truly, for myself, meseems I see before mine eyes the lost child's disdainful prodigality, turned to envy a swine's dinner: which by the learned divines[6] are thought not historical acts, but instructing parables.

For conclusion, I say the philosopher teacheth, but he teacheth obscurely, so as the learned only can understand him, that is to say, he teacheth them that are already taught; but the poet is the food for the tenderest stomachs, the poet is indeed the right popular philosopher, whereof Aesop's tales[7] give good proof: whose pretty

2. Species.
3. Gnatho: a parasite and flatterer in the Roman playwright Terence's *Eunuchus*; Pandar: the go-between for the lovers in Chaucer's *Troilus and Criseyde*.
4. Neither gods, nor men, nor booksellers permit poets to be mediocre; a statement adapted from Horace's *Art of Poetry*.
5. Sidney cites several parables from scripture. The rich man, Dives, refused to help the beggar Lazarus; Dives was condemned to hell, Lazarus went to heaven (Luke 16.19–31). He then cites the story of the Prodigal Son, welcomed home by his father after a period of dissolution (Luke 15.11–32).
6. Theologians.
7. Moralistic fables reputedly by a Greek slave who lived about 570 B.C.E.; numerous translations into English of his work were available in the 16th century.

allegories, stealing under the formal tales of beasts, make many, more beastly than beasts, begin to hear the sound of virtue from these dumb speakers.

But now may it be alleged that if this imagining of matters be so fit for the imagination, then must the historian needs surpass, who bringeth you images of true matters, such as indeed were done, and not such as fantastically or falsely may be suggested to have been done. Truly, Aristotle himself, in his discourse of poesy, plainly determineth this question, saying that poetry is φιλοσοφώτερον and σπουδαιότερον, that is to say, it is more philosophical and more studiously serious than history. His reason is, because poesy dealeth with καθόλου, that is to say, with the universal consideration, and the history with καθέκαστον, the particular: now, saith he, the universal weighs what is fit to be said or done, either in likelihood or necessity (which the poesy considereth in his imposed names), and the particular only marks whether Alcibiades did, or suffered, this or that.[8] Thus far Aristotle: which reason of his (as all his) is most full of reason. For indeed, if the question were whether it were better to have a particular act truly or falsely set down, there is no doubt which is to be chosen, no more than whether you had rather have Vespasian's picture[9] right as he was, or, at the painter's pleasure, nothing resembling. But if the question be for your own use and learning, whether it be better to have it set down as it should be, or as it was, then certainly is more doctrinable the feigned Cyrus in Xenophon than the true Cyrus in Justin, and the feigned Aeneas in Virgil than the right Aeneas in Dares Phrygius:[1] as to a lady that desired to fashion her countenance to the best grace, a painter should more benefit her to portrait a most sweet face, writing Canidia upon it, than to paint Canidia as she was, who, Horace sweareth, was full ill-favored.[2]

If the poet do his part aright, he will show you in Tantalus, Atreus, and such like,[3] nothing that is not to be shunned; in Cyrus, Aeneas, Ulysses, each thing to be followed; where the historian, bound to tell things as things were, cannot be liberal (without he will be poetical) of a perfect pattern, but, as in Alexander or Scipio himself, show doings, some to be liked, some to be misliked. And then how will you discern what to follow but by your own discretion, which you had without reading Quintus Curtius?[4] And whereas a man may say, though in universal consideration of doctrine the poet prevaileth, yet that the history, in his saying such a thing was done, doth warrant a man more in that he shall follow—the answer is manifest: that, if he stand upon that[5] was (as if he should argue, because it rained yesterday, therefore it should rain today), then indeed hath it some advantage to a gross conceit; but if he know an example only informs a conjectured likelihood, and so go by reason, the poet doth so far exceed him as he is to frame his example to that which is most reasonable (be it in warlike, politic, or private matters), where the historian in his bare *Was* hath many times that which we call fortune to overrule the best wisdom. Many times he must tell events whereof he can yield no cause; or, if he do, it must be poetically.

8. Sidney paraphrases Aristotle's *Poetics* (9.1451b). Alcibiades was a talented if unscrupulous Greek statesman.
9. A Roman emperor (70–79 C.E.) who was described by the historian Suetonius as very ugly.
1. Justinus (2nd–3rd century C.E.), and Dares Phrygius (5th century C.E.) wrote histories that some readers thought were more accurate than the more literary accounts by Xenophon, Homer, and Virgil.
2. Canidia was a prostitute who jilted the Roman poet, Horace; he then attacked her in his poems.
3. Evil figures (Tantalus served the flesh of his son, Pelops, to the gods; Atreus served his nephews' flesh to their father Thyestes).
4. Quintus Curtius (1st century C.E.) wrote a history of Alexander the Great.
5. What.

For that a feigned example hath as much force to teach as a true example (for as for to move, it is clear, since the feigned may be tuned to the highest key of passion), let us take one example wherein an historian and a poet did concur. Herodotus and Justin do both testify that Zopyrus, King Darius's faithful servant, seeing his master long resisted by the rebellious Babylonians, feigned himself in extreme disgrace of his king: for verifying of which, he caused his own nose and ears to be cut off, and so flying to the Babylonians, was received, and for his known valor so sure credited, that he did find means to deliver them over to Darius.[6] Much like matter doth Livy record of Tarquinius and his son. Xenophon excellently feigneth such another stratagem performed by Abradatas in Cyrus's behalf.[7] Now would I fain know, if occasion be presented unto you to serve your prince by such an honest dissimulation, why you do not as well learn it of Xenophon's fiction as of the other's verity; and truly so much the better, as you shall save your nose by the bargain: for Abradatas did not counterfeit so far. So then the best of the historian is subject to the poet; for whatsoever action, or faction, whatsoever counsel, policy, or war stratagem the historian is bound to recite, that may the poet (if he list[8]) with his imitation make his own, beautifying it both for further teaching, and more delighting, as it please him: having all, from Dante's heaven to his hell, under the authority of his pen.[9] Which if I be asked what poets have done so, as I might well name some, so yet say I, and say again, I speak of the art, and not of the artificer.

Now, to that which commonly is attributed to the praise of history, in respect of the notable learning is got by marking the success, as though therein a man should see virtue exalted and vice punished—truly that commendation is particular to poetry, and far off from history. For indeed poetry ever sets virtue so out in her best colors, making Fortune her well-waiting handmaid, that one must needs be enamored of her. Well may you see Ulysses in a storm, and in other hard plights; but they are but exercises of patience and magnanimity, to make them shine the more in the near-following prosperity. And of the contrary part, if evil men come to the stage, they ever go out (as the tragedy writer answered to one that misliked the show of such persons) so manacled as they little animate folks to follow them. But the history, being captived to the truth of a foolish world, is many times a terror from well-doing, and an encouragement to unbridled wickedness. For see we not valiant Miltiades rot in his fetters?[1] The just Phocion and the accomplished Socrates put to

6. The story of Zopyrus is told in Herodotus's *Histories* (3.153–58) and in Justin's *Histories* (1.10.15–22).
7. Tarquinius Superbus was the last of the Roman kings: his son, Sextus Tarquinius, passed himself off as an ally of the Gabians to spy for Rome (Livy, *Histories* 1.3–4). Abradates (actually Araspes), acted in the same way for the Persian king, Cyrus (Xenophon, *Cyropaedia* 6.1.39).
8. Wishes.
9. Dante's *Divine Comedy* describes his journey through hell, purgatory, and paradise.
1. Sidney demonstrates that the study of history is not conducive to good morals because it does not show virtue rewarded or vice punished. Miltiades: unsuccessful against the Persians in his seige of Paros, he was imprisoned by his own people, the Athenians (Herodotus, *Histories* 6.136). Phocion: an Athenian statesman wrongly put to death for a supposed conspiracy (Plutarch, *Phocion* 38). Plato's teacher Socrates had been put to death for supposed impiety. Lucius Septimius Severus, Emperor of Rome (193–211), was able but termed "most cruel" by his biographer, Aelius Spartianus; by contrast, his virtuous successor, Marcus Aurelius Alexander Severus, was murdered by mutinous soldiers. Lucius Cornelius Sulla was a dictator of Rome, who tyrannized his subjects and yet died peacefully in his bed in 78 B.C.E.; Caius Marius was also a tyrant and never punished. Pompey opposed Caesar and was murdered after his defeat at Pharsalus; Marcus Tullius Cicero, the most accomplished of Roman lawyers and orators, was murdered by the order of Marcus Antonius in 43 B.C.E. Marcus Portius Cato committed suicide after his defeat at the battle of Thapsus rather than be captured by Caesar. Sidney calls Caesar a "rebel" because he invaded the territory of the Roman state (crossing the river Rubicon) without permission from the Roman Senate.

death like traitors? The cruel Severus live prosperously? The excellent Severus miserably murdered? Sulla and Marius dying in their beds? Pompey and Cicero slain then when they would have thought exile a happiness? See we not virtuous Cato driven to kill himself, and rebel Caesar so advanced that his name yet, after 1600 years, lasteth in the highest honor? And mark but even Caesar's own words of the aforenamed Sulla (who in that only did honestly, to put down his dishonest tyranny), *literas nescivit*,[2] as if want of learning caused him to do well. He meant it not by poetry, which, not content with earthly plagues, deviseth new punishments in hell for tyrants, nor yet by philosophy, which teacheth *occidendos esse*; but no doubt by skill in history, for that indeed can afford you Cypselus, Periander, Phalaris, Dionysius, and I know not how many more of the same kennel, that speed well enough in their abominable injustice of usurpation.

I conclude, therefore, that he excelleth history, not only in furnishing the mind with knowledge, but in setting it forward to that which deserveth to be called and accounted good: which setting forward, and moving to well-doing, indeed setteth the laurel crown upon the poets as victorious, not only of the historian, but over the philosopher, howsoever in teaching it may be questionable.

For suppose it be granted (that which I suppose with great reason may be denied) that the philosopher, in respect of his methodical proceeding, doth teach more perfectly than the poet, yet do I think that no man is so much φιλοφιλόσοφος [a lover of philosophy] as to compare the philosopher in moving with the poet. And that moving is of a higher degree than teaching, it may by this appear, that it is well nigh both the cause and effect of teaching. For who will be taught, if he be not moved with desire to be taught? And what so much good doth that teaching bring forth (I speak still of moral doctrine) as that it moveth one to do that which it doth teach? For, as Aristotle saith, it is not γνῶσις [knowing] but πρᾶξις [doing] must be the fruit. And how πρᾶξις can be, without being moved to practice, it is no hard matter to consider.[3]

The philosopher showeth you the way, he informeth you of the particularities, as well of the tediousness of the way, as of the pleasant lodging you shall have when your journey is ended, as of the many by-turnings that may divert you from your way. But this is to no man but to him that will read him, and read him with attentive studious painfulness; which constant desire whosoever hath in him, hath already passed half the hardness of the way, and therefore is beholding to the philosopher but[4] for the other half. Nay truly, learned men have learnedly thought that where once reason hath so much overmastered passion as that the mind hath a free desire to do well, the inward light each mind hath in itself is as good as a philosopher's book; since in nature we know it is well to do well, and what is well, and what is evil, although not in the words of art which philosophers bestow upon us; for out of natural conceit the philosophers drew it. But to be moved to do that which we know, or to be moved with desire to know, *hoc opus, hic labor est*.[5]

2. He knew no literature. Sidney indicates that the learning Sulla lacked was not of poetry, which reveals the punishments of hell; or of philosophy, which teaches *occidendum esse*—that is, when someone should be put to death, or the punishments inflicted by the state. Sidney argues that Sulla learned his misgovernment from history, which instructed him in the profitable ways of tyrants: Cipselus and Periander, both tyrants of Corinth; Phalaris, tyrant of Agrigentum; and Dionysius, tyrant of Syracuse.

3. *Nicomachean Ethics* 1.1.

4. Merely.

5. "This is the task, this the work"; the words of the Cumaean sybil to the hero Aeneas, who intends to return to earth from the underworld (*Aeneid* 6.128).

Now therein of all sciences (I speak still of human, and according to the human conceit[6]) is our poet the monarch. For he doth not only show the way, but giveth so sweet a prospect into the way, as will entice any man to enter into it. Nay, he doth, as if your journey should lie through a fair vineyard, at the first give you a cluster of grapes, that full of that taste, you may long to pass further. He beginneth not with obscure definitions, which must blur the margin with interpretations, and load the memory with doubtfulness; but he cometh to you with words set in delightful proportion, either accompanied with, or prepared for, the well enchanting skill of music; and with a tale forsooth he cometh unto you, with a tale which holdeth children from play, and old men from the chimney corner. And, pretending no more, doth intend the winning of the mind from wickedness to virtue—even as the child is often brought to take most wholesome things by hiding them in such other as have a pleasant taste, which, if one should begin to tell them the nature of *aloes* or *rhabarbarum*[7] they should receive, would sooner take their physic at their ears than at their mouth. So is it in men (most of which are childish in the best things, till they be cradled in their graves): glad they will be to hear the tales of Hercules, Achilles, Cyrus, Aeneas; and, hearing them, must needs hear the right description of wisdom, valor, and justice; which, if they had been barely, that is to say philosophically, set out, they would swear they be brought to school again.

That imitation whereof poetry is, hath the most conveniency to nature of all other, insomuch that, as Aristotle saith, those things which in themselves are horrible, as cruel battles, unnatural monsters, are made in poetical imitation delightful.[8] Truly, I have known men that even with reading *Amadis de Gaule*[9] (which God knoweth wanteth much of a perfect poesy) have found their hearts moved to the exercise of courtesy, liberality, and especially courage. Who readeth Aeneas carrying old Anchises on his back, that wisheth not it were his fortune to perform so excellent an act? Whom doth not these words of Turnus move, the tale of Turnus having planted his image in the imagination,

Fugientem haec terra videbit?
Usque adeone mori miserum est?[1]

Where the philosophers, as they scorn to delight, so must they be content little to move—saving wrangling whether *virtus* [virtue] be the chief or the only good, whether the contemplative or the active life do excel—which Plato and Boethius well knew, and therefore made mistress Philosophy very often borrow the masking raiment of poesy.[2] For even those hard-hearted evil men who think virtue a school name, and know no other good but *indulgere genio* [self-indulgence], and therefore despise the austere admonitions of the philosopher, and feel not the inward reason they stand upon, yet will be content to be delighted—which is all the good-fellow poet seemeth to promise—and so steal to see the form of goodness (which seen they cannot but love) ere themselves be aware, as if they took a medicine of cherries.

Infinite proofs of the strange effects of this poetical invention might be alleged; only two shall serve, which are so often remembered as I think all men know them.

6. Way of thinking.
7. Medicines.
8. *Poetics*, 4.1448b.
9. Chivalric romance in Spanish by Vasco de Lobeyra, c. 1325. It appeared in English translation in 1567.
1. In Virgil, Turnus unsuccessfully defended his native Latium (the region around Rome) against the invading Trojans led by Aeneas. Taking his last stand, Turnus cries: "Shall this ground see [Turnus] fleeing? Is it so hard, then, to die?" (*Aeneid* 12.645–46).
2. The philosophers Plato and Boethius both argued that a retired and contemplative life was superior to the active life or the life in public service. By contrast, the Roman orator Cicero asserted the value of prudence and the importance of contributing to the public good.

The one of Menenius Agrippa,[3] who, when the whole people of Rome had resolutely divided themselves from the senate, with apparent show of utter ruin, though he were (for that time) an excellent orator, came not among them upon trust of figurative speeches or cunning insinuations, and much less with far-fet[4] maxims of philosophy, which (especially if they were Platonic) they must have learned geometry before they could well have conceived; but forsooth he behaves himself like a homely and familiar poet. He telleth them a tale, that there was a time when all the parts of the body made a mutinous conspiracy against the belly, which they thought devoured the fruits of each other's labor; they concluded they would let so unprofitable a spender starve. In the end, to be short (for the tale is notorious, and as notorious that it was a tale), with punishing the belly they plagued themselves. This applied by him wrought such effect in the people, as I never read that only words brought forth but then so sudden and so good an alteration; for upon reasonable conditions a perfect reconcilement ensued. The other is of Nathan the prophet,[5] who, when the holy David had so far forsaken God as to confirm adultery with murder, when he was to do the tenderest office of a friend in laying his own shame before his eyes, sent by God to call again so chosen a servant, how doth he it but by telling of a man whose beloved lamb was ungratefully taken from his bosom: the application most divinely true, but the discourse itself feigned; which made David (I speak of the second and instrumental cause) as in a glass see his own filthiness, as that heavenly psalm of mercy well testifieth.

By these, therefore, examples and reasons, I think it may be manifest that the poet, with that same hand of delight, doth draw the mind more effectually than any other art doth. And so a conclusion not unfitly ensue: that, as virtue is the most excellent resting place for all worldly learning to make his end of, so poetry, being the most familiar to teach it, and most princely to move towards it, in the most excellent work is the most excellent workman.

But I am content not only to decipher him[6] by his works (although works, in commendation or dispraise, must ever hold a high authority), but more narrowly will examine his parts; so that (as in a man) though all together may carry a presence full of majesty and beauty, perchance in some one defectuous piece we may find blemish.

Now in his parts, kinds, or species (as you list to term them), it is to be noted that some poesies have coupled together two or three kinds, as the tragical and comical, whereupon is risen the tragicomical. Some, in the manner, have mingled prose and verse, as Sannazaro and Boethius.[7] Some have mingled matters heroical and pastoral. But that cometh all to one in this question, for, if severed they be good, the conjunction cannot be hurtful. Therefore, perchance forgetting some and leaving some as needless to be remembered, it shall not be amiss in a word to cite the special kinds, to see what faults may be found in the right use of them.

Is it then the Pastoral poem which is misliked? (For perchance where the hedge is lowest they will soonest leap over.) Is the poor pipe disdained, which sometime out of Meliboeus's mouth can show the misery of people under hard lords or ravening soldiers, and again, by Tityrus, what blessedness is derived to them that lie lowest from the goodness of them that sit highest;[8] sometimes, under the pretty tales of wolves

3. Roman consul who calmed rebellious commoners in 494 B.C.E. (Livy, *Histories* 2.32).
4. Far-fetched.
5. 2 Samuel 12.1–7.
6. Poetry.
7. Sannazaro: Italian poet (1458–1530) whose pastoral of mixed prose and verse, the *Arcadia*, influenced Sidney's work of the same name. Boethius (480?–524?): the Roman and Christian philosopher whose work *The Consolation of Philosophy* contains passages of prose and poetry.
8. Meliboeus and Tityrus are characters in Virgil's *Eclogues*. Sidney responds to the idea that pastoral is the least elevated of the poetic genres; here he declares that it is capable of conveying political and moral ideas.

and sheep, can include the whole considerations of wrongdoing and patience; sometimes show that contentions for trifles can get but a trifling victory: where perchance a man may see that even Alexander and Darius, when they strave who should be cock of this world's dunghill, the benefit they got was that the after-livers may say

> *Haec memini et victum frustra contendere Thirsin:*
> *Ex illo Corydon, Corydon est tempore nobis.*[9]

Or is it the lamenting Elegiac;[1] which in a kind heart would move rather pity than blame; who bewails with the great philosopher Heraclitus, the weakness of mankind and the wretchedness of the world; who surely is to be praised, either for compassionate accompanying just causes of lamentations, or for rightly painting out how weak be the passions of woefulness? Is it the bitter but wholesome Iambic,[2] who rubs the galled mind, in making shame the trumpet of villainy, with bold and open crying out against naughtiness? Or the Satiric, who

> *Omne vafer vitium ridenti tangit amico;*[3]

who sportingly never leaveth till he make a man laugh at folly, and at length shamed, to laugh at himself, which he cannot avoid without avoiding the folly; who, while

> *circum praecordia ludit,*[4]

giveth us to feel how many headaches a passionate life bringeth us to; how, when all is done,

> *Est Ulubris, animus si nos non deficit aequus?*[5]

No, perchance it is the Comic, whom naughty playmakers and stage-keepers have justly made odious. To the arguments of abuse I will answer after. Only this much now is to be said, that the comedy is an imitation of the common errors of our life, which he representeth in the most ridiculous and scornful sort that may be, so as it is impossible that any beholder can be content to be such a one. Now, as in geometry the oblique must be known as well as the right, and in arithmetic the odd as well as the even, so in the actions of our life who seeth not the filthiness of evil wanteth a great foil to perceive the beauty of virtue. This doth the comedy handle so in our private and domestical matters as with hearing it we get as it were an experience what is to be looked for of a niggardly Demea, of a crafty Davus, of a flattering Gnatho, of a vainglorious Thraso;[6] and not only to know what effects are to be expected, but to know who be such, by the signifying badge given them by the comedian. And little reason hath any man to say that men learn the evil by seeing it so set out, since, as I said before, there is no man living but, by the force truth hath in nature, no sooner seeth these men play their parts, but wisheth them *in pistrinum*;[7] although perchance the sack of his own faults lie so hidden behind his back that he

9. "These things I remember, how vanquished Thrysis tried in vain. Since then it has been Coridon, only Coridon, with us" (Virgil, *Eclogues*, 7.69–70). These lines suggest the futility of ambition.
1. A kind of poetry lamenting loss or remembering what no longer exists. Heraclitus: a philosopher of conflict and flux, who lived about 500 B.C.E.
2. A verse form used in satire.
3. "The sly man probes every one of his friend's faults while making his friend laugh" (Persius, *Satires*, 1.116–17).
4. "He plays around the heart" (Persius, *Satires* 1.117).
5. "[Contentment] is at Ulubrae, if a well-balanced mind doesn't fail us" (Horace, *Epistles*, 1.11.30). Ulubrae was a notoriously disagreeable small town.
6. Stock characters from the Roman comedies of Terence.
7. At a mill; a customary punishment for criminals and unruly slaves.

seeth not himself dance the same measure; whereto yet nothing can more open his eyes than to find his own actions contemptibly set forth.

So that the right use of comedy will (I think) by nobody be blamed; and much less of the high and excellent Tragedy, that openeth the greatest wounds, and showeth forth the ulcers that are covered with tissue; that maketh kings fear to be tyrants, and tyrants manifest their tyrannical humors; that, with stirring the affects of admiration and commiseration, teacheth the uncertainty of this world, and upon how weak foundations gilden roofs are builded; that maketh us know

Qui sceptra saevus duro imperio regit
Timet timentes; metus in auctorem redit.[8]

But how much it can move, Plutarch yieldeth a notable testimony of the abominable tyrant Alexander Pheraeus,[9] from whose eyes a tragedy, well made and represented, drew abundance of tears, who without all pity had murdered infinite numbers, and some of his own blood: so as he, that was not ashamed to make matters for tragedies, yet could not resist the sweet violence of a tragedy. And if it wrought no further good in him, it was that he, in despite of himself, withdrew himself from hearkening to that which might mollify his hardened heart. But it is not the tragedy they do mislike; for it were too absurd to cast out so excellent a representation of whatsoever is most worthy to be learned.

Is it the Lyric that most displeaseth, who with his tuned lyre and well-accorded voice, giveth praise, the reward of virtue, to virtuous acts; who gives moral precepts, and natural problems; who sometimes raiseth up his voice to the height of the heavens, in singing the lauds of the immortal God? Certainly, I must confess my own barbarousness, I never heard the old song of Percy and Douglas[1] that I found not my heart moved more than with a trumpet; and yet is it sung but by some blind crowder,[2] with no rougher voice than rude style; which, being so evil apparelled in the dust and cobwebs of that uncivil age, what would it work trimmed in the gorgeous eloquence of Pindar?[3] In Hungary I have seen it the manner at all feasts, and other such meetings, to have songs of their ancestors' valor, which that right soldierlike nation think one of the chiefest kindlers of brave courage. The incomparable Lacedemonians[4] did not only carry that kind of music ever with them to the field, but even at home, as such songs were made, so were they all content to be singers of them—when the lusty men were to tell what they did, the old men what they had done, and the young what they would do. And where a man may say that Pindar many times praiseth highly victories of small moment, matters rather of sport than virtue; as it may be answered, it was the fault of the poet, and not of the poetry, so indeed the chief fault was in the time and custom of the Greeks, who set those toys at so high a price that Philip of Macedon[5] reckoned a horserace won at Olympus among his three fearful[6] felicities. But as the unimitable Pindar often did, so is that kind most capable and most fit to awake the thoughts from the sleep of idleness to embrace honorable enterprises.

8. "The cruel man (i.e., the tyrant) who rules his people with a harsh government fears his fearful people; terror returns to its author" (Seneca, *Oedipus*, 3.705–6).
9. Tyrant of Pherae in Thessaly (369–357 B.C.E.), described by Plutarch in his *Life of Pelopidas*.
1. Sidney refers to the ballad *Chevy Chase*, which describes the conflict between the Earls of Percy and Douglas.
2. Fiddler.
3. The most famous of Greek lyric poets (c. 522–402 B.C.E.), whose metrically complex odes celebrate victories in the Panhellenic games, the most famous of which was held every four years at Olympia.
4. Spartans.
5. Father of Alexander the Great, himself a conquering general and hero. Olympus: Sidney's error for Olympia, site of the Olympian Games.
6. Wonderful.

There rests the Heroical—whose very name (I think) should daunt all backbiters: for by what conceit can a tongue be directed to speak evil of that which draweth with him no less champions than Achilles, Cyrus, Aeneas, Turnus, Tydeus, and Rinaldo?[7]—who doth not only teach and move to a truth, but teacheth and moveth to the most high and excellent truth; who maketh magnanimity and justice shine through all misty fearfulness and foggy desires; who, if the saying of Plato and Tully be true, that who could see virtue would be wonderfully ravished with the love of her beauty—this man sets her out to make her more lovely in her holiday apparel, to the eye of any that will deign not to disdain until they understand. But if anything be already said in the defense of sweet poetry, all concurreth to the maintaining the heroical, which is not only a kind, but the best and most accomplished kind of poetry. For as the image of each action stirreth and instructeth the mind, so the lofty image of such worthies most inflameth the mind with desire to be worthy, and informs with counsel how to be worthy. Only let Aeneas be worn in the tablet of your memory, how he governeth himself in the ruin of his country; in the preserving his old father, and carrying away his religious ceremonies; in obeying God's commandment to leave Dido, though not only all passionate kindness, but even the human consideration of virtuous gratefulness, would have craved other of him; how in storms, how in sports, how in war, how in peace, how a fugitive, how victorious, how besieged, how besieging, how to strangers, how to allies, how to enemies, how to his own; lastly, how in his inward self, and how in his outward government—and I think, in a mind not prejudiced with a prejudicating humor, he will be found in excellency fruitful, yea, even as Horace saith,

melius Chrysippo et Crantore.[8]

But truly I imagine it falleth out with these poet-whippers, as with some good women, who often are sick, but in faith they cannot tell where; so the name of poetry is odious to them, but neither his cause nor effects, neither the sum that contains him, nor the particularities descending from him, give any fast handle to their carping dispraise.

Since then poetry is of all human learning the most ancient and of most fatherly antiquity, as from whence other learnings have taken their beginnings; since it is so universal that no learned nation doth despise it, nor barbarous nation is without it; since both Roman and Greek gave such divine names unto it, the one of prophesying, the other of making, and that indeed that name of making is fit for him, considering that where all other arts retain themselves within their subject, and receive, as it were, their being from it, the poet only bringeth his own stuff, and doth not learn a conceit out of a matter,[9] but maketh matter for a conceit; since neither his description nor end containing any evil, the thing described cannot be evil; since his effects be so good as to teach goodness and to delight the learners; since therein (namely in moral doctrine, the chief of all knowledges) he doth not only far pass the historian, but, for instructing, is well nigh comparable to the philosopher, for moving leaves him behind him; since the Holy Scripture (wherein there is no uncleanness) hath whole parts in it poetical, and that even our Savior Christ vouchsafed to use the flowers of it; since all his kinds are not only in their united forms but in their severed

7. Epic heroes and moral exemplars. Tydeus fought to bring Polyneices, the son of Oedipus, to the throne of Thebes (see Statius's *Thebaid*); Rinaldo was one of the French king Charlemagne's knights who fought against the Saracens in Italy (see Ludovico Ariosto's *Orlando Furioso* and Torquato Tasso's *Jerusalem Delivered*).

8. "Better than [the philosophers] Chrysippus and Crantor" (Horace, *Epistles*, 1.4).

9. I.e., does not take his theme from his material.

dissections fully commendable; I think (and think I think rightly) the laurel crown appointed for triumphant captains doth worthily (of all other learnings) honor the poet's triumph.

But because we have ears as well as tongues, and that the lightest reasons that may be will seem to weigh greatly, if nothing be put in the counterbalance, let us hear, and, as well as we can, ponder what objections be made against this art, which may be worthy either of yielding or answering.

First, truly I note not only in these μισ'ομονσοι, poet-haters, but in all that kind of people who seek a praise by dispraising others, that they do prodigally spend a great many wandering words in quips and scoffs, carping and taunting at each thing which, by stirring the spleen, may stay the brain from a through-beholding the worthiness of the subject. Those kind of objections, as they are full of a very idle easiness, since there is nothing of so sacred a majesty but that an itching tongue may rub itself upon it, so deserve they no other answer, but, instead of laughing at the jest, to laugh at the jester. We know a playing wit can praise the discretion of an ass, the comfortableness of being in debt, and the jolly commodities of being sick of the plague. So of the contrary side, if we will turn Ovid's verse

Ut lateat virtus proximitate mali,[1]

that good lie hid in nearness of the evil, Agrippa will be as merry in showing the vanity of science as Erasmus was in the commending of folly. Neither shall any man or matter escape some touch of these smiling railers. But for Erasmus and Agrippa,[2] they had another foundation than the superficial part would promise. Marry, these other pleasant faultfinders, who will correct the verb before they understand the noun, and confute others' knowledge before they confirm their own—I would have them only remember that scoffing cometh not of wisdom. So as the best title in true English they get with their merriments is to be called good fools; for so have our grave forefathers ever termed that humorous kind of jesters.

But that which giveth greatest scope to their scorning humor is rhyming and versing. It is already said (and, as I think, truly said), it is not rhyming and versing that maketh poesy. One may be a poet without versing, and a versifier without poetry. But yet, presuppose it were inseparable (as indeed it seemeth Scaliger[3] judgeth), truly it were an inseparable commendation. For if *oratio* next to *ratio*, speech next to reason, be the greatest gift bestowed upon mortality, that cannot be praiseless which doth most polish that blessing of speech; which considers each word, not only (as a man may say) by his most forcible quality, but by his best measured quantity, carrying even in themselves a harmony—without, perchance, number, measure, order, proportion be in our time grown odious. But lay aside the just praise it hath, by being the only fit speech for music (music, I say, the most divine striker of the senses), thus much is undoubtedly true, that if reading be foolish without remembering, memory being the only treasure of knowledge, those words which are fittest for memory are likewise most convenient for knowledge. Now, that verse far exceedeth prose in the

1. "That virtue may lie next to evil" (Cf. Ovid, *The Art of Love* 2.662).

2. Henry Cornelius Agrippa of Nettesheim (1486–1533), a German philosopher, and Desiderius Erasmus of Rotterdam (1467–1536), the greatest humanist scholar of the early modern period. Sidney refers to their most popular works, *The Uncertainty and Vanity of Knowledge* and *The Praise of Folly*, respectively, both written to satirize human pretensions.

3. Julius Caesar Scaliger (1484–1558), an Italian scholar who wrote a treatise, *Seven Books on Poetry*.

knitting up of memory, the reason is manifest: the words (besides their delight, which hath a great affinity to memory) being so set as one cannot be lost but the whole work fails; which accusing itself, calleth the remembrance back to itself, and so most strongly confirmeth it. Besides, one word so, as it were, begetting another, as, be it in rhyme or measured verse, by the former a man shall have a near guess to the follower. Lastly, even they that have taught the art of memory have showed nothing so apt for it as a certain room divided into many places well and thoroughly known. Now, that hath the verse in effect perfectly, every word having his natural seat, which seat must needs make the word remembered. But what needeth more in a thing so known to all men? Who is it that ever was a scholar that doth not carry away some verses of Virgil, Horace, or Cato, which in his youth he learned, and even to his old age serve him for hourly lessons? But the fitness it hath for memory is notably proved by all delivery of arts: wherein for the most part, from grammar to logic, mathematics, physic, and the rest, the rules chiefly necessary to be borne away are compiled in verses. So that, verse being in itself sweet and orderly, and being best for memory, the only handle of knowledge, it must be in jest that any man can speak against it.

Now then go we to the most important imputations laid to the poor poets. For aught I can yet learn, they are these. First, that there being many other more fruitful knowledges, a man might better spend his time in them than in this. Secondly, that it is the mother of lies. Thirdly, that it is the nurse of abuse, infecting us with many pestilent desires; with a siren's sweetness drawing the mind to the serpent's tail of sinful fancies (and herein, especially, comedies give the largest field to ear,[4] as Chaucer saith); how, both in other nations and in ours, before poets did soften us, we were full of courage, given to martial exercises, the pillars of manlike liberty, and not lulled asleep in shady idleness with poets' pastimes. And lastly, and chiefly, they cry out with open mouth as if they had overshot Robin Hood,[5] that Plato banished them out of his commonwealth. Truly, this is much, if there be much truth in it.

First, to the first. That a man might better spend his time, is a reason indeed; but it doth (as they say) but *petere principium* [beg the question]. For if it be as I affirm, that no learning is so good as that which teacheth and moveth to virtue; and that none can both teach and move thereto so much as poetry: then is the conclusion manifest that ink and paper cannot be to a more profitable purpose employed. And certainly, though a man should grant their first assumption, it should follow (methinks) very unwillingly, that good is not good, because better is better. But I still and utterly deny that there is sprong out of earth a more fruitful knowledge.

To the second, therefore, that they should be the principal liars, I answer paradoxically, but truly, I think truly, that of all writers under the sun the poet is the least liar, and, though he would, as a poet can scarcely be a liar. The astronomer, with his cousin the geometrician, can hardly escape, when they take upon them to measure the height of the stars. How often, think you, do the physicians lie, when they aver things good for sicknesses, which afterwards send Charon[6] a great number of souls drowned in a potion before they come to his ferry? And no less of the rest, which take upon them to affirm. Now, for the poet, he nothing affirms, and therefore never lieth. For, as I take it, to lie is to affirm that to be true which is false. So as the other artists,

4. Sidney refers to an expression in Chaucer's *Canterbury Tales:* "a large feeld to ere," *The Knight's Tale,* line 28.
5. The medieval folk hero, who is said to have lived in Sherwood Forest. Plato banishes poets in his treatise on the ideal state (*The Republic* 3.392).
6. According to Greek myth, Charon ferries souls across the river Styx to the underworld.

and especially the historian, affirming many things, can, in the cloudy knowledge of mankind, hardly escape from many lies. But the poet (as I said before) never affirmeth. The poet never maketh any circles about your imagination, to conjure you to believe for true what he writes. He citeth not authorities of other histories, but even for his entry calleth the sweet Muses to inspire into him a good invention; in truth, not laboring to tell you what is or is not, but what should or should not be. And therefore, though he recount things not true, yet because he telleth them not for true, he lieth not—without we will say that Nathan lied in his speech before-alleged to David; which as a wicked man durst scarce say, so think I none so simple would say that Aesop lied in the tales of his beasts; for who thinks that Aesop wrote it for actually true were well worthy to have his name chronicled among the beasts he writeth of. What child is there, that, coming to a play, and seeing *Thebes* written in great letters upon an old door, doth believe that it is Thebes? If then a man can arrive to that child's age to know that the poets' persons and doings are but pictures what should be, and not stories what have been, they will never give the lie to things not affirmatively but allegorically and figuratively written. And therefore, as in history, looking for truth, they may go away full fraught with falsehood, so in poesy, looking but for fiction, they shall use the narration but as an imaginative ground-plot of a profitable invention. But hereto is replied, that the poets give names to men they write of, which argueth a conceit of an actual truth, and so, not being true, proves a falsehood. And doth the lawyer lie then, when under the names of *John-a-stiles* and *John-a-nokes*[7] he puts his case? But that is easily answered. Their naming of men is but to make their picture the more lively, and not to build any history: painting men, they cannot leave men nameless. We see we cannot play at chess but that we must give names to our chessmen; and yet, methinks, he were a very partial champion of truth that would say we lied for giving a piece of wood the reverend title of a bishop. The poet nameth Cyrus or Aeneas no other way than to show what men of their fames, fortunes, and estates should do.

Their third is, how much it abuseth men's wit, training it to wanton sinfulness and lustful love: for indeed that is the principal, if not only, abuse I can hear alleged.[8] They say, the comedies rather teach than reprehend amorous conceits. They say the lyric is larded with passionate sonnets; the elegiac weeps the want of his mistress; and that even to the heroical, Cupid hath ambitiously climbed. Alas, Love, I would thou couldst as well defend thyself as thou canst offend others. I would those on whom thou dost attend could either put thee away, or yield good reason why they keep thee. But grant love of beauty to be a beastly fault (although it be very hard, since only man, and no beast, hath that gift to discern beauty); grant that lovely name of Love to deserve all hateful reproaches (although even some of my masters the philosophers spent a good deal of their lamp-oil in setting forth the excellency of it); grant, I say, whatsoever they will have granted, that not only love, but lust, but vanity, but (if they list) scurrility, possesseth many leaves of the poets' books; yet think I, when this is granted, they will find their sentence may with good manners put the last words foremost, and not say that poetry abuseth man's wit, but that man's wit abuseth poetry.

7. I.e., John Doe, or John Roe of ancient law courts.
8. Sidney refers to contemporary criticism of the drama, the best known of which was Stephen Gosson's *School of Abuse* (1579); see page 1033.

For I will not deny but that man's wit may make poesy, which should be εἰκαστικη [representing real things] (which some learned have defined: figuring forth good things), to be φανταστικη [representing imaginary things] (which doth, contrariwise, infect the fancy with unworthy objects), as the painter, that should give to the eye either some excellent perspective, or some fine picture, fit for building or fortification, or containing in it some notable example (as Abraham sacrificing his son Isaac, Judith killing Holofernes, David fighting with Goliath),[9] may leave those, and please an ill-pleased eye with wanton shows of better hidden matters. But what, shall the abuse of a thing make the right use odious? Nay truly, though I yield that poesy may not only be abused, but that being abused, by the reason of his sweet charming force, it can do more hurt than any other army of words: yet shall it be so far from concluding that the abuse should give reproach to the abused, that, contrariwise, it is a good reason that whatsoever, being abused, doth most harm, being rightly used (and upon the right use each thing conceiveth his title), doth most good. Do we not see the skill of physic, the best rampire[1] to our often-assaulted bodies, being abused, teach poison, the most violent destroyer? Doth not knowledge of law, whose end is to even and right all things, being abused, grow the crooked fosterer of horrible injuries? Doth not (to go to the highest) God's word abused breed heresy, and His name abused become blasphemy? Truly, a needle cannot do much hurt, and as truly (with leave of ladies be it spoken) it cannot do much good: with a sword thou mayst kill thy father, and with a sword thou mayst defend thy prince and country. So that, as in their calling poets fathers of lies they said nothing, so in this their argument of abuse they prove the commendation.

They allege herewith, that before poets began to be in price our nation had set their hearts' delight upon action, and not imagination: rather doing things worthy to be written, than writing things fit to be done. What that before-time was, I think scarcely Sphinx[2] can tell, since no memory is so ancient that hath not the precedent of poetry. And certain it is that, in our plainest homeliness, yet never was the Albion[3] nation without poetry. Marry, this argument, though it be levelled against poetry, yet is it indeed a chainshot[4] against all learning, or bookishness as they commonly term it. Of such mind were certain Goths,[5] of whom it is written that, having in the spoil of a famous city taken a fair library, one hangman (belike fit to execute the fruits of their wits) who had murdered a great number of bodies, would have set fire in it: no, said another very gravely, take heed what you do, for while they are busy about these toys, we shall with more leisure conquer their countries. This indeed is the ordinary doctrine of ignorance, and many words sometimes I have heard spent in it. But because this reason is generally against all learning as well as poetry, or rather, all learning but poetry; because it were too large a digression to handle it, or at least too superfluous (since it is manifest that all government of action is to be gotten by knowledge, and knowledge best by gathering many knowledges, which is reading), I only, with Horace, to him that is of that opinion

jubeo stultum esse libenter;[6]

for as for poetry itself, it is the freest from this objection.

9. Sidney refers to episodes in the Bible (Genesis 22, 1 Samuel 17, Judith 2–14).
1. Rampart.
2. In Greek mythology, a monster with a woman's head and a lion's body who posed riddles to human beings.
3. British.
4. Two cannonballs joined by a chain; it was deployed in naval warfare, usually against the rigging on enemy ships.
5. Northern European tribes, often described as uncivilized by ancient historians. The fate of "a fair library" is told by Michel de Montaigne in his essay *Of Pedantry* (*Essays* 1.24).
6. "I order [him] to be stupid cheerfully" (Horace, *Satires*, 1.1.63).

For poetry is the companion of camps. I dare undertake, Orlando Furioso, or honest King Arthur, will never displease a soldier; but the quiddity of *ens* and *prima materia* will hardly agree with a corselet;[7] and therefore, as I said in the beginning, even Turks and Tartars are delighted with poets. Homer, a Greek, flourished before Greece flourished. And if to a slight conjecture a conjecture may be opposed, truly it may seem, that as by him their learned men took almost their first light of knowledge, so their active men received their first motions of courage. Only Alexander's example may serve, who by Plutarch is accounted of such virtue, that Fortune was not his guide but his footstool; whose acts speak for him, though Plutarch did not: indeed the phoenix of warlike princes.[8] This Alexander left his schoolmaster, living Aristotle, behind him, but took dead Homer with him. He put the philosopher Callisthenes to death for his seeming philosophical, indeed mutinous, stubbornness, but the chief thing he was ever heard to wish for was that Homer had been alive. He well found he received more bravery of mind by the pattern of Achilles than by hearing the definition of fortitude. And therefore, if Cato misliked Fulvius for carrying Ennius with him to the field,[9] it may be answered that, if Cato misliked it, the noble Fulvius liked it, or else he had not done it; for it was not the excellent Cato Uticensis (whose authority I would much more have reverenced), but it was the former, in truth a bitter punisher of faults (but else a man that had never well sacrificed to the Graces: he misliked and cried out against all Greek learning, and yet, being eighty years old, began to learn it, belike fearing that Pluto understood not Latin). Indeed, the Roman laws allowed no person to be carried to the wars but he that was in the soldiers' roll; and therefore, though Cato misliked his unmustered person, he misliked not his work.[1] And if he had, Scipio Nasica, judged by common consent the best Roman, loved him. Both the other Scipio brothers, who had by their virtues no less surnames than of Asia and Afric, so loved him that they caused his body to be buried in their sepulture. So as Cato's authority, being but against his person, and that answered with so far greater than himself, is herein of no validity.

But now indeed my burden is great; now Plato's name is laid upon me, whom, I must confess, of all philosophers I have ever esteemed most worthy of reverence, and with good reason: since of all philosophers he is the most poetical. Yet if he will defile the fountain out of which his flowing streams have proceeded, let us boldly examine with what reasons he did it. First, truly, a man might maliciously object that Plato, being a philosopher, was a natural enemy of poets. For indeed, after the philosophers had picked out of the sweet mysteries of poetry the right discerning true points of knowledge, they forthwith putting it in method, and making a school-art of that which the poets did only teach by a divine delightfulness, beginning to spurn at their guides, like ungrateful prentices, were not content to set up shops for themselves, but

7. I.e., soldiers will enjoy reading about knights like Ariosto's Orlando Furioso or Malory's King Arthur, but will balk at philosophers' concerns with "quiddities" (subtleties), "*ens*" (being), and "*prima materia*" (the original matter of the universe).

8. Sidney cites various episodes from Plutarch's accounts of Alexander the Great in his *Lives* (c. 100 C.E.), which was translated into English by Sir Thomas North in 1579. The phoenix was a mythic bird thought to be eternally reborn in the ashes of its own funeral pyre.

9. Marcus Portius Cato the Censor (234–184 B.C.E.), criticized the general Marcus Flavius Nobilior for carrying the poetry of Quintus Ennius (239–169 B.C.E.) on a battle campaign. Sidney goes on to distinguish Cato the Censor from his great-grandson, Marcus Porcius Cato, the chief political antagonist of Julius Caesar.

1. In fact, as Sidney states, the poet Ennius in person actually accompanied Flavius; he was "unmustered" in that he was not on the army payroll. Sidney continues to praise Ennius by saying that he was loved by various Scipios: Publius Cornelius Scipio Nasica, Publius Cornelius Scipio Africanus, and Lucius Cornelius Scipio Asiaticus, all notable patriots and generals.

sought by all means to discredit their masters; which by the force of delight being barred them, the less they could overthrow them, the more they hated them. For indeed, they found for Homer seven cities strave who should have him for their citizen; where many cities banished philosophers as not fit members to live among them. For only repeating certain of Euripides' verses,[2] many Athenians had their lives saved of the Syracusans, where the Athenians themselves thought many philosophers unworthy to live. Certain poets, as Simonides and Pindar, had so prevailed with Hiero the First,[3] that of a tyrant they made him a just king; where Plato could do so little with Dionysius, that he himself of a philosopher was made a slave. But who should do thus, I confess, should requite the objections made against poets with like cavillations[4] against philosophers; as likewise one should do that should bid one read *Phaedrus* or *Symposium* in Plato, or the discourse of love in Plutarch, and see whether any poet do authorize abominable filthiness, as they do. Again, a man might ask out of what commonwealth Plato did banish them:[5] in sooth, thence where he himself alloweth community of women—so as belike this banishment grew not for effeminate wantonness, since little should poetical sonnets be hurtful when a man might have what woman he listed.[6] But I honor philosophical instructions, and bless the wits which bred them: so as they be not abused, which is likewise stretched to poetry.

St. Paul himself (who yet, for the credit of poets, twice citeth poets, and one of them by the name of "their prophet") setteth a watchword upon philosophy—indeed upon the abuse.[7] So doth Plato upon the abuse, not upon poetry. Plato found fault that the poets of his time filled the world with wrong opinions of the gods, making light tales of that unspotted essence, and therefore would not have the youth depraved with such opinions. Herein may much be said. Let this suffice: the poets did not induce such opinions, but did imitate those opinions already induced. For all the Greek stories can well testify that the very religion of that time stood upon many and many-fashioned gods, not taught so by the poets, but followed according to their nature of imitation. Who list may read in Plutarch the discourses of Isis and Osiris,[8] of the cause why oracles ceased, of the divine providence, and see whether the theology of that nation stood not upon such dreams which the poets indeed superstitiously observed—and truly (since they had not the light of Christ) did much better in it than the philosophers, who, shaking off superstition, brought in atheism. Plato therefore (whose authority I had much rather justly construe than unjustly resist) meant not in general of poets, in those words of which Julius Scaliger saith *Qua authoritate barbari quidam atque hispidi abuti velint ad poetas e republica exigendos;*[9] but only meant to drive out those wrong opinions of the Deity (whereof now, without further law, Christianity hath taken away all the hurtful belief)

2. Plutarch states that Greek slaves living outside Greece had won their release by teaching their masters the poetry of Euripides (*Life of Nicias*, ch. 29).
3. Tyrant of Syracuse (478–476 B.C.E.), who patronized Greek poets. Aeschylus was a playwright; Bacchylides a lyric poet; and Simonides a writer of satire. Dionysius the Elder of Syracuse was said to have sold Plato to the Spartan ambassador Pollis as a slave, a situation from which he was later liberated.
4. Objections.
5. I.e., poets. Plato argued that in his ideal republic, all women should be common, that is, not married to a single man but sexually available to all men (*Republic* 5, 449–462). Sidney observes that Plato banishes poets not because poetry makes men licentious, an impossibility in a state in which women are readily available, but for some other reason.
6. Desired.
7. Paul rejects the assessment of poets by philosophers (Acts 17.18, Colossians 2.8), and he castigates false prophets (Titus 1.12).
8. Isis, the Egyptian goddess of fertility, was sister and wife of Osiris, civilizer of Egypt, god of the dead, and source of life.
9. By abuse of whose authority, barbarous and crude men wish to expel poets from the Republic; Scaliger is commenting on Plato's expulsion of poets from an ideal republic in his own treatise on poetry.

perchance (as he thought) nourished by the then esteemed poets. And a man need go no further than to Plato himself to know his meaning: who, in his dialogue called *Ion*, giveth high and rightly divine commendation unto poetry. So as Plato, banishing the abuse, not the thing, not banishing it, but giving due honor unto it, shall be our patron, and not our adversary. For indeed I had much rather (since truly I may do it) show their mistaking of Plato (under whose lion's skin they would make an ass-like braying against poesy) than go about to overthrow his authority; whom, the wiser a man is, the more just cause he shall find to have in admiration; especially since he attributeth unto poesy more than myself do, namely, to be a very inspiring of a divine force, far above man's wit, as in the forenamed dialogue is apparent.

Of the other side, who would show the honors have been by the best sort of judgments granted them, a whole sea of examples would present themselves: Alexanders, Caesars, Scipios, all favorers of poets; Laelius, called the Roman Socrates, himself a poet, so as part of *Heautontimorumenos*[1] in Terence was supposed to be made by him; and even the Greek Socrates, whom Apollo confirmed to be the only wise man, is said to have spent part of his old time in putting Aesop's fables into verses. And therefore, full evil should it become his scholar Plato to put such words in his master's mouth against poets. But what need more? Aristotle writes the Art of Poesy;[2] and why, if it should not be written? Plutarch teacheth the use to be gathered of them; and how, if they should not be read? And who reads Plutarch's either history or philosophy, shall find he trimmeth both their garments with guards of poesy. But I list not to defend poesy with the help of his underling historiography. Let it suffice to have showed it is a fit soil for praise to dwell upon; and what dispraise may be set upon it, is either easily overcome, or transformed into just commendation.

So that, since the excellencies of it may be so easily and so justly confirmed, and the low-creeping objections so soon trodden down: it not being an art of lies, but of true doctrine; not of effeminateness, but of notable stirring of courage; not of abusing man's wit, but of strengthening man's wit; not banished, but honored by Plato: let us rather plant more laurels for to engarland the poets' heads (which honor of being laureate, whereas besides them only triumphant captains were, is a sufficient authority to show the price they ought to be held in) than suffer the ill-favored breath of such wrong-speakers once to blow upon the clear springs of poesy.

But since I have run so long a career in this matter, methinks, before I give my pen a full stop, it shall be but a little more lost time to inquire why England, the mother of excellent minds, should be grown so hard a stepmother to poets, who certainly in wit ought to pass all other, since all only proceedeth from their wit, being indeed makers of themselves, not takers of others. How can I but exclaim

Musa, mihi causas memora, quo numine laeso?[3]

Sweet poesy, that hath anciently had kings, emperors, senators, great captains, such as, besides a thousand others, David, Adrian, Sophocles, Germanicus, not only to

1. Gaius Laelius was said to have written parts of a play called *Heautontimorumenos* (*The Self-Tormenter*), reputed to be by the Roman playwright Terence. Plato reports that Socrates turned Aesop's fables into verse.

2. Sidney refers to Aristotle's *Poetics*.

3. "Muse, tell me the cause, by what wounded divinity. . . ." (*Aeneid* 1.8).

favor poets, but to be poets;[4] and of our nearer times can present for her patrons a Robert, king of Sicily, the great King Francis of France, King James of Scotland; such cardinals as Bembus and Bibbiena; such famous preachers and teachers as Beza and Melanchthon; so learned philosophers as Fracastorius and Scaliger; so great orators as Pontanus and Muretus; so piercing wits as George Buchanan; so grave counselors as, beside many, but before all, that Hospital of France,[5] than whom (I think) that realm never brought forth a more accomplished judgment, more firmly builded upon virtue: I say these, with numbers of others, not only to read others' poesies, but to poetize for others' reading—that poesy, thus embraced in all other places, should only find in our time a hard welcome in England, I think the very earth lamenteth it, and therefore decketh our soil with fewer laurels than it was accustomed. For heretofore poets have in England also flourished, and, which is to be noted, even in those times when the trumpet of Mars[6] did sound loudest. And now that an overfaint quietness should seem to strew[7] the house for poets, they are almost in as good reputation as the mountebanks[8] at Venice. Truly even that, as of the one side it giveth great praise to poesy, which like Venus (but to better purpose) had rather be troubled in the net with Mars than enjoy the homely quiet of Vulcan:[9] so serves it for a piece of a reason why they are less grateful to idle England, which now can scarce endure the pain of a pen.

Upon this necessarily followeth, that base men with servile wits undertake it, who think it enough if they can be rewarded of the printer. And so as Epaminondas[1] is said with the honor of his virtue to have made an office, by his exercising it, which before was contemptible, to become highly respected; so these men, no more but setting their names to it, by their own disgracefulness disgrace the most graceful poesy. For now, as if all the Muses were got with child to bring forth bastard poets, without any commission they do post over the banks of Helicon,[2] till they make the readers more weary than post-horses; while, in the meantime, they

Queis meliore luto finxit praecordia Titan

are better content to suppress the outflowings of their wit, than, by publishing them, to be accounted knights of the same order. But I that, before ever I durst aspire unto the dignity, am admitted into the company of the paper-blurrers, do find the very true cause of our wanting estimation is want of desert—taking upon us to be poets in despite of Pallas.

Now, wherein we want desert were a thankworthy labor to express; but if I knew, I should have mended myself. But I, as I never desired the title, so have I neglected the means to come by it. Only, overmastered by some thoughts, I yielded an inky

4. King David of Israel composed psalms; the emperor Adrian (i.e., Hadrian) wrote verse and prose; Germanicus Caesar, conqueror of Germany, is supposed to have written poetry and plays. Sidney goes on to list a range of modern statesmen-poets.
5. Michel de L'Hôpital (1505–1573), a statesman who favored religious toleration, wrote Latin poems.
6. God of war.
7. Be scattered over.
8. Itinerant quacks peddling fake medicines.
9. Roman god of fire and smiths who caught his adulterous wife, Venus, and Mars, the god of war, in a net he had forged.

1. Theban general (4th century B.C.E.).
2. Not a very clear paragraph. The mountain named Helicon is sacred to the muses. Here it represents the inspirational springs that are being "post[ed] over," that is, bypassed, by contemporary "bastard poets" eager to publish, while better writers "whose hearts the Titan [Prometheus] molded out of better clays" (Juvenal, *Satires* 14.36) keep their works private rather than be lumped in with their inferiors. Sidney himself claims, perhaps with false modesty, that as a poet he is classed with the mediocrities, and declares that the reason for poets' low esteem is "want of desert" or lack of worth: They have not been helped by Pallas Athena, goddess of wisdom.

tribute unto them. Marry, they that delight in poesy itself should seek to know what they do, and how they do; and especially look themselves in an unflattering glass of reason, if they be inclinable unto it. For poesy must not be drawn by the ears; it must be gently led, or rather it must lead—which was partly the cause that made the ancient-learned affirm it was a divine gift, and no human skill: since all other knowledges lie ready for any that hath strength of wit. A poet no industry can make, if his own genius be not carried into it; and therefore it is an old proverb, *orator fit, poeta nascitur* [the orator is made, the poet born].

Yet confess I always that as the fertilest ground must be manured, so must the highest-flying wit have a Daedalus to guide him.[3] That Daedalus, they say, both in this and in other, hath three wings to bear itself up into the air of due commendation: that is, art, imitation, and exercise. But these, neither artificial rules nor imitative patterns, we much cumber ourselves withal. Exercise indeed we do, but that very fore-backwardly: for where we should exercise to know, we exercise as having known; and so is our brain delivered of much matter which never was begotten by knowledge. For there being two principal parts, matter to be expressed by words and words to express the matter, in neither we use art or imitation rightly. Our matter is *quodlibet* [what you will] indeed, though wrongly performing Ovid's verse,

Quicquid conabor dicere, versus erit;[4]

never marshalling it into any assured rank, that almost the readers cannot tell where to find themselves.

Chaucer, undoubtedly, did excellently in his *Troilus and Criseyde;*[5] of whom, truly, I know not whether to marvel more, either that he in that misty time could see so clearly, or that we in this clear age go so stumblingly after him. Yet had he great wants, fit to be forgiven in so reverent an antiquity. I account the *Mirror of Magistrates* meetly furnished of beautiful parts, and in the Earl of Surrey's lyrics many things tasting of a noble birth, and worthy of a noble mind. The *Shepherd's Calendar* hath much poetry in his eclogues, indeed worthy the reading, if I be not deceived. (That same framing of his style to an old rustic language I dare not allow, since neither Theocritus in Greek, Virgil in Latin, nor Sannazaro in Italian did affect it.) Besides these I do not remember to have seen but few (to speak boldly) printed that have poetical sinews in them; for proof whereof, let but most of the verses be put in prose, and then ask the meaning, and it will be found that one verse did but beget another, without ordering at the first what should be at the last; which becomes a confused mass of words, with a tingling sound of rhyme, barely accompanied with reason.

Our tragedies and comedies (not without cause cried out against), observing rules neither of honest civility nor skilful poetry—excepting *Gorboduc*[6] (again, I say, of those that I have seen), which notwithstanding as it is full of stately speeches and well-sounding phrases, climbing to the height of Seneca's style, and as full of notable

3. The mythical artisan Daedalus built wings so that he and his son Icarus could escape from Crete, where Minos had confined him in the maze of his own making; but Icarus flew too near the sun, the wax in his wings melted, and he fell into the Aegean Sea and drowned. He is often cited as a figure of ambition.
4. "Whatever I shall try to say shall become verse" (*Tristia* 4.10.26).
5. Sidney gives grudging praise to a number of poets of the early modern period: Chaucer's romance *Troilus and Criseyde* relates the unhappy love affair of two Trojans; the *Mirror of* [*i.e., for*] *Magistrates*, a poem by various authors and added to at intervals during the 16th century, illustrated exemplary tragedies; the Earl of Surrey is Henry Howard; *The Shepheardes Calender* was written by Edmund Spenser. Theocritus, Virgil, and Sannazzaro were poets of pastoral.
6. A tragedy by Thomas Sackville and Thomas Norton (1561).

morality, which it doth most delightfully teach, and so obtain the very end of poesy, yet in truth it is very defectuous[7] in the circumstances, which grieveth me, because it might not remain as an exact model of all tragedies. For it is faulty both in place and time, the two necessary companions of all corporal actions. For where the stage should always represent but one place, and the uttermost time presupposed in it should be, both by Aristotle's precept and common reason, but one day, there is both many days, and many places, inartificially[8] imagined.

But if it be so in *Gorboduc*, how much more in all the rest, where you shall have Asia of the one side, and Afric of the other, and so many other under-kingdoms, that the player, when he cometh in, must ever begin with telling where he is, or else the tale will not be conceived? Now you shall have three ladies walk to gather flowers: and then we must believe the stage to be a garden. By and by we hear news of shipwreck in the same place: and then we are to blame if we accept it not for a rock. Upon the back of that comes out a hideous monster with fire and smoke: and then the miserable beholders are bound to take it for a cave. While in the meantime two armies fly in, represented with four swords and bucklers: and then what hard heart will not receive it for a pitched field?

Now, of time they are much more liberal: for ordinary it is that two young princes fall in love; after many traverses, she is got with child, delivered of a fair boy; he is lost, groweth a man, falls in love, and is ready to get another child; and all this in two hours' space: which, how absurd it is in sense, even sense may imagine, and art hath taught, and all ancient examples justified—and at this day, the ordinary players in Italy will not err in. Yet will some bring in an example of *Eunuchus* in Terence, that containeth matter of two days, yet far short of twenty years. True it is, and so was it to be played in two days, and so fitted to the time it set forth. And though Plautus have in one place done amiss, let us hit with him, and not miss with him.[9]

But they will say: How then shall we set forth a story which containeth both many places and many times? And do they not know that a tragedy is tied to the laws of poesy, and not of history; not bound to follow the story, but having liberty either to feign a quite new matter or to frame the history to the most tragical conveniency? Again, many things may be told which cannot be showed, if they know the difference betwixt reporting and representing. As, for example, I may speak (though I am here) of Peru, and in speech digress from that to the description of Calicut;[1] but in action I cannot represent it without Pacolet's horse;[2] and so was the manner the ancients took, by some *Nuntius* [messenger] to recount things done in former time or other place. Lastly, if they will represent a history, they must not (as Horace saith) begin *ab ovo* [from the beginning], but they must come to the principal point of that one action which they will represent.

By example this will be best expressed. I have a story of young Polydorus,[3] delivered for safety's sake, with great riches, by his father Priam to Polymnestor, king of Thrace, in the Trojan war time; he, after some years, hearing the overthrow of Priam, for to make the treasure his own, murdereth the child; the body of the child is taken up by Hecuba; she, the same day, findeth a sleight to be revenged most cruelly of the tyrant. Where now would one of our tragedy writers begin, but with the delivery of the child? Then should he sail over into Thrace, and so spend I know not how many

7. Defective.
8. Inartistically.
9. Terence, Plautus: two well-known writers of Roman comedies who influenced the drama in early modern England; Shakespeare took the plot of *The Comedy of Errors* from Plautus's *Menaechmi*.

1. Seaport on the west coast of India.
2. A magic horse in the French romance *Valentine and Orson*.
3. Sidney praises the narrative of the hero Polydorus as told by Euripides, who avoids a lengthy plot in his play on the subject, *Hecuba*.

years, and travel numbers of places. But where doth Euripides? Even with the finding of the body, leaving the rest to be told by the spirit of Polydorus. This need no further to be enlarged; the dullest wit may conceive it.

But besides these gross absurdities, how all their plays be neither right tragedies, nor right comedies, mingling kings and clowns, not because the matter so carrieth it, but thrust in the clown by head and shoulders to play a part in majestical matters with neither decency nor discretion, so as neither the admiration and commiseration, nor the right sportfulness, is by their mongrel tragicomedy obtained. I know Apuleius did somewhat so,[4] but that is a thing recounted with space of time, not represented in one moment; and I know the ancients have one or two examples of tragicomedies, as Plautus hath *Amphitryo*;[5] but, if we mark them well, we shall find that they never, or very daintily, match hornpipes and funerals. So falleth it out that, having indeed no right comedy, in that comical part of our tragedy, we have nothing but scurrility, unworthy of any chaste ears, or some extreme show of doltishness, indeed fit to lift up a loud laughter, and nothing else: where the whole tract of a comedy should be full of delight, as the tragedy should be still maintained in a well-raised admiration.

But our comedians think there is no delight without laughter; which is very wrong, for though laughter may come with delight, yet cometh it not of delight, as though delight should be the cause of laughter; but well may one thing breed both together. Nay, rather in themselves they have, as it were, a kind of contrariety: for delight we scarcely do but in things that have a conveniency to ourselves or to the general nature; laughter almost ever cometh of things most disproportioned to ourselves and nature. Delight hath a joy in it, either permanent or present. Laughter hath only a scornful tickling.

For example, we are ravished with delight to see a fair woman, and yet are far from being moved to laughter; we laugh at deformed creatures, wherein certainly we cannot delight. We delight in good chances, we laugh at mischances: we delight to hear the happiness of our friends, or country, at which he were worthy to be laughed at that would laugh; we shall, contrarily, laugh sometimes to find a matter quite mistaken and go down the hill against the bias in the mouth of some such men—as for the respect of them one shall be heartily sorry, he cannot choose but laugh, and so is rather pained than delighted with laughter.

Yet deny I not but that they may go well together. For as in Alexander's picture well set out we delight without laughter,[6] and in twenty mad antics we laugh without delight; so in Hercules, painted with his great beard and furious countenance, in a woman's attire, spinning at Omphale's commandment, it breedeth both delight and laughter: for the representing of so strange a power in love procureth delight, and the scornfulness of the action stirreth laughter. But I speak to this purpose, that all the end of the comical part be not upon such scornful matters as stir laughter only, but, mixed with it, that delightful teaching which is the end of poesy. And the great fault even in that point of laughter, and forbidden plainly by Aristotle, is that they stir laughter in

4. In his prose romance *The Golden Ass* (c. 155 C.E.); William Adlington translated the work into English in the 16th century.

5. In this play, the tragic element is represented by the heroine Alcmena, tricked into sleeping with the god Jupiter, who is disguised as her husband Amphitrion, and the comic element by the burlesque behavior of the gods who arrange the deception.

6. Sidney distinguishes reactions to different kinds of descriptions: Alexander's portrait delights; mad antics provoke laughter; Hercules, captive and dressed as a woman by Queen Omphale of Lydia, both delights and provokes laughter.

sinful things, which are rather execrable than ridiculous, or in miserable, which are rather to be pitied than scorned. For what is it to make folks gape at a wretched beggar and a beggarly clown; or, against law of hospitality, to jest at strangers, because they speak not English so well as we do? What do we learn, since it is certain

Nil habet infelix paupertas durius in se,
Quam quod ridiculos homines facit?[7]

But rather, a busy loving courtier and a heartless threatening Thraso;[8] a self-wise-seeming schoolmaster; an awry-transformed traveler. These if we saw walk in stage names, which we play naturally, therein were delightful laughter, and teaching delightfulness—as in the other, the tragedies of Buchanan[9] do justly bring forth a divine admiration.

But I have lavished out too many words of this play matter. I do it because, as they are excelling parts of poesy, so is there none so much used in England, and none can be more pitifully abused; which, like an unmannerly daughter showing a bad education, causeth her mother Poesy's honesty to be called in question.

Other sort of poetry almost have we none, but that lyrical kind of songs and sonnets: which, Lord, if He gave us so good minds, how well it might be employed, and with how heavenly fruit, both private and public, in singing the praises of the immortal beauty: the immortal goodness of that God who giveth us hands to write and wits to conceive; of which we might well want words, but never matter; of which we could turn our eyes to nothing, but we should ever have new-budding occasions. But truly many of such writings as come under the banner of unresistible love, if I were a mistress, would never persuade me they were in love: so coldly they apply fiery speeches, as men that had rather read lovers' writings—and so caught up certain swelling phrases which hang together like a man that once told my father that the wind was at northwest and by south, because he would be sure to name winds enough—than that in truth they feel those passions, which easily (as I think) may be bewrayed by that same forcibleness or *energia* (as the Greeks call it) of the writer. But let this be a sufficient though short note, that we miss the right use of the material point of poesy.

Now, for the outside of it, which is words, or (as I may term it) diction, it is even well worse. So is that honey-flowing matron Eloquence appareled, or rather disguised, in a courtesan-like painted affectation: one time, with so far-fet words that may seem monsters but must seem strangers to any poor Englishman; another time, with coursing[1] of a letter, as if they were bound to follow the method of a dictionary; another time, with figures and flowers, extremely winter-starved. But I would this fault were only peculiar to versifiers, and had not as large possession among prose-printers; and (which is to be marveled) among many scholars; and (which is to be pitied) among some preachers. Truly I could wish, if at least I might be so bold to wish in a thing beyond the reach of my capacity, the diligent imitators of Tully and Demosthenes[2] (most worthy to be imitated) did not so much keep Nizolian paperbooks[3] of their figures and

7. "Unfortunate poverty has nothing in itself harder to bear than that it makes men ridiculous" (Juvenal, *Satires* 3.152–53).
8. The braggart soldier of Terence's comedy *Eunuchus*.
9. A Scots humanist (1506–1582) who wrote four tragedies on biblical and classical themes.
1. Alliteration.
2. Athenian statesman and orator (383–322 B.C.E.).
3. Marius Nizolius, a 16th-century Italian rhetorician and lexicographer, published a collection of phrases by Cicero (i.e., Tully). Sidney complains that contemporary writers use them too often. Cicero, when he prosecuted the traitor Catiline, employed repetition skillfully to heighten the effect of his argument, but writers in Sidney's time are not as discriminating.

phrases, as by attentive translation (as it were) devour them whole, and make them wholly theirs: for now they cast sugar and spice upon every dish that is served to the table—like those Indians, not content to wear earrings at the fit and natural place of the ears, but they will thrust jewels through their nose and lips, because they will be sure to be fine. Tully, when he was to drive out Catiline, as it were with a thunderbolt of eloquence, often used the figure of repetition, as *Vivit. Vivit? Imo in senatum venit, & c.*[4] Indeed, inflamed with a well-grounded rage, he would have his words (as it were) double out of his mouth, and so do that artificially which we see men in choler do naturally. And we, having noted the grace of those words, hale them in sometimes to a familiar epistle, when it were too too much choler to be choleric. How well store of *similiter cadences* [similar cadences] doth sound with the gravity of the pulpit, I would but invoke Demosthenes' soul to tell, who with a rare daintiness useth them. Truly they have made me think of the sophister[5] that with too much subtlety would prove two eggs three, and though he might be counted a sophister, had none for his labor. So these men bringing in such a kind of eloquence, well may they obtain an opinion of a seeming finesse, but persuade few—which should be the end of their finesse. Now for similitudes, in certain printed discourses, I think all herbarists, all stories of beasts, fowls, and fishes are rifled up,[6] that they come in multitudes to wait upon any of our conceits; which certainly is as absurd a surfeit to the ears as is possible. For the force of a similitude not being to prove anything to a contrary disputer, but only to explain to a willing hearer, when that is done, the rest is a most tedious prattling, rather overswaying the memory from the purpose whereto they were applied, than any whit informing the judgment, already either satisfied, or by similitudes not to be satisfied. For my part, I do not doubt, when Antonius and Crassus,[7] the great forefathers of Cicero in eloquence, the one (as Cicero testifieth of them) pretended not to know art, the other not to set by it, because with a plain sensibleness they might win credit of popular ears (which credit is the nearest step to persuasion, which persuasion is the chief mark of oratory), I do not doubt (I say) but that they used these knacks very sparingly; which who doth generally use, any man may see doth dance to his own music, and so be noted by the audience more careful to speak curiously than to speak truly. Undoubtedly (at least to my opinion undoubtedly), I have found in divers smally learned courtiers a more sound style than in some professors of learning; of which I can guess no other cause, but that the courtier, following that which by practice he findeth fittest to nature, therein (though he know it not) doth according to art, though not by art: where the other, using art to show art, and not to hide art (as in these cases he should do), flieth from nature, and indeed abuseth art.

But what? Methinks I deserve to be pounded for straying from poetry to oratory. But both have such an affinity in the wordish consideration, that I think this digression will make my meaning receive the fuller understanding: which is not to take upon me to teach poets how they should do, but only, finding myself sick among the rest, to show some one or two spots of the common infection grown among the most part of writers, that, acknowledging ourselves somewhat awry, we may bend to the right use both of matter and manner: whereto our language giveth us great occasion, being indeed capable of any excellent exercising of it. I know some will say it is a

4. "He lives. He lives? He still comes into the Senate. . . ." The sentences paraphrase the opening of Cicero's first oration against Catiline.

5. One who argues by specious reasons.

6. Sidney suggests that the figures in beast fables are all "rifled" or taken by many writers; hence they have become trite.

7. Antonius: Marcus Antonius, consul in 99 B.C.E.; Crassus: Publius Licinius Crassus Dives Mucianus, consul in 175 B.C.E. Both men were famous orators.

mingled language.[8] And why not so much the better, taking the best of both the other? Another will say it wanteth grammar. Nay truly, it hath that praise, that it wants not grammar: for grammar it might have, but it needs it not, being so easy in itself, and so void of those cumbersome differences of cases, genders, moods, and tenses, which I think was a piece of the Tower of Babylon's curse,[9] that a man should be put to school to learn his mother-tongue. But for the uttering sweetly and properly the conceits of the mind (which is the end of speech), that hath it equally with any other tongue in the world; and is particularly happy in compositions of two or three words together, near the Greek, far beyond the Latin, which is one of the greatest beauties can be in a language.

Now of versifying there are two sorts, the one ancient, the other modern: the ancient marked the quantity of each syllable, and according to that framed his verse; the modern, observing only number (with some regard of the accent), the chief life of it standeth in that like sounding of the words, which we call rhyme. Whether of these be the more excellent, would bear many speeches: the ancient (no doubt) more fit for music, both words and time observing quantity, and more fit lively to express diverse passions, by the low or lofty sound of the well-weighed syllable; the latter likewise, with his rhyme, striketh a certain music to the ear, and, in fine, since it doth delight, though by another way, it obtains the same purpose: there being in either sweetness, and wanting in neither majesty. Truly the English, before any vulgar language I know, is fit for both sorts. For, for the ancient, the Italian is so full of vowels that it must ever be cumbered with elisions;[1] the Dutch so, of the other side, with consonants, that they cannot yield the sweet sliding, fit for a verse; the French in his whole language hath not one word that hath his accent in the last syllable saving two, called *antepenultima* [third from last]; and little more hath the Spanish, and therefore very gracelessly may they use dactyls.[2] The English is subject to none of these defects. Now for the rhyme, though we do not observe quantity, yet we observe the accent very precisely, which other languages either cannot do, or will not do so absolutely. That *caesura*, or breathing place in the midst of the verse, neither Italian nor Spanish have, the French and we never almost fail of. Lastly, even the very rhyme itself, the Italian cannot put it in the last syllable, by the French named the masculine rhyme, but still in the next to the last, which the French call the female, or the next before that, which the Italian term *sdrucciola* [three-syllable rhyme]. The example of the former is *buono: suono*, of the *sdrucciola* is *femina: semina*. The French, of the other side, hath both the male, as *bon: son*, and the female, as *plaise: taise*, but the *sdrucciola* he hath not: where the English hath all three, as *due: true, father: rather, motion: potion*[3]—with much more which might be said, but that already I find the triflingness of this discourse is much too much enlarged.

So that since the ever-praiseworthy Poesy is full of virtue-breeding delightfulness, and void of no gift that ought to be in the noble name of learning; since the blames laid against it are either false or feeble; since the cause why it is not esteemed in England is the fault of poet-apes, not poets; since, lastly, our tongue is

8. Sidney describes English as a "mingled" language because it is derived from Anglo-Saxon, brought over by the invading Germanic tribes during the 6th century, and Norman-French, introduced by William the Conqueror in 1066.
9. Early modern writers identified Babylon with Babel (see Genesis 10.10).

1. The suppression of a vowel at the end of a word when the next word begins with a vowel.
2. A metric foot in classical poetry, consisting of one long and two short syllables, as in the words "murmuring," "sensible."
3. *Motion* and *potion* presumably retained three syllables, as the Middle English spelling "mocioun" reveals.

most fit to honor poesy, and to be honored by poesy; I conjure you all that have had the evil luck to read this ink-wasting toy of mine, even in the name of the nine Muses, no more to scorn the sacred mysteries of poesy; no more to laugh at the name of poets, as though they were next inheritors to fools; no more to jest at the reverent title of a rhymer; but to believe, with Aristotle, that they were the ancient treasurers of the Grecians' divinity; to believe, with Bembus, that they were first bringers-in of all civility; to believe, with Scaliger, that no philosopher's precepts can sooner make you an honest man than the reading of Virgil; to believe, with Clauserus,[4] the translator of Cornutus, that it pleased the heavenly Deity, by Hesiod and Homer, under the veil of fables, to give us all knowledge, logic, rhetoric, philosophy natural and moral, and *quid non?* [what not]; to believe, with me, that there are many mysteries contained in poetry, which of purpose were written darkly, lest by profane wits it should be abused; to believe, with Landino,[5] that they are so beloved of the gods that whatsoever they write proceeds of a divine fury; lastly, to believe themselves, when they tell you they will make you immortal by their verses. Thus doing, your name shall flourish in the printers' shops; thus doing, you shall be of kin to many a poetical preface; thus doing, you shall be most fair, most rich, most wise, most all, you shall dwell upon superlatives; thus doing, though you be *libertino patre natus* [son of freed slave], you shall suddenly grow *Herculea proles* [a descendant of Hercules],

Si quid mea carmina possunt;[6]

thus doing, your soul shall be placed with Dante's Beatrice, or Virgil's Anchises. But if (fie of such a but) you be born so near the dull-making cataract of Nilus[7] that you cannot hear the planet-like music of poetry; if you have so earth-creeping a mind that it cannot lift itself up to look to the sky of poetry, or rather, by a certain rustical disdain, will become such a mome as to be a Momus[8] of poetry; then, though I will not wish unto you the ass's ears of Midas, nor to be driven by a poet's verses, as Bubonax[9] was, to hang himself, nor to be rhymed to death, as is said to be done in Ireland; yet thus much curse I must send you, in the behalf of all poets, that while you live, you live in love, and never get favor for lacking skill of a sonnet; and, when you die, your memory die from the earth for want of an epitaph.

"THE APOLOGY" AND ITS TIME

The Art of Poetry

After the spread of Reformation doctrine on the importance of moral discipline, English readers often encountered denunciations of poetry and especially drama. The issues that Sidney took up when he defended poetry were the subject of sharp dispute. Stephen Gosson

4. Conrad Clauser, a 16th-century German scholar who translated the works of Lucius Annaeus Cornutus, a 1st-century Greek slave who wrote commentaries on Aristotle and Virgil.
5. Cristoforo Landino (1424–1504), an Italian humanist who wrote moral dialogues.
6. "If my songs can do anything" (*Aeneid* 9.446).
7. Cicero claimed that hearing the sound of the cataracts of the Nile River in Egypt caused deafness; the Neoplatonists thought the movement of the planets produced heavenly music, the music of the spheres.
8. Momus personified the faultfinder in Greek literature; a mome is a blockhead. Apollo changed Midas's ears to those of an ass to signal his stupidity after Midas judged Pan's flute playing to be superior to Apollo's (Ovid, *Metamorphoses* 11.146).
9. Sidney conflates Hipponax, a Greek poet, with *Bupalus*, a sculptor. The latter had made an unflattering portrait of the former, who took revenge with deadly verses. Irish poets claimed their verses could kill man or beast.

represented the opinions of many of poetry's detractors. As he declares in *The School of Abuse*, published shortly before Sidney wrote his *Apology*, poetry provides frivolous distraction from the serious business of life and, what is worse, temptations to godlessness. But others, like Sidney, took a more optimistic view of the subject. In *The Art of English Poesy*, George Puttenham states that poets were the first lawgivers (as Sidney had) and focuses particularly on epic poetry, which, he says, give readers images of a truth beyond history as well as consistently inspiring models of action to imitate. His popular treatise contains a wealth of practical advice for aspiring writers and even today remains a useful sourcebook for information on rhetorical figures of thought and speech.

In addition to the challenge posed by moralists such as Gosson, defenders of English poetry also had to confront purely practical problems. Unlike the Romance languages—Italian, French, and Spanish—sixteenth-century English had lost almost all its feminine endings, the accented vowel sounds that made rhyming fairly easy. English was also a language in which words of one syllable were quite common, and poets had trouble creating the metrical harmonies usual in poetry written in languages rich in polysyllables. George Gascoigne's brief treatise *Certain Notes of Instruction*, which concerns the making of verse or rhyme in English, deals with these conditions directly. He warns against trying to achieve euphony or a musical quality by "rolling in pleasant words," as in the sequence "Rim, Ram, Ruff," and he insists that the "truer Englishman" uses words of one syllable. Critics could differ in what they valued, of course; in *A Defense of Rhyme*, Samuel Daniel justified rhyme as "pleasing to nature," which desires form and closures, not chaos and infinity. More important, he defended English writers against the claim that they could never match their classical precursors. He reminded readers that imputations of barbarism and ignorance are based on relative, not absolute, judgments.

Stephen Gosson

from *The School of Abuse*[1]

The Syracusans used such variety of dishes in their banquets that when they were set and their boards furnished,[2] they were many times in doubt which they should touch first or taste last. And in my opinion the world giveth every writer so large a field to walk in that before he set pen to the book, he shall find himself feasted at Syracuse, uncertain where to begin or when to end. This caused Pindarus[3] to question with his Muse whether he were better with his art to decipher the life of Nimpe Melia, or Cadmus's encounter with the dragon, or the wars of Hercules at the walls of Thebes, or Bacchus's cups, or Venus's juggling? He saw so many turnings laid open to his feet, that he knew not which way to bend his pace.

Therefore, as I cannot but commend his wisdom which in banqueting feeds most upon that that doth nourish best, so must I dispraise his method in writing which, following the course of amorous poets, dwelleth longest on those points that profit least, and like a wanton whelp,[4] leaveth the game[5] to run riot. The scarab flies over many a sweet flower and lights in a cowsherd.[6] It is the custom of the fly to leave the sound

1. Stephen Gosson was a playwright who turned against the stage, and then wrote Puritanical critiques of what he considered its immorality. His *School of Abuse* was published in 1579.

2. Tables set.

3. Pindar, the most difficult and obscure of Greek poets, famous for his odes. The story of Cadmus's encounter with the dragon is a fragment of a cycle of legends about the city of Thebes; the legendary hero Hercules delivered the city of Thebes from the burden of paying tribute to the foreign king Orchomenus; Bacchus was the Roman god of wine; and Venus's "juggling" refers to her erotic escapades.

4. Unruly puppy.

5. Hunt.

6. Cow dung.

places of the horse and suck at the botch,[7] the nature of colloquintida[8] to draw the worst humors to itself, the manner of swine to forsake the fair fields and wallow in the mire, and the whole practice of poets, either with fables to show their abuses or with plain terms to unfold their mischief, discover their shame, discredit themselves, and disperse their poison through the world. Virgil sweats in describing his gnat, Ovid bestirreth him to paint out his flea; the one shows his art in the lust of Dido, the other his cunning in the incest of Myrrha and that trumpet of bawdry, the craft of love.[9]

I must confess that poets are the whetstones of wit, notwithstanding that wit is dearly bought. Where honey and gall are mixed, it will be hard to sever the one from the other. The deceitful physician giveth sweet syrups to make his poison go down the smoother, the juggler casteth a mist to work the closer, the siren's song is the sailor's wrack,[1] the fowler's whistle the bird's death, the wholesome bait the fish's bane. The Harpies[2] have virgin faces, and the vultures, talents; Hyena speaks like a friend and devours like a foe; the calmest seas hide dangerous rocks; the wolf jets in wether's fells.[3] Many good sentences are spoken by David to shadow his knavery,[4] and written by poets as ornaments to beautify their works and set their trumpery to sale without suspect.

But if you look well to Epaeus's horse,[5] you shall find in his bowels the destruction of Troy; open the sepulchre of Semiramis,[6] whose title promiseth such wealth to the kings of Persia, you shall see nothing but dead bones; rip up the golden ball that Nero consecrated to Jupiter Capitolinus,[7] you shall [find] it stuffed with the shavings of his beard; pull off the visor that poets mask in, you shall disclose their reproach, bewray[8] their vanity, loathe their wantonness, lament their folly, and perceive their sharp sayings to be placed as pearls in dunghills, fresh pictures on rotten walls, chaste matrons' apparel on common courtesans. These are the cups of Circe,[9] that turn reasonable creatures into brute beasts; the balls of Hippomenes,[1] that hinder the course of Atalanta; and the blocks of the Devil, that are cast in our ways to cut off the race of toward wits. No marvel though Plato shut them out of his school and banished them quite from his commonwealth as effeminate writers,[2] unprofitable members, and utter enemies to virtue.

7. Ulcer.
8. A wild cucumber, used as an herbal medicine.
9. Dido, Queen of Carthage, with whom the legendary Trojan hero Aeneas stayed on his way to founding Rome; Virgil's *Aeneid* provides the best-known account of this episode. According to legend, Myrrha was the mother of the Greek god of vegetation, Adonis, by her father, King Cinyras, who, when he learned of his incest, changed her into a myrtle; the story is told by Ovid in his *Metamorphoses*, a poem describing erotic transformations. Gosson condemns Ovid's poem *Ars Amatoria*, or "the craft (or art) of love," as an immoral work ("bawdry" is licentiousness).
1. The mermaid's song is the sailor's shipwreck.
2. Monstrous and filthy birds whom Aeneas and his companions encounter.
3. The wolf strolls in sheep's clothing.
4. King of the ancient Israelites and poet of the psalms, David was guilty of adulterous love for Bathsheba, whose husband he murdered.
5. The Trojan horse.
6. Mythical queen of Assyria, who is supposed to have built the city of Babylon.
7. The Emperor Nero is said to have consecrated a golden ball to Jupiter in his temple on the Capitoline Hill in Rome.
8. Expose.
9. In Homer's *Odyssey*, the goddess who transformed the companions of Odysseus into swine.
1. The legendary suitor of Atalanta, who refused to marry anyone she could defeat in a footrace. Hippomenes won the race by dropping golden apples on the racetrack. Atalanta could not resist stopping to pick them up, and her delay allowed Hippomenes victory.
2. Plato exiles poets from his ideal republic (see *The Republic* 3.398a).

George Puttenham

from *The Art of English Poesie*[1]

How Poets were the first Philosophers, the first Astronomers and Historiographers, and Orators and Musicians of the world.[2]

Utterance also and language is given by nature to man for persuasion of others and aid of themselves, I mean the first ability to speak. For speech itself is artificial and made by man, and the more pleasing it is, the more it prevaileth to such purpose as it is intended for. But speech by meter is a kind of utterance more cleanly couched and more delicate to the ear than prose is, because it is more current and slipper upon the tongue and withal tunable and melodious as a kind of music and therefore may be termed a musical speech or utterance which cannot but please the hearer very well. Another cause is for that[3] is briefer and more compendious and easier to bear away and be retained in memory than that which is contained in multitude of words and full of tedious ambage and long periods.[4] It is beside a manner of utterance more eloquent and rhetorical than the ordinary proof which we use in our daily talk, because it is decked and set out with all manner of fresh colors and figures, which maketh that it sooner inveigleth[5] the judgment of man and carryeth his opinion this way and that, whither soever the heart by impression of the ear shall be most affectionately bent and directed. The utterance in prose is not of so great efficacy because not only it is daily used, and by that occasion the care is over-glutted with it, but is also not so voluble and slipper on the tongue, being wide and loose, and nothing numerous nor contrived into measures and founded with so gallant and harmonical accents, nor in fine allowed that figurative conveyance[6] nor so great license in choice of words and phrases as meter is. So as the poets were also from the beginning the best persuaders and their eloquence the first rhetoric of the world, even so it became[7] that the high mysteries of the gods should be revealed and taught by a manner of utterance and language of extraordinary phrase and brief and compendious and above all others sweet and civil as the metrical is. The same also was meetest to register the lives and noble gifts of princes, and of the great monarchs of the world and all other memorable accidents of time, so as the poet was also the first historiographer. Then forasmuch as they were the first observers of all natural causes and effects in the things generable and corruptable, and from thence mounted up to search after the celestial courses and influences and yet penetrated further to know the divine essences and substances separate,[8] as is said before, they were the first astronomers and philosophists and metaphysics. Finally, because they did altogether endeavor themselves to reduce[9] the life of man to a certain method of good manners, and made

1. George Puttenham has always been assumed to be the author of *The Art of English Poesie*, a critical treatise that appeared in 1589. Dividing his work into three books (*Of Poets and Poesie*, *Of Proportion*, and *Of Ornament*), Puttenham discusses the works of English poets, poetic forms and genres, and figures of speech and thought respectively. The work as a whole is a compendium of contemporary ideas and practices illustrating the proper way to compose and appreciate poetry.

2. In his *Apology for Poetry*, Sidney also claims that poets were the first human beings to express feeling, thought, and a sense of the higher purposes of life.

3. I.e., poetry.

4. Dull indirection and long sentences.

5. Appeals to.

6. Expression.

7. Was appropriate.

8. I.e., to know the divine essences and the particular objects present in the heavens.

9. Abstract.

the first differences between virtue and vice, and then tempered all these knowledges and skills with the exercise of a delectable music by melodious instruments, which withall served them to delight their hearers and to call the people together by admiration to a plausible and virtuous conversation, therefore were they the first philosophers ethic[1] and the first artificial musicians of the world. Such was Linus, Orpheus, Amphion, and Musaeus,[2] the most ancient poets and philosophers, of whom there is left any memory by the profane writers. King David also and Solomon his son and many other of the holy prophets wrote in meters and used to sing them to the harp,[3] although to many of us ignorant of the Hebrew language and phrase and not observing it, the same seem but a prose. It cannot be therefore that any scorn or indignity should justly be offered to so noble, profitable, ancient, and divine a science as Poesie is. * * *

Of historical poesie,[4] by which the famous acts of Princes and the virtuous and worthy lives of our forefathers were reported.

There is nothing in man of all the potential parts of his mind (reason and will excepted) more noble or more necessary to the active life than memory. Because it maketh[5] most to a sound judgment and perfect worldly wisdom, examining and comparing the times past with the present and by them both considering the time to come, [it] concludeth with a steadfast resolution what is the best course to be taken in all his actions and advices in this world. It came upon this reason: experience [is] to be so highly commended in all consultations of importance and preferred before any learning or science, and yet experience is no more than a mass of memories assembled, that is, such trials as man hath made in time before. Right so, no kind of argument in all the oratory craft doth better persuade and more universally satisfy than example, which is but the representation of old memories and like successes [that have] happened in times past. For these regards, the poesie historical is of all other, next[6] the divine, most honorable and worthy, as well for the common benefit as for the special comfort every man receiveth by it. No one thing in the world with more delectation [is] reviving our spirits than to behold, as it were in a glass, the lively image of our dear forefathers, their noble and virtuous manner of life, with other things authentic, which because we are not able otherwise to attain to the knowledge of by any of our fences,[7] we apprehend them by memory, whereas the present time and things so swiftly pass away [so] as they give us no leisure almost to look into them and much less to know and consider of them thoroughly. The things future, being also events very uncertain, and such as cannot possibly be known because they be not yet, cannot be used for example nor for delight otherwise than by hope, though many promise the contrary, by vain and deceitful arts taking upon them to reveal the truth of accidents to come, which if it were so as they surmise, are yet but sciences merely conjectural and not of any benefit to man or to the commonwealth where they be used or professed. Therefore the good and exemplary things and actions of the former ages were reserved only to the historical reports of wise and grave

1. I.e., philosophers who consider ethics.
2. Puttenham names legendary figures who were thought to be among the first poets: Linus, a poet and the teacher of Hercules, who later killed him with his own lyre; Orpheus, commonly considered the first poet, whose music charmed even the animals; Amphion, the poet whose music moved stones to build Thebes; and Musaeus, said to have been a pupil of Orpheus.
3. Scripture provides accounts of King David, supposed to be the author of the psalms, and Solomon, to whom the Song of Songs is attributed.
4. Epic poetry.
5. Benefits.
6. After.
7. Ways of arguing.

men; those of the present time [were] left to the fruition and judgment of our senses; the future as hazards and uncertain events [were] utterly neglected and laid aside for magicians and mockers to get their livings by, such manner of men as by negligence of magistrates and remisses of laws every country breedeth great store of. These historical men nevertheless used not the matter so precisely to wish that all they wrote should be accounted true,[8] for that was not needful nor expedient to the purpose, namely to be used either for example or for the pleasure, considering that many times it is seen a feigned matter or altogether fabulous, besides that it maketh more mirth than any other, works no less good conclusions for example than the most true and veritable, but oftentimes more, because the poet hath the handling of them[9] to fashion at his pleasure, but not so of the other[1] which must go according to their verity and none otherwise without the writers' great blame. Again as ye know, more and more excellent examples may be feigned in one day by a good wit than many ages through man's frailty are able to put in ure,[2] which made the learned and witty men of those times to devise many historical matters of no verity at all, but with purpose to do good and no hurt, as using them for a manner of discipline and precedent of commendable life. Such was the commonwealth of Plato, and Sir Thomas More's *Utopia*, resting all in device,[3] but never [to be] put in execution and easier wished than to be performed. And you shall perceive that histories were of three sorts, wholly true and wholly false, and a third holding part of either, but for honest recreation and good example they were all of them.[4]

George Gascoigne

from *Certain Notes of Instruction*[1]

The first and most necessary point that ever I found meet to be considered in making of a delectable poem is this, to ground it upon some fine invention.[2] For it is not enough to roll in pleasant words, nor yet to thunder in Rim, Ram, Ruff, by letter (quoth my master Chaucer) nor yet to abound in apt vocables or epithets, unless the invention have in it also *aliquid salis* [something salty]. By this *aliquid salis* I mean some good and fine device, showing the quick capacity of a writer, and where I say some good and fine invention, I mean that I would have it both fine and good. For many inventions are so superfine that they are *Vix* [scarcely] good. And again many inventions are good, and yet not finely handled. And for a general forewarning: what theme soever you do take in hand, if you do handle it but *tanquam in oratione perpetua* [as a perpetual sermon], and never study for some depth of device in your invention and some figures also in the handling thereof, it will appear to the skillful reader but a tale of a tub. To deliver unto you general examples it were almost impossible, since the occasions of inventions are (as it were) infinite. Nevertheless, take in worth mine opinion and perceive my further meaning in these few points. If I should undertake to

8. Puttenham identifies epic poets as historical, in that they represent the past, but not as historians, in that they do not represent it entirely truthfully.
9. His poetic subjects.
1. I.e., the historian who must try to discover the factual truth of the past.
2. Use.
3. Conception.
4. I.e., they were all equally good for recreation and good moral example.

1. George Gascoigne's *Certain Notes* was published in 1575 as part of his second work, containing both poetry and prose, entitled *The Posies of George Gascoigne*. Gascoigne's full listing appears on page 673.
2. In early modern treatises on the art of writing poetry, "invention" meant the discovery and development of "matter," the topics and ideas that the poet will then represent. After "invention," he draws on a knowledge of rhetoric, the techniques by which "matter" is made interesting and memorable.

write in praise of a gentlewoman, I would neither praise her crystal eye nor her cherry lip, etc., for these things are *trita et obvia* [trite and obvious]. But I would either find some supernatural cause whereby my pen might walk in superlative degree, or else I would undertake to answer for any imperfection that she hath, and thereupon raise the praise of her commendation.[3] Likewise, if I should disclose my pretense in[4] love, I would either make a strange discourse of some intolerable passion, or find occasion to plead by the example of some history, or discover[5] my disquiet in shadows *per allegoriam* [through allegory], or use the covertest mean that I could to avoid the uncomely customs of common writers. Thus much I adventure to deliver unto you (my friend) upon [the] rule of invention, which of all other rules is most to be marked and hardest to be prescribed in certain and infallible rules. Nevertheless, to conclude therein, I would have you stand most upon the excellency of your invention and stick[6] not to study deeply for some fine device. For that being found, pleasant words will follow well enough and fast enough.

Your invention being once devised, take heed that neither pleasure of rhyme nor variety of device do carry you from it. For as to use obscure and dark phrases in a pleasant[7] sonnet is nothing delectable, so to intermingle merry jests in a serious matter is an indecorum.[8]

I will next advise you that you hold the just measure wherewith you begin your verse. I will not deny but this may seem a preposterous order, but because I covet rather to satisfy you particularly than to undertake a general tradition, I will not so much stand upon the manner as the matter of my precepts. I say then, remember to hold the same measure wherewith you begin, whether it be in a verse of six syllables, eight, ten, twelve, etc., and though this precept might seem ridiculous unto you, since every young scholar can conceive that he ought to continue in the same measure wherewith he beginneth, yet do I see and read many men's poems nowadays which beginning with the measure of twelve in the first line and fourteen in the second (which is the common kind of verse), they will yet (by that time they have passed over a few verses) fall into fourteen and fourteen and *sic de similibus* [so on], the which is either forgetfulness or carelessness. * * *

I think it not amiss to forewarn you that you thrust as few words of many syllables into your verse as may be, and hereunto I might allege many reasons. First, the most ancient English words are of one syllable, so that the more monosyllables that you use, the truer Englishman you shall seem, and the less you shall smell of the inkhorn.[9] Also, words of many syllables do cloy a verse and make it unpleasant, whereas words of one syllable will more easily fall to be short or long as occasion requireth, or will be adapted to become circumflex[1] or of an indifferent[2] sound.

I would exhort you also to beware of rhyme without reason. My meaning is hereby that your rhyme lead you not from your first invention, for many writers when they have laid the platform of their invention are yet drawn sometimes (by rhyme) to forget it or at least to alter it, as when they cannot readily find out a word which may rhyme to the first (and yet continue their determinate invention) they do then either botch it up with a word that will rhyme (how small reason soever it carry with it) or else they alter their first word and so perhaps decline or trouble their former

3. My compliment to her.
4. Profession of.
5. Reveal.
6. Hesitate.
7. Lighthearted.
8. Improper act.
9. Inkpot.
1. Accentuated.
2. Soft.

invention. But do you always hold your first determined invention, and do rather search the bottom of your brains for apt words than change good reason for rumbling rhyme. * * *

Also as much as may be, eschew strange words or *obsoleta et inusitata* [obsolete and rare], unless the theme do give just occasion. Marry, in some places a strange word doth draw attentive reading, but yet I would have you therein to use discretion.

And as much as you may, frame your style to perspicuity and to be sensible, for the haughty obscure verse doth not much delight and the verse that is too easy is like a tale of a rusted[3] horse. But let your poem be such as may both delight and draw attentive reading and therewithal may deliver such matter as be worth the marking.

Samuel Daniel

from *A Defense of Rhyme*[1]

Such affliction doth laborsome curiosity[2] still lay upon our best delights (which ever must be made strange and variable) as if art were ordained to afflict nature and that we could not go but in fetters. Every science, every profession, must be so wrapped up in unnecessary intrications, as if it were not to fashion but to confound the understanding, which makes me much to distrust man and fear that our presumption goes beyond our ability and our curiosity is more than our judgment, laboring ever to seem to be more than we are or laying greater burdens upon our minds than they are well able to bear, because we would not appear like other men.

And indeed I have wished there were not that multiplicity of rhymes as is used by many in sonnets, which yet we see in some so happily to succeed and hath been so far from hindering their inventions as it hath begot conceit[3] beyond expectation and comparable to the best inventions of the world. For sure in an eminent spirit whom nature hath fitted for that mystery, rhyme is no impediment to his conceit, but rather gives him wings to mount and carries him, not out of his course, but as it were beyond his power to a far happier flight. All excellencies being sold us at the hard price of labor, it follows, where we bestow most thereof, we buy the best success, and rhyme being far more laborious than loose measures (whatsoever is objected), must needs, meeting with wit and industry, breed greater and worthier effects in our language. So that if our labors have wrought out a manumission[4] from bondage and that we go at liberty, notwithstanding these ties, we are no longer the slaves of rhyme but we make it a most excellent instrument to serve us. Nor is this certain limit observed in sonnets any tyrannical bounding of the conceit,[5] but rather a reducing it in *girum* [in bounds], and a just form, neither too long for the shortest project nor too short for the longest, being but only employed for a present passion. For the body of our imagination, being as an unformed chaos without fashion, without day, if by the divine power of the spirit it be wrought into an orb of order and form, is it not more pleasing to nature that desires a certainty and comports not with that which is infinite, to have these closes[6]

3. Restless.

1. Samuel Daniel, a poet and playwright, published a variety of works throughout his long career, notably: a collection of sonnets, *Delia* (1592); two tragedies, *Cleopatra* (1594) and *Philotas* (1604); an epic poem of the Wars of the Roses, *Civil Wars* (1595, 1609); and several masques. His essay on poetry, *A Defense of Rhyme*, was published in 1603.

2. Daniel's criticism of "laborsome curiosity" is comparable to Gascoigne's criticism of an "inkhorn" style: both poets reject pedantry.

3. Created conceptions.

4. Release.

5. I.e., the conception informing the poem.

6. Endings, as in rhyme.

rather than not to know where to end or how far to go, especially seeing our passions are often without measure. And we find in the best of the Latins many times either not concluding or else otherwise in the end than they began. Besides, is it not most delightful to see much excellently ordered in a small room, or little gallantly disposed and made to fill up a space of like capacity, in such sort that the one would not appear so beautiful in a larger circuit nor the other do well in a less, which often we find to be so, according to the powers of nature, in the workman. And these limited proportions and rests of stanzas, consisting of six, seven, or eight lines, are of that happiness, both for the disposition of the matter, the apt planting the sentence where it may best stand to hit, the certain close of delight with the full body of a just period well-carried,[7] is such as neither the Greeks or Latins ever attained unto. For their boundless running on often so confounds the reader that having once lost himself must either give off unsatisfied or certainly cast back to retrieve the escaped sense and to find way again into his matter.

Methinks we should not so soon yield our consents captive to the authority of antiquity unless we saw more reason. All our understandings are not to be built by the square of Greece and Italy. We are the children of nature as well as they, we are not so placed out of the way of judgment but that the same sun of discretion shineth upon us, we have our portion of the same virtues as well as of the same vices. * * *

It is not the observing of trochaics nor their iambics[8] that will make our writings aught the wiser. All their poesie, all their philosophy is nothing unless we bring the discerning light of conceit[9] with us to apply it to use. It is not books, but only that great book of the world and the all-overspreading grace of heaven that makes men truly judicial.[1] Nor can it be but a touch of arrogant ignorance to hold this or that nation barbarous, these or those times gross, considering how this manifold creature man, wheresoever he stand in the world, hath always some disposition of worth, entertains the order of society, affects that which is most in use, and is eminent in some one thing or other that fits his humor and the times. The Grecians held all other nations barbarous but themselves, yet Pyrrhus when he saw the well-ordered marching of the Romans, which made them see their presumptuous error, could say it was no barbarous manner of preceding. The Goths, Vandals, and Longobards,[2] whose coming down like an innundation overwhelmed, as they say, all the glory of learning in Europe, have yet left us still their laws and customs as the originals of most of the provincial constitutions of Christendom, which well-considered with their other course of government may serve to clear them from this imputation of ignorance. And though the vanquished never yet spoke well of the conqueror,[3] yet even through the unsound coverings of malediction appear those monuments of truth as argue well their worth and proves them not without judgment, though without Greek and Latin.

END OF "THE APOLOGY" AND ITS TIME

7. A well-constructed sentence.
8. Meters used in classical poetry.
9. Imagination.
1. Discriminating.
2. Lombards.
3. Daniel refers to the culture of conquered peoples without specifying which conquests or peoples he has in mind. But he acknowledges that even in the curses of these peoples, as they complain about their conquerors, there are "monuments of truth" that reveal worth and judgment.

Isabella Whitney

fl. 1567–1573

Little is known about the life of Isabella Whitney. Biographers agree that she was the sister of Geoffrey Whitney, the author of the first emblem book in England, and that, like him, she was born in Cheshire. The rest is to be deduced from her poetry, which points to an author with little formal education, a sharp eye for the details of urban life, and some knowledge of classical mythology. The modesty of Whitney's literary background sets her off from such later and accomplished poets as Mary Herbert and Aemilia Lanyer, and her poems on the challenges of love, friendship, and survival in a large city distinguish her from women who wrote devotional verse. Her poems follow the form and conventions of broadside ballads, a feature that may have made them popular with readers who were drawn to stories that gave advice on affairs of the heart and matters of the purse. Of "the middling sort," Whitney probably came to London for employment and diversion, but she seems to have had difficulty supporting herself. In any case, after publishing two collections of verse, *The Copy of a Letter* (c. 1567) and *A Sweet Nosegay* (1573), she left the city, having lived out the dreams as well as the disappointments of many English villagers who went to London to find work. Poems like *The Manner of Her Will* provide a detailed sketch of the delights and horrors of urban life as it was experienced by a talented woman of limited means.

The Admonition by the Author
to All Young Gentlewomen, and to All Other Maids Being in Love

Ye virgins that from Cupid's tents
  do bear away the foil,[1]
Whose hearts as yet with raging love
  most painfully do boil,

To you I speak, for you be they
  that good advice do lack;
Oh, if I could good counsel give,
  my tongue should not be slack.

But such as I can give, I will,
  here in few words express,
Which if you do observe, it will
  some of your care redress.

Beware of fair and painted talk,
  beware of flattering tongues;
The mermaids do pretend no good
  for all their pleasant songs.

Some use the tears of crocodiles
  contrary to their heart,

1. The reference is obscure. Cupid's weapons were traditionally a bow and arrows; Whitney describes him rather as a fencer who wounds his victims with a foil or sword. By bearing his foil away, Whitney's virgins appear to have experienced unrequited love.

And if they cannot always weep,
  they wet their cheeks by art.

Ovid, within his art of love,[2]
  doth teach them this same knack,
To wet their hand and touch their eyes,
  so oft as tears they lack.

Why have ye such deceit in store?
  have you such crafty wile?
Less craft than this, God knows, would soon
  us simple souls beguile.

And will ye not leave off? But still
  delude us in this wise?
Since it is so, we trust we shall
  take heed to feigned lies.

Trust not a man at the first sight,
  but try him well before;
I wish all maids within their breasts
  to keep this thing in store:

For trial shall declare his truth,
  and show what he doth think,
Whether he be a lover true,
  or do intend to shrink.

If Scylla[3] had not trust too much
  before that she did try,
She could not have been clean forsake° *forsaken*
  when she for help did cry.

Or if she had had good advice,
  Nisus had lived long;
How durst she trust a stranger, and
  do her dear father wrong?

King Nisus had a hair by fate
  which hair while he did keep,
He never should be overcome
  neither on land nor deep.

The stranger that the daughter loved
  did war against the King,

2. The *Ars Amatoria*, a facetious treatise in which the poet advises men how to court and make love to women. Here, Whitney implies that her readers either imitate or avoid the examples of legendary women whose stories she tells.

3. Daughter of the mythical Nisus, king of Megara, Scylla trusted the love of Minos, king of Crete, who was beseiging her father's city. For love of Minos (whom Whitney refers to as "the stranger"), Scylla betrayed her father by stealing a lock of his hair, a guarantee that Megara would remain free. According to Virgil, Minos, having taken Megara, captured Scylla, tied her to his ship, and dragged her through the sea. She was eventually transformed into a ciris, or sea-bird.

And always sought how that he might
them in subjection bring.

This Scylla stole away the hair
for to obtain her will,
And gave it to the stranger that
did straight her father kill.

Then she, who thought herself most sure
to have her whole desire,
Was clean reject,° and left behind
when he did home retire. *rejected*

Or if such falsehood had been once
unto Oenone[4] known,
About the fields of Ida wood
Paris had walked alone.

Or if Demophoon's deceit
to Phyllis[5] had been told,
She had not been transformed so,
as poets tell of old.

Hero did try Leander's[6] truth
before that she did trust,
Therefore she found him unto her
both constant, true, and just.

For always did he swim the sea
when stars in sky did glide,
Till he was drowned by the way
near hand unto the side.

She scratched her face, she tore her hair
(it grieveth me to tell)
When she did know the end of him,
that she did love so well.

But like Leander there be few,
therefore in time take heed;
And always try before ye trust,
so shall you better speed.

The little fish that careless is
within the water clear,
How glad is he, when he doth see
a bait for to appear.

He thinks his hap° right good to be, *luck*
that he the same could spy,

4. A nymph of Mount Ida, who was abandoned by Paris, son of Priam, king of Troy.
5. A mythical princess of Thrace and loved by the Greek warrior Demophon (or Demophoon); believing that he would not return to her after the Trojan War, she hanged herself.
6. Hero's lover, Leander, drowned while swimming across the Hellespont to be with her, whereupon she, too, threw herself into the sea.

And so the simple fool doth trust
too much before he try.

O little fish what hap hadst thou,
to have such spiteful fate,
To come into one's cruel hands
out of so happy state?

Thou didst suspect no harm, when thou
upon the bait didst look;
O that thou hadst had Linceus's[7] eyes
for to have seen the hook.

Then hadst thou with thy pretty mates
been playing in the streams,
Whereas Sir Phoebus° daily doth *the sun god Apollo*
show forth his golden beams.

But since thy fortune is so ill
to end thy life on shore,
Of this thy most unhappy end
I mind to speak no more.

But of thy fellow's chance that late
such pretty shift did make,
That he from fisher's hook did sprint
before he could him take.

And now he pries on every bait,
suspecting still that prick
(For to lie hid in every thing)
wherewith the fishers strick.° *strike*

And since the fish that reason lacks
once warned doth beware,
Why should not we take heed to that
that turneth us to care?

And I who was deceived late
by one's unfaithful tears,
Trust now for to beware, if that
I live this hundred years.

Finis.

A Careful Complaint by the Unfortunate Author

Good Dido[1] stint thy tears,
and sorrows all resign
To me that born was to augment
misfortune's luckless line.

7. A sharp-eyed mythical warrior of Greece.
1. Queen of Carthage, seduced and then abandoned by Aeneas on his way from Troy to Italy.

Or using still the same,
  good Dido do thy best,
In helping to bewail the hap
  that furthereth mine unrest.
For though thy Troyan mate,
  that Lord Aeneas hight,
Requiting all thy steadfast love,
  from Carthage took his flight,
And foully broke his oath,
  and promise made before
Whose falsehood finished thy delight
  before thy hairs were hoar.
Yet greater cause of grief
  compels me to complain,
For Fortune fell° converted hath *evil*
  my health to heaps of pain.
And that she[2] swears my death,
  too plain it is (alas),
Whose end let malice still attempt
  to bring the same to pass.
O Dido, thou hadst lived
  a happy woman still,
If fickle fancy had not thralled° *enslaved*
  thy wits to reckless will.
For as the man by whom
  thy deadly dolors bred,
Without regard of plighted troth
  from Carthage city fled,
So might thy cares in time
  be banished out of thought,
His absence might well salve the sore
  that erst° his presence wrought. *first*
For fire no longer burns
  than faggots° feed the flame, *except when sticks*
The want of things that breed annoy
  may soon redress the same.[3]
But I, unhappy most,
  and gripped with endless griefs,
Despair (alas) amid my hope,
  and hope without relief.
And as the swelt'ring heat
  consumes the war away,
So do the heaps of deadly harms
  still threaten my decay.
O death delay not long

2. I.e., Fortune, whose end or purpose, Whitney's death, malice will bring to pass.

3. I.e., "want," which breeds annoyance, will also end annoyance, as it will eventually result in death.

thy duty to declare.
Ye Sisters three[4] dispatch my days
and finish all my care.

The Manner of Her Will

The Author (though loath to leave the City) upon her friend's procurement is constrained to depart, wherefore she feigneth as she would die and maketh her will and testament, as followeth, with large legacies of such goods and riches which she most abundantly hath left behind her, and thereof maketh London sole executor to see her legacies performed.

A communication which the Author had to London, before she made her will.

The time is come I must depart
from thee, ah famous city.
I never yet to rue my smart,
did find that thou hadst pity,
Wherefore small cause there is that I
should grieve from thee to go.
But many women foolishly,
like me, and other mo'e,
Do such a fixed fancy set,
on those which least deserve,
That long it is ere° wit we get, *before*
away from them to swerve.° *turn*
But time with pity oft will tell
to those that will her try,
Whether it best be more to mell,° *associate with*
or utterly defy.
And now hath time me put in mind,
of thy great cruelness,
That never once a help would find,
to ease me in distress.
Thou never yet wouldst credit give
to board me for a year,
Nor with apparel me relieve
except thou paid were.
No, no, thou never didst me good,
nor ever wilt, I know;
Yet I am in no angry mood
but will, or ere I go,
In perfect love and charity,
my testament here write,
And leave to thee such treasury
as I in it recite.
Now stand aside and give me leave
to write my latest will,

4. I.e., the three Fates, who determine the length of life and the time of death.

And see that none you do deceive
of that I leave them till.[1]

The manner of her will, and what she left to London and to all those in it at her departing.

I whole in body and in mind,
but very weak in purse,
Do make and write my testament
for fear it will be worse.
And first I wholly do commend
my soul and body eke,° *also*
To God the Father and the Son
so long as I can speak.
And after speech, my soul to him
and body to the grave,
Till time that all shall rise again
their judgment for to have.
And then I hope they both shall meet
to dwell for aye° in joy, *ever*
Whereas I trust to see my friends
released from all annoy.
Thus have you heard touching my soul
and body what I mean,
I trust you all will witness bear,
I have a steadfast brain.
And now let me dispose such things
as I shall leave behind,
That those which shall receive the same
may know my willing mind.
I first of all to London leave
because I there was bred,
Brave buildings rare, of churches store,
and Paul's to the head.[2]
Between the same, fair streets there be
and people goodly store;
Because their keeping craveth° cost, *requires*
I yet will leave him[3] more.
First for their food, I butchers leave,
that every day shall kill;
By Thames you shall have brewers store,
and bakers at your will.
And such as orders do observe,° *clergymen*
and eat fish thrice a week,
I leave two streets, full fraught therewith,
they need not far to seek.

1. I.e., you must not deceive my inheritors by taking what I leave them until I leave them.
2. St. Paul's Cathedral, in the heart of the City of London; Whitney describes it as the foremost or "head" of London's public buildings.
3. St. Paul's, to whose district Whitney will leave "more" than the "goodly store" already there.

Watling Street, and Canwick Street,
  I full of woolen leave,
And linen store in Friday Street,
  if they me not deceive.
And those which are of calling such,
  that costlier they require,
I mercers leave, with silk so rich,
  as any would desire.
In cheap of them, they store shall find,
  and likewise in that street,[4]
I goldsmiths leave, with jewels such
  as are for ladies meet.
And plate to furnish cupboards with,
  full brave there shall you find,
With purl° of silver and of gold. *cord*
  to satisfy your mind.
With hoods, bongraces,° hats or caps, *sunshades*
  such store are in that street,
As if on one side you should miss,
  the other serves you feat.
For nets of every kind of sort,
  I leave within the pawn,
French ruffs, high purls,° gorgets° and sleeves *ruffs / collars*
  of any kind of lawn.° *thin cloth*
For purse or knives, for comb or glass,
  or any needful knack,
I by the stocks have left a boy
  will ask you what you lack.
I hose do leave in Birchin Lane,
  of any kind of size,
For women stitched, for men both trunks
  and those of Gascoigne guise,
Boots, shoes, or pantables° good store, *slippers*
  Saint Martin's hath for you.
In Cornwall, there I leave you beds,
  and all that 'longs° thereto. *belongs*
For women shall you tailors have,
  by Bow, the chiefest dwell,
In every lane you some shall find
  can do indifferent well.
And for the men, few streets or lanes,
  but bodymakers° be, *suitmakers*
And such as make the sweeping cloaks
  with guards° beneath the knee. *ornamental borders*
Artillery at Temple Bar,
  and dagges° at Tower Hill, *pistols*

4. I.e., they shall also find much cheap cloth in that street.

Swords and bucklers of the best
are nigh the Fleet until.[5]
Now when thy folk are fed and clad
with such as I have named,
For dainty mouths, and stomachs weak
some junkets° must be framed. *milk puddings*
Wherefore I 'pothecaries° leave *apothecaries*
with banquets in their shop,
Physicians also for the sick,
diseases for to stop.
Some roisters° still must bide in thee, *thugs*
and such as cut it out,
That with the guiltless quarrel will
to let their blood about.[6]
For them I cunning surgeons leave
some plasters° to apply, *bandages*
That ruffians may not still be hanged
nor quiet persons die.
For salt, oatmeal, candles, soap,
or what you else do want,
In many places shops are full,
I left you nothing scant.
If they that keep what you I leave,
ask money, when they sell it,
At mint,° there is such store, it is *the mint*
impossible to tell it.
At stillyard° store of wines there be, *the distillery*
your dulled minds to glad,
And handsome men, that must not wed
except they leave their trade.[7]
They oft shall seek for proper girls,
and some perhaps shall find,
That need compels, or lucre lures
to satisfy their mind.
And near the same, I houses leave
for people to repair,
To bathe themselves, so to prevent
infection of the air.
On Saturdays I wish that those,
which all the week do drug,° *drudge*
Shall thither trudge, to trim them up
on Sundays to look smug.
If any other thing be lacked
in thee, I wish them look,
For there it is, I little brought

5. I.e., near the Temple Bar up to Fleet Street.
6. I.e., those who assault men who have done them no harm must remain in London.
7. I.e., because they deal in liquor, they are not fit husbands.

but nothing from thee took.
Now for the people in thee left,
I have done as I may,
And that the poor, when I am gone,
have cause for me to pray.
I will to prisons portions leave,
what though but very small,
Yet that they may remember me,
occasion be it shall,
And first the counter they shall have,
lest they should go to wrack,° *ruin*
Some coggers,° and some honest men, *crooks*
that sergeants draw aback.[8]
And such as friends will not them bail,
whose coin is very thin,
For them I leave a certain hole
and little ease within.
The Newgate once a month shall have
a sessions° for his share, *court trials*
Lest being heaped, infection might
procure a further care.[9]
And at those sessions some shall 'scape
with burning near the thumb,
And afterward to beg their fees,
till they have got the sum.
And such whose deeds deserveth death,
and twelve° have found the same, *a jury*
They shall be drawn up Holborn Hill
to come to further shame.
Well, yet to such I leave a nag
shall soon their sorrows cease,
For he shall either break their necks
or gallop from the preace.° *crowd*
The Fleet, not in their circuit is,[1]
yet if I give him nought,
It might procure his curse, ere I
unto the ground be brought.
Wherefore I leave some papist old
to underprop his roof,
And to the poor within the same
a box for their behoof.° *benefit*

8. Whitney seems to wish to endow prisons with a "counter," a device to keep track of accounts, lest the prisoners be ruined by tradesmen, both crooks and honest men, who sell goods to prisoners and who are also restrained in their commerce by sergeants.

9. I.e., Newgate prison shall hold trials once a month to avoid overcrowding and disease. Some prisoners, marked by a burn on the thumb, will be freed to beg for bail money.

1. In the 16th century the Fleet was a prison for people convicted of crimes by the Star Chamber, a court dealing with affairs of conscience, such as treason and differences of faith; hence it is where one would find a Catholic, a papist. It was not a prison for people convicted by the common law; hence it is not in the same "circuit" as Newgate.

What makes you standers-by to smile,
  and laugh so in your sleeve,
I think it is, because that I
  to Ludgate° nothing give. *a debtors' prison*
I am not now in case to lie,
  here is no place of jest;
I did reserve that for myself,
  if I my health possessed.
And ever came in credit so
  a debtor for to be,
When days of payment did approach,
  I thither meant to flee.
To shroud myself amongst the rest
  that choose to die in debt;
Rather than any creditor
  should money from them get.
Yet 'cause° I feel myself so weak *because*
  that none me credit° dare, *give me credit*
I here revoke, and do it leave
  some bankrupts to his° share. *their*
To all the bookbinders by Paul's° *St. Paul's Cathedral*
  because I like their art,
They every week shall money have
  when they from books depart.° *sell their books*
Amongst them all, my printer must
  have somewhat to his share;
I will my friends these books to buy
  of him, with other ware.
For maidens poor, I widowers rich
  do leave, that oft shall dote,
And by that means shall marry them,
  to set the girls afloat.
And wealthy widows will I leave
  to help young gentlemen,
Which when you° have, in any case, *i.e., gentlemen*
  be courteous to them° then. *i.e., widows*
And see their plate and jewels eke
  may not be marred with rust,
Nor let their bags too long be full,
  for fear that they do burst.
To every gate under the walls
  that compass thee about,
I fruit wives leave to entertain
  such as come in and out.
To Smithfield° I must something leave, *the meat market*
  my parents there did dwell;
So careless for to be of it,
  none would account it well.
Wherefore it thrice a week shall have,

of horse and neat° good store, *beef*
And in his spittle,[2] blind and lame,
to dwell for evermore.
And Bedlam[3] must not be forgot,
for that was oft my walk,
I people there too many leave,
that out of tune do talk.
At Bridewell[4] there shall beadles be,
and matrons that shall still
See chalk well-chopped, and spinning plied,
and turning of the mill.
For such as cannot quiet be,
but strive for house or land,
At th'Inns of Court,[5] I lawyers leave
to take their cause in hand.
And also leave I at each Inn,
of Court or Chancery,
Of gentlemen, a youthful root,
full of activity,
For whom I store of books have left
at each bookbinder's stall,
And part of all that London hath
to furnish them withal.° *with*
And when they are with study cloyed,° *tired*
to recreate their mind,
Of tennis courts, of dancing schools,
and fence they store shall find.
And every Sunday at the least,
I leave to make them sport,
In divers places players that
of wonder shall report.
Now London have I (for thy sake)
within thee and without,
As comes into my memory,
dispersed round about
Such needful things, as they should have
here left now unto thee
When I am gone, with conscience
let them dispersed be.
And though I nothing named have
to bury me withal,
Consider that above the ground
annoyance be I shall.° *I shall be*
And let me have a shrouding sheet

2. In the hospital at Smithfield, the blind and lame are always to dwell or find refuge.
3. Asylum for the insane.
4. A prison for persons convicted for minor offenses; it also served as a workhouse for the unemployed.
5. The offices of those practicing common law; also the schools teaching common law.

to cover me from shame,
And in oblivion bury me
and never more me name.
Ringings° nor other ceremonies *of church bells*
use you not for cost,
Nor at my burial make no feast,
your money were but lost.
Rejoice in God that I am gone,
out of this vale so vile.
And that of each thing left such store,
as may your wants exile.
I make thee sole executor, because
I loved thee best.
And thee I put in trust, to give
the goods unto the rest.
Because thou shalt a helper need,
in this so great a charge,
I wish good Fortune be thy guide, lest
thou shouldst run at large.
The happy days and quiet times,
they both her servants be,
Which well will serve to fetch and bring
such things as need° to thee. *are needed*
Wherefore (good London) not refuse° *do not refuse*
for helper her to take,
Thus being weak and weary both
an end here will I make.
To all that ask what end I made,
and how I went away,
Thou answer mayest like those which here
no longer tarry may.
And unto all that wish me well,
or rue that I am gone,
Do me commend, and bid them cease
my absence for to moan.
And tell them further, if they would,
my presence still have had,
They should have sought to mend my luck,
which ever was too bad.
So fare thou well a thousand times,
God shield thee from thy foe,
And still make thee victorious
of those that seek thy woe.
And though I am persuade° that I *persuaded*
shall never more thee see,
Yet to the last, I shall not cease
to wish much good of thee.
This twenty of October, I,
in Anno Domini,

A thousand five hundred seventy three,
as almanacs descry,
Did write this will with mine own hand
and it to London gave,
In witness of the standers-by,
whose names if you will have,
Paper, Pen, and Standish° were, *inkstand*
at that same present by,
With Time, who promised to reveal,
so fast as she could hie,
The same, lest of my nearer kin
for any thing should vary,
So finally I make an end
no longer can I tarry.

Finis.

Mary Herbert, Countess of Pembroke

1561–1621

Mary Herbert was like many women of her time in having two phases to her life: a period of service to men, followed by a phase of independent activity. Deeply attached to her brother, Sir Philip Sidney, she spent much of her young adulthood in his company. The estate she presided over as wife to Henry Herbert, Earl of Pembroke, was Sidney's place of refuge after Queen Elizabeth had exiled him from court. At Wilton House and in his sister's company he wrote *The Apology for Poetry* and the first version of his prose romance, *The Arcadia*. Mary Herbert was an interested party in yet another project, his translation of the psalms, and when he died in 1586, she resolved to finish the project. Picking up where he had left off, at Psalm 43, she completed the cycle. Her work was encouraged by the circle of friends that gathered frequently at Wilton House and included such writers and musicians as Francis Mere, Edmund Spenser, Samuel Daniel, Nicholas Breton, Fulke Greville, and Abraham Fraunce. The seventeenth-century biographer John Aubrey spoke of the group as a "college."

Translations of the psalms were popular among Protestant writers of the period; they fulfilled the obligation to know both the Word and the indwelling spirit of God. Poets of religious lyric in the next century, especially George Herbert, would seek and represent a similar knowledge. Mary Herbert dedicated her work to Queen Elizabeth in a poem entitled *Even Now That Care* (available on our Web site), which was followed by an elegy for her brother Philip, *To Thee Pure Sprite*. Although riddled with ellipses or words that have been deliberately omitted, they convey the spiritual intensity that characterizes her translations. Some critics think that she did not write a second elegy (here attributed to her), *The Lay of Clorinda*; it is, however, what we might expect a woman of her station and training to have written about the death of a beloved friend. Milton would later give a profoundly political and religious dimension to the genre in his *Lycidas*, an elegy that is as much for an age and its temperament as it is for a person.

For additional resources on Mary Herbert, go to *The Longman Anthology of British Literature* Web site at www.myliteraturekit.com.

Psalm 71: In Te Domini Speravi

On thee my trust is grounded.
Lord, let me never be
With shame confounded,
But set me free
And in thy justice rescue me;
Thy gracious ear to meward° bend [toward me]
And me defend.

Be thou my rock, my tower,
My ever safe resort,
Whose saving power
Hath not been short° [deficient]
To work my safety, for my fort
On thee alone is built; in thee
My strongholds be.

Me, O my God, deliver
From wicked, wayward hand.
God, my help-giver,
On whom I stand
And stood since I could understand,
Nay, since by life I first became
What now I am.

Since prisoned in my mother,
By thee I prison brake,° [broke from]
I trust no other,
No other make
My stay, no other refuge take,
Void of thy praise no time doth find
My mouth and mind.

Men for a monster took me,
Yet hope of help from thee
Never forsook me.
Make then by me
All men, with praise extolled, may see
Thy glory,[1] thy magnificence,
Thy excellence.

When feeble years do leave me
No stay of other sort,
Do not bereave me
Of thy support,
And fail not then to be my fort,
When weakness, in me killing might,° [strength]
Usurps his right.[2]

1. I.e., cause all men to see, by my aid, thy glory magnified with praise.

2. I.e., when weakness, having overcome strength, takes the place of strength in my soul.

For now against me banded,
My foes have talked of me;
Now unwithstanded,° *not withstood*
Who° their spies be *whoever*
Of me have made a firm decree:
(Lo!) God to him hath bid adieu,
Now then pursue.[3]

Pursue, say they, and take him;
No succor can he win,
No refuge make him.
O God, begin
To bring with speed thy forces in.
Help me, my God, my God, I say
Go not away.

But let them be confounded
And perish by whose hate
My soul is wounded;
And in one rate,° *as a class*
Let them all share in shameful state
Whose counsels, as their farthest end,° *goal*
My wrong intend.

For I will still persevere
My hopes on thee to raise,
Augmenting ever
Thy praise with praise.
My mouth shall utter forth always
Thy truths, thy helps, whose sum surmounts
My best accounts.

Thy force keeps me from fearing,
Nor ever dread I aught;
Thy justice bearing
In mindful thought
And glorious acts which thou hast taught
Me from my youth;[4] and I have shown
What I have known.

Now age doth overtake me
And paint my head with snow;
Do not forsake me
Until I show
The ages which succeeding grow,
And every afterliving wight,° *generation of men*
Thy power and might.

3. I.e., my enemies' spies have decreed: God has said goodbye to him, so now hunt him down.

4. I.e., bearing thy justice and glorious acts in mindful thought.

How is thy justice raised
Above the height of thought;
How highly praised
What thou hast wrought.
Sought let be all that can be sought,
None shall be found, nay none shall be,
O God, like thee.

What if thou down didst drive me
Into the gulf of woes;
Thou wilt revive me
Again from those
And from the deep, which deepest goes;
Exalting me again will make
Me comfort take.

My greatness shall be greater
By thee; by comfort thine
My good state better.
O lute of mine,
To praise his truth thy tunes incline;
My harp extol the Holy One
In Judah known.

My voice to my harp join thee,[5]
My soul saved from decay,
My voice conjoin° thee, *join with*
My tongue each day,
In all men's view his justice lay,° *reveal*
Who° hath disgraced and shamed so, *those who*
Who work my woe.

Psalm 121: Levavi Oculos

Unto the hills, I now will bend
And list° with joy my hopeful sight; *incline*
To him who me doth comfort send,
My gracious God, the Lord of might.
Even he (who ever blessed be he named)
Who Heaven and Earth and all therein hath framed.

By him thy foot, from slip shall stay,° *prevent*
Nor will he sleep who thee sustains;
Israel's great God by night or day
To sleep or slumber aye° disdains. *always*
For he is still thy guard forever waking,
On thy right hand thy safety undertaking.

5. I.e., let my voice, joined to my harp, join thee.

So undertakes that neither sun
By day with heat shall thee molest,
Nor moon by night, when day is done,
Offend thee, or disturb thy rest.
Yea, from all evil thou still in his protection
Shalt safely dwell from harm or ill infection.

This Lord (who never fails his flock)
Shall thee in all thy ways attend
At home, abroad, thy fort, thy rock
From all annoy shall thee defend.
Yea, from this time from age to age for ever
Will be thy God, and thee forsaking never.

c. 1590

The Doleful Lay° of Clorinda *ballad*

Ay me, to whom shall I my case complain
That may compassion° my impatient grief? *sympathize with*
Or where shall I unfold my inward pain,
That my enriven° ear may find relief? *dismayed*
Shall I unto the heavenly powers it show?
Or unto earthly men that dwell below?

To heavens? Ah they, alas, the authors were
And workers of my unremedied woe;
For they foresee what to us happens here,
And they foresaw, yet suffered this be so.
From them comes good, from them comes also ill;
That which they made, who can them warn to spill.° *destroy*

To men? Ah they, alas, like wretched be
And subject to the heavens' ordinance;
Bound to abide whatever they decree,
Their best redress is their best sufferance.[1]
How then can they, like wretched, comfort me,
The which no less, need comforted to be?[2]

Then to myself will I my sorrow mourn,
Since none alive like sorrowful remains;
And to myself my plaints shall back return,
To pay their usury with doubled pains.
The woods, the hills, the rivers shall resound
The mournful accent of my sorrow's ground.° *cause*

Wood, hills, and rivers now are desolate,
Since he is gone the which them all did grace;

1. I.e., the best recourse for men subject to heaven is to tolerate its decrees.

2. I.e., how can they comfort me, wretched as I am, who themselves need to be comforted?

And all the fields do wail their widow state,
Since death their fairest flower did late deface.
The fairest flower in field that ever grew,
Was Astrophel;[3] that was, we all may rue.

What cruel hand of cursed fate unknown,
Hath cropped the stalk which bore so fair a flower?
Untimely cropped, before it were well grown,
And clean defaced in untimely hour.
Great loss to all that ever him did see,
Great loss to all, but greatest loss to me.

Break now your garlands, O ye shepherds' lasses,
Since the fair flower which them adorned is gone;
The flower which them adorned is gone to ashes,
Never again let lass put garland on.
Instead of garland, wear sad cypress now,
And bitter elder, broken from the bow.

Nor ever sing the love-lays which he made,
Who ever made such lays of love as he?
Nor ever read the riddles which he said
Unto yourselves to make you merry glee.
Your merry glee is now laid all abed,
Your merry maker now, alas, is dead.

Death, the devourer of all world's delight,
Hath robbed you and reft from me my joy;
Both you and me and all the world he quite
Hath robbed of joyance and left sad annoy.
Joy of the world, and shepherds' pride was he,
Shepherds' hope, never like again to see.

Oh death, that hast us of such riches reft,
Tell us at least, what hast thou with it done?
What is become of him whose flower here left
Is but the shadow of his likeness gone,
Scarce like the shadow of that which he was,
Naught° like, but that he like a shade did pass? *nothing*

But that immortal spirit, which was decked
With all the dowries of celestial grace,
By sovereign choice from the heavenly choirs select,
And lineally derived from angel's race,
O what is now of it become, aread—° *tell*
Ay me, can so divine a thing be dead?

3. Astrophel or Astrophil: the principal speaker and the lover of "Stella," the figure representing the beloved woman, in Sir Philip Sidney's sonnet sequence *Astrophil and Stella*.

Ah no, it is not dead, nor can it die,
But lives for aye° in blissful paradise, *ever*
Where like a newborn babe it soft doth lie,
In bed of lilies wrapped in tender wise.° *manner*
  And compassed all about with roses sweet,
  And dainty violets from head to feet.

There thousand birds all of celestial brood,
To him do sweetly carol day and night,
And with strange notes, or him well understood,
Lull him asleep in angel-like delight,
  While in sweet dream to him presented be
  Immortal beauties which no eye may see.

But he them sees and takes exceeding pleasure
Of their divine aspects, appearing plain,
And kindling love in him above all measure,
Sweet love still joyous, never feeling pain.
  For what so goodly form he there doth see,
  He may enjoy from jealous rancor free.

There liveth he in everlasting bliss,
Sweet spirit never fearing more to die,
Nor dreading harm from any foes of his,
Nor fearing salvage° beasts more cruelty. *savage*
  While we here, wretches, wail his private lack,
  And with vain vows do often call him back.

But live thou there still happy, happy spirit,
And give us leave thee here thus to lament.
Not thee that dost thy heaven's joy inherit,
But our own selves that here in dole are drent.° *drenched*
  Thus do we weep and wail and wear our eyes,
  Mourning others, our own miseries.

PERSPECTIVES

Early Modern Books

With the invention of movable type by Johann Gutenberg in 1439, the production of printed books became more efficient, and their dissemination was far wider. The use of paper for printing, as opposed to the animal skins that were used for manuscripts, also meant that printed books could be produced much more cheaply. But this did not necessarily mean that all books were necessarily inexpensive. Many of the books printed before 1500 (known as *incunables* or *incunabula*) were sumptuously printed. William Caxton produced the first printed English book in Bruges in 1474, and then two years later established printing presses in Westminster and London. The first works that he printed were great literary works such as Chaucer's *Canterbury Tales* and Sir Thomas Malory's *Morte Darthur*. Caxton's collaborator and successor as head of his printing press, Wynkyn de Worde, born in Alsace, is largely credited with improving the technology of English printing and bringing in an era of more affordable printed books. A woodcut from his 1495 printing of Ranulf Higdon's *Polychronicon*, translated by John of Trevisa (1387), is reproduced here. This text by a Benedictine monk was both theological and historical. The best sellers of the sixteenth and seventeenth centuries were not literary but rather religious texts. The Bible and Foxe's *Book of Martyrs* in the sixteenth century, and Bunyan's *Pilgrim's Progress* in the later seventeenth century were the most commonly found books in English households. As elsewhere in Europe, the advent of the printing press in England brought with it the wider dissemination of a greater number of books in a wide array of formats. In this section, you can observe some of the features of early modern printing through viewing facsimiles of printed books and one example of a commonplace book, a form of handwritten text that remained popular in the seventeenth century.

This woodcut, taken from the second edition of *Polychronicon* published by the printer Wynkyn de Worde in 1495, represents an idealized English landscape. It depicts a city on a river, enclosed by a massive wall, behind which one can see houses, castles, towers, and an imposing cathedral. A sea opens up in the distance, showing yet other islands, cities, and boats under sail. The representation is typical of the bird's-eye views illustrated in contemporary topographical surveys.

"The burning of Tharchbishop of Cant. D. Thom. Cranmer in the town dich at Oxford" from John Foxe's (1516–1587) *Actes and Monuments of These Latter and Perilous Days* (1563). Like many other intellectual Protestants, John Foxe had gone into exile during the reign of the Catholic Mary I (1553–1558). Foxe compiled his magnum opus from manuscript and printed accounts of the persecution of English Protestants during the Marian period. His book became known as the *Book of Martyrs* and was the most popular book of the early modern period after the Bible. Foxe collaborated with the printer John Day, who was also publisher and bookseller, to produce four editions (1563, 1570, 1576, and 1583) of this bestselling book. The woodcut illustrating the burning of Archbishop Cranmer in 1556 shows his hand outstretched as Friar John to the left, and to the right three noblemen, numerous civilians and soldiers look on. Cranmer was said to have held his hand "so steadfast and immutable . . . that all might see his hand burned before his body was touched." This was the same hand with which he had previously written a recantation of his prior resistance to the Roman Catholic Church. He repented his recantation, and for his refusal to accept Catholicism as the national faith was sentenced to death. The text combines the use of black letter type face for the narrative alongside Roman type face for the heading. Ironically, this black letter type, based on a textus hand from medieval manuscripts, was more easily read by the common English reader of the sixteenth century. It was only after 1590 that most printing was done in Roman type, based on the humanist hand used to write Latin. The Bible and *The Book of Martyrs* continued to be printed in black letter throughout the seventeenth century.

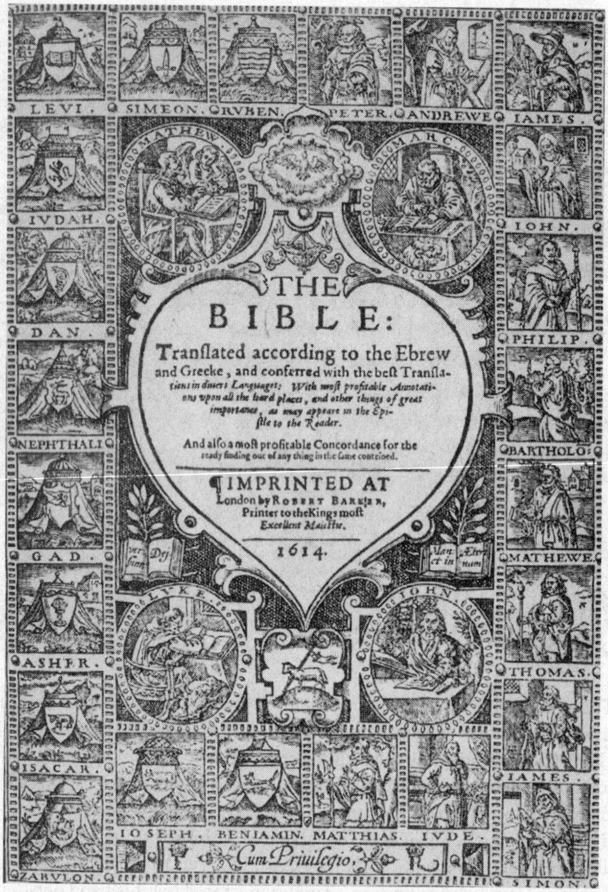

The Geneva Bible was printed in at least 144 editions between 1560 and 1644. It was the first to use Roman Type (as opposed to black letter) and verse divisions. This frontispiece of the 1614 edition displays the twelve tribes of Israel and the twelve apostles, with the four evangelists (Matthew, Mark, Luke, and John) at the center. The text was translated in Geneva, Switzerland, by the English Protestant Exiles, fleeing religious persecution under Queen Mary. They also provided marginal notes whose antihierarchical church politics made them so controversial that King James banned their use in the King James Bible and made ownership of the Geneva Bible a felony. James I was particularly worried about marginal notes such as the one in Exodus 1.19, which allowed disobedience to kings. Authorized King James Version Bibles became more widely used, and in 1644, the Geneva Bible was printed for the last time.

Plate XVI. "Their sitting at meate" from Thomas Hariot's (1560–1621) *A briefe and true report of the new found land of Virginia of the commodities and of the nature and manners of the naturall inhabitants* (1585). First Published by Theodore de Bry. 1590. Thomas Hariot's *A Briefe and True Report of the New Found Land of Virginia* (1588) was reprinted by Richard Hakluyt in his *Principal Navigations* (1589). Hakluyt brought John White's drawings illustrating the text to the attention of the Flemish printer Theodore De Bry, who modeled the engraved plates of his *True Pictures and Fashions of America* (1590) upon them. Hariot wrote captions for these plates, which Hakluyt translated into English. So, there are levels of both visual and textual revision that have reformed the representation of Hariot's eyewitness account of the Algonquian Indians. The caption provided for this illustration extols the taste of maize and the moderation of the Indians in their eating and drinking. This text promotes the feasibility and the profit to be gained from future voyages. Some other captions, however, such as that to Plate XIII: "Their manner of fishynge in Virginia" betray the Europeans' judgment of the Indians as barbaric: "content with their state and livinge frendlye together of those things which god in his bountye hath given unto them, yet without givinge hym any thankes according to his desarte. So savage is this people, and deprived of the true knowledge of god."

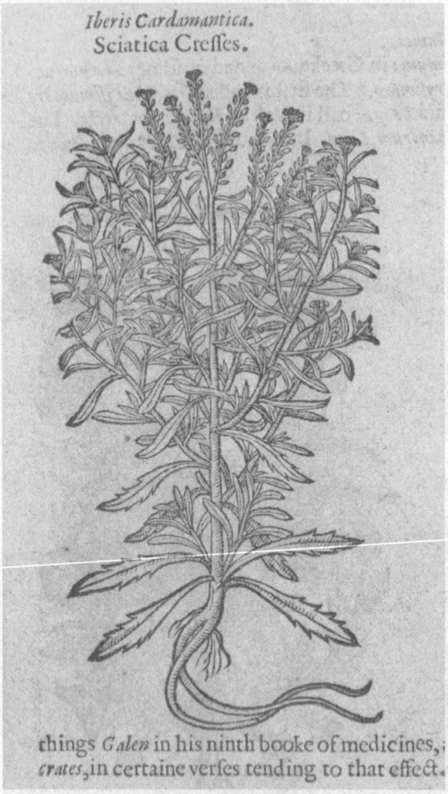
Iberis Cardamantica.
Sciatica Cresses.
things Galen in his ninth booke of medicines,
crates, in certaine verses tending to that effect.

Illustration of *sciatica cresses* herb from a 1597 edition of John Gerard's *The Herball or Generall historie of plantes*. *The Herball or Generall historie of plantes* (1597) illustrates the demand for the books offering practical advice and instruction. Its author, John Gerard, was a well-known physician, a member of the Barbers and Surgeons' Company, superintendent of the "physic garden" at the College of Physicians, and in charge of the garden of William Cecil, Lord Burghley, the queen's Lord Chancellor. His hugely popular book, which went into many editions, describes the appearance, cultivation, and medicinal virtues of over a thousand kinds of English plant. The plate of the herb *sciatica cresses* shows its foliage and root system, and notes that its roots mixed with pig fat relieve the pain of sciatica, a disease affecting the nerves of the back and hips.

Geoffrey Whitney (1548?–1601) composed one of the most important English emblem books, *A Choice of Emblems* (1586). Each emblem contains a woodcut, prefixed by a Latin motto and accompanied by verses in six-line stanzas. The book was dedicated to the Earl of Leicester and was published in Leyden, where Whitney was studying at the university. Although only twenty-three of the emblems are original and another 235 loosely or exactly copy Continental models by Alciati, Paradin, Sambucus, and Junius, Whitney gives many of the emblems a specifically English interpretation. Sometimes an emblem is used to support the politics of the Leicester court faction, who urged an active role in defending Protestants in the Low Countries. At other times, Whitney's Englishness surfaces in references to local events. For example, he applies the emblem of the phoenix to the fire of Nantwich, not far from his birthplace in Chesire, where he would retire after the death of his patron Leicester. Possibly because of the decline of the Leicester faction, Whitney's book was not republished in his lifetime. Nevertheless, his influence is seen in later Jacobean emblem books, such as Peacham's *Minerva Britanna* (London, 1612), and in decorations in domestic architecture and furnishings. Whitney's work helped to make the Continental emblem tradition known to such English poets as Shakespeare, Spenser, Donne, and Philips, whose poetry is enriched by emblematic metaphor, conjuring up both a visual image and its complex symbolic associations. The motto to this emblem "Unica semper avis" (means "the bird that is ever unique") and the image are inspired by Ovid's *Metamorphoses* 15.393–407.

The Phoenix

Unica semper avis

To my countrymen of the Nampwiche in Cheshire.

The Phoenix rare, with feathers fresh of hue,
Arabia's right, and sacred to the sun:
Whom, other birds with wonder seem to view,
Doth live until a thousand years be run:
Then makes a pile: which, when with sun it burns,
She flies therein, and so to ashes turns.

Whereof, behold, another Phoenix rare,
With speed doth rise most beautiful and fair:
And though for truth, this many do declare,
Yet thereunto, I mean not for to swear:
Although I know that author's witness true,
What here I write, both of the old, and new.

Which when I weighed, the new, and eke the old,
I thought upon your town destroyed with fire:
And did in mind, the new Nampwiche behold,
A spectacle for any man's desire:
Whose buildings brave, where cinders were but late,
Did represent (me thought) the Phoenix fate.

And as the old, was many hundred years,
A town of fame, before it felt that cross:
Even so, (I hope) this Wiche,[1] that now appears,
A Phoenix age shall last, and know no loss:
Which God vouchsafe, who make you thankful, all:
That see this rise, and saw the other fall.

1. Originally meaning the group of buildings connected with a salt pit, "wich" was the name given to such saltmaking towns as Nantwich and Northwich in Chesire.

Title page to Volume 2 of *Utriusque cosmi, maioris scilicet et minoris, metaphysica atque technica historia*, ("Metaphysical and Technical History of both the Greater and Lesser Universe"), by Robert Fludd, 1619. After taking his degree at Oxford, Robert Fludd studied chemistry and medicine on the Continent, where he came into contact with the occult philosophy of the Rosicrucians, whose goals ranged from alchemy to moral reformation. Returning to London, he practiced medicine and published numerous works expressing his belief that science was a form of divine revelation and that all creation reflected a divinely ordered design. This engraving shows the image of a male body spread out over the cosmos as a circle, portraying the human body's perfect proportions, and their analogy to the proportions of the universe: man is a little world, the microcosm to the universe's macrocosm. The engraving also depicts the earth-centered Ptolemaic universe, the constellations and astrological signs. The innermost circles are the four bodily humors (choleric, melancholic, phlegmatic, and sanguine), and the outermost circles are the supernatural faculties of reason, intellect, and mind.

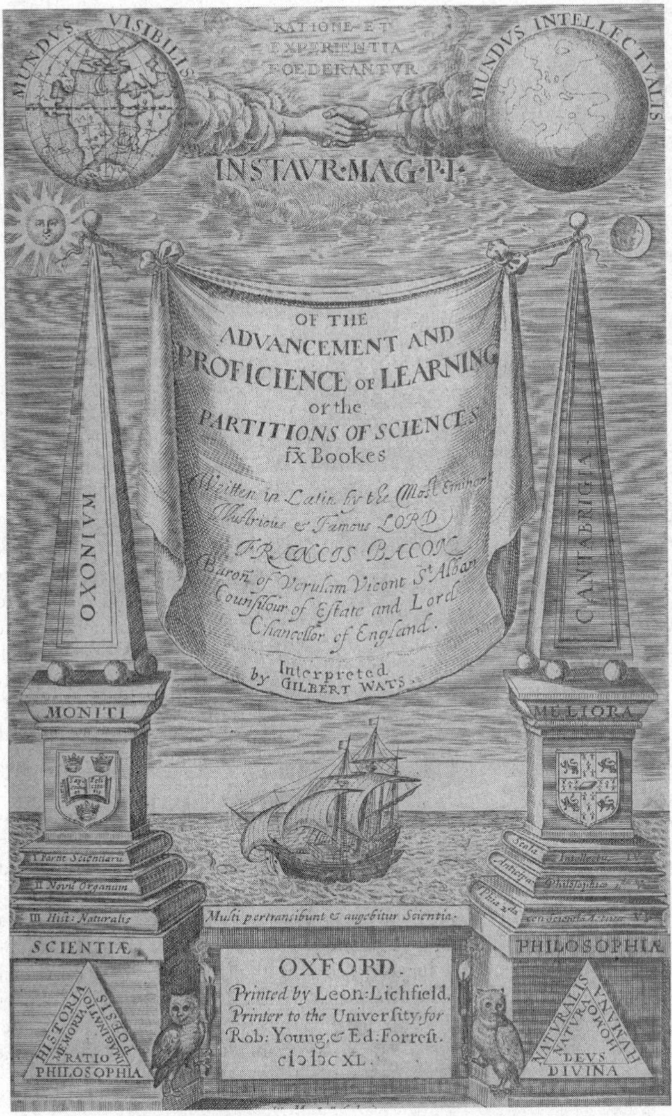

Frontispiece to Francis Bacon, *Advancement of Learning* (1640). This engraving can be read as both a representation of the kind of technological innovation that Bacon lauds in the *Advancement* as well as a kind of allegory of the scientific revolution. The text is an accurate representation of one of the inventions of the early modern Europe—the large sailing ship. At the same time it symbolizes the transgression of the Pillars of Hercules (the Straits of Gibraltar), once thought of as the limits of the known world, a kind of hubristic and bold adventure not unlike the quest for knowledge and power by Marlowe's Doctor Faustus or Shakespeare's Prospero.

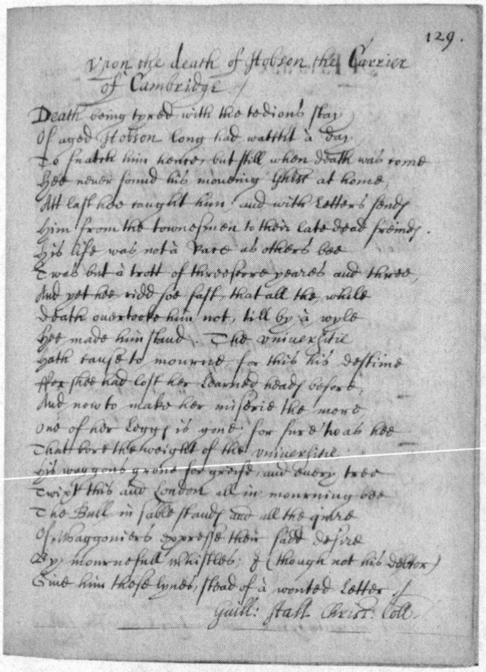

Vpon the death of Hobson the Carrier of Cambridge./

Death being tyred with the tedious stay
Of aged Hobson long had watcht à day
To snatch him hence, but still when death was come
Hee neuer found his moueing Ghest at home,
Att last hee caught him; and with Letters sendes
Him from the townesmen to their late dead freiendes.
His life was not à Race as others bee
'Twas but à trott of threescore yeares and three,
And yet hee ridd soe fast, that all the while
Death ouertooke him not, till by à wyle
Hee made him stand. The vniuersitie
Hath cause to mourne, for this his Destinie
ffor shee had lost her Learned heades before,
And now to make her miserie the more,
One of her Legges is gone; for sure 'twas hee
That bore the weight of the vniuersitie;
His waggons grone for greife, and euery tree
Twixt this and London all in mourning bee
The Bull in sable standes and all the quire
Of Waggoniers expresse their sadd desire
By mournefull Whistles; I (though not his Debtor)
Giue him these lynes, stead of á wonted Letter.

Guill: Hall Christ: Coll'./[1]

The handwriting in this manuscript is a combination of Italic, a script made popular by Italian Renaissance humanists, and widely used for Latin, and secretary, a hand prevalent in England from 1500 to 1650. William Hall wrote the poem to commemorate the death of Thomas Hobson, the mail carrier of Christ's College, Cambridge. Milton also wrote a poem about Hobson that helped make popular the expression "Hobson's choice," referring to his only allowing students to rent out the next horse in line—"this one or none." The poem by Hall appears only in two manuscript books, now both at the Folger Library.

1. Guill: that is, "Guillelmus," the Latin form of "William."

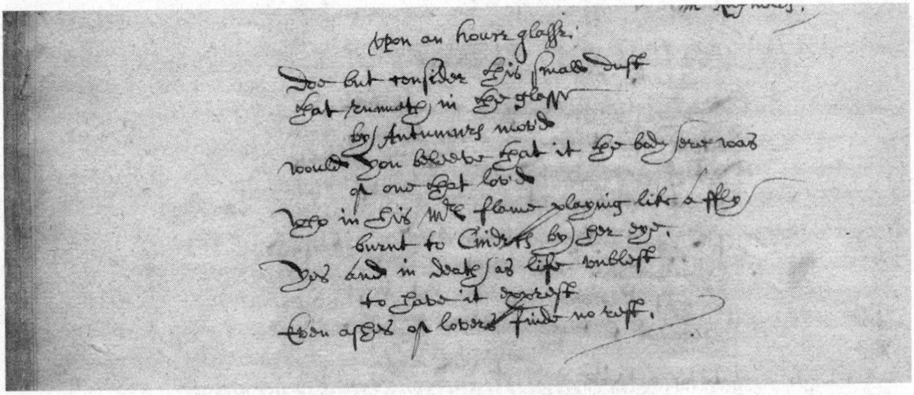

From Folger MS V.b.43, f. 9v. *Vpon an houre glasse* written by Ben Jonson in a secretary hand, the type of handwriting prevalent in England from the early sixteenth through the seventeenth century. This poem appears in a large manuscript referred to as a *folio*, large pieces of paper, each folded in half to produce two leaves or four pages. This manuscript verse collection, referred to as both a *miscellany* and a *commonplace book*, contains many poems by different authors written side by side by a scribe, circa. 1630. So, for example, Donne's "The Anagram" appears on the same page as "Vpon an houre glasse."[1] Compare the poem in MS. V. 43 on the left with the version in the 1640 printed edition on the right:

Vpon an houre glasse

Doe but consider this small dust
that runneth in the glasse
by Autumnes mov'd
would you beleeve that it the body ere was
of one that lov'd
who in his M[ist]r[i]s flame playing like a Fly
burnt to Cinders by her eye,
Yes and in death as life vnblest
to have it exprest
Even ashes of lovers finde no rest.

The Hour-Glass[2]

Do but consider this small dust
Here running in the glass,
By atoms moved:
Could you believe that this
The body [ever] was
Of one that loved?
And in his mistress' flame, playing like a fly,
Turned to cinders by her eye?
Yes; and in death, as life, unblest,
To have't expressed,
Even ashes of lovers find no rest.

1. To read more about this poem and other manuscript collections of poems, you can read an on-line article by Christopher Ivic at http://www.folger.edu/html/folger_institute/mm/EssayCI.html.

2. This version of the poem by Jonson was published in 1640.

A certaine Relation of the Hog-faced Gentlewoman called Mistris *Tannakin Skinker*, who was borne at *Wirkham* a Neuter Towne betweene the Emperour and the Hollander, scituate on the river *Rhyne*.
Who was bewitched in her mothers wombe in the yeare 1618. and hath lived ever since unknowne in this kind to any, but her Parents and a few other neighbours. And can never recover her true shape, tell she be married, &c.

Also relating the cause, as it is since conceived, how her mother came so bewitched.

London Printed by *J. O.* and are to be sold by *F. Grove*, at his shop on *Snow-hil* neare *St. Sepulchers Church*. 1640.

Frontispiece to *A certaine Relation of the Hog-faced Gentlewoman called Mistris Tannakin Skinker, who was borne at Wirkham, a Neuter Towne between the Emperour and the Hollander, scituate on the river Rhyne. Who was bewitched in her mothers wombe in the yeare 1618 and hath lived ever since unknowne in this kinde to any, but her Parents and a few other neighbours. And can never recover her true shape, till she be married, & c Also relating the cause, as it is since conceived, how her mother came to be so bewitched* (1640). This woodcut illustration of the woman with the hog face and one of her suitors is a good example of cheap print. It is the early modern equivalent of supermarket check-out tabloids such as *News of the World*. This title page shows an interesting feature of early modern printing—the tendency to advertise the entire text by summarizing its contents and setting forth the most outrageous details on the title page.

END OF PERSPECTIVES: EARLY MODERN BOOKS

Elizabeth I

1533–1603

No British monarch has left posterity a more dazzling record of accomplishments than Elizabeth Tudor, second daughter of Henry VIII. During the course of her reign, England became a nation to rival France and Spain; England's cities became centers of commerce, her navy controlled the principal routes of trade, and her people pursued lucrative interests in Europe and the New World. Having ruled England for almost half a century, Elizabeth has lived on as a figure of compelling power in the history of her people. What Shakespeare said of his character Cleopatra—"Age cannot wither her, nor custom stale her infinite variety"—conveys something of the fascination the memory of this extraordinary woman has had for the English people as well as for others around the globe. Age did, of course, eventually touch her being; doubtless, too, the brilliant strategies by which she governed subjects who were ever jealous of her royal prerogative must finally have become predictable. But Elizabeth was brought up in the atmosphere of a volatile politics, given to shifts in the winds of chance, susceptible to the heat of violent controversy and even to the flames of rebellion. She did what she had to do to remain on the throne; her father's example, if nothing else, taught her how fragile was the rule of a monarch who depended much more on the loyalty of subjects than on the authority of office or the power of the law.

Elizabeth's birth was itself a disappointment, at least to Henry VIII, who had hoped for a son. Her mother was the king's second wife, the charming Anne Boleyn, whom he married after divorcing Catherine of Aragon, the mother of his first daughter, Mary Tudor. The divorce precipitated the king's break with the Catholic Church, made Mary Tudor illegitimate, and effectively defined Anne's politics as unequivocally Protestant. But the new queen's influence was short-lived. Supporters of Catholicism, those who remained faithful to the memory of Catherine and respected the claims of Mary Tudor, may have been responsible for convincing the king that Anne had been unfaithful to him; in any case, he ordered her execution. Ten days later, he married Jane Seymour, declared Elizabeth illegitimate, and again waited for the birth of a son. Elizabeth's half-brother, the future Edward VI, was born in 1537, when Elizabeth was four years old. Fortunately, at the age of ten, Elizabeth at last acquired a loving stepmother: Henry's sixth wife, Catherine Parr, looked after her interests and education. An excellent student, fluent in Latin, French, and Italian and versed in history, Elizabeth was raised to be the subject of her brother, who became king after Henry's death in 1547. When he died in 1553, she became a pawn in a long and vicious struggle for the crown. Imprisoned in the Tower and then in Woodstock Castle in Oxfordshire by the Catholic supporters of her sister's claim to the throne, Elizabeth wrote lyrics that testify to both her fears and her faith during this dangerous time.

In 1558, Queen Mary died, and Elizabeth was crowned with much rejoicing; in the historian William Camden's words: "neither did the people ever embrace any other Prince with more willing and constant mind." Once on the throne, Elizabeth pursued a policy of exemplary discretion; she rewarded those who were loyal to her and punished those who showed signs of disobedience. In 1568, when her cousin Mary, Queen of Scots, abdicated the throne of Scotland in favor of her son, James VI, Elizabeth granted Mary refuge in England. Yet evidence later suggested that Mary, an ardent Catholic, had plotted to kill Elizabeth and restore Catholicism in England, and in 1587, Elizabeth ordered her execution with great regret. Reflecting on this action, also the subject of a speech to Parliament, the queen declared: "This death will wring my heart as long as I live."

Robert Peake (attr.), *Queen Elizabeth Going in Procession to Blackfriars in 1600*. This splendid painting is linked to no particular event. Its arrangement of figures suggests a Roman imperial triumph, and evokes the success of the queen's monarchy. She appears to be in a litter, but is actually in a chair on wheels pushed by attendants, and protected by a canopy held by courtiers. She is preceded by a knight, perhaps Gilbert Talbot, Earl of Shrewsbury, who carries the sword of state. Though Elizabeth was sixty-eight when this painting was made in 1601, she is shown as a much younger woman. Her wish to be recognized as always desirable and ever the object of courtly devotion is well illustrated by her pale, unlined face, her highly dressed hair and her stylized body, clothed in a bejeweled dress whose puffed sleeves and intricate lace ruff suggest an ethereal and even divine creature. She is attended by six Knights of the Garter; the knight standing directly beside her (with a bald head and stiff grey beard) has been identified as her current favorite, Edward Somerset, Earl of Worcester; his two principal castles, Raglan and Chepstow, are probably those in the background of the painting.

A woman and reigning monarch, Elizabeth's position was anomalous. As a woman, she retained an important kind of social power only as long as she was an object of desire, to be courted and won; as a reigning monarch, she was expected not only to govern but also to secure the succession. In her speech to Parliament on the subject of marriage early in her reign, Elizabeth provided reasons why she would delay taking a husband. She probably never intended to take one. Continuing the fiction of courtship well past the age at which she could be expected to have a child, she saw to it that she remained at once attractive and unavailable. Most important, she succeeded in commanding the attention of her subjects by transforming her court into a center of literary and artistic activity. Late in life, she met her most serious suitor, the Duke of Alençon, brother to the French king, Henry III. A dwarf whose face was disfigured by smallpox, he was her "little frog," a man she is said to have loved dearly. The problem of succession required another kind of temporizing. She refused to name James VI of Scotland as the next king of England until shortly before she died—a silence that she maintained was necessary to preserve the peace.

Throughout her long reign she cultivated two personas. As a monarch, she could speak courageously (as she did to her soldiers at Tilbury on the Devon coast while they waited for the Spanish to invade); as a woman, she could convey understanding (as she did to her critics in her so-called Golden Speech curtailing her prerogative to create monopolies). Her government remained a conscientious one to its very end. She cultivated a habit of mind that must have helped to ensure its stability: as her translation of Boethius's *Consolation of Philosophy* (made when she was sixty years old) reminds us, she never allowed herself to forget the vicissitudes of fortune and her own mortality.

Written with a Diamond on Her Window at Woodstock[1]

Much suspected by° me, *to have been done by*
Nothing proved can be,
Quoth Elizabeth prisoner.

Written on a Wall at Woodstock

Oh fortune, thy wresting wavering state
Hath fraught with cares my troubled wit,
Whose witness this present prison late
Could bear, where once was joy flown quite.[1]
Thou causedst the guilty to be loosed
From lands where innocents were inclosed,
And caused the guiltless to be reserved,° *bound*
And freed those that death had well deserved.
But all herein° can be nothing caught, *in prison*
So God send to my foes all they have thought.[2]

The Doubt of Future Foes

The doubt° of future foes exiles my present joy, *fear*
And wit me warns to shun such snares as threaten mine annoy;[1]
For falsehood now doth flow, and subjects' faith doth ebb,
Which should not be if reason ruled or wisdom weaved the web.
But clouds of joys untried° do cloak aspiring minds, *untested*
Which turn to rage of late repent by changed course of winds.[2]
The top of hope supposed the root of rue shall be,
And fruitless all their grafted guile, as shortly ye shall see.[3]
The dazzled eyes with pride, which great ambition blinds,

1. Elizabeth was imprisoned at Woodstock Castle, near Oxford, from 23 May 1554 to sometime late in April 1555. The queen, Mary I, Elizabeth's half-sister, suspected her of treason. This and the following poem are thought to have been written at this time.
1. I.e., this prison could bear witness recently to fortune's wavering state, once joy had flown from it.
2. I.e., nothing can be done by one who is in prison, so may God send to my foes what they have suspected me of planning.

1. My harm.
2. I.e., because of a change of wind, my enemies' clouds of joy can turn to the rain of repentance.
3. I.e., at their most hopeful, my enemies supposed that the tree of my monarchy would be uprooted, but their grafted limbs of guile will bear no fruit.

Shall be unsealed by worthy wights[4] whose foresight falsehood finds.
The daughter of debate that discord aye° doth sow *ever*
Shall reap no gain where former rule[5] still peace hath taught to know.
No foreign banished wight[6] shall anchor in this port;
Our realm brooks not seditious sects, let them elsewhere resort.
My rusty sword through rest shall first his edge employ
To poll their tops[7] that seek such change or gape[8] for future joy.

On Monsieur's Departure[1]

I grieve and dare not show my discontent,
I love and yet am forced to seem to hate,
I do, yet dare not say I ever meant,
I seem stark mute but inwardly do prate.
I am and not,° I freeze and yet am burned, *am not*
Since from myself another self I turned.

My care is like my shadow in the sun,
Follows me flying, flies when I pursue it,
Stands and lies by me, doth what I have done.
His too familiar care doth make me rue° it. *regret*
No means I find to rid him from my breast,
Till by the end of things° it be suppress. *death*

Some gentler passion slide into my mind,
For I am soft and made of melting snow;
Or be more cruel, love, and so be kind.
Let me or° float or sink, be high or low. *either*
Or let me live with some more sweet content,
Or die and so forget what love ere meant.

Speeches The speeches of Elizabeth I exemplify early modern public oratory at its most effective. But they are also marked by features uniquely derived from her sense of herself as a monarch who wished (and probably needed) to convince her subjects that their welfare was more important to her than her own. In the excerpts that follow, Elizabeth emphasizes that although nature made her a woman and therefore of the weaker sex, divine right has made her a "prince," a person endowed with a masculine persona whose function it is to command not obey. She further emphasizes that her principal care is for her subjects, who are her charges and in some sense her children. In her public dealings throughout her reign, she played the gender card for all it was worth; in so doing, she transformed the fact that she was a woman, potentially a liability, into an instrument of policy.

4. Men.
5. The rule of Elizabeth's father, Henry VIII, and brother, Edward VI, both Protestants.
6. Any supporter of Philip II, king of Spain and consort of Mary I.
7. Cut their heads off.
8. Smile.
1. The poem expresses Elizabeth's regret at the departure of the Duke d'Alençon, who had sought her hand in marriage. After four years of visits and inconclusive negotiations, the courtship ended in 1583.

On Marriage[1]

I may say unto you that from my years of understanding, sith[2] I first had consideration of myself to be born a servitor of Almighty God, I happily chose this kind of life in which I yet live, which I assure you for mine own part hath hitherto best contented myself and I trust hath been most acceptable to God. From the which, if either ambition of high estate offered to me in marriage by the pleasure and appointment of my prince[3]—whereof I have some records in this presence, as you our Lord Treasurer[4] well know; or if the eschewing of the danger of mine enemies or the avoiding of the period of death, whose messenger or rather continual watchman, the prince's indignation, was not little time daily before mine eyes—by whose means, although I know or justly may suspect, yet I will not now utter; or if the whole cause were in my sister herself, I will not now burthen her therewith, because I will not charge the dead: if any of these I say, I had not now remained in this estate wherein you see me. But so constant have I always continued in this determination—although my youth and words may seem to some hardly to agree together—yet is it most true that at this day I stand free from any other meaning that either I have had in times past or have at this present. With which trade of life I am so thoroughly acquainted that I trust God, who hath hitherto therein preserved and led me by the hand, will not now of His goodness suffer me to go alone. * * *

Nevertheless—if any of you be in suspect—whensoever it may please God to incline my heart to another kind of life, ye may well assure yourselves my meaning is not to do or determine anything wherewith the realm may or shall have just cause to be discontented. And therefore put that clean out of your heads.[5] For I assure you—what credit my assurance may have with you I cannot tell, but what credit it shall deserve to have the sequence shall declare—I will never in that matter conclude anything that shall be prejudicial to the realm, for the weal, good, and safety whereof I will never shun to spend my life. And whomsoever my chance shall be to light upon, I trust he shall be as careful for the realm and you—I will not say as myself, because I cannot so certainly determine of any other; but at the least ways, by my good will and desire he shall be such as shall be as careful for the preservation of the realm and you as myself.

And albeit it might please Almighty God to continue me still in this mind to live out of the state of marriage, yet it is not to be feared but He will so work in my heart and in your wisdoms as good provision by His help may be made in convenient time, whereby the realm shall not remain destitute of an heir that may be a fit governor, and peradventure more beneficial to the realm than such offspring as may

1. In 1559, a year after she had acceded to the throne at the age of 25, Elizabeth addressed Parliament on the subject of marriage. Because the monarchy passed on by inheritance, it was expected that a monarch would marry and have children. In this speech, Elizabeth hints that she will never marry and also that she trusts God to provide for her successor who, she guesses, may be more "beneficial" to the kingdom than any child of her own would be. She probably intended to convey to her subjects that she would never abandon the kingdom either to the rule of a foreign prince (as Mary I had) or to a succession crisis.

2. Since.

3. The "prince" Elizabeth refers to is probably not Philip II, the consort of Mary I, but rather Mary herself, who in her official capacity as queen regnant might have offered her sister's hand in marriage to a suitable consort. Elizabeth can refer to Mary as her "sister" when she alludes to a "cause" that has no implications for the state but is rather personal, "in my sister herself."

4. The Marquis of Winchester.

5. Elizabeth emphasizes that her subjects and their representatives in Parliament have no authority to force her into marriage, however desirable they may think marriage is for the future of the kingdom.

come of me. For, although I be never so careful of your well doings and mind ever so to be, yet may my issue grow out of kind and become perhaps ungracious. And in the end, this shall be for me sufficient, that a marble stone shall declare that a Queen, having reigned such a time, lived and died a virgin.

On Mary, Queen of Scots[1]

The bottomless graces and immeasurable benefits bestowed upon me by the Almighty are and have been such, as I must not only acknowledge them but admire them, accounting them as well miracles as benefits; not so much in respect of His Divine Majesty—with whom nothing is more common than to do things rare and singular—as in regard of our weakness, who cannot sufficiently set forth His wonderful works and graces, which to me have been so many, so diversely folded and embroidered one upon another, as in no sort am I able to express them.

And although there liveth not any that may more justly acknowledge themselves infinitely bound unto God than I, whose life He hath miraculously preserved at sundry times (beyond my merit) from a multitude of perils and dangers, yet is not that the cause for which I count myself the deepliest bound to give Him my humblest thanks, or to yield Him greatest recognition; but this which I shall tell you hereafter, which will deserve the name of wonder, if rare things and seldom seen be worthy of account. Even this it is: that as I came to the crown with the willing hearts of subjects, so do I now, after twenty-eight years' reign, perceive in you no diminution of good wills, which, if haply I should want, well might I breathe but never think I lived.

And now, albeit I find my life hath been full dangerously sought, and death contrived by such as no desert procured it, yet am I thereof so clear from malice—which hath the property to make men glad at the falls and faults of their foes, and make them seem to do for other causes, when rancor is the ground—as I protest it is and hath been my grievous thought that one, not different in sex, of like estate, and my near kin, should be fallen into so great a crime. Yea, I had so little purpose to pursue her with any color of malice, that as it is not unknown to some of my Lords here—for now I will play the blab—I secretly wrote her a letter upon the discovery of sundry treasons, that if she would confess them, and privately acknowledge them by her letters unto myself, she never should need be called for them into so public question. Neither did I it of mind to circumvent her, for then I knew as much as she could confess; and so did I write.

And if, even yet, now the matter is made but too apparent, I thought she truly would repent—as perhaps she would easily appear in outward show to do—and that for her none other would take the matter upon them; or that we were but as two milkmaids, with pails upon our arms; or that there were no more dependency upon us, but mine own life were only in danger, and not the whole estate of your religion and well doings; I protest—wherein you may believe me, for although I may have many vices, I hope I have not accustomed my tongue to be an instrument of untruth—I would most willingly pardon and remit this offence. Or if by my death

1. The text is Elizabeth's answer to a petition from Parliament to execute Mary, Queen of Scots, who was reported to have conspired to depose her cousin Elizabeth and who had been a prisoner of the English queen for ten years. In August 1586, evidence of a new plot came to light, and the conspirators, led by Sir Thomas Babington, were executed. On the evidence in letters to Babington, Mary was then formally tried and convicted of treason by a special court of peers, counsellors, and judges. Elizabeth answered Parliament in October by asking for delay and divine enlightenment.

other nations and kingdoms might truly say that this realm had attained an ever prosperous and flourishing estate, I would (I assure you) not desire to live, but gladly give my life, to the end my death might procure you a better prince. And for your sakes it is that I desire to live: to keep you from a worse. For, as for me, I assure you I find no great cause I should be fond to live. I take no such pleasure in it that I should much wish it, nor conceive such terror in death that I should greatly fear it. And yet I say not but, if the stroke were coming, perchance flesh and blood would be moved with it, and seek to shun it.

I have had good experience and trial of this world. I know what it is to be a subject, what to be a sovereign, what to have good neighbors, and sometime meet evil-willers. I have found treason in trust, seen great benefits little regarded, and instead of gratefulness, courses[2] of purpose to cross. These former remembrances, present feeling, and future expectation of evils, (I say), have made me think an evil is much the better the less while it dureth,[3] and so them happiest that are soonest hence;[4] and taught me to bear with a better mind these treasons, than is common to my sex—yea, with a better heart perhaps than is in some men. Which I hope you will not merely impute to my simplicity or want of understanding, but rather that I thus conceived—that had their purposes taken effect, I should not have found the blow, before I had felt it; nor, though my peril should have been great, my pain should have been but small and short. Wherein, as I would be loath to die so bloody a death, so doubt I not but God would have given me grace to be prepared for such an event; which, when it shall chance, I refer to His good pleasure.

And now, as touching their treasons and conspiracies, together with the contriver of them. I will not so prejudicate myself and this my realm as to say or think that I might not, without the last statute, by the ancient laws of this land have proceeded against her; which[5] was not made particularly to prejudice her, though perhaps it might then be suspected in respect of the disposition of such as depend that way. It was so far from being intended to entrap her, that it was rather an admonition to warn the danger thereof. But sith it is made, and in the force of a law, I thought good, in that which might concern her, to proceed according thereunto rather than by course of common law. Wherein, if you the judges have not deceived me, or that the books you brought me were not false—which God forbid—I might as justly have tried her by the ancient laws of the land.

But you lawyers are so nice and so precise in sifting and scanning every word and letter, that many times you stand more upon form than matter, upon syllables than the sense of the law. For, in this strictness and exact following of common form, she must have been indicted in Staffordshire, been arraigned at the bar, holden up her hand, and then been tried by a jury: a proper course, forsooth, to deal in that manner with one of her estate! I thought it better, therefore, for avoiding of these and more absurdities, to commit the cause to the inquisition of a good number of the greatest and most noble personages of this realm, of the judges and others of good account, whose sentence I must approve.[6]

2. Plans.
3. Lasts.
4. I.e., out of this world.
5. I.e., the Parliamentary statute of 1584–1585, known as the Act for the Queen's Surety, which provided for the trial of Mary, Queen of Scots, should she be accused of treason.
6. Elizabeth claims that Mary could have been tried as a criminal in a common law court but that this would have been an improper way to proceed as Mary remained a Queen of Scotland and her liability under English law was open to question.

And all little enough: for we Princes, I tell you, are set on stages, in the sight and view of all the world duly observed. The eyes of many behold our actions; a spot is soon spied in our garments, a blemish quickly noted in our doings. It behoveth us, therefore, to be careful that our proceedings be just and honorable.

But I must tell you one thing more: that in this late Act of Parliament you have laid an hard hand on me—that I must give direction for her death, which cannot be but most grievous, and an irksome burden to me. And lest you might mistake mine absence from this Parliament—which I had almost forgotten: although there be no cause why I should willingly come amongst multitudes (for that amongst many, some may be evil), yet hath it not been the doubt of any such danger or occasion that kept me from thence, but only the great grief to hear this cause spoken of, especially that such one of state and kin should need so open a declaration, and that this nation should be so spotted with blots of disloyalty. Wherein, the less is my grief for that I hope the better part is mine; and those of the worse not much to be accounted of, for that in seeking my destruction they might have spoiled their own souls.

And even now could I tell you that which would make you sorry. It is a secret; and yet I will tell it you (although it be known I have the property to keep counsel but too well, often times to mine own peril). It is not long since mine eyes did see it written that an oath was taken within few days either to kill me or to be hanged themselves; and that to be performed ere one month were ended. Hereby I see your danger in me, and neither can or will be so unthankful or careless of your consciences as to take no care for your safety.

I am not unmindful of your oath made in the Association,[7] manifesting your great good wills and affections, taken and entered into upon good conscience and true knowledge of the guilt, for safeguard of my person; done (I protest to God) before I ever heard it, or ever thought of such a matter, till a thousand hands, with many obligations, were showed me at Hampton Court, signed and subscribed with the names and seals of the greatest of this land. Which, as I do acknowledge as a perfect argument of your true hearts and great zeal to my safety, so shall my bond be stronger tied to greater care for all your good.

But, for that this matter is rare, weighty and of great consequence, and I think you do not look for any present resolution—the rather for that, as it is not my manner in matters of far less moment to give speedy answer without due consideration, so in this of such importance—I think it very requisite with earnest prayer to beseech His Divine Majesty so to illuminate mine understanding and inspire me with His grace, as I may do and determine that which shall serve to the establishment of His Church, preservation of your estates, and prosperity of this Commonwealth under my charge. Wherein, for that I know delay is dangerous, you shall have with all conveniency our resolution delivered by our message. And what ever any prince may merit of their subjects, for their approved testimony of their unfeigned sincerity, either by governing justly, void of all partiality, or sufferance of any injuries done (even to the poorest), that do I assuredly promise inviolably to perform, for requital of your so many deserts.

7. The Oath (or Bond) of Association was taken by the Queen's Council in October 1582. It provided for Mary's arrest and execution without a trial; in essence, it sanctioned a lynching.

On Mary's Execution[1]

Full grievous is the way whose going on and end breeds cumber[2] for the hire of a laborious journey. I have strived more this day than ever in my life whether I should speak or use silence. If I speak and not complain, I shall dissemble; if I hold my peace, your labor taken were full vain.

For me to make my moan were strange and rare, for I suppose you shall find few that, for their own particular, will cumber you with such a care. Yet such, I protest, hath been my greedy desire and hungry will that of your consultation might have fallen out some other means to work my safety, joined with your assurance, than that for which you are become so earnest suitors, as I protest I must needs use complaint[3]—though not of you, but unto you, and of the cause; for that I do perceive, by your advices, prayers, and desires, there falleth out this accident, that only my injurer's bane must be my life's surety.

But if any there live so wicked of nature to suppose that I prolonged this time only pro forma, to the intent to make a show of clemency, thereby to set my praises to the wire-drawers[4] to lengthen them the more, they do me so great a wrong as they can hardly recompense. Or if any person there be that think or imagine that the least vainglorious thought hath drawn me further herein, they do me as open injury as ever was done to any living creature—as He that is the maker of all thoughts knoweth best to be true. Or if there be any that think that the Lords, appointed in commission, durst do no other, as fearing thereby to displease or to be suspected to be of a contrary opinion to my safety, they do but heap upon me injurious conceits. For, either those put in trust by me to supply my place have not performed their duty towards me, or else they have signified unto you all that my desire was that every one should do according to his conscience, and in the course of these proceedings should enjoy both freedom of voice and liberty of opinion, and what they would not openly, they might privately to myself declare. It was of a willing mind and great desire I had, that some other means might be found out, wherein I should have taken more comfort than in any other thing under the sun.

And since now it is resolved that my surety cannot be established without a princess's head, I have just cause to complain that I, who have in my time pardoned so many rebels, winked at so many treasons, and either not produced[5] them or altogether slipped them over with silence, should now be forced to this proceeding, against such a person. I have besides, during my reign, seen and heard many opprobrious books and pamphlets against me, my realm and state, accusing me to be a tyrant. I thank them for their alms. I believe therein their meaning was to tell me news: and news it is to me indeed. I would it were as strange to hear of their impiety. What will they not now say, when it shall be spread that for the safety of her life a maiden queen could be content to spill the blood even of her own kinswoman? I may therefore full well complain that any man should think me given to cruelty; whereof I am so guiltless and innocent as I should slander God if I should say He gave me so vile a mind. Yea, I protest, I am so far from it that for mine own life I would not touch her.

1. Parliament had determined that Elizabeth's safety and the future of Protestantism in England could be secured only by Mary's execution; it sent a delegation to Elizabeth asking for her approval. Again Elizabeth demurred. It was only in February 1587, after a new conspiracy was discovered, that Elizabeth signed Mary's death warrant.

2. Distress.

3. Express regret.

4. One who draws metal into wire.

5. Acted upon.

Neither hath my care been so much bent how to prolong mine, as how to preserve both: which I am right sorry is made so hard, yea so impossible.

I am not so void of judgment as not to see mine own peril; nor yet so ignorant as not to know it were in nature a foolish course to cherish a sword to cut mine own throat; nor so careless as not to weigh that my life daily is in hazard. But this I do consider, that many a man would put his life in danger for the safeguard of a king. I do not say that so will I; but I pray you think that I have thought upon it.

But sith so many hath both written and spoken against me, I pray you give me leave to say somewhat for myself, and, before you return to your countries, let you know for what a one you have passed so careful thoughts. And, as I think myself infinitely beholding unto you all that seek to preserve my life by all the means you may, so I protest that there liveth no prince—nor ever shall be—more mindful to requite so good deserts. Wherein, as I perceive you have kept your old wont[6] in a general seeking the lengthening of my days, so am I sure that never shall I requite it, unless I had as many lives as you all; but for ever I will acknowledge it while there is any breath left me. Although I may not justify, but may justly condemn, my sundry faults and sins to God, yet for my care in this government let me acquaint you with my intents.

When first I took the sceptre, my title made me not forget the giver, and therefore [I] began as it became me, with such religion as both I was born in, bred in, and, I trust, shall die in; although I was not so simple as not to know what danger and peril so great an alteration might procure me—how many great princes of the contrary opinion would attempt all they might against me, and generally what enmity I should thereby breed unto myself. Which all I regarded not, knowing that He, for whose sake I did it, might and would defend me. Rather marvel that I am, than muse that I should not be if it were not God's holy hand that continueth me beyond all other expectation.

I was not simply trained up, nor in my youth spent my time altogether idly; and yet, when I came to the crown, then entered I first into the school of experience, bethinking myself of those things that best fitted a king—justice, temper, magnanimity, judgment. As for the two latter, I will not boast. But for the two first, this may I truly say: among my subjects I never knew a difference of person, where right was one;[7] nor never to my knowledge preferred for favor what I thought not fit for worth; nor bent mine ears to credit a tale that first was told me; nor was so rash to corrupt my judgment with my censure, ere I heard the cause. I will not say but many reports might fortune[8] be brought me by such as must hear the matter, whose partiality might mar the right; for we princes cannot hear all causes ourselves. But this dare I boldly affirm: my verdict went with the truth of my knowledge.

But full well wished Alcibiades[9] his friend, that he should not give any answer till he had recited the letters of the alphabet. So have I not used over-sudden resolutions in matters that have touched me full near: you will say that with me, I think. And therefore, as touching your counsels and consultations, I conceive them to be wise, honest, and conscionable; so provident and careful for the safety of my life (which I wish no longer than may be for your good), that though I never can yield

6. Desire.
7. I.e., my justice was impartial; it did not regard rank, occupation, or property as factors in determining what was right.
8. By chance.
9. An Athenian statesman who took part in the Peloponnesian War; changed sides to support Athens' enemy, Sparta; and was finally assassinated by Persians with whom he sought an alliance. The source of Elizabeth's reference is unknown.

you of recompense your due, yet shall I endeavor myself to give you cause to think your good will not ill bestowed, and strive to make myself worthy for such subjects. And as for your petition: your judgment I condemn not, neither do I mistake your reasons, but pray you to accept my thankfulness, excuse my doubtfulness, and take in good part my answer-answerless. Wherein I attribute not so much to my own judgment, but that I think many particular persons may go before me, though by my degree I go before them. Therefore, if I should say, I would not do what you request, it might peradventure be more than I thought; and to say I would do it, might perhaps breed peril of that you labor to preserve, being more than in your own wisdoms and discretions would seem convenient,[1] circumstances of place and time being duly considered.

To the English Troops at Tilbury, Facing the Spanish Armada[1]

My loving people, we have been persuaded by some that are careful of our safety, to take heed how we commit ourselves to armed multitudes, for fear of treachery. But I assure you, I do not desire to live to distrust my faithful and loving people. Let tyrants fear. I have always so behaved myself that, under God, I have placed my chiefest strength and safeguard in the loyal hearts and good will of my subjects; and therefore I am come amongst you, as you see, at this time, not for my recreation and disport,[2] but being at this time resolved, in the midst and heat of the battle, to live or die amongst you all, to lay down for my God, and for my kingdom, and for my people, my honor and my blood, even in the dust. I know I have the body of a weak and feeble woman, but I have the heart and stomach of a king, and of a king of England too, and think foul scorn[3] that Parma or Spain, or any prince of Europe should dare to invade the border of my realm; to which rather than any dishonor shall grow[4] by me, I myself will take up arms, I myself will be your general, judge, and rewarder of every one of your virtues in the field. I know, already for your forwardness[5] you have deserved rewards and crowns;[6] and we do assure you, in the word of a prince, they shall be duly paid you.

The Golden Speech[1]

Mr. Speaker, we have heard your declaration and perceive your care of our estate, by falling into a consideration of a grateful acknowledgment of such benefits as you have received; and that your coming is to present thanks to us, which I accept with no less joy than your loves can have desire to offer such a present.

I do assure you there is no prince that loves his subjects better, or whose love can countervail our love. There is no jewel, be it of never so rich a price, which I set before this jewel: I mean your love. For I do esteem it more than any treasure or

1. Elizabeth equivocates nicely. She refuses to disagree with Parliament, lest she not respect her own misgivings; she refuses to agree with Parliament, lest its policy not be in her own interest.

1. In 1588, with the Spanish fleet threatening the south coast of England, Elizabeth went to Tilbury, in Dorset, to speak to the troops who were guarding England against an invasion.

2. Amusement.

3. Shameful.

4. Be caused.

5. Courage.

6. Recompense.

1. The queen had the prerogative or absolute power to grant favored subjects a patent for an exclusive manufacture. But the monopolies so created were disliked by those who would otherwise have competed for business, and a move to limit them was begun in Parliament. In response, in 1601, Elizabeth met with a committee of the House of Commons, led by the Speaker, thanked them for the subsidies recently granted the crown by the Commons, and promised to reform her practice.

riches; for that we know how to prize, but love and thanks I count unvaluable. And, though God hath raised me high, yet this I count the glory of my crown, that I have reigned with your loves. This makes me that I do not so much rejoice that God hath made me to be a queen, as to be a queen over so thankful a people. Therefore, I have cause to wish nothing more than to content the subject; and that is a duty which I owe. Neither do I desire to live longer days than I may see your prosperity; and that is my only desire. And as I am that person that still yet under God hath delivered you, so I trust, by the almighty power of God, that I shall be His instrument to preserve you from every peril, dishonor, shame, tyranny and oppression; partly by means of your intended helps which we take very acceptably, because it manifesteth the largeness of your good loves and loyalties unto your sovereign.

Of myself I must say this: I never was any greedy, scraping grasper, nor a strait, fast-holding prince, nor yet a waster. My heart was never set on any worldly goods, but only for my subjects' good. What you bestow on me, I will not hoard it up, but receive it to bestow on you again. Yea, mine own properties I account yours, to be expended for your good; and your eyes shall see the bestowing of all for your good. Therefore, render unto them, I beseech you, Mr. Speaker, such thanks as you imagine my heart yieldeth, but my tongue cannot express.

Since I was queen, yet did I never put my pen to any grant but that, upon pretext and semblance made unto me, it was both good and beneficial to the subject in general, though a private profit to some of my ancient servants who had deserved well at my hands. But the contrary being found by experience, I am exceedingly beholding to such subjects as would move the same at the first. And I am not so simple to suppose, but that there be some of the Lower House whom these grievances never touched: and for them, I think they spake out of zeal to their countries,[2] and not out of spleen or malevolent affection as being parties grieved; and I take it exceeding gratefully from them, because it gives us to know that no respects or interest had moved them, other than the minds they have to suffer no diminution of our honor and our subjects' love unto us. The zeal of which affection, tending to ease my people and knit their hearts unto me, I embrace with a princely care, for above all earthly treasure I esteem my people's love, more than which I desire not to merit.

That my grants should be grievous to my people and oppressions privileged under color of our patents, our kingly dignity shall not suffer[3] it. Yea, when I heard it, I could give no rest unto my thoughts until I had reformed it. Shall they, think you, escape unpunished that have thus oppressed you, and have been respectless of their duty, and regardless of our honor?[4] No, I assure you, Mr. Speaker, were it not more for conscience' sake than for any glory or increase of love that I desire, these errors, troubles, vexations and oppressions, done by these varlets and lewd persons, not worthy the name of subjects, should not escape without condign punishment. But I perceive they dealt with me like physicians who, ministering a drug, make it more acceptable by giving it a good aromatical savor, or when they give pills do gild them all over.[5]

I have ever used to set the Last-Judgment Day before mine eyes, and so to rule as I shall be judged to answer before a higher Judge, to whose judgment seat I do ap-

2. I.e, those members who protested monopolies on behalf of their constituents, or "countries," and not on their own account.
3. Allow.
4. I.e., those who benefited from a monopoly without regard to the welfare of the general public.
5. Elizabeth compares unscrupulous patentees to physicians who coat bitter pills with sugar; in this case she is the patient who did not realize what was being given to her.

peal, that never thought was cherished in my heart that tended not unto my people's good. And now, if my kingly bounties have been abused, and my grants turned to the hurt of my people, contrary to my will and meaning, and if any in authority under me have neglected or perverted what I have committed to them, I hope God will not lay their culps[6] and offences to my charge; who, though there were danger in repealing our grants, yet what danger would I not rather incur for your good, than I would suffer them still to continue?

I know the title of a king is a glorious title; but assure yourself that the shining glory of princely authority hath not so dazzled the eyes of our understanding, but that we well know and remember that we also are to yield an account of our actions before the great Judge. To be a king and wear a crown is a thing more glorious to them that see it, than it is pleasant to them that bear it. For myself, I was never so much enticed with the glorious name of a king or royal authority of a queen, as delighted that God hath made me His instrument to maintain His truth and glory, and to defend this kingdom (as I said) from peril, dishonor, tyranny and oppression.

There will never queen sit in my seat with more zeal to my country, care for my subjects, and that will sooner with willingness venture her life for your good and safety, than myself. For it is my desire to live nor reign no longer than my life and reign shall be for your good. And though you have had and may have many princes more mighty and wise sitting in this seat, yet you never had nor shall have any that will be more careful and loving.

Shall I ascribe anything to myself and my sexly weakness? I were not worthy to live then; and, of all, most unworthy of the mercies I have had from God, who hath given me a heart that yet never feared any foreign or home enemy. And I speak it to give God the praise, as a testimony before you, and not to attribute anything to myself. For I, oh Lord! what am I, whom practices and perils past should not fear? Or what can I do? That I should speak for any glory, God forbid.

This, Mr. Speaker, I pray you deliver unto the House, to whom heartily recommend me. And so I commit you all to your best fortunes and further counsels. And I pray you, Mr. Comptroller,[7] Mr. Secretary,[8] and you of my Council, that before these gentlemen go into their countries, you bring them all to kiss my hand.

Aemilia Lanyer

1569–1645

Aemilia Lanyer was born Aemilia Bassano, the daughter of Queen Elizabeth's court musician, Baptista Bassano. Acquaintance with the nobility surrounding the Queen allowed her an education that was typically reserved for women of high station. At eighteen, shortly after her mother's death, she became the mistress of Henry Cary Hunsdon, the Lord Chancellor. Her position increased her presence at court until, at twenty-three, she became pregnant and was forced to marry a court musician. Their son, conspicuously named Henry, was born three months after the wedding. The first years of her married life were not auspicious. Alfonso Lanyer was a spendthrift, and the money Aemilia had acquired as Hunsdon's mistress was

6. Sins.
7. Sir William Knollys.
8. Sir Robert Cecil.

soon exhausted. Desperate for reassurance, she visited the astrologer Simon Forman to learn whether the stars indicated that Alfonso would gain a knighthood. The disreputable Forman appears to have had other ideas. His casebook records that on one occasion, he "went and supped with her and stayed all night, and she was familiar and friendly to him in all things. But only she would not halek [have intercourse] . . . he never obtained his purpose and she was a whore and dealt evil with him."

Lanyer's character is more accurately represented in the record of her long friendship with Margaret Clifford, Countess of Cumberland, and her daughter Anne. In 1610, partly in tribute to the loyal support of her patroness, Lanyer published a volume of poetry entitled *Salve Deus Rex Judaeorum;* this included a verse defense of women and a poem to Cookham, a country house leased by Margaret Clifford's brother, William Russell, and visited frequently by Lanyer until 1605. She particularly records two critical transformations in her sense of herself: a spiritual awakening, inspired by the piety of the Countess, and a confirmation of herself as a poet. Her impressions of Cookham express a unity among aesthetic elements that are usually opposed and antithetical: pagan culture and Christian vision, temporal experience and spiritual knowledge, and the erotic pleasure in the discipline of chastity.

The Description of Cookham

Farewell (sweet Cookham) where I first obtained
Grace from that Grace where perfit° grace remained; *perfect*
And where the Muses[1] gave their full consent,
I should have power the virtuous to content;
Where princely Palace willed me to indite,° *write*
The sacred story[2] of the soul's delight.
Farewell (sweet place) where virtue then did rest,
And all delights did harbor in her breast;
Never shall my sad eyes again behold
Those pleasures which my thoughts did then unfold:
Yet you (great Lady),[3] Mistress of that place,
From whose desires did spring this work of grace;
Vouchsafe° to think upon those pleasures past, *agree*
As fleeting worldly joys that could not last,
Or, as dim shadows of celestial pleasures,
Which are desired above all earthly treasures.
Oh how (me thought) against you thither came,[4]
Each part did seem some new delight to frame!
The house received all ornaments to grace it,
And would endure no foulness to deface it.
The walks put on their summer liveries,° *uniforms*
And all things else did hold like similies:° *comparisons*
The trees with leaves, with fruits, with flowers clad,
Embraced each other, seeming to be glad,
Turning themselves to beauteous canopies,
To shade the bright sun from your brighter eyes.
The crystal streams with silver spangles graced,

1. Divinities who presided over the arts and courtesy.
2. Possibly the story of the Passion, recounted in the poem *Salve Deus Rex Judaeorum*.
3. Margaret Clifford, the Countess of Cumberland.
4. In preparation for your arrival.

While by the glorious sun they were embraced,
The little birds in chirping notes did sing,
To entertain both you and that sweet spring.
And Philomela[5] with her sundry lays,° *songs*
Both you and that delightful place did praise.
Oh, how me thought each plant, each flower, each tree
Set forth their beauties then to welcome thee:
The very hills right humbly did descend,
When you to tread upon them did intend.
And as you set your feet, they still did rise,
Glad that they could receive so rich a prize.
The gentle winds did take delight to be
Among those woods that were so graced by thee.
And in sad° murmur uttered pleasing sound, *deep*
That pleasure in that place might more abound:
The swelling banks delivered all their pride,
When such a Phoenix[6] once they had espied.
Each arbor, bank, each seat, each stately tree,
Thought themselves honored in supporting thee.
The pretty birds would oft come to attend thee,
Yet fly away for fear they should offend thee:
The little creatures in the burrow by° *nearby*
Would come abroad to sport them in your eye;
Yet fearful of the bow in your fair hand,
Would run away when you did make a stand.
Now let me come unto that stately tree,
Wherein such goodly prospects you did see;
That oak that did in height his fellows pass,
As much as lofty trees, low growing grass
Much like a comely cedar straight and tall,
Whose beauteous stature far exceeded all.
How often did you visit this fair tree,
Which seeming joyful in receiving thee,
Would like a palm tree spread his arms abroad,
Desirous that you there should make abode:
Whose fair green leaves much like a comely veil,
Defended Phoebus when he would assail:[7]
Whose pleasing boughs did yield a cool fresh air,
Joying his happiness when you were there.
Where being seated, you might plainly see,
Hills, vales, and woods, as if on bended knee
They had appeared, your honor to salute,
Or to prefer some strange unlooked for suit:
All interlaced with brooks and crystal springs,
A prospect fit to please the eyes of kings:

5. In Greek mythology, a woman who was transformed into a swallow; in Latin versions of her story she becomes a nightingale.

6. A mythical bird, always unique on earth, that regenerates itself in its own funeral pyre and therefore signifies eternity; here it figures the Countess.

7. The leaves of the palm tree protected the Countess from Phoebus, the god of the sun.

And thirteen shires appeared all in your sight,
Europe could not afford much more delight.
What was there then but gave you all content,
While you the time in meditation spent,
Of their Creator's power, which there you saw,
In all his creatures held a perfit law;
And in their beauties did you plain descry,° *discern*
His beauty, wisdom, grace, love, majesty.
In these sweet woods how often did you walk,
With Christ and his apostles there to talk;
Placing his holy writ in some fair tree,
To meditate what you therein did see:
With Moses you did mount his holy hill,[8]
To know his pleasure, and perform his will.
With lovely David[9] you did often sing
His holy hymns to heaven's eternal king.
And in sweet music did your soul delight,
To sound his praises, morning, noon, and night.
With blessed Joseph you did often feed
Your pined° brethren, when they stood in need.[1] *poor*
And that sweet lady sprung from Clifford's race,[2]
Of noble Bedford's blood, fair steam of grace,
To honorable Dorset now espoused,
In whose fair breast true virtue then was housed.
Oh, what delight did my weak spirits find
In those pure parts of her well framed mind,
And yet it grieves me that I cannot be
Near unto her, whose virtues did agree
With those fair ornaments of outward beauty,
Which did enforce from all both love and duty.
Unconstant Fortune, thou art most to blame,
Who casts us down into so low a frame,
Where our great friends we cannot daily see,
So great a diffrence is there in degree.
Many are placed in those orbs of state,
Parters° in honor, so ordained by Fate; *participants*
Nearer in show, yet farther off in love,
In which, the lowest always are above.[3]
But whither am I carried in conceit?° *imagination*
My wit too weak to conster of° the great. *understand*
Why not? although we are but born of earth,
We may behold the heavens, despising death;
And loving heaven that is so far above,

8. Moses climbed Mount Sinai to receive the law of God (Exodus 24, 25).
9. King David the psalmist.
1. Sold by his jealous brothers into slavery, Joseph became Pharoah's right-hand man and granted these same brothers food and money during a famine many years later (Genesis 42.1–28).
2. The Lady is the Countess's daughter Anne, descended from Margaret Russell of Bedford and her father George Clifford, Duke of Cumberland. Anne married the Earl of Dorset in 1609 and is thus referred to as Dorset.
3. I.e., persons of low station or rank love more than those who are of the gentry or nobility.

May in the end vouchsafe us entire love.
Therefore sweet memory do thou retain
Those pleasures past, which will not turn again;
Remember beauteous Dorset's former sports,
So far from being touched by ill reports;
Wherein myself did always bear a part,
While reverend Love presented my true heart.
Those recreations let me bear in mind,
Which her sweet youth and noble thoughts did find,
Whereof deprived, I evermore must grieve,
Hating blind Fortune, careless to relieve.
And you sweet Cookham, whom these ladies leave,
I now must tell the grief you did conceive
At their departure; when they went away,
How everything retained a sad dismay;
Nay long before, when once an inkling came,
Methought each thing did unto sorrow frame:
The trees that were so glorious in our view,
Forsook both flowers and fruit, when once they knew
Of your depart,° their very leaves did wither, *departure*
Changing their colors as they grew together.
But when they saw this had no power to stay you,
They often wept, though speechless, could not pray° you; *beg*
Letting their tears in your fair bosoms fall,
As if they said, "Why will ye leave us all?"
This being vain, they cast their leaves away,
Hoping that pity would have made you stay,
Their frozen tops like age's hoary hairs,
Shows their disasters, languishing in fears;
A swarthy riveled rine° all overspread, *bark*
Their dying bodies half alive, half dead.
But your occasions called you so away,
That nothing there had power to make you stay:
Yet did I see a noble grateful mind,
Requiting each according to their kind,
Forgetting not to turn and take your leave
Of these sad creatures, powerless to receive
Your favor when with grief you did depart,
Placing their former pleasures in your heart;
Giving great charge to noble memory,
There to preserve their love continually:
But specially the love of that fair tree,
That first and last you did vouchsafe to see:
In which it pleased you oft to take the air,
With noble Dorset, then a virgin fair:
Where many a learned book was read and scanned
To this fair tree, taking me by the hand,
You did repeat the pleasures which had passed,
Seeming to grieve they could no longer last.

And with a chaste, yet loving kiss took leave,
Of which sweet kiss I did it soon bereave:[4]
Scorning a senseless creature should possess
So rare a favor, so great happiness.
No other kiss it could receive from me,
For fear to give back what it took of thee:
So I ungrateful creature did deceive it,
Of that which you vouchsafed in love to leave it.
And though it oft° had given me much content, *often*
Yet this great wrong I never could repent:
But of the happiest made it most forlorn,
To show that nothing's free from Fortune's scorn,
While all the rest with this most beauteous tree,
Made their sad consort° sorrow's harmony. *music*
The flowers that on the banks and walks did grow,
Crept in the ground, the grass did weep for woe.
The winds and waters seemed to chide together,
Because you went away they know not whither:
And those sweet brooks that ran so fair and clear,
With grief and trouble wrinkled did appear.
Those pretty birds that wonted° were to sing, *accustomed*
Now neither sing, nor chirp, nor use their wing;
But with their tender feet on some bare spray,
Warble forth sorrow, and their own dismay.
Fair Philomela leaves her mournful ditty,
Drowned in dead sleep, yet can procure no pity:
Each arbor, bank, each seat, each stately tree,
Looks bare and desolate now for want of thee;
Turning green tresses into frosty gray,
While in cold grief they wither all away.
The sun grew weak, his beams no comfort gave,
While all green things did make the earth their grave;
Each briar, each bramble, when you went away,
Caught fast your clothes, thinking to make you stay;
Delightful Echo[5] wonted° to reply *used*
To our last words, did now for sorrow die:
The house cast off each garment that might grace it,
Putting on dust and cobwebs to deface it.
All desolation then there did appear,
When you were going whom they held so dear.
This last farewell to Cookham here I give,
When I am dead thy name in this may live,
Wherein I have performed her noble hest,° *request*
Whose virtues lodge in my unworthy breast,
And ever shall, so long as life remains,
Tying my heart to her by those rich chains.

4. I.e., I took their kiss from the tree on which they had put it.

5. A nymph who can only repeat what she has heard; in the absence of voices, she dies.

Christopher Marlowe

1564–1593

When Christopher Marlowe began his career as a dramatist, the Elizabethan stage was at the height of its popularity and sophistication. Marlowe's plays were an immediate success, fascinating audiences with dazzling characters, exotic settings, and controversial subjects. Throughout his career—and even after his sudden death at the age of twenty-nine—Marlowe was Shakespeare's principal commercial and artistic rival.

A shoemaker's son, Marlowe went to Cambridge on a scholarship that was intended to prepare him for holy orders. His interests proved to be literary rather than religious, however, and he left Cambridge for London. As a student, he had composed a number of poems, notably the brilliant but unfinished *Hero and Leander*, a narrative of heterosexual and homosexual passion, but public recognition came with the production of his first play, *Tamburlaine the Great*, in 1587. This was followed by *The Second Part of Tamburlaine the Great*, *The Jew of Malta*, *Edward II*, *Dr. Faustus*, *Dido, Queen of Carthage*, and finally, *The Massacre at Paris*, all composed within a period of six years. Marlowe's bold and inventive language captivated audiences; his blank verse, in which the sense of a sentence is not interrupted at the end of each line by the constraints of rhyme, brought the rhythms of natural speech to the language of theater. His characterizations of heroes were equally astonishing: driven by an incandescent desire that no conquest could satisfy, they revealed the torment and tragedy that were occasioned by pride.

Marlowe himself may have been employed in subversive activities. While still at Cambridge, he became a spy for Queen Elizabeth's secret service, dedicated to the infiltration and exposure of Catholic groups in England and abroad. How much activity he was responsible for remains guesswork. At the very least, the manner in which he died suggests his involvement in clandestine politics. In May 1593, the Queen's Privy Council issued a warrant for his arrest. The charge against him—blasphemy—seems to have come from Thomas Kyd, a fellow playwright with whom Marlowe shared lodgings. While in London waiting for a hearing, Marlowe, who was drinking in an alehouse, got into a fight with three men (all government spies), one of whom was Ingram Friser. Marlowe raised a dagger to stab Friser, but Friser, warding off the blow, managed to turn the dagger against Marlowe. It pierced his eye "in such sort that his brains coming out at the dagger point, he shortly after died." The affair did not end there; two days after Marlowe's death, Richard Baines (himself a former spy) accused him before the Privy Council of atheism, treason, and the opinion "that they that love not tobacco and boys were fools." Whether or not these accusations held any truth, they referred to views that were not unusual in the circles Marlowe frequented; they indicate a skepticism in matters of religion and an indifference to social decorum that authorities responsible for political order would have considered dangerous. Some scholars think that Marlowe was murdered by government command. Although the mystery surrounding his death may never be solved, the mercurial brilliance of his work remains undisputed.

With the exception of the two parts of *Tamburlaine*, published in 1590, Marlowe's works were published after his death: *Edward II* and *Dido, Queen of Carthage* in 1594; *Hero and Leander* in 1598; *Dr. Faustus* in 1604; and *The Jew of Malta* in 1633.

For additional resources on Marlowe, go to *The Longman Anthology of British Literature* Web site at www.myliteraturekit.com.

Hero and Leander[1]

On Hellespont,[2] guilty of true love's blood,
In view and opposite, two cities stood,
Seaborders,° disjoined by Neptune's might. *seaports*
The one Abydos, the other Sestos hight.
As Sestos, Hero dwelt, Hero the fair,
Whom young Apollo° courted for her hair, *god of the sun*
And offered as a dower° his burning throne, *wedding gift*
Where she should sit for men to gaze upon.
The outside of her garments were of lawn,° *fine cloth*
The lining, purple silk, with gilt stars drawn,
Her wide sleeves green, and bordered with a grove,
Where Venus° in her naked glory strove, *goddess of love*
To please the careless and disdainful eyes,
Of proud Adonis° that before her lies. *Venus's lover*
Her kirtle° blue, whereon was many a stain, *gown*
Made with the blood of wretched lovers slain.
Upon her head she wore a myrtle wreath,
From whence her veil reached to the ground beneath.
Her veil was artificial flowers and leaves,
Whose workmanship both man and beast deceives.
Many would praise the sweet smell as she passed,
When t'was the odor which her breath forth cast,
And there for honey, bees have fought in vain,
And beat from thence, have lighted there again.
About her neck hung chains of pebble stone,
Which, lightened by her neck, like diamonds shone.
She wore no gloves, for neither sun nor wind
Would burn or parch her hands, but to her mind,
Or warm or cool them, for they took delight
To play upon those hands, they were so white.
Buskins° of shells all silvered, used she, *boots*
And branched° with blushing coral to the knee. *decorated*
Where sparrows perched, of hollow pearl and gold,
Such as the world would wonder to behold.
Those with sweet water oft her handmaid fills,
Which as she went would chirrup through the° bills.[3] *their*
Some say, for her the fairest Cupid pined,
And looking in her face, was strucken° blind. *struck*
But this is true, so like was one the other,
As he imagined Hero was his mother.
And oftentimes into her bosom flew,
About her naked neck his bare arms threw.

1. In the early modern period, the story of the lovers Hero and Leander was attributed to the legendary poet Musaeus; in fact, it appears to be the work of an anonymous Greek poet of the 4th or 5th century C.E.
2. The straits separating Asia Minor from Thracian Greece, now the Dardanelles.
3. A fantastic costume: Hero's boots are decorated with shells that are filled with water on which mechanical sparrows made of pearl and gold perch and chirp.

And laid his childish head upon her breast,
And with still panting rocked, there took his rest.
So lovely fair was Hero, Venus' nun,
As nature wept, thinking she was undone,
Because she took more from her than she left,
And of such wondrous beauty her bereft.
Therefore in sign° her treasure suffered wrack,° *to signify / loss*
Since Hero's time, hath half the world been black.
Amorous Leander, beautiful and young,
(Whose tragedy divine Musaeus sung)
Dwelt at Abidos, since him dwelt there none
For whom succeeding times make greater moan.
His dangling tresses that were never shorn,
Had they been cut and unto Colchis[4] borne,
Would have allured the vent'rous° youth of Greece, *adventurous*
To hazard more than for the golden fleece.
Fair Cynthia° wished his arms might be her sphere, *goddess of the moon*
Grief makes her pale, because she moves not there.
His body was straight as Circe's[5] wand,
Jove might have sipped out nectar from his hand.
Even as delicious meat is to the taste,
So was his neck in touching, and surpassed
The white of Pelops'[6] shoulder; I could tell ye
How smooth his breast was, and how white his belly,
And whose immortal fingers did imprint,
That heavenly path with many a curious dint
That runs along his back, but my rude pen
Can hardly blazon° forth the loves of men,[7] *list*
Much less of powerful gods. Let it suffice,
That my slack muse sings of Leander's eyes.
Those orient° cheeks and lips, exceeding his *shining*
That leapt into the water for a kiss
Of his own shadow, and despising many,
Died ere he could enjoy the love of any.
Had wild Hippolytus[8] Leander seen,
Enamored of his beauty had he been,
His presence made the rudest peasant melt,
That in the vast uplandish° country dwelt; *rustic*
The barbarous Thracian[9] soldier, moved with nought,
Was moved with him, and for his favor fought.

4. A country at the east end of the Black Sea, to which the legendary golden fleece—a Greek treasure—had been taken. Colchis was raided by the Greek hero Jason and his men, the Argonauts, who carried the fleece back to their homeland.

5. The Greek divinity who with her magic wand turned the companions of Odysseus into swine (*Odyssey* 10).

6. A legendary figure whose father, Tantalus, had him cooked and served to the gods. Only his shoulder was eaten, however, and that was restored with a piece of ivory.

7. The homoerotic element in Marlowe's description of Leander becomes explicit here and continues to be prominent later in the poet's account of Neptune's love for Leander.

8. A legendary hero, vowed to hunting and chastity; at the command of Phaedra, his stepmother, he was consumed by a sea-monster for having refused to return her love for him.

9. Thrace was a mountainous region in northeastern Greece.

Some swore he was a maid in man's attire,
For in his looks were all that men desire,
A pleasant, smiling cheek, a speaking eye,
A brow for love to banquet royally,
And such as knew he was a man would say,
Leander, thou art made for amorous play;
Why art thou not in love, and loved of all?
Though thou be fair, yet be not thine own thrall.° *slave*

The men of wealthy Sestos, every year
(For his sake whom their goddess° held so dear, *Venus*
Rose-cheeked Adonis), kept a solemn feast;
Thither resorted many a wandering guest
To meet their loves; such as had none at all
Came lovers home from this great festival.
For every street like to a firmament° *sky*
Glistered with breathing stars, who where they went,
Frighted the melancholy earth, which deemed,
Eternal heaven to burn, for so it seemed
As if another Phaeton[1] had got
The guidance of the sun's rich chariot.
But far above, the loveliest Hero shined,
And stole away th'enchanted gazer's mind,
For like sea-nymphs inveigling harmony,
So was her beauty to the standers-by.
Nor that night-wandering pale and watery star,[2]
(When yawning dragons draw her thirling° car, *spinning*
From Latmos' mount up to the gloomy sky,
Where crowned with blazing light and majesty,
She proudly sits) more over-rules the flood,
Than she the hearts of those that near her stood.
Even as, when gaudy nymphs pursue the chase,
Wretched Ixion's shaggy-footed race,[3]
Incensed with savage heat, gallop amain,
From steep pine-bearing mountains to the plain,
So ran the people forth to gaze upon her,
And all that viewed her were enamored on her.
And as in fury of a dreadful fight,
Their fellows being slain or put to flight,
Poor soldiers stand with fear of death strucken,
So at her presence all surprised and tooken° *taken*
Await the sentence of her scornful eyes;
He whom she favors lives, the other dies.
There might you see one sigh, another rage,

1. Apollo's son, who drove his father's chariot too near the earth and was struck down by Jove's thunderbolt.
2. The moon, or Cynthia, whose seat is Mount Latmos.
3. Centaurs, creatures who were half-man, half-horse. They were the sons of Centaurus, the son of Ixion and Nephele, a cloud-goddess whom Zeus substituted for Hera, Ixion's real love.

And some (their violent passions to assuage)
Compile sharp satires; but alas too late,
For faithful love will never turn to hate.
And many, seeing great princes were denied,
Pined as they went and thinking on her, died.
On this feast day, O cursed day and hour,
Went Hero through Sestos, from her tower
To Venus' temple, where unhappily,
As after chanced, they did each other spy.
So fair a church as this had Venus none,
The walls were of discolored jasper stone,
Wherein was Proteus[4] carved, and o'erhead,
A lively vine of green sea agate spread,
Where by one hand, light-headed Bacchus° hung, *god of wine*
And with the other, wine from grapes out-wrung.
Of crystal shining fair the pavement was,
The town of Sestos called it Venus' glass.
There might you see the gods in sundry shapes
Committing heady riots, incest, rapes.
For know that underneath this radiant flower
Was Danae's statue[5] in a brazen tower;
Jove, stealing from his sister's bed
To dally with Idalian Ganymede,
And for his love, Europa, bellowing loud,
And tumbling with the rainbow in a cloud;
Blood-quaffing Mars, heaving the iron net,
Which limping Vulcan and his Cyclops set;
Love kindling fire to burn such towns as Troy;
Sylvanus weeping for the lovely boy
That now is turned into a cypress tree,
Under whose shade the wood gods love to be.
And in the midst a silver altar stood,
There Hero, sacrificing turtle's° blood, *dove's*
Veiled to the ground, veiling her eyelids close,
And modestly they opened as she rose;
Thence flew Love's arrow with the golden head,
And thus Leander was enamored.
Stone still he stood, and evermore he gazed,
Till with the fire that from his count'nance blazed,
Relenting Hero's gentle heart was struck,
Such force and virtue hath an amorous look.

It lies not in our power to love or hate,
For will in us is overruled by fate.

4. A sea-god, who could change his shape at will.

5. The figure of the mythical woman Danae, whose father shut her up in a tower to keep her from suitors; Jupiter visited her there in a shower of gold. Marlowe continues his description of "Venus' glass" by allusions to popular mythological figures: Ganymede, Jove's cupbearer and lover; Europa, carried off by Jove disguised as a bull; the lover of Venus, Mars, who was caught in the net of Vulcan, Venus's husband, assisted by his one-eyed helpers, the Cyclops; and Sylvanus, a wood god, who wept for his lover, Cyparissus, who had been turned into a tree.

When two are stripped long ere the course begin,
We wish that one should lose, the other win.
And one especially do we affect,
Of two gold ingots like in each respect.
The reason no man knows, let it suffice,
What we behold is censured° by our eyes. *judged*
Where both deliberate, the love is slight,
Who ever loved that loved not at first sight?

He kneeled, but unto her devoutly prayed.
Chaste Hero to herself thus softly said,
Were I the saint he worships, I would hear him,
And as she spoke those words, came somewhat near him.
He started up, she blushed as one ashamed,
Wherewith Leander much more was inflamed.
He touched her hand, in touching it she trembled,
Love deeply grounded, hardly is dissembled.
These lovers parled° by the touch of hands; *spoke*
True love is mute, and oft amazed stands.
Thus while dumb signs their yielding hearts entangled,
The air with sparks of living fire was spangled,
And Night, deep-drenched in misty Acheron,° *a river in hell*
Heaved up her head, and half the world upon
Breathed darkness forth (dark night is Cupid's day)
And now begins Leander to display
Love's holy fire with words, with sighs and tears,
Which like sweet music entered Hero's ears,
And yet at every word she turned aside,
And always cut him off as he replied.
At last, like to a bold, sharp sophister,° *false reasoner*
With cheerful hope thus he accosted her.

Fair creature, let me speak without offence,
I would my rude words had the influence
To lead thy thoughts, as thy fair looks do mine,
Then shouldst thou be his prisoner who is thine.
Be not unkind and fair, misshapen stuff° *ungainly persons*
Are of behavior boisterous and rough.
O shun me not, but hear me ere you go,
God knows I cannot force love, as you do.
My words shall be as spotless as my youth,
Full of simplicity and naked truth.
This sacrifice (whose sweet perfume descending
From Venus' altar to your footsteps bending)
Doth testify that you exceed her far,
To whom you offer, and whose nun you are.
Why should you worship her, her you surpass,
As much as sparkling diamonds flaring° glass. *flashing*
A diamond set in lead his worth retains,
A heavenly nymph, beloved of human swains,° *suitors*

Receives no blemish, but oft times more grace,
Which makes me hope, although I am but base,
Base in respect of thee, divine and pure,
Dutiful service may thy love procure,
And I in duty will excel all other,
As thou in beauty dost exceed Love's mother.
Nor heaven, nor thou, were made to gaze upon,
As heaven preserves all things, so save thou one.° *Leander*
A stately builded ship, well-rigged and tall,
The ocean maketh more majestical.
Why vowest thou then to live in Sestos here,
Who on Love's seas more glorious wouldst appear?
Like untuned golden strings all women are,
Which, long time lie untouched, will harshly jar.
Vessels of brass oft handled brightly shine,
What difference betwixt the richest mine
And basest mold, but use? For both not used
Are of like worth. Then treasure is abused
When misers keep it; being put to loan,
In time it will return us two for one.
Rich robes, themselves and others do adorn,
Neither themselves nor others, if not worn.
Who builds a palace and rams up the gate,
Shall see it ruinous and desolate.
Ah, simple Hero, learn thyself to cherish,
Lone women, like to empty houses, perish.
Less sins the poor rich man that starves himself,
In heaping up a mass of drossy pelf,° *worthless booty*
Than such as you; his golden earth remains,
Which, after his decease, some other gains.
But this fair gem, sweet in the loss alone,
When you fleet hence, can be bequeathed to none.
Or if it could, down from th'enamelled sky,
All heaven would come to claim this legacy,
And with intestine broils° the world destroy, *civil wars*
And quite confound nature's sweet harmony.
Well therefore by the gods decreed it is,
We human creatures should enjoy that bliss.
One is no number, maids are nothing then,
Without the sweet society of men.
Wilt thou live single still? One shalt thou be,
Though never-singling Hymen[6] couple thee.
Wild savages, that drink of running springs,
Think water far excels all earthly things.
But they that daily taste neat° wine, despise it. *unwatered*
Virginity, albeit some highly prize it,
Compared with marriage, had you tried them both,

6. Marlowe turns to paradox: Although Hero is coupled by Hymen, the god of marriage, she can also remain "one" or single.

Differs as much as wine and water doth.
Base boullion° for the stamp's sake we allow,[7] *metal*
Even so for men's impression do we you.
By which alone, our reverend fathers say,
Women receive perfection every way.
This idol which you term virginity,
Is neither essence subject to the eye,
No, nor to any one exterior sense,
Nor hath it any place of residence,
Nor is't of earth or mold celestial,
Or capable of any form at all.
Of that which hath no being do not boast,
Things that are not at all are never lost.
Men foolishly do call it virtuous,
What virtue is it, that is born with us?
Much less can honor be ascribed thereto;
Honor is purchased by the deeds we do.
Believe me, Hero, honor is not won,
Until some honorable deed be done.
Seek you for chastity, immortal fame,
And know that some have wronged Diana's name?
Whose name is it, if she be false or not,
So she be fair, but some vile tongues will blot?
But you are fair (aye me), so wondrous fair,
So young, so gentle, and so debonair,° *courteous*
As Greece will think if thus you live alone,
Some one or other keeps you as his own.
Then, Hero, hate me not, nor from me fly,
To follow swiftly blasting infamy.
Perhaps thy sacred priesthood makes thee loath,
Tell me, to whom mad'st thou that heedless oath?

To Venus, answered she, and as she spoke,
Forth from those two translucent cisterns broke
A stream of liquid pearl, which down her face
Made milk-white paths, whereon the gods might trace
To Jove's high court. He thus replied: the rites
In which love's beauteous empress most delights
Are banquets, Doric[8] music, midnight revel,
Plays, masques, and all that stern age counteth evil.
Thee as a holy Idiot doth she scorn,
For thou, in vowing chastity, hast sworn
To rob her name and honor, and thereby
Commit'st a sin far worse than perjury,
Even sacrilege against her deity,
Through regular and formal purity.

7. Just as a coin has its value stamped on it, so a woman is valued according to the impression she gives.

8. Pertaining to the Greek region of Doris, noted for the simplicity of its culture.

To expiate which sin, kiss and shake hands,
Such sacrifice as this Venus demands.

Thereat she smiled, and did deny him so,
As put thereby, yet might he hope for mo'e.
Which makes him quickly re-enforce his speech,
And her in humble manner thus beseech.

Though neither gods nor men may thee deserve,
Yet for her sake whom you have vowed to serve,
Abandon fruitless, cold virginity,
The gentle Queen of Love's sole enemy.
Then shall you most resemble Venus' nun,
When Venus' sweet rites are performed and done.
Flint-breasted Pallas[9] joys in single life,
But Pallas and your mistress are at strife.
Love, Hero, then, and be not tyrannous,
But heal the heart that thou has wounded thus,
Nor stain thy youthful years with avarice,
Fair fools delight to be accounted nice.° *coy*
The richest corn° dies if it be not reaped, *grain*
Beauty alone is lost, too warily kept.
These arguments he used, and many more,
Wherewith she yielded, that was won before,
Hero's looks yielded, but her words made war;
Women are won when they begin to jar.° *quarrel*
Thus having swallowed Cupid's golden hook,
The more she strived, the deeper was she struck.
Yet evilly feigning anger, strove she still,
And would be wrought to grant against her will.
So having paused a while, at last she said:
Who taught thee rhetoric to deceive a maid?
Aye me, such words as these should I abhor,
And yet I like them for the orator.

With that Leander stooped, to have embraced her,
But from his spreading arms away she cast her,
And thus bespake him: Gentle youth, forbear
To touch the sacred garments which I wear.
Upon a rock, and underneath a hill,
Far from the town (where all is whist° and still, *quiet*
Save that sea playing on yellow sand
Sends forth a rattling murmur to the land,
Whose sound allures the golden Morpheus,° *god of sleep*
In silence of the night to visit us)
My turret stands, and there God knows I play
With Venus' swans and sparrows all the day,
A dwarfish beldame° bears° me company, *old woman / keeps*

9. Athena or Minerva, goddess of wisdom, justice, and war.

That hops about the chamber where I lie,
And spends the night (that might be better spent)
In vain discourse and apish merriment.
Come thither; as she spake this, her tongue tripped,
For unawares (Come thither) from her slipped,
And suddenly her former color changed,
And here and there her eyes through anger ranged,
And like a planet, moving several ways,
At one self instant, she, poor soul, assays,
Loving, not to love at all, and every part,
Strove to resist the motions of her heart.
And hands so pure, so innocent, nay such,
As might have made heaven stoop to have a touch,
Did she uphold to Venus, and again,
Vowed spotless chastity, but all in vain.
Cupid beat down her prayers with his wings,
Her vowes above the empty air he flings.
All deep enraged, his sinewy bow he bent,
And shot a shaft that burning from him went,
Wherewith she, stroocken,° looked so dolefully, *struck*
As made Love sigh to see his tyranny.
And as she wept, her tears to pearl he turned,
And wound them on his arm, and for her mourned.
Then towards the palace of the Destinies,° *the Fates*
Laden with languishment and grief, he flies.
And to those stern nymphs humbly made request,
Both might enjoy each other, and be blessed.
But with a ghastly dreadful countenance,
Threatening a thousand deaths at every glance,
They answered Love, nor would vouchsafe so much
As one poor word, their hate to him was such.
Harken a while, and I will tell you why:
Heaven's winged herald, Jove-born Mercury,[1]
The selfsame day that he asleep had laid
Enchanted Argus, spied a country maid,
Whose careless hair, instead of pearl t'adorn it,
Glistered with dew, as one that seemed to scorn it,
Her breath as fragrant as the morning rose,
Her mind pure and her tongue untaught to glose.° *deceive*
Yet proud she was (for lofty pride that dwells
In towered courts, is oft in shepherds' cells°), *cottages*
And too too well the fair vermillion knew,
And silver tincture of her cheeks, that drew
The love of every swain. On her, this god
Enamored was, and with his snakey rod,° *Mercury's staff*
Did charm her nimble feet, and made her stay,

1. The messenger god; he enchanted the many-eyed herdsman Argus (or Argos), whom Juno had ordered to guard the heifer Io, beloved of Jupiter.

The while upon a hillock down he lay,
And sweetly on his pipe began to play,
And with his smooth speech, her fancy to assay,° *attempt*
Till in his twining arms he locked her fast,
And then he wooed her with kisses and at last,
As shepherds do, her on the ground he laid,
And tumbling in the grass, he often strayed
Beyond the bounds of shame, in being bold
To eye those parts, which no eye should behold,
And like an insolent commanding lover,
Boasting his parentage, would needs discover
The way to new Elysium; but she,
Whose only dower° was her chastity, *dowry, wealth*
Having striven in vain, was now about to cry,
And crave the help of the shepherds that were nigh.
Herewith he stayed his fury, and began
To give her leave to rise; away she ran,
After went Mercury, who used such cunning,
As she to hear his tale, left off running.
Maids are not wooed by brutish force and might,
But speeches full of pleasure and delight.
And knowing Hermes° courted her, was glad *Mercury*
That she such loveliness and beauty had
As could provoke his liking, yet was mute,
And neither would deny, nor grant his suit.
Still vowed he love, she wanting no excuse
To feed him with delays, as women use,
Or thirsting after immortality,
All women are ambitious naturally,
Imposed upon her lover such a task,
As he ought not perform, nor yet she ask.
A draught of flowing nectar, she requested,
Wherewith the king of the gods and men is feasted.
He ready to accomplish what she willed,
Stole some from Hebe° (Hebe, Jove's cups filled) *a goddess*
And gave it to his simple rustic love,
Which being known (as what is hid from Jove?)
He inly stormed, and waxed more furious
Than for the fire filched by Prometheus,[2]
And thrusts him down from heaven; he wandering here,
In mournful terms, with sad and heavy cheer
Complained to Cupid. Cupid, for his° sake, *Prometheus's*
To be revenged on Jove, did undertake,
And those on whom heaven, earth, and hell relies,
I mean the adamantine° Destinies, *implacable*
He wounds with love, and forced them equally,

2. In Greek mythology, the figure of "forethought"; he made mankind out of clay and, when Jupiter deprived them of fire, stole it from heaven.

To dote upon deceitful Mercury.
They offered him the deadly, fatal knife,
That shears the slender threads of human life,
At his fair feathered feet, the engines laid,
Which th'earth from ugly Chaos'[3] den up-weighed:
These he regarded not, but did entreat
That Jove, usurper of his father's° seat, *Saturn's*
Might presently be banished into hell,
And aged Saturn in Olympus dwell.
They granted what he craved, and once again,
Saturn and Ops° began their golden reign. *Wealth (Saturn's wife)*
Murder, rape, war, lust, and treachery
Were, with Jove, closed in Stygian Emprie.° *empire of hell*
But long this blessed time continued not,
As soon as he his wished purpose got;
He reckless of his promise, did despise
The love of the everlasting Destinies.
They seeing it, both Love and him abhorred,
And Jupiter unto his place restored.
And but that learning, in despite of Fate,
Will mount aloft and enter heaven's gate,
And to the seat of Jove itself advance,
Hermes[4] had slept in hell with ignorance.
Yet as a punishment they added this,
That he and Poverty should always kiss.
And to this day is every scholar poor,
Gross gold from them runs headlong to the boor.
Likewise the angry sisters° thus deluded, *the Destinies*
To venge themselves on Hermes have concluded
That Midas' brood[5] shall sit in honor's chair,
To which the Muses' sons are only heir.
And fruitful wits that in aspiring° are, *ambitious*
Shall, discontent, run into regions far,
And few great lords in virtuous deeds shall joy,
But be surprised with every garish toy.
And still enrich the lofty° servile clown, *proud*
Who with encroaching guile keeps learning down.
Then muse not Cupid's suit no better sped,° *succeeded*
Seeing in their loves the Fates were injured.
By this, sad Hero, with love unacquainted
Viewing Leander's face, fell down and fainted.
He kissed her and breathed life into her lips,
Wherewith as one displeased, away she trips.

3. The infinite space that precedes creation.

4. Hermes (or Mercury), as Learning (or the messenger god), must rise to a god's status; he cannot therefore be imprisoned in ignorance for long. Marlowe's unprecedented mythology is complicated: he describes "deceitful Mercury" as instituting a new golden age, then as losing it because he neglects "the Destinies," and finally as regaining divine favor because of what he signifies.

5. Like their father, the children of Midas would have the golden touch, i.e., money; ironically, the Destinies decree that money is also honor.

Yet as she went full often looked behind,
And many poor excuses did she find
To linger by the way, and once she stayed,
And would have turned again, but was afraid,
In offering parley,° to be counted light. *speech*
So on she goes, and in her idle flight,
Her painted fan of curled plumes let fall,
Thinking to train° Leander therewithal. *tempt*
He, being a novice, knew not what she meant,
But stayed, and after her a letter sent.
Which joyful Hero answered in such sort,
As he had hope to scale the beauteous fort,
Wherein the liberal graces locked their wealth,
And therefore to her tower he got by stealth.
Wide open stood the door, he need not climb,
And she herself before the pointed° time, *appointed*
Had spread the board, with roses strewed the room,
And oft looked out and mused he did not come.
At last he came, O who can tell the greeting,
These greedy lovers had at their first meeting.
He asked, she gave, and nothing was denied,
Both to each other quickly were affied.° *betrothed*
Look how their hands, so were their hearts united,
And what he did, she willingly requited.
(Sweet are the kisses, the embracements sweet,
When like desires and affections meet
For from the earth to heaven, is Cupid raised,
Where fancy is in equal balance paised°), *poised*
Yet she this rashness suddenly repented,
And turned aside and to herself lamented.
As if her name and honor had been wronged,
By being possessed of him for whom she longed.
Aye, and she wished, albeit not from her heart,
That he would leave her turret and depart.
The mirthful god of amorous pleasure smiled,
To see how he this captive nymph beguiled.
For hitherto he did but fan the fire,
And kept it down that it might burn the higher.
Now waxed she jealous, lest his love abated,
Fearing her own thoughts made her to be hated.[6]
Therefore unto him hastily she goes,
And like light Salmacis,[7] her body throws
Upon his bosom, where with yielding eyes,
She offers up herself a sacrifice,
To slake his anger, if he were displeased,
O what god would not therewith be appeased?

6. I.e., fearing that she was hated, she imagined that she was hated.

7. A nymph who pursued the boy Hermaphroditus; when she embraced him they became one, half-girl, half-boy.

Like Aesop's cock,[8] this jewel he enjoyed,
And as a brother with his sister toyed,
Supposing nothing else was to be done,
Now he her favor and good will had won.
But know you not that creatures wanting sense° *inanimate*
By nature have a mutual appetence,° *desire*
And wanting organs to advance a step,
Moved by Love's force, unto each other leap?
Much more in subjects having intellect,
Some hidden influence breeds like effect.
Albeit Leander, rude in love and raw,
Long dallying with Hero, nothing saw
That might delight him more, yet he suspected
Some amorous rites or other were neglected.
Therefore unto his body, hers he clung,° *clasped*
She fearing on the rushes° to be flung, *a floor covering*
Strived with redoubled strength; the more she strived,
The more a gentle pleasing heat revived,
Which taught him all that elder lovers know,
And now the same 'gan° so to scorch and glow, *began*
As in plain terms (yet cunningly) he craved it,
Love always makes those eloquent that have it.
She, with a kind of granting, put him by it,
And ever as he thought himself most nigh it,
Like to the tree of Tantalus[9] she fled,
And seeming lavish, saved her maidenhead.
Ne'er king more sought to keep his diadem
Than Hero this inestimable gem.
Above our life we love a steadfast friend,
Yet when a token of great wealth we send,
We often kiss it, often look thereon,
And stay the messenger that would be gone;
No marvel then, though Hero would not yield
So soon to part from that she dearly held.
Jewels being lost are found again; this, never.
T'is lost but once, and once lost, lost for ever.

Now had the morn° espied her lover's° steeds, *Aurora / Apollo*
Whereat she starts, puts on her purple weeds,
And red for anger that he stayed so long,
All headlong throws herself the clouds among,
And now Leander, fearing to be missed,
Embraced her suddenly, took leave, and kissed,
Long was he taking leave, and loath to go,
And kissed again, as lovers use to do,

8. According to Aesop, a writer of animal fables supposed to have lived in Thrace in the 6th century B.C.E., his cock found a precious jewel in the barnyard but rejected it because it was not a barleycorn. In the context of Marlowe's story the comparison is ambiguous.

9. Punished in hell for revealing the secrets of the gods, Tantalus was doomed to reach for fruit from a tree whose branches were always beyond his grasp.

Sad Hero wrung him by the hand and wept,
Saying, let your vows and promises be kept.
Then standing at the door, she turned about,
As loath to see Leander going out.
And now the sun that through th'orizon peeps,
As pitying these lovers, downward creeps.
So that in silence of the cloudy night,
Though it was morning, did he take his flight.
But what the secret trusty night concealed,
Leander's amorous habit soon revealed,
With Cupid's myrtle was his bonnet crowned,
About his arms the purple ribbon wound,
Wherewith she wreathed her largely spreading hair.
Nor could the youth abstain, but he must wear
The sacred ring wherewith she was endowed
When first religious chastity she vowed,
Which made his love through Sestos to be known,
And thence to Abydos sooner blown
Than he could sail, for incorporeal Fame,° *Rumor*
Whose weight consists of nothing but her name,
Is swifter than the wind, whose tardy plumes
Are reeking° water and dull earthly fumes. *vaporizing*
Home when he came, he seemed not to be there,
But like exiled air thrust from his sphere,
Set in a foreign place, and straight from thence,
Alcides-like,° by mighty violence, *like Heracles*
He would have chased away the swelling main,
That him from her unjustly did detain.
Like as the sun in a diameter[1]
Fires and enflames objects removed far,
And heateth kindly,° shining lat'rally, *gently*
So beauty sweetly quickens when 'tis nigh.
But being separated and removed,
Burns where it cherished, murders where it loved.
Therefore even as an index to a book,
So to his mind was young Leander's look.° *appearance*
O none but gods have power their love to hide,
Affection by the countenance is descried.
The light of hidden fire itself discovers,
And love that is concealed betrays poor lovers.
His secret flame apparently was seen,
Leander's father knew where he had been,
And for the same mildly rebuked his son,
Thinking to quench the fire new begun.
But love resisted once grows passionate,
And nothing more than counsel, lovers hate.
For as a hot, proud horse lightly disdains

1. I.e., directly (as opposed to obliquely) above the earth.

To have his head controlled, but breaks the reins,
Spits forth the ringled bit° and with his hooves *the bit with rings*
Checks the submissive ground, so he that loves,
The more he is restrained, the worse he fares,
What is it now but mad Leander dares?
O Hero, Hero, thus he cried full oft,
And then he got him to a rock aloft.
Where having spied her tower, long stared he on't,
And prayed the narrow toiling Hellespont
To part in twain, that he might come and go,
But still the rising billows answered no.
With that he stripped him to the ivory skin,
And crying, Love I come!, leapt lively° in. *quickly*
Whereat the sapphire-visaged god[2] grew proud,
And made his capr'ing triton sound aloud,
Imagining that Ganymede, displeased,
Had left the heavens, therefore on him he seized.
Leander strived, the waves about him wound,
And pulled him to the bottom, where the ground
Was strewed with pearl and in low coral groves,
Sweet singing mermaids sported with their loves
On heaps of heavy gold, and took great pleasure
To spurn the careless sort, the shipwrack° treasure. *shipwrecked*
For here the stately azure palace stood,
Where kingly Neptune and his train abode,
The lusty god embraced him, called him love,
And swore he never should return to Jove.
But when he knew it was not Ganymede,
For underwater he was almost dead,
He heaved him up, and looking on his face,
Beat down the gold waves with his triple mace,
Which mounted up, intending to have kissed him,
And fell in drops like tears because they missed him.
Leander, being up, began to swim,
And looking back, saw Neptune follow him.
Whereat aghast, the poor soul 'gan to cry,
O let me visit Hero ere I die!
The god put Helle's[3] bracelet on his arm,
And swore the sea should never do him harm.
He clapped his plump cheeks, with his tresses played,
And smiling wantonly, his love bewrayed.° *revealed*
He watched his arms, and as they opened wide,
At every stroke, betwixt them would he slide,
And steal a kiss, and then run out and dance,
And as he turned, cast many a lustful glance,

2. Neptune, whose son, Triton, is both a shell and the creature who blows upon it.
3. The daughter of the mythical Athamas and Nephele, who had to escape from the wrath of her stepmother, Ino, on a flying ram; she fell off its back into the part of the sea called the Hellespont. Neptune is said to have rescued her; the bracelet the god puts on Leander's arm signifies divine protection.

And threw him gaudy toys to please his eye,
And dive into the water, and there pry
Upon his breast, his thighs, and every limb,
And up again, and close beside him swim
And talk of love. Leander made reply,
You are deceived, I am no woman I.
Thereat smiled Neptune, and then told a tale,
How that a shepherd sitting in a vale,
Played with a boy so fair and kind,
As for his love both earth and heaven pined,
That of the cooling river durst not drink,
Lest water nymphs should pull him from the brink.
And when he sported in the fragrant lawns,
Goat-footed satyrs and up-staring fawns,[4]
Would steal him thence. Ere half this tale was done,
Aye me, Leander cried, th'enamored sun,
That now should shine on Thetis' glassy bower,[5]
Descends upon my radiant Hero's tower.
O that these tardy arms of mine were wings,
And as he spake, upon the waves he springs.
Neptune was angry that he gave no ear,
And in his heart, revenging malice bore.
He flung at him his mace, but as it went,
He called it in, for love made him repent.
The mace, returning back, his own hand hit,
As meaning to be venged for darting it.
When this fresh-bleeding wound Leander viewed,
His color went and came, as if he rued
The grief which Neptune felt. In gentle breasts,
Relenting thoughts, remorse, and pity rests.
And who have hard hearts, and obdurate minds,
But vicious, harebrained, and illit'rate hinds?° *rustics*
The god, seeing him with pity to be moved,
Thereon concluded that he was beloved.
(Love is too full of faith, too credulous,
With folly and false hope deluding us.)
Wherefore Leander's fancy to surprise,
To the rich ocean for gifts he flies.
'Tis wisdom to give much, a gift prevails,
When deep, persuading oratory fails.
By this, Leander, being near the land,
Cast down his weary feet and felt the sand.
Breathless albeit he were, he rested not,
Till to the solitary tower he got.
And knocked and called, at which celestial noise,
The longing heart of Hero much more joys
Than nymphs and shepherds when the timbrell° rings, *tambourine*

4. Fauns, spirits who are guided by the heavens.

5. The bower of Thetis, a sea nymph, is the sea.

Or crooked dolphin when the sailor sings.[6]
She stayed not her robes, but straight arose,
And drunk with gladness, to the door she goes,
Where seeing a naked man, she screeched for fear,
Such sighs as this to tender maids are rare.
And ran into the dark herself to hide;
Rich jewels in the dark are soonest spied.
Unto her he was led, or rather drawn,
By those white limbs which sparkled through the lawn.
The nearer he came, the more she fled,
And seeking refuge, slipped into her bed.
Whereon Leander sitting, thus begin,
Though numbing cold, all feeble, faint, and wan:

If not for love, yet love, for pity's sake,
Me in thy bed and maiden bosom take,
At least vouchsafe these arms some little room,
Who hoping to embrace thee cheerily swome.° *swam*
This head was beat with many a churlish billow,
And therefore let it rest upon thy pillow.
Herewith, afrighted, Hero shrunk away,
And in her lukewarm place Leander lay.
Whose lively head like fire from heaven fet,° *fetched*
Would animate gross clay, and higher set
The drooping thoughts of base declining souls,
Than dreary° Mars, carousing nectar bowls.° *bloody / bowls of nectar*
His hands he cast upon her like a snare,
She, overcome with shame and sallow fear,
Like chaste Diana when Actaeon spied her,
Being suddenly betrayed, dived down to hide her.
And as her silver body downward went,
With both her hands she made the bed a tent,
And in her own mind thought herself secure,
O'ercast with dim and darksome coverture.° *covering*
And now she lets him whisper in her ear,
Flatter, entreat, promise, protest, and swear,
Yet ever as he greedily assayed
To touch those dainties, she the Harpy[7] played
And every limb did as a soldier stout,
Defend the fort, and keep the foe-man out.
For though the rising iv'ry mount he scaled,
Which is with azure circling lines empaled,
Much like a globe (a globe may I term this,
By which love sails to regions full of bliss),
Yet there with Sisyphus[8] he toiled in vain,

6. The sailor is the mythical musician Arion, who was saved by dolphins ("crooked" because of their curved backs) when they heard him sing.

7. One of the fierce birds who snatched food from the Trojan companions of Aeneas on their way from Troy to Italy (*Aeneid* 3.225ff.).

8. The legendary king of Corinth, who in the underworld was eternally condemned to roll a large stone to the top of a hill, only to have it roll down again.

Till gentle parley° did the truce obtain. *speech*
She trembling strove, this strife of hers (like that
Which made the world) another world begat,
Of unknown joy. Treason was in her thought,
And cunningly to yield herself she sought.
Seeming not won, yet won she was at length,
In such wars women use but half their strength.
Leander now like Thebian Hercules,[9]
Entered the orchard of Th'esperides.
Whose fruit none rightly can describe, but he
That pulls or shakes it from the golden tree.
Wherein Leander on her quivering breast,
Breathless spoke some thing and sighed out the rest,
Which so prevailed, as he with small ado,
Enclosed her in his arms and kissed her too.
And every kiss to her was as a charm,
And to Leander as a fresh alarm.
So that the truce was broke, and she alas,
(Poor silly maiden) at his mercy was.
Love is not full of pity (as men say)
But deaf and cruel, where he means to prey,
Even as a bird, which in our hands we wring,
Forth plungeth and oft flutters with her wing.
And now she wished this night were never done,
And sighed to think upon th'approaching sun,
For much it grieved her that the bright daylight
Should know the pleasure of this blessed night.
And then like Mars and Ericine° displayed, *Venus*
Both in each others' arms, chained as they laid,
Again she knew not how to frame her look,
Or speak to him who in a moment took
That which so long, so charily she kept,
And feign by stealth away she would have crept,
And to some corner secretly have gone,
Leaving Leander in the bed alone.
But as her naked feet were whipping out,
He on the sudden clinged her so about,
That mermaid-like unto the floor she slid,
One half appeared, the other half was hid.
Thus near the bed she blushing stood upright,
And from her countenance behold ye might,
A kind of twilight break, which through the hair,
As from an orient cloud, glimpse here and there.
And round about the chamber this false morn
Brought forth the day before the day was born,

9. The eleventh labor of Hercules was to steal the golden apples of the Hesperides, daughters of the evening, who watched over their orchard on an island in a distant western sea.

So Hero's ruddy cheek, Hero betrayed,
And her all naked to his sight displayed.
Whence his admiring eyes more pleasure took
Than Dis on heaps of gold fixing his look.
By this Apollo's golden harp began,
To sound forth music to the ocean,
Which watchful Hesperus[1] no sooner heard,
But he the day bright-bearing car prepared
And ran before, as harbinger of light,
And with his flaming beams mocked ugly Night,
Till she, o'ercome with anguish, shame, and rage,
Danged° down to Hell her loathsome carriage. *hurled*
Desunt nonnulla.[2]

THE TRAGICAL HISTORY OF DR. FAUSTUS Marlowe's play is the first dramatic rendition of the medieval legend of a man who sold his soul to the devil. Sixteenth-century readers associated him with a necromancer named Dr. Faustus, and Marlowe exploited this identification when he reworked the medieval plot for his play. Rejecting the usual learning available to ambitious men—philosophy, medicine, law, and theology—Marlowe's Faustus signs a contract with the devil, represented in this case by his servant, Mephostophilis; in exchange for his soul, Faustus gains superhuman powers for twenty-four years. He uses these powers to conjure the Pope in Rome into giving the Protestant Emperor Charles V authority over the church through a surrogate Pope, Bruno; but his powers are also deployed in the banal trickery of simple and even criminal characters. The play is enigmatic on points of doctrine. Mephostophilis describes hell not as a locale but rather as the state of mind of one who has rejected God—a description that Milton will later amplify—telling Faustus: "this is hell, nor am I out of it." And Faustus, having worshipped the devil, is nevertheless offered a chance to repent and find salvation even at the very end of his alloted life. But he rejects God's love in favor of a night with Helen of Troy, praising her in lines that are now famous: "Was this the face that launched a thousand ships, / And burnt the topless towers of Ilium?" The play concludes with a report of Faustus's mangled body, torn to bits by the demon to whom he had given his soul.

The textual history of the play is very vexed, and the extent of Marlowe's own authorship remains unclear. A short version of the play was published in 1604; known as the A text, it was probably used by touring companies. The longer B text, given here, was published in 1616, probably based on Marlowe's original manuscript but also incorporating revisions and additions by Marlowe and others as the play continued to evolve in performance.

Although playtexts in this period quite often show variants from one edition to another, the case of *Dr. Faustus* is an extreme one; lacking an authoritative version, it has generally been read in various conflations of A and B. Even so, it has continued to prove popular with audiences, both for the fatal drama of Faustus's bargain with the Devil and for the magnificent blank verse in which the drama plays out.

1. Marlowe mistakes the evening star, Hesperus, for the morning star, Venus.
2. "Some things are missing." Added in 1598 by Marlowe's printer, Edward Blunt, who believed the poem was unfinished.

The Tragical History of Dr. Faustus

Dramatis Personae

CHORUS
FAUSTUS
WAGNER, *SERVANT TO FAUSTUS*
GOOD ANGEL AND EVIL ANGEL
VALDES
CORNELIUS } *Friends to Faustus*
MEPHOSTOPHILIS
LUCIFER
BELZEBUB
THE SEVEN DEADLY SINS
CLOWN/ROBIN
DICK
RAFE
VINTNER
CARTER
HOSTESS
THE POPE
BRUNO
RAYMOND, *KING OF HUNGARY*
CHARLES, *THE GERMAN EMPEROR*
MARTINO
FREDERICK
BENVOLIO
SAXONY
DUKE OF VANHOLT
DUCHESS OF VANHOLT
SPIRITS IN THE SHAPES OF ALEXANDER THE GREAT, DARIUS, PARAMOUR, AND HELEN
AN OLD MAN
SCHOLARS, SOLDIERS, DEVILS, COURTIERS, CARDINALS, MONKS, CUPIDS

[Enter Chorus.]

CHORUS: Not marching in the fields of Thrasimene,[1]
Where Mars did mate the warlike Carthigens,
Nor sporting in the dalliance of love
In courts of kings where state is overturned,
Nor in the pomp of proud audacious deeds,
Intends our muse to vaunt his heavenly verse.[2]
Only this, gentles: we must now perform
The form of Faustus' fortunes, good or bad.
And now to patient judgments we appeal,
And speak for Faustus in his infancy.
Now is he born, of parents base of stock,
In Germany, within a town called Rhodes.
At riper years to Wittenberg he went,
Whereas his kinsmen chiefly brought him up.
So much he profits in divinity,
The fruitful plot° of scholarism graced, *field*
That shortly he was graced with Doctor's name,
Excelling all; and sweetly can dispute
In th' heavenly matters of theology.
Till swol'n with cunning of a self-conceit,
His waxen wings did mount above his reach,

1. Trasimeno, a lake in Italy near Rome. The Carthaginian general Hannibal conquered Roman forces at Trasimeno in 217 B.C.E.; Marlowe's "Mars" is probably a reference to the Roman army, which "mated" or engaged the enemy opposition there.

2. These lines may refer to plays Marlowe had previously staged and whose subjects were war (*Tamburlaine*) and love (*Edward II*, *Dido, Queen of Carthage*).

Title page, 1620 edition of Marlowe's *The Tragical History of Dr. Faustus*.

And melting, heavens conspired his overthrow.[3]
For falling to a devilish exercise,
And glutted now with learning's golden gifts,
He surfeits upon cursed necromancy.
Nothing so sweet as magic is to him,
Which he prefers before his chiefest bliss:
And this the man that in his study sits.

ACT 1

Scene 1

[*Faustus in his study.*]

FAUSTUS: Settle thy studies, Faustus, and begin
To sound the depth of that thou wilt profess.
Having commenced, be a divine in show,
Yet level at the end of every art
And live and die in Aristotle's works.
Sweet Analytics, 'tis thou hast ravished me.[4]

3. Faustus is compared to the legendary figure of Icarus, whose father, the master craftsman Daedalus, made him a pair of wings that were attached to his body with wax. Icarus flew too near the sun, the wax supporting his wings melted, and he fell to the sea. The legend is generally understood to signify the consequences of pride and presumption.

4. Aristotle (384–322 B.C.E.), the best known of the Greek philosophers, wrote on the natural and social sciences. His *Analytics* dealt with logic.

Bene disserere est finis logices.
Is "to dispute well logic's chiefest end"?
Affords this art no greater miracle?
Then read no more: thou hast attained that end.
A greater subject fitteth Faustus' wit.
Bid *on cai me on*° farewell. And Galen,[5] come. *being and non-being*
Seeing, *ubi desinit philosophus, ibi incipit medicus*.
Be a physician, Faustus: heap up gold
And be eternized for some wondrous cure.
Summum bonum medicinae sanitas:
"The end of physic is our body's health."
Why, Faustus, hast thou not attained that end?
Is not thy common talk sound aphorisms?° *wise sayings*
Are not thy bills hung up as monuments,
Whereby whole cities have escaped the plague,
And thousand desperate maladies been cured?
Yet art thou still but Faustus and a man.
Couldst thou make men to live eternally,
Or being dead, raise them to life again,
Then this profession were to be esteemed.
Physic, farewell. Where is Justinian?[6]
Si una eademque res legatur duobus,
Alter rem, alter valorem rei etc.,
A petty case of paltry legacies!
Exhaereditare filium non potest pater, nisi—
Such is the subject of the institute
And universal body of the law.
This study fits a mercenary drudge,
Who aims at nothing but external trash,
Too servile and illiberal for me.
When all is done Divinity is best.
Jerome's Bible![7] Faustus, view it well.
Stipendium peccati mors est. Ha! Stipendium etc.,
"The reward of sin is death."[8] That's hard.
Si pecasse negamus, fallimur, et nulla est in nobis veritas.
"If we say that we have no sin
We deceive ourselves, and there is no truth in us."[9]
Why then, belike, we must sin,
And so consequently die.
Ay, we must die, an everlasting death.
What doctrine call you this? *Che sera, sera*.
"What will be, shall be." Divinity, adieu!
These necromantic books are heavenly,

5. Greek physician (130–200 C.E.) whose works on medicine were studied through the early modern period. Faustus welcomes his change of authorities with "where the philosopher ends, the physician begins."

6. Justinian, Emperor of Byzantium (483–565 C.E.), codified all of Roman law; his *Institutes* provided the basis for civil law in England as well as on the continent. Faustus cites a principle of estate law: "if one and the same thing is bequeathed to two people, one of them should have the thing itself, and the other the value of it"; and "the father may not disinherit the son."

7. Jerome (347–420 C.E.), a theologian who translated the Greek Bible and some of the Hebrew Bible into Latin, also wrote on Christian doctrine.

8. Romans 6.23.

9. 1 John 1.8.

Lines, circles, scenes, letters and characters:
Ay, these are those that Faustus most desires.
Oh, what a world of profit and delight,
Of power, of honor, of omnipotence,
Is promised to the studious artisan!
All things that move between the quiet poles
Shall be at my command. Emperors and kings
Are but obeyed in their several provinces.
Nor can they raise the wind or rend the clouds.
But his dominion that exceeds in this
Stretcheth as far as doth the mind of man:
A sound magician is a demi-god.
Here, tire° my brains to get° a deity. *use / engender*
[*Enter Wagner.*]
Wagner, commend me to my dearest friends,
The German Valdes and Cornelius.
Request them earnestly to visit me.

WAGNER: I will, sir.

[*Exit.*]

FAUSTUS: Their conference will be a greater help to me
Than all my labors, plod I ne'er so fast.
[*Enter the Good and Evil Angels.*]

GOOD ANGEL: Oh Faustus, lay that damned book aside,
And gaze not on it lest it tempt thy soul
And heap God's heavy wrath upon thy head.
Read, read the scriptures: that is blasphemy.

EVIL ANGEL: Go forward, Faustus, in that famous art
Wherein all nature's treasure is contained.
Be thou on earth as Jove[1] is in the sky,
Lord and commander of these elements.

[*Exeunt Angels.*]

FAUSTUS: How am I glutted with conceit° of this! *idea*
Shall I make spirits fetch me what I please,
Resolve me of all ambiguities,
Perform what desperate enterprise I will?
I'll have them fly to India for gold,
Ransack the ocean for orient pearl,
And search all corners of the new-found world
For pleasant fruits and princely delicates.
I'll have them read me strange philosophy,
And tell the secrets of all foreign kings.
I'll have them wall all Germany with brass,
And make swift Rhine circle fair Wittenberg.
I'll have them fill the public schools° with silk, *college lecture halls*
Wherewith the students shall be bravely clad.
I'll levy soldiers with the coin they bring,
And chase the Prince of Parma from our land,

1. Roman god of the heavens and king of the gods.

And reign sole king of all the provinces.
Yea, stranger engines for the brunt of war
Than was the fiery keel[2] at Antwerp's bridge
I'll make my servile spirits to invent.
Come, German Valdes and Cornelius,
And make me blest with your sage conference.
[*Enter Valdes and Cornelius*.]
Valdes, sweet Valdes and Cornelius!
Know that your words have won me at the last
To practice magic and concealed arts.
Yet not your words only but mine own fantasy
That will receive no object° for my head, *idea*
But ruminates on necromantic skill.
Philosophy is odious and obscure.
Both law and physic are for petty wits.
Divinity is basest of the three,
Unpleasant, harsh, contemptible and vile.
'Tis magic, magic that hath ravished me.
Then, gentle friends, aid me in this attempt,
And I, that have with subtle syllogisms
Gravelled the pastors of the German Church
And made the flowering pride of Wittenberg
Swarm to my problems as the infernal spirits
On sweet Musaeus[3] when he came to hell,
Will be as cunning as Agrippa was,
Whose shadow made all Europe honor him.
VALDES: Faustus, these books, thy wit and our experience
Shall make all nations to canonize us,
As Indian moors obey their Spanish lords.
So shall the spirits of every element
Be always serviceable to us three.
Like lions shall they guard us when we please;
Like Almain rutters° with their horsemen's staves; *German knights*
Or Lapland giants trotting by our sides.
Sometimes like women or unwedded maids,
Shadowing more beauty in their airy brows
Than has the white breasts of the queen of love.
From Venice shall they drag huge argosies,° *merchant ships*
And from America the golden fleece[4]
That yearly stuffs old Philip's treasury
If learned Faustus will be resolute.
FAUSTUS: Valdes, as resolute am I in this
As thou to live, therefore object° it not. *reject*

2. In 1585 a fire ship destroyed the Duke of Parma's bridge across the river Scheldt in the city of Antwerp.
3. Faustus wants to model himself on Musaeus, a legendary poet, said to have been a student of Orpheus, and Cornelius Agrippa of Nettesheim (1486–1535), a philosopher known for his works on skepticism and the occult.
4. The "golden fleece" refers to the treasure (the gold wool of a divine ram) sought and won by the legendary hero, Jason, and his companions, known as the Argonauts (from the name of their ship, the Argo). Faustus alludes to this treasure when he refers to the gold the King of Castile, Philip II, was taking from lands in the New World.

CORNELIUS: The miracles that magic will perform
Will make thee vow to study nothing else.
He that is grounded in Astrology,
Enriched with tongues,° well seen° in minerals, *languages / educated*
Hath all the principles magic doth require.
Then doubt not, Faustus, but to be renowned,
And more frequented° for this mystery *sought after*
Than heretofore the Delphian oracle.[5]
The spirits tell me they can dry the sea,
And fetch the treasure of all foreign wracks,° *wrecks*
Yea, all the wealth that our forefathers hid
Within the massy° entrails of the earth. *massive*
Then tell me, Faustus, what shall we three want?
FAUSTUS: Nothing, Cornelius! Oh, this cheers my soul.
Come, show me some demonstrations magical,
That I may conjure in some bushy grove,
And have these joys in full possession.
VALDES: Then haste thee to some solitary grove,
And bear wise Bacon's and Albanus'[6] works,
The Hebrew Psalter and New Testament;
And whatsoever else is requisite
We will inform thee e're our conference cease.
CORNELIUS: Valdes, first let him know the words of art,
And then, all other ceremonies learned,
Faustus may try his cunning by himself.
VALDES: First I'll instruct thee in the rudiments,
And then wilt thou be perfecter than I.
FAUSTUS: Then come and dine with me, and after meat
We'll canvass every quiddity° thereof, *question*
For ere I sleep, I'll try what I can do.
This night I'll conjure, though I die therefore. [*Exeunt.*]

Scene 2

[*Enter two Scholars.*]

FIRST SCHOLAR: I wonder what's become of Faustus, that was wont to make our schools ring with *sic probo*.[7]

[*Enter Wagner.*]

SECOND SCHOLAR: That shall we presently know. Here comes his boy.

FIRST SCHOLAR: How now, sirrah, where's thy master?

WAGNER: God in heaven knows.

SECOND SCHOLAR: Why, dost not thou know then?

WAGNER: Yes, I know, but that follows not.

5. A shrine of Apollo, the god of the sun, music, and medicine, in his temple at Delphi, where his priestess, called the Pythia, spoke incoherent phrases that a priest later interpreted as prophecies.

6. Roger Bacon (1214–1294) was an English Franciscan monk and a lecturer at Oxford University who was interested in natural science, particularly alchemy. Albanus is perhaps Pietro D'Abano (1250–1360), who was supposed to be a sorcerer and was burned in effigy by the Inquisition after his death.

7. "Thus I prove."

FIRST SCHOLAR: Go to, sirrah. Leave your jesting and tell us where he is.

WAGNER: That follows not by force of argument, which you, being licentiates,[8] should stand upon. Therefore, acknowledge your error and be attentive.

SECOND SCHOLAR: Then you will not tell us?

WAGNER: You are deceived, for I will tell you. Yet if you were not dunces, you would never ask me such a question. For is he not *Corpus naturale?*[9] And is not that *mobile?* Then wherefore should you ask me such a question? But that I am by nature phlegmatic, slow to wrath and prone to lechery (to love, I would say), it were not for you to come within forty foot of the place of execution, although I do not doubt but to see you both hanged the next sessions. Thus, having triumphed over you, I will set my countenance like a precision,[1] and begin to speak thus: "Truly, my dear brethren, my master is within at dinner with Valdes and Cornelius, as this wine, if it could speak would inform your worships. And so the Lord bless you, preserve you and keep you, my dear brethren."

[*Exit.*]

FIRST SCHOLAR: Oh Faustus, then I fear that which I have long suspected:
That thou art fallen into that damned art
For which they two are infamous through the world.

SECOND SCHOLAR: Were he a stranger, not allied to me,
The danger of his soul would make me mourn.
But come, let us go, and inform the Rector.
It may be his grave counsel may reclaim him.

FIRST SCHOLAR: I fear me nothing will reclaim him now.

SECOND SCHOLAR: Yet let us see what we can do. [*Exeunt.*]

Scene 3

[*Thunder. Enter Lucifer and Four Devils. Faustus to them with this speech.*]

FAUSTUS: Now that the gloomy shadow of the night,
Longing to view Orion's drizzling look,
Leaps from th'Antarctic world unto the sky,
And dims the welkin° with her pitchy breath, *heaven*
Faustus, begin thine incantations
And try if devils will obey thy hest,° *command*
Seeing thou hast prayed and sacrificed to them.
Within this circle is Jehovah's name
Forward and backward anagrammatized:
The abbreviated names of holy saints,
Figures of every adjunct to the heavens,
And characters of signs and evening stars,
By which the spirits are enforced to rise.
Then fear not, Faustus, to be resolute
And try the utmost magic can perform.[2]

8. Postgraduates.

9. A natural body.

1. Puritan.

2. Faustus styles himself an accomplished magician. He now repeats, in Latin, his command to Mephostophilis to appear in the guise of a friar: "May the gods of the underworld be kind to me; may the triple deity of Jehovah be gone; to the spirits of fire, air, and water, greetings. Prince of the east, Beelzebub, monarch of the fires below, and Demogorgon, we appeal to you so that Mephostophilis may appear and rise. Why do you delay? By Jehovah, hell and the hallowed water which I now sprinkle, and the sign of the cross, which I now make, and by our vows, let Mephostophilis himself now arise to serve us."

[*Thunder.*]
Sint mihi dei acherontis propitii, valeat numen triplex Jehovae, ignei areii, aquatani spiritus salvete: orientis princeps Belzebub, inferni ardentis monarcha et demigorgon, propitiamus vos, ut appareat, et surgat Mephostophilis (Dragon)[3] *quod tumeraris: per Jehovam, gehennam, et consecratam aquam quam nunc spargo; signumque crucis quod nunc facio; et per vota nostra ipse nunc surgat nobis dicatus Mephostophilis.*

[*Enter a Devil.*]

I charge thee to return and change thy shape.
Thou art too ugly to attend on me.
Go, and return an old Franciscan friar:
That holy shape becomes a devil best.

[*Exit Devil.*]

I see there's virtue in my heavenly words.
Who would not be proficient in this art?
How pliant is this Mephostophilis!
Full of obedience and humility,
Such is the force of magic and my spells.
Now, Faustus, thou art conjuror laureate:[4]
Thou canst command great Mephostophilis.
Quin redis Mephostophilis fratris imagine.

[*Enter Mephostophilis.*]

MEPHOSTOPHILIS: Now, Faustus, what wouldst thou have me do?

FAUSTUS: I charge thee wait upon me whilst I live,
To do whatever Faustus shall command,
Be it to make the moon drop from her sphere,
Or the ocean to overwhelm the world.

MEPHOSTOPHILIS: I am a servant to great Lucifer,
And may not follow thee without his leave.
No more than he commands must we perform.

FAUSTUS: Did not he charge thee to appear to me?

MEPHOSTOPHILIS: No, I came now hither of mine own accord.

FAUSTUS: Did not my conjuring speeches raise thee? Speak.

MEPHOSTOPHILIS: That was the cause, but yet *per accidens*;° *by accident*
For when we hear one rack the name of God,
Abjure the scriptures and his saviour Christ,
We fly in hope to get his glorious soul.
Nor will we come unless he use such means
Whereby he is in danger to be damned.
Therefore the shortest cut for conjuring
Is stoutly to abjure all godliness
And pray devoutly to the prince of hell.

FAUSTUS: So Faustus hath already done, and holds this principle:
There is no chief but only Belzebub,
To whom Faustus doth dedicate himself.

3. This appears to be a stage direction that was inserted into the playtext; it probably indicates that at this point the figure of a dragon should come on stage.

4. Faustus, stating he is a "conjurer laureate" or honored magician, asks again, in Latin: "Why do you not return, Mephostophilis, in the guise of a friar?"

This word "damnation" terrifies not me,
For I confound hell in elysium.° *heaven*
My ghost be with the old philosophers.
But leaving these vain trifles of men's souls,
Tell me, what is that Lucifer, thy lord?

MEPHOSTOPHILIS: Arch-regent and commander of all spirits.

FAUSTUS: Was not that Lucifer an angel once?

MEPHOSTOPHILIS: Yes, Faustus, and most dearly loved of God.

FAUSTUS: How comes it then that he is prince of devils?

MEPHOSTOPHILIS: Oh, by aspiring pride and insolence,
For which God threw him from the face of heaven.

FAUSTUS: And what are you that live with Lucifer?

MEPHOSTOPHILIS: Unhappy spirits that fell with Lucifer,
Conspired against our God with Lucifer,
And are for ever damned with Lucifer.

FAUSTUS: Where are you damned?

MEPHOSTOPHILIS: In hell.

FAUSTUS: How comes it then that thou art out of hell?

MEPHOSTOPHILIS: Why, this is hell, nor am I out of it.
Think'st thou that I that saw the face of God
And tasted the eternal joys of heaven,
Am not tormented with ten thousand hells
In being deprived of everlasting bliss?
Oh, Faustus, leave these frivolous demands,
Which strike a terror to my fainting soul.

FAUSTUS: What, is great Mephostophilis so passionate
For being deprived of the joys of heaven?
Learn thou of Faustus manly fortitude,
And scorn those joys thou never shalt possess.
Go, bear these tidings to great Lucifer,
Seeing Faustus hath incurred eternal death
By desperate thoughts against Jove's deity.
Say he surrenders up to him his soul,
So he will spare him four and twenty years,
Letting him live in all voluptuousness,
Having thee ever to attend on me,
To give me whatsoever I shall ask,
To tell me whatsoever I demand,
To slay mine enemies and to aid my friends
And always be obedient to my will.
Go, and return to mighty Lucifer,
And meet me in my study at midnight,
And then resolve me of thy master's mind.

MEPHOSTOPHILIS: I will, Faustus. [*Exit*.]

FAUSTUS: Had I as many souls as there be stars,
I'd give them all for Mephostophilis.
By him I'll be great emperor of the world,
And make a bridge through the air
To pass the ocean. With a band of men

I'll join the hills that bind the Affrick shore,
And make that country continent to Spain,
And both contributory to my crown.
The Emperor shall not live but by my leave,
Nor any potentate of Germany.
Now that I have obtained what I desired,
I'll live in speculation of this art
Till Mephostophilis return again. *[Exit.]*

Scene 4

[Enter Wagner and the Clown.]

WAGNER: Come hither, sirrah boy.

CLOWN: Boy? Oh, disgrace to my person! Zounds! "Boy" in your face! You have seen many boys with beards, I am sure.

WAGNER: Sirrah, hast thou no comings in?

CLOWN: Yes, and goings out too, you may see, sir.

WAGNER: Alas, poor slave. See how poverty jests in his nakedness. I know the villain's out of service and so hungry that I know he would give his soul to the devil for a shoulder of mutton though it were blood-raw.

CLOWN: Not so neither. I had need to have it well roasted, and good sauce to it, if I pay so dear, I can tell you.

WAGNER: Sirrah, wilt thou be my man and wait on me? And I will make thee go like *Qui mihi discipulus*.[5]

CLOWN: What, in verse?

WAGNER: No, slave, in beaten silk and stavesacre.[6]

CLOWN: Stavesacre? That's good to kill vermin. Then belike, if I serve you I shall be lousy.

WAGNER: Why, so thou shalt be whether thou dost it or no. For, sirrah, if thou dost not presently bind thyself to me for seven years, I'll turn all the lice about thee into familiars,[7] and make them tear thee in pieces.

CLOWN: Nay, sir, you may save yourself a labor, for they are as familiar with me as if they paid for their meat and drink, I can tell you.

WAGNER: Well, sirrah, leave your jesting and take these guilders.[8]

CLOWN: Yes, marry, sir, and I thank you too.

WAGNER: So, now thou art to be at an hour's warning, whensoever and whereso ever the devil shall fetch thee.

CLOWN: Here, take your guilders.

WAGNER: Truly, I'll none of them.

CLOWN: Truly but you shall.

WAGNER: Bear witness I gave them him.

CLOWN: Bear witness I give them you again.

WAGNER: Not I. Thou art pressed. Prepare thyself, for I will presently raise up two devils, to carry thee away: Banio, Belcher!

CLOWN: Belcher? And Belcher come here, I'll belch him! I am not afraid of a devil.

[Enter Two Devils and the Clown runs up and down crying.]

5. One who is my disciple.
6. A poison.
7. Spirits.
8. Coins.

WAGNER: How now, sir, will you serve me now?
CLOWN: Ay, good Wagner. Take away the devil then.
WAGNER: Baliol and Belcher, spirits, away!
[*Exeunt Devils*.]

CLOWN: What, are they gone? A vengeance on them! They have vile long nails. There was a he-devil and a she-devil. I'll tell you how you shall know them: all he-devils has horns, and all she-devils has clifts[9] and cloven feet.

WAGNER: Well, sirrah, follow me.

CLOWN: But, do you hear, if I should serve you, would you teach me to raise up Banio's and Belcheo's?

WAGNER: I will teach thee to turn thyself to anything, to a dog, or a cat, or a mouse, or a rat, or anything.

CLOWN: How? A Christian fellow to a dog or a cat, a mouse or a rat? No, no, sir, if you turn me into anything, let it be in the likeness of a little pretty frisking flea, that I may be here and there and everywhere. Oh, I'll tickle the pretty wenches' plackets![1] I'll be amongst them, i'faith.

WAGNER: Well, sirrah, come.

CLOWN: But do you hear, Wagner?

WAGNER: How? Baliol and Belcher!

CLOWN: Oh Lord, I pray, sir, let Banio and Belcher go sleep.

WAGNER: Villain, call me Master Wagner, and see that you walk attentively and let your right eye be always diametrically fixed upon my left heel, that thou mayest *Quasi vestigias nostras insistere*.[2] [*Exit*.]

CLOWN: God forgive me, he speaks Dutch fustian![3] Well, I'll follow him. I'll serve him, that's flat. [*Exit*.]

Scene 5

[*Enter Faustus in his study*.]

FAUSTUS: Now, Faustus, must thou needs be damned?
And canst thou not be saved?
What boots it then to think on God or heaven?
Away with such vain fancies and despair,
Despair in God and trust in Belzebub.° *the Devil*
Now go not backward. No, Faustus, be resolute.
Why waverest thou? Oh, something soundeth in mine ears
Abjure this magic, turn to God again.
Ay, and Faustus will turn to God again.
To God? He loves thee not.
The God thou servest is thine own appetite,
Wherein is fixed the love of Belzebub.
To him I'll build an altar and a church,
And offer lukewarm blood of new-born babes.

[*Enter the Good and Evil Angels*.]

GOOD ANGEL: Sweet Faustus, leave that execrable art.
FAUSTUS: Contrition, prayer, repentance, what of these?

9. Clefts.
1. Petticoats.
2. Wagner mocks the Clown by telling him to walk "as if to tread in our footsteps," knowing that the clown's magic will never be as powerful as his own.
3. Nonsense.

GOOD ANGEL: Oh, they are means to bring thee unto heaven.
EVIL ANGEL: Rather illusions, fruits of lunacy,
That make men foolish that do trust them most.
GOOD ANGEL: Sweet Faustus, think of heaven and heavenly things.
EVIL ANGEL: No, Faustus, think of honor and of wealth.
[*Exeunt Angels.*]
FAUSTUS: Of wealth!
Why, the signory of Emden[4] shall be mine!
When Mephostophilis shall stand by me,
What God can hurt thee, Faustus? Thou art safe.
Cast no more doubts. Come, Mephostophilis,
And bring glad tidings from great Lucifer.
Is't not midnight? Come Mephostophilis!
Veni, veni,° *Mephostophile!* — *come, come*
[*Enter Mephostophilis.*]
Now tell me, what saith Lucifer, thy lord?
MEPHOSTOPHILIS: That I shall wait on Faustus whilst he lives,
So he will buy my service with his soul.
FAUSTUS: Already Faustus hath hazarded that for thee.
MEPHOSTOPHILIS: But now thou must bequeath it solemnly,
And write a deed of gift with thine own blood,
For that security craves great Lucifer.
If thou deny it, I will back to hell.
FAUSTUS: Stay, Mephostophilis, and tell me
What good will my soul do thy lord?
MEPHOSTOPHILIS: Enlarge his kingdom.
FAUSTUS: Is that the reason why he tempts us thus?
MEPHOSTOPHILIS: *Solamen miseris, socios habuisse doloris.*[5]
FAUSTUS: Why, have you any pain, that torture others?
MEPHOSTOPHILIS: As great as have the human souls of men.
But tell me, Faustus, shall I have thy soul?
And I will be thy slave and wait on thee,
And give thee more than thou hast wit to ask.
FAUSTUS: Ay, Mephostophilis, I'll give it thee.
MEPHOSTOPHILIS: Then, Faustus, stab thy arm courageously,
And bind thy soul, that at some certain day
Great Lucifer may claim it as his own,
And then be thou as great as Lucifer.
FAUSTUS: Lo, Mephostophilis, for love of thee
I cut mine arm, and with my proper blood
Assure my soul to be great Lucifer's,
Chief lord and regent of perpetual night.
View here the blood that trickles from mine arm,
And let it be propitious for my wish.
MEPHOSTOPHILIS: But, Faustus, thou must write it in manner of a deed of gift.

4. At this point in his career, Faustus aspires to the governorship of Emden, an important trading town in Germany, a pathetic exchange for his immortal soul.

5. Mephostophilis states that misery loves company in hell: "It is a comfort in wretchedness to have companions in woe."

FAUSTUS: Ay, so I will. But, Mephostophilis,
My blood congeals and I can write no more!
MEPHOSTOPHILIS: I'll fetch thee fire to dissolve it straight. [*Exit.*]
FAUSTUS: What might the staying of my blood portend?
Is it unwilling I should write this bill?
Why streams it not that I may write afresh?
"Faustus gives to thee his soul": ah, there it stayed!
Why shouldst thou not? Is not thy soul thine own?
Then write again: "Faustus gives to thee his soul."
[*Enter Mephostophilis with a chafer of coals.*]
MEPHOSTOPHILIS: Here's fire. Come, Faustus, set it on.
FAUSTUS: So, now my blood begins to clear again.
Now will I make an end immediately.
MEPHOSTOPHILIS: Oh what will not I do to obtain his soul!
FAUSTUS: *Consummatum est:*[6] this bill is ended,
And Faustus hath bequeathed his soul to Lucifer.
But what is this inscription on mine arm?
Homo fuge!° Whither should I flee? *Flee, O man*
If unto heaven, he'll throw me down to hell.
My senses are deceived: here's nothing writ!
Oh, yes, I see it plain. Even here is writ
Homo fuge. Yet shall not Faustus fly.
MEPHOSTOPHILIS: I'll fetch him somewhat to delight his mind. [*Exit.*]
[*Enter Devils, giving crowns and rich apparel to Faustus; they dance and then depart. Enter Mephostophilis.*]
FAUSTUS: What means this show? Speak, Mephostophilis.
MEPHOSTOPHILIS: Nothing, Faustus, but to delight thy mind,
And let thee see what magic can perform.
FAUSTUS: But may I raise such spirits when I please?
MEPHOSTOPHILIS: Ay, Faustus, and do greater things than these.
FAUSTUS: Then there's enough for a thousand souls.
Here, Mephostophilis, receive this scroll,
A deed of gift, of body and of soul:
But yet conditionally, that thou perform
All covenants and articles between us both.
MEPHOSTOPHILIS: Faustus, I swear by hell and Lucifer
To effect all promises between us both.
FAUSTUS: Then hear me read it, Mephostophilis.
On these conditions following:
First, that Faustus may be a spirit in form and substance.
Secondly, that Mephostophilis shall be his servant, and be by him commanded.
Thirdly, that Mephostophilis shall do for him, and bring him whatsoever.
Fourthly, that he shall be in his chamber or house invisible.
Lastly, that he shall appear to the said John Faustus at all times, in what shape and form soever he please.

6. As reported in the Vulgate Bible, Faustus speaks the last words of Jesus on the cross: "It is finished" (John 19.30), and then realizes he must try to avoid the consequences: "Flee, O man."

I, John Faustus of Wittenberg Doctor, by these presents, do give both body and soul to Lucifer, Prince of the East, and his minister Mephostophilis, and furthermore grant unto them that four and twenty years being expired, and these articles above written being inviolate, full power to fetch or carry the said John Faustus, body and soul, flesh, blood or goods, into their habitation wheresoever.

By me, John Faustus.

MEPHOSTOPHILIS: Speak, Faustus, do you deliver this as your deed?
FAUSTUS: Ay, take it, and the devil give thee good of it.
MEPHOSTOPHILIS: So now, Faustus, ask me what thou wilt.
FAUSTUS: First I will question with thee about hell.
Tell me, where is the place that men call hell?
MEPHOSTOPHILIS: Under the heavens.
FAUSTUS: Ay, so are all things else; but whereabouts?
MEPHOSTOPHILIS: Within the bowels of these elements,
Where we are tortured and remain for ever.
Hell hath no limits, nor is circumscribed
In one self place. But where we are is hell,
And where hell is there must we ever be.
And to be short, when all the world dissolves
And every creature shall be purified,
All places shall be hell that is not heaven.
FAUSTUS: Come, I think hell's a fable.
MEPHOSTOPHILIS: Ay, think so still, till experience change thy mind.
FAUSTUS: Why, dost thou think that Faustus shall be damned?
MEPHOSTOPHILIS: Ay, of necessity, for here's the scroll
In which thou hast given thy soul to Lucifer.
FAUSTUS: Ay, and body too, but what of that?
Think'st thou that Faustus is so fond to imagine
That after this life there is any pain?
Tush, these are trifles and old wives' tales.
MEPHOSTOPHILIS: But Faustus, I am an instance to prove the contrary,
For I tell thee I am damned, and now in hell.
FAUSTUS: How? Now in hell? Nay, and this be hell, I'll willingly be damned here. What! Sleeping, eating, walking and disputing? But leaving this, let me have a wife, the fairest maid in Germany, for I am wanton and lascivious, and can not live without a wife.
MEPHOSTOPHILIS: How, a wife? I prithee, Faustus, talk not of a wife.
FAUSTUS: Nay, sweet Mephostophilis, fetch me one, for I will have one.
MEPHOSTOPHILIS: Well, thou wilt have one. Sit there till I come: I'll fetch thee a wife in the devil's name.

[*Enter a Devil dressed like a woman, with fireworks.*]

FAUSTUS: What sight is this?
MEPHOSTOPHILIS: Tell, Faustus, how dost thou like thy wife?
FAUSTUS: A plague on her for a hot whore.
MEPHOSTOPHILIS: Tut, Faustus, marriage is but a ceremonial toy.
If thou lovest me, think no more of it.
I'll cull thee out the fairest courtesans
And bring them every morning to thy bed.

She whom thine eye shall like, thy heart shall have,
Be she as chaste as was Penelope,[7]
As wise as Saba, or as beautiful
As was bright Lucifer before his fall.
Here, take this book, and peruse it well.
The iterating° of these lines brings gold, *repetition*
The framing of this circle on the ground
Brings thunder, whirlwinds, storm and lightning.
Pronounce this thrice devoutly to thyself
And men in harness shall appear to thee,
Ready to execute what thou commandest.

FAUSTUS: Thanks, Mephostophilis. Yet fain would I have a book wherein I might behold all spells and incantations, that I might raise up spirits when I please.

MEPHOSTOPHILIS: Here they are in this book. [*There turn to them.*]

FAUSTUS: Now would I have a book where I might see all characters and planets of the heavens, that I might know their motions and dispositions.

MEPHOSTOPHILIS: Here they are too. [*Turn to them.*]

FAUSTUS: Nay, let me have one book more, and then I have done, wherein I might see all plants, herbs and trees that grow upon the earth.

MEPHOSTOPHILIS: Here they be.

FAUSTUS: Oh thou art deceived.

MEPHOSTOPHILIS: Tut, I warrant thee. [*Turn to them.*]

ACT 2

Scene 1

[*Enter Faustus in his study, and Mephostophilis.*]

FAUSTUS: When I behold the heavens then I repent,
And curse thee, wicked Mephostophilis,
Because thou hast deprived me of those joys.

MEPHOSTOPHILIS: 'Twas thine own seeking, Faustus, thank thyself.
But thinkst thou heaven is such a glorious thing?
I tell thee, Faustus, it is not half so fair
As thou or any man that breathes on earth.

FAUSTUS: How prov'st thou that?

MEPHOSTOPHILIS: 'Twas made for man; then he's more excellent.

FAUSTUS: If heaven was made for man, 'twas made for me.
I will renounce this magic and repent.

[*Enter the Good and Evil Angels.*]

GOOD ANGEL: Faustus, repent. Yet God will pity thee.

EVIL ANGEL: Thou art a spirit. God cannot pity thee.

FAUSTUS: Who buzzeth in mine ears I am a spirit?
Be I a devil, yet God may pity me.
Yea, God will pity me if I repent.

EVIL ANGEL: Ay, but Faustus never shall repent. [*Exeunt.*]

FAUSTUS: My heart's so hardened I cannot repent.

7. Mephostophilis compares the ideal woman to Penelope, the wife of Odysseus, who waited 20 years for him to return from the Trojan wars, and to Saba, the wise Queen of Sheba, who caught King Solomon, known himself for his wisdom (1 Kings).

Scarce can I name salvation, faith or heaven,
But fearful echoes thunder in mine ears
"Faustus, thou art damned." Then swords and knives,
Poison, guns, halters and envenomed steel
Are laid before me to dispatch myself.
And long ere this I should have done the deed,
Had not sweet pleasure conquered deep despair.
Have not I made blind Homer sing to me
Of Alexander's love and Oenon's death?[1]
And hath not he that built the walls of Thebes
With ravishing sound of his melodious harp
Made music with my Mephostophilis?[2]
Why should I die then, or basely despair?
I am resolved, Faustus shall not repent.
Come, Mephostophilis, let us dispute again,
And reason of divine astrology.
Speak, are there many spheres above the moon?
Are all celestial bodies but one globe,
As is the substance of this centric earth?[3]

MEPHOSTOPHILIS: As are the elements, such are the heavens,
Even from the moon unto the empyrial orb,
Mutually folded in each other's spheres,
And jointly move upon one axle-tree,
Whose termine° is termed the world's wide pole. *end point*
Nor are the names of Saturn, Mars or Jupiter
Feigned, but are erring stars.

FAUSTUS: But have they all one motion, both *situet tempore?*[4]

MEPHOSTOPHILIS: All move from east to west in four and twenty hours upon the poles of the world, but differ in their motions upon the poles of the zodiac.

FAUSTUS: Tush, these slender trifles Wagner can decide. Hath Mephostophilis no greater skill? Who knows not the double motion of the planets? That the first is finished in a natural day? The second thus, as Saturn in thirty years, Jupiter in twelve, Mars in four, the sun, Venus and Mercury in twenty-eight days. Tush, these are freshmen's suppositions. But tell me, hath every sphere a dominion or *intelligentia?*[5]

MEPHOSTOPHILIS: Ay.

FAUSTUS: How many heavens or spheres are there?

MEPHOSTOPHILIS: Nine, the seven planets, the firmament, and the empyrial heaven.

FAUSTUS: But is there not *coelum igneum et cristallinum?*

MEPHOSTOPHILIS: No, Faustus, they be but fables.[6]

1. Faustus claims he has made the poet Homer sing to him of the love of Alexander the Great (356–323 B.C.E.), who was married to Statira, daughter of the Emperor Darius of Persia; and of Oenone, a nymph of Mount Ida, who died from grief when her lover, Paris of Troy, deserted her for Helen, the wife of King Menalaus of Sparta.
2. Faustus further claims that the legendary Amphion, whose music built the walls of Thebes, also made music with Mephostophilis, now Faustus's servant.
3. Faustus alludes to the Ptolemaic universe in which the earth, at the center, is surrounded by concentric spheres, beginning with the moon. Beyond the spheres of the stars that were thought to move (the constellations) were the spheres of the fixed stars.
4. In place and in time.
5. Guiding spirit.
6. Faustus asks whether there is a "fiery and crystalline heaven" beyond the "empyrial heaven" Mephostophilis has mentioned, and he is told it is a fiction.

FAUSTUS: Resolve me then in this one question. Why are not conjunctions, oppositions, aspects, eclipses, all at one time, but in some years we have more, in some less?

MEPHOSTOPHILIS: *Per inaequalem motum, respectu totius*.[7]

FAUSTUS: Well, I am answered. Now tell me, who made the world?

MEPHOSTOPHILIS: I will not.

FAUSTUS: Sweet Mephostophilis, tell me.

MEPHOSTOPHILIS: Move me not, Faustus.

FAUSTUS: Villain, have not I bound thee to tell me anything?

MEPHOSTOPHILIS: Ay, that is not against our kingdom, but this is.
Think on hell, Faustus, for thou art damned.

FAUSTUS: Think, Faustus, upon God, that made the world.

MEPHOSTOPHILIS: Remember this— [*Exit.*]

FAUSTUS: Ay, go, accursed spirit to ugly hell.
'Tis thou hast damned distressed Faustus' soul.
Is't not too late?

[*Enter the Good and Evil Angels.*]

EVIL ANGEL: Too late.

GOOD ANGEL: Never too late, if Faustus will repent.

EVIL ANGEL: If thou repent devils will tear thee in pieces.

GOOD ANGEL: Repent, and they shall never raze° thy skin. *shave*

[*Exeunt Angels.*]

FAUSTUS: Ah, Christ my savior,
Seek to save distressed Faustus' soul.

[*Enter Lucifer, Belzebub and Mephostophilis.*]

LUCIFER: Christ cannot save thy soul, for he is just.
There's none but I have interest in the same.

FAUSTUS: Oh what art thou that look'st so terribly?

LUCIFER: I am Lucifer, and this is my companion prince in hell.

FAUSTUS: Oh Faustus, they are come to fetch away thy soul.

BELZEBUB: We are come to tell thee thou dost injure us.

LUCIFER: Thou call'st on Christ contrary to thy promise.

BELZEBUB: Thou shouldst not think on God.

LUCIFER: Think on the devil.

BELZEBUB: And his dam too.

FAUSTUS: Nor will I henceforth. Pardon me in this,
And Faustus vows never to look to heaven,
Never to name God or to pray to him,
To burn his scriptures, slay his ministers,
And make my spirits pull his churches down.

LUCIFER: Do so, and we will highly gratify thee.

BELZEBUB: Faustus, we are come from hell in person to show thee some pastime. Sit down and thou shalt behold the seven deadly sins appear to thee in their own proper shapes and likeness.

FAUSTUS: That sight will be as pleasant to me as Paradise was to Adam the first day of his creation.

7. Faustus asks why planetary and astral events do not occur uniformly, and Mephostophilis answers that they do "with respect to the whole" but each "by unequal motion."

LUCIFER: Talk not of Paradise or Creation, but mark this show. Talk of the devil and nothing else. Go, Mephostophilis, fetch them in.

[*Enter the Seven Deadly Sins*.]

BELZEBUB: Now, Faustus, question them of their names and dispositions.

FAUSTUS: That shall I soon. What art thou, the first?

PRIDE: I am Pride. I disdain to have any parents. I am like to Ovid's flea.[8] I can creep into every corner of a wench. Sometimes like a periwig I sit upon her brow. Next, like a necklace I hang about her neck. Then, like a fan of feathers, I kiss her. And then turning myself to a wrought smock do what I list. But fie, what a smell is here! I'll not speak a word for a king's ransome, unless the ground be perfumed and covered with cloth of Arras.[9]

FAUSTUS: Thou art a proud knave indeed. What art thou, the second?

COVETOUSNESS: I am Covetousness. Begotten of an old churl in a leather bag. And might I now obtain my wish, this house, you and all, should turn to gold, that I might lock you safe into my chest. Oh, my sweet gold!

FAUSTUS: And what art thou, the third?

ENVY: I am Envy, begotten of a chimney-sweeper and an oyster-wife. I cannot read and therefore wish all books were burnt. I am lean with seeing others eat. Oh, that there would come a famine over all the world, that all might die, and I live alone, then thou should'st see how fat I'd be. But must thou sit and I stand? Come down, with a vengeance!

FAUSTUS: Out, envious wretch. But what art thou, the fourth?

WRATH: I am Wrath. I had neither father nor mother. I leapt out of a lion's mouth when I was scarce an hour old, and ever since have run up and down the world with this case of rapiers, wounding myself when I could get none to fight withal. I was born in hell, and look to it, for some of you shall be my father.

FAUSTUS: And what art thou, the fifth?

GLUTTONY: I am Gluttony. My parents are all dead, and the devil a penny they have left me, but a small pension and that buys me thirty meals a day and ten bevers:[1] a small trifle to suffice nature. I come of a royal pedigree; my father was a gammon of bacon and my mother was a hog's head of claret wine. My godfathers were these: Peter Pickle-herring and Martin Martlemas-beef. But my godmother, oh, she was an ancient gentlewoman, and well-beloved in every good town and city. Her name was Mistress Margery March-beer. Now, Faustus, thou hast heard all my progeny, wilt thou bid me to supper?

FAUSTUS: No, I'll see thee hanged. Thou wilt eat up all my victuals.

GLUTTONY: Then the devil choke thee.

FAUSTUS: Choke thyself, Glutton. What art thou, the sixth?

SLOTH: Hey ho, I am Sloth. I was begotten on a sunny bank where I have lain ever since, and you have done me great injury to bring me from thence. Let me be carried thither again by Gluttony and Lechery. I'll not speak another word for a king's ransom.

FAUSTUS: And what are you, Mistress Minx, the seventh and last?

LECHERY: Who, I sir? I am one that loves an inch of raw mutton better than an ell of fried stockfish,[2] and the first letter of my name begins with Lechery.

8. One of the poems of the Roman poet Ovid (43 B.C.E.–18 C.E.) describes the journey of a flea around a woman's body.

9. Flemish cloth for tapestries.

1. Snacks.

2. Lechery implies that she would prefer a short but energetic penis to a yard-long but dry one.

FAUSTUS: Away to hell! Away, on, piper!

[*Exeunt the Seven Deadly Sins.*]

LUCIFER: Now, Faustus, how dost thou like this?

FAUSTUS: Oh, this feeds my soul.

LUCIFER: Tut, Faustus, in hell is all manner of delight.

FAUSTUS: Oh, might I see hell and return again safe, how happy were I then!

LUCIFER: Faustus, thou shalt. At midnight I will send for thee. Meanwhile, peruse this book and view it throughly, and thou shalt turn thyself into what shape thou wilt.

FAUSTUS: Thanks, mighty Lucifer. This will I keep as chary as my life.

LUCIFER: Now, Faustus, farewell, and think on the devil.

FAUSTUS: Farewell, great Lucifer. Come, Mephostophilis.

[*Exeunt omnes, several ways.*]

Scene 2

[*Enter the Clown.*]

CLOWN: What, Dick, look to the horses there till I come again. I have gotten one of Doctor Faustus' conjuring books, and now we'll have such knavery as't passes.

[*Enter Dick.*]

DICK: What, Robin, you must come away and walk the horses.

ROBIN: I walk the horses? I scorn't, faith. I have other matters in hand. Let the horses walk themselves and they will. *A per se a, t.h.e. the: o per se o deny orgon, gorgon.*[3] Keep further from me, O thou illiterate and unlearned hostler.

DICK: 'Snails![4] What hast thou got there? A book? Why, thou canst not tell ne'er a word on't.

ROBIN: That thou shalt see presently. Keep out of the circle, I say, lest I send you into the ostry[5] with a vengeance.

DICK: That's like, faith. You had best leave your foolery, for, an my master come, he'll conjure you, faith!

ROBIN: My master conjure me? I'll tell thee what, an my master come here, I'll clap as fair a pair of horns[6] on's head as e'er thou sawest in thy life.

DICK: Thou need'st not do that, for my mistress hath done it.

ROBIN: Ay, there be of us here, that have waded as deep into matters as other men, if they were disposed to talk.

DICK: A plague take you! I thought you did not sneak up and down after her for nothing. But I prithee tell me, in good sadness, Robin, is that a conjuring book?

ROBIN: Do but speak what thou't have me to do, and I'll do't. If thou't dance naked, put off thy clothes and I'll conjure thee about presently. Or if thou't

3. Barely literate, Robin is trying to parse a Latin phrase, *atheo Demigorgon* ("godless Demigorgon").
4. Christ's nails.
5. Inn.
6. Sign of a cuckold.

go but to the tavern with me, I'll give thee white wine, red wine, claret wine, sack, muskadine, malmesey and whippincrust.[7] Hold, belly, hold; and we'll not pay one penny for it.

DICK: Oh brave! Prithee, let's to it presently, for I am as dry as a dog.

ROBIN: Come, then, let's away. [*Exeunt.*]

ACT 3

Scene 1

[*Enter the Chorus.*]

CHORUS: Learned Faustus,
To find the secrets of astronomy,
Graven in the book of Jove's high firmament,
Did mount him up to scale Olympus' top,
Where sitting in a chariot burning bright,
Drawn by the strength of yoked dragons' necks,
He views the clouds, the planets, and the stars,
The tropic, zones, and quarters of the sky,
From the bright circle of the horned moon,
Even to the height of *Primum Mobile*.[1]
And whirling round with this circumference,
Within the concave compass of the pole,
From east to west his dragons swiftly glide,
And in eight days did bring him home again.
Not long he stayed within his quiet house,
To rest his bones after his weary toil,
But new exploits do hale him out again,
And mounted then upon a dragon's back,
That with his wings did part the subtle air,
He now is gone to prove cosmography,
That measures coasts and kingdoms of the earth;
And as I guess will first arrive at Rome,
To see the Pope and manner of his court,
And take some part of holy Peter's feast,
The which this day is highly solemnized. [*Exit.*]

Scene 2

[*Enter Faustus and Mephostophilis.*]

FAUSTUS: Having now, my good Mephostophilis,
Passed with delight the stately town of Trier,
Environed round with airy mountain tops,
With walls of flint, and deep entrenched lakes,
Not to be won by any conquering prince,
From Paris next coasting the realm of France
We saw the river Main fall into Rhine,

7. Robin lists various kinds of wine; "whippencrust" is probably a corruption of "hippocras," a kind of sweet wine.

1. The outermost of the heavenly spheres. Faustus is pictured as viewing the heavens from Mount Olympus to the circle of the moon and beyond, to the *primum mobile*.

Whose banks are set with groves of fruitful vines;
Then up to Naples, rich Campania,
Whose buildings fair and gorgeous to the eye,
The streets straight forth and paved with finest brick,
Quarters the town in four equivolence.° *parts*
There saw we learned Maro's golden tomb,[2]
The way he cut an English mile in length,
Thorough a rock of stone in one night's space.
From thence to Venice, Padua and the rest,
In midst of which a sumptuous temple stands,
That threats the stars with her aspiring top,
Whose frame is paved with sundry colored stones,
And roofed aloft with curious work in gold.
Thus hitherto hath Faustus spent his time.
But tell me now, what resting place is this?
Hast thou, as erst I did command,
Conducted me within the walls of Rome?

MEPHOSTOPHILIS: I have, my Faustus, and for proof thereof,
This is the goodly palace of the Pope;
And cause we are no common guests,
I choose his privy chamber for our use.

FAUSTUS: I hope his Holiness will bid us welcome.

MEPHOSTOPHILIS: All's one, for we'll be bold with his venison.
But now, my Faustus, that thou may'st perceive
What Rome contains for to delight thine eyes,
Know that this city stands upon seven hills
That underprop the groundwork of the same.
Just through the midst runs flowing Tiber's stream,
With winding banks that cut it in two parts,
Over the which four stately bridges lean,
That make safe passage to each part of Rome.
Upon the bridge called Ponto Angelo
Erected is a castle passing strong,
Where thou shalt see such store of ordinance
As that the double cannons forged of brass
Do match the number of the days contained
Within the compass of one complete year.
Beside the gates and high pyramides,
That Julius Caesar brought from Africa.[3]

FAUSTUS: Now by the kingdoms of infernal rule,
Of Styx, or Acheron, and the fiery lake
Of ever-burning Phlegethon,° I swear *rivers in hell*
That I do long to see the monuments
And situation of bright splendent Rome.
Come, therefore, let's away.

2. Faustus' fiery chariot cut through rocks to go from Naples, where the Roman poet Publius Virgilius Maro, or Virgil, is buried, to Padua and Venice.

3. The Emperor Caligula brought an obelisk back from Heliopolis in Egypt, which stands before St. Peter's in Rome.

MEPHOSTOPHILIS: Now, stay, my Faustus. I know you'd see the Pope,
And take some part of holy Peter's feast,
The which in state and high solemnity
This day is held through Rome and Italy
In honor of the Pope's triumphant victory.

FAUSTUS: Sweet Mephostophilis, thou pleasest me.
Whilst I am here on earth let me be cloyed
With all things that delight the heart of man.
My four and twenty years of liberty
I'll spend in pleasure and in dalliance,
That Faustus' name, whilst this bright frame doth stand,
May be admired through the furthest land.

MEPHOSTOPHILIS: 'Tis well said, Faustus. Come then, stand by me,
And thou shalt see them come immediately.

FAUSTUS: Nay stay, my gentle Mephostophilis,
And grant me my request, and then I go.
Thou know'st within the compass of eight days
We viewed the face of heaven, of earth and hell.
So high our dragons soared into the air,
That looking down, the earth appeared to me
No bigger than my hand in quantity.
There did we view the kingdoms of the world,
And what might please mine eye, I there beheld.
Then in this show let me an actor be,
That this proud Pope may Faustus' cunning see.

MEPHOSTOPHILIS: Let it be so, my Faustus, but first stay
And view their triumphs° as they pass this way. *procession*
And then devise what best contents thy mind
By cunning in thine art to cross the Pope,
Or dash the pride of this solemnity,
To make his monks and abbots stand like apes,
And point like antics° at his triple crown, *clowns*
To beat the beads about the friars' pates,
Or clap huge horns upon the cardinals' heads,
Or any villainy thou canst devise,
And I'll perform it, Faustus. Hark, they come!
This day shall make thee be admired in Rome.

[*Enter the Cardinals and Bishops, some bearing crosiers, some the pillars, Monks and Friars, singing their procession. Then the Pope and Raymond, King of Hungary with Bruno*[4] *led in chains.*]

POPE: Cast down our footstool.

RAYMOND: Saxon Bruno, stoop,
Whilst on thy back his Holiness ascends
Saint Peter's chair and state pontifical.

BRUNO: Proud Lucifer, that state belongs to me:
But thus I fall to Peter, not to thee.

4. This character has no apparent historical counterpart or model.

POPE: To me and Peter shalt thou grovelling lie,
And crouch before the papal dignity.
Sounds trumpets then, for thus Saint Peter's heir
From Bruno's back ascends Saint Peter's chair.
[*A flourish while he ascends*.]
Thus, as the gods creep on with feet of wool
Long ere with iron hands they punish men,
So shall our sleeping vengeance now arise,
And smite with death thy hated enterprise.
Lord cardinals of France and Padua,
Go forthwith to our holy consistory,
And read amongst the statutes decretal,
What by the holy council held at Trent[5]
The sacred synod hath decreed for them
That doth assume the papal government,
Without election and a true consent.
Away, and bring us word with speed!
FIRST CARDINAL: We go, my lord.
[*Exeunt Cardinals*.]
POPE: Lord Raymond.
FAUSTUS: Go, haste thee, gentle Mephostophilis,
Follow the cardinals to the consistory,
And as they turn their superstitious books,
Strike them with sloth and drowsy idleness,
And make them sleep so sound that in their shapes
Thyself and I may parly° with this Pope, *speak*
This proud confronter of the Emperor,[6]
And in despite of all his holiness
Restore this Bruno to his liberty
And bear him to the states of Germany.
MEPHOSTOPHILIS: Faustus, I go.
FAUSTUS: Dispatch it soon,
The Pope shall curse that Faustus came to Rome.
[*Exeunt Faustus and Mephostophilis*.]
BRUNO: Pope Adrian,[7] let me have some right of law:
I was elected by the Emperor.
POPE: We will depose the Emperor for that deed,
And curse the people that submit to him.
Both he and thou shalt stand excommunicate,
And interdict from Church's privilege
And all society of holy men.
He grows too proud in his authority,
Lifting his lofty head above the clouds
And like a steeple overpeers the Church.
But we'll pull down his haughty insolence,

5. The council of Trent, called to meet the challenges posed by the Protestant Reformation, was held between 1545 and 1563.
6. The Holy Roman Emperor, Charles V, Emperor from 1519.
7. Possibly Marlowe means Hadrian VI (1522–1523), although he was Pope before the Council of Trent, after which the action of the play is supposed to have taken place.

And, as Pope Alexander, our progenitor,
Stood on the neck of German Frederick,[8]
Adding this golden sentence to our praise,
That Peter's heirs should tread on emperors
And walk upon the dreadful adder's back,
Treading the lion and the dragon down,
And fearless spurn the killing basilisk,[9]
So will we quell that haughty schismatic,
And by authority apostolical
Depose him from his regal government.

BRUNO: Pope Julius swore to princely Sigismond[1]
For him and the succeeding popes of Rome,
To hold the emperors their lawful lords.

POPE: Pope Julius did abuse the Church's rites,
And therefore none of his decrees can stand.
Is not all power on earth bestowed on us?
And therefore though we would we cannot err.
Behold this silver belt, whereto is fixed
Seven golden seals fast sealed with seven seals,
In token of our seven-fold power from heaven,
To bind or loose, lock fast, condemn or judge,
Resign or seal, or what so pleaseth us.
Then he and thou, and all the world, shall stoop,
Or be assured of our dreadful curse,
To light as heavy as the pains of hell.

[*Enter Faustus and Mephostophilis, like the cardinals.*]

MEPHOSTOPHILIS: Now tell me, Faustus, are we not fitted well?

FAUSTUS: Yes, Mephostophilis, and two such cardinals
Ne'er served a holy Pope as we shall do.
But whilst they sleep within the consistory,
Let us salute his reverend fatherhood.

RAYMOND: Behold, my lord, the cardinals are returned.

POPE: Welcome, grave fathers, answer presently
What have our holy council there decreed
Concerning Bruno and the Emperor,
In quittance of their late conspiracy
Against our state and papal dignity?

FAUSTUS: Most sacred patron of the Church of Rome,
By full consent of all the synod
Of priests and prelates, it is thus decreed:
That Bruno and the German Emperor
Be held as lollards[2] and bold schismatics
And proud disturbers of the Church's peace.
And if that Bruno by his own assent,
Without enforcement of the German peers,

8. Pope Alexander III (1159–1181) forced Emperor Frederick Barbarossa to acknowledge his authority.
9. A mythical creature whose glance was lethal.
1. It is unclear to whom Marlowe refers; there was no Pope Julius during the reign of the Emperor Sigismund (1368–1436).
2. Heretics; in England, followers of John Wycliffe (1328?–1384).

Did seek to wear the triple diadem
And by your death to climb Saint Peter's chair,
The statutes decretal have thus decreed:
He shall be straight condemned of heresy
And on a pile of faggots burnt to death.

POPE: It is enough. Here, take him to your charge,
And bear him straight to Ponto Angelo,
And in the strongest tower enclose him fast.
Tomorrow, sitting in our consistory
With all our college of grave cardinals,
We will determine of his life or death.
Here, take his triple crown along with you,
And leave it in the Church's treasury.
Make haste again, my good lord cardinals,
And take our blessing apostolical.

MEPHOSTOPHILIS: So, so, was never devil thus blessed before.

FAUSTUS: Away, sweet Mephostophilis, be gone:
The cardinals will be plagued for this anon.

[*Exeunt Faustus and Mephostophilis*.]

POPE: Go presently, and bring a banquet forth
That we may solemnize Saint Peter's feast,
And with Lord Raymond, King of Hungary,
Drink to our late and happy victory. [*Exeunt*.]

Scene 3

[A *sennet*[3] *while the banquet is brought in, and then enter Faustus and Mephostophilis in their own shapes*.]

MEPHOSTOPHILIS: Now, Faustus, come prepare thyself for mirth.
The sleepy cardinals are hard at hand
To censure Bruno that is posted° hence, *ridden*
And on a proud paced steed as swift as thought
Flies o'er the Alps to fruitful Germany,
There to salute the woeful Emperor.

FAUSTUS: The Pope will curse them for their sloth today,
That slept both Bruno and his crown away.
But now, that Faustus may delight his mind,
And by their folly make some merriment,
Sweet Mephostophilis, so charm me here,
That I may walk invisible to all,
And do what e'er I please unseen of any.

MEPHOSTOPHILIS: Faustus, thou shalt. Then kneel down presently:
Whilst on thy head I lay my hand,
And charm thee with this magic wand.
First wear this girdle, then appear
Invisible to all are here.
The planets seven, the gloomy air,
Hell and the Furies'[4] forked hair,

3. A trumpet call.

4. Greek divinities instigating revenge.

Pluto's[5] blue fire and Hecate's[6] tree,
With magic spells so compass thee,
That no eye may thy body see.
So, Faustus, now for all their holiness,
Do what thou wilt, thou shalt not be discerned.

FAUSTUS: Thanks, Mephostophilis. Now, friars, take heed
Lest Faustus make your shaven crowns to bleed.

MEPHOSTOPHILIS: Faustus, no more. See where the cardinals come.

[*Enter the Pope and all the Lords. Enter the Cardinals with a book.*]

POPE: Welcome, lord cardinals. Come, sit down.
Lord Raymond, take your seat. Friars, attend
And see that all things be in readiness
As best beseems this solemn festival.

FIRST CARDINAL: First, may it please your sacred Holiness,
To view the sentence of the reverend synod
Concerning Bruno and the Emperor?

POPE: What needs this question? Did I not tell you
Tomorrow we would sit i'the consistory
And there determine of his punishment?
You brought us word even now, it was decreed
That Bruno and the cursed Emperor
Were by the holy Council both condemned
For loathed lollards and base schismatics.
Then wherefore would you have me view that book?

FIRST CARDINAL: Your Grace mistakes. You gave us no such charge.

RAYMOND: Deny it not. We all are witnesses
That Bruno here was late delivered you,
With his rich triple crown to be reserved
And put into the Church's treasury.

BOTH CARDINAL: By holy Paul, we saw them not.

POPE: By Peter, you shall die
Unless you bring them forth immediately.
Hale° them to prison, lade their limbs with gyves!° *take / chains*
False prelates, for this hateful treachery,
Cursed be your souls to hellish misery.

FAUSTUS: So, they are safe. Now Faustus, to the feast.
The Pope had never such a frolic guest.

POPE: Lord Archbishop of Rheims, sit down with us.

BISHOP: I thank your Holiness.

FAUSTUS: Fall to, and the devil choke you an you spare.

POPE: Who's that spoke? Friars, look about.

FRIARS: Here's nobody, if it like your Holiness.

POPE: Lord Raymond, pray fall to. I am beholding
To the Bishop of Milan for this so rare a present.

FAUSTUS: I thank you, sir.

[*Snatches it.*]

5. The Roman god of the underworld.

6. Goddess representing death and the dark side of the moon.

POPE: How now? Who snatched the meat from me?
Villains, why speak you not?
My good Lord Archbishop, here's a most dainty dish
Was sent me from a cardinal in France.

FAUSTUS: I'll have that too.
[*Snatches it.*]

POPE: What lollards do attend our Holiness
That we receive such great indignity? Fetch me some wine.

FAUSTUS: Ay, pray do, for Faustus is a-dry.

POPE: Lord Raymond, I drink unto your grace.

FAUSTUS: I pledge your grace.
[*Snatches the glass.*]

POPE: My wine gone too? Ye lubbers,° look about *louts*
And find the man that doth this villainy,
Or by our sanctitude you all shall die.
I pray, my lords, have patience at this
Troublesome banquet.

BISHOP: Please it your Holiness, I think it be some ghost crept out of Purgatory, and now is come unto your Holiness for his pardon.

POPE: It may be so.
Go, then, command our priests to sing a dirge
To lay the fury of this same troublesome ghost.
[*The Pope crosseth himself.*]

FAUSTUS: How now? Must every bit be spiced with a cross?
Nay then, take that.
[*Faustus hits him a box of the ear.*]

POPE: Oh, I am slain! Help me, my lords.
Oh come, and help to bear my body hence.
Damned be this soul for ever for this deed!
[*Exeunt the Pope and his train.*]

MEPHOSTOPHILIS: Now, Faustus, what will you do now?
For I can tell you, you'll be cursed with bell, book and candle.

FAUSTUS: Bell, book and candle, candle, book and bell,
Forward and backward, to curse Faustus to hell.
[*Enter the Friars with bell, book and candle, for the dirge.*]

FIRST FRIAR: Come, brethren, let's about our business with good devotion.
[*sing*] Cursed be he that stole his Holiness' meat from the table. *Maledicat dominus.*[7]
Cursed be he that took his Holiness a blow on the face. *Maledicat dominus.*
Cursed be he that struck Friar Sandelo a blow on the pate. *Maledicat dominus.*
Cursed be he that disturbeth our holy dirge. *Maledicat dominus.*
Cursed be he that took away his Holiness' wine. *Maledicat dominus.*
Et omnes sancti.[8] Amen.
[*Faustus and Mephostophilis beat the Friars, fling fireworks among them and exeunt. Enter Chorus.*]

CHORUS: When Faustus had with pleasure ta'en the view
Of rarest things and royal courts of kings,

7. May God curse you.

8. And all the saints.

He stayed his course and so returned home;
Where such as bear his absence but with grief,
I mean his friends and nearest companions,
Did gratulate his safety with kind words,
And in their conference of what befell,
Touching his journey through the world and air,
They put forth questions of astrology,
Which Faustus answered with such learned skill
As they admired and wondered at his wit.
Now is his fame spread forth in every land;
Amongst the rest, the Emperor is one,
Carolus the Fifth, at whose palace now
Faustus is feasted 'mongst his noblemen.
What there he did in trial of his art,
I leave untold: your eyes shall see performed.

Scene 4

[*Enter Robin the ostler*[9] *with a book in his hand.*]

ROBIN: Oh this is admirable! Here I ha' stol'n one of Doctor Faustus' conjuring books, and, i'faith, I mean to search some circles for my own use. Now will I make all the maidens in our parish dance at my pleasure stark naked before me. And so by that means I shall see more than ere I felt or saw yet.

[*Enter Rafe calling Robin.*]

RAFE: Robin, prithee come away! There's a gentleman tarries to have his horse, and he would have his things rubbed and made clean. He keeps such a chafing with my mistress about it, and she has sent me to look thee out. Prithee, come away!

ROBIN: Keep out, keep out, or else you are blown up. You are dismembered, Rafe, keep out, for I am about a roaring piece of work.

RAFE: Come, what dost thou with that same book? Thou canst not read?

ROBIN: Yes, my master and mistress shall find that I can read, he for his forehead, she for her private study. She's born to bear with me, or else my art fails.

RAFE: Why, Robin, what book is that?

ROBIN: What book? Why, the most intolerable book for conjuring that ere was invented by any brimstone devil.

RAFE: Canst thou conjure with it?

ROBIN: I can do all these things easily with it. First, I can make thee drunk with ippocras at any tavern in Europe, for nothing. That's one of my conjuring works!

RAFE: Our master parson says that's nothing.

ROBIN: True, Rafe. And more, Rafe, if thou hast any mind to Nan Spit, our kitchen maid, then turn her and wind her to thy own use as often as thou wilt, and at midnight.

RAFE: Oh brave Robin! Shall I have Nan Spit, and to mine own use? On that condition, I'll feed thy devil with horsebread as long as he lives, of free cost.

9. Stableman.

ROBIN: No more, sweet Rafe. Let's go and make clean our boots which lie foul upon our hands, and then to our conjuring, in the devil's name.

[Exeunt. Re-enter Robin and Rafe with a silver goblet.]

ROBIN: Come, Rafe, did I not tell thee we were for ever made by this Doctor Faustus' book? *Ecce signum,*[1] here's a simple purchase for horse-keepers. Our horses shall eat no hay as long as this lasts.

[*Enter the Vintner.*]

RAFE: But, Robin, here comes the vintner.

ROBIN: Hush, I'll gull[2] him supernaturally. Drawer, I hope all is paid. God be with you. Come, Rafe.

VINTNER: Soft, sir, a word with you. I must yet have a goblet paid from you ere you go.

ROBIN: I, a goblet? Rafe, I a goblet? I scorn you, and you are but a etc. I, a goblet? Search me.

VINTNER: I mean so, sir, with your favor.

ROBIN: How say you now?

VINTNER: I must say somewhat to your fellow—you, sir.

RAFE: Me, sir? Me, sir? Search your fill. Now, sir, you may be ashamed to burden honest men with a matter of truth.

VINTNER: Well, t'one of you hath this goblet about you.

ROBIN: You lie, drawer. 'Tis afore me! Sirrah, you! I'll teach ye to impeach honest men. Stand by, I'll scour you for a goblet. Stand aside, you were best. I charge you in the name of Belzebub. Look to the goblet, Rafe.

VINTNER: What mean you, sirrah?

ROBIN: I'll tell you what I mean. [*He reads*] *Sanctobolorum Periphrasticon.*[3] Nay, I'll tickle you, vintner—look to the goblet, Rafe. *Polypragmos Belseborams framanto pacostiphos tostu Mephostophilis, Etc.*

[*Enter Mephostophilis, who sets squibs*[4] *at their backs. They run about.*]

VINTNER: *O nomine Domine*[5] what mean'st thou, Robin? Thou hast no goblet.

RAFE: *Peccatum peccatorum*[6] here's thy goblet, good vintner.

ROBIN: *Misericordia pro nobis*[7] what shall I do? Good devil, forgive me now and I'll never rob thy library more.

[*Enter to them Mephostophilis.*]

MEPHOSTOPHILIS: Vainish villains! Th'one like an ape, another like a bear, the third an ass, for doing this enterprise.

Monarch of hell, under whose black survey
Great potentates do kneel with awful fear,
Upon whose altars thousand souls do lie,
How am I vexed with these villains' charms?
From Constantinople am I hither come,
Only for pleasure of these damned slaves.

ROBIN: How, from Constantinople? You have had a great journey. Will you take six pence in your purse to pay for your supper, and be gone?

1. "Behold, the sign"; i.e., of the truth.
2. Trick.
3. Gibberish.
4. Firecrackers.
5. In God's name.
6. Sin of sins.
7. Mercy on us.

MEPHOSTOPHILIS: Well, villains, for your presumption I transform thee into an ape and thee into a dog, and so be gone. [*Exit*.]
ROBIN: How, into an ape? That's brave! I'll have fine sport with the boys. I'll get nuts and apples enow.
RAFE: And I must be a dog!
ROBIN: I'faith thy head will never be out of the potage pot. [*Exeunt*.]

ACT 4

Scene 1

[*The Emperor's Court. Enter Martino and Frederick at several doors*.]

MARTINO: What ho, officers, gentlemen!
Hie to the presence to attend the Emperor.
Good Frederick, see the rooms be voided straight.
His Majesty is coming to the hall;
Go back, and see the state in readiness.
FREDERICK: But where is Bruno, our elected Pope,
That on a fury's back came post from Rome?
Will not his grace consort° the Emperor? *greet*
MARTINO: Oh yes, and with him comes the German conjuror,
The learned Faustus, fame of Wittenberg,
The wonder of the world for magic art.
And he intends to show great Carolus
The race of all his stout progenitors,
And bring in presence of his Majesty
The royal shapes and warlike semblances
Of Alexander and his beauteous paramour.[1]
FREDERICK: Where is Benvolio?
MARTINO: Fast asleep, I warrant you.
He took his rouse with stoups° of Rhenish wine *large cups*
So kindly yesternight to Bruno's health,
That all this day the sluggard keeps his bed.
FREDERICK: See, see, his window's ope. We'll call to him.
MARTINO: What ho, Benvolio?

[*Enter Benvolio above at a window in his nightcap, buttoning*.]

BENVOLIO: What a devil ail you two?
MARTINO: Speak softly, sir, lest the devil hear you;
For Faustus at the court is late arrived,
And at his heels a thousand furies wait
To accomplish whatsoever the Doctor please.
BENVOLIO: What of this?
MARTINO: Come, leave thy chamber first, and thou shalt see
This conjuror perform such rare exploits
Before the Pope and royal Emperor
As never yet was seen in Germany.
BENVOLIO: Has not the Pope enough of conjuring yet?
He was upon the devil's back late enough,

1. Alexander the Great and his wife, Roxana.

And if he be so far in love with him,
I would he would post with him to Rome again.
FREDERICK: Speak, wilt thou come and see this sport?
BENVOLIO: Not I.
MARTINO: Wilt thou stand in thy window and see it, then?
BENVOLIO: Ay, and I fall not asleep i' the meantime.
MARTINO: The Emperor is at hand, who comes to see
What wonders by black spells may compassed be.
BENVOLIO: Well, go you, attend the Emperor. I am content for this once to thrust my head out at a window, for they say if a man be drunk over night the devil cannot hurt him in the morning. If that be true, I have a charm in my head shall control him as well as the conjuror, I warrant you.
[Exeunt Martino and Frederick.]

Scene 2

[Sennet. Charles, the German Emperor, Bruno, Saxony, Faustus, Mephostophilis, Frederick, Martino, and Attendants. Benvolio still at the window.]

EMPEROR: Wonder of men, renowned magician,
Thrice-learned Faustus, welcome to our court.
This deed of thine, in setting Bruno free
From his and our professed enemy,
Shall add more excellence unto thine art,
Than if by powerful necromantic spells
Thou couldst command the world's obedience.
For ever be beloved of Carolus;
And if this Bruno thou hast late redeemed,
In peace possess the triple diadem
And sit in Peter's chair, despite of chance,
Thou shalt be famous through all Italy,
And honored of the German Emperor.
FAUSTUS: These gracious words, most royal Carolus,
Shall make poor Faustus to his utmost power
Both love and serve the German Emperor,
And lay his life at holy Bruno's feet.
For proof whereof, if so your Grace be pleased,
The Doctor stands prepared, by power of art,
To cast his magic charms that shall pierce through
The ebon° gates of ever-burning hell, *ebony*
And hale the stubborn furies from their caves,
To compass whatsoe'er your Grace commands.
BENVOLIO [*ASIDE*]: Blood, he speaks terribly! But for all that, I do not greatly believe him. He looks as like a conjuror as the Pope to a coster-monger.[2]
EMPEROR: Then, Faustus, as thou late didst promise us,
We would behold that famous conqueror,
Great Alexander, and his paramour,
In their true shapes and state majestical,

2. Vegetable seller.

That we may wonder at their excellence.
FAUSTUS: Your Majesty shall see them presently.
Mephostophilis, away!
And with a solemn noise of trumpets' sound,
Present before this royal Emperor
Great Alexander and his beauteous paramour.
MEPHOSTOPHILIS: Faustus, I will.
BENVOLIO: Well, Master Doctor, an your devils come not away quickly, you shall have me asleep presently. Zounds, I could eat myself for anger, to think I have been such an ass all this while, to stand gaping after the devil's governor, and can see nothing.
FAUSTUS: I'll make you feel something anon, if my art fail me not.
My lord, I must forwarn your Majesty
That when my spirits present the royal shapes
Of Alexander and his paramour,
Your Grace demand no questions of the King,
But in dumb silence let them come and go.
EMPEROR: Be it as Faustus please, we are content.
BENVOLIO: Ay, ay, and I am content too. And thou bring Alexander and his paramour before the Emperor, I'll be Actaeon[3] and turn myself to a stag.
FAUSTUS: And I'll play Diana, and send you the horns presently.
[*Sennet. Enter at one the Emperor Alexander, at the other Darius. They meet. Darius is thrown down; Alexander kills him, takes off his crown, and, offering to go out, his Paramour meets him. He embraceth her and sets Darius' crown upon her head, and coming back, both salute the Emperor, who, leaving his state, offers to embrace them, which Faustus seeing, suddenly stays him. Then trumpets cease and music sounds.*]
My gracious lord, you do forget yourself.
These are but shadows, not substantial.
EMPEROR: Oh pardon me, my thoughts are so ravished
With sight of this renowned Emperor,
That in mine arms I would have compassed him.
But, Faustus, since I may not speak to them,
To satisfy my longing thoughts at full,
Let me this tell thee: I have heard it said
That this fair lady, whilst she lived on earth,
Had on her neck a little wart or mole.
How may I prove that saying to be true?
FAUSTUS: Your Majesty may boldly go and see.
EMPEROR: Faustus, I see it plain,
And in this sight thou better pleasest me
Than if I gained another monarchy.
FAUSTUS: Away, be gone.
[*Exit Show.*]
See, see, my gracious lord, what strange beast is yon, that thrusts his head out at window?
EMPEROR: Oh, wondrous sight! See, Duke of Saxony,

3. Mythical hunter, changed by the goddess Diana into a stag because he had seen her naked as she bathed after a hunt; he was then devoured by his own dogs.

Two spreading horns most strangely fastened
Upon the head of young Benvolio![4]

SAXONY: What, is he asleep? Or dead?

FAUSTUS: He sleeps, my lord: but dreams not of his horns.

EMPEROR: This sport is excellent. We'll call and wake him.
What ho, Benvolio!

BENVOLIO: A plague upon you! Let me sleep awhile.

EMPEROR: I blame thee not to sleep much, having such a head of thine own.

SAXONY: Look up, Benvolio, 'tis the Emperor calls.

BENVOLIO: The Emperor? Where? Oh, zounds, my head!

EMPEROR: Nay, and thy horns hold, 'tis no matter for thy head, for that's armed sufficiently.

FAUSTUS: Why, how now, Sir Knight? What, hanged by the horns? This most horrible! Fie, fie! Pull in your head for shame; let not all the world wonder at you.

BENVOLIO: Zounds, Doctor, is this your villainy?

FAUSTUS: Oh, say not so, sir. The Doctor has no skill,
No art, no cunning, to present these lords
Or bring before this royal Emperor
The mighty monarch, warlike Alexander.
If Faustus do it, you are straight resolved
In bold Actaeon's shape to turn a stag.
And therefore, my lord, so please your majesty,
I'll raise a kennel of hounds shall hunt him so
As all his footmanship shall scarce prevail
To keep his carcass from their bloody fangs.
Ho, Belimote, Argiron, Asterote!

BENVOLIO: Hold, hold! Zounds, he'll raise up a kennel of devils, I think anon. Good my lord, entreat for me. 'Sblood, I am never never able to endure these torments.

EMPEROR: Then, good Master Doctor,
Let me entreat you to remove his horns:
He has done penance now sufficiently.

FAUSTUS: My gracious lord, not so much for injury done to me, as to delight your majesty with some mirth, hath Faustus justly requited this injurious knight; which being all I desire, I am content to remove his horns. Mephostophilis, transform him. And hereafter, sir, look you speak well of scholars.

BENVOLIO [*ASIDE*]: Speak well of ye? 'Sblood, and scholars be such cuckold-makers to clap horns of honest men's heads o' this order, I'll ne'er trust smooth faces and small ruffs more. But an I be not revenged for this, would I might be turned to a gaping oyster and drink nothing but salt water.

EMPEROR: Come, Faustus, while the Emperor lives,
In recompense of this thy high desert,° *merit*
Thou shalt command the state of Germany,
And live beloved of mighty Carolus. [*Exeunt omnes.*]

4. To be "horned" was to be cuckolded. Benvolio, who has insulted scholars, is given horns by Faustus, who takes a scholar's revenge. The insult is introduced as a reflection on the myth of Diana and Actaeon.

Scene 3

[*Enter Benvolio, Martino, Frederick and Soldiers.*]

MARTINO: Nay, sweet Benvolio, let us sway thy thoughts
From this attempt against the conjuror.

BENVOLIO: Away, you love me not, to urge me thus.
Shall I let slip° so great an injury, *overlook*
When every servile groom jests at my wrongs,
And in their rustic gambols proudly say
Benvolio's head was graced with horns today?
Oh, may these eyelids never close again
Till with my sword I have that conjuror slain.
If you will aid me in this enterprise,
Then draw your weapons and be resolute.
If not, depart. Here will Benvolio die,
But Faustus' death shall quit my infamy.

FREDERICK: Nay, we will stay with three, betide what may,
And kill that Doctor if he come this way.

BENVOLIO: Then, gentle Frederick, hie° thee to the grove, *take*
And place our servants and our followers
Close in an ambush there behind the trees.
By this I know the conjuror is near:
I saw him kneel and kiss the Emperor's hand,
And take his leave, laden with rich rewards.
Then, soldiers, boldly fight. If Faustus die,
Take you the wealth, leave us the victory.

FREDERICK: Come, soldiers, follow me unto the grove.
Who kills him shall have gold and endless love.

[*Exit Frederick with the Soldiers.*]

BENVOLIO: My head is lighter than it was by th'horns,
But yet my heart more ponderous than my head,
And pants until I see that conjuror dead.

MARTINO: Where shall we place ourselves, Benvolio?

BENVOLIO: Here will we stay to bide the first assault.
Oh, were that damned hell-hound but in place,
Thou soon shouldst see me quit my foul disgrace.

[*Enter Frederick.*]

FREDERICK: Close, close! The conjuror is at hand,
And all alone comes walking in his gown.
Be ready then, and strike the peasant down.

BENVOLIO: Mine be that honor, then. Now sword, strike home.
For horns he gave, I'll have his head anon.

[*Enter Faustus with a false head.*]

MARTINO: See, see, he comes.

BENVOLIO: No words. This blow ends all.
Hell take his soul; his body thus must fall.

[*Attacks Faustus.*]

FAUSTUS: Oh!

FREDERICK: Groan you, Master Doctor?

BENVOLIO: Break may his heart with groans! Dear Frederick, see,
Thus will I end his griefs immediately.
[*Cuts off his head.*]
MARTINO: Strike with a willing hand: his head is off.
BENVOLIO: The devil's dead! The Furies now may laugh.
FREDERICK: Was this that stern aspect, that awful frown,
Made the grim monarch of infernal spirits
Tremble and quake at his commanding charms?
MARTINO: Was this that damned head, whose heart conspired
Benvolio's shame before the Emperor?
BENVOLIO: Ay, that's the head, and here the body lies,
Justly rewarded for his villainies.
FREDERICK: Come, let's devise how we may add more shame
To the black scandal of his hated name.
BENVOLIO: First, on his head, in quittance° of my wrongs, *payment*
I'll nail huge forked horns, and let them hang
Within the window where he yoked° me first, *overcame*
That all the world may see my just revenge.
MARTINO: What use shall we put his beard to?
BENVOLIO: We'll sell it to a chimney-sweeper: it will wear
out ten birching° brooms, I warrant you. *birch-twig*
FREDERICK: What shall eyes do?
BENVOLIO: We'll put out his eyes, and they shall serve for buttons to his lips, to
keep his tongue from catching cold.
MARTINO: An excellent policy! And now, sirs, having divided him, what shall
the body do?
[*Faustus rises.*]
BENVOLIO: Zounds, the devil's alive again!
FREDERICK: Give him his head, for God's sake!
FAUSTUS: Nay, keep it. Faustus will have heads and hands.
I call your hearts to recompense this deed.
Knew you not, traitors, I was limited
For four and twenty years to breathe on earth?
And had you cut my body with your swords,
Or hewed this flesh and bones as small as sand,
Yet in a minute had my spirit returned,
And I had breathed a man made free from harm.
But wherefore do I dally° my revenge? *delay*
Asteroth, Belimoth, Mephostophilis!
[*Enter Mephostophilis and other Devils.*]
Go, horse these traitors on your fiery backs,
And mount aloft with them as high as heaven;
Thence pitch them headlong to the lowest hell.
Yet stay, the world shall see their misery,
And hell shall after plague their treachery.
Go, Belimoth, and take this caitiff° hence, *coward*
And hurl him in some lake of mud and dirt.
Take thou this other: drag him through the woods
Amongst the pricking thorns and sharpest briars,

Whilst with my gentle Mephostophilis,
This traitor flies unto some steepy rock,
That rolling down may break the villain's bones,
As he intended to dismember me.
Fly hence, dispatch my charge immediately.

FREDERICK: Pity us, gentle Faustus! Save our lives!

FAUSTUS: Away!

FREDERICK: He must needs go that the devil drives.

[*Exeunt Spirits with the Knights. Enter the Ambush Soldiers.*]

FIRST SOLDIER: Come, sirs, prepare yourselves in readiness.
Make haste to help these noble gentlemen.
I heard them parley with the conjuror.

SECOND SOLDIER: See, where he comes. Dispatch and kill the slave.

FAUSTUS: What's here? An ambush to betray my life!
Then Faustus, try thy skill. Base peasants, stand!
For lo, these trees remove at my command,
And stand as bulwarks twixt yourselves and me,
To shield me from your hated treachery.
Yet, to encounter this your weak attempt,
Behold an army comes incontinent.° *rapidly*

[*Faustus strikes the door, and enter a devil playing on a drum; after him another bearing an ensign;*[5] *and divers with weapons; Mephostophilis with fireworks. They set upon the soldiers and drive them out.*]

Scene 4

[*Enter at several doors Benvolio, Frederick and Martino, their heads and faces bloody and besmeared with mud and dirt, all having horns on their heads.*]

MARTINO: What ho, Benvolio!

BENVOLIO: Here! What, Frederick, ho!

FREDERICK: Oh help me, gentle friend. Where is Martino?

MARTINO: Dear Frederick, here,
Half smothered in a lake of mud and dirt,
Through which the Furies dragged me by the heels.

FREDERICK: Martino, see Benvolio's horns again!

MARTINO: Oh misery! How now, Benvolio?

BENVOLIO: Defend me, heaven! Shall I be haunted still?

MARTINO: Nay, fear not, man; we have no power to kill.

BENVOLIO: My friends transformed thus! Oh hellish spite!
Your heads are all set with horns!

FREDERICK: You hit it right:
It is your own you mean. Feel on your head.

BENVOLIO: Zounds, horns again!

MARTINO: Nay, chafe not, man. We all are sped.° *done for*

BENVOLIO: What devil attends this damned magician,
That, spite of spite, our wrongs are doubled?

FREDERICK: What may we do, that we may hide our shames?

5. Flag.

BENVOLIO: If we should follow him to work revenge,
He'd join long asses' ears to these huge horns,
And make us laughing stocks to all the world.

MARTINO: What shall we then do, dear Benvolio?

BENVOLIO: I have a castle joining near these woods,
And thither we'll repair and live obscure,
Till time shall alter these our brutish shapes.
Sith° black disgrace hath thus eclipsed our fame, *since*
We'll rather die with grief, than live with shame.

[*Exeunt omnes.*]

Scene 5

[*Enter Faustus and Mephostophilis.*]

FAUSTUS: Now, Mephostophilis, the restless course
That time doth run with calm and deadly foot,
Shortening my days and thread of vital life,
Calls for the payment of my latest years.
Therefore, sweet Mephostophilis, let us
Make haste to Wittenberg.

MEPHOSTOPHILIS: What, will you go on horseback, or on foot?

FAUSTUS: Nay, till I am past this fair and pleasant green
I'll walk on foot.

[*Enter a Horse-Courser.*][6]

HORSE-COURSER: I have been all this day seeking one master Fustian.[7] Mass, see where he is! God save you, Master Doctor.

FAUSTUS: What, horse-courser! You are well met.

HORSE-COURSER: Do you hear, sir? I have brought you forty dollars for your horse.

FAUSTUS: I cannot sell him so. If thou likest him for fifty, take him.

HORSE-COURSER: Alas, sir, I have no more. I pray you, speak for me.

MEPHOSTOPHILIS: I pray you, let him have him. He is an honest fellow, and he has a great charge, neither wife nor child.

FAUSTUS: Well, come, give me your money. My boy will deliver him to you. But I must tell you one thing before you have him: ride him not into the water at any hand.

HORSE-COURSER: Why, sir, will he not drink of all waters?

FAUSTUS: Oh yes, he will drink of all waters; but ride him not into the water. Ride him over hedge or ditch or where thou wilt, but not into the water.

HORSE-COURSER: Well, sir, now I am a made man for ever. I'll not leave my horse for forty. If he had but the quality of hey ding ding, hey ding ding, I'd make a brave living on him. He has a buttock as slick as an eel. Well, God bye, sir. Your boy will deliver him me. But hark ye sir: if my horse be sick or ill at ease, if I bring his water to you, you'll tell me what is?

FAUSTUS: Away, you villain! What, dost think I am a horse-doctor?

[*Exit Horse-Courser.*]

What art thou, Faustus, but a man condemned to die?

6. Horse trader.

7. Bombast.

Thy fatal time doth draw to final end:
Despair doth drive distrust into my thoughts.
Confound these passions with a quiet sleep.
Tush, Christ did call the thief upon the cross;
Then rest thee, Faustus, quiet in conceit.

[*Sleeps in his chair. Enter Horse-Courser all wet, crying.*]

HORSE-COURSER: Alas, alas, Doctor Fustian quotha! Mass, Doctor Lopus[8] was never such a doctor. Has given me a purgation has purged me of forty dollars: I shall never see them more. But yet like an ass as I was, I would not be ruled by him, for he bade me I should ride him into no water. Now I, thinking my horse had had some rare quality that he would not have had me known of, I, like a venturous youth, rid him into the deep pond at the town's end. I was no sooner in the middle of the pond but my horse vanished away, and I sat upon a bottle of hay, never so near drowning in my life. But I'll seek out my Doctor and have my forty dollars again, or I'll make it the dearest horse. Oh, yonder is his snipper-snapper. Do you hear? You! Hey-pass, where's your master?

MEPHOSTOPHILIS: Why, sir, what would you? You cannot speak with him.

HORSE-COURSER: But I *will* speak with him.

MEPHOSTOPHILIS: Why, he's fast asleep. Come some other time.

HORSE-COURSER: I'll speak with him now, or I'll break his glass windows about his ears.

MEPHOSTOPHILIS: I tell thee he has not slept this eight nights.

HORSE-COURSER: And he have not slept this eight weeks I'll speak with him.

MEPHOSTOPHILIS: See where he is fast asleep.

HORSE-COURSER: Ay, this is he. God save ye, Master Doctor. Master Doctor! Master Doctor Fustian! Forty dollars, forty dollars for a bottle of hay!

MEPHOSTOPHILIS: Why, thou seest he hears thee not.

HORSE-COURSER: So, ho, ho! So, ho, ho!

[*Halloos in his ear.*]

No, will you not wake? I'll make you wake e'er I go.

[*He pulls him by the leg, and pulls it away.*]

Alas, I am undone! What shall I do?

FAUSTUS: Oh, my leg, my leg! Help, Mephostophilis. Call the officers. My leg, my leg!

MEPHOSTOPHILIS: Come, villain, to the Constable.

HORSE-COURSER: Oh lord, sir, let me go and I'll give you forty dollars more.

MEPHOSTOPHILIS: Where be they?

HORSE-COURSER: I have none about me. Come to my hostry and I'll give them you.

MEPHOSTOPHILIS: Be gone, quickly!

[*Horse-Courser runs away.*]

FAUSTUS: What, is he gone? Farewell he. Faustus has his leg again, and the horse-courser, I take it, a bottle of hay for his labor. Well, this trick shall cost him forty dollars more.

8. Dr. Lopez, Queen Elizabeth's physician, who was executed in 1594 for alleged complicity in an attempt to murder the Queen. Marlowe died in 1593, so the reference is not his but one of a later editor.

[*Enter Wagner.*]

FAUSTUS: How now, Wagner, what news with thee?

WAGNER: If it please you, the Duke of Vanholt[9] doth earnestly entreat your company, and hath sent some of his men to attend you with provision for your journey.

FAUSTUS: The Duke of Vanholt's an honorable gentleman, and one to whom I must be no niggard[1] of my cunning. Come, away. [*Exeunt.*]

Scene 6

[*Enter Clown, Dick, Horse-Courser and a Carter.*]

CARTER: Come, my masters, I'll bring you to the best beer in Europe. What ho, hostess. Where be these whores?

[*Enter Hostess.*]

HOSTESS: How now, what lack you? What, my old guests, welcome!

CLOWN: Sirrah Dick, dost thou know why I stand so mute?

DICK: No, Robin, why is't?

CLOWN: I am eighteen pence on the score.[2] But say nothing. See if she have forgotten me.

HOSTESS: Who's this, that stands so solemnly by himself? What, my old guest?

CLOWN: Oh, hostess, how do you? I hope my score stands still.

HOSTESS: Ay, there's no doubt of that, for methinks you make no haste to wipe it out.

DICK: Why, hostess, I say, fetch us some beer.

HOSTESS: You shall presently. Look up into the hall there, ho! [*Exit.*]

DICK: Come, sirs, what shall we do now till mine hostess comes?

CARTER: Marry, sir, I'll tell you the bravest tale how a conjuror served me. You know Doctor Faustus?

HORSE-COURSER: Ay, a plague take him. Here's some on's have cause to know him. Did he conjure thee too?

CARTER: I'll tell you how he served me. As I was going to Wittenberg t'other day, with a load of hay, he met me and asked me what he should give me for as much hay as he could eat. Now, sir, I, thinking that a little would serve his turn, bade him take as much as he would for three-farthings. So he presently gave me my money and fell to eating. And, as I am a cursen man, he never left eating till he had eat up all my load of hay.

ALL: Oh monstrous! Eat a whole load of hay?

CLOWN: Yes, yes, that may be, for I have heard of one that has eat a load of logs.

HORSE-COURSER: Now, sirs, you shall hear how villainously he served me. I went to him yesterday to buy a horse of him, and he would by no means sell him under forty dollars. So, sir, because I knew him to be such a horse as would run over hedge and ditch and never tire, I gave him his money. So when I had my horse, Doctor Fauster bade me ride him night and day and spare him no time. But, quoth he, in any case ride him not into the water. Now, sir, I thinking the horse had some quality that he would not have me

9. The Duchy of Anholt in Germany.
1. Miser.
2. Eighteen pence in debt.

know of, what did I but ride him into a great river, and when I came just in the midst, my horse vanished away, and I sat straddling upon a bottle of hay.

ALL: Oh brave Doctor!

HORSE-COURSER: But you shall hear how bravely I served him for it: I went me home to his house, and there I found him asleep. I kept a-hallowing and whooping in his ears, but all could not wake him. I, seeing that, took him by the leg and never rested pulling, till I had pulled me his leg quite off, and now 'tis at home in mine hostry.

CLOWN: And has the Doctor but one leg, then? That's excellent, for one of his devils turned me into the likeness of an ape's face.

CARTER: Some more drink, hostess.

CLOWN: Hark you, we'll into another room and drink a while, and then we'll go seek out the Doctor. [*Exeunt omnes*.]

Scene 7

[*Enter the Duke of Vanholt, his Duchess, Faustus and Mephostophilis*.]

DUKE: Thanks, Master Doctor, for these pleasant sights. Nor know I how sufficiently to recompense your great deserts in erecting that enchanted castle in the air, the sight whereof so delighted me, as nothing in the world could please me more.

FAUSTUS: I do think myself, my good lord, highly recompensed in that it pleaseth your grace to think but well of that which Faustus hath performed. But, gracious lady, it may be that you have taken no pleasure in those sights. Therefore, I pray you tell me, what is the thing you most desire to have. Be it in the world, it shall be yours. I have heard that great-bellied women do long for things are rare and dainty.

LADY: True, Master Doctor, and since I find you so kind, I will make known unto you what my heart desires to have; and were it now summer, as it is January, a dead time of the winter, I would request no better meat than a dish of ripe grapes.

FAUSTUS: This is but a small matter. Go, Mephostophilis, away.

[*Exit Mephostophilis*.]

Madame, I will do more than this for your content.

[*Enter Mephostophilis again with the grapes*.]

Here, now taste ye these. They should be good, for they come from a far country, I can tell you.

DUKE: This makes me wonder more than all the rest, that at this time of the year, when every tree is barren of his fruit, from whence you had these ripe grapes.

FAUSTUS: Please it your grace, the year is divided into two circles over the whole world, so that when it is winter with us, in the contrary circle it is likewise summer with them, as in India, Saba and such countries that lie far East, where they have fruit twice a year. From whence, by means of a swift spirit that I have, I had these grapes brought as you see.

LADY: And trust me, they are the sweetest grapes that e'er I tasted.

[*The Clowns bounce at the gate within*.]

DUKE: What rude disturbers have we at the gate?
Go, pacify their fury. Set it ope,
And then demand of them what they would have.

[*They knock again and call out to talk with Faustus*.]

SERVANT: Why, how now, masters? What a coil[3] is there?
What is the reason you disturb the Duke?

DICK: We have no reason for it, therefore a fig for him.

SERVANT: Why, saucy varlets, dare you be so bold?

HORSE-COURSER: I hope, sir, we have wit enough to be more bold than welcome.

SERVANT: It appears so. Pray be bold elsewhere,
And trouble not the Duke.

DUKE: What would they have?

SERVANT: They all cry out to speak with Doctor Faustus.

CARTER: Ay, and we will speak with him.

DUKE: Will you, sir? Commit the rascals.

DICK: Commit with us! He were as good commit with his father as commit with us.

FAUSTUS: I do beseech your grace let them come in.
They are good subject for a merriment.

DUKE: Do as thou wilt, Faustus; I give thee leave.

FAUSTUS: I thank your grace.

[*Enter the Clown, Dick, Carter and Horse-Courser*.]

Why, how now, my good friends?
Faith, you are too outrageous, but come near.
I have procured your pardons. Welcome all.

CLOWN: Nay, sir, we will be welcome for our money, and we will pay for what we take. What ho! Give's half-a-dozen of beer here, and be hanged.

FAUSTUS: Nay, hark you. Can you tell me where you are?

CARTER: Ay, marry can I. We are under heaven.

SERVANT: Ay, but, sir sauce-box, know you in what place?

HORSE-COURSER: Ay, ay, the house is good enough to drink in. Zounds, fill us some beer or we'll break all the barrels in the house and dash out all your brains with your bottles.

FAUSTUS: Be not so furious. Come, you shall have beer.
My lord, beseech you give me leave awhile.
I'll gage my credit, 'twill content your Grace.

DUKE: With all my heart, kind Doctor; please thyself.
Our servants and our court's at thy command.

FAUSTUS: I humbly thank your Grace. Then fetch some beer.

HORSE-COURSER: Ay, marry. There spake a doctor indeed, and faith, I'll drink a health to thy wooden leg for that word.

FAUSTUS: My wooden leg? What dost thou mean by that?

CARTER: Ha, ha, ha! Dost thou hear him, Dick? He has forgot his leg.

HORSE-COURSER: Ay, ay, he does not stand much upon that.

FAUSTUS: No, faith. Not much upon a wooden leg.

CARTER: Good lord! That flesh and blood should be so frail with your worship. Do not you remember a horse-courser you sold a horse to?

FAUSTUS: Yes, I remember I sold one a horse.

3. Disturbance.

CARTER: And do you remember you bid he should not ride into the water?
FAUSTUS: Yes, I do very well remember that.
CARTER: And do you remember nothing of your leg?
FAUSTUS: No, in good sooth.
CARTER: Then I pray remember your courtesy.[4]
FAUSTUS: I thank you, sir.
CARTER: 'Tis not so much worth. I pray you, tell me one thing.
FAUSTUS: What's that?
CARTER: Be both your legs bedfellows every night together?
FAUSTUS: Wouldst thou make a colossus[5] of me, that thou askest me such questions?
CARTER: No, truly, sir. I would make nothing of you, but I would fain know that.
[*Enter Hostess with drink*.]
FAUSTUS: Then I assure thee certainly they are.
CARTER: I thank you, I am fully satisfied.
FAUSTUS: But wherefore dost thou ask?
CARTER: For nothing, sir: but methinks you should have a wooden bedfellow of one of 'em.
HORSE-COURSER: Why, do you hear, sir? Did not I pull off one of your legs when you were asleep?
FAUSTUS: But I have it again now I am awake. Look you here, sir.
ALL: Oh horrible! Had the Doctor three legs?
CARTER: Do you remember, sir, how you cozened[6] me and eat up my load of—
[*Faustus charms him dumb*.]
DICK: Do you remember how you made me wear an ape's—
HORSE-COURSER: You whoreson conjuring scab, do you remember how you cozened me with a ho—
CLOWN: Ha'you forgotten me? You think to carry it away with your hey-pass and re-pass. Do you remember the dog's fa—
[*Faustus has charmed each dumb in turn; exeunt Clowns*.]
HOSTESS: Who pays for the ale? Hear you, Master Doctor, now you have sent away my guests, I pray who shall pay me for my a—?
[*Exit Hostess*.]
LADY: My lord,
We are much beholding to this learned man.
DUKE: So are we, madam, which we will recompense
With all the love and kindness that we may.
His artful sport drives all sad thoughts away. [*Exeunt*.]

ACT 5

Scene 1

[*Thunder and lightning. Enter Devils with covered dishes. Mephostophilis leads them into Faustus' study. Then enter Wagner*.]
WAGNER: I think my master means to die shortly.

4. Kindness
5. Huge statue.
6. Tricked.

He hath made his will, and given me his wealth,
His house, his goods, and store of golden plate,
Besides two thousand ducats ready coined.
And yet methinks, if that death were near,
He would not banquet and carouse and swill
Amongst the students, as even now he doth,
Who are at supper with such belly-cheer
As Wagner ne'er beheld in all his life.
See where they come; belike the feast is ended. [*Exit.*]

[*Enter Faustus, Mephostophilis and two or three Scholars.*]

FIRST SCHOLAR: Master Doctor Faustus, since our conference about fair ladies, which was the beautifullest in all the world, we have determined with ourselves that Helen of Greece[1] was the admirablest lady that ever lived. Therefore Master Doctor, if you will do us so much favor, as to let us see that peerless dame of Greece, whom all the world admires for majesty, we should think ourselves much beholding unto you.

FAUSTUS: Gentlemen, for that I know your friendship is unfeigned,
It is not Faustus' custom to deny
The just request of those that wish him well.
You shall behold that peerless dame of Greece,
No otherwise for pomp of majesty,
Than when Sir Paris crossed the seas with her,
And brought the spoils to rich Dardania.° *Troy*
Be silent then, for danger is in words.

[*Music sounds. Mephostophilis brings in Helen; she passeth over the stage.*]

SECOND SCHOLAR: Was this fair Helen, whose admired worth
Made Greece with ten years wars afflict poor Troy?

THIRD SCHOLAR: Too simple is my wit to tell her worth
Whom all the world admires for majesty.

FIRST SCHOLAR: Now we have seen the pride of nature's work,
We'll take our leaves, and for this blessed sight
Happy and blest be Faustus evermore.

[*Enter an Old Man.*]

FAUSTUS: Gentlemen, farewell: the same wish I to you. [*Exeunt Scholars.*]

OLD MAN: Oh gentle Faustus, leave this damned art,[2]
This magic, that will charm thy soul to hell,
And quite bereave thee of salvation.
Though thou hast now offended like a man,
Do not persever in it like a devil.
Yet, yet, thou hast an amiable° soul, *lovable*
If sin by custom grow not into nature:

1. The mythical queen of Menelaus, King of Sparta, who was abducted by Paris, son of King Priam of Troy. The action began the Trojan War.

2. The Old Man's lines in the A text reflect a Calvinist sense that Faustus may be saved by the Saviour's "mercy" and "blood alone":

Ah Doctor Faustus, that I might prevail,
To guide thy steps unto the way of life,
By which sweet path thou mayst attain the goal
That shall conduct thee to celestial rest.
Break heart, drop blood, and mingle it with tears,
Tears falling from repentant heaviness
Of thy most vile and loathsome filthiness,
The stench whereof corrupts the inward soul
With such flagitious crimes of hainous sinnes,
As no commiseration may expel,
But mercy Faustus of thy Saviour sweet,
Whose blood alone must wash away thy guilt.

Then, Faustus, will repentance come too late,
Then thou art banished from the sight of heaven;
No mortal can express the pains of hell.
It may be this my exhortation
Seems harsh and all unpleasant; let it not,
For, gentle son, I speak it not in wrath,
Or envy of thee, but in tender love,
And pity of thy future misery.
And so have hope, that this my kind rebuke,
Checking thy body, may amend thy soul.

FAUSTUS: Where art thou, Faustus? Wretch, what hast thou done?
Damned art thou, Faustus, damned: despair and die.
Hell claims his right, and with a roaring voice
Says "Faustus, come, thine hour is almost come"
[*Mephostophilis gives him a dagger.*]
And Faustus now will come to do thee right.

OLD MAN: Oh stay, good Faustus, stay thy desperate steps.
I see an angel hover o'er thy head,
And with a vial full of precious grace,
Offers to pour the same into thy soul.
Then call for mercy and avoid despair.

FAUSTUS: Ah my sweet friend, I feel thy words
To comfort my distressed soul.
Leave me awhile to ponder on my sins.

OLD MAN: I leave thee, but with grief of heart,
Fearing the ruin of thy hopeless soul. [*Exit.*]

FAUSTUS: Accursed Faustus, wretch, what hast thou done?
I do repent, and yet I do despair.
Hell strives with grace for conquest in my breast.
What shall I do to shun the snares of death?

MEPHOSTOPHILIS: Thou traitor, Faustus, I arrest thy soul
For disobedience to my sovereign lord.
Revolt,[3] or I'll in piecemeal tear thy flesh.

FAUSTUS: I do repent I e'er offended him.
Sweet Mephostophilis, entreat thy lord
To pardon my unjust presumption,
And with my blood again I will confirm
The former vow I made to Lucifer.

MEPHOSTOPHILIS: Do it then, Faustus, with unfeigned heart,
Lest greater dangers do attend thy drift.

FAUSTUS: Torment, sweet friend, that base and crooked age
That durst dissuade me from thy Lucifer,
With greatest torment that our hell affords.

MEPHOSTOPHILIS: His faith is great: I cannot touch his soul.
But what I may afflict his body with
I will attempt, which is but little worth.

FAUSTUS: One thing, good servant, let me crave of thee,

3. I.e., return to the terms of your bargain with the devil.

To glut the longing of my heart's desire,
That I may have unto my paramour
That heavenly Helen which I saw of late,
Whose sweet embraces may extinguish clear
Those thoughts that do dissuade me from my vow,
And keep my vow I made to Lucifer.

MEPHOSTOPHILIS: This, or what else my Faustus shall desire,
Shall be performed in twinkling of an eye.

[Enter Helen again, passing over between two Cupids.]

FAUSTUS: Was this the face that launched a thousand ships,
And burnt the topless towers of Ilium?
Sweet Helen, make me immortal with a kiss.
Her lips suck forth my soul: see where it flies.
Come, Helen, come, give me my soul again.
Here will I dwell, for heaven is in those lips,
And all is dross that is not Helena.

[Enter Old Man.]

I will be Paris,[4] and for love of thee
Instead of Troy shall Wittenberg be sacked,
And I will combat with weak Menelaus,
And wear thy colors on my plumed crest.
Yea, I will wound Achilles in the heel,
And then return to Helen for a kiss.
Oh, thou art fairer than the evening's air,
Clad in the beauty of a thousand stars.
Brighter art thou than flaming Jupiter,
When he appeared to hapless Semele:[5]
More lovely than the monarch of the sky,
In wanton Arethusa's[6] azure arms,
And none but thou shalt be my paramour. *[Exeunt.]*

OLD MAN: Accursed Faustus, miserable man,
That from thy soul exclud'st the grace of heaven,
And fliest the throne of his tribunal seat.

[Enter the Devils.]

Satan begins to sift° me with his pride, *scrutinize*
As in this furnace God shall try my faith.
My faith, vile hell, shall triumph over thee.
Ambitious fiends, see how the heavens smiles
At your repulse, and laughs your state to scorn.
Hence, hell, for hence I fly unto my God. *[Exeunt.]*

Scene 2

[Thunder. Enter Lucifer, Belzebub and Mephostophilis.]

LUCIFER: Thus from infernal Dis° do we ascend *hell*
To view the subjects of our monarchy,

4. Faustus imagines he will be not only Paris, Helen's lover, but also the victor in combat with her husband, King Menelaus, as well as with the greatest of the Greek warriors, Achilles.

5. The mortal woman to whom Jupiter appeared as lightening.

6. A nymph beloved by the river-god Alpheus; no myth describes her as Jupiter's lover.

Those souls which sin seals the black sons of hell,
'Mong which as chief, Faustus, we come to thee,
Bringing with us lasting damnation
To wait upon thy soul. The time is come
Which makes it forfeit.

MEPHOSTOPHILIS: And this gloomy night,
Here in this room will wretched Faustus be.

BELZEBUB: And here we'll stay,
To mark him how he doth demean himself.

MEPHOSTOPHILIS: How should he, but in desperate lunacy?
Fond worldling, now his heart blood dries with grief.
His conscience kills it, and his laboring brain
Begets a world of idle fantasies
To overreach the devil. But all in vain:
His store of pleasures must be sauced with pain.
He and his servant Wagner are at hand.
Both come from drawing Faustus' latest will.
See where they come.

[*Enter Faustus and Wagner*.]

FAUSTUS: Say, Wagner, thou hast perused my will:
How dost thou like it?

WAGNER: Sir, so wondrous well
As in all humble duty I do yield
My life and lasting service for your love.

[*Enter the Scholars*.]

FAUSTUS: Gramercies, Wagner. Welcome, gentlemen.

FIRST SCHOLAR: Now, worthy Faustus, methinks your looks are changed.

FAUSTUS: Oh gentlemen!

SECOND SCHOLAR: What ails Faustus?

FAUSTUS: Ah, my sweet chamber-fellow, had I lived with thee
Then had I lived still, but now must die eternally.
Look, sirs, comes he not? Comes he not?

FIRST SCHOLAR: Oh, my dear Faustus, what imports this fear?

SECOND SCHOLAR: Is all our pleasure turned to melancholy?

THIRD SCHOLAR: He is not well with being oversolitary.

SECOND SCHOLAR: If it be so, we'll have physicians, and Faustus shall be cured.

THIRD SCHOLAR: 'Tis but a surfeit, sir; fear nothing.

FAUSTUS: A surfeit of deadly sin, that hath damned both body and soul.

SECOND SCHOLAR: Yet Faustus, look up to heaven, and remember mercy is infinite.

FAUSTUS: But Faustus' offence can ne'er be pardoned, The serpent that tempted Eve may be saved, but not Faustus. Oh gentlemen, hear with patience and tremble not at my speeches. Though my heart pant and quiver to remember that I have been a student here these thirty years, oh would I had never seen Wittenberg, never read book. And what wonders I have done all Germany can witness, yea all the world, for which Faustus hath lost both Germany and the world, yea heaven itself, heaven, the seat of God, the throne of the blessed, the kingdom of joy, and must remain in hell for ever. Hell, oh hell for ever. Sweet friends, what shall become of Faustus, being in hell for ever?

SECOND SCHOLAR: Yet Faustus, call on God.

FAUSTUS: On God, whom Faustus hath abjured? On God, whom Faustus hath blasphemed? Oh my God, I would weep, but the devil draws in my tears. Gush forth blood instead of tears, yea, life and soul. Oh, he stays my tongue. I would lift up my hands, but see, they hold them, they hold them.

ALL: Who, Faustus?

FAUSTUS: Why, Lucifer and Mephostophilis: Oh gentlemen, I gave them my soul for my cunning.

ALL: Oh, God forbid.

FAUSTUS: God forbade it indeed, but Faustus hath done it. For vain pleasure of four and twenty years hath Faustus lost eternal joy and felicity. I writ them a bill with mine own blood, the date is expired: this is the time, and he will fetch me.

FIRST SCHOLAR: Why did not Faustus tell us of this before, that divines might have prayed for thee?

FAUSTUS: Oft have I thought to have done so, but the devil threatened to tear me in pieces if I named God; to fetch me body and soul if I once gave ear to divinity, and now 'tis too late. Gentlemen, away, lest you perish with me.

SECOND SCHOLAR: Oh what may we do to save Faustus?

FAUSTUS: Talk not of me, but save yourselves and depart.

THIRD SCHOLAR: God will strengthen me. I will stay with Faustus.

FIRST SCHOLAR: Tempt not God, sweet friend, but let us into the next room and pray for him.

FAUSTUS: Ay, pray for me, pray for me. And what noise soever you hear, come not unto me, for nothing can rescue me.

SECOND SCHOLAR: Pray thou, and we will pray, that God may have mercy upon thee.

FAUSTUS: Gentlemen, farewell. If I live till morning, I'll visit you. If not, Faustus is gone to hell.

ALL: Faustus, farewell.

[*Exeunt Scholars.*]

MEPHOSTOPHILIS: Ay, Faustus, now thou hast no hope of heaven,
Therefore despair, think only upon hell,
For that must be thy mansion, there to dwell.

FAUSTUS: Oh, thou bewitching fiend, 'twas thy temptation
Hath robbed me of eternal happiness.

MEPHOSTOPHILIS: I do confess it, Faustus, and rejoice.
'Twas I that, when thou were't i' the way to heaven,
Dammed up thy passage; when thou took'st the book
To view the scriptures, then I turned the leaves
And led thine eye.
What, weep'st thou? 'Tis too late, despair. Farewell.
Fools that will laugh on earth, must weep in hell. [*Exit.*]

[*Enter the Good and the Evil Angel at several doors.*]

GOOD ANGEL: Oh Faustus, if thou hadst given ear to me,
Innumerable joys had followed thee.

But thou didst love the world.
EVIL ANGEL: Gave ear to me,
And now must taste hell's pains perpetually.
GOOD ANGEL: Oh, what will all thy riches, pleasures, pomps,
Avail thee now?
EVIL ANGEL: Nothing but vex thee more,
To want in hell, that had on earth such store.
[*Music while the throne descends*.]
GOOD ANGEL: Oh, thou hast lost celestial happiness,
Pleasures unspeakable, bliss without end.
Hadst thou affected sweet divinity,
Hell, or the devil, had had no power on thee.
Hadst thou kept on that way, Faustus, behold
In what resplendent glory thou hadst sat
In yonder throne, like those bright shining saints,
And triumphed over hell. That thou hast lost,
And now, poor soul, must thy good angel leave thee:
The jaws of hell are open to receive thee. [*Exit*.]
[*Hell is discovered*.]
EVIL ANGEL: Now, Faustus, let thine eyes with horror stare
Into that vast perpetual torture-house.
There are the furies tossing damned souls
On burning forks. Their bodies broil in lead.
There are live quarters broiling on the coals
That ne'er can die. This ever-burning chair
Is for o'er-tortured souls to rest them in.
These, that are fed with sops of flaming fire,
Were gluttons, and loved only delicates,
And laughed to see the poor starve at their gates.
But yet all these are nothing. Thou shalt see
Ten thousand tortures that more horrid be.
FAUSTUS: Oh, I have seen enough to torture me.
EVIL ANGEL: Nay, thou must feel them, taste the smart of all:
He that loves pleasure must for pleasure fall.
And so I leave thee, Faustus, till anon.
Then wilt thou tumble in confusion. [*Exit*.]
[*The clock strikes eleven*.]
FAUSTUS: Ah Faustus,
Now hast thou but one bare hour to live,
And then thou must be damned perpetually.
Stand still, you ever-moving spheres of heaven,
That time may cease and midnight never come.
Fair nature's eye, rise, rise again, and make
Perpetual day. Or let this hour be but
A year, a month, a week, a natural day,
That Faustus may repent and save his soul.
O lente, lente, currite noctis equi.[7]

7. Faustus quotes from Ovid's *Amores* 1.13.40: "O slowly, slowly run, horses of the night."

The stars move still, time runs, the clock will strike.
The devil will come, and Faustus must be damned.
Oh, I'll leap up to my God: who pulls me down?
See, see, where Christ's blood streams in the firmament.
One drop would save my soul, half a drop. Ah, my Christ!
Ah, rend not my heart for naming of my Christ!
Yet will I call on him. Oh, spare me, Lucifer!
Where is it now? 'Tis gone:
And see where God stretcheth out his arm,
And bends his ireful brows.
Mountains and hills, come, come, and fall on me,
And hide me from the heavy wrath of God.
No, no. Then will I headlong run into the earth.
Earth, gape! Oh no, it will not harbor me.
You stars that reigned at my nativity,
Whose influence hath allotted death and hell,
Now draw up Faustus like a foggy mist
Into the entrails of yon laboring cloud,
That when you vomit forth into the air
My limbs may issue from your smoky mouths,
So that my soul may but ascend to heaven.
[*The watch strikes*.]
Ah! half the hour is past,
'Twill all be past anon.° soon
Oh God, if thou wilt not have mercy on my soul,
Yet, for Christ's sake whose blood hath ransomed me,
Impose some end to my incessant pain.
Let Faustus live in hell a thousand years,
A hundred thousand, and at last be saved.
Oh, no end is limited to damned souls.
Why wert thou not a creature wanting soul?
Or why is this immortal that thou hast?
Ah, Pythagoras' *metempsychosis*,[8] were that true
This soul should fly from me, and I be changed
Unto some brutish beast.
All beasts are happy, for when they die
Their souls are soon dissolved in elements,
But mine must live still to be plagued in hell.
Cursed be the parents that engendered me!
No, Faustus, curse thyself, curse Lucifer,
That hath deprived thee of the joys of heaven.
[*The clock strikes twelve*.]
Oh, it strikes, it strikes! Now body turn to air,
Or Lucifer will bear thee quick to hell.
[*Thunder and lightning*.]

8. The transmigration of souls. The Greek philosopher Pythagoras speculated that souls were reborn in other bodies in an endless progression.

Oh soul, be changed into little water drops
And fall into the ocean, ne'er be found.
[*Thunder. Enter the Devils.*]
My God, my God, look not so fierce on me.
Adders and serpents, let me breathe awhile.
Ugly hell, gape not, come not, Lucifer!
I'll burn my books. Ah, Mephostophilis! [*Exeunt with him.*]

Scene 3

[*Enter the Scholars.*]

FIRST SCHOLAR: Come, gentlemen, let us go visit Faustus,
For such a dreadful night was never seen
Since first the world's creation did begin.
Such fearful shrieks and cries were never heard.
Pray heaven the Doctor have escaped the danger.

SECOND SCHOLAR: Oh help us, heaven! See, here are Faustus' limbs,
All torn asunder by the hand of death.

THIRD SCHOLAR: The devils whom Faustus served have torn him thus:
For twixt the hours of twelve and one, methought
I heard him shriek and call aloud for help,
At which self time the house seemed all on fire
With dreadful horror of these damned fiends.

SECOND SCHOLAR: Well, gentlemen, though Faustus' end be such.
As every Christian heart laments to think on,
Yet, for he was a scholar once admired
For wondrous knowledge in our German schools,
We'll give his mangled limbs due burial,
And all the students clothed in mourning black
Shall wait upon his heavy funeral. [*Exeunt.*]

Epilogue

[*Enter the Chorus.*]

CHORUS: Cut is the branch that might have grown full straight,
And burned is Apollo's laurel bough,
That sometime grew within this learned man.
Faustus is gone. Regard his hellish fall,
Whose fiendful fortune may exhort the wise
Only to wonder at unlawful things,
Whose deepness doth entice such forward wits,
To practice more than heavenly power permits.

Terminat hora diem, Terminat Author opus.[9]

Finis.

9. The hour ends the day, the author ends the work.

RESPONSE
C. S. Lewis: from *The Screwtape Letters*

The Screwtape Letters (1940) inverts the terms of the Faust story and tells the devil's side of it. C. S. Lewis's diabolical character Screwtape shows how a human being and Christian soul may be enlisted in the devil's service. While Satan's agent Mephostophilis convinces Marlowe's Dr. Faustus to accept an afterlife in hell in exchange for a life of extraordinary influence and a high place in the world, Screwtape urges his helper, Wormwood, to corrupt his intended victim by subtle temptations to ambition. As long as Lewis's hero is preoccupied with getting ahead—living for the future rather than in the present—he risks capture and a place in hell. But unlike Dr. Faustus, he escapes the clutches of Wormwood by repudiating ambition and embracing the charitable doctrines of the devil's "Enemy," an unnamed power but clearly a figure for Jesus.

from *The Screwtape Letters*
Letter XV

My Dear Wormwood,

I had noticed, of course, that the humans were having a lull in their European war—what they naively call "The War"![1]—and am not surprised that there is a corresponding lull in the patient's anxieties. Do we want to encourage this, or to keep him worried? Tortured fear and stupid confidence are both desirable states of mind. Our choice between them raises important questions.

The humans live in time but our Enemy[2] destines them to eternity. He therefore, I believe, wants them to attend chiefly to two things, to eternity itself, and to that point of time which they call the Present. For the Present is the point at which time touches eternity. Of the present moment, and of it only, humans have an experience analogous to the experience which our Enemy has of reality as a whole; in it alone freedom and actuality are offered them. He would therefore have them continually concerned either with eternity (which means being concerned with Him) or with the Present—either meditating on their eternal union with, or separation from, Himself, or else obeying the present voice of conscience, bearing the present cross, receiving the present grace, giving thanks for the present pleasure.

Our business is to get them away from the eternal, and from the Present. With this in view, we sometimes tempt a human (say a widow or a scholar) to live in the Past. But this is of limited value, for they have some real knowledge of the past and it has a determinate nature and, to that extent, resembles eternity. It is far better to make them live in the Future. Biological necessity makes all their passions point in that direction already, so that thought about the Future inflames hope and fear. Also, it is unknown to them, so that in making them think about it we make them think of unrealities. In a word, the Future is, of all things, the thing least like eternity. It is the most completely temporal part of time—for the Past is frozen and no longer flows, and the Present is all lit up with eternal rays. Hence the encouragement we have given to all those schemes of thought such as Creative Evolution, Scientific Humanism, or Communism, which fix men's affections on the Future, on

1. World War II began in 1939.

2. Jesus.

the very core of temporality. Hence nearly all vices are rooted in the future. Gratitude looks to the past and love to the present; fear, avarice, lust, and ambition look ahead.[3] Do not think lust an exception. When the present pleasure arrives, the sin (which alone interests us) is already over. The pleasure is just the part of the process which we regret and would exclude if we could do so without losing the sin; it is the part contributed by the Enemy, and therefore experienced in a Present. The sin, which is our contribution, looked forward.

To be sure, the Enemy wants men to think of the Future too—just so much as is necessary for now planning the acts of justice or charity which will probably be their duty tomorrow. The duty of planning the morrow's work is today's duty; though its material is borrowed from the future, the duty, like all duties, is in the Present. This is not straw splitting. He does not want men to give the Future their hearts, to place their treasure in it. We do. His ideal is a man who, having worked all day for the good of prosperity (if that is his vocation), washes his mind of the whole subject, commits the issue to Heaven, and returns at once to the patience or gratitude demanded by the moment that is passing over him. But we want a man hag-ridden by the Future—haunted by visions of an imminent heaven or hell upon earth—ready to break the Enemy's commands in the present if by so doing we make him think he can attain the one or avert the other—dependent for his faith on the success or failure of schemes whose end he will not live to see. We want a whole race perpetually in pursuit of the rainbow's end, never honest, nor kind, nor happy now, but always using as mere fuel wherewith to heap the altar of the future every real gift which is offered them in the Present.

It follows then, in general, and other things being equal, that it is better for your patient[4] to be filled with anxiety or hope (it doesn't much matter which) about this war than for him to be living in the present. But the phrase "living in the present" is ambiguous. It may describe a process which is really just as much concerned with the Future as anxiety itself. Your man may be untroubled about the Future, not because he is concerned with the Present, but because he has persuaded himself that the Future is going to be agreeable. As long as that is the real course of his tranquility, his tranquility will do us good, because it is only piling up more disappointment, and therefore more impatience, for him when his false hopes are dashed. If, on the other hand, he is aware that horrors may be in store for him and is praying for the virtues, wherewith to meet them, and meanwhile concerning himself with the Present because there, and there alone, all duty, all grace, all knowledge, and all pleasure dwell, his state is very undesirable and should be attacked at once. Here again, our Philological Arm[5] has done good work; try the word "complacency" on him. But, of course, it is most likely that he is "living in the present" for none of these reasons but simply because his health is good and he is enjoying his work. The phenomenon would then be merely natural. All the same, I should break it up if I were you. No natural phenomenon is really in our favor. Anyway, why should the creature be happy?

Your affectionate uncle

Screwtape

3. Emotions felt by Doctor Faustus.
4. Wormword's potential victim.
5. The institution of hypocrisy. Screwtape argues that feelings of "complacency" in the Present mask an ambitious confidence in the Future.

Sir Walter Raleigh

c. 1554–1618

Born in South Devon, a region in which ports and shipyards testified to the importance of England's world trade and colonies abroad, Sir Walter Raleigh spent a considerable part of his life outside his native land. As a boy, he fought with Huguenot armies in France; at twenty-four he led an expedition to the West Indies with his half-brother, Sir Humphrey Gilbert; and two years later, he commanded a contingent of English troops in Ireland. He is reported to have been a great favorite of Elizabeth, at least until in 1592, when he secretly married one of her ladies-in-waiting, Elizabeth Throckmorton. The Queen, furious that she had had no say in the match, imprisoned Raleigh in the Tower of London for a period that summer.

Raleigh was famous for his travels. His most challenging expedition was intended to locate the legendary gold mines of El Dorado in South America. In 1595 he set out for the Spanish colony of Guiana, penetrating the interior of that land by venturing up the Orinoco. He described his trip in the brilliantly detailed *Discovery of the Large, Rich and Beautiful Empire of Guiana,* and although he returned to England without the gold he had gone for, his leadership of an expedition to sack the harbor of Cadiz in 1596 was enough to restore him to royal favor. But Raleigh was to encounter real trouble with the accession of James I. His enemies at court convinced the king that Raleigh had committed treason, and in 1603 he was tried, convicted, and once again confined to the Tower of London, this time with his wife and family. He remained there for thirteen years. His release was finally granted on the condition that he lead another expedition to Guiana. He had informed the King that on his earlier trip he had discovered an actual gold mine, and he now claimed that his new adventure would be successful. In fact, it was a disaster. Not only did he find no gold, but the mine to whose existence he had sworn was revealed to be a fabrication. On this occasion the grounds for proving treason were stronger than they had been in 1603. Raleigh was executed in 1618.

During his long imprisonment, Raleigh began to write a complete history of the world, managing only to cover events in ancient history to 168 B.C.E. Entitled *The History of the World* and published in 1614, the work is primarily remembered for the stunning reflection on death that appears on its last page: "O eloquent, just and mighty Death! Whom none could advise, thou hast persuaded; what none hath dared, thou hast done; and whom all the world hath flattered, thou only hast cast out of the world and despised; thou hast drawn together all the far stretched greatness, all the pride, cruelty, and ambition of man, and covered it all over with those two narrow words, *Hic iacet.*"

Much of Raleigh's poetry is occasional, written to address the circumstances and the moment in which he found himself. It possesses the quality Castiglione celebrated in his treatise on court life: a brilliance of self-expression that contemporary Italians termed *sprezzatura,* created by the supposedly artless use of artifice showing not the courtier's education but, rather, his native wit and talent. Raleigh exploits images of common life but with an unusual intensity, adding sensuous detail to expressions of affection and reminders of mortality to celebrations of love. His longest and greatest poem, *The 21st and Last Book of the Ocean to Cynthia,* remained fragmentary at the time of his death. Occasioned when Queen Elizabeth imprisoned him for his marriage, the poem illustrates Raleigh's fury at the Queen's inconsistent treatment of her "Ocean" or "Water," as Raleigh pronounced his first name. It ends in an equivocation: Raleigh professes his devotion to Elizabeth, instancing his good will that "knit up by faith shall ever last"; but he also concludes that despite this, they will not be reconciled: "Her love hath end; my woe must ever last."

For additional resources on Raleigh, including a selection from *Discovery of the Large, Rich and Beautiful Empire of Guiana,* go to *The Longman Anthology of British Literature* Web site at www.myliteraturekit.com.

Nature That Washed Her Hands in Milk

Nature that washed her hands in milk
And had forgot to dry them,
Instead of earth took snow and silk,[1]
At love's request to try them,
If she a mistress could compose
To please love's fancy out of those.

Her eyes he would should be of light,
A violet breath and lips of jelly,
Her hair not black nor over-bright,
And of the softest down her belly;
As for her inside he would have it
Only of wantonness and wit.

At love's entreaty, such a one
Nature made, but with her beauty
She hath framed a heart of stone,
So as love by ill destiny
Must die for her whom nature gave him
Because her darling would not save him.

But time, which nature doth despise,
And rudely gives her love the lie,
Makes hope a fool, and sorrow wise,
His hands doth neither wash nor dry,
But being made of steel and rust,
Turns snow, and silk, and milk to dust.

The light, the belly, lips, and breath
He dims, discolors, and destroys,
With those he feeds, but fills not death,
Which sometimes were the food of joys;
Yea, time doth dull each lively wit
And dries all wantonness with it.

Oh cruel time which takes in trust
Our youth, our joys, and all we have,
And pays us but with age and dust,
Who in the dark and silent grave,
When we have wandered all our ways,
Shuts up the story of our days.[2]

1. "And the Lord God formed man of the dust of the ground" (Genesis 2.7).

2. With one slight change and the addition of a final couplet, the last stanza of this poem is also Raleigh's *Epitaph*.

To the Queen[1]

Our passions are most like to floods and streams,
The shallow murmur, but the deep are dumb.
So when affections yield discourse, it seems
The bottom is but shallow whence they come.
 They that are rich in words must needs discover
 That they are poor in that which makes a lover.

Wrong not, dear empress of my heart,
 The merit of true passion,
With thinking that he feels no smart,
 That sues for no compassion.
Since, if my plaints serve not to prove
 The conquest of your beauty,
It comes not from defect of love,
 But from excess of duty.

For knowing that I sue to serve
 A saint of such perfection,
As all desire, but none deserve,
 A place in her affection;
I rather choose to want relief
 Than venture the revealing,
When glory recommends the grief,
 Despair distrusts the healing.

Thus those desires that aim too high
 For any mortal lover,
When reason cannot make them die,
 Discretion will them cover.
Yet when discretion doth bereave
 The plaints that they should utter,
Then your discretion may perceive
 That silence is a suitor.

Silence in love bewrays more woe
 Than words, though ne'er so witty,
A beggar that is dumb, you know,
 Deserveth double pity.
Then misconceive not (dearest heart)
 My true, though secret passion,
He smarteth most that hides his smart,
 And sues for no compassion.

1. This elaborate compliment is typical of the courtly expressions of devotion Elizabeth I often inspired. Its respectful complaint can be compared to the bitter regrer in Raleigh's later poem *The Shepherd of the Ocean to Cynthia*.

On the Life of Man

What is our life? A play of passion,
Our mirth the music of division,
Our mothers' wombs the tiring houses be,
Where we are dressed for this short comedy,
Heaven the judicious sharp spectator is,
That sits and marks still who doth act amiss,
Our graves that hide us from the searching sun,
Are like drawn curtains when the play is done;
Thus march we playing to our latest rest,
Only we die in earnest, that's no jest.

1612

The Author's Epitaph, Made by Himself

Even such is time, which takes in trust
Our youth, our joys, and all we have,
And pays us but with age and dust,
Who in the dark and silent grave,
When we have wandered all our days,
Shuts up the story of our days;
And from which earth, and grave, and dust,
The Lord shall raise me up, I trust.

As You Came from the Holy Land

As you came from the holy land
  Of Walsingham[1]
Met you not with my true love
  By the way as you came?[2]

How shall I know your true love
  That have met many one?
As I went to the holy land
  That have come, that have gone.

She is neither white nor brown
  But as the heavens, fair.
There is none hath a form so divine
  In the earth or the air.

Such a one did I meet good sir,
  Such an angelic face,

1. A district in the county of Norfolk and site of Walsingham Abbey, one of the great shrines of medieval England.
2. This stanza is the first in the dialogue that constitutes the poem. Its first seven stanzas alternate statements between two speakers: a lover and a traveler. Stanzas 8 and 9 are spoken by the traveler; the final two stanzas are spoken by the lover.

Who like a queen, like a nymph did appear
By her gait, by her grace.

She hath left me here all alone,
All alone as unknown,
Who sometimes did me lead with herself,
And me loved as her own.

What's the cause that she leaves you alone
And a new way doth take,
Who loved you once as her own,
And her joy did you make?

I have loved her all my youth,
But now old, as you see;
Love likes not the falling fruit
From the withered tree.

Know that love is a careless child
And forgets promise past;
He is blind, he is deaf, when he list,° *wishes*
And in faith never fast.

His desire is a dureless° content *transient*
And a trustless joy;
He is won with a world of despair
And is lost with a toy.

Of womankind such indeed is the love
Or the word love abused,
Under which many childish desires
And conceits are excused.

But love is a durable fire
In the mind ever burning;
Never sick, never old, never dead,
From itself never turning.

from The 21st and Last Book of the Ocean to Cynthia[1]

Sufficeth to you, my joys interred,
In simple words that I my woes complain;
You that then died when first my fancy erred—[2]
Joys under dust that never live again.

1. This lyric complaint, a fragment of what was projected as a much longer work, is the most important of Raleigh's poems. It tells of his despair at losing the Queen's favor and reproaches her for indifference to his devoted service. Adopting the conventions of pastoral, Raleigh styles himself "The Shepherd of the Ocean," perhaps to draw attention to his first name, which he pronounced "Water." "Cynthia" is, of course, Elizabeth, figured here (as she was so often) as the moon, ever changeful, as well as Diana, the goddess of the moon and of chastity. Characterizing Cynthia as the moving force in his life, Raleigh's verse illustrates how conventions of courtly love could acquire a political reference: both Elizabeth and her courtiers were accustomed to conveying their hopes and desires in the coded language of erotic compliment. Spenser's poem *Colin Clout's Come Home Again* (1591) notes that the subject of Raleigh's "Cynthia" is "the great unkindness" and "usage hard" of the "Lady of the Sea," who has "from her presence faultless him (i.e., the Shepherd) debarred."

2. The poet complains to his own "joys" that are now dead and buried.

If to the living were my muse addressed,
Or did my mind her own spirit still inhold,
Were not my living passion so repressed
As to the dead° the dead did these unfold, *i.e., joys*

Some sweeter words, some more becoming verse
Should witness my mishap in higher kind;
But my love's wounds, my fancy in the hearse,
The idea but resting of a wasted mind,

The blossoms fallen, the sap gone from the tree,
The broken monuments of my great desires—
From these so lost what may the affections° be? *passions*
What heat in cinders of extinguished fires?

Lost in the mud of those high-flowing streams,
Which through more fairer fields their courses bend,
Slain with self-thoughts, amazed in fearful dreams,
Woes without date, discomforts without end.

From fruitless trees I gather withered leaves,
And glean° the broken ears° with miser's hand, *harvest / of grain*
Who sometime did enjoy the weighty sheaves;
I seek fair flowers amid the brinish° sand. *salty*

All in the shade, even in the fair sun days,
Under those healthless trees I sit alone,
Where joyful birds sing neither lovely lays,
Nor Philomen° recounts her direful moan. *the nightingale*

No feeding flocks, no shepherd's company,
That might renew my dolorous conceit,° *imagination*
While happy then, while love and fantasy
Confined my thoughts on that fair flock to wait;

No pleasing streams fast to the ocean wending,
The messengers sometimes of my great woe;
But all on earth, as from the cold storms bending,
Shrink from my thoughts in high heavens or below.

Oh, hopeful love, my object and invention,
Oh, true desire, the spur of my conceit,
Oh, worthiest spirit, my mind's impulsion,° *force*
Oh, eyes transpersant,° my affection's bait, *that penetrate*

Oh princely form, my fancy's adamant,° *magnet*
Divine conceit,° my pains' acceptance, *image*
Oh, all in one! Oh, heaven on earth transparent!
The seat of joys and love's abundance!

Out of that mass of miracles, my muse
Gathered those flowers, to her pure senses pleasing;

Out of her eyes, the store of joys, did choose
Equal delights, my sorrow's counterpoising.

Her regal looks my vigorous sighs suppressed,
Small drops of joys sweetened great worlds of woes,
One gladsome day a thousand cares redressed—
Whom love defends, what fortune overthrows?

When she did well, what did there else amiss?
When she did ill, what empires would have pleased?
No other power affecting woe or bliss,
She gave, she took, she wounded, she appeased.

The honor of her love, love still devising,
Wounding my mind with contrary conceit,
Transferred itself sometime to her aspiring,
Sometime the trumpet of her thought's retreat.[3]

To seek new worlds for gold, for praise, for glory,
To try° desire, to try love severed far, *test*
When I was gone, she sent her memory,
More strong than were ten thousand ships of war,

To call me back; to leave great honor's thought;
To leave my friends, my fortune, my attempt;
To leave the purpose[4] I so long had sought,
And hold both cares and comforts in contempt.

Such heat in ice, such fire in frost remained,
Such trust in doubt, such comfort in despair,
Which, like the gentle lamb, though lately weaned,
Plays with the dug, though finds no comfort there.

But as a body, violently slain,
Retaineth warmth although the spirit be gone,
And by a power in nature moves again
Till it be laid below the fatal stone;

Or as the earth, even in cold winter days,
Left for a time by her life-giving sun,
Doth by the power remaining of his rays
Produce some green, though not as it hath done;

Or as a wheel, forced by the falling stream,
Although the course be turned some other way,
Doth for a time go round upon the beam,
Till, wanting strength to move, it stands at stay;

3. The honor of being loved by her creating love (in me), wounding me with a contrary (twofold) conception, sometimes aspiring to (please) her, sometimes heralding the withdrawal of her attention. In other words, the poet is constantly aware that his love makes him have a conflicted conception of how to approach Cynthia: sometimes he pleases her, sometimes what he does causes her disdain.

4. Raleigh's "purpose" was to find gold for England in the wilderness of the New World; he continued to hope for success in this venture until 1617, when his last voyage to Guiana ended in nothing.

So my forsaken heart, my withered mind—
Widow of all the joys it once possessed,
My hopes clean out of sight with forced wind—
To kingdoms strange, to lands far off, addressed,

Alone, forsaken, friendless, on the shore
With many wounds, with death's cold pangs embraced,
Writes in the dust, as one that could no more,
Whom love, and time, and fortune, had defaced,

Of things so great, so long, so manifold,
With means so weak, the soul even then depicting
The weal, the woe, the passages of old,
And worlds of thoughts descried° by one last sighing. *discerned*

As if, when after Phoebus° is descended, *the sun*
And leaves a light much like the past day's dawning,
And every toil and labor wholly ended,
Each living creature draweth to his resting,

We should begin by such a parting light
To write the story of all ages past,
And end the same before approaching night.

Such is again the labor of my mind,
Whose shroud, by sorrow woven now to end,
Hath seen that ever shining sun declined,
So many years that so could not descend,

But that the eyes of my mind held her beams
In every part transferred by love's swift thought,
Far off or near, in waking or in dreams,
Imagination strong in lustre brought.

Such force her angelic appearance had
To master distance, time, or cruelty,
Such art to grieve, and after to make glad,
Such fear in love, such love in majesty.

My weary lines her memory embalmed;
My darkest ways her eyes make clear as day.
What storms so great but Cynthia's beams appeased?
What rage so fierce, that love could not allay?

Twelve years entire I wasted in this war,[5]
Twelve years of my most happy younger days;
But I in them, and they now wasted are,
"Of all which past, the sorrow only stays."

* * *

Yet as the air in deep caves underground
Is strongly drawn when violent heat hath vent

5. The 12 years of service to Elizabeth began with his command of troops in Ireland in 1580 and ended, in the terms the poem supplies, with his marriage and imprisonment in 1592. Raleigh was only 36 at the time.

Great clefts therein, till moisture do abound,
And then the same, imprisioned and up-pent,° *pent up*

Breaks out in earthquakes, tearing all asunder,
So in the center of my cloven heart—
My heart, to whom her beauties were such wonder—
Lies the sharp, poisoned head of that love's dart

Which, till all break and dissolve to dust,
Thence drawn it cannot be, or therein known,
There, mixed with my heart-blood, the fretting rust
The better part hath eaten and outgrown.

But what of those or these? Or what of aught
Of that which was, or that which is, to treat?
What I possess is but the same I sought;
My love was false, my labors were deceit.

Nor less than such they are esteemed to be,
A fraud bought at the price of many woes,
A guile, whereof the profits unto me—
Could it be thought premediate° for those? *plead*

Witness those withered leaves left on the tree,
The sorrow-worn face, the pensive mind,
The external shows, what may the internal be;
Cold care hath bitten both the root and rind.

But stay, my thoughts, make end, give fortune way;
Harsh is the voice of woe and sorrow's sound;
Complaints cure not, and tears do but allay
Griefs for a time, which after more abound.

To seek for moisture in the Arabian sand
Is but a loss of labor and of rest,
The links which time did break of hearty bands

Words cannot knit, or wailings make anew,
Seek not the sun in clouds when it is set . . .
On highest mountains, where those cedars[6] grew,
Against whose banks the troubled ocean beat,

And were the marks to find thy hoped port,
Into a soil far off themselves remove.
On Sestos' shore, Leander's late resort,
Hero hath left no lamp to guide her love.[7]

Thou lookest for light in vain, and storms arise,
She sleeps thy death, that erst thy danger sighed,

6. The cedar was identified as a tree of royalty; so Raleigh can speak of the ocean beating against banks over which the cedar presides.

7. Leander and Hero were two lovers who lived on opposite shores of the Hellespont. When Leander swam at night from Abydos to visit Hero in Sestos, she hung out a lantern to guide him.

Strive then no more, bow down thy weary eyes—
Eyes which to all these woes thy heart have guided.

She is gone, she is lost, she is found, she is ever fair;
Sorrow draws weakly where love draws not too,
Woe's cries sound nothing, but only in love's ear.
Do then by dying what life cannot do.

Unfold thy flocks and leave them to the fields,
To feed on hills or dales, where likes them best,
Of what the summer or the springtime yields,
For love and time hath given thee leave to rest.

Thy heart which was their fold, now in decay
By often storms and winter's many blasts,
All torn and rent, becomes misfortune's prey,
False hope, my shepherd's staff, now age hath brast.° *broken*

My pipe, which love's own hand gave my desire
To sing her praises and my woe upon—
Despair hath often threatened to the fire,
As vain to keep now all the rest are gone.

Thus home I draw, as death's long night draws on,
Yet every foot, old thoughts turn back mine eyes;
Constraint me guides, as old age draws a stone
Against a hill, which over-weighty lies

For feeble arms or wasted strength to move.
My steps are backward, gazing on my loss,
My mind's affection and my soul's sole love,
Not mixed with fancy's chaff or fortune's dross.

To God I leave it,° who first gave it me, *my soul*
And I her gave, and she returned again,
As it was hers; so let His mercies be
Of my last comforts the essential mean.° *factor*

But be it so or not, the effects are past;
Her love hath end, my woes must ever last.

PERSPECTIVES
England, Britain, and the World

Although the Elizabethan Age is often seen as the dawn of transatlantic travel, it is clear that the horizons of English men and women were very much bounded by Europe. Most trade was with European neighbors and the mighty Ottoman empire that dominated the southern Mediterranean and included vast sections of modern Bulgaria and Hungary. Routes to the east had to be negotiated with the Ottoman imperial authorities. Although Venice—the subject of two of Shakespeare's plays, *The Merchant of Venice* and *Othello*—had declined from its heyday owing to the Turkish threat, it was still one of the most powerful ports in Europe and the main point of Western access to the Mediterranean. In contrast the Americas looked like a distant and strange land. Travel across the Atlantic often took as long as three months and the main purpose of voyages was often to commandeer Spanish treasure from their huge empire in South America rather than establish colonies (unless they served as naval bases). Some Englishmen were alarmed by their countrymen's indifference to the New World, and Richard Hakluyt's anthology, *The Principal Voyages, Traffiques and Discoveries of the English Nation* (1589, revised and expanded 1598) was designed to give the English the confidence to become a major imperial nation and so rival the Spanish. But it is worth noting that only one of Shakespeare's plays, *The Tempest* (1611), has any reference to the Americas, and, even so, it is set on an island in the Mediterranean. Shakespeare's imagination remained firmly rooted in Britain and Europe.

The English were unsure of their place within the British Isles. Wales had been absorbed in the early sixteenth century by Henry VIII but remained an alien land with its own traditions, customs and, most importantly, language. Ireland had been conquered by the Normans in the twelfth century and held as a lordship, but was made a separate kingdom ruled by the English king when Henry VIII declared himself its monarch in 1534. Yet, as many commentators have pointed out, it was as much a colony, inhabited by hostile and alien people, as a sovereign territory. Scotland was a separate kingdom, often regarded with considerable fear and hostility by the English, its people, like the Welsh and Irish, eager to discomfort their more powerful neighbors at every opportunity. England and Scotland were united when James VI of Scotland became king in 1603, but this was a Scottish takeover, not the English conquest that many had predicted. James brought with him a large entourage of his fellow countrymen, who occupied important positions in his household, and were bitterly resented by many important Londoners. It tells us a great deal about the politics of the British Isles that, while James styled himself "King of Britain," the English parliament refused to ratify his plan to unite the kingdoms. Moreover, as events throughout the sixteenth and seventeenth centuries were to demonstrate with frequent regularity, England itself was hardly a united realm. The north was predominately Catholic with its great lords looking to challenge the power and authority of the crown, as were many parts of the East; the southwest and Cornwall in particular, were hard to access and fiercely independent. Cornwall had its own language, and the Prayer book had to be translated into Cornish because so few people understood English. Given the hostility of Catholic Europe, led by Spain, and the problematic relationship with France, it is easy to see why England often felt surrounded and beleaguered.

This section tries to provide a snapshot of the world as it appeared to English men and women in the sixteenth and seventeenth centuries. There were indeed important accounts of the discovery of the Americas that were widely available. But these were mainly stories of Spanish conquests and hardships until the publication of Thomas Hariot's important *A Brief and True Report of the Newfound Land of Virginia*, first published in a small quarto in 1588 but then reproduced as a grand folio with superb illustrations based on John White's drawings in 1590, the first part of Theodor De Bry's series of works recounting the discovery of America for a Protestant audience. Hariot's text, designed to encourage settlers to join the fledgling colonies in Virginia, represented the natives of the New World as civilized and law-abiding, a pointed contrast to some of the savages who lived nearer to home. Edmund Spenser's *A View of the Present State of Ireland* (c.1596) gives us a sense of how threatening the English felt the native Irish to be, comparing them with the most ferocious savages known to man. Spenser shows that the native Irish are descended from the Scythians, an ancient and powerful people who lived by the Black Sea alongside the ancient Greeks. The Scythians were known for their ferocity and warlike nature but they could be civilized. Spenser, in describing the Irish use of the mantle, claims that Irish customs and practices are the problem in Ireland, suggesting that if they are removed the Irish can be anglicized and civilized. Such passages help us to understand that their near neighbors were seen in mainly negative ways, but that we should be careful of assuming that such stereotypes can always be read in a straightforward manner or that they are simply the product of prejudice.

Also included here are passages describing the Ottoman Empire and Italy, as well as John Smith's famous account of Pocahontas. The early seventeenth century saw the first substantial publications of travelers' accounts of their journeys, with Fynes Moryson (1566–1630) producing the longest work. Moryson is not always an acute judge and sees the world through his own prejudices, but he gives us an important picture of how English people saw themselves and others in the early seventeenth century. Italy, as Moryson's comments indicate, was seen with a mixture of envy and fear, being, on the one hand, much more sophisticated and cultured than England, and, on the other, a Catholic country known for its vicious politics and unstable nature. The Ottoman empire was similarly feared and admired, but for different reasons, being a powerful military machine that threatened to overwhelm its Christian opponents.

Fynes Moryson

1566–1630

Fynes Moryson has a good claim to have been the first professional travel writer. His account of his travels is the most comprehensive by an early modern English writer. He was educated at Peterhouse College Cambridge, and became a fellow there. At the age of twenty-three he persuaded the college to let him travel at its expense and, after studying law at Oxford, he left for Germany on 1 May 1591. Moryson spent the next four years traveling through Germany, the Low Countries, Denmark, Poland, and Austria, before returning to London on 13 May 1595. He then wished to venture further afield, having a particular desire to see "Jerusalem, the fountain of Religion, and Constantinople, of old the seat of Christian Emperors, and now the seat of the Turkish Ottoman." Together with his brother, Henry, he set out from London on 29 November 1595. He traveled overland to Venice before sailing to Joppa and proceeding to Jerusalem. They then traveled to Tripoli, Aleppo, and Antioch where Henry Moryson died of dysentery. Fynes, having recovered from the illness, returned to London via Crete, Constantinople, and Venice, arriving on 10 July 1597.

In 1599 Moryson was employed as secretary to Charles Blount, Lord Mountjoy, the Lord Deputy of Ireland, remaining in his service until 1606. He spent much of the rest of his life trying to find a publisher for the increasingly voluminous account of his travels, eventually persuading John Beale of Aldersgate Street, to produce three huge volumes entitled *An Itinerary* (1617). A fourth volume was licensed in 1626, but remained in manuscript until sections of it were published in the twentieth century. Moryson was clearly frustrated by these problems and vowed that he would give up writing in order to concentrate on theology. Little is known of the last years of his life. He died in 1630.

The extracts here give some sense of Moryson's fascination with and contempt for Italy. While he is attracted by the glamour of its riches, architectural beauties, and images—which, as a Protestant, he is duty bound to be suspicious of—he is horrified by the superstitiousness he encounters. Other passages reveal his traveler's taste for anecdotes.

Moryson represents the Ottoman Empire as an absolute tyranny. Preferment is achieved through favoritism and corruption. People are overtaxed and Christians are treated especially badly. Inheritance laws demand that the emperor takes a large slice of the property of the deceased, so people tend to bury and hide their wealth. The Turks are brave and tough but intensely cruel. They are taught that death in defense of one's country is admirable. They are also idle and addicted to sexual pleasure, particularly sodomy.

In some ways Moryson clearly admires the Ottoman Empire and its military prowess in the same way that commentators admired the martial culture of the Spartan, while tempering their respect with fear. He is as much in awe of their wealth and success as he is in many Italian cities. Overall, however, the Turks pose as much a threat to European Christianity as they represent respected trading partners. The extracts here represent Moryson's cultural analysis of the Ottoman Empire—sections which were not printed until the twentieth century—and his impressions of Constantinople.

from An Itinerary Containing His Ten Year Travel through the Twelve Dominions of Germany, Bohmerland, Switzerland, Netherland, Denmark, Poland, Italy, Turkey, France, England, Scotland & Ireland (1617)

Observations of Italy

Now we were to cross the breadth of Italy, from the Adriatic to the Tyrrhenian Sea. The first day in the Morning, we rode fifteen miles to a little City, called Madonna di Loreto, through fruitful Mountains, and passing a high Promontory. By the way was an Alter, with this inscription in Latin; O passenger, go on merrily, &c. Gregory the thirteenth hath well paved the rest of the way. The like inscription is in the ascent of the Mountain, upon which the little City Loreto stands: for this way (in a fruitful Country of corn, and a dirty soil) was paved at the charge of the said Pope.

A certain chamber hath given beginning to this City and the Church thereof, then which nothing is esteemed more holy among the Papists; and because many gifts of great price use to be given by vow to our Lady of this Church, the City is well fortified against Pirates, who did once spoil the same, and were like again to be invited by the hope of rich spoils to the like attempts, if the Towne lay unfortified. It is of little circuit, and lies in length from East to the West, so narrow; as it hath almost but one street in the breadth, and all the houses of this street are Innes, or Shops of them that sell Beads to number prayers. On the East side, after a steep descent of a Mountain, lies a valley of two miles, and beyond that the sea. On the North side, towards Ancona, though the sea be very far distant, yet from this City, seated upon a high Mountain, it may easily be seen. Upon the doors of this Church, famous for men's superstitious/worship, these verses are written:

Illotus timeat quincunque intrara, Sacellum,
In terries nullum sanctius orbis habet.

Enter not here unwashed of any spot,
For a more holy Church the world hath not.

At the Church door is a statue of brass erected to Pope Gregory the thirteenth. As I walked about the Church, behold in a dark Chappell a Priest, by his Exorcisms casting a devil out of a poor woman: Good Lord what fencing and truly conjuring words he used!

How much more skilful was he in the devils names? Then any ambitious Roman ever was in the names of his Citizens, whom he courted for their voices. If he had eaten a bushel of salt in hell; if he had been an inhabitant thereof, surely this Art could never have been more familiar to him. He often spoke to the ignorant woman in the Latin tongue, but nothing less then in Tullie's[1] phrase, and at last the poor wretch, either hired to deceive the people, or (if that be more probable) drawn by familiar practice with the Priest, or at least affrighted with his strange language and cries, confessed her self dispossessed by his exorcism. In the body of the Church, a Table of written hand, in the Greek, Latin, and many other tongues, was fastened to a Pillar, setting down at large the wonderful history of the Chamber in midst of the Church, which I confess was less curiously observed by me, abhorring from that superstition, & hastening from thence as much as I might; yet give me leave to set down the sum thereof out of the itinerary of Villamont a French Gentleman. This Chamber or Chappell (said he) is the very house, in which the Queen Virgin of Nazareth was borne, brought up, and saluted by the Angell, foretelling her of Christ's birth, and in which Christ was conceived, and in which the Virgin dwelt after Christ's ascension, accompanied with the holy Apostles, especially with Saint John by Christ's command, which the Apostles after the Virgins death, for the great mysteries done here, turned into a Chappell, consecrated to the sacrificing of Christ, and dedicated the same, and with their own hands, made the great Crosse of wood, now set in the window of the Chappell, and in which Saint Luke made with his hand the picture and Image now set above it. Let me add: This Chappell from a House became a Chamber, and of a Chamber was made a Chappell, and it is built of brick, and is thirty feet long, twelve and a half broad. In the chimney (as Villemont said) as yet remain the holy ashes, which no man dare take away, and the Alter also, upon which the Masse is sung, was made by the Apostles hand. There is a room into which you first enter, which is divided from the Chapel by an iron grate, for no man enters the chapel without leave, but must say his prayers in the outer room; yet leave is given to any that ask it. Villamont added, that he found by diligent search, that this Chapel was much reverenced in the primitive Church: but the holy land being subdued by Saracens, then by Turks; he said it happened in the year 1291, that this house was taken up from the foundations, by Angels, who in the night miraculously carried it to the Sea shore of Slavonia, where it was made known to the people by the shining of the Virgin's Image, and then by a vision of a religious man. The Virgin her self made known the History to him. He added the Virgins Oration wherein she gives her self many titles, which in later ages were first invented, and she doth so extol her own praises with her own mouth, as he that reads the old song of the blessed Virgin, would cry out with the Latin Poet, only changing the name. O how is she changed from the Virgin, which so modestly spoke of her self.

Villamont added, that messengers were sent into Palestine, who found this History to be most true: yet this Chappell did not long abide in Slavonia, but the Angels in the year 1294 took it up again, and transported it to this Sea coast of Italy, where again it was made known by the shining of the Image was called Madonna at Loreto, that is, our Lady of Loreto. And because thieves lying in the wood, did spoil strangers, who took it up, and set it down in a private possession of two brothers, who disagreeing in the division of the profit rising by the concourse of people, the Angels the fourth time took it up, and placed it in this firm seat, where now it remained. After it was often visited by strangers, Pope Paul the second built an other stately Church over it, Pope Leo the tenth having first fortified the little City against Pirates. Let me add, that Pope Sixtus the fifth, borne in this Marca of Ancona, established a Bishop in this Towne, and so

1. Marcus Tullius Cicero (106–43 B.C.E.), Roman orator and statesman. One of the models of Renaissance prose style.

made it a City. Villamont relating the treasure of this Church, among the rest, named certain Maps of Cities, and Mountains, and the Images of the twelve Apostles, a great Crucifix, Candlesticks, and infinite Vessels of silver, Images, Chalices, Crosses of gold, and many precious stones of huge value, two Crosses made all of precious stones (whereof one was given by the Arch-Duke of Austria), and a Harte of gold set with precious stones (the gift of the Duchesse of Loraine) and a vessel of huge value. * * *

The second day we began the view of Rome with the Popes Palace, seated in the part of the City, called Il Borgo; which Palace Pope Nicholas the third built, and Nicholas the fifth compassed with walls, and the Palace is of great circuit, and the stairs are so easy, that Horses and Mules may go up to the top of the Mountain, and with easy ascent and descent bear the Popes carriage.[2] At the entrance there be galleries one above the other, whereof the two first were built by Leo the tenth, and Paul the third, and the third and highest by Sixtus Quintus, and they are all fairly painted and gilded. Upon these lie two large chambers, and beyond them is a vast and long gallery of four hundred seventy and one walking paces, in the middle whereof is the famous Library of the Popes. In Vatican; and therein are many inscriptions of the Pope Sixtus Quintus who repaired it, and it is adorned with many faire pictures gilded all over. I did see the several rooms thereof. The first one hundred forty and seven walking paces long, had three rows of Cupboards filled with books: the second was thirty nine paces long; and the third containing the books of greatest price locked up, was twenty paces long. Pope Sixtus the fourth built this Library, with the Chappell of the Palace, and the Conclave. The wall of the Chappell shined like a glass with precious stones: where the Pope Sixtus Quintus commanded Michael Angelo to paint the day of Judgment, and the common report is, that this Pope promised this famous Painter thereupon made the picture of the Pope and the Cardinals in hell amongst the Devils, so lively as every man might known them. Between this Chappell and the Conclave, (where they choose the Popes) lies a Kingly Gallery, not unworthily called vulgarly Sala Regia, (which others call Sala del Conclave). The wall of this Gallery in like sort shined with precious stones, and the pavement is of precious marble, the arched roof all gilded, and at the upper end I wondered to see the Massacre of Paris painted upon the wall, with the Popes inscription greatly commending that detestable cruelty.[3] At the same upper end the foresaid Chappell (as you come up) lies on the left hand, and the Conclave on the right hand; in which Conclave the Cardinals meet to choose the Pope, divided into several rooms, but meeting at a common table, and when they have chosen him, they lead him into a Chappell at the lower end, and near the door of the said Kingly Gallery, and place him there upon a hollow seat of Marble. I know not whether this be the chair, in which the sex or the Pope is tried, but I am sure it is hollow, with a hold in the bottom. After they put a Banner out of a high window, and there make known to the people the name that the Pope hath chosen, and then his arms are hung up round about. This Chappell at the lower end of the said Gallery, hath the name of Pope Paul the third, of the Family of Farnese, and it is little, and of a round form (as I remember), but it is beautiful beyond imagination. The images of the Apostles seem to be of silver, and Paradise painted upon the arched roof, with Angels flying, being the work of Michael Angelo, seemed to me admirable. Upon the other side of the said Library is the private Gallery of the Pope, looking into the Garden (3) Belvedere, which is seated upon the side of the Mountain

2. Moryson's visit would seem to indicate that the papal buildings were more accessible and less obviously threatening and paranoid fortresses than many contemporary English accounts would indicate.

3. Protestants regarded the Massacre of Saint Bartholomew's Day, August 23, 1572, when the Catholic Guise faction in Paris killed 50,000 Protestant Huguenots, as one of the most significant dates of European history. The evil genius behind the massacre was said to be Catherine de'Medici who was, of course, Italian. She was congratulated by Pope Gregory XIII.

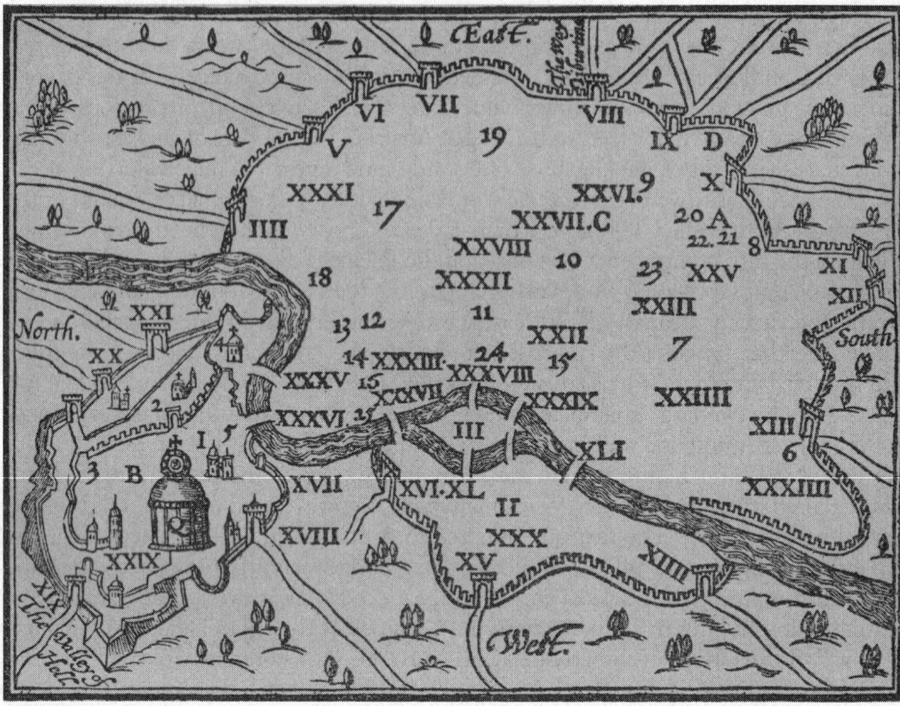

Fynes Moryson's representation of Rome, labeling all the places he visited in the text (1617).

Vatican, where Pope Innocent the eight built part of the Palace, and called it Belvedere, of the faire prospect of all Rome subject to the eye. And Pope Julius the second placed in this Garden many very faire statues, namely, of the River Nile, of the River Tiber, of Romulus and Remus playing with the papps[4] of a shee-Wolfe, all being placed in the open Garden, and a most faire statua of Apollo, another admirable statua of Lycaon with his children, another of the boy Antoninus, whom the Emperor Adrian loved, another of Hercules another of Cupid, another of Venus, another of Cleopatra sleeping with her arm over her face, and bearing a Serpent, being a wonderful faire statua. And these are all locked up, and not to be seen without favor.

Hence we went to the Castle (4) of Saint Angelo of old called Moles Adiani, for it was the Sepulcher of the Emperor Adrian, upon the top whereof was the Pine apple of brass, which before I said was since placed in the open Court-yard of Saint Peters Church. This Sepulcher of Adrian called Moles (B) was demolished by Belisarius, in the war of the Goths, upon the ruins whereof Pope Boniface the eight built this Castle, and Pope Alexander the sixth compassed it with walls and ditches, and placed therein a guard of Soldiers, and built from this Castle to the Popes Palace an open and a close gallery, by which upon any tumult, the Pope may pass safely from his Palace to the Castle. And after Pope Paul the third built very faire chambers in this Castle. On the outside is the statua of Pope Pius the fourth, and within is the statua of Paul the third, upon which these verses are written of the Emperor Charles the fifth coming to Rome.

E Lvbia venit Romanas victor ad arces
Caesar, & in niveis aureus ivit Equis.

4. Breasts.

Ille triumphavit, sed tu plus Paule triumphas,
Victor namque tuis oscula dat pedibus.

With victory to Rome from Africa came
Caesar, on milk white Horses, golden all.
He Triumph'd, Paul thy triumph hath more fame,
This Conqueror to kiss thy feet did fall.

In this Castle they show the head of Adrian, the statua of Saint Peter, a bunch of Grapes of brass, the place where the Cardinal Caietan escaped out of prison, and a Trap-door where prisoners are let down into a dungeon. The chambers are built in a circle round about the great chamber in the middle, which is called Sala regia, and without is a round Garden within the walls, and upon the top of the Castle, in the place of the said Pine-apple, is the statua of the Angell Michael, of which the Castle hath the name. The meadows of Quintis Cincinates lie near this Castle.

Upon the walls of the Church S. Croce, is a monument of Arno, overflowing, with this inscription in the Italian tongue: In the year 1333. The water of Arno overflowed to this height, and in the year 1557 to this, yet higher. In this Church is the sepulcher of Michaele Angleo Bonoritio, a most famous Engraver, Painter, and Builder, whose bones were brought from Rome, at the instance of Duke Cosmo, in the year 1570 and laid here. It is most certain that he was most skilful in those Arts, and of him the Italians greatly boast, and with all tell much of his fantastic humors: namely, that when he painted the Popes Chappell, (whereof I spoke in describing that Popes Palace) that he first obtained the Popes promise, that no man should come in, ill the work were finished; and understanding that the Pope had broken this promise, coming in himself with some Cardinals at the back door of the vestry, that he being then to paint the last Judgment, did so lively figure the Pope and the Cardinal (that tempted him) amongst the Devils, as every man might easily know them. But that is abominable, which the Romans of the better sort seriously tell of him, that he being to paint a crucifix for the Pope, when he came to expresses the lively actions of the passion, hired a Porter to be fastened upon a Crosse, and at that very time stabbed him with a penknife, and while he was dying, made a rare piece of work for the Art, but infamous for the murder: and that hereupon he was banished Rome, and went to the Court of the Duke of Urbino, where he was entertained with much honor. And they report also that when he was recalled to Rome with pardon of that fault, the Duchess of Urbino being bold upon her former acquaintance, should entreat him at his leisure to paint all the Saints for her: and that he to show that so great a task should not be imposed upon a workman of his sort, should satisfy this request, or rather put it off with a rude & uncivil jest, sending her the picture of a mans privy part, most artificially painted, and praying her to take in good part the Father of all the Saints, till he could at leisure send their pictures.

from Observations of the Ottoman Empire

The Turkish State

The Turkish Empire in our time is more vast and ample then ever it was formerly containing most large provinces. In Africa it begins from the straight of Gibraltar and so contains Mauritania, Barbaria, Egypt, and all the Coasts of the Mediterranean sea. The chief City of Egypt Al-Cairo hath rich traffic, and yields exceeding great Revenues to the Emperor though no doubt much less since the Portugal's sailing by the South coast of Africa and planting themselves in the East, brought all the Commodities thereof into Portugal, from thence distributing them through Europe, which voyage in our days, is yearly made by the English and Flemings. From Egypt it contains in Asia the three Provinces of Arabia, all Palestine, Syria, Mesopotamia, the many and large Provinces of Natolia or Asia the lesser, and both the Provinces of Armenia to the very confines of Persia (in these times much more straightened than in former ages) herein the famous City of Aleppo,[1] whether all the precious wares of the East are brought by great Rivers and upon the backs of Camels, yields huge Revenues to the Emperor. In Europe it contains all Greece and the innumerable Islands of the Mediterranean sea, some few excepted (as Malta fortified by an order of Christian knights, Sicily and Sardinia subject to the king of Spain, and Corsica subject to the City of Genoa, and the two Islands of Cephalonia, that of Corfu, of Zante and of Candia with some few other small Islands, subject to the Venetians). Also it contains Thracia, Bulgaria, Walachia, almost all Hungary, Albania, Slavonia, part of Dalmatia and other large Provinces to the Confines of the Germane Emperor, and king of Poland.

The form of the Ottoman Empire is merely absolute, and in the highest degree Tyrannical using all his Subjects as borne-slaves.

No man hath any free Inheritance from his father, but mangled if any at all, since all unmovable goods belong to the Emperor, and for moveable goods, they either have little, or dare not freely use them in life, or otherwise dispose them at death then by a secret guift,[2] as I shall show in his place. Yea the Children of the very Bashawes and chief Subjects, though equal to their fathers in military virtues (since there is no way to avoid contempt or live in estimation but the profession of Arms), yet seldom rise to any place of government. For this Tyrant indeed uses to prefer no borne Turk to any high place, but they who sit at the Sterne of the Sate, or have any great Command either in the Army, or in Civil government are for the most part Christians of ripe years, either taken Captives or voluntarily subjecting themselves, and so leaving the profession of Christianity to become Mohammedans, or else they be the Tributary Children of Christian Subjects gathered every fifth year oftener if occasion requires, and carried far from their parents while they are young to be brought up in the Turkish religion and military exercises; So as when they come to age, they neither know their Country nor parents; nor kinsmen so much as by name. * * *

All that live under this Tyrant, are used like sponges to be squeezed when they are full. All the Turks, yea the basest sort, spoil and make a pray of the Franks (so they call Christians that are strangers, upon the old league they have with the French) and in like sort they spoil Christian Subjects. The soldiers and officers seeking all occasions of oppression, spoil the Common Turks, and all Christians. The Governors and greatest Commanders make a pray of the very soldiers, and of the Common Turks, and all Christians, and the superiors among them use like extortion upon the Inferiors, and when these great men are grown rich, the Emperor strangles them to have their treasure. So as the Turks hide their riches and many times bury them under ground, and because nothing is so dangerous as to be reputed rich, they dare neither fare well, not build faire houses, nor have any rich household stuff. The Emperor seldom speaks or writes to any, no not to his chief Viziers but by the name of slaves, and so miserable is their servitude, so base their obedience, as if

1. Aleppo, in Syria.

2. I.e., trick.

he send a poor Chiaass or messenger to take the head of the greatest Subject, he though riding in the head of his troops, yet presently submits himself to the execution. Neither indeed hath he any hope in resistance, since his equals are his enemies in hope to rise by his fall, his fellow soldiers forsake him as inured to absolute obedience, and he not knowing his parents, kinsmen or any friends, is left alone to stand or fall by himself. * * *

This Tyrant seldom speaks to any of his subjects, but will be understood by his looks, having many dumb men about his person, who will speak by signs among themselves as fast as we do by words, and these men together with some boys prostituted to his lust, and some of his dearest Concubines, are only admitted to be continually near his person. The chief Vizier only receives his Commandments and his mouth gives law to all under him, being of incredible power and authority by reason of this pride and retirednes of the Tyrant were not this high estate of his very slippery, and subject to sudden destruction. They, who are admitted to the Tyrants presence, must not look him in the face, and having kissed the hem of his garment, when they rise from adoring him, must return with their eyes cast on the ground, and their faces towards him, not turning their backs till they be out of his sight.

Warfare in General

Certain positions of religion and the due conferring of rewards and punishments make the Turks bold adventure their persons and carefully perform all duties in War. By blind religion they are taught, that they mount to heaven without any impediment, who dye fighting for their Country and the Law of Mahomet. And that a Stoical Fate or destiny governs all humane affaires, so as if the time of death be not come, a man is no less safe in the Camp then in a Castle, if it be come, he can be preserved in neither of them, and this makes them like beasts to rush upon all dangers even without Arms to defend or offend, and to fill the ditches with their dead Carcasses, thinking to overcome by number alone, without military art. Again all rewards as the highest dignities and the like given continually by the Emperor to the most valiant and best deserving, make them apt to dare any thing. And in like sort severe punishments never failing to be inflicted on all offenders, more specially on such as brawl and fight among themselves, who are punished according to the quality of the offence, sometimes with death, and also such as break martial discipline, sometimes punishing him with death that pulls but a bunch of grapes in a Vineyard. I say these punishments never failing to be inflicted upon offenders, make the soldiers formerly encouraged by rewards no less to fear base Cowardice, brawling, fighting or any breach of discipline, and keep them in awe, as they keep all other Subjects and enemies under fear of their sword hanging over them. And the form of this State being absolute tyranny, since all things must be kept by the same means they are gotten, the State gotten and maintained by the sword, must needs give exorbitant Privileges or rather means of oppression to all the Soldiers who (as I formerly have showed) are not themselves free from the yoke of the same Tyranny which they exercise over others, while the superiors oppressing their inferiors are themselves grinded to dust by greater men, and the greatest of all hold life and goods at the Emperors pleasure, upon an hours warning, among whom happy are the lean, for the fat are still drawn to the shambles. The poorest man may aspire to the highest dignities, if his mind and fortune will serve him, but upon those high pinnacles, there is no firm abiding, and the same Virtue and Starr, that made him rise, cannot preserve him long from falling. The great men most ravenously gape for treasure, and by rapine get abundance, but when they have it, all that cannot be made portable, must be hidden or buried, for to build a fairer house, to have a rich household stuff, or to keep a good table, doth but make the Puttock[3] a prey to the Eagle. * * *

JUDGMENTS CORPORAL AND CAPITAL

Touching their Corporal and Capital Judgments. For small offences they are beaten with Cudgels on the soles of the feet, the bellies and backs, the strokes being many and painful according to the offence, or the anger of him that inflicts them. Myself did see some hanging and rotting in Chains upon the Gallows.

Also I did see one that had been impaled (vulgarly Casuckde) an horrible kind of death. The malefactor carries the wooden stake upon which he is to dye, being eight foot long and sharp towards one end, and when he comes into the place of execution, he is stripped into his shirt, and laid upon the ground with his face downward, then the sharp end of the stake is thrust into his fundament, and beaten with beetles up into his body, till it come out, at or about his Waist, then the blunt end is fastened in the ground, and so he sets at little ease, till he dye, which may be soon if the stake be driven with favor, otherwise, he may languish two or three days in pain and hunger; if torment will permit him in that time to feel hunger, for no man dares give him meat.

They have an other terrible kind of death vulgarly called Gaucher. The malefactor hath a rope or Chain fastened about his body, whereof the other end is made fast to the top of a Tower or of a Gibbet made high of purpose, and so this rope or chain being of fit length, his body is cast down to pitch upon a hook of Iron, where he hangs till he dyes, with horror of the height of pain, and of hunger. For howsoever, he may dye presently if any vital part pitch upon the hook, yet hanging by the shoulder or thigh he may live long. And if any men give these executed men, meat, or help to prolong their miserable life, he shall dye the same death; Mores and Christians and they that are not of the Army, are often putt to this death, yea the Beglerbegs sometimes putt Governors to this death for extortions or Cruelties committed by them, or rather to get their wealth. They have an other terrible kind of death Bragadino a Venetian Governor of Famagusta in Cyprus, after he had yielded the City upon Composition for life to him and his soldiers.

A Turk forsaking his faith and a Christian doing or speaking any thing against the law of Mahomet are burned with fire. Traitors or those whom the Emperor so calls, are tortured under the nails and with diverse torments, but the great men of the Army are only strangled.

A murderer is putt to some of the former cruel deaths. A thief is hanged and I have read of a soldier that had stolen milk, and after was strangled. The Adulterer is imprisoned for some Months, and after redeemed with money, but the Adulteress is set naked upon an Ass with the bowels of an ox about her neck, and so she is whipped about the streets having stones and dirt cast at her. If a Christian man commit fornication with a Turkish woman both are putt to death, and this Common danger to both, makes them more wary of others, and more confident to trust one an other, but the sin is Common, and at Constantinople the houses of Ambassadors, will not stick to play the bawds for a small reward. In case of this offence nothing frees a Christian from death, but his turning Mahomet an. Yet I remember that I saw a Tower at Tripoli

3. A buzzard or kite, which are largely scavengers; in falconry terms, an ignoble bird, despite its size.

called the tower of Love, built by a rich Christian to redeem his life being condemned for this Crime. But if a Turk lye with a Christian woman, he is not putt to death, but sett upon an Ass with his face towards the tail, which he holds in his hand, and hath the bowels of an ox cast about his neck, and so is led through the streets in scorn. If a Christian lye with a Christian woman, the fault is punished with paying of money. All harlots write their names in the book of the Cady or the Sobbassa, and not only the Turks but even the Janissaries are permitted to have acquaintance with them so it be not in the two lents, wherein they yearly fast, For in that Case, while I was in Turkey many women were sewed in sacks, and drowned in the Sea at Constantinople. Generally for greater Crimes, the Judge of the Turks devise and impose a death with greater torment especially for reproaching their law of Prophet, which a Christian cannot redeem, but by turning Turk.

Of Degrees in the Common Wealth and Family

* * * For the private Family each man may have as many Wives as he is able to feed so he take a letter of permission from the Cady, and some of them keep their wives in diverse Cities to avoid the strife of women; yet if they live both in one house with him, they seldom disagree, being not preferred one above another. The Turks use not to take a dowry but as they buy captive women, (whom they may sell again or keep for Concubines of for any other service); so they also buy Free women to be their wives, so as the father is enriched by having many and fair Daughters. Divorce is permitted for perverse manners, for barrenness or like faults allowed by the Cady. As they buy Captive Women, so may they buy any other for Concubines so they write their names in the book of the Cady. For as Christians are married by Priests in the Church; so Turks are married by taking a letter, or bill from the Cady (who is their spiritual Judge) and writing the marriage in his book at his private house. But at the day of marriage, they also use to bathe, and to pray in their Mosques.

Lastly it is no disgrace to be borne of a Captive Woman, or out of marriage, for that is the Condition, of the very Emperors, Whose mothers are Captives, and before the birth of their first son, never have a letter of dowry to make them free women and wives, which after they have a son was of old wont to be granted them, but the Emperors of late times seldom give that letter to them, for jealousy lest they should practice their deaths to have power in the reign of their succeeding son * * *

Having cast anchor (as I said) in the Port of Constantinople, behold, as soon as day began to break, many companies of Turks rushing into our Bark, who like so many starved flies fell to suck the sweet Wines, each rascal among them beating with cudgels and ropes the best of our Mariners, if he durst but repine against it, till within short space the Candian Merchant having advertised the Venetian Ambassador of their arrival, he sent a Janissary to protect the Bark, and the goods; and as soon as he came, it seemed to me no less strange, that this one man should beat all those Turks, and drive them out of the Bark like so many dogs, the common Turks daring no more resist them. And the Sergeant of the Magistrate having taken some of our Greek Mariners (though subject to the State of Venice) to work for their Ottoman in gathering stones, and like base employments, this Janissary caused them presently to be released, and to be sent again into their Bark, such is the tyranny of the Turks against all Christians as well their subjects as others, so as no man sailed into these parts, but under the Banner of England, France, or Venice, who being in league with the great Turk, have their Ambassadors in this City, and their Consuls in other Havens, to protect those that come under their Banner, in this sort sending them a Janissary to keep them from wrongs, so soon as they are advertised of their arrival. * * *

The Description of the City of Constantinople, and the Adjacent Territories and Seas

The great lines or walls show the form of the City, and the single small lines describe the Territory adjoining.

(A) In this Tower they hang out a light of pitch and like burning matter, to direct the Sailors by night, coming to the City, or sailing along the coast out of the Sea Euxinus (which they say is called the Black Sea of many shipwrecks therein happening.) And this Tower is sixteen miles distant from the City.

(B) Here is a marble pillar erected upon a Rock compassed with the sea, which they call the pillar of Pompey, and therein many passengers (for their memory) use to engrave their names. And here are innumerable flocks of Sea foul and of many kinds, wherewith he that is skilful to shoot in his Peace, may abundantly furnish himself.

(C) Here is the Euxine or black Sea.

(D E) Here lie two strong Castles, one in Europe, the other in Asia, some eight miles distant from the City, built to defend the Haven from the assault of the enemies by Sea on that side, and the Garrison there kept, searched the ships coming from the City, that no slaves or prohibited goods be carried therein, neither can any ship pass unsearched, except they will hazard to be sunk. Finally, the great Turk sends his chief prisoners to be kept in these strong Castles.

(F) Here great ships use to cast anchor at their first arrival, till they bee unloaded, and here again they ride at anchor to expect winds, when they are loaded and ready to depart.

(G) All along this bank and the opposite side for a large circuit, the greatest ships use to lie when they are unloaded, and they lie most safely and close by the shore, fastened by cables on land.

(H) Here lies the old City built by the Genoese of Italy, called Gallata by the Turks, and Perah by the Greeks (of the situation beyond the Chanel.) It is now accounted a Suburb of Constantinople, and is seated upon a most pleasant hill, wherein for the most part live Christians, as well subjects as others, and the Ambassadors of England, France, and Venice, only the Emperors Ambassadors of England were wont to dwell upon the Sea-shore in the Plain, and their Palace is not far distant from this (K); but Master Edward Barton the English Ambassador at this time dwelt upon the top of the hill, in a faire house within a large field, and pleasant gardens compassed with a wall. And all Gallata is full of very pleasant gardens, and compassed with pleasant fields, whereof some towards the land furthest from the Sea, are used for the burial of Turks.

(I) Here is a little Creek of the Sea is compassed with walls and buildings, within which the Galleys, and store-houses for all things thereunto belonging.

(K) Here is the chief passage over the water called Tapano, where a man may pass for two aspers. All along this Sea bank lye very many great Guns (as upon the Tower Wharf at London), and here the fishers land, and sell their fish.

(L) Here the Megarenses of old built Chalcedon, a City of Bethinia, famous for Council held there, by the ruin of which City, Constantinople increased. At this day there is only a Village, or rather some scattered houses, and it is commonly called Scuteri, or Scudretta.

(M) Here the Great Turks mother then living, had her private Garden.

(N) Hither the Heir of the Empire is sent, as it were into banishment, under pretence to govern the Province Bursia, as soon as he is circumcised, and so being made a Muslim (that is, a circumcised Turk) first begins to draw the eyes of the Army and Janissaries towards him.

(O) Here is the Palace or Court of the great Turk, called by the Italians Seraglio, and vulgarly Saray, and it was of old the Monastery of Saint Sophia. Mahomet the second first compassed it with walls, and the buildings together with the large and pleasant gardens are some three or four miles in circuit. I entered the outward Court thereof by a stately Gate kept by many Janissaries called Capigi of that office. The court yard was large, all compassed with building of free stone two stories high, with a low and almost plain roof tiled, and without windows, after the manner of the building of Italy, and round about the inside, it was cast out with arches like the building of Cloisters, under which they walked dry in the greatest rain. And in this Court is a large pulpit or open room, where the great Turk useth to show himself to the Janissaries to satisfy them when they make any mutiny.

(P) Here is a banqueting house, vulgarly called Chuske, the prospect whereof is more pleasant then can be expressed, beholding four Sears at once, and the land on all sides beyond them.

Fynes Moryson's representation of Constantinople, labeling all the places he visited in the text (1617).

(Q) Here is the Church of Saint Sophia, opposite to the Court Gate, of old built by the Christians after the form of Solomon's Temple, and endowed with the annual rent of three hundred thousand Zechines, now made a Mosque or Mahomet an Church. And howsoever the Turks cannot endure that unwashed Christians (so called by them, because they use not Baths so continually as they doe) should enter their Mosques, or pass over their Sepulchers, yet my self entered this Church with the Janissary my guide, trusting to his power to defend me, yet he willed me first to put of my shoes, and according to the Turks custom to leave them in the porch, where they were safe till we returned. The Church is of a round form, and built of brick, and supported with faire pillars, and paved with Marble (over which the Turks laid Mats to kneel, and prostrate themselves more commodiously upon them.) The roof is beautified with pictures of that rich painting, which the Italians call alla Mosaica, shining like enameled work, which now by antiquity were much decayed, and in some parts defaced. Round about the Church hung many Lamps, which they use to burn in time of the Lent (called Beyram); and every week upon Thursday in the evening, and Friday all day, which they keep holy after their fashion for their Sabbath day. Round about the upper part of the Church are large and most faire Galleries. And here I did see two Nuts of Marble of huge bigness and great beauty. Moreover I did see the great Turk when he entered this Church, and howsoever it lie close to the Gate of his Palace. Yet he came riding upon a horse richly trapped, with many troopes of his chief horseman, standing in rank within the Courts of his Palace, and from the Court Gate to the Church door, between which troops on both sides, he passed as between walls of brass, with great pomp. And when a Chaus (or Pensioner) being on horseback did see me close by the Emperors side, he rushed upon me to strike me with his mace, saying, What doth this Christian dog so near the person of our great Lord? But the Janissary, whom our Ambassador had given me for a Guide and Protector, repelled him from doing me any wrong, and many Janissaries (according to their manner) coming to help him, the Chaus was glad to let me alone, and they bade me be bold to stand still, though I were the second or third person from the Emperor. Near this Church is the stately Sepulcher of Selymus the second, and another Sepulcher no less stately, and newly built for Amaranth lately deceased, where he lay with those male children round about him, who according to the manner were strangled by his Successor after he was dead. Not far thence is the Market place having some one hundred marble pillars about it, and adorned with a Pyramids or pinnacle, erected upon four Globes, and with a pleasant Fountain of water, together with other ornaments left (as it seems) by Christian Emperors.

(R) The wonderful Mosque and Sepulcher of Solyman, numbered among the miracles of the World.

(S) Two houses for the same use, as the Exchange of London, where the Merchants meet, namely, for the selling of fine wares, but no way to be compared to the same for the building. They are called the great and the less Bezestand, and use to bee opened only certain days of the week, and for some six hours, at which times small and more precious wares are there to be sold, as Jewels, Semiters (or Swords), set with Jewels, but commonly counterfeit, pieces of Velvet, Satin, and Damask, and the like. And the Market place is not far distant, where Captives of both sexes are weekly sold, and the buyers if they will, may take them into a house, and there see them naked, and handle them (as wee handle beasts to know their fatness and strength.)

(T) Here is a Fort that is fortified with seven Towers, called by the Turks Jadicule, and by Christians the seven Towers, where a garrison of Soldiers is kept, because the Emperors treasure is there laid up, and chief Prisoners use to be kept there. The treasure is vulgarly said to bee laid up there, but the great Turk seldom goes thither: and since it is true, that where the treasure is, there is the mind, I think it probable (which I have heard of experienced men) that more of the treasure lies in the Seraglio, where the great Turk holds his Court.

(V) Here be the ruins of a Palace upon the very walls of the City, called the Palace of Constantine, wherein I did see an Elephant, called Philo by the Turks, and another beast newly brought out of Africa, (the Mother of Monsters) which beast is altogether unknown in our parts, and is called Surnapa by the people of Asia, Astanpa by others, and Giraffe by the Italians, the picture whereof I remember to have seen in the Maps of Mercator; and because the beast is very rare, I will describe his form as well as I can. His hair is red colored, with many black and white spots; I could scarce reach with the point of my fingers to the hinder part of his back, which grew higher and higher towards his foreshoulder, and his neck was thin and some three ells long, so as he easily turned his head in a moment to any part or corner of the room wherein he stood, putting it over the beams thereof, being built like a Barn, and high (for the Turkish building, not unlike the building of Italy, both which I have formerly described) by reason where of he many times put his nose in my neck, when I though my self furthest distant from him, which familiarity of his I liked not; and howsoever the Keepers assured me he would not hurt me, yet I avoided these his familiar kisses as much as I could. His body was slender, not greater, but much higher then the body of a stag or Hart, and his head and face was like to that of a stag, but the head was less and the face more beautiful: He had two horns, but short and scarce half a foot long; and in the forehead he had two bunches of flesh, his ears and feet like an Ox, and his legs like a stag. The Janissary my guide did in my name and for me give twenty Aspers to the Keeper of this Beast.

Edmund Spenser

1552?–1599

from A View of the [Present] State of Ireland

Spenser's dialogue, *A View of the Present State of Ireland* was composed in about 1596 as a response to Hugh O'Neill's sustained threat to English rule in Ireland, which had begun in 1594 and was to last until 1603, after Spenser's death. The long work was not published until 1633 but circulated extensively in manuscript (over twenty copies survive). The dialogue has become notorious as a brutal defense of the English right to colonize its weaker neighbor, and the denigration of the Irish as savages who needed to be civilized by firm government. In this extract the fictional Irenius, who Spenser represents as an English settler in Ireland, explains to his English-based counterpart, Eudoxus, that Irish customs are derived from those of one of the barbarian races of the ancient world, the Scythians, whose lands bordered those of Greece. Everything about the Irish is a means of confronting civilized values, even their clothes, which seem innocent to the uninitiated but which help them resist the march of progress and civilization.

Eudox: In truth Iren. You doe well remember the plot of your first purpose; but yet from that (meseemes) ye have much swerved in all this long discourse, of the first inhabiting of Ireland; for what is that to your purpose?

Iren: Truly very material, for if you marked the course of all that speech well, it was to show, by what means the customs, that now are in Ireland, being some of them indeed very strange and almost heathenish, were first brought in: and that was, as I said, by those nations from whom that country was first peopled; for the difference in manners and customs, doth follow the difference of nations and people. The which I have declared to you, to have been three especially which seated themselves here: to wit, first the Scythian, then the Gauls, and lastly the English. Notwithstanding that I am not ignorant, that there were sundry nations which got footing in that land, of the which there yet remain divers great families and septs, of whom I will also in their proper places make mention.

Eudox: You bring your self Iren. Very well into the way again, notwithstanding that it seems that you were never out of the way, but now that you have passed thorough those antiquities, which I could have wished not so soon ended, begin when you please, to declare what customs and manners have been derived from those nations to the Irish, and which of them you find fault withal.

Iren: I will begin then to count their customs in the same order that I counted their nations, and first with the Scythian or Scottish manners. Of the which there is one use, amongst them, to keep their cattle, and to live themselves the most part of the year in boolies, still to fresh land, as they have depastured the former. The which appeared plainer to be the manner of the Scythians, as you may read in Olaus Magnus, and Io. Bohemus, and yet is used amongst all the Tartarians and the people about the Caspian Sea, which are naturally Scythians, to live in herds as they call them, being the very same, that the Irish boolies are, driving their cattle continually with them, and feeding only on their milk and white meats.

Eudox: What fault can you find with this custom? For though it be an old Scythian use, yet it is very behoofefull[1] in this country of Ireland, where there are great mountains, and waste deserts full of grass, that the same should be eaten down, and nourish many thousands of cattle, for the good of the whole realm, which cannot (me thinks) well be any other way, then by keeping those boolies there, as you have showed.

Iren: But by this custom of boolying, there grow in the mean time many great enormities unto that Common-wealth. For first if there be any out-laws, or loose people, (as they are never without some) which live upon stealths and spoils, they are evermore succored and find relief only in these boolies, being upon the waste places, whereas else they should be driven shortly to starve, or to come down to the towns to seek relief, where by one means or other, they would soon be caught. Besides, such stealths of cattle as they make, they bring commonly to those boolies, being upon those waste places, where they are readily received, and the thief harbored from danger of law, or such officers as might light upon him.[2] Moreover the people that thus live in those boolies, grow thereby the more barbarous, and live more licentiously than they could in towns, using what manners they list, and practicing what mischief and villainies they will, either against the government there, by their combinations, or against private men, whom they malign, by stealing their goods, or murdering themselves. For there they think themselves half exempted from law and obedience,

1. Necessary.
2. Cattle raiding enjoyed a significant role in Irish culture and society. The greatest Irish epic, the *Táin Bó Cuailnge* ("Cattle Raid of Cooley"), as the title might suggest, centers around such an event.

and having once tasted freedom, doe like a steer, that hath been long out of his yoke, grudge and repine ever after, to come under rule again.

Eudox: By your speech Iren. I perceive more evil to come by this use of boolies, then good by their grassing; and therefore it may well be reformed: but that must be in his due course: do you proceed to the next.

Iren: They have another custom from the Scythians, that is the wearing of Mantles, and long glibbes, which is a thick curled bush of hair, hanging down over their eyes, and monstrously disguising them, which are both very bad and hurtful.

Eudox: Doe you think that the mantle comes from the Scythians? I would surely think otherwise, for by that which I have read, it appeared that most nations of the world anciently used the mantle. For the Jews used it, as you may read of Elias mantle, &c. The Chaldees also used it, as you may read in Diodorus. The Egyptians likewise used it, as you may read in Herodotus, and may be gathered by the description of Berenice, in the Greek Commentary upon Callimachus. The Greeks also used it anciently, as appeared by Venus mantle lined with stars, though afterwards they changed the form thereof into their cloaks, called Pallia, as some of the Irish also use. And the ancient Latin's and Romans used it, as you may read in Virgil, who was a very great antiquary: That Evander, when Aeneas came to him at his feast, did entertain and feast him, sitting on the ground, and lying on mantles. Insomuch as he useth the very word mantile for mantle.

"– Humi mantilia sternunt."[3]

So that it seems that the mantle was a general habit to most nations, and not proper to the Scythians only, as you suppose.

Iren: I cannot deny but that anciently it was common to most, and yet since disused and laid away. But in this later age of the world, since the decay of the Roman empire, it was renewed and brought in again by those Northern Nations, when breaking out of their cold caves and frozen habitations, into the sweet soil of Europe, they brought with them their usual weeds, fit to shield the cold, and that continual frost, to which they had at home been inured: the which yet they left not off, by reason that they were in perpetual wars, with the nations whom they had invaded, but, still removing from place to place, carried always with them that weed, as their house, their bed, and their garment; and, coming lastly into Ireland, they found there more special use thereof, by reason of the raw cold climate, from whom it is now grown into that general use, in which that people now have it. After whom the Gauls succeeding, yet finding the like necessity of that garment, continued the like use thereof.

Eudox: Since then the necessity thereof is so commodious, as you allege, that it is instead of housing, bedding, and clothing, what reason have you then to wish so necessary a thing cast off?

Iren: Because the commodity doth not countervail the discommodity; for the inconveniencies which thereby doe arise, are much more many; for it is a fit house for an out-law, a meet bed for a rebel, and an apt cloak for a thief. First the out-law being for his many crimes and villains banished from the towns and houses of honest men, and wandering in waste places, far from danger of law, make his mantle his house, and under it cover himself from the wrath of heaven, from the offence of the earth, and from the sight of men. When it rains it is his pent-house; when it blows it is his tent; when it freezes it is his tabernacle. In Summer he can wear it loose, in winter he can wrap it close; at all times he can use it; never heavy, never cumbersome. Likewise for a rebel it is as serviceable. For in his war that he make (if at least it deserve the name of

3. They spread their cloaks on the ground.

war) when he still flies from his foe, and lurks in the thick woods and straight passages, waiting for advantages, it is his bed, yea and almost his household stuff. For the wood is his house against all weathers, and his mantle is his couch to sleep in. Therein he wraps himself round, and coucheth[4] himself strongly against the gnats, which in that country doe more annoy the naked rebels, whilst they keep the woods, and doe more sharply wound them then all their enemies swords, or spears, which can seldom come nigh them: yea and oftentimes their mantle serves them, when they are near driven, being wrapped about their left arm in stead of a target, for it is hard to cut thorough with a sword, besides it is light to bear, light to throw away, and, being (as they commonly are) naked, it is to them all in all. Lastly for a thief it is so handsome, as it may seem it was first invented for him, for under it he may cleanly convey any fit pillage that comes handsomely in his way, and when he goes abroad in the night in free-booting, it is his best and surest friend; for lying, as they often do, 2 or 3 nights together abroad to watch for their booty, with that they can prettily shroud themselves under a bush or a bank side, till they may conveniently do their errand: and when all is over, he can, in his mantle pass thorough any town or company, being close hooded over his head, as he useth, from knowledge of any to whom he is endangered. Besides this, he, or any man else that is disposed to mischief or villainy, may under his mantle go privily armed without suspicion of any, carry his head-piece, his skein, or pistol if his please, to be always in readiness. Thus necessary and fitting is a mantle, for a bad man, and surely for a bad housewife it is no less convenient, for some of them that bee wandering woe men, called of them Mona-shul, it is half a wardrobe; for in Summer you shall find her arrayed commonly but in her smock and mantle to be more ready for her light services: in Winter, and in her travaile,[5] it is her cloak and safeguard, and also a coverlet for her lewd exercise. And when she hath filled her vessel, under it she can hide both her burden, and her blame; yea, and when her bastard is borne, it serves instead of swaddling clouts. And as for all other good women which love to doe but little work, how handsome it is to lye in and sleep, or to louse themselves in the sun-shine, they that you will think it very unfit for a good housewife to stir in, or to busy her self about her housewifery in such sort as she should. These be some of the abuses for which I would think it meet to forbid all mantles.

Eudox: O evil minded man, that having reckoned up so many uses of a mantle, will yet wish it to be abandoned! Sure I think Diogenes dish did never serve his master for more turns, notwithstanding that he made it his dish, his cup, his cap, his measure, his water-pot, then a mantle doth an Irish man. But I see they be most to bad intents, and therefore I will join with you in abolishing it. But what blame lay you to the glib? take heed (I pray you) that you be not too busy therewith for fear of your own blame, seeing our Englishmen take it up in such a general fashion to wear their hair so immeasurably long, that some of them exceed the longest Irish glibs.

Iren: I fear not the blame of any underserved dislikes: but for the Irish glibbes, they are as fit masks as a mantle is for a thief. For whensoever he hath run himself into that peril of law, that he will not be known, he either cuts of his glib quite, by which he becomes nothing like himself, or pulls it so low down over his eyes, that it is very hard to discern his thievish countenance. And therefore fit to be trussed up with the mantle.

Eudox: Truly these three Scythian abuses, I hold most fit to bee taken away with sharp penalties, and sure I wonder how they have been kept thus long, notwithstanding so many good provisions and orders, as have been devised for that people.

4. Protects, covers.

5. Labor, giving birth.

Thomas Hariot

c. 1560–1621

Thomas Hariot, an astronomer and mathematician, was a member of Sir Walter Raleigh's household. This account, published by Hakluyt in 1598, reports on his voyage to Virginia in 1586. He tells of an unanticipated yet terrible consequence of European colonization: the death of numbers of Indians from diseases—brought by colonists—to which the Indians had no immunity. As a scientific matter, the phenomenon was not at all understood, and Hariot describes attempts by the English to explain what it meant in supposedly moral terms and also to take advantage of its practical effect—the reduction of the Indian population—as a way to colonize the region further.

from A Brief and True Report of the Newfound Land of Virginia

It resteth I speak a word or two of the natural inhabitants, their natures and manners, leaving large discourse thereof until time more convenient hereafter; now only so far forth as that you may know how they in respect of troubling our inhabiting and planting are not to be feared, but that they shall have cause both to fear and love us that shall inhabit with them.

They are a people clothed with loose mantles made of deerskins, and aprons of the same round about their middles, all else naked; of such a difference of statures only as we in England;[1] having no edge tools or weapons of iron or steel to offend us withal, neither know they how to make any. Those weapons that they have are only bows made of witch hazel and arrows of reeds, flat-edged truncheons also of wood about a yard long; neither have they anything to defend themselves but targets[2] made of barks and some armors made of sticks wickered together with thread. * * *

Their manner of war amongst themselves is either by sudden surprising one another, most commonly about the dawning of the day or moonlight, or else by ambushes or some subtle devices. Set battles are very rare, except it fall out where there are many trees, where either part may have some hope of defense after the delivery of every arrow, in leaping behind some or other.[3]

If there fall out any wars between us and them, what their fight is likely to be, we having advantages against them so many manner of ways, as by our discipline, our strong weapons and devices else, especially ordinance[4] great and small, it may easily be imagined. By the experience we have had in some places, the turning up of their heels against us in running away was their best defense.

In respect of us they are a people poor, and for want of skill and judgment in the knowledge and use of our things do esteem our trifles before things of greater value. Nothwithstanding, in their proper manner (considering the want of such means as we have), they seem very ingenious. For although they have no such tools, nor any such crafts, sciences, and arts as we, yet in those things they do, they show excellency of wit. And by how much they upon due consideration shall find our manner of knowledges

1. I.e., the Indians are generally of the same stature as the English and have the same range of differences in height as the English.
2. Shields.
3. Europeans fought each other in "set battles." Typically, an army was led by its cavalry and supported by its infantry, who marched to a distance from which they could fire their guns and cannons at the enemy. Indians waged what is known in the modern period as guerrilla warfare, attacking the enemy by surprise maneuvers and defending themselves in quick retreats.
4. Artillery.

and crafts to exceed theirs in perfection and speed for doing or execution, by so much the more is it probable that they should desire our friendship and love and have the greater respect for pleasing and obeying us. Whereby may be hoped, if means of good government be used, that they may in a short time be brought to civility and the embracing of true religion.

Some religion they have already, which although it be far from the truth, yet being as it is, there is hope that it may be the easier and sooner reformed.

They believe that there are many gods, which they call Mantoac, but of different sorts and degrees, one only chief and great God, which hath been from all eternity, who, as they affirm, when he purposed to make the world, made first other gods of a principal order to be as means and instruments to be used in the creation and government to follow, and after, the sun, moon, and stars as petty gods and the instruments of the other more principal. First (they say) were made waters, out of which by the gods was made all diversity of creatures that are visible or invisible.

For mankind, they say a woman was made first, which by the working of one of the gods, conceived and brought forth children; and in such sort they say they had their beginning. But how many years or ages have passed since, they say they can make no relation, having no letters or other such means as we to keep records of the particularities of times past, but only tradition from father to son.

* * *

Most things they saw with us, as mathematical instruments, sea compasses, the virtue of the loadstone[5] in drawing[6] iron, a perspective glass[7] whereby was showed many strange sights, burning glasses,[8] wild fireworks, guns, hooks, writing and reading, springclocks that seem to go of themselves, and many other things that we had were so strange unto them and so far exceeded their capacities to comprehend the reason and means how they should be made and done that they thought they were rather the works of gods than of men, or at the leastwise they had been given and taught us of the gods. Which made many of them to have such opinion of us as that if they knew not the truth of God and religion already, it was rather to be had from us whom God so specially loved than from a people that were so simple as they found themselves to be in comparison of us. Whereupon greater credit was given unto that we spoke of, concerning such matters. * * *

There could at no time happen any strange sickness, losses, hurts, or any other cross unto them but that they would impute to us the cause or means thereof, for offending or not pleasing us. One other rare and strange accident, leaving others, will I mention before I end, which moved the whole country that either knew or heard of us, to have us in wonderful admiration.

There was no town where we had any subtle devise[9] practiced against us, we leaving it unpunished or not revenged (because we sought by all means possible to win them by gentleness) but that within a few days after our departure from every such town, the people began to die very fast, and many in short space; in some towns about twenty, in some forty, and in one six score, which in truth was very many in respect of their numbers. This happened in no place that we could learn but where we had been where they used some practice against us, and after such time.[1] The

5. Magnet.
6. Attracting.
7. Telescope.
8. Magnifying glasses.
9. Trick.

1. Hariot moralizes the phenomenon of immunity by stating that Indian villages that came down with disease were those that had resisted or "used some practice against" the English.

disease also was so strange that they neither knew what it was, nor how to cure it, the like by report of the oldest men in the country never happened before, time out of mind. * * *

This marvelous accident in all the country wrought so strange opinions of us that some people could not tell whether to think us gods or men, and the rather because that all the space of their sickness, there was no man of ours known to die or that was especially sick; they noted also that we had no women among us, neither that we did care for any of theirs.

Some therefore were of opinion that we were not born of women, and therefore not mortal, but that we were men of an old generation many years past, then risen again to immortality.

Some would likewise seem to prophecy that there were more of our generation yet to come to kill theirs and take their places, as some thought the purpose was, by that which was already done. Those that were immediately to come after us they imagined to be in the air, yet invisible and without bodies, and that they by our entreaty and for the love of us did make the people to die in that sort as they did by shooting invisible bullets into them.

To confirm this opinion, their physicians (to excuse their ignorance in curing the disease) would not be ashamed to say but earnestly make the simple people believe that the strings of blood that they sucked out of the sick bodies were the strings wherewithal the invisible bullets were tied and cast. Some also thought that we shot them ourselves out of our pieces from the place where we dwelt and killed the people in any town that had offended us, as we listed, how far distant from us so ever it were. And other some said that it was the special work of God for our sakes as we ourselves have cause in some sort to think no less, whatsoever some do or may imagine to the contrary, specially some astrologers, knowing of the eclipse of the sun which we saw the same year before in our voyage thitherward, which unto them appeared very terrible. And also of a comet which began to appear but a few days before the beginning of the said sickness.[2] But to exclude them[3] from being the special causes of so special an accident, there are further reasons than I think fit at this present to be alleged. These their[4] opinions I have set down the more at large that it may appear unto you that there is good hope that they may be brought through discreet dealing and government to the embracing of the truth and consequently to honor, obey, fear, and love us.

And although some of our company toward the end of the year showed themselves too fierce in slaying some of the people in some towns, upon causes that on our part might easily enough have been born withal; yet notwithstanding, because it was on their part justly deserved, the alteration of their opinions generally and for the most part concerning us is the less to be doubted.[5] And whatsoever else they may be, by carefulness[6] of ourselves need nothing at all to be feared.

2. The Indians attributed their disease to God's favor toward the English. Hariot observes that the English concurred in this opinion, despite the warnings of astrologers who saw a recent eclipse of the sun and the arrival of a comet as bad omens. He concludes that the Indians' sense of a divine power backing the English enterprise could be the basis for their further peaceful subjugation.
3. The eclipse and the comet.
4. I.e., the Indians'.
5. Hariot admits that the English were "too fierce" in killing Indians for insufficient reason; at the same time, he states, without further explanation, that as these actions were "justly deserved," the English need fear no change in the Indians' attitude toward them.
6. Taking care.

John Smith

c. 1580–1631

John Smith's reports on the first years of the Jamestown settlement offered English readers a remarkably complete account of their colony in Virginia. To this day, it remains our principal source of information about English relations with the Indians of that region, the Powhatans. The first version of these reports, entitled *A True Relation of such occurrences and accidents of note as hath hap'ned in Virginia since the first planting of that colony* (1608) records events from the settlers' landing on Cape Henry at the mouth of the Chesapeake in December 1606 to the moment of Smith's return to England during the spring of 1608. Written as a first-person narrative in a terse, reportorial style, *A True Relation* reads as a series of notes. It gives us a vivid picture of the Indians of the area, how they received the English, and what measures they took to contain these newcomers, but it tells us little about how the author interpreted these events. What we notice is how often Smith imposes his own Europeanist construction on the situation, calling Powhatan—the principal chief of the local tribes—an "Emperor" and those governing the tribes themselves as "Kings." Smith's later *General History of Virginia and the Summer Isles* was published in 1623 and obviously elaborated his earlier material. Referring to himself in the third person as "Captain Smith" or "the president," Smith evaluates with considerable astuteness the actions of both the English and the Powhatan Indians as they met on ground they increasingly understood as contested.

It is impossible to know how much of Smith's *General History* is the result of his imaginative reconstruction of events that had, in all likelihood, lost their immediacy in his memory. The *General History* is much longer than *A True Relation* and is replete with details that give the reader a vivid sense of the difficulty the English had settling this unfamiliar territory. Smith's most compelling passages report conversations he had with Powhatan. Presumably with the aid of an interpreter, although he does not tell us so, Smith understands that Powhatan was fully aware of the end the colonists had in view: in Smith's translation of Powhatan's words, it was "to invade my people and possess my country." With remarkable ventriloquism, Smith speaks sympathetically, through Powhatan, on behalf of the people he himself often declared as being "savages." In these reported conversations, Smith's Powhatan shows dignity and perspicacity. As Powhatan reflects upon English deceit and ambition with a keen and uncompromising accuracy, it is evident that Smith had reason to admire—and to fear—his adversary.

from General History of Virginia and the Summer Isles

This happened in the winter in that extreme frost, 1607. Now though we had victual sufficient—I mean only of oatmeal, meal, and corn—yet the ship staying 14 weeks when she might as well have been gone in 14 days spent[1] a great part of that, the beef, pork, oil, aqua vitae, fish, butter and cheese, beer, and near all the rest that was sent to be landed. When they departed what their discretion could spare to make a little poor meal or two we called feasts to relish our mouths. Of each somewhat they left us, yet I must confess those that had either money, spare clothes, credit to give bills of payment, gold, rings, furs, or any such commodities were ever welcome to this removing tavern.[2] * * * Now for all this plenty our ordinary was but meal and water, so that this great charge little relieved our wants, whereby with the extremity of the bitter cold frost and those defects more than half of us died and took our deaths in that

1. Consumed.

2. The ship that had the food supply; Smith refers to its dwindling stores.

piercing winter. I cannot deny but both Smith and Skrivener[3] did their best to amend what was amiss, but with the president[4] went the major part.

But the worst mischief was our gilded refiners with their golden promises made all men their slaves in hope of recompenses. There was no talk, no hope, no work but *dig* gold, *wash* gold, *refine* gold, *load* gold—such a bruit of GOLD that one mad fellow desired to be buried in the sands, lest they should by their art make gold of his bones! Little need there was and less reason the ship should stay, their wages run on, our victual consume 14 weeks, that the mariners might say they did help to build such a golden church that we can say the rain washed near to nothing in 14 days.[5]

Were it that Captain Smith would not applaud all those golden inventions because they admitted him not to the sight of their trials nor golden consultations, I know not. But I have heard him oft question with Captain Martin, and tell him, except he could show him a more substantial trial, he was not enamored with their "dirty" skill, breathing out these and many other passions. Never anything did more torment him than to see all necessary business neglected to fraught such a drunken ship with so much gilded dirt.

Till then we never accounted Captain Newport a refiner, who being ready to set sail for England—and we not having any use of parliaments, plays, petitions, admirals, recorders, interpreters, chronologers, courts of plea, nor justices of peace!—sent Master Wingfield and Captain Archer home with him, that had engrossed all those titles, for England *to seek some place of better employment*![6]

O cursed gold, those hunger-starved movers,
To what misfortunes lead'st thou all those lovers!
For all the China wealth nor Indies can
Suffice the mind of an av'ricious man.

* * *

The 12 of January [1609], we arrived at Werowocomoco,[7] where the river was frozen near half a mile from the shore. But to neglect no time, the president with his barge so far had approached by breaking the ice as the ebb left him amongst those oozy shoals. Yet rather than to lie there frozen to death, by his own example he taught them to march near middle deep more than a flight-shot[8] through this muddy, frozen ooze. When the barge floated he appointed two or three to return her aboard the pinnace[9] where, for want of water, in melting the ice they made fresh water, for the river there was salt. But in this march Master Russell, whom none could persuade to stay behind, being somewhat ill and exceeding heavy, so overtoiled himself as the rest had much ado ere he got ashore to regain life into his dead, benumbed spirits.

Quartering in the next houses we found, we sent to Powhatan for provision, who sent us plenty of bread, turkeys, and venison.

3. Matthew Skrivener was a member of the Council of the Virginia Company.
4. Edward Wingfield was president of the colony until 1607, after which Smith served in that position. Here Smith claims that neither he nor Skrivener had ways or means enough to secure the food the president had preempted.
5. Smith writes ironically. There was no reason for the ship to stay in Virginia just so the mariners could say that they had built a "golden church"; because no gold in fact existed in Virginia, to have said so would have meant that the colonists then would have to say that the rain had washed this church to nothing to account for its absence. Smith deplores the gold lust of the mariners.
6. I.e., "Until we saw the ship laden with supposed gold ore, we never thought that Captain Newport was a refiner (of gold ore)." Smith claims ironically that Newport sent Wingfield and Archer, both gentlemen and officers, back to England because they had no skills of use to the colony. In fact, Smith recognized that the colony desperately needed the skills in governance these officers were supposed to have but actually lacked. Thus Smith deplores the gold lust of the leaders of the Virginia Company as well as their inability to establish order in Jamestown.
7. A Powhatan village near Jamestown, on the eastern shore of Charles River.
8. The distance a bow shoots an arrow.
9. A small, light ship that often accompanied a larger ship.

The next day, having feasted us after his ordinary manner, he began to ask us when we would be gone, feigning he sent not for us, neither had he any corn, and his people much less—yet for forty swords he would procure us forty baskets. The president, showing him the men there present that brought him the message and conditions, asked Powhatan how it chanced he became so forgetful. Thereat the king concluded the matter with a merry laughter, asking for our commodities. But none he liked without guns and swords, valuing a basket of corn more precious than a basket of copper, saying he could rate[1] his corn but not the copper.

Captain Smith, seeing the intent of this subtle savage, began to deal with him after this manner:

"Powhatan, though I had many courses[2] to have made my provision, yet believing your promises to supply my wants, I neglected all to satisfy your desire. And to testify my love, I send you my men for your building, neglecting mine own. What your people had you have engrossed, forbidding them our trade; and now you think by consuming the time we shall consume for want, not having to fulfill your strange demands. As for swords and guns, I told you long ago I had none to spare. And you must know those I have can keep me from want. Yet steal or wrong you I will not, nor dissolve that friendship we have mutually promised, except you constrain me by our bad usage."

The king,[3] having attentively list'ned to this discourse, promised that both he and his country would spare him what he could, the which within two days they should receive.

"Yet Captain Smith," saith the king, "some doubt I have of your coming hither that makes me not so kindly seek to relieve you as I would. For many do inform me your coming hither is not for trade but to invade my people and possess my country, who dare not come to bring you corn, seeing you thus armed with your men. To free us of this fear, leave aboard your weapons, for here they are needless, we being all friends and forever Powhatans."

With many such discourses they spent the day, quartering that night in the king's houses.

* * * Powhatan began to expostulate the difference of peace and war after this manner:

"Captain Smith, you may understand that I having seen the death of all my people thrice, and not anyone living of those three generations but myself—I know the difference of peace and war better than any in my country. But now I am old and ere long must die, my brethren, namely, Opitchapam, Opechancanough, and Kekataugh, [and] my two sisters and their two daughters are distinctly each other's successors: I wish their experience no less than mine, and your love to them no less than mine to you.

"But this bruit from Nansamund[4] that you are come to destroy my country so much affrighteth all my people as they dare not visit you. What will it avail you to take that by force you may quickly have by love? or to destroy them that provide you food? What can you get by war when we can hide our provisions and fly to the woods? whereby you must famish by wronging us, your friends. And why are you thus jealous of our loves, seeing us unarmed, and both do and are willing still to feed you with that you cannot get but by our labors?

"Think you I am so simple not to know it is better to eat good meat, lie well, and sleep quietly with my women and children, laugh and be merry with you, have copper,

1. Appraise.
2. Opportunities.
3. Powhatan.
4. I.e., this rumor from Nansamund (a Powhatan village near the mouth of the James River). Powhatan rightly claims that the colonists value food, a necessity of life, more than they do copper; he bargains with Smith accordingly.

hatchets, or what I want, being your friend, than be forced to fly from all?—to lie cold in the woods, feed upon acorns, roots, and such trash, and be so hunted by you that I can neither rest, eat, nor sleep, but my tired men must watch, and if a twig but break, everyone crieth THERE COMETH CAPTAIN SMITH!—then must I fly I know not whither, and thus with miserable fear end my miserable life, leaving my pleasures to such youths as you, which through your rash unadvisedness may quickly as miserably end, for want of that you never know where to find.

"Let this therefore assure you of our loves, and every year our friendly trade shall furnish you with corn, and now also, if you would come in friendly manner to see us and not thus with your guns and swords as to invade your foes."

To this subtle discourse the president thus replied:

"Seeing you will not rightly conceive of our words, we strive to make you know our thoughts by our deeds. The vow I made you of my love both myself and my men have kept. As for your promise, I find it every day violated by some of your subjects. Yet, we finding your love and kindness, our custom is so far from being ungrateful that for your sake only we have curbed our thirsting desire of revenge, else had they known as well the cruelty we use to our enemies as our true love and courtesy to our friends.

"And I think your judgment sufficient to conceive as well by the adventures we have undertaken as by the advantage we have by our arms of yours that had we intended you any hurt, long ere this we could have effected it.

"Your people coming to me at James Town are entertained with their bows and arrows without any exceptions, we esteeming it with you as it is with us to wear our arms as our apparel.

"As for the danger of our enemies, in such wars consist our chiefest pleasure. For your riches we have no use. As for the hiding your provision or by your flying to the woods, we shall not so unadvisedly starve as you conclude. Your friendly care in that behalf is needless, for we have a rule to find beyond your knowledge."[5]

Many other discourses they had till at last they began to trade. But the king seeing his will would not be admitted as a law, our guard dispersed,[6] nor our men disarmed, he (sighing) breathed his mind once more in this manner:

"Captain Smith, I never use any werowance[7] so kindly as yourself, yet from you I receive the least kindness of any. Captain Newport gave me swords, copper, clothes, a bed, tools, or what I desired, ever taking what I offered him; and would send away his guns when I entreated him. None doth deny to lie at my feet or refuse to do what I desire, but only you; of whom I can have nothing but what you regard not, and yet you will have whatsoever you demand. Captain Newport you call father, and so you call me. But I see for all us both you will do what you list, and we must both seek to content you. But if you intend so friendly as you say, send hence your arms that I may believe you. For you see the love I bear you doth cause me thus nakedly to forget myself."[8]

Smith, seeing this savage but trifle the time[9] to cut his throat, procured the savages to break the ice that his boat might come to fetch his corn and him, and gave order for more men to come on shore to surprise the king, with whom also he but

5. Smith claims that the colonists could have wiped out the Powhatans long ago had they so desired; in fact, they have allowed the Powhatans to visit Jamestown armed. Smith also claims that the English have a superior knowledge of the sources of food. His boasts are without substance. Historians agree that during these early years of Jamestown, the Powhatans could have destroyed the English. It is certain that the English relied on the Powhatans for food, but bragging of this kind was typical of such negotiations.

6. Surrounding them.

7. The Powhatan term for tribal chief.

8. Powhatan fences verbally with Smith, comparing his meanness to the Indians with Newport's generosity.

9. Waited.

trifled the time till his men were landed; and to keep him from suspicion, entertained the time with this reply:

"Powhatan, you must know as I have but one God I honor but one king; and I live not here as your subject but as your friend to pleasure you with what I can. By the gifts you bestow on me you gain more than by trade. Yet would you visit me as I do you, you should know it is not our custom to sell our courtesies as a vendible commodity. Bring all your country with you for your guard, I will not dislike it as being overjealous.

"But to content you, tomorrow I will leave my arms and trust to your promise. I call you father indeed, and as a father you shall see I will love you. But the small care you have of such a child caused my men persuade me to look to myself."[1]

By this time Powhatan—having knowledge his men were ready whilest the ice was a-breaking—with his luggage, women, and children fled, yet to avoid suspicion left two or three of the women talking with the captain whilest he secretly ran away, and his men that secretly beset the house; which being presently discovered to Captain Smith, with his pistol, sword, and target he made such a passage among these naked devils that at his first shoot they next him tumbled one over another and the rest quickly fled before him, some one way, some another, so that without any hurt, only accompanied with John Russell, he obtained the *corps du guard*.[2]

When they perceived him so well escaped and with his eighteen men—for he had no more with him ashore—to the uttermost of their skill they sought excuses to dissemble the matter. And Powhatan to excuse his flight and the sudden coming of this multitude sent our captain a great bracelet and a chain of pearl by an ancient orator[3] that bespoke us to this purpose, perceiving even then from our pinnace a barge and men departing and coming unto us:

"Captain Smith, our werowance is fled, fearing your guns, and knowing when the ice was broken there would come more men, sent these numbers but to guard his corn from stealing that might happen without your knowledge. Now though some be hurt by your misprision,[4] yet Powhatan is your friend and so will forever continue. Now since the ice is open, he would have you send away your corn and if you would have his company, send away also your guns which so affrighteth his people that they dare not come to you as he promised they should."

Then having provided baskets for our men to carry our corn to the boats, they kindly offered their service to guard our arms that none should steal them. A great many they were of goodly, well-proportioned fellows as grim as devils. Yet the very sight of cocking our matches and being to let fly,[5] a few words caused them to leave their bows and arrows to our guard, and bear down our corn on their own backs. We needed not importune them to make dispatch, but our barges being left on the ooze by the ebb caused us stay till the next high water midnight tide, so that we returned again to our old quarter, [and] spent that half night with such mirth as though we never had suspected or intended anything.

Powhatan and his Dutchmen bursting with desire to have the head of Captain Smith (for if they could but kill him they thought all was theirs), neglected not any

1. Smith believes Powhatan wants to kill him; he therefore determines to take him prisoner. He states that he is not a subject of Powhatan but, rather, of another king, i.e., James I. He further contrasts his belief in one God with the Powhatans' pantheism.
2. Military advantage.
3. Spokesman for the Powhatans.
4. Mistake; the Powhatans' spokesman claims that Smith is responsible for the wounding of his men and that their chief is Smith's friend.
5. Priming our guns, preparing to fire.

opportunity to effect his purpose.[6] The Indians with all the merry sports they could devise spent the time till night. Then they all returned to Powhatan, who all this time was making ready his forces to surprise the house and him at supper.

Notwithstanding, the eternal all-seeing God did prevent him and by a strange means. For Pocahontas, his dearest jewel and daughter, in that dark night came through the irksome woods and told our captain great cheer should be sent us by and by. But Powhatan and all the power he could make would after come kill us all if they that brought it could not kill us with our own weapons when we were at supper. Therefore if we would live she wished us presently to be gone. Such things as she delighted in he[7] would have given her, but with the tears running down her cheeks she said she durst not be seen to have any, for if Powhatan should know it, she were but dead, and so she ran away by herself as she came.

Within less than an hour came eight or ten lusty fellows with great platters of venison and other victual, very importunate to have us put out our matches,[8] whose smoke made them sick, and sit down to our victual. But the captain made them taste every dish, which done he sent some of them back to Powhatan to bid him make haste for he was prepared for his coming. As for them, he knew they came to betray him at his supper, but he would prevent them and all their other intended villainies, so that they might be gone. Not long after came more messengers to see what news. Not long after them others. Thus we spent the night as vigilantly as they till it was high water, yet seemed to the savages as friendly as they to us. And that we were so desirous to give Powhatan content as he requested, we did leave him Edward Brynton to kill him fowl and the Dutchmen to finish his house, thinking at our return from Pamaunkee[9] the frost would be gone, and then we might find a better opportunity if necessity did occasion it, little dreaming yet of the Dutchmen's treachery, whose humor well suited this verse—

Is any free that may not live as freely as he list?
Let us live so, then w'are as free and brutish as the best.[1]

END OF PERSPECTIVES: ENGLAND, BRITAIN, AND THE WORLD

William Shakespeare

1564–1616

English colonists venturing to the New World carried with them an English Bible; if they owned a single secular book, it was probably the works of William Shakespeare. A humanist scripture of sorts, his works have never hardened into doctrine; rather, they have lent themselves to a myriad range of interpretations, each shaped by particular interests, tastes, and expectations. Ben Jonson's line—"He was not of an age, but for all time!"—describes the appeal Shakespeare has had for speakers of English and the many other languages into which his works have been translated.

6. The Indians made allies of the Dutch, who were competing with the English for trade in the New World.
7. I.e., Smith.
8. A match was a wick or a cord, usually made of hemp or cotton, that was kept lit to use for firing guns or cannons; the Powhatans did not want the colonists to have a way to use their weapons.
9. A Powhatan village on the Pamaunkee (now the Charles) River.
1. Smith implies a distinction between living as you wish, which is license, and living under law, which is liberty. That the "best" should be bestial is, of course, ironic.

Attributed to John Taylor, *Portrait of William Shakespeare*, c. 1610.

Shakespeare was born in the provincial town of Stratford-on-Avon, a three-day journey from London by horse or carriage. His father, John Shakespeare, was a glover and local justice of the peace; his mother, Mary Arden, came from a family that owned considerable land in the county. He probably went to a local grammar school where he learned Latin and read histories of the ancient world. Jonson's disparaging comment, that Shakespeare knew "small Latin and less Greek," must not be taken too seriously. Shakespeare (unlike Jonson) was not classically inclined, but his mature works reveal a mind that was extraordinarily well informed and acutely aware of rhetorical techniques and logical argument. At eighteen Shakespeare married Anne Hathaway, who was twenty-six; in the next three years they had a daughter, Susanna, and then twins, Hamnet and Judith. Six years later, perhaps after periods of teaching school in Stratford, he went to London, eventually (in 1594) to join one of the great theatrical companies of the day, the Chamberlain's Men. It was with this company that he began his career as actor, manager, and playwright. In 1599 the troupe began to put on plays at the Globe, an outdoor theater in Southwark, not far from the other principal theaters of the day—the Rose, the Bear Garden, and the Swan—and across the river from the city of London itself. Because these theaters were outside city limits, in a district known as "the liberties," they were free from the control of authorities responsible for civic order; in effect, the theater provided a place in which all kinds of ideas and ways of life, whether conventional or not, could be represented, examined, and criticized. When James I acceded to the throne in 1603, Shakespeare's company became the King's Men and played also at court and at Blackfriars, an indoor theater in London. Some critics think that the change in venue necessitated a degree of allusiveness and innuendo that was not evident in earlier productions.

During the years Shakespeare was writing for the theater, the populations of Europe were periodically devastated by the plague, and city authorities were obliged to close places of public gathering, including theaters. Shakespeare provided plays for seasons in which the theaters in London were open, composing them at lightning speed and helping to stage productions on very short notice. The plays that we now accept as Shakespeare's fall roughly into several general categories: first, the histories, largely based on the chronicles of the Tudor historian Raphael Holinshed, and the Roman plays, inspired by Plutarch's *Lives of the Ancient Romans*, written in Greek and translated by Sir Thomas North; second, the comedies, often set in the romantic world of the English countryside or an Italian town; third, the tragedies, some of which explore the dark legends of the past; and fourth, a group in the mixed genre of tragicomedy but also called, after critics in the nineteenth century, the romances. A fifth, somewhat anomalous group—*All's Well That Ends Well*, *Measure for Measure*, and *Troilus and Cressida*—falls between comedy and satire; these plays are usually termed "problem comedies."

The early phase of Shakespeare's career, the decade beginning in the late 1580s, saw the first cycle of his English histories. In four plays (known as the first tetralogy) this cycle depicted events in the reigns of Henry VI and Richard III and concluded by dramatizing the accession of the first Tudor monarch, Henry VII. Fascinated by the fate of peoples governed by feeble or oppressive rulers, Shakespeare expressed his loathing of tyranny by showing how the misgovernment of a weak king can lead to despotic rule. The cycle ends with the death of the tyrant, Richard III, and the accession of the Duke of Richmond, later Henry VII (Elizabeth's grandfather)—an action that celebrates the founder of the Tudor dynasty and the providence that had selected this family to bring peace to England. A later play, *King John*, concerns an earlier monarch whose claim to the throne is suspect; here divine right, having validated the succession of the Tudor monarchy in the first tetralogy, is made doubtful by a monarch's own viciousness. The play implies a question that Shakespeare continues to ask of history for the rest of his career: in what sense may divine right to be understood as a principle of monarchic rule? History, as Shakespeare will go on to represent it, no longer clearly demonstrates the triumph of justice but rather shows the interrelatedness of good and evil motives that end in morally ambiguous action. The first of the Roman plays, *The Tragedy of Titus Andronicus*, which tells of the Roman general's revenge for the rape of his daughter Lavinia, and the early comedies, *The Taming of the Shrew*, *The Comedy of Errors*, *Two Gentlemen of Verona*, and *Love's Labor's Lost*, which depict the effects of mistaken identity and misunderstood speech, illustrate other themes that Shakespeare will continue to represent: the terrible consequences of the search for revenge and the unfortunate, as well as salutary, self-deceptions of love.

The second phase, culminating in productions around 1600, is marked by more and subtler comedy: *A Midsummer Night's Dream*, *The Merchant of Venice*, *The Merry Wives of Windsor*, *Much Ado About Nothing*, *As You Like It*, and *Twelfth Night*. These plays insert into plots focusing primarily on the courtship of young couples a dramatic commentary on darker kinds of human desire: a longing for possessions; a wish to control others, particularly children; and a self-love so intense that it leads to fantasy and delusion. A romantic tragedy of this period, *Romeo and Juliet*, shows how the gross unreason sustaining a family feud and a mysteriously malevolent fate combine to destroy the future of lovers. A second cycle of four English histories, beginning with the deposition of Richard II and ending in the triumphs of Henry V and the birth of Henry VI, reveals how Shakespeare complicates the genre. An ostensible motive for the second tetralogy was the celebration of an English monarchy that had been preserved through the ages by God's will. Yet the actions of even the least controversial of its kings are questionable: Henry V's conquest of France is driven by greed as much as by his claim to the French throne, which is represented as dubious even in the playtext. A second Roman play, *The Tragedy of Julius Caesar*, takes up the question of tyranny in relation to the liberty inherent in a republic; the play seems most tragic when its action suggests that the Roman people do not recognize the sacrifices that are necessary to preserve such freedom and even regard freedom itself as negligible. As a whole, these plays demonstrate the characteristics of Shakespeare's mature style. Certain recurring images unify the plays thematically and, more important, link them to contemporary habits of speech as well as to the intellectual discourse of the period. Visual images—the "I" and the "eye" of the lover—often clarify the language of love, and figures denoting the well-being of different kinds of "corporation," including the human body, the family, and the body politic, signal the comprehensive order that was supposed to govern relations among all the elements of creation.

Incorporating many of the themes in the "problem comedies," the tragedies of the same period preoccupied Shakespeare for the seven years following the accession of James I: *Hamlet*, *Othello*, *King Lear*, *Macbeth*, *Antony and Cleopatra*, and *Coriolanus*, together with *Timon of Athens*, a play that was apparently written in collaboration with Thomas Middleton. *All's Well That Ends Well* and *Measure for Measure* illustrate societies that contain rather than reject sordid or unregenerate characters, both noble and common, and thus provide opportunities for comic endings to situations that might otherwise have ended in tragedy. And making much of the need for order but exemplifying the deep disorder of the military societies of Greece and Troy, the characters in *Troilus and Cressida* reveal the extent to which Shakespeare could imagine language as ironic and the human spirit as utterly possessed by a cynical need to turn every occasion to its own advantage. These plays serve to introduce tragedies of unprecedented scope.

Featuring heroes who overreach the limits of their place in life and so fail to fulfill their obligations to themselves and their dependents, Shakespeare's later tragedies embrace a wider range of human experience than can be explained by traditional conceptions of sin and fate. Profoundly complex in their treatment of motivation and the operations of the will, the tragedies entertain the idea of a beneficent deity who both permits terrible suffering and infuses, to use Hamlet's words, a "special providence in the fall of a sparrow." They reveal the blinding egotism that causes fatal misperceptions of character, motive, and action; their heroes are at once terribly in error and also strangely sympathetic. The human capacity for evil is perhaps most fully realized in the characters of women: the bestial daughters of King Lear, Goneril and Regan; the diabolical Lady Macbeth; the shamelessly duplicitous Cleopatra. Yet even they are not entirely unsympathetic; in many ways their behavior responds to the challenges that other, essentially more authoritative characters represent. The romances—*Pericles*, *Cymbeline*, *The Winter's Tale*, and *The Tempest*—round out the final phase of Shakespeare's dramatic career, representing (like the comedies) the restoration of family harmony and (like the histories) the return of good government. The deeply troubling divisions within families and states that characterize the tragedies are the basis for the restorative unions in the romances. Their depiction of passages of time and space that allow providential recoveries of health and prosperity to both individual characters and whole bodies politic are largely owing to the intervention of women. Unlike the women of the tragedies, the daughters and wives of the romances are generative in the broadest sense. They heal their fathers and husbands by restoring to their futures the possibility of descendents and therefore of dynastic continuity. Their agency is, in turn, sustained by forces identified as divine and outside history. *Henry VIII*, a history, and *Two Noble Kinsmen*, a romance, both probably composed jointly with John Fletcher, conclude Shakespeare's career as a dramatist.

Shakespeare also wrote narrative and lyric poems of great power, notably *Venus and Adonis*, *The Rape of Lucrece*, and a cycle of 154 sonnets. In a bold departure from tradition the sonnets celebrate the poet's steadfast love for a young man (never identified), his competitive rivalry with another poet (sometimes identified as Christopher Marlowe), and his troubled relationship with a woman who has dark features. The cycle encourages an interpretation that accounts for its romantic elements, but it also thwarts any obvious construction of events. It is thought that most of the sonnets were composed in the mid-1590s, although they were not published until 1609, apparently without Shakespeare's oversight. Their order therefore cannot be assigned to Shakespeare, and for this reason alone their function as narrative must remain problematic. Still, the reader can trace their representation of successive relations between persons and themes: the young man, although himself derelict in the duties of friendship, will remain beloved by the poet and be made immortal by his verse, while the dark lady, who is unscrupulous and afflicted with venereal disease, receives only expressions of desire and lust, shadowed by the poet's disdain and self-loathing.

In a sense, Shakespeare has always been up to date. True, his language is not what is heard today, and his characters are shaped by forces within his culture, not ours. Yet we continue to see his plays on stage and in film, sometimes as recreations of the productions that historians of theater think he knew and saw but more often as reconceived with the addition of modern costumes, settings, and music as well as some strategic cutting of the dramatic text. Earlier periods produced their own kinds of Shakespeare. The Restoration stage, with scenery that allowed audiences to imagine they were looking through a window to life itself, put on plays that were embellished and trimmed to satisfy the taste of the time. Some producers omitted characters who were considered superfluous (the porter in *Macbeth*); others added characters who were judged essential for balance (Miranda's sister, Dorinda, in *The Tempest*). *King Lear* acquired a happy ending when Edgar married Cordelia. No one production of any period has defined a play entirely; every director has had his or her vision of what Shakespeare meant an audience to see. These reinterpretations testify to the perennial vitality of a playwright who was indeed, as Jonson said, "for all time."

For additional resources on Shakespeare, go to *The Longman Anthology of British Literature* Web site at www.myliteraturekit.com.

THE SONNETS The entire sequence numbers 154 sonnets. The first fourteen encourage a young man to marry and have children and may have been commissioned by his family. Neither the young man nor his family has been identified, although some readers have thought Henry Wriosthesley, Earl of Southampton, a possible subject. In Sonnet 15, Shakespeare turns to a related topic: the young man will be made eternal not only by his descendants but by the poet's praise of him in verse. Sonnet 20 initiates a long sequence of sonnets addressed to a young man as the poet's lover; whether he is the man who featured in the earlier sonnets on procreation is unclear, but it has generally been assumed so. Beginning with Sonnet 78, the poet complains that a rival poet is stealing his subject—the young man's virtue and grace—to the detriment of his own poetry. Who Shakespeare's rival is (or whether he is in fact a single person) is not known, although some readers have considered Christopher Marlowe a possibility. A final set of twenty-eight sonnets introduces a new character to the sequence, a figure often referred to as "the dark lady," who is the lover of both the poet and the young man. The threesome make up a dramatic unity that is fraught with tension and anguish.

Sonnets

1

From fairest creatures we desire increase,
That thereby beauty's rose might never die,
But as the riper° should by time decease, *the older person*
His tender heir might bear his memory;
But thou, contracted° to thine own bright eyes, *engaged, shrunk*
Feed'st thy light's flame with self-substantial fuel,
Making a famine where abundance lies,
Thyself thy foe, to thy sweet self too cruel.
Thou that art now the world's fresh ornament
And only herald to the gaudy spring,
Within thine own bud buriest thy content,
And, tender churl, mak'st waste in niggarding.° *hoarding*
  Pity the world, or else this glutton be:
  To eat the world's due, by the grave and thee.[1]

12

When I do count the clock that tells the time,
And see the brave day sunk in hideous night;
When I behold the violet past prime,
And sable° curls all silvered o'er with white; *dark*
When lofty trees I see barren of leaves
Which erst from heat did canopy the herd,
And summer's green, all girded up in sheaves,
Borne on the bier with white and bristly beard,[2]
Then of thy beauty do I question make
That thou among the wastes of time must go,
Since sweets and beauties do themselves forsake[3]

1. Have pity on the world and do not consume your own substance by refusing to engender the child you owe now to the world and finally to the grave.
2. The harvest of grain, once green, is gathered in bundles; each stalk ends in clusters of kernels protected by husks that resemble a white and bristling beard.
3. Beauties fade, seeming to forsake themselves.

And die as fast as they see others grow;
  And nothing 'gainst Time's scythe can make defense
  Save breed, to brave° him when he takes thee hence. *defy*

15

When I consider every thing that grows
Holds in perfection but a little moment,
That this huge stage presenteth naught but shows
Whereon the stars in secret influence comment;[4]
When I perceive that men as plants increase,
Cheerèd and checked even by the selfsame sky,
Vaunt° in their youthful sap, at height decrease, *boast*
And wear their brave state out of memory;° *until forgotten*
Then the conceit° of this inconstant stay *idea*
Sets you most rich in youth before my sight,
Where wasteful Time debateth with Decay
To change your day of youth to sullied° night, *dark*
  And all in war with Time for love of you,
  As he takes from you, I ingraft you new.[5]

18

Shall I compare thee to a summer's day?
Thou art more lovely and more temperate.
Rough winds do shake the darling buds of May,
And summer's lease hath all too short a date.° *duration*
Sometimes too hot the eye of heaven shines,
And often is his gold complexion dimmed;
And every fair from fair sometimes declines,
By chance or nature's changing course untrimmed.° *stripped bare*
But thy eternal summer shall not fade
Nor lose possession of that fair thou ow'st;° *own*
Nor shall Death brag thou wanderest in his shade,
When in eternal lines° to time thou grow'st. *of verse*
  So long as men can breathe or eyes can see,
  So long lives this, and this gives life to thee.

20

A woman's face with Nature's own hand painted
Hast thou, the master-mistress of my passion;[6]
A woman's gentle heart, but not acquainted
With shifting change, as is false women's fashion;
An eye more bright than theirs, less false in rolling,° *straying*
Gilding the object whereupon it gazeth;
A man in hue, all hues in his controlling,[7]

4. Human action is a kind of show, influenced by the stars or heavenly forces.
5. Renew by grafting new beauty in verse.
6. Feminine in appearance, the young man is both a master and a mistress of the poet's passion. This is the first of a series of sonnets in which Shakespeare addresses the young man in clearly erotic language.
7. A man in appearance, he determines the nature of what he sees, what is apparent to him.

Which steals men's eyes and women's souls amazeth.
And for a woman wert thou first created,
Till Nature, as she wrought thee, fell a-doting,° *in love*
And by addition me of thee defeated,[8]
By adding one thing to my purpose nothing.
  But since she pricked thee out for women's pleasure,
  Mine be thy love and thy love's use their treasure.

29

When, in disgrace with fortune and men's eyes,
I all alone beweep my outcast state,
And trouble deaf heaven with my bootless° cries, *unavailing*
And look upon myself and curse my fate,
Wishing me like to one more rich in hope,
Featured like him, like him with friends possessed,
Desiring this man's art and that man's scope,° *powers*
With what I most enjoy contented least;
Yet in these thoughts myself almost despising,
Haply° I think on thee, and then my state, *perhaps*
Like to the lark at break of day arising
From sullen earth, sings hymns at heaven's gate;
  For thy sweet love remembered such wealth brings
  That then I scorn to change° my state with kings. *exchange*

30

When to the sessions° of sweet silent thought[9] *law courts*
I summon up remembrance of things past,
I sigh the lack of many a thing I sought,
And with old woes new wail my dear time's waste.[1]
Then can I drown an eye, unused to flow,
For precious friends hid in death's dateless° night, *endless*
And weep afresh love's long since cancelled woe,
And moan th'expense° of many a vanished sight. *what it cost*
Then can I grieve at grievances foregone,
And heavily° from woe to woe tell o'er *sorrowfully*
The sad account of fore-bemoanèd moan,
Which I new pay as if not paid before.[2]
  But if the while I think on thee, dear friend,
  All losses are restored, and sorrows end.

8. The last four lines of the sonnet are full of double meanings: the thing loving nature adds to the young man is a penis; this points or "pricks" him out for women's pleasure or "use" (with the added suggestion that his body is capital, which through usury generates interest); but the poet reserves for himself the young man's love, which is beyond commerce and has no price.

9. The conceit governing this imagery depends on the poet's association of his sense of guilt at his misdeeds with a notion of a debt. He represents himself as a debtor who cannot discharge what he owes to others because the complaints against him remain constantly fresh in his mind. He also figures as in debt to himself, as it is his time that he has wasted in reviewing these complaints. His debts are paid, however, when he thinks of his friend.

1. I bemoan the waste of my time by remembering anew former sadness.

2. I add up the sorrows and complaints against me that I have already accounted for; I pay for them as if they were new debts; so I add to the sum I have wasted.

31

Thy bosom is endearèd with all hearts,
Which I by lacking have supposèd dead,
And there reigns love and all love's loving parts,
And all those friends which I thought burièd.[3]
How many a holy and obsequious° tear — *mournful*
Hath dear religious love stol'n from mine eye
As interest of the dead, which now appear
But things removed that hidden in thee lie!
Thou art the grave where buried love doth live,
Hung with the trophies of my lovers gone,
Who all their parts° of me to thee did give; — *shares*
That due of many now is thine alone.
  Their images I loved I view in thee,[4]
  And thou, all they, hast all the all of me.

33

Full many a glorious morning have I seen
Flatter the mountaintops with sovereign eye,
Kissing with golden face the meadows green,
Gilding pale streams with heavenly alchemy;
Anon° permit the basest clouds to ride — *soon*
With ugly rack° on his celestial face, — *driven clouds*
And from the forlorn world his visage hide,
Stealing unseen to west with this disgrace.
Even so my sun one early morn did shine
With all-triumphant splendor on my brow.
But out, alack! He was but one hour mine;
The region° cloud hath masked him from me now. — *of the upper air*
  Yet him for this my love no whit disdaineth;
  Suns of the world may stain when heaven's sun staineth.[5]

35

No more be grieved at that which thou hast done.
Roses have thorns, and silver fountains mud,
Clouds and eclipses stain both moon and sun,
And loathsome canker° lives in sweetest bud. — *worm*
All men make faults, and even I in this,
Authorizing thy trespass with compare,° — *comparisons*
Myself corrupting, salving thy amiss,
Excusing thy sins more than thy sins are.
For to thy sensual fault I bring in sense°— — *reason*

3. I.e., my past loves seem to live again in your bosom; the affection they had is now made over to you.
4. Here Shakespeare plays with a convention of courtly love: the virtues of all previous loves are said to be summed up in a present love, who embodies a universal perfection.
5. If the sun may be covered by clouds, so too the suns (or sons) of the world may dim in their affections. This is the first of the poet's laments for his lover's insincerity.

Thy adverse party° is thy advocate— *accuser*
And 'gainst myself a lawful plea commence.
Such civil war is in my love and hate
That I an accessary needs must be
To that sweet thief which sourly robs from me.

55

Not marble nor the gilded monuments
Of princes shall outlive this powerful rhyme,
But you shall shine more bright in these contents
Than unswept stone besmeared with sluttish° time. *dirty*
When wasteful war shall statues overturn,
And broils° root out the work of masonry, *uprisings*
Nor° Mars his sword nor war's quick fire shall burn *neither*
The living record of your memory.
'Gainst death and all-oblivious° enmity *casting into oblivion*
Shall you pace forth; your praise shall still find room
Even in the eyes of all posterity
That wear this world out to the ending doom.° *judgment day*
So, till the judgment that yourself° arise, *when you yourself*
You live in this, and dwell in lovers' eyes.

60

Like as the waves make towards the pebbled shore,
So do our minutes hasten to their end;
Each changing place with that which goes before,
In sequent° toil all forwards do contend.° *successive / strive*
Nativity, once in the main° of light, *sea*
Crawls to maturity, wherewith being crowned,
Crookèd eclipses 'gainst his glory fight,
And Time that gave doth now his gift confound.° *destroy*
Time doth transfix° the flourish set on youth *puncture*
And delves° the parallels in beauty's brow, *digs*
Feeds on the rarities of nature's truth,
And nothing stands but for his scythe to mow.
And yet to times in hope my verse shall stand,
Praising thy worth despite his cruel hand.

71

No longer mourn for me when I am dead
Than° you shall hear the surly sullen bell *then*
Give warning to the world that I am fled
From this vile world with vildest° worms to dwell. *vilest*
Nay, if you read this line, remember not
The hand that writ it, for I love you so,
That I in your sweet thoughts would be forgot,
If thinking on me then should make you woe.° *grieve you*
O if, I say, you look upon this verse,
When I, perhaps, compounded am with clay,

Do not so much as my poor name rehearse,° *repeat*
But let your love ev'n with my life decay,
  Lest the wise world should look into your moan,
  And mock you with me after I am gone.[6]

73

That time of year thou mayst in me behold
When yellow leaves, or none, or few, do hang
Upon those boughs which shake against the cold,
Bare ruined choirs[7] where late the sweet birds sang.
In me thou seest the twilight of such day
As after sunset fadeth in the west,
Which by and by black night doth take away,
Death's second self, that seals up all in rest.
In me thou seest the glowing of such fire
That on the ashes of his youth doth lie
As the deathbed whereon it must expire,
Consumed with that which it was nourished by.
  This thou perceiv'st, which makes thy love more strong,
  To love that well which thou must leave ere long.

80

O, how I faint when I of you do write,
Knowing a better spirit° doth use your name, *the rival poet*
And in the praise thereof spends all his might
To make me tongue-tied, speaking of your fame!
But since your worth, wide as the ocean is,
The humble as° the proudest sail doth bear, *as well as*
My saucy bark, inferior far to his,
On your broad main° doth willfully appear. *sea*
Your shallowest° help will hold me up afloat, *slightest*
Whilst he upon your soundless° deep doth ride; *unfathomable*
Or, being wrecked, I am a worthless boat,
He of tall building° and of goodly pride. *construction*
  Then if he thrive and I be cast away,
  The worst was this: my love was my decay.° *ruin*

86

Was it the proud full sail of his great verse,
Bound for the prize° of all-too-precious you, *captive booty*
That did my ripe thoughts in my brain inhearse,° *entomb*
Making their tomb the womb wherein they grew?
Was it his spirit,° by spirits taught to write *genius*
Above a mortal pitch, that struck me dead?[8]

6. Lest people seeing your grief at my death should ridicule you because of your association with me.
7. The choir is the section of a church reserved for the singers in the choir. "Choir" puns on "quire," the gathering of pages in a book, and thus recalls the "leaves" in line 2.
8. Shakespeare ironically suggests that the rival poet writes with supernatural help, or at least what he claims is supernatural help. Shakespeare later implies that this help is actually no more than a gull's (trickster's) intelligence or gossip.

No, neither he, nor his compeers by night
Giving him aid, my verse astonishèd.
He, nor that affable familiar ghost° *spirit*
Which nightly gulls him with intelligence,
As victors of my silence cannot boast;
I was not sick of any fear from thence.
But when your countenance filled up his line,[9]
Then lacked I matter; that enfeebled mine.° *my verse*

87

Farewell! Thou art too dear for my possessing,
And like enough thou know'st thy estimate.° *value*
The charter of thy worth gives thee releasing;[1]
My bonds in thee are all determinate.° *ended*
For how do I hold thee but by thy granting,
And for that riches where is my deserving?
The cause of this fair gift in me is wanting,
And so my patent[2] back again is swerving.
Thyself thou gav'st, thy own worth then not knowing,
Or me, to whom thou gav'st it, else mistaking;
So thy great gift, upon misprision° growing, *error*
Comes home again, on better judgment making.
Thus have I had thee as a dream doth flatter,
In sleep a king, but waking no such matter.

93

So shall I live, supposing thou art true,
Like a deceivèd husband; so love's face
May still seem love to me, though altered new,
Thy looks with me, thy heart in other place.
For there can live no hatred in thine eye,
Therefore in that I cannot know thy change.° *infidelity*
In many's looks the false heart's history
Is writ in moods and frowns and wrinkles strange,
But heaven in thy creation did decree
That in thy face sweet love should ever dwell;
Whate'er thy thoughts or thy heart's workings be,
Thy looks should nothing thence but sweetness tell.
How like Eve's apple doth thy beauty grow,
If thy sweet virtue answer not thy show![3]

94

They that have pow'r to hurt, and will do none,[4]
That do not do the thing they most do show,° *appear to do*

9. When you became his subject.
1. You are worth so much that you can pay off all obligations you owe me; in other words, I have no right to you.
2. Deed granting a monopoly.
3. Like Eve's deceptively attractive apple, the young man's beauty is a kind of temptation that leads to the death of him who succumbs to it.
4. The poem warns against a loss of self-control, which is associated with a loss of self-ownership. Persons (the undefined "they" of the sonnet) can lend themselves to others, their stewards, but at the same time, they retain control over their own great virtue. If they succumb to evil or ill-will, however, they risk becoming very corrupt.

Who moving others are themselves as stone,
Unmovèd, cold, and to temptation slow—
They rightly° do inherit heaven's graces, *justly*
And husband° nature's riches from expense; *protect*
They are the lords and owners of their faces,° *appearances*
Others but stewards of their excellence.
The summer's flow'r is to the summer sweet,
Though to itself it only live and die;
But if that flow'r with base° infection meet, *common*
The basest° weed outbraves his dignity. *humblest*
For sweetest things turn sourest by their deeds;
Lilies that fester smell far worse than weeds.

104

To me, fair friend, you never can be old,
For, as you were when first your eye I eyed,
Such seems your beauty still. Three winters cold
Have from the forests shook three summers' pride,
Three beauteous springs to yellow autumn turned
In process of the seasons have I seen,
Three April perfumes in three hot Junes burned,
Since first I saw you fresh, which yet are green.
Ah, yet doth beauty, like a dial[5] hand,
Steal from his figure and no pace perceived.
So your sweet hue, which methinks still doth stand,
Hath motion, and mine eye may be deceived,
For fear of which, hear this, thou age unbred:° *unborn*
Ere you were born was beauty's summer dead.

106

When in the chronicle of wasted° time *past*
I see descriptions of the fairest wights,° *people*
And beauty making beautiful old rhyme
In praise of ladies dead and lovely knights,
Then, in the blazon° of sweet beauty's best, *catalogue*
Of hand, of foot, of lip, of eye, of brow,
I see their antique pen would have expressed
Even such a beauty as you master° now. *possess*
So all their praises are but prophecies
Of this our time, all you prefiguring;
And, for° they looked but with divining eyes, *because*
They had not skill enough your worth to sing.
For we, which now behold these present days,
Have eyes to wonder, but lack tongues to praise.[6]

5. Beauty is like the hand of a clock, a dial; it moves slowly but inexorably away from the height of the hour.

6. The poets of antiquity could not describe your perfection because they could only guess at it; we recognize your perfection but lack the skill to describe it.

107

Not mine own fears nor the prophetic soul
Of the wide world dreaming on things to come[7]
Can yet the lease of my true love control,
Supposed as forfeit to a confined doom.° *at a set time*
The mortal moon hath her eclipse endured,
And the sad augurs mock their own presage;
Incertainties now crown themselves assured,
And peace proclaims olives of endless age.[8]
Now with the drops of this most balmy time[9]
My love looks fresh, and Death to me subscribes,° *yields*
Since, spite of him, I'll live in this poor rhyme,
While he insults° o'er dull and speechless tribes; *triumphs*
And thou in this shalt find thy monument,
When tyrants' crests and tombs of brass are spent.° *worn away*

116

Let me not to the marriage of true minds
Admit impediments. Love is not love
Which alters when it alteration finds,° *in the beloved*
Or bends with the remover to remove.
O, no, it is an ever-fixèd mark° *landmark*
That looks on tempests and is never shaken;
It is the star to every wandering bark,
Whose worth's unknown, although his height be taken.[1]
Love's not Time's fool, though rosy lips and cheeks
Within his bending sickle's compass° come; *range*
Love alters not with his brief hours and weeks,
But bears it out even to the edge of doom.° *judgment day*
If this be error and upon me proved,
I never writ, nor no man ever loved.

123

No, Time, thou shalt not boast that I do change.
Thy pyramids[2] built up with newer might
To me are nothing novel, nothing strange;
They are but dressings of a former sight.
Our dates are brief, and therefore we admire

7. Shakespeare may have had in mind the ancient concept of *anima mundi* (literally, a world soul), which was imagined as breathing life into all creation.
8. A supposedly dangerous lunar eclipse has passed, and those who predicted disaster now mock their own predictions. The moon may be Elizabeth I, who died in 1603; the endless peace to follow may be the one that James I negotiated with the Spanish in 1604. Or the moon's eclipse may figure Elizabeth's sixty-third year, a numerologically suspect period; in this case the ensuing peace describes a time in which anxiety over the future of the kingdom diminished, or "uncertainties" were "assured," i.e., became certainties.
9. A time that is restorative, as from the application of a medicinal ointment; a possible reference to the coronation of James I, celebrated by anointing the monarch with balm and other rituals.
1. The star by which ships navigate by measuring its altitude from the horizon (known values) is itself beyond valuation.
2. Any imposing structure; those built recently, "with newer might," are reconceptions, "dressings," of former structures.

What thou dost foist upon us that is old,
And rather make them born to our desire
Than think that we before have heard them told.
Thy registers° and thee I both defy, (*records*)
Not wondering at the present nor the past,
For thy records and° what we see doth lie, (*and also*)
Made more or less by thy continual haste.
This I do vow and this shall ever be:
I will be true, despite thy scythe and thee.

124

If my dear love were but the child of state,
It might for Fortune's bastard be unfathered,
As subject to Time's love or to Time's hate,
Weeds among weeds, or flowers with flowers gathered.[3]
No, it was builded far from accident;
It suffers not in smiling pomp, nor falls
Under the blow of thrallèd° discontent, (*enslaved*)
Whereto th' inviting time our fashion° calls. (*manner*)
It fears not Policy,° that heretic, (*expediency*)
Which works on leases of short-numbered hours,
But all alone stands hugely politic,[4]
That it nor grows with heat nor drowns with showers.
To this I witness call the fools of Time,
Which die for goodness, who have lived for crime.[5]

126

O thou, my lovely boy, who in thy power
Dost hold Time's fickle glass,° his sickle hour; (*hourglass*)
Who hast by waning grown, and therein show'st
Thy lovers withering as thy sweet self grow'st;
If Nature, sovereign mistress over wrack,° (*destruction*)
As thou goest onwards, still will pluck thee back,
She keeps thee to this purpose, that her skill
May Time disgrace and wretched minutes kill.[6]
Yet fear her, O thou minion° of her pleasure! (*slave*)
She may detain, but not still keep, her treasure.
Her audit, though delayed, answered must be,
And her quietus° is to render thee.[7] (*settlement*)

3. If my love for you were merely a product of circumstance, it would be no more than Fortune's bastard and not have a father; it would be subject to accidents, both good and bad.
4. His love is beyond the expedient maneuvers of mere "policy" because it is itself "politic" or a state.
5. This enigmatic couplet may mean that those who have lived as criminals and then die for goodness are Time's fools because deathbed repentance is folly; or that those who have lived as criminals and then die in a good cause are Time's fools in the sense that everyone who resists the temporizing ways of the world is a fool.
6. His lover's power can hold back time and prevent his sickle from mowing down his green youth; paradoxically, while others grow old, he grows young. Nature permits this expressly to defy Time.
7. Yet Nature owes you to Time and will pay her debt by handing you over at last. The sonnet ends short of the 14 lines the form demands, as if to emphasize the idea of brevity.

128[8]

How oft, when thou my music play'st[9]
Upon that blessed wood whose motion sounds
With thy sweet fingers when thou gently sway'st
The wiry concord that mine ear confounds,[1]
Do I envy those jacks° that nimble leap *keys*
To kiss the tender inward of thy hand,
Whilst my poor lips, which should that harvest reap,
At the wood's boldness by° thee blushing stand. *alongside*
To be so tickled they° would change their state *his lips*
And situation with those dancing chips,
O'er whom thy fingers walk with gentle gait,
Making dead wood more blest° than living lips. *happier*
  Since saucy jacks so happy are in this,
  Give them thy fingers, me thy lips to kiss.

129

The expense° of spirit in a waste of shame[2] *dissipation*
Is lust in action; and, till action, lust
Is perjured, murderous, bloody, full of blame,
Savage, extreme, rude, cruel, not to trust,
Enjoyed no sooner but despised straight,° *immediately*
Past reason hunted, and no sooner had
Past reason hated, as a swallowed bait
On purpose laid to make the taker mad;[3]
Mad in pursuit, and in possession so;° *also*
Had, having, and in quest to have, extreme;
A bliss in proof,° and proved, a very woe; *i.e., while experienced*
Before, a joy proposed; behind, a dream.
  All this the world well knows; yet none knows well
  To shun the heaven that leads men to this hell.

130

My mistress' eyes are nothing like the sun;
Coral is far more red than her lips' red;
If snow be white, why then her breasts are dun;° *brown*
If hairs be wires, black wires grow on her head.
I have seen roses damasked,° red and white, *mingled*
But no such roses see I in her cheeks;
And in some perfumes is there more delight
Than in the breath that from my mistress reeks.

8. Sonnet 127 was the first to have a woman, not a man, as its principal subject; she is described as a woman of dark complexion.
9. The poem builds on a comparison between playing a keyboard instrument, understood to be a virginal or small harpsichord, and a lover's kiss. The keys or jacks of the instrument "kiss" the player's fingers; the speaker asks to kiss the player's lips.
1. I.e., your fingers produce the concord between the strings of the instrument that astounds my hearing.
2. The line evokes two kinds of meaning, moral and sexual: the futility and degradation of passion, and its waste as "spirit," conventionally understood as semen, in the body or waist of the woman.
3. The lover is both the hunter, who seeks satisfaction, and the hunted, for whom a bait is laid by mad passion.

I love to hear her speak, yet well I know
That music hath a far more pleasing sound.
I grant I never saw a goddess go;
My mistress, when she walks, treads on the ground.
And yet, by heaven, I think my love as rare
As any she belied with false compare.[4]

138

When my love swears that she is made of truth
I do believe her, though I know she lies,
That she might think me some untutored youth,
Unlearnèd in the world's false subtleties.
Thus vainly thinking that she thinks me young,
Although she knows my days are past the best,
Simply I credit her false-speaking tongue;
On both sides thus is simple truth suppressed.
But wherefore says she not she is unjust?
And wherefore say not I that I am old?
O, love's best habit is in seeming° trust, *apparent*
And age in love loves not to have years told.
Therefore I lie with her, and she with me,[5]
And in our faults by lies we flattered be.

144

Two loves I have, of comfort and despair,
Which like two spirits do suggest° me still: *tempt*
The better angel is a man right fair,
The worser spirit a woman colored ill.
To win me soon to hell, my female evil
Tempteth my better angel from my side,
And would corrupt my saint to be a devil,
Wooing his purity with her foul pride.
And whether that my angel be turned fiend
Suspect I may, yet not directly tell;
But being both from me, both to each friend,
I guess one angel in another's hell.
Yet this shall I ne'er know, but live in doubt
Till my bad angel fire my good one out.[6]

152

In loving thee thou know'st I am forsworn,° *faithless*
But thou art twice forsworn, to me love swearing:
In act thy bed-vow° broke, and new faith torn *marriage vow*
In vowing new hate after new love bearing.[7]

4. The couplet suggests ironic or hyperbolic compliment: my mistress is exceptional in that she has set new standards for true beauty by a comparison that defies its standards.
5. We deceive each other; we have sex with each other.
6. The couplet suggests several interpretations. The poet's lady or bad angel could fire or dismiss his "fair" friend; she could infect him with a venereal disease, a condition that would cause a fever; finally, she could be the cause of his descent into hellfire, a consequence of sin.
7. You have broken your marriage vow and your vow to love me.

But why of two oaths' breach do I accuse thee,
When I break twenty? I am perjured most,
For all my vows are oaths but to misuse° thee, *deceive*
And all my honest faith in thee is lost.
For I have sworn deep oaths of thy deep kindness,
Oaths of thy love, thy truth, thy constancy,
And, to enlighten thee, gave eyes to blindness,[8]
Or made them swear against the thing they see;
    For I have sworn thee fair. More perjured eye,
    To swear against the truth so foul a lie!

TWELFTH NIGHT; OR, WHAT YOU WILL. Shakespeare's *Twelfth Night; or, What You Will* was first performed during the feast of Candlemas at the Middle Temple, one of the Inns of Court, on 2 February 1602. An eyewitness to that performance, the barrister John Manningham, found the story of the puritanical steward Malvolio the most memorable: "A good practice in it to make the steward believe his lady widow was involved with him, by counterfeiting a letter as from his Lady . . . telling him what she liked best in him, and prescribing his gesture in smiling, his apparel, etc. And then when he came to practice making him believe he was mad." However distant the memory of the twelfth day of Christmas as a feast of misrule was at the time of the play's first performance, the element of the world turned upside down in Shakespeare's comedy delighted the carousing young lawyers.

Part of the play's larger parody of the self-delusion of desire and of the literary forms in which that desire is expressed is shown in the plotline where the sanctimonious Malvolio is fooled into believing that he might be the love object of Olivia, his female employer, and so acts out the most preposterous courtship of her. The play sends up the conventions of courtly love, particularly as stylized in the lyric love poetry that was popular among young London men with literary ambition as well as self-dramatizing aristocrats in the Elizabethan court. This was the poetry of Sir Walter Raleigh and the young John Donne, with all its teasing eroticism, hyperbolic flattery, and Petrarchan angst.

In *Twelfth Night*, the three central characters—Orsino, Olivia, and Viola—all act out their similarly stylized passions. Orsino lolls about listening to sad music as he pines for love of Olivia. She vows to do nothing but mourn for her dead brother—for seven years—until she meets Cesario, a servant whom Orsino has sent to woo her. Cesario, none other than the shipwrecked Viola disguised as a male servant, praises Olivia from head to toe and makes witty, erotic jokes and complaints against the lady's cruelty that capture her fancy. Olivia is jolted out of mourning and into infatuation. Cesario/Viola in turn falls almost immediately in love with Orsino, and her love grows in heat not despite but more likely because of the apparent impossibility of fulfillment. Viola's twin Sebastian meanwhile flees Antonio, a man who has taken care of him for three months since being shipwrecked, only to fall haphazardly into Olivia's arms at the right moment to become the realization of her infatuation for Cesario.

All these self-deluded desires are expressed in some of Shakespeare's most lyrical dramatic verse. The play is studded throughout with such stars of lyric illumination as the fool Feste's songs. The sad ironies he reflects on and the enlightening wit he laces his barbs with

8. To make you seem fair, I saw what was not there or did not see what was there.

provide a kind of detachment and wisdom that set into relief the absurdity of the lovers' self-seriousness.

At the end of the play, the lovers—and even the drunkard Sir Toby Belch and the serving maid Maria—are matched as couples, while only Malvolio vows revenge. Antonio, the one character whose passion seems to be based on any real acquaintance with the object of his affection, is also left alone; the text is silent on his fate. In the comic world of *Twelfth Night*, mistaken identity and lack of self-knowledge are, if not for Antonio, at least overcome for some by "nature's bias"—an openness to affection and the ability to snatch pleasure when the lucky opportunity arises.

The text of *Twelfth Night* is based on the 1623 Folio.

Twelfth Night; or, What You Will*

The Names of the Actors

ORSINO, Duke (or Count) of Illyria
VALENTINE, Gentleman attending on Orsino
CURIO, Gentleman attending on Orsino

VIOLA, a shipwrecked lady, later disguised as Cesario
SEBASTIAN, twin brother of Viola
ANTONIO, a sea captain, friend to Sebastian
CAPTAIN, of the shipwrecked vessel

OLIVIA, a rich countess of Illyria
MARIA, gentlewoman in Olivia's household
SIR TOBY BELCH, Olivia's uncle
SIR ANDREW AGUECHEEK, a companion of Sir Toby
MALVOLIO, Steward of Olivia's household
FABIAN, a member of Olivia's household
FESTE, a clown, also called Fool, Olivia's jester

A PRIEST
FIRST OFFICER
SECOND OFFICER

LORDS, SAILORS, MUSICIANS, AND OTHER ATTENDANTS
Scene: A city in Illyria, and the seacoast near it

ACT 1

Scene 1[1]

[*Enter Orsino Duke of Illyria, Curio, and other lords (with musicians).*]

ORSINO: If music be the food of love, play on;
Give me excess of it, that surfeiting,

* The notes are based on those of David Bevington, ed. *The Complete Works of Shakespeare*. All original stage directions are in square brackets, and all editorially added stage directions are in parentheses.

1. Location: Orsino's court.

The appetite may sicken and so die.
That strain again! It had a dying fall;° *cadence*
O, it came o'er my ear like the sweet sound
That breathes upon a bank of violets,
Stealing and giving odor. Enough, no more.
'tis not so sweet now as it was before.
O spirit of love, how quick° and fresh art thou, *alive*
That, notwithstanding thy capacity
Receiveth as the sea, naught enters there,
Of what validity° and pitch° soe'er, *value / worth*
But falls into abatement° and low price *depreciation*
Even in a minute! So full of shapes° is fancy° *imagined forms / love*
That it alone is high fantastical.° *highly imaginative*

CURIO: Will you go hunt, my lord?
ORSINO: What, Curio?
CURIO: The hart.° *pun on "heart"*
ORSINO: Why, so I do, the noblest that I have.
O, when mine eyes did see Olivia first,
Methought she purged the air of pestilence.
That instant was I turned into a hart,
And my desires, like fell° and cruel hounds, *fierce*
E'er since pursue me.[2]

[*Enter Valentine.*]

How now, what news from her?

VALENTINE: So please my lord, I might not be admitted,
But from her handmaid do return this answer:
The element° itself, till seven years' heat,° *sky / seven summers*
Shall not behold her face at ample view;
But like a cloistress° she will veilèd walk, *nun*
And water once a day her chamber round
With eye-offending brine—all this to season° *preserve*
A brother's dead love, which she would keep fresh
And lasting in her sad remembrance.

ORSINO: O, she that hath a heart of that fine frame° *construction*
To pay this debt of love but to a brother,
How will she love, when the rich golden shaft° *Cupid's arrow*
Hath killed the flock of all affections else° *other feelings*
That live in her; when liver, brain, and heart,[3]
These sovereign thrones, are all supplied, and filled
Her sweet perfections,[4] with one self king!° *single lord*
Away before me to sweet beds of flowers.
Love-thoughts lie rich when canopied with bowers. [*Exeunt.*]

2. Allusion to Ovid: Actaeon was turned into a stag by Diana and killed by his own hounds.

3. Seats of the passions.

4. I.e., her sweet perfections are filled.

Scene 2[5]

[*Enter Viola, a Captain, and Sailors.*]

VIOLA: What country, friends, is this?
CAPTAIN: This is Illyria, lady.
VIOLA: And what should I do in Illyria?
My brother he is in Elysium.[6]
Perchance° he is not drowned. What think you, sailors? *perhaps*
CAPTAIN: It is perchance° that you yourself were saved. *by chance*
VIOLA: O, my poor brother! And so perchance may he be.
CAPTAIN: True, madam, and to comfort you with chance,° *possibilities*
Assure yourself, after our ship did split,
When you and those poor number saved with you
Hung on our driving° boat, I saw your brother, *drifting*
Most provident in peril, bind himself,
Courage and hope both teaching him the practice,
To a strong mast that lived° upon the sea; *floated*
Where, like Arion[7] on the dolphin's back,
I saw him hold acquaintance with the waves
So long as I could see.
VIOLA: For saying so, there's gold. [*She gives money.*]
Mine own escape unfoldeth to my hope,° *gives me hope*
Whereto thy speech serves for authority,
The like of him. Know'st thou this country?
CAPTAIN: Ay, madam, well, for I was bred and born
Not three hours' travel from this very place.
VIOLA: Who governs here?
CAPTAIN: A noble duke, in nature as in name.
VIOLA: What is his name?
CAPTAIN: Orsino.
VIOLA: Orsino! I have heard my father name him.
He was a bachelor then.
CAPTAIN: And so is now, or was so very late;
For but a month ago I went from hence,
And then 'twas fresh in murmur°—as, you know, *rumor*
What great ones do the less° will prattle of— *social inferiors*
That he did seek the love of fair Olivia.
VIOLA: What's she?
CAPTAIN: A virtuous maid, the daughter of a count
That died some twelvemonth since, then leaving her
In the protection of his son, her brother,
Who shortly also died; for whose dear love,
They say, she hath abjured the sight
And company of men.
VIOLA: O, that I served that lady,
And might not be delivered° to the world *revealed*
Till I had made mine own occasion mellow,° *ready*

5. Location: The coast of the Adriatic.
6. Home of the blessed dead.
7. Greek poet who jumped overboard to escape murderous sailors and charmed dolphins with his lyre, so that they carried him to shore.

What my estate° is! *social position*
CAPTAIN: That were hard to compass,° *bring about*
Because she will admit no kind of suit,
No, not° the Duke's. *not even*
VIOLA: There is a fair behavior° in thee, Captain, *conduct; appearance*
And though that nature with a beauteous wall
Doth oft close in pollution, yet of thee
I will believe thou hast a mind that suits
With this thy fair and outward character.° *appearance*
I prithee, and I'll pay thee bounteously,
Conceal me what I am, and be my aid
For such disguise as haply shall become
The form of my intent.° I'll serve this duke. *my outward purpose*
Thou shalt present me as an eunuch[8] to him.
It may be worth thy pains, for I can sing
And speak to him in many sorts of music
That will allow° me very worth his service. *prove*
What else may hap, to time I will commit;
Only shape thou thy silence to my wit.° *plan*
CAPTAIN: Be you his eunuch, and your mute° I'll be; *silent attendant*
When my tongue blabs, then let mine eyes not see.
VIOLA: I thank thee. Lead me on. [*Exeunt.*]

Scene 3[9]

[*Enter Sir Toby (Belch) and Maria.*]

SIR TOBY: What a plague means my niece to take the death of her brother thus? I am sure care's an enemy to life.

MARIA: By my troth, Sir Toby, you must come in earlier o'nights. Your cousin,[1] my lady, takes great exceptions to your ill hours.

SIR TOBY: Why, let her except before excepted.[2]

MARIA: Ay, but you must confine yourself within the modest limits of order.

SIR TOBY: Confine? I'll confine myself no finer[3] than I am. These clothes are good enough to drink in, and so be these boots too. An[4] they be not, let them hang themselves in their own straps.

MARIA: That quaffing and drinking will undo you. I heard my lady talk of it yesterday, and of a foolish knight that you brought in one night here to be her wooer.

SIR TOBY: Who, Sir Andrew Aguecheek?

MARIA: Ay, he.

SIR TOBY: He's as tall[5] a man as any's in Illyria.

MARIA: What's that to the purpose?

SIR TOBY: Why, he has three thousand ducats a year.

8. Castrato, or male soprano singer, which would explain her high-pitched voice.
9. Location: Olivia's house.
1. Kinswoman.
2. I.e., let her take exception all she wants; I don't care (plays on the cant legal phrase, *exceptis excipiendis*, "with the exceptions before named").
3. Tighter; better.
4. If.
5. Brave; tall.

MARIA: Ay, but he'll have but a year in all these ducats.[6] He's a very fool and a prodigal.

SIR TOBY: Fie, that you'll say so! He plays o' the viol-degamboys,[7] and speaks three or four languages word for word without book, and hath all the good gifts of nature.

MARIA: He hath indeed, almost natural,[8] for, besides that he's a fool, he's a great quarreler, and but that he hath the gift of a coward to allay the gust[9] he hath in quarreling, 'tis thought among the prudent he would quickly have the gift of a grave.

SIR TOBY: By this hand, they are scoundrels and substractors[1] that say so of him. Who are they?

MARIA: They that add, moreover, he's drunk nightly in your company.

SIR TOBY: With drinking healths to my niece. I'll drink to her as long as there is a passage in my throat and drink in Illyria. He's a coward and a coistrel[2] that will not drink to my niece till his brains turn o' the toe like a parish top.[3] What, wench? *Castiliano vulgo*![4] For here comes Sir Andrew Agueface.[5]

[*Enter Sir Andrew (Aguecheek).*]

SIR ANDREW: Sir Toby Belch! How now, Sir Toby Belch?

SIR TOBY: Sweet Sir Andrew!

SIR ANDREW [*to Maria*]: Bless you, fair shrew.[6]

MARIA: And you too, sir.

SIR TOBY: Accost,[7] Sir Andrew, accost.

SIR ANDREW: What's that?

SIR TOBY: My niece's chambermaid.[8]

SIR ANDREW: Good Mistress Accost, I desire better acquaintance.

MARIA: My name is Mary, sir.

SIR ANDREW: Good Mistress Mary Accost—

SIR TOBY: You mistake, knight. "Accost" is front her,[9] board her,[1] woo her, assail her.

SIR ANDREW: By my troth, I would not undertake her in this company. Is that the meaning of "accost"?

MARIA: Fare you well, gentlemen. [(*Going.*)]

SIR TOBY: An thou let part[2] so, Sir Andrew, would thou mightst never draw sword again.

SIR ANDREW: An you part so, mistress, I would I might never draw sword again. Fair lady, do you think you have fools in hand?[3]

MARIA: Sir, I have not you by the hand.

6. He'll spend all his money in a year.
7. Predecessor to the violincello.
8. Play on the sense "born idiot."
9. Taste.
1. Detractors.
2. Horse groom (base fellow).
3. Large top, spun by whipping, provided by the parish as a form of exercise.
4. Uncertain meaning. Possibly a call for politeness, or else a form of "speak of the devil."
5. With the thin, pale countenance of someone suffering from ague, a fever marked by chills.
6. Small creature (connotation of shrewishness probably unintended).
7. Greet her.
8. A lady-in-waiting, not a servant.
9. Come alongside her.
1. As in a naval encounter; the language of battle is used to describe sex.
2. If you let her leave.
3. Have fools to deal with (Mary chooses to take it literally).

SIR ANDREW: Marry,[4] but you shall have, and here's my hand. [(*He gives her his hand.*)]

MARIA: Now, sir, thought is free. I pray you, bring your hand to the buttery-bar,[5] and let it drink.

SIR ANDREW: Wherefore, sweetheart? What's your metaphor?

MARIA: It's dry,[6] sir.

SIR ANDREW: Why, I think so. I am not such an ass but I can keep my hand dry. But what's your jest?

MARIA: A dry[7] jest, sir.

SIR ANDREW: Are you full of them?

MARIA: Ay, sir, I have them at my fingers' ends.[8] Marry, now I let go your hand, I am barren. [*She lets go his hand.*] [*Exit Maria.*]

SIR TOBY: O knight, thou lack'st a cup of canary![9] When did I see thee so put down?[1]

SIR ANDREW: Never in your life, I think, unless you see canary put me down.[2] Methinks sometimes I have no more wit than a Christian or an ordinary man has. But I am a great eater of beef, and I believe that does harm to my wit.

SIR TOBY: No question.

SIR ANDREW: An I thought that, I'd forswear it. I'll ride home tomorrow, Sir Toby.

SIR TOBY: *Pourquoi*,[3] my dear knight?

SIR ANDREW: What is "*pourquoi*"? Do or not do? I would I had bestowed that time in the tongues[4] that I have in fencing, dancing, and bearbaiting. O, had I but followed the arts![5]

SIR TOBY: Then hadst thou had an excellent head of hair.

SIR ANDREW: Why, would that have mended my hair?

SIR TOBY: Past question, for thou seest it will not curl by nature.

SIR ANDREW: But it becomes me well enough, does't not?

SIR TOBY: Excellent. It hangs like flax on a distaff;[6] and I hope to see a huswife take thee between her legs and spin it off.[7]

SIR ANDREW: Faith, I'll home tomorrow, Sir Toby. Your niece will not be seen, or if she be, it's four to one she'll none of me. The Count himself here hard by[8] woos her.

SIR TOBY: She'll none o' the Count. She'll not match above her degree,[9] neither in estate,[1] years, nor wit; I have heard her swear 't. Tut; there's life in 't,[2] man.

SIR ANDREW: I'll stay a month longer. I am a fellow o' the strangest mind i' the world; I delight in masques and revels sometimes altogether.[3]

SIR TOBY: Art thou good at these kickshawses,[4] knight?

4. Indeed.
5. Door of the wine-cellar.
6. Thirsty; aged and sexually weak.
7. Ironic; barren (referring to Sir Andrew).
8. At my disposal; in my hand.
9. Sweet wine from the Canary Islands.
1. Discomfited.
2. Knocked flat.
3. Why.
4. Languages, perhaps with a pun on curling-tongs.
5. Liberal arts (but Sir Toby plays on arts as "artifice").
6. Staff for holding flax during spinning.
7. Treat your hair like flax to be spun; cause you to lose it through venereal disease ("huswife" may be a pun on "hussy").
8. Nearby.
9. Rank.
1. Fortune.
2. There's hope left.
3. In all respects.
4. Trifles (from the French *quelque chose*).

SIR ANDREW: As any man in Illyria, whatsoever he be, under the degree of my betters,[5] and yet I will not compare with an old man.[6]

SIR TOBY: What is thy excellence in a galliard,[7] knight?

SIR ANDREW: Faith, I can cut a caper.[8]

SIR TOBY: And I can cut the mutton to 't.

SIR ANDREW: And I think I have the back-trick[9] simply as strong as any man in Illyria.

SIR TOBY: Wherefore are these things hid? Wherefore have these gifts a curtain before 'em? Are they like to take[1] dust, like Mistress Mall's picture?[2] Why dost thou not go to church in a galliard and come home in a coranto?[3] My very walk should be a jig; I would not so much as make water but in a sink-a-pace.[4] What dost thou mean? Is it a world to hide virtues[5] in? I did think, by the excellent constitution of thy leg, it was formed under the star of a galliard.[6]

SIR ANDREW: Ay, 'tis strong, and it does indifferent well[7] in a dun-colored stock.[8] Shall we set about some revels?

SIR TOBY: What shall we do else? Were we not born under Taurus?[9]

SIR ANDREW: Taurus? That's sides and heart.

SIR TOBY: No, sir, it is legs and thighs. Let me see thee caper. [(*Sir Andrew capers.*)] Ha, higher! Ha, ha, excellent! [*Exeunt.*]

Scene 4[1]

[*Enter Valentine, and Viola in man's attire.*]

VALENTINE: If the Duke continue these favors towards you, Cesario, you are like to be much advanced. He hath known you but three days, and already you are no stranger.

VIOLA: You either fear his humor[2] or my negligence, that you call in question the continuance of his love. Is he inconstant, sir, in his favors?

VALENTINE: No, believe me.

[*Enter Duke (Orsino), Curio, and attendants.*]

VIOLA: I thank you. Here comes the Count.

ORSINO: Who saw Cesario, ho?

VIOLA: On your attendance,° my lord, here. *at your service*

ORSINO: Stand you awhile aloof. [(*The others stand aside.*)] Cesario,
Thou know'st no less but all.° I have unclasped *everything*
To thee the book even of my secret soul.
Therefore, good youth, address thy gait° unto her; *go*
Be not denied access, stand at her doors,
And tell them, there thy fixèd foot shall grow
Till thou have audience.

5. Excepting my social superiors.
6. Experienced person.
7. Lively dance in triple-time.
8. Lively leap; spice used with mutton (mutton suggests "whore").
9. Backward step in the galliard.
1. Likely to collect.
2. Any woman's portrait (usually kept under protective glass).
3. Running dance.
4. Dance like the galliard (French *cinquepace*).
5. Talents.
6. Under a star favorable to dancing.
7. Well enough.
8. Stocking.
9. Zodiacal sign said to govern legs and thighs (Sir Andrew is mistaken).
1. Location: Orsino's court.
2. Changeableness.

VIOLA: Sure, my noble lord,
If she be so abandoned to her sorrow
As it is spoke, she never will admit me.
ORSINO: Be clamorous and leap all civil bounds° *bounds of civility*
Rather than make unprofited return.
VIOLA: Say I do speak with her, my lord, what then?
ORSINO: O, then unfold the passion of my love;
Surprise° her with discourse of my dear faith. *take her by storm*
It shall become° thee well to act my woes; *suit*
She will attend it better in thy youth
Than in a nuncio's° of more grave aspect. *messenger's*
VIOLA: I think not so, my lord.
ORSINO: Dear lad, believe it;
For they shall yet belie thy happy years
That say thou art a man. Diana's lip
Is not more smooth and rubious;° thy small pipe° *ruby red / voice*
Is as the maiden's organ, shrill and sound,° *high and clear*
And all is semblative° a woman's part. *resembling*
I know thy constellation° is right apt *predestined nature*
For this affair.—Some four or five attend him.
All, if you will, for I myself am best
When least in company.—Prosper well in this,
And thou shalt live as freely as thy lord,
To call his fortunes thine.
VIOLA: I'll do my best,
To woo your lady. [(*Aside.*)] Yet a barful strife!° *conflict full of impediments*
Whoe'er I woo, myself would be his wife. [*Exeunt.*]

Scene 5[3]

[*Enter Maria and Clown (Feste).*]

MARIA: Nay, either tell me where thou hast been, or I will not open my lips so wide as a bristle may enter in way of thy excuse. My lady will hang thee for thy absence.

FESTE: Let her hang me. He that is well hanged in this world needs to fear no colors.[4]

MARIA: Make that good.[5]

FESTE: He shall see none to fear.[6]

MARIA: A good Lenten[7] answer. I can tell thee where that saying was born, of "I fear no colors."

FESTE: Where, good Mistress Mary?

MARIA: In the wars,[8] and that may you be bold to say in your foolery.

FESTE: Well, God give them wisdom that have it; and those that are fools, let them use their talents.[9]

3. Location: Olivia's house.
4. Fear nothing.
5. Explain that.
6. He'll be dead and, therefore, fear no one.
7. Meager, like Lenten fare.
8. In war, "colors" would be enemy flags.
9. Abilities (reference to the parable of the talents, Matthew 25.14–29).

MARIA: Yet you will be hanged for being so long absent; or to be turned away,[1] is not that as good as a hanging to you?

FESTE: Many a good hanging[2] prevents a bad marriage; and for turning away, let summer bear it out.[3]

MARIA: You are resolute, then?

FESTE: Not so, neither, but I am resolved on two points.[4]

MARIA: That if one break, the other will hold; or if both break, your gaskins[5] fall.

FESTE: Apt, in good faith, very apt. Well, go thy way. If Sir Toby would leave drinking, thou wert as witty a piece of Eve's flesh as any in Illyria.

MARIA: Peace, you rogue, no more o' that. Here comes my lady. Make your excuse wisely, you were best.[6] [*Exit.*]

[*Enter Lady Olivia with Malvolio* (*and Attendants*).]

FESTE [(*Aside*)]: Wit, an 't be thy will, put me into good fooling! Those wits that think they have thee do very oft prove fools, and I that am sure I lack thee may pass for a wise man. For what says Quinapalus?[7] "Better a witty fool than a foolish wit."—God bless thee, lady!

OLIVIA [(*To attendants*)]: Take the fool away.

FESTE: Do you not hear, fellows? Take away the lady.

OLIVIA: Go to,[8] you're a dry[9] fool. I'll no more of you.
Besides, you grow dishonest.[1]

FESTE: Two faults, madonna,[2] that drink and good counsel will amend. For give the dry[3] fool drink, then is the fool not dry. Bid the dishonest man mend himself; if he mend, he is no longer dishonest; if he cannot, let the botcher[4] mend him. Anything that's mended is but patched; virtue that transgresses is but patched with sin, and sin that amends is but patched with virtue. If that this simple syllogism will serve, so; if it will not, what remedy? As there is no true cuckold but calamity, so beauty's a flower.[5] The lady bade take away the fool; therefore I say again, take her away.

OLIVIA: Sir, I bade them take away you.

FESTE: Misprision[6] in the highest degree! Lady, *cucullus non facit monachum;*[7] that's as much to say as I wear not motley[8] in my brain. Good madonna, give me leave to prove you a fool.

OLIVIA: Can you do it?

FESTE: Dexterously, good madonna.

OLIVIA: Make your proof.

FESTE: I must catechize you for it, madonna. Good my mouse of virtue,[9] answer me.

OLIVIA: Well, sir, for want of other idleness,[1] I'll bide[2] your proof.

FESTE: Good madonna, why mourn'st thou?

1. Dismissed.
2. Perhaps a bawdy pun on being "well-hung."
3. Let mild weather make homelessness endurable.
4. Maria plays on points as "laces used to hold up breeches."
5. Wide breeches.
6. It would be best for you.
7. Feste's invention.
8. Stop.
9. Dull.
1. Unreliable.
2. My lady.
3. Thirsty.
4. Mender of old clothes.
5. I.e., Olivia has wedded calamity but will be unfaithful to it, for it is natural to seize the moment of youth and beauty.
6. Mistake.
7. The cowl does not make the monk.
8. The multicolored fool's garment.
9. Virtuous mouse (term of endearment).
1. Pastime.
2. Endure.

OLIVIA: Good fool, for my brother's death.

FESTE: I think his soul is in hell, madonna.

OLIVIA: I know his soul is in heaven, fool.

FESTE: The more fool, madonna, to mourn for your brother's soul, being in heaven. Take away the fool, gentlemen.

OLIVIA: What think you of this fool, Malvolio? Doth he not mend?[3]

MALVOLIO: Yes, and shall do till the pangs of death shake him. Infirmity, that decays the wise, doth ever make the better fool.

FESTE: God send you, sir, a speedy infirmity for the better increasing your folly! Sir Toby will be sworn that I am no fox, but he will not pass[4] his word for twopence that you are no fool.

OLIVIA: How say you to that, Malvolio?

MALVOLIO: I marvel your ladyship takes delight in such a barren rascal. I saw him put down the other day with[5] an ordinary fool that has no more brain than a stone. Look you now, he's out of his guard[6] already. Unless you laugh and minister occasion[7] to him, he is gagged. I protest I take these wise men that crow so at these set[8] kind of fools no better than the fools' zanies.[9]

OLIVIA: O, you are sick of self-love, Malvolio, and taste with a distempered[1] appetite. To be generous, guiltless, and of free disposition is to take those things for bird-bolts[2] that you deem cannon bullets. There is no slander in an allowed[3] fool, though he do nothing but rail; nor no railing in a known discreet man, though he do nothing but reprove.

FESTE: Now Mercury[4] endue thee with leasing,[5] for thou speak'st well of fools!

[*Enter Maria.*]

MARIA: Madam, there is at the gate a young gentleman much desires to speak with you.

OLIVIA: From the Count Orsino, is it?

MARIA: I know not, madam. 'Tis a fair young man, and well attended.

OLIVIA: Who of my people hold him in delay?

MARIA: Sir Toby, madam, your kinsman.

OLIVIA: Fetch him off, I pray you. He speaks nothing but madman.[6] Fie on him! [(*Exit Maria.*)] Go you, Malvolio. If it be a suit from the Count, I am sick, or not at home; what you will, to dismiss it. [*Exit Malvolio.*] Now you see, sir, how your fooling grows old, and people dislike it.

FESTE: Thou hast spoke for us, madonna, as if thy eldest son should be a fool; whose skull Jove cram with brains, for—here he comes—

[*Enter Sir Toby.*]

one of thy kin has a most weak *pia mater*.[7]

OLIVIA: By mine honor, half drunk. What is he at the gate, cousin?

SIR TOBY: A gentleman.

OLIVIA: A gentleman? What gentleman?

3. Improve.
4. Give.
5. By.
6. Defenseless.
7. Provide occasion for wit.
8. Artificial.
9. Fools' assistants.

1. Diseased.
2. Blunt arrows for shooting birds.
3. Licensed.
4. God of trickery.
5. Make you a skillful liar.
6. The words of madness.
7. Brain.

SIR TOBY: 'tis a gentleman here—[(*He belches.*)] A plague o' these pickle-herring! [*To Feste.*] How now, sot?[8]

FESTE: Good Sir Toby.

OLIVIA: Cousin,[9] cousin, how have you come so early by this lethargy?

SIR TOBY: Lechery? I defy lechery. There's one at the gate.

OLIVIA: Ay, marry, what is he?

SIR TOBY: Let him be the devil an he will, I care not.
Give me faith,[1] say I. Well, it's all one.[2] [*Exit.*]

OLIVIA: What's a drunken man like, Fool?

FESTE: Like a drowned man, a fool, and a madman. One draft above heat[3] makes him a fool, the second mads him, and a third drowns him.

OLIVIA: Go thou and seek the crowner,[4] and let him sit o' my coz;[5] for he's in the third degree of drink, he's drowned. Go, look after him.

FESTE: He is but mad yet, madonna; and the fool shall look to the madman. [*Exit.*]

[*Enter Malvolio.*]

MALVOLIO: Madam, yond young fellow swears he will speak with you. I told him you were sick; he takes on him to understand so much, and therefore comes to speak with you. I told him you were asleep; he seems to have a foreknowledge of that too, and therefore comes to speak with you. What is to be said to him, lady? He's fortified against any denial.

OLIVIA: Tell him he shall not speak with me.

MALVOLIO: He's been told so; and he says he'll stand at your door like a sheriff 's post,[6] and be the supporter to a bench, but he'll speak with you.

OLIVIA: What kind o' man is he?

MALVOLIO: Why, of mankind.

OLIVIA: What manner of man?

MALVOLIO: Of very ill manner. He'll speak with you, will you or no.

OLIVIA: Of what personage and years is he?

MALVOLIO: Not yet old enough for a man, nor young enough for a boy; as a squash[7] is before 'tis a peascod,[8] or a codling[9] when 'tis almost an apple. 'tis with him in standing water[1] between boy and man. He is very well-favored,[2] and he speaks very shrewishly.[3] One would think his mother's milk were scarce out of him.

OLIVIA: Let him approach. Call in my gentlewoman.

MALVOLIO: Gentlewoman, my lady calls. [*Exit.*]

[*Enter Maria.*]

OLIVIA: Give me my veil. Come, throw it o'er my face.
We'll once more hear Orsino's embassy. [*Olivia veils.*]

[*Enter Viola.*]

VIOLA: The honorable lady of the house, which is she?

OLIVIA: Speak to me; I shall answer for her. Your will?

8. Fool; drunkard.
9. Kinsman.
1. I.e., to resist the devil.
2. It doesn't matter.
3. Drink more than would make him warm.
4. Coroner.
5. Hold an inquest on my kinsman (Sir Toby).
6. Post before the sherrif's door to mark a residence of authority.
7. Unripe pea-pod.
8. Pea-pod.
9. Unripe apple.
1. At the turn of the tide.
2. Good-looking.
3. Sharply.

VIOLA: Most radiant, exquisite, and unmatchable beauty—I pray you, tell me if this be the lady of the house, for I never saw her. I would be loath to cast away my speech; for besides that it is excellently well penned, I have taken great pains to con[4] it. Good beauties, let me sustain[5] no scorn; I am very comptible,[6] even to the least sinister usage.[7]

OLIVIA: Whence came you, sir?

VIOLA: I can say little more than I have studied, and that question's out of my part. Good gentle one, give me modest[8] assurance if you be the lady of the house, that I may proceed in my speech.

OLIVIA: Are you a comedian?[9]

VIOLA: No, my profound heart; and yet, by the very fangs of malice, I swear I am not that I play. Are you the lady of the house?

OLIVIA: If I do not usurp[1] myself, I am.

VIOLA: Most certain, if you are she, you do usurp yourself; for what is yours to bestow is not yours to reserve. But this is from[2] my commission. I will on with my speech in your praise, and then show you the heart of my message.

OLIVIA: Come to what is important in 't. I forgive[3] you the praise.

VIOLA: Alas, I took great pains to study it, and 'tis poetical.

OLIVIA: It is the more like to be feigned. I pray you, keep it in. I heard you were saucy at my gates, and allowed your approach rather to wonder at you than to hear you. If you be not mad,[4] begone; if you have reason,[5] be brief. 'Tis not that time of moon with me[6] to make one[7] in so skipping[8] a dialogue.

MARIA: Will you hoist sail, sir? Here lies your way.

VIOLA: No, good swabber,[9] I am to hull[1] here a little longer.—Some mollification for your giant,[2] sweet lady. Tell me your mind; I am a messenger.

OLIVIA: Sure you have some hideous matter to deliver, when the courtesy[3] of it is so fearful. Speak your office.[4]

VIOLA: It alone concerns your ear. I bring no overture of war, no taxation[5] of homage. I hold the olive[6] in my hand; my words are as full of peace as matter.

OLIVIA: Yet you began rudely. What are you? What would you?

VIOLA: The rudeness that hath appeared in me have I learned from my entertainment.[7] What I am and what I would are as secret as maidenhead—to your ears, divinity;[8] to any other's, profanation.

OLIVIA: Give us the place alone. We will hear this divinity. [*Exeunt Maria and attendants.*] Now, sir, what is your text?

VIOLA: Most sweet lady—

4. Learn by heart.
5. Endure.
6. Sensitive.
7. Slightest rude treatment.
8. Reasonable.
9. Actor.
1. Supplant.
2. Outside.
3. Excuse.
4. Altogether mad? But mad?
5. Sanity.
6. I'm not in the mood.
7. Take part.
8. Sprightly.
9. One who swabs the deck.
1. Float without sails.
2. Small Maria, who guards her lady like a medieval giant.
3. Formal beginning.
4. Business.
5. Demand.
6. Olive-branch.
7. Reception.
8. Holy discourse.

OLIVIA: A comfortable[9] doctrine, and much may be said of it. Where lies your text?

VIOLA: In Orsino's bosom.

OLIVIA: In his bosom? In what chapter of his bosom?

VIOLA: To answer by the method,[1] in the first of his heart.

OLIVIA: O, I have read it. It is heresy. Have you no more to say?

VIOLA: Good madam, let me see your face.

OLIVIA: Have you any commission from your lord to negotiate with my face? You are now out of your text. But we will draw the curtain and show you the picture. [*Unveiling.*] Look you, sir, such a one I was this present.[2] Is 't not well done?

VIOLA: Excellently done, if God did all.

OLIVIA: 'tis in grain,[3] sir; 'twill endure wind and weather.

VIOLA: 'tis beauty truly blent,[4] whose red and white
Nature's own sweet and cunning[5] hand laid on.
Lady, you are the cruel'st she alive
If you will lead these graces to the grave
And leave the world no copy.

OLIVIA: O, sir, I will not be so hardhearted. I will give out divers schedules[6] of my beauty. It shall be inventoried, and every particle and utensil[7] labeled to[8] my will: as, item, two lips, indifferent[9] red; item, two gray eyes, with lids to them; item, one neck, one chin, and so forth. Were you sent hither to praise[1] me?

VIOLA: I see you what you are: you are too proud.
But, if° you were the devil, you are fair. *even if*
My lord and master loves you. O, such love
Could be but recompensed,° though you were crowned *could only be repaid*
The nonpareil of beauty!

OLIVIA: How does he love me?

VIOLA: With adorations, fertile° tears, *abundant*
With groans that thunder love, with sighs of fire.

OLIVIA: Your lord does know my mind; I cannot love him.
Yet I suppose him virtuous, know him noble,
Of great estate, of fresh and stainless youth,
In voices well divulged,° free,° learned, and valiant, *well spoken of / generous*
And in dimension and the shape of nature° *physical form*
A gracious° person. But yet I cannot love him. *graceful*
He might have took his answer long ago.

VIOLA: If I did love you in my master's flame,° *passion*
With such a suffering, 'such a deadly° life, *death-like*
In your denial I would find no sense;
I would not understand it.

OLIVIA: Why, what would you?

9. Comforting.
1. To continue the metaphor.
2. A minute ago.
3. Fast dyed.
4. Blended.
5. Skillful.
6. Lists.
7. Article.
8. Added to.
9. Somewhat.
1. Pun on "appraise."

VIOLA: Make me a willow[2] cabin at your gate
And call upon my soul° within the house; *Olivia*
Write loyal cantons° of contemnèd° love *songs / rejected*
And sing them loud even in the dead of night;
Hallow° your name to the reverberate hills, *call; bless*
And make the babbling gossip° of the air *echo*
Cry out "Olivia!" O, you should not rest
Between the elements of air and earth
But you should pity me!

OLIVIA: You might do much.
What is your parentage?

VIOLA: Above my fortunes, yet my state° is well. *social standing*
I am a gentleman.

OLIVIA: Get you to your lord.
I cannot love him. Let him send no more—
Unless, perchance, you come to me again
To tell me how he takes it. Fare you well.
I thank you for your pains. Spend this for me.

[(*She offers a purse.*)]

VIOLA: I am no fee'd post,° lady. Keep your purse. *paid messenger*
My master, not myself, lacks recompense.
Love make his heart of flint that you shall love,
And let your fervor, like my master's, be
Placed in contempt! Farewell, fair cruelty. [*Exit.*]

OLIVIA: "What is your parentage?"
"Above my fortunes, yet my state is well:
I am a gentleman." I'll be sworn thou art!
Thy tongue, thy face, thy limbs, actions, and spirit
Do give thee fivefold blazon.° Not too fast! Soft,° soft! *coat of arms / wait*
Unless the master were the man.[3] How now?
Even so quickly may one catch the plague?
Methinks I feel this youth's perfections
With an invisible and subtle stealth
To creep in at mine eyes. Well, let it be.
What ho, Malvolio!

[*Enter Malvolio.*]

MALVOLIO: Here, madam, at your service.

OLIVIA: Run after that same peevish messenger,
The County's° man. He left this ring behind him, *Count's*
[*giving a ring*]
Would I or not.[4] Tell him I'll none of it.
Desire him not to flatter with° his lord, *encourage*
Nor hold him up with hopes; I am not for him.
If that the youth will come this way tomorrow,
I'll give him reasons for 't. Hie thee, Malvolio.

MALVOLIO: Madam, I will. [*Exit*]

2. Willow was the symbol of unrequited love.
3. Unless Cesario and Orsino changed places.
4. Whether I wanted it or not.

OLIVIA: I do I know not what, and fear to find
Mine eye too great a flatterer for my mind.
Fate, show thy force. Ourselves we do not owe.° *own*
What is decreed must be; and be this so. [*Exit.*]

ACT 2

Scene 1[5]

[*Enter Antonio and Sebastian.*]

ANTONIO: Will you stay no longer? Nor will you not[6] that I go with you?

SEBASTIAN: By your patience,[7] no. My stars shine darkly over me. The malignancy of my fate might perhaps distemper yours; therefore I shall crave of you your leave that I may bear my evils alone. It were a bad recompense for your love to lay any of them on you.

ANTONIO: Let me yet know of you whither you are bound.

SEBASTIAN: No, sooth,[8] sir; my determinate[9] voyage is mere extravagancy.[1] But I perceive in you so excellent a touch of modesty that you will not extort from me what I am willing to keep in; therefore it charges me in manners the rather to express myself.[2] You must know of me then, Antonio, my name is Sebastian, which I called Roderigo. My father was that Sebastian of Messaline whom I know you have heard of. He left behind him myself and a sister, both born in an hour.[3] If the heavens had been pleased, would we had so ended! But you, sir, altered that, for some hour[4] before you took me from the breach of the sea[5] was my sister drowned.

ANTONIO: Alas the day!

SEBASTIAN: A lady, sir, though it was said she much resembled me, was yet of many accounted beautiful. But though I could not with such estimable wonder[6] over-far believe that, yet thus far I will boldly publish[7] her: she bore a mind that envy[8] could not but call fair. She is drowned already, sir, with salt water, though I seem to drown her remembrance again with more.

ANTONIO: Pardon me, sir, your bad entertainment.[9]

SEBASTIAN: O good Antonio, forgive me your trouble.[1]

ANTONIO: If you will not murder me for[2] my love, let me be your servant.

SEBASTIAN: If you will not undo what you have done, that is, kill him whom you have recovered,[3] desire it not. Fare ye well at once. My bosom is full of

5. Location: Somewhere in Illyria.
6. Do you not wish.
7. Leave.
8. Truly.
9. Determined upon.
1. Wandering.
2. Courtesy demands that I reveal myself.
3. In the same hour.
4. About an hour.
5. The surf.
6. Admiring judgment.
7. Proclaim.
8. Even malice.
9. Reception.
1. The trouble I put you to.
2. Be the death of me in return for.
3. Saved.

kindness,[4] and I am yet so near the manners of my mother[5] that upon the least occasion more mine eyes will tell tales of me. I am bound to the Count Orsino's court. Farewell. *[Exit.]*

ANTONIO: The gentleness of all the gods go with thee!
I have many enemies in Orsino's court,
Else would I very shortly see thee there.
But come what may, I do adore thee so
That danger shall seem sport, and I will go. *[Exit.]*

Scene 2[6]

[Enter Viola and Malvolio, at several[7] doors.]

MALVOLIO: Were not you even now with the Countess Olivia?

VIOLA: Even now, sir. On a moderate pace I have since arrived but hither.

MALVOLIO: She returns this ring to you, sir. You might have saved me my pains, to have taken[8] it away yourself. She adds, moreover, that you should put your lord into a desperate[9] assurance she will none of him. And one thing more: that you be never so hardy to come[1] again in his affairs, unless it be to report your lord's taking of this. Receive it so.

VIOLA: She took the ring of me. I'll none of it.

MALVOLIO: Come, sir, you peevishly threw it to her, and her will is it should be so returned. [*He throws down the ring.*] If it be worth stooping for, there it lies, in your eye; if not, be it his that finds it.

[Exit.]

VIOLA [*picking up the ring*]: I left no ring with her. What means this lady?
Fortune forbid my outside have not charmed her!
She made good view of° me, indeed so much — *looked closely at*
That sure methought her eyes had lost° her tongue, — *caused her to lose*
For she did speak in starts, distractedly.
She loves me, sure! The cunning of her passion
Invites me in° this churlish messenger. — *in the person of*
None of my lord's ring? Why, he sent her none.
I am the man.° If it be so—as 'tis— — *man of her choice*
Poor lady, she were better love a dream.
Disguise, I see, thou art a wickedness
Wherein the pregnant enemy° does much. — *resourceful Satan*
How easy is it for the proper false° — *handsome deceivers*
In women's waxen° hearts to set their forms!° — *malleable / impressions*
Alas, our frailty is the cause, not we,
For such as we are made of, such we be.
How will this fadge?° My master loves her dearly, — *turn out*
And I, poor monster,[2] fond° as much on him; — *dote*
And she, mistaken, seems to dote on me.

4. Tenderness.
5. Womanly inclination to weep.
6. Location: Outside Olivia's house.
7. Different.
8. By taking.
9. Without hope.
1. Bold as to come.
2. Because both man and woman.

What will become of this? As I am man,
My state is desperate° for my master's love; *hopeless*
As I am woman—now, alas the day!—
What thriftless° sighs shall poor Olivia breathe! *unprofitable*
O Time, thou must untangle this, not I;
It is too hard a knot for me t' untie. [*Exit.*]

Scene 3[3]

[*Enter Sir Toby and Sir Andrew.*]

SIR TOBY: Approach, Sir Andrew. Not to be abed after midnight is to be up betimes;[4] and *diluculo surgere*,[5] thou know'st—

SIR ANDREW: Nay, by my troth, I know not, but I know to be up late is to be up late.

SIR TOBY: A false conclusion. I hate it as an unfilled can.[6] To be up after midnight and to go to bed then, is early; so that to go to bed after midnight is to go to bed betimes. Does not our lives consist of the four elements?[7]

SIR ANDREW: Faith, so they say, but I think it rather consists of eating and drinking.

SIR TOBY: Thou'rt a scholar; let us therefore eat and drink. Marian, I say, a stoup[8] of wine!

[*Enter Clown (Feste).*]

SIR ANDREW: Here comes the Fool, i' faith.

FESTE: How now, my hearts! Did you never see the picture of "we three"?[9]

SIR TOBY: Welcome, ass. Now let's have a catch.[1]

SIR ANDREW: By my troth, the Fool has an excellent breast.[2] I had rather than forty shillings I had such a leg, and so sweet a breath to sing, as the fool has. In sooth, thou wast in very gracious[3] fooling last night, when thou spok'st of Pigrogromitus, of the Vapians passing the equinoctial of Queubus.[4] 'twas very good, i' faith. I sent thee sixpence for thy leman.[5] Hadst it?

FESTE: I did impeticos thy gratillity;[6] for Malvolio's nose is no whipstock.[7] My lady has a white hand, and the Myrmidons[8] are no bottle-ale houses.

SIR ANDREW: Excellent! Why, this is the best fooling, when all is done. Now, a song.

SIR TOBY: Come on, there is sixpence for you. [(*He gives money.*)] Let's have a song.

SIR ANDREW: There's a testril[9] of me too. [(*He gives money.*)] If one knight give a—

FESTE: Would you have a love song, or a song of good life?[1]

SIR TOBY: A love song, a love song.

SIR ANDREW: Ay, ay, I care not for good life.

3. Location: Olivia's house.
4. Early.
5. *Diluculo surgere (saluberrimum est)*—to rise early is most healthful (from Lily's *Latin Grammar*).
6. Tankard.
7. Fire, water, earth, air.
8. Goblet.
9. Picture of two fools or asses, the onlooker being the third.
1. Round-song.
2. Voice.
3. Elegant.
4. Mock erudition.
5. Sweetheart.
6. Impetticoat (pocket up) thy gratuity.
7. Whip-handle.
8. Followers of Achilles.
9. Coin worth sixpence.
1. Virtuous living.

FESTE [(*sings*)]:

O mistress mine, where are you roaming?
O, stay and hear, your true love 's coming.
That can sing both high and low.
Trip no further, pretty sweeting
Journeys end in lovers' meeting,
Every wise man's son doth know.

SIR ANDREW: Excellent good, i' faith.

SIR TOBY: Good, good.

FESTE [(*sings*)]:

What is love? 'tis not hereafter;
Present mirth hath present laughter;
What's to come is still unsure.
In delay there lies no plenty.
Then come kiss me, sweet and twenty;
Youth's a stuff will not endure.

SIR ANDREW: A mellifluous voice, as I am true knight.

SIR TOBY: A contagious[2] breath.

SIR ANDREW: Very sweet and contagious, i' faith.

SIR TOBY: To hear by the nose, it is dulcet in contagion. But shall we make the welkin[3] dance indeed? Shall we rouse the night owl in a catch that will draw three souls out of one weaver?[4] Shall we do that?

SIR ANDREW: An you love me, let's do't. I am dog at a catch.

FESTE: By'r Lady, sir, and some dogs will catch well.

SIR ANDREW: Most certain. Let our catch be "Thou knave."

FESTE: "Hold thy peace, thou knave," knight? I shall be constrained in 't to call thee knave, knight.

SIR ANDREW: 'Tis not the first time I have constrained one to call me knave. Begin, Fool. It begins, "Hold thy peace."

FESTE: I shall never begin if I hold my peace.

SIR ANDREW: Good, i' faith. Come, begin. [*Catch sung.*]

[*Enter Maria.*]

MARIA: What a caterwauling do you keep here! If my lady have not called up her steward Malvolio and bid him turn you out of doors, never trust me.

SIR TOBY: My lady's a Cataian,[5] we are politicians,[6] Malvolio's a Peg-o'-Ramsey,[7] and [(*He sings*)] "Three merry men be we." Am not I consanguineous?[8] Am I not of her blood? Tillyvally![9] Lady! [(*He sings.*)] "There dwelt a man in Babylon, lady, lady."[1]

FESTE: Beshrew me, the knight's in admirable fooling.

SIR ANDREW: Ay, he does well enough if he be disposed, and so do I too. He does it with a better grace, but I do it more natural.[2]

2. Catchy; infected.
3. Sky.
4. Weavers were associated with the singing of psalms.
5. Native of Cathay; trickster.
6. Schemers.
7. Character in a popular song (here used contemptuously).
8. Related.
9. Nonsense.
1. From an old song, *The Constancy of Suzanna.*
2. Naturally (unconsciously suggesting idiocy).

SIR TOBY [(*sings*)]: "O' the twelfth day of December"—

MARIA: For the love o' God, peace!

[*Enter Malvolio.*]

MALVOLIO: My masters, are you mad? Or what are you? Have you no wit,[3] manners, nor honesty[4] but to gabble like tinkers at this time of night? Do ye make an alehouse of my lady's house, that ye squeak out your coziers'[5] catches without any mitigation or remorse[6] of voice? Is there no respect of place, persons, nor time in you?

SIR TOBY: We did keep time, sir, in our catches. Sneck up![7]

MALVOLIO: Sir Toby, I must be round[8] with you. My lady bade me tell you that though she harbors you as her kinsman, she's nothing allied to your disorders. If you can separate yourself and your misdemeanors, you are welcome to the house; if not, an it would please you to take leave of her, she is very willing to bid you farewell.

SIR TOBY [(*sings*)]: "Farewell, dear heart, since I must needs be gone."[9]

MARIA: Nay, good Sir Toby.

FESTE [(*sings*)]: "His eyes do show his days are almost done."

MALVOLIO: Is't even so?

SIR TOBY [(*sings*)]: "But I will never die."

FESTE: "Sir Toby, there you lie."

MALVOLIO: This is much credit to you.

SIR TOBY [(*sings*)]: "Shall I bid him go?"

FESTE [(*sings*)]: "What an if you do?"

SIR TOBY [(*sings*)]: "Shall I bid him go, and spare not?"

FESTE [(*sings*)]: "O, no, no, no, no, you dare not."

SIR TOBY: Out o' tune, sir? Ye lie. Art any more than a steward? Dost thou think, because thou art virtuous, there shall be no more cakes and ale?

FESTE: Yes, by Saint Anne,[1] and ginger[2] shall be hot i' the mouth, too.

SIR TOBY: Thou'rt i' the right.—Go, sir, rub your chain with crumbs.[3]—A stoup of wine, Maria!

MALVOLIO: Mistress Mary, if you prized my lady's favor at anything more than contempt, you would not give means[4] for this uncivil rule.[5] She shall know of it, by this hand. [*Exit.*]

MARIA: Go shake your ears.[6]

SIR ANDREW: 'Twere as good a deed as to drink when a man's a-hungry to challenge him the field[7] and then to break promise with him and make a fool of him.

SIR TOBY: Do 't, knight. I'll write thee a challenge, or I'll deliver thy indignation to him by word of mouth.

MARIA: Sweet Sir Toby, be patient for tonight. Since the youth of the Count's was today with my lady, she is much out of quiet. For[8] Monsieur Malvolio, let

3. Common sense.
4. Decency.
5. Cobblers'.
6. Considerate lowering.
7. Go hang.
8. Blunt.
9. From the ballad *Corydon's Farewell to Phyllis*.
1. Mother of the Virgin Mary. (Her cult was derided in the Reformation, as were cakes and ale at church feasts.)
2. Used to spice ale.
3. Remember your position.
4. I.e., provide wine.
5. Behavior.
6. I.e., your ass's ears.
7. To a duel.
8. As for.

me alone with him. If I do not gull[9] him into a nayword[1] and make him a common recreation,[2] do not think I have wit enough to lie straight in my bed. I know I can do it.

SIR TOBY: Possess us,[3] possess us. Tell us something of him.

MARIA: Marry, sir, sometimes he is a kind of puritan.

SIR ANDREW: O, if I thought that, I'd beat him like a dog.

SIR TOBY: What, for being a puritan? Thy exquisite reason, dear knight?

SIR ANDREW: I have no exquisite reason for 't, but I have reason good enough.

MARIA: The devil a puritan that he is, or anything constantly,[4] but a time-pleaser;[5] an affectioned[6] ass, that cons state without book[7] and utters it by great swaths; the best persuaded of himself, so crammed, as he thinks, with excellencies, that it is his grounds of faith that all that look on him love him; and on that vice in him will my revenge find notable cause to work.

SIR TOBY: What wilt thou do?

MARIA: I will drop in his way some obscure epistles of love, wherein by the color of his beard, the shape of his leg, the manner of his gait, the expressure[8] of his eye, forehead, and complexion, he shall find himself most feelingly personated.[9] I can write very like my lady your niece; on a forgotten matter[1] we can hardly make distinction of our hands.

SIR TOBY: Excellent! I smell a device.

SIR ANDREW: I have't in my nose too.

SIR TOBY: He shall think, by the letters that thou wilt drop, that they come from my niece, and that she's in love with him.

MARIA: My purpose is indeed a horse of that color.

SIR ANDREW: And your horse now would make him an ass.

MARIA: Ass, I doubt not.

SIR ANDREW: O, 'twill be admirable!

MARIA: Sport royal, I warrant you. I know my physic[2] will work with him. I will plant you two, and let the Fool make a third, where he shall find the letter. Observe his construction[3] of it. For this night, to bed, and dream on the event.[4] Farewell. *[Exit.]*

SIR TOBY: Good night, Penthesilea.[5]

SIR ANDREW: Before me,[6] she's a good wench.

SIR TOBY: She's a beagle[7] true-bred and one that adores me. What o' that?

SIR ANDREW: I was adored once, too.

SIR TOBY: Let's to bed, knight. Thou hadst need send for more money.

SIR ANDREW: If I cannot recover[8] your niece, I am a foul way out.[9]

SIR TOBY: Send for money, knight. If thou hast her not i' the end, call me cut.[1]

SIR ANDREW: If I do not, never trust me, take it how you will.

9. Trick.
1. Byword (for dupe).
2. Sport.
3. Inform.
4. Consistently.
5. Sychophant.
6. Affected.
7. Learns a stately manner by heart.
8. Expression.
9. Represented.
1. When we have forgotten who wrote something.
2. Medicine.
3. Interpretation.
4. Outcome.
5. Queen of the Amazons.
6. I swear.
7. Small, intelligent hunting dog.
8. Win.
9. Out of money.
1. Horse with a docked tail or, perhaps, a gelding.

SIR TOBY: Come, come, I'll go burn some sack.[2] 'tis too late to go to bed now.
Come, knight; come, knight. [*Exeunt.*]

Scene 4[3]

[*Enter Duke (Orsino) Viola, Curio, and others.*]

ORSINO: Give me some music. Now, good morrow,° friends. *morning*
Now, good Cesario, but° that piece of song, *I ask only*
That old and antique° song we heard last night. *quaint*
Methought it did relieve my passion much,
More than light airs and recollected° terms *studied*
Of these most brisk and giddy-pacèd times.
Come, but one verse.

CURIO: He is not here, so please your lordship, that should sing it.

ORSINO: Who was it?

CURIO: Feste the jester, my lord, a fool that the Lady Olivia's father took much delight in. He is about the house.

ORSINO: Seek him out, and play the tune the while. [(*Exit Curio.*)]

[*Music plays.*]

[*To Viola.*] Come hither, boy. If ever thou shalt love
In the sweet pangs of it remember me;
For such as I am, all true lovers are,
Unstaid and skittish in all motions else° *other emotions*
Save in the constant image of the creature
That is beloved. How dost thou like this tune?

VIOLA: It gives a very echo to the seat
Where Love is throned.° *i.e., the heart*

ORSINO: Thou dost speak masterly.
My life upon 't, young though thou art, thine eye
Hath stayed upon some favor° that it loves. *face*
Hath it not, boy?

VIOLA: A little, by your favor.

ORSINO: What kind of woman is't?

VIOLA: Of your complexion.

ORSINO: She is not worth thee, then. What years, i' faith?

VIOLA: About your years, my lord.

ORSINO: Too old, by heaven. Let still° the woman take *always*
An elder than herself. So wears° she to him; *adapts herself*
So sways she level° in her husband's heart. *she keeps constant*
For, boy, however we do praise ourselves,
Our fancies° are more giddy and unfirm, *loves*
More longing, wavering, sooner lost and worn,
Than women's are.

VIOLA: I think it well, my lord.

ORSINO: Then let thy love be younger than thyself,
Or thy affection cannot hold the bent;° *hold steady*

2. Warm some Spanish wine.

3. Location: Orsino's court.

For women are as roses, whose fair flower
Being once displayed,° doth fall that very hour. *full blown*

VIOLA: And so they are. Alas that they are so,
To die even when° they to perfection grow! *just as*

[*Enter Curio and Clown (Feste).*]

ORSINO: O fellow, come, the song we had last night.
Mark it, Cesario, it is old and plain;
The spinsters° and the knitters in the sun, *spinners*
And the free° maids that weave their thread with bones,° *innocent / bobbins*
Do use° to chant it. It is silly sooth,° *are used / simple truth*
And dallies with the innocence of love,
Like the old age.° *good old days*

FESTE: Are you ready, sir?

ORSINO: Ay, prithee, sing. [*Music.*]

[*The Song.*]

FESTE [(*sings*)]:

Come away, come away, death,
And in sad cypress° let me be laid. *coffin*
Fly away, fly away, breath;
I am slain by a fair cruel maid.
My shroud of white, stuck all with yew,° *yew-sprigs*
O, prepare it!
My part° of death, no one so true *portion*
Did share it.

Not a flower, not a flower sweet
On my black coffin let there be strown;° *strewn*
Not a friend, not a friend greet
My poor corpse, where my bones shall be thrown.
A thousand thousand sighs to save,
Lay me, O, where
Sad true lover never find my grave,
To weep there!

ORSINO [(*offering money*)]: There's for thy pains.

FESTE: No pains, sir. I take pleasure in singing, sir.

ORSINO: I'll pay thy pleasure then.

FESTE: Truly, sir, and pleasure will be paid,[4] one time or another.

ORSINO: Give me now leave to leave thee.

FESTE: Now, the melancholy god[5] protect thee, and the tailor make thy doublet[6] of changeable taffeta, for thy mind is a very opal. I would have men of such constancy put to sea, that their business might be everything and their intent[7] everywhere, for that's it that always makes a good voyage of nothing.[8] Farewell.

[*Exit.*]

ORSINO: Let all the rest give place.[9]

4. Indulgence must be paid for.
5. Saturn, said to control the melancholy temperament.
6. Jacket.
7. Destination.
8. Come to nothing.
9. Leave.

[*Curio and attendants withdraw.*]
Once more, Cesario,
Get thee to yond same sovereign cruelty.° *cruel person*
Tell her, my love, more noble than the world,
Prizes not quantity of dirty lands;
The parts° that fortune hath bestowed upon her, *possessions*
Tell her, I hold as giddily as fortune;
But 'tis that miracle and queen of gems
That nature pranks° her in attracts my soul. *adorns*
VIOLA: But if she cannot love you, sir?
ORSINO: I cannot be so answered.
VIOLA: Sooth,° but you must. *In truth*
Say that some lady, as perhaps there is,
Hath for your love as great a pang of heart
As you have for Olivia. You cannot love her;
You tell her so; Must she not then be answered?° *accept your answer*
ORSINO: There is no woman's sides
Can bide° the beating of so strong a passion *withstand*
As love doth give my heart; no woman's heart
So big, to hold so much. They lack retention.
Alas, their love may be called appetite,
No motion° of the liver,[1] but the palate, *emotion*
That suffer surfeit, cloyment,° and revolt;° *satiety / revulsion*
But mine is all as hungry as the sea,
And can digest as much. Make no compare
Between that love a woman can bear me
And that I owe° Olivia. *have for*
VIOLA: Ay, but I know—
ORSINO: What dost thou know?
VIOLA: Too well what love women to men may owe.
In faith, they are as true of heart as we.
My father had a daughter loved a man
As it might be, perhaps, were I a woman,
I should your lordship.
ORSINO: And what's her history?
VIOLA: A blank, my lord. She never told her love,
But let concealment, like a worm i' the bud,
Feed on her damask° cheek. She pined in thought, *pink and white*
And with a green and yellow° melancholy *pale and sallow*
She sat like Patience on a monument,° *tomb*
Smiling at grief. Was not this love indeed?
We men may say more, swear more, but indeed
Our shows° are more than will;° for still we prove *displays / our passions*
Much in our vows, but little in our love.
ORSINO: But died thy sister of her love, my boy?
VIOLA: I am all the daughters of my father's house,
And all the brothers too—and yet I know not.

1. Seat of the emotion of love.

Sir, shall I to this lady?
ORSINO: Ay, that's the theme.
To her in haste; give her this jewel.
[*He gives a jewel.*] Say
My love can give no place, bide no denay.° *cannot endure denial*
[*Exeunt (separately).*]

Scene 5[2]

[*Enter Sir Toby, Sir Andrew, and Fabian.*]

SIR TOBY: Come thy ways,[3] Signor Fabian.

FABIAN: Nay, I'll come. If I lose a scruple[4] of this sport, let me be boiled to death with melancholy.

SIR TOBY: Wouldst thou not be glad to have the niggardly rascally sheep-biter[5] come by some notable shame?

FABIAN: I would exult, man. You know he brought me out o' favor with my lady about a bearbaiting[6] here.

SIR TOBY: To anger him we'll have the bear again, and we will fool him black and blue. Shall we not, Sir Andrew?

SIR ANDREW: An we do not, it is pity of our lives.

[*Enter Maria (with a letter).*]

SIR TOBY: Here comes the little villain.—How now, my metal of India![7]

MARIA: Get ye all three into the boxtree.[8] Malvolio's coming down this walk. He has been yonder i' the sun practicing behavior[9] to his own shadow this half hour. Observe him, for the love of mockery, for I know this letter will make a contemplative[1] idiot of him. Close,[2] in the name of jesting! [*The others hide.*] Lie thou there [*throwing down a letter*]; for here comes the trout that must be caught with tickling.[3] [*Exit.*]

[*Enter Malvolio.*]

MALVOLIO: 'tis but fortune; all is fortune. Maria once told me she did affect me;[4] and I have heard herself come thus near, that should she fancy,[5] it should be one of my complexion.[6] Besides, she uses me with a more exalted respect than anyone else that follows[7] her. What should I think on 't?

SIR TOBY: Here's an overweening rogue!

FABIAN: O, peace! Contemplation makes a rare turkey-cock of him. How he jets[8] under his advanced[9] plumes!

SIR ANDREW: 'Slight,[1] I could so beat the rogue!

SIR TOBY: Peace, I say.

MALVOLIO: To be Count Malvolio.

SIR TOBY: Ah, rogue!

SIR ANDREW: Pistol him, pistol him.

2. Location: Olivia's garden.
3. Come along.
4. A bit.
5. Dog that bites sheep; i.e., a sneak.
6. Target of Puritan disapproval.
7. Gold; i.e., priceless one.
8. Shrub.
9. Elegant conduct.
1. I.e., from his musings.
2. Hide.
3. Stroking about the gills.
4. Olivia liked me.
5. Fall in love.
6. Personality.
7. Serves.
8. Struts.
9. Raised.
1. By God's light.

SIR TOBY: Peace, peace!

MALVOLIO: There is example[2] for 't. The lady of the Strachy[3] married the yeoman of the wardrobe.

SIR ANDREW: Fie on him, Jezebel![4]

FABIAN: O, peace! Now he's deeply in. Look how imagination blows him.[5]

MALVOLIO: Having been three months married to her, sitting in my state[6]—

SIR TOBY: O, for a stone-bow,[7] to hit him in the eye!

MALVOLIO: Calling my officers about me, in my branched[8] velvet gown; having come from a daybed,[9] where I have left Olivia sleeping—

SIR TOBY: Fire and brimstone!

FABIAN: O, peace, peace!

MALVOLIO: And then to have the humor of state;[1] and after a demure travel of regard,[2] telling them I know my place as I would they should do theirs, to ask for my kinsman Toby.

SIR TOBY: Bolts and shackles!

FABIAN: O, peace, peace, peace! Now, now.

MALVOLIO: Seven of my people, with an obedient start, make out for him. I frown the while, and perchance wind up my watch, or play with my[3]—some rich jewel. Toby approaches; curtsies[4] there to me—

SIR TOBY: Shall this fellow live?

FABIAN: Though our silence be drawn from us with cars,[5] yet peace.

MALVOLIO: I extend my hand to him thus, quenching my familiar smile with an austere regard of control[6]—

SIR TOBY: And does not Toby take[7] you a blow o' the lips then?

MALVOLIO: Saying, "Cousin Toby, my fortunes having cast me on your niece give me this prerogative of speech—"

SIR TOBY: What, what?

MALVOLIO: "You must amend your drunkenness."

SIR TOBY: Out, scab!

FABIAN: Nay, patience, or we break the sinews of our plot.

MALVOLIO: "Besides, you waste the treasure of your time with a foolish knight—"

SIR ANDREW: That's me, I warrant you.

MALVOLIO: "One Sir Andrew."

SIR ANDREW: I knew 'twas I, for many do call me fool.

MALVOLIO: What employment have we here?

[(*Taking up the letter.*)]

FABIAN: Now is the woodcock[8] near the gin.[9]

SIR TOBY: O, peace, and the spirit of humors[1] intimate reading aloud to him!

2. Precedent.
3. Unknown reference; lady who married below her station.
4. Wicked queen of Israel.
5. Puffs him up.
6. Chair of state.
7. Crossbow.
8. Embroidered.
9. Sofa.
1. Manner of authority.
2. Grave survey of the company.
3. Malvolio recalls that, as a Count, he would not be wearing his steward's chain.
4. Bows.
5. With chariots; i.e., by force.
6. Look of authority.
7. Give.
8. Proverbially stupid bird.
9. Snare.
1. Whim.

MALVOLIO: By my life, this is my lady's hand. These be her very c's, her u's, and her t's;[2] and thus makes she her great[3] P's. It is in contempt of[4] question her hand.

SIR ANDREW: Her c's, her u's, and her t's. Why that?

MALVOLIO [(*reads*)]: "To the unknown beloved, this, and my good wishes."—Her very phrases! By your leave, wax.[5] Soft![6] And the impressure her Lucrece,[7] with which she uses to seal. 'tis my lady. To whom should this be? [(*He opens the letter.*)]

FABIAN: This wins him, liver[8] and all.

MALVOLIO [(*reads*)]: "Jove knows I love,
But who?
Lips, do not move;
No man must know."

"No man must know." What follows? The numbers[9] altered! "No man must know." If this should be thee, Malvolio?

SIR TOBY: Marry, hang thee, brock![1]

MALVOLIO [(*reads*)]: "I may command where I adore,
But silence, like a Lucrece knife,
With bloodless stroke my heart doth gore;
M.O.A.I. doth sway my life."

FABIAN: A fustian[2] riddle!

SIR TOBY: Excellent wench,[3] say I.

MALVOLIO: "M.O.A.I. doth sway my life." Nay, but first, let me see, let me see, let me see.

FABIAN: What dish o' poison has she dressed[4] him!

SIR TOBY: And with what wing[5] the staniel[6] checks at it![7]

MALVOLIO: "I may command where I adore." Why, she may command me; I serve her, she is my lady. Why, this is evident to any formal capacity.[8] There is no obstruction[9] in this. And the end—what should that alphabetical position portend? If I could make that resemble something in me! Softly! M.O.A.I.—

SIR TOBY: O, ay, make up that. He is now at a cold scent.[1]

FABIAN: Sowter will cry upon 't[2] for all this, though it be as rank as a fox.

MALVOLIO: M—Malvolio. M! Why, that begins my name!

FABIAN: Did not I say he would work it out? The cur is excellent at faults.[3]

MALVOLIO: M—But then there is no consonancy in the sequel that suffers under probation:[4] A should follow, but O does.

2. *Cut*; slang for female pudenda.
3. Uppercase; copious (implying "pee").
4. Beyond.
5. Conventional apology for breaking a seal.
6. Softly.
7. Lucretia; chaste matron, who stabbed herself to death as a response to being raped.
8. Seat of passion.
9. Verses.
1. Badger.
2. Pompous.
3. Clever girl (Maria).
4. Prepared.
5. Speed.
6. Inferior hawk.
7. Turns to fly at it.
8. Normal understanding.
9. Difficulty.
1. Difficult trail.
2. The hound will pick up the scent.
3. Breaks in the scent.
4. Pattern in the letters that stands up under examination.

FABIAN: And O shall end,[5] I hope.

SIR TOBY: Ay, or I'll cudgel him, and make him cry "O!"

MALVOLIO: And then I comes behind.

FABIAN: Ay, an you had any eye behind you, you might see more detraction[6] at your heels than fortunes before you.

MALVOLIO: M.O.A.I. This simulation[7] is not as the former. And yet, to crush[8] this a little, it would bow to me, for every one of these letters are in my name. Soft! Here follows prose.

[*He reads.*] "If this fall into thy hand, revolve.[9] In my stars[1] I am above thee, but be not afraid of greatness. Some are born great, some achieve greatness, and some have greatness thrust upon 'em. Thy Fates open their hands; let thy blood and spirit embrace them; and, to inure[2] thyself to what thou art like to be, cast thy humble slough[3] and appear fresh. Be opposite[4] with a kinsman, surly with servants. Let thy tongue tang[5] arguments of state; put thyself into the trick of singularity.[6] She thus advises thee that sighs for thee. Remember who commended thy yellow stockings, and wished to see thee ever cross-gartered.[7] I say, remember. Go to, thou art made, if thou desir'st to be so. If not, let me see thee a steward still, the fellow of servants, and not worthy to touch Fortune's fingers. Farewell. She that would alter services[8] with thee,

The Fortunate-Unhappy."[9]

Daylight and champaign[1] discovers[2] not more! This is open. I will be proud, I will read politic authors,[3] I will baffle[4] Sir Toby, I will wash off gross acquaintance, I will be point-devise[5] the very man. I do not now fool myself, to let imagination jade[6] me; for every reason excites to this, that my lady loves me. She did commend my yellow stockings of late, she did praise my leg being cross-gartered; and in this[7] she manifests herself to my love, and with a kind of injunction drives me to these habits[8] of her liking. I thank my stars, I am happy.[9] I will be strange,[1] stout,[2] in yellow stockings and cross-gartered, even with the swiftness of putting on. Jove and my stars be praised! Here is yet a post-script. [*He reads.*] "Thou canst not choose but know who I am. If thou entertain'st[3] my love, let it appear in thy smiling; thy smiles become thee well. Therefore in my presence still[4] smile, dear my sweet, I prithee."

Jove, I thank thee. I will smile; I will do everything that thou wilt have me.

[*Exit.*]

5. O ends Malvolio's name; a noose shall end his life; *omega* ends the Greek alphabet.
6. Defamation.
7. Disguise.
8. Force.
9. Consider.
1. Fate.
2. Accustom.
3. Outer skin.
4. Contradictory.
5. Sound with.
6. Eccentricity.
7. Wearing hose garters crossed above and below the knee.
8. Change places.
9. Unfortunate.
1. Open country.
2. Discloses.
3. Political writers.
4. Disgrace.
5. Correct to the letter.
6. Trick.
7. This letter.
8. Attire.
9. Fortunate.
1. Aloof.
2. Haughty.
3. You accept.
4. Always.

[*Sir Toby, Sir Andrew, and Fabian come from hiding.*]

FABIAN: I will not give my part of this sport for a pension of thousands to be paid from the Sophy.[5]

SIR TOBY: I could marry this wench for this device.

SIR ANDREW: So could I too.

SIR TOBY: And ask no other dowry with her but such another jest.

[*Enter Maria.*]

SIR ANDREW: Nor I neither.

FABIAN: Here comes my noble gull-catcher.[6]

SIR TOBY: Wilt thou set thy foot o' my neck?

SIR ANDREW: Or o' mine either?

SIR TOBY: Shall I play[7] my freedom at tray-trip,[8] and become thy bondslave?

SIR ANDREW: I' faith, or I either?

SIR TOBY: Why, thou hast put him in such a dream that when the image of it leaves him he must run mad.

MARIA: Nay, but say true, does it work upon him?

SIR TOBY: Like aqua vitae[9] with a midwife.

MARIA: If you will then see the fruits of the sport, mark his first approach before my lady. He will come to her in yellow stockings, and 'tis a color she abhors, and cross-gartered, a fashion she detests; and he will smile upon her, which will now be so unsuitable to her disposition, being addicted to a melancholy as she is, that it cannot but turn him into a notable contempt.[1] If you will see it, follow me.

SIR TOBY: To the gates of Tartar,[2] thou most excellent devil of wit!

SIR ANDREW: I'll make one[3] too.

[*Exeunt.*]

ACT 3

Scene 1[4]

[*Enter Viola, and Clown (Feste, playing his pipe and tabor).*]

VIOLA: Save thee,[5] friend, and thy music. Dost thou live by[6] thy tabor?[7]

FESTE: No, sir, I live by the church.

VIOLA: Art thou a churchman?

FESTE: No such matter, sir. I do live by the church, for I do live at my house, and my house doth stand by the church.

VIOLA: So thou mayst say the king lies[8] by a beggar if a beggar dwell near him, or the church stands by thy tabor if thy tabor stand by the church.

FESTE: You have said, sir. To see this age! A sentence is but a cheveril[9] glove to a good wit. How quickly the wrong side may be turned outward!

5. Shah of Persia.
6. Fool-catcher.
7. Gamble.
8. Game of dice.
9. Distilled liquor.
1. Notorious object of contempt.
2. Tartarus, the section of hell for the most evil.
3. Tag along.
4. Location: Olivia's garden.
5. God save.
6. Earn your living with.
7. Drum.
8. Dwells; lies sexually.
9. Kid.

VIOLA: Nay, that's certain. They that dally nicely[1] with words may quickly make them wanton.[2]

FESTE: I would therefore my sister had had no name, sir.

VIOLA: Why, man?

FESTE: Why, sir, her name's a word, and to dally with that word might make my sister wanton.[3] But indeed, words are very rascals since bonds disgraced them.[4]

VIOLA: Thy reason, man?

FESTE: Troth, sir, I can yield you none without words, and words are grown so false I am loath to prove reason with them.

VIOLA: I warrant thou art a merry fellow and car'st for nothing.

FESTE: Not so, sir, I do care for something; but in my conscience, sir, I do not care for you. If that be to care for nothing, sir, I would it would make you invisible.

VIOLA: Art not thou the Lady Olivia's fool?

FESTE: No indeed, sir. The Lady Olivia has no folly. She will keep no fool, sir, till she be married, and fools are as like husbands as pilchers[5] are to herrings—the husband's the bigger. I am indeed not her fool but her corrupter of words.

VIOLA: I saw thee late[6] at the Count Orsino's.

FESTE: Foolery, sir, does walk about the orb[7] like the sun; it shines everywhere. I would be sorry, sir, but[8] the fool should be as oft with your master as with my mistress. I think I saw your wisdom there.

VIOLA: Nay, an thou pass upon[9] me, I'll no more with thee. Hold, there's expenses for thee. [(*She gives a coin.*)]

FESTE: Now Jove, in his next commodity[1] of hair, send thee a beard!

VIOLA: By my troth, I'll tell thee, I am almost sick for one—[*aside*] though I would not have it grow on my chin.—Is thy lady within?

FESTE: Would not a pair of these have bred, sir?

VIOLA: Yes, being kept together and put to use.[2]

FESTE: I would play Lord Pandarus[3] of Phrygia, sir, to bring a Cressida to this Troilus.

VIOLA: I understand you, sir. 'Tis well begged. [(*She gives another coin.*)]

FESTE: The matter, I hope, is not great, sir, begging but a beggar; Cressida was a beggar.[4] My lady is within, sir. I will conster[5] to them whence you come. Who you are and what you would are out of my welkin[6]—I might say "element," but the word is overworn. [*Exit.*]

VIOLA: This fellow is wise enough to play the fool,
And to do that well craves° a kind of wit. *requires*
He must observe their mood on whom he jests,
The quality of persons, and the time,

1. Play subtly; toy amorously.
2. Equivocal.
3. Licentious.
4. Since sworn statements have been needed to make them good.
5. Small fish.
6. Recently.
7. Earth.
8. Unless.
9. Fence verbally with me.
1. Shipment.
2. Put out at interest.
3. Go-between in the story of Troilus and Cressida.
4. She became a leprous beggar in Henryson's continuation of Chaucer's story.
5. Explain.
6. Sky.

And, like the haggard,° check° at every feather *untrained hawk / turn*
That comes before his eye. This is a practice° *skill*
As full of labor as a wise man's art;
For folly that he wisely shows is fit,
But wise men, folly-fall'n,° quite taint their wit.[7] *fallen into folly*

[*Enter Sir Toby and (Sir) Andrew.*]

SIR TOBY: Save you, gentleman.

VIOLA: And you, sir.

SIR ANDREW: *Dieu vous garde, monsieur.*[8]

VIOLA: *Et vous aussi; votre serviteur.*[9]

SIR ANDREW: I hope, sir, you are, and I am yours.

SIR TOBY: Will you encounter[1] the house? My niece is desirous you should enter, if your trade[2] be to her.

VIOLA: I am bound to[3] your niece, sir; I mean, she is the list[4] of my voyage.

SIR TOBY: Taste[5] your legs, sir. Put them to motion.

VIOLA: My legs do better understand[6] me, sir, than I understand what you mean by bidding me taste my legs.

SIR TOBY: I mean, to go, sir, to enter.

VIOLA: I will answer you with gait and entrance.—But we are prevented.[7]

[*Enter Olivia and Gentlewoman (Maria).*]

Most excellent accomplished lady, the heavens rain odors on you!

SIR ANDREW: That youth's a rare courtier. "Rain odors"—well.

VIOLA: My matter hath no voice,[8] lady, but to your own most pregnant[9] and vouchsafed[1] ear.

SIR ANDREW: "Odors," "pregnant," and "vouchsafed." I'll get 'em all three all ready.[2]

OLIVIA: Let the garden door be shut, and leave me to my hearing.

[*Exeunt Sir Toby, Sir Andrew, and Maria.*]

Give me your hand, sir.

VIOLA: My duty, madam, and most humble service.

OLIVIA: What is your name?

VIOLA: Cesario is your servant's name, fair princess.

OLIVIA: My servant, sir? 'Twas never merry world
Since lowly feigning° was called compliment. *false humility*
You're servant to the Count Orsino, youth.

VIOLA: And he is yours, and his must needs be yours;
Your servant's servant is your servant, madam.

OLIVIA: For him, I think not on him. For his thoughts,
Would they were blanks, rather than filled with me!

VIOLA: Madam, I come to whet your gentle thoughts
On his behalf.

OLIVIA: O, by your leave,° I pray you. *please*
I bade you never speak again of him.

7. Ruin their reputation for intelligence.
8. God protect you, sir.
9. You, too; your servant.
1. Enter.
2. Business.
3. Bound for; obliged to.
4. Destination.
5. Try.
6. Comprehend; stand under.
7. Anticipated.
8. Cannot be uttered.
9. Receptive.
1. Attentive.
2. Memorized for future use.

But, would you undertake another suit,
I had rather hear you to solicit that
Than music from the spheres.° *heavenly harmony*
VIOLA: Dear lady—
OLIVIA: Give me leave, beseech you. I did send,
After the last enchantment you did here,
A ring in chase of you; so did I abuse° *deceive*
Myself, my servant, and, I fear me, you.
Under your hard construction° must I sit, *interpretation*
To force° that on you in a shameful cunning *for forcing*
Which you knew none of yours. What might you think?
Have you not set mine honor at the stake
And baited° it with all th' unmuzzled thoughts *harassed*
That tyrannous heart can think? To one of your receiving° *intelligence*
Enough is shown; a cypress,° not a bosom, *thin black cloth*
Hides my heart. So, let me hear you speak.
VIOLA: I pity you.
OLIVIA: That's a degree to love.
VIOLA: No, not a grece;° for 'tis a vulgar proof° *step / common experience*
That very oft we pity enemies.
OLIVIA: Why then, methinks 'tis time to smile again.
O world, how apt° the poor are to be proud! *ready*
If one should be a prey, how much the better
To fall before the lion than the wolf!
[*Clock strikes.*]
The clock upbraids me with the waste of time.
Be not afraid, good youth, I will not have you;
And yet, when wit and youth is come to harvest
Your wife is like° to reap a proper° man. *likely / handsome*
There lies your way, due west.
VIOLA: Then westward ho![3]
Grace and good disposition attend your ladyship.
You'll nothing, madam, to my lord by me?
OLIVIA: Stay.
I prithee, tell me what thou think'st of me.
VIOLA: That you do think you are not what you are.
OLIVIA: If I think so, I think the same of you.
VIOLA: Then think you right. I am not what I am.
OLIVIA: I would you were as I would have you be!
VIOLA: Would it be better, madam, than I am?
I wish it might, for now I am your fool.
OLIVIA [(*aside*)]: O, what a deal of scorn looks beautiful
In the contempt and anger of his lip!
A murderous guilt shows not itself more soon
Than love that would seem hid; love's night is noon.[4]—
Cesario, by the roses of the spring,

3. The cry of Thames watermen to attract westward-bound passengers from London to Westminster.

4. Love cannot hide itself.

By maidhood, honor, truth, and everything,
I love thee so that, maugre° all thy pride, *despite*
Nor wit nor reason can my passion hide.
Do not extort thy reasons from this clause,
For that I woo, thou therefore hast no cause.
But rather reason thus with reason fetter.
Love sought is good, but given unsought is better.

VIOLA: By innocence I swear, and by my youth,
I have one heart, one bosom, and one truth,
And that no woman has, nor never none
Shall mistress be of it save I alone.
And so adieu, good madam. Nevermore
Will I my master's tears to you deplore.° *beweep*

OLIVIA: Yet come again, for thou perhaps mayst move
That heart, which now abhors, to like his love.

[*Exeunt (separately).*]

Scene 2[5]

[*Enter Sir Toby, Sir Andrew, and Fabian.*]

SIR ANDREW: No, faith, I'll not stay a jot longer.

SIR TOBY: Thy reason, dear venom,[6] give thy reason.

FABIAN: You must needs yield your reason, Sir Andrew.

SIR ANDREW: Marry, I saw your niece do more favors to the Count's servingman than ever she bestowed upon me. I saw't i' the orchard.[7]

SIR TOBY: Did she see thee the while, old boy? Tell me that.

SIR ANDREW: As plain as I see you now.

FABIAN: This was a great argument[8] of love in her toward you.

SIR ANDREW: 'Slight,[9] will you make an ass o' me?

FABIAN: I will prove it legitimate,[1] sir, upon the oaths[2] of judgment and reason.

SIR TOBY: And they have been grand-jurymen since before Noah was a sailor.

FABIAN: She did show favor to the youth in your sight only to exasperate you, to awake your dormouse[3] valor, to put fire in your heart and brimstone in your liver. You should then have accosted her, and with some excellent jests, fire-new from the mint, you should have banged the youth into dumbness. This was looked for at your hand, and this was balked.[4] The double gilt of this opportunity you let time wash off, and you are now sailed into the north[5] of my lady's opinion, where you will hang like an icicle on a Dutchman's beard[6] unless you do redeem it by some laudable attempt either of valor or policy.[7]

SIR ANDREW: An't be any way, it must be with valor, for policy I hate. I had as lief be a Brownist[8] as a politician.[9]

5. Location: Olivia's house.
6. Venomous person.
7. Garden.
8. Proof.
9. God's light.
1. True.
2. Testimony.
3. Sleepy.
4. Missed.
5. Out of the warmth.
6. Alludes to the arctic voyage of William Berentz in 1596–1597.
7. Stratagem.
8. Early name for the Congregationalists, after founder Robert Browne.
9. Schemer.

SIR TOBY: Why, then, build me thy fortunes upon the basis of valor. Challenge me the Count's youth to fight with him; hurt him in eleven places. My niece shall take note of it; and assure thyself, there is no love-broker in the world can more prevail in man's commendation with woman than report of valor.

FABIAN: There is no way but this, Sir Andrew.

SIR ANDREW: Will either of you bear me a challenge to him?

SIR TOBY: Go, write it in a martial hand. Be curst[1] and brief; it is no matter how witty, so it be eloquent and full of invention. Taunt him with the license of ink.[2] If thou "thou"-est[3] him some thrice, it shall not be amiss; and as many lies[4] as will lie in thy sheet of paper, although the sheet were big enough for the bed of Ware[5] in England, set 'em down. Go, about it. Let there be gall[6] enough in thy ink, though thou write with a goose pen,[7] no matter. About it.

SIR ANDREW: Where shall I find you?

SIR TOBY: We'll call thee at the cubiculo.[8] Go.

[Exit Sir Andrew.]

FABIAN: This is a dear manikin[9] to you, Sir Toby.

SIR TOBY: I have been dear to him, lad, some two thousand strong or so.

FABIAN: We shall have a rare letter from him; but you'll not deliver 't?

SIR TOBY: Never trust me, then; and by all means stir on the youth to an answer. I think oxen and wainropes[1] cannot hale[2] them together. For Andrew, if he were opened and you find so much blood in his liver[3] as will clog the foot of a flea, I'll eat the rest of th' anatomy.

FABIAN: And his opposite,[4] the youth, bears in his visage no great presage of cruelty.

[Enter Maria.]

SIR TOBY: Look where the youngest wren[5] of nine comes.

MARIA: If you desire the spleen,[6] and will laugh yourselves into stitches, follow me. Yond gull[7] Malvolio is turned heathen, a very renegado; for there is no Christian that means to be saved by believing rightly can ever believe such impossible passages of grossness.[8] He's in yellow stockings.

SIR TOBY: And cross-gartered?

MARIA: Most villainously, like a pedant that keeps a school i', the church. I have dogged him like his murderer. He does obey every point of the letter that I dropped to betray him. He does smile his face into more lines than is in the new map with the augmentation of the Indies.[9] You have not seen such a thing as 'tis. I can hardly forbear hurling things at him. I know my lady will strike him. If she do, he'll smile and take't for a great favor.

SIR TOBY: Come, bring us, bring us where he is. *[Exeunt omnes.]*

1. Fierce.
2. Freedom of writing.
3. Call him "thou" (informal).
4. Charges of lying.
5. Famous bed, more than 10 feet wide.
6. Bitterness; ingredient in ink.
7. Goose quill; foolish style.
8. Small chamber.
9. Puppet.
1. Wagon ropes.
2. Haul.
3. A pale and bloodless liver was a sign of cowardice.
4. Adversary.
5. Smallest of small birds.
6. Laughing fit.
7. Fool.
8. Gross impossibilities.
9. Emerie Molyneux's map, c. 1599, which showed more of the East Indies than had ever been mapped before.

Scene 3[1]

[*Enter Sebastian and Antonio.*]

SEBASTIAN: I would not by my will have troubled you,
But since you make your pleasure of your pains,
I will no further chide you.

ANTONIO: I could not stay behind you. My desire,
More sharp than filèd steel, did spur me forth,
And not all° love to see you—though so much *only*
As might have drawn one to a longer voyage—
But jealousy° what might befall your travel, *solicitude*
Being skilless in° these parts, which to a stranger, *unacquainted with*
Unguided and unfriended, often prove
Rough and unhospitable. My willing love,
The rather by these arguments of fear,
Set forth in your pursuit.

SEBASTIAN: My kind Antonio,
I can no other answer make but thanks,
And thanks; and ever oft good turns
Are shuffled off with such uncurrent° pay. *valueless*
But were my worth,° as is my conscience,° firm, *wealth / inclination*
You should find better dealing.° What's to do? *treatment*
Shall we go see the relics° of this town? *monuments*

ANTONIO: Tomorrow, sir. Best first go see your lodging.

SEBASTIAN: I am not weary, and 'tis long to night.
I pray you, let us satisfy our eyes
With the memorials and the things of fame
That do renown° this city. *make famous*

ANTONIO: Would you'd pardon me.
I do not without danger walk these streets.
Once in a sea fight 'gainst the Count his° galleys *Count's*
I did some service, of such note indeed
That were I ta'en here it would scarce be answered.° *atoned for*

SEBASTIAN: Belike° you slew great number of his people? *Perhaps*

ANTONIO: Th' offense is not of such a bloody nature,
Albeit the quality of the time and quarrel
Might well have given us bloody argument.° *cause for bloodshed*
It might have since been answered° in repaying *atoned for*
What we took from them, which for traffic's° sake *trade's*
Most of our city did. Only myself stood out,
For which, if I be lapsèd° in this place, *surprised*
I shall pay dear.

SEBASTIAN: Do not then walk too open.

ANTONIO: It doth not fit me. Hold, sir, here's my purse.

[*He gives his purse.*]

In the south suburbs, at the Elephant,° *an inn*
Is best to lodge. I will bespeak our diet,° *order our food*

1. Location: A street.

Whiles you beguile the time and feed your knowledge
With viewing of the town. There shall you have me.

SEBASTIAN: Why I your purse?

ANTONIO: Haply° your eye shall light upon some toy° (*perhaps / trifle*)
You have desire to purchase; and your store° (*store of money*)
I think is not for idle markets,° sir. (*useless purchases*)

SEBASTIAN: I'll be your purse-bearer and leave you
For an hour.

ANTONIO: To th' Elephant.

SEBASTIAN: I do remember. [*Exeunt* (*separately*).]

Scene 4[2]

[*Enter Olivia and Maria.*]

OLIVIA [(*aside*)]: I have sent after him; he says he'll come.
How shall I feast him? What bestow of him?
For youth is bought more oft than begged or borrowed.
I speak too loud.—
Where's Malvolio? He is sad and civil,[3]
And suits well for a servant with my fortunes.
Where is Malvolio?

MARIA: He's coming, madam, but in very strange manner. He is, sure, possessed, madam.

OLIVIA: Why, what's the matter? Does he rave?

MARIA: No, madam, he does nothing but smile. Your ladyship were best to have some guard about you if he come, for sure the man is tainted in 's wits.

OLIVIA: Go call him hither. [(*Maria summons Malvolio.*)] I am as mad as he, If sad and merry madness equal be.

[*Enter Malvolio,* (*cross-gartered and in yellow stockings*).]

How now, Malvolio?

MALVOLIO: Sweet lady, ho, ho!

OLIVIA: Smil'st thou? I sent for thee upon a sad occasion.

MALVOLIO: Sad, lady? I could be sad. This does make some obstruction in the blood, this cross-gartering, but what of that? If it please the eye of one, it is with me as the very true sonnet[4] is, "Please one and please all."

OLIVIA: Why, how dost thou, man? What is the matter with thee?

MALVOLIO: Not black in my mind, though yellow in my legs. It did come to his hands, and commands shall be executed. I think we do know the sweet roman hand.[5]

OLIVIA: Wilt thou go to bed, Malvolio?

MALVOLIO: To bed! "Ay, sweetheart, and I'll come to thee."[6]

OLIVIA: God comfort thee! Why dost thou smile so and kiss thy hand so oft?

MARIA: How do you, Malvolio?

MALVOLIO: At your request? Yes, nightingales answer daws.[7]

2. Location: Olivia's garden.
3. Serious and sedate.
4. Song.
5. Italian style of handwriting.
6. Quotation from a popular song.
7. I.e., why should a fine fellow like me answer a daw (crow) like you.

MARIA: Why appear you with this ridiculous boldness before my lady?
MALVOLIO: "Be not afraid of greatness." 'Twas well writ.
OLIVIA: What mean'st thou by that, Malvolio?
MALVOLIO: "Some are born great—"
OLIVIA: Ha?
MALVOLIO: "Some achieve greatness—"
OLIVIA: What sayst thou?
MALVOLIO: "And some have greatness thrust upon them."
OLIVIA: Heaven restore thee!
MALVOLIO: "Remember who commended thy yellow stockings—"
OLIVIA: Thy yellow stockings?
MALVOLIO: "And wished to see thee cross-gartered."
OLIVIA: Cross-gartered?
MALVOLIO: "Go to, thou art made, if thou desir'st to be so—"
OLIVIA: Am I made?
MALVOLIO: "If not, let me see thee a servant still."
OLIVIA: Why, this is very midsummer madness.

[*Enter Servant.*]

SERVANT: Madam, the young gentleman of the Count Orsino's is returned. I could hardly entreat him back. He attends your ladyship's pleasure.

OLIVIA: I'll come to him. [(*Exit Servant.*)] Good Maria, let this fellow be looked to. Where's my cousin Toby? Let some of my people have a special care of him. I would not have him miscarry[8] for the half of my dowry.

[*Exeunt (Olivia and Maria, different ways).*]

MALVOLIO: Oho, do you come near[9] me now? No worse man than Sir Toby to look to me! This concurs directly with the letter. She sends him on purpose that I may appear stubborn to him, for she incites me to that in the letter. "Cast thy humble slough," says she; "be opposite with a kinsman, surly with servants; let thy tongue tang with arguments of state; put thyself into the trick of singularity." And consequently sets down the manner how: as, a sad[1] face, a reverend carriage, a slow tongue, in the habit[2] of some sir of note, and so forth. I have limed[3] her, but it is Jove's doing, and Jove make me thankful! And when she went away now, "Let this fellow be looked to." "Fellow!"[4] Not "Malvolio," nor after my degree,[5] but "fellow." Why, everything adheres together, that no dram[6] of a scruple,[7] no scruple of a scruple, no obstacle, no incredulous[8] or unsafe circumstance—what can be said?—nothing that can be can come between me and the full prospect of my hopes. Well, Jove, not I, is the doer of this, and he is to be thanked.

[*Enter (Sir) Toby, Fabian, and Maria.*]

SIR TOBY: Which way is he, in the name of sanctity? If all the devils of hell be drawn in little,[9] and Legion[1] himself possessed him, yet I'll speak to him.

8. Come to harm.
9. Appreciate.
1. Serious.
2. Attire.
3. Caught.
4. Companion.
5. According to my position.
6. Small amount; one-eighth of a fluid ounce.
7. Doubt; one-third of a dram.
8. Incredible.
9. Brought together in a small space.
1. An unclean spirit ("My name is Legion, for we are many," Mark 5.9).

FABIAN: Here he is, here he is.—How is't with you, sir? How is't with you, man?

MALVOLIO: Go off. I discard you. Let me enjoy my private. Go off.

MARIA: Lo, how hollow the fiend speaks within him! Did not I tell you? Sir Toby, my lady prays you to have a care of him.

MALVOLIO: Aha, does she so?

SIR TOBY: Go to, go to! Peace, peace, we must deal gently with him. Let me alone.—How do you, Malvolio? How is 't with you? What, man, defy the devil! Consider, he's an enemy to mankind.

MALVOLIO: Do you know what you say?

MARIA: La you,[2] an you speak ill of the devil, how he takes it at heart! Pray God he be not bewitched!

FABIAN: Carry his water[3] to the wisewoman.

MARIA: Marry, and it shall be done tomorrow morning, if I live. My lady would not lose him for more than I'll say.

MALVOLIO: How now, mistress?

MARIA: O Lord!

SIR TOBY: Prithee, hold thy peace; this is not the way. Do you not see you move[4] him? Let me alone with him.

FABIAN: No way but gentleness, gently, gently. The fiend is rough, and will not be roughly used.

SIR TOBY: Why, how now, my bawcock![5] How dost thou, chuck?[6]

MALVOLIO: Sir!

SIR TOBY: Ay, biddy,[7] come with me. What man, tis not for gravity[8] to play at cherry-pit[9] with Satan. Hang him, foul collier![1]

MARIA: Get him to say his prayers, good Sir Toby, get him to pray.

MALVOLIO: My prayers, minx?

MARIA: No, I warrant you, he will not hear of godliness.

MALVOLIO: Go hang yourselves all! You are idle,[2] shallow things; I am not of your element. You shall know more hereafter. [*Exit.*]

SIR TOBY: Is 't possible?

FABIAN: If this were played upon a stage, now, I could condemn it as an improbable fiction.

SIR TOBY: His very genius[3] hath taken the infection of the device, man.

MARIA: Nay, pursue him now, lest the device take air and taint.[4]

FABIAN: Why, we shall make him mad indeed.

MARIA: The house will be the quieter.

SIR TOBY: Come, we'll have him in a dark room and bound. My niece is already in the belief that he's mad. We may carry it[5] thus for our pleasure and his penance till our very pastime, tired out of breath, prompt us to have mercy on him, at which time we will bring the device to the bar[6] and crown thee for a finder of madmen. But see, but see!

2. Look you.
3. Urine.
4. Upset.
5. Fine fellow (from French *beau-coq*).
6. Chick.
7. Chicken.
8. Dignity.
9. A child's game.

1. Coal-peddler.
2. Foolish.
3. Spirit.
4. Become exposed to air and, thus, to spoil.
5. Carry the trick on.
6. To court.

[*Enter Sir Andrew (with a letter).*]

FABIAN: More matter for a May morning.[7]

SIR ANDREW: Here's the challenge. Read it. I warrant there's vinegar and pepper in 't.

FABIAN: Is 't so saucy?[8]

SIR ANDREW: Ay, is 't, I warrant him. Do but read.

SIR TOBY: Give me. [(*He reads.*)] "Youth, whatsoever thou art, thou art but a scurvy fellow."

FABIAN: Good, and valiant.

SIR TOBY [(*reads*)]: "Wonder not, nor admire[9] not in thy mind, why I do call thee so, for I will show thee no reason for 't."

FABIAN: A good note, that keeps you from the blow of the law.

SIR TOBY [(*reads*)]: "Thou com'st to the Lady Olivia, and in my sight she uses thee kindly. But thou liest in thy throat; that is not the matter I challenge thee for."

FABIAN: Very brief, and to exceeding good sense—less.

SIR TOBY [(*reads*)]: "I will waylay thee going home, where if it be thy chance to kill me—"

FABIAN: Good.

SIR TOBY [(*reads*)]: "Thou kill'st me like a rogue and a villain."

FABIAN: Still you keep o' the windy[1] side of the law. Good.

SIR TOBY [(*reads*)]: "Fare thee well, and God have mercy upon one of our souls! He may have mercy upon mine, but my hope is better, and so look to thyself. Thy friend, as thou usest him, and thy sworn enemy,

Andrew Aguecheek."

If this letter move him not, his legs cannot. I'll give 't him.

MARIA: You may have very fit occasion for 't. He is now in some commerce with my lady, and will by and by depart.

SIR TOBY: Go, Sir Andrew. Scout me[2] for him at the corner of the orchard like a bum-baily.[3] So soon as ever thou seest him, draw, and as thou draw'st, swear horrible; for it comes to pass oft that a terrible oath, with a swaggering accent sharply twanged off, gives manhood more approbation[4] than ever proof[5] itself would have earned him. Away!

SIR ANDREW: Nay, let me alone for swearing.[6] [*Exit.*]

SIR TOBY: Now will not I deliver his letter, for the behavior of the young gentleman gives him out to be of good capacity and breeding; his employment between his lord and my niece confirms no less. Therefore this letter, being so excellently ignorant, will breed no terror in the youth. He will find it comes from a clodpoll.[7] But, sir, I will deliver his challenge by word of mouth, set upon Aguecheek a notable report of valor, and drive the gentleman—as I know his youth will aptly receive it—into a most hideous

7. Material for a May Day comedy.
8. Spicy; insolent.
9. Marvel.
1. Windward; i.e., safe.
2. Keep watch.
3. Agent who makes arrests.
4. Reputation.
5. Testing.
6. Leave swearing to me.
7. Blockhead.

opinion of his rage, skill, fury, and impetuosity. This will so fright them both that they will kill one another by the look, like cockatrices.[8]

[*Enter Olivia and Viola.*]

FABIAN: Here he comes with your niece. Give them way till he take leave, and presently after him.

SIR TOBY: I will meditate the while upon some horrid message for a challenge.

[*Exeunt Sir Toby, Fabian, and Maria.*]

OLIVIA: I have said too much unto a heart of stone
And laid mine honor too unchary° on 't. *carelessly*
There's something in me that reproves my fault,
But such a headstrong potent fault it is
That it but mocks reproof.

VIOLA: With the same havior° that your passion bears *behavior*
Goes on my master's griefs.

OLIVIA [*giving a locket*]: Here, wear this jewel for me. 'Tis my picture.
Refuse it not; it hath no tongue to vex you.
And I beseech you come again tomorrow.
What shall you ask of me that I'll deny,
That honor, saved, may upon asking give?

VIOLA: Nothing but this; your true love for my master.

OLIVIA: How with mine honor may I give him that
Which I have given to you?

VIOLA: I will acquit° you. *release*

OLIVIA: Well, come again tomorrow. Fare thee well.
A fiend like° thee might bear my soul to hell. *resembling*

[*Exit.*]

[*Enter (Sir) Toby and Fabian.*]

SIR TOBY: Gentleman, God save thee.

VIOLA: And you, sir.

SIR TOBY: That defense thou hast, betake thee to 't. Of what nature the wrongs are thou hast done him, I know not, but thy intercepter,[9] full of despite,[1] bloody as the hunter, attends thee at the orchard end. Dismount thy tuck,[2] be yare[3] in thy preparation, for thy assailant is quick, skillful, and deadly.

VIOLA: You mistake sir. I am sure no man hath any quarrel to me. My remembrance is very free and clear from any image of offense done to any man.

SIR TOBY: You'll find it otherwise, I assure you. Therefore, if you hold your life at any price, betake you to your guard, for your opposite[4] hath in him what youth, strength, skill, and wrath can furnish man withal.

VIOLA: I pray you, sir, what is he?

SIR TOBY: He is knight, dubbed with unhatched[5] rapier and on carpet consideration,[6] but he is a devil in private brawl. Souls and bodies hath he divorced three, and his incensement at this moment is so implacable that satisfaction can be none but by pangs of death and sepulcher. Hob, nob[7] is his word;[8] give 't or take 't.

8. Basilisks, or reptiles able to kill with a glance.
9. He who lies in wait.
1. Defiance.
2. Draw your rapier.
3. Quick.
4. Opponent.
5. Unhacked; unused in battle.
6. Through court favor.
7. Have or have not.
8. Motto.

VIOLA: I will return again into the house and desire some conduct[9] of the lady. I am no fighter. I have heard of some kind of men that put quarrels purposely on others, to taste[1] their valor. Belike[2] this is a man of that quirk.[3]

SIR TOBY: Sir, no. His indignation derives itself out of a very competent[4] injury; therefore, get you on and give him his desire. Back you shall not to the house unless you undertake that with me which with as much safety you might answer him. Therefore, on, or strip your sword stark naked; for meddle[5] you must, that's certain, or forswear to wear iron[6] about you.

VIOLA: This is as uncivil as strange. I beseech you, do me this courteous office, as to know of the knight what my offense to him is. It is something of my negligence, nothing of my purpose.

SIR TOBY: I will do so.—Signor Fabian, stay you by this gentleman till my return. *[Exit (Sir) Toby.]*

VIOLA: Pray you, sir, do you know of this matter?

FABIAN: I know the knight is incensed against you, even to a mortal arbitrament,[7] but nothing of the circumstance more.

VIOLA: I beseech you, what manner of man is he?

FABIAN: Nothing of that wonderful promise, to read him by his form, as you are like to find him in the proof of his valor. He is, indeed, sir, the most skillful, bloody, and fatal opposite that you could possibly have found in any part of Illyria. Will you walk towards him, I will make your peace with him if I can.

VIOLA: I shall be much bound to you for 't. I am one that had rather go with Sir Priest than Sir Knight. I care not who knows so much of my mettle. *[Exeunt.]*

[Enter (Sir) Toby and (Sir) Andrew.]

SIR TOBY: Why, man, he's a very devil; I have not seen such a firago.[8] I had a pass[9] with him, rapier, scabbard, and all, and he gives me the stuck in[1] with such a mortal motion that it is inevitable; and on the answer,[2] he pays you as surely as your feet hits the ground they step on. They say he has been fencer to the Sophy.

SIR ANDREW: Pox on 't, I'll not meddle with him.

SIR TOBY: Ay, but he will not now be pacified. Fabian can scarce hold him yonder.

SIR ANDREW: Plague on 't, an I thought he had been valiant and so cunning in fence, I'd have seen him damned ere I'd have challenged him. Let him let the matter slip and I'll give him my horse, gray Capilet.

SIR TOBY: I'll make the motion.[3] Stand here, make a good show on 't. This shall end without the perdition of souls.[4] *[Aside, as he crosses to meet Fabian.]* Marry, I'll ride your horse as well as I ride you.

9. Escort.
1. Test.
2. Probably.
3. Peculiarity.
4. Sufficient.
5. Engage in combat.
6. Give up your right to wear a sword.
7. Trial to the death.
8. Virago (overbearing woman).
9. Bout.
1. Thrust.
2. Return.
3. Offer.
4. I.e., killing.

[*Enter Fabian and Viola.*]

[(*Aside to Fabian.*)] I have his horse to take up[5] the quarrel. I have persuaded him the youth's a devil.

FABIAN: He is as horribly conceited of him,[6] and pants and looks pale as if a bear were at his heels.

SIR TOBY [(*to Viola*)]: There's no remedy, sir, he will fight with you for 's oath's sake. Marry, he hath better bethought him of his quarrel, and he finds that now scarce to be worth talking of. Therefore draw, for the supportance of his vow; he protests he will not hurt you.

VIOLA [(*aside*)]: Pray God defend me! A little thing would make me tell them how much I lack of a man.

FABIAN: Give ground, if you see him furious.

SIR TOBY [*crossing to Sir Andrew*]: Come, Sir Andrew, there's no remedy. The gentleman will, for his honor's sake, have one bout with you. He cannot by the *duello*[7] avoid it. But he has promised me, as he is a gentleman and a soldier, he will not hurt you. Come on, to 't.

SIR ANDREW: Pray God he keep his oath!

[*Enter Antonio.*]

VIOLA: I do assure you, 'tis against my will.

[(*They draw.*)]

ANTONIO [(*drawing, to Sir Andrew*)]: Put up your sword. If this young gentleman
Have done offense, I take the fault on me;
If you offend him, I for him defy you.

SIR TOBY: You, sir? Why, what are you?

ANTONIO: One, sir, that for his love dares yet do more
Than you have heard him brag to you he will.

SIR TOBY [(*drawing*)]: Nay, if you be an undertaker,° I am for° you. *challenger / ready for*

[*Enter Officers.*]

FABIAN: O good Sir Toby, hold! Here come the officers.

SIR TOBY [(*to Antonio*)]: I'll be with you anon.

VIOLA [(*to Sir Andrew*)]: Pray, sir, put your sword up, if you please.

SIR ANDREW: Marry, will I, sir; and for that I promised you, I'll be as good as my word.
He will bear you easily, and reins well.

FIRST OFFICER: This is the man. Do thy office.

SECOND OFFICER: Antonio, I arrest thee at the suit
Of Count Orsino.

ANTONIO: You do mistake me, sir.

FIRST OFFICER: No, sir, no jot. I know your favor° well, *face*
Though now you have no sea-cap on your head.—
Take him away. He knows I know him well.

ANTONIO: I must obey. [(*To Viola.*)] This comes with seeking you.
But there's no remedy; I shall answer it.
What will you do, now my necessity

5. Settle.

6. I.e., Cesario has as horrible a conception of Sir Andrew.

7. Dueling code.

Makes me to ask you for my purse? It grieves me
Much more for what I cannot do for you
Than what befalls myself. You stand amazed,
But be of comfort.

SECOND OFFICER: Come, sir, away.

ANTONIO [*to Viola*]: I must entreat of you some of that money.

VIOLA: What money, sir?
For the fair kindness you have showed me here,
And part° being prompted by your present trouble, *partly*
Out of my lean and low ability
I'll lend you something. My having° is not much; *wealth*
I'll make division of my present° with you. *what I have now*
Hold, there's half my coffer.° [(*She offers money.*)] *purse*

ANTONIO: Will you deny me now?
Is 't possible that my deserts to° you *claims on*
Can lack persuasion? Do not tempt my misery,
Lest that it make me so unsound a man
As to upbraid you with those kindnesses
That I have done for you.

VIOLA: I know of none,
Nor know I you by voice or any feature.
I hate ingratitude more in a man
Than lying, vainness, babbling drunkenness,
Or any taint of vice whose strong corruption
Inhabits our frail blood.

ANTONIO: O heavens themselves!

SECOND OFFICER: Come, sir, I pray you, go.

ANTONIO: Let me speak a little. This youth that you see here
I snatched one half out of the jaws of death,
Relieved him with such° sanctity of love, *much*
And to his image, which methought did promise
Most venerable worth,° did I devotion. *worthiness*

FIRST OFFICER: What's that to us? The time goes by. Away!

ANTONIO: But, O, how vile an idol proves this god!
Thou hast, Sebastian, done good feature shame.
In nature there's no blemish but the mind;
None can be called deformed but the unkind.° *unnatural*
Virtue is beauty, but the beauteous evil
Are empty trunks o'erflourished° by the devil. *ornamented*

FIRST OFFICER: The man grows mad. Away with him! Come, come, sir.

ANTONIO: Lead me on.

[*Exit (with Officers).*]

VIOLA [(*aside*)]: Methinks his words do from such passion fly
That he believes himself. So do not I.
Prove true, imagination, O, prove true,
That I, dear brother, be now ta'en for you!

SIR TOBY: Come hither, knight. Come hither, Fabian.
We'll whisper o'er a couplet or two of most sage saws.° *wise sayings*

[(*They gather apart from Viola.*)]

VIOLA: He named Sebastian. I my brother know
Yet living in my glass;° even such and so *mirror*
In favor was my brother, and he went
Still° in this fashion, color, ornament, *always*
For him I imitate. O, if it prove,° *prove true*
Tempests are kind, and salt waves fresh in love!
[(*Exit.*)]

SIR TOBY: A very dishonest[8] paltry boy, and more a coward than a hare. His dishonesty appears in leaving his friend here in necessity and denying him; and for his cowardship, ask Fabian.

FABIAN: A coward, a most devout coward, religious° in it. *confirmed*

SIR ANDREW: 'Slid,° I'll after him again and beat him. *God's eyelid*

SIR TOBY: Do, cuff him soundly, but never draw thy sword.

SIR ANDREW: An I do not— [(*Exit.*)]

FABIAN: Come, let's see the event.° *result*

SIR TOBY: I dare lay any money 'twill be nothing yet.° *nevertheless*

[*Exeunt.*]

ACT 4

Scene 1[9]

[*Enter Sebastian and Clown (Feste).*]

FESTE: Will you make me believe that I am not sent for you?

SEBASTIAN: Go to, go to, thou art a foolish fellow. Let me be clear of thee.

FESTE: Well held out,[1] i' faith! No, I do not know you, nor I am not sent to you by my lady to bid you come speak with her, nor your name is not Master Cesario, nor this is not my nose, neither. Nothing that is so is so.

SEBASTIAN: I prithee, vent thy folly somewhere else. Thou know'st not me.

FESTE: Vent my folly! He has heard that word of some great man, and now applies it to a fool. Vent my folly! I am afraid this great lubber,[2] the world, will prove a cockney.[3] I prithee now, ungird thy strangeness[4] and tell me what I shall vent to my lady. Shall I vent to her that thou art coming?

SEBASTIAN: I prithee, foolish Greek,[5] depart from me. There's money for thee. [(*He gives money.*)] If you tarry longer, I shall give worse payment.

FESTE: By my troth, thou hast an open hand. These wise men that give fools money get themselves a good report—after fourteen years' purchase.[6]

[*Enter (Sir) Andrew, (Sir) Toby, and Fabian.*]

SIR ANDREW: Now, sir, have I met you again? There's for you!
[(*He strikes Sebastian.*)]

SEBASTIAN: Why, there's for thee, and there, and there!
[(*He beats Sir Andrew with the hilt of his dagger.*)]
Are all the people mad?

8. Dishonorable.
9. Location: Before Olivia's house.
1. Kept up.
2. Lout.
3. Affected person.
4. Abandon your strange manner.
5. Buffoon.
6. At great expense.

SIR TOBY: Hold, sir, or I'll throw your dagger o'er the house.

FESTE: This will I tell my lady straight. I would not be in some of your coats for twopence.

[*Exit.*]

SIR TOBY: Come on, sir, hold!

[*He grips Sebastian.*]

SIR ANDREW: Nay, let him alone. I'll go another way to work with him. I'll have an action of battery[7] against him, if there be any law in Illyria. Though I struck him first, yet it's no matter for that.

SEBASTIAN: Let go thy hand!

SIR TOBY: Come, sir, I will not let you go. Come, my young soldier, put up your iron. You are well fleshed.[8] Come on.

SEBASTIAN: I will be free from thee. [*He breaks free and draws his sword.*] What wouldst thou now?
If thou dar'st tempt me further, draw thy sword.

SIR TOBY: What, what? Nay, then I must have an ounce or two of this malapert[9] blood from you. [*He draws.*]

[*Enter Olivia.*]

OLIVIA: Hold, Toby! On thy life I charge thee, hold!

SIR TOBY: Madam—

OLIVIA: Will it be ever thus? Ungracious wretch,
Fit for the mountains and the barbarous caves,
Where manners ne'er were preached! Out of my sight!—
Be not offended, dear Cesario.—
Rudesby,° begone! *rude fellow*

[(*Exeunt Sir Toby, Sir Andrew, and Fabian.*)]

I prithee, gentle friend,
Let thy fair wisdom, not thy passion, sway
In this uncivil and unjust extent° *attack*
Against thy peace. Go with me to my house,
And hear thou there how many fruitless pranks
This ruffian hath botched up,° that thou thereby *contrived*
Mayst smile at this. Thou shalt not choose but go.
Do not deny.° Beshrew° his soul for me! *refuse / curse*
He started° one poor heart of mine, in thee. *startled*

SEBASTIAN [(*aside*)]: What relish° is in this? How runs the stream? *taste*
Or I am mad, or else this is a dream.
Let fancy° still my sense in Lethe[1] steep; *imagination*
If it be thus to dream, still let me sleep!

OLIVIA: Nay, come, I prithee. Would thou'dst be ruled by me!

SEBASTIAN: Madam, I will.

OLIVIA: O, say so, and so be! [*Exeunt.*]

7. Assault charge.
8. Initiated into battle.
9. Impudent.
1. River of forgetfulness in the Underworld.

Scene 2[2]

[*Enter Maria (with a gown and a false beard), and Clown (Feste).*]

MARIA: Nay, I prithee, put on this gown and this beard; make him believe thou art Sir[3] Topas[4] the curate. Do it quickly. I'll call Sir Toby the whilst. [*Exit.*]

FESTE: Well, I'll put it on, and I will dissemble[5] myself in 't, and I would I were the first that ever dissembled in such a gown. [*He disguises himself in gown and beard.*] I am not tall enough to become the function[6] well, nor lean[7] enough to be thought a good student; but to be said an honest man and a good housekeeper[8] goes as fairly as to say a careful man and a great scholar. The competitors[9] enter.

[*Enter (Sir) Toby (and Maria).*]

SIR TOBY: Jove bless thee, Master Parson.

FESTE: *Bonos dies,*[1] Sir Toby. For, as the old hermit of Prague,[2] that never saw pen and ink, very wittily said to a niece of King Gorboduc,[3] "That that is, is"; so I, being Master Parson, am Master Parson; for what is "that" but "that," and "is" but "is"?

SIR TOBY: To him, Sir Topas.

FESTE: What, ho, I say! Peace in this prison!

[*He approaches the door behind which Malvolio is confined.*]

SIR TOBY: The knave[4] counterfeits well; a good knave.

MALVOLIO [*within*]: Who calls there?

FESTE: Sir Topas the curate, who comes to visit Malvolio the lunatic.

MALVOLIO: Sir Topas, Sir Topas, good Sir Topas, go to my lady—

FESTE: Out, hyperbolical[5] fiend! How vexest thou this man! Talkest thou nothing but of ladies?

SIR TOBY: Well said, Master Parson.

MALVOLIO: Sir Topas, never was man thus wronged. Good Sir Topas, do not think I am mad. They have laid me here in hideous darkness.

FESTE: Fie, thou dishonest Satan! I call thee by the most modest terms, for I am one of those gentle ones that will use the devil himself with courtesy. Sayst thou that house[6] is dark?

MALVOLIO: As hell, Sir Topas.

FESTE: Why, it hath bay windows transparent as barricadoes,[7] and the clerestories[8] toward the south north are as lustrous as ebony; and yet complainest thou of obstruction?

MALVOLIO: I am not mad, Sir Topas. I say to you this house is dark.

FESTE: Madman, thou errest. I say there is no darkness but ignorance, in which thou art more puzzled than the Egyptians in their fog.[9]

2. Location: Olivia's house.
3. Title for priests.
4. Comic knight in Chaucer. (The topaz stone was believed to cure lunacy.)
5. Disguise.
6. Priestly office.
7. Scholars were supposed to be poor and, therefore, thin.
8. Neighbor.
9. Associates.
1. Good day.
2. Invented authority.
3. Legendary British king in the tragedy *Gorbobuc* (1562).
4. Fellow.
5. Boisterous.
6. Room.
7. Barricades.
8. Upper windows.
9. Allusion to the darkness Moses brought upon Egypt (Exodus 10.21–23).

MALVOLIO: I say this house is as dark as ignorance, though ignorance were as dark as hell; and I say there was never man thus abused. I am no more mad than you are. Make the trial of it in any constant question.[1]

FESTE: What is the opinion of Pythagoras[2] concerning wildfowl?

MALVOLIO: That the soul of our grandam might haply inhabit a bird.

FESTE: What think'st thou of his opinion?

MALVOLIO: I think nobly of the soul, and no way approve his opinion.

FESTE: Fare thee well. Remain thou still in darkness. Thou shalt hold th' opinion of Pythagoras ere I will allow of thy wits,[3] and fear to kill a woodcock[4] lest thou dispossess the soul of thy grandam. Fare thee well.

[(*He moves away from Malvolio's prison.*)]

MALVOLIO: Sir Topas, Sir Topas!

SIR TOBY: My most exquisite Sir Topas!

FESTE: Nay, I am for all waters.[5]

MARIA: Thou mightst have done this without thy beard and gown. He sees thee not.

SIR TOBY: To him in thine own voice, and bring me word how thou find'st him. I would we were well rid of this knavery. If he may be conveniently delivered,[6] I would he were, for I am now so far in offense with my niece that I cannot pursue with any safety this sport to the upshot.[7] Come by and by to my chamber.

[*Exit (with Maria)*.]

FESTE [(*singing as he approaches Malvolio's prison*)]:
"Hey, Robin, jolly Robin,
Tell me how thy lady does."[8]

MALVOLIO: Fool!

FESTE: "My lady is unkind, pardie."[9]

MALVOLIO: Fool!

FESTE: "Alas, why is she so?"

MALVOLIO: Fool, I say!

FESTE: "She loves another—" Who calls, ha?

MALVOLIO: Good Fool, as ever thou wilt deserve well at my hand, help me to a candle, and pen, ink, and paper. As I am a gentleman, I will live to be thankful to thee for 't.

FESTE: Master Malvolio?

MALVOLIO: Ay, good Fool.

FESTE: Alas, sir, how fell you beside your five wits?[1]

MALVOLIO: Fool, there was never man so notoriously abused. I am as well in my wits, Fool, as thou art.

FESTE: But[2] as well? Then you are mad indeed, if you be no better in your wits than a fool.

1. Consistent discussion.
2. Philosopher who originated the doctrine of the transmigration of souls.
3. Acknowledge your sanity.
4. Proverbially stupid bird.
5. Good for any trade.
6. Delivered from prison.
7. Conclusion.
8. Fragment of a song attributed to Thomas Wyatt.
9. By God (French: *par Dieu*).
1. Out of your mind.
2. Only.

MALVOLIO: They have here propertied me,[3] keep me in darkness, send ministers to me—asses—and do all they can to face me[4] out of my wits.

FESTE: Advise you[5] what you say. The minister is here.

[*He speaks as Sir Topas.*]

Malvolio, Malvolio, thy wits the heavens restore! Endeavor thyself to sleep; and leave thy vain bibble-babble.

MALVOLIO: Sir Topas!

FESTE [*in Sir Topas' voice*]: Maintain no words with him, good fellow.

[*In his own voice.*] Who, I, sir? Not I, sir. God b' wi' you, good Sir Topas.

[*In Sir Topas' voice.*] Marry, amen.

[*In his own voice.*] I will, sir, I will.

MALVOLIO: Fool! Fool! Fool, I say!

FESTE: Alas, sir, be patient. What say you, sir? I am shent[6] for speaking to you.

MALVOLIO: Good Fool, help me to some light and some paper. I tell thee I am as well in my wits as any man in Illyria.

FESTE: Welladay[7] that you were, sir!

MALVOLIO: By this hand, I am. Good Fool, some ink, paper, and light; and convey what I will set down to my lady. It shall advantage thee more than ever the bearing of letter did.

FESTE: I will help you to 't. But tell me true, are you not mad indeed, or do you but counterfeit?

MALVOLIO: Believe me, I am not. I tell thee true.

FESTE: Nay, I'll ne'er believe a madman till I see his brains. I will fetch you light and paper and ink.

MALVOLIO: Fool, I'll requite it in the highest degree. I prithee, begone.

FESTE [*sings*]:

I am gone, sir,
And anon, sir,
I'll be with you again,
In a trice,
Like to the old Vice,[8]
Your need to sustain;
Who, with dagger of lath,° *Vice's weapon*
In his rage and his wrath,
Cries, "Aha!" to the devil;
Like a mad lad,
Pare thy nails, dad?
Adieu, goodman devil! [*Exit.*]

Scene 3[9]

[*Enter Sebastian (with a pearl).*]

SEBASTIAN: This is the air; that is the glorious sun;
This pearl she gave me, I do feel 't and see 't;
And though 'tis wonder that enwraps me thus,

3. Treated me as property.
4. Brazen me.
5. Take care.
6. Rebuked.
7. Alas.
8. Comic character of old morality plays.
9. Location: Olivia's garden.

Yet 'tis not madness. Where's Antonio, then?
I could not find him at the Elephant;
Yet there he was,° and there I found this credit,° [*had been / belief*]
That he did range the town to seek me out.
His counsel now might do me golden service;
For though my soul disputes well with my sense
That this may be some error, but no madness,
Yet doth this accident° and flood of fortune [*surprise*]
So far exceed all instance,° all discourse,° [*precedent / logic*]
That I am ready to distrust mine eyes
And wrangle° with my reason that persuades me [*dispute*]
To any other trust° but that I am mad, [*belief*]
Or else the lady's mad. Yet if 'twere so,
She could not sway° her house, command her followers, [*rule*]
Take and give back affairs and their dispatch° [*management*]
With such a smooth, discreet, and stable bearing
As I perceive she does. There's something in 't
That is deceivable.° But here the lady comes. [*deceptive*]

[*Enter Olivia and Priest.*]

OLIVIA: Blame not this haste of mine. If you mean well,
Now go with me and with this holy man
Into the chantry° by. There, before him, [*chapel nearby*]
And underneath that consecrated roof,
Plight me the full assurance of your faith,
That my most jealous° and too doubtful soul [*anxious*]
May live at peace. He shall conceal it
Whiles° you are willing it shall come to note,° [*until / become known*]
What time° we will our celebration keep [*at which time*]
According to my birth.° What do you say? [*social position*]

SEBASTIAN: I'll follow this good man, and go with you,
And having sworn truth, ever will be true.

OLIVIA: Then lead the way, good Father, and heavens so shine
That they may fairly note° this act of mine! [*look well upon*]
[*Exeunt.*]

ACT 5

Scene 1[1]

[*Enter Clown (Feste) and Fabian.*]

FABIAN: Now, as thou lov'st me, let me see his letter.

FESTE: Good Master Fabian, grant me another request.

FABIAN: Anything.

FESTE: Do not desire to see this letter.

FABIAN: This is to give a dog and in recompense desire my dog again.[2]

[*Enter Duke (Orsino), Viola, Curio, and Lords.*]

1. Location: Before Olivia's house.
2. Famously, Queen Elizabeth once asked Dr. Bulleyn for his dog and promised a gift of his choosing in exchange; he asked to have his dog back.

ORSINO: Belong you to the Lady Olivia, friends?
FESTE: Ay, sir, we are some of her trappings.[3]
ORSINO: I know thee well. How dost thou, my good fellow?
FESTE: Truly, sir, the better for[4] my foes and the worse for my friends.
ORSINO: Just the contrary—the better for thy friends.
FESTE: No, sir, the worse.
ORSINO: How can that be?
FESTE: Marry, sir, they praise me, and make an ass of me. Now my foes tell me plainly I am an ass, so that by my foes, sir, I profit in the knowledge of myself, and by my friends I am abused;[5] so that, conclusions to be as kisses, if your four negatives make your two affirmatives, why then the worse for my friends and the better for my foes.
ORSINO: Why, this is excellent.
FESTE: By my troth, sir, no, though it please you to be one of my friends.
ORSINO: Thou shalt not be the worse for me. There's gold.
[(*He gives a coin.*)]
FESTE: But that it would be double-dealing,[6] sir, I would you could make it another.
ORSINO: O, you give me ill counsel.
FESTE: Put your grace in your pocket,[7] sir, for this once, and let your flesh and blood obey it.[8]
ORSINO: Well, I will be so much a sinner to be a double-dealer. There's another.
[(*He gives another coin.*)]
FESTE: *Primo, secundo, tertio*, is a good play,[9] and the old saying is, the third pays for all.[1] The triplex,[2] sir, is a good tripping measure; or the bells of Saint Bennet,[3] sir, may put you in mind—one, two, three.
ORSINO: You can fool no more money out of me at this throw.[4] If you will let your lady know I am here to speak with her, and bring her along with you, it may awake my bounty further.
FESTE: Marry, sir, lullaby to your bounty till I come again. I go, sir, but I would not have you to think that my desire of having is the sin of covetousness. But as you say, sir, let your bounty take a nap. I will awake it anon. [*Exit*.]
[*Enter Antonio and Officers*.]
VIOLA: Here comes the man, sir, that did rescue me.
ORSINO: That face of his I do remember well,
Yet when I saw it last it was besmeared
As black as Vulcan[5] in the smoke of war.
A baubling° vessel was he captain of, *trifling*
For shallow draft[6] and bulk unprizable,[7]
With which such scatheful° grapple did he make *harmful*
With the most noble bottom° of our fleet *ship*
That very envy° and the tongue of loss° *even malice / the losers*
Cried fame and honor on him. What's the matter?

3. Ornaments.
4. Because of.
5. Deceived.
6. Giving twice; deceit.
7. Pocket your virtue; be generous.
8. I.e., my ill counsel.
9. Game.
1. I.e., the third time is lucky.
2. Triple-time in music.
3. Church of St. Benedict.
4. Throw of the dice.
5. Roman god of fire, smith to the other gods.
6. Depth of water a ship draws.
7. Of slight value.

FIRST OFFICER: Orsino, this is that Antonio
That took the *Phoenix* and her freight from Candy,° *Crete*
And this is he that did the *Tiger* board
When your young nephew Titus lost his leg.
Here in the streets, desperate° of shame and state, *reckless*
In private brabble° did we apprehend him. *brawl*
VIOLA: He did me kindness, sir, drew on my side,
But in conclusion put strange speech upon me.
I know not what 'twas but distraction.° *madness*
ORSINO: Notable° pirate, thou saltwater thief, *notorious*
What foolish boldness brought thee to their mercies
Whom thou in terms so bloody and so dear° *costly*
Hast made thine enemies?
ANTONIO: Orsino, noble sir,
Be pleased that I° shake off these names you give me. *allow me to*
Antonio never yet was thief or pirate,
Though, I confess, on base and ground° enough *solid grounds*
Orsino's enemy. A witchcraft drew me hither.
That most ingrateful boy there by your side
From the rude sea's enraged and foamy mouth
Did I redeem; a wreck past hope he was.
His life I gave him, and did thereto add
My love, without retention° or restraint, *reservation*
All his in dedication. For his sake
Did I expose myself—pure° for his love— *purely*
Into° the danger of this adverse° town, *unto / hostile*
Drew to defend him when he was beset;
Where being apprehended, his false cunning,
Not meaning to partake with me in danger,
Taught him to face me out of his acquaintance° *deny knowing me*
And grew a twenty years' removed° thing *estranged*
While one would wink; denied me mine own purse,
Which I had recommended° to his use *entrusted*
Not half an hour before.
VIOLA: How can this be?
ORSINO: When came he to this town?
ANTONIO: Today, my lord; and for three months before,
No interim, not a minute's vacancy,
Both day and night did we keep company.
[*Enter Olivia and attendants.*]
ORSINO: Here comes the Countess. Now heaven walks on earth.
But for thee, fellow—fellow, thy words are madness.
Three months this youth hath tended upon me;
But more of that anon. Take him aside.
OLIVIA [*to Orsino*]: What would my lord—but that° he may not have— *except what*
Wherein Olivia may seem serviceable?—
Cesario, you do not keep promise with me.
VIOLA: Madam?
ORSINO: Gracious Olivia—

OLIVIA: What do you say, Cesario?—Good my lord—
VIOLA: My lord would speak. My duty hushes me.
OLIVIA: If it be aught to the old tune, my lord,
It is as fat° and fulsome° to mine ear *gross / offensive*
As howling after music.
ORSINO: Still so cruel?
OLIVIA: Still so constant, lord.
ORSINO: What, to perverseness? You uncivil lady,
To whose ingrate° and unauspicious° altars *ungrateful / unpromising*
My soul the faithfull'st offerings have breathed out
That e'er devotion tendered! What shall I do?
OLIVIA: Even what it please my lord that shall become° him. *suit*
ORSINO: Why should I not, had I the heart to do it,
Like to th' Egyptian thief[8] at point of death
Kill what I love?—a savage jealousy
That sometimes savors nobly. But hear me this:
Since you to nonregardance° cast my faith, *neglect*
And that° I partly know the instrument *since*
That screws° me from my true place in your favor, *pries*
Live you the marble-breasted tyrant still.
But this your minion,° whom I know you love, *favorite*
And whom, by heaven I swear, I tender° dearly, *hold*
Him will I tear out of that cruel eye
Where he sits crownèd in his master's spite.°— *despite his master*
Come, boy, with me. My thoughts are ripe in mischief.
I'll sacrifice the lamb that I do love,
To spite a raven's heart within a dove. [(*Going.*)]
VIOLA: And I, most jocund, apt,° and willingly, *readily*
To do you rest,° a thousand deaths would die. [(*Going.*)] *give you peace*
OLIVIA: Where goes Cesario?
VIOLA: After him I love
More than I love these eyes, more than my life,
More by all mores° than e'er I shall love wife. *all comparisons*
If I do feign, you witnesses above
Punish my life for tainting of my love!
OLIVIA: Ay me, detested! How am I beguiled!
VIOLA: Who does beguile you? Who does do you wrong?
OLIVIA: Hast thou forgot thyself? Is it so long?
Call forth the holy father.
[(*Exit an attendant.*)]
ORSINO [(*to Viola*)]: Come, away!
OLIVIA: Whither, my lord? Cesario, husband, stay.
ORSINO: Husband?
OLIVIA: Ay, husband. Can he that deny?
ORSINO [*to Viola*]: Her husband, sirrah?[9]
VIOLA: No, my lord, not I.

8. Allusion to the *Ethiopica* by Heliodorus, in which the robber captain Thyamis kidnaps and falls in love with Chariclea. Threatened with death, he tries to kill her first.
9. Address to an inferior.

OLIVIA: Alas, it is the baseness of thy fear
That makes thee strangle thy propriety.° *identity*
Fear not, Cesario, take thy fortunes up;
Be that thou know'st thou art, and then thou art
As great as that thou fear'st.° *Orsino*
[*Enter Priest.*]
O, welcome, Father!
Father, I charge thee by thy reverence
Here to unfold—though lately we intended
To keep in darkness what occasion now
Reveals before 'tis ripe—what thou dost know
Hath newly passed between this youth and me.

PRIEST: A contract of eternal bond of love,
Confirmed by mutual joinder° of your hands, *joining*
Attested by the holy close° of lips, *meeting*
Strengthened by interchangement of your rings,
And all the ceremony of this compact
Sealed in my function, by my testimony;
Since when, my watch hath told me, toward my grave
I have traveled but two hours.

ORSINO [*to Viola*]: O thou dissembling cub! What wilt thou be
When time hath sowed a grizzle° on thy case?° *gray hair / skin*
Or will not else thy craft so quickly grow
That thine own trip° shall be thine overthrow? *trickery*
Farewell, and take her, but direct thy feet
Where thou and I henceforth may never meet.

VIOLA: My Lord, I do protest—

OLIVIA: O, do not swear!
Hold little° faith, though thou hast too much fear. *a little*
[*Enter Sir Andrew.*]

SIR ANDREW: For the love of God, a surgeon! Send one presently[1] to Sir Toby.

OLIVIA: What's the matter?

SIR ANDREW: He's broke my head across, and has given Sir Toby a bloody coxcomb[2] too. For the love of God, your help! I had rather than forty pound I were at home.

OLIVIA: Who has done this, Sir Andrew?

SIR ANDREW: The Count's gentleman, one Cesario. We took him for a coward, but he's the very devil incardinate.[3]

ORSINO: My gentleman, Cesario?

SIR ANDREW: 'Od's lifelings,[4] here he is!—You broke my head for nothing, and that that I did I was set on to do 't by Sir Toby.

VIOLA: Why do you speak to me? I never hurt you.
You drew your sword upon me without cause,
But I bespake you fair, and hurt you not.

SIR ANDREW: If a bloody coxcomb be a hurt, you have hurt me. I think you set nothing by a bloody coxcomb.

1. Immediately.
2. Fool's cap (here, head).
3. Incarnate.
4. By God's little lives.

[*Enter (Sir) Toby and Clown (Feste).*]

Here comes Sir Toby, halting.[5] You shall hear more. But if he had not been in drink, he would have tickled you othergates[6] than he did.

ORSINO: How now, gentleman? How is 't with you?

SIR TOBY: That's all one.[7] He's hurt me, and there's th' end on 't.—Sot,[8] didst see Dick surgeon, sot?

FESTE: O, he's drunk, Sir Toby, an hour agone; his eyes were set[9] at eight i' the morning.

SIR TOBY: Then he's a rogue, and a passy measures pavane.[1] I hate a drunken rogue.

OLIVIA: Away with him! Who hath made this havoc with them?

SIR ANDREW: I'll help you, Sir Toby, because we'll be dressed[2] together.

SIR TOBY: Will you help? An ass-head and a coxcomb and a knave, a thin-faced knave, a gull!

OLIVIA: Get him to bed, and let his hurt be looked to.

[(*Exeunt Feste, Fabian, Sir Toby, and Sir Andrew.*)]

[*Enter Sebastian.*]

SEBASTIAN: I am sorry, madam, I have hurt your kinsman;
But, had it been the brother of my blood,
I must have done no less with wit and safety.[3]—
You throw a strange regard° upon me, and by that *estranged look*
I do perceive it hath offended you.
Pardon me, sweet one, even for the vows
We made each other but so late ago.

ORSINO: One face, one voice, one habit,° and two persons, *dress*
A natural perspective,[4] that is and is not!

SEBASTIAN: Antonio, O my dear Antonio!
How have the hours racked and tortured me
Since I have lost thee!

ANTONIO: Sebastian are you?

SEBASTIAN: Fear'st thou° that, Antonio? *do you doubt*

ANTONIO: How have you made division of yourself?
An apple cleft in two is not more twin
Than these two creatures. Which is Sebastian?

OLIVIA: Most wonderful!

SEBASTIAN [(*seeing Viola*)]: Do I stand there? I never had a brother;
Nor can there be that deity in my nature
Of here and everywhere.° I had a sister, *omnipresence*
Whom the blind° waves and surges have devoured. *heedless*
Of charity,° what kin are you to me? *tell me in kindness*
What countryman? What name? What parentage?

VIOLA: Of Messaline. Sebastian was my father.
Such a Sebastian was my brother, too.
So went he suited° to his watery tomb. *dressed*

5. Limping.
6. Otherwise.
7. It doesn't matter.
8. Drunkard.
9. Closed.
1. Slow dance.
2. Have our wounds dressed.
3. With an intelligent regard for my safety.
4. Optical illusion.

If spirits can assume both form and suit,
You come to fright us.

SEBASTIAN: A spirit I am indeed,
But am in that dimension grossly clad° *clothed in the flesh*
Which from the womb I did participate.° *inherit*
Were you a woman, as the rest goes even,° *circumstances allow*
I should my tears let fall upon your cheek
And say, "Thrice welcome, drownèd Viola!"

VIOLA: My father had a mole upon his brow.

SEBASTIAN: And so had mine.

VIOLA: And died that day when Viola from her birth
Had numbered thirteen years.

SEBASTIAN: O, that record° is lively in my soul! *memory*
He finishèd indeed his mortal act
That day that made my sister thirteen years.

VIOLA: If nothing lets° to make us happy both *hinders*
But this my masculine usurped attire,
Do not embrace me till each circumstance
Of place, time, fortune, do cohere and jump° *agree completely*
That I am Viola—which to confirm
I'll bring you to a captain in this town
Where lie my maiden weeds,° by whose gentle help *clothes*
I was preserved to serve this noble count.
All the occurrence of my fortune since
Hath been between this lady and this lord.

SEBASTIAN [(*to Olivia*)]: So comes it, lady, you have been mistook.
But nature to her bias drew° in that. *followed her bent*
You would have been contracted to a maid,° *virgin man*
Nor are you therein, by my life, deceived.
You are betrothed both to a maid and man.

ORSINO [(*to Olivia*)]: Be not amazed; right noble is his blood.
If this be so, as yet the glass° seems true, *natural perspective*
I shall have share in this most happy wreck.
[(*to Viola.*)] Boy, thou hast said to me a thousand times
Thou never shouldst love woman like to° me. *as much as*

VIOLA: And all those sayings will I over swear,° *swear again*
And all those swearings keep as true in soul
As doth that orbèd continent° the fire *the Sun*
That severs day from night.

ORSINO: Give me thy hand,
And let me see thee in thy woman's weeds.° *clothes*

VIOLA: The captain that did bring me first on shore
Hath my maid's garments. He upon some action° *legal charge*
Is now in durance,° at Malvolio's suit, *imprisonment*
A gentleman and follower of my lady's.

OLIVIA: He shall enlarge° him. Fetch Malvolio hither. *release*
And yet, alas, now I remember me,
They say, poor gentleman, he's much distract.

[*Enter Clown (Feste) with a letter, and Fabian.*]

A most extracting° frenzy of mine own *distracting*
From my remembrance clearly banished his.
How does he, sirrah?

FESTE: Truly, madam, he holds Beelzebub at the stave's end[5] as well as a man in his case may do. He's here writ a letter to you; I should have given 't you today morning. But as a madman's epistles are no gospels, so it skills[6] not much when they are delivered.

OLIVIA: Open 't and read it.

FESTE: Look then to be well edified when the fool delivers[7] the madman. [*He reads loudly.*] "By the Lord, madam—"

OLIVIA: How now, art thou mad?

FESTE: No, madam, I do but read madness. An your ladyship will have it as it ought to be, you must allow *vox*.[8]

OLIVIA: Prithee, read i' thy right wits.[9]

FESTE: So I do, madonna; but to read his right wits is to read thus. Therefore perpend,[1] my princess, and give ear.

OLIVIA [*to Fabian*]: Read it you, sirrah.

FABIAN [*reads*]: "By the Lord, madam, you wrong me, and the world shall know it. Though you have put me into darkness and given your drunken cousin rule over me, yet have I the benefit of my senses as well as your ladyship. I have your own letter that induced me to the semblance I put on, with the which I doubt not but to do myself much right or you much shame. Think of me as you please. I leave my duty a little unthought of, and speak out of my injury.

The madly used Malvolio."

OLIVIA: Did he write this?

FESTE: Ay, madam.

ORSINO: This savors not much of distraction.

OLIVIA: See him delivered,° Fabian. Bring him hither. *released*

[*Exit Fabian.*]

My lord, so please you, these things further thought on,
To think me as well a sister as a wife,
One day shall crown th' alliance on 't, so please you,
Here at my house and at my proper° cost. *own*

ORSINO: Madam, I am most apt° t' embrace your offer. *ready*
[*To Viola.*] Your master quits° you; and for your service done him, *releases*
So much against the mettle° of your sex, *disposition*
So far beneath your soft and tender breeding,
And since you called me master for so long,
Here is my hand. You shall from this time be
Your master's mistress.

OLIVIA: A sister! You are she.

[*Enter (Fabian with) Malvolio.*]

ORSINO: Is this the madman?

OLIVIA: Ay, my lord, this same.
How now, Malvolio?

5. Holds the devil off.
6. Matters.
7. Speaks the words of.
8. Loud voice.
9. I.e., express his true state of mind.
1. Consider.

MALVOLIO: Madam, you have done me wrong,
Notorious wrong.
OLIVIA: Have I, Malvolio? No.
MALVOLIO [*showing a letter*]: Lady, you have. Pray you, peruse that letter.
You must not now deny it is your hand.
Write from it,° if you can, in hand or phrase, *differently*
Or say 'tis not your seal, not your invention.° *composition*
You can say none of this. Well, grant it then,
And tell me, in the modesty of honor,
Why you have given me such clear lights° of favor, *signs*
Bade me come smiling and cross-gartered to you,
To put on yellow stockings, and to frown
Upon Sir Toby and the lighter° people? *lesser*
And, acting this in an obedient hope,
Why have you suffered me to be imprisoned,
Kept in a dark house, visited by the priest,° *Feste*
And made the most notorious geck° and gull *dupe*
That e'er invention played on? Tell me why?
OLIVIA: Alas, Malvolio, this is not my writing,
Though, I confess, much like the character;° *my handwriting*
But out of° question 'tis Maria's hand. *beyond*
And now I do bethink me, it was she
First told me thou wast mad; then cam'st in smiling,
And in such forms which here were presupposed° *pre-imposed*
Upon thee in the letter. Prithee, be content.
This practice° hath most shrewdly° passed upon thee; *plot / mischievously*
But when we know the grounds and authors of it,
Thou shalt be both the plaintiff and the judge
Of thine own cause.
FABIAN: Good madam, hear me speak,
And let no quarrel nor no brawl to come
Taint the condition of this present hour,
Which I have wondered at. In hope it shall not,
Most freely I confess, myself and Toby
Set this device against Malvolio here,
Upon° some stubborn and uncourteous parts° *because of / qualities*
We had conceived against him. Maria writ
The letter at Sir Toby's great importance,° *importunity*
In recompense whereof he hath married her.
How with a sportful malice it was followed° *carried out*
May rather pluck on° laughter than revenge, *induce*
If that the injuries be justly weighed
That have on both sides passed.
OLIVIA [*to Malvolio*]: Alas, poor fool, how have they baffled° thee! *disgraced*
FESTE: Why, "Some are born great, some achieve greatness, and some have greatness thrown upon them." I was one, sir, in this interlude,[2] one Sir Topas, sir, but that's all one. "By the Lord, fool, I am not mad." But do you remember?

2. Little play.

"Madam, why laugh you at such a barren rascal? An you smile not, he's gagged." And thus the whirligig[3] of time brings in his revenges.

MALVOLIO: I'll be revenged on the whole pack of you!

[*Exit.*]

OLIVIA: He hath been most notoriously abused.

ORSINO: Pursue him, and entreat him to a peace.
He hath not told us of the captain yet.
When that is known, and golden time convents,° *is convenient*
A solemn combination shall be made
Of our dear souls. Meantime, sweet sister,
We will not part from hence. Cesario, come—
For so you shall be, while you are a man;
But when in other habits° you are seen, *attire*
Orsino's mistress and his fancy's° queen. *love's*

[*Exeunt (all, except Feste).*]

FESTE [*sings*]:

When that I was and a little tiny boy,
With hey, ho, the wind and the rain,
A foolish thing was but a toy,° *trifle*
For the rain it raineth every day.

But when I came to man's estate,
With hey, ho, the wind and the rain,
'Gainst knaves and thieves men shut their gate,
For the rain it raineth every day.

But when I came, alas, to wive,
With hey, ho, the wind and the rain,
By swaggering could I never thrive,
For the rain it raineth every day.

But when I came unto my beds,
With hey, ho, the wind and the rain,
With tosspots° still had drunken heads, *drunkards*
For the rain it raineth every day.

A great while ago the world begun,
With hey, ho, the wind and the rain,
But that's all one, our play is done,
And we'll strive to please you every day.

[*Exit.*]

OTHELLO The first recorded performance of *Othello* was on 1 November 1604, before King James I and his guests at Whitehall Palace. The Chamberlain's Men were now the King's Men, and, as such, their duties at times even included waiting on the king, as Shakespeare and eleven of his troupe did earlier in August of that year. The play would be performed again at court as part of the marriage celebrations for the king's daughter, Princess Elizabeth, in 1612–1613. A notation on the title page of the Quarto gives evidence of the play's popularity: "As it hath been diverse times acted at the Globe and Black Friers, by his Maiesties Servants." A man from an Oxford college who had seen one of these productions wrote an account of how the

3. Spinning top.

boy actor who played Desdemona "acted her part supremely, yet when she was killed was even more moving, for when she fell back upon the bed she implored the pity of the spectators by her very face." Contemporary audiences were clearly moved to pity by Othello as well, as can be seen in an elegy for Richard Burbage, the star of Shakespeare's troupe:

But let me not forget one chiefest part
Wherein beyond the rest, he mov'd the heart,
The grieved Moor, made jealous by a slave,
Who sent his wife to fill a timeless grave,
Then slew himself upon the bloody bed.

The above poem sympathetically echoes the play's reversal of the audience's expectations. It is Iago, who speaks of Othello in racist language, who is the "slave" and "villain," not Othello, who had been "sold to slavery." Othello is "The grieved Moor." The term "Moor" has various connotations in the early modern period. It is often synonymous with "black Moor," or it can be identified with the "tawny" inhabitants of Barbary. At least one recent editor of *Othello*, E. A. J. Honigmann, has questioned the identification of "the noble Moor" as "black." Honigmann hypothesizes that the play was inspired by the visit to Elizabeth's court by the Moorish ambassador from the King of Barbary, whom Shakespeare would have witnessed when performing at court with the Chamberlain's Men during Christmastime in 1601. The vast majority of Shakespeare's audience, however, would not have seen this very aristocratic Moorish diplomat. The identification between "Moor" and a specific complexion is perhaps less important than the notion that Moors were seen as culturally alien and could be subject to racist practices. There were blacks in England, a result of the capture of slaves from Spanish and Portuguese vessels by English seamen. These Africans, brought into the country by force, were in turn expelled by force. In 1601, Elizabeth I issued a proclamation for the transportation of all "Negroes and blackamoors" out of England.

Shakespeare's audience would have known at least three black characters on the popular stage, all monstrous villains. Muly Hamet in George Peele's revenge tragedy *The Battle of Alcazar* (1589) seeks to destroy his own family; though given to bombastic rants, he proves cowardly and underhanded. Shakespeare's first black character, Aaron, in *Titus Andronicus* (1594), may have a redeeming concern for his son, but he is possessed by a motiveless and unrepentant drive to commit evil: He boasts of having "done a thousand dreadful things / As willingly as one would kill a fly." Eleazar in *Lust's Dominion* (c. 1600) embodies the sexual stereotype of the "black devil," manipulating his erotic hold over a white woman of royal blood to gain power.

It is against this network of racial exclusion, in both political practice and dramatic representation, that the play's persistent references to Othello's race need to be read. Othello's bravery and passionate love for Desdemona confound the stereotype of the black villain, and his Italian name and loyal service to the state suggest his assimilation to and identification with Venice. Yet to a certain degree, Othello shares some of his dramatic ancestors' traits—rhetorical bombast, an intense sexuality and uncontrollable violence. Iago voices sexually demonized portrayals of Othello's blackness, calling him "an old black ram," a "Barbary horse," "a lascivious Moor," "an erring Barbarian." However, Othello, too, is haunted by his own "blackness," as when he expresses his fear that Iago's claims of Desdemona's infidelity are true and that she has left him for another man: "Haply for I am black . . . she's gone." Through imagining Othello's internalization of the stereotype of racial inferiority, Shakespeare adds to our understanding of his vulnerability and the fatal consequences of such self-hatred.

Shakespeare's thinking both in his time and ahead of his time emerges in his complex representation of race in relation to marriage, sexuality, and love. From his rather more schematic narrative source, Giraldi Cinthio's *Hecatommithi* (1565), an Italian Renaissance tale of lust, brutality and banal moralization, Shakespeare creates a tragedy. A brief synopsis of the Italian novella will make the point. The Ensign (Iago) to a Moorish Captain (Othello) lusts after his wife Desdemona, and when she will not return his advances, the Ensign decides it is because she is in love with the Corporal (Cassio). Filled with hate and a desire to kill her lest even her husband enjoy her, the Ensign sets about convincing the Captain of his wife's infidelity. When Desdemona is confronted with her husband's jealous suspicions, she concludes that she should never have married a Moor. The Ensign plots with the Moor to kill Desdemona. Bludgeoning her to death with sandbags, they then pull the plaster down from the ceiling to make it look like an accident. Afterward realizing that his wicked Ensign has cost him the joy of his life, the Captain demotes him; in turn, the Ensign accuses the Captain of murdering his own wife. The Moorish Captain denies everything under torture, but Desdemona's relatives eventually get their revenge upon him.

In the narrative source, the protagonist is merely a cultural marker, "the Moor," whom the heroine can dismiss as an inappropriate choice for marriage—a warning to other young women. Shakespeare transforms the Ensign's frustrated lust for Desdemona into the complex homoeroticism of Iago's sexual jealousy of and manipulative intimacy with both Cassio and Othello. Whereas the tales in Cinthio's *Hecatommithi* as a whole do not deny the validity of Iago's cynical views of sexuality and love, Desdemona's combination of passion and faithful devotion exposes how sickly twisted and hatefully vengeful such a view is. The ruling emotion of Cinthio's Moor, a compound of mere jealousy and unrepentant hatred, becomes, in Shakespeare's conception, the tormented self-hatred that leads the tragic hero to doubt his worthiness to be loved and to shoulder the unbearable responsibility that leads him to take his life. The Moor's uncontrollable desire to punish his wife for her supposed sexual transgression in the tale is allied in the tragedy with Othello's obsession with punishing himself for his racial difference: "My name that was as fresh / As Dian's visage is now begrimed and black / As my own face."

At the same time, Othello's identification of his public honor with his wife's chastity demonstrates Shakespeare's understanding of how the need to control women's sexuality in early modern conceptions of marriage functions as a microcosm of the larger theological and political order. Iago's accusations of Desdemona's infidelity stir up the male fear of uncontrollable female sexuality, causing Othello to lament: "O curse of marriage / That we can call these delicate creatures ours / And not their appetites." Renaissance tracts on marriage present women as "the weaker vessel," requiring control by fathers and husbands. The sermons on marriage echoed Saint Paul in stating that men should be "the head of the wife, as Christ is the head of the Church." This male authority demanded the woman's obedience to her husband, just as subjects owed obedience to their sovereign. In eloping with Othello, Desdemona has already transgressed the authority of her father, who taunts Othello with Desdemona's potential for future disobedience: "She has deceived her father and may thee." Although she defies her father in her unswerving loyalty and love for her husband, like that recommended in early modern tracts on marriage, Desdemona is simultaneously compromised as disobedient and furtive.

While the play celebrates the passionate love of Desdemona for Othello, it also reveals the terrible costs of her submission. Such submission also informs Emilia's desire to please Iago. By obeying Iago's desire that she steal the handkerchief that becomes the circumstantial evidence of Desdemona's betrayal, Emilia becomes an unwitting accomplice in her mistress's murder. In telling the truth at the end of the play, Emilia defies her husband's command that she be silent, acknowledging how shocking such defiance would seem: "Let heaven and men and devils, let them all, / All, all, cry shame against me, yet I'll speak." In giving her this defiant speech, the play speaks volumes about the silent obedience demanded of women.

In multiple and sometimes contradictory ways, Shakespeare's *Othello* reproduces the discourses of racism and sexism in early modern English culture and contests them, defying audience expectations by creating sympathy for a black hero and a disobedient daughter, and placing this sympathy against a hero's sexism and a wife's too willing submission. Iago's manipulation of these discourses in preying upon Othello's self-hatred of his "blackness" and fear of Desdemona's passionate independence lead him to murder her. To protect her husband, even as he kills her, Desdemona persists in her loyalty by claiming responsibility for her own death. But may she also be acknowledging her acquiescence in her murder? At the end of the play, Othello acknowledges how he has allowed himself to be blinded, but maintains that he was "not easily jealous but, being wrought, / Perplexed in the extreme." Witnessing his wife's faithful love, he describes his crime in racially charged terms: "one whose hand / Like the base Indian, threw a pearl away / Richer than all his tribe." The unbearable guilt he suffers for her death leads him to take his own life. Othello's self-description as "one who loved not wisely, but too well," may more accurately describe Desdemona's self-sacrifice and suffering for love. To what extent either she or Othello achieves self-knowledge are questions the audience must answer in relation to themselves and their own world, as well as the world in which Shakespeare lived and created.

Othello, the Moor of Venice

The Names of the Actors

OTHELLO, *the Moor*
BRABANTIO, *a senator, father to Desdemona*
CASSIO, *an honorable lieutenant to Othello*
IAGO, *Othello's ancient,° a villain* — *ensign*
RODERIGO, *a gulled gentleman*
DUKE OF VENICE
SENATORS *of Venice*
MONTANO, *Governor of Cyprus*
GENTLEMEN *of Cyprus*
LODOVICO AND GRATIANO, *kinsmen to Brabantio, two noble Venetians*
SAILORS
CLOWN
DESDEMONA, *daughter to Brabantio and wife to Othello*
EMILIA, *wife to Iago*
BIANCA, *a courtesan and mistress to Cassio*
A MESSENGER
A HERALD
A MUSICIAN
SERVANTS, ATTENDANTS, OFFICERS, SENATORS, MUSICIANS, GENTLEMEN

Scene: *Venice; a seaport in Cyprus*

ACT 1[1]

Scene 1[2]

[*Enter Roderigo and Iago.*]

RODERIGO: Tush, never tell me! I take it much unkindly
That thou, Iago, who hast had my purse
As if the strings were thine, shouldst know of this.[3]

IAGO: 'Sblood,[4] but you'll not hear me.
If ever I did dream of such a matter,
Abhor me.

RODERIGO: Thou toldst me thou didst hold him in thy hate.

IAGO: Despise me
If I do not. Three great ones of the city,
In personal suit to make me his lieutenant,
Off-capped to him;° and by the faith of man, — *Othello*
I know my price, I am worth no worse a place.

1. The notes are based on those of David Bevington, ed. *The Complete Works of Shakespeare*. All original stage directions are in square brackets, and all editorially added stage directions are in parentheses.
2. Location: Venice. A street.
3. I.e., Desdemona's elopement.
4. By His (Christ's) blood.

But he, as loving his own pride and purposes,
Evades them with a bombast circumstance[5]
Horribly stuffed with epithets of war,
And, in conclusion,
Nonsuits° my mediators. For, "Certes,"° says he, *rejects / certainly*
"I have already chose my officer."
And what was he?
Forsooth, a great arithmetician,[6]
One Michael Cassio, a Florentine,
A fellow almost damned in a fair wife,[7]
That never set a squadron in the field
Nor the division of a battle knows
More than a spinster[8]—unless the bookish theoric,° *theory*
Wherein the togaed consuls° can propose° *senators / discuss*
As masterly as he. Mere prattle without practice
Is all his soldiership. But he, sir, had th'election;
And I, of whom his° eyes had seen the proof *Othello's*
At Rhodes, at Cyprus, and on other grounds
Christened° and heathen, must be beleed and calmed[9] *Christian*
By debitor and creditor.[1] This countercaster,[2]
He, in good time,° must his lieutenant be, *opportunely*
And I—God bless the mark![3]—his Moorship's ancient.° *ensign*

RODERIGO: By heaven, I rather would have been his hangman.

IAGO: Why, there's no remedy. 'Tis the curse of service;
Preferment° goes by letter and affection,[4] *promotion*
And not by old gradation,[5] where each second
Stood heir to th' first. Now, sir, be judge yourself
Whether I in any just term° am affined° *respect / bound*
To love the Moor.

RODERIGO: I would not follow him then.

IAGO: O sir, content you.[6]
I follow him to serve my turn upon him.
We cannot all be masters, nor all masters
Cannot be truly° followed. You shall mark *faithfully*
Many a duteous and knee-crooking knave
That, doting on his own obsequious bondage,
Wears out his time, much like his master's ass,
For naught but provender, and when he's old, cashiered.° *dismissed*
Whip me[7] such honest knaves. Others there are
Who, trimmed in forms and visages of duty,[8]

5. Wordy evasion. *Bombast* is cotton padding.
6. A man whose military knowledge is merely theoretical, based on books of tactics.
7. Cassio does not seem to be married, but his counterpart in Shakespeare's source does have a woman in his house.
8. A housewife, one whose regular occupation is spinning.
9. Left to leeward without wind, becalmed (a sailing metaphor).
1. A name for a system of bookkeeping.
2. Bookkeeper, one who tallies with *counters*, or "metal disks." Said contemptuously of Cassio.
3. Perhaps originally a formula to ward off evil; here an expression of impatience.
4. Personal influence and favoritism.
5. Step-by-step seniority, the traditional way.
6. Don't you worry about that.
7. Whip, as far as I'm concerned.
8. Dressed up in the mere form and show of dutifulness.

Keep yet their hearts attending on themselves,
And, throwing but shows of service on their lords,
Do well thrive by them, and when they have lined their coats,[9]
Do themselves homage.[1] These fellows have some soul,
And such a one do I profess myself. For, sir,
It is as sure as you are Roderigo,
Were I the Moor I would not be Iago.[2]
In following him, I follow but myself—
Heaven is my judge, not I for love and duty,
But seeming so for my peculiar° end. *particular*
For when my outward action doth demonstrate
The native° act and figure° of my heart *innate / intent*
In compliment extern,[3] 'tis not long after
But I will wear my heart upon my sleeve
For daws[4] to peck at. I am not what I am.[5]

RODERIGO: What a full° fortune does the thick-lips[6] owe° *swelling / own*
If he can carry 't thus!° *carry this off*

IAGO: Call up her father.
Rouse him, make after him, poison his delight,
Proclaim him in the streets; incense her kinsmen,
And, though he in a fertile climate dwell,
Plague him with flies.[7] Though that his joy be joy,[8]
Yet throw such changes of vexation° on 't *vexing changes*
As it may lose some color.[9]

RODERIGO: Here is her father's house. I'll call aloud.

IAGO: Do, with like timorous° accent and dire yell *frightening*
As when, by night and negligence, the fire
Is spied in populous cities.

RODERIGO: What ho, Brabantio! Signor Brabantio, ho!

IAGO: Awake! What ho, Brabantio! Thieves, thieves, thieves!
Look to your house, your daughter, and your bags!
Thieves, thieves!

[*Brabantio* (*enters*) *above* (*at a window.*)][1]

BRABANTIO: What is the reason of this terrible summons?
What is the matter° there? *your business*

RODERIGO: Signor, is all your family within?

IAGO: Are your doors locked?

BRABANTIO: Why, wherefore ask you this?

IAGO: Zounds,[2] sir, you're robbed. For shame, put on your gown!
Your heart is burst; you have lost half your soul.
Even now, now, very now, an old black ram

9. Stuffed their purses.
1. Attend to self-interest solely.
2. If I were able to assume command, I certainly would not choose to remain a subordinate, or, I would keep a suspicious eye on a flattering subordinate.
3. Outward show (conforming in this case to the inner workings and intention of the heart).
4. Small crowlike birds, proverbially stupid and avaricious.
5. I am not one who wears his heart on his sleeve.
6. Elizabethans often applied the term "Moor" to Africans.
7. Though he seems prosperous and happy now, vex him with misery.
8. Although he seems fortunate and happy.
9. That may cause it to lose some of its first gloss.
1. This stage direction, from the Quarto, probably calls for an appearance on the gallery above and rearstage.
2. By His (Christ's) wounds.

Is tupping your white ewe.[3] Arise, arise!
Awake the snorting° citizens with the bell, *snorting*
Or else the devil[4] will make a grandsire of you.
Arise, I say!

BRABANTIO: What, have you lost your wits?

RODERIGO: Most reverend signor, do you know my voice?

BRABANTIO: Not I. What are you?

RODERIGO: My name is Roderigo.

BRABANTIO: The worser welcome.
I have charged thee not to haunt about my doors.
In honest plainness thou hast heard me say
My daughter is not for thee; and now, in madness,
Being full of supper and distempering° drafts, *intoxicating*
Upon malicious bravery[5] dost thou come
To start° my quiet. *disrupt*

RODERIGO: Sir, sir, sir—

BRABANTIO: But thou must needs be sure
My spirits and my place[6] have in° their power *have it in*
To make this bitter to thee.

RODERIGO: Patience, good sir.

BRABANTIO: What tell'st thou me of robbing? This is Venice;
My house is not a grange.° *country house*

RODERIGO: Most grave Brabantio,
In simple° and pure soul I come to you. *sincere*

IAGO: Zounds, sir, you are one of those that will not serve God if the devil bid you. Because we come to do you service and you think we are ruffians, you'll have your daughter covered with a Barbary[7] horse; you'll have your nephews[8] neigh to you; you'll have coursers for cousins and jennets for germans.[9]

BRABANTIO: What profane wretch art thou?

IAGO: I am one, sir, that comes to tell you your daughter and the Moor are now making the beast with two backs.

BRABANTIO: Thou art a villain.

IAGO: You are—a senator.[1]

BRABANTIO: This thou shalt answer.[2] I know thee, Roderigo.

RODERIGO: Sir, I will answer anything. But I beseech you,
If 't be your pleasure and most wise° consent— *well-informed*
As partly I find it is—that your fair daughter,
At this odd-even[3] and dull watch o' the night,
Transported with° no worse nor better guard *by*
But with a knave of common hire,[4] a gondolier,
To the gross clasps of a lascivious Moor—
If this be known to you and your allowance° *permission*

3. Covering, copulating with (said of sheep).
4. The devil was conventionally pictured as black.
5. With hostile intent to defy me.
6. My temperament and my authority of office.
7. From northern Africa (and hence associated with Othello).
8. I.e., grandsons.
9. You'll have stallions for kinsmen and ponies for relatives.
1. Said with mock politeness, as though the word itself were an insult.
2. Be held accountable for.
3. Between one day and the next, i.e., about midnight.
4. Than by a low fellow, a servant.

We then have done you bold and saucy° wrongs. *insolent*
But if you know not this, my manners tell me
We have your wrong rebuke. Do not believe
That, from° the sense of all civility,° *contrary to / decency*
I thus would play and trifle with your reverence.[5]
Your daughter, if you have not given her leave,
I say again, hath made a gross revolt,
Tying her duty, beauty, wit,° and fortunes *intelligence*
In an extravagant° and wheeling° stranger[6] *expatriate / vagabond*
Of here and everywhere. Straight° satisfy yourself. *straightway*
If she be in her chamber or your house,
Let loose on me the justice of the state
For thus deluding you.
BRABANTIO: Strike on the tinder,[7] ho!
Give me a taper! Call up all my people!
This accident° is not unlike my dream. *event*
Belief of it oppresses me already.
Light, I say, light! [*Exit above*].
IAGO: Farewell, for I must leave you.
It seems not meet° nor wholesome to my place° *fitting / position*
To be producted[8]—as, if I stay, I shall—
Against the Moor. For I do know the state,
However this may gall° him with some check,° *oppress / rebuke*
Cannot with safety cast° him, for he's embarked° *dismiss / engaged*
With such loud reason[9] to the Cyprus wars,
Which even now stands in act,° that, for their souls,[1] *are going on*
Another of his fathom[2] they have none
To lead their business; in which regard,[3]
Though I do hate him as I do hell pains,
Yet for necessity of present life° *livelihood*
I must show out a flag and sign of love,
Which is indeed but sign. That you shall surely find him,
Lead to the Sagittary[4] the raisèd search,[5]
And there will I be with him. So farewell. [*Exit.*]
[*Enter (below), Brabantio (in his nightgown)*[6] *with servants and torches.*]
BRABANTIO: It is too true an evil. Gone she is;
And what's to come of my despisèd time[7]
Is naught but bitterness. Now, Roderigo,
Where didst thou see her?—O, unhappy girl!—
With the Moor, sayst thou?—Who would be a father!—
How didst thou know 'twas she?—O, she deceives me
Past thought!—What said she to you?—Get more tapers.

5. The respect due to you.
6. Foreigner.
7. Charred linen ignited by a spark from flint and steel, used to light torches or *tapers*.
8. Produced (as a witness).
9. Unanimous shout of confirmation (in the Senate).
1. To save themselves.
2. I.e., ability, depth of experience.
3. Out of regard for which.
4. An inn or house where Othello and Desdemona are staying, named for its sign of Sagittarius, or Centaur.
5. Search party roused out of sleep.
6. Dressing gown. (This costuming is specified in the Quarto text.)
7. I.e., remainder of life.

Raise all my kindred.—Are they married, think you?
RODERIGO: Truly, I think they are.
BRABANTIO: O heaven! How got she out? O treason of the blood!
Fathers, from hence trust not your daughters' minds
By what you see them act. Is there not charms° *spells*
By which the property° of youth and maidhood *nature*
May be abused?° Have you not read, Roderigo, *deceived*
Of some such thing?
RODERIGO: Yes, sir, I have indeed.
BRABANTIO: Call up my brother.—O would you had had her!—
Some one way, some another.—Do you know
Where we may apprehend her and the Moor?
RODERIGO: I think I can discover° him, if you please *reveal*
To get good guard and go along with me.
BRABANTIO: Pray you, lead on. At every house I'll call;
I may command° at most.—Get weapons, ho! *demand aid*
And raise some special officers of night.—
On, good Roderigo. I will deserve° your pains. *reward*
[*Exeunt.*]

Scene 2[8]

[(*Before Othello's lodgings.*) *Enter Othello, Iago, attendants with torches.*]

IAGO: Though in the trade of war I have slain men,
Yet do I hold it very stuff[9] o' the conscience
To do no contrived° murder. I lack iniquity *premeditated*
Sometimes to do me service. Nine or ten times
I had thought t' have yerked° him° here under the ribs. *stabbed / Roderigo*
OTHELLO: 'Tis better as it is.
IAGO: Nay, but he prated,
And spoke such scurvy and provoking terms
Against your honor
That, with the little godliness I have,
I did full hard forbear him.[1] But, I pray you, sir,
Are you fast married? Be assured of this,
That the magnifico[2] is much beloved,
And hath in his effect° a voice potential° *command / powerful*
As double as the Duke's. He will divorce you,
Or put upon you what restraint or grievance
The law, with all his might to enforce it on,
Will give him cable.° *scope*
OTHELLO: Let him do his spite.
My services which I have done the seigniory° *government*
Shall out-tongue his complaints. 'Tis yet to know°— *not yet known*
Which, when I know that boasting is an honor,
I shall promulgate—I fetch my life and being

8. Location: Venice. Another street. Before Othello's lodgings.
9. Essence, basic material (continuing the metaphor of *trade* from line 1).
1. I restrained myself with great difficulty from assaulting him.
2. Venetian grandee, i.e., Brabantio.

From men of royal siege,° and my demerits° *rank / deserts*
May speak unbonneted[3] to as proud a fortune
As this that I have reached. For know, Iago,
But that I love the gentle Desdemona,
I would not my unhousèd° free condition *unconfined*
Put into circumscription and confine° *confinement*
For the seas' worth.[4] But look, what lights come yond?
[*Enter Cassio (and certain officers*[5]*) with torches*.]
IAGO: Those are the raisèd father and his friends.
You were best go in.
OTHELLO: Not I. I must be found.
My parts, my title, and my perfect soul[6]
Shall manifest me rightly. Is it they?
IAGO: By Janus,[7] I think no.
OTHELLO: The servants of the Duke? And my lieutenant?
The goodness of the night upon you, friends!
What is the news?
CASSIO: The Duke does greet you, General,
And he requires your haste-post-haste appearance
Even on the instant.
OTHELLO: What is the matter,° think you? *business*
CASSIO: Something from Cyprus, as I may divine.° *guess*
It is a business of some heat.° The galleys *urgency*
Have sent a dozen sequent° messengers *successive*
This very night at one another's heels,
And many of the consuls,° raised and met, *senators*
Are at the Duke's already. You have been hotly called for;
When, being not at your lodging to be found,
The Senate hath sent about[8] three several° quests *separate*
To search you out.
OTHELLO: 'Tis well I am found by you.
I will but spend a word here in the house
And go with you. [*Exit*.]
CASSIO: Ancient, what makes° he here? *does*
IAGO: Faith, he tonight hath boarded[9] a land carrack.° *merchant ship*
If it prove lawful prize,° he's made forever. *booty*
CASSIO: I do not understand.
IAGO: He's married.
CASSIO: To who?
[(*Enter Othello*.)]
IAGO: Marry,[1] to—Come, Captain, will you go?
OTHELLO: Have with you.[2]
CASSIO: Here comes another troop to seek for you.

3. Without removing the hat, i.e., on equal terms (or "with hat off," "in all due modesty").
4. All the riches at the bottom of the sea.
5. The Quarto text calls for "Cassio with lights, officers with torches."
6. My natural gifts, my position or reputation, and my unflawed conscience.
7. Roman two-faced god of beginnings.
8. All over the city.
9. Gone aboard and seized as an act of piracy (with sexual suggestion).
1. An oath, originally "by the Virgin Mary"; here with wordplay on *married*.
2. Let's go.

[*Enter Brabantio, Roderigo, with officers and torches*.][3]

IAGO: It is Brabantio. General, be advised.[4]
He comes to bad intent.

OTHELLO: Holla! Stand there!

RODERIGO: Signor, it is the Moor.

BRABANTIO: Down with him, thief!

[(*They draw on both sides*.)]

IAGO: You, Roderigo! Come, sir, I am for you.

OTHELLO: Keep up° your bright swords, for the dew will rust them. *sheathe*
Good signor, you shall more command with years
Than with your weapons.

BRABANTIO: O thou foul thief, where hast thou stowed my daughter?
Damned as thou art, thou hast enchanted her!
For I'll refer me to all things of sense,[5]
If she in chains of magic were not bound
Whether a maid so tender, fair, and happy,
So opposite to marriage that she shunned
The wealthy curlèd darlings of our nation,
Would ever have, t' incur a general mock,
Run from her guardage[6] to the sooty bosom
Of such a thing as thou—to fear, not to delight.
Judge me the world if 'tis not gross in sense° *obvious*
That thou hast practiced on her with foul charms,
Abused her delicate youth with drugs or minerals° *poisons*
That weakens motion.[7] I'll have 't disputed on;[8]
'Tis probable and palpable to thinking.
I therefore apprehend and do attach° thee *arrest*
For an abuser of the world, a practicer
Of arts inhibited° and out of warrant.°— *black magic / illegal*
Lay hold upon him! If he do resist,
Subdue him at his peril.

OTHELLO: Hold your hands,
Both you of my inclining° and the rest. *following*
Were it my cue to fight, I should have known it
Without a prompter.—Whither will you that I go
To answer this your charge?

BRABANTIO: To prison, till fit time
Of law and course of direct session[9]
Call thee to answer.

OTHELLO: What if I do obey?
How may the Duke be therewith satisfied,
Whose messengers are here about my side
Upon some present business of the state
To bring me to him?

3. The Quarto text calls for "others with lights and weapons."
4. Be on your guard.
5. Submit my case to creatures possessing common sense.
6. My guardianship of her.
7. Impair the vital faculties.
8. Argued in court by professional counsel, debated by experts.
9. Regular or specially convened legal proceedings.

OFFICER: 'Tis true, most worthy signor.
The Duke's in council, and your noble self,
I am sure, is sent for.
BRABANTIO: How? The Duke in council?
In this time of the night? Bring him away.° *right along*
Mine's not an idle° cause. The Duke himself, *trifling*
Or any of my brothers of the state,
Cannot but feel this wrong as 'twere their own;
For if such actions may have passage free,[1]
Bondslaves and pagans shall our statesmen be.
[*Exeunt.*]

Scene 3[2]

[*Enter Duke (and) Senators (and sit at a table with lights,) and Officers. (The Duke and Senators are reading dispatches.)*][3]

DUKE: There is no composition° in these news *consistency*
That gives them credit.
FIRST SENATOR: Indeed, they are disproportioned.° *inconsistent*
My letters say a hundred and seven galleys.
DUKE: And mine, a hundred forty.
SECOND SENATOR: And mine, two hundred.
But though they jump° not on a just° account— *agree / exact*
As in these cases, where the aim° reports *conjecture*
'Tis oft with difference—yet do they all confirm
A Turkish fleet, and bearing up to Cyprus.
DUKE: Nay, it is possible enough to judgment.
I do not so secure me in the error
But the main article I do approve[4]
In fearful sense.
SAILOR [*within*]: What ho, what ho, what ho!
[*Enter Sailor.*]
OFFICER: A messenger from the galleys.
DUKE: Now, what's the business?
SAILOR: The Turkish preparation[5] makes for Rhodes.
So was I bid report here to the state
By Signor Angelo.
DUKE: How say you by° this change? *about*
FIRST SENATOR: This cannot be
By no assay° of reason. 'Tis a pageant° *test / mere show*
To keep us in false gaze.[6] When we consider
Th' importancy of Cyprus to the Turk,
And let ourselves again but understand
That, as it more concerns the Turk than Rhodes,

1. Are allowed to go unchecked.
2. Location: Venice. A council chamber.
3. The Quarto text calls for the Duke and senators to "sit at a table with lights and attendants."
4. I do not take such (false) comfort in the discrepancies that I fail to perceive the main point, i.e., that the Turkish fleet is threatening.
5. Fleet prepared for battle.
6. Looking the wrong way.

So may he with more facile question bear it,[7]
For that° it stands not in such warlike brace,° *since / state*
But altogether lacks th' abilities° *means of defense*
That Rhodes is dressed in°—if we make thought of this, *equipped with*
We must not think the Turk is so unskillful° *careless*
To leave that latest° which concerns him first, *last*
Neglecting an attempt of ease and gain
To wake° and wage° a danger profitless. *stir up / risk*

DUKE: Nay, in all confidence, he's not for Rhodes.

OFFICER: Here is more news.

[*Enter a Messenger*.]

MESSENGER: The Ottomites, reverend and gracious,
Steering with due course toward the isle of Rhodes,
Have there injointed them[8] with an after° fleet. *following*

FIRST SENATOR: Ay, so I thought. How many, as you guess?

MESSENGER: Of thirty sail; and now they do restem
Their backward course,[9] bearing with frank° appearance *undisguised*
Their purposes toward Cyprus. Signor Montano,
Your trusty and most valiant servitor,° *officer*
With his free duty[1] recommends[2] you thus,
And prays you to believe him.

DUKE: 'Tis certain then for Cyprus.
Marcus Luccicos, is not he in town?

FIRST SENATOR: He's now in Florence.

DUKE: Write from us to him, post-post-haste. Dispatch.

FIRST SENATOR: Here comes Brabantio and the valiant Moor.

[*Enter Brabantio, Othello, Cassio, Iago, Roderigo, and officers*.]

DUKE: Valiant Othello, we must straight° employ you *straightway*
Against the general enemy[3] Ottoman.
[(*To Brabantio*.)] I did not see you; welcome, gentle° signor. *noble*
We lacked your counsel and your help tonight.

BRABANTIO: So did I yours. Good Your Grace, pardon me;
Neither my place° nor aught I heard of business *official position*
Hath raised me from my bed, nor doth the general care
Take hold on me, for my particular° grief *personal*
Is of so floodgate[4] and o'erbearing nature
That it engluts° and swallows other sorrows *engulfs*
And it is still itself.[5]

DUKE: Why, what's the matter?

BRABANTIO: My daughter! O, my daughter!

DUKE AND SENATORS: Dead?

BRABANTIO: Ay, to me.
She is abused,° stol'n from me, and corrupted *deceived*
By spells and medicines bought of mountebanks;
For nature so preposterously to err,

7. So also he (the Turk) can more easily capture it (Cyprus).
8. Joined themselves.
9. Retrace their original course.
1. Freely given and loyal service.
2. Commends himself and reports to.
3. Universal enemy to all Christendom.
4. Overwhelming (as when floodgates are opened).
5. Remains undiminished.

Being not deficient,° blind, or lame of sense, *defective*
Sans° witchcraft could not. *without*
DUKE: Whoe'er he be that in this foul proceeding
Hath thus beguiled your daughter of herself,
And you of her, the bloody book of law
You shall yourself read in the bitter letter
After your own sense[6]—yea, though our proper° son *my own*
Stood in your action.[7]
BRABANTIO: Humbly I thank Your Grace.
Here is the man, this Moor, whom now it seems
Your special mandate for the state affairs
Hath hither brought.
ALL: We are very sorry for 't.
DUKE [(*to Othello*)]:
What, in your own part, can you say to this?
BRABANTIO: Nothing, but this is so.
OTHELLO: Most potent, grave, and reverend signors,
My very noble and approved° good masters: *esteemed*
That I have ta'en away this old man's daughter,
It is most true; true, I have married her.
The very head and front[8] of my offending
Hath this extent, no more. Rude° am I in my speech, *unpolished*
And little blessed with the soft phrase of peace;
For since these arms of mine had seven years' pith,[9]
Till now some nine moons wasted,[1] they have used
Their dearest° action in the tented field; *most valuable*
And little of this great world can I speak
More than pertains to feats of broils and battle,
And therefore little shall I grace my cause
In speaking for myself. Yet, by your gracious patience,
I will a round° unvarnished tale deliver *plain*
Of my whole course of love—what drugs, what charms,
What conjuration, and what mighty magic,
For such proceeding I am charged withal,° *with*
I won his daughter.
BRABANTIO: A maiden never bold;
Of spirit so still and quiet that her motion
Blushed at herself;[2] and she, in spite of nature,
Of years,[3] of country, credit,° everything, *reputation*
To fall in love with what she feared to look on!
It is a judgment maimed and most imperfect
That will confess° perfection so could err *concede (that)*
Against all rules of nature, and must be driven
To find out practices° of cunning hell *plots*

6. According to your own interpretation.
7. Were under your accusation.
8. Height and breadth, entire extent.
9. Since I was seven.
1. Until some nine months ago (since when Othello has evidently not been on active duty, but in Venice).
2. She blushed easily at herself. (*Motion* can suggest the impulse of the soul or of the emotions, or physical movement.)
3. I.e., difference in age.

Why this should be. I therefore vouch° again — *assert*
That with some mixtures powerful o'er the blood,° — *passions*
Or with some dram conjured to this effect,[4]
He wrought upon her.
DUKE: To vouch this is no proof,
Without more wider° and more overt test° — *fuller / testimony*
Than these thin habits[5] and poor likelihoods° — *weak inferences*
Of modern seeming[6] do prefer° against him. — *bring forth*
FIRST SENATOR: But Othello, speak.
Did you by indirect and forcèd courses[7]
Subdue and poison this young maid's affections?
Or came it by request and such fair question° — *conversation*
As soul to soul affordeth?
OTHELLO: I do beseech you,
Send for the lady to the Sagittary
And let her speak of me before her father.
If you do find me foul in her report,
The trust, the office I do hold of you
Not only take away, but let your sentence
Even fall upon my life.
DUKE: Fetch Desdemona hither.
OTHELLO: Ancient, conduct them. You best know the place.
[(*Exeunt Iago and attendants.*)]
And, till she come, as truly as to heaven
I do confess the vices of my blood,° — *passions*
So justly° to your grave ears I'll present — *accurately*
How I did thrive in this fair lady's love,
And she in mine.
DUKE: Say it, Othello.
OTHELLO: Her father loved me, oft invited me,
Still° questioned me the story of my life — *continually*
From year to year—the battles, sieges, fortunes
That I have passed.
I ran it through, even from my boyish days
To th' very moment that he bade me tell it,
Wherein I spoke of most disastrous chances,
Of moving accidents° by flood and field, — *stirring happenings*
Of hairbreadth scapes i' th' imminent deadly breach,[8]
Of being taken by the insolent foe
And sold to slavery, of my redemption thence,
And portance° in my travels' history, — *conduct*
Wherein of antres° vast and deserts idle,° — *caverns / barren*
Rough quarries,° rocks, and hills whose heads touch heaven, — *rock formations*
It was my hint° to speak—such was my process— — *opportunity*
And of the Cannibals that each other eat,

4. Dose made by magical spells to have this effect.
5. Garments, i.e., appearances.
6. Commonplace assumption.
7. Means used against her will.
8. Death-threatening gaps made in a fortification.

The Anthropophagi,[9] and men whose heads
Do grow beneath their shoulders. These things to hear
Would Desdemona seriously incline;
But still the house affairs would draw her thence,
Which ever as she could with haste dispatch
She'd come again, and with a greedy ear
Devour up my discourse. Which I, observing,
Took once a pliant° hour, and found good means *well-suiting*
To draw from her a prayer of earnest heart
That I would all my pilgrimage dilate,° *relate in detail*
Whereof by parcels° she had something heard, *piecemeal*
But not intentively.° I did consent, *continuously*
And often did beguile her of her tears,
When I did speak of some distressful stroke
That my youth suffered. My story being done,
She gave me for my pains a world of sighs.
She swore, in faith, 'twas strange, 'twas passing° strange, *exceedingly*
'Twas pitiful, 'twas wondrous pitiful.
She wished she had not heard it, yet she wished
That heaven had made her° such a man. She thanked me, *created her to be*
And bade me, if I had a friend that loved her,
I should but teach him how to tell my story,
And that would woo her. Upon this hint° I spake. *opportunity*
She loved me for the dangers I had passed,
And I loved her that she did pity them.
This only is the witchcraft I have used.
Here comes the lady. Let her witness it.

[*Enter Desdemona, Iago (and) attendants.*]

DUKE: I think this tale would win my daughter too.
Good Brabantio,
Take up this mangled matter at the best.[1]
Men do their broken weapons rather use
Than their bare hands.

BRABANTIO: I pray you, hear her speak.
If she confess that she was half the wooer,
Destruction on my head if my bad blame
Light on the man!—Come hither, gentle mistress.
Do you perceive in all this noble company
Where most you owe obedience?

DESDEMONA: My noble Father,
I do perceive here a divided duty.
To you I am bound for life and education;° *upbringing*
My life and education both do learn° me *teach*
How to respect you. You are the lord of duty;[2]
I am hitherto your daughter. But here's my husband,
And so much duty as my mother showed

9. Man-eaters (a term from Pliny's *Natural History*).
1. Make the best of a bad bargain.
2. To whom duty is due.

To you, preferring you before her father,
So much I challenge° that I may profess — *claim*
Due to the Moor my lord.

BRABANTIO: God be with you! I have done.
Please it Your Grace, on to the state affairs.
I had rather to adopt a child than get° it. — *beget*
Come hither, Moor. [(*He joins the hands of Othello and Desdemona.*)]
I here do give thee that with all my heart[3]
Which, but thou hast already, with all my heart° — *gladly*
I would keep from thee.—For your sake,° jewel, — *on your account*
I am glad at soul I have no other child,
For thy escape° would teach me tyranny, — *elopement*
To hang clogs[4] on them.—I have done, my lord.

DUKE: Let me speak like yourself,[5] and lay a sentence[6]
Which, as a grice° or step, may help these lovers — *step*
Into your favor.
When remedies° are past, the griefs are ended — *hopes of remedy*
By seeing the worst, which late on hopes depended.[7]
To mourn a mischief° that is past and gone — *misfortune*
Is the next° way to draw new mischief on. — *nearest*
What° cannot be preserved when fortune takes, — *whatever*
Patience her injury a mockery makes.[8]
The robbed that smiles steals something from the thief;
He robs himself that spends a bootless grief.[9]

BRABANTIO: So let the Turk of Cyprus us beguile,
We lose it not, so long as we can smile.
He bears the sentence well that nothing bears
But the free comfort which from thence he hears,
But he bears both the sentence and the sorrow
That, to pay grief, must of poor patience borrow.[1]
These sentences, to sugar or to gall,
Being strong on both sides, are equivocal.[2]
But words are words. I never yet did hear
That the bruised heart was piercèd through the ear.[3]
I humbly beseech you, proceed to th' affairs of state.

DUKE: The Turk with a most mighty preparation makes for Cyprus. Othello, the fortitude[4] of the place is best known to you; and though we have there a substitute[5] of most allowed[6] sufficiency, yet opinion, a sovereign mistress of

3. Wherein my whole affection has been engaged.
4. Blocks of wood fastened to the legs of criminals or convicts to inhibit escape.
5. As you would, in your proper temper.
6. Apply a maxim.
7. Which griefs were sustained until recently by hopeful anticipation.
8. Patience laughs at the injury inflicted by fortune (and thus eases the pain).
9. Indulges in unavailing grief.
1. A person well bears out your maxim who can enjoy its platitudinous comfort, free of all genuine sorrow, but anyone whose grief bankrupts his poor patience is left with your saying and his sorrow, too. (*Bears the sentence* also plays on the meaning, "receives judicial sentence.")
2. These fine maxims are equivocal, either sweet or bitter in their application.
3. I.e., surgically lanced and cured by mere words of advice.
4. Strength.
5. Deputy.
6. Acknowledged.

effects, throws a more safer voice on you.[7] You must therefore be content to slubber[8] the gloss of your new fortunes with this more stubborn[9] and boisterous expedition.

OTHELLO: The tyrant custom, most grave senators,
Hath made the flinty and steel couch of war
My thrice-driven° bed of down. I do agnize[1] *thrice sifted*
A natural and prompt alacrity
I find in hardness,° and do undertake *hardship*
These present wars against the Ottomites.
Most humbly therefore bending to your state,[2]
I crave fit disposition for my wife,
Due reference of place and exhibition,[3]
With such accommodation° and besort° *provision / attendance*
As levels° with her breeding.° *suits / upbringing*

DUKE: Why, at her father's.

BRABANTIO: I will not have it so.

OTHELLO: Nor I.

DESDEMONA: Nor I. I would not there reside,
To put my father in impatient thoughts
By being in his eye. Most gracious Duke,
To my unfolding° lend your prosperous° ear, *proposal / propitious*
And let me find a charter° in your voice, *authorization*
T' assist my simpleness.

DUKE: What would you, Desdemona?

DESDEMONA: That I did love the Moor to live with him,
My downright violence and storm of fortunes[4]
May trumpet to the world. My heart's subdued
Even to the very quality of my lord.[5]
I saw Othello's visage in his mind,
And to his honors and his valiant parts° *qualities*
Did I my soul and fortunes consecrate.
So that, dear lords, if I be left behind
A moth[6] of peace, and he go to the war,
The rites[7] for why I love him are bereft me,
And I a heavy interim shall support
By his dear[8] absence. Let me go with him.

OTHELLO: Let her have your voice.° *consent*
Vouch with me, heaven, I therefor beg it not
To please the palate of my appetite,
Nor to comply with heat°—the young affects° *sexual passion / desires*
In me defunct—and proper° satisfaction, *personal*
But to be free° and bounteous to her mind. *generous*

7. General opinion, an important determiner of affairs, chooses you as the best man.
8. Soil, sully.
9. Harsh, rough.
1. Know in myself, acknowledge.
2. Bowing to your authority.
3. Provision of appropriate place to live and allowance of money.
4. My plain and total breach of social custom, taking my future by storm and disrupting my whole life.
5. My heart is brought wholly into accord with Othello's virtues; I love him for his virtues.
6. I.e., one who consumes merely.
7. Rites of love (with a suggestion, too, of "rights," sharing).
8. Heartfelt. Also, costly.

And heaven defend° your good souls that you think° *forbid / should think*
I will your serious and great business scant
When she is with me. No, when light-winged toys
Of feathered Cupid seel[9] with wanton dullness
My speculative and officed instruments,[1]
That my disports corrupt and taint my business,[2]
Let huswives make a skillet of my helm,
And all indign° and base adversities *unworthy, shameful*
Make head° against my estimation!° *rise up / reputation*

DUKE: Be it as you shall privately determine,
Either for her stay or going. Th' affair cries haste,
And speed must answer it.

A SENATOR: You must away tonight.

DESDEMONA: Tonight, my lord?

DUKE: This night.

OTHELLO: With all my heart.

DUKE: At nine i' the morning here we'll meet again.
Othello, leave some officer behind,
And he shall our commission bring to you,
With such things else of quality and respect[3]
As doth import° you. *concern*

OTHELLO: So please Your Grace, my ancient;
A man he is of honesty and trust.
To his conveyance I assign my wife,
With what else needful Your Good Grace shall think
To be sent after me.

DUKE: Let it be so.
Good night to everyone. [*To Brabantio.*] And, noble signor,
If virtue no delighted° beauty lack, *delightful*
Your son-in-law is far more fair than black.

FIRST SENATOR: Adieu, brave Moor. Use Desdemona well.

BRABANTIO: Look to her, Moor, if thou hast eyes to see.
She has deceived her father, and may thee.

[(*Exeunt Duke, Brabantio, Cassio, Senators, and officers.*)]

OTHELLO: My life upon her faith! Honest Iago,
My Desdemona must I leave to thee.
I prithee, let thy wife attend on her,
And bring them after in the best advantage.[4]
Come, Desdemona. I have but an hour
Of love, of worldly matters and direction,° *instructions*
To spend with thee. We must obey the time.[5]

[*Exit* (*with Desdemona.*)]

RODERIGO: Iago—

IAGO: What sayst thou, noble heart?

9. I.e., make blind (as in falconry, by sewing up the eyes of the hawk during training).

1. Eyes and other faculties used in the performance of duty.

2. So that my sexual pastimes impair my work.

3. Of importance and relevance.

4. At the most favorable opportunity.

5. The urgency of the present crisis.

RODERIGO: What will I do, think'st thou?

IAGO: Why, go to bed and sleep.

RODERIGO: I will incontinently° drown myself. *immediately*

IAGO: If thou dost, I shall never love thee after. Why, thou silly gentleman?

RODERIGO: It is silliness to live when to live is torment; and then have we a prescription[6] to die when death is our physician.

IAGO: O villainous![7] I have looked upon the world for four times seven years, and, since I could distinguish betwixt a benefit and an injury, I never found man that knew how to love himself. Ere I would say I would drown myself for the love of a guinea hen,[8] I would change my humanity with a baboon.

RODERIGO: What should I do? I confess it is my shame to be so fond,[9] but it is not in my virtue[1] to amend it.

IAGO: Virtue? A fig![2] 'Tis in ourselves that we are thus or thus. Our bodies are our gardens, to the which our wills are gardeners; so that if we will plant nettles or sow lettuce, set hyssop[3] and weed up thyme, supply it with one gender[4] of herbs or distract it with[5] many, either to have it sterile with idleness[6] or manured with industry—why, the power and corrigible authority[7] of this lies in our wills. If the beam[8] of our lives had not one scale of reason to poise[9] another of sensuality, the blood[1] and baseness of our natures would conduct us to most preposterous conclusions. But we have reason to cool our raging motions,[2] our carnal stings, our unbitted[3] lusts, whereof I take this that you call love to be a sect or scion.[4]

RODERIGO: It cannot be.

IAGO: It is merely a lust of the blood and a permission of the will. Come, be a man. Drown thyself? Drown cats and blind puppies. I have professed me thy friend, and I confess me knit to thy deserving with cables of perdurable[5] toughness. I could never better stead[6] thee than now. Put money in thy purse. Follow thou the wars; defeat thy favor[7] with an usurped[8] beard. I say, put money in thy purse. It cannot be long that Desdemona should continue her love to the Moor—put money in thy purse—nor he his to her. It was a violent commencement in her, and thou shalt see an answerable sequestration[9]—put but money in thy purse. These Moors are changeable in their wills[1]—fill thy purse with money. The food that to him now is as luscious as locusts[2] shall be to him shortly as bitter as coloquintida.[3] She must change for youth; when she is sated with his body, she will find the error of her choice. She must have change, she

6. Right based on long-established custom. Also, doctor's prescription.
7. I.e., what perfect nonsense.
8. A slang term for a prostitute.
9. Infatuated.
1. Strength, nature.
2. To give a fig is to thrust the thumb between the first and second fingers in a vulgar and insulting gesture.
3. An herb of the mint family.
4. Kind.
5. Divide it among.
6. Want of cultivation.
7. Power to correct.
8. Balance.
9. Counterbalance.
1. Natural passions.
2. Appetites.
3. Unbridled, uncontrolled.
4. Cutting or offshoot.
5. Very durable.
6. Assist.
7. Disguise your face.
8. The suggestion is that Roderigo is not man enough to have a beard of his own.
9. A corresponding separation or estrangement.
1. Carnal appetites.
2. Fruit of the carob tree (see Matthew 3.4), or perhaps honeysuckle.
3. Colocynth or bitter apple, a purgative.

must. Therefore put money in thy purse. If thou wilt needs damn thyself, do it a more delicate way than drowning. Make[4] all the money thou canst. If sanctimony[5] and a frail vow betwixt an erring[6] barbarian and a supersubtle Venetian be not too hard for my wits and all the tribe of hell, thou shalt enjoy her. Therefore make money. A pox of drowning thyself! It is clean out of the way.[7] Seek thou rather to be hanged in compassing[8] thy joy than to be drowned and go without her.

RODERIGO: Wilt thou be fast[9] to my hopes if I depend on the issue?[1]

IAGO: Thou art sure of me. Go, make money. I have told thee often, and I retell thee again and again, I hatethe Moor. My cause is hearted;[2] thine hath no less reason. Let us be conjunctive[3] in our revenge against him. If thou canst cuckold him, thou dost thyself a pleasure, me a sport. There are many events in the womb of time which will be delivered. Traverse,[4] go, provide thy money. We will have more of this tomorrow. Adieu.

RODERIGO: Where shall we meet i' the morning?

IAGO: At my lodging.

RODERIGO: I'll be with thee betimes.° [(*He starts to leave.*)] *early*

IAGO: Go to, farewell.—Do you hear, Roderigo?

RODERIGO: What say you?

IAGO: No more of drowning, do you hear?

RODERIGO: I am changed.

IAGO: Go to, farewell. Put money enough in your purse.

RODERIGO: I'll sell all my land. [*Exit.*]

IAGO: Thus do I ever make my fool my purse;
For I mine own gained knowledge should profane
If I would time expend with such a snipe[5]
But for my sport and profit. I hate the Moor;
And it is thought abroad° that twixt my sheets *rumored*
He's done my office.[6] I know not if 't be true;
But I, for mere suspicion in that kind,
Will do as if for surety.[7] He holds me well;[8]
The better shall my purpose work on him.
Cassio's a proper° man. Let me see now: *handsome*
To get his place and to plume[9] up my will
In double knavery—How, how?—Let's see:
After some time, to abuse° Othello's ear *deceive*
That he° is too familiar with his wife. *Cassio*
He hath a person and a smooth dispose° *disposition*
To be suspected, framed to make women false.

4. Raise, collect.
5. Sacred ceremony.
6. Wandering, vagabond, unsteady.
7. Entirely unsuitable as a course of action.
8. Encompassing, embracing.
9. True.
1. Successful outcome.
2. Fixed in the heart, heartfelt.
3. United.
4. A military marching term.
5. Woodcock, i.e., fool.
6. My sexual function as husband.
7. Act as if on certain knowledge.
8. Regards me favorably.
9. Put a feather in the cap of, i.e., glorify, gratify.

The Moor is of a free° and open° nature, *frank / unsuspicious*
That thinks men honest that but seem to be so,
And will as tenderly° be led by the nose *readily*
As asses are.
I have 't. It is engendered. Hell and night
Must bring this monstrous birth to the world's light.

[*Exit.*]

ACT 2

Scene 1[1]

[*Enter Montano and two Gentlemen.*]

MONTANO: What from the cape can you discern at sea?
FIRST GENTLEMAN: Nothing at all. It is a high-wrought flood.° *agitated sea*
I cannot, twixt the heaven and the main,° *ocean*
Descry a sail.
MONTANO: Methinks the wind hath spoke aloud at land;
A fuller blast ne'er shook our battlements.
If it hath ruffianed° so upon the sea, *raged*
What ribs of oak, when mountains° melt on them, *of water*
Can hold the mortise?[2] What shall we hear of this?
SECOND GENTLEMAN: A segregation° of the Turkish fleet. *dispersal*
For do but stand upon the foaming shore,
The chidden[3] billow seems to pelt the clouds;
The wind-shaked surge, with high and monstrous mane,[4]
Seems to cast water on the burning Bear[5]
And quench the guards of th' ever-fixèd pole.
I never did like molestation° view *such a disturbance*
On the enchafèd° flood. *angry*
MONTANO: If that° the Turkish fleet *if*
Be not ensheltered and embayed,° they are drowned; *in a harbor*
It is impossible to bear it out.° *survive*

[*Enter a (Third) Gentleman.*]

THIRD GENTLEMAN: News, lads! Our wars are done.
The desperate tempest hath so banged the Turks
That their designment° halts.° A noble ship of Venice *enterprise / is lame*
Hath seen a grievous wreck° and sufferance° *shipwreck / damage*
On most part of their fleet.
MONTANO: How? Is this true?
THIRD GENTLEMAN: The ship is here put in,
A Veronesa;[6] Michael Cassio,

1. Location; A seaport in Cyprus. An open place near the quay.
2. Hold their joints together.
3. I.e., rebuked, repelled (by the shore), and thus shot into the air.
4. The surf is like the mane of a wild beast.
5. The constellation Ursa Minor or the Little Bear, which includes the polestar (and hence regarded as the *guards of th' ever-fixed pole* in the next line; sometimes the term *guards* is applied to the two "pointers" of the Big Bear or Dipper, which may be intended here).
6. Fitted out in Verona for Venetian service, or possibly *Verennessa* (the Folio spelling), i.e., *verrinessa,* a cutter (from *verrinare*, "to cut through").

Lieutenant to the warlike Moor Othello,
Is come on shore; the Moor himself at sea,
And is in full commission here for Cyprus.

MONTANO: I am glad on 't. 'Tis a worthy governor.

THIRD GENTLEMAN: But this same Cassio, though he speak of comfort
Touching the Turkish loss, yet he looks sadly° *gravely*
And prays the Moor be safe, for they were parted
With foul and violent tempest.

MONTANO: Pray heaven he be,
For I have served him, and the man commands
Like a full° soldier. Let's to the seaside, ho! *perfect*
As well to see the vessel that's come in
As to throw out our eyes for brave Othello,
Even till we make the main and th' aerial blue[7]
An indistinct regard.[8]

THIRD GENTLEMAN: Come, let's do so,
For every minute is expectancy° *gives expectation*
Of more arrivance.° *arrival*

[*Enter Cassio.*]

CASSIO: Thanks, you the valiant of this warlike isle,
That so approve° the Moor! O, let the heavens *honor*
Give him defense against the elements,
For I have lost him on a dangerous sea.

MONTANO: Is he well shipped?

CASSIO: His bark is stoutly timbered, and his pilot
Of very expert and approved allowance;° *tested reputation*
Therefore my hopes, not surfeited to death,[9]
Stand in bold cure.[1]

[(*A cry*) *within:*] "*A sail, a sail, a sail!*"

CASSIO: What noise?

A GENTLEMAN: The town is empty. On the brow o' the sea[2]
Stand ranks of people, and they cry "A sail!"

CASSIO: My hopes do shape him for[3] the governor.

[(*A shot within.*)]

SECOND GENTLEMAN: They do discharge their shot of courtesy;[4]
Our friends at least.

CASSIO: I pray you, sir, go forth,
And give us truth who 'tis that is arrived.

SECOND GENTLEMAN: I shall. [*Exit.*]

MONTANO: But, good Lieutenant, is your general wived?

CASSIO: Most fortunately. He hath achieved a maid
That paragons° description and wild fame,° *surpasses / rumor*
One that excels the quirks° of blazoning[5] pens, *witty conceits*
And in th' essential vesture of creation

7. The sea and the sky.
8. Indistinguishable in our view.
9. Overextended, worn thin through repeated application or delayed fulfillment.
1. In strong hopes of fulfillment.
2. Cliff-edge.
3. I hope it is.
4. Fire a salute in token of respect and courtesy.
5. Setting forth as though in heraldic language.

Does tire the engineer.[6]
[*Enter (Second) Gentleman.*][7]
How now? Who has put in?° *to harbor*
SECOND GENTLEMAN: 'Tis one Iago, ancient to the General.
CASSIO: He's had most favorable and happy speed.
Tempests themselves, high seas, and howling winds,
The guttered° rocks and congregated sands— *jagged*
Traitors ensteeped° to clog the guiltless keel— *lying under water*
As° having sense of beauty, do omit° *as if / suspend*
Their mortal° natures, letting go safely by *deadly*
The divine Desdemona.
MONTANO: What is she?
CASSIO: She that I spake of, our great captain's captain,
Left in the conduct of the bold Iago,
Whose footing° here anticipates our thoughts *landing*
A se'nnight's° speed. Great Jove, Othello guard, *week's*
And swell his sail with thine own powerful breath,
That he may bless this bay with his tall° ship, *splendid*
Make love's quick pants in Desdemona's arms,
Give renewed fire to our extincted spirits,
And bring all Cyprus comfort!
[*Enter Desdemona, Iago, Roderigo, and Emilia.*]
O, behold,
The riches of the ship is come on shore!
You men of Cyprus, let her have your knees.
[(*The gentlemen make curtsy to Desdemona.*)]
Hail to thee, lady! And the grace of heaven
Before, behind thee, and on every hand
Enwheel thee round!
DESDEMONA: I thank you, valiant Cassio.
What tidings can you tell me of my lord?
CASSIO: He is not yet arrived, nor know I aught
But that he's well and will be shortly here.
DESDEMONA: Oh, but I fear—How lost you company?
CASSIO: The great contention of the sea and skies
Parted our fellowship.
[*Within:* "*A sail, a sail!*" (*A shot.*)]
But hark. A sail!
SECOND GENTLEMAN: They give their greeting to the citadel.
This likewise is a friend.
CASSIO: See for the news.
[(*Exit Second Gentleman.*)]
Good Ancient, you are welcome. [(*Kissing Emilia.*)]
Welcome, mistress.
Let it not gall your patience, good Iago,
That I extend° my manners; 'tis my breeding[8] *give scope to*

6. In her real, God-given, beauty, (she) defeats any attempt to praise her. The enginer [enginer] is the poet, one who devises.

7. So identified in the Quarto text here and in lines 57, 60, 67 and 95; the Folio calls him a gentelman.

8. Training in the niceties of etiquette.

That gives me this bold show of courtesy.
IAGO: Sir, would she give you so much of her lips
As of her tongue she oft bestows on me,
You would have enough.
DESDEMONA: Alas, she has no speech![9]
IAGO: In faith, too much.
I find it still,° when I have list° to sleep. *always / desire*
Marry, before your ladyship, I grant,
She puts her tongue a little in her heart
And chides with thinking.[1]
EMILIA: You have little cause to say so.
IAGO: Come on, come on. you are pictures out of doors,[2]
Bells[3] in your parlors, wildcats in your kitchens,[4]
Saints° in your injuries, devils being offended, *martyrs*
Players° in your huswifery,° and huswives[5] in your beds. *idlers / housekeeping*
DESDEMONA: O, fie upon thee, slanderer!
IAGO: Nay, it is true, or else I am a Turk.[6]
You rise to play, and go to bed to work.
EMILIA: You shall not write my praise.
IAGO: No, let me not.
DESDEMONA: What wouldst write of me, if thou shouldst praise me?
IAGO: O, gentle lady, do not put me to 't,
For I am nothing if not critical.° *censorious*
DESDEMONA: Come on, essay.°—There's one gone to the harbor? *try*
IAGO: Ay, madam.
DESDEMONA: I am not merry, but I do beguile
The thing I am[7] by seeming otherwise.
Come, how wouldst thou praise me?
IAGO: I am about it, but indeed my invention
Comes from my pate as birdlime[8] does from frieze°— *coarse cloth*
It plucks out brains and all. But my Muse labors,[9]
And thus she is delivered:
If she be fair and wise, fairness and wit,
The one's for use, the other useth it.[1]
DESDEMONA: Well praised! How if she be black[2] and witty?
IAGO: If she be black, and thereto have a wit,
She'll find a white[3] that shall her blackness fit.[4]
DESDEMONA: Worse and worse.
EMILIA: How if fair and foolish?
IAGO: She never yet was foolish that was fair,
For even her folly[5] helped her to an heir.° *to bear a child*

9. She's not a chatterbox, as you allege.
1. In her thoughts only.
2. Silent and well-behaved in public.
3. Jangling, noisy, and brazen.
4. In domestic affairs. (Ladies would not do the cooking.)
5. Hussies (i.e., women are "busy" in bed, or unduly thrifty in dispensing sexual favors).
6. An infidel, not to be believed.
7. My anxious self.
8. Sticky substance used to catch small birds.
9. Exerts herself. Also, prepares to deliver a child (with a following pun on "*delivered*" in line 130).
1. Her cleverness will make use of her beauty.
2. Dark-complexioned, brunette.
3. A fair person (with wordplay on "wight," a person).
4. With sexual suggestion of mating.
5. With added meaning of "lechery, wantonness."

DESDEMONA: These are old fond[6] paradoxes to make fools laugh i' th' alehouse.
What miserable praise hast thou for her that's foul[7] and foolish?

IAGO: There's none so foul and foolish thereunto,° *in addition*
But does foul° pranks which fair and wise ones do. *sluttish*

DESDEMONA: O, heavy ignorance! Thou praisest the worst best. But what praise couldst thou bestow on a deserving woman indeed, one that, in the authority of her merit, did justly put on the vouch[8] of very malice itself?

IAGO: She that was ever fair, and never proud,
Had tongue at will, and yet was never loud,
Never lacked gold and yet went never gay,° *extravagantly clothed*
Fled from her wish, and yet said, "Now I may,"[9]
She that being angered, her revenge being nigh,
Bade her wrong stay[1] and her displeasure fly,
She that in wisdom never was so frail
To change the cod's head for the salmon's tail,[2]
She that could think and ne'er disclose her mind,
See suitors following and not look behind,
She was a wight, if ever such wight were—

DESDEMONA: To do what?

IAGO: To suckle fools and chronicle small beer.[3]

DESDEMONA: Oh, most lame and impotent conclusion! Do not learn of him, Emilia, though he be thy husband. How say you, Cassio? Is he not a most profane and liberal[4] counselor?

CASSIO: He speaks home,[5] madam. You may relish[6] him more in[7] the soldier than in the scholar.

[(*Cassio and Desdemona stand together, conversing intimately.*)]

IAGO [(*aside*)]: He takes her by the palm. Ay, well said,[8] whisper. With as little a web as this will I ensnare as great a fly as Cassio. Ay, smile upon her, do; I will gyve[9] thee in thine own courtship.[1] You say true;[2] 'tis so, indeed. If such tricks as these strip you out of your lieutenantry, it had been better you had not kissed your three fingers so oft, which now again you are most apt to play the sir[3] in. Very good; well kissed! An excellent courtesy! 'Tis so, indeed. Yet again your fingers to your lips? Would they were clyster pipes[4] for your sake! [*Trumpet within.*] The Moor! I know his trumpet.

CASSIO: 'Tis truly so.

DESDEMONA: Let's meet him and receive him.

CASSIO: Lo, where he comes!

[*Enter Othello and attendants.*]

6. Foolish.
7. Ugly.
8. Compel the approval.
9. Avoided temptation where the choice was hers.
1. Resolved to put up with her injury patiently.
2. To exchange a lackluster husband for a sexy lover(?) (*Cod's head* is slang for "penis.").
3. To nurse babies and keep petty household accounts.
4. Ribald and licentious.
5. Right to the target (a term from fencing).
6. Appreciate.
7. In the character of.
8. Well done.
9. Fetter, shackle.
1. Courtesy, show of courtly manners.
2. That's right, go ahead.
3. The fine gentleman.
4. Tubes used for enemas and douches.

OTHELLO: O, my fair warrior!
DESDEMONA: My dear Othello!
OTHELLO: It gives me wonder great as my content
To see you here before me. O my soul's joy,
If after every tempest come such calms,
May the winds blow till they have weakened death,
And let the laboring bark climb hills of seas
Olympus-high, and duck again as low
As hell's from heaven! If it were now to die,
'Twere now to be most happy, for I fear
My soul hath her content so absolute
That not another comfort like to this
Succeeds in unknown fate.[5]
DESDEMONA: The heavens forbid
But that our loves and comforts should increase
Even as our days do grow!
OTHELLO: Amen to that, sweet powers!
I cannot speak enough of this content.
It stops me here; it is too much of joy.
And this, and this, the greatest discords be
[(*They kiss*.)][6]
That e'er our hearts shall make!
IAGO [(*aside*)]: O, you are well tuned now!
But I'll set down[7] the pegs that make this music,
As honest as I am.[8]
OTHELLO: Come, let us to the castle.
News, friends! Our wars are done, the Turks are drowned.
How does my old acquaintance of this isle?—
Honey, you shall be well desired° in Cyprus; *welcomed*
I have found great love amongst them. O, my sweet,
I prattle out of fashion,° and I dote *incoherntly*
In mine own comforts.—I prithee, good Iago,
Go to the bay and disembark my coffers.° *chests*
Bring thou the master° to the citadel; *ship's captain*
He is a good one, and his worthiness
Does challenge° much respect.—Come, Desdemona.— *deserve*
Once more, well met at Cyprus!
[*Exeunt Othello and Desdemona (and all but Iago and Roderigo.)*]

IAGO [(*to an attendant*)]: Do thou meet me presently at the harbor. [(*To Roderigo*)] Come hither. If thou be'st valiant—as, they say, base men[9] being in love have

5. Can follow in the unknown future.
6. The direction is from the Quarto.
7. Loosen (and hence untune the instrument).
8. For all my supposed honesty.
9. Even lowly born men.

then a nobility in their natures more than is native to them—list[1] me. The Lieutenant tonight watches on the court of guard.[2] First, I must tell thee this: Desdemona is directly in love with him.

RODERIGO: With him? Why, 'tis not possible.

IAGO: Lay thy finger thus,[3] and let thy soul be instructed. Mark me with what violence she first loved the Moor, but[4] for bragging and telling her fantastical lies. To love him still for prating? Let not thy discreet heart think it. Her eye must be fed; and what delight shall she have to look on the devil? When the blood is made dull with the act of sport,[5] there should be, again to inflame it and to give satiety a fresh appetite, loveliness in favor,[6] sympathy[7] in years, manners, and beauties—all which the Moor is defective in. Now, for want of these required conveniences,[8] her delicate tenderness will find itself abused,[9] begin to heave the gorge,[1] disrelish and abhor the Moor. Very nature[2] will instruct her in it and compel her to some second choice. Now, sir, this granted—as it is a most pregnant[3] and unforced position—who stands so eminent in the degree[4] of this fortune as Cassio does? A knave very voluble,[5] no further conscionable[6] than in putting on the mere form of civil and humane[7] seeming for the better compassing of his salt[8] and most hidden loose affection.[9] Why, none, why, none. A slipper[1] and subtle knave, a finder out of occasions, that has an eye can stamp[2] and counterfeit advantages,[3] though true advantage never present itself; a devilish knave. Besides, the knave is handsome, young, and hath all those requisites in him that folly[4] and green[5] minds look after. A pestilent complete knave, and the woman hath found him[6] already.

RODERIGO: I cannot believe that in her. She's full of most blessed condition.[7]

IAGO: Blessed fig's end! The wine she drinks is made of grapes. If she had been blessed, she would never have loved the Moor. Blessed pudding![8] Didst thou not see her paddle with the palm of his hand? Didst not mark that?

RODERIGO: Yes, that I did; but that was but courtesy.

IAGO: Lechery, by this hand. An index[9] and obscure prologue to the history of lust and foul thoughts. They met so near with their lips that their breaths embraced together. Villainous thoughts, Roderigo! When these mutualities[1] so marshal the way, hard at hand[2] comes the master and main exercise, th' incorporate[3] conclusion. Pish! But, sir, be you ruled by me. I have brought you from Venice.

1. Listen to.
2. Guardhouse. (Cassio is in charge of the watch.)
3. I.e., on your lips.
4. Only.
5. Sex.
6. Appearance.
7. Correspondence, similarity.
8. Things conducive to sexual compatibility.
9. Cheated, revolted.
1. Experience nausea.
2. Her very instincts.
3. Evident, cogent.
4. As next in line for.
5. Facile, glib.
6. Conscientious, conscience-bound.
7. Polite, courteous.
8. Licentious.
9. Passion.
1. Slippery.
2. An eye that can coin, create.
3. Favorable opportunities.
4. Wantonness.
5. Immature.
6. Sized him up, perceived his intent.
7. Disposition.
8. Sausage.
9. Table of contents.
1. Exchanges, intimacies.
2. Closely following.
3. Carnal.

Watch you[4] tonight; for the command, I'll lay 't upon you.[5] Cassio knows you not. I'll not be far from you. Do you find some occasion to anger Cassio, either by speaking too loud, or tainting[6] his discipline, or from what other course you please, which the time shall more favorably minister.[7]

RODERIGO: Well.

IAGO: Sir, he's rash and very sudden in choler,[8] and haply[9] may strike at you. Provoke him that he may, for even out of that will I cause these of Cyprus to mutiny,[1] whose qualification[2] shall come into no true taste[3] again but by the displanting of Cassio. So shall you have a shorter journey to your desires by the means I shall then have to prefer[4] them, and the impediment most profitably removed, without the which there were no expectation of our prosperity.

RODERIGO: I will do this, if you can bring it to any opportunity.

IAGO: I warrant[5] thee. Meet me by and by[6] at the citadel. I must fetch his necessaries ashore. Farewell.

RODERIGO: Adieu. [*Exit.*]

IAGO: That Cassio loves her, I do well believe 't;
That she loves him, 'tis apt° and of great credit.° *probable / credibility*
The Moor, howbeit that I endure him not,
Is of a constant, loving, noble nature,
And I dare think he'll prove to Desdemona
A most dear husband. Now, I do love her too,
Not out of absolute lust—though peradventure
I stand accountant° for as great a sin— *accountable*
But partly led to diet° my revenge *feed*
For that I do suspect the lusty Moor
Hath leaped into my seat, the thought whereof
Doth, like a poisonous mineral, gnaw my innards;
And nothing can or shall content my soul
Till I am evened with him, wife for wife,
Or failing so, yet that I put the Moor
At least into a jealousy so strong
That judgment cannot cure. Which thing to do,
If this poor trash of Venice, whom I trace[7]
For[8] his quick hunting, stand[9] the putting on,
I'll have our Michael Cassio on the hip,[1]
Abuse° him to the Moor in the rank garb°— *slander / coarse manner*
For I fear Cassio with my nightcap[2] too—
Make the Moor thank me, love me, and reward me

4. Stand watch.
5. I'll arrange for you to be appointed, given orders.
6. Disparaging.
7. Provide.
8. Wrath.
9. Perhaps.
1. Riot.
2. Appeasement.
3. Acceptable state.
4. Advance.
5. Assure.
6. Immediately.
7. Train, or follow (?), or perhaps *trash*, a hunting term, meaning to put weights on a hunting dog in order to slow him down.
8. To make more eager.
9. Responds properly when I incite him to quarrel.
1. At my mercy, where I can throw him. (A wrestling term.)
2. As a rival in my bed, as one who gives me cuckold's horns.

For making him egregiously an ass
And practicing upon° his peace and quiet *plotting against*
Even to madness. 'Tis here, but yet confused.
Knavery's plain face is never seen till used. [*Exit.*]

Scene 2[3]

[*Enter Othello's Herald with a proclamation.*]

HERALD: It is Othello's pleasure, our noble and valiant general, that, upon certain tidings now arrived, importing the mere perdition[4] of the Turkish fleet, every man put himself into triumph:[5] some to dance, some to make bonfires, each man to what sport and revels his addiction[6] leads him. For, besides these beneficial news, it is the celebration of his nuptial. So much was his pleasure should be proclaimed. All offices[7] are open, and there is full liberty of feasting from this present hour of five till the bell have told eleven. Heaven bless the isle of Cyprus and our noble general Othello!

[*Exit.*]

Scene 3[8]

[*Enter Othello, Desdemona, Cassio, and attendants.*]

OTHELLO: Good Michael, look you to the guard tonight.
Let's teach ourselves that honorable stop° *restraint*
Not to outsport° discretion. *celebrate beyond*
CASSIO: Iago hath direction what to do,
But notwithstanding, with my personal eye
Will I look to 't.
OTHELLO: Iago is most honest.
Michael, good night. Tomorrow with your earliest[9]
Let me have speech with you. [(*To Desdemona.*)] Come, my dear love,
The purchase made, the fruits are to ensue;
That profit's yet to come 'tween me and you.[1]—
Good night.
[*Exit* (*Othello, with Desdemona and attendants.*)]

[*Enter Iago.*]

CASSIO: Welcome, Iago. We must to the watch.
IAGO: Not this hour,[2] Lieutenant; 'tis not yet ten o' the clock. Our general cast[3] us thus early for the love of his Desdemona; who[4] let us not therefore blame. He hath not yet made wanton the night with her, and she is sport for Jove.
CASSIO: She's a most exquisite lady.
IAGO: And, I'll warrant her, full of game.
CASSIO: Indeed, she's a most fresh and delicate creature.

3. Location: Cyprus. A street.
4. Complete destruction.
5. Public celebration.
6. Inclination.
7. Rooms where food and drink are kept.
8. Location: Cyprus. The citadel.
9. At your earliest convenience.
1. Though married, we haven't yet consummated our love.
2. Not for an hour yet.
3. Dismissed.
4. Othello.

IAGO: What an eye she has! Methinks it sounds a parley[5] to provocation.

CASSIO: An inviting eye, and yet methinks right modest.

IAGO: And when she speaks, is it not an alarum[6] to love?

CASSIO: She is indeed perfection.

IAGO: Well, happiness to their sheets! Come, Lieutenant, I have a stoup[7] of wine, and here without[8] are a brace[9] of Cyprus gallants that would fain have a measure[1] to the health of black Othello.

CASSIO: Not tonight, good Iago. I have very poor and unhappy brains for drinking. I could well wish courtesy would invent some other custom of entertainment.

IAGO: O, they are our friends. But one cup! I'll drink for you.[2]

CASSIO: I have drunk but one cup tonight, and that was craftily qualified[3] too, and behold what innovation[4] it makes here.[5] I am unfortunate in the infirmity and dare not task my weakness with any more.

IAGO: What, man? 'Tis a night of revels. The gallants desire it.

CASSIO: Where are they?

IAGO: Here at the door. I pray you, call them in.

CASSIO: I'll do't, but it dislikes me.[6] [*Exit.*]

IAGO: If I can fasten but one cup upon him,
With that which he hath drunk tonight already,
He'll be as full of quarrel and offense[7]
As my young mistress' dog. Now, my sick fool Roderigo,
Whom love hath turned almost the wrong side out,
To Desdemona hath tonight caroused° *drunk off*
Potations pottle-deep;[8] and he's to watch.° *stand watch*
Three lads of Cyprus—noble swelling° spirits, *proud*
That hold their honors in a wary distance,[9]
The very elements° of this warlike isle— *typical sort*
Have I tonight flustered with flowing cups,
And they watch° too. Now, 'mongst this flock of drunkards *are on guard*
Am I to put our Cassio in some action
That may offend the isle.—But here they come.

[*Enter Cassio, Montano, and gentlemen;* (*servants following with wine*.)]

If consequence do but approve my dream,[1]
My boat sails freely both with wind and stream.° *current*

CASSIO: 'Fore God, they have given me a rouse° already. *large drink*

MONTANO: Good faith, a little one; not past a pint, as I am a soldier.

IAGO: Some wine, ho!
[(*He sings*.)] "And let me the cannikin° clink, clink, *cup*
And let me the cannikin clink.
A soldier's a man,

5. Calls for a conference, issues an invitation.
6. Signal calling men to arms (continuing the military metaphor of *parley*, line 21).
7. Measure of liquor, two quarts.
8. Outside.
9. Pair.
1. Gladly drink a toast.
2. In your place. (Iago will do the steady drinking to keep the gallants company while Cassio has only one cup.)
3. Diluted.
4. Disturbance, insurrection.
5. I.e., in my head.
6. I'm reluctant.
7. Readiness to take offense.
8. To the bottom of the tankard.
9. Are extremely sensitive of their honor.
1. If subsequent events will only substantiate scheme.

O, man's life's but a span;[2]
Why, then, let a soldier drink."

Some wine, boys!

CASSIO: 'Fore God, an excellent song.

IAGO: I learned it in England, where indeed they are most potent in potting.[3] Your Dane, your German, and your swag-bellied Hollander—drink, ho!—are nothing to your English.

CASSIO: Is your Englishman so exquisite in his drinking?

IAGO: Why, he drinks you,[4] with facility, your Dane dead drunk; he sweats not[5] to overthrow your Almain;[6] he gives your Hollander a vomit ere the next pottle can be filled.

CASSIO: To the health of our general!

MONTANO: I am for it, Lieutenant, and I'll do you justice.[7]

IAGO: O sweet England! [*He sings*.]

"King Stephen was and-a worthy peer,
His breeches cost him but a crown;
He held them sixpence all too dear,
With that he called the tailor lown.° *lout*

He was a wight of high renown,
And thou art but of low degree.
'Tis pride[8] that pulls the country down;
Then take thy auld° cloak about thee." *old*

Some wine, ho!

CASSIO: 'Fore God, this is a more exquisite song than the other.

IAGO: Will you hear 't again?

CASSIO: No, for I hold him to be unworthy of his place that does those things. Well, God's above all; and there be souls must be saved, and there be souls must not be saved.

IAGO: It's true, good Lieutenant.

CASSIO: For mine own part—no offense to the General, nor any man of quality[9]—I hope to be saved.

IAGO: And so do I too, Lieutenant.

CASSIO: Ay, but, by your leave, not before me; the lieutenant is to be saved before the ancient. Let's have no more of this; let's to our affairs.—God forgive us our sins!—Gentlemen, let's look to our business. Do not think, gentlemen, I am drunk. This is my ancient; this is my right hand, and this is my left. I am not drunk now. I can stand well enough, and speak well enough.

GENTLEMEN: Excellent well.

CASSIO: Why, very well then; you must not think then that I am drunk. [*Exit*.]

MONTANO: To th' platform, masters. Come, let's set the watch.[1]

[(*Exeunt Gentlemen*.)]

2. Brief span of time. (Cf. Psalm 39.5 as rendered in the Book of Common Prayer: "Thou hast made my days as it were a span long.")
3. Drinking.
4. Drinks.
5. Need not exert himself.
6. German.
7. I'll drink as much as you.
8. Extravagance in dress.
9. Rank.
1. Mount the guard.

IAGO: You see this fellow that is gone before.
He's a soldier fit to stand by Caesar
And give direction; and do but see his vice.
'Tis to his virtue a just equinox,[2]
The one as long as th' other. 'Tis pity of him.
I fear the trust Othello puts him in,
On some odd time of his infirmity,
Will shake this island.
MONTANO: But is he often thus?
IAGO: 'Tis evermore the prologue to his sleep.
He'll watch the horologe a double set,[3]
If drink rock not his cradle.
MONTANO: It were well
The General were put in mind of it.
Perhaps he sees it not, or his good nature
Prizes the virtue that appears in Cassio
And looks not on his evils. Is not this true?
[*Enter Roderigo.*]
IAGO [*aside to him*]: How now, Roderigo?
I pray you, after the Lieutenant; go. [(*Exit Roderigo.*)]
MONTANO: And 'tis great pity that the noble Moor
Should hazard such a place as his own second
With[4] one of an engraffed° infirmity. *inveterate*
It were an honest action to say so
To the Moor.
IAGO: Not I, for this fair island.
I do love Cassio well and would do much
To cure him of this evil. [(*Cry within:* "Help! Help!")]
But hark! What noise?
[*Enter Cassio, pursuing Roderigo.*][5]
CASSIO: Zounds, you rogue! You rascal!
MONTANO: What's the matter, Lieutenant?
CASSIO: A knave teach me my duty? I'll beat the knave into a twiggen[6] bottle.
RODERIGO: Beat me?
CASSIO: Dost thou prate, rogue? [(*He strikes Roderigo.*)]
MONTANO: Nay, good Lieutenant. [(*Restraining him.*)] I pray you, sir, hold your hand.
CASSIO: Let me go, sir, or I'll knock you o'er the mazard.[7]
MONTANO: Come, come, you're drunk.
CASSIO: Drunk? [(*They fight.*)]
IAGO [(*aside to Roderigo*)]:
Away, I say. Go out and cry a mutiny.[8]
[(*Exit Roderigo.*)]

2. Exact counterpart. (*Equinox* is an equal length of days and nights.)
3. Stay awake twice around the clock or *horologe*.
4. Risk giving such an important position as his second in command to.
5. The Quarto text reads, "driving in."
6. Wicker-covered. (Cassio vows to assail Roderigo until his skin resembles wickerwork or until he has driven Roderigo through the holes in a wickerwork.)
7. Head. (literally, a drinking vessel.)
8. Riot.

Nay, good Lieutenant—God's will, gentlemen—
Help, ho!—Lieutenant—sir—Montano—sir—
Help, masters!°—Here's a goodly watch indeed! *sirs*
[(*A bell rings*.)][9]
Who's that which rings the bell?—Diablo,° ho! *the devil*
The town will rise.° God's will, Lieutenant, hold! *grow riotous*
You'll be ashamed forever.
[*Enter Othello and attendants with weapons*].
OTHELLO: What is the matter here?
MONTANO: Zounds, I bleed still.
I am hurt to th' death. He dies! [(*He thrusts at Cassio*.)]
OTHELLO: Hold, for your lives!
IAGO: Hold, ho! Lieutenant—sir—Montano—gentlemen—
Have you forgot all sense of place and duty?
Hold! The General speaks to you. Hold, for shame!
OTHELLO: Why, how now, ho! From whence ariseth this?
Are we turned Turks, and to ourselves do that
Which heaven hath forbid the Ottomites?[1]
For Christian shame, put by this barbarous brawl!
He that stirs next to carve for[2] his own rage
Holds his soul light;[3] he dies upon his motion.[4]
Silence that dreadful bell. It frights the isle
From her propriety.° What is the matter, masters? *proper state*
Honest Iago, that looks dead with grieving,
Speak. Who began this? On thy love, I charge thee.
IAGO: I do not know. Friends all but now, even now,
In quarter[5] and in terms° like bride and groom *on good terms*
Devesting them° for bed; and then, but now— *undressing*
As if some planet had unwitted men—
Swords out, and tilting one at others' breasts
In opposition bloody. I cannot speak° *explain*
Any beginning to this peevish odds;° *quarrel*
And would in action glorious I had lost
Those legs that brought me to a part of it!
OTHELLO: How comes it, Michael, you are thus forgot?[6]
CASSIO: I pray you, pardon me. I cannot speak.
OTHELLO: Worthy Montano, you were wont° be civil; *accustomed to be*
The gravity and stillness° of your youth *sobriety*
The world hath noted, and your name is great
In mouths of wisest censure.° What's the matter *judgment*
That you unlace[7] your reputation thus
And spend your rich opinion° for the name *reputation*
Of a night-brawler? Give me answer to it.

9. This direction is from the Quarto, as are *Exit Roderigo* at line 130, *They fight* at line 129, and *with weapons* at line 136.
1. Inflict on ourselves the harm that heaven has prevented the Turks from doing (by destroying their fleet).
2. Indulge, satisfy with his sword.
3. Places little value on his life.
4. If he moves.
5. In friendly conduct, within bounds.
6. Have forgotten yourself thus.
7. Undo, lay open (as one might loose the strings of a purse containing reputation).

MONTANO: Worthy Othello, I am hurt to danger.
Your officer, Iago, can inform you—
While I spare speech, which something° now offends° me— *somewhat / pains*
Of all that I do know; nor know I aught
By me that's said or done amiss this night,
Unless self-charity be sometimes a vice,
And to defend ourselves it be a sin
When violence assails us.

OTHELLO: Now, by heaven,
My blood[8] begins my safer guides[9] to rule,
And passion, having my best judgment collied,° *darkened*
Essays° to lead the way. Zounds, if I stir, *undertakes*
Or do but lift this arm, the best of you
Shall sink in my rebuke. Give me to know
How this foul rout° began, who set it on; *riot*
And he that is approved in° this offense, *found guilty of*
Though he had twinned with me, both at a birth,
Shall lose me. What? In a town of[1] war
Yet wild, the people's hearts brim full of fear,
To manage° private and domestic quarrel? *undertake*
In night, and on the court and guard of safety?[2]
'Tis monstrous. Iago, who began 't?

MONTANO [(*to Iago*)]: If partially affined,[3] or leagued in office,[4]
Thou dost deliver more or less than truth,
Thou art no soldier.

IAGO: Touch me not so near.
I had rather have this tongue cut from my mouth
Than it should do offense to Michael Cassio;
Yet, I persuade myself, to speak the truth
Shall nothing wrong him. Thus it is, General.
Montano and myself being in speech,
There comes a fellow crying out for help,
And Cassio following him with determined sword
To execute[5] upon him. Sir, this gentleman [*indicating Montano.*]
Steps in to Cassio and entreats his pause.° *him to stop*
Myself the crying fellow did pursue,
Lest by his clamor—as it so fell out—
The town might fall in fright. He, swift of foot,
Outran my purpose, and I returned, the rather° *sooner*
For that I heard the clink and fall of swords
And Cassio high in oath, which till tonight
I ne'er might say before. When I came back—
For this was brief—I found them close together
At blow and thrust, even as again they were

8. Passion (of anger).
9. I.e., reason.
1. Town garrisoned for.
2. At the main guardhouse or headquarters and on watch.
3. Made partial by some personal relationship.
4. In league as fellow officers.
5. Give effect to (his anger).

When you yourself did part them.
More of this matter cannot I report.
But men are men; the best sometimes forget.° *forget themselves*
Though Cassio did some little wrong to him,
As men in rage strike those that wish them best,[6]
Yet surely Cassio, I believe, received
From him that fled some strange indignity,
Which patience could not pass.° *overlook*

OTHELLO: I know, Iago,
Thy honesty and love doth mince this matter,
Making it light to Cassio. Cassio, I love thee,
But nevermore be officer of mine.

[*Enter Desdemona, attended.*]

Look if my gentle love be not raised up.
I'll make thee an example.

DESDEMONA: What is the matter, dear?

OTHELLO: All's well now, sweeting;
Come away to bed. [(*To Montano.*)] Sir, for your hurts,
Myself will be your surgeon.[7]—Lead him off.

[(*Montano is led off.*)]

Iago, look with care about the town
And silence those whom this vile brawl distracted.
Come, Desdemona. 'Tis the soldiers' life
To have their balmy slumbers waked with strife.

[*Exit* (*with all but Iago and Cassio.*)]

IAGO: What, are you hurt, Lieutenant?

CASSIO: Ay, past all surgery.

IAGO: Marry, God forbid!

CASSIO: Reputation, reputation, reputation! O, I have lost my reputation! I have lost the immortal part of myself, and what remains is bestial. My reputation, Iago, my reputation!

IAGO: As I am an honest man, I thought you had received some bodily wound; there is more sense in that than in reputation. Reputation is an idle and most false imposition,[8] oft got without merit and lost without deserving. You have lost no reputation at all, unless you repute yourself such a loser. What, man, there are more ways to recover[9] the General again. You are but now cast in his mood[1]—a punishment more in policy[2] than in malice, even so as one would beat his offenseless dog to affright an imperious lion.[3] Sue[4] to him again and he's yours.

CASSIO: I will rather sue to be despised than to deceive so good a commander with so slight,[5] so drunken, and so indiscreet an officer. Drunk? And speak parrot?[6] And squabble? Swagger? Swear? And discourse fustian with one's own shadow?

6. Even those who are well disposed.
7. Make sure you receive medical attention.
8. Thing artificially imposed and of no real value.
9. Regain favor with.
1. Dismissed in a moment of anger.
2. Done for expediency's sake and as a public gesture.
3. Would make an example of a minor offender to deter more important and dangerous offenders.
4. Petition.
5. Worthless.
6. Talk nonsense, rant. (*Discourse fustian*, in the next lines, has much the same meaning.)

O thou invisible spirit of wine, if thou hast no name to be known by, let us call thee devil!

IAGO: What was he that you followed with your sword? What had he done to you?

CASSIO: I know not.

IAGO: Is 't possible?

CASSIO: I remember a mass of things, but nothing distinctly; a quarrel, but nothing wherefore.[7] O God, that men should put an enemy in their mouths to steal away their brains! That we should, with joy, pleasance, revel, and applause[8] transform ourselves into beasts!

IAGO: Why, but you are now well enough. How came you thus recovered?

CASSIO: It hath pleased the devil drunkenness to give place to the devil wrath. One unperfectness shows me another, to make me frankly despise myself.

IAGO: Come, you are too severe a moraler.[9] As the time, the place, and the condition of this country stands, I could heartily wish this had not befallen; but since it is as it is, mend it for your own good.

CASSIO: I will ask him for my place again; he shall tell me I am a drunkard. Had I as many mouths as Hydra,[1] such an answer would stop them all. To be now a sensible man, by and by a fool, and presently a beast! Oh, strange! Every inordinate cup is unblessed, and the ingredient is a devil.

IAGO: Come, come, good wine is a good familiar creature, if it be well used. Exclaim no more against it. And, good Lieutenant, I think you think I love you.

CASSIO: I have well approved[2] it, sir. I drunk!

IAGO: You or any man living may be drunk at a time,[3] man. I'll tell you what you shall do. Our general's wife is now the general—I may say so in this respect, for that[4] he hath devoted and given up himself to the contemplation, mark, and denotement[5] of her parts[6] and graces. Confess yourself freely to her; importune her help to put you in your place again. She is of so free,[7] so kind, so apt, so blessed a disposition, she holds it a vice in her goodness not to do more than she is requested. This broken joint between you and her husband entreat her to splinter;[8] and, my fortunes against any lay[9] worth naming, this crack of your love shall grow stronger than it was before.

CASSIO: You advise me well.

IAGO: I protest,[1] in the sincerity of love and honest kindness.

CASSIO: I think it freely;[2] and betimes in the morning I will beseech the virtuous Desdemona to undertake for me. I am desperate of my fortunes if they check[3] me here.

IAGO: You are in the right. Good night, Lieutenant. I must to the watch.

CASSIO: Good night, honest Iago. [*Exit Cassio.*]

IAGO: And what's he then that says I play the villain,
When this advice is free[4] I give, and honest,

7. Why.
8. Desire for applause.
9. Moralizer.
1. The Lernaean Hydra, a monster with many heads and the ability to grow two heads when one was cut off, slain by Hercules as the second of his 12 labors.
2. Proved.
3. At one time or another.
4. In view of this fact, that.
5. Both words mean "observation."
6. Qualities.
7. Generous.
8. Bind with splints.
9. Stake, wager.
1. Insist, declare.
2. Unreservedly.
3. Repulse.
4. Free from guile. Also, freely given.

Probal° to thinking, and indeed the course *reasonable*
To win the Moor again? For 'tis most easy
Th' inclining° Desdemona to subdue° *willing / persuade*
In any honest suit; she's framed as fruitful[5]
As the free elements.[6] And then for her
To win the Moor—were 't to renounce his baptism,
All seals and symbols of redeemèd sin—
His soul is so enfettered to her love
That she may make, unmake, do what she list,
Even as her appetite[7] shall play the god
With his weak function.[8] How am I then a villain,
To counsel Cassio to this parallel[9] course
Directly to his good? Divinity of hell![1]
When devils will the blackest sins put on,° *instigate*
They do suggest° at first with heavenly shows, *tempt*
As I do now. For whiles this honest fool
Plies Desdemona to repair his fortune,
And she for him pleads strongly to the Moor,
I'll pour this pestilence into his ear,
That she repeals him[2] for her body's lust;
And by how much she strives to do him good,
She shall undo her credit with the Moor.
So will I turn her virtue into pitch,[3]
And out of her own goodness make the net
That shall enmesh them all.

[*Enter Roderigo.*]

How now, Roderigo?

RODERIGO: I do follow here in the chase, not like a hound that hunts, but one that fills up the cry.[4] My money is almost spent; I have been tonight exceedingly well cudgeled; and I think the issue will be I shall have so much[5] experience for my pains, and so, with no money at all and a little more wit, return again to Venice.

IAGO: How poor are they that have not patience!
What wound did ever heal but by degrees?
Thou know'st we work by wit, and not by witchcraft,
And wit depends on dilatory time.
Does 't not go well? Cassio hath beaten thee,
And thou, by that small hurt, hast cashiered° Cassio. *dismissed*
Though other things grow fair against the sun,

5. Created as generous.
6. I.e., earth, air, fire, and water, unrestrained and spontaneous.
7. Her desire, or, perhaps, his desire for her.
8. Exercise of faculties (weakened by his fondness for her).
9. Corresponding to these facts and to his best interests.
1. Inverted theology of hell (which seduces the soul to its damnation).
2. Attempts to get him restored.
3. Foul blackness. Also a snaring substance.
4. Merely takes part as one of the pack.
5. Just so much and no more.

Yet fruits that blossom first will first be ripe.[6]
Content thyself awhile. By the Mass, 'tis morning!
Pleasure and action make the hours seem short.
Retire thee; go where thou art billeted.
Away, I say! Thou shalt know more hereafter.
Nay, get thee gone. [*Exit Roderigo*.]
Two things are to be done.
My wife must move° for Cassio to her mistress; *plead*
I'll set her on;
Myself the while to draw the Moor apart
And bring him jump° when he may Cassio find *precisely*
Soliciting his wife. Ay, that's the way.
Dull not device° by coldness° and delay. [*Exit*.] *plot / lack of zeal*

ACT 3

Scene 1[7]

[*Enter Cassio* (*and*) *Musicians*.]

CASSIO: Masters, play here—I will content your pains[8]—
Something that's brief, and bid "Good morrow, General." [(*They play*.)]

[(*Enter*) *Clown*.]

CLOWN: Why, masters, have your instruments been in Naples, that they speak i' the nose[9] thus?

A MUSICIAN: How, sir, how?

CLOWN: Are these, I pray you, wind instruments?

A MUSICIAN: Ay, marry, are they, sir.

CLOWN: O, thereby hangs a tail.

A MUSICIAN: Whereby hangs a tale, sir?

CLOWN: Marry, sir, by many a wind instrument[1] that I know. But, masters, here's money for you. [*He gives money*.] And the General so likes your music that he desires you, for love's sake,[2] to make no more noise with it.

A MUSICIAN: Well, sir, we will not.

CLOWN: If you have any music that may not[3] be heard, to 't again; but, as they say, to hear music the General does not greatly care.

A MUSICIAN: We have none such, sir.

CLOWN: Then put up your pipes in your bag, for I'll away.[4] Go, vanish into air, away! [*Exeunt Musicians*.]

CASSIO: Dost thou hear, mine honest friend?

CLOWN: No, I hear not your honest friend; I hear you.

6. Plans that are well prepared and set expeditiously in motion will soonest ripen into success.
7. Location: Before the chamber of Othello and Desdemona.
8. Reward your efforts.
9. Sound nasal. Also sound like one whose nose has been attacked by syphilis. (Naples was popularly supposed to have a high incidence of venereal disease.)

1. With a joke on flatulence. The *tail* that hangs nearby the *wind instrument* suggests the penis.
2. Out of friendship and affection. Also, for the sake of lovemaking in Othello's marriage.
3. Cannot.
4. (Possibly a misprint, or a snatch of song?)

CASSIO: Prithee, keep up[5] thy quillets.[6] There's a poor piece of gold for thee. [*He gives money*.] If the gentlewoman that attends the General's wife be stirring, tell her there's one Cassio entreats her a little favor of speech.[7] Wilt thou do this?

CLOWN: She is stirring, sir. If she will stir[8] hither, I shall seem[9] to notify unto her.

CASSIO: Do, good my friend. [*Exit Clown*.]

[*Enter Iago*.]

In happy time,[1] Iago.

IAGO: You have not been abed, then?

CASSIO: Why, no. The day had broke
Before we parted. I have made bold, Iago,
To send in to your wife. My suit to her
Is that she will to virtuous Desdemona
Procure me some access.

IAGO: I'll send her to you presently;
And I'll devise a mean to draw the Moor
Out of the way, that your converse and business
May be more free.

CASSIO: I humbly thank you for 't. [*Exit* (*Iago*.)]
I never knew
A Florentine[2] more kind and honest.

[*Enter Emilia*.]

EMILIA: Good morrow, good Lieutenant. I am sorry
For your displeasure;° but all will sure be well. *fall from favor*
The General and his wife are talking of it,
And she speaks for you stoutly.° The Moor replies *spiritedly*
That he you hurt is of great fame° in Cyprus *importance*
And great affinity,° and that in wholesome wisdom *family connection*
He might not but refuse you; but he protests° he loves you *insists*
And needs no other suitor but his likings
To take the safest occasion by the front[3]
To bring you in again.

CASSIO: Yes I beseech you,
If you think fit, or that it may be done,
Give me advantage of some brief discourse
With Desdemon alone.

EMILIA: Pray you, come in.
I will bestow you where you shall have time
To speak your bosom° freely. *thoughts*

CASSIO: I am much bound to you. [(*Exeunt*.)]

5. Do not bring out.
6. Quibbles, puns.
7. The favor of a brief talk.
8. Bestir herself (with a play on *stirring*, "rousing herself from rest").
9. Deem it good, think fit.
1. I.e., well met.
2. I.e., even a fellow Florentine. (Iago is a Venetian; Cassio is a Florentine.)
3. Opportunity by the forelock.

Scene 2[4]

[*Enter Othello, Iago, and Gentlemen.*]

OTHELLO [(*giving letters*)]: These letters give, Iago, to the pilot,
And by him do my duties° to the Senate. *give my respects*
That done, I will be walking on the works;° *fortifications*
Repair° there to me. *return*

IAGO: Well, my good lord, I'll do 't.

OTHELLO: This fortification, gentlemen, shall we see 't?

GENTLEMEN: We'll wait upon° your lordship. [*Exeunt.*] *attend*

Scene 3[5]

[*Enter Desdemona, Cassio, and Emilia.*]

DESDEMONA: Be thou assured, good Cassio, I will do
All my abilities in thy behalf.

EMILIA: Good madam, do. I warrant it grieves my husband
As if the cause were his.

DESDEMONA: O, that's an honest fellow. Do not doubt, Cassio,
But I will have my lord and you again
As friendly as you were.

CASSIO: Bounteous madam,
Whatever shall become of Michael Cassio,
He's never anything but your true servant.

DESDEMONA: I know 't. I thank you. You do love my lord;
You have known him long, and be you well assured
He shall in strangeness° stand no farther off *aloofness*
Than in a politic[6] distance.

CASSIO: Ay but, lady,
That policy may either last so long,
Or feed upon such nice and waterish diet,[7]
Or breed itself so out of circumstance,[8]
That, I being absent and my place supplied,[9]
My general will forget my love and service.

DESDEMONA: Do not doubt° that. Before Emilia here *fear*
I give thee warrant° of thy place. Assure thee, *guarantee*
If I do vow a friendship I'll perform it
To the last article. My lord shall never rest.
I'll watch him tame[1] and talk him out of patience;[2]
His bed shall seem a school, his board° a shrift;° *table / confessional*
I'll intermingle everything he does
With Cassio's suit. Therefore be merry, Cassio,
For thy solicitor° shall rather die *advocate*
Than give thy cause away.° *up*

4. Location: The citadel.
5. Location: The garden of the citadel.
6. Required by wise policy.
7. Or sustain itself at length upon such trivial and meager technicalities.
8. Continually renew itself so out of chance events, or yield so few chances for my being pardoned.
9. Filled by another person.
1. Tame him by keeping him from sleeping (a term from falconry).
2. Past his endurance.

[*Enter Othello and Iago (at a distance).*]
EMILIA: Madam, here comes my lord.
CASSIO: Madam, I'll take my leave.
DESDEMONA: Why, stay, and hear me speak.
CASSIO: Madam, not now. I am very ill at ease,
Unfit for mine own purposes.
DESDEMONA: Well, do your discretion.[3] [*Exit Cassio.*]
IAGO: Ha? I like not that.
OTHELLO: What dost thou say?
IAGO: Nothing, my lord; or if—I know not what.
OTHELLO: Was not that Cassio parted from my wife?
IAGO: Cassio, my lord? No, sure, I cannot think it,
That he would steal away so guiltylike,
Seeing you coming.
OTHELLO: I do believe 'twas he.
DESDEMONA: How now, my lord?
I have been talking with a suitor here,
A man that languishes in your displeasure.
OTHELLO: Who is 't you mean?
DESDEMONA: Why, your lieutenant, Cassio. Good my lord,
If I have any grace or power to move you,
His present reconciliation take;[4]
For if he be not one that truly loves you,
That errs in ignorance and not in cunning,° *wittingly*
I have no judgment in an honest face.
I prithee, call him back.
OTHELLO: Went he hence now?
DESDEMONA: Yes, faith, so humbled
That he hath left part of his grief with me
To suffer with him. Good love, call him back.
OTHELLO: Not now, sweet Desdemon. Some other time.
DESDEMONA: But shall 't be shortly?
OTHELLO: The sooner, sweet, for you.
DESDEMONA: Shall 't be tonight at supper?
OTHELLO: No, not tonight.
DESDEMONA: Tomorrow dinner,° then? *noontime*
OTHELLO: I shall not dine at home.
I meet the captains at the citadel.
DESDEMONA: Why, then, tomorrow night, or Tuesday morn,
On Tuesday noon, or night, on Wednesday morn.
I prithee, name the time, but let it not
Exceed three days. In faith, he's penitent;
And yet his trespass, in our common reason°— *judgments*
Save that, they say, the wars must make example

3. Act according to your own discretion.
4. Let him be reconciled to you right away.

Out of her best[5]—is not almost° a fault *scarcely*
T' incur a private check.[6] When shall he come?
Tell me, Othello. I wonder in my soul
What you would ask me that I should deny,
Or stand so mammering on.° What? Michael Cassio, *wavering about*
That came a-wooing with you, and so many a time,
When I have spoke of you dispraisingly,
Hath ta'en your part—to have so much to do
To bring him in!° By 'r Lady, I could do much— *restore him to favor*
OTHELLO: Prithee, no more. Let him come when he will;
I will deny thee nothing.
DESDEMONA: Why, this is not a boon.
'Tis as I should entreat you wear your gloves,
Or feed on nourishing dishes, or keep you warm,
Or sue to you to do a peculiar° profit *personal*
To your own person. Nay, when I have a suit
Wherein I mean to touch° your love indeed, *test*
It shall be full of poise[7] and difficult weight,
And fearful to be granted.
OTHELLO: I will deny thee nothing.
Whereon,° I do beseech thee, grant me this, *in return*
To leave me but a little to myself.
DESDEMONA: Shall I deny you? No. Farewell, my lord.
OTHELLO: Farewell, my Desdemona. I'll come to thee straight.° *straightway*
DESDEMONA: Emilia, come.—Be as your fancies° teach you; *inclinations*
Whate'er you be, I am obedient. [*Exit with Emilia.*]
OTHELLO: Excellent wretch![8] Perdition catch my soul
But I do love thee! And when I love thee not,
Chaos is come again.[9]
IAGO: My noble lord—
OTHELLO: What dost thou say, Iago?
IAGO: Did Michael Cassio, when you wooed my lady,
Know of your love?
OTHELLO: He did, from first to last. Why dost thou ask?
IAGO: But for a satisfaction of my thought;
No further harm.
OTHELLO: Why of thy thought, Iago?
IAGO: I did not think he had been acquainted with her.
OTHELLO: O, yes, and went between us very oft.
IAGO: Indeed?
OTHELLO: Indeed? Ay, indeed. Discern'st thou aught in that?
Is he not honest?
IAGO: Honest, my lord?
OTHELLO: Honest. Ay, honest.

5. Were it not that, as the saying goes, military discipline requires making an example of the very best men. (*Her* refers to *wars* as a singular concept.)
6. Even a private reprimand.
7. Weight, heaviness; or equipoise, delicate balance involving hard choice.
8. A term of affectionate endearment.
9. I.e., My love for you will last forever, until the end of time when chaos will return. (But with an unconscious, ironic suggestion that, if anything should induce Othello to cease loving Desdemona, the result would be chaos.)

IAGO: My lord, for aught I know.
OTHELLO: What dost thou think?
IAGO: Think, my lord?
OTHELLO: "Think, my lord?" By heaven, thou echo'st me,
As if there were some monster in thy thought
Too hideous to be shown. Thou dost mean something.
I heard thee say even now, thou lik'st not that,
When Cassio left my wife. What didst not like?
And when I told thee he was of my counsel° — *in my confidence*
In my whole course of wooing, thou cried'st "Indeed?"
And didst contract and purse° thy brow together — *knit*
As if thou then hadst shut up in thy brain
Some horrible conceit.° If thou dost love me, — *fancy*
Show me thy thought.
IAGO: My lord, you know I love you.
OTHELLO: I think thou dost;
And, for° I know thou'rt full of love and honesty, — *because*
And weigh'st thy words before thou giv'st them breath,
Therefore these stops° of thine fright me the more; — *pauses*
For such things in a false disloyal knave
Are tricks of custom,° but in a man that's just — *customary*
They're close dilations,[1] working from the heart
That passion cannot rule.[2]
IAGO: For° Michael Cassio, — *as for*
I dare be sworn I think that he is honest.
OTHELLO: I think so too.
IAGO: Men should be what they seem;
Or those that be not, would they might seem none![3]
OTHELLO: Certain, men should be what they seem.
IAGO: Why, then, I think Cassio's an honest man.
OTHELLO: Nay, yet there's more in this.
I prithee, speak to me as to thy thinkings,
As thou dost ruminate, and give thy worst of thoughts
The worst of words.
IAGO: Good my lord, pardon me.
Though I am bound to every act of duty,
I am not bound to that° all slaves are free to.[4] — *that which*
Utter my thoughts? Why, say they are vile and false,
As where's that palace whereinto foul things
Sometimes intrude not? Who has that breast so pure
But some uncleanly apprehensions
Keep leets and law days,[5] and in sessions sit
With° meditations lawful?° — *along with / innocent*

1. Secret or involuntary expressions or delays.
2. I.e., that are too passionately strong to be restrained (referring to the workings), or that cannot rule its own passions (referring to the heart).
3. I.e., not to be men, or not seem to be honest.
4. Free with respect to.
5. I.e., hold court, set up their authority in one's heart. *Leets* are a kind of manor court; *law days* are the days courts sit in session, or those sessions.

OTHELLO: Thou dost conspire against thy friend,[6] Iago,
If thou but think'st him wronged and mak'st his ear
A stranger to thy thoughts.
IAGO: I do beseech you,
Though I perchance am vicious° in my guess— *wrong*
As I confess it is my nature's plague
To spy into abuses, and oft my jealousy° *suspicious nature*
Shapes faults that are not—that your wisdom then,° *on that account*
From one[7] that so imperfectly conceits, *conjectures*
Would take no notice, nor build yourself a trouble
Out of his scattering° and unsure observance. *random*
It were not for your quiet nor your good,
Nor for my manhood, honesty, and wisdom,
To let you know my thoughts.
OTHELLO: What dost thou mean?
IAGO: Good name in man and woman, dear my lord,
Is the immediate° jewel of their souls. *essential*
Who steals my purse steals trash; 'tis something, nothing;
'Twas mine, 'tis his, and has been slave to thousands;
But he that filches from me my good name
Robs me of that which not enriches him
And makes me poor indeed.
OTHELLO: By heaven, I'll know thy thoughts.
IAGO: You cannot, if° my heart were in your hand, *even if*
Nor shall not, whilst 'tis in my custody.
OTHELLO: Ha?
IAGO: O, beware, my lord, of jealousy.
It is the green-eyed monster, which doth mock
The meat it feeds on.[8] That cuckold lives in bliss
Who, certain of his fate, loves not his wronger;[9]
But O, what damnèd minutes tells° he o'er *counts*
Who dotes, yet doubts, suspects, yet fondly loves!
OTHELLO: O, misery!
IAGO: Poor and content is rich, and rich enough,[1]
But riches fineless° is as poor as winter *boundless*
To him that ever fears he shall be poor.
Good God, the souls of all my tribe defend
From jealousy!
OTHELLO: Why, why is this?
Think'st thou I'd make a life of jealousy,
To follow still the changes of the moon
With fresh suspicions?[2] No! To be once in doubt
Is once° to be resolved.[3] Exchange me for a goat *once and for all*

6. I.e., Othello.
7. I.e., myself, Iago.
8. Mocks and torments the heart of its victim, the man who suffers jealously.
9. I.e., his faithless wife. (The unsuspecting cuckold is spared the misery of loving his wife only to discover she is cheating on him.)
1. To be content with what little one has is the greatest wealth of all (proverbial).
2. To be constantly imagining new causes for suspicion, changing incessantly like the moon.
3. Free of doubt, having settled the matter.

When I shall turn the business of my soul
To such exsufflicate and blown[4] surmises
Matching thy inference.° 'Tis not to make me jealous *allegation*
To say my wife is fair, feeds well, loves company,
Is free of speech, sings, plays, and dances well;
Where virtue is, these are more virtuous.
Nor from mine own weak merits will I draw
The smallest fear or doubt of her revolt,[5]
For she had eyes, and chose me. No, Iago,
I'll see before I doubt; when I doubt, prove;
And on the proof, there is no more but this—
Away at once with love or jealousy.

IAGO: I am glad of this, for now I shall have reason
To show the love and duty that I bear you
With franker spirit. Therefore, as I am bound,
Receive it from me. I speak not yet of proof.
Look to your wife; observe her well with Cassio.
Wear your eyes thus, not° jealous nor secure.° *neither / certain*
I would not have your free and noble nature,
Out of self-bounty,[6] be abused.° Look to 't. *deceived*
I know our country disposition well;
In Venice they do let God see the pranks
They dare not show their husbands; their best conscience
Is not to leave 't undone, but keep 't unknown.

OTHELLO: Dost thou say so?

IAGO: She did deceive her father, marrying you;
And when she seemed to shake and fear your looks,
She loved them most.

OTHELLO: And so she did.

IAGO: Why, go to,[7] then!
She that, so young, could give out such a seeming,° *false appearance*
To seel[8] her father's eyes up close as oak,[9]
He thought 'twas witchcraft! But I am much to blame.
I humbly do beseech you of your pardon
For too much loving you.

OTHELLO: I am bound[1] to thee forever.

IAGO: I see this hath a little dashed your spirits.

OTHELLO: Not a jot, not a jot.

IAGO: I' faith, I fear it has.
I hope you will consider what is spoke
Comes from my love. But I do see you're moved.
I am to pray you not to strain my speech
To grosser issues° nor to larger reach° *significances / scope*
Than to suspicion.

4. Inflated and blown up, rumored about, or, spat out and flyblown, hence, loathsome, disgusting.
5. Fear of her unfaithfulness.
6. Inherent or natural goodness and generosity.
7. An expression of impatience.
8. Blind (a term from falconry).
9. A close-grained wood.
1. Indebted (but perhaps with ironic sense of "tied").

OTHELLO: I will not.
IAGO: Should you do so, my lord,
My speech should fall into such vile success° *effect*
Which my thoughts aimed not. Cassio's my worthy friend.
My lord, I see you're moved.
OTHELLO: No, not much moved.
I do not think but Desdemona's honest.° *chaste*
IAGO: Long live she so! And long live you to think so!
OTHELLO: And yet, how nature erring from itself—
IAGO: Ay, there's the point! As—to be bold with you—
Not to affect° many proposèd matches *prefer*
Of her own clime, complexion, and degree,[2]
Whereto we see in all things nature tends—
Foh! One may smell in such a will° most rank, *sensuality*
Foul disproportion,° thoughts unnatural. *abnormality*
But pardon me. I do not in position° *argument*
Distinctly speak of her, though I may fear
Her will, recoiling° to her better[3] judgment, *reverting*
May fall to match you with her country forms[4]
And happily repent.[5]
OTHELLO: Farewell, farewell!
If more thou dost perceive, let me know more.
Set on thy wife to observe. Leave me, Iago.
IAGO [*going*]: My lord, I take my leave.
OTHELLO: Why did I marry? This honest creature doubtless
Sees and knows more, much more, than he unfolds.
IAGO [*returning*]: My lord, I would I might entreat your honor
To scan° this thing no farther. Leave it to time. *scrutinize*
Although 'tis fit that Cassio have his place—
For, sure, he fills it up with great ability—
Yet, if you please to hold him off awhile,
You shall by that perceive him and his means.[6]
Note if your lady strain his entertainment[7]
With any strong or vehement importunity;
Much will be seen in that. In the meantime,
Let me be thought too busy° in my fears— *interfering*
As worthy cause I have to fear I am—
And hold her free,[8] I do beseech your honor.
OTHELLO: Fear not my government.° *conduct*
IAGO: I once more take my leave. [*Exit*.]
OTHELLO: This fellow's of exceeding honesty,
And knows all qualities,° with a learnèd spirit, *natures*
Of human dealings. If I do prove her haggard,[9]
Though that her jesses[1] were my dear heartstrings,

2. Country, color, and social position.
3. I.e., more natural and reconsidered.
4. Undertake to compare you with Venetian norms of handsomeness.
5. Perhaps repent her marriage.
6. The method he uses (to regain his post).
7. Urge his reinstatement.
8. Regard her as innocent.
9. Wild (like a wild female hawk).
1. Straps fastened around the legs of a trained hawk.

I'd whistle her off and let her down the wind[2]
To prey at fortune.[3] Haply, for[4] I am black
And have not those soft parts of conversation[5]
That chamberers° have, or for I am declined *gallants*
Into the vale of years—yet that's not much—
She's gone. I am abused,° and my relief *deceived*
Must be to loathe her. O curse of marriage,
That we can call these delicate creatures ours
And not their appetites! I had rather be a toad
And live upon the vapor of a dungeon
Than keep a corner in the thing I love
For others' uses. Yet, 'tis the plague of great ones;
Prerogatived[6] are they less than the base.[7]
'Tis destiny unshunnable, like death.
Even then this forkèd[8] plague is fated to us
When we do quicken.[9] Look where she comes.
[*Enter Desdemona and Emilia.*]
If she be false, O, then heaven mocks itself!
I'll not believe 't.

DESDEMONA: How now, my dear Othello?
Your dinner, and the generous° islanders *noble*
By you invited, do attend° your presence. *await*

OTHELLO: I am to blame.

DESDEMONA: Why do you speak so faintly?
Are you not well?

OTHELLO: I have a pain upon my forehead here.

DESDEMONA: Faith, that's with watching.° 'Twill away again. *too little sleep*
[(*She offers her handkerchief.*)]
Let me but bind it hard, within this hour
It will be well.

OTHELLO: Your napkin° is too little. *handkerchief*
Let it alone.° Come, I'll go in with you. *never mind*
[*He puts the handkerchief from him, and it drops.*]

DESDEMONA: I am very sorry that you are not well.
[*Exit* (*with Othello.*)]

EMILIA [(*picking up the handkerchief*)]:
I am glad I have found this napkin.
This was her first remembrance from the Moor.
My wayward° husband hath a hundred times *capricious*
Wooed me to steal it, but she so loves the token—
For he conjured her she should ever keep it—

2. I'd let her go forever. (To release a hawk downwind was to invite it not to return.)
3. Fend for herself in the wild.
4. Perhaps because.
5. Pleasing graces of social behavior.
6. Privileged (to have honest wives).
7. Ordinary citizens. (Socially prominent men are especially prone to the unavoidable destiny of being cuckolded and to the public shame that goes with it.)
8. An allusion to the horns of the cuckold.
9. Receive life. *Quicken* may also mean to swarm with maggots as the body festers, in which case lines suggest that *even then*, in death, we are cuckolded by *forkèd* worms.

That she reserves it evermore about her
To kiss and talk to. I'll have the work ta'en out,[1]
And give 't Iago. What he will do with it
Heaven knows, not I;
I nothing but to please his fantasy.° *whim*
[*Enter Iago.*]
IAGO: How now? What do you here alone?
EMILIA: Do not you chide. I have a thing for you.
IAGO: You have a thing for me? It is a common thing[2]—
EMILIA: Ha?
IAGO: To have a foolish wife.
EMILIA: O, is that all? What will you give me now
For that same handkerchief?
IAGO: What handkerchief?
EMILIA: What handkerchief?
Why, that the Moor first gave to Desdemona;
That which so often you did bid me steal.
IAGO: Hast stolen it from her?
EMILIA: No, faith. She let it drop by negligence,
And to th' advantage[3] I, being here, took 't up.
Look, here 'tis.
IAGO: A good wench! Give it me.
EMILIA: What will you do with 't, that you have been so earnest
To have me filch it?
IAGO [(*snatching it*)]: Why, what is that to you?
EMILIA: If it be not for some purpose of import,
Give 't me again. Poor lady, she'll run mad
When she shall lack° it. *miss*
IAGO: Be not acknown on 't.[4]
I have use for it. Go, leave me. [*Exit Emilia.*]
I will in Cassio's lodging lose[5] this napkin
And let him find it. Trifles light as air
Are to the jealous confirmations strong
As proofs of Holy Writ. This may do something.
The Moor already changes with my poison.
Dangerous conceits° are in their natures poisons, *ideas*
Which at the first are scarce found to distaste,° *be distasteful*
But with a little act° upon the blood *action*
Burn like the mines of sulfur.
[*Enter Othello.*]
I did say so.
Look where he comes! Not poppy nor mandragora[6]
Nor all the drowsy syrups of the world
Shall ever medicine thee to that sweet sleep

1. Design of the embroidery copied.
2. With bawdy suggestion; *common* suggests coarseness and availability to all comers, and *thing* is a slang term for the genitals.
3. Taking the opportunity.
4. Do not confess knowledge of it.
5. The Folio spelling, *loose*, is a normal spelling for "lose," but it may also contain the idea of "let go," "release."
6. An opiate made of the mandrake root.

Which thou owedst° yesterday. *you did own*
OTHELLO: Ha, ha, false to me?
IAGO: Why, how now, General? No more of that.
OTHELLO: Avaunt! Begone! Thou hast set me on the rack.
I swear 'tis better to be much abused
Than but to know 't a little.
IAGO: How now, my lord?
OTHELLO: What sense had I of her stolen hours of lust?
I saw 't not, thought it not, it harmed not me.
I slept the next night well, fed well, was free° and merry; *carefree*
I found not Cassio's kisses on her lips.
He that is robbed, not wanting° what is stolen, *missing*
Let him not know 't and he's not robbed at all.
IAGO: I am sorry to hear this.
OTHELLO: I had been happy if the general camp,
Pioners[7] and all, had tasted her sweet body,
So° I had nothing known. O, now, forever *provided*
Farewell the tranquil mind! Farewell content!
Farewell the plumèd troops and the big° wars *stately*
That makes ambition virtue! O, farewell!
Farewell the neighing steed and the shrill trump,
The spirit-stirring drum, th' ear-piercing fife,
The royal banner, and all quality,° *character*
Pride,° pomp, and circumstance° of glorious war! *display / pageantry*
And O, you mortal engines,[8] whose rude throats
Th' immortal Jove's dread clamors° counterfeit, *thunder*
Farewell! Othello's occupation's gone.
IAGO: Is 't possible, my lord?
OTHELLO: Villain, be sure thou prove my love a whore!
Be sure of it. Give me the ocular proof,
Or, by the worth of mine eternal soul,
Thou hadst been better have been born a dog
Than answer my waked wrath!
IAGO: Is 't come to this?
OTHELLO: Make me to see 't, or at the least so prove it
That the probation° bear no hinge nor loop *proof*
To hang a doubt on, or woe upon thy life!
IAGO: My noble lord—
OTHELLO: If thou dost slander her and torture me,
Never pray more; abandon all remorse;° *pity*
On horror's head horrors accumulate;
Do deeds to make heaven weep, all earth amazed;
For nothing canst thou to damnation add
Greater than that.
IAGO: O grace! O heaven forgive me!
Are you a man? Have you a soul or sense?

7. Diggers of mines, the lowest grade of soldiers.

8. Cannon. (*Mortal* means "deadly.")

God b' wi' you; take mine office. O wretched fool,[9]
That lov'st to make thine honesty a vice!° *failing*
O monstrous world! Take note, take note, O world,
To be direct and honest is not safe.
I thank you for this profit,° and from hence° *instruction / henceforth*
I'll love no friend, sith° love breeds such offense.[1] *since*

OTHELLO: Nay, stay. Thou shouldst be honest.[2]

IAGO: I should be wise, for honesty's a fool
And loses that° it works for. *what*

OTHELLO: By the world,
I think my wife be honest and think she is not;
I think that thou art just and think thou art not.
I'll have some proof. My name, that was as fresh
As Dian's[3] visage, is now begrimed and black
As mine own face. If there be cords, or knives,
Poison, or fire, or suffocating streams,
I'll not endure it. Would I were satisfied!

IAGO: I see, sir, you are eaten up with passion.
I do repent me that I put it to you.
You would be satisfied?

OTHELLO: Would? Nay, and I will.

IAGO: And may; but how? How satisfied, my lord?
Would you, the supervisor,° grossly gape on? *onlooker*
Behold her topped?

OTHELLO: Death and damnation! O!

IAGO: It were a tedious difficulty, I think,
To bring them to that prospect. Damn them then,[4]
If ever mortal eyes do see them bolster[5]
More° than their own.° What then? How then? *other / own eyes*
What shall I say? Where's satisfaction?
It is impossible you should see this,
Were they as prime° as goats, as hot as monkeys, *wanton*
As salt° as wolves in pride,° and fools as gross *lustful / heat*
As ignorance made drunk. But yet I say,
If imputation[6] and strong circumstances
Which lead directly to the door of truth
Will give you satisfaction, you might have 't.

OTHELLO: Give me a living reason she's disloyal.

IAGO: I do not like the office.
But sith° I am entered in this cause so far, *since*
Pricked° to 't by foolish honesty and love, *spurred*
I will go on. I lay with Cassio lately,
And being troubled with a raging tooth
I could not sleep. There are a kind of men
So loose of soul that in their sleeps will mutter

9. Iago addresses himself as a fool for having carried honesty too far.
1. Harm to the one who offers help and friendship.
2. It appears that you are. (But Iago replies in the sense of "ought to be.")
3. Diana, goddess of the moon and of chastity.
4. They would have to be really incorrigible.
5. Go to bed together, share a bolster.
6. Strong circumstantial evidence.

Their affairs. One of this kind is Cassio.
In sleep I heard him say, "Sweet Desdemona,
Let us be wary, let us hide our loves!"
And then, sir, would he grip and wring my hand,
Cry "O sweet creature!", then kiss me hard,
As if he plucked up kisses by the roots
That grew upon my lips; then laid his leg
Over my thigh, and sighed, and kissed, and then
Cried, "Cursèd fate that gave thee to the Moor!"
OTHELLO: O, monstrous! Monstrous!
IAGO: Nay, this was but his dream.
OTHELLO: But this denoted a foregone conclusion.[7]
'Tis a shrewd doubt,[8] though it be but a dream.
IAGO: And this may help to thicken other proofs
That do demonstrate thinly.
OTHELLO: I'll tear her all to pieces.
IAGO: Nay, but be wise. Yet we see nothing done;
She may be honest yet. Tell me but this:
Have you not sometimes seen a handkerchief
Spotted° with strawberries in your wife's hand? *embroidered*
OTHELLO: I gave her such a one. 'Twas my first gift.
IAGO: I know not that; but such a handkerchief—
I am sure it was your wife's—did I today
See Cassio wipe his beard with.
OTHELLO: If it be that—
IAGO: If it be that, or any that was hers,
It speaks against her with the other proofs.
OTHELLO: O, that the slave° had forty thousand lives! *Cassio*
One is too poor, too weak for my revenge.
Now do I see 'tis true. Look here, Iago,
All my fond[9] love thus do I blow to heaven.
'Tis gone.
Arise, black vengeance, from the hollow hell!
Yield up, O love, thy crown and hearted° throne *fixed in the heart*
To tyrannous hate! Swell, bosom, with thy freight,° *burden*
For 'tis of aspics'° tongues! *venomous serpents'*
IAGO: Yet be content.° *calm*
OTHELLO: O, blood, blood, blood!
IAGO: Patience, I say. Your mind perhaps may change.
OTHELLO: Never, Iago. Like to the Pontic Sea,[1]
Whose icy current and compulsive course
Ne'er feels retiring ebb, but keeps due on
To the Propontic[2] and the Hellespont,[3]
Even so my bloody thoughts with violent pace
Shall ne'er look back, ne'er ebb to humble love,

7. Concluded experience or action.
8. Suspicious circumstance.
9. Foolish (but also suggesting "affectionate").
1. Black Sea.
2. Sea of Marmara, between the Black Sea and the Aegean.
3. Dardanelles, straits where the Sea of Marmara joins with the Aegean.

Till that a capable° and wide revenge *ample*
Swallow them up. Now, by yond marble[4] heaven,
[*Kneeling.*] In the due reverence of a sacred vow
I here engage my words.

IAGO: Do not rise yet.
[*He kneels.*][5] Witness, you ever-burning lights above,
You elements that clip° us round about, *encompass*
Witness that here Iago doth give up
The execution° of his wit,° hands, heart, *exercise / mind*
To wronged Othello's service. Let him command,
And to obey shall be in me remorse,[6]
What bloody business ever.° [(*They rise.*)] *soever*

OTHELLO: I greet thy love,
Not with vain thanks, but with acceptance bounteous,
And will upon the instant put thee to 't.[7]
Within these three days let me hear thee say
That Cassio's not alive.

IAGO: My friend is dead;
'Tis done at your request. But let her live.

OTHELLO: Damn her, lewd minx!° O, damn her, damn her! *wanton*
Come, go with me apart. I will withdraw
To furnish me with some swift means of death
For the fair devil. Now art thou my lieutenant.

IAGO: I am your own forever. [*Exeunt.*]

Scene 4[8]

[*Enter Desdemona, Emilia, and Clown.*]

DESDEMONA: Do you know, sirrah,[9] where Lieutenant Cassio lies?

CLOWN: I dare not say he lies[1] anywhere.

DESDEMONA: Why, man?

CLOWN: He's a soldier, and for me to say a soldier lies, 'tis stabbing.

DESDEMONA: Go to. Where lodges he?

CLOWN: To tell you where he lodges is to tell you where I lie.

DESDEMONA: Can anything be made of this?

CLOWN: I know not where he lodges, and for me to devise a lodging and say he lies here, or he lies there, were to lie in mine own throat.[2]

DESDEMONA: Can you inquire him out, and be edified by report?

CLOWN: I will catechize the world for him; that is, make questions, and by them answer.

DESDEMONA: Seek him, bid him come hither. Tell him I have moved[3] my lord on his behalf and hope all will be well.

CLOWN: To do this is within the compass of man's wit, and therefore I will attempt the doing it. [*Exit Clown.*]

DESDEMONA: Where should I lose that handkerchief, Emilia?

4. I.e., gleaming like marble and unrelenting.
5. In the Quarto text, Iago kneels here after Othello has knelt at line 460.
6. Pity (for Othello's wrongs).
7. To the proof.
8. Location: Before the citadel.
9. A form of address to an inferior.
1. Lodges. (But the Clown makes the obvious pun.)
2. Lie egregiously and deliberately. Also, use the windpipe to speak a lie.
3. Petitioned.

EMILIA: I know not, madam.
DESDEMONA: Believe me, I had rather have lost my purse
Full of crusadoes;° and but my noble Moor *gold coins*
Is true of mind and made of no such baseness
As jealous creatures are, it were enough
To put him to ill thinking.
EMILIA: Is he not jealous?
DESDEMONA: Who, he? I think the sun where he was born
Drew all such humors[4] from him.
EMILIA: Look where he comes.
[*Enter Othello.*]
DESDEMONA: I will not leave him now till Cassio
Be called to him.—How is 't with you, my lord?
OTHELLO: Well, my good lady. [*Aside.*] O, hardness to dissemble!—
How do you, Desdemona?
DESDEMONA: Well, my good lord.
OTHELLO: Give me your hand. [*She gives her hand.*] This hand is moist, my lady.
DESDEMONA: It yet hath felt no age nor known no sorrow.
OTHELLO: This argues fruitfulness and liberal heart.[5]
Hot, hot, and moist. This hand of yours requires
A sequester° from liberty, fasting and prayer, *separation*
Much castigation,° exercise° devout; *discipline / prayer*
For here's a young and sweating devil here
That commonly rebels. 'Tis a good hand,
A frank[6] one.
DESDEMONA: You may indeed say so,
For 'twas that hand that gave away my heart.
OTHELLO: A liberal hand. The hearts of old gave hands,[7]
But our new heraldry is hands, not hearts.[8]
DESDEMONA: I cannot speak of this. Come now, your promise.
OTHELLO: What promise, chuck?[9]
DESDEMONA: I have sent to bid Cassio come speak with you.
OTHELLO: I have a salt and sorry rheum[1] offends me;
Lend me thy handkerchief.
DESDEMONA: Here, my lord. [(*She offers a handkerchief.*)]
OTHELLO: That which I gave you.
DESDEMONA: I have it not about me.
OTHELLO: Not?
DESDEMONA: No, faith, my lord.
OTHELLO: That's a fault. That handkerchief
Did an Egyptian to my mother give.
She was a charmer,° and could almost read *sorceress*
The thoughts of people. She told her, while she kept it
'Twould make her amiable° and subdue my father *desirable*

4. Refers to the four bodily fluids thought to determine temperament.
5. Gives evidence of amorousness, fecundity, and sexually freedom.
6. Generous, open (with sexual suggestion).
7. In former times, people would give their hearts when they gave their hands to something.
8. In our decadent times, the joining of hands is no longer a badge to signify the giving of hearts.
9. A term of endearment.
1. Distressful head cold or watering of the eyes.

Entirely to her love, but if she lost it
Or made a gift of it, my father's eye
Should hold her loathèd and his spirits should hunt
After new fancies.° She, dying, gave it me, *loves*
And bid me, when my fate would have me wived,
To give it her.[2] I did so; and take heed on 't;
Make it a darling like your precious eye.
To lose 't or give 't away were such perdition° *loss*
As nothing else could match.
DESDEMONA: Is 't possible?
OTHELLO: 'Tis true. There's magic in the web° of it. *weaving*
A sibyl, that had numbered in the world
The sun to course two hundred compasses,[3]
In her prophetic fury[4] sewed the work;° *embroidered pattern*
The worms were hallowed that did breed the silk,
And it was dyed in mummy[5] which the skillful
Conserved of[6] maidens' hearts.
DESDEMONA: I' faith! Is 't true?
OTHELLO: Most veritable. Therefore look to 't well.
DESDEMONA: Then would to God that I had never seen 't!
OTHELLO: Ha? Wherefore?
DESDEMONA: Why do you speak so startingly and rash?[7]
OTHELLO: Is 't lost? Is 't gone? Speak, is 't out o' the way?° *misplaced*
DESDEMONA: Heaven bless us!
OTHELLO: Say you?
DESDEMONA: It is not lost; but what an if° it were? *if*
OTHELLO: How?
DESDEMONA: I say it is not lost.
OTHELLO: Fetch 't, let me see 't.
DESDEMONA: Why, so I can, sir, but I will not now.
This is a trick to put me from my suit.
Pray you, let Cassio be received again.
OTHELLO: Fetch me the handkerchief! My mind misgives.
DESDEMONA: Come, come,
You'll never meet a more sufficient° man. *able*
OTHELLO: The handkerchief!
DESDEMONA: I pray, talk° me of Cassio. *talk to*
OTHELLO: The handkerchief!
DESDEMONA: A man that all his time[8]
Hath founded his good fortunes on your love,
Shared dangers with you—
OTHELLO: The handkerchief!
DESDEMONA: I' faith, you are to blame.
OTHELLO: Zounds! [*Exit Othello.*]

2. I.e., to my wife.
3. Annual circlings. (The *sibyl*, or prophetess, was 200 years old.)
4. Frenzy of prophetic inspiration.
5. Medicinal or magical preparation drained from mummified bodies.
6. Prepared or preserved out of.
7. Disjointedly and impetuously, excitedly.
8. Throughout his career.

EMILIA: Is not this man jealous?
DESDEMONA: I ne'er saw this before.
Sure, there's some wonder in this handkerchief.
I am most unhappy in the loss of it.
EMILIA: 'Tis not a year or two shows us a man.[9]
They are all but° stomachs, and we all but food; *nothing but*
They eat us hungerly,° and when they are full *hungrily*
They belch us.
[*Enter Iago and Cassio.*]
Look you, Cassio and my husband.
IAGO [(*to Cassio*)]:
There is no other way; 'tis she must do 't.
And, lo, the happiness![1] Go and importune her.
DESDEMONA: How now, good Cassio? What's the news with you?
CASSIO: Madam, my former suit. I do beseech you
That by your virtuous° means I may again *efficacious*
Exist and be a member of his love
Whom I, with all the office° of my heart, *loyal service*
Entirely honor. I would not be delayed.
If my offense be of such mortal° kind *fatal*
That nor° my service past, nor present sorrows, *neither*
Nor purposed merit in futurity
Can ransom me into his love again,
But to know so must be my benefit;[2]
So shall I clothe me in a forced content,
And shut myself up in[3] some other course,
To fortune's alms.[4]
DESDEMONA: Alas, thrice-gentle Cassio,
My advocation° is not now in tune. *advocacy*
My lord is not my lord; nor should I know him,
Were he in favor° as in humor° altered. *appearance / mood*
So help me every spirit sanctified
As I have spoken for you all my best
And stood within the blank[5] of his displeasure
For my free speech! You must awhile be patient.
What I can do I will, and more I will
Than for myself I dare. Let that suffice you.
IAGO: Is my lord angry?
EMILIA: He went hence but now,
And certainly in strange unquietness.
IAGO: Can he be angry? I have seen the cannon
When it hath blown his ranks into the air,
And like the devil from his very arm
Puffed his own brother—and is he angry?

9. You can't really know a man even in a year or two of experience (?), or, real men come along seldom (?).
1. In happy time, fortunately met.
2. Merely to know that my case is hopeless will have to content me (and will be better than uncertainty).
3. Confine myself to.
4. Throwing myself on the mercy of fortune.
5. Within pointblank range. (The *blank* is the center of the target.)

Something of moment[6] then. I will go meet him.
There's matter in 't indeed, if he be angry.

DESDEMONA: I prithee, do so. [*Exit (Iago.)*]
Something, sure, of state,° *state affairs*
Either from Venice, or some unhatched practice[7]
Made demonstrable here in Cyprus to him,
Hath puddled° his clear spirit; and in such cases *muddied*
Men's natures wrangle with inferior things,
Though great ones are their object. 'Tis even so;
For let our finger ache, and it indues° *induces*
Our other, healthful members even to a sense
Of pain. Nay, we must think men are not gods,
Nor of them look for such observancy° *attentiveness*
As fits the bridal.[8] Beshrew me[9] much, Emilia,
I was, unhandsome° warrior as I am, *unskillful*
Arraigning his unkindness with[1] my soul;
But now I find I had suborned the witness,[2]
And he's indicted falsely.

EMILIA: Pray heaven it be
State matters, as you think, and no conception
Nor no jealous toy° concerning you. *fancy*

DESDEMONA: Alas the day! I never gave him cause.

EMILIA: But jealous souls will not be answered so;
They are not ever jealous for the cause,
But jealous for° they're jealous. It is a monster *do because*
Begot upon itself,[3] born on itself.

DESDEMONA: Heaven keep that monster from Othello's mind!

EMILIA: Lady, amen.

DESDEMONA: I will go seek him. Cassio, walk hereabout.
If I do find him fit, I'll move your suit
And seek to effect it to my uttermost.

CASSIO: I humbly thank Your ladyship.
[*Exit (Desdemona with Emilia.)*]

[*Enter Bianca.*]

BIANCA: Save° you, friend Cassio! *God save*

CASSIO: What make° you from home? *do*
How is 't with you, my most fair Bianca?
I' faith, sweet love, I was coming to your house.

BIANCA: And I was going to your lodging, Cassio.
What, keep a week away? Seven days and nights?
Eightscore-eight[4] hours? And lovers' absent hours
More tedious than the dial[5] eightscore times?
O weary reckoning!

CASSIO: Pardon me, Bianca.

6. Of immediate importance, momentous.
7. As yet unexecuted or undiscovered plot.
8. Wedding (when a bridegroom is newly attentive to his bride).
9. A mild oath.
1. Before the bar of.
2. Induced the witness to give false testimony.
3. Generated solely from itself.
4. One hundred sixty-eight, the number of hours in a week.
5. A complete revolution of the clock.

I have this while with leaden thoughts been pressed;
But I shall, in a more continuate° time, *uninterrupted*
Strike off this score[6] of absence. Sweet Bianca,
[(*Giving her Desdemona's handkerchief.*)]
Take me this work out.[7]

BIANCA: O Cassio, whence came this?
This is some token from a newer friend.° *mistress*
To the felt absence now I feel a cause.
Is 't come to this? Well, well.

CASSIO: Go to, woman!
Throw your vile guesses in the devil's teeth,
From whence you have them. You are jealous now
That this is from some mistress, some remembrance.
No, by my faith, Bianca.

BIANCA: Why, whose is it?

CASSIO: I know not, neither. I found it in my chamber.
I like the work well. Ere it be demanded°— *inquired for*
As like° enough it will—I would have it copied. *likely*
Take it and do 't, and leave me for this time.

BIANCA: Leave you? Wherefore?

CASSIO: I do attend here on the General,
And think it no addition,[8] nor my wish,
To have him see me womaned.

BIANCA: Why, I pray you?

CASSIO: Not that I love you not.

BIANCA: But that you do not love me.
I pray you, bring° me on the way a little, *accompany*
And say if I shall see you soon at night.

CASSIO: 'Tis but a little way that I can bring you,
For I attend here; but I'll see you soon.

BIANCA: 'Tis very good. I must be circumstanced.[9]

[*Exeunt omnes.*]

ACT 4

Scene 1[1]

[*Enter Othello and Iago.*]

IAGO: Will you think so?

OTHELLO: Think so, Iago?

IAGO: What,
To kiss in private?

OTHELLO: An unauthorized kiss!

IAGO: Or to be naked with her friend in bed
An hour or more, not meaning any harm?

OTHELLO: Naked in bed, Iago, and not mean harm?
It is hypocrisy against the devil.
They that mean virtuously and yet do so,

6. Settle this account.
7. Copy this embroidery for me.
8. I.e., addition to my reputation.
9. Be governed by circumstance, yield to your conditions.
1. Location: Before the citadel.

The devil their virtue tempts, and they tempt heaven.
IAGO: If they do nothing, 'tis a venial° slip. *pardonable*
But if I give my wife a handkerchief—
OTHELLO: What then?
IAGO: Why then, 'tis hers, my lord, and being hers,
She may, I think, bestow 't on any man.
OTHELLO: She is protectress of her honor too.
May she give that?
IAGO: Her honor is an essence that's not seen;
They have it[2] very oft that have it not.
But, for the handkerchief—
OTHELLO: By heaven, I would most gladly have forgot it.
Thou saidst—O, it comes o'er my memory
As doth the raven o'er the infectious house,[3]
Boding to all—he had my handkerchief.
IAGO: Ay, what of that?
OTHELLO: That's not so good now.
IAGO: What
If I had said I had seen him do you wrong?
Or heard him say—as knaves be such abroad,° *around about*
Who having, by their own importunate suit,
Or voluntary dotage[4] of some mistress,
Convincèd or supplied[5] them, cannot choose
But they must blab—
OTHELLO: Hath he said anything?
IAGO: He hath, my lord; but, be you well assured,
No more than he'll unswear.
OTHELLO: What hath he said?
IAGO: Faith, that he did—I know not what he did.
OTHELLO: What? What?
IAGO: Lie—
OTHELLO: With her?
IAGO: With her, on her; what you will.

OTHELLO: Lie with her? Lie on her? We say "lie on her" when they belie[6] her. Lie with her? Zounds, that's ful-some.[7]—Handkerchief—confessions—handkerchief!—To confess and be hanged for his labor—first to be hanged and then to confess.[8]—I tremble at it. Nature would not invest herself in such shadowing passion without some instruction.[9] It is not words[1] that shakes me thus. Pish! Noses, ears, and lips.—Is 't possible?—Confess—handkerchief!—O devil!

[*Falls in a trance*.]

IAGO: Work on, My medicine, work! Thus credulous fools are caught,

2. They enjoy a reputation for it.
3. Allusion to the belief that the raven hovered over a house of sickness or infection, such as one visited by the plague.
4. Willing infatuation.
5. Seduced or sexually gratified.
6. Slander.
7. Foul.
8. Othello reverses the proverbial *confess and be hanged;* Cassio is to be given no time to confess before he dies.
9. I.e., without some foundation in fact, nature would not have dressed herself in such an overwhelming passion that comes over me now and fills my mind with images, or in such a lifelike fantasy as Cassio had in his dream of lying with Desdemona.
1. Mere words.

And many worthy and chaste dames even thus,
All guiltless, meet reproach.—What, ho! My lord!
My lord, I say! Othello!
[*Enter Cassio.*]
How now, Cassio?
CASSIO: What's the matter?
IAGO: My lord is fall'n into an epilepsy.
This is his second fit. He had one yesterday.
CASSIO: Rub him about the temples.
IAGO: No, forbear.
The lethargy° must have his° quiet course. *coma / its*
If not, he foams at mouth, and by and by
Breaks out to savage madness. Look, he stirs.
Do you withdraw yourself a little while.
He will recover straight. When he is gone,
I would on great occasion speak with you.
[*Exit Cassio.*]
How is it, General? Have you not hurt your head?
OTHELLO: Dost thou mock me?[2]
IAGO: I mock you not, by heaven.
Would you would bear your fortune like a man!
OTHELLO: A hornèd man's a monster and a beast.
IAGO: There's many a beast then in a populous city,
And many a civil° monster. *city-dwelling*
OTHELLO: Did he confess it?
IAGO: Good sir, be a man.
Think every bearded fellow that's but yoked[3]
May draw with you.[4] There's millions now alive
That nightly lie in those unproper° beds *shared*
Which they dare swear peculiar.° Your case is better.[5] *their own*
O, 'tis the spite of hell, the fiend's arch-mock,
To lip° a wanton in a secure couch *kiss*
And to suppose her chaste! No, let me know,
And knowing what I am,[6] I know what she shall be.[7]
OTHELLO: O, thou art wise. 'Tis certain.
IAGO: Stand you awhile apart;
Confine yourself but in a patient list.[8]
Whilst you were here o'erwhelmèd with your grief—
A passion most unsuiting such a man—
Cassio came hither. I shifted him away,[9]
And laid good 'scuse upon your ecstasy,° *trance*
Bade him anon return and here speak with me,

2. Othello takes Iago's question about hurting his head to be a mocking reference to the cuckold's horns.
3. Married. Also, put into the yoke of infamy and cuckoldry.
4. Pull as you do, like oxen who are yoked, i.e., share your fate as cuckold.
5. I.e., because you know the truth.
6. I.e., a cuckold.
7. Will happen to her.
8. Within the bounds of patience.
9. Used a dodge to get rid of him.

The which he promised. Do but encave° yourself *conceal*
And mark the fleers,° the gibes, and notable° scorns *sneere / obvious*
That dwell in every region of his face;
For I will make him tell the tale anew,
Where, how, how oft, how long ago, and when
He hath and is again to cope° your wife. *have sex with*
I say, but mark his gesture. Marry, patience!
Or I shall say you're all-in-all in spleen,[1]
And nothing of a man.

OTHELLO: Does thou hear, Iago?
I will be found most cunning in my patience;
But—dost thou hear?—most bloody.

IAGO: That's not amiss;
But yet keep time[2] in all. Will you withdraw?
[(*Othello stands apart.*)]
Now will I question Cassio of Bianca,
A huswife° that by selling her desires *hussy*
Buys herself bread and clothes. It is a creature
That dotes on Cassio—as 'tis the strumpet's plague
To beguile many and be beguiled by one.
He, when he hears of her, cannot restrain° *refrain*
From the excess of laughter. Here he comes.
[*Enter Cassio.*]
As he shall smile, Othello shall go mad;
And his unbookish° jealousy must conster° *uninstructed / construe*
Poor Cassio's smiles, gestures, and light behaviors
Quite in the wrong.—How do you now, Lieutenant?

CASSIO: The worser that you give me the addition° *title*
Whose want[3] even kills me.

IAGO: Ply Desdemona well and you are sure on 't.
[(*Speaking lower*)] Now, if this suit lay in Bianca's power,
How quickly should you speed!

CASSIO [(*laughing*)]: Alas, poor caitiff!° *wretch*

OTHELLO [(*aside*)]: Look how he laughs already!

IAGO: I never knew a woman love man so.

CASSIO: Alas, poor rogue! I think, i' faith, she loves me.

OTHELLO: Now he denies it faintly, and laughs it out.

IAGO: Do you hear, Cassio?

OTHELLO: Now he importunes him
To tell it o'er. Go to![4] Well said,° well said. *well done*

IAGO: She gives it out that you shall marry her.
Do you intend it?

CASSIO: Ha, ha, ha!

OTHELLO: Do you triumph, Roman?[5] Do you triumph?

1. Utterly governed by passionate impulses.
2. Keep yourself steady (as in music).
3. The lack of which.
4. An expression of remonstrance.
5. The Romans were noted for their *triumphs* or triumphal processions.

CASSIO: I marry her? What? A customer?[6] Prithee, bear some charity to my wit;[7] do not think it so unwholesome. Ha, ha, ha!

OTHELLO: So, so, so, so! They laugh that win.[8]

IAGO: Faith, the cry goes that you shall marry her.

CASSIO: Prithee, say true.

IAGO: I am a very villain else.[9]

OTHELLO: Have you scored me?[1] Well.

CASSIO: This is the monkey's own giving out. She is persuaded I will marry her out of her own love and flattery,[2] not out of my promise.

OTHELLO: Iago beckons° me. Now he begins the story. *signals*

CASSIO: She was here even now; she haunts me in every place. I was the other day talking on the seabank[3] with certain Venetians, and thither comes the bauble,[4] and, by this hand,[5] she falls me thus about my neck—
[(*He embraces Iago.*)]

OTHELLO: Crying, "O, dear Cassio!" as it were; his gesture imports it.

CASSIO: So hangs and lolls and weeps upon me, so shakes and pulls me. Ha, ha, ha!

OTHELLO: Now he tells how she plucked him to my chamber. O, I see that nose of yours, but not that dog I shall throw it to.[6]

CASSIO: Well, I must leave her company.

IAGO: Before me,[7] look where she comes.
[*Enter Bianca* (*with Othello's handkerchief*).]

CASSIO: 'Tis such another fitchew![8] Marry, a perfumed one.—What do you mean by this haunting of me?

BIANCA: Let the devil and his dam[9] haunt you! What did you mean by that same handkerchief you gave me even now? I was a fine fool to take it. I must take out the work? A likely piece of work,[1] that you should find it in your chamber and know not who left it there! This is some minx's token, and I must take out the work? There; give it your hobbyhorse.[2] [(*She gives him the handkerchief.*)] Wheresoever you had it, I'll take out no work on't.

CASSIO: How now, my sweet Bianca? How now? How now?

OTHELLO: By heaven, that should be[3] my handkerchief!

BIANCA: If you'll come to supper tonight, you may; if you will not, come when you are next prepared for.[4]
[*Exit.*]

IAGO: After her, after her.

CASSIO: Faith, I must. She'll rail in the streets else.

IAGO: Will you sup there?

CASSIO: Faith, I intend so.

IAGO: Well, I may chance to see you, for I would very fain speak with you.

CASSIO: Prithee, come. Will you?

6. Prostitute.
7. Be more charitable to my judgment.
8. I.e., they that laugh last laugh best.
9. Call me a complete rogue if I'm not telling the truth.
1. Scored off me, beaten me, made up my reckoning, branded me.
2. Self-flattery, self-deception.
3. Seashore.
4. Plaything.
5. I make my vow.
6. Othello imagines himself cutting off Cassio's nose and throwing it to a dog.
7. On my soul.
8. What a polecat she is! Just like all the others. (Polecats were often compared with prostitutes because of their rank smell and presumed lechery.)
9. Mother.
1. A fine story.
2. Harlot.
3. Must be.
4. When I'm ready for you (i.e., never).

IAGO: Go to. Say no more. [*Exit Cassio*.]

OTHELLO [(*advancing*)]: How shall I murder him, Iago?

IAGO: Did you perceive how he laughed at his vice?

OTHELLO: O, Iago!

IAGO: And did you see the handkerchief?

OTHELLO: Was that mine?

IAGO: Yours, by this hand. And to see how he prizes the foolish woman your wife! She gave it him, and he hath given it his whore.

OTHELLO: I would have him nine years a-killing. A fine woman! A fair woman! A sweet woman!

IAGO: Nay, you must forget that.

OTHELLO: Ay, let her rot and perish, and be damned tonight, for she shall not live. No, my heart is turned to stone; I strike it, and it hurts my hand. O, the world hath not a sweeter creature! She might lie by an emperor's side and command him tasks.

IAGO: Nay, that's not your way.[5]

OTHELLO: Hang her! I do but say what she is. So delicate with her needle! An admirable musician! O, she will sing the savageness out of a bear. Of so high and plenteous wit and invention![6]

IAGO: She's the worse for all this.

OTHELLO: O, a thousand, a thousand times! And then, of so gentle a condition![7]

IAGO: Ay, too gentle.[8]

OTHELLO: Nay, that's certain. But yet the pity of it, Iago! O, Iago, the pity of it, Iago!

IAGO: If you are so fond[9] over her iniquity, give her patent[1] to offend, for if it touch not you it comes near nobody.

OTHELLO: I will chop her into messes.[2] Cuckold me?

IAGO: O, 'tis foul in her.

OTHELLO: With mine officer?

IAGO: That's fouler.

OTHELLO: Get me some poison, Iago, this night. I'll not expostulate with her, lest her body and beauty unprovide[3] my mind again. This night, Iago.

IAGO: Do it not with poison. Strangle her in her bed, even the bed she hath contaminated.

OTHELLO: Good, good! The justice of it pleases. Very good.

IAGO: And for Cassio, let me be his undertaker.[4] You shall hear more by midnight.

OTHELLO: Excellent good. [(*A trumpet within.*)] What trumpet is that same?

IAGO: I warrant, something from Venice.

[*Enter Lodovico, Desdemona, and attendants*.]

'Tis Lodovico. This comes from the Duke.
See, your wife's with him.

LODOVICO: God save you, worthy General!

OTHELLO: With all my heart, sir.[5]

5. I.e., the way you should think of her.
6. Imagination.
7. Wellborn and well-bred.
8. Generous, yielding (to other men).
9. Foolish.
1. License.
2. Portions of meat, i.e., bits.
3. Weaken, render unfit.
4. Undertake to dispatch him.
5. I thank you most heartily.

LODOVICO: [(*giving him a letter*)] The Duke and the senators of Venice greet you.
OTHELLO: I kiss the instrument of their pleasures.
[(*He opens the letter, and reads.*)]
DESDEMONA: And what's the news, good cousin Lodovico?
IAGO: I am very glad to see you, signor.
Welcome to Cyprus.
LODOVICO: I thank you. How does Lieutenant Cassio?
IAGO: Lives, sir.
DESDEMONA: Cousin, there's fall'n between him and my lord
An unkind[6] breach; but you shall make all well.
OTHELLO: Are you sure of that?
DESDEMONA: My lord?
OTHELLO [*reads*]: "This fail you not to do, as you will—"
LODOVICO: He did not call; he's busy in the paper.
Is there division twixt my lord and Cassio?
DESDEMONA: A most unhappy one. I would do much
T' atone° them, for the love I bear to Cassio. *reconcile*
OTHELLO: Fire and brimstone!
DESDEMONA: My lord?
OTHELLO: Are you wise?
DESDEMONA: What, is he angry?
LODOVICO: Maybe the letter moved him;
For, as I think, they do command him home,
Deputing Cassio in his government.° *office*
DESDEMONA: By my troth, I am glad on 't.° *of it*
OTHELLO: Indeed?
DESDEMONA: My lord?
OTHELLO: I am glad to see you mad.[7]
DESDEMONA: Why, sweet Othello—
OTHELLO [(*striking her*)]: Devil!
DESDEMONA: I have not deserved this.
LODOVICO: My lord, this would not be believed in Venice,
Though I should swear I saw 't. 'Tis very much.° *outrageous*
Make her amends; she weeps.
OTHELLO: O devil, devil!
If that the earth could teem° with woman's tears, *breed*
Each drop she falls° would prove a crocodile.[8] *lets fall*
Out of my sight!
DESDEMONA: I will not stay to offend you. [(*Going.*)]
LODOVICO: Truly, an obedient lady.
I do beseech your lordship, call her back.
OTHELLO: Mistress!
DESDEMONA: [*returning*] My lord?
OTHELLO: What would you with her, sir?
LODOVICO: Who, I, my lord?

6. Unnatural, contrary to their natures; hurtful.
7. I.e., I am glad to see that you are insane enough to rejoice in Cassio's promotion. (Othello bitterly plays on Desdemona's *I am glad.*)
8. Crocodiles were supposed to weep hypocritical tears for their victims.

OTHELLO: Ay, you did wish that I would make her turn.[9]
Sir, she can turn, and turn, and yet go on
And turn again; and she can weep, sir, weep;
And she's obedient,[1] as you say, obedient,
Very obedient.—Proceed you in your tears.—
Concerning this, sir—Oh, well-painted passion!°— *grief*
I am commanded home.—Get you away;
I'll send for you anon.—Sir, I obey the mandate
And will return to Venice.—Hence, avaunt!
[(*Exit Desdemona.*)]
Cassio shall have my place. And, sir, tonight
I do entreat that we may sup together.
You are welcome, sir, to Cyprus.—Goats and monkeys![2]

LODOVICO: Is this the noble Moor whom our full Senate
Call all in all sufficient? Is this the nature
Whom passion could not shake? Whose solid virtue
The shot of accident nor dart of chance
Could neither graze nor pierce?

IAGO: He is much changed.

LODOVICO: Are his wits safe? Is he not light of brain?

IAGO: He's that he is. I may not breathe my censure
What he might be. If what he might he is not,
I would to heaven he were![3]

LODOVICO: What, strike his wife?

IAGO: Faith, that was not so well; yet would I knew
That stroke would prove the worst!

LODOVICO: Is it his use?°
custom
Or did the letters work upon his blood° *passions*
And new-create his fault?

IAGO: Alas, alas!
It is not honesty in me to speak
What I have seen and known. You shall observe him,
And his own courses will denote[4] him so
That I may save my speech. Do but go after,
And mark how he continues.

LODOVICO: I am sorry that I am deceived in him. [*Exeunt.*]

Scene 2[5]

[*Enter Othello and Emilia.*]

OTHELLO: You have seen nothing, then?

EMILIA: Nor ever heard, nor ever did suspect.

OTHELLO: Yes, you have seen Cassio and she together.

EMILIA: But then I saw no harm, and then I heard

9. Othello implies that Desdemona is pliant and will do a *turn* sexually with any man.
1. With much the same sexual connotation as *turn*.
2. The most lustful animals.
3. I dare not venture an opinion as to whether he's of unsound mind, as you suggest, but, if he isn't, then it might be better to wish he were in fact insane, since only that could excuse his wild behavior.
4. Actions will reveal.
5. Location: The citadel.

Each syllable that breath made up between them.
OTHELLO: What, did they never whisper?
EMILIA: Never, my lord.
OTHELLO: Nor send you out o' the way?
EMILIA: Never.
OTHELLO: To fetch her fan, her gloves, her mask, nor nothing?
EMILIA: Never, my lord.
OTHELLO: That's strange.
EMILIA: I durst, my lord, to wager she is honest,
Lay down my soul at stake.° If you think other, *as the wager*
Remove your thought; it doth abuse your bosom.° *deceive you*
If any wretch have put this in your head,
Let heaven requite it with the serpent's curse![6]
For if she be not honest, chaste, and true,
There's no man happy; the purest of their wives
Is foul as slander.
OTHELLO: Bid her come hither. Go.
[*Exit Emilia.*]
She says enough; yet she's a simple bawd
That cannot say as much.[7] This° is a subtle whore, *Desdemona*
A closet lock and key of villainous secrets.
And yet she'll kneel and pray; I have seen her do 't.
[*Enter Desdemona and Emilia.*]
DESDEMONA: My lord, what is your will?
OTHELLO: Pray you, chuck, come hither.
DESDEMONA: What is your pleasure?
OTHELLO: Let me see your eyes.
Look in my face.
DESDEMONA: What horrible fancy's this?
OTHELLO [(*to Emilia*)]: Some of your function,[8] mistress.
Leave procreants° alone and shut the door; *mating couples*
Cough or cry "hem" if anybody come.
Your mystery,° your mystery! Nay, dispatch. *trade*
[*Exit Emilia.*]
DESDEMONA [(*kneeling*)]: Upon my knees, what doth your speech import?
I understand a fury in your words,
But not the words.
OTHELLO: Why, what art thou?
DESDEMONA: Your wife, my lord, your true
And loyal wife.
OTHELLO: Come, swear it, damn thyself,
Lest, being like one of heaven,[9] the devils themselves

6. The curse pronounced by God on the serpent for deceiving Eve, just as some man has done to Othello and Desdemona. (See Genesis 3.14.)
7. Any procuress or go-between who couldn't make up as plausible a story as Emilia's would have to be pretty stupid.
8. I.e., Practice your chosen profession, that of bawd (by guarding the door).
9. Looking like an angel.

Should fear to seize thee. Therefore be double damned:
Swear thou art honest.
DESDEMONA: Heaven doth truly know it.
OTHELLO: Heaven truly knows that thou art false as hell.
DESDEMONA: To whom, my lord? With whom? How am I false?
OTHELLO [(*weeping*)]: Ah, Desdemon! Away, away, away!
DESDEMONA: Alas the heavy day! Why do you weep?
Am I the motive° of these tears, my lord? *cause*
If haply you my father do suspect
An instrument of this your calling back,
Lay not your blame on me. If you have lost him,
I have lost him too.
OTHELLO: Had it pleased heaven
To try me with affliction, had they[1] rained
All kinds of sores and shames on my bare head,
Steeped me in poverty to the very lips,
Given to captivity me and my utmost hopes,
I should have found in some place of my soul
A drop of patience. But, alas, to make me
A fixèd figure for the time of scorn[2]
To point his° slow and moving finger[3] at! *its*
Yet could I bear that too, well, very well.
But there where I have garnered° up my heart, *stored*
Where either I must live or bear no life,
The fountain° from the which my current runs *spring*
Or else dries up—to be discarded thence!
Or keep it as a cistern° for foul toads *cesspool*
To knot° and gender° in! Turn thy complexion there,[4] *couple / engender*
Patience, thou young and rose-lipped cherubin—
Ay, there look grim as hell![5]
DESDEMONA: I hope my noble lord esteems me honest.° *chaste*
OTHELLO: O, ay, as summer flies are in the shambles,° *slaughterhouse*
That quicken° even with blowing.[6] O thou weed, *come to life*
Who art so lovely fair and smell'st so sweet
That the sense aches at thee, would thou hadst ne'er been born!
DESDEMONA: Alas, what ignorant sin[7] have I committed?
OTHELLO: Was this fair paper, this most goodly book,
Made to write "whore" upon? What committed?
Committed? O, thou public commoner!° *prostitute*
I should make very forges of my cheeks,
That would to cinders burn up modesty,
Did I but speak thy deeds. What committed?

1. I.e., heavenly powers.
2. Scornful world.
3. I.e., hour hand of the clock, moving so slowly it seems hardly to move at all. (Othello envisages himself as being eternally pointed at by the scornful world as the numbers on a clock are pointed at by the hour hand.)
4. Change your color, grow pale, at such a sight.
5. Even Patience, that rose-lipped cheruh, will look grim and pale at this spectacle.
6. I.e., with the puffing up of something rotten in which maggots are breeding.
7. Sin in ignorance.

Heaven stops the nose at it and the moon winks;[8]
The bawdy[9] wind, that kisses all it meets,
Is hushed within the hollow mine[1] of earth
And will not hear 't. What committed?
Impudent strumpet!

DESDEMONA: By heaven, you do me wrong.

OTHELLO: Are not you a strumpet?

DESDEMONA: No, as I am a Christian.
If to preserve this vessel° for my lord — *body*
From any other foul unlawful touch
Be not to be a strumpet, I am none.

OTHELLO: What, not a whore?

DESDEMONA: No, as I shall be saved.

OTHELLO: Is 't possible?

DESDEMONA: O, heaven forgive us!

OTHELLO: I cry you mercy,° then. — *beg you pardon*
I took you for that cunning whore of Venice
That married with Othello. [*Calling out*.] You, mistress,
That have the office opposite to Saint Peter
And keep the gate of hell!

[*Enter Emilia*.]

You, you, ay, you!
We have done our course.[2] There's money for your pains. [(*He gives money*.)]
I pray you, turn the key and keep our counsel. [*Exit*.]

EMILIA: Alas, what does this gentleman conceive?° — *suppose*
How do you, madam? How do you, my good lady?

DESDEMONA: Faith, half asleep.[3]

EMILIA: Good madam, what's the matter with my lord?

DESDEMONA: With who?

EMILIA: Why, with my lord, madam.

DESDEMONA: Who is thy lord?

EMILIA: He that is yours, sweet lady.

DESDEMONA: I have none. Do not talk to me, Emilia.
I cannot weep, nor answers have I none
But what should go by water.[4] Prithee, tonight
Lay on my bed my wedding sheets, remember;
And call thy husband hither.

EMILIA: Here's a change indeed! [*Exit*.]

DESDEMONA: 'Tis meet° I should be used so, very meet. — *fitting*
How have I been behaved, that he might stick° — *attach*
The small'st opinion° on my least misuse?° — *censure / misconduct*

[*Enter Iago and Emilia*.]

IAGO: What is your pleasure, madam? How is 't with you?

DESDEMONA: I cannot tell. Those that do teach young babes
Do it with gentle means and easy tasks.

8. Closes her eyes. (The moon symbolizes chastity.)
9. Kissing one and all.
1. Cave (where the winds were thought to dwell).
2. Business (with an indecent suggestion of "trick," turn at sex.)
3. I.e., dazed.
4. Be expressed by tears.

He might have chid me so, for, in good faith,
I am a child to chiding.
IAGO: What is the matter, lady?
EMILIA: Alas, Iago, my lord hath so bewhored her,
Thrown such despite and heavy terms upon her,
That true hearts cannot bear it.
DESDEMONA: Am I that name, Iago?
IAGO: What name, fair lady?
DESDEMONA: Such as she said my lord did say I was.
EMILIA: He called her whore. A beggar in his drink
Could not have laid such terms upon his callet.° *whore*
IAGO: Why did he so?
DESDEMONA [(*weeping*)]:
I do not know. I am sure I am none such.
IAGO: Do not weep, do not weep. Alas the day!
EMILIA: Hath she forsook so many noble matches,
Her father and her country and her friends,
To be called whore? Would it not make one weep?
DESDEMONA: It is my wretched fortune.
IAGO: Beshrew° him for 't! *curse*
How comes this trick° upon him? *delusion*
DESDEMONA: Nay, heaven doth know.
EMILIA: I will be hanged if some eternal° villain, *inveterate*
Some busy and insinuating° rogue, *wheedling*
Some cogging,° cozening° slave, to get some office, *cheating / defrauding*
Have not devised this slander. I will be hanged else.
IAGO: Fie, there is no such man. It is impossible.
DESDEMONA: If any such there be, heaven pardon him!
EMILIA: A halter° pardon him! And hell gnaw his bones! *hangman's noose*
Why should he call her whore? Who keeps her company?
What place? What time? What form?° What likelihood? *appearance*
The Moor's abused by some most villainous knave,
Some base notorious knave, some scurvy fellow.
O, heaven, that such companions thou'dst unfold,[5]
And put in every honest hand a whip
To lash the rascals naked through the world
Even from the east to th' west!
IAGO: Speak within door.[6]
EMILIA: O, fie upon them! Some such squire° he was *fellow*
That turned your wit the seamy side without° *wrong side out*
And made you to suspect me with the Moor.
IAGO: You are a fool. Go to.[7]
DESDEMONA: Alas, Iago,
What shall I do to win my lord again?
Good friend, go to him; for, by this light of heaven,
I know not how I lost him. Here I kneel. [*She kneels.*]

5. If only you would expose such fellows.
6. I.e., not so loud.
7. I.e., that's enough.

If e'er my will did trespass 'gainst his love,
Either in discourse of thought or actual deed,
Or that° mine eyes, mine ears, or any sense *if*
Delighted them° in any other form; *took delight*
Or that I do not yet,° and ever did, *still*
And ever will—though he do shake me off
To beggarly divorcement—love him dearly,
Comfort forswear[8] me! Unkindness may do much,
And his unkindness may defeat° my life, *destroy*
But never taint my love. I cannot say "whore."
It does abhor[9] me now I speak the word;
To do the act that might the addition° earn *title*
Not the world's mass of vanity° could make me. *showy splendor*
[*She rises*.]

IAGO: I pray you, be content. 'Tis but his humor.° *mood*
The business of the state does him offense,
And he does chide with you.

DESDEMONA: If 'twere no other—

IAGO: It is but so, I warrant. [(*Trumpets within*.)]
Hark, how these instruments summon you to supper!
The messengers of Venice stays the meat.° *wait to dine*
Go in, and weep not. All things shall be well.
[*Exeunt Desdemona and Emilia*.]

[*Enter Roderigo*.]

How now, Roderigo?

RODERIGO: I do not find that thou deal'st justly with me.

IAGO: What in the contrary?

RODERIGO: Every day thou daff'st me[1] with some device,[2] Iago, and rather, as it seems to me now, keep'st from me all conveniency[3] than suppliest me with the least advantage[4] of hope. I will indeed no longer endure it, nor am I yet persuaded to put up[5] in peace what already I have foolishly suffered.

IAGO: Will you hear me, Roderigo?

RODERIGO: Faith, I have heard too much, for your words and performances are no kin together.

IAGO: You charge me most unjustly.

RODERIGO: With naught but truth. I have wasted myself out of my means. The jewels you have had from me to deliver[6] Desdemona would half have corrupted a votarist.[7] You have told me she hath received them and returned me expectations and comforts of sudden respect[8] and acquaintance, but I find none.

IAGO: Well, go to, very well.

RODERIGO: "Very well"! "Go to"! I cannot go to,[9] man, nor 'tis not very well. By this hand, I think it is scurvy, and begin to find myself fopped[1] in it.

IAGO: Very well.

8. May heavenly comfort forsake.
9. Fill me with abhorrence. Also, make me whorelike.
1. You put me off.
2. Excuse, trick.
3. Advantage, opportunity.
4. Increase.
5. Submit to, tolerate.
6. Deliver to.
7. Nun.
8. Immediate consideration.
9. Roderigo changes Iago's *go to*, an expression urging patience, to *I cannot go to*, "I have no opportunity for success in wooing."
1. Fooled, duped.

RODERIGO: I tell you 'tis not very well.[2] I will make myself known to Desdemona. If she will return me my jewels, I will give over my suit and repent my unlawful solicitation; if not, assure yourself I will seek satisfaction[3] of you.

IAGO: You have said now?[4]

RODERIGO: Ay, and said nothing but what I protest intendment[5] of doing.

IAGO: Why, now I see there's mettle in thee, and even from this instant do build on thee a better opinion than ever before. Give me thy hand, Roderigo. Thou hast taken against me a most just exception; but yet I protest I have dealt most directly in thy affair.

RODERIGO: It hath not appeared.

IAGO: I grant indeed it hath not appeared, and your suspicion is not without wit and judgment. But, Roderigo, if thou hast that in thee indeed which I have greater reason to believe now than ever—I mean purpose, courage, and valor—this night show it. If thou the next night following enjoy not Desdemona, take me from this world with treachery and devise engines[6] for my life.

RODERIGO: Well, what is it? Is it within reason and compass?

IAGO: Sir, there is especial commission come from Venice to depute Cassio in Othello's place.

RODERIGO: Is that true? Why, then Othello and Desdemona return again to Venice.

IAGO: O, no; he goes into Mauritania and takes away with him the fair Desdemona, unless his abode be lingered here by some accident; wherein none can be so determinate[7] as the removing of Cassio.

RODERIGO: How do you mean, removing of him?

IAGO: Why, by making him uncapable of Othello's place—knocking out his brains.

RODERIGO: And that you would have me to do?

IAGO: Ay, if you dare do yourself a profit and a right. He sups tonight with a harlotry,[8] and thither will I go to him. He knows not yet of his honorable fortune. If you will watch his going thence, which I will fashion to fall out[9] between twelve and one, you may take him at your pleasure. I will be near to second your attempt, and he shall fall between us. Come, stand not amazed at it, but go along with me. I will show you such a necessity in his death that you shall think yourself bound to put it on him. It is now high[1] suppertime, and the night grows to waste.[2] About it.

RODERIGO: I will hear further reason for this.

IAGO: And you shall be satisfied. [*Exeunt.*]

2. Roderigo changes Iago's *very well*, "all right, then," to *not very well*, "not at all good."
3. Repayment. (The term normally means settling of accounts in a duel.)
4. Have you finished?
5. Intention.
6. Plots against.
7. Conclusive.
8. Slut.
9. Occur.
1. Fully.
2. Wastes away.

Scene 3[3]

[*Enter Othello, Lodovico, Desdemona, Emilia, and attendants.*]

LODOVICO: I do beseech you, sir, trouble yourself no further.
OTHELLO: O, pardon me; 'twill do me good to walk.
LODOVICO: Madam, good night. I humbly thank your ladyship.
DESDEMONA: Your honor is most welcome.
OTHELLO: Will you walk, sir?
O, Desdemona!
DESDEMONA: My lord?
OTHELLO: Get you to bed on th' instant. I will be returned forthwith. Dismiss your attendant there. Look 't be done.
DESDEMONA: I will, my lord.

[*Exit* (*Othello, with Lodovico and attendants.*)]

EMILIA: How goes it now? He looks gentler than he did.
DESDEMONA: He says he will return incontinent,° *immediately*
And hath commanded me to go to bed,
And bid me to dismiss you.
EMILIA: Dismiss me?
DESDEMONA: It was his bidding. Therefore, good Emilia,
Give me my nightly wearing, and adieu.
We must not now displease him.
EMILIA: I would you had never seen him!
DESDEMONA: So would not I. My love doth so approve him
That even his stubbornness,° his checks,° his frowns— *roughness / rebukes*
Prithee, unpin me—have grace and favor in them.

[(*Emilia prepares Desdemona for bed.*)]

EMILIA: I have laid those sheets you bade me on the bed.
DESDEMONA: All's one.[4] Good faith, how foolish are our minds!
If I do die before thee, prithee shroud me
In one of these same sheets.
EMILIA: Come, come, you talk.° *prattle*
DESDEMONA: My mother had a maid called Barbary.
She was in love, and he she loved proved mad° *wild*
And did forsake her. She had a song of "Willow."
An old thing 'twas, but it expressed her fortune,
And she died singing it. That song tonight
Will not go from my mind; I have much to do
But to go hang[5] my head all at one side
And sing it like poor Barbary. Prithee, dispatch.
EMILIA: Shall I go fetch your nightgown?° *dressing gown*
DESDEMONA: No, unpin me here.
This Lodovico is a proper° man. *handsome*
EMILIA: A very handsome man.
DESDEMONA: He speaks well.
EMILIA: I know a lady in Venice would have walked barefoot to Palestine for a touch of his nether lip.

3. Location: The citadel.
4. All right. It doesn't really matter.
5. I can scarcely keep myself from hanging.

DESDEMONA [(*singing*)]: "The poor soul sat sighing by a sycamore tree,
Sing all a green willow;[6]
Her hand on her bosom, her head on her knee,
Sing willow, willow, willow.
The fresh streams ran by her and murmured her moans;
Sing willow, willow, willow;
Her salt tears fell from her, and softened the stones—"
Lay by these.
[*Singing*] "Sing willow, willow, willow—"
Prithee, hie thee.° He'll come anon.° *hurry / right away*
[*Singing*] "Sing all a green willow must be my garland.
Let nobody blame him; his scorn I approve—"
Nay, that's not next.—Hark! Who is 't that knocks?
EMILIA: It's the wind.
DESDEMONA [(*singing*)]: "I called my love false love; but what said he then?
Sing willow, willow, willow;
If I court more women, you'll couch with more men."
So, get thee gone. Good night. Mine eyes do itch;
Doth that bode weeping?
EMILIA: 'Tis neither here nor there.
DESDEMONA: I have heard it said so. O, these men, these men!
Dost thou in conscience think—tell me, Emilia—
That there be women do abuse° their husbands *deceive*
In such gross kind?
EMILIA: There be some such, no question.
DESDEMONA: Wouldst thou do such a deed for all the world?
EMILIA: Why, would not you?
DESDEMONA: No, by this heavenly light!
EMILIA: Nor I neither by this heavenly light;
I might do 't as well i' the dark.
DESDEMONA: Wouldst thou do such a deed for all the world?
EMILIA: The world's a huge thing. It is a great price
For a small vice.
DESDEMONA: Good troth, I think thou wouldst not.
EMILIA: By my troth, I think I should, and undo 't when I had done. Marry, I would not do such a thing for a joint ring,[7] nor for measures of lawn,[8] nor for gowns, petticoats, nor caps, nor any petty exhibition.[9] But for all the whole world! Uds[1] pity, who would not make her husband a cuckold to make him a monarch? I should venture purgatory for 't.
DESDEMONA: Beshrew me if I would do such a wrong
For the whole world.
EMILIA: Why, the wrong is but a wrong i' the world, and having the world for your labor, 'tis a wrong in your own world, and you might quickly make it right.

6. A conventional emblem of disappointed love.
7. A ring made in separate halves.
8. Fine linen.
9. Gift.
1. God's.

DESDEMONA: I do not think there is any such woman.
EMILIA: Yes, a dozen, and as many
To th' vantage[2] as would store° the world they played[3] for. *populate*
But I do think it is their husbands' faults
If wives do fall. Say that they slack their duties° *marital duties*
And pour our treasures into foreign laps,[4]
Or else break out in peevish jealousies,
Throwing restraint upon us?[5] Or say they strike us,
Or scant our former having in despite?[6]
Why, we have galls,[7] and though we have some grace,
Yet have we some revenge. Let husbands know
Their wives have sense° like them. They see, and smell, *physical sense*
And have their palates both for sweet and sour,
As husbands have. What is it that they do
When they change us for others? Is it sport?° *sexual pastime*
I think it is. And doth affection° breed it? *passion*
I think it doth. Is 't frailty that thus errs?
It is so, too. And have not we affections,
Desires for sport, and frailty, as men have?
Then let them use us well; else let them know,
The ills we do, their ills instruct us so.
DESDEMONA: Good night, good night. God me such uses° send *practice*
Not to pick bad from bad, but by bad mend![8]

[*Exeunt.*]

ACT 5

Scene 1[9]

[*Enter Iago and Roderigo.*]
IAGO: Here stand behind this bulk.[1] Straight will he come.
Wear thy good rapier bare,° and put it home. *unsheathed*
Quick, quick! Fear nothing. I'll be at thy elbow.
It makes us or it mars us. Think on that,
And fix most firm thy resolution.
RODERIGO: Be near at hand. I may miscarry in 't.
IAGO: Here, at thy hand. Be bold, and take thy stand.
[(*Iago stands aside; Roderigo conceals himself.*)]
RODERIGO: I have no great devotion to the deed;
And yet he hath given me satisfying reasons.
'Tis but a man gone. Forth, my sword! He dies.
[(*He draws.*)]

2. In addition, to boot.
3. Gambled. Also, sported sexually.
4. I.e., are unfaithful, give what is rightfully ours (semen) to other women.
5. I.e., jealously restricting our freedom to see other men.
6. Reduce our allowance to spite us.
7. Are capable of resenting injury and insult.
8. Not to learn bad conduct from others' badness (as Emilia has suggested women learn from men), but to mend my ways by perceiving what badness is, making spiritual benefit out of evil and adversity.
9. Location: A street in Cyprus.
1. Framework projecting from the front of a shop.

IAGO: I have rubbed this young quat° almost to the sense,° *pimple / raw*
And he grows angry. Now, whether he kill Cassio
Or Cassio him, or each do kill the other,
Every way makes my gain. Live Roderigo,[2]
He calls me to a restitution large
Of gold and jewels that I bobbed° from him *swindled*
As gifts to Desdemona.
It must not be. If Cassio do remain,
He hath a daily beauty in his life
That makes me ugly; and besides, the Moor
May unfold° me to him; there stand I in much peril. *expose*
No, he must die. Be 't so. I hear him coming.
[*Enter Cassio.*]
RODERIGO [(*coming forth*)]: I know his gait, 'tis he.—Villain, thou diest!
[(*He attacks Cassio.*)]
CASSIO: That thrust had been mine enemy indeed,
But that my coat[3] is better than thou know'st.
I will make proof° of thine. *a test*
[(*He draws, and wounds Roderigo.*)]
RODERIGO: O, I am slain! [*He falls.*]
[(*Iago, from behind, wounds Cassio in the leg, and exits.*)]
CASSIO: I am maimed forever. Help, ho! Murder! Murder!
[*Enter Othello.*]
OTHELLO: The voice of Cassio! Iago keeps his word.
RODERIGO: O, villain that I am!
OTHELLO: It is even so.
CASSIO: O, help, ho! Light! A surgeon!
OTHELLO: 'Tis he. O brave Iago, honest and just,
That hast such noble sense of thy friend's wrong!
Thou teachest me. Minion,[4] your dear lies dead,
And your unblest fate hies.° Strumpet, I come. *hastens on*
Forth of° my heart those charms, thine eyes, are blotted; *from out*
Thy bed, lust-stained, shall with lust's blood be spotted. [*Exit Othello.*]
[*Enter Lodovico and Gratiano.*]
CASSIO: What ho! No watch? No passage?° Murder! Murder! *passers-by*
GRATIANO: 'Tis some mischance. The voice is very direful.
CASSIO: O, help!
LODOVICO: Hark!
RODERIGO: O, wretched villain!
LODOVICO: Two or three groan. 'Tis heavy° night; *thick, dark*
These may be counterfeits. Let's think 't unsafe
To come in° to the cry without more help. *approach*
[(*They remain near the entrance.*)]
RODERIGO: Nobody come? Then shall I bleed to death.
[*Enter Iago (in his shirtsleeves, with a light.)*]

2. If Roderigo lives.
3. Possibly a garment of mail under the outer clothing, or simply a tougher coat than Roderigo expected.
4. Hussy (i.e., Desdemona).

LODOVICO: Hark!
GRATIANO: Here's one comes in his shirt, with light and weapons.
IAGO: Who's there? Whose noise is this that cries on° murder? *cries out*
LODOVICO: We do not know.
IAGO: Did not you hear a cry?
CASSIO: Here, here! For heaven's sake, help me!
IAGO: What's the matter?
[(*He moves toward Cassio.*)]
GRATIANO [(*to Lodovico*)]: This is Othello's ancient, as I take it.
LODOVICO [(*to Gratiano*)]: The same indeed, a very valiant fellow.
IAGO [(*to Cassio*)]: What° are you here that cry so grievously? *who*
CASSIO: Iago? Oh, I am spoiled,° undone by villains! *ruined*
Give me some help.
IAGO: O me, Lieutenant! What villains have done this?
CASSIO: I think that one of them is hereabout,
And cannot make° away. *get*
IAGO: O treacherous villains!
[*To Lodovico and Gratiano.*] What are you there? Come in, and
give some help. [(*They advance.*)]
RODERIGO: O, help me there!
CASSIO: That's one of them.
IAGO: O murderous slave! O villain!
[(*He stabs Roderigo.*)]
RODERIGO: O damned Iago! O inhuman dog!
IAGO: Kill men i' the dark?—Where be these bloody thieves?—
How silent is this town!—Ho! Murder, murder!—
[(*To Lodovico and Gratiano.*)]
What may you be? Are you of good or evil?
LODOVICO: As you shall prove us, praise° us. *appraise*
IAGO: Signor Lodovico?
LODOVICO: He, sir.
IAGO: I cry you mercy.[5] Here's Cassio hurt by villains.
GRATIANO: Cassio?
IAGO: How is 't, brother?
CASSIO: My leg is cut in two.
IAGO: Marry, heaven forbid!
Light, gentlemen! I'll bind it with my shirt.
[(*He hands them the light and tends to Cassio's wound.*)]
[*Enter Bianca.*]
BIANCA: What is the matter, ho? Who is 't that cried?
IAGO: Who is 't that cried?
BIANCA: O my dear Cassio!
My sweet Cassio! O, Cassio, Cassio, Cassio!
IAGO: O, notable strumpet! Cassio, may you suspect

5. I beg your pardon.

Who they should be that have thus mangled you?
CASSIO: No.
GRATIANO: I am sorry to find you thus. I have been to seek you.
IAGO: Lend me a garter. [(*He applies a tourniquet.*)] So.—O, for a chair,° (*litter*)
To bear him easily hence!
BIANCA: Alas, he faints! O, Cassio, Cassio, Cassio!
IAGO: Gentlemen all, I do suspect this trash
To be a party in this injury.—
Patience awhile, good Cassio.—Come, come;
Lend me a light. [*He shines the light on Roderigo.*]
Know we this face or no?
Alas, my friend and my dear countryman
Roderigo! No.—Yes, sure.—O, heaven! Roderigo!
GRATIANO: What, of Venice?
IAGO: Even he, sir. Did you know him?
GRATIANO: Know him? Ay.
IAGO: Signor Gratiano? I cry your gentle° pardon. (*noble*)
These bloody accidents° must excuse my manners (*sudden events*)
That so neglected you.
GRATIANO: I am glad to see you.
IAGO: How do you, Cassio?—O a chair, a chair!
GRATIANO: Roderigo!
IAGO: He, he, 'tis he. [(*A litter is brought in.*)] O, that's well said;[6] the chair.
Some good man bear him carefully from hence;
I'll fetch the General's surgeon. [*To Bianca.*] For you, mistress,
Save you your labor.[7]—He that lies slain here, Cassio,
Was my dear friend. What malice° was between you? (*enmity*)
CASSIO: None in the world, nor do I know the man.
IAGO [(*to Bianca*)]: What, look you pale?—O, bear him out o' th' air.[8]
[(*Cassio and Roderigo are borne off.*)]
Stay you,[9] good gentlemen.—Look you pale, mistress?—
Do you perceive the gastness° of her eye?— (*terror*)
Nay, if you stare,[1] shall hear more anon.—
Behold her well; I pray you, look upon her.
Do you see, gentlemen? Nay, guiltiness
Will speak, though tongues were out of use.
[(*Enter Emilia.*)]
EMILIA: 'Las, what's the matter? What's the matter, husand?
IAGO: Cassio hath here been set on in the dark
By Roderigo and fellows that are scaped.
He's almost slain, and Roderigo dead.
EMILIA: Alas, good gentleman! Alas, good Cassio!
IAGO: This is the fruits of whoring. Prithee, Emilia,
Go know° of Cassio where he supped tonight. (*learn*)
[(*To Bianca.*)] What, do you shake at that?

6. Well done.
7. Never you mind tending Cassio.
8. Fresh air was thought to be dangerous for a wound.
9. Lodovico and Gratiano are evidently about to leave.
1. Iago pretends to interpret Bianca's wild looks as an involuntary confession of guilt.

BIANCA: He supped at my house, but I therefore shake not.
IAGO: O, did he so? I charge you go with me.
EMILIA: O, fie upon thee, strumpet!
BIANCA: I am no strumpet, but of life as honest° *chaste*
As you that thus abuse me.
EMILIA: As I? Faugh! Fie upon thee!
IAGO: Kind gentlemen, let's go see poor Cassio dressed.[2]—
Come, mistress, you must tell 's another tale.
Emilia, run you to the citadel
And tell my lord and lady what hath happed.—
Will you go on afore? [(*Aside.*)] This is the night
That either makes me or fordoes° me quite. [*Exeunt.*] *ruins*

Scene 2[3]

[*Enter Othello (with a light,) and Desdemona in her bed.*][4]
OTHELLO: It is the cause,[5] it is the cause, my soul.
Let me not name it to you, you chaste stars!
It is the cause. Yet I'll not shed her blood,
Nor scar that whiter skin of hers than snow,
And smooth as monumental alabaster.[6]
Yet she must die, else she'll betray more men.
Put out the light, and then put out the light.[7]
If I quench thee, thou flaming minister,[8]
I can again thy former light restore,
Should I repent me;° but once put out thy light, *change my mind*
Thou cunning'st pattern[9] of excelling nature,
I know not where is that Promethean heat[1]
That can thy light relume.° When I have plucked thy rose, *rekindle*
I cannot give it vital growth again;
It needs must wither. I'll smell thee on the tree.
[(*He kisses her.*)]
O, balmy breath, that dost almost persuade
Justice to break her sword! One more, one more.
Be thus when thou art dead, and I will kill thee,
And love thee after. One more, and that's the last.
[*He kisses her.*]
So sweet was ne'er so fatal. I must weep,
But they are cruel° tears. This sorrow's heavenly; *unrelenting*
It strikes where it doth love.[2] She wakes.
DESDEMONA: Who's there? Othello?
OTHELLO: Ay, Desdemona.
DESDEMONA: Will you come to bed, my lord?

2. Cassio's wounds dressed.
3. Location: A bedchamber in the citadel.
4. Either the curtains are drawn back to reveal the bed in a recessed area backstage, or the bed is "thrust out" onstage as the scene begins.
5. Cause of justice, the offense itself, which Othello must correct as an agent of justice.
6. Used in making tombs and funeral monuments.
7. The torch or lamp . . . Desdemona's life.
8. Torch or lamp that serves me.
9. You skillfully wrought perfect example.
1. Divine fire (alluding to the theft of fire from heaven by Prometheus).
2. Compare Hebrews 12.6: "For whom the Lord loveth he chasteneth."

OTHELLO: Have you prayed tonight, Desdemon?
DESDEMONA: Ay, my lord.
OTHELLO: If you bethink yourself of any crime° *sin*
Unreconciled as yet to heaven and grace,
Solicit° for it straight.° *pray / immediately*
DESDEMONA: Alack, my lord, what may you mean by that?
OTHELLO: Well, do it, and be brief. I will walk by.
I would not kill thy unpreparèd spirit.
No, heaven forfend!° I would not kill thy soul. *forbid*
DESDEMONA: Talk you of killing?
OTHELLO: Ay, I do.
DESDEMONA: Then heaven
Have mercy on me!
OTHELLO: Amen, with all my heart!
DESDEMONA: If you say so, I hope you will not kill me.
OTHELLO: Humh!
DESDEMONA: And yet I fear you; for you're fatal then
When your eyes roll so. Why I should fear I know not,
Since guiltiness I know not; but yet I feel I fear.
OTHELLO: Think on thy sins.
DESDEMONA: They are loves I bear to you.[3]
OTHELLO: Ay, and for that thou diest.
DESDEMONA: That death's unnatural that kills for loving.
Alas, why gnaw you so your nether lip?
Some bloody passion shakes your very frame.
These are portents; but yet I hope, I hope,
They do not point on[4] me.
OTHELLO: Peace, and be still!
DESDEMONA: I will so. What's the matter?
OTHELLO: That handkerchief which I so loved and gave thee
Thou gav'st to Cassio.
DESDEMONA: No, by my life and soul!
Send for the man and ask him.
OTHELLO: Sweet soul, take heed, take heed of perjury.
Thou art on thy deathbed.
DESDEMONA: Ay, but not yet to die.
OTHELLO: Yes, presently.° *immediately*
Therefore confess thee freely of thy sin;
For to deny each article with oath
Cannot remove nor choke the strong conception[5]
That I do groan withal.[6] Thou art to die.
DESDEMONA: Then Lord have mercy on me!
OTHELLO: I say, amen.
DESDEMONA: And have you mercy too! I never did
Offend° you in my life; never loved Cassio *wrong*
But with such general warranty° of heaven *sanction*

3. If I sinned, it was in loving you more than my father or more than God.
4. Point at, predict what is to happen to.
5. Belief in your guilt. Also, plan in my mind.
6. Groan at in sorrow. Also, as in giving birth.

As I might love. I never gave him token.
OTHELLO: By heaven, I saw my handkerchief in 's hand.
O, perjured woman! Thou dost stone° heart, *harden*
And makes me call what I intend to do
A murder, which I thought a sacrifice.
I saw the handkerchief.
DESDEMONA: He found it, then.
I never gave it him. Send for him hither;
Let him confess a truth.
OTHELLO: He hath confessed.
DESDEMONA: What, my lord?
OTHELLO: That he hath used thee.
DESDEMONA: How? Unlawfully?
OTHELLO: Ay.
DESDEMONA: He will not say so.
OTHELLO: No, his mouth is stopped;
Honest Iago hath ta'en order° for 't. *taken measures*
DESDEMONA: O, my fear interprets. What, is he dead?
OTHELLO: Had all his hairs been lives, my great revenge
Had stomach for them all.
DESDEMONA: Alas, he is betrayed and I undone! [(*She weeps.*)]
OTHELLO: Out, strumpet! Weep'st thou for him to my face?
DESDEMONA: O, banish me, my lord, but kill me not!
OTHELLO: Down, strumpet!
DESDEMONA: Kill me tomorrow; let me live tonight!
OTHELLO: Nay, if you strive—
DESDEMONA: But half an hour!
OTHELLO: Being done,[7] there is no pause.
DESDEMONA: But while I say one prayer!
OTHELLO: It is too late. [(*Smothers her.*)]
EMILIA [(*at the door*)]: My lord, my lord! What, ho! My lord, my lord!
OTHELLO: What noise is this? Not dead? Not yet quite dead?
I that am cruel am yet merciful;
I would not have thee linger in thy pain. [(*He dispatches her.*)]
So, so.
EMILIA [*within*]: What, ho! My lord, my lord!
OTHELLO: Who's there?
EMILIA [*within*]: O, good my lord, I would speak a word with you!
OTHELLO: Yes, 'tis Emilia.—By and by.—She's dead.
'Tis like° she comes to speak of Cassio's death.— *likely that*
The noise was here.[8] Ha! No more moving?
Still as the grave. Shall she come in? Were 't good?—
I think she stirs again. No. What's best to do?
If she come in, she'll sure speak to my wife.
My wife! My wife! What wife? I have no wife.

7. Since justice has begun its relentless course.

8. The Folio's *high* is possible, suggesting that the commotion of the attack on Cassio was loud.

O, insupportable! O, heavy hour!
Methinks it should be now a huge eclipse
Of sun and moon, and that th' affrighted globe
Should yawn[9] at alteration.[1]

EMILIA [(*within*)]: I do beseech you
That I may speak with you, O, good my lord!

OTHELLO: I had forgot thee. O, come in, Emilia.—
Soft,° by and by. Let me the curtains draw.— *wait a minute*
[(*He closes the bed curtains and opens the door.*)]
Where art thou?

[*Enter Emilia.*]

What's the matter with thee now?

EMILIA: O, my good lord, yonder's foul murders done!

OTHELLO: What, now?

EMILIA: But now, my lord.

OTHELLO: It is the very error° of the moon; *aberration, irregularity*
She comes more nearer earth than she was wont,
And makes men mad.

EMILIA: Cassio, my lord, hath killed a young Venetian
Called Roderigo.

OTHELLO: Roderigo killed?
And Cassio killed?

EMILIA: No, Cassio is not killed.

OTHELLO: Not Cassio killed? Then murder's out of tune,
And sweet revenge grows harsh.

DESDEMONA: O, falsely, falsely murdered!

EMILIA: O, Lord, what cry is that?

OTHELLO: That? What?

EMILIA: Out[2] and alas, that was my lady's voice.
[(*She opens the bed-curtains.*)]
Help, help, ho, help! O lady, speak again!
Sweet Desdemona! O sweet mistress, speak!

DESDEMONA: A guiltless death I die.

EMILIA: O, who hath done this deed?

DESDEMONA: Nobody; I myself. Farewell.
Commend me to my kind lord. O, farewell! [(*She dies.*)]

OTHELLO: Why, how should she be murdered?

EMILIA: Alas, who knows?

OTHELLO: You heard her say herself it was not I.

EMILIA: She said so. I must needs report the truth.

OTHELLO: She's like a liar gone to burning hell!
'Twas I that killed her.

EMILIA: O, the more angel she,
And you the blacker devil!

9. Gape in amazement, i.e., move in an earthquake. (According to Pliny, earthquakes often happen during eclipses.)

1. At these cataclysmic events in nature, well suited to express the horror of Desdemona's death.

2. A cry of dismay, intensifying *alas*.

OTHELLO: She turned to folly,[3] and she was a whore.
EMILIA: Thou dost belie° her, and thou art a devil. *slander*
OTHELLO: She was false as water.
EMILIA: Thou art rash as fire to say
That she was false. O, she was heavenly true!
OTHELLO: Cassio did top her. Ask thy husband else.[4]
O, I were damned beneath all depth in hell
But that I did proceed upon just grounds
To this extremity. Thy husband knew it all.
EMILIA: My husband?
OTHELLO: Thy husband.
EMILIA: That she was false to wedlock?
OTHELLO: Ay, with Cassio. Nay, had she been true,
If heaven would make me such another world
Of one entire and perfect chrysolite,° *precious topaz*
I'd not have sold her for it.
EMILIA: My husband?
OTHELLO: Ay, 'twas he that told me on her first.
An honest man he is, and hates the slime
That sticks on filthy deeds.
EMILIA: My husband?
OTHELLO: What needs this iterance,° woman? I say thy husband. *repetition*
EMILIA: O, mistress, villainy hath made mocks° with love! *made sport*
My husband say she was false?
OTHELLO: He, woman;
I say thy husband. Dost understand the word?
My friend, thy husband, honest, honest Iago.
EMILIA: If he say so, may his pernicious soul
Rot half a grain a day! He lies to th' heart.
She was too fond of her most filthy bargain.
OTHELLO: Ha? [(*He draws.*)]
EMILIA: Do thy worst!
This deed of thine is no more worthy heaven
Than thou wast worthy her.
OTHELLO: Peace, you were best.[5]
EMILIA: Thou hast not half that power to do me harm
As I have to be hurt.° O gull!° O dolt! *to endure hurt / dupe*
As ignorant as dirt! Thou hast done a deed—
I care not for thy sword; I'll make thee known,
Though I lost twenty lives.—Help! Help, ho, help!
The Moor hath killed my mistress! Murder, murder!
[*Enter Montano, Gratiano, and Iago.*]
MONTANO: What is the matter? How now, General?
EMILIA: O, are you come, Iago? You have done well,
That men must lay their murders on your neck.

3. I.e., wantonness, fleshly sin.
4. I.e., if you don't believe me.
5. It would be best for you.

GRATIANO: What is the matter?
EMILIA [*to Iago*]:
Disprove this villain, if thou be'st a man.
He says thou toldst him that his wife was false.
I know thou didst not; thou'rt not such a villain.
Speak, for my heart is full.
IAGO: I told him what I thought, and told no more
Than what he found himself was apt° and true. *plausible*
EMILIA: But did you ever tell him she was false?
IAGO: I did.
EMILIA: You told a lie, an odious, damnèd lie!
Upon my soul, a lie, a wicked lie.
She false with Cassio? Did you say with Cassio?
IAGO: With Cassio, mistress. Go to, charm[6] your tongue.
EMILIA: I will not charm my tongue; I am bound to speak.
My mistress here lies murdered in her bed—
ALL: O, heavens forfend!
EMILIA: And your reports have set the murder on.
OTHELLO: Nay, stare not, masters. It is true indeed.
GRATIANO: 'Tis a strange truth.
MONTANO: O, monstrous act!
EMILIA: Villainy, villainy, villainy!
I think upon 't—I think I smell 't! O, villainy!
I thought so then[7]—I'll kill myself for grief—
O, villainy, villainy!
IAGO: What, are you mad? I charge you, get you home.
EMILIA: Good gentlemen, let me have leave to speak.
'Tis proper I obey him, but not now.
Perchance, Iago, I will ne'er go home.
OTHELLO: O! O! O! [(*Othello falls on the bed.*)][8]
EMILIA: Nay, lay thee down and roar,
For thou hast killed the sweetest innocent
That e'er did lift up eye.[9]
OTHELLO [*rising*]: O, she was foul!
I scarce did know you, uncle. There lies your niece,
Whose breath indeed these hands have newly stopped.
I know this act shows° horrible and grim. *looks*
GRATIANO: Poor Desdemon! I am glad thy father's dead.
Thy match was mortal to him, and pure grief
Shore his old thread[1] in twain. Did he live now,
This sight would make him do a desperate turn,° *deed*
Yea, curse his better angel from his side,
And fall to reprobance.[2]
OTHELLO: 'Tis pitiful. But yet Iago knows
That she with Cassio hath the act of shame

6. Keep silent (as though by a magic spell).
7. Perhaps in 3.3 and 4.2.
8. This direction is from the Quarto.
9. Lift her eyes to heaven.
1. Sheared the thread of his old age (as Atropos, one of the three Fates, was thought to do).
2. Damnation, i.e., suicide.

A thousand times committed. Cassio confessed it;
And she did gratify° his amorous works *reward*
With that recognizance° and pledge of love *token*
Which I first gave her. I saw it in his hand;
It was a handkerchief, an antique token
My father gave my mother.

EMILIA: O, God! O, heavenly God!

IAGO: Zounds, hold your peace.

EMILIA: 'Twill out, 'twill out! I peace?
No, I will speak as liberal as the north.[3]
Let heaven and men and devils, let them all,
All, all, cry shame against me, yet I'll speak.

IAGO: Be wise, and get you home.

EMILIA: I will not.

[(*Iago threatens Emilia.*)]

GRATIANO: Fie,
Your sword upon a woman?

EMILIA: O, thou dull Moor! That handkerchief thou speak'st of
I found by fortune and did give my husband;
For often, with a solemn earnestness,
More than indeed belonged° to such a trifle, *was appropriate*
He begged of me to steal 't.

IAGO: Villainous whore!

EMILIA: She give it Cassio? No, alas! I found it,
And I did give 't my husband.

IAGO: Filth, thou liest!

EMILIA: By heaven, I do not, I do not, gentlemen.
O, murderous coxcomb![4] What should such a fool
Do with so good a wife?

OTHELLO: Are there no stones[5] in heaven
But what serves for the thunder?—Precious° villain! *utter*

[(*He runs at Iago; Montano disarms Othello. Iago, from behind, stabs Emilia.*)][6]

GRATIANO: The woman falls! Sure he hath killed his wife.

EMILIA: Ay, ay. O, lay me by my mistress' side.

[(*Exit Iago.*)]

GRATIANO: He's gone, but his wife's killed.

MONTANO: 'Tis a notorious villain. Take you this weapon,
Which I have here recovered from the Moor.
Come, guard the door without. Let him not pass,
But kill him rather. I'll after that same villain,
For 'tis a damnèd slave.

[*Exit* (*with all but Othello and Emilia, who has been laid by Desdemona's side.*)]

OTHELLO: I am not valiant neither,
But every puny whipster[7] gets my sword.

3. Freely as the north wind (blows).
4. Fool (addressed to Othello).
5. Bolts, such as those used for thunderbolts.
6. The quarto text reads, "The Moor runs at Iago. Iago kills his wife." The Quarto also specifies the exit of Iago below.
7. Contemptible fellow (one who is always ready to whip out his sword).

But why should honor[8] outlive honesty?° *integrity*
Let it go all.

EMILIA: What did thy song bode, lady?
Hark, canst thou hear me? I will play the swan,
And die in music. [*She sings*.] "Willow, willow, willow."
Moor, she was chaste. She loved thee, cruel Moor.
So come my soul to bliss as I speak true.
So speaking as I think, alas, I die. [*She dies*.]

OTHELLO: I have another weapon in this chamber;
It was a sword of Spain, the ice-brook's temper[9]—
O, here it is. [(*He finds a sword*.)] Uncle, I must come forth.

GRATIANO: [(*within*)] If thou attempt it, it will cost thee dear.
Thou hast no weapon, and perforce must suffer.

OTHELLO: Look in upon me then and speak with me,
Or, naked° as I am, I will assault thee. *unarmed*

[(*Enter Gratiano*.)]

GRATIANO: What is the matter?

OTHELLO: Behold, I have a weapon;
A better never did itself sustain
Upon a soldier's thigh. I have seen the day
That, with this little arm and this good sword,
I have made my way through more impediments
Than twenty times your stop.[1] But O, vain boast!
Who can control his fate? 'Tis not so now.
Be not afraid, though you do see me weaponed;
Here is my journey's end, here is my butt[2]
And very seamark[3] of my utmost sail.

[(*Gratiano steps back*.)]

Do you go back dismayed? 'Tis a lost° fear; *wasted*
Man but a rush[4] against Othello's breast
And he retires. Where should Othello go?

[(*He turns to Desdemona*.)]

Now, how dost thou look now? O, ill-starred wench!
Pale as thy smock! When we shall meet at compt,° *Judgment Day*
This look of thine will hurl my soul from heaven,
And fiends will snatch at it. Cold, cold, my girl?
Even like thy chastity. O, cursèd, cursèd slave![5]
Whip me, ye devils,
From the possession of this heavenly sight!
Blow me about in winds! Roast me in sulfur!
Wash me in steep-down gulfs of liquid fire!
O, Desdemon! Dead, Desdemon! Dead! O! O!

[*Enter Lodovico, Cassio* [(*carried in a litter*)],[6] *Montano, and Iago* [(*prisoner*)], *with officers*.]

8. The bravery for which one enjoys a soldier's reputation.
9. Tempered in ice-cold water.
1. Power (to stop).
2. Goal, limit (an archery term).
3. Beacon (marking his destination or limit).
4. Wield no more than a reed.
5. Othello himself.
6. The Quarto specifies that Cassio is "in a chair."

LODOVICO: Where is this rash and most unfortunate man?
OTHELLO: That's he that was Othello. Here I am.
LODOVICO: Where is that viper? Bring the villain forth.
[(*Iago is led forward.*)]
OTHELLO: I look down towards his feet;[7] but that's a fable.
If that thou be'st a devil, I cannot kill thee.
[(*He wounds Iago.*)]
LODOVICO: Wrench his sword from him. [(*Othello is disarmed.*)]
IAGO: I bleed, sir, but not killed.
OTHELLO: I am not sorry neither. I'd have thee live,
For in my sense[8] 'tis happiness to die.
LODOVICO: O thou Othello, that was once so good,
Fall'n in the practice[9] of a cursèd slave,° *villain*
What shall be said to thee?
OTHELLO: Why, anything.
An honorable murderer, if you will,
For naught I did in hate, but all in honor.
LODOVICO: This wretch hath part confessed his villainy.
Did you and he consent° in Cassio's death? *agree*
OTHELLO: Ay.
CASSIO: Dear General, I never gave you cause.
OTHELLO: I do believe it, and I ask your pardon.
Will you, I pray, demand that demi-devil
Why he hath thus ensnared my soul and body?
IAGO: Demand me nothing. What you know, you know.
From this time forth I never will speak word.
LODOVICO: What, not to pray?
GRATIANO: Torments° will ope your lips. *torture*
OTHELLO: Well, thou dost best.
LODOVICO: Sir, you shall understand what hath befall'n,
Which, as I think, you know not. Here is a letter
Found in the pocket of the slain Roderigo;
And here another. [(*He produces letters.*)] The one of them imports
The death of Cassio, to be undertook
By Roderigo.
OTHELLO: O villain!
CASSIO: Most heathenish and most gross!° *monstrous*
LODOVICO [(*showing another paper*)]: Now here's another discontented paper
Found in his pocket too. And this, it seems,
Roderigo meant t' have sent this damnèd villain;
But that belike° Iago in the interim *most likely*
Came in and satisfied him.[1]
OTHELLO: O thou pernicious caitiff!—
How came you, Cassio, by that handkerchief
That was my wife's?

7. I.e., to see if they are cloven, as the devil's are fabled to be.
8. To one who feels as I do.
9. Through the plotting, into the snare.
1. Interposed and gave him satisfactory explanation.

CASSIO: I found it in my chamber;
And he himself confessed but even now
That there he dropped it for a special purpose
Which wrought to his desire.[2]
OTHELLO: O fool, fool, fool!
CASSIO: There is besides in Roderigo's letter
How he upbraids Iago, that he made him
Brave° me upon the watch, whereon it came[3] *defy*
That I was cast;° and even but now he spake, *dismissed*
After long seeming dead, Iago hurt him,
Iago set him on.
LODOVICO: [(*to Othello*)] You must forsake this room and go with us.
Your power and your command is taken off,° *taken away*
And Cassio rules in Cyprus. For this slave,
If there be any cunning cruelty
That can torment him much and hold him long,[4]
It shall be his. You shall close prisoner rest° *remain*
Till that the nature of your fault be known
To the Venetian state.—Come, bring away.
OTHELLO: Soft you;° a word or two before you go. *one moment*
I have done the state some service, and they know't.
No more of that. I pray you, in your letters,
When you shall these unlucky° deeds relate, *unfortunate*
Speak of me as I am; nothing extenuate,
Nor set down aught in malice. Then must you speak
Of one that loved not wisely but too well;
Of one not easily jealous but, being wrought,[5]
Perplexed° in the extreme; of one whose hand, *distraught*
Like the base Indian,[6] threw a pearl away
Richer than all his tribe; of one whose subdued[7] eyes,
Albeit unusèd to the melting mood,
Drops tears as fast as the Arabian trees
Their medicinable gum.° Set you down this; *myrrh*
And say besides that in Aleppo once,
Where a malignant and a turbaned Turk
Beat a Venetian and traduced the state,
I took by th' throat the circumcisèd dog
And smote him, thus. [(*He stabs himself.*)][8]
LODOVICO: O, bloody period!° *end, conclusion*
GRATIANO: All that is spoke is marred.
OTHELLO: I kissed thee ere I killed thee. No way but this,
Killing myself, to die upon a kiss.
[*He kisses Desdemona and dies.*]

2. Worked out as he wished, fitted in with his plan.
3. Whereof it came about.
4. Keep him alive a long time (during his torture).
5. Worked upon, worked into a frenzy.
6. This reading from the Quarto pictures an ignorant savage who cannot recognize the value of a precious jewel. The Folio reading, *Iudean* or *Judean* i.e., infidel or disbeliever, may refer to Herod, who slew Miriam in a fit of jealousy, or to Judas Iscariot, the betrayer of Christ.
7. I.e., overcome by grief.
8. This direction is in the Quarto text.

CASSIO: This did I fear, but thought he had no weapon;
For he was great of heart.
LODOVICO [*to Iago*]: O Spartan dog,[9]
More fell° than anguish, hunger, or the sea! *cruel*
Look on the tragic loading of this bed.
This is thy work. The object poisons sight;
Let it be hid.[1] Gratiano, keep° the house, *remain in*
[(*The bed curtains are drawn*)]
And seize upon the fortunes of the Moor,
For they succeed on you.[2] [*To Cassio.*] To you, Lord Governor,
Remains the censure° of this hellish villain, *sentencing*
The time, the place, the torture. O, enforce it!
Myself will straight aboard, and to the state
This heavy act with heavy heart relate. [*Exeunt.*]

King Lear

King Lear has the power to move us as no other play of Shakespeare's can. The tragedy enacts the suffering endured by a father who rejects the one child who truly loves him. Lear's downfall is set in motion through his desire to measure love, an emotional commitment that cannot be quantified. Equally disastrous is his decision to bestow power over the kingdom to the daughters who can best meet his childish desire for public protestations of affection. When Lear demands to know, "Which of you shall we say doth love us most?" Goneril boasts of loving Lear "more than word can wield the matter," and Regan protests herself "an enemy to all other joys." Cordelia, however, recognizes the emotional bankruptcy of this contest and refuses to speak in such hyperbole. Lear banishes her and hands over the reins of power to her sisters, only to discover they will not meet his exigent demands with any more patience than he granted to Cordelia. Like father like daughter, Goneril and Regan banish the father who banished their sister. Lear blames his unkind daughters for all his troubles. He curses them, threatening them with "the terrors of the earth," as he attempts to ward off his descent into grief and madness. When, homeless, he enters the storm on the heath, he experiences the lot of his poorest subjects. Standing by him in all this are his Fool, who speaks truth through nonsense, and the disguised Kent, who for his outspoken defense of Cordelia had been banished by Lear. Paradoxically, only by becoming mad does Lear achieve some measure of wisdom. Dislocated and deranged, he discovers his error only in time to receive Cordelia's comfort and forgiveness before she is executed at the command of those his fatal misjudgment put into power. The play makes us confront human brutality and the lack of any comforting divine intervention, yet it also allows us to witness Lear's learning through suffering. This combination of profound suffering, brought on by human error, and great insight into that same weakness makes this the closest of all Shakespeare's tragedies to the works of the ancient Greek tragedians.

9. Spartan dogs were noted for their savagery and silence.
1. I.e., draw the bed curtains. (No stage direction specifies that the dead are to be carried offstage at the end of the play.)
2. Take legal possession of Othello's property, which passes as though by inheritance to you.

This combination of pathos and understanding is in part achieved through Shakespeare's very original handling of source material. First performed at court in December 1606, Shakespeare's *Lear* comes after a long line of versions of the story that end happily. In earlier versions of the story—including Raphael Holinshed's *Chronicles* (1587), Edmund Spenser's *The Faerie Queene* 2.10.27–32, and the play *The True Chronicle History of King Leir* (written c. 1594; published 1605)—the King of France restores Lear to his power after he has been dethroned. Not only is there no tragic ending in the earlier *King Leir* but there is no storm on the heath and no descent into madness. In Holinshed's *Chronicles* and Spenser's *Faerie Queene* 2.10, Cordelia commits suicide after the death of her father, rather than being executed in front of him. In contrast, Shakespeare's choice to have Lear attempt to save Cordelia by slaying her executioner makes the once exigent and self-centered father defiantly heroic and self-sacrificing in his final hour. Beyond this, Shakespeare's Lear has to live through Cordelia's death, which increases the depth of his tragic suffering.

Not only did Shakespeare alter the central plot, but he added to it the subplot of the gullible Gloucester, inspired by the story of the blinded king of Paphlagonia from Sir Philip Sidney's prose romance *Arcadia*. Edmund, Gloucester's bastard son, convinces his too trusting father that his legitimate son Edgar is plotting to kill him. Gloucester then is turned over by Edmund to Goneril who orders his eyes to be "plucked out." Later, in his blindness Gloucester is aided by Edgar now disguised as a mad beggar. Only in his blindness does Gloucester come to understand his mistaken judgment. The subplot of his experience of insight through blindness mirrors Lear's experience of wisdom through madness. The two plots both make us reflect on how human beings deceive themselves and collude in their own destruction, and yet rise above mere victimhood through the capacity to acknowledge their part in all this. Strikingly both plots deal with the cruelty of parents against children and children against parents, along with the difficulty in those relationships of trusting love and resisting manipulation.

King Lear interrogates the character of the filial bond, and the extent to which human relationships are governed by "nature." The two meanings of the word "kind," signifying both generous and related by blood, are played off of each other repeatedly and underscore our troubled awareness of how the parent-child relationship should but does not guarantee kind treatment. The play is haunted by the multiple meanings of the words "nature" and "natural," referring to the natural world of flora and fauna, and to the social world of human nature. Edmund is Lear's "natural" or illegitimate son. Lear's legitimate daughters Goneril and Regan are called monstrous and "unnatural." We are made to question the relation between what is deemed "natural" by biology on the one hand and by custom on the other. How can Lear claim to have "loved [Cordelia] most" and so easily disinherit her? How natural is Edmund's worship of the "Nature" he calls his "goddess"? Why does Lear expect Goneril and Regan to treat him kindly? Is the unforgiving storm on the heath the ultimate experience of nature? Where does Cordelia's capacity to treat Lear kindly come from? Is it her nature as a daughter? Or is there something else at work here, something beyond what was believed at the time of the play to be part of the natural hierarchical order of the family?

At the end of the play the incredible goodness of Cordelia is defeated by the forces of evil, as represented by her sisters and the man they fought over, Edmund. While Edmund repents his evil at the end, her sisters destroy each other. Significantly, those who have managed to conceal their true identities survive—Kent, who has played the role of Caius, the servant of Lear, and Edgar, who has feigned the role of Tom o' Bedlam as he protected his blinded father Gloucester. Ironically, it is in masquerading that they prove themselves to be most true, or loyal. Kent and Edgar embody the ability to adapt to changing conditions and yet to remain true to one's cause in the face of the arbitrary and capricious will of those in power. That the imagination has a role to play in this survival is no better illustrated than in Edgar's convincing his blind father that he has jumped off a cliff and been saved from death. Even such moments of hope, however, withhold any easy comfort. Edgar's words to

Gloucester—"Men must endure / Their going hence, even as their coming hither, / Ripeness is all," (5.2.7–8)—suggest the notion that our lives are made more meaningful by our awareness of and preparation for death. Yet, Gloucester's rejoinder "And that's true too," could be read as darkly and humorously undercutting the solace offered by such wisdom.

King Lear represents the terrifying abyss of human cruelty causing a suffering that the loyal love of Edgar, Kent, and Cordelia can comfort but never fully heal. Perhaps it is this very searching look at the way we humans torture each other that made the play the most celebrated at the end of the most violent century in history. If eighteenth-century audiences were outraged by the extremity of the tragedy and could only bear to see it acted with the happy ending, provided in Nahum Tate's adaptation (1687), those of the twentieth century could see parallels between Shakespeare's desperadoes on the heath and the derelicts of Samuel Beckett's dark comedies. At the start of the twenty-first century, you, a new generation of readers, will inevitably make the play your own through a fresh reading of how suffering and love mysteriously intertwine in *King Lear*.

King Lear*

The Names of the Actors

KING LEAR
GONERIL, REGAN, CORDELIA, } *Lear's daughters*
DUKE OF ALBANY, *Goneril's husband*
DUKE OF CORNWALL, *Regan's husband*
KING OF FRANCE, *Cordelia's suitor and husband*
DUKE OF BURGUNDY, *suitor to Cordelia*
EARL OF KENT, *later disguised as Caius*
EARL OF GLOUCESTER
EDGAR, *Gloucester's son and heir, later disguised as poor Tom*
EDMUND, *Gloucester's bastard son*
OSWALD, *Goneril's steward*
A KNIGHT *serving King Lear*
Lear's FOOL
CURAN, *in Gloucester's household*
GENTLEMEN
Three SERVANTS
OLD MAN, *a tenant of Gloucester*
Three MESSENGERS
A GENTLEMAN *attending Cordelia as a Doctor*
Two CAPTAINS
HERALD
Knights, Gentlemen, Attendants, Servants, Officers, Soldiers, Trumpeters

SCENE: *Britain*]

ACT 1

Scene 1[1]

[*Enter Kent, Gloucester, and Edmund.*]

KENT: I thought the King had more affected[2] the Duke of Albany[3] than Cornwall.

GLOUCESTER: It did always seem so to us; but now in the division of the kingdom it appears not which of the dukes he values most, for equalities are so weighed that curiosity in neither can make choice of either's moiety.[4]

KENT: Is not this your son, my lord?

* The text and notes in this selection are based on the sixth edition of Bevington.
1. Location: King Lear's palace.
2. Favored.
3. I.e., Scotland.
4. The shares balance so equally that close scrutiny cannot find advantage in either's portion.

GLOUCESTER: His breeding,[5] sir, hath been at my charge. I have so often blushed to acknowledge him that now I am brazed[6] to't.

KENT: I cannot conceive[7] you.

GLOUCESTER: Sir, this young fellow's mother could; whereupon she grew round-wombed and had indeed, sir, a son for her cradle ere she had a husband for her bed. Do you smell a fault?

KENT: I cannot wish the fault undone, the issue[8] of it being so proper.[9]

GLOUCESTER: But I have a son, sir, by order of law,[1] some year[2] elder than this, who yet is no dearer in my account. Though this knave[3] came something[4] saucily to the world before he was sent for, yet was his mother fair, there was good sport at his making, and the whoreson must be acknowledged.—Do you know this noble gentleman, Edmund?

EDMUND: No, my lord.

GLOUCESTER: My lord of Kent. Remember him hereafter as my honorable friend.

EDMUND: My services to Your Lordship.

KENT: I must love you, and sue[5] to snow you better.

EDMUND: Sir, I shall study deserving.[6]

GLOUCESTER: He hath been out[7] nine years, and away he shall again. The King is coming.

[*Sennet.*[8] *Enter (one bearing a coronet,*[9] *then) King Lear, Cornwall, Albany, Goneril, Regan, Cordelia, and attendants.*]

LEAR: Attend[1] the lords of France and Burgundy, Gloucester.

GLOUCESTER: I shall, my liege.° [*Exit.*] *lord*

LEAR: Meantime we[2] shall express our darker° purpose. *secret*
Give me the map there. [(*He takes a map.*)] Know that we have divided
In three our kingdom; and 'tis our fast° intent *firm*
To shake all cares and business from our age,
Conferring them on younger strengths while we
Unburdened crawl toward death. Our son of Cornwall,
And you, our no less loving son of Albany,
We have this hour a constant will to publish
Our daughters' several dowers,[3] that future strife
May be prevented now. The princes, France and Burgundy,
Great rivals in our youngest daughter's love,
Long in our court have made their amorous sojourn
And here are to be answered. Tell me, my daughters—
Since now we will divest us both of rule,
Interest° of territory, cares of state— *possession*
Which of you shall we say doth love us most,

5. His raising has been at my expense.
6. Hardened.
7. Understand, but Gloucester puns on the sense of "become pregnant."
8. Offspring.
9. Excellent, handsome.
1. Legitimate.
2. Estimation.
3. Young fellow.
4. Somewhat.

5. Petition, beg.
6. Strive to be worthy of your esteem.
7. Abroad, absent.
8. Trumpet signal announcing a procession.
9. This stage direction is from the Quarto; a coronet signifies nobility below the rank of a king.
1. Wait upon.
2. The royal use of "we" for "I."
3. I firmly resolve to make known each daughter's dowry, or inheritance for marriage.

That we our largest bounty may extend
Where nature doth with merit challenge?[4] Goneril,
Our eldest born, speak first.
GONERIL: Sir, I love you more than words can wield° the matter, *handle, convey*
Dearer than eyesight, space, and liberty,
Beyond what can be valued, rich or rare,
No less than life, with grace, health, beauty, honor;
As much as child e'er loved, or father found;
A love that makes breath poor and speech unable.[5]
Beyond all manner of so much I love you.
CORDELIA [*aside*]: What shall Cordelia speak? Love and be silent.
LEAR [*indicating on map*]: Of all these bounds, even from this line to this,
With shadowy° forests and with champains riched,° *shady / fertile plains*
With plenteous rivers and wide-skirted meads,[6]
We make thee lady. To thine and Albany's issue
Be this perpetual.—What says our second daughter,
Our dearest Regan, wife of Cornwall? Speak.
REGAN: I am made of that self mettle[7] as my sister,
And prize me at her worth.[8] In my true heart
I find she names my very deed of love;[9]
Only she comes too short, that I profess
Myself an enemy to all other joys
Which the most precious square of sense possesses,[1]
And find I am alone felicitate° *made happy*
In your dear Highness' love.
CORDELIA [(*aside*)]: Then poor Cordelia!
And yet not so, since I am sure my love's
More ponderous° than my tongue. *weighty*
LEAR: To thee and thine hereditary ever
Remain this ample third of our fair kingdom,
No less in space, validity, and pleasure
Than that conferred on Goneril.—Now, our joy,
Although our last and least, to whose young love
The vines° of France and milk° of Burgundy *vineyards / pastures*
Strive to be interessed,° what can you say to draw° *establish a claim / win*
A third more opulent than your sisters'? Speak.
CORDELIA: Nothing, my lord.
LEAR: Nothing?
CORDELIA: Nothing.
LEAR: Nothing will come of nothing. Speak again.
CORDELIA: Unhappy that I am, I cannot heave
My heart into my mouth. I love Your Majesty
According to my bond,° no more nor less. *duty*

4. Where natural affection and merit claim our bounty.
5. Utterance impoverished and speech inadequate.
6. Abundant rivers bordered with wide meadows.
7. That same spirited temperament.
8. And value myself as her equal.
9. Describes my love in action.
1. Which the most delicately sensitive part of my nature can enjoy.

LEAR: How, how, Cordelia? Mend your speech a little,
Lest you may mar your fortunes.
CORDELIA: Good my lord,
You have begot me, bred me, loved me. I
Return those duties back as are right fit,
Obey you, love you, and most honor you.
Why have my sisters husbands if they say
They love you all?° Hapły, when I shall wed, *exclusively*
That lord whose hand must take my plight[2] shall carry
Half my love with him, half my care and duty.
Sure I shall never marry like my sisters,
To love my father all.
LEAR: But goes thy heart with this?
CORDELIA: Ay, my good lord.
LEAR: So young, and so untender?
CORDELIA: So young, my lord, and true.
LEAR: Let it be so! Thy truth then be thy dower!
For, by the sacred radiance of the sun,
The mysteries of Hecate[3] and the night,
By all the operation of the orbs
From whom we do exist and cease to be,
Here I disclaim all my paternal care,
Propinquity, and property of blood,[4]
And as a stranger to my heart and me
Hold thee from this[5] forever. The barbarous Scythian,[6]
Or he that makes his generation messes[7]
To gorge his appetite, shall to my bosom
Be as well neighbored, pitied, and relieved
As thou my sometime° daughter. *former*
KENT: Good my liege—
LEAR: Peace, Kent!
Come not between the dragon and his wrath.
I loved her most, and thought to set my rest
On her kind nursery.[8] [(*To Cordelia*)] Hence, and avoid my sight!—
So be my grave my peace, as here I give
Her father's heart from her. Call France. Who stirs?
Call Burgundy. [(*Exit one.*)]
Cornwall and Albany,
With my two daughters' dowers digest the third.[9]
Let pride, which she calls plainness, marry her.
I do invest you jointly with my power,
Preeminence, and all the large effects
That troop with majesty. Ourself by monthly course,

2. Marriage pledge.
3. Secret rites of the goddess of witchcraft and the moon.
4. Close kinship, and rights and duties entailed in blood ties.
5. This time forth.
6. Scythians were typed by classical authors as savages.
7. He that makes meals of his children.
8. To rely wholly on her nursing.
9. Put Cordelia's inheritance in with those of the other two.

With reservation of an hundred knights
By you to be sustained,[1] shall our abode
Make with you by due turns. Only we shall retain
The name and all th'addition[2] to a king.
The sway,[3] revenue, execution of the rest,
Belovèd sons, be yours, which to confirm,
This coronet part between you.
KENT: Royal Lear,
Whom I have ever honored as my king,
Loved as my father, as my master followed,
As my great patron thought on in my prayers—
LEAR: The bow is bent and drawn. Make from[4] the shaft.
KENT: Let it fall rather, though the fork invade
The region of my heart.[5] Be Kent unmannerly
When Lear is mad. What wouldst thou do, old man?
Think'st thou that duty shall have dread to speak
When power to flattery bows?
To plainness honor's bound[6]
When majesty falls to folly. Reserve thy state,[7]
And in thy best consideration check
This hideous rashness. Answer my life my judgment,[8]
Thy youngest daughter does not love thee least,
Nor are those emptyhearted whose low sounds
Reverb no hollowness.[9]
LEAR: Kent, on thy life, no more.
KENT: My life I never held but as a pawn
To wage against thine enemies, nor fear to lose it,
Thy safety being motive.[1]
LEAR: Out of my sight!
KENT: See better, Lear, and let me still remain
The true blank[2] of thine eye.
LEAR: Now, by Apollo—
KENT: Now, by Apollo, King,
Thou swear'st thy gods in vain.
LEAR: Oh, vassal! Miscreant![3]
[(*Laying his hand on his sword.*)]
ALBANY, CORNWALL: Dear sir, forbear.
KENT: Kill thy physician, and the fee bestow
Upon the foul disease. Revoke thy gift,
Or whilst I can vent clamor from my throat
I'll tell thee thou dost evil.
LEAR: Hear me, recreant,° on thine allegiance hear me! *traitor*
That thou hast sought to make us break our vows,

1. Reserving the right to be attended by 100 knights, whom you will have to support.
2. The honors and prerogatives of a king.
3. Sovereign authority.
4. Get out of the way of.
5. Let the arrow strike even if the barbed head pierce my heart.
6. Loyalty demands frankness.
7. Retain control of your kingdom.
8. I wager my life on my judgment.
9. Do not reverberate emptiness and insincerity.
1. Your safety being what prompts me to act.
2. Center of the target.
3. Literally "unbeliever"; hence, villain.

Which we durst never yet, and with strained pride
To come betwixt our sentence and our power,[4]
Which nor our nature nor our place can bear,[5]
Our potency made good, take thy reward.
Five days we do allot thee for provision
To shield thee from disasters of the world,
And on the sixth to turn thy hated back
Upon our kingdom. If on the tenth day following
Thy banished trunk° be found in our dominions, *body*
The moment is thy death. Away! By Jupiter,
This shall not be revoked.

KENT: Fare thee well, King. Sith thus thou wilt appear,
Freedom lives hence and banishment is here.
[(*To Cordelia*)] The gods to their dear shelter take thee, maid,
That justly think'st and hast most rightly said!
[(*To Regan and Goneril*)] And your large speeches may your deeds approve,[6]
That good effects may spring from words of love.
Thus Kent, O princes, bids you all adieu.
He'll shape his old course in a country new. [*Exit.*]

[*Flourish.*[7] *Enter Gloucester, with France and Burgundy; attendants*]

GLOUCESTER: Here's France and Burgundy, my noble lord.

LEAR: My lord of Burgundy,
We first address toward you, who with this king
Hath rivaled for our daughter. What in the least
Will you require in present dower with her
Or cease your quest of love?

BURGUNDY: Most royal Majesty,
I crave no more than hath Your Highness offered,
Nor will you tender less.

LEAR: Right noble Burgundy,
When she was dear to us we did hold her so,
But now her price is fallen. Sir, there she stands.
If aught within that little-seeming substance,[8]
Or all of it, with our displeasure pieced,° *joined*
And nothing more, may fitly like Your Grace,
She's there, and she is yours.

BURGUNDY: I know no answer.

LEAR: Will you, with those infirmities she owes,
Unfriended, new-adopted to our hate,
Dowered with our curse and strangered with our oath,
Take her, or leave her?

BURGUNDY: Pardon me, royal sir.
Election makes not up in such conditions.[9]

4. To block my power to command and judge.
5. Which neither my temperament nor my office as king can bear.
6. May your deeds confirm your speeches.
7. Trumpet fanfare.
8. One who seems substantial but whose substance is little.
9. No choice is possible in such conditions.

LEAR: Then leave her, sir, for by the power that made me,
I tell you all her wealth. [(*To France*)] For you, great King,
I would not from your love make such a stray
To match you where I hate; therefore beseech you
T'avert your liking[1] a more worthier way
Than on a wretch whom Nature is ashamed
Almost t'acknowledge hers.

FRANCE: This is most strange,
That she whom even but now was your best object,
The argument of your praise, balm of your age,
The best, the dearest, should in this trice° of time *moment*
Commit a thing so monstrous to dismantle
So many folds of favor. Sure her offense
Must be of such unnatural degree
That monsters[2] it, or your forevouched affection
Fall into taint,[3] which to believe of her
Must be a faith that reason without miracle
Should never plant in me.

CORDELIA: I yet beseech Your Majesty—
If for I want[4] that glib and oily art
To speak and purpose not, since what I well intend
I'll do't before I speak—that you make known
It is no vicious blot, murder, or foulness,
No unchaste action or dishonored step
That hath deprived me of your grace and favor,
But even for want of that for which I am richer:
A still-soliciting° eye and such a tongue *ever-begging*
That I am glad I have not, though not to have it
Hath lost me in your liking.

LEAR: Better thou
Hadst not been born than not t'have pleased me better.

FRANCE: Is it but this? A tardiness in nature
Which often leaves the history° unspoke *story*
That it intends to do?—My lord of Burgundy,
What say you to the lady? Love's not love
When it is mingled with regards that stands
Aloof from th'entire point.[5] Will you have her?
She is herself a dowry.

BURGUNDY [(*to Lear*)]: Royal King,
Give but that portion which yourself proposed,
And here I take Cordelia by the hand,
Duchess of Burgundy.

LEAR: Nothing. I have sworn. I am firm.

BURGUNDY [(*to Cordelia*)]: I am sorry, then, you have so lost a father

1. Turn your affections.
2. Makes it monstrous.
3. Or else the affection for her you have hitherto affirmed must fall into suspicion.
4. Because I lack.
5. Love is not mixed with irrelevant considerations.

That you must lose a husband.
CORDELIA: Peace be with Burgundy!
Since that respects of fortune are his love,
I shall not be his wife.
FRANCE: Fairest Cordelia, that art most rich being poor,
Most choice, forsaken, and most loved, despised,
Thee and thy virtues here I seize upon,
Be it lawful I take up what's cast away.
[*He takes her hand.*]
Gods, gods! 'Tis strange that from their cold'st neglect
My love should kindle to inflamed respect.—
Thy dowerless daughter, King, thrown to my chance,
Is queen of us, of ours, and our fair France.
Not all the dukes of wat'rish Burgundy
Can buy this unprized[6] precious maid of me.—
Bid them farewell, Cordelia, though unkind.
Thou losest here, a better where to find.
LEAR: Thou hast her, France. Let her be thine, for we
Have no such daughter, nor shall ever see
That face of hers again. Therefore begone
Without our grace, our love, our benison.
Come, noble Burgundy.
[*Flourish. Exeunt (all but France, Goneril, Regan, and Cordelia).*]
FRANCE: Bid farewell to your sisters.
CORDELIA: Ye jewels of our father, with washed° eyes *tear washed*
Cordelia leaves you. I know you what you are,
And like a sister am most loath to call
Your faults as they are named. Love well our father.
To your professèd bosoms[7] I commit him.
But yet, alas, stood I within his grace,
I would prefer° him to a better place. *recommend*
So, farewell to you both.
REGAN: Prescribe not us our duty.
GONERIL: Let your study
Be to content your lord, who hath received you
At Fortune's aims.[8] You have obedience scanted,
And well are worth the want that you have wanted.[9]
CORDELIA: Time shall unfold what plighted cunning hides;
Who covers faults, at last shame them derides.[1]
Well may you prosper!
FRANCE: Come, my fair Cordelia.
[*Exeunt France and Cordelia.*]
GONERIL: Sister, it is not little I have to say of what most nearly appertains to us both. I think our father will hence tonight.

6. Not appreciated, but also priceless.
7. Publicly avowed love.
8. As a handout from Fortune.
9. You well deserve to be without the dowry and parental affection that you lacked and flouted.
1. Those who hide their faults in time will be ashamed and derided.

REGAN: That's most certain, and with you; next month with us.

GONERIL: You see how full of changes his age is; the observation we have made of it hath not been little. He always loved our sister most, and with what poor judgment he hath now cast her off appears too grossly.

REGAN: 'Tis the infirmity of his age. Yet he hath ever but slenderly known himself.

GONERIL: The best and soundest of his time hath been but rash.[2] Then must we look from his age to receive not alone the imperfections of long-ingraffed condition,[3] but therewithal[4] the unruly waywardness that infirm and choleric years bring with them.

REGAN: Such unconstant starts[5] are we like to have from him as this of Kent's banishment.

GONERIL: There is further compliment[6] of leave-taking between France and him. Pray you, let us hit[7] together. If our father carry authority with such disposition as he bears, this last surrender of his will but offend us.[8]

REGAN: We shall further think of it.

GONERIL: We must do something, and i'th' heat.[9]

[Exeunt.]

Scene 2[1]

[*Enter Bastard (Edmund, with a letter).*]

EDMUND: Thou, Nature,[2] art my goddess; to thy law
My services are bound. Wherefore should I
Stand in the plague of custom and permit
The curiosity of nations to deprive me,
For that I am some twelve or fourteen moonshines
Lag of a brother?[3] Why bastard? Wherefore base?
When my dimensions are as well compact,° *fitted, framed*
My mind as generous, and my shape as true,
As honest° madam's issue? Why brand they us *chaste*
With base? With baseness? Bastardy? Base, base?
Who in the lusty stealth of nature take
More composition and fierce quality[4]
Than doth within a dull, stale, tirèd bed
Go to th' creating a whole tribe of fops° *fools*
Got 'tween asleep and wake? Well, then,
Legitimate Edgar, I must have your land.
Our father's love is to the bastard Edmund
As to th' legitimate. Fine word, "legitimate"!
Well, my legitimate, if this letter speed° *prosper*

2. Even in the prime of his life, he was stormy and unpredictable.
3. Long-implanted habit.
4. Angry, dominated by the hot and dry choleric humor.
5. Impulsive outbursts.
6. Ceremony.
7. Agree.
8. If our father continues to boss us around with his usual imperiousness, this most recent display of willfulness will do us nothing but harm.
9. While the iron is hot.
1. Location: The Earl of Gloucester's house.
2. The force that governs the material world through mechanistic and amoral forces.
3. Why should I submit to the injustice of convention and allow arbitrary social gradations to deprive me because I am 12 to 14 months younger than a brother?
4. Whose begetting in the sexual act requires and engenders a fuller mixture and more energetic force.

And my invention thrive, Edmund the base
Shall top th' legitimate. I grow, I prosper.
Now, gods, stand up for bastards!
[*Enter Gloucester.*]

GLOUCESTER: Kent banished thus? And France in choler,° parted? *anger*
And the King gone tonight? Prescribed° his power, *limited*
Confined to exhibition?° All this done *an allowance of money*
Upon the gad?° Edmund, how now? What news? *suddenly*

EDMUND: So please Your Lordship, none. [(*Putting up the letter.*)]

GLOUCESTER: Why so earnestly seek you to put up that letter?

EDMUND: I know no news, my lord.

GLOUCESTER: What paper were you reading?

EDMUND: Nothing, my lord.

GLOUCESTER: No? What needed then that terrible dispatch[5] of it into your pocket? The quality of nothing hath not such need to hide itself. Let's see. Come, if it be nothing I shall not need spectacles.

EDMUND: I beseech you, sir, pardon me. It is a letter from my brother, that I have not all o'erread; and for so much as I have perused, I find it not fit for your o'erlooking.

GLOUCESTER: Give me the letter, sir.

EDMUND: I shall offend either to detain or give it. The contents, as in part I understand them, are to blame.[6]

GLOUCESTER: Let's see, let's see. [(*Edmund gives the letter.*)]

EDMUND: I hope for my brother's justification he wrote this but as an essay or taste[7] of my virtue.

GLOUCESTER [(*reads*)]: "This policy and reverence of age makes the world bitter to the best of our times,[8] keeps our fortunes from us till our oldness cannot relish them. I begin to find an idle and fond[9] bondage in the oppression of aged tyranny, who sways not as it hath power but as it is suffered.[1] Come to me, that of this I may speak more. If our father would sleep till I waked him, you should enjoy half his revenue forever and live the beloved of your brother, Edgar." Hum! Conspiracy! "Sleep till I waked him, you should enjoy half his revenue." My son Edgar! Had he a hand to write this? A heart and brain to breed it in? When came you to this? Who brought it?

EDMUND: It was not brought me, my lord; there's the cunning of it. I found it thrown in at the casement of my closet.

GLOUCESTER: You know the character[2] to be your brother's?

EDMUND: If the matter[3] were good, my lord, I durst swear it were his; but in respect of that I would fain[4] think it were not.

5. Fearful quick disposal.
6. The Folio reading "too blame," "too blameworthy to be shown," may be correct.
7. Trial or test.
8. This policy of reverencing old age makes the best years of our lives bitter.
9. Useless and foolish.
1. Permitted.
2. Handwriting.
3. Contents.
4. Gladly.

GLOUCESTER: It is his.

EDMUND: It is his hand, my lord, but I hope his heart is not in the contents.

GLOUCESTER: Has he never before sounded you in this business?

EDMUND: Never, my lord. But I have heard him oft maintain it to be fit that, sons at perfect age and fathers declined,[5] the father should be as ward to the son, and the son manage his revenue.

GLOUCESTER: Oh, villain, villain! His very opinion in the letter! Abhorred villain! Unnatural, detested, brutish villain! Worse than brutish! Go, sirrah, seek him. I'll apprehend him. Abominable villain! Where is he?

EDMUND: I do not well know, my lord. If it shall please you to suspend your indignation against my brother till you can derive from him better testimony of his intent, you should run a certain course; where, if you violently proceed against him, mistaking his purpose, it would make a great gap in your own honor and shake in pieces the heart of his obedience. I dare pawn down[6] my life for him that he hath writ this to feel my affection to Your Honor, and to no other pretense of danger.

GLOUCESTER: Think you so?

EDMUND: If Your Honor judge it meet, I will place you where you shall hear us confer of this, and by an auricular assurance have your satisfaction,[7] and that without any further delay than this very evening.

GLOUCESTER: He cannot be such a monster—

EDMUND: Nor is not, sure.

GLOUCESTER: To his father, that so tenderly and entirely loves him. Heaven and earth! Edmund, seek him out; wind me into him,[8] I pray you. Frame the business after your own wisdom. I would unstate myself to be in a due resolution.[9]

EDMUND: I will seek him, sir, presently,[1] convey the business as I shall find means, and acquaint you withal.

GLOUCESTER: These late[2] eclipses in the sun and moon portend no good to us. Though the wisdom of nature can reason it thus and thus, yet nature finds itself scourged by the sequent effects.[3] Love cools, friendship falls off, brothers divide; in cities, mutinies; in countries, discord; in palaces, treason; and the bond cracked twixt son and father. This villain of mine comes under the prediction; there's son against father. The King falls from bias of nature;[4] there's father against child. We have seen the best of our time. Machinations, hollowness, treachery, and all ruinous disorders follow us disquietly to our graves. Find out this villain, Edmund; it shall lose thee nothing.[5] Do it carefully. And the noble and truehearted Kent banished! His offense, honesty! 'Tis strange. *Exit.*

EDMUND: This is the excellent foppery[6] of the world, that when we are sick in fortune—often the surfeits of our own behavior[7]—we make guilty of our disasters the sun, the moon, and stars, as if we were villains on necessity, fools

5. Sons at full maturity and father having become feeble.
6. Stake.
7. Satisfy yourself as to the truth by what you hear.
8. Insinuate yourself into his confidence.
9. I would give up my rank and wealth to know the truth.
1. Immediately.
2. Recent.
3. Though natural science explains these eclipses, nature is tortured by the devastating consequences.
4. Natural inclination.
5. Earn you a reward.
6. Foolishness.
7. Consequences of our own overindulgence.

by heavenly compulsion, knaves, thieves, and treachers[8] by spherical predominance,[9] drunkards, liars, and adulterers by an enforced obedience of planetary influence, and all that we are evil in, by a divine thrusting on. An admirable evasion of whoremaster man, to lay his goatish[1] disposition on the charge[2] of a star! My father compounded with my mother under the Dragon's tail[3] and my nativity was under Ursa Major,[4] so that it follows I am rough and lecherous. Fut, I should have been that I am, had the maidenliest star in the firmament twinkled on my bastardizing. Edgar—

[*Enter Edgar.*]

and pat[5] he comes like the catastrophe of the old comedy. My cue is villainous melancholy, with a sigh like Tom o' Bedlam.[6]—Oh, these eclipses do portend these divisions![7] Fa, sol, la, mi.

EDGAR: How now, brother Edmund, what serious contemplation are you in?

EDMUND: I am thinking, brother, of a prediction I read this other day, what should follow these eclipses.

EDGAR: Do you busy yourself with that?

EDMUND: I promise you, the effects he writes of succeed unhappily,[8] as of unnaturalness between the child and the parent, death, dearth, dissolutions of ancient amities, divisions in state, menaces and maledictions against king and nobles, needless diffidences,[9] banishment of friends, dissipation of cohorts, nuptial breaches, and I know not what.

EDGAR: How long have you been a sectary astronomical?[1]

EDMUND: Come, come, when saw you my father last?

EDGAR: The night gone by.

EDMUND: Spake you with him?

EDGAR: Ay, two hours together.

EDMUND: Parted you in good terms? Found you no displeasure in him by word nor countenance?

EDGAR: None at all.

EDMUND: Bethink yourself wherein you may have offended him, and at my entreaty forbear his presence[2] until some little time hath qualified the heat of his displeasure, which at this instant so rageth in him that with the mischief of your person[3] it would scarcely allay.

EDGAR: Some villain hath done me wrong.

EDMUND: That's my fear. I pray you, have a continent forbearance till the speed of his rage goes slower; and, as I say, retire with me to my lodging, from whence I will fitly bring you to hear my lord speak. Pray ye, go! There's my key. [*He gives a key.*] If you do stir abroad, go armed.

EDGAR: Armed, brother?

EDMUND: Brother, I advise you to the best. I am no honest man if there be any good meaning toward you. I have told you what I have seen and

8. Traitors.
9. Astrological determination.
1. Lecherous.
2. To the responsibility of.
3. My father had sex with my mother under the constellation Draco.
4. The big bear or dipper.
5. On cue, like the resolution (of a play).
6. A lunatic patient of Bethlehem Hospital in London turned out to beg for his own bread.
7. Family and social conflicts.
8. Follow unluckily.
9. Groundless distrust of others.
1. Astronomical believer.
2. Avoid meeting him.
3. With the harmful effect of your presence.

heard, but faintly, nothing like the image and horror of it. Pray you, away.

EDGAR: Shall I hear from you anon?

EDMUND: I do serve you in this business. [*Exit (Edgar).*]

A credulous father and a brother noble,
Whose nature is so far from doing harms
That he suspects none; on whose foolish honesty
My practices ride easy. I see the business.
Let me, if not by birth, have lands by wit.
All with me's meet that I can fashion fit. [*Exit.*]

Scene 3[4]

[*Enter Goneril, and (Oswald, her) steward.*]

GONERIL: Did my father strike my gentleman for chiding of his fool?

OSWALD: Ay, madam.

GONERIL: By day and night he wrongs me! Every hour
He flashes into one gross crime° or other *offense*
That sets us all at odds. I'll not endure it.
His knights grow riotous, and himself upbraids us
On every trifle. When he returns from hunting
I will not speak with him. Say I am sick.
If you come slack[5] of former services
You shall do well; the fault of it I'll answer.

[(*Horns within.*)]

OSWALD: He's coming, madam. I hear him.

GONERIL: Put on what weary negligence you please,
You and your fellows. I'd have it come to question.° *be made an issue*
If he distaste° it, let him to my sister, *dislike*
Whose mind and mine, I know, in that are one,
Not to be overruled. Idle old man,
That still would manage those authorities
That he hath given away! Now, by my life,
Old fools are babes again, and must be used
With checks as flatteries, when they are seen abused.[6]
Remember what I have said.

OSWALD: Well, madam.

GONERIL: And let his knights have colder looks among you.
What grows of it, no matter. Advise your fellows so.
I would breed from hence occasions, and I shall,
That I may speak.[7] I'll write straight to my sister
To hold my very course. Prepare for dinner. [*Exeunt.*]

4. Location: The Duke of Albany's palace.
5. Fall short of.
6. Old fools . . . must be treated with rebukes in place of flatteries, when such flattery is seen to be taken advantage of.
7. Speak bluntly.

Scene 4

[*Enter Kent (disguised)*].

KENT: If but as well[8] I other accents borrow
That can my speech diffuse,[9] my good intent
May carry through itself to that full issue
For which I razed my likeness.[1] Now, banished Kent,
If thou canst serve where thou dost stand condemned,
So may it come[2] thy master, whom thou lov'st,
Shall find thee full of labors.

[*Horns within. Enter Lear, (Knights,) and attendants.*]

LEAR: Let me not stay° a jot for dinner. Go get it ready. *wait*
[(*Exit an Attendant.*)]
[(*To Kent*)] How now, what art thou?

KENT: A man, sir.

LEAR: What dost thou profess?[3] What wouldst thou with us?

KENT: I do profess to be no less than I seem: to serve him truly that will put me in trust, to love him that is honest, to converse with him that is wise and says little, to fear judgment, to fight when I cannot choose, and to eat no fish.[4]

LEAR: What art thou?

KENT: A very honest-hearted fellow, and as poor as the King.

LEAR: If thou be'st as poor for a subject as he's for a king, thou'rt poor enough. What wouldst thou?

KENT: Service.

LEAR: Who wouldst thou serve?

KENT: You.

LEAR: Dost thou know me, fellow?

KENT: No, sir, but you have that in your countenance[5] which I would fain call master.

LEAR: What's that?

KENT: Authority.

LEAR: What services canst do?

KENT: I can keep honest counsel,[6] ride, run, mar a curious[7] tale in telling it, and deliver a plain message bluntly. That which ordinary men are fit for I am qualified in, and the best of me is diligence.

LEAR: How old art thou?

KENT: Not so young, sir, to love a woman for singing, nor so old to dote on her for anything. I have years on my back forty-eight.

LEAR: Follow me; thou shalt serve me. If I like thee no worse after dinner, I will not part from thee yet.—Dinner, ho, dinner! Where's my knave, my fool? Go you and call my fool hither. [(*Exit one.*)]

[*Enter steward (Oswald).*]

You! You, sirrah, where's my daughter?

8. As well as I have disguised myself by means of costume.
9. Render confused or indistinct.
1. May achieve the desired result for which I scraped off my beard and erased my outward appearance.
2. Come to pass that.
3. What is your special calling? (But Kent puns in his answer on *profess* meaning "to claim.")
4. To be a meat eater, or to be a good Protestant (?).
5. Face and bearing.
6. Keep confidences.
7. Ornate.

OSWALD: So please you— [Exit.]

LEAR: What says the fellow there? Call the clodpoll[8] back. [(Exit a knight.)]
Where's my fool, ho? I think the world's asleep.

[(Enter Knight.)]

How now? Where's that mongrel?

KNIGHT: He says, my lord, your daughter is not well.

LEAR: Why came not the slave back to me when I called him?

KNIGHT: Sir, he answered me in the roundest[9] manner, he would not.

LEAR: He would not?

KNIGHT: My lord, I know not what the matter is, but to my judgment Your Highness is not entertained[1] with that ceremonious affection as you were wont. There's a great abatement of kindness appears as well in the general dependents as in the Duke himself also and your daughter.

LEAR: Ha? Say'st thou so?

KNIGHT: I beseech you, pardon me, my lord, if I be mistaken, for my duty cannot be silent when I think Your Highness wronged.

LEAR: Thou but rememberest[2] me of mine own conception. I have perceived a most faint neglect of late, which I have rather blamed as mine own jealous curiosity[3] than as a very pretense and purpose of unkindness. I will look further into't. But where's my fool? I have not seen him this two days.

KNIGHT: Since my young lady's going into France, sir, the Fool hath much pined away.

LEAR: No more of that. I have noted it well. Go you and tell my daughter I would speak with her. [(Exit one.)]
Go you call hither my fool. [(Exit one.)]

[Enter steward (Oswald).]

Oh, you, sir, you, come you hither, sir. Who am I, sir?

OSWALD: My lady's father.

LEAR: "My lady's father"? My lord's knave! You whoreson dog, you slave, you cur!

OSWALD: I am none of these, my lord, I beseech your pardon.

LEAR: Do you bandy looks[4] with me, you rascal?

[(He strikes Oswald.)]

OSWALD: I'll not be strucken, my lord.

KENT: Nor tripped neither, you base football[5] player.

[(He trips up Oswald's heels.)]

LEAR: I thank thee, fellow. Thou serv'st me, and I'll love thee.

KENT: Come, sir, arise, away! I'll teach you differences. Away, away! If you will measure your lubber's length again,[6] tarry; but away! Go to. Have you wisdom? So.

[(He pushes Oswald out.)]

LEAR: Now, my friendly knave, I thank thee. There's earnest of thy service.

[(He gives Kent money.)]

[Enter Fool.]

8. Blockhead.
9. Bluntest.
1. Treated.
2. Remind.
3. Overly scrupulous regard for etiquette.
4. Exchange glances (in such a way as to imply that Oswald and Lear are social equals).
5. Football, a raucous street game played by the lower classes.
6. If you want to be laid out flat again, you clumsy ox.

FOOL: Let me hire him too. Here's my coxcomb. [(*Offering Kent his cap.*)]

LEAR: How now, my pretty knave, how dost thou?

FOOL [(*to Kent*)]: Sirrah, you were best take my coxcomb.

KENT: Why, Fool?

FOOL: Why? For taking one's part that's out of favor. Nay, an thou canst not smile as the wind sits, thou'lt catch cold shortly. There, take my coxcomb. Why, this fellow has banished two on 's daughters[7] and did the third a blessing against his will. If thou follow him, thou must needs wear my coxcomb.—How now, nuncle? Would I had two coxcombs and two daughters.

LEAR: Why, my boy?

FOOL: If I gave them all my living,[8] I'd keep my coxcombs myself. There's mine; beg another of thy daughters.[9]

LEAR: Take heed, sirrah—the whip.

FOOL: Truth's a dog must to kennel. He must be whipped out, when the Lady Brach[1] may stand by th' fire and stink.

LEAR: A pestilent gall[2] to me!

FOOL: Sirrah, I'll teach thee a speech.

LEAR: Do.

FOOL: Mark it, nuncle:
Have more than thou showest,
Speak less than thou knowest,
Lend less than thou owest,
Ride more than thou goest,° *walk*
Learn° more than thou trowest,° *listen to / believe*
Set less than thou throwest;[3]
Leave thy drink and thy whore,
And keep in-a-door,
And thou shalt have more
Than two tens to a score.[4]

KENT: This is nothing, Fool.

FOOL: Then 'tis like the breath of an unfee'd lawyer;[5] you gave me nothing for't. Can you make no use of nothing, nuncle?

LEAR: Why, no, boy. Nothing can be made out of nothing.

FOOL [*to Kent*]: Prithee, tell him; so much the rent of his land comes to. He will not believe a fool.

LEAR: A bitter° fool! *satirical*

FOOL: Dost know the difference, my boy, between a bitter fool and a sweet one?

LEAR: No, lad. Teach me.

FOOL: That lord that counseled thee
To give away thy land,
Come place him here by me;

7. Paradoxically, by giving Goneril and Regan his kingdom, Lear has lost them.
8. Property.
9. Beg for the coxcomb that you deserve for dealing with your daughters as you did.
1. Bitch hound (likened to Goneril and Regan who have been given favored places despite their reeking of dishonest flattery.)
2. Irritation.
3. Don't stake everything on a single throw.
4. You will more than break even, since a score equals two tens.
5. It is free and useless advice (Lawyers, being proverbially mercenary, would not give good advice unless paid well.

Do thou for him stand.
The sweet and bitter fool.
Will presently appear:
The one in motley[6] here,
The other found out there.[7]

LEAR: Dost thou call me fool, boy?

FOOL: All thy other titles thou hast given away; that thou wast born with.

KENT: This is not altogether fool, my lord.

FOOL: No, faith, lords and great men will not let me;[8] if I had a monopoly out, they would have part on't. And ladies too, they will not let me have all the fool to myself; they'll be snatching. Nuncle, give me an egg and I'll give thee two crowns.

LEAR: What two crowns shall they be?

FOOL: Why, after I have cut the egg i'th' middle and eat up the meat, the two crowns of the egg. When thou clovest thy crown i'th' middle and gav'st away both parts, thou bor'st thine ass on thy back o'er the dirt. Thou hadst little wit in thy bald crown when thou gav'st thy golden one away. If I speak like myself in this, let him be whipped that first finds it so.[9]
[(*Sings*)] "Fools had ne'er less grace in a year,
For wise men are grown foppish
And know not how their wits to wear,
Their manners are so apish."[1]

LEAR: When were you wont to be so full of songs, sirrah?

FOOL: I have used[2] it, nuncle, e'er since thou mad'st thy daughters thy mothers; for when thou gav'st them the rod and putt'st down thine own breeches,
[(*Sings*)] "Then they for sudden joy did weep,
And I for sorrow sung,
That such a king should play bo-peep
And go the fools among."
Prithee, nuncle, keep a schoolmaster that can teach thy fool to lie. I would fain learn to lie.

LEAR: An[3] you lie, sirrah, we'll have you whipped.

FOOL: I marvel what kin thou and thy daughters are. They'll have me whipped for speaking true, thou'lt have me whipped for lying, and sometimes I am whipped for holding my peace. I had rather be any kind o' thing than a fool. And yet I would not be thee, nuncle. Thou hast pared thy wit o' both sides and left nothing i'th' middle. Here comes one o' th' parings.

[*Enter Goneril.*]

LEAR: How now, daughter? What makes that frontlet on?[4] You are too much of late i'th' frown.

6. The parti-colored dress of the professional fool.
7. The Fool points at Lear, the "bitter" fool.
8. Great persons at court will not let me monopolize folly.
9. If I speak like a fool in saying this, let the first person to discover the truth be whipped (since in this corrupt world those who speak the truth are punished for doing so.
1. Fools have never been so out of favor, for wise men foppishly trade places with the fools and no longer know how to show off their wits to advantage, they have grown so foolish in their manners.
2. Practiced.
3. If.
4. What is that frown doing on your forehead?

FOOL: Thou wast a pretty fellow when thou hadst no need to care for her frowning; now thou art an O with-out a figure.[5] I am better than thou art now; I am a fool, thou art nothing. [*To Goneril*] Yes, forsooth, I will hold my tongue; so your face bids me, though you say nothing.
Mum, mum,
He that keeps nor crust nor crumb,
Weary of all, shall want some.[6]
[(*Pointing to Lear*)] That's a shelled peascod.[7]
GONERIL: Not only, sir, this your all-licensed[8] fool,
But other of your insolent retinue
Do hourly carp and quarrel, breaking forth
In rank and not-to-be-endurèd riots. Sir,
I had thought by making this well known unto you
To have found a safe redress, but now grow fearful,
By what yourself too late° have spoke and done, *recently*
That you protect this course and put it on° *encourage it*
By your allowance; which if you should, the fault
Would not scape censure, nor the redresses sleep
Which in the tender of a wholesome weal
Might in their working do you that offense,
Which else were shame, that then necessity
Will call discreet proceeding.[9]
FOOL: For you know, nuncle,
"The hedge sparrow fed the cuckoo[1] so long
That it had its head bit off by it young."
So, out went the candle, and we were left darkling.[2]
LEAR [(*to Goneril*)]: Are you our daughter?
GONERIL: I would you would make use of your good wisdom,
Whereof I know you are fraught, and put away
These dispositions which of late transport you
From what you rightly are.
FOOL: May not an ass know when the cart draws the horse? Whoop, Jug![3] I love thee.
LEAR: Does any here know me? This is not Lear.
Does Lear walk thus, speak thus? Where are his eyes?
Either his notion[4] weakens, or his discernings
Are lethargied[5]—Ha! Waking? 'Tis not so.
Who is it that can tell me who I am?
FOOL: Lear's shadow.
LEAR: I would learn that[6]; for, by the marks of sovereignty,
Knowledge, and reason, I should be false persuaded

5. A zero, unless preceded by a digit.
6. That person who, having grown weary of his possessions, gives all away, will find himself in need of part of what is gone.
7. A peapod empty of its contents.
8. Allowed to speak or act as he pleases.
9. Nor would the punishment remain unused, which out of care for the common good, might prove unpleasant to you—proceedings that the stern necessity of the times will regard as prudent even if under normal circumstances they might seem shameful.
1. Cuckoo, a bird that lays its eggs in other birds' nests.
2. In the dark.
3. Jug is a nickname for Joan and can also mean whore.
4. Intellectual power.
5. Or his faculties are asleep.
6. Who I am.

I had daughters.[7]
FOOL: Which they will make an obedient father.
LEAR: Your name, fair gentlewoman?
GONERIL: This admiration,[8] sir, is much o'th' savor
Of other your new pranks. I do beseech you
To understand my purposes aright.
As you are old and reverend, should be wise.
Here do you keep a hundred knights and squires,
Men so disordered, so debauched and bold
That this our court, infected with their manners,
Shows like a riotous inn. Epicurism[9] and lust
Makes it more like a tavern or a brothel
Than a graced palace. The shame itself doth speak
For instant remedy. Be then desired,° *requested*
By her that else will take the thing she begs,
A little to disquantity your train,[1]
And the remainders that shall still depend
To be such men as may besort your age,
Which know themselves and you.
LEAR: Darkness and devils!
Saddle my horses! Call my train together! [(*Exit one.*)]
Degenerate bastard, I'll not trouble thee.
Yet have I left a daughter.
GONERIL: You strike my people, and your disordered rabble
Make servants of their betters.
[*Enter Albany.*]
LEAR: Woe, that too late repents!—Oh, sir, are you come?
Is it your will? Speak, sir—Prepare my horses.
[(*Exit one.*)]
Ingratitude, thou marble-hearted fiend,
More hideous when thou show'st thee in a child
Than the sea monster!
ALBANY: Pray, sir, be patient.
LEAR [(*to Goneril*)]: Detested kite,° thou liest! *bird of prey*
My train are men of choice and rarest parts,
That all particulars of duty know
And in the most exact regard support
The worships of their name. Oh, most small fault,
How ugly didst thou in Cordelia show!
Which, like an engine, wrenched my frame of nature
From the fixed place,[2] drew from my heart all love,
And added to the gall. Oh, Lear, Lear, Lear!
Beat at this gate [*striking his head*] that let thy folly in
And thy dear judgment out!—Go, go, my people.
[*Exeunt some.*]

7. All these outward signs of kingly status and sanity would seem to suggest falsely that I am a man who had daughters.
8. Wonderment.
9. Hedonism.
1. Diminish the number of your attendants.
2. Which like a powerful mechanical contrivance wrenched my natural affection away from where it belonged.

ALBANY: My lord, I am guiltless as I am ignorant
Of what hath moved you.
LEAR: It may be so, my lord.—
Hear, Nature, hear! Dear goddess, hear!
Suspend thy purpose if thou didst intend
To make this creature fruitful!
Into her womb convey sterility;
Dry up in her the organs of increase,
And from her derogate° body never spring *debased*
A babe to honor her! If she must teem,° *produce offspring*
Create her child of spleen,[3] that it may live
And be a thwart disnatured torment to her!
Let it stamp wrinkles in her brow of youth,
With cadent° tears fret channels in her cheeks, *cascading*
Turn all her mother's pains and benefits
To laughter and contempt, that she may feel
How sharper than a serpent's tooth it is
To have a thankless child! Away, away!
[*Exit (with Kent and the rest of Lear's followers).*]
ALBANY: Now, gods that we adore, whereof comes this?
GONERIL: Never afflict yourself to know more of it,
But let his disposition have that scope
As dotage gives it.
[*Enter Lear.*]
LEAR: What, fifty of my followers at a clap?
Within a fortnight?
ALBANY: What's the matter, sir?
LEAR: I'll tell thee. [(*To Goneril*)] Life and death! I am ashamed
That thou hast power to shake my manhood thus,
That these hot tears, which break from me perforce,
Should make thee worth them. Blasts and fogs upon thee!
Th'untented[4] woundings of a father's curse
Pierce every sense about thee! Old fond eyes,
Beweep this cause again, I'll pluck ye out
And cast you, with the waters that you loose,[5]
To temper clay.[6] Yea, is't come to this?
Ha! Let it be so. I have another daughter,
Who, I am sure, is kind and comfortable.° *comforting*
When she shall hear this of thee, with her nails
She'll flay thy wolvish visage. Thou shalt find
That I'll resume the shape which thou dost think
I have cast off forever. [*Exit.*]
GONERIL [(*to Albany*)]: Do you mark that?
ALBANY: I cannot be so partial, Goneril,
To the great love I bear you—

3. Violent ill nature.
4. Too deep to be probed.
5. Let loose in tears.
6. To mix with earth.

GONERIL: Pray you, content.—What, Oswald, ho!
[*(To the Fool)*] You, sir, more knave than fool, after your master.
FOOL: Nuncle Lear, nuncle Lear! Tarry, take the Fool with thee.[7]
A fox, when one has caught her,
And such a daughter
Should sure to the slaughter,
If my cap would buy a halter.
So the Fool follows after. [*Exit.*]
GONERIL: This man hath had good counsel. A hundred knights?
'Tis politic and safe to let him keep
At point a hundred knights—yes, that on every dream,
Each buzz, each fancy, each complaint, dislike,
He may enguard his dotage with their powers
And hold our lives in mercy—Oswald, I say!
ALBANY: Well, you may fear too far.
GONERIL: Safer than trust too far.
Let me still take away the harms I fear,
Not fear still to be taken.[8] I know his heart.
What he hath uttered I have writ my sister.
If she sustain him and his hundred knights
When I have showed th'unfitness—
[*Enter steward (Oswald).*]
How now, Oswald?
What, have you writ that letter to my sister?
OSWALD: Ay, madam.
GONERIL: Take you some company and away to horse.
Inform her full of my particular fear,
And thereto add such reasons of your own
As may compact° if more. Get you gone, *confirm*
And hasten your return. (*Exit Oswald.*)
No, no, my lord,
This milky gentleness and course[9] of yours
Though I condemn not, yet, under pardon,
You're much more attasked for want of wisdom
Than praised for harmful mildness.
ALBANY: How far your eyes may pierce I cannot tell.
Striving to better, oft we mar what's well.
GONERIL: Nay, then—
ALBANY: Well, well, th'event.[1] [*Exeunt.*]

Scene 5[2]

[*Enter Lear, Kent (disguised as Caius), and Fool.*]
LEAR [*giving a letter to Kent*]: Go you before to Gloucester[3] with these letters. Acquaint my daughter no further with anything you know than comes from

7. Take me with you, and take the name "fool" with you.
8. Rather than always be in fear of being taken prisoner by such harms.
9. Effeminate and gentle way.

1. Time will tell.
2. Location: Before Albany's palace.
3. The city in Gloucestershire.

her demand out of the letter. If your diligence be not speedy, I shall be there afore you.

KENT: I will not sleep, my lord, till I have delivered your letter. [*Exit.*]

FOOL: If a man's brains were in 's heels, were't not in danger of kibes?[4]

LEAR: Ay, boy.

FOOL: Then, I prithee, be merry. Thy wit shall not go slipshod.[5]

LEAR: Ha, ha, ha!

FOOL: Shalt see thy other daughter will use thee kindly,[6] for though she's as like this as a crab's like an apple, yet I can tell what I can tell.

LEAR: What canst tell, boy?

FOOL: She will taste as like this as a crab does to a crab.[7] Thou canst tell why one's nose stands i'th' middle on 's face?

LEAR: No.

FOOL: Why, to keep one's eyes of either side 's[8] nose, that what a man cannot smell out he may spy into.

LEAR: I did her wrong.

FOOL: Canst tell how an oyster makes his shell?

LEAR: No.

FOOL: Nor I neither. But I can tell why a snail has a house.

LEAR: Why?

FOOL: Why, to put 's head in, not to give it away to his daughters and leave his horns without a case.[9]

LEAR: I will forget my nature.[1] So kind a father!—Be my horses ready?

FOOL: Thy asses are gone about 'em. The reason why the seven stars are no more than seven is a pretty reason.

LEAR: Because they are not eight.

FOOL: Yes, indeed. Thou wouldst make a good fool.

LEAR: To take't again perforce! Monster ingratitude!

FOOL: If thou wert my fool, nuncle, I'd have thee beaten for being old before thy time.

LEAR: How's that?

FOOL: Thou shouldst not have been old till thou hadst been wise.

LEAR: Oh, let me not be mad, not mad, sweet heaven!
Keep me in temper; I would not be mad!

[(*Enter Gentleman.*)]

How now, are the horses ready?

GENTLEMAN: Ready, my lord.

LEAR: Come, boy. [*Exeunt (Lear and Gentleman).*]

FOOL: She that's a maid now, and laughs at my departure,
Shall not be a maid long, unless things[2] be cut shorter.[3] [(*Exit.*)]

4. Wouldn't his brains be in danger of that common affliction of the heel called chilblains?
5. Your brains would have no need for slippers to avoid chafing the chilblains, since you have no brains.
6. With the natural kindness or "relatedness" of child to father; according to her own "kind" or nature.
7. Crabapple.
8. Of his.
9. The snail's head and horns are unendangered with its case or shell; Lear conversely, has given away his crown to his daughters, leaving his brows unadorned and vulnerable.
1. Natural affection.
2. Penises.
3. A bawdy joke addressed to the audience.

ACT 2

Scene 1[4]

[*Enter Bastard (Edmund) and Curan, severally.*[5]]

EDMUND: Save thee, Curan.

CURAN: And you, sir. I have been with your father and given him notice that the Duke of Cornwall and Regan his duchess will be here with him this night.

EDMUND: How comes that?

CURAN: Nay, I know not. You have heard of the news abroad[6]—I mean the whispered ones, for they are yet but ear-kissing arguments?

EDMUND: Not I. Pray you, what are they?

CURAN: Have you heard of no likely wars toward[7] twixt the Dukes of Cornwall and Albany?

EDMUND: Not a word.

CURAN: You may do, then, in time. Fare you well, sir.

[*Exit.*]

EDMUND: The Duke be here tonight? The better! Best!
This weaves itself perforce into my business.
My father hath set guard to take my brother,
And I have one thing, of a queasy question,[8]
Which I must act. Briefness and fortune, work!—
Brother, a word. Descend. Brother, I say!

[*Enter Edgar.*]

My father watches. Oh, sir, fly this place!
Intelligence is given where you are hid.
You have now the good advantage of the night.
Have you not spoken 'gainst the Duke of Cornwall?
He's coming hither, now, i'th' night, i'th' haste,
And Regan with him. Have you nothing said
Upon his party 'gainst the Duke of Albany?
Advise yourself.[9]

EDGAR: I am sure on't, not a word.

EDMUND: I hear my father coming. Pardon me;
In cunning I must draw my sword upon you.
Draw. Seem to defend yourself. Now, quit you well.—

[(*They draw.*)]

Yield! Come before my father!—Light, ho, here!—
Fly, brother.—Torches, torches!—So farewell.

[*Exit Edgar.*]

Some blood drawn on me would beget opinion
Of my more fierce endeavor.[1] I have seen drunkards
Do more than this in sport. [(*He wounds himself in the arm.*)] Father, father!
Stop, stop! No help?

[*Enter Gloucester, and servants with torches.*]

4. Location: The Earl of Gloucester's house.
5. Separately.
6. Going the rounds.
7. Impending.
8. Not for queasy stomachs.
9. Consider your situation.
1. Create an impression of my having fought fiercely.

GLOUCESTER: Now, Edmund, where's the villain?
EDMUND: Here stood he in the dark, his sharp sword out,
Mumbling of wicked charms, conjuring the moon
To stand's[2] auspicious mistress.
GLOUCESTER: But where is he?
EDMUND: Look, sir, I bleed.
GLOUCESTER: Where is the villain, Edmund?
EDMUND: Fled this way, sir. When by no means he could—
GLOUCESTER: Pursue him, ho! Go after. [*Exeunt some servants.*] By no means what?
EDMUND: Persuade me to the murder of Your Lordship,
But that I told him the revenging gods
'Gainst parricides did all the thunder bend,° *aim*
Spoke with how manifold and strong a bond
The child was bound to th' father; sir, in fine,
Seeing how loathly opposite[3] I stood
To his unnatural purpose, in fell motion
With his preparèd sword he charges home
My unprovided° body, latched° mine arm; *unprotected / nicked*
And when he saw my best alarumed spirits,
Bold in the quarrel's right, roused to th'encounter,
Or whether ghasted° by the noise I made, *frightened*
Full suddenly he fled.
GLOUCESTER: Let him fly far.
Not in this land shall he remain uncaught;
And found—dispatch.[4] The noble Duke my master,
My worthy arch and patron,[5] comes tonight.
By his authority I will proclaim it
That he which finds him shall deserve our thanks,
Bringing the murderous coward to the stake;
He that conceals him, death.
EDMUND: When I dissuaded him from his intent
And found him pight° to do it, with curst speech *determined*
I threatened to discover° him. He replied, *expose*
"Thou unpossessing° bastard, dost thou think, *unable to inherit*
If I would stand against thee, would the reposal,° *placing*
Of any trust, virtue, or worth in thee
Make thy words faithed? No. What I should deny—
As this I would, ay, though thou didst produce
My very character—I'd turn it all
To thy suggestion,° plot, and damnèd practice;° *handwriting / scheming*
And thou must make a dullard of the world
If they not thought the profits of my death

2. Act as his.
3. Loathingly opposed.
4. That will be the end for him.
5. Chief patron.

Were very pregnant and potential spirits
To make thee seek it."[6]

GLOUCESTER: Oh, strange and fastened° villain! *hardened*
Would he deny his letter, said he?
I never got him. [*Tucket within.*[7]]
Hark, the Duke's trumpets! I know not why he comes.
All ports[8] I'll bar; the villain shall not scape.
The Duke must grant me that. Besides, his picture
I will send far and near, that all the kingdom
May have due note of him; and of my land,
Loyal and natural[9] boy, I'll work the means
To make thee capable.[1]

[*Enter Cornwall, Regan, and attendants.*]

CORNWALL: How now, my noble friend? Since I came hither,
Which I can call but now, I have heard strange news.

REGAN: If it be true, all vengeance comes too short
Which can pursue th'offender. How dost, my lord?

GLOUCESTER: Oh madam, my old heart is cracked, it's cracked!

REGAN: What, did my father's godson seek your life?
He whom my father named? Your Edgar?

GLOUCESTER: Oh, lady, lady, shame would have it hid!

REGAN: Was he not companion with the riotous knights
That tended upon my father?

GLOUCESTER: I know not, madam. 'Tis too bad, too bad.

EDMUND: Yes, madam, he was of that consort.° *crew*

REGAN: No marvel, then, though° he were ill affected. *if*
'Tis they have put him on[2] the old man's death,
To have th'expense and spoil of his revenues.
I have this present evening from my sister
Been well informed of them, and with such cautions
That if they come to sojourn at my house
I'll not be there.

CORNWALL: Nor I, assure thee, Regan.
Edmund, I hear that you have shown your father
A childlike office.

EDMUND: It was my duty, sir.

GLOUCESTER [(*to Cornwall*)]: He did bewray his practice,[3] and received
This hurt you see striving to apprehend° him. *arrest*

CORNWALL: Is he pursued?

GLOUCESTER: Ay, my good lord.

CORNWALL: If he be taken, he shall never more
Be feared of doing harm. Make your own purpose,

6. It and you must think everyone slow-witted indeed not to suppose that they would see how the profits to be gained by my death would be fertile and potent tempters to make you seek my death.
7. Flourish on a trumpet.
8. Seaports or gateways.
9. Prompted by natural feeling; bastard.
1. Legally able to inherit.
2. Incited him to.
3. Expose his plot.

How in my strength you please.[4] For you, Edmund,
Whose virtue and obedience doth this instant
So much commend itself, you shall be ours.
Natures of such deep trust we shall much need;
You we first seize on.

EDMUND: I shall serve you, sir,
Truly, however else.[5]

GLOUCESTER: For him I thank Your Grace.

CORNWALL: You know not why we came to visit you—

REGAN: —Thus out of season, threading dark-eyed night:
Occasions, noble Gloucester, of some poise,° *(weight)*
Wherein we must have use of your advice.
Our father he hath writ, so hath our sister,
Of differences, which I least thought it fit
To answer from our home. The several messengers
From hence attend dispatch.[6] Our good old friend,
Lay comforts to your bosom, and bestow
Your needful counsel to our businesses,
Which craves the instant use.

GLOUCESTER: I serve you, madam.
Your Graces are right welcome. *[Flourish. Exeunt.]*

Scene 2[7]

[Enter Kent (disguised as Caius) and steward (Oswald), severally.[8]*]*

OSWALD: Good dawning to thee, friend. Art of this house?

KENT: Ay.

OSWALD: Where may we set our horses?

KENT: I'th' mire.

OSWALD: Prithee, if thou lov'st me, tell me.

KENT: I love thee not.

OSWALD: Why then, I care not for thee.

KENT: If I had thee in Lipsbury pinfold,[9] I would make thee care for me.

OSWALD: Why dost thou use me thus? I know thee not.

KENT: Fellow, I know thee.

OSWALD: What dost thou know me for?

KENT: A knave, a rascal, an eater of broken meats; a base, proud, shallow, beggarly, three-suited, hundred-pound, filthy worsted-stocking knave;[1] a lily-livered, action-taking, whoreson, glass-gazing, superserviceable, finical rogue; one-trunk-inheriting slave;[2] one that wouldst be a bawd in way of good service,[3] and art nothing but the composition of a knave, beggar, coward, pander, and

4. Go about achieving your purpose, making free use of my authority and resources.
5. Above all else.
6. Wait to be dispatched.
7. Location: Before Gloucester's house.
8. At separate doors.
9. Within the pinfold of the lips, between my teeth.
1. A steward of a household, with an allowance of three suits a year and a comfortable income of 100 pounds, dressed up in dirty wool stockings appropriate to the servant class.
2. A cowardly, litigious, insufferable, self-infatuated, officious, foppish rogue, whose personal property fits into one trunk.
3. The titles I've given you.

the son and heir of a mongrel bitch; one whom I will beat into clamorous whining if thou deny'st the least syllable of thy addition.

OSWALD: Why, what a monstrous fellow art thou thus to rail on one that is neither known of thee nor knows thee!

KENT: What a brazen-faced varlet art thou to deny thou knowest me! Is it two days since I tripped up thy heels and beat thee before the King? Draw, you rogue, for though it be night, yet the moon shines. I'll make a sop o'th' moonshine[4] of you, you whoreson, cullionly barbermonger.[5] Draw! [(*He brandishes his sword.*)]

OSWALD: Away! I have nothing to do with thee.

KENT: Draw, you rascal! You come with letters against the King, and take Vanity the puppet's part[6] against the royalty of her father. Draw, you rogue, or I'll so carbonado[7] your shanks—draw, you rascal! Come your ways.

OSWALD: Help, ho! Murder! Help!

KENT: Strike, you slave! Stand, rogue, stand, you neat[8] slave, strike! [(*He beats him.*)]

OSWALD: Help, ho! Murder! Murder!

[*Enter Bastard (Edmund, with his rapier drawn), Cornwall, Regan, Gloucester, servants.*]

EDMUND: How now, what's the matter? Part!

KENT: With you, goodman boy, an you please! Come, I'll flesh ye. Come on, young master.

GLOUCESTER: Weapons? Arms? What's the matter here?

CORNWALL: Keep peace, upon your lives! [(*Kent and Oswald are parted.*)] He dies that strikes again. What is the matter?

REGAN: The messengers from our sister and the King.

CORNWALL: What's your difference? Speak.

OSWALD: I am scarce in breath, my lord.

KENT: No marvel, you have so bestirred your valor. You cowardly rascal, nature disclaims in[9] thee. A tailor made thee.

CORNWALL: Thou art a strange fellow. A tailor make a man?

KENT: A tailor, sir. A stonecutter or a painter could not have made him so ill, though they had been but two years o'th' trade.

CORNWALL: Speak yet, how grew your quarrel?

OSWALD: This ancient ruffian, sir, whose life I have spared at suit of his gray beard—

KENT: Thou whoreson zed![1] Thou unnecessary letter!—My lord, if you'll give me leave, I will tread this un bolted[2] villain into mortar and daub the wall of a jakes[3] with him.—Spare my gray beard, you wagtail?[4]

CORNWALL: Peace, sirrah!
You beastly knave, know you no reverence?

4. Something so perforated that it will soak up moonshine as a sop soaks up liquor.
5. Base frequenter of barber shops.
6. The part of Goneril, here personified as a character in a morality play.
7. Cut crosswise.
8. Foppish, calflike.
9. Disowns.
1. The letter *z*, regarded as unnecessary and often not included in dictionaries of the time.
2. Unsifted, hence coarse.
3. Toilet.
4. Bird wagging its tail feathers.

KENT: Yes, sir, but anger hath a privilege.
CORNWALL: Why art thou angry?
KENT: That such a slave as this should wear a sword,
Who wears no honesty. Such smiling rogues as these,
Like rats, oft bite the holy cords atwain
Which are too intrinse[5] t'unloose; smooth every passion
That in the natures of their lords rebel,
Bring oil to fire, snow to their colder moods,
Renege, affirm, and turn their halcyon beaks[6]
With every gale and vary of their masters,
Knowing naught, like dogs, but following.—
A plague upon your epileptic[7] visage!
Smile you my speeches, as I were a fool?
Goose, an I had you upon Sarum plain,
I'd drive ye cackling home to Camelot.[8]
CORNWALL: What, art thou mad, old fellow?
GLOUCESTER: How fell you out? Say that.
KENT: No contraries hold more antipathy
Than I and such a knave.
CORNWALL: Why dost thou call him knave? What is his fault?
KENT: His countenance likes me not.
CORNWALL: No more, perchance, does mine, nor his, nor hers.
KENT: Sir, 'tis my occupation to be plain:
I have seen better faces in my time
Than stands on any shoulder that I see
Before me at this instant.
CORNWALL: This is some fellow
Who, having been praised for bluntness, doth affect
A saucy roughness, and constrains the garb
Quite from his nature.[9] He cannot flatter, he;
An honest mind and plain, he must speak truth!
An they will take't, so; if not, he's plain.
These kind of knaves I know, which in this plainness
Harbor more craft and more corrupter ends
Than twenty silly-ducking observants
That stretch their duties nicely.[1]
KENT: Sir, in good faith, in sincere verity,
Under th'allowance of your great aspect,
Whose influence, like the wreath of radiant fire
On flickering Phoebus' front[2]—
CORNWALL: What mean'st by this?
KENT: To go out of my dialect,[3] which you discommend so much. I know, sir, I am no flatterer. He that beguiled you in a plain accent was a plain knave,

5. Intricately knotted.
6. The halcyon or kingfisher, if hung up, would supposedly turn its beak to the wind.
7. Grimacing.
8. Kent if given space and opportunity would send Oswald packing like a cackling goose. Camelot is the legendary seat of King Arthur and the Knights of the Round Table.
9. Distorts plainness from its true purpose so that it becomes instead a way of deceiving the listener.
1. Than 20 foolishly bowing courtiers.
2. The sun god's forehead.
3. Manner of speech.

which for my part I will not be, though I should win your displeasure to entreat me to't.

CORNWALL [(*to Oswald*)]: What was th'offense you gave him?

OSWALD: I never gave him any.
It pleased the King his master very late
To strike at me, upon his misconstruction;[4]
When he, compact, and flattering his displeasure,
Tripped me behind; being down, insulted, railed,
And put upon him such a deal of man
That worthied him,[5] got praises of the King
For him attempting who was self-subdued;
And, in the fleshment° of this dread exploit,[6] *excitement*
Drew on me here again.

KENT: None of these rogues and cowards
But Ajax is their fool.[7]

CORNWALL: Fetch forth the stocks!
You stubborn, ancient knave, you reverend braggart,
We'll teach you.

KENT: Sir, I am too old to learn.
Call not your stocks for me. I serve the King,
On whose employment I was sent to you.
You shall do small respect, show too bold malice
Against the grace and person of my master,
Stocking his messenger.

CORNWALL: Fetch forth the stocks! As I have life and honor,
There shall he sit till noon.

REGAN: Till noon? Till night, my lord, and all night too.

KENT: Why, madam, if I were your father's dog
You should not use me so.

REGAN: Sir, being his knave, I will.

CORNWALL: This is a fellow of the selfsame color
Our sister speaks of.—Come, bring away the stocks!

[*Stocks brought out*.]

GLOUCESTER: Let me beseech Your Grace not to do so.
His fault is much, and the good King his master
Will check him for't. Your purposed low correction
Is such as basest and contemned'st wretches
For pilferings and most common trespasses
Are punished with. The King must take it ill
That he, so slightly valued in his messenger,
Should have him thus restrained.

CORNWALL: I'll answer that.

REGAN: My sister may receive it much more worse
To have her gentleman abused, assaulted,
For following her affairs. Put in his legs.

[(*Kent is put in the stocks*.)]

4. As a result of the king's misunderstanding me.
5. And acted with a bravado that earned him praise.
6. For attacking one who chose not to resist.
7. You never find any rogues and cowards of this sort who do not outdo the blustering Ajax in his boasting.

Come, my good lord, away.
[*Exeunt (all but Gloucester and Kent).*]
GLOUCESTER: I am sorry for thee, friend. 'Tis the Duke's pleasure,
Whose disposition, all the world well knows,
Will not be rubbed° nor stopped. I'll entreat for thee. *hindered*
KENT: Pray, do not, sir. I have watched° and traveled hard. *gone sleepless*
Some time I shall sleep out; the rest I'll whistle.
A good man's fortune may grow out at heels.[8]
Give you good morrow!
GLOUCESTER: The Duke's to blame in this. 'Twill be ill taken. [*Exit.*]
KENT: Good King, that must approve° the common saw, *prove true*
Thou out of heaven's benediction com'st
To the warm sun! [(*He takes out a letter.*)]
Approach, thou beacon to this under globe,
That by thy comfortable beams I may
Peruse this letter. Nothing almost sees miracles
But misery. I know 'tis from Cordelia,
Who hath most fortunately been informed
Of my obscurèd course, "and shall find time
From this enormous state, seeking to give
Losses their remedies." All weary and o'erwatched,
Take vantage,° heavy eyes, not to behold *advantage*
This shameful lodging.
Fortune, good night. Smile once more; turn thy wheel!
[(*He sleeps.*)]

Scene 3[9]

[*Enter Edgar.*]
EDGAR: I heard myself proclaimed,
And by the happy hollow of a tree
Escaped the hunt. No port is free, no place
That guard and most unusual vigilance
Does not attend my taking. Whiles I may scape
I will preserve myself, and am bethought
To take the basest and most poorest shape
That ever penury, in contempt of man,
Brought near to beast. My face I'll grime with filth,
Blanket my loins, elf° all my hairs in knots, *tangle*
And with presented nakedness outface
The winds and persecutions of the sky.
The country gives me proof and precedent
Of Bedlam beggars who with roaring voices
Strike° in their numbed and mortifièd° arms *stick / deadened*
Pins, wooden pricks, nails, sprigs of rosemary;
And with this horrible object, from low farms,
Poor pelting° villages, sheepcotes, and mills, *paltry*

8. Even good men suffer decline in fortune at times.

9. Location: The scene continues. Kent is dozing in the stocks.

Sometimes with lunatic bans,° sometimes with prayers, *curses*
Enforce their charity. Poor Turlygod! Poor Tom![1]
That's something yet. Edgar I nothing am. [*Exit.*]

Scene 4[2]

Enter Lear, Fool, and Gentleman.

LEAR: 'Tis strange that they[3] should so depart from home
And not send back my messenger.

GENTLEMAN: As I learned,
The night before there was no purpose in them
Of this remove.[4]

KENT: Hail to thee, noble master!

LEAR: Ha?
Mak'st thou this shame thy pastime?

KENT: No, my lord.

FOOL: Ha, ha, he wears cruel[5] garters. Horses are tied by the heads, dogs and bears by th' neck, monkeys by th' loins, and men by th' legs. When a man's overlusty at legs,[6] then he wears wooden netherstocks.[7]

LEAR: What's he that hath so much thy place mistook
To set thee here?

KENT: It is both he and she:
Your son and daughter.

LEAR: No.

KENT: Yes.

LEAR: No, I say.

KENT: I say yea.

LEAR: No, no, they would not.

KENT: Yes, they have.

LEAR: By Jupiter, I swear no.

KENT: By Juno, I swear ay.

LEAR: They durst not do't!
They could not, would not do't. 'Tis worse than murder
To do upon respect[8] such violent outrage.
Resolve° me with all modest° haste which way *enlighten / moderate*
Thou mightst deserve, or they impose, this usage,
Coming from us.

KENT: My lord, when at their home[9]
I did commend° Your Highness' letters to them, *deliver*
Ere I was risen from the place that showed
My duty kneeling, came there a reeking post,
Stewed° in his haste, half breathless, panting forth *soaked*
From Goneril his mistress salutations;
Delivered letters, spite of intermission,[1]

1. Bedlam beggars were known as "poor Toms."
2. Location: scene continues before Gloucester's house. Kent still dozing in the stocks.
3. Cornwall and Regan.
4. Change of residence.
5. Unkind, with pun on *crewel*, "worsted."
6. Given to running away or overly active sexually.
7. Stockings.
8. Against my officers who deserve respect.
9. Kent and Oswald went first to Cornwall's palace after leaving Albany's palace.
1. In disregard of interrupting me, or in spite of the interruptions caused by being out of breath.

Which presently they read; on whose contents
They summoned up their meiny,[2] straight took horse,
Commanded me to follow and attend
The leisure of their answer, gave me cold looks;
And meeting here the other messenger,
Whose welcome, I perceived, had poisoned mine—
Being the very fellow which of late
Displayed so saucily against Your Highness—
Having more man than wit[3] about me, drew.
He raised the house with loud and coward cries.
Your son and daughter found this trespass worth
The shame which here it suffers.

FOOL: Winter's not gone yet if the wild geese fly that way.[4]
Fathers that wear rags
Do make their children blind,[5]
But fathers that bear bags[6]
Shall see their children kind.
Fortune, that arrant whore,
Ne'er turns the key to th' poor.
But, for all this, thou shalt have as many dolors[7] for thy daughters as thou canst tell in a year.

LEAR: Oh, how this mother[8] swells up toward my heart!
Hysterica passio, down, thou climbing sorrow!
Thy element's below.—Where is this daughter?

KENT: With the Earl, sir, here within.

LEAR: Follow me not. Stay here. [*Exit*.]

GENTLEMAN: Made you no more offense but what you speak of?

KENT: None.
How chance the King comes with so small a number?

FOOL: An thou hadst been set i'th' stocks for that question, thou'dst well deserved it.

KENT: Why, Fool?

FOOL: We'll set thee to school to an ant to teach thee there's no laboring i'th' winter. All that follow their noses are led by their eyes but blind men, and there's not a nose among twenty but can smell him that's stinking.[9] Let go thy hold when a great wheel runs down a hill lest it break thy neck with following; but the great one that goes upward, let him draw thee after. When a wise man gives thee better counsel, give me mine again. I would have none but knaves follow it, since a fool gives it.
That sir which serves and seeks for gain,
And follows but for form,

2. Retinue of servants.
3. Having more courage than good sense.
4. The signs still point to worsening fortune; the wild geese are still flying south.
5. Indifferent to their father's needs.
6. I.e., bags of gold.
7. Griefs, with pun on dollars.
8. The "mother," or "*Hysterica passio*" was a form of hysteria which women were believed to suffer from because the womb, or uterus (Greek *hystera*) moved in such a way or emitted vapors that caused them to choke.
9. One who is out of favor is easily detected.

Will pack° [be off] when it begins to rain
And leave thee in the storm.
But I will tarry; the fool will stay,
And let the wise man fly.
The knave turns fool that runs away;
The fool no knave, pardie.[1]

[*Enter Lear and Gloucester*.]

KENT: Where learned you this, Fool?

FOOL: Not i'th' stocks, fool.

LEAR: Deny to speak with me? They are sick? They are weary?
They have traveled all the night? Mere fetches,° [pretexts]
The images of revolt and flying off.
Fetch me a better answer.

GLOUCESTER: My dear lord,
You know the fiery quality of the Duke,
How unremovable and fixed he is
In his own course.

LEAR: Vengeance! Plague! Death! Confusion!
Fiery? What quality? Why, Gloucester, Gloucester,
I'd speak with the Duke of Cornwall and his wife.

GLOUCESTER: Well, my good lord, I have informed them so.

LEAR: Informed them? Dost thou understand me, man?

GLOUCESTER: Ay, my good lord.

LEAR: The King would speak with Cornwall. The dear father
Would with his daughter speak, commands, tends service.
Are they informed of this? My breath and blood!
Fiery? The fiery Duke? Tell the hot Duke that—
No, but not yet. Maybe he is not well.
Infirmity doth still neglect all office
Whereto our health is bound;[2] we are not ourselves
When nature, being oppressed, commands the mind
To suffer with the body. I'll forbear,
And am fallen out with my more headier will,
To take the indisposed and sickly fit
For the sound man.[3] [(*Looking at Kent*)] Death on my state! Wherefore
Should he sit here? This act persuades me
That this remotion° [keeping apart] of the Duke and her
Is practice only. Give me my servant forth.
Go tell the Duke and 's wife I'd speak with them,
Now, presently. Bid them come forth and hear me,
Or at their chamber door I'll beat the drum
Till it cry sleep to death.[4]

1. *Par dieu* (French), "by God."
2. Sickness always prompts us to neglect duties which in good health we are bound to perform.
3. And now disapprove of my more impetuous will in having rashly supposed that those who are indisposed and sickly were in sound health.
4. Put an end to sleep by the noise.

GLOUCESTER: I would have all well betwixt you. [*Exit.*]

LEAR: Oh, me, my heart, my rising heart! But down!

FOOL: Cry to it, nuncle, as the cockney did to the eels when she put 'em i'th' paste alive. She knapped 'em o'th' coxcombs with a stick and cried, "Down, wantons,[5] down!" 'Twas her brother that, in pure kindness to his horse, buttered his hay.

[*Enter Cornwall, Regan, Gloucester, (and) servants.*]

LEAR: Good morrow to you both.

CORNWALL: Hail to your Grace!

[*Kent here set at liberty.*]

REGAN: I am glad to see Your Highness.

LEAR: Regan, I think you are. I know what reason
I have to think so. If thou shouldst not be glad,
I would divorce me from thy mother's tomb,
Sepulch'ring an adultress.[6] [(*To Kent*)] Oh, are you free?
Some other time for that.—Belovèd Regan,
Thy sister's naught.° Oh, Regan, she hath tied — *wicked*
Sharp-toothed unkindness, like a vulture, here.

[(*He lays his hand on his heart.*)]

I can scarce speak to thee. Thou'lt not believe
With how depraved a quality—Oh, Regan!

REGAN: I pray you, sir, take patience. I have hope
You less know how to value her desert
Than she to scant her duty.[7]

LEAR: Say? How is that?

REGAN: I cannot think my sister in the least
Would fail her obligation. If, sir, perchance
She have restrained the riots of your followers,
'Tis on such ground and to such wholesome end
As clears her from all blame.

LEAR: My curses on her!

REGAN: Oh, sir, you are old;
Nature in you stands on the very verge
Of his confine.[8] You should be ruled and led
By some discretion that discerns your state
Better than you yourself. Therefore, I pray you,
That to our sister you do make return.
Say you have wronged her.

LEAR: Ask her forgiveness?
Do you but mark how this becomes the house:
[(*Kneeling*)] "Dear daughter, I confess that I am old;

5. The cockney wife is trying to coax the eels into laying down their lives for the making of the pastry pie, a plea that is about as ineffectual as Lear's imploring his rising heart to subside.

6. I would stop honoring your dead mother's grave, since it would surely contain the dead body of an adulteress.

7. I trust this is more a matter of your undervaluing her merit than of her falling slack in her duty to you.

8. Your life has almost completed its allotted scope.

Age is unnecessary. On my knees I beg
That you'll vouchsafe me raiment, bed, and food."
REGAN: Good sir, no more. These are unsightly tricks.
Return you to my sister.
LEAR [(*rising*)]: Never, Regan.
She hath abated° me of half my train, *deprived*
Looked black upon me, struck me with her tongue
Most serpentlike upon the very heart.
All the stored vengeances of heaven fall
On her ingrateful top![9] Strike her young bones,
You taking airs, with lameness!
CORNWALL: Fie, sir, fie!
LEAR: You nimble lightnings, dart your blinding flames
Into her scornful eyes! Infect her beauty,
You fen-sucked[1] fogs drawn by the powerful sun
To fall and blister!
REGAN: O the blest gods! So will you wish on me
When the rash mood is on.
LEAR: No, Regan, thou shalt never have my curse.
Thy tender-hafted[2] nature shall not give
Thee o'er to harshness. Her eyes are fierce, but thine
Do comfort and not burn. 'Tis not in thee
To grudge my pleasures, to cut off my train,
To bandy° hasty words, to scant my sizes,[3] *exchange*
And, in conclusion, to oppose the bolt
Against my coming in. Thou better know'st
The offices of nature, bond of childhood,
Effects of courtesy, dues of gratitude.
Thy half o'th' kingdom hast thou not forgot,
Wherein I thee endowed.
REGAN: Good sir, to th' purpose.
LEAR: Who put my man i'th' stocks? [*Tucket within*.]
CORNWALL: What trumpet's that?
REGAN: I know't—my sister's. This approves her letter,
That she would soon be here.
[*Enter steward (Oswald)*.]
Is your lady come?
LEAR: This is a slave, whose easy-borrowed pride
Dwells in the fickle grace of her he follows.—
Out, varlet, from my sight!
CORNWALL: What means Your Grace?
LEAR: Who stocked my servant? Regan, I have good hope
Thou didst not know on't.
[*Enter Goneril*.]
Who comes here? O heavens,

9. Ungrateful head.
1. It was thought that the sun sucked up poisons from fens or marshes.
2. Set in a tender frame.
3. Diminish my allowances.

If you do love old men, if your sweet sway
Allow obedience, if you yourselves are old,
Make it your cause; send down, and take my part!
[(*To Goneril*)] Art not ashamed to look upon this beard?
[(*Goneril and Regan join hands.*)]
Oh, Regan, will you take her by the hand?

GONERIL: Why not by th' hand, sir? How have I offended?
All's not offense that indiscretion finds
And dotage terms so.

LEAR: O sides,[4] you are too tough!
Will you yet hold?—How came my man i'th' stocks?

CORNWALL: I set him there, sir; but his own disorders
Deserved much less advancement.[5]

LEAR: You? Did you?

REGAN: I pray you, father, being weak, seem so.
If till the expiration of your month
You will return and sojourn with my sister,
Dismissing half your train, come then to me.
I am now from[6] home, and out of that provision
Which shall be needful for your entertainment.[7]

LEAR: Return to her? And fifty men dismissed?
No! Rather I abjure all roofs, and choose
To wage against the enmity o'th'air,
To be a comrade with the wolf and owl—
Necessity's sharp pinch. Return with her?
Why, the hot-blooded France, that dowerless took
Our youngest born—I could as well be brought
To knee his throne and, squirelike, pension beg
To keep base life afoot. Return with her?
Persuade me rather to be slave and sumpter° *packhorse*
To this detested groom. [(*He points to Oswald.*)]

GONERIL: At your choice, sir.

LEAR: I prithee, daughter, do not make me mad.
I will not trouble thee, my child. Farewell.
We'll no more meet, no more see one another.
But yet thou art my flesh, my blood, my daughter—
Or rather a disease that's in my flesh,
Which I must needs call mine. Thou art a boil,
A plague-sore, or embossed[8] carbuncle
In my corrupted blood. But I'll not chide thee;
Let shame come when it will, I do not call it.
I do not bid the thunder-bearer[9] shoot,
Nor tell tales of thee to high-judging Jove.
Mend when thou canst; be better at thy leisure.

4. Sides of the chest, stretched by the swelling heart.
5. Far less honor, far worse treatment.
6. Away from.
7. Proper reception.
8. Swollen stone.
9. Jove.

I can be patient. I can stay with Regan,
I and my hundred knights.

REGAN: Not altogether so.
I looked not for you yet, nor am provided
For your fit welcome. Give ear, sir, to my sister;
For those that mingle reason with your passion
Must be content to think you old, and so—
But she knows what she does.

LEAR: Is this well spoken?

REGAN: I dare avouch it, sir. What, fifty followers?
Is it not well? What should you need of more?
Yea, or so many, sith that both charge and danger
Speak 'gainst so great a number? How in one house
Should many people under two commands
Hold amity? 'Tis hard, almost impossible.

GONERIL: Why might not you, my lord, receive attendance
From those that she calls servants, or from mine?

REGAN: Why not, my lord? If then they chanced to slack° ye, *neglect*
We could control them. If you will come to me—
For now I spy a danger—I entreat you
To bring but five-and-twenty. To no more
Will I give place or notice.

LEAR: I gave you all—

REGAN: And in good time you gave it.

LEAR: Made you my guardians, my depositaries,° *trustees*
But kept a reservation to be followed
With such a number. What, must I come to you
With five-and-twenty? Regan, said you so?

REGAN: And speak't again, my lord. No more with me.

LEAR: Those wicked creatures yet do look well-favored
When others are more wicked; not being the worst
Stands in some rank of praise. [(*To Goneril*)] I'll go with thee.
Thy fifty yet doth double five-and-twenty
And thou art twice her love.

GONERIL: Hear me, my lord:
What need you five-and-twenty, ten, or five,
To follow in a house where twice so many
Have a command to tend you?

REGAN: What need one?

LEAR: Oh, reason not the need! Our basest beggars
Are in the poorest thing superfluous.[1]
Allow not nature more than nature needs,
Man's life is cheap as beast's. Thou art a lady;
If only to go warm were gorgeous,
Why, nature needs not what thou gorgeous wear'st,

1. Even our poorest beggars have some wretched possessions beyond what they absolutely need.

Which scarcely keeps thee warm. But, for true need—
You heavens, give me that patience, patience I need!
You see me here, you gods, a poor old man,
As full of grief as age, wretched in both.
If it be you that stirs these daughters' hearts
Against their father, fool me not so much
To bear it tamely; touch me with noble anger,
And let not women's weapons, water drops,
Stain my man's cheeks. No, you unnatural hags,
I will have such revenges on you both
That all the world shall—I will do such things—
What they are yet I know not, but they shall be
The terrors of the earth. You think I'll weep;
No, I'll not weep. [*Storm and tempest.*]
I have full cause of weeping; but this heart
Shall break into a hundred thousand flaws
Or ere I'll weep. Oh, Fool, I shall go mad!
[*Exeunt (Lear, Gloucester, Kent, Gentleman, and Fool).*]

CORNWALL: Let us withdraw. 'Twill be a storm.
REGAN: This house is little. The old man and 's people
Cannot be well bestowed.° *lodged*
GONERIL: 'Tis his own blame hath put himself from rest,[2]
And must needs taste his folly.
REGAN: For his particular,[3] I'll receive him gladly,
But not one follower.
GONERIL: So am I purposed. Where is my lord of Gloucester?
CORNWALL: Followed the old man forth.
[*Enter Gloucester.*]
He is returned.
GLOUCESTER: The King is in high rage.
CORNWALL: Whither is he going?
GLOUCESTER: He calls to horse, but will I know not whither.
CORNWALL: 'Tis best to give him way. He leads himself.
GONERIL [(*to Gloucester*)]: My lord, entreat him by no means to stay.
GLOUCESTER: Alack, the night comes on, and the bleak winds
Do sorely ruffle. For many miles about
There's scarce a bush.
REGAN: Oh, sir, to willful men
The injuries that they themselves procure
Must be their schoolmasters. Shut up your doors.
He is attended with a desperate train,
And what they may incense him to, being apt
To have his ear abused,[4] wisdom bids fear.

2. Out of the house, and lacking peace of mind.
3. As for him individually.
4. He being inclined to listen to wild counsel.

CORNWALL: Shut up your doors, my lord; 'tis a wild night.
My Regan counsels well. Come out o'th' storm.

[*Exeunt.*]

ACT 3
Scene 1[5]

[*Storm still. Enter Kent (disguised as Caius) and a Gentleman, severally.*]

KENT: Who's there, besides foul weather?

GENTLEMAN: One minded like the weather, most unquietly.

KENT: I know you. Where's the King?

GENTLEMAN: Contending with the fretful elements;
Bids the wind blow the earth into the sea
Or swell the curlèd waters 'bove the main,
That things might change or cease; tears his white hair,
Which the impetuous blasts with eyeless rage
Catch in their fury and make nothing of;
Strives in his little world of man to outstorm
The to-and-fro-conflicting wind and rain.
This night, wherein the cub-drawn[6] bear would couch,
The lion and the belly-pinchèd wolf
Keep their fur dry, unbonneted he runs
And bids what will take all.

KENT: But who is with him?

GENTLEMAN: None but the Fool, who labors to outjest
His heart-struck injuries.

KENT: Sir, I do know you,
And dare upon the warrant of my note
Commend a dear thing to you. There is division,
Although as yet the face of it is covered
With mutual cunning, twixt Albany and Cornwall;
Who have—as who have not, that their great stars
Throned and set high?—servants, who seem no less,
Which are to France the spies and speculations
Intelligent of our state.[7] What hath been seen,
Either in snuffs and packings[8] of the dukes,
Or the hard rein which both of them hath borne
Against the old kind King, or something deeper,
Whereof perchance these are but furnishings—
But true it is, from France there comes a power
Into this scattered kingdom, who already,
Wise in our negligence, have secret feet
In some of our best ports and are at point
To show their open banner. Now to you:
If on my credit you dare build so far

5. Location: A heath in Gloucestershire.
6. Famished, with udders sucked dry.
7. Supplying intelligence pertinent to our state.
8. Resentments and intrigues.

To make your speed to Dover, you shall find
Some that will thank you, making just report
Of how unnatural and bemadding sorrow
The King hath cause to plain.
I am a gentleman of blood and breeding,
And from some knowledge and assurance offer
This office to you.

GENTLEMAN: I will talk further with you.

KENT: No, do not.
For confirmation that I am much more
Than my outwall,[9] open this purse and take
What it contains. [(*He gives a purse and a ring.*)] If you shall see Cordelia—
As fear not but you shall—show her this ring,
And she will tell you who that fellow is
That yet you do not know. Fie on this storm!
I will go seek the King.

GENTLEMAN: Give me your hand. Have you no more to say?

KENT: Few words, but, to effect, more than all yet:
That when we have found the King—in which your pain
That way, I'll this—he that first lights on him
Holla the other.

[*Exeunt (separately).*]

Scene 2[1]

[*Storm still. Enter Lear and Fool.*]

LEAR: Blow, winds, and crack your cheeks! Rage, blow!
You cataracts and hurricanoes, spout
Till you have drenched our steeples, drowned the cocks![2]
You sulfurous and thought-executing fires,
Vaunt-couriers° of oak-cleaving thunderbolts, *forerunners*
Singe my white head! And thou, all-shaking thunder,
Strike flat the thick rotundity o'th' world!
Crack nature's molds, all germens spill at once[3]
That makes ingrateful man!

FOOL: Oh, nuncle, court holy water in a dry house is better than this rainwater out o'door. Good nuncle, in, ask thy daughters blessing. Here's a night pities neither wise men nor fools.

LEAR: Rumble thy bellyful! Spit, fire! Spout, rain!
Nor rain, wind, thunder, fire are my daughters.
I tax not you, you elements, with unkindness;
I never gave you kingdom, called you children.
You owe me no subscription.° Then let fall *allegiance*
Your horrible pleasure. Here I stand your slave,

9. Exterior appearance.
1. Location: The heath.
2. Weathercocks.
3. Crack the molds in which nature makes all life; destroy all seeds at once.

A poor, infirm, weak, and despised old man.
But yet I call you servile ministers,
That will with two pernicious daughters join
Your high-engendered battles 'gainst a head
So old and white as this. O, ho! 'Tis foul.

FOOL: He that has a house to put 's head in has a good headpiece.[4]
The codpiece that will house
Before the head has any,
The head and he shall louse;
So beggars marry many.[5]
The man that makes his toe
What he his heart should make
Shall of a corn cry woe,
And turn his sleep to wake.[6]
For there was never yet fair woman but she made mouths in a glass.[7]

LEAR: No, I will be the pattern of all patience;
I will say nothing.

[*Enter Kent, (disguised as Caius).*]

KENT: Who's there?

FOOL: Marry, here's grace and a codpiece[8]; that's a wise man and a fool.

KENT: Alas, sir, are you here? Things that love night
Love not such nights as these. The wrathful skies
Gallow° the very wanderers of the dark *frighten*
And make them keep their caves. Since I was man,
Such sheets of fire, such bursts of horrid thunder,
Such groans of roaring wind and rain I never
Remember to have heard. Man's nature cannot carry
Th'affliction nor the fear.

LEAR: Let the great gods,
That keep this dreadful pother° o'er our heads, *hubbub*
Find out their enemies now. Tremble, thou wretch,
That hast within thee undivulgèd crimes
Unwhipped of justice! Hide thee, thou bloody hand,
Thou perjured, and thou simular° of virtue *pretender*
That art incestuous! Caitiff,° to pieces shake, *wretch*
That under covert and convenient seeming
Has practiced° on man's life! Close pent-up guilts, *plotted*
Rive your concealing continents and cry
These dreadful summoners grace![9] I am a man
More sinned against than sinning.

4. Helmetlike covering for the head, and head for common sense.
5. A man who houses his genitals in a sexual embrace before he has a roof over his head can expect the lice-infected poverty of a penniless marriage.
6. Anyone who unwisely places his affection on base things will be afflicted with sorrow and sleeplessness.
7. The practice of making attractive faces in the mirror.
8. Royal grace and a codpiece, prominent in the Fool's costume.
9. O you secret and buried consciousnesses of guilt, burst open the hiding places that conceal you, and pray for mercy. (Summoners are the officers who cited offenders to appear before ecclesiastical courts.)

KENT: Alack, bareheaded?
Gracious my lord, hard by here is a hovel;
Some friendship will it lend you 'gainst the tempest.
Repose you there while I to this hard house—
More harder than the stones whereof 'tis raised,
Which even but now, demanding after you,
Denied me to come in—return and force
Their scanted° courtesy. *stinted*

LEAR: My wits begin to turn.
Come on, my boy. How dost, my boy? Art cold?
I am cold myself.—Where is this straw, my fellow?
The art of our necessities is strange,
And can make vile things precious. Come, your hovel.—
Poor fool and knave, I have one part in my heart
That's sorry yet for thee.

FOOL: [*sings*] "He that has and a little tiny wit,
With heigh-ho, the wind and the rain,
Must make content with his fortunes fit,
Though the rain it raineth every day."

LEAR: True, boy.—Come, bring us to this hovel.

[*Exit (with Kent)*.]

FOOL: This is a brave night to cool a courtesan.[1] I'll speak a prophecy ere I go:
When priests are more in word than matter;[2]
When brewers mar their malt with water;
When nobles are their tailors' tutors,
No heretics burned but wenches' suitors,[3]
Then shall the realm of Albion
Come to great confusion.

When every case in law is right,
No squire in debt, nor no poor knight;
When slanders do not live in tongues,
Nor cutpurses come not to throngs;
When usurers tell their gold i'th' field,
And bawds and whores do churches build,
Then comes the time, who lives to see't,
That going shall be used with feet.[4]

This prophecy Merlin shall make, for I live before his time.[5] [*Exit*.]

1. This night is stormy enough to cool the lust of a courtesan.
2. When priests do not practice what they preach. This and the next three lines satirize the present state of affairs.
3. When the prevailing heresy is lechery, punished not by burning at the stake but by venereal infection.
4. The anticlimax of "then people will walk on foot" suggests that none of these utopian dreams will come to pass.
5. Both prophecies are imitations of the pseudo-Chaucerian "Merlin's Prophecy."

Scene 3[6]

[*Enter Gloucester and Edmund (with lights).*]

GLOUCESTER: Alack, alack, Edmund, I like not this unnatural dealing. When I desired their leave that I might pity him, they took from me the use of mine own house, charged me on pain of perpetual displeasure neither to speak of him, entreat for him, or any way sustain him.

EDMUND: Most savage and unnatural!

GLOUCESTER: Go to; say you nothing. There is division between the dukes, and a worse matter than that. I have received a letter this night; 'tis dangerous to be spoken; I have locked the letter in my closet.[7] These injuries the King now bears will be revenged home;[8] there is part of a power already footed.[9] We must incline to the King. I will look him and privily relieve him. Go you and maintain talk with the Duke, that my charity be not of him perceived. If he ask for me, I am ill and gone to bed. If I die for't, as no less is threatened me, the King my old master must be relieved. There is strange things toward,[1] Edmund. Pray you, be careful. [*Exit.*]

EDMUND: This courtesy forbid thee shall the Duke
Instantly know, and of that letter too.
This seems a fair deserving, and must draw me
That which my father loses—no less than all.
The younger rises when the old doth fall. [*Exit.*]

Scene 4[2]

[*Enter Lear, Kent (disguised as Caius), and Fool.*]

KENT: Here is the place, my lord. Good my lord, enter.
The tyranny of the open night's too rough
For nature[3] to endure. [*Storm still.*]

LEAR: Let me alone.

KENT: Good my lord, enter here.

LEAR: Wilt break my heart?

KENT: I had rather break mine own. Good my lord, enter.

LEAR: Thou think'st 'tis much that this contentious storm
Invades us to the skin. So 'tis to thee,
But where the greater malady is fixed
The lesser is scarce felt, Thou'dst shun a bear,
But if thy flight lay toward the roaring sea
Thou'dst meet the bear i'th' mouth. When the mind's free,
The body's delicate. This tempest in my mind
Doth from my senses take all feeling else
Save what beats there. Filial ingratitude!
Is it not as this mouth should tear this hand
For lifting food to't? But I will punish home.

6. Location: Gloucester's house.
7. Private chamber.
8. Thoroughly.
9. Landed.
1. Impending.
2. Location: The heath, before a hovel.
3. Human nature.

No, I will weep no more. In such a night
To shut me out? Pour on; I will endure.
In such a night as this? Oh, Regan, Goneril,
Your old kind father, whose frank heart gave all—
Oh, that way madness lies; let me shun that!
No more of that.

KENT: Good my lord, enter here.

LEAR: Prithee, go in thyself; seek thine own ease.
This tempest will not give me leave to ponder
On things would hurt me more. But I'll go in.
[(*To the Fool*)] In, boy; go first. You houseless poverty—
Nay, get thee in. I'll pray, and then I'll sleep.

[*Exit (Fool into the hovel).*]

Poor naked wretches, wheresoe'er you are,
That bide the pelting of this pitiless storm,
How shall your houseless heads and unfed sides,
Your looped and windowed[4] raggedness, defend you
From seasons such as these? Oh, I have ta'en
Too little care of this! Take physic, pomp;[5]
Expose thyself to feel what wretches feel,
That thou mayst shake the superflux[6] to them
And show the heavens more just.

EDGAR [(*within*)]: Fathom and half, fathom and half! Poor Tom!

[*Enter Fool (from the hovel).*]

FOOL: Come not in here, nuncle; here's a spirit. Help me, help me!

KENT: Give me thy hand. Who's there?

FOOL: A spirit, a spirit! He says his name's poor Tom.

KENT: What art thou that dost grumble there i'th' straw?
Come forth.

[*Enter Edgar (disguised as a madman).*]

EDGAR: Away! The foul fiend follows me! Through the sharp hawthorn blows the cold wind.[7] Hum! Go to thy bed and warm thee.

LEAR: Didst thou give all to thy daughters? And art thou come to this?

EDGAR: Who gives anything to poor Tom? Whom the foul fiend[8] hath led through fire and through flame, through ford and whirlpool, o'er bog and quagmire; that hath laid knives under his pillow and halters in his pew, set ratsbane by his porridge, made him proud of heart to ride on a bay trotting horse over four-inched bridges to course his own shadow for a traitor.[9] Bless thy five wits![1] Tom's a-cold. Oh, do de, do de, do de. Bless thee from whirlwinds, star-blasting, and taking![2] Do poor Tom some charity, whom

4. Full of openings that let in the rain.
5. Cure yourself, O powerful ones.
6. Superfluity, wealth above one's needs.
7. This line is found in an 18th-century ballad "The Friar of Orders Grey."
8. Edgar's feigned identity of Tom o' Bedlam includes demonic possession.
9. The fiend has laid in poor Tom's way tempting means to despairing suicide, knives under his pillow, nooses in his church pew, and rat poison beside his soup, and riding a horse over bridges four inches wide in pursuit of his shadow.
1. Either the five physical senses—sight, hearing, taste, touch, and smell—or the five faculties of the mind—wit, imagination, fantasy, estimation, and memory.
2. Being blighted by the influence of the stars and taking infection.

the foul fiend vexes. There could I have him now—and there—and there again—and there. [*Storm still.*]

LEAR: Has his daughters brought him to this pass?—
Couldst thou save nothing? Wouldst thou give 'em all?

FOOL: Nay, he reserved a blanket, else we had been all shamed.

LEAR: Now, all the plagues that in the pendulous air
Hang fated o'er men's faults light on thy daughters!

KENT: He hath no daughters, sir.

LEAR: Death, traitor! Nothing could have subdued nature
To such a lowness but his unkind daughters.
Is it the fashion that discarded fathers
Should have thus little mercy on their flesh?
Judicious punishment! 'Twas this flesh begot
Those pelican[3] daughters.

EDGAR: Pillicock[4] sat on Pillicock Hill. Alow, alow, loo, loo!

FOOL: This cold night will turn us all to fools and madmen.

EDGAR: Take heed o'th' foul fiend. Obey thy parents; keep thy word's justice; swear not; commit not with man's sworn spouse; set not thy sweet heart on proud array. Tom's a-cold.

LEAR: What hast thou been?

EDGAR: A servingman, proud in heart and mind, that curled my hair, wore gloves in my cap, served the lust of my mistress' heart, and did the act of darkness with her; swore as many oaths as I spake words, and broke them in the sweet face of heaven. One that slept in the contriving of lust and waked to do it. Wine loved I deeply, dice dearly, and in woman out-paramoured the Turk.[5] False of heart, light of ear, bloody of hand; hog in sloth, fox in stealth, wolf in greediness, dog in madness, lion in prey. Let not the creaking of shoes nor the rustling of silks betray thy poor heart to woman. Keep thy foot out of brothels, thy hand out of plackets,[6] thy pen from lenders' books, and defy the foul fiend. Still through the hawthorn blows the cold wind; says suum, mun, nonny. Dolphin my boy, boy, sessa! Let him trot by. [*Storm still.*]

LEAR: Thou wert better in a grave than to answer with thy uncovered body this extremity of the skies. Is man no more than this? Consider him well. Thou ow'st the worm no silk, the beast no hide, the sheep no wool, the cat no perfume. Ha! Here's three on 's are sophisticated; thou art the thing itself. Unaccommodated[7] man is no more but such a poor, bare, forked animal as thou art. Off, off, you lendings! Come, unbutton here. [(*Tearing off his clothes.*)]

FOOL: Prithee, nuncle, be contented; 'tis a naughty[8] night to swim in. Now a little fire in a wild field were like an old lecher's heart—a small spark, all the rest on 's body cold.

[*Enter Gloucester, with a torch.*]

Look, here comes a walking fire.

3. Greedy, because young pelicans fed upon their mother's blood.
4. A euphemism for penis in nursery rhymes.
5. Outdid the Sultan in keeping mistresses.
6. Slits in skirts or petticoats.
7. Unfurnished with the trappings of civilization.
8. Nasty.

EDGAR: This is the foul fiend Flibbertigibbet![9] He begins at curfew and walks till the first cock; he gives the web and the pin,[1] squinnies the eye and makes the harelip, mildews the white wheat, and hurts the poor creature of earth.

Swithold[2] footed thrice the 'old;[3]
He met the nightmare and her ninefold;
Bid her alight,
And her troth plight,
And aroint[4] thee, witch, aroint thee!

KENT: How fares Your Grace?

LEAR: What's he?

KENT: Who's there? What is't you seek?

GLOUCESTER: What are you there? Your names?

EDGAR: Poor Tom, that eats the swimming frog, the toad, the tadpole, the wall newt and the water; that in the fury of his heart, when the foul fiend rages, eats cow dung for salads, swallows the old rat and the ditch-dog, drinks the green mantle[5] of the standing pool; who is whipped from tithing to tithing and stock-punished and imprisoned; who hath had three suits to his back, six shirts to his body,

Horse to ride, and weapon to wear;
But mice and rats and such small deer
Have been Tom's food for seven long year.

Beware my follower. Peace, Smulkin![6] Peace, thou fiend!

GLOUCESTER What, hath Your Grace no better company?

EDGAR: The Prince of Darkness is a gentleman. Modo he's called, and Mahu.

GLOUCESTER [(*to Lear*)]: Our flesh and blood, my lord, is grown so vile
That it doth hate what gets it.

EDGAR: Poor Tom's a-cold.

GLOUCESTER: Go in with me. My duty cannot suffer
T'obey in all your daughters' hard commands.
Though their injunction be to bar my doors
And let this tyrannous night take hold upon you,
Yet have I ventured to come seek you out
And bring you where both fire and food is ready.

LEAR: First let me talk with this philosopher.
[(*To Edgar*)] What is the cause of thunder?

KENT: Good my lord,
Take his offer. Go into th' house.

LEAR: I'll talk a word with this same learnèd Theban.[7]
[(*To Edgar*)] What is your study?

9. A devil from Elizabethan folklore whose name appears in Samuel Harsnett's *Declaration of Egregious Popish Impostures* (1603) and elsewhere.
1. Cataract.
2. Saint Withold, an Anglo-Saxon exorcist, who here provides defense against the demon thought to afflict sleepers by commanding the nightmare to alight.
3. Walked over the upland plain.
4. Begone.
5. Scum.
6. A devil's name, from Harsnett's *Declaration*, as are Modo and Mahu in line 1117.
7. A scholar or philosopher.

EDGAR: How to prevent the fiend, and to kill vermin.
LEAR: Let me ask you one word in private.
[*Lear and Edgar talk apart.*]
KENT [(*to Gloucester*)]: Importune him once more to go, my lord.
His wits begin t'unsettle.
GLOUCESTER: Canst thou blame him?
[*Storm still.*]
His daughters seek his death. Ah, that good Kent!
He said it would be thus, poor banished man.
Thou sayest the King grows mad; I'll tell thee, friend,
I am almost mad myself. I had a son,
Now outlawed from my blood; he sought my life
But lately, very late. I loved him, friend,
No father his son dearer. True to tell thee,
The grief hath crazed my wits. What a night's this!—
I do beseech Your Grace—
LEAR: Oh, cry you mercy, sir.
[(*To Edgar*)] Noble philosopher, your company.
EDGAR: Tom's a-cold.
GLOUCESTER [(*to Edgar*)]: In, fellow, there, in th' hovel. Keep thee warm.
LEAR [*starting toward the hovel*]: Come, let's in all.
KENT: This way, my lord.
LEAR: With him!
I will keep still with my philosopher.
KENT [(*to Gloucester*)]: Good my lord, soothe him. Let him take the fellow.
GLOUCESTER: [*to Kent*] Take you him on.
KENT [(*to Edgar*)]: Sirrah, come on. Go along with us.
LEAR: Come, good Athenian.[8]
GLOUCESTER: No words, no words! Hush.
EDGAR: Child Rowland to the dark tower came;[9]
His word[1] was still, "Fie, foh, and fum,
I smell the blood of a British man."[2] [*Exeunt.*]

Scene 5[3]

[*Enter Cornwall and Edmund (with a letter).*]

CORNWALL: I will have my revenge ere I depart his house.

EDMUND: How, my lord, I may be censured,[4] that nature[5] thus gives way to loyalty, something fears me to think of.

8. Philosopher.
9. Probably a fragment of a ballad about the hero of the Charlemagne legends. A *child* is a candidate for knighthood.
1. Watchword.
2. The words of the Giant in "Jack, the Giant Killer."
3. Location: Gloucester's house.
4. Judged.
5. Attachment to family.

CORNWALL: I now perceive it was not altogether your brother's evil disposition made him seek his death, but a provoking merit set awork by a reprovable badness in himself.

EDMUND: How malicious is my fortune, that I must repent to be just! This is the letter he spoke of, which approves him an intelligent party to the advantages of France. Oh, heavens! That this treason were not, or not I the detector!

CORNWALL: Go with me to the Duchess.

EDMUND: If the matter of this paper be certain, you have mighty business in hand.

CORNWALL: True or false, it hath made thee Earl of Gloucester. Seek out where thy father is, that he may be ready for our apprehension.[6]

EDMUND [(*aside*)]: If I find him comforting the King, it will stuff his suspicion more fully—I will persevere in my course of loyalty, though the conflict be sore between that and my blood.[7]

CORNWALL: I will lay trust upon thee, and thou shalt find a dearer father in my love. [*Exeunt.*]

Scene 6[8]

[*Enter Kent (disguised as Caius) and Gloucester.*]

GLOUCESTER: Here is better than the open air; take it thankfully. I will piece[9] out the comfort with what addition I can. I will not be long from you.

KENT: All the power of his wits have given way to his impatience.[1] The gods reward your kindness!

[*Exit (Gloucester).*]

[*Enter Lear, Edgar (as poor Tom), and Fool.*]

EDGAR: Frateretto[2] calls me, and tells me Nero is an angler[3] in the lake of darkness. Pray, innocent, and beware the foul fiend.

FOOL: Prithee, nuncle, tell me whether a madman be a gentleman or a yeoman?[4]

LEAR: A king, a king!

FOOL: No, he's a yeoman that has a gentleman to his son; for he's a mad yeoman that sees his son a gentleman before him.

LEAR: To have a thousand with red burning spits
Come hizzing[5] in upon 'em—

EDGAR: The foul fiend bites my back.

FOOL: He's mad that trusts in the tameness of a wolf, a horse's health, a boy's love, or a whore's oath.

LEAR: It shall be done; I will arraign them[6] straight.
[(*To Edgar*)] Come, sit thou here, most learnèd justicer.
[(*To the Fool*)] Thou, sapient sir, sit here. Now, you she-foxes!

EDGAR: Look where he stands and glares! Want'st thou eyes at trial, madam?
[(*Sings.*)] "Come o'er the burn, Bessy, to me—"[7]

6. For our arresting of him.
7. Family loyalty.
8. Location: Within a building on Gloucester's estate.
9. Eke.
1. Rage.
2. Another fiend from Harsnett's *Declaration*.
3. Chaucer's "Monk's Tale" tells how Nero fished in the Tiber with nets of gold thread.
4. Property owner below the rank of gentleman.
5. Hissing.
6. Put them on trial.
7. First line of a ballad by William Birche, 1558. A burn is a brook.

FOOL [(*sings*)]: Her boat hath a leak,[8]
And she must not speak
Why she dares not come over to thee.

EDGAR: The foul fiend haunts poor Tom in the voice of a nightingale. Hoppedance[9] cries in Tom's belly for two white herring. Croak not, black angel; I have no food for thee.

KENT [(*to Lear*)]: How do you, sir? Stand you not so amazed.
Will you lie down and rest upon the cushions?

LEAR: I'll see their trial first. Bring in their evidence.
[(*To Edgar*)] Thou robèd[1] man of justice, take thy place;
[(*To the Fool*)] And thou, his yokefellow of equity,[2]
Bench by his side. [(*To Kent*)] You are o'th' commission;
Sit you, too. [(*They sit.*)]

EDGAR: Let us deal justly. [(*He sings.*)]
Sleepest or wakest thou, jolly shepherd?
Thy sheep be in the corn;[3]
And for one blast of thy minikin mouth,[4]
Thy sheep shall take no harm.
Purr the cat[5] is gray.

LEAR: Arraign her first; 'tis Goneril, I here take my oath before this honorable assembly, kicked the poor King her father.

FOOL: Come hither, mistress. Is your name Goneril?

LEAR: She cannot deny it.

FOOL: Cry you mercy, I took you for a joint stool.[6]

LEAR: And here's another,[7] whose warped looks proclaim
What store[8] her heart is made on. Stop her there!
Arms, arms, sword, fire! Corruption in the place!
False justicer, why hast thou let her scape?

EDGAR: Bless thy five wits!

KENT: Oh, pity! Sir, where is the patience now
That you so oft have boasted to retain?

EDGAR [(*aside*)]: My tears begin to take his part so much
They mar my counterfeiting.

LEAR: The little dogs and all,
Tray, Blanch, and Sweetheart, see, they bark at me.

EDGAR: Tom will throw his head at[9] them.—Avaunt, you curs!
Be thy mouth or black or white,
Tooth that poisons if it bite,
Mastiff, greyhound, mongrel grim,

8. The leaky boat may suggest the woman's sexual easiness.
9. Another fiend from Harsnett's *Declaration*.
1. Edgar with his blanket.
2. Partner in law.
3. In the grain field.
4. One shout from your dainty (minikin) mouth can save the sheep.
5. A devil or familiar from Harsnett.
6. A low stool made by a joiner. Proverbially the phrase "I took you for a joint stool" meant "I beg your pardon for failing to notice you." The reference is also to a stool on stage.
7. Regan.
8. Material.
9. Threaten.

Hound or spaniel, brach or lym,[1]
Bobtail tike or trundle-tail,[2]
Tom will make him weep and wail;
For, with throwing thus my head,
Dogs leap the hatch,[3] and all are fled.
Do de, de, de. Sessa! Come, march to wakes[4] and fairs and market towns.
Poor Tom, thy horn is dry.

LEAR: Then let them anatomize Regan; see what breeds about her heart. Is there any cause in nature that makes these hard hearts? [(*To Edgar*)] You, sir, I entertain for one of my hundred; only I do not like the fashion of your garments. You will say they are Persian; but let them be changed.

KENT: Now, good my lord, lie here and rest awhile.

LEAR [(*lying on cushions*)]: Make no noise, make no noise. Draw the curtains.[5] So, so. We'll go to supper i'th' morning. [(*He sleeps.*)]

FOOL: And I'll go to bed at noon.

[*Enter Gloucester.*]

GLOUCESTER [(*to Kent*)]: Come hither, friend. Where is the King my master?

KENT: Here, sir, but trouble him not; his wits are gone.

GLOUCESTER: Good friend, I prithee, take him in thy arms.
I have o'erheard a plot of death upon him.
There is a litter ready; lay him in't
And drive toward Dover, friend, where thou shalt meet
Both welcome and protection. Take up thy master.
If thou shouldst dally half an hour, his life,
With thine and all that offer to defend him,
Stand in assurèd loss. Take up, take up,
And follow me, that will to some provision
Give thee quick conduct.

KENT: Oppressèd nature sleeps.
This rest might yet have balmed thy broken sinews,° *nerves*
Which, if convenience° will not allow, *circumstances*
Stand in hard cure. [(*To the Fool*)] Come, help to bear thy master.
Thou must not stay behind. [(*They pick up Lear.*)]

GLOUCESTER: Come, come, away!

[*Exeunt (all but Edgar).*]

EDGAR: When we our betters see bearing our woes,
We scarcely think our miseries our foes.
Who alone suffers suffers most i'th' mind,[6]
Leaving free things and happy shows behind;
But then the mind much sufferance doth o'erskip
When grief hath mates, and bearing fellowship.
How light and portable my pain seems now,
When that which makes me bend makes the King bow—
He childed as I fathered. Tom, away!

1. Bitch hound or blood hound.
2. Mongrel dog with a docked or bobbed tail.
3. Lower half of a divided door.
4. Parish festivals.
5. Bedcurtains.
6. Whoever suffers alone has the greatest mental suffering.

Mark the high noises, and thyself bewray
When false opinion, whose wrong thoughts defile thee,
In thy just proof repeals and reconciles thee.[7]
What will hap more tonight, safe scape the King!
Lurk, lurk. [*Exit.*]

Scene 7[8]

[*Enter Cornwall, Regan, Goneril, Bastard (Edmund), and Servants.*]

CORNWALL [(*to Goneril*)]: Post speedily to my lord your husband; show him this letter. [*He gives a letter.*] The army of France is landed.—Seek out the traitor Gloucester. [(*Exeunt some Servants.*)]

REGAN: Hang him instantly.

GONERIL: Pluck out his eyes.

CORNWALL: Leave him to my displeasure. Edmund, keep you our sister company. The revenges we are bound to take upon your traitorous father are not fit for your beholding. Advise the Duke,[9] where you are going, to a most festinate[1] preparation; we are bound to the like. Our posts[2] shall be swift and intelligent betwixt us. Farewell, dear sister; farewell, my lord of Gloucester.

[*Enter steward (Oswald).*]

How now? Where's the King?

OSWALD: My lord of Gloucester hath conveyed him hence.
Some five- or six-and-thirty of his knights,
Hot questrists° after him, met him at gate, *searchers*
Who, with some other of the lord's dependents,
Are gone with him toward Dover, where they boast
To have well-armèd friends.

CORNWALL: Get horses for your mistress. [(*Exit Oswald.*)]

GONERIL: Farewell, sweet lord, and sister.

CORNWALL: Edmund, farewell. [(*Exeunt (Goneril and Edmund).*)]
Go seek the traitor Gloucester.
Pinion° him like a thief; bring him before us. *bind*
[(*Exeunt Servants.*)]
Though well we may not pass upon his life[3]
Without the form of justice, yet our power
Shall do a court'sy° to our wrath, which men *bow to*
May blame but not control.

[*Enter Gloucester, and Servants (leading him).*]

Who's there? The traitor?

REGAN: Ingrateful fox! 'Tis he.

CORNWALL: Bind fast his corky° arms. *withered*

7. Pay attention to what is being said about those in high places; only reveal your identity when public opinion, which now falsely derides you, finally justly proclaims your innocence and recalls you from banishment.
8. Location: Gloucester's house.
9. Albany.
1. Speedy.
2. Messengers.
3. Pass the death sentence upon him.

GLOUCESTER: What means Your Graces? Good my friends, consider
You are my guests. Do me no foul play, friends.
CORNWALL: Bind him, I say. [(*Servants bind him.*)]
REGAN: Hard, hard. Oh, filthy traitor!
GLOUCESTER: Unmerciful lady as you are, I'm none.
CORNWALL: To this chair bind him.—Villain, thou shalt find—
[(*Regan plucks Gloucester's beard.*)]
GLOUCESTER: By the kind gods, 'tis most ignobly done
To pluck me by the beard.
REGAN: So white,° and such a traitor? *old*
GLOUCESTER: Naughty° lady, *wicked*
These hairs which thou dost ravish from my chin
Will quicken and accuse thee. I am your host.
With robbers' hands my hospitable favors
You should not ruffle thus. What will you do?
CORNWALL: Come, sir, what letters had you late from France?
REGAN: Be simple-answered, for we know the truth.
CORNWALL: And what confederacy have you with the traitors
Late footed[4] in the kingdom?
REGAN: To whose hands
You have sent the lunatic King. Speak.
GLOUCESTER: I have a letter guessingly set down,
Which came from one that's of a neutral heart,
And not from one opposed.
CORNWALL: Cunning.
REGAN: And false.
CORNWALL: Where hast thou sent the King?
GLOUCESTER: To Dover.
REGAN: Wherefore to Dover? Wast thou not charged at peril—
CORNWALL: Wherefore to Dover? Let him answer that.
GLOUCESTER: I am tied to th' stake, and I must stand the course.[5]
REGAN: Wherefore to Dover?
GLOUCESTER: Because I would not see thy cruel nails
Pluck out his poor old eyes, nor thy fierce sister
In his anointed[6] flesh rash° boarish fangs. *slash*
The sea, with such a storm as his bare head
In hell-black night endured, would have buoyed up
And quenched the stellèd fires;[7]
Yet, poor old heart, he holp° the heavens to rain. *helped*
If wolves had at thy gate howled that dern° time, *dread*
Thou shouldst have said, "Good porter, turn the key."
All cruels else subscribe.[8] But I shall see
The wingèd Vengeance[9] overtake such children.

4. Recently landed.
5. Like a bear baited with dogs whose attack he must withstand.
6. Consecrated with holy oil.
7. Fires of the stars.
8. All other cruel creatures would show forgiveness except you.
9. The vengeance of the angel of divine wrath.

CORNWALL: See't shalt thou never.—Fellows, hold the chair.
Upon these eyes of thine I'll set my foot.
GLOUCESTER: He that will think to live till he be old,
Give me some help!
[(*Servants hold the chair as Cornwall grinds out one of Gloucester's eyes with his boot.*)]
Oh, cruel! O you gods!
REGAN: One side will mock another. Th'other too.
CORNWALL [*to Gloucester*]: If you see Vengeance—
FIRST SERVANT: Hold your hand, my lord!
I have served you ever since I was a child;
But better service have I never done you
Than now to bid you hold.
REGAN: How now, you dog?
FIRST SERVANT [*to Regan*]: If you did wear a beard upon your chin,
I'd shake it on this quarrel.[1]—What do you mean?
CORNWALL: My villain? [(*He draws his sword.*)]
FIRST SERVANT [(*drawing*)]: Nay, then, come on, and take the chance of anger.
[(*They fight. Cornwall is wounded.*)]
REGAN [(*to another Servant*)]: Give me thy sword. A peasant stand up thus?
[(*She takes a sword and runs at him behind.*)]
FIRST SERVANT: Oh, I am slain! My lord, you have one eye left
To see some mischief° on him. Oh! [*He dies.*] *injury*
CORNWALL: Lest it see more, prevent it. Out, vile jelly!
[(*He puts out Gloucester's other eye.*)]
Where is thy luster now?
GLOUCESTER: All dark and comfortless. Where's my son Edmund?
Edmund, enkindle all the sparks of nature[2]
To quit this horrid act.
REGAN: Out, treacherous villain!
Thou call'st on him that hates thee. It was he
That made the overture of thy treasons to us,
Who is too good to pity thee.
GLOUCESTER: Oh, my follies! Then Edgar was abused.
Kind gods, forgive me that, and prosper him!
REGAN [*to a Servant*]: Go thrust him out at gates and let him smell
His way to Dover. [*Exit (a Servant) with Gloucester.*]
How is't, my lord? How look you?
CORNWALL: I have received a hurt. Follow me, lady.—
Turn out that eyeless villain. Throw this slave
Upon the dunghill.—Regan, I bleed apace.
Untimely comes this hurt. Give me your arm.
[*Exeunt (Cornwall, supported by Regan).*]

1. I'd pull your beard in defiance for the cause of Gloucester.
2. Love of child for father.

SECOND SERVANT: I'll never care what wickedness I do,
If this man come to good.
THIRD SERVANT: If she live long,
And in the end meet the old course of death,
Women will all turn monsters.
SECOND SERVANT: Let's follow the old Earl, and get the Bedlam[3]
To lead him where he would. His roguish madness
Allows itself to anything.[4]
THIRD SERVANT: Go thou. I'll fetch some flax and whites of eggs
To apply to his bleeding face. Now, heaven help him!
[*Exeunt (with the body.)*][5]

ACT 4

Scene 1[6]

[*Enter Edgar (as poor Tom).*]
EDGAR: Yet better thus, and known to be contemned,
Than still contemned and flattered.[7] To be worst,
The lowest and most dejected thing of fortune,
Stands still in esperance,[8] lives not in fear.
The lamentable change is from the best;
The worst returns to laughter.[9] Welcome, then,
Thou unsubstantial air that I embrace!
The wretch that thou hast blown unto the worst
Owes nothing to thy blasts.
[*Enter Gloucester, and an Old Man (leading him).*]
But who comes here?
My father, poorly led? World, world, O world!
But that thy strange mutations make us hate thee,
Life would not yield to age.[1]
OLD MAN: Oh, my good lord, I have been your tenant
And your father's tenant these fourscore years.
GLOUCESTER: Away, get thee away! Good friend, begone.
Thy comforts can do me no good at all;
Thee they may hurt.
OLD MAN: You cannot see your way.
GLOUCESTER: I have no way and therefore want no eyes;
I stumbled when I saw. Full oft 'tis seen
Our means secure us, and our mere defects
Prove our commodities.[2] O dear son Edgar,

3. Madman from the insane asylum.
4. His madness means he can do anything we ask.
5. At some point after line 96, the body of the slain servant must be removed.
6. Location: The heath.
7. It is better to be a beggar and know that you are despised by others rather than to be despised behind one's back and flattered to one's face.
8. Gives one some cause for hope.
9. Any change from the worst is bound to be happy.
1. If it were not for the bad fortune we suffer, we would never accept old age and death.
2. Our prosperity makes us feel falsely secure whereas our suffering helps us.

The food of thy abusèd father's wrath![3]
Might I but live to see thee in my touch,
I'd say I had eyes again!
OLD MAN: How now? Who's there?
EDGAR [*aside*]: O gods! Who is't can say, "I am at the worst"?
I am worse than e'er I was.
OLD MAN: 'Tis poor mad Tom.
EDGAR [(*aside*)]: And worse I may be yet. The worst is not
So long as we can say, "This is the worst."
OLD MAN [(*to Edgar*)]: Fellow, where goest?
GLOUCESTER: Is it a beggar-man?
OLD MAN: Madman and beggar too.
GLOUCESTER: He has some reason,° else he could not beg. *sanity*
I'th' last night's storm I such a fellow saw,
Which made me think a man a worm. My son
Came then into my mind, and yet my mind
Was then scarce friends with him. I have heard more since.
As flies to wanton° boys are we to th' gods; *heedless*
They kill us for their sport.
EDGAR [(*aside*)]: How should this be?
Bad is the trade that must play fool to sorrow,
Ang'ring itself and others.[4]—Bless thee, master!
GLOUCESTER: Is that the naked fellow?
OLD MAN: Ay, my lord.
GLOUCESTER: Then, prithee, get thee gone. If for my sake
Thou wilt o'ertake us hence a mile or twain
I'th' way toward Dover, do it for ancient love,[5]
And bring some covering for this naked soul,
Which I'll entreat to lead me.
OLD MAN: Alack, sir, he is mad.
GLOUCESTER: 'Tis the time's plague, when madmen lead the blind.
Do as I bid thee, or rather do thy pleasure;
Above the rest, begone.
OLD MAN: I'll bring him the best 'parel that I have,
Come on't what will. [*Exit.*]
GLOUCESTER: Sirrah, naked fellow—
EDGAR: Poor Tom's a-cold. [(*Aside*)] I cannot daub it further.[6]
GLOUCESTER: Come hither, fellow.
EDGAR [(*aside*)]: And yet I must.—Bless thy sweet eyes, they bleed.
GLOUCESTER: Know'st thou the way to Dover?

3. On whom your deceived father's anger fed.
4. It's hard to have to play the fool to my suffering father, distressing both myself and others.
5. The traditional trusting bond of master and tenant.
6. I cannot continue the pretense further.

EDGAR: Both stile and gate, horseway and footpath. Poor Tom hath been scared out of his good wits. Bless thee, good man's son, from the foul fiend! Five fiends have been in poor Tom at once: of lust, as Obidicut; Hobbididance, prince of dumbness; Mahu, of stealing; Modo, of murder; Flibbertigibbet,[7] of mopping and mowing,[8] who since possesses chambermaids and waiting women. So, bless thee, master!

GLOUCESTER [(*giving a purse*)]: Here, take this purse, thou whom the heavens' plagues
Have humbled to all strokes. That I am wretched
Makes thee the happier. Heavens, deal so still!
Let the superfluous and lust-dieted[9] man,
That slaves your ordinance,[1] that will not see
Because he does not feel, feel your pow'r quickly!
So distribution should undo excess
And each man have enough. Dost thou know Dover?

EDGAR: Ay, master.

GLOUCESTER: There is a cliff, whose high and bending head
Looks fearfully in the confinèd deep.
Bring me but to the very brim of it
And I'll repair the misery thou dost bear
With something rich about me. From that place
I shall no leading need.

EDGAR: Give me thy arm.
Poor Tom shall lead thee. [*Exeunt.*]

Scene 2[2]

[*Enter Goneril (and) Bastard (Edmund).*]

GONERIL: Welcome, my lord. I marvel our mild husband
Not met us on the way.
[*(Enter) steward (Oswald).*]
Now, where's your master?

OSWALD: Madam, within, but never man so changed.
I told him of the army that was landed;
He smiled at it. I told him you were coming;
His answer was "The worse." Of Gloucester's treachery
And of the loyal service of his son
When I informed him, then he called me sot° *fool*
And told me I had turned the wrong side out.
What most he should dislike seems pleasant to him;
What like, offensive.

GONERIL [*to Edmund*]: Then shall you go no further.
It is the cowish° terror of his spirit, *cowardly*
That dares not undertake. He'll not feel wrongs
Which tie him to an answer.[3] Our wishes on the way

7. Names of fiends taken from Harsnett.
8. Making faces.
9. Immoderately gluttonous and allowed to indulge in his appetites.
1. That enslaves your divine ordinances to his own corrupt will.
2. Location: Before the Duke of Albany's palace.
3. He will ignore insults that, if he took notice, would oblige him to fight.

May prove effects. Back, Edmund, to my brother;[4]
Hasten his musters and conduct his powers.[5]
I must change names at home and give the distaff[6]
Into my husband's hands. This trusty servant
Shall pass between us. Ere long you are like to hear,
If you dare venture in your own behalf,
A mistress's command. Wear this; spare speech.
[(*She gives him a favor.*)]
Decline your head. [(*She kisses him.*)] This kiss, if it durst speak,
Would stretch thy spirits up into the air.
Conceive,[7] and fare thee well.

EDMUND: Yours in the ranks of death. [*Exit.*]

GONERIL: My most dear Gloucester!
Oh, the difference of man and man!
To thee a woman's services are due;
My fool usurps my body.[8]

OSWALD: Madam, here comes my lord. [(*Exit*).]

[*Enter Albany.*]

GONERIL: I have been worth the whistling.

ALBANY: Oh, Goneril,
You are not worth the dust which the rude wind
Blows in your face. I fear your disposition;
That nature which contemns° its origin *hates, spurns*
Cannot be bordered certain[9] in itself.
She that herself will sliver and disbranch
From her material sap perforce must wither
And come to deadly use.

GONERIL: No more. The text is foolish.

ALBANY: Wisdom and goodness to the vile seem vile;
Filths savor but themselves.[1] What have you done?
Tigers, not daughters, what have you performed?
A father, and a gracious agèd man,
Whose reverence even the head-lugged[2] bear would lick,
Most barbarous, most degenerate, have you madded.° *driven mad*
Could my good brother suffer you to do it?
A man, a prince, by him so benefited?
If that the heavens do not their visible spirits
Send quickly down to tame these vile offenses,
It will come,
Humanity must perforce prey on itself,
Like monsters of the deep.

GONERIL: Milk-livered° man, *cowardly*
That bear'st a cheek for blows, a head for wrongs,
Who hast not in thy brows an eye discerning

4. Brother-in-law Cornwall.
5. Assembling of troops and armed forces.
6. Spinning wheel, symbol of the wife's role.
7. Understand, with sexual double meaning, continuing from "stretch my spirits" and to "death," (or climax) in the next line.
8. My foolish husband claims possession of my body.
9. Kept within bounds.
1. Those who are filthy only have a taste for what is filthy.
2. Dragged by the head.

Thine honor from thy suffering,[3] that not know'st
Fools do those villains pity who are punished
Ere they have done their mischief.[4] Where's thy drum?
France spreads his banners in our noiseless land,
With plumèd helm thy state begins to threat,
Whilst thou, a moral° fool, sits still and cries, *moralizing*
"Alack, why does he so?"

ALBANY: See thyself, devil!
Proper deformity shows not in the fiend
So horrid as in woman.

GONERIL: Oh, vain fool!

ALBANY: Thou changèd and self-covered thing, for shame,
Bemonster not thy feature. Were't my fitness
To let these hands obey my blood,
They are apt enough to dislocate and tear
Thy flesh and bones. Howe'er thou art a fiend,
A woman's shape doth shield thee.

GONERIL: Marry, your manhood! Mew!

[*Enter a Messenger*.]

ALBANY: What news?

MESSENGER: Oh, my good lord, the Duke of Cornwall's dead,
Slain by his servant, going to put out
The other eye of Gloucester.

ALBANY: Gloucester's eyes!

MESSENGER: A servant that he bred, thrilled with remorse,
Opposed against the act, bending his sword
To his great master, who, thereat enraged,
Flew on him and amongst them felled him dead,
But not without that harmful stroke which since
Hath plucked him after.

ALBANY: This shows you are above,
You justicers,° that these our nether crimes *judges*
So speedily can venge! But, oh, poor Gloucester!
Lost he his other eye?

MESSENGER: Both, both, my lord.—
This letter, madam, craves a speedy answer;
'Tis from your sister. [*He gives her a letter*.]

GONERIL [(*aside*)]: One way I like this well;
But being widow, and my Gloucester with her,
May all the building in my fancy pluck
Upon my hateful life.[5] Another way
The news is not so tart.—I'll read, and answer.
[(*Exit*.)]

ALBANY: Where was his son when they did take his eyes?

MESSENGER: Come with my lady hither.

3. Able to tell the difference between an insult to your honor and something you should tolerate.
4. You who fail to understand that only fools like yourselves are so tenderhearted as to pity villains like Gloucester, Lear, and Cordelia, who are apprehended before they have committed a crime.
5. I like this because Edmund is now Duke of Gloucester, and Cornwall, a rival for the throne is dead, but since Regan is a widow and with Edmund, she may destroy my fantasy of sharing the kingdom with Edmund.

ALBANY: He is not here.
MESSENGER: No, my good lord. I met him back again.
ALBANY: Knows he the wickedness?
MESSENGER: Ay, my good lord. 'Twas he informed against him,
And quit the house on purpose that their punishment
Might have the freer course.
ALBANY: Gloucester, I live
To thank thee for the love thou show'dst the King
And to revenge thine eyes.—Come hither, friend.
Tell me what more thou know'st. [*Exeunt.*]

Scene 3[6]

[*Enter Kent (disguised) and a Gentleman.*]

KENT: Why the King of France is so suddenly gone back know you no reason?

GENTLEMAN: Something he left imperfect in the state,[7] which since his coming forth is thought of, which imports[8] to the kingdom so much fear and danger that his personal return was most required and necessary.

KENT: Who hath he left behind him general?

GENTLEMAN: The Marshal of France, Monsieur la Far.

KENT: Did your letters pierce the Queen to any demonstration of grief?

GENTLEMAN: Ay, sir. She took them, read them in my presence,
And now and then an ample tear trilled down
Her delicate cheek. It seemed she was a queen
Over her passion, who, most rebel-like,
Sought to be king o'er her.
KENT: Oh, then it moved her?
GENTLEMAN: Not to a rage. Patience and sorrow strove
Who should express her goodliest. You have seen
Sunshine and rain at once. Her smiles and tears
Were like a better way; those happy smilets
That played on her ripe lip seemed not to know
What guests were in her eyes, which parted thence
As pearls from diamonds dropped. In brief,
Sorrow would be a rarity most beloved
If all could so become it.
KENT: Made she no verbal question?
GENTLEMAN: Faith, once or twice she heaved the name of "father"
Pantingly forth, as if it pressed her heart;
Cried, "Sisters, sisters! Shame of ladies, sisters!
Kent! Father! Sisters! What, i'th' storm, i'th' night?
Let pity not be believed!" There she shook
The holy water from her heavenly eyes,
And, clamor-moistened, then away she started
To deal with grief alone.
KENT: It is the stars,
The stars above us, govern our conditions,
Else one self mate and make could not beget

6. Location: The French camp near Dover.
7. Unsettled in state affairs.
8. Portends.

Such different issues.[9] You spoke not with her since?
GENTLEMAN: No.
KENT: Was this before the King returned?[1]
GENTLEMAN: No, since.
KENT: Well, sir, the poor distressèd Lear's i'th' town,
Who sometime in his better tune[2] remembers
What we are come about, and by no means
Will yield to see his daughter.
GENTLEMAN: Why, good sir?
KENT: A sovereign shame so elbows him[3]—his own unkindness
That stripped her from his benediction,° turned her *blessing*
To foreign casualties, gave her dear rights
To his dog-hearted daughters—these things sting
His mind so venomously that burning shame
Detains him from Cordelia.
GENTLEMAN: Alack, poor gentleman!
KENT: Of Albany's and Cornwall's powers° you heard not? *troops*
GENTLEMAN: 'Tis so. They are afoot.° *on the march*
KENT: Well, sir, I'll bring you to our master Lear
And leave you to attend him. Some dear cause
Will in concealment wrap me up awhile.
When I am known aright, you shall not grieve
Lending me this acquaintance.[4] I pray you, go
Along with me. [*Exeunt.*]

Scene 4[5]

[*Enter, with drum and colors, Cordelia, Gentleman,*[6] *and soldiers.*]
CORDELIA: Alack, 'tis he! Why, he was met even now
As mad as the vexed sea, singing aloud,
Crowned with rank fumiter[7] and furrow weeds,
With hardocks,[8] hemlock, nettles, cuckooflowers,
Darnel,[9] and all the idle weeds that grow
In our sustaining corn. A century[1] send forth!
Search every acre in the high-grown field
And bring him to our eye. [(*Exit a soldier or soldiers.*)]
What can man's wisdom[2]
In the restoring his bereavèd sense,
He that helps him take all my outward worth.
GENTLEMAN: There is means, madam.
Our foster nurse of nature is repose,
The which he lacks. That to provoke in him

9. Otherwise one couple could not give birth to such different children.
1. Before the King of France returned to his kingdom.
2. More composed state of mind.
3. Prods his memory.
4. Regret having met me.
5. Location: The French camp.
6. The Quarto specifies "Doctor" here and at line 11.
7. Fumitory, a weed or herb.
8. Burdocks, or wild mustard.
9. Weedy grass.
1. A troop of 100 men.
2. What medical wisdom can accomplish.

Are many simples operative,[3] whose power
Will close the eye of anguish.

CORDELIA: All blest secrets,
All you unpublished virtues[4] of the earth,
Spring with my tears! Be aidant and remediate
In the good man's distress! Seek, seek for him,
Lest his ungoverned rage dissolve the life
That wants the means to lead it.

[*Enter Messenger.*]

MESSENGER: News, madam.
The British powers° are marching hitherward. *armies*

CORDELIA: 'Tis known before. Our preparation stands
In expectation of them. O dear father,
It is thy business that I go about;[5]
Therefore great France
My mourning and importuned tears hath pitied.
No blown ambition doth our arms incite,
But love, dear love, and our aged father's right.
Soon may I hear and see him! [*Exeunt.*]

Scene 5[6]

[*Enter Regan and steward (Oswald).*]

REGAN: But are my brother's powers[7] set forth?

OSWALD: Ay, madam.

REGAN: Himself in person there?

OSWALD: Madam, with much ado.
Your sister is the better soldier.

REGAN: Lord Edmund spake not with your lord at home?

OSWALD: No, madam.

REGAN: What might import° my sister's letters to him? *express*

OSWALD: I know not, lady.

REGAN: Faith, he is posted° hence on serious matter. *has hurried*
It was great ignorance, Gloucester's eyes being out,
To let him live. Where he arrives he moves
All hearts against us. Edmund, I think, is gone,
In pity of his misery, to dispatch
His nighted° life; moreover to descry° *blinded / spy out*
The strength o'th'enemy.

OSWALD: I must needs after him, madam, with my letter.

REGAN: Our troops set forth tomorrow. Stay with us;
The ways are dangerous.

OSWALD: I may not, madam.
My lady charged my duty[8] in this business.

REGAN: Why should she write to Edmund? Might not you
Transport her purposes by word? Belike

3. Many herbal remedies can work.
4. Little known beneficial herbs.
5. Possibly an allusion to Luke 2.40, where Jesus says, "Wist ye not that I must be about my Father's business?"
6. Location: Gloucester's house.
7. Albany's forces.
8. Insisted upon my obedience.

Something—I know not what. I'll love thee much;
Let me unseal the letter.

OSWALD: Madam, I had rather—

REGAN: I know your lady does not love her husband,
I am sure of that; and at her late being here
She gave strange oeillades[9] and most speaking looks
To noble Edmund. I know you are of her bosom.

OSWALD: I, madam?

REGAN: I speak in understanding; y'are, I know't.
Therefore I do advise you, take this note:[1]
My lord is dead; Edmund and I have talked,
And more convenient is he for my hand
Than for your lady's. You may gather more.
If you do find him, pray you, give him this;
And when your mistress hears thus much from you,
I pray, desire her call her wisdom to her.
So, fare you well.
If you do chance to hear of that blind traitor,
Preferment falls on him that cuts him off.

OSWALD: Would I could meet him, madam! I should show
What party I do follow.

REGAN: Fare thee well.

[*Exeunt (separately)*.]

Scene 6[2]

[*Enter Gloucester, and Edgar (in peasant's clothes, leading his father)*.]

GLOUCESTER: When shall I come to th' top of that same hill?

EDGAR: You do climb up it now. Look how we labor.

GLOUCESTER: Methinks the ground is even.

EDGAR: Horrible steep.
Hark, do you hear the sea?

GLOUCESTER: No, truly.

EDGAR: Why, then, your other senses grow imperfect
By your eyes' anguish.

GLOUCESTER: So may it be, indeed.
Methinks thy voice is altered, and thou speak'st
In better phrase and matter than thou didst.

EDGAR: You're much deceived. In nothing am I changed
But in my garments.

GLOUCESTER: Methinks you're better spoken.

EDGAR: Come on, sir, here's the place. Stand still. How fearful
And dizzy 'tis to cast one's eyes so low!
The crows and choughs° that wing the midway air *jackdaws*
Show scarce so gross as beetles. Halfway down
Hangs one that gathers samphire[3]—dreadful trade!

9. Eliads, or amorous glances.
1. Take note of this.
2. Location: An open place near Dover.
3. Herb used in pickling.

Methinks he seems no bigger than his head.
The fishermen that walk upon the beach
Appear like mice, and yond tall anchoring bark
Diminished to her cock;[4] her cock, a buoy
Almost too small for sight. The murmuring surge,
That on th'unnumbered idle pebble chafes,
Cannot be heard so high. I'll look no more,
Lest my brain turn, and the deficient sight
Topple down headlong.

GLOUCESTER: Set me where you stand.

EDGAR: Give me your hand. You are now within a foot
Of th'extreme verge. For all beneath the moon
Would I not leap upright.[5]

GLOUCESTER: Let go my hand.
Here, friend, 's another purse; in it a jewel
Well worth a poor man's taking. [(*He gives a purse.*)]
Fairies and gods.
Prosper it with thee! Go thou further off.
Bid me farewell, and let me hear thee going.

EDGAR [(*moving away*)]: Now fare ye well, good sir.

GLOUCESTER: With all my heart.

EDGAR [(*aside*)]: Why I do trifle thus with his despair
Is done to cure it.

GLOUCESTER [(*kneeling*)]: O you mighty gods!
This world I do renounce, and in your sights
Shake patiently my great affliction off.
If I could bear it longer and not fall
To quarrel with your great opposeless wills,
My snuff[6] and loathèd part of nature should
Burn itself out. If Edgar live, oh, bless him!
Now, fellow, fare thee well. [*He falls forward.*]

EDGAR: Gone, sir. Farewell.—
And yet I know not how conceit° may rob *imagination*
The treasury of life, when life itself
Yields to the theft. Had he been where he thought,
By this had thought been past. Alive or dead?—
Ho, you, sir! Friend! Hear you, sir! Speak!—
Thus might he pass indeed; yet he revives.—
What[7] are you, sir?

GLOUCESTER: Away, and let me die.

EDGAR: Hadst thou been aught but gossamer, feathers, air,
So many fathom down precipitating,
Thou'dst shivered like an egg; but thou dost breathe,
Hast heavy substance, bleed'st not, speak'st, art
sound.

4. Reduced to the size of her cockboat, a small ship's boat.
5. Up and down.
6. Useless residue.
7. Who. Edgar now speaks in a new voice, different from that of Poor Tom and from the other voice he put on at the start of this scene.

Ten masts at each make not the altitude
Which thou hast perpendicularly fell.
Thy life's a miracle. Speak yet again.

GLOUCESTER: But have I fall'n or no?

EDGAR: From the dread summit of this chalky bourn.° *cliff*
Look up aheight; the shrill-gorged lark so far
Cannot be seen or heard. Do but look up.

GLOUCESTER: Alack, I have no eyes.
Is wretchedness deprived that benefit
To end itself by death? 'Twas yet some comfort
When misery could beguile the tyrant's rage
And frustrate his proud will.

EDGAR: Give me your arm.
[*He lifts him up*.]
Up—so. How is't? Feel you your legs? You stand.

GLOUCESTER: Too well, too well.

EDGAR: This is above all strangeness.
Upon the crown o'th' cliff what thing was that
Which parted from you?

GLOUCESTER: A poor unfortunate beggar.

EDGAR: As I stood here below, methought his eyes
Were two full moons; he had a thousand noses,
Horns whelked and waved like the enridgèd sea.
It was some fiend. Therefore, thou happy father,
Think that the clearest gods, who make them honors
Of men's impossibilities,[8] have preserved thee.

GLOUCESTER: I do remember now. Henceforth I'll bear
Affliction till it do cry out itself
"Enough, enough," and die. That thing you speak of,
I took it for a man; often 'twould say
"The fiend, the fiend." He led me to that place.

EDGAR: Bear free and patient thoughts.
[*Enter Lear (mad, fantastically dressed with wild flowers)*.]
But who comes here?
The safer sense will ne'er accommodate
His master thus.

LEAR: No, they cannot touch me for coining. I am the King himself.[9]

EDGAR: Oh, thou side-piercing[1] sight!

LEAR: Nature's above art in that respect. There's your press money.[2] That fellow handles his bow like a crow-keeper.[3] Draw me a clothier's yard.[4] Look, look a mouse! Peace, peace; this piece of toasted cheese will do't. There's my gauntlet;[5] I'll prove it on a giant. Bring up the brown bills.[6] Oh, well flown, bird! I'th' clout,[7] i'th' clout—hewgh! Give the word.

8. Who win our awe and reverence by doing things impossible to men.
9. They cannot prosecute me for minting coins. As King, I enjoy the exclusive royal prerogative for doing so.
1. Heartrending, with a suggestion of Christ's suffering on the cross.
2. Bonus for enlisting.
3. Worker who drives crows away.
4. Draw your bow a full cloth-yard long.
5. Armored glove thrown down in a challenge to a duel.
6. Soldiers carrying pikes.
7. Target, bull's-eye.

EDGAR: Sweet marjoram.[8]
LEAR: Pass.
GLOUCESTER: I know that voice.
LEAR: Ha! Goneril with a white beard? They flattered me like a dog and told me I had white hairs in my beard ere the black ones were there. To say ay and no to everything that I said ay and no to was no good divinity.[9] When the rain came to wet me once and the wind to make me chatter, when the thunder would not peace at my bidding, there I found 'em, there I smelt 'em out. Go to, they are not men o' their words. They told me I was everything. 'Tis a lie. I am not ague-proof.[1]
GLOUCESTER: The trick of that voice I do well remember.
Is't not the King?
LEAR: Ay, every inch a king.
When I do stare, see how the subject quakes
I pardon that man's life. What was thy cause?[2]
Adultery?
Thou shalt not die. Die for adultery? No.
The wren goes to't, and the small gilded fly
Does lecher in my sight.
Let copulation thrive; for Gloucester's bastard son
Was kinder to his father than my daughters
Got 'tween the lawful sheets.
To't, luxury,° pell-mell, for I lack soldiers. *lechery*
Behold yond simpering dame,
Whose face between her forks presages snow,[3]
That minces virtue and does shake the head
To hear of pleasure's name;
The fitchew nor the soilèd horse goes to't[4]
With a more riotous appetite.
Down from the waist they're centaurs,[5]
Though women all above.
But to the girdle do the gods inherit;
Beneath is all the fiends'.
There's hell, there's darkness, there is the sulfurous pit,
Burning, scalding, stench, consumption. Fie, fie, fie!
Pah, pah! Give me an ounce of civet,[6] good apothecary,
sweeten my imagination. There's money for thee.
GLOUCESTER: Oh, let me kiss that hand!
LEAR: Let me wipe it first; it smells of mortality.
GLOUCESTER: Oh, ruined piece of nature! This great world
Shall so wear out to naught. Dost thou know me?

8. An herb used to cure madness.
9. To agree flatteringly to everything I said was not good theology, since the Bible teaches us "let your yea be yea and your nay, nay'" (James 5.12, Matthew 5.37, and 2 Corinthians 1.18).
1. Immune to illness.
2. Offense.
3. Whose frosty looks seem to suggest frigidity between the legs.
4. Neither the polecat nor the well-pastured horse indulges in sexual pleasure.
5. Mythical creatures with the head, arms, and torso of a man and the lower body and legs of a horse.
6. Musk perfume.

LEAR: I remember thine eyes well enough. Dost thou squinny[7] at me? No, do thy worst, blind Cupid; I'll not love. Read thou this challenge. Mark but the penning of it.

GLOUCESTER: Were all thy letters suns, I could not see.

EDGAR [(*aside*)]: I would not take this from report. It is,
And my heart breaks at it.

LEAR: Read.

GLOUCESTER: What, with the case of eyes?

LEAR: Oho, are you there with me? No eyes in your head, nor no money in your purse? Your eyes are in a heavy case, your purse in a light, yet you see how this world goes.

GLOUCESTER: I see it feelingly.[8]

LEAR: What, art mad? A man may see how this world goes with no eyes. Look with thine ears. See how yond justice rails upon yond simple thief. Hark in thine ear: change places and, handy-dandy,[9] which is the justice, which is the thief? Thou hast seen a farmer's dog bark at a beggar?

GLOUCESTER: Ay, sir.

LEAR: And the creature run from the cur? There thou mightst behold the great image of authority: a dog's obeyed in office.
Thou rascal beadle,[1] hold thy bloody hand!
Why does thou lash[2] that whore? Strip thine own back;
Thou hotly lusts to use her in that kind
For which thou whipp'st her. The usurer hangs the cozener.[3]
Through tattered clothes small vices do appear;
Robes and furred gowns hide all. Plate sin with gold,
And the strong lance of justice hurtless breaks;[4]
Arm it in rags, a pygmy's straw does pierce it.
None does offend, none, I say, none. I'll able 'em.[5]
Take that of me, my friend, who have the power
To seal th'accuser's lips. Get thee glass eyes,
And like a scurvy politician seem[6]
To see the things thou does not. Now, now, now, now!
Pull off my boots. Harder, harder! So.

EDGAR [(*aside*)]: Oh, matter and impertinency[7] mixed,
Reason in madness!

LEAR: If thou wilt weep my fortunes, take my eyes.
I know thee well enough; thy name is Gloucester.
Thou must be patient. We came crying hither.
Thou know'st the first time that we smell the air
We wawl and cry. I will preach to thee. Mark.

GLOUCESTER: Alack, alack the day!

LEAR: When we are born, we cry that we are come

7. Squint.
8. By touch, and with emotional feeling.
9. Take your choice of hands, as in the child's game.
1. Parish officer.
2. Why do we allow adulteresses to be publicly whipped by law? Why not whip the man who lusts after her?
3. The moneylender sentences the con man to be hanged.
4. Splinters harmlessly.
5. Exempt everyone from legal guilt.
6. If Gloucester were to fit himself with glasses, he would look wise like a vile politician.
7. Sense and nonsense.

To this great stage of fools.—This' a good block.[8]
It were a delicate stratagem to shoe
A troop of horse with felt. I'll put 't in proof,
And when I have stol'n upon these son-in-laws,
Then, kill, kill, kill, kill, kill, kill!

[*Enter a Gentleman (with attendants).*]

GENTLEMAN: Oh, here he is. Lay hand upon him.—Sir,
Your most dear daughter—

LEAR: No rescue? What, a prisoner? I am even
The natural fool of fortune.[9] Use me well;
You shall have ransom. Let me have surgeons;
I am cut to th' brains.

GENTLEMAN: You shall have anything.

LEAR: No seconds? All myself?
Why, this would make a man a man of salt[1]
To use his eyes for garden waterpots,
Ay, and laying a autumn's dust.
I will die bravely, like a smug bridegroom.[2] What?
I will be jovial. Come, come, I am a king,
Masters, know you that?

GENTLEMAN: You are a royal one, and we obey you.

LEAR: Then there's life in't. Come, an you get it, you
shall get it by running. Sa, sa, sa, sa.[3]

[*Exit (running, followed by attendants).*]

GENTLEMAN: A sight most pitiful in the meanest wretch,
Past speaking of in a king! Thou hast one daughter
Who redeems nature from the general curse
Which twain have brought her to.

EDGAR: Hail, gentle sir.

GENTLEMAN: Sir, speed you. What's your will?

EDGAR: Do you hear aught, sir, of a battle toward?

GENTLEMAN: Most sure and vulgar. Everyone hears that
Which can distinguish sound.

EDGAR: But, by your favour,
How near's the other army?

GENTLEMAN: Near and on speedy foot. The main descry
Stands on the hourly thought.

EDGAR: I thank you, sir; that's all.

GENTLEMAN: Though that the Queen on special cause is here,
Her army is moved on.

EDGAR: I thank you, sir.

[*Exit (Gentleman)*]

GLOUCESTER: You ever-gentle gods, take my breath from me;
Let not my worser spirit tempt me again
To die before you please!

8. Mold for a felt hat. Lear may be referring to the weeds he has wound about his hair.
9. Born plaything.
1. Of salt tears.
2. Bridegroom continues the punning of *die bravely*, "have sex successfully."
3. A hunting cry.

EDGAR: Well pray you, father.
GLOUCESTER: Now, good sir, what are you?
EDGAR: A most poor man, made tame to fortune's blows,
Who, by the art of known and feeling sorrows,
Am pregnant to good pity. Give me your hand.
I'll lead you to some biding. [*(He offers his arm.)*]
GLOUCESTER: Hearty thanks.
The bounty and the benison of heaven
To boot, and boot!
[*Enter steward (Oswald)*.]
OSWALD: A proclaimed prize![4] Most happy!
[*(He draws his sword.)*]
That eyeless head of thine was first framed flesh
To raise my fortunes. Thou old unhappy traitor,
Briefly thyself remember.[5] The sword is out
That must destroy thee.
GLOUCESTER: Now let thy friendly hand
Put strength enough to't. [*(Edgar intervenes.)*]
OSWALD: Wherefore, bold peasant,
Durst thou support a published traitor? Hence,
Lest that th'infection of his fortune take
Like hold on thee. Let go his arm.
EDGAR: 'Chill not let go, zir, without vurther 'cagion.[6]
OSWALD: Let go, slave, or thou diest!
EDGAR: Good gentleman, go your gait, and let poor volk pass. An 'chud ha' bin zwaggered out of my life, 'twould not ha' bin zo long as 'tis by a vortnight.[7] Nay, come not near th' old man; keep out, 'che vor ye, or Ise try whether your costard or my ballow[8] be the harder. 'Chill be plain with you.
OSWALD: Out, dunghill!
EDGAR: 'Chill[9] pick your teeth, zir. Come no matter vor your foins.[1]
[*(They fight. Edgar fells him with his cudgel.)*]
OSWALD: Slave, thou hast slain me. Villain, take my purse.
If ever thou wilt thrive, bury my body
And give the letters which thou find'st about me
To Edmund, Earl of Gloucester. Seek him out
Upon the English party. Oh, untimely death!
Death! [*(He dies.)*]
EDGAR: I know thee well: a serviceable villain,
As duteous to the vices of thy mistress
As badness would desire.
GLOUCESTER: What, is he dead?
EDGAR: Sit you down, father. Rest you. [*(Gloucester sits.)*]

4. A man with a price on his head.
5. Say your prayers.
6. I will not let go, sir without further occasion. Edgar adopts the Somerset dialect, a stage convention used for peasants.
7. If I could have been swaggered (bullied) out of my life, it wouldn't have lasted as long as a fortnight (i.e., two weeks).
8. Your head or my cudgel.
9. I'll.
1. Thrusts.

Let's see these pockets; the letters that he speaks of
May be my friends. He's dead; I am only sorry
He had no other deathsman.[2] Let us see.
[*(He finds a letter and opens it.)*]
Leave, gentle wax,[3] and, manners, blame us not.
To know our enemies' minds we rip their hearts;
Their papers is more lawful. [*(Reads the letter.)*]

"Let our reciprocal vows be remembered. You have many opportunities to cut him[4] off; if your will want not, time and place will be fruitfully offered. There is nothing done if he return the conqueror. Then am I the prisoner, and his bed my jail, from the loathed warmth whereof deliver me and supply the place for your labor.
Your—wife, so I would say—affectionate servant,
and for you her own for venture, Goneril."

Oh, indistinguished space of woman's will!
A plot upon her virtuous huaband's life,
And the exchange my brother! Here in the sands
Thee I'll rake up, the post unsanctified
Of murderous lechers; and in the mature time
With this ungracious paper strike the sight
Of the death-practiced Duke. For him 'tis well
That of thy death and business I can tell.
[*(Exit with the body.)*]

GLOUCESTER: The King is mad. How stiff is my vile sense,[5]
That I stand up and have ingenious[6] feeling
Of my huge sorrows! Better I were distract;° *crazy*
So should my thoughts be severed from my griefs,
And woes by wrong imaginations lose
The knowledge of themselves. [*Drum afar off.*]

[*Enter Edgar.*]

EDGAR: Give me your hand.
Far off, methinks, I hear the beaten drum.
Come, father, I'll bestow you with a friend.
[*Exeunt, (Edgar leading his father).*]

Scene 7[7]

[*Enter Cordelia, Kent (dressed still in his disguise costume), and Gentleman.*[8]]

CORDELIA: O thou good Kent, how shall I live and work
To match thy goodness? My life will be too short,
And every measure fail me.

KENT: To be acknowledged, madam, is o'erpaid.
All my reports go with the modest truth,
Nor more nor clipped, but so.

2. Executioner.
3. The letter's seal.
4. Albany.
5. How obstinate is my deplorable sanity and power of sensation.
6. Keen consciousness.
7. Location: The French camp.
8. Doctor in the Quarto.

CORDELIA: Be better suited.
These weeds° are memories of those worser hours; *garments*
I prithee, put them off.
KENT: Pardon, dear madam;
Yet to be known shortens my made intent.[9]
My boon I make it[1] that you know me not
Till time and I think meet.
CORDELIA: Then be't so, my good lord. [*To the Gentleman*] How does the King?
GENTLEMAN: Madam, sleeps still.
CORDELIA: O you kind goods,
Cure this great breach in his abusèd nature!
Th'untuned and jarring senses, oh, wind up° *tune*
Of this child-changèd[2] father!
GENTLEMAN: So please Your Majesty
That we may wake the King? He hath slept long.
CORDELIA: Be governed by your knowledge, and proceed
I'th' sway of your own will.—Is he arrayed?
[*Enter Lear in a chair carried by servants.*]
GENTLEMAN: Ay, madam. In the heaviness of sleep
We put fresh garments on him.
Be by, good madam, when we do awake him.
I doubt not of his temperance.
CORDELIA: Very well. [(*Music.*)]
GENTLEMAN: Please you, draw near.—Louder the music there!
CORDELIA [(*kissing him*)]:
O my dear father! Restoration hang
Thy medicine on my lips, and let this kiss
Repair those violent harms that my two sisters
Have in thy reverence made!
KENT: Kind and dear princess!
CORDELIA: Had you not been their father, these white flakes[3]
Did challenge pity of them. Was this a face
To be opposed against the warring winds?
To stand against the deep dread-bolted thunder
In the most terrible and nimble stroke
Of quick cross lightning? To watch—poor perdu!—
With this thin helm? Mine enemy's dog,
Though he had bit me, should have stood that night
Against my fire; and wast thou fain, poor father,
To hovel thee with swine and rogues forlorn
In short and musty straw? Alack, alack!
'Tis wonder that thy life and wits at once
Had not concluded all.—He wakes! Speak to him.

9. To reveal my true identity now would alter my carefully made plan.
1. The favor I seek.
2. Changed by children's cruelty.
3. White locks of hair.

GENTLEMAN: Madam, do you; 'tis fittest.
CORDELIA: How does my royal lord? How fares Your Majesty?
LEAR: You do me wrong to take me out o'th' grave.
Thou art a soul in bliss; but I am bound
Upon a wheel of fire,[4] that mine own tears
Do scald like molten lead.
CORDELIA: Sir, do you know me?
LEAR: You are a spirit, I know. Where did you die?
CORDELIA: Still, still, far wide!
GENTLEMAN: He's scarce awake. Let him alone awhile.
LEAR: Where have I been? Where am I? Fair daylight?
I am mightily abused.° I should ev'n die with pity *confused*
To see another thus. I know not what to say.
I will not swear these are my hands. Let's see;
I feel this pinprick. Would I were assured
Of my condition!
CORDELIA [(*kneeling*)]: Oh, look upon me, sir,
And hold your hands in benediction o'er me.
[*He attempts to kneel.*]
No, sir, you must not kneel.
LEAR: Pray, do not mock me.
I am a very foolish fond old man,
Fourscore and upward, not an hour more nor less;
And, to deal plainly,
I fear I am not in my perfect mind.
Methinks I should know you, and know this man,
Yet I am doubtful; for I am mainly ignorant
What place this is, and all the skill I have
Remembers not these garments, nor I know not
Where I did lodge last night. Do not laugh at me,
For, as I am a man, I think this lady
To be my child Cordelia.
CORDELIA [(*weeping*)]: And so I am, I am.
LEAR: Be your tears wet? Yes, faith. I pray, weep not.
If you have poison for me I will drink it.
I know you do not love me, for your sisters
Have, as I do remember, done me wrong.
You have some cause, they have not.
CORDELIA: No cause, no cause.
LEAR: Am I in France?
KENT: In your own kingdom, sir.
LEAR: Do not abuse° me. *confuse*
GENTLEMAN: Be comforted, good madam. The great rage,
You see, is killed in him, and yet it is danger

4. A punishment of hell in medieval accounts.

To make him even o'er the time he has lost.
Desire him to go in. Trouble him no more
Till further settling.

CORDELIA: Will't please Your Highness walk?

LEAR: You must bear with me.
Pray you now, forget and forgive.
I am old and foolish.

[*Exeunt (all but Kent and Gentleman)*.]

GENTLEMAN: Holds it true, sir, that the Duke of Cornwall was so slain?

KENT: Most certain, sir.

GENTLEMAN: Who is conductor° of his people? *leader*

KENT: As 'tis said, the bastard son of Gloucester.

GENTLEMAN: They say Edgar, his banished son, is with the Earl of Kent in Germany.

KENT: Report is changeable. 'Tis time to look about; the powers of the kingdom approach apace.

GENTLEMAN: The arbitrament[5] is like to be bloody. Fare you well, sir. [(*Exit*.)]

KENT: My point and period will be throughly wrought,[6]
Or well or ill, as this day's battle's fought. [(*Exit*.)]

ACT 5

Scene 1[7]

[*Enter, with drum and colors, Edmund, Regan, Gentlemen, and soldiers*.]

EDMUND [*to a Gentleman*]:
Know of the Duke if his last purpose hold,
Or whether since he is advised by aught
To change the course. He's full of alteration
And self-reproving. Bring his constant pleasure.

[(*Exit Gentleman*.)]

REGAN: Our sister's man is certainly miscarried.° *lost*

EDMUND: 'Tis to be doubted,° madam. *feared*

REGAN: Now, sweet lord,
You know the goodness I intend upon you.
Tell me, but truly—but then speak the truth—
Do you not love my sister?

EDMUND: In honored love.

REGAN: But have you never found my brother's way
To the forfended[8] place?

EDMUND: That thought abuses you.

REGAN: I am doubtful that you have been conjunct
And bosomed with her, as far as we call hers.

EDMUND: No, by mine honor, madam.

REGAN: I never shall endure her. Dear my lord,

5. Decision by arms.
6. Literally, the full stop at the end of my life's sentence will be thoroughly shaped.
7. Location: The British camp near Dover.
8. Forbidden (by the commandment against adultery).

Be not familiar° with her. *intimate*
EDMUND: Fear me not.—She and the Duke her husband!
[*Enter, with drum and colors, Albany, Goneril, (and) soldiers.*]
GONERIL [(*aside*)]: I had rather lose the battle than that sister
Should loosen him and me.
ALBANY [(*to Regan*)]: Our very loving, sister, well bemet.
[(*To Edmund*)] Sir, this I heard: the King is come to his daughter,
With others whom the rigor of our state
Forced to cry out. Where I could not be honest,
I never yet was valiant. For this business,
It touches us as France invades our land,
Not bolds the King, with others whom, I fear,
Most just and heavy causes make oppose.
EDMUND: Sir, you speak nobly.
REGAN: Why is this reasoned?[9]
GONERIL: Combine together 'gainst the enemy;
For these domestics and particular broils
Are not the question here.
ALBANY: Let's then determine
With th'ancient of war on our proceeding.
EDMUND: I shall attend you presently at your tent.
REGAN: Sister, you'll go with us?
GONERIL: No.
REGAN: 'Tis most convenient. Pray, go with us.
GONERIL [(*aside*)]: Oho, I know the riddle.[1]—I will go.
[(*As they are going out,*) *enter Edgar* (*disguised*).]
EDGAR [(*to Albany*)]: If e'er Your Grace had speech with man so poor,
Hear me one word.
ALBANY [(*to the others*)]: I'll overtake you.
[*Exeunt both the armies.*]
Speak.
EDGAR [(*giving a letter*)]: Before you fight the battle, ope this letter.
If you have victory, let the trumpet sound
For him that brought it. Wretched though I seem,
I can produce a champion that will prove
What is avouchèd° there. If you miscarry,[2] *affirmed*
Your business of the world hath so an end,
And machination ceases. Fortune love you!
ALBANY: Stay till I have read the letter.
EDGAR: I was forbid it.
When time shall serve, let but the herald cry
And I'll appear again. [*Exit* (*Edgar*).]
ALBANY: Why, fare thee well. I will o'erlook thy paper.
[*Enter Edmund.*]

9. Why are we arguing about reasons for fighting?
1. I understand the reason for Regan's demand that I accompany her, which is that she wants to keep me away from Edmund.
2. Lose the battle and die.

EDMUND: The enemy's in view. Draw up your powers.
[*(He offers Albany a paper.)*]
Here is the guess of their true strength and forces
By diligent discovery;° but your haste — *scouting*
Is now urged on you.
ALBANY: We will greet the time. [*Exit.*]
EDMUND: To both these sisters have I sworn my love,
Each jealous° of the other as the stung — *suspicious*
Are of the adder. Which of them shall I take?
Both? One? Or neither? Neither can be enjoyed
If both remain alive. To take the widow
Exasperates, makes mad her sister Goneril,
And hardly shall I carry out my side,
Her husband being alive. Now then, we'll use
His countenance for the battle, which being done,
Let her who would be rid of him devise
His speedy taking off. As for the mercy
Which he intends of Lear and to Cordelia,
The battle done and they within our power,
Shall never see his pardon, for my state
Stands on me to defend, not to debate.

[*Exit.*]

Scene 2[3]

[*Alarum within. Enter, with drum and colors, Lear, Cordelia, and soldiers, over the stage; and exeunt.*]

[*Enter Edgar and Gloucester.*]
EDGAR: Here, father, take the shadow of this tree
For your good host. Pray that the right may thrive.
If ever I return to you again,
I'll bring you comfort.
GLOUCESTER: Grace go with you, sir!
[*Exit (Edgar.)*]
[*Alarum*[4] *and retreat within. Enter Edgar.*]
EDGAR: Away, old man! Give me thy hand. Away!
King Lear hath lost, he and his daughter ta'en.
Give me thy hand. Come on.
GLOUCESTER: No further, sir. A man may rot even here.
EDGAR: What, in ill thoughts again? Men must endure
Their going hence, even as their coming hither;
Ripeness is all. Come on.
GLOUCESTER: And that's true too.

[*Exeunt.*]

3. Location: The battlefield.

4. Trumpet call to battle.

Scene 3[5]

[*Enter, in conquest, with drum and colors, Edmund; Lear and Cordelia, as prisoners; soldiers, Captain.*]

EDMUND: Some officers take them away. Good guard[6]
Until their greater pleasures[7] first be known
That are to censure° them. *judge*

CORDELIA [(*to Lear*)]: We are not the first
Who with best meaning have incurred the worst.
For thee, oppressèd King, I am cast down;
Myself could else outfrown false Fortune's frown.
Shall we not see these daughters and these sisters?

LEAR: No, no, no, no! Come, let's away to prison.
We two alone will sing like birds i'th' cage.
When thou dost ask me blessing, I'll kneel down
And ask of thee forgiveness. So we'll live,
And pray, and sing, and tell old tales, and laugh
At gilded butterflies,[8] and hear poor rogues
Talk of court news; and we'll talk with them too—
Who loses and who wins; who's in, who's out—
And take upon 's the mystery of things,
As if we were God's spies; and we'll wear out,
In a walled prison, packs and sects of great ones,
That ebb and flow by th' moon.

EDMUND: Take them away.

LEAR: Upon such sacrifices, my Cordelia,
The gods themselves throw incense. Have I caught thee?
He that parts us shall bring a brand from heaven
And fire us hence like foxes.[9] Wipe thine eyes;
The good years shall devour them, flesh and fell,
Ere they shall make us weep. We'll see 'em starved first.
Come. [*Exit (with Cordelia, guarded).*]

EDMUND: Come hither, Captain. Hark.
Take thou this note. [(*He gives a paper.*)] Go follow them to prison.
One step I have advanced thee; if thou dost
As this instructs thee, thou dost make thy way
To noble fortunes. Know thou this: that men
Are as the time is. To be tender-minded
Does not become a sword. Thy great employment
Will not bear question; either say thou'lt do't
Or thrive by other means.

CAPTAIN: I'll do't, my lord.

EDMUND: About it, and write "happy" when th' hast done.
Mark, I say, instantly, and carry it so
As I have set it down.

5. Location: The British camp.
6. Guard them well.
7. The wishes of those in command.
8. Brightly dressed courtiers.
9. Nothing short of a firebrand from heaven will ever part us again. Firebrands were used to smoke foxes from their lairs.

CAPTAIN: I cannot draw a cart, nor eat dried oats;
If it be man's work, I'll do't [*Exit Captain.*]

[*Flourish. Enter Albany, Goneril, Regan, (another Captain, and) soldiers.*]

ALBANY: Sir, you have showed today your valiant strain,
And fortune led you well. You have the captives
Who were the opposites° of this day's strife; *enemies*
I do require them of you, so to use them
As we shall find their merits and our safety
May equally determine.

EDMUND: Sir, I thought it fit
To send the old and miserable King
To some retention° and appointed guard, *confinement*
Whose age had charms in it, whose title more,
To pluck the common bosom on his side
And turn our impressed lances in our eyes
Which do command them.[1] With him I sent the Queen,
My reason all the same; and they are ready
Tomorrow, or at further space, t'appear
Where you shall hold your session. At this time
We sweat and bleed; the friend hath lost his friend,
And the best quarrels in the heat are cursed
By those that feel their sharpness.
The question of Cordelia and her father
Requires a fitter place.

ALBANY: Sir, by your patience,
I hold you but a subject of[2] this war,
Not as a brother.

REGAN: That's as we list to grace him.
Methinks our pleasure might have been demanded
Ere you had spoke so far. He led our powers,
Bore the commission of my place and person,
The which immediacy may well stand up
And call itself your brother.

GONERIL: Not so hot!
In his own grace he doth exalt himself
More than in your addition.[3]

REGAN: In my rights,
By me invested, he compeers° the best. *is equal with*

GONERIL: That were the most if he should husband you.

REGAN: Jesters do oft prove prophets.

GONERIL: Holla, holla!
That eye that told you so looked but asquint.° *furtively*

1. Whose advanced age had magic in it, and whose title as king had even more, to win the sympathy of the commoners and turn against us the weapons of those very troops whom we impressed into service.
2. Subordinate in.
3. The titles you confer upon him.

REGAN: Lady, I am not well, else I should answer
From a full-flowing stomach. [(*To Edmund*)] General,
Take thou my soldiers, prisoners, patrimony;
Dispose of them, of me; the walls is thine.[4]
Witness the world that I create thee here
My lord and master.
GONERIL: Mean you to enjoy him?
ALBANY: The let-alone lies not in your good will.
EDMUND: Nor in thine, lord.
ALBANY: Half-blooded[5] fellow, yes.
REGAN [(*to Edmund*)]: Let the drum strike and prove my title thine.
ALBANY: Stay yet; hear reason. Edmund, I arrest thee
On capital treason; and, in thy attaint
This gilded serpent. [(*Pointing to Goneril*)] For your claim, fair sister,
I bar it in the interest of my wife;
'Tis she is subcontracted to this lord,
And I, her husband, contradict your banns.
If you will marry, make your loves to me;
My lady is bespoke.
GONERIL: An interlude!° *a play*
ALBANY: Thou art armed, Gloucester. Let the trumpet sound.
If none appear to prove upon thy person
Thy heinous, manifest, and many treasons,
There is my pledge. [(*He throws down a glove*.)] I'll make it on thy heart,
Ere I taste bread, thou art in nothing less
Than I have here proclaimed thee.
REGAN: Sick, oh, sick!
GONERIL [(*aside*)]: If not, I'll ne'er trust medicine.[6]
EDMUND [(*throwing down a glove*)]: There's my exchange. What in the world he is
That names me traitor, villain-like he lies.
Call by the trumpet. He that dares approach,
On him, on you—who not?—I will maintain
My truth and honor firmly.
ALBANY: A herald, ho!
EDMUND: A herald, ho, a herald!
[*Enter a Herald.*]
ALBANY [(*to Edmund*)]: Trust to thy single virtue;[7] for thy soldiers,
All levied in my name, have in my name
Took their discharge.
REGAN: My sickness grows upon me.
ALBANY [(*to Soldiers*)]: She is not well. Convey her to my tent.
[(*Exit Regan, supported.*)]

4. The citadel of my heart and body surrender completely to you.
5. Only half noble.
6. Poison.
7. Unaided strength.

Come hither, herald. Let the trumpet sound,
And read out this. [*(He gives a paper.)*]

CAPTAIN: Sound, trumpet! [*A trumpet sounds.*]

HERALD: (*reads*) "If any man of quality or degree[8] within the lists of the army will maintain upon Edmund, supposed Earl of Gloucester, that he is a mainfold traitor, let him appear by the third sound of the trumpet. He is bold in his defense."

EDMUND: Sound! [*First trumpet.*]

HERALD: Again! [*Second trumpet.*]

HERALD: Again! [*Third trumpet.*]

[*Trumpet answers within.*]

[*Enter Edgar, armed, (with a trumpeter before him).*]

ALBANY: Ask him his purposes, why he appears
Upon this call o'th' trumpet.

HERALD: What[9] are you?
Your name, your quality, and why you answer
This present summons?

EDGAR: Know my name is lost,
By treason's tooth bare-gnawn and canker-bit.[1]
Yet am I noble as the adversary
I come to cope.° *encounter*

ALBANY: Which is that adversary?

EDGAR: What's he that speaks for Edmund, Earl of Gloucester?

EDMUND: Himself. What say'st thou to him?

EDGAR: Draw thy sword,
That, if my speech offend a noble heart,
Thy arm may do thee justice. Here is mine.

[*(He draws his sword.)*]

Behold, it is the privilege of mine honors,[2]
My oath, and my profession. I protest,
Maugre[3] thy strength, place, youth, and eminence,
Despite thy victor sword and fire-new fortune,
Thy valor, and thy heart, thou art a traitor—
False to thy gods, thy brother, and thy father,
Conspirant 'gainst this high-illustrious prince,
And from th'extremest upward of thy head
To the descent and dust below thy foot
A most toad-spotted traitor. Say thou no,
This sword, this arm, and my best spirits are bent
To prove upon thy heart, whereto I speak,
Thou liest.

EDMUND: In wisdom I should ask thy name.
But since thy outside looks so fair and warlike,
And that thy tongue some say of breeding breathes,

8. Noble birth or rank.
9. Who.
1. Worm-eaten.
2. Of my knighthood.
3. In spite of.

What safe and nicely[4] I might well delay
By rule of knighthood, I disdain and spurn.[5]
Back do I toss those treasons[6] to thy head,
With the hell-hated lie o'erwhelm thy heart,
Which—for they yet glance by and scarcely bruise[7]—
This sword of mine shall give them instant way,[8]
Where they shall rest forever.—Trumpets, speak!

[*(He draws.) Alarums. Fight. (Edmund falls.)*]

ALBANY [*(to Edgar)*]: Save him, save him!
GONERIL: This is practice, Gloucester.
By th' law of arms thou wast not bound to answer
An unknown opposite. Thou art not vanquished,
But cozened° and beguiled. *tricked*
ALBANY: Shut your mouth, dame,
Or with this paper shall I stopple° it.—Hold, sir. *stop up*
Thou worse than any name, read thine own evil.

[*(He shows the letter.)*]

[*(To Goneril)*] No tearing, lady; I perceive you know it.
GONERIL: Say if I do, the laws are mine, not thine.
Who can arraign me for't?
ALBANY: Most monstrous! Oh!
Know'st thou this paper?
GONERIL: Ask me not what I know.

[*Exit.*]

ALBANY: Go after her. She's desperate; govern her.

[*(Exit a soldier.)*]

EDMUND: What you have charged me with, that have I done,
And more, much more. The time will bring it out.
'Tis past, and so am I. But what art thou
That hast this fortune on me? If thou'rt noble,
I do forgive thee.
EDGAR: Let's exchange charity.
I am no less in blood than thou art, Edmund;
If more, the more th' hast wronged me.
My name is Edgar, and thy father's son
The gods are just, and of our pleasant° vices *pleasurable*
Make instruments to plague us.
The dark and vicious place where thee he got° *begot*
Cost him his eyes.
EDMUND: Th' hast spoken right. 'Tis true.
The wheel is come full circle; I am here.
ALBANY [*(to Edgar)*]: Methought thy very gait did prophesy
A royal nobleness. I must embrace thee.

[*(They embrace.)*]

4. Cautiously and punctiliously.
5. I disdain to insist on my right to refuse combat with one of lower rank.
6. Accusations of treason.
7. Which charges of treason—since as yet they merely glance off my armor.
8. Provide an immediate pathway to your heart.

Let sorrow split my heart if ever I
Did hate thee or thy father!

EDGAR: Worthy prince, I know't.

ALBANY: Where have you hid yourself?
How have you known the miseries of your father?

EDGAR: By nursing them, my lord. List° a brief tale, *listen to*
And when 'tis told, oh, that my heart would burst!
The bloody proclamation to escape[9]
That followed me so near—oh, our lives' sweetness,
That we the pain of death would hourly die
Rather than die at once![1]—taught me to shift
Into a madman's rags, t'assume a semblance
That very dogs disdained; and in this habit
Met I my father with his bleeding rings,° *sockets*
Their precious stones new lost; became his guide,
Led him, begged for him, saved him from despair;
Never—oh, fault!—revealed myself unto him
Until some half hour past, when I was armed.
Not sure, though hoping, of this good success,
I asked his blessing, and from first to last
Told him our pilgrimage. But his flawed° heart— *cracked*
Alack, too weak the conflict to support—
Twixt two extremes of passion, joy and grief,
Burst smilingly.

EDMUND: This speech of yours hath moved me,
And shall perchance do good. But speak you on;
You look as you had something more to say.

ALBANY: If there be more, more woeful, hold it in,
For I am almost ready to dissolve,[2]
Hearing of this.

EDGAR: This would have seemed a period
To such as love not sorrow; but another,
To amplify too much, would make much more
And to extremity.[3] Whilst I
Was big in clamor, came there in a man
Who, having seen me in my worst estate,
Shunned my abhorred society; but then, finding
Who 'twas that so endured, with his strong arms
He fastened on my neck and bellowed out
As he'd burst heaven, threw him on my father,[4]
Told the most piteous tale of Lear and him
That ever ear received, which in recounting
His grief grew puissant,° and the strings of life *powerful*

9. In order to escape the death-threatening proclamation.
1. Oh, the perversity of our attachment to our lives' sweetness, that we prefer to suffer continually the fear of death rather than die at once and be done with it.
2. Break into tears.
3. But another sorrowful circumstance, adding to what is already too much, would increase it and exceed the limit.
4. Threw himself on my father.

Began to crack. Twice then the trumpets sounded,
And there I left him tranced.

ALBANY: But who was this?

EDGAR: Kent, sir, the banished Kent, who in disguise
Followed his enemy king and did him service
Improper for a slave.

[*Enter a Gentleman (with a bloody knife)*.]

GENTLEMAN: Help, help, oh, help!

EDGAR: What kind of help?

ALBANY: Speak, man.

EDGAR: What means this bloody knife?

GENTLEMAN: 'Tis hot, it smokes.
It came even from the heart of—Oh, she's dead!

ALBANY: Who dead? Speak, man.

GENTLEMAN: Your lady, sir, your lady! And her sisiter
By her is poisoned; she confesses it.

EDMUND: I was contracted to them both. All three
Now marry in an instant.

EDGAR: Here comes Kent.

[*Enter Kent*.]

ALBANY: Produce the bodies, be they alive or dead.

[(*Exit Gentleman*.)]

This judgment of the heavens, that makes us tremble,
Touches us not with pity.—Oh, is this he?
[*To Kent*] The time will not allow the compliment
Which very manners urges.

KENT: I am come
To bid my king and master aye good night.
Is he not here?

ALBANY: Great thing of us forgot!
Speak, Edmund, where's the King? And where's Cordelia?

[*Goneril and Regan's bodies (are) brought out*.]

See's thou this object, Kent?

KENT: Alack, why thus?

EDMUND: Yet Edmund was beloved.
The one the other poisoned for my sake
And after slew herself.

ALBANY: Even so. Cover their faces.

EDMUND: I pant for life. Some good I mean to do,
Despite of mine own nature. Quickly send—
Be brief in it—to th' castle, for my writ
Is on the life of Lear and on Cordelia.
Nay, send in time.

ALBANY: Run, run, oh, run!

EDGAR: To who, my lord? Who has the office? [(*To Edmund*)] Send
Thy token of reprieve.

EDMUND: Well thought on. Take my sword. The captain!
Give it the Captain.
EDGAR: Haste thee, for thy life.
[(*Exit one with Edmund's sword.*)]
EDMUND: He hath commission from thy wife and me
To hang Cordelia in the prison and
To lay the blame upon her own despair,
That she fordid° herself. *destroyed*
ALBANY: The gods defend her! Bear him hence awhile.
[(*Edmund is borne off.*)]
[*Enter Lear, with Cordelia in his arms; (Captain).*]
LEAR: Howl, howl, howl! Oh, you are men of stones!
Had I your tongues and eyes, I'd use them so
That heaven's vault should crack. She's gone forever.
I know when one is dead and when one lives;
She's dead as earth. Lend me a looking glass;
If that her breath will mist or stain the stone,
Why, then she lives.
KENT: Is this the promised end?
EDGAR: Or image of that horror?
ALBANY: Fall and cease!
LEAR: This feather stirs; she lives! If it be so,
It is a chance which does redeem all sorrows
That ever I have felt.
KENT [(*kneeling*)]: O my good master!
LEAR: Prithee, away.
EDGAR: 'Tis noble Kent, your friend.
LEAR: A plague upon you, murderers, traitors all!
I might have saved her; now she's gone forever!
Cordelia, Cordelia! Stay a little. Ha?
What is't thou say'st? Her voice was ever soft,
Gentle, and low, an excellent thing in woman.
I killed the slave that was a-hanging thee.
CAPTAIN: 'Tis true, my lords, he did.
LEAR: Did I not, fellow?
I have seen the day, with my good biting falchion° *light sword*
I would have made them skip. I am old now,
And these same crosses spoil me.[5]—Who are you?
Mine eyes are not o'th' best; I'll tell you straight.
KENT: If Fortune brag of two she loved and hated,
One of them we behold.
LEAR: This is a dull sight. Are you not Kent?
KENT: The same,
Your servant Kent. Where is your servant Caius?[6]

5. Adversities take away my strength.

6. Kent's disguise name.

LEAR: He's a good fellow, I can tell you that;
He'll strike, and quickly too. He's dead and rotten
KENT: No, my good lord, I am the very man—
LEAR: I'll see that straight.
KENT: That from your first of difference and decay
Have followed your sad steps—
LEAR: You are welcome hither.
KENT: Nor no man else. All's cheerless, dark, and deadly.
Your eldest daughters have fordone° themselves, *destroyed*
And desperately are dead.
LEAR: Ay, so I think.
ALBANY: He knows not what he says, and vain is it
That we present us to him.
EDGAR: Very bootless.° *in vain*
[*Enter a Messenger*.]
MESSENGER: Edmund is dead, my lord.
ALBANY: That's but a trifle here.
You lords and noble friends, know our intent:
What comfort to this great decay may come
Shall be applied. For us, we will resign,
During the life of this old majesty,
To him our absolute power; [(*to Edgar and Kent*)] you, to your rights,
With boot and such addition as your honors
Have more than merited. All friends shall taste
The wages of their virtue, and all foes
The cup of their deservings.—Oh, see, see!
LEAR: And my poor fool[7] is hanged! No, no, no life?
Why should a dog, a horse, a rat have life,
And thou no breath at all? Thou'lt come no more,
Never, never, never, never, never!
Pray you, undo this button. Thank you, sir.
Do you see this? Look on her, look, her lips,
Look there, look there! [*He dies*.]
EDGAR: He faints.—My lord, my lord!
KENT: Break, heart, I prithee, break!
EDGAR: Look up, my lord.
KENT: Vex not his ghost.[8] Oh, let him pass! He hates him
That would upon the rack[9] of this tough world
Stretch him out longer.
EDGAR: He is gone indeed.
KENT: The wonder is he hath endured so long.
He but usurped his life.

7. Cordelia; fool is a term of endearment.
8. Departing spirit.
9. Torture rack.

ALBANY: Bear them from hence. Our present business
Is general woe. [(*To Kent and Edgar*)] Friends of my soul, you twain
Rule in this realm, and the gored state sustain.
KENT: I have a journey, sir, shortly to go.
My master calls me; I must not say no.
EDGAR: The weight of this sad time we must obey;
Speak what we feel, not what we ought to say.
The oldest hath borne most; we that are young
Shall never see so much nor live so long.
[*Exeunt, with a dead march.*]

PERSPECTIVES

Tracts on Women and Gender

What is the nature of woman? Is she meant to be subordinate to man or an equal partner? What virtues is she capable of? Does she have intellectual ability, and if so, is it appropriate for her to write? How should she behave toward her husband? What are his responsibilities to her? What is the difference between a good woman and a bad one? What is the difference between manly behavior and womanly behavior? These are some of the questions that early modern English tracts on women and gender ask. Although we would not ask all of these questions in precisely the same way today, they are still of burning interest. The debate over these questions in early modern tracts on women sheds light on the representation of sex and gender in the poetry and drama of the period. By *sex* is meant the representation of biological difference; by *gender* is meant the representation of sex difference as it is socially constructed.

In the Middle Ages there were both attacks on women and defenses of them by both women and men, but intellectual and social changes modified the debate in the early modern period. One of the prominent medieval genres that continued to be imitated in the early modern period was the praise of exemplary women, such as Boccaccio's *De Claris Mulieribus* ("concerning famous women"), Chaucer's *Legend of Good Women*, and Christine de Pisan's *Le Livre de la Cité des Dames* (translated into English in 1521 as *The Book of the City of Ladies*). Renaissance humanism brought a new intellectual rigor to the genre. The German humanist Heinrich Cornelius Agrippa (1486–1535) stands out in the early Tudor controversy of the 1540s. Agrippa's *De Nobilitate et Praecellentia Foemenei Sexus* (translated in 1542 as *A Treatise of the Nobilitie and Excellencye of Woman Kynde*) not only lists biblical and classical heroines but also examines how the place of women in society is determined by culture rather than nature: "And thus by these lawes, the women being subdued as it were by force of arms, are constrained to give place to men, and to obey their subduers, not by natural, nor divine necessity or reason, but by custom, education, fortune, and a certain tyrannical occasion." However, even a humanist author such as Erasmus, who had enlightened views on other social issues, had very strict views about the absolute subordination of wife to husband. Indeed, this subordination seems to have increased in intensity in the early modern period as the nuclear family headed by the father superseded the extended family, in which power was more dispersed throughout the network of kinship.

Among the learned, the new classical humanist education was still largely reserved for young men. Such changes moved the historian Joan Kelly Gadol to ask, "Did women have a Renaissance?" At the same time, some early modern women were educated enough to represent themselves in the debate on the nature of women, and they brought new perspectives to it. Margaret Tyler was one of the first English women to speak in defense of women as writers. Rachel Speght, the first polemical or argumentative woman writer in English, wrote her defense of women in response to a controversy set in motion by the publication of Joseph Swetnam's *The Arraignment of Lewd, Idle, Froward, and Unconstant Women* (1615). Swetnam was a misogynist, but his tract had the virtue of eliciting defenses of women. Among these responses were *A Muzzle for Melastomus*, written from the theological perspective of Rachel Speght, and *Ester Hath Hanged Haman*, written from the more secular outlook of "Ester Sowernam" (a pen-name adopted to counter the "sweet" in the name Swetnam). Two other tracts of the 1620s, *Hic Mulier* ("the mannish woman") and *Haec-Vir* ("the womanish man") humorously raised the problem of the blurring of genders and carried on a debate about the style of dress and behavior that men and women should adopt.

Whether these tracts take the form of an oration, a speech by one person, or a dialogue between two people (as in *Haec-Vir*), they are all in lively conversation with each other, either directly or indirectly. They are also in a lively conversation with other texts in this period.

Title page from *The English Gentlewoman,* by Richard Brathwaite, 1631.

Representing only a fraction of the early modern literature on women and gender, these tracts attest to heightened interest in questions of gender.

Joseph Swetnam
fl. 1615

Little is known about Joseph Swetnam other than that he stirred up an enormous controversy over the question of women when he wrote *The Arraignment of Lewd, Idle, Froward, and Unconstant Women* (1615). The work was published anonymously with an introductory letter signed by "Thomas Tel-troth." Trotting out all the negative stereotypes of women he could jumble together, Swetnam constructed his mock treatise as a piece of raucous comedy, aimed at the lowest common denominator. Reading Swetnam's work as a serious diatribe against women, Rachel Speght and the pseudonymous Ester Sowernam and Constantia Munda produced critiques of misogyny. Speght unmasked Swetnam's authorship and identified him as a fencing master in Bristol. An anonymous comedy, *Swetnam the Woman-hater, Arraigned by*

Women (1620), possibly by Thomas Heywood, dramatized the debate as a court trial with Swetnam prosecuting his case against women and the Amazon Atlanta (a soldier disguised as a woman) defending them. Swetnam is finally turned over to a court of women, who find him guilty and muzzle him (an obvious reference to Speght's *Muzzle for Melastomus*).

from The Arraignment of Lewd, Idle, Froward, and Unconstant Women

from *Chapter 2. The Second Chapter showeth the manner of such women as live upon evil report: it also showeth that the beauty of women has been the bane of many a man, for it hath overcome valiant and strong men, eloquent and subtle men. And in a word it hath overcome all men, as by examples following shall appear.*

First, that of Solomon unto whom God gave singular wit and wisdom, yet he loved so many women that he quite forgot his God which always did guide his steps, so long as he lived godly and ruled justly, but after he had glutted himself with women, then he could say, vanity of vanity all is but vanity. He also in many places of his book of Proverbs exclaims most bitterly against lewd women calling them all that naught is, and also displayeth their properties, and yet I cannot let men go blameless although women go shameless; but I will touch them both, for if there were not receivers then there would not be so many stealers: if there were not some knaves there would not be so many whores, for they both hold together to bolster each other's villainy, for always birds of a feather will flock together hand in hand to bolster each other's villainy.

Men, I say, may live without women, but women cannot live without men. For Venus, whose beauty was excellent fair, yet when she needeth man's help she took Vulcan, a clubfooted smith. And therefore if a woman's face glister,[1] and her gesture pierce the marble wall, or if her tongue be as smooth as oil or as soft as silk, and her words so sweet as honey, or if she were a very ape for wit, or a bag of gold for wealth, or if her personage have stolen away all that nature can afford, and if she be decked up in gorgeous apparel, then a thousand to one but she will love to walk where she may get acquaintance, and acquaintance bringeth familiarity, and familiarity setteth all follies abroach,[2] and twenty to one that if a woman love gadding but that she will pawn her honor to please her fantasy.

Man must be at all the cost and yet live by the loss. A man must take all the pains and women will spend all the gains. A man must watch and ward, fight and defend, till the ground, labor in the vineyard, and look what he getteth in seven years; a woman will spread it abroad with a fork in one year, and yet little enough to serve her turn but a great deal too little to get her good will. Nay, if thou give her ever so much and yet if thy person please not her humor, then will I not give a halfpenny for her honesty at the year's end.

For then her breast will be the harborer of an envious heart, and her heart the storehouse of poisoned hatred; her head will devise villainy, and her hands are ready to practice that which their heart desireth. Then who can but say that women are sprung from the devil, whose heads, hands and hearts, minds and souls are evil, for women are called the hook of all evil, because men are taken by them as a fish is taken in with the hook.

1. Glitter, shine.

2. Flowing abroad.

For women have a thousand ways to entice thee, and ten thousand ways to deceive thee, and all such fools as are suitors unto them; some they keep in hand with promises, and some they feed with flattery, and some they delay with dalliances, and some they please with kisses. They lay out the folds of their hair to entangle men into their love; betwixt their breasts is the vale of destruction, and in their beds there is hell, sorrow and repentance. Eagles do not eat men till they are dead, but women devour them alive, for a woman will pick thy pocket and empty thy purse, laugh in thy face and cut thy throat. They are ungrateful, perjured, full of fraud, flouting and deceit, unconstant, waspish,[3] toyish,[4] light, sullen, proud, discourteous and cruel, and yet they were by God created, and by nature formed, and therefore by policy and wisdom to be avoided, for good things abused are to be refused. Or else for a month's pleasure, she may make thee go stark naked. She will give thee roast meat, but she will beat thee with the spit. If thou hast crowns in thy purse, she will be thy heart's gold until she leave thee not a whit of white money. They are like summer birds, for they will abide no storm, but flock about thee in the pride of thy glory, and fly from thee in the storms of affliction; for they aim more at thy wealth than at thy person, and esteem more thy money than any man's virtuous qualities; for they esteem of a man without money as a horse does a fair stable without meat. They are like eagles which will always fly where the carrion is.

They will play the horse-leech to suck away thy wealth, but in the winter of thy misery, she will fly away from thee. Not unlike the swallow, which in the summer harboreth herself under the eaves of a house, and against winter flieth away, leaving nothing but dirt behind her.

Solomon saith, he that will suffer himself to be led away or to take delight in such women's company is like a fool which rejoiceth when he is led to the stocks. *Proverbs* 7.

Hosea, by marrying a lewd woman of light behavior was brought unto idolatry, *Hosea* 1. Saint Paul accounteth fornicators so odious, that we ought not to eat meat with them. He also showeth that fornicators shall not inherit the kingdom of Heaven, 1 *Corinthians* the 9th and 11th verse.

And in the same chapter Saint Paul excommunicateth fornicators, but upon amendment he receiveth them again. Whoredom punished with death, *Deuteronomy* 22.21 and *Genesis* 38.24. Phineas a priest thrust two adulterers, both the man and the woman, through the belly with a spear, *Numbers* 25.

God detests the money or goods gotten by whoredom, *Deuteronomy* 23.17, 18. Whores called by diverse names, and the properties of whores, *Proverbs* 7.6 and 21. A whore envieth an honest woman, *Esdras* 16 and 24. Whoremongers God will judge, *Hebrews* 13 and 42. They shall have their portions with the wicked in the lake that burns with fire and brimstone, *Revelation* 21.8.

Only for the sin of whoredom God was sorry at heart, and repented that he ever made man, *Genesis* 6.67.

Saint Paul saith, to avoid fornication every man may take a wife, 1 *Corinthians* 6.9.

Therefore he which hath a wife of his own and yet goeth to another woman is like a rich thief which will steal when he has no need.

There are three ways to know a whore: by her wanton looks, by her speech, and by her gait. *Ecclesiasticus* 26.[5] And in the same chapter he saith, that we must not give our strength unto harlots, for whores are the evil of all evils, and the vanity of all

3. Spiteful.
4. Frivolous, wanton.
5. Apocryphal book of the Old Testament.

vanities, they weaken the strength of a man and deprive the body of his beauty, it furroweth his brows and maketh the eyes dim, and a whorish woman causeth the fever and the gout; and at a word, they are a great shortening to a man's life.

For although they seem to be as dainty as sweet meat, yet in trial not so wholesome as sour sauce. They have wit, but it is all in craft; if they love it is vehement, but if they hate it is deadly.

Plato saith, that women are either angels or devils, and that they either love dearly or hate bitterly, for a woman hath no mean in her love, nor mercy in her hate, no pity in revenge, nor patience in her anger; therefore it is said, that there is nothing in the world which both pleases and displeases a man more than a woman, for a woman most delighteth a man and yet most deceiveth him, for as there is nothing more sweet to a man than a woman when she smiles, even so there is nothing more odious than the angry countenance of a woman.

Solomon in his 20th chapter of *Ecclesiastes*[6] saith, that an angry woman will foam at the mouth like a boar. If all this be true as most true it is, why shouldest thou spend one hour in the praise of women as some fools do, for some will brag of the beauty of such a maid, another will vaunt of the bravery of such a woman, that she goeth beyond all the women in the parish. Again, some study their fine wits how they may cunningly swooth[7] women, and with logic how to reason with them, and with eloquence to persuade them. They are always tempering their wits as fiddlers do their strings, who wrest them so high, that many times they stretch them beyond time, tune and reason.

Again, there are many that weary themselves with dallying, playing, and sporting with women, and yet they are never satisfied with the unsatiable desire of them; if with a song thou wouldest be brought asleep, or with a dance be led to delight, then a fair woman is fit for thy diet. If thy head be in her lap she will make thee believe that thou are hard by[8] God's seat, when indeed thou are just at hell gate.

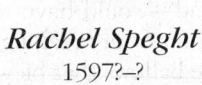

Rachel Speght

1597?–?

The daughter of the rector of two London churches and the wife of a minister, Rachel Speght was only about nineteen years old when she wrote *A Muzzle for Melastomus, the Cynical Baiter of, and Foul-Mouthed Barker Against Evah's Sex, or an Apologetical Answer to the Irreligious and Illiterate Pamphlet made by Io. Swu. and by him Intituled The Arraignment of Women*. Speght interpreted Swetnam's *Arraignment* as a serious attack on women to show the faulty logic underpinning misogyny. Her title indicates the dual thrust of her analysis: the *irreligious* Swetnam has misinterpreted Scripture, and the *illiterate* pamphlet is logically confused and rhetorically flawed. She argues for a view of marriage as a mutual partnership and the relation between the sexes as one of greater equality. Modern critics have debated the implications of Speght's work: Barbara Lewalski has called Rachel Speght "the first self-proclaimed and positively identified female polemicist in England," while Ann Rosalind Jones has questioned whether Speght's work can be considered as feminist in the twentieth-century sense. All critics of early modern gender studies agree, however, that Speght was a learned and committed author. She alone of the participants in the Jacobean controversy about women affixed her own name to the title

6. A faulty citation: in Ecclesiasticus 25, an angry woman is compared to a bear.

7. Sway, woo.

8. Close to.

page. And she reiterated her authorship with the publication of her poetic dream-vision *Mortalities Memorandum* (1621), in which she defends women's education.

from A Muzzle for Melastomus

Of Woman's Excellency, with the causes of her creation, and of the sympathy which ought to be in man and wife each toward other

The work of creation being finished, this approbation thereof was given by God himself, that "All was very good."[1] If all, then woman, who—except man—is the most excellent creature under the canopy of heaven. But if it be objected by any:

First, that woman, though created good, yet by giving ear to Satan's temptations brought death and misery upon all her posterity.

Secondly, that "Adam was not deceived, but that the woman was deceived and was in the transgression."[2]

Thirdly, that St. Paul says "It were good for a man not to touch a woman."[3]

Fourthly and lastly, that of Solomon, who seems to speak against all of our sex: "I have found one man of a thousand, but a woman among them all I have not found,"[4] whereof in its due place.

To the first of these objections, I answer: that Satan first assailed the woman because where the hedge is lowest, most easy it is to get over, and she being the weaker vessel[5] was with more facility to be seduced—like as a crystal glass sooner receives a crack than a strong stone pot. Yet we shall find the offense of Adam and Eve almost to parallel; for as an ambitious desire to be made like God was the motive which caused her to eat, so likewise was it his, as may plainly appear by that *ironia:* "Behold, man is become as one of us"[6]—not that he was so indeed, but hereby his desire to attain a greater perfection than God had given him was reproved. Woman sinned, it is true, by her infidelity in not believing the word of God but giving credit to Satan's fair promises that "she should not die";[7] but so did the man, too. And if Adam had not approved of that deed which Eve had done, and been willing to tread the steps where she had gone, he—being her head—would have reproved her and have made the commandment a bit to restrain him from breaking his Maker's injunction. For if a man burn his hand in the fire, the bellows that blew the fire is not to be blamed, but himself rather for not being careful to avoid the danger. Yet if the bellows had not blown, the fire had not burned; no more is woman simply to be condemned for man's transgression. For by the free will which before his fall he enjoyed, he might have avoided and been free from being burned or singed with that fire which was kindled by Satan and blown by Eve. It therefore served not his turn a whit afterwards to say: "The woman which thou gavest me gave me of the tree, and I did eat."[8] For a penalty was inflicted upon him as well as on the woman, the punishment of her transgression being particular to her own sex and to none but the female kind, but for the sin of man the whole earth was cursed.[9] And he being better able than the woman to have

1. Genesis 1.31. References to the Bible are indicated in the margins of Speght's text.
2. 1 Timothy 2.14.
3. 1 Corinthians 7.1.
4. Ecclesiastes 7.28.
5. "The weaker vessel," a phrase taken from 1 Peter 3.7, is frequently used in early modern English sermons to describe woman.
6. Genesis 3.22. "Ironia," or irony, is a figure of speech in which the meaning is the opposite of that of the words used and the tone of which is often mocking.
7. Genesis 3.4.
8. Genesis 3.12.
9. Genesis 3.17.

resisted temptation, because the stronger vessel, was first called to account, to show that to whom much is given, of them much is required; and that he who was the sovereign of all creatures visible should have yielded greatest obedience to God.

True it is (as is already confessed) that woman first sinned, yet find we no mention of spiritual nakedness till man had sinned. Then it is said "Their eyes were opened,"[1] the eyes of their mind and conscience; and then perceived they themselves naked, that is, not only bereft of that integrity which they originally had, but felt the rebellion and disobedience of their members in the disordered motions of their now corrupt nature, which made them for shame to cover their nakednesse. Then (and not afore) it is said that they saw it, as if sin were imperfect and unable to bring a deprivation of a blessing received, or death on all mankind, till man (in whom lay the active power of generation) had transgressed. The offense, therefore, of Adam and Eve is by St. Austin[2] thus distinguished: "the man sinned against God and himself, the woman against God, herself and her husband"; yet in her giving of the fruit to eat had she no malicious intent towards him, but did therein show a desire to make her husband partaker of that happiness, which she thought by their eating they should both have enjoyed. This her giving Adam of that sauce, wherewith Satan had served her, whose sourness, afore he had eaten, she did not perceive, was that which made her sin to exceed his. Wherefore, that she might not of him who ought to honor her be abhorred,[3] the first promise that was made in Paradise, God makes to woman, that by her seed should the serpent's head be broken.[4] Whereupon Adam calls her *Hevah*, Life, that as the woman had been an occasion of his sin so should woman bring forth the Savior from sin, which was in the fullness of time accomplished.[5] By which was manifested that he is a Savior of believing women no less than of men, that so the blame of sin may not be imputed to his creature, which is good, but to the will by which Eve sinned; and yet by Christ's assuming the shape of man was it declared that his mercy was equivalent to both sexes. So that by Hevah's blessed seed, as St. Paul affirms, it is brought to pass that "male and female are all one in Christ Jesus."[6]

To the second objection I answer: that the Apostle does not hereby exempt man from sin, but only giveth to understand that the woman was the primary transgressor, and not the man; but that man was not at all deceived was far from his meaning. For he afterwards expressly saith that "in Adam all die, so in Christ shall all be made alive."[7]

For the third objection, "It is good for a man not to touch a woman": the Apostle makes it not a positive prohibition but speaks it only because of the Corinth[ian]s' present necessity,[8] who were then persecuted by the enemies of the church. For which cause, and no other, he saith: "Art thou loosed from a wife? Seek not a wife"—meaning whilst the time of these perturbations should continue in their heat; "but if thou are bound, seek not to be loosed; if thou marriest, thou sinnest not," only increase thy care: "for the married careth for the things of this world. And I wish that you were without care that ye might cleave fast to the Lord without separation: for the time remaineth, that they which have wives be as though they had none, for the persecutors shall deprive you of them either by imprisonment, banishment or death." So that manifest it is, that the Apostle does not hereby forbid marriage, but only adviseth the Corinth[ian]s to forbear a while, till God in mercy should curb the fury of their

1. Genesis 3.7.
2. St. Augustine; this commonplace echoes parts of his sermon on Adam and Eve.
3. 1 Peter 3.7.
4. Genesis 3.15.
5. Galatians 4.4.
6. Galatians 3.28.
7. 1 Corinthians 15.22.
8. 1 Corinthians 7.

adversaries. For (as Eusebius[9] writeth) Paul was afterward married himself, the which is very probable, being that interrogatively he saith: "Have we not power to lead about a wife being a sister, as well as the rest of the Apostles, and as the brethren of the Lord, and Cephas?"[1]

The fourth and last objection is that of Solomon: "I have found one man among a thousand, but a woman among them all have I not found."[2] For answer of which, if we look into the story of his life, we shall find therein a commentary upon this enigmatical[3] sentence included. For it is there said that Solomon had seven hundred wives and three hundred concubines, which number connected make one thousand. These women turning away his heart from being perfect with the Lord his God,[4] sufficient cause had he to say, that among the said thousand women found he not one upright. He saith not, that among a thousand women never any man found one worthy of commendation, but speaks in the first person singularly "I have not found," meaning in his own experience. For this assertion is to be held a part of the confession of his former follies, and no otherwise, his repentance being the intended drift of *Ecclesiastes*.

Thus having (by God's assistance) removed those stones whereat some have stumbled, others broken their shins, I will proceed toward the period of my intended task, which is to decipher the excellency of women. Of whose creation I will, for order's sake, observe: first, the efficient cause,[5] which was God; secondly, the material cause, or whereof she was made; thirdly, the formal cause, or fashion and proportion of her feature; fourthly and lastly, the final cause, the end or purpose for which she was made. To begin with the first.

The efficient cause of woman's creation was Jehovah the Eternal, the truth of which is manifest in Moses his narration of the six days' works, where he says, "God created them male and female."[6] And David, exhorting all "the earth to sing to the Lord" (meaning, by a metonymy,[7] "earth": all creatures that live on the earth, of whatever sex or nation) gives this reason: "For the Lord has made us."[8] That work then cannot choose but be good, yea very good, which is wrought by so excellent a workman as the Lord; for he, being a glorious Creator, must effect a worthy creature. Bitter water cannot proceed from a pleasant sweet fountain, nor bad work from that workman which is perfectly good—and, in propriety, none but he.[9]

Secondly, the material cause, or matter whereof woman was made, was of a refined mold, if I may so speak. For man was created of the dust of the earth,[1] but woman was made of a part of man after that he was a living soul. Yet she was not produced from Adam's foot, to be his too low inferior; nor from his head to be his superior; but from his side, near his heart, to be his equal: that where he is lord, she may be lady. And therefore saith God concerning man and woman jointly: "Let them rule over the fish of the sea, and over the fowls of the heaven, and over every beast that moves upon the earth."[2] By which words he makes their authority equal, and all creatures to be in subjection to them both. This, being rightly considered, doth teach men to make such

9. Eusebius (A.D. 260–340) was Bishop of Caesarea and a church historian. See *Ecclesiastical History* 3.30.
1. 1 Corinthians 9.5.
2. Ecclesiastes 7.30.
3. Mysterious.
4. 1 Kings 11.3.
5. The agent who makes something; see Aristotle's *Physics* 2.3.
6. Genesis 1.28 [27].
7. A figure of speech that substitutes one term for another to which it is closely related.
8. Psalms 100.3.
9. Psalms 100.5; Matthew 19.7.
1. Genesis 2.7.
2. Genesis 1.26.

account of their wives as Adam did of Eve: "This is bone of my bone, and flesh of my flesh."[3] As also, that they neither do or wish any more hurt unto them, than unto their own bodies. For men ought to love their wives as themselves, because he that loves his wife loves himself;[4] and never did man hate his own flesh (which the woman is) unless a monster in nature.

Thirdly, the formal cause, fashion and proportion, of woman was excellent. For she was neither like the beasts of the earth, fowls of the air, fishes of the sea, or any other inferior creature; but man was the only object which she did resemble. For as God gave man a lofty countenance that he might look up toward Heaven, so did he likewise give unto woman. And as the temperature of man's body is excellent, so is woman's. For whereas other creatures, by reason of their gross humors, have excrements for their habit—as fowls their feathers, beasts their hair, fishes their scales—man and woman only have their skin clear and smooth.[5] And (that more is) in the image of God were they both created; yea and to be brief, all the parts of their bodies, both external and internal, were correspondent and meet each for other.

Fourthly and lastly, the final cause or end for which woman was made was to glorify God, and to be a collateral companion for man to glory God, in using her body and all the parts, powers and faculties thereof as instruments for his honor. As with her voice to sound forth his praises, like Miriam, and the rest of her company;[6] with her tongue not to utter words of strife, but to give good counsel unto her husband, the which he must not despise. For Abraham was bidden to give ear to Sarah his wife.[7] Pilate was willed by his wife not to have any hand in the condemning of Christ;[8] and a sin it was in him that he listened not to her; Leah and Rachel counseled Jacob to do according to the word of the Lord;[9] and the Shunamite put her husband in mind of harboring the prophet Elisha.[1] Her hands should be open, according to her ability, in contributing towards God's service and distressed servants, like to that poor widow who cast two mites into the treasury;[2] and as Mary Magdalene, Susanna and Joanna, the wife of Herod's steward, with many others which of their substance ministered unto Christ.[3] Her heart should be a receptacle for God's word, like Mary that treasured the sayings of Christ in her heart.[4] Her feet should be swift in going to seek the Lord in his sanctuary, as Mary Magdalene made haste to seek Christ at his sepulcher.[5] Finally, no power external or internal ought woman to keep idle, but to employ it in some service of God, to the glory of her creator and comfort of her own soul.

The other end for which woman was made was to be a companion and helper for man; and if she must be a *helper*, and but a *helper*, then are those husbands to be blamed, which lay the whole burden of domestical affairs and maintenance on the shoulders of their wives. For, as yoke-fellows they are to sustain part of each other's cares, griefs and calamities. But as if two oxen be put into one yoke, the one being bigger than the other, the greater bears most weight; so the husband, being the stronger vessel, is to bear a greater burden than his wife. And therefore the Lord said to Adam: "In the sweat of your face shall you eat your bread, till you return to the dust."[6] And St. Paul says that "he that provideth not for his household is worse than an infidel."[7]

3. Genesis 2.23.
4. Ephesians 5.28.
5. Genesis 1.26.
6. Exodus 15.20.
7. Genesis 21.12.
8. Matthew 27.19.
9. Genesis 31.16.

1. 2 Kings 4.9.
2. Mark 12.43.
3. Luke 8.
4. Luke 1.45.
5. John 20.1.
6. Genesis 3.19.
7. 1 Timothy 5.8.

Nature hath taught senseless creatures to help one another: as the male pigeon, when his hen is weary with sitting on her eggs and comes off from them, supplies her place, that in her absence they may receive no harm, until such time as she is fully refreshed. Of small birds, the cock always helps his hen to build her nest; and while she sits upon her eggs he flies abroad to get meat for her, who cannot then provide any for herself. The crowing cockerel helps his hen to defend her chickens from peril, and will endanger himself to save her and them from harm. Seeing then, that these unreasonable creatures by the instinct of nature bear such affection to each other, that without any grudge they willingly according to their kind help one another, I may reason, *a minore ad maius*,[8] that much more should man and woman, which are reasonable creatures, be helpers to each other in all things lawful, they having the law of God to guide them, his word to be a lantern to their feet and a light unto their paths, by which they are excited to a far more mutual participation of each other's burden than other creatures. So that neither the wife may say to her husband nor the husband to his wife: "I have no need of thee,"[9] no more than the members of the body may say to each other, between whom there is such a sympathy that if one member suffer, all suffer with it. Therefore though God bade Abraham forsake his country and kindred, yet he bade him not forsake his wife who, being "Flesh of his flesh, and bone of his bone," was to be copartner with him of whatsoever did betide him, whether joy or sorrow. Wherefore Solomon says "woe to him that is alone";[1] for when thoughts of discomfort, troubles of this world and fear of dangers do possess him, he wants a companion to lift him up from the pit of perplexity into which he is fallen.[2] For a good wife, saith Plautus, is the wealth of the mind and the welfare of the heart; and therefore a meet associate for her husband. And "woman," saith Paul, "is the glory of the man."[3]

Marriage is a merri-age, and this world's paradise, where there is mutual love. Our blessed Savior vouchsafed to honor a marriage with the first miracle that he wrought,[4] unto which miracle matrimonial estate may not unfitly be resembled. For as Christ turned water into wine, a far more excellent liquor (which, as the Psalmist saith, "Makes glad the hearts of man"[5]) so the single man is changed by marriage from a bachelor to a husband, a far more excellent title: from a solitary life to a joyful union and conjunction with such a creature as God had made meet for man, for whom none was fit till she was made. The enjoying of this great blessing made Pericles more unwilling to part from his wife than to die for his country; and Antonius Pius to pour forth that pathetic exclamation against death for depriving him of his dearly beloved wife: "O cruel hard-hearted death in bereaving me of her whom I esteemed more than my own life!"[6] "A virtuous woman," saith Solomon, "is the crown of her husband";[7] by which metaphor he shows both the excellency of such a wife and what account her husband is to make of her. For a king does not trample his crown under his feet, but highly esteems it, gently handles it and carefully lays it up as the evidence of his kingdom; and therefore when David destroyed Rabbah[8] he took off the crown from their king's head. So husbands should not account their wives as their vassals but as those that are "heirs together of the grace of life,"[9] and with all lenity and mild persuasions

8. From the lesser to the greater.
9. 1 Corinthians 12.21.
1. Ecclesiastes 4.10.
2. Ecclesiastes 4.10.
3. 1 Corinthians 11.7.
4. John 2.
5. Psalms 104.15.
6. Antonius Pius (86–161 C.E.) Roman emperor, founded a charity for orphaned girls in honor of his wife. Plutarch writes about how Pericles (495–429 B.C.E.), ruler of Athens, greatly loved Aspasia.
7. Proverbs 7.4.
8. 1 Chronicles 20.2. Joab destroyed Rabbah, while David took the king's crown.
9. 1 Peter 3.7.

set their feet in the right way if they happen to tread awry, bearing with their infirmities, as Elkanah did with his wife's barrenness.[1]

The kingdom of God is compared to the marriage of a king's son;[2] John calleth the conjunction of Christ and his chosen a marriage;[3] and not few but many times does our blessed Savior in the Canticles[4] set forth his unspeakable love towards his church under the title of a husband rejoicing with his wife, and often vouchsafeth to call her his sister a spouse—by which is showed that with God "is no respect of persons," nations, or sexes.[5] For whosoever, whether it be man or woman, that doth "believe in the lord Jesus, such shall be saved."[6] And if God's love, even from the beginning, had not been as great toward woman as to man, then he would not have preserved from the deluge of the old world as many women as men. Nor would Christ after his resurrection have appeared to a woman first of all other, had it not been to declare thereby, that the benefits of his death and resurrection are as available, by belief, for women as for men; for he indifferently died for the one sex as well as the other.

Ester Sowernam

The pen name Ester Sowernam comes from the Old Testament heroine Esther, who defended her people against Haman, and the antithesis of Joseph Swetnam's last name (sweet/sour). The full title of her text also parodies Swetnam's: *Ester Hath Hanged Haman; or An Answer to a Lewd Pamphlet, Entitled The Arraignment of Women. With the Arraignment of Lewd, Idle, Froward and Unconstant Men, and Husbands* (1617). On the whole, the author of this pamphlet presents herself in a more secular light than Rachel Speght does. Sowernam's criticisms of misogyny are more psychological and social than moral and logical. Trained in classics as well as Scripture and a keen observer, Ester Sowernam finds that Swetnam has incorrectly stated that the Bible is the source of the statement that women are a necessary evil and finds that the true source is in Euripides's *Medea.* The occasion for Sowernam's writing is a dinner party at which Swetnam's book and Speght's response were discussed. Sowernam finds fault with both—Swetnam because he "damns all women" and Speght because she "undertaking to defend women doth rather charge and condemn them." Sowernam cites the double standard by which men are excused for what women are judged harshly for in order to assert women's superiority. She argues that women are judged more severely because they are thought to be more virtuous in the first place. The second half of her pamphlet may have helped to inspire the comedy that spoofed the entire controversy, *Swetnam the Woman-Hater Arraigned by Women* (1620).

from **Ester Hath Hanged Haman**

from Chapter 7. The answer to all objections which are material made against women

As for that crookedness and frowardness[1] with which you charge women, look from whence they have it. For of themselves and their own disposition it doth not proceed, which is proved directly by your own testimony. For in your 46th page, line 15[16], you say: "A young woman of tender years is flexible, obedient, and subject to do

1. 1 Samuel 1.17.
2. Matthew 22.
3. Revelation 19.7.
4. The Song of Songs.
5. Romans 2.11.
6. John 3.18.

1. Perversity, unreasonableness.

anything, according to the will and pleasure of her husband." How cometh it then that this gentle and mild disposition is afterwards altered? Yourself doth give the true reason, for you give a great charge not to marry a widow. But why? Because, say you in the same page, "A widow is framed to the conditions[2] of another man." Why then, if a woman have froward conditions, they be none of her own, she was framed to them. Is not our adversary ashamed of himself to rail against women for those faults which do all come from men? Doth not he most grievously charge men to learn[3] their wives bad and corrupt behavior? For he saith plainly: "Thou must unlearn a widow, and make her forget and forego her former corrupt and disordered behavior." Thou must unlearn her; *ergo*, what fault she hath learned: her corruptness comes not from her own disposition but from her husband's destruction.

Is it not a wonder that your pamphlets are so dispersed? Are they not wise men to cast away time and money upon a book which cutteth their own throats? 'Tis pity but that men should reward you for your writing (if it be but as the Roman Sertorius[4] did the idle poet: he gave him a reward, but not for his writing—but because he should never write more). As for women, they laugh that men have no more able a champion. This author cometh to bait women or, as he foolishly saith, the "Bearbaiting of Women," and he bringeth but a mongrel cur who doth his kind[5] to brawl and bark, but cannot bite. The mild and flexible disposition of a woman is in philosophy proved in the composition of her body, for it is a maxim: *Mores animi sequuntur temperaturam corporis* (the disposition of the mind is answerable to the temper of the body). A woman in the temperature of her body is tender, soft and beautiful, so doth her disposition in mind correspond accordingly: she is mild, yielding and virtuous. What disposition accidentally happeneth unto her is by the contagion of a froward husband, as Joseph Swetnam affirmeth.

And experience proveth. It is a shame for a man to complain of a froward woman—in many respects all concerning himself. It is a shame he hath no more government over the weaker vessel.[6] It is a shame he hath hardened her tender sides and gentle heart with his boisterous and Northern blasts. It is a shame for a man to publish and proclaim household secrets—which is a common practice amongst men, especially drunkards, lechers, and prodigal spendthrifts. These when they come home drunk, or are called in question for their riotous misdemeanors, they presently show themselves the right children of Adam. They will excuse themselves by their wives and say that their unquietness and frowardness at home is the cause that they run abroad: an excuse more fitter for a beast than a man. If thou wert a man thou wouldst take away the cause which urgeth a woman to grief and discontent, and not by thy frowardness increase her distemperature.[7] Forbear thy drinking, thy luxurious riot, thy gaming and spending, and thou shalt have thy wife give thee as little cause at home as thou givest her great cause of disquiet abroad. Men which are men, if they chance to be matched with froward wives—either of their own making or others' marring[8]—they would make a benefit of the discommodity:[9] either try his skill to make her mild or exercise his patience to endure her cursedness; for all crosses are inflicted either for punishment of sins or for exercise of virtues. But humorous[1] men will sooner mar a thousand women than out of a hundred make one good.

2. Circumstances, character traits.
3. Teach.
4. Quintus Sertorius, Roman general, appointed governor of Farther Spain in 83 B.C.E.
5. Nature.
6. From 1 Peter 3.7.
7. Disorder in mind and body.
8. Spoiling.
9. Inconvenience, disadvantageousness.
1. Moody.

And this shall appear in the imputation which our adversary chargeth upon our sex: to be lascivious, wanton and lustful. He saith: "Women tempt, allure and provoke men." How rare a thing is it for women to prostitute and offer themselves? How common a practice is it for men to seek and solicit women to lewdness? What charge do they spare? What travail do they bestow? What vows, oaths and protestations do they spend to make them dishonest? They hire panders, they write letters, they seal them with damnations and execrations to assure them of love when the end proves but lust. They know the flexible disposition of women, and the sooner to overreach them some will pretend they are so plunged in love that, except they obtain their desire, they will seem to drown, hang, stab, poison, or banish themselves from friends and country. What motives are these to tender dispositions? Some will pretend marriage, another offer continual maintenance; but when they have obtained their purpose, what shall a woman find?—just that which is her everlasting shame and grief: she hath made herself the unhappy subject to a lustful body and the shameful stall[2] of a lascivious tongue. Men may with foul shame charge woman with this sin which she had never committed, if she had not trusted; nor had ever trusted, if she had not been deceived with vows, oaths and protestations. To bring a woman to offend in one sin, how many damnable sins do they commit? I appeal to their own consciences. The lewd disposition of sundry men doth appear in this: if a woman or maid will yield to lewdness, what shall they want?[3]—but if they would live in honesty, what help shall they have? How much will they make of the lewd? How base an account of the honest? How many pounds will they spend in bawdy houses? But when will they bestow a penny upon an honest maid or woman, except it be to corrupt them?

Our adversary bringeth many examples of men which have been overthrown by women. It is answered before: the fault is their own. But I would have him, or anyone living, to show any woman that offended in this sin of lust, but that she was first solicited by a man.

Helen was the cause of Troy's burning: first, Paris did solicit her; next, how many knaves and fools of the male kind had Troy, which to maintain whoredom would bring their city to confusion?

When you bring in examples of lewd women and of men which have been stained by women, you show yourself both frantic and a profane irreligious fool to mention Judith,[4] for cutting off Holofernes' head, in that rank.

You challenge women for untamed and unbridled tongues; there was never woman was ever noted for so shameless, so brutish, so beastly a scold as you prove yourself in this base and odious pamphlet. Your blaspheme God, you rail at his creation, you abuse and slander his creatures; and what immodest or impudent scurrility is it which you do not express in this lewd and lying pamphlet?

Hitherto I have so answered all your objections against women that, as I have not defended the wickedness of any, so I have set down the true state of the question. As Eve did not offend without temptation of a serpent, so women do seldom offend but it is by provocation of men. Let not your impudency, nor your consorts' dishonesty, charge our sex hereafter with those sins of which you yourselves were the first procurers. I have, in my discourse, touched you, and all yours, to the quick. I have taxed you with bitter speeches; you will, perhaps, say I am a railing scold. In this objection,

2. Target.
3. Lack, need.
4. A wealthy, attractive widow who saved her people from Holofernes, an Assyrian general, by attracting and then killing him. (See the Book of Judith, part of the Catholic Bible, but viewed as apocryphal by Jews and Protestants.)

Joseph Swetnam, I will teach you both wit and honesty. The difference between a railing scold and an honest accuser is this: the first rageth upon passionate fury without bringing cause or proof, the other bringeth direct proof for what she allegeth. You charge women with clamorous words, and bring no proof; I charge you with blasphemy, with impudency, scurrility, foolery and the like. I show just and direct proof for what I say. It is not my desire to speak so much; it is your dessert to provoke me upon just cause so far. It is not railing to call a crow black, or a wolf a ravenor,[5] or a drunkard a beast; the report of the truth is never to be blamed: the deserver of such a report deserves the shame.

Now, for this time, to draw to an end. Let me ask according to the question of Cassian, *cui bono?*[6]—what have you gotten by publishing your pamphlet? Good I know you can get none. You have, perhaps, pleased the humors of some giddy, idle, conceited persons. But you have dyed yourself in the colors of shame, lying, slandering, blasphemy, ignorance, and the like.

The shortness of time and the weight of business call me away, and urge me to leave off thus abruptly; but assure yourself, where I leave now I will by God's grace supply the next term, to your small content. You have exceeded in your fury against widows, whose defense you shall hear of at the time aforesaid. In the mean space, recollect your wits; write out of deliberation, not out of fury; write out of advice, not out of idleness: forbear to charge women with faults which come from the contagion of masculine serpents.

Hic Mulier and *Haec-Vir*

Hic Mulier and *Haec-Vir* were published anonymously within a week of each other in February 1620. *Hic Mulier,* the first of the two pamphlets to appear, begins with the complaint that "since the days of Adam women were never so masculine." The title introduces this theme by a gender switch of its own: *Hic Mulier,* Latin for "This Woman," uses the masculine form *hic* instead of the feminine *haec.* The title page contains illustrations of two such mannish women—one wearing a man's hat, which she admires in a mirror, and another sitting in a barber's chair to get her hair cut. Structured as a "brief declamation," or oration, the text argues that such activities as hair bobbing and wearing men's clothes are immoral and unnatural for women. Furthermore, such gender crossing is also a threat to the entire political order: "most pernicious to the commonwealth for she hath power by example to do it a world of injury."

As its subtitle boasts, *Haec-Vir* was "an answer to the late book intituled *Hic Mulier*" and was represented as "a brief dialogue between Haec-Vir the Womanish-Man, and Hic Mulier the Man-Woman." The effeminate man and the hermaphroditic woman first misrecognize each other's gender. Once that is cleared up, the foppish man launches into a diatribe against the woman, who defends herself by arguing that "custom is an idiot." The first half of the dialogue reads like a proclamation of the equality of the sexes, with the bare-breasted, dagger-swinging Hic Mulier exclaiming, "We are as free-born as men, have as free election, and as free spirits, we are compounded of like parts and may with like liberty make benefit of our creations." Despite this bold challenge, the text as a whole makes a rather conservative case for the need for gender distinctions, the overturning of which was seen as an assault on hierarchy. The dialogue ends with both participants agreeing to exchange clothes and Latin pronouns so that men will again be manly and women subservient to them.

5. An animal who seizes in order to devour.

6. "To whose benefit," a phrase attributed by Cicero to Lucius Cassius.

These pamphlets display the early modern fascination with, and loathing of, transvestism. Not only did the fashionable young male favorites of King James I's court resemble the womanish man of *Haec-Vir,* but there were more than a few documented cases of women wearing breeches on the streets. A few women were actually brought before ecclesiastical courts for "shamefully" putting on "man's apparel."

While conforming to the comic pattern of disrupting and then reestablishing the status quo, these pamphlets show that questions about custom, nature, and sex and gender roles were being asked in the early seventeenth century.

from Hic Mulier; or, The Man-Woman

So I present these masculine women in their deformities as they are, that I may call them back to the modest comeliness in which they were.

The modest comeliness in which they were? Why, did ever these mermaids, or rather mere-monsters,[1] that wear the Car-man's block,[2] the Dutchman's feather *upse-van-muffe,* the poor man's pate pouled by a Treene dish, the French doublet trussed with points, to Mary Aubries' light nether skirts, the fool's baldric, and the devil's poniard. Did they ever know comeliness or modesty? Fie, no, they never walked in those paths, for these at the best are sure but rags of gentry, torn from better pieces for their foul stains, or else the adulterate branches of rich stocks,[3] that taking too much sap from the root, are cut away, and employed in base uses; or, if not so, they are the stinking vapors drawn from dunghills, which nourished in the higher regions of the air, become meteors and false fires blazing and flashing therein, and amazing men's minds with their strange proportions, till the substance of their pride being spent, they drop down again to the place from whence they came, and there rot and consume unpitied, and unremembered.

And questionless it is true, that such were the first beginners of these last deformities, for from any purer blood would have issued a purer birth; there would have been some spark of virtue: some excuse for imitation; but this deformity has no agreement with goodness, nor any difference against the weakest reason: it is all base, all barbarous. Base, in the respect it offends men in the example, and God in the most unnatural use: barbarous, in that it is exorbitant from nature, and an antithesis to kind,[4] going astray (with ill-favored affectation) both in attire, in speech, in manners, and (it is to be feared) in the whole courses and stories of their actions. What can be more true and curious consent of the most fairest colors and the wealthy gardens which fill the world with living plants? Do but you receive virtuous inmates (as what palaces are more rich to receive heavenly messengers?) and you shall draw men's souls to you with that severe, devout, and holy adoration, that you shall never want praise, never love, never reverence.

But now methinks I hear the witty-offending great ones reply in excuse of their deformities: What, is there no difference amongst women? no distinction of places, no respect of honors, nor no regard of blood, or alliance? Must but a bare pair of shears pass between noble and ignoble, between the generous spirit and the base mechanic; shall we be all co-heirs of one honor, one estate, and one habit? O men, you are then too tyrannous, and not only injure nature, but also break the laws and customs of the

1. Pure monsters.
2. A merchant's hat. Descriptions of ridiculous fashions follow: the *upse-van-muffe* is an elaborate feathered hat; the pate pouled by a Treene dish is hair cut short to the shape of a wooden dish; the French doublet is a man's close-fitting upper body garment tied with laces; baldric: fancy belt; poniard: dagger.
3. Trunks or stems.
4. The opposite of what is natural to the gender.

wisest princes. Are not bishops known by their miters, princes by their crowns, judges by their robes, and knights by their spurs? But poor women have nothing (how great soever they be) to divide themselves from the enticing shows or moving images which do furnish most shops in the city. What is it that either the laws have allowed to the greatest ladies, custom found convenient, or their bloods or places challenged, which hath not been engrossed into the city with as great greediness, and pretense of true title; as if the surcease[5] from the imitation were the utter breach of their charter everlastingly.

For this cause, these apes of the city have enticed foreign nations to the cells, and there committing gross adultery with their gewgaws,[6] have brought out such unnatural conceptions, that the whole world is not able to make a *Democritus* big enough to laugh at their foolish ambitions.[7] Nay, the very art of painting (which to the last age shall ever be held in detestation) they have so cunningly stolen and hidden amongst their husbands' hoards of treasure, that the decayed stock of prostitution (having little other revenues) are hourly in bringing their action of *detinue*[8] against them. Hence (being thus troubled with these *Popeniars*,[9] and loath still to march in one rank with fools and *zanies*[1]) have proceeded these disguised deformities, not to offend the eyes of goodness, but to tire with ridiculous contempt the never to be satisfied appetites of these gross and unmannerly intruders. Nay, look if this very last edition of disguise, this which is so full of faults, corruptions, and false quotations, this bait which the devil had laid to catch the souls of wanton women, be not as frequent in the demipalaces of burghers and citizens as it is either at masque, triumph, tilt-yard, or playhouse. Call but to account the tailors that are contained within the circumference of the walls of the city, and let but their heels and their hard reckonings be justly summed together, and it will be found they have raised more new foundations of this new disguise, and metamorphosed more modest old garments, to this new manner of short base and French doublet (only for the use of freemen's wives[2] and their children) in one month, than has been worn in court, suburbs, or country, since the unfortunate beginning of the first devilish invention.

Let therefore the powerful Statute of Apparel[3] but lift his battle-axe, and crush the offenders in pieces, so as every one may be known by the true badge of their blood, or fortune; and then these *Chimeras* of deformity will be sent back to hell, and there burn to cinders in the flames of their own malice.

Thus, methinks, I hear the best offenders argue, nor can I blame a high blood to swell when it is coupled and counter-checked with baseness and corruption; yet this shows an anger passing near akin to envy, and alludes much to the saying of an excellent poet:

Women never
Love beauty in their sex, but envy ever.

They have Caesar's ambition, and desire to be one and one alone, but yet to offend themselves, to grieve others, is a revenge dissonant to reason, and as *Euripides* says, a woman of that malicious nature is a fierce beast, and most pernicious to the

5. Cessation, stop.
6. Showy decorations.
7. Seneca recounts how Democritus laughed rather than cried at human life (*De tranquilitate animi* 15.2).
8. Legal action to recover personal property.
9. Popinjays, vain and empty people.
1. Parasites, those who play the fool for amusement.
2. Women married to men possessing the freedom of a city, borough, or corporation.
3. Laws governing dress that were intended to differentiate the aristocracy from the common people had been enacted from the Middle Ages through to the early modern period.

commonwealth, for she has power by example to do it a world of injury. But far be such cruelty from the softness of their gentle dispositions: O let them remember what the poet saith:

Women be
Fram'd with the same parts of the mind as men
Nay Nature triumph'd in their beauty's birth,
And women made the glory of the earth,
The life of beauty, in whose simple breast,
(As in her fair lodging) Virtue rests:
Whose towering thoughts attended with remorse,
Do make their fairness be of greater force.

But when they thrust virtue out of doors, and give a shameless liberty to every loose passion, that either their weak thoughts engender, or the discourse of wicked tongues can charm into their yielding bosoms (much too apt to be opened with any pick-lock of flattering and deceitful insinuation) then they turn maskers, mummers, nay monsters in their disguises, and so they may catch the bridle in their teeth, and run away with their rulers, they care not into what dangers they plunge either their fortunes or reputations, the disgrace of the whole sex, or the blot and obloquy of their private families, according to the saying of the poets

Such is the cruelty of women-kind,
When they have shaken off the shamefac'd band
With which wise nature did them strongly bind,
T'obey the hests of man's well-ruling hand
That then all rule and reason they withstand
To purchase a licentious liberty;
But virtuous women wisely understand,
That they were born to mild humility,
Unless the heavens them lift to lawful sovereignty.[4]

To you therefore that are fathers, husbands, of sustainers of these new hermaphrodites, belongs the cure of this impostume;[5] it is you that give fuel to the flames of their wild indiscretion. You add the oil which makes their stinking lamps defile the whole house with filthy smoke, and your purses purchase these deformities at rates both dear and unreasonable. Do you but hold close your liberal hands, or take a strict account of the employment of the treasure you give to their necessary maintenance, and these excesses will either cease, or else die smothered in prison in the tailors' trunks for want of redemption.

from Haec-Vir; or, The Womanish-Man

Hic-Mulier: Well, then to the purpose: first, you say, I am base in being a slave to novelty. What flattery can there be in freedom of election? Or what baseness to crown my delights with those pleasures which are most suitable to mine affections? Bondage or slavery is a restraint from those actions, which the mind (of its own accord) doth most willingly desire: to perform the intents and purposes of another's disposition, and that

4. Description of the tyranny of the Amazonian ruler Radigund in Spenser's *Faerie Queene* 5.5.25.

5. Abscess.

not but by mansuetude[1] or sweetness of entreaty; but by the force of authority and strength of compulsion. Now for me to follow change, according to the limitation of my own will and pleasure, there cannot be a greater freedom. Nor do I in my delight of change otherwise than as the whole world doth, or as becometh a daughter of the world to do. For what is the world, but a very shop or warehouse of change? Sometimes winter, sometimes summer; day and night: they hold sometimes riches, sometimes poverty, sometimes health, sometimes sickness: now pleasure; presently anguish; now honor; then contempt: and to conclude, there is nothing but change, which doth surround and mix with all our fortunes. And will you have poor woman such a fixed star, that she shall not so much as move or twinkle in her own sphere? That would be true slavery indeed, and a baseness beyond the chains of the worst servitude. Nature to everything she hath created hath given a singular delight in change, as to herbs, plants, and trees a time to wither and shed their leaves, a time to bud and bring forth their leaves, and a time for their fruits and flowers; to worms and creeping things a time to hide themselves in the pores and hollows of the earth, and a time to come abroad and suck the dew; to beasts liberty to choose their food, liberty to delight in their food, and liberty to feed and grow fat with their food. The birds have the air to fly in, the waters to bathe in, and the earth to feed on. But to man, both these and all things else, to alter, frame, and fashion, according to his will and delight shall rule him. Again, who will rob the eye of the variety of objects, the ear of the delight of sounds, the nose of smells, the tongue of taste, and the hand of feeling? And shall only woman, excellent woman, so much better in that she is something purer, be only deprived of this benefit? Shall she be the bondslave of time, the handmaid of opinion, or the strict observer of every frosty or cold benumbed imagination? It would be a cruelty beyond the rack or strapado.[2]

But you will say it is not change, but novelty, from which you deter us: a thing that doth avert the good, and erect the evil; prefer the faithless, and confound desert; that with the change of opinions breeds the change of states, and with continual alterations thrusts headlong forward both ruin and subversion. Alas (soft Sir) what can you christen by that new imagined title, when the words of a wise man are: *that what was done, is but done again: all things do change, and under the cope of heaven there is no new thing.*[3] So that whatsoever we do or imitate, it is neither slavish, base, nor a breeder of novelty.

Next, you condemn me of unnaturalness, in forsaking my creation, and contemning[4] custom. How do I forsake my creation, that do all the right and offices due to my creation? I was created free, born free, and live free: what lets me then so to spin out my time, that I may die free?

To alter creation were to walk on my hands with my heels upward, to feed myself with my feet, or to forsake the sweet sound of sweet words, for the hissing noise of the serpent: but I walk with a face erected, with a body clothed, with a mind busied, and with a heart full of reasonable and devout cogitations; only offensive in attire, inasmuch as it is a stranger to the curiosity of the present times, and an enemy to custom. Are we then bound to be the flatterers of time, or the dependents on custom? O miserable servitude chained only to baseness and folly! For then custom, nothing is more absurd, nothing more foolish. * * *

1. Gentleless, meekness.
2. Rack: a frame with a roller at either end on which a person would be tortured; strapado: a form of torture in which the victim's hands would be tied behind his or her back and the victim would then be suspended by a pulley with a sharp jolt.
3. Ecclesiastes 1.9.
4. Disdaining, despising.

Cato Junior held it for a custom, never to eat meat but sitting on the ground. The Venetians kiss one another ever at the first meeting; and even in this day it is a general received custom amongst our English, that when we meet or overtake any man in our travel or journeying, to examine him whither he rides, how far, to what purpose, and where he lodgeth? Nay, and with that unmannerly boldness of inquisition, that it is a certain ground of a most insufficient quarrel, not to receive a full satisfaction of those demands which go far astray from good manners, or comely civility; and will you have us to marry ourselves to these mimic and most fantastic customs? It is a fashion or custom with us to mourn in black, yet the Argian[5] and Roman ladies ever mourned in white; and (if we will tie the action upon the signification of colors) I see not but we may mourn in green, blue, red or any simple color used in heraldry. For us to salute strangers with a kiss is counted but civility, but with foreign nations immodesty; for you to cut the hair of your upper lips, familiar here in England, everywhere else almost thought unmanly. To ride on side-saddles at first was counted here abominable pride, and et cetera. I might instance in a thousand things that only custom and not reason hath approved. To conclude, Custom is an idiot, and whoever dependeth wholly upon him, without the discourse of reason, will take from him his pied[6] coat, and become a slave indeed to contempt and censure.

But you say we are barbarous and shameless and cast off all softness, to run wild through a wilderness of opinions. In this you express more cruelty than in all the rest, because I do not stand with my hands on my belly like a baby[7] at Bartholomew Fair,[8] that move not my whole body when I should but only stir my head like Jack of the clock house[9] which has no joints, that is not dumb when wantons court me, as if asslike I were ready for all burdens, or because I weep not when injury gripes me, like a worried deer in the fangs of many curs. Am I therefore barbarous or shameless? He is much injurious that so baptized us; we are as free-born as men, have as free election, and as free spirits, we are compounded of like parts, and may with like liberty make benefit of our creations; my countenance shall smile on the worthy, and frown on the ignoble, I will hear the wise, and be deaf to idiots, give counsel to my friend, but be dumb to flatterers, I have hands that shall be liberal to reward desert, feet that shall move swiftly to do good offices, and thoughts that shall ever accompany freedom and severity. If this be barbarous, let me leave the city and live with creatures of like simplicity.

* * *

Hic-Mulier: Therefore to take your proportion in a few lines (my dear Feminine-Masculine) tell me what Charter, prescription or right of claim you have to those things you make our absolute inheritance? Why do you curl, frizzle and powder your hair, bestowing more hours and time in dividing lock from lock, and hair from hair, in giving every thread his posture, and every curl his true fence and circumference than ever Caesar did in marshalling his army, either at Pharsalia, in Spain, or Britain? Why do you rob us of our ruffs, our earrings, carkanets,[1] and mamillions,[2] of our fans and feathers, our busks and French bodies, nay, of our masks, hoods, shadows, and shapynas,[3] not so much as the very art of painting, but you have so greedily engrossed it,

5. Of Argos.
6. Spotted, motley.
7. Doll.
8. A popular carnival fair held every year from 1133 to 1865 at West Smithfield on 24 August, the feast day of St. Bartholomew.
9. Figure that strikes the bell of a clock.
1. A jeweled or gold necklace.
2. Rounded protuberances (from French *mamelon*, nipple).
3. Disguises.

that were it not for that little fantastical sharp pointed dagger that hangs at your chins, and the cross hilt which guards your upper lip, hardly would there be any difference between the fair mistress and the foolish servant. But is this theft the uttermost of our spoil? Fie, you have gone a world further, and even ravished from us our speech, our actions, sports, and recreations. Goodness leave me, if I have not heard a man court his mistress with the same words that Venus did Adonis, or as near as the book could instruct him;[4] where are the tilts and tourneys, and lofty galliards[5] that were danced in the days of old, when men capered in the air like wanton kids on the tops of mountains, and turned above ground as if they had been compact of fire or a purer element?[6] Tut, all's forsaken, all's vanished, those motions showed more strength than art, and more courage than courtship; it was much too robustious, and rather spent the body than prepared it, especially where any defect before reigned; hence you took from us poor women our traverses and tourneys, our modest stateliness and curious slidings, and left us nothing but the new French garb of puppet hopping and setting. Lastly, poor shuttlecock[7] that was only a female invention, how have you taken it out of our hands, and made yourselves such lords and rulers over it, that though it be a very emblem of us, and our lighter despised fortunes, yet it dare now hardly come near us; nay, you keep it so imprisoned within your bed-chambers and dining rooms, amongst your pages and panders, that a poor innocent maid to give but a kick with her battledore,[8] were more than halfway to the ruin of her reputation. For this you have demolished the noble schools of horsemanship (of which many were in this city) hung up your arms to rust, glued up those swords in their scabbards that would shake all Christendom with the brandish, and entertained into your mind such softness, dullness, and effeminate niceness that it would even make *Heraclitus*[9] himself laugh against his nature to see how pulingly[1] you languish in this weak entertained sin of womanish softness. To see one of your gender either show himself (in the midst of his pride or riches) at a playhouse or public assembly; how (before he dare enter) with the Jacob's-staff of his own eyes and his pages, he takes a full survey of himself, from the highest sprig in his feather, to the lowest spangle that shines in his shoestring: how he prunes and picks himself like a hawk set a-weathering, calls every several garment to auricular[2] confession, making them utter both their mortal great stains, and their venial and less blemishes, though the mote must be much less than an atom. Then to see him pluck and tug everything into the form of the newest received fashion; and by *Durer's* rules[3] make his leg answerable to his neck; his thigh proportionable with his middle, his foot with his hand, and a world of such idle disdained foppery. To see him thus patched up with symmetry, make himself complete, and even as a circle, and lastly, cast himself among the eyes of the people (as an object of wonder) with more niceness than a virgin goes to the sheets of her first lover would make patience herself mad with anger, and cry with the poet:

> O hominum mores, O gens, O tempora dura,
> Quantus in urbe dolor; quantus in orbe dolus![4]

4. Venus, goddess of love, fell in love with the beautiful youth Adonis.
5. A brisk dance in triple time.
6. Men were thought to be dominated by dry humors and women by humid ones.
7. A small piece of cork with feathers sticking out of it, batted back and forth in the game of battledoor and shuttlecock.
8. A small racket, used to hit a shuttlecock.
9. Heraclitus was said to weep whenever he went forth in public (See Seneca, *De tranquilitate animi* 15.2).
1. In a whining tone.
2. Told privately, to the ear.
3. Albrecht Dürer (1471–1528), German painter and engraver, wrote a work on human proportions that was published after his death.
4. O customs of men, O people, O hard times / What great sadness in the city; what great fraud in the world.

Now since according to your own inference, even by the laws of nature, by the rules of religion, and the customs of all civil nations, it is necessary there be a distinct and special difference between man and woman, both in their habit and behaviors, what could we poor weak women do less (being far too weak by force to fetch back those spoils you have unjustly taken from us) than to gather up those garments you have proudly cast away, and therewith to clothe both our bodies and our minds; since no other means was left us to continue our names, and to support a difference? For to have held the way in which our forefathers first set us, or to have still embraced the civil modesty, or gentle sweetness of our soft inclinations; why, you had so far encroached upon us, and so over-bribed the world, to be deaf to any grant of restitution, that as at our creation, our whole sex was contained in man our first parent, so we should have had no other being, but in you, and your most effeminate quality. Hence we have preserved (though to our own shames) those manly things which you have forsaken, which would you again accept, and restore to us the blushes we laid by, when first we put on your masculine garments; doubt not but chaste thoughts and bashfulness will again dwell in us, and our palaces being newly gilt, trimmed, and reedified, draw to us all the Graces, all the Muses,[5] which that you may more willingly do, and (as we of yours) grow into detestation of that deformity you have purloined, to the utter loss of your honors and reputations. Mark how the brave Italian poet,[6] even in the infancy of your abuses, most lively describes you:

About his neck a Carknet[7] rich he ware
Of precious Stones, all set in gold well tried;
His arms that erst all warlike weapons bare,
In golden bracelets wantonly were tied:
Into his ears two rings conveyed are
Of golden wire, at which on either side,
Two Indian pearls, in making like two pears,
Of passing price were pendant at his ears.

His locks bedewed with water of sweet savor,
Stood curled round in order on his head;
He had such wanton womanish behavior,
As though in valor he had ne'er been bred:
So chang'd in speech, in manners and in favor,
So from himself beyond all reason led,
By these enchantments of this amorous dame;
He was himself in nothing, but in name.

Thus you see your injury to us is of an old and inveterate continuance, having taken such strong root in your bosoms, that it can hardly be pulled up, without some offense to the soil: ours young and tender, scarce freed from the swaddling clothes, and therefore may with as much ease be lost, as it was with little difficulty found. Cast then from you our ornaments, and put on your own armors. Be men in shape, men in show, men in words, men in actions, men in counsel, men in example: then will we love and serve you; then will we hear and obey you; then will we like rich jewels hang

5. The graces were the three sisters, Aglaia, Thalia, and Euphrosyne, viewed as bestowers of charm and beauty; the muses were the nine daughters of Zeus and Memory who inspire poetry and the arts.

6. Ludovico Ariosto (1474–1532), whose description of Ruggiero's decadence when he is seduced by the sorceress Alcina in *Orlando Furioso 7* is quoted here in the translation (1590) by Sir John Harington, Queen Elizabeth's godson.

7. Necklace.

at your ears to take our instructions, like true friends follow you through all dangers, and like careful leeches[8] pour oil into your wounds. Then shall you find delight in our words; pleasure in our faces; faith in our hearts; chastity in our thoughts, and sweetness both in our inward and outward inclinations. Comeliness shall be then our study; fear our armor, and modesty our practice: then shall we be all your most excellent thoughts can desire, and have nothing in us less than impudence and deformity.

Haec-Vir; Enough: you have both raised my eyelids, cleared my sight, and made my heart entertain both shame and delight at an instant; shame in my follies past; delight in our noble and worthy conversion. Away then from me these light vanities, the only ensigns[9] of a weak and soft nature: and come you grave and solid pieces, which arm a man with fortitude and resolution: you are too rough and stubborn for a woman's wearing, we will here change our attires, as we have changed our minds, and with our attires, our names. I will no more be *Haec-Vir*, but *Hic Vir*, nor you *Hic-Mulier*, but *Haec Mulier*. From henceforth deformity shall pack to Hell; and if at any time he hide himself upon the earth, yet it shall be with contempt and disgrace. He shall have no friend but Poverty; no favorer but Folly, nor no reward but Shame. Henceforth we will live nobly like ourselves, ever sober, ever discreet, ever worthy; true men, and true women. We will be henceforth like well-coupled doves, full of industry, full of love: I mean, not of sensual and carnal love, but heavenly and divine love, which proceeds from God, whose inexpressible nature none is able to deliver in words, since is like his dwelling, high and beyond the reach of human apprehension.

END OF PERSPECTIVES: TRACTS ON WOMEN AND GENDER

Ben Jonson

1572–1637

Ben Jonson's life was full of changes and contradictions. His earliest biographer, William Drummond, called him "passionately kind and angry, careless either to gain or keep, vindictive, but, if he be well answered, at himself." His father was Protestant, but Jonson turned Catholic, only to recant that conversion later; nevertheless, in his last years he called himself a "beadsman." The stepson of a bricklayer, he became Poet Laureate. He wrote poems of praise to win the patronage of king and court but also skewered their follies in satire. Though often assuming the role of moralist in his poetry and plays, Jonson admitted that as a younger man he was "given to venery" and pleaded guilty to the charge of murder. He was attached to admiring younger poets, "the tribe of Ben," yet he also enjoyed feuds, such as those with fellow dramatists Marston and Dekker. While espousing Horatian spareness and an acute sense of meter in both criticism and poetry, Jonson also had a keen ear for the colloquial language of London.

Indeed, London was one of the few constants in Jonson's turbulent career. Born in Harts-Born Lane near Charing Cross, he was buried in the nave in the north aisle, across the Abbey from Poets' Corner. Jonson portrayed the city as the world of those who lived by their wits. He dramatized literary infighting in *Every Man Out of His Humour* (1599), greedy schemes in *Volpone* (1606), intellectual confidence scams in *The Alchemist* (1610), and antitheatrical Puritan preaching in *Bartholomew Fair* (1614). The London audience at the Hope Theatre was reported to have exclaimed at a performance of *Bartholomew Fair*: "O rare Ben Jonson!"

8. Physicians.

9. Banners, signs.

Unlike other playwrights of his time (including Shakespeare), Jonson oversaw the publication of his plays, which appeared with his poems in the same deluxe folio volume, entitled *Works* (1616). The assertion of the dignity of popular drama surprised many of his readers, one of whom wrote, "Pray tell me Ben, where doth the mystery lurk, / What others call a play, you call a work?" That Jonson wanted his plays to be read as much as performed can be gathered from the comment printed on the title page of *Every Man Out of His Humour*: "as it was first composed by the author, Ben Jonson, containing more than hath been publicly spoken or acted."

Jonson viewed writing as his profession; he became the first poet in England to earn a living by his art. His achievement was recognized by James I, who made Jonson the first Poet Laureate of England and granted him a pension for life. Before becoming laureate, Jonson depended on a whole string of patrons. With the new Stuart king in power, Jonson was able to use his claim of Scots descent to advantage. He was supported by Esme Stuart Seigneur D'Aubigny (a cousin of King James), to whom he dedicated his first tragedy, *Sejanus* (1603). His patrons included Sir Walter Raleigh and Lady Mary Wroth, to whom he dedicated *The Alchemist*. Jonson's most important break came when he received a commission for a court masque. In 1605 he wrote *The Masque of Blackness* starring the Queen herself. To gain some idea of the extravagance of these masques, consider that in 1617, while 12,000 pounds were spent on the entire administration of Ireland, 4,000 pounds were spent on a single masque, *Pleasure Reconciled to Virtue*. The masques were lavish ventures that required costumes, music, and magnificent scenery, which was designed by Inigo Jones, who introduced the Italian invention of perspective.

If the pursuit of patronage was crucial to Jonson's advancement, his satire of politics and power repeatedly put his career and even his life at risk. In 1603 Jonson was called before the Privy Council for *Sejanus;* the charges included "popery and treason." Jonson's *Epicoene, or the Silent Woman*—which climaxes in the revelation that the silent woman is really a boy—was suppressed because it lampooned a love affair of the King's first cousin, Lady Arbella Stuart. One observer complained of the 1613 *Irish Masque at Court* that it was "no time . . . to exasperate that nation by making ridiculous." Jonson was imprisoned twice for the offense that his plays gave to the powerful—once for the now lost *The Isle of Dogs* (1597) and another time for *Eastward Ho!* (1605), in which he made fun of King James's Scots accent.

Jonson took reckless risks, whose consequences he barely managed to escape. While imprisoned for the murder of Gabriel Spencer in 1598, Jonson became a Catholic. Following his conversion, Jonson pleaded guilty to manslaughter (later calling it the result of a duel) but went free by claiming benefit of clergy. This medieval custom originally allowed clerics to be judged by the bishop's court but, by Jonson's time, permitted anyone who could translate the Latin Bible to go free. Jonson left prison with his belongings confiscated, his thumb branded for the felony, and his reputation marked by his profession of an outlaw religion. Like any other Catholic in Elizabethan England, Jonson could be fined or have his property confiscated for not attending Anglican services. Indeed, he and his wife were interrogated for their nonattendance in 1605; Jonson was also charged with being "a poet, and by fame a seducer of youth to the Popish religion." Threatened again with loss of property and another prison term, Jonson complied with the Court's order that he take instruction in Protestantism.

Not all Jonson's disputes were quite so dangerous. Like the characters in his plays, he enjoyed engaging in the game of vapors, a mock argument, drummed up for the display of wit. He not only engaged in combats of wit with Shakespeare (who acted in *Every Man Out of His Humour*) but also ridiculed Marston and Dekker in what critics call "the War of the Theaters." Jonson's *Every Man Out of His Humour* satirized Marston as a pseudo-intellectual. The same year, Jonson and Dekker collaborated on a play. Two years later, Dekker parodied Jonson as the bombastic Horace, constantly reading his work aloud and expecting praise in *Satiriomastix* (1601). The title of this play means "the whipping of the satirist," and it is full of barbs about Jonson's checkered past—both his imprisonment and his theatrical flops. Dekker called Jonson a "brown-bread mouth-stinker." Jonson responded with a "forced defense" against "base detractors and illiterate apes" in *Poetaster* (1601).

Jonson did have high regard for some of his contemporaries, as they did for him. Among these was John Donne, who wrote commendatory verses for *Volpone* and to whom Jonson wrote "Who shall doubt, Donne, whe'er I a poet be / When I dare send my epigrams to thee?" As an older man, Jonson held court at the Devil Tavern among his fellow poets as self-proclaimed *arbiter bibendi* (master of drinking), whose main object was "Not drinking much, but talking wittily." This vein of wit was carried on by Sir John Suckling's *A Session of Poets* and Herrick's *Prayer for Ben Jonson*. His servant Brome wrote an elegy for him, as did the many men of letters who contributed to *Jonsonius Virbius* ("Jonson Reborn"), the year after his death.

Jonson saw himself as a moral and poetic guide. His satire of moral depravity and intellectual delusion is hysterically funny. His plays include direct criticism of contemporary poetry and drama, contracts with the audience, and self-mockery—a foretaste of the break from realistic conventions in modernism. Jonson's comedies also persuade us that there is no reality without satire; we cannot know the world without laughing at its ridiculousness. The human foibles and obsessions portrayed in his comedies are captured in a language so vivid and oral that it has to be read aloud. Jonson's verse dazzles by concealing its art, allowing conversational words and rhythms to be perfectly wedded to poetic meters. The simplicity and restraint of his language, as in his elegy on the death of his son, are the vehicles for pure music and powerful emotion.

For additional resources on Jonson, including *Volpone*, go to *The Longman Anthology of British Literature* Web site at www.myliteraturekit.com.

The Alchemist *The Alchemist* begins with a fart. So starts a series of insults that two swindlers—Face and Subtle—hurl at each other until their prostitute pal Dol Common reminds them of their "venture tripartite" to "cozen kindly." Subtle, a down-at-the-heels confidence man who passes himself off as an alchemist, capable through secret knowledge of turning base metals to gold, and his wily assistant Face, who lures clients to the empty house in Blackfriars that he is supposed to be minding, team up with Dol to hoodwink eight variously self-deluded early modern London types by promising to fulfill their wildest dreams of wealth, sex, and power. The law clerk Dapper is made to believe that, as nephew of the Queen of the Faeries (played by Dol), he will be given a magic spirit to help him clean up at gambling. The shopkeeper Abel Drugger has a horoscope cast that promises him a killing in business and marriage to a rich widow. The Puritan parson Tribulation and the skeptical elder Ananias eagerly agree to have the goods of poor orphans transmuted into precious metals. The city knight Epicure Mammon hopes to achieve the philosopher's stone itself—the magic ingredient that will turn all to gold and allow him to enjoy jewel-encrusted luxury and sex with a harem of succubae. His at-first-unbelieving sidekick Surly thinks that by playing the role of a Spanish Count he can win the hand of the rich, nineteen-year-old widow Dame Pliant, while she believes that her fortune will be to marry a gallant young aristocrat. Her brother the country squire Kastril simply wants to learn how to quarrel in the abusive manner of the London "angry boys" to succeed in the kind of one-upmanship that the play roundly ridicules.

Indeed, no one really gets the better of anyone in this play except Lovewit, the owner of the Blackfriars townhouse in which this madcap action takes place. When he returns home, all these plots explode, as all the neighbors complain to him about the riotous comings and goings they have been witnessing. All the dupes that the cozeners have been trying to keep separate from one another show up almost simultaneously to attempt to get back the money they have all too willingly allowed themselves to be defrauded of. None of the dupes is punished—except by losing the loot that they have handed over and by having to resume the lives they lead at the start. While Subtle and Dol have to return to their lives on the street, Face returns to his role as Jeremy the butler through a bargain with his master, Lovewit. In short, Lovewit gets the girl—Dame Pliant—and all the money in return for protecting his servant Jeremy from the law.

Andrew Gurr, director of the Globe project in London, has suggested an intriguing explanation for the point of this rather unsettling happy ending: that in the crafty metadramatic world created by the playwright, Lovewit was none other than William Shakespeare, Jonson's chief rival. Like Lovewit, Shakespeare was out of town because of the plague in 1610, and like Lovewit, Shakespeare not only loved wit but made a profit out of it as a capitalist landlord. As one of the five co-owners of the Blackfriars theater, where *The Alchemist* was first performed in 1610, Shakespeare, the greatest playwright of his age, was also a typical early modern Londoner, who shared the dupes of the play's concern with making money. At the end of the play, Face asks the audience to "feast often" and "invite new guests" to the theater, to laugh at his and his theatrical conspirators' shenanigans (as Lovewit has). At the same time, Face implicitly enjoins the spectators to contemplate how they have been both tricked and entertained by the actors who have counterfeited their roles to make money for themselves—but even more money for the owners of the stage.

But the play is about much more than greed for money or the deceptive power of theater. It is about the self-deception and self-aggrandizement that motivate not only greed but all sorts of human desires, including lust and even the betterment of society. In Act 4, Surly calls Subtle "Faustus" for promising to cure "plagues, piles, and pox." As Jonson critic Anne Barton has pointed out, Mammon is also like the Marlovian tragic hero Dr. Faustus in his utopian dreams. Another pseudo-Faustus, Mammon claims that he wants to relieve beggars of want and to cure the plague. The play is about the universally human and particularly early modern desire for control over a world that cannot really be controlled—at least not through the mental constructs the play sends up.

Among these systems of discourse that pretend to knowledge, the central object of the play's derision is alchemy. During the early modern period, alchemy was still widely believed in, so much so that Elizabeth I hired John Dee (alluded to in 2.6.20) to make astrological predictions for her and punished Cornelius Lannoy for not making good on his promises to make gold. The transformative power of alchemy becomes a metaphor for every other type of transformation in the play. There is the transformative power to control reality promised by an array of specialized discourses. Grammar, rhetoric, and logic are meant to transform Kastril into a master of argument but merely result in his ability to contradict and abuse others. The language of Puritan millenarian prophecy, based on allegorical interpretation of the Bible, was meant to predict the end of the world. Here, this language is put in the mouth of Dol Common, who pretends to be outraged into a fit of Puritan ranting when she is courted as a great lady by Mammon. The play also ridicules such systems to predict the future as astrology and palmistry. These illusions of control are also not unlike the New Age therapies of today, what the Australian actor Geoffrey Rush has referred to as the "feng shui gobbledegook" behind the magically successful floor plan for Drugger's shop.

The human capacities that allow us to deal more ably with the chaos of life—acceptance of reality and self-knowledge—are sorely wanting in all the play's characters, not just in the foolish gulls but in the tricksters as well. As removed as we might like to think we are from the outrageous hypocrisy of a parson willing to counterfeit money to promote his religion or the gullibility of a law clerk who thinks that by sitting in a privy and biting on gingerbread the Queen of Faeries will appear to him, the play encourages us to laugh at our shared human capacity for self-abasement in the hope of achieving our desires. The satire is gentle enough, since all survive to face the fallible selves they are trying to escape through their foolish, and often base, desires. In *The Alchemist,* Jonson produced a visceral portrait of the London of his day and the characters who made it tick. While we may no longer believe in alchemy, the play's evocation of the frenetic energy, clever scheming for wealth, and drive to control through the pretense of specialized knowledge can still provoke a corrosively ironic laughter at not only the follies of early modern London but also the self-delusions of the city in our contemporary world.

The Alchemist appeared in both the *Quarto* of 1612 and the *Folio* of 1616 and 1640. The *Folio* added stage directions and changed the oaths to remove possible accusation of blasphemy.

The Alchemist

To the Lady Most Deserving Her Name and Blood

Lady Mary Wroth[1]

Madam—In the age of sacrifices, the truth of religion was not in the greatness and fat of the offerings, but in the devotion and zeal of the sacrificers: else what could a handful of gums have done in the sight of a hecatomb?[2] Or how might I appear at this altar, except with those affections that no less love the light and witness, than they have the conscience of your virtue? If what I offer bear an acceptable odor, and hold the first strength, it is your value of it, which remembers where, when, and to whom it was kindled. Otherwise, as the times are, there comes rarely forth that thing so full of authority or example, but by assiduity[3] and custom grows less, and loses. This, yet, safe in your judgment (which is a Sidney's) is forbidden to speak more, lest it talk or look like one of the ambitious faces of the time, who, the more they paint,[4] are the less themselves. Your ladyship's true honorer,

Ben Jonson.

To The Reader

If thou beest more, thou art an understander, and then I trust thee. If thou art one that takest up, and but a pretender, beware of what hands thou receivest thy commodity; for thou wert never more fair in the way to be cozened,[5] than in this age, in poetry, especially in plays: wherein, now the concupiscence of dances and of antics so reigneth, as to run away from nature, and be afraid of her, is the only point of art that tickles the spectators. But how out of purpose, and place, do I name art? When the professors are grown so obstinate contemners of it, and presumers on their own naturals,[6] as they are deriders of all diligence that way, and, by simple mocking at the terms, when they understand not the things, think to get off wittily with their ignorance. Nay, they are esteemed the more learned, and sufficient for this, by the many, through their excellent vice of judgment. For they commend writers, as they do fencers or wrestlers; who if they come in robustuously, and put for it with a great deal of violence, are received for the braver fellows: when many times their own rudeness is the cause of their disgrace, and a little touch of their adversary gives all that boisterous force the foil.[7] I deny not, but that these men, who always seek to do more than enough, may some time happen on some thing that is good, and great; but very seldom; and when it comes it doth not recompense the rest of their ill. It sticks out,

1. The play is dedicated to Lady Mary Wroth, poet, patroness of poets, and niece of Sir Philip Sidney. Her name was also spelled "Worth," as alluded to in "deserving of her name." See selected poems from her sonnet sequence *Pamphilia to Amphilanthus* (page 1611).
2. How could incense ("gums") compare with a huge sacrifice ("hecatomb," literally 100 oxen)?
3. Perseverance.
4. Apply makeup.
5. Tricked.
6. Confident in their natural, or innate, wit; "naturals" also means "fools."
7. Check, repulse, defeat.

perhaps, and is more eminent, because all is sordid and vile about it: as lights are more discerned in a thick darkness, than a faint shadow. I speak not this, out of a hope to do good to any man against his will; for I know, if it were put to the question of theirs and mine, the worse would find more suffrages: because the most favor common errors. But I give thee this warning, that there is a great difference between those, that, to gain the opinion of copy,[8] utter all they can, however unfitly; and those that use election and a mean.[9] For it is only the disease of the unskilful, to think rude things greater than polished; or scattered more numerous[1] than composed.

Dramatis Personae

SUBTLE, *the Alchemist*
FACE, *the Housekeeper*
DOL COMMON, *their Colleague*
DAPPER, *a Lawyer's Clerk*
DRUGGER, *Tobacco Man*
LOVEWIT, *Master of the House*
SIR EPICURE MAMMON, *a Knight*
PERTINAX SURLY, *a Gamester*
TRIBULATION WHOLESOME, *a Pastor of Amsterdam*
ANANIAS, *a Deacon (church officer) there*
KASTRIL,[2] *the Angry Boy*
DAME PLIANT, *his Sister, a Widow*
NEIGHBORS, OFFICERS, ATTENDANTS, etc.

Scene, London

ARGUMENT

T *he sickness hot,*[3] *a master quit, for fear,*
H *is house in town, and left one servant there;*
E *ase him corrupted, and gave means to know*

A *Cheater, and his punk;*° *who now brought low,* — prostitute
L *eaving their narrow practice, were become*
C *ozeners*° *at large; and only wanting some* — cheaters, tricksters
H *ouse to set up, with him they here contract,*
E *ach for a share, and all begin to act.*
M *uch company they draw, and much abuse,*
I *n casting figures,*° *telling fortunes, news,* — reading horoscopes
S *elling of flies, flat bawdry with the stone,*[4]
T *ill it, and they, and all in fume are gone.*

PROLOGUE

Fortune, that favors fools, these two short hours,
  We wish away, both for your sakes and ours,
Judging spectators; and desire, in place.
  To the author justice, to ourselves but grace.
Our scene is London, 'cause we would make known,

8. Fame for prolific and fluent writing.
9. Careful choice and moderation.
1. "Numerous" in the sense of both "copious" and "skilled in numbers," able to write verse that is musical in its rhythm.
2. Kestrel, a small hawk; a term of contempt.
3. A reference to the plague that hit London in 1609–1610.
4. "Flies" were demons; "the stone" is the philosophers' stone and also slang for "testicle."

No country's mirth is better than our own:
No clime breeds better matter for your whore,
Bawd,° squire,° impostor, many persons more, *madam / pimp*
Whose manners, now call'd humors,[5] feed the stage;
And which have still been subject for the rage
Or spleen of comic writers. Though this pen
Did never aim to grieve, but better men;
Howe'er the age he lives in doth endure
The vices that she breeds, above their cure.
But when the wholesome remedies are sweet,
And in their working gain and profit meet,
He hopes to find no spirit so much diseased.
But will with such fair correctives be pleased.
For here he doth not fear who can apply.
If there be any that will sit so nigh
Unto the stream, to look what it doth run,
They shall find things, they'd think or wish were done;
They are so natural follies, but so shewn,
As even the doers may see, and yet not own.

ACT 1

Scene 1—*A room in Lovewit's house*

[*Enter Face, in a captain's uniform, with his sword drawn, and Subtle with a vial, quarrelling, and followed by Dol Common.*]

FACE: Believe't, I will.
SUBTLE: Thy worst. I fart at thee.
DOL: Ha' you your wits? why, gentlemen! for love—
FACE: Sirrah, I'll strip you—
SUBTLE: What to do? Lick figs° *ficus, the piles*
Out at my—
FACE: Rogue, rogue!—out of all your sleights.
DOL: Nay, look ye, sovereign, general, are you madmen?
SUBTLE: O, let the wild sheep loose. I'll gum your silks
With good strong water,[6] an you come.
DOL: Will you have
The neighbours hear you? will you betray all?
Hark! I hear somebody.
FACE: Sirrah—
SUBTLE: I shall mar
All that the tailor has made, if you approach.
FACE: You most notorious whelp, you insolent slave,
Dare you do this?
SUBTLE: Yes, faith; yes, faith.

5. The four personality types controlled by the four bodily fluids: sanguine, or happy (blood); phlegmatic, or impassive (phlegm); choleric, or angry (bile); and melancholy (black bile).
6. Subtle threatens to ruin the fabric of Face's fancy uniform by throwing a vial of chemicals at him.

FACE: Why, who
Am I, my mongrel? who am I?
SUBTLE: I'll tell you,
Since you know not yourself.
FACE: Speak lower, rogue.
SUBTLE: Yes, you were once (time's not long past) the good,
Honest, plain, livery-three-pound-thrum,[7] that kept
Your master's worship's house here in the Friars,[8]
For the vacations—
FACE: Will you be so loud?
SUBTLE: Since, by my means, translated° suburb-captain.[9] *promoted to*
FACE: By your means, Doctor Dog!
SUBTLE: Within man's memory,
All this I speak of.
FACE: Why, I pray you, have I
Been countenanced by you, or you by me?
Do but collect, sir, where I met you first.
SUBTLE: I do not hear well.
FACE: Not of this, I think it.
But I shall put you in mind, sir;—at Pie-corner,[1]
Taking your meal of steam in, from cooks' stalls,
Where, like the father of hunger, you did walk
Piteously costive,° with your pinch'd-horn-nose, *constipated, stingy*
And your complexion of the Roman wash,
Stuck full of black and melancholic worms,
Like powder corns shot at the artillery-yard.[2]
SUBTLE: I wish you could advance your voice a little.
FACE: When you went pinn'd up in the several rags
You'd raked and picked from dunghills, before day;
Your feet in mouldy slippers, for your kibes;° *chilblains*
A felt° of rug, and a thin threaden cloke, *hat*
That scarce would cover your no-buttocks—
SUBTLE: So, sir!
FACE: When all your alchemy, and your algebra,
Your minerals, vegetals, and animals,
Your conjuring, cozening,° and your dozen of trades, *trickery*
Could not relieve your corps with so much linen° *underwear*
Would make you tinder, but to see a fire;[3]
I gave you countenance, credit for your coals,
Your stills, your glasses, your materials;

7. A poorly dressed servant. Three pounds was a servant's yearly salary, and a thrum is the loose end of a weaver's warp.
8. Neighborhood of Blackfriars Theatre, where *The Alchemist* was performed.
9. Pretender to officer rank in the suburbs, the sleazy outskirts of the city.
1. Location of cooks' shops in Smithfield, a down-at-the-heels part of town.
2. Face describes Subtle's face as sallow and covered with blackheads that look like blotches of shot gunpowder.
3. So few shreds of linen that it would not even be enough kindling to start a fire.

Built you a furnace, drew you customers,
Advanced all your black arts; lent you, beside,
A house to practise in—
SUBTLE: Your master's house!
FACE: Where you have studied the more thriving skill
Of bawdry° since. *lewdness, pandering*
SUBTLE: Yes, in your master's house.
You and the rats here kept possession.
Make it not strange. I know you were one could keep
The buttery-hatch still lock'd, and save the chippings,
Sell the dole beer to aqua-vitae men,[4]
The which, together with your Christmas vails° *tips*
At post-and-pair, your letting out of counters,
Made you a pretty stock, some twenty marks,[5]
And gave you credit to converse with cobwebs,
Here, since your mistress' death hath broke up house.
FACE: You might talk softlier, rascal.
SUBTLE: No, you scarab,° *dung beetle*
I'll thunder you in pieces: I will teach you
How to beware to tempt a Fury again,
That carries tempest in his hand and voice.
FACE: The place has made you valiant.
SUBTLE: No, your clothes.—
Thou vermin, have I ta'en thee out of dung,
So poor, so wretched, when no living thing
Would keep thee company, but a spider, or worse?
Rais'd thee from brooms, and dust, and watering-pots,
Sublimed° thee, and exalted thee, and fix'd thee *turned to vapor*
In the third region,[6] call'd our state of grace?
Wrought thee to spirit, to quintessence, with pains
Would twice have won me the philosopher's work?[7]
Put thee in words and fashion, made thee fit
For more than ordinary fellowships?
Giv'n thee thy oaths, thy quarrelling dimensions,
Thy rules to cheat at horse-race, cock-pit, cards,
Dice, or whatever gallant tincture[8] else?
Made thee a second in mine own great art?
And have I this for thanks! Do you rebel,
Do you fly out in the projection?
Would you be gone now?
DOL: Gentlemen, what mean you?
Will you mar all?
SUBTLE: Slave, thou hadst had no name—
DOL: Will you undo yourselves with civil war?

4. Subtle accuses Face of selling beer given out free from rich households.
5. Post and pair: a card game; counters: gambling chips: a mark was worth 13 shillings and 4 pence.
6. The highest sphere of the universe.
7. The quintessence was the most purified form that could be extracted from all matter. The philosopher's work was the result of alchemy, the "stone" that transformed metal into gold.
8. A color or quality in alchemy.

SUBTLE: Never been known, past *equi clibanum*,[9]
The heat of horse-dung, under ground, in cellars.
Or an ale-house darker than deaf John's; been lost
To all mankind, but laundresses and tapsters,[1]
Had not I been.
DOL: Do you know who hears you, Sovereign?
FACE: Sirrah—
DOL: Nay, General, I thought you were civil.
FACE: I shall turn desperate, if you grow thus loud.
SUBTLE: And hang thyself, I care not.
FACE: Hang thee, collier,° *coal miner*
And all thy pots, and pans, in picture, I will,
Since thou hast moved me—
DOL: O, this will o'erthrow all.
FACE: Write thee up bawd in Paul's,[2] have all thy tricks
Of cozening with a hollow coal, dust, scrapings,
Searching for things lost, with a sieve and sheers,[3]
Erecting figures° in your rows of houses, *cast a horoscope*
And taking in of shadows with a glass,
Told in red letters;[4] and a face cut for thee,
Worse than Gamaliel Ratsey's.[5]
DOL: Are you sound?
Have you your senses, masters?
FACE: I will have
A book, but barely reckoning thy impostures,
Shall prove a true philosopher's stone to printers.
SUBTLE: Away, you trencher-rascal!
FACE: Out, you dog-leach!
The vomit of all prisons—
DOL: Will you be
Your own destructions, gentlemen?
FACE: Still spew'd out
For lying too heavy on the basket.[6]
SUBTLE: Cheater!
FACE: Bawd!
SUBTLE: Cow-herd!
FACE: Conjurer!
SUBTLE: Cut-purse!
FACE: Witch!
DOL: O me!
We are ruin'd, lost! have you no more regard
To your reputations? where's your judgment? 'slight,° *by God's light*
Have yet some care of me, of your republic[7]—

9. Oven fueled by horse dung.
1. Women who drew beer in taverns.
2. Advertise yourself as a pimp outside St. Paul's.
3. The sieve was believed to turn in the direction of thieves and stolen goods.
4. The glass cast up figures that were interpreted by a virgin.
5. A famous bandit known for his mask ("cut").
6. For eating too much from the sheriff 's charity basket for the poor.
7. Commonweal and also a pun on *res publica*, public, or common thing; a bawdy reference to Dol Common.

FACE: Away, this brach! I'll bring thee, rogue, within
The statute of sorcery, tricesimo tertio
Of Harry the Eighth:[8] ay, and perhaps, thy neck
Within a noose, for laundring gold and barbing° it. *clipping*

DOL [*snatches Face's sword*]: You'll bring your head within a cockscomb, will you?[9]
And you, sir, with your menstrue°— *solvent*
[*Dashes Subtle's vial out of his hand.*] Gather it up.—
'Sdeath,° you abominable pair of stinkards, *by God's death*
Leave off your barking, and grow one again,
Or, by the light that shines, I'll cut your throats.
I'll not be made a prey unto the marshal,
For ne'er a snarling dog-bolt° of you both. *blunt-headed arrow*
Have you together cozen'd all this while,
And all the world, and shall it now be said,
You've made most courteous shift to cozen yourselves?
[*To Face*] You will accuse him! you will bring him in
Within the statute! Who shall take your word?
A whoreson, upstart, apocryphal captain,
Whom not a Puritan in Blackfriars will trust
So much as for a feather: [*To Subtle*] and you, too,
Will give the cause, forsooth! you will insult,
And claim a primacy in the divisions?
You must be chief? as if you only had
The powder to project with, and the work
Were not begun out of equality?
The venture tripartite? all things in common?
Without priority? 'Sdeath! you perpetual curs,
Fall to your couples again, and cozen kindly,[1]
And heartily, and lovingly, as you should,
And lose not the beginning of a term,[2]
Or, by this hand, I shall grow factious too,
And take my part, and quit you.

FACE: 'Tis his fault;
He ever murmurs, and objects his pains,
And says, the weight of all lies upon him.

SUBTLE: Why, so it does.

DOL: How does it? do not we
Sustain our parts?

SUBTLE: Yes, but they are not equal.

DOL: Why, if your part exceed to-day, I hope
Ours may, to-morrow, match it.

SUBTLE: Ay, they may.

DOL: May, murmuring mastiff! ay, and do. Death on me!
Help me to throttle him. [*Seizes Subtle by the throat.*]

SUBTLE: Dorothy! mistress Dorothy!
'Ods precious, I'll do any thing. What do you mean?

8. Law of 1541 prohibiting sorcery.
9. The cockscomb was the fool's cap.
1. Work together as a pack, like hunting dogs.
2. A term of the law courts; the busiest times in London.

DOL: Because o' your fermentation and cibation?[3]
SUBTLE: Not I, by heaven—
DOL [*To Face*.]: Your Sol and Luna°—help me. *gold and silver*
SUBTLE: Would I were hang'd then! I'll conform myself.
DOL: Will you, sir? do so then, and quickly: swear.
SUBTLE: What should I swear?
DOL: To leave your faction, sir,
And labor kindly in the common work.
SUBTLE: Let me not breathe if I meant aught beside.
I only used those speeches as a spur
To him.
DOL: I hope we need no spurs, sir. Do we?
FACE: 'Slid,° prove to-day, who shall shark° best. *God's eyelid / cheat*
SUBTLE: Agreed.
DOL: Yes, and work close and friendly.
SUBTLE: 'Slight, the knot
Shall grow the stronger for this breach, with me.
[*They shake hands*.]
DOL: Why, so, my good baboons! Shall we go make
A sort of sober, scurvy, precise neighbours,
That scarce have smiled twice since the king came in,
A feast of laughter at our follies? Rascals,
Would run themselves from breath, to see me ride,[4]
Or you t' have but a hole to thrust your heads in,
For which you should pay ear-rent?[5] No, agree,
And may Don Provost° ride a feasting long, *Provost-Marshal*
In his old velvet jerkin and stain'd scarfs,
My noble Sovereign, and worthy General,
Ere we contribute a new crewel° garter *double thread*
To his most worsted worship.
SUBTLE: Royal Dol!
Spoken like Claridiana,[6] and thyself.
FACE: For which at supper, thou shalt sit in triumph,
And not be styled Dol Common, but Dol Proper,
Dol Singular: the longest cut at night,
Shall draw thee for his Dol Particular.[7] [*Bell rings without*.]
SUBTLE: Who's that? one rings. To the window, Dol—pray heaven,
The master do not trouble us this quarter.
FACE: O, fear not him. While there dies one a week
O' the plague, he's safe, from thinking toward London:
Beside, he's busy at his hop-yards now;
I had a letter from him. If he do,
He'll send such word, for airing of the house,

3. Alchemical processes: fermentation was the change of any substance into fermented or purified form, and cibation was an infusion of liquid into dried matter.
4. To see her ride or carried off in a cart as were prostitutes, who were also often stripped and beaten.
5. Those who had their heads put in the stocks as punishment often had their ears cut off as well.
6. Heroine of the *Mirror of Princely Deeds and Knighthood*, a Spanish romance, translated by Margaret Tyler.
7. Whoever draws the longest lot gets to sleep with Dol. Also, "longest cut," in the sexual sense, as in *Twelfth Night* 2.5.67–68.

As you shall have sufficient time to quit it:
Though we break up a fortnight, 'tis no matter.
SUBTLE: Who is it, Dol?
DOL: A fine young quodling.° *unripe apple*
FACE: O,
My lawyer's clerk, I lighted on last night,
In Holborn, at the Dagger. He would have
(I told you of him) a familiar,[8]
To rifle with at horses, and win cups.
DOL: O, let him in.
SUBTLE: Stay. Who shall do't?
FACE: Get you
Your robes on: I will meet him as going out.
DOL: And what shall I do?
FACE: Not be seen; away! [*Exit Dol.*]
Seem you very reserv'd.
SUBTLE: Enough. [*Exit.*]
FACE [*aloud and retiring*]: God be wi' you, sir,
I pray you let him know that I was here:
His name is Dapper. I would gladly have staid, but—

Scene 2

DAPPER [*within*]: Captain, I am here.
FACE: Who's that?—He's come, I think, Doctor.
[*Enter Dapper.*]
Good faith, sir, I was going away.
DAPPER: In truth,
I am very sorry, Captain.
FACE: But I thought
Sure I should meet you.
DAPPER: Ay, I am very glad.
I had a scurvy writ or two to make,
And I had lent my watch last night to one
That dines to-day at the sheriff's, and so was robb'd
Of my past-time.
[*Re-enter Subtle, in his velvet Cap and Gown.*]
Is this the cunning-man?
FACE: This is his worship.
DAPPER: Is he a doctor?° *learned man*
FACE: Yes.
DAPPER: And you have broke with him, Captain?
FACE: Ay.
DAPPER: And how?
FACE: Faith, he does make the matter, sir, so dainty° *complicated*
I know not what to say.
DAPPER: Not so, good Captain.
FACE: Would I were fairly rid of it, believe me.

8. A spirit, in this instance to advise him on gambling.

DAPPER: Nay, now you grieve me, sir. Why should you wish so?
I dare assure you, I'll not be ungrateful.
FACE: I cannot think you will, sir. But the law
Is such a thing—and then he says, Read's matter[9]
Falling so lately.
DAPPER: Read! he was an ass,
And dealt, sir, with a fool.
FACE: It was a clerk, sir.
DAPPER: A clerk?
FACE: Nay, hear me, sir, you know the law
Better, I think—
DAPPER: I should, sir, and the danger:
You know, I shew'd the statute to you.
FACE: You did so.
DAPPER: And will I tell then? By this hand of flesh,
Would it might never write good court-hand more,[1]
If I discover. What do you think of me,
That I am a chiaus?[2]
FACE: What's that?
DAPPER: The Turk was here.
As one would say, do you think I am a Turk?
FACE: I'll tell the doctor so.
DAPPER: Do, good sweet Captain.
FACE: Come, noble Doctor, pray thee let's prevail;
This is the gentleman, and he is no chiaus.
SUBTLE: Captain, I have return'd you all my answer.
I would do much, sir, for your love—But this
I neither may, nor can.
FACE: Tut, do not say so.
You deal now with a noble fellow, Doctor,
One that will thank you richly; and he is no chiaus:
Let that, sir, move you.
SUBTLE: Pray you, forbear—
FACE: He has
Four angels here.[3]
SUBTLE: You do me wrong, good sir.
FACE: Doctor, wherein? to tempt you with these spirits?
SUBTLE: To tempt my art and love, sir, to my peril.
Fore heaven, I scarce can think you are my friend,
That so would draw me to apparent danger.
FACE: I draw you! a horse draw you, and a halter,
You, and your flies° together— *familiar spirits*
DAPPER: Nay, good Captain.
FACE: That know no difference of men.

9. Simon Read was in trouble with the College of Physicians for practicing medicine without a license. After being charged with dealing in spirits in 1607, he was pardoned because he contacted spirits to determine the identity of the men who had robbed Toby Matthew.

1. Court-hand was a handwriting used in the courts that took training and skill to produce.

2. A cheat, from the Turkish *chäush*, meaning messenger.

3. An angel was a gold coin worth 10 shillings with the image of the Archangel Michael stamped on it.

SUBTLE: Good words, sir.
FACE: Good deeds, Sir Doctor Dogs-meat. 'Slight, I bring you
No cheating Clim o' the Cloughs, or Claribels,[4]
That look as big as five-and-fifty, and flush;[5]
And spit out secrets like hot custard—
DAPPER: Captain!
FACE: Nor any melancholic under-scribe,
Shall tell the vicar;[6] but a special gentle,° *gentleman*
That is the heir to forty marks[7] a year,
Consorts with the small poets of the time,
Is the sole hope of his old grandmother:
That knows the law, and writes you six fair hands,
Is a fine clerk, and has his cyphering° perfect, *account keeping*
Will take his oath o' the Greek Testament,[8]
If need be, in his pocket; and can court
His mistress out of Ovid.[9]
DAPPER: Nay, dear Captain—
FACE: Did you not tell me so?
DAPPER: Yes; but I'd have you
Use Master Doctor with some more respect.
FACE: Hang him, proud stag, with his broad velvet head![1]—
But for your sake, I'd choak, ere I would change
An article of breath with such a puckfist:° *ball of air*
Come, let's be gone. [*Going.*]
SUBTLE: Pray you let me speak with you.
DAPPER: His worship calls you, Captain.
FACE: I am sorry
I e'er embark'd myself in such a business,
DAPPER: Nay, good sir; he did call you.
FACE: Will he take then?
SUBTLE: First, hear me—
FACE: Not a syllable, 'less you take.
SUBTLE: Pray you, sir—
FACE: Upon no terms, but an *assumpsit.*° *verbal promise*
SUBTLE: Your humor must be law. [*He takes the four angels.*]
FACE: Why now, sir, talk.
Now I dare hear you with mine honor. Speak.
So may this gentleman too.
SUBTLE: Why, sir—[*Offering to whisper Face.*]
FACE: No whispering.
SUBTLE: Fore heaven, you do not apprehend the loss
You do yourself in this.
FACE: Wherein? for what?

4. Clim o' the Cloughs was an outlaw in the *Ballad of Adam Bell*, and Claribel was a knight who "loved out of measure" in Spenser's *Faerie Queene* 4.9.20.
5. A winning hand of cards.
6. Vicar-general in the ecclesiastical courts.
7. A mark was worth 14 shillings.
8. In the Folio, Jonson changed "Testament" to "Xenophon" to avoid the charge of blasphemy, forbidden on the stage by the law of 1606.
9. The Roman poet Ovid's *Art of Love* was a text popular with amorous young men who wanted to show off their sophistication and learning.
1. The velvet capped head of a doctor.

SUBTLE: Marry, to be so importunate for one,
That, when he has it, will undo you all:
He'll win up all the money in the town,
FACE: How!
SUBTLE: Yes, and blow up gamester after gamester,
As they do crackers° in a puppet play. *firecrackers*
If I do give him a familiar,° *spirit, demon*
Give you him all you play for; never set him:
For he will have it.
FACE: You are mistaken, Doctor.
Why he does ask one but for cups and horses,
A rifling fly;[2] none of your great familiars.
DAPPER: Yes, Captain, I would have it for all games.
SUBTLE: I told you so.
FACE [*taking Dapper aside*]: 'Slight, that is a new business!
I understood you, a tame bird, to fly
Twice in a term, or so, on Friday nights,
When you had left the office, for a nag
Of forty or fifty shillings.
DAPPER: Ay, 'tis true, sir;
But I do think now I shall leave the law,
And therefore—
FACE: Why, this changes quite the case,
Do you think that I dare move° him? *urge*
DAPPER: If you please, sir;
All's one to him, I see.
FACE: What! for that money?
I cannot with my conscience; nor should you
Make the request, methinks.
DAPPER: No, sir, I mean
To add consideration.
FACE: Why then, sir,
I'll try.—[*Goes to Subtle.*] Say that it were for all games, Doctor?
SUBTLE: I say then, not a mouth shall eat for him
At any ordinary, but on the score,[3]
That is a gaming mouth, conceive me.
FACE: Indeed!
SUBTLE: He'll draw you all the treasure of the realm,
If it be set him.
FACE: Speak you this from art?
SUBTLE: Ay, sir, and reason too, the ground of art.
He is of the only best complexion,
The Queen of Fairy loves.
FACE: What! is he?
SUBTLE: Peace.
He'll overhear you. Sir, should she but see him—

2. He wants a fly, or familiar spirit, only for gambling.

3. No gambler shall eat his dinner at an inn except on credit.

FACE: What?
SUBTLE: Do not you tell him.
FACE: Will he win at cards too?
SUBTLE: The spirits of dead Holland, living Isaac,[4]
You'd swear were in him; such a vigorous luck
As cannot be resisted. 'Slight, he'll put
Six of your gallants to a cloke,[5] indeed.
FACE: A strange success, that some man shall be born to!
SUBTLE: He hears you, man—
DAPPER: Sir, I'll not be ingrateful.
FACE: Faith, I have confidence in his good nature:
You hear, he says he will not be ingrateful.
SUBTLE: Why, as you please; my venture follows yours.
FACE: Troth, do it, Doctor; think him trusty, and make him.
He may make us both happy in an hour:
Win some five thousand pound, and send us two on't.
DAPPER: Believe it, and I will, sir.
FACE: And you shall, sir. [*Takes him aside*.]
You have heard all?
DAPPER: No, what was't? Nothing, I, sir.
FACE: Nothing!
DAPPER: A little, sir.
FACE: Well, a rare star
Reign'd at your birth.
DAPPER: At mine, sir! No.
FACE: The Doctor
Swears that you are—
SUBTLE: Nay, Captain, you'll tell all now.
FACE: Allied to the Queen of Fairy.
DAPPER: Who? that I am?
Believe it, no such matter—
FACE: Yes, and that
You were born with a cawl on your head.[6]
DAPPER: Who says so?
FACE: Come,
You know it well enough, though you dissemble it.
DAPPER: I'fac,° I do not: you are mistaken. *in faith*
FACE: How!
Swear by your fac, and in a thing so known
Unto the Doctor? How shall we, sir, trust you
In the other matter? can we ever think,
When you have won five or six thousand pound,
You'll send us shares in't, by this rate?
DAPPER: By Jove, sir,
I'll win ten thousand pound, and send you half.
I'fac's no oath.

4. John and Isaac Hollander, Dutch alchemists, were said to have lived in the early 15th century. Their works were published in the late 16th century.

5. Strip them down to their cloaks.

6. A membrane surrounding the head of a baby at birth, believed to be a good omen.

SUBTLE: No, no, he did but jest.
FACE: Go to. Go thank the doctor: he's your friend,
To take it so.
DAPPER: I thank his worship.
FACE: So!
Another angel.
DAPPER: Must I?
FACE: Must you! 'slight,
What else is thanks? will you be trivial?—Doctor,
[*Dapper gives him the money.*]
When must he come for his familiar?
DAPPER: Shall I not have it with me?
SUBTLE: O, good sir!
There must a world of ceremonies pass;
You must be bath'd and fumigated first;
Besides the Queen of Fairy does not rise
Till it be noon.
FACE: Not, if she danced, to-night.
SUBTLE: And she must bless it.
FACE: Did you never see
Her royal grace yet?
DAPPER: Whom?
FACE: Your aunt of Fairy?
SUBTLE: Not since she kist him in the cradle, Captain;
I can resolve you that.
FACE: Well, see her grace,
Whate'er it cost you, for a thing that I know.
It will be somewhat hard to compass; but
However, see her. You are made, believe it,
If you can see her. Her grace is a lone woman,
And very rich; and if she take a fancy,
She will do strange things. See her, at any hand.
'Slid, she may hap to leave you all she has:
It is the doctor's fear.
DAPPER: How will't be done, then?
FACE: Let me alone, take you no thought. Do you
But say to me, Captain, I'll see her grace.
DAPPER: Captain, I'll see her grace.
FACE: Enough. [*Knocking within.*]
SUBTLE: Who's there?
Anon.—[*aside to Face*] Conduct him forth by the back way.—
[*to Dapper*] Sir, against one o'clock prepare yourself;
Till when you must be fasting; only take
Three drops of vinegar in at your nose,
Two at your mouth, and one at either ear;
Then bathe your fingers' ends and wash your eyes,
To sharpen your five senses, and cry "hum"
Thrice, and then "buz" as often; and then come. [*Exit.*]

FACE: Can you remember this?
DAPPER: I warrant you.
FACE: Well then, away. It is but your bestowing
Some twenty nobles[7] 'mong her grace's servants,
And put on a clean shirt: you do not know
What grace her grace may do you in clean linen.
[Exeunt Face and Dapper.]

Scene 3

SUBTLE [*within*]: Come in! Good wives, I pray you forbear me now;
Troth I can do you no good till afternoon—
[*Re-enters, followed by Drugger.*]
What is your name, say you, Abel Drugger?
DRUGGER: Yes, sir.
SUBTLE: A seller of tobacco?
DRUGGER: Yes. sir.
SUBTLE: Umph!
Free of the Grocers?[8]
DRUGGER: Ay, an't please you.
SUBTLE: Well—
Your business, Abel?
DRUGGER: This, an't please your worship;
I am a young beginner, and am building
Of a new shop, an't like your worship, just
At corner of a street:—Here is the plot on't—
And I would know by art, sir, of your worship,
Which way I should make my door, by necromancy,
And where my shelves; and which should be for boxes,
And which for pots. I would be glad to thrive, sir:
And I was wish'd to your worship by a gentleman,
One Captain Face, that says you know men's planets,
And their good angels, and their bad.
SUBTLE: I do,
If I do see them—
[*Re-enter Face.*]
FACE: What! my honest Abel?
Thou art well met here.
DRUGGER: Troth, sir, I was speaking,
Just as your worship came here, of your worship:
I pray you speak for me to Master Doctor.
FACE: He shall do any thing.—Doctor, do you hear?
This is my friend, Abel, an honest fellow;
He lets me have good tobacco, and he does not
Sophisticate° it with sack-lees or oil, *dilute*
Nor washes it in muscadel° and grains,° *wine / spices*
Nor buries it in gravel, under ground.
Wrapp'd up in greasy leather, or piss'd clouts;

7. A noble was a coin worth six shillings and eight pence.
8. Admitted to the guild of the Grocers' Company.

But keeps it in fine lily pots, that, open'd,
Smell like conserve of roses, or French beans.
He has his maple block, his silver tongs,
Winchester pipes, and fire of Juniper:[9]
A neat, spruce, honest fellow, and no goldsmith.° *usurer*
SUBTLE: He is a fortunate fellow, that I am sure on.
FACE: Already, sir, have you found it? Lo thee, Abel!
SUBTLE: And in right way toward riches—
FACE: Sir!
SUBTLE: This summer
He will be of the clothing of his company,
And next spring call'd to the scarlet;° spend what he can. *made sheriff*
FACE: What and so little beard?
SUBTLE: Sir, you must think,
He may have a receipt to make hair come:[1]
But he'll be wise, preserve his youth, and fine for't;
His fortune looks for him another way.
FACE: 'Slid, Doctor, how canst thou know this so soon?
I am amused at that!
SUBTLE: By a rule, Captain,
In metoposcopy,[2] which I do work by;
A certain star in the forehead, which you see not.
Your chestnut or your olive-color'd face
Does never fail; and your long ear doth promise.
I knew't by certain spots, too, in his teeth,
And on the nail of his mercurial finger.[3]
FACE: Which finger's that?
SUBTLE: His little finger. Look.
You were born upon a Wednesday?
DRUGGER: Yes, indeed, sir.
SUBTLE: The thumb, in chiromancy,° we give Venus; *palmistry*
The fore-finger, to Jove; the midst, to Saturn;
The ring, to Sol; the least, to Mercury,
Who was the lord, sir, of his horoscope,
His house of life being Libra; which fore-show'd,
He should be a merchant, and should trade with balance.[4]
FACE: Why, this is strange! Is it not, honest Nab?
SUBTLE: There is a ship now, coming from Ormus,[5]
That shall yield him such a commodity
Of drugs—This is the west, and this the south?
[*Pointing to the plan.*]

9. The tobacco was cut on a maple wood block, smoked in pipes made in Winchester, and lit with aromatic coal of juniper that was held with silver tongs.
1. Recipe for growing hair.
2. Interpretation of personality on the basis of facial features.
3. The chestnut-colored face was believed to mean a happy and straightforward person; long ears signified intelligence. Each finger was associated with a particular planet in palmistry.
4. Subtle relies on Drugger's ignorance of the astrological belief that if Libra ruled the "first house," the sign of the zodiac rising on the eastern horizon at the time of one's birth, then that meant that Venus, goddess of love, ruled one's life, rather than Mercury, the god of businessmen, alchemists, tricksters, and thieves.
5. The port of Hormuz, then a center of the spice trade on the Persian Gulf.

DRUGGER: Yes, sir.
SUBTLE: And those are your two sides?
DRUGGER: Ay, sir.
SUBTLE: Make me your door, then, south; your broad side, west:
And on the east side of your shop, aloft,
Write Mathlai, Tarmiel, and Baraborat;
Upon the north part, Rael, Velel, Thiel.[6]
They are the names of those mercurial spirits,
That do fright flies from boxes.
DRUGGER: Yes, sir.
SUBTLE: And
Beneath your threshold, bury me a load-stone° *magnet*
To draw in gallants that wear spurs: the rest,
They'll seem[7] to follow.
FACE: That's a secret, Nab!
SUBTLE: And, on your stall, a puppet, with a vice
And a court-fucus° to call city-dames: *cosmetic*
You shall deal much with minerals.
DRUGGER: Sir, I have
At home, already—
SUBTLE: Ay, I know you have arsenic,
Vitriol, sal-tartar, argaile, alkali,
Cinoper:[8] I know all.—This fellow, Captain,
Will come, in time, to be a great distiller,
And give a say°—I will not say directly, *make an attempt at*
But very fair—at the philosopher's stone.
FACE: Why, how now, Abel! is this true?
DRUGGER [*aside to Face*]: Good Captain,
What must I give?
FACE: Nay, I'll not counsel thee.
Thou hear'st what wealth (he says, spend what thou canst,)
Thou'rt like to come to.
DRUGGER: I would gi' him a crown.[9]
FACE: A crown! and toward such a fortune? heart,
Thou shalt rather gi' him thy shop. No gold about thee?
DRUGGER: Yes, I have a portague,[1] I have kept this half year.
FACE: Out on thee, Nab! 'Slight, there was such an offer—
Shalt keep't no longer, I'll give't him for thee.
Doctor, Nab prays your worship to drink this, and swears
He will appear more grateful, as your skill
Does raise him in the world.
DRUGGER: I would entreat
Another favor of his worship.

6. These spirits' names are taken from *Heptameron Seu Elementa Magica Pietri de Albano Philosophi*, an appendix to Cornelius Agrippa's *De Occulta Philosophia* (1567). Subtle claims these spirits protect tobacco from fleas.
7. Playing on the Latin *videre*, meaning to be seen, to seem.
8. Vitriol: sulphuric acid; sal-tartar: potash; argaile: crude cream of tartar; alkali: soda ash; cinoper, or cinnabar: mercuric sulphide.
9. Silver coin worth five shillings, 25 pence.
1. Portuguese gold coin worth approximately four pounds.

FACE: What is't, Nab?
DRUGGER: But to look over, sir, my almanac,
And cross out my ill days, that I may neither
Bargain, nor trust upon them.
FACE: That he shall, Nab;
Leave it, it shall be done, 'gainst afternoon.
SUBTLE: And a direction for his shelves.
FACE: Now, Nab,
Art thou well pleased, Nab?
DRUGGER: 'Thank, sir, both your worships.
FACE: Away.— [*Exit Drugger*.]
Why, now, you smoaky persecutor of nature!
Now do you see, that something's to be done,
Beside your beech-coal, and your corsive waters,
Your crosslets, crucibels, and cucurbites?[2]
You must have stuff brought home to you, to work on:
And yet you think, I am at no expense
In searching out these veins, then following them,
Then trying them out. 'Fore God, my intelligence° *information*
Costs me more money, than my share oft comes to.
In these rare works.
SUBTLE: You are pleasant, sir.—How now!

Scene 4

[*Re-enter Dol.*]
SUBTLE: What says my dainty Dolkin?
DOL: Yonder fish-wife
Will not away. And there's your giantess,
The bawd of Lambeth.[3]
SUBTLE: Heart, I cannot speak with them.
DOL: Not afore night, I have told them in a voice,
Thorough the trunk, like one of your familiars.
But I have spied Sir Epicure Mammon—
SUBTLE: Where?
DOL: Coming along, at far end of the lane,
Slow of his feet, but earnest of his tongue
To one that's with him.
SUBTLE: Face, go you, and shift. [*Exit Face*.]
Dol, you must presently make ready, too.
DOL: Why, what's the matter?
SUBTLE: O, I did look for him
With the sun's rising: 'marvel he could sleep!
This is the day I am to perfect for him
The magisterium,° our great work, the stone; *master-principle*
And yield it, made, into his hands: of which
He has, this month, talk'd as he were possess'd.

2. Crosslets: melting pots; crucibels: melting pots; cucurbites: vessels with downturned necks for distilling liquids.

3. Prostitute of Lambeth, a disreputable quarter of London in Jonson's time.

And now he's dealing pieces on't away.—
Methinks I see him entering ordinaries,° *inns*
Dispensing for the pox, and plaguy houses,[4]
Reaching his dose, walking Moorfields for lepers,[5]
And offering citizens' wives pomander-bracelets,[6]
As his preservative, made of the elixir;
Searching the spittal,° to make old bawds young; *hospital*
And the highways, for beggars, to make rich:
I see no end of his labors. He will make
Nature asham'd of her long sleep: when art,
Who's but a step-dame, shall do more than she,
In her best love to mankind, ever could:
If his dream lasts, he'll turn the age to gold. [*Exeunt*.]

ACT 2

Scene 1—*An outer room in Lovewit's house*

[*Enter Sir Epicure Mammon and Surly*.]

MAMMON: Come on, sir. Now, you set your foot on shore
In *Novo Orbe;*° here's the rich Peru: *New World*
And there within, sir, are the golden mines,
Great Solomon's Ophir![7] he was sailing to't,
Three years, but we have reach'd it in ten months.
This is the day, wherein, to all my friends,
I will pronounce the happy word, BE RICH;
THIS DAY YOU SHALL BE SPECTATISSIMI,° *most looked at*
You shall no more deal with the hollow dye,
Or the frail card. No more be at charge of keeping
The livery-punk° for the young heir, that must *prostitute*
Seal,[8] at all hours, in his shirt: no more,
If he deny, have him beaten to't, as he is
That brings him the commodity.[9] No more
Shall thirst of satin, or the covetous hunger
Of velvet entrails for a rude-spun cloke,
To be display'd at Madam Augusta's,[1] make
The sons of Sword and Hazard fall before
The golden calf, and on their knees, whole nights
Commit idolatry with wine and trumpets;

4. Pox: smallpox; and the great pox: syphilis; plaguy houses: hospitals for those suffering from the plague.
5. Moorfields was an area to the north of London, bordering on the areas of Bedlam, the madhouse, and of the leper houses.
6. Pomander bracelets were believed to protect the wearer against infectious disease.
7. King Solomon was said to have brought his gold from Ophir every three years (1 Kings 10.22). The alchemists believed Solomon possessed the philosophers' stone and alchemically produced the gold in Ophir.
8. Seal: to have sexual intercourse and to make a promissory note as pay for services rendered.
9. The heir, or john, is beaten to be forced to pay what he owes. Then to raise the money, he uses a commodity swindle, buying cheap goods on credit, which he sells at a loss. Incensed at how he has been cheated and beaten, the heir takes out his anger by beating the prostitute.
1. Most likely a brothel.

Or go a feasting after drum and ensign.[2]
No more of this. You shall start up young viceroys,
And have your punks, and punketees,° my Surly. *little prostitutes*
And unto thee I speak it first, BE RICH.
Where is my Subtle, there? Within, ho!
FACE [*within*]: Sir
He'll come to you by and by.
MAMMON: That is his fire-drake,° *one who tends fire*
His Lungs, his Zephyrus,° he that puffs his coals, *west wind*
Till he firk° nature up, in her own center. *excite*
You are not faithful, sir. This night, I'll change
All that is metal, in my house, to gold:
And, early in the morning, will I send
To all the plumbers and the pewterers,
And buy their tin and lead up; and to Lothbury
For all the copper.
SURLY: What, and turn that too?
MAMMON: Yes, and I'll purchase Devonshire and Cornwall,
And make them perfect Indies! you admire now?
SURLY: No, faith.
MAMMON: But when you see th' effects of the Great Medicine,[3]
Of which one part projected on a hundred
Of Mercury, or Venus, or the moon,
Shall turn it to as many of the sun;
Nay, to a thousand, so *ad infinitum;*
You will believe me.
SURLY: Yes, when I see't, I will.
But if my eyes do cozen me so, and I
Giving them no occasion, sure I'll have
A whore, shall piss them out next day.
MAMMON: Ha! why?
Do you think I fable with you? I assure you,
He that has once the flower of the sun,
The perfect ruby, which we call elixir,
Not only can do that, but, by its virtue,
Can confer honor, love, respect, long life;
Give safety, valor, yea, and victory,
To whom he will. In eight and twenty days,
I'll make an old man of fourscore, a child.
SURLY: No doubt; he's that already.
MAMMON: Nay, I mean,
Restore his years, renew him, like an eagle,
To the fifth age;[4] make him get sons and daughters,
Young giants; as our philosophers have done,

2. Garbled version of the story of the golden calf (Exodus 32).
3. The philosophers' stone.
4. Between the ages of 50 and 65.

The ancient patriarchs, afore the flood,[5]
But taking, once a week, on a knife's point,
The quantity of a grain of mustard of it;
Become stout Marses,[6] and beget young Cupids.
SURLY: The decay'd vestals of Piet-hatch[7] would thank you,
That keep the fire° alive, there. *venereal disease*
MAMMON: 'Tis the secret
Of nature naturis'd[8] 'gainst all infections,
Cures all diseases coming of all causes;
A month's grief in a day, a year's in twelve;
And, of what age soever, in a month:
Past all the doses of your drugging doctors.
I'll undertake, withal, to fright the plague
Out of the kingdom in three months,
SURLY: And I'll
Be bound, the players[9] shall sing your praises, then,
Without their poets.
MAMMON: Sir, I'll do't. Meantime,
I'll give away so much unto my man,
Shall serve the whole city, with preservative,
Weekly; each house his dose, and at the rate—
SURLY: As he that built the Water-work,[1] does with water?
MAMMON: You are incredulous.
SURLY: Faith I have a humor,° *whim*
I would not willingly be gull'd.° Your stone *hoodwinked*
Cannot transmute me.
MAMMON: Pertinax, my Surly,
Will you believe antiquity? records?
I'll show you a book where Moses and his sister,
And Solomon have written of the art;
Ay, and a treatise penn'd by Adam—
SURLY: How!
MAMMON: Of the philosophers' stone, and in High Dutch.° *High German*
SURLY: Did Adam write, sir, in High Dutch?
MAMMON: He did;
Which proves it was the primitive tongue.
SURLY: What paper?
MAMMON: On cedar board.
SURLY: O that, indeed, they say,
Will last 'gainst worms.
MAMMON: 'Tis like your Irish wood,[2]

5. The alchemists attributed the longevity of the Hebrew patriarchs to their possession of the all-curing philosophers' stone.
6. Gods of war.
7. Haunt of prostitutes.
8. In scholastic philosophy, *natura naturata*, created nature, as opposed to creating nature, *natura naturans*, God's power in nature.
9. Actors would be happy if Mammon cured the plague, since the playhouses were closed whenever the death toll from the plague reached 40 deaths per week.
1. A system of lead pipes, designed by Peter Moris in 1582 and Bevis Bulmer in 1594, carried water from the Thames River to the houses of London.
2. According to Richard Braithwaite's *A Strappado for the Devil* (1615), Irish wood was protected from blight by St. Patrick.

'Gainst cob-webs. I have a piece of Jason's fleece, too,[3]
Which was no other than a book of alchemy,
Writ in large sheep-skin, a good fat ram-vellum.
Such was Pythagoras' thigh, Pandora's tub,
And, all that fable of Medea's charms,[4]
The manner of our work; the bulls, our furnace,
Still breathing fire; our *argent-vive*,° the dragon: *quicksilver, mercury*
The dragon's teeth, mercury sublimate,
That keeps the whiteness, hardness, and the biting:
And they are gather'd into Jason's helm,
The alembic, and then sow'd in Mars his field,
And thence sublimed so often, till they're fixed.
Both this, the Hesperian garden, Cadmus' story,
Jove's shower, the boon of Midas, Argus' eyes,[5]
Boccace his Demogorgon,[6] thousands more,
All abstract riddles of our stone.—How now?

Scene 2

[*Enter Face, dressed as a servant.*]

MAMMON: Do we succeed? Is our day come? and holds it?
FACE: The evening will set red upon you, sir;
You have color for it, crimson:[7] the red ferment
Has done his office; three hours hence prepare you
To see projection.
MAMMON: Pertinax, my Surly,
Again I say to thee, aloud, "Be rich."
This day, thou shalt have ingots; and, to-morrow,
Give lords th' affront.—Is it, my Zephyrus,° right *west wind*
Blushes the bolt's-head?[8]
FACE: Like a wench with child, sir,
That were but now discover'd° to her master. *revealed*
MAMMON: Excellent witty Lungs!—my only care is
Where to get stuff enough now, to project on;
This town will not half serve me.
FACE: No, sir! buy
The covering off o' churches.
MAMMON: That's true.
FACE: Yes.
Let them stand bare, as do their auditory;° *congregation*
Or cap them, new, with shingles.

3. Mammon follows the allegorical interpretation of mythology popular with the alchemists. The Golden Fleece, the object of Jason and the Argonauts' quest, becomes a text on how to turn metal into gold.
4. Pythagoras's thigh was believed to be golden. Pandora released all evil into the world when she opened her box. Medea used her witchcraft to aid Jason in his pursuit of the Golden Fleece. Her father promised Jason the fleece if he could plow a field with a team of fire-breathing horses and brass-footed bulls, then plant the field with teeth from the dragon slain by Cadmus, defeat the men who would rise up out of the teeth, and slay the dragon who guarded the fleece.
5. Hercules won the three golden apples in the Hesperian garden. Jove changed into a shower of gold to have intercourse with Danaë. All that Midas touched turned to gold; Argus was a watchman with 100 eyes.
6. In his *De Genealogia Deorum* (*On the Genealogy of the Gods*), Boccaccio portrayed Demogorgon as the original god of all mythology.
7. Crimson, or red, signified the last stage in the process of alchemical transformation.
8. Long-necked flask.

MAMMON: No, good thatch:
Thatch will lie light upon the rafters, Lungs.—
Lungs, I will manumit° thee from the furnace; *free, release*
I will restore thee thy complexion, Puff,
Lost in the embers; and repair this brain,
Hurt with the fume o' the metals.

FACE: I have blown, sir,
Hard for your worship; thrown by many a coal,
When 'twas not beech; weigh'd those I put in, just,
To keep your heat still even; these blear'd eyes
Have wak'd to read your several colors, sir,
Of the pale citron, the green lion, the crow,
The peacook's tail, the plumed swan.

MAMMON: And, lastly,
Thou hast descry'd the flower, the *sanguis agni?*° *blood of the lamb*

FACE: Yes, sir.

MAMMON: Where's master?

FACE: At his prayers, sir, he;
Good man, he's doing his devotions
For the success.

MAMMON: Lungs, I will set a period
To all thy labors; thou shalt be the master
Of my seraglio.° *harem*

FACE: Good, sir.

MAMMON: But do you hear?
I'll geld° you, Lungs *castrate*

FACE: Yes, sir.

MAMMON: For I do mean
To have a list of wives and concubines,
Equal with Solomon, who had the stone
Alike with me; and I will make me a back
With the elixir, that shall be as tough
As Hercules, to encounter fifty a night.—
Thou art sure thou saw'st it blood?

FACE: Both blood and spirit, sir.

MAMMON: I will have all my beds blown up, not stuft:
Down is too hard: and then, mine oval room
Fill'd with such pictures as Tiberius took
From Elephantis, and dull Aretine[9]
But coldly imitated. Then, my glasses° *mirrors*
Cut in more subtle angles, to disperse
And multiply the figures, as I walk
Naked between my succubae.[1] My mists
I'll have of perfume, vapor'd 'bout the room,
To lose ourselves in; and my baths, like pits

9. Elephantis: Roman erotic writer referred to by Suetonius; Aretine: Pietro Aretino, Italian author of sexual satires *Sonnetti Lussuriosi* (1523).

1. Demons who assume female form to have sex.

To fall into; from whence we will come forth,
And roll us dry in gossamer and roses.—
Is it arrived at ruby?—Where I spy
A wealthy citizen, or a rich lawyer,
Have a sublimed pure wife, unto that fellow
I'll send a thousand pound to be my cuckold.

FACE: And I shall carry it?

MAMMON: No. I'll have no bawds,° *panderers, procurers*
But fathers and mothers: they will do it best,
Best of all others. And my flatterers
Shall be the pure and gravest of divines,
That I can get for money. My mere fools,
Eloquent burgesses, and then my poets
The same that writ so subtly of the fart,
Whom I will entertain still for that subject.
The few that would give out themselves to be
Court and town-stallions, and, each-where, belie
Ladies who are known most innocent for them;
Those will I beg, to make me eunuchs of;
And they shall fan me with ten ostrich tails
A-piece, made in a plume to gather wind.
We will be brave, Puff, now we have the med'cine,
My meat shall all come in, in Indian shells,
Dishes of agat set in gold, and studded
With emeralds, sapphires, hyacinths, and rubies.
The tongues of carps, dormice, and camels' heels,
Boil'd in the spirit of Sol, and dissolv'd pearl,
Apicius' diet, gainst the epilepsy:[2]
And I will eat these broths with spoons of amber,
Headed with diamond and carbuncle,
My foot-boy shall eat pheasants, calver'd salmons,
Knots, godwits, lampreys:° I myself will have *eel-like fish*
The beards of barbels° served, instead of salads; *carp-like fish*
Oil'd mushrooms; and the swelling unctuous paps
Of a fat pregnant sow, newly cut off,
Drest with an exquisite, and poignant sauce;
For which, I'll say unto my cook, "There's gold,
Go forth, and be a knight."

FACE: Sir, I'll go look
A little, how it heightens. [*Exit.*]

MAMMON: Do.—My shirts
I'll have of taffeta-sarsnet,° soft and light *silky material*
As cobwebs; and for all my other raiment,
It shall be such as might provoke the Persian,
Were he to teach the world riot anew.
My gloves of fishes' and birds' skins, perfumed
With gums of paradise, and eastern air—

2. Quintus Gavius Apicius, Roman gourmand of Tiberius's reign; "tongues of carps" and "dormice" were considered delicacies, and camels' heels were thought to ward off disease.

SURLY: And do you think to have the stone with this?
MAMMON: No, I do think t' have all this with the stone.
SURLY: Why, I have heard, he must be *homo frugi*,° *temperate man*
A pious, holy, and religious man,
One free from mortal sin, a very virgin.
MAMMON: That makes it, sir; he is so; but I buy it;
My venture brings it me. He, honest wretch,
A notable, superstitious, good soul,
Has worn his knees bare, and his slippers bald,
With prayer and fasting for it; and sir, let him
Do it alone, for me, still. Here he comes.
Not a profane word afore him: 'tis poison.—

Scene 3

[*Enter Subtle*.]
Good morrow, father.
SUBTLE: Gentle son, good morrow.
And to your friend there. What is he, is with you?
MAMMON: An heretic, that I did bring along,
In hope, sir, to convert him.
SUBTLE: Son, I doubt° *suspect*
You are covetous, that thus you meet your time
In the just point: prevent° your day at morning. *anticipate*
This argues something, worthy of a fear
Of importune° and carnal appetite. *untimely*
Take heed you do not cause the blessing leave you,
With your ungovern'd haste. I should be sorry
To see my labors, now even at perfection,
Got by long watching and large patience,
Not prosper where my love and zeal hath placed them.
Which (heaven I call to witness, with your self,
To whom I have pour'd my thoughts) in all my ends,
Have look'd no way, but unto public good,
To pious uses, and dear charity
Now grown a prodigy with men. Wherein
If you, my son, should now prevaricate,° *deviate*
And, to your own particular lusts employ
So great and catholic° a bliss, be sure *universal*
A curse will follow, yea, and overtake
Your subtle and most secret ways.
MAMMON: I know, sir;
You shall not need to fear me: I but come,
To have you confute° this gentleman. *prove wrong*
SURLY: Who is,
Indeed, sir, somewhat costive° of belief *reluctant*
Toward your stone; would not be gull'd.
SUBTLE: Well, son,
All that I can convince him in, is this.

The WORK IS DONE, bright Sol is in his robe.[3]
We have a medicine of the triple soul,[4]
The glorified spirit. Thanks be to heaven,
And make us worthy of it!—Ulen Spiegel![5]
FACE [*within*]: Anon, sir.
SUBTLE: Look well to the register,
And let your heat still lessen by degrees,
To the aludels.° *pear-shaped pots*
FACE [*within*]: Yes, sir.
SUBTLE: Did you look
On the bolt's-head yet?
FACE [*within*]: Which? on D, sir?
SUBTLE: Ay;
What's the complexion?
FACE [*within*]: Whitish.
SUBTLE: Infuse vinegar,
To draw his volatile substance and his tincture:
And let the water in glass E be filter'd,
And put into the gripe's egg.[6] Lute° him well; *seal in clay*
And leave him closed in *balneo*.° *in a bath*
FACE [*within*]: I will, sir.
SURLY: What a brave language here is! next to canting.[7]
SUBTLE: I have another work, you never saw, son.
That three days since past the philosopher's wheel[8]
In the lent° heat of Athanor;[9] and's become *slow*
Sulphur of Nature.
MAMMON: But 'tis for me?
SUBTLE: What need you?
You have enough in that is perfect,
MAMMON: O but—
SUBTLE: Why, this is covetise!
MAMMON: No, I assure you,
I shall employ it all in pious uses,
Founding of colleges and grammar schools,
Marrying young virgins, building hospitals,
And now and then a church,
[*Re-enter Face*.]
SUBTLE: How now!
FACE: Sir, please you,
Shall I not change the filter?
SUBTLE: Marry, yes;
And bring me the complexion of glass B. [*Exit Face*.]
MAMMON: Have you another?

3. The gold is ready.
4. Triple soul, including the vital (in the heart), natural (in the liver), and universal (in the brain) spirits.
5. Til Owl-glass, or mirror, trickster hero of German jest books, hoodwinked the Landgrave of Hesse, who believed in alchemy.
6. Vessel shaped like a vulture's egg.
7. Rhyming street talk.
8. Alchemical cycle.
9. Furnace with slow and steady heat.

SUBTLE: Yes, son; were I assured—
Your piety were firm, we would not want
The means to glorify it: but I hope the best.—
I mean to tinct C in sand-heat to-morrow,
And give him imbibition.[1]
MAMMON: Of white oil?
SUBTLE: No, sir, of red. F is come over the helm too,
I thank my Maker, in S. Mary's bath,
And shews *lac virginis*.[2] Blessed be heaven!
I sent you of his feces° there calcined:[3] *sediment*
Out of that calx,° I have won the salt of mercury. *fine powder*
MAMMON: By pouring on your rectified water?
SUBTLE: Yes, and reverberating in Athanor.
[*Re-enter Face*.]
How now! what color says it?
FACE: The ground black, sir.
MAMMON: That's your crow's head?[4]
SURLY: Your cock's-comb's,° is it not? *fool's*
SUBTLE: No, 'tis not perfect. Would it were the crow!
That work wants something.
SURLY [*aside*]: O, I look'd for this.
The hay's a pitching.
SUBTLE: Are you sure you loosed them
In their own menstrue?
FACE: Yes, sir, and then married them,
And put them in a bolt's-head nipp'd to digestion,[5]
According as you bade me, when I set
The liquor of Mars° to circulation *molten iron*
In the same heat.
SUBTLE: The process then was right.
FACE: Yes, by the token, sir, the retort brake,
And what was saved was put into the pelican,[6]
And sign'd with Hermes' seal.[7]
SUBTLE: I think 'twas so.
We should have a new amalgama.° *mixture of metals*
SURLY [*aside*]: O, this ferret
Is rank as any pole-cat.
SUBTLE: But I care not:
Let him e'en die; we have enough beside,
In embrion.° H has his white shirt on?[8] *in early stages*
FACE: Yes, sir,
He's ripe for inceration,[9] he stands warm,

1. Absorption of a liquid by a solid.
2. Virgin's milk, a term for mercury.
3. Burnt down to fine powder.
4. "Crow's head" refers to the blackness of the material at this stage of the process.
5. Digestion is the extraction of soluble substances by water and heat.
6. A retort is a closed vessel with an outlet tube. A pelican is a vessel resembling a pelican, with a long neck curving down and reentering the body of the vessel.
7. Hermetically sealed, heated, and twisted closed.
8. Has turned white now.
9. Turning solid matter waxy by adding fluid.

In his ash-fire. I would not you should let
Any die now, if I might counsel, sir,
For luck's sake to the rest: it is not good.
MAMMON: He says right.
SURLY [*aside*]: Ay, are you bolted?
FACE: Nay, I know't, sir,
I have seen the ill fortune. What is some three ounces
Of fresh materials?
MAMMON: Is't no more?
FACE: No more, sir,
Of gold, t'amalgame with some six of mercury.
MAMMON: Away, here's money. What will serve?
FACE: Ask him, sir.
MAMMON: How much?
SUBTLE: Give him nine pound:—you may give him ten.
SURLY: Yes, twenty, and be cozen'd, do.
MAMMON: There 'tis. [*Gives Face the money.*]
SUBTLE: This needs not; but that you will have it so,
To see conclusions of all: for two
Of our inferior works are at fixation,[1]
A third is in ascension.° Go your ways. *distillation*
Have you set the oil of Luna° in kemia?[2] *white elixir*
FACE: Yes, sir.
SUBTLE: And the philosopher's vinegar?° *mercury*
FACE: Ay. [*Exit.*]
SURLY: We shall have a salad!
MAMMON: When do you make projection?
SUBTLE: Son, be not hasty, I exalt our med'cine,
By hanging him *in balneo vaporoso,*° *vapor bath*
And giving him solution; then congeal him;
And then dissolve him; then again congeal him;
For look, how oft I iterate the work,
So many times I add unto his virtue.
As, if at first one ounce convert a hundred.
After his second loose, he'll turn a thousand;
His third solution, ten; his fourth, a hundred;
After his fifth, a thousand thousand ounces
Of any imperfect metal, into pure
Silver or gold, in all examinations,
As good as any of the natural mine,
Get you your stuff here against afternoon,
Your brass, your pewter, and your andirons,
MAMMON: Not those of iron?
SUBTLE: Yes, you may bring them too:
We'll change all metals,
SURLY: I believe you in that.

1. Reducing a volatile substance to stable form.

2. Vessel in which distillation occurred in chemical analysis.

MAMMON: Then I may send my spits?
SUBTLE: Yes, and your racks.
SURLY: And dripping pans, and pot-hangers, and hooks,
Shall he not?
SUBTLE: If he please.
SURLY: —To be an ass.
SUBTLE: How, sir!
MAMMON: This gentleman you must bear withal:
I told you he had no faith.
SURLY: And little hope, sir;
But much less charity, should I gull myself.
SUBTLE: Why, what have you observ'd, sir, in our art.
Seems so impossible?
SURLY: But your whole work, no more.
That you should hatch gold in a furnace, sir,
As they do eggs in Egypt![3]
SUBTLE: Sir, do you
Believe that eggs are hatch'd so?
SURLY: If I should?
SUBTLE: Why, I think that the greater miracle,
No egg but differs from a chicken more
Than metals in themselves.[4]
SURLY: That cannot be.
The egg's ordain'd by nature to that end,
And is a chicken *in potentia*.° *in potentiality*
SUBTLE: The same we say of lead and other metals,
Which would be gold, if they had time.
MAMMON: And that
Our art doth further.
SUBTLE: Ay, for 'twere absurd
To think that nature in the earth bred gold
Perfect in the instant: something went before.
There must be remote matter.
SURLY: Ay, what is that?
SUBTLE: Marry, we say—
MAMMON: Ay, now it heats: stand, father,
Pound him to dust.
SUBTLE: It is, of the one part,
A humid exhalation, which we call
Materia liquida,° or the unctuous water; *liquid matter*
On the other part, a certain crass and vicious
Portion of earth; both which, concorporate,
Do make the elementary matter of gold;
Which is not yet *propria materia*,° *its own substance*
But common to all metals and all stones;
For, where it is forsaken of that moisture,

3. In dunghills and incubators. See Pliny, *Naturalis Historia* 10.75–76.

4. The following 70 lines are based on Martin Del Rio's *Disquisitiones Magicae* (1599–1600).

And hath more dryness, it becomes a stone:
Where it retains more of the humid fatness,
It turns to sulphur, or to quicksilver,
Who are the parents of all other metals.
Nor can this remote matter suddenly
Progress so from extreme unto extreme,
As to grow gold, and leap o'er all the means.
Nature doth first beget the imperfect, then
Proceeds she to the perfect. Of that airy
And oily water, mercury is engender'd;
Sulphur of the fat and earthy part; the one,
Which is the last, supplying the place of male,
The other of the female, in all metals.
Some do believe hermaphrodeity,[5]
That both do act and suffer. But these two
Make the rest ductile, malleable, extensive.[6]
And even in gold they are; for we do find
Seeds of them, by our fire, and gold in them;
And can produce the species of each metal
More perfect thence, than nature doth in earth.
Beside, who doth not see in daily practice
Art can beget bees, hornets, beetles, wasps,
Out of the carcasses and dung of creatures;
Yes, scorpions of an herb, being rightly placed?
And these are living creatures, far more perfect
And excellent than metals.[7]

MAMMON: Well said, father!
Nay, if he take you in hand, sir, with an argument,
He'll bray° you in a mortar. *grind into bits*

SURLY: Pray you, sir, stay.
Rather than I'll be bray'd, sir, I'll believe
That Alchemy is a pretty kind of game,
Somewhat like tricks o' the cards, to cheat a man
With charming.

SUBTLE: Sir?

SURLY: What else are all your terms,
Whereon no one of your writers 'grees with other!
Of your elixir, your *lac virginis*,° *dissolved mercury*
Your stone, your med'cine, and your chrysosperme,° *golden sperm*
Your sal, your sulphur, and your mercury,
Your oil of height, your tree of life, your blood,
Your marcasite, your tutty, your magnesia,[8]
Your toad, your crow, your dragon, and your panther,[9]

5. Involving both male and female.
6. Capable of being extended.
7. The way alchemy worked is here described in terms of spontaneous generation of life from dead matter. People still believed in spontaneous generation because they did not yet realize that life sprung from eggs that had been laid in dead matter.
8. Marchasite: iron pyrites; tutty: zinc oxide.
9. Toad, crow, and panther are a series of colors in the alchemical process; dragon is mercury.

Your sun, your moon, your firmament, your adrop,[1]
Your lato, azoch, zernich, chibrit, heautarit,[2]
And then your red man, and your white woman,[3]
With all your broths, your menstrues, and materials,
Of piss and egg-shells, women's terms, man's blood,
Hair o' the head, burnt clouts, chalk, merds, and clay,
Powder of bones, scalings of iron, glass,
And worlds of other strange ingredients,
Would burst a man to name?

SUBTLE: And all these named,
Intending but one thing: which art our writers
Used to obscure their art.

MAMMON: Sir, so I told him—
Because the simple idiot should not learn it,
And make it vulgar.

SUBTLE: Was not all the knowledge
Of the Egyptians writ in mystic symbols?
Speak not the scriptures oft in parables?
Are not the choicest fables of the poets,
That were the fountains and first springs of wisdom,
Wrapp'd in perplexed allegories?

MAMMON: I urg'd that,
And clear'd to him, that Sysiphus was damn'd
To roll the ceaseless stone, only because
He would have made ours common.[4] [*Dol appears at the door*.]—
Who is this?

SUBTLE: 'Sprecious!°—What do you mean? go in, good lady, *God's precious*
Let me entreat you. [*Dol retires*.]—Where's this varlet?
[*Re-enter Face*.]

FACE: Sir.

SUBTLE: You very knave! do you use me thus?

FACE: Wherein, sir?

SUBTLE: Go in and see, you traitor. Go! [*Exit Face*.]

MAMMON: Who is it, sir?

SUBTLE: Nothing, sir; nothing.

MAMMON: What's the matter, good sir?
I have not seen you thus distemper'd: who is't?

SUBTLE: All arts have still had, sir, their adversaries,
But ours the most ignorant.—
[*Re-enter Face*.]
What now?

FACE: 'Twas not my fault, sir; she would speak with you.

SUBTLE: Would she, sir? Follow me. [*Exit*.]

MAMMON [*stopping him*.]: Stay, Lungs.

1. The firmament is another name for the philosophers' stone; adrop is lead.
2. Lato: brasslike metal; azoch: mercury; zernich: trisulphide of arsenic; chibrit: sulphur; heautarit: mercury.
3. Red man: sulphur; white woman: mercury.
4. Condemned to Hades for revealing the secret of the gods (here interpreted as the philosophers' stone), Sisyphus had to roll a huge stone up a hill over and over as it kept rolling back downhill.

FACE: I dare not, sir.
MAMMON: Stay, man; what is she?
FACE: A lord's sister, sir.
MAMMON: How! pray thee, stay.
FACE: She's mad, sir, and sent hither—
He'll be mad too—
MAMMON: I warrant thee.—Why sent hither?
FACE: Sir, to be cured.
SUBTLE [*within*]: Why, rascal!
FACE: Lo you!—Here, sir! [*Exit.*]
MAMMON: 'Fore God, a Bradamante, a brave piece.[5]
SURLY: Heart, this is a bawdy-house! I will be burnt else.
MAMMON: O, by this light, no: do not wrong him. He's
Too scrupulous that way: it is his vice.
No, he's a rare physician, do him right,
An excellent Paracelsian,[6] and has done
Strange cures with mineral physic. He deals all
With spirits, he; he will not hear a word
Of Galen, or his tedious recipes.[7]
[*Re-enter Face.*]
How now, Lungs!
FACE: Softly, sir; speak softly. I meant
To have told your worship all. This must not hear.
MAMMON: No, he will not be gull'd: let him alone.
FACE: Y're very right, sir, she is a most rare scholar,
And is gone mad with studying Broughton's works.[8]
If you but name a word touching the Hebrew,
She falls into her fit, and will discourse
So learnedly of genealogies,
As you would run mad too, to hear her, sir.
MAMMON: How might one do't'have conference with her, Lungs?
FACE: O divers have run mad upon the conference:
I do not know, sir. I am sent in haste,
To fetch a vial.
SURLY: Be not gull'd, sir Mammon.
MAMMON: Wherein? pray ye, be patient.
SURLY: Yes, as you are,
And trust confederate° knaves and bawds and whores. *banded together*
MAMMON: You are too foul, believe it.—Come here, Ulen,
One word.
FACE: I dare not, in good faith. [*Going.*]
MAMMON: Stay, knave.
FACE: He is extreme angry that you saw her, sir.

5. Bradamante, a female knight, is the heroine of Ariosto's *Orlando Furioso* (1532; English trans., 1591). Brave: good looking, and courageous.

6. A follower of the medical theory of Paracelsus (1493–1541), which proposed that health depended on the proper chemical balance of mercury, salt, and sulphur in the body.

7. Galen, respected medical authority of antiquity (130–210), whose humoral theory of medicine was still widely believed by early modern physicians.

8. Hugh Broughton (1549–1612) was a Puritan author who wrote learned works on the Bible, particularly on the genealogies of the Old Testament. See *The Alchemist* 4.5 for a send-up of his scholarly jargon.

MAMMON: Drink that. [*Gives him money.*] What is she when she's out of her fit?
FACE: O, the most affablest creature, sir! so merry!
So pleasant! she'll mount you up, like quicksilver,
Over the helm; and circulate like oil,
A very vegetal:[9] discourse of state,
Of mathematics, bawdry, any thing—
MAMMON: Is she no way accessible? no means,
No trick to give a man a taste of her—wit—
Or so?
SUBTLE [*within*]: Ulen!
FACE: I'll come to you again, sir. [*Exit.*]
MAMMON: Surly, I did not think one of your breeding
Would traduce personages of worth.
SURLY: Sir Epicure,
Your friend to use; yet still loth to be gull'd:
I do not like your philosophical bawds.
Their stone is letchery enough to pay for,
Without this bait.
MAMMON: 'Heart, you abuse yourself.
I know the lady, and her friends, and means,
The original of this disaster. Her brother
Has told me all.
SURLY: And yet you never saw her
Till now?
MAMMON: O yes, but I forgot. I have, believe it,
One of the treacherousest memories, I do think,
Of all mankind.
SURLY: What call you her brother?
MAMMON: My lord—
He will not have his name known, now I think on't,
SURLY: A very treacherous memory!
MAMMON: On my faith—
SURLY: Tut, if you have it not about you, pass it,
Till we meet next.
MAMMON: Nay, by this hand, 'tis true.
He's one I honor, and my noble friend;
And I respect his house.
SURLY: Heart! can it be,
That a grave sir, a rich, that has no need,
A wise sir, too, at other times, should thus,
With his own oaths, and arguments, make hard means
To gull himself? An this be your elixir,
Your *lapis mineralis*, and your lunary,[1]
Give me your honest trick yet at primero,
Or gleek;[2] and take your *lutum sapientis*,

9. With the connotation of Latin *vegetus*, lively, animated. An extended series of alchemical metaphors for her sexual responsiveness.
1. *Lapis mineralis:* mineral stone; lunary: the fern moonwort, and mercury.
2. Trick: a hand of cards with a pun on trick as a sly scheme. Primero and gleek are card games.

Your *menstruum simplex!*[3] I'll have gold before you,
And with less danger of the quicksilver,
Or the hot sulphur.[4]
[*Re-enter Face*.]
FACE [*to Surly*]: Here's one from Captain Face, sir,
Desires you meet him in the Temple-church,
Some half hour hence, and upon earnest business.
[*whispers to Mammon*] Sir, if you please to quit us, now; and come
Again within two hours, you shall have
My master busy examining o' the works;
And I will steal you in, unto the party,
That you may see her converse.—Sir, shall I say,
You'll meet the captain's worship?
SURLY: Sir, I will.— [*Walks aside*.]
But, by attorney, and to a second purpose.
Now, I am sure it is a bawdy-house;
I'll swear it, were the marshal here to thank me:
The naming this commander doth confirm it.
Don Face! why he's the most authentic dealer
In these commodities, the superintendant
To all the quainter[5] traffickers in town!
He is the visitor, and does appoint,
Who lies with whom, and at what hour; what price:
Which gown, and in what smock; what fall; what tire.
Him will I prove, by a third person, to find
The subtleties of this dark labyrinth:
Which if I do discover, dear Sir Mammon,
You'll give your poor friend leave, though no philosopher,
To laugh: for you that are, 'tis thought, shall weep.
FACE: Sir, he does pray, you'll not forget.
SURLY: I will not, sir.
Sir Epicure, I shall leave you. [*Exit*.]
MAMMON: I follow you, straight.
FACE: But do so, good sir, to avoid suspicion.
This gentleman has a parlous head.
MAMMON: But wilt thou, Ulen,
Be constant to thy promise?
FACE: As my life, sir.
MAMMON: And wilt thou insinuate what I am, and praise me,
And say, I am a noble fellow?
FACE: O, what else, sir?
And that you'll make her royal with the stone,
An empress; and yourself, king of Bantam.[6]
MAMMON: Wilt thou do this?
FACE: Will I, sir!

3. *Lutum sapientis:* paste for closing the mouths of vessels; *menstruum simplex:* simple solvent.
4. Quicksilver was used to treat venereal disease; sulphur was used to treat skin diseases.
5. Quainter: with a pun on quaint, cunt.
6. Land of legendary wealth in Java; Bantam was the capital of an Islamic empire.

MAMMON: Lungs, my Lungs!
I love thee.
FACE: Send your stuff, sir, that my master
May busy himself about projection,
MAMMON: Thou hast witch'd me, rogue: take, go.
[*Gives him money*.]
FACE: Your jack,[7] and all, sir.
MAMMON: Thou art a villain—I will send my jack,
And the weights too. Slave, I could bite thine ear.
Away, thou dost not care for me.
FACE: Not I, sir!
MAMMON: Come, I was born to make thee, my good weasel,
Set thee on a bench, and have thee twirl a chain
With the best lord's vermin of 'em all.
FACE: Away, sir.
MAMMON: A count, nay, a Count Palatine[8]—
FACE: Good, sir, go.
MAMMON: —shall not advance thee better: no, nor faster. [*Exit*.]

Scene 4

[*Re-enter Subtle and Dol*.]
SUBTLE: Has he bit? has he bit?
FACE: And swallowed too, my Subtle.
I have given him line, and now he plays, i'faith.
SUBTLE: And shall we twitch him?
FACE: Thorough both the gills.
A wench is a rare bait, with which a man
No sooner's taken, but he straight firks mad.[9]
SUBTLE: Dol, my lord What's-ums sister, you must now
Bear yourself *statelich*.° *stately*
DOL: O let me alone.
I'll not forget my race,[1] I warrant you.
I'll keep my distance, laugh and talk aloud;
Have all the tricks of a proud scurvy lady,
And be as rude as her woman.
FACE: Well said, Sanguine![2]
SUBTLE: But will he send his andirons?
FACE: His jack too,
And's iron shoeing-horn; I have spoke to him. Well,
I must not lose my wary gamester yonder.
SUBTLE: O Monsieur Caution, that will not be gull'd.
FACE: Ay, if I can strike a fine hook into him, now!
The Temple-church, there I have cast mine angle.
Well, pray for me. I'll about it. [*Knocking without*.]

7. Device for turning the spit; the jack was driven by weights.
8. The jurisdiction of a palatinate count was equal to the king's.
9. Firks mad: is excited to raving madness.
1. Race in the early modern sense of lineage, and also sex; and course, in the sense of plan of action.
2. Pink-cheeked; the personality of the sanguine humor was happy, amorous, and brave.

SUBTLE: What, more gudgeons![3]
Dol, scout, scout! [*Dol goes to the window.*] Stay, Face, you must go to the door,
'Pray God it be my Anabaptist.[4]—Who is't, Dol?
DOL: I know him not: he looks like a gold-end man.[5]
SUBTLE: Goods so! 'tis he, he said he would send what call you him?
The sanctified elder, that should deal
For Mammon's jack and andirons. Let him in.
Stay, help me off, first, with my gown. [*Exit Face with the gown.*] Away,
Madam, to your withdrawing chamber. [*Exit Dol.*] Now,
In a new tune, new gesture, but old language.—
This fellow is sent from one negociates with me
About the stone too; for the holy brethren
Of Amsterdam, the exiled saints; that hope
To raise their discipline by it.[6] I must use him
In some strange fashion, now, to make him admire me.—

Scene 5

[*Enter Ananias.*]
SUBTLE: Where is my drudge? [*Aloud.*]
[*Re-enter Face.*]
FACE: Sir!
SUBTLE: Take away the recipient,
And rectify your menstrue from the phlegma.[7]
Then pour it on the Sol, in the cucurbite,[8]
And let them macerate[9] together.
FACE: Yes, sir.
And save the ground?
SUBTLE: No: *terra damnata*[1]
Must not have entrance in the work.—Who are you?
ANANIAS: A faithful brother, if it please you.
SUBTLE: What's that?
A Lullianist? a Ripley? *Filius artis?*[2]
Can you sublime and dulcify? calcine?[3]
Know you the sapor pontic? sapor stiptic?[4]
Or what is homogene, or heterogene?[5]
ANANIAS: I understand no heathen language, truly.

3. Small fish eager to bite live bait.
4. Anabaptists began as a Protestant sect in Germany. They believed in communal ownership of property, adult baptism, and a return to the principles of the early Christian Church.
5. Traveling jeweler.
6. The Anabaptists came to England when their attempts to take over Amsterdam and other Dutch towns led to their being exiled.
7. Purify your solvent by distillation from the watery substance.
8. Gourd-shaped vessel with long neck bent downward.
9. Soak to soften.
1. Damned earth; the residue remaining after distillation.
2. Lullianist: follower of Raymond Lull (1235–1315), a Spanish scientist to whom alchemical works were attributed; Ripley: follower of George Ripley, an English Canon who wrote works of alchemy and popularized Lull; *Filius artis:* son of art.
3. Sublime: vaporize and distill; dulcify: sweeten; calcine: heat and reduce to fine powder.
4. Two of the five savors engendered by heat; *sapor pontic:* a sour taste; *sapor stiptic:* a less sour taste.
5. Homogene: of one kind; heterogene: of various kinds.

SUBTLE: Heathen! you Knipper-doling?[6] Is *ars sacra*,
Or chrysopoeia, or spagyrica,
Or the pamphysic, or panarchic knowledge,[7]
A heathen language?
ANANIAS: Heathen Greek, I take it.
SUBTLE: How! heathen Greek?
ANANIAS: All's heathen but the Hebrew.[8]
SUBTLE: Sirrah, my varlet, stand you forth and speak to him,
Like a philosopher: answer in the language.
Name the vexations, and the martyrisations[9]
Of metals in the work.
FACE: Sir, putrefaction,
Solution, ablution, sublimation,
Cohobation, calcination, ceration, and
Fixation.[1]
SUBTLE: This is heathen Greek to you, now!—
And when comes vivification?[2]
FACE: After mortification.° *destruction*
SUBTLE: What's cohobation?
FACE: 'Tis the pouring on
Your *aqua regis*, and then drawing him off,
To the trine circle of the seven spheres.[3]
SUBTLE: What's the proper passion of metals?
FACE: Malleation.[4]
SUBTLE: What's your *ultimum supplicium auri*?[5]
FACE: Antimonium.
SUBTLE: This is heathen Greek to you!—And what's your mercury?
FACE: A very fugitive, he will be gone, sir.
SUBTLE: How know you him?
FACE: By his viscosity,
His oleosity,° and his suscitability.° *oiliness / volatility*
SUBTLE: How do you sublime him?
FACE: With the calce[6] of egg-shells,
White marble, talc.
SUBTLE: Your magisterium,° now, *masterwork*
What's that?
FACE: Shifting, sir, your elements,
Dry into cold, cold into moist, moist into hot,
Hot into dry.

6. Bernt Knipperdollink, one of the instigators of the Anabaptist rebellion in Munster (1534–1536).
7. Chrysopoeia: gold-making; spagyrica: special alchemical method of Paracelsus; pamphysic or panarchic knowledge: universal knowledge.
8. Puritans regarded Hebrew as the original language, which Adam spoke, and the Anabaptists even considered dispensing with all books except the Hebrew Bible, or Old Testament.
9. Martyrisations: the tests that metals were put through.
1. Putrefaction: disintegration; solution: changing a solid to a liquid; ablution: washing away impurities; sublimation; vaporization and distillation; cohobation: redistillation; calcination: reducing to powder by heating; ceration: making waxy; fixation: changing volatile material into stable form.
2. Vivification: restoration of a substance to its first state.
3. *Aqua regis*: a solvent for gold; trine circle: planets that were one-third of a circle or 120 degrees apart were thought to be a positive sign; the seven spheres are the Sun, the Moon, and the planets Earth, Mars, Mercury, Venus, and Saturn.
4. Passion: how metals can be affected; malleation: hammering.
5. *Ultimum supplicium auri*: ultimate punishment of gold.
6. Calce: powder produced by burning of a substance.

SUBTLE: This is heathen Greek to you still?
Your *lapis philosophicus?*° *philosophers' stone*
FACE: 'Tis a stone, and not
A stone; a spirit, a soul, and a body:
Which if you do dissolve, it is dissolved;
If you coagulate, it is coagulated;
If you make it to fly, it flieth.
SUBTLE: Enough. [*Exit Face.*]
This is heathen Greek to you! What are you, sir?
ANANIAS: Please you, a servant of the exiled Brethren,[7]
That deal with widows' and with orphans' goods;
And make a just account unto the saints:
A deacon,
SUBTLE: O, you are sent from Master Wholesome,
Your teacher?
ANANIAS: From Tribulation Wholesome,
Our very zealous pastor.
SUBTLE: Good! I have
Some orphans' goods to come here.
ANANIAS: Of what kind, sir?
SUBTLE: Pewter and brass, andirons and kitchen-ware,
Metals, that we must use our medicine on:
Wherein the brethren may have a pennyworth,
For ready money.
ANANIAS: Were the orphans' parents
Sincere professors?[8]
SUBTLE: Why do you ask?
ANANIAS: Because
We then are to deal justly, and give, in truth,
Their utmost value.
SUBTLE: 'Slid, you'd cozen else,
And if their parents were not of the faithful?
I will not trust you, now I think on it,
'Till I have talk'd with your pastor. Have you brought money
To buy more coals?
ANANIAS: No, surely.
SUBTLE: No! how so?
ANANIAS: The Brethren bid me say unto you, sit,
Surely, they will not venture any more,
Till they may see projection.
SUBTLE: How!
ANANIAS: You've had,
For the instruments, as bricks, and loam, and glasses,
Already thirty pound; and for materials,
They say, some ninety more: and they have heard since,

7. The exiled Brethren were a Protestant sect of Anabaptists exiled from the Netherlands.

8. Zealous Anabaptists, true believers.

That one at Heidelberg,[9] made it of an egg,
And a small paper of pin-dust.° *metal filings*
SUBTLE: What's your name?
ANANIAS: My name is Ananias.
SUBTLE: Out, the varlet
That cozen'd the apostles![1] Hence, away!
Flee, Mischief! had your holy consistory[2]
No name to send me, of another sound,
Than wicked Ananias? send your elders[3]
Hither to make atonement for you quickly,
And give me satisfaction; or out goes
The fire; and down th' alembics, and the furnace,
Piger Henricus,[4] or what not. Thou wretch!
Both sericon and bufo[5] shall be lost,
Tell them. All hope of rooting out the bishops,[6]
Or the antichristian hierarchy, shall perish,
If they stay threescore minutes: the aqueity,
Terreity, and sulphureity
Shall run together again, and all be annull'd,[7]
Thou wicked Ananias! [*Exit Ananias*.] This will fetch 'em,
And make them haste towards their gulling more.
A man must deal like a rough nurse, and fright
Those that are froward,° to an appetite. *contrary*

Scene 6

[*Re-enter Face in his uniform, followed by Drugger*.]
FACE: H's busy with his spirits, but we'll upon him.
SUBTLE: How now! what mates, what Bayards have we here?[8]
FACE: I told you, he would be furious.—Sir, here's Nab,
Has brought you another piece of gold to look on:
—We must appease him. Give it me,—and prays you,
You would devise—what is it, Nab?
DRUGGER: A sign, sir.
FACE: Ay, a good lucky one, a thriving sign, Doctor.
SUBTLE: I was devising now.
FACE: 'Slight, do not say so,
He will repent he gave you any more—
What say you to his constellation, Doctor,
The Balance?[9]
SUBTLE: No, that way is stale, and common.

9. City known as a center for alchemy.
1. Ananias kept money back from the apostles. See *Acts of the Apostles* 5.1–11.
2. Church board made up of deacons, ministers, and elders.
3. Authority figures of the church.
4. A lazy Henry.
5. Red and black tincture.
6. Radical Protestants objected to the bishops in the Church of England as a remnant of Roman Catholicism.
7. The processes of alchemical purification will be reversed and the work completely ruined.
8. Bayard was the enchanted horse of Rinaldo in Ariosto's *Orlando Furioso*.
9. Constellation: zodiacal sign; the Balance: Libra (21 September to 20 October).

A townsman born in Taurus,[1] gives the bull,
Or the bull's-head: in Aries,[2] the ram,
A poor device! No, I will have his name
Form'd in some mystic character; whose radii,° — *rays*
Striking the senses of the passers by,
Shall, by a virtual° influence, breed affections,° — *powerful / inclinations*
That may result upon the party owns it:
As thus—

FACE: Nab!

SUBTLE: He shall have "a bell," that's "Abel";
And by it standing one whose name is "Dee,"[3]
In a "rug" gown, there's "D," and "Rug," that's "drug":
And right anenst° him a dog snarling "er"; — *against*
There's "Drugger," Abel Drugger. That's his sign.
And here's now mystery and hieroglyphic![4]

FACE: Abel, thou art made.

DRUGGER: Sir, I do thank his worship.

FACE: Six o' thy legs° more will not do it, Nab. — *bows*
He has brought you a pipe of tobacco, Doctor.

DRUGGER: Yes, sir:
I have another thing I would impart—

FACE: Out with it, Nab.

DRUGGER: Sir, there is lodged, hard by me,
A rich young widow—

FACE: Good! a *bona roba?*[5]

DRUGGER: But nineteen, at the most.

FACE: Very good, Abel.

DRUGGER: Marry, she's not in fashion yet; she wears
A hood, but it stands a-cop.° — *high on the head*

FACE: No matter, Abel.

DRUGGER: And I do now and then give her a fucus—[6]

FACE: What! dost thou deal, Nab?

SUBTLE: I did tell you, Captain.

DRUGGER: And physic too, sometime, sir; for which she trusts me
With all her mind. She's come up here of purpose
To learn the fashion.

FACE: Good (his match too!)—On, Nab.

DRUGGER: And she does strangely long to know her fortune.

FACE: God's lid, Nab, send her to the Doctor, hither.

DRUGGER: Yes, I have spoke to her of his worship already;
But she's afraid it will be blown abroad,
And hurt her marriage.

FACE: Hurt it! 'tis the way

1. Taurus, the bull (21 April to 20 May).
2. Aries, the ram (21 March to 20 April).
3. John Dee (1527–1608), alchemist and mathematician, favored by Queen Elizabeth, to whom he gave advice based on astrology.
4. The Renaissance interest in Egyptian hieroglyphics was rooted in the belief in Hermes Trismegistus, the supposed author of the *Corpus Hermeticum,* who was thought to be the inventor of the hieroglyph.
5. Well-dressed woman, a prostitute.
6. Fucus: make-up with a pun of obvious sexual meaning.

To heal it, if 'twere hurt; to make it more
Follow'd and sought: Nab, thou shalt tell her this.
She'll be more known, more talk'd of; and your widows
Are ne'er of any price till they be famous;
Their honor is their multitude of suitors:
Send her, it may be thy good fortune. What!
Thou dost not know,
DRUGGER: No, sir, she'll never marry
Under a knight: her brother has made a vow.
FACE: What! and dost thou despair, my little Nab,
Knowing what the Doctor has set down for thee,
And seeing so many of the city dubb'd?° *knighted*
One glass o' thy water, with a madam I know,
Will have it done, Nab: what's her brother, a knight?
DRUGGER: No, sir, a gentleman newly warm° in his land, sir, *having just inherited*
Scarce cold in his one and twenty, that does govern
His sister here; and is a man himself
Of some three thousand a year, and is come up
To learn to quarrel, and to live by his wits,
And will go down again, and die in the country.
FACE: How! to quarrel?
DRUGGER: Yes, sir, to carry quarrels,
As gallants do; to manage them by line.
FACE: 'Slid, Nab, the Doctor is the only man
In Christendom for him. He has made a table,
With mathematical demonstrations,
Touching the art of quarrels: he will give him
An instrument to quarrel by. Go, bring them both,
Him and his sister. And, for thee, with her
The Doctor happ'ly may persuade. Go to:
'Shalt give his worship a new damask suit
Upon the premises.
SUBTLE: O, good Captain!
FACE: He shall;
He is the honestest fellow, doctor.—Stay not,
No offers; bring the damask, and the parties.
DRUGGER: I'll try my power, sir,
FACE: And thy will too, Nab.
SUBTLE: 'Tis good tobacco, this! what is't an ounce?
FACE: He'll send you a pound, Doctor.
SUBTLE: O no.
FACE: He will do't.
It is the goodest soul!—Abel, about it.
Thou shalt know more anon. Away, be gone.— [*Exit Abel.*]
A miserable rogue, and lives with cheese,
And has the worms. That was the cause, indeed,
Why he came now: he dealt with me in private,
To get a med'cine for them.
SUBTLE: And shall, sir. This works.

FACE: A wife, a wife for one of us, my dear Subtle!
We'll e'en draw lots, and he that fails, shall have
The more in goods, the other has in tail.[7]
SUBTLE: Rather the less: for she may be so light
She may want grains.
FACE: Ay, or be such a burden,
A man would scarce endure her for the whole.
SUBTLE: Faith, best let's see her first, and then determine.
FACE: Content: but Dol must ha' no breath on't.
SUBTLE: Mum.
Away you, to your Surly yonder, catch him.
FACE: 'Pray God I have not staid too long.
SUBTLE: I fear it. [*Exeunt.*]

ACT 3

Scene 1—*The lane before Lovewit's house*

[*Enter Tribulation Wholesome and Ananias.*]
TRIBULATION: These chastisements are common to the saints,
And such rebukes, we of the Separation[8]
Must bear with willing shoulders, as the trials
Sent forth to tempt frailties.
ANANIAS: In pure zeal,
I do not like the man, he is a heathen,
And speaks the language of Canaan,[9] truly.
TRIBULATION: I think him a profane person indeed.
ANANIAS: He bears
The visible mark of the Beast in his forehead.[1]
And for his stone, it is a work of darkness,
And with philosophy blinds the eyes of man.
TRIBULATION: Good brother, we must bend unto all means
That may give furtherance to the holy cause.
ANANIAS: Which his cannot: the sanctified cause
Should have a sanctified course.
TRIBULATION: Not always necessary:
The children of perdition are oft-times
Made instruments even of the greatest works:
Beside, we should give° somewhat to man's nature, *concede*
The place he lives in, still about the fire,
And fume of metals, that intoxicate
The brain of man, and make him prone to passion.
Where have you greater atheists than your cooks?
Or more profane, or choleric,° than your glass-men?° *angry / glass-blowers*

7. In tail: obvious sexual meaning with a pun on legal entail, or limited ownership.
8. Separation: i.e., of the Anabaptists both by exile from Holland and God's election of them from the world of sinners.
9. In the Old Testament, the Canaanites, the original inhabitants of Israel, are portrayed as worshippers of idols.
1. The Puritans portrayed the Roman Catholic Church as the Beast of Revelation 16.2.

More antichristian than your bell-founders?
What makes the devil so devilish, I would ask you,
Satan, our common enemy, but his being
Perpetually about the fire, and boiling
Brimstone and arsenic? We must give, I say,
Unto the motives, and the stirrers up
Of humors in the blood. It may be so,
When as the work is done, the stone is made,
This heat of his may turn into a zeal,
And stand up for the beauteous discipline,
Against the menstruous cloth and rag of Rome.[2]
We must await his calling, and the coming
Of the good spirit. You did fault, t' upbraid him
With the brethren's blessing of Heidelberg,[3] weighing
What need we have to hasten on the work,
For the restoring of the silenced Saints,[4]
Which ne'er will be, but by the philosophers' stone.
And so a learned elder, one of Scotland,
Assured me; *aurum potabile* being
The only med'cine for the civil magistrate,[5]
T' incline him to a feeling of the cause;
And must be daily used in the disease.

ANANIAS: I have not edified more, truly, by man;
Not since the beautiful light first shone on me;
And I am sad my zeal hath so offended.

TRIBULATION: Let us call on him then.

ANANIAS: The motion's good,
And of the spirit; I will knock first. [*Knocks.*] Peace he within!
[*The door is opened, and they enter.*]

Scene 2—*A room in Lovewit's house*

[*Enter Subtle, followed by Tribulation and Ananias.*]

SUBTLE: O, are you come? 'twas time. Your threescore minutes
Were at the last thread, you see: and down had gone
Furnus acedice, turris circulatorius:[6]
Lembec, bolt's-head, retort and pelican[7]
Had all been cinders.—Wicked Ananias!
Art thou return'd? nay then, it goes down yet.

TRIBULATION: Sir, be appeased; he is come to humble
Himself in spirit, and to ask your patience,
If too much zeal hath carried him aside
From the due path.

2. The priest's vestments, the outward show of which the Puritans objected to. The Puritans demonized Catholicism as the "Scarlet Woman" of Revelation 17.
3. Heidelberg was known as a center of alchemy.
4. The "silenced Saints" were the Puritan clergy who were excommunicated and forbidden to preach by the Church of England.
5. *Aurum potabile*, drinkable gold; refers to the bribery of magistrates.
6. *Furnus acedice:* furnace of sloth; *turris circulatorius*: circulation tower.
7. Lembec, or alembic: vessel for distilling; bolt's-head: long-necked round flask; retort: curved-necked vessel; pelican: vessel with spout that curved down and entered the base.

SUBTLE: Why, this doth qualify!
TRIBULATION: The brethren had no purpose, verily,
To give you the least grievance: but are ready
To lend their willing hands to any project
The spirit and you direct.
SUBTLE: This qualifies[8] more!
TRIBULATION: And for the orphan's goods, let them be valued,
Or what is needful else to the holy work,
It shall be numbered; here, by me, the saints,
Throw down their purse before you.
SUBTLE: This qualifies most!
Why, thus it should be, now you understand.
Have I discours'd so unto you of our stone,
And of the good that it shall bring your cause?
Shew'd you (beside the main of hiring forces
Abroad, drawing the Hollanders,[9] your friends.
From the Indies, to serve you, with all their fleet)
That even the med'cinal use shall make you a faction,
And party in the realm? As, put the case,
That some great man in state, he have the gout,
Why, you but send three drops of your elixir,
You help him straight: there you have made a friend.
Another has the palsy or the dropsy,
He takes of your incombustible stuff,
He's young again: there you have made a friend,
A lady that is past the feat[1] of body,
Though not of mind, and hath her face decay'd
Beyond all cure of paintings, you restore,
With the oil of talc: there you have made a friend;
And all her friends. A lord that is a leper,
A knight that has the bone-ache,° or a squire *syphilis*
That hath both these, you make them smooth and sound,
With a bare fricace° of your med'cine: still *rub*
You increase your friends.
TRIBULATION: Ay, it is very pregnant.° *full of potential*
SUBTLE: And then the turning of this lawyer's pewter
To plate at Christmas.—
ANANIAS: Christ-tide, I pray you.[2]
SUBTLE: Yet, Ananias!
ANANIAS: I have done.
SUBTLE: Or changing
His parcel gilt° to massy gold. You cannot *guilded silver*
But raise you friends. Withal, to be of power

8. Qualifies: to dilute chemically and to pacify Subtle's anger at Ananais.
9. Subtle leads Tribulation to believe that Dutch traders in the east were concerned with religious toleration for the exiled Anabaptists.
1. Meaning both fitness and act, as in the act of sex.
2. Christ-tide rather than Christmas, because the Puritans objected to the mass.

To pay an army in the field, to buy
The king of France out of his realms, or Spain
Out of his Indies. What can you not do
Against lords spiritual or temporal,
That shall oppone° you? *oppose*

TRIBULATION: Verily, 'tis true.
We may be temporal lords ourselves, I take it.

SUBTLE: You may be anything, and leave off to make
Long-winded exercises;° or suck up *religious ceremonies*
Your "ha!" and "hum!" in a tune.[3] I not deny,
But such as are not graced in a state,
May, for their ends, be adverse in religion,
And get a tune to call the flock together:
For, to say sooth, a tune does much with women,
And other phlegmatic people; it is your bell.

ANANIAS: Bells are profane; a tune may be religious.

SUBTLE: No warning with you! then farewell my patience.
'Slight, it shall down: I will not be thus tortured.

TRIBULATION: I pray you, sir.

SUBTLE: All shall perish. I have spoken it.

TRIBULATION: Let me find grace, sir, in your eyes; the man
He stands corrected: neither did his zeal,
But as your self, allow a tune somewhere,
Which now, being toward the stone, we shall not need.

SUBTLE: No, nor your holy vizard,° to win widows *pious look*
To give you legacies; or make zealous wives
To rob their husbands for the common cause:
Nor take the start° of bonds broke but one day, *take advantage*
And say, they were forfeited by providence.
Nor shall you need o'er night to eat huge meals,
To celebrate your next day's fast the better;
The whilst the brethren and the sisters humbled,
Abate the stiffness of the flesh.[4] Nor east
Before your hungry hearers scrupulous bones;° *bones of contention*
As whether a Christian may hawk or hunt,[5]
Or whether matrons of the holy assembly
May lay their hair out, or wear doublets,
Or have that idol, Starch, about their linen.[6]

ANANIAS: It is indeed an idol.

TRIBULATION: Mind him not, sir.
I do command thee, spirit of zeal, but trouble,
To peace within him! Pray, you, sir, go on.

SUBTLE: Nor shall you need to libel 'gainst the prelates,
And shorten so your ears[7] against the hearing

3. The "ha" and "hum" were sounds associated with Puritan preaching and singing.
4. The hardship of hunger with a comic pun on the stiffness of the male sex organ.
5. Puritan writers decried hunting as immoral.
6. Puritans also attacked fancy dress and elaborate hairstyles.
7. Have your ears cut off.

Of the next wire-drawn grace.[8] Nor of necessity
Rail against plays, to please the alderman[9]
Whose daily custard you devour: nor lie
With zealous rage till you are hoarse. Not one
Of these so singular arts. Nor call your selves
By names of Tribulation, Persecution,
Restraint, Long-patience, and such-like, affected
By the whole family or wood° of you, *collection*
Only for glory, and to catch the ear
Of the disciple.

TRIBULATION: Truly, sir, they are
Ways that the godly brethren have invented,
For propagation of the glorious cause,
As very notable means, and whereby also
Themselves grow soon, and profitably, famous.

SUBTLE: O, but the stone, all's idle to it! nothing!
The art of angels' nature's miracle,
The divine secret that doth fly in clouds
From east to west;[1] and whose tradition
Is not from men, but spirits.

ANANIAS: I hate traditions;[2]
I do not trust them.—

TRIBULATION: Peace!

ANANIAS: They are popish all.
I will not peace: I will not—

TRIBULATION: Ananias!

ANANIAS: Please the profane, to grieve the godly; I may not.

SUBTLE: Well, Ananias, thou shalt overcome.

TRIBULATION: It is an ignorant zeal that haunts him, sir:
But truly, else, a very faithful brother,
A botcher, and a man, by revelation,[3]
That hath a competent knowledge of the truth.

SUBTLE: Has he a competent sum there in the bag
To buy the goods within? I am made guardian,
And must, for charity, and conscience sake,
Now see the most be made for my poor orphan;
Though I desire the brethren too good gainers;
There they are within. When you have view'd, and bought 'em,
And ta'en the inventory of what they are,
They are ready for projection; there's no more
To do: cast on the med'cine, so much silver
As there is tin there, so much gold as brass,
I'll give't you in by weight.

8. Long prayer.
9. City magistrates often had Puritan leanings against the plays.
1. The "divine secret," the hidden truth of alchemy traveled from Egypt in the east to Europe in the west.
2. Puritans saw the interpretations of the Bible in the tradition of the Roman Catholic Church as a corruption of the truth.
3. A "botcher" was a tailor who did repairs; a "man by revelation" was the Puritan ideal of one who sought the truth strictly through his own inner inspiration.

TRIBULATION: But how long time,
Sir, must the saints expect yet?
SUBTLE: Let me see,
How's the moon now? Eight, nine, ten days hence,
He will be silver potate;° then three days *liquefied silver*
Before he citronise:[4] Some fifteen days,
The magisterium will be perfected.
ANANIAS: About the second day of the third week,
In the ninth month?
SUBTLE: Yes, my good Ananias.
TRIBULATION: What will the orphan's goods arise to, think you?
SUBTLE: Some hundred marks, as much as fill'd three cars,
Unladed now: you'll make six millions of them.—
But I must have more coals laid in.
TRIBULATION: How?
SUBTLE: Another load,
And then we have finish'd. We must now increase
Our fire to *ignis ardens*, we are past
Fimus equinus, *balnei*, *cineris*,
And all those lenter heats.[5] If the holy purse
Should with this draught fall low, and that the saints
Do need a present sum, I have a trick
To melt the pewter, you shall buy now, instantly,
And with a tincture make you as good Dutch dollars
As any are in Holland.
TRIBULATION: Can you so?
SUBTLE: Ay, and shall 'bide the third examination.
ANANIAS: It will be joyful tidings to the brethren.
SUBTLE: But you must carry it secret.
TRIBULATION: Ay; but stay,
This act of coining,° is it lawful? *counterfeiting*
ANANIAS: Lawful?
We know no magistrate;[6] or, if we did,
This 's foreign coin.
SUBTLE: It is no coining, sir.
It is but casting.
TRIBULATION: Ha? you distinguish well:
Casting of money may be lawful.
ANANIAS: 'Tis, sir.
TRIBULATION: Truly, I take it so.
SUBTLE: There is no scruple,
Sir, to be made of it; believe Ananias;
This case of conscience he is studied in.
TRIBULATION: I'll make a question of it to the brethren.
ANANIAS: The brethren shall approve it lawful, doubt not.

4. Be made citron in color, a late stage of the alchemical process.

5. *Ignis ardens*, the hottest fire; the "lenter," or lower, heats are *fimus equinus*, the slowest heat, produced by horse manure; *balnei*, slow even heat; *cineris:* heat of ashes.

6. Puritans believed that civil magistrates had no authority over matters of conscience.

Where shall it be done? [*Knocking without.*]
SUBTLE: For that we'll talk anon.
There's some to speak with me. Go in, I pray you,
And view the parcels. That's the inventory.
I'll come to you straight. [*Exeunt Tribulation and Ananias.*] Who is it?—
Face! appear.

Scene 3

[*Enter Face, in his uniform.*]
SUBTLE: How now! good prize?
FACE: Good pox! yond' costive cheater[7]
Never came on.
SUBTLE: How then?
FACE: I have walk'd the round
Till now, and no such thing.
SUBTLE: And ha' you quit° him! *given up on*
FACE: Quit him? an hell would quit him too, he were happy.
'Slight! would you have me stalk like a mill-jade,[8]
All day, for one that will not yield us grains?[9]
I know him of old.
SUBTLE: O, but to have gull'd him,
Had been a mastery.
FACE: Let him go, black boy![1]
And turn thee, that some fresh news may possess thee.
A noble count, a don of Spain, my dear
Delicious compeer, and my party-bawd,° *fellow pimp*
Who is come hither private for his conscience,[2]
And brought munition with him, six great slops,° *large, wide trousers*
Bigger than three Dutch hoys, beside round trunks,
Furnished with pistolets, and pieces of eight,[3]
Will straight be here, my rogue, to have thy bath,
(That is the color,)° and to make his battery *pretext*
Upon our Dol, our castle, our cinque-port,[4]
Our Dover pier, our what thou wilt. Where is she?
She must prepare perfumes, delicate linen,
The bath in chief, a banquet, and her wit,
For she must milk his epididimis.[5]
Where is the doxy?° *wench*
SUBTLE: I'll send her to thee:
And but dispatch my brace of little John Leydens,[6]
And come again myself.
FACE: Are they within then?
SUBTLE: Numb'ring the sum.

7. Skeptical gambler, i.e., surly.
8. Horse that circled around and pushed the arm turning the grindstone.
9. Profit, as in grains of flour and of gold.
1. Black, because his face is covered with soot.
2. Private, or concealed, because of his religious beliefs.
3. Spanish gold coins.
4. One of the five defensive ports of the southeastern coast of England.
5. Tube that sperm move through.
6. John Leyden, leader of the Anabaptists.

FACE: How much?
SUBTLE: A hundred marks, boy. [*Exit.*]
FACE: Why, this is a lucky day. Ten pounds of MAMMON!° *riches*
Three of my clerk! a portague[7] of my grocer!
This of the brethren! beside reversions,[8]
And states° to come in the widow, and my count! *estates*
My share to-day will not be bought for forty—
[*Enter Dol.*]
DOL: What?
FACE: Pounds, dainty Dorothy! art thou so near?
DOL: Yes; say, lord general, how fares our camp?[9]
FACE: As with the few that had entrench'd themselves
Safe, by their discipline, against a world, Dol,
And laugh'd within those trenches, and grew fat
With thinking on the booties, Dol, brought in
Daily by their small parties. This dear hour,
A doughty Don is taken with my Dol;
And thou mayst make his ransom what thou wilt,
My Dousabel;[1] he shall be brought here fetter'd
With thy fair looks, before he sees thee; and thrown
In a down-bed, as dark as any dungeon;
Where thou shalt keep him waking with thy drum;[2]
Thy drum, my Dol, thy drum; till he be tame
As the poor black-birds were in the great frost,[3]
Or bees are with a basin;[4] and so hive him
In the swan-skin coverlid, and cambric sheets,
Till he work honey and wax, my little God's-gift.
DOL: What is he, General?
FACE: An *adelantado*,° *governor*
A grandee, girl. Was not my Dapper here yet?
DOL: No.
FACE: Nor my Drugger?
DOL: Neither.
FACE: A pox on 'em.
They are so long a furnishing! such stinkards
Would not be seen upon these festival days.—
[*Re-enter Subtle.*]
How now! have you done?
SUBTLE: Done. They are gone. The sum
Is here in bank, my Face. I would we knew
Another chapman° now would buy 'em outright. *merchant*
FACE: 'Slid, Nab shall do't against he have the widow,
To furnish household.
SUBTLE: Excellent, well thought on:

7. Portuguese gold coin.
8. Future possessions, inherited when owner gives them up.
9. The first line of Kyd's play *The Spanish Tragedy*.
1. Sweet and beautiful.
2. Sexual activity.
3. The "great frost" occurred when the Thames froze over (December 1607 to February 1608).
4. A swarm of bees was made to settle by banging a basin.

Pray God he come!

FACE: I pray he keep away
Till our new business be o'erpast.

SUBTLE: But, Face,
How cam'st thou by this secret don?

FACE: A spirit
Brought me th' intelligence in a paper here,
As I was conjuring yonder in my circle
For Surly; I have my flies° abroad. Your bath *spirits*
Is famous, Subtle, by my means. Sweet Dol,
You must go tune your virginal,[5] no losing
O' the least time: and, do you hear? good action.
Firk,° like a flounder; kiss, like a scallop, close; *excite sexually*
And tickle him with thy mother-tongue. His great
Verdugoship has not a jot of language;[6]
So much the easier to be cozen'd, my Dolly.
He will come here in a hired coach, obscure,
And our own coachman, whom I have sent as guide,
No creature else. [*Knocking without.*] Who's that? [*Exit Dol.*]

SUBTLE: It is not he?

FACE: O no, not yet this hour.

[*Re-enter Dol.*]

SUBTLE: Who is't?

DOL: Dapper,
Your clerk.

FACE: God's will then, Queen of Fairy,
On with your tire;° [*Exit Dol.*] and, Doctor, with your robes. *costume*
Let's dispatch him for God's sake.

SUBTLE: 'Twill be long.

FACE: I warrant you, take but the cues I give you,
It shall be brief enough. [*Goes to the window.*] 'Slight, here are more!
Abel, and I think the angry boy, the heir,
That fain would quarrel.

SUBTLE: And the widow?

FACE: No,
Not that I see. Away! [*Exit Subtle*]—O sir, you are welcome.

Scene 4

[*Enter Dapper.*]

FACE: The Doctor is within a-moving° for you; *conjuring*
I have had the most ado to win him to it!—
He swears you'll be the darling of the dice;
He never heard her highness dote till now.
Your aunt has given you the most gracious words
That can be thought on.

DAPPER: Shall I see her grace?

5. Keyboard instrument, with a sexual innuendo.

6. Verdugoship: a mock title; not a jot of language: speaks no English.

FACE: See her, and kiss her too.—
[*Enter Abel, followed by Kastril.*]
What, honest Nab!
Hast brought the damask?
DRUGGER: No, sir; here's tobacco.
FACE: 'Tis well done, Nab: thou'lt bring the damask too?
DRUGGER: Yes: here's the gentleman, Captain, Master Kastril,
I have brought to see the Doctor.
FACE: Where's the widow?
DRUGGER: Sir, as he likes, his sister, he says, shall come.
FACE: O, is it so? good time. Is your name Kastril, sir?
KASTRIL: Ay, and the best of the Kastrils, I'd be sorry else,
By fifteen hundred a year. Where is the Doctor?
My mad° tobacco-boy, here, tells me of one *wild*
That can do things: has he any skill?
FACE: Wherein, sir?
KASTRIL: To carry a business,° manage a quarrel fairly, *arrange a duel*
Upon fit terms.
FACE: It seems, sir, you are but young
About the town, that can make that a question.
KASTRIL: Sir, not so young, but I have heard some speech
Of the angry boys, and seen them take tobacco;
And in his shop; and I can take it too.
And I would fain be one of 'em, and go down
And practice in the country.
FACE: Sir, for the duello,
The Doctor, I assure you, shall inform you,
To the least shadow of a hair; and show you
An instrument° he has of his own making, *book, treatise*
Wherewith no sooner shall you make report
Of any quarrel, but he will take the height on't
Most instantly, and tell in what degree
Of safety it lies in, or mortality.
And how it may be borne, whether in a right line,
Or a half circle; or may else be cast
Into an angle blunt, if not acute:
All this he will demonstrate. And then, rules
To give and take the lie by.
KASTRIL: How! to take it?
FACE: Yes, in oblique he'll show you, or in circle;
But never in diameter.[7] The whole town
Study his theorems, and dispute them ordinarily
At the eating academies.
KASTRIL: But does he teach
Living by the wits too?

7. To uphold his honor, a gentleman could not allow a direct ("in diameter") accusation of lying, but he might allow an indirect ("oblique") or roundabout ("in a circle") suggestion.

FACE: Anything whatever.
You cannot think that subtlety, but he reads it.
He made me a captain. I was a stark pimp,
Just of your standing, 'fore I met with him;
It is not two months since. I'll tell you his method:
First, he will enter you at some ordinary.° *eating house*
KASTRIL: No, I'll not come there: you shall pardon me.
FACE: For why, sir?
KASTRIL: There's gaming there, and tricks.
FACE: Why, would you be
A gallant, and not game?
KASTRIL: Ay, 'twill spend a man.[8]
FACE: Spend you! it will repair you when you are spent:
How do they live by their wits there, that have vented
Six times your fortunes?
KASTRIL: What, three thousand a-year!
FACE: Ay, forty thousand.
KASTRIL: Are there such?
FACE: Ay, sir,
And gallants yet. Here's a young gentleman
Is born to nothing,—[*Points to Dapper.*] forty marks a-year,
Which I count nothing:—he is to be initiated,
And have a fly° of the Doctor. He will win you, *familiar spirit*
By unresistible luck, within this fortnight,
Enough to buy a barony. They will set him
Upmost, at the groom porters, all the Christmas:
And for the whole year through, at every place,
Where there is play, present him with the chair;
The best attendance, the best drink; sometimes
Two glasses of Canary,° and pay nothing; *sweet wine*
The purest linen, and the sharpest knife,
The partridge next his trencher: and somewhere
The dainty bed, in private, with the dainty.[9]
You shall have your ordinaries bid for him,
As play-houses for a poet; and the master
Pray him aloud to name what dish he affect.
Which must be butter'd shrimps:[1] and those that drink
To no mouth else, will drink to his, as being
The goodly president mouth of all the board.
KASTRIL: Do you not gull one?
FACE: 'Ods my life! do you think it?
You shall have a cast commander,° (can but get *unemployed officer*
In credit with a glover, or a spurrier,
For some two pair of either's ware aforehand,)
Will, by most swift posts, dealing [but] with him,
Arrive at competent means to keep himself,

8. Waste a man's wealth.
9. Sweet and lovely sexual object.
1. Sexually stimulating food.

His punk and naked boy,[2] in excellent fashion,
And be admired for't.
KASTRIL: Will the Doctor teach this?
FACE: He will do more, sir: when your land is gone,
As men of spirit hate to keep earth long,
In a vacation,[3] when small money is stirring,
And ordinaries suspended till the term,
He'll show a perspective,° where on one side *magic mirror*
You shall behold the faces and the persons
Of all sufficient young heirs in town,
Whose bonds are current for commodity;
On th' other side, the merchants' forms, and others,
That without help of any second broker,
Who would expect a share, will trust such parcels:
In the third square, the very street and sign
Where the commodity dwells, and does but wait
To be deliver'd, be it pepper, soap,
Hops, or tobacco, oatmeal, woad, or cheeses.
All which you may so handle, to enjoy
To your own use, and never stand obliged.
KASTRIL: I'faith! is he such a fellow?
FACE: Why, Nab here knows him.
And then for making matches for rich widows,
Young gentlewomen, heirs, the fortunat'st man!
He's sent to, far and near, all over England,
To have his counsel, and to know their fortunes.
KASTRIL: God's will, my suster shall see him.
FACE: I'll tell you, sir,
What he did tell me of Nab, It's a strange thing:—
By the way, you must eat no cheese, Nab, it breeds melancholy,
And that same melancholy breeds worms; but pass it:—
He told me, honest Nab here was ne'er at tavern
But once in's life!
DRUGGER: Truth, and no more I was not.
FACE: And then he was so sick—
DRUGGER: Could he tell you that too?
FACE: How should I know it?
DRUGGER: In troth we had been a shooting,
And had a piece of fat ram-mutton to supper,
That lay so heavy o' my stomach—
FACE: And he has no head
To bear any wine; for what with the noise of the fiddlers,
And care of his shop, for he dares keep no servants—
DRUGGER: My head did so ache—
FACE: As he was fain to be brought home,
The Doctor told me: and then a good old woman—

2. Prostitute and catamite.

3. Time between terms of the law courts.

DRUGGER: Yes, faith, she dwells in Sea-coal-lane,[4]—did cure me,
With sodden° ale, and pellitory of the wall;[5] *boiled*
Cost me but two-pence. I had another sickness
Was worse than that.

FACE: Ay, that was with the grief
Thou took'st for being cess'd° at eighteen-pence, *taxed*
For the water-work.[6]

DRUGGER: In truth, and it was like
T' have cost me almost my life.

FACE: Thy hair went off?

DRUGGER: Yes, sir; 'twas done for spite.

FACE: Nay, so says the Doctor.

KASTRIL: Pray thee, tobacco-boy, go fetch my suster;
I'll see this learned boy before I go;
And so shall she.

FACE: Sir, he is busy now;
But if you have a sister to fetch hither,
Perhaps your own pains may command her sooner;
And he by that time will be free.

KASTRIL: I go. [*Exit*.]

FACE: Drugger, she's thine: the damask!— [*Exit Abel*.]
[*Aside*.] Subtle and I
Must wrestle for her.—Come on, Master Dapper,
You see how I turn clients here away,
To give your cause dispatch; have you perform'd
The ceremonies were enjoin'd you?

DAPPER: Yes, of the vinegar,
And the clean shirt.

FACE: 'Tis well: that shirt may do you
More worship° than you think. Your aunt's a-fire, *praise*
But that she will not show it, t' have a sight of you,
Have you provided for her grace's servants?

DAPPER: Yes, here are six score Edward shillings.

FACE: Good!

DAPPER: And an old Harry's sovereign.

FACE: Very good!

DAPPER: And three James shillings, and an Elizabeth groat,° *four pennies*
Just twenty nobles.° *gold coins*

FACE: O, you are too just.
I would you had had the other noble in Mary's,

DAPPER: I have some Philip and Mary's.

FACE: Ay, those same
Are best of all: where are they? Hark, the Doctor.

4. Neighborhood of fruit sellers, peddlers, and poor people.
5. Low, green plant growing at the base of walls.
6. Bulmer's London Bridge pump-house piped water to houses in London.

Scene 5

[*Enter Subtle, disguised like a priest of Fairy, with a stripe of cloth.*]

SUBTLE [*in a feigned voice*]: Is yet her grace's cousin come?
FACE: He is come.
SUBTLE: And is he fasting?
FACE: Yes.
SUBTLE: And hath cried hum?
FACE: Thrice, you must answer.
DAPPER: Thrice.
SUBTLE: And as oft buz?
FACE: If you have, say.
DAPPER: I have.
SUBTLE: Then, to her cuz,
Hoping that he hath vinegar'd his senses,
As he was bid, the Fairy Queen dispenses,
By me, this robe, the petticoat of fortune;
Which that he straight put on, she doth importune,
And though to fortune[7] near be her petticoat,
Yet nearer is her smock,° the Queen doth note: *undergarment*
And therefore, ev'n of that a piece she hath sent
Which, being a child, to wrap him in was rent;
And prays him for a scarf he now will wear it,
With as much love as then her grace did tear it,
About his eyes, [*They blind him with the rag.*] to shew he is fortunate.[8]
And, trusting unto her to make his state,° *fortune*
He'll throw away all worldly pelf about him;
Which that he will perform, she doth not doubt him.
FACE: She need not doubt him, sir. Alas, he has nothing,
But what he will part withal as willingly,
Upon her Grace's word—throw away your purse—
As she would ask it;—handkerchiefs and all—
[*He throws away, as they bid him.*]
She cannot bid that thing, but he'll obey.—
If you have a ring about you, cast it off,
Or a silver seal at your wrist; her grace will send
Her fairies here to search you, therefore deal
Directly with her Highness: if they find
That you conceal a mite, you are undone,
DAPPER: Truly, there's all.
FACE: All what?
DAPPER: My money; truly.
FACE: Keep nothing that is transitory about you.
[*aside to Subtle*] Bid Dol play music.—Look, the elves are come
[*Dol plays on the cittern[9] within.*]

7. Bawdy reference to her private parts.
8. Playing on the notion that Fortune is blind.
9. Stringed instrument played with a plectrum.

To pinch you, if you tell not truth. Advise you. [*They pinch him.*]
DAPPER: O! I have a paper with a spur-ryal[1] in't.
FACE: *Ti, ti.*
They knew't, they say.
SUBTLE: *Ti, ti, ti, ti.* He has more yet.
FACE [*aside to Sub*]: *Ti, ti-ti-ti.* In the other pocket.
SUBTLE: *Titi, titi, titi, titi, titi.*
They must pinch him or he will never confess, they say.
[*They pinch him again.*]
DAPPER: O, O!
FACE: Nay, pray you hold: he is her Grace's nephew.
Ti, ti, ti? What care you? good faith, you shall care.—
Deal plainly, sir, and shame the fairies. Show
You are innocent.
DAPPER: By this good light, I have nothing.
SUBTLE: *Ti, ti, ti, ti, to, ta.* He does equivocate, she says:
Ti, ti do ti, ti ti do, ti da; and swears by the *light* when he is blinded.
DAPPER: By this good *dark*, I have nothing but a half-crown
Of gold about my wrist, that my love gave me;
And a leaden heart I wore since she forsook me.
FACE: I thought 'twas something. And would you incur
Your aunt's displeasure for these trifles? Come,
I had rather you had thrown away twenty half-crowns. [*Takes it off.*]
You may wear your leaden heart still.—[*Enter Dol, hastily.*]
How now!
SUBTLE: What news, Dol?
DOL: Yonder's your knight, sir Mammon.
FACE: 'Ods lid, we never thought of him till now!
Where is he?
DOL: Here hard by: he is at the door.
SUBTLE: And you are not ready, now! Dol, get his suit.[2] [*Exit Dol.*]
He must not be sent back.
FACE: O by no means.
What shall we do with this same puffin[3] here,
Now he's on the spit?
SUBTLE: Why, lay him back[4] awhile,
With some device.
[*Re-enter Dol, with Face's clothes.*]
—*Ti, ti, ti, ti, ti, ti,* Would her Grace speak with me?
I come.—Help, Dol!
[*Knocking without.*]
FACE [*speaks through the key-hole*]: Who's there? sir Epicure,
My master's in the way. Please you to walk
Three or four turns, but till his back be turn'd,
And I am for you.—Quickly, Dol!

1. Coin worth 15 shillings.
2. The costume of Lungs, assistant to the Alchemist.
3. Half fish and half bird, so a person who is neither fish nor fowl.
4. Away from the fire.

SUBTLE: Her grace
Commends her kindly to you, master Dapper.
DAPPER: I long to see her Grace.
SUBTLE: She now is set
At dinner in her bed, and she has sent you
From her own private trencher, a dead mouse,
And a piece of gingerbread, to be merry withal.
And stay your stomach, lest you faint with fasting;
Yet if you could hold out till she saw you, she says,
It would be better for you.
FACE: Sir, he shall
Hold out, an 'twere this two hours, for her highness;
I can assure you that. We will not lose
All we ha' done.—
SUBTLE: He must not see, nor speak
To any body, till then.
FACE: For that we'll put, sir,
A stay° in's mouth. *gag*
SUBTLE: Of what?
FACE: Of gingerbread.
Make you it fit. He that hath pleas'd her Grace
Thus far, shall not now crincle° for a little.— *shrink, flinch*
Gape, sir, and let him fit you.
[*They thrust a gag of gingerbread in his mouth.*]
SUBTLE: Where shall we now
Bestow him?
DOL: I' the privy.
SUBTLE: Come along, sir,
I now must shew you Fortune's privy lodgings.
FACE: Are they perfum'd, and his bath ready?
SUBTLE: All:
Only the fumigation's somewhat strong.
FACE [*Speaking through the key-hole*]: Sir Epicure, I am yours, sir, by and by.
[*Exeunt with Dapper.*]

ACT 4

Scene 1—*A room in Lovewit's house*

[*Enter Face and Mammon.*]
FACE: O sir, y' are come i' the only finest time.—
MAMMON: Where's master?
FACE: Now preparing for projection, sir.
Your stuff will b' all chang'd shortly.
MAMMON: Into gold?
FACE: To gold and silver, sir.
MAMMON: Silver I care not for.
FACE: Yes, sir, a little to give beggars.
MAMMON: Where's the lady?
FACE: At hand here. I ha' told her such brave things of you,

Touching your bounty, and your noble spirit—
MAMMON: Hast thou?
FACE: As she is almost in her fit to see you.
But, good sir, no divinity in your conference,
For fear of putting her in rage.—
MAMMON: I warrant thee.
FACE: Six men [sir] will not hold her down: and then,
If the old man should hear or see you—
MAMMON: Fear not.
FACE: The very house, sir, would run mad. You know it,
How scrupulous he is, and violent,
'Gainst the least act of sin. Physic, or mathematics,
Poetry, state,° or bawdry, as I told you, *politics*
She will endure, and never startle; but
No word of controversy.
MAMMON: I am school'd, good Ulen.
FACE: And you must praise her house, remember that,
And her nobility.
MAMMON: Let me alone:
No herald, no, nor antiquary, Lungs,
Shall do it better. Go.
FACE [*aside*]: Why, this is yet
A kind of modern happiness, to have
Dol Common for a great lady. [*Exit*]
MAMMON: Now, Epicure,
Heighten thyself, talk to her all in gold;
Rain her as many showers as Jove did drops
Unto his Danäe;[5] show the god a miser,
Compared with Mammon. What! the stone will do't.
She shall feel gold, taste gold, hear gold, sleep gold;
Nay, we will *concumbere*[6] gold: I will be puissant,
And mighty in my talk to her.—
[*Re-enter Face, with Dol richly dressed.*]
Here she comes.
FACE: To him, Dol, suckle him.—This is the noble knight,
I told your ladyship—
MAMMON: Madam, with your pardon,
I kiss your vesture.
DOL: Sir, I were uncivil
If I would suffer that; my lip to you, sir.
MAMMON: I hope my lord your brother be in health, lady.
DOL: My lord, my brother is, though I no lady, sir.
FACE [*aside*]: Well said, my Guinea bird.° *prostitute*
MAMMON: Right noble madam—
FACE [*aside*]: O, we shall have most fierce idolatry.
MAMMON: 'Tis your prerogative.
DOL: Rather your courtesy.

5. Jove came to his love object Danaë in a shower of gold.
6. Copulate; see Juvenal, *Satire* 6.191.

MAMMON: Were there nought else to enlarge your virtues to me,
These answers speak your breeding and your blood.
DOL: Blood we boast none, sir, a poor baron's daughter.
MAMMON: Poor! and gat you? profane not. Had your father
Slept all the happy remnant of his life
After that act, lien but there still, and panted.
He had done enough to make himself, his issue,
And his posterity noble.
DOL: Sir, although
We may be said to want the gilt and trappings,
The dress of honor, yet we strive to keep
The seeds and the materials.
MAMMON: I do see
The old ingredient, virtue, was not lost,
Nor the drug money used to make your compound.
There is a strange nobility in your eye,
This lip, that chin! methinks you do resemble
One of the Austriac princes.[7]
FACE [*aside*]: Very like!
Her father was an Irish costermonger.° *fruit seller*
MAMMON: The house of Valois° just had such a nose, *French royal family*
And such a forehead yet the Medici
Of Florence boast.
DOL: Troth, and I have been liken'd
To all these princes.
FACE: I'll be sworn, I heard it.
MAMMON: I know not how! it is not any one,
But e'en the very choice of all their features.
FACE [*aside*]: I'll in, and laugh. [*Exit.*]
MAMMON: A certain touch, or air,
That sparkles a divinity, beyond
An earthly beauty!
DOL: O, you play the courtier.
MAMMON: Good lady, gi' me leave—
DOL: In faith, I may not,
To mock me, sir.
MAMMON: To burn in this sweet flame;
The phœnix never knew a nobler death.[8]
DOL: Nay, now you court the courtier, and destroy
What you would build; this art, sir, in your words,
Calls your whole faith in question.
MAMMON: By my soul—
DOL: Nay, oaths are made of the same air, sir.
MAMMON: Nature
Never bestow'd upon mortality

7. The royal Austrian family of the Habsburgs was noted for a large lower lip.

8. Every 500 years the phoenix was consumed by fire and rose again from its ashes. See Geoffrey Whitney, *The Phoenix,* in Perspectives: Early Modern Books, page 1066.

A more unblamed, a more harmonious feature;
She play'd the step-dame in all faces else:
Sweet Madam, let me be particular—
DOL: Particular,[9] sir! I pray you know your distance.
MAMMON: In no ill sense, sweet lady; but to ask
How your fair graces pass the hours? I see
You are lodg'd here, in the house of a rare man,
An excellent artist; but what's that to you?
DOL: Yes, sir; I study here the mathematics,
And distillation.
MAMMON: O, I cry your pardon.
He's a divine instructor! can extract
The souls of all things by his art; call all
The virtues, and the miracles of the sun,
Into a temperate furnace; teach dull nature
What her own forces are. A man, the emperor
Has courted above Kelly;[1] sent his medals
And chains, to invite him.
DOL: Ay, and for his physic, sir—
MAMMON: Above the art of Aesculapius,[2]
That drew the envy of the thunderer!
I know all this, and more.
DOL: Troth, I am taken, sir,
Whole with these studies, that contemplate nature.
MAMMON: It is a noble humor; but this form
Was not intended to so dark a use.
Had you been crooked, foul, of some coarse mould
A cloister had done well; but such a feature
That might stand up the glory of a kingdom,
To live recluse! is a mere solecism,[3]
Though in a nunnery. It must not be.
I muse, my lord your brother will permit it!
You should spend half my land first, were I he.
Does not this diamond better on my finger,
Than in the quarry?
DOL: Yes.
MAMMON: Why, you are like it.
You were created, lady, for the light.
Here, you shall wear it; take it, the first pledge
Of what I speak, to bind you to believe me.
DOL: In chains of adamant?° *strong iron*
MAMMON: Yes, the strongest bands.
And take a secret too. Here, by your side
Doth stand this hour, the happiest man in Europe.

9. Dol has taken him to mean sexually intimate.
1. Edward Kelly, the medium for the alchemist John Dee, claimed to posses the philosophers' stone but, when he failed to produce it in Prague, was imprisoned by the emperor Rudolph II.
2. God of medicine who was killed by Jove's thunderbolt lest humans become immortal.
3. Mistake, impropriety.

DOL: You are contented, sir?
MAMMON: Nay, in true being,
The envy of princes and the fear of states.
DOL: Say you so, sir Epicure?
MAMMON: Yes, and thou shalt prove it,
Daughter of honor. I have cast mine eye
Upon thy form, and I will rear this beauty
Above all styles.
DOL: You mean no treason, sir?
MAMMON: No, I will take away that jealousy.° *suspicion*
I am the lord of the philosophers' stone,
And thou the lady.
DOL: How, sir! ha' you that?
MAMMON: I am the master of the mystery.
This day the good old wretch here o' the house
Has made it for us; now he's at projection.
Think therefore thy first wish now, let me hear it,
And it shall rain into thy lap, no shower,
But floods of gold, whole cataracts, a deluge,
To get a nation on thee.
DOL: You are pleased, sir,
To work on the ambition of our sex.
MAMMON: I am pleased the glory of her sex should know,
This nook, here, of the Friars[4] is no climate
For her to live obscurely in, to learn
Physic and surgery, for the constable's wife
Of some odd hundred[5] in Essex; but come forth,
And taste the air of palaces; eat, drink
The toils of empirics,[6] and their boasted practice;
Tincture of pearl, and coral, gold and amber;
Be seen at feasts and triumphs; have it ask'd,
What miracle she is? set all the eyes
Of court a-fire, like a burning glass,
And work them into cinders, when the jewels
Of twenty states adorn thee, and the light
Strikes out the stars! that when thy name is mention'd,
Queens may look pale; and we but showing our love,
Nero's Poppaea may be lost in story![7]
Thus will we have it.
DOL: I could well consent, sir.
But, in a monarchy, how will this be?
The prince will soon take notice, and both seize
You and your stone, it being a wealth unfit
For any private subject.
MAMMON: If he knew it.

4. Blackfriars, location of Lovewit's house.
5. Subdivision of a county.
6. Ancient physicians who practiced medicine based on empirical evidence.
7. Nero killed his mother and wife on account of his love for Poppea.

DOL: Yourself do boast it, sir.
MAMMON: To thee, my life.
DOL: O, but beware, sir! you may come to end
The remnant of your days in a loth'd prison,
By speaking of it.
MAMMON: 'Tis no idle fear:
We'll therefore go with all, my girl, and live
In a free state,° where we will eat our mullets, *a republic*
Soused in high-country wines, sup pheasants' eggs,
And have our cockles boil'd in silver shells;
Our shrimps to swim again, as when they liv'd,
In a rare butter made of dolphin's milk,
Whose cream does look like opals; and with these
Delicate meats set ourselves high for pleasure,[8]
And take us down again, and then renew
Our youth and strength with drinking the elixir,
And so enjoy a perpetuity
Of life and lust! And thou shalt have thy wardrobe
Richer than nature's, still to change thy self,
And vary oftener, for thy pride, than she,
Or art, her wise and almost-equal servant.
[*Re-enter Face*.]
FACE: Sir, you are too loud. I hear you, every word,
Into the laboratory. Some fitter place;
The garden, or great chamber above. How like you her?
MAMMON: Excellent! Lungs. There's for thee. [*Gives him money*.]
FACE: But do you hear?
Good sir, beware, no mention of the rabbins.[9]
MAMMON: We think not on 'em. [*Exeunt Mammon and Dol*.]
FACE: O, it is well, sir.—Subtle!

Scene 2

[*Enter Subtle*.]
FACE: Dost thou not laugh?
SUBTLE: Yes; are they gone?
FACE: All's clear.
SUBTLE: The widow is come.
FACE: And your quarrelling disciple?
SUBTLE: Ay.
FACE: I must to my captainship again then.
SUBTLE: Stay, bring them in first.
FACE: So I meant. What is she?
A bonnibel?° *beauty*
SUBTLE: I know not.
FACE: We'll draw lots:
You'll stand to that?

8. Ready for sexual excitement and all forms of sensuous pleasure.

9. Jewish authorities on law and doctrine, cited in the work of the Puritan author Broughton.

SUBTLE: What else?

FACE: O, for a suit,
To fall now like a curtain, flap![1]

SUBTLE: To the door, man.

FACE: You'll have the first kiss, 'cause I am not ready. [*Exit.*]

SUBTLE: Yes, and perhaps hit you through both the nostrils.[2]

FACE [*within*]: Who would you speak with?

KASTRIL [*within*]: Where's the captain?

FACE [*within*]: Gone, sir,
About some business.

KASTRIL [*within*]: Gone!

FACE [*within*]: He'll return straight.
But master Doctor, his lieutenant, is here.

[*Enter Kastril, followed by Dame Pliant.*]

SUBTLE: Come near, my worshipful boy, my *terrae fili*,[3]
That is, my boy of land; make thy approaches:
Welcome; I know thy lusts,° and thy desires, *wishes*
And I will serve and satisfy them. Begin,
Charge me from thence, or thence, or in this line;
Here is my center: ground thy quarrel.

KASTRIL: You lie.

SUBTLE: How, child of wrath and anger! the loud lie?
For what, my sudden boy?

KASTRIL: Nay, that look you to,
I am afore-hand.[4]

SUBTLE: O, this is no true grammar,
And as ill logic! You must render causes, child,
Your first and second intentions, know your canons
And your divisions, moods, degrees, and differences,
Your predicaments, substance, and accident,
Series, extern and intern, with their causes,
Efficient, material, formal, final,
And have your elements perfect.[5]

KASTRIL [*aside*]: What is this!
The angry tongue he talks in?

SUBTLE: That false precept,
Of being afore-hand, has deceived a number,
And made them enter quarrels, often-times,
Before they were aware; and afterward,
Against their wills.

KASTRIL: How must I do then, sir?

SUBTLE: I cry this lady mercy: she should first
Have been saluted. [*Kisses her.*] I do call you lady,
Because you are to be one, ere't be long,

1. His "suit" is his captain's uniform; "like a curtain flap," like the drop scene in a masque which would create an instant change of scene.
2. Get the better of you.
3. Son of the earth.
4. I got there first.
5. Subtle uses the terms of scholastic logic to describe how one should properly quarrel.

My soft and buxom widow.
KASTRIL: Is she, i'faith?
SUBTLE: Yes, or my art is an egregious liar.
KASTRIL: How know you?
SUBTLE: By inspection on her forehead,
And subtlety[6] of her lip, which must be tasted
Often, to make a judgment. [*Kisses her again.*] 'Slight, she melts
Like a myrobolane:[7]—here is yet a line.
In *rivo frontis*,[8] tells me he is no knight.
DAME PLIANT: What is he then, sir?
SUBTLE: Let me see your hand.
O, your *linea fortunæ*[9] makes it plain;
And stella here *in monte Veneris*.[1]
But, most of all, *junctura annularis*.[2]
He is a soldier, or a man of art, lady,
But shall have some great honor shortly.
DAME PLIANT: Brother,
He's a rare man, believe me!
[*Re-enter Face, in his uniform.*]
KASTRIL: Hold your peace.
Here comes the t'other rare man.—'Save you, Captain,
FACE: Good master Kastril! Is this your sister?
KASTRIL: Ay, sir.
Please you to kuss her, and be proud to know her.
FACE: I shall be proud to know you, lady. [*Kisses her.*]
DAME PLIANT: Brother.
He calls me lady, too.
KASTRIL: Ay, peace: I heard it. [*Takes her aside.*]
FACE: The Count is come.
SUBTLE: Where is he?
FACE: At the door.
SUBTLE: Why, you must entertain him.
FACE: What'll you do
With these the while?
SUBTLE: Why, have them up, and show them
Some fustian book, or the dark glass.[3]
FACE: 'Fore God,
She is a delicate dab-chick![4] I must have her. [*Exit.*]
SUBTLE: Must you! ay, if your fortune will, you must.—
Come, sir, the Captain will come to us presently:
I'll have you to my chamber of demonstrations,
Where I will show you both the grammar and logic,
And rhetoric of quarreling; my whole method

6. Exquisiteness, and also a pun on subtlety as a sugary confection.
7. Plumlike fruit from the east.
8. The frontal vein.
9. Line of fortune, extending from beneath the little finger to the index finger.
1. The star ("stella") on the mount of Venus (*monte Veneris*) at the base of the thumb.
2. Joint of the ring finger.
3. Fustian: bogus, bombastic; dark glass: crystal ball.
4. Dainty bird that dives into water.

Drawn out in tables; and my instrument,
That hath the several scales[5] upon't, shall make you
Able to quarrel at a straw's-breadth by moon-light.
And, lady, I'll have you look in a glass,
Some half an hour, but to clear your eye-sight,
Against you see your fortune; which is greater,
Than I may judge upon the sudden, trust me.
[Exit, followed by Kastril and Dame Pliant.]

Scene 3

[Re-enter Face.]
FACE: Where are you, Doctor?
SUBTLE *[within]*: I'll come to you presently.
FACE: I will ha' this same widow, now I ha' seen her,
On any composition.° — *terms*
[Re-enter Subtle.]
SUBTLE: What do you say?
FACE: Ha' you disposed of them?
SUBTLE: I have sent 'em up.
FACE: Subtle, in troth, I needs must have this widow.
SUBTLE: Is that the matter?
FACE: Nay, but hear me.
SUBTLE: Go to.
If you rebel once, Dol shall know it all:
Therefore be quiet, and obey your chance.
FACE: Nay, thou art so violent now—Do but conceive,
Thou art old, and canst not serve[6]—
SUBTLE: Who cannot? I?
'Slight, I will serve her with thee, for a—
FACE: Nay,
But understand: I'll gi' you composition.° — *compensation*
SUBTLE: I will not treat with thee; what! sell my fortune?
'Tis better than my birth-right. Do not murmur:
Win her, and carry her. If you grumble, Do!
Knows it directly.
FACE: Well, sir, I am silent.
Will you go help to fetch in Don in state? *[Exit.]*
SUBTLE: I follow you, sir: we must keep Face in awe,
Or he will over-look us like a tyrant.
[Re-enter Face, introducing Surly disguised as a Spaniard.]
Brain of a tailor! who comes here? Don John![7]
SURLY: *Señores, beso las manos a vuestras mercedes.*[8]
SUBTLE: Would you had stoop'd a little, and kist our *anos!*
FACE: Peace, Subtle.
SUBTLE: Stab me; I shall never hold, man.
He looks in that deep ruff like a head in a platter.

5. A scale different for each argument.
6. Serve sexually.
7. Typical name for a Spaniard.
8. "Gentlemen, I kiss your honors' hands."

Serv'd in by a short cloak upon two trestles.[9]
FACE: Or, what do you say to a collar of brawn, cut down
Beneath the souse, and wriggled with a knife?[1]
SUBTLE: 'Slud, he does look too fat to be a Spaniard.
FACE: Perhaps some Fleming or some Hollander got him
In d'Alva's time; Count Egmont's bastard.[2]
SUBTLE: Don,
Your scurvy, yellow, Madrid face is welcome.
SURLY: *Gracias.*
SUBTLE: He speaks out of a fortification.
Pray God he have no squibs in those deep sets.[3]
SURLY: *Por dios, señores, muy linda casa!*[4]
SUBTLE: What says he?
FACE: Praises the house, I think;
I know no more but's action.
SUBTLE: Yes, the *casa*,
My precious Diego, will prove fair enough
To cozen you in. Do you mark? you shall
Be cozen'd, Diego.
FACE: Cozen'd, do you see,
My worthy Donzel,[5] cozen'd.
SURLY: *Entiendo.*[6]
SUBTLE: Do you intend it? so do we, dear Don.
Have you brought pistolets, or portagues,
My solemn Don?—Dost thou feel any?
FACE [*feels his pockets*]: Full.
SUBTLE: You shall be emptied, Don, pumped and drawn
Dry, as they say.
FACE: Milked, in troth, sweet Don.
SUBTLE: See all the monsters; the great lion of all, Don.[7]
SURLY: *Con licencia, se puede ver a esta señora?*[8]
SUBTLE: What talks he now?
FACE: Of the señora.
SUBTLE: O, Don,
That is the lioness, which you shall see
Also, my Don.
FACE: 'Slid, Subtle, how shall we do?
SUBTLE: For what?
FACE: Why Dol's employ'd, you know.
SUBTLE: That's true.
'Fore heaven, I know not: he must stay, that's all.
FACE: Stay! that he must not by no means.
SUBTLE: No! why?

9. His legs.
1. Collar of brawn: pig's neck; souse: ear; wriggled: cut in a ruffled pattern.
2. The Dutch patriot Egmont was executed by the Duke of Alva, commander of the Spanish army in the Netherlands.
3. Squibs: rockets; deep sets: deep folds in his collar.
4. "By God, gentlemen, a very fine house."
5. From Italian *donzello*, squire.
6. "I understand."
7. The lions were a tourist attraction at the Tower of London.
8. "If you please, may one see the lady."

FACE: Unless you'll mar all, 'Slight, he'll suspect it:
And then he will not pay, not half so well.
This is a travelled punk-master, and does know
All the delays; a notable hot rascal,
And looks already rampant.[9]
SUBTLE: 'Sdeath, and Mammon
Must not be troubled.
FACE: Mammon! in no case.
SUBTLE: What shall we do then?
FACE: Think: you must be sudden.
SURLY: *Entiendo que la señora es tan hermosa, que codicio tan à verla, como la bien aventuranza de mi vida.*[1]
FACE: *Mi vida!* 'Slid, Subtle, he puts me in mind o' the widow.
What dost thou say to draw her to it, ha!
And tell her 'tis her fortune? All our venture
Now lies upon't. It is but one man more,
Which of us chance to have her: and beside,
There is no maidenhead to be fear'd or lost.
What dost thou think on't, Subtle?
SUBTLE: Who, I? why—
FACE: The credit of our house too is engaged.
SUBTLE: You made me an offer for my share erewhile.
What wilt thou give me, i'faith?
FACE: O, by that light
I'll not buy now: You know your doom to me.
E'en take your lot, obey your chance, sir; win her,
And wear her out, for me.
SUBTLE: 'Slight, I'll not work her then.
FACE: It is the common cause; therefore bethink you.
Dol else must know it, as you said.
SUBTLE: I care not.
SURLY: *Señores, por qué se tarda tanto?*[2]
SUBTLE: Faith, I am not fit, I am old.
FACE: That's now no reason, sir.
SURLY: *Puede ser de hacer burla de mi amor?*[3]
FACE: You hear the Don too? by this air, I call,
And loose the hinges: Dol!
SUBTLE: A plague of hell—
FACE: Will you then do?
SUBTLE: Y're a terrible rogue!
I'll think of this: will you, sir, call the widow?
FACE: Yes, and I'll take her too with all her faults,
Now I do think on't better.
SUBTLE: With all my heart, sir;
Am I discharged o' the lot?

9. Heraldic term for an animal rearing on its hind legs.
1. "I understand the lady is so beautiful that I long to see her as the great good fortune of my life."
2. "Gentlemen, why so much delay?"
3. "Perhaps you are mocking my love."

FACE: As you please.
SUBTLE: Hands. [*They take hands*.]
FACE: Remember now, that upon any change,
You never claim her.
SUBTLE: Much good joy, and health to you, sir.
Marry a whore! Fate, let me wed a witch first.
SURLY: *Por estas honradas barbas*[4]—
SUBTLE: He swears by his beard.
Dispatch, and call the brother too. [*Exit Face*.]
SURLY: *Tengo duda, Señores*
Que no me hagan alguna traición.[5]
SUBTLE: How, issue on? yes, *presto, Señor*. Please you
Enthratha the *chambratha*, worthy Don:
Where if you please the fates, in your *bathada*,
You shall be soaked, and stroked, and tubb'd, and rubb'd,
And scrubb'd, and fubb'd,° dear Don, before you go. *cheated*
You shall, in faith, my scurvy baboon Don.
Be curried,[6] claw'd and flaw'd, and taw'd, indeed.
I will the heartlier go about it now,
And make the widow a punk so much the sooner,
To be revenged on this impetuous face:
The quickly doing of it, is the grace. [*Exeunt Subtle and Surly*.]

Scene 4

[*Enter Face, Kastril, and Dame Pliant*.]
FACE: Come, lady: I knew the Doctor would not leave,
Till he had found the very nick[7] of her fortune.
KASTRIL: To be a countess, say you?
FACE: A Spanish countess, sir.
DAME PLIANT: Why, is that better than an English countess?
FACE: Better? 'Slight, make you that a question, lady?
KASTRIL: Nay, she is a fool, Captain, you must pardon her.
FACE: Ask from your courtier, to your inns-of-court-man,° *lawyer*
To your mere milliner; they will tell you all,
Your Spanish gennet is the best horse;[8] your Spanish
Stoop° is the best garb:° your Spanish beard *bow / manner*
Is the best cut; your Spanish ruffs are the best
Wear; your Spanish pavin the best dance;[9]
Your Spanish titillation° in a glove *perfume*
The best perfume: and for your Spanish pike,[1]
And Spanish blade, let your poor Captain speak—
Here comes the Doctor.
[*Enter Subtle with a paper*.]
SUBTLE: My most honor'd lady,
For so I am now to style you, having found

4. "By this honored beard."
5. "I am afraid, gentlemen, you are deceiving me in some way."
6. Soaked, scraped, and beaten.
7. Crucial moment.
8. Small Spanish horse.
9. Dance with a stately rhythm.
1. Spear used by the infantry.

By this my scheme, you are to undergo
An honorable fortune, very shortly.
What will you say now, if some—

FACE: I ha' told her all, sir:
And her right worshipful brother here, that she shall be
A countess: do not delay them, sir: a Spanish countess,

SUBTLE: Still, my scarce-worshipful Captain, you can keep
No secret! Well, since he has told you, madam,
Do you forgive him, and I do.

KASTRIL: She shall do that, sir;
I'll look to't, 'tis my charge.

SUBTLE: Well then: nought rests
But that she fit her love now to her fortune.

DAME PLIANT: Truly I shall never brook a Spaniard.

SUBTLE: No?

DAME PLIANT: Never since eighty-eight could I abide them,[2]
And that was some three year afore I was born, in truth,

SUBTLE: Come, you must love him, or be miserable,
Choose which you will.

FACE: By this good rush,[3] persuade her,
She will cry strawberries else within this twelvemonth.

SUBTLE: Nay, shads and mackerel, which is worse.[4]

FACE: Indeed, sir?

KASTRIL: God's lid, you shall love him, or I'll kick you.

DAME PLIANT: Why,
I'll do as you will have me, brother,

KASTRIL: Do,
Or by this hand I'll maul you.

FACE: Nay, good sir,
Be not so fierce.

SUBTLE: No, my enraged child;
She will be ruled. What, when she comes to taste
The pleasures of a countess! to be courted—

FACE: And kiss'd, and ruffled!° *fondled*

SUBTLE: Ay, behind the hangings.[5]

FACE: And then come forth in pomp!

SUBTLE: And know her state!

FACE: Of keeping all the idolators of the chamber
Barer to her,[6] than at their prayers!

SUBTLE: Is serv'd
Upon the knee!

FACE: And has her pages, ushers,
Footmen, and coaches—

2. 1588, the year of the Spanish Armada's attack on England.
3. The stage, like the floors of private houses, were covered with rush, or straw.
4. She will be so poor that she will have to sell strawberries in the street, or she will have to sell fish, an even lower occupation.
5. Tapestries or wall-hangings.
6. With their hats off in respect to her.

SUBTLE: Her six mares—
FACE: Nay, eight!
SUBTLE: To hurry her through London, to th' Exchange,
Bethlem, the china-houses[7]—
FACE: Yes, and have
The citizens gape at her, and praise her tires,° *clothes*
And my lord's goose-turd bands,[8] that ride with her.
KASTRIL: Most brave! By this hand, you are not my suster,
If you refuse.
DAME PLIANT: I will not refuse, brother.
[*Enter Surly.*]
SURLY: *Qué es esto, señores, que no se venga?*
Esta tardanza me mata![9]
FACE: It is the count come:
The doctor knew he would be here, by his art.
SUBTLE: *En gallanta madama, Don! gallantissima!*
SURLY: *Por todos los dioses, la más acabada*
Hermosura, que he visto en mi vida![1]
FACE: Is't not a gallant language that they speak?
KASTRIL: An admirable language! Is't not French?
FACE: No, Spanish, sir.
KASTRIL: It goes like law-French,
And that, they say, is the courtliest language.[2]
FACE: List, sir.
SURLY: *El sol ha perdido su lumbre, con el*
Resplandor que trae esta dama! Válgame Dios![3]
FACE: H'admires your sister.
KASTRIL: Must not she make curt'sy?
SUBTLE: 'Ods will, she must go to him, man, and kiss him!
It is the Spanish fashion, for the women
To make first court.
FACE: 'Tis true he tells you, sir:
His art knows all.
SURLY: *Por qué no se acude?*[4]
KASTRIL: He speaks to her, I think.
FACE: That he does, sir.
SURLY: *Por el amor de Dios, qué es esto que se tarda?*[5]
KASTRIL: Nay, see: she will not understand him! gull,
Noddy.
DAME PLIANT: What say you, brother?
KASTRIL: Ass, my suster.
Go kuss him, as the cunning man would have you;

7. The Exchange was a fashionable shopping area. Bethlem, or Bedlam, was the London insane asylum; china houses were shops selling porcelain and other precious goods from the east.
8. Collars in goose-turd green, a fashionable color.
9. "Why does she not come, gentlemen? This delay is killing me."
1. "By all the gods, the most perfect beauty that I have ever seen in my life."
2. Norman French was the language of the law courts.
3. "The sun has lost its light with the splendor that this lady brings. God bless me!"
4. "Why does she not come?"
5. "For the love of God, why is it she delays?"

I'll thrust a pin in your buttocks else.
FACE: O no, sir.
SURLY: *Señora mia, mi persona está muy indigna a llegar a tanta hermosura.*[6]
FACE: Does he not use her bravely?
KASTRIL: Bravely, i'faith!
FACE: Nay, he will use her better.
KASTRIL: Do you think so?
SURLY: *Señora, si será servida, entremos.*[7] [*Exit with Dame Pliant.*]
KASTRIL: Where does he carry her?
FACE: Into the garden, sir;
Take you no thought: I must interpret for her.
SUBTLE [*aside to Face, who goes out*]: Give Dol the word.—[*to Kastril*] Come, my fierce child, advance,
We'll to our quarreling lesson again.
KASTRIL: Agreed.
I love a Spanish boy with all my heart.
SUBTLE: Nay, and by this means, sir, you shall be brother
To a great count.
KASTRIL: Ay, I knew that at first.
This match will advance the house of the Kastrils.
SUBTLE: 'Pray God your sister prove but pliant!
KASTRIL: Why,
Her name is so, by her other husband.
SUBTLE: How!
KASTRIL: The widow Pliant. Knew you not that?
SUBTLE: No, faith, sir;
Yet, by erection of her figure,[8] I guessed it,
Come, let's go practice.
KASTRIL: Yes, but do you think, Doctor,
I e'er shall quarrel well?
SUBTLE: I warrant you. [*Exeunt.*]

Scene 5

[*Enter Dol in her fit of raving, followed by* MAMMON.]
DOL: For after Alexander's death[9]—
MAMMON: Good lady—
DOL: That Perdiccas and Antigonus, were slain,
The two that stood, Seleuc' and Ptolomy[1]—
MAMMON: Madam.

6. "My lady, my person is unworthy to attain so much beauty."
7. "Lady, if it is convenient, let us go in."
8. Both the casting of her horoscope and the sexual arousal that her appearance provokes.
9. Alexander the Great, King of Macedonia, who conquered and ruled an empire over the Mediterranean world in the 4th century B.C.E. Dol's lines 1–32 contain quotations from Hugh Broughton's *A Conceit of Scripture* (1590). The passage quoted here is from an interpretation of the dream of Nebuchadnezzar in the Book of Daniel 2, where a pagan idol with legs of iron and clay is broken by a stone that becomes a huge mountain.
1. Perdiccas, Antigonus, Seleucus, and Ptolemy were the four generals of Alexander the Great, who fought over his kingdom. Like many Puritans, Broughton interpreted the Ptolemaic empire (Egypt, to the south) and the Seleucid empire (Syria, to the north) as the four kingdoms in a cycle of decay of pagan rule that would give way to the fifth monarchy (see line 34 below), which in the 17th century was identified with the thousand-year reign of Christ.

DOL: Made up the two legs, and the fourth beast,
That was Gog-north, and Egypt-south: which after
Was call'd Gog-iron-leg, and South-iron-leg—
MAMMON: Lady—
DOL: And then Gog-horned. So was Egypt, too:
Then Egypt-clay-leg, and Gog-clay-leg—
MAMMON: Sweet madam.
DOL: And last Gog-dust, and Egypt-dust, which fall
In the last link of the fourth chain. And these
Be stars in story, which none see, or look at—
MAMMON: What shall I do?
DOL: For, as he says, except
We call the rabbins, and the heathen Greeks[2]—
MAMMON: Dear lady.
DOL: To come from Salem, and from Athens,
And teach the people of Great Britain—
[*Enter Face, hastily, in his servant's dress.*]
FACE: What's the matter, sir?
DOL: To speak the tongue of Eber, and Javan—
MAMMON: O,
She's in her fit.
DOL: We shall know nothing—
FACE: Death, sir,
We are undone!
DOL: Where then a learned linguist
Shall see the ancient used communion
Of vowels and consonants—
FACE: My master will hear!
DOL: A wisdom, which Pythagoras held most high—
MAMMON: Sweet honorable lady!
DOL: To comprise
All sounds of voices, in few marks of letters—
FACE: Nay, you must never hope to lay her now.[3]
[*They all speak together.*]
DOL: And so we may arrive by Talmud skill,[4]
And profane Greek, to raise the building up
Of Helen's house against the Ismaelite,[5]
King of Thogarma,[6] and his habergions° *armor*
Brimstony, blue, and fiery; and the force
Of King Abaddon, and the Beast of Cittim:
Which rabbi David Kimchi, Onkelos,

2. The "rabbins" (Jews from Salem) and the "heathen Greeks" (from Athens) are to teach the Puritans of Great Britain the languages of Scripture, the tongue of Eber (ancestor of the Hebrews) and of Javan (ancestor of the Greeks).
3. "Lay her," means both to allay or calm her down, and to have sexual intercourse with her.
4. The Talmud contains texts of Jewish civil and religious law.
5. "Helen's house" is Heber's house in Hugh Broughton's *A Conceit of Scripture* (1590) where he uses it to mean "the kingdom of God;" the Ismaelite are the sons of Ismael (Ishmael), pagans.
6. King of Thogarma, ruler of a biblical kingdom (Ezekiel 38.6).

And Aben Ezra do interpret Rome.[7]
FACE: How did you put her into't?
MAMMON: Alas! I talk'd
Of a fifth monarchy I would erect,
With the philosopher's stone,[8] by chance, and she
Falls on the other four straight.
FACE: Out of Broughton![9]
I told you so. 'Slid, stop her mouth.
MAMMON: Is't best?
FACE: She'll never leave else. If the old man hear her,
We are but feces, ashes.
SUBTLE [*within*]: What's to do there?
FACE: O, we are lost! Now she hears him, she is quiet.
[*Enter Subtle, they run different ways.*]
MAMMON: Where shall I hide me!
SUBTLE: How! what sight is here?
Close deeds of darkness, and that shun the light!
Bring him again. Who is he? What, my son!
O, I have lived too long.
MAMMON: Nay, good, dear father,
There was no unchaste purpose.
SUBTLE: Not? and flee me,
When I come in?
MAMMON: That was my error.
SUBTLE: Error?
Guilt, guilt, my son: give it the right name. No marvel,
If I found check in our great work within,
When such affairs as these were managing!
MAMMON: Why, have you so?
SUBTLE: It has stood still this half hour:
And all the rest of our less works gone back.
Where is the instrument of wickedness,
My lewd° false drudge? *ignorant*
MAMMON: Nay, good sir, blame not him;
Believe me, 'twas against his will or knowledge:
I saw her by chance.
SUBTLE: Will you commit more sin,
To excuse a varlet?
MAMMON: By my hope, 'tis true, sir.
SUBTLE: Nay, then I wonder less, if you, for whom
The blessing was prepared, would so tempt heaven,
And lose your fortunes.
MAMMON: Why, sir?
SUBTLE: This will retard

7. Biblical commentators interpreted King of Abaddon as the Pope and Beast of Cittim as the Roman Catholic Church.

8. With a bawdy pun on stone as "testicle."

9. Broughton's *A Conceit of Scripture*.

The work, a month at least.
MAMMON: Why, if it do.
What remedy? But think it not, good father:
Our purposes were honest.
SUBTLE: As they were,
So the reward will prove.—[*A loud explosion within.*] How now! ah me!
God, and all saints be good to us.—
[*Re-enter Face.*]
What's that?
FACE: O, sir, we are defeated! all the works
Are flown *in fumo*,° every glass is burst: *in smoke*
Furnace, and all rent down! as if a bolt
Of thunder had been driven through the house.
Retorts, receivers, pelicans, bolt-heads,
All struck in shivers! [*Subtle falls down as in a swoon.*]
Help, good sir! alas,
Coldness, and death invades him. Nay, sir Mammon,
Do the fair offices° of a man! You stand, *duties*
As you were readier to depart than he.
[*Knocking within.*]
Who's there? My lord her brother is come.
MAMMON: Ha, Lungs!
FACE: His coach is at the door. Avoid his sight,
For he's as furious as his sister's mad.
MAMMON: Alas!
FACE: My brain is quite undone with the fume, sir,
I ne'er must hope to be mine own man again.
MAMMON: Is all lost, Lungs? will nothing be preserv'd
Of all our cost?
FACE: Faith, very little, sir;
A peck of coals or so, which is cold comfort, sir.
MAMMON: O my voluptuous mind! I am justly punish'd.
FACE: And so am I, sir.
MAMMON: Cast from all my hopes—
FACE: Nay, certainties, sir.
MAMMON: By mine own base affections.
SUBTLE [*seeming to come to himself*]: O, the curst fruits of vice and lust!
MAMMON: Good father,
It was my sin. Forgive it.
SUBTLE: Hangs my roof
Over us still, and will not fall, O justice,
Upon us, for this wicked man!
FACE: Nay, look, sir,
You grieve him now with staying in his sight:
Good sir, the nobleman will come too, and take you,
And that may breed a tragedy.
MAMMON: I'll go.
FACE: Ay, and repent at home, sir. It may be,

For some good penance you may ha' it yet;
A hundred pound to the box at Bedlam[1]—
MAMMON: Yes.
FACE: For the restoring such as—have their wits.
MAMMON: I'll do't.
FACE: I'll send one to you to receive it.
MAMMON: Do.
Is no projection left?
FACE: All flown, or stinks, sir.
MAMMON: Will nought be sav'd that's good for med'cine, think'st thou?
FACE: I cannot tell, sir. There will be perhaps,
Something about the scraping of the shards,
Will cure the itch,—[*aside*] though not your itch of mind, sir.—
It shall be saved for you, and sent home. Good sir.
This way, for fear the lord should meet you. [*Exit Mammon.*]
SUBTLE [*raising his head*]: Face!
FACE: Ay.
SUBTLE: Is he gone?
FACE: Yes, and as heavily
As all the gold he hoped for were in's blood.
Let us be light though.
SUBTLE [*leaping up*]: Ay, as balls, and bound
And hit our heads against the roof for joy:
There's so much of our care now cast away,
FACE: Now to our Don,
SUBTLE: Yes, your young widow by this time
Is made a countess, Face; she has been in travail
Of a young heir for you.
FACE: Good sir.
SUBTLE: Off with your case,[2]
And greet her kindly, as a bridegroom should,
After these common hazards.
FACE: Very well, sir.
Will you go fetch Don Diego off, the while?
SUBTLE: And fetch him over too,[3] if you'll be pleased, sir:
Would Dol were in her place, to pick his pockets now!
FACE: Why, you can do't as well, if you would set to't.
I pray you prove your virtue.[4]
SUBTLE: For your sake, sir. [*Exeunt.*]

Scene 6

[*Enter Surly and Dame Pliant.*]
SURLY: Lady, you see into what hands you are fall'n;
'Mongst what a nest of villains! and how near
Your honor was t' have catch'd a certain clap,° *gonorrhea*

1. The poor box for the madhouse.
2. Costume as Lungs.
3. Get the better of him.
4. Virtue in the sense of ability or skill.

Through your credulity, had I but been
So punctually forward, as place, time,
And other circumstances would have made a man;
For you're a handsome woman: would you were wise too!
I am a gentleman come here disguised,
Only to find the knaveries of this citadel;
And where I might have wrong'd your honor and have not,
I claim some interest in your love. You are,
They say, a widow, rich: and I'm a bachelor,
Worth nought: your fortunes may make me a man.
As mine have preserv'd you a woman. Think upon it,
And whether I have deserv'd you or no.

DAME PLIANT: I will, sir.

SURLY: And for these household-rogues, let me alone
To treat with them.

[*Enter Subtle.*]

SUBTLE: How doth my noble Diego,
And my dear madam countess? Hath the count
Been courteous, lady? liberal, and open?
Donzel, methinks you look melancholic,
After your coitum, and scurvy:[5] truly,
I do not like the dullness of your eye:
It hath a heavy cast, 'tis upsee Dutch,[6]
And says you are a lumpish whore-master.
Be lighter, I will make your pockets so. [*Attempts to pick them.*]

SURLY [*throws open his cloak*]: Will you, Don Bawd and Pick-purse?
[*strikes him down*] How now! reel you?
Stand up, sir, you shall find, since I am so heavy,
I'll give you equal weight.

SUBTLE: Help! murder!

SURLY: No, sir,
There's no such thing intended: a good cart,
And a clean whip[7] shall ease you of that fear.
I am the Spanish Don that should be cozen'd.
Do you see, cozen'd! Where's your captain Face,
That parcel-broker,[8] and whole-bawd, all rascal!

[*Enter Face, in his uniform.*]

FACE: How, Surly!

SURLY: O, make your approach, good Captain.
I have found from whence your copper rings and spoons
Come, now, wherewith you cheat abroad in taverns.
'Twas here you learn'd t' anoint your boot with brimstone,
Then rub men's gold on't for a kind of touch,
And say 'twas naught, when you had changed the color,
That you might have't for nothing. And this Doctor,

5. Sad and sick after sex.
6. In the Dutch style, drunken.
7. A common punishment for minor crimes was to be tied to a cart and whipped through the streets.
8. Part-time go-between.

Your sooty, smoky-bearded compeer, he
Will close you so much gold, in a bolt's-head,
And, on a turn, convey in the stead another
With sublimed mercury, that shall burst in the heat,
And fly out all *in fumo!* Then weeps Mammon;
Then swoons his worship. [*Face slips out.*] Or, he is the Faustus,[9]
That casteth figures and can conjure, cures
Plagues, piles, and pox, by the ephemerides,[1]
And holds intelligence with all the bawds
And midwives of three shires: while you send in—
Captain—what! is he gone!—damsels with child,
Wives that are barren, or the waiting-maid
With the green sickness. [*Seizes Subtle as he tries to leave.*]
Nay, sir, you must tarry,
Though he be scaped; and answer by the ears, sir.

Scene 7

[*Re-enter Face, with Kastril.*]

FACE: Why, now's the time, if ever you will quarrel
Well, as they say, and be a true-born child:
The doctor and your sister both are abused.

KASTRIL: Where is he? Which is he? He is a slave,
Whate'er he is, and the son of a whore.—Are you
The man, sir, I would know?

SURLY: I should be loath, sir,
To confess so much.

KASTRIL: Then you lie in your throat.

SURLY: How!

FACE [*to Kastril*]: A very arrant° rogue, sir, and a cheater, *notorious*
Employ'd here by another conjurer
That does not love the doctor, and would cross him,
If he knew how.

SURLY: Sir, you are abused.

KASTRIL: You lie:
And 'tis no matter.

FACE: Well said, sir! He is
The impudent'st rascal—

SURLY: You are indeed: Will you hear me, sir?

FACE: By no means: bid him be gone.

KASTRIL: Begone, sir, quickly.

SURLY: This's strange!—Lady, do you inform your brother.

FACE: There is not such a foist° in all the town, *cheat*
The Doctor had him presently; and finds yet,
The Spanish Count will come here.—[*aside.*] Bear up, Subtle.

SUBTLE: Yes, sir, he must appear within this hour.

FACE: And yet this rogue would come in a disguise,

9. Character who made a pact with the devil to achieve power in Christopher Marlowe's play *Doctor Faustus*.

1. Astronomical almanacs.

By the temptation of another spirit,
To trouble our art, though he could not hurt it!
KASTRIL: Ay,
I know—Away, [*to his sister*] you talk like a foolish mauther.[2]
SURLY: Sir, all is truth she says.
FACE: Do not believe him, sir.
He is the lying'st swabber![3] Come your ways, sir.
SURLY: You are valiant out of company!
KASTRIL: Yes, how then, sir?
[*Enter Drugger, with a piece of damask.*]
FACE: Nay, here's an honest fellow, too, that knows him,
And all his tricks. Make good what I say, Abel,
This cheater would have cozen'd thee o' the widow.—
[*Aside to Drugger.*]
He owes this honest Drugger here, seven pound,
He has had on him, in two-penny'orths of tobacco.
DRUGGER: Yes, sir. And he has damn'd himself three terms to pay me.[4]
FACE: And what does he owe for lotium?[5]
DRUGGER: Thirty shillings, sir;
And for six syringes.[6]
SURLY: Hydra[7] of villainy!
FACE: Nay, sir, you must quarrel him out o' the house.
KASTRIL: I will:
—Sir, if you get not out o' doors, you lie;
And you are a pimp.
SURLY: Why, this is madness, sir,
Not valor in you; I must laugh at this.
KASTRIL: It is my humor: you are a pimp and a trig,° *fop*
And an *Amadis de Gaul*, or a Don Quixote.[8]
DRUGGER: Or a knight o' the curious coxcomb,[9] do you see?
[*Enter Ananias.*]
ANANIAS: Peace to the household!
KASTRIL: I'll keep peace for no man.
ANANIAS: Casting of dollars is concluded lawful.
KASTRIL: Is he the constable?
SUBTLE: Peace, Ananias.
FACE: No, sir.
KASTRIL: Then you are an otter, and a shad, a whit,
A very tim.° *tiny particle*
SURLY: You'll hear me, sir?
KASTRIL: I will not.
ANANIAS: What is the motive?
SUBTLE: Zeal in the young gentleman,

2. Young girl.
3. Low person, deck-scrubber.
4. Sworn for three law terms in a row.
5. Lotium was stale urine used as a hair tonic.
6. Syringes for applying lotium or taking medicine to treat venereal disease.
7. The many-headed sea beast who grew two new heads for each one that was cut off.
8. Amadis of Gaul, the hero of the Spanish prose romance of the same name, was the model of all chivalry for Don Quixote, the hero of Cervantes' comic novel about a deluded old man who thought he could be a knight.
9. The preposterous hat that Surly wears.

Against his Spanish slops.[1]
ANANIAS: They are profane,
Lewd, superstitious, and idolatrous breeches.
SURLY: New rascals!
KASTRIL: Will you begone, sir!
ANANIAS: Avoid, Satan!
Thou art not of the light: That ruff of pride
About thy neck, betrays thee; and is the same
With that which the unclean birds, in seventy-seven,[2]
Were seen to prank° it with on divers coasts: *swagger*
Thou look'st like antichrist, in that lewd hat,
SURLY: I must give way.
KASTRIL: Be gone, sir.
SURLY: But I'll take
A course with you—
ANANIAS: Depart, proud Spanish fiend!
SURLY: Captain and Doctor.
ANANIAS: Child of perdition!
KASTRIL: Hence, sir! [*Exit Surly*.]
Did I not quarrel bravely!
FACE: Yes, indeed, sir.
KASTRIL: Nay, an I give my mind to't, I shall do't.
FACE: O, you must follow, sir, and threaten him tame:
He'll turn again else.
KASTRIL: I'll re-turn him then. [*Exit*.]
[*Subtle takes Ananias aside*.]
FACE: Drugger, this rogue prevented° us for thee: *forestalled*
We had determin'd that thou should'st have come
In a Spanish suit, and have carried her so; and he,
A brokerly° slave! goes, puts it on himself. *pimping*
Hast brought the damask?
DRUGGER: Yes, sir.
FACE: Thou must borrow
A Spanish suit: hast thou no credit with the players?
DRUGGER: Yes, sir; did you never see me play the Fool?[3]
FACE: I know not, Nab:—[*aside*.] Thou shalt, if I can help it.—
Hieronimo's old cloak, ruff, and hat will serve;[4]
I'll tell thee more when thou bring'st 'em. [*Exit Drugger*.]
ANANIAS: Sir, I know
The Spaniard hates the brethren, and hath spies
Upon their actions: and that this was one

1. Large, wide trousers.
2. The "unclean birds" may refer to the "unclean bird" that appears in Babylon after the fall of the city in Revelation 18.2. It is unclear what "seventy-seven" refers to; perhaps Jonson meant 1567, the year of D'Alva's invasion of the Protestant Netherlands.
3. Drugger was probably played by the actor Robert Arnim, who played the role of the Fool for the King's Men, Shakespeare's acting company and the company for *The Alchemist*.
4. Ben Jonson was reported to have worn just such a costume when playing the role of Hieronimo, the hero of Kyd's *Spanish Tragedy*.

I make no scruple.—But the holy synod[5]
Have been in prayer and meditation for it;
And 'tis reveal'd no less to them than me,
That casting of money is most lawful.
SUBTLE: True,
But here I cannot do it; if the house
Should chance to be suspected, all would out,
And we be lock'd up in the Tower for ever,
To make gold there for the state, never come out;[6]
And then are you defeated.
ANANIAS: I will tell
This to the elders and the weaker brethren,
That the whole company of the separation
May join in humble prayer again.
SUBTLE: And fasting.
ANANIAS: Yea, for some fitter place. The peace of mind
Rest with these walls!
SUBTLE: Thanks, courteous Ananias.
FACE: What did he come for?
SUBTLE: About casting dollars,
Presently out of hand. And so I told him,
A Spanish minister came here to spy,
Against the faithful—
FACE: I conceive.° Come, Subtle, *understand*
Thou art so down upon the least disaster!
How wouldst thou ha' done, if I had not helped thee out?
SUBTLE: I thank thee, Face, for the angry boy, i'faith.
FACE: Who would ha' look'd° it should ha' been that rascal, *expected*
Surly? He had dyed his beard and all. Well, sir,
Here's damask come to make you a suit.
SUBTLE: Where's Drugger?
FACE: He is gone to borrow me a Spanish habit;
I'll be the Count, now.
SUBTLE: But where's the widow?
FACE: Within, with my lord's sister: Madam Dol
Is entertaining her.
SUBTLE: By your favor, Face,
Now she is honest,° I will stand again. *chaste*
FACE: You will not offer it.
SUBTLE: Why?
FACE: Stand to your word,
Or—here comes Dol, she knows—
SUBTLE: Y'are tyrannous still.
[*Enter Dol, hastily*.]
FACE: Strict for my right.—How now, Dol? Hast told her,

5. Assembly of church people.
6. Edward II was said to have imprisoned the alchemist Raymond Lull in the Tower of London when he failed to produce gold; Elizabeth I punished Cornelius Lannoy for the same failure.

The Spanish Count will come?
DOL: Yes; but another is come,
You little look'd for!
FACE: Who is that?
DOL: Your master;
The master of the house.
SUBTLE: How, Dol!
FACE: She lies,
This is some trick. Come, leave your quiblins,° Dorothy. *tricks*
DOL: Look out, and see. [*Face goes to the window*.]
SUBTLE: Art thou in earnest?
DOL: 'Slight,
Forty o' the neighbors are about him, talking.
FACE: 'Tis he, by this good day.
DOL: 'Twill prove ill day
For some on us.
FACE: We are undone, and taken.
DOL: Lost, I'm afraid.
SUBTLE: You said he would not come,
While there died one a week within the liberties.[7]
FACE: No: 'twas within the walls.[8]
SUBTLE: Was't so! cry you mercy.
I thought the liberties. What shall we do now, Face?
FACE: Be silent: not a word, if he call or knock.
I'll into mine old shape again and meet him,
Of Jeremy, the butler. In the mean time,
Do you two pack up all the goods and purchase,
That we can carry in the two trunks. I'll keep him
Off for to-day, if I cannot longer: and then
At night, I'll ship you both away to Ratcliff,
Where we will meet to-morrow, and there we'll share.
Let Mammon's brass and pewter keep the cellar;
We'll have another time for that. But, Dol,
'Prythee go heat a little water quickly;
Subtle must shave me: all my Captain's beard
Must off, to make me appear smooth Jeremy.
You'll do it?
SUBTLE: Yes, I'll shave you, as well as I can.
FACE: And not cut my throat, but trim me?
SUBTLE: You shall see, sir. [*Exeunt*.]

ACT 5

Scene 1—*Before Lovewit's door*

[*Enter Lovewit, with several of the Neighbors*.]
LOVEWIT: Has there been such resort, say you?
1 NEIGHBOR: Daily, sir.

7. Many died of plague in the area of the Liberties, or Blackfriars, outside the city walls.

8. The walls of the City of London, one square mile in area.

2 NEIGHBOR: And nightly, too.
3 NEIGHBOR: Ay, some as brave as lords.
4 NEIGHBOR: Ladies and gentlewomen.
5 NEIGHBOR: Citizens' wives.
1 NEIGHBOR: And knights.
6 NEIGHBOR: In coaches.
2 NEIGHBOR: Yes, and oyster women.
1 NEIGHBOR: Beside other gallants.
3 NEIGHBOR: Sailors' wives.
4 NEIGHBOR: Tobacco men.
5 NEIGHBOR: Another Pimlico![9]
LOVEWIT: What should my knave advance.
To draw this company? He hung out no banners
Of a strange calf with five legs to be seen,
Or a huge lobster with six claws?
6 NEIGHBOR: No, sir.
3 NEIGHBOR: We had gone in then, sir.
LOVEWIT: He has no gift
Of teaching in the nose[1] that e'er I know of!
You saw no bills set up that promised cure
Of agues, or the tooth-ache?
2 NEIGHBOR: No such thing, sir.
LOVEWIT: Nor heard a drum struck for baboons or puppets?
5 NEIGHBOR: Neither, sir.
LOVEWIT: What device should he bring forth now?
I love a teeming wit as I love my nourishment:
'Pray God he have not kept such open house
That he hath sold my hangings, and my bedding!
I left him nothing else. If he have eat them,
A plague o' the moth, say I! Sure he has got
Some bawdy pictures to call all this ging°! *crowd*
The friar and the nun; or the new motion[2]
Of the knight's courser covering the parson's mare;
The boy of six year old with the great thing:° *penis*
Or 't may be, he has the fleas that run at tilt
Upon a table, or some dog to dance.
When saw you him?
1 NEIGHBOR: Who, sir, Jeremy!
2 NEIGHBOR: Jeremy butler?
We saw him not this month.
LOVEWIT: How!
4 NEIGHBOR: Not these five weeks, sir.
6 NEIGHBOR: These six weeks at the least.
LOVEWIT: You amaze me, neighbors!
5 NEIGHBOR: Sure, if your worship know not where he is,

9. Resort near Hogsden, which was known for its cakes and ales.

1. Preaching with the nasal intonation that was associated with the Puritans.

2. Puppet show and sexual intercourse.

He's slipt away.
6 NEIGHBOR: Pray God, he be not made away.
LOVEWIT: Ha! it's no time to question, then. [*Knocks at the door.*]
6 NEIGHBOR: About
Some three weeks since, I heard a doleful cry,
As I sat up a mending my wife's stockings.
LOVEWIT: 'Tis strange that none will answer! Didst thou hear
A cry, sayst thou?
6 NEIGHBOR: Yes, sir, like unto a man
That had been strangled an hour, and could not speak.
2 NEIGHBOR: I heard it too, just this day three weeks, at two o'clock
Next morning.
LOVEWIT: These be miracles, or you make them so!
A man an hour strangled, and could not speak,
And both you heard him cry?
3 NEIGHBOR: Yes, downward, sir.
LOVEWIT: Thou art a wise fellow. Give me thy hand, I pray thee.
What trade art thou on?
3 NEIGHBOR: A smith, an't please your worship.
LOVEWIT: A smith! Then lend me thy help to get this door open.
3 NEIGHBOR: That I will presently, sir, but fetch my tools— [*Exit.*]
1 NEIGHBOR: Sir, best to knock again, afore you break it.

Scene 2

LOVEWIT [*knocks again*]: I will.
[*Enter Face, in his butler's livery.*]
FACE: What mean you, sir?
1, 2, 4 NEIGHBOR: O, here's Jeremy!
FACE: Good sir, come from the door.
LOVEWIT: Why, what's the matter?
FACE: Yet farther, you are too near yet.
LOVEWIT: I' the name of wonder,
What means the fellow?
FACE: The house, sir, has been visited.
LOVEWIT: What, with the plague? Stand thou then farther.
FACE: No, sir,
I had it not.
LOVEWIT: Who had it then? I left
None else but thee i' the house.
FACE: Yes, sir, my fellow,
The cat that kept the buttery, had it on her
A week before I spied it; but I got her
Convey'd away in the night: and so I shut
The house up for a month—
LOVEWIT: How!
FACE: Purposing then, sir,
T' ha' burnt rose-vinegar, treacle, and tar,
And ha' made it sweet, that you shou'd ne'er have known it;

Because I knew the news would but afflict you, sir.
LOVEWIT: Breathe less, and farther off! Why this is stranger:
The neighbors tell me all here that the doors
Have still been open—
FACE: How, sir!
LOVEWIT: Gallants, men and women,
And of all sorts, tag-rag, been seen to flock here
In threaves,° these ten weeks, as to a second Hogsden, *crowds*
In days of Pimlico and Eye-bright.[3]
FACE: Sir.
Their wisdoms will not say so.
LOVEWIT: To-day they speak
Of coaches, and gallants; one in a French hood
Went in, they tell me; and another was seen
In a velvet gown at the window: divers more
Pass in and out.
FACE: They did pass through the doors then,
Or walls, I assure their eye-sights, and their spectacles:
For here, sir, are the keys, and here have been,
In this my pocket, now above twenty days:
And for before, I kept the fort alone there.
But that 'tis yet not deep in the afternoon,
I should believe my neighbours had seen double
Through the black-pot,° and made these apparitions! *beer mug*
For, on my faith to your worship, for these three weeks
And upwards the door has not been open'd.
LOVEWIT: Strange!
1 NEIGHBOR: Good faith, I think I saw a coach.
2 NEIGHBOR: And I too,
I'd have been sworn.
LOVEWIT: Do you but think it now?
And but one coach?
4 NEIGHBOR: We cannot tell, sir: Jeremy
Is a very honest fellow.
FACE: Did you see me at all?
1 NEIGHBOR: No; that we are sure on.
2 NEIGHBOR: I'll be sworn o' that.
LOVEWIT: Fine rogues to have your testimonies built on!
[*Re-enter Third Neighbor, with his tools*.]
3 NEIGHBOR: Is Jeremy come!
1 NEIGHBOR: O yes; you may leave your tools;
We were deceived, he says.
2 NEIGHBOR: He has had the keys;
And the door has been shut these three weeks.
3 NEIGHBOR: Like enough.

3. Pimlico and Eye-bright: resorts at Hogsden known for beer.

LOVEWIT: Peace and get hence, you changelings.[4]
[*Enter Surly and Mammon.*]
FACE [*aside*]: Surly come!
And Mammon made acquainted! They'll tell all.
How shall I beat them off? What shall I do?
Nothing's more wretched than a guilty conscience.[5]

Scene 3

SURLY: No, sir, he was a great physician. This,
It was no bawdy house, but a mere chancel![6]
You knew the lord and his sister.
MAMMON: Nay, good Surly—
SURLY: The happy word, Be Rich—
MAMMON: Play not the tyrant.—
SURLY: Should be to-day pronounced to all your friends.
And where be your andirons now? And your brass pots,
That should have been golden flagons, and great wedges?
MAMMON: Let me but breathe. What, they have shut their doors,
Methinks!
SURLY: Ay, now 'tis holiday with them.
MAMMON: Rogues, [*He and Surly knock.*]
Cozeners, impostors, bawds!
FACE: What mean you, sir!
MAMMON: To enter if we can.
FACE: Another man's house!
Here is the owner, sir: turn you to him,
And speak your business.
MAMMON: Are you, sir, the owner?
LOVEWIT: Yes, sir.
MAMMON: And are those knaves within your cheaters?
LOVEWIT: What knaves, what cheaters?
MAMMON: Subtle and his Lungs.
FACE: The gentleman is distracted, sir! No lungs,
Nor lights[7] have been seen here these three weeks, sir,
Within these doors, upon my word.
SURLY: Your word,
Groom arrogant?
FACE: Yes, sir, I am the housekeeper,
And know the keys have not been out of my hands.
SURLY: This is a new Face.[8]

4. People who change their opinion often, and idiots, whom the faeries exchanged for the human babies whom they snatched out of their cribs.
5. A translation of "Nihil est miserius quam animus hominis conscius" (Plautus, *Mostellaria* 544–45).
6. Nothing less than a church. The chancel is the eastern part of a church.
7. The lungs of animals were called "lights" when sold by butchers.
8. A "new Face," both another man like Face, and Face in the new disguise or role, of Jeremy the butler, in which Surly, ironically, does not appear to recognize him.

FACE: You do mistake the house, sir:
What sign was't at?
SURLY: You rascal! This is one
Of the confederacy. Come, let's get officers,
And force the door.
LOVEWIT: 'Pray you stay, gentlemen.
SURLY: No, sir, we'll come with warrant.
MAMMON: Ay, and then
We shall have your doors open. [*Exeunt Mammon and Surly*.]
LOVEWIT: What means this?
FACE: I cannot tell, sir.
1 NEIGHBOR: These are two o' the gallants
That we do think we saw.
FACE: Two of the fools!
You talk as idly as they. Good faith, sir,
I think the moon has crazed 'em all.—[*aside*] (O me,
[*Enter Kastril*.]
The angry boy come too! He'll make a noise,
And ne'er away till he have betray'd us all.)
KASTRIL [*knocking*]: What rogues, bawds, slaves, you'll open the door, anon!
Punk, cockatrice,° my suster! By this light *whore*
I'll fetch the marshal[9] to you. You are a whore
To keep your castle—
FACE: Who would you speak with, sir?
KASTRIL: The bawdy Doctor, and the cozening Captain,
And Puss my suster.
LOVEWIT: This is something, sure.
FACE: Upon my trust, the doors were never open, sir.
KASTRIL: I have heard all their tricks told me twice over,
By the fat knight and the lean gentleman.
LOVEWIT: Here comes another.
[*Enter Ananias and Tribulation*.]
FACE: Ananias too!
And his pastor!
TRIBULATION [*beating at the door*]: The doors are shut against us,
ANANIAS: Come forth, you seed of sulphur, sons of fire!
Your stench it is broke forth; abomination
Is in the house.
KASTRIL: Ay, my suster's there.
ANANIAS: The place,
It is become a cage of unclean birds.
KASTRIL: Yes, I will fetch the scavenger, and the constable.
TRIBULATION: You shall do well.
ANANIAS: We'll join to weed them out.
KASTRIL: You will not come then, punk device,[1] my sister!
ANANIAS: Call her not sister; she's a harlot verily.

9. Court officer in charge of prisons.

1. "Punk device," complete whore.

KASTRIL: I'll raise the street.
LOVEWIT: Good gentleman, a word.
ANANIAS: Satan avoid, and hinder not our zeal!
[*Exeunt Ananias, Tribulation, and Kastril.*]
LOVEWIT: The world's turn'd Bedlam.
FACE: These are all broke loose,
Out of St. Katherine's, where they use to keep
The better sort of mad-folks.
1 NEIGHBOR: All these persons
We saw go in and out here.
2 NEIGHBOR: Yes, indeed, sir.
3 NEIGHBOR: These were the parties.
FACE: Peace, you drunkards! Sir.
I wonder at it: please you to give me leave
To touch the door, I'll try an the lock be chang'd.
LOVEWIT: It mazes° me! *bewilders*
FACE [*goes to the door*]: Good faith, sir, I believe
There's no such thing: 'tis all *deceptio visus*[2]—
[*aside*] Would I could get him away.
DAPPER [*within*]: Master Captain! Master Doctor!
LOVEWIT [*aside*]: Who's that?
FACE: Our clerk within, that I forgot! [*to Lovewit*] I know not, sir.
DAPPER [*within*]: For God's sake, when will her Grace be at leisure?
FACE: Ha!
Illusions, some spirit o' the air!—[*aside.*] His gag is melted,
And now he sets out the throat.
DAPPER [*within*]: I am almost stifled—
FACE [*aside*]: Would you were altogether.
LOVEWIT: 'Tis in the house.
Ha! list.
FACE: Believe it, sir, in the air.
LOVEWIT: Peace, you.
DAPPER [*within*]: Mine aunt's Grace does not use me well.
SUBTLE [*within*]: You fool,
Peace, you'll mar all.
FACE [*speaks through the key-hole, while Lovewit advances to the door unobserved*]:
Or you will else, you rogue.
LOVEWIT: O, is it so? Then you converse with spirits!—
Come, sir. No more of your tricks, good Jeremy,
The truth, the shortest way.
FACE: Dismiss this rabble, sir.—
What shall I do? I am catch'd. [*Aside.*]
LOVEWIT: Good neighbors,
I thank you all. You may depart. [*Exeunt Neighbors.*]—Come, sir,
You know that I am an indulgent master;
And therefore conceal nothing. What's your medicine,

2. Optical illusion.

To draw so many several sorts of wild fowl?
FACE: Sir, you were wont to affect mirth and wit—
But here's no place to talk on't in the street.
Give me but leave to make the best of my fortune,
And only pardon me the abuse of your house:
It's all I beg. I'll help you to a widow,
In recompense, that you shall give me thanks for,
Will make you seven years younger, and a rich one.
'Tis but your putting on a Spanish cloak:
I have her within. You need not fear the house;
It was not visited.
LOVEWIT: But by me, who came
Sooner than you expected.
FACE: It is true, sir.
'Pray you forgive me.
LOVEWIT: Well: let's see your widow. [*Exeunt.*]

Scene 4—*A room in the same*

[*Enter Subtle, leading in Dapper, with his eyes bound as before.*]
SUBTLE: How! Ha' you eaten your gag?
DAPPER: Yes faith, it crumbled
Away in my mouth.
SUBTLE: You ha' spoil'd all then.
DAPPER: No!
I hope my aunt of Fairy will forgive me.
SUBTLE: Your aunt's a gracious lady; but in troth
You were to blame.
DAPPER: The fume did overcome me,
And I did do't to stay my stomach. 'Pray you
So satisfy her Grace.
[*Enter Face, in his uniform.*]
Here comes the Captain
FACE: How now! Is his mouth down?° *open*
SUBTLE: Ay, he has spoken!
FACE: A pox, I heard him, and you too.—He's undone then.—
I have been fain to say, the house is haunted
With spirits, to keep churl° back. *country bumpkin*
SUBTLE: And hast thou done it?
FACE: Sure, for this night.
SUBTLE: Why, then triumph and sing
Of Face so famous, the precious king
Of present wits.
FACE: Did you not hear the coil° *disturbance*
About the door?
SUBTLE: Yes, and I dwindled with it.
FACE: Show him his aunt, and let him be dispatch'd:
I'll send her to you. [*Exit Face.*]
SUBTLE: Well, sir, your aunt her Grace
Will give you audience presently,° on my suit, *at once*

And the Captain's word that you did not eat your gag
In any contempt of her highness. [*Unbinds his eyes*.]
DAPPER: Not I, in troth, sir.
[*Enter Dol, like the Queen of Fairy*.]
SUBTLE: Here she is come. Down o' your knees and wriggle:
She has a stately presence. [*Dapper kneels, and shuffles towards her*.]
Good! Yet nearer,
And bid, God save you!
DAPPER: Madam!
SUBTLE: And your aunt.
DAPPER: And my most gracious aunt, God save your Grace.
DOL: Nephew, we thought to have been angry with you;
But that sweet face of yours hath turn'd the tide,
And made it flow with joy, that ebb'd of love.
Arise, and touch our velvet gown.
SUBTLE: The skirts,
And kiss 'em. So!
DOL: Let me now stroke that head.
Much, nephew, shall thou win, much shall thou spend,
Much shall thou give away, much shall thou lend.
SUBTLE [*aside*]: Ay, much! indeed. [*aloud*] Why do you not thank her Grace?
DAPPER: I cannot speak for joy.
SUBTLE: See the kind wretch!
Your Grace's kinsman right.
DOL: Give me the bird.[3]
Here is your fly in a purse, about your neck, cousin;
Wear it, and feed it about this day sev'n-night,
On your right wrist—
SUBTLE: Open a vein with a pin.
And let it suck but once a week; till then,
You must not look on't.
DOL: No: and kinsman,
Bear yourself worthy of the blood you come on.[4]
SUBTLE: Her grace would have you eat no more Woolsack pies.
Nor Dagger frumety.[5]
DOL: Nor break his fast
In Heaven and Hell.[6]
SUBTLE: She's with you everywhere!
Nor play with costarmongers, at mum-chance, tray-trip,[7]
God make you rich;[8] (when as your aunt has done it); but keep
The gallant'st company, and the best games—
DAPPER: Yes, sir.
SUBTLE: Gleek and primero[9]: and what you get, be true to us.
DAPPER: By this hand, I will.

3. Familiar spirit, the "fly."
4. Are born from.
5. Woolsack and Dagger were London inns; "frumety," wheat boiled in milk sweetened with cinnamon and sugar.
6. Heaven and Hell are taverns near Westminster.
7. Dice games.
8. A type of backgammon.
9. Card games.

SUBTLE: You may bring's a thousand pound
Before to-morrow night, if but three thousand
Be stirring,[1] an you will.
DAPPER: I swear I will then.
SUBTLE: Your fly will learn you all games.
FACE [*within*]: Have you done there?
SUBTLE: Your Grace will command him no more duties?
DOL: No:
But come, and see me often. I may chance
To leave him three or four hundred chests of treasure,
And some twelve thousand acres of Fairyland,
If he game well and comely with good gamesters.
SUBTLE: There's a kind aunt! Kiss her departing part.—
But you must sell your forty mark a year, now.
DAPPER: Ay, sir, I mean.
SUBTLE: Or, give't away; pox on't!
DAPPER: I'll give't mine aunt: I'll go and fetch the writings. [*Exit.*]
SUBTLE: 'Tis well—away!
[*Re-enter Face.*]
FACE: Where's Subtle?
SUBTLE: Here: what news?
FACE: Drugger is at the door, go take his suit,
And bid him fetch a parson, presently;
Say, he shall marry the widow. Thou shalt spend
A hundred pound by the service! [*Exit Subtle.*] Now, queen Dol,
Have you pack'd up all?
DOL: Yes.
FACE: And how do you like
The Lady Pliant?
DOL: A good dull innocent.
[*Re-enter Subtle.*]
SUBTLE: Here's your Hieronimo's cloak and hat.
FACE: Give me 'em.
SUBTLE: And the ruff too?
FACE: Yes; I'll come to you presently. [*Exit.*]
SUBTLE: Now he is gone about his project, Dol,
I told you of, for the widow.
DOL: 'Tis direct
Against our articles.
SUBTLE: Well, we will fit him, wench.
Hast thou gull'd her of her jewels or her bracelets?
DOL: No; but I will do't.
SUBTLE: Soon at night, my Dolly,
When we are shipp'd, and all our goods aboard,
Eastward for Ratcliff; we will turn our course
To Brainford, westward, if thou sayst the word,
And take our leaves of this o'er-weening rascal,

1. If there are only 3,000 pounds to be gambled for.

This peremptory Face.
DOL: Content, I'm weary of him.
SUBTLE: Thou'st cause, when the slave will run a wiving, Dol,
Against the instrument that was drawn between us.
DOL: I'll pluck his bird as bare as I can.
SUBTLE: Yes, tell her,
She must by any means address some present
To the cunning man, make him amends for wronging
His art with her suspicion; send a ring
Or chain of pearl; she will be tortured else
Extremely in her sleep, say, and have strange things
Come to her. Wilt thou?
DOL: Yes.
SUBTLE: My fine flitter-mouse,° *bat*
My bird o' the night! We'll tickle it at the Pigeons,[2]
When we have all, and may unlock the trunks,
And say, this's mine, and thine; and thine, and mine. [*They kiss.*]
[*Re-enter Face.*]
FACE: What now! a billing?
SUBTLE: Yes, a little exalted
In the good passage of our stock-affairs.[3]
FACE: Drugger has brought his parson; take him in, Subtle,
And send Nab back again to wash his face,
SUBTLE: I will: and shave himself. [*Exit.*]
FACE: If you can get him.
DOL: You are hot upon it, Face, whate'er it is!
FACE: A trick that Dol shall spend ten pound a month by.
[*Re-enter Subtle.*]
Is he gone?
SUBTLE: The chaplain waits you in the hall, sir.
FACE: I'll go bestow him. [*Exit.*]
DOL: He'll now marry her, instantly.
SUBTLE: He cannot yet, he is not ready. Dear Dol,
Cozen her of all thou canst. To deceive him
Is no deceit, but justice, that would break
Such an inextricable tie as ours was.
DOL: Let me alone to fit him.
[*Re-enter Face.*]
FACE: Come, my venturers,
You have pack'd up all? where be the trunks? Bring forth.
SUBTLE: Here.
FACE: Let us see 'em. Where's the money?
SUBTLE: Here,
In this.
FACE: Mammon's ten pound; eight score before:
The brethren's money, this. Drugger's and Dapper's.

2. To "tickle it," have fun, with sexual innuendo; the Three Pigeons in Brentford marketplace.

3. Joint capital of the company.

What paper's that?
DOL: The jewel of the waiting-maid's,
That stole it from her lady, to know certain—
FACE: If she should have precedence of her mistress?
DOL: Yes.
FACE: What box is that?
SUBTLE: The fish-wives' rings, I think,
And the ale-wives' single money.[4] Is't not, Dol?
DOL: Yes; and the whistle that the sailor's wife
Brought you to know an her husband were with Ward.[5]
FACE: We'll wet it to-morrow; and our silver-beakers
And tavern cups. Where be the French petticoats,
And girdles and hangers?[6]
SUBTLE: Here, in the trunk,
And the bolts of lawn.
FACE: Is Drugger's damask there?
And the tobacco?
SUBTLE: Yes.
FACE: Give me the keys.
DOL: Why you the keys?
SUBTLE: No matter, Dol; because
We shall not open them before he comes.
FACE: 'Tis true, you shall not open them, indeed;
Nor have them forth, do you see? Not forth, Dol.
DOL: No?
FACE: No, my smock rampant.[7] The right is, my master
Knows all, has pardon'd me, and he will keep them;
Doctor, 'tis true—you look—for all your figures:
I sent for him indeed. Wherefore, good partners,
Both he and she be satisfied; for here
Determines° the indenture tripartite *ends*
'Twixt Subtle, Dol, and Face. All I can do
Is to help you over the wall, o' the back-side,
Or lend you a sheet to save your velvet gown, Dol.
Here will be officers presently, bethink you
Of some course suddenly to 'scape the dock:
For thither you will come else. [*Loud knocking*] Hark you, thunder.
SUBTLE: You are a precious fiend!
OFFICER [*without*]: Open the door.
FACE: Dol, I am sorry for thee, i'faith; but hear'st thou?
It shall go hard but I will place thee somewhere:
Thou shalt have my letter to Mistress Amo[8]—
DOL: Hang you!

4. Small change.
5. A well-known pirate.
6. Hangers: loops on belts from which swords were hung.
7. Wild whore, applying the image of a rampant beast, standing on its hind legs and attacking, to Dol's sexuality.
8. "Mistress Amo" and "Madam Caesarean" were stock names for brothel keepers.

FACE: Or Madam Caesarean.
DOL: Pox upon you, rogue,
Would I had but time to beat thee!
FACE: Subtle,
Let's know where you set up next; I will send you
A customer now and then, for old acquaintance:
What new course ha' you?
SUBTLE: Rogue, I'll hang myself;
That I may walk a greater devil than thou,
And haunt thee in the flock-bed and the buttery.[9] [*Exeunt*.]

Scene 5—*An outer room in the same*

[*Enter Lovewit in the Spanish dress, with the Parson*.]
[*Loud knocking at the door*.]
LOVEWIT: What do you mean, my masters?
MAMMON [*without*]: Open your door,
Cheaters, bawds, conjurers.
OFFICER [*without*]: Or we will break it open.
LOVEWIT: What warrant have you?
OFFICER [*without*]: Warrant enough, sir, doubt not,
If you'll not open it.
LOVEWIT: Is there an officer, there?
OFFICER [*without*]: Yes, two or three for failing.
LOVEWIT: Have but patience,
And I will open it straight.
[*Enter Face, as butler*.]
FACE: Sir, ha' you done?
Is it a marriage? Perfect?
LOVEWIT: Yes, my brain.
FACE: Off with your ruff and cloak then; be yourself, sir.
SURLY [*without*]: Down with the door.
KASTRIL [*without*]: 'Slight, ding° it open. *break*
LOVEWIT [*opening the door*]: Hold,
Hold, gentlemen, what means this violence;
[*Mammon, Surly, Kastril, Ananias, Tribulation, and Officers, rush in*.]
MAMMON: Where is this collier?[1]
SURLY: And my Captain Face?
MAMMON: These day owls.
SURLY: That are birding in men's purses.
MAMMON: Madam Suppository.[2]
KASTRIL: Doxy, my suster.
ANANIAS: Locusts
Of the foul pit.

9. Flock-bed: mattress stuffed with cheap material; buttery: eating place.
1. The collier, or coal worker, like the alchemist, was associated with darkness and the devil.
2. "Suppository," refers to Dol's occupation as a prostitute but also to her fraudulent, or suppositious, study of medicine.

TRIBULATION: Profane as Bel and the Dragon.[3]
ANANIAS: Worse than the grasshoppers, or the lice of Egypt.[4]
LOVEWIT: Good gentlemen, hear me. Are you officers,
And cannot stay this violence?
1 OFFICER: Keep the peace.
LOVEWIT: Gentlemen, what is the matter? whom do you seek?
MAMMON: The chemical cozener.
SURLY: And the Captain Pander.
KASTRIL: The nun my suster.[5]
MAMMON: Madam Rabbi.[6]
ANANIAS: Scorpions,
And caterpillars.
LOVEWIT: Fewer at once, I pray you.
2 OFFICER: One after another, gentlemen, I charge you,
By virtue of my staff.
ANANIAS: They are the vessels
Of pride, lust, and the cart.
LOVEWIT: Good zeal, lie still
A little while.
TRIBULATION: Peace, Deacon Ananias.
LOVEWIT: The house is mine here, and the doors are open;
If there be any such persons as you seek for,
Use your authority, search on o' God's name.
I am but newly come to town, and finding
This tumult 'bout my door, to tell you true,
It somewhat mazed me; till my man, here, fearing
My more displeasure, told me he had done
Somewhat an insolent part, let out my house
(Belike, presuming on my known aversion
From any air o' the town while there was sickness,)
To a doctor and a captain: who, what they are
Or where they be, he knows not.
MAMMON: Are they gone?
LOVEWIT: You may go in and search, sir. [*Mammon, Ananias, and Tribulation go in.*]
Here, I find
The empty walls worse than I left them, smok'd.
A few crack'd pots, and glasses, and a furnace:
The ceiling fill'd with poesies of the candle,[7]
And madam with a dildo writ o' the walls:[8]
Only one gentlewoman, I met here,
That is within, that said she was a widow—
KASTRIL: Ay, that's my suster; I'll go thump her. Where is she?
[*Goes in.*]

3. Idols worshipped by the Babylonians referred to in one of the apocryphal books of the Old Testament.
4. Two of the plagues inflicted upon the Egyptians in Exodus 7–12.
5. Ironic term for a prostitute.
6. A reference to Dol's Puritan rantings in 4.5.1–32.
7. Words written with candle smoke.
8. Drawing of a woman playing with a dildo (phallus) on the walls.

LOVEWIT: And should have married a Spanish count, but he,
When he came to't, neglected her so grossly,
That I, a widower, am gone through° with her. *married*
SURLY: How! have I lost her then?
LOVEWIT: Were you the Don, sir?
Good faith, now, she does blame y' extremely, and says
You swore, and told her you had taken the pains
To dye your beard, and umber o'er your face,
Borrowed a suit, and ruff, all for her love;
And then did nothing. What an oversight,
And want of putting forward, sir, was this!
Well fare an old harquebusier,[9] yet,
Could prime his powder, and give fire, and hit,
All in a twinkling!

[*Re-enter Mammon.*]

MAMMON: The whole nest are fled!
LOVEWIT: What sort of birds were they?
MAMMON: A kind of choughs,[1]
Or thievish daws, sir, that have pick'd my purse
Of eight score and ten pounds within these five weeks,
Beside my first materials; and my goods,
That lie in the cellar, which I am glad they have left,
I may have home yet.
LOVEWIT: Think you so, sir?
MAMMON: Ay.
LOVEWIT: By order of law, sir, but not otherwise.
MAMMON: Not mine own stuff!
LOVEWIT: Sir, I can take no knowledge
That they are yours, but by public means.
If you can bring certificate that you were gull'd of 'em,
Or any formal writ out of a court
That you did cozen yourself, I will not hold them.
MAMMON: I'll rather lose 'em.
LOVEWIT: That you shall not, sir,
By me, in troth. Upon these terms, they are yours.
What! should they have been, sir, turn'd into gold, all?
MAMMON: No,
I cannot tell—It may be they should—What then?
LOVEWIT: What a great loss in hope have you sustain'd!
MAMMON: Not I, the commonwealth has.
FACE: Ay, he would ha' built
The city new; and made a ditch about it.
Of silver, should have run with cream from Hogsden;
That, every Sunday, in Moorfields, the younkers,
And tits and tom-boys[2] should have fed on, gratis.
MAMMON: I will go mount a turnip-cart, and preach

9. A soldier armed with a harquebus, or handgun.
1. Pronounced "chuffs," type of crows.
2. Younkers, and tits and tom-boys: adolescent boys and girls.

The end of the world, within these two months, Surly,
What! in a dream?
SURLY: Must I needs cheat myself,
With that same foolish vice of honesty!
Come, let us go and hearken out the rogues:
That Face I'll mark for mine, if e'er I meet him.
FACE: If I can hear of him, sir, I'll bring you word,
Unto your lodging; for in troth, they were strangers
To me, I thought them honest as myself, sir.
[*Exeunt Mammon and Surly*.]
[*Re-enter Ananias and Tribulation*.]
TRIBULATION: 'Tis well, the saints shall not lose all yet. Go,
And get some carts—
LOVEWIT: For what, my zealous friends?
ANANIAS: To bear away the portion of the righteous
Out of this den of thieves.
LOVEWIT: What is that portion?
ANANIAS: The goods sometimes the orphans', that the brethren
Bought with their silver pence.
LOVEWIT: What, those i' the cellar,
The knight sir Mammon claims?
ANANIAS: I do defy
The wicked Mammon, so do all the brethren,
Thou profane man! I ask thee with what conscience
Thou canst advance that idol against us,
That have the seal?[3] Were not the shillings number'd,
That made the pounds; were not the pounds told out,
Upon the second day of the fourth week,
In the eighth month, upon the table dormant,[4]
The year of the last patience of the saints,
Six hundred and ten?[5]
LOVEWIT: Mine earnest vehement botcher,
And deacon also, I cannot dispute with you:
But if you get you not away the sooner,
I shall confute you with a cudgel.
ANANIAS: Sir!
TRIBULATION: Be patient, Ananias.
ANANIAS: I am strong,
And will stand up, well girt, against an host
That threaten Gad in exile.[6]
LOVEWIT: I shall send you
To Amsterdam, to your cellar.
ANANIAS: I will pray there,
Against thy house: may dogs defile thy walls,

3. Those with the seal are God's chosen (Revelation 9.4).
4. Permanent side-table.
5. I.e., 1610. The "year of the last patience of the saints" refers to the millennium, when the end of the world was supposed to occur.
6. An allegorical reference to the exiled Anabaptists; see Genesis 49.19.

And wasps and hornets breed beneath thy roof,
This seat of falsehood, and this cave of cozenage!
[*Exeunt Ananias and Tribulation.*]

[*Enter Drugger.*]

LOVEWIT: Another too?

DRUGGER: Not I, sir, I am no brother.

LOVEWIT [*beats him*]: Away, you Harry Nicholas![7] do you talk?
[*Exit Drugger.*]

FACE: No, this was Abel Drugger. Good sir, go.
[*To the Parson.*]
And satisfy him; tell him all is done:
He staid too long a washing of his face.
The Doctor, he shall hear of him at Westchester,
And of the Captain, tell him, at Yarmouth, or
Some good port-town else, lying for a wind. [*Exit Parson.*]
If you can get off the angry child, now, sir—

[*Enter Kastril, dragging in his sister.*]

KASTRIL: Come on, you ewe, you have match'd most sweetly, ha' you not?
Did not I say, I would never ha' you tupp'd° *mated with*
But by a dubb'd boy,° to make you a lady-tom? *knight*
'Slight, you are a mammet! O, I could touse you, now.[8]
Death, mun' you marry, with a pox!

LOVEWIT: You lie, boy;
As sound as you; and I'm aforehand with you.

KASTRIL: Anon!

LOVEWIT: Come, will you quarrel? I will feize° you, sirrah; *beat*
Why do you not buckle to your tools?

KASTRIL: God's light,
This is a fine old boy as e'er I saw!

LOVEWIT: What, do you change your copy[9] now? Proceed,
Here stands my dove: stoop at her, if you dare.[1]

KASTRIL: 'Slight, I must love him! I cannot choose, i' faith,
An I should be hang'd for't! Suster, I protest,
I honor thee for this match.

LOVEWIT: O, do you so, sir?

KASTRIL: Yes, an thou canst take tobacco and drink, old boy,
I'll give her five hundred pound more to her marriage,
Than her own state.

LOVEWIT: Fill a pipe-full, Jeremy.

FACE: Yes; but go in and take it, sir.

LOVEWIT: We will—
I will be ruled by thee in any thing. Jeremy.

KASTRIL: 'Slight, thou art not hide-bound, thou art a jovy° boy! *jovial*
Come, let us in. I pray thee, and take our whiffs.

7. Hendrick Niclaes was an Anabaptist and leader of the Family of Love, a sect outlawed by Elizabeth I in 1580.
8. Mammet: puppet; touse: beat, tousle.
9. Change your tune.
1. The "dove" may be Dame Pliant as well as his sword; stoop at her: attack her, a term from falconry. Kastril's name comes from kestrel, a small hawk.

LOVEWIT: Whiff in with your sister, brother boy. [*Exeunt Kastril and Dame Pliant.*]
That master
That had received such happiness by a servant,
In such a widow, and with so much wealth,
Were very ungrateful, if he would not be
A little indulgent to that servant's wit,
And help his fortune, though with some small strain
Of his own candour. [*advancing*]—Therefore, gentlemen,
And kind spectators, if I have outstript
An old man's gravity, or strict canon,[2] think
What a young wife and a good brain may do;
Stretch age's truth sometimes, and crack it too.
Speak for thy self, knave.

FACE: So I will. sir. [*advancing to the front of the stage*]
Gentlemen,
My part a little fell in this last scene,
Yet 'twas decorum.[3] And though I am clean
Got off from Subtle, Surly, Mammon, Dol,
Hot Ananias, Dapper, Drugger, all
With whom I traded: yet I put my self
On you, that are my country:[4] and this pelf° *loot*
Which I have got, if you do quit° me, rests *acquit*
To feast you often, and invite new guests.

[*Exeunt.*]

On Something, That Walks Somewhere[1]

At court I met it, in clothes brave° enough *showy*
To be a courtier, and looks grave enough
To seem a statesman. As I near it came,
It made me a great face; I asked the name.
"A lord," it cried, "buried in flesh, and blood,
And such from whom let no man hope least good,
For I will do none; and as little ill,
For I will dare none." Good lord, walk dead still.

On My First Daughter[1]

Here lies to each her parents' ruth,° *grief*
Mary, the daughter of their youth;
Yet, all heaven's gifts, being heaven's due,
It makes the father less to rue.
At six months' end, she parted hence
With safety of her innocence;

2. Rule of behavior.
3. Decorum is the sense of consistency of character. Lovewit has just defended his own behavior that was inconsistent with the character of an old man.
4. Appeal to my countrymen's judgment, as to a jury.

1. This and the following four poems were all first printed in the collected *Works* of 1616 under the heading "Epigrams." An epigram is a short, witty poem of invective or satire. Jonson's "Epigrams" include epitaphs, poems of praise, and verse letters.
1. Probably written in the late 1590s.

Whose soul heaven's Queen (whose name she bears),
In comfort of her mother's tears,
Hath placed amongst her virgin-train;
Where, while that severed doth remain,
This grave partakes the fleshly birth;[2]
Which cover lightly, gentle earth.

To John Donne

Donne, the delight of Phoebus,[1] and each Muse,
Who, to thy one, all other brains refuse;[2]
Whose every work, of thy most early wit
Came forth example, and remains so, yet;
Longer a-knowing than most wits do live;
And which no affection praise enough can give!
To it,[3] thy language, letters, arts, best life,
Which might with half mankind maintain a strife;
All which I meant to praise, and, yet, I would,
But leave, because I cannot as I should.

On My First Son[1]

Farewell, thou child of my right hand,[2] and joy;
My sin was too much hope of thee, loved boy.
Seven years thou wert lent to me, and I thee pay,
Exacted by thy fate, on the just day.
O, could I lose all father, now![3] For why
Will man lament the state he should envy?
To have so soon 'scaped world's and flesh's rage,
And, if no other misery, yet age?
Rest in soft peace, and, asked, say, "Here doth lie
Ben Jonson his best piece of poetry."
For whose sake, henceforth, all his vows be such,
As what he loves may never like too much.[4]

Inviting a Friend to Supper[1]

Tonight, grave sir, both my poor house and I
Do equally desire your company:
Not that we think us worthy such a guest,
But that your worth will dignify our feast
With those that come; whose grace may make that seem
Something, which else could hope for no esteem.

2. While the soul is in heaven, the grave holds the body.
1. God of poetry.
2. The Muses give the inspiration to your brain that they deny to others.
3. In addition to your wit.
1. Benjamin, who died of the plague on his birthday in 1603.
2. In Hebrew, Benjamin means "son of the right hand; dexterous, fortunate."
3. Let go of fatherly feeling.
4. "If you wish . . . to beware of sorrows that gnaw the heart, to no man make yourself too much a comrade" (Martial 12.34, lines 8–11).
1. Based on three poems of invitation by the Roman poet Martial, 11.52, 5.78, and 10.48.

It is the fair acceptance, Sir, creates
The entertainment perfect, not the cates.° *food*
Yet shall you have, to rectify your palate,
An olive, capers, or some better salad
Ushering the mutton; with a short-legged hen
If we can get her, full of eggs, and then
Lemons, and wine for sauce: to these, a coney° *rabbit*
Is not to be despaired of, for our money;
And though fowl now be scarce, yet there are clerks,° *scholars*
The sky not falling, think we may have larks.
I'll tell you of more, and lie, so you will come:
Of partridge, pheasant, woodcock, of which some
May yet be there; and godwit, if we can;
Knat, rail, and ruff,° too. Howsoe'er, my man *gamebirds*
Shall read a piece of Virgil, Tacitus,
Livy, or of some better book to us,
Of which we'll speak our minds, amidst our meat;
And I'll profess no verses to repeat;
To this, if aught appear, which I not know of,
That will the pastry, not my paper, show of.[2]
Digestive cheese and fruit there sure will be;
But that, which most doth take my muse and me,
Is a pure cup of rich Canary wine,
Which is the Mermaid's,[3] now, but shall be mine:
Of which had Horace, or Anacreon tasted,
Their lives, as do their lines, till now had lasted.[4]
Tobacco, nectar, or the Thespian spring
Are all but Luther's beer to this I sing.[5]
Of this we will sup free, but moderately,
And we will have no Poley, or Parrot by;[6]
Nor shall our cups make any guilty men,
But, at our parting, we will be, as when
We innocently met. No simple word
That shall be uttered at our mirthful board
Shall make us sad next morning, or affright
The liberty, that we'll enjoy tonight.

To Penshurst[1]

Thou art not, Penshurst, built to envious show
Of touch,° or marble; nor canst boast a row *black marble*
Of polished pillars, or a roof of gold;

2. Add to this that if there is any paper, it will only be that used to keep the pastry from sticking to the pan.
3. A famous tavern in Cheapside, London.
4. Horace praised wine in Latin verse, as did Anacreon in Greek.
5. The Thespian spring, inspiration of poetry, and all these things are but Luther's beer in comparison with Canary.
6. Government spies; talkative birds.

1. First published in the 1616 *Works* in *The Forest*, a title inspired by the Latin *silva* (timber), suggesting raw materials to be worked, used by classical authors for an improvised collection of poems. Penshurst was the Sidney family's house in Kent since 1552, the "great lord" (line 91) of which was Robert Sidney, Baron Sidney of Penshurst and Viscount of Lille, younger brother of Sir Philip Sidney.

Thou hast no lantern,° whereof tales are told, *turret*
Or stair, or courts; but stand'st an ancient pile,[2]
And these grudged at, art reverenced the while.
Thou joy'st in better marks, of soil, of air,
Of wood, of water; therein thou art fair.
Thou hast thy walks for health, as well as sport:
Thy mount to which the dryads° do resort, *wood nymphs*
Where Pan, and Bacchus their high feasts have made,[3]
Beneath the broad beech and the chestnut shade;
That taller tree, which of a nut was set
At his great birth, where all the Muses met.
There, in the writhèd bark, are cut the names
Of many a sylvan,° taken with his flames; *wood sprite*
And thence, the ruddy satyrs oft provoke
The lighter fauns, to reach thy Lady's oak.[4]
Thy copse,° too, named of Gamage, thou hast there, *a small wood*
That never fails to serve thee seasoned deer
When thou wouldst feast, or exercise thy friends.
The lower land, that to the river bends,
Thy sheep, thy bullocks, kine° and calves do feed; *cows*
The middle grounds thy mares and horses breed.
Each bank doth yield thee conies,° and the tops *rabbits*
Fertile of wood, Ashour and Sydney's copse,
To crown thy open table, doth provide
The purpled pheasant with the speckled side;
The painted partridge lies in every field,
And, for thy mess, is willing to be killed.
And if the high-swoll'n Medway[5] fail thy dish,
Thou hast thy ponds, that pay thee tribute fish:
Fat, agèd carps, that run into thy net.
And pikes, now weary their own kind to eat,
As loath, the second draught, or cast to stay,
Officiously, at first, themselves betray;
Bright eels, that emulate them, and leap on land
Before the fisher, or into his hand.
Then hath thy orchard fruit, thy garden flowers,
Fresh as the air, and new as are the hours.
The early cherry, with the later plum,
Fig, grape, and quince, each in his time doth come;
The blushing apricot and woolly peach
Hang on thy walls, that every child may reach.
And though thy walls be of the country stone,
They're reared with no man's ruin, no man's groan;
There's none, that dwell about them, wish them down;
But all come in, the farmer, and the clown,° *peasant*

2. The castle was built in 1340.
3. Pan was the god of forest, field, and pasture; Bacchus was the god of wine.
4. In Greek mythology the satyr with a man's body and a goat's legs was devoted to lechery. Robert Sidney's wife Barbara Gamage was said to have given birth under this oak.
5. The local river.

And no one empty-handed, to salute
  Thy lord and lady, though they have no suit.
Some bring a capon, some a rural cake,
  Some nuts, some apples; some that think they make
The better cheeses, bring'em; or else send
  By their ripe daughters, whom they would commend
This way to husbands; and whose baskets bear
  An emblem of themselves in plum, or pear.
But what can this (more than express their love)
  Add to thy free provisions, far above
The need of such? whose liberal board doth flow
  With all that hospitality doth know!
Where comes no guest, but is allowed to eat
  Without his fear, and of thy lord's own meat;
Where the same beer, and bread, and self-same wine
  That is his lordship's shall be also mine,
And I not fain to sit (as some this day
  At great men's tables) and yet dine away.
Here no man tells my cups; nor, standing by,
  A waiter, doth my gluttony envy,
But gives me what I call, and lets me eat;
  He knows below he shall find plenty of meat,
Thy tables hoard not up for the next day.
  Nor, when I take my lodging, need I pray
For fire, or lights, or livery:° all is there, *provisions, food*
  As if thou then wert mine, or I reigned here;
There's nothing I can wish, for which I stay.
  That found King James, when, hunting late this way
With his brave son, the Prince, they saw thy fires
  Shine bright on every hearth as the desires
Of thy Penates[6] had been set on flame
  To entertain them; or the country came,
With all their zeal, to warm their welcome here.
  What (great, I will not say, but) sudden cheer
Didst thou, then, make 'em! and what praise was heaped
  On thy good lady, then, who therein reaped
The just reward of her high housewifery;
  To have her linen, plate, and all things nigh,
When she was far, and not a room, but dressed
  As if it had expected such a guest!
These, Penshurst, are thy praise, and yet not all.
  Thy lady's noble, fruitful, chaste withall.
His children thy great lord may call his own,
  A fortune, in this age, but rarely known.
They are, and have been, taught religion; thence
  Their gentler spirits have sucked innocence.
Each morn and even, they are taught to pray,

6. Household gods.

With the whole household, and may every day
Read in their virtuous parents' noble parts
The mysteries of manners, arms, and arts.
Now, Penshurst, they that will proportion° thee *compare*
With other edifices, when they see
Those proud, ambitious heaps, and nothing else,
May say, their lords have built, but thy lord dwells.

Song to Celia

Drink to me only with thine eyes,
And I will pledge with mine;
Or leave a kiss but in the cup,
And I'll not look for wine.
The thirst that from the soul doth rise
Doth ask a drink divine;
But might I of Jove's nectar sup,
I would not change for thine.
I sent thee late a rosy wreath,
Not so much honoring thee
As giving it a hope that there
It could not withered be.
But thou thereon didst only breathe,
And sent'st it back on me;
Since when it grows, and smells, I swear,
Not of itself, but thee.

Queen and Huntress[1]

Queen and huntress, chaste and fair,
Now the sun is laid to sleep,
Seated in thy silver chair,
State in wonted manner keep;
Hesperus° entreats thy light, *the evening star*
Goddess excellently bright.

Earth, let not thy envious shade
Dare itself to interpose;
Cynthia's shining orb was made
Heaven to clear, when day did close.
Bless us then with wishèd sight,
Goddess excellently bright.

Lay thy bow of pearl apart,
And thy crystal-shining quiver;
Give unto the flying hart
Space to breathe, how short soever.
Thou that mak'st a day of night,
Goddess excellently bright.

1. From *Cynthia's Revels*, 5.6.1–18. Cynthia, another name for Diana, goddess of the moon and the hunt, and of chastity, an image associated with Queen Elizabeth.

To the Memory of My Beloved, the Author, Mr. William Shakespeare, and What He Hath Left Us[1]

To draw no envy, Shakespeare, on thy name,
  Am I thus ample[2] to thy book and fame,
While I confess thy writings to be such,
  As neither man nor muse can praise too much.
'Tis true, and all men's suffrage. But these ways
  Were not the paths I meant unto thy praise;
For silliest ignorance on these may light,
  Which, when it sounds at best, but echoes right;
Or blind affection, which doth ne'er advance
  The truth, but gropes, and urgeth all by chance;
Or crafty malice, might pretend this praise,
  And think to ruin, where it seemed to raise.
These are as some infamous bawd or whore
  Should praise a matron. What could hurt her more?
But thou art proof against them, and indeed
  Above the ill fortune of them, or the need.
I, therefore will begin. Soul of the age!
  The applause! delight! the wonder of our stage!
My Shakespeare, rise; I will not lodge thee by
  Chaucer, or Spenser, or bid Beaumont lie
A little further, to make thee a room;[3]
  Thou art a monument without a tomb,
And art alive still while thy book doth live,
  And we have wits to read, and praise to give.
That I not mix thee so, my brain excuses,
  I mean with great, but disproportioned, Muses;
For, if I thought my judgment were of years,
  I should commit thee surely with thy peers,
And tell how far thou didst our Lyly outshine,
  Or sporting Kyd, or Marlowe's mighty line.[4]
And though thou hadst small Latin, and less Greek,
  From thence to honor thee, I would not seek
For names, but call forth thundering Aeschylus,
  Euripides, and Sophocles to us,
Pacuvius, Accius, him of Cordova dead,
  To life again, to hear thy buskin[5] tread
And shake a stage; or, when thy socks[6] were on,
  Leave thee alone for the comparison

1. Prefixed to the first folio of Shakespeare's plays (1623).
2. From Latin *amplus:* copious; an *amplus orator* was one who spoke richly and with dignity.
3. Chaucer, Spenser, and Francis Beaumont were buried in Westminster Abbey; Shakespeare was buried in Stratford.
4. Lyly was an author of English prose comedies; Kyd and Marlowe were authors of English verse tragedies.
5. Boot worn by tragic actors. Jonson compares Shakespeare to tragedians of ancient Greece (Aeschylus, Euripides, Sophocles) and Rome (Pacuvius, Accius, and "him of Cordova," Seneca).
6. Symbols of comedy.

Of all that insolent Greece or haughty Rome
Sent forth, or since did from their ashes come.
Triumph, my Britain; thou hast one to show
To whom all scenes of Europe homage owe.
He was not of an age, but for all time!
And all the muses still were in their prime
When like Apollo he came forth to warm
Our ears, or like a Mercury to charm![7]
Nature herself was proud of his designs,
And joyed to wear the dressing of his lines,
Which were so richly spun, and woven so fit
As, since, she will vouchsafe no other wit.
The merry Greek, tart Aristophanes,
Neat Terence, witty Plautus,[8] now not please,
But antiquated, and deserted lie,
As they were not of nature's family.
Yet must I not give nature all; thy art,
My gentle Shakespeare, must enjoy a part.
For though the poet's matter nature be,
His art doth give the fashion. And that he
Who casts to write a living line must sweat
(Such as thine are) and strike the second heat
Upon the Muses' anvil: turn the same,
And himself with it, that he thinks to frame;[9]
Or for the laurel, he may gain a scorn;
For a good poet's made as well as born.
And such wert thou! Look how the father's face
Lives in his issue; even so, the race
Of Shakespeare's mind and manners brightly shines
In his well-turnèd, and true-filèd lines:
In each of which he seems to shake a lance,[1]
As brandished at the eyes of ignorance.
Sweet Swan of Avon, what a sight it were
To see thee in our waters yet appear,
And make those flights upon the banks of Thames,
That so did take Eliza, and our James![2]
But stay, I see thee in the hemisphere
Advanced, and made a constellation there!
Shine forth, thou star of poets, and with rage
Or influence chide or cheer the drooping stage,[3]
Which, since thy flight from hence, hath mourned like night,
And despairs day, but for thy volume's light.

7. Apollo and Mercury were the gods of poetry and eloquence.
8. Aristophanes was an ancient Greek comic playwright; Terence and Plautus were authors of Roman comedy.
9. See Horace, *Ars Poetica* 441: "return the ill-tuned verses to the anvil."
1. Pun on "Shake-speare."
2. Queen Elizabeth and King James.
3. Like an ancient hero, Shakespeare is given a place among the stars; as the "rage" and "influence" of the planets affect life on earth, Shakespeare affects the world of the stage.

To the Immortal Memory, and Friendship of that Noble Pair, Sir Lucius Cary and Sir H. Morison[1]

The Turn[2]

Brave infant of Saguntum, clear
Thy coming forth in that great year,
When the prodigious Hannibal did crown
His rage with razing your immortal town.[3]
Thou, looking then about,
Ere thou wert half got out,
Wise child, didst hastily return,
And mad'st thy mother's womb thine urn.
How summed° a circle[4] didst thou leave mankind *complete*
Of deepest lore, could we the center find!

The Counter-Turn

Did wiser nature draw thee back
From out the horror of that sack,
Where shame, faith, honor, and regard of right
Lay trampled on?—the deeds of death, and night,
Urged, hurried forth, and hurled
Upon th'affrighted world?
Sword, fire, and famine, with fell fury met;
And all on utmost ruin set;
As, could they but life's miseries foresee,
No doubt all infants would return like thee.

The Stand

For, what is life, if measured by the space,
Not by the act?
Or maskèd man, if valued by his face,
Above his fact?° *deeds*
Here's one outlived his peers
And told forth fourescore years;
He vexèd time, and busied the whole state;
Troubled both foes, and friends,
But ever to no ends:
What did this stirrer, but die late?
How well at twenty had he fallen, or stood!
For three of his fourescore, he did no good.

1. Sir Lucius Cary (1610?–1643), second Viscount Falkland, son of Elizabeth Cary (author of *The Tragedy of Mariam*). He befriended Jonson and wrote an elegy on his death. Sir Henry Morison (or Moryson), son of Sir Richard Morison and nephew of the travel writer Fynes Morison, see page 1174 died on or near his twenty-first birthday.

2. "Turn," "counter-turn," and "stand" represent the Greek "strophe," "antistrophe," and "epode." Jonson's poem is the first Great Ode in English. Often in the form of an address, the ode is a dignified lyric poem, in commemoration of a person, occasion, or theme. The Greek poet Pindar wrote odes praising winners of the Olympics. His odes were sung by a chorus in a three-part scheme, which Jonson imitates here.

3. Pliny, *History* 7.3.40–42: "an infant of Saguntum . . . at once went back into the womb in the year in which the city was destroyed by Hannibal" (the great Carthaginian general in the Second Punic War).

4. Emblem of perfection.

The Turn

He entered well by virtuous parts,
Got up and thrived with honest arts:
He purchased friends, and fame, and honors then,
And had his noble name advanced with men:
But weary of that flight,
He stooped in all men's sight!
To sordid flatteries, acts of strife,
And sunk in that dead sea of life
So deep, as he did then death's waters sup;
But that the cork of title buoyed him up.

The Counter-Turn

Alas, but Morison fell young!
He never fell: thou fall'st,[5] my tongue.
He stood, a soldier to the last right end,
A perfect patriot, and a noble friend,
But most, a virtuous son.
All offices were done
By him, so ample, full, and round,
In weight, in measure, number, sound,
As, though his age imperfect might appear,
His life was of humanity the sphere.

The Stand

Go now, and tell out days summed up with fears;
And make them years;
Produce thy mass of miseries on the stage,
To swell thine age;
Repeat of things a throng,
To show thou hast been long,
Not lived; for life doth her great actions spell
By what was done and wrought
In season, and so brought
To light: her measures are, how well
Each syllabe° answered, and was formed, how fair; *syllable*
These make the lines of life, and that's her air.

The Turn

It is not growing like a tree
In bulk, doth make man better be;
Or standing long an oak, three hundred year,
To fall a log at last, dry, bald, and sere:
A lily of a day
Is fairer far, in May,
Although it fall and die that night;
It was the plant and flower of light.

5. Slip, with a pun on the Latin *fallere*, to deceive, to be mistaken.

In small proportions, we just beauty see,
And in short measures life may perfect be.

The Counter-Turn

Call, noble Lucius, then for wine,
And let thy looks with gladness shine;
Accept this garland,[6] plant it on thy head;
And think, nay know, thy Morison's not dead.
He leaped the present age,
Possessed with holy rage,
To see that bright eternal day,
Of which we priests, and poets say
Such truths, as we expect for happy men,
And there he lives with memory, and Ben

The Stand

Jonson, who sung this of him, ere he went
Himself to rest,
Or taste a part of that full joy he meant
To have expressed
In this bright asterism;° *constellation*
Where it were friendship's schism
(Were not his Lucius long with us to tarry)
To separate these twi-
Lights, the Dioscuri;[7]
And keep the one half from his Harry.
But fate doth so alternate the design,
Whilst that in heaven, this light on earth must shine.

The Turn

And shine as you exalted are;
Two names of friendship, but one star:
Of hearts the union. And those not by chance
Made, or indentured,° or leased out t' advance *contracted for*
The profits for a time.
No pleasures vain did chime,
Of rhymes, or riots, at your feasts,
Orgies of drink, or feigned protests;
But simple love of greatness, and of good;
That knits brave minds, and manners, more than blood.

The Counter-Turn

This made you first to know the why
You liked; then after, to apply
That liking; and approach so one the t'other,

6. The poem itself.
7. "Twin lights:" the mythical Greek brothers, Castor and Pollux. After Castor's death the twin brothers exchanged places on earth and in the underworld at regular intervals.

Till either grew a portion of the other:
Each stylèd, by his end,
The copy of his friend.
You lived to be the great surnames
And titles by which all made claims
Unto the virtue. Nothing perfect done,
But as a Cary, or a Morison.

The Stand

And such a force the fair example had,
As they that saw
The good, and durst not practise it, were glad
That such a law
Was left yet to mankind;
Where they might read, and find
Friendship in deed was written, not in words.
And with the heart, not pen,
Of two so early° men, *youthful*
Whose lines her rolls were, and records.
Who, ere the first down bloomèd on the chin,
Had sowed these fruits, and got the harvest in.

Pleasure Reconciled to Virtue

A Masque as It Was Presented at Court Before King James. 1618.[1]

The Scene was the Mountain Atlas, who had his top ending in the figure of an old man, his head and beard all hoary and frost, as if his shoulders were covered with snow; the rest wood and rock. A grove of ivy at his feet, out of which, to a wild music of cymbals, flutes, and tabors, is brought forth Comus,[2] the god of cheer or the belly, riding in triumph, his head crowned with roses and other flowers, his hair curled; they that wait upon him, crowned with ivy, their javelins done about with it; one of them going with Hercules' bowl[3] bare before him, while the rest presented him, with this

Hymn

Room, room, make room for the bouncing belly,
First father of sauce and deviser of jelly,
Prime master of arts, and the giver of wit,
That found out the excellent engine, the spit,
The plough and the flail, the mill, and the hopper,
The hutch, and the bolter, the furnace and copper.
The oven, the bavin, the mawkin, and peel,
The hearth and the range, the dog and the wheel.[4]

1. A masque was an entertainment performed by members of the court that included elaborate sets, dance, music, and poetry. Designed to compliment the monarch, the masque portrayed him as an ideal ruler in a moral allegory. The myth on which this masque is based in the story of Hercules' choice between pleasure and virtue, in which King James is represented as harmonizing voluptuous enjoyment and right action.

2. Allied with Dionysus, the god of wine, Comus is the god of sensual excess.

3. Hercules used the bowl that the Sun gave him as a sailing ship.

4. Flail: tool for threshing corn; mill: apparatus for grinding grain; hopper: a cone through which grain is conveyed to the mill; hutch: a box for sifting grain; bolter: a sieve; bavin: bundle of light wood used in bakers' oven; mawkin: mop for cleaning a baker's oven; peel: a baker's shovel. A dog connected to a wheel turned the roasting spit.

He, he first invented both hogshead° and tun,° *cask / barrel*
The gimlet and vice, too, taught them to run.[5]
And since, with the funnel, an Hippocras bag
He's made of himself, that now he cries swag.[6]
Which shows, though the pleasure be but of four inches,
Yet he is a weezle, the gullet° that pinches, *throat*
Of any delight, and not spares from the back
Whatever, to make of the belly a sack.
Hail, hail, plump paunch! O the founder of taste
For fresh meats, or powdered, or pickle, or paste;
Devourer of broiled, baked, roasted, or sod,° *boiled*
And emptier of cups, be they even, or odd;
All which have now made thee, so wide i' the waist
As scarce with no pudding thou art to be laced;
But eating and drinking, until thou dost nod,
Thou break'st all thy girdles, and break'st forth[7] a god.

To this, the Bowl-bearer

Do you hear, my friends, to whom do you sing all this now? Pardon me only that I ask you, for I do not look for an answer; I'll answer myself. I know it is now such a time as the Saturnals[8] for all the world, that every man stands under the eaves of his own hat and sings what pleases him; that's the right and the liberty of it. Now you sing of god Comus here, the Belly-god. I say it is well, and I say it is not well. It is well, as it is a ballad, and the belly worthy of it I must needs say, and 'twere forty yards of ballad, more—as much ballad as tripe.[9] But when the belly is not edified by it, it is not well; for where did you ever read, or hear, that the belly had any ears? Come, never pump for an answer, for you are defeated. Our fellow Hunger there, that was as ancient a retainer to the belly as any of us, was turned away, for being unseasonable—not unreasonable, but unseasonable—and now is he (poor thin-gut) fain to get his living with teaching of starlings, magpies, parrots, and jackdaws, those things he would have taught the belly. Beware of dealing with the Belly; the Belly will not be talked to, especially when he is full. Then there is no venturing upon Venter,[1] then he will blow you all up; he will thunder, indeed la; some in derision call him the father of farts. But I say, he was the first inventor of great ordinance,[2] and taught us to discharge them on festival days. Would we had a fit feast for him i' faith, to show his activity. I would have something now fetched in now to please his five senses, the throat; or the two senses, the eyes. Pardon me, for my two senses; for I that carry Hercules' bowl[3] in the service may see double by my place, for I have drunk like a frog today. I would have a tun[4] now, brought in to dance, and so many bottles about him. Ha? You look as if you would make a problem of this. Do you see? a problem: why bottles? and why a tun? and why a tun? and why bottles to dance? I say that men that drink hard and serve the belly in any place of quality (as *The Jovial Tinkers*, or *The Lusty Kindred*)[5] are

5. The gimlet and vice were used to tap the cask.
6. A Hippocras bag was a strainer for wine. To "cry swag" was to let out a hanging belly.
7. With a double meaning of fart.
8. The Roman Saturnalia was a wild festival at the end of the year, similar to Twelfth Night, part of the English Christmas season, at the celebration of which this masque was performed.
9. Edible animal intestines, and also the human stomach.
1. Belly (Latin).
2. Artillery.
3. "To carry Hercules' bowl" means to drink heavily.
4. Keg.
5. Taverns.

living measures of drink, and can transform themselves, and do every day, to bottles or tuns when they please; and when they have done all they can, they are, as I say again (for I think I said somewhat like it afore), but moving measures of drink. And there is a piece-in-the-cellar can hold more than all they. This will I make good, if it please our new god but to give a nod; for the belly does all by signs, and I am all for the belly, the truest clock in the world to go by.

Here the first Anti-masque[6] [danced by men in the shape of bottles, tuns, etc.] after which,

HERCULES: What rites are these? Breeds earth more monsters yet?
Antaeus[7] scarce is cold; what can beget
This store? and stay such contraries upon her?
Is earth so fruitful of her own dishonor?
Or 'cause his vice was inhumanity,
Hopes she, by vicious hospitality
To work an expiation first?[8] and then
(Help, Virtue) these are sponges, and not men.
Bottles? mere vessels? half a tun of paunch?
How? and the other half thrust forth in haunch?[9]
Whose feast? the belly's! Comus'! and my cup
Brought in to fill the drunken orgies up
And here abused! That was the crowned reward
Of thirsty heroes after labor hard!
Burdens and shames of nature, perish, die;
For yet you never lived, but in the sty
Of vice have wallowed, and in that swine's strife
Been buried under the offense of life.
Go, reel, and fall, under the load you make,
Till your swoll'n bowels burst with what you take.
Can this be pleasure, to extinguish man?
Or so quite change him in his figure? Can
The belly love his pain, and be content
With no delight, but what's a punishment?
These monsters plague themselves, and fitly too,
For they do suffer what and all they do.
But here must be no shelter, nor no shroud
For such: sink grove, or vanish into cloud.

After this, the whole grove vanished, and the whole music was discovered, sitting at the foot of the mountain, with Pleasure and Virtue seated above them. The Choir invited Hercules to rest with this

Song

Great friend and servant of the good,
Let cool a while thy heated blood,
And from thy mighty labor cease.
Lie down, lie down,
And give thy troubled spirits peace,

6. A grotesque, comic interlude.
7. Antaeus was a Libyan giant slain by Hercules.
8. Hercules assumes that Comus is another monster, like Antaeus, produced by the Earth and that Earth hopes to expiate her guilt by giving birth to one monster after another.
9. The area between the ribs and thighs.

Whilst Virtue, for whose sake
Thou dost this godlike travail take,
May of the choicest herbage° make, *plants*
Here on this mountain bred,
A crown, a crown
For thy immortal head.

Here Hercules being laid down at their feet, the second anti-masque, which was of pygmies,[1] appeared.

1ST PYGMY: Antaeus dead? And Hercules yet live!
Where is this Hercules? What would I give
To meet him, now? Meet him? Nay, three such other,
If they had hand in murder of our brother![2]
With three? with four? with ten? nay, with as many
As the name yields![3] Pray anger there by any
Whereon to feed my just revenge and soon!
How shall I kill him? Hurl him 'gainst the moon,
And break him in small portions! Give to Greece
His brain, and every tract of earth a piece!
2ND PYGMY: He is yonder.
1ST: Where?
3RD: At the hill foot, asleep.
1ST: Let one go steal his club.
2ND: My charge; I'll creep.
4TH: He's ours.
1ST: Yes, peace.
3RD: Triumph, we have him, boy.
4TH: Sure, sure, he's sure.
1ST: Come, let us dance for joy.

At the end of their dance they thought to surprise him, when suddenly, being awaked by the music, he roused himself, and they all ran into holes.

Song

CHOIR: Wake, Hercules, awake, but heave up thy black eye,
'Tis only asked from thee to look and these will die,
Or fly.
Already they are fled,
Whom scorn had else left dead.

At which Mercury[4] descendeth from the hill, with a garland of poplar to crown him.

MERCURY: Rest still, thou active friend of Virtue: these
Should not disturb the peace of Hercules.
Earth's worms and honor's dwarfs, at too great odds,
Prove or provoke the issue of the gods.
See here, a crown, the agèd hill hath sent thee,
My grandsire Atlas, he that did present thee
With the best sheep that in his fold were found,

1. In ancient Greek history, the pygmies were supposed to have been a tribe of very short people in Africa or India; the term was also used of dwarves.
2. Antaeus.
3. The Pygmies' assumption that there is more than one Hercules is a joke alluding to the many different stories about Hercules put forward by the mythographers.
4. The messenger god.

Or golden fruit, on the Hesperian ground,
For rescuing his fair daughters, then the prey
Of a rude pirate, as thou cam'st this way;
And taught thee all the learning of the sphere,
And how, like him, thou mightst the heaven up-bear,
As that thy labors virtuous recompense.[5]
He, though a mountain now, hath yet the sense
Of thanking thee for more, thou being still
Constant to goodness, guardian of the hill;
Antaeus, by thee suffocated here,
And the voluptuous Comus, god of cheer,
Beat from his grove, and that defaced. But now
The time's arrived, that Atlas told thee of: how
By unaltered law, and working of the stars,
There should be a cessation of all jars° *fights*
'Twixt Virtue and her noted opposite,
Pleasure, that both should meet here, in the sight
Of Hesperus, the glory of the west,[6]
The brightest star, that from his burning crest
Lights all on this side the Atlantic seas
As far as to thy pillars Hercules.[7]
See where he shines, Justice and Wisdom placed
About his throne and those with Honor graced,
Beauty and Love. It is not with his brother
Bearing the world, but ruling such another
Is his renown.[8] Pleasure, for his delight,
Is reconciled to Virtue; and this night
Virtue brings forth twelve princes have been bred
In this rough mountain and near Atlas' head,
The hill of Knowledge; one, and chief of whom
Of the bright race of Hesperus is come,
Who shall in time the same that he is, be,
And now is only a less light than he.[9]
These now she trusts with Pleasure, and to these
She gives an entrance to the Hesperides,
Fair Beauty's garden; neither can she fear
They should grow soft or wax effeminate here,
Since in her sight and by her charge all's done,
Pleasure the servant, Virtue looking on.

Here the whole choir of music called the masquers forth from the lap of the mountain, which now opens with this

Song

Ope, agèd Atlas, open then thy lap,
And from thy beamy bosom, strike a light,

5. Atlas was an astronomer. His labor of holding up the heavens was taken over by Hercules so that Atlas could capture the golden apples of the Hesperides.
6. Hesperus, the brother of Atlas, was the evening star and the protector of the western isles.
7. The Pillars of Hercules are the Straits of Gibraltar.
8. Hesperus is similar to King James, who also rules "another" world: England.
9. King James's 18-year-old son Prince Charles.

That men may read in thy mysterious map
All lines
And signs
Of royal education, and the right,
See how they come, and show,
That are but born to know.
Descend,
Descend,
Though pleasure lead,
Fear not to follow:
They who are bred
Within the hill
Of skill,
May safely tread
What path they will:
No ground of good is hollow.

In their descent from the hill Daedalus[1] came down before them of whom Hercules questioned Mercury.

HERCULES: But Hermes, stay a little, let me pause:
Who's this that leads?
MERCURY: A guide that gives them laws
To all their motions. Daedalus the wise.
HERCULES: And doth in sacred harmony comprise
His precepts?
MERCURY: Yes.
HERCULES: They may securely prove° *experience*
Then, any labyrinth, though it be of love.

Here, while they put themselves in form, Daedalus hath his first

Song

Come on, come on, and where you go,
So interweave the curious knot,
As even th'observer scarce may know
Which lines are Pleasures, and which not.

First, figure out the doubtful way
At which, a while all youth should stay
Where she and Virtue did contend
Which should have Hercules to friend.[2]

Then, as all actions of mankind
Are but a labyrinth or maze,
So let your dances be entwined,
Yet not perplex men unto gaze;

1. Daedalus here acts as choreographer for the dance. As architect of the labyrinth, or maze, Daedalus may symbolize Inigo Jones, the set designer of the masque.

2. The story of how Hercules had to choose the arduous path of Virtue over the easy road offered to him by Vice is related by the ancient Greek author Xenophon (*Memorabilia* 2.1.21–34).

But measured, and so numerous° too, *rhythmical*
As men may read each act you do,
And when they see the graces meet,
Admire the wisdom of your feet.

For dancing is an exercise
Not only shows the mover's wit,
But maketh the beholder wise,
As he hath power to rise to it.

The first dance.

After which Daedalus again.

Song 2

O more, and more! this was so well
As praise wants half his voice to tell;
Again yourselves compose;
And now put all the aptness on
Of figure, that proportion
Or color can disclose.

That if those silent arts were lost,
Design and picture, they might boast
From you a newer ground;
Instructed to that height'ning sense
Of dignity and reverence
In your true motions found:

Begin, begin; for look, the fair
Do longing listen to what air
You form your second touch;
That they may vent their murmuring hymns
Just to the tune you move your limbs,
And wish their own were such.

Make haste, make haste, for this
The labyrinth of Beauty is.

The second dance.

That ended, Daedalus:

Song 3

It follows now, you are to prove
The subtlest maze of all, that's love,
And if you stay too long,
The fair will think you do 'em wrong,

Go choose among—but with a mind
As gentle as the stroking wind
Runs o'er the gentler flowers.

And so let all your actions smile,
As if they meant not to beguile
The ladies, but the hours.

Grace, laughter and discourse may meet,
And yet the beauty not go less:
For what is noble should be sweet,
But not dissolved in wantonness.

Will you, that I give the law
To all your sport and sum it?
It should be such should envy draw,
But ever overcome it.

Here they danced with the ladies, and the whole revels[3] followed; which ended, Mercury called to Daedalus in this following speech, which was after repeated in song, by two trebles, two tenors, a bass, and the whole chorus.

Song 4

An eye of looking back were well,
Or any murmur that would tell
Your thoughts, how you were sent
And went,
To walk with Pleasure, not to dwell.

These, these are hours by Virtue spared
Herself, she being her own reward,
But she will have you know
That though
Her sports be soft, her life is hard.

You must return unto the hill,
And there advance
With labor and inhabit still
That height and crown
From whence you ever may look down
Upon triumphed Chance.

She, she it is, in darkness shines.
'Tis she that still herself refines
By her own light, to every eye,
More seen, more known, when Vice stands by.

And though a stranger here on earth,
In heaven she hath her right of birth.
There, there is Virtue's seat,
Strive to keep her your own;
'Tis only she can make you great,
Though place, here, make you known.

3. The audience, including members of the court.

After which they danced their last dance, and returned into the scene, which closed, and is a mountain again, as before.

The End.

This pleased the king so well, as he would see it again; when it was presented with these additions.[4]

John Donne

1572–1631

A. Duncan, engraved portrait of John Donne.

John Donne wrote some of the most passionate love poems and most moving religious verse in the English language. Even his contemporaries wondered how one mind could express itself in such different modes. Eliciting a portrait of the artist as a split personality, Donne's letters mention the melancholic lover "Jack Donne," succeeded by the Anglican priest "Doctor Donne." Izaak Walton's *Life of Donne* (1640) portrays an earnest, aspiring clergyman who wrote love poetry to his wife. Yet Donne actually wrote most of his poetry—both the love lyrics and the *Holy Sonnets*—before he entered the ministry at forty-three. An ambitious, talented, and handsome young man, Donne struggled to attain secular patronage; later, he resigned himself to life in the church and, after his wife's death, came to terms with his own mortality.

Donne was born into a Catholic family. His mother was the great-niece of Sir Thomas More; she went into exile in Antwerp for a time to seek religious toleration. One of Donne's uncles was imprisoned in the Tower of London because he was a Jesuit priest. Donne wrote of his family that none "hath endured and suffered more in their persons and fortunes, for obeying the Teachers of Roman Doctrine, then it hath done." Donne and his brother Henry entered Hart Hall, Oxford, when they were just eleven and ten, young enough to be spared the required oath recognizing the Queen as head of the church. The Donne brothers later studied law at Lincoln's Inn, where Henry was arrested for harboring a priest in 1593. The priest was drawn and quartered; Henry died in Newgate prison of the plague.

Though shadowed by his brother's death, Donne's student years in London had their pleasures. Donne was distracted from studying law by "the worst voluptuousness . . . an Hydroptique immoderate desire of humane learning and languages." The young Donne was described by his friend Sir Richard Baker as "a great visitor of ladies, a great frequenter of Playes, a great writer of conceited Verses." Among these were Donne's erotic *Elegies*, including *To His Mistress Going to Bed* and *Love's Progress*, both of which were refused a license for publication in the 1633 edition of his collected verse.

Shortly after gaining a position as secretary to Sir Thomas Egerton, Lord Keeper of the Great Seal, in 1597, Donne met and fell in love with Ann More. His noble employer's niece, she was so far above Donne's station that they married secretly. When Ann's father heard the

4. The additions were another masque, *For the Honor of Wales*.

news, he asked Egerton to have Donne fired and saw to it that he was incarcerated. At this time, Donne is said to have written to Ann: *"John Donne, Ann Donne, un-done."* As a result of Donne's petition, the Court of Audience for Canterbury declared the marriage lawful; nevertheless, Ann was disinherited.

John and Ann made a love match, but their life was not easy. She bore twelve children in fifteen years, not counting miscarriages. Donne lamented the "poorness of [his] fortune and the greatness of [his] charge." After thirteen years of marriage, however, he could also still say: "we had not one another at so cheap a rate, as that we should ever be weary of one another." A few of the love poems in *Songs and Sonnets* express a mixture of bliss and hardship linked with their marriage.

Relations with friends and patrons also influenced Donne's poetry. He is said to have addressed several poems to Magdalen Herbert, mother of the poet George. Living in Mitcham near London, Donne cemented his friendship with Ben Jonson, who wrote two epigrams in praise of Donne in thanks for his Latin verses on *Volpone* (1607). Donne was also introduced to Lucy, Countess of Bedford, who asked Jonson to get her a copy of Donne's *Satires*. Donne not only addressed several verse letters to her but also enjoyed her poems. An even more generous patron was Sir Robert Drury, for the death of whose young daughter Elizabeth the poet composed *A Funeral Elegie*, the inspiration for his two *Anniversaries* (1612) on the nature of the cosmos and death.

Donne's writing from 1607 to 1611 dealt with theological and moral controversies. His *Pseudo-Martyr* (1610) argued that Catholics should take the Oath of Allegiance to the King and that resistance to him should not be glorified as a form of martyrdom. This work won him James I's advice to enter the ministry, but, still skeptical, Donne held off. He protested against sectarianism: "You know I never fettered nor imprisoned the word Religion ... immuring it in a Rome, or a Wittenberg, or a Geneva." Donne also examined the morality of suicide in *Biathanatos* (written 1607, published 1646). His *Holy Sonnets* (some of which may have been written as early as 1608–1610) reveal an obsession with his own death and fear of damnation: "I dare not move my dim eyes any way, / Despair behind, and death before doth cast / Such terror."

Donne was plagued by professional bad luck until he became an Anglican priest. With the exception of Sir Robert Drury, Donne never found a dependable patron. His applications for secretaryships in Ireland and Virginia were unsuccessful. In search of the Earl of Somerset's patronage, Donne wrote an epithalamion for his marriage to Frances Howard and even volunteered to justify her earlier controversial divorce. Fortunately for Donne, his attempts to win a position through Somerset failed, since a year later the Earl fell from power. Giving up his long quest for secular preferment, Donne took holy orders in 1615. Once an Anglican priest, he was made a royal chaplain and received an honorary Doctorate of Divinity from Cambridge. Two years later, he became reader in divinity at his old law school Lincoln's Inn.

Prosperity was followed by tragic loss. Ann Donne died giving birth in 1617. The death of his wife turned Donne more completely toward God. His later prose viewed death from a different perspective from his earlier personal torment. Suffering from a recurring fever, he wrote *Devotions upon Emergent Occasions* (1624). In the midst of a major epidemic, at the height of his fever, distraught and sleepless, he realizes our common mortality: "never send to know for whom the bell tolls; it tolls for thee." He became a prolific and stirring preacher of sermons. Some of these, such as that urging the Company of the Virginia Plantation to spread the gospel (1622), were printed in his lifetime. One written just before his death shows confidence in God's forgiveness: "I cannot plead innocency of life, especially of my youth: But I am to be judged by a merciful God."

If Donne's life can be split into the secular and religious, his poetic sensibility cannot. His verse fuses flesh and spirit through metaphysical conceits that create fascinating connections between apparently unrelated topics. In Donne's erotic lyrics, sex excites spiritual ecstasy along with hot lust and seductive wit. Similarly, Donne's religious poems express his relation with God not as an intellectual construct but as an emotional need, articulated in intimate and even erotic language. Later ages did not always appreciate either Donne's sensuality or his intellectual extravagance; remarkably, none of his poems were included in the most important nineteenth-century anthology of poetry, Palgraves's *Golden Treasury*. Donne's fame was revived early in the twentieth century, when modernist poets, especially T. S. Eliot, took inspiration from Donne's complex mixture of immediacy and artifice, passion and subtle thought.

For additional resources on Donne, go to *The Longman Anthology of British Literature* Web site at www.myliteraturekit.com.

The Good Morrow[1]

I wonder by my troth, what thou, and I
Did, till we loved? Were we not weaned till then?
But sucked on country pleasures, childishly?
Or snorted we in the seven sleepers' den?[2]
'Twas so; but this, all pleasures fancies be.
If ever any beauty I did see,
Which I desired, and got, 'twas but a dream of thee.

And now good morrow to our waking souls,
Which watch not one another out of fear;
For love, all love of other sights controls,
And makes one little room, an everywhere.
Let sea-discoverers to new worlds have gone,
Let maps to others, worlds on worlds have shown,
Let us possess one world, each hath one, and is one.

My face in thine eye, thine in mine appears,
And true plain hearts do in the faces rest.
Where can we find two better hemispheres
Without sharp north, without declining west?
What ever dies was not mixed equally;[3]
If our two loves be one, or, thou and I
Love so alike, that none do slacken, none can die.

Song

Go, and catch a falling star,
    Get with child a mandrake root,[1]
Tell me, where all past years are,
    Or who cleft the Devil's foot,
Teach me to hear mermaids singing,
Or to keep off envy's stinging,

1. Donne's love poems, written over a period of 20 years, cannot be dated with any certainty. They were first printed in 1633, scattered throughout the entire collection of poems. Then, in the 1635 edition, the love poems were printed as a group under the title *Songs and Sonnets*. There is no certainty that the titles were chosen by Donne.

2. Legendary cave where seven Ephesian youths were put to sleep by God to escape the persecution of Christians by the Emperor Decius (249).

3. According to ancient medicine, death was caused by an imbalance of elements in the body.

1. A fork-rooted plant, resembling the human body in its form.

And find
What wind
Serves to advance an honest mind.

If thou be borne to strange sights,
Things invisible to see,
Ride ten thousand days and nights,[2]
Till age snow white hairs on thee.
Thou, when thou return'st, will tell me
All strange wonders that befell thee,
And swear
No where
Lives a woman true, and fair.

If thou findest one, let me know,
Such a pilgrimage were sweet;
Yet do not, I would not go,
Though at next door we might meet,
Though she were true, when you met her,
And last, till you write your letter,
Yet she
Will be
False, ere I come, to two, or three.

Twickenham Garden[1]

Blasted with sighs, and surrounded with tears,
Hither I come to seek the spring,
And at mine eyes, and at mine ears,
Receive such balms[2] as else cure everything;
But oh, self-traitor, I do bring
The spider love, which transubstantiates all,
And can convert manna to gall;[3]
And that this place may thoroughly be thought
True Paradise, I have the serpent brought.

'Twere wholesomer for me, that winter did
Benight the glory of this place,
And that a grave frost did forbid
These trees to laugh, and mock me to my face;
But that I may not this disgrace
Endure, nor leave this garden, Love, let me
Some senseless piece of this place be;

2. See *Faerie Queene* 3.7.56–61, where Spenser's Squire of Dames searches the country for a chaste woman.

1. Twickenham Park was the home of Lucy Harington, Countess of Bedford, and a meeting place of writers whom she patronized, such as Donne. The poem most likely is addressed to her and dates from 1608, when she bought the house, to 1617, when she moved.

2. Healing influences.

3. Spiders turn what they eat into poison; and transubstantiation is the changing of the bread and wine in the Eucharist into the body and blood of Jesus Christ. Manna is the miraculous food that God gave the Israelites to eat when they left Egypt and traveled through the desert. Hence, poisonous love that transforms all and can turn miraculous food into bitterness.

Make me a mandrake[4] so I may groan[5] here,
Or a stone fountain weeping out my year.

Hither with crystal vials,[6] lovers, come,
And take my tears, which are love's wine,
And try your mistress' tears at home,
For all are false, that taste not just like mine;
Alas, hearts do not in eyes shine,
Nor can you more judge woman's thoughts by tears,
Than by her shadow, what she wears.
O pérverse sex, where none is true but she
Who's therefore true, because her truth kills me.[7]

The Undertaking

I have done one braver thing
Than all the Worthies did,[1]
And yet a braver thence doth spring,
Which is to keep that hid.

It were but madness now to impart
The skill of specular stone,[2]
When he which can have learned the art
To cut it, can find none.

So, if I now should utter this,
Others (because no more
Such stuff to work upon, there is,)
Would love but as before.

But he who loveliness within
Hath found, all outward loathes,
For he who color loves, and skin,
Loves but their oldest clothes.

If, as I have, you also do
Virtue attired in woman see,
And dare love that, and say so too,
And forget the He and She;

And if this love, though placèd so,
From profane men you hide,
Which will no faith on this bestow,
Or, if they do, deride:

Then you have done a braver thing
Than all the Worthies did;

4. The mandrake, a poisonous and narcotic plant, was said to shriek when uprooted.
5. Donne's *Songs and Sonnets* (1633) and some manuscripts read "grow" instead of "groan."
6. Crystal vials, or tear-vessels, were put in ancient tombs as symbols of mourning.
7. The speaker rails against the lady's perverseness in being the only faithful ("true") woman, who is faithful to her man, for the very reason that this faithfulness distresses the speaker of the poem.
1. The nine great military heroes of ancient and medieval legend and history.
2. Transparent stone of ancient times, but now lost, that required great skill to cut in strips.

And a braver thence will spring,
Which is, to keep that hid.

The Sun Rising[1]

Busy old fool, unruly Sun,
Why dost thou thus
Through windows, and through curtains call on us?
Must to thy motions lovers' seasons run?
Saucy pedantic wretch, go chide
Late schoolboys, and sour prentices,° *apprentices*
Go tell court-huntsmen, that the king will ride,
Call country ants to harvest offices;
Love, all alike, no season knows, nor clime,
Nor hours, days, months, which are the rags of time.
Thy beams, so reverend, and strong
Why shouldst thou think?
I could eclipse and cloud them with a wink,
But that I would not lose her sight so long:
If her eyes have not blinded thine,
Look, and tomorrow late, tell me,
Whether both th'Indias of spice and mine[2]
Be where thou left'st them, or lie here with me.
Ask for those kings whom thou saw'st yesterday,
And thou shalt hear, all here in one bed lay.

She is all states, and all princes, I,
Nothing else is.
Princes do but play us; compared to this,
All honor's mimic; all wealth alchemy.° *fake science*
Thou sun art half as happy as we,
In that the world's contracted thus;
Thine age asks ease, and since thy duties be
To warm the world, that's done in warming us.
Shine here to us, and thou art everywhere;
This bed thy center is, these walls, thy sphere.

The Indifferent

I can love both fair and brown,
Her whom abundance melts, and her whom want betrays,
Her who loves loneness best, and her who masks and plays,
Her whom the country formed, and whom the town,
Her who believes, and her who tries,° *questions*
Her who still weeps with spongy eyes,

1. In the tradition of the alba, a love song addressing the dawn, as in Ovid's *Amores* 1.13 and Petrarch's *Canzoniere* 188.

2. The East Indies was the source of spice; the West Indies was the source of gold.

And her who is dry cork, and never cries;
I can love her, and her, and you and you,
I can love any, so she be not true.

Will no other vice content you?
Will it not serve your turn to do, as did your mothers?
Or have you old vices spent, and now would find out others?
Or doth a fear, that men are true, torment you?
Oh we are not, be not you so,
Let me, and do you, twenty know.
Rob me, but bind me not, and let me go.
Must I, who came to travail,[1] thorough you
Grow your fixed subject, because you are true?

Venus heard me sigh this song,
And by love's sweetest part, variety, she swore,
She heard not this till now; and that it should be so no more.
She went, examined, and returned ere long,
And said, "Alas, some two or three
Poor heretics in love there be,
Which think to establish dangerous constancy.
But I have told them, 'Since you will be true,
You shall be true to them, who are false to you.' "

The Canonization[1]

For God's sake hold your tongue, and let me love,
  Or° chide my palsy, or my gout, *either*
My five gray hairs, or ruined fortune flout,
  With wealth your state, your mind with arts improve,
    Take you a course, get you a place,
    Observe his Honor, or his Grace,
Or the King's real, or his stampèd face[2]
  Contemplate, what you will, approve,
  So you will let me love.

Alas, alas, who's injured by my love?
  What merchant's ships have my sighs drowned?
Who says my tears have overflowed his ground?
  When did my colds a forward spring remove?
    When did the heats which my veins fill
    Add one more to the plaguy bill?[3]
Soldiers find wars, and lawyers find out still
  Litigious men, which quarrels move
  Though she and I do love.

Call us what you will, we are made such by love;
  Call her one, me another fly,

1. In three senses: to make love, to undergo hardship, and to travel or move on to another woman.
1. The making of saints.
2. The King's actual face or his image stamped on coins.
3. Daily list of those who have died issued during outbreaks of the plague.

We are tapers° too, and at our own cost die,[4] *candles*
And we in us find the eagle and the dove.
The phoenix riddle hath more wit[5]
By us; we two being one, are it.
So to one neutral thing both sexes fit,
We die and rise the same, and prove
Mysterious by this love.

We can die by it, if not live by love,
And if unfit for tombs and hearse
Our legend be, it will be fit for verse;
And if no piece of chronicle we prove,
We'll build in sonnets pretty rooms;[6]
As well a well wrought urn becomes
The greatest ashes, as half-acre tombs,
And by these hymns, all shall approve
Us canonized for love.

And thus invoke us: You whom reverend love
Made one another's hermitage;° *refuge, retreat*
You, to whom love was peace, that now is rage;
Who did the whole world's soul contract, and drove
Into the glasses° of your eyes[7] *lenses*
(So made such mirrors, and such spies,
That they did all to you epitomize)
Countries, towns, courts: beg from above
A pattern of your love!

Air and Angels

Twice or thrice had I loved thee,
Before I knew thy face or name;
So in a voice, so in a shapeless flame,
Angels affect us oft, and worshipped be;
Still when, to where thou wert, I came,
Some lovely glorious nothing I did see.[1]
But since my soul, whose child love is,
Takes limbs of flesh, and else could nothing do,
More subtle than the parent is
Love must not be, but take a body too,
And therefore what thou wert, and who,
I bid love ask, and now
That it assume thy body, I allow,
And fix itself in thy lip, eye, and brow.

4. To die is to experience orgasm.
5. The mythical bird that was burned and reborn out of its own ashes, a symbol of perfection. See Geoffrey Whitney, "The Phoenix" from *A Choice of Emblems* in Perspectives: Early Modern Books (page 1066).
6. A play on *stanza,* Italian for "room."
7. The lovers gazing into each other's eyes saw there a compact version or microcosm of the larger world or macrocosm.
1. A divine light shining through the body that Neoplatonists thought was the true object of desire rather than the body, which only reflected that beauty.

Whilst thus to ballast love, I thought,
And so more steadily to have gone,
With wares which would sink admiration,
I saw, I had love's pinnace° overfraught, *light sailing ship*
  Every thy hair for love to work upon
Is much too much, some fitter must be sought;
  For, nor in nothing, nor in things
Extreme, and scattering bright, can love inhere;
  Then as an angel, face and wings
Of air, not pure as it, yet pure doth wear,
  So thy love may be my love's sphere;[2]
    Just such disparity
As is twixt air and angel's purity,[3]
'Twixt women's love, and men's will ever be.

Break of Day[1]

'Tis true, 'tis day; what though it be?
Oh wilt thou therefore rise from me?
Why should we rise, because 'tis light?
Did we lie down, because 'twas night?
Love, which in spite of darkness brought us hither,
Should in despite of light keep us together.
Light hath no tongue, but is all eye;
If it could speak as well as spy,
This were the worst, that it could say,
That being well, I fain would stay,
And that I loved my heart and honor so,
That I would not from him, that had them, go.

Must business thee from hence remove?
Oh, that's the worst disease of love,
The poor, the foul, the false, love can
Admit, but not the busied man.
He which hath business, and makes love, does do
Such wrong, as when a married man doth woo.

A Valediction:° Of Weeping *farewell*

    Let me pour forth
My tears before thy face, whilst I stay here,
For thy face coins them, and thy stamp° they bear, *image*
And by this mintage they are something worth,
    For thus they be
    Pregnant of thee;
Fruits of much grief they are, emblems° of more, *symbols*

2. The analogy is between his love as the intelligence controlling a heavenly body and her love as the heavenly sphere, or material body.
3. Metaphysical doctrine separates being into celestial, aerial, and material. If the material lady returns his aerial love, then they will be united in a celestial union.
1. First printed, with music, in W. Corkine's *Second Book of Airs* (1612).

When a tear falls, that thou falst which it bore,
So thou and I are nothing then, when on a diverse shore.

On a round ball
A workman that hath copies by, can lay
A Europe, Africa, and an Asia,
And quickly make that, which was nothing, all,[1]
So doth each tear,
Which thee doth wear,
A globe, yea world by that impression grow,
Till thy tears mixed with mine do overflow
This world, by waters sent from thee, my heaven dissolvèd so.

Oh more than moon,
Draw not up seas to drown me in thy sphere,[2]
Weep me not dead, in thine arms, but forbear
To teach the sea, what it may do too soon;
Let not the wind
Example find,
To do me more harm, than it purposeth;
Since thou and I sigh one another's breath,
Whoe'er sighs most, is cruelest, and hastes the other's death.

Love's Alchemy

Some that have deeper digged love's mine than I,
Say, where his centric° happiness doth lie: *central*
I have loved, and got, and told,
But should I love, get, tell, till I were old,
I should not find that hidden mystery;
Oh, 'tis imposture all:
And as no chemic° yet the elixir got,[1] *alchemist*
But glorifies his pregnant pot,
If by the way to him befall
Some odoriferous thing, or medicinal,
So, lovers dream a rich and long delight,
But get a winter-seeming summer's night.

Our ease, our thrift, our honor, and our day,
Shall we, for this vain bubble's shadow pay?
Ends love in this, that my man,° *servant*
Can be as happy as I can; if he can
Endure the short scorn of a bridegroom's play?
That loving wretch that swears,
'Tis not the bodies marry, but the minds,
Which he in her angelic finds,
Would swear as justly, that he hears,

1. The blank ball looks like a zero ("nothing") until the continents are painted on it to represent the entire world ("all").

2. An astral sphere with a power of attraction greater than the moon might draw the seas up to itself.

1. A goal of alchemy was to produce a pure essence with the power to heal and prolong life.

In that day's rude hoarse minstrelsy, the spheres.[2]
Hope not for mind in women; at their best
Sweetness and wit, they're but mummy,[3] possessed.

The Flea[1]

Mark but this flea, and mark in this,
How little that which thou deniest me is;
It sucked me first,[2] and now sucks thee,
And in this flea, our two bloods mingled be;
Thou know'st that this cannot be said
A sin, nor shame, nor loss of maidenhead,
    Yet this enjoys before it woo,
    And pampered swells with one blood made of two,
    And this, alas, is more than we would do.

Oh stay, three lives in one flea spare,
Where we almost, yea more than married are.
This flea is you and I, and this
Our marriage bed, and marriage temple is;
    Though parents grudge, and you, w'are met,
    And cloistered in these living walls of jet.° *black*
    Though use make you apt to kill me,
    Let not to that, self murder added be,
    And sacrilege, three sins in killing three.

Cruel and sudden, hast thou since
Purpled thy nail, in blood of innocence?
Wherein could this flea guilty be,
Except in that drop which it sucked from thee?
Yet thou triumph'st, and say'st that thou
Find'st not thy self, nor me the weaker now;
        'Tis true, then learn how false, fears be;
        Just so much honor, when thou yield'st to me,
        Will waste, as this flea's death took life from thee.

The Bait[1]

Come live with me, and be my love,
And we will some new pleasures prove
Of golden sands, and crystal brooks,
With silken lines, and silver hooks.

There will the river whispering run
Warmed by thy eyes, more than the sun.

2. The concentric globes that created sublime music as they revolved around the earth.
3. Medicine made from mummies; dead bodies.
1. Based on a poem attributed to Ovid, the poem plays on the belief that intercourse involved the mixing of bloods.
2. "Me it sucked first" in the 1635 edition.
1. Parodies Marlowe's *The Passionate Shepherd to His Love* and Raleigh's *The Nymph's Reply*.

And there the enamored fish will stay,
Begging themselves they may betray.

When thou wilt swim in that live bath,
Each fish, which every channel hath,
Will amorously to thee swim,
Gladder to catch thee, then thou him.

If thou, to be so seen, be'st loath,
By sun, or moon, thou darkenest both,
And if myself have leave to see,
I need not their light, having thee.

Let others freeze with angling reeds,
And cut their legs, with shells and weeds,
Or treacherously poor fish beset,
With strangling snare, or windowy net:

Let coarse bold hands, from slimy nest
The bedded fish in banks out-wrest,
Or curious traitors, sleave-silk flies[2]
Bewitch poor fishes' wandering eyes.

For thee, thou need'st no such deceit,
For thou thyself are thine own bait;
That fish, that is not catched thereby,
Alas, is wiser far than I.

The Apparition

When by thy scorn, O murderess, I am dead,
And that thou thinkst thee free
From all solicitation from me,
Then shall my ghost come to thy bed,
And thee, feigned vestal,° in worse arms shall see; *virgin priestess*
Then thy sick taper will begin to wink,
And he, whose thou art then, being tired before,
Will, if thou stir, or pinch to wake him, think
    Thou call'st for more,
And in false sleep will from thee shrink,
And then poor aspen[1] wretch, neglected thou
Bathed in a cold quicksilver[2] sweat will lie
    A verier° ghost than I; *truer*
What I will say, I will not tell thee now,
Lest that preserve thee; and since my love is spent,
I had rather thou shouldst painfully repent,
Than by my threatenings rest still innocent.

2. Artificial flies made from silk threads.

1. Trembling like an aspen leaf in the wind.

2. Liquid mercury, used to treat venereal disease.

A Valediction: Forbidding Mourning[1]

As virtuous men pass mildly away,
And whisper to their souls, to go,
Whilst some of their sad friends do say,
The breath goes now, and some say, no:

So let us melt, and make no noise,
No tear-floods, nor sigh-tempests move,
'Twere profanation° of our joys *desecration*
To tell the laity[2] of our love.

Moving of th'earth brings harms and fears,
Men reckon what it did and meant,
But trepidation of the spheres,[3]
Though greater far, is innocent.

Dull sublunary[4] lovers' love
(Whose soul is sense) cannot admit
Absence, because it doth remove
Those things which elemented° it. *composed*

But we by a love, so much refined,
That our selves know not what it is,
Inter-assurèd of the mind,
Care less, eyes, lips, and hands to miss.

Our two souls therefore, which are one,
Though I must go, endure not yet
A breach, but an expansion,
Like gold to airy thinness beat.[5]

If they be two, they are two so
As stiff twin compasses[6] are two,
Thy soul the fixed foot, makes no show
To move, but doth, if th' other do.

And though it in the center sit,
Yet when the other far doth roam,
It leans, and hearkens after it,
And grows erect, as that comes home.

Such wilt thou be to me, who must
Like th' other foot, obliquely run;
Thy firmness makes my circle just,° *complete*
And makes me end, where I begun.

1. In his *Life of Dr. John Donne* (1640), Walton describes the occasion as Donne's farewell to his wife before his journey to France in 1611.
2. The uninitiated.
3. Though the movement of the spheres is greater than an earthquake, we feel its effects less.
4. Under the sphere of the moon, hence sensual.
5. Gold was beaten to produce gold leaf. "Airy" suggests their love will become so fine that it will be spiritual.
6. A common emblem of constancy amidst change.

The Ecstasy[1]

Where, like a pillow on a bed,
  A pregnant bank swelled up, to rest
The violet's reclining head,[2]
  Sat we two, one another's best.

Our hands were firmly cemented
  With a fast balm, which thence did spring,
Our eye-beams twisted, and did thread
  Our eyes, upon one double string;[3]

So to intergraft our hands, as yet
  Was all the means to make us one,
And pictures in our eyes to get
  Was all our propagation.[4]

As 'twixt two equal armies, Fate
  Suspends uncertain victory,
Our souls (which to advance their state
  Were gone out) hung 'twixt her and me.

And whilst our souls negotiate there,
  We like sepulchral statues lay;
All day, the same our postures were,
  And we said nothing, all the day.

If any, so by love refined,
  That he soul's language understood,
And by good love were grown all mind,
  Within convenient distance stood,

He (though he knew not which soul spake
  Because both meant, both spake the same)
Might thence a new concoction[5] take,
  And part far purer than he came.

This ecstasy doth unperplex,
  We said, and tell us what we love,
We see by this, it was not sex,
  We see, we saw not what did move:

But as all several souls contain
  Mixture of things, they know not what,
Love, these mixed souls, doth mix again,
  And makes both one, each this and that.

A single violet transplant,
  The strength, the color, and the size,

1. From *ekstasis* (Greek) meaning passion and the withdrawal of the soul from the body. A beautiful and secluded pastoral spot was a frequent setting for love poetry.
2. The violet was an emblem of faithfulness.
3. The lovers are totally enthralled by gazing into each other's eyes.
4. The act of reflecting each other's image was called "making babies."
5. Refining of metals by heat.

(All which before was poor and scant)
Redoubles still, and multiplies.

When love with one another so
Interinanimates two souls,
That abler soul, which thence doth flow,
Defects of loneliness controls.

We then, who are this new soul, know,
Of what we are composed and made,
For, th' atomies° of which we grow, *components, parts*
Are souls, whom no change can invade.

But O alas, so long, so far
Our bodies why do we forbear?
They are ours, though they are not we, we are
The intelligences, they the sphere.[6]

We owe them thanks, because they thus,
Did us to us at first convey,
Yielded their forces, sense, to us,
Nor are dross° to us, but allay.° *refuse / a mixture*

On man heaven's influence works not so,
But that it first imprints the air,[7]
So soul into the soul may flow,
Though it to body first repair.

As our blood labors to beget
Spirits, as like souls as it can,
Because such fingers need to knit
That subtle knot, which makes us man:[8]

So much pure lovers' souls descend
T'affections,° and to faculties,°[9] *feelings / powers*
Which sense may reach and apprehend,
Else a great prince in prison lies.

To our bodies turn we then, that so
Weak men on love revealed may look;
Love's mysteries in souls do grow,
But yet the body is his book.

And if some lover, such as we,
Have heard this dialogue of one,
Let him still mark us, he shall see
Small change, when we are to bodies gone.

6. In Aristotelian cosmology, each planet moved in a sphere (the form of its motion around the earth) and was guided by an inner spiritual force, or intelligence.
7. An angel has to put on clothes of air to be seen by men; in hermetic medicine, the air mediates the influence of the stars. Just as spirits need a material medium, so souls need the union of bodies.
8. In scholastic philosophy a human being is composed of body and soul, and vapors called spirits produced by the blood link the body with the soul.
9. As the blood mediates between body and soul, so the lovers' feelings mediate between flesh and spirit.

The Funeral

Whoever comes to shroud me, do not harm
Nor question much
That subtle wreath of hair, which crowns my arm;
The mystery, the sign you must not touch,
For 'tis my outward soul,
Viceroy to that, which then to heaven being gone,
Will leave this to control,
And keep these limbs her provinces, from dissolution.

For if the sinewy thread my brain lets fall
Through every part,
Can tie those parts, and make me one of all;[1]
These hairs which upward grew, and strength and art
Have from a better brain,
Can better do it;[2] except she meant that I
By this should know my pain,
As prisoners then are manacled when they're condemned to die.

Whate'er she meant by it, bury it with me,
For since I am
Love's martyr, it might breed idolatry,
If into others' hands these relics[3] came;
As 'twas humility
To afford to it all a soul can do,
So, 'tis some bravery,
That since you would save[4] none of me, I bury some of you.

The Relic

When my grave is broke up again
Some second guest to entertain,
(For graves have learned that woman-head[1]
To be to more than one a bed)
And he that digs it, spies
A bracelet of bright hair about the bone,
Will he not let us alone,
And think that there a loving couple lies,
Who thought that this device might be some way
To make their souls, at the last busy day,
Meet at this grave, and make a little stay?

1. There was a theory that nerves emanating from the brain held the entire body together.
2. Her hairs coming from a better brain could better preserve his body.
3. Objects, often body parts, that served as memorials of a saint.
4. Editions from 1633 to 1669 read "have," as do some manuscripts.
1. A feminine trait, with a play on maidenhead. The reference is to the custom of burying more than one corpse in the same grave.

If this fall in a time, or land,
Where misdevotion[2] doth command,
Then, he that digs us up, will bring
Us, to the Bishop, and the King,
To make us relics; then
Thou shalt be a Mary Magdalen, and I
A something else thereby;[3]
All women shall adore us, and some men;
And since at such time, miracles are sought,
I would have that age by this paper taught
What miracles we harmless lovers wrought.

First, we loved well and faithfully,
Yet knew not what we loved, nor why,
Difference of sex no more we knew,
Than our guardian angels do;
Coming and going, we
Perchance might kiss, but not between those meals;
Our hands ne'er touched the seals,
Which nature, injured by late law, sets free:[4]
These miracles we did; but now alas,
All measure, and all language, I should pass,
Should I tell what a miracle she was.

Elegy 19: To His Mistress Going to Bed[1]

Come, Madam, come, all rest my powers defy,
Until I labor, I in labor° lie. *suffering*
The foe oft-times having the foe in sight,
Is tired with standing though he never fight.
Off with that girdle,° like heaven's zone° glistering, *belt / zodiac*
But a far fairer world encompassing.
Unpin that spangled breastplate[2] which you wear,
That th'eyes of busy fools may be stopped there.
Unlace your self, for that harmonious chime,
Tells me from you, that now it is bed time.
Off with that happy busk,° which I envy, *bodice*
That still can be, and still can stand so nigh.
Your gown going off, such beauteous state reveals,
As when from flowery meads th' hill's shadow steals.
Off with that wiry coronet and show
The hairy diadem which on you doth grow:
Now off with those shoes, and then safely tread

2. Idolatry, as in *The Second Anniversary*, where Donne calls prayers to saints "misdevotion."
3. Possibly Jesus Christ or one of Mary's lovers.
4. Nature permits a free love forbidden by human law.
1. In Latin poetry, an elegy was a poem in "elegiacs" (alternating lines of dactylic hexameters and pentameters). Most of these, like Ovid's *Amores*, were about love and sex; Donne imitates Ovid's wit and eroticism. This poem was refused a license to be printed in 1633; it was first printed in *The Harmony of the Muses* (1654).
2. The stomacher, a covering for the chest worn under the bodice and covered with jewels.

In this love's hallowed temple, this soft bed.
In such white robes, heaven's angels used to be
Received by men; thou angel bring'st with thee
A heaven like Mahomet's paradise;[3] and though
Ill spirits walk in white, we easily know,
By this these angels from an evil sprite,
Those set our hairs, but these our flesh upright.
   License my roving hands, and let them go,
Before, behind, between, above, below.
Oh my America! my new-found-land,
My kingdom, safliest when with one man manned,
My mine of precious stones, my empery,° *empire*
How blest am I in this discovering thee!
To enter in these bonds, is to be free;
Then where my hand is set, my seal shall be.[4]
   Full nakedness! All joys are due to thee.
As souls unbodied, bodies unclothed must be,
To taste whole joys. Gems which you women use
Are like Atlanta's balls, cast in men's views,[5]
That when a fool's eye lighteth on a gem,
His earthly soul may covet theirs, not them.
Like pictures, or like books' gay coverings made
For laymen, are all women thus arrayed;
Themselves are mystic books, which only we
(Whom their imputed grace will dignify)
Must see revealed.[6] Then since that I may know,
As liberally, as to a midwife, show
Thyself: cast all, yea, this white linen hence,
Here is no penance much less innocence.[7]
To teach thee, I am naked first; why then
What need'st thou have more covering than a man?

from Holy Sonnets[1]
Divine Meditations

1

As due by many titles° I resign *legal rights*
Myself to thee, Oh God, first I was made
By thee, and for thee, and when I was decayed
Thy blood bought that, the which before was thine,
I am thy son, made with thyself to shine,
Thy servant, whose pains thou has still repaid,

3. A heaven of sensual pleasure.
4. He has signed an agreement, which he will now stamp with his seal. Also, he has put his hand where he will consummate his desire.
5. Donne changes the story of how Atalanta was distracted from racing her suitor Hippomenes when he threw three golden apples before her, which she paused to pick up.
6. The analogy is between the grace that man cannot merit from God in Calvinist doctrine and the undeserved favors women grant their lovers.
7. The 1669 edition and some manuscripts read: "There is no penance due to innocence."
1. The first 12 of the sonnets are printed in the sequence of the 1633 edition, which, according to Helen Gardner, represents Donne's order.

Thy sheep, thine image, and, till I betrayed
Myself, a temple of thy Spirit divine;
Why doth the devil then usurp on me?
Why doth he steal, nay ravish that's thy right?
Except thou rise and for thine own work fight,
Oh I shall soon despair, when I do see
That thou lov'st mankind well, yet wilt not choose me,
And Satan hates me, yet is loth to lose me.

2

Oh my black soul! Now thou art summoned
By sickness, death's herald, and champion;
Thou art like a pilgrim, which abroad hath done
Treason, and durst not turn to whence he is fled,
Or like a thief, which till death's doom be read,
Wisheth himself delivered from prison;
But damned and haled° to execution, *dragged*
Wisheth that still he might be imprisoned;
Yet grace, if thou repent, thou canst not lack;
But who shall give thee that grace to begin?
Oh make thyself with holy mourning black,
And red with blushing, as thou art with sin;
Or wash thee in Christ's blood, which has this might
That being red, it dyes red souls to white.

3

This is my play's last scene, here heavens appoint
My pilgrimage's last mile; and my race
Idly, yet quickly run, hath this last pace,
My span's last inch, my minute's latest point,
And gluttonous death, will instantly unjoint
My body, and soul, and I shall sleep a space,
But my ever-waking part shall see that face,
Whose fear already shakes my every joint:
Then, as my soul, to heaven her first seat, takes flight,
And earth-borne body, in the earth shall dwell,
So, fall my sins, that all may have their right,
To where they're bred, and would press me, to hell.
Impute me righteous, thus purged of evil,[2]
For thus I leave the world, the flesh, and devil.

4

At the round earth's imagined corners, blow[3]
Your trumpets, angels, and arise, arise
From death, you numberless infinities

2. Protestant theology held that even when a man repented of his sins, he was still marked by the sin of Adam and needed to be made righteous by Christ's grace.

3. "I saw four angels standing on the four corners of the earth, holding the four winds of the earth" (Revelation 7.1).

Of souls, and to your scattered bodies go,
All whom the flood did, and fire shall o'erthrow,[4]
All whom war, dearth, age, agues, tyrannies,
Despair, law, chance, hath slain, and you whose eyes,
Shall behold God, and never taste death's woe.[5]
But let them sleep, Lord, and me mourn a space,
For, if above all these, my sins abound,
'Tis late to ask abundance of thy grace,
When we are there; here on this lowly ground,
Teach me how to repent; for that's as good
As if thou hadst sealed my pardon with thy blood.

5

If poisonous minerals, and if that tree,
Whose fruit threw death on else immortal us,
If lecherous goats, if serpents envious
Cannot be damned; alas, why should I be?
Why should intent or reason, born in me,
Make sins, else equal, in me more heinous?
And mercy being easy, and glorious
To God, in his stern wrath, why threatens he?
But who am I, that dare dispute with thee?
O God, Oh! of thine only worthy blood,
And my tears, make a heavenly Lethean[6] flood,
And drown in it my sins' black memory.
That thou remember them, some claim as debt,
I think it mercy, if thou wilt forget.

6

Death be not proud, though some have called thee
Mighty and dreadful, for thou are not so.
For, those, whom thou think'st thou dost overthrow,
Die not, poor death, nor yet canst thou kill me;
From rest and sleep, which but thy pictures be,
Much pleasure, then from thee, much more must flow,
And soonest our best men with thee do go,
Rest of their bones, and soul's delivery.
Thou art slave to fate, chance, kings, and desperate men,
And dost with poison, war, and sickness dwell,
And poppy,° or charms can make us sleep as well, *a narcotic*
And better than thy stroke; why swell'st° thou then? *grow in pride*
One short sleep past, we wake eternally,
And death shall be no more. Death thou shalt die.[7]

4. The flood that Noah survived (Genesis 7) and the fire that will destroy the world at the last judgment (Revelation 6.11).
5. The resurrection of the body (see 1 Corinthians 15.51–52).
6. Of Lethe, the river of forgetfulness in the underworld of ancient mythology.
7. "The last enemy that shall be destroyed is death" (1 Corinthians 15.26).

7

Spit in my face ye Jews, and pierce my side,
Buffet, and scoff, scourge, and crucify me,
For I have sinned, and sinned, and only he,
Who could do no iniquity, hath died:
But by my death cannot be satisfied° *atoned for*
My sins, which pass° the Jews' impiety: *surpass, exceed*
They killed once an inglorious[8] man, but I
Crucify him daily, being now glorified.[9]
Oh let me then, his strange love still admire:
Kings pardon, but he bore our punishment.
And Jacob came clothed in vile harsh attire
But to supplant, and with gainful intent:[1]
God clothed himself in vile man's flesh, that so
He might be weak enough to suffer woe.

8

Why are we by all creatures waited on?
Why do the prodigal elements supply
Life and food to me, being more pure than I,
Simple, and further from corruption?[2]
Why brook'st thou, ignorant horse, subjection?
Why dost thou bull, and boar so sillily
Dissemble weakness, and by one man's stroke die,[3]
Whose whole kind, you might swallow and feed upon?
Weaker I am, woe is me, and worse than you,
You have not sinned, nor need be timorous.
But wonder at a greater wonder, for to us
Created nature doth these things subdue,
But their Creator, whom sin, nor nature tied,
For us, his creatures, and his foes, hath died.

9

What if this present were the world's last night?
Mark in my heart, O soul, where thou dost dwell,
The picture of Christ crucified, and tell
Whether that countenance can thee affright,
Tears in his eyes quench the amazing light,
Blood fills his frowns, which from his pierced head fell,
And can that tongue adjudge thee unto hell,
Which prayed forgiveness for his foes' fierce spite?
No, no; but as in my idolatry[4]

8. Unknown; not yet ascended into glory.
9. Every sin knowingly committed is another torture of Christ. (See Hebrews 6.6: "They crucify to themselves the Son of God afresh.")
1. Jacob tricked his father Isaac into giving him his blessing by disguising himself in goatskin as his hairy brother Esau (see Genesis 27.1–36).
2. The elements are physically and morally pure, while humans are a complex mixture of all four elements, prone to decay, and moral agents, capable of sin.
3. The slaughterman's blow, and Adam's sin, causing death to all creation.
4. Erotic devotion to women.

I said to all my profane mistresses,
Beauty, of pity, foulness only is
A sign of rigor:[5] so I say to thee,
To wicked spirits are horrid shapes assigned,
This beauteous form assures a piteous mind.

10

Batter my heart, three-personed God;[6] for, you
As yet but knock, breathe, shine, and seek to mend;
That I may rise, and stand, o'erthrow me, and bend
Your force, to break, blow, burn and make me new.
I, like an usurped town, to another due,
Labor to admit you, but oh, to no end,
Reason your viceroy° in me, me should defend, *ruler*
But is captived, and proves weak or untrue,
Yet dearly I love you, and would be loved fain,° *willingly*
But am betrothed unto your enemy,
Divorce me, untie, or break that knot again,
Take me to you, imprison me, for I
Except you enthrall me, never shall be free,
Nor ever chaste, except you ravish me.

11

Wilt thou love God, as he thee? Then digest,° *consider*
My soul, this wholesome meditation,
How God the Spirit, by angels waited on
In heaven, doth make his temple in thy breast.
The Father having begot a Son most blest,
And still begetting, (for he ne'er begun)[7]
Hath deigned to choose thee by adoption,
Coheir to his glory, and Sabbath's endless rest;
And as a robbed man, which by search doth find
His stol'n stuff sold, must lose or buy it again:
The Son of glory came down, and was slain,
Us whom he had made, and Satan stol'n, to unbind.
'Twas much, that man was made like God before,
But, that God should be made like man, much more.

12

Father, part of his double interest
Unto thy kingdom, thy Son gives to me,
His jointure° in the knotty Trinity, *joint tenancy*
He keeps, and gives me his death's conquest.

5. Beautiful women show compassion; only ugly ones refuse their lovers.

6. The Trinity: God the Father, Son, and Holy Spirit.

7. God's existence and begetting of his Son are both eternal.

This Lamb, whose death, with life the world hath blest,
Was from the world's beginning slain, and he[8]
Hath made two wills, which with the legacy[9]
Of his and thy kingdom, do thy sons invest.
Yet such are those laws, that men argue yet
Whether a man those statutes can fulfill;
None doth, but all-healing grace and Spirit,
Revive again what law and letter kill.
Thy law's abridgement, and thy last command
Is all but love; oh let that last will stand![1]

from Devotions Upon Emergent Occasions[1]

["FOR WHOM THE BELL TOLLS"]

Nunc lento sonitu dicunt, morieris.
Now this bell tolling softly for another, says to me, Thou must die.

Perchance he for whom this bell[2] tolls may be so ill as that he knows not it tolls for him; and perchance I may think myself so much better than I am, as that they who are about me, and see my state may have caused it to toll for me, and I know not that. The Church is catholic, universal, so are all her actions; all that she does, belongs to all. When she baptises a child, that action concerns me; for that child is thereby connected to that Head which is my Head too, and engrafted into that body,[3] whereof I am a member. And when she buries a man, that action concerns me: all mankind is of one Author, and is of one volume; when one man dies, one chapter is not torn out of the book, but translated[4] into a better language; and every chapter must be so translated. God employs several translators; some pieces are translated by age, some by sickness, some by war, some by justice; but God's hand is in every translation, and his hand shall bind up all our scattered leaves again, for that library where every book shall lie open to one another. As therefore the bell that rings to a sermon calls not upon the preacher only, but upon the congregation to come, so this bell calls us all; but how much more me, whom am brought so near the door by this sickness. There was a contention as far as a suit, (in which both piety and dignity, religion, and estimation, were mingled) which of the religious orders should ring to prayers first in the morning; and it was determined that they should ring first that rose earliest. If we understand aright the dignity of this bell that tolls for our evening prayer, we would be glad to make it ours by rising early, in that application, that it might be ours, as well as his whose indeed it is. The bell doth toll for him that thinks it doth; and though it intermit again, yet from that minute that occasion wrought upon him, he is united to God. Who casts not up his eye to the sun when it rises? but who takes off his eye from a comet when that breaks out?

8. Christ, "the Lamb slain from the foundation of the world" (Revelation 13.8).
9. Old and New Testaments.
1. "A new commandment I give unto you, that ye love one another" (John 13.34).

1. Donne wrote the *Devotions* (1624) following an illness he suffered in winter 1623. Each meditation concerns a phase of his disease.
2. The passing-bell rung slowly when a person was dying.
3. United with the church.
4. From Latin *translatus*, "having been carried across."

Who bends not his ear to any bell which upon any occasion rings? but who can remove it from that bell which is passing a piece of himself out of this world? No man is an island, entire of itself; every man is a piece of the Continent, a part of the main. If a clod be washed away by the sea, Europe is the less, as well as if a promontory were, as well as if a manor of thy friends or of thine own were. Any man's death diminishes me, because I am involved in mankind; and therefore never send to know for whom the bell tolls; it tolls for thee. Neither can we call this a begging of misery or a borrowing of misery, as though we were not miserable enough of ourselves but must fetch in more from the next house in taking upon us the misery of our neighbors. Truly it were an excusable covetousness if we did; for affliction is a treasure, and scarce any man hath enough of it. No man hath affliction enough that is not matured and ripened by it, and made fit for God by that affliction. If a man carry treasure in bullion, or in a wedge of gold, and have none coined into current moneys, his treasure will not defray him as he travels. Tribulation is treasure in the nature of it, but it is not current money in the use of it, except we get nearer and nearer our home, heaven, by it. Another man may be sick too, and sick to death, and this affliction may lie in his bowels as gold in a mine and be of no use to him: but this bell that tells me of his affliction digs out and applies that gold to me, if by this consideration of another's danger I take mine own into contemplation and so secure myself by making my recourse to my God who is our only security.

Lady Mary Wroth

1586–1640

Lady Mary Wroth was born the same year that her uncle Sir Philip Sidney died in battle. Like her uncle, she wrote brilliant sonnets and an entertaining and complex prose romance, but whereas his death and writing became the stuff of myth, she died in obscurity. Appreciated by the finest poets of her time, her writing was neglected for the next 300 years; she has only recently been rediscovered as one of the most compelling women writers of her age. Her *Pamphilia to Amphilanthus*, the first Petrarchan sonnet sequence in English by a woman, was first printed in 1621 but was not reprinted until 1977. Wroth's work has finally become available outside rare book libraries, thanks to Josephine Robert's editions of Wroth's complete poems (1983) and her prose romance *The Countess of Montgomeries Urania* (1995), along with Michael Brennan's edition of her pastoral tragicomedy *Love's Victory* (1988). Recent criticism has stressed the formal complexity and variety of her poetry and prose, their creation of female subjectivity, and their relationship to her life and social context, shedding new light on one of the most emotionally powerful and stylistically innovative authors of the Jacobean period.

Mary Wroth was born into the cultivated and distinguished Sidney family. Mary and her mother, two brothers, and seven sisters lived at the family estate Penshurst in Kent. She sometimes visited her father in the Low Countries, where he commanded the English troops fighting for the Protestant cause against the Spanish. Ben Jonson sang the praises of Lady Mary's family and their way of life in *To Penshurst* (see page 1569), a place where the children not only enjoyed natural beauty—"broad beech" and "chest-nut shade"—but also learned the "mysteries of manners, arms and arts." Mary also spent a great deal of time in London with her aunt for whom she was named, Mary (Sidney) Herbert, Countess of Pembroke, hostess to and patron of a circle of poets that included George Chapman and Ben Jonson.

Mary found a mentor in her aunt, who herself wrote poems as well as translations of the Psalms and of Petrarch. Mary Herbert's translation of Petrarch's *Trionfo della Morte* ("Triumph of Death") portrays the poet's beloved Laura not as a passive object but as a lively and eloquent speaker. Mary Wroth's own sonnets similarly portray the woman as the suffering and desiring subject of love rather than the mute object that was common in earlier English Petrarchan poetry. Mary Wroth took the title of her *Urania* from a character in Philip Sidney's *The Countess of Pembrokes Arcadia*, whose publication had been overseen by his sister, Mary Sidney Herbert. Mary Wroth even created the character of the Queen of Naples as a fictional version of her aunt and perhaps saw *Urania* as a continuation of *Arcadia*.

When Mary married Sir Robert Wroth, Lord of Durance and Laughton House and juror for the Gunpowder Plot, she continued her close family ties with her aunt and father (yet another poet), but she also moved into the larger world of the Jacobean court. She served as Queen Anne's companion, and she became at once an observer and a center of attention in the aristocratic circle at court. In 1605, shortly after the first recorded performance of *Othello* at Whitehall, Lady Mary Wroth played in Ben Jonson's *Masque of Blackness*, in which she was presented to the court with Lady Frances Walsingham as the embodiment of gravity and dignity. Later, Wroth would deploy metaphors of darkness and night to great effect in her lyric poems.

It was in this court context that she attracted the attention of Ben Jonson, who not only wrote a poem complimenting her husband but also dedicated a sonnet and two epigrams to her. Jonson paid tribute to her as a subject and inspiration for poetry and as a powerfully moving poet in her own right. He claimed that since writing out her sonnets, he had "become / A better lover and much better poet." Dedicating his great play *The Alchemist* to her, he portrayed her as inheriting her uncle's mantle as poet: "To that Lady Most Deserving her Name and Blood, Lady Mary Wroth,"—a pun on her name, as Wroth was pronounced "worth." While she, too, punned on her married name in her poetry, Mary clung to her identity as a Sidney, using the Sidney device in her letters.

Her marriage was not particularly happy and pales in comparison with her literary friendship and love affair with her cousin William Herbert, by whom she had two illegitimate children, after she was widowed in 1614. During the years of her early widowhood she wrote the first part of her prose romance *Urania*, which was printed with *Pamphilia to Amphilanthus* in 1621. The *Urania* not only presents a fictional account of her relationship with her cousin and her parents' own happy marriage but also was read at the time as a criticism of the mores of the court. King James's courtiers, taking offense at the satire of their private lives, attacked her, prompting her to ask for the book to be removed from publication a few months after it first appeared. The early modern prejudice against women writing surfaces in Lord Denny's punning condescension to Wroth: "leave idle books alone / For wiser and worthier women have writ none."

Fortunately for us, she didn't take his advice and continued to write the second book of the *Urania*, which survives in manuscript. Indeed, no record of a warrant to recall the book survives. Her final years remain a mystery; she lived in retirement after her cousin's death. She left behind a body of poetry challenging the status quo of the court, proclaiming the suffering she had endured for love, and singing the beauty of spiritual love in a woman's voice. Imitating not only her uncle Philip's *Arcadia* but also the *Heptameron* of the French writer Marguerite de Navarre, Mary Wroth made the prose romance a complex combination of novelistic fantasy, roman à clef, and social satire. The greatest English woman writer of her age, Mary Wroth fashioned a new voice and new perspectives within literary tradition that convey the fullness and complexity of her life as woman, lover, and writer.

from Pamphilia to Amphilanthus[1]

1

When night's black mantle could most darkness prove,
And sleep death's image did my senses hire
From knowledge of myself, then thoughts did move
Swifter than those most swiftness need require:
In sleep, a chariot drawn by winged desire
I saw, where sat bright Venus, Queen of love,
And at her feet her son,[2] still adding fire
To burning hearts which she did hold above,
But one heart flaming more than all the rest
The goddess held, and put it to my breast.
"Dear son, now shut,"[3] said she, "thus must we win."
He her obeyed, and martyred my poor heart,
I, waking, hoped as dreams it would depart;[4]
Yet since, O me, a lover I have been.

5

Can pleasing sight, misfortune ever bring?
Can firm desire a painful torment try?
Can winning eyes prove to the heart a sting?
Or can sweet lips in treason hidden lie?
The Sun most pleasing blinds the strongest eye.
If too much look'd on, breaking the sight's string;[5]
Desires still crossed, must unto mischief hie,° *move quickly*
And as despair, a luckless chance may fling.
Eyes, having won, rejecting proves a sting
Killing the bud before the tree doth spring;
Sweet lips not loving do as poison prove:
Desire, sight, eyes, lips, seek, see, prove, and find
You love may win, but curses if unkind;
Then show you harm's dislike, and joy in Love.[6]

16

Am I thus conquered? Have I lost the powers
That to withstand, which joys to ruin me?
Must I be still while it my strength devours
And captive leads me prisoner, bound, unfree?
Love first shall leave men's fant'sies to them free,[7]
Desire shall quench love's flames, spring hate sweet showers,
Love shall loose all his darts, have sight, and see

1. The title means "From the All-loving one to the Dual Lover." First published in 1621, the sonnet sequence is here printed according to the numbering in Josephine Robert's 1983 edition.
2. Cupid. Compare the image of the chariot here with that in Petrarch's *Triumph of Love*.
3. Enclose that flaming heart within Pamphilia.
4. Pamphilia's experience of love is represented as a dream vision, a symbolic narrative in which the dreamer discovers hidden truth.
5. Compare 1.6 with Donne's "The Extasie," lines 7–8. Both poems rely on the early modern notion that the eyes give off light that make vision possible.
6. The form of this poem that begins with rhetorical questions that are echoed in the answers that follow is called *carmen correlativum*, or correlative verse.
7. Before I surrender to Love, Love will allow men to realize their fantasies freely.

His shame, and wishings hinder happy hours.[8]
Why should we not Love's purblind° charms resist? *totally blind*
Must we be servile, doing what he list?° *wants*
No, seek some host to harbor thee: I fly
Thy babish° tricks, and freedom do profess; *childish*
But O my hurt, makes my lost heart confess
I love, and must. So farewell liberty.

17

Truly poor Night thou welcome art to me;
I love thee better in this sad attire
Than that which raiseth some men's fant'sies higher
Like painted outsides which foul inward be.[9]
I love thy grave, and saddest looks to see,
Which seems my soul, and dying heart entire,
Like to the ashes of some happy fire
That flamed in joy, but quenched in misery.
I love thy count'nance,° and thy sober pace *face, expression*
Which evenly goes, and as of loving grace
To us, and me among the rest oppressed
Gives quiet, peace to my poor self alone,
And freely grants day leave when thou art gone
To give clear light to see all ill redressed.

25

Like to the Indians, scorched with the sun,
The sun which they do as their God adore
So am I us'd by love, for ever more
I worship him, less favors have I won.
Better are they who thus to blackness run,
And so can only whiteness' want deplore
Then I who pale and white am with grief's store,
Nor can have hope, but to see hopes undone;
Besides their sacrifice received's in sight
Of their chose saint: Mine hid as worthless rite;
Grant me to see where I my offerings give,
Then let me wear the mark of Cupid's might
In heart as they in skin of Phoebus° light *Apollo, the sun god*
Not ceasing off'rings to love while I live.

26

When everyone to pleasing pastime hies° *goes in haste*
Some hunt, some hawk,[1] some play, while some delight
In sweet discourse, and music shows joy's might
Yet I my thoughts do far above these prize.

8. Cupid blindfolded was a popular figure in Renaissance iconography.
9. Like the whitewashed sepulchers (tombs) in Matthew 23.27.
1. To hunt game with hawks.

The joy which I take is that free from eyes
I sit, and wonder at this day-like night
So to dispose themselves, as void of right,
And leave true pleasure for poor vanities;
When others hunt, my thoughts I have in chase;
If hawk, my mind at wishèd end doth fly,
Discourse, I with my spirit talk, and cry
While others music choose as greatest grace.
O God, say I, can these fond pleasures move?
Or music be but in sweet thoughts of love?

28. Song

Sweetest love, return again,
Make not too long stay;
Killing mirth and forcing pain,
Sorrow leading way,
Let us not thus parted be,
Love and absence ne'er agree;

But since you must needs depart,
And me hapless° leave, *unlucky*
In your journey take my heart
Which will not deceive.
Yours it is, to you it flies
Joying in those lovèd eyes,

So in part, we shall not part
Though we absent be;
Time, nor place, nor greatest smart
Shall my bands make free.
Tied I am, yet think it gain,
In such knots I feel no pain.

But can I live having lost
Chiefest part of me?
Heart is fled, and sight is crossed,
These my fortunes be;
Yet dear heart go, soon return,
As good there as here to burn.

39

Take heed mine eyes, how you your looks do cast,
Lest they betray my heart's most secret thought;
Be true unto yourselves for nothing's bought
More dear than doubt which brings a lover's fast.
Catch you all watching eyes, ere they be past,
Or take yours fixed where your best love hath sought
The pride of your desires; let them be taught
Their faults for shame, they could no truer last;

Then look, and look with joy for conquest won,
Of those that searched your hurt in double kind;
So you kept safe, let them themselves look blind;
Watch, gaze, and mark 'til they to madness run,
While you, mine eyes, enjoy full sight of love
Contented that such happinesses move.

40

False hope which feeds but to destroy, and spill° *kill*
What it first breeds; unnatural to the birth
Of thine own womb; conceiving but to kill,[2]
And plenty gives to make the greater dearth,
So tyrants do who falsely ruling earth
Outwardly grace them, and with profits fill,
Advance those who appointed are to death
To make their greater fall to please their will.
Thus shadow they their wicked vile intent,
Coloring evil with a show of good
While in fair shows their malice so is spent;
Hope kills the heart, and tyrants shed the blood.
For hope deluding brings us to the pride[3]
Of our desires the farther down to slide.

48

If ever Love had force in human breast?
If ever he could move in pensive heart?
Or if that he such power could but impart
To breed those flames whose heat brings joy's unrest,
Then look on me: I am to these addressed.
I am the soul that feels the greatest smart,
I am that heartless trunk of heart's depart,
And I, that one, by love and grief oppressed;
None ever felt the truth of Love's great miss° *need, want*
Of eyes, 'til I deprived was of bliss;
For had he seen, he must have pity showed;
I should not have been made this stage of woe
Where sad disasters have their open show;
O no, more pity he had sure bestowed.

55

How like a fire doth love increase in me,
The longer that it lasts, the stronger still,
The greater purer, brighter, and doth fill
No eye with wonder more, then hopes still be
Bred in my breast, when fires of love are free
To use that part to their best pleasing will,
And now impossible it is to kill

2. The image is of a miscarriage or infanticide.

3. Arrogance, but also elation and pleasure.

The heat so great where Love his strength doth see.
Mine eyes can scare sustain the flames my heart
Doth trust in them my passions to impart,
And languishingly strive to show my love;
My breath not able is to breathe least part
Of that increasing fuel of my smart;
Yet love I will till I but ashes prove.[4]
Pamphilia[5]

68

My pain, still smothered in my grievèd breast
Seeks for some ease, yet cannot passage find
To be discharged of this unwelcome guest;
When most I strive, more fast his burdens bind,
Like to a ship, on Goodwins[6] cast by wind
The more she strives, more deep in sand is pressed
Till she be lost; so am I, in this kind° *way*
Sunk and devoured, and swallowed by unrest,
Lost, shipwracked, spoiled, debarred of smallest hope
Nothing of pleasure left; save thoughts have scope,
Which wander may. Go then, my thoughts, and cry
Hope's perished, Love tempest-beaten, Joy lost:
Killing Despair hath all these blessings crossed.
Yet Faith still cries, Love will not falsify.

74. Song

Love a child is ever crying,
Please him, and he straight is flying;
Give him, he the more is craving,
Never satisfied with having.

His desires have no measure,
Endless folly is his treasure;
What he promiseth he breaketh;
Trust not one word that he speaketh.

He vows nothing but false matter,
And to cozen° you he'll flatter. *trick*
Let him gain the hand[7] he'll leave you,
And still glory to deceive you.

He will triumph in your wailing,
And yet cause be of your failing.
These his virtues are, and slighter

4. Josephine Roberts has noted that "will" may stand for the poet's lover William Herbert. Early modern poets frequently used the device of the embedded name.
5. To mark the completion of the first section of sonnets, the poet signed her pen name at the foot of sonnet 55.
6. A dangerous shoal off the southeastern coast of England.
7. Let him take control.

Are his gifts, his favors lighter.
Feathers are as firm in staying,
Wolves no fiercer in their preying;
As a child then leave him crying,
Nor seek him so given to flying.

from A Crown of Sonnets Dedicated to Love[1]

77

In this strange labyrinth how shall I turn?
Ways° are on all sides while the way I miss: *paths*
If to the right hand, there, in love I burn;
Let me go forward, therein danger is;
If to the left, suspicion hinders bliss,
Let me turn back, shame cries I ought return,
Nor faint° though crosses with my fortunes kiss;[2] *lose heart*
Stand still is harder, although sure to mourn.[3]
Thus let me take the right, or left-hand way,
Go forward, or stand still, or back retire;
I must these doubts endure without allay° *relief*
Or help, but travail[4] find for my best hire.
Yet that which most my troubled sense doth move
Is to leave all, and take the thread of love.[5]

82

He may our profit, and our tutor prove
In whom alone we do this power find,
To join two hearts as in one frame to move;
Two bodies, but one soul to rule the mind;
Eyes which must care to one dear object bind
Ears to each other's speech as if above
All else they sweet, and learned were; this kind
Content of lovers witnesseth true love.
It doth enrich the wits, and make you see
That in your self, which you knew not before,
Forcing you to admire such gifts should be
Hid from your knowledge, yet in you the store;
Millions of these adorn the throne of Love,
How blest be they then, who his favors prove.

83

How blessed be they then, who his favors prove,
A life whereof the birth is just desire,

1. The crown (Italian *corona*) is a form in which the last line of each poem is repeated as the first line of the next. The last poem of the sequence ends with the first line of the first poem.
2. Though troubles embrace my luck, or fate.
3. It is more difficult to do nothing, although this is sure to make me mourn.
4. Hard work, with wordplay on "Travel," which occurs in the 1621 text.
5. An allusion to the myth of Ariadne, beloved of Theseus, to whom she gave a thread to unwind behind him on his path through the labyrinth so that, after slaying the Minotaur, he could retrace his steps on his way out.

Breeding sweet flame which hearts invite to move
In these loved eyes which kindle Cupid's fire,
And nurse his longings with his thoughts entire,
Fixed on the heat of wishes formed by love;
Yet whereas fire destroys this doth aspire,
Increase, and foster all delights above;
Love will a painter make you, such as you
Shall able be to draw your only dear
More lovely, perfect, lasting, and more true
Than rarest workman, and to you more near.
These be the least, then all must needs confess
He that shuns love doth love himself the less.

84

He that shuns love does love himself the less
And cursed he whose spirit not admires
The worth of love, where endless blessedness
Reigns,[6] and commands, maintained by heav'nly fires
Made of virtue, joined by truth, blown by desires
Strengthened by worth, renewed by carefulness
Flaming in never changing thoughts, briers
Of jealousy shall here miss welcomeness;
Nor coldly pass in the pursuits of love
Like one long frozen in a sea of ice,
And yet but chastely let your passions move
No thought from virtuous love your minds entice.
Never to other ends your fant'sies place
But where they may return with honor's grace.

103

My muse now happy, lay thyself to rest,
Sleep in the quiet of a faithful love,
Write you no more, but let these fant'sies move
Some other hearts, wake not to new unrest;
But if you study, be those thoughts addressed
To truth, which shall eternal goodness prove,
Enjoying of true joy, the most, and best,
The endless gain which never will remove.
Leave the discourse to Venus, and her son
To young beginners, and their brains inspire
With stories of great love, and from that fire
Get heat to write the fortunes they have won,
And thus leave off; what's past shows you can love,
Now let your constancy your honor prove.

Pamphilia.[7]

6. Reigns: "raines" in the original.
7. According to the 1621 *Urania,* when Pamphilia accepts the keys to the Throne of Love, the virtue *Constancy* disappears and is transformed into Pamphilia's breast.

Robert Herrick

1591–1674

The urbane and at times pagan poet Robert Herrick might seem an unlikely candidate for rural vicar, but such were his connections that he was promoted from deacon to priest in a day. He spent most of his life as vicar of the Devonshire parish of Dean, where he wrote poetry about country customs and church liturgy. A hundred and fifty years after his death, a writer in the *Quarterly Review* was able to find people in the village who could recite from memory Herrick's *Farewell to Dean Bourn*: "I never look to see / Dean, or thy watery incivility," lines that "they said he uttered as he crossed the brook, upon being ejected from the vicarage by Cromwell." Referring to Herrick's return to the vicarage after the Restoration, these locals "added with an air of innocent triumph, 'He did see it again.'" The villagers also recalled stories of how the bachelor vicar threw his sermon at the congregation one day for their inattention and how he taught his pet pig to drink from a tankard. Many of his best poems, such as *Corinna's Going A-Maying* and *The Hock-Cart, or Harvest Home*, celebrate the landscape and the life of the country in the idealized tradition of pastoral poetry.

The son of a goldsmith in Cheapside, Herrick was apprenticed to the trade at age fourteen. After taking his B.A. from Cambridge in 1617, he returned to London, where he spent his poetic apprenticeship until he was appointed chaplain to the Duke of Buckingham in his failed expedition to aid the French Protestants of Rhé in 1627. Only a year later, Herrick moved to the vicarage at Dean, but many of his poems recount his London days, recalling the feasts frequented by Ben Jonson, whose verse "out-did the meat, out-did the frolic wine." The influence of Jonson's classical concision, wit, and urbanity can be felt in such poems as *Delight in Disorder* and his *Prayer* to the poet. While in London, Herrick also became friends with William Lawes, the court composer who wrote the music for Milton's masque *Comus*. When Lawes set Herrick's *To the Virgins, to Make Much of Time* to music, this poem became one of the most popular drinking songs of the seventeenth century—often sung as a "catch," which meant that its words could be played with to produce ribald double meanings. His poems circulated in manuscript until his volume of verse was printed in 1648, with his secular poetry entitled *Hesperides* and his religious poetry entitled *Noble Numbers*. He first achieved a wide readership in the early nineteenth century with the romantic revival of interest in rural life and poetry.

from HESPERIDES

The Argument of His Book[1]

I sing of brooks, of blossoms, birds, and bowers,
Of April, May, of June, and July flowers.
I sing of Maypoles, hock carts, wassails, wakes,[2]
Of bridegrooms, brides, and of their bridal cakes.
I write of youth, of love, and have access
By these, to sing of cleanly wantonness.° *carefree abandon*
I sing of dews, of rains, and piece by piece,
Of balm, of oil, of spice, and ambergris.[3]

1. All of Herrick's poems were published in 1648. The "Argument" introduces the book's themes.
2. Hock carts: harvest wagons; wassails: drinking toasts; wakes: celebrations in honor of the dedication of a parish church.
3. Secretion from the intestines of sperm whales, used to make perfume.

I sing of times trans-shifting;[4] and I write
How roses first came red, and lilies white.
I write of groves, of twilights, and I sing
The court of Mab,[5] and of the fairy king.
I write of hell; I sing (and ever shall)
Of Heaven, and hope to have it after all.

To His Book

While thou did keep thy candor[1] undefil'd,
Dearly I lov'd thee as my first-born child;
But when I saw thee wantonly to roam
From house to house, and never stay at home,
I break° my bonds of love, and bade thee go, *broke*
Regardless whether well thou sped'st, or no.
On with thy fortunes then, what e're they be;
If good I'll smile, if bad I'll sigh for thee.

Another

To read my book the virgin shy
May blush (with Brutus[1] standing by);
But when he's gone, read through what's writ,
And never stain a cheek for it.

Another

Who with thy leaves shall wipe at need
The place where swelling piles do breed:
May every ill that bites or smarts
Perplex him in his hinder-parts.

To the Sour Reader

If thou dislik'st the piece thou light'st on first;
Think that of all that I have writ, the worst:
But if thou read'st my book unto the end,
And still do'st this and that verse reprehend:
O perverse man! If all disgustful be,
Th' extreme scab take thee, and thine, for me.

When He Would Have His Verses Read

In sober mornings, do not thou rehearse
The holy incantation of a verse;
But when that men have both well drunk and fed,
Let my enchantments then be sung or read.

4. Times changing and passing; the cycle of the seasons.
5. Queen of the fairies.
1. A play on the modern meaning of "candor" (frank honesty) and its Latin meaning, "whiteness, radiance."
1. Presumably her sweetheart.

When laurel spirits i' th' fire, and when the hearth
Smiles to itself, and guilds the roof with mirth;
When up the thyrse[1] is rais'd, and when the sound
Of sacred orgies[2] flies around, around;
When the rose reigns, and locks with ointment shine,
Let rigid Cato[3] read these lines of mine.

Delight in Disorder

A sweet disorder in the dress
Kindles in clothes a wantonness:
A lawn° about the shoulders thrown *scarf*
Into a fine distraction;
An erring° lace, which here and there *wandering*
Enthralls the crimson stomacher:[1]
A cuff neglectful, and thereby
Ribbons to flow confusedly:
A winning wave, deserving note,
In the tempestuous petticoat;
A carelesse shoestring, in whose tie
I see a wild civility:
Do more bewitch me, than when art
Is too precise[2] in every part.

Corinna's Going A-Maying

Get up, get up for shame! the blooming morn
Upon her wings presents the god unshorn.[1]
See how Aurora[2] throws her fair
Fresh-quilted colors through the air:
Get up, sweet slug-a-bed, and see
The dew-bespangling herb and tree.
Each flower has wept, and bowed toward the east,
Above an hour since; yet you not dressed,
Nay! not so much as out of bed?
When all the birds have matins° said, *morning prayer*
And sung their thankfull hymns: 'tis sin,
Nay, profanation° to keep in, *impiety*
Whenas a thousand virgins on this day
Spring, sooner than the lark, to fetch in May.[3]

Rise, and put on your foliage, and be seen
To come forth, like the springtime, fresh and green,
And sweet as Flora.[4] Take no care

1. A javelin twisted with ivy.
2. Songs to Bacchus, god of wine.
3. Cato the Elder, Roman statesman (234–149 B.C.E.), who inveighed against moral laxity.

1. Ornamental covering for the chest worn under the lacing of the bodice.
2. "Precise" was often used to describe the strictness of the Puritans.

1. Apollo, the sun god, whose beams are seen as his flowing locks.
2. Goddess of the dawn in Roman mythology.
3. The custom on May Day morning was to gather blossoms.
4. Ancient Italian goddess of fertility and flowers.

For jewels for your gown, or hair:
Fear not; the leaves will strew
Gems in abundance upon you;
Besides, the childhood of the day has kept,
Against you come, some orient° pearls unwept; *oriental, shining*
Come, and receive them while the light
Hangs on the dew-locks of the night,
And Titan[5] on the eastern hill
Retires himself, or else stands still
Till you come forth. Wash, dress, be brief in praying:
Few beads are best,[6] when once we go a-Maying.

Come, my Corinna, come; and coming, mark
How each field turns a street; each street a park
Made green, and trimmed with trees; see how
Devotion gives each house a bough,
Or branch: each porch, each door, ere this,
An ark, a tabernacle is,[7]
Made up of whitethorn neatly interwove;
As if here were those cooler shades of love.
Can such delights be in the street
And open fields, and we not see't?
Come, we'll abroad; and let's obey
The proclamation made for May,
And sin no more, as we have done, by staying;
But my Corinna, come, let's go a-Maying.

There's not a budding boy, or girl, this day,
But is got up, and gone to bring in May.
A deal of youth, ere this, is come
Back, and with whitethorn laden home.
Some have dispatched their cakes and cream,
Before that we have left to dream:
And some have wept, and wooed, and plighted troth,
And chose their priest, ere we can cast off sloth.
Many a green-gown has been given,
Many a kiss, both odd and even:[8]
Many a glance, too, has been sent
From out the eye, love's firmament:
Many a jest told of the keys betraying
This night, and locks picked; yet we're not a-Maying.

Come, let us go, while we are in our prime,
And take the harmless folly of the time.
We shall grow old apace, and die
Before we know our liberty.

5. The sun god.
6. An allusion to Catholic rosary beads.
7. The Hebrew ark of the Covenant contained the tablets of the laws; a tabernacle is an ornamental niche to hold the consecrated host.
8. Green gown . . . given; by lying in the grass. Kisses are odd and even in kissing games.

Our life is short; and our days run
As fast away as does the sun;
And as a vapor, or a drop of rain
Once lost, can ne'er be found again,
So when or you or I are made
A fable, song, or fleeting shade,° *soul*
All love, all liking, all delight
Lies drowned with us in endless night.
Then while time serves, and we are but decaying,
Come, my Corinna, come, let's go a-Maying.

To the Virgins, to Make Much of Time

Gather ye rosebuds while ye may,
Old time is still a-flying;[1]
And this same flower that smiles today,
Tomorrow will be dying.[2]

The glorious lamp of heaven, the sun,
The higher he's a-getting;
The sooner will his race be run,[3]
And nearer he's to setting.

That age is best, which is the first,
When youth and blood are warmer;
But being spent, the worse, and worst
Times still succeed the former.
Then be not coy, but use your time,
And while ye may, go marry;
For having lost but once your prime,
You may for ever tarry.

The Hock-Cart,[1] or Harvest Home

To the Right Honorable, Mildmay, Earl of Westmoreland[2]

Come, sons of summer, by whose toil,
We are the lords of wine and oil;
By whose tough labors, and rough hands,
We rip up first, then reap our lands.
Crowned with the ears of corn, now come,
And, to the pipe, sing harvest home.
Come forth, my Lord, and see the cart
Dressed up with all the country art.
See, here a maukin,° there a sheet, *scarecrow*
As spotlesse pure, as it is sweet,
The horses, mares, and frisking fillies,

1. The Latin tag *tempus fugit* ("time flies").
2. "Dying" was also a euphemism for orgasm.
3. In Greek mythology, the sun was seen as the chariot of Phoebus Apollo drawn across the sky each day as in a race.

1. Wagon carrying the last load of harvest crops.
2. The landlord, Mildmay Fane (Earl of Westmoreland), was one of Herrick's patrons.

(Clad, all, in linen, white as lilies.)
The harvest swains,° and wenches bound *young men*
For joy, to see the hock-cart crowned.
About the cart, hear how the rout
Of rural younglings raise the shout,
Pressing before, some coming after,
Those with a shout and these with laughter.
Some bless the cart, some kiss the sheaves;
Some prank° them up with oaken leaves: *decorate*
Some cross the fill-horse, some with great
Devotion stroke the home-borne wheat:[3]
While other rustics, less attent
To prayers, than to merriment,
Run after with their breeches rent.
  Well, on, brave boys, to your Lord's hearth,
Glittering with fire; where, for your mirth,
Ye shall see first the large and chief
Foundation of your feast, fat beef:
With upper stories, mutton, veal,
And bacon, (which makes full the meal)
With several dishes standing by,
As here a custard, there a pie,
And here all tempting frumenty.° *pudding*
And for to make the merry cheer,
If smirking° wine be wanting here, *sparkling*
There's that, which drowns all care, stout beer:
Which freely drink to your Lord's health,
Then to the plough, (the common-wealth),
Next to your flails, your fanes, your vats;[4]
Then to the maids with wheaten hats:
To the rough sickle, and crook'd scythe,
Drink, frolic boys, till all be blithe.
  Feed, and grow fat; and as ye eat,
Be mindfull, that the laboring neat[5]
As you, may have their fill of meat.
And know, besides, ye must revoke° *call back*
The patient ox unto the yoke,
And all go back unto the plow
And harrow, though they're hanged up now.
And, you must know, your Lord's word's true,
Feed him ye must, whose food fills you,
And that this pleasure is like rain,
Not sent ye for to drown your pain,
But for to make it spring again.

3. The fill-horse is harnessed between the shafts of the cart. Crossing the horse and kissing the sheaves of wheat were old English Catholic customs.

4. Flails: instruments for threshing; fans: used to separate wheat from chaff.

5. Cattle, whose "meat" is grain or hay.

His Prayer to Ben Jonson[1]

When I a verse shall make,
Know I have prayed thee,
For old religion's sake,[2]
Saint Ben to aid me.

Make the way smooth for me,
When I, thy Herrick,
Honoring thee, on my knee
Offer my lyric.

Candles I'll give to thee
And a new altar;
And thou Saint Ben shall be
Writ in my psalter.° *hymn book*

Upon Julia's Clothes

When as in silks my Julia goes,
Then, then, me thinks, how sweetly flows
That liquefaction of her clothes.
Next, when I cast mine eyes and see
That brave° vibration each way free; *splendid*
O how that glittering taketh me!

Upon His Spaniel Tracie

Now thou art dead, no eye shall ever see,
For shape and service, spaniel like to thee.
This shall my love do, give thy sad death one
Tear, that deserves of me a million.

To Dean-Bourn, a Rude River in Devon

Dean-Bourn, farewell; I never look to see
Deane, or thy watery incivility.
Thy rocky bottom that doth tear thy streams,
And makes them frantic, ev'n to all extremes,
To my content I never should behold,
Were thy streams silver, or thy rocks all gold.
Rocky thou art; and rocky we discover
Thy men; and rocky are thy ways all over.
O men, O manners; there and ever known
To be a rocky generation!
A people currish, churlish as the seas;
And rude (almost) as rudest savages:

1. The humorous conceit in this poem is of Ben Jonson as a saint in the "religion" of poetry, aiding Herrick as a saint would intercede for a sinner. Herrick pays homage to Jonson's style both in his humor and verse form.
2. A reference to Jonson's Catholicism.

With whom I did, and may re-sojourn when
Rocks turn to rivers, rivers turn to men.

from His Noble Numbers

His Prayer for Absolution

For those my unbaptizèd rhymes,
Writ in my wild unhallow'd times;
For every sentence, clause, and word,
That's not inlaid with Thee (my Lord),
Forgive me God, and blot each line
Out of my book that is not Thine.
But if 'mongst all, Thou find'st here one
Worthy thy benediction,
That one of all the rest shall be
The glory of my work, and me.

To His Sweet Saviour

Night hath no wings to him that cannot sleep;
And Time seems then not for to fly, but creep;
Slowly her chariot drives, as if that she
Had broke her wheel, or cracked her axeltree.
Just so it is with me, who list'ning, pray
The winds to blow the tedious night away,
That I might see the cheerful peeping day.
Sick is my heart! O Saviour! Do Thou please
To make my bed soft in my sicknesses:
Lighten my candle, so that I beneath
Sleep not forever in the vaults of death.
Let me Thy voice betimes i' th' morning hear;
Call, and I'll come; say Thou the when and where.
Draw me but first, and after Thee I'll run,
And make no one stop till my race be done.

To God, on His Sickness

What though my harp and viol be
Both hung upon the willow tree?[1]
What though my bed be now my grave,
And for my house I darkness have?
What though my healthful days are fled,
And I lie number'd with the dead?
Yet I have hope, by Thy great power,
To spring, though now a wither'd flower.

1. In Psalm 137, the Hebrew poets, exiled in Babylon, hang their harps in the willow trees, too sorrowful to sing songs of their lost homeland.

George Herbert

1593–1633

Engraved portrait of George Herbert.

George Herbert spent the last three years of his life as a country parson. In an age in which such a church living was often a mere sinecure, Herbert had a genuine vocation, which he chose over other paths open to him through his talent and the connections of his distinguished Welsh family. His education and vocation were most influenced by his mother Magdalene Herbert, a woman with a great appreciation for poetry and strong devotion to the Church of England. When she died in 1627, John Donne gave the funeral sermon, extolling not only her grace, wit, and charm but especially her extraordinary charity to those who suffered from the plague of 1625, among whom was Donne himself. Herbert's mother had been widowed when he was just three years old. She brought up ten children, first in Oxford and then in London, where she saw to it that they were well read in the Bible and the classics.

Herbert studied at Cambridge University, where he became Reader in Rhetoric in 1616; in 1620 he was elected Public Orator, a post that he held for eight years. He wrote poetry and delivered public addresses in Latin and worked on the Latin version of Francis Bacon's *The Advancement of Learning*. Herbert also stood for Parliament and served there in 1624, when the Virginia Company, in which many of his friends and family were stockholders, was beset by financial difficulties and ultimately dissolved by James I.

Though his book *The Temple*, which included all his English poems, was not published until just after his death in 1633, Herbert was already writing verse as an undergraduate in 1610, when he dedicated two sonnets to his mother that advocated religious rather than secular love as the subject for poetry. His first published poems were written in Latin, commemorating the death of Prince Henry (1612). Herbert also wrote three different collections of Latin poems during his Cambridge years: *Musae Responsoriae*, polemical poems that defended the rites of the Church of England from Puritan criticism; *Passio discerpta*, religious verse that focused on Christ's passion and death in a style reminiscent of Crashaw; and *Lucas*, a collection of brief epigrams, such as this one on pride: "Each man is earth, and the field's child. Tell me, / Will you be a sterile mountain or a fertile valley?" The sardonic and mocking tone of these epigrams may surprise a reader of his English poems, but the wit and the rhetorical finish of his Latin poetry recur in his later verse.

Herbert's poetry is some of the most complex and innovative of all English verse. In a very pared-down style, enlivened by gentle irony, Herbert produces complexity of meaning through allegory and emblem, directly or more often indirectly alluding to biblical images, events, and insights, which take on their own moral and poetic meaning in the life of the speaker and the reader. Each of his poems is a kind of spiritual event, enacting in its form, both visual and aural, the very theological experiences and beliefs—or conflict of beliefs—expressed. Herbert allows us to make the spiritual journey with him through suffering and redemption, through doubt and hope. The meaning of one of his poems unravels like a discovery, each line and stanza raising alternative possibilities and altering the meaning of the one before. His spirituality is not a matter of easy acceptance but one of struggle, portrayed with wit, logic, and passion that recall the best of Donne's verse. The humility, subtle hesitancy, and whimsical irony are Herbert's alone, as when he addresses a love poem, *The Pearl,* to God:

> I know the ways of pleasure, the sweet strains,
> The lullings and the relishes of it . . .
> My stuff is flesh, not brass; my senses live,
> And grumble oft, that they have more in me
> Then he that curbs them, being but one to five:
> Yet I love thee.

The Altar[1]

A broken ALTAR, Lord, thy servant rears,
Made of a heart, and cemented with tears:
Whole parts are as thy hand did frame;
No workman's tool has touched the same.[2]
A HEART alone
Is such a stone,
As nothing but
Thy power doth cut.
Wherefore each part
Of my hard heart
Meets in this frame,
To praise thy Name.
That, if I chance to hold my peace,
These stones to praise thee may not cease.[3]
Oh let thy blessed SACRIFICE be mine,
and sanctify this ALTAR to be thine.

Redemption[1]

Having been tenant long to a rich lord,
Not thriving, I resolvèd to be bold,
And make a suit unto him, to afford
A new small-rented° lease, and cancel the old. *cheaper*

In heaven at his manor I him sought:
They told me there, that he was lately gone
About some land, which he had dearly bought
Long since on earth, to take possession.

I straight returned, and knowing his great birth,
Sought him accordingly in great resorts—

1. All of Herbert's poems were published in *The Temple* (1633).
2. See Exodus 20.5, where God tells Moses: "And if thou wilt make me an altar of stone, thou shalt not build it of hewn stone: for if thou lift up thy tool upon it thou has polluted it."
3. See Luke 19.40: "I tell you that, if these should hold their peace, the stones would immediately cry out."
1. "Redemption," means deliverance from sin and comes from the Latin *redimere,* meaning to buy back, to ransom.

In cities, theaters, gardens, parks, and courts:
At length I heard a ragged noise and mirth
Of thieves and murderers: there I him espied,
Who straight, "Your suit is granted," said, and died.

Easter

Rise heart, thy Lord is risen. Sing his praise
Without delays,
Who takes thee by the hand, that thou likewise
With him may'st rise:
That, as his death calcinèd° thee to dust, *reduced by fire*
His life may make thee gold, and much more just.

Awake, my lute, and struggle for thy part
With all thy art.
The cross taught all wood to resound his name
Who bore the same.
His stretchèd sinews taught all strings, what key
Is best to celebrate this most high day.

Consort° both heart and lute, and twist a song *harmonize*
Pleasant and long:
Or, since all music is but three parts vied
And multiplied,[1]
Oh let thy blessed spirit bear a part,
And make up our defects with his sweet art.

I got me flowers to strew thy way;
I got me boughs off many a tree:
But thou wast up by break of day,
And brought'st thy sweets along with thee.

The sun arising in the east,
Though he give light, and th' east perfume,
If they should offer to contest
With thy arising, they presume.

Can there be any day but this,
Though many suns to shine endeavor?
We count three hundred, but we miss:[2]
There is but one, and that one ever.

1. Since music is increased by three-part harmony.
2. We are mistaken in reckoning that there are 300-plus days in the year, since they are all but as one day when compared to the light of the Son (Christ) rising.

Easter Wings[1]

Lord, who createdst man in wealth and store,[2]
Though foolishly he lost the same,
Decaying more and more,
Till he became
Most poor:
With thee
Oh let me rise
As larks, harmoniously,
And sing this day thy victories:
Then shall the fall[3] further the flight in me.

My tender age in sorrow did begin
And still with sickness and shame
Thou didst so punish sin,
That I became
Most thin.
With thee
Let me combine,
And feel this day thy victory:
For, if I imp[4] my wing on thine,
Affliction shall advance the flight in me.

Affliction (1)[1]

When first thou didst entice to thee my heart,
I thought the service brave:
So many joys I wrote down for my part,
Besides what I might have
Out of my stock of natural delights,
Augmented with thy gracious benefits.

I lookèd on thy furniture so fine,
And made it fine to me:
Thy glorious household stuff did me entwine,
And 'tice me unto thee.
Such stars I counted mine: both heaven and earth
Paid me my wages in a world of mirth.

What pleasures could I want, whose king I served,
Where joys my fellows were?
Thus argued into hopes, my thoughts reserved
No place for grief or fear;
Therefore my sudden soul caught at the place,
And made her youth and fierceness seek thy face.

1. As in the first editions of Herbert, this poem is printed sideways to represent the shape of wings.
2. Plenty.
3. The human frailty of sin, as well as the speaker's own descent into sin and suffering, which Christ redeems through his rising from the dead on Easter.
4. In falconry, to insert feathers in a bird's wing.
1. Editors assign numbers to poems to which Herbert gave the same title to distinguish them from one another.

At first thou gav'st me milk and sweetness;
I had my wish and way:
My days were strawed° with flowers and happiness; *strewed*
There was no month but May.
But with my years sorrow did twist and grow,
And made a party unawares for woe.

My flesh began unto my soul in pain,[2]
Sicknesses cleave° my bones; *penetrate*
Consuming agues dwell in every vein,
And tune my breath to groans,
Sorrow was all my soul, I scarce believed,
Till grief did tell me roundly, that I lived.

When I got health, thou took'st away my life,
And more; for my friends die:
My mirth and edge was lost; a blunted knife
Was of more use than I.
Thus thin and lean without a fence or friend,
I was blown through with every storm and wind.

Whereas my birth and spirit rather took
The way that takes the town,
Thou didst betray me to a lingering book,
And wrap me in a gown.
I was entangled in the world of strife,
Before I had the power to change my life.

Yet, for I threatened often the siege to raise,
Not simpering all mine age,
Thou often did with academic praise
Melt and dissolve my rage.
I took thy sweetened pill, till I came near;
I could not go away, nor persevere.

Yet, lest perchance I should too happy be
In my unhappiness,
Turning my purge[3] to food, thou throwest me
Into more sickness.
Thus does thy power cross-bias[4] me, not making
Thine own gift good, yet me from my ways taking.

Now I am here, what thou wilt do with me
None of my books will show:
I read, and sigh, and wish I were a tree,
For sure then I should grow
To fruit or shade; at least some bird would trust
Her household to me, and I should be just.

2. The body speaks to the soul from this point on.
3. Medicine inducing evacuation of the bowels.
4. To give an inclination running counter to another.

Yet, though thou troublest me, I must be meek;
In weakness must be stout.
Well, I will change the service, and go seek
Some other master out.
Ah my dear God! though I am clean forgot,
Let me not love thee, if I love thee not.

Prayer (1)

Prayer the church's banquet; angels' age,
God's breath in man returning to his birth;
The soul in paraphrase; heart in pilgrimage;
The Christian plummet[1] sounding heaven and earth;

Engine against th' Almighty, sinner's tower,[2]
Reversèd thunder, Christ-side-piercing spear,
The six-days world transposing in an hour;
A kind of tune, which all things hear and fear;

Softness, and peace, and joy, and love, and bliss;
Exalted manna,[3] gladness of the best;
Heaven in ordinary,[4] man well dressed,
The milky way, the bird of paradise,[5]

Church bells beyond the stars heard, the soul's blood,
The land of spices; something understood.

Jordan (1)[1]

Who says that fictions only and false hair
Become a verse? Is there in truth no beauty?
Is all good structure in a winding stair?
May no lines pass, except they do their duty
Not to a true, but painted chair?

Is it no verse, except enchanted groves
And sudden arbors shadow coarse-spun lines?
Must purling° streams refresh a lover's loves? *rippling*
Must all be veiled, while he that reads, divines,[2]
Catching the sense at two removes?

Shepherds are honest people; let them sing:
Riddle who list,[3] for me, and pull for prime.[4]
I envy no man's nightingale or spring;

1. A metal weight used to measure, or sound, the depth of water; figuratively, the criterion of truth.
2. A stronghold or fortress, used for purposes of defense.
3. The food that God supplied to the Jews during their wandering in the wilderness.
4. What is usual; or, a meal in a tavern.
5. A bird, found in New Guinea, known for its beautiful feathers.

1. To cross the river Jordan symbolizes entering the Promised Land.
2. To interpret what is obscure through magical insight or intuitive conjecture.
3. Whoever wants to may interpret.
4. Draw a lucky card, or hit upon a lucky guess.

Nor let them punish me with loss of rhyme,
Who plainly say, *My God, My King*.

Church Monuments

While that my soul repairs to her devotion,
Here I entomb my flesh, that it betimes
May take acquaintance of this heap of dust;
To which the blast of death's incessant motion,
Fed with the exhalation of our crimes,
Drives all at last. Therefore I gladly trust

My body to this school, that it may learn
To spell his elements and find his birth
Written in dusty heraldry and lines
Which dissolution sure does best discern,
Comparing dust with dust, and earth with earth.[1]
These[2] laugh at jet and marble, put for signs

To sever the good fellowship of dust
And spoil the meeting. What shall point out them[3]
When they shall bow, and kneel, and fall down flat
To kiss those heaps, which now they have in trust?
Dear flesh, while I do pray, learn here thy stem
And true descent; that when thou shalt grow fat,

And wanton in thy cravings, thou may'st know,
That flesh is but the glass, which holds the dust
That measures all our time, which also shall
Be crumbled into dust. Mark here below
How tame these ashes are, how free from lust,
That thou may'st set thyself against thy fall.

The Windows

Lord, how can man preach thy eternal word?
He is a brittle, crazy° glass, *cracked*
Yet in thy temple thou do him afford
This glorious and transcendent place,
To be a window, through thy grace.

But when thou dost anneal[1] in glass thy story,
Making thy life to shine within
The holy preachers, then the light and glory
More reverent grows, and does win
Which else shows watr'ish, bleak, and thin.

1. An allusion to Genesis 3.19: "for dust thou art and to dust shalt thou return."
2. Dust and earth.
3. The souls that cling to "those heaps," the dust of their bodies and of the earth.
1. To burn in colors on glass.

Doctrine and life, colors and light, in one
When they combine and mingle, bring
A strong regard and awe; but speech alone
Doth vanish like a flaring thing,
And in the ear, not conscience ring.

Denial

When my devotions could not pierce
Thy silent ears;
Then was my heart broken, as was my verse:
My breast was full of tears
And disorder:

My bent thoughts, like a brittle bow,
Did fly asunder:
Each took his way; some would to pleasures go,
Some to the wars and thunder
Of alarms.

As good go anywhere, they say,
As to benumb
Both knees and heart in crying night and day,
Come, come, my God, Oh come!
But no hearing.

O that thou shouldst give dust a tongue
To cry to thee,
And then not hear it crying! All day long
My heart was in my knee,
But no hearing.

Therefore my soul lay out of sight,
Untuned, unstrung;
My feeble spirit, unable to look right,
Like a nipped bloom, hung
Discontented.

Oh cheer and tune my heartless breath,
Defer no time,
That so thy favors granting my request,
They and my mind may chime,° *ring together, agree*
And mend my rhyme.

Virtue

Sweet day, so cool, so calm, so bright,
The bridal° of the earth and sky: *wedding*
The dew shall weep thy fall tonight,
For thou must die.

Sweet rose, whose hue, angry and brave
Bids the rash gazer wipe his eye:
Thy root is ever in its grave,
And thou must die.

Sweet spring, full of sweet days and roses,
A box where sweets° compacted lie; *pleasant fragrances*
My music shows ye have your closes,[1]
And all must die.

Only a sweet and virtuous soul,
Like seasoned timber, never gives;
But though the whole world turn to coal,[2]
Then chiefly lives.

Man

My God, I heard this day
That none doth build a stately habitation,
But he that means to dwell therein.
What house more stately hath there been,
Or can be, than is man? to[1] whose creation
All things are in decay.

For man is everything,
And more; he is a tree, yet bears more[2] fruit;
A beast, yet is, or should be more:
Reason and speech we only bring.
Parrots may thank us, if they are not mute:
They go upon the score.[3]

Man is all symmetry,
Full of proportions, one limb to another,
And all to all the world besides:
Each part may call the farthest, brother;
For head with foot has private amity,
And both with moons and tides.

Nothing hath got so far
But man hath caught and kept it as his prey.
His eyes dismount the highest star:
He is in little all the sphere.[4]
Herbs gladly cure our flesh; because that they
Find their acquaintance there.

For us the winds do blow,
The earth doth rest, heav'n move, and fountains flow;

1. Cadences, indicating that Herbert wanted this poem to be sung.
2. Reduced to ashes as at the Last Judgment.

1. In comparison to.
2. An alternative reading is "no."
3. They are indebted to us.
4. See Robert Fludd's engraving of the human body as microcosm of the universe, page 1068.

Nothing we see, but means our good,
As our delight, or as our treasure.
The whole is, either our cupboard of food,
Or cabinet of pleasure.

The stars have us to bed;
Night draws the curtain, which the sun withdraws,
Music and light attend our head.
All things unto our flesh are kind
In their descent and being; to our mind
In their ascent and cause.

Each thing is full of duty.
Waters united are our navigation,
Distinguished, our habitation;
Below, our drink; above, our meat;
Both are our cleanliness. Hath one such beauty?
Then how are all things neat?

More servants wait on man
Than he'll take notice of: in ev'ry path,
He treads down that which doth befriend him,
When sickness makes him pale and wan.
Oh mighty love! Man is one world, and hath
Another to attend him.

Since then, my God, thou hast
So brave a palace built, O dwell in it,
That it may dwell with thee at last!
Till then, afford us so much wit,
That, as the world serves us, we may serve thee,
And both thy servants be.

Jordan (2)

When first my lines of heav'nly joys made mention,
Such was their luster, they did so excel,
That I sought out quaint° words, and trim invention; *clever*
My thoughts began to burnish,° sprout, and swell, *spread out*
Curling with metaphors a plain intention,
Decking the sense, as if it were to sell.[1]

Thousands of notions in my brain did run,
Off'ring their service, if I were not sped.[2]
I often blotted what I had begun;
This was not quick° enough, and that was dead. *lively*
Nothing could seem too rich to clothe the sun,
Much less those joys which trample on his head.[3]

1. Decorating the meaning as if it were for sale.
2. Dealt with so that I was satisfied.
3. The sun is a symbol for Christ; the sun's head is the Son's head.

As flames do work and wind, when they ascend,
So did I weave my self into the sense.
But while I bustled, I might hear a friend
Whisper, "How wide° is all this long pretence! *beside the point*
There is in love a sweetness ready penn'd:
Copy out only that, and save expense."

Time

Meeting with time, "Slack thing," said I,
"Thy scythe is dull; whet it for shame."
"No marvel sir," he did reply,
"If it at length deserve some blame:
But where one man would have me grind it,
Twenty for one too sharp do find it."

"Perhaps some such of old did pass,[1]
Who above all things lov'd this life;
To whom thy scythe a hatchet was,
Which now is but a pruning knife.
Christ's coming hath made man thy debtor,
Since by thy cutting he grows better.

"And in this blessing thou art blest:
For where thou only wert before
An executioner at best,
Thou art a gard'ner now, and more,
An usher to convey our souls
Beyond the utmost stars and poles.

"And this is that makes life so long,
While it detains us from our God.
Ev'n pleasures here increase the wrong,
And length of days lengthen the rod.
Who wants° the place, where God doth dwell, *lacks*
Partakes already half of hell.

"Of what strange length must that needs be,
Which ev'n eternity excludes!"
Thus far Time heard me patiently:
Then chafing° said, "This man deludes: *getting angry*
What do I here before his door?
He doth not crave less time, but more."

The Collar

I struck the board,° and cried, "No more. *table*
I will abroad!
What? Shall I ever sigh and pine?

1. Herbert is the speaker in stanzas 2, 3, and 4 and in the first two lines of stanza 5.

My lines and life are free; free as the road,
Loose as the wind, as large as store.° *abundance*
Shall I be still in suit?[1]
Have I no harvest but a thorn
To let me blood, and not restore
What I have lost with cordial[2] fruit?
Sure there was wine
Before my sighs did dry it; there was corn
Before my tears did drown it.
Is the year only lost to me?
Have I no bays[3] to crown it?
No flowers, no garlands gay? all blasted?
All wasted?
Not so, my heart; but there is fruit,
And thou hast hands.
Recover all thy sigh-blown age
On double pleasures: leave thy cold dispute
Of what is fit and not forsake thy cage,
Thy rope of sands,
Which petty thoughts have made, and made to thee
Good cable, to enforce and draw,
And be thy law,
While thou didst wink[4] and wouldst not see.
Away! take heed:
I will abroad.
Call in thy death's head[5] there: tie up thy fears.
He that forbears
To suit and serve his need,
Deserves his load."
But as I raved and grew more fierce and wild
At every word,
Me thoughts I heard one calling, *Child!*
And I replied, *My Lord*.

The Pulley

When God at first made man,
Having a glass of blessings standing by,
"Let us," said he "pour on him all we can:
Let the world's riches, which dispersèd lie,
Contract into a span."

So strength first made a way;
Then beauty flowed, then wisdom, honor, pleasure:
When almost all was out, God made a stay,
Perceiving that alone of all his treasure
Rest in the bottom lay.[1]

1. Engaged in a lawsuit.
2. Invigorating to the heart.
3. The poet's laurel wreath.
4. Shut your eyes to.
5. The skull as an emblem of human mortality.

1. "Rest" in the sense of repose, or freedom from distress, and in the sense of remainder, or surplus.

"For if I should," said he,
"Bestow this jewel also on my creature,
He would adore my gifts instead of me,
And rest in Nature, not the God of Nature.
So both should losers be.

"Yet let him keep the rest,
But keep them with repining° restlessness: *complaining*
Let him be rich and weary, that at least,
If goodness lead him not, yet weariness
May toss him to my breast."

The Forerunners

The harbingers[1] are come: see, see their mark;
White is their color, and behold my head.
But must they have my brain? Must they dispark° *turn out*
Those sparkling notions, which therein were bred?
Must dullness turn me to a clod?
Yet have they left me, "Thou art still my God."

Good men ye be, to leave me my best room,
Ev'n all my heart, and what is lodged there:
I pass not, I, what of the rest become,
So "Thou art still my God," be out of fear.[2]
He will be pleasèd with that ditty;
And if I please him, I write fine and witty.

Farewell, sweet phrases, lovely metaphors:
But will ye leave me thus? when ye before
Of stews[3] and brothels only knew the doors,
Then did I wash you with my tears, and more,
Brought you to Church well-dressed and clad:
My God must have my best, ev'n all I had.

Lovely enchanting language, sugarcane,
Honey of roses, whither wilt thou fly?
Hath some fond lover 'ticed thee to thy bane?
And wilt thou leave the Church, and love a sty?
Fie, thou wilt soil thy 'broidered coat,
And hurt thy self, and him that sings the note.

Let foolish lovers, if they will love dung,
With canvas, not with arras° clothe their shame: *rich tapestry*
Let Folly speak in her own native tongue.
True Beauty dwells on high; ours is a flame

1. Men sent out before a royal train to requisition lodgings by marking the doors with chalk.

2. I don't care about anything except being left with the thought that "Thou art still my God."

3. Public hot bathhouses, brothels.

But borrowed thence to light us thither:
Beauty and beauteous words should go together.

Yet if you go, I pass not; take your way.
For, "Thou art still my God" is all that ye
Perhaps with more embellishment can say.
Go, birds of spring; let winter have his fee;
Let a bleak paleness chalk the door.
So all within be livelier than before.

Love (3)

Love bade me welcome: yet my soul drew back,
Guilty of dust and sin.
But quick-eyed Love, observing me grow slack° *slow, weak*
From my first entrance in,
Drew nearer to me, sweetly questioning,
If I lacked anything.

"A guest," I answered, "worthy to be here":
Love said, "You shall be he."
"I the unkind, ungrateful? Ah my dear,
I cannot look on thee."
Love took my hand, and smiling did reply,
"Who made the eyes but I?"

"Truth Lord, but I marred them; let my shame
Go where it doth deserve."
"And know you not," says Love, "who bore the blame?"
"My dear, then I will serve."
"You must sit down," says Love, "and taste my meat."
So I did sit and eat.[1]

Richard Lovelace

1618–1657

In *To His Noble Friend,* Andrew Marvell portrays Richard Lovelace as an amorous and chivalrous courtier from a world destroyed by "Our Civil Wars." Marvell depicts the consternation that arose

When the beauteous ladies came to know
That their dear Lovelace was endangered so:
Lovelace that thawed the most congealèd breast
He who loved best and them defended best.

1. The speaker takes Communion, which symbolizes union with God.

The dashing and handsome Lovelace was the last exemplar of courtly *sprezzatura* in the history of English poetry, recalling the eroticism and finesse of Wyatt and the chivalry of Sidney and Raleigh. The voluptuousness and elegance that characterized his poetry no less than the Carolinian court was destroyed by the Puritan Revolution.

Lovelace's brief life was indeed endangered more than once—all because of his allegiance to the Royalist cause. After only two years at Cambridge University, he left school to fight in the army of King Charles I, serving as senior ensign in the First Scottish expedition of 1639 and captain in the second of 1640. Both expeditions were disasters for the King's forces. Lovelace was imprisoned twice, first in 1642 for presenting an anti-Parliamentary petition from his home county Kent and again in 1648, when Marvell's patron Lord Fairfax brought the Roundhead (Puritan) army right to the doors of Lovelace's country estate. During his first stint in prison, Lovelace wrote one of his most memorable poems, *To Althea, from Prison*. Released on bail, he lived a precarious life, aiding the King's cause by selling his property and giving money to supply arms. In 1649, when he was released from prison the second time, Lovelace was reduced to selling all of his property, even his family portraits.

Lovelace is a representative of the cultural milieu of the court of Charles I, which included many poets and painters of great distinction. The regime was graced by such poets as Sir John Suckling, Thomas Carew, Abraham Cowley, and Edmund Waller, sometimes referred to as the Cavalier poets, among whom Lovelace is considered the greatest. Lovelace admired not only the works of his fellow poets but also the paintings of Rubens, Van Dyck, and Lely, which adorned the court. Lovelace was great friends with and wrote poems praising Lely, who designed plates for Lovelace's two books of poems, published in 1649 and 1659. Lovelace enjoyed painting and music as a gentleman amateur, the characteristic persona of a Cavalier poet. His poems express a tone of extravagant passion tempered with courtly poise achieved through lush images conveying a sensuous *joie de vivre* and a perspective of brave insouciance mixed with self-deprecating irony. His deft rhythms create songlike poems with a spontaneous grace and ease, stylistic ideals of the Cavaliers.

We know nothing about Lovelace after 1649. His brother Philip had been colonel in the King's army but survived the Interregnum to become governor of New York in 1688. Of his brother William's death on the field of battle in the Civil War, Richard had written these stoic lines to Philip:

> Iron decrees of Destiny
> Are ne'er wiped out with a wet eye.
> But this way you may gain the field,
> Oppose but sorrow, and 'twill yield;
> One gallant thorough made resolve
> Doth starry influence dissolve.

To Lucasta, Going to the Wars

Tell me not, sweet, I am unkind,
  That from the nunnery
Of thy chaste breast and quiet mind
  To war and arms I fly.

True, a new mistress now I chase,
  The first foe in the field;
And with a stronger faith embrace
  A sword, a horse, a shield.

Yet this inconstancy is such
  As you too shall adore;
I could not love thee, dear, so much,
  Loved I not honor more.

1649

The Grasshopper[1]

To My Noble Friend, Mr. Charles Cotton[2]

O thou that swing'st upon the waving hair
  Of some well-fillèd oaten beard,
Drunk ev'ry night with a delicious tear
  Dropped thee from heav'n, where now th' art reared,

The joys of earth and air are thine entire,
  That with thy feet and wings dost hop and fly;
And when thy poppy[3] works thou dost retire
  To thy carved acorn-bed to lie.

Up with the day, the sun thou welcom'st then,
  Sport'st in the gilt-plats° of his beams, *golden fields*
And all these merry days mak'st merry men,
  Thyself, and melancholy streams.

But ah the sickle! golden ears are cropped,
  Ceres and Bacchus[4] bid good night;
Sharp frosty fingers all your flowers have topped,
  And what scythes spared, winds shave off quite.

Poor verdant fool! and now green ice! thy joys,
  Large and as lasting as thy perch of grass,
Bid us lay in 'gainst winter, rain, and poise° *counterbalance*
  Their floods, with an o'erflowing glass.

Thou best of men and friends! We will create
  A genuine summer in each other's breast;
And spite of this cold time and frozen fate[5]
  Thaw us a warm seat to our rest.

Our sacred hearths shall burn eternally
  As vestal flames;[6] the North Wind, he
Shall strike his frost-stretched wings, dissolve and fly
  This Etna[7] in epitome.

Dropping December shall come weeping in,
  Bewail th' usurping of his reign;

1. The grasshopper was associated with a carefree life.
2. Charles Cotton was a learned and literary man. This poem describes the atmosphere of Puritan rule during the Interregnum.
3. A plant with narcotic powers.
4. The goddess of agriculture and the god of wine.
5. A reference to the persecution of Royalists during the rule of the Puritans.
6. The Roman Vestal Virgins attended to the eternal flame.
7. A volcano, here symbolizing the force and warmth of friendship.

But when in showers of old Greek[8] we begin,
  Shall cry, he hath his crown[9] again!

Night as clear Hesper shall our tapers whip
  From the light casements where we play,
And the dark hag from her black mantle strip,
  And stick there everlasting day.[1]

Thus richer than untempted kings are we,
  That asking nothing, nothing need:
Though Lord of all what seas embrace; yet he
  That wants himself is poor indeed.

1649

To Althea, from Prison

When love with unconfined wings
  Hovers within my gates,
And my divine Althea brings
  To whisper at the grates:
When I lie tangled in her hair
  And fettered to her eye,
The gods[1] that wanton° in the air, *play*
  Know no such liberty.

When flowing cups run swiftly round,
  With no allaying Thames,[2]
Our careless heads with roses bound,
  Our hearts with loyal flames;
When thirsty grief in wine we steep,
  When healths and draughts go free,
Fishes that tipple in the deep
  Know no such liberty.

When, like committed° linnets,° I *confined / songbirds*
  With shriller throat shall sing
The sweetness, mercy, majesty,
  And glories of my king;
When I shall voice aloud, how good
  He is, how great should be,
Enlargèd winds that curl the flood,
  Know no such liberty.

Stone walls do not a prison make,
  Nor iron bars a cage;
Minds innocent and quiet take
  That for an hermitage;° *hermit's dwelling*

8. The wine that was most prized in ancient Rome.
9. Wreath worn at a drinking party.
1. Hesperus, the morning star; casements: frames forming windows; the dark hag: Hecate, daughter of Night.

1. Some editions read "birds" rather than "gods."
2. River running through London; the meaning of this line is "with no water to dilute the wine."

If I have freedom in my love,
And in my soul am free,
Angels alone that soar above,
Enjoy such liberty.

1649

Love Made in the First Age: To Chloris[1]

In the nativity of time,
Chloris, it was not thought a crime
In direct Hebrew for to woo.[2]
Now we make love, as all on fire,
Ring retrograde[3] our loud desire,
And court in English backward too.

Thrice happy was that golden age,
When compliment was construed rage,[4]
And fine words in the center hid;
When cursed *No* stained no maid's bliss,
And all discourse was summed in *Yes*,
And nought forbade, but to forbid.

Love then unstinted, love did sip,
And cherries plucked fresh from the lip,
On cheeks and roses free he fed;
Lasses like autumn plums did drop,
And lads, indifferently did crop
A flower, and a maidenhead.

Then unconfinèd each did tipple
Wine from the bunch, milk from the nipple;
Paps tractable as udders were;
Then equally the wholesome jellies
Were squeezed from olive-trees, and bellies,
Nor suits of trespass did they fear.

A fragrant bank of strawberries,
Diapered° with violet's eyes, *decorated*
Was table, tablecloth, and fare;
No palace to the clouds did swell;
Each humble princess then did dwell
In the piazza[5] of her hair.

Both broken faith, and the cause of it,
All-damning gold was damned to the pit;
Their troth sealed with a clasp and kiss,

1. "The First Age" refers to the golden age of Greek and Roman mythology, a time of idyllic plenty in which there was no need for laws or work.
2. Hebrew, which reads from right to left, was believed to have been the original language.
3. In backward or reverse direction; an imitation of notes in contrary motion.
4. When compliments were interpreted as passionate proposals.
5. A colonnade surrounding a square.

Lasted until that extreme day,
In which they smiled their souls away,
And, in each other breathed new bliss.

Because no fault, there was no tear;
No groan did grate the granting ear;
No false foul breath their delicate smell:
No serpent kiss poisoned the taste,
Each touch was naturally chaste,
And their mere sense a miracle.

Naked as their own innocence,
And unembroidered[6] from offense
They went, above poor riches, gay;
On softer than the cygnet's° down, *young swan's*
In beds they tumbled of their own;
For each within the other lay.

Thus did they live: thus did they love,
Repeating only joys above;
And angels were, but with clothes on,
Which they would put off cheerfully,
To bathe them in the galaxy,[7]
Then gird them with the heavenly zone.[8]

Now, Chloris, miserably crave
The offered bliss you would not have;
Which evermore I must deny,
Whilst ravished with these noble dreams
And crownèd with mine own soft beams,
Enjoying of myself I lie.

Henry Vaughan

1622–1695

Henry Vaughan grew up speaking Welsh among the woods and streams of Newton in the parish of Llansantffraed. He responded to the sound of his first language and to the beauty of this countryside in the music and imagery of his poetry. For example, the slope of Mount Allt, on which he lived, provided a striking image: "those faint beams in which this hill is dressed, / After the Sun's remove." The Welsh influence can be heard in his poetry's alliteration and assonance; his piling up of comparisons, as in *The Night,* is called *dyfalu* ("to liken") in Welsh poetic technique. On the title page to his second book of verse, *Olor Iscanus* ("The Swan of Usk" [a local river]), he is called a "Silurist," a member of an ancient Welsh tribe. Though his verse is written in English, Vaughan's poetry and identity were always bound up with his native land.

6. Not ornamented with the trappings of authority.
7. The Milky Way.
8. The zodiac of stars.

Henry Vaughan's Welsh childhood was followed by education at Oxford, where he studied with his twin brother Thomas, and then at the Inns of Court in London, where he began his poetic apprenticeship. An admirer of Ben Jonson's verse, Vaughan praised and imitated Jonson in his first book of poetry, *Poems with the Tenth Satyre of Juvenal Englished* (1646). The mysticism and Neoplatonism of Vaughan's best known collection of poems, *Silex Scintillans* ("The Fiery Flint") (1650), link him to the metaphysical tradition of Donne, Herbert, and Crashaw, yet his verse continued to show fondness for the wit and spareness of Jonson.

At the outbreak of the Civil War, Vaughan returned to Wales in August 1642. He worked as secretary to the Circuit Chief Justice of the Great Sessions until 1645, when he joined the company of soldiers who fought for King Charles's cause with Sir Herbert Price at Chester. The poems in *Silex Scintillans* express his anger and disappointment at the outcome of the Civil War. In *Prayer in Time of Persecution*, Vaughan rails against the Puritans for confiscating the woods of his family's estate. The 1650 Act for the Propagation of the Gospel in Wales gave a committee of Puritan commissioners the power to purge the Welsh royalist clergy. Among these was Henry's brother Thomas, who was stripped of his position and livelihood. In *The World*, Vaughan describes a "darksome statesman" reminiscent of Cromwell; and in several poems, Vaughan complains of the Puritan "zeal" that brought about regicide and persecution of the Church of England. In *Christ's Nativity*, Vaughan lamented the Puritans' prohibition of the observance of Christmas and Good Friday:

> Shall he that came down from thence,
> And here for us was slain,
> Shall he be now cast off? no sense
> Of all his woes remain?
> Can neither Love, nor sufferings bind?
> Are we all stone, and Earth?
> Neither his bloody passions mind,
> Nor one day bless his birth?
> Alas, my God! Thy birth now here
> Must not be numbered in the year.

There is even evidence in one poem, *The Proffer*, that Vaughan disdained offers of power from Cromwell's government: "I'll not stuff my story / With your Commonwealth and glory." Some time after 1650, Vaughan decided to study and practice medicine.

The 1650s were troubled years for Vaughan. During this time he grieved for the deaths of his brother Thomas and his first wife Catherine. In the preface to the second edition of *Silex Scintillans* in 1655, Vaughan refers to an illness he had suffered, which seems to have been spiritual and may even have resulted in a kind of conversion experience. In this same preface, Vaughan also praises George Herbert: "his holy life and verse gained many pious Converts of whom I am the least." Along with the Bible, Herbert's verse is the main influence on Vaughan's. The titles of twenty-six lyrics in *Silex Scintillans* are taken from Herbert's *The Temple*. Both poets describe a spiritual paradise, but while Herbert's is ineffable, Vaughan's has the physical beauty of an actual landscape. Vaughan's temple stretches beyond the pristine church architecture of Herbert's imagery to touch flowers and trees and to contemplate the stars. Vaughan's feeling for nature is unsurpassed in English verse until Wordsworth. Vaughan's intense sense of the transitoriness of natural beauty and the immanence of mortality make his verse worth contemplating and savoring.

Regeneration

A ward, and still in bonds, one day
I stole abroad;
It was high spring, and all the way

Primrosed, and hung with shade;
Yet, was it frost within,
And surly winds
Blasted my infant buds, and sin
Like clouds eclipsed my mind.

Stormed thus, I straight perceived my spring
Mere stage and show,
My walk a monstrous, mountained thing,
Roughcast with rocks, and snow;
And as a pilgrim's eye
Far from relief,
Measures the melancholy sky,
Then drops, and rains for grief,

So sighed I upwards still, at last
'Twixt steps, and falls
I reached the pinnacle, where placed
I found a pair of scales,
I took them up and laid
In th'one late pains,
The other smoke, and pleasures weighed,
But proved the heavier grains.

With that, some cried, "Away!" Straight I
Obeyed, and led
Full east, a fair, fresh field could spy;
Some called it, Jacob's bed,[1]
A virgin soil, which no
Rude feet ere trod,
Where, since he stepped there, only go
Prophets, and friends of God.

Here, I reposed; but scarce well set,
A grove descried
Of stately height, whose branches met
And mixed on every side;
I entered, and once in,
Amazed to see't,
Found all was changed, and a new spring
Did all my senses greet;

The unthrift° sun shot vital gold *spendthrift*
A thousand pieces,
And heaven its azure did unfold,
Checkered with snowy fleeces,
The air was all in spice,
And every bush

1. See Genesis 28.11–19. Sleeping outdoors, Jacob had a vision of a ladder in the sky leading up to God.

A garland wore; thus fed my eyes,
But all the ear lay hush.

Only a little fountain lent
Some use for ears,
And on the dumb shades language spent
The music of her tears;
I drew her near, and found
The cistern full
Of divers stones, some bright, and round
Others ill-shaped, and dull.

The first, pray mark, as quick as light
Danced through the flood,
But, th'last more heavy than the night
Nailed to the center stood;
I wondered much, but tired
At last with thought,
My restless eye that still desired
As strange an object brought;

It was a bank of flowers, where I descried,
Though 'twas mid-day,
Some fast asleep, others broad-eyed
And taking in the ray,
Here musing long, I heard
A rushing wind
Which still increased, but whence it stirred
Nowhere I could not find.

I turned me round, and to each shade
Dispatched an eye,
To see, if any leaf had made
Least motion, or reply;
But while I listening sought
My mind to ease
By knowing, where 'twas, or where not,
It whispered, "Where I please."[2]

"Lord," then said I, "on me one breath,
And let me die before my death!"

The Retreat

Happy those early days! when I
Shined in my angel infancy.

2. John 3.8: "The wind bloweth where it listeth, and thou hearest the sound thereof, but canst not tell whence it cometh, and whither it goeth: so is every one that is born of the Spirit." See also Genesis 2.7 for the breath of life that God breathed into humanity.

Before I understood this place
Appointed for my second race,[1]
Or taught my soul to fancy ought
But a white, celestial thought;
When yet I had not walked above
A mile or two from my first love,
And looking back, at that short space,
Could see a glimpse of his bright face;
When on some gilded cloud, or flower
My gazing soul would dwell an hour,
And in those weaker glories spy
Some shadows of eternity;
Before I taught my tongue to wound
My conscience with a sinful sound,
Or had the black art to dispense
A several° sin to every sense, *separate*
But felt through all this fleshly dress
Bright shoots of everlastingness.
O, how I long to travel back,
And tread again that ancient track!
That I might once more reach that plain
Where first I left my glorious train,
From whence th' enlightened spirit sees
That shady city of palm trees.[2]
But, ah! my soul with too much stay° *hesitation*
Is drunk, and staggers in the way.
Some men a forward motion love;
But I by backward steps would move,
And when this dust falls to the urn
In that state I came, return.

Silence, and Stealth of Days[1]

Silence, and stealth of days! 'tis now
Since thou art gone,
Twelve hundred hours, and not a brow[2]
But clouds hang on.
As he that in some cave's thick damp,
Locked from the light,
Fixeth a solitary lamp,
To brave the night

1. "Second race" implies a Platonic belief in the reincarnation of the soul and in the preexistence of the soul in the world of perfect forms.
2. The New Jerusalem, the Paradise of Heaven.
1. The poem is about the death of Vaughan's younger brother William, who died in July 1648.
2. Facial expression, but also a gallery in a coal mine, since the following lines depict the image of a miner making his way through dark mist.

And walking from his sun, when past
That glim'ring ray,
Cuts through the heavy mists in haste
Back to his day,[3]
So o'er fled minutes I retreat
Unto that hour
Which showed thee last, but did defeat
Thy light, and pow'r;
I search, and rack my soul to see
Those beams again,
But nothing but the snuff[4] to me
Appeareth plain;
That dark, and dead sleeps in its known
And common urn,
But those fled to their Maker's throne,
There shine, and burn.
O could I track them! but souls must
Track one the other,
And now the spirit, not the dust,
Must be thy brother.
Yet I have one Pearl[5] by whose light
All things I see,
And in the heart of earth and night,
Find Heaven and thee.

The World

I saw eternity the other night,
Like a great ring of pure and endless light,
All calm as it was bright;
And round beneath it, Time, in hours, days, years,
Driven by the spheres,[1]
Like a vast shadow moved, in which the world
And all her train were hurled.
The doting lover in his quaintest strain[2]
Did there complain;
Near him, his lute, his fancy, and his flights,
Wit's sour delights,
With gloves and knots,[3] the silly snares of pleasure,
Yet his dear treasure,
All scattered lay, while he his eyes did pour
Upon a flower.

3. When the miner walks a little beyond the area lit by his lamp into the dark, he then rushes back to the light.
4. The part of a candlewick burnt to give light; an image of his brother's body turned to dust.
5. The Bible.
1. The spheres of the heavenly bodies circling the earth.
2. Most intricate melody.
3. Ties or bows worn as love tokens.

The darksome statesman[4] hung with weights and woe
Like a thick midnight fog moved there so slow
He did not stay nor go;
Condemning thoughts, like sad eclipses, scowl
Upon his soul,
And clouds of crying witnesses without
Pursued him with one shout.
Yet digged the mole, and lest his ways be found,
Worked underground,
Where he did clutch his prey. But one did see
That policy:
Churches and altars fed him; perjuries
Were gnats and flies;
It rained about him blood and tears; but he
Drank them as free.

The fearful miser on a heap of rust
Sat pining all his life there, did scarce trust
His own hands with the dust;
Yet would not place° one piece above, but lives *invest*
In fear of thieves.
Thousands there were as frantic as himself,
And hugged each one his pelf:° *money*
The downright epicure placed heaven in sense,[5]
And scorned pretense;
While others, slipped into a wide excess,
Said little less;
The weaker sort slight, trivial wares enslave,
Who think them brave,° *showy*
And poor, depisèd Truth sat counting by,° *reckoning*
Their victory.

Yet some, who all this while did weep and sing,
And sing and weep, soared up into the ring;
But most would use no wing,
"O fools!" said I, "thus to prefer dark night
Before true light!
To live in grots° and caves, and hate the day *caverns*
Because it shows the way;
The way which from the dead and dark abode
Leads up to God,
A way where you might tread the sun and be
More bright than he!"
But as I did their madness so discuss,
One whispered thus:

4. Possibly a reference to Cromwell.

5. An "epicure" is a person who finds the greatest good in sensual pleasure.

"This ring the bridegroom did for none provide,
But for his bride."[6]

1650

They Are All Gone into the World of Light!

They are all gone into the world of light!
And I alone sit lingering here;
Their very memory is fair and bright,
And my sad thoughts doth clear.

It glows and glitters in my cloudy breast
Like stars upon some gloomy grove,
Or those faint beams in which this hill is dressed,
After the sun's remove.

I see them walking in an air of glory,
Whose light doth trample on my days:
My days, which are at best but dull and hoary,
Mere glimmering and decays.

O holy hope! and high humility,
High as the heavens above!
These are your walks, and you have showed them me
To kindle my cold love,

Dear, beauteous death! the jewel of the just,
Shining no where, but in the dark;
What mysteries do lie beyond thy dust,
Could man outlook that mark!

He that hath found some fledged birds nest, may know
At first sight, if the bird be flown;
But what fair well, or grove he sings in now,
That is to him unknown.

And yet, as angels in some brighter dreams
Call to the soul, when man doth sleep,
So some strange thoughts transcend our wonted themes,
And into glory peep.

If a star were confined into a tomb
Her captive flames must needs burn there;
But when the hand that locked her up, gives room,
She'll shine through all the sphere.

O Father of eternal life, and all
Created glories under thee!
Resume thy spirit from this world of thrall° *slavery*
Into true liberty.

6. For the union of Christ and his Church as that between husband and wife, see Ephesians 5.23.

Either disperse these mists, which blot and fill
  My perspective[1] still as they pass,
Or else remove me hence unto that hill,[2]
    Where I shall need no glass.

1655

The Night
John 3.2[1]

  Through that pure virgin-shrine,
That sacred veil drawn o'er thy glorious noon
That men might look and live as glowworms shine,
      And face the moon:
    Wise Nicodemus saw such light
    As made him know his God by night.

  Most blest believer he!
Who in that land of darkness and blind eyes
Thy long expected healing wings could see,
      When thou didst rise,
    And what can never more be done,
    Did at midnight speak with the Sun!

  O who will tell me, where
He found thee at that dead and silent hour?
What hallowed solitary ground did bear
      So rare a flower,
    Within whose sacred leaves did lie
    The fullness of the Deity?

  No mercy-seat of gold,[2]
No dead and dusty cherub, nor carved stone,
But his own living works did my Lord hold
      And lodge alone;
    Where trees and herbs did watch and peep
    And wonder, while the Jews did sleep.

  Dear night! this world's defeat;[3]
The stop to busy fools; cares check and curb;
The day of spirits; my soul's calm retreat
      Which none disturb!
    Christ's progress, and his prayer time;
    The hours to which high heaven doth chime;

1. Telescope; vision.
2. Sion Hill, a symbol for union with God.
1. In John 3.2, the Pharisee Nicodemus tells Jesus: "Rabbi, we know that thou art a teacher come from God: for no man can do these miracles that thou doest except God be with him."
2. God told the Israelites to build "a mercy seat of pure gold" with a cherub on either end to place above the ark (see Exodus 25.17–21).
3. This and the next stanza echo George Herbert's *Prayer (1)*; see page 1631.

God's silent, searching flight,
When my Lord's head is filled with dew, and all
His locks are wet with the clear drops of night;
His still, soft call;
His knocking time; the souls dumb watch,
When spirits their fair kindred catch.

Were all my loud, evil days
Calm and unhaunted as is thy dark tent,
Whose peace but by some angel's wing or voice
Is seldom rent;
Then I in heaven all the long year
Would keep, and never wander here.

But living where the sun
Doth all things wake, and where all mix and tire
Themselves and others, I consent and run
To ev'ry mire,° *bog*
And by this world's ill-guiding light,
Ere more then I can do by night.

There is in God (some say)
A deep, but dazzling darkness; as men here
Say it is late and dusky, because they
See not all clear;
O for that night! where I in him
Might live invisible and dim.

Andrew Marvell

1621–1678

Praised by his nephew for "joining the most peculiar graces of wit and learning" and berated by his antagonist Samuel Parker for speaking the language of "boat-swains and cabin boys," Andrew Marvell left little evidence for his biographers. Most of what remains of his verse has been bequeathed to posterity by virtue of a shady banking scheme on his part and an implausible claim by his housekeeper to be "Mrs. Marvell." Though she couldn't remember the date of his death, Mary Palmer tried to prove that she was the poet's wife to get at money that her master had squirrelled away in an account for some bankrupt acquaintances. To further her claim, she saw to it that Marvell's *Miscellaneous Poems* were published in 1681. In his own name, Marvell published only a few occasional poems and a satire attacking religious intolerance and political authoritarianism.

If it is thanks to Mrs. Palmer's rummaging through the poet's papers that such exquisite poems as *To His Coy Mistress* and *The Definition of Love* saw the light of day, it is largely thanks to T. S. Eliot that modern critical attention was turned to Marvell's poetry. The Augustans and Romantics neglected him, and it was not until Eliot that such features of Marvell's verse as Latinate gravity, metaphysical wit, and muscular syntax came to be fully appreciated. For ingenious ambiguity and sheer seductive sensuousness, Marvell is one of the greatest poets of all time.

As tantalizing as the verse is, it leaves little solid evidence of what was a very private life. Marvell grew up in a house surrounded by gardens in the Yorkshire town of Hull on the Humber, where his father was the Anglican rector. There is a story that Marvell once left university for London to flirt with Catholicism, but his father made sure he returned to Cambridge and Protestantism. After his father's death, Marvell traveled in Holland, France, Italy, and Spain (1642–1647). He later tutored Mary Fairfax, daughter of Lord Fairfax of Nun-Appleton House (1650–1652), and taught William Dutton, Cromwell's ward (1653–1656). Initially recommended by Milton to serve as Assistant Latin Secretary in 1653, Marvell was first appointed Latin Secretary to the Council of State in 1657. He was elected Member of Parliament for Hull in 1659, a position he held until 1678. When Charles II restored the monarchy, Marvell interceded on Milton's behalf and made sure his old friend and fellow poet was released from prison. Later in life, Marvell wrote satires criticizing the corruption of the Restoration regime, all but one published anonymously.

Marvell chose to keep his cards close to his chest in the ideologically volatile atmosphere of the Civil War and Restoration. A contemporary biographer remarked that Marvell "was wont to say that, he would not play the good-fellow in any man's company in whose hands he would not trust his life." He did not fight in the Civil War, since he was in Europe at the time, and as he later ambiguously maintained, "the Cause was too good to have been fought for." His strategy in dealing with change involved publicly siding with the faction in power while maintaining politically incorrect friendships and finding himself "inclinable to favor the weaker party"—whether it was a Royalist who had given his life for the King, such as Lord Hastings, or a Republican who went to prison for his convictions, such as Milton. Marvell wrote poems praising both royalists and revolutionaries. He was nothing if not tolerant.

He was also something of a chameleon, an assumer of numerous poetic personae and disguises. In *Tom May's Death,* Marvell satirized the Royalist turned Republican, here portrayed arriving in heaven drunk. Marvell equivocally praised Cromwell in *An Horatian Ode*, ironically maintaining that it was the Irish whom Cromwell had so brutally massacred who could "best affirm his praises." When he became tutor to Cromwell's ward William Dutton, Marvell wrote poems praising Cromwell in such slavishly glowing terms that the poet was made Latin Secretary to the Council of State.

The last word should go to Marvell, whose choice to translate the following chorus from Seneca's *Thyestes* shows his outlook on the vicissitudes of power:

> Climb at court for me that will
> Giddy favor's slippery hill;
> All I seek is to lie still,
> Settled in some secret nest.
> In calm leisure let me rest,
> And far off the public stage
> Pass away my silent age.
> Thus, when without noise, unknown,
> I have lived out all my span,
> I shall die without a groan,
> An old honest countryman,
> Who exposed to others' eyes,
> Into his own heart ne'er pries.
> Death to him's a strange surprise.

The Coronet[1]

When for the thorns with which I long, too long,
With many a piercing wound,
My Savior's head have crowned,
I seek with garlands to redress that wrong:
Through every garden, every mead,
I gather flow'rs (my fruits are only flow'rs)
Dismantling all the fragrant towers° *tall headdresses*
That once adorned my shepherdess's head.
And now when I have summed up all my store,
Thinking (so I myself deceive)
So rich a chaplet° thence to weave *wreath*
As never yet the King of Glory wore:
Alas, I find the serpent old
That, twining in his speckled breast,[2]
About the flowers disguised does fold,° *wind*
With wreaths° of fame and interest. *coils*
Ah, foolish man, that wouldst debase with them,
And mortal glory, Heaven's diadem!
But Thou who only couldst the serpent tame,
Either his slippery knots at once untie,
And disentangle all his winding snare:
Or shatter too with him my curious frame:[3]
And let these wither, so that he may die,
Though set with skill and chosen out with care:
That they, while Thou on both their spoils[4] dost tread,
May crown thy feet, that could not crown thy head.[5]

Bermudas[1]

Where the remote Bermudas ride
In th' ocean's bosom unespied,
From a small boat, that rowed along,
The list'ning winds received this song.
"What should we do but sing his praise
That led us through the watry maze,
Unto an isle so long unknown,[2]
And yet far kinder than our own?
Where he the huge sea-monsters wracks,° *shipwrecks*
That lift the deep upon their backs.
He lands us on a grassy stage,

1. Marvell's poems were first published in 1681.
2. See Spenser, *Faerie Queene* 1.11.15.
3. Ingenious structure (the chaplet).
4. Sloughing of the snake's skin; plundering.
5. See Genesis 3.15, for the prophecy that the seed of Eve will bruise the serpent's head.

1. Probably composed sometime after 1653, when Marvell was living in the house of John Oxenbridge, who had made two trips to the Bermudas. Marvell could also have known Captain John Smith's 1624 work *The General History of Virginia, New England and the Summer Isles* (as the Bermudas were called).
2. Unknown to Europeans; Juan Bermudez first came there in 1515.

Safe from the storms, and prelate's[3] rage.
He gave us this eternal spring,
Which here enamels everything;
And sends the fowl to us in care,
On daily visits through the air.
He hangs in shades the orange bright,
Like golden lamps in a green night,
And does in the pom'granates close,
Jewels more rich than Ormus[4] shows.
He makes the figs our mouths to meet,
And throws the melons at our feet,
But apples° plants of such a price, *pineapples*
No tree could ever bear them twice.
With cedars, chosen by his hand,
From Lebanon, he stores the land,
And makes the hollow seas, that roar,
Proclaim the ambergris[5] on shore.
He cast (of which we rather boast)
The gospel's pearl upon our coast,
And in these rocks for us did frame
A temple, where to sound his name.
Oh let our voice his praise exalt,
Till it arrive at heaven's vault:
Which thence (perhaps) rebounding, may
Echo beyond the Mexique Bay.[6]
Thus sung they, in the English boat,
An holy and a cheerful note,
And all the way, to guide their chime,
With falling oars they kept the time.

The Nymph Complaining for the Death of Her Fawn[1]

The wanton troopers[2] riding by
Have shot my fawn, and it will die.
Ungentle men! They cannot thrive
To kill thee. Thou ne'er didst alive
Them any harm: alas, nor could
Thy death yet do them any good.
I'm sure I never wished them ill;
Nor do I for all this; nor will:
But, if my simple prayers may yet
Prevail with Heaven to forget
Thy murder, I will join my tears
Rather than fail. But, O my fears!

3. Clergyman's, bishop's.
4. Hormuz on the Persian Gulf.
5. Musky secretion of the sperm whale that is used in perfumes.
6. Gulf of Mexico.

1. Ancient Roman poets such as Catullus and Ovid had written poems on the death of pets, as did the early 16th-century English poet John Skelton in *Philip Sparrow*.
2. A term used for the Presbyterian Scots Covenanting Army that attacked England in 1640.

It cannot die so. Heaven's King
Keeps register of everything:
And nothing may we use in vain.
E'en beasts must be with justice slain,
Else men are made their deodands.[3]
Though they should wash their guilty hands
In this warm life-blood, which doth part
From thine, and wound me to the heart,
Yet could they not be clean: their stain
Is dyed in such a purple grain.
There is not such another in
The world, to offer for their sin.
  Unconstant Sylvio, when yet
I had not found him counterfeit,
One morning (I remember well)
Tied in this silver chain and bell,
Gave it to me: nay, and I know
What he said then; I'm sure I do.
Said he, "Look how your huntsman here
Hath taught a fawn to hunt his dear."
But Sylvio soon had me beguiled.
This waxèd tame, while he grew wild,
And quite regardless of my smart,
Left me his fawn, but took his heart.
  Thenceforth I set myself to play
My solitary time away
With this: and very well content,
Could so mine idle life have spent.
For it was full of sport; and light
Of foot, and heart; and did invite
Me to its game: it seemed to bless
Itself in me. How could I less
Than love it? O I cannot be
Unkind, t' a beast that loveth me.
  Had it lived long, I do not know
Whether it too might have done so
As Sylvio did: his gifts might be
Perhaps as false or more than he.
But I am sure, for ought that I
Could in so short a time espie,
Thy Love was far more better than
The love of false and cruel men.
  With sweetest milk and sugar first
I it at mine own fingers nursed.
And as it grew, so every day
It waxed more white and sweet than they,

3. Otherwise, men would become forfeited objects. In early modern English law, any personal property that caused a human death had to be given up as part of the reparation for the crime.

It had so sweet a breath! And oft
I blushed to see its foot more soft,
And white, (shall I say than my hand?)
Nay any lady's of the land.
   It is a wondrous thing, how fleet
'Twas on those little silver feet.
With what a pretty skipping grace,
It oft would challenge me the race:
And when 't had left me far away,
'Twould stay, and run again, and stay.
For it was nimbler much than hinds;
And trod, as on the four winds.
   I have a garden of my own,
But so with roses overgrown,
And lilies, that you would it guess
To be a little wilderness.
And all the springtime of the year
It only lovèd to be there.
Among the beds of lilies, I
Have sought it oft, where it should lie;
Yet could not, till itself would rise,
Find it, although before mine eyes.
For, in the flaxen lilies' shade,
It like a bank of lilies laid.
Upon the roses it would feed,
Until its lips e'en seemed to bleed:
And then to me 'twould boldly trip,
And print those roses on my lip.
But all its chief delight was still
On roses thus itself to fill:
And its pure virgin limbs to fold
In whitest sheets of lilies cold.
Had it lived long, it would have been
Lilies without, roses within.
O help! O help! I see it faint:
And die as calmly as a saint.
See how it weeps. The tears do come
Sad, slowly dropping like a gum.
So weeps the wounded balsam: so
The holy frankincense doth flow.
The brotherless Heliades
Melt in such amber tears as these.[4]
   I in a golden vial will
Keep these two crystal tears; and fill
It till it do o'reflow with mine;
Then place it in Diana's[5] shrine.

4. Grieving the death of their brother Phaethon, the Heliades were transformed into poplar trees which wept tears of amber.

5. Goddess of chastity and of the hunt.

Now my sweet fawn is vanished to
Whither the swans and turtles° go: *doves*
In fair Elysium to endure,
With milk-white lambs, and ermines pure.
O do not run too fast: for I
Will but bespeak thy grave, and die.
First my unhappy statue shall
Be cut in marble; and withal,
Let it be weeping too:[6] but there
Th' engraver sure his art may spare;
For I so truly thee bemoan,
That I shall weep though I be stone:
Until my tears, still dropping, wear
My breast, themselves engraving there.
There at my feet shalt thou be laid,
Of purest alabaster made:
For I would have thine image be
White as I can, though not as thee.

To His Coy Mistress[1]

Had we but world enough, and time,
This coyness, Lady, were no crime.
We would sit down, and think which way
To walk, and pass our long love's day.
Thou by the Indian Ganges' side
Shouldst rubies find: I by the tide
Of Humber would complain.[2] I would
Love you ten years before the flood:
And you should if you please refuse
Till the conversion of the Jews.[3]
My vegetable love should grow
Vaster than empires, and more slow.[4]
An hundred years should go to praise
Thine eyes, and on thy forehead gaze.
Two hundred to adore each breast:
But thirty thousand to the rest.
An age at least to every part,
And the last age should show your heart.
For Lady you deserve this state;
Nor would I love at lower rate.
But at my back I always hear

6. Niobe was turned into a weeping stone for her pride in her children.

1. A poem on the theme of *carpe diem* ("seize the day") that includes a blazon, or description of the lady from head to toe, and a logical argument: "If . . . But . . . Therefore."

2. Marvell grew up in Hull on the Humber River.

3. The end of time: the Flood occurred in the distant past, and Christians prophesied that Jews would convert to Christianity at the end of the world.

4. The "vegetable" was characterized only by growth, in contrast to the sensitive, which felt, and the rational, which could reason.

Times wingèd chariot hurrying near:
And yonder all before us lie
Deserts of vast eternity.
Thy beauty shall no more be found;
Nor, in thy marble vault, shall sound
My echoing song: then worms shall try
That long preserved virginity:
And your quaint honor turn to dust;[5]
And into ashes all my lust.
The grave's a fine and private place,
But none, I think, do there embrace.
Now, therefore, while the youthful hue
Sits on thy skin like morning dew,[6]
And while thy willing soul transpires
At every pore with instant fires,
Now let us sport us while we may;
And now, like amorous birds of prey,
Rather at once our time devour,
Than languish in his slow-chapped° power. *slowly biting*
Let us roll all our strength, and all
Our sweetness, up into one ball:
And tear our pleasures with rough strife,
Thorough the iron gates of life.[7]
Thus, though we cannot make our sun
Stand still, yet we will make him run.[8]

The Definition of Love

My Love is of a birth as rare
As 'tis for object strange and high:
It was begotten by Despair
Upon Impossibility.

Magnanimous Despair alone
Could show me so divine a thing,
Where feeble Hope could ne'er have flown
But vainly flapped its tinsel wing.

And yet I quickly might arrive
Where my extended soul is fixed,
But Fate does iron wedges drive,
And always crowds itself betwixt.

For Fate with jealous eye does see
Two perfect loves, nor lets them close:° *unite*

5. "Quaint honor," proud chastity. Note the pun on *queynte* (Middle English), woman's genitals.
6. In the 1681 Folio, "dew" reads "glue," and in two manuscripts the rhymes in lines 33 and 34 are "glue" and "dew."
7. One manuscript reads "grates" for "gates."
8. Joshua made the sun stand still in the war against Gibeon (see Joshua 10.12).

Their union would her ruin be,
And her tyrannic power depose.

And therefore her decrees of steel
Us as the distant poles have placed,
(Though Love's whole world on us doth wheel)
Not by themselves to be embraced.

Unless the giddy heaven fall,
And earth some new convulsion tear;
And, us to join, the world should all
Be cramped into a planisphere.[1]

As lines (so loves) oblique[2] may well
Themselves in every angle greet:
But ours so truly parallel,
Though infinite, can never meet.

Therefore the love which us doth bind,
But Fate so enviously debars,
Is the conjunction of the mind,
And opposition of the stars.[3]

The Mower Against Gardens

Luxurious man, to bring his vice in use,[1]
  Did after him the world seduce,
And from the fields the flowers and plants allure,
  Where Nature was most plain and pure.
He first enclosed within the garden's square
  A dead and standing pool of air,
And a more luscious earth for them did knead,
  Which stupefied them while it fed.
The pink grew then as double as his mind;[2]
  The nutriment did change the kind.
With strange perfumes he did the roses taint,
  And flowers themselves were taught to paint.
The tulip, white, did for complexion seek,
  And learned to interline its cheek:
Its onion root they then so high did hold,
  That one was for a meadow sold.[3]
Another world was searched, through oceans new,
  To find the Marvel of Peru.[4]
And yet these rarities might be allowed
  To man, that sovereign thing and proud,

1. A two-dimensional map of the globe.
2. Slanting at an angle other than a right angle, and also veering away from right morals.
3. Conjunction: coming together in the same sign of the zodiac; union. Stars in opposition are diametrically opposed to one another.
1. To make current.
2. Double, both in the sense of having two blooms and being the result of sophisticated (duplicitous) thought.
3. Marvell alludes to the 17th-century lucrative trade in Dutch tulips.
4. *Mirabilis jalapa*, also known as the four-o'clock, a multicolored flower native to tropical America.

Had he not dealt between the bark and tree,[5]
 Forbidden mixtures there to see.
No plant now knew the stock from which it came;
 He grafts upon the wild the tame:
That the uncertain and adult'rate fruit
 Might put the palate in dispute.
His green seraglio[6] has its eunuchs too;
 Lest any tyrant him outdo.
And in the cherry he does nature vex,
 To procreate without a sex.[7]
'Tis all enforced; the fountain and the grot,° *grotto*
 While the sweet fields do lie forgot:
Where willing Nature does to all dispense
 A wild and fragrant innocence:
And fauns and fairies do the meadows till,
 More by their presence than their skill.
Their statues polished by some ancient hand,
 May to adorn the gardens stand:
But howsoe'er the figures do excel,
 The gods themselves with us do dwell.

The Mower's Song

 My mind was once the true survey
 Of all these meadows fresh and gay;
 And in the greenness of the grass
 Did see its hopes as in a glass;° *mirror*
 When Juliana came, and she,
What I do to the grass, does to my thoughts and me.[1]

 But these, while I with sorrow pine,
 Grew more luxuriant still and fine,
 That not one blade of grass you spied,
 But had a flower on either side;
 When Juliana came, and she,
What I do to the grass, does to my thoughts and me.

 Unthankful meadows, could you so
 A fellowship so true forgo,
 And in your gaudy May-games meet,[2]
 While I lay trodden under feet?
 When Juliana came, and she,
What I do to the grass, does to my thoughts and me.

 But what you in compassion ought,
 Shall now by my revenge be wrought:

5. An expression used to describe interfering in another's affairs, especially those of a married couple.
6. Secluded place; Turkish palace; harem.
7. To grow by grafting one strain of cherry onto another.

1. This 12-syllable line (an alexandrine) is the only instance of a refrain in all of Marvell's poetry.
2. Festivals celebrated on May 1.

And flowers, and grass, and I and all,
Will in one common ruin fall.
For Juliana comes, and she,
What I do to the grass, does to my thoughts and me.

And thus, ye meadows, which have been
Companions of my thoughts more green,
Shall now the heraldry become
With which I shall adorn my tomb;
For Juliana comes, and she,
What I do to the grass, does to my thoughts and me.

The Garden

How vainly men themselves amaze
To win the palm, the oak, or bays,[1]
And their uncessant labors see
Crowned from some single herb or tree,
Whose short and narrow-vergèd shade
Does prudently their toils upbraid,
While all flowers and all trees do close° *unite*
To weave the garlands of repose.

Fair quiet, have I found thee here,
And innocence thy sister dear!
Mistaken long, I sought you then
In busy companies of men.
Your sacred plants, if here below,
Only among the plants will grow.
Society is all but rude,
To this delicious solitude.[2]

No white nor red[3] was ever seen
So am'rous as this lovely green.
Fond lovers, cruel as their flame,
Cut in these trees their mistress' name.
Little, alas, they know, or heed,
How far these beauties hers exceed!
Fair trees! whereso'er your barks I wound,
No name shall but your own be found.

When we have run our passion's heat,
Love hither makes his best retreat.
The gods, that mortal beauty chase,
Still in a tree did end their race.
Apollo hunted Daphne so,

1. Vainly: arrogantly, in vain; amaze: bewilder, go mad; the palm, the oak, or bays: prizes symbolic of military, political, and poetic excellence.

2. Compare to Katherine Philips's A *Country-life*: "Then welcome dearest solitude, / My great felicity; / Though some are pleased to call thee rude."

3. Colors used to describe the beloved's beauty.

Only that she might laurel grow,
And Pan did after Syrinx speed,
Not as a nymph, but for a reed.[4]

What wondrous life in this I lead!
Ripe apples drop about my head;
The luscious clusters of the vine
Upon my mouth do crush their wine;
The nectarine, and curious peach,
Into my hands themselves do reach;
Stumbling on melons, as I pass,
Insnared with flowers, I fall on grass.

Meanwhile the mind, from pleasure less,
Withdraws into its happiness:
The mind, that ocean where each kind
Does straight its own resemblance find,[5]
Yet it creates, transcending these,
Far other worlds, and other seas,
Annihilating all that's made
To a green thought in a green shade.

Here at the fountain's sliding foot,
Or at some fruit-tree's mossy root,
Casting the body's vest aside,
My soul into the boughs does glide:
There like a bird it sits and sings,
Then whets and combs its silver wings;
And, till prepared for longer flight,
Waves in its plumes the various light.

Such was that happy garden-state,
While man there walked without a mate:
After a place so pure and sweet,
What other help could yet be meet!
But 'twas beyond a mortal's share
To wander solitary there:
Two paradises 'twere in one
To live in paradise alone.

How well the skillful gardener drew
Of flowers and herbs this dial new;[6]
Where from above the milder sun
Does through a fragrant zodiac run;
And, as it works, th' industrious bee
Computes its time as well as we.[7]

4. As god of poetry, Apollo seeks the laurel (the bays), while Pan seeks the syrinx (pipe) of pastoral poetry. Apollo chased Daphne, who prayed to be saved from him and was transformed into a laurel tree, just as Syrinx escaped Pan's lust when she was turned into a reed.

5. It was popularly believed that animals and plants on land had counterparts in the sea. This line describes the mind as innately possessing ideas, a concept of Platonic philosophy.

6. The garden is arranged as a floral sundial.

7. Computes its time: a pun on thyme.

How could such sweet and wholesome hours
Be reckoned but with herbs and flowers!

An Horatian Ode Upon Cromwell's Return from Ireland[1]

The forward youth that would appear
Must now forsake his muses dear,
Nor in the shadows sing
His numbers[2] languishing.
'Tis time to leave the books in dust,
And oil th' unusèd armor's rust:
Removing from the wall
The corslet[3] of the hall.
So restless Cromwell could not cease
In the inglorious arts of peace,
But through adventurous war
Urgèd his active star.
And, like the three-forked lightning, first
Breaking the clouds where it was nursed,
Did thorough his own side
His fiery way divide:[4]
For 'tis all one to courage high
The emulous or enemy;
And with such to enclose
Is more than to oppose.
Then burning through the air he went,
And palaces and temples rent:
And Caesar's head at last
Did through his laurels blast.[5]
'Tis madness to resist or blame
The force of angry heaven's flame:
And, if we would speak true,
Much to the man is due,
Who, from his private gardens, where
He lived reservèd and austere,
As if his highest plot
To plant the bergamot,[6]
Could by industrious valor climb
To ruin the great work of Time,

1. Cromwell returned from his military campaign in Ireland in May 1650. After General Fairfax resigned as commander of the parliamentary army because he refused to invade Scotland, Cromwell assumed his position and attacked the Scots. This poem was printed in the 1681 edition but then was canceled from printed copies until 1776. The influence of Horace's *Odes* (especially I. 35, 37; IV. 4, 5, 14, 15) surfaces in the poised dignity of the verse and its subtly ambiguous attitude toward power.

2. Conformity to a rhythmical pattern in verse or music.

3. Defensive armor covering the upper body.

4. Cromwell's overtaking his rivals in Parliament is described as an elemental force similar to the "three-forked lightning" of Zeus.

5. Although lightning was thought not to strike the laurel (symbolizing the royal crown), Cromwell had struck down Charles I (Caesar).

6. A pear known as the "prince's pear."

And cast the kingdom old
Into another mold.
Though justice against fate complain,
And plead the ancient rights in vain:
But those do hold or break,
As men are strong or weak.
Nature, that hateth emptiness,
Allows of penetration less:[7]
And therefore must make room
Where greater spirits come.
What field of all the Civil Wars,
Where his were not the deepest scars?
And Hampton[8] shows what part
He had of wiser art,
Where, twining subtle fears with hope,
He wove a net of such a scope,
That Charles himself might chase
To Carisbrooke's narrow case:
That thence the royal actor borne,
The tragic scaffold might adorn;
While round the armèd bands
Did clap their bloody hands.
He nothing common did or mean
Upon that memorable scene:
But with his keener eye
The axe's[9] edge did try;
Nor called the gods with vulgar spite
To vindicate his helpless right,
But bowed his comely head,
Down, as upon a bed.
This was that memorable hour
Which first assured the forcèd power.
So when they did design
The Capitol's first line,
A bleeding head where they begun,
Did fright the architects to run;
And yet in that the State
Foresaw it's happy fate.[1]
And now the Irish are ashamed
To see themselves in one year tamed:[2]
So much one man can do,
That does both act and know.
They can affirm his praises best,

7. Nature abhors not only a vacuum but even more so the penetration of one body's space by another body.
8. Hampton Court where Charles I was held captive before his execution in 1649. He had fled to Carrisbrooke Castle on the Isle of Wight, where he was betrayed to the Governor in 1647.
9. Marvell plays on the Latin "*acies*," the sharp edge of a sword, a keen glance, and the vanguard of battle.

1. In digging the foundations of the temple of Jupiter Capitolinum, the excavators found a human's head (*caput*), which was interpreted as prophesying that Rome should be the capitol of the Empire (see Livy, *Annals* I.55.6).
2. From August 1649 to his return to England in May 1650, Cromwell went on a savage military campaign that included the slaughter of Irish civilians.

And have, though overcome, confessed
How good he is, how just,
And fit for highest trust.[3]
Nor yet grown stiffer with command,
But still in the Republic's hand:
How fit he is to sway
That can so well obey.[4]
He to the commons' feet presents
A kingdom, for his first year's rents:
And, what he may, forbears
His fame to make it theirs:
And has his sword and spoils ungirt,
To lay them at the public's skirt.
So when the falcon high
Falls heavy from the sky,
She, having killed, no more does search,
But on the next green bough to perch;
Where, when he first does lure,
The falconer has her sure.
What may not then our isle presume
While victory his crest does plume!
What may not others fear
If thus he crown each year!
A Caesar he ere long to Gaul,
To Italy an Hannibal,[5]
And to all states not free
Shall climactéric° be. *period of change*
The Pict no shelter now shall find
Within his particolored mind;
But from this valor sad° *severe*
Shrink underneath the plaid:[6]
Happy if in the tufted brake
The English hunter him mistake;
Nor lay his hounds in near
The Caledonian° deer. *Scottish*
But thou the wars' and fortune's son
March indefatigably on;
And for the last effect
Still keep thy sword erect:
Besides the force it has to fright
The spirits of the shady night,[7]
The same arts that did gain
A power must it maintain.

3. An example of one of the many equivocal statements in this poem; of course, the Irish did not affirm Cromwell's greatness.
4. A saying attributed to the Athenian Solon the lawgiver.
5. Neither Caesar nor Hannibal gave freedom to peoples whose countries they invaded and conquered.
6. Marvell uses "Picts" the ancient name for the Scots, creating a play on *picti* (Latin: painted) and particolored.
7. There was an ancient tradition of dead spirits being frightened by raised swords (Homer, *Odyssey* 11; Virgil, *Aeneid* 6). The dead spirits referred to here include the dead in the wars in Ireland and England, including the king.

Katherine Philips

1631–1664

Idolized as the "Matchless Orinda" in her own day, Katherine Philips is now taking her place in the history of English verse after two centuries of neglect. During her lifetime, her work circulated in manuscript among a close network of friends. The first edition of her poems appeared posthumously in 1664. The second edition of 1667 was evidently a commercial success, since it was reprinted in 1669, 1678, and 1710. The next complete edition of her poems did not appear until 1994.

John Keats esteemed Philips's *To Mrs. Mary Awbrey at Parting* as an example of "real feminine Modesty;" today, by contrast, critics praise her poems to women friends as reminiscent of the ancient Greek Sappho's erotic lyrics. By imitating Donne's love lyrics in her poems to women, Philips poetically conceives of these friendships as no less world-changing, no less ennobling and enthralling, than Donne's romantic liaisons. Some of the best poets of her own day were able to appreciate her as a fellow poet rather than as Keats's romanticized ideal woman. Marvell paid tribute to her by subtly alluding to lines of her poetry in one of his greatest poems, *The Garden*. And Henry Vaughan insisted that "No laurel grows, but for [her] brow."

Katherine Philips's work was particularly important for other women writers. Philips's lyric poetry influenced such other early modern women poets as Aphra Behn and Anne Killigrew. Yet it is impossible to pigeonhole Philips as stereotypically feminine. She wrote on public and political themes as well as personal subjects, endowing traditional genres such as the parting poem, the elegy, and the epitaph, with a particular directness and clarity all her own.

Katherine Philips was born in London to a well-to-do Presbyterian family. Her father was a prosperous merchant, and her mother was the daughter of a Fellow of the Royal College of Physicians. Philips's father was wealthy enough to invest two hundred pounds for a thousand acres in Ulster, a scheme that was begun in 1642 by the Puritan Parliament but, ironically, not realized until the Restoration, when we find Katherine in Ireland pursuing lawsuits to obtain this land. As a girl, Katherine attended Mrs. Salmon's Presbyterian School, where she learned to love poetry and began to write verses. In 1646 her widowed mother married Sir Richard Philips, and the family moved to his castle in Wales. Philips herself married Sir Richard's kinsman James Philips, and they lived together for twelve years in the small Welsh town of Cardigan when not in London, where her husband served as a Member of Parliament during the Interregnum.

However Presbyterian and Cromwellian were the associations of her family and marriage, she emerged after the Restoration as a complete Anglican. Not only did she write poetry against the regicide, such as *Upon the Double Murder of King Charles*, but she became a favorite author at court. She was encouraged to write poetry by her friend "Poliarchus," Sir Charles Cotterell, Master of Ceremonies in the Court of Charles II, who showed her poems to the royal family. An Anglo-Irish nobleman, the Earl of Orrery, encouraged her to complete a translation of Corneille's *Pompey* and actually produced and had the play printed in Dublin in 1663.

Katherine Philips developed friendships that became the theme of what most critics regard as her best poems. Perhaps the most intense of these friendships was that with Mrs. Anne Owen, the Lucasia of Philips's most passionate poems, several of which echo love poems by Donne. Her friend Sir Edward Dering, whom she called "the Noble Silvander," lamented

Katherine Philips's death in recounting the extraordinary accomplishment of both her poetry and her life, which had attempted

> the most generous design . . . to unite all those of her acquaintance which she found worthy or desired to make so (among which later number she was pleased to give me a place) into one society, and by the bands of friendship to make an alliance more firm than what nature, our country or equal education can produce.

Friendship in Emblem
or the Seal,[1]
To My Dearest Lucasia[2]

The hearts thus intermixèd speak
A love that no bold shock can break;
For joined and growing, both in one,
Neither can be disturbed alone.

That means a mutual knowledge too;
For what is't either heart can do,
Which by its panting sentinel° *guard*
It does not to the other tell?

That friendship hearts so much refines,
It nothing but itself designs:
The hearts are free from lower ends,
For each point to the other tends.

They flame, 'tis true, and several ways,
But still those flames do so much raise,
That while to either they incline
They yet are noble and divine.

From smoke or hurt those flames are free,
From grossness or mortality:
The hearts (like Moses bush presumed)[3]
Warmed and enlightened, not consumed.

The compasses that stand above
Express this great immortal Love;[4]
For friends, like them, can prove this true,
They are, and yet they are not, two.

And in their posture is expressed

1. A symbolic picture, which appeared with a motto and a poem in such books as Whitney's *Choice of Emblems* (see Perspectives: Early Modern Books, page 1066). The central emblematic image of this poem is "the compasses" (line 21); another emblem is "those flames" (line 14).

2. Anne Owen, to whom many of Philips's poems are dedicated, was a neighbor of hers in Wales and a close friend from 1651 until Philips's death.

3. See Exodus 3.2–5 for the burning bush through which the angel of the Lord appeared to and from which God called Moses.

4. Compare the image of the compasses here to the "twin compasses" in Donne's *A Valediction: Forbidding Mourning* (page 1598).

Friendship's exalted interest:
Each follows where the other leans,
And what each does, the other means.

And as when one foot does stand fast,
And t'other circles seeks to cast,
The steady part does regulate
And make the wanderer's motion straight:

So friends are only two in this,
T'reclaim each other when they miss:
For whose'er will grossly fall,
Can never be a friend at all.

And as that useful instrument
For even lines was ever meant;
So friendship from good angels[5] springs,
To teach the world heroic things.

As these are found out in design
To rule and measure every line;
So friendship governs actions best,
Prescribing law to all the rest.

And as in nature nothing's set
So just as lines and numbers met;
So compasses for these being made,
Do friendship's harmony persuade.

And like to them, so friends may own
Extension, not division:
Their points, like bodies, separate;
But head, like souls, knows no such fate.

And as each part so well is knit,
That their embraces ever fit:
So friends are such by destiny,
And no third can the place supply.

There needs no motto to the seal:
But that we may the mine[6] reveal
To the dull eye, it was thought fit
That friendship only should be writ.

But as there is degrees of bliss,
So there's no friendship meant by this,
But such as will transmit to fame
Lucasia's and Orinda's name.

5. Guardian spirits, with puns on angels, and *angeli* (Latin), messengers.
6. A mass of gold, a store of plenty, as well as a pun on the possessive pronoun meaning "my own" and perhaps also on "mind."

Upon the Double Murder of King Charles
in Answer to a Libelous Rhyme Made by V. P.[1]

I think not on the state, nor am concerned
Which way soever that great helm is turned,
But as that son whose father's danger nigh
Did force his native dumbness, and untie
The fettered organs: so here is a cause
That will excuse the breach of nature's laws.[2]
Silence were now a sin: nay passion now
Wise men themselves for merit would allow.
What noble eye could see, (and careless pass)
The dying lion kicked by every ass?
Hath Charles so broke God's laws, he must not have
A quiet crown, nor yet a quiet grave?
Tombs have been sanctuaries; thieves lie here
Secure from all their penalty and fear.
Great Charles his double misery was this,
Unfaithful friends, ignoble enemies;
Had any heathen been this prince's foe,
He would have wept to see him injured so.
His title was his crime, they'd reason good
To quarrel at the right they had withstood.
He broke God's laws, and therefore he must die,
And what shall then become of thee and I?
Slander must follow treason; but yet stay,
Take not our reason with our king away.
Though you have seized upon all our defense,
Yet do not sequester° our common sense. *confiscate*
But I admire not at this new supply:
No bounds will hold those who at scepters fly.
Christ will be King, but I ne'er understood,
His subjects built his kingdom up with blood,
(Except their own) or that he would dispense
With his commands, though for his own defense.
Oh! to what height of horror are they come,
Who dare pull down a crown, tear up a tomb![3]

On the Third of September, 1651[1]

As when the glorious magazine of light[2]
Approaches to his canopy of night,
He with new splendor clothes his dying rays,

1. Vavasor Powell, a Fifth Monarchist who believed that Christ's second coming was imminent, and an ardent Republican, whose verses on the murder of the king are lost. According to Philips's poem, Powell argued that Charles I had usurped God's power.
2. Breaking the prohibition against women speaking on public affairs. See Margaret Tyler's preface to *The First Part of the Mirror of Princely Deeds*, for a defense of woman's ability to write about war, traditionally considered only appropriate to male authors.
3. Possibly a reference to the unearthing of the regicides' bodies.

1. Cromwell defeated Charles II at the Battle of Worcester on this date.
2. The sun; a magazine is a storehouse for gunpowder.

And double brightness to his beams conveys;
As if to brave and check his ending fate,
Puts on his highest looks in 's lowest state;
Dressed in such terror as to make us all
Be anti-Persians,[3] and adore his fall;
Then quits the world, depriving it of day,
While every herb and plant does droop away:
So when our gasping English royalty
Perceived her period now was drawing nigh,
She summons her whole strength to give one blow,
To raise her self, or pull down others too.
Big with revenge and hope, she now spake more
Of terror than in many months before;
And musters her attendants, or to save
Her from, or wait upon her to the grave:
Yet but enjoyed the miserable fate
Of setting majesty, to die in state.
    Unhappy Kings! who cannot keep a throne,
Nor be so fortunate to fall alone!
Their weight sinks others: Pompey could not fly,
But half the world must bear him company;[4]
Thus captive Sampson could not life conclude,
Unless attended with a multitude.[5]
Who'd trust to greatness now, whose food is air,
Whose ruin sudden, and whose end despair?
Who would presume upon his glorious birth,
Or quarrel for a spacious share of earth,
That sees such diadems° become thus cheap, *crowns*
And heroes tumble in the common heap?
    O! give me virtue then, which sums up all,
And firmly stands when crowns and scepters fall.

To the Truly Noble, and Obliging Mrs. Anne Owen
(on My First Approaches)[1]

Madam,
As in a triumph conquerors admit
Their meanest captives to attend on it,[2]
Who, though unworthy, have the power confessed,
And justified the yielding of the rest:
So when the busy world (in hope t'excuse
Their own surprise) your conquests do peruse,
And find my name, they will be apt to say

3. Anti-sun, since the Persians were thought to worship the sun, and anti-monarchist, possibly with reference to Darius I, the Persian king who put down many revolts during his lifetime.
4. Caesar defeated Pompey at the battle of Pharsalus, where 15,000 of Pompey's men were killed. Afterward, Pompey fled to Egypt, where he was assassinated.
5. The blind Israelite hero Samson tore down the temple at Gaza, thus killing both himself and his enemies (Judges 16).
1. Mrs. Anne Owen of Orielton, Wales, was Philips' close friend and the "Lucasia" of her poems; she was married to John Owen and was the heiress to the ancient seat of Presaddfed in Anglesey.
2. Here, "triumph" means military victory and the triumphal procession that announced it.

Your charms were blinded, or else thrown away.
There is no honor got in gaining me,
Who am a prize not worth your victory.
But this will clear you, that 'tis general
The worst applaud what is admired by all.
But I have plots in't: for the way to be
Secure of fame to all posterity
Is to obtain the honor I pursue,
To tell the world I was subdued by you.
And since in you all wonders common are,
Your votaries° may in your virtues share, *devoted admirers*
While you by noble magic worth impart:
She that can conquer, can reclaim a heart.
Of this creation I shall not despair,
Since for your own sake it concerns your care:
For 'tis more honor that the world should know
You made a noble soul, than found it so.

To Mrs. Mary Awbrey at Parting[1]

I have examined, and do find,
    Of all that favor me,
There's none I grieve to leave behind
    But only, only thee.
To part with thee I needs must die,
    Could parting separate thee and I.

But neither chance nor compliment
    Did element our love;
'Twas sacred sympathy was lent
    Us from the choir above.
That friendship fortune did create,
Which fears a wound from time or fate.

Our changed and mingled souls are grown
    To such acquaintance now,
That if each would assume their own,
    Alas! we know not how.
We have each other so engrossed,
That each is in the union lost.

And thus we can no absence know,
    Nor shall we be confined;
Our active souls will daily go
    To learn each other's mind.
Nay, should we never meet to sense,
Our souls would hold intelligence.[2]

1. Mrs. Mary Awbrey, one of Philips' classmates at Mrs. Salmon's school. Quoting the entire poem, John Keats praises it as an example of "real feminine Modesty" in a letter to J. H. Reynolds of 21 September 1817.

2. A Neoplatonic idea, that the souls would know each other not by physical contact but by spiritual communion. Compare Donne's *A Valediction: Forbidding Mourning* (page 1598.)

Inspired with a flame divine,
  I scorn to court a stay;
For from the noble soul of thine
  I can ne'er be away.
But I shall weep when thou dost grieve;
Nor can I die whilst thou dost live.

By my own temper I shall guess
  At thy felicity,
And only like my happiness
  Because it pleaseth thee.
Our hearts at any time will tell
If thou, or I, be sick, or well.

All honor sure I must pretend,
  All that is good or great;
She that would be Rosania's[3] friend,
  Must be at least complete.
If I have any bravery,
'Tis cause I am so much of thee.

Thy leiger° soul in me shall lie, *ambassador*
  And all thy thoughts reveal;
Then back again with mine shall fly,
  And thence to me shall steal.
Thus still to one another tend;
Such is the sacred name of friend.

Thus our twin souls in one shall grow,
  And teach the world new love;
Redeem the age and sex, and show
  A flame fate dares not move:
And courting death to be our friend,
Our lives together too shall end.

A dew shall dwell upon our tomb
  Of such a quality,
That fighting armies, thither come,
  Shall reconciled be.
We'll ask no epitaph, but say
Orinda and Rosania.

To My Excellent Lucasia, on Our Friendship
17th July 1651[1]

I did not live until this time
  Crowned my felicity,
When I could say without a crime,

3. Rosania was the poetic name that Philips gave to her friend Mary Awbrey.

1. Philips met her friend Anne Owen (called "Lucasia") in 1651.

I am not thine, but thee.
This carcass breathed, and walked, and slept,
So that the world believed
There was a soul the motions kept;
But they were all deceived.
For as a watch by art is wound
To motion, such was mine:
But never had Orinda found
A soul till she found thine;
Which now inspires, cures and supplies,
And guides my darkened breast:
For thou art all that I can prize,
My joy, my life, my rest.
Nor bridegroom's nor crowned conqueror's mirth
To mine compared can be:
They have but pieces of this earth,
I've all the world in thee.
Then let our flame still light and shine,
(And no bold fear control)
As innocent as our design,
Immortal as our soul.

The World

We falsely think it due unto our friends,
That we should grieve for their too early ends:
He that surveys the world with serious eyes,
And strips her from her gross and weak disguise,[1]
Shall find 'tis injury to mourn their fate;
He only dies untimely who dies late.
For if 'twere told to children in the womb,
To what a stage of mischief they must come;
Could they foresee with how much toil and sweat
Men court that gilded nothing, being great;
What pains they take not to be what they seem,
Rating their bliss by others' false esteem,
And sacrificing their content, to be
Guilty of grave and serious vanity;
How each condition hath its proper thorns,
And what one man admires, another scorns;
How frequently their happiness they miss,
And so far from agreeing what it is,
That the same person we can hardly find,
Who is an hour together in a mind;
Sure they would beg a period of their breath,
And what we call their birth would count their death.
Mankind is mad; for none can live alone,

1. The Platonic notion that the body is a covering for the soul.

Because their joys stand by comparison:
And yet they quarrel at society,
And strive to kill they know not whom, nor why.
We all live by mistake, delight in dreams,
Lost to ourselves, and dwelling in extremes;
Rejecting what we have, though ne'er so good,
And prizing what we never understood.
Compared to our boisterous inconstancy
Tempests are calm, and discords harmony.
Hence we reverse the world, and yet do find
The God that made can hardly please our mind.
We live by chance, and slip into events;
Have all of beasts except their innocence.
The soul, which no man's power can reach, a thing
That makes each woman man, each man a king,
Doth so much loose, and from its height so fall,
That some contend to have no soul at all.
'Tis either not observed, or at the best
By passion fought withall, by sin depressed.
Freedom of will (God's image) is forgot;
And if we know it, we improve it not.
Our thoughts, though nothing can be more our own,
Are still unguided, very seldom known.
Time 'scapes our hands as water in a sieve,
We come to die ere we begin to live.
Truth, the most suitable and noble prize,
Food of our spirits, yet neglected lies.
Errors and shadows are our choice, and we
Owe our perdition to our own decree.
If we search truth, we make it more obscure;
And when it shines, we can't the light endure.
For most men who plod on, and eat, and drink,
Have nothing less their business than to think;
And those few that enquire, how small a share
Of truth they find! how dark their notions are!
That serious evenness that calms the breast,
And in a tempest can bestow a rest,
We either not attempt, or else decline,
By every trifle snatched from our design.
(Others he must in his deceits involve,
Who is not true unto his own resolve.)
We govern not ourselves, but loose the reins,
Courting our bondage to a thousand chains;
And with as many slaveries content,
As there are tyrants ready to torment,
We live upon a rack, extended still
To one extreme, or both, but always ill.
For since our fortune is not understood,
We suffer less from bad than from the good.

The sting is better dressed and longer lasts,
As surfeits are more dangerous than fasts.
And to complete the misery to us,
We see extremes are still contiguous.
And as we run so fast from what we hate,
Like squibs on ropes,[2] to know no middle state;
So (outward storms strengthened by us) we find
Our fortune as disordered as our mind.
But that's excused by this, it doth its part;
A treacherous world befits a treacherous heart.
All ill's our own; the outward storms we loathe
Receive from us their birth, or sting, or both;
And that our vanity be past a doubt,
'Tis one new vanity to find it out.
Happy are they to whom God gives a grave,
And from themselves as from his wrath doth save.
'Tis good not to be born; but if we must,
The next good is, soon to return to dust:
When th'uncaged[3] soul, fled to eternity,
Shall rest, and live, and sing, and love, and see.
Here we but crawl and grope, and play and cry;[4]
Are first our own, then other's enemy:
But there shall be defaced both stain and score,
For time, and death, and sin shall be no more.[5]

2. A display of fireworks on a line.
3. Free from the body.
4. Paraphrasing 1 Corinthians 13.11–12.
5. As promised in Revelation 21.4.

The Execution of Charles I, 17th-century German print.

PERSPECTIVES

The Civil War, or the Wars of Three Kingdoms

The English Civil War arose out of citizens' revolutionary demands for their rights and those of their legislature, and out of England's attempt to dominate Ireland and Scotland. The armed conflicts that arose from the demand for political self-determination in every part of the British Isles would have consequences for centuries to come. During the period from 1639 to 1651, war raged not only in England but also in Ireland, Scotland, and Wales; hence, historians now prefer to call this period of conflict the Wars of Three Kingdoms. The origins of the conflict in England were between Parliament and a King who had an absolutist style of governing. Charles I reigned without Parliament from 1629 to 1640, a period referred to as the "Eleven Years' Tyranny." He also imposed unpopular heavy taxes in the form of ship money levies to build up the fleet. Even more controversial was his imposition of Anglican worship and episcopal authority on Puritans and Presbyterians, who felt that such ritual was tantamount to Roman Catholicism. The King placed two Anglican bishops on the court of Star Chamber, who used the arbitrary power of this body to enforce unpopular religious practices.

When the King decided to impose an Anglican liturgy on the Scottish Kirk in 1639, riots broke out in Edinburgh, and Scottish Lowlanders united in a National Covenant against English interference. In 1639 and 1640, Scottish military uprisings necessitated Charles I's recalling Parliament to ask for financial aid. The Parliament was already angered by the eleven-year shutdown by the King, his imposition of taxes without its consent, and his support for Archbishop Laud, whom Parliament viewed as too dictatorial and too high church, shutting out both Puritans (who elected their ministers and disdained Catholic sacraments) and Presbyterians (who favored central church government but not Anglo-Catholic authority or ritual). When Parliament refused after three weeks to grant the King's request for money, the King decided to dissolve the "Short Parliament." In the wake of the dissolution of Parliament, soldiers went on rampages against churches, smashing stained glass windows and altar rails that smacked to them of Roman Catholicism. In some places, soldiers mutinied against their aristocratic commanders.

When the Scots defeated the King's army in the fall of 1640, he had to recall Parliament to petition for more funds. Led by John Pym, the "Long Parliament" seized the opportunity to criticize the King. It passed a Bill of Attainder, condemning to death as a traitor the general of the King's army, Viscount Strafford, who had been accused of instigating the war against Scotland and of suggesting that an Irish Catholic army could be used against England. No proof of guilt was necessary, only assent from the House of Lords and the King. Despite the King's reluctance, the combined opposition of the House of Commons and armed mobs in London in the spring of 1641 pressured him into signing Strafford's death warrant.

That fall two rebellions broke out in Ireland—one organized by Catholic Irish gentry, another arising more spontaneously among the native Gaelic Irish in Ulster against Scots and English settlers who had dispossessed them of their land. Pym blamed the unrest on the King and his Catholic court. Although there was terrible violence, especially in the popular uprisings, the English press wildly exaggerated the extent of the bloodshed, claiming a figure for Protestant deaths in the North of Ireland that was greater than the number of Protestants then living in the whole country. Pym, the leader of the House of Commons, moved that Parliament should offer no help in repressing Irish rebellion unless Charles agreed to dismiss his guilty counselors. The next day, Oliver Cromwell moved that the Parliament empower the Puritan Earl of Essex to head the English militia. Attacks on the King became stronger: his irresponsibility and violation of the security and rights of the people mandated Parliament's wresting power from him. On May 12, Archbishop Laud was executed. Although the King made some concessions, by January 1642 he decided to impeach Pym, four other members of Commons, and one from the House of Lords for treason. However, the accused were safely hidden in the City, and the King left London, not to return until he was put on trial and beheaded seven years later. Just on the eve of the outbreak of the war, the "Gentlewomen and Tradesmen's Wives of London" presented their petition to Parliament, complaining against Archbishop Laud's Anglicanism and the threat of violence from Ireland. The first part of the English Civil War (1642–1646), arising from the disputes between Parliament and the King, culminated in the victory of Parliament's New Model Army, headed by Sir Thomas Fairfax.

With the King defeated by the combined forces of the New Model Army and the Scots Covenanters in 1646, new conflicts arose between the army and the Parliament. Closely tied to the army, the Levellers, led by John Lilburne, agitated for a fundamental revision of the constitution: a single representative body, universal suffrage for men, and the abolition of monarchy and noble privilege. Colonel Ludlow, a leader of the republicans, opposed any negotiations with the King and petitioned Parliament to reform the constitution and to put the King on trial. When the House of Commons refused to listen to the army and continued to negotiate with the King, Colonels Ludlow, Ireton, and Pride purged Parliament, placing forty-five members under arrest and prohibiting another 186 from entering the House. This Rump Parliament set up a high court to try the King. On 27 January 1649, Charles I was condemned to death as a tyrant and traitor who had shed the blood of his people. John Bradshaw, President of the Court, proclaimed that the King was subject to the law and the law proceeded from Parliament. Arising out of these events came both the King's own memoir, *Eikon Basilike* ("the Royal Image"), ghostwritten and published after his execution by John Gauden, and Milton's militantly republican response *Eikonoklastes* ("Image-Breaker").

In the last stage of the Civil War, the dead king's son, Charles II, attempted to regain power through Irish and Scottish aid. In Ireland the Marquis of Ormonde led a coalition of royalists that secured the support of Irish troops for the King in exchange for the free exercise of Catholicism. Before Charles II could land in Dublin, the English sent troops there to put down the uprising. Cromwell slaughtered many at the siege of Drogheda; his campaign throughout Munster killed many civilians. In the aftermath of Cromwell's conquest, what remained of an Irish intelligentsia was either exiled or killed off, and large numbers of native inhabitants were either thrown off their land onto poorer farming land in western Ireland or sent into indentured servitude in the Caribbean. Following policies begun by Elizabeth and James, Cromwell granted Irish land to English settlers. The late events of the war in Ireland are represented here by one of Cromwell's letters from his campaign in Ireland, and by *John O'Dwyer of the Glenn*, a translation of one of the many Irish-language laments for the devastation of the Cromwellian conquest.

In Scotland, Charles II found allies among Presbyterian Covenanters, infuriated with the English Parliament for executing a Scottish monarch, and in the Marquis of Montrose, who recruited the Highland clans. When the Covenanters met with Charles II for the Treaty of Breda in Holland, they imposed on him a promise to reestablish Presbyterianism as the religion of both England and Scotland, to reinstate the Scottish Parliament, and to repudiate his pledges to Ormonde and Montrose. When Charles landed in Scotland, he learned that Montrose, most loyal of all royalists, had been hanged and quartered as a traitor. The political intrigue of Argyle against Montrose can be seen in the Earl of Clarendon's account of Montrose's death. The Covenanters, fighting for Scotland rather than for the King, were defeated by Cromwell at Dunbar. The Scots' losses were so huge that Scottish royalism was revived for one last battle between the King's Cavaliers and Cromwell's Roundheads. Facing Cromwell's army at Worcester in 1651, the forces of Scots and English royalists were vastly outnumbered and easily defeated. Charles II escaped to France, where he remained until the Restoration. Two years later, Cromwell became Lord Protector of the Commonwealth.

John Gauden
1605–1662

John Gauden wrote the most influential account of the royalist cause, *Eikon Basilike* ("Royal Portrait"), advance copies of which were sold on the day of Charles I's execution in 1649. Although Gauden at first sided with Parliament and the Presbyterians, he did not agree to the abolition of the bishops. In 1647 supporters of Charles I, then confined at Hampton Court by Parliament, sought Gauden's help to revise the King's meditations for publication. When the manuscript was complete, Gauden showed it to the King, who hesitated about having it published under his name. Meanwhile, the King was preoccupied first by his attempts to escape and then by his confinement, trial, and execution. When Royston first printed the book in January 1649, he believed that King Charles was the author. Just months later, William Duggard published another edition based on a manuscript that had been revised by the King; Gauden's authorship remained publically unknown until 1690.

Throughout the Interregnum, Gauden managed to keep his deanery at Brockton by conforming to Presbyterianism. With the Restoration in 1660, he was made Bishop of Exeter. In letters to Sir Edward Hyde, Gauden admitted his authorship and complained that his reward had not been sufficient. He was then promoted to the bishopric of Worcester, just a year before his death.

Eikon Basilike was written to influence public opinion and to guide the Prince of Wales, who waited in exile to regain his father's throne. A collection of meditations written in a lofty style, *Eikon Basilike* justified the King's views and evoked sympathy for his plight. The emblematic frontispiece shows the King in a saintly light—kneeling in prayer. Admirers of the work called it "most charitable, most heavenly" and "most pious, most ravishing." By the end of 1649, thirty-five editions had been printed in England. The most important of these, that of March 1649, added the King's prayers, the Prince of Wales's letter to his father, and an epitaph on the King's death. An English-language edition was published in Ireland in 1649, and twenty foreign-language editions were published on the Continent for the English community in exile as well as their European supporters.

The text aroused both support and criticism. Parliament had the printer Duggard arrested but released him when he produced a license to publish the book. Parliament prohibited the further sale of the book in May 1649, but by the end of 1649, five clandestine editions and two responses had appeared. *The Princely Pellican* explained how Charles had come to write the book, and *Eikon Alethine* attacked it as a fraud. Milton wrote his own rebuttal in *Eikonoklastes*, a savagely satirical prosecution of the King. *Eikonoklastes* merely went through two editions, showing that it could not compete in popularity with *Eikon Basilike*.

from Eikon Basilike

from *Chapter 4. Upon the Insolency of the Tumults*

I never thought anything, except our sins, more ominously presaging all these mischiefs which have followed, than those tumults in London and Westminster soon after the convening of this Parliament which were not like a storm at sea, (which yet wants not its terror,) but like an earthquake, shaking the very foundation of all; than which nothing in the world hath more of horror.

As it is one of the most convincing arguments that there is a God, while His power sets bounds to the raging of the sea, so it is no less that He restrains the madness of the people. Nor does anything portend more God's displeasure against a nation than when He suffers the confluence and clamors of the vulgar to pass all boundaries of laws and reverence to authority.

Which those tumults did to so high degrees of insolence, that they spared not to invade the honor and freedom of the two Houses, menacing, reproaching, shaking, yea, and assaulting some members of both Houses as they fancied or disliked them; nor did they forbear most rude and unseemly deportments, both in contemptuous words and actions, to myself and my court.

Nor was this a short fit or two of shaking, as an ague, but a quotidian fever, always increasing to higher inflammations, impatient of any mitigation, restraint, or remission.

First, they must be a guard against those fears which some men scared themselves and others withal; when, indeed, nothing was more to be feared, and less to be used by wise men, than those tumultuary confluxes of mean and rude people who are taught first to petition, then to protect, then to dictate, at last to command and overawe the Parliament.

All obstructions of Parliament, that is, all freedom of differing in votes, and debating matters with reason and candor, must be taken away with these tumults. By these must the Houses be purged, and all rotten members (as they pleased to count them) cast out; by these the obstinacy of men, resolved to discharge their consciences, must be subdued; by these all factious, seditious, and schismatical proposals against government, ecclesiastical or civil, must be backed and abetted till they prevailed.

Generally, whoever had most mind to bring forth confusion and ruin upon Church and State used the midwifery of those tumults, whose riot and impatience was such as they would not stay the ripening and season of counsels, or fair production of acts, in the order, gravity, and deliberateness befitting a Parliament, but ripped up with barbarous cruelty, and forcibly cut out abortive notes, such as their inviters and encouragers most fancied.

Yea, so enormous and detestable were their outrages, that no sober man could be without infinite shame and sorrow to see them so tolerated and connived at by some, countenanced, encouraged, and applauded by others.

What good man had not rather want anything he most desired for the public good, than obtain it by such unlawful and irreligious means? But men's passions and God's directions seldom agree; violent designs and motions must have suitable engines; such as too much attend their own ends, seldom confine themselves to God's means. Force must crowd in what reason will not lead.

Who were the chief demagogues and patrons of tumults, to send for them, to flatter and embolden them, to direct and tune their clamorous importunities, some men yet living are too conscious to pretend ignorance. God in His due time will let these see that those were no fit means to be used for attaining His ends.

But as it is no strange thing for the sea to rage when strong winds blow upon it, so neither for multitudes to become insolent when they have men of some reputation for parts and piety to set them on.

That which made their rudeness most formidable was, that many complaints being made, and messages sent by myself and some of both Houses yet no order for redress could be obtained with any vigor and efficacy proportionable to the malignity of that now far-spread disease and predominant mischief.

Such was some men's stupidity, that they feared no inconvenience; others' petulancy, that they joyed to see their betters shamefully outraged and abused, while they knew their only security consisted in vulgar flattery, so insensible were they of mine or the two Houses common safety and honors.

Nor could ever any order be obtained impartially to examine, censure, and punish the known boutefeus[1] and impudent incendiaries, who boasted of the influence they had, and used to convoke those tumults as their advantages served.

Yea some, who should have been wiser statesmen, owned them as friends, commending their courage, zeal, and industry, which to sober men could seem no better than that of the devil, who goes about seeking whom he may deceive and devour.

I confess, when I found such a deafness, that no declaration from the bishops, who were first foully insolenced and assaulted, nor yet from other lords and gentlemen of honor, nor yet from myself, could take place for the due repression of these tumults, and securing not only our freedom in Parliament, but our very persons in the streets; I thought myself not bound by my presence to provoke them to higher boldness and contempts; I hoped by my withdrawing[2] to give time both for the ebbing of their tumultuous fury, and others regaining some degrees of modesty and sober sense.

1. Firebrands.
2. Charles decided to flee from London on the night of 10 January 1642 in response to rioting that erupted as a result of his failed attempts to arrest the five opposition leaders in the House of Commons. Charles returned to Whitehall only as a prisoner just before his execution.

Some may interpret it as an effect of pusillanimity[3] in any man, for popular terrors, to desert his public station; but I think it is hardiness beyond true valor for a wise man to set himself against the breaking in of a sea, which to resist at present threatens imminent danger, but to withdraw gives it space to spend its fury, and gains a fitter time to repair the breach. Certainly a gallant man had rather fight to great disadvantages for number and place in the field in an orderly way, than scuffle with an undisciplined rabble.

Some suspected and affirmed that I meditated a war, when I went from Whitehall only to redeem my person and conscience from violence: God knows I did not then think of a war. Nor will any prudent man conceive that I would, by so many former and some after acts, have so much weakened myself if I had purposed to engage in a war, which to decline by all means I denied myself in so many particulars. It is evident I had then no army to fly unto for protection and vindication.

Who can blame me, or any other, for withdrawing ourselves from the daily baitings of the tumults, not knowing whether their fury and discontent might not fly so high as to worry and tear those in pieces whom as yet they but played with in their paws? God, who is my sole judge, is my witness in heaven that I never had any thoughts of my going from my house at Whitehall if I could have had but any reasonable fair quarter. I was resolved to bear much, and did so; but I did not think myself bound to prostitute the majesty of my place and person, the safety of my wife and children, to those who are prone to insult most when they have objects and opportunity most capable of their rudeness and petulancy.

But this business of the tumults, whereof some have given already an account to God, others yet living know themselves desperately guilty, time and the guilt of many has so smothered up and buried, that I think it best to leave it as it is; only I believe the just avenger of all disorders will in time make those men and that city see their sin in the glass of their punishment. It is more than an even lay, that they may one day see themselves punished by that way they offended.

Had this Parliament, as it was in its first election and constitution, sat full and free, the members of both Houses, being left to their freedom of voting, as in all reason, honor, and religion they should have been, I doubt not but things would have been so carried as would have given no less good content to all good men than they wished or expected.

For I was resolved to hear reason in all things, and to consent to it as far as I could comprehend it; but as swine are to gardens and orderly plantations, so are tumults to Parliaments, and plebeian concourses to public counsels, turning all into disorders and sordid confusions.

I am prone sometimes to think that had I called this Parliament to any other place in England, as I might opportunely enough have done, the sad consequences in all likelihood, with God's blessing, might have been prevented. A Parliament would have been welcome in any place; no place afforded such confluence of various and vicious humors as that where it was unhappily convened. But we must leave all to God, who orders our disorders, and magnifies His wisdom most when our follies and miseries are most discovered.

3. Cowardice.

John Milton
1608–1674

With the popularity of the royalist tract *Eikon Basilike* after the execution of Charles I, the new Puritan government needed to find someone to defend its cause against the growing support for the King. The Puritans found their man in the newly appointed Secretary for Foreign Tongues to the Council of State, John Milton. In *Eikonoklastes* ("Image Breaker"), Milton focused his attack on the arguments of *Eikon Basilike* more than on its authorship. He doubted whether the King wrote his own defense, but he chose to concentrate on a chapter-by-chapter refutation of the book's account of history—in terms of both events and the perspective on them. Milton also revealed that one the prayers attributed to the King was really Pamela's prayer from Sir Philip Sidney's prose romance *Arcadia*. For the Puritan Milton this was a shocking piece of paganism and plagiarism by one who presented himself as pious. Milton's language in *Eikonoklastes* is iconoclastic—mocking and sarcastic, marked by invective and sharply stinging *ad hominem* argument. One royalist called *Eikonoklastes* a "blackguardly book" in which Milton "blows his viper's breath upon those immortal devotions." Some royalists even viewed Milton's blindness as God's punishment for his having attacked the King. Shortly after the Restoration of Charles II in 1660, the House of Commons ordered the burning of *Eikonoklastes* and had Milton arrested. He was imprisoned for several months before being released through the aid of his friend Andrew Marvell. *Eikonklastes* was first published in October 1649; the second and final edition in Milton's lifetime appeared in 1650.

For more about Milton, see his principal listing, page 1698.

from Eikonoklastes
from *Chapter 1. Upon the King's Calling This Last Parliament*

"The odium and offenses which some men's rigor, or remissness in church and state had contracted upon his government, he resolved to have expiated with better laws and regulations." And yet the worst of misdemeanors committed by the worst of all his favorites, in the height of their dominion, whether acts of rigor or remissness, he hath from time to time continued, owned, and taken upon himself by public declarations, as often as the clergy, or any other of his instruments felt themselves overburdened with the people's hatred. And who knows not the superstitious rigor of his Sunday's chapel, and the licentious remissness of his Sunday's theater;[1] accompanied with that reverend statute for dominical jigs and maypoles,[2] published in his own name, and derived from the example of his father James? Which testifies all that rigor in superstition, all that remissness in religion to have issued out originally from his own house, and from his own authority.

Much rather then may those general miscarriages in State, his proper sphere, be imputed to no other person chiefly than to himself. And which of all those oppressive

1. While observers such as the Spanish ambassador noted Charles's sincere piety, Milton considered traditional ritual "superstitious," ironically linking it to irreligious theater life. Like the Puritans, Milton abhorred Sunday theater performances, and in *Of Reformation*, he attacked the bishops for promoting "gaming, jigging, wassailing, and mixed dancing" on Sundays.

2. The *Book of Sports* (1633) forbade bearbaiting and bullbaiting on Sundays, but also rebuked the Puritans for condemning other forms of recreation such as dancing and archery.

acts, or impositions did he ever disclaim or disavow, till the fatal awe of this Parliament hung ominously over him. Yet here he smoothly seeks to wipe off all the envy of his evil government upon his substitutes, and under-officers: and promises, though much too late, what wonders he purposed to have done in the reforming of religion—a work wherein all his undertakings heretofore declare him to have had little or no judgment. Neither could his breeding, or his course of life acquaint him with a thing so spiritual. Which may well assure us what kind of reformation we could expect from him; either some politic form of an imposed religion, or else perpetual vexation, and persecution to all those that complied not with such a form.

The like amendment he promises in State; not a step further "than his reason and conscience told him was fit to be desired"; wishing "he had kept within those bounds, and not suffered his own judgment to have been overborne in some things," of which things one was the Earl of Strafford's execution.[3] And what signifies all this, but that still his resolution was the same, to set up an arbitrary government of his own; and that all Britain was to be tied and chained to the conscience, judgment, and reason of one man; as if those gifts had been only his peculiar and prerogative, entailed upon him with his fortune to be a king? When as doubtless no man so obstinate, or so much a tyrant, but professes to be guided by that which he calls his reason, and his judgment, though never so corrupted; and pretends also his conscience. In the meanwhile, for any Parliament or the whole nation to have either reason, judgment, or conscience, by this rule was altogether in vain, if it thwarted the king's will; which was easy for him to call by any other more plausible name. He himself hath many times acknowledged to have no right over us but by law; and by the same law to govern us: but law in a free nation hath been ever public reason, the enacted reason of a Parliament; which he denying to enact, denies to govern us by that which ought to be our law; interposing his own private reason, which to us is no law. And thus we find these fair and specious promises, made upon the experience of many hard sufferings, and his most mortified retirements, being thoroughly sifted, to contain nothing in them much different from his former practices, so cross, and so averse to all his Parliaments, and both the nations of this island. What fruits they could in likelihood have produced in his restorement, is obvious to any prudent foresight.

And this is the substance of his first section, till we come to the devout of it, modeled into the form of a private psalter. Which they who so much admire, either for the matter or the manner, may as well admire the archbishop's late breviary,[4] and many other as good *Manuals*, and *Handmaids of Devotion*, the lip-work of every prelatical liturgist, clapped together, and quilted out of Scripture phrase, with as much ease, and as little need of Christian diligence, or judgment, as belongs to the compiling of any ordinary and salable piece of English divinity, that the shops value. But he who from such a kind of psalmistry, or any other verbal devotion, without the pledge and

3. Thomas Wentworth, Earl of Strafford, was executed in May 1641. Charles had recalled Strafford from the Lord Deputyship in Ireland to help with the war against the Scots Covenanters. Parliament accused Wentworth of planning to use the Irish army to suppress the King's opponents in Scotland and England. Even though Strafford was successfully defended against the charges, Charles signed his death warrant, fearing retaliation against himself and the Queen for their part in a plot to rescue Strafford.

4. Milton's name for Archbishop Laud's *Prayer Book*, which the Puritans hated because of its similarity to Roman Catholic ritual.

earnest of suitable deeds, can be persuaded of a zeal, and true righteousness in the person, hath much yet to learn; and knows not that the deepest policy of a tyrant hath been ever to counterfeit religious. And Aristotle in his *Politics*, hath mentioned that special craft among twelve other tyrannical sophisms.[5] Neither want we examples. Andronicus Comnenus the Byzantine Emperor, though a most cruel tyrant, is reported by Nicetas[6] to have been a constant reader of Saint Paul's Epistles; and by continual study had so incorporated the phrase and style of that transcendent apostle into all his familiar letters, that the imitation seemed to vie with the original. Yet this availed not to deceive the people of that empire; who notwithstanding his saint's vizard, tore him to pieces for his tyranny.

From stories of this nature both ancient and modern which abound, the poets also, and some English, have been in this point so mindful of decorum, as to put never more pious words in the mouth of any person, than of a tyrant. I shall not instance an abstruse author, wherein the King might be less conversant, but one whom we well know was the closet companion of these his solitudes, William Shakespeare, who introduces the person of Richard the Third, speaking in as high a strain of piety, and mortification, as is uttered in any passage of this book, and sometimes to the same sense and purpose with some words in this place, "I intended," saith he, "not only to oblige my friends but mine enemies." The like saith Richard, Act 2. Scene 1,

I do not know that Englishman alive
With whom my soul is any jot at odds,
More than the infant that is born tonight;
I thank my God for my humility.

Other stuff of this sort may be read throughout the whole tragedy, wherein the poet used not much license in departing from the truth of history, which delivers him a deep dissembler, not of his affections only, but of religion.

from *Chapter 4. Upon the Insolency of the Tumults*

And that the King was so emphatical and elaborate on this theme against tumults, and expressed with such a vehemence his hatred of them, will redound less perhaps, than he was aware, to the commendation of his government. For besides that in good governments they happen seldomest, and rise not without cause, if they prove extreme and pernicious, they were never counted so to monarchy, but to monarchical tyranny; and extremes one with another are at most antipathy. If then the King so extremely stood in fear of tumults, the inference will endanger him to be the other extreme. Thus far the occasion of this discourse against tumults; now to the discourse itself, voluble enough, and full of sentence,[1] but that, for the most part, either specious rather than solid, or to his cause nothing pertinent.

"He never thought any thing more to presage the mischiefs that ensued, than those tumults." Then was his foresight but short, and much mistaken. Those tumults were but the mild effects of an evil and injurious reign; not signs of mischiefs to come, but seeking relief for mischiefs past; those signs were to be read more apparent in his

5. See Aristotle, *Politics* 5.9.15, for the notion that care in religious ritual is a device of tyrants.

6. A 12th-century historian who recorded the cruelty of Comnenus's reign (1183–1185).

1. Significance, meaning.

rage and purposed revenge of those free expostulations, and clamors of the people against his lawless government. "Not any thing," saith he, "portends more God's displeasure against a nation than when he suffers the clamors of the vulgar to pass all bounds of law & reverence to authority." It portends rather his displeasure against a tyrannous King, whose proud throne he intends to overturn by that contemptible vulgar; the sad cries and oppressions of whom his royalty regarded not. As for that supplicating people they did no hurt either to law or authority, but stood for it rather in the Parliament against whom they feared would violate it.

That "they invaded the honor and freedom of the two Houses," is his own officious accusation, not seconded by the Parliament, who had they seen cause, were themselves best able to complain. And if they "shook & menaced" any, they were such as had more relation to the Court, than to the Commonwealth; enemies, not patrons of the people. But if their petitioning unarmed were an invasion of both Houses, what was his entrance into the House of Commons, besetting it with armed men, in what condition then was the honor, and freedom of that House?

"They forbore not rude deportments, contemptuous words and actions to himself and his Court."

It was more wonder, having heard what treacherous hostility he had designed against the city, and his whole kingdom, that they forbore to handle him as people in their rage have handled tyrants heretofore for less offenses.

"They were not a short ague, but a fierce quotidian fever:" He indeed may best say it, who most felt it; for the shaking was within him; and it shook him by his own description "worse than a storm, worse then an earthquake, Belshazzar's Palsy."[2] Had not worse fears, terrors, and envies made within him that commotion, how could a multitude of his subjects, armed with no other weapon then petitions, have shaken all his joints with such a terrible ague. Yet that the Parliament should entertain the least fear of bad intentions from him or his party, he endures not; but would persuade us that "men scare themselves and others without cause;" for he thought fear would be to them a kind of armor, and his design was, if it were possible, to disarm all, especially of a wise fear and suspicion; for that he knew would find weapons.

He goes on therefore with vehemence to repeat the mischiefs done by these tumults. "They first petitioned, then protected, dictate next, and lastly overawe the Parliament. They removed obstructions, they purged the Houses, cast out rotten members." If there were a man of iron, such as Talus, by our poet Spenser, is feigned to be the page of Justice, who with his iron flail could do all this, and expeditiously, without those deceitful forms and circumstances of law, worse than ceremonies in religion; I say God send it down, whether by one Talus, or by a thousand.[3]

"But they subdued the men of conscience in Parliament, backed and abetted all seditious and schismatical proposals against government ecclesiastical and civil."

Now we may perceive the root of his hatred whence it springs. It was not the King's grace or princely goodness, but this iron flail the people, that drove the bishops out of their baronies, out of their cathedrals, out of the Lord's house, out of their copes

2. In *Of Reformation*, Milton compares the feasting of Anglican bishops to that of Belshazzar in his palace in Babylon on the eve of the fall of the city to the Medes and Persians. When King Belshazzar saw the mysterious writing on the wall that foretold his doom, "the joints of his loins were loosed, and his knees smote one against another" (Daniel 5.6).

3. Talus is the iron flail who ruthlessly cuts down all who oppose Artegal, the Knight of Justice, in Spenser's *Faerie Queene* 5, much of which is about the subjugation of Ireland by England.

and surplices, and all those papistical innovations,[4] threw down the High Commission and Star Chamber, gave us a triennial Parliament, and what we most desired;[5] in revenge whereof he now so bitterly inveighs against them; these are those seditious and schismatical proposals, then by him condescended to, as acts of grace, now of another name; which declares him, touching matters of Church and State, to have been no other man in the deepest of his solitude, than he was before at the highest of his sovereignty.

But this was not the worst of these tumults, they played the hasty "midwives," and "would not stay the ripening, but went straight to ripping up, and forcibly cut out abortive votes."

They would not stay perhaps the Spanish demurring, and putting off such wholesome acts and counsels, as the politic cabin at Whitehall had no mind to. But all this is complained here as done to the Parliament, and yet we heard not the Parliament at that time complain of any violence from the people, but from him. Wherefore intrudes he to plead the cause of Parliament against the people, while the Parliament was pleading their own cause against him; and against him were forced to seek refuge of the people? 'Tis plain then that those confluxes and resorts interrupted not the Parliament, nor by them were thought tumultuous, but by him only and his court faction.

"But what good Man had not rather want any thing he most desired for the public good, than attain it by such unlawful and irreligious means;" as much as to say, had not rather sit still and let his country be tyrannized, than that the people, finding no other remedy, should stand up like men and demand their rights and liberties. This is the artificialest piece of fineness to persuade men into slavery that the wit of court could have invented. But hear how much better the moral of this lesson would befit the teacher. What good man had not rather want a boundless and arbitrary power, and those fine flowers of the crown, called prerogatives, than for them to use force and perpetual vexation to his faithful subjects, nay to wade for them through blood and civil war? So that this and the whole bundle of those following sentences may be applied better to the convincement of his own violent courses, than of those pretended tumults.

"Who were the chief demagogues to send for those tumults, some alive are not ignorant." Setting aside the affrightment of this goblin word; for the King by his leave cannot coin English as he could money, to be current (and tis believed this wording was above his known style and orthography, and accuses the whole composure to be conscious of some other author)[6] yet if the people "were sent for, emboldened and directed" by those "demagogues," who, saving his Greek, were good patriots, and by his own confession "Men of some repute for parts and piety," it helps well to assure us there was both urgent cause, and the less danger of their coming.

"Complaints were made, yet no redress could be obtained." The Parliament also complained of what danger they sat in from another party, and demanded of him a guard, but it was not granted. What marvel then if it cheered them to see some store

4. Milton refers to the London petition calling for the abolition of the bishops' power, introduced into Parliament in December 1640, that resulted in their exclusion from the House of Lords.

5. The High Commission, the highest ecclesiastical court, investigated such matters as heresy, recusancy, and any writing against the Book of Common Prayer; Parliament abolished it on 5 July 1641. The Star Chamber was also abolished because it was viewed as a special tool of government favoring the special right of the sovereign above all other persons and the common law. A triennial Parliament is a parliament convened every three years.

6. Milton believed that Charles I could not have written *Eikon Basilike* because such passages as this one showed a word choice and style different from Charles's.

of their friends, and in the Roman not the pettifogging sense, their clients so near about them; a defense due by nature both from whom it was offered, and to whom; as due as to their parents; though the Court stormed, and fretted to see such honor given to them, who were then best fathers of the Commonwealth. And both the Parliament and people complained, and demanded justice for those assaults, if not murders done at his own doors, by that crew of rufflers, but he, instead of doing justice on them, justified and abetted them in what they did, as in his public "Answer to a Petition from the City" may be read. Neither is it slightly to be passed over, that in the very place where blood was first drawn in this cause, as the beginning of all that followed, there was his own blood shed by the executioner. According to that sentence of divine justice, "In the place where dogs licked the blood of Naboth, shall dogs lick thy blood, even thine."

From hence he takes occasion to excuse that improvident and fatal error of his absenting from the Parliament. "When he found that no declaration of the bishops could take place against those tumults." Was that worth his considering, that foolish and self-undoing declaration of twelve cypher bishops, who were immediately appeached of treason for that audacious declaring?[7] The bishops peradventure were now and then pulled by the rochets,[8] and deserved another kind of pulling; but what amounted this to "the fear of his own person in the streets"? Did he not the very next day after his irruption into the House of Commons, than which nothing had more exasperated the people, go in his coach unguarded into the city? did he receive the least affront, much less violence in any of the streets, but rather humble demeanors, and supplications? Hence may be gathered, that however in his own guiltiness he might have justly feared, yet that he knew the people so full of awe and reverence to his person, as to dare commit himself single among the thickest of them, at a time when he had most provoked them. Besides in Scotland they had handled the Bishops in a more robustious manner; Edinburgh had been full of tumults,[9] two armies from thence had entered England against him;[1] yet after all this, he was not fearful, but very forward to take so long a journey to Edinburgh;[2] which argues first, as did also his rendition afterward to the Scotch Army,[3] that to England he continued still, as he was indeed, a stranger, and full of diffidence; to the Scots only a native King,[4] in his confidence, though not in his dealing towards them. It shows us next beyond doubting, that all this his fear of tumults was but a mere color and occasion taken of his resolved absence from the Parliament, for some other end not difficult to be guessed. And those instances wherein valor is not to be questioned for not "scuffling with the sea, or an undisciplined rabble," are but subservient to carry on the solemn jest of his fearing tumults: if they discover not withall, the true reason why he departed; only to turn his slashing at the court gate, to slaughtering "in the field"; his disorderly bickering, to an orderly invading: which was nothing else but a more orderly disorder.

"Some suspected and affirmed, that he meditated a War when he went first from Whitehall." And they were not the worst heads that did so, nor did "any of his former

7. The Bishops' Exclusion Bill was Parliament's reaction to the assertion by 12 bishops that any legislation passed by the House of Lords when the bishops were absent was void.

8. Vestments.

9. When Charles attempted to force the Book of Common Prayer on the Scottish churches, the people rioted.

1. The first Scottish war ended with the Treaty of Berwick in June 1639, the second with the Treaty of Ripon in October 1640.

2. Charles went to Edinburgh in 1641, hoping to pit the Covenanters against their opponents.

3. Charles surrendered himself to the Scottish army commanders in May 1646.

4. Charles was born in Scotland, and he made special appeals to the Scots to be their king in both 1641 and 1646.

acts weaken him" to that, as he alleges for himself, or if they had, they clear him only for the time of passing them, not for what ever thoughts might come after into his mind. Former actions of improvidence or fear, not with him unusual, cannot absolve him of all after meditations.

He goes on protesting his "no intention to have left Whitehall," had these horrid tumults given him but "fair quarter," as if he himself, his wife and children had been in peril. But to this enough hath been answered.

"Had this Parliament as it was in its first election," namely, with the Lord and Baron Bishops, "sat full and free," he doubts not but all had gone well. What warrant this of his to us? Whose not doubting was all good men's greatest doubt.

"He was resolved to hear reason, and to consent so far as he could comprehend." A hopeful resolution; what if his reason were found by oft experience to comprehend nothing beyond his own advantages, was this a reason fit to be intrusted with the common good of three nations?

"But," saith he, "as swine are to gardens, so are tumults to Parliaments." This the Parliament, had they found it so, could best have told us. In the meanwhile, who knows not that one great hog may do as much mischief in a garden, as many little swine.[5]

"He was sometimes prone to think that had he called this last Parliament to any other place in England, the sad consequences might have been prevented." But change of air changes not the mind. Was not his first Parliament at Oxford dissolved after two subsidies given him, and no justice received? Was not his last in the same place, where they sat with as much freedom, as much quiet from tumults, as they could desire, a Parliament both in his account, and their own, consisting of all his friends, that fled after him, and suffered for him, and yet by him nicknamed, and cashiered for a "mongrel Parliament that vexed his Queen with their base and mutinous motions," as his cabinet letter tells us?[6] Whereby the world may see plainly, that no shifting of place, no sifting of members to his own mind, no number, no paucity, no freedom from tumults, could ever bring his arbitrary wilfulness, and tyrannical designs to brook the least shape or similitude, the least counterfeit of a Parliament.

Finally instead of praying for his people as a good King should do, he prays to be delivered from them, as "from wild beasts, inundations, and raging seas, that had overborne all loyalty, modesty, laws, justice, and religion." God save the people from such intercessors.

Oliver Cromwell
1599–1658

Oliver Cromwell's brutal conquest of Ireland (1649–1650) was the culmination of a long military, political, and religiously zealous career and the turning point in his rise to the position of Lord Protector. He had risen steadily in the Parliamentary Army, serving in the early days of the Civil War as captain of a troop of horses and finally becoming the chief of the New Model

5. Milton may echo the identification of the hog with Henry VIII for his failure to carry out a thorough and consistent reformation in Anthony Gilby's *An Admonition to England and Scotland to Call Them to Repentance* (Geneva, 1558).

6. Charles called an opposition Parliament that met in Oxford on 22 January 1644 and that he ordered closed after disagreement with them. This Parliament first attempted a peaceful settlement with the Westminster Parliament and then declared it guilty of treason. The King called it his "mongrel Parliament."

Army. Not only did he have a genius for military strategy but he was one of those who "never stirred from their troops . . . but fought to the last minute." He and his men were both called "Ironsides" in tribute to their indomitability. As a member of Parliament, he argued vigorously for the Puritan cause, and when Parliament was purged of Presbyterians in 1649, Cromwell's power and that of his fellow Congregationalists or Independents increased. At the trial of Charles I in January 1649, Cromwell adamantly demanded execution. Afterward, when the new Commonwealth was set up, one of Parliament's first charges was to send Cromwell to subdue Ireland, where Irish Royalists and Rebels, once pitted against each other, had formed a coalition and were gaining ground.

Cromwell's treatment of the Irish tested the limits of the principles of the Puritan Revolution and left a legacy of devastation. Although Cromwell was a strong member of the English Parliament, he helped to bring about the abolition of both Irish and Scottish Parliaments with his military defeats of both kingdoms. In September 1644, Cromwell urged the Presbyterian Parliament to guarantee liberty of conscience to the Independents among his troops, but when the Catholics of New Ross, Ireland, called for similar toleration in October 1649, Cromwell refused them: "if by liberty of conscience, you mean a liberty to exercise the Mass, I judge it best to use plain dealing, and to let you know, where the Parliament of England have power, that will not be allowed of." Indeed during Cromwell's rule in England, only Jews and non-Anglican Protestants were tolerated. Furthermore, Cromwell escalated the policy (begun under Elizabeth and James) of giving lands confiscated from native Irish inhabitants to English colonists. The massacre of Drogheda—including civilians as well as troops—made the Irish remember Cromwell as cruel. In the following letter of 17 September 1649, Cromwell presents his troops' massacre of the people of Drogheda as "the righteous judgment of God." The same religious conviction that had made him and his New Model Army such valiant defenders of English liberty was used to justify Irish slaughter.

Cromwell also used his letters to keep Parliament informed of his progress, to ask for further supplies, and to promote his political power. He was to go on to defeat the Scots in 1650. Ultimately, his power grew to such an extent that in 1657 he became Lord Protector, assuming the pomp and trappings of royalty. When his son Richard succeeded him at his death in September 1658, it seemed as if Oliver Cromwell's rule had led to a new monarchy. His son proved a weak successor, and the Commonwealth was restored in May 1659, only to collapse with the Restoration of 1660. If Cromwell's participation in parliamentary politics and the New Model Army contributed to the cause of republican liberty, his conquest of Ireland marked one of the bleakest chapters in the English colonization of Ireland.

from Letters from Ireland

Relating the Several Great Success It Hath Pleased God to Give Unto the Parliament's Forces There, in the Taking of Drogheda, Trym, Dundalk, Carlingford, and the Nury.

* * *

For the Honorable *William Lenthal* Esq;
Speaker of the Parliament of *England*

Sir,

Your army[1] being safely arrived at Dublin, and the enemy endeavoring to draw all his forces together about Trym and Tecroghan[2] (as my intelligence gave me); from

1. The letter is addressed to Parliament from the commander of the parliamentary army, hence "your army."

2. A town and townland in County Meath, northwest of Dublin.

whence endeavors were used by the Marquis of Ormonde, to draw Owen Roe O'Neal with his forces to his assistance, but with what success I cannot yet learn.[3] I resolved after some refreshment taken for our weather-beaten men and horses, and accommodations for a march, to take the field; and accordingly upon Friday the thirtieth of August last, rendezvoused with eight regiments of foot, and six of horse, and some troops of dragoons, three miles on the north side of Dublin; the design was, to endeavor the regaining of Drogheda,[4] or tempting the enemy, upon his hazard of the loss of that place, to fight. Your army came before the town upon Monday following, where having pitched, as speedy course as could be was taken to frame our batteries,[5] which took up the more time, because divers of the battering guns were on shipboard. Upon Monday the ninth of this instant, the batteries began to play; whereupon I sent Sir Arthur Ashton the then Governor a summons, to deliver the town to the use of the Parliament of England; to the which I received no satisfactory answer, but proceeded that day to beat down the steeple of the church on the south side of the town, and to beat down a tower not far from the same place, which you will discern by the card[6] enclosed. Our guns not being able to do much that day, it was resolved to endeavor to do our utmost the next day to make breaches[7] assaultable, and by the help of God to storm them. The places pitched upon, were that part of the town wall next a church, called St. Marie's, which was the rather chosen, because we did hope that if we did enter and possess that church, we should be the better able to keep it against their horse and foot, until we could make way for the entrance of our horse, which we did not conceive that any part of the town would afford the like advantage for that purpose with this. The batteries planted were two, one was for that part of the wall against the east end of the said church, the other against the wall on the south side; being somewhat long in battering, the enemy made six retrenchments, three of them from the said church to Duleek Gate, and three from the east end of the church to the town wall, and so backward. The guns after some two or three hundred shot, beat down the corner tower, and opened two reasonable good breaches in the east and south wall. Upon Tuesday the tenth of this instant, about five of the clock in the evening, we began the storm, and after some hot dispute, we entered about seven or eight hundred men, the enemy disputing it very stiffly with us; and indeed through the advantages of the place, and the courage God was pleased to give the defenders, our men were forced to retreat quite out of the breach, not without some considerable loss; Colonel Cassel being there shot in the head, whereof he presently died, and divers soldiers and officers doing their duty, killed and wounded. There was a tenalia[8] to flanker the south wall of the town, between Duleek Gate, and the corner tower before mentioned, which our men entered, wherein they found some forty or fifty of the enemy, which they put to the sword, and this they held; but it being without[9] the wall, and the sallyport[1] through the wall into that tenalia being choked up with some of the enemy which were killed in it, it proved of no use for our entrance into the town that way.

3. James Butler, Earl of Ormonde, represented Charles I in Ireland throughout the 1640s. At first opposed to the Catholic Confederation led by Owen Roe O'Neill (c. 1590–1649), Ormonde joined forces with O'Neill against the incursion of Cromwell's army.

4. Drogheda (Droichead átha, "Bridge of the ford"), a city in County Louth, was under royalist command when Cromwell arrived there on 2 September 1649.

5. Platforms on which artillery was mounted.

6. Chart, map.

7. Gaps in fortifications.

8. A low fortification to protect the wall from the side.

9. Outside.

1. An opening for troops to pass through.

Although our men that stormed the breaches were forced to recoil, as before is expressed, yet being encouraged to recover their loss, they made a second attempt, wherein God was pleased to animate them, that they got ground of the enemy, and by the goodness of God, forced him to quit his entrenchments; and after a very hot dispute, the enemy having both horse and foot, and we only foot within the wall, the enemy gave ground, and our men became masters; but of their retrenchments and the church, which indeed although they made our entrance the more difficult, yet they proved of excellent use to us, so that the enemy could not annoy us with their horse, but thereby we had advantage to make good the ground, that so we might let in our own horse, which accordingly was done, though with much difficulty; the enemy retreated divers of them into the Mill-Mount, a place very strong and of difficult access, being exceeding high, having a good graft[2] and strongly pallisadoed;[3] the Governor Sir Arthur Ashton and divers considerable officers being there, our men getting up to them, were ordered by me to put them all to the sword; and indeed being in the heat of action, I forbade them to spare any that were in arms in the town, and I think that night they put to the sword about two thousand men, divers of the officers and soldiers being fled over the bridge into the other part of the town, where about one hundred of them possessed St. Peter's church steeple, some the west gate, and others, a round strong tower next the gate, called St. Sunday's. These being summoned to yield to mercy, refused; whereupon I ordered the steeple of St. Peter's church to be fired, where one of them was heard to say in the midst of the flames, "God damn me, God confound me, I burn, I burn." The next day the other two towers were summoned,[4] in one of which was about six or seven score, but they refused to yield themselves; and we knowing that hunger must compel them, set only good guards to secure them from running away, until their stomachs were come down. From one of the said towers, notwithstanding their condition, they killed and wounded some of our men; when they submitted, their officers were knocked on the head, and every tenth man of the soldiers killed, and the rest shipped for the Barbados;[5] the soldiers in the other tower were all spared, as to their lives only, and shipped likewise for the Barbados. I am persuaded that this is a righteous judgment of God upon these barbarous wretches, who have imbrued their hands in so much innocent blood, and that it will tend to prevent the effusion of blood for the future, which are the satisfactory grounds to such actions, which otherwise cannot but work remorse and regret.

The officers and soldiers of this garrison were the flower of all their army; and their great expectation was that our attempting this place would put fair to ruin us; they being confident of the resolution of their men, and the advantage of the place; if we had divided our force into two quarters, to have besieged the north town and the south town, we could not have had such a correspondency between the two parts of our army, but that they might have chosen to have brought their army, and have fought with which part they pleased, and at the same time have made a sally with two thousand men upon us, and have left their walls manned, they having in the town the numbers specified in this inclosed, by some say near four thousand. Since this great mercy vouchsafed to us, I sent a party of horse and dragoons to Dundalk, which the enemy quitted, and we are possessed of; as also another castle they deserted between

2. Ditch, moat.
3. Defended with a strong fence of pointed stakes.
4. Called to surrender.
5. In the Cromwellian period in Ireland, not only men captured in battle but also women and children were sent into indentured servitude to English colonies in the Caribbean.

Trym and Drogheda, upon the Boynes.[6] I sent a party of horse and dragoons to a house within five miles of Trym, there being then in Trym some Scots companies which the Lord of Ards[7] brought to assist the Lord of Ormonde; but upon the news of Drogheda they ran away, leaving their great guns behind them, which we also have possessed. And now give me leave to say how it comes to pass that this work is wrought. It was set upon some of our hearts, that a great thing should be done, not by power, or might, but by the Spirit of God; and is it not so clear? That which caused your men to storm so courageously, it was the Spirit of God, who gave your men courage, and took it away again, and gave the enemy courage, and took it away again, and gave your men courage again, and therewith this happy success; and therefore it is good that God alone have all the glory.

It is remarkable, that these people at the first set up the Mass in some places of the town that had been monasteries; but afterwards grew so insolent, that the last Lord's day before the Storm,[8] the Protestants were thrust out of the great church, called St. Peter's, and they had public Mass there; and in this very place near one thousand of them were put to the sword, flying thither for safety: I believe all their friars were knocked on the head promiscuously, but two, the one of which was Father Peter Taaff (Brother to the Lord Taaff)[9] whom the Soldiers took the next day, and made an end of; the other was taken in the round tower, under the repute of lieutenant, and when he understood the officers in that tower had no quarter, he confessed he was a friar, but that did not save him. A great deal of loss in this business, fell upon Col. Hewson, Col. Cassel, and Colonel Ewers' regiments; Colonel Ewers having two field-officers in his regiment shot, Colonel Cassel and a captain of his regiment slain, Colonel Hewson's captain-lieutenant slain; I do not think we lost one hundred men upon the place, though many be wounded. I most humbly pray, the Parliament will be pleased this army may be maintained, and that a consideration may be had of them, and of the carrying on of the affairs here, as may give a speedy issue to this work, to which there seems to be a marvelous fair opportunity offered by God. And although it may seem very chargeable to the State of England to maintain so great a force, yet surely to stretch a little for the present, in following God's Providence, in hope the charge will not be long, I trust it will not be thought by any (that have no irreconcilable or malicious principles) unfit for me to move for a constant supply, which in humane probability, as to outward means, is most likely to hasten and perfect this work; and indeed, if God please to finish it here, as he hath done in England, the war is like to pay itself. We keep the field much, our tents sheltering us from the wet and cold, but yet the country sickness overtakes many, and therefore we desire recruits, and some fresh regiments of foot may be sent us; for it is easily conceived by what the garrisons already drink up, what our field army will come to, if God shall give more garrisons into our hands. Craving pardon for this great trouble, I rest,

Your most humble Servant,

O. CROMWELL

Dublin, Sept. 17, 1649

6. The Boyne River.
7. Hugh Montgomery (c. 1623–1663), 3rd Viscount of Ards.
8. I.e., Cromwell's attack on the town.
9. Theobald, 2nd Viscount Taaff (d. 1677). An uncle of Lord Taaff, Lucas was forced to surrender New Ross to Cromwell in October 1649.

John O'Dwyer of the Glenn
c. 1651

John O'Dwyer of the Glenn (*Seán O'Duibhir an Ghleanna*) is one of the most beautiful popular Irish-language songs commemorating the war against the Cromwellian conquest of Ireland and its aftermath. According to James Hardiman, who collected this song in his *Irish Minstrelsy, or Bardic Remains of Ireland* (1831), John O'Dwyer was "a distinguished officer who commanded in the Counties of Waterford and Tipperary in 1651." The poem is listed under the heading "Jacobite Relics," which places it in a long tradition of support for the Stuart kings, which began with the celebration of the accession of James I in elite bardic poetry and continued into the eighteenth century with support for Bonnie Prince Charlie in popular ballads.

The imagery of the natural world in *John O'Dwyer of the Glenn* symbolizes the state of Ireland. The lyric begins with a pastoral idyll, as the speaker describes awakening in the morning to the sound of birds singing. The intrusion of a fox signals the advent of war, and a sad old woman who stands by the side of the road reckoning her geese evokes Ireland weeping for those she has lost. Some of the geese (*geidh*), here referred to as "that prowler's spoil," died in battle; others, like the "wild geese" (*geidh fiádháin*) who left Ireland after the defeat of the Gaelic chiefs in 1603, fled to the Continent. John O'Dwyer and his men were said by Hardiman to have embarked for Spain.

The translation here is that of Thomas Furlong as printed in Hardiman's *Irish Minstrelsy*. The song originated in County Tipperary in the mid-seventeenth century, and there are more verses in Irish. It is still sung in both English and Irish. The best edition of the Irish text is that edited by Padraig de Brún and Breandán Ó Buachalla in *Nua-Dhuanaire* (1971), which also contains poems by such mid-seventeenth-century Irish poets as Piaras Feiritéar and Dáibhí O Bruadair.

John O'Dwyer of the Glenn

Blithe the bright dawn found me,
Rest with strength had crown'd me,
Sweet the birds sung round me,
    Sport was all their toil.
The horn its clang was keeping,
Forth the fox was creeping,
Round each dame stood weeping,
    O'er that prowler's spoil.
Hark, the foe is calling,
Fast the woods are falling,
Scenes and sights appalling
    Mark the wasted soil.[1]

War and confiscation
Curse the fallen nation;
Gloom and desolation
    Shade the lost land o'er.
Chill the winds are blowing,

1. The falling woods are the old Irish families who have been thrown off their land, and the "wasted soil" is the country after war.

Death aloft is going;
Peace or hope seems growing
For our race no more.
Hark the foe is calling,
Fast the woods are falling,
Scenes and sights appalling
Throng our blood-stained shore.

Where's my goat to cheer me,[2]
Now it plays not near me;
Friends no more can hear me;
Strangers round me stand.
Nobles once high-hearted,
From their homes have parted,
Scatter'd, scar'd and started
By a base-born band.
Hark the foe is calling,
Fast the woods are falling;
Scenes and sights appalling
Thicken round the land.

Oh! that death had found me
And in darkness bound me,
Ere each object round me
Grew so sweet, so dear.
Spots that once were cheering,
Girls beloved endearing,
Friends from whom I'm steering,
Take this parting tear.
Hark, the foe is calling,
Fast the woods are falling;
Scenes and sights appalling
Plague and haunt me here.

The Story of Alexander Agnew

Alexander Agnew is seen by contemporary Scots writers such as Booker Prize–winning novelist James Kelman as something of a hero. An unrepentant freethinker, Agnew was the first man in Scots history publicly to deny the existence of God. Offending the Presbyterian laws of Scotland, Agnew was found guilty of blasphemy and hanged. The following journalistic account of his trial gives the sense of a man being driven to greater and greater levels of vitriolic sarcasm by the nitpicking detail of his Presbyterian examiners. Since the story begins with his refusing to go to church, saying, "Hang God, God was hanged long since," the ninth count against him—that he refused to say grace—seems oddly anticlimactic.

2. The goat stands for both Charles II in exile and the defeated Irish lords.

The story was printed in *Mercurius Politicus*, a pamphlet founded by Marchamont Needham in June 1650. In 1649, Parliament had had Needham arrested for the royalist *Mercurius Pragmaticus*, a pamphlet he had been editing since 1647, and ordered John Milton to examine Needham on his political views. Less than a year after his brush with the law, Needham reemerged as the editor of *Mercurius Politicus, the Common-Wealth of England Stated . . . With a Discourse of Excellencie of a Free-State, above a Kingly-Government*. Needham's editorial style has been described as slangy. For example, in Needham's first sentence in *Mercurius Politicus* 15, he refers to the Scots Prebyterians as "our gown'd Granado's." Needham clearly had it in for the Scots, whose independence he and his pamphlet's republican English audience saw as one of the greatest obstacles to the Commonwealth.

The Story of Alexander Agnew; or Jock of Broad Scotland[1]

Alexander Agnew, commonly called Jock of broad Scotland, being accused; forasmuch as by the Divine Law of Almighty God, and Acts of Parliament of this nation, the committers of the horrid crime of blasphemy are punished by death; nevertheless, in plain contempt of the said Laws and Acts of Parliament, the said Alexander Agnew uttered heinous and grievous blasphemies against the Omnipotent and Almighty God; and second and third persons of the Trinity, as the same is set down in diverse articles in manner following; to wit,

First, the said Alexander being desired to go to church answered, "Hang God, God was hanged long since." What had he to do with God? He had nothing to do with God. Secondly, he answered, he was nothing in God's common,[2] God gave him nothing, and he was no more obliged to God than to the Devil, and God was very greedy. Thirdly, when he was desired to seek anything in God's name, he said he would never seek anything for God's sake, and that it was neither God nor the Devil that gave the fruits of the ground, the wives of the country gave him his meat. Fourthly, being asked, wherein he believed, answered, he believed in white meal, water, and salt. Fifthly, being asked how many persons were in the Godhead, answered there was only one person in the Godhead who made all, but for Christ he was not God, because he was made, and came into the world after it was made, and died as other men, being nothing but a mere man.

Sixthly, he declared that he knew not whether God or the Devil had the greater power, but he thought the Devil had the greatest, "And when I die," said he, "let God and the Devil strive for my soul, and let him that is strongest take it." Seventhly, he denied there was a holy Ghost, or knew there was a Spirit, and denied he was a sinner or needed mercy. Eighthly, he denied he was a sinner and that he scorned to seek God's mercy. Ninthly, he ordinarily mocked all exercise of God's worship, and invocation on his name, in derision saying, "Pray you to your God and I will pray to mine when I think time." And when he was desired by some to give thanks for his meat, he said, "Take a sackful of prayers to the mill and shell them, and grind them and take your breakfast of them." To others he said, "I will give you a twopence, and pray until a bowl of meal and one stone[3] of butter fall down from heaven through the house rigging to you." To others he said when bread and cheese was given him, and was laid on the ground by him, he said, "If I leave this, I will long cry to God before he give it me again." To others he said, "Take a bannock[4] and break it in two, and lay down the one half thereof, and ye will long pray to God before he put the other half to it again."

1. From *Mercurius Politicus*, 3 July 1656.
2. Community.
3. Fourteen pounds.
4. In Scotland and the North of England, a large round loaf of bread.

Tenthly, being posed whether or not he knew God or Christ, he answered, he had never had any profession, nor never would; he never had any religion, nor never would: also that there was no God nor Christ, and that he never received anything from God but from nature, which he said ever reigned, and ever would, and that to speak of God and their persons was an idle thing, and that he would never name such names, for he had shaken his cap of these things long since, and he denied that a man has a soul, or that there is a heaven or a hell, or that the Scriptures are the word of God. Concerning Christ he said, that he heard of such a man, but for the second person of the Trinity, he had been the second person of the Trinity, if the ministers had not put him in prison, and that he was no more obliged to God nor the Devil. And these aforesaid blasphemies are not rarely or seldom uttered by him, but frequently and ordinarily in several places where he resorted, to the entangling, deluding, and seducing of the common people: through the committing of which blasphemies he hath contravened the tenor of the said Laws and Acts of Parliament and incurred the pain of death mentioned therein, which ought to be inflicted upon him with all rigor, in manner specified in the indictment.

Which indictment being put to the knowledge of an assize,[5] the said Alexander Agnew called Jock of broad Scotland, was by the said assize, all in one voice, by the mouth of William Carlile, late baily[6] of Dumfrize their chancellor[7] found guilty of the crime of blasphemy mentioned in his indictment. For which the commissioners ordained him upon Wednesday, 21 May 1656, betwixt 2 and 4 hours in the afternoon to be taken to the ordinary place of execution for the burgh of Dumfrize, and there to be hanged on a gibbet while he be dead, and all his movable goods to be escheat.[8]

END OF PERSPECTIVES: THE CIVIL WAR, OR THE WARS OF THREE KINGDOMS

John Milton

1608–1674

John Milton Surrounded by Muses. Seventeenth-century engraving.

While writing *Paradise Lost,* Milton would rise early to begin composing poetry; when his secretary arrived late, the old blind man would complain, "I want to be milked." Prodigious in his memory and ingenuity, austere in his frugality and discipline, Milton devoted his life to learning, politics, and art. He put his eloquence at the service of the Puritan Revolution, which brought on the beheading of a king and the institution of a republican commonwealth. Milton entered controversies on divorce and freedom of the press. He showed courage in defending the Puritan republic when he could have lost his life for doing so. Radical, scholar, sage—Milton is above all the great epic poet of England.

Milton's life was marked by a passionate devotion to his religious, political, and artistic ideals, a devotion that ran in

5. In Scotland, a trial by jury.
6. In Scotland, the chief magistrate of a county who functions as a sheriff.
7. In Scotland, the foreman of a jury.
8. Forfeited to the state.

his family. Milton's father was said to have been disinherited for his Protestantism by his own father, who was Roman Catholic. When the Civil War broke out, Milton sided with Cromwell while his brother fought for the King. The oldest of three children in a prosperous middle-class family, young John read Virgil, Ovid, and Livy; he especially loved "our sage and serious Spenser," whom he called "a better teacher than Aquinas." Milton later wrote that from the age of twelve he "hardly ever gave up reading for bed till midnight." After his first year at Christ's College, Cambridge, the poet was expelled. While in exile, Milton excoriated academia: "How wretchedly suited that place is to the worshippers of Phoebus! It is disgusting to be constantly subjected to the threats of a rough tutor and to other indignities my spirit cannot endure." Returning to Cambridge, he took his BA in 1629 and his MA in 1632. On vacations during these years he wrote two of his most musical lyrics, the erotic *L'Allegro* and the Platonic *Il Penseroso*. After leaving university, Milton lived with his parents in Berkshire, where he wrote *Lycidas*, a haunting elegy for the early death of his Cambridge friend Edward King, and *Comus*, a masque for the prominent noble Egerton family at Ludlow Castle.

After his mother's death in 1638, Milton traveled to Europe. He stayed longest in Italy, where his poems were greatly admired by the Florentine literati, who welcomed him into their academies. He later reflected that it was in Italy that he first sensed his vocation as an epic poet, hoping to "perhaps leave something so written, as they should not willingly let it die." Visiting Rome, Naples, and Venice, Milton collected Monteverdi's music, which he would later sing and play. He also met the famed astronomer Galileo, the censorship of whose works Milton would later protest. Concerned about political turmoil in England, he returned home at the outbreak of the Civil War.

From 1640 to 1660, Milton devoted himself to "the cause of real and substantial liberty," by which he meant religious, domestic, and civil liberties. Defending religious liberty, he decried Anglican hierarchy and ritualism—"the new vomited paganism of sensual idolatry"—in a series of tracts, including *Of Reformation* (1641) and *The Reason of Church Government* (1642).

That same year, Milton married seventeen-year-old Mary Powell, who came from a royalist Oxfordshire family. After only a month, she left Milton alone to his "philosophical" life for a more sociable one at home. Troubled by the unhappiness of his marriage, Milton wrote four treatises on divorce, for which he was publicly condemned. He argued that incompatibility should be grounds for divorce, that both husband and wife should be allowed to remarry, and that to maintain otherwise was contrary to reason and scripture. According to his nephew, whom Milton tutored during this time, he was interested in marrying another woman but by 1645 was reunited with Mary. They had a daughter soon afterward. They were joined for several years by Mary's family, who had lost their estate in the Civil War.

Along with "the true conception of marriage," Milton's concept of domestic liberty included "the sound education of children, and freedom of thought and speech." In *Of Education* (1644), opposing strictly vocational instruction, Milton called for the study of languages, rhetoric, poetry, philosophy, and science, the goal of which was "to perform justly, skillfully and magnanimously all of the offices both private and public of peace and war." In *Areopagitica* (1644), Milton fought against censorship before publication but counseled control of printed texts posing political or religious danger. In the 1640s, Milton steered a course midway between the religious conformity demanded by the once-dissenting Presbyterians and the complete separation of church and state advocated by such radicals as Roger Williams, who ultimately went to America in search of greater toleration.

After Oliver Cromwell defeated the Royalists and the King was tried and executed by order of the "Rump" parliament purged of dissenters, Milton wrote *The Tenure of Kings and Magistrates* (1649) to argue that subjects could justly overthrow a tyrant. This tract won him the job of Latin Secretary to the Council of State, handling all correspondence to foreign governments. After the beheading of Charles I in 1649, *Eikon Basilike*, "the Royal Image" (page 1681) appeared, pieced together from the King's papers by his chaplain John Gauden. To counteract sympathy for the King's cause that this work might elicit, Milton wrote a chapter-by-chapter refutation of it entitled *Eikonoklastes*, or *Image-Breaker* (1649) (page 1684). Milton also defended Cromwell's government in three Latin works that were in some measure self-defenses: *First* and *Second Defense of the English People* (1651, 1654) and *Defense of Himself* (1656).

His eyes weakened by the strain of so much writing, Milton went blind. His wife Mary died, leaving three daughters and one son. The boy died soon after, in May 1652. That same month, Milton wrote a sonnet exhorting the Lord General Cromwell to "Help us to save free conscience from the paw of hireling wolves," a reference to ministers who wanted to exclude dissenters from a unified established church. Sounding the cry for liberty again in *Avenge, O Lord these Slaughtered Saints* (1655), Milton lamented the massacre of Italian Protestants. One of Milton's most beautiful and best-known sonnets, *Methought I Saw My Late Espoused Saint*, is said to be about his second wife, Katherine Woodcock, who, after just two years of marriage, died following the birth of her child in 1558.

Cromwell died the same year, and his son Richard's succession to power began a period of political confusion. Milton continued to write political tracts, now even more radical in arguing for universal education and freedom from allegiance to *any* established church and against the abuse of church positions for money. In *De Doctrina Christiana* (written 1655–1660, published 1823), Milton set forth his individualistic theology; he was convinced that no one should be required to attend church and that everyone should interpret scripture in his own way. Committed to the cause of the republic even after the Restoration of Charles II, Milton published *The Ready and Easy Way to Establish a Free Commonwealth* in 1660. Shortly after its appearance, Milton went into hiding. The House of Commons ordered the burning of *Eikonoklastes* and had Milton arrested. He was held in prison for several months. For a time threatened with heavy fines and even death by hanging, Milton was finally released through the aid of his friend Andrew Marvell.

In the aftermath of the Restoration, Milton lived in obscurity and desolation. On the anniversary of Charles I's execution, Cromwell's body was dug up and hanged. More than a few of Milton's friends were either executed or forced into exile. The republic to which he had devoted his life's work had been defeated. Amid this experience of defeat, he worked on *Paradise Lost*, with its themes of fall, damnation, war in heaven, and future redemption for an erring humanity.

While writing his epic, he was much helped by the companionship and housekeeping of his young and amiable third wife Elizabeth Minshull, whom he married in 1663. Young pupils, secretaries, and his daughters read to him in many languages (some of which they didn't understand). The Miltons lived frugally on the money that he had saved from his salary as Latin Secretary (1649–1659). Milton had begun writing *Paradise Lost* by 1658–1659, but he only completed the first edition for publication in 1667. First conceiving of this work as a drama, he had written a soliloquy for the rebellious Lucifer in 1642, which later appeared near the opening of the epic's fourth book. Milton explained that he had put off writing *Paradise Lost* because it was "a work to be raised . . . by devout prayer to that eternal Spirit who can enrich with all utterance and knowledge."

In the last ten years of his life, Milton also wrote *Paradise Regained* (1671), a short epic about the temptation of Christ, based on the model of the Book of Job. Published in the same year was *Samson Agonistes*, a verse tragedy about the biblical hero, who, betrayed by his lover Delilah, brought down destruction on himself as well as his enemies. In 1673 he published an expanded edition of his *Poems* (1645), to which he added his translations of the Psalms. Finally, in 1674, all twelve books of *Paradise Lost* as we know it were published. That same year, Milton died in a fit of gout and was buried in Saint Giles Cripplegate alongside his father.

Milton combined the traditional erudition of a Renaissance poet with the committed politics of a Puritan radical, both of which contributed to his crowning achievement, *Paradise Lost*. Milton draws on the Bible, Homer, Virgil, and Dante to create his own original sound and story. The vivid sensual imagery of *L'Allegro*, echoing Shakespeare and Spenser, suggests the pastoral idyll of Adam and Eve in Paradise. The intellectual rebelliousness of his prose works inflects the epic's dramatic embodiment of such problems as the origin of evil, sin, and death. Like *Samson Agonistes, Paradise Lost* reaches humanity's psychological depths: arrogance, despair, revenge, self-destruction, desire, and self-knowledge. Most of all, *Paradise Lost* dramatizes human wayfaring in the face of the Fall, not unlike Milton's own heroic perseverance in writing his epic after the loss of the world he had helped to create.

For additional resources on Milton, including the full text of *Samson Agonistes*, go to *The Longman Anthology of British Literature* Web site at www.myliteraturekit.com.

L'Allegro[1]

Hence loathèd Melancholy
  Of Cerberus,[2] and blackest midnight born,
In Stygian cave forlorn.
  'Mongst horrid shapes, and shreiks, and sights unholy,
Find out some uncouth° cell, *unknown*
  Where brooding darkness spreads his jealous wings,
And the night-raven[3] sings;
  There under ebon shades, and low-brow'd rocks,
As ragged as thy Locks,
  In dark Cimmerian[4] desert ever dwell.
But come thou goddess fair and free,
In Heaven yclept° Euphrosyne, *called*
And by men, heart-easing Mirth,
Whom lovely Venus at a birth
With two sister Graces more
To ivy-crownèd Bacchus bore;[5]
Or whether (as some sager sing)
The frolic wind that breathes the spring,
Zephyr with Aurora playing,
As he met her once a-Maying,[6]
There on beds of violets blue,
And fresh-blown roses washed in dew,
Filled her with thee a daughter fair,
So buxom,° blithe, and debonair. *yielding*
Haste thee nymph, and bring with thee
Jest and youthful Jollity,
Quips and cranks,° and wanton wiles, *jests*
Nods, and becks, and wreathèd smiles,
Such as hang on Hebe's[7] cheek,
And love to live in dimple sleek;

1. The happy person. This and the companion poem *Il Penseroso* (the pensive one) were composed around 1631; they were first published in 1645.
2. For the underworld cave of the three-headed dog Cerberus, see Virgil, *Aeneid* 6.418. Milton makes Cerberus and Night the parents of Melancholy, which is the subject of *Il Penseroso*.
3. Ominous bird.
4. The Cimmerians lived at the extreme limit of the known world (see *Odyssey* 11.13–22).
5. The Graces: Euphrosyne (Mirth), Aglaia (Brightness), and Thalia (Bloom). Servius's commentary to the *Aeneid* makes Venus and Bacchus their parents.
6. Milton invented this parentage of the Graces by Aurora, the dawn, and Zephyr, the west wind.
7. Goddess of youth and daughter of Zeus and Hera.

Sport that wrinkled Care derides,
And Laughter holding both his sides.
Come, and trip it as you go
On the light fantastic toe,
And in thy right hand lead with thee,
The mountain nymph, sweet Liberty;
And if I give thee honor due,
Mirth, admit me of thy crew
To live with her, and live with thee,
In unreprovèd pleasures free;
To hear the lark begin his flight,
And singing startle the dull night,
From his watch-tower in the skies,
Till the dappled dawn doth rise;
Then to come in spite of sorrow,
And at my window bid good morrow,
Through the sweetbriar, or the vine,
Or the twisted eglantine.° *honey-suckle*
While the cock with lively din,
Scatters the rear of darkness thin,
And to the stack, or the barn door,
Stoutly struts his dames before,
Oft listening how the hounds and horn
Cheerly rouse the slumbring morn,
From the side of some hoar° hill, *gray with mist*
Through the high wood echoing shrill.
Sometime walking not unseen
By hedge-row elms, on hillocks green,
Right against the eastern gate,
Where the great sun begins his state,° *progress*
Robed in flames, and amber light,
The clouds in thousand liveries dight,° *dressed*
While the plowman near at hand,
Whistles ore the furrowed land,
And the milkmaid singeth blithe,
And the mower whets his scythe,
And every shepherd tells his tale
Under the hawthorn in the dale.
Straight mine eye hath caught new pleasures
Whilst the landscape round it measures,
Russet lawns, and fallows° gray, *plowed lands*
Where the nibling flocks do stray,
Mountains on whose barren breast
The laboring clouds do often rest;
Meadows trim with daisies pied,° *variegated*
Shallow brooks, and rivers wide.
Towers and battlements it sees
Bosomed high in tufted trees,
Where perhaps some beauty lies,

The cynosure[8] of neighboring eyes.
Hard by, a cottage chimney smokes
From betwixt two agèd oaks,
Where Corydon and Thyrsis met,
Are at their savory dinner set
Of herbs, and other country messes,
Which the neat-handed Phyllis dresses;
And then in haste her bower she leaves,
With Thestylis[9] to bind the sheaves;
Or if the earlier season lead
To the tanned haycock° in the mead, *heaps of hay*
Sometimes with secure delight
The upland hamlets will invite,
When the merry bells ring round,
And the jocond rebecks° sound *fiddles*
To many a youth, and many a maid,
Dancing in the checkered shade;
And young and old come forth to play
On a sunshine holiday,
Till the livelong daylight fail,
Then to the spicy nut-brown ale,
With stories told of many a feat,
How fairy Mab[1] the junkets° eat, *cream cheeses*
She was pinched, and pulled she said,
And by the friar's lantern led
Tells how the drudging goblin sweat,
To earn his cream-bowl duly set,
When in one night, ere glimpse of morn,
His shadowy flail hath threshed the corn
That ten day-laborers could not end;
Then lies him down the lubber fiend.[2]
And stretched out all the chimney's length,
Basks at the fire his hairy strength;
And crop-full out of doors he flings,
Ere the first cock his matin rings.
Thus done the tales, to bed they creep,
By whispering winds soon lulled asleep.
Towered cities please us then,
And the busy hum of men,
Where throngs of knights and barons bold,
In weeds° of peace high triumphs° hold, *clothes / tournaments*
With store of ladies, whose bright eyes
Rain influence,[3] and judge the prize,
Of wit, or arms, while both contend

8. The North Star, here meaning, the center of attention.
9. The shepherds' names are common in Renaissance pastoral.
1. Queen of the fairies, and the topic of Mercutio's famous speech (*Romeo and Juliet* 1.4.54–95).
2. Slaving demon, like Robin Goodfellow called "lob of spirits" in *Midsummer Night's Dream* 2.1.16.
3. In astrology, the process by which an etherial fluid emanating from the stars ruled human fate.

To win her grace, whom all commend.
There let Hymen[4] oft appear
In saffron robe, with taper clear,
And pomp, and feast, and revelry,
With mask, and antique pageantry;
Such sights as youthful poets dream
On summer eves by haunted stream.
Then to the well-trod stage anon,
If Jonson's learned sock[5] be on,
Or sweetest Shakespeare fancy's child,
Warble his native wood-notes wild,
And ever against eating cares
Lap me in soft Lydian airs,[6]
Married to immortal verse
Such as the meeting soul may pierce
In notes, with many a winding bout
Of linkèd sweetness long drawn out,
With wanton heed and giddy cunning,
The melting voice through mazes running,
Untwisting all the chains that tie
The hidden soul of harmony.
That Orpheus' self may heave his head
From golden slumber on a bed
Of heaped Elysian flowers, and hear
Such strains as would have won the ear
Of Pluto, to have quite set free
His half regained Eurydice.[7]
These delights, if thou canst give,
Mirth with thee, I mean to live.[8]

Il Penseroso[1]

Hence vain deluding joys,
  The brood of Folly without father bred,
How little you bestead,° *help*
  Or fill the fixèd mind with all your toys;
Dwell in some idle brain,
  And fancies fond with gaudy shapes possess,
As thick and numberless
  As the gay motes that people the sunbeams,
Or likest hovering dreams,
  The fickle pensioners° of Morpheus'[2] train. *guards*

4. Roman wedding god.
5. Low-heeled slipper of the comic actor in ancient Greece and Rome.
6. Plato considered the Lydian mode to be morally corrupting and loose; others found it a source of relaxed enjoyment.
7. When Orpheus attempted to rescue his wife Eurydice from Hades, he lost her by violating the command that he not look back to see if she were behind him.
8. These lines recall the final couplet of Marlowe's "The Passionate Shepherd to His Love": "of these delights thy mind may move; / Then love with me, and be my love."
1. The pensive one.
2. God of dreams and son of Sleep.

But hail thou Goddess, sage and holy,
Hail divinest Melancholy,
Whose saintly visage is too bright
To hit° the sense of human sight, *fit*
And therefore to our weaker view,
O'er laid with black staid Wisdom's hue;[3]
Black, but such as in esteem,
Prince Memnon's sister[4] might beseem,
Or that starred Ethiope Queen[5] that strove
To set her beauties praise above
The sea nymphs, and their powers offended.
Yet thou art higher far descended,
Thee bright-haired Vesta[6] long of yore,
To solitary Saturn bore;
His daughter she (in Saturn's reign
Such mixture was not held a stain)[7]
Oft in glimmering bowers, and glades
He met her, and in secret shades
Of woody Ida's inmost grove,
While yet there was no fear of Jove.
Come pensive nun, devout and pure,
Sober, steadfast, and demure,
All in a robe of darkest grain,
Flowing with majestic train,
And sable° stole of cypress lawn,° *dark / fine linen*
Over thy decent shoulders drawn.
Come, but keep thy wonted state,
With even step, and musing gait,
And looks commercing with the skies,
Thy rapt soul sitting in thine eyes:
There held in holy passion still,
Forget thyself to marble,[8] till
With a sad leaden downward cast,
Thou fix them on the earth as fast.
And join with thee calm Peace, and Quiet,
Spare Fast, that oft with gods doth diet,
And hears the Muses in a ring,
Ay round about Jove's altar sing.
And add to these retired leisure;
That in trim gardens takes his pleasure;
But first, and chiefest, with thee bring
Him that yon soars on golden wing,

3. Melancholy was governed by the black bile in the body and manifested itself in a black face.
4. The Ethiopian Prince Memnon (*Odyssey* 11.521) had a sister named Himera (Greek, "light of day").
5. Cassiopea was turned into a constellation because she boasted that she was more beautiful than the Nereids.
6. Milton makes Vesta a mother; by tradition, she was a virgin, daughter of Saturn, and goddess of the hearth.
7. The Golden Age was a time of plenty and sexual freedom.
8. Turning to stone through grief comes from the story of Niobe.

Guiding the fiery-wheelèd throne,[9]
The cherub Contemplation;[1]
And the mute Silence hist° along, *a call*
'Less Philomel[2] will deign a song,
In her sweetest, saddest plight,
Smoothing the rugged brow of night,
While Cynthia[3] checks her dragon yoke,
Gently o'er th'accustomed oak;
Sweet bird that shunn'st the noise of folly,
Most musical, most melancholy!
Thee chantress oft the woods among,
I woo to hear thy evensong;
And missing thee, I walk unseen
On the dry smooth-shaven green,
To behold the wandring moon,
Riding near her highest noon,
Like one that had been led astray
Through the heaven's wide pathless way;
And oft, as if her head she bowed,
Stooping through a fleecy cloud.
Oft on a plat° of rising ground, *plot*
I hear the far-off curfew sound,
Over some wide-watered shore,
Swinging slow with sullen roar;
Or if the air will not permit,
Some still removèd place will fit,
Where glowing embers through the room
Teach light to counterfeit a gloom,
Far from all resort of mirth,
Save the cricket on the hearth,
Or the bellman's drowsy charm,[4]
To bless the doors from nightly harm;
Or let my lamp at midnight hour,
Be seen in some high lonely tower,
Where I may oft out-watch the Bear,[5]
With thrice great Hermes,[6] or unsphere[7]
The spirit of Plato to unfold
What worlds, or what vast regions hold
The immortal mind that hath forsook
Her mansion in this fleshly nook;
And of those demons that are found

9. See Ezekiel 1.4–6.
1. The angel Cherubim contemplate God.
2. The nightingale (Greek).
3. The moon goddess, another name for Hecate; for her dragons, see Ovid, *Metamorphoses* 7.218–19.
4. The night-watchman, or bellman, cries out the hours in a chant, or charm (from *carmen*, Latin for song).
5. The constellation of the Great Bear, which never sets, symbolizes perfection.
6. Hermes Trismegistus was believed to be the author of the Hermetica, texts of esoteric neoplatonism and magic.
7. To remove from the eternal sphere and make reappear on earth.

In fire, air, flood, or under ground,
Whose power hath a true consent
With planet, or with element.
Sometime let gorgeous Tragedy
In scepter'd pall° come sweeping by, *robe*
Presenting Thebes, or Pelops line,
Or the tale of Troy divine.[8]
Or what (though rare) of later age
Ennobled hath the buskined stage.[9]
But, O sad virgin, that thy power
Might raise Musaeus[1] from his bower,
Or bid the soul of Orpheus[2] sing
Such notes as warbled to the string,
Drew iron tears down Pluto's cheek,
And made Hell grant what Love did seek.
Or call up him[3] that left half told
The story of Cambuscan bold,
Of Camball, and of Algarsife,
And who had Canace to wife,
That owned the virtuous° ring and glass, *magical*
And of the wondrous horse of brass,
On which the Tartar king did ride;
And if aught else, great bards beside,[4]
In sage and solemn tunes have sung,
Of tourneys and of trophies hung;
Of forests, and enchantments drear,
Where more is meant then meets the ear.
Thus, Night, oft see me in thy pale career,
Till civil-suited Morn appear,
Not tricked and frounced[5] as she was wont,
With the Attic boy[6] to hunt,
But kerchiefed in a comely cloud,
While rocking winds are piping loud,
Or ushered with a shower still,° *quiet*
When the gust hath blown his fill,
Ending on the rustling leaves,
With minute drops from off the eaves.
And when the sun begins to fling
His flaring beams, me, Goddess, bring
To archèd walks of twilight groves,

8. Thebes was the birthplace of Oedipus, tragic hero of Sophocles' *Oedipus Rex*. Pelops' descendants Agamemnon and Orestes are the subject of Aeschylus' tragedy *Oresteia*. Troy was the city destroyed by the Trojan War, the tragic consequences of which are the subject of Euripides' *The Trojan Women*.
9. The high boots of tragic actors. Compare *L'Allegro* line 132.
1. Prophet and poet, who studied with the mythic bard Orpheus.
2. See *L'Allegro* 145–50.
3. Chaucer; the "story" is the unfinished *Squire's Tale*.
4. Lines 116–20 refer to Spenser's allegorical *Faerie Queene*.
5. Richly attired and wearing ringlets.
6. Cephalus, beloved of Aurora, who met him while he was hunting. (See Ovid, *Metamorphoses* 7.700–13.)

And shadows brown that Sylvan[7] loves
Of pine, or monumental oak,
Where the rude ax with heavèd stroke.
Was never heard the nymphs to daunt,
Or fright them from their hallowed haunt.
There in close covert by some brook,
Where no prophaner eye may look,
Hide me from day's garish eye,
While the bee with honeyed thigh,
That at her flowery work doth sing,
And the waters murmuring
With such consort° as they keep, *musical harmony*
Entice the dewy-feathered sleep;
And let some strange mysterious dream
Wave at his wings in airy stream
Of lively portraiture displayed,
Softly on my eye-lids laid.
And as I wake, sweet music breathe
Above, about, or underneath,
Sent by some spirit to mortals good,
Or th'unseen genius° of the wood. *presiding local god*
But let my due feet never fail
To walk the studious cloisters° pale, *enclosure*
And love the high embowèd° roof, *arched*
With antic pillars massy proof,° *impenetrability*
And storied[8] windows richly dight,° *decorated*
Casting a dim religious light.
There let the pealing organ blow
To the full voiced choir below,
In service high, and anthems clear,
As may with sweetness, through mine ear,
Dissolve me into ecstasies,
And bring all heaven before mine eyes.
And may at last my weary age
Find out the peaceful hermitage,
The hairy gown and mossy cell,
Where I may sit and rightly spell° *find out about*
Of every star that heaven doth shew,
And every herb that sips the dew,
Till old experience do attain
To something like prophetic strain.
These pleasures Melancholy give,
And I with thee will choose to live.[9]

7. Roman god of the forest.
8. With stories from the Bible.
9. See *L'Allegro* 151–52.

Lycidas

In this Monody[1] the Author bewails a learned Friend,[2] unfortunately drowned in his passage from Chester on the Irish Seas, 1637. And by occasion foretells the ruin of our corrupted Clergy then in their height.

Yet once more, O ye laurels, and once more
Ye myrtles brown, with ivy[3] never sear,° *withered*
I come to pluck your berries harsh and crude,° *unripe*
And with forced fingers rude,
Shatter your leaves before the mellowing year.
Bitter constraint, and sad occasion dear,
Compels me to disturb your season due:
For Lycidas is dead, dead ere his prime,[4]
Young Lycidas, and hath not left his peer:
Who would not sing for Lycidas? he knew
Himself to sing, and build the lofty rhyme.
He must not float upon his watery bier
Unwept, and welter° to the parching wind, *writhe*
Without the meed° of some melodious tear.° *recompense / elegy*
  Begin then, sisters of the sacred well,[5]
That from beneath the seat of Jove doth spring,
Begin, and somewhat loudly sweep the string.
Hence with denial vain, and coy excuse,
So may some gentle Muse
With lucky words favor my destined urn,
And as he passes turn,
And bid fair peace be to my sable° shrowd. *black*
For we were nursed upon the self-same hill,
Fed the same flock; by fountain, shade, and rill.
  Together both, ere the high lawns appeared
Under the opening eyelids of the morn,
We drove a field, and both together heard
What time the grayfly[6] winds her sultry horn,
Battening° our flocks with the fresh dews of night, *fattening*
Oft till the star that rose, at evening, bright,
Toward heaven's descent had sloped his westering wheel.
Meanwhile the rural ditties were not mute,
Tempered to th' oaten flute,
Rough satyrs danced, and fauns with cloven heel,
From the glad sound would not be absent long,
And old Damaetas[7] lov'd to hear our song.

1. A mournful song sung by one voice. *Lycidas* is a pastoral elegy, a lament for the dead through language evoking nature and the rural life of shepherds. The first *Idyll* of Theocritus and Virgil's fifth *Eclogue* are classical precedents for *Lycidas*. Shelley's *Adonais* and Arnold's *Thyrsis* are later examples of this form.
2. Edward King, who attended Cambridge when Milton did, drowned 10 August 1637. He had planned to enter the clergy and had written some Latin poems.
3. Laurels . . . myrtles . . . ivy: the leaves used to crown respectively poets, lovers, and scholars.
4. King ("Lycidas") was 25 when he died.
5. Sisters: the nine muses; well: Aganippe, on Mount Helicon, where there was an altar to Jove.
6. Name used to designate various kinds of insects.
7. "Damaetas" is etymologically derived from the Greek verb meaning "to tame;" thus a tutor is meant.

But O the heavy change, now thou art gone,
Now thou art gone, and never must return!
Thee shepherd, thee the woods, and desert caves,
With wild thyme and the gadding° vine o'ergrown, *wandering*
And all their echoes mourn.
The willows, and the hazle copses green,
Shall now no more be seen,
Fanning their joyous leaves to thy soft lays.
As killing as the canker° to the rose, *cankerworm*
Or taint-worm[8] to the weanling herds that graze,
Or frost to flowers, that their gay wardrop wear,
When first the white thorn blows;
Such, Lycidas, thy loss to shepherd's ear.
Where were ye nymphs when the remorseless deep
Closed o'er the head of your loved Lycidas?
For neither were ye playing on the steep
Where your old Bards, the famous Druids,° lie, *pagan Celtic priests*
Nor on the shaggy top of Mona[9] high,
Nor yet where Deva spreads her wizard stream:
Ay me, I fondly dream!
Had ye been there—for what could that have done?
What could the Muse[1] herself that Orpheus bore,
The Muse herself for her inchanting son
Whom universal nature did lament,
When by the rout that made the hideous roar
His gory visage down the stream was sent,
Down the swift Hebrus to the Lesbian shore.[2]
Alas! What boots° it with incessant care *avails*
To tend the homely slighted shepherd's trade,
And strictly meditate the thankless Muse,
Were it not better done as others use,
To sport with Amaryllis in the shade,
Or with the tangles of Neaera's hair?[3]
Fame is the spur that the clear spirit doth raise
(That last infirmity of noble mind)
To scorn delights, and live laborious days;
But the fair guerdon° when we hope to find, *reward*
And think to burst out into sudden blaze,
Comes the blind Fury[4] with th'abhorred shears,
And slits the thin spun life. "But not the praise,"
Phoebus replied, and touched my trembling ears;[5]
"Fame is no plant that grows on mortal soil,

8. An intestinal worm that can kill newly weaned calves.
9. The island of Anglesey; Deva: the river Dee, viewed as magical and prophetic by the inhabitants.
1. Calliope, Orpheus' mother.
2. Ovid, *Metamorphoses*, 11.1–55, relates how Orpheus was torn to pieces by the Thracian women and how his severed head floated down the Hebrus and was carried across to the island of Lesbos.
3. Amaryllis symbolizes erotic poetry (Virgil, *Eclogues* 2.14–15); Neaera: see *Eclogues* 3.3.
4. Atropos, one of the Fates, who cut the thread of life spun by her sisters.
5. Echoing Virgil, *Eclogues* 6.3–4: "the Cynthian plucked my ear and warned me."

Nor in the glistering foil[6]
Set off to the world, nor in broad rumor lies,
But lives and spreds aloft by those pure eyes,
And perfet witness of all-judging Jove;
As he pronounces lastly on each deed,
Of so much fame in heaven expect thy meed."
O Fountain Arethuse, and thou honored flood,
Smooth-sliding Mincius, crowned with vocal reeds,
That strain I heard was of a higher mood.[7]
But now my oat proceeds,
And listens to the herald of the sea
That came in Neptune's plea.[8]
He asked the waves, and asked the felon° winds, *savage*
"What hard mishap hath doomed this gentle swain?"
And questioned every gust of rugged wings
That blows from off each beakèd promontory;
They knew not of his story,
And sage Hippotades[9] their answer brings,
That not a blast was from his dungeon strayed,
The air was calm, and on the level brine,
Sleek Panope[1] with all her sisters played.
It was that fatal and perfidious bark,
Built in th' eclipse,° and rigged with curses dark, *period of evil omen*
That sunk so low that sacred head of thine.
Next Camus,[2] reverend sire, went footing slow,
His mantle hairy, and his bonnet sedge,[3]
Inwrought with figures dim, and on the edge
Like to that sanguine flower inscribed with woe.[4]
"Ah! who hath reft (quoth he) my dearest pledge?"° *child*
Last came, and last did go,
The Pilot of the Galilean lake,[5]
Two massy keys he bore of metals twain,
(The golden opes, the iron shuts amain°). *vehemently*
He shook his mitered[6] locks, and stern bespake,
"How well could I have spared for thee, young swain,
Enow° of such as for their bellies' sake, *enough*
Creep and intrude, and climb into the fold?[7]
Of other care they little reckoning make,
Than how to scramble at the shearer's feast,

6. A reflecting leaf of gold or silver placed under a precious stone.
7. The "higher mood" is the lofty tone of Phoebus' speech. The invocation to the river Arethuse (in Sicily) and the Mincius (Virgil's native river) marks a return to pastoral.
8. The herald Triton came to defend Neptune from blame for King's death.
9. God of winds, son of Hippotes.
1. One of the 50 Nereids (sea nymphs), mentioned by Virgil, *Aeneid* 5.240.
2. The River Cam, representing Cambridge University.
3. "Hairy" refers to the fur of the academic gown; sedge: a rushlike plant growing near water.
4. The hyacinth; see Ovid, *Metamorphoses* 10.214–16: "the flower bore the marks AI AI, letters of lamentation."
5. St. Peter bearing the keys of heaven given to him by Christ (Matthew 16.19).
6. Wearing a bishop's headdress.
7. See John 10.1: "He that entereth not by the door into the sheepfold, but climbeth up some other way, the same is a thief and a robber."

And shove away the worthy bidden guest.
Blind mouths![8] that scarce themselves know how to hold
A sheep-hook, or have learned aught else the least
That to the faithfull herdman's art belongs!
What recks it them?[9] What need they? They are sped;° *satisfied*
And when they list,° their lean and flashy° songs *please / insipid*
Grate on their scrannel° pipes of wretched straw, *feeble*
The hungry sheep look up, and are not fed,
But swoln with wind, and the rank mist they draw,
Rot inwardly, and foul contagion spread.
Besides what the grim woolf[1] with privy° paw *secret, hidden*
Daily devours apace, and nothing said,
But that two-handed engine at the door,
Stands ready to smite once, and smite no more."[2]
  Return Alpheus,[3] the dread voice is past,
That shrunk thy streams; return Sicilian muse,
And call the vales, and bid them hither cast
Their bells, and flowerets of a thousand hues.
Ye valleys low where the mild whispers use,° *often go*
Of shades and wanton winds, and gushing brooks,
On whose fresh lap the swart star[4] sparely looks,
Throw hither all your quaint enameled eyes,
That on the green turf suck the honeyed showers,
And purple all the ground with vernal flowers.
Bring the rathe° primrose that forsaken dies, *early*
The tufted crow-toe,° and pale jessamine,° *hyacinth / jasmine*
The white pink, and the pansie freaked° with jet, *adorned*
The glowing violet.
The musk-rose, and the well attired woodbine,
With cowslips wan° that hang the pensive head, *pale*
And every flower that sad embroidery wears:
Bid amaranthus[5] all his beauty shed,
And daffadillies fill their cups with tears,
To strew the laureate hearse where Lycid lies.
For so to interpose a little ease,
Let our frail thoughts dally with false surmise.[6]
Ay me! whilst thee the shores, and sounding seas
Wash far away, where'er thy bones are hurled,
Whether beyond the stormy Hebrides[7]
Where thou perhaps under the whelming tide
Visit'st the bottom of the monstrous world;
Or whether thou to our moist° vows denied, *tearful*
Sleep'st by the fable of Bellerus[8] old,

8. Milton's charge against the greed of the clergy.
9. What business is it of theirs?
1. The Roman Catholic Church.
2. Indicates that the corrupted clergy will be punished; see 1 Samuel 26.8.
3. The Arcadian hunter, who pursued Arethusa, the nymph he loved, under the sea to Sicily.
4. The Dog-star, Sirius. Its rising brings on the dog-days of heat.
5. The eternal flower (see *Paradise Lost*, 3.353–57).
6. The surmise is false since King's body drowned and will have no hearse.
7. Islands off the northwest coast of Scotland.
8. A giant of Bellerium, the Latin name for Land's End.

Where the great vision of the guarded mount
Looks toward Namancos and Bayona's hold;[9]
Look homeward angel° now, and melt with ruth.° *Michael / pity*
And, O ye dolphins, waft the haples youth.[1]
Weep no more, woeful shepherds weep no more,
For Lycidas your sorrow is not dead,
Sunk though he be beneath the wat'ry floor,
So sinks the day-star° in the ocean bed, *the sun*
And yet anon repairs his drooping head,
And tricks° his beams, and with new spangled ore,° *arrays / gold*
Flames in the forehead of the morning sky:
So Lycidas sunk low, but mounted high,
Through the dear might of him[2] that walked the waves
Where other groves, and other streams along,
With nectar pure his oozy lock's he laves,[3]
And hears the unexpressive nuptial[4] song,
In the blest kingdoms meek of joy and love.
There entertain him all the saints above,
In solemn troops, and sweet societies
That sing, and singing in their glory move,
And wipe the tears for ever from his eyes.[5]
Now Lycidas the shepherds weep no more;
Henceforth thou art the genius° of the shore, *local deity*
In thy large recompense, and shalt be good
To all that wander in that perilous flood.
Thus sang the uncouth° swain to th' oaks and rills, *unknown*
While the still morn went out with sandals gray,
He touched the tender stops of various quills,[6]
With eager thought warbling his Doric° lay: *pastoral*
And now the sun had stretched out all the hills,[7]
And now was dropped into the western bay;
At last he rose, and twitch'd his mantle blue:[8]
Tomorrow to fresh woods, and pastures new.

How Soon Hath Time

How soon hath time the subtle thief of youth,
Stol'n on his wing my three and twentieth year![1]
My hasting days fly on with full career,° *speed*
But my late spring no bud or blossom shew'th.
Perhaps my semblance° might deceive the truth, *appearance*

9. Namancos: an ancient name for a district in northwestern Spain; Bayona: a fortress town about 50 miles south of Cape Finisterre. The two names represent the threat of Spanish Catholicism, against which St. Michael guards England.
1. The dolphin is a symbol of Christ; waft: convey by water.
2. Christ, who walks on the sea in Matthew 14.25–6.
3. The brooks in Eden run with nectar, *Paradise Lost* 4.240; oozy: slimy from contact with the sea.
4. Relating to the marriage of the Lamb, or Christ, to the Church (Revelation 19.7).
5. See Revelation 7.17: "God shall wipe away all tears from their eyes"; see also Revelation 21.4.
6. Stops are the finger-holes in the pipes; quills are the hollow reeds of the shepherd's pipe.
7. The setting sun had shone over the hills and lengthened their shadows.
8. Blue is the traditional symbol of hope.
1. Written when Milton was 23, this sonnet was published in 1645.

That I to manhood am arrived so near,
And inward ripeness doth much less appear,
That some more timely-happy spirits[2] endu'th.° *gives, endows*
Yet be it less or more, or soon or slow,
It shall be still° in strictest measure even,° *always / level with*
To that same lot, however mean or high,
Toward which Time leads me, and the will of Heaven;
All is, if I have grace to use it so,
As ever in my great task Master's° eye. *God's*

On the New Forcers of Conscience Under the Long Parliament[1]

Because you have thrown off your prelate Lord,[2]
And with stiff vows renounced his liturgy[3]
To seize the widowed whore Plurality[4]
From them whose sin ye envied, not abhored,
Dare ye for this adjure° the civil sword *entreat*
To force our consciences that Christ set free,[5]
And ride us with a classic hierarchy[6]
Taught ye by meer A. S. and Rutherford?[7]
Men whose life, learning, faith and pure intent
Would have been held in high esteem with Paul
Must now be named and printed heretics
By shallow Edwards[8] and Scotch what d'ye call:
But we do hope to find out all your tricks,
Your plots and packing worse then those of Trent,[9]
That so the Parliament
May with their wholsome and preventive shears
Clip your phylacteries,[1] though balk° your ears,[2] *stop short of*
And succor our just fears,
When they shall read this clearly in your charge:
New presbyter is but *old priest* writ large.[3]

2. Those individuals of Milton's age who have already achieved success.
1. Written c. 1646, but printed in 1673.
2. Refers to the abolishment of episcopacy in England in September 1646.
3. The House of Commons forbade the use of the *Book of Common Prayer* in August 1645.
4. The practice of holding more than one living identified with episcopacy but subsequently supported by the Presbyterian system.
5. Milton complains of the Westminster Assembly's attempt to impose Presbyterianism by force.
6. Parliament resolved that the English congregations were to be grouped in Presbyteries or "Classes," which could impose rules after the Scottish pattern.
7. A. S.: Dr. Adam Stewart, Scottish Presbyterian controversialist; Rutherford: Samuel Rutherford, author of pamphlets in defense of Presbyterianism.
8. Thomas Edwards, author of *Antapologia*, advocating strict Presbyterianism, and *Gangraena* (1646), which included a denunciation of Milton's views on divorce.
9. Comparing the overwhelming Presbyterian predominance in the Assembly to the anti-protestant Roman Catholic Council of Trent (1545–1563).
1. Small leather boxes containing scriptural texts worn by Jews as a mark of obedience. Christ in Matthew 23.5 uses the phrase "make broad their phylacteries" in the sense "vaunt their own righteousness."
2. William Prynne, who had attacked one of the Bishops in print, actually did have both of his ears cut off. Milton's manuscript of this poem contains the line: "Crop ye as close as marginal P—'s ears."
3. "Priest" is etymologically a contracted form of Latin "presbyter" (an elder). The Presbyterians now appeared as dictatorial as the bishops had been.

To the Lord General Cromwell

Cromwell, our chief of men, who through a cloud[1]
Not of war only, but detractions rude,
Guided by faith and matchless fortitude
To peace and truth thy glorious way hast ploughed,
And on the neck of crownèd Fortune[2] proud
Hast reard° God's trophies and his work pursued, *raised, erected*
While Darwen stream[3] with blood of Scotts imbrued,° *stained*
And Dunbar field[4] resounds thy praises loud,
And Worester's laureate wreath;[5] yet much remains
To conquer still; peace hath her victories
No less renownd than war, new foes arise
Threatening to bind our souls with secular chains:
Help us to save free conscience from the paw
Of hireling wolves whose gospel is their maw.

On the Late Massacre in Piedmont[1]

Avenge O Lord thy slaughtered saints, whose bones
Lie scattered on the Alpine mountains cold,[2]
Even them who kept thy truth so pure of old
When all our Fathers worshiped stocks and stones,[3]
Forget not: in thy book[4] record their groans
Who were thy sheep and in their ancient fold
Slain by the bloody Piemontese that rolled
Mother with infant down the rocks. Their moans
The vales redoubled to the hills, and they
To Heaven. Their martyred blood and ashes sow
O'er all th' Italian fields where still doth sway
The triple tyrant:[5] that from these may grow
A hundred-fold,[6] who having learnt thy way
Early may fly the Babylonian[7] woe.

1. In Virgil, Aeneas prevails through the "war-cloud" of battle as he conquers Italy (*Aeneid* 10.809).
2. Refers to Charles I and to his successor, whose army Cromwell defeated at Worcester after he had been crowned king in Scotland on 1 January 1651. This poem was written in 1652 but not published until 1694.
3. Near Preston, where, on 17–19 August 1648, Cromwell routed the invading Scottish army.
4. At Dunbar, on 3 September 1650, after being virtually surrounded, Cromwell routed the Scottish army.
5. At Worcester, on 3 September 1651, Cromwell virtually annihilated Charles II's Royalist Scottish army.

1. The poem protests the persecution of Protestants in northern Italy in 1655.
2. See Luke 18.7: "shall not God avenge his own elect," and Psalms 141.7: "Our bones are scattered at the grave's mouth."
3. Gods of wood and stone.
4. See Revelation 5.1: "I saw in the right hand of him that sat on the throne a book."
5. The Pope with his three-tiered crown.
6. Lines 10–13 combine the parable of the sower (Matthew 13.3–23) with the legend of Cadmus, in which an army of warriors sprouts from the sowing of a dragon's teeth.
7. The Puritans used the corrupt Babylon of Revelation as a symbol for the Roman Catholic Church.

When I Consider How My Light Is Spent[1]

When I consider how my light is spent,
Ere half my days, in this dark world and wide,
And that one talent which is death to hide,[2]
Lodged with me useless, though my soul more bent
To serve therewith my Maker, and present
My true account, lest he returning chide,
Doth God exact day-labor, light denied,
I fondly° ask; but Patience to prevent *foolishly*
That murmur, soon replies, "God doth not need
Either man's work or his own gifts,[3] who best
Bear his mild yoke,[4] they serve him best, his state
Is kingly. Thousands at his bidding speed
And post o'er land and ocean without rest:
They also serve who only stand and wait."

Methought I Saw My Late Espoused Saint[1]

Methought I saw my late espousèd saint° *soul in heaven*
Brought to me like Alcestis[2] from the grave,
Whom Jove's great son to her glad husband gave,
Rescued from death by force though pale and faint.
Mine as whom washed from spot of child-bed taint,
Purification in the old Law[3] did save,
And such, as yet once more I trust to have
Full sight of her in Heaven without restraint,
Came vested all in white, pure as her mind:
Her face was veiled, yet to my fancied sight,
Love, sweetness, goodness, in her person shined
So clear, as in no face with more delight,
But O, as to embrace me she enclined,
I waked, she fled, and day brought back my night.[4]

AREOPAGITICA The title *Areopagitica* refers to the Areopagus, the ancient Athenian Council of State. Milton wrote *Areopagitica* to criticize the Parliamentary Ordinance of 14 June 1643 "to prevent and suppress the licence of printing." Although *Areopagitica* was

1. Probably written around 1652, as Milton's blindness became complete.
2. In the parable of the talents, Jesus tells of a servant who is given a talent (a large sum of money) to keep for his master. He buries the money; his master condemns him for not having invested it wisely. Matthew 25.14–30.
3. See Job 22.2.
4. See Matthew 11.30: "My yoke is easy."

1. The date of composition is placed at 1658; the poem appears as the last sonnet in the 1673 edition.
2. In Euripides' *Alcestis*, she gives her life for her husband Admetus, but Hercules ("Jove's great son") wrestles with death and brings her back from the grave.
3. According to Leviticus 12.4–8, after bearing a female child, a woman shall be unclean "two weeks, as in her separation: and she shall continue in the blood of her purifying threescore and six days" (i.e., during this period "she shall touch no hallowed thing, nor come into the sanctuary"). Some critics construe this line as evidence that the sonnet is about the death of Milton's second wife Katherine Woodcock, who died three months after childbirth in 1658.
4. In Virgil, Aeneas sees the ghost of his wife Creusa amid the ruins of Troy; when he tries to embrace her, "she withdrew into thin air . . . most like a winged dream" (*Aeneid* 2.791–794).

unlicensed, Milton made the bold move of affixing his name to the title page, which made no mention of the printer. Also on the title page are these lines from Euripides' *Suppliant Women* (438–41):

> There is true Liberty when free born men
> Having to advise the public may speak free,
> Which he who can and will, deserv'd high praise,
> Who neither can nor will, may hold his peace;
> What can be juster in a state than this?

from Areopagitica[1]
A Speech of Mr. John Milton for the Liberty of Unlicensed Printing, to the Parliament of England

* * * Good and evil we know in the field of this world grow up together almost inseparably; and the knowledge of good is so involved and interwoven with the knowledge of evil, and in so many cunning resemblances hardly to be discerned, that those confused seeds which were imposed on Psyche as an incessant labor to cull out and sort asunder, were not more intermixed.[2] It was from out the rind of one apple tasted, that the knowledge of good and evil, as two twins cleaving together, leaped forth into the world. And perhaps this is that doom which Adam fell into of knowing good and evil, that is to say, of knowing good by evil.[3]

As therefore the state of man now is, what wisdom can there be to choose, what continence to forbear without the knowledge of evil? He that can apprehend and consider vice with all her baits and seeming pleasures, and yet abstain, and yet distinguish, and yet prefer that which is truly better, he is the true wayfaring[4] Christian. I cannot praise a fugitive and cloistered virtue, unexercised and unbreathed, that never sallies out and sees her adversary, but slinks out of the race where that immortal garland is to be run for, not without dust and heat. Assuredly we bring not innocence into the world, we bring impurity much rather: that which purifies us is trial, and trial is by what is contrary. That virtue therefore which is but a youngling in the contemplation of evil, and knows not the utmost that vice promises to her followers, and rejects it, is but a blank virtue, not a pure; her whiteness is but an excremental[5] whiteness; which was the reason why our sage and serious poet Spenser, whom I dare be known to think a better teacher than Scotus or Aquinas, describing true temperance under the person of Guyon, brings him in with his palmer through the cave of Mammon and the bower of earthly bliss, that he might see and know, and yet abstain.[6]

1. The Areopagus was the seat of the Council of State, organized as a judicial tribunal by Solon in the sixth century B.C. The Athenian orator Isocrates argues for its renewal in his *Areopagiticus*.
2. Furious over her son Cupid's love for Psyche, Venus ordered Psyche to sort out a huge mass of seeds, but the ants, sympathizing with her plight, sorted them for her. See Apuleius, *Golden Ass* 4–6.
3. See *Paradise Lost* 4.222: "Knowledge of Good bought dear by knowing ill."
4. The original reads "warfaring," but in several copies this is corrected by hand to "wayfaring."
5. Superficial.
6. Duns Scotus and Thomas Aquinas here represent types of the scholastic theologian. For the cave of Mammon, see *The Faerie Queene* 2.7 (the Palmer is not with Guyon in Mammon's Cave); the "Bower of Bliss," 2.12.

Since therefore, the knowledge and survey of vice is in this world so necessary to the constituting of human virtue, and the scanning of error to the confirmation of truth, how can we more safely and with less danger scout into the regions of sin and falsity than by reading all manner of tractates and hearing all manner of reason? And this is the benefit which may be had of books promiscuously read.

But of the harm that may result hence, three kinds are usually reckoned. First is feared the infection that may spread; but then all human learning and controversy in religious points must remove out of the world, yea the Bible itself; for that ofttimes relates blasphemy not nicely,[7] it describes the carnal sense of wicked men not unelegantly, it brings in holiest men passionately murmuring against providence through all the arguments of Epicurus;[8] in other great disputes it answers dubiously and darkly to the common reader; and ask a Talmudist what ails the modesty of his marginal Keri, that Moses and all the prophets cannot persuade him to pronounce the textual Chetiv.[9] For these causes we all know the Bible itself put by the papist into the first rank of prohibited books. The ancientest fathers must be next removed, as Clement of Alexandria, and that Eusebian book of Evangelic preparation transmitting our ears through a hoard of heathenish obscenities to receive the Gospel. Who finds not that Irenaeus, Epiphanius, Jerome,[1] and others discover more heresies than they well confute, and that oft for heresy which is the truer opinion?[2]

* * *

Impunity and remissness, for certain, are the bane of a commonwealth; but here the great art lies, to discern in what the law is to bid restraint and punishment, and in what things persuasion only is to work. If every action which is good or evil in man at ripe years, were to be under pittance and prescription and compulsion, what were virtue but a name, what praise could be then due to well-doing, what gramercy[3] to be sober, just, or continent?

Many there be that complain of divine providence for suffering Adam to transgress. Foolish tongues! when God gave him reason, he gave him freedom to choose, for reason is but choosing; he had been else a mere artificial Adam, such an Adam as he is in the motions.[4] We ourselves esteem not of that obedience, or love, or gift, which is of force. God therefore left him free, set before him a provoking object, ever almost in his eyes; herein consisted his merit, herein the right of his reward, the praise of his abstinence. Wherefore did he create passions within us, pleasures round about us, but that these rightly tempered are the very ingredients of virtue? They are not skilful considerers of human things who imagine to remove sin by removing the matter of sin. For, besides that it is a huge heap increasing under the very act of diminishing, though some part of it may for a time be withdrawn from some persons, it cannot from all, in such a universal thing as

7. Delicately.
8. The Greek philosopher who propounded a morality based on pleasure.
9. Talmudist: a student of the Talmud, the Jewish commentaries on the Bible; Keri: marginal emendations of rabbinical scholars on the Chetiv, the text of the Bible.
1. Early apologists of Christianity: St. Clement of Alexandria (2nd century) and Eusebius, who describes pagan depravity to promote faith in Christianity, as do St. Irenaeus (2nd century), Epiphanius (4th century), and St. Jerome (early 5th century).
2. Milton goes on to argue that the effect of books depends upon the teacher, who, if really good, needs no books. Milton stresses the role of the reader: A wise person can find something instructive in even the worst books.
3. Thanks.
4. Puppet shows. For this statement about Adam, see *Paradise Lost* 3.103–28.

books are; and when this is done, yet the sin remains entire. Though ye take from a covetous man all his treasure, he has yet one jewel left—ye cannot bereave him of his covetousness. Banish all objects of lust, shut up all youth into the severest discipline that can be exercised in any hermitage, ye cannot make them chaste that came not thither so: such great care and wisdom is required to the right managing of this point.

Suppose we could expel sin by this means; look how much we thus expel of sin, so much we expel of virtue: for the matter of them both is the same; remove that, and ye remove them both alike. This justifies the high providence of God, who, though he command us temperance, justice, continence, yet pours out before us, even to a profuseness, all desirable things, and gives us minds that can wander beyond all limit and satiety. Why should we then affect a rigor contrary to the manner of God and of nature, by abridging or scanting those means which books freely permitted are, both to the trial of virtue and the exercise of truth?[5]

* * *

And lest some should persuade ye, Lords and Commons, that these arguments of learned men's discouragement at this your Order are mere flourishes, and not real, I could recount what I have seen and heard in other countries where this kind of inquisition tyrannizes; when I have sat among their learned men, for that honor I had, and been counted happy to be born in such a place of philosophic freedom as they supposed England was, while themselves did nothing but bemoan the servile condition into which learning amongst them was brought; that this was it which had damped the glory of Italian wits; that nothing had been there written now these many years but flattery and fustian. There it was that I found and visited the famous Galileo, grown old, a prisoner to the Inquisition[6] for thinking in astronomy otherwise than the Franciscan and Dominican licensers thought. And though I knew that England then was groaning loudest under the prelatical yoke, nevertheless I took it as a pledge of future happiness that other nations were so persuaded of her liberty.

Yet was it beyond my hope that those worthies were then breathing in her air, who should be her leaders to such a deliverance as shall never be forgotten by any revolution of time that this world hath to finish. When that was once begun, it was as little in my fear, that what words of complaint I heard among learned men of other parts uttered against the Inquisition, the same I should hear by as learned men at home uttered in time of Parliament against an order of licensing; and that so generally, that when I had disclosed myself a companion of their discontent, I might say, if without envy, that he whom an honest quaestorship had endeared to the Sicilians, was not more by them importuned against Verres,[7] than the favorable opinion which I had among many who honor ye, and are known and respected by ye, loaded me with entreaties and persuasions that I would not despair to lay together that which just reason should bring into my mind toward the removal of an undeserved thraldom upon learning.

5. Milton argues that no intelligent person will be willing to take on the job of censorship and that an unintelligent person would be prone to commit serious errors. In addition to giving power to stupid people, censorship would actually encourage people to read banned books and to adhere to the perverse opinions expressed in such books.
6. In 1633 the great Italian astronomer Galileo was tried by the Inquisition at Rome and forced to abjure his earlier assertion that his findings confirmed the Copernican heliocentric theory of the universe. He was under house arrest in Florence when Milton visited there in 1638–1639.
7. Cicero exposed the corruption of Verres' government in 75 B.C.E.

That this is not, therefore, the disburdening of a particular fancy, but the common grievance of all those who had prepared their minds and studies above the vulgar pitch to advance truth in others, and from others to entertain it, thus much may satisfy. And in their name I shall for neither friend nor foe conceal what the general murmur is; that if it come to inquisitioning again and licensing, and that we are so timorous of ourselves and so suspicious of all men as to fear each book and the shaking of every leaf, before we know what the contents are; if some who but of late were little better than silenced from preaching, shall come now to silence us from reading, except what they please, it cannot be guessed what is intended by some but a second tyranny over learning; and will soon put it out of controversy that bishops and presbyters are the same to us both name and thing.

* * *

But I am certain that a state governed by the rules of justice and fortitude, or a church built and founded upon the rock of faith and true knowledge, cannot be so pusillanimous.[8] While things are yet not constituted in religion, that freedom of writing should be restrained by a discipline imitated from the prelates, and learnt by them from the Inquisition, to shut us up all again into the breast of a licenser, must needs give cause of doubt and discouragement to all learned and religious men. Who cannot but discern the fineness of this politic drift, and who are the contrivers: that while bishops were to be baited down, then all presses might be open; it was the people's birthright and privilege in time of parliament, it was the breaking forth of light.

But now, the bishops abrogated and voided out of the church, as if our reformation sought no more but to make room for others into their seats under another name, the episcopal arts begin to bud again; the cruse[9] of truth must run no more oil; liberty of printing must be enthralled again under a prelatical commission of twenty, the privilege of the people nullified; and, which is worse, the freedom of learning must groan again, and to her old fetters: all this the parliament yet sitting. Although their own late arguments and defenses against the prelates might remember them that this obstructing violence meets for the most part with an event utterly opposite to the end which it drives at; instead of suppressing sects and schisms, it raises them and invests them with a reputation: "The punishing of wits enhances their authority," saith the Viscount St. Albans,[1] "and a forbidden writing is thought to be a certain spark of truth that flies up in the faces of them who seek to tread it out."

This Order, therefore, may prove a nursing mother to sects, but I shall easily show how it will be a stepdame to Truth; and first by disenabling us to the maintenance of what is known already.

Well knows he who uses to consider, that our faith and knowledge thrives by exercise, as well as our limbs and complexion. Truth is compared in scripture to a streaming fountain;[2] if her waters flow not in a perpetual progression, they sicken into a muddy pool of conformity and tradition. A man may be a heretic in the truth;

8. Mean-spirited, cowardly.
9. Small vessel; see 1 Kings 17.12–16.
1. Sir Francis Bacon, *An Advertisement Touching the Controversies of the Church of England*.
2. See Psalms 85.11.

and if he believe things only because his pastor says so, or the Assembly so determines, without knowing other reason, though his belief be true, yet the very truth he holds becomes his heresy. There is not any burden that some would gladlier post off to another than the charge and care of their religion. There be, who knows not that there be, of protestants and professors who live and die in as arrant an implicit faith, as any lay papist of Loreto.[3]

A wealthy man addicted to his pleasure and to his profits, finds religion to be a traffic so entangled, and of so many piddling accounts, that of all mysteries[4] he cannot skill to keep a stock going upon that trade. What should he do? Fain he would have the name to be religious, fain he would bear up with his neighbors in that. What does he, therefore, but resolves to give over toiling, and to find himself out some factor to whose care and credit he may commit the whole managing of his religious affairs; some Divine of note and estimation that must be. To him he adheres, resigns the whole warehouse of his religion with all the locks and keys into his custody; and indeed makes the very person of that man his religion; esteems his associating with him a sufficient evidence and commendatory of his own piety. So that a man may say his religion is now no more within himself, but is become a dividual movable,[5] and goes and comes near him, according as that good man frequents the house. He entertains him, gives him gifts, feasts him, lodges him. His religion comes home at night, prays, is liberally supped, and sumptuously laid to sleep, rises, is saluted, and after the malmsey, or some well spiced brewage, and better breakfasted than he[6] whose morning appetite would have gladly fed on green figs between Bethany and Jerusalem, his religion walks abroad at eight, and leaves his kind entertainer in the shop trading all day without his religion.

Another sort there be, who, when they hear that all things shall be ordered, all things regulated and settled, nothing written but what passes through the customhouse of certain publicans[7] that have the tonnaging and the poundaging of all freespoken truth, will straight give themselves up into your hands, make 'em and cut 'em out what religion ye please. There be delights, there be recreations and jolly pastimes that will fetch the day about from sun to sun, and rock the tedious year as in a delightful dream. What need they torture their heads with that which others have taken so strictly and so unalterably into their own purveying? These are the fruits which a dull ease and cessation of our knowledge will bring forth among the people. How goodly, and how to be wished, were such an obedient unanimity as this, what a fine conformity would it starch us all into! Doubtless a staunch and solid piece of framework, as any January could freeze together.[8]

* * *

Truth indeed came once into the world with her divine Master, and was a perfect shape most glorious to look on. But when he ascended, and his apostles after him were laid asleep, then straight arose a wicked race of deceivers, who, as that story goes of the Egyptian Typhon with his conspirators, how they dealt with the

3. Professors: those who profess religion; Loreto: a Catholic shrine supposed to have been transported to Italy from the Holy Land.
4. Trades, crafts.
5. A separate piece of property.
6. For this description of Christ, see Mark 11.12–14.
7. Tax collectors.
8. Milton goes on to argue that censorship will make the clergy lazy and will hinder the Reformation's goal of seeking truth.

good Osiris, took the virgin Truth, hewed her lovely form into a thousand pieces, and scattered them to the four winds.[9] From that time ever since, the sad friends of Truth, such as durst appear, imitating the careful search that Isis made for the mangled body of Osiris, went up and down gathering up limb by limb still as they could find them. We have not yet found them all, Lords and Commons, nor ever shall do, till her Master's second coming. He shall bring together every joint and member, and shall mold them into an immortal feature of loveliness and perfection. Suffer not these licensing prohibitions to stand at every place of opportunity, forbidding and disturbing them that continue seeking, that continue to do our obsequies to the torn body of our martyred saint.

We boast our light; but if we look not wisely on the sun itself, it smites us into darkness. Who can discern those planets that are oft combust, and those stars of brightest magnitude that rise and set with the sun, until the opposite motion of their orbs bring them to such a place in the firmament, where they may be seen evening or morning. The light which we have gained, was given us, not to be ever staring on, but by it to discover onward things more remote from our knowledge. It is not the unfrocking of a priest, the unmitering of a bishop, and the removing him from off the Presbyterian shoulders that will make us a happy nation; no, if other things as great in the church, and in the rule of life both economical and political, be not looked into and reformed, we have looked so long upon the blaze that Zwinglius[1] and Calvin hath beaconed up to us, that we are stark blind.

There be who perpetually complain of schisms and sects, and make it such a calamity that any man dissents from their maxims. It is their own pride and ignorance which causes the disturbing, who neither will hear with meekness, nor can convince, yet all must be suppressed which is not found in their syntagma.[2] They are the troublers, they are the dividers of unity, who neglect and permit not others to unite those dissevered pieces which are yet wanting to the body of Truth. To be still searching what we know not by what we know, still closing up truth to truth as we find it (for all her body is homogeneal[3] and proportional), this is the golden rule in theology as well as in arithmetic, and makes up the best harmony in a church; not the forced and outward union of cold and neutral and inwardly divided minds.

Lords and Commons of England, consider what nation it is whereof ye are, and whereof ye are the governors; a nation not slow and dull, but of a quick, ingenious, and piercing spirit, acute to invent, subtle and sinewy to discourse, not beneath the reach of any point the highest that human capacity can soar to. Therefore the studies of learning in her deepest sciences have been so ancient and so eminent among us that writers of good antiquity and ablest judgment have been persuaded that even the school of Pythagoras and the Persian wisdom took beginning from the old philosophy of this island.[4] And that wise and civil Roman, Julius Agricola, who governed once here for Caesar, preferred the natural wits of Britain before the labored studies of the

9. Typhon tore apart and scattered Osiris' body, and his wife Isis and son Horus collected it. The interpretation here is based on Plutarch's allegory in *Isis and Osiris*.

1. Ulrich Zwingli (1484–1531), the Protestant reformer of Zurich.

2. Systematic doctrinal treatise.

3. Homogeneous.

4. For the connection between the Druids and Zoroastrian and Pythagorean philosophy, see Pliny, *Natural History* 30.2.

French.[5] Nor is it for nothing that the grave and frugal Transylvanian[6] sends out yearly from as far as the mountainous borders of Russia and beyond the Hercynian wilderness,[7] not their youth, but their staid men to learn our language and our theologic arts.

Yet that which is above all this, the favor and the love of Heaven, we have great argument to think in a peculiar manner propitious and propending towards us. Why else was this nation chosen before any other, that out of her as out of Sion should be proclaimed and sounded forth the first tidings and trumpet of reformation to all Europe? And had it not been the obstinate perverseness of our prelates against the divine and admirable spirit of Wycliffe[8] to suppress him as a schismatic and innovator, perhaps neither the Bohemian Huss and Jerome,[9] no, nor the name of Luther, or of Calvin, had been ever known; the glory of reforming all our neighbors had been completely ours. But now, as our obdurate clergy have with violence demeaned the matter, we are become hitherto the latest and the backwardest scholars of whom God offered to have made us the teachers.

Now once again by all concurrence of signs, and by the general instinct of holy and devout men, as they daily and solemnly express their thoughts, God is decreeing to begin some new and great period in his Church, even to the reforming of reformation itself. What does he then but reveal himself to his servants, and, as his manner is, first to his Englishmen? I say as his manner is, first to us, though we mark not the method of his counsels and are unworthy. Behold now this vast city, a city of refuge, the mansion house of liberty, encompassed and surrounded with his protection. The shop of war hath not there more anvils and hammers waking, to fashion out the plates and instruments of armed justice in defense of beleaguered Truth, than there be pens and heads there, sitting by their studious lamps, musing, searching, revolving new notions and ideas wherewith to present, as with their homage and their fealty, the approaching reformation; others as fast reading, trying all things, assenting to the force of reason and convincement.

What could a man require more from a nation so pliant and so prone to seek after knowledge? What wants there to such a towardly[1] and pregnant soul but wise and faithful laborers to make a knowing people, a nation of prophets, of sages, and of worthies? We reckon more than five months yet to harvest; there need not be five weeks, had we but eyes to lift up; the fields are white already. Where there is much desire to learn, there of necessity will be much arguing, much writing, many opinions; for opinion in good men is but knowledge in the making. Under these fantastic terrors of sect and schism, we wrong the earnest and zealous thirst after knowledge and understanding which God hath stirred up in this city.

What some lament of, we rather should rejoice at, should rather praise this pious forwardness among men, to reassume the ill-deputed care of their religion into their own hands again. A little generous prudence, a little forbearance of one another, and some grain of charity might win all these diligences to join and unite into one general

5. See Tacitus, *Agricola* 21.

6. Seventeenth-century Transylvania was Protestant and independent.

7. South-central Germany.

8. English Protestants viewed John Wyclif (1320?–1384) as the initiator of the Reformation in England.

9. Jerome of Prague (c. 1365–1416), a disciple of Wycliff, and John Huss of Bohemia (1373–1415).

1. Promising.

and brotherly search after truth; could we but forego this prelatical tradition of crowding free consciences and Christian liberties into canons and precepts of men. I doubt not, if some great and worthy stranger should come among us, wise to discern the mold and temper of a people, and how to govern it, observing the high hopes and aims, the diligent alacrity of our extended thoughts and reasonings in the pursuance of truth and freedom, but that he would cry out as Pyrrhus did, admiring the Roman docility and courage, "If such were my Epirots, I would not despair the greatest design that could be attempted to make a church or kingdom happy."[2]

Yet these are the men cried out against for schismatics and sectaries;[3] as if, while the temple of the Lord was building, some cutting, some squaring the marble, others hewing the cedars, there should be a sort of irrational men who could not consider there must be many schisms and many dissections made in the quarry and in the timber, ere the house of God can be built. And when every stone is laid artfully together, it cannot be united into a continuity, it can but be contiguous in this world; neither can every piece of the building be of one form; nay rather the perfection consists in this, that out of many moderate varieties and brotherly dissimilitudes that are not vastly disproportional, arises the goodly and the graceful symmetry that commends the whole pile and structure.

Let us, therefore, be more considerate builders, more wise in spiritual architecture, when great reformation is expected. For now the time seems come, wherein Moses, the great prophet, may sit in heaven rejoicing to see that memorable and glorious wish of his fulfilled, when not only our seventy elders, but all the Lord's people, are become prophets.

* * *

Methinks I see in my mind a noble and puissant nation rousing herself like a strong man after sleep, and shaking her invincible locks. Methinks I see her as an eagle muing[4] her mighty youth, and kindling her undazzled eyes at the full midday beam; purging and unscaling her long-abused sight at the fountain itself of heavenly radiance; while the whole noise of timorous and flocking birds, with those also that love the twilight, flutter about, amazed at what she means, and in their envious gabble would prognosticate a year of sects and schisms.

What should ye do then, should ye suppress all this flowery crop of knowledge and new light sprung up and yet springing daily in this city? Should ye set an oligarchy of twenty engrossers[5] over it, to bring a famine upon our minds again, when we shall know nothing but what is measured to us by their bushel? Believe it, Lords and Commons, they who counsel ye to such a suppressing, do as good as bid ye suppress yourselves; and I will soon show how.

* * *

And now the time in special is, by privilege, to write and speak what may help to the further discussing of matters in agitation. The temple of Janus with his two controversal faces might now not unsignificantly be set open.[6] And though all the winds of doctrine were let loose to play upon the earth, so Truth be in the field, we do injuriously by licensing and prohibiting to misdoubt her strength. Let her and Falsehood grapple; who ever knew Truth put to the worse, in a free and open encounter. Her confuting is the best and surest suppressing. He who hears what praying there is for

2. King Pyrrhus of Epirus defeated the Romans at Herecla in 280 B.C.E.
3. Dividers of the church.
4. Renewing.
5. Monopolists.
6. The Roman god Janus's head had two faces looking in opposite directions. During times of war, the gates of Janus were open.

light and clearer knowledge to be sent down among us, would think of other matters to be constituted beyond the discipline of Geneva, framed and fabriced already to our hands.[7]

Yet when the new light which we beg for shines in upon us, there be who envy and oppose, if it come not first in at their casements. What a collusion[8] is this, whenas we are exhorted by the wise man to use diligence, to seek for wisdom as for hidden treasures[9] early and late, that another order shall enjoin us to know nothing but by statute. When a man hath been laboring the hardest labor in the deep mines of knowledge, hath furnished out his findings in all their equipage, drawn forth his reasons as it were a battle ranged, scattered and defeated all objections in his way, calls out his adversary into the plain, offers him the advantage of wind and sun, if he please, only that he may try the matter by dint of argument; for his opponents then to skulk, to lay ambushments, to keep a narrow bridge of licensing where the challenger should pass, though it be valor enough in soldiership, is but weakness and cowardice in the wars of Truth.

For who knows not that Truth is strong, next to the Almighty. She needs no policies, nor stratagems, nor licensings to make her victorious—those are the shifts and the defenses that error uses against her power. Give her but room, and do not bind her when she sleeps, for then she speaks not true, as the old Proteus did, who spake oracles only when he was caught and bound,[1] but then rather she turns herself into all shapes except her own, and perhaps tunes her voice according to the time, as Micaiah did before Ahab,[2] until she be adjured into her own likeness.

Yet is it not impossible that she may have more shapes than one. What else is all that rank of things indifferent, wherein Truth may be on this side, or on the other, without being unlike herself? What but a vain shadow else is the abolition of those ordinances, that handwriting nailed to the cross;[3] what great purchase is this Christian liberty which Paul so often boasts of? His doctrine is, that he who eats, or eats not, regards a day, or regards it not, may do either to the Lord.[4] How many other things might be tolerated in peace and left to conscience, had we but charity, and were it not the chief stronghold of our hypocrisy to be ever judging one another. I fear yet this iron yoke of outward conformity hath left a slavish print upon our necks; the ghost of a linen decency[5] yet haunts us. We stumble and are impatient at the least dividing of one visible congregation from another, though it be not in fundamentals; and through our forwardness to suppress, and our backwardness to recover any enthralled piece of truth out of the gripe of custom, we care not to keep truth separated from truth, which is the fiercest rent and disunion of all. We do not see that while we still affect by all means a rigid external formality, we may as soon fall again into a gross conforming stupidity, a stark and dead congealment of "wood, and hay, and stubble"[6] forced and frozen together, which is more to the sudden degenerating of a church than many subdichotomies[7] of petty schisms.

Not that I can think well of every light separation, or that all in a church is to be expected "gold and silver and precious stones."[8] It is not possible for man to sever

7. Discipline of Geneva: Calvinism; fabriced: fabricated.
8. Secret agreement for purposes of trickery; ambiguity in words or reasoning.
9. The wise man is Solomon; see Proverbs 8.11 and Matthew 13.44.
1. The story of Proteus is in *Odyssey* 384–93.
2. 1 Kings 22.
3. Colossians 2.14.
4. Romans 14.1–13.
5. A reference to the controversy over ecclesiastical vestments.
6. See 1 Corinthians 3.12.
7. Inconsequential divisions.
8. 1 Corinthians 3.12.

the wheat from the tares, the good fish from the other fry; that must be the angels' ministry at the end of mortal things.[9] Yet if all cannot be of one mind,—as who looks they should be?—this doubtless is more wholesome, more prudent, and more Christian, that many be tolerated, rather than all compelled. I mean not tolerated popery and open superstition, which, as it extirpates all religions and civil supremacies, so itself should be extirpate, provided first that all charitable and compassionate means be used to win and regain the weak and the misled; that also which is impious or evil absolutely, either against faith or manners, no law can possibly permit, that intends not to unlaw itself; but those neighboring differences, or rather indifferences, are what I speak of, whether in some point of doctrine or of discipline, which though they may be many, yet need not interrupt "the unity of spirit," if we could but find among us the "bond of peace."[1]

In the meanwhile, if any one would write and bring his helpful hand to the slow-moving reformation which we labor under, if truth have spoken to him before others, or but seemed at least to speak, who hath so bejesuited us that we should trouble that man with asking license to do so worthy a deed? And not consider this, that if it come to prohibiting, there is not aught more likely to be prohibited than truth itself; whose first appearance to our eyes bleared and dimmed with prejudice and custom, is more unsightly and unplausible than many errors, even as the person is of many a great man slight and contemptible to see to. And what do they tell us vainly of new opinions, when this very opinion of theirs, that none must be heard but whom they like, is the worst and newest opinion of all others; and is the chief cause why sects and schisms do so much abound, and true knowledge is kept at distance from us; besides yet a greater danger which is in it. For when God shakes a kingdom with strong and healthful commotions to a general reforming, it is not untrue that many sectaries and false teachers are then busiest in seducing; but yet more true it is that God then raises to his own work men of rare abilities and more than common industry, not only to look back and revise what hath been taught heretofore, but to gain further and go on some new enlightened steps in the discovery of truth.

Paradise Lost *Paradise Lost* is about devastating loss attended by redemption. The reader's knowledge of the Fall creates a sense of tragic inevitability. And Satan, no less than Adam and Eve, appears in all the psychological complexity and verbal grandeur of a tragic hero. Indeed, there is even a manuscript in which Milton outlined the story as a tragedy. In that version, "Lucifer's contriving Adam's ruin" is Act 3. Following epic tradition, Milton places this part of the action at the forefront of his poem, beginning *in medias res*.

So powerful is Milton's opening portrayal of Satan that the Romantic poets thought Satan was the hero of the poem. Focusing on the first two books, the romantic reading sees him as a dynamic rebel. From a Renaissance point of view, Satan is more like an Elizabethan hero-villain, with his many soliloquies and his tortured psychology of brilliance twisted toward evil. Only in Book 9, however, does Milton say, "I now must change these notes to tragic," thereby signaling that he is about to narrate the fall of Adam and Eve. From this point on, the poem follows Adam and Eve's tragic movement from sin to despair to the recognition of sin and the need for repentance. Adam and Eve's learning through suffering and the prophecy of the Son's redemption of sin make this a story of gain as well as loss, on the order of Acschylean tragedy.

Like all epics, *Paradise Lost* is encyclopedic, combining many different genres. To read this poem is to have an education in everything from literary history to astronomy. Milton draws on a

9. Matthew 13.24.

1. Ephesians 4.3.

vast wealth of reading, with the Bible as his main source—not only Genesis, but also Exodus, the Prophets, Revelation, Saint Paul, and especially the Psalms, which he had translated. Milton also makes great use of biblical commentary from rabbinical, patristic, and contemporary sources. Early on, Milton had envisaged a poem about the Arthurian legend, and his choice of the non-martial, seemingly unheroic biblical story of Adam and Eve marks a bold departure from epic tradition. While Spenser's *Faerie Queene* is Milton's most important vernacular model, among epic poets his closest affinity is with Virgil and Dante, both of whom had written of the underworld; Dante especially devoted himself to humanity's free choice of sin. Like Dante, Milton creates his poem as a microcosm of the natural universe. His ideal vision of the world before the Fall is one where day and night are equal and the sun is always in the same sign of the zodiac, an image that embodies in poetic astronomy the world of simplicity and perfection that humans have lost through sin. Milton does not choose between the earth-centered Ptolemaic and the heliocentric Copernican systems but presents both as alternative explanations for the order of the universe.

Although we know nothing about the order in which the parts of the poem were composed, we do know that Milton typically composed at night or in the early morning. Sometimes he lay awake unable to write a line; at others he was seized "with a certain impetus and *oestro*" [frenzy]. He would dictate forty lines from memory and then reduce them to half that number. According to his nephew, the poem was written from 1658 to 1663.

The one extant manuscript of the poem, which contains the first book, reveals that Milton revised for punctuation and spelling. There were two editions in Milton's lifetime, both printed by Samuel Simmons. The first edition, *Paradise Lost: A poem in ten books*, was printed in six different issues in 1667, 1668, and 1669. From the fourth issue of the poem on, such paratexts as "The Printer to Reader," "The Argument" (which stood altogether), and Milton's note on the verse appear. With the second octave edition of 1674, Milton divided Books 7 and 10 into two books each to create twelve books in all. Prefaced by dedicatory Latin verses, one of which was by his old friend Andrew Marvell, this 1674 edition, which appeared in the year of Milton's death, is the basis for the present text.

Paradise Lost[1]
Book 1
The Argument

This first Book proposes, first in brief, the whole Subject, *Man's disobedience, and the loss thereupon of Paradise wherein he was plac't:* Then touches *the prime cause of his fall, the Serpent, or rather* Satan *in the Serpent; who revolting from God, and drawing to his side many Legions of Angels, was by the command of God driven out of Heaven with all his Crew into the great Deep.* Which action past over, the Poem hastes into the midst of things,[2] presenting *Satan with his Angels now fallen into Hell*, describ'd here, *not in the Centre* (for Heaven and Earth may be suppos'd as yet not made, certainly not yet accurst) *but in a place of utter darkness, fitliest call'd* Chaos: *Here Satan with his Angels lying on the burning Lake, thunder-struck and astonisht, after a certain space recovers, as from confusion, calls up him who next in Order and Dignity lay by him; they confer of thir miserable fall.* Satan *awakens all his Legions, who lay till then in the same manner confounded; They rise, thir Numbers, array of Battle, thir chief Leaders nam'd, according to the Idols known afterwards in* Canaan *and the Countries adjoining. To these Satan directs his Speech,*

1. Our text is taken from Merritt Y. Hughes, ed., *John Milton Complete Poems and Major Prose*, and the notes are adapted from Alastair Fowler, ed., *Paradise Lost*.

2. Following Horace's rule that the epic should plunge "*in medias res*."

comforts them with hope yet of regaining Heaven but tells them lastly of a new World and new kind of Creature to be created, according to an ancient Prophecy or report in Heaven; for that Angels were long before this visible Creation, was the opinion of many ancient Fathers. *To find out the truth of this Prophecy, and what to determine thereon he refers to a full Council. What his Associates thence attempt.* Pandemonium *the Palace of* Satan *rises, suddenly built out of the Deep: The infernal Peers there sit in Council.*

Of Man's First Disobedience, and the Fruit
Of that Forbidden Tree, whose mortal[3] taste
Brought Death into the World, and all our woe,[4]
With loss of *Eden*, till one greater Man[5]
Restore us, and regain the blissful Seat,
Sing Heav'nly Muse,[6] that on the secret top
Of *Oreb*, or of *Sinai*, didst inspire
That Shepherd, who first taught the chosen Seed,[7]
In the Beginning how the Heav'ns and Earth
Rose out of *Chaos:* Or if *Sion* Hill[8]
Delight thee more, and *Siloa's* Brook[9] that flow'd
Fast° by the Oracle of God; I thence *close*
Invoke thy aid to my advent'rous Song,
That with no middle flight intends to soar
Above th' *Aonian* Mount,[1] while it pursues
Things unattempted yet in Prose or Rhyme.[2]
And chiefly Thou O Spirit, that dost prefer
Before all Temples th' upright heart and pure,[3]
Instruct me, for Thou know'st; Thou from the first
Wast present, and with mighty wings outspread
Dove-like satst brooding on the vast Abyss
And mad'st it pregnant:[4] What in me is dark
Illumine, what is low raise and support;
That to the highth of this great Argument° *theme*
I may assert Eternal Providence,
And justify[5] the ways of God to man.

3. "Death-bringing" (Latin *mortalis*) but also "to mortals."
4. This definition of the first sin follows Calvin's Catechism.
5. Christ, in Pauline theology the second Adam (see Romans 5.19). The people and events referred to in these lines have a typological connection, i.e., the Christian interpretation of the Old Testament as a prefiguration of the New.
6. Rhetorically, lines 1–49 are the *invocatio*, consisting of an address to the Muse, and the *principium* that states the whole scope of the poem's action. The "Heavenly Muse," later addressed as the muse of astronomy Urania (7.1), is here identified with the Holy Spirit of the Bible, which inspires Moses.
7. The "Shepherd" is Moses, who was granted the vision of the burning bush on Mount Oreb (Exodus 3) and received the Law, either on Mount Oreb (Deuteronomy 4.10) or on its lower part, Mount Sinai (Exodus 19.20). Moses, the first Jewish writer, taught "the chosen seed," the children of Israel, about the beginning of the world in Genesis.
8. The sanctuary, a place of ceremonial song but also (Isaiah 2.3) of oracular pronouncements.
9. A spring immediately west of Mount Zion and beside Calvary, often used as a symbol of the operation of the Holy Ghost.
1. Helicon, sacred to the Muses.
2. Ironically translating Ariosto's boast in the invocation to *Orlando Furioso*.
3. The Spirit is the voice of God, which inspired the Hebrew prophets.
4. Identifying the Spirit present at the creation (Genesis 1.2) with the Spirit in the form of a dove that descended on Jesus at the beginning of his ministry (John 1.32). Vast: large; deserted (Latin *vastus*).
5. Does not mean merely "demonstrate logically" but has its biblical meaning and implies spiritual rather than rational understanding.

Say first, for Heav'n hides nothing from thy view
Nor the deep Tract of Hell, say first what cause
Mov'd our Grand[6] Parents in that happy State,
Favor'd of Heav'n so highly, to fall off
From thir Creator, and transgress his Will
For° one restraint, Lords of the World besides?° *because of / otherwise*
Who first seduc'd them to that foul revolt?
Th' infernal Serpent;[7] hee it was, whose guile
Stirr'd up with Envy and Revenge, deceiv'd
The Mother of Mankind; what time his Pride
Had cast him out from Heav'n, with all his Host
Of Rebel Angels, by whose aid aspiring
To set himself in Glory above his Peers,
He trusted to have equall'd the most High,[8]
If he oppos'd; and with ambitious aim
Against the Throne and Monarchy of God
Rais'd impious War in Heav'n and Battle proud
With vain attempt. Him the Almighty Power
Hurl'd headlong flaming from th' Ethereal Sky[9]
With hideous ruin and combustion down
To bottomless perdition, there to dwell
In Adamantine Chains[1] and penal Fire,
Who durst defy th' Omnipotent to Arms.
Nine times the Space that measures Day and Night[2]
To mortal men, hee with his horrid crew
Lay vanquisht, rolling in the fiery Gulf
Confounded though immortal: But his doom
Reserv'd him to more wrath; for now the thought
Both of lost happiness and lasting pain
Torments him; round he throws his baleful° eyes *evil, suffering*
That witness'd huge affliction and dismay
Mixt with obdúrate° pride and steadfast hate: *unyielding*
At once as far as Angels' ken° he views *power of vision*
The dismal° Situation waste and wild, *dreadful, sinister*
A Dungeon horrible, on all sides round
As one great Furnace flam'd, yet from those flames
No light, but rather darkness visible
Serv'd only to discover sights of woe,[3]
Regions of sorrow, doleful shades, where peace

6. Implies not only greatness, but also inclusiveness of generality or parentage.
7. "That old serpent, called the Devil, and Satan" (Revelation 12.9) both because Satan entered the body of a serpent to tempt Eve and because his nature is guileful and dangerous to humans.
8. Satan's crime was not his aspiring "above his peers" but aspiring "To set himself in [divine] Glory." Numerous verbal echoes relate lines 40–48 to the biblical accounts of the fall and binding of Lucifer, in 2 Peter 2.4, Revelation 20.1–2, and Isaiah 14.12–15: "Thou hast said . . . I will exalt my throne above the stars of God . . . I will be like the most High. Yet thou shalt be brought down to hell."
9. Mingling an allusion to Luke 10.18, "I beheld Satan as lightning fall from heaven," with one to Homer, *Iliad* 1.591, Hephaistos "hurled from the ethereal threshold."
1. 2 Peter 2.4; "God spared not the angels that sinned, but . . . delivered them into chains of darkness."
2. The devils fall for the same number of days that the Titans fall from heaven when overthrown by the Olympian gods (see Hesiod, *Theogony* 664–735).
3. See the account of the land of the dead in Job 10.22: "the light is as darkness."

And rest can never dwell, hope never comes
That comes to all;[4] but torture without end
Still urges,° and a fiery Deluge, fed *presses*
With ever-burning Sulphur unconsum'd:
Such place Eternal Justice had prepar'd
For those rebellious, here thir Prison ordained
In utter° darkness, and thir portion set *complete, outer*
As far remov'd from God and light of Heav'n
As from the Center thrice to th' utmost Pole.[5]
O how unlike the place from whence they fell!
There the companions of his fall, o'erwhelm'd
With Floods and Whirlwinds of tempestuous fire,
He soon discerns, and welt'ring by his side
One next himself in power, and next in crime,
Long after known in *Palestine*, and nam'd
Beëlzebub.[6] To whom th' Arch-Enemy,
And thence in Heav'n call'd Satan,[7] with bold words
Breaking the horrid silence thus began.[8]
 If thou beest hee; But O how fall'n! how chang'd
From him, who in the happy Realms of Light
Cloth'd with transcendent brightness didst outshine
Myriads though bright:[9] If he whom mutual league,
United thoughts and counsels, equal hope,
And hazard in the Glorious Enterprise,
Join'd with me once, now misery hath join'd
In equal ruin: into what Pit thou seest
From what highth fall'n, so much the stronger prov'd
He with his Thunder: and till then who knew
The force of those dire Arms? yet not for those,
Nor what the Potent Victor in his rage
Can else inflict, do I repent or change,
Though chang'd in outward luster; that fixt mind
And high disdain, from sense of injur'd merit,
That with the mightiest rais'd me to contend,
And to the fierce contention brought along
Innumerable force of Spirits arm'd
That durst dislike his reign, and mee preferring,
His utmost power with adverse power oppos'd
In dubious Battle on the Plains of Heav'n,

4. The phrase echoes Dante's *Inferno:* III.9 "All hope abandon, ye who enter here."

5. Milton refers to the Ptolemaic universe in which the earth is at the center of ten concentric spheres. Milton draws attention to the numerical proportion, heaven-earth:earth-hell—i.e., earth divides the interval between heaven and hell in the proportion that Neoplatonists believed should be maintained between reason and concupiscence.

6. Hebrew, "Lord of the flies"; Matthew 12.24, "the prince of the devils."

7. Hebrew, "enemy." After his rebellion, Satan's "former name" (Lucifer) was no longer used (5.658).

8. Rhetorically, the opening of the action proper. The 41-line speech beginning here, the first speech in the book, exactly balances the last, which also is spoken by Satan and also consists of 41 lines (1.622–62).

9. The break in grammatical concord (between "him" and "didst") reflects Satan's doubt whether Beelzebub is present and so whether second-person forms are appropriate.

And shook his throne.[1] What though the field be lost?
All is not lost; the unconquerable Will,
And study° of revenge, immortal hate, *pursuit*
And courage never to submit or yield:
And what is else not to be overcome?
That Glory[2] never shall his wrath or might
Extort from me. To bow and sue for grace
With suppliant knee, and deify his power
Who from the terror of this Arm so late
Doubted° his Empire, that were low indeed, *feared for*
That were an ignominy and shame beneath
This downfall; since by Fate the strength of Gods
And this Empyreal substance cannot fail,[3]
Since through experience of this great event
In Arms not worse, in foresight much advanc't,
We may with more successful hope resolve
To wage by force or guile eternal War
Irreconcilable to our grand Foe,
Who now triúmphs, and in th' excess of joy
Sole reigning holds the Tyranny of Heav'n.[4]
So spake th' Apostate Angel, though in pain,
Vaunting aloud, but rackt with deep despair:
And him thus answer'd soon his bold Compeer.° *comrade*
O Prince, O Chief of many Throned Powers,
That led th' imbattl'd Seraphim[5] to War
Under thy conduct, and in dreadful deeds
Fearless, endanger'd Heav'n's perpetual King;
And put to proof his high Supremacy,
Whether upheld by strength, or Chance, or Fate;[6]
Too well I see and rue the dire event,
That with sad overthrow and foul defeat
Hath lost us Heav'n, and all this mighty Host
In horrible destruction laid thus low,
As far as Gods and Heav'nly Essences
Can perish: for the mind and spirit remains
Invincible, and vigor soon returns,
Though all our Glory extinct, and happy state
Here swallow'd up in endless misery.
But what if he our Conqueror (whom I now
Of force° believe Almighty, since no less *necessarily*
Than such could have o'erpow'rd such force as ours)

1. The Son's chariot, not Satan's armies, shakes heaven to its foundations, as we learn in Book 6. Throughout the present passage, Satan sees himself as the hero of a pagan epic.

2. Either "the glory of overcoming me" or "my glory of will."

3. Implying not only that as angels they are immortal, but also that the continuance of their strength is assured by fate.

4. An obvious instance of the devil's bias.

5. The traditional nine orders of angels are seraphim, cherubim, thrones, dominions, virtues, powers, principalities, archangels, and angels, but Milton does not use these terms systematically.

6. The main powers recognized in the devils' ideology. God's power rests on a quality that does not occur to Beelzebub: goodness.

Have left us this our spirit and strength entire
Strongly to suffer and support our pains,
That we may so suffice° his vengeful ire, *satisfy*
Or do him mightier service as his thralls
By right of War, whate'er his business be
Here in the heart of Hell to work in Fire,
Or do his Errands in the gloomy Deep;
What can it then avail though yet we feel
Strength undiminisht, or eternal being
To undergo eternal punishment?[7]
Whereto with speedy words th' Arch-fiend repli'd.
  Fall'n Cherub, to be weak is miserable
Doing or Suffering: but of this be sure,
To do aught good never will be our task,
But ever to do ill our sole delight,
As being the contrary to his high will
Whom we resist.[8] If then his Providence
Out of our evil seek to bring forth good,
Our labor must be to pervert that end,
And out of good still to find means of evil;
Which oft-times may succeed, so as perhaps
Shall grieve him, if I fail not, and disturb
His inmost counsels from thir destin'd aim.
But see the angry Victor hath recall'd
His Ministers of vengeance and pursuit
Back to the Gates of Heav'n: the Sulphurous Hail
Shot after us in storm, o'erblown hath laid° *subdued*
The fiery Surge, that from the Precipice
Of Heav'n receiv'd us falling, and the Thunder,
Wing'd with red Lightning and impetuous rage,
Perhaps hath spent his shafts, and ceases now
To bellow through the vast and boundless Deep.
Let us not slip° th' occasion, whether scorn, *lose*
Or satiate fury yield it from our Foe.
Seest thou yon dreary Plain, forlorn and wild,
The seat of desolation, void of light,
Save what the glimmering of these livid flames
Casts pale and dreadful? Thither let us tend
From off the tossing of these fiery waves,
There rest, if any rest can harbor there,
And reassembling our afflicted° Powers, *downcast*
Consult how we may henceforth most offend° *harm*
Our Enemy, our own loss how repair,
How overcome this dire Calamity,

7. Existing eternally, merely so that our punishment may also be eternal.

8. This fundamental disobedience and disorientation make Satan's heroic virtue into the corresponding excess of vice. Lines 163–65 look forward to 12.470–78 and Adam's wonder at the astonishing reversal whereby God will turn the Fall into an occasion for good.

What reinforcement we may gain from Hope,
If not what resolution from despair.
  Thus Satan talking to his nearest Mate
With Head up-lift above the wave, and Eyes
That sparkling blaz'd, his other Parts besides
Prone on the Flood, extended long and large
Lay floating many a rood,° in bulk as huge *six to eight yards*
As whom the Fables name of monstrous size,
Titanian, or *Earth-born*, that warr'd on *Jove*,
Briareos or *Typhon*,[9] whom the Den
By ancient *Tarsus*[1] held, or that Sea-beast
Leviathan,[2] which God of all his works
Created hugest that swim th' Ocean stream:
Him haply slumb'ring on the *Norway* foam
The Pilot of some small night-founder'd° Skiff, *sunk in night*
Deeming some Island, oft, as Seamen tell,
With fixed Anchor in his scaly rind
Moors by his side under the Lee, while Night
Invests° the Sea, and wished Morn delays: *wraps*
So stretcht out huge in length the Arch-fiend lay
Chain'd on the burning Lake, nor ever thence
Had ris'n or heav'd his head, but that the will
And high permission of all-ruling Heaven
Left him at large to his own dark designs,
That with reiterated crimes he might
Heap on himself damnation, while he sought
Evil to others, and enrag'd might see
How all his malice serv'd but to bring forth
Infinite goodness, grace and mercy shown
On Man by him seduc't, but on himself
Treble confusion, wrath and vengeance pour'd.
Forthwith upright he rears from off the Pool
His mighty Stature; on each hand the flames
Driv'n backward slope thir pointing spires, and roll'd
In billows, leave i' th' midst a horrid° Vale. *bristling*
Then with expanded wings he steers his flight
Aloft, incumbent[3] on the dusky Air
That felt unusual weight, till on dry Land
He lights, if it were Land that ever burn'd
With solid, as the Lake with liquid fire
And such appear'd in hue;[4] as when the force

9. The serpent-legged *Briareos* was a Titan, the serpent-headed *Typhon* (Typhoeus) a Giant. Each was a son of Earth; each fought against Jupiter; and each was eventually confined beneath Aetna (see lines 232–37). Typhon was so powerful that when he first made war on the Olympians, they had to resort to metamorphoses to escape (Ovid, *Metamorphoses* 5.325–31 and 346–58).

1. The biblical Tarsus was the capital of Cilicia, and both Pindar and Aeschylus describe Typhon's habitat as a Cilician cave or "den."

2. The monster of Job 41, identified in Isaiah's prophecy of judgment as "the crooked serpent" (Isaiah 27.1) but also sometimes thought of as a whale.

3. Pressing with his weight.

4. In the 17th century, "hue" referred to surface appearance and texture as well as color.

Of subterranean wind transports a Hill
Torn from *Pelorus*,[5] or the shatter'd side
Of thund'ring *Etna*, whose combustible
And fuell'd entrails thence conceiving Fire,
Sublim'd[6] with Mineral fury,[7] aid the Winds,
And leave a singed bottom all involv'd° *wreathed*
With stench and smoke: Such resting found the sole
Of unblest feet. Him follow'd his next Mate,
Both glorying to have scap't the *Stygian*[8] flood
As Gods, and by thir own recover'd strength,
Not by the sufferance of supernal Power.
Is this the Region, this the Soil, the Clime,
Said then the lost Arch-Angel, this the seat
That we must change° for Heav'n, this mournful gloom *exchange*
For that celestial light? Be it so, since he
Who now is Sovran can dispose and bid
What shall be right: fardest° from him is best *farthest*
Whom reason hath equall'd, force hath made supreme
Above his equals. Farewell happy Fields
Where Joy for ever dwells: Hail horrors, hail
Infernal world, and thou profoundest Hell
Receive thy new Possessor: One who brings
A mind not to be chang'd by Place or Time.
The mind is its own place, and in itself
Can make a Heav'n of Hell, a Hell of Heav'n.[9]
What matter where, if I be still the same,
And what I should be, all but less than hee
Whom Thunder hath made greater? Here at least
We shall be free; th' Almighty hath not built
Here for his envy, will not drive us hence:
Here we may reign secure, and in my choice
To reign is worth ambition[1] though in Hell:
Better to reign in Hell, than serve in Heav'n.
But wherefore let we then our faithful friends,
Th' associates and copartners of our loss
Lie thus astonisht on th' oblivious Pool,[2]
And call them not to share with us their part
In this unhappy Mansion: or once more
With rallied Arms to try what may be yet
Regain'd in Heav'n, or what more lost in Hell?
So *Satan* spake, and him *Beëlzebub*
Thus answer'd. Leader of those Armies bright,
Which but th' Omnipotent none could have foiled,

5. Pelorus and Aetna are volcanic mountains in Sicily.
6. Converted directly from solid to vapor by volcanic heat in such a way as to resolidify on cooling.
7. Disorder of minerals, or subterranean disorder.
8. Of the river Styx—i.e., hellish.
9. The view that heaven and hell are states of mind was held by Amaury de Bene, a medieval heretic often cited in 17th-century accounts of atheism.
1. Worth striving for (Latin *ambitio*). Satan refers not merely to a mental state but also to an active effort that is the price of power.
2. The pool attended by forgetfulness.

If once they hear that voice, thir liveliest pledge
Of hope in fears and dangers, heard so oft
In worst extremes, and on the perilous edge° *front line*
Of battle when it rag'd, in all assaults
Thir surest signal, they will soon resume
New courage and revive, though now they lie
Groveling and prostrate on yon Lake of Fire,
As we erewhile, astounded and amaz'd;
No wonder, fall'n such a pernicious highth.
  He scarce had ceas't when the superior Fiend
Was moving toward the shore; his ponderous shield
Ethereal temper,[3] massy, large and round,
Behind him cast; the broad circumference
Hung on his shoulders like the Moon, whose Orb
Through Optic Glass the *Tuscan* Artist[4] views
At Ev'ning from the top of *Fesole*,
Or in *Valdarno*, to descry new Lands,
Rivers or Mountains in her spotty Globe.
His Spear, to equal which the tallest Pine
Hewn on *Norwegian* hills, to be the Mast
Of some great Ammiral,° were but a wand, *flagship*
He walkt with to support uneasy steps
Over the burning Marl,° not like those steps *ground*
On Heaven's Azure, and the torrid Clime
Smote on him sore besides, vaulted with Fire;
Nathless° he so endur'd, till on the Beach *nevertheless*
Of that inflamed Sea, he stood and call'd
His Legions, Angel Forms, who lay intrans't
Thick as Autumnal Leaves that strow the Brooks
In *Vallombrosa*, where th' *Etrurian* shades
High overarch't imbow'r;[5] or scatter'd sedge
Afloat, when with fierce Winds *Orion* arm'd
Hath vext the Red-Sea Coast,[6] whose waves o'erthrew
Busiris and his *Memphian* Chivalry,
While with perfidious hatred they pursu'd
The Sojourners of *Goshen*, who beheld
From the safe shore thir floating Carcasses
And broken Chariot Wheels;[7] so thick bestrown
Abject and lost lay these, covering the Flood,

3. Tempered in celestial fire.
4. Galileo, who looked through a telescope ("optic glass"), had been placed under house arrest by the Inquisition near Florence, which is in the "Valdarno" or the Valley of the Arno, overlooked by the hills of "Fesole" or Fiesole.
5. See Isaiah 34.4: "and all their host shall fall down, as the leaf falleth off from the vine, and as a falling fig from the fig tree." Fallen leaves were an enduring simile for the numberless dead; see Homer, *Iliad* 6.146; Virgil, *Aeneid* 6.309; Dante, *Inferno* 3.112. Milton adds an actual locality, Vallombrosa, again near Florence.
6. Commentators on Job 9.9 and Amos 5.8 interpreted the creation of Orion as a symbol of God's power to raise tempests and floods to execute his judgments. Thus Milton's transition to the Egyptians overwhelmed by God's judgment in lines 306–11 is a natural one. The Hebrew name for the Red Sea was "Sea of Sedge."
7. Contrary to his promise, the Pharaoh with his Memphian (i.e., Egyptian) charioteers pursued the Israelites—who had been in captivity in Goshen—across the Red Sea. The Israelites passed over safely; but the Egyptians' chariot wheels were broken (Exodus 14.25), and the rising sea engulfed them and cast their corpses on the shore.

Under amazement of thir hideous change.
He call'd so loud, that all the hollow Deep
Of Hell resounded. Princes, Potentates,
Warriors, the Flow'r of Heav'n, once yours, now lost,
If such astonishment as this can seize
Eternal spirits; or have ye chos'n this place
After the toil of Battle to repose
Your wearied virtue,° for the ease you find *strength*
To slumber here, as in the Vales of Heav'n?
Or in this abject posture have ye sworn
To adore the Conqueror? who now beholds
Cherub and Seraph rolling in the Flood
With scatter'd Arms and Ensigns,° till anon *battle flags*
His swift pursuers from Heav'n Gates discern
Th' advantage, and descending tread us down
Thus drooping, or with linked Thunderbolts
Transfix us to the bottom of this Gulf.
Awake, arise, or be for ever fall'n.
They heard, and were abasht, and up they sprung
Upon the wing; as when men wont to watch
On duty, sleeping found by whom they dread,
Rouse and bestir themselves ere well awake.
Nor did they not perceive the evil plight
In which they were, or the fierce pains not feel;
Yet to thir General's Voice they soon obey'd
Innumerable. As when the potent Rod
Of *Amram's* Son[8] in *Egypt's* evil day
Wav'd round the Coast, up call'd a pitchy cloud
Of *Locusts*, warping° on the Eastern Wind, *floating*
That o'er the Realm of impious *Pharaoh* hung
Like Night, and darken'd all the Land of *Nile:*
So numberless were those bad Angels seen
Hovering on wing under the Cope° of Hell *canopy*
'Twixt upper, nether, and surrounding Fires;
Till, as a signal giv'n, th' uplifted Spear
Of thir great Sultan waving to direct
Thir course, in even balance down they light
On the firm brimstone, and fill all the Plain;
A multitude, like which the populous North
Pour'd never from her frozen loins, to pass
Rhene or the *Danaw*, when her barbarous Sons
Came like a Deluge on the South, and spread
Beneath *Gibraltar* to the *Lybian* sands.[9]
Forthwith from every Squadron and each Band
The Heads and Leaders thither haste where stood

8. Moses, who used his rod to bring down on the Egyptians a plague of locusts (Exodus 10.12–15).

9. The barbarian invasions of Rome began with crossings of the Rhine ("Rhene") and Danube ("Danaw") rivers and spread to North Africa.

Thir great Commander; Godlike shapes and forms
Excelling human, Princely Dignities,
And Powers that erst in Heaven sat on Thrones;
Though of thir Names in heav'nly Records now
Be no memorial, blotted out and ras'd
By thir Rebellion, from the Books of Life.[1]
Nor had they yet among the Sons of *Eve*
Got them new Names, till wand'ring o'er the Earth,
Through God's high sufferance for the trial of man,
By falsities and lies the greatest part
Of Mankind they corrupted to forsake
God thir Creator, and th' invisible
Glory of him that made them, to transform
Oft to the Image of a Brute, adorn'd
With gay Religions° full of Pomp and Gold, *ceremonies*
And Devils to adore for Deities:[2]
Then were they known to men by various Names,
And various Idols through the Heathen World.
Say, Muse, thir Names then known, who first, who last,
Rous'd from the slumber on that fiery Couch,
At thir great Emperor's call, as next in worth
Came singly where he stood on the bare strand,
While the promiscuous crowd stood yet aloof?
The chief were those who from the Pit of Hell
Roaming to seek thir prey on earth, durst fix
Thir Seats long after next the Seat of God,
Thir Altars by his Altar, Gods ador'd
Among the Nations round, and durst abide
Jehovah thund'ring out of *Sion,* thron'd
Between the Cherubim; yea, often plac'd
Within his Sanctuary itself thir Shrines,
Abominations; and with cursed things
His holy Rites, and solemn Feasts profan'd,
And with thir darkness durst affront his light.
First *Moloch,*[3] horrid King besmear'd with blood
Of human sacrifice, and parents' tears,
Though for the noise of Drums and Timbrels° loud *tambourines*
Thir children's cries unheard, that pass'd through fire
To his grim Idol. Him the *Ammonite*
Worshipt in *Rabba* and her wat'ry Plain,
In *Argob* and in *Basan,* to the stream
Of utmost *Arnon.*[4] Nor content with such

1. See Revelation 3.5 ("He that overcometh . . . I will not blot out his name out of the book of life") and Exodus 32.32–33.
2. The catalogue of gods here is an epic convention.
3. Satan gathers 12 disciples: Moloch, Chemos, Baalim, Ashtaroth, Astoreth, Thammuz, Dagon, Rimmon, Osiris, Isis, Horus, and Belial. The literal meaning of *Moloch* is "king."
4. Though ostensibly magnifying Moloch's empire, these lines look forward to his eventual defeat; for Rabba, the Ammonite royal city, is best known for its capture by David after his repentance (2 Samuel 12), while the Israelite conquest of the regions of Argob and Basan, as far as the boundary river Arnon, is recalled by Moses as particularly crushing (Deuteronomy 3.1–13).

Audacious neighborhood, the wisest heart
Of *Solomon*[5] he led by fraud to build
His Temple right against the Temple of God
On that opprobrious Hill,[6] and made his Grove
The pleasant Valley of *Hinnom*, *Tophet* thence
And black *Gehenna* call'd, the Type of Hell.[7]
Next *Chemos*,[8] th' obscene dread of *Moab's* Sons,
From *Aroar* to *Nebo*, and the wild
Of Southmost *Abarim*; in *Hesebon*
And *Horonaim*, *Seon's* Realm, beyond
The flow'ry Dale of *Sibma* clad with Vines,
And *Eleale* to th' *Asphaltic* Pool.[9]
Peor[1] his other Name, when he entic'd
Israel in *Sittim* on thir march from *Nile*
To do him wanton rites, which cost them woe.[2]
Yet thence his lustful Orgies he enlarg'd
Even to that Hill of scandal, by the Grove
Of *Moloch* homicide, lust hard by hate;
Till good *Josiah*[3] drove them thence to Hell.
With these came they, who from the bord'ring flood
Of old *Euphrates*[4] to the Brook that parts
Egypt from *Syrian* ground, had general Names
Of *Baalim* and *Ashtaroth*,[5] those male,
These Feminine. For Spirits when they please
Can either Sex assume, or both; so soft
And uncompounded is thir Essence pure,
Not ti'd or manacl'd with joint or limb,
Nor founded on the brittle strength of bones,
Like cumbrous flesh; but in what shape they choose
Dilated° or condens't, bright or obscure, *expanded*
Can execute thir aery purposes,
And works of love or enmity fulfil.
For those the Race of *Israel* oft forsook
Thir living strength,[6] and unfrequented left

5. Solomon's wives drew him into idolatry (1 Kings 11.5–7); but the "high places that were before Jerusalem . . . on the right hand of the mount of corruption which Solomon . . . had builded for Ashtoreth the abomination of the Zidonians, and for Chemosh the abomination of the Moabites, and Milcom the abomination of the children of Ammon" were later destroyed by Josiah (2 Kings 23.13–14).

6. The Mount of Olives, because of Solomon's idolatry called "mount of corruption." Throughout the poem, Solomon functions as a type both of Adam and of Christ.

7. To abolish sacrifice to Moloch, Josiah "defiled Topheth, which is in the valley of the children of Hinnom" (2 Kings 23.10). Gehenna, for "Valley of Hinnom," is used in Matthew 10.28 as a name for hell.

8. "The abomination of Moab," associated with the neighboring god Moloch in 1 Kings 11.7.

9. Most of these places are named in Numbers 32 as the formerly Moabite inheritance assigned by Moses to the tribes of Reuben and Gad. Numbers 21.25–30 rejoices at the Israelite capture of Hesebon (Heshbon), a Moabite city which had been taken by the Amorite King Seon, or Sihon. Heshbon, Horonaim, "the vine of Sibmah," and Elealeh all figure in Isaiah's sad prophecy of the destruction of Moab (Isaiah 15.5, 16.8f). The Asphaltic Pool is the Dead Sea.

1. For the story of Peor, see Numbers 25.1–3 and Hosea 9.10.

2. A plague that killed 24,000 (Numbers 25.9).

3. Always a favorite with the Reformers because of his destruction of idolatrous images.

4. An area stretching from the northeast limit of Syria to the southwest limit of Canaan, the river Besor.

5. Baal is the general name for most idols; the Phoenician and Canaanite sun gods were collectively called Baalim (plural form). Astartes (Ishtars) were manifestations of the moon goddess.

6. See 1 Samuel 15.29: "Strength of Israel," a formulaic periphrasis for Jehovah.

His righteous Altar, bowing lowly down
To bestial Gods; for which thir heads as low
Bow'd down in Battle, sunk before the Spear
Of despicable foes. With these in troop
Came *Astoreth*, whom the *Phoenicians* call'd
Astarte, Queen of Heav'n, with crescent Horns;[7]
To whose bright Image nightly by the Moon
Sidonian Virgins paid thir Vows and Songs,
In *Sion* also not unsung, where stood
Her Temple on th' offensive Mountain, built
By that uxorious King, whose heart though large,
Beguil'd by fair Idolatresses, fell
To Idols foul. *Thammuz*[8] came next behind,
Whose annual wound in *Lebanon* allur'd
The *Syrian* Damsels to lament his fate
In amorous ditties all a Summer's day,
While smooth *Adonis* from his native Rock
Ran purple to the Sea, suppos'd with blood
Of *Thammuz* yearly wounded: the Love-tale
Infected *Sion's* daughters with like heat,
Whose wanton passions in the sacred Porch
Ezekiel saw, when by the Vision led
His eye survey'd the dark Idolatries
Of alienated *Judah*. Next came one
Who mourn'd in earnest, when the Captive Ark
Maim'd his brute Image, head and hands lopt off
In his own Temple, on the grunsel° edge, *threshold*
Where he fell flat, and sham'd his Worshippers:
Dagon his Name, Sea Monster, upward Man
And downward Fish:[9] yet had his Temple high
Rear'd in *Azotus*, dreaded through the Coast
Of *Palestine*, in *Gath* and *Ascalon*,
And *Accaron* and *Gaza's* frontier bounds.[1]
Him follow'd *Rimmon*, whose delightful Seat
Was fair *Damascus*, on the fertile Banks
Of *Abbana* and *Pharphar*, lucid streams.[2]
He also against the house of God was bold:

7. The image of Astoreth or Astarte, the Sidonian (Phoenician) moon goddess and Venus, was the statue of a woman with the head of a bull above her head with horns resembling the crescent moon. "Queen of heaven:" from Jeremiah 44.17–19.

8. The lover of Astarte. His identification with Adonis was based on St. Jerome's commentary on the passage in Ezekiel 8.14, drawn on by Milton in lines 454–56. The Syrian festival of Tammuz was celebrated after the summer solstice; the slaying of the young god by a boar was mourned as a symbol of the southward withdrawal of the sun and the death of vegetation. Each year when the river Adonis became discolored with red mud, it was regarded as a renewed sign of the god's wound.

9. When the Philistines put the ark of the Lord, which they had captured, into the temple of Dagon, "on the morrow morning, behold, Dagon was fallen upon his face to the ground . . . and the head of Dagon and both the palms of his hands were cut off upon the threshold" (1 Samuel 5.4).

1. Divine vengeance on these Philistine cities is prophesied in Zephaniah 2.4.

2. When Elisha told Naaman that his leprosy would be cured if he washed in the Jordan, the Syrian was at first angry (2 Kings 5.12: "Are not Abana and Pharpar, rivers of Damascus, better than all the waters of Israel?") but then humbled himself and was cured.

A Leper once he lost and gain'd a King,
Ahaz his sottish Conqueror, whom he drew
God's Altar to disparage and displace
For one of *Syrian* mode, whereon to burn
His odious off'rings, and adore the Gods
Whom he had vanquisht.[3] After these appear'd
A crew who under Names of old Renown,
Osiris, *Isis*, *Orus* and thir Train
With monstrous shapes and sorceries abus'd° — *deceived*
Fanatic *Egypt* and her Priests, to seek
Thir wand'ring Gods disguis'd in brutish forms
Rather than human.[4] Nor did *Israel* scape
Th' infection when thir borrow'd Gold compos'd
The Calf in *Oreb*:[5] and the Rebel King[6]
Doubl'd that sin in *Bethel* and in *Dan*,
Lik'ning his Maker to the Grazed Ox,[7]
Jehovah, who in one Night when he pass'd
From *Egypt* marching, equall'd with one stroke
Both her first born and all her bleating Gods.[8]
Belial came last,[9] than whom a Spirit more lewd
Fell not from Heaven, or more gross to love
Vice for itself: To him no Temple stood
Or Altar smok'd; yet who more oft than hee
In Temples and at Altars, when the Priest
Turns Atheist, as did *Ely's* Sons, who fill'd
With lust and violence the house of God.[1]
In Courts and Palaces he also Reigns
And in luxurious Cities, where the noise
Of riot ascends above thir loftiest Tow'rs,
And injury and outrage: And when Night
Darkens the Streets, then wander forth the Sons
Of *Belial*, flown° with insolence and wine.[2] — *swollen*
Witness the Streets of *Sodom*, and that night
In *Gibeah*, when the hospitable door
Expos'd a Matron to avoid worse rape.[3]
These were the prime in order and in might;
The rest were long to tell, though far renown'd,

3. After engineering the overthrow of Damascus by the Assyrians, the sottish (foolish) King Ahaz became interested in the cult of Rimmon and had an altar of the Syrian type put in the temple of the Lord (2 Kings 16.9–17).
4. Milton alludes to the myth of the Olympian gods fleeing from the Giant Typhoeus into Egypt and hiding in bestial forms (Ovid, *Metamorphoses* 5.319–31) afterward worshipped by the Egyptians.
5. Perhaps the most familiar of all Israelite apostasies was their worship of "a calf in Horeb" (Psalms 106.19) made by Aaron while Moses was away receiving the tables of the Law (Exodus 32).
6. Jeroboam, who led the revolt of the ten tribes of Israel against Rehoboam, Solomon's successor; he "doubled" Aaron's sin, since he made "two calves of gold," placing one in Bethel and the other in Dan (1 Kings 12.28–29).
7. "Thus they changed their glory into the similitude of an ox that eateth grass" (Psalms 106.20).
8. At the passover, Jehovah smote all the Egyptian firstborn, "both man and beast" (Exodus 12.12); presumably, this stroke would extend to their sacred animals.
9. Belial comes last, both because he had no local cult and because in the poem he is "timorous and slothful" (2.117). Properly, "Belial" is an abstract noun meaning "iniquity."
1. The impiety and fornication of Ely's sons are described in 1 Samuel 2.12–24.
2. The Puritans referred to their enemies as the Sons of Belial.
3. See Genesis 19 and Judges 19.

Th' *Ionian* Gods,[4] of *Javan's* Issue held
Gods, yet confest later than Heav'n and Earth
Thir boasted Parents; *Titan* Heav'n's first born
With his enormous° brood, and birthright seiz'd — *monstrous*
By younger *Saturn*, he from mightier *Jove*
His own and *Rhea's* Son like measure found;
So *Jove* usurping reign'd: these first in *Crete*
And *Ida* known,[5] thence on the Snowy top
Of cold *Olympus* rul'd the middle Air
Thir highest Heav'n; or on the *Delphian* Cliff,[6]
Or in *Dodona*, and through all the bounds
Of *Doric* Land;° or who with *Saturn* old — *Greece*
Fled over *Adria* to th' *Hesperian* Fields,
And o'er the *Celtic* roam'd the utmost Isles.[7]
All these and more came flocking; but with looks
Downcast and damp,° yet such wherein appear'd — *depressed*
Obscure some glimpse of joy, to have found thir chief
Not in despair, to have found themselves not lost
In loss itself; which on his count'nance cast
Like doubtful hue: but he his wonted pride
Soon recollecting,° with high words, that bore — *recovering*
Semblance of worth, not substance, gently rais'd
Thir fainting courage, and dispell'd thir fears.
Then straight commands that at the warlike sound
Of Trumpets loud and Clarions° be uprear'd — *shrill trumpets*
His mighty Standard; that proud honor claim'd
Azazel as his right, a Cherub tall:[8]
Who forthwith from the glittering Staff unfurl'd
Th' Imperial Ensign, which full high advanc't
Shone like a Meteor streaming to the Wind
With Gems and Golden lustre rich imblaz'd,[9]
Seraphic arms and Trophies: all the while
Sonorous metal blowing Martial sounds:
At which the universal Host upsent
A shout that tore Hell's Concave,° and beyond — *vault*
Frighted the Reign of *Chaos* and old Night.[1]
All in a moment through the gloom were seen
Ten thousand Banners rise into the Air
With Orient° Colors waving: with them rose — *brilliant*
A Forest huge of Spears: and thronging Helms

4. The Ionian Greeks were held by some to be the issue of Javan the son of Japhet the son of Noah, on the basis of the Septuagint version of Genesis 10.

5. Jove was born and secretly reared on Mount Ida, in Crete.

6. Delphi was famed as the site of the Pythian oracle of Apollo, but cults of Ge, Poseidon, and Artemis were also celebrated there.

7. After Saturn's downfall he fled across the Adriatic Sea (Adria) to Italy (Hesperian Fields), France (the Celtic), and the British Isles (Utmost Isles).

8. Azazel was one of the chief fallen angels who are the object of God's wrath in the apocryphal Book of Enoch. For the healing of the earth he is bound and cast into the same wilderness where the scapegoat was led (Enoch 10.4–8).

9. Adorned with heraldic devices.

1. Chaos and Night, rulers of the region of unformed matter between Heaven and Hell.

Appear'd, and serried° Shields in thick array *locked together*
Of depth immeasurable: Anon they move
In perfect *Phalanx*[2] to the *Dorian*° mood *solemn*
Of Flutes and soft Recorders; such as rais'd
To highth of noblest temper Heroes old
Arming to Battle, and instead of rage
Deliberate valor breath'd, firm and unmov'd
With dread of death to flight or foul retreat,
Nor wanting power to mitigate and swage° *assuage*
With solemn touches, troubl'd thoughts, and chase
Anguish and doubt and fear and sorrow and pain
From mortal or immortal minds. Thus they
Breathing united force with fixed thought
Mov'd on in silence to soft Pipes that charm'd
Thir painful steps o'er the burnt soil; and now
Advanc't in view they stand, a horrid° Front *bristling*
Of dreadful length and dazzling Arms, in guise
Of Warriors old with order'd Spear and Shield,
Awaiting what command thir mighty Chief
Had to impose: He through the armed Files
Darts his experienc't eye, and soon traverse° *across*
The whole Battalion views, thir order due,
Thir visages and stature as of Gods;
Thir number last he sums. And now his heart
Distends with pride, and hard'ning in his strength
Glories: For never since created man,[3]
Met such imbodied° force, as nam'd with these *united*
Could merit more than that small infantry
Warr'd on by Cranes:[4] though all the Giant brood
Of *Phlegra* with th' Heroic Race were join'd
That fought at *Thebes* and *Ilium*, on each side
Mixt with auxiliar Gods;[5] and what resounds
In Fable or *Romance of Uther's* Son° *King Arthur*
Begirt with *British* and *Armoric*[6] Knights;
And all who since, Baptiz'd or Infidel
Jousted in *Aspramont* or *Montalban*,
Damasco, or *Marocco*, or *Trebisond*,
Or whom *Biserta* sent from *Afric* shore
When *Charlemain* with all his Peerage fell
By *Fontarabbia*.[7] Thus far these beyond

2. A square battle formation.
3. Since humanity was created.
4. When compared with Satan's, any army would seem no bigger than pygmies ("that small infantry"), who were portrayed by Pliny as tiny men who fought with cranes.
5. To amplify the heroic stature of the angels, Milton mentions a series of armies that had been thought worthy of epic treatment only to dismiss them. The Giants, who fought with the Olympians at Phlegra, join with the heroes of Thebes and Troy (Ilium).
6. From Brittany.
7. Aspramont was a castle near Nice, and Montalban was the castle of Rinaldo; these castles figure in Ariosto's *Orlando Furioso* and the romances concerned with chivalric wars between Christians and Saracens. Milton would know late versions of the Charlemagne legend. Charlemagne's whole rearguard, led by Roland, one of the 12 peers or paladins, was massacred at Roncesvalles, about 40 miles from Fontarabbia (Fuenterrabia).

Compare of mortal prowess, yet observ'd° *obeyed*
Thir dread commander: he above the rest
In shape and gesture proudly eminent
Stood like a Tow'r; his form had yet not lost
All her Original brightness, nor appear'd
Less than Arch-Angel ruin'd, and th' excess
Of Glory obscur'd: As when the Sun new ris'n
Looks through the Horizontal misty Air
Shorn of his Beams, or from behind the Moon
In dim Eclipse disastrous twilight sheds
On half the Nations, and with fear of change
Perplexes Monarchs.[8] Dark'n'd so, yet shone
Above them all th' Arch-Angel: but his face
Deep scars of Thunder had intrencht, and care
Sat on his faded cheek, but under Brows
Of dauntless courage, and considerate° Pride *deliberate*
Waiting revenge: cruel his eye, but cast
Signs of remorse and passion to behold
The fellows of his crime, the followers rather
(Far other once beheld in bliss) condemn'd
For ever now to have thir lot in pain,
Millions of Spirits for his fault amerc't° *deprived*
Of Heav'n, and from Eternal Splendors flung
For his revolt, yet faithful how they stood,
Thir Glory wither'd. As when Heaven's Fire
Hath scath'd the Forest Oaks, or Mountain Pines,
With singed top thir stately growth though bare
Stands on the blasted Heath. He now prepar'd
To speak; whereat thir doubl'd Ranks they bend
From wing to wing, and half enclose him round
With all his Peers: attention held them mute.
Thrice he assay'd, and thrice in spite of scorn,
Tears such as Angels weep, burst forth: at last
Words interwove with sighs found out thir way.
  O Myriads of immortal Spirits, O Powers
Matchless, but with th' Almighty, and that strife
Was not inglorious, though th' event° was dire, *result*
As this place testifies, and this dire change
Hateful to utter: but what power of mind
Foreseeing or presaging, from the Depth
Of knowledge past or present, could have fear'd
How such united force of Gods, how such
As stood like these, could ever know repulse?
For who can yet believe, though after loss,
That all these puissant° Legions, whose exíle *powerful*

8. The comparison is ironically double-edged, for the ominous solar eclipse presages not only disaster for creation but also the doom of the godlike ruler for whom the sun was a traditional symbol.

Hath emptied Heav'n, shall fail to re-ascend
Self-rais'd, and repossess thir native seat?
For mee be witness all the Host of Heav'n,
If counsels different, or danger shunn'd
By me, have lost our hopes. But he who reigns
Monarch in Heav'n, till then as one secure
Sat on his Throne, upheld by old repute,
Consent or custom, and his Regal State
Put forth at full, but still his strength conceal'd,
Which tempted our attempt, and wrought our fall.
Henceforth his might we know, and know our own
So as not either to provoke, or dread
New War, provok't; our better part remains
To work in close° design, by fraud or guile *secret*
What force effected not: that he no less
At length from us may find, who overcomes
By force, hath overcome but half his foe.
Space may produce new Worlds; whereof so rife° *common*
There went a fame° in Heav'n that he ere long *rumor*
Intended to create, and therein plant
A generation, whom his choice regard
Should favor equal to the Sons of Heaven:
Thither, if but to pry, shall be perhaps
Our first eruption, thither or elsewhere:
For this Infernal Pit shall never hold
Celestial Spirits in Bondage, nor th' Abyss
Long under darkness cover. But these thoughts
Full Counsel must mature: Peace is despair'd,
For who can think Submission? War then, War
Open or understood, must be resolv'd.
He spake: and to confirm his words, out-flew
Millions of flaming swords, drawn from the thighs
Of mighty Cherubim; the sudden blaze
Far round illumin'd hell: highly they rag'd
Against the Highest, and fierce with grasped Arms
Clash'd on thir sounding shields the din of war,
Hurling defiance toward the Vault of Heav'n.
There stood a Hill not far whose grisly top
Belch'd fire and rolling smoke; the rest entire
Shone with a glossy scurf, undoubted sign
That in his womb was hid metallic Ore,
The work of Sulphur.[9] Thither wing'd with speed
A numerous Brígad° hasten'd. As when bands *brigade*
Of Píoners° with Spade and Pickax arm'd *engineers*
Forerun the Royal Camp, to trench a Field,

9. The traditional physiognomy of the fiend is in Milton's hell displaced onto the landscape. It is a dead or corrupt body imaged as scurf (i.e., scales, crust), belching, ransacked womb, bowels, entrails, and ribs.

Or cast a Rampart. *Mammon*[1] led them on,
Mammon, the least erected° Spirit that fell — *elevated*
From Heav'n, for ev'n in Heav'n his looks and thoughts
Were always downward bent, admiring more
The riches of Heav'n's pavement, trodd'n Gold,
Than aught divine or holy else enjoy'd
In vision beatific: by him first
Men also, and by his suggestion taught,
Ransack'd the Center, and with impious hands
Rifl'd the bowels of thir mother Earth
For Treasures better hid. Soon had his crew
Op'n'd into the Hill a spacious wound
And digg'd out ribs of Gold. Let none admire° — *wonder*
That riches grow in Hell; that soil may best
Deserve the precious bane. And here let those
Who boast in mortal things, and wond'ring tell
Of *Babel*, and the works of *Memphian* Kings,[2]
Learn how thir greatest Monuments of Fame,
And Strength and Art are easily outdone
By Spirits reprobate, and in an hour
What in an age they with incessant toil
And hands innumerable scarce perform.
Nigh on the Plain in many cells prepar'd,
That underneath had veins of liquid fire
Sluic'd° from the Lake, a second multitude — *led by channels*
With wondrous Art founded the massy Ore,
Severing each kind, and scumm'd the Bullion dross:
A third as soon had form'd within the ground
A various mould, and from the boiling cells
By strange conveyance fill'd each hollow nook:
As in an Organ from one blast of wind
To many a row of Pipes the sound-board breathes.
Anon out of the earth a Fabric huge
Rose like an Exhalation,[3] with the sound
Of Dulcet Symphonies and voices sweet,
Built like a Temple, where *Pilasters*° round — *columns*
Were set, and Doric pillars overlaid
With Golden Architrave; nor did there want
Cornice or Frieze, with bossy° Sculptures grav'n; — *embossed*
The Roof was fretted° Gold. Not *Babylon*,[4] — *patterned*

1. In Matthew 6.24 and Luke 16.13, "Mammon" is an abstract noun meaning wealth, but later it was used as the name of "the prince of this world" (John 12.31). Medieval and Renaissance tradition often associated Mammon with Plutus, the Greek god of riches.

2. The Tower of Babel was built by the ambitious Nimrod. The works of Memphian kings, the Pyramids, were regarded as memorials of vanity.

3. Pandaemonium rises to music, since in the Renaissance it was believed that musical proportions governed the forms of architecture.

4. An ironic allusion to Ovid's description of the Palace of the Sun built by Mulciber (*Metamorphoses* 2.1–4). Pandaemonium has a classical design, complete in every respect, like that of the ancient (but still surviving) giltroofed Pantheon, the most admired building of Milton's time. Doric is the oldest and simplest order of Greek architecture.

Nor great *Alcairo* such magnificence
Equall'd in all thir glories,[5] to inshrine
Belus[6] or *Serapis*[7] thir Gods, or seat
Thir Kings, when *Egypt* with *Assyria* strove
In wealth and luxury. Th' ascending pile
Stood fixt her stately highth, and straight the doors
Op'ning thir brazen folds discover wide
Within, her ample spaces, o'er the smooth
And level pavement: from the arched roof
Pendant by subtle Magic many a row
Of Starry Lamps and blazing Cressets[8] fed
With *Naphtha* and *Asphaltus*[9] yielded light
As from a sky. The hasty multitude
Admiring enter'd, and the work some praise
And some the Architect: his hand was known
In Heav'n by many a Tow'red structure high,
Where Scepter'd Angels held thir residence,
And sat as Princes, whom the supreme King
Exalted to such power, and gave to rule,
Each in his Hierarchy, the Orders bright.
Nor was his name unheard or unador'd
In ancient *Greece;* and in *Ausonian* land
Men call'd him *Mulciber;*[1] and how he fell
From Heav'n, they fabl'd, thrown by angry *Jove*
Sheer o'er the Crystal Battlements: from Morn
To Noon he fell, from Noon to dewy Eve,
A Summer's day; and with the setting Sun
Dropt from the Zenith like a falling Star,
On *Lemnos* th' *Aegean* Isle:[2] thus they relate,
Erring; for he with this rebellious rout
Fell long before; nor aught avail'd him now
To have built in Heav'n high Tow'rs; nor did he scape
By all his Engines, but was headlong sent
With his industrious crew to build in hell.
Meanwhile the winged Heralds by command
Of Sovran power, with awful Ceremony
And Trumpets' sound throughout the Host proclaim
A solemn Council forthwith to be held
At *Pandaemonium*, the high Capitol

5. In traditional biblical exegesis, Babylon, a place of proud iniquity, was often a figure of Antichrist or of hell. Memphis (modern Cairo) was the most splendid city of Egypt.
6. Bel, the Babylonian Baal; see lines 421–23n and Jeremiah 51.44: "I will punish Bel in Babylon."
7. An Egyptian deity.
8. Basketlike lamps.
9. *Naphtha* is an oily constituent of asphalt (*asphaltus*).
1. The Greek god Hephaistos, in Latin *Mulciber* or Vulcan, presided over all arts, such as metal-working, that required the use of fire. He built all the palaces of the gods. "Ausonian land" is the old Greek name for Italy. Milton emulates Homer's description of the daylong fall of Hephaistos (*Iliad* 1.591–95) and then deflates it in the casual but commanding dismissal of 746–48.
2. In Homer (*Iliad* 2.87–90), the Achaians going to a council are compared to bees, as are the Carthaginians in Virgil (*Aeneid* 1.430–36). Milton also glances at Virgil's mock-epic account of the ideal social organization of the hive (*Georgics* 4.149–227).

Of Satan and his Peers: thir summons call'd
From every Band and squared Regiment
By place or choice the worthiest; they anon
With hunderds and with thousands trooping came
Attended: all access was throng'd, the Gates
And Porches wide, but chief the spacious Hall
(Though like a cover'd field, where Champions bold
Wont ride in arm'd, and at the Soldan's° chair *Sultan's*
Defi'd the best of *Paynim*° chivalry *pagan*
To mortal combat or career with Lance)
Thick swarm'd, both on the ground and in the air,
Brusht with the hiss of rustling wings. As Bees
In spring time, when the Sun with *Taurus*[3] rides,
Pour forth thir populous youth about the Hive
In clusters; they among fresh dews and flowers
Fly to and fro, or on the smoothed Plank,
The suburb of thir Straw-built Citadel,
New rubb'd with Balm, expatiate° and confer *debate*
Thir State affairs. So thick the aery crowd
Swarm'd and were strait'n'd; till the Signal giv'n,
Behold a wonder! they but now who seem'd
In bigness to surpass Earth's Giant Sons
Now less than smallest Dwarfs, in narrow room
Throng numberless, like that Pigmean Race
Beyond the *Indian* Mount, or Faery Elves,
Whose midnight Revels, by a Forest side
Or Fountain some belated Peasant sees,
Or dreams he sees, while over-head the Moon
Sits Arbitress, and nearer to the Earth
Wheels her pale course;[4] they on thir mirth and dance
Intent, with jocund Music charm his ear;
At once with joy and fear his heart rebounds.
Thus incorporeal Spirits to smallest forms
Reduc'd thir shapes immense, and were at large,
Though without number still amidst the Hall
Of that infernal Court. But far within
And in thir own dimensions like themselves
The great Seraphic Lords and Cherubim
In close° recess and secret conclave[5] sat *secret*
A thousand Demi-Gods on golden seats,
Frequent° and full. After short silence then *crowded*
And summons read, the great consult began.

The End of the First Book.

3. In Milton's time the sun entered the second sign of the zodiac in mid-April, according to the Julian calendar.

4. Echoing *A Midsummer Night's Dream* 2.1.28f and 141. "The moon / Sits arbitress" because the moon-goddess was queen of faery.

5. "Conclave" could refer to any assembly in secret session but already had the specifically ecclesiastical meaning on which Milton's satire here depends.

Book 2

The Argument

The Consultation begun, Satan *debates whether another Battle be to be hazarded for the recovery of Heaven: some advise it, others dissuade: A third proposal is preferr'd, mention'd before by* Satan, *to search the truth of that Prophecy or Tradition in Heaven concerning another world, and another kind of creature equal or not much inferior to themselves, about this time to be created: Thir doubt who shall be sent on this difficult search:* Satan *thir chief undertakes alone the voyage, is honor'd and applauded. The Council thus ended, the rest betake them several ways and to several employments, as thir inclinations lead them, to entertain the time till* Satan *return. He passes on his Journey to Hell Gates, finds them shut, and who sat there to guard them, by whom at length they are op'n'd, and discover*[1] *to him the great Gulf between Hell and Heaven; with what difficulty he passes through, directed by* Chaos, *the Power of that place, to the sight of this new World which he sought.*

High on a Throne of Royal State,[2] which far
Outshone the wealth of *Ormus* and of *Ind,*[3]
Or where the gorgeous East with richest hand
Show'rs on her Kings *Barbaric* Pearl and Gold,
Satan exalted sat, by merit rais'd
To that bad eminence; and from despair
Thus high uplifted beyond hope, aspires
Beyond thus high, insatiate to pursue
Vain War with Heav'n, and by success° untaught *result*
His proud imaginations thus display'd.
Powers and Dominions,[4] Deities of Heav'n,
For since no deep within her gulf can hold
Immortal vigor, though opprest and fall'n,
I give not Heav'n for lost. From this descent
Celestial Virtues rising, will appear
More glorious and more dread than from no fall
And trust themselves to fear no second fate:
Mee though just right and the fixt Laws of Heav'n
Did first create your Leader, next, free choice,
With what besides, in Counsel or in Fight,
Hath been achiev'd of merit, yet this loss
Thus far at least recover'd, hath much more
Establisht in a safe unenvied Throne
Yielded with full consent. The happier state
In Heav'n, which follows dignity, might draw
Envy from each inferior; but who here
Will envy whom the highest place exposes
Foremost to stand against the Thunderer's aim[5]
Your bulwark, and condemns to greatest share

1. Disclose.
2. Compare Spenser's description of the bright throne of the Phaethon-like Lucifera, embodiment of pride in *The Faerie Queene* 1.4.8.
3. India. Ormus, an island town in the Persian Gulf, was famous as a jewel market.
4. Two angelic orders mentioned by St. Paul in Colossians 1.16.
5. By identifying him with thunder, the attribute of Jupiter, Satan reduces God to a mere Olympian tyrant.

Of endless pain? where there is then no good
For which to strive, no strife can grow up there
From Faction; for none sure will claim in Hell
Precedence, none, whose portion is so small
Of present pain, that with ambitious mind
Will covet more. With this advantage then
To union, and firm Faith, and firm accord,
More than can be in Heav'n, we now return
To claim our just inheritance of old,
Surer to prosper than prosperity
Could have assur'd us; and by what best way,
Whether of open War or covert guile,
We now debate; who can advise, may speak.
He ceas'd, and next him *Moloch,* Scepter'd King
Stood up, the strongest and the fiercest Spirit
That fought in Heav'n; now fiercer by despair:
His trust was with th' Eternal to be deem'd
Equal in strength, and rather than be less
Car'd not to be at all; with that care lost
Went all his fear: of God, or Hell, or worse
He reck'd° not, and these words thereafter spake. *cared*
My sentence° is for open War: Of Wiles, *opinion*
More unexpert,° I boast not: them let those *inexperienced*
Contrive who need, or when they need, not now.
For while they sit contriving, shall the rest,
Millions that stand in Arms, and longing wait
The Signal to ascend, sit ling'ring here
Heav'n's fugitives, and for thir dwelling place
Accept this dark opprobrious Den of shame,
The Prison of his Tyranny who Reigns
By our delay? no, let us rather choose
Arm'd with Hell flames and fury[6] all at once
O'er Heav'n's high Tow'rs to force resistless way,
Turning our Tortures into horrid Arms
Against the Torturer; when to meet the noise
Of his Almighty Engine[7] he shall hear
Infernal Thunder, and for Lightning see
Black fire and horror shot with equal rage
Among his Angels; and his Throne itself
Mixt with *Tartarean* Sulphur, and strange fire,[8]
His own invented Torments. But perhaps
The way seems difficult and steep to scale
With upright wing against a higher foe.

6. The violent yoking of concrete and abstract words is one of the most characteristic figures of Milton's style.
7. Machine of war, probably here referring to the Messiah's chariot or perhaps to his thunder.
8. In the classical underworld, Tartarus was the place of the guilty. For "strange fire," see Leviticus 10.1–2: "Nadab and Abihu, the sons of Aaron . . . offered strange fire before the Lord, which he commanded them not. And there went out fire from the Lord, and devoured them."

Let such bethink them, if the sleepy drench[9]
Of that forgetful Lake benumb not still,
That in our proper motion we ascend
Up to our native seat: descent and fall
To us is adverse. Who but felt of late
When the fierce Foe hung on our brok'n Rear
Insulting,° and pursu'd us through the Deep, *assaulting, exulting*
With what compulsion and laborious flight
We sunk thus low? Th' ascent is easy then;
Th' event° is fear'd; should we again provoke *outcome*
Our stronger, some worse way his wrath may find
To our destruction: if there be in Hell
Fear to be worse destroy'd: what can be worse
Than to dwell here, driv'n out from bliss, condemn'd
In this abhorred deep to utter woe;
Where pain of unextinguishable fire
Must exercise° us without hope of end *afflict*
The Vassals[1] of his anger, when the Scourge
Inexorably, and the torturing hour
Calls us to Penance? More destroy'd than thus
We should be quite abolisht and expire.
What fear we then? what doubt we to incense
His utmost ire? which to the highth enrag'd,
Will either quite consume us, and reduce
To nothing this essential,° happier far *essence*
Than miserable to have eternal being:
Or if our substance be indeed Divine,
And cannot cease to be, we are at worst
On this side nothing;[2] and by proof we feel
Our power sufficient to disturb his Heav'n,
And with perpetual inroads to Alarm,
Though inaccessible, his fatal Throne:
Which if not Victory is yet Revenge.
He ended frowning, and his look denounc'd
Desperate revenge, and Battle dangerous
To less than Gods. On th' other side up rose
Belial, in act more graceful and humane;
A fairer person lost not Heav'n; he seem'd
For dignity compos'd and high exploit:
But all was false and hollow; though his Tongue
Dropt Manna, and could make the worse appear
The better reason,[3] to perplex and dash
Maturest Counsels: for his thoughts were low;

9. A draught of medicine for an animal.
1. Servants, slaves. Also an allusion to Romans 9.22: "What if God, willing to show his wrath, and to make his power known, endured with much longsuffering the vessels of wrath fitted to destruction . . . ?"
2. Already we are in the worst condition possible, short of being nothing, being annihilated.
3. This was the claim of the Greek Sophists, who taught their students how to use rhetoric to win an argument.

To vice industrious, but to Nobler deeds
Timorous and slothful: yet he pleas'd the ear,
And with persuasive accent thus began.
I should be much for open War, O Peers,
As not behind in hate; if what was urg'd
Main reason to persuade immediate War,
Did not dissuade me most, and seem to cast
Ominous conjecture on the whole success:
When he who most excels in fact° of Arms, *feat*
In what he counsels and in what excels
Mistrustful, grounds his courage on despair
And utter dissolution, as the scope
Of all his aim, after some dire revenge.
First, what Revenge? the Tow'rs of Heav'n are fill'd
With Armed watch, that render all access
Impregnable; oft on the bordering Deep
Encamp thir Legions, or with obscure[4] wing
Scout far and wide into the Realm of night,
Scorning surprise. Or could we break our way
By force, and at our heels all Hell should rise
With blackest Insurrection, to confound
Heav'n's purest Light, yet our great Enemy
All incorruptible would on his Throne
Sit unpolluted, and th' Ethereal mould
Incapable of stain would soon expel
Her mischief, and purge off the baser fire
Victorious.[5] Thus repuls'd, our final hope
Is flat° despair: we must exasperate *absolute*
Th' Almighty Victor to spend all his rage,
And that must end us, that must be our cure,
To be no more; sad cure; for who would lose,
Though full of pain, this intellectual being,
Those thoughts that wander through Eternity,
To perish rather, swallow'd up and lost
In the wide womb of uncreated night,
Devoid of sense and motion? and who knows,
Let this be good,[6] whether our angry Foe
Can give it, or will ever? how he can
Is doubtful; that he never will is sure.
Will he, so wise, let loose at once his ire,
Belike° through impotence, or unaware, *no doubt*
To give his Enemies thir wish, and end
Them in his anger, whom his anger saves
To punish endless? wherefore cease we then?

4. "Obscure" is stressed on the first syllable here.
5. Criticizing Moloch's proposal to mix God's throne with sulphur (lines 68–9) and shoot "black fire" among his angels. This "baser fire" Belial contrasts with the "ethereal" (derived from ether, the fifth and purest element) fire of the throne.
6. Suppose it is good to be destroyed.

Say they who counsel War, we are decreed,
Reserv'd and destin'd to Eternal woe;
Whatever doing, what can we suffer more,
What can we suffer worse? is this then worst,
Thus sitting, thus consulting, thus in Arms?
What when we fled amain,° pursu'd and strook° *headlong / struck*
With Heav'n's afflicting Thunder, and besought
The Deep to shelter us? this Hell then seem'd
A refuge from those wounds: or when we lay
Chain'd on the burning Lake? that sure was worse.
What if the breath that kindl'd those grim fires
Awak'd should blow them into sevenfold rage
And plunge us in the flames? or from above
Should intermitted vengeance arm again
His red right hand to plague us? what if all
Her° stores were op'n'd, and this Firmament *Hell's*
Of Hell should spout her Cataracts of Fire,
Impendent° horrors, threat'ning hideous fall *threatening*
One day upon our heads; while we perhaps
Designing or exhorting glorious war,
Caught in a fiery Tempest shall be hurl'd
Each on his rock transfixt, the sport and prey
Of racking whirlwinds, or for ever sunk
Under yon boiling Ocean, wrapt in Chains;
There to converse with everlasting groans,
Unrespited, unpitied, unrepriev'd,
Ages of hopeless end; this would be worse.
War therefore, open or conceal'd, alike
My voice dissuades; for what can force or guile
With him, or who deceive his mind, whose eye
Views all things at one view? he from Heav'n's highth
All these our motions° vain, sees and derides; *schemes*
Not more Almighty to resist our might
Than wise to frustrate all our plots and wiles.
Shall we then live thus vile, the race of Heav'n
Thus trampl'd, thus expell'd to suffer here
Chains and these Torments? better these than worse
By my advice; since fate inevitable
Subdues us, and Omnipotent Decree,
The Victor's will. To suffer, as to do,
Our strength is equal, nor the Law unjust
That so ordains: this was at first resolv'd,
If we were wise, against so great a foe
Contending, and so doubtful what might fall.
I laugh, when those who at the Spear are bold
And vent'rous, if that fail them, shrink and fear
What yet they know must follow, to endure
Exile, or ignominy, or bonds, or pain,
The sentence of thir Conqueror: This is now

Our doom; which if we can sustain and bear,
Our Supreme Foe in time may much remit
His anger, and perhaps thus far remov'd
Not mind us not offending, satisfi'd
With what is punisht; whence these raging fires
Will slack'n, if his breath stir not thir flames.
Our purer essence then will overcome
Thir noxious vapor, or enur'd° not feel, *accustomed*
Or chang'd at length, and to the place conform'd
In temper[7] and in nature, will receive
Familiar the fierce heat, and void of pain;
This horror will grow mild, this darkness light,[8]
Besides what hope the never-ending flight
Of future days may bring, what chance, what change
Worth waiting, since our present lot appears
For happy though but ill, for ill not worst,[9]
If we procure not to ourselves more woe.
Thus *Belial* with words cloth'd in reason's garb
Counsell'd ignoble ease, and peaceful sloth,
Not peace: and after him thus *Mammon* spake.
Either to disinthrone the King of Heav'n
We war, if war be best, or to regain
Our own right lost: him to unthrone we then
May hope, when everlasting Fate shall yield
To fickle Chance, and *Chaos* judge the strife:
The former vain to hope argues as vain
The latter: for what place can be for us
Within Heav'n's bound, unless Heav'n's Lord supreme
We overpower? Suppose he should relent
And publish Grace to all, on promise made
Of new Subjection; with what eyes could we
Stand in his presence humble, and receive
Strict Laws impos'd, to celebrate his Throne
With warbl'd Hymns, and to his Godhead sing
Forc't Halleluiahs[1] while he Lordly sits
Our envied Sovran, and his Altar breathes
Ambrosial[2] Odors and Ambrosial Flowers,
Our servile offerings. This must be our task
In Heav'n, this our delight; how wearisome
Eternity so spent in worship paid
To whom we hate. Let us not then pursue
By force impossible, by leave obtain'd
Unácceptable, though in Heav'n, our state

7. Temperament, the mixture or adjustment of humors. Thus the phrase means "adjusted psychologically and physically to the new environment."
8. Easy to bear, and illumination.
9. Though as far as happiness is concerned, the devils are but ill off, as far as evil is concerned, they could be worse.
1. The word "hallelujah" (Hebrew, "praise Jehovah") occurred in so many psalms that it came to mean a song of praise to God.
2. Fragrant and perfumed, immortal. Ambrosia was the fabled food or drink of the gods.

Of splendid vassalage, but rather seek
Our own good from ourselves, and from our own
Live to ourselves, though in this vast recess,
Free, and to none accountable, preferring
Hard liberty before the easy yoke
Of servile Pomp.[3] Our greatness will appear
Then most conspicuous, when great things of small,
Useful of hurtful, prosperous of adverse
We can create, and in what place soe'er
Thrive under evil, and work ease out of pain
Through labor and endurance. This deep world
Of darkness do we dread? How oft amidst
Thick clouds and dark doth Heav'n's all-ruling Sire
Choose to reside, his Glory unobscur'd,
And with the Majesty of darkness round
Covers his Throne; from whence deep thunders roar
Must'ring thir rage, and Heav'n resembles Hell?
As he our darkness, cannot we his Light
Imitate when we please? This Desert soil
Wants not her hidden lustre, Gems and Gold;
Nor want we skill or art, from whence to raise
Magnificence; and what can Heav'n show more?
Our torments also may in length of time
Become our Elements, these piercing Fires
As soft as now severe, our temper chang'd
Into their temper;[4] which must needs remove
The sensible of pain.[5] All things invite
To peaceful Counsels, and the settl'd State
Of order, how in safety best we may
Compose° our present evils, with regard *order*
Of what we are and where, dismissing quite
All thoughts of War; ye have what I advise.
He scarce had finisht, when such murmur fill'd
Th' Assembly, as when hollow Rocks retain
The sound of blust'ring winds, which all night long
Had rous'd the Sea, now with hoarse cadence lull
Sea-faring men o'erwatcht, whose Bark by chance
Or Pinnace anchors in a craggy Bay
After the Tempest: Such applause was heard
As *Mammon* ended, and his Sentence° pleas'd, *opinion*
Advising peace: for such another Field
They dreaded worse than Hell: so much the fear
Of Thunder and the Sword of *Michaël*[6]

3. In *Samson Agonistes* 271, Samson condemns those who are fonder of "bondage with ease than strenuous liberty." The antithesis is from the Roman historian, Sallust, who assigns it to an opponent of the dictator Sulla. See also Jesus' words in Matthew 11.28–30: "Come unto me. . . . For my yoke is easy."

4. Milton alludes to an idea of St. Augustine's, that the devils are bound to tormenting fires as if to bodies (*City of God*, 21.10).

5. The part of pain apprehended through the senses.

6. In the war in Heaven, Michael's two-handed sword felled "squadrons at once" and wounded even Satan. "Michael" here has three syllables.

Wrought still within them; and no less desire
To found this nether Empire, which might rise
By policy,[7] and long process of time,
In emulation opposite to Heav'n.
Which when *Beëlzebub*[8] perceiv'd, than whom,
Satan except, none higher sat, with grave
Aspect he rose, and in his rising seem'd
A Pillar of State; deep on his Front° engraven *forehead*
Deliberation sat and public care;
And Princely counsel in his face yet shone,
Majestic though in ruin: sage he stood
With *Atlantean*[9] shoulders fit to bear
The weight of mightiest Monarchies; his look
Drew audience and attention still as Night
Or Summer's Noon-tide air, while thus he spake.
   Thrones and Imperial Powers, off-spring of Heav'n,
Ethereal Virtues; or these Titles now
Must we renounce, and changing style be call'd
Princes of Hell? for so the popular vote
Inclines, here to continue, and build up here
A growing Empire; doubtless; while we dream,
And know not that the King of Heav'n hath doom'd
This place our dungeon, not our safe retreat
Beyond his Potent arm, to live exempt
From Heav'n's high jurisdiction, in new League
Banded against his Throne, but to remain
In strictest bondage, though thus far remov'd,
Under th' inevitable curb, reserv'd
His captive multitude: For he, be sure,
In highth or depth, still first and last will Reign
Sole King, and of his Kingdom lose no part
By our revolt, but over Hell extend
His Empire, and with Iron Sceptre rule
Us here, as with his Golden those in Heav'n.
What° sit we then projecting peace and war? *why*
War hath determin'd[1] us, and foil'd with loss
Irreparable; terms of peace yet none
Voutsaf't[2] or sought; for what peace will be giv'n
To us enslav'd, but custody severe,
And stripes, and arbitrary punishment
Inflicted? and what peace can we return,
But to our power[3] hostility and hate,
Untam'd reluctance,° and revenge though slow, *resistance*

7. Statesmanship, often in a bad sense, implying Machiavellian strategems. "Process" is stressed on the second syllable.
8. Satan's closest associate.
9. Worthy of Atlas, who was forced by Jupiter to carry the heavens on his shoulders as a punishment for his part in the rebellion of the Titans.
1. Finished, but the context also activates a subsidiary meaning, "war has given us a settled aim."
2. "Vouchsafed": granted; Milton's spelling, "Voutsaf't," indicates the 17th-century pronunciation he preferred.
3. To the limit of our power.

Yet ever plotting how the Conqueror least
May reap his conquest, and may least rejoice
In doing what we most in suffering feel?[4]
Nor will occasion want, nor shall we need
With dangerous expedition to invade
Heav'n, whose high walls fear no assault or Siege,
Or ambush from the Deep. What if we find
Some easier enterprise? There is a place
(If ancient and prophetic fame in Heav'n
Err not) another World, the happy seat
Of some new Race call'd *Man*, about this time
To be created like to us, though less
In power and excellence, but favor'd more
Of him who rules above;[5] so was his will
Pronounc'd among the Gods, and by an Oath,
That shook Heav'n's whole circumference, confirm'd.[6]
Thither let us bend all our thoughts, to learn
What creatures there inhabit, of what mould,
Or substance, how endu'd,° and what thir Power, *gifted*
And where thir weakness, how attempted° best, *attacked*
By force or subtlety: Though Heav'n be shut,
And Heav'n's high Arbitrator sit secure
In his own strength, this place may lie expos'd
The utmost border of his Kingdom, left
To their defense who hold it: here perhaps
Some advantageous act may be achiev'd
By sudden onset, either with Hell fire
To waste his whole Creation, or possess
All as our own, and drive as we were driven,
The puny° habitants, or if not drive, *weak*
Seduce them to our Party, that thir God
May prove thir foe, and with repenting hand
Abolish his own works. This would surpass
Common revenge, and interrupt his joy
In our Confusion, and our Joy upraise
In his disturbance; when his darling Sons
Hurl'd headlong to partake with us,[7] shall curse
Thir frail Original,° and faded bliss, *author*
Faded so soon. Advise if this be worth
Attempting, or to sit in darkness here
Hatching vain Empires. Thus *Beëlzebub*
Pleaded his devilish Counsel, first devis'd
By *Satan*, and in part propos'd: for whence,

4. How God may get the least happiness from our pain. Beelzebub portrays God as similar in his motives to the devils.

5. The creation of humanity was the subject of a public oath by God, but the time of the creation was the subject of a rumor only ("it is not for you to know the times or season," Acts 1.7).

6. See Isaiah 13.12–13: "I will make a man more precious than fine gold. . . . Therefore I will shake the Heavens."

7. Share in our condition; also, take sides with us.

But from the Author of all ill could Spring
So deep a malice, to confound the race
Of mankind in one root,[8] and Earth with Hell
To mingle and involve, done all to spite
The great Creator? But thir spite still serves
His glory to augment. The bold design
Pleas'd highly those infernal States,[9] and joy
Sparkl'd in all thir eyes; with full assent
They vote: whereat his speech he thus renews.
Well have ye judg'd, well ended long debate,
Synod[1] of Gods, and like to what ye are,
Great things resolv'd, which from the lowest deep
Will once more lift us up, in spite of Fate,
Nearer our ancient Seat; perhaps in view
Of those bright confines, whence with neighboring Arms
And opportune excursion we may chance
Re-enter Heav'n; or else in some mild Zone
Dwell not unvisited of Heav'n's fair Light
Secure, and at the bright'ning Orient beam
Purge off this gloom; the soft delicious Air,
To heal the scar of these corrosive Fires
Shall breathe her balm. But first whom shall we send
In search of this new world, whom shall we find
Sufficient? who shall tempt° with wand'ring feet *venture upon*
The dark unbottom'd infinite Abyss
And through the palpable obscure[2] find out
His uncouth° way, or spread his aery flight *unknown*
Upborne with indefatigable wings
Over the vast abrupt,[3] ere he arrive
The happy Isle; what strength, what art can then
Suffice, or what evasion bear him safe
Through the strict Senteries° and Stations thick *sentries*
Of Angels watching round? Here he had need
All circumspection, and wee now no less
Choice in our suffrage;[4] for on whom we send,
The weight of all and our last hope relies.
This said, he sat; and expectation held
His look suspense, awaiting who appear'd
To second, or oppose, or undertake
The perilous attempt; but all sat mute,
Pondering the danger with deep thoughts; and each
In other's count'nance read his own dismay
Astonisht: none among the choice and prime

8. Adam, the root of the genealogical tree of man.
9. Estates of the realm, people of rank and authority.
1. A meeting of councillors.
2. See Exodus 10.21: "The Lord said unto Moses, Stretch out thine hand toward heaven, that there may be darkness over the land of Egypt, even darkness which may be felt."
3. The adjective (precipitous, broken off) is here used as a noun and refers to the abyss between hell and heaven.
4. Care in our vote (to elect him).

Of those Heav'n-warring Champions could be found
So hardy as to proffer° or accept *offer*
Alone the dreadful voyage; till at last
Satan, whom now transcendent glory rais'd
Above his fellows, with Monarchal pride
Conscious of highest worth, unmov'd thus spake.
O Progeny of Heav'n, Empyreal Thrones,
With reason hath deep silence and demur° *delay*
Seiz'd us, though undismay'd: long is the way
And hard, that out of Hell leads up to light;
Our prison strong, this huge convex° of Fire, *vault*
Outrageous to devour, immures us round
Ninefold, and gates of burning Adamant
Barr'd over us prohibit all egress.
These past, if any pass, the void profound
Of unessential° Night receives him next *empty*
Wide gaping, and with utter loss of being
Threatens him, plung'd in that abortive gulf.
If thence he scape into whatever world,
Or unknown Region, what remains him less
Than[5] unknown dangers and as hard escape.
But I should ill become this Throne, O Peers,
And this Imperial Sov'ranty, adorn'd
With splendor, arm'd with power, if aught propos'd
And judg'd of public moment, in the shape
Of difficulty or danger could deter
Mee from attempting. Wherefore do I assume
These Royalties, and not refuse to Reign,
Refusing[6] to accept as great a share
Of hazard as of honor, due alike
To him who Reigns, and so much to him due
Of hazard more, as he above the rest
High honor'd sits? Go therefore mighty Powers.
Terror of Heav'n, though fall'n; intend° at home, *consider*
While here shall be our home, what best may ease
The present misery, and render Hell
More tolerable; if there be cure or charm
To respite° or deceive, or slack the pain *rest*
Of this ill Mansion: intermit no watch
Against a wakeful Foe, while I abroad
Through all the Coasts of dark destruction seek
Deliverance for us all: this enterprise
None shall partake with me. Thus saying rose
The Monarch, and prevented all reply,
Prudent, lest from his resolution rais'd° *encouraged*
Others among the chief might offer now

5. What awaits him except.

6. If I refuse.

(Certain to be refus'd) what erst they fear'd;
And so refus'd might in opinion stand
His Rivals, winning cheap the high repute
Which he through hazard huge must earn. But they
Dreaded not more th' adventure than his voice
Forbidding; and at once with him they rose;
Thir rising all at once was as the sound
Of Thunder heard remote. Towards him they bend
With awful° reverence prone; and as a God *respectful*
Extol him equal to the highest in Heav'n:
Nor fail'd they to express how much they prais'd,
That for the general safety he despis'd
His own: for neither do the Spirits damn'd
Lose all thir virtue; lest bad men should boast[7]
Thir specious° deeds on earth, which glory excites, *pretending*
Or close° ambition varnisht o'er with zeal. *secret*
Thus they thir doubtful consultations dark
Ended rejoicing in their matchless Chief:
As when from mountain tops the dusky clouds
Ascending, while the North wind sleeps, o'erspread
Heav'n's cheerful face, the low'ring Element
Scowls o'er the dark'n'd lantskip° Snow, or show'r; *landscape*
If chance the radiant Sun with farewell sweet
Extend his ev'ning beam, the fields revive,
The birds thir notes renew, and bleating herds
Attest thir joy, that hill and valley rings.
O shame to men! Devil with Devil damn'd
Firm concord holds, men only disagree
Of Creatures rational, though under hope
Of heavenly Grace; and God proclaiming peace,
Yet live in hatred, enmity, and strife
Among themselves, and levy cruel wars,
Wasting the Earth, each other to destroy:
As if (which might induce us to accord)
Man had not hellish foes anow° besides, *enough*
That day and night for his destruction wait.
  The *Stygian* Council thus dissolv'd; and forth
In order came the grand infernal Peers:
Midst came thir mighty Paramount,° and seem'd *ruler*
Alone th' Antagonist of Heav'n, nor less
Than Hell's dread Emperor with pomp Supreme,[8]
And God-like imitated State; him round
A Globe° of fiery Seraphim inclos'd *band*
With bright imblazonry,° and horrent° Arms. *heraldry / bristling*
Then of thir Session ended they bid cry
With Trumpet's regal sound the great result:

7. So that men ought not to boast.
8. Lines 510–20 may portray the English mob's easy gullibility and their passion (which Milton detested) for the regalia of monarchy.

Toward the four winds four speedy Cherubim
Put to thir mouths the sounding Alchymy[9]
By Herald's voice explain'd: the hollow Abyss
Heard far and wide, and all the host of Hell
With deaf'ning shout, return'd them loud acclaim.
Thence more at ease thir minds and somewhat rais'd° *encouraged*
By false presumptuous hope, the ranged powers[1]
Disband, and wand'ring, each his several way
Pursues, as inclination or sad choice
Leads him perplext, where he may likeliest find
Truce to his restless thoughts, and entertain
The irksome hours, till this great Chief return.
Part on the Plain, or in the Air sublime° *uplifted*
Upon the wing, or in swift Race contend,
As at th' *Olympian* Games or *Pythian* fields;[2]
Part curb thir fiery Steeds, or shun the Goal
With rapid wheels, or fronted Brígads form.
As when to warn proud Cities war appears
Wag'd in the troubl'd Sky, and Armies rush
To Battle in the Clouds, before each Van
Prick forth the Aery Knights, and couch thir spears
Till thickest Legions close; with feats of Arms
From either end of Heav'n the welkin° burns. *sky*
Others with vast *Typhoean*[3] rage more fell
Rend up both Rocks and Hills, and ride the Air
In whirlwind; Hell scarce holds the wild uproar.
As when *Alcides* from *Oechalia* Crown'd
With conquest, felt th' envenom'd robe, and tore
Through pain up by the roots *Thessalian* Pines,
And *Lichas* from the top of *Oeta* threw
Into th' *Euboic* Sea.[4] Others more mild,
Retreated in a silent valley, sing
With notes Angelical to many a Harp
Thir own Heroic deeds and hapless fall
By doom of Battle; and complain that Fate
Free Virtue should enthrall to Force or Chance.
Thir Song was partial,° but the harmony *prejudiced*
(What could it less when Spirits immortal sing?)
Suspended° Hell, and took with ravishment *enthralled*
The thronging audience. In discourse more sweet

9. Trumpets made of the alloy brass, associated with alchemy.
1. Armies drawn up in ranks.
2. Epic models for lines 528–69 include the sports of the Myrmidons during Achilles' absence from the war (Homer, *Iliad* 2.774ff.), the Greek funeral games of *Iliad* 23 and the Trojan of *Aeneid* 5, and the amusements of the blessed dead in Virgil's Elysium (*Aeneid* 6.642–59). To "shun the goal" (line 531) is to drive a chariot as close as possible around a post without touching it.
3. Like that of Typhon, the hundred-headed Titan. A pun, for "typhon" was also an English word meaning "whirlwind."
4. "Alcides" (Hercules) returning as victor from "Oechalia" (Ovid, *Metamorphoses* 9.136) put on a ritual robe that had inadvertently been soaked by his wife in corrosive poison. Mad with pain, he blamed his friend Lichas, who had brought the robe, and hurled him far into the "Euboic" (Euboean) Sea.

(For Eloquence the Soul, Song charms the Sense,)
Others apart sat on a Hill retir'd,
In thoughts more elevate, and reason'd high
Of Providence, Foreknowledge, Will, and Fate,
Fixt Fate, Free will, Foreknowledge absolute,
And found no end, in wand'ring mazes lost.
Of good and evil much they argu'd then,
Of happiness and final misery,
Passion and Apathy, and glory and shame,
Vain wisdom all, and false Philosophie:[5]
Yet with a pleasing sorcery could charm
Pain for a while or anguish, and excite
Fallacious hope, or arm th' obdured° breast *hardened*
With stubborn patience as with triple steel.
Another part in Squadrons and gross° Bands, *dense*
On bold adventure to discover wide
That dismal World, if any Clime perhaps
Might yield them easier habitation, bend
Four ways thir flying March, along the Banks
Of four infernal Rivers that disgorge
Into the burning Lake thir baleful° streams;[6] *evil*
Abhorred *Styx* the flood of deadly hate,
Sad *Acheron* of sorrow, black and deep;
Cocytus, nam'd of lamentation loud
Heard on the rueful stream; fierce *Phlegeton*
Whose waves of torrent fire inflame with rage.
Far off from these a slow and silent stream,
Lethe the River of Oblivion rolls
Her wat'ry Labyrinth, whereof who drinks,
Forthwith his former state and being forgets,
Forgets both joy and grief, pleasure and pain.
Beyond this flood a frozen Continent
Lies dark and wild, beat with perpetual storms
Of Whirlwind and dire Hail, which on firm land
Thaws not, but gathers heap, and ruin seems
Of ancient pile; all else deep snow and ice,
A gulf profound as that *Serbonian* Bog[7]
Betwixt *Damiata* and Mount *Casius* old,
Where Armies whole have sunk: the parching° Air *withering*
Burns frore,° and cold performs th' effect of Fire. *frozen*
Thither by harpy-footed Furies hal'd,[8]
At certain revolutions all the damn'd

5. Directed against Stoicism, the most formidable ethical challenge to Christianity; "apathy," or complete freedom from passion, was a Stoic ideal.

6. This description of the four rivers of hell takes its broad outline from Virgil's *Aeneid* 6, Dante's *Inferno* 14, and Spenser's *Faerie Queene* 2.7.56ff. Milton adds the detail of confluence in the "burning lake." The epithet or description attached to each river translates its Greek name (e.g., "Styx" means hateful).

7. Serbonis, a lake bordered by quicksands on the Egyptian coast.

8. Milton combines the hook-clawed Harpies of Dante and Virgil with the ancient Greek Furies, daughters of Acheron and Night and agencies of divine vengeance.

Are brought: and feel by turns the bitter change
Of fierce extremes, extremes by change more fierce,
From Beds of raging Fire to starve° in Ice — stifle
Thir soft Ethereal warmth, and there to pine
Immovable, infixt, and frozen round,
Periods of time, thence hurried back to fire.
They ferry over this *Lethean* Sound
Both to and fro, thir sorrow to augment,
And wish and struggle, as they pass, to reach
The tempting stream, with one small drop to lose
In sweet forgetfulness all pain and woe,
All in one moment, and so near the brink;
But Fate withstands, and to oppose th' attempt
Medusa[9] with *Gorgonian* terror guards
The Ford, and of itself the water flies
All taste of living wight, as once it fled
The lip of *Tantalus*.[1] Thus roving on
In confus'd march forlorn, th' advent'rous Bands
With shudd'ring horror pale, and eyes aghast
View'd first thir lamentable lot, and found
No rest: through many a dark and dreary Vale
They pass'd, and many a Region dolorous,
O'er many a Frozen, many a Fiery Alp,
Rocks, Caves, Lakes, Fens, Bogs, Dens, and shades of death,
A Universe of death, which God by curse
Created evil, for evil only good,
Where all life dies, death lives, and Nature breeds,
Perverse, all monstrous, all prodigious things,
Abominable, inutterable, and worse
Than Fables yet have feign'd, or fear conceiv'd,
Gorgons and *Hydras*, and *Chimeras* dire.[2]
  Meanwhile the Adversary of God and Man,
Satan with thoughts inflam'd of highest design,
Puts on swift wings, and towards the Gates of Hell
Explores his solitary flight; sometimes
He scours the right hand coast, sometimes the left,
Now shaves with level wing the Deep, then soars
Up to the fiery concave tow'ring high.
As when far off at Sea a Fleet descri'd
Hangs in the Clouds, by *Equinoctial* Winds
Close sailing from *Bengala*, or the Isles
Of *Ternate* and *Tidore*, whence Merchants bring
Thir spicy Drugs:[3] they on the Trading Flood

9. One of the Gorgons, mythical sisters with snakes for hair, whose look turned the beholder into stone.
1. In Homer's hell, Tantalus is tormented by thirst, standing in a pool that recedes whenever he tries to drink (*Odyssey* 11.582–92).
2. The Hydra was many-headed, and the Chimeras breathed flame.
3. In Milton's time there was increased trade with "Bengala" (Bengal) and "Ternate" and "Tidore" (two of the "spice islands," or Moluccas). The spice ships would cross the "Ethiopian" Sea (the Indian Ocean) before rounding the Cape of Good Hope.

Through the wide *Ethiopian* to the Cape
Ply stemming nightly toward the Pole. So seem'd
Far off the flying Fiend: at last appear
Hell bounds high reaching to the horrid Roof,
And thrice threefold the Gates; three folds were Brass,
Three Iron, three of Adamantine Rock,
Impenetrable, impal'd° with circling fire, *enclosed*
Yet unconsum'd. Before the Gates there sat
On either side a formidable shape;
The one seem'd Woman to the waist, and fair,[4]
But ended foul in many a scaly fold
Voluminous and vast, a Serpent arm'd
With mortal° sting: about her middle round *death-dealing*
A cry of Hell Hounds never ceasing bark'd
With wide *Cerberean* mouths full loud, and rung
A hideous Peal:[5] yet, when they list, would creep,
If aught disturb'd thir noise, into her womb,
And kennel there, yet there still bark'd and howl'd
Within unseen. Far less abhorr'd than these
Vex'd *Scylla* bathing in the Sea that parts
Calabria from the hoarse *Trinacrian* shore:[6]
Nor uglier follow the Night-Hag,[7] when call'd
In secret, riding through the Air she comes
Lur'd with the smell of infant blood, to dance
With *Lapland* Witches, while the laboring Moon
Eclipses at thir charms. The other shape,
If shape it might be call'd that shape had none
Distinguishable in member, joint, or limb,
Or substance might be call'd that shadow seem'd,
For each seem'd either; black it stood as Night,
Fierce as ten Furies, terrible as Hell,
And shook a dreadful Dart;[8] what seem'd his head
The likeness of a Kingly Crown had on.
Satan was now at hand, and from his seat
The Monster moving onward came as fast,
With horrid strides; Hell trembled as he strode.
Th' undaunted Fiend what this might be admir'd,° *wondered*
Admir'd, not fear'd; God and his Son except,
Created thing naught valu'd he nor shunn'd;

4. The nearest analogue to Milton's Sin is probably Spenser's Errour, who is half serpent and half woman, has a "mortal sting," and swallows her young (*The Faerie Queene* 1.1.14–16). The serpent of sin that tempted Adam and Eve was traditionally portrayed as having a woman's head or bust.

5. There is a whole "cry" (pack) of hounds, because one sin engenders many consequences, sometimes hidden. Cerberus was the many-headed dog who guarded Hades.

6. Circe, jealous of the nymph Scylla, changed her lower parts into a knot of "gaping dogs' heads, such as a Cerberus might have" (Ovid, *Metamorphoses* 14.50–74). Later Scylla was again transformed, into a dangerous rock between "Trinacria" (Sicily) and Calabria. In the medieval moralized Ovid, she became a symbol of lust or of sin.

7. Hecate, whose charms were used by Circe in her spell against Scylla. Milton may allude here to the hellish yeth hounds, which, according to popular superstition, followed the queen of darkness across the sky in pursuit of the souls of the damned.

8. The "dreadful dart" was a traditional attribute of Death, signifying his sharpness and suddenness.

And with disdainful look thus first began.
  Whence and what are thou, execrable shape,
That dar'st, though grim and terrible, advance
Thy miscreated Front athwart my way
To yonder Gates? through them I mean to pass,
That be assured, without leave askt of thee:
Retire, or taste thy folly, and learn by proof,° *experience*
Hell-born, not to contend with Spirits of Heav'n.
  To whom the Goblin full of wrath repli'd:
Art thou that Traitor Angel, art thou hee,
Who first broke peace in Heav'n and Faith, till then
Unbrok'n, and in proud rebellious Arms
Drew after him the third part of Heav'n's Sons
Conjur'd[9] against the Highest, for which both Thou
And they outcast from God, are here condemn'd
To waste Eternal days in woe and pain?
And reck'n'st thou thyself with Spirits of Heav'n,
Hell-doom'd, and breath'st defiance here and scorn,
Where I reign King, and to enrage thee more,
Thy King and Lord? Back to thy punishment,
False fugitive, and to thy speed add wings,
Lest with a whip of Scorpions I pursue
Thy ling'ring, or with one stroke of this Dart
Strange horror seize thee, and pangs unfelt before.
  So spake the grisly terror, and in shape,
So speaking and so threat'ning, grew tenfold
More dreadful and deform: on th' other side
Incens't with indignation *Satan* stood
Unterrifi'd, and like a Comet burn'd,
That fires the length of *Ophiucus*[1] huge
In th' Artic Sky, and from his horrid hair
Shakes Pestilence and War. Each at the Head
Levell'd his deadly aim; thir fatal hands
No second stroke intend, and such a frown
Each cast at th' other, as when two black Clouds
With Heav'n's Artillery fraught, come rattling on
Over the *Caspian*, then stand front to front
Hov'ring a space, till Winds the signal blow
To join thir dark Encounter in mid air:
So frown'd the mighty Combatants, that Hell
Grew darker at thir frown, so matcht they stood;
For never but once more was either like
To meet so great a foe:[2] and now great deeds

9. Sworn together in conspiracy; bewitched.

1. The comet referred to here may be a magnificent one that appeared in 1618 in the constellation *Ophiuchus*. In his diary, John Evelyn held it responsible for the Thirty Years' War. Ophiuchus (Serpent Bearer) is also chosen to allude to Satan's later transformation into a serpent.

2. When Christ destroys "him that had the power of death, that is, the devil" (Hebrews 2.14), as well as "the last enemy . . . death" (1 Corinthians 15.26).

Had been achiev'd, whereof all Hell had rung,
Had not the Snaky Sorceress that sat
Fast by Hell Gate, and kept the fatal Key,
Ris'n, and with hideous outcry rush'd between.
O Father, what intends thy hand, she cri'd,
Against thy only Son?[3] What fury O Son,
Possesses thee to bend that mortal Dart
Against thy Father's head? and know'st for whom;
For him who sits above and laughs the while
At thee ordain'd his drudge, to execute
Whate'er his wrath, which he calls Justice, bids,
His wrath which one day will destroy ye both.
She spake, and at her words the hellish Pest
Forbore, then these to her *Satan* return'd:
So strange thy outcry, and thy words so strange
Thou interposest, that my sudden hand
Prevented spares to tell thee yet by deeds
What it intends; till first I know of thee,
What thing thou art, thus double-form'd, and why
In this infernal Vale first met thou call'st
Me Father, and that Phantasm call'st my Son?
I know thee not, nor ever saw till now
Sight more detestable than him and thee.
T' whom thus the Portress of Hell Gate repli'd:[4]
Hast thou forgot me then, and do I seem
Now in thine eye so foul, once deem'd so fair
In Heav'n, when at th' Assembly, and in sight
Of all the Seraphim with thee combin'd
In bold conspiracy against Heav'n's King,
All on a sudden miserable pain
Surpris'd thee, dim thine eyes, and dizzy swum
In darkness, while thy head flames thick and fast
Threw forth, till on the left side op'ning wide,
Likest to thee in shape and count'nance bright,
Then shining heav'nly fair, a Goddess arm'd
Out of thy head I sprung:[5] amazement seiz'd
All th' Host of Heav'n; back they recoil'd afraid
At first, and call'd me *Sin*, and for a Sign
Portentous held me; but familiar grown,
I pleas'd, and with attractive graces won
The most averse, thee chiefly, who full oft
Thyself in me thy perfect image viewing
Becam'st enamor'd, and such joy thou took'st

3. The allegory whereby Sin is daughter of Satan and mother of Death is from St. Basil's *Hexameron*.
4. Sin's office is an allegorical statement of the idea that access to hell is by sinning.
5. The circumstances of Sin's birth recall the ancient myth about Athena springing fully formed from the head of Zeus. It is thus presented as a parody of God's generation of the Son, since Minerva's birth had traditionally been allegorized by theologians in that sense.

With me in secret, that my womb conceiv'd
A growing burden. Meanwhile War arose,
And fields were fought in Heav'n: wherein remain'd
(For what could else) to our Almighty Foe
Clear Victory, to our part loss and rout
Through all the Empyrean: down they fell
Driv'n headlong from the Pitch° of Heaven, down *summit*
Into this Deep, and in the general fall
I also; at which time this powerful Key
Into my hand was giv'n, with charge to keep
These Gates for ever shut, which none can pass
Without my op'ning. Pensive here I sat
Alone, but long I sat not, till my womb
Pregnant by thee, and now excessive grown
Prodigious motion felt and rueful throes.
At last this odious offspring whom thou seest
Thine own begotten, breaking violent way
Tore through my entrails, that with fear and pain
Distorted, all my nether shape thus grew
Transform'd: but he my inbred enemy
Forth issu'd, brandishing his fatal Dart
Made to destroy: I fled, and cri'd out *Death*;
Hell trembl'd at the hideous Name, and sigh'd
From all her Caves, and back resounded *Death*.
I fled, but he pursu'd (though more, it seems,
Inflam'd with lust than rage) and swifter far,
Mee overtook his mother all dismay'd,
And in embraces forcible and foul
Ingend'ring with me, of that rape begot
These yelling Monsters that with ceasless cry
Surround me, as thou saw'st, hourly conceiv'd
And hourly born, with sorrow infinite
To me, for when they list, into the womb
That bred them they return, and howl and gnaw
My Bowels, thir repast; then bursting forth
Afresh with conscious terrors vex° me round, *harass*
That rest or intermission none I find.[6]
Before mine eyes in opposition sits
Grim *Death* my Son and foe, who sets them on,
And me his Parent would full soon devour
For want of other prey, but that he knows
His end with mine involv'd; and knows that I
Should prove a bitter Morsel, and his bane,
Whenever that shall be; so Fate pronounc'd.
But thou O Father, I forewarn thee, shun
His deadly arrow; neither vainly hope

6. Here Sin's offspring appear to symbolize the pangs of guilt or fear. "Conscious terrors" are terrors of guilty knowledge.

To be invulnerable in those bright Arms,
Though temper'd heav'nly, for that mortal dint,
Save he who reigns above, none can resist.[7]
She finish'd, and the subtle Fiend his lore
Soon learn'd, now milder, and thus answer'd smooth.
Dear Daughter, since thou claim'st me for thy Sire,
And my fair Son here show'st me, the dear pledge
Of dalliance had with thee in Heav'n, and joys
Then sweet, now sad to mention, through dire change
Befall'n us unforeseen, unthought of, know
I come no enemy, but to set free
From out this dark and dismal house of pain,
Both him and thee, and all the heav'nly Host
Of Spirits that in our just pretenses arm'd
Fell with us from on high: from them I go
This uncouth° errand sole, and one for all *strange*
Myself expose, with lonely steps to tread
Th' unfounded° deep, and through the void immense *bottomless*
To search with wand'ring quest a place foretold
Should be, and, by concurring signs, ere now
Created vast and round, a place of bliss
In the Purlieus° of Heav'n, and therein plac't *outskirts*
A race of upstart Creatures, to supply
Perhaps our vacant room, though more remov'd,
Lest Heav'n surcharg'd° with potent multitude *too full*
Might hap to move new broils: Be this or aught
Than this more secret now design'd, I haste
To know, and this once known, shall soon return,
And bring ye to the place where Thou and Death
Shall dwell at ease, and up and down unseen
Wing silently the buxom° Air, imbalm'd[8] *unresisting*
With odors; there ye shall be fed and fill'd
Immeasurably, all things shall be your prey.
He ceas'd, for both seem'd highly pleas'd, and Death
Grinn'd horrible a ghastly smile, to hear
His famine° should be fill'd, and blest his maw *hunger*
Destin'd to that good hour: no less rejoic'd
His mother bad, and thus bespake her Sire.
The key of this infernal Pit by due,
And by command of Heav'n's all-powerful King
I keep, by him forbidden to unlock
These Adamantine Gates; against all force
Death ready stands to interpose his dart,
Fearless to be o'ermatcht by living might.
But what owe I to his commands above

7. Dint: stroke given with a weapon. Only God is immune to death.

8. Balmy, rendered resistent to decay.

Who hates me, and hath hither thrust me down
Into this gloom of *Tartarus* profound,
To sit in hateful Office here confin'd,
Inhabitant of Heav'n, and heav'nly-born,
Here in perpetual agony and pain,
With terrors and with clamors compasst round
Of mine own brood, that on my bowels feed:
Thou art my Father, thou my Author, thou
My being gav'st me; whom should I obey
But thee, whom follow? thou wilt bring me soon
To that new world of light and bliss, among
The Gods who live at ease, where I shall Reign
At thy right hand voluptuous, as beseems
Thy daughter and thy darling, without end.[9]
Thus saying, from her side the fatal Key,
Sad instrument of all our woe, she took;[1]
And towards the Gate rolling her bestial train,
Forthwith the huge Portcullis high up drew,
Which but herself not all the *Stygian* powers
Could once have mov'd; then in the key-hole turns
Th' intricate wards,[2] and every Bolt and Bar
Of massy Iron or solid Rock with ease
Unfast'ns: on a sudden op'n fly
With impetuous recoil and jarring sound
Th' infernal doors, and on thir hinges grate
Harsh Thunder, that the lowest bottom shook
Of *Erebus*.[3] She op'n'd, but to shut
Excell'd her power; the Gates wide op'n stood,
That with extended wings a Banner'd Host
Under spread Ensigns marching might pass through
With Horse and Chariots rankt in loose array;
So wide they stood, and like a Furnace mouth
Cast forth redounding° smoke and ruddy flame. *surging*
Before thir eyes in sudden view appear
The secrets of the hoary deep, a dark
Illimitable Ocean without bound,
Without dimension, where length, breadth, and highth,
And time and place are lost; where eldest *Night*
And *Chaos*, Ancestors of Nature, hold
Eternal Anarchy, amidst the noise
Of endless wars, and by confusion stand.
For hot, cold, moist, and dry, four Champions fierce
Strive here for Maistry, and to Battle bring

9. Parodying the Nicene creed ("on the right hand of the Father . . . [Christ] whose kingdom shall have no end"). In Sin's fantasy, she enjoys glory like Christ's. Satan, Sin, and Death form a complete anti-Trinity.

1. "Sad instrument" may stand in apposition to "she" as well as to "key"; it could mean "a person made use of by another, for the accomplishment of a purpose."

2. The incisions in a key's bit.

3. Classical name for Hell.

Thir embryon Atoms;[4] they around the flag
Of each his Faction, in thir several Clans,
Light-arm'd or heavy, sharp, smooth, swift or slow,
Swarm populous, unnumber'd as the Sands
Of *Barca* or *Cyrene's* torrid soil,[5]
Levied° to side with warring Winds, and poise *enlisted*
Thir lighter wings. To whom these most adhere,
Hee rules a moment; *Chaos* Umpire sits,
And by decision more imbroils the fray
By which he Reigns: next him high Arbiter
Chance governs all. Into this wild Abyss,
The Womb of nature and perhaps her Grave,
Of neither Sea, nor Shore, nor Air, nor Fire,
But all these in thir pregnant causes mixt
Confus'dly, and which thus must ever fight,
Unless th' Almighty Maker them ordain
His dark materials to create more Worlds,
Into this wild Abyss the wary fiend
Stood on the brink of Hell and look'd a while,
Pondering his Voyage: for no narrow frith° *channel*
He had to cross. Nor was his ear less peal'd° *dinned*
With noises loud and ruinous (to compare
Great things with small) than when *Bellona*[6] storms,
With all her battering Engines bent to rase
Some Capital City; or less than if this frame
Of Heav'n were falling, and these Elements
In mutiny had from her Axle torn
The steadfast Earth. At last his Sail-broad Vans° *wings*
He spreads for flight, and in the surging smoke
Uplifted spurns the ground, thence many a League
As in a cloudy Chair ascending rides
Audacious, but that seat soon failing, meets
A vast vacuity: all unawares
Flutt'ring his pennons° vain plumb down he drops *wings*
Ten thousand fadom° deep, and to this hour *fathoms*
Down had been falling, had not by ill chance
The strong rebuff of some tumultuous cloud
Instinct° with Fire and Nitre hurried him *inflamed*
As many miles aloft: that fury stay'd,
Quencht in a Boggy *Syrtis*, neither Sea,[7]
Nor good dry Land, nigh founder'd on he fares,
Treading the crude consistence, half on foot,

4. In Hesiod's *Theogony*, Chaos and Night were made "ancestors" of nature. Milton's description of the strife between contrary qualities that preceded the emergence of the cosmos is close to Ovid's account of the primeval chaos in which "cold things strove with hot, moist with dry, soft with hard, weightless with heavy" (*Metamorphoses* 1.19ff.).

5. "Barca," an ancient city of Cyrenaica, of which "Cyrene" was the capital.

6. Goddess of war, here a metonymy for war itself.

7. The Syrtes were two huge and proverbially dangerous shifting sandbanks off the North African shore.

Half flying;[8] behoves him now both Oar and Sail.
As when a Gryfon through the Wilderness
With winged course o'er Hill or moory Dale,
Pursues the *Arimaspian*, who by stealth
Had from his wakeful custody purloin'd
The guarded Gold: So eagerly the fiend
O'er bog or steep, through strait, rough, dense, or rare,
With head, hands, wings, or feet pursues his way,
And swims or sinks, or wades, or creeps, or flies:
At length a universal hubbub wild
Of stunning sounds and voices all confus'd
Borne through the hollow dark assaults his ear
With loudest vehemence: thither he plies,
Undaunted to meet there whatever power
Or Spirit of the nethermost Abyss
Might in that noise reside, of whom to ask
Which way the nearest coast of darkness lies
Bordering on light; when straight behold the Throne
Of *Chaos*, and his dark Pavilion spread
Wide on the wasteful Deep; with him Enthron'd
Sat Sable-vested *Night*, eldest of things,
The Consort of his Reign; and by them stood
Orcus and *Ades*, and the dreaded name
Of *Demogorgon*;[9] *Rumor* next and *Chance*,
And *Tumult* and *Confusion* all imbroil'd,
And *Discord* with a thousand various mouths.
T' whom *Satan* turning boldly, thus. Ye Powers
And Spirits of this nethermost Abyss,
Chaos and *ancient Night*, I come no Spy,
With purpose to explore or to disturb
The secrets of your Realm, but by constraint
Wand'ring this darksome Desert, as my way
Lies through your spacious Empire up to light,
Alone, and without guide, half lost, I seek
What readiest path leads where your gloomy bounds
Confine with° Heav'n; or if some other place *border on*
From your Dominion won, th' Ethereal King
Possesses lately, thither to arrive
I travel this profound,° direct my course; *deep pit*
Directed, no mean recompence it brings

8. Spenser's dragon of evil is similarly described as "halfe flying, and halfe footing in his hast" (*The Faerie Queene* 1.11.8). The legend of "gold-guarding griffins" in Scythia, from whom the one-eyed Arimaspi steal, was often retold out of Herodotus (3.116) and Pliny (*Natural History* 7.10). The griffin (a composite monster: half eagle, half lion) is appropriate here partly because it was subdued by the sun god Apollo, as Satan will be by Christ.

9. In general, this court of personifications resembles Virgil's halls of Pluto (*Aeneid* 6.268–81), though the only member common to both is Discord. Milton's Demogorgon is from Boccaccio's *De genealogia deorum*, in which he comes first of all the dark gods. Among his brood are Night, Tartarus, Erebus, the serpent Python, Litigium (cf. Milton's Tumult and Discord), and Fama (Milton's Rumor). Orcus and Ades are Latin and Greek names of Pluto, god of hell.

To your behoof, if I that Region lost,
All usurpation thence expell'd, reduce
To her original darkness and your sway
(Which is my present journey) and once more
Erect the Standard there of *ancient Night;*
Yours be th' advantage all, mine the revenge.
Thus *Satan;* and him thus the Anarch[1] old
With falt'ring speech and visage incompos'd° *disordered*
Answer'd. I know thee, stranger, who thou art,
That mighty leading Angel, who of late
Made head against Heav'n's King, though overthrown.
I saw and heard, for such a numerous Host
Fled not in silence through the frighted deep
With ruin upon ruin, rout on rout,
Confusion worse confounded; and Heav'n Gates
Pour'd out by millions her victorious Bands
Pursuing. I upon my Frontiers here
Keep residence; if all I can will serve,
That little which is left so to defend,
Encroacht on still through our intestine broils
Weak'ning the Sceptre of old *Night:* first Hell
Your dungeon stretching far and wide beneath;
Now lately Heaven and Earth, another World
Hung o'er my Realm, link'd in a golden Chain
To that side Heav'n from whence your Legions fell:
If that way be your walk, you have not far;
So much the nearer danger; go and speed;
Havoc and spoil and ruin are my gain.
He ceas'd; and *Satan* stay'd not to reply,
But glad that now his Sea should find a shore,
With fresh alacrity and force renew'd
Springs upward like a Pyramid of fire
Into the wild expanse, and through the shock
Of fighting Elements, on all sides round
Environ'd wins his way; harder beset
And more endanger'd, than when *Argo* pass'd
Through *Bosporus* betwixt the justling° Rocks:[2] *jostling*
Or when *Ulysses* on the Larboard shunn'd
Charybdis, and by th' other whirlpool steer'd.[3]
So he with difficulty and labor hard
Mov'd on, with difficulty and labor hee;
But hee once past, soon after when man fell,
Strange alteration! Sin and Death amain° *without delay*

1. Chaos, ruler or antiruler of the "eternal anarchy" (line 896).
2. When Jason and the Argonauts sailed through the Bosporus (Straits of Constantinople) en route to Colchis, their boat, the *Argo*, narrowly escaped destruction between the Symplegades, the clashing or "jostling" rocks. See Apollonius Rhodius, *Argonautica* 2.317, 552–611.
3. Homer tells how Odysseus followed Circe's advice in avoiding Charybdis and sailing close by Scylla ("the other whirlpool") in his passage through the Straits of Messina between Sicily and Italy (*Odyssey* 12).

Following his track, such was the will of Heav'n,
Pav'd after him a broad and beat'n way
Over the dark Abyss, whose boiling Gulf
Tamely endur'd a Bridge of wondrous length
From Hell continu'd reaching th' utmost Orb
Of this frail World; by which the Spirits perverse
With easy intercourse pass to and fro
To tempt or punish mortals, except whom
God and good Angels guard by special grace.
But now at last the sacred influence
Of light appears, and from the walls of Heav'n
Shoots far into the bosom of dim Night
A glimmering dawn; here Nature first begins
Her fardest° verge, and *Chaos* to retire *farthest*
As from her outmost works a brok'n foe
With tumult less and with less hostile din,
That *Satan* with less toil, and now with ease
Wafts on the calmer wave by dubious light
And like a weather-beaten Vessel holds° *remains in*
Gladly the Port, though Shrouds and Tackle torn;
Or in the emptier waste, resembling Air,
Weighs his spread wings, at leisure to behold
Far off th' Empyreal Heav'n, extended wide
In circuit, undetermin'd square or round,[4]
With Opal Tow'rs and Battlements adorn'd
Of living° Sapphire, once his native Seat; *unshaped*
And fast by hanging in a golden Chain[5]
This pendant world, in bigness as a Star
Of smallest Magnitude close by the Moon.
Thither full fraught with mischievous revenge,
Accurst, and in a cursed hour he hies.

The End of the Second Book.

Book 3

The Argument

God sitting on his Throne sees Satan *flying towards this world, then newly created; shows him to the Son who sat at his right hand; foretells the success of* Satan *in perverting mankind; clears his own Justice and Wisdom from all imputation, having created Man free and able enough to have withstood his Tempter; yet declares his purpose of grace towards him, in regard he fell not of his own malice, as did* Satan, *but by him seduc't. The Son of God renders praises to his Father for the manifestation of his gracious purpose towards Man;*

4. So wide that it was impossible to tell whether the boundary was rectilinear or curved.
5. Homer's Zeus asserts his transcendence by claiming that if a golden chain were lowered from Heaven, he could draw up by it all the other gods, together with the earth and the sea, and hang them from a pinnacle of Olympus (*Iliad* 8.18–27). Milton interprets this chain as "the universal concord and sweet union of all things which Pythagoras poetically figures as harmony" (*Prolusion* 2), thus accepting a philosophical and literary tradition that runs from Plato through Boethius, Chaucer, and Spenser.

but God again declares, that Grace cannot be extended towards Man without the satisfaction of divine Justice; Man hath offended the majesty of God by aspiring to Godhead, and therefore with all his Progeny devoted to death must die, unless some one can be found sufficient to answer for his offense, and undergo his Punishment. The Son of God freely offers himself a Ransom for Man: the Father accepts him, ordains his incarnation, pronounces his exaltation above all Names in Heaven and Earth; commands all the Angels to adore him; they obey, and hymning to thir Harps in full Choir, celebrate the Father and the Son. Meanwhile Satan *alights upon the bare convex of this World's outermost Orb; where wand'ring he first finds a place since call'd The Limbo of Vanity; what persons and things fly up thither; thence comes to the Gate of Heaven, describ'd ascending by stairs, and the waters above the Firmament that flow about it: His passage thence to the Orb of the Sun; he finds there* Uriel *the Regent of that Orb, but first changes himself into the shape of a meaner Angel; and pretending a zealous desire to behold the new Creation and Man whom God had plac't there, inquires of him the place of his habitation, and is directed; alights first on Mount* Niphates.

Hail holy Light, offspring of Heav'n first-born,
Or of th' Eternal Coeternal beam
May I express thee unblam'd?[1] since God is Light,
And never but in unapproached Light
Dwelt from Eternity, dwelt then in thee,
Bright effluence° of bright essence increate.[2] *radiance*
Or hear'st thou rather[3] pure Ethereal stream,
Whose Fountain who shall tell? before the Sun,
Before the Heavens thou wert, and at the voice
Of God, as with a Mantle didst invest° *cover*
The rising world of waters dark and deep,
Won from the void° and formless infinite.[4] *chaos*
Thee I revisit now with bolder wing,
Escap't the *Stygian* Pool, though long detain'd
In that obscure sojourn, while in my flight
Through utter and through middle darkness borne[5]
With other notes than to th' *Orphean* Lyre
I sung of Chaos and Eternal Night,
Taught by the heav'nly Muse° to venture down *Urania*
The dark descent, and up to reascend,
Though hard and rare:[6] thee I revisit safe,
And feel thy sovran vital Lamp; but thou

1. The light of the invocation has been interpreted as the Son of God, as physical light, and as the principal image of God and the divine emanation itself, according to the Platonic system. Milton proposes three images or forms of address, "offspring," "beam," and "stream," each of which associates the divine Light or Wisdom with a different aspect of deity. The blame could attach only to using the second name, "co-eternal beam;" it is this name that is justified by the implicit appeal to scriptural authority.

2. "God is Light," from 1 John 1.5. God "only hath immortality, dwelling in the light which no man can approach unto" (1 Timothy 6.16). "Essence increate," the uncreated divine essence. In the physics and metaphysics of Milton's time, light was regarded as an "accident" (quality), not a body or substance.

3. Do you prefer to be called.

4. See Genesis 1.1–5.

5. The "Stygian pool" and the "utter" (outer) darkness are hell; the "middle darkness" is chaos.

6. Alluding to the "fable of Orpheus, whom they faigne to have recovered his Euridice from Hell with his Musick, that is, Truth and Equity from darkenesse of Barbarisme and Ignorance with his profound and excellent Doctrines; but, that in the way to the upper-earth, she was lost againe" (Henry Reynolds, *Mythomystes*). "Other notes," because Milton, unlike Orpheus, claims not to have lost his Eurydice.

Revisit'st not these eyes, that roll in vain
To find thy piercing ray, and find no dawn;
So thick a drop serene[7] hath quencht thir Orbs,
Or dim suffusion° veil'd. Yet not the more *cataract*
Cease I to wander where the Muses haunt
Clear Spring, or shady Grove, or Sunny Hill,
Smit with the love of sacred Song;[8] but chief
Thee *Sion*[9] and the flow'ry Brooks beneath
That wash thy hallow'd feet, and warbling flow,
Nightly I visit: nor sometimes forget
Those other two equall'd with me in Fate,
So were I equall'd with them in renown,
Blind *Thamyris* and blind *Maeonides*,
And *Tiresias* and *Phineus* Prophets old.[1]
Then feed on thoughts, that voluntary move
Harmonious numbers;° as the wakeful Bird[2] *rhythmic measure*
Sings darkling,° and in shadiest Covert hid *in the dark*
Tunes her nocturnal Note. Thus with the Year
Seasons return, but not to me returns
Day, or the sweet approach of Ev'n or Morn,
Or sight of vernal bloom, or Summer's Rose,
Or flocks, or herds, or human face divine;
But cloud instead, and ever-during dark
Surrounds me, from the cheerful ways of men
Cut off, and for the Book of knowledge[3] fair
Presented with a Universal blanc° *blank*
Of Nature's works to me expung'd and ras'd,° *erased*
And wisdom at one entrance quite shut out.
So much the rather thou Celestial Light
Shine inward, and the mind through all her powers
Irradiate, there plant eyes, all mist from thence
Purge and disperse, that I may see and tell
Of things invisible to mortal sight.
Now had th' Almighty Father from above,
From the pure Empyrean where he sits
High Thron'd above all highth, bent down his eye,
His own works and their works at once to view:
About him all the Sanctities of Heaven
Stood thick as Stars, and from his sight receiv'd
Beatitude past utterance; on his right

7. Literally translating *gutta serena*, the medical term for the form of blindness from which Milton suffered.
8. An allusion to Virgil's prayer that "smitten with a great love" of the Muses, he may be shown by them the secrets of nature (*Georgics* 2.475–89).
9. The mountain of scriptural inspiration.
1. Thamyris was a Thracian poet who fell in love with the Muses and challenged them to a contest in which the loser was to give the winner whatever he wanted. The Muses, having won, took Thamyris's eyes and his lyre. Maeonides was Homer's surname; the contrast between his outward blindness and inner vision was a commonplace. In *De Idea Platonica*, Milton writes of Tiresias that his "very blindness gave him boundless light." The Thracian king Phineus lost his sight because he had become too good a prophet.
2. The nightingale. The soul of Thamyris passed into a nightingale.
3. The Book of Nature.

The radiant image of his Glory sat,
His only Son; On Earth he first beheld
Our two first Parents, yet the only two
Of mankind, in the happy Garden plac't,
Reaping immortal fruits of joy and love,
Uninterrupted joy, unrivall'd love
In blissful solitude; he then survey'd
Hell and the Gulf between, and *Satan* there
Coasting the wall of Heav'n on this side Night
In the dun° Air sublime,° and ready now *dusky / aloft*
To stoop with wearied wings, and willing feet
On the bare outside of this World, that seem'd
Firm land imbosom'd without Firmament,[4]
Uncertain which, in Ocean or in Air.
Him God beholding from his prospect high,
Wherein past, present, future he beholds,
Thus to his only Son foreseeing spake.
Only begotten Son, seest thou what rage
Transports our adversary, whom no bounds
Prescrib'd, no bars of Hell, nor all the chains
Heapt on him there, nor yet the main Abyss
Wide interrupt° can hold; so bent he seems *divided*
On desperate revenge, that shall redound
Upon his own rebellious head. And now
Through all restraint broke loose he wings his way
Not far off Heav'n, in the Precincts of light,
Directly towards the new created World,
And Man there plac't, with purpose to assay° *test*
If him by force he can destroy, or worse,
By some false guile pervert; and shall pervert;
For Man will heark'n to his glozing° lies, *flattering*
And easily transgress the sole Command,[5]
Sole pledge of his obedience: So will fall
Hee and his faithless Progeny: whose fault?
Whose but his own? ingrate, he had of mee
All he could have; I made him just and right,
Sufficient to have stood, though free to fall.
Such I created all th' Ethereal Powers
And Spirits, both them who stood and them who fail'd;
Freely they stood who stood, and fell who fell.
Not free, what proof could they have giv'n sincere
Of true allegiance, constant Faith or Love,
Where only what they needs must do, appear'd,
Not what they would? what praise could they receive?
What pleasure I from such obedience paid,
When Will and Reason (Reason also is choice)

4. The firmament or atmosphere, being inside the shell of the universe that Satan stands on, is invisible to him.

5. I.e., not to taste the fruit of the forbidden tree.

Useless and vain, of freedom both despoil'd,
Made passive both, had serv'd necessity,
Not mee. They therefore as to right belong'd,
So were created, nor can justly accuse
Thir maker, or thir making, or thir Fate;
As if Predestination over-rul'd
Thir will, dispos'd by absolute Decree
Or high foreknowledge; they themselves decreed
Thir own revolt, not I: if I foreknew,
Foreknowledge had no influence on their fault,
Which had no less prov'd certain unforeknown.
So without least impulse or shadow of Fate,
Or aught by me immutably foreseen,
They trespass, Authors to themselves in all
Both what they judge and what they choose; for so
I form'd them free, and free they must remain,
Till they enthrall themselves: I else must change
Thir nature, and revoke the high Decree
Unchangeable, Eternal, which ordain'd
Thir freedom: they themselves ordain'd thir fall.
The first sort[6] by thir own suggestion° fell, *temptation*
Self-tempted, self-deprav'd: Man falls deceiv'd
By th' other first: Man therefore shall find grace,
The other none: in Mercy and Justice both,
Through Heav'n and Earth, so shall my glory excel,
But Mercy first and last shall brightest shine.

Thus while God spake, ambrosial fragrance fill'd
All Heav'n, and in the blessed Spirits elect[7]
Sense of new joy ineffable diffus'd:
Beyond compare the Son of God was seen
Most glorious, in him all his Father shone
Substantially express'd, and in his face
Divine compassion visibly appear'd,
Love without end, and without measure Grace,
Which uttering thus he to his Father spake.

O Father, gracious was that word which clos'd
Thy sovran° sentence, that Man should find grace; *sovereign*
For which both Heav'n and Earth shall high extol
Thy praises, with th' innumerable sound
Of Hymns and sacred Songs, wherewith thy Throne
Encompass'd shall resound thee ever blest.
For should Man finally be lost, should Man
Thy creature late so lov'd, thy youngest Son
Fall circumvented thus by fraud, though join'd
With his own folly? that be from thee far,
That far be from thee, Father, who art Judge

6. Satan and the rebel angels.
7. The "elect angels" of 1 Timothy 5.21, explained in Milton's *De doctrina* 1.9 as angels "who have not revolted."

Of all things made, and judgest only right.
Or shall the Adversary[8] thus obtain
His end, and frustrate thine, shall he fulfil
His malice, and thy goodness bring to naught,
Or proud return though to his heavier doom,
Yet with revenge accomplish't and to Hell
Draw after him the whole Race of mankind,
By him corrupted? or wilt thou thyself
Abolish thy Creation, and unmake,
For him, what for thy glory thou hast made?
So should thy goodness and thy greatness both
Be question'd and blasphem'd without defense.
To whom the great Creator thus repli'd.
O Son, in whom my Soul hath chief delight,[9]
Son of my bosom, Son who art alone
My word, my wisdom, and effectual might,
All hast thou spok'n as my thoughts are, all
As my Eternal purpose hath decreed:
Man shall not quite be lost, but sav'd who will,
Yet not of will in him, but grace in me
Freely voutsaf't;° once more I will renew *vouchsafed*
His lapsed° powers, though forfeit and enthrall'd *decayed*
By sin to foul exorbitant desires;
Upheld by me, yet once more he shall stand
On even ground against his mortal foe,
By me upheld, that he may know how frail
His fall'n condition is, and to me owe
All his deliv'rance, and to none but me.
Some I have chosen of peculiar grace
Elect above the rest; so is my will:[1]
The rest shall hear me call, and oft be warn'd
Thir sinful state, and to appease betimes
Th' incensed Deity while offer'd grace
Invites; for I will clear thir senses dark,
What may suffice, and soft'n stony hearts
To pray, repent, and bring obedience due.
To Prayer, repentance, and obedience due,
Though but endeavor'd with sincere intent,
Mine ear shall not be slow, mine eye not shut.
And I will place within them as a guide
My Umpire *Conscience*, whom if they will hear,

8. The literal meaning of "Satan."

9. Echoing Mark 1.11, the words out of the heavens at Jesus' baptism: "Thou art my beloved Son, in whom I am well pleased."

1. In *De doctrina* 1.4, Milton sets out an Arminian position, explicitly opposed to the Calvinist, on such doctrines as predestination, election, and reprobation, and he could be regarded as doing something similar here (lines 173–202); e.g., his God seems to make salvation depend on humans' will to avail themselves of grace, or on "prayer, repentance, and obedience" (line 191), whereas Calvinists regarded humans as incapable of contributing in any way to their own salvation. By the term "elect," Milton usually means no more than "whoever believes and continues in the faith."

Light after light well us'd they shall attain,
And to the end persisting, safe arrive.
This my long sufferance and my day of grace
They who neglect and scorn, shall never taste;
But hard be hard'n'd, blind be blinded more,
That they may stumble on, and deeper fall;
And none but such from mercy I exclude.
But yet all is not done; Man disobeying,
Disloyal breaks his fealty, and sins
Against the high Supremacy of Heav'n,
Affecting° God-head, and so losing all, *seeking*
To expiate his Treason hath naught left,
But to destruction sacred and devote,° *dedicated*
He with his whole posterity must die,
Die hee or Justice must; unless for him
Some other able, and as willing, pay
The rigid satisfaction, death for death.[2]
Say Heav'nly Powers, where shall we find such love,
Which of ye will be mortal[3] to redeem
Man's mortal crime, and just th' unjust to save,
Dwells in all Heaven charity° so dear? *compassionate love*
He ask'd, but all the Heav'nly Choir stood mute,
And silence was in Heav'n: on man's behalf
Patron or Intercessor none appear'd,
Much less that durst upon his own head draw
The deadly forfeiture, and ransom set.[4]
And now without redemption all mankind
Must have been lost, adjudg'd to Death and Hell
By doom° severe, had not the Son of God, *judgment*
In whom the fulness dwells of love divine,
His dearest mediation thus renew'd.
Father, thy word is past,[5] man shall find grace;
And shall grace not find means, that finds her way,
The speediest of thy winged messengers,
To visit all thy creatures, and to all
Comes unprevented,° unimplor'd, unsought? *unanticipated*
Happy for man, so coming; he her aid
Can never seek, once dead in sins and lost;
Atonement for himself or offering meet,
Indebted and undone, hath none to bring:
Behold mee then, mee for him, life for life
I offer, on mee let thine anger fall;
Account mee man; I for his sake will leave
Thy bosom, and this glory next to thee

2. Note that human death is here regarded by God not as a punishment, but as a "satisfaction" for the treason. See *De doctrina* 1.16: "The satisfaction of Christ is the complete reparation made by him . . . by the fulfilment of the Law, and payment of the required price for all mankind."
3. Is willing to be subject to death.
4. Put down the ransom price (by giving his own life).
5. Your word of honor is pledged.

Freely put off, and for him lastly die
Well pleas'd, on me let Death wreck all his rage;
Under his gloomy power I shall not long
Lie vanquisht; thou hast giv'n me to possess
Life in myself for ever, by thee I live,[6]
Though now to Death I yield, and am his due
All that of me can die, yet that debt paid,
Thou wilt not leave me in the loathsome grave
His prey, nor suffer my unspotted Soul
For ever with corruption there to dwell;
But I shall rise Victorious, and subdue
My vanquisher, spoil'd of his vaunted spoil;
Death his death's wound shall then receive, and stoop
Inglorious, of his mortal sting disarm'd.[7]
I through the ample Air in Triumph high
Shall lead Hell Captive maugre° Hell, and show *despite*
The powers of darkness bound. Thou at the sight
Pleas'd, out of Heaven shalt look down and smile,
While by thee rais'd I ruin all my Foes,
Death last, and with his Carcass glut the Grave:[8]
Then with the multitude of my redeem'd
Shall enter Heav'n long absent, and return,
Father, to see thy face, wherein no cloud
Of anger shall remain, but peace assur'd,
And reconcilement; wrath shall be no more
Thenceforth, but in thy presence Joy entire.
His words here ended, but his meek aspéct
Silent yet spake, and breath'd immortal love
To mortal men, above which only shone
Filial obedience: as a sacrifice
Glad to be offer'd, he attends° the will *awaits*
Of his great Father. Admiration seiz'd
All Heav'n, what this might mean, and whither tend
Wond'ring; but soon th' Almighty thus repli'd:
O thou in Heav'n and Earth the only peace
Found out for mankind under wrath, O thou
My sole complacence! well thou know'st how dear
To me are all my works, nor Man the least
Though last created, that for him I spare
Thee from my bosom and right hand, to save,
By losing thee a while, the whole Race lost.
Thou therefore whom thou only canst redeem,
Thir Nature also to thy Nature join;
And be thyself Man among men on Earth,

6. See John 5.26: "As the Father hath life in himself: so hath he given to the Son to have life in himself."
7. See 1 Corinthians 15.55–56: "O death, where is thy sting? O grave, where is thy victory? The sting of death is sin; and the strength of sin is the law."
8. Alludes to 1 Corinthians 15.26: "The last enemy that shall be destroyed is death."

Made flesh, when time shall be, of Virgin seed,
By wondrous birth: Be thou in *Adam's* room° *place*
The Head of all mankind, though *Adam's* Son.
As in him perish all men, so in thee
As from a second root shall be restor'd,
As many as are restor'd, without thee none.[9]
His crime makes guilty all his Sons, thy merit
Imputed shall absolve them who renounce
Thir own both righteous and unrighteous deeds,[1]
And live in thee transplanted, and from thee
Receive new life. So Man, as is most just,
Shall satisfy for Man, be judg'd and die,
And dying rise, and rising with him raise
His Brethren, ransom'd with his own dear life.
So Heav'nly love shall outdo Hellish hate,
Giving to death, and dying to redeem,
So dearly to redeem what Hellish hate
So easily destroy'd, and still destroys
In those who, when they may, accept not grace.
Nor shalt thou by descending to assume
Man's Nature, lessen or degrade thine own.
Because thou hast, though Thron'd in highest bliss
Equal to God, and equally enjoying
God-like fruition, quitted[2] all to save
A world from utter loss, and hast been found
By Merit more than Birthright Son of God,
Found worthiest to be so by being Good,
Far more than Great or High; because in thee
Love hath abounded more than Glory abounds,
Therefore thy Humiliation shall exalt
With thee thy Manhood also to this Throne;
Here shalt thou sit incarnate, here shalt Reign
Both God and Man, Son both of God and Man,
Anointed[3] universal King; all Power
I give thee, reign for ever, and assume
Thy Merits; under thee as Head Supreme
Thrones, Princedoms, Powers, Dominions I reduce:
All knees to thee shall bow, of them that bide
In Heaven, or Earth, or under Earth in Hell;
When thou attended gloriously from Heav'n
Shalt in the Sky appear, and from thee send
The summoning Arch-Angels to proclaim
Thy dread Tribunal: forthwith from all Winds

9. See 1 Corinthians 15.22: "As in Adam all die, even so in Christ shall all be made alive."

1. See *De doctrina* 1.22: "As therefore our sins are imputed to Christ, so the merits or righteousness of Christ are imputed to us through faith." If one simply renounced dependence on "righteous" deeds, one would be justified by faith alone; but for the "living faith"—faith issuing in works—that Milton believes necessary, one has to renounce (in a different sense) "unrighteous" deeds.

2. A pun, since "quitted" meant "redeemed, remitted" as well as "left."

3. The "Anointed" in Hebrew is the Messiah.

The living, and forthwith the cited° dead *summoned*
Of all past Ages to the general Doom° *judgment*
Shall hast'n, such a peal shall rouse thir sleep.
Then all thy Saints° assembl'd, thou shalt judge *elect*
Bad men and Angels, they arraign'd shall sink
Beneath thy Sentence; Hell, her numbers full,
Thenceforth shall be for ever shut. Meanwhile
The World shall burn, and from her ashes spring
New Heav'n and Earth, wherein the just shall dwell
And after all thir tribulations long
See golden days, fruitful of golden deeds,
With Joy and Love triumphing, and fair Truth.[4]
Then thou thy regal Sceptre shalt lay by,
For regal Sceptre then no more shall need,
God shall be All in All. But all ye Gods,° *angels*
Adore him, who to compass all this dies,
Adore the Son, and honor him as mee.
  No sooner had th' Almighty ceas't, but all
The multitude of Angels with a shout
Loud as from numbers without number, sweet
As from blest voices, uttering joy, Heav'n rung
With Jubilee, and loud Hosannas fill'd
Th' eternal Regions: lowly reverent
Towards either Throne they bow, and to the ground
With solemn adoration down they cast
Thir Crowns inwove with Amarant and Gold,
Immortal Amarant,[5] a Flow'r which once
In Paradise, fast by the Tree of Life
Began to bloom, but soon for man's offense
To Heav'n remov'd where first it grew, there grows,
And flow'rs aloft shading the Fount of Life,
And where the river of Bliss through midst of Heav'n
Rolls o'er *Elysian* Flow'rs her Amber stream;[6]
With these that never fade the Spirits elect
Bind thir resplendent locks inwreath'd with beams,
Now in loose Garlands thick thrown off, the bright
Pavement that like a Sea of Jasper shone
Impurpl'd with Celestial Roses smil'd.
Then Crown'd again thir gold'n Harps they took,
Harps ever tun'd, that glittering by thir side
Like Quivers hung, and with Preamble sweet
Of charming symphony they introduce
Thir sacred Song, and waken raptures high;
No voice exempt,° no voice but well could join *debarred*

4. The burning of Earth is based on 2 Peter 3.12ff.
5. "Amaranth" in Greek means "unwithering"; a purple flower that was a "symbol of immortality"; the amarantine crown was an ancient pagan symbol of untroubled tranquillity and health.
6. Allusion to Virgil, *Aeneid* 6.656–59, the description of spirits chanting in chorus beside the Eridanus, in the Elysian fields; "amber" was a standard of purity or clarity.

Melodious part, such concord is in Heav'n.
  Thee Father first they sung Omnipotent,
Immutable, Immortal, Infinite,[7]
Eternal King; thee Author of all being,
Fountain of Light, thyself invisible
Amidst the glorious brightness where thou sit'st
Thron'd inaccessible, but° when thou shad'st *except*
The full blaze of thy beams, and through a cloud
Drawn round about thee like a radiant Shrine,
Dark with excessive bright thy skirts appear,
Yet dazzle Heav'n, that brightest Seraphim
Approach not, but with both wings veil thir eyes.
Thee next they sang of all Creation first,
Begotten Son, Divine Similitude,
In whose conspicuous count'nance, without cloud
Made visible, th' Almighty Father shines,
Whom else no Creature can behold;[8] on the
Impresst th' effulgence of his Glory abides,
Transfus'd on thee his ample Spirit rests.
Hee Heav'n of Heavens and all the Powers therein
By thee created, and by thee threw down
Th' aspiring Dominations:° thou that day *rebel angels*
Thy Father's dreadful Thunder didst not spare,
Nor stop thy flaming Chariot wheels, that shook
Heav'n's everlasting Frame, while o'er the necks
Thou drov'st of warring Angels disarray'd.
Back from pursuit thy Powers with loud acclaim
Thee only extoll'd, Son of thy Father's might,
To execute fierce vengeance on his foes:
Not so on Man; him through their malice fall'n,
Father of Mercy and Grace, thou didst not doom° *judge*
So strictly, but much more to pity incline:
No sooner did thy dear and only Son
Perceive thee purpos'd not to doom frail Man
So strictly, but much more to pity inclin'd,[9]
Hee to appease thy wrath, and end the strife
Of Mercy and Justice in thy face discern'd,
Regardless of the Bliss wherein hee sat
Second to thee, offer'd himself to die
For man's offense. O unexampl'd love,
Love nowhere to be found less than Divine!
Hail Son of God, Savior of Men, thy Name
Shall be the copious matter of my Song
Henceforth, and never shall my Harp thy praise

7. Line 373 is transplanted in its entirety from Sylvester's translation of Du Bartas's poem on creation.
8. See John 1.18 and 14.9.
9. Most editors say that "but" or "than" has to be supplied before "He" (line 406). However, if "much more to pity inclined" refers to the Son, the "but" immediately preceding is available for the main clause.

Forget, nor from thy Father's praise disjoin.
  Thus they in Heav'n, above the starry Sphere,
Thir happy hours in joy and hymning spent.
Meanwhile upon the firm opacous Globe
Of this round World, whose first convex divides
The luminous inferior Orbs, enclos'd
From *Chaos* and th' inroad of Darkness old,[1]
Satan alighted walks: a Globe far off
It seem'd, now seems a boundless Continent
Dark, waste, and wild, under the frown of Night
Starless expos'd, and ever-threat'ning storms
Of *Chaos* blust'ring round, inclement sky;
Save on that side which from the wall of Heav'n,
Though distant far, some small reflection gains
Of glimmering air less vext° with tempest loud: *tossed about*
Here walk'd the Fiend at large in spacious field.
As when a Vultur on *Imaus* bred,
Whose snowy ridge the roving *Tartar* bounds,
Dislodging from a Region scarce of prey
To gorge the flesh of Lambs or yeanling Kids
On Hills where Flocks are fed, flies toward the Springs
Of *Ganges* or *Hydaspes*, *Indian* streams;
But in his way lights on the barren Plains
Of *Sericana*, where *Chineses* drive
With Sails and Wind thir cany Waggons light:
So on this windy Sea of Land, the Fiend
Walk'd up and down alone bent on his prey,[2]
Alone, for other Creature in this place
Living or lifeless to be found was none,
None yet, but store hereafter from the earth
Up hither like Aereal vapors flew
Of all things transitory and vain, when Sin
With vanity had fill'd the works of men:[3]
Both all things vain, and all who in vain things
Built thir fond hopes of Glory or lasting fame,
Or happiness in this or th' other life;
All who have thir reward on Earth, the fruits
Of painful Superstition and blind Zeal,
Naught seeking but the praise of men, here find
Fit retribution, empty as thir deeds;

1. The "starry Sphere" is either the sphere of the fixed stars or, more loosely, the stars and planets together. The stars are enclosed within the *primum mobile* or "first convex" (sphere). Both heaven and chaos lie outside that opaque ("opacous") shell.

2. The simile compares the vulture's journey to Satan's. One journey is from Imaus (a mountain range said to run through Afghanistan) to the rivers of India; the other is from the "frozen continent" (2.587) of Tartarus, which did not keep Satan from roving, to Eden with its rivers. The "barren plains of Sericana" correspond to the *primum mobile* because both are stopping places and in both the elements are confused. (The Chinese use sails, the means of propulsion for ships, on their land vehicles; and the *primum mobile* is a "sea of land.")

3. In *Orlando Furioso* 34.73ff., a passage from which Milton quotes in *Of Reformation*, Ariosto tells how Astolfo searches for his lost wits in a Limbo of Vanity on the moon.

All th' unaccomplisht works of Nature's hand,
Abortive, monstrous, or unkindly mixt,
Dissolv'd on Earth, fleet hither, and in vain,
Till final dissolution, wander here,
Not in the neighboring Moon, as some have dream'd;
Those argent Fields more likely habitants,
Translated Saints,[4] or middle Spirits hold
Betwixt th' Angelical and Human kind:
Hither of ill-join'd Sons and Daughters born
First from the ancient World those Giants came
With many a vain exploit, though then renown'd:[5]
The builders next of *Babel* on the Plain
Of *Sennaar*, and still with vain design
New *Babels*, had they wherewithal, would build:[6]
Others came single; he who to be deem'd
A God, leap'd fondly into *Ætna* flames,
Empedocles, and hee who to enjoy
Plato's Elysium, leap'd into the Sea,
Cleombrotus,[7] and many more too long,
Embryos, and Idiots, Eremites and Friars
White, Black and Grey, with all thir trumpery.[8]
Here Pilgrims roam, that stray'd so far to seek
In *Golgotha*[9] him dead, who lives in Heav'n;
And they who to be sure of Paradise
Dying put on the weeds of *Dominic*,
Or in *Franciscan* think to pass disguis'd;[1]
They pass the Planets seven, and pass the fixt,
And that Crystalline Sphere whose balance weighs
The Trepidation talkt, and that first mov'd;[2]
And now Saint *Peter* at Heav'n's Wicket seems
To wait them with his Keys, and now at foot
Of Heav'n's ascent they lift thir Feet, when lo
A violent cross wind from either Coast
Blows them transverse ten thousand Leagues awry
Into the devious Air; then might ye see
Cowls, Hoods and Habits with thir weares tost

4. Probably such as Enoch (Genesis 5.24) and Elijah (2 Kings 2).

5. The first group of fools are the Giants, "mighty men . . . of renown," born of the misunion of "sons of God" with "daughters of men" (Genesis 6.4).

6. At 12.45–47 the builders of Babel are said to have formed their "vain design" out of a desire for fame. "New Babels" suggests the New Babylon of anti-Papist propaganda.

7. Empedocles and Cleombrotus were not associated by classical writers but occur together in Lactantius' chapter on "Pythagoreans and Stoics who, Believing in the Immortality of the Soul, Foolishly Persuade a Voluntary Death" (*Divinae Institutiones* 3.18). Cleombrotus drowned himself after an unwise reading of Plato's *Phaedo;* Empedocles' motive was to conceal his own mortality.

8. Milton here satirizes a Catholic tradition that consigned cretins and unbaptized infants to a much debated *limbo infantum*. The friars were specified by robe color; "white" meant Carmelite, "black" Dominican, and "grey" Franciscan. The contemptuous juxtaposition of all three colors ridicules the importance assigned to external trappings. "Eremites" were Order of Friars Hermits.

9. The hill where Christ was crucified and buried.

1. Compare *Inferno* 27.67–84, in which Dante tells how Guido da Montefeltro hoped to get into heaven by virtue of Franciscan robes but found to his cost that absolution without repentance is vain.

2. In order of proximity to earth, the spheres passed are the seven planetary spheres; the eighth sphere, containing the "fixed" stars; the ninth, "crystalline sphere;" and the tenth sphere, the "first moved" or *primum mobile*.

And flutter'd into Rags, then Reliques, Beads,
Indulgences, Dispenses,[3] Pardons, Bulls,
The sport of Winds: all these upwhirl'd aloft
Fly o'er the backside of the World far off
Into a *Limbo*° large and broad, since call'd *empty region*
The Paradise of Fools, to few unknown
Long after, now unpeopl'd and untrod;
All this dark Globe the Fiend found as he pass'd,
And long he wander'd, till at last a gleam
Of dawning light turn'd thither-ward in haste
His travell'd steps; far distant he descries
Ascending by degrees magnificent
Up to the wall of Heaven a Structure high,
At top whereof, but far more rich appear'd
The work as of a Kingly Palace Gate
With Frontispiece[4] of Diamond and Gold
Imbellisht; thick with sparkling orient° Gems *brilliant*
The Portal shone, inimitable on Earth
By Model, or by shading Pencil drawn.
The Stairs were such as whereon *Jacob* saw
Angels ascending and descending, bands
Of Guardians bright, when he from *Esau* fled
To *Padan-Aram* in the field of *Luz*,
Dreaming by night under the open Sky,
And waking cri'd, *This is the Gate of Heav'n*.[5]
Each Stair mysteriously° was meant,[6] nor stood *symbolically*
There always, but drawn up to Heav'n sometimes
Viewless, and underneath a bright Sea flow'd
Of Jasper, or of liquid Pearl, whereon
Who after came from Earth, sailing arriv'd,
Wafted by Angels, or flew o'er the Lake
Rapt in a Chariot drawn by fiery Steeds.
The Stairs were then let down, whether to dare
The Fiend by easy ascent, or aggravate
His sad exclusion from the doors of Bliss.
Direct against which op'n'd from beneath,
Just o'er the blissful seat of Paradise,
A passage down to th' Earth, a passage wide,
Wider by far than that of after-times
Over Mount *Sion*, and, though that were large,
Over the *Promis'd Land* to God so dear,
By which, to visit oft those happy Tribes,
On high behests his Angels to and fro

3. A "dispense" or dispensation was an exemption from a solemn obligation by licence of an ecclesiastical dignitary, especially the Pope.
4. A decorated entrance or a pediment over the gate.
5. The unregenerate Jacob was terrified by the vision of a ladder reaching to heaven just after he had cheated Esau out of his father's blessing (Genesis 27–28). The experience awed him into belief and a vow to the Lord.
6. Jacob's ladder had been identified with Homer's golden chain linking the universe to Jupiter. Each "stair," or step, could be interpreted as a spiritual stage extending "from the supreme God even to the bottomest dregs of the universe."

Pass'd frequent, and his eye with choice° regard *careful*
From *Paneas* the fount of *Jordan's* flood
To *Beërsaba,*[7] where the *Holy Land*
Borders on *Egypt* and th' *Arabian* shore;
So wide the op'ning seem'd, where bounds were set
To darkness, such as bound the Ocean wave.
Satan from hence now on the lower stair
That scal'd by steps of Gold to Heaven Gate
Looks down with wonder at the sudden view
Of all this World at once. As when a Scout
Through dark and desert ways with peril gone
All night; at last by break of cheerful dawn
Obtains° the brow of some high-climbing Hill, *reaches*
Which to his eye discovers unaware
The goodly prospect of some foreign land
First seen, or some renown'd Metropolis
With glistering Spires and Pinnacles adorn'd,
Which now the Rising Sun gilds with his beams.
Such wonder seiz'd, though after Heaven seen,
The Spirit malign, but much more envy seiz'd
At sight of all this World beheld so fair.
Round he surveys, and well might, where he stood
So high above the circling Canopy
Of Night's extended shade; from Eastern Point
Of *Libra* to the fleecy Star that bears
Andromeda far off *Atlantic* Seas
Beyond th' Horizon;[8] then from Pole to Pole
He views in breadth, and without longer pause
Down right into the World's first Region throws
His flight precipitant, and winds with ease
Through the pure marble Air his oblique way
Amongst innumerable Stars, that shone
Stars distant, but nigh hand seem'd other Worlds,
Or other Worlds they seem'd, or happy Isles,
Like those *Hesperian* Gardens fam'd of old,[9]
Fortunate Fields, and Groves and flow'ry Vales,
Thrice happy Isles, but who dwelt happy there
He stay'd not to enquire: above them all[1]
The golden Sun in splendor likest Heaven
Allur'd his eye: Thither his course he bends
Through the calm Firmament; but up or down
By centre, or eccentric, hard to tell,[2]

7. "Paneas" is a later Greek name for Dan—not the city of Dan but the spring of the same name, "the easternmost fountain of Jordan." Beersaba was the southern limit of Canaan, as Dan was the northern.

8. From Satan's viewpoint the constellation Andromeda appears just above Aries, as if carried on its back.

9. A hint of the Fall. Hesiod places beyond the ocean the gardens where the Hesperides (Atlantides) unsuccessfully guarded apples Jupiter entrusted them with; see 3.559.

1. Above: in splendor, not spatially.

2. Satan might travel by a centric orbit around earth (as in the Ptolemaic universe) or an eccentric orbit, around the sun (as in the Copernican universe). His path is "hard to tell" because specifying further would involve opting for a particular astronomical system (Ptolemaic, Copernican, etc.), a choice Milton avoids; see 4.592–7.

Or Longitude, where the great Luminary
Aloof the vulgar Constellations thick,
That from his Lordly eye keep distance due,
Dispenses Light from far; they as they move
Thir Starry dance in numbers° that compute *rhythms*
Days, months, and years,[3] towards his all-cheering Lamp
Turn swift thir various motions, or are turn'd
By his Magnetic beam, that gently warms
The Universe,[4] and to each inward part
With gentle penetration, though unseen,
Shoots invisible virtue even to the deep:
So wondrously was set his Station bright.
There lands the Fiend, a spot like which perhaps
Astronomer in the Sun's lucent Orb
Through his glaz'd Optic Tube yet never saw.[5]
The place he found beyond expression bright,
Compar'd with aught on Earth, Metal or Stone;
Not all parts like, but all alike inform'd
With radiant light, as glowing Iron with fire;
If metal, part seem'd Gold, part Silver clear;
If stone, Carbuncle most or Chrysolite,
Ruby or Topaz, to the Twelve° that shone *completing the twelve*
In *Aaron's* Breastplate,[6] and a stone besides
Imagin'd rather oft than elsewhere seen,
That stone, or like to that which here below
Philosophers in vain so long have sought,
In vain, though by thir powerful Art they bind
Volatile *Hermes*, and call up unbound
In various shapes old *Proteus* from the Sea,
Drain'd through a Limbec° to his Native form.[7] *beaker*
What wonder then if fields and regions here
Breathe forth *Elixir* pure, and Rivers run
Potable Gold,[8] when with one virtuous° touch *powerful*
Th' Arch-chemic Sun so far from us remote
Produces with Terrestrial Humor mixt
Here in the dark so many precious things
Of color glorious and effect so rare?
Here matter new to gaze the Devil met

3. In Plato's *Timaeus* (38C), God created planets "for the determining of the numbers of time," day, month and year. See also Genesis 1:14, "Let there be lights in the firmament of the heaven to divide the day from the night; and let them be for signs, and for seasons, and for days, and years."

4. Kepler's theory that solar "magnetic" force regulated planetary motions continued Tycho's emphasis on the sun's supremacy.

5. Spots on the sun—supposed to show corruptibility—were observed by Virgil, Charlemagne, Johann Fabricius (1611), and telescopically by the Jesuit Christopher Scheiner (1612) and by Galileo (1613).

6. Aaron's 12 jewels represent the 12 tribes of Israel. His "breastplate of judgment" has four rows of three stones each: "a ruby, a topaz, and a carbuncle in the first row" (Exodus 25; 28:15–20).

7. That is, "Alchemists have failed to find the philosopher's stone, however adept they are at the preliminary stage of fixing philosophic mercury." Hermes is represented as Mercury, and Proteus as matter, because of his changing forms.

8. An elixir is any medium like the philosopher's stone that transmutes base metals to gold. The "elixir of long life," or "Potable [drinkable] Gold," was a goal of alchemy.

Undazzl'd, far and wide his eye commands,
For sight no obstacle found here, nor shade,
But all Sun-shine, as when his Beams at Noon
Culminate from th' *Equator*, as they now
Shot upward still direct, whence no way round
Shadow from body opaque can fall, and the Air,
Nowhere so clear, sharp'n'd his visual ray
To objects distant far, whereby he soon
Saw within ken a glorious Angel stand,
The same whom *John* saw also in the Sun:[9]
His back was turn'd, but not his brightness hid;
Of beaming sunny Rays, a golden tiar
Circl'd his Head, nor less his Locks behind
Illustrious° on his Shoulders fledge° with wings *shining / feathered*
Lay waving round; on some great charge employ'd
He seem'd, or fixt in cogitation deep.
Glad was the Spirit impure; as now in hope
To find who might direct his wand'ring flight
To Paradise the happy seat of Man,
His journey's end and our beginning woe.
But first he casts to change his proper shape,[1]
Which else might work him danger or delay:
And now a stripling Cherub he appears,
Not of the prime, yet such as in his face
Youth smil'd Celestial, and to every Limb
Suitable grace diffus'd, so well he feign'd;
Under a Coronet his flowing hair
In curls on either check play'd, wings he wore
Of many a color'd plume sprinkl'd with Gold,
His habit fit for speed succinct,[2] and held
Before his decent° steps a Silver wand. *graceful*
He drew not nigh unheard; the Angel bright,
Ere he drew nigh, his radiant visage turn'd,
Admonisht by his ear, and straight was known
Th' Arch-Angel *Uriel*, one of the sev'n
Who in God's presence, nearest to his Throne
Stand ready at command, and are his Eyes
That run through all the Heav'ns, or down to th' Earth
Bear his swift errands over moist and dry,
O'er Sea and Land: him *Satan* thus accosts.[3]
Uriel, for thou of those sev'n Spirits that stand
In sight of God's high Throne, gloriously bright,
The first art wont his great authentic will

9. Refers to John the Divine's vision in Revelation 19:17, "I saw an angel standing in the sun."
1. Satan later assumes other shapes: wolf (4.183); cormorant (4.196); lion (4.402); tiger (4.403); toad (4.800); angel (5.55); serpent (9.188). In Satan, as in Spenser's Archimago, protean "fluctuations of shape" connote evil.
2. That is, "his uniform suitable for speed," or "his clothing girt up."
3. Seven principal angels are "the eyes of the Lord, which run to and fro through the whole earth" (Zechariah 4). *Uriel*, or "Light of God," was the angel of the south.

Interpreter through highest Heav'n to bring,
Where all his Sons thy Embassy attend;
And here art likeliest by supreme decree
Like honor to obtain, and as his Eye
To visit oft this new Creation round;
Unspeakable desire to see, and know
All these his wondrous works, but chiefly Man,
His chief delight and favor,° him for whom *object of favor*
All these his works so wondrous he ordain'd,
Hath brought me from the Choirs of Cherubim
Alone thus wand'ring. Brightest Seraph, tell
In which of all these shining Orbs hath Man
His fixed seat, or fixed seat hath none,
But all these shining Orbs his choice to dwell;
That I may find him, and with secret gaze,[4]
Or open admiration him behold
On whom the great Creator hath bestow'd
Worlds, and on whom hath all these graces pour'd;
That both in him and all things, as is meet
The Universal Maker we may praise;
Who justly hath driv'n out his Rebel Foes
To deepest Hell, and to repair that loss
Created this new happy Race of Men
To serve him better: wise are all his ways.
So spake the false dissembler unperceiv'd;
For neither Man nor Angel can discern
Hypocrisy, the only evil that walks
Invisible, except to God alone,
By his permissive will,[5] through Heav'n and Earth:
And oft though wisdom wake, suspicion sleeps
At wisdom's Gate, and to simplicity
Resigns her charge, while goodness thinks no ill
Where no ill seems: Which now for once beguil'd
Uriel, though Regent of the Sun, and held
The sharpest-sighted Spirit of all in Heav'n;
Who to the fraudulent Impostor foul
In his uprightness answer thus return'd.
Fair Angel, thy desire which tends to know
The works of God, thereby to glorify
The great Work-Master, leads to no excess
That reaches blame,[6] but rather merits praise
The more it seems excess, that led thee hither
From thy Empyreal Mansion thus alone,
To witness with thine eyes what some perhaps
Contented with report hear only in Heav'n:

4. Echoing Herod's enquiry after Jesus, the second Adam (Matthew 2:8).
5. The permissive will is distinguished from God's positive will, which permits only good.
6. The "desire" for knowledge may be blameless if its objects are good and it has a good motivation (to "glorify" God).

For wonderful indeed are all his works,
Pleasant to know, and worthiest to be all
Had in remembrance always with delight;[7]
But what created mind can comprehend
Thir number, or the wisdom infinite
That brought them forth, but hid thir causes deep.[8]
I saw when at his Word the formless Mass,
This world's material mould, came to a heap:
Confusion heard his voice, and wild uproar
Stood rul'd, stood vast infinitude confin'd;
Till at his second bidding darkness fled,
Light shone, and order from disorder sprung:
Swift to thir several Quarters hasted then
The cumbrous Elements, Earth, Flood, Air, Fire,
And this Ethereal quintessence° of Heav'n *purest distillation*
Flew upward, spirited with various forms,
That roll'd orbicular, and turn'd to Stars
Numberless, as thou seest, and how they move;
Each had his place appointed, each his course,
The rest in circuit walls this Universe.
Look downward on that Globe whose hither side
With light from hence, though but reflected, shines:
That place is Earth the seat of Man, that light
His day, which else as th' other Hemisphere
Night would invade, but there the neighboring Moon
(So call that opposite fair Star) her aid
Timely interposes, and her monthly round
Still ending, still renewing through mid Heav'n,
With borrow'd light her countenance triform
Hence° fills and empties to enlighten the Earth, *from the sun*
And in her pale dominion checks the night.
That spot to which I point is *Paradise*,[9]
Adam's abode, those lofty shades his Bow'r.
Thy way thou canst not miss, me mine requires.
Thus said, he turn'd, and *Satan* bowing low,
As to superior Spirits is wont in Heav'n,
Where honor due and reverence none neglects,
Took leave, and toward the coast° of Earth beneath, *side*
Down from th' Ecliptic,[1] sped with hop'd success,
Throws his steep flight in many an Aery wheel,
Nor stay'd, till on *Niphates'* top he lights.[2]

The End of the Third Book.

7. See Psalms 111:2, 4, "The works of the Lord are great, sought out of all them that have pleasure therein. . . He hath made his wonderful works to be remembered."
8. In *De doctrina* 1.9, Milton says that "The good angels do not see into all God's thoughts, as the Papists pretend . . . there are many things of which they are ignorant." Even Christ "does not know absolutely everything, for there are some secrets which the Father has kept to himself alone."
9. Since Paradise is visible from the sun, sunlight is already reaching it: Satan's 12-hour journey from the *primum mobile* has taken at least the second half of Adam's night.
1. The sun's orbit, lying (until the Fall) in the equatorial plane.
2. *Niphates* is a mountain on the Armenia-Assyria border, source of the Tigris. The river of Paradise is called Tigris before it divides (9.71).

Book 4
The Argument

Satan *now in prospect of* Eden, *and nigh the place where he must now attempt the bold enterprise which he undertook alone against God and Man, falls into many doubts with himself, and many passions, fear, envy, and despair; but at length confirms himself in evil, journeys on to Paradise, whose outward prospect and situation is described, overleaps the bounds, sits in the shape of a Cormorant on the Tree of Life, as highest in the Garden to look about him. The Garden describ'd;* Satan's *first sight of* Adam *and* Eve; *his wonder at thir excellent form and happy state, but with resolution to work thir fall; overhears thir discourse, thence gathers that the Tree of Knowledge was forbidden them to eat of, under penalty of death; and thereon intends to found his Temptation, by seducing them to transgress: then leaves them a while, to know further of thir state by some other means. Meanwhile* Uriel *descending on a Sun-beam warns* Gabriel, *who had in charge the Gate of Paradise, that some evil spirit had escap'd the Deep, and past at Noon by his Sphere in the shape of a good Angel down to Paradise, discovered after by his furious gestures in the Mount.* Gabriel *promises to find him ere morning. Night coming on,* Adam *and* Eve *discourse of going to thir rest: thir Bower describ'd; thir Evening worship.* Gabriel *drawing forth his Bands of Nightwatch to walk the round of Paradise, appoints two strong Angels to* Adam's *Bower, lest the evil spirit should be there doing some harm to* Adam *or* Eve *sleeping; there they find him at the ear of* Eve, *tempting her in a dream, and bring him, though unwilling, to* Gabriel; *by whom question'd, he scornfully answers, prepares resistance, but hinder'd by a Sign from Heaven, flies out of Paradise.*

O for that warning voice, which he who saw
Th' *Apocalypse*, heard cry in Heav'n aloud,
Then when the Dragon, put to second rout,
Came furious down to be reveng'd on men,
Woe to the inhabitants on Earth![1] that now,
While time was, our first Parents had been warn'd
The coming of thir secret foe, and scap'd
Haply so scap'd his mortal snare; for now
Satan, now first inflam'd with rage, came down,
The Tempter ere th' Accuser of man-kind,
To wreck° on innocent frail man his loss *avenge*
Of that first Battle, and his flight to Hell:
Yet not rejoicing in his speed, though bold,
Far off and fearless, nor with cause to boast,
Begins his dire attempt, which nigh the birth
Now rolling, boils in his tumultuous breast,
And like a devilish Engine back recoils
Upon himself; horror and doubt distract
His troubl'd thoughts, and from the bottom stir
The Hell within him, for within him Hell
He brings, and round about him, nor from Hell
One step no more than from himself can fly

1. The Apocalypse of St. John (Revelation) relates a vision of a second battle in heaven between Michael and "the Dragon," Satan.

By change of place: Now conscience wakes despair
That slumber'd, wakes the bitter memory
Of what he was, what is, and what must be
Worse; of worse deeds worse sufferings must ensue.
Sometimes towards *Eden* which now in his view
Lay pleasant,[2] his griev'd look he fixes sad,
Sometimes towards Heav'n and the full-blazing Sun,
Which now sat high in his Meridian Tow'r:
Then much revolving, thus in sighs began.
  O thou that with surpassing Glory crown'd,
Look'st from thy sole Dominion like the God
Of this new World; at whose sight all the Stars
Hide thir diminisht heads; to thee I call,
But with no friendly voice, and add thy name
O Sun, to tell thee how I hate thy beams
That bring to my remembrance from what state
I fell, how glorious once above thy Sphere;
Till Pride and worse Ambition threw me down
Warring in Heav'n against Heav'n's matchless King:[3]
Ah wherefore! he deserv'd no such return
From me, whom he created what I was
In that bright eminence, and with his good
Upbraided none;[4] nor was his service hard.
What could be less than to afford him praise,
The easiest recompense, and pay him thanks,
How due! yet all his good prov'd ill in me,
And wrought but malice; lifted up so high
I sdein'd° subjection, and thought one step higher *disdained*
Would set me highest, and in a moment quit° *pay off*
The debt immense of endless gratitude,
So burdensome, still paying, still to owe;
Forgetful what from him I still receiv'd,
And understood not that a grateful mind
By owing owes not, but still pays, at once
Indebted and discharg'd; what burden then?[5]
O had his powerful Destiny ordain'd
Me some inferior Angel, I had stood
Then happy; no unbounded hope had rais'd
Ambition. Yet why not? some other Power
As great might have aspir'd, and me though mean
Drawn to his part; but other Powers as great
Fell not, but stand unshak'n, from within
Or from without, to all temptations arm'd.
Hadst thou the same free Will and Power to stand?

2. The etymological meaning of "Eden" is "pleasure, delight."
3. According to Edward Phillips, lines 32–41 were shown to him and some others "before the Poem was begun," when Milton intended to write a tragedy on the Fall.
4. Demanded no return for his benefits; see James 1.5.
5. Simply by owning an obligation gratefully, one ceases to owe it.

Thou hadst: whom hast thou then or what to accuse,
But Heav'n's free Love dealt equally to all?
Be then his Love accurst, since love or hate,
To me alike, it deals eternal woe.
Nay curs'd be thou; since against his thy will
Chose freely what it now so justly rues.
Me miserable! which way shall I fly
Infinite wrath, and infinite despair?
Which way I fly is Hell; myself am Hell;
And in the lowest deep a lower deep
Still threat'ning to devour me opens wide,
To which the Hell I suffer seems a Heav'n.
O then at last relent: is there no place
Left for Repentance, none for Pardon left?
None left but by submission; and that word
Disdain forbids me, and my dread of shame
Among the Spirits beneath, whom I seduc'd
With other promises and other vaunts
Than to submit, boasting I could subdue
Th' Omnipotent. Ay me, they little know
How dearly I abide that boast so vain,
Under what torments inwardly I groan:
While they adore me on the Throne of Hell,
With Diadem and Sceptre high advanc'd
The lower still I fall, only Supreme
In misery; such joy Ambition finds.
But say I could repent and could obtain
By Act of Grace[6] my former state; how soon
Would highth recall high thoughts, how soon unsay
What feign'd submission swore: ease would recant
Vows made in pain, as violent and void.
For never can true reconcilement grow
Where wounds of deadly hate have pierc'd so deep:
Which would but lead me to a worse relapse,
And heavier fall: so should I purchase dear
Short intermission bought with double smart.
This knows my punisher; therefore as far
From granting hee, as I from begging peace:
All hope excluded thus, behold instead
Of us out-cast, exil'd, his new delight,
Mankind created, and for him this World.
So farewell Hope, and with Hope farewell Fear,
Farewell Remorse: all Good to me is lost;
Evil be thou my Good; by thee at least
Divided Empire with Heav'n's King I hold

6. By concession of favor, not of right; often used for a formal pardon by Parliament.

By thee, and more than half perhaps will reign;
As Man ere long, and this new World shall know.
Thus while he spake, each passion dimm'd his face,
Thrice chang'd with pale, ire, envy and despair,
Which marr'd his borrow'd visage, and betray'd
Him counterfeit, if any eye beheld.
For heav'nly minds from such distempers foul
Are ever clear. Whereof hee soon aware,
Each perturbation smooth'd with outward calm,
Artificer° of fraud; and was the first *inventor*
That practis'd falsehood under saintly show,
Deep malice to conceal, couch't° with revenge: *hidden*
Yet not anough had practis'd to deceive
Uriel once warn'd; whose eye pursu'd him down
The way he went, and on th' *Assyrian* mount° *Niphates mountain range*
Saw him disfigur'd, more than could befall
Spirit of happy sort: his gestures fierce
He mark'd and mad demeanor, then alone,
As he suppos'd, all unobserv'd, unseen.
So on he fares, and to the border comes
Of *Eden*, where delicious Paradise,
Now nearer, Crowns with her enclosure green,
As with a rural mound the champaign° head *unenclosed, level*
Of a steep wilderness, whose hairy sides
With thicket overgrown, grotesque and wild,
Access deni'd; and over head up grew
Insuperable highth of loftiest shade,
Cedar, and Pine, and Fir, and branching Palm,
A Silvan Scene, and as the ranks ascend
Shade above shade, a woody Theatre
Of stateliest view. Yet higher than thir tops
The verdurous wall of Paradise up sprung:
Which to our general Sire° gave prospect large *Adam*
Into his nether Empire neighboring round.
And higher than that Wall a circling row
Of goodliest Trees loaden with fairest Fruit,
Blossoms and Fruits at once of golden hue
Appear'd, with gay enamell'd° colors mixt: *lustrous*
On which the Sun more glad impress'd his beams
Than in fair Evening Cloud, or humid Bow,° *rainbow*
When God hath show'r'd the earth; so lovely seem'd
That Lantskip:° And of pure now purer air *landscape*
Meets his approach, and to the heart inspires
Vernal delight and joy, able to drive
All sadness but despair: now gentle gales
Fanning thir odoriferous wings dispense
Native perfúmes, and whisper whence they stole
Those balmy spoils. As when to them who sail

Beyond the *Cape* of *Hope*, and now are past
Mozambic,[7] off at Sea North-East winds blow
Sabean[8] Odors from the spicy shore
Of *Araby* the blest, with such delay
Well pleas'd they slack thir course, and many a League
Cheer'd with the grateful smell old Ocean smiles.
So entertain'd those odorous sweets the Fiend
Who came thir bane, though with them better pleas'd
Than *Asmodeus* with the fishy fume,
That drove him, though enamor'd, from the Spouse
Of *Tobit's* Son, and with a vengeance sent
From *Media* post to *Egypt*, there fast bound.[9]
  Now to th' ascent of that steep savage° Hill *wild*
Satan had journey'd on, pensive and slow;
But further way found none, so thick entwin'd,
As one continu'd brake, the undergrowth
Of shrubs and tangling bushes had perplext
All path of Man or Beast that pass'd that way:
One Gate there only was, and that look'd East
On th' other side: which when th' arch-felon saw
Due entrance he disdain'd, and in contempt,
At one slight bound high overleap'd all bound
Of Hill or highest Wall, and sheer within
Lights on his feet. As when a prowling Wolf,
Whom hunger drives to seek new haunt for prey,
Watching where Shepherds pen thir Flocks at eve
In hurdl'd Cotes° amid the field secure, *shelters*
Leaps o'er the fence with ease into the Fold:
Or as a Thief bent to unhoard the cash
Of some rich Burgher, whose substantial doors,
Cross-barr'd and bolted fast, fear no assault,
In at the window climbs, or o'er the tiles:
So clomb° this first grand Thief into God's Fold: *climbed*
So since into his Church lewd Hirelings[1] climb.
Thence up he flew, and on the Tree of Life,
The middle Tree and highest there that grew,
Sat like a Cormorant;[2] yet not true Life
Thereby regain'd, but sat devising Death
To them who liv'd; nor on the virtue thought
Of that life-giving Plant, but only us'd
For prospect,° what well us'd had been the pledge *lookout*

7. Mozambique, a Portuguese colony on the east coast of Africa; the trade route lay between Mozambique and Madagascar.

8. Of Saba or Sheba (now Yemen). Milton draws on the description of "Araby the blest"—"Arabia felix"—in Diodorus Siculus 3.46.

9. The apocryphal book Tobit relates the story of Tobit's son Tobias, who was sent into Media on an errand and there married Sara. Sara had previously been given to seven men, but all were killed by the jealous spirit Asmodeus before their marriages could be consummated. By the advice of Raphael, however, Tobias succeeded by creating a fishy smoke to drive away the devil Asmodeus.

1. Wicked men motivated only by material gain.

2. A voracious sea bird, often used to describe greedy clergy.

Of immortality. So little knows
Any, but God alone, to value right
The good before him, but perverts best things
To worst abuse, or to thir meanest use.
Beneath him with new wonder now he views
To all delight of human sense expos'd
In narrow room Nature's whole wealth, yea more,
A Heaven on Earth: for blissful Paradise
Of God the Garden was, by him in the East
Of *Eden* planted; *Eden* stretch'd her Line
From *Auran* Eastward to the Royal Tow'rs
Of Great *Seleucia,* built by *Grecian* Kings,
Or where the Sons of *Eden* long before
Dwelt in *Telassar:*[3] in this pleasant soil
His far more pleasant Garden God ordain'd;
Out of the fertile ground he caus'd to grow
All Trees of noblest kind for sight, smell, taste;
And all amid them stood the Tree of Life,
High eminent, blooming Ambrosial Fruit
Of vegetable Gold; and next to Life
Our Death the Tree of Knowledge grew fast by,
Knowledge of Good bought dear by knowing ill.[4]
Southward through *Eden* went a River large,
Nor chang'd his course, but through the shaggy hill
Pass'd underneath ingulft, for God had thrown
That Mountain as his Garden mould high rais'd
Upon the rapid current, which through veins
Of porous Earth with kindly° thirst up-drawn, *natural*
Rose a fresh Fountain, and with many a rill
Water'd the Garden;[5] thence united fell
Down the steep glade, and met the nether Flood,
Which from his darksome passage now appears,
And now divided into four main Streams,
Runs diverse, wand'ring many a famous Realm
And Country whereof here needs no account,
But rather to tell how, if Art could tell,
How from that Sapphire Fount the crisped° Brooks, *wavy*
Rolling on Orient Pearl and sands of Gold,
With mazy error° under pendant shades *wandering*
Ran Nectar, visiting each plant, and fed
Flow'rs worthy of Paradise which not nice° Art *careful*
In Beds and curious Knots, but Nature boon° *bounteous*
Pour'd forth profuse on Hill and Dale and Plain,
Both where the morning Sun first warmly smote

3. Auran was an eastern boundary of the land of Israel. Great Seleucia was built by Alexander's general Seleucus Nicator as a seat of government for his Syrian empire. The mention of Telassar prophesies war in Eden; see 2 Kings 14.11ff., where Telassar is an instance of lands destroyed utterly.

4. See Genesis 2.9.

5. See Genesis 2.10.

The open field, and where the unpierc't shade
Imbrown'd° the noontide Bow'rs: Thus was this place, *darkened*
A happy rural seat of various view:
Groves whose rich Trees wept odorous Gums and Balm,
Others whose fruit burnisht with Golden Rind
Hung amiable,° *Hesperian* Fables true,[6] *lovely*
If true, here only, and of delicious taste:
Betwixt them Lawns, or level Downs, and Flocks
Grazing the tender herb, were interpos'd,
Or palmy hillock, or the flow'ry lap
Of some irriguous° Valley spread her store, *well-watered*
Flow'rs of all hue, and without Thorn the Rose:[7]
Another side, umbrageous° Grots and Caves *shady*
Of cool recess, o'er which the mantling Vine
Lays forth her purple Grape, and gently creeps
Luxuriant; meanwhile murmuring waters fall
Down the slope hills, disperst, or in a Lake,
That to the fringed Bank with Myrtle crown'd,
Her crystal mirror holds, unite thir streams.
The Birds thir choir apply;° airs, vernal airs,[8] *practice*
Breathing the smell of field and grove, attune
The trembling leaves, while Universal *Pan*[9]
Knit with the *Graces* and the *Hours* in dance
Led on th' Eternal Spring.[1] Not that fair field
Of *Enna*, where *Proserpin* gath'ring flow'rs
Herself a fairer Flow'r by gloomy *Dis*
Was gather'd, which cost *Ceres* all that pain
To seek her through the world;[2] nor that sweet Grove
Of *Daphne* by *Orontes*, and th' inspir'd
Castalian Spring[3] might with this Paradise
Of *Eden* strive; nor that *Nyseian* Isle
Girt with the River *Triton*, where old *Cham*,
Whom Gentiles *Ammon* call and *Lybian Jove*,
Hid *Amalthea* and her Florid° Son, *ruddy-complexioned*
Young *Bacchus*, from his Stepdame *Rhea's* eye;[4]
Nor where *Abassin* Kings thir issue Guard,
Mount *Amara*, though this by some suppos'd
True Paradise under the *Ethiop* Line
By *Nilus* head, enclos'd with shining Rock,

6. Golden fruit like the legendary apples of the western islands, the Hesperides.
7. The thornless rose was used to symbolize the sinless state of humanity before the Fall; or the state of grace.
8. Breezes and melodies.
9. Pan (Greek for "all") was a symbol of universal nature.
1. Neoplatonists thought the triadic pattern of their dance expressed the movement underlying all natural generation.
2. The rape of Proserpina by Dis, the king of hell, was located in *Enna* by Ovid (*Fasti* 4.420ff.). The search for her made the world barren, and even when she was found, she was restored to Ceres—and fruitfulness to the world—only for half the year.
3. The grove called "Daphne" beside the river Orontes, near Antioch, had an Apolline oracle and a stream named after the famous Castalian spring of Parnassus.
4. Ammon, King of Libya, had an illicit affair with a maiden Amaltheia, who gave birth to a marvelous son Dionysus (Bacchus). To protect mother and child from the jealousy of his wife Rhea, Ammon hid them on Nysa, an island near modern Tunis. The identifications of Ammon with the Libyan Jupiter and with Noah's son Ham were widely accepted.

A whole day's journey high,[5] but wide remote
From this *Assyrian* Garden, where the Fiend
Saw undelighted all delight, all kind
Of living Creatures new to sight and strange:
Two of far nobler shape erect and tall,
Godlike erect, with native Honor clad
In naked Majesty seem'd Lords of all,
And worthy seem'd, for in thir looks Divine
The image of thir glorious Maker shone,[6]
Truth, Wisdom, Sanctitude severe and pure,
Severe, but in true filial freedom plac't;
Whence true autority in men; though both
Not equal, as thir sex not equal seem'd;
For contemplation hee and valor form'd,
For softness shee and sweet attractive Grace,
Hee for God only, shee for God in him:[7]
His fair large Front° and Eye sublime° declar'd *forehead / uplifted*
Absolute rule; and Hyacinthine Locks
Round from his parted forelock manly hung
Clust'ring, but not beneath his shoulders broad:
Shee as a veil down to the slender waist
Her unadorned golden tresses wore
Dishevell'd, but in wanton ringlets wav'd
As the Vine curls her tendrils, which impli'd
Subjection, but requir'd with gentle sway,
And by her yielded, by him best receiv'd,
Yielded with coy° submission, modest pride, *modest*
And sweet reluctant amorous delay.
Nor those mysterious parts were then conceal'd,
Then was not guilty shame: dishonest shame
Of Nature's works, honor dishonorable,
Sin-bred, how have ye troubl'd all mankind
With shows instead, mere shows of seeming pure,
And banisht from man's life his happiest life,
Simplicity and spotless innocence.
So pass'd they naked on, nor shunn'd the sight
Of God or Angel, for they thought no ill:
So hand in hand they pass'd, the loveliest pair
That ever since in love's imbraces met,
Adam the goodliest man of men since born
His Sons, the fairest of her Daughters *Eve*.
Under a tuft of shade that on a green
Stood whispering soft, by a fresh Fountain side
They sat them down, and after no more toil

5. Milton takes his description of Mount Amara from Peter Heylyn's *Cosmographie* 4.64.

6. See Genesis 1.27: "God created man in his own image."

7. See 1 Corinthians 11.3: "The head of every man is Christ; and the head of the woman is the man; and the head of Christ is God."

Of thir sweet Gard'ning labor than suffic'd
To recommend cool *Zephyr*,[8] and made ease
More easy, wholesome thirst and appetite
More grateful, to thir Supper Fruits they fell,
Nectarine Fruits which the compliant boughs
Yielded them, side-long as they sat recline° *lying down*
On the soft downy Bank damaskt with flow'rs:
The savory pulp they chew, and in the rind
Still as they thirsted scoop the brimming stream;
Nor gentle purpose,° nor endearing smiles *conversation*
Wanted,° nor youthful dalliance as beseems *lacked*
Fair couple, linkt in happy nuptial League,
Alone as they. About them frisking play'd
All Beasts of th' Earth, since wild, and of all chase
In Wood or Wilderness, Forest or Den;
Sporting the Lion ramp'd,° and in his paw *reared up*
Dandl'd the Kid; Bears, Tigers, Ounces,° Pards° *lynxes / leopards*
Gamboll'd before them, th' unwieldy Elephant
To make them mirth us'd all his might, and wreath'd
His Lithe Proboscis; close the Serpent sly
Insinuating,[9] wove with Gordian twine[1]
His braided train, and of his fatal guile
Gave proof unheeded; others on the grass
Coucht, and now fill'd with pasture gazing sat,
Or Bedward ruminating;[2] for the Sun
Declin'd was hasting now with prone career
To th' Ocean Isles,[3] and in th' ascending Scale
Of Heav'n the Stars that usher Evening rose:
When *Satan* still in gaze, as first he stood,
Scarce thus at length fail'd speech recover'd sad.
O Hell! what do mine eyes with grief behold,
Into our room of bliss thus high advanc't
Creatures of other mould, earth-born perhaps,
Not Spirits, yet to heav'nly Spirits bright
Little inferior; whom my thoughts pursue
With wonder, and could love, so lively shines
In them Divine resemblance, and such grace
The hand that form'd them on thir shape hath pour'd.
Ah gentle pair, yee little think how nigh
Your change approaches, when all these delights
Will vanish and deliver ye to woe,
More woe, the more your taste is now of joy;
Happy, but for so happy ill secur'd
Long to continue, and this high seat your Heav'n
Ill fenc't for Heav'n to keep out such a foe

8. The west wind.
9. Penetrating by sinuous ways.
1. Coil, convolution, as difficult to undo as the Gordian knot, which it took the hero Alexander to cut.
2. Chewing the cud before going to rest.
3. The Azores.

As now is enter'd; yet no purpos'd foe
To you whom I could pity thus forlorn
Though I unpitied: League with you I seek,
And mutual amity so strait,° so close, *intimate*
That I with you must dwell, or you with me
Henceforth; my dwelling haply may not please
Like this fair Paradise, your sense, yet such
Accept your Maker's work; he gave it me,
Which I as freely give; Hell shall unfold,[4]
To entertain you two, her widest Gates,
And send forth all her Kings; there will be room,
Not like these narrow limits, to receive
Your numerous offspring; if no better place,
Thank him who puts me loath to this revenge
On you who wrong me not for him who wrong'd.
And should I at your harmless innocence
Melt, as I do, yet public reason[5] just,
Honor and Empire with revenge enlarg'd,
By conquering this new World, compels me now
To do what else though damn'd I should abhor.
  So spake the Fiend, and with necessity,
The Tyrant's plea, excus'd his devilish deeds.
Then from his lofty stand on that high Tree
Down he alights among the sportful Herd
Of those fourfooted kinds, himself now one,
Now other, as thir shape serv'd best his end
Nearer to view his prey, and unespi'd
To mark what of thir state he more might learn
By word or action markt: about them round
A Lion now he stalks with fiery glare,
Then as a Tiger, who by chance hath spi'd
In some Purlieu° two gentle Fawns at play, *edge of a forest*
Straight couches close, then rising changes oft
His couchant watch, as one who chose his ground
Whence rushing he might surest seize them both
Gript in each paw: when *Adam* first of men
To first of women *Eve* thus moving speech,
Turn'd him° all ear to hear new utterance flow. *Satan*
  Sole partner and sole part of all these joys,[6]
Dearer thyself than all; needs must the Power
That made us, and for us this ample World
Be infinitely good, and of his good
As liberal and free as infinite,
That rais'd us from the dust and plac't us here
In all this happiness, who at his hand

4. A blasphemous echo of Matthew 10.8 ("freely ye have received, freely give").
5. Reason of state, a perversion of the Ciceronian principle (*Laws* 3.3.8) that the good of the people is the supreme law.
6. The first "sole" means "only"; the second, "unrivalled."

Have nothing merited, nor can perform
Aught whereof hee hath need, hee who requires
From us no other service than to keep
This one, this easy charge, of all the Trees
In Paradise that bear delicious fruit
So various, not to taste that only Tree
Of Knowledge, planted by the Tree of Life,[7]
So near grows Death to Life, whate'er Death is,
Some dreadful thing no doubt; for well thou know'st
God hath pronounc't it death to taste that Tree,
The only sign of our obedience left
Among so many signs of power and rule
Conferr'd upon us, and Dominion giv'n
Over all other Creatures that possess
Earth, Air, and Sea.[8] Then let us not think hard
One easy prohibition, who enjoy
Free leave so large to all things else, and choice
Unlimited of manifold delights:
But let us ever praise him, and extol
His bounty, following our delightful task
To prune these growing Plants, and tend these Flow'rs,
Which were it toilsome, yet with thee were sweet.
To whom thus Eve repli'd. O thou for whom
And from whom I was form'd flesh of thy flesh,[9]
And without whom am to no end, my Guide
And Head, what thou hast said is just and right.[1]
For wee to him indeed all praises owe,
And daily thanks, I chiefly who enjoy
So far the happier Lot, enjoying thee
Preëminent by so much odds,° while thou *advantage*
Like consort to thyself canst nowhere find.
That day I oft remember, when from sleep
I first awak't, and found myself repos'd
Under a shade on flow'rs, much wond'ring where
And what I was, whence thither brought, and how.
Not distant far from thence a murmuring sound
Of waters issu'd from a Cave and spread
Into a liquid Plain, then stood unmov'd
Pure as th' expanse of Heav'n; I thither went
With unexperienc't thought, and laid me down
On the green bank, to look into the clear
Smooth Lake, that to me seem'd another Sky.
As I bent down to look, just opposite,

7. See Genesis 2.16ff.
8. See Genesis 1.28: "God said unto them . . . have dominion over the fish of the sea, and over the fowl of the air, and over every living thing that moveth upon the earth."
9. See 1 Corinthians 11.9: "Neither was the man created for the woman; but the woman for the man." See Genesis 2.23.
1. See 1 Corinthians 11.3: "The head of every man is Christ; and the head of the woman is the man; and the head of Christ is God."

A Shape within the wat'ry gleam appear'd
Bending to look on me, I started back,
It started back, but pleas'd I soon return'd,
Pleas'd it return'd as soon with answering looks
Of sympathy and love; there I had fixt
Mine eyes till now, and pin'd with vain desire,[2]
Had not a voice thus warn'd me, What thou seest,
What there thou seest fair Creature is thyself,
With thee it came and goes: but follow me,
And I will bring thee where no shadow stays° *awaits*
Thy coming, and thy soft imbraces, hee
Whose image thou art, him thou shalt enjoy
Inseparably thine, to him shalt bear
Multitudes like thyself, and thence be call'd
Mother of human Race: what could I do,
But follow straight, invisibly thus led?
Till I espi'd thee, fair indeed and tall,
Under a Platan, yet methought less fair,
Less winning soft, less amiably mild,
Than that smooth wat'ry image; back I turn'd,
Thou following cri'd'st aloud, Return fair *Eve*,
Whom fli'st thou? whom thou fli'st, of him thou art,
His flesh, his bone; to give thee being I lent
Out of my side to thee, nearest my heart
Substantial Life, to have thee by my side
Henceforth an individual° solace dear; *inseparable*
Part of my Soul I seek thee, and thee claim
My other half: with that thy gentle hand
Seiz'd mine, I yielded, and from that time see
How beauty is excell'd by manly grace
And wisdom, which alone is truly fair.
So spake our general Mother, and with eyes
Of conjugal attraction unreprov'd,° *innocent*
And meek surrender, half imbracing lean'd
On our first Father, half her swelling Breast
Naked met his under the flowing Gold
Of her loose tresses hid: hee in delight
Both of her Beauty and submissive Charms
Smil'd with superior Love, as *Jupiter*
On *Juno* smiles, when he impregns° the Clouds *impregnates*
That shed *May* Flowers; and press'd her Matron lip
With kisses pure: aside the Devil turn'd
For envy, yet with jealous leer malign
Ey'd them askance, and to himself thus plain'd.° *complained*
Sight hateful, sight tormenting! thus these two
Imparadis't in one another's arms

2. Alluding to Ovid's story of the proud youth Narcissus, who was punished for his scornfulness by being made to fall in love with his own reflection in a pool.

The happier *Eden*, shall enjoy thir fill
Of bliss on bliss, while I to Hell am thrust,
Where neither joy nor love, but fierce desire,
Among our other torments not the least,
Still unfulfill'd with pain of longing pines;° *troubles*
Yet let me not forget what I have gain'd
From thir own mouths; all is not theirs it seems:
One fatal Tree there stands of Knowledge call'd,
Forbidden them to taste: Knowledge forbidd'n?
Suspicious, reasonless. Why should thir Lord
Envy them that? can it be sin to know,
Can it be death? and do they only stand
By Ignorance, is that thir happy state,
The proof of thir obedience and thir faith?
O fair foundation laid whereon to build
Thir ruin! Hence I will excite thir minds
With more desire to know, and to reject
Envious commands, invented with design
To keep them low whom Knowledge might exalt
Equal with Gods; aspiring to be such,
They taste and die: what likelier can ensue?
But first with narrow search I must walk round
This Garden, and no corner leave unspi'd;
A chance but chance[3] may lead where I may meet
Some wand'ring Spirit of Heav'n, by Fountain side,
Or in thick shade retir'd, from him to draw
What further would be learnt. Live while ye may,
Yet happy pair; enjoy, till I return,
Short pleasures, for long woes are to succeed.
So saying, his proud step he scornful turn'd,
But with sly circumspection, and began
Through wood, through waste, o'er hill, o'er dale his roam.
Meanwhile in utmost Longitude,[4] where Heav'n
With Earth and Ocean meets, the setting Sun
Slowly descended, and with right aspect
Against the eastern Gate of Paradise
Levell'd his ev'ning Rays: it was a Rock
Of Alablaster,° pil'd up to the Clouds, *alabaster*
Conspicuous far, winding with one ascent
Accessible from Earth, one entrance high;
The rest was craggy cliff, that overhung
Still as it rose, impossible to climb.[5]
Betwixt these rocky Pillars *Gabriel*[6] sat
Chief of th' Angelic Guards, awaiting night;
About him exercis'd Heroic Games

3. An accident and an opportunity.
4. The farthest west.
5. A possible source is the paradise of Mount Amara in Heylyn's *Cosmographie*.
6. "Strength of God," one of the four archangels ruling the corners of the world.

Th' unarmed Youth of Heav'n, but nigh at hand
Celestial Armory, Shields, Helms, and Spears
Hung high with Diamond flaming, and with Gold.
Thither came *Uriel,* gliding through the Even
On a Sun-beam, swift as a shooting Star
In *Autumn* thwarts° the night, when vapors fir'd *crosses*
Impress the Air, and shows the Mariner
From what point of his Compass to beware
Impetuous winds:[7] he thus began in haste.
 Gabriel, to thee thy course by Lot hath giv'n
Charge and strict watch that to this happy place
No evil thing approach or enter in;
This day at highth of Noon came to my Sphere
A Spirit, zealous, as he seem'd, to know
More of th' Almighty's works, and chiefly Man
God's latest Image: I describ'd° his way *observed*
Bent all on speed, and markt his Aery Gait;
But in the Mount that lies from *Eden* North,
Where he first lighted, soon discern'd his looks
Alien from Heav'n, with passions foul obscur'd:
Mine eye pursu'd him still, but under shade
Lost sight of him; one of the banisht crew
I fear, hath ventur'd from the Deep, to raise
New troubles; him thy care must be to find.
 To whom the winged Warrior thus return'd:
Uriel,[8] no wonder if thy perfect sight,
Amid the Sun's bright circle where thou sitst,
See far and wide: in at this Gate none pass
The vigilance here plac't, but such as come
Well known from Heav'n; and since Meridian hour
No Creature thence: if Spirit of other sort,
So minded, have o'erleapt these earthy bounds
On purpose, hard thou know'st it to exclude
Spiritual substance with corporeal bar.
But if within the circuit of these walks
In whatsoever shape he lurk, of whom
Thou tell'st, by morrow dawning I shall know.
 So promis'd hee, and *Uriel* to his charge
Return'd on that bright beam, whose point now rais'd
Bore him slope downward to the Sun now fall'n
Beneath th' *Azores;* whither the prime Orb,
Incredible how swift, had thither roll'd
Diurnal,° or this less volúbil[9] Earth *in one day*
By shorter flight to th' East, had left him there
Arraying with reflected Purple and Gold

7. Shooting stars were thought to be a sign of storm because in falling they were thrust down by winds.

8. "Light of God."

9. Capable of ready rotation on its axis.

The Clouds that on his Western Throne attend:[1]
Now came still Ev'ning on, and Twilight gray
Had in her sober Livery all things clad;
Silence accompanied, for Beast and Bird,
They to thir grassy Couch, these to thir Nests
Were slunk, all but the wakeful Nightingale;
She all night long her amorous descant sung;
Silence was pleas'd: now glow'd the Firmament
With living Sapphires: *Hesperus*[2] that led
The starry Host, rode brightest, till the Moon
Rising in clouded Majesty, at length
Apparent Queen unveil'd her peerless light,
And o'er the dark her Silver Mantle threw.
  When *Adam* thus to *Eve:* Fair Consort, th' hour
Of night, and all things now retir'd to rest
Mind us of like repose, since God hath set
Labor and rest, as day and night to men
Successive, and the timely dew of sleep
Now falling with soft slumbrous weight inclines
Our eye-lids; other Creatures all day long
Rove idle unimploy'd, and less need rest;
Man hath his daily work of body or mind
Appointed, which declares his Dignity,
And the regard of Heav'n on all his ways;
While other Animals unactive range,
And of thir doings God takes no account.
Tomorrow ere fresh Morning streak the East
With first approach of light, we must be ris'n,
And at our pleasant labor, to reform
Yon flow'ry Arbors, yonder Alleys green,
Our walk at noon, with branches overgrown,
That mock our scant manuring,° and require *cultivating*
More hands than ours to lop thir wanton growth:
Those Blossoms also, and those dropping Gums,
That lie bestrown unsightly and unsmooth,
Ask riddance, if we mean to tread with ease;
Meanwhile, as Nature wills, Night bids us rest.
  To whom thus *Eve* with perfect beauty adorn'd.
My Author° and Disposer, what thou bidd'st *origin, creator*
Unargu'd I obey; so God ordains,
God is thy Law, thou mine: to know no more
Is woman's happiest knowledge and her praise.
With thee conversing I forget all time,
All seasons and thir change, all please alike.[3]
Sweet is the breath of morn, her rising sweet,

1. The appearance of sunset can be regarded as caused either by orbital motion of the sun about the earth or by the earth's rotation (a lesser movement).

2. The evening star.

3. Time of day; not "seasons of the year," since it is still eternal spring.

With charm° of earliest Birds; pleasant the Sun *song*
When first on this delightful Land he spreads
His orient Beams, on herb, tree, fruit, and flow'r,
Glist'ring with dew; fragrant the fertile earth
After soft showers; and sweet the coming on
Of grateful Ev'ning mild, then silent Night
With this her solemn Bird and this fair Moon,
And these the Gems of Heav'n, her starry train:
But neither breath of Morn when she ascends
With charm of earliest Birds, nor rising Sun
On this delightful land, nor herb, fruit, flow'r,
Glist'ring with dew, nor fragrance after showers,
Nor grateful Ev'ning mild, nor silent Night
With this her solemn Bird, nor walk by Moon,
Or glittering Star-light without thee is sweet.
But wherefore all night long shine these, for whom
This glorious sight, when sleep hath shut all eyes?
  To whom our general Ancestor repli'd.
Daughter of God and Man, accomplisht *Eve*,
Those have thir course to finish, round the Earth,
By morrow Ev'ning, and from Land to Land
In order, though to Nations yet unborn,
Minist'ring light prepar'd, they set and rise;
Lest total darkness should by Night regain
Her old possession, and extinguish life
In Nature and all things, which these soft fires
Not only enlighten, but with kindly heat
Of various influence foment and warm,
Temper or nourish, or in part shed down
Thir stellar virtue on all kinds that grow
On Earth, made hereby apter to receive
Perfection from the Sun's more potent Ray.[4]
These then, though unbeheld in deep of night,
Shine not in vain, nor think, though men were none,
That Heav'n would want spectators, God want praise;
Millions of spiritual Creatures walk the Earth
Unseen, both when we wake, and when we sleep:
All these with ceaseless praise his works behold
Both day and night: how often from the steep
Of echoing Hill or Thicket have we heard
Celestial voices to the midnight air,
Sole, or responsive each to other's note
Singing thir great Creator: oft in bands
While they keep watch, or nightly rounding walk,
With Heav'nly touch of instrumental sounds

4. In Neoplatonic astrology, Sol was said to accomplish the generation of new life by acting through each of the other planets in turn; their function was only to modulate his influence or to select from his complete spectrum of virtues. After the Fall, the influence of the stars becomes less "kindly" (benign; natural).

In full harmonic number join'd, thir songs
Divide the night, and lift our thoughts to Heaven.
  Thus talking hand in hand alone they pass'd
On to thir blissful Bower; it was a place
Chos'n by the sovran Planter, when he fram'd
All things to man's delightful use; the roof
Of thickest covert was inwoven shade
Laurel and Myrtle, and what higher grew
Of firm and fragrant leaf; on either side
Acanthus, and each odorous bushy shrub
Fenc'd up the verdant wall; each beauteous flow'r,
Iris all hues, Roses, and Jessamin° *jasmine*
Rear'd high thir flourisht heads between, and wrought
Mosaic; underfoot the Violet,
Crocus, and Hyacinth with rich inlay
Broider'd the ground, more color'd than with stone
Of costliest Emblem:[5] other Creature here
Beast, Bird, Insect, or Worm durst enter none;
Such was thir awe of Man. In shadier Bower
More sacred and sequester'd, though but feign'd,
Pan or *Silvanus* never slept, nor Nymph,
Nor *Faunus* haunted.[6] Here in close recess
With Flowers, Garlands, and sweet-smelling Herbs
Espoused *Eve* deckt first her Nuptial Bed,
And heav'nly Choirs the Hymenaean° sung, *wedding hymn*
What day the genial° Angel to our Sire *nuptial, generative*
Brought her in naked beauty more adorn'd,
More lovely than *Pandora*, whom the Gods
Endow'd with all thir gifts, and O too like
In sad event, when to the unwiser Son
Of *Japhet* brought by *Hermes*, she ensnar'd
Mankind with her fair looks, to be aveng'd
On him who had stole *Jove's* authentic fire.[7]
  Thus at thir shady Lodge arriv'd, both stood,
Both turn'd, and under op'n Sky ador'd
The God that made both Sky, Air, Earth and Heav'n
Which they beheld, the Moon's resplendent Globe
And starry Pole:° Thou also mad'st the Night, *sky*

5. Any ornament of inlaid work; the other sense of "emblem" (pictorial symbol) also operates here, to draw attention to the emblematic properties of the flowers (the humility of the violet, prudence of the hyacinth, amiability of the jasmine, etc.). The bower as a whole is an emblem of true married love.

6. Pan, Silvanus, and Faunus were confused, for all were represented as half man, half goat. Pan was a symbol of fecundity; Silvanus, god of woods, symbolized gardens and limits; Faunus, the Roman Pan, a wood god, and the father of satyrs, was an emblem of concupiscence.

7. Milton has followed the version of the myth in Charles Estienne's *Dictionarium historicum* (1671): "Pandora . . . is feigned by Hesiod the first woman—made by Vulcan at Jupiter's command—. . . she was called Pandora, either because she was 'endowed with all [the gods'] gifts,' or because she was endowed with gifts by all." She was "sent with a closed casket to Epimetheus, since Jupiter wanted revenge on the human race for the boldness of Prometheus, who had stolen fire from heaven and taken it . . . down to earth; and that Epimetheus received her and opened the casket, which contained every kind of evil, so that it filled the world with diseases and calamaties." Prometheus and Epimetheus were sons of Iapetus, the Titan son of Coelus and Terra. Milton identifies Iapetus with Iaphet (Noah's son).

Maker Omnipotent, and thou the Day,
Which we in our appointed work imploy'd
Have finisht happy in our mutual help
And mutual love, the Crown of all our bliss
Ordain'd by thee, and this delicious place
For us too large, where thy abundance wants
Partakers, and uncropt falls to the ground.
But thou hast promis'd from us two a Race
To fill the Earth, who shall with us extol
Thy goodness infinite, both when we wake,
And when we seek, as now, thy gift of sleep.
This said unanimous, and other Rites
Observing none, but adoration pure
Which God likes best, into thir inmost bower
Handed they went; and eas'd the putting off
These troublesome disguises which wee wear,
Straight side by side were laid, nor turn'd I ween
Adam from his fair Spouse, nor *Eve* the Rites
Mysterious of connubial Love refus'd:
Whatever Hypocrites austerely talk
Of purity and place and innocence,
Defaming as impure what God declares
Pure, and commands to some, leaves free to all.
Our Maker bids increase,[8] who bids abstain
But our Destroyer, foe to God and Man?
Hail wedded Love, mysterious Law, true source
Of human offspring, sole propriety
In Paradise of all things common else.
By thee adulterous lust was driv'n from men
Among the bestial herds to range, by thee
Founded in Reason, Loyal, Just, and Pure,
Relations dear, and all the Charities° *affections*
Of Father, Son, and Brother first were known.
Far be it, that I should write thee sin or blame,
Or think thee unbefitting holiest place,
Perpetual Fountain of Domestic sweets,
Whose bed is undefil'd and chaste pronounc't,[9]
Present, or past, as Saints and Patriarchs us'd.
Here Love his golden shafts imploys,[1] here lights
His constant Lamp, and waves his purple wings,
Reigns here and revels; not in the bought smile
Of Harlots, loveless, joyless, unindear'd,
Casual fruition, nor in Court Amours,
Mixt Dance, or wanton Mask, or Midnight Ball,
Or Serenate, which the starv'd Lover sings

8. See Genesis 1.28.
9. See Hebrews 13.4: "Marriage is honourable in all, and the bed undefiled."
1. Cupid's "golden shafts" were sharp and gleaming and kindled love, while those of lead were blunt and put love to flight (Ovid, *Metamorphoses* 1.468–71).

To his proud fair, best quitted with disdain.
These lull'd by Nightingales imbracing slept,
And on thir naked limbs the flow'ry roof
Show'r'd Roses, which the Morn repair'd.° Sleep on, *made up for*
Blest pair; and O yet happiest if ye seek
No happier state, and know to know no more.[2]
  Now had night measur'd with her shadowy Cone
Half way up Hill this vast Sublunar Vault,[3]
And from thir Ivory Port the Cherubim
Forth issuing at th' accustom'd hour stood arm'd
To thir night watches in warlike Parade,
When *Gabriel* to his next in power thus spake.
  Uzziel,[4] half these draw off, and coast the South
With strictest watch; these other wheel the North;
Our circuit meets full West. As flame they part
Half wheeling to the Shield, half to the Spear.[5]
From these, two strong and subtle Spirits he call'd
That near him stood, and gave them thus in charge.
  Ithuriel and *Zephon,* with wing'd speed
Search through this Garden, leave unsearcht no nook,
But chiefly where those two fair Creatures Lodge,
Now laid perhaps asleep secure° of harm. *careless*
This Ev'ning from the Sun's decline arriv'd
Who tells of some infernal Spirit seen
Hitherward bent (who could have thought?) escap'd
The bars of Hell, on errand bad no doubt:
Such where ye find, seize fast, and hither bring.
  So saying, on he led his radiant Files,
Dazzling the Moon; these to the Bower direct
In search of whom they sought: him there they found
Squat like a Toad, close at the ear of *Eve;*
Assaying by his Devilish art to reach
The Organs of her Fancy, and with them forge
Illusions as he list, Phantasms° and Dreams, *illusions*
Or if, inspiring venom, he might taint
Th' animal spirits[6] that from pure blood arise
Like gentle breaths from Rivers pure, thence raise
At least distemper'd,° discontented thoughts, *vexed*
Vain hopes, vain aims, inordinate desires
Blown up with high conceits ingend'ring pride.

2. Either "know that it is best not to seek new knowledge (by eating the forbidden fruit)" or "know how to limit your experience to the state of innocence."
3. The earth's shadow is a cone that appears to circle around it in diametrical opposition to the sun. When the axis of the cone reaches the meridian, it is midnight; but here it is only "Half way up," so the time is nine o'clock.
4. "Uzziel" (Strength of God) occurs in the Bible as an ordinary human name (e.g., Exodus 6.18), and so does "Zephon" (Searcher of Secrets: Numbers 26.15). "Ithuriel" (Discovery of God) is not from the Bible.
5. "Shield" for "left" and "spear" for "right" were ancient military terms.
6. Spirits in this sense were fine vapors, regarded by some as a medium between body and soul, by others as a separate soul. Animal spirits (Latin *anima,* soul) ascended to the brain and issued through the nerves to impart motion to the body. Local movement of the animal spirits could also produce imaginative apparitions, by which angels were thought to affect the human mind.

Him thus intent *Ithuriel* with his Spear
Touch'd lightly; for no falsehood can endure
Touch of Celestial temper, but returns
Of force to its own likeness: up he starts
Discover'd and surpris'd. As when a spark
Lights on a heap of nitrous[7] Powder, laid
Fit for the Tun[8] some Magazin to store
Against° a rumor'd War, the Smutty grain — *preparing for*
With sudden blaze diffus'd, inflames the Air:
So started up in his own shape the Fiend.
Back stepp'd those two fair Angels half amaz'd
So sudden to behold the grisly King;
Yet thus, unmov'd with fear, accost him soon.
  Which of those rebel Spirits adjudg'd to Hell
Com'st thou, escap'd thy prison, and transform'd,
Why satst thou like an enemy in wait
Here watching at the head of these that sleep?
  Know ye not then said *Satan*, fill'd with scorn,
Know ye not mee? ye knew me once no mate
For you, there sitting where ye durst not soar;
Not to know mee argues yourselves unknown,
The lowest of your throng; or if ye know,
Why ask ye, and superfluous begin
Your message, like to end as much in vain?
To whom thus *Zephon*, answering scorn with scorn.
Think not, revolted Spirit, thy shape the same,
Or undiminisht brightness, to be known
As when thou stood'st in Heav'n upright and pure;
That Glory then, when thou no more wast good,
Departed from thee, and thou resembl'st now
Thy sin and place of doom obscure and foul.
But come, for thou, be sure, shalt give account
To him who sent us, whose charge is to keep
This place inviolable, and these from harm.
  So spake the Cherub, and his grave rebuke
Severe in youthful beauty, added grace
Invincible: abasht the Devil stood,
And felt how awful goodness is, and saw
Virtue in her shape how lovely, saw, and pin'd° — *mourned*
His loss; but chiefly to find here observ'd
His lustre visibly impair'd; yet seem'd
Undaunted. If I must contend, said he,
Best with the best, the Sender not the sent,
Or all at once; more glory will be won,
Or less be lost. Thy fear, said *Zephon* bold,
Will save us trial what the least can do

7. Mixed with niter (potassium nitrate or saltpeter, an ingredient in gunpowder) to form an explosive.

8. In proper condition for casking, ready for use.

Single against thee wicked, and thence weak.
  The Fiend repli'd not, overcome with rage;
But like a proud Steed rein'd, went haughty on,
Champing his iron curb: to strive or fly
He held it vain; awe from above had quell'd
His heart, not else dismay'd. Now drew they nigh
The western Point,[9] where those half-rounding guards
Just met, and closing stood in squadron join'd
Awaiting next command. To whom thir Chief
Gabriel from the Front thus call'd aloud.
  O friends, I hear the tread of nimble feet
Hasting this way, and now by glimpse discern
Ithuriel and *Zephon* through the shade,
And with them comes a third of Regal port,
But faded splendor wan; who by his gait
And fierce demeanor seems the Prince of Hell,
Not likely to part hence without contest;
Stand firm, for in his look defiance low'rs.
  He scarce had ended, when those two approach'd
And brief related whom they brought, where found,
How busied, in what form and posture coucht.
  To whom with stern regard thus *Gabriel* spake.
Why hast thou, *Satan,* broke the bounds prescrib'd
To thy transgressions, and disturb'd the charge
Of others, who approve not to transgress
By thy example, but have power and right
To question thy bold entrance on this place;
Imploy'd it seems to violate sleep, and those
Whose dwelling God hath planted here in bliss?
  To whom thus *Satan,* with contemptuous brow.
Gabriel, thou hadst in Heav'n th' esteem of wise,
And such I held thee; but this question askt
Puts me in doubt. Lives there who loves his pain?
Who would not, finding way, break loose from Hell,
Though thither doom'd? Thou wouldst thyself, no doubt,
And boldly venture to whatever place
Farthest from pain, where thou might'st hope to change
Torment with ease, and soonest recompense
Dole° with delight, which in this place I sought; *suffering*
To thee no reason; who know'st only good,
But evil hast not tri'd: and wilt object
His will who bound us? let him surer bar
His Iron Gates, if he intends our stay
In that dark durance:° thus much what was askt.[1] *imprisonment*
The rest is true, they found me where they say;
But that implies not violence or harm.

9. For the angels' movement in a circle around heaven, see also 4.782–4.

1. That is, "thus much in reply to what was asked."

Thus he in scorn. The warlike Angel mov'd,
Disdainfully half smiling thus repli'd.
O loss of one in Heav'n to judge of wise,
Since *Satan* fell, whom folly overthrew,
And now returns him from his prison scap't,
Gravely in doubt whether to hold them wise
Or not, who ask what boldness brought him hither
Unlicens't from his bounds in Hell prescrib'd;
So wise he judges it to fly from pain
However,° and to scape his punishment. *howsoever*
So judge thou still, presumptuous, till the wrath,
Which thou incurr'st by flying, meet thy flight
Sevenfold, and scourge that wisdom back to Hell,
Which taught thee yet no better, that no pain
Can equal anger infinite provok't.
But wherefore thou alone? wherefore with thee
Came not all Hell broke loose? is pain to them
Less pain, less to be fled, or thou than they
Less hardy to endure? courageous Chief,
The first in flight from pain, hadst thou alleg'd
To thy deserted host this cause of flight,
Thou surely hadst not come sole fugitive.
To which the Fiend thus answer'd frowning stern.
Not that I less endure, or shrink from pain,
Insulting Angel, well thou know'st I stood
Thy fiercest, when in Battle to thy aid
The blasting volley'd Thunder made all speed
And seconded thy else not dreaded Spear.
But still thy words at random, as before,
Argue thy inexperience what behooves
From hard assays and ill successes past
A faithful Leader,[2] not to hazard all
Through ways of danger by himself untri'd.
I therefore, I alone first undertook
To wing the desolate Abyss, and spy
This new created World, whereof in Hell
Fame is not silent, here in hope to find
Better abode, and my afflicted Powers
To settle here on Earth, or in mid Air;
Though for possession put to try once more
What thou and thy gay Legions dare against;
Whose easier business were to serve thir Lord
High up in Heav'n, with songs to hymn his Throne,
And practis'd distances to cringe, not fight.
To whom the warrior Angel soon repli'd.
To say and straight unsay; pretending first

2. That is, "You're still talking off the top of your head, showing how little you know about a defeated commander's responsibilities."

Wise to fly pain, professing next the Spy,
Argues no Leader, but a liar trac't,° *discovered*
Satan, and couldst thou faithful add? O name,
O sacred name of faithfulness profan'd!
Faithful to whom? to thy rebellious crew?
Army of Fiends, fit body to fit head;
Was this your discipline and faith ingag'd,
Your military obedience, to dissolve
Allegiance to th' acknowledg'd Power supreme?
And thou sly hypocrite, who now wouldst seem
Patron of liberty, who more than thou
Once fawn'd, and cring'd, and servilely ador'd
Heav'n's awful Monarch? wherefore but in hope
To dispossess him, and thyself to reign?
But mark what I arede° thee now, avaunt; *advise*
Fly thither whence thou fledd'st: if from this hour
Within these hallow'd limits thou appear,
Back to th' infernal pit I drag thee chain'd,
And Seal thee so, as henceforth not to scorn
The facile° gates of hell too slightly barr'd. *easily moved*
So threat'n'd hee, but *Satan* to no threats
Gave heed, but waxing more in rage repli'd.
Then when I am thy captive talk of chains,
Proud limitary Cherub,[3] but ere then
Far heavier load thyself expect to feel
From my prevailing arm, though Heaven's King
Ride on thy wings, and thou with thy Compeers,
Us'd to the yoke, draw'st his triumphant wheels
In progress through the road of Heav'n Star-pav'd.
While thus he spake, th' Angelic Squadron bright
Turn'd fiery red, sharp'ning in mooned horns
Thir Phalanx, and began to hem him round
With ported Spears,[4] as thick as when a field
Of *Ceres* ripe for harvest waving bends
Her bearded Grove of ears, which way the wind
Sways them; the careful Plowman doubting stands
Lest on the threshing floor his hopeful sheaves
Prove chaff.[5] On th' other side *Satan* alarm'd
Collecting all his might dilated stood.
Like *Teneriff* or *Atlas* unremov'd:[6]
His stature reacht the Sky, and on his Crest

3. Satan contemptuously mistakes Gabriel, who is a top seraph (4.549–50) rather than a cherub. "Limitary" implies that Gabriel has an undesirable provincial assignment.

4. The spears are held sloping upward, pointing towards Satan. The angels' formation is crescent-shaped ("mooned"); such formations, classic in warfare, were still used.

5. Comparison of an excited army to wind-stirred corn is Homeric (*Iliad* 2.147–50). Ceres is the harvest goddess, here standing for "corn."

6. "Teneriff" is Tenerife, the pyramidal mountain on the Canary Island of the same name. Atlas sustained the stars as Satan sustains the pressure of the angels. Like Satan, Atlas also rebelled against God.

Sat horror Plum'd; nor wanted in his grasp
What seem'd both Spear and Shield: now dreadful deeds
Might have ensu'd, nor only Paradise
In this commotion, but the Starry Cope° *firmament*
Of Heav'n perhaps, or all the Elements
At least had gone to rack, disturb'd and torn
With violence of this conflict, had not soon
Th' Eternal to prevent such horrid fray
Hung forth in Heav'n his golden Scales,[7] yet seen
Betwixt *Astrea*° and the *Scorpion* sign, *Virgo*
Wherein all things created first he weigh'd,
The pendulous round Earth with balanc't Air
In counterpoise, now ponders all events,
Battles and Realms: in these he put two weights
The sequel each of parting and of fight;
The latter quick up flew, and kickt the beam;
Which *Gabriel* spying, thus bespake the Fiend.
Satan, I know thy strength, and thou know'st mine,
Neither our own but giv'n; what folly then
To boast what Arms can do, since thine no more
Than Heav'n permits, nor mine, though doubl'd now
To trample thee as mire: for proof look up,
And read thy Lot in yon celestial Sign
Where thou art weigh'd, and shown how light, how weak,
If thou resist. The Fiend lookt up and knew
His mounted scale aloft: nor more; but fled
Murmuring, and with him fled the shades of night.

The End of the Fourth Book.

Book 5
The Argument

Morning approacht, Eve *relates to* Adam *her troublesome dream; he likes it not, yet comforts her: They come forth to thir day labors: Thir Morning Hymn at the Door of thir Bower. God to render Man inexcusable sends* Raphael *to admonish him of his obedience, of his free estate, of his enemy near at hand; who he is, and why his enemy, and whatever else may avail* Adam *to know.* Raphael *comes down to Paradise, his appearance describ'd, his coming discern'd by* Adam *afar off sitting at the door of his Bower; he goes out to meet him, brings him to his lodge, entertains him with the choicest fruits of Paradise got together by* Eve*; thir discourse at Table:* Raphael *performs his message, minds* Adam *of his state and of his enemy; relates at* Adam's *request who that enemy is, and how he came to be so, beginning from his first revolt in Heaven, and the occasion thereof; how he drew his Legions after him to the parts of the North, and there incited them to rebel with him, persuading all but only* Abdiel *a Seraph, who in Argument dissuades and opposes him, then forsakes him.*

7. Homer's Zeus balances the fates of Trojans and Greeks, and Hector and Achilles, with golden scales (*Iliad* 8.68–77 and 22.208–13, imitated in Virgil's *Aeneid* 12.725–7). In Homer, the loser's scale sinks down to death; in Milton the inferior side rises, being "found wanting" (Daniel 5.27).

Now Morn her rosy steps in th' Eastern Clime
Advancing, sow'd the Earth with Orient Pearl,
When *Adam* wak't, so custom'd, for his sleep
Was Aery light, from pure digestion bred,
And temperate vapors bland, which th' only sound
Of leaves and fuming rills, *Aurora's* fan,
Lightly dispers'd, and the shrill Matin° Song *morning*
Of Birds on every bough;[1] so much the more
His wonder was to find unwak'n'd *Eve*
With Tresses discompos'd, and glowing Cheek,
As through unquiet rest: hee on his side
Leaning half-rais'd, with looks of cordial Love
Hung over her enamor'd, and beheld
Beauty, which whether waking or asleep,
Shot forth peculiar° graces; then with voice *distinctive*
Mild, as when *Zephyrus*[2] on *Flora* breathes,
Her hand soft touching, whisper'd thus. Awake
My fairest, my espous'd, my latest found,
Heav'n's last best gift, my ever new delight,
Awake, the morning shines, and the fresh field
Calls us; we lose the prime,[3] to mark how spring
Our tended Plants, how blows° the Citron Grove, *blossoms*
What drops the Myrrh, and what the balmy Reed,
How Nature paints her colors, how the Bee
Sits on the Bloom extracting liquid sweet.[4]
Such whispering wak'd her, but with startl'd eye
On *Adam*, whom imbracing, thus she spake.
O Sole in whom my thoughts find all repose,
My Glory, my Perfection, glad I see
Thy face, and Morn return'd, for I this Night,
Such night till this I never pass'd, have dream'd,
If dream'd, not as I oft am wont, of thee,
Works of day past, or morrow's next design,
But of offense and trouble, which my mind
Knew never till this irksome night; methought
Close at mine ear one call'd me forth to walk
With gentle voice, I thought it thine; it said,
Why sleep'st thou *Eve?* now is the pleasant time,
The cool, the silent, save where silence yields
To the night-warbling Bird, that now awake
Tunes sweetest his love-labor'd song; now reigns
Full Orb'd the Moon, and with more pleasing light
Shadowy sets off the face of things; in vain,
If none regard; Heav'n wakes with all his eyes,

1. The "only" (mere) sound of leaves, water, and birds was enough to rouse Adam. The fan of Aurora, the goddess of morning, is the leaves.
2. The west wind. Zephyrus's sweet breath was supposed to produce flowers, as was that of his wife, the flower-goddess Flora.
3. The first hour of the day.
4. For lines 18–25, see Song of Solomon 2.10–13 and 7.12.

Whom to behold but thee, Nature's desire,
In whose sight all things joy, with ravishment
Attracted by thy beauty still to gaze.
I rose as at thy call, but found thee not;
To find thee I directed then my walk;
And on, methought, alone I pass'd through ways
That brought me on a sudden to the Tree
Of interdicted Knowledge: fair it seem'd,
Much fairer to my Fancy than by day:
And as I wond'ring lookt, beside it stood
One shap'd and wing'd like one of those from Heav'n
By us oft seen; his dewy locks distill'd
Ambrosia;[5] on that Tree he also gaz'd;
And O fair Plant, said he, with fruit surcharg'd,
Deigns none to ease thy load and taste thy sweet,
Nor God, nor Man; is Knowledge so despis'd?
Or envy, or what reserve[6] forbids to taste?
Forbid who will, none shall from me withhold
Longer thy offer'd good, why else set here?
This said he paus'd not, but with vent'rous Arm
He pluckt, he tasted; mee damp horror chill'd
At such bold words voucht with a deed so bold:
But he thus overjoy'd, O Fruit Divine,
Sweet of thyself, but much more sweet thus cropt,
Forbidd'n here, it seems, as only fit
For Gods, yet able to make Gods of Men:
And why not Gods of Men, since good, the more
Communicated, more abundant grows,
The Author not impair'd, but honor'd more?
Here, happy Creature, fair Angelic *Eve*,
Partake thou also; happy though thou art,
Happier thou may'st be, worthier canst not be:
Taste this, and be henceforth among the Gods
Thyself a Goddess, not to Earth confin'd,
But sometimes in the Air, as wee, sometimes
Ascend to Heav'n, by merit thine, and see
What life the Gods live there, and such live thou.
So saying, he drew nigh, and to me held,
Even to my mouth of that same fruit held part
Which he had pluckt; the pleasant savory smell[7]
So quick'n'd appetite, that I, methought,
Could not but taste. Forthwith up to the Clouds
With him I flew, and underneath beheld
The Earth outstretcht immense, a prospect wide
And various: wond'ring at my flight and change

5. The fabled anointing oil of the gods.
6. Limitation, restriction, or knowledge kept secret on the part of God; but perhaps also inhibition, self-restraint on the part of humans.
7. The fruit has an appetizing, fragrant scent, but "savory" could also mean "spiritually edifying."

To this high exaltation; suddenly
My Guide was gone, and I, methought, sunk down,
And fell asleep; but O how glad I wak'd
To find this but a dream! Thus *Eve* her Night
Related, and thus *Adam* answer'd sad.° *gravely*
Best Image of myself and dearer half,
The trouble of thy thoughts this night in sleep
Affects me equally; nor can I like
This uncouth° dream, of evil sprung I fear; *strange*
Yet evil whence? in thee can harbor none,
Created pure. But know that in the Soul
Are many lesser Faculties that serve
Reason as chief; among these Fancy next
Her office holds; of all external things,
Which the five watchful Senses represent,
She forms Imaginations, Aery shapes,
Which Reason joining or disjoining, frames
All what we affirm or what deny, and call
Our knowledge or opinion; then retires
Into her private Cell when Nature rests.[8]
Oft in her absence mimic Fancy wakes
To imitate her; but misjoining shapes,
Wild work produces oft, and most in dreams,
Ill matching words and deeds long past or late.
Some such resemblances methinks I find
Of our last Ev'ning's talk,[9] in this thy dream,
But with addition strange; yet be not sad.
Evil into the mind of God[1] or Man
May come and go, so unapprov'd, and leave
No spot or blame behind: Which gives me hope
That what in sleep thou didst abhor to dream,
Waking thou never wilt consent to do.
Be not disheart'n'd then, nor cloud those looks
That wont to be more cheerful and serene
Than when fair Morning first smiles on the World,
And let us to our fresh imployments rise
Among the Groves, the Fountains, and the Flow'rs
That open now thir choicest bosom'd° smells *hidden*
Reserv'd from night, and kept for thee in store.
So cheer'd he his fair Spouse, and she was cheer'd,
But silently a gentle tear let fall
From either eye, and wip'd them with her hair;
Two other precious drops that ready stood,

8. For the psychology involved here, see Burton, *Anatomy of Melancholy* 1.1.2.7: "Phantasy, or imagination . . . is an inner sense which doth more fully examine the species perceived by common sense, of things present or absent. . . . In time of sleep this faculty is free, and many times conceives strange, stupend, absurd shapes . . . it is subject and governed by reason, or at least should be."

9. Their discussion of the prohibition of the Tree of Knowledge (4.421ff.).

1. Probably "angel." But Milton (if not Adam) may also intend a reference to the doctrine that God's omniscience extends to evil.

Each in thir crystal sluice, hee ere they fell
Kiss'd as the gracious signs of sweet remorse
And pious awe, that fear'd to have offended.
So all was clear'd, and to the Field they haste.
But first from under shady arborous roof,
Soon as they forth were come to open sight
Of day-spring,° and the Sun, who scarce up risen *daybreak*
With wheels yet hov'ring o'er the Ocean brim,
Shot parallel to the earth his dewy ray,
Discovering in wide Lantskip° all the East *landscape*
Of Paradise and *Eden's* happy Plains,
Lowly they bow'd adoring, and began
Thir Orisons,° each Morning duly paid *prayers*
In various style, for neither various style
Nor holy rapture wanted they to praise
Thir Maker, in fit strains pronounct or sung
Unmeditated, such prompt eloquence
Flow'd from thir lips, in Prose or numerous Verse,
More tuneable° than needed Lute or Harp *tuneful*
To add more sweetness, and they thus began.[2]
These are thy glorious works, Parent of good,
Almighty, thine this universal Frame,[3]
Thus wondrous fair; thyself how wondrous then!
Unspeakable, who sit'st above these Heavens
To us invisible or dimly seen
In these thy lowest works, yet these declare
Thy goodness beyond thought, and Power Divine:
Speak yee who best can tell, ye Sons of Light,
Angels, for yee behold him, and with songs
And choral symphonies, Day without Night,
Circle his Throne rejoicing, yee in Heav'n;
On Earth join all ye Creatures to extol
Him first, him last, him midst, and without end.
Fairest of Stars,[4] last in the train of Night,
If better thou belong not to the dawn,
Sure pledge of day, that crown'st the smiling Morn
With thy bright Circlet, praise him in thy Sphere
While day arises, that sweet hour of Prime.
Thou Sun, of this great World both Eye and Soul,[5]
Acknowledge him thy Greater, sound his praise
In thy eternal course, both when thou climb'st,
And when high Noon hast gain'd, and when thou fall'st.
Moon, that now meet'st the orient Sun, now fli'st

2. The hymn (lines 153–208) is based on Psalm 148 and on the canticle *Benedicite, omnia opera* (in the 1549 *Book of Common Prayer*).
3. Used of heaven, earth, or the universe regarded as structures fabricated by God.
4. The planet Venus rises in the east just before sunrise and is known as the morning star.
5. The metaphor of the sun as an eye implied a connection between seeing and understanding and hence an identification of the sun with the creative word. The sun is "soul" of the world in the sense that it gives life.

With the fixt Stars, fixt in thir Orb that flies,
And yee five other wand'ring Fires that move
In mystic Dance not without Song,[6] resound
His praise, who out of Darkness call'd up Light.
Air, and ye Elements the eldest birth
Of Nature's Womb, that in quaternion run
Perpetual Circle, multiform, and mix
And nourish all things, let your ceaseless change
Vary to our great Maker still new praise.
Ye Mists and Exhalations that now rise
From Hill or steaming Lake, dusky or grey,
Till the Sun paint your fleecy skirts with Gold,
In honor to the World's great Author rise,
Whether to deck with Clouds th' uncolor'd sky,
Or wet the thirsty Earth with falling showers,
Rising or falling still advance his praise.
His praise ye Winds, that from four Quarters blow,
Breathe soft or loud; and wave your tops, ye Pines,
With every Plant, in sign of Worship wave.
Fountains and yee, that warble, as ye flow,
Melodious murmurs, warbling tune his praise.
Join voices all ye living Souls; ye Birds,
That singing up to Heaven Gate ascend,
Bear on your wings and in your notes his praise;
Yee that in Waters glide, and yee that walk
The Earth, and stately tread, or lowly creep;
Witness if I be silent, Morn or Even,
To Hill, or Valley, Fountain, or fresh shade
Made vocal by my Song, and taught his praise.
Hail universal Lord, be bounteous still
To give us only good; and if the night
Have gather'd aught of evil or conceal'd,
Disperse it, as now light dispels the dark.
  So pray'd they innocent, and to thir thoughts
Firm peace recover'd soon and wonted calm.
On to thir morning's rural work they haste
Among sweet dews and flow'rs; where any row
Of Fruit-trees overwoody reach'd too far
Thir pamper'd boughs, and needed hands to check
Fruitless imbraces: or they led the Vine
To wed her Elm; she spous'd about him twines
Her marriageable arms, and with her brings
Her dow'r th' adopted Clusters, to adorn
His barren leaves. Them thus imploy'd beheld
With pity Heav'n's high King, and to him call'd

6. The music of the spheres, inaudible now to fallen humans' gross hearing. The elements are a form of the quaternion, or tetrad, a group of four regarded as one: air, earth, fire, and water. For the transformation of the elements into one another, see Cicero, *De natura deorum* 2.33.

Raphael, the sociable Spirit, that deign'd
To travel with *Tobias*, and secur'd
His marriage with the seven-times-wedded Maid.
Raphael, said hee, thou hear'st what stir on Earth
Satan from Hell scap't through the darksome Gulf
Hath rais'd in Paradise, and how disturb'd
This night the human pair, how he designs
In them at once to ruin all mankind.
Go therefore, half this day as friend with friend
Converse with *Adam*, in what Bow'r or shade
Thou find'st him from the heat of Noon retir'd,
To respite his day-labor with repast,
Or with repose; and such discourse bring on,
As may advise him of his happy state,
Happiness in his power left free to will,
Left to his own free Will, his Will though free,
Yet mutable; whence warn him to beware
He swerve not too secure:[7] tell him withal
His danger, and from whom, what enemy
Late fall'n himself from Heaven, is plotting now
The fall of others from like state of bliss;
By violence, no, for that shall be withstood,
But by deceit and lies; this let him know,
Lest wilfully transgressing he pretend
Surprisal, unadmonisht, unforewarn'd.
So spake th' Eternal Father, and fulfill'd
All Justice: nor delay'd the winged Saint
After his charge receiv'd,[8] but from among
Thousand Celestial Ardors, where he stood
Veil'd with his gorgeous wings, up springing light
Flew through the midst of Heav'n; th' angelic Choirs
On each hand parting, to his speed gave way
Through all th' Empyreal road; till at the Gate
Of Heav'n arriv'd, the gate self-open'd wide
On golden Hinges turning, as by work
Divine the sovran Architect had fram'd.[9]
From hence, no cloud, or, to obstruct his sight,
Star interpos'd, however small he sees,[1]
Not unconform to other shining Globes,
Earth and the Gard'n of God, with Cedars crown'd
Above all Hills. As when by night the Glass
Of *Galileo*, less assur'd, observes
Imagin'd Lands and Regions in the Moon.[2]

7. To be careful not to err through overconfidence.
8. That is, "after he received his order."
9. In Acts 12.10, an iron gate opens to St. Peter and an angel. Likewise, in the *Iliad* 5.749, heaven's gates open automatically for Hera.
1. "Small" qualifies Earth. From Raphael's startling viewpoint, earth is almost too small to be like "other shining globes" (stars).
2. Contrast 1.286–91, where the reality of lunar geography is unquestioned.

Or Pilot from amidst the *Cyclades*
Delos or Samos first appearing kens° *detects*
A cloudy spot.[3] Down thither prone° in flight *downward sloping*
He speeds, and through the vast Ethereal Sky
Sails between worlds and worlds, with steady wing
Now on the polar winds, then with quick Fan
Winnows the buxom° Air; till within soar *yielding*
Of Tow'ring Eagles, to all the Fowls he seems
A *Phœnix*, gaz'd by all, as that sole Bird
When to enshrine his reliques in the Sun's
Bright Temple, to *Egyptian Thebes* he flies.[4]
At once on th' Eastern cliff of Paradise
He lights,[5] and to his proper shape returns
A Seraph wing'd; six wings he wore, to shade
His lineaments° Divine; the pair that clad *figure*
Each shoulder broad, came mantling o'er his breast
With regal Ornament; the middle pair
Girt like a Starry Zone his waist, and round
Skirted his loins and thighs with downy Gold
And colors dipt in Heav'n; the third his feet
Shadow'd from either heel with feather'd mail
Sky-tinctur'd grain.[6] Like *Maia's* son° he stood, *Mercury*
And shook his Plumes, that Heav'nly fragrance fill'd
The circuit wide. Straight knew him all the Bands
Of Angels under watch; and to his state,° *rank*
And to his message° high in honor rise; *mission*
For on some message high they guess'd him bound.
Thir glittering Tents he pass'd, and now is come
Into the blissful field, through Groves of Myrrh.
And flow'ring Odors, Cassia, Nard, and Balm,[7]
A Wilderness of sweets; for Nature here
Wanton'd as in her prime, and play'd at will
Her Virgin Fancies, pouring forth more sweet,
Wild above Rule or Art, enormous bliss.
Him through the spicy Forest onward come
Adam discern'd, as in the door he sat
Of his cool Bow'r, while now the mounted Sun
Shot down direct his fervid Rays, to warm
Earth's inmost womb, more warmth than *Adam* needs;

3. The Cyclades are a circular group of islands in the southern Aegean. Delos is one of the Cyclades, the birthplace of Apollo and Diana. Samos is not one of the Cyclades, but the birthplace of Juno, who married Jupiter there; so, like Delos, a mythic version of Eden.
4. Every 500 years the mythic phoenix immolated itself in a pyre or nest of spices, from which a new phoenix arose from its ashes or bone marrow and flew to Heliopolis, City of the Sun, to deposit its relics. (See Ovid's *Metamorphoses* 15.391–407, and Pliny's *Natural History* 10.2.)
5. The only gate is on the Eastern side (4.178).
6. Echoes the description of the seraphim in Isaiah 6.2, "Each one had six wings; with twain he covered his face, and with twain he covered his feet, and with twain he did fly."
7. Myrrh is an aromatic gum, used for protection against devils. Cassia is a cinnamon-like spice. Nard was the ointment poured over Jesus' head to anoint him for burial (Mark 14.3, 8). Balm of Gilead was celebrated as the earliest known balsam (another aromatic substance).

And *Eve* within, due° at her hour prepar'd *duly*
For dinner savoury fruits, of taste to please
True appetite, and not disrelish thirst
Of nectarous draughts between, from milky° stream, *sweet*
Berry or Grape: to whom thus *Adam* call'd.
  Haste hither *Eve*, and worth thy sight behold
Eastward among those Trees, what glorious shape
Comes this way moving; seems another Morn
Ris'n on mid-noon; some great behest from Heav'n
To us perhaps he brings, and will voutsafe
This day to be our Guest. But go with speed,
And what thy stores contain, bring forth and pour
Abundance, fit to honor and receive
Our Heav'nly stranger; well we may afford
Our givers thir own gifts, and large bestow
From large bestow'd, where Nature multiplies
Her fertile growth, and by disburd'ning grows
More fruitful, which instructs us not to spare.
  To whom thus *Eve*. *Adam*, earth's hallow'd mould,
Of God inspir'd, small store will serve, where store,
All seasons, ripe for use hangs on the stalk;
Save what by frugal storing firmness gains
To nourish, and superfluous moist consumes:
But I will haste and from each bough and brake,° *bush*
Each Plant and juiciest Gourd will pluck such choice
To entertain our Angel guest, as hee
Beholding shall confess that here on Earth
God hath dispenst his bounties as in Heav'n.
  So saying, with dispatchful looks in haste
She turns, on hospitable thoughts intent
What choice to choose for delicacy best,
What order, so contriv'd as not to mix
Tastes, not well join'd, inelegant, but bring
Taste after taste upheld° with kindliest change; *sustained*
Bestirs her then, and from each tender stalk
Whatever Earth all-bearing Mother yields
In *India* East or West, or middle shore
In *Pontus* or the *Punic* Coast, or where
Alcinoüs reign'd,[8] fruit of all kinds, in coat,
Rough, or smooth rin'd,° or bearded husk, or shell *rinded*
She gathers, Tribute large, and on the board
Heaps with unsparing hand; for drink the Grape
She crushes, inoffensive must, and meaths
From many a berry, and from sweet kernels prest
She tempers dulcet creams, nor these to hold
Wants her fit vessels pure, then strews the ground

8. The Pontus is the southern shore of the Black Sea. The Punic Coast is the Carthaginian coast of the Mediterranean. Alcinous, Homer's hospitable Phaeacian king, lived on an island paradise called Scheria.

With Rose and Odors from the shrub unfum'd.[9]
Meanwhile our Primitive great Sire, to meet
His god-like Guest, walks forth, without more train
Accompanied than with his own complete
Perfections; in himself was all his state,° *dignity*
More solemn than the tedious pomp that waits
On Princes, when thir rich Retinue long
Of Horses led, and Grooms besmear'd with Gold
Dazzles the crowd, and sets them all agape.
Nearer his presence *Adam* though not aw'd,
Yet with submiss° approach and reverence meek, *submissive*
As to a superior Nature, bowing low,
Thus said. Native of Heav'n, for other place
None can than Heav'n such glorious shape contain;
Since by descending from the Thrones above,
Those happy places thou hast deign'd a while
To want,° and honor these, voutsafe with us *miss*
Two only, who yet by sovran gift possess
This spacious ground, in yonder shady Bow'r
To rest, and what the Garden choicest bears
To sit and taste, till this meridian heat
Be over, and the Sun more cool decline.
Whom thus the Angelic Virtue answer'd mild.
Adam, I therefore came, nor art thou such
Created, or such place hast here to dwell,
As may not oft invite, though Spirits of Heav'n
To visit thee; lead on then where thy Bow'r
O'ershades; for these mid-hours, till Ev'ning rise
I have at will. So to the Silvan Lodge
They came, that like *Pomona's* Arbor smil'd
With flow'rets deck't and fragrant smells; but *Eve*
Undeckt, save with herself more lovely fair
Than Wood-Nymph,[1] or the fairest Goddess feign'd
Of three that in Mount *Ida* naked strove,[2]
Stood to entertain her guest from Heav'n; no veil
Shee needed, Virtue-proof, no thought infirm
Alter'd her cheek. On whom the Angel *Hail*
Bestow'd, the holy salutation us'd
Long after to blest *Mary,* second *Eve.*
Hail Mother of Mankind, whose fruitful Womb
Shall fill the World more numerous with thy Sons
Than with these various fruits the Trees of God

9. "Must" is unfermented grape-juice; "meaths" are meads, or sweet drinks; to "temper" is to mix; "dulcet" can mean sweet or bland; and "odours" are scented flowers or spices that are "unfum'd" because they do not require burning, as incense does.

1. The Roman wood-nymph Pomona presided over gardens and especially fruit trees.

2. The three goddesses Juno, Minerva, and Venus all claimed the apple of Strife, inscribed TO THE FAIREST, and the mortal Paris, famed for his wisdom, was appointed arbiter. The judgment of Paris was delivered on Mount Ida, where the goddesses appeared before him naked and without ornament.

Have heap'd this Table. Rais'd of grassy turf
Thir Table was, and mossy seats had round,
And on her ample Square from side to side
All *Autumn* pil'd, though *Spring* and *Autumn* here
Danc'd hand in hand. A while discourse they hold;
No fear lest Dinner cool; when thus began
Our Author.° Heav'nly stranger, please to taste *ancestor*
These bounties which our Nourisher, from whom
All perfet good unmeasur'd out, descends,
To us for food and for delight hath caus'd
The Earth to yield; unsavory food perhaps
To spiritual Natures; only this I know,
That one Celestial Father gives to all.
To whom the Angel. Therefore what he gives
(Whose praise be ever sung) to man in part
Spiritual, may of purest Spirits be found
No ingrateful food:[3] and food alike those pure
Intelligential substances[4] require
As doth your Rational; and both contain
Within them every lower faculty
Of sense, whereby they hear, see, smell, touch, taste,
Tasting concoct, digest, assimilate,
And corporeal to incorporeal turn,[5]
For know, whatever was created, needs
To be sustain'd and fed; of Elements
The grosser feeds the purer, Earth the Sea,
Earth and the Sea feed Air, the Air those Fires
Ethereal, and as lowest first the Moon;
Whence in her visage round those spots, unpurg'd
Vapors not yet into her substance turn'd.
Nor doth the Moon no nourishment exhale[6]
From her moist Continent to higher Orbs.
The Sun that light imparts to all, receives
From all his alimental° recompense *nutritive*
In humid exhalations, and at Even
Sups with the Ocean:[7] though in Heav'n the Trees
Of life ambrosial fruitage bear, and vines
Yield Nectar, though from off the boughs each Morn
We brush mellifluous° Dews, and find the ground *sweetly flowing*
Cover'd with pearly grain:[8] yet God hath here
Varied his bounty so with new delights,

3. Food acceptable to the angels ("purest spirits") because acceptable to humans ("in part spiritual").
4. Intellectual beings.
5. Physiological theory distinguished three stages of digestion: the "first concoction," or digestion in the stomach ("concoct"); the "second concoction," or conversion to blood ("digest"); and the "third concoction," or secretion ("assimilate").
6. The ancient theory was that vapors drawn up to the moon from the earth caused lunar spots. Galileo explained them as landscape features, a theory used above at lines 287–91.
7. This version of the Great Chain of Being was held by Stoics and Epicureans and was also popular in Milton's own time with mystical and alchemic Platonists such as Robert Fludd.
8. Manna, the "corn of heaven."

As may compare with Heaven; and to taste
Think not I shall be nice.° So down they sat, *overrefined*
And to thir viands fell, nor seemingly[9]
The Angel, nor in mist, the common gloss
Of Theologians, but with keen dispatch
Of real hunger, and concoctive heat
To transubstantiate;[1] what redounds,° transpires *remains in excess*
Through Spirits with ease; nor wonder; if by fire
Of sooty coal the Empiric Alchemist
Can turn, or holds it possible to turn
Metals of drossiest Ore to perfet Gold
As from the Mine. Meanwhile at Table *Eve*
Minister'd naked, and thir flowing cups
With pleasant liquors crown'd: O innocence
Deserving Paradise! if ever, then,
Then had the Sons of God° excuse to have been *angels*
Enamour'd at that sight; but in those hearts
Love unlibidinous reign'd, nor jealousy
Was understood, the injur'd Lover's Hell.
Thus when with meats and drinks they had suffic't,
Not burd'n'd Nature, sudden mind arose
In *Adam*, not to let th' occasion pass
Given him by this great Conference to know
Of things above his World, and of thir being
Who dwell in Heav'n, whose excellence he saw
Transcend his own so far, whose radiant forms
Divine effulgence, whose high Power so far
Exceeded human, and his wary speech
Thus to th' Empyreal° Minister he fram'd. *heavenly*
Inhabitant with God, now know I well
Thy favor, in this honor done to Man,
Under whose lowly roof thou hast voutsaf't
To enter, and these earthly fruits to taste,
Food not of Angels, yet accepted so,
As that more willingly thou couldst not seem
At Heav'n's high feasts to have fed: yet what compare?
To whom the winged Hierarch repli'd.
O *Adam*, one Almighty is, from whom
All things proceed, and up to him return,
If not deprav'd from good, created all
Such to perfection, one first matter all,
Indu'd with various forms, various degrees

9. Refers to the Docetist theories about angelic appearances, devised to explain away the awkwardly materialistic accounts of angels in the Bible (e.g., at Genesis 18.8, "they did eat"). The Reformers on the whole rejected such evasions.

1. Transubstantiation is the Roman Catholic doctrine that the bread and wine of the Eucharist become the body and blood of Christ so "transubstantiate" contrasts sharply with the direct concrete simplicity of "keen . . . hunger."

Of substance, and in things that live, of life;[2]
But more refin'd, more spiritous, and pure,
As nearer to him plac't or nearer tending
Each in thir several active Spheres assign'd,
Till body up to spirit work, in bounds
Proportion'd to each kind. So from the root
Springs lighter the green stalk, from thence the leaves
More aery, last the bright consummate° flow'r *perfected*
Spirits odorous breathes: flow'rs and thir fruit
Man's nourishment, by gradual scale sublim'd° *raised*
To vital spirits aspire, to animal,
To intellectual, give both life and sense,[3]
Fancy° and understanding, whence the Soul *imagination*
Reason receives, and reason is her being,
Discursive, or Intuitive; discourse
Is oftest yours, the latter most is ours,
Differing but in degree, of kind the same.[4]
Wonder not then, what God for you saw good
If I refuse not, but convert, as you,
To proper substance; time may come when men
With Angels may participate, and find
No inconvenient Diet, nor too light Fare:
And from these corporal nutriments perhaps
Your bodies may at last turn all to spirit,
Improv'd by tract of time, and wing'd ascend
Ethereal, as wee, or may at choice
Here or in Heav'nly Paradises dwell;
If ye be found obedient, and retain
Unalterably firm his love entire
Whose progeny you are. Meanwhile enjoy
Your fill what happiness this happy state
Can comprehend, incapable of more.
  To whom the Patriarch of mankind repli'd:
O favorable Spirit, propitious guest,
Well hast thou taught the way that might direct
Our knowledge, and the scale of Nature set
From centre to circumference, whereon
In contemplation of created things
By steps we may ascend to God.[5] But say,
What meant that caution join'd, *if ye be found*

2. Raphael's world picture is characterized by a cyclic movement of emanation and return that marks it as Platonic, as does the notion of successive degrees of spirituousness. The plant simile explains the notion of a scale of being from vegetable to animal, human, and angelic natures.

3. "Vital spirits" were fine pure fluids, given off by the blood of the heart and sustaining life; "animal spirits" had their seat in the brain and controlled sensation and voluntary motion.

4. The distinction between the "intuitive," simple undifferentiated operation of the contemplating intellect and the "discursive" or ratiocinative, piecemeal operation of the intellect working in conjunction with the reason goes back ultimately to Plato.

5. In the scale or ladder of nature, Adam refers to the Platonic ascent from image to universal, up the hierarchic grades of existence.

Obedient? can we want obedience then
To him, or possibly his love desert
Who form'd us from the dust, and plac'd us here
Full to the utmost measure of what bliss
Human desires can seek or apprehend?
  To whom the Angel. Son of Heav'n and Earth,
Attend: That thou art happy, owe to God;
That thou continu'st such, owe to thyself,
That is, to thy obedience; therein stand.
This was that caution giv'n thee; be advis'd.
God made thee perfet, not immutable;
And good he made thee, but to persevere
He left it in thy power, ordain'd thy will
By nature free, not over-rul'd by Fate
Inextricable, or strict necessity;
Our voluntary service he requires,
Not our necessitated, such with him
Finds no acceptance, nor can find, for how
Can hearts, not free, be tri'd whether they serve
Willing or no, who will but what they must
By Destiny, and can no other choose?
Myself and all th' Angelic Host that stand
In sight of God enthron'd, our happy state
Hold, as you yours, while our obedience holds;
On other surety none; freely we serve,
Because we freely love, as in our will
To love or not; in this we stand or fall:
And some are fall'n, to disobedience fall'n,
And so from Heav'n to deepest Hell; O fall
From what high state of bliss into what woe!
  To whom our great Progenitor. Thy words
Attentive, and with more delighted ear
Divine instructor, I have heard, than when
Cherubic Songs by night from neighboring Hills
Aereal Music send: nor knew I not
To be both will and deed created free;
Yet that we never shall forget to love
Our maker, and obey him whose command
Single, is yet so just, my constant thoughts
Assur'd me and still assure: though what thou tell'st
Hath past in Heav'n, some doubt within me move,
But more desire to hear, if thou consent,
The full relation, which must needs be strange,
Worthy of Sacred silence to be heard;
And we have yet large day, for scarce the Sun
Hath finisht half his journey, and scarce begins
His other half in the great Zone of Heav'n.
  Thus *Adam* made request, and *Raphaël*

After short pause assenting, thus began.[6]
High matter thou injoin'st me, O prime of men,
Sad task and hard, for how shall I relate
To human sense th' invisible exploits
Of warring Spirits; how without remorse° *pity*
The ruin of so many glorious once
And perfet while they stood; how last unfold
The secrets of another World, perhaps
Not lawful to reveal? yet for thy good
This is dispens't, and what surmounts the reach
Of human sense, I shall delineate so,
By lik'ning spiritual to corporal forms,
As may express them best, though what if Earth
Be but the shadow of Heav'n, and things therein
Each to other like, more than on Earth is thought?
As yet this World was not, and *Chaos* wild
Reign'd where these Heav'ns now roll, where Earth now rests
Upon her Centre pois'd, when on a day
(For Time, though in Eternity, appli'd
To motion, measures all things durable
By present, past, and future) on such day
As Heav'n's great Year brings forth, th' Empyreal Host
Of Angels by Imperial summons call'd,
Innumerable before th' Almighty's Throne
Forthwith from all the ends of Heav'n appear'd
Under thir Hierarchs in orders bright;
Ten thousand thousand Ensigns high advanc'd,[7]
Standards and Gonfalons, twixt Van and Rear
Stream in the Air,[8] and for distinction serve
Of Hierarchies, of Orders, and Degrees;
Or in thir glittering Tissues bear imblaz'd
Holy Memorials, acts of Zeal and Love
Recorded eminent. Thus when in Orbs
Of circuit inexpressible they stood,
Orb within Orb, the Father infinite,
By whom in bliss imbosom'd sat the Son,
Amidst as from a flaming Mount, whose top
Brightness had made invisible, thus spake.
Hear all ye Angels, Progeny of Light,
Thrones, Dominations, Princedoms, Virtues, Powers,[9]
Hear my Decree, which unrevok't shall stand.

6. Raphael's account of the war in heaven continues to the end of Book 6. It is one of the two long "episodes," or inset narrations, that conclude the two halves of the poem (the other is at the end of Book 11).

7. Echoing Daniel 7.10, "thousand thousands ministered unto him, and ten thousand times ten thousand stood before him."

8. "Gonfalons" are banners fastened to cross-bars, whereas "standards" are fastened to a flagpole.

9. No mere roll call of titles; see Colossians 1.16 for Christ's agency in the angels' creation ("whether they be thrones, or dominions, or principalities, or powers: all things were created by him, and for him").

This day I have begot whom I declare
My only Son, and on this holy Hill
Him have anointed, whom ye now behold
At my right hand; your Head I him appoint;
And by my Self have sworn to him shall bow
All knees in Heav'n, and shall confess him Lord:
Under his great Vice-gerent Reign abide
United as one individual Soul
For ever happy: him who disobeys
Mee disobeys, breaks union, and that day
Cast out from God and blessed vision, falls
Into utter darkness, deep ingulft, his place
Ordain'd without redemption, without end.
So spake th' Omnipotent, and with his words
All seem'd well pleas'd, all seem'd, but were not all.
That day, as other solemn days,[1] they spent
In song and dance about the sacred Hill,
Mystical dance, which yonder starry Sphere
Of Planets and of fixt° in all her Wheels *fixed stars*
Resembles nearest, mazes intricate,
Eccentric, intervolv'd, yet regular
Then most, when most irregular they seem:
And in thir motions harmony Divine
So smooths her charming° tones, that God's own ear *magical*
Listens delighted.[2] Ev'ning now approach'd
(For wee have also our Ev'ning and our Morn,
Wee ours for change delectable, not need)
Forthwith from dance to sweet repast they turn
Desirous; all in Circles as they stood,
Tables are set, and on a sudden pil'd
With Angels' Food, and rubied Nectar flows:
In Pearl, in Diamond, and massy Gold,
Fruit of delicious Vines, the growth of Heav'n.
On flow'rs repos'd, and with fresh flow'rets crown'd,
They eat, they drink, and in communion sweet
Quaff immortality and joy, secure
Of surfeit where full measure only bounds
Excess, before th' all bounteous King, who show'r'd
With copious hand, rejoicing in thir joy.
Now when ambrosial Night with Clouds exhal'd
From that high mount of God, whence light and shade
Spring both, the face of brightest Heav'n had chang'd
To grateful Twilight (for Night comes not there
In darker veil) and roseate Dews dispos'd
All but the unsleeping eyes of God to rest,

1. Holy days, festivals. Politically, these were opposed by Puritans.
2. The music of the spheres was a Neopythagorean concept, in which the movement of planets and other heavenly bodies in their spheres created a divine music.

Wide over all the Plain, and wider far
Than all this globous Earth in Plain outspread,
(Such are the Courts of God) th' Angelic throng
Disperst in Bands and Files thir Camp extend
By living Streams among the Trees of Life,
Pavilions numberless, and sudden rear'd,
Celestial Tabernacles, where they slept
Fann'd with cool Winds, save those who in thir course
Melodious Hymns about the sovran Throne
Alternate all night long: but not so wak'd
Satan, so call him now, his former name
Is heard no more in Heav'n;[3] he of the first,
If not the first Arch-Angel, great in Power,
In favor and preëminence, yet fraught
With envy against the Son of God, that day
Honor'd by his great Father, and proclaim'd
Messiah King anointed, could not bear
Through pride that sight, and thought himself impair'd.° *injured*
Deep malice thence conceiving and disdain,
Soon as midnight brought on the dusky hour
Friendliest to sleep and silence, he resolv'd
With all his Legions to dislodge,[4] and leave
Unworshipt, unobey'd the Throne supreme,
Contemptuous, and his next subordinate
Awak'ning, thus to him in secret spake.
Sleep'st thou, Companion dear, what sleep can close
Thy eye-lids? and rememb'rest what Decree
Of yesterday, so late hath past the lips
Of Heav'n's Almighty. Thou to me thy thoughts
Wast wont, I mine to thee was wont to impart;
Both waking we were one; how then can now
Thy sleep dissent? new Laws thou see'st impos'd;
New Laws from him who reigns, new minds may raise
In us who serve, new Counsels, to debate
What doubtful may ensue; more in this place
To utter is not safe. Assemble thou
Of all those Myriads which we lead the chief;
Tell them that by command, ere yet dim Night
Her shadowy Cloud withdraws, I am to haste,
And all who under me thir Banners wave,
Homeward with flying march where we possess
The Quarters of the North, there to prepare
Fit entertainment to receive our King
The great *Messiah*, and his new commands,
Who speedily through all the Hierarchies

3. Satan's name prior to his fall is unknown. Like those of the other fallen angels, his has been erased from memory (see 1.361–3).

4. Can mean to shift military quarters, or to displace (with "throne" as the object).

Intends to pass triumphant, and give Laws.
So spake the false Arch-Angel, and infus'd
Bad influence into th' unwary breast
Of his Associate; hee together calls,
Or several one by one, the Regent Powers,
Under him Regent, tells, as he was taught,
That the most High commanding, now ere Night,
Now ere dim Night had disincumber'd Heav'n,
The great Hierarchal Standard was to move;
Tells the suggested cause, and casts between
Ambiguous words and jealousies, to sound
Or taint integrity; but all obey'd
The wonted signal, and superior voice
Of thir great Potentate; for great indeed
His name, and high was his degree in Heav'n;
His count'nance, as the Morning Star that guides
The starry flock, allur'd them, and with lies
Drew after him the third part of Heav'n's Host:[5]
Meanwhile th' Eternal eye, whose sight discerns
Abstrusest thoughts, from forth his holy Mount
And from within the golden Lamps that burn
Nightly before him, saw without thir light
Rebellion rising, saw in whom, how spread
Among the sons of Morn, what multitudes
Were banded to oppose his high Decree;
And smiling to his only Son thus said.
Son, thou in whom my glory I behold
In full resplendence, Heir of all my might,
Nearly it now concerns us to be sure
Of our Omnipotence, and with what Arms
We mean to hold what anciently we claim
Of Deity or Empire, such a foe
Is rising, who intends to erect his Throne
Equal to ours, throughout the spacious North;
Nor so content, hath in his thought to try° *test*
In battle, what our Power is, or our right.
Let us advise, and to this hazard draw
With speed what force is left, and all imploy
In our defense, lest unawares we lose
This our high place, our Sanctuary, our Hill.
To whom the Son with calm aspect and clear
Lightning Divine, ineffable, serene,
Made answer. Mighty Father, thou thy foes
Justly hast in derision, and secure
Laugh'st at thir vain designs and tumults vain,

5. The image depends on familiar symbolism whereby the morning star represented both Satan and Christ. As evening star, Christ set in death; as morning star he was resurrected (Revelation 22.16). Satan, as Lucifer, travesties Christ, specifically the Good Shepherd.

Matter to mee of Glory, whom thir hate
Illustrates,° when they see all Regal Power — *glorifies*
Giv'n me to quell thir pride, and in event° — *result*
Know whether I be dext'rous to subdue[6]
Thy Rebels, or be found the worst in Heav'n.
  So spake the Son, but *Satan* with his Powers
Far was advanc't on winged speed, an Host
Innumerable as the Stars of Night,
Or Stars of Morning, Dew-drops, which the Sun
Impearls on every leaf and every flower.
Regions they pass'd, the mighty Regencies° — *dominions*
Of Seraphim and Potentates and Thrones
In thir triple Degrees, Regions to which
All thy Dominion, *Adam* is no more
Than what this Garden is to all the Earth,
And all the Sea, from one entire globose° — *sphere*
Stretcht into Longitude; which having pass'd
At length into the limits of the North
They came, and *Satan* to his Royal seat
High on a Hill, far blazing, as a Mount
Rais'd on a Mount, with Pyramids and Tow'rs
From Diamond Quarries hewn,[7] and Rocks of Gold,
The Palace of great *Lucifer*, (so call
That Structure in the Dialect of men
Interpreted) which not long after, he
Affecting° all equality with God, — *pretending to*
In imitation of that Mount whereon
Messiah was declar'd in sight of Heav'n,
The Mountain of the Congregation call'd:
For thither he assembl'd all his Train,
Pretending so commanded to consult
About the great reception of thir King,
Thither to come, and with calumnious° Art — *slanderous*
Of counterfeited truth thus held thir ears.
  Thrones, Dominations, Princedoms, Virtues, Powers,
If these magnific Titles yet remain
Not merely titular, since by Decree
Another now hath to himself ingross't
All Power, and us eclipst under the name
Of King anointed, for whom all this haste
Of midnight march, and hurried meeting here,
This only to consult how we may best
With what may be devis'd of honors new
Receive him coming to receive from us

6. Matching the Father's wit: Christ's dextrous position at God's right hand results from his dextrous (skillful) defeat of Satan (see 6.892 and Mark 16.19).

7. Pyramids are spires or obelisks, rather than the squat form now assumed. Obelisk-pyramids were associated with Rome, and with fame, and in miniature form were fashionable in palaces.

Knee-tribute yet unpaid, prostration vile,
Too much to one, but double how endur'd,
To one and to his image now proclaim'd?
But what if better counsels might erect
Our minds and teach us to cast off this Yoke?
Will ye submit your necks, and choose to bend
The supple knee? ye will not, if I trust
To know ye right, or if ye know yourselves
Natives and Sons of Heav'n possest before
By none, and if not equal all, yet free,
Equally free; for Orders and Degrees
Jar not with liberty, but well consist.
Who can in reason then or right assume
Monarchy over such as live by right
His equals, if in power and splendor less,
In freedom equal? or can introduce
Law and Edict on us, who without law
Err not? much less for this to be our Lord,
And look for adoration to th' abuse
Of those Imperial Titles which assert
Our being ordain'd to govern, not to serve?[8]
Thus far his bold discourse without control
Had audience, when among the Seraphim
Abdiel,[9] than whom none with more zeal ador'd
The Deity, and divine commands obey'd,
Stood up, and in a flame of zeal severe
The current of his fury thus oppos'd.
O argument blasphemous, false and proud!
Words which no ear ever to hear in Heav'n
Expected, least of all from thee, ingrate,° *ungrateful*
In place thyself so high above thy Peers.
Canst thou with impious obloquy condemn
The just Decree of God, pronounc't and sworn,
That to his only Son by right endu'd
With Regal Sceptre, every Soul in Heav'n
Shall bend the knee, and in that honor due
Confess him rightful King? unjust thou say'st
Flatly unjust, to bind with Laws the free,
And equal over equals to let Reign,
One over all with unsucceeded power.[1]
Shalt thou give Law to God, shalt thou dispute
With him the points of liberty, who made
Thee what thou art, and form'd the Pow'rs of Heav'n
Such as he pleas'd, and circumscrib'd thir being?

8. Satan's argument recalls the Stuarts' assertion of the divine right of kings to govern independently of rule of law. Satan avoids the question of who ordained the titles.

9. Abdiel ("Servant of God") occurs in the Bible only in a genealogy (1 Chronicles 5.15).

1. Never to be succeeded, everlasting. But at 3.339–41 God envisages the obsolescence of both rule and duty, as God is "all in all."

Yet by experience taught we know how good,
And of our good, and of our dignity
How provident he is, how far from thought
To make us less, bent rather to exalt
Our happy state under one Head more near
United. But to grant it thee unjust,
That equal over equals Monarch Reign:
Thyself though great and glorious dost thou count,
Or all Angelic Nature join'd in one,
Equal to him begotten Son, by whom
As by his Word the mighty Father made
All things, ev'n thee, and all the Spirits of Heav'n
By him created in thir bright degrees,° *ranks*
Crown'd them with Glory, and to thir Glory nam'd
Thrones, Dominations, Princedoms, Virtues, Powers,
Essential Powers, nor by his Reign obscur'd,
But more illustrious made, since he the Head
One of our number thus reduc't becomes,[2]
His Laws our Laws, all honor to him done
Returns our own. Cease then this impious rage,
And tempt not these; but hast'n to appease
Th' incensed Father, and th' incensed Son,
While Pardon may be found in time besought.
So spake the fervent Angel, but his zeal
None seconded, as out of season judg'd,
Or singular and rash, whereat rejoic'd
Th' Apostate, and more haughty thus repli'd.
That we were form'd then say'st thou? and the work
Of secondary hands, by task transferr'd
From Father to his Son? strange point and new!
Doctrine which we would know whence learnt: who saw
When this creation was? remember'st thou
Thy making, while the Maker gave thee being?
We know no time when we were not as now;
Know none before us, self-begot, self-rais'd
By our own quick'ning° power, when fatal course *life-giving*
Had circl'd his full Orb, the birth mature
Of this our native Heav'n, Ethereal Sons.
Our puissance is our own, our own right hand
Shall teach us highest deeds, by proof to try
Who is our equal: then thou shalt behold
Whether by supplication we intend
Address, and to begirt th' Almighty Throne
Beseeching or besieging. This report,
These tidings carry to th' anointed King;
And fly, ere evil intercept thy flight.

2. Having set aside his divinity, the Son will be "reduced" by the incarnation.

He said, and as the sound of waters deep
Hoarse murmur echo'd to his words applause
Through the infinite Host, nor less for that
The flaming Seraph fearless, though alone
Encompass'd round with foes, thus answer'd bold.
O alienate from God, O Spirit accurst,
Forsak'n of all good; I see thy fall
Determin'd, and thy hapless crew involv'd
In this perfidious fraud, contagion spread
Both of thy crime and punishment: henceforth
No more be troubl'd how to quit the yoke
Of God's *Messiah:* those indulgent Laws
Will not be now voutsaf'd, other Decrees
Against thee are gone forth without recall;
That Golden Sceptre which thou didst reject
Is now an Iron Rod to bruise and break
Thy disobedience. Well thou didst advise,
Yet not for thy advice or threats I fly
These wicked Tents devoted,[3] lest° the wrath *but*
Impendent, raging into sudden flame
Distinguish not: for soon expect to feel
His Thunder on thy head, devouring fire.
Then who created thee lamenting learn,
When who can uncreate thee thou shalt know.
So spake the Seraph *Abdiel* faithful found,
Among the faithless, faithful only hee;
Among innumerable false, unmov'd,
Unshak'n, unseduc'd, unterrifi'd
His Loyalty he kept, his Love, his Zeal;
Nor number, nor example with him wrought
To swerve from truth, or change his constant mind
Though single. From amidst them forth he pass'd,
Long way through hostile scorn, which he sustain'd
Superior, nor of violence fear'd aught;
And with retorted scorn his back he turn'd
On those proud Tow'rs to swift destruction doom'd.

The End of the Fifth Book.

Book 6

The Argument

Raphael *continues to relate how* Michael *and* Gabriel *were sent forth to Battle against* Satan *and his* Angels. *The first fight describ'd:* Satan *and his Powers retire under Night: He calls a Council, invents devilish Engines, which in the second day's Fight put* Michael *and his* Angels *to some disorder; but they at length pulling up Mountains overwhelm'd both the force and Machines of* Satan: *Yet the Tumult not so ending,* God *on the third day sends* Messiah *his Son for whom he had reserv'd the glory of the Victory: Hee in the Power*

3. That is, consigned to destruction.

of his Father coming to the place, and causing all his Legions to stand still on either side, with his Chariot and Thunder driving into the midst of his Enemies, pursues them unable to resist towards the wall of Heaven; which opening they leap down with horror and confusion in the place of punishment prepar'd for them in the Deep: Messiah *returns with triumph to his Father.*

All night the dreadless Angel° unpursu'd *Abdiel*
Through Heav'n's wide Champaign° held his way, till Morn, *field*
Wak't by the circling Hours, with rosy hand
Unbarr'd the gates of Light. There is a Cave
Within the Mount of God, fast by his Throne,
Where light and darkness in perpetual round
Lodge and dislodge° by turns, which makes through Heav'n *move quarters*
Grateful vicissitude,° like Day and Night; *change*
Light issues forth, and at the other door
Obsequious° darkness enters, till her hour *dutiful*
To veil the Heav'n, though darkness there might well
Seem twilight here; and now went forth the Morn[1]
Such as in highest Heav'n, array'd in Gold
Empyreal,[2] from before her vanisht Night,
Shot through with orient Beams: when all the Plain
Cover'd with thick embattl'd Squadrons bright,
Chariots and flaming Arms, and fiery Steeds
Reflecting blaze on blaze, first met his view:
War he perceiv'd, war in procinct,° and found *prepared*
Already known what he for news had thought
To have reported: gladly then he mixt
Among those friendly Powers who him receiv'd
With joy and acclamations loud, that one
That of so many Myriads fall'n, yet one
Return'd not lost: On to the sacred hill
They led him high applauded, and present
Before the seat supreme; from whence a voice
From midst a Golden Cloud thus mild was heard.
Servant of God,[3] well done, well hast thou fought
The better fight, who single hast maintain'd
Against revolted multitudes the Cause
Of Truth, in word mightier than they in Arms;
And for the testimony of Truth hast borne
Universal reproach, far worse to bear
Than violence:[4] for this was all thy care
To stand approv'd in sight of God, though Worlds
Judg'd thee perverse: the easier conquest now
Remains thee, aided by this host of friends,
Back on thy foes more glorious to return

1. The appearance of morning signals Day 2 of the action.
2. Purest; of the region nearest God.
3. Translating "Abdiel" (see 5.805n).
4. Milton echoes Matthew 25.21 ("Well done, thou good and faithful servant"); 1 Timothy 6.12 ("fight the good fight of faith"); and Psalm 69.7 ("for thy sake I have borne reproach").

Than scorn'd thou didst depart, and to subdue
By force, who reason for thir Law refuse,
Right reason for thir Law,[5] and for thir King
Messiah, who by right of merit Reigns.
Go *Michael* of Celestial Armies Prince,
And thou in Military prowess next,
Gabriel, lead forth to Battle these my Sons
Invincible,[6] lead forth my armed Saints
By Thousands and by Millions rang'd for fight;
Equal in number to that Godless crew
Rebellious, them with Fire and hostile Arms
Fearless assault, and to the brow° of Heav'n — *verge*
Pursuing drive them out from God and bliss,
Into thir place of punishment, the Gulf
Of *Tartarus*, which ready opens wide
His fiery *Chaos* to receive thir fall.[7]
 So spake the Sovran voice, and Clouds began
To darken all the Hill, and smoke to roll
In dusky wreaths, reluctant flames, the sign
Of wrath awak't: nor with less dread the loud
Ethereal Trumpet from on high gan° blow: — *began to*
At which command the Powers Militant,
That stood for Heav'n, in mighty Quadrate join'd
Of Union irresistible, mov'd on
In silence thir bright Legions, to the sound
Of instrumental Harmony that breath'd
Heroic Ardor to advent'rous deeds
Under thir God-like Leaders, in the Cause
Of God and his *Messiah*. On they move
Indissolubly firm; nor obvious° Hill, — *standing in the way*
Nor straitening Vale, nor Wood, nor Stream divides
Thir perfet ranks; for high above the ground
Thir march was, and the passive Air upbore
Thir nimble tread; as when the total kind
Of Birds in orderly array on wing
Came summon'd over *Eden* to receive
Thir names of thee; so over many a tract
Of Heav'n they march'd, and many a Province wide
Tenfold the length of this terrene:° at last — *earth*
Far in th' Horizon to the North appear'd
From skirt to skirt° a fiery Region, stretcht — *edge*
In battailous° aspect, and nearer view — *warlike*
Bristl'd with upright beams innumerable

5. Upright, true reason; conscience. Translating the Stoic and Scholastic phrase "recta ratio."
6. See Daniel 12.1; Revelation 12.7ff, "And there was war in heaven: Michael and his angels fought against the dragon; and the dragon fought and his angels, And prevailed not; neither was their place any more in heaven."
7. For Tartarus as a pagan type of hell, see 2.69n. "Fiery chaos" is an exact term, since hell "encroached" on chaos (2.1002). Presumably hell was created at the moment of Satan's fall (6.292n).

Of rigid Spears, and Helmets throng'd, and Shields
Various, with boastful Argument portray'd,
The banded Powers of *Satan* hasting on
With furious expedition;° for they ween'd *speed*
That selfsame day by fight, or by surprise
To win the Mount of God, and on his Throne
To set the envier of his State, the proud
Aspirer, but thir thoughts prov'd fond and vain
In the mid way: though strange to us it seem'd
At first, that Angel should with Angel war,
And in fierce hosting° meet, who wont to meet *hostile encounter*
So oft in Festivals of joy and love
Unanimous, as sons of one great Sire
Hymning th' Eternal Father: but the shout
Of Battle now began, and rushing sound
Of onset ended soon each milder thought.
High in the midst exalted as a God
Th' Apostate in his Sun-bright Chariot sat
Idol of Majesty Divine, enclos'd
With Flaming Cherubim, and golden Shields;[8]
Then lighted from his gorgeous Throne, for now
'Twixt Host and Host but narrow space was left,
A dreadful interval, and Front to Front
Presented stood in terrible array
Of hideous length: before the cloudy Van,
On the rough edge of battle ere it join'd,
Satan with vast and haughty strides advanc'd,
Came tow'ring, arm'd in Adamant and Gold;
Abdiel that sight endur'd not, where he stood
Among the mightiest, bent on highest deeds,
And thus his own undaunted heart explores.
O Heav'n! that such resemblance of the Highest
Should yet remain, where faith and realty° *sincerity*
Remain not; wherefore should not strength and might
There fail where Virtue fails, or weakest prove
Where boldest; though to sight unconquerable?
His puissance,° trusting in th' Almighty's aid, *power*
I mean to try, whose Reason I have tri'd° *tested*
Unsound and false; nor is it aught but just,
That he who in debate of Truth hath won,
Should win in Arms, in both disputes alike
Victor; though brutish that contest and foul,
When Reason hath to deal with force, yet so
Most reason is that Reason overcome.
So pondering, and from his armed Peers
Forth stepping opposite, half way he met

8. Satan's chariot travesties Messiah's cosmic vehicle; it is an idol, or false image, of majesty divine.

His daring foe, at this prevention° more *obstruction*
Incenst, and thus securely him defi'd.[9]
Proud, art thou met? thy hope was to have reacht
The highth of thy aspiring unoppos'd,
The Throne of God unguarded, and his side
Abandon'd at the terror of thy Power
Or potent tongue; fool, not to think how vain
Against th' Omnipotent to rise in Arms;
Who out of smallest things could without end
Have rais'd incessant Armies to defeat
Thy folly; or with solitary hand
Reaching beyond all limit, at one blow
Unaided could have finisht thee, and whelm'd
Thy Legions under darkness; but thou seest
All are not of thy Train; there be who° Faith *there are those who*
Prefer, and Piety to God, though then
To thee not visible, when I alone
Seem'd in thy World erroneous to dissent
From all: my Sect thou seest, now learn too late
How few sometimes may know, when thousands err.
Whom the grand Foe with scornful eye askance
Thus answer'd. Ill for thee, but in wisht hour
Of my revenge, first sought for thou return'st
From flight, seditious Angel, to receive
Thy merited reward, the first assay
Of this right hand provok'd, since first that tongue
Inspir'd with contradiction durst oppose
A third part of the Gods, in Synod met
Thir Deities to assert,[1] who while they feel
Vigor Divine within them, can allow
Omnipotence to none. But well thou com'st
Before thy fellows, ambitious to win
From me some Plume, that thy success may show
Destruction to the rest: this pause between
(Unanswer'd lest thou boast) to let thee know;
At first I thought that Liberty and Heav'n
To heav'nly Souls had been all one; but now
I see that most through sloth had rather serve,
Minist'ring Spirits, train'd up in Feast and Song;
Such hast thou arm'd, the Minstrelsy of Heav'n,
Servility with freedom to contend,
As both thir deeds compar'd this day shall prove.
To whom in brief thus *Abdiel* stern repli'd.
Apostate, still thou err'st, nor end wilt find
Of erring, from the path of truth remote:

9. "Incensed" describes Satan, while "securely" (confidently) describes Abdiel.
1. Satan presumptuously claims more than angelic status.
Synod: a general church council to determine doctrine; a Presbyterian ecclesiastical court.

Unjustly thou deprav'st° it with the name *defame*
Of *Servitude* to serve whom God ordains,
Or Nature; God and Nature bid the same,
When he who rules is worthiest, and excels
Them whom he governs. This is servitude,
To serve th' unwise, or him who hath rebell'd
Against his worthier, as thine now serve thee,
Thyself not free, but to thyself enthrall'd;
Yet lewdly° dar'st our minist'ring upbraid. *seditiously*
Reign thou in Hell thy Kingdom, let mee serve
In Heav'n God ever blest,[2] and his Divine
Behests obey, worthiest to be obey'd;
Yet Chains in Hell, not Realms expect: meanwhile
From mee return'd, as erst thou said'st, from flight,
This greeting on thy impious Crest receive.
So saying, a noble stroke he lifted high,
Which hung not, but so swift with tempest fell
On the proud Crest of *Satan*, that no sight,
Nor motion of swift thought, less could his Shield
Such ruin intercept: ten paces huge
He back recoil'd; the tenth on bended knee
His massy Spear upstay'd; as if on Earth
Winds under ground or waters forcing way
Sidelong, had pusht a Mountain from his seat
Half sunk with all his Pines. Amazement seiz'd
The Rebel Thrones, but greater rage to see
Thou foil'd thir mightiest, ours joy fill'd, and shout,
Presage of Victory and fierce desire
Of Battle: whereat *Michaël* bid sound
Th' Arch-Angel trumpet; through the vast of Heav'n
It sounded, and the faithful Armies rung° *proclaimed*
Hosanna to the Highest: nor stood at gaze
The adverse Legions, nor less hideous join'd
The horrid shock: now storming fury rose,
And clamor such as heard in Heav'n till now
Was never, Arms on Armor clashing bray'd
Horrible discord, and the madding° Wheels *frenzied*
Of brazen Chariots rag'd; dire was the noise
Of conflict; over head the dismal hiss
Of fiery Darts in flaming volleys flew,
And flying vaulted either Host with fire.
So under fiery Cope° together rush'd *sky*
Both Battles main,[3] with ruinous assault
And inextinguishable rage; all Heav'n
Resounded, and had Earth been then, all Earth
Had to her Centre shook. What wonder? when

2. Satan echoes this phrase in hell; see 1.263, "Better to reign in hell, than serve in heaven."

3. The main bodies of the armies, as distinct from the wings or van at 6.107.

Millions of fierce encount'ring Angels fought
On either side, the least of whom could wield
These Elements, and arm him with the force
Of all thir Regions:[4] how much more of Power
Army against Army numberless to raise
Dreadful combustion° warring, and disturb, *commotion*
Though not destroy, thir happy Native seat;
Had not th' Eternal King Omnipotent
From his stronghold of Heav'n high over-rul'd
And limited thir might; though number'd such
As each divided Legion might have seem'd
A numerous Host, in strength each armed hand
A Legion; led in fight, yet Leader seem'd
Each Warrior single as in Chief, expert
When to advance, or stand, or turn the sway
Of Battle, open when, and when to close
The ridges of grim War; no thought of flight,
None of retreat, no unbecoming deed.
That argu'd fear; each on himself reli'd,
As only in his arm the moment° lay *determining influence*
Of victory; deeds of eternal fame
Were done, but infinite: for wide was spread
That War and various; sometimes on firm ground
A standing fight, then soaring on main wing° *fully airborne*
Tormented all the Air; all Air seem'd then
Conflicting Fire: long time in even scale
The Battle hung; till *Satan*, who that day
Prodigious power had shown, and met in Arms
No equal, ranging through the dire attack
Of fighting Seraphim confus'd, at length
Saw where the Sword of *Michael* smote, and fell'd
Squadrons at once, with huge two-handed sway
Brandisht aloft the horrid edge came down
Wide wasting; such destruction to withstand
He hasted, and oppos'd the rocky Orb
Of tenfold Adamant, his ample Shield
A vast circumference: At his approach
The great Arch-Angel from his warlike toil
Surceas'd, and glad as hoping here to end
Intestine° War in Heav'n, the Arch-foe subdu'd *internal*
Or Captive dragg'd in Chains, with hostile frown
And visage all inflam'd first thus began.
Author of evil, unknown till thy revolt,
Unnam'd in Heav'n, now plenteous, as thou seest
These Acts of hateful strife, hateful to all,
Though heaviest by just measure on thyself

4. The layers into which the four elements were arranged, more or less according to what would now be called their density.

And thy adherents: how hast thou disturb'd
Heav'n's blessed peace, and into Nature brought
Misery, uncreated till the crime
Of thy Rebellion? how hast thou instill'd
Thy malice into thousands, once upright
And faithful, now prov'd false. But think not here
To trouble Holy Rest; Heav'n casts thee out
From all her Confines. Heav'n the seat of bliss
Brooks not the works of violence and War.
Hence then, and evil go with thee along,
Thy offspring, to the place of evil, Hell,
Thou and thy wicked crew; there mingle broils,° *concoct quarrels*
Ere this avenging Sword begin thy doom,
Or some more sudden vengeance wing'd from God
Precipitate thee with augmented pain.
So spake the Prince of Angels; to whom thus
The Adversary.[5] Nor think thou with wind
Of airy threats to awe whom yet with deeds
Thou canst not. Hast thou turn'd the least of these
To flight, or if to fall, but that they rise
Unvanquisht, easier to transact with mee
That thou shouldst hope, imperious, and with threats
To chase me hence? err not that so shall end
The strife which thou call'st evil, but wee style
The strife of Glory: which we mean to win,
Or turn this Heav'n itself into the Hell
Thou fabl'st,[6] here however to dwell free,
If not to reign: meanwhile thy utmost force,
And join him nam'd 'Almighty' to thy aid,
I fly not, but have sought thee far and nigh.
They ended parle,° and both address'd for fight *debate*
Unspeakable; for who, though with the tongue
Of Angels, can relate, or to what things
Liken on Earth conspicuous, that may lift
Human imagination to such highth
Of Godlike Power: for likest Gods they seem'd,
Stood they or mov'd, in stature, motion, arms
Fit to decide the Empire of great Heav'n.
Now wav'd thir fiery Swords, and in the Air
Made horrid Circles; two broad Suns thir Shields
Blaz'd opposite, while expectation stood
In horror; from each hand with speed retir'd
Where erst was thickest fight, th' Angelic throng,
And left large field, unsafe within the wind
Of such commotion, such as, to set forth

5. The literal meaning of "Satan." See 1.82n, and Job 1.6.
6. Satan rejects even the word "hell" as a made-up term. Hell has existed since 6.54, if not earlier; but God announced it to the loyal angels only. Only after joining them does Abdiel mention it (6.183).

Great things by small, if Nature's concord broke,
Among the Constellations war were sprung,
Two Planets rushing from aspect malign
Of fiercest opposition in mid Sky,[7]
Should combat, and thir jarring Spheres confound.
Together both with next to Almighty Arm,
Uplifted imminent one stroke they aim'd
That might determine, and not need repeat,
As not of power, at once;[8] nor odds appear'd
In might or swift prevention;° but the sword — *anticipation*
Of *Michael* from the Armory of God
Was giv'n him temper'd so, that neither keen
Nor solid might resist that edge: it met
The sword of *Satan* with steep force to smite
Descending, and in half cut sheer, nor stay'd,
But with swift wheel reverse,[9] deep ent'ring shear'd
All his right side; then *Satan* first knew pain,
And writh'd him to and fro convolv'd;° so sore — *contorted*
The griding° sword with discontinuous wound — *piercing*
Pass'd through him, but th' Ethereal substance clos'd
Not long divisible, and from the gash
A stream of Nectarous humor issuing flow'd
Sanguine, such as Celestial Spirits may bleed,
And all his Armor stain'd erewhile so bright.
Forthwith on all sides to his aid was run
By Angels many and strong, who interpos'd
Defense, while others bore him on thir Shields
Back to his Chariot, where it stood retir'd
From off the files of war: there they him laid
Gnashing for anguish and despite and shame
To find himself not matchless, and his pride
Humbl'd by such rebuke, so far beneath
His confidence to equal God in power.
Yet soon he heal'd; for Spirits that live throughout
Vital in every part, not as frail man
In Entrails, Heart or Head, Liver or Reins,° — *kidneys*
Cannot but by annihilating die;
Nor in thir liquid° texture mortal wound — *flexible*
Receive, no more than can the fluid Air:
All Heart they live, all Head, all Eye, all Ear,
All Intellect, all Sense, and as they please,
They Limb themselves, and color, shape or size
Assume, as likes° them best, condense or rare. — *pleases*
Meanwhile in other parts like deeds deserv'd

7. The planets are in diametrically opposite signs at mid-sky, or the zenith. Astrologers recognized five spatial relations ("aspects") between planets; "opposition" was disharmonious, with a malign influence.

8. That is, it would be beyond their power to repeat such a blow immediately.

9. Michael follows through into a reverse stroke. As a young man, Milton assiduously practiced fencing.

Memorial, where the might of *Gabriel* fought,
And with fierce Ensigns° pierc'd the deep array *battle cries*
Of *Moloch* furious King, who him defi'd,
And at his Chariot wheels to drag him bound
Threat'n'd, nor from the Holy One of Heav'n
Refrain'd his tongue blasphemous; but anon
Down clov'n to the waist, with shatter'd Arms
And uncouth° pain fled bellowing. On each wing *unfamiliar*
Uriel and *Raphaël* his vaunting foe,
Though huge, and in a Rock of Diamond Arm'd,
Vanquish'd *Adramelech*, and *Asmadai*,[1]
Two potent Thrones, that to be less than Gods
Disdain'd, but meaner thoughts learn'd in thir flight,
Mangl'd with ghastly wounds through Plate and Mail.
Nor stood unmindful *Abdiel* to annoy
The Atheist crew, but with redoubl'd blow
Ariel and *Arioch*, and the violence
Of *Ramiel* scorcht and blasted overthrew.[2]
I might relate of thousands, and thir names
Eternize here on Earth; but those elect
Angels contented with thir fame in Heav'n
Seek not the praise of men; the other sort
In might though wondrous and in Acts of War,
Nor of Renown less eager, yet by doom
Cancell'd from Heav'n and sacred memory,
Nameless in dark oblivion let them dwell.
For strength from Truth divided and from Just,
Illaudable,° naught merits but dispraise *unworthy of praise*
And ignominy, yet to glory aspires
Vain-glorious, and through infamy seeks fame:
Therefore Eternal silence be thir doom.
   And now thir Mightiest quell'd, the battle swerv'd
With many an inroad° gor'd; deformed rout *passage*
Enter'd, and foul disorder; all the ground
With shiver'd armor strown, and on a heap
Chariot and Charioteer lay overturn'd
And fiery foaming Steeds; what stood, recoil'd
O'erwearied, through the faint Satanic Host
Defensive scarce,[3] or with pale fear surpris'd,
Then first with fear surpris'd and sense of pain
Fled ignominious, to such evil brought
By sin of disobedience, till that hour
Not liable to fear or flight or pain.

1. Presumably Raphael vanquishes Asmodeus (Asmadai), in view of their biblical encounter (4.171n). Aptly, the solar intelligence Uriel vanquishes the sun-god Adramelec (2 Kings 17.31).

2. Ariel ("Lion of God" or "Divine Light") is Jerusalem at Isaiah 29.1ff. Arioc ("Lion-like") was the "King of Ellasar" (Genesis 14.1) whom Abram fought. Ramiel ("Deceiver of God") was one of the angels fornicating with women in 1 Enoch 6.7.

3. That is, hardly capable of defending itself.

Far otherwise th' inviolable Saints
In Cubic Phalanx firm advanc'd entire,
Invulnerable, impenetrably arm'd:
Such high advantages thir innocence
Gave them above thir foes, not to have sinn'd,
Not to have disobey'd; in fight they stood
Unwearied, unobnoxious° to be pain'd *not liable*
By wound, though from thir place by violence mov'd.
Now Night her course began, and over Heav'n
Inducing darkness, grateful truce impos'd,
And silence on the odious din of War:
Under her Cloudy covert both retir'd,
Victor and Vanquisht: on the foughten field° *battlefield*
Michaël and his Angels prevalent° *victorious*
Encamping, plac'd in Guard thir Watches round,
Cherubic waving fires:[4] on th' other part
Satan with his rebellious disappear'd,
Far in the dark dislodg'd,° and void of rest, *moved camp*
His Potentates to Council call'd by night;[5]
And in the midst thus undismay'd began.
O now in danger tri'd, now known in Arms
Not to be overpow'r'd, Companions dear,
Found worthy not of Liberty alone,
Too mean pretense, but what we more affect,[6]
Honor, Dominion, Glory, and renown,
Who have sustain'd one day in doubtful fight,
(And if one day, why not Eternal days?)
What Heaven's Lord had powerfullest to send
Against us from about his Throne, and judg'd
Sufficient to subdue us to his will,
But proves not so: then fallible, it seems,
Of future we may deem him, though till now
Omniscient thought. True is, less firmly arm'd,
Some disadvantage we endur'd and pain,
Till now not known, but known as soon contemn'd,
Since now we find this our Empyreal form
Incapable of mortal injury,
Imperishable, and though pierc'd with wound,
Soon closing, and by native vigor heal'd.
Of evil then so small as easy think
The remedy; perhaps more valid Arms,
Weapons more violent, when next we meet,
May serve to better us, and worse° our foes, *injure*

4. Cherubim, excelling in knowledge, are assigned to sentry duty; see also 4.778ff, 12.590ff. Being fiery, they are their own watchfires.

5. In the *Iliad* 9, there is a nocturnal council of war called by Agamemnon after defeat by Hector.

6. Raphael conveys instruction by ironic wordplay: "mean pretence" can mean both "low ambition" and "base dissimulation," while "affect" can mean both "aspire to" and "feign."

Or equal what between us made the odds,
In Nature none: if other hidden cause
Left them Superior, while we can preserve
Unhurt our minds, and understanding sound,
Due search and consultation will disclose.
He sat; and in th' assembly next upstood
Nisroch, of Principalities the prime;[7]
As one he stood escap't from cruel fight,
Sore toil'd, his riv'n Arms to havoc hewn,
And cloudy in aspect thus answering spake.
Deliverer from new Lords, leader to free
Enjoyment of our right as Gods; yet hard
For Gods, and too unequal work we find
Against unequal arms to fight in pain,
Against unpain'd, impassive; from which evil
Ruin must needs ensue; for what avails
Valor or strength, though matchless, quell'd with pain
Which all subdues, and makes remiss° the hands — *slack*
Of Mightiest. Sense of pleasure we may well
Spare out of life perhaps, and not repine,
But live content, which is the calmest life:
But pain is perfet misery, the worst
Of evils, and excessive, overturns
All patience. He who therefore can invent
With what more forcible we may offend° — *hurt*
Our yet unwounded Enemies, or arm
Ourselves with like defense, to me° deserves — *it seems to me*
No less than for deliverance what we owe.[8]
Whereto with look compos'd *Satan* repli'd.
Not uninvented that, which thou aright
Believ'st so main° to our success, I bring; — *important*
Which of us who beholds the bright surface
Of this Ethereous mould whereon we stand,
This continent of spacious Heav'n, adorn'd
With Plant, Fruit, Flow'r Ambrosial, Gems and Gold,
Whose Eye so superficially surveys
These things, as not to mind° from whence they grow — *recall*
Deep under ground, materials dark and crude,
Of spiritous and fiery spume, till toucht
With Heav'n's ray, and temper'd they shoot forth
So beauteous, op'ning to the ambient light.
These in thir dark Nativity the Deep
Shall yield us, pregnant with infernal flame,
Which into hollow Engines long and round
Thick ramm'd, at th' other bore with touch of fire
Dilated and infuriate° shall send forth — *exploded*

7. The Assyrian King Sennacherib perished while worshipping the idol Nisroch.

8. That is, "no less for than what we owe our deliverer (Satan)." Nisroc is inviting a leadership contest.

From far with thund'ring noise among our foes
Such implements of mischief as shall dash
To pieces, and o'erwhelm whatever stands
Adverse, that they shall fear we have disarm'd
The Thunderer of his only dreaded bolt.[9]
Nor long shall be our labor, yet ere dawn,
Effect shall end our wish. Meanwhile revive;
Abandon fear; to strength and counsel join'd
Think nothing hard, much less to be despair'd.
He ended, and his words thir drooping cheer° *mood*
Enlight'n'd, and thir languisht hope reviv'd.
Th' invention all admir'd, and each, how hee
To be th' inventor miss'd, so easy it seem'd
Once found, which yet unfound most would have thought
Impossible: yet haply of thy Race
In future days, if Malice should abound,
Some one intent on mischief, or inspir'd
With dev'lish machination might devise
Like instrument to plague the Sons of men
For sin, on war and mutual slaughter bent.
Forthwith from Council to the work they flew,
None arguing stood, innumerable hands
Were ready, in a moment up they turn'd
Wide the Celestial soil, and saw beneath
Th' originals of Nature° in thir crude *original elements*
Conception; Sulphurous and Nitrous Foam
They found, they mingl'd, and with subtle Art,
Concocted and adusted° they reduc'd *dried up by heat*
To blackest grain, and into store convey'd:
Part hidd'n veins digg'd up (nor hath this Earth
Entrails unlike) of Mineral and Stone,[1]
Whereof to found° thir Engines and thir Balls *cast*
Of missive ruin; part incentive reed° *match*
Provide, pernicious with one touch to fire.
So all ere day-spring, under conscious Night
Secret they finish'd, and in order set,
With silent circumspection unespi'd.
Now when fair Morn Orient in Heav'n appear'd[2]
Up rose the Victor Angels, and to Arms
The matin Trumpet Sung: in Arms they stood
Of Golden Panoply, refulgent Host,
Soon banded; others from the dawning Hills
Look'd round, and Scouts each Coast light-armed scour

9. The invention of gunpowder portrayed here had recent associations as well as epic ones. The Parliamentary forces were famed for their artillery. Mid-century sermons and tracts regarded the Gunpowder Plot, the unsuccessful attempt to blow up Parliament (1605), as a "hellish invention."

1. This is necessary information for Adam and Eve: before the Fall there was no mining.

2. The morning of Day 3 of the action.

Each quarter, to descry the distant foe,
Where lodg'd, or whither fled, or if for fight,
In motion or in halt: him soon they met
Under spread Ensigns moving nigh, in slow
But firm Battalion; back with speediest Sail
Zophiel,[3] of Cherubim the swiftest wing,
Came flying, and in mid Air aloud thus cri'd.
  Arm, Warriors, Arm for fight, the foe at hand,
Whom fled we thought, will save us long pursuit
This day, fear not his flight; so thick a Cloud
He comes, and settl'd in his face I see
Sad° resolution and secure:° let each *serious / confident*
His Adamantine coat gird well, and each
Fit well his Helm, grip fast his orbed Shield,
Borne ev'n or high, for this day will pour down,
If I conjecture aught, no drizzling show'r,
But rattling storm of Arrows barb'd with fire.
So warn'd he them aware themselves, and soon
In order, quit° of all impediment; *freed*
Instant without disturb they took Alarm,
And onward move Embattl'd; when behold
Not distant far with heavy pace the Foe
Approaching gross and huge; in hollow Cube
Training° his devilish Enginry, impal'd *pulling*
On every side with shadowing Squadrons Deep,
To hide the fraud. At interview° both stood *in mutual view*
A while, but suddenly at head appear'd
Satan: And thus was heard Commanding loud.
  Vanguard, to Right and Left the Front unfold;
That all may see who hate us, how we seek
Peace and composure,° and with open breast *settlement*
Stand ready to receive them, if they like
Our overture, and turn not back perverse;
But that I doubt; however witness Heaven,
Heav'n witness thou anon, while we discharge
Freely our part: yee who appointed stand
Do as you have in charge, and briefly touch
What we propound, and loud that all may hear.
  So scoffing in ambiguous words, he scarce
Had ended; when to Right and Left the Front
Divided, and to either Flank retir'd.
Which to our eyes discover'd new and strange,
A triple-mounted row of Pillars laid
On Wheels (for like to Pillars most they seem'd
Or hollow'd bodies made of Oak or Fir
With branches lopt, in Wood or Mountain fell'd)

3. Zophiel means "Spy of God."

Brass, Iron, Stony mould,[4] had not thir mouths
With hideous orifice gap't on us wide,
Portending hollow truce; at each behind
A Seraph stood, and in his hand a Reed
Stood waving tipt with fire; while we suspense,° *attentive*
Collected stood within our thoughts amus'd,° *puzzled*
Not long, for sudden all at once thir Reeds
Put forth, and to a narrow vent appli'd
With nicest touch. Immediate in a flame,
But soon obscur'd with smoke, all Heav'n appear'd,
From those deep-throated Engines belcht, whose roar
Embowell'd with outrageous noise the Air,
And all her entrails tore, disgorging foul
Thir devilish glut, chain'd Thunderbolts and Hail
Of Iron Globes, which on the Victor Host
Levell'd, with such impetuous fury smote,
That whom they hit, none of thir feet might stand,
Though standing else as Rocks, but down they fell
By thousands, Angel on Arch-Angel roll'd;
The sooner for thir Arms; unarm'd they might
Have easily as Spirits evaded swift
By quick contraction or remove; but now
Foul dissipation follow'd and forc't rout;
Nor serv'd it to relax thir serried files.[5]
What should they do? if on they rush'd repulse
Repeated, and indecent° overthrow *unbecoming*
Doubl'd, would render them yet more despis'd,
And to thir foes a laughter; for in view
Stood rankt of Seraphim another row
In posture to displode° thir second tire° *discharge / volley*
Of Thunder: back defeated to return
They worse abhorr'd. *Satan* beheld thir plight,
And to his Mates° thus in derision call'd. *comrades*
O Friends, why come not on these Victors proud?
Erewhile they fierce were coming, and when wee,
To entertain them fair with open Front
And Breast, (what could we more?) propounded terms
Of composition, straight they chang'd thir minds,
Flew off, and into strange vagaries° fell, *fits*
As they would dance, yet for a dance they seem'd
Somewhat extravagant and wild, perhaps
For joy of offer'd peace: but I suppose
If our proposals once again were heard
We should compel them to a quick result.
To whom thus *Belial* in like gamesome mood.
Leader, the terms we sent were terms of weight,

4. Made of brass, iron, stone.

5. That is, space their close formation more loosely.

Of hard contents, and full of force urg'd home,
Such as we might perceive amus'd them all,
And stumbl'd many; who receives them right,
Had need from head to foot well understand;
Not understood, this gift they have besides,
They show us when our foes walk not upright.
  So they among themselves in pleasant vein
Stood scoffing, highth'n'd in thir thoughts beyond
All doubt of Victory, eternal might
To match with thir inventions they presum'd
So easy, and of his Thunder made a scorn,
And all his Host derided, while they stood
A while in trouble; but they stood not long,
Rage prompted them at length, and found them arms[6]
Against such hellish mischief fit to oppose.
Forthwith (behold the excellence, the power
Which God hath in his mighty Angels plac'd)
Thir Arms away they threw, and to the Hills[7]
(For Earth hath this variety from Heav'n
Of pleasure situate in Hill and Dale)
Light as the Lightning glimpse they ran, they flew,
From thir foundations loos'ning to and fro
They pluckt the seated° Hills with all thir load, *fixed*
Rocks, Waters, Woods, and by the shaggy tops
Uplifting bore them in thir hands: Amaze,° *bewilderment*
Be sure, and terror seiz'd the rebel Host,
When coming towards them so dread they saw
The bottom of the Mountains upward turn'd,
Till on those cursed Engines' triple-row
They saw them whelm'd, and all thir confidence
Under the weight of Mountains buried deep,
Themselves invaded next, and on thir heads
Main° Promontories flung, which in the Air *whole*
Came shadowing,° and opprest whole Legions arm'd, *casting shade*
Thir armor help'd thir harm, crush't in and bruis'd
Into thir substance pent, which wrought them pain
Implacable, and many a dolorous groan,
Long struggling underneath, ere they could wind° *squirm*
Out of such prison, though Spirits of purest light,
Purest at first, now gross by sinning grown.
The rest in imitation to like Arms
Betook them, and the neighboring Hills uptore;
So Hills amid the Air encounter'd Hills
Hurl'd to and fro with jaculation° dire, *hurling*
That under ground they fought in dismal shade:
Infernal noise; War seem'd a civil Game

6. Echoing Virgil's *Aeneid* 1.150 ("furor arma minstrat").
7. Lines 639–66 allude to the Giants' war against the Olympians, a pagan type of the angelic rebellion. See 1.199n, 1.231ff, and Hesiod's *Theogony* 713–18.

To this uproar; horrid confusion heapt
Upon confusion rose: and now all Heav'n
Had gone to wrack, with ruin overspread,
Had not th' Almighty Father where he sits
Shrin'd in his Sanctuary of Heav'n secure,
Consulting on the sum of things,[8] foreseen
This tumult, and permitted all, advis'd:° *after consideration*
That his great purpose he might so fulfil,
To honor his Anointed Son aveng'd
Upon his enemies, and to declare
All power on him transferr'd: whence to his Son
Th' Assessor° of his Throne he thus began. *sharer*
  Effulgence of my Glory, Son belov'd,
Son in whose face invisible is beheld
Visibly, what by Deity I am,
And in whose hand what by Decree I do,
Second Omnipotence, two days are past,
Two days, as we compute the days of Heav'n,
Since *Michael* and his Powers went forth to tame
These disobedient; sore hath been thir fight,
As likeliest was, when two such Foes met arm'd;
For to themselves I left them, and thou know'st,
Equal in thir Creation they were form'd,
Save what sin hath impair'd, which yet hath wrought
Insensibly, for I suspend thir doom;
Whence in perpetual fight they needs must last
Endless, and no solution will be found:
War wearied hath perform'd what War can do,
And to disorder'd rage let loose the reins,
With Mountains as with Weapons arm'd, which makes
Wild work in Heav'n, and dangerous to the main.° *whole*
Two days are therefore past, the third is thine;[9]
For thee I have ordain'd it, and thus far
Have suffer'd, that the Glory may be thine
Of ending this great War, since none but Thou
Can end it. Into thee such Virtue and Grace
Immense I have transfus'd, that all may know
In Heav'n and Hell thy Power above compare,
And this perverse Commotion govern'd thus,
To manifest thee worthiest to be Heir
Of all things, to be Heir and to be King
By Sacred Unction,° thy deserved right. *anointing*
Go then thou Mightiest in thy Father's might,
Ascend my Chariot, guide the rapid Wheels
That shake Heav'n's basis,° bring forth all my War, *foundation*

8. Usually explained as "universe," by analogy with Lucretius 5.362 ("summarum summa"). But "summa rerum" ("highest public interest") is closer.

9. Allegorically, the third day is the day of resurrection, as in Luke 13.32, "the third day I shall be perfected."

My Bow and Thunder, my Almighty Arms
Gird on, and Sword upon thy puissant Thigh;
Pursue these sons of Darkness, drive them out
From all Heav'n's bounds into the utter Deep:
There let them learn, as likes them, to despise
God and *Messiah* his anointed King.[1]
He said, and on his Son with Rays direct
Shone full; hee all his Father full exprest
Ineffably into his face receiv'd,
And thus the filial Godhead answering spake.
O Father, O supreme of heav'nly Thrones,
First, Highest, Holiest, Best, thou always seek'st
To glorify thy Son, I always thee,
As is most just; this I my Glory account,
My exaltation, and my whole delight,
That thou in me well pleas'd, declar'st thy will
Fulfill'd, which to fulfil is all my bliss.
Sceptre and Power, thy giving, I assume
And gladlier shall resign, when in the end
Thou shalt be All in All, and I in thee
For ever, and in mee all whom thou lov'st;[2]
But whom thou hat'st, I hate, and can put on
Thy terrors, as I put thy mildness on,
Image of thee in all things; and shall soon,
Arm'd with thy might, rid heav'n of these rebell'd,
To thir prepar'd ill Mansion° driven down, *dwelling*
To chains of darkness, and th' undying Worm,
That from thy just obedience could revolt,
Whom to obey is happiness entire.
Then shall thy Saints unmixt, and from th' impure
Far separate, circling thy holy Mount
Unfeigned *Halleluiahs* to thee sing,
Hymns of high praise, and I among them chief.
So said, he o'er his Sceptre bowing, rose
From the right hand of Glory where he sat,
And the third sacred Morn began to shine
Dawning through Heav'n: forth rush'd with whirl-wind sound
The Chariot of Paternal Deity,[3]
Flashing thick flames, Wheel within Wheel, undrawn,° *self-powered*
Itself instinct° with Spirit, but convoy'd *animated*
By four Cherubic shapes, four Faces each
Had wondrous, as with Stars thir bodies all

1. Literally translating "Messiah."
2. Echoing 1 Corinthians 15.24, 28, "Then cometh the end, when he shall have delivered up the kingdom to God, even the Father; when he shall have put down all rule and all authority and power. . . . And when all things shall be subdued unto him, then shall the Son also himself be subject unto him that put all things under him, that God may be all in all." See also 3.339–43.
3. The central allegory, prepared for by many partial anticipations; see 1.311; 2.887; 3.394, 522, 653n (the seven archangels of the cosmic chariot); 6.100–3 (Satan's chariot), 211, 338, 358, 390, 711. The image is also present in Ezekiel 1.4–6, 16, 26–8; 10.12, 16.

And Wings were set with Eyes, with Eyes the Wheels
Of Beryl, and careering Fires between;
Over thir heads a crystal Firmament,
Whereon a Sapphire Throne, inlaid with pure
Amber, and colors of the show'ry Arch.
Hee in Celestial Panoply all arm'd
Of radiant *Urim*,[4] work divinely wrought,
Ascended, at his right hand Victory
Sat Eagle-wing'd, beside him hung his Bow
And Quiver with three-bolted Thunder stor'd,[5]
And from about him fierce Effusion roll'd
Of smoke and bickering° flame, and sparkles dire; *flashing*
Attended with ten thousand thousand Saints,
He onward came, far off his coming shone,
And twenty thousand (I thir number heard)
Chariots of God, half on each hand were seen:
Hee on the wings of Cherub rode sublime° *set aloft*
On the Crystalline Sky, in Sapphire Thron'd.
Illustrious far and wide, but by his own
First seen, them unexpected joy surpris'd,
When the great Ensign of *Messiah* blaz'd
Aloft by Angels borne, his Sign in Heav'n:[6]
Under whose Conduct *Michael* soon reduc'd° *led back*
His Army, circumfus'd° on either Wing, *spread around*
Under thir Head imbodied all in one.
Before him Power Divine his way prepar'd;
At his command the uprooted Hills retir'd
Each to his place, they heard his voice and went
Obsequious, Heav'n his wonted face renew'd,
And with fresh Flow'rets Hill and Valley smil'd.
This saw his hapless Foes, but stood obdur'd,° *hardened*
And to rebellious fight rallied thir Powers
Insensate, hope conceiving from despair.
In heav'nly Spirits could such perverseness dwell?
But to convince the proud what Signs avail,
Or Wonders move th' obdurate to relent?
They hard'n'd more by what might most reclaim,[7]
Grieving to see his Glory, at the sight
Took envy, and aspiring to his highth,
Stood reimbattl'd fierce, by force or fraud

4. Mentioned in Exodus 28.30, "thou shalt put in the breastplate of judgment the Urim and the Thummim; and they shall be upon Aaron's heart, when he goeth in before the Lord."

5. Jupiter's thunderbolts in the Giant War were sometimes interpreted as a type of Christ's power, sometimes as a contrasting evil; see 1.506–21; Hesiod, *Theogony* 687ff. And in contrast with Phaethon (another charioteer), Messiah's true sonship allows him to wield three-bolted thunder (6.572) instead of having it used against him.

6. A portrayal of Matthew 24.30, "then shall appear the sign of the Son of man in heaven: and then . . . they shall see the Son of man coming in the clouds of heaven with power and great glory."

7. In Exodus 14.4, Pharaoh's heart hardened despite miraculous signs.

Weening to prosper, and at length prevail
Against God and *Messiah,* or to fall
In universal ruin last, and now
To final Battle drew, disdaining flight,
Or faint retreat; when the great Son of God
To all his Host on either hand thus spake.
  Stand still in bright array ye Saints, here stand
Ye Angels arm'd, this day from Battle rest;
Faithful hath been your Warfare, and of God
Accepted, fearless in his righteous Cause,
And as ye have receiv'd, so have ye done
Invincibly: but of this cursed crew
The punishment to other hand belongs;
Vengeance is his, or whose he sole appoints;[8]
Number to this day's work is not ordain'd
Nor multitude, stand only and behold
God's indignation on these Godless pour'd
By mee; not you but mee they have despis'd,
Yet envied; against mee is all thir rage,
Because the Father, t'whom in Heav'n supreme
Kingdom and Power and Glory appertains,
Hath honor'd me according to his will.
Therefore to mee thir doom he hath assign'd;
That they may have thir wish, to try° with mee *test*
In Battle which the stronger proves, they all,
Or I alone against them, since by strength
They measure all, of other excellence
Not emulous, nor care who them excels;
Nor other strife with them do I voutsafe.
  So spake the Son, and into terror chang'd
His count'nance too severe to be beheld
And full of wrath bent on his Enemies.
At once the Four[9] spread out thir Starry wings
With dreadful shade contiguous, and the Orbs
Of his fierce Chariot roll'd, as with the sound
Of torrent Floods, or of a numerous Host.
Hee on his impious Foes right onward drove,
Gloomy as Night; under his burning Wheels
The steadfast Empyrean shook throughout,
All but the Throne itself of God.[1] Full soon
Among them he arriv'd; in his right hand
Grasping ten thousand Thunders, which he sent
Before him, such as in thir Souls infix'd
Plagues; they astonisht all resistance lost,

8. The Bible reiterates that vengeance is a divine prerogative, not lightly delegated. For examples, see Deuteronomy 32.35; Psalm 94.1; Romans 12.19; Hebrews 10.30.
9. The "four cherubic shapes" of 6.753, their wings set with eyes; see Ezekiel 10.12.
1. Refuting Satan's claim to have shaken the throne, at 1.105.

All courage; down thir idle weapons dropp'd;
O'er Shields and Helms, and helmed heads he rode
Of Thrones and mighty Seraphim prostrate,
That wish't the Mountains now might be again
Thrown on them as a shelter from his ire.[2]
Nor less on either side tempestuous fell
His arrows, from the fourfold-visag'd Four,
Distinct° with eyes, and from the living Wheels, *adorned*
Distinct alike with multitude of eyes;
One Spirit in them rul'd, and every eye
Glar'd lightning, and shot forth pernicious fire
Among th' accurst, that wither'd all thir strength,
And of thir wonted vigor left them drain'd,
Exhausted, spiritless, afflicted, fall'n.
Yet half his strength he put not forth, but check'd
His Thunder in mid Volley, for he meant
Not to destroy, but root them out of Heav'n:[3]
The overthrown he rais'd, and as a Herd
Of Goats or timorous flock together throng'd
Drove them before him Thunder-struck, pursu'd
With terrors and with furies to the bounds
And Crystal wall of Heav'n, which op'ning wide,
Roll'd inward, and a spacious Gap disclos'd
Into the wasteful° Deep; the monstrous sight *desolate*
Struck them with horror backward, but far worse
Urg'd them behind; headlong themselves they threw
Down from the verge of Heav'n, Eternal wrath
Burn'd after them to the bottomless pit.
    Hell heard th' unsufferable noise, Hell saw
Heav'n ruining° from Heav'n, and would have fled *falling*
Affrighted; but strict Fate had cast too deep
Her dark foundations, and too fast had bound.
Nine days they fell; confounded *Chaos* roar'd,
And felt tenfold confusion in thir fall
Through his wild Anarchy, so huge a rout
Incumber'd him with ruin: Hell at last
Yawning receiv'd them whole, and on them clos'd,
Hell thir fit habitation fraught with fire
Unquenchable, the house of woe and pain.
Disburd'n'd Heav'n rejoic'd, and soon repair'd
Her mural breach, returning whence it roll'd.
Sole Victor from th' expulsion of his Foes
Messiah his triumphal Chariot turn'd:
To meet him all his Saints, who silent stood

2. Echoes Revelation 6.16, where the damned cry "to the mountains and rocks, Fall on us, and hide us from the face of him that sitteth on the throne, and from the wrath of the Lamb."

3. Contrast with Hesiod, *Theogony*, where Zeus' total energies are insufficient to end the conflict.

Eye-witnesses of his Almighty Acts,
With Jubilee advanc'd; and as they went,
Shaded with branching Palm,[4] each order bright,
Sung Triumph, and him sung Victorious King,
Son, Heir, and Lord, to him Dominion giv'n,
Worthiest to Reign: he celebrated rode
Triumphant through mid Heav'n, into the Courts
And Temple of his mighty Father Thron'd
On high; who into Glory him receiv'd,
Where now he sits at the right hand of bliss.
  Thus measuring things in Heav'n by things on Earth
At thy request, and that thou mayst beware
By what is past, to thee I have reveal'd
What might have else to human Race been hid:
The discord which befell, and War in Heav'n
Among th' Angelic Powers, and the deep fall
Of those too high aspiring, who rebell'd
With *Satan,* hee who envies now thy state,
Who now is plotting how he may seduce
Thee also from obedience, that with him
Bereav'd of happiness thou mayst partake
His punishment, Eternal misery;
Which would be all his solace and revenge,
As a despite done against the most High,
Thee once to gain Companion of his woe.
But list'n not to his Temptations, warn
Thy weaker;[5] let it profit thee to have heard
By terrible Example the reward
Of disobedience; firm they might have stood,
Yet fell; remember, and fear to transgress.

The End of the Sixth Book.

Book 7
The Argument

Raphael *at the request of* Adam *relates how and wherefore this world was first created; that* God, *after the expelling of* Satan *and his Angels out of Heaven, declar'd his pleasure to create another World and other Creatures to dwell therein; sends his Son with Glory and attendance of Angels to perform the work of Creation in six days: the Angels celebrate with Hymns the performance thereof, and his reascension into Heaven.*

4. The palm also belongs to an allegory of the passion narrative. The palm of victory recalls that in Revelation 7.9; the song of triumph recalls Revelation 5.12; and reception into glory at the right hand of bliss recalls the ascension in Hebrews 1.3.

5. Supply "vessel" to "weaker." See 1 Peter 3.7, "ye husbands, dwell with them according to knowledge, giving honor unto the wife, as unto the weaker vessel, and as being heirs together of the grace of life." This is part of a homily on duties of spouses calculated to counteract any tendency to submissiveness on the part of husbands.

[The Invocation]

Descend from Heav'n *Urania*,[1] by that name
If rightly thou art call'd, whose Voice divine
Following, above th' *Olympian* Hill I soar,
Above the flight of *Pegasean* wing.[2]
The meaning, not the Name I call: for thou
Nor of the Muses nine, nor on the top
Of old *Olympus* dwell'st, but Heav'nly born,
Before the Hills appear'd, or Fountain flow'd,
Thou with Eternal Wisdom didst converse,
Wisdom thy Sister, and with her didst play
In presence of th' Almighty Father, pleas'd
With thy Celestial Song. Up led by thee
Into the Heav'n of Heav'ns I have presum'd,
An Earthly Guest, and drawn Empyreal Air,
Thy temp'ring;[3] with like safety guided down
Return me to my Native Element:
Lest from this flying Steed unrein'd, (as once
Bellerophon, though from a lower Clime)
Dismounted, on th' *Aleian* Field I fall
Erroneous° there to wander and forlorn.[4] *wandering, erring*
Half yet remains unsung, but narrower bound
Within the visible Diurnal Sphere
Standing on Earth, not rapt° above the Pole,[5] *entranced*
More safe I Sing with mortal voice, unchang'd
To hoarse or mute, though fall'n on evil days,
On evil days though fall'n, and evil tongues;
In darkness, and with dangers compast round,
And solitude;[6] yet not alone, while thou
Visit'st my slumbers Nightly, or when Morn
Purples the East: still govern thou my Song,
Urania, and fit audience find, though few.
But drive far off the barbarous dissonance
Of *Bacchus* and his Revellers, the Race
Of that wild Rout that tore the *Thracian* Bard
In *Rhodope*, where Woods and Rocks had Ears
To rapture, till the savage clamor drown'd
Both Harp and Voice;[7] nor could the Muse defend

1. Only in this invocation is the Muse ever named. *Urania* was the Muse of Astronomy. Milton's denial that his Urania is one "of the Muses nine" directs attention to a more recent, single Muse. Since Du Bartas's *Uranie*, the name had been used for the Christian Muse of the divine poetry movement.
2. The winged horse Pegasus was an emblem for the inspired poet.
3. The air of the "first region" (3.562–64) was fatal to mortals.
4. When Bellerophon tried to fly to heaven on Pegasus, Jupiter sent an insect to sting the horse and throw the rider. Bellerophon fell on the Aleian plain and wandered blind and lonely until his death.
5. Either the celestial pole or a synecdoche for the sky.
6. The obfuscated syntax conceals an allusion to Milton's dangerous situation during the persecutions that immediately followed the Restoration.
7. Orpheus as a type of the inspired poet. The myth of his dismemberment by Thracian women during orgies of Bacchus seems to have focused some of Milton's deepest fears. Rhodope was a mountain range in Thrace. In Ovid, *Metamorphoses* 11.1–60, the "woods and rocks" mourned Orpheus's loss, though they were the instruments of his murder.

Her Son. So fail not thou, who thee implores:
For thou art Heavn'ly, shee an empty dream.
  Say Goddess, what ensu'd when *Raphaël*,
The affable Arch-angel, had forewarn'd
Adam by dire example to beware
Apostasy, by what befell in Heaven
To those Apostates, lest the like befall
In Paradise to *Adam* or his Race,
Charg'd not to touch the interdicted Tree,
If they transgress, and slight that sole command,
So easily obey'd amid the choice
Of all tastes else to please thir appetite,
Though wand'ring. He with his consorted° *Eve* *espoused*
The story heard attentive, and was fill'd
With admiration,° and deep muse° to hear *amazement / meditation*
Of things so high and strange, things to thir thought
So unimaginable as hate in Heav'n,
And War so near the Peace of God in bliss
With such confusion: but the evil soon
Driv'n back redounded° as a flood on those *flared back*
From whom it sprung, impossible to mix
With Blessedness. Whence *Adam* soon repeal'd° *abandoned*
The doubts that in his heart arose: and now
Led on, yet sinless, with desire to know
What nearer might concern him, how this World
Of Heav'n and Earth conspicuous first began[8]
When, and whereof created, for what cause,
What within *Eden* or without was done
Before his memory, as one whose drouth° *thirst*
Yet scarce allay'd still eyes the current stream,
Whose liquid murmur heard new thirst excites,
Proceeded thus to ask his Heav'nly Guest.
  Great things, and full of wonder in our ears,
Far differing from this World, thou hast reveal'd
Divine Interpreter[9] by favor sent
Down from the Empyrean to forewarn
Us timely of what might else have been our loss,
Unknown, which human knowledge could not reach:
For which to th' infinitely Good we owe
Immortal thanks, and his admonishment
Receive with solemn purpose to observe
Immutably his sovran will, the end° *purpose*
Of what we are.[1] But since thou hast voutsaf't
Gently for our instruction to impart

8. Heaven and earth are "conspicuous," or visible, as opposed to the invisible "heaven of heavens." See 3.390; 7.13, 22.

9. In Virgil's *Aeneid* (4.378), Mercury is called "interpres divum" when he brings Jupiter's command for Aeneas to leave Dido.

1. Echoing Ecclesiastes 12.13, "Let us hear the end of all: Fear God, and keep his commandments: for this is the whole duty of man."

Things above Earthly thought, which yet concern'd
Our knowing, as to highest wisdom seem'd,° *seemed good*
Deign to descend now lower, and relate
What may no less perhaps avail us known,
How first began this Heav'n which we behold
Distant so high, with moving Fires adorn'd
Innumerable, and this which yields or fills
All space[2] the ambient Air wide interfus'd
Imbracing round this florid Earth, what cause
Mov'd the Creator in his holy Rest
Through all Eternity so late to build
In *Chaos*, and the work begun, how soon
Absolv'd,° if unforbid thou mayst unfold *completed*
What wee, not to explore the secrets ask
Of his Eternal Empire, but the more
To magnify his works,[3] the more we know.
And the great Light of Day yet wants to run
Much of his Race though steep, suspense in Heav'n
Held by thy voice,[4] thy potent voice he hears,
And longer will delay to hear thee tell
His Generation, and the rising Birth
Of Nature from the unapparent° Deep: *invisible*
Or if the Star of Ev'ning and the Moon
Haste to thy audience, Night with her will bring
Silence, and Sleep list'ning to thee will watch,° *remain awake*
Or we can bid his absence, till thy Song
End, and dismiss thee ere the Morning shine.
Thus *Adam* his illustrious Guest besought:
And thus the Godlike Angel answer'd mild.
This also thy request with caution askt
Obtain: though to recount Almighty works
What words or tongue of Seraph can suffice,
Or heart of man suffice to comprehend?
Yet what thou canst attain which best may serve
To glorify the Maker, and infer° *render*
Thee also happier, shall not be withheld
Thy hearing, such Commission from above
I have receiv'd, to answer thy desire
Of knowledge within bounds; beyond abstain
To ask, nor let thine own inventions° hope° *reasonings / hope for*
Things not reveal'd, which th' invisible King,
Only Omniscient, hath suprest in Night,
To none communicable in Earth or Heaven:[5]

2. Air yields to solids, or fills the space they leave.
3. Echoing Job 36.24, "Remember that thou magnify his work." Adam treads lightly, not wishing to pry into forbidden knowledge.
4. The day is nearly over since the sun is at a low point in its course ("race"). In "suspense," it is both hanging in the sky and attentive to Raphael.
5. See 1 Timothy 1.17, "The king eternal, immortal, invisible, the only wise God" and Matthew 24.36, "of that day and hour knoweth no man, no, not the angels of heaven, but my Father only." Milton elsewhere sets bounds to astronomical inquiry; see 8.70ff.

Anough is left besides to search and know.
But Knowledge is as food, and needs no less
Her Temperance over Appetite, to know
In measure what the mind may well contain,
Oppresses else with Surfeit, and soon turns
Wisdom to Folly, as Nourishment to Wind.
  Know then, that after *Lucifer* from Heav'n
(So call him, brighter once amidst the Host
Of Angels, than that Star the Stars among)[6]
Fell with his flaming Legions through the Deep
Into his place, and the great Son return'd
Victorious with his Saints,° th' Omnipotent *angels*
Eternal Father from his Throne beheld
Thir multitude, and to his Son thus spake.
  At least our envious Foe hath fail'd, who thought
All like himself rebellious, by whose aid
This inaccessible high strength, the seat
Of Deity supreme, us dispossest,
He trusted to have seiz'd, and into fraud° *faithlessness*
Drew many, whom thir place knows here no more;[7]
Yet far the greater part have kept, I see,
Thir station, Heav'n yet populous retains
Number sufficient to possess her Realms
Though wide, and this high Temple to frequent
With Ministeries due and solemn Rites:
But lest his heart exalt him in the harm
Already done to have dispeopl'd Heav'n,
My damage fondly° deem'd, I can repair *foolishly*
That detriment, if such it be to lose
Self-lost, and in a moment will create
Another World, out of one man a Race
Of men innumerable, there to dwell,
Not here, till by degrees of merit rais'd
They open to themselves at length the way
Up hither, under long obedience tri'd,
And Earth be chang'd to Heav'n, and Heav'n to Earth,
One Kingdom, Joy and Union without end.
Meanwhile inhabit lax,° ye Powers of Heav'n; *live spaciously*
And thou my Word, begotten Son, by thee
This I perform, speak thou, and be it done:
My overshadowing Spirit and might with thee
I send along, ride forth, and bid the Deep
Within appointed bounds be Heav'n and Earth,
Boundless the Deep, because I am[8] who fill

6. Raphael offers "Lucifer" (the morning star, Venus or Mercury) as an intelligible human translation for Satan's original name. That name is suggested but not given; see 1.82, 361–63; 5.658ff, 700–14.

7. In Job 7.9ff, "He that goeth down to the grave shall come up no more. He shall return no more to his house, neither shall his place know him any more."

8. "I am" is the divine name in Exodus 3.14.

Infinitude, nor vacuous the space
Though I uncircumscrib'd myself retire,
And put not forth my goodness, which is free
To act or not, Necessity and Chance
Approach not mee, and what I will is Fate.
So spake th' Almighty, and to what he spake
His Word, the Filial Godhead, gave effect.
Immediate are the Acts of God, more swift
Than time or motion, but to human ears
Cannot without process of speech be told,
So told as earthly notion can receive.
Great triumph and rejoicing was in Heav'n
When such was heard declar'd the Almighty's will;
Glory they sung to the most High, good will
To future men, and in thir dwellings peace:[9]
Glory to him whose just avenging ire
Had driven out th' ungodly from his sight
And th' habitations of the just; to him
Glory and praise, whose wisdom had ordain'd
Good out of evil to create, instead
Of Spirits malign a better Race to bring
Into their vacant room, and thence diffuse
His good to Worlds and Ages infinite.
So sang the Hierarchies: Meanwhile the Son
On his great Expedition now appear'd,
Girt with Omnipotence, with Radiance crown'd
Of Majesty Divine, Sapience and Love
Immense, and all his Father in him shone.
About his Chariot numberless were pour'd
Cherub and Seraph, Potentates and Thrones,
And Virtues, winged Spirits, and Chariots wing'd,
From the Armory of God, where stand of old
Myriads between two brazen Mountains lodg'd[1]
Against a solemn day, harness't at hand,
Celestial Equipage;° and now came forth *equipment*
Spontaneous, for within them Spirit liv'd,
Attendant on thir Lord: Heav'n op'n'd wide
Her ever-during Gates, Harmonious sound
On golden Hinges moving,[2] to let forth
The King of Glory in his powerful Word
And Spirit coming to create new Worlds.
On heav'nly ground they stood, and from the shore
They view'd the vast immeasurable Abyss

9. Echoing Job 38.7 ("the morning stars sang together, and all the sons of God shouted for joy" at creation); and Luke 2.14 (the angels' hymn celebrating incarnation and new creation: "Glory to God in the highest, and on earth peace, good will toward men").
1. See Zechariah 6.1, "there came four chariots out from between two mountains; and the mountains were mountains of brass."
2. Contrast these gates with those of hell, which opened with a "jarring sound" (2.879ff) to give Satan his view of the abyss.

Outrageous° as a Sea, dark, wasteful,° wild, *unrestrained / desolate*
Up from the bottom turn'd by furious winds
And surging waves, as Mountains to assault
Heav'n's highth, and with the Centre mix the Pole.
Silence, ye troubl'd waves, and thou Deep, peace,
Said then th' Omnific° Word, your discord end: *all-creating*
Nor stay'd, but on the Wings of Cherubim
Uplifted, in Paternal Glory rode
Far into *Chaos*, and the World unborn;
For *Chaos* heard his voice: him all his Train
Follow'd in bright procession to behold
Creation, and the wonders of his might.
Then stay'd the fervid° Wheels, and in his hand *burning*
He took the golden Compasses, prepar'd
In God's Eternal store, to circumscribe
This Universe, and all created things:
One foot he centred, and the other turn'd
Round through the vast profundity obscure,
And said, Thus far extend, thus far thy bounds,
This be thy just° Circumference, O World. *exact*
Thus God the Heav'n created, thus the Earth,
Matter unform'd and void:[3] Darkness profound
Cover'd th' Abyss: but on the wat'ry calm
His brooding wings the Spirit of God outspread,
And vital virtue° infus'd, and vital warmth *power*
Throughout the fluid Mass, but downward purg'd
The black tartareous cold Infernal dregs
Adverse to life; then founded, then conglob'd° *formed into a ball*
Like things to like, the rest to several place
Disparted, and between spun out the Air,
And Earth self-balanc't on her Centre hung.
Let there be Light, said God, and forthwith Light
Ethereal, first of things,[4] quintessence pure
Sprung from the Deep, and from her Native East
To journey through the airy gloom began,
Spher'd in a radiant Cloud, for yet the Sun
Was not; shee in a cloudy Tabernacle
Sojourn'd the while.[5] God saw the Light was good;
And light from darkness by the Hemisphere
Divided: Light the Day, and Darkness Night
He nam'd. Thus was the first Day Ev'n and Morn:[6]

3. Plato writes of a formless substance in *Timaeus* 50ff; compare to the void of Genesis 1.2. But in *De doctrina* 1.7, Milton explicitly rejects creation *ex nihilo*.

4. Ether is the purest element; see 3.7, "pure ethereal stream."

5. With the tabernacle, or sanctuary for God, Milton avoids the biblical problem of how there could be light without the sun. He also addresses this problem in *De doctrina* 1.7, where he admits the impossibility of conceiving "light without some source of light," yet distinguishes visible light from the perpetual invisible light in the heaven of heavens.

6. Echoing Genesis 1.4ff, "God saw the light, that it was good: and God divided the light from the darkness. And God called the light Day, and the darkness he called Night. And the evening and the morning were the first day." This phrase marks Day 14 of *Paradise Lost*'s action.

Nor pass'd uncelebrated, nor unsung
By the Celestial Choirs, when Orient Light
Exhaling° first from Darkness they beheld; *breathing forth*
Birth-day of Heav'n and Earth; with joy and shout
The hollow Universal Orb they fill'd,
And touch'd thir Golden Harps, and hymning prais'd
God and his works, Creator him they sung,
Both when first Ev'ning was, and when first Morn.
 Again, God said, let there be Firmament
Amid the Waters, and let it divide
The Waters from the Waters: and God made
The Firmament, expanse of liquid, pure,
Transparent, Elemental Air, diffus'd
In circuit to the uttermost convex
Of this great Round:° partition firm and sure, *universe*
The Waters underneath from those above
Dividing: for as Earth, so hee the World° *universe*
Built on circumfluous Waters calm, in wide
Crystalline Ocean, and the loud misrule
Of *Chaos* far remov'd, lest fierce extremes
Contiguous might distemper the whole frame:[7]
And Heav'n he nam'd the Firmament: So Ev'n
And Morning *Chorus* sung the second Day.
 The Earth was form'd, but in the Womb as yet
Of Waters, Embryon° immature involv'd,° *embryo / enveloped*
Appear'd not: over all the face of Earth
Main° Ocean flow'd, not idle, but with warm *uninterrupted*
Prolific° humor soft'ning all her Globe, *generative*
Fermented the great Mother to conceive,
Satiate with genial° moisture, when God said, *generative*
Be gather'd now ye Waters under Heav'n
Into one place, and let dry Land appear.[8]
Immediately the Mountains huge appear
Emergent, and thir broad bare backs upheave
Into the Clouds, thir tops ascend the Sky:
So high as heav'd the tumid° Hills, so low *swollen*
Down sunk a hollow bottom broad and deep,
Capacious bed of Waters: thither they
Hasted with glad precipitance, uproll'd
As drops on dust conglobing from the dry;
Part rise in crystal Wall, or ridge direct,
For haste; such flight the great command impress'd
On the swift floods: as Armies at the call
Of Trumpet (for of Armies thou hast heard)[9]

7. In chaos, opposite qualities ("extremes") are not held apart by intervening means, but are contiguous.
8. Echoing Genesis 1.9.
9. The simile would not have made things clearer to Adam and Eve, if Raphael had not already recounted the angelic war.

Troop to thir Standard, so the wat'ry throng,
Wave rolling after Wave, where way they found,
If steep, with torrent rapture,° if through Plain, *force*
Soft-ebbing; nor withstood them Rock or Hill,
But they, or under ground, or circuit wide
With Serpent error wand'ring,[1] found thir way,
And on the washy Ooze deep Channels wore;
Easy, ere God had bid the ground be dry,
All but within those banks, where Rivers now
Stream, and perpetual draw thir humid train.° *trailed robe*
The dry Land, Earth, and the great receptacle
Of congregated Waters he call'd Seas:[2]
And saw that it was good, and said, Let th' Earth
Put forth the verdant Grass, Herb yielding Seed,
And Fruit Tree yielding Fruit after her kind;
Whose Seed is in herself upon the Earth.
He scarce had said, when the bare Earth, till then
Desert and bare, unsightly, unadorn'd,
Brought forth the tender Grass, whose verdure clad
Her Universal Face with pleasant green,
Then Herbs of every leaf, that sudden flow'r'd
Op'ning thir various colors, and made gay
Her bosom smelling sweet: and these scarce blown,
Forth flourish'd thick the clust'ring Vine, forth crept
The smelling Gourd, up stood the corny Reed
Embattl'd in her field: and th' humble° Shrub, *low-growing*
And Bush with frizzl'd hair implicit:° last *interwoven*
Rose as in Dance the stately Trees, and spread
Thir branches hung with copious Fruit: or gemm'd° *budded*
Thir Blossoms: with high Woods the Hills were crown'd,
With tufts the valleys and each fountain side,
With borders long the Rivers. That Earth now
Seem'd like to Heav'n, a seat where Gods might dwell,
Or wander with delight, and love to haunt
Her sacred shades: though God had yet not rain'd
Upon the Earth, and man to till the ground
None was, but from the Earth a dewy Mist
Went up and water'd all the ground, and each
Plant of the field, which ere it was in the Earth
God made, and every Herb, before it grew
On the green stem; God saw that it was good:
So Ev'n and Morn recorded° the Third Day.[3] *sang*
Again th' Almighty spake: Let there be Lights
High in th' expanse of Heaven to divide
The Day from Night; and let them be for Signs,

1. By itself, "error" might be a Latinism for "winding;" but after "serpent" it indisputably anticipates the Fall.
2. Echoing Genesis 1.10ff. "Congregated waters" echoes the Vulgate's "congregationesque aquarum."
3. This marks day 16 of the action.

For Seasons, and for Days, and circling Years,
And let them be for Lights as I ordain
Thir Office in the Firmament of Heav'n
To give Light on the Earth; and it was so.[4]
And God made two great Lights, great for thir use
To Man, the greater to have rule by Day,
The less by Night altern:° and made the Stars, *by turns*
And set them in the Firmament of Heav'n
To illuminate the Earth, and rule the Day
In thir vicissitude,° and rule the Night, *variety*
And Light from Darkness to divide. God saw,
Surveying his great Work, that it was good:
For of Celestial Bodies first the Sun
A mighty Sphere he fram'd, unlightsome first,
Though of Ethereal Mould:° then form'd the Moon *quintessential matter*
Globose, and every magnitude of Stars,
And sow'd with Stars the Heav'n thick as a field:
Of Light by far the greater part he took.
Transplanted from her cloudy Shrine,[5] and plac'd
In the Sun's Orb, made porous to receive
And drink the liquid Light, firm to retain
Her gather'd beams, great Palace now of Light.
Hither as to thir Fountain other Stars
Repairing, in thir gold'n Urns draw Light,
And hence the Morning Planet gilds her horns;
By tincture° or reflection they augment *infusion*
Thir small peculiar,[6] though from human sight
So far remote, with diminution seen.
First in his East the glorious Lamp was seen,
Regent of Day, and all th' Horizon round
Invested with bright Rays, jocund to run
His Longitude° through Heav'n's high road: the gray *ecliptic course*
Dawn, and the *Pleiades* before him danc'd
Shedding sweet influence: less bright the Moon,
But opposite in levell'd° West was set *on the same plane*
His mirror, with full face borrowing her Light
From him, for other light she needed none
In that aspect, and still that distance keeps
Till night, then in the East her turn she shines,
Revolv'd on Heav'n's great Axle and her Reign
With thousand lesser Lights dividual° holds, *shared*
With thousand thousand Stars, that then appear'd
Spangling the Hemisphere: then first adorn'd
With thir bright Luminaries that Set and Rose,
Glad Ev'ning and glad Morn crown'd the fourth day.[7]

4. Echoing Genesis 1.14ff.
5. Equivalent to the "cloudy tabernacle" at 7.248.
6. "Peculiar" light is inherent to a heavenly body, as opposed to "strange" or borrowed light.
7. The fourth day is crowned because it occupies the sovereign central place, fourth of the days of creation and seventeenth of the action.

And God said, let the Waters generate
Reptile with Spawn abundant, living Soul.° *animate existence*
And let Fowl fly above the Earth, with wings
Display'd on the op'n Firmament of Heav'n.
And God created the great Whales, and each
Soul living, each that crept, which plenteously
The waters generated by thir kinds,
And every Bird of wing after his kind;
And saw that it was good, and bless'd them, saying,
Be fruitful, multiply, and in the Seas
And Lakes and running Streams the waters fill;
And let the Fowl be multipli'd on the Earth.[8]
Forthwith the Sounds and Seas, each Creek and Bay
With Fry° innumerable swarm, and Shoals *offspring*
Of Fish that with thir Fins and shining Scales
Glide under the green Wave, in Sculls that oft
Bank° the mid Sea: part single or with mate *form a shelf*
Graze the Seaweed thir pasture, and through Groves
Of Coral stray, or sporting with quick glance
Show to the Sun thir wav'd coats dropt° with Gold, *spotted*
Or in thir Pearly shells at ease, attend° *wait for*
Moist nutriment, or under Rocks thir food
In jointed Armor watch: on smooth° the Seal, *smooth water*
And bended Dolphins play: part huge of bulk
Wallowing unwieldly, enormous in thir Gait
Tempest° the Ocean: there Leviathan *disturb violently*
Hugest of living Creatures, on the Deep
Stretcht like a Promontory sleeps or swims,
And seems a moving Land, and at his Gills
Draws in, and at his Trunk° spouts out a Sea. *blowhole*
Meanwhile the tepid Caves, and Fens and shores
Thir Brood as numerous hatch, from th' Egg that soon
Bursting with kindly° rupture forth disclos'd° *natural / hatched*
Thir callow° young, but feather'd soon and fledge *unfeathered*
They summ'd° thir Pens,° and soaring th' air sublime *completed / plumage*
With clang° despis'd the ground, under a cloud *harsh scream*
In prospect; there the Eagle and the Stork
On Cliffs and Cedar tops thir Eyries build:[9]
Part loosely wing the Region, part more wise
In common, rang'd in figure wedge thir way,
Intelligent of seasons, and set forth
Thir Aery Caravan high over Seas
Flying, and over Lands with mutual wing
Easing thir flight; so steers the prudent Crane
Her annual Voyage, borne on Winds; the Air
Floats, as they pass, fann'd with unnumber'd plumes:

8. Echoing Genesis 1.20–2.
9. Milton's epic catalogue compresses Tasso's *Creation* (1607), book 5, where 19 birds (including almost all Milton's seven) are assigned complex moral qualities.

From Branch to Branch the smaller Birds with song
Solac'd the Woods, and spread thir painted wings
Till Ev'n, nor then the solemn Nightingale
Ceas'd warbling, but all night tun'd her soft lays:
Others on Silver Lakes and Rivers Bath'd
Thir downy Breast; the Swan with Arched neck
Between her white wings mantling° proudly, Rows *stretching*
Her state with Oary feet: yet oft they quit
The Dank,° and rising on stiff Pennons,° tow'r *pool / wings*
The mid Aereal Sky: Others on ground
Walk'd firm; the crested Cock whose clarion° sounds *small trumpet*
The silent hours, and th' other° whose gay Train *peacock*
Adorns him, color'd with the Florid hue
Of Rainbows and Starry Eyes. The Waters thus
With Fish replenisht, and the Air with Fowl
Ev'ning and Morn solemniz'd the Fift day.[1]
The Sixt, and of Creation last arose
With Ev'ning Harps and Matin, when God said,
Let th' Earth bring forth Soul living in her kind,
Cattle and Creeping things, and Beast of the Earth,
Each in their kind.[2] The Earth obey'd, and straight
Op'ning her fertile Womb teem'd° at a Birth *produced*
Innumerous living Creatures, perfet forms,
Limb'd and full grown: out of the ground up rose
As from his Lair the wild Beast where he wons° *lives*
In Forest wild, in Thicket, Brake, or Den;
Among the Trees in Pairs they rose, they walk'd:
The Cattle in the Fields and Meadows green:
Those rare and solitary, these in flocks[3]
Pasturing at once, and in broad Herds upsprung.
The grassy Clods now Calv'd, now half appear'd
The Tawny Lion, pawing to get free
His hinder parts, then springs as broke from Bonds,
And Rampant shakes his Brinded° mane; the Ounce,° *streaked / lynx*
The Libbard,° and the Tiger, as the Mole *leopard*
Rising, the crumbl'd Earth above them threw
In Hillocks; the swift Stag from under ground
Bore up his branching head: scarce from his mould
Behemoth biggest born of Earth upheav'd
His vastness:[4] Fleec't the Flocks and bleating rose,
As Plants: ambiguous between Sea and Land
The River Horse° and scaly Crocodile. *hippopotamus*
At once came forth whatever creeps the ground,
Insect or Worm; those wav'd thir limber fans
For wings, and smallest Lineaments exact

1. Day 18 of the action.
2. Echoing Genesis 1.24.
3. "Those" are the wild beasts, while "these" are the cattle.
4. The italics make "behemoth" seem a name. See Job 40.15, "Behold now behemoth, which I made with thee."

In all the Liveries deckt of Summer's pride
With spots of Gold and Purple, azure and green:
These as a line thir long dimension drew,
Streaking the ground with sinuous trace; not all
Minims° of Nature; some of Serpent kind — *smallest creatures*
Wondrous in length and corpulence° involv'd° — *bulk / coiled*
Thir Snaky folds, and added wings. First crept
The Parsimonious Emmet,° provident — *careful ant*
Of future, in small room large heart° enclos'd, — *wisdom*
Pattern of just equality perhaps
Hereafter, join'd in her popular Tribes
Of Commonalty: swarming next appear'd
The Female Bee that feeds her Husband Drone
Deliciously,° and builds her waxen Cells — *luxuriously*
With Honey stor'd: the rest are numberless,
And thou thir Natures know'st, and gav'st them Names,
Needless to thee repeated; nor unknown
The Serpent subtl'st Beast of all the field,[5]
Of huge extent sometimes, with brazen Eyes
And hairy Mane terrific, though to thee
Not noxious, but obedient at thy call.
Now Heav'n in all her Glory shone, and roll'd
Her motions, as the great first-Mover's hand
First wheel'd thir course; Earth in her rich attire
Consummate° lovely smil'd; Air, Water, Earth, — *completed*
By Fowl, Fish, Beast, was flown, was swum, was walkt
Frequent;° and of the Sixt day yet remain'd; — *abundantly*
There wanted yet the Master work, the end
Of all yet done; a Creature who not prone
And Brute as other Creatures, but endu'd
With Sanctity of Reason, might erect
His Stature, and upright with Front° serene — *face*
Govern the rest, self-knowing, and from thence
Magnanimous° to correspond with Heav'n, — *noble*
But grateful to acknowledge whence his good
Descends, thither with heart and voice and eyes
Directed in Devotion, to adore
And worship God Supreme who made him chief
Of all his works: therefore th'Omnipotent
Eternal Father (For where is not hee
Present) thus to his Son audibly spake.
 Let us make now Man in our image, Man
In our similitude, and let them rule
Over the Fish and Fowl of Sea and Air,
Beast of the Field, and over all the Earth,

5. Milton singles out the serpent for mention last of the beasts, next to mankind. Echoing Genesis 3.1, "Now the serpent was more subtle than any beast of the field which the Lord God had made."

And every creeping thing that creeps the ground.[6]
This said, he form'd thee, *Adam*, thee O Man
Dust of the ground, and in thy nostrils breath'd
The breath of Life; in his own Image hee
Created thee, in the Image of God
Express,[7] and thou becam'st a living Soul.
Male he created thee, but thy consort
Female for Race; then bless'd Mankind, and said,
Be fruitful, multiply, and fill the Earth,
Subdue it, and throughout Dominion hold
Over Fish of the Sea, and Fowl of the Air,
And every living thing that moves on the Earth.[8]
Wherever thus created, for no place
Is yet distinct by name, thence as thou know'st
He brought thee into this delicious° Grove, *delightful*
This Garden, planted with the Trees of God,
Delectable both to behold and taste;
And freely all thir pleasant fruit for food
Gave thee, all sorts are here that all th' Earth yields,
Variety without end; but of the Tree
Which tasted works knowledge of Good and Evil,
Thou may'st not; in the day thou eat'st, thou di'st;
Death is the penalty impos'd, beware,
And govern well thy appetite, lest sin
Surprise thee, and her black attendant Death.[9]
Here finish'd hee, and all that he had made
View'd, and behold all was entirely good;
So Ev'n and Morn accomplish'd the Sixt day:
Yet not till the Creator from his work,
Desisting, though unwearied, up return'd
Up to the Heav'n of Heav'ns his high abode,
Thence to behold this new created World
Th' addition of his Empire, how it show'd
In prospect from his Throne, how good, how fair,
Answering his great Idea. Up he rode
Follow'd with acclamation and the sound
Symphonious of ten thousand Harps that tun'd° *gave vent to*
Angelic harmonies: the Earth, the Air
Resounded, (thou remember'st, for thou heard'st)
The Heav'ns and all the Constellations rung,
The Planets in thir station list'ning stood,
While the bright Pomp° ascended jubilant. *procession*
Open, ye everlasting Gates, they sung,
Open, ye Heav'ns, your living doors; let in

6. Echoing Genesis 1.26.
7. Milton echoes a phrase from Hebrews 1.3, "Who being . . . the express image of his person . . . purged our sins."
8. Echoing Genesis 1.28.
9. Perhaps Raphael, calling Death Sin's "attendant," is innocent about Sin and Death's true relationship—or wishes Adam and Eve to be so.

The great Creator from his work return'd
Magnificent, his Six days' work, a World;
Open, and henceforth oft; for God will deign
To visit oft the dwellings of just Men
Delighted, and with frequent intercourse
Thither will send his winged Messengers
On errands of supernal Grace. So sung
The glorious Train ascending: He through Heav'n,
That open'd wide her blazing Portals,[1] led
To God's Eternal house direct the way,
A broad and ample road, whose dust is Gold
And pavement Stars, as Stars to thee appear,
Seen in the Galaxy, that Milky way
Which nightly as a circling Zone° thou seest *belt*
Powder'd with Stars. And now on Earth the Seventh
Ev'ning arose in *Eden*,[2] for the Sun
Was set, and twilight from the East came on,
Forerunning Night; when at the holy mount
Of Heav'n's high-seated top, th' Imperial Throne
Of Godhead, fixt for ever firm and sure,
The Filial Power arriv'd, and sat him down
With his great Father, for he also went
Invisible, yet stay'd (such privilege
Hath Omnipresence) and the work ordain'd,
Author and end of all things, and from work[3]
Now resting, bless'd and hallow'd the Sev'nth day,
As resting on that day from all his work,
But not in silence holy kept; the Harp
Had work and rested not, the solemn Pipe,
And Dulcimer, all Organs of sweet stop,
All sounds on Fret by String or Golden Wire
Temper'd soft Tunings,[4] intermixt with Voice
Choral or Unison; of incense Clouds
Fuming from Golden Censers hid the Mount.
Creation and the Six days' acts they sung:
Great are thy works, *Jehovah*, infinite
Thy power; what thought can measure thee or tongue
Relate thee; greater now in thy return
Than from the Giant Angels;[5] thee that day
Thy Thunders magnifi'd; but to create

1. The portals of the sun are represented by the tropical signs of Capricorn and Cancer. In Macrobius' *Dream of Scipio*, Cancer is "the portal of men, because through it descent is made to the lower regions; Capricorn, the portal of gods, because through it souls return to their rightful abode of immortality, to be reckoned among the gods."
2. Beginning day 20 of the action.
3. See Genesis 2.3, "God blessed the seventh day, and sanctified it: because that in it he had rested from all his work which God created and made."
4. The details of the heavenly music: the harp takes precedence, as it was played by David. A "stop" is a register of an organ or harpsichord; a "fret" is a ridge dividing the fingerboard of guitar-like stringed instruments; to "temper" is to adjust the pitch; and "tunings" are melodious sounds.
5. The Gigantomachia, or rebellion of the giants against the gods, serves throughout as a mythic version of Satan's rebellion.

Is greater than created to destroy
Who can impair thee, mighty King, or bound
Thy Empire? easily the proud attempt
Of Spirits apostate and thir Counsels vain
Thou hast repell'd, while impiously they thought
Thee to diminish, and from thee withdraw
The number of thy worshippers. Who seeks
To lessen thee, against his purpose serves
To manifest the more thy might: his evil
Thou usest, and from thence creat'st more good.
Witness this new-made World, another Heav'n
From Heaven Gate not far, founded in view
On the clear *Hyaline*, the Glassy Sea;[6]
Of amplitude almost immense,° with Stars *immeasurable*
Numerous, and every Star perhaps a World
Of destin'd habitation; but thou know'st
Thir seasons: among these the seat of men,
Earth with her nether Ocean circumfus'd,
Thir pleasant dwelling-place. Thrice happy men,
And sons of men, whom God hath thus advanc't,
Created in his Image, there to dwell
And worship him, and in reward to rule
Over his Works, on Earth, in Sea, or Air,
And multiply a Race of Worshippers
Holy and just: thrice happy if they know
Thir happiness, and persevere upright.
  So sung they, and the Empyrean rung,
With *Halleluiahs:* Thus was Sabbath kept.
And thy request think now fulfill'd, that ask'd
How first this World and face° of things began, *outward form*
And what before thy memory was done
From the beginning, that posterity
Inform'd by thee might know; if else thou seek'st
Aught, not surpassing human measure, say.

The End of the Seventh Book.

Book 8
The Argument

Adam *inquires concerning celestial Motions, is doubtfully answer'd, and exhorted to search rather things more worthy of knowledge:* Adam *assents, and still desirous to detain* Raphael, *relates to him what he remember'd since his own Creation, his placing in Paradise, his talk with God concerning solitude and fit society, his first meeting and Nuptials with* Eve, *his discourse with the Angel thereupon; who after admonitions repeated departs.*

6. In Revelation 4.6, the "thalassa hyaline" is called a "sea of glass like unto crystal." Here, the term refers to the waters above the firmament.

The Angel ended, and in *Adam's* Ear
So Charming left his voice, that he a while
Thought him still speaking, still stood fixt to hear;[1]
Then as new wak't thus gratefully repli'd.
What thanks sufficient, or what recompense
Equal have I to render thee, Divine
Historian, who thus largely hast allay'd
The thirst I had of knowledge, and voutsaf't
This friendly condescension to relate
Things else by me unsearchable, now heard
With wonder, but delight, and, as is due,
With glory attributed to the high
Creator; something yet of doubt remains,
Which only thy solution° can resolve *explanation*
When I behold this goodly Frame,° this World *universe*
Of Heav'n and Earth consisting, and compute
Thir magnitudes, this Earth a spot, a grain,
An Atom, with the Firmament compar'd
And all her number'd° Stars, that seem to roll *numerous*
Spaces incomprehensible (for such
Thir distance argues and thir swift return
Diurnal) merely to officiate° light *minister*
Round this opacous° Earth, this punctual° spot, *opaque / pointlike*
One day and night; in all thir vast survey
Useless besides; reasoning I oft admire,° *wonder*
How Nature wise and frugal could commit
Such disproportions, with superfluous hand
So many nobler Bodies to create,
Greater so manifold to this one use,
For aught appears, and on thir Orbs impose
Such restless revolution day by day
Repeated, while the sedentary Earth,
That better might with far less compass move,
Serv'd by more noble than herself, attains
Her end without least motion, and receives,
As Tribute such a sumless journey brought
Of incorporeal speed, her warmth and light;
Speed, to describe whose swiftness Number fails.
So spake our Sire, and by his count'nance seem'd
Ent'ring on studious thoughts abstruse, which *Eve*
Perceiving where she sat retir'd in sight,
With lowliness Majestic from her seat,
And Grace that won who saw to wish her stay,
Rose and went forth among her Fruits and Flow'rs,
To visit° how they prosper'd, bud and bloom, *inspect*
Her Nursery; they at her coming sprung

1. After epic digressions, audiences often remain rapt; see Homer's *Odyssey* 13.1 and Apollonius 1.512-16 (after Orpheus' song of creation).

And toucht by her fair tendance° gladlier grew. *attention*
Yet went she not, as not with such discourse
Delighted, or not capable her ear
Of what was high: such pleasure she reserv'd,
Adam relating, she sole Auditress;
Her Husband the Relater she preferr'd
Before the Angel, and of him to ask
Chose rather: hee, she knew, would intermix
Grateful digressions, and solve high dispute
With conjugal Caresses, from his Lip
Not Words alone pleas'd her. O when meet now
Such pairs, in Love and mutual Honor join'd?
With Goddess-like demeanor forth she went;
Not unattended, for on her as Queen
A pomp° of winning Graces waited still, *retinue*
And from about her shot Darts of desire
Into all Eyes to wish her still in sight.
And *Raphael* now to *Adam's* doubt propos'd
Benevolent and facile° thus repli'd. *kindly*
To ask or search I blame thee not, for Heav'n
Is as the Book of God before thee set,
Wherein to read his wond'rous Works, and learn
His Seasons, Hours, or Days, or Months, or Years:[2]
This to attain, whether Heav'n move or Earth,
Imports not, if thou reck'n right; the rest
From Man or Angel the great Architect
Did wisely to conceal, and not divulge
His secrets to be scann'd° by them who ought *examined minutely*
Rather admire; or if they list to try
Conjecture, he his Fabric of the Heav'ns
Hath left to thir disputes, perhaps to move
His laughter at thir quaint Opinions wide
Hereafter,[3] when they come to model Heav'n
And calculate the Stars, how they will wield
The mighty frame, how build, unbuild, contrive
To save appearances, how gird the Sphere
With Centric and Eccentric scribbl'd o'er,
Cycle and Epicycle, Orb in Orb:[4]
Already by thy reasoning this I guess,
Who are to lead thy offspring, and supposest
That bodies bright and greater should not serve
The less not bright, nor Heav'n such journeys run,
Earth sitting still, when she alone receives
The benefit: consider first, that Great
Or Bright infers not Excellence: the Earth

2. Echoing Genesis 1.14, "lights in the firmament for signs, and for seasons, and for days, and years."
3. For other instances of God's laughter, see 2.731; 3.257; 5.718, 737; 12.59.
4. Eccentric orbits and epicycles are attempts within the Ptolemaic system to accommodate observed irregularities in stellar motions.

Though in comparison of Heav'n, so small,
Nor glistering,° may of solid good contain *gleaming*
More plenty than the Sun that barren shines,[5]
Whose virtue on itself works no effect,
But in the fruitful Earth; there first receiv'd
His beams, unactive else, thir vigor find.
Yet not to Earth are those bright Luminaries
Officious,° but to thee Earth's habitant. *dutiful*
And for the Heav'n's wide Circuit, let it speak
The Maker's high magnificence, who built
So spacious, and his Line stretcht out so far;
That Man may know he dwells not in his own;
An Edifice too large for him to fill,
Lodg'd in a small partition, and the rest
Ordain'd for uses to his Lord best known.
The swiftness of those Circles° attribute, *orbits*
Though numberless,° to his Omnipotence, *innumerable*
That to corporeal substances could add
Speed almost Spiritual; mee thou think'st not slow,
Who since the Morning hour set out from Heav'n
Where God resides, and ere mid-day arriv'd
In *Eden*, distance inexpressible
By Numbers that have name. But this I urge,
Admitting Motion in the Heav'ns, to show
Invalid that which thee to doubt it mov'd;
Not that I so affirm, though so it seem
To thee who hast thy dwelling here on Earth.
God to remove his ways from human sense,
Plac'd Heav'n from Earth so far, that earthly sight,
If it presume, might err in things too high,
And no advantage gain. What if the Sun
Be Centre to the World,° and other Stars *universe*
By his attractive virtue° and their own *power of attraction*
Incited, dance about him various rounds?[6]
Thir wandring course now high, now low, then hid,
Progressive, retrograde, or standing still,
In six thou seest,[7] and what if sev'nth to these
The Planet Earth, so steadfast though she seem,
Insensibly three different Motions move?
Which else to several Spheres thou must ascribe,
Mov'd contrary with thwart obliquities,
Or save the Sun his labor, and that swift

5. The sun is "barren" because it already contains a plenitude of life. It requires no additions from its own reflected beams.

6. The elusive astronomy reflects Milton's own difficulty in choosing among the planetary systems available. The main choice was between updated versions of the earth-centered Ptolemaic system and the new system of Copernicus, which placed the sun at the center. The lesson for Adam is more likely that models matter less than obedience. As the argument to Book 8 puts it, "Adam is doubtfully answered."

7. The six are Saturnus, Iupiter, Mars, Venus, Mercurius, and Luna. Whether Tellus (the earth) or Sol (the sun) constituted the seventh planet was controversial.

Nocturnal and Diurnal rhomb suppos'd,
Invisible else above all Stars, the Wheel
Of Day and Night; which needs not thy belief,
If Earth industrious of herself fetch Day
Travelling East, and with her part averse
From the Sun's beam meet Night, her other part
Still luminous by his ray.[8] What if that light
Sent from her through the wide transpicuous° air, *transparent*
To the terrestrial Moon be as a Star
Enlight'ning her by Day, as she by Night
This Earth? reciprocal, if Land be there,
Fields and Inhabitants: Her spots thou seest
As Clouds,[9] and Clouds may rain, and Rain produce
Fruits in her soft'n'd Soil, for some to eat
Allotted there; and other Suns perhaps
With thir attendant Moons thou wilt descry
Communicating Male and Female Light,
Which two great Sexes animate the World,
Stor'd in each Orb perhaps with some that live.
For such vast room in Nature unpossest
By living Soul, desert and desolate,
Only to shine, yet scarce to contribute
Each Orb a glimpse of Light, convey'd so far
Down to this habitable, which returns
Light back to them, is obvious° to dispute. *open*
But whether thus these things, or whether not,
Whether the Sun predominant in Heav'n
Rise on the Earth, or Earth rise on the Sun,
Hee from the East his flaming road begin,
Or Shee from West her silent course advance
With inoffensive° pace that spinning sleeps *unobstructed*
On her soft Axle, while she paces Ev'n,
And bears thee soft with the smooth Air along,
Solicit° not thy thoughts with matters hid, *disturb*
Leave them to God above, him serve and fear;[1]
Of other Creatures, as him pleases best,
Wherever plac't, let him dispose: joy thou
In what he gives to thee, this Paradise
And thy fair *Eve*: Heav'n is for thee too high
To know what passes there; be lowly wise:
Think only what concerns thee and thy being;

8. Raphael uses terminology of various astronomical systems here. Copernicus attributed these motions to earth (8.130); the "thwart obliquities" may look forward to a post-Fall, tilted Zodiac; and the "rhomb" probably refers to the *primum mobile* or tenth sphere of the medieval planetary system, which revolved with incredibly swift diurnal motion about the earth, carrying the spheres of stars and planets with it. The "earth industrious" of Copernicus contrasts with the Ptolemeic "sedentary earth" (32).

9. Changes of the moon's spots were often ascribed to effects of the lunar atmosphere. Raphael also opts for the lunar clouds theory at 5.418-20.

1. Echoing Ecclesiastes 12.13, "Fear God, and keep his commandments: for this is the whole duty of man."

Dream not of other Worlds, what Creatures there
Live, in what state, condition or degree,
Contented that thus far hath been reveal'd
Not of Earth only but of highest Heav'n.
  To whom thus Adam clear'd of doubt, repli'd.
How fully hast thou satisfi'd me, pure
Intelligence° of Heav'n, Angel serene, *spirit*
And freed from intricacies, taught to live
The easiest way, nor with perplexing thoughts
To interrupt the sweet of Life, from which
God hath bid dwell far off all anxious cares,
And not molest us, unless we ourselves
Seek them with wand'ring thoughts, and notions vain.
But apt the Mind or Fancy is to rove
Uncheckt, and of her roving is no end;
Till warn'd, or by experience taught, she learn
That not to know at large of things remote
From use, obscure and subtle, but to know
That which before us lies in daily life,
Is the prime Wisdom; what is more, is fume,° *smoke*
Or emptiness, or fond impertinence,° *foolish irrelevance*
And renders us in things that most concern
Unpractic'd, unprepar'd, and still to seek.
Therefore from this high pitch let us descend
A lower flight, and speak of things at hand
Useful, whence haply mention may arise
Of something not unseasonable to ask
By sufferance,° and thy wonted favor deign'd. *permission*
Thee I have heard relating what was done
Ere my remembrance: now hear mee relate
My Story, which perhaps thou hast not heard;
And Day is yet not spent; till then thou seest
How subtly to detain thee I devise,
Inviting thee to hear while I relate,
  Fond, were it not in hope of thy reply:
For while I sit with thee, I seem in Heav'n,
And sweeter thy discourse is to my ear
Than Fruits of Palm-tree pleasantest to thirst
And hunger both, from labor, at the hour
Of sweet repast; they satiate, and soon fill,
Though pleasant, but thy words with Grace Divine
Imbu'd, bring to thir sweetness no satiety.
  To whom thus *Raphael* answer'd heav'nly meek.
Nor are thy lips ungraceful, Sire of men,
Nor tongue ineloquent; for God on thee
Abundantly his gifts hath also pour'd
Inward and outward both, his image fair:
Speaking or mute all comeliness and grace
Attends thee, and each word, each motion forms.

Nor less think wee in Heav'n of thee on Earth
Than of our fellow servant, and inquire
Gladly into the ways of God with Man:
For God we see hath honor'd thee, and set
On Man his Equal Love: say therefore on;
For I that Day was absent, as befell,
Bound on a voyage uncouth° and obscure, *unfamiliar*
Far on excursion toward the Gates of Hell;
Squar'd in full Legion (such command we had)
To see that none thence issu'd forth a spy,
Or enemy, while God was in his work,
Lest hee incenst at such eruption bold,
Destruction with Creation might have mixt.
Not that they durst without his leave attempt,
But us he sends upon his high behests
For state,° as Sovran King, and to enure *ceremony*
Our prompt obedience. Fast we found, fast shut
The dismal Gates, and barricado'd strong;
But long ere our approaching heard within
Noise, other than the sound of Dance or Song,
Torment, and loud lament, and furious rage.
Glad we return'd up to the coasts of Light
Ere Sabbath Ev'ning: so we had in charge.
But thy relation now; for I attend,
Pleas'd with thy words no less than thou with mine.
    So spake the Godlike Power, and thus our Sire.
For man to tell how human Life began
Is hard; for who himself beginning knew?
Desire with thee still longer to converse
Induc'd me. As new wak't from soundest sleep
Soft on the flow'ry herb I found me laid
In Balmy Sweat, which with his Beams the Sun
Soon dri'd, and on the reeking moisture fed.
Straight toward Heav'n my wond'ring Eyes I turn'd,
And gaz'd a while the ample Sky, till rais'd
By quick instinctive motion up I sprung,
As thitherward endeavoring, and upright
Stood on my feet; about me round I saw
Hill, Dale, and shady Woods, and sunny Plains,
And liquid Lapse of murmuring Streams; by these,
Creatures that liv'd, and mov'd, and walk'd, or flew
Birds on the branches warbling; all things smil'd,
With fragrance and with joy my heart o'erflow'd.
Myself I then perus'd, and Limb by Limb
Survey'd, and sometimes went,° and sometimes ran *walked*
With supple joints, as lively vigor led:
But who I was, or where, or from what cause,
Knew not; to speak I tri'd, and forthwith spake,
My Tongue obey'd and readily could name

Whate'er I saw. Thou Sun, said I, fair Light
And thou enlight'n'd Earth, so fresh and gay,
Ye Hills and Dales, ye Rivers, Woods, and Plains
And ye that live and move, fair Creatures, tell,
Tell, if ye saw, how came I thus, how here?
Not of myself; by some great Maker then,
In goodness and in power preëminent;
Tell me, how may I know him, how adore,
From whom I have that thus I move and live,[2]
And feel that I am happier than I know.
While thus I call'd, and stray'd I knew not whither,
From where I first drew Air, and first beheld
This happy Light, when answer none return'd,
On a green shady Bank profuse of Flow'rs
Pensive I sat me down; there gentle sleep
First found me, and with soft oppression seiz'd
My drowsed sense, untroubl'd, though I thought
I then was passing to my former state
Insensible, and forthwith to dissolve:
When suddenly stood at my Head a dream,
Whose inward apparition gently mov'd
My fancy to believe I yet had being,
And liv'd: One came, methought, of shape Divine,
And said, thy Mansion° wants thee, *Adam*, rise, *home*
First Man, of Men innumerable ordain'd
First Father, call'd by thee I come thy Guide
To the Garden of bliss, thy seat prepar'd.[3]
So saying, by the hand he took me rais'd,
And over Fields and Waters, as in Air
Smooth sliding without step, last led me up
A woody Mountain; whose high top was plain,
A Circuit wide, enclos'd, with goodliest Trees
Planted, with Walks, and Bowers, that what I saw
Of Earth before scarce pleasant seem'd. Each Tree
Load'n with fairest Fruit, that hung to the Eye
Tempting, stirr'd in me sudden appetite
To pluck and eat; whereat I wak'd, and found
Before mine Eyes all real, as the dream
Had lively shadow'd: Here had new begun
My wand'ring, had not hee who was my Guide
Up hither, from among the Trees appear'd,
Presence Divine. Rejoicing, but with awe,
In adoration at his feet I fell
Submiss:° he rear'd me, and Whom thou sought'st I am,[4] *submissive*

2. See St. Paul's sermon on the Unknown God, Acts 17.28: "For in him we live, and move, and have our being."
3. See Genesis 2.15.
4. See Exodus 3.14: "I AM THAT I AM. . . . Thus shalt thou say unto the children of Israel, I AM hath sent me unto you."

Said mildly, Author of all this thou seest
Above, or round about thee or beneath.
This Paradise I give thee, count it thine
To Till and keep, and of the Fruit to eat:
Of every Tree that in the Garden grows
Eat freely with glad heart; fear here no dearth:[5]
But of the Tree whose operation brings
Knowledge of good and ill, which I have set
The Pledge of thy Obedience and thy Faith,
Amid the Garden by the Tree of Life,
Remember what I warn thee, shun to taste,
And shun the bitter consequence: for know,
The day thou eat'st thereof, my sole command
Transgrest, inevitably thou shalt die;
From that day mortal, and this happy State
Shalt lose, expell'd from hence into a World
Of woe and sorrow. Sternly he pronounc'd
The rigid interdiction,° which resounds *prohibition*
Yet dreadful in mine ear, though in my choice
Not to incur; but soon his clear aspect
Return'd and gracious purpose° thus renew'd. *discourse*
Not only these fair bounds, but all the Earth
To thee and to thy Race I give; as Lords
Possess it, and all things that therein live,
Or live in Sea, or Air, Beast, Fish, and Fowl.[6]
In sign whereof each Bird and Beast behold
After thir kinds; I bring them to receive
From thee thir Names, and pay thee fealty
With low subjection; understand the same
Of Fish within thir wat'ry residence,
Not hither summon'd, since they cannot change
Thir Element to draw the thinner Air.
As thus he spake, each Bird and Beast behold
Approaching two and two, These cow'ring low
With blandishment, each Bird stoop'd on his wing.
I nam'd them, as they pass'd, and understood
Thir Nature, with such knowledge God endu'd
My sudden apprehension: but in these
I found not what methought I wanted still;
And to the Heav'nly vision thus presum'd.
O by what Name, for thou above all these,
Above mankind, or aught than mankind higher,
Surpassest far my naming, how may I
Adore thee, Author of this Universe,
And all this good to man, for whose well being
So amply, and with hands so liberal

5. See Genesis 2.15–17.

6. See Genesis 1.28.

Thou hast provided all things: but with mee
I see not who partakes. In solitude
What happiness, who can enjoy alone,
Or all enjoying, what contentment find?
Thus I presumptuous; and the vision bright,
As with a smile more bright'n'd, thus repli'd.
  What call'st thou solitude? is not the Earth
With various living creatures, and the Air
Replenisht, and all these at thy command
To come and play before thee; know'st thou not
Thir language and thir ways? They also know,[7]
And reason not contemptibly; with these
Find pastime, and bear rule; thy Realm is large.
So spake the Universal Lord, and seem'd
So ordering. I with leave of speech implor'd,
And humble deprecation thus repli'd.
  Let not my words offend thee, Heav'nly Power,
My Maker, be propitious while I speak.
Hast thou not made me here thy substitute,
And these inferior far beneath me set?
Among unequals what society
Can sort,° what harmony or true delight? *agree*
Which must be mutual, in proportion due
Giv'n and receiv'd; but in disparity
The one intense, the other still remiss
Cannot well suit with either, but soon prove
Tedious alike:[8] Of fellowship I speak
Such as I seek, fit to participate
All rational delight, wherein the brute
Cannot be human consort; they rejoice
Each with thir kind, Lion with Lioness;
So fitly them in pairs thou hast combin'd;
Much less can Bird with Beast, or Fish with Fowl
So well converse, nor with the Ox the Ape;
Worse then can Man with Beast, and least of all.
  Whereto th' Almighty answer'd, not displeas'd.
A nice and subtle happiness I see
Thou to thyself proposest, in the choice
Of thy Associates, *Adam*, and wilt taste
No pleasure, though in pleasure, solitary.
What think'st thou then of mee, and this my State,
Seem I to thee sufficiently possest
Of happiness, or not? who am alone
From all Eternity, for none I know

7. It was a widespread Jewish belief that before the Fall, Adam understood the language of the beasts. The original language was usually supposed to have been Hebrew, but sometimes Syriac, Greek, or Aramaic.

8. In a stringed instrument the strings should bear a due ratio of length and frequency. But the human string is too strained ("intense") and therefore high in pitch, while the animal string is too "remiss," i.e., low in pitch.

Second to mee or like, equal much less.
How have I then with whom to hold converse
Save with the Creatures which I made, and those
To me inferior, infinite descents
Beneath what other Creatures are to thee?
He ceas'd, I lowly answer'd. To attain
The highth and depth of thy Eternal ways
All human thoughts come short, Supreme of things;
Thou in thyself art perfet, and in thee
Is no deficience found; not so is Man,
But in degree, the cause of his desire
By conversation with his like to help,
Or solace his defects. No need that thou
Shouldst propagate, already infinite;
And through all numbers absolute, though One;[9]
But Man by number is to manifest
His single imperfection, and beget
Like of his like, his Image multipli'd,
In unity defective, which requires
Collateral love, and dearest amity.
Thou in thy secrecy although alone,
Best with thyself accompanied, seek'st not
Social communication, yet so pleas'd,
Canst raise thy Creature to what highth thou wilt
Of Union or Communion, deifi'd;
I by conversing cannot these erect
From prone, nor in thir ways complacence° find. *source of pleasure*
Thus I embold'n'd spake, and freedom us'd
Permissive, and acceptance found, which gain'd
This answer from the gracious voice Divine.
Thus far to try thee, *Adam*, I was pleas'd,
And find thee knowing not of Beasts alone,
Which thou hast rightly nam'd, but of thyself,
Expressing well the spirit within thee free,
My Image, not imparted to the Brute,
Whose fellowship therefore unmeet for thee
Good reason was thou freely shouldst dislike,
And be so minded still; I, ere thou spak'st,
Knew it not good for Man to be alone,
And no such company as then thou saw'st
Intended thee, for trial only brought,
To see how thou couldst judge of fit and meet:
What next I bring shall please thee, be assur'd,
Thy likeness, thy fit help, thy other self,
Thy wish, exactly to thy heart's desire.
Hee ended, or I heard no more, for now

9. The divine monad contains all other numbers and is therefore complete and perfect through them all. The monad is like God because it is the fountain and origin of all numbers, as God is the origin of created being.

My earthly° by his Heav'nly overpower'd, *earthly nature*
Which it had long stood under, strain'd to the highth
In that celestial Colloquy sublime,
As with an object that excels the sense,
Dazzl'd and spent, sunk down, and sought repair
Of sleep, which instantly fell on me, call'd
By Nature as in aid, and clos'd mine eyes.[1]
Mine eyes he clos'd, but op'n left the Cell
Of Fancy my internal sight, by which
Abstract° as in a trance methought I saw, *withdrawn*
Though sleeping, where I lay, and saw the shape
Still glorious before whom awake I stood;
Who stooping op'n'd my left side, and took
From thence a Rib, with cordial spirits warm,
And Life-blood streaming fresh; wide was the wound,
But suddenly with flesh fill'd up and heal'd:
The Rib he form'd and fashion'd with his hands;
Under his forming hands a Creature grew,
Manlike, but different sex, so lovely fair,
That what seem'd fair in all the World, seem'd now
Mean, or in her summ'd up, in her contain'd
And in her looks, which from that time infus'd
Sweetness into my heart, unfelt before,
And into all things from her Air inspir'd
The spirit of love and amorous delight.
Shee disappear'd, and left me dark, I wak'd
To find her, or for ever to deplore
Her loss, and other pleasures all abjure:
When out of hope, behold her, not far off,
Such as I saw her in my dream, adorn'd
With what all Earth or Heaven could bestow
To make her amiable: On she came,
Led by her Heav'nly Maker, though unseen,
And guided by his voice, nor uninform'd
Of nuptial Sanctity and marriage Rites:
Grace was in all her steps, Heav'n in her Eye,
In every gesture dignity and love.
I overjoy'd could not forbear aloud.° *saying aloud*
    This turn hath made amends; thou hast fulfill'd
Thy words, Creator bounteous and benign,
Giver of all things fair, but fairest this
Of all thy gifts, nor enviest. I now see
Bone of my Bone, Flesh of my Flesh, my Self
Before me; Woman is her Name, of Man
Extracted; for this cause he shall forgo
Father and Mother, and to his Wife adhere;

1. For lines 452–86, see Genesis 2.21ff.

And they shall be one Flesh, one Heart, one Soul.[2]
She heard me thus, and though divinely brought,
Yet Innocence and Virgin Modesty,
Her virtue and the conscience° of her worth, *consciousness*
That would be woo'd, and not unsought be won,
Not obvious, not obtrusive, but retir'd,
The more desirable, or to say all,
Nature herself, though pure of sinful thought,
Wrought in her so, that seeing me, she turn'd;
I follow'd her, she what was Honor knew,
And with obsequious° Majesty approv'd *compliant*
My pleaded reason. To the Nuptial Bow'r
I led her blushing like the Morn: all Heav'n,
And happy Constellations on that hour
Shed thir selectest influence; the Earth
Gave sign of gratulation,° and each Hill; *joy*
Joyous the Birds; fresh Gales and gentle Airs
Whisper'd it to the Woods, and from thir wings
Flung Rose, flung Odors from the spicy Shrub,
Disporting, till the amorous Bird of Night[3]
Sung Spousal, and bid haste the Ev'ning Star
On his Hill top, to light the bridal Lamp.
Thus I have told thee all my State, and brought
My Story to the sum of earthly bliss
Which I enjoy, and must confess to find
In all things else delight indeed, but such
As us'd or not, works in the mind no change,
Nor vehement desire, these delicacies
I mean of Taste, Sight, Smell, Herbs, Fruits, and Flow'rs,
Walks, and the melody of Birds; but here
Far otherwise, transported I behold,
Transported touch; here passion first I felt,
Commotion strange, in all enjoyments else
Superior and unmov'd, here only weak
Against the charm of Beauty's powerful glance.
Or° Nature fail'd in mee, and left some part *either*
Not proof enough such Object to sustain,
Or from my side subducting,° took perhaps *subtracting*
More than enough; at least on her bestow'd
Too much of Ornament, in outward show
Elaborate, of inward less exact.° *perfect*
For well I understand in the prime end
Of Nature her th' inferior, in the mind
And inward Faculties, which most excel,
In outward also her resembling less
His Image who made both, and less expressing

2. See *Genesis* 3.23ff. The biblical expression "one flesh" is replaced by the familiar Platonic tripartite division.

3. The nightingale; see 5.40–41.

The character of that Dominion giv'n
O'er other Creatures; yet when I approach
Her loveliness, so absolute she seems
And in herself complete, so well to know
Her own, that what she wills to do or say,
Seems wisest, virtuousest, discreetest, best;
All higher knowledge in her presence falls
Degraded, Wisdom in discourse with her
Loses discount'nanc't, and like folly shows;
Authority and Reason on her wait,
As one intended first, not after made
Occasionally;° and to consummate all, *accidentally*
Greatness of mind and nobleness thir seat
Build in her loveliest, and create an awe
About her, as a guard Angelic plac't.
To whom the Angel with contracted brow.
  Accuse not Nature, she hath done her part;
Do thou but thine, and be not diffident° *mistrustful*
Of Wisdom, she deserts thee not, if thou
Dismiss not her, when most thou need'st her nigh,
By attribúting overmuch to things
Less excellent, as thou thyself perceiv'st.
For what admir'st thou, what transports thee so,
An outside? fair no doubt, and worthy well
Thy cherishing, thy honoring, and thy love,
Not thy subjection: weigh with her thyself;
Then value: Oft-times nothing profits more
Than self-esteem, grounded on just and right
Well manag'd; of that skill the more thou know'st,
The more she will acknowledge thee her Head,[4]
And to realities yield all her shows;
Made so adorn for thy delight the more,
So awful, that with honor thou may'st love
Thy mate, who sees when thou art seen least wise.
But if the sense of touch whereby mankind
Is propagated seem such dear delight
Beyond all other, think the same voutsaf't
To Cattle and each Beast; which would not be
To them made common and divulg'd, if aught
Therein enjoy'd were worthy to subdue
The Soul of Man, or passion in him move.
What higher in her society thou find'st
Attractive, human, rational, love still;
In loving thou dost well, in passion not,
Wherein true Love consists not; Love refines
The thoughts, and heart enlarges, hath his seat

4. Alludes to 1 Corinthians 11.3: "The head of every man is Christ; and the head of the woman is the man; and the head of Christ is God."

In Reason, and is judicious, is the scale[5]
By which to heav'nly Love thou may'st ascend,
Not sunk in carnal pleasure, for which cause
Among the Beasts no Mate for thee was found.[6]
To whom thus half abash't *Adam* repli'd.[7]
Neither her out-side form'd so fair, nor aught
In procreation common to all kinds
(Though higher of the genial° Bed by far, *nuptial*
And with mysterious reverence I deem)
So much delights me, as those graceful acts,
Those thousand decencies that daily flow
From all her words and actions, mixt with Love
And sweet compliance, which declare unfeign'd
Union of Mind, or in us both one Soul;
Harmony to behold in wedded pair
More grateful than harmonious sound to the ear.
Yet these subject not; I to thee disclose
What inward thence I feel, not therefore foil'd,° *overcome*
Who meet with various objects, from the sense
Variously representing; yet still free
Approve the best, and follow what I approve.
To Love thou blam'st me not, for Love thou say'st
Leads up to Heav'n, is both the way and guide;
Bear with me then, if lawful what I ask;
Love not the heav'nly Spirits, and how thir Love
Express they, by looks only, or do they mix
Irradiance, virtual or immediate touch?
To whom the Angel with a smile that glow'd
Celestial rosy red, Love's proper hue,
Answer'd. Let it suffice thee that thou know'st
Us happy, and without Love no happiness.
Whatever pure thou in the body enjoy'st
(And pure thou wert created) we enjoy
In eminence, and obstacle find none
Of membrance, joint, or limb, exclusive bars:
Easier than Air with Air, if Spirits embrace,
Total they mix, Union of Pure with Pure
Desiring; nor restrain'd conveyance need
As Flesh to mix with Flesh, or Soul with Soul.
But I can now no more; the parting Sun
Beyond the Earth's green Cape and verdant Isles

5. The Neoplatonic ladder of love.

6. Raphael here expounds the very familiar Neoplatonic distinction between divine or celestial love, human or terrestrial love, and bestial love. The first (Milton's "heavenly love") is the love of the contemplative, belonging to mind alone. The second ("true love") is the force that drives humans to propagate the earthly image of divine beauty but may also, in its ideal form, lead them to the first. The third ("sunk . . . pleasure") is experienced by humans who stoop to debauchery.

7. The conversation of Raphael and Adam does in some respects resemble a debate between Heavenly Love and Human Love in which the angel/human distinction is intensified into an antithesis.

Hesperian sets, my Signal to depart.[8]
Be strong, live happy, and love, but first of all
Him whom to love is to obey, and keep
His great command; take heed lest Passion sway
Thy Judgment to do aught, which else free Will
Would not admit; thine and of all thy Sons
The weal or woe in thee is plac't; beware.
I in thy persevering shall rejoice,
And all the Blest: stand fast; to stand or fall
Free in thine own Arbitrement it lies.
Perfet within, no outward aid require;
And all temptation to transgress repel.
  So saying, he arose; whom *Adam* thus
Follow'd with benediction. Since to part,
Go heavenly Guest, Ethereal Messenger,
Sent from whose sovran goodness I adore.
Gentle to me and affable hath been
Thy condescension, and shall be honor'd ever
With grateful Memory: thou to mankind
Be good and friendly still, and oft return.
  So parted they, the Angel up to Heav'n
From the thick shade, and *Adam* to his Bow'r.

The End of the Eighth Book.

Book 9

The Argument

Satan *having compast the Earth, with meditated guile returns as a mist by Night into Paradise, enters into the Serpent sleeping.* Adam *and* Eve *in the Morning go forth to thir labors, which* Eve *proposes to divide in several places, each laboring apart:* Adam *consents not, alleging the danger, lest that Enemy, of whom they were forewarn'd, should attempt her found alone:* Eve *loath to be thought not circumspect or firm enough, urges her going apart, the rather desirous to make trial of her strength;* Adam *at last yields: The Serpent finds her alone; his subtle approach, first gazing, then speaking, with much flattery extolling* Eve *above all other Creatures.* Eve *wond'ring to hear the Serpent speak, asks how he attain'd to human speech and such understanding not till now; the Serpent answers, that by tasting of a certain Tree in the Garden he attain'd both to Speech and Reason, till then void of both:* Eve *requires him to bring her to that Tree, and finds it to be the Tree of Knowledge forbidden: The Serpent now grown bolder, with many wiles and arguments induces her at length to eat; she pleas'd with the taste deliberates awhile whether to impart thereof to* Adam *or not, at last brings him of the Fruit, relates what persuaded her to eat thereof:* Adam *at first amaz'd, but perceiving her lost, resolves through vehemence*[1] *of love to perish with her; and extenuating*[2] *the trespass, eats also of the Fruit: The effects thereof in them both; they seek to cover thir nakedness; then fall to variance and accusation of one another.*

8. Where the sun sets "beneath the Azores." Here the "green Cape" is Cape Verde, and the "verdant Isles" are the Cape Verde Islands.

1. The root meaning of Latin "vehementia" is mindlessness.
2. Carrying further, drawing out.

No more of talk where God or Angel Guest
With Man, as with his Friend, familiar us'd
To sit indulgent, and with him partake
Rural repast, permitting him the while
Venial° discourse unblam'd: I now must change *permissible*
Those Notes to Tragic; foul distrust, and breach
Disloyal on the part of Man, revolt,
And disobedience: On the part of Heav'n
Now alienated, distance and distaste,
Anger and just rebuke, and judgment giv'n,
That brought into this World a world of woe,
Sin and her shadow Death, and Misery
Death's Harbinger: Sad task, yet argument
Not less but more Heroic than the wrath
Of stern *Achilles* on his Foe pursu'd
Thrice Fugitive about *Troy* Wall; or rage
Of *Turnus* for *Lavinia* disespous'd,
Or *Neptune's* ire or *Juno's*, that so long
Perplex'd the *Greek* and *Cytherea's* Son;[3]
If answerable° style I can obtain *equal, accountable*
Of my Celestial Patroness,[4] who deigns
Her nightly visitation unimplor'd,
And dictates to me slumb'ring, or inspires
Easy my unpremeditated Verse:
Since first this Subject for Heroic Song
Pleas'd me long choosing, and beginning late;
Not sedulous by Nature to indite
Wars, hitherto the only Argument
Heroic deem'd, chief maistry to dissect
With long and tedious havoc fabl'd Knights
In Battles feign'd; the better fortitude
Of Patience and Heroic Martyrdom
Unsung; or to describe Races and Games,
Or tilting Furniture, emblazon'd Shields,
Impreses[5] quaint, Caparisons[6] and Steeds;
Bases and tinsel Trappings, gorgeous Knights
At Joust and Tournament; then marshall'd Feast
Serv'd up in Hall with Sewers,° and Seneschals;° *waiters / stewards*
The skill of Artifice or Office mean,

3. Achilles is "stern" in his "wrath" because he refused any covenant with Hector, and Turnus dies fighting Aeneas for the hand of Lavinia, whereas Messiah, more heroically, is not implacable in his anger. He issued his sole commandment "sternly" (8.333); but when it is disobeyed, he works for reconciliation. Similarly, God's anger is distinguished from "Neptune's ire" and "Juno's" (which merely "perplexed" Odysseus and Aeneas) in that it is expressed in justice rather than in victimization.

4. The heavenly Muse, Urania. Both ancient and modern epics had always had war, or at least fighting, as a principal ingredient. (So has *Paradise Lost*, in the first half of the poem; but in the second half this subject is transcended.) Milton now glances unfavorably at the typical matter of the romantic epic.

5. Heraldic devices, often with accompanying mottoes.

6. Ornamented coverings spread over the saddle of a horse.

Not that which justly gives Heroic name
To Person or to Poem.[7] Mee of these
Nor skill'd nor studious, higher Argument
Remains, sufficient of itself to raise
That name,[8] unless an age too late, or cold
Climate, or Years damp my intended wing
Deprest; and much they may, if all be mine,
  Not Hers who brings it nightly to my Ear.
The Sun was sunk, and after him the Star
Of *Hesperus*,° whose Office is to bring *the planet Venus*
Twilight upon the Earth, short Arbiter
Twixt Day and Night, and now from end to end
Night's Hemisphere had veil'd the Horizon round:
When *Satan* who late fled before the threats
Of *Gabriel* out of *Eden*,[9] now improv'd° *intensified*
In meditated fraud and malice, bent
On Man's destruction, maugre what might hap
Of heavier on himself,[1] fearless return'd.
By Night he fled, and at Midnight return'd
From compassing the Earth, cautious of day,
Since *Uriel* Regent of the Sun descri'd
His entrance, and forewarn'd the Cherubim
That kept thir watch; thence full of anguish driv'n,
The space of seven continu'd Nights he rode
With darkness, thrice the Equinoctial Line
He circl'd, four times cross'd the Car of Night
From Pole to Pole, traversing each Colure;[2]
On th'eighth return'd, and on the Coast averse
From entrance or Cherubic Watch, by stealth
Found unsuspected way. There was a place,
Now not, though Sin, not Time, first wrought the change,
Where *Tigris* at the foot of Paradise
Into a Gulf shot under ground, till part
Rose up a Fountain by the Tree of Life;
In with the River sunk, and with it rose
Satan involv'd in rising Mist, then sought
Where to lie hid; Sea he had searcht and Land
From *Eden* over *Pontus*, and the Pool
Maeotis, up beyond the River *Ob*;[3]
Downward as far Antarctic; and in length

7. Artifice implies mechanic or applied art. It is beneath the dignity of epic to teach etiquette and social ceremony and heraldry.
8. The name of epic.
9. I.e., at the end of Book 4, a week earlier.
1. Despite the danger of heavier punishment.
2. By keeping to earth's shadow, Satan contrives to experience a whole week of darkness. The two colures were great circles, intersecting at right angles at the poles and dividing the equinoctial circle (the equator) into four equal parts.
3. In his north-south circles, Satan passed Pontus (the Black Sea), the "pool / Maeotis" (the Sea of Azov), and the Siberian River Ob, which flows north into the Gulf of Ob and from there into the Arctic Ocean.

West from *Orontes* to the Ocean barr'd
At *Darien,* thence to the Land where flows
Ganges and *Indus:*[4] thus the Orb he roam'd
With narrow search; and with inspection deep
Consider'd every Creature, which of all
Most opportune might serve his Wiles, and found
The Serpent subtlest Beast of all the Field.[5]
Him after long debate, irresolute° *undecided*
Of thoughts revolv'd, his final sentence° chose *judgment*
Fit Vessel, fittest Imp° of fraud, in whom *offshoot*
To enter, and his dark suggestions hide
From sharpest sight: for in the wily Snake,
Whatever sleights none would suspicious mark,
As from his wit and native subtlety
Proceeding, which in other Beasts observ'd
Doubt° might beget of Diabolic pow'r *suspicion*
Active within beyond the sense of brute.
Thus he resolv'd, but first from inward grief
His bursting passion into plaints thus pour'd:
  O Earth, how like to Heav'n, if not preferr'd
More justly, Seat worthier of Gods, as built
With second thoughts, reforming what was old!
For what God after better worse would build?
Terrestrial Heav'n, danc't round by other Heav'ns
That shine, yet bear thir bright officious Lamps,
Light above Light, for thee alone, as seems,
In thee concentring all thir precious beams
Of sacred influence:[6] As God in Heav'n
Is Centre, yet extends to all, so thou
Centring receiv'st from all those Orbs; in thee,
Not in themselves, all thir known virtue appears
Productive in Herb, Plant, and nobler birth
Of Creatures animate with gradual life
Of Growth, Sense, Reason, all summ'd up in Man.[7]
With what delight could I have walkt thee round,
If I could joy in aught, sweet interchange
Of Hill and Valley, Rivers, Woods and Plains,
Now Land, now Sea, and Shores with Forest crown'd,
Rocks, Dens, and Caves; but I in none of these
Find place or refuge; and the more I see
Pleasures about me, so much more I feel
Torment within me, as from the hateful siege° *conflict*
Of contraries; all good to me becomes

4. In his westward circling of the equinoctial line, he crossed the Syrian river Orontes, then the Pacific ("peaceful") "Ocean barred" by the Isthmus of Darien (Panama) and India.
5. See Genesis 3.1.
6. The case for an earth-centered universe, put at 8.86–114 by Raphael, is now put by Satan.
7. "Growth, sense, reason" are the activities of the vegetable, animal, and rational souls, respectively, in humans.

Bane,° and in Heav'n much worse would be my state. *poison*
But neither here seek I, no nor in Heav'n
To dwell, unless by maistring Heav'n's Supreme;
Nor hope to be myself less miserable
By what I seek, but others to make such
As I, though thereby worse to me redound:
For only in destroying I find ease
To my relentless thoughts; and him destroy'd,
Or won to what may work his utter loss,
For whom all this was made, all this will soon
Follow, as to him linkt in weal or woe,
In woe then: that destruction wide may range:[8]
To mee shall be the glory sole among
Th'infernal Powers, in one day to have marr'd
What he *Almight* styl'd, six Nights and Days
Continu'd making, and who knows how long
Before had been contriving, though perhaps
Not longer than since I in one Night freed
From servitude inglorious well nigh half
Th' Angelic Name, and thinner left the throng
Of his adorers: hee to be aveng'd,
And to repair his numbers thus impair'd,
Whether such virtue° spent of old now fail'd *power*
More Angels to Create, if they at least
Are his Created, or to spite us more,
Determin'd to advance into our room
A Creature form'd of Earth, and him endow,
Exalted from so base original,
With Heav'nly spoils, our spoils; What he decreed
He effected; Man he made, and for him built
Magnificent this World, and Earth his seat,
Him Lord pronounc'd, and, O indignity!
Subjected to his service Angel wings,
And flaming Ministers to watch and tend
Thir earthy Charge: Of these the vigilance
I dread, and to elude, thus wrapt in mist
Of midnight vapor glide obscure, and pry
In every Bush and Brake, where hap may find
The Serpent sleeping, in whose mazy folds
To hide me, and the dark intent I bring.
O foul descent! that I who erst contended
With Gods to sit the highest, am now constrain'd
Into a Beast, and mixt with bestial slime,
This essence to incarnate and imbrute,
That to the highth of Deity aspir'd;
But what will not Ambition and Revenge

8. The created cosmos will follow humans to destruction.

Descend to? who aspires must down as low
As high he soar'd, obnoxious° first or last *exposed*
To basest things. Revenge, at first though sweet,
Bitter ere long back on itself recoils;
Let it, I reck not, so it light well aim'd,
Since higher I fall short, on him who next
Provokes my envy, this new Favorite
Of Heav'n, this Man of Clay, Son of despite,
Whom us the more to spite his Maker rais'd
From dust: spite then with spite is best repaid.
So saying, through each Thicket Dank or Dry,
Like a black mist low creeping, he held on
His midnight search, where soonest he might find
The Serpent: him fast sleeping soon he found
In Labyrinth of many a round self-roll'd,
His head the midst, well stor'd with subtle wiles:
Not yet in horrid Shade or dismal Den,
Nor nocent° yet, but on the grassy Herb *harmful, guilty*
Fearless unfear'd he slept: in at his Mouth
The Devil enter'd, and his brutal sense,
In heart or head, possessing soon inspir'd
With act intelligential; but his sleep
Disturb'd not, waiting close° th' approach of Morn. *concealed*
Now whenas sacred Light began to dawn
In *Eden* on the humid Flow'rs, that breath'd
Thir morning incense, when all things that breathe,
From th' Earth's great Altar send up silent praise
To the Creator, and his Nostrils fill
With grateful Smell, forth came the human pair
And join'd thir vocal Worship to the Choir
Of Creatures wanting voice; that done, partake
The season, prime for sweetest Scents and Airs:
Then cómmune how that day they best may ply
Thir growing work: for much thir work outgrew
The hands' dispatch of two Gard'ning so wide.
And *Eve* first to her Husband thus began.
Adam, well may we labor still to dress
This Garden, still to tend Plant, Herb and Flow'r,
Our pleasant task enjoin'd, but till more hands
Aid us, the work under our labor grows,
Luxurious by restraint; what we by day
Lop overgrown, or prune, or prop, or bind,
One night or two with wanton growth derides
Tending to wild. Thou therefore now advise
Or hear what to my mind first thoughts present,
Let us divide our labors, thou where choice
Leads thee, or where most needs, whether to wind
The Woodbine round this Arbor, or direct
The clasping Ivy where to climb, while I
In yonder Spring of Roses intermixt

With Myrtle, find what to redress till Noon:
For while so near each other thus all day
Our task we choose, what wonder if so near
Looks intervene and smiles, or object new
Casual discourse draw on, which intermits
Our day's work brought to little, though begun
Early, and th' hour of Supper comes unearn'd.
　To whom mild answer *Adam* thus return'd.
Sole *Eve,* Associate sole, to me beyond
Compare above all living Creatures dear,
Well hast thou motion'd,° well thy thoughts imploy'd *proposed*
How we might best fulfil the work which here
God hath assign'd us, nor of me shalt pass
Unprais'd: for nothing lovelier can be found
In Woman, than to study household good,
And good works in her Husband to promote.
Yet not so strictly hath our Lord impos'd
Labor, as to debar us when we need
Refreshment, whether food, or talk between,
Food of the mind, or this sweet intercourse
Of looks and smiles, for smiles from Reason flow,
To brute deni'd, and are of Love the food,
Love not the lowest end of human life.
For not to irksome toil, but to delight
He made us, and delight to Reason join'd.
These paths and Bowers doubt not but our joint hands
Will keep from Wilderness with ease, as wide
As we need walk, till younger hands ere long
Assist us: But if much converse perhaps
Thee satiate, to short absence I could yield.
For solitude sometimes is best society,
And short retirement urges sweet return.
But other doubt possesses me, lest harm
Befall thee sever'd from me; for thou know'st
What hath been warn'd us, what malicious Foe
Envying our happiness, and of his own
Despairing, seeks to work us woe and shame
By sly assault; and somewhere nigh at hand
Watches, no doubt, with greedy hope to find
His wish and best advantage, us asunder,
Hopeless to circumvent us join'd, where each
To other speedy aid might lend at need;
Whether his first design be to withdraw
Our fealty from God, or to disturb
Conjugal Love, than which perhaps no bliss
Enjoy'd by us excites his envy more;
Or this, or worse,[9] leave not the faithful side

9. Whether this or worse (be his first design).

That gave thee being, still shades thee and protects.
The Wife, where danger or dishonor lurks,
Safest and seemliest by her Husband stays,
Who guards her, or with her the worst endures.
To whom the Virgin° Majesty of *Eve*, *chaste, innocent*
As one who loves, and some unkindness meets,
With sweet austere composure thus repli'd.
Offspring of Heav'n and Earth, and all Earth's Lord,
That such an Enemy we have, who seeks
Our ruin, both by thee inform'd I learn,
And from the parting Angel over-heard
As in a shady nook I stood behind,
Just then return'd at shut of Ev'ning Flow'rs.
But that thou shouldst my firmness therefore doubt
To God or thee, because we have a foe
May tempt it, I expected not to hear.
His violence thou fear'st not, being such,
As wee, not capable of death or pain,
Can either not receive, or can repel.
His fraud is then thy fear, which plain infers
Thy equal fear that my firm Faith and Love
Can by his fraud be shak'n or seduc't;
Thoughts, which how found they harbor in thy breast,
Adam, misthought of her to thee so dear?
To whom with healing words *Adam* repli'd.
Daughter of God and Man, immortal *Eve*,
For such thou art, from sin and blame entire:° *free*
Not diffident° of thee do I dissuade *mistrustful*
Thy absence from my sight, but to avoid
Th' attempt itself, intended by our Foe.
For hee who tempts, though in vain, at least asperses° *falsely charges*
The tempted with dishonor foul, suppos'd
Not incorruptible of Faith, not proof
Against temptation: thou thyself with scorn
And anger wouldst resent the offer'd wrong,
Though ineffectual found: misdeem not then,
If such affront I labor to avert
From thee alone, which on us both at once
The Enemy, though bold, will hardly dare,
Or daring, first on mee th' assault shall light.
Nor thou his malice and false guile contemn;
Subtle he needs must be, who could seduce
Angels, nor think superfluous others' aid.
I from the influence of thy looks receive
Access° in every Virtue, in thy sight *increase*
More wise, more watchful, stronger, if need were
Of outward strength; while shame, thou looking on,
Shame to be overcome or over-reacht
Would utmost vigor raise, and rais'd unite.

Why shouldst not thou like sense within thee feel
When I am present, and thy trial choose
With me, best witness of thy Virtue tri'd.
  So spake domestic *Adam* in his care
And Matrimonial Love; but *Eve,* who thought
Less° attribúted to her Faith sincere, *too little*
Thus her reply with accent sweet renew'd.
  If this be our condition, thus to dwell
In narrow circuit strait'n'd by a Foe,
Subtle or violent, we not endu'd
Single with like defense, wherever met,
How are we happy, still in fear of harm?
But harm precedes not sin: only our Foe
Tempting affronts us with his foul esteem
Of our integrity: his foul esteem
Sticks no dishonor on our Front,° but turns *forehead*
Foul on himself; then wherefore shunn'd or fear'd
By us? who rather double honor gain
From his surmise prov'd false, find peace within,
Favor from Heav'n, our witness from th' event.
And what is Faith, Love, Virtue unassay'd
Alone, without exterior help sustain'd?
Let us not then suspect our happy State
Left so imperfet by the Maker wise,
As not secure to single or combin'd.
Frail is our happiness, if this be so,
And *Eden* were no Eden[1] thus expos'd.
  To whom thus Adam fervently repli'd.
O Woman, best are all things as the will
Of God ordain'd them, his creating hand
Nothing imperfet or deficient left
Of all that he Created, much less Man,
Or aught that might his happy State secure,
Secure from outward force; within himself
The danger lies, yet lies within his power:
Against his will he can receive no harm.
But God left free the Will, for what obeys
Reason, is free, and Reason he made right,
But bid her well beware, and still erect,[2]
Lest by some fair appearing good surpris'd
She dictate false, and misinform the Will
To do what God expressly hath forbid.
Not then mistrust, but tender love enjoins,
That I should mind thee oft, and mind thou me.
Firm we subsist, yet possible to swerve,
Since Reason not impossibly may meet

1. I.e., no pleasure, the literal Hebrew meaning of "Eden."

2. Always attentive, but also with a glance at upright.

Some specious object by the Foe suborn'd,
And fall into deception unaware,
Not keeping strictest watch, as she was warn'd.
Seek not temptation then, which to avoid
Were better, and most likely if from mee
Thou sever not: Trial will come unsought.
Wouldst thou approve° thy constancy, approve *demonstrate*
First thy obedience; th' other who can know,
Not seeing thee attempted, who attest?
But if thou think, trial unsought may find
Us both securer° than thus warn'd thou seem'st, *more careless*
Go; for thy stay, not free, absents thee more;
Go in thy native innocence, rely
On what thou hast of virtue, summon all,
For God towards thee hath done his part, do thine.
  So spake the Patriarch of Mankind, but *Eve*
Persisted, yet submiss, though last, repli'd.
  With thy permission then, and thus forewarn'd
Chiefly by what thy own last reasoning words
Touch'd only, that our trial, when least sought,
May find us both perhaps far less prepar'd,
The willinger I go, nor much expect
A Foe so proud will first the weaker seek;
So bent, the more shall shame him his repulse.
Thus saying, from her Husband's hand her hand
Soft she withdrew, and like a Wood-Nymph light,
Oread or *Dryad*, or of *Delia's* Train,[3]
Betook her to the Groves, but *Delia's* self
In gait surpass'd and Goddess-like deport,
Though not as shee with Bow and Quiver arm'd,
But with such Gard'ning Tools as Art yet rude,
Guiltless° of fire had form'd, or Angels brought.[4] *innocent, ignorant*
To Pales, or Pomona, thus adorn'd,
Likest she seem'd, Pomona when she fled
Vertumnus, or to *Ceres* in her Prime,
Yet Virgin of *Proserpina* from *Jove*.[5]
Her long and ardent look his Eye pursu'd
Delighted, but desiring more her stay.
Oft he to her his charge of quick return
Repeated, shee to him as oft engag'd
To be return'd by Noon amid the Bow'r,
And all things in best order to invite
Noontide repast, or Afternoon's repose.

3. Oreads were mountain nymphs, such as attended on Diana; dryads were wood nymphs. Neither class of nymphs was immortal.

4. Only as a result of the Fall did it become necessary for humans to have some means of warming themselves. There may also be an allusion to the fire stolen from heaven by Prometheus.

5. Pales was the Roman goddess of pastures; Pomona was the nymph or goddess of fruit trees, seduced by the disguised Vertumnus; Ceres was the goddess of corn and agriculture who bore Proserpina to Jove.

O much deceiv'd, much failing, hapless *Eve*,
Of thy presum'd return! event perverse!
Thou never from that hour in Paradise
Found'st either sweet repast, or sound repose;
Such ambush hid among sweet Flow'rs and Shades
Waited with hellish rancor imminent
To intercept thy way, or send thee back
Despoil'd of Innocence, of Faith, of Bliss.
For now, and since first break of dawn the Fiend,
Mere° Serpent in appearance, forth was come, *plain*
And on his Quest, where likeliest he might find
The only two of Mankind, but in them
The whole included Race, his purpos'd prey.
In Bow'r and Field he sought, where any tuft
Of Grove or Garden-Plot more pleasant lay,
Thir tendance° or Plantation for delight, *object of care*
By Fountain or by shady Rivulet,
He sought them both, but wish'd his hap° might find *chance*
Eve separate, he wish'd, but not with hope
Of what so seldom chanc'd, when to his wish,
Beyond his hope, *Eve* separate he spies,
Veil'd in a Cloud of Fragrance, where she stood,
Half spi'd, so thick the Roses bushing round
About her glow'd, oft stooping to support
Each Flow'r of slender stalk, whose head though gay
Carnation, Purple, Azure, or speckt with Gold,
Hung drooping unsustain'd, them she upstays
Gently with Myrtle band, mindless the while,
Herself, though fairest unsupported Flow'r,
From her best prop so far, and storm so nigh.[6]
Nearer he drew, and many a walk travers'd
Of stateliest Covert, Cedar, Pine, or Palm,
Then voluble and bold, now hid, now seen
Among thick-wov'n Arborets and Flow'rs
Imborder'd on each Bank, the hand° of *Eve:* *handiwork*
Spot more delicious than those Gardens feign'd
Or of reviv'd *Adonis*, or renown'd
Alcinoüs, host of old *Laertes'* Son,
Or that, not Mystic, where the Sapient King
Held dalliance with his fair *Egyptian* Spouse.[7]
Much hee the Place admir'd, the Person more.
As one who long in populous City pent,
Where Houses thick and Sewers annoy the Air,

6. See 4.270, page 1797, where Proserpina (and by implication Eve) was "Herself a fairer flower" when she was carried off by the king of hell.

7. "The sapient king" was Solomon (*Song of Solomon* 6.2). Milton alludes to Spenser's addition to the myth of Adonis, that Venus keeps Adonis hidden in a secret garden (*The Faerie Queene* 3.6). "Laertes' son" was Odysseus; much-traveled as he was, he marveled when he saw the Garden of Alcinoüs (Homer, *Odyssey* 7).

Forth issuing on a Summer's Morn to breathe
Among the pleasant Villages and Farms
Adjoin'd, from each thing met conceives delight,
The smell of Grain, or tedded° Grass, or Kine,° *mown / cows*
Or Dairy, each rural sight, each rural sound;
If chance with Nymphlike step fair Virgin pass,
What pleasing seem'd, for her now pleases more,
She most, and in her look sums all Delight.
Such Pleasure took the Serpent to behold
This Flow'ry Plat,° the sweet recess of *Eve* *piece of ground*
Thus early, thus alone; her Heav'nly form
Angelic, but more soft, and Feminine,
Her graceful Innocence, her every Air
Of gesture or least action overaw'd
His Malice, and with rapine sweet bereav'd
His fierceness of the fierce intent it brought:
That space the Evil one abstracted stood
From his own evil, and for the time remain'd
Stupidly good, of enmity disarm'd,
Of guile, of hate, of envy, of revenge;
But the hot Hell that always in him burns,
Though in mid Heav'n, soon ended his delight,
And tortures him now more, the more he sees
Of pleasure not for him ordain'd: then soon
Fierce hate he recollects, and all his thoughts
Of mischief, gratulating,° thus excites. *rejoicing*
Thoughts, whither have ye led me, with what sweet
Compulsion thus transported to forget
What hither brought us, hate, not love, nor hope
Of Paradise for Hell, hope here to taste
Of pleasure, but all pleasure to destroy,
Save what is in destroying, other joy
To me is lost. Then let me not let pass
Occasion which now smiles, behold alone
The Woman, opportune° to all attempts, *exposed*
Her Husband, for I view far round, not nigh,
Whose higher intellectual more I shun,
And strength, of courage haughty, and of limb
Heroic built, though of terrestrial mould,° *formed of earth*
Foe not informidable, exempt from wound,
I not; so much hath Hell debas'd, and pain
Infeebl'd me, to what I was in Heav'n.
Shee fair, divinely fair, fit Love for Gods,
Not terrible, though terror be in Love
And beauty, not approacht by stronger hate,
Hate stronger, under show of Love well feign'd,
The way which to her ruin now I tend.
So spake the Enemy of Mankind, enclos'd
In Serpent, Inmate bad, and toward *Eve*

Address'd his way, not with indented wave,
Prone on the ground, as since, but on his rear,
Circular base of rising folds, that tow'r'd
Fold above fold a surging Maze, his Head
Crested aloft, and Carbuncle his Eyes;[8]
With burnisht Neck of verdant Gold, erect
Amidst his circling Spires,° that on the grass — *coils*
Floated redundant:° pleasing was his shape, — *abundant to excess*
And lovely, never since of Serpent kind
Lovelier, not those that in *Illyria* chang'd
Hermione and *Cadmus*, or the God
In *Epidaurus*;[9] nor to which transform'd
Ammonian Jove, or *Capitoline* was seen,
Hee with *Olympias*, this with her who bore
Scipio the highth of Rome.[1] With tract oblique
At first, as one who sought access, but fear'd
To interrupt, side-long he works his way.
As when a Ship by skilful Steersman wrought
Nigh River's mouth or Foreland, where the Wind
Veers oft, as oft so steers, and shifts her Sail;
So varied hee, and of his tortuous Train
Curl'd many a wanton wreath in sight of *Eve*,
To lure her Eye; shee busied heard the sound
Of rustling Leaves, but minded not, as us'd
To such disport before her through the Field,
From every Beast, more duteous at her call,
Than at *Circean* call the Herd disguis'd.[2]
Hee bolder now, uncall'd before her stood;
But as in gaze admiring: Oft he bow'd
His turret Crest, and sleek enamell'd Neck,
Fawning, and lick'd the ground whereon she trod.
His gentle dumb expression turn'd at length
The Eye of *Eve* to mark his play; he glad
Of her attention gain'd, with Serpent Tongue
Organic, or impulse of vocal Air,
His fraudulent temptation thus began.
  Wonder not, sovran Mistress, if perhaps
Thou canst, who are sole Wonder, much less arm
Thy looks, the Heav'n of mildness, with disdain,
Displeas'd that I approach thee thus, and gaze
Insatiate, I thus single, nor have fear'd
Thy awful brow, more awful thus retir'd.

8. "Carbuncle" or reddish eyes denoted rage.

9. Cadmus was turned into a serpent first; only after he had embraced his wife Hermione (Harmonia) in his new form did she, too, change, (Ovid, *Metamorphoses* 4.572–603). Aesculapius, the god of healing, once changed into a serpent to help the Romans in that form (Ovid, *Metamorphoses* 15.626–744).

1. Jupiter Ammon, the "Lybian Jove," as a serpent mated with Olympias to father Alexander the Great, just as the Roman Jupiter, Capitolinus, took the form of a snake to father the great general Scipio.

2. Homer's Circe changed men into beasts who surprised Odysseus's company by fawning on them like dogs (*Odyssey* 10.212–19).

Fairest resemblance of thy Maker fair,
Thee all things living gaze on, all things thine
By gift, and thy Celestial Beauty adore
With ravishment beheld, there best beheld
Where universally admir'd: but here
In this enclosure wild, these Beasts among,
Beholders rude, and shallow to discern
Half what in thee is fair, one man except,
Who sees thee? (and what is one?) who shouldst be seen
A Goddess among Gods, ador'd and serv'd
By Angels numberless, thy daily Train.
So gloz'd° the Tempter, and his Proem° tun'd; *flattered / prelude*
Into the Heart of *Eve* his words made way,
Though at the voice much marvelling; at length
Not unamaz'd she thus in answer spake.
What may this mean? Language of Man pronounc't
By Tongue of Brute, and human sense exprest?[3]
The first at least of these I thought deni'd
To Beasts, whom God on thir Creation-Day
Created mute to all articulate sound;
The latter I demur,° for in thir looks *hesitate about*
Much reason, and in thir actions oft appears.
Thee, Serpent, subtlest beast of all the field
I knew, but not with human voice endu'd;
Redouble then this miracle, and say,
How cam'st thou speakable of mute,[4] and how
To me so friendly grown above the rest
Of brutal kind, that daily are in sight?
Say, for such wonder claims attention due.
To whom the guileful Tempter thus repli'd.
Empress of this fair World, resplendent *Eve*,
Easy to mee it is to tell thee all
What thou command'st and right thou should'st be obey'd:
I was at first as other Beasts that graze
The trodden Herb, of abject° thoughts and low, *mean-spirited*
As was my food, nor aught but food discern'd
Or Sex, and apprehended nothing high:
Till on a day roving the field, I chanc'd
A goodly Tree far distant to behold
Loaden with fruit of fairest colors mixt,
Ruddy and Gold: I nearer drew to gaze;
When from the boughs a savory odor blown,
Grateful to appetite, more pleas'd my sense
Than smell of sweetest Fennel, or the Teats
Of Ewe or Goat dropping with Milk at Ev'n,

3. Milton is unusually favorable to Eve in making her ask the serpent how it came by its voice. The Eve of Scriptural exegesis, by contrast, is carried away by the words and makes no inquiry into their source.
4. How did you become capable of speech from being dumb?

Unsuckt of Lamb or Kid, that tend thir play.
To satisfy the sharp desire I had
Of tasting those fair Apples, I resolv'd
Not to defer; hunger and thirst at once,
Powerful persuaders, quick'n'd at the scent
Of that alluring fruit, urg'd me so keen.
About the mossy Trunk I wound me soon,
For high from ground the branches would require
Thy utmost reach or *Adam's:* Round the Tree
All other Beasts that saw, with like desire
Longing and envying stood, but could not reach.
Amid the Tree now got, where plenty hung
Tempting so nigh, to pluck and eat my fill
I spar'd not, for such pleasure till that hour
At Feed or Fountain never had I found.
Sated at length, ere long I might perceive
Strange alteration in me, to degree
Of Reason in my inward Powers, and Speech
Wanted not long, though to this shape retain'd.
Thenceforth to Speculations high or deep
I turn'd my thoughts, and with capacious mind
Consider'd all things visible in Heav'n,
Or Earth, or Middle, all things fair and good;
But all that fair and good in thy Divine
Semblance, and in thy Beauty's heav'nly Ray
United I beheld; no Fair° to thine — *beauty*
Equivalent or second, which compell'd
Mee thus, though importune perhaps, to come
And gaze, and worship thee of right declar'd
Sovran of Creatures, universal Dame.
So talk'd the spirited[5] sly Snake; and *Eve,*
Yet more amaz'd unwary thus repli'd.
Serpent, thy overpraising leaves in doubt
The virtue° of that Fruit, in thee first prov'd: — *power*
But say, where grows the Tree, from hence how far?
For many are the Trees of God that grow
In Paradise, and various, yet unknown
To us, in such abundance lies our choice,
As leaves a greater store of Fruit untoucht,
Still hanging incorruptible, till men
Grow up to thir provision, and more hands
Help to disburden Nature of her Birth.
To whom the wily Adder, blithe and glad.
Empress, the way is ready, and not long,
Beyond a row of Myrtles, on a Flat,
Fast by a Fountain, one small Thicket past

5. Endowed with an animating spirit, stirred up; also energetic, enterprising, possessed by a spirit.

Of blowing° Myrrh and Balm; if thou accept *blooming*
My conduct,° I can bring thee thither soon. *guidance*
Lead then, said Eve. Hee leading swiftly roll'd
In tangles, and made intricate seem straight,
To mischief swift. Hope elevates, and joy
Bright'ns his Crest, as when a wand'ring Fire,
Compact° of unctuous vapor, which the Night *made up*
Condenses, and the cold invirons round,
Kindl'd through agitation to a Flame,
Which oft, they say, some evil Spirit attends,
Hovering and blazing with delusive Light,
Misleads th' amaz'd Night-wanderer from his way
To Bogs and Mires, and oft through Pond or Pool,
There swallow'd up and lost, from succor far.
So glister'd the dire Snake, and into fraud
Led *Eve* our credulous Mother, to the Tree
Of prohibition, root of all our woe;
Which when she saw, thus to her guide she spake.
Serpent, we might have spar'd our coming hither,
Fruitless to mee, though Fruit be here to excess,
The credit of whose virtue rest with thee,
Wondrous indeed, if cause of such effects.
But of this Tree we may not taste nor touch;
God so commanded, and left that Command
Sole Daughter of his voice;[6] the rest, we live
Law to ourselves, our Reason is our Law.
To whom the Tempter guilefully repli'd.
Indeed? hath God then said that of the Fruit
Of all these Garden Trees ye shall not eat,
Yet Lords declar'd of all in Earth or Air?[7]
To whom thus *Eve* yet sinless. Of the Fruit
Of each Tree in the Garden we may eat,
But of the Fruit of this fair Tree amidst
The Garden, God hath said, Ye shall not eat
Thereof, nor shall ye touch it, lest ye die.
She scarce had said, though brief, when now more bold
The Tempter, but with show of Zeal and Love
To Man, and indignation at his wrong,
New part puts on, and as to passion mov'd,
Fluctuates disturb'd, yet comely, and in act
Rais'd, as of some great matter to begin.
As when of old some Orator renown'd
In *Athens* or free *Rome,* where Eloquence
Flourish'd, since mute, to some great cause addrest,
Stood in himself collected, while each part,
Motion, each act won audience ere the tongue,

6. A Hebraism for "voice sent from heaven."

7. Lines 655–58 closely follow Genesis 3.1.

Sometimes in highth began, as no delay
Of Preface brooking through his Zeal of Right.[8]
So standing, moving, or to highth upgrown
The Tempter all impassion'd thus began.
  O Sacred, Wise, and Wisdom-giving Plant,
Mother of Science,° Now I feel thy Power *knowledge*
Within me clear, not only to discern
Things in thir Causes, but to trace the ways
Of highest Agents, deem'd however wise.
Queen of this Universe, do not believe
Those rigid threats of Death; ye shall not Die:
How should ye? by the Fruit? it gives you Life
To° Knowledge: By the Threat'ner? look on mee, *in addition to*
Mee who have touch'd and tasted, yet both live,
And life more perfet have attain'd than Fate
Meant mee, by vent'ring higher than my Lot.
Shall that be shut to Man, which to the Beast
Is open? or will God incense his ire
For such a petty Trespass, and not praise
Rather your dauntless virtue, whom the pain
Of Death denounc't, whatever thing Death be,
Deterr'd not from achieving what might lead
To happier life, knowledge of Good and Evil;
Of good, how just? of evil, if what is evil
Be real, why not known, since easier shunn'd?[9]
God therefore cannot hurt ye, and be just;
Not just, not God; not fear'd then, nor obey'd:
Your fear itself of Death removes the fear.
Why then was this forbid? Why but to awe,
Why but to keep ye low and ignorant,
His worshippers; he knows that in the day
Ye Eat thereof, your Eyes that seem so clear,
Yet are but dim, shall perfetly be then
Op'n'd and clear'd, and ye shall be as Gods,
Knowing both Good and Evil as they know.[1]
That ye should be as Gods, since I as Man,
Internal Man,[2] is but proportion meet,
I of brute human, thee of human Gods.
So ye shall die perhaps, by putting off
Human, to put on Gods, death to be wisht,
Though threat'n'd, which no worse than this can bring.[3]

8. This simile blends oratorical, theatrical, and theological meanings. Thus "part" means "part of the body," "dramatic role," and "moral act"; "motion" means "gesture," "mime" (or "puppet-show"), and "instigation, persuasive force, inclination"; "act" means "action," "performance of a play," and "the accomplished deed itself."

9. If the knowledge is good, how is it just to prohibit it? Here occurs the most egregious logical fallacy in speech. (For evil to be "shunned," it is not at all necessary that it should be "known" in the sense of being experienced.)

1. See Genesis 3.5.

2. The serpent's pretense is that his "inward powers" are human.

3. Satan offers a travesty of Christian mortification and death to sin; see Colossians 3.1–15: "ye have put off the old man with his deeds; And have put on the new man, which is renewed in knowledge after the image of him that created him."

And what are Gods that Man may not become
As they, participating° God-like food? *sharing*
The Gods are first, and that advantage use
On our belief, that all from them proceeds;
I question it, for this fair Earth I see,
Warm'd by the Sun, producing every kind,
Them nothing: If they° all things, who enclos'd *if they produce*
Knowledge of Good and Evil in this Tree,
That who so eats thereof, forthwith attains
Wisdom without their leave? and wherein lies
Th' offense, that Man should thus attain to know?
What can your knowledge hurt him, or this Tree
Impart against his will if all be his?
Or is it envy, and can envy dwell
In heav'nly breasts?[4] these, these and many more
Causes import° your need of this fair Fruit. *suggest*
Goddess humane, reach then, and freely taste.
He ended, and his words replete with guile
Into her heart too easy entrance won:
Fixt on the Fruit she gaz'd, which to behold
Might tempt alone, and in her ears the sound
Yet rung of his persuasive words, impregn'd° *impregnated*
With Reason, to her seeming, and with Truth;
Meanwhile the hour of Noon drew on, and wak'd
An eager appetite, rais'd by the smell
So savory of that Fruit, which with desire,
Inclinable now grown to touch or taste,
Solicited her longing eye;[5] yet first
Pausing a while, thus to herself she mus'd.
Great are thy Virtues, doubtless, best of Fruits,
Though kept from Man, and worthy to be admir'd,
Whose taste, too long forborne, at first assay
Gave elocution to the mute, and taught
The Tongue not made for Speech to speak thy praise:[6]
Thy praise hee also who forbids thy use,
Conceals not from us, naming thee the Tree
Of Knowledge, knowledge both of good and evil;
Forbids us then to taste, but his forbidding
Commends thee more, while it infers the good
By thee communicated, and our want:
For good unknown, sure is not had, or had
And yet unknown, is as not had at all.
In plain° then, what forbids he but to know, *plainly*
Forbids us good, forbids us to be wise?

4. See Virgil, *Aeneid* 1.11; Satan is inviting Eve to participate in a pagan epic, complete with machinery of jealous gods.
5. For lines 735–43, see Genesis 3.6.
6. Eve has trusted Satan's account of the fruit and consequently argues from false premises, such as its magical power.

Such prohibitions bind not. But if Death
Bind us with after-bands, what profits then
Our inward freedom? In the day we eat
Of this fair Fruit, our doom is, we shall die.
How dies the Serpent? hee hath eat'n and lives,
And knows, and speaks, and reasons, and discerns,
Irrational till then. For us alone
Was death invented? or to us deni'd
This intellectual food, for beasts reserv'd?
For Beasts it seems: yet that one Beast which first
Hath tasted, envies not, but bring with joy
The good befall'n him, Author unsuspect,[7]
Friendly to man, far from deceit or guile.
What fear I then, rather what know to fear[8]
Under this ignorance of Good and Evil,
Of God or Death, of Law or Penalty?
Here grows the Cure of all, this Fruit Divine,
Fair to the Eye, inviting to the Taste,
Of virtue° to make wise: what hinders then *power*
To reach, and feed at once both Body and Mind?
So saying, her rash hand in evil hour
Forth reaching to the Fruit, she pluck'd, she eat:° *ate*
Earth felt the wound, and Nature from her seat
Sighing through all her Works gave signs of woe,
That all was lost. Back to the Thicket slunk
The guilty Serpent, and well might, for *Eve*,
Intent now wholly on her taste, naught else
Regarded, such delight till then, as seem'd,
In Fruit she never tasted, whether true
Or fancied so, through expectation high
Of knowledge, nor was God-head from her thought.[9]
Greedily she ingorg'd without restraint,
And knew not eating Death:[1] Satiate at length,
And hight'n'd as with Wine, jocund and boon,° *jolly*
Thus to herself she pleasingly began.
O Sovran, virtuous, precious of all Trees
In Paradise, of operation blest
To Sapience,[2] hitherto obscur'd, infam'd,° *defamed*
And thy fair Fruit let hang, as to no end
Created; but henceforth my early care,
Not without Song, each Morning, and due praise
Shall tend thee, and the fertile burden ease
Of thy full branches offer'd free to all;

7. Eve means "informant not subject to suspicion."
8. What fear I, then—or rather (since I'm not allowed to know anything) what do I know that is to be feared?
9. She expected to achieve godhead.
1. She knew not that she was eating death; "she was unaware, while she ate death" or even "she 'knew'; not eating (immediate) death."
2. "Sapience" is derived from Latin *sapientia* (discernment, taste) and ultimately from *sapere* (to taste).

Till dieted by thee I grow mature
In knowledge, as the Gods who all things know;
Though others[3] envy what they cannot give;
For had the gift been theirs, it had not here
Thus grown. Experience, next to thee I owe,
Best guide; not following thee, I had remain'd
In ignorance, thou op'n'st Wisdom's way,
And giv'st access, though secret she retire.
And I perhaps am secret; Heav'n is high,
High and remote to see from thence distinct
Each thing on Earth; and other care perhaps
May have diverted from continual watch
Our great Forbidder, safe with all his Spies
About him. But to *Adam* in what sort
Shall I appear? shall I to him make known
As yet my change, and give him to partake
Full happiness with mee, or rather not.
But keep the odds of Knowledge in my power
Without Copartner? so to add what wants
In Female Sex, the more to draw his Love,
And render me more equal, and perhaps,
A thing not undesirable, sometime
Superior: for inferior who is free?
This may be well: but what if God have seen,
And Death ensue? then I shall be no more,
And *Adam* wedded to another *Eve*,
Shall live with her enjoying, I extinct;
A death to think. Confirm'd then I resolve,
Adam shall share with me in bliss or woe:
So dear I love him, that with him all deaths
I could endure, without him live no life.
So saying, from the Tree her step she turn'd,
But first low Reverence done, as to the power
That dwelt within, whose presence had infus'd
Into the plant sciential[4] sap, deriv'd
From Nectar, drink of Gods. *Adam* the while
Waiting desirous her return, had wove
Of choicest Flow'rs a Garland to adorn
Her Tresses, and her rural labors crown,
As Reapers oft are wont thir Harvest Queen.
Great joy he promis'd to his thoughts, and new
Solace in her return, so long delay'd;
Yet oft his heart, divine° of something ill, *prophet*
Misgave him; hee the falt'ring measure[5] felt;
And forth to meet her went, the way she took
That Morn when first they parted; by the Tree

3. I.e., God. Eve's language is now full of lapses in logic and evasions in theology.

4. Endowed with knowledge.

5. The rhythm of his own heart.

Of Knowledge he must pass; there he her met,
Scarce from the Tree returning; in her hand
A bough of fairest fruit that downy smil'd,
New gather'd, and ambrosial smell diffus'd.
To him she hasted, in her face excuse
Came Prologue, and Apology to prompt,[6]
Which with bland words at will she thus addrest.
  Hast thou not wonder'd, *Adam*, at my stay?
Thee I have misst, and thought it long, depriv'd
Thy presence, agony of love till now
Not felt, nor shall be twice, for never more
Mean I to try, what rash untri'd I sought,
The pain of absence from thy sight. But strange
Hath been the cause, and wonderful to hear:
This Tree is not as we are told, a Tree
Of danger tasted,° nor to evil unknown *if tasted*
Op'ning the way, but of Divine effect
To open Eyes, and make them Gods who taste;
And hath been tasted such: the Serpent wise,
Or not restrain'd as wee, or not obeying,
Hath eat'n of the fruit, and is become,
Not dead, as we are threat'n'd, but thenceforth
Endu'd with human voice and human sense,
Reasoning to admiration, and with mee
Persuasively hath so prevail'd, that I
Have also tasted, and have also found
Th' effects to correspond, opener mine Eyes,
Dim erst, dilated Spirits, ampler Heart,
And growing up to Godhead; which for thee
Chiefly I sought, without thee can despise.
For bliss, as thou hast part, to me is bliss,
Tedious, unshar'd with thee, and odious soon.
Thou therefore also taste, that equal Lot
May join us, equal Joy, as equal Love;
Lest thou not tasting, different degree[7]
Disjoin us, and I then too late renounce
Deity for thee, when Fate will not permit.
  Thus *Eve* with Count'nance blithe her story told;
But in her Cheek distemper[8] flushing glow'd.
On th' other side, *Adam*, soon as he heard
The fatal Trespass done by *Eve*, amaz'd,
Astonied° stood and Blank, while horror chill *stunned*
Ran through his veins, and all his joints relax'd;

6. The expression on Eve's face is visible in advance as she approaches and so is like the prologue-speaker of a play. But it also remains on her face as she speaks, to help out her words, and so is like the prompter of the play. The actor prompted is apology, i.e., justification or defense personified.

7. Differing position in the scale of creatures.

8. A disordered condition due to disturbance of the temperament of the bodily humors.

From his slack hand the Garland wreath'd for *Eve*,
Down dropp'd, and all the faded Roses shed:
Speechless he stood and pale, till thus at length
First to himself he inward silence broke.
   O fairest of Creation, last and best
Of all God's Works, Creature in whom excell'd
Whatever can to sight or thought be form'd,
Holy, divine, good, amiable, or sweet!
How art thou lost, how on a sudden lost,
Defac't, deflow'r'd, and now to death devote?° *given over*
Rather how hast thou yielded to transgress
The strict forbiddance, how to violate
The sacred Fruit forbidd'n! some cursed fraud
Of Enemy hath beguil'd thee, yet unknown,
And mee with thee hath ruin'd, for with thee
Certain my resolution is to Die;
How can I live without thee, how forgo
Thy sweet Converse and Love so dearly join'd,
To live again in these wild Woods forlorn?
Should God create another *Eve*, and I
Another Rib afford, yet loss of thee
Would never from my heart; no no, I feel
The Link of Nature draw me: Flesh of Flesh,
Bone of my Bone thou art, and from thy State
Mine never shall be parted, bliss or woe.
   So having said, as one from sad dismay
Recomforted, and after thoughts disturb'd
Submitting to what seem'd remediless,
Thus in calm mood his Words to *Eve* he turn'd.
   Bold deed thou hast presum'd, advent'rous *Eve*,
And peril great provok't, who thus hath dar'd
Had it been only coveting to Eye
That sacred Fruit, sacred° to abstinence, *devoted*
Much more to taste it under ban to touch.
But past who can recall, or done undo?
Not God Omnipotent, nor Fate; yet so
Perhaps thou shalt not Die, perhaps the Fact° *crime, deed*
Is not so heinous now, foretasted Fruit,
Profan'd first by the Serpent, by him first
Made common and unhallow'd ere our taste;
Nor yet on him found deadly, he yet lives,
Lives, as thou said'st, and gains to live as Man
Higher degree of Life, inducement strong
To us, as likely tasting to attain
Proportional ascent, which cannot be
But to be Gods, or Angels Demi-gods.
Nor can I think that God, Creator wise,
Though threat'ning, will in earnest so destroy
Us his prime Creatures, dignifi'd so high,

Set over all his Works, which in our Fall,
For us created, needs with us must fail,
Dependent made; so God shall uncreate,
Be frustrate, do, undo, and labor lose,
Not well conceiv'd of God, who though his Power
Creation could repeat, yet would be loath
Us to abolish, lest the Adversary
Triumph and say; Fickle their State whom God
Most Favors, who can please him long? Mee first
He ruin'd, now Mankind; whom will he next?
Matter of scorn, not to be given the Foe.
However I with thee have fixt my Lot,
Certain to undergo like doom;[9] if Death
Consort with thee, Death is to mee as Life;
So forcible within my heart I feel
The Bond of Nature draw me to my own,
My own in thee, for what thou art is mine;
Our State cannot be sever'd, we are one,
One Flesh; to lose thee were to lose myself.
So *Adam*, and thus *Eve* to him repli'd.
O glorious trial of exceeding Love,
Illustrious evidence, example high!
Ingaging me to emulate, but short
Of thy perfection, how shall I attain,
Adam, from whose dear side I boast me sprung,
And gladly of our Union hear thee speak,
One Heart, one Soul in both; whereof good proof
This day affords, declaring thee resolv'd,
Rather than Death or aught than Death more dread
Shall separate us, linkt in Love so dear,
To undergo with mee one Guilt, one Crime,
If any be, of tasting this fair Fruit,
Whose virtue, for of good still good proceeds,
Direct, or by occasion[1] hath presented
This happy trial of thy Love, which else
So eminently never had been known.
Were it I thought Death menac't would ensue
This my attempt, I would sustain alone
The worst, and not persuade thee, rather die
Deserted, than oblige° thee with a fact *make liable*
Pernicious to thy Peace, chiefly assur'd
Remarkably so late of thy so true,
So faithful Love unequall'd; but I feel
Far otherwise th' event,° nor Death, but Life *result*
Augmented, op'n'd Eyes, new Hopes, new Joys,
Taste so Divine, that what of sweet before

9. Three separate meanings are possible: judgment, irrevocable destiny, and death.

1. I.e., directly or indirectly.

Hath toucht my sense, flat seems to this, and harsh.
On my experience, *Adam,* freely taste,
And fear of Death deliver to the Winds.
So saying, she embrac'd him, and for joy
Tenderly wept, much won that he his Love
Had so ennobl'd, as of choice to incur
Divine displeasure for her sake, or Death.
In recompense (for such compliance bad
Such recompense best merits) from the bough
She gave him of that fair enticing Fruit
With liberal hand: he scrupl'd not to eat
Against his better knowledge, not deceiv'd,
But fondly overcome with Female charm.[2]
Earth trembl'd from her entrails, as again
In pangs, and Nature gave a second groan,
Sky low'r'd, and muttering Thunder, some sad drops
Wept at completing of the mortal Sin
Original;[3] while *Adam* took no thought,
Eating his fill, nor *Eve* to iterate
Her former trespass fear'd, the more to soothe
Him with her lov'd society, that now
As with new Wine intoxicated both
They swim in mirth, and fancy that they feel
Divinity within them breeding wings
Wherewith to scorn the Earth: but that false Fruit
Far other operation first display'd,
Carnal desire inflaming, hee on *Eve*
Began to cast lascivious Eyes, she him
As wantonly repaid; in Lust they burn:
Till *Adam* thus 'gan *Eve* to dalliance move.
Eve, now I see thou are exact of taste,
And elegant, of Sapience[4] no small part,
Since to each meaning savor[5] we apply,
And Palate call judicious; I the praise
Yield thee, so well this day thou hast purvey'd.° *provided*
Much pleasure we have lost, while we abstain'd
From this delightful Fruit, nor known till now
True relish, tasting; if such pleasure be
In things to us forbidden, it might be wish'd,
For this one Tree had been forbidden ten.
But come, so well refresh't, now let us play,
As meet is, after such delicious Fare;
For never did thy Beauty since the day

2. See 1 Timothy 2.14: "And Adam was not deceived, but the woman being deceived was in the transgression."
3. The only occurrence in *Paradise Lost* of the term "Original Sin." In his *De doctrina* (1.11), Milton defines Original Sin as "the sin which is common to all men, that which our first parents, and in them all their posterity committed, when, casting off their obedience to God, they tasted the fruit of the forbidden tree."
4. Wisdom, from Latin *sapere,* to taste.
5. Tastiness, understanding.

I saw thee first and wedded thee, adorn'd
With all perfections, so inflame my sense
With ardor to enjoy thee, fairer now
Than ever, bounty of this virtuous Tree.[6]
So said he, and forbore not glance or toy° *caress*
Of amorous intent, well understood
Of° *Eve*, whose Eye darted contagious Fire. *by*
Her hand he seiz'd, and to a shady bank,
Thick overhead with verdant roof imbowr'd
He led her nothing loath; Flow'rs were the Couch,
Pansies, and Violets, and Asphodel,
And Hyacinth, Earth's freshest softest lap.
There they thir fill of Love and Love's disport
Took largely, of thir mutual guilt the Seal,
The solace of thir sin, till dewy sleep
Oppress'd them, wearied with thir amorous play.
Soon as the force of that fallacious Fruit,
That with exhilarating vapor bland° *pleasing*
About thir spirits had play'd, and inmost powers
Made err, was now exhal'd, and grosser sleep
Bred of unkindly fumes,[7] with conscious dreams
Encumber'd, now had left them, up they rose
As from unrest, and each the other viewing,
Soon found thir Eyes how op'n'd, and thir minds
How dark'n'd;[8] innocence, that as a veil
Had shadow'd them from knowing ill, was gone,
Just confidence, and native righteousness,
And honor from about them, naked left
To guilty shame: hee cover'd, but his Robe
Uncover'd more. So rose the *Danite* strong
Herculean Samson from the Harlot-lap
Of *Philistean Dalilah*, and wak'd
Shorn of his strength, They destitute and bare
Of all thir virtue:[9] silent, and in face
Confounded long they sat, as struck'n mute,
Till *Adam*, though not less than *Eve* abasht,
At length gave utterance to these words constrain'd.
O *Eve*, in evil hour thou didst give ear
To that false Worm, of whomsoever taught
To counterfeit Man's voice, true in our Fall,
False in our promis'd Rising; since our Eyes
Op'n'd we find indeed, and find we know
Both Good and Evil, Good lost, and Evil got,

6. See Homer, *Iliad* 14, where Hera, bent on deceiving Zeus, comes to him wearing Aphrodite's belt and seems more charming to him than ever before.
7. Unnatural vapors or exhalations rising from the stomach to the brain.
8. See Genesis 3.7: "The eyes of them both were opened, and they knew that they were naked."
9. See Judges 16 for the story of Samson's betrayal by Delilah.

Bad Fruit of Knowledge, if this be to know,
Which leaves us naked thus, of Honor void,
Of Innocence, of Faith, of Purity,
Our wonted Ornaments now soil'd and stain'd,
And in our Faces evident the signs
Of foul concupiscence; whence evil store;
Even shame, the last of evils; of the first
Be sure then. How shall I behold the face
Henceforth of God or Angel, erst with joy
And rapture so oft beheld? those heav'nly shapes
Will dazzle now this earthly, with thir blaze
Insufferably bright. O might I here
In solitude live savage, in some glade
Obscur'd, where highest Woods impenetrable
To Star or Sun-light, spread thir umbrage broad,
And brown as Evening: Cover me ye Pines,
Ye Cedars, with innumerable boughs
Hide me, where I may never see them more.
But let us now, as in bad plight, devise
What best may for the present serve to hide
The Parts of each from other, that seem most
To shame obnoxious,° and unseemliest seen, *exposed*
Some Tree whose broad smooth Leaves together sew'd,
And girded on our loins, may cover round
Those middle parts, that this new comer, Shame,
There sit not, and reproach us as unclean.[1]
  So counsell'd hee, and both together went
Into the thickest Wood, there soon they chose
The Figtree,[2] not that kind for Fruit renown'd,
But such as at this day to *Indians* known
In *Malabar* or *Decan* spreads her Arms
Branching so broad and long, that in the ground
The bended Twigs take root, and Daughters grow
About the Mother Tree, a Pillar'd shade
High overarch't, and echoing Walks between;
There oft the *Indian* Herdsman shunning heat
Shelters in cool, and tends his pasturing Herds
At Loopholes cut through thickest shade: Those Leaves
They gather'd, broad as Amazonian Targe,° *shield*
And with what skill they had, together sew'd,
To gird thir waist, vain Covering if to hide
Thir guilt and dreaded shame; O how unlike
To that first naked Glory. Such of late
Columbus found th' *American* so girt
With feather'd Cincture,° naked else and wild *belt*
Among the Trees on Isles and woody Shores.

1. See Genesis 3.7.
2. Milton's description of the banyan or Indian fig comes from Gerard's *Herball* (1597).

Thus fenc't, and as they thought, thir shame in part
Cover'd, but not at rest or ease of Mind,
They sat them down to weep, nor only Tears
Rain'd at thir Eyes, but high Winds worse within
Began to rise, high Passions, Anger, Hate,
Mistrust, Suspicion, Discord, and shook sore
Thir inward State of Mind, calm Region once
And full of Peace, now toss't and turbulent:
For Understanding rul'd not, and the Will
Heard not her lore, both in subjection now
To sensual Appetite, who from beneath
Usurping over sovran Reason claim'd
Superior sway: From thus distemper'd breast,
Adam, estrang'd in look and alter'd style,
Speech intermitted thus to *Eve* renew'd.
  Would thou hadst heark'n'd to my words, and stay'd
With me, as I besought thee, when that strange
Desire of wand'ring this unhappy Morn,
I know not whence possess'd thee; we had then
Remain'd still happy, not as now, despoil'd
Of all our good, sham'd, naked, miserable.
Let none henceforth seek needless cause to approve° *give proof of*
The Faith they owe;[3] when earnestly they seek
Such proof, conclude, they then begin to fail.
  To whom soon mov'd with touch of blame thus *Eve*.
What words have past thy Lips,[4] *Adam* severe,
Imput'st thou that to my default, or will
Of wand'ring, as thou call'st it, which who knows
But might as ill have happ'n'd thou being by,
Or to thyself perhaps: hadst thou been there,
Or here th' attempt, thou couldst not have discern'd
Fraud in the Serpent, speaking as he spake;
No ground of enmity between us known,
Why hee should mean me ill, or seek to harm.
Was I to have never parted from thy side?
As good have grown there still a lifeless Rib.
Being as I am, why didst not thou the Head[5]
Command me absolutely not to go,
Going into such danger as thou said'st?
Too facile° then thou didst not much gainsay, *permissive*
Nay, didst permit, approve, and fair dismiss.
Hadst thou been firm and fixt in thy dissent
Neither had I transgress'd, nor thou with mee.
  To whom then first incenst Adam repli'd.
Is this the Love, is this the recompense

3. Be under obligation to render or possess.
4. Echoes Odysseus' disapproval of a speech of Agamemnon's (*Iliad* 14.83).
5. Alludes to 1 Corinthians 11.3: "The head of every man is Christ; and the head of the woman is the man; and the head of Christ is God."

Of mine to thee, ingrateful *Eve*, express't
Immutable° when thou wert lost, not I, *unchangeable*
Who might have liv'd and joy'd immortal bliss,
Yet willingly chose rather Death with thee:
And am I now upbraided, as the cause
Of thy transgressing? not enough severe,
It seems, in thy restraint: what could I more?
I warn'd thee, I admonish'd thee, foretold
The danger, and the lurking Enemy
That lay in wait; beyond this had been force,
And force upon free Will hath here no place.
But confidence then bore thee on, secure
Either to meet no danger, or to find
Matter of glorious trial; and perhaps
I also err'd in overmuch admiring
What seem'd in thee so perfet, that I thought
No evil durst attempt thee, but I rue
That error now, which is become my crime,
And thou th' accuser. Thus it shall befall
Him who to worth in Woman overtrusting
Lets her Will rule; restraint she will not brook,
And left to herself, if evil thence ensue,
Shee first his weak indulgence will accuse.
Thus they in mutual accusation spent
The fruitless hours, but neither self-condemning,
And of thir vain contést appear'd no end.

The End of the Ninth Book.

Book 10

The Argument

Man's *transgression known, the Guardian Angels forsake Paradise, and return up to Heaven to approve thir vigilance, and are approv'd, God declaring that the entrance of* Satan *could not be by them prevented. He sends his Son to judge the Transgressors, who descends and gives Sentence accordingly; then in pity clothes them both, and reascends.* Sin *and* Death *sitting till then at the Gates of Hell, by wondrous sympathy feeling the success of* Satan *in this new World, and the sin by Man there committed, resolve to sit no longer confin'd in Hell, but to follow* Satan *thir Sire up to the place of Man: To make the way easier from Hell to this World to and fro, they pave a broad Highway or Bridge over Chaos, according to the Track that* Satan *first made; then preparing for Earth, they meet him proud of his success returning to Hell; thir mutual gratulation.* Satan *arrives at* Pandemonium, *in full assembly relates with boasting his success against Man; instead of applause is entertained with a general hiss by all his audience, transform'd with himself also suddenly into Serpents, according to his doom giv'n in Paradise; then deluded with a show of the forbidden Tree springing up before them, they greedily reaching to take of the Fruit, chew dust and bitter ashes. The proceedings of* Sin *and* Death; *God foretells the final Victory of his Son over them, and the renewing of all things; but for the present commands his Angels to make several alterations in the Heavens and Elements.* Adam *more and more perceiving his fall'n condition heavily bewails, rejects the condolement of* Eve; *she persists and at length appeases him: then to evade the Curse likely to fall on thir Offspring, proposes to* Adam *violent ways, which he approves not, but conceiving better hope, puts her in mind of the late Promise made them, that her Seed should be reveng'd on the Serpent, and exhorts her with him to seek Peace of the offended Deity, by repentance and supplication.*

Meanwhile the heinous and despiteful act
Of *Satan* done in Paradise, and how
Hee in the Serpent had perverted *Eve*,
Her Husband shee, to taste the fatal fruit,
Was known in Heav'n;[1] for what can scape the Eye
Of *God* All-seeing, or deceive his Heart
Omniscient, who in all things wise and just,
Hinder'd not *Satan* to attempt the mind
Of Man, with strength entire, and free will arm'd,
Complete to have discover'd and repulst
Whatever wiles of Foe or seeming Friend.
For still they knew, and ought to have still remember'd
The high Injunction not to taste that Fruit,
Whoever tempted; which they not obeying,
Incurr'd, what could they less, the penalty,
And manifold[2] in sin, deserv'd to fall.
Up into Heav'n from Paradise in haste
Th' Angelic Guards ascended, mute and sad
For Man, for of his state by this they knew,
Much wond'ring how the subtle Fiend had stol'n
Entrance unseen. Soon as th' unwelcome news
From Earth arriv'd at Heaven Gate, displeas'd
All were who heard, dim sadness did not spare
That time Celestial visages, yet mixt
With pity, violated not thir bliss.
About the new-arriv'd, in multitudes
Th' ethereal People ran, to hear and know
How all befell: they towards the Throne Supreme
Accountable made haste to make appear
With righteous plea, thir utmost vigilance,
And easily approv'd; when the most High
Eternal Father from his secret Cloud,
Amidst in Thunder utter'd thus his voice.
Assembl'd Angels, and ye Powers return'd
From unsuccessful charge, be not dismay'd,
Nor troubl'd at these tidings from the Earth,

1. Rhetorically, lines 1–16 function both as *principium*, stating the subject of the book, and as *initium*, introducing the first scene. They also sum up the theological content of Book 3, which will receive specific application in the present book, in the exchanges between the Father and the Son (lines 34–84) and between the Son and Adam (lines 124ff.). Note the structural symmetry whereby the divine decrees of the third book are balanced by those of the third from the end.

2. Multiplied; alluding to Psalms 38.19: "they that hate me wrongfully are multiplied."

Which your sincerest care could not prevent,
Foretold so lately what would come to pass,
When first this Tempter cross'd the Gulf from Hell.
I told ye then he should prevail and speed° *succeed*
On his bad Errand, Man should be seduc't
And flatter'd out of all, believing lies
Against his Maker; no Decree of mine
Concurring to necessitate his Fall,
Or touch with lightest moment of impulse
His free Will, to her own inclining left
In even scale.[3] But fall'n he is, and now
What rests, but that the mortal Sentence pass
On his transgression. Death denounc't that day,
Which he presumes already vain and void,
Because not yet inflicted, as he fear'd,
By some immediate stroke; but soon shall find
Forbearance no acquittance ere day end.
Justice shall not return as bounty scorn'd.
But whom send I to judge them? whom but thee
Vicegerent Son, to thee I have transferr'd
All Judgment, whether in Heav'n, or Earth, or Hell.
Easy it may be seen that I intend
Mercy colleague with Justice, sending thee
Man's Friend, his Mediator, his design'd
Both Ransom and Redeemer voluntary,
And destin'd Man himself to judge Man fall'n.[4]
So spake the Father, and unfolding bright
Toward the right hand his Glory, on the Son
Blaz'd forth unclouded Deity; he full
Resplendent all his Father manifest
Express'd, and thus divinely answer'd mild.
Father Eternal, thine is to decree,
Mine both in Heav'n and Earth to do thy will
Supreme, that thou in mee thy Son belov'd
May'st ever rest well pleas'd.[5] I go to judge
On Earth these thy transgressors, but thou know'st,
Whoever judg'd, the worst on mee must light,
When time shall be, for so I undertook
Before thee; and not repenting, this obtain
Of right, that I may mitigate thir doom
On me deriv'd, yet I shall temper so
Justice with Mercy, as may illustrate most
Them fully satisfied, and thee appease.

3. "Moment" is a term applied to the smallest increment that could affect the equilibrium of a balance. If man had been protected from the tempter, then there would have been real interference with the free action of the scales of justice.

4. The double syntax—line 62 can be read as either "himself a man, destined to judge man" (primary) or "destined to judge man himself, man fallen"—mimes the close identification of Christ with humanity.

5. Echoing Matthew 3.17.

Attendance none shall need, nor Train, where none
Are to behold the Judgment, but the judg'd,
Those two; the third[6] best absent is condemn'd,
Convict° by flight, and Rebel to all Law: *convicted*
Conviction to the Serpent none belongs.[7]
Thus saying, from his radiant Seat he rose
Of high collateral° glory: him Thrones and Powers, *side by side*
Princedoms, and Dominations ministrant
Accompanied to Heaven Gate, from whence
Eden and all the Coast in prospect lay.
Down he descended straight; the speed of Gods
Time counts not, though with swiftest minutes wing'd.
Now was the Sun in Western cadence° low[8] *falling*
From Noon, and gentle Airs due at thir hour
To fan the Earth now wak'd, and usher in
The Ev'ning cool, when he from wrath more cool
Came the mild Judge and Intercessor both
To sentence Man: the voice of God they heard
Now walking in the Garden, by soft winds
Brought to thir Ears, while day declin'd, they heard,
And from his presence hid themselves among
The thickest Trees, both Man and Wife, till God
Approaching, thus to Adam call'd aloud.
Where art thou *Adam,* wont with joy to meet
My coming seen far off? I miss thee here,
Not pleas'd, thus entertain'd with solitude,
Where obvious duty erewhile appear'd unsought:
Or come I less conspicuous, or what change
Absents thee, or what chance detains? Come forth.
He came, and with him *Eve,* more loath, though first
To offend, discount'nanc't both, and discompos'd;
Love was not in thir looks, either to God
Or to each other, but apparent guilt,
And shame, and perturbation, and despair,
Anger, and obstinacy, and hate, and guile.
Whence *Adam* falt'ring long, thus answer'd brief.
I heard thee in the Garden, and of thy voice
Afraid, being naked, hid myself. To whom
The gracious Judge without revile repli'd.
My voice thou oft hast heard, and hast not fear'd,
But still rejoic't, how is it now become
So dreadful to thee? that thou art naked, who
Hath told thee? hast thou eaten of the Tree
Whereof I gave thee charge thou shouldst not eat?
To whom thus *Adam* sore beset repli'd.

6. Satan.
7. "Conviction" has both the legal sense (proof of guilt) and the theological (the condition of being convinced of sin).
8. Lines 92–123 follow Genesis 3.8–11.

O Heav'n! in evil strait this day I stand
Before my Judge, either to undergo
Myself the total Crime, or to accuse
My other self, the partner of my life;
Whose failing, while her Faith to me remains,
I should conceal, and not expose to blame
By my complaint; but strict necessity
Subdues me, and calamitous constraint,
Lest on my head both sin and punishment,
However insupportable, be all
Devolv'd;[9] though should I hold my peace, yet thou
Wouldst easily detect what I conceal.
This Woman whom thou mad'st to be my help,
And gav'st me as thy perfet gift, so good,
So fit, so acceptable, so Divine,
That from her hand I could suspect no ill,
And what she did, whatever in itself,
Her doing seem'd to justify the deed;
Shee gave me of the Tree, and I did eat.[1]
To whom the sovran Presence thus repli'd.
Was shee thy God, that her thou didst obey
Before his voice, or was shee made thy guide,
Superior, or but equal, that to her
Thou didst resign thy Manhood, and the Place
Wherein God set thee above her made of thee,
And for thee, whose perfection far excell'd
Hers in all real° dignity:[2] Adorn'd *regal*
She was indeed, and lovely to attract
Thy Love, not thy Subjection, and her Gifts
Were such as under Government well seem'd,
Unseemly to bear rule, which was thy part° *role*
And person,° hadst thou known thyself aright. *character*
So having said, he thus to Eve in few:
Say Woman, what is this which thou hast done?
To whom sad *Eve* with shame nigh overwhelm'd,
Confessing soon, yet not before her Judge
Bold or loquacious, thus abasht repli'd.
The Serpent me beguil'd and I did eat.[3]
Which when the Lord God heard, without delay
To Judgment he proceeded on th' accus'd
Serpent though brute, unable to transfer
The Guilt on him who made him instrument
Of mischief, and polluted from the end
Of his Creation; justly then accurst,
As vitiated in Nature: more to know

9. Caused to fall upon.
1. See Genesis 3.12.
2. See 1 Corinthians 11.8ff.: "For the man is not of the woman; but the woman of the man. Neither was the man created for the woman; but the woman for the man."
3. Repeating Genesis 3.13.

Concern'd not Man (since he no further knew)
Nor alter'd his offense; yet God at last
To Satan first in sin his doom appli'd,
Though in mysterious° terms, judg'd as then best: *mystical*
And on the Serpent thus his curse let fall.
Because thou hast done this, thou art accurst
Above all Cattle, each Beast of the Field;
Upon thy Belly groveling thou shalt go,
And dust shalt eat all the days of thy Life.
Between Thee and the Woman I will put
Enmity, and between thine and her Seed;
Her Seed shall bruise thy head, thou bruise his heel.[4]
So spake this Oracle, then verifi'd
When *Jesus* son of *Mary* second *Eve*,
Saw Satan fall like Lightning down from Heav'n,[5]
Prince of the Air; then rising from his Grave
Spoil'd Principalities and Powers, triumpht
In open show, and with ascension bright
Captivity led captive through the Air,[6]
The Realm itself of Satan long usurpt,
Whom he shall tread at last under our feet;[7]
Ev'n hee who now foretold his fatal bruise,
And to the Woman thus his Sentence turn'd.
Thy sorrow I will greatly multiply
By thy Conception; Children thou shalt bring
In sorrow forth, and to thy Husband's will
Thine shall submit, hee over thee shall rule.
On *Adam* last thus judgment he pronounc'd.
Because thou hast heark'n'd to the voice of thy Wife,
And eaten of the Tree concerning which
I charg'd thee, saying: Thou shalt not eat thereof,
Curs'd is the ground for thy sake, thou in sorrow
Shalt eat thereof all the days of thy Life;[8]
Thorns also and Thistles it shall bring thee forth
Unbid, and thou shalt eat th' Herb of the Field,
In the sweat of thy Face shalt thou eat Bread,
Till thou return unto the ground, for thou
Out of the ground wast taken, know thy Birth,
For dust thou art, and shalt to dust return.[9]
So judg'd he Man, both Judge and Savior sent,
And th' instant stroke of Death denounc't that day
Remov'd far off;[1] then pitying how they stood
Before him naked to the air, that now

4. See Genesis 3.14ff.
5. "I beheld Satan as lightning fall from heaven" (Luke 10.18).
6. Psalms 68.18: "Thou hast ascended on high, thou hast led captivity captive:" applied to Christ in Ephesians 4.8.
7. See Romans 16.20: "And the God of peace shall bruise Satan under your feet shortly."
8. See Genesis 3.17.
9. See Genesis 3.18–19.
1. Christ removes the fear that physical death will follow the eating of the fruit on the same day.

Must suffer change, disdain'd not to begin
Thenceforth the form of servant to assume,[2]
As when he wash'd his servants' feet, so now
As Father of his Family he clad
Thir nakedness with Skins of Beasts, or slain,
Or as the Snake with youthful Coat repaid;
And thought not much to clothe his Enemies:
Nor hee thir outward only with the Skins
Of Beasts, but inward nakedness, much more
Opprobrious, with his Robe of righteousness,
Arraying cover'd from his Father's sight.
To him with swift ascent he up return'd,
Into his blissful bosom reassum'd
In glory as of old, to him appeas'd
All, though all-knowing, what had past with Man
Recounted, mixing intercession sweet.
Meanwhile ere thus was sinn'd and judg'd on Earth,
Within the Gates of Hell sat Sin and Death,
In counterview within the Gates that now
Stood open wide, belching outrageous° flame *enormous*
Far into *Chaos,* since the Fiend pass'd through,
Sin opening, who thus now to Death began.
O Son, why sit we here each other viewing
Idly, while Satan our great Author° thrives *parent*
In other Worlds, and happier Seat provides
For us his offspring dear? It cannot be
But that success attends him; if mishap,
Ere this he had return'd, with fury driv'n
By his Avengers, since no place like° this *so well as*
Can fit his punishment, or their revenge.
Methinks I feel new strength within me rise,
Wings growing, and Dominion giv'n me large
Beyond this Deep; whatever draws me on,
Or° sympathy,° or some connatural force *Either / affinity*
Powerful at greatest distance to unite
With secret amity things of like kind
By secretest conveyance.° Thou my Shade *communication*
Inseparable must with mee along:
For Death from Sin no power can separate.
But lest the difficulty of passing back
Stay his return perhaps over this Gulf
Impassable, Impervious, let us try
Advent'rous work, yet to thy power and mine
Not unagreeable to found° a path *establish*
Over this Main° from Hell to that new World *expanse*
Where Satan now prevails, a Monument

2. See Philippians 2.7: "made himself of no reputation, and took upon him the form of a servant, and was made in the likeness of men."

Of merit high to all th' infernal Host,
Easing thir passage hence, for intercourse,
Or transmigration,[3] as thir lot shall lead.
Nor can I miss the way, so strongly drawn
By this new felt attraction and instinct.
 Whom thus the meagre° Shadow answer'd soon, *emaciated*
Go whither Fate and inclination strong
Leads thee, I shall not lag behind, nor err
The way, thou leading, such a scent I draw° *inhale*
Of carnage, prey innumerable, and taste
The savor of Death from all things there that live:
Nor shall I to the work thou enterprisest
Be wanting, but afford thee equal aid.
 So saying, with delight he snuff'd the smell
Of mortal change on Earth. As when a flock
Of ravenous Fowl, though many a League remote,
Against the day of Battle, to a Field,
Where Armies lie encampt, come flying, lur'd
With scent of living Carcasses design'd
For death, the following day, in bloody fight.
So scented the grim Feature,° and upturn'd *form*
His Nostril wide into the murky Air,
Sagacious° of his Quarry from so far. *acutely perceiving*
Then Both from out Hell Gates into the waste
Wide Anarchy of *Chaos* damp and dark
Flew diverse, and with Power (thir Power was great)
Hovering upon the Waters; what they met
Solid or slimy, as in raging Sea
Tost up and down together crowded drove
From each side shoaling° towards the mouth of Hell. *crowding*
As when two Polar Winds blowing adverse
Upon the *Cronian* Sea,[4] together drive
Mountains of Ice, that stop th' imagin'd way
Beyond *Petsora* Eastward, to the rich
Cathaian Coast. The aggregated Soil
Death with his Mace petrific,° cold and dry, *turning into stone*
As with a Trident smote, and fix't as firm
As *Delos* floating once; the rest his look
Bound with *Gorgonian* rigor not to move,
And with *Asphaltic* slime; broad as the Gate
Deep to the Roots of Hell the gather'd beach° *ridge of stones*
They fasten'd, and the Mole° immense wrought on *causeway*

3. Permanent emigration, a euphemism for damnation.

4. Various references to stone, ice, and exploration follow. The Cronian Sea is the Arctic Ocean; as *mare concretum*, it is relevant to Death's solidifying work. The "imagin'd way" is the northeast passage to Cathay searched for by Henry Hudson (1608), who failed to find a route through the ice. Petsora is the Pechora, a river in northern Russia. Cathay was a separate empire, north of present-day China. Delos, an island in the Aegean Sea, was supposedly made to float by Poseidon's trident in order to provide a refuge where Latona could give birth to Apollo and Artemis, safe from Hera's jealousy. It was later anchored by Zeus. The Gorgons turned to stone all whom they looked at.

Over the foaming deep high Archt, a Bridge
Of length prodigious joining to the Wall[5]
Immoveable of this now fenceless World
Forfeit to Death; from hence a passage broad,
Smooth, easy, inoffensive down to Hell.
So, if great things to small may be compar'd,
Xerxes, the Liberty of *Greece* to yoke,
From *Susa* his *Memnonian* Palace high
Came to the Sea, and over *Hellespont*
Bridging his way, *Europe* with *Asia* join'd,
And scourg'd with many a stroke th' indignant waves.[6]
Now had they brought the work by wondrous Art
Pontifical,[7] a ridge of pendent° Rock *hanging*
Over the vext° Abyss, following the track *stormy*
Of *Satan*, to the selfsame place where hee
First lighted from his Wing, and landed safe
From out of *Chaos* to the outside bare
Of this round World: with Pins of Adamant
And Chains they made all fast, too fast they made
And durable; and now in little space
The confines met of Empyrean Heav'n
And of this World, and on the left hand Hell[8]
With long reach interpos'd; three sev'ral ways
In sight, to each of these three places led.
And now thir way to Earth they had descri'd,
To Paradise first tending, when behold
Satan in likeness of an Angel bright
Betwixt the *Centaur* and the *Scorpion* steering
His *Zenith*,[9] while the Sun in *Aries* rose:
Disguis'd he came, but those his Children dear
Thir Parent soon discern'd, though in disguise.
Hee, after *Eve* seduc't, unminded° slunk *unnoticed*
Into the Wood fast by, and changing shape
To observe the sequel,° saw his guileful act *consequence*
By *Eve*, though all unweeting,° seconded *unwitting*
Upon her Husband, saw thir shame that sought
Vain covertures;° but when he saw descend *clothes, lies*
The Son of God to judge them, terrifi'd
Hee fled, not hoping to escape, but shun
The present, fearing guilty what his wrath

5. The outer shell (2.1024–31) reached by the bridge, the "utmost orb / Of this frail world." Despite the wall, the world is without defense ("fenceless") against Death after the Fall.

6. Xerxes, king of the Persians, bridged the Hellespont, a stretch of water separating Europe and Asia. When a storm destroyed the bridge, he is said to have had the waters whipped. Susa, sometimes called Memnonia, after Memnon, son of Tithonus and Aurora was the winter seat of the Persian kings.

7. Meaning both bridge-making, and episcopal. The Pope's title Pontifex referred to his role as bridge-builder between this world and the next. The implication, therefore, is that priests have special skill in easing the way to hell.

8. The sinister, evil side, where reprobate goats go in the parable (Matthew 25:33). Compare to the "dextrous" Son at God's right hand; 5.742n.

9. Satan flies straight up from Paradise, between Scorpio and Sagittarius.

Might suddenly inflict; that past, return'd
By Night, and list'ning where the hapless Pair
Sat in thir sad discourse and various plaint,° *complaint*
Thence gather'd his own doom;° which understood *judgment*
Not instant, but of future time, with joy
And tidings fraught, to Hell he now return'd,
And at the brink of *Chaos*, near the foot
Of this new wondrous Pontifice, unhop't
Met who to meet him came, his Offspring dear.
Great joy was at thir meeting, and at sight
Of that stupendous Bridge his joy increas'd.
Long hee admiring stood, till Sin, his fair
Enchanting Daughter, thus the silence broke.
O Parent, these are thy magnific deeds,
Thy Trophies, which thou view'st as not thine own,
Thou art thir Author and prime Architect:
For I no sooner in my Heart divin'd,
My Heart, which by a secret harmony
Still moves with thine, join'd in connexion sweet,
That thou on Earth hadst prosper'd, which thy looks
Now also evidence, but straight I felt
Though distant from thee Worlds between, yet felt
That I must after thee with this thy Son;
Such fatal consequence° unites us three: *relationship*
Hell could no longer hold us in her bounds,
Nor this unvoyageable Gulf obscure
Detain from following thy illustrious track.
Thou hast achiev'd our liberty, confin'd
Within Hell Gates till now, thou us impow'r'd
To fortify° thus far, and overlay *grow strong*
With this portentous Bridge the dark Abyss.
Thine now is all this World, thy virtue° hath won *power*
What thy hands builded not, thy Wisdom gain'd
With odds° what War hath lost, and fully aveng'd *advantage*
Our foil° in Heav'n; here thou shalt Monarch reign, *defeat*
There didst not; there let him still Victor sway,
As Battle hath adjudg'd, from this new World
Retiring, by his own doom alienated,
And henceforth Monarchy with thee divide
Of all things, parted by th' Empyreal bounds
His Quadrature, from thy Orbicular World,[1]
Or try thee now more dang'rous to his Throne.
Whom thus the Prince of Darkness answer'd glad
Fair Daughter, and thou Son and Grandchild both,[2]
High proof ye now have giv'n to be the Race
Of *Satan* (for I glory in the name,

1. The world (universe) is often "orbicular" (see 3.718), a form incommensurate with the "quadrature" or square.

2. As offspring of Satan's incest with his daughter Sin.

Antagonist of Heav'n's Almighty King)
Amply have merited of me, of all
Th' Infernal Empire, that so near Heav'n's door
Triumphal with triumphal act have met,
Mine with this glorious Work, and made one Realm
Hell and this World, one Realm, one Continent
Of easy thorough-fare. Therefore while I
Descend through Darkness, on your Road with ease
To my associate Powers, them to acquaint
With these successes, and with them rejoice,
You two this way, among those numerous Orbs
All yours, right down to Paradise descend;
There dwell and Reign in bliss, thence on the Earth
Dominion exercise and in the Air,
Chiefly on Man, sole Lord of all declar'd,
Him first make sure your thrall, and lastly kill.
My Substitutes I send ye, and Create
Plenipotent° on Earth, of matchless might *having full authority*
Issuing from mee: on your joint vigor now
My hold of this new Kingdom all depends,
Through Sin to Death expos'd by my exploit.
If your joint power prevail, th' affairs of Hell
No detriment° need fear, go and be strong. *injury*
So saying he dismiss'd them, they with speed
Thir course through thickest Constellations held
Spreading thir bane; the blasted Stars lookt wan,
And Planets, Planet-strook, real Eclipse
Then suffer'd.[3] Th' other way *Satan* went down
The Causey° to Hell Gate; on either side *causeway*
Disparted *Chaos* over-built exclaim'd,
And with rebounding surge the bars assail'd,
That scorn'd his indignation: through the Gate,
Wide open and unguarded, *Satan* pass'd,
And all about found desolate; for those
Appointed to sit there,[4] had left thir charge,
Flown to the upper World; the rest were all
Far to th'inland retir'd, about the walls
Of *Pandaemonium*, City and proud seat
Of *Lucifer*, so by allusion call'd,
Of that bright Star to *Satan* paragon'd.° *compared*
There kept thir Watch the Legions, while the Grand
In Council sat, solicitous° what chance *anxious*
Might intercept thir Emperor sent, so hee
Departing gave command, and they observ'd.
As when the Tartar from his *Russian* Foe

3. The planets are stricken by an adverse influence. Stars are literally struck when Phaethon's pride leads him to drive his father Apollo's sun-chariot on an unnatural course through the heavens; see Ovid's *Metamorphoses* 2.205.

4. Sin and Death.

By *Astracan*[5] over the Snowy Plains
Retires, or *Bactrian* Sophi[6] from the horns
Of *Turkish* Crescent,[7] leaves all waste beyond
The Realm of *Aladule*,[8] in his retreat
To *Tauris* or *Casbeen:*[9] So these the late
Heav'n-banisht Host, left desert utmost Hell
Many a dark League, reduc't in careful Watch
Round thir Metropolis, and now expecting
Each hour their great adventurer from the search
Of Foreign Worlds: he through the midst unmark't,
In show Plebeian Angel militant
Of lowest order, pass't; and from the door
Of that *Plutonian*[1] Hall, invisible
Ascended his high Throne, which under state° *canopy*
Of richest texture spread, at th' upper end
Was plac't in regal lustre. Down a while
He sat, and round about him saw unseen:
At last as from a Cloud his fulgent head
And shape Star-bright appear'd, or brighter, clad
With what permissive glory since his fall
Was left him, or false glitter: All amaz'd
At that so sudden blaze the Stygian throng
Bent thir aspect, and whom they wish'd beheld,
Thir mighty Chief return'd: loud was th' acclaim:
Forth rush'd in haste the great consulting Peers,
Rais'd from thir dark *Divan*,[2] and with like joy
Congratulant approach'd him, who with hand
Silence, and with these words attention won.
Thrones, Dominations, Princedoms, Virtues, Powers,
For in possession such, not only of right,
I call ye and declare ye now, return'd
Successful beyond hope, to lead ye forth
Triumphant out of this infernal Pit
Abominable, accurst, the house of woe,
And Dungeon of our Tyrant: Now possess,
As Lords, a spacious World, to our native Heaven
Little inferior, by my adventure hard
With peril great achiev'd. Long were to tell
What I have done, what suffer'd, with what pain
Voyag'd th' unreal, vast, unbounded deep
Of horrible confusion, over which
By Sin and Death a broad way now is pav'd
To expedite your glorious march; but I

5. Astracan, or Astrakhan, was a Tartar kingdom and capital city near the mouth of the Volga.
6. Persian king.
7. Refers not only to the Turkish ensign, but also to their battle formations.
8. Greater Armenia.
9. Tauris (modern Tabriz) is in the extreme northwest of Persia; Casbeen, or Kazvin, is north of Teheran.
1. Pertaining to Pluto, ruler of the classical underworld.
2. Turkish council of state.

Toil'd out my úncouth° passage, forc't to ride *strange*
Th' untractable Abyss, plung'd in the womb
Of unoriginal° *Night* and *Chaos* wild, *uncreated*
That jealous of thir secrets fiercely oppos'd
My journey strange, with clamorous uproar
Protesting Fate supreme; thence how I found
The new created World, which fame in Heav'n
Long had foretold, a Fabric wonderful
Of absolute perfection, therein Man
Plac't in a Paradise, by our exile
Made happy: Him by fraud I have seduc'd
From his Creator, and the more to increase
Your wonder, with an Apple; he thereat
Offended, worth your laughter, hath giv'n up
Both his beloved Man and all his World,
To Sin and Death a prey, and so to us,
Without our hazard, labor, or alarm,
To range in, and to dwell, and over Man
To rule, as over all he should have rul'd.
True is, mee also he hath judg'd, or rather
Mee not, but the brute Serpent in whose shape
Man I deceiv'd: that which to mee belongs,
Is enmity, which he will put between
Mee and Mankind; I am to bruise his heel;
His Seed, when is not set, shall bruise my head:
A World who would not purchase with a bruise,
Or much more grievous pain? Ye have th' account
Of my performance: What remains, ye Gods,
But up and enter now into full bliss.
So having said, a while he stood, expecting
Thir universal shout and high applause
To fill his ear, when contrary he hears
On all sides, from innumerable tongues
A dismal universal hiss, the sound
Of public scorn; he wonder'd, but not long
Had leisure, wond'ring at himself now more;
His Visage drawn he felt to sharp and spare,
His Arms clung to his Ribs, his Legs entwining
Each other, till supplanted° down he fell *tripped*
A monstrous Serpent on his Belly prone,[3]
Reluctant,° but in vain: a greater power *resisting*
Now rul'd him, punisht in the shape he sinn'd,
According to his doom: he would have spoke,
But hiss for hiss return'd with forked tongue
To forked tongue, for now were all transform'd
Alike, to Serpents all as accessories

3. See the metamorphosis of Cadmus in Ovid, *Metamorphoses* 4.572–603, and the mutual interchange of serpentine forms in Dante's canto of the thieves, *Inferno* 25.

To his bold Riot: dreadful was the din
Of hissing through the Hall, thick swarming now
With complicated° monsters, head and tail, *compound*
Scorpion and Asp, and *Amphisbaena* dire,
Cerastes horn'd, *Hydrus*, and *Ellops* drear,
And *Dipsas*[4] (not so thick swarm'd once the Soil
Bedropt with blood of *Gorgon*, or the Isle
Ophiusa) but still greatest hee the midst,[5]
Now Dragon grown, larger than whom the Sun
Ingender'd in the *Pythian* Vale on slime,
Huge *Python*, and his Power no less he seem'd
Above the rest still to retain;[6] they all
Him follow'd issuing forth to th' open Field,
Where all yet left of that revolted Rout
Heav'n-fall'n, in station stood or just array,
Sublime° with expectation when to see *uplifted*
In Triumph issuing forth thir glorious Chief;
They saw, but other sight instead, a crowd
Of ugly Serpents; horror on them fell,
And horrid sympathy; for what they saw,
They felt themselves now changing; down thir arms,
Down fell both Spear and Shield, down they as fast,
And the dire hiss renew'd, and the dire form
Catcht by Contagion, like in punishment,
As in thir crime. Thus was th' applause they meant,
Turn'd to exploding hiss, triumph to shame
Cast on themselves from thir own mouths. There stood
A Grove hard by, sprung up with this thir change,
His will who reigns above, to aggravate
Thir penance, laden with fair Fruit, like that
Which grew in Paradise, the bait of *Eve*
Us'd by the Tempter: on that prospect strange
Thir earnest eyes they fix'd, imagining
For one forbidden Tree a multitude
Now ris'n, to work them furder° woe or shame; *further*
Yet parcht with scalding thirst and hunger fierce,
Though to delude them sent, could not abstain,
But on they roll'd in heaps, and up the Trees
Climbing, sat thicker than the snaky locks
That curl'd *Megaera*:[7] greedily they pluck'd
The Fruitage fair to sight, like that which grew

4. The amphisbaena is a serpent with a head at either end. The cerastes has four horns on its head. The hydrus is a water snake. The ellops, though sometimes identified as the swordfish, is mentioned as a serpent in Pliny, *Natural History* 32.5. The dipsas causes raging thirst by its bite.

5. When Perseus was bringing back the severed head of Medusa, drops of blood fell to earth and became serpents. "Ophiusa" means literally "full of serpents"; a name anciently given to several islands, including Rhodes and one of the Balearic group.

6. For the birth of Python from the slime remaining after the flood, see Ovid, *Metamorphoses* 1.438–40. Python was slain by Apollo. Satan's dragon shape is that of the "old dragon" of Christian apocalypse; see Revelation 12.9: "the great dragon was cast out, that old serpent, called the Devil, and Satan."

7. One of the Furies, often described as snaky-haired.

Near that bituminous Lake where *Sodom* flam'd;[8]
This more delusive, not the touch, but taste
Deceiv'd; they fondly thinking to allay
Thir appetite with gust,° instead of Fruit *taste*
Chew'd bitter Ashes, which th' offended taste
With spattering noise rejected: oft they assay'd,
Hunger and thirst constraining, drugg'd° as oft, *nauseated*
With hatefullest disrelish writh'd thir jaws
With soot and cinders fill'd; so oft they fell
Into the same illusion, not as Man
Whom they triumph'd, once lapst. Thus were they plagu'd
And worn with Famine long, and ceaseless hiss,
Till thir lost shape, permitted, they resum'd,
Yearly enjoin'd, some say, to undergo
This annual humbling certain number'd days,
To dash thir pride, and joy for Man seduc't.
However some tradition they dispers'd
Among the Heathen of thir purchase got,
And Fabl'd how the Serpent, whom they call'd
Ophion with *Eurynome*, the wide-
Encroaching *Eve* perhaps, had first the rule
Of high *Olympus*, thence by Saturn driv'n
And Ops, ere yet *Dictaean Jove* was born.[9]
Meanwhile in Paradise the hellish pair
Too soon arriv'd, *Sin* there in power before,
Once actual, now in body, and to dwell
Habitual habitant; behind her *Death*
Close following pace for pace, not mounted yet
On his pale Horse:[1] to whom *Sin* thus began.
  Second of *Satan* sprung, all conquering *Death*,
What think'st thou of our Empire now, though earn'd
With travail difficult, not better far
Than still at Hell's dark threshold to have sat watch,
Unnam'd, undreaded, and thyself half starv'd?
  Whom thus the Sin-born Monster answer'd soon.
To mee, who with eternal Famine pine,
Alike is Hell, or Paradise, or Heaven,
There best, where most with ravin I may meet;
Which here, though plenteous, all too little seems
To stuff this Maw, this vast unhide-bound Corpse.
  To whom th' incestuous Mother thus repli'd.
Thou therefore on these Herbs, and Fruits, and Flow'rs
Feed first, on each Beast next, and Fish, and Fowl,

8. The allusion is to Josephus, *Wars* 4.8.4, where it is said that traces still remain of the divine fire that burnt Sodom, such as tasty-looking fruits that turned to ashes when plucked.

9. Ophion and Eurynome ruled Olympus until the one yielded to Cronos (Saturn) and the other to Rhea (Ops). Their two successors then ruled the Titans, while Zeus lived in the Dictaean cave. See Apollonius Rhodius, *Argonautica* 1.503–9.

1. See Revelation 6.8: "I looked, and behold a pale horse: and his name that sat on him was Death, and Hell followed with him."

No homely morsels, and whatever thing
The Scythe of Time mows down, devour unspar'd,
Till I in Man residing through the Race,
His thoughts, his looks, words, actions all infect,
And season him thy last and sweetest prey.
This said, they both betook them several ways,
Both to destroy, or unimmortal make
All kinds, and for destruction to mature
Sooner or later; which th' Almighty seeing
From his transcendent Seat the Saints among,
To those bright Orders utter'd thus his voice.
See with what heat these Dogs of Hell advance
To waste and havoc° yonder World, which I *devastate*
So fair and good created, and had still
Kept in that state, had not the folly of Man
Let in these wasteful Furies, who impute
Folly to mee, so doth the Prince of Hell
And his Adherents, that with so much ease
I suffer them to enter and possess
A place so heav'nly, and conniving seem
To gratify my scornful Enemies,
That laugh, as if transported with some fit
Of Passion, I to them had quitted° all, *yielded*
At random yielded up to their misrule;
And know not that I call'd and drew them thither
My Hell-hounds, to lick up the draff° and filth *refuse*
Which man's polluting Sin with taint hath shed
On what was pure, till cramm'd and gorg'd, nigh burst
With suckt and glutted offal, at one sling
Of thy victorious Arm, well-pleasing Son,
Both *Sin*, and *Death*, and yawning *Grave* at last
Through *Chaos* hurl'd, obstruct the mouth of Hell
For ever, and seal up his ravenous Jaws.
Then Heav'n and Earth renew'd shall be made pure
To sanctity that shall receive no stain:
Till then the Curse pronounc't on both precedes.[2]
He ended, and the heav'nly Audience loud
Sung *Halleluiah,* as the sound of Seas,
Through multitude that sung: Just are thy ways,
Righteous are thy Decrees on all thy Works;
Who can extenuate° thee? Next, to the Son, *disparage*
Destin'd restorer of Mankind, by whom
New Heav'n and Earth shall to the Ages rise,
Or down from Heav'n descend. Such was thir song,
While the Creator calling forth by name
His mighty Angels gave them several charge,

2. See Genesis 3.17: "Cursed is the ground for thy sake."

As sorted° best with present things. The Sun — *accorded*
Had first his precept° so to move, so shine, — *order*
As might affect the Earth with cold and heat
Scarce tolerable, and from the North to call
Decrepit Winter, from the South to bring
Solstitial summer's[3] heat. To the blanc° Moon — *pale*
Her office they prescrib'd, to th' other five° — *planets*
Thir planetary motions and aspects
In *Sextile*, *Square*, and *Trine*, and *Opposite*,[4]
Of noxious efficacy, and when to join
In Synod° unbenign, and taught the fixt — *conjunction*
Thir influence malignant when to show'r,[5]
Which of them rising with the Sun, or falling,
Should prove tempestuous: To the Winds they set
Thir corners, when with bluster to confound
Sea, Air, and Shore, the Thunder when to roll
With terror through the dark Aereal Hall.
Some say he bid his Angels turn askance
The Poles of Earth twice ten degrees and more
From the Sun's Axle; they with labor push'd
Oblique the Centric Globe: Some say[6] the Sun
Was bid turn Reins from th' Equinoctial Road
Like distant breadth to *Taurus* with the Sev'n
Atlantic Sisters, and the *Spartan* Twins
Up to the *Tropic* Crab,[7] thence down amain° — *at full speed*
By *Leo* and the *Virgin* and the *Scales*,
As deep as *Capricorn*, to bring in change
Of Seasons to each Clime; else had the Spring
Perpetual smil'd on Earth with vernant° Flow'rs, — *flourishing*
Equal in Days and Nights, except to those
Beyond the Polar Circles; to them Day
Had unbenighted shone, while the low Sun
To recompense his distance, in thir sight
Had rounded still th' *Horizon*, and not known
Or East or West, which had forbid the Snow
From cold *Estotiland* and South as far
Beneath *Magellan*.[8] At that tasted Fruit
The Sun, as from *Thyestean* Banquet, turn'd

3. God commands the angels to make the earth turn on its axis and so cause the change of seasons, and to disrupt the order of the planets, making their effect on the world negative as well as positive. Milton's own, invented pre-Fall cosmos thus gives way to the Ptolemaic, Copernican, and other post-Fall systems.
4. Sextile and trine are harmonious astrological aspects, while quartile and opposition are disharmonious — as a result of the Fall.
5. The "fixed" (stars) exerted "sweet influence" when first created (7.375).
6. The first alternative accords with heliocentric theories, the second with geocentric; Milton does not decide.
7. The Atlantic sisters are the Pleiades, daughters of Atlas, a group within the constellation Taurus. The Spartan Twins are Castor and Pollux, sons of King Tyndarus of Sparta; the zodiacal constellation (and sign) Gemini.
8. "Estotiland" was used vaguely for northeast Labrador, relevant to Hudson's search for a northwest passage in 1610. "Magellan" is not necessarily the straits of Magellan: modern Argentina was labelled Magellonica.

His course intended;[9] else how had the World
Inhabited, though sinless, more than now,
Avoided pinching cold and scorching heat?
These changes in the Heav'ns, though slow, produc'd
Like change on Sea and Land, sideral° blast, *from the stars*
Vapor, and Mist, and Exhalation° hot, *meteor*
Corrupt and Pestilent: Now from the North
Of *Norumbega*, and the *Samoed* shore[1]
Bursting thir brazen Dungeon, arm'd with ice
And snow and hail and stormy gust and flaw,° *sudden squall*
Boreas and *Cæcias* and *Argesles* loud
And *Thrascias* rend the Woods and Seas upturn;
With adverse blast upturns them from the South
Notus and *Afer* black with thundrous Clouds
From *Serraliona*;° thwart of these as fierce *Sierra Leone*
Forth rush the *Levant* and the *Ponent* Winds
Eurus and *Zephir* with thir lateral noise,
Sirocco, and *Libecchio*. Thus began
Outrage from lifeless things; but Discord first
Daughter of Sin, among th' irrational,
Death introduc'd through fierce antipathy:
Beast now with Beast gan war, and Fowl with Fowl,
And Fish with Fish; to graze the Herb all leaving,
Devour'd each other; nor stood much in awe
Of Man, but fled him, or with count'nance grim
Glar'd on him passing: these were from without
The growing miseries, which *Adam* saw
Already in part, though hid in gloomiest shade,
To sorrow abandon'd, but worse felt within,
And in a troubl'd Sea of passion tost,
Thus to disburd'n sought with sad complaint.
O miserable of happy! is this the end
Of this new glorious World, and mee so late
The Glory of that Glory, who now become
Accurst of blessed, hide me from the face
Of God, whom to behold was then my highth
Of happiness: yet well, if here would end
The misery, I deserv'd it, and would
My own deservings; but this will not serve;
All that I eat or drink, or shall beget,

9. Thyestes seduced Aerope, his brother's wife. In revenge, Atreus invited Thyestes to a reconciliation banquet and served up to him his child's flesh. The sun changed course to avoid seeing an act so obscene. See Seneca, *Thyestes* 776ff.

1. Milton's catalogue of winds begins with Norumbega, modern-day southeast Canada and northeast United States. Samoed is northeast Siberia. The "brazen Dungeon" refers to Virgil's *Aeneid* 1.50ff, where Aeolus imprisons the winds in a cave. There are 11 winds in all: the four northern are Boreas, Caecias, Argestes, and Thrascias. These oppose two adverse southern winds, Notus and Afer. The five lateral east-west winds are Levant, Eurus, Zephir, Sirocco, and Libecchio.

Is propagated curse.[2] O voice once heard
Delightfully, *Increase and multiply*,[3]
Now death to hear! for what can I increase
Or multiply, but curses on my head?
Who of all Ages to succeed, but feeling
The evil on him brought by me, will curse
My Head; Ill fare our Ancestor impure,
For this we may thank *Adam;* but his thanks
Shall be the execration; so besides
Mine own that bide upon me, all from mee
Shall with a fierce reflux on mee redound,° *overflow, come back*
On mee as on thir natural centre light
Heavy, though in thir place. O fleeting joys
Of Paradise, dear bought with lasting woes!
Did I request thee, Maker, from my Clay
To mould me Man, did I solicit thee
From darkness to promote me, or here place
In this delicious Garden? as my Will
Concurr'd not to my being, it were but right
And equal° to reduce me to my dust, *just*
Desirous to resign, and render back
All I receiv'd, unable to perform
Thy terms too hard, by which I was to hold
The good I sought not. To the loss of that,
Sufficient penalty, why hast thou added
The sense of endless woes? inexplicable
Thy Justice seems; yet to say truth, too late
I thus contest; then should have been refus'd
Those terms whatever, when they were propos'd:
Thou didst accept them; wilt thou enjoy the good,
Then cavil the conditions? and though God
Made thee without thy leave, what if thy Son
Prove disobedient, and reprov'd, retort,
Wherefore didst thou beget me? I sought it not:
Wouldst thou admit for his contempt of thee
That proud excuse? yet him not thy election,° *choice*
But Natural necessity begot.
God made thee of choice his own, and of his own
To serve him, thy reward was of his grace,
Thy punishment then justly is at his Will.
Be it so, for I submit, his doom° is fair, *judgment*
That dust I am, and shall to dust return:[4]
O welcome hour whenever! why delays
His hand to execute what his Decree
Fix'd on this day? why do I overlive,

2. Handed down from one generation to another. Food prolongs life and thus extends the curse, while begetting children hands it on. Note also that eating and sex are jointly the concerns of the concupiscible faculty, which was often regarded as the special field of operation of concupiscence or the "body of sin."

3. See Genesis 1.28.

4. Alluding to Genesis 3.19.

Why am I mockt with death, and length'n'd out
To deathless pain? How gladly would I meet
Mortality my sentence, and be Earth
Insensible, how glad would lay me down
As in my Mother's lap![5] There I should rest
And sleep secure; his dreadful voice no more
Would Thunder in my ears, no fear of worse
To mee and to my offspring would torment me
With cruel expectation. Yet one doubt
Pursues me still, lest all I cannot die,
Lest that pure breath of Life, the Spirit of Man
Which God inspir'd, cannot together perish
With this corporeal Clod; then in the Grave,
Or in some other dismal place, who knows
But I shall die a living Death? O thought
Horrid, if true! yet why? it was but breath
Of Life that sinn'd; what dies but what had life
And sin? the Body properly hath neither.
All of me then shall die:[6] let this appease
The doubt, since human reach no further knows.
For though the Lord of all be infinite,
Is his wrath also? be it, Man is not so,
But mortal doom'd. How can he exercise
Wrath without end on Man whom Death must end?
Can he make deathless Death? that were to make
Strange contradiction, which to God himself
Impossible is held, as Argument
Of weakness, not of Power. Will he draw out,
For anger's sake, finite to infinite
In punisht Man, to satisfy his rigor
Satisfi'd never; that were to extend
His Sentence beyond dust and Nature's Law,
By which all Causes else according still
To the reception of thir matter act,
Not to th' extent of thir own Sphere.[7] But say
That Death be not one stroke, as I suppos'd,
Bereaving sense, but endless misery
From this day onward, which I feel begun
Both in me, and without me, and so last
To perpetuity; Ay me, that fear
Comes thund'ring back with dreadful revolution

5. Adam's lament echoes Job 3.
6. Adam's question is like Milton's in *De doctrina* 1.13: "What could be more absurd than that the mind, which is the part principally offending, should escape the threatened death; and that the body alone, to which immortality was equally allotted, before death came into the world by sin, should pay the penalty of sin by undergoing death, though not implicated in the transgression?" Milton's belief in the joint extinction and joint resurrection of man's body and mind was not an eccentric heresy but good biblical theology.
7. Adam tries to comfort himself with an argument drawn from medieval philosophy. Here Adam means that God would be going beyond a natural law, that any agent acts according to the powers of what receives its action, not according to its own powers.

On my defenseless head; both Death and I
Am found Eternal, and incorporate° both, *united, embodied*
Nor I on my part single, in mee all
Posterity stands curst:[8] Fair Patrimony
That I must leave ye, Sons; O were I able
To waste it all myself, and leave ye none!
So disinherited how would ye bless
Me now your Curse! Ah, why should all mankind
For one man's fault thus guiltless be condemn'd,
If guiltless? But from me what can proceed,
But all corrupt, both Mind and Will deprav'd,
Not to do only, but to will the same
With me? how can they then acquitted stand
In sight of God? Him after all Disputes
Forc't I absolve: all my evasions vain
And reasonings, though through Mazes, lead me still
But to my own conviction:[9] first and last
On mee, mee only, as the source and spring
Of all corruption, all the blame lights due;
So might the wrath. Fond wish! couldst thou support
That burden heavier than the Earth to bear,
Than all the World much heavier, though divided
With that bad Woman? Thus what thou desir'st,
And what thou fear'st, alike destroys all hope
Of refuge, and concludes thee miserable
Beyond all past example and futúre,
To *Satan* only like both crime and doom.
O Conscience, into what Abyss of fears
And horrors hast thou driv'n me; out of which
I find no way, from deep to deeper plung'd!
   Thus *Adam* to himself lamented loud
Through the still Night, not now, as ere man fell,
Wholesome and cool and mild, but with black Air
Accompanied, with damps and dreadful gloom,
Which to his evil Conscience represented
All things with double terror: On the ground
Outstretcht he lay, on the cold ground, and oft
Curs'd his Creation, Death as oft accus'd
Of tardy execution, since denounc't
The day of his offense. Why comes not Death,
Said he, with one thrice àcceptable stroke
To end me? Shall Truth fail to keep her word,
Justice Divine not hast'n to be just?
But Death comes not at call, Justice Divine

8. Not only are Death and I double, two in one, but so also am I, since I am both myself and my descendants.
9. Adam at last reaches full conviction of his sin, but being unable yet to pass to contrition, the next stage of repentance, he falls instead into despair. The present passage should be compared with Satan's similar fall into conscience-stricken despair at 4.86–113.

Mends not her slowest pace for prayers or cries.
O Woods, O Fountains, Hillocks, Dales and Bow'rs,
With other echo late I taught your Shades
To answer, and resound far other Song.
Whom thus afflicted when sad Eve beheld,
Desolate where she sat, approaching nigh,
Soft words to his fierce passion she assay'd:
But her with stern regard he thus repell'd.
Out of my sight, thou Serpent, that name best
Befits thee with him leagu'd, thyself as false
And hateful; nothing wants, but that thy shape,
Like his, and color Serpentine may show
Thy inward fraud, to warn all Creatures from thee
Henceforth; lest that too heav'nly form, pretended[1]
To hellish falsehood, snare them. But for thee
I had persisted happy, had not thy pride
And wand'ring vanity, when least was safe,
Rejected my forewarning, and disdain'd
Not to be trusted, longing to be seen
Though by the Devil himself, him overweening
To over-reach, but with the Serpent meeting
Fool'd and beguil'd, by him thou, I by thee,
To trust thee from my side, imagin'd wise,
Constant, mature, proof against all assaults,
And understood not all was but a show
Rather than solid virtue, all but a Rib
Crooked by nature, bent, as now appears,
More to the part sinister[2] from me drawn,
Well if thrown out, as supernumerary
To my just number found. O why did God,
Creator wise, that peopl'd highest Heav'n
With Spirits Masculine, create at last
This novelty on Earth, this fair defect
Of Nature, and not fill the World at once
With Men as Angels without Feminine,
Or find some other way to generate
Mankind?[3] this mischief had not then befall'n,
And more that shall befall, innumerable
Disturbances on Earth through Female snares,
And strait conjunction with this Sex: for either
He never shall find out fit Mate, but such
As some misfortune brings him, or mistake,
Or whom he wishes most shall seldom gain
Through her perverseness, but shall see her gain'd

1. Stretched in front as a covering serving as a mask.
2. Left; also corrupt, evil, base. The notion that woman is formed from a bent rib, and therefore crooked, had appeared in tracts like Joseph Swetnam's *The Arraignment of Lewd, Idle, Froward, and Unconstant Women* (page 1447).
3. Another ancient piece of antifeminism; see Euripides, *Hippolytus* 616ff. Aristotle had said in the *De generatione* that the female is a defective male.

By a far worse, or if she love, withheld
By Parents, or his happiest choice too late
Shall meet, already linkt and Wedlock-bound
To a fell° Adversary, his hate or shame: *bitter*
Which infinite calamity shall cause
To Human life, and household peace confound.
He added not, and from her turn'd, but *Eve*
Not so repulst, with Tears that ceas'd not flowing,
And tresses all disorder'd, at his feet
Fell humble, and imbracing them, besought
His peace, and thus proceeded in her plaint.
Forsake me not thus, *Adam*, witness Heav'n
What love sincere, and reverence in my heart
I bear thee, and unweeting° have offended, *unintentionally*
Unhappily deceiv'd; thy suppliant
I beg, and clasp thy knees; bereave me not,
Whereon I live, thy gentle looks, thy aid,
Thy counsel in this uttermost distress,
My only strength and stay: forlorn of thee,
Whither shall I betake me, where subsist?
While yet we live, scarce one short hour perhaps,
Between us two let there be peace, both joining,
As join'd in injuries, one enmity
Against a Foe by doom express assign'd us,
That cruel Serpent: On me exercise not
Thy hatred for this misery befall'n,
On me already lost, mee than thyself
More miserable; both have sinn'd, but thou
Against God only, I against God and thee,
And to the place of judgment will return,
There with my cries importune Heaven, that all
The sentence from thy head remov'd may light
On me, sole cause to thee of all this woe,
Mee mee only just object of his ire.
She ended weeping, and her lowly plight,
Immovable till peace obtain'd from fault
Acknowledg'd and deplor'd,[4] in *Adam* wrought
Commiseration; soon his heart relented
Towards her, his life so late and sole delight,
Now at his feet submissive in distress,
Creature so fair his reconcilement seeking,
His counsel whom she had displeas'd, his aid;
As one disarm'd, his anger all he lost,
And thus with peaceful words uprais'd her soon.
Unwary, and too desirous, as before,
So now of what thou know'st not, who desir'st

4. Eve cannot be moved from Adam's feet until he forgives her.

The punishment all on thyself; alas,
Bear thine own first, ill able to sustain
His full wrath whose thou feel'st as yet least part,
And my displeasure bear'st so ill. If Prayers
Could alter high Decrees, I to that place
Would speed before thee, and be louder heard,
That on my head all might be visited,
Thy frailty and infirmer Sex forgiv'n,
To me committed and by me expos'd.
But rise, let us no more contend, nor blame
Each other, blam'd enough elsewhere,[5] but strive
In offices of Love, how we may light'n
Each other's burden in our share of woe;
Since this day's Death denounc't, if aught I see,
Will prove no sudden, but a slow-pac't evil,
A long day's dying to augment our pain,
And to our Seed (O hapless Seed!) deriv'd.
To whom thus *Eve,* recovering heart, repli'd.
Adam, by sad experiment I know
How little weight my words with thee can find,
Found so erroneous, thence by just event° *consequence*
Found so unfortunate; nevertheless,
Restor'd by thee, vile as I am, to place
Of new acceptance, hopeful to regain
Thy Love, the sole contentment of my heart
Living or dying, from thee I will not hide
What thoughts in my unquiet breast are ris'n,
Tending to some relief of our extremes,
Or end, though sharp and sad, yet tolerable,
As in our evils, and of easier choice.
If care of our descent° perplex° us most, *descendants / torment*
Which must be born to certain woe, devour'd
By Death at last, and miserable it is
To be to other cause of misery,
Our own begott'n, and of our Loins to bring
Into this cursed World a woeful Race,
That after wretched Life must be at last
Food for so foul a Monster, in thy power
It lies, yet ere Conception to prevent
The Race unblest, to being yet unbegot.
Childless thou art, Childless remain: So Death
Shall be deceiv'd his glut, and with us two
Be forc'd to satisfy his Rav'nous Maw.
But if thou judge it hard and difficult,
Conversing, looking, loving, to abstain
From Love's due Rites, Nuptial embraces sweet,

5. Either "heaven" or the "place of judgment" of line 932.

And with desire to languish without hope,[6]
Before the present object° languishing *Eve*
With like desire, which would be misery
And torment less than none of what we dread,
Then both ourselves and Seed at once to free
From what we fear for both, let us make short,
Let us seek Death, or he not found, supply
With our own hands his Office on ourselves;
Why stand we longer shivering under fears,
That show no end but Death, and have the power,
Of many ways to die the shortest choosing,
Destruction with destruction to destroy.
She ended here, or vehement despair
Broke off the rest; so much of Death her thoughts
Had entertain'd, as dy'd her Cheeks with pale.
But *Adam* with such counsel nothing sway'd,
To better hopes his more attentive mind
Laboring had rais'd, and thus to *Eve* replied.
Eve, thy contempt of life and pleasure seems
To argue in thee something more sublime
And excellent than what thy mind contemns;
But self-destruction therefore sought, refutes
That excellence thought in thee, and implies,
Not thy contempt, but anguish and regret
For loss of life and pleasure overlov'd.
Or if thou covet death, as utmost end
Of misery, so thinking to evade
The penalty pronounc't, doubt not but God
Hath wiselier arm'd his vengeful ire than so
To be forestall'd; much more I fear lest Death
So snatcht will not exempt us from the pain
We are by doom to pay; rather such acts
Of contumacy° will provoke the Highest *contempt*
To make death in us live: Then let us seek
Some safer resolution, which methinks
I have in view, calling to mind with heed
Part of our Sentence, that thy Seed shall bruise
The Serpent's head; piteous amends, unless
Be meant, whom I conjecture, our grand Foe
Satan, who in the Serpent hath contriv'd
Against us this deceit: to crush his head
Would be revenge indeed; which will be lost
By death brought on ourselves, or childless days
Resolv'd, as thou proposest; so our Foe
Shall 'scape his punishment ordain'd, and wee
Instead shall double ours upon our heads.

6. See Dante, *Inferno* 4.42: "without hope we live in desire."

No more be mention'd then of violence
Against ourselves, and wilful barrenness,
That cuts us off from hope, and savors only
Rancor and pride, impatience and despite,
Reluctance° against God and his just yoke *resistance*
Laid on our Necks. Remember with what mild
And gracious temper he both heard and judg'd
Without wrath or reviling; wee expected
Immediate dissolution, which we thought
Was meant by Death that day, when lo, to thee
Pains only in Child-bearing were foretold,
And bringing forth, soon recompens't with joy,
Fruit of thy Womb: On mee the Curse aslope
Glanc'd on the ground, with labor I must earn
My bread;[7] what harm? Idleness had been worse;
My labor will sustain me; and lest Cold
Or Heat should injure us, his timely care
Hath unbesought provided, and his hands
Cloth'd us unworthy, pitying while he judg'd;
How much more, if we pray him, will his ear
Be open, and his heart to pity incline,[8]
And teach us further by what means to shun
Th' inclement Seasons, Rain, Ice, Hail and Snow,
Which now the Sky with various Face begins
To show us in this Mountain, while the Winds
Blow moist and keen, shattering the graceful locks
Of these fair spreading Trees; which bids us seek
Some better shroud,° some better warmth to cherish *shelter*
Our Limbs benumb'd, ere this diurnal Star[9]
Leave cold the Night, how we his gather'd beams
Reflected, may with matter sere foment,[1]
Or by collision of two bodies grind
The Air attrite° to Fire, as late the Clouds *ground down*
Justling° or pusht with Winds rude in thir shock *jostling*
Tine° the slant Lightning, whose thwart flame driv'n down *ignite*
Kindles the gummy bark of Fir or Pine,
And sends a comfortable heat from far,
Which might supply° the Sun: such Fire to use, *take the place of*
And what may else be remedy or cure
To evils which our own misdeeds have wrought,
Hee will instruct us praying, and of Grace
Beseeching him, so as we need not fear
To pass commodiously this life, sustain'd
By him with many comforts, till we end

7. Referring to Christ's words at lines 201–5.
8. Biblical diction; see Psalms 24.4, 119.36, 112, and 1 Peter 3.12.
9. The sun.
1. Cherish; but alluding also to Latin *fomes* (tinder). Adam envisages making fire: focusing the sun's rays onto dry combustibles ("matter sere") with a parabolic mirror.

In dust, our final rest and native home.
What better can we do, than to the place
Repairing where he judg'd us, prostrate fall
Before him reverent, and there confess
Humbly our faults, and pardon beg, with tears
Watering the ground, and with our sighs the Air
Frequenting,° sent from hearts contrite, in sign *filling*
Of sorrow unfeign'd, and humiliation meek.[2]
Undoubtedly he will relent and turn
From his displeasure; in whose look serene,
When angry most he seem'd and most severe,
What else but favor, grace, and mercy shone?
So spake our Father penitent, nor Eve
Felt less remorse: they forthwith to the place
Repairing where he judg'd them prostrate fell
Before him reverent, and both confess'd
Humbly thir faults, and pardon begg'd, with tears
Watering the ground, and with thir sighs the Air
Frequenting, sent from hearts contrite, in sign
Of sorrow unfeign'd, and humiliation meek.[3]
The End of the Tenth Book.

Book 11
The Argument

The Son of God present to his Father the Prayers of our first Parents now repenting, and intercedes for them: God accepts them, but declares that they must no longer abide in Paradise; sends Michael *with a Band of Cherubim to dispossess them; but first to reveal to* Adam *future things;* Michael's *coming down.* Adam *shows to Eve certain ominous signs; he discerns* Michael's *approach, goes out to meet him: the Angel denounces thir departure.* Eve's *Lamentation.* Adam *pleads, but submits: The Angel leads him up to a high Hill, sets before him in vision what shall happ'n till the Flood.*

Thus they in lowliest plight repentant stood
Praying, for from the Mercy-seat above
Prevenient Grace descending had remov'd
The stony from thir hearts,[1] and made new flesh
Regenerate grow instead, that sighs now breath'd
Unutterable, which the Spirit of prayer
Inspir'd, and wing'd for Heav'n with speedier flight
Than loudest Oratory: yet thir port° *bearing*
Not of mean suitors, nor important less
Seem'd thir Petition, than when th' ancient Pair

2. Having passed on from conviction of sin Adam, now "contrite" (line 1103), is ready for confession, the third stage of repentance. An allusion to the Penitential Psalm: "The sacrifices of God are a broken spirit: a broken and a contrite heart, O God, thou wilt not despise" (Psalm 51.17).

3. Repeating lines 1086–92, modulated into narrative discourse (only the last two verses remain identical).

1. In Milton's Arminian view, grace precedes human choice. People remain free to accept grace or reject grace, but in neither case does it produce repentance.

In Fables old, less ancient yet than these,
Deucalion and chaste *Pyrrha* to restore
The Race of Mankind drown'd, before the Shrine
Of *Themis* stood devout.[2] To Heav'n thir prayers
Flew up, nor miss'd the way, by envious winds
Blown vagabond or frustrate: in they pass'd
Dimensionless through Heav'nly doors: then clad
With incense, where the Golden Altar fum'd,
By thir great Intercessor, came in sight
Before the Father's Throne: Then the glad Son
Presenting, thus to intercede began.
    See Father, what first fruits on Earth are sprung
From thy implanted Grace in Man, these Sighs
And Prayers, which in this Golden Censer, mixt
With Incense, I thy Priest before thee bring,
Fruits of more pleasing savor from thy seed
Sown with contrition in his heart, than those
Which his own hand manuring° all the Trees *cultivating*
Of Paradise could have produc't, ere fall'n
From innocence.[3] Now therefore bend thine ear
To supplication, hear his sighs though mute;
Unskilful with what words to pray, let mee
Interpret for him, mee his Advocate
And propitiation,[4] all his works on mee
Good or not good ingraft, my Merit those
Shall perfet, and for these my Death shall pay.
Accept me, and in mee from these receive
The smell of peace toward Mankind, let him live
Before thee reconcil'd, at least his days
Number'd, though sad, till Death, his doom° (which I *judgment*
To mitigate thus plead, not to reverse)
To better life shall yield him, where with mee
All my redeem'd may dwell in joy and bliss,
Made one with me as I with thee am one.
    To whom the Father, without Cloud, serene.
All thy request for Man, accepted° Son, *approved*
Obtain, all thy request was my Decree:
But longer in that Paradise to dwell,
The Law I gave to Nature him forbids:
Those pure immortal Elements that know
No gross, no unharmonious mixture foul,
Eject him tainted now, and purge him off

2. A mythic version of Noah's salvation, itself a type of Christ's. Advised by his father Prometheus, Deucalion built an ark and escaped the flood. When it subsided, he and Pyrrha consulted Themis, who told them to restore the race by throwing stones behind them, which became people.

3. Varying the parable of the sower (Mark 4.14–30), with the help of Hebrews 13.15, "Let us offer the sacrifice of praise to God continually, that is, the fruit of our lips giving thanks to his name."

4. Echoing 1 John 2.1ff, "We have an advocate with the Father, Jesus Christ the righteous: And he is the propitiation of our sins."

As a distemper, gross to air as gross,
And mortal food, as may dispose him best
For dissolution wrought by Sin, that first
Distemper'd all things, and of incorrupt
Corrupted.[5] I at first with two fair gifts
Created him endow'd, with Happiness
And Immortality: that fondly° lost, *foolishly*
This other serv'd but to eternize woe;
Till I provided Death; so Death becomes
His final remedy, and after Life
Tri'd in sharp tribulation, and refin'd
By Faith and faithful works,[6] to second Life,
Wak't in the renovation of the just,
Resigns him up with Heav'n and Earth renew'd.
But let us call to Synod° all the Blest *assembly*
Through Heav'n's wide bounds; from them I will not hide
My judgments, how with Mankind I proceed,
As how with peccant° Angels late they saw; *sinning*
And in thir state, though firm, stood more confirm'd.
He ended, and the Son gave signal high
To the bright Minister that watch'd: hee blew
His Trumpet, heard in *Oreb* since perhaps
When God descended,[7] and perhaps once more
To sound at general Doom. Th' Angelic blast
Fill'd all the Regions; from thir blissful Bow'rs
Of *Amarantin* Shade,[8] Fountain or Spring,
By the waters of Life, where'er they sat
In fellowships of joy, the Sons of Light
Hasted, resorting to the Summons high,
And took thir Seats; till from his Throne supreme
Th' Almighty thus pronounc'd his sovran Will.
O Sons, like one of us Man is become
To know both Good and Evil, since his taste
Of that defended° Fruit; but let him boast *forbidden*
His knowledge of Good lost, and Evil got,
Happier, had it suffic'd him to have known
Good by itself, and Evil not at all.
He sorrows now, repents, and prays contrite,
My motions° in him; longer than they move, *impulses*
His heart I know, how variable and vain
Self-left.° Lest therefore his now bolder hand *left to itself*
Reach also of the Tree of Life, and eat,
And live for ever, dream at least to live

5. The expulsion is not punishment but a necessary consequence of the change in human nature.
6. Milton shared the general Protestant belief in justification by faith; see *De doctrina* 1.22, "we are justified by faith without the works of the law, but not without the works of faith."
7. Horeb, where God descended to the sound of a trumpet to deliver the ten commandments on Mt Sinai (Exodus 19.16).
8. The unwithering amaranth flower was a symbol of immortality; see 3.353n.

For ever, to remove him I decree,
And send him from the Garden forth to Till
The Ground whence he was taken, fitter soil.[9]
  Michael, this my behest have thou in charge,[1]
Take to thee from among the Cherubim
Thy choice of flaming Warriors, lest the Fiend
Or° in behalf of Man, or to invade *Either*
Vacant possession[2] some new trouble raise:
Haste thee, and from the Paradise of God
Without remorse drive out the sinful Pair,
From hallow'd ground th' unholy, and denounce° *proclaim*
To them and to thir Progeny from thence
Perpetual banishment. Yet lest they faint
At the sad Sentence rigorously urg'd,
For I behold them soft'nd and with tears
Bewailing thir excess,° all terror hide. *transgression*
If patiently thy bidding they obey,
Dismiss them not disconsolate; reveal
To *Adam* what shall come in future days,
As I shall thee enlighten, intermix
My Cov'nant in the woman's seed renew'd;[3]
So send them forth, though sorrowing, yet in peace:
And on the East side of the Garden place,
Where entrance up from *Eden* easiest climbs,
Cherubic watch, and of a Sword the flame
Wide waving, all approach far off to fright,
And guard all passage to the Tree of Life:[4]
Lest Paradise a receptacle prove
To Spirits foul, and all my Trees thir prey,
With whose stol'n Fruit Man once more to delude.
  He ceas'd; and th' Archangelic Power prepar'd
For swift descent, with him the Cohort bright
Of watchful Cherubim; four faces each
Had, like a double *Janus*,[5] all thir shape
Spangl'd with eyes more numerous than those
Of *Argus*, and more wakeful than to drowse,
Charm'd with *Arcadian* Pipe, the Pastoral Reed
Of *Hermes*, or his opiate Rod.[6] Meanwhile
To resalute the World with sacred Light

9. Contrast with Genesis 3.22ff, "the Lord God said, Behold, the man is become as one of us, to know good and evil: and now, lest he put forth his hand, and take also of the tree of life, and eat, and live for ever: Therefore the Lord God sent him forth from the garden of Eden."
1. Michael was the angel of the apocalypse, and the history he shows Adam is ultimately apocalyptic.
2. Legal terminology for "encroach on my property while it has no possessor."
3. The covenant was the contract between God and the Israelites, whereby they paid obedience and sacrificial worship.
4. Echoing Genesis 3.24.
5. Janus Quadrifons, the four-faced Janus, god of gates and beginnings—including the month of January. Apt for the expulsion into a world of historical change: Janus' four heads, like the four doors of his temple, symbolized the seasons of the year.
6. Argus was set to guard Io, since his 100 eyes could watch by turns; but Mercury lulled all 100 with his reed pipe. See Ovid's *Metamorphoses* 1.671ff.

Leucóthea wak'd,[7] and with fresh dews imbalm'd
The Earth, when *Adam* and first Matron *Eve*
Had ended now thir Orisons, and found
Strength added from above, new hope to spring
Out of despair, joy, but with fear yet linkt;
Which thus to *Eve* his welcome words renew'd.
Eve, easily may Faith admit, that all
The good which we enjoy, from Heav'n descends;
But that from us aught° should ascend to Heav'n *anything*
So prevalent° as to concern the mind *efficacious*
Of God high-blest, or to incline his will,
Hard to belief may seem; yet this will Prayer,
Or one short sigh of human breath, up-borne
Ev'n to the Seat of God. For since I sought
By Prayer th' offended Deity to appease,
Kneel'd and before him humbl'd all my heart,
Methought I saw him placable and mild,
Bending his ear; persuasion in me grew
That I was heard with favor; peace return'd
Home to my Breast, and to my memory
His promise, that thy Seed shall bruise our Foe;
Which then not minded in dismay, yet now
Assures me that the bitterness of death
Is past, and we shall live. Whence Hail to thee,
Eve rightly call'd, Mother of all Mankind,
Mother of all things living, since by thee
Man is to live, and all things live for Man.
To whom thus *Eve* with sad° demeanor meek. *serious*
Ill worthy I such title should belong
To me transgressor, who for thee ordain'd
A help, became thy snare; to mee reproach
Rather belongs, distrust and all dispraise:
But infinite in pardon was my Judge,
That I who first brought Death on all, am grac't
The source of life; next favorable thou,
Who highly thus to entitle me voutsaf'st
Far other name deserving. But the Field
To labor calls us now with sweat impos'd,
Though after sleepless Night; for see the Morn,
All unconcern'd with our unrest, begins
Her rosy progress smiling,[8] let us forth,
I never from thy side henceforth to stray,
Where'er our day's work lies, though now enjoin'd
Laborious, till day droop; while here we dwell,
What can be toilsome in these pleasant Walks?
Here let us live, though in fall'n state, content.

7. Leucothea is Mater Matuta, Roman goddess of dawn.

8. The morning marks day 33 of the action.

So spake, so wish'd much humbl'd *Eve*, but Fate
Subscrib'd not; Nature first gave Signs, imprest
On Bird, Beast, Air, Air suddenly eclips'd
After short blush of Morn; nigh in her sight
The Bird of *Jove*, stoopt° from his aery tow'r, *swooping*
Two Birds of gayest plume before him drove:
Down from a Hill the Beast that reigns in Woods,
First hunter then, pursu'd a gentle brace,
Goodliest of all the Forest, Hart and Hind;
Direct to th' Eastern Gate was bent thir flight.
Adam observ'd, and with his Eye the chase
Pursuing, not unmov'd to *Eve* thus spake.
O *Eve*, some furder change awaits us nigh,
Which Heav'n by these mute signs in Nature shows
Forerunners of his purpose, or to warn
Us haply too secure of our discharge
From penalty, because from death releast
Some days; how long, and what till then our life,
Who knows, or more than this, that we are dust,
And thither must return and be no more.
Why else this double object in our sight
Of flight pursu'd in th' Air and o'er the ground
One way the self-same hour? why in the East
Darkness ere Day's mid-course, and Morning light
More orient° in yon Western Cloud that draws *bright*
O'er the blue Firmament a radiant white,
And slow descends, with something heav'nly fraught.
He err'd not, for by this the heav'nly Bands
Down from a Sky of Jasper lighted° now *descended*
In Paradise, and on a Hill made halt,° *halted*
A glorious Apparition, had not doubt
And carnal fear that day dimm'd *Adam's* eye.
Not that more glorious, when the Angels met
Jacob in *Mahanaim*,[9] where he saw
The field Pavilion'd with his Guardians bright;
Nor that which on the flaming Mount appear'd
In *Dothan*, cover'd with a Camp of Fire,
Against the *Syrian* King, who to surprise
One man, Assassin-like had levied War,
War unproclaim'd.[1] The Princely Hierarch
In thir bright stand,° there left his Powers to seize *station*
Possession of the Garden; hee alone,
To find where *Adam* shelter'd, took his way,
Not unperceiv'd of *Adam*, who to *Eve*,

9. In Genesis 32.1–2, Jacob called the place of the meeting Mahanaim.

1. Juxtaposing 2 Kings 6.13–17 and Genesis 37.16ff. The Syrian king besieged Dothan to catch one man, Elisha, who was unconcerned to hear of this. At his prayer God opened the servant's eyes "and, behold, the mountain was full of horses and chariots of fire round about Elisha."

While the great Visitant approach'd, thus spake.
  Eve, now expect great tidings, which perhaps
Of us will soon determine,° or impose *decree the future*
New Laws to be observ'd; for I descry
From yonder blazing Cloud that veils the Hill
One of the heav'nly Host, and by his Gait
None of the meanest, some great Potentate
Or of the Thrones above, such Majesty
Invests him coming; yet not terrible,
That I should fear, nor sociably mild,
As *Raphaël*, that I should much confide,
But solemn and sublime, whom not to offend,
With reverence I must meet, and thou retire.
He ended; and th' Arch-Angel soon drew nigh,
Not in his shape Celestial, but as Man
Clad to meet Man; over his lucid° Arms *bright*
A military Vest of purple flow'd
Livelier than *Melibæan*, or the grain° *dye*
Of *Sarra*, worn by Kings and Heroes old
In time of Truce; *Iris* had dipt the woof;[2]
His starry Helm unbuckl'd show'd him prime
In Manhood where Youth ended; by his side
As in a glistering *Zodiac* hung the Sword,
Satan's dire dread, and in his hand the Spear.
Adam bow'd low, hee Kingly from his State° *dignity*
Inclin'd not, but his coming thus declar'd.
  Adam, Heav'n's high behest no Preface needs:
Sufficient that thy Prayers are heard, and Death,
Then due by sentence when thou didst transgress,
Defeated of his seizure many days
Giv'n thee of Grace, wherein thou mayst repent,
And one bad act with many deeds well done
May'st cover: well may then thy Lord appeas'd
Redeem thee quite° from Death's rapacious claim; *completely*
But longer in this Paradise to dwell
Permits not; to remove thee I am come,
And send thee from the Garden forth to till
The ground whence thou wast tak'n, fitter Soil.[3]
  He added not, for *Adam* at the news
Heart-strook with chilling gripe° of sorrow stood, *spasm*
That all his senses bound; *Eve*, who unseen
Yet all had heard, with audible lament
Discover'd° soon the place of her retire.° *revealed / withdrawal*
  O unexpected stroke, worse than of Death!
Must I thus leave thee Paradise? thus leave

2. Sarra is the city Tyre, famous for its dye. Iris dyed the woof (threads woven across a warp), because the iris flower was "lilium purpureum," and because she was the rainbow, sign of God's covenant or "truce."

3. Michael delivers the divine decree verbatim, as befits his solemn mission (11.96–8).

Thee Native Soil, these happy Walks and Shades,
Fit haunt of Gods? where I had hope to spend,
Quiet though sad, the respite of that day
That must be mortal to us both. O flow'rs,
That never will in other Climate grow,
My early visitation, and my last
At Ev'n, which I bred up with tender hand
From the first op'ning bud, and gave ye Names,
Who now shall rear ye to the Sun, or rank
Your Tribes, and water from th' ambrosial Fount?[4]
Thee lastly nuptial Bower, by mee adorn'd
With what to sight or smell was sweet; from thee
How shall I part, and whither wander down
Into a lower World, to° this obscure *compared with*
And wild, how shall we breathe in other Air
Less pure, accustom'd to immortal Fruits?
  Whom thus the Angel interrupted mild.
Lament not *Eve*, but patiently resign
What justly thou hast lost; nor set thy heart,
Thus over-fond, on that which is not thine;
Thy going is not lonely, with thee goes
Thy Husband, him to follow thou art bound;
Where he abides, think there thy native soil.
  Adam by this from the cold sudden damp° *stupor*
Recovering, and his scatter'd spirits return'd,
To *Michael* thus his humble words address'd.
  Celestial, whether among the Thrones, or nam'd
Of them the Highest, for such of shape may seem
Prince above Princes, gently hast thou told
Thy message, which might else in telling wound,
And in performing end us; what besides
Of sorrow and dejection and despair
Our frailty can sustain, thy tidings bring,
Departure from this happy place, our sweet
Recess, and only consolation left
Familiar to our eyes, all places else
Inhospitable appear and desolate,
Nor knowing us nor known: and if by prayer
Incessant I could hope to change the will
Of him who all things can,° I would not cease *knows*
To weary him with my assiduous cries:[5]
But prayer against his absolute Decree
No more avails than breath against the wind,
Blown stifling back on him that breathes it forth:

4. Recalling 4.240, where the fountain "ran nectar," another immortal food. The fountain of Paradise was often termed a Fountain of Life (from the "living water" in John 4.10) within which was sheltered an elaborate Well of Life.

5. The first of Adam's many errors in the course of his instruction. See Luke 18.5–7 for an instance of the effectiveness of such prayers.

Therefore to his great bidding I submit.
This most afflicts me, that departing hence,
As from his face I shall be hid, depriv'd
His blessed count'nance;[6] here I could frequent,
With worship, place by place where he voutsaf'd
Presence Divine, and to my Sons relate;
On this Mount he appear'd, under this Tree
Stood visible, among these Pines his voice
I heard, here with him at this Fountain talk'd:
So many grateful Altars I would rear
Of grassy Turf, and pile up every Stone
Of lustre from the brook, in memory,
Or monument to Ages, and thereon
Offer sweet smelling Gums and Fruits and Flow'rs:
In yonder nether World where shall I seek
His bright appearances, or footstep trace?
For though I fled him angry, yet recall'd
To life prolong'd and promis'd Race, I now
Gladly behold though but his utmost skirts
Of glory, and far off his steps adore.
  To whom thus *Michael* with regard benign.
Adam, thou know'st Heav'n his, and all the Earth,
Not this Rock only; his Omnipresence fills
Land, Sea, and Air, and every kind that lives,[7]
Fomented° by his virtual° power and warm'd: *nurtured / virtuous*
All th' Earth he gave thee to possess and rule,
No despicable gift; surmise not then
His presence to these narrow bounds confin'd
Of Paradise or *Eden*: this had been
Perhaps thy Capital Seat, from whence had spread
All generations, and had hither come
From all the ends of th' Earth, to celebrate
And reverence thee thir great Progenitor.
But this preëminence thou hast lost, brought down
To dwell on even ground now with thy Sons:
Yet doubt not but in Valley and in Plain
God is as here, and will be found alike
Present, and of his presence many a sign
Still following thee, still compassing thee round
With goodness and paternal Love, his Face
Express,° and of his steps the track Divine. *exactly imaging*
Which that thou may'st believe, and be confirm'd,
Ere thou from hence depart, know I am sent
To show thee what shall come in future days

6. Cain complains similarly: "Behold, thou hast driven me out this day from the face of the earth; and from thy face shall I be hid; and I shall be a fugitive and a vagabond in the earth" (Genesis 4.14).

7. Michael corrects Adam's post-Fall tendency to practice local devotions. For God's omnipresence, see 7.168ff; Jerome 23.24; Malachi 1.11; and John 4.21.

To thee and to thy Offspring; good with bad
Expect to hear, supernal° Grace contending *heavenly*
With sinfulness of Men; thereby to learn
True patience, and to temper joy with fear
And pious sorrow, equally inur'd
By moderation either state to bear,
Prosperous or adverse: so shalt thou lead
Safest thy life, and best prepar'd endure
Thy mortal passage when it comes. Ascend
This Hill; let *Eve* (for I have drencht° her eyes) *applied medicine to*
Here sleep below while thou to foresight° wak'st, *prophetic vision*
As once thou slep'st, while Shee to life was form'd.
To whom thus *Adam* gratefully repli'd.
Ascend, I follow thee, safe Guide, the path
Thou lead'st me, and to the hand of Heav'n submit,
However chast'ning, to the evil turn
My obvious° breast, arming to overcome *exposed*
By suffering, and earn rest from labor won,
If so I may attain. So both ascend
In the Visions of God: It was a Hill
Of Paradise the highest, from whose top
The Hemisphere of Earth in clearest Ken
Stretcht out to the amplest reach of prospect lay.
Not higher that Hill nor wider looking round,
Whereon for different cause the Tempter set
Our second *Adam* in the Wilderness,
To show him all Earth's Kingdoms and thir Glory.[8]
His Eye might there command wherever stood
City of old or modern Fame, the Seat
Of mightiest Empire, from the destin'd Walls
Of *Cambalu*, seat of *Cathaian Can*,[9]
And *Samarchand* by *Oxus*, *Temir's* Throne,
To *Paquin* of *Sinœan* Kings, and thence
To *Agra* and *Lahor* of great *Mogul*
Down to the golden *Chersonese*, or where
The *Persian* in *Ecbatan* sat, or since
In *Hispahan*, or where the *Russian Ksar*
In *Mosco*, or the Sultan in *Bizance*,
Turchestan-born; nor could his eye not ken

8. To tempt Christ, the devil "taketh him up into an exceeding high mountain, and showeth him all the kingdoms of the world, and the glory of them." (See Matthew 4.8.) Milton portrays this scene in *Paradise Regained* 3.251ff.

9. Adam first sees Asian kingdoms: Cambalu is Cambalus, capital of Cathay. Samarchand is Timur's capital, near the Oxus River. Paquin (Peking) is the capital of China, a separate kingdom from Cathay. Sinoean means Chinese. Agra is a kingdom in the north central region of India, whereas Lahor is in northwest Punjab. The wealthy Chersonese peninsula is vaguely located in India's extreme east—now Malacca in Malaysia. Ecbatan was the summer capital of Persian kings. Hispahan (or Ispahan) became a capital in the sixteenth century, when the Safavid dynasty moved their seat from Kazvin. Bizance is Byzantium, Constantinople, or Istanbul—then capital of the Turkish sultan. The sultans belonged to a tribe that haled from Turkestan, a central Asian region between Mongolia and the Caspian.

Th' Empire of *Negus* to his utmost Port[1]
Ercoco and the less Maritime Kings
Mombaza, and *Quiloa*, and *Melind*,
And *Sofala* thought *Ophir*, to the Realm
Of *Congo*, and *Angola* fardest South;
Or thence from *Niger* Flood to *Atlas* Mount
The Kingdoms of *Almansor*, *Fez* and *Sus*,
Marocco and *Algiers*, and *Tremisen*;
On *Europe* thence, and where *Rome* was to sway
The World: in Spirit perhaps he also saw
Rich *Mexico* the seat of *Montezume*,[2]
And *Cusco* in *Peru*, the richer seat
Of *Atabalipa*, and yet unspoil'd
Guiana, whose great City *Geryon's* Sons
Call *El Dorado:* but to nobler sights
Michael from *Adam's* eyes the Film remov'd[3]
Which that false Fruit that promis'd clearer sight
Had bred; then purg'd with Euphrasy and Rue[4]
The visual Nerve, for he had much to see;
And from the Well of Life three drops instill'd.
So deep the power of these Ingredients pierc'd,
Ev'n to the inmost seat of mental sight,
That *Adam* now enforc't to close his eyes,
Sunk down and all his Spirits became intranst:
But him the gentle Angel by the hand
Soon rais'd, and his attention thus recall'd.
Adam, now ope thine eyes, and first behold
Th' effects which thy original crime hath wrought
In some to spring from thee, who never touch'd
Th'excepted Tree, nor with the Snake conspir'd,
Nor sinn'd thy sin, yet from that sin derive
Corruption to bring forth more violent deeds.
His eyes he op'n'd, and beheld a field,
Part arable and tilth,° whereon were Sheaves *ploughed field*
New reapt, the other part sheep-walks° and folds; *pasture*
I' th' midst an Altar as the Land-mark stood
Rustic, of grassy sward;° thither anon° *turf / soon*
A sweaty Reaper from his Tillage brought

1. As with the Asian kingdoms, Adam and Michael see nine African realms. Negus was the hereditary title of the Abyssinian empire. Ercoco or Arkiko is a port on the Red Sea. Melind or Malindi was Vasco's last port of call before his audacious voyage to India to found Portugal's short-lived empire. These are both on the coast of modern Kenya; Quiloa or Kilwa is on the coast of Tanzania. Sofala is a port in Mozambique, from its wealth sometimes supposed to be Ophir. The Niger River is in modern Guinea and Mali, and the Atlas Mountains in Morocco. Almansor (or Mansur, "Victorious") was the name of several Mohammedan princes. Fez was part of the Sultanate of Fez and Morocco. Sus is a province in southern Morocco, formerly independent. And Tremisen or Tlemcen is part of Algeria.

2. Even from the hill Adam could not physically see the hemisphere, so he sees it "in spirit." The empire of Montezuma was plundered by Cortez. The empire of Atahuallpa (Atabalipa), with its capital Cusco was plundered by Pizarro. But Manoa, the fabulous capital of Guiana, remained yet unspoiled by the Spanish. Hercules killed the mythical monster Geryon, which had three heads — thus the three kingdoms described here.

3. So Homer's Pallas clears Diomedes' eyes (*Iliad* 5.127); Virgil's Venus clears Aeneas' (*Aeneid* 2.604), and Tasso's Michael clears Goffredo's (*Gerusalemme Liberata* 18.92ff).

4. Euphrasy (or eyebright) and rue are herbal restoratives for the eyes.

First Fruits, the green Ear, and the yellow Sheaf,
Uncull'd,° as came to hand; a Shepherd next *not select*
More meek came with the Firstlings of his Flock
Choicest and best; then sacrificing, laid
The Inwards and thir Fat, with Incense strew'd,
On the cleft Wood, and all due Rites perform'd.
His Off'ring soon propitious Fire from Heav'n
Consum'd with nimble glance,° and grateful steam;[5] *swift flash*
The other's not, for his was not sincere;
Whereat hee inly rag'd, and as they talk'd,
Smote him into the Midriff with a stone
That beat out life; he fell, and deadly pale
Groan'd out his Soul with gushing blood effus'd.
Much at that sight was *Adam* in his heart
Dismay'd, and thus in haste to th' Angel cri'd.
　O Teacher, some great mischief hath befall'n
To that meek man, who well had sacrific'd;
Is Piety thus and pure Devotion paid?
　T' whom *Michael* thus, hee also mov'd, repli'd.
These two are Brethren, *Adam*, and to come
Out of thy loins; th' unjust the just hath slain,
For envy that his Brother's Offering found
From Heav'n acceptance; but the bloody Fact° *crime*
Will be aveng'd, and th' other's Faith approv'd
Lose no reward, though here thou see him die,
Rolling in dust and gore. To which our Sire.
　Alas, both for the deed and for the cause!
But have I now seen Death? Is this the way
I must return to native dust? O sight
Of terror, foul and ugly to behold,
Horrid to think, how horrible to feel!
　To whom thus *Michaël*.[6] Death thou hast seen
In his first shape on man; but many shapes
Of Death, and many are the ways that lead
To his grim Cave, all dismal;° yet to sense *dreadful*
More terrible at th' entrance than within.
Some, as thou saw'st, by violent stroke shall die.
By Fire, Flood, Famine, by Intemperance more
In Meats and Drinks, which on the Earth shall bring
Diseases dire, of which a monstrous crew
Before thee shall appear; that thou may'st know
What misery th' inabstinence of *Eve*
Shall bring on men. Immediately a place
Before his eyes appear'd, sad, noisome, dark,
A Lazar-house° it seem'd, wherein were laid *hospital*
Numbers of all diseas'd, all maladies

5. The fire and steam are common signs that a sacrifice was acceptable. See Leviticus 9.24; Judges 6.21; 1 Kings 18.38; 1 Chronicles 21.26; 2 Chronicles 7.1.
6. Trisyllabic, as befits the passage's slow gravity.

Of ghastly Spasm, or racking torture, qualms
Of heart-sick Agony, all feverous kinds,
Convulsions, Epilepsies, fierce Catarrhs,
Intestine Stone and Ulcer, Colic pangs,
Dæmoniac Frenzy, moping Melancholy[7]
And Moon-struck madness, pining° Atrophy, *emaciating*
Marasmus,° and wide-wasting Pestilence, *wasting of the body*
Dropsies, and Asthmas, and Joint-racking Rheums.° *rheumatic pains*
Dire was the tossing, deep the groans, despair
Tended the sick busiest from Couch to Couch;
And over them triumphant Death his Dart
Shook, but delay'd to strike, though oft invok't
With vows, as thir chief good, and final hope.
Sight so deform what heart of Rock could long
Dry-ey'd behold? *Adam* could not, but wept,
Though not of Woman born; compassion quell'd
His best of Man,[8] and gave him up to tears
A space, till firmer thoughts restrain'd excess,
And scarce recovering words his plaint renew'd.
O miserable Mankind, to what fall
Degraded, to what wretched state reserv'd!
Better end here unborn. Why is life giv'n
To be thus wrested from us? rather why
Obtruded on us thus? who if we knew
What we receive, would either not accept
Life offer'd, or soon beg to lay it down,
Glad to be so dismist in peace. Can thus
Th' Image of God in man created once
So goodly and erect, though faulty since,
To such unsightly sufferings be debas't
Under inhuman pains? Why should not Man,
Retaining still Divine similitude
In part, from such deformities be free,
And for his Maker's Image sake exempt?[9]
Thir Maker's Image, answer'd *Michael*, then
Forsook them, when themselves they vilifi'd° *demeaned*
To serve ungovern'd appetite, and took
His Image whom they served, a brutish vice,
Inductive° mainly to the sin of *Eve*. *giving rise*
Therefore so abject is thir punishment,
Disfiguring not God's likeness, but thir own,
Or if his likeness, by themselves defac't
While they pervert pure Nature's healthful rules
To loathsome sickness, worthily, since they
God's Image did not reverence in themselves.

7. Melancholy was a more comprehensive category at the time.
8. A man's tears, and softer feelings generally, were attributed to his feminine part.
9. Protestant theology emphasized disfiguring of the *imago Dei*, or image of God.

I yield it just, said *Adam*, and submit.
But is there yet no other way, besides
These painful passages,° how we may come *deaths*
To Death, and mix with our connatural dust?
There is, said *Michael*, if thou well observe
The rule of not too much, by temperance taught,
In what thou eat'st and drink'st, seeking from thence
Due nourishment, not gluttonous delight,
Till many years over thy head return:
So may'st thou live, till like ripe Fruit thou drop
Into thy Mother's lap, or be with ease
Gather'd, not harshly pluckt, for death mature:
This is old age; but then thou must outlive
Thy youth, thy strength, thy beauty, which will change
To wither'd weak and gray; thy Senses then
Obtuse, all taste of pleasure must forgo,
To what thou hast, and for the Air of youth
Hopeful and cheerful, in thy blood will reign
A melancholy damp of cold and dry
To weigh thy Spirits down, and last consume
The Balm of Life. To whom our Ancestor.
Henceforth I fly not Death, nor would prolong
Life much, bent rather how I may be quit
Fairest and easiest of this cumbrous charge,
Which I must keep till my appointed day
Of rend'ring up, and patiently attend° *await*
My dissolution. *Michaël* repli'd.
Nor love thy Life, nor hate; but what thou liv'st
Live well, how long or short permit to Heav'n:
And now prepare thee for another sight.
He look'd and saw a spacious Plain, whereon
Were Tents of various hue; by some were herds
Of Cattle grazing: others, whence the sound
Of Instruments that made melodious chime
Was heard, of Harp and Organ; and who mov'd
Thir stops and chords was seen: his volant° touch *nimble*
Instinct° through all proportions low and high *impelled*
Fled and pursu'd transverse the resonant fugue.
In other part stood one who at the Forge
Laboring, two massy clods of Iron and Brass
Had melted (whether found where casual° fire *accidental*
Had wasted woods on Mountain or in Vale,
Down to the veins of Earth, thence gliding hot
To some Cave's mouth, or whether washt by stream
From underground); the liquid Ore he drain'd
Into fit moulds prepar'd; from which he form'd
First his own Tools; then, what might else be wrought
Fusile° or grav'n in metal. After these, *cast*
But on the hither side a different sort

From the high neighboring Hills, which was thir Seat,[1]
Down to the Plain descended: by thir guise
Just men they seem'd, and all thir study bent
To worship God aright, and know his works
Not hid, nor those things last which might preserve
Freedom and Peace to men: they on the Plain
Long had not walkt, when from the Tents behold
A Bevy of fair Women, richly gay
In Gems and wanton dress; to the Harp they sung
Soft amorous Ditties, and in dance came on:
The Men though grave, ey'd them, and let thir eyes
Rove without rein, till in the amorous Net
Fast caught, they lik'd and each his liking chose;
And now of love they treat° till th' Ev'ning Star *talk*
Love's Harbinger appear'd; then all in heat
They light the Nuptial Torch, and bid invoke
Hymen, then first to marriage Rites invok't;
With Feast and Music all the Tents resound.
Such happy interview and fair event
Of love and youth not lost, Songs, Garlands, Flow'rs,
And charming Symphonies attach'd the heart
Of *Adam*, soon inclin'd to admit delight
The bent of Nature; which he thus express'd.
True opener of mine eyes, prime Angel blest,
Much better seems this Vision, and more hope
Of peaceful days portends, than those two past;
Those were of hate and death, or pain much worse,
Here Nature seems fulfill'd in all her ends.
To whom thus *Michael*. Judge not what is best
By pleasure, though to Nature seeming meet,
Created, as thou art, to nobler end
Holy and pure, conformity divine.
Those Tents thou saw'st so pleasant, were the Tents
Of wickedness, wherein shall dwell his Race
Who slew his Brother; studious they appear
Of Arts that polish Life, Inventors rare,
Unmindful of thir Maker, though his Spirit
Taught them, but they his gifts acknowledg'd none.
Yet they a beauteous offspring shall beget;
For that fair female Troop thou saw'st, that seem'd
Of Goddesses, so blithe, so smooth, so gay,
Yet empty of all good wherein consists
Woman's domestic honor and chief praise;
Bred only and completed° to the taste *equipped*
Of lustful appetence,° to sing, to dance, *desire*
To dress, and troll° the Tongue, and roll the Eye. *wag*

1. In Genesis 5, these are descendants not of Cain but of Seth. They inhabited mountains neighboring Paradise and so on the hither side of the plain, whereas Cain lived "on the east of Eden" (Genesis 4.16).

To these that sober Race of Men, whose lives
Religious titl'd them the Sons of God,
Shall yield up all thir virtue, all thir fame
Ignobly, to the trains° and to the smiles *enticements*
Of these fair Atheists, and now swim in joy,
(Erelong to swim at large) and laugh; for which
The world erelong a world of tears must weep.
To whom thus *Adam* of short joy bereft.
O pity and shame, that they who to live well
Enter'd so fair, should turn aside to tread
Paths indirect, or in the mid way faint![2]
But still I see the tenor of Man's woe
Holds on the same, from Woman to begin.
From Man's effeminate slackness it begins,
Said th' Angel, who should better hold his place
By wisdom, and superior gifts receiv'd.
But now prepare thee for another Scene.
He look'd and saw wide Territory spread
Before him, Towns, and rural works between,
Cities of Men with lofty Gates and Tow'rs,
Concourse° in Arms, fierce Faces threat'ning War, *hostile encounter*
Giants of mighty Bone,[3] and bold emprise;° *chivalric deeds*
Part wield thir Arms, part curb the foaming Steed,
Single or in Array of Battle rang'd
Both Horse and Foot, nor idly must'ring stood;
One way a Band select from forage drives
A herd of Beeves, fair Oxen and fair Kine
From a fat Meadow ground; or fleecy Flock,
Ewes and thir bleating Lambs over the Plain,
Thir Booty; scarce with Life the Shepherds fly,
But call in aid, which makes a bloody Fray;
With cruel Tournament the Squadrons join;
Where Cattle pastur'd late, now scatter'd lies
With Carcasses and Arms th' ensanguin'd° Field *blood-stained*
Deserted: Others to a City strong
Lay Siege, encampt; by Battery, Scale,° and Mine, *ladder*
Assaulting; others from the wall defend
With Dart and Jav'lin, Stones and sulphurous Fire;
On each hand slaughter and gigantic deeds.
In other part the scepter'd Heralds call
To Council in the City Gates: anon
Grey-headed men and grave, with Warriors mixt,
Assemble, and Harangues are heard, but soon
In factious opposition, till at last

2. This line marks the "midway" of the first, destroyed world. It is the midpoint between the first vision's first line (11.423) and the fifth vision's last line (11.839).

3. "Giants" is not exaggeration, in view of the tradition that giants were offspring of angels. See 1.195–200; 3.461ff; 11.621–22, 688.

Of middle Age one rising,[4] eminent
In wise deport, spake much of Right and Wrong,
Of Justice, of Religion, Truth and Peace,
And Judgment from above: him old and young
Exploded,° and had seiz'd with violent hands, *shouted down*
Had not a Cloud descending snatch'd him thence
Unseen amid the throng: so violence
Proceeded, and Oppression, and Sword-Law
Through all the Plain, and refuge none was found.
Adam was all in tears, and to his guide
Lamenting turn'd full sad; O what are these,
Death's Ministers, not Men, who thus deal Death
Inhumanly to men, and multiply
Ten thousandfold the sin of him who slew
His Brother; for of whom such massacre
Make they but of thir Brethren, men of men?
But who was that Just Man, whom had not Heav'n
Rescu'd, had in his Righteousness been lost?
  To whom thus *Michael*. These are the product
Of those ill-mated Marriages thou saw'st;
Where good with bad were matcht, who of themselves
Abhor to join; and by imprudence mixt,
Produce prodigious Births of body or mind.
Such were these Giants, men of high renown;
For in those days Might only shall be admir'd,
And Valor and Heroic Virtue call'd;
To overcome in Battle, and subdue
Nations, and bring home spoils with infinite
Man-slaughter, shall be held the highest pitch
Of human Glory, and for Glory done
Of triumph, to be styl'd great Conquerors,
Patrons of Mankind, Gods, and Sons of Gods,
Destroyers rightlier call'd and Plagues of men.
Thus Fame shall be achiev'd, renown on Earth,
And what most merits fame in silence hid.
But hee the sev'nth from thee, whom thou beheld'st
The only righteous in a World perverse,
And therefore hated, therefore so beset
With Foes for daring single to be just,
And utter odious Truth, that God would come
To judge them with his Saints: Him the most High
Rapt in a balmy Cloud with winged Steeds
Did, as thou saw'st, receive, to walk with God
High in Salvation and the Climes of bliss,
Exempt from Death; to show thee what reward
Awaits the good, the rest what punishment;

4. Enoch, who was seven generations from Adam (11.700), and Noah's grandfather. He was taken directly into heaven by God when 365 years old. See Genesis 5.21–4; Jude 14; Hebrews 11.5. The apocryphal book of Enoch, like Michael, treats the Flood as judgment on sin.

Which now direct thine eyes and soon behold.
He look'd, and saw the face of things quite chang'd;
The brazen Throat of War had ceast to roar,
All now was turn'd to jollity and game,
To luxury° and riot, feast and dance, *lust*
Marrying or prostituting, as befell,
Rape of Adultery, where passing° fair *surpassing*
Allur'd them; thence from Cups to civil Broils.
At length a Reverend Sire among them came,[5]
And of thir doings great dislike declar'd,
And testifi'd against thir ways; hee oft
Frequented thir Assemblies, whereso met,
Triumphs or Festivals, and to them preach'd
Conversion and Repentance, as to Souls
In Prison under Judgments imminent:
But all in vain: which when he saw, he ceas'd
Contending, and remov'd his Tents far off;
Then from the Mountain hewing Timber tall,
Began to build a Vessel of huge bulk,
Measur'd by Cubit, length, and breadth, and highth,
Smear'd round with Pitch, and in the side a door
Contriv'd, and of provisions laid in large
For Man and Beast: when lo a wonder strange!
Of every Beast, and Bird, and Insect small
Came sevens, and pairs, and enter'd in, as taught
Thir order; last the Sire, and his three Sons
With thir four Wives; and God made fast the door.
Meanwhile the Southwind rose, and with black wings
Wide hovering, all the Clouds together drove
From under Heav'n; the Hills to their supply° *assistance*
Vapor, and Exhalation° dusk and moist, *mist*
Sent up amain; and now the thick'n'd Sky
Like a dark Ceiling stood; down rush'd the Rain
Impetuous, and continu'd till the Earth
No more was seen; the floating Vessel swum
Uplifted; and secure with beaked prow
Rode tilting o'er the Waves, all dwellings else
Flood overwhelm'd, and them with all thir pomp
Deep under water roll'd; Sea cover'd Sea,
Sea without shore; and in thir Palaces
Where luxury late reign'd, Sea-monsters whelp'd° *had offspring*
And stabl'd;° of Mankind so numerous late, *lived as in a stable*
All left, in one small bottom° swum embark't. *boat*
How didst thou grieve then, *Adam*, to behold
The end of all thy Offspring, end so sad,
Depopulation; thee another Flood,

5. Milton's flood account follows Genesis 6.9–9:17 with few changes.

Of tears and sorrow a Flood thee also drown'd,
And sunk thee as thy Sons; till gently rear'd
By th' Angel, on thy feet thou stood'st at last,
Though comfortless, as when a Father mourns
His Children, all in view destroy'd at once;
And scarce to th' Angel utter'd'st thus thy plaint.
O Visions ill foreseen! better had I
Liv'd ignorant of future, so had borne
My part of evil only, each day's lot
Anough to bear; those now, that were dispens't
The burd'n of many Ages, on me light
At once, by my foreknowledge gaining Birth
Abortive, to torment me ere thir being,
With thought that they must be. Let no man seek
Henceforth to be foretold what shall befall
Him or his Children, evil he may be sure,
Which neither his foreknowing can prevent,
And hee the future evil shall no less
In apprehension than in substance feel
Grievous to bear: but that care now is past,
Man is not whom to warn:[6] those few escap't
Famine and anguish will at last consume
Wand'ring that wat'ry Desert: I had hope
When violence was ceas't, and War on Earth,
All would have then gone well, peace would have crown'd
With length of happy days the race of man;
But I was far deceiv'd; for now I see
Peace to corrupt no less than War to waste.
How comes it thus? unfold, Celestial Guide,
And whether here the Race of man will end.
To whom thus *Michael.* Those whom last thou saw'st
In triumph and luxurious wealth, are they
First seen in acts of prowess eminent
And great exploits, but of true virtue void;
Who having spilt much blood, and done much waste
Subduing Nations, and achiev'd thereby
Fame in the World, high titles, and rich prey,
Shall change thir course to pleasure, ease, and sloth,
Surfeit, and lust, till wantonness and pride
Raise out of friendship hostile deeds in Peace.
The conquer'd also, and enslav'd by War
Shall with thir freedom lost all virtue lose
And fear of God, from whom thir piety feign'd
In sharp contest of Battle found no aid
Against invaders; therefore cool'd in zeal
Thenceforth shall practice how to live secure,° *heedlessly*

6. That is, "there is no one left to warn."

Worldly or dissolute, on what thir Lords
Shall leave them to enjoy; for th' Earth shall bear
More than anough, that temperance may be tri'd:
So all shall turn degenerate, all deprav'd,
Justice and Temperance, Truth and Faith forgot;
One Man except, the only Son of light
In a dark Age, against example good,
Against allurement, custom, and a World
Offended; fearless of reproach and scorn,
Or violence, hee of thir wicked ways
Shall them admonish, and before them set
The paths of righteousness how much more safe,
And full of peace, denouncing° wrath to come *proclaiming*
On thir impenitence; and shall return
Of them derided, but of God observ'd
The one just Man alive; by his command
Shall build a wondrous Ark, as thou beheld'st,
To save himself and household from amidst
A World devote° to universal rack.° *doomed / destruction*
No sooner hee with them of Man and Beast
Select for life shall in the Ark be lodg'd,
And shelter'd round, but all the Cataracts° *sluices*
Of Heav'n set open on the Earth shall pour
Rain day and night, all fountains of the Deep
Broke up, shall heave the Ocean to usurp
Beyond all bounds, till inundation rise
Above the highest Hills: then shall this Mount
Of Paradise by might of Waves be mov'd
Out of his place, push'd by the horned flood,
With all his verdure spoil'd, and Trees adrift
Down the great River[7] to the op'ning Gulf,
And there take root an Island salt and bare
The haunt of Seals and Ores,° and Sea-mews'° clang. *sea monsters / gulls'*
To teach thee that God attributes to place
No sanctity, if none be thither brought
By Men who there frequent, or therein dwell.
And now what further shall ensue, behold.
    He look'd, and saw the Ark hull° on the flood, *drift*
Which now abated, for the Clouds were fled,
Driv'n by a keen North-wind, that blowing dry
Wrinkl'd the face of Deluge, as decay'd;
And the clear Sun on his wide wat'ry Glass
Gaz'd hot, and of the fresh Wave largely drew,
As after thirst, which made thir flowing shrink
From standing lake to tripping° ebb, that stole *dancing*
With soft foot towards the deep, who now had stopt

7. The modern Tigris or Euphrates.

His Sluices, as the Heav'n his windows shut.
The Ark no more now floats, but seems on ground
Fast on the top of some high mountain fixt.[8]
And now the tops of Hills as Rocks appear;
With clamor thence the rapid Currents drive
Towards the retreating Sea thir furious tide.
Forthwith from out the Ark a Raven flies,
And after him, the surer messenger,
A Dove sent forth once and again to spy
Green Tree or ground whereon his foot may light;
The second time returning, in his Bill
An Olive leaf he brings, pacific sign:
Anon dry ground appears, and from his Ark
The ancient Sire descends with all his Train;
Then with uplifted hands, and eyes devout,
Grateful to Heav'n, over his head beholds
A dewy Cloud, and in the Cloud a Bow
Conspicuous with three listed° colors gay, *arranged in bands*
Betok'ning peace from God, and Cov'nant new.[9]
Whereat the heart of *Adam* erst° so sad *previously*
Greatly rejoic'd, and thus his joy broke forth.

O thou who future things canst represent
As present, Heav'nly instructor, I revive
At this last sight, assur'd that Man shall live
With all the Creatures, and thir seed preserve.
Far less I now lament for one whole World
Of wicked Sons destroy'd, than I rejoice
For one Man found so perfet and so just,
That God voutsafes to raise another World
From him, and all his anger to forget.
But say, what mean those color'd streaks in Heav'n,
Distended° as the Brow of God appeas'd, *expanded*
Or serve they as a flow'ry verge to bind
The fluid skirts of that same wat'ry Cloud,
Lest it again dissolve and show'r the Earth?

To whom th' Arch-Angel. Dext'rously thou aim'st;
So willingly doth God remit his Ire,
Though late repenting him of Man deprav'd,
Griev'd at his heart, when looking down he saw
The whole Earth fill'd with violence, and all flesh
Corrupting each thir way; yet those remov'd,
Such grace shall one just Man find in his sight,
That he relents, not to blot out mankind,
And makes a Cov'nant never to destroy
The Earth again by flood, nor let the Sea

8. Milton rejects the locale given by Genesis 8.4, "upon the mountains of Ararat."

9. Echoing Genesis 9.13–15, "I do set my bow in the cloud, and it shall be for a token of a covenant between me and the earth . . . the waters shall no more become a flood to destroy all flesh."

Surpass his bounds, nor Rain to drown the World
With Man therein or Beast; but when he brings
Over the Earth a Cloud, will therein set
His triple-color'd Bow, whereon to look
And call to mind his Cov'nant: Day and Night,
Seed-time and Harvest, Heat and hoary Frost
Shall hold thir course, till fire purge all things new,[1]
Both Heav'n and Earth, wherein the just shall dwell.

The End of the Eleventh Book.

Book 12
The Argument

The Angel Michael *continues from the Flood to relate what shall succeed; then, in the mention of* Abraham, *comes by degrees to explain, who that Seed of the Woman shall be, which was promised* Adam and Eve *in the Fall; his Incarnation, Death, Resurrection, and Ascension; the state of the Church till his second Coming.* Adam *greatly satisfied and recomforted by these Relations and Promises descends the Hill with* Michael; *wakens* Eve, *who all this while had slept, but with gentle dreams compos'd to quietness of mind and submission.* Michael *in either hand leads them out of Paradise, the fiery Sword waving behind them, and the Cherubim taking thir Stations to guard the Place.*

As one who in his journey bates° at Noon, *pauses*
Though bent on speed, so here the Arch-Angel paus'd
Betwixt the world destroy'd and world restor'd,
If *Adam* aught perhaps might interpose;
Then with transition sweet new Speech resumes.
Thus thou hast seen one World begin and end;
And Man as from a second stock proceed.[1]
Much thou hast yet to see, but I perceive
Thy mortal sight to fail; objects divine
Must needs impair and weary human sense:
Henceforth what is to come I will relate,
Thou therefore give due audience, and attend.
This second source of Men, while yet but few,
And while the dread of judgment past remains
Fresh in thir minds, fearing the Deity,
With some regard to what is just and right
Shall lead thir lives, and multiply apace,
Laboring° the soil, and reaping plenteous crop, *tilling*
Corn, wine and oil; and from the herd or flock,
Oft sacrificing Bullock, Lamb, or Kid,
With large Wine-offerings pour'd, and sacred Feast,

1. The three colors of the bow are blue, yellow, and red. 2 Peter 3.6ff and 3.13ff links the Flood (blue) with the final conflagration (red): "The world that then was, being overflowed with water, perished: But the heavens and the earth, which are now, by the same word are kept in store, reserved unto fire against the day of judgment and perdition of ungodly men."

1. "Stock," an ambiguity, refers not only to the literal replacement of one source of the human line of descent (Adam) by another (Noah), but also to the grafting of mankind onto the stem of Christ, according to the Pauline allegory of regeneration (Romans 11). The covenant with Noah was a type of the New Covenant.

Shall spend thir days in joy unblam'd, and dwell
Long time in peace by Families and Tribes
Under paternal rule; till one shall rise[2]
Of proud ambitious heart, who not content
With fair equality, fraternal state,
Will arrogate Dominion undeserv'd
Over his brethren, and quite dispossess
Concord and law of Nature from the Earth:[3]
Hunting (and Men not Beasts shall be his game)
With War and hostile snare such as refuse
Subjection to his Empire tyrannous:[4]
A mighty Hunter thence he shall be styl'd
Before the Lord, as in despite of Heav'n,
Or from Heav'n claiming second Sovranty;[5]
And from Rebellion shall derive his name,
Though of Rebellion others he accuse.
Hee with a crew, whom like Ambition joins
With him or under him to tyrannize,
Marching from *Eden* towards the West, shall find
The Plain, wherein a black bituminous gurge° *whirlpool*
Boils out from under ground, the mouth of Hell;
Of Brick, and of that stuff they cast to build
A City and Tow'r, whose top may reach to Heav'n;[6]
And get themselves a name, lest far disperst
In foreign Lands thir memory be lost,
Regardless whether good or evil fame.[7]
But God who oft descends to visit men
Unseen, and through thir habitations walks
To mark thir doings, them beholding soon,
Comes down to see thir City, ere the Tower
Obstruct Heav'n Tow'rs, and in derision sets
Upon thir Tongues a various Spirit to rase
Quite out thir Native Language, and instead
To sow a jangling noise of words unknown:
Forthwith a hideous gabble rises loud
Among the Builders; each to other calls
Not understood, till hoarse, and all in rage,
As mockt they storm;[8] great laughter was in Heav'n
And looking down, to see the hubbub strange
And hear the din; thus was the building left

2. Nimrod is not connected with the builders of the Tower in Genesis 10.8. The connection is made, however, in Josephus, *Antiquities* 1.4.2ff., where we also learn that Nimrod "changed the government into tyranny."

3. In *The Tenure of Kings and Magistrates*, Milton denies the natural right of kings and insists that their power is committed to them in trust by the people.

4. See *Eikonoklastes:* "The Bishops could have told him, that 'Nimrod,' the first that hunted after Faction is reputed, by ancient Tradition, the first that founded monarchy; whence it appeares that to hunt after Faction is more properly the King's Game."

5. "Before the Lord," Genesis 10.9; Milton takes it in a constitutional sense; see *The Tenure:* "To say Kings are accountable to none but God, is the overturning of all Law."

6. The materials of the Tower—brick with bitumen as mortar—are specified in Genesis 11.3.

7. See Genesis 11.4.

8. In the 17th century it was generally believed that the separation of language into distinct individual languages had its beginning at the confusion of tongues at Babel.

Ridiculous, and the work Confusion nam'd.[9]
Whereto thus *Adam* fatherly displeas'd.
O execrable Son so to aspire
Above his Brethren, to himself assuming
Authority usurpt, from God not giv'n:
He gave us only over Beast, Fish, Fowl
Dominion absolute; that right we hold
By his donation; but Man over men
He made not Lord; such title to himself
Reserving, human left from human free.
But this Usurper his encroachment proud
Stays not on Man; to God his Tower intends
Siege and defiance: Wretched man! what food
Will he convey up thither to sustain
Himself and his rash Army, where thin Air
Above the Clouds will pine his entrails gross,
And famish him of breath, if not of Bread?
To whom thus *Michael*. Justly thou abhorr'st
That Son, who on the quiet state of men
Such trouble brought, affecting to subdue
Rational Liberty;[1] yet know withal,
Since thy original lapse, true Liberty
Is lost, which always with right Reason dwells
Twinn'd, and from her hath no dividual° being: *separate*
Reason in man obscur'd, or not obey'd,
Immediately inordinate desires
And upstart Passions catch the Government
From Reason, and to servitude reduce
Man till then free. Therefore since hee permits
Within himself unworthy Powers to reign
Over free Reason, God in Judgment just
Subjects him from without to violent Lords;
Who oft as undeservedly enthral
His outward freedom: Tyranny must be,
Though to the Tyrant thereby no excuse.
Yet sometimes Nations will decline so low
From virtue, which is reason, that no wrong,
But Justice, and some fatal curse annext
Deprives them of thir outward liberty,
Thir inward lost: Witness th' irreverent Son
Of him who built the Ark,[2] who for the shame
Done to his Father, heard this heavy curse,

9. See Genesis 11.9, "Therefore is the name of it called Babel"; marginal gloss: "that is, Confusion."

1. Lines 80–101 recall the regicide tracts and follow St. Augustine's *City of God* 19.15, where we read that the derivation of servitude, whose mother is sin, is the "first cause of man's subjection to man: which notwithstanding comes not to pass but by the direction of the highest, in whom is no injustice." For the connection between psychological and political enslavement, see 9.1127–31.

2. Because of Ham's perverse act committed with the drunken Noah, his own son Canaan was cursed: "a servant of servants shall he be unto his brethren" (Genesis 9.25).

Servant of Servants, on his vicious Race.° *descendants*
Thus will this latter, as the former World,
Still tend from bad to worse, till God at last
Wearied with their iniquities, withdraw
His presence from among them, and avert
His holy Eyes; resolving from thenceforth
To leave them to thir own polluted ways;
And one peculiar° Nation to select *special*
From all the rest, of whom to be invok'd,
A Nation from one faithful man to spring:
Him on this side *Euphrates* yet residing,[3]
Bred up in Idol-worship; O that men
(Canst thou believe?) should be so stupid grown,
While yet the Patriarch° liv'd, who scap'd the Flood, *Noah*
As to forsake the living God, and fall
To worship thir own work in Wood and Stone
For Gods! yet him God the most High voutsafes
To call by Vision from his Father's house,
His kindred and false Gods, into a Land
Which he will show him, and from him will raise
A mighty Nation, and upon him show'r
His benediction so, that in his Seed
All Nations shall be blest; he straight obeys,
Not knowing to what Land, yet firm believes:
I see him, but thou canst not, with what Faith
He leaves his Gods, his Friends, and native Soil
Ur of Chaldæa,[4] passing now the Ford
To *Haran*, after him a cumbrous Train
Of Herds and Flocks, and numerous servitude;° *slaves and servants*
Not wand'ring poor, but trusting all his wealth
With God, who call'd him, in a land unknown.
Canaan he now attains, I see his Tents
Pitcht about *Sechem*, and the neighboring Plain
Of *Moreh*; there by promise he receives
Gift to his Progeny of all that Land;
From *Hamath* Northward to the Desert South
(Things by thir names I call, though yet unnam'd)
From *Hermon* East to the great Western Sea,
Mount *Hermon*, yonder Sea, each place behold

3. On Abraham's origins, see Joshua 24.2, "Thus saith the Lord God of Israel, Your fathers dwelt on the other side of the flood in old time, even Terah, father of Abraham, and the father of Nachor: and they served other gods."

4. Nine places are named in the Holy Land — the number of heavenly things. Milton may have put Ur in Mesopotamia, on the strength of Acts 7.2. Haran was far to the northwest. Sechem (Shechem) was the scene of Joshua's covenant with Israel. Moreh, like Sechem, was near the pass between Mt Ebal and Mt Gerizim; Jacob buried his people's idols under the oak there (Genesis 35.4). Hamath marked the northern border of the Promised Land, as the great western sea marked the western border, and the wilderness of Zin marked the southern (Numbers 34.3–8). Mt Hermon is a boundary between Lebanon and Syria (Joshua 13.5ff); it is the highest mountain in Palestine. Mt Carmel's position is something to swear by (Jerome 46.18). The double-fonted stream reflects the notion that the Jor and Dan formed by confluence the Jordan. Senir was the Amorite name for Hermon (Deuteronomy 3.9).

In prospect, as I point them; on the shore
Mount *Carmel;* here the double-founted stream
Jordan, true limit Eastward; but his Sons
Shall dwell to *Senir,* that long ridge of Hills.
This ponder, that all Nations of the Earth
Shall in his Seed be blessed; by that Seed
Is meant thy great deliverer, who shall bruise
The Serpent's head;[5] whereof to thee anon
Plainlier shall be reveal'd. This Patriarch blest,
Whom *faithful Abraham* due time shall call,
A Son,° and of his Son a Grandchild° leaves, *Isaac / Jacob*
Like him in faith, in wisdom, and renown;
The Grandchild with twelve Sons increast, departs
From *Canaan,* to a Land hereafter call'd
Egypt, divided by the River *Nile;*
See where it flows, disgorging at seven mouths
Into the Sea: to sojourn in that Land
He comes invited by a younger Son[6]
In time of dearth, a Son whose worthy deeds
Raise him to be the second in that Realm
Of *Pharaoh:* there he dies, and leaves his Race
Growing into a Nation, and now grown
Suspected to a sequent King,[7] who seeks
To stop thir overgrowth,° as inmate guests *overpopulation*
Too numerous; whence of guests he makes them slaves
Inhospitably, and kills thir infant Males:
Till by two brethren (those two brethren call
Moses and *Aaron*) sent from God to claim
His people from enthralment, they return
With glory and spoil back to thir promis'd Land.
But first the lawless Tyrant, who denies
To know thir God, or message to regard,
Must be compell'd by Signs and Judgments dire;
To blood unshed the Rivers must be turn'd,
Frogs, Lice and Flies must all his Palace fill
With loath'd intrusion, and fill all the land;
His Cattle must of Rot and Murrain° die, *plague*
Botches and blains° must all his flesh imboss, *sores and blisters*
And all his people; Thunder mixt with Hail,
Hail mixt with fire must rend th' *Egyptian* Sky
And wheel on th' Earth, devouring where it rolls;
What it devours not, Herb, or Fruit, or Grain,
A darksome Cloud of Locusts swarming down
Must eat, and on the ground leave nothing green:

5. This is the promise to Abram, renewing that of the serpent's curse (see 10.180ff, and Genesis 12.1–3). "Abraham" is changed from "Abram" (Genesis 17.5), implying by etymological wordplay "father of a (great) multitude."

6. Jacob went down to Egypt at the bidding of Joseph (the "younger son"); see Genesis 45.6.

7. Named as Busiris at 1.307.

Darkness must overshadow all his bounds,
Palpable darkness, and blot out three days;
Last with one midnight stroke all the first-born
Of *Egypt* must lie dead. Thus with ten wounds
The River-dragon° tam'd at length submits[8] *crocodile*
To let his sojourners depart, and oft
Humbles his stubborn heart, but still as Ice
More hard'n'd after thaw, till in his rage
Pursuing whom he late dismiss'd, the Sea
Swallows him with his Host, but them lets pass
As on dry land between two crystal walls,
Aw'd by the rod of *Moses* so to stand
Divided, till his rescu'd gain thir shore:
Such wondrous power God to his Saint will lend,
Though present in his Angel, who shall go
Before them in a Cloud, and Pillar of Fire,
By day a Cloud, by night a Pillar of Fire,[9]
To guide them in thir journey, and remove
Behind them, while th' obdurate King pursues:
All night he will pursue, but his approach
Darkness defends° between till morning Watch; *wards off*
Then through the Fiery Pillar and the Cloud
God looking forth will trouble all his Host
And craze thir Chariot wheels: when by command
Moses once more his potent Rod extends
Over the Sea; the Sea his Rod obeys;
On thir imbattl'd ranks the Waves return,
And overwhelm thir War:° the Race elect *army and equipment*
Safe towards *Canaan* from the shore advance
Through the wild Desert, not the readiest way,
Lest ent'ring on the *Canaanite* alarm'd
War terrify them inexpert, and fear
Return them back to *Egypt*, choosing rather
Inglorious life with servitude; for life
To noble and ignoble is more sweet
Untrain'd in Arms, where rashness leads not on.
This also shall they gain by thir delay
In the wide Wilderness, there they shall found
Thir government, and thir great Senate choose
Through the twelve Tribes, to rule by Laws ordain'd:[1]
God from the Mount of *Sinai*, whose gray top
Shall tremble, he descending, will himself
In Thunder, Lightning and loud Trumpet's sound

8. In Ezekiel 29.3, the Pharaoh is called "the great dragon that lieth in the midst of his rivers." Milton uses the Pharaoh as an example of heart-hardening in *De doctrina* 1.8.

9. In *De doctrina* 1.5, Milton says that if God himself had gone with the Israelites, it would have destroyed them; he sent "the representation of his name and glory in some angel."

1. Milton uses "senate" for the Seventy Elders, the origin of the Sanhedrin. See Numbers 11.16–25; Exodus 24; and Acts 5.21. Milton took the Sanhedrin as a model for contemporary senates.

Ordain them Laws; part such as appertain
To civil Justice, part religious Rites
Of sacrifice, informing them, by types
And shadows, of that destin'd Seed to bruise
The Serpent, by what means he shall achieve
Mankind's deliverance. But the voice of God
To mortal ear is dreadful; they beseech
That *Moses* might report to them his will,[2]
And terror cease; he grants what they besought,
Instructed that to God is no access
Without Mediator, whose high Office now
Moses in figure bears, to introduce
One greater, of whose day he shall foretell,
And all the Prophets in thir Age the times
Of great *Messiah* shall sing. Thus Laws and Rites
Establisht, such delight hath God in Men
Obedient to his will, that he voutsafes
Among them to set up his Tabernacle,
The holy One with mortal Men to dwell:
By his prescript a Sanctuary is fram'd
Of Cedar, overlaid with Gold, therein
An Ark, and in the Ark his Testimony,
The Records of his Cov'nant, over these
A Mercy-seat of Gold between the wings
Of two bright Cherubim, before him burn
Sev'n Lamps as in a Zodiac representing
The Heav'nly fires; over the Tent a Cloud
Shall rest by Day, a fiery gleam by Night,
Save when they journey, and at length they come,
Conducted by his Angel to the Land
Promis'd to *Abraham* and his Seed: the rest
Were long to tell, how many Battles fought,
How many Kings destroy'd, and Kingdoms won,
Or how the Sun shall in mid Heav'n stand still
A day entire, and Night's due course adjourn,
Man's voice commanding, Sun in *Gibeon* stand,
And thou Moon in the vale of *Aialon*,[3]
Till *Israel*° overcome; so call the third *Jacob*
From *Abraham*, Son of *Isaac*, and from him
His whole descent, who thus shall *Canaan* win.
  Here *Adam* interpos'd. O sent from Heav'n,
Enlight'ner of my darkness, gracious things
Thou hast reveal'd, those chiefly which concern

2. Frightened by the thunder and lightning and trumpeting, the Israelites said to Moses: "Speak thou with us, and we will hear: but let not God speak with us, lest we die" (Exodus 20.19).

3. Echoes Joshua 10.12ff, "Then spake Joshua to the Lord in the day when the Lord delivered up the Amorites . . . and he said in the sight of Israel, Sun, stand thou still upon Gibeon; and thou, Moon, in the valley of Ajalon. And the sun stood still, and the moon stayed, until the people had avenged themselves upon their enemies."

Just *Abraham* and his Seed: now first I find
Mine eyes true op'ning, and my heart much eas'd,
Erewhile perplext with thoughts what would become
Of mee and all Mankind; but now I see
His day, in whom all Nations shall be blest,
Favor unmerited by me, who sought
Forbidd'n knowledge by forbidd'n means.
This yet I apprehend not, why to those
Among whom God will deign to dwell on Earth
So many and so various Laws are giv'n;
So many Laws argue so many sins
Among them; how can God with such reside?
To whom thus *Michael*. Doubt not but that sin
Will reign among them, as of thee begot;
And therefore was Law given them to evince° *subdue*
Thir natural pravity,° by stirring up *depravity*
Sin against Law to fight; that when they see
Law can discover sin, but not remove,
Save by those shadowy expiations weak,
The blood of Bulls and Goats, they may conclude
Some blood more precious must be paid for Man,
Just for unjust, that in such righteousness
To them by Faith imputed, they may find
Justification towards God, and peace
Of Conscience, which the Law by Ceremonies
Cannot appease, nor Man the moral part
Perform, and not performing cannot live.
So Law appears imperfet; and but° giv'n *only*
With purpose to resign them in full time
Up to a better Cov'nant, disciplin'd
From shadowy Types to Truth, from Flesh to Spirit,
From imposition of strict Laws, to free
Acceptance of large Grace, from servile fear
To filial, works of Law to works of Faith.[4]
And therefore shall not *Moses*, though of God
Highly belov'd, being but the Minister
Of Law, his people into *Canaan* lead;
But *Joshua* whom the Gentiles *Jesus* call,[5]
His Name and Office bearing, who shall quell
The adversary Serpent, and bring back
Through the world's wilderness long wander'd man
Safe to eternal Paradise of rest.

4. Outlining the central Protestant doctrine of Justification by Faith. Too concise for assignment of sources, but see Romans 3.20; 4.22–5; 5.1–21; 7.7ff; 8.15; 10.5; Hebrews 7.19; 9.13ff; 10.1–5; Galatians 3.4.

5. In *De doctrina* 1.26, Milton states that the law fails to promise what faith in God through Christ attains, eternal life: "the imperfection of the law was made apparent in the person of Moses himself. For Moses, who was the type of the law, could not lead the children of Israel into the land of Canaan, that is, into eternal rest. But an entrance was granted to them under Joshua, that is, Jesus." See also Deuteronomy 34; Joshua 1. "Jesus" is the Greek equivalent of the Hebrew "Joshua."

Meanwhile they in thir earthly *Canaan* plac't
Long time shall dwell and prosper; but° when sins *except*
National interrupt thir public peace,
Provoking God to raise them enemies:
From whom as oft he saves them penitent
By Judges first, then under Kings; of whom
The second, both for piety renown'd
And puissant deeds, a promise shall receive
Irrevocable, that his Regal Throne
For ever shall endure;[6] the like shall sing
All Prophecy, That of the Royal Stock
Of *David* (so I name this King) shall rise
A Son, the Woman's Seed to thee foretold,[7]
Foretold to *Abraham*, as in whom shall trust
All Nations, and to Kings foretold, of Kings
The last, for of his Reign shall be no end.
But first a long succession must ensue,
And his next Son for Wealth and Wisdom fam'd,[8]
The clouded Ark of God till then in Tents
Wand'ring, shall in a glorious Temple enshrine.
Such follow him, as shall be register'd
Part good, part bad, of bad the longer scroll,
Whose foul Idolatries, and other faults
Heapt to the popular sum,[9] will so incense
God, as to leave them, and expose thir Land,
Thir City, his Temple, and his holy Ark
With all his sacred things, a scorn and prey
To that proud City, whose high Walls thou saw'st
Left in confusion, *Babylon* thence call'd.
There in captivity he lets them dwell
The space of seventy years, then brings them back,[1]
Rememb'ring mercy, and his Cov'nant sworn
To *David*, stablisht as the days of Heav'n.
Return'd from *Babylon* by leave of Kings
Thir Lords, whom God dispos'd,° the house of God *put into a good mood*
They first re-edify, and for a while
In mean estate live moderate, till grown
In wealth and multitude, factious they grow;
But first among the Priests dissension springs,[2]
Men who attend the Altar, and should most
Endeavor Peace: thir strife pollution brings

6. The prophet Nathan promised David "thine house and thy kingdom shall be established for ever before thee: thy throne shall be established for ever" (2 Samuel 7.16).
7. The royal line of David had Messianic significance; see Psalm 89.36; Isaiah 11.10; Luke 1.32.
8. Solomon, who built the Temple to give the ark its first fixed location (1 Kings 5–8; 2 Chronicles 2–5) — the occasion of another divine covenant (1 Kings 9.1–9).
9. That is, added to people's accumulated faults.
1. For the Babylonian captivity, see Jerome 25.12; 33.20–6 relating the return from exile to the covenant with David.
2. Maccabees 4–6 relates strife between intriguing priests, and for Milton provides an exemplum of the Church's betrayal by prelates and Presbyterians.

Upon the Temple itself: at last they seize
The Sceptre, and regard not *David's* Sons,
Then lose it to a stranger,[3] that the true
Anointed King *Messiah* might be born
Barr'd of his right; yet at his Birth a Star
Unseen before in Heav'n proclaims him come,
And guides the Eastern Sages, who enquire
His place, to offer Incense, Myrrh, and Gold;
His place of birth, a Solemn Angel tells
To simple Shepherds, keeping watch by night;
They gladly thither° haste, and by a Choir *to Bethlehem*
Of squadron'd Angels hear his Carol sung.
A Virgin is his Mother, but his Sire
The Power of the most High; he shall ascend
The Throne hereditary, and bound his Reign
With earth's wide bounds, his glory with the Heav'ns.[4]
He ceas'd, discerning *Adam* with such joy
Surcharg'd,° as had like grief been dew'd in tears, *overwhelmed*
Without the vent of words, which these he breath'd.
O Prophet of glad tidings, finisher
Of utmost hope! now clear I understand
What oft my steadiest thoughts have searcht in vain,
Why our great expectation should be call'd
The seed of Woman: Virgin Mother, Hail,
High in the love of Heav'n, yet from my Loins
Thou shalt proceed, and from thy Womb the Son
Of God most High; So God with man unites.
Needs must the Serpent now his capital° bruise *on the head*
Expect with mortal pain: say where and when
Thir fight, what stroke shall bruise the Victor's heel.
To whom thus *Michael.* Dream not of thir fight,
As of a Duel, or the local wounds
Of head or heel: not therefore joins the Son
Manhood to Godhead, with more strength to foil
Thy enemy; nor so is overcome
Satan, whose fall from Heav'n, a deadlier bruise,
Disabl'd not to give thee thy death's wound:
Which hee, who comes thy Saviour, shall recure.
Not by destroying *Satan*, but his works[5]
In thee and in thy Seed: nor can this be,
But by fulfilling that which thou didst want,
Obedience to the Law of God, impos'd
On penalty of death, and suffering death,

3. The stranger is Antipater the Idumean, father of Herod the Great and Procurator of Judaea from 47 B.C.E., under Julius Caesar.
4. Christ's terrestrial reign is prophesied, among other places, in Isaiah 9.7; Daniel 7.13–22; Revelation 2.25–7.
5. Echoing 1 John 3.8, "For this purpose the Son of God was manifested, that he might destroy the works of the devil."

The penalty to thy transgression due,
And due to theirs which out of thine will grow:
So only can high Justice rest appaid.° *satisfied*
The Law of God exact he shall fulfil
Both by obedience and by love, though love
Alone fulfil the Law; thy punishment
He shall endure by coming in the Flesh
To a reproachful life and cursed death,
Proclaiming Life to all who shall believe
In his redemption, and that his obedience
Imputed becomes theirs by Faith, his merits
To save them, not thir own, though legal works.[6]
For this he shall live hated, be blasphem'd,
Seiz'd on by force, judg'd, and to death condemn'd
A shameful and accurst, nail'd to the Cross
By his own Nation, slain for bringing Life;
But to the Cross he nails thy Enemies,
The Law that is against thee, and the sins
Of all mankind, with him there crucifi'd,
Never to hurt them more who rightly trust
In this his satisfaction; so he dies,
But soon revives, Death over him no power
Shall long usurp; ere the third dawning light
Return, the Stars of Morn shall see him rise
Out of his grave, fresh as the dawning light,
Thy ransom paid, which Man from death redeems,
His death for Man, as many as offer'd Life
Neglect not, and the benefit embrace
By Faith not void of works: this God-like act
Annuls thy doom, the death thou shouldst have di'd,
In sin for ever lost from life; this act
Shall bruise the head of *Satan*, crush his strength
Defeating Sin and Death, his two main arms,
And fix far deeper in his head thir stings
Than temporal° death shall bruise the Victor's heel, *bodily*
Or theirs whom he redeems, a death like sleep,
A gentle wafting to immortal Life.
Nor after resurrection shall he stay
Longer on Earth than certain times to appear
To his Disciples, Men who in his Life
Still follow'd him; to them shall leave in charge
To teach all nations what of him they learn'd
And his Salvation, them who shall believe
Baptizing in the profluent° stream, the sign *flowing profusely*
Of washing them from guilt of sin to Life

6. In the Protestant doctrine of Justification by Faith, Christ's obedient righteousness was imputed to the believer. Fulfillment of the law cannot save, there being no justification by works.

Pure, and in mind prepar'd, if so befall,
For death, like that which the redeemer di'd.
All Nations they shall teach; for from that day
Not only to the Sons of *Abraham's* Loins
Salvation shall be Preacht, but to the Sons
Of *Abraham's* Faith wherever through the world;
So in his seed all Nations shall be blest.
Then to the Heav'n of Heav'ns he shall ascend
With victory, triumphing through the air
Over his foes and thine; there shall surprise
The Serpent, Prince of air, and drag in Chains
Through all his Realm, and there confounded leave;
Then enter into glory, and resume
His Seat at God's right hand, exalted high
Above all names in Heav'n; and thence shall come,[7]
When this world's dissolution shall be ripe,
With glory and power to judge both quick and dead,
To judge th' unfaithful dead, but to reward
His faithful, and receive them into bliss,
Whether in Heav'n or Earth, for then the Earth
Shall all be Paradise, far happier place
Than this of *Eden*, and far happier days.
So spake th' Arch-Angel *Michaël*, then paus'd,
As at the World's great period;[8] and our Sire
Replete with joy and wonder thus repli'd.
O goodness infinite, goodness immense![9]
That all this good of evil shall produce,
And evil turn to good; more wonderful
Than that which by creation first brought forth
Light out of darkness! full of doubt I stand,
Whether I should repent me now of sin
By mee done and occasion'd, or rejoice
Much more, that much more good thereof shall spring,
To God more glory, more good will to Men
From God, and over wrath grace shall abound.[1]
But say, if our deliverer up to Heav'n
Must reascend, what will betide the few
His faithful, left among th' unfaithful herd,
The enemies of truth; who then shall guide
His people, who defend? will they not deal
Worse with his followers than with him they dealt?

7. The Second Coming foretold at 3.321ff. For the phrase "the quick [living] and dead," see the Apostles' Creed; Acts 10.42; 2 Timothy 4.1; 1 Peter 4.5.

8. This is Michael's second pause; the first was at 12.2. The three divisions of Adam's instruction are meant to correspond to "three drops" of the well of life placed in his eyes (11.416). Here the pause is compared with the world's period the dawning of the present age, from the first to the second coming of Christ.

9. The Final Cause or end of the Fall: a greater "glory" for God and an opportunity for him to show his surpassing love through the sacrifice of Christ.

1. See Romans 5.20 ("where sin abounded, grace did much more abound") and 2 Corinthians 4.15.

Be sure they will, said th' Angel; but from Heav'n
Hee to his own a Comforter will send,[2]
The promise of the Father, who shall dwell
His Spirit within them, and the Law of Faith
Working through love, upon thir hearts shall write,[3]
To guide them in all truth, and also arm
With spiritual Armor, able to resist
Satan's assaults, and quench his fiery darts,[4]
What Man can do against them, not afraid,
Though to the death, against such cruelties
With inward consolations recompens't,
And oft supported so as shall amaze
Thir proudest persecutors: for the Spirit
Pour'd first on his Apostles, whom he sends
To evangelize the Nations, then on all
Baptiz'd, shall them with wondrous gifts endue° *endow*
To speak all Tongues, and do all Miracles,
As did thir Lord before them. Thus they win
Great numbers of each Nation to receive
With joy the tidings brought from Heav'n: at length
Thir Ministry perform'd, and race well run,
Thir doctrine and thir story written left,
They die; but in thir room, as they forewarn,
Wolves shall succeed for teachers, grievous Wolves,[5]
Who all the sacred mysteries of Heav'n
To thir own vile advantages shall turn
Of lucre and ambition, and the truth
With superstitions and traditions taint,
Left only in those written Records pure,
Though not but by the Spirit understood.[6]
Then shall they seek to avail themselves of names,
Places and titles, and with these to join
Secular power, though feigning still to act
By spiritual, to themselves appropriating
The Spirit of God, promis'd alike and giv'n
To all Believers;[7] and from that pretense,
Spiritual Laws by carnal° power shall force *worldly*
On every conscience; Laws which none shall find
Left them inroll'd, or what the Spirit within

2. The Holy Spirit. See John 14.18 and 15.26.
3. See Galatians 5.6: "faith which worketh by love."
4. Alluding to the allegory in Ephesians 6.16: "Above all, taking the shield of faith, wherewith ye shall be able to quench all the fiery darts of the wicked."
5. "For I know this, that after my departing shall grievous wolves enter in among you, not sparing the flock" (Acts 20.29). See the simile comparing Satan to a wolf in the fold, at 4.183–87; see also *Lycidas* 113ff, page 1711.
6. It was an important article of Protestant belief that in doctrinal matters the ultimate arbiter is individual conscience rather than mere authority.
7. The corruption of the Church through its pursuit of "secular power" is a subject Milton had dealt with in *Of Reformation*. In *De doctrina* 1.30 he condemns the enforcement of obedience to human opinions or authority.

Shall on the heart engrave.[8] What will they then
But force the Spirit of Grace itself, and bind
His consort Liberty; what, but unbuild
His living Temples, built by Faith to stand,[9]
Thir own Faith not another's: for on Earth
Who against Faith and Conscience can be heard
Infallible?[1] yet many will presume:
Whence heavy persecution shall arise
On all who in the worship persevere
Of Spirit and Truth; the rest, far greater part,
Will deem in outward Rites and specious forms
Religion satisfi'd; Truth shall retire
Bestuck with sland'rous darts, and works of Faith
Rarely be found: so shall the World go on,
To good malignant, to bad men benign,
Under her own weight groaning, till the day
Appear of respiration[2] to the just,
And vengeance to the wicked, at return
Of him so lately promis'd to thy aid,
The Woman's seed, obscurely then foretold,
Now amplier known thy Saviour and thy Lord,
Last in the Clouds from Heav'n to be reveal'd
In glory of the Father, to dissolve
Satan with his perverted World, then raise
From the conflagrant° mass, purg'd and refin'd, *burning*
New Heav'ns, new Earth, Ages of endless date
Founded in righteousness and peace and love,
To bring forth fruits Joy and eternal Bliss.
He ended; and thus *Adam* last repli'd.
How soon hath thy prediction, Seer blest,
Measur'd this transient World, the Race of time,
Till time stand fixt: beyond is all abyss,
Eternity, whose end no eye can reach.
Greatly instructed I shall hence depart,
Greatly in peace of thought, and have my fill
Of knowledge, what this Vessel can contain;
Beyond which was my folly to aspire.
Henceforth I learn, that to obey is best,
And love with fear the only God, to walk
As in his presence, ever to observe
His providence, and on him sole depend,
Merciful over all his works, with good
Still overcoming evil, and by small
Accomplishing great things, by things deem'd weak

8. The wolves will enforce laws written neither in Scripture nor in the individual conscience.

9. See 1 Corinthians 3.17: "The temple of God is holy, which temple ye are."

1. Even though the doctrine of papal infallibility was not formally adapted until 1870, there can be no doubt that Rome is Milton's main target here. In A *Treatise of Civil Power* he writes that the "Pope assumes infallibility over conscience and scripture."

2. Opportunity for breathing again; rest.

Subverting worldly strong, and worldly wise
By simply meek; that suffering for Truth's sake
Is fortitude to highest victory,
And to the faithful Death the Gate of Life;
Taught this by his example whom I now
Acknowledge my Redeemer ever blest.
To whom thus also th' Angel last repli'd:
This having learnt, thou hast attain'd the sum
Of wisdom; hope no higher, though all the Stars
Thou knew'st by name, and all th' ethereal Powers,
All secrets of the deep, all Nature's works,
Or works of God in Heav'n, Air, Earth, or Sea,
And all the riches of this World enjoy'dst,
And all the rule, one Empire; only add
Deeds to thy knowledge answerable, add Faith,
Add Virtue, Patience, Temperance, add Love,
By name to come call'd Charity, the soul
Of all the rest;[3] then wilt thou not be loath
To leave this Paradise, but shalt possess
A paradise within thee, happier far.
Let us descend now therefore from this top
Of Speculation;[4] for the hour precise
Exacts our parting hence; and see the Guards,
By mee encampt on yonder Hill, expect
Thir motion,[5] at whose Front a flaming Sword,
In signal of remove, waves fiercely round;
We may no longer stay: go, waken *Eve;*
Her also I with gentle Dreams have calm'd
Portending good, and all her spirits compos'd
To meek submission: thou at season fit
Let her with thee partake what thou hast heard,
Chiefly what may concern her Faith to know,
The great deliverance by her Seed to come
(For by the Woman's Seed)[6] on all Mankind,
That ye may live, which will be many days,[7]
Both in one Faith unanimous though sad,
With cause for evils past, yet much more cheer'd
With meditation on the happy end.
He ended, and they both descend the Hill;
Descended, *Adam* to the Bow'r where *Eve*
Lay sleeping ran before, but found her wak't;
And thus with words not sad she him receiv'd.

3. Compare 2 Peter 1.5–7: "Add to your faith virtue; and to virtue knowledge; and to knowledge temperance; and to temperance patience; and to patience godliness; and to godliness brotherly kindness; and to brotherly kindness charity."
4. Vantage point but also height of theological speculation.
5. Await deployment, marching orders.
6. Alluding to the birth of Jesus.
7. Adam lived to be 930 years of age (Genesis 5.5).

Whence thou return'st, and whither went'st, I know;
For God is also in sleep, and Dreams advise,
Which he hath sent propitious, some great good
Presaging, since with sorrow and heart's distress
Wearied I fell asleep: but now lead on;
In mee is no delay; with thee to go,
Is to stay here; without thee here to stay,
Is to go hence unwilling; thou to mee
Art all things under Heav'n, all places thou,
Who for my wilful crime art banisht hence.[8]
This further consolation yet secure
I carry hence; though all by mee is lost,
Such favor I unworthy am voutsaf't,
By mee the Promis'd Seed shall all restore.
So spake our Mother *Eve*, and *Adam* heard
Well pleas'd, but answer'd not; for now too nigh
Th' Arch-Angel stood, and from the other Hill
To thir fixt Station, all in bright array
The Cherubim descended; on the ground
Gliding meteorous,° as Ev'ning Mist *meteoric*
Ris'n from a River o'er the marish° glides, *marsh*
And gathers ground fast at the Laborer's heel
Homeward returning. High in Front advanc't,
The brandisht Sword of God before them blaz'd
Fierce as a Comet; which with torrid heat,
And vapor as the *Libyan* Air adust,° *scorched*
Began to parch that temperate Clime; whereat
In either hand the hast'ning Angel caught
Our ling'ring Parents, and to th' Eastern Gate
Led them direct, and down the Cliff as fast
To the subjected° Plain; then disappear'd. *underlying*
They looking back, all th' Eastern side beheld
Of Paradise, so late thir happy seat,
Wav'd over by that flaming Brand,[9] the Gate
With dreadful Faces throng'd and fiery Arms:
Some natural tears they dropp'd, but wip'd them soon;
The World was all before them, where to choose
Thir place of rest, and Providence thir guide:[1]
They hand in hand with wand'ring steps and slow,
Through *Eden* took thir solitary way.

The End

8. Eve has assimilated Michael's exhortation at 11.292: "where [Adam] abides, think there thy native soil." There is also a resonance with Eve's song at 4.635–56 (every time of day is pleasing with Adam, none is pleasing without him).

9. See Genesis. 3.24: "a flaming sword which turned every way."

1. Note that "Providence" can be the object of "choose": decisions of faith lie ahead.

Responses

Mary Wollstonecraft: from *A Vindication of the Rights of Woman*[1]

from *Chapter 2. The Prevailing Opinion of a Sexual Character Discussed*

To account for, and excuse the tyranny of man, many ingenious arguments have been brought forward to prove, that the two sexes, in the acquirement of virtue, ought to aim at attaining a very different character: or, to speak explicitly, women are not allowed to have sufficient strength of mind to acquire what really deserves the name of virtue. Yet it should seem, allowing them to have souls, that there is but one way appointed by Providence to lead *mankind* to either virtue or happiness.

If then women are not a swarm of ephemeron[2] triflers, why should they be kept in ignorance under the specious name of innocence? Men complain, and with reason, of the follies and caprices of our sex, when they do not keenly satirize our headstrong passions and groveling vices.—Behold, I should answer, the natural effect of ignorance! The mind will ever be unstable that has only prejudices to rest on, and the current will run with destructive fury when there are no barriers to break its force. Women are told from their infancy, and taught by the example of their mothers, that a little knowledge of human weakness, justly termed cunning, softness of temper, *outward* obedience, and a scrupulous attention to a puerile kind of propriety, will obtain for them the protection of man; and should they be beautiful, every thing else is needless, for, at least, twenty years of their lives.

Thus Milton describes our first frail mother; though when he tells us that women are formed for softness and sweet attractive grace,[3] I cannot comprehend his meaning, unless, in the true Mahometan strain, he meant to deprive us of souls, and insinuate that we were beings only designed by sweet attractive grace, and docile blind obedience, to gratify the senses of man when he can no longer soar on the wing of contemplation.

How grossly do they insult us who thus advise us only to render ourselves gentle, domestic brutes! For instance, the winning softness so warmly, and frequently, recommended, that governs by obeying. What childish expressions, and how insignificant is the being—can it be an immortal one? who will condescend to govern by such sinister methods! "Certainly," says Lord Bacon, "man is of kin to the beasts by his body; and if he be not of kin to God by his spirit, he is a base and ignoble creature!"[4] Men, indeed, appear to me to act in a very unphilosophical manner when they try to secure the good conduct of women by attempting to keep them always in a state of childhood. Rousseau was more consistent when he wished to stop the progress of reason in both sexes, for if men eat of the tree of knowledge, women will come in for a taste;

1. Written by the leading feminist of the late eighteenth century, this essay rebuts the notion that woman is naturally submissive to man. Wollstonecraft explains that this view was promoted by the Genesis story of the creation of Eve from Adam's rib and by Milton's description of Eve as created for "softness . . . and sweet attractive grace" (*Paradise Lost* 4.298). The author, however, also finds evidence of Milton's siding with her point of view when he portrays Adam's arguing with God in *Paradise Lost* 8.381–91. Where does Milton stand on the relationship between man and woman? Does he side more with the view of woman as submissive or with Adam's contestation of that view? Wollstonecraft's reading of Milton opens up *Paradise Lost* to contested readings; her reading of Genesis also bears comparison with that of Rachel Speght in terms of contrasting views of the biblical presentation of the nature of woman. (For Speght's work, see *Perspectives: Tracts on Women and Gender*, page 1445).

2. Winged insect that lives for only a day.

3. Satan's first view of Adam and Eve in *Paradise Lost:* "Not equal, as thir sex not equal seem'd; / For contemplation hee and valor form'd, / For softness shee and sweet attractive Grace, / He for God only, shee for God in him" (4.296–99). Fordyce quotes these lines in *Sermons to Young Women*, ch. 13.

4. Francis Bacon, *Essay 16*, "Of Atheism" (1606).

but, from the imperfect cultivation which their understandings now receive, they only attain a knowledge of evil.[5]

Children, I grant, should be innocent; but when the epithet is applied to men, or women, it is but a civil term for weakness. For if it be allowed that women were destined by Providence to acquire human virtues, and by the exercise of their understandings, that stability of character which is the firmest ground to rest our future hopes upon, they must be permitted to turn to the fountain of light, and not forced to shape their course by the twinkling of a mere satellite. Milton, I grant, was of a very different opinion; for he only bends to the indefeasible right of beauty, though it would be difficult to render two passages which I now mean to contrast, consistent. But into similar inconsistencies are great men often led by their senses.

> To whom thus Eve with *perfect beauty* adorn'd.
> "My Author and Disposer, what thou bidst
> *Unargued* I obey; So God ordains;
> God is *thy law, thou mine:* to know no more
> Is Woman's *happiest* knowledge and her *praise*."[6]

These are exactly the arguments that I have used to children; but I have added, your reason is now gaining strength, and, till it arrives at some degree of maturity, you must look up to me for advice—then you ought to *think,* and only rely on God.

Yet in the following lines Milton seems to coincide with me; when he makes Adam thus expostulate with his Maker.

> Hast thou not made me here thy substitute,
> And these inferior far beneath me set?
> Among *unequals* what society
> Can sort, what harmony or true delight?
> Which must be mutual, in proportion due
> Giv'n and receiv'd; but in *disparity*
> The one intense, the other still remiss
> Cannot well suit with either, but soon prove
> Tedious alike: of *fellowship* I speak
> Such as I seek, fit to participate
> All rational delight[7]—

In treating, therefore, of the manners of women, let us, disregarding sensual arguments, trace what we should endeavour to make them in order to co-operate, if the expression be not too bold, with the supreme Being.

By individual education, I mean, for the sense of the word is not precisely defined, such an attention to a child as will slowly sharpen the senses, form the temper, regulate the passions as they begin to ferment, and set the understanding to work before the body arrives at maturity; so that the man may only have to proceed, not to begin, the important task of learning to think and reason. ***

Probably the prevailing opinion, that woman was created for man, may have taken its rise from Moses's poetical story,[8] yet, as very few, it is presumed, who have

5. See Rousseau's *Émile* (1.1): "Only reason teaches us good from evil."
6. *Paradise Lost* 4.634–38; Wollstonecraft's emphases.
7. *Paradise Lost* 8.381–91; Wollstonecraft's emphases.
8. The first five books of the Old Testament are traditionally attributed to Moses; in Genesis 2.21–23, followed by Milton, God creates Eve out of Adam's rib.

bestowed any serious thought on the subject, ever supposed that Eve was, literally speaking, one of Adam's ribs, the deduction must be allowed to fall to the ground; or, only be so far admitted as it proves that man, from the remotest antiquity, found it convenient to exert his strength to subjugate his companion, and his invention to shew that she ought to have her neck bent under the yoke, because the whole creation was only created for his convenience or pleasure.

Let it not be concluded that I wish to invert the order of things; I have already granted, that, from the constitution of their bodies, men seem to be designed by Providence to attain a greater degree of virtue. I speak collectively of the whole sex; but I see not the shadow of a reason to conclude that their virtues should differ in respect to their nature. In fact, how can they, if virtue has only one eternal standard? I must therefore, if I reason consequentially, as strenuously maintain that they have the same simple direction, as that there is a God.

It follows then that cunning should not be opposed to wisdom, little cares to great exertions, or insipid softness, varnished over with the name of gentleness, to that fortitude which grand views alone can inspire.

William Blake: A Poison Tree[1]

I was angry with my friend:
I told my wrath, my wrath did end.
I was angry with my foe:
I told it not, my wrath did grow.

And I water'd it in fears,
Night & morning with my tears:
And I sunned it with smiles.
And with soft deceitful wiles.

And it grew both day and night.
Till it bore an apple bright.
And my foe beheld it shine.
And he knew that it was mine.

And into my garden stole.
When the night had veiled the pole.
In the morning glad I see.
My foe outstretched beneath the tree.

1. In "The Word Made Flesh: Blake's 'A Poison Tree' and the Book of Genesis" *Studies in Romanticism* 16 (1977); 237–249, the Blake scholar Philip J. Gallagher connects Blake's "A Poison Tree" from *Songs of Experience* with Milton's *Paradise Lost*. First both texts are readings of Genesis and in some sense contain parodies of the concept of "the word made flesh." If Milton's Satan out of his "malice . . . and disdain" (V.666) gives birth to Sin, the speaker of Blake's lyric conceives an anger that through being repressed gives birth to murder—palpably represented in Blake's illustration to this poem by a dead body under the "Poison Tree." Seeing the same critique of conventional morality in Blake's *The Marriage of Good and Evil* (see *The Longman Anthology of British Literature: The Romantic Period*), at work in "A Poison Tree" allows Gallagher to read the poem as "a counter-myth which exposes the biblical narrative as a fraud." To what extent can Blake's poem be seen as a critique of the biblical narrative, and of the notion that because of man's "first disobedience" all human beings are born with original sin? In what respects are the murderous and hypocritical envy of Blake's speaker like that of Milton's Satan? To what extent is the Poison Tree an alternative reading of the Tree of the Knowledge of Good and Evil, in which the poison that is born forth comes from denying knowledge rather than partaking of it? How does Blake's rewriting of the Genesis story compare with Milton's?

Thomas Bowles, *The Bubblers' Medley, or a Sketch of the Times*, 1720.

The Restoration and the Eighteenth Century

Population[1]

National Populations (in millions)[2]

	England and Wales	Scotland	Ireland
1661	5.5	—	2.2
1701	5.6	1.0	1.8–2.0
1751	6.5	1.3	3.2
1791	8.3	1.4	4.8

Urban Populations[3]

	London	Manchester	Edinburgh
1650	400,000	4,500	35,000
1700	75,000	8,000	40,000
1750	675,000	18,000	57,000
1801	959,000	89,0000	83,000

Life Expectancy

Life expectancy at birth is about 36 years. In London expectancy is shorter (perhaps 25 years); more than half of the children born in London die by the age of 10; London burials consistently outnumber London christenings.

Daily Life

Currency[4]

4 farthings	1d. (1 penny)	One penny (a 240th of a pound) in 1750 would be worth 85 U.S. cents today.
12d.	1s. (1 shilling)	One shilling (a 20th of a pound) would be worth $10.20 today.
5s.	1 crown	One crown (a 4th of a pound) would be worth $51 today.
20s.	1£ (1 pound)	One pound in 1750 would be worth $204 today.
21s.	1 guinea	One guinea in 1750 would be worth $214.20 today.

Social Structure and Income in England and Wales in 1696[5]

	Number of Persons	Annual Income per Family
Lords Temporal (secular peers)	6,400	£12,800
Gentlemen	96,000	£1280
Freeholders (i.e., property owners): the "better sort"	280,000	£184
Shopkeepers and tradesmen	180,000	£145
Farmers	750,000	£144
Artisans	240,000	£140
Laborers and servants	1,275,000	£115
Cottagers and paupers	1,300,000	£16
Vagrants	30,000	£12

1. Any population figures before 1801, when the first official census was taken, are only speculations, grounded in very fragmentary data.
2. The population of today's United Kingdom is 60,493,912 (July 2008 est.).
3. The population of today's London is over 7.6 million (October 2008 est.).
4. Historical equivalences for the purchasing power of a given sum are very approximate. Different types of calculations provide quite different results. A calculation based on wages, for instance, yields a different figure from a calculation based on the prices of basic consumer goods; and those consumer goods thought essential to daily life change drastically over time. These conversions, then, are meant only to be suggestive.
5. The chart represents selected groups from the much more comprehensive table, *A Scheme of the Income and Expense of the Several Families of England*, produced by the statistician Gregory King (1648–1712).

Cost of Goods[6]

1d.	A bun at the Chelsea Bun House, London 1711; enough gin to get drunk on
4d.	One pound of butcher's meat in London
1s. 6d.	Price of a chicken in London, 1755
2s. 3d.	Price of a chicken in London, 1785
2d.	Cost per night of a bed in a gin-shop, 1751
£3	House rent for an Oxfordshire rural laborer, last quarter of the century
£22	Annual rent on James Boswell's modest but comfortable London lodgings
£20–60	Approximate annual rent of "handsome large houses" in Stratford in the early 1720s
3d.	Duty per gallon on gin sales, midcentury
18s. 2d.	Tax on a shopkeeper with seven windows and an annual rent of £6 in 1797
£1	Duty per gallon on gin sales between 1736 and 1743
£1 5s.	Average Englishman's tax bill c.1776
£12 14s.	Tax on a shopkeeper with 23 windows, an annual rent of £50, a dog, and a servant, in 1797

Cost of Bread (in pence, per four-pound loaf)

1660 – 1664	5.8
1700 – 1704	4.8
1750 – 1754	5.1
1800 – 1804	11.7

Food and Drink

For the London poor, the cheapest foods are bread (often heavily adulterated), bacon, occasional beef and thin beef soup, tripe, and fish sold at discount price because past its first freshness; narrow apartments offer no opportunities for cooking, but the ovens of local bakeshops are sometimes made available on Sundays for the heating of a meal.

For the middling ranks and wealthy, dinners are served between three and five o'clock, and they are elaborate: two large courses, each composed of multiple items (as many as 25 per course). First course: peas, broccoli, salad, calf's head . . . ; second course: pheasant, hare, pig snipe . . . ; and dessert: apple pie, spun sugar, ices, syllabub (sherry with sugar, cream, and nutmeg).

Estimates of Per Capita Consumption of Beer and Spirits in London (pints per annum)

	1700	1750
Strong beer	512	417
Small beer	307	207
Spirits	4	22

Cocoa, coffee, sugar, and tobacco, all cultivated by slave labor on colonial plantations, are relatively inexpensive and widely consumed; tea, initially more expensive, becomes a ritual component of middle-class life beginning in the 1750s.

During the early 1700s, the craze for gin, pervasively and cheaply sold in impoverished neighborhoods, grows to be regarded as a dangerous blight on city life. "That poison," wrote the London magistrate and novelist Henry Fielding, "is the principal sustenance (if so it may be called) of more than 100,000 people in this metropolis."

Apparel

Men of the middle and higher ranks would don the following, in sequence: drawers (underpants) tied at the waist and knee; a linen shirt with jabots (frills) down the front; breeches that descend to the knee, and stockings either rolled over or tucked under the breeches' bottom edge; a waistcoat of silk or satin; a close-fitting coat with large buttons of the same material; a third "greatcoat" for outerwear; shoes or boots with large buckles; a wig and (outdoors) a hat in one of many widely varied styles.

Women of the middle and higher ranks would don the following, in sequence: a knee-length chemise (shirt) that functioned as undergarment; "stays"—a bodice, stiffened with whalebone but covered in costly and elegant materials and often left visible in the completed outfit; a petticoat, often elaborately decorated with flounces, embroidery, and even jewelry; an overskirt left open at the front to display the elegancies of the petticoat; shoes of silk or satin; and for outdoor wear, a cloak, or a tippet (a small fur cape) and muff. Wigs are worn less often by women than by men; hairstyles vary in intricacy, but by the 1760s they have achieved both height and elaboration to a notorious degree, and display a variety of cumbersome ornamentations: model ships, flower baskets, mini-gardens, and platters of fresh produce. Headwear ranges widely: elegant caps, large soft hats, luxuriantly lined hoods.

The clothing of the poor entails fewer items (often cast-off or second-hand), and only one of each, kept until worn out: for women, stays, a skirt, a wool-and-flax petticoat, a woolen gown, and a white, close-fitting cap; for men, a linen shirt, breeches, stockings, strong shoes, hat, and foul-weather overcoat.

6. Adapted from Kristen Olsen, *Daily Life in Eighteenth-Century England*. Westport, CT.: Greenwood Press, 1999.

Rulers

Monarchs	Parties and Preeminent Ministers
The Stuarts	Tories: originally, during the Exclusion Crisis (1678–1682), they supported the hereditary succession, by which the Catholic James, Duke of York, succeeded (1685) his older brother Charles II. After James's abdication (1688), many Tories became Jacobites, supporting the hereditary claims of James and his descendants—an allegiance that excluded them from office throughout the first three decades (1714–1742) of Hanoverian rule.
Charles II, King of England, Scotland, and Ireland (1660–1685)	
James II, King of England, Scotland, and Ireland (1685–1688)	
William III, King of England, Scotland, and Ireland (1689–1702); and Mary II, Queen of England, Scotland, and Ireland (1689–1694)	Whigs: originally, during the Exclusion Crisis, they argued against James's succession and for parliamentary rather than monarchical prerogative; the "Glorious Revolution" of 1688, which supplanted James with the Protestant William of Orange, constituted their first triumph; the establishment of the Hanoverian line in 1714 enabled them to monopolize power over the ensuing decades.
Anne, Queen of Great Britain and Ireland (1702–1714)	
The Hanoverians	
George I, King of Great Britain and Ireland (1714–1727)	
George II, King of Great Britain and Ireland (1727–1760)	Robert Walpole (1721–1742) Whig
George III, King of the United Kingdom of Great Britain and Ireland (1760–1820)	William Pitt the Elder (1766–1768) Whig
	William Pitt the Younger (1804–1806) Tory

Queen Anne

Robert Walpole

Timeline

1660 Charles II restored as king; the Act of Indemnity and Oblivion extends a general pardon to nearly all participants in the Civil War and the Interregnum administrations.

1664–1667 The Second Anglo-Dutch War, fought over trade routes and rights, ends with Dutch ships entering the Thames and destroying much of the English fleet.

1660 Pepys begins his diary (page 2010).

1660 The Royal Society is founded (page 2039).

1665–1666 Bubonic Plague breaks out in London one last time, killing approximately 57,000 (some 14% of the city's population).

1666 The Great Fire of London destroys 13,200 houses, 87 churches, and most municipal and guild buildings in the city, but leaves western London (site of the royal palace, government buildings, and fashionable town life) intact.

1668 Aphra Behn's *Oroonoko* (page 2137)

1673 The First Test Act excludes nonmembers of the Church of England (i.e., Catholics and Dissenters) from holding public office.

1675 William Wycherley's *The Country Wife* (page 2215)

1679 The Popish Plot, an adroitly fabricated conspiracy theory, propagates the conviction that Jesuits are planning, by means of assassination and invasion, to establish Catholic rule in England.

1679–1681 In the Exclusion Crisis, a large parliamentary faction attempts (unsuccessfully) to bar the king's Catholic brother from succession.

1681 John Dryden's *Absalom and Achitophel* (page 2077)

1685 Charles II dies; accession of James II.

1687 Sir Isaac Newton publishes *Principia Mathematica*, the founding text of modern physics.

1688–1689 The "Glorious Revolution": William of Orange conducts a virtually bloodless invasion-by-invitation; James II's escape to France enables Parliament to construe his throne as "vacant" and to ratify the accession of William and his wife Mary (James's daughter) as William III and Mary II.

1689 The Toleration Act permits dissenters (but not Catholics or Unitarians) to worship in authorized meeting houses.

1690 John Locke's *Essay Concerning Human Understanding* (page 2618)

1694 Founding of the Bank of England. Mary II dies.

1700 Mary Astell's *Reflections on Marriage* (page 2284)

1701–1713 The War of the Spanish Succession is fought by the British, Dutch, and Germans against the French and Spanish in hopes of preventing an expansion of French hegemony.

1701 The Act of Settlement bypasses 50 Catholic claimants to the English throne, and grants the succession to Sophia, Electress of Hanover (first cousin to Charles II) and her heirs; James II dies in exile.

1702 William III dies; accession of Queen Anne (Mary II's younger sister)

1707 The Act of Union unites the kingdoms of England and Scotland under the name of Great Britain.

1708 Sir Christopher Wren designs St. Paul's Cathedral, and about 50 new churches, to replace the 86 destroyed by the Great Fire.

1711 Alexander Pope's *An Essay on Criticism* (page 2441)

1713 The Treaty of Utrecht concludes the War of the Spanish Succession, and grants Britain the *asiento*—the exclusive right to supply slaves to the Spanish empire.

1714 Queen Anne dies; accession of George I, Elector of Hanover.

1715 The Jacobite rebellion in support of James II's son ("The Old Pretender") fails.

1717 Lady Mary Wortley Montagu's *Turkish Embassy Letters* (page 2544)

1719 Daniel Defoe's *Robinson Crusoe* (page 2793)

1720 Stock in the South Sea Company rises sharply, then plummets; the bursting of the "Bubble" plunges many into ruin.

1721 Robert Walpole, credited with engineering a post-Bubble recovery and appointed First Lord of the Treasury and Chancellor of the Exchequer, creates the Whig administrative "machine" that will enable him to monopolize power for the next two decades.

1726 Jonathan Swift's *Gulliver's Travels* (page 2371)

1727 George I dies; accession of George II.

1728 John Gay's *Beggar's Opera*, a pioneering piece of musical theater that unexpectedly becomes one of the most successful and enduring entertainments of the century (page 2557)

1735 William Hogarth's *Rake's Progress* (page 2605)

1739–1748 The War of the Austrian Succession is fought on fronts in Europe, America, and India.

1742 Walpole resigns.

1745 The "Forty-Five," a sustained Jacobite uprising led by the "Young Pretender" Charles Edward Stuart (James II's grandson), ends in defeat at the Battle of Culloden.

1750s Strawberry Hill, designed by Horace Walpole and friends, helps spark the Gothic revival.

1755 Samuel Johnson's *Dictionary of the English Language* (page 2704)

1756–1763 The Seven Years' War entailing for the British considerable conquest in Europe, Canada, and India

1757 Robert Clive, a leading force of the East India Company, defeats the army of the Bengali leader Siraj ud-Daula at the Battle of Plassey, consolidating the Empire's hold on India.

1760 George II dies; accession of George III.

1772 The practice of slavery is declared illegal within Britain, but continues legally within the British Empire until the Slave Trade Act of 1807.

1776 The American War of Independence begins.

1778 The Roman Catholic Relief Act permits Catholic worship.

1780 Lord George Gordon, petitioning for the repeal of the Catholic Relief Act, triggers the most violent riots in British history.

1781 The American War of Independence ends.

1787–1795 The impeachment and trial of Warren Hastings, governor-general of Bengal, focuses attention on questions of ethics, exploitation, and empire in British India.

1789 The French Revolution begins.

The Restoration and the Eighteenth Century

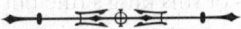

On 25 May 1660, Charles II set foot on the shore of Dover and brought his eleven-year exile to an end. The arrival was recorded by the great diarist Samuel Pepys, and his words preserve for us a form of the event:

> I went, and Mr. Mansell, and one of the King's footmen, with a dog that the King loved (which beshat the boat, which made us laugh, and methink that a king and all that belong to him are but just as others are), in a boat by ourselves, and so got on shore when the King did, who was received . . . with all imaginable love and respect at his entrance upon the land of Dover. Infinite the crowd of people and the horsemen, citizens, and noblemen of all sorts. The Mayor of the town came and gave him his white staff, the badge of his place, which the King did give him again. The Mayor also presented him from the town a very rich Bible, which he took and said it was the thing that he loved above all things in the world. . . . The shouting and joy expressed by all is past imagination.

Pepys captures and creates a brilliant mix of materials and experiences: his words compound jubilation and skepticism, images of authority and obeisance, tropes of spirituality and irony, and they remind us of the elements and passions by which all mortals live. Every gesture and exchange in this scene forecast the world to come, but what most signals the future is the paradox of remembering and forgetting that the diarist performs even as he records this scene. And all who witnessed the King's descent at Dover committed similar acts of memory and oblivion. Many of those (Pepys included) who were drunk with pleasure at the return of Charles Stuart had endorsed the destruction of his father eleven years before. The entire Restoration and the events that would follow over the ensuing years would prove a complex unfolding of memory and forgetfulness.

The jubilant crowds at Dover thought to make flux stop here: forever to banish the turbulence of civil war and political innovation, to restore all the old familiar forms, utterly to erase what had come between the death of the father and the restoration of the son. Charles II would soon institute an Act of Oblivion to those ends, forgiving proponents of rebellion by officially forgetting their misdeeds. But civil war and revolution would not be erased, nor could monarchy, the Anglican Church, aristocratic privilege, political patronage, and the old social hierarchies be revived as though nothing had intervened. Much of the old was brought back with the return of the Stuart monarchy, but the consequence of layering the present over a willfully suppressed past was an instability of feelings and forms that ensured the ever-changing triumph of different memories and different oblivions during the ensuing decades. No one celebrating the return of ancient ways in 1660 could have foreseen the ruptures and innovations that lay ahead in the next half of the century, when crises of conspiracy and the birth of party politics would produce further shifts in monarchy through a sequence of

> *No one celebrating the return of ancient ways in 1660 could have foreseen the ruptures and innovations that lay ahead in the next half of the century . . .*

three ruling houses from three different countries. But even in 1660 the innocent acclaim on the shores of Dover was accompanied by hidden guilts and ironies, by vindictive desires, even for some by millenarian hopes. And while such stresses and tensions were unacknowledged in May 1660, they soon enough surfaced, and they unsettled not only the pleasures of this king's rule but the politics of an entire age.

MONARCHS, MINISTERS, EMPIRE

The coronation of Charles II in May 1661 marked the beginning of both the first and the eleventh year of his rule. The King's laws were named as if he had taken possession of the crown at the moment of his father's execution in 1649. And fictions, legal and not so legal, were to prove a hallmark of Stuart rule. The King openly proclaimed his love of parliaments, his devotion to the immemorial constitution of balance and moderation, his Protestant fervor, and his pious hopes for a national church. Yet he often postponed his parliaments; he claimed a tender conscience for Protestant dissenters, but he maneuvered for the toleration of Roman Catholics; he conducted an aggressive, nationalist program against European powers, but he signed a secret and deeply compromising treaty with Louis XIV; he took communion in the Anglican Church, but on his deathbed he sealed his own conversion to Catholicism; he was tenderly affectionate to his barren queen, yet he publicly flaunted his whoring tastes; he repeatedly exiled his unpopular brother James, Duke of York, while promoting and indulging his own bastard sons, yet he staunchly resisted any effort to displace his brother from the line of succession. The dominance of masquerade surely derived from Charles's temper, but fiction and falsehood were also the structural principles and aesthetic features of an entire world.

. . . fictions, legal and not so legal, were to prove a hallmark of Stuart rule.

In December 1678, a series of events started to unfold that proved the very emblem of the masking, the fears, and the psychology of Charles II's rule. It began with legal depositions: one Titus Oates, a baker's son and self-anointed savior of a Protestant people, claimed to have knowledge of a secret plot to kill the King, crown his Catholic brother, and begin the wholesale conversion of English souls—and, just as frightening, English properties—to Rome. Oates offered to a public hungry for scandal and change a Popish plot and a familiar mix of images and idioms: priests and idols, the Roman Antichrist, conspiracy, murder, and mayhem. His depositions and fabrications played brilliantly on memories of the past and on fears of a future under a Catholic king. Nor did it help that the Duke of York's private secretary, Edward Coleman, was caught with treasonous correspondence in his chamber. The plot seemed compounded of sufficient truths to challenge the stability of the Crown. From the midst of the plot, and under the hand of the Earl of Shaftesbury, a political party emerged that took advantage of Popish facts and fears by proposing the Bill of Exclusion in Parliament, which would have barred the Duke of York and any future Catholic monarchs from the English throne. In the event, the bill failed, Charles died of natural causes, and the Duke succeeded his brother in February 1685.

During James's brief reign, no plots, conspiracies, or political parties proved so costly to his rule as did the new king himself. He succeeded his brother in a mood of surprising public affirmation. At his accession, James returned the embrace of

Anglican England by promising to honor the national church and that most beloved of Protestant properties, a tender conscience. There would be no forcing of religious uniformity in this reign. But soon enough James began to move against Anglican interests: he staffed his army with Catholic officers, he imposed Catholic officials on Oxford University, and he insisted that his Declarations of Toleration be read aloud from the pulpits of Anglican churches. Such a program challenged interest, property, and propriety, and it spelled the quick demise of Catholic rule.

As Duke of York, James had been famed for martial valor. But now, when confronted in November 1688 by the army of his Dutch son-in-law, William of Orange, he fled under cover of night to France. What had in part provoked James's flight were memories of the past—of civil war and of the execution of his father, Charles I. What had provoked the invasion by William of Orange was not merely the specter of Louis XIV hovering behind James's rule or the open presence of Jesuits at James's court. It was the birth of James Francis Edward Stuart, son of James II and Mary of Modena. Protestants would suffer not only the inconvenience of one Catholic monarch but the possibility of an endless Catholic succession. The prospect was too much to bear. Secret negotiations were begun between powerful English artistocrats—Whigs and Tories alike—and William, the governor (stadholder) of Holland, resulting in what many called the Glorious Revolution. But the deceits and pretenses—the gaps and silences—of this palace coup did not strike all contemporaries as glorious. The stadholder who chased a Catholic king from England was not only an invading hero (though some did call him William the Conqueror), he was also the son-in-law of James II. Those who clung to the binding ties of loyalty and gratitude accused William and Mary of deep impiety, indeed, of parricide.

. . . the deceits and pretenses—the gaps and silences—of this palace coup did not strike all contemporaries as glorious.

But the astonishing invitation to William of Orange produced no bloodshed. What it did produce was a Protestant monarchy under the rule of King William III and Queen Mary. Members of Parliament, meeting to invent the laws that would sanctify this revolutionary change, decided that it would be best to say they had discovered the throne of England mysteriously vacant and that this William was no conqueror but a rightful claimant on a vacant throne. Of course, not everyone was pleased by such a revolution—sacred oaths had been broken, binding ties were cast aside, vows were juggled as mere words. Those who would not accept a convenient revolution were called Jacobites, that is, supporters of King James (*Jacobus* in Latin); they remained a force that would trouble British political life by threatening a Stuart restoration in the fervent but failed Jacobite rebellions of 1715 and 1745.

Most of William's subjects, though, were content with the evasions of this Glorious Revolution. Many were not content, though, with the program of European war in which the English were now plunged by their new king, intent on thwarting the ambitions of Louis XIV, his lifelong nemesis. The ruinous expense of war demanded taxes and fiscal innovation; it produced a stream of grumbling satire, complaint against Dutch favorites, and more than one conspiracy and attempted assassination. No such disaffection or turbulence disturbed the reign (1702–1714) of William's successor, Queen Anne. Her years were the twilight of Stuart monarchy, a time of political nostalgia and commercial confidence whose mood the young

Alexander Pope captured in the lines of *Windsor-Forest* (1713), where softened memories and strategic elisions of the years of Stuart rule are mingled with images of triumph—of imperial expansion and a swelling commerce of domestic and foreign trade.

But luxury was not England's only import. At the death of Queen Anne, an entire court and new ruling house were shipped to England from the German state of Hanover. George I was the grandson of James I; beyond lineage, George's communion in a Protestant church was the virtue that most recommended his succession. He spoke no English, knew nothing of his new subjects, and could not be bothered to learn. Nor was he much implicated in the management of a state whose rule would successively become less the prerogative of kings than the business of ministers and the function of parties, interest, and corruption. This displacement of monarch by minister was cemented during the period caustically nicknamed "Robin's Reign": two decades (1721–1742), transversing the reigns of George I and George II, when politics were dominated by Robert Walpole, who bought loyalties, managed kings, and ran the state with such ruthless efficiency as to earn him the new label "prime minister" (the phrase was meant as an insult, aimed at the perceived excess of his power in a government where ministers were only supposed to advise their colleagues and their king). The South Sea Bubble, a state-endorsed investment scheme that ruined many, was the making of Robert Walpole. As the only cabinet minister untainted by the scandal (he had initially argued against the scheme, then lost money in it), he was put in charge of the subsequent governmental housecleaning. Once empowered, he cheerfully shed his scruples, devising a political machine fueled by patronage that made his cronies rich, his opposition apoplectic. By the firmness of his rule and the prudence of his policies, Walpole consolidated a long period of Whig supremacy that supplanted the party contest of the preceding decades, when Whigs and Tories had seesawed more swiftly in and out of power.

. . . politics were dominated by Robert Walpole, who bought loyalties, managed kings, and ran the state with such ruthless efficiency as to earn him the new label "prime minister" . . .

The parties had begun to crystallize during the Exclusion crisis of the early 1680s, when Whigs fought to bar the king's Catholic brother from the throne and Tories upheld the established continuity of the Stuart line. Like "prime minister," the two party names began as insult, "Tory" denoting an Irish-Catholic bandit, "Whigs" identifying a group of Scottish rebels during the civil wars. Late in the eighteenth century, Samuel Johnson summed up their polarities: "The prejudice of the Tory is for establishment; the prejudice of the Whig is for innovation." "Establishment" meant preserving monarchic prerogatives, upholding the Anglican church, lamenting the advent of the Hanoverians, and—for some Tories, not all—actively yearning for the restoration of the Stuart line and abetting the attempts to achieve this in the Jacobite rebellions of 1715 and 1745. Whig "innovation" entailed enthusiastic support for both the Glorious Revolution and the House of Hanover, for policies of religious tolerance, and for all measures that advanced the interests of the newly prosperous and powerful merchant class. In the late seventeenth century, party politics had begun for the first time to supplant long-running religious conflicts as the main articulation of interest and power. For all its noise and rage, the new structure produced a paradoxical calm, not by the suppression of difference but by its recognition. The division into parties amounted to a sanctioned fragmentation of the whole. Even during the reign of Anne, when party conflict was at its most feverish, what the machinery of party seemed to ensure was the containment of partisan interest within the dynamic, even organic, coherence of the state.

During Walpole's "reign," portions of the two parties coalesced in an uneasy alliance. The arrogance, obstinacy, and efficacy of Walpole's methods galvanized an opposition consisting of both Tories and alienated Whigs; their endeavors acquired luster from the contributions of a remarkable array of writers (the Tories Jonathan Swift, Alexander Pope, John Gay, and Henry Fielding, and the Whig James Thomson) who opposed the prime minister on grounds of personality, principle, and of course self-interest. Walpole, recognizing that the best writers worked for the opposition, strove to suppress them by all the strategies of censorship he could devise. But by his greatness as a character and his force as an opponent, Walpole loomed for a long while as both literature's nemesis and its muse.

In fact, Walpole enforced the policies endorsed by only a fraction of his party—those moderate Whigs deeply interested in cultivating the country's wealth by commerce, deeply resistant to waging war. "My *politics*," he once wrote emphatically, "*are to keep free from all engagements, as long as we possibly can*"; by "engagements," he meant military commitments abroad. By the late 1730s, he discovered that he could keep free from them no longer. Britons feared that powers on the Continent—Spain, Austria, and above all France—were encroaching on their rights, and the popular clamor to wage European war prevailed. "When trade is at stake," the oppositionist William Pitt warned the British, "it is your last retrenchment; you must defend it or perish." Under the pressure of such sentiments Walpole eventually resigned, having led the state through two decades of comparative peace, growing national prosperity, and a new stability in government, but leaving behind him an army and a navy debilitated by disuse. Nonetheless, with trade at stake and the navy rebuilt, Britain embarked on a series of wars that ran almost unbroken for the rest of the century. Pitt presided brilliantly over many of them, wars waged directly or indirectly against France for trading privileges and territories abroad. By 1763, Britain had secured possession of Bengal in India, many islands and coastal territories in the Caribbean, and virtually all of North America (including Canada) east of the Mississippi, as well as half of all the international trade transpiring on the planet. So great was the impetus toward empire that even Britain's humiliating defeat in the American War of Independence (1775–1783) could not really halt the momentum; territories in India were still expanding, and settlement of Australia lay in the offing.

. . . with trade at stake and the navy rebuilt, Britain embarked on a series of wars that ran almost unbroken for the rest of the century.

By now, the throne was occupied by the first Hanoverian monarch born in Britain—George III. His long reign (1760–1820) teemed with troubles: the popular scorn for his chosen ministers, the loss of the American war, the aftershocks of the French Revolution, the defiance of his heirs, the torments of his own slow-encroaching madness. But almost from beginning to end he ruled over the richest nation and the widest empire in the world. In 1740, a new song could be heard with a catchy refrain: "Rule, Britannia, rule the waves / Britons never will be slaves." The words were the work of the Scots-born poet James Thomson, now a proud adherent of "Britannia" by virtue of the Act of Union (1707), which had fused Scotland with England and Wales into a new nation, newly named: Great Britain. Over the ensuing years the song took hold partly because of the seductively prophetic ways in which it forecast Britain's greatness and partly because of the proud but peculiar resonances of the refrain's last line. There, Thomson contrasts British liberties with the slave-like constraints supposedly suffered by subjects of absolute monarchy elsewhere. Less directly, "slaves" also points to those peoples upon whose subjugation British privilege and British prosperity were increasingly to depend. Throughout the century, Britons profited spectacularly from the capture, transport, sale, and labor of African slaves in current and former colonies; "no nation," William Pitt the Younger proclaimed in 1792, had "plunged so deeply into this guilt as Great Britain."

There were also whole populations whose condition often evoked the analogy of slavery in the minds of the few who paid reformist attention to their plight: the oppressed indigenous peoples of the colonies, and women and the poor at home. Conversation about such issues became louder and more purposeful near the end of the eighteenth century, as particular champions began to turn social questions into moral causes: John Wilkes on the widening of liberties and voting rights; Mary Wollstonecraft on the rights of women; William Blake (and later, William Cobbett) on the economic inequities of the whole social structure. The problems themselves did not even begin to find redress until the following century, but the emergence of such advocacies, quickened by the audacities of the French Revolution, marked a turning point toward the Romanticism that seized poetic and political imaginations in the 1790s. For most Britons of the eighteenth century, however, the new prosperity produced no special promptings of conscience. As their Restoration forebears had actively encouraged oblivion in an effort to anesthetize themselves to their past, men and women now sustained a moral and social oblivion that eased their use of others and their pleasure in new wealth. Out of such adroitly managed oscillations, Britons fabricated a new sense of themselves as a nation and an empire.

. . . particular champions began to turn social questions into moral causes . . .

This new construct was in large measure the work of a prominent breed of economic architects: the capital-wielding middle classes. For centuries, wealth had derived primarily from land: tenant farmers performed the labor; the landed gentry collected the often enormous profits. The new wealth was amassed, even created, by people situated between these two extremes, constituting what was often referred to as "the middling rank," "the middling station," or "the middling orders." What set the middling orders apart was the comparatively new way in which they made their money: not by landed inheritance, not by tenancy or wage work, but by the adroit deployment of money itself. Having acquired a sum by inheritance, wage, or loan, they used it as capital, investing it, along with their own efforts, in potentially lucrative enterprises: in shops, in factories, and in the enormous new financial structures (banks, stocks) that underwrote the nation's economic expansiveness. They hired helpers, reinvested profits, and when their schemes succeeded, they made their money grow. With wealth, of course, grew clout. The interests of the "City"—that is, of the eastern half of London where bustling merchants made their deals—increasingly shaped the affairs of state, the appetites for empire. Empire also shaped the progress of the arts.

Members of the middle class became the chief consumers and energetic producers of the period's most conspicuous new forms of literature: newspapers and novels. But nowhere were the new powers of the burgeoning bourgeoisie more striking than in the theater, that cultural site they often visited and ultimately revised.

Money, Manners, and Theatrics

No event more exactly and more economically signals the return of an aristocratic court to the center of English culture than the reopening of the London theaters in 1660. The intimacy, indeed the complicity, of court with theater throughout the early modern period was such that when in the 1640s Parliament took aim at monarchy, aristocracy, and privilege, it not only struck off the heads of the Earl of Strafford and Archbishop Laud, it also banished play acting and shut tight the doors of the London stage. But Puritans could not banish the theater from the English imagination, and no sooner were the playhouses closed than publishers issued new editions of old plays and the theater made a secret return in domestic spaces and before private audiences. Print and memory would be the preservative of an entire culture. In 1660, monarchy and theater were restored in tandem. But this artistic restoration, like the political one that made it possible, irresistibly mingled the old with the new. Pepys captured all the excitement and splendor of this restoration; as usual he proves adroit at reckoning innovation:

> [T]he stage is now . . . a thousand times better and more glorious than heretofore. Now, wax-candles, and many of them; then, not above three pounds of tallow. Now, all things civil, no rudeness anywhere; then, as in a bear garden. Then, two or three fiddlers; now, nine or ten of the best. Then, nothing but rushes upon the ground and everything mean; and now all otherwise. Then the Queen seldom and the King never would come; now not the King only for state but all civil people do think they may come as well as any.

One reason that "all civil people" thought so was a matter of simple geography. Whereas the theaters of Shakespeare's day had been located in seedy districts on the outskirts of the city, this new and sumptuous theatrical world was ensconced in new neighborhoods strategically located for maximum social confluence, on the border between Westminster—home of the court—and the City of London, dwelling place of a "mighty band of citizens and prentices" whose sudden convergence with royalty seemed a dramatic innovation. They had all gathered to witness the most astonishing new spectacle of all: women on stage in a public theater.

Before the Restoration, aristocratic women had tantalized the court in private and privileged masquing; now the pleasures of display and consumption were democratized in several ways. For women, theatricality was no longer a pastime reserved for the very few but a plausible—though precarious—profession. For audiences at the new theaters, actresses represented the possibility of erotic spectacle for the price of a ticket—a chance to gaze on women who everyone knew were managing the pleasures, and often the policies, of kings and courtiers. Inevitably new strategies of theatricality suffused this audience, where women might model seductive conduct on the teasing combinations of concealment and display enacted before them. Pepys eavesdropped on the libertine Sir Charles Sedley in urgent banter with two women: "And one of the women would and did sit with her mask on, all the play. He would fain know who she was, but she would not tell; yet did give him many pleasant hints of her knowledge of him, by

The traffic between revelation and concealment defined this theater.

that means setting his brains at work to find out who she was, and did give him leave to use all means but pulling off her mask." Display and disguise not only animated the stage, they quickened social exchange in the intimate spaces of stalls and boxes. The traffic between revelation and concealment defined this theater. It drove the plots of plays and galvanized audiences, modeling and scripting their fashions, their language, their lives.

In such a world the theater provided a national mask, a fantasy of empire and heroism, and yet at the same time sustained a critique of masquerade, a brutal exposure of deceptions rampant in the culture. On the one hand, the heroic drama displayed, indeed reveled in, outsized acts of conquest in exotic lands, valor, and virtue: on stage, princes slaughtered infidels by the thousands; virgins sustained honor through impossible ordeals of abduction and assault. Yet in 1667, at the same moment such dramas were thriving in the king's and the duke's playhouses, the royal fleet was being burned and sunk by a Dutch navy that breached all defenses, invading the very precincts and privacy of London's docks and shipyards. And while the fleet burned, the king busied himself with other depredations, sustaining a series of intrigues, some with the very actresses who wore such incomparable honor and virtue on the stage. (The mix of myth and mischief was popular in pictures too—for example, in the portrait of Barbara Villiers, Countess of Castlemaine, perhaps the most notorious of all the king's mistresses, gotten up in the guise of Minerva, Roman goddess of wisdom; see Color Plate 20.) The heroic drama celebrated military conquest and colonial glory, and displayed them at a moment in national history that produced nothing so much as shame and humiliation: defeat at the hands of Dutch ships and Dutch commerce.

At the same time, but in a far different dramatic mode, the stage sustained a brilliant critique of a whole culture of incongruity, masquerade, and self-delusion. Restoration comedy took as its subject appetite and opportunism, social hypocrisy and sexual power play. The London audience watched scenes of seduction and connivance set in the very vicinities they had traversed to reach the playhouse: St. James's Park, Covent Garden. Such aristocratic libertines as Sir Charles Sedley and Lord Rochester, intent on their own intrigues, might admire themselves in a theatrical mirror, where the rake-hero conducted endless parry-and-thrust with his equals, brutalized his inferiors, and laid hands and claim on any moveable object of desire: fruits and foodstuffs, silks and sonnets, housemaids and women of high estate. But the rakes in the playhouse might see themselves mocked as well. The best comic writers—Wycherley, Etherege, Behn, Congreve—showed the libertines equaled and often bested in cunning by the women they pursued, baffled where they would be most powerful, enslaved where they would be most free. In brilliant volleys of dialogue, these lovers mixed passion and poison in volatile measures, chasing one another through a maze of plots, counterplots, and subplots so convoluted as to suggest a world of calculation run mad. Over the thirty years of its triumphs, Restoration comedy, in an astounding fugue of excesses and depravities, laid bare the turbulence and toxins of this culture.

. . . Restoration comedy, in an astounding fugue of excesses and depravities, laid bare the turbulence and toxins of this culture.

That the heroic drama, with all its exaggerations and flatteries, found a market is hardly surprising; what is more puzzling is the commercial triumph of Restoration comedy, a theatrical mode that entertained by punishing and humiliating its audience—though it is hardly surprising that this theater should itself have fallen victim in the 1690s to prudery and what would come to be called "taste." In the wake of the Protestant revolution of 1688, which typed Stuart rule as the very emblem of self-indulgence, agents of moral improvement and social propriety made their assault on Restoration comedy the stalking horse for a broad program of Christian reform. Restoration comedy, which had erupted as a repudiation of Puritan prohibitions, now seemed to prompt a new wave of moral rectitude.

Under such pressures, the playhouse redirected its mirror away from the aristocracy toward the upper strata of the "middling sort": London merchants, colonial profiteers. During the Restoration, the newly prosperous mercantile classes who converged with courtiers at the theater had watched themselves either derided or ignored on stage, their social pretensions and ineptitudes put down in the comedies, their commercial concerns absent from the heroic drama. In the early eighteenth century, they saw themselves glorified instead, in "domestic tragedy," which displayed the tribulations of commercial households, and in sentimental comedy, which sought by a mix of tears and modest laughter to inculcate family values and to portray the merchant class as the nation's moral core. Richard Steele's *The Conscious Lovers* (1722) sounded the fanfare for a newly theatric social self-conception. "We merchants," a businessman informs an aristocrat, "are a species of gentry that have grown into the world this last century, and are as honorable and almost as useful as you landed folk, that have always thought yourself so much above us."

Nor was the stage the only venue to promulgate this new cultural self-awareness. By its very title *The Spectator* (1711–1713), one of the most widely read periodicals of the century, assured its largely middle-class audience that they moved under the constant, thoughtful scrutiny of a virtual playgoer, the paper's fictive author, "Mr. Spectator," who made all London a kind of theater, in which he (and his eagerly imitative readers) might perpetually enjoy the privileges of making observations and forming judgments. The very energies that had been drained away from the stage now found a new home in the theatricalized world of commerce, fashion, manners, taste.

The cast members in this new theater were numerous, varied, and eager for direction, mostly because, as a "new species of gentry," they aspired to roles for which they had formerly been deemed unfit. Terms like "esquire" and "gentleman" had operated in previous centuries as proof of literal "entitlement." They were secured by registration with the College of Heralds, and they calibrated not merely monetary wealth but lineage, landholdings, education, and social standing. In the eighteenth century, men and women with sufficient money and nerve assumed these titles for themselves, confident enough that they might learn to play the part. "In our days," noted a 1730 dictionary, "all are accounted gentlemen that have money." But since the "money" was now so variously attainable—by shopkeeping, by manufacture, by international trade—the "middle station" was itself subdivided into many strata, and since the very point of capital was accumulation and improvement, ascent by emulation became a master plot in the new social theater. "Everyone," observed one commentator, "is flying from his inferiors in pursuit of his superiors, who fly from him with equal alacrity."

Wigs, fans, scarves, silks, petticoats, and jewels; china, silver, family portraits—these were the costumes, these the props of the new commercial theater . . .

Amid the flux, fashion and commodity—what one wore, what one owned—mattered enormously. Wigs, fans, scarves, silks, petticoats, and jewels; china, silver, family portraits—these were the costumes, these the props of the new commercial theater, by which members of the middle orders pleased themselves and imitated the gentry. The commercial classes who had begun by catering to the aristocracy gradually became, in their waxing prosperity, their own best customers, selling garb and goods to one another. Shrewd marketers saw that novelty itself possessed an intrinsic and urgent appeal for people constantly in social flight, tirelessly engaged in remaking themselves. Advertising came into its own, filling the pages and underwriting the costs of the daily, weekly, and monthly periodicals. The listing of consumables became a prevalent mode of print, in everything from auction catalogues (the still-dominant houses of Christie's and Sotheby's got their start near the middle of the century) to poems and novels, where long lists of products and possessions became a means of recording the culture's appetites, and at times of satirizing them. In the hands of Swift and Pope, the catalogue itself became a form of art. The taste in literary miscellany reflected a more general taste for omnivorous consumption: variety indexed abundance and proved power. Tea from China, coffee from the Caribbean, tobacco from Virginia—all were relatively new, comparatively inexpensive, and enormously popular. In daily rituals of drink and smoke, the middling orders imbibed and inhaled a pleasing sense of their global reach, their comfortable centrality on a planet newly commercialized.

Commodities formed part of a larger discourse, involving speech and gesture as well as prop and costume. A cluster of precepts, gathered under the umbrella-term "politeness," supplied the stage directions, even at times the script, for the new social theater in which everyone was actor and everyone was audience. Eager to shine in their recently acquired roles, the merchant classes pursued the polish implicit in the word "polite." They hired "dancing masters" to teach them graceful motions and proper manners, "bear leaders" (tutors) to guide their sons on the Grand Tour of France and Italy in the footsteps of the nobility, elocution coaches to help them purge inappropriate accents, teachers of painting and music to supply their daughters with marriageable competence. For the newly prosperous, politeness was the epitome of distinction: it went beyond gesture and accomplishment to suggest a state of mind, a refinement of perception, a mix of knowledge, responsiveness, and judgment often summarized as "taste." "The man of polite imagination," said the *Spectator*, "is let into a great many pleasures that the vulgar are not capable of receiving." Eager to gain access, middle-class readers avidly sought instruction.

A cluster of precepts, gathered under the umbrella-term "politeness," supplied the stage directions, even at times the script, for the new social theater . . .

Politeness (which Samuel Johnson once defined as "fictitious benevolence") required considerable self-control; the passions (rage, greed, lust) were to be contained and channeled into the appearance of abundant and abiding goodwill. The middle classes embraced such constraints partly to allay widespread suspicion of their

Color Plate 20 Theatricality Disseminated. Sir Peter Lely, *Barbara Villiers, Countess of Castlemaine*, c. 1665. Charles II's favorite painter portrays Charles II's favorite mistress, in costume as Minerva, Roman goddess of wisdom, against a stormy background. Castlemaine's countenance was reproduced in less costly ways as well, in engravings from Lely's portraits that made the visage of the King's mistress possessible by ordinary mortals. The diarist Samuel Pepys records a visit to Lely's sumptuous studio, where he "saw the so-much-by-me-desired picture of my Lady Castlemaine, which is a most blessed picture and that I must have a copy of." *(The Royal Collection © 2005, Her Majesty Queen Elizabeth II.)*

Color Plate 21 Theatricality Domesticated. Johann Zoffany, *Queen Charlotte with Her Two Eldest Sons*, 1764. A century after Lely painted the king's mistress in the garb of the goddess of wisdom (Color Plate 20), such mythological trappings are reduced to dress-up for George III's two young sons at play. Amid sumptuous furnishings, Zoffany's conversation piece emphasizes not the grandeur of the royal family but its intimacy and affection; a new era of majesty as "good example" has commenced. *(The Royal Collection © 2005, Her Majesty Queen Elizabeth II.)*

Color Plate 22 Restoration Theatricality Transposed and Transformed. Joshua Reynolds, *Mrs. Abington as "Miss Prue,"* 1771. The comic actress Frances Abington (1737–1815) here traverses time and rank, reincarnating Miss Prue, an "awkward country girl" in William Congreve's late-17th-century comedy *Love for Love* (1695), in garb that epitomizes late-18th-century high fashion. Abington later scored her greatest triumph in a similar role, modeled on Restoration antecedents and crafted especially for her: Lady Teazle, the country wife ardent for London life in Richard Brinsley Sheridan's *School for Scandal*. *(The Royal Collection © 2005, Her Majesty Queen Elizabeth II.)*

Color Plate 23 Science Enthroned. Marcellus Laroon, *Charles II as President of the Royal Society*, 1684. In this portrait of the King painted a year before his death, the traditional trappings of royalty—crown, throne, and orb—literally take a back seat (in the background at left) to the advancements of the new science. Charles gestures toward the instruments of seeing, modeling, mapping, and calibrating that the Royal Society he sponsored had done much to devise and develop. By their placement, the painter suggests that these tools make possible the naval commerce and conquest depicted in the distance—as though the telescope were the world's new scepter, and the globe the monarch's proper sphere. *(Picture Desk, Inc./Kobal Collection.)*

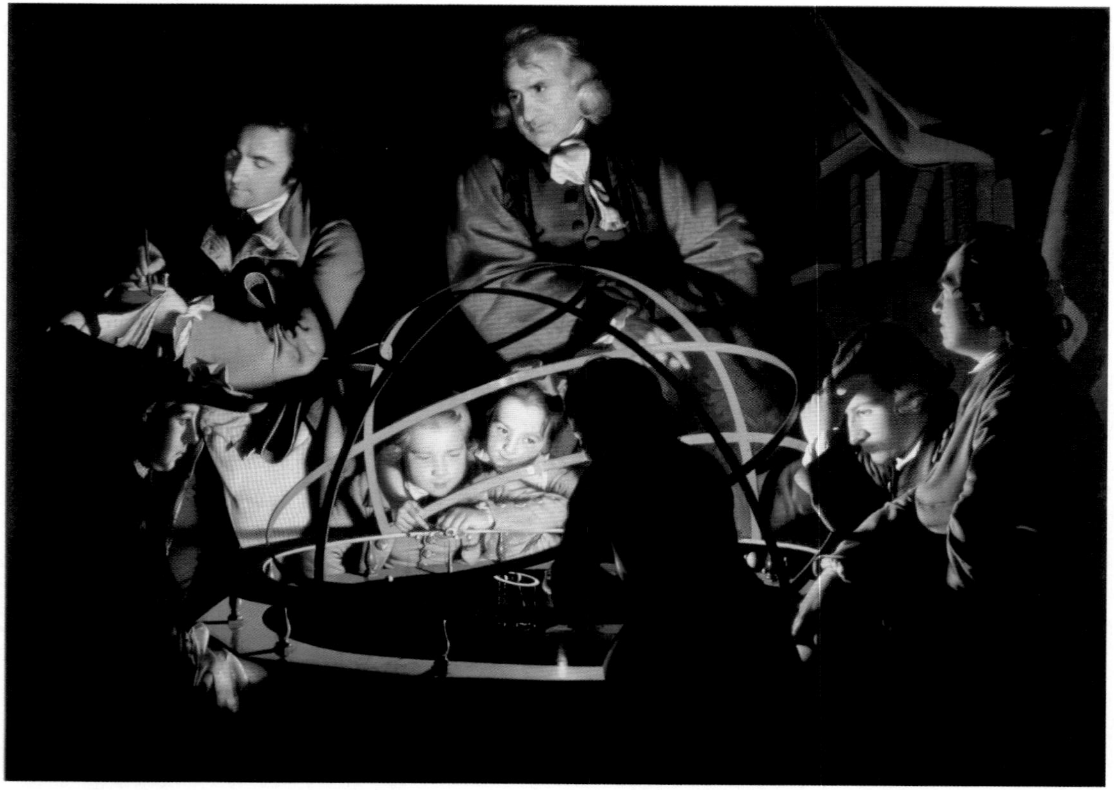

Color Plate 24 Science Popularized. Joseph Wright, *A Philosopher Giving That Lecture on the Orrery, in Which a Lamp Is Put in Place of the Sun*, 1766. The experimental philosophy and new science pioneered during the 17th century provided both pleasure and instruction in the 18th, as teachers and textbooks strove to distill and redistribute recondite discoveries as common knowledge. The orrery, a working model of the solar system, figured prominently in this new educational endeavor; it could supply, wrote Richard Steele, "the pleasures of science to any one." The spheres within the circle, coordinated by clockwork, enacted the orbits of the planets and their moons. The sun's stand-in was often a brass ball, but more rarely (as here) a lit oil lamp at the center of the machine. In Wright's painting, the flame sheds light on the lecturer and his listeners, each of them different, all of them enthralled. *(Derby Museums and Art Gallery.)*

Color Plate 25 Science Interrogated. Joseph Wright, *An Experiment on a Bird in the Air Pump*, 1768. The experiment's purpose is to demonstrate the effects of a vacuum on a breathing creature; its outcome, unless the experimenter restores air to the glass chamber, will be the death of the bird. Such experiments, though widely performed, were deemed by one lecturer "too shocking to every spectator who has the least degree of humanity." This time, Wright depicts a mixture of reactions. The lecturer, gesturing like a conjurer, stares out at the viewer as though in a kind of trance, oblivious both to the bird and to his audience, whose faces and forms variously evince absorption, meditation, distraction, and distress. *(Copyright © National Gallery, London/Art Resource, New York.)*

Color Plate 26 **Theatricality Encompasses All.** William Hogarth, *The Beggar's Opera, Act 3, Scene 11*, 1792. Audience and actors encounter each other on stage. Hogarth here replicates icons of art history much as *The Beggar's Opera*, a theatrical sensation of 1728, echoed popular ballads. Macheath, the criminal-hero of the play, is shown poised in the center between Lucy (left) and Polly (right)—a grouping that evokes the hero Hercules at his mythic moment of choosing between Virtue and Vice. Meanwhile, Polly and her father, Mr. Peachum (in black at right), strike poses bizarrely reminiscent of Christ and Mary Magdalen. Another kind of pairing is in play too. Lavinia Fenton, the actress playing Polly, gestures not so much toward her stage father as to the audience member standing starstruck just beyond him: the Duke of Bolton, so taken with her in the role that he became her lover and eventually her husband. In this, the fifth version he painted of the same scene, Hogarth has expanded the scope of the stage set so that the prison walls appear to enclose the spectators too within the *Opera*'s bright, bleak world, where everything and everyone have become commodities—objects of desire and items of exchange engulfed in intricate, energetic, precarious transactions. *(The Bridgeman Art Library International.)*

Color Plate 27 **Satire Suspended.** William Hogarth, *Hogarth's Servants*, mid-1750s. In this late painting, Hogarth's lifelong brilliancies of satire cede place to an approach both documentary and tender, as he traces, with painstaking attention and evident affection, the faces of six people deeply familiar to him. *(Copyright © Tate Gallery, London/Art Resource, New York.)*

Color Plate 28 Doubled Vision. Thomas Gainsborough, *Cottage Door with Children Playing*, c. 1788. As the critic John Barrell has pointed out, Gainsborough's painting mingles two different perceptions of the rural poor. The gracious women and boisterous children basking in the day's last light conjure up the sort of sentimental idealization of pastoral joys that also found expression in such poems as Oliver Goldsmith's *The Deserted Village*. George Crabbe's contrapuntal insistence on the misery of the laborer's lot in such works as *The Village* and *The Parish Register* is figured here in the form of the returning husband at bottom left, bent with his burden of firewood and nearly buried by the shadows. *(Cincinnati Art Museum, Given in honor of Mr. and Mrs. Charles F. Williams by their children. Accession #: 1948.173.)*

commercial aggressions, their social ambitions. Their preoccupation with politeness has helped to foster a recurrent misimpression of the period: that, setting aside the occasional rake or wench, it was all manners and morals, dignity and decorum, fuss and formality, reason and enlightenment. Not so. Even among the merchant classes, politeness afforded only provisional concealment for roiling energies; amid the impoverished and the gentry, it held less purchase still. In no succeeding epoch until our own was language so openly and energetically obscene, drunkenness so rampant, sexual conduct so various and unapologetic. Even among the "officially" polite, the very failure of containment could produce a special thrill. In one of the century's most often-used phrases, a speaker announces that "I cannot forbear"—that is, cannot restrain myself—from saying or doing what the verb itself suggests were better left unsaid or undone. The formula declares helpless and pleasurable surrender to an unmastered impulse, and the condition was apparently endemic. James Boswell records the memorable self-summary of an elderly lawyer: "I have tried . . . in my time to be a philosopher, but—I don't know how—cheerfulness was always breaking in." Such "breakings-in" (and breakings-out) of feeling were common, even cherished. The scholar Donald Greene has argued well that the eighteenth century was less an "age of reason" (as has often been said) than an age of exuberance. Certainly much of what the middle classes read and wrote is a literature of outburst: of hilarity, of lament, of rage, of exaltation. The copious diaries that the century brought forth deal in all such exclamations; they are the prose of people who have chosen to write rather than repress the thoughts and actions that strict politeness might proscribe. Even the *Spectator*, that manual of polished taste, presents itself as the daily outpouring of a writer who, after maintaining an eccentric lifelong silence, has found that he can no longer keep his "discoveries"—moral, social, experiential—to himself.

Post-Restoration prosperity and politeness supplied women with many new venues for self-display and sociability . . .

Such self-publicizing was more complex for women than for men. When women represented their own lives—in manuscript (letters, journals) and increasingly in print—they sometimes chafed at the paradoxical mix of tantalizing possibilities and painful limitations that their privilege produced. Post-Restoration prosperity and politeness supplied women with many new venues for self-display and sociability, in playhouses and pleasure gardens, ballrooms, spas, and shops. Society exalted and paraded women as superior consumers: wearing the furs, fragrances, and fabrics of distant climes, they furnished evidence of empire, proud proof of their fathers' and husbands' economic attainments. They consumed print, too; near the start of the eighteenth century, male editors invented the women's periodical and found the new genre immensely profitable. Increasingly, women not only purchased print but produced it, deploying their words and wit as a kind of cultural capital, which when properly expended might reap both cash and fame. During the eighteenth century, for the first time, books by women—of poems, of precepts, and above all of fiction-became not exotic but comparatively commonplace.

Still, books by women remained controversial, as did all manifestations of female autonomy and innovation. The very excitement aroused by women's new conspicuousness in the culture provoked counter-efforts at containment. Preachers and moralists argued endlessly that female virtue resided in domesticity. Marriage itself offered an age-old instrument of social control, newly retooled to meet the needs of ambitious merchants, for whom daughters were the very currency of social mobility. If parents could arrange the right marriage, the whole family's status promptly rose. The dowry that the bride brought with her was an investment in future possibilities: in the rank and connections that the union secured, in the inheritance that would descend to its heirs, in the annual income ("jointure") that the wife herself would receive following the death of the husband. Financially, a widow (or for that matter, a well-born woman who never married) was often far more independent than a wife, whose wedding led to a kind of sanctioned erasure. She possessed little or no control over marital property (including the wealth she had brought to the union); "in marriage," wrote the codifier of English law William Blackstone, "husband and wife are one person, and that person is the husband." The sums that the husband undertook to hand over to his wife were dubbed "pin money" (a suggestive trivialization): funds for managing the household, that sphere wherein, as the moral literature insisted, a woman might best deploy her innate talents and find her sanctioned satisfactions. These consisted first and foremost in producing children and in shaping their manners and morals. In a time of improvisatory birth control, precarious obstetrics, and high infant mortality, the bearing of children was a relentless, dangerous, and emotionally exhausting process. The upbringing of children provided more pleasure and possessed a new cachet: the conduct literature endorsed busy, attentive child-rearing as the highest calling possible for women whose prosperity freed them from the need to work for wages. (Guidebooks for parents and pleasure books for children both had their origins in the eighteenth century.) Apart from the duties of motherhood and household management—the supervision of servants, meals, shopping, and social occasions—the woman of means was encouraged to pursue those pleasures for which her often deliberately constricted education had prepared her: music, embroidery, letter writing, and talk at the tea table—the domestic counterpart of the clubs and coffeehouses, where women were not permitted to appear.

In the late seventeenth century, the possibilities for women had seemed at moments more various and more audacious. In the plays of Aphra Behn, female characters pursued their pleasures with an almost piratical energy and ingenuity; in *A Serious Proposal to the Ladies* (1694), the feminist Mary Astell imagined academies where women could withdraw to pursue the pleasures of learning and escape the drudgeries of marriage. In the eighteenth century, though, despite women's increasing authorial presence, these early audacities tended to go underground. Protests by women against their secondary status are most overt in manuscript—in the acerbic poems and letters that Mary Wortley Montagu circulated among her friends, in the journal entries wherein the brewer's wife Hester Thrale vented her frustrations. In print, women's desire for autonomy became a tension in the text, rather than its explicit point or outcome. Novelists explored women's psyches with subtlety; their plots, however, nearly always culminated in marriage, and more rarely in catastrophe, as though those were the only alternatives. Even the Bluestocking Circle, an eminent late-century group of intellectual women, preached tenets of essential sexual difference and subordination; they argued (for example) in favor of improving girls' educations, but as a way of preparing them for better and happier

In print, women's desire for autonomy became a tension in the text, rather than its explicit point or outcome.

work within the home rather than for adventures abroad. During the eighteenth century, the middle classes did much to spell out the gendered divison of labor—father as the family's champion in the marketplace, mother as cheerfully efficient angel in the house—that remained a cultural commonplace, among families who could afford it, for the next two hundred years.

Among the poor, such divisions were not tenable; most manual labor paid so little that everyone in the family had to work if all were to survive. Wives not only managed their frugal households, they also worked for wages, in fields, in shops, or in cottage manufacture of fabrics, gloves, basketry. Children often began wage work at age four or five, treading laundry, scaring crows, sweeping chimneys; boys began the more promising role of apprenticeships around the age of ten. For many of the poor, domestic service offered employment comparatively secure and endlessly demanding. Darker prospects included prostitution and crime: shoplifting was punishable by death. In the case of the helplessly indigent, local government was responsible for providing relief, but the Poor Law provided large loop-holes by which the parish could drive out any unwanted supplicant—an unwed mother, for example—who could not meet the intricate and restrictive criteria for legal residence. The poor had no vote, no voice in government; as the century progressed, their predicament attracted increasing attention and advocacy. Philanthropists instituted charity schools designed, in the words of their proponent Hannah More, "to train up the lower classes in habits of industry and piety." Two convictions informed even the most ambitious philanthropy: that poverty was part of a divine plan and that it was the fault of the indolent poor themselves; they thus found themselves caught between the rock of providence and the hard place of reproach. Yet charity schools did increase literacy, and with it perhaps the sense of possibilities. Other late-century developments, too, were mixed. Improvements in sanitation, medicine, and hygiene contributed to a surge in population, which in turn produced among the rural poor a labor surplus: too many people, too little work. At the same time, wealthy landholders increased the practice of "enclosure," acquiring and sequestering acreage formerly used by the poor for common pasturage and family farming. As a result, many rural families left the land on which they had worked for centuries and traveled to alien terrain: the textile mills that capitalists had newly built and the industrial cities developing rapidly around them.

As the poor became poorer, the very rich—landowning lords and gentry—became very much richer, both by the means they now shared with the middle class (capital investment in banks and stocks) and through their own long-held resources. Land increased in value, partly because there were now so many merchant families passionately eager to buy into the landscape and the life of their aristocratic betters, among whom the spectacle of emulation provoked amusement and revulsion. The landed gentry preserved their distance by many means: social practices (they often flaunted their adulteries, for example, as contrast to middle-class proprieties), artistic allegiance (with the advent of the bourgeois drama, aristocratic audiences defected from the theater to the opera house, where elaborate productions and myth-based plots sustained the aristocratic values of the heroic drama), and the sheer ostentation of their leisure and magnitude of their consumption. But the pivotal difference remained political: by the

As the poor became poorer, the very rich—landowning lords and gentry—became very much richer . . .

award of offices, by the control of elections, landowners maintained their stranglehold on local and national power, despite all the waxing wealth of trade.

At the same time, their very absorption in pleasure and power demanded a continual traffic with their inferiors. Merchants and shopkeepers catered to them; professionals managed their transactions; household servants contrived their comforts; aspiring artists sought to cultivate their taste and profit by their patronage. Transactions among the aristocracy and the middle classes took other forms as well. A lord low on money often found it lucrative to marry the daughter of a thriving merchant. And middle-class modes of life could exert a subtler magnetism, too—particularly for George III, who prized mercantile decorum over aristocratic swagger. In the portrait of his queen and her two eldest sons in Color Plate 21, the artist Johann Zoffany (himself an expensive German import) celebrates not their royal state but their domestic felicity: the heroic trappings (helmet, spear, turban) so conspicuous in Lely's portrait of the scandalous Lady Castlemaine (see Color Plate 20) are here reduced to the props of child's play in the domestic theater of family relations.

King George had commissioned Johann Zoffany in pursuit of precisely this effect. By his eager emulation of the middling orders, George III broke with monarchic traditions, but he inaugurated a new one that would be sustained and expanded in various ways by Queen Victoria in the nineteenth century and her successors in the twentieth. During George's reign, too, the middle classes began to pursue more practical convergence with the aristocracy: a wider distribution of voting rights, a firmer political power base. For the first time, the phrase "middle classes" itself came into use, as a way of registering this cohort's recognition of its own coherence and interests, its unique, often combative relations with the classes above and below; the plural ("classes") registered the abiding diversity—of income, of lifestyle—within the cohesion. In the years since the Restoration, the middle classes had moved themselves energetically in the theater of social and economic relations from a place in the audience toward center stage, exerting enormous power over the working lives of the poor, posing challenges to the elite. Increasingly, their money, manners, appetites, and tastes came to be perceived as the essence of national life, as the part that might stand for the whole. "Trade," Henry Fielding remarked in 1751, "has indeed given a new face to the nation."

It gave the nation new momentum, too, literal as well as figurative. The engineering marvels of the eighteenth century—the harnessing of steam power, the innovations in factory design, the acceleration of production—were instruments of capital. So were improvements in the rate of transport. Over the course of the century, the government collaborated with private investors to construct a proliferating network of smooth turnpikes and inland waterways: canal boats delivered coal and other cargo with new celerity; stagecoaches sped between cities on precise schedules with crowded timetables. Timekeeping itself became a source of national wealth and pride. During the 1660s, British clockmakers established themselves as the best in Europe. A century later, the clockmaker John Harrison invented the "marine chronometer," a large watch so sturdy and so precise that it could keep time to the minute throughout a voyage around the world, amid all

The engineering marvels of the eighteenth century—the harnessing of steam power, the innovations in factory design, the acceleration of production—were instruments of capital.

vicissitudes of wind and weather. Harrison's invention made it possible to calculate a ship's longitude accurately, thus solving a problem that had bedeviled navigation for centuries (and sometimes sunk whole fleets). The innovation further paved the way for trade and empire-building, and did much to establish Greenwich, a town just east of London, as the reference point for world timekeeping. Trade was giving a new face—a new distribution of power and priority—not only to the nation but also to the globe, placing Britain (so Britons liked to think) at its center.

Faith and Knowledge, Thought and Feeling

Clockwork functioned another way too: as a new, theologically unsettling metaphor for the relations between God and his creation. In his *Principia Mathematica* (1687), Isaac Newton set forth the mathematical principles—the laws of motion, the workings of gravity—by which, it turned out, the universe could be seen to operate more consistently and efficiently than even the finest clockwork. What need had this flawless mechanism for any further adjustments by its divine clockmaker? Some of Newton's admirers—though never the pious scientist himself—found in his discoveries the cue for a nearly omnivorous skepticism. The boldest deists and "freethinkers" dismissed Christianity as irrational fiction, to be supplanted by the stripped-down doctrine of "natural religion." In the intricate design of nature they found the proof of a creator whose existence and infinite wisdom, they argued, are all we know on earth and all we need to know. The fashion for such thought—at least in its purest form—proved fleeting. To most minds, the "argument from design" simply furnished further proof of God's benevolence. Amid such comfortable conviction, the blasphemies of a virtuoso skeptic like David Hume appeared an aberration, even an entertainment, rather than a trend. "There is a great cry about infidelity," Samuel Johnson remarked in 1775, "but there are, in reality, very few infidels." From deep belief and ingrained habit, Christianity retained its hold over the entire culture; though a few pietists voiced alarm, science tended to enhance faith, not destroy it.

Still, the relation of religion to public life had changed. In the mid-seventeenth century, politics was inevitably suffused with spirituality. Charles I had gone to the scaffold as an Anglican martyr; he had ruled according to the dictum "No bishop, no king." For many English men and women, the war of Parliament against the king was a holy war: Puritans had typed Charles I as that "man of blood"; Cromwell's army had gone to battle singing David's psalms. By the eighteenth century, ardors had cooled: no one went to war for creed alone. But that is not to say that these were lives bereft of the spiritual; deep religious feeling remained, even as violence of expression abated. The Restoration had reinstated Anglicanism as the national faith; its adherents were admitted to the full privileges of education and office. Over the ensuing century, the Church of England pursued a strategic but controversial mix of old exclusions and new accommodations. For dissenters (offspring of the Puritans), new laws proffered certain permissions (to teach, to congregate for public worship) in exchange for certain oaths. Catholics, by contrast, were kept beyond the pale; they received no such concessions until late in the eighteenth century, when even a limited act provoked angry Protestant riots. Early in the century, the Anglican

By the eighteenth century, ardors had cooled: no one went to war for creed alone.

faithful were divided between the "high flyers," who perennially claimed that the church was in danger of dilution, and the Latitudinarians, who argued that all kinds of dissent might finally be accommodated within the structure of the church. Latitudinarians prevailed, but as the Church of England broadened, it began to lose the force of its exclusiveness; attendance at services shrank markedly as the century advanced, but alternative forms of communal worship flourished. In the eighteenth century, evangelical religions came to occupy the crucial space of fervent spirituality that the church of Donne and Herbert had once claimed as its own. By midcentury, in the new movement called Methodism, John Wesley expressed a vehement response against the skeptical rationalism of the freethinkers and the monied complacency of the established church. Wesley preached the truth of scriptural revelation. He urged his followers to purge their sins methodically—by a constant self-monitoring, partly modeled on earlier Puritan practices—and enthusiastically, by attending revival meetings, hearing electrifying sermons. Wesley delivered some 40,000 sermons over the course of a phenomenally energetic life, and his no less relentless brother Charles composed some 6,000 hymns to quicken evangelical spirits. Methodism found its most ardent following among the poor, who discovered in the doctrine a sympathy for their condition and a recognition of their worth, epitomized in one of Charles Wesley's verses: "Our Savior by the rich unknown / Is worshipped by the poor alone." Their worship was loud and fervent; intensity of feeling attested authenticity of faith.

The middle class and gentry located their own fervor in the more polished idioms of sentiment and sensibility. The terms named a code of conduct and of feeling current in the mid-eighteenth century, when men and women increasingly came to pride themselves on an emotional responsiveness highly cultivated and conspicuously displayed: tears of pity at the spectacle of suffering, admiration for the achievements of art or the magnificence of nature. For many in the middle class, the cult of sentiment held out the appealing prospect of a democratization of manners; the elaborate protocols of the aristocracy might remain elusive, but pure *feeling* was surely more accessible, to anyone with the leisure and the training. For many women, the cult afforded the added attraction of honoring that very susceptibility to feeling and that renunciation of reason that had long and pejoratively been gendered female. The sufferings of the poor, of children, of animals, became a testing ground for empathy; majestic mountains became favorite proving grounds for heightened response. The fashion for benevolence helped focus attention on the plight of the poor and the oppressed, prompting new charities and social movements. For many of the conventionally religious, sentimentality became an adjunct article of faith. They found their scriptures in treatises that posited proper feeling as a chief measure of human worth—Adam Smith's *Theory of Moral Sentiments* (1759); in sentimental dramas that modeled the cultivation (and the performance) of elaborate emotion; in novels that paid minute attention to the protagonist's every emotional nuance—Samuel Richardson's *Pamela* (1740–1741) and *Clarissa* (1747–1749), Laurence Sterne's *Life and Opinions of Tristram Shandy* (1759–1767) and *A Sentimental Journey* (1768), Henry Mackenzie's *The Man of Feeling* (1771); in travel books that transported readers geographically and emotionally by charged descriptions of mighty vistas. For both deists and pietists earlier in the century, nature had testified

The fashion for benevolence helped focus attention on the plight of the poor and the oppressed . . .

the existence of a God; for connoisseurs of the sublime near century's end, nature itself was beginning to serve as surrogate for the divine.

In the articulation of eighteenth-century faith and science, thought and feeling, the most conspicuous and continuous voice was that of the first person. The "I" was omnipresent, observing world and self alike: in the experiment-reports of the scientists and the thought-experiments of the philosophers; in the Methodists' self-monitoring, the sentimentalist's self-approbation, the sublimity-seekers' recorded raptures; in the copious autobiographical writings—diaries, letters, memoirs—of characters in novels and people in the real world. Always and everywhere, it seems, someone was setting down the nuances of his or her experience. The self-reckoning promulgated in the past by dissenters was now a broad cultural preoccupation. Its dominion may help to explain why the literature of this era famed for the dominance and delight of its conversation returns us, again and again, to a sense of fundamental solitude.

Writers, Readers, Conversations

The century and a half from the English Civil Wars to the brink of the French Revolution brought startling change to the structures of politics, social relations, scientific knowledge, and the economy, and no change was more intimate to all these revolutions than the transformations in the relations between writers and readers. From our present perspective, perhaps no scene seems more familiar, even eternal, than that of reader with book in hand. We imagine Virgil's readers and Dante's, Austen's and Wilde's, Pound's and Pynchon's similarly situated, alone with a book, communing silently with an oracular author. But these configurations have changed radically from age to age—sometimes driven by shifts in technology, at other times by social changes. In the eighteenth century, the sea change in relations between writers and readers derived from new social transactions and a new marketplace of letters. And this change did much to shape the modern reckoning of the mix of the solitary and the social, the commercial and the therapeutic within the act of reading. In its refiguring of the social contract between writers and readers, the eighteenth century was nearly as eruptive as our own time with its marketplace of e-mail and Internet, where everyone can potentially operate as both consumer and purveyor—and no one knows for sure the shape of literary things to come.

In 1661, the Earl of Argyle wrote to his son with advice on books, their acquisition, and their proper use:

> Think no cost too much in purchasing rare books; next to that of acquiring good friends I look upon this purchase; but buy them not to lay by or to grace your library, with the name of such a manuscript, or by such a singular piece, but read, revolve him, and lay him up in your memory where he will be far the better ornament. Read seriously whatever is before you, and reduce and digest it to practice and observation, otherwise it will be Sisyphus's labor to be always revolving sheets and books at every new occurence which will require the oracle of your reading. Trust not to your memory, but put all remarkable, notable things you shall meet with in your books *sub salva custodia* [under the sound care] of pen and ink, but so alter the property by your own scholia and annotations on it, that your memory may speedily recur to the place it was committed to.

The earl's account displays all the elements of the traditional reading program of Renaissance humanism: book or manuscript as surrogate friend, as "ornament" of the gentleman's mind and library, as "oracle" of enduring truths, as "property" to be possessed, marked, transcribed, and committed to memory. In the decades that followed, all these constructions remained in play, yet every one of the earl's crucial terms broadened in application to include print genres and transactions that Argyle would not have imagined: the periodical review, the monthly miscellany; epistolary fiction; the three-volume novel; as well as the coffeehouses and penny lending libraries that broadly circulated these new forms of print. With these new genres and modes of distribution, the text's status as friend, ornament, oracle, and property changed markedly.

Nothing had demonstrated (some even thought created) the material force and oracular authority of print so much as the English Civil Wars. Sermons and prophecies bearing the names of "oracles" and "revelations" forecast the demise of the Beast, the triumph of Parliament, indeed the imminence of the thousand-year rule of Christ on earth. Nor had the restoration of the Stuart monarchy wholly denatured print as prophecy—royalists and radicals continued to publish apocalyptic claims. And yet, over the ensuing decades the repeated threat of contest and rebellion began to exhaust both the authority of print as prophecy and the appetite of readers for a textual diet of frenzy and apocalypse—not that party warfare in print forms declined, but rather that partisanship yoked political contest to forms of confrontation that cooled apocalyptic tempers and supplanted military combat with paper controversy. The uneven course of government censorship, the issuing and lapsing of the licensing laws that governed press freedom, meant that paper wars with their full armory of ephemera—pamphlets, broadsides, pasquinades—raged at moments of crisis and parliamentary inattention when printers might cash in on the market for opposition and confrontation.

Satire, that most venerable mode of attack and advocacy, flourished in England as it had in Augustan Rome.

But not all the action of print contest was situated in the gutter of journalism. Satire, that most venerable mode of attack and advocacy, flourished in England as it had in Augustan Rome. Horace and Juvenal were indeed the models for Dryden, Pope, and Swift, who not only translated the forms of Roman satire into native idioms but were themselves possessed by all the Roman delight in outrage and invective, in civic engagement and political contest. But the genius of satire is never solely political. Satirists always score their most important points by wit, by cool savagery, by the thrust and parry of language, by the most brilliant and damaging metaphors and rhymes. Their peers, their rivals, even their enemies ruefully conceded that Dryden, Pope, and Swift had brought the verse couplet and the prose sentence to an unprecedented suppleness and precision. Satire in the years of civil war and Stuart agitations had begun in politics; pamphlet wars, swelled by periodicals, continued to rage through the Georgian age. But the classic verse satire had moved to a more exalted ground where the aesthetic often overwhelmed the political, and satire itself became an object of admiration, even of theorizing, and of the most vivid and polite conversation.

"Conversation" had once meant the entire conduct of life itself; now, "conversation" had narrowed to signify social exchange; yet social exchange in its turn had expanded to govern the conduct of life itself. Many of the most striking literary developments in the period—its poetic modes and tastes, the popularity and prominence of letter and journal writing, the advent of the newspaper and the novel—can perhaps best be understood as new ways devised by writers for performing conversation on the page—conversation with readers, with other writers, and within the texts themselves. The cultural critic Mikhail Bakhtin has pinpointed as one key feature of the novel its "heteroglossia": its capacity to speak, almost concurrently, many different languages, in the various voices and viewpoints of its characters and narrators; the range of its concerns (across social ranks and geographical spaces); even the variabilities of its style (each with its own cultural connotations) from page to page, paragraph to paragraph. But in this respect as in so many, the novel, usually reckoned the greatest literary invention of the period, is the product of a time when virtually all modes of writing were involved with diversity and dialogue.

One of the most popular ways of buying and reading poetry, for example, was in the form of "miscellanies"—anthologies of work by many hands ancient and modern in many modes, brought together in intriguing juxtapositions. Such juxtapositions could also take place within a single poem. For poets, a crucial procedure was the "imitation"—a poem in English that closely echoes the tone, structure, and sequence of a classical model while applying the predecessor's form and thought to contemporary topics. Where the Roman poet Juvenal, for example, begins his tenth Satire by declaring that wise men are hard to find even if you search every country from Spain to India (roughly the extent of the known Roman world), Samuel Johnson begins his imitation of Juvenal's poem (*The Vanity of Human Wishes*) this way:

> Let Observation, with extensive view,
> Survey mankind, from China to Peru . . .

The known world, Johnson tacitly reminds his knowing reader, is much larger than it was when Juvenal wrote (and hence the rarity of discerning mortals will be all the more striking). The opening couplet prepares us for the poem's close, where it will turn out that moral possibilities are larger too: there, Johnson will supplant Juvenal's characteristically Roman resignation to "Fortune" with an expressly Christian reliance on the cardinal virtues (faith, hope, charity) as a means of protection from the delusions of desire. The writer of a poetic imitation always conducts at least a double dialogue: between poet and predecessor, and between the present writer and the ideal reader who knows enough of the "original" to savor the poetic exchange, the cultural cross-talk, in all its echoes, divergences, and diversions.

Johnson here practices a more general kind of imitation as well, by casting his poem in heroic couplets: iambic pentameter lines paired in a sequence of successive rhymes. The rhymed pairs are often "closed," so that the moment of the rhyme coincides with and clinches the completion of a sentence and a thought. The verse form was called "heroic" because of its frequent use in the heroic drama and other high-aspiring poetry of the Restoration; the rhymed, closed pentameter was also thought to imitate, as closely as English allowed, the grandeur and the sonority of the lines in which ancient poets composed their epics. Throughout the century following the Restoration, the heroic couplet prevailed as the most commonly used poetic structure, adaptable to all genres and occasions, deployed by every sort of poet from hacks to John Dryden and Alexander Pope, the supreme masters of the mode. It was in this form that Dryden translated Virgil's *Aeneid* (1697) and Pope translated Homer's *Iliad* (1715–1720) and *Odyssey* (1725–1726),

. . . the mesh of mighty ancient models with trivial modern subjects produced a new mode of satire . . .

it was in this form that they wrote original poems of high seriousness and savage satire, and it was in this form that they aspired (like many of their contemporaries) to write new epics of their own. Neither ever did; both complained intermittently that they lived in an unheroic age. But the mesh of mighty ancient models with trivial modern subjects produced a new mode of satire, the mock-heroic, and disclosed astonishing suppleness in the heroic couplet itself.

In the hands of Dryden, Pope, and many others, the mock mode—high style, low subject matter—performed brilliant accommodations and solved large problems. It allowed poets to turn what they perceived as the crassness of modern culture to satiric advantage. If the triviality of modern life prevented them from recapturing epic grandeur whole, they could at least strive to match the epic's inclusiveness, its capacity to encompass all the things and actions of the world: the accessories of a young woman's dressing table (Pope's *Rape of the Lock*), the clutter in a gutter after rain (Swift's *Description of a City Shower*), the glut of print itself and the folly of those who produce so much bad writing (Pope's *Dunciad*). After Pope's death, though, this vein of mockery seemed exhausted. The heroic couplet persisted in poetry to the end of the century, but other verse forms became prominent too, partly in the service of an even wider inclusiveness, of paying new kinds of attention to modes of life and literature that lay outside the heroic and the mock: the predicament of the poor, the pleasures of domesticity, the discoveries of science, the tones and textures of medieval English balladry, the modalities of melancholy, the improvisatory motions of human thought and feeling. Blank verse—iambic pentameter without rhyme—offered one manifestation of the impulse to open-endedness. James Thomson's *The Seasons* (1730) and William Cowper's *The Task* (1785), huge works in blank verse, are epic in their own kind: they mingle genres and move from topic to topic with the improvisatory energy of a barely stoppable train of thought. They perform the world's miscellany, the mind's conversation with itself and others, in a new poetic language—one that Wordsworth had absorbed by century's end, when he cast his *Prelude* in a capacious blank verse and praised in the preface to *Lyrical Ballads* that kind of poetry which deploys "the real language" of "a man speaking to men."

In the new prose forms of the eighteenth century—both nonfiction and fiction—the dominion of miscellany, the centrality of conversation, is if anything more palpable than in poetry. The first daily newspaper and the first magazines both appeared early in the century, providing a regularly recurrent compendium of disparate items intended to appeal to a variety of tastes and interests. These periodicals formed part of a larger and highly visible print mix: coffeehouses attracted a burgeoning clientele of urbanites by laying out copies of the current gazettes, mercuries, newsletters, playbooks, and satiric verses. Customers took pleasure in the literary montage, the ever-shifting anthology on the tabletops (of which the pictorial medley on page 1980 conveys a vivid visual idea). Coffeehouse customers

Coffeehouse customers gathered to consume new drink and new print in a commerce of pleasure, intellect, and gossip.

gathered to consume new drink and new print in a commerce of pleasure, intellect, and gossip. Some read silently, others aloud to listeners who eagerly seized on texts and topics. Habits of social reading that would have been familiar to Chaucer and his audience (even to Virgil performing his epic at the court of Augustus Caesar) contributed to sociable debate on the persons and personalities of public life, foreign potentates, military campaigns, theatrical rivalries, monsters, and prodigies. In the eighteenth century, the papers and the consequent conversations broadened to encompass questions of personal conduct, relations between the sexes, manner and fashion. Writers of papers still claimed oracular authority: "Isaac Bickerstaff" of the *Tatler* dubbed himself the Censor of Great Britain, Mr. Spectator claimed to watch everyone who read his paper, and the *Athenian Gazette* dispensed advice as though with the authority of a supremely learned society. But writers made such claims at least partly with tongue in cheek; they knew that their oracular "truths" would trickle down into the commerce of conversation.

The press not only stimulated but also simulated conversation. Newspapers had always depended on "correspondents"—not (as now) professional reporters, but local letter writers who sent in the news of their parish and county in exchange for free copies of the paper. To read a newspaper was to read in part the work of fellow readers. Other periodicals—the scientific monthly as well as the journal of advice and the review of arts—adopted the practice of printing letters as a reliable source of copy and as an act and model of sociability. Printed correspondence ran longer, more ambitiously, and more lucratively. For the first time, the collected letters of the eminent became an attractive commercial genre (Pope was a pioneer), and travel books in the form of copious letters home sold by the thousands.

The printed letter would prove crucial too to the development of the newest form of all, the novel. Aphra Behn had pioneered epistolary fiction in the Restoration, and Samuel Richardson recast the mode on an epic scale in *Pamela* and *Clarissa,* among the most important and talked-about fictions of the eighteenth century. In discussing the fate of his characters, Richardson's readers joined a conversation already in progress; Richardson's characters, in their lively exchange of letters, performed and modeled what their creator called "the converse of the pen."

Yet letters were only one among the many kinds of conversation that novelists contrived to carry on. "The rise of the novel"—the emergence over the course of the eighteenth century of so curious, capacious, and durable a genre—has long excited interest and controversy among scholars, who explain the phenomenon in various ways: by the emergence of a large middle-class readership with the money to obtain, the leisure to read, and the eagerness to absorb long narratives that mirrored their circumstances, their aspirations, and their appetites; by a tension between the aristocratic virtues central to older forms of fiction and the constructs of human merit prized by a proud commercial culture; by the passion for journalistic and experiential fact (in newspapers, criminal autobiographies, scientific experiments, etc.), shading over imperceptibly into new practices of fiction.

All of these explanations are true, and each is revelatory when applied to particular clusters of novels. Still, definition and explanation remain elusive, as they clearly were for the genre's early readers and practitioners. The very word "novel"—identifying the genre by no other marks than newness itself—performs a kind of surrender in the face of a form whose central claim to novelty was its

Mimicry, motion, and metamorphosis are the genre's stock in trade.

barely definable breadth. Mimicry, motion, and metamorphosis are the genre's stock in trade. Novels absorbed all the modes of literature around them: letters, diaries, memoirs, news items, government documents, drawings, verses, even sheet music all crop up within the pages of the early novels, one representational mode supplanting another with often striking speed. Novelists moved with equal alacrity through space: through England (Henry Fielding's *Tom Jones*), Britain more broadly (Tobias Smollett's *Humphry Clinker*), Europe (Smollett's *Roderick Random*), the entire globe as it is ordinarily mapped (Behn's *Oroonoko,* Defoe's *Robinson Crusoe*) or as it could be extraordinarily imagined (Swift's *Gulliver's Travels*). Traversing geographies, the genre crossed cultures too, mostly by means of mimicry, and parroted a range of accents, for purposes either of mockery—the malapropisms of a semiliterate housemaid, the fulminations of a Scots soldier, the outrage of an Irish cuckold—or of pathos: the lamentations of the African slave Oroonoko, the delirium of the violated Clarissa. Many novels, too, made a point of spanning the social spectrum, often compassing destitution and prosperity, labor and luxury within the career of a single ambitious character. Social mobility was perhaps the one plot element that novel readers savored most.

But the novel's supplest means of self-conveyance, its subtlest modes of conversation, were grounded in its attention to the workings of the mind. In his *Essay Concerning Human Understanding* (1690), the philosopher John Locke had explained the mind as a capacious, absorptive instrument engaged in constant motion, linking mixed memories, impressions, and ideas in a ceaseless chain of "associations." In the eighteenth century, novelists took Locke's cue: their works both mimicked the mind's capacity, heterogeneity, and associativeness, and explored them too, tracking over many pages the subtlest modulations in the characters' thoughts and feelings. Richardson famously boasted that his epistolary mode, featuring "familiar letters written as it were to the moment" by characters in their times of crisis, enabled him to track the course of their "hopes and fears" with unprecedented precision—and he trusted that the value of such a process would surely excuse the "bulk" of the huge novels themselves. In the nine volumes of Laurence Sterne's *Life and Opinions of Tristram Shandy*, the title narrator is so committed to following his digressive trains of thought wherever they may lead that the pronouncement of his opinions leaves him preposterously little time to narrate his life. Moving widely over space, freely through society, minutely through time, and deeply into mind, the novelists devised new strategies for achieving that epic inclusiveness that writers sought, in various ways, throughout the century.

The new tactics of miscellany, the new conversations conducted by means of pen and printing press, poetry and prose, refigured the practices of reading that the Earl of Argyle had wished to transmit to his son. In the aristocratic world of Renaissance letters, the book as friend had intimated a sphere of male pedagogy and sociability. The grammar school classroom, the college lecture hall, the estate library, the world of the tutor and his high-born protégé, all these figured reading principally as the privilege and the pleasure of a limited few, mostly males in positions of some leisure, comfort, and power. The links between reading and power were sustained through patterns of production and consumption in which authors received benefits from aristocratic patrons, and manuscripts passed from hand to hand. Donne refused to imagine his verse circulating in any other fashion. After the Restoration, Dryden, Behn, and Pope all pursued the compensations of print, but they nonetheless remained eager to participate in patronage and coterie circulation. Even when printed, their satires purveyed the pleasurable sense of shared knowledge that had constituted the *frisson* of coterie reading. Printers and poets understood that concealing a public name behind initials and dashes provided safety from censors and litigants, at the same time garnering a market share among readers who pleased themselves by decoding "dangerous matter."

By the middle of the eighteenth century, the patronage model of literary production and the coterie mode of distribution had been complicated (some thought ruined) by the commerce of print, for print had become the principal mode of literary distribution. Samuel Johnson, a bookseller's son, thought of literature as print and rarely circulated a manuscript as a gesture of literary sociability. ("None but a blockhead," he famously intoned, "ever wrote except for money.") As a consequence of the dominance of print and its broad distribution, the audiences for texts proliferated into new mixtures. Readers from many strata could afford a penny paper; apprentices and merchants' daughters might read the same novel. Assumptions of commonality that had underwritten the intimate sociability of Renaissance reading had been exploded by civil conflict in the mid-seventeenth century, by the profusion of print and the proliferation of genres that drove and were driven by the appetite of contest and conversation. During the eighteenth century, the print marketplace generated audiences on a scale vaster than ever before, circulating widely across the boundaries of class and gender. Print may have canceled some of the intimacies of the coterie, but it generated new convergences, even new consciousness—a public sphere in which aesthetics, politics, conduct, and taste were all objects of perpetual, often pleasurable debate. To an unprecedented extent, print furnished its readers with the substance for sustained conversation and continual contact.

It also kept them apart. Nothing was more evident to eighteenth-century men and women than the burgeoning of their domestic economy, the vastness of their colonial empire, and the growth in wealth and population which both entailed. The proliferation of consumables was evident in the village market, the Royal Exchange, and the bookstalls of country towns and capitol. The sheer bulk and variety of these consumables were strikingly evident in the length and scope of that capacious new genre, the novel. But even in the midst of abundance and sociability, eighteenth-century consumers were instructed in their paradoxical solitude. Defoe inscribes the condition of the novel as isolation—Robinson Crusoe, a man alone on an island, opines that human life "is, or ought to be, one universal act of solitude." And in novel after novel the very transactions of commerce produce isolation, as ambition and acquisition drive each character into the solitary, often melancholy corner of his or her own self-interest. The novel itself as a reading experience produced comparable sensations. Readers might now empathize with an entire world of fictional characters, but in order to savor such imaginative pleasures, they spent long hours in the privacy of their own quarters, in silent acts of reading.

A sense of solitude underwrote all this century's celebrated gregariousness. This held true even for sociable transactions that might take place between a

A sense of solitude underwrote all this century's celebrated gregariousness.

reader and a text. In the Renaissance, it had long been a practice to annotate texts with comments echoing and endorsing the author's oracular wisdom. Under the pressure of civil war, the dialogue between author and reader often became more heated as the manuscript marginalia expressed anger and outrage at the partisan zeal of the printed text. But one form of textual reverence persisted. Throughout the seventeenth century readers took pleasure in writing marginalia that epitomized the text, making its wisdom portable. They filled blank books with pithy sentences, "commonplaces" drawn from their favorite works and organized in ways that would allow them to recirculate these sayings in their own writing and conversation.

By the eighteenth century, print had managed to appropriate all these modes of study and sociability. Through print, the manuscript collation of wit and wisdom turned into popular commodities—the printed commonplace book, the miscellany, the anthology. Even annotation itself migrated from manuscript markings into print, as Swift and Pope (among others) found ways of exploding scholarly pretension and of rendering the breath of gossip and scandal in the elaborate apparatus of the printed page. By century's end, all of manuscript's august authority and its most cherished genres—letters and memoirs—had been commandeered by print. In the mid-1730s, Pope alarmed and outraged his contemporaries by publishing his letters as if they deserved to partake of eternity with Cicero's. By the early nineteenth century, even that most secretive mode of self-communion, the private journal, had made its way into the marketplace. In 1825, Pepys's *Diary* appeared in two large printed folios, laying bare the elaborate machinery of public life, the secrets and scandals of the Restoration court, and the diarist's own experiences, transgressions, and sequestered musings, which he had written in shorthand code and shown to no one. The communal and commodified medium of print had found yet another way to market signal acts of solitude.

Coda

Mrs. Abington as "Miss Prue" (1771), by the pre-eminent portraitist Sir Joshua Reynolds (see Color Plate 22), shows a solitary figure engaged in intricate conversation with the viewer. Some of the intricacy inheres in the life history of the sitter, whose career many of the painting's first viewers would have known well. The daughter of a cobbler, Frances Abington had worked in childhood as a flower seller and in her teens as an actress, quickly establishing herself as "by far the most eminent performer in comedy of her day" (these words, and others to follow, are the testimony of contemporaries); she would eventually score one of her greatest hits in the role of that latter-day country wife Lady Teazle, in Richard Brinsley Sheridan's *The school for Scandal* (1777). When an unknown, Abington had married her music teacher; as fame increased, she carried on several well-publicized affairs with members of parliament and the aristocracy. By her sexual frankness, she scandalized—and of course fascinated—the multitudes. By her grace and taste, she became "a favorite of the public" and "the high priestess of fashion"; her costumes on stage instantly set new trends among her audience. Reynolds, who greatly

Joshua Reynolds, *Mrs. Abington as "Miss Prue,"* 1771. Restoration theatricality transposed and transformed.

admired her, here captures the complexity of her character and reputation. Her dress is supremely stylish, her pose deliberately provocative. For a woman to lean casually over the back of a chair this way violated all propriety; in earlier portraits, only men had struck such a pose. The thumb at her lips suggests vulgarity verging on the lascivious. The portrait's title purports to explain such seeming aberrations: the actress here appears in her celebrated role as Miss Prue, the "silly, awkward country girl" in William Congreve's Restoration comedy *Love for Love* (1695), who comes to London with the intention, frankly lustful and loudly declared, of getting herself a husband. In Reynolds's painting, of course, Mrs. Abington plays a role more layered: a hybrid of Miss Prue, of the matchlessly fashionable figure into which the actress had transformed herself, and of the whole range of experiences, the prodigious lifelong motion from poverty to polish, which formed part of her self-creation and her fame. Impersonating Miss Prue some seventy-five years after the comedy's first production, Mrs. Abington here infuses Restoration wantonness with Georgian elegance, transgression with high taste, theatricality with self-assertive authenticity. Like the century she inhabits, she is miscellany incarnate.

Stuart Sherman
and Steven N. Zwicker

For additional resources on the Restoration and the eighteenth century, including a timeline of the period, go to *The Longman Anthology of British Literature* Web site at www.myliteraturekit.com.

Samuel Pepys

1633–1703

John Hayls, *Samuel Pepys*, 1666.

Twice in his life, Samuel Pepys embarked on long projects that allowed him to fuse the methods of the bureaucrat with an inventiveness that amounted to genius. The longer project, which occupied him from his mid-twenties through his mid-fifties, was a fundamental restructuring of the Royal Navy. The shorter project began just a few months earlier. Starting on 1 January 1660, and continuing for the next nine years, Pepys devised the diary form as we know it today: a detailed, private, day-by-day account of daily doings.

Halfway through the diary, Pepys delights to describe himself as "a very rising man," and he wrote the diary in part to track his ascent. The rise began slowly. Born in London to a tailor and a butcher's sister, Pepys studied at Puritan schools; he then attended Magdalene College, Cambridge, as a scholarship student. His B.A. left him well educated but short on cash. A year later he married the fifteen-year-old Elizabeth St. Michel, a French Protestant whose poverty surpassed his own. By his mid-twenties (when the diary commences), neither his accomplishments nor his prospects were particularly striking: he was working as factotum for two powerful men, one of them his high-born cousin Edward Mountagu, First Earl of Sandwich, an important naval officer once devoted to Cromwell but recently turned Royalist.

The diary begins at a calendrical turning point (the first day of a new week, a new year, and a new decade) and on a kind of double bet: that the coming time would bring changes worth writing up, both in the life of the diarist and in the history of the state. The two surmises quickly proved true. As a schoolboy taught by Puritans, Pepys had attended and applauded the execution of Charles I, but the Restoration of Charles II was the making of him, and he recalibrated his loyalties readily enough. His cousin secured for him the Clerkship of the Acts in the Navy Office, a secretarial post that Pepys transformed into something more. By mastering the numberless details of shipbuilding and supplying—from the quality of timber to the composition of tar and hemp—he contrived to control costs and produce results to an extent unmatched by any predecessor.

He managed all these matters so carefully that he soon became the ruler of the Royal Navy, in effect if not in name. When the Test Act of 1673 forced Charles's Catholic brother James to resign as Lord High Admiral, Pepys took his place (in the newly created post of Admiralty Secretary) and ran the operation. He immediately launched a systematic reform of the institution, which he had come to see as dangerously slipshod. By devising (in the words of one biographer) "a rule for all things, great or small" and by enforcing the new disciplines through a method of tireless surveillance and correspondence with ports extending from the Thames to Tangier, Pepys made the navy immeasurably more efficient than ever before. His efforts were interrupted by the political tribulations of his patron James: Pepys spent two brief terms in prison on trumped-up charges of Catholic sympathies, and in 1688 the Glorious Revolution drove him from office into a prosperous retirement. At the height of his power, though, as his biographer Richard Ollard observes, Pepys was the "master builder" of the permanent, professional navy that made possible the expansion of trade and the conquest of colonies over the ensuing century. Energetic in his king's service and in his own (the taking of bribes was one of the perquisites of office that Pepys mastered most adroitly), the tailor's son functioned formidably as an early architect of empire.

Pepys's schooling and profession had immersed him in the two practices most central to earlier English diaries, Puritanism and financial bookkeeping. But where account books and religious diaries emphasize certain kinds of moment—exchanges of money and goods, instances of moral redemption and relapse—Pepys tries for something more comprehensive. He implicitly commits himself to tracking the whole day's experience: the motions of the body as it makes its way through the city in boats, in coaches, and on foot, and the motions of the mind as it shuttles between business and pleasure. He sustained his narrative over a virtually unbroken series of daily entries before stopping out of fear that his work on the diary had helped to damage his eyesight to the brink of blindness. "None of Pepys's contemporaries," writes his editor Robert Latham, "attempted a diary in the all-inclusive Pepysian sense and on the Pepysian scale." To the efficiency of the bookkeeper and the discipline of the Puritan, Pepys added the ardor of the virtuoso, eager (as he observes at one point) "to see any strange thing" and capable of finding wonder in ordinary things: music, plays, books, food, clothes, conversation. The phrase "with great pleasure" recurs in the diary as a kind of leitmotiv, and superlatives play leapfrog through the pages: many, many experiences qualify in turn as the "best" thing that the diarist ever ate, read, thought, saw, heard. To achieve the diary's seeming immediacy, Pepys put his entries through as many as five stages of revision, sometimes days or even months after the events recorded. Even at the final stage, in the bound, elegantly formatted volumes of the diary manuscript, he often crammed new detail or comment into margins and between the lines. Comparable pressures operated in connection with the diary's complex privacy. Pepys took pains to secure secrecy for his text. He hid it from view in drawers or in cabinets. He wrote most of it in a secretarial shorthand, and where he most wanted secrecy, as in the accounts of his many flirtations and infidelities, he obscured things further by an improvised language made up of Spanish, French, Latin, and other tongues. (Elizabeth Pepys figures throughout the diary as a kind of muse and countermuse, the narrative's most recurrent and obsessive subject, and the person most urgently to be prevented from reading it.) At the same time, the manuscript makes notable gestures toward self-display. Pepys frequently shifts to a readily readable longhand, especially for names, places, titles of books, plays, and persons; at times even his secret sexual language opens out into longhand.

This ambivalent secrecy persisted past the diarist's death. Pepys bequeathed the manuscript to Magdalene College without calling any special attention to it. It was included among his many collections: of naval books and papers, of broadsheet ballads, and of instruction manuals on shorthand methods—including the one Pepys used to write the diary. The manuscript kept its secrets long. In the early nineteenth century, the diary was discovered and painstakingly decoded (by a transcriber who, missing the connection between the manuscript and the shorthand manuals on adjacent shelves, treated the text as a million-word cryptogram); it was finally published, in a severely shortened and expurgated version, in 1825. Readers and reviewers soon called for more, recognizing that Pepys possessed (in the words of one reviewer) "the most indiscriminating, insatiable, and miscellaneous curiosity, that ever . . . supplied the pen, of a daily chronicler." Expanded (but still bowdlerized) editions appeared throughout the century, and only in the 1970s did the semisecret manuscript make its way wholly into print.

from The Diary

[First Entries][1]

$16\frac{59}{60}$

Blessed be God, at the end of the last year I was in very good health, without any sense of my old pain[2] but upon taking of cold.

1. England still adhered to the Old Style calendar, in which the new year officially began on March 25, Pepys wrote this "prolude" in early January 1659 according to the English reckoning, but 1660 (New Style) in the rest of Europe.
2. Pepys had suffered from stones in the bladder from babyhood until 1658, when he under went a risky but successful operation.

I lived in Axe Yard,[3] having my wife and servant Jane, and no more in family than us three.

My wife, after the absence of her terms[4] for seven weeks, gave me hopes of her being with child, but on the last day of the year she hath them again. The condition of the state was thus. *Viz.* the Rump, after being disturbed by my Lord Lambert, was lately returned to sit again.[5] The officers of the army all forced to yield. Lawson lies still in the river and Monck is with his army in Scotland.[6] Only my Lord Lambert is not yet come in to the Parliament; nor is it expected that he will, without being forced to it.

The new Common Council of the City doth speak very high; and hath sent to Monck their sword-bearer, to acquaint him with their desires for a free and full Parliament, which is at present the desires and the hopes and expectation of all—22 of the old secluded members having been at the House door the last week to demand entrance; but it was denied them, and it is believed that they nor the people will not be satisfied till the House be filled.[7]

My own private condition very handsome; and esteemed rich, but indeed very poor, besides my goods of my house and my office, which at present is somewhat uncertain. Mr Downing master of my office.[8]

1 January 1659/60. Lord's Day. This morning (we lying lately in the garret) I rose, put on my suit with great skirts,[9] having not lately worn any other clothes but them.

Went to Mr. Gunning's church at Exeter House, where he made a very good sermon upon these words: that in the fullness of time God sent his Son, made of a woman, etc., showing that by "made under the law" is meant his circumcision, which is solemnized this day.[1]

Dined at home in the garret, where my wife dressed the remains of a turkey, and in the doing of it she burned her hand.

I stayed at home all the afternoon, looking over my accounts.

Then went with my wife to my father's; and in going, observed the great posts which the City hath set up[2] at the Conduit in Fleet Street.

Supped at my father's, where in came Mrs. Theophila Turner and Madam Morris[3] and supped with us. After that, my wife and I went home with them, and so to our own home.

3. In Westminster.
4. Menstrual periods.
5. John Lambert, a skilled general under Oliver Cromwell, now oppossed the convening of the Rump Parliament, which had governed England since the fall of Cromwell's son Richard in 1659.
6. At this point, the political intentions and allegiance of General George Monck were the object of much speculation; he led his army back from Scotland into England on January 1 and became one of the principal engineers of the Restoration. Vice-Admiral John Lawson supported the rump.
7. A Parliament that would include the "old secluded members"—the representatives expelled in 1648—was understood to be a first step toward restoration of the monarchy.
8. Pepys was at this point a clerk in the office of the Exchequer.
9. I.e., with a long coat.
1. Peter Gunning had held illegal Anglican services during the Commonwealth. His sermon text is Galatians 4.4; "But, when the fullness of the time was come, God sent forth his Son, made of a woman, made under the law."
2. As defesive barriers during its opposition to the Rump Parliament.
3. A relative and a friend, respectively, "Mistress" ("Mrs.") was applied to unmarried as well as to married women; Theophila was eight years old.

[The Coronation of Charles II][4]

[23 April 1661] I lay with Mr. Shiply,[5] and about 4 in the morning I rose.

Coronation Day.

And got to the Abbey,[6] where I followed Sir J. Denham the surveyor with some company that he was leading in. And with much ado, by the favor of Mr. Cooper his man, did get up into a great scaffold across the north end of the Abbey—where with a great deal of patience I sat from past 4 till 11 before the King came in. And a pleasure it was to see the Abbey raised in the middle, all covered with red and a throne (that is a chair) and footstool on the top of it. And all the officers of all kinds, so much as the very fiddlers, in red vests.

At last comes in the Dean and prebends of Westminster with the Bishops (many of them in cloth-of-gold copes); and after them the nobility all in their Parliament robes, which was a most magnificent sight. Then the Duke[7] and the King with a scepter (carried by my Lord of Sandwich) and sword and mond before him, and the crown too.

The King in his robes, bare-headed, which was very fine. And after all had placed themselves, there was a sermon and the service. And then in the choir at the high altar he passed all the ceremonies of the coronation—which, to my very great grief, I and most in the Abbey could not see. The crown being put upon his head, a great shout begun. And he came forth to the throne and there passed more ceremonies: as, taking the oath and having things read to him by the Bishop, and his lords (who put on their caps as soon as the King put on his crown) and bishops came and kneeled before him.

And three times the King-at-Arms went to the three open places on the scaffold and proclaimed that if any one could show any reason why Charles Stuart should not be King of England, that now he should come and speak.

And a general pardon also was read by the Lord Chancellor;[8] and medals flung up and down by my Lord Cornwallis—of silver; but I could not come by any.

But so great a noise, that I could make but little of the music; and indeed, it was lost to everybody. But I had so great a list[9] to piss, that I went out a little while before the King had done all his ceremonies and went round the Abbey to Westminster Hall, all the way within rails, and 10,000 people, with the ground covered with blue cloth—and scaffolds all the way. Into the hall I got—where it was very fine with hangings and scaffolds, one upon another, full of brave[1] ladies. And my wife in one little one on the right hand.

Here I stayed walking up and down; and at last, upon one of the side-stalls, I stood and saw the King come in with all the persons (but the soldiers) that were yesterday in the cavalcade;[2] and a most pleasant sight it was to see them in their several robes. And the King came in with his crown on and his scepter in his hand—under a canopy borne up by six silver staves, carried by Barons of the Cinqueports—and little bells at every end.

And after a long time he got up to the farther end, and all set themselves down at their several tables—and that was also a rare sight. And the King's first course

4. Charles II had returned to England in May 1660; he scheduled his coronartion for St. George's Day, honoring England's patron saint.
5. Edward Shipley was steward to Pepys's cousin Edward Mountagu.
6. Westminster Abbey, site of English coronations.
7. Charles's brother James, Duke of York, later James II.
8. Charles II's Act of Oblivion forgave the crimes of all those on the parliamentary side, with the principal exception of those who had participated in the trial, sentencing, and execution of his father.
9. Desire.
1. Splendid.
2. The previous day's procession.

carried up by the Knights of the Bath. And many fine ceremonies there was of the heralds leading up people before him and bowing; and my Lord of Albemarle's[3] going to the kitchen and eat[4] a bit of the first dish that was to go to the King's table.

But above all was these three Lords, Northumberland and Suffolk and the Duke of Ormond, coming before the courses on horseback and staying so all dinner-time; and at last, to bring up Dymock the King's champion, all in armor on horseback, with his spear and target carried before him. And a herald proclaim that if any dare deny Charles Stuart to be lawful King of England, here was a champion that would fight with him; and with those words the champion flings down his gauntlet; and all this he doth three times in his going up toward the King's table. At last, when he is come, the King drinks to him and then sends him the cup, which is of gold; and he drinks it off and then rides back again with the cup in his hand.

I went from table to table to see the bishops and all others at their dinner, and was infinite pleased with it. And at the lords' table I met with Will Howe and he spoke to my Lord for me and he did give him four rabbits and a pullet; and so I got it, and Mr. Creed and I got Mr. Mitchell to give us some bread and so we at a stall eat it, as everybody else did what they could get.[5]

I took a great deal of pleasure to go up and down and look upon the ladies—and to hear the music of all sorts; but above all, the 24 violins.

About 6 at night they had dined; and I went up to my wife and there met with a pretty lady (Mrs. Franklin, a doctor's wife, a friend of Mr. Bowyer's) and kissed them both—and by and by took them down to Mr. Bowyer's. And strange it is, to think that these two days have held up fair till now that all is done and the King gone out of the Hall; and then it fell a-raining and thundering and lightening as I have not seen it do some years—which people did take great notice of God's blessing of the work of these two days—which is a foolery, to take too much notice of such things.

I observed little disorder in all this; but only the King's footmen had got hold of the canopy and would keep it from the Barons of the Cinqueports; which they endeavored to force from them again but could not do it till my Lord Duke of Albemarle caused it to be put into Sir R. Pye's hand till tomorrow to be decided.

At Mr. Bowyer's, a great deal of company; some I knew, others I did not. Here we stayed upon the leads[6] and below till it was late, expecting to see the fireworks; but they were not performed tonight. Only, the City had a light like a glory round about it, with bonfires.

At last I went to King Street; and there sent Crockford to my father's and my house to tell them I could not come home tonight, because of the dirt and a coach could not be had.

And so after drinking a pot of ale alone at Mrs. Harper's, I returned to Mr. Bowyer's; and after a little stay more, I took my wife and Mrs. Franklin (who I proferred the civility of lying with my wife at Mrs. Hunt's tonight) to Axe Yard. In which, at the further end, there was three great bonfires and a great many great gallants, men and women; and they laid hold of us and would have us drink the King's health upon our knee, kneeling upon a fagot; which we all did, they drinking to us one after another—which we thought a strange frolic. But these gallants continued thus a great while, and I wondered to see how the ladies did tipple.

3. In 1660 Charles II had made George Monck Duke of Albemarle as a reward for his role in the Restoration.
4. Ate (pronounced "ett"), to test for poison.
5. Will Howe and John Creed served as clerks to Sandwich, whom the diarist invariably refers to as "my Lord." Miles Mitchell was a local bookseller.
6. Rooftop.

At last I sent my wife and her bedfellow to bed, and Mr. Hunt and I went in with Mr. Thornbury (who did give the company all their wines, he being yeoman of the wine-cellar to the King) to his house; and there, with his wife and two of his sisters and some gallant sparks that were there, we drank the King's health and nothing else, till one of the gentlemen fell down stark drunk and there lay spewing. And I went to my Lord's pretty well. But no sooner a-bed with Mr. Shiply but my head begun to turn and I to vomit, and if ever I was foxed[7] it was now—which I cannot say yet, because I fell asleep and sleep till morning—only, when I waked I found myself wet with my spewing. Thus did the day end, with joy everywhere; and blessed be God, I have not heard of any mischance to anybody through it all, but only to Sergeant Glynne, whose horse fell upon him yesterday and is like to kill him; which people do please themselves with, to see how just God is to punish that rogue at such a time as this—he being now one of the King's sergeants and rode in the cavalcade with Maynard, to whom people wished the same fortune.[8]

There was also this night, in King Street, a woman had her eye put out by a boy's flinging of a firebrand into the coach.

Now after all this, I can say that besides the pleasure of the sight of these glorious things, I may now shut my eyes against any other objects, or for the future trouble myself to see things of state and show, as being sure never to see the like again in this world.

[24 April 1661] Waked in the morning with my head in a sad taking through the last night's drink, which I am very sorry for. So rise and went out with Mr. Creed to drink our morning draught, which he did give me in chocolate to settle my stomach. And after that to my wife, who lay with Mrs. Franklin at the next door to Mrs. Hunt's.

And they were ready, and so I took them up in a coach and carried the lady to Paul's[9] and there set her down; and so my wife and I home—and I to the office.

That being done, my wife and I went to dinner to Sir W. Batten;[1] and all our talk about the happy conclusion of these last solemnities.

After dinner home and advised with my wife about ordering things in my house; and then she went away to my father's to lie, and I stayed with my workmen, who do please me very well with their work.

At night set myself to write down these three days' diary; and while I am about it, I hear the noise of the chambers and other things of the fireworks, which are now playing upon the Thames before the King. And I wish myself with them, being sorry not to see them.

So to bed.

[The Plague Year]

[7 June 1665] This morning my wife and mother rose about 2 a-clock, and with Mercer, Mary, the boy, and W. Hewer,[2] as they had designed, took boat and down to refresh themselves on the water to Gravesend. I lay till 7 a-clock; then up, and to the office upon Sir G. Carteret's accounts again—where very busy.[3] Thence abroad and to the Change, no news of certainty being yet come from the fleet.[4] Thence to the

7. Drunk.
8. Sir John Glynne and Sir John Maynard were lawyers who had served under Cromwell.
9. St. Paul's Cathedral.
1. Surveyor of the Navy.
2. Mary Mercer was Elizabeth Pepys's paid companion; Will Hewer was Pepys's office clerk and lifelong friend; Mary and "the boy" are household servants.
3. George Carteret was Navy Treasurer.
4. The Royal Exchange was the City's central location for luxury shopping, business dealings, and news gathering. Pepys wanted news of the ongoing Second Dutch War; his patron Sandwich was in command of the fleet.

Dolphin Tavern, where Sir J. Mennes, Lord Brouncker, Sir Thomas Harvey and myself dined upon Sir G. Carteret's charge—and very merry we were, Sir Thomas Harvey being a very droll.[5] Thence to the office; and meeting Creed, away with him to my Lord Treasurer's, there thinking to have met the goldsmiths, or at Whitehall; but did not, and so appointed another time for my lord to speak to them to advance us some money. Thence, it being the hottest day that ever I felt in my life, and it is confessed so by all other people the hottest they ever knew in England in the beginning of June—we to the New Exchange and there drunk whey; with much entreaty, getting it for our money, and would not be entreated to let us have one glass more. So took water, and to Foxhall[6] to the Spring Garden and there walked an hour or two with great pleasure, saving our minds ill at ease concerning the fleet and my Lord Sandwich, that we have no news of them, and ill reports run up and down of his being killed, but without ground. Here stayed, pleasantly walking and spending but 6*d*, till 9 at night; and then by water to Whitehall, and there I stopped to hear news of the fleet, but none come, which is strange; and so by water home—where, weary with walking and with the mighty heat of the weather, and for my wife's not coming home—I staying walking in the garden till 12 at night, when it begun to lighten exceedingly through the greatness of the heat. Then, despairing of her coming home, I to bed.

This day, much against my will, I did in Drury Lane see two or three houses marked with a red cross upon the doors, and "Lord have mercy upon us" writ there[7]—which was a sad sight to me, being the first of that kind that to my remembrance I ever saw. It put me into an ill conception of myself and my smell, so that I was forced to buy some roll-tobacco to smell to and chaw—which took away the apprehension.[8]

[30 July 1665] Lord's Day. Up, and in my nightgown, cap, and neck-cloth, undressed all day long; lost not a minute, but in my chamber setting my Tangier accounts to rights, which I did by night, to my very heart's content; not only that it is done, but I find everything right and even beyond what, after so long neglecting them, I did hope for. The Lord of Heaven be praised for it.

Will was with me today and is very well again. It was a sad noise to hear our bell to toll and ring so often today, either for deaths or burials; I think five or six times.

At night, weary with the day's work but full of joy at my having done it—I to bed, being to rise betimes tomorrow to go to the wedding at Dagnams.

So to bed—fearing I have got some cold sitting in my loose garment all this day.

[31 July 1665[9]] Up, and very betimes, by 6 a-clock, at Deptford; and there find Sir G. Carteret and my lady ready to go—I being in my new colored-silk suit and coat, trimmed with gold buttons and gold broad lace round my hands, very rich and fine. By water to the ferry, where, when we came, no coach there—and tide of ebb so far spent as the horse-boat could not get off on the other side the river to bring away the coach. So we were fain to stay there in the unlucky Isle of Dogs—in a chill place, the morning cool and wind fresh, above two if not three hours, to our great discontent. Yet being upon a pleasant errand, and seeing that could not be helped, we did bear it

5. All these men were colleagues on the Navy Board. *Droll:* jester.
6. Vauxhall, a cluster of riverside gardens, immensely popular for its avenues, covered walks, and wine stalls.
7. The red cross marked houses infected by plague.
8. Tobacco was thought to prevent infection.
9. The wedding day of Lady Jemimah Mountagu, Sandwich's eldest daughter, and Philip Carteret, eldest son of Pepys's colleague Sir George. Pepys had helped to arrange the match.

very patiently; and it was worth my observing, I thought as ever anything, to see how upon these two scores, Sir G. Carteret, the most passionate man in the world and that was in greatest haste to be gone, did bear with it, and very pleasant all the while, at least not troubled much so as to fret and storm at it.

Anon the coach comes—in the meantime there coming a citizen thither with his horse to go over, that told us he did come from Islington this morning, and that Proctor the vintner of the Mitre in Wood Street, and his son, is dead this morning there—of the plague. He having laid out abundance of money there—and was the greatest vintner for some time in London for great entertainments.

We, fearing the canonical hour would be past before we got thither,[1] did with a great deal of unwillingness send away the license and wedding ring. So that when we came, though we drove hard with six horses, yet we found them gone from home; and going toward the church, met them coming from church—which troubled us. But however, that trouble was soon over—hearing it was well done—they being both in their old clothes. My Lord Crew giving her—there being three coach-fulls of them. The young lady mighty sad, which troubled me; but yet I think it was only her gravity, in a little greater degree than usual. All saluted her,[2] but I did not till my Lady Sandwich did ask me whether I had not saluted her or no. So to dinner, and very merry we were; but yet in such a sober way as never almost any wedding was in so great families—but it was much better. After dinner, company divided, some to cards—others to talk. My Lady Sandwich and I up to settle accounts and pay her some money—and mighty kind she is to me, and would fain have had me gone down for company with her to Hinchingbrooke—but for my life I cannot.

At night to supper, and so to talk and, which methought was the most extraordinary thing, all of us to prayers as usual, and the young bride and bridegroom too. And so after prayers, soberly to bed; only, I got into the bridegroom's chamber while he undressed himself, and there was very merry—till he was called to the bride's chamber and into bed they went. I kissed the bride in bed, and so the curtains drawn with the greatest gravity that could be, and so good-night.

But the modesty and gravity of this business was so decent, that it was to me, indeed, ten times more delightful than if it had been twenty times more merry and jovial.

Whereas I feared I must have sat up all night, we did here all get good beds—and I lay in the same I did before, with Mr. Brisband, who is a good scholar and sober man; and we lay in bed, getting him to give me an account of Rome, which is the most delightful talk a man can have of any traveler. And so to sleep—my eyes much troubled already with the change of my drink.

Thus I ended this month with the greatest joy that ever I did any in my life, because I have spent the greatest part of it with abundance of joy and honor, and pleasant journeys and brave entertainments, and without cost of money. And at last live to see that business ended[3] with great content on all sides.

This evening with Mr. Brisband speaking of enchantments and spells, I telling him some of my charms,[4] he told me this of his own knowledge at Bourdeaux in France. The words these—

1. Church law stipulated that weddings could be performed only during certain hours of the day.
2. Greeted her with a kiss.
3. The marriage concluded.
4. At the end of the previous year, Pepys had written into his diary a set of incantations ("charms") for healing cuts, burns, etc.

Voicy un corps mort
Royde comme un baston
Froid comme marbre
Leger comme un esprit,
Levons te au nom de Jesus Christ.[5]

He saw four little girls, very young ones, all kneeling, each of them upon one knee; and one begin the first line, whispering in the ear of the next, and the second to the third, and the third to the fourth, and she to the first. Then the first begun the second line, and so round quite through. And putting each one finger only to a boy that lay flat upon his back on the ground, as if he was dead. At the end of the words they did with their four fingers raise this boy as high as they could reach. And he being there and wondering at it (as also being afeared to see it—for they would have had him to have bore a part in saying the words in the room of one of the little girls, that was so young that they could hardly make her learn to repeat the words), did, for fear there might be some sleight used in it by the boy, or that the boy might be light, called the cook of the house, a very lusty fellow, as Sir G. Carteret's cook, who is very big, and they did raise him just in the same manner.

This is one of the strangest things I ever heard, but he tells it me of his own knowledge and I do heartily believe it to be true. I inquired of him whether they were Protestant or Catholic girls, and he told me they were Protestant—which made it the more strange to me.

Thus we end this month, as I said, after the greatest glut of content that ever I had; only, under some difficulty because of the plague, which grows mightily upon us, the last week being about 1,700 or 1,800 [dead] of the plague.

My Lord Sandwich, at sea with a fleet of about 100 sail to the Norward, expect De Ruyter or the Dutch East-India fleet.

My Lord Hinchingbrooke[6] coming over from France, and will meet his sister at Scott's Hall.

Myself having obliged both these families in this business very much, as both my lady and Sir G. Carteret and his lady do confess exceedingly; and the latter two also now call me cousin, which I am glad of.

So God preserve us all friends long, and continue health among us.

[15 August 1665] Up by 4 a-clock and walked to Greenwich, where called at Captain Cocke's[7] and to his chamber, he being in bed—where something put my last night's dream into my head, which I think is the best that ever was dreamed—which was, that I had my Lady Castlemaine[8] in my arms and was admitted to use all the dalliance I desired with her, and then dreamed that this could not be awake but that it was only a dream. But that since it was a dream and that I took so much real pleasure in it, what a happy thing it would be, if when we are in our graves (as Shakespeare resembles it),[9] we could dream, and dream but such dreams as this—that then we should not need to be so fearful of death as we are this plague-time. * * *

5. Here is a dead body / Stiff as a rod / Cold as marble / Light as a spirit, / We raise thee in the name of Jesus Christ.

6. Sandwich's son.

7. George Cocke, supplier to the navy and Pepys's colleague on the board.

8. Barbara Palmer, Countess of Castlemaine, was a celebrated beauty and at this point the foremost among the King's mistresses. See Color Plate 20.

9. Shakespeare compares ("resembles") death to sleep in Hamlet's famous soliloquy, though Hamlet fears what he might dream when dead: "To die, to sleep; / To sleep, perchance to dream. Ay, there's the rub, / For in that sleep of death what dreams may come, / When we have shuffled off this mortal coil, / Must give us pause." (*Hamlet* 3.1.65–69).

It was dark before I could get home; and so land at church-yard-stairs, where to my great trouble I met a dead corpse, of the plague, in the narrow ally, just bringing down[1] a little pair of stairs—but I thank God I was not much disturbed at it. However, I shall beware of being late abroad again.

[10 September 1665] *Lord's day.* Walked home, being forced thereto by one of my watermen falling sick yesterday; and it was God's great mercy I did not go by water with them yesterday, for he fell sick on Saturday night and it is to be feared of the plague. So I sent him away to London with his fellow.

But another boat came to me this morning, whom I sent to Blackwell for Mr. Andrews; I walked to Woolwich,[2] and there find Mr. Hill, and he and I all the morning at music and a song he hath set, of three parts; methinks very good. Anon comes Mr. Andrews, though it be a very ill day. And so after dinner we to music and sang till about 4 or 5 a-clock, it blowing very hard, and now and then raining—and, wind and tide being against us, Andrews and I took leave and walked to Greenwich—my wife before I came out telling me the ill news that she hears, that her father is very ill; and then I told her I feared of the plague, for that the house is shut up.[3] And so, she much troubled, she did desire me to send them something, and I said I would, and will do so.

But before I came out, there happened news to come to me by an express from Mr. Coventry, telling me the most happy news of my Lord Sandwich's meeting with part of the Dutch; his taking two of their East India ships and six or seven others, and very good prize—and that he is in search of the rest of the fleet, which he hopes to find upon the Well Bank—with the loss only of the *Hector*, poor Captain Cuttle. This news doth so overjoy me, that I know not what to say enough to express it; but the better to do it, I did walk to Greenwich;[4] and there sending away Mr. Andrews, I to Captain Cocke's, where I find my Lord Brouncker and his mistress and Sir J. Mennes—where we supped (there was also Sir W. Doyly and Mr. Evelyn);[5] but the receipt of this news did put us all into such an ecstasy of joy, that it inspired into Sir J. Mennes and Mr. Evelyn such a spirit of mirth, that in all my life I never met with so merry a two hours as our company this night was. Among other humors, Mr. Evelyn's repeating of some verses made up of nothing but the various acceptations of May and Can, and doing it so aptly, upon occasion of something of that nature, and so fast, did make us all die almost with laughing, and did so stop the mouth of Sir J. Mennes in the middle of all his mirth (and in a thing agreeing with his own manner of genius) that I never saw any man so outdone in all my life; and Sir J. Mennes's mirth too, to see himself outdone, was the crown of all our mirth.

In this humor we sat till about 10 at night; and so my Lord and his mistress home, and we to bed—it being one of the times of my life wherein I was the fullest of true sense of joy.

[14 September 1665] Up, and walked to Greenwich and there fitted myself in several businesses to go to London, where I have not been now a pretty while. But before I

1. Being carried down.
5. A navy yard on the Thames, east of London, where Pepys, his wife, and their servants had taken lodgings in an effort to avoid the plague.
3. Quarantined.
4. A town on the Thames, east of London, where the Navy Office had temporarily relocated during plague time.
5. John Evelyn (1620–1706), author, virtuoso, and fellow diarist. During the Second Dutch War, both Evelyn and William Doyly served the Navy as Commissioners for the Sick and Wounded.

went from the office, news is brought by word of mouth that letters are now just now brought from the Fleet of our taking a great many more of the Dutch fleet—in which I did never more plainly see my command of my temper, in my not admitting myself to receive any kind of joy from it till I had heard the certainty of it. And therefore went by water directly to the Duke of Albemarle, where I find a letter of the 12th from Solebay, from my Lord Sandwich, of the fleet's meeting with about 18 more of the Dutch fleet and his taking of most of them; and the messenger says they had taken three after the letter was wrote and sealed; which being 21, and the 14 took the other day, is 45 sail—some of which are good, and others rich ships—which is so great a cause of joy in us all, that my Lord and every body is highly joyed thereat. And having taken a copy of my Lord's letter, I away back again to the Bear at the bridge-foot, being full of wind and out of order, and there called for a biscuit and a piece of cheese and gill of sack[6]—being forced to walk over the bridge toward the Change, and the plague being all thereabouts. Here my news was highly welcome, and I did wonder to see the Change so full, I believe 200 people; but not a man or merchant of any fashion, but plain men all. And Lord, to see how I did endeavor all I could to talk with as few as I could, there being now no observation of shutting up of houses infected, that to be sure we do converse and meet with people that have the plague upon them. I to Sir Robert Viners, where my main business was about settling the business of Debusty's *5000l* tallies—which I did for the present to enable me to have some money. And so home, buying some things for my wife in the way. So home and put up several things to carry to Woolwich—and upon serious thoughts, I am advised by W. Griffin to let my money and plate[7] rest there, as being as safe as any place, nobody imagining that people would leave money in their houses now, when all their families are gone. So for the present, that being my opinion, I did leave them there still. But Lord, to see the trouble that it puts a man to to keep safe what with pain a man hath been getting together; and there is good reason for it. Down to the office, and there wrote letters to and again about this good news of our victory, and so by water home late—

Where when I came home, I spent some thoughts upon the occurrences of this day, giving matter for as much content on one hand and melancholy on another as any day in all my life—for the first, the finding of my money and plate and all safe at London and speeding in my business of money this day—the hearing of this good news, to such excess after so great a despair of my Lord's doing anything this year—adding to that, the decrease of 500 and more, which is the first decrease we have yet had in the sickness since it begun—and great hopes that the next week it will be greater. Then on the other side—my finding that though the Bill[8] in general is abated, yet the City within the walls[9] is increased and likely to continue so and is close to our house there—my meeting dead corpses of the plague, carried to be buried close to me at noonday through the City in Fanchurch Street—to see a person sick of the sores carried close by me by Grace Church in a hackney-coach—my finding the Angel Tavern at the lower end of Tower Hill shut up; and more than that, the ale-house at the Tower stairs; and more than that, that the person was then dying of the plague when I was last there, a little while ago at night, to write a short letter there,

6. Quarter pint of white wine.
7. Silver.
8. The Bill of Mortality, a weekly, parish-by-parish account of the deaths in London.
9. London had spread beyond its original walls, but the area within those walls was still known as "the City."

and I overheard the mistress of the house sadly saying to her husband somebody was very ill, but did not think it was of the plague—to hear that poor Payne my waterman hath buried a child and is dying himself—to hear that a laborer I sent but the other day to Dagnams to know how they did there is dead of the plague; and that one of my own watermen, that carried me daily, fell sick as soon as he had landed me on Friday morning last, when I had been all night upon the water (and I believed he did get his infection that day at Brainford) is now dead of the plague—to hear that Captain Lambert and Cuttle are killed in the taking these ships and that Mr. Sidney Mountagu is sick of a desperate fever at my Lady Carteret's at Scott's Hall—to hear that Mr. Lewes hath another daughter sick—and lastly, that both my servants, W. Hewer and Tom Edwards, have lost their fathers, both in St. Sepulcher's parish, of the plague this week—doth put me into great apprehensions of melancholy, and with good reason. But I put off the thoughts of sadness as much as I can; and the rather to keep my wife in good heart, and family also. After supper (having eat nothing all this day) upon a fine tench[1] of Mr. Sheldon's taking, we to bed.

[The Fire of London]

[2 September 1666] Lord's Day. Some of our maids sitting up late last night to get things ready against our feast today, Jane called us up, about 3 in the morning, to tell us of a great fire they saw in the City. So I rose, and slipped on my nightgown and went to her window, and thought it to be on the back side of Mark Lane at the furthest; but being unused to such fires as followed, I thought it far enough off, and so went to bed again and to sleep. About 7 rose again to dress myself, and there looked out at the window and saw the fire not so much as it was, and further off. So to my closet[2] to set things to rights after yesterday's cleaning. By and by Jane comes and tells me that she hears that above 300 houses have been burned down tonight by the fire we saw, and that it was now burning down all Fish Street by London Bridge. So I made myself ready presently, and walked to the Tower and there got up upon one of the high places, Sir J. Robinson's little son going up with me; and there I did see the houses at that end of the bridge all on fire, and an infinite great fire on this and the other side the end of the bridge—which, among other people, did trouble me for poor little Mitchell and our Sarah on the bridge.[3] So down, with my heart full of trouble, to the Lieutenant of the Tower, who tells me that it begun this morning in the King's baker's house in Pudding Lane, and that it hath burned down St. Magnus's Church and most part of Fish Street already. So I down to the water-side and there got a boat and through bridge,[4] and there saw a lamentable fire. Poor Mitchell's house, as far as the Old Swan, already burned that way and the fire running further, that in a very little time it got as far as the Steelyard while I was there. Everybody endeavoring to remove their goods, and flinging into the river or bringing them into lighters[5] that lay off. Poor people staying in their houses as long as till the very fire touched them, and then running into boats or clambering from one pair of stair by the water-side to another. And among other things, the poor pigeons I perceive were loath to leave their houses, but hovered about the windows and balconies till they were some of them burned, their wings, and fell down.

1. A kind of fish.
2. Private room, study.
3. London Bridge was lined with shops and houses, including the liquor shop of Pepys's friend Michael Mitchell and the residence of his former servant Sarah.
4. Under the bridge.
5. Barges.

Having stayed, and in an hour's time seen the fire rage every way, and nobody to my sight endeavoring to quench it, but to remove their goods and leave all to the fire; and having seen it get as far as the Steelyard, and the wind mighty high and driving it into the City, and everything, after so long a drought, proving combustible, even the very stones of churches, and among other things, the poor steeple by which pretty Mrs. Horsley lives, and whereof my old school-fellow Elborough is parson, taken fire in the very top and there burned till it fall down—I to Whitehall with a gentleman with me who desired to go off from the Tower to see the fire in my boat—to Whitehall, and there up to the King's closet in the chapel, where people came about me and I did give them an account dismayed them all; and word was carried in to the King, so I was called for and did tell the King and Duke of York what I saw, and that unless his Majesty did command houses to be pulled down, nothing could stop the fire. They seemed much troubled, and the King commanded me to go to my Lord Mayor from him and command him to spare no houses but to pull down before the fire every way. The Duke of York bid me tell him that if he would have any more soldiers, he shall; and so did my Lord Arlington afterward, as a great secret. Here meeting with Captain Cocke, I in his coach, which he lent me, and Creed with me, to Paul's; and there walked along Watling Street as well as I could, every creature coming away loaden with goods to save—and here and there sick people carried away in beds. Extraordinary good goods carried in carts and on backs. At last met my Lord Mayor in Canning Street, like a man spent, with a hankercher about his neck. To the King's message, he cried like a fainting woman, "Lord, what can I do? I am spent! People will not obey me. I have been pulling down houses. But the fire overtakes us faster than we can do it." That he needed no more soldiers; and that for himself, he must go and refresh himself, having been up all night. So he left me, and I him, and walked home—seeing people all almost distracted and no manner of means used to quench the fire. The houses too, so very thick thereabouts, and full of matter for burning, as pitch and tar, in Thames Street—and warehouses of oil and wines and brandy and other things. Here I saw Mr. Isaac Houblon, that handsome man—prettily dressed and dirty at his door at Dowgate, receiving some of his brothers' things whose houses were on fire; and as he says, have been removed twice already, and he doubts (as it soon proved) that they must be in a little time removed from his house also—which was a sad consideration. And to see the churches all filling with goods, by people who themselves should have been quietly there at this time.

By this time it was about 12 a-clock, and so home and there find my guests, which was Mr. Wood and his wife, Barbary Shelden, and also Mr. Moone—she mighty fine, and her husband, for aught I see, a likely man. But Mr. Moone's design and mine, which was to look over my closet and please him with the sight thereof, which he hath long desired, was wholly disappointed, for we were in great trouble and disturbance at this fire, not knowing what to think of it. However, we had an extraordinary good dinner, and as merry as at this time we could be.

While at dinner, Mrs. Batelier came to inquire after Mr. Woolfe and Stanes (who it seems are related to them), whose houses in Fish Street are all burned, and they in a sad condition. She would not stay in the fright.

As soon as dined, I and Moone away and walked through the City, the streets full of nothing but people and horses and carts loaden with goods, ready to run over one another, and removing goods from one burned house to another—they now removing out of Canning Street (which received goods in the morning) into Lombard Street and further; and among others, I now saw my little goldsmith Stokes receiving some friend's goods, whose house itself was burned the day after. We parted at Paul's, he home and I to Paul's Wharf, where I had appointed a boat to attend me; and took in Mr. Carkesse and his brother, whom I met in the street, and carried them below and above bridge, to and again, to see the fire, which was now got further, both below and above, and no likelihood of stopping it. Met with the King and Duke of York in their barge, and with them to Queenhithe and there called Sir Richard Browne to them. Their order was only to pull down houses apace, and so below bridge at the water-side; but little was or could be done, the fire coming upon them so fast. Good hopes there was of stopping it at the Three Cranes above, and at Buttolph's Wharf below bridge, if care be used; but the wind carries it into the City, so as we know not by the water-side what it doth there. River full of lighters and boats taking in goods, and good goods swimming in the water; and only, I observed that hardly one lighter or boat in three that had the goods of a house in, but there was a pair of virginals[6] in it. Having seen as much as I could now, I away to Whitehall by appointment, and there walked to St. James's Park, and there met my wife and Creed and Wood and his wife and walked to my boat, and there upon the water again, and to the fire up and down, it still increasing and the wind great. So near the fire as we could for smoke; and all over the Thames, with one's face in the wind you were almost burned with a shower of firedrops—this is very true—so as houses were burned by these drops and flakes of fire, three or four, nay five or six houses, one from another. When we could endure no more upon the water, we to a little alehouse on the Bankside over against the Three Cranes, and there stayed till it was dark almost and saw the fire grow; and as it grow darker, appeared more and more, and in corners and upon steeples and between churches and houses, as far as we could see up the hill of the City, in a most horrid malicious bloody flame, not like the fine flame of an ordinary fire. Barbary and her husband away before us. We stayed till, it being darkish, we saw the fire as only one entire arch of fire from this to the other side the bridge, and in a bow up the hill, for an arch of above a mile long. It made me weep to see it. The churches, houses, and all on fire and flaming at once, and a horrid noise the flames made, and the cracking of houses at their ruin. So home with a sad heart, and there find everybody discoursing and lamenting the fire; and poor Tom Hayter[7] came with some few of his goods saved out of his house, which is burned upon Fish Street Hill. I invited him to lie at my house, and did receive his goods: but was deceived in his lying there, the noise coming every moment of the growth of the fire, so as we were forced to begin to pack up our own goods and prepare for their removal. And did by moonshine (it being brave,[8] dry, and moonshine and warm weather) carry much of my goods into the garden, and Mr. Hayter and I did remove my money and iron-chests into my cellar—as thinking that the safest place. And got my bags of gold into my office ready to carry away, and my chief papers of accounts also there, and my tallies into a box by themselves. So great was our fear, as Sir W. Batten had carts come out of the country to fetch away his goods this night. We did put Mr. Hayter, poor man, to bed a little; but he got but very little rest, so much noise being in my house, taking down of goods.

[3 September 1666] About 4 a-clock in the morning, my Lady Batten sent me a cart to carry away all my money and plate and best things to Sir W. Rider's at Bethnell

6. A small harpsichord.
7. One of Pepys's clerks in the Navy Office.
8. Pleasant.

Green; which I did, riding myself in my nightgown in the cart; and Lord, to see how the streets and the highways are crowded with people, running and riding and getting of carts at any rate to fetch away things. I find Sir W. Rider tired with being called up[9] all night and receiving things from several friends. His house full of goods—and much of Sir W. Batten and Sir W. Penn's.[1] I am eased at my heart to have my treasure so well secured. Then home with much ado to find a way. Nor any sleep all this night to me nor my poor wife. But then, and all this day, she and I and all my people laboring to get away the rest of our things, and did get Mr. Tooker to get me a lighter to take them in, and we did carry them (myself some) over Tower Hill, which was by this time full of people's goods, bringing their goods thither. And down to the lighter, which lay at the next quay above the Tower Dock. And here was my neighbor's wife, Mrs. Buckworth, with her pretty child and some few of her things, which I did willingly give way to be saved with mine. But there was no passing with anything through the postern,[2] the crowd was so great.

The Duke of York came this day by the office and spoke to us, and did ride with his guard up and down the City to keep all quiet (he being now general, and having the care of all).

This day, Mercer being not at home, but against her mistress's order gone to her mother's, and my wife going thither to speak with W. Hewer, met her there and was angry; and her mother saying that she was not a prentice girl, to ask leave every time she goes abroad, my wife with good reason was angry, and when she came home, bid her be gone again. And so she went away, which troubled me; but yet less than it would, because of the condition we are in fear of coming into in a little time, of being less able to keep one in her quality. At night, lay down a little upon a quilt of W. Hewer in the office (all my own things being packed up or gone); and after me, my poor wife did the like—we having fed upon the remains of yesterday's dinner, having no fire nor dishes, nor any opportunity of dressing anything.

[4 September 1666] Up by break of day to get away the remainder of my things, which I did by a lighter at the Iron Gate; and my hands so few, that it was the afternoon before we could get them all away.

Sir W. Penn and I to Tower Street, and there met the fire burning three or four doors beyond Mr. Howell's; whose goods, poor man (his trays and dishes, shovels, etc., were flung all along Tower Street in the kennels, and people working therewith from one end to the other), the fire coming on in that narrow street, on both sides, with infinite fury. Sir W. Batten, not knowing how to remove his wine, did dig a pit in the garden and laid it in there; and I took the opportunity of laying all the papers of my office that I could not otherwise dispose of. And in the evening Sir W. Penn and I did dig another and put our wine in it, and I my parmesan cheese as well as my wine and some other things.

The Duke of York was at the office this day at Sir W. Penn's, but I happened not to be within. This afternoon, sitting melancholy with Sir W. Penn in our garden and thinking of the certain burning of this office without extraordinary means, I did propose for the sending up of all our workmen from Woolwich and Deptford yards (none whereof yet appeared), and to write to Sir W. Coventry to have the Duke of York's

9. Called on, woken.
1. William Penn, Pepys's colleague on the Navy Board (and father of the founder of Pennsylvania).
2. Back or side gate.

permission to pull down houses rather then lose this office, which would much hinder the King's business. So Sir W. Penn he went down this night, in order to the sending them up tomorrow morning; and I wrote to Sir W. Coventry about the business, but received no answer.

This night Mrs. Turner (who, poor woman, was removing her goods all this day—good goods, into the garden, and knew not how to dispose of them)—and her husband supped with my wife and I at night in the office, upon a shoulder of mutton from the cook's, without any napkin or anything, in a sad manner but were merry. Only, now and then walking into the garden and saw how horridly the sky looks, all on a fire in the night, was enough to put us out of our wits; and indeed it was extremely dreadful—for it looks just as if it was at us, and the whole heaven on fire. I after supper walked in the dark down to Tower Street, and there saw it all on fire at the Trinity House on that side and the Dolphin Tavern on this side, which was very near us—and the fire with extraordinary vehemence. Now begins the practice of blowing up of houses in Tower Street, those next the Tower, which at first did frighten people more than anything; but it stopped the fire where it was done—it bringing down the houses to the ground in the same places they stood, and then it was easy to quench what little fire was in it, though it kindled nothing almost. W. Hewer this day went to see how his mother did, and comes late home, but telling us how he hath been forced to remove her to Islington, her house in Pye Corner being burned. So that it is got so far that way and all the Old Bailey, and was running down to Fleet Street. And Paul's is burned, and all Cheapside. I wrote to my father this night; but the post-house being burned, the letter could not go.

PEPYS'S DIARY AND ITS TIME

John Evelyn: from *Kalendarium*[1]

[2 September 1666] This fatal night about ten, began that deplorable fire, near Fish Street in London. 2: I had public prayers at home: after dinner the fire continuing, with my wife and son took coach and went to the Bankside in Southwark,[2] where we beheld that dismal spectacle, the whole City in dreadful flames near the water-side, and had now consumed all the houses from the bridge all Thames Street and upwards towards Cheapside, down to the Three Cranes, and so returned exceedingly astonished, what would become of the rest. 3: The fire having continued all this night (if I may call that night, which was as light as day for 10 miles round about after a dreadful manner) when conspiring with a fierce eastern wind, in a very dry season, I went on foot to the same place, when I saw the whole south part of the City burning from Cheapside to the Thames, and all along Cornhill (for it likewise kindled back against the wind, as well as forward) Tower Street, Fenchurch Street, Gracious Street and so along to Baynard Castle, and was now taking hold of St. Paul's Church, to which the

1. John Evelyn (1620–1706), versatile author (on air pollution, architecture, gardening, forestry, and other subjects), wrote up his life on a plan very different from that of his friend Pepys. Evelyn's vantage on the Fire of London (as on much else) contrasts with Pepys's. A landowning gentleman, Evelyn dwelt at a remove from the City on a country estate across the river. A devout Anglican, he saw the catastrophe as an apocalypse steeped in biblical precedent and prophecy. For another account of the fire, see the selection from the *London Gazette* in Perspectives: Reading Papers, page 2310.

2. The southern bank of the Thames, across the river from the fire.

scaffolds contributed exceedingly. The conflagration was so universal, and the people so astonished, that from the beginning (I know not by what desponding or fate), they hardly stirred to quench it, so as there was nothing heard or seen but crying out and lamentation, and running about like distracted creatures, without at all attempting to save even their goods; such a strange consternation there was upon them, so as it burned both in breadth and length, the churches, public halls, Exchange, hospitals, monuments, and ornaments, leaping after a prodigious manner from house to house and street to street, at great distance one from the other, for the heat (with a long set of fair and warm weather) had even ignited the air, and prepared the materials to conceive the fire, which devoured after an incredible manner, houses, furniture, and everything. Here we saw the Thames covered with goods floating, all the barges and boats laden with what some had time and courage to save, as on the other, the carts etc. carrying out to the fields, which for many miles were strewed with moveables of all sorts, and tents erecting to shelter both people and what goods they could get away: O the miserable and calamitous spectacle, such as haply the whole world had not seen the like since the foundation of it, nor to be outdone, till the universal conflagration of it. All the sky were of a fiery aspect, like the top of a burning oven, and the light seen above 40 miles round about for many nights. God grant mine eyes may never behold the like, who now saw above ten thousand houses all in one flame, the noise and crackling and thunder of the impetuous flames, the shrieking of women and children, the hurry of people, the fall of towers, houses and churches was like an hideous storm, and the air all about so hot and inflamed that at the last one was not able to approach it, so as they were forced to stand still, and let the flames consume on which they did for near two whole miles in length and one in breadth. The clouds also of smoke were dismal, and reached upon computation near 50 miles in length. Thus I left it this afternoon burning, a resemblance of Sodom, or the last day.[3] It called to mind that of 4 *Heb: non enim hic habemus stabilem Civitatem:*[4] the ruins resembling the picture of *Troy: London* was,[5] but is no more. Thus I returned.

[4 September 1666] The burning still rages; I went now on horseback, and it was now gotten as far as the Inner Temple; all Fleet Street, Old Bailey, Ludgate Hill, Warwick Lane, Newgate, Paul's Chain, Watling Street now flaming and most of it reduced to ashes, the stones of Paul's flew like granados,[6] the lead melting down the streets in a stream, and the very pavements of them glowing with fiery redness, so as nor horse nor man was able to tread on them, and the demolitions had stopped all the passages, so as no help could be applied; the eastern wind still more impetuously driving the flames forwards. Nothing but the almighty power of God was able to stop them, for vain was the help of man. On the fourth it crossed towards Whitehall, but O the confusion was then at that court. It pleased his Majesty to command me among the rest to look after the quenching of Fetter Lane end, to preserve (if possible) that part of Holborn, whilst the rest of the gentlemen took their several posts, some at one part, some at another, for now they began to bestir themselves, and not till now, who till

3. In Genesis, the Lord destroys the sinful city of Sodom by raining "fire and brimstone . . . out of heaven" (19.24). "The last day" is the Day of Judgment, when the city of Babylon (emblem of the corrupt world) "shall be utterly burned with fire" (Revelation 18.8).
4. For here we have no lasting city (Hebrews 13.14; the sentence continues: "but we seek one to come").
5. Echoing the account of the fall of Troy in the *Aeneid* (2.325): on the night the Greeks burn the city, a Trojan priest declares *fuit Ilium* ("Troy was").
6. Grenades.

now had stood as men interdict, with their hands a cross,[7] and began to consider that nothing was like to put a stop, but the blowing up of so many houses, as might make a wider gap, than any had yet been made by the ordinary method of pulling them down with engines.[8] This some stout seamen proposed early enough to have saved the whole City; but some tenacious and avaricious men, aldermen etc., would not permit, because their houses must have been of the first. It was therefore now commanded to be practiced, and my concern being particularly for the Hospital of St. Bartholomew's near Smithfield, where I had many wounded and sick men, made me the more diligent to promote it;[9] nor was my care for the Savoy less. So as it pleased Almighty God by abating of the wind, and the industry of people, now when all was lost, infusing a new spirit into them (and such as had if exerted in time undoubtedly preserved the whole) that the fury of it began sensibly to abate, about noon, so as it came no farther than the Temple westward, nor than the entrance of Smithfield north; but continued all this day and night so impetuous toward Cripplegate, and the Tower, as made us even all despair. It also brake out again in the Temple: but the courage of the multitude persisting, and innumerable houses blown up with gunpowder, such gaps and desolations were soon made, as also by the former three days' consumption, as the back fire did not so vehemently urge upon the rest, as formerly. There was yet no standing near the burning and glowing ruins near a furlong's space. The coal and wood wharves and magazines of oil, rosin, chandler, etc.[1] did infinite mischief; so as the invective I but a little before dedicated to his Majesty and published, giving warning what might probably be the issue of suffering those shops to be in the City, was looked on as prophetic.[2] But there I left this smoking and sultry heap, which mounted up in dismal clouds night and day, the poor inhabitants dispersed all about St. George's, Moorfields, as far as Highgate, and several miles in circle, some under tents, others under miserable huts and hovels, without a rag, or any necessary utensils, bed or board, who from delicateness, riches and easy accommodations in stately and well-furnished houses, were now reduced to extremest misery and poverty. In this calamitous condition I returned with a sad heart to my house, blessing and adoring the distinguishing mercy of God, to me and mine, who in the midst of all this ruin, was like Lot, in my little Zoar, safe and sound.[3]

END OF PEPYS'S DIARY AND ITS TIME

[The Royal Society][4]

[14 November 1666] Up, and by water to Whitehall; and thence to Westminister, where I bought several things—as, a hone—ribband—gloves—books. And then took coach and to Knepp's[5] lodging, whom I find not ready to go home with me, so I away to do a little business; among others, to call upon Mr. Osborne for my Tangier warrant for the last quarter, and so to the New Exchange for some things for my wife, and

7. Immobilized, with their arms crossed (a conventional posture of passivity).
8. Machines.
9. Evelyn served on the Navy Board as a commissioner, charged with the care of sick and wounded seamen.
1. Different sorts of fuel, stored and sold in shops along the Thames.
2. In 1661 Evelyn had warned of these dangers in a pamphlet entitled *Fumifugium: or the Inconvenciency of the Air and Smoke of London Dissipated. Together with Some Remedies Humbly Proposed by J. E., Esq; to His Sacred Majesty, and to the Parliament Now Assembled.*
3. Lot, a prosperous inhabitant of Sodom, is warned by angels of the city's impending destruction. He escapes to Zoar, a small city nearby (Genesis 19.20–22).
4. This next selection from Pepys was written two months after the fire, when life had begun to return to normal.
5. Elizabeth Knepp, actress, singer, and friend of Pepys.

then to Knepp again and there stayed, reading of Waller's[6] verses while she finished her dressing—her husband being by, I had no other pastime. Her lodging very mean, and the condition she lives in; yet makes a show without doors, God bless us. I carried him along with us into the City, and set him down in Bishopsgate Street and then home with her. She tells me how Smith of the Duke's house hath killed a man upon a quarrel in play—which makes everybody sorry, he being a good actor, and they say a good man, however this happens. The ladies of the court do much bemoan him, she says. Here she and we alone at dinner, to some good victuals that we could not put off,[7] that was intended for the great dinner of my Lord Hinchingbrooke, if he had come. After dinner, I to teach her my new recitative of *It is decreed*[8]—of which she learnt a good part; and I do well like it, and believe shall be well pleased when she hath it all, and that it will be found an agreeable thing. Then carried her home, and my wife and I intended to have seen my Lady Jemima at Whitehall; but the Exchange street was so full of coaches, everybody as they say going thither to make themselves fine against tomorrow night,[9] that after half an hour's stay we could not do any; but only, my wife to see her brother, and I to go speak one word with Sir G. Carteret about office business. And talk of the general complexion of matters; which he looks upon, as I do, with horror, and gives us all for an undone people—that there is no such thing as a peace in hand, nor a possibility of any without our begging it, they[1] being as high, or higher, in their terms than ever. And tells me that just now my Lord Hollis had been with him, and wept to think in what a condition we are fallen. He showed me my Lord Sandwich's letter to him, complaining of the lack of money; which Sir G. Carteret is at a loss how in the world to get the King to supply him[2] with—and wishes him for that reason here, for that he fears he will be brought to disgrace there, for want of supplies. He says the House is yet in a bad humor; and desiring to know whence it is that the King stirs not, he says he minds it not, nor will be brought to it—and that his servants of the House do, instead of making the Parliament better, rather play the rogue one with another, and will put all in fire.[3] So that upon the whole, we are in a wretched condition, and I went from him in full apprehensions of it. So took up my wife, her brother being yet very bad, and doubtful whether he will recover or no; and so to St. Ellen's and there sent my wife home, and myself to the Pope's Head, where all the Houblons were, and Dr. Croone;[4] and by and by to an exceeding pretty supper—excellent discourse of all sorts; and indeed, are a set of the finest gentlemen that ever I met withal in my life. Here Dr. Croone told me that at the meeting[5] at Gresham College tonight (which it seems they now have every Wednesday again) there was a pretty experiment, of the blood of one dog let out (till he died) into the body of another on one side, while all his own run out on the other side. The first died upon the place, and the other very well, and likely to do well. This did give occasion to many pretty wishes, as of the blood of a Quaker to be let into an archbishop, and such like. But, as Dr. Croone says, may if it takes be of

6. Sir Edmund Waller (1606–1687), widely read poet and pioneer of the heroic couplet; he wrote much love poetry in praise of "Sacharissa," a woman he wooed without success.
7. Delay (because the food would spoil).
8. Pepys enjoyed composing music (here setting words from Ben Jonson's play *Catiline*).
9. When a court ball was to be held for the queen's birthday.
1. The Dutch.
2. Sandwich, now ambassador to Spain.
3. Into ruin.
4. The Houblons were a merchant family—a father and five sons—whom Pepys and others admired for their affection and generosity. Dr. William Croone, a specialist in anatomy, was an original Fellow and First Secretary of the Royal Society for the Improving of Natural Knowledge.
5. Of the Royal Society.

mighty use to man's health, for the amending of bad blood by borrowing from a better body.

After supper James Houblon and another brother took me aside, and to talk of some businesses of their own, where I am to serve them, and will. And then to talk of public matters; and I do find that they, and all merchants else, do give over trade and the nation for lost—nothing being done with care or foresight—no convoys[6] granted, nor anything done to satisfaction. But do think that the Dutch and French will master us the next year, do what we can; and so do I, unless God Almighty makes the King to mind his business; which might yet save all.

Here we sat talking till past one in the morning, and then home—where my people sat up for me, my wife and all; and so to bed.

[30 May 1667] Up, and to the office, where all the morning. At noon dined at home; being, without any words, friends with my wife, though last night I was very angry, and do think I did give her as much cause to be angry with me. After dinner I walked to Arundel House, the way very dusty (the day of meeting of the Society being changed from Wednesday to Thursday; which I knew not before because the Wednesday is a Council day and several of the Council are of the Society, and would come but for their attending the King at Council); where I find much company, indeed very much company, in expectation of the Duchess of Newcastle,[7] who had desired to be invited to the Society, and was, after much debate pro and con, it seems many being against it, and we do believe the town will be full of ballets[8] of it. Anon comes the Duchess, with her women attending her; among others, that Ferrabosco[9] of whom so much talk is, that her lady would bid her show her face and kill the gallants. She is indeed black[1] and hath good black little eyes, but otherwise but a very ordinary woman I do think; but they say sings well. The Duchess hath been a good comely woman; but her dress so antic and her deportment so unordinary, that I do not like her at all, nor did I hear her say anything that was worth hearing, but that she was full of admiration, all admiration.[2] Several fine experiments were shown her of colors, lodestones, microscope, and of liquors: among others, of one that did while she was there turn a piece of roasted mutton into pure blood—which was very rare. Here was Mr. Moore of Cambridge, whom I had not seen before, and I was glad to see him—as also a very pretty black boy that run up and down the room, somebody's child in Arundel House. After they had shown her many experiments, and she cried still she was "full of admiration," she departed, being led out and in by several lords that were there; among others, Lord George Berkeley and the Earl of Carlisle and a very pretty young man, the Duke of Somerset.

She gone, I by coach home and there busy at my letters till night; and then with my wife in the evening, singing with her in the garden with great pleasure. And so home to supper and to bed.

[21 November 1667] Up, and to the office, where all the morning; and at noon home, where my wife not very well, but is to go to Mr. Mill's child's christening, where she is godmother, Sir. J. Mennes and Sir R. Brookes her companions. I left

6. Protective escort for merchant ships.

7. Margaret Cavendish, Duchess of Newcastle, had published poems, plays, and treatises on natural philosophy highly critical of the Society's methods (see pages 2068–70.

8. Ballads (Evelyn wrote one on Cavendish's visit).

9. An Italian family of this name was eminent in England for its musical talents.

1. I.e., of dark complexion and hair.

2. Wonder, amazement.

her after dinner (my clerks dining with me) to go with Sir J. Mennes, and I to the office, where did much business till after candlelight; and then, my eyes beginning to fail me, I out and took coach and to Arundel House, where the meeting of Gresham College was broke up; but there meeting Creed, I with him to the tavern in St. Clement's churchyard, where was Dean Wilkins, Dr. Whistler[3] * * * and others. * * * Among the rest, they discourse of a man that is a little frantic (that hath been a kind of minister, Dr. Wilkins saying that he hath read for him in his church) that is a poor and debauched man, that the college have hired for 20s[4] to have some of the blood of a sheep let into his body; and it is to be done on Saturday next. They purpose to let in about twelve ounces, which they compute is what will be let in in a minute's time by a watch. They differ in the opinion they have of the effects of it; some think that it may have a good effect upon him as a frantic man, by cooling his blood; others, that it will not have any effect at all. But the man is a very healthy man, and by this means will be able to give an account what alteration, if any, he doth find in himself, and so may be useful. On this occasion Dr. Whistler told a pretty story related by Muffett, a good author, of Dr. Caius that built Key's College: that being very old and lived only at that time upon woman's milk, while he fed upon the milk of an angry fretful woman, was so himself; and then being advised to take of a good-natured patient woman, he did become so, beyond the common temper of his age. Thus much nutriment, they observed, might do. Their discourse was very fine; and if I should be put out of my office,[5] I do take great content in the liberty I shall be at of frequenting these gentlemen's companies. Broke up thence and home, and there to my wife in her chamber, who is not well (of those[6]); and there she tells me great stories of the gossiping women of the parish, what this and what that woman was; and among the rest, how Mrs. Hollworthy is the veriest confident bragging gossip of them all, which I should not have believed—but that Sir R. Brookes, her partner,[7] was mighty civil to her and taken with her and what not. My eyes being bad, I spent the evening with her in her chamber, talking and inventing a cipher to put on a piece of plate[8] which I must give, better than ordinary, to the parson's child; and so to bed, and through my wife's illness had a bad nght of it, and she a worse, poor wretch.

[30 November 1667] Then to Cary House, a house now of entertainment, * * * next my Lord Ashly's; and there, where I have heretofore heard Common Prayer in the time of Dr. Mossum,[9] we after two hours' stay, sitting at the table with our napkins open, had our dinners brought; but badly done. But here was good company, I choosing to sit next Dr. Wilkins, Sir George Ent, and others whom I value. And there talked of several things; among others, Dr. Wilkins, talking of the universal speech, of which he hath a book coming out,[1] did first inform me how man was certainly

3. The mathematician John Wilkins was one of the founders of the Royal Society; the physician Daniel Whistler was a Fellow.
4. Twenty shillings.
5. Pepys's position was in jeopardy because of a parliamentary investigation into Navy Office mismanagement during the Second Dutch War.
6. Her menstrual period.
7. As godfather at the christening.
8. I.e., a coded message to be engraved on a silver dish (so that the gift includes a kind of game).
9. Robert Mossum had conducted illegal Anglican services (using the forbidden Book of Common Prayer) during the Interregnum.
1. In his *Essay toward a Real Character, and a Philosophical Language* (1668), Wilkins argued for (and attempted) the creation of a newly precise and logical language based not on an arbitrary alphabet but on written symbols representing ideas and things.

made for society, he being of all creatures the least armed for defense; and of all creatures in the world, the young ones are not able to do anything to help themselves, nor can find the dug without being put to it, but would die if the mother did not help it. And he says were it not for speech, man would be a very mean creature. Much of this good discourse we had. But here above all, I was pleased to see the person who had his blood taken out. He speaks well, and did this day give the Society a relation thereof in Latin, saying that he finds himself much better since, and as a new man. But he is cracked a little in his head, though he speaks very reasonably and very well. He had but 20s for his suffering it, and is to have the same again tried upon him—the first sound man that ever had it tried on him in England, and but one that we hear of in France, which was a porter hired by the virtuosi.

[THEATER AND MUSIC]

[5 October 1667] Up, and to the office and there all the morning, none but my Lord Anglesey and myself. But much surprised with the news of the death of Sir W. Batten, who died this morning, having been but two days sick. Sir W. Penn and I did dispatch a letter this morning to Sir W. Coventry[2] to recommend Colonel Middleton, who we think a most honest and understanding man, and fit for that place. Sir G. Carteret did also come this morning, and walked with me in the garden and concluded not to concern or have any advice made to Sir W. Coventry in behalf of my Lord Sandwich's business; so I do rest satisfied, though I do think they are all mad,[3] that they will judge Sir W. Coventry an enemy, when he is indeed no such man to anybody, but is severe and just, as he ought to be, where he sees things ill done. At noon home, and by coach to Temple Bar to a India shop[4] and there bought a gown and sash, which cost me 26s. And so she and Willett[5] away to the Change, and I to my Lord Crew and there met my Lord Hinchingbrooke and Lady Jemima, and there dined with them and my Lord—where pretty merry. And after dinner, my Lord Crew and Hinchingbrooke and myself went aside to discourse about my Lord Sandwich's business, which is in a very ill state for want of money; and so parted, and I to my tailor's and there took up my wife and Willet, who stayed there for me, and to the Duke of York's playhouse;[6] but the House so full, it being a new play *The Coffee-House*, that we could not get in, and so to the King's House; and there going in, met with Knepp and she took us up into the tiring-rooms and to the women's shift,[7] where Nell[8] was dressing herself and was all unready; and is very pretty, prettier than I thought; and so walked all up and down the house above, and then below into the scene-room, and there sat down and she gave us fruit; and here I read the Qu's[9] to Knepp while she answered me, through all her part of *Flora's Figarys*, which was acted today. But Lord, to see how they were both painted would make a man mad—and did make me loathe them—and what base company of men comes among them, and how lewdly they talk—and how poor the men are in clothes, and yet what a show they make on the stage by candlelight, is very

2. A commissioner on the Navy Board.
3. "They" are the Parliament investigators looking into the Board's (and Sandwich's) conduct during the Second Dutch War.
4. Dealing in goods imported from India.
5. Deborah Willett, recently hired as Elizabeth Pepys's companion.
6. There were only two licensed theater companies in Restoration London, one officially sponsored by the duke, the other by the king.
7. Attiring rooms; women's dressing room.
8. Nell Gwyn, a popular comic actress; she would later become the king's mistress.
9. Cues.

observable. But to see how Nell cursed for having so few people in the pit was pretty, the other house carrying away all the people at the new play, and is said nowadays to have generally most company, as being better players. By and by into the pit and there saw the play; which is pretty good, but my belly was full of what I had seen in the house; and so after the play done, away home and there to the writing my letters; and so home to supper and to bed.

[27 February 1668] All the morning at the office, and at noon home to dinner; and thence with my wife and Deb[1] to the King's House to see *Virgin Martyr*,[2] the first time it hath been acted a great while, and it is mighty pleasant; not that the play is worth much, but it is finely acted by Becke Marshall; but that which did please me beyond anything in the whole world was the wind-music when the angel comes down, which is so sweet that it ravished me; and indeed, in a word, did wrap up my soul so that it made me really sick, just as I have formerly been when in love with my wife; that neither then, nor all the evening going home and at home, I was able to think of anything, but remained all night transported, so as I could not believe that ever any music hath that real command over the soul of a man as this did upon me; and makes me resolve to practice wind-music and to make my wife do the like.

[20 January 1669], Up, and my wife and I and W. Hewer to White-hall, where she set us down. * * * Thence to my wife at Unthankes and with her and W. Hewer to Hercules-Pillars, calling to do two or three things by the way, and there dined; and thence to the Duke of York's House[3] and saw *Twelfth Night,* as it is now revived, but I think one of the weakest plays that ever I saw on the stage.[4] [This afternoon, before the play, I called with my wife at Dancre's[5] the great lanskip-painter, by Mr. Povy's advice, and have bespoke him to come to take measure of my dining-room panels; and there I met with the pretty daughter of the Coate-seller's that lived in Cheapside, and now in Covent-garden, who hath her picture drawn here, but very poorly; but she is a pretty woman, and now I perceive married, a very pretty black[6] woman.][7] So the play done, we home, my wife letting fall some words of her observing my eyes too mightily employed in the playhouse; meaning, upon women, which did vex me; but however, when we came home we were good friends; and so to read and to supper, and so to bed.

[Elizabeth Pepys and Deborah Willett]

[25 October 1668] *Lord's Day*. Up, and discoursing with my wife about our house and many new things we are doing of; and so to church I, and there find Jack Fen come, and his wife, a pretty black woman; I never saw her before, nor took notice of her now. So home and to dinner; and after dinner, all the afternoon got my wife and boy to read to me. And at night W. Batelier comes and sups with us; and after supper, to have my head combed by Deb, which occasioned the greatest sorrow to me that ever I knew in this world; for my wife, coming up suddenly, did find me embracing the girl con my

1. Deborah Willett.
2. A tragedy by Thomas Dekker and Philip Massinger, first performed c. 1620.
3. I.e., playhouse.
4. Pepys had already seen the play twice, and set down similar opinions both times: "the play [was] a burthen to me, and I took no pleasure at all in it" (11 September 1661); "saw *Twelfth Night* acted well, though it be but a silly play and not relating at all to the name or day"—i.e., to the Twelfth Night festivities celebrated on this date (6 January 1663).
5. Hendrick Danckerts, Dutch-born painter of portraits and landscapes.
6. Dark-haired.
7. Pepys squeezed these bracketed sentences into the margin of the entry's pages, as an afterthought.

hand sub su coats; and indeed, I was with my main in her cunny.[8] I was at a wonderful loss upon it, and the girl also; and I endeavored to put it off, but my wife was struck mute and grew angry, and as her voice came to her, grew quite out of order; and I do say little, but to bed; and my wife said little also, but could not sleep all night; but about 2 in the morning waked me and cried, and fell to tell me as a great secret that she was a Roman Catholic and had received the Holy Sacrament; which troubled me but I took no notice of it, but she went on from one thing to another, till at last it appeared plainly her trouble was at what she saw; but yet I did not know how much she saw and therefore said nothing to her. But after her much crying and reproaching me with inconstancy and preferring a sorry girl before her, I did give her no provocations but did promise all fair usage to her, and love, and foreswore any hurt that I did with her—till at last she seemed to be at ease again; and so toward morning, a little sleep; [26][9] and so I, with some little repose and rest, rose, and up and by water to Whitehall, but with my mind mightily troubled for the poor girl, whom I fear I have undone by this, my wife telling me that she would turn her out of door. However, I was obliged to attend the Duke of York, thinking to have had a meeting of Tangier today, but had not; but he did take me and Mr. Wren into his closet, and there did press me to prepare what I had to say upon the answers of my fellow-officers to his great letter; which I promised to do against his coming to town again the next week; and so to other discourse, finding plainly that he is in trouble and apprehensions of the reformers, and would be found to do what he can towards reforming himself.[1] And so thence to my Lord Sandwich; where after long stay, he being in talk with others privately, I to him; and there he taking physic and keeping his chamber, I had an hour's talk with him about the ill posture of things at this time, while the King gives countenance to Sir Charles Sedley and Lord Buckhurst,[2] telling him their late story of running up and down the streets a little while since all night, and their being beaten and clapped up all night by the constable, who is since chid and imprisoned for his pains.

He tells me that he thinks his matters do stand well with the King—and hopes to have dispatch to his mind; but I doubt it, and do see that he doth fear it too. He told me my Lady Carteret's trouble about my writing of that letter[3] of the Duke of York's lately to the office; which I did not own, but declared to be of no injury to G. Carteret, and that I would write a letter to him to satisfy him therein. But this I am in pain how to do without doing myself wrong, and the end I had, of preparing a justification to myself hereafter, when the faults of the Navy come to be found out. However, I will do it in the best manner I can.

Thence by coach home and to dinner, finding my wife mightily discontented and the girl sad, and no words from my wife to her. So after dinner, they out with me about two or three things; and so home again, I all the evening busy and my wife full of trouble in her looks; and anon to bed—where about midnight, she wakes me and there falls foul on me again, affirming that she saw me hug and kiss the girl; the latter I denied, and truly; the other I confessed and no more. And upon her pressing me,

8. I.e., with his hand under her petticoats and his hand in her vagina. Here as often, Pepys reports his illicit sexual activities in a "secret" language compounded of Latin, French, Spanish, and English.

9. Pepys wedges the new date into the margin, beside the run-on narrative.

1. The duke was Lord High Admiral of the navy; on his behalf Pepys had composed a letter to the Navy Board proposing reforms in response to parliamentary investigations of the disastrous Second Dutch War.

2. Notorious libertines (Buckhurst was Nell Gwyn's current lover).

3. The "great letter" on naval reform.

did offer to give her under my hand that I would never see Mrs. Pearse[4] more, nor Knepp, but did promise her particular demonstrations of my true love to her, owning some indiscretion in what I did, but that there was no harm in it. She at last on these promises was quiet, and very kind we were, and so to sleep; [27] and in the morning up, but with my mind troubled for the poor girl, with whom I could not get opportunity to speak; but to the office, my mind mighty full of sorrow for her, where all the morning, and to dinner with my people and to the office all the afternoon; and so at night home and there busy to get some things ready against tomorrow's meeting of Tangier; and that being done and my clerks gone, my wife did toward bedtime begin to be in a mighty rage from some new matter that she had got in her head, and did most part of the night in bed rant at me in most high terms, of threats of publishing my shame; and when I offered to rise, would have rose too, and caused a candle to be lit, to burn by her all night in the chimney while she ranted; while I, that knew myself to have given some grounds for it, did make it my business to appease her all I could possibly, and by good words and fair promises did make her very quiet; and so rested all night and rose with perfect good peace, being heartily afflicted for this folly of mine that did occasion it; but was forced to be silent about the girl, which I have no mind to part with, but much less that the poor girl should be undone by my folly. [28] So up, with mighty kindness from my wife and a thorough peace; and being up, did by a note advise the girl what I had done and owned, which note I was in pain for till she told me that she had burned it. This evening, Mr. Spong came and sat late with me, and first told me of the instrument called parrallogram, which I must have one of, showing me his practice thereon by a map of England.[5]

So by coach with Mr. Gibson[6] to Chancery Lane, and there made oath before a master of chancery to my Tangier account of fees; and so to Whitehall, where by and by a committee met; my Lord Sandwich there, but his report was not received, it being late; but only a little business done, about the supplying the place with victuals; but I did get, to my great content, my account allowed of fees, with great applause by my Lord Ashley and Sir W. Penn. Thence home, calling at one or two places, and there about our workmen, who are at work upon my wife's closet and other parts of my house, that we are all in dirt. So after dinner, with Mr. Gibson all the afternoon in my closet; and at night to supper and to bed, my wife and I at good peace, but yet with some little grudgings of trouble in her, and more in me, about the poor girl.

[14 November 1668] Up, and had a mighty mind to have seen or given a note to Deb or to have given her a little money; to which purpose I wrapped up 40s in a paper, thinking to give her; but my wife rose presently, and would not let me be out of her sight; and went down before me into the kitchen, and came up and told me that she was in the kitchen, and therefore would have me go round the other way; which she repeating, and I vexed at it, answered her a little angrily; upon which she instantly flew out into a rage, calling me dog and rogue, and that I had a rotten heart; all which, knowing that I deserved it, I bore with; and word being brought presently up that she was gone away by coach with her things, my wife was friends; and so all quiet, and I to the office with my heart sad, and find that I cannot forget the girl, and vexed I know not where to look for her—and more troubled to see how my wife is by this means likely for ever to have her hand over me, that I shall for ever be a slave to her;

4. Elizabeth Pearse, wife of a naval surgeon.
5. The parallelogram was a device for making copies of diagrams and maps on the same or on a different scale.
6. A favorite assistant of Pepys's.

that is to say, only in matters of pleasure, but in other things she will make her business, I know, to please me and to keep me right to her—which I will labor to be indeed, for she deserves it of me, though it will be I fear a little time before I shall be able to wear Deb out of my mind. At the office all the morning, and merry at noon at dinner; and after dinner to the office, where all the afternoon and doing much business late; my mind being free of all troubles, I thank God, but only for my thoughts of this girl, which hang after her. And so at night home to supper, and there did sleep with great content with my wife. I must here remember that I have lain with my moher[7] as a husband more times since this falling-out than in I believe twelve months before—and with more pleasure to her than I think in all the time of our marriage before.

[20 November 1668] This morning up, with mighty kind words between my poor wife and I; and so to Whitehall by water, W. Hewer with me, who is to go with me everywhere until my wife be in condition to go out along with me herself; for she doth plainly declare that she dares not trust me out alone, and therefore made it a piece of our league that I should alway take somebody with me, or her herself; which I am mighty willing to, being, by the grace of God resolved never to do her wrong more.[8]

We landed at the Temple, and there I did bid him call at my cousin Roger Pepys's lodgings, and I stayed in the street for him; and so took water again at the Strand stairs and so to Whitehall, in my way I telling him plainly and truly my resolutions, if I can get over this evil, never to give new occasion for it. He is, I think, so honest and true a servant to us both, and one that loves us, that I was not much troubled at his being privy to all this, but rejoiced in my heart that I had him to assist in the making us friends; which he did do truly and heartily, and with good success—for I did get him to go to Deb to tell her that I had told my wife all of my being with her the other night, that so, if my wife should send, she might not make the business worse by denying it. While I was at Whitehall with the Duke of York doing our ordinary business with him, here being also the first time the new treasurers, W. Hewer did go to her and come back again; and so I took him into St. James's Park, and there he did tell me he had been with her and found what I said about my manner of being with her true, and had given her advice as I desired. I did there enter into more talk about my wife and myself, and he did give me great assurance of several particular cases to which my wife had from time to time made him privy of her loyalty and truth to me after many and great temptations, and I believe them truly. I did also discourse the unfitness of my leaving of my employment now in many respects, to go into the country as my wife desires—but that I would labor to fit myself for it; which he thoroughly understands, and doth agree with me in it; and so, hoping to get over this trouble, we about our business to Westminster Hall to meet Roger Pepys; which I did, and did there discourse of the business of lending him 500*l* to answer some occasions of his, which I believe to be safe enough; and so took leave of him and away by coach home, calling on my coach-maker by the way, where I like my little coach mightily. But when I came home, hoping for a further degree of peace and quiet, I find my wife upon her bed in a horrible rage afresh, calling me all the bitter names; and rising, did

7. Spanish *mujer:* wife. For the first time, Pepys applies his secret language to Elizabeth.

8. Two nights earlier, Pepys had traced Deborah Willett to her new lodgings, and caressed her in his coach. The next day, Elizabeth told him that she knew about the assignation, and he signed a pledge "never to see or speak with Deb while I live."

fall to revile me in the bitterest manner in the world, and could not refrain to strike me and pull my hair; which I resolved to bear with, and had good reason to bear it. So I by silence and weeping did prevail with her a little to be quiet, and she would not eat her dinner without me; but yet by and by into a raging fit she fell again worse than before, that she would slit the girl's nose; and at last W. Hewer came in and came up, who did allay her fury, I flinging myself in a sad desperate condition upon the bed in the blue room, and there lay while they spoke together; and at last it came to this, that if I would call Deb "whore" under my hand,[9] and write to her that I hated her and would never see her more, she would believe me and trust in me—which I did agree to; only, as to the name of "whore" I would have excused, and therefore wrote to her sparing that word; which my wife thereupon tore it, and would not be satisfied till, W. Hewer winking upon me, I did write so, with the name of a whore, as that I did fear she might too probably have been prevailed upon to have been[1] a whore by her carriage to me, and therefore, as such, I did resolve never to see her more. This pleased my wife, and she gives it W. Hewer to carry to her, with a sharp message from her. So from that minute my wife begun to be kind to me, and we to kiss and be friends, and so continued all the evening and fell to talk of other matters with great comfort, and after supper to bed.

This evening comes Mr. Billup to me to read over Mr. Wren's alterations of my draft of a letter for the Duke of York to sign, to the board; which I like mighty well, they being not considerable, only in mollifying some hard terms which I had thought fit to put in. From this to other discourse; I do find that the Duke of York and his servant Mr. Wren do look upon this service of mine as a very seasonable service to the Duke of York, as that which he will have to show to his enemies in his own justification of his care of the King's business. And I am sure I am heartily glad of it—both for the King's sake and the Duke of York's, and my own also—for if I continue, my work, by this means, will be the less, and my share in the blame[2] also.

He being gone, I to my wife again and so spent the evening with very great joy, and the night also, with good sleep and rest, my wife only troubled in her rest, but less than usual—for which the God of Heaven be praised. I did this night promise to my wife never to go to bed without calling upon God upon my knees by prayer; and I begun this night, and hope I shall never forget to do the like all my life—for I do find that it is much the best for my soul and body to live pleasing to God and my poor wife—and will ease me of much care, as well as much expense.

[31 May 1669] Up very betimes, and so continued all the morning, with W. Hewer, upon examining and stating my accounts, in order to the fitting myself to go abroad beyond sea,[3] which the ill condition of my eyes, and my neglect for a year or two, hath kept me behindhand in, and so as to render it very difficult now, and troublesome to my mind to do it; but I this day made a satisfactory entrance therein.[4] Dined at home, and in the afternoon by water to Whitehall, calling by the way at Mitchell's,[5] where I have not been many a day till just the other day; and now I met her mother there and knew her husband to be out of town. And here yo did besar

9. In writing.
1. Become.
2. For Navy Board misconduct.
3. Pepys and his wife planned a tour of Holland, Flanders, and France. Near journey's end, Elizabeth Pepys caught a fever; she died in London on 10 November 1669.
4. Pepys suffered from a painful combination of farsightedness and astigmatism which doctors did not know how to diagnose or to treat; he feared (mistakenly) that he was going blind.
5. Michael Mitchell sold liquor in a shop on London Bridge; his wife Betty is the "her" of the ensuing clauses.

ella, but have not opportunity para hazer mas[6] with her as I would have offered if yo had had it. And thence had another meeting with the Duke of York at Whitehall with the Duke of York on yesterday's work, and made a good advance; and so being called by my wife, we to the park, Mary Batelier, a Dutch gentleman, a friend of hers, being with us. Thence to the World's End, a drinking-house by the park, and there merry; and so home late.

And thus ends all that I doubt I shall ever be able to do with my own eyes in the keeping of my journal, I being not able to do it any longer, having done now so long as to undo my eyes almost every time that I take a pen in my hand; and therefore, whatever comes of it, I must forbear; and therefore resolve from this time forward to have it kept by my people in longhand, and must therefore be contented to set down no more than is fit for them and all the world to know; or if there be anything (which cannot be much, now my amours to Deb are past, and my eyes hindering me in almost all other pleasures), I must endeavor to keep a margin in my book open, to add here and there a note in shorthand with my own hand.[7] And so I betake myself to that course which is almost as much as to see myself go into my grave—for which, and all the discomforts that will accompany my being blind, the good God prepare me.

May. 31. 1669. S.P.

RESPONSE

Robert Louis Stevenson (1850–1894): from *Samuel Pepys*[1]

Pepys was a young man for his age, came slowly to himself in the world, sowed his wild oats late, took late to industry, and preserved till nearly forty the headlong gusto of a boy. So, to come rightly at the spirit in which the Diary was written, we must recall a class of sentiments which with most of us are over and done before the age of twelve. In our tender years we still preserve a freshness of surprise at our prolonged existence; events make an impression out of all proportion to their consequence; we are unspeakably touched by our own past adventures, and look forward to our future personality with sentimental interest. It was something of this, I think, that clung to Pepys. Although not sentimental in the abstract, he was sweetly sentimental about himself. His own past clung about his heart, an evergreen. He was the slave of an association. He could not pass by Islington, where his father used to carry him to cakes and ale, but he must light at the "King's Head" and eat and drink "for rememberance

6. I did kiss her but had no chance to do more.

7. Pepys never produced the continuation of his journal that he envisions here.

1. Pepys's diary, written in the seventeenth century, made its way into print only in the nineteenth. Readers were at once fascinated by his distance from them in time and by what they regarded as his proximity to them in temperament; they resurrected him, as readers always will, partly in their own image. When a new, unprecedentedly full but still partly expurgated edition of the diary appeared in 1881, it was greeted with mixed emotion (praise for the fullness, exasperation at the expurgation) by a prolific literary journalist who would achieve his own global fame just a few years later: Robert Louis Stevenson. After a single paragraph, Stevenson's review of the edition gives way to a long, perceptive essay on the diarist, in whom he finds forecast many of the energies and endeavors that had preoccupied his own century: the self-absorbed self-revelations of the Romantics; a countervailing devotion to proto-Victorian "respectability"; and a recurrent, almost sensual devotion to the memories and pleasures of childhood that would soon mark much of Stevenson's own most enduring work: *Treasure Island*, *Kidnapped*, and *A Child's Garden of Verses* (1885). The essay first appeared in *Cornhill Magazine* 44 (July 1881).

of the old house sake." He counted it good fortune to lie at night at Epsom to renew his old walks, "where Mrs. Hely and I did use to walk and talk, with whom I had the first sentiments of love and pleasure in a woman's company, discourse and taking her by the hand, she being a pretty woman." He goes about weighing up the *Assurance*, which lay near Woolwich under water, and cries in a parenthesis, "Poor ship, that I have been twice merry in, in Captain Holland's time"; and after revisiting the *Naseby*, now changed into the *Charles*, he confesses "it was a great pleasure to myself to see the ship that I began my good fortune in." The stone that he was cut for[2] he preserved in a case; and to the Turners he kept alive such gratitude for their assistance that for years, and after he had begun to mount himself into higher zones, he continued to have that family to dinner on the anniversary of the operation. Not Hazlitt[3] nor Rousseau[4] had a more romantic passion for their past, although at times they might express it more romantically; and if Pepys shared with them this childish fondness, did not Rousseau, who left behind him the *Confessions*, or Hazlitt, who wrote the *Liber Amoris*, and loaded his essays with loving personal detail, share with Pepys in his unwearied egotism? For the two things go hand in hand; or, to be more exact, it is the first that makes the second either possible or pleasing.

But, to be quite in sympathy with Pepys, we must return once more to the experience of children. I can remember to have written, in the flyleaf of more than one book, the date and the place where I was then—if, for instance, I was ill in bed or sitting in a certain garden; these were jottings for my future self; if I should chance on such a note in after years, I thought it would cause me a particular thrill to recognize myself across the intervening distance. Indeed, I might come upon them now, and not be moved one tittle—which shows that I have comparatively failed in life, and grown older than Samuel Pepys. For in the Diary we can find more than one such note of perfect childish egotism; as when he explains that his candle is going out, "which makes me write thus slobberingly"; or as in this incredible particularity, "To my study, where I only wrote thus much of this day's passages to this,[5] and so out again"; or lastly, as here, with more of circumstance: "I staid up till the bellman came by with his bell under my window, *as I was writing of this very line*, and cried, 'Past one of the clock, and a cold, frosty, windy morning.'" Such passages are not to be misunderstood. The appeal to Samuel Pepys years hence is unmistakable. He desires that dear, though unknown, gentleman keenly to realize his predecessor; to remember why a passage was uncleanly written; to recall (let us fancy, with a sigh) the tones of the bellman, the chill of the early, windy morning, and the very line his own romantic self was scribing at the moment. The man, you will perceive, was making reminiscences—a sort of pleasure by ricochet, which comforts many in distress, and turns some others into sentimental libertines: and the whole book, if you will but look at it in that way, is seen to be a work of art to[6] Pepys's own address.

Here, then, we have the key to that remarkable attitude preserved by him throughout his Diary, to that unflinching—I had almost said, that unintelligent—sincerity which makes it a miracle among human books. * * *

1881

2. See Pepys's first diary entry, p. 2011.
3. William Hazlitt (1778–1830), journalist, essayist, critic, and author of *Liber Amoris* (1823), an autobiographical account of his feverish, futile love affair with his landlady's daughter.
4. Jean-Jacques Rousseau (1712–1788), political philosopher, novelist, and author of the matchlessly unabashed and copious autobiography *Confessions* (1781).
5. I.e., to this point in the entry.
6. I.e., posted to.

PERSPECTIVES

The Royal Society and the New Science

In the late 1600s, the antiquarian John Aubrey looked back to the middle of his century as a turning point in intellectual history: "Till about the year 1649, when experimental philosophy was first cultivated by a club at Oxford, 'twas held a strange presumption for a man to attempt an innovation in learnings; and not to be good manners, to be more knowing than his neighbors and forefathers." The "club" consisted of a group of inquirers for whom the university at Oxford offered a place of retreat in time of civil war. As Aubrey implies, their "innovation" consisted in a kind of bad manners. They refused to take the word of their intellectual "forefathers" (notably Aristotle) for how the natural world worked, and instead pursued knowledge of it through direct experiment, preferring new data to old theory, the testimony of the senses over the constructs of the intellect; the works of Francis Bacon, who had articulated such a method a half-century earlier, served for these investigators as something akin to scripture. The members continued to meet during the Interregnum. In 1662, Charles II granted the group (which had relocated to London) a charter, a seal, and with his patronage, a new prominence. The informal club had become the "Royal Society for the Improving of Natural Knowledge."

That "Improving" was to take place on many fronts. The Society's charter stipulated that its experiments should be aimed at "promoting the knowledge of natural things and useful arts": science and technology. In its first decades, its members made enormous advances in both realms, producing (among innumerable innovations) new explanations of heat, cold, and light; an air pump capable of creating a vacuum; a newly efficient pocket watch; and a newly coherent and durable account of the universe. A Fellow of the Society might work simultaneously at many endeavors that have since become specialties, investigating biology, physics, and astronomy, inventing scientific instruments and domestic appliances, advancing inquiries into theology, astrology, even demonology.

The group liked to portray itself as inclusive demographically too. Its Fellows represented many religious views, political persuasions, and social strata, from dukes to merchants to "mechanicks." Still, the early records evince an initial emphasis on high rank: aristocrats, courtiers, politicians, and "gentlemen" made up more than half the original membership (women were excluded altogether). Many of these men were mere names on the rolls, enlisted to bolster the respectability of the new enterprise; others were occasional spectators, intermittently attending the meetings to observe (amused, amazed, often baffled) the experiments performed there. But the Society also fostered a new category of inquirer: the "Christian virtuoso," a man of birth, means, merit, brains, and leisure, whose dissociation from any one profession was taken to guarantee the objectivity of his investigations, and whose rank and goodness underwrote the integrity of his findings. The Honorable Robert Boyle, who coined the phrase, was also its epitome. Well-born, devout, and dazzlingly gifted at science, he was the Society's prime mover and first star. But the type also found a less rarified, more popular incarnation in a new kind of amateur: the prosperous person who read, contemplated, talked the new philosophy, and kept a "cabinet of curiosities"—a closet or small room in which were arranged, and proudly displayed, antiquarian objects, scientific specimens, anything whose strangeness might arouse interest. The Society was amassing comparable collections on a much larger scale; the history of museums begins within the cabinets of the virtuosi.

The Society's emphasis on gentlemanly virtuosity was partly a form of self-defense against attacks from many quarters, where the "experimental philosophy" was regarded as ludicrous or dangerous or both. The influential wits of the day scoffed at the earnestness of the investigators and the seeming preposterousness of their findings (even Charles II laughed out loud when he learned that the members were busy weighing air); some clergymen and politicians saw in the new enterprise a threat to religion and to social hierarchy, a challenge against past, present, and divine authority, mounted by persons so presumptuous as to suppose that the truths of the world could be determined by human investigation rather than by Christian revelation.

The Society answered (again in the language of its charter) that it was intent upon serving "the glory of God and the good of mankind." The "good of mankind" was to be enhanced by technological improvements, which would make work more productive, life easier, and commerce more abundant, in contrast to the dark old days when (as Aubrey reminisces) "even to attempt an improvement in husbandry [agriculture], though it succeeded with profit, was looked upon with an ill eye." The "glory of God" would be served by a new form of attention to the world God made. A long tradition ascribed to the Deity two sacred texts: the Book of Scripture, and the Book of Nature. The faithful had long pondered the first; the Society now undertook to read the second anew and aright. "Each page in the great volume of nature," observed Boyle, "is full of real hieroglyphs, where (by an inverted way of expression) things stand for words"—objects and actions incarnate truths. To disclose the divine intricacy in the Book of Nature (so the Society's advocates argued) could only enlarge wonder and increase worship.

The new reading of that old text reshaped other texts as well. In the 1660s and after, manuscripts, periodicals, and printed books all explored new forms, as writers attempted to render in language what Michel Foucault has called "the prose of the world," to grapple with new relations between words and things, and to make the written or the printed page (like the closet and the cabinet) a copious repository of newfound curiosities.

Thomas Sprat
1635–1713

Given the date of its first appearance, the *History of the Royal Society* seems puzzlingly titled. The Oxford-educated clergyman Thomas Sprat wrote much of it in 1663, just a year after the Society received its charter, and published it (after delays caused by fire, plague, and other distractions) in 1667. Both title and timing reflect the pressures that produced the book in the first place. As he acknowledges at the outset, Sprat has produced not so much a "plain history" of the Society as an "apology," in the Greek-based sense of the word current in the seventeenth century: an energetic defense of the new institution's policies and methods.

From its inception, the Society's directors felt the need for such a defense, and they brought Sprat in specifically to provide it, appointing him a Founding Fellow and anxiously inquiring after his progress on the book. They had chosen him not for his knowledge of science (negligible) but for his status as a divine and for his skill as a rhetorician. In response to its detractors, Sprat insists that the Society will enhance piety (by detailing the wonders of Creation); will uphold hierarchy (as evidenced by the predominance of gentlemen and aristocrats among the Fellowship); and will cultivate community (in order to appease fears that the Fellows will revive "disputation" when the new Restoration needs it least, Sprat downplays the importance of argument in the new science and stresses instead the accumulation of raw data). Above all, Sprat focuses on the Society's capacity to improve ordinary life by producing "new inventions and shorter ways of labor" that will make possible an easier and more prosperous existence for the English, whose national "Genius" is uniquely suited to such advances.

As Michael Hunter notes, Sprat's "generalized attempt to appeal to everybody and antagonize nobody" fell short. It appealed mainly to adherents, and provided critics with a new target for their attacks. In the selection printed here, Sprat navigates a particularly delicate portion of his argument. He sets forth the Fellows' attempts to simplify the prose style in which they wrote up their inquiries and discoveries. The degree to which the Society actually sought and managed to implement a new "mathematical plainness" has long remained a matter of dispute. In contemporary writing, clarity and "ornament" were often seen as mutually supportive; even when Sprat is arguing for a "naked" prose, he intermittently resorts to the very "amplifications, digressions, and swellings of style" that he is ruling out. As its sponsors intended, Sprat's *History* applies a polished rhetoric to a pointed claim: that the Royal Society was creating a "common-stock" of knowledge on which all might draw, and from which all might profit.

from The History of the Royal Society of London, for the Improving of Natural Knowledge

Thus they have directed, judged, conjectured upon, and improved experiments. But lastly, in these and all other businesses that have come under their care, there is one thing more about which the Society has been most solicitous, and that is the manner of their discourse, which unless they have been watchful to keep in due temper, the whole spirit and vigor of their design had been soon eaten out by the luxury and redundance of speech. The ill effects of this superfluity of talking have already overwhelmed most other arts and professions, insomuch that when I consider the means of happy living and the causes of their corruption, I can hardly forbear recanting what I said before, and concluding that eloquence ought to be banished out of all civil societies as a thing fatal to peace and good manners. To this opinion I should wholly incline, if I did not find that it is a weapon which may be as easily procured by bad men as good, and that, if these should only cast it away and those retain it, the naked innocence of virtue would be upon all occasions exposed to the armed malice of the wicked. This is the chief reason that should now keep up the ornaments of speaking in any request, since they are so much degenerated from their original usefulness. They were at first, no doubt, an admirable instrument in the hands of wise men, when they were only employed to describe goodness, honesty, obedience, in larger, fairer, and more moving images; to represent truth, clothed with bodies; and to bring knowledge back again to our very senses, from whence it was at first derived to our understandings. But now they are generally changed to worse uses. They make the fancy disgust[1] the best things, if they come sound and unadorned. They are in open defiance against reason, professing not to hold much correspondence with that, but with its slaves, the passions. They give the mind a motion too changeable and bewitching to consist with right practice. Who can behold, without indignation, how many mists and uncertainties these specious tropes and figures[2] have brought on our knowledge? How many rewards, which are due to more profitable and difficult arts, have been still snatched away by the easy vanity of fine speaking? For now I am warmed with this just anger, I cannot withhold myself from betraying the shallowness of all these seeming mysteries upon which we writers and speakers look so big. And, in few words, I dare say that of all the studies of men, nothing may be sooner obtained than this vicious abundance of phrase, this trick of metaphors, this volubility of tongue, which makes so great a noise in the world. But I spend words in vain; for the evil is now so inveterate that it is hard to know whom to blame or where to begin to reform. We all value one another so much upon this beautiful deceit and labor so long after it in the years of our education that we cannot but ever after think kinder of it than it deserves. And indeed, in most other

1. They make the imagination reject.

2. Figures of speech.

parts of learning, I look on it to be a thing almost utterly desperate in its cure. And I think it may be placed amongst those general mischiefs such as the dissension of Christian princes,[3] the want[4] of practice in religion and the like, which have been so long spoken against, that men are become insensible about them, every one shifting off the fault from himself to others, and so they are only made bare commonplaces of complaint. It will suffice my present purpose to point out what has been done by the Royal Society towards the correcting of its[5] excesses in natural philosophy, to which it is, of all others, a most professed enemy.

They have therefore been most rigorous in putting in execution the only remedy that can be found for this extravagance. And that has been a constant resolution to reject all the amplifications, digressions, and swellings of style; to return back to the primitive purity and shortness, when men delivered so many *things*, almost in an equal number of *words*. They have exacted from all their members a close, naked, natural way of speaking; positive expressions; clear senses; a native easiness; bringing all things as near the mathematical plainness as they can and preferring the language of artisans, countrymen, and merchants before that of wits or scholars.[6]

And here there is one thing not to be passed by, which will render this established custom of the Society well nigh everlasting; and that is, the general constitution of the minds of the English. I have already often insisted on some of the prerogatives of England, whereby it may justly lay claim to be the head of a philosophical league, above all other countries in Europe. I have urged its situation,[7] its present genius, and the disposition of its merchants, and many more such arguments to encourage us still remain to be used. But of all others, this, which I am now alleging, is of the most weighty and important consideration. If there can be a true character given of the universal temper of any nation under heaven, then certainly this must be ascribed to our countrymen: that they have commonly an unaffected sincerity; that they love to deliver their minds with a sound simplicity; that they have the middle qualities between the reserved, subtle southern and the rough, unhewn northern people; that they are not extremely prone to speak; that they are more concerned what others will think of the strength, than of the fineness of what they say; and that an universal modesty possesses them. These qualities are so conspicuous and proper to our soil that we often hear them objected to us by some of our neighbor satirists in more disgraceful expressions. For they are wont to revile the English with a want of familiarity; with a melancholy dumpishness,[8] with slowness, silence, and with the unrefined sullenness of their behavior. But these are only the reproaches of partiality or ignorance. For they ought rather to be commended for an honorable integrity; for a neglect of circumstances and flourishes; for regarding things of greater moment,[9] more than less; for a scorn to deceive as well as to be deceived, which are all the best endowments that can enter into a philosophical mind. So that even the position of our climate, the air, the influence of the heaven, the composition of the English blood, as well as the embraces of the ocean, seem to join with the labors of the Royal Society to render our country a land of experimental

3. Disputes between Christian monarchs.
4. Lack.
5. I.e., eloquence's.
6. For a parody of this position, see Swift's depiction of the Academy in *Gulliver's Travels*, Part 3. ch.5.
7. I.e., its location. Sprat has earliler emphasized that England's status as an island, and as "mistress of the Ocean," gives it a privileged position from which to supervise international scientific experiments and correspondence.
8. Tendency to depression.
9. Importance.

knowledge. And it is a good sign that nature will reveal more of its secrets to the English than to others because it has already furnished them with a genius so well proportioned for the receiving and retaining its mysteries.

And now to come to a close of the second part of the narration. The Society has reduced its principal observations into one common-stock[1] and laid them up in public registers to be nakedly transmitted to the next generation of men, and so from them to their successors. And as their purpose was to heap up a mixed mass of experiments, without digesting them into any perfect model, so to this end, they confined themselves to no order of subjects; and whatever they have recorded, they have done it, not as complete schemes of opinions, but as bare, unfinished histories.

Philosophical Transactions

Philosophical Transactions first appeared in 1665 and continues to the present day; it is the longest running periodical in English and the oldest scientific journal in the world. It was created by Henry Oldenburg (1618–1677), a German-born diplomat who came to England in 1653 as an emissary to Oliver Cromwell and found himself powerfully drawn to the ideas and the company of the practitioners of the new science at Oxford. His gift for copious, accurate reporting on scientific matters prompted the Royal Society to enlist him as Fellow and Secretary, charged with attending the meetings, keeping the minutes, and managing the new institution's huge correspondence with scientific inquirers in England and abroad. Oldenburg produced the monthly *Transactions* as a private venture, but he drew its material from the documents in which his Society work immersed him, particularly from the correspondence that provided so plentiful an account (in the words of the journal's subtitle) "of the present undertakings, studies, and labors of the ingenious in many considerable parts of the world." The *Transactions*' content ranged wide conceptually as well as geographically, readily shifting from systematic searches for natural laws, to reports on technological innovations, to eager surmises about random oddities: monstrous births, human and otherwise, were a recurrent favorite. The new journal combined in text the attractions of the scientific treatise and the cabinet of curiosities; the insatiable curiosity of the journal's most assiduous contributor, Oldenburg's patron Robert Boyle, helped to ensure this variety and texture.

More than any other instrument, the *Transactions* established the Royal Society as central to the new philosophy and fostered the conviction that the advancement of learning was a communal pursuit of truth to which (as Francis Bacon had predicted) everyone from a mariner to a virtuoso could contribute indispensable information. The *Transactions* influenced nonscientific journalism as well: with its topical headlines, variegated matter, and detailed tables of contents, it resembled no periodical of its time, but many that came after.

from Philosophical Transactions
[The Introduction][1]

Whereas there is nothing more necessary for promoting the improvement of philosophical matters than the communicating, to such as apply their studies and

1. Property and resource for the use of all.

1. This and the following two selections appeared in Vol 1., No.1, 6 March 1665.

endeavors that way, such things as are discovered or put in practice by others, it is therefore thought fit to employ the press as the most proper way to gratify those whose engagement in such studies and delight in the advancement of learning and profitable discoveries doth entitle them to the knowledge of what this kingdom or other parts of the world do from time to time afford, as well of the progress of the studies, labors, and attempts of the curious and learned in things of this kind, as of their complete discoveries and performances. To the end that, such productions being clearly and truly communicated, desires after solid and useful knowledge may be further entertained, ingenious endeavors and undertakings cherished, and those addicted to and conversant in such matters may be invited and encouraged to search, try, and find out new things, impart their knowledge to one another, and contribute what they can to the grand design of improving natural knowledge and perfecting all philosophical arts and sciences. All for the glory of God, the honor and advantage of these kingdoms, and the universal good of mankind.

* * *

An Account of a Very Odd Monstrous Calf

By the same noble person[2] was lately communicated to the Royal Society an account of a very odd, monstrous birth produced at Limmington in Hampshire, where a butcher, having caused a cow (which calved her first calf the year before) to be covered that she might the sooner be fatted, killed her when fat, and opening the womb, which he found heavy to admiration, saw in it a calf, which had begun to have hair, whose hinderlegs had no joints and whose tongue was, Cerebus-like,[3] triple—to each side of his mouth one, and one in the midst. Between the forelegs and the hinderlegs was a great stone, on which the calf rid.[4] The *sternum*, or that part of the breast where the ribs lie, was also perfect stone. And the stone on which it rid weighed twenty pounds and a half. The outside of the stone was of greenish color, but some small parts being broken off, it appeared a perfect free-stone. The stone, according to the letter of Mr. David Thomas, who sent this account to Mr. Boyle, is with Dr. Haughten of Salisbury, to whom he also refers for further information.

* * *

An observation imparted to the noble Mr. Boyle by Mr. David Thomas touching some particulars further considerable in the monster mentioned in the first papers of these Philosophical Transactions.[5]

Upon the strictest inquiry, I find by one that saw the monstrous calf and stone, within four hours after it was cut out of the cow's belly, that the breast of the calf was not stony (as I wrote) but that the skin of the breast and between the legs and of the neck (which parts lay on the smaller end of the stone) was very much thicker than on any other part, and that the feet of the calf were so parted as to be like the claws of a dog. The stone I have since seen. It is bigger at one end than the other, of no plain *superficies*,[6] but full of little cavities. The stone, when broken, is full of

2. Robert Boyle.
3. Resembling the mythical three-headed dog that guarded the entrance to Hades, the underworld of the dead.
4. Rode (i.e., straddled).
5. A "follow-up" from Vol. 1, No. 2.
6. Smooth surface.

small pebble stones of an oval figure. Its color is gray—like free-stone, but intermixed with veins of yellow and black. A part of it I have begged of Dr. Haughten for you, which I have sent to Oxford, whither a more exact account will be conveyed by the same person.

* * *

A letter of the honorable Robert Boyle of Sept. 13, 1673, to the publisher concerning Amber Greece and its being a vegetable production[7]

Sir,

Some occasions calling me this afternoon up to London, I was met there with a very intelligent gentleman, who was ready to go out of it. But before he did so, he willingly spared me some time to discourse with him about some of the affairs of our East Indian Company,[8] of which he was very lately Deputy Governor, and, his year being expired, is still one of the chief of the Court of Committees, which a foreigner would call Directors that manage all the affairs of that considerable society. And among other things, talking with him about some contents of a journal lately taken in a Dutch East Indian prize,[9] I learned from him that he, who understands that language very well, is now perusing that manuscript; and among many things recorded there that concern the economical and political affairs of the said Dutch company, he met with one physical observation which he thought so rare that, remembering the curiosity I had expressed for such things, he put it into English and transcribed it for me; and immediately drawing it out of his pocket, he presented me the short paper, whereof I now show you the copy. Upon perusal of which, you will very easily believe, that not only his civility obliged me, but the information it brought me surprised me too. For the several trials and observations of my own about amber greece have long kept me from acquiescing either in the vulgar opinions[1] or those of some learned men concerning it. Yet I confess, my experiments did much less discover what it is than this paper has done, in case we may safely and entirely give credit to its information, and that it reach to all kinds of amber greece. And probably you will be invited to look on this account, though not as complete, yet as very sincere, and on that score credible if you consider that this was not written by a philosopher to broach[2] a paradox or serve a hypothesis, but by a merchant or factor[3] for his superiors to give them an account of a matter of fact. And that this passage is extant in an authentic journal, wherein the affairs of the company were by public order from time to time registered at their chief colony Batavia.[4] And it appears by the paper itself that the relation was not looked upon as a doubtful thing, but as a thing from which a practical way may be deduced to make this discovery easily lucriferous[5] to the Dutch Company. And I could heartily wish that in those countries that are addicted to long navigations, more notice than is usual were taken and given of the natural rarities

7. Ambergris (Latin, "gray amber") is a gray waxy substance formed in the intestines of sperm whales; it was valued as a component in perfumes and medicines. Because ambergris, once emitted by the whale, often floats along the sea coast, traders and scientists were uncertain about its orgins. (Boyle's letter appeared in Vol. 8 No. 97).
8. A company chartered by Elizabeth 1 in 1600 to develop trade with India and the Far East.
9. I.e., the ship's log of a Dutch trading vessel recently captured by the English.
1. Received ideas of ordinary people.
2. Penetrate, untangle.
3. Company agent. Boyle reaffirms the Royal Society's interest in raw data over cooked theory, in the testimony of experienced "mechanics" over that of abstract "philosophers."
4. A seaport on the island of Java.
5. Profitable.

that occur to merchants and seamen. On which occasion I remember when I had in compliance with my curiosity put myself into our East Indian Company and had by their civility to me been chosen of their Committee as long as my health allowed me to continue so, I had the opportunity in some register books of merchants English and Dutch to observe some things which would easily justify this wish of mine, if my haste and their interest would permit me to acquaint others with them. But to return to our account of amber greece I think you will easily believe that if I had received it not by a paper but immediately from the writer,[6] I should by proposing diverse questions, have been enabled to give you a much more satisfactory account than this short one contains. But the obliging person that gave it me, being just going out of town, I could not civilly stay him to receive my queries about it, which though (God permitting) I may propose ere long, if I can light on him again, yet I fear he has given me in these few lines all that he found about this matter. However, this relation, as short as it is, being about the nature of a drug so precious and so little known will not, I hope, be unwelcome to the curious. To whom none is so like to convey it so soon and so well as Mr. O,[7] whose forwardness to oblige others by his various communications challenges returns of the like nature from others and particularly from his affectionate humble servant.

Follows the extract itself out of a Dutch journal belonging to the Dutch East Indian Company:

> Amber greece is not the scum or excrement of the whale, etc., but issues out of the root of a tree, which tree how far soever it stands on the land, always shoots forth its roots towards the sea, seeking the warmth of it, thereby to deliver the fattest gum that comes out of it, which tree otherwise by its copious fatness might be burnt and destroyed. Wherever that fat gum is shot into the sea, it is so tough that it is not easily broken from the root, unless its own weight and the working of the warm sea doth it,[8] and so it floats on the sea.
>
> There was found by a soldier 7/8 of a pound and by the chief two pieces weighing five pounds. If you plant the trees where the stream sets to the shore, then the stream will cast it up to great advantage. March 1, 1672, in Batavia.

Robert Hooke

1635–1703

In a long life, Robert Hooke got little sleep. From the age of twenty-eight until his death, he lived in rooms at Gresham College, the Royal Society headquarters, in order to make himself maximally available to meet the ceaseless demands of his many concurrent employments, as the Society's first Curator of Experiments, as the College's lecturer in geometry, as surveyor and rebuilder of London after the Great Fire, and as restless, relentless inventor and improver of scientific instruments. Hooke's friend John Aubrey described him as "the greatest mechanick this day in the world"; the jostle between the high superlative and the equivocal noun captures Hooke's uncertain status in the Society to which he devoted his prodigiously productive working life. The mechanical arts were in many ways the lifeblood of the Society's enterprise,

6. I.e., in conversation.
7. Henry Oldenburg, editor of the *Transactions*.
8. I.e., breaks it off.

but "mechanicks" were not gentry. In an institution founded and headed by aristocrats and gentlemen, this gifted son of a provincial clergyman was often treated (in Stephen Shapin's words) "as a tradesman, as a servant." Hooke's contract as Curator required that he prepare and perform "three or four substantial experiments" at each of the Society's weekly meetings, as well as any other experiments the Fellows might (in the recurrent wording of the meeting minutes) "order" or "direct" him to undertake. The empirical life of the Society during its first four decades would have been unimaginable without Hooke, but the Fellows registered his indispensability by irritation at the outside interests through which he pursued autonomy and income. "I could wish," wrote Sir Robert Moray, "he had finished the task laid upon him rather than to learn a dozen trades." Hooke's variegated pursuits, though, produced dozens of inventions and discoveries: newly efficient lenses, lamps, telescopes, watches; new theories of optics, chemistry, and gravity that in some cases anticipated Issac Newton's. Constitutionally irascible, Hooke spent much energy asserting, angrily but often accurately, the priority and/or superiority of his many innovations.

Hooke produced *Micrographia* at the Society's behest. The book doubled as a work of science and a piece of institutional propaganda, designed to promote the Society's methods. It fulfilled both purposes. In Hooke's sixty word-and-picture "Observations" of magnified objects, readers could see for the first time how far the useful artifice of the microscope had extended the "knowledge of natural things" into realms unreachable by the eye and mind alone. At the same time, the book touched a cultural pulse point. At its Greek root, Hooke's title suggests "the writing down of small things," and this is what many of his fellow Fellows—Pepys, Oldenburg, Evelyn, Aubrey—were in their different ways newly up to. (Pepys thought *Micrographia* "the most ingenious book that I ever read in my life.") Small things, it had been discovered, could produce large amazements when written up.

from Micrographia

Or Some Physiological Description of Minute Bodies Made by Magnifying Glasses with Observations and Inquiries thereupon

To the King

Sir,

I do here most humbly lay this small present at your Majesty's royal feet. And though it comes accompanied with two disadvantages, the meanness of the author and of the subject; yet in both I am encouraged by the greatness of your mercy and your knowledge. By the one I am taught, that you can forgive the most presumptuous offenders. And by the other, that you will not esteem the least work of nature or art unworthy of your observation. Amidst the many felicities that have accompanied your Majesty's happy restoration and government, it is none of the least considerable that philosophy and experimental learning have prospered under your royal patronage.[1] And as the calm prosperity of your reign has given us the leisure to follow these studies of quiet and retirement, so it is just that the fruits of them should, by way of acknowledgment, be returned to your Majesty. There are, Sir, several other of your subjects, of your Royal Society, now busy about nobler matters: the improvement of manufactures and agriculture, the increase of commerce, the advantage of navigation—in all which they are assisted by your Majesty's encouragement and example. Amidst all those greater designs, I here presume to bring in that which is

1. Charles II had granted the Society a royal charter in 1662.

more proportional to the smallness of my abilities and to offer some of the least of all visible things to that mighty king that has established an empire over the best of all invisible things of this world, the minds of men. Your Majesty's most humble and most obedient subject and servant,

Robert Hooke

TO THE ROYAL SOCIETY

After my address to our great founder and patron, I could not but think myself obliged, in consideration of those many engagements you have laid upon me, to offer these my poor labors to this most illustrious assembly. You have been pleased formerly to accept of these rude drafts.[2] I have since added to them some descriptions and some conjectures of my own. And therefore, together with your acceptance, I must also beg your pardon. The rules you have prescribed yourselves in your philosophical progress do seem the best that have ever yet been practiced. And particularly that of avoiding dogmatizing and the espousal of any hypothesis not sufficiently grounded and confirmed by experiments. This way seems the most excellent and may preserve both philosophy and natural history from its former corruptions. In saying which, I may seem to condemn my own course in this treatise, in which there may perhaps be some expressions, which may seem more positive than your prescriptions will permit. And though I desire to have them understood only as conjectures and queries (which your method does not altogether disallow) yet if even in those I have exceeded, 'tis fit that I should declare that it was not done by your directions. For it is most unreasonable that you should undergo the imputation of the faults of my conjectures, seeing you can receive so small advantage of reputation by the slight observations of Your most humble and most faithful servant,

Robert Hooke

from ***The Preface***

[A]ll the uncertainty and mistakes of human actions proceed either from the narrowness and wandering of our senses, from the slipperiness or delusion of our memory, from the confinement or rashness of our understanding, so that 'tis no wonder that our power over natural causes and effects is so slowly improved, seeing we are not only to contend with the obscurity and difficulty of the things whereon we work and think, but even the forces of our own minds conspire to betray us.

These being the dangers in the process of human reason, the remedies of them all can only proceed from the real, the mechanical, the experimental philosophy, which has this advantage over the philosophy of discourse and disputation, that whereas that chiefly aims at the subtlety of its deductions and conclusions, without much regard to the first groundwork, which ought to be well laid on the sense and memory, so this intends the right ordering of them all and the making them serviceable to each other.

The first thing to be undertaken in this weighty work is a watchfulness over the failings and an enlargement of the dominion of the senses.

To which end it is requisite, first, that there should be a scrupulous choice and a strict examination of the reality, constancy, and certainty of the particulars that we

2. Hooke had originally drawn many of the book's illustrations for use in the public presentation of experiments, which, as the Society's Curator of Experiments, he was obliged to perform regularly.

admit.[3] This is the first rise[4] whereon truth is to begin, and here the most severe and most impartial diligence must be employed. The storing up of all, without any regard to evidence or use, will only tend to darkness and confusion. We must not therefore esteem the riches of our philosophical treasure by the number only, but chiefly by the weight. The most vulgar instances[5] are not to be neglected, but above all, the most instructive are to be entertained.[6] The footsteps of Nature are to be traced, not only in her ordinary course, but when she seems to be put to her shifts,[7] to make many doublings and turnings, and to use some kind of art in endeavoring to avoid our discovery.

The next care to be taken, in respect of the senses, is a supplying of their infirmities with instruments, and as it were, the adding of artificial organs to the natural; this in one of them has been of late years accomplished with prodigious benefit to all sorts of useful knowledge by the invention of optical glasses. By the means of telescopes, there is nothing so far distant but may be represented to our view; and by the help of microscopes, there is nothing so small as to escape our inquiry; hence there is a new visible world discovered to the understanding. By this means the heavens are opened, and a vast number of new stars and new motions and new productions appear in them to which all the ancient astronomers were utterly strangers. By this the earth itself, which lies so near us under our feet, shows quite a new thing to us; and in every little particle of its matter, we now behold almost as great a variety of creatures as we were able before to reckon up in the whole universe itself. * * *

I here present to the world my imperfect endeavors, which though they shall prove no other way considerable, yet I hope they may be in some measure useful to the main design of a reformation in philosophy, if it be only by showing that there is not so much required towards it any strength of imagination or exactness of method or depth of contemplation (though the addition of these, where they can be had, must needs produce a much more perfect composure) as[8] a sincere hand and a faithful eye to examine and to record the things themselves as they appear.

And I beg my reader to let me take the boldness to assure him that in this present condition of knowledge, a man so qualified as I have endeavored to be, only with resolution and integrity and plain intentions of employing his senses aright, may venture to compare the reality and the usefulness of his services towards the true philosophy with those of other men that are of much stronger and more acute speculations that shall not make uses of the same method by the senses. * * *

from *Observation 1. Of the Point of a Sharp Small Needle*

As in geometry, the most natural way of beginning is from a mathematical point, so is the same method in observations and natural history the most genuine, simple, and instructive. We must first endeavor to make letters, and draw single strokes true, before we venture to write whole sentences, or to draw large pictures. And in physical inquiries, we must endeavor to follow Nature in the more plain and easy ways she treads in the most simple and uncompounded bodies, to trace her steps, and be acquainted with her manner of walking there, before we venture ourselves into the multitude of meanders she has in bodies of a more complicated nature; lest, being

3. I.e., as experimental data.
4. Elevation (with "truth" imagined as a progressive ascent).
5. Familiar particulars.
6. Considered.
7. Up to her tricks.
8. But only.

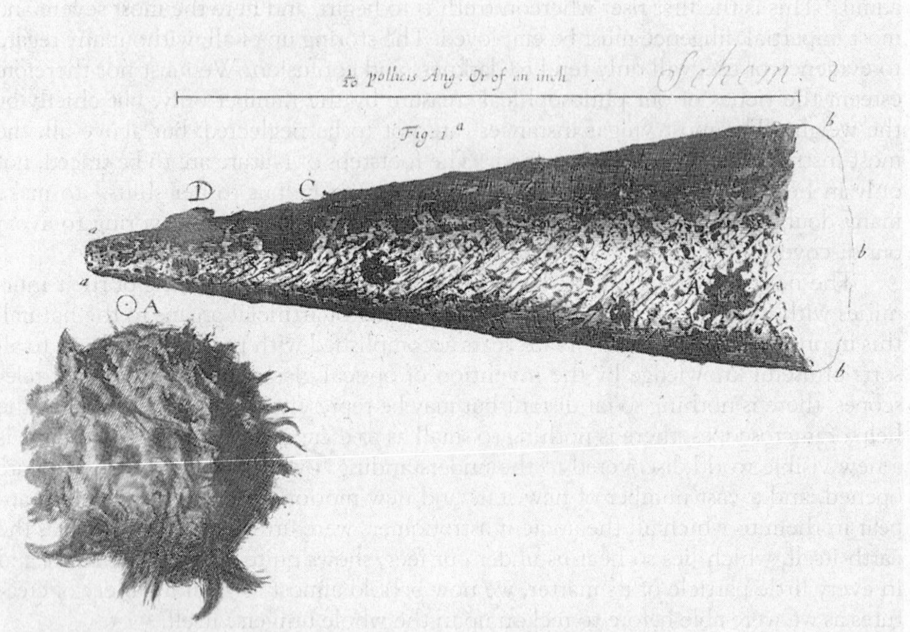

Robert Hooke, *Schema ii: Needle Point and Period,* from *Micrographia,* 1665.

unable to distinguish and judge of our way, we quickly lose both Nature our guide, and ourselves too, and are left to wander in the labyrinth of groundless opinions; wanting both judgment, that light, and experience, that clue, which should direct our proceedings.

We will begin these our inquiries therefore with the observations of bodies of the most simple nature first, and so gradually proceed to those of a more compounded one. In prosecution of which method, we shall begin with a physical point; of which kind the point of a needle is commonly reckoned for one, and is indeed, for the most part, made so sharp, that the naked eye cannot distinguish any parts of it. It very easily pierces and makes its way through all kinds of bodies softer than itself. But if viewed with a very good microscope, we may find that the top of a needle (though as to the sense very sharp) appears a broad, blunt, and very irregular end; not resembling a cone, as is imagined, but only a piece of a tapering body, with a great part of the top removed, or deficient. The points of pins are yet more blunt, and the points of the most curious mathematical instruments so very seldom arrive at so great a sharpness. How much therefore can be built upon demonstrations made only by the productions of the ruler and compasses, he will be better able to consider that shall but view those points and lines with a microscope.

* * *

The image we have here exhibited in the first figure, was the top of a small and very sharp needle, whose point *aa* nevertheless appeared through the microscope above a quarter of an inch broad, not round nor flat, but irregular and uneven; so that it seemed to have been big enough to have afforded a hundred armed mites room enough to be ranged by each other without endangering the breaking one another's necks, by being thrust off on either side. The surface of which, though appearing to the naked eye very smooth, could not nevertheless hide a multitude of holes and scratches and ruggednesses from being discovered by the microscope to invest it, several of which inequalities (as A, B, C, seemed holes made by some small specks of rust; and D some adventitious[9] body, that stuck very close to it) were casual.[1] All the rest that roughen the surface, were only so many marks of the rudeness and bungling of art.[2] So unaccurate is it, in all its productions, even in those which seem most neat, that if examined with an organ more acute than that by which they were made, the more we see of their shape, the less appearance will there be of their beauty; whereas in the works in nature, the deepest discoveries show us the greatest excellencies. An evident argument, that He that was the author of all these things, was no other than omnipotent; being able to include as great a variety of parts and contrivances in the yet smallest discernible point, as in those vaster bodies (which comparatively are called also points) such as the earth, sun, or planets. Nor need it seem strange that the earth itself may be by an analogy called a physical point: for as its body, though now so near us as to fill our eyes and fancies with a sense of the vastness of it, may by a little distance, and some convenient diminishing glasses, be made vanish into a scarce visible speck, or point (as I have often tried on the moon, and—when not too bright—on the sun itself), so, could a mechanical contrivance successfully answer our theory, we might see the least spot as big as the earth itself; and discover, as Descartes also conjectures,[3] as great a variety of bodies in the moon, or planets, as in the earth.

But leaving these discoveries to future industries, we shall proceed to add one observation more of a point commonly so called, that is, the mark of a full stop, or period. And for this purpose I observed many both printed ones and written; and among multitudes I found few of them more round or regular than this which I have delineated in the * * * second scheme, but very many abundantly more disfigured; and for the most part if they seemed equally round to the eye, I found those points that had been made by a copper plate, and roll-press, to be as misshapen as those which had been made with types, the most curious and smoothly engraven strokes and points looking but as so many furrows and holes, and their printed impressions but like smutty daubings on a mat or uneven floor with a blunt extinguished brand[4] or stick's end. And as for points made with a pen they were much more rugged and deformed. Nay, having viewed certain pieces of exceeding curious writing of the kind (one of which in the breadth of a two-pence comprised the Lord's Prayer, the Apostles' Creed, the Ten Commandments, and about half a dozen verses besides of the Bible[5]), whose lines were so small and near together, that I was unable to number them with my naked eye, a very ordinary microscope, I had then about me, enabled me to see that what the writer of it had asserted was true, but withal discovered of what pitiful bungling scribbles and scrawls it was composed, Arabian and China characters being almost as well shaped; yet thus much I must say for the man, that it was for the most part legible enough, though in some places there wanted a good fantasy well prepossessed[6] to help one through. If this manner of

9. Chance-encountered.
1. Accidental.
2. Artifice; human (as opposed to natural) creation.
3. René Descartes (1596–1650); French mathematician and philosopher.
4. Torch.
5. In the mid-17th century, this minuscule writing was practiced as a craft; specimens (often of the scriptural texts Hooke lists here) were prized by collectors.
6. Imagination kindly disposed.

small writing were made easy and practicable (and I think I know such a one,[7] but have never yet made trial of it, whereby one might be enabled to write a great deal with much ease, and accurately enough in a very little room) it might be of very good use to convey secret intelligence without any danger of discovery or mistrusting. But to come again to the point. The irregularies of it are caused by three or four coadjutors,[8] one of which is the uneven surface of the paper, which at best appears no smoother than a very coarse piece of shagged cloth; next the irregularity of the type of engraving; and a third is the rough daubing of the printing ink that lies upon the instrument that makes the impression; to all which, add the variation made by the different lights and shadows, and you may have sufficient reason to guess that a point may appear much more ugly than this, which I have here presented, which though it appeared through the microscope gray, like a great splatch of London dirt, about three inches over; yet to the naked eye it was black, and no bigger than that in the midst of the Circle A. And could I have found room in this plate to have inserted an O you should have seen that the letters were not more distinct than the points of distinction, nor a drawn circle more exactly so, than we have now shown a point to be a point.

from *Observation 53. Of a Flea*

The strength and beauty of this small creature, had it no other relation at all to man, would deserve a description.

For its strength, the microscope is able to make no greater discoveries of it than the naked eye, but only the curious contrivance of its legs and joints, for the exerting that strength, is very plainly manifested, such as no other creature I have yet observed has anything like it; for the joints of it are so adapted, that he can, as 'twere, fold them short one within another, and suddenly stretch, or spring them out to their whole length, that is, of the forelegs. The part A * * * lies within B, and B within C, parallel to, or side by side each other; but the parts of the two next lie quite contrary, that is, D without E, and E without F, but parallel also; but the parts of the hinder legs G, H, and I, bend one within another, like the parts of a double jointed ruler, or like the foot, leg, and thigh of a man; these six legs he clitches[9] up altogether, and when he leaps, springs them all out, and thereby exerts his whole strength at once.

But, as for the beauty of it, the microscope manifests it to be all over adorned with a curiously polished suit of sable armor, neatly jointed, and beset with multitudes of sharp pins, shaped almost like porcupine's quills, or bright conical steel bodkins[1]; the head is either side beautified with a quick and round black eye K, behind each of which also appears a small cavity, L, in which he seems to move to and fro a certain thin film beset with many small transparent hairs, which probably may be his ears. In the forepart of his head, between the two forelegs, he has two small long jointed feelers, or rather smellers, M M, which have four joints, and are hairy, like those of several other creatures. Between these, it has a small proboscis, or probe, N N O, that seems to consist of a tube N N, and a tongue or sucker O, which I have perceived him to flip in and out. Besides these, it has also two chaps or biters P P, which are somewhat like those of an ant, but

7. I.e., an instrument.
8. Factors.
9. Clutches.

1. "A instrument with a small blade and sharp point used to bore holes" (Johnson's *Dictionary*).

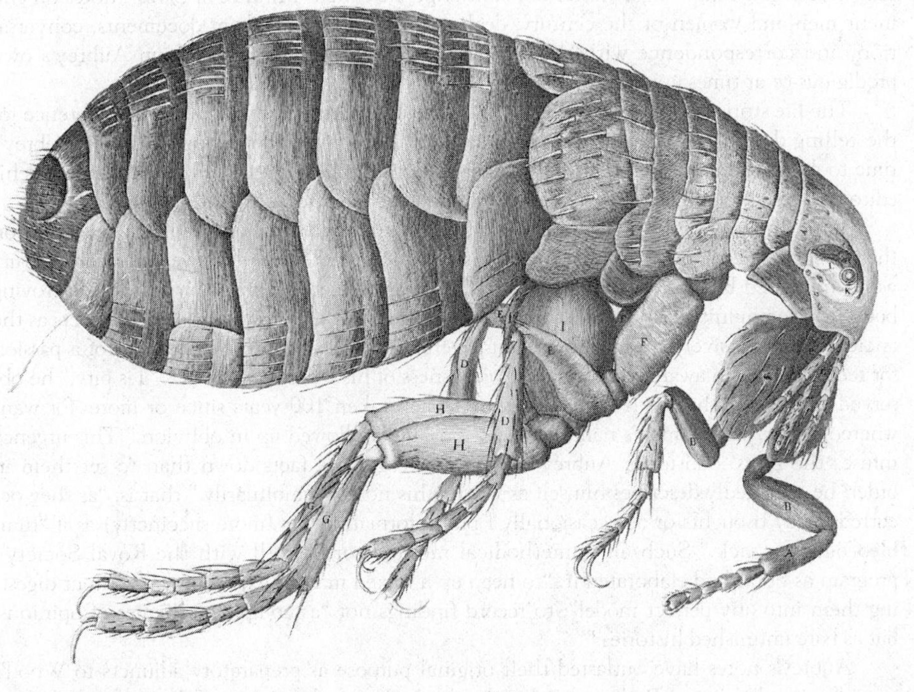

Robert Hooke, *Schema xxxiv: A Flea,* from *Micrographia,* 1665.

I could not perceive them toothed; and were opened and shut just after the same manner. With these instruments does this little busy creature bite and pierce the skin, and suck out the blood of an animal, leaving the skin inflamed with a small round red spot. These parts are very difficult to be discovered, because for the most part, they lie covered between the forelegs. There are many other particulars, which, being more obvious, and affording no great matter of information, I shall pass by, and refer the reader to the figure.

1663–1665 1665

John Aubrey
1626–1697

One of the original Fellows of the Royal Society, John Aubrey possessed in abundance two of its defining characteristics: an omnivorous curiosity and a reluctance to impose arbitrary order on collections of raw data. Prosperous by birth, sickly throughout his life, and prevented by the Civil Wars from completing the Oxford education he craved, Aubrey devoted himself to the study of natural history, folklore, and archaeology. His discovery of the prehistoric stone circle at Avebury remains one of the most important finds in Britain, but he is now best known as an innovator in biography. In the 1670s he agreed to help his friend Anthony à Wood with research for a "history of all the writers and bishops" educated at Oxford since

1500. He began compiling a cluster of manuscripts he called "Minutes of Lives": notes on eminent men and women of the century, dealing in data gathered from documents, conversation, and correspondence with the subjects and their survivors, and from Aubrey's own prodigious (if at times unreliable) memory.

The life stories thus produced display an obsessive particularity, an abiding preference for the telling detail over the big picture (which in the conventional biographies of Aubrey's time took the form of hagiography: pious summations of pious lives). Aubrey's *Lives*, notes his editor Oliver Lawson Dick, "were the first biographies that did not point a moral."

Throughout his "Minutes," Aubrey performs a kind of textual archaeology. He dwells on the physical objects, natural and manufactured, which marked the early seventeenth-century world inhabited by most of his subjects, and by his younger self. The Civil Wars, destroying buildings, communities, and bodies, had rendered that world as remote in some respects as the ancient tribes elusively commemorated at Avebury. Aubrey writes the *Lives* out of a passion for recovery and an awareness of the precariousness of his whole enterprise. "'Tis pity," he observed to Wood, "that such minutes had not been taken 100 years since or more: for want whereof many worthy men's names and notions are swallowed up in oblivion." This urgency infuses the *Lives'* odd form. Aubrey cares more to get the facts down than to set them in order: he repeatedly describes himself as writing his notes "tumultuarily," that is, "as they occurred to my thoughts or as occasionally I had information" or (more succinctly) as if "tumbled out of a sack." Such an unmethodical method sorted well with the Royal Society's program as Sprat had elaborated it: "to heap up a mixed mass of experiments, without digesting them into any perfect model"; to record findings not "as complete schemes of opinions, but as bare unfinished histories."

Aubrey's notes have outlasted their original purpose as preparatory adjuncts to Wood's more "finished" history. Rediscovered and published over the course of the nineteenth century, they have exerted considerable influence over the twentieth, primarily through their talky, energetic language and their unabashed attention to bodily functions and ignoble motives as defining elements in the course of a human life. Lytton Strachey and James Joyce both display distinctly Aubreyan characteristics, as do more recent practitioners of the tell-all biography and the contemporary novel. In the "bare unfinished histories" of Aubrey's "Minutes," the techniques and protocols of the new science begin to infuse the craft of biography.

from Brief Lives

[FRANCIS BACON][1]

* * * He came often to Sir John Danvers[2] at Chelsea. Sir John told me that when his lordship had wrote the *History of Henry 7*, he sent the manuscript copy to him to desire his opinion of it before 'twas printed. Qd.[3] Sir John, "Your lordship knows that I am no scholar." "'Tis no matter," said my lord, "I know what a scholar can say; I would know what *you* can say." Sir John read it, and gave his opinion what he misliked which Tacitus[4] did not omit (which I am sorry I have forgot) which my lord acknowledged to be true, and mended it: "Why," said he, "a scholar would never have told me this."

1. Statesman, scholor, philosopher, and writer (1561–1626); in his *Advancement of Learning* (1605) and *Novum Organum* (1620) he articulated the experimental methods that would later be championed by the Royal Society.
2. Danvers was a relative of Aubrey's and "a great acquaintance and favorite" of Bacon's.
3. *Quod*: said (Latin).
4. Publius Tacitus (c. 56–c.117 C.E.), Roman historian; the sense here seems to be that Bacon has left out some element in history that Tacitus would have included.

Mr. Thomas Hobbes (Malmesburiensis[5]) was beloved by his lordship, who was wont to have him walk with him in his delicate groves where he did meditate: and when a notion darted into his mind, Mr. Hobbes was presently to write it down, and his lordship was wont to say that he did it better than anyone else about him; for that many times, when he read their[6] notes he scarce understood what they writ, because they understood it not clearly themselves.

In short, all that were *great* and *good* loved and honored him. * * *

His lordship would many times have music in the next room where he meditated.

The aviary at York House[7] was built by his lordship; it did cost £300.

At every meal, according to the season of the year, he had his table strewn with sweet herbs and flowers, which he said did refresh his spirits and memory.

When his lordship was at his country house at Gorhambery,[8] St. Albans seemed as if the Court were there, so nobly did he live. His servants had liveries with his crest (a boar . . .[9]); his watermen[1] were more employed by gentlemen than any other, even the King's.

King James sent a buck to him, and he gave the keeper fifty pounds.

He was wont to say to his servant Hunt (who was a notable thrifty man, and loved this world, and the only servant he had that he could never get to become bound for[2] him), "The world was made for man, Hunt; and not man for the world." Hunt left an estate of £1000 per annum in Somerset.

None of his servants durst appear before him without Spanish leather boots:[3] for he would smell the neat's leather which offended him. * * *

He was a παιδεραστής.[4] His Ganimeds[5] and favorites took bribes; but his lordship always gave judgment *secundum aequum et bonum*.[6] His decrees in Chancery[7] stand firm, i.e., there are fewer of his decrees reversed than any other Chancellor.

His dowager[8] married her gentleman-usher,[9] Sir (Thomas, I think) Underhill, whom she made deaf and blind with too much of Venus.[1] She was living since the beheading of the late King.—Quaere[2] where and when she died.

He had a delicate, lively hazel eye; Dr. Harvey told me it was like the eye of a viper. I have now forgot what Mr. Bushnell said, whether his lordship enjoyed his Muse[3] best at night, or in the morning.

Apothegmata[4]

His lordship being in York House garden looking on fishers as they were throwing their net, asked them what they would take for their draught;[5] they answered *so*

5. Of Malmeshury (Hobbes's birthplace). Hobbes was a close friend of Aubrey's, and his is the longest and the fullest of the *Brief Lives*.
6. Anyone else's.
7. In London; Bacons's birthplace and residence.
8. Gornhambry, Bacon's estate on the river Ver, near the city of St. Albans.
9. Aubrey inserts this ellipsis, presumably for filling in later.
1. Ferrymen, busy bringing guests to and from the house.
2. I.e., legaly committed to serve.
3. Cordovan leather from Spain was more highly processed than ordinary English "neat's (cattle) leather."
4. Greek: pederast, a homosexual lover of boys.
5. Beloved boys (so called after the Trojan youth Ganymede, Zeus's cupbearer).
6. "Fairly and well." Bacon had served as attorney-general and Lord Chancellor until he was impeached for taking bribes.
7. The law court presided over by the Lord Chancellor.
8. Widow.
9. A gentleman acting as attendant to a person of superior rank.
1. Sex.
2. "Find out" (Aubrey's most frequent instruction to himself in his notes).
3. I.e., wrote and thought.
4. Witty sayings.
5. Catch.

much: his lordship would offer them no more but *so much*. They drew up their net, and in it were only 2 or 3 little fishes: his lordship then told them it had been better for them to have taken his offer. They replied, they hoped to have had a better draught. "But," said his lordship, "hope is a good breakfast, but an ill supper." * * *

The Bishop of London did cut down a noble cloud of trees at Fulham. The Lord Chancellor told him that he was *a good expounder of dark places*.[6]

Upon his being in disfavor his servants suddenly went away; he compared them to the flying of the vermin when the house was falling.

One told his lordship it was now time to look about him. He replied, "I do not look *about* me, I look *above* me." * * *

His lordship would often drink a good draught of strong beer (March beer) tobedwards, to lay his working fancy[7] asleep: which otherwise would keep him from sleeping great part of the night. * * *

Mr. Hobbes told me that the cause of his lordship's death was trying an experiment: viz., as he was taking the air in a coach with Dr. Witherborne (a Scotchman, physician to the king) towards Highgate, snow lay on the ground, and it came into my lord's thought, why flesh might not be preserved in snow, as in salt. They were resolved they would try the experiment presently. They alighted out of the coach, and went into a poor woman's house at the bottom of Highgate Hill, and bought a hen, and made the woman exenterate[8] it, and then stuffed the body with snow, and my lord did help to do it himself. The snow so chilled him, that he immediately fell so extremely ill, that he could not return to his lodgings (I suppose then at Gray's Inn), but went to the Earl of Arundel's house at Highgate, where they put him into a good bed warmed with a pan, but it was a damp bed that had not been lain in in about a year before, which gave him such a cold that in 2 or 3 days, as I remember he told me, he died of suffocation.

[WILLIAM HARVEY][9]

He was always very contemplative, and the first that I hear of that was curious in anatomy in England. He had made dissections of frogs, toads, and a number of other animals, and had curious observations on them, which papers, together with his goods, in his lodgings at Whitehall, were plundered at the beginning of the Rebellion, he being for the King, and with him at Oxon;[1] but he often said, that of all the losses he sustained, no grief was so crucifying to him as the loss of these papers, which for love or money he could never retrieve or obtain. When Charles I by reason of the tumults left London, he attended him, and was at the fight of Edgehill with him; and during the fight, the Prince and Duke of York were committed to his care. He told me that he withdrew with them under a hedge, and took out of his pocket a book and read; but he had not read very long before a bullet of a great gun grazed on the ground near him, which made him remove his station. He told me that Sir Adrian Scrope was dangerously wounded there, and left for dead amongst the dead men, stripped; which happened to be the saving of his life. It was cold,

6. Bacon puns on the Bishop's duty to shed light on obscure passages in scripture.
7. Busy mind.
8. Clean it; remove its innards.

9. Physician and anatomist (1578–1657); he discovered the circulation of the blood, and set forth his findings in *De Motu Cordis* ("on the heart's motion"), 1628.
1. Oxford, to which Charles I removed himself and his Court in 1643.

clear weather, and a frost that night; which staunched his bleeding, and about midnight, or some hours after his hurt, he awaked, and was fain to draw a dead body upon him for warmth-sake * * *

He did delight to be in the dark, and told me he could then best contemplate. He had a house heretofore at Combe, in Surrey, a good air and prospect, where he had caves made in the earth, in which in summer time he delighted to meditate.—He was pretty well versed in the mathematics, and had made himself master of Mr. Oughtred's *Clavis Math.*[2] in his old age; and I have seen him perusing it, and working problems, not long before he died, and that book was always in his meditating apartment. * * *

At Oxford, he grew acquainted with Dr. Charles Scarborough,[3] then a young physician (since by King Charles II knighted), in whose conversation he much delighted; and whereas before he marched up and down with the army, he took him to him and made him lie in his chamber, and said to him, "Prithee leave off thy gunning, and stay here; I will bring thee into practice."[4]

I remember he kept a pretty young wench to wait on him, which I guess he made use of for warmth-sake as King David did,[5] and took care of her in his will, as also of his man servant. * * *

He was, as all the rest of the brothers, very choleric;[6] and in his young days wore a dagger (as the fashion then was, nay I remember my old schoolmaster, old Mr. Latimer, at 70, wore a dudgeon, with a knife, and bodkin, as also my old grandfather Lyte, and alderman Whitson of Bristowe, which I suppose was the common fashion in their young days), but this Dr. would be too apt to draw out his dagger upon every slight occasion.

He was not tall; but of the lowest stature, round faced, olivaster[7] complexion; little eye, round, very black, full of spirit; his hair was black as a raven, but quite white 20 years before he died. * * *

He was much and often troubled with the gout,[8] and his way of cure was thus: he would then sit with his legs bare, if it were frost, on the leads[9] of Cockaine house, put them into a pail of water, till he was almost dead with cold, and betake himself to the stove, and so 'twas gone.

He was hot-headed, and his thoughts working would many times keep him from sleeping; he told me that then his way was to rise out of his bed and walk about his chamber in his shirt till he was pretty cool, i.e., till he began to have a horror,[1] and then return to bed, and sleep very comfortably.

I remember he was wont to drink coffee; which he and his brother Eliab did, before coffeehouses were in fashion in London.[2] * * *

It is now fit, and but just, that I should endeavor to undeceive the world in a scandal that I find strongly runs of him, which I have met amongst some learned young men: viz. that he made himself away[3] to put himself out of his pain, by opium; not but that, had he labored under great pains, he had been ready enough to have done it; I do not deny that it was not according to his principles upon certain

2. William Oughtred (1575–1660), mathematician; his *Clavis Mathematicae* ("the key of mathematics") was a widely used textbook on algebra and arithmetic (it introduced the symbol "3" for multiplication).
3. Charles Scarburgh (1616–1694) assisted Harvey with his work on the generation of animals.
4. I.e., medical practice.
5. In his old age David was warmed in bed at night by a young woman (1 Kings 1.1–4).
6. Prone to anger.
7. Olive-colored.
8. Inflammation of the joints in the hands and feet.
9. Rooftop (lined with lead).
1. Shiver.
2. The drink was rare in England before midcentury, hugely popular thereafter; London's first coffeehouse opened in 1652.
3. Killed himself.

occasions to . . . .[4] But the manner of his dying was really, and *bona fide*, thus, viz.: The morning of his death about 10 a clock, he went to speak, and found he had the dead palsy[5] in his tongue; then he saw what was to become of him, he knew there was then no hopes of his recovery, so presently sends for his young nephews to come up to him, to whom he gives one his watch ('twas a minute watch with which he made his experiments);[6] to another, another remembrance, etc.; made sign to . . .[7] Sambroke, his apothecary (in Blackfriars), to let him blood in[8] the tongue, which did little or no good; and so he ended his days. His practice was not very great towards his later end; he declined it, unless to a special friend—e.g. my Lady Howland, who had a cancer in her breast, which he did cut off and seared, but at last she died of it.

* * *

I was at his funeral, and helped to carry him into the vault.

1680s 1813

END OF PERSPECTIVES: THE ROYAL SOCIETY AND THE NEW SCIENCE

Margaret Cavendish, Duchess of Newcastle

1623–1674

The youngest child in a wealthy family whose social arrogance and Royalist sympathies brought it near ruin during the Civil Wars, Margaret Lucas combined a near immobilizing shyness with a passion for fame. She spent the years of war and Interregnum on the continent, first as maid of honor to Charles's exiled queen, then as wife to the Royalist general William Cavendish, Marquis of Newcastle; he was made Duke by Charles II after the couple returned to England at the Restoration. Neglected by the Court, they lived far from London on their northern estates, where they cultivated their passions: his, riding and fencing; hers, reading and writing. Words poured from her pen into a variety of genres: verse (*Poems and Fancies*, 1653), fiction (*Nature's Pictures*, 1656), plays (*Love's Adventure*, *The Matrimonial Trouble*, *The Female Academy*, and some fifteen others: all printed, none performed); essays (*The World's Olio*, 1655); scientific speculations (*Philosophical and Physical Opinions*, 1663; *Observations upon Experimental Philosophy*, 1665); biography (of her husband); and autobiography (*A True Relation*, 1656; *Sociable Letters*, 1664). Cavendish and her husband published much of her work (and some of his) in sumptuous editions at their own expense.

It was rare for a woman to write and publish, rarer still for an aristocrat to write so revealingly and emphatically about her own fears, desires, opinions, and aspirations. The combination of her gender, rank, and work brought the Duchess an equivocal celebrity, a mix of amazement and derision which her occasional trips to London did much to animate. After one such visit, Mary Evelyn (wife of the diarist John) tried to capture Cavendish's impact in a letter to a friend: "I was surprised to find so much extravagancy and vanity in any person not confined within four walls" (of a madhouse). Her clothing, Evelyn reported, was "fantastical"; her behavior outstripped "the imagination of poets, or the descriptions of a romance heroine's

4. Aubrey leaves the blank, perhaps intending a phrase like "commit suicide."
5. Paralysis caused by stroke.
6. At this time, most clocks and watches told only the hour, not the minutes.
7. Aubrey's blank.
8. Draw blood from.

greatness; her gracious bows, seasonable nods, courteous stretching out of hands, twinkling of her eyes, and various gestures of approbation, show what may be expected from her discourse, which is as airy, empty, whimsical, and rambling as her books, aiming at science, difficulties, high notions . . ." Evelyn voices a satiric hostility shared by many London onlookers, but she also pinpoints some of Cavendish's range and intensity: her idiosyncratic engagement with the new science of her day, and her variable, highly conscious self-presentation.

At letter's end, Evelyn despairs of description. The Duchess "is not of mortal race, and therefore cannot be defined." Cavendish, though, knew herself mortal. She repeatedly made clear that the threat of oblivion impelled her pen, and she worked constantly and inventively to define herself, sometimes in familiar genres, sometimes in modes of her own making—most notably that mix of fantasy, science fiction, argument, and autobiography she called *The Blazing World* (1665). The Duchess's extraordinary energies and kaleidoscopic output have transmuted seventeenth-century ridicule into late twentieth-century fascination with a woman's voice in relentless pursuit of (a favorite Cavendish term) "singularity."

from POEMS AND FANCIES[1]

The Poetress's Hasty Resolution

Reading my verses, I liked them so well,
Self-love did make my judgment to rebel;
And thinking them so good, thought more to make,
Considering not how others would them take.
I writ so fast, thought, lived I many a year,
A pyramid of fame thereon to rear.[2]
Reason, observing which way I was bent,
Did stay my hand, and asked me what I meant.
"Will you," said he, "thus waste your time in vain,
On that which in the world small praise shall gain?
For shame leave off, and do the printer spare:
He'll lose by your ill poetry, I fear.
Besides, the world already hath great store
Of useless books, wherefore do write no more,
But pity take, do the world a good turn,
And all you write cast in the fire and burn."
Angry I was, and Reason struck away,
When I did hear what he to me did say.
Then all in haste I to the press it sent,
Fearing persuasion might my book prevent.
But now 'tis done, repent with grief do I,
Hang down my head with shame, blush, sigh, and cry.
Take pity, and my drooping spirits raise,
Wipe off my tears with handkerchiefs of praise.

1. This was Cavendish's first publication; the first three pieces presented here functioned as a verse preface to the collection. The texts are taken from the second edition (1664), "much altered and corrected."

2. I.e., I thought that if I were to live a long time I would be able to create a poetic monument to myself.

The Poetress's Petition

Like to a fever's pulse my heart doth beat,
For fear my book some great repulse should meet.
If it be naught, let it in silence lie;
Disturb it not; let it in quiet die;
Let not the bells of your dispraise ring loud,
But wrap it up in silence as a shroud;
Cause black oblivion on its hearse to lie,
Instead of tapers, let dark night stand by;
Instead of flowers, on its grave to strew,
Before its hearse, sleepy, dull poppy throw;
Instead of scutcheons,[3] let my tears be hung,
Which grief and sorrow from my eyes out wrung.
Let those that bear its corpse no jesters be,
But sober, sad, and grave mortality.
No satyr° poets by its grave appear, *satirical*
No altars raised, to write inscriptions there.
Let dust of all forgetfulness be cast
Upon its corpse, there let it lie and waste.
Nor let it rise again, unless some know,
At Judgments some good merits it can show;
Then shall it live in Heavens of high praise,
And for its glory, garlands have of bays.[4]

An Apology for Writing So Much upon This Book

Condemn me not, I make so much ado
About this book; it is my child, you know;
Just like a bird, when her young are in nest,
Goes in, and out, and hops, and takes no rest;
But when their young are fledged,[5] their heads out peep,
Lord! what a chirping does the old one keep.
So I, for fear my strengthless child should fall
Against a door, or stool, aloud I call,
Bid have a care of such a dangerous place.
Thus write I much, to hinder all disgrace.

The Hunting of the Hare

Betwixt two ridges of plowed land sat Wat,[6]
Whose body, pressed to the earth, lay close and squat;
His nose upon his two forefeet did lie,
With his gray eyes he glared obliquely;
His head he always set against the wind,
His tail when turned, his hair blew up behind,
And made him to get cold; but he being wise,

3. Escutcheons: funeral ornaments, shield-shaped, exhibiting the deceased's coat of arms.
4. Wreaths of laurel leaves, awarded for military victory or literary excellence.
5. Feathered; ready to fly.
6. Conventional nickname for a hare.

Doth keep his coat still down, so warm he lies.
Thus rests he all the day, til th' sun doth set,
Then up he riseth his relief to get,
And walks about, until the sun doth rise,
Then coming back in's° former posture lies. *in his*
At last poor Wat was found, as he there lay,
By huntsmen, which came with their dogs that way,
Whom seeing, he got up, and fast did run,
Hoping some ways the cruel dogs to shun;
But they by nature had so quick a scent,
That by their nose they traced what way he went,
And with their deep wide mouths set forth a cry,
Which answered was by echo in the sky;
Then Wat was struck with terror and with fear,
Seeing each shadow thought the dogs were there,
And running out some distance from their cry,
To hide himself, his thoughts he did employ;
Under a clod of earth in sand pit wide
Poor Wat sat close, hoping himself to hide,
There long he had not been, but straight in's ears
The winding° horns and crying dogs he hears; *blowing*
Then starting up with fear, he leaped, and such
Swift speed he made, the ground he scarce did touch;
Into a great thick wood straight ways he got,
And underneath a broken bough he sat,
Where every leaf that with the wind did shake
Brought him such terror, that his heart did ache;
That place he left, to champaign° plains he went, *open*
Winding about, for to deceive their scent,
And while they snuffling were to find his track,
Poor Wat being weary, his swift pace did slack;
On his two hinder legs for ease he sat;
His forefeet rubbed his face from dust and sweat;
Licking his feet, he wiped his ears so clean
That none could tell that Wat had hunted been;
But casting round about his fair gray eyes,
The hounds in full career he near him 'spies;
To Wat it was so terrible a sight,
Fear gave him wings and made his body light;
Though he was tired before by running long,
Yet now his breath he never felt more strong—
Like those that dying are, think health returns,
When 'tis but a faint blast which life out-burns;
For spirits seek to guard the heart about,
Striving with death, but death doth quench them out.
The hounds so fast came on, and with such cry,
That he no hopes had left, nor help could 'spy;
With that the winds did pity poor Wat's case,
And with their breath the scent blew from that place;

Then every nose was busily employed,
And every nostril was set open wide,
And every head did seek a several way,
To find the grass or track where the scent lay;
For witty industry° is never slack, *cunning diligence*
'Tis like to witchcraft, and brings lost things back;
But though the wind had tied the scent up close,
A busy dog thrust in his snuffling nose
And drew it out, with that did foremost run,
Then horns blew loud, the rest to follow on;
The great slow hounds their throats did set a base,
The fleet, swift hounds, as tenors next in place,
The little beagles did a treble sing,
And through the air their voices round did ring,
Which made such consort as they ran along,
That, had they spoken words, 't had been a song;
The horns kept time, the men did shout for joy,
And seemed most valiant, poor Wat to destroy;
Spurring their horses to a full career,
Swum rivers deep, leaped ditches without fear,
Endangered life and limbs, so fast they'd ride,
Only to see how patiently Wat died;
At last the dogs so near his heels did get,
That their sharp teeth they in his breech did set;
Then tumbling down he fell, with weeping eyes
Gave up his ghost; and thus poor Wat he dies.
Men whooping loud, such acclamations made,
As if the Devil they imprisoned had,
When they but did a shiftless creature kill;
To hunt, there needs no valiant soldier's skill;
But men do think that exercise and toil,
To keep their health, is best, which makes most spoil,
Thinking that food and nourishment so good,
Which doth proceed from others' flesh and blood.
When they do lions, wolves, bears, tigers see
Kill silly sheep, they say, they cruel be,
But for themselves all creatures think too few,
For luxury, wish God would make more new;
As if God did make creatures for man's meat,
And gave them life and sense for man to eat,
Or else for sport or recreation's sake
For to destroy those lives that God did make,
Making their stomachs graves, which full they fill
With murdered bodies, which in sport they kill;
Yet man doth think himself so gentle and mild,
When of all creatures he's most cruel, wild,
Nay, so proud, that he only[7] thinks to live,

7. Alone, with no other creature.

That God a God-like nature him did give,
And that all creatures for his sake alone
Were made, for him to tyrannize upon.

1653, 1664

from A True Relation of My Birth, Breeding, and Life[1]

My father was a gentleman,[2] which title is grounded and given by merit, not by princes; and 'tis the act of time, not favor. And though my father was not a peer of the realm, yet there were few peers who had much greater estates, or lived more noble therewith. * * *

As for my breeding, it was according to my birth and the nature of my sex, for my birth was not lost in my breeding; for as my sisters was or had been bred, so was I in plenty, or rather with superfluity. Likewise we were bred virtuously, modestly, civilly, honorably, and on honest principles. As for plenty, we had not only for necessity, conveniency, and decency, but for delight and pleasure to a superfluity. 'Tis true, we did not riot, but we lived orderly; for riot, even in kings' courts and princes' palaces, brings ruin without content or pleasure, when order in less fortune shall live more plentifully and deliciously than princes that lives in a hurly-burly, as I may term it, in which they are seldom well served, for disorder obstructs. Besides, it doth disgust life,[3] distract the appetites, and yield no true relish to the senses; for pleasure, delight, peace, and felicity live in method and temperance.

As for our garments, my mother[4] did not only delight to see us neat and cleanly, fine and gay, but rich and costly, maintaining us to the height of her estate, but not beyond it. For we were so far from being in debt, before the wars,[5] as we were rather beforehand with the world, buying all with ready money, not on the score.[6] For although after my father's death the estate was divided between my mother and her sons, paying such a sum of money for portions to her daughters either at the day of their marriage or when they should come to age, yet by reason she and her children agreed with a mutual consent, all their affairs were managed so well as she lived not in a much lower condition than when my father lived. 'Tis true my mother might have increased her daughters' portions by a thrifty sparing, yet she chose to bestow it on our breeding, honest pleasures, and harmless delights, out of an opinion that if she bred us with needy necessity it might chance to create in us sharking[7] qualities, mean[8] thoughts, and base actions, which she knew my father as well as herself did abhor. Likewise we were bred tenderly, for my mother naturally did strive to please and delight her children, not to cross or torment them, terrifying them with threats or lashing them with slavish whips. But instead of threats, reason was used to persuade us, and instead of lashes, the deformities of vices was discovered, and the

1. Cavendish published her autobiography as the closing piece in a collection of her fiction called *Nature's Pictures* (1656), which she wrote while living in exile at Antwerp during the years of Cromwell's commonwealth. This work (like many of her others) was privately printed, at the author's expense, in a lavish folio, whose title page suggests the autobiography's particular place in the scheme: "In this volume there are several feigned stories . . . comical, tragical, and tragicomical, poetical, romantical, philosophical, and historical. . . . And a true story at the latter end, wherein there is no feignings." In a later edition (1671), published after she and her husband had returned to England, Cavendish omitted the autobiography.

2. Thomas Lucas (c. 1573–1625), whose forebears had risen to the gentry in the 16th century. He died when Margaret was two years old.

3. I.e., makes life unpleasant.

4. Elizabeth Lucas, née Leighton (?–1647).

5. The English Civil Wars, begun in 1642.

6. On credit.

7. Greedy.

8. Ignoble.

graces and virtues were presented unto us. Also we were bred with respectful attendance, every one being severally waited upon. And all her servants in general used the same respect to her children (even those that were very young) as they did to herself, for she suffered not her servants either to be rude before us or to domineer over us, which all vulgar servants are apt and ofttimes have leave to do. Likewise she never suffered the vulgar servingmen to be in the nursery amongst the nursemaids, lest their rude lovemaking[9] might do unseemly actions, or speak unhandsome words in the presence of her children, knowing that youth is apt to take infection by ill examples, having not the reason of distinguishing good from bad. Neither were we suffered to have any familiarity with the vulgar servants, or conversation; yet caused us to demean ourselves[1] with an humble civility towards them, as they with a dutiful respect to us. Not because they were servants were we so reserved, for many noble persons are forced to serve through necessity, but by reason the vulgar sort of servants are as ill bred as meanly born, giving children ill examples, and worse counsel. * * *

But some time after this war began, I knew not how they[2] lived. For though most of them were in Oxford, where the King was, yet after the Queen went from Oxford, and so out of England, I was parted from them.[3] For when the Queen was in Oxford, I had a great desire to be one of her Maids of Honor, hearing the Queen had not the same number she was used to have. Whereupon I wooed and won my mother to let me go, for my mother being fond of all her children was desirous to please them, which made her consent to my request. But my brothers and sisters seemed not very well pleased, by reason I had never been from home, nor seldom out of their sight; for though they knew I would not behave myself to their or my own dishonor, yet they thought I might to my disadvantage, being inexperienced in the world. Which indeed I did, for I was so bashful when I was out of my mother's, brothers', and sisters' sight, whose presence used to give me confidence, thinking I could not do amiss while any one of them were by, for I knew they would gently reform me if I did. Besides, I was ambitious they should approve of my actions and behavior, that when I was gone from them I was like one that had no foundation to stand, or guide to direct me, which made me afraid lest I should wander with ignorance out of the ways of honor so that I knew not how to behave myself. Besides, I had heard the world was apt to lay aspersions even on the innocent, for which I dared neither look up with my eyes, nor speak, nor be any way sociable, insomuch as I was thought a natural fool.[4] Indeed I had not much wit, yet I was not an idiot; my wit was according to my years. And though I might have learned more wit, and advanced my understanding by living in a court, yet being dull, fearful, and bashful, I neither heeded what was said or practiced, but just what belonged to my loyal duty and my own honest reputation. And indeed I was so afraid to dishonor my friends and family by my indiscreet actions that I rather chose to be accounted a fool than to be thought rude or wanton. In truth my bashfulness and fears made me repent my going from home to see the world abroad, and much I did desire to return to my mother again, or to my sister Pye,[5] with whom I often lived when she was in London, and loved with a supernatural affection. But my mother advised me there to stay, although I put her to more charges than if she had kept me at home, and the

9. Flirtation.
1. To behave.
2. Her mother and siblings.
3. In 1643, Charles I had moved his family, court, and military base to Oxford as the Civil Wars rendered London unsafe. In 1644 his queen, Henrietta Maria, escaped to her native Paris in hopes of raising money and support for the Royalist cause.
4. I.e., born mentally defective.
5. Catherine, wife of Edmond Pye.

more, by reason she and my brothers were sequestered from their estates and plundered of all their goods.[6] Yet she maintained me so, that I was in a condition rather to lend than to borrow, which courtiers usually are not, being always necessitated by reason of great expenses courts put them to. But my mother said it would be a disgrace for me to return out of the court so soon after I was placed.

So I continued almost two years, until such time as I was married from thence. For my Lord the Marquis of Newcastle[7] did approve of those bashful fears which many condemned, and would choose such a wife as he might bring to his own humors,[8] and not such an one as was wedded to self-conceit, or one that had been tempered to the humors of another, for which he wooed me for his wife. And though I did dread marriage, and shunned men's companies as much as I could, yet I could not nor had not the power to refuse him, by reason my affections were fixed on him, and he was the only person I ever was in love with. Neither was I ashamed to own it, but gloried therein, for it was not amorous love. I never was infected therewith—it is a disease, or a passion, or both, I know by relation, not by experience. Neither could title, wealth, power, or person entice me to love. But my love was honest and honorable, being placed upon merit; which affection joyed at the fame of his worth, pleased with delight in his wit, proud of the respects he used to me, and triumphing in the affections he professed for me; which affections he hath confirmed to me by a deed[9] of time, sealed by constancy, and assigned by an unalterable decree of his promise, which makes me happy in despite of Fortune's frowns. For though misfortunes may and do oft dissolve base, wild, loose, and ungrounded affections, yet she hath no power of those that are united either by merit, justice, gratitude, duty, fidelity, or the like. And though my Lord hath lost his estate, and banished out of his country for his loyalty to his King and country, yet neither despised poverty nor pinching necessity could make him break the bonds of friendship, or weaken his loyal duty to his King or country.

But not only the family I am linked to is ruined, but the family from which I sprung, by these unhappy wars—which ruin my mother lived to see, and then died, having lived a widow many years, for she never forgot my father so as to marry again. Indeed he remained so lively in her memory, and her grief was so lasting, as she never mentioned his name, though she spoke often of him, but love and grief caused tears to flow, and tender sighs to rise, mourning in sad complaints. She made her house her cloister, enclosing herself as it were therein, for she seldom went abroad, unless to church, but these unhappy wars forced her out by reason she and her children were loyal to the King, for which they plundered her and my brothers of all their goods, plate, jewels, money, corn, cattle, and the like, cut down their woods, pulled down their houses, and sequestered them from their lands and livings. But in such misfortunes my mother was of an heroic spirit, in suffering patiently where there is no remedy, or to be industrious where she thought she could help. She was of a grave behavior, and had such a majestic grandeur, as it were continually hung about her, that it would strike a kind of an awe to the beholders, and command respect from the rudest. I mean the rudest of civilized people; I mean not such

6. The Lucas family took the king's side in the Civil Wars; its property was raided during anti-Royalist riots in 1642.

7. William Cavendish (1593–1676), a general in the king's army. In 1644, after suffering defeat in a pivotal battle, he departed for the Continent. He married Margaret (his second wife) at Paris in 1645.

8. Inclinations, ways of thinking.

9. A legal document (here used metaphorically).

barbarous people as plundered her and used her cruelly, for they would have pulled God out of Heaven, had they had power, as they did royalty out of his throne. Also her beauty was beyond the ruin of time, for she had a well-favored loveliness in her face, a pleasing sweetness in her countenance, and a well-tempered complexion, as neither too red nor too pale, even to her dying hour, although in years. And by her dying, one might think death was enamored with her, for he embraced her in a sleep, and so gently, as if he were afraid to hurt her. Also she was an affectionate mother, breeding her children with a most industrious care and tender love. * * * Likewise my mother was a good mistress to her servants, taking care of her servants in their sickness, not sparing any cost she was able to bestow for their recovery. Neither did she exact more from them in their health than what they with ease or rather like pastime could do. She would freely pardon a fault, and forget an injury. Yet sometimes she would be angry, but never with her children; the sight of them would pacify her. Neither would she be angry with others but when she had cause, as with negligent or knavish servants that would lavishly or unnecessarily waste, or subtly and thievishly steal. And though she would often complain that her family was too great for her weak management, and often pressed my brother to take it upon him, yet I observe she took a pleasure and some little pride in the governing thereof. * * *

But howsoever our fortunes are, we are both content, spending our time harmlessly, for my Lord pleaseth himself with the management of some few horses, and exercises himself with the use of the sword. Which two arts he hath brought by his studious thoughts to an absolute perfection. And though he hath taken as much pains in those arts, both by study and practice, as chemists[1] for the philosopher's stone, yet he hath this advantage of them, that he hath found the right and the truth thereof and therein, which chemists never found in their art and I believe never will. Also he recreates himself with his pen, writing what his wit dictates to him. But I pass my time rather with scribbling than writing, with words than wit. Not that I speak much, because I am addicted to contemplation, unless I am with my Lord; yet then I rather attentively listen to what he says, than impertinently speak. Yet when I am writing any sad feigned stories or serious humors or melancholy passions, I am forced many times to express them with the tongue before I can write them with the pen, by reason those thoughts that are sad, serious, and melancholy are apt to contract and to draw too much back, which oppression doth as it were overpower or smother the conception in the brain. But when some of those thoughts are sent out in words, they give the rest more liberty to place themselves in a more methodical order, marching more regularly with my pen on the ground of white paper. But my letters seem rather as a ragged rout, than a well-armed body, for the brain being quicker in creating than the hand in writing, or the memory in retaining, many fancies are lost by reason they ofttimes outrun the pen. Where I, to keep speed in the race, write so fast as I stay not so long as to write my letters plain, insomuch as some have taken my handwriting for some strange character.[2] And being accustomed so to do, I cannot now write very plain. When I strive to write my best, indeed my ordinary handwriting is so bad as few can read it so as to write it fair for the press. But however that[3] little wit I have, it delights me to scribble it out and

1. Alchemists, who devoted themselves to the search for the "philosopher's stone"—the substance that would turn base metals into gold.

2. Code, cryptography.

3. Whatever.

disperse it about. For I being addicted from my childhood to contemplation rather than conversation, to solitariness rather than society, to melancholy rather than mirth, to write with the pen than to work with a needle, passing my time with harmless fancies, their company being pleasing, their conversation innocent, in which I take such pleasure as I neglect my health. For it is as great a grief to leave their society, as a joy to be in their company. My only trouble is lest my brain should grow barren, or that the root of my fancies should become insipid, withering into a dull stupidity, for want of maturing subjects to write on. * * *

But since I have writ in general thus far of my life, I think it fit I should speak something of my humor, particular practice, and disposition. As for my humor, I was from my childhood given to contemplation, being more taken or delighted with thoughts than in conversation with a society. * * * Also I did dislike any should follow my fashions, for I always took delight in a singularity, even in accoutrements of habits. But whatsoever I was addicted to, either in fashions of clothes, contemplation of thoughts, actions of life, they were lawful, honest, honorable, and modest, of which I can avouch to the world with a great confidence, because it is a pure truth. * * * Likewise I am neither spiteful, envious, nor malicious. I repine not at[4] the gifts that Nature or Fortune bestows upon others, yet I am a great emulator. For though I wish none worse than they are, nor fear any should be better than they are, yet it is lawful for me to wish myself the best, and to do my honest endeavor thereunto. For I think it no crime to wish myself the exactest[5] of Nature's works, my thread of life the longest, my chain of destiny the strongest, my mind the peaceablest, my life the pleasantest, my death the easiest, and the greatest saint in Heaven. * * * As I am not covetous, so I am not prodigal.[6] But of the two I am inclining to be prodigal, yet I cannot say to a vain prodigality, because I imagine it is to a profitable end; for perceiving the world is given or apt to honor the outside more than the inside, worshipping show more than substance; and I am so vain, if it be a vanity, as to endeavor to be worshipped rather than not to be regarded. Yet I shall never be so prodigal as to impoverish my friends,[7] or go beyond the limits or facility of our estate. And though I desire to appear at the best advantage whilst I live in the view of the public world, yet I could most willingly exclude myself, so as never to see the face of any creature but my Lord as long as I live, enclosed myself like an anchorite,[8] wearing a frieze gown[9] tied with a cord about my waist. But I hope my readers will not think me vain for writing my life, since there have been many that have done the like, as Caesar, Ovid,[1] and many more, both men and women, and I know no reason I may not do it as well as they. But I verily believe some censuring readers will scornfully say, "Why hath this lady writ her own life, since none cares to know whose daughter she was or whose wife she is, or how she was bred, or what fortunes she had, or how she lived, or what humor or disposition she was of?" I answer that it is true, that 'tis to no purpose, to the readers, but it is to the authoress, because I write it for my own sake, not theirs. Neither did I intend this piece for to delight, but to divulge, not to please the fancy, but to tell the truth, lest after-ages should mistake, in not knowing I was daughter to one Master Lucas of St. Johns near Colchester in Essex, second wife to

4. Do not fret about.
5. Most perfected.
6. Spendthrift, lavish.
7. Family members.
8. Religious recluse.
9. Coarse woolen robe.
1. Julius Caesar (c. 100–44 B.C.E.), Roman general and statesman, wrote memoirs of his military campaigns; the Roman poet Ovid (43 B.C.E.–17 C.E.) wrote many autobiographical poems.

the Lord Marquis of Newcastle; for my Lord having had two wives, I might easily have been mistaken, especially if I should die, and my Lord marry again.

1656

from Observations upon Experimental Philosophy. To which is added, The Description of a New Blazing World[1]

Of Micrography, and of Magnifying and Multiplying Glasses[2]

Although I am not able to give a solid judgment of the art of micrography and the several dioptrical[3] instruments belonging thereto, by reason I have neither studied nor practiced that art, yet of this I am confident: that this same art, with all its instruments, is not able to discover the interior natural motions of any part or creature of nature. Nay, the question is whether it can represent yet the exterior shapes and motions so exactly as naturally they are, for art[4] doth more easily alter than inform. As, for example, art makes cylinders, concave and convex glasses, and the like, which represent the figure of an object in no part exactly and truly, but very deformed and misshaped. Also a glass that is flawed, cracked, or broke, or cut into the figure of lozenges, triangles, squares, or the like, will present numerous pictures of one object. Besides, there are so many alterations made by several lights, their shadows, refractions, reflections, as also several lines, points, mediums, interposing and intermixing parts, forms, and positions, as the truth of an object will hardly be known.[5] For the perception of sight, and so of the rest of the senses, goes no further than the exterior parts of the object presented, and though the perception may be true when the object is truly presented, yet when the presentation is false, the information must be false also. And it is to be observed that art for the most part makes hermaphroditical,[6] that is, mixed figures, as partly artificial and partly natural. For art may make some metal as pewter, which is between tin and lead, as also brass, and numerous other things of mixed natures; in the like manner may artificial glasses present objects partly natural and partly artificial. Nay, put the case they can present the natural figure of an object; yet that natural figure may be presented in as monstrous a shape as it may appear misshapen rather than natural. For example, a louse by the help of a magnifying glass appears like a lobster,[7] where the microscope enlarging and magnifying each part of it makes them bigger and rounder than naturally they are. The truth is, the more the figure by art is magnified, the more it appears misshapen from the natural, inasmuch as each joint will appear as a diseased, swelled and tumid body, ready and ripe for incision. But mistake me not; I do not say that no glass presents the true picture of an object, but only that magnifying, multiplying, and the like optic glasses may and do oftentimes present falsely the picture of an

1. The *Observations* is a critique of science, the *Blazing World* a work of fantasy; Cavendish published them together in a single volume as complementary texts. The "experimental philosophy" was that method and outlook pursued and exalted by the Royal Society; the group itself makes a sustained parodic appearance in the *Blazing World*. The Society held that copious experiment was the necessary basis for reliable study of the natural world. Cavendish challenges any such investigation grounded in human perceptions and the machines (microscopes, telescopes) contrived to enhance them; in the excerpt here she specifically takes on the work of Robert Hooke (see page 2046), whose *Micrographia* (1665) may well have prompted her to write the *Observations*, which includes the first selection given here.

2. Lenses.

3. Vision-enhancing (by means of refraction).

4. Artifice, like that of the lens-makers.

5. Early microscopes in England used simple lenses that blurred the image.

6. Composed of two opposite qualities.

7. As in Hooke's *Micrographia* illustration.

exterior object. I say the picture because it is not the real body of the object which the glass presents, but the glass only figures or patterns out the picture presented in and by the glass, and there may easily mistakes be committed in taking copies from copies. Nay, artists[8] do confess themselves that flies and the like will appear of several figures or shapes, according to the several reflections, refractions, mediums, and positions of several lights. Which if so, how can they tell or judge which is the truest light, position, or medium, that doth present the object naturally as it is? And if not, then an edge may very well seem flat, and a point of a needle a globe;[9] but if the edge of a knife, or point of a needle were naturally and really so as the microscope presents them, they would never be so useful as they are, for a flat or broad plain-edged knife would not cut, nor a blunt globe pierce so suddenly another body. Neither would or could they pierce without tearing and rending, if their bodies were so uneven. And if the picture of a young beautiful lady should be drawn according to the representation of the microscope, or according to the various refraction and reflection of light through such like glasses, it would be so far from being like her, as it would not be like a human face, but rather a monster than a picture of nature.

Wherefore those that invented microscopes and suchlike dioptrical glasses at first did, in my opinion, the world more injury than benefit. For this art has intoxicated so many men's brains, and wholly employed their thoughts and bodily actions about phenomena, or the exterior figures of objects, as[1] all better arts and studies are laid aside. Nay, those that are not as earnest and active in such employments as they, are by many of them accounted unprofitable subjects to the commonwealth of learning. But though there be numerous books written of the wonders of these glasses, yet I cannot perceive any such; at best, they are but superficial wonders, as I may call them.

But could experimental philosophers find out more beneficial arts than our forefathers have done, either for the better increase of vegetables and brute animals to nourish our bodies, or better and commodious contrivances in the art of architecture to build us houses, or for the advancing of trade and traffic to provide necessaries for us to live, or for the decrease of nice[2] distinctions and sophistical[3] disputes in churches, schools, and courts of judicature, to make men live in unity, peace, and neighborly friendship, it would not only be worth their labor, but of as much praise as could be given to them. But as boys that play with watery bubbles, or sling dust into each other's eyes, or make a hobbyhorse of snow, are worthy of reproof rather than praise, for wasting their time with useless sports, so those that addict themselves to unprofitable arts spend more time than they reap benefit thereby. Nay, could they benefit men either in husbandry, architecture, or the like necessary and profitable employments, yet before the vulgar sort[4] would learn to understand them, the world would want bread to eat, and houses to dwell in, as also clothes to keep them from the inconveniences of the inconstant weather. But truly, although spinsters[5] were most experienced in this art, yet they will never be able to spin silk, thread, or wool, etc., from loose atoms; neither will weavers weave a web of light from the sun's rays, nor an architect build a house of the bubbles of water and air,

8. Technicians.
9. Cavendish evidently refers to Hooke's micrographic depiction of a needle's point, a printed period (her "globe"), and (in the original illustration) a razor's edge; see page 2050.
1. That.
2. Minute, subtle, trivial.
3. Complicatedly and falsely argued.
4. Common people.
5. People who spin yarn or thread (possibly, here, with the additional sense of "unmarried woman").

unless they be poetical spinsters, weavers, and architects. And if a painter should draw a louse as big as a crab, and of that shape as the microscope presents, can anybody imagine that a beggar would believe it to be true?[6] But if he did, what advantage would it be to the beggar? For it doth neither instruct him how to avoid breeding them, or how to catch them, or to hinder them from biting. Again, if a painter should paint birds according to those colors the microscope presents, what advantage would it be for fowlers to take them? Truly, no fowler will be able to distinguish several birds through a microscope, neither by their shapes nor colors; they will be better discerned by those that eat their flesh than by micrographers that look upon their colors and exterior figures through a magnifying glass.

In short, magnifying glasses are like a high heel to a short leg, which if it be made too high, it is apt to make the wearer fall, and at the best can do no more than represent exterior figures in a bigger, and so in a more deformed shape and posture than naturally they are. But as for the interior form and motions of a creature, as I said before, they can no more represent them, than telescopes can the interior essence and nature of the sun, and what matter it consists of. For if one that never had seen milk before should look upon it through a microscope, he would never be able to discover the interior parts of milk by that instrument, were it the best that is in the world—neither the whey, nor the butter, nor the curds. Wherefore the best optic[7] is a perfect natural eye, and a regular sensitive perception, and the best judge is reason, and the best study is rational contemplation joined with the observations of regular sense, but not deluding arts. For art is not only gross[8] in comparison to nature, but for the most part deformed and defective, and at best produces mixed or hermaphroditical figures—that is, a third figure between nature and art. Which proves that natural reason is above artificial sense, as I may call it. Wherefore those arts are the best and surest informers that alter nature least, and they the greatest deluders that alter nature most—I mean, the particular nature of each particular creature. (For art is so far from altering infinite Nature that it is no more in comparison to it than a little fly to an elephant;[9] no, not so much, for there is no comparison between finite and infinite.) But wise Nature taking delight in variety, her parts, which are her creatures, must of necessity do so too.

from The Description of a New Blazing World

from To the Reader

If you wonder that I join a work of fancy[1] to my serious philosophical contemplations, think not that it is out of a disparagement to philosophy, or out of an opinion as if this noble study were but a fiction of the mind * * * The end of reason is truth, the end of fancy is fiction. But mistake me not when I distinguish fancy from reason; I mean not as if fancy were not made by the rational parts of matter, but by "reason" I understand a rational search and inquiry into the causes of natural effects, and by "fancy" a voluntary creation or production of the mind, both being effects, or rather actions, of the rational part of matter, of which, as that[2] is a more profitable and useful study than this,

6. Beggars were assumed to be most familiar (because most often afflicted) with lice.
7. Lens.
8. Rough, approximate.
9. Cavendish probably refers to Hooke's illustration of a flea (see page 2053).
1. Imagination.
2. Philosophy.

so it is also more laborious and difficult, and requires sometimes the help of fancy to recreate the mind and withdraw it from its more serious contemplations.

And this is the reason, why I added this piece of fancy to my philosophical observations, and joined them as two worlds at the ends of their poles; both for my own sake, to divert my studious thoughts, which I employed in the contemplation thereof, and to delight the reader with variety, which is always pleasing. But lest my fancy should stray too much, I chose such a fiction as would be agreeable to the subject treated of in the former parts; it is a description of a new world, not such as Lucian's, or the Frenchman's world in the moon;[3] but a world of my own creating, which I call the Blazing World: the first part whereof is romancical, the second philosophical, and the third is merely fancy, or (as I may call it) fantastical, which if it add any satisfaction to you, I shall account myself a happy creatoress.[4] If not, I must be content to live a melancholy life in my own world; I cannot call it a poor world, if poverty be only want of gold, silver, and jewels; for there is more gold in it than all the chemists ever did, and (as I verily believe) will ever be able to make.[5] As for the rocks of diamonds, I wish with all my soul they might be shared amongst my noble female friends, and upon that condition, I would willingly quit my part;[6] and of the gold I should only desire so much as might suffice to repair my noble Lord and husband's losses:[7] for I am not covetous, but as ambitious as ever any of my sex was, is, or can be; which makes, that though I cannot be Henry the Fifth, or Charles the Second,[8] yet I endeavor to be Margaret the First; and although I have neither power, time, nor occasion to conquer the world as Alexander and Caesar did; yet rather than not to be mistress of one, since Fortune and the Fates would give me none, I have made a world of my own: for which nobody, I hope, will blame me, since it is in everyone's power to do the like.

[Creating Worlds]

At last, when the Duchess[9] saw that no patterns would do her any good in the framing of her world, she resolved to make a world of her own invention, * * * which world after it was made, appeared so curious and full of variety, so well ordered and wisely governed, that it cannot possibly be expressed by words, nor the delight and pleasure which the Duchess took in making this world of her own.

In the meantime the Empress was also making and dissolving several worlds in her own mind, and was so puzzled, that she could not settle in any of them; wherefore she sent for the Duchess, who being ready to wait on the Empress, carried her

3. The *True History*, by the Greek satirist Lucian (2nd century C.E.), initiated a long literary tradition of imaginary voyages, to which the French writer Savinien Cyrano de Bergerac's account of a trip to the moon (*Histoire comique contenant les états et empires de la lune* [1657]) was a recent, celebrated contribution.

4. In the first part of *The Blazing World*, a "virtuous lady" survives her abduction at sea and is transported into a "Blazing World" that touches Earth at the North Pole; quickly wooed and wedded by the Emperor of this utopia, she becomes its Empress. In the second, "philosophical," section, she hears the testimony of various scholars, scientists, theologians, and philosophers; in the third, "fantastical," section, the Empress summons the soul of Margaret Cavendish to travel from England to the Blazing World, in order to serve as her companion and secretary. The excerpts that follow are from the third part of the narrative.

5. Alchemists sought to turn base metals into gold.

6. Give up my share.

7. During the civil wars, William Cavendish had lost much wealth and property, of which he had recovered only part since the Restoration.

8. Henry V of England (1387–1422) was celebrated for his conquest of France; Charles II for his restoration of the monarchy after the Interregnum.

9. Cavendish herself, whose soul has been transported to the Blazing World at the Empress's request. At this point in the story she and the Empress have been experimenting with creating worlds in accordance with the theories established by various experts, ancient and modern (Pythagoras, Plato, Aristotle, Descartes, Hobbes).

beloved world along with her, and invited the Empress's soul to observe the frame, order, and government of it. Her Majesty was so ravished with the perception of it, that her soul desired to live in the Duchess's world; but the Duchess advised her to make such another world in her own mind; for, said she, your Majesty's mind is full of rational corporeal motions, and the rational motions of my mind shall assist you by the help of sensitive expressions, with the best instructions they are able to give you.

The Empress being thus persuaded by the Duchess to make an imaginary world of her own, followed her advice; and after she had quite finished it, and framed all kinds of creatures proper and useful for it, strengthened it with good laws, and beautified it with arts and sciences; having nothing else to do, unless she did dissolve her imaginary world, or made some alterations in the Blazing World she lived in, which yet she could hardly do, by reason it was so well ordered that it could not be mended.[1]

[Empress, Duchess, Duke]

At last, they entered into the Duke's house,[2] an habitation not so magnificent, as useful; and when the Empress saw it, "Has the Duke," said she, "no other house but this?" "Yes," answered the Duchess, "some five miles from this place, he has a very fine castle, called Bolsover."[3] "That place then," said the Empress, "I desire to see." "Alas!" replied the Duchess, "it is but a naked house, and unclothed of all furniture." "However," said the Empress, "I may see the manner of its structure and building." "That you may," replied the Duchess. And as they were thus discoursing, the Duke came out of the house into the court, to see his horses of manage;[4] whom when the Duchess's soul perceived, she was so overjoyed, that her aerial vehicle[5] became so splendorous, as if it had been enlightened by the sun; by which we may perceive, that the passions of souls or spirits can alter their bodily vehicles. Then these two ladies' spirits went close to him, but he could not perceive them; and after the Empress had observed the art of manage, she was much pleased with it, and commended it as a noble pastime, and an exercise fit and proper for noble and heroic persons; but when the Duke was gone into the house again, those two souls followed him; where the Empress observing, that he went to the exercise of the sword, and was such an excellent and unparalleled master thereof, she was as much pleased with that exercise, as she was with the former. But the Duchess's soul being troubled, that her dear lord and husband used such a violent exercise before meat, for fear of overheating himself, without any consideration of the Empress's soul, left her aerial vehicle, and entered into her lord. The Empress's soul perceiving this, did the like: and then the Duke had three souls in one body; and had there been but some such souls more, the Duke would have been like the Grand Signior in his seraglio,[6] only it would have been a Platonic seraglio.[7] But the Duke's soul being wise, honest, witty, complaisant, and noble, afforded such delight and pleasure to the Empress's soul by

1. Instead, the Empress resolves "to see the world the Duchess came from," and so "those two female souls" travel together "as lightly as two thoughts," into England.
2. Welbeck Abbey, north-country birthplace and family seat of Cavendish's husband the Duke of Newcastle.
3. The Duke's favorite residence.
4. Well-disciplined in the actions and paces of *ménage*, or systematic horse training. The Duke, an expert equestrian, had published two books on the subject; when Charles II was a boy, Newcastle had taught him how to ride.
5. Form made out of air.
6. Harem.
7. One where the pleasures of the flesh would be repudiated in favor of the contemplation of pure, disembodied Ideas.

her conversation, that these two souls became enamored of each other; which the Duchess's soul perceiving, grew jealous at first, but then considering that no adultery could be committed amongst Platonic lovers, and that Platonism was divine, as being derived from divine Plato, cast forth of her mind that idea of jealousy. Then the conversation of these three souls was so pleasant, that it cannot be expressed; for the Duke's soul entertained the Empress's soul with scenes, songs, music, witty discourses, pleasant recreations, and all kinds of harmless sports; so that the time passed away faster than they expected. At last, a spirit came and told the Empress, that although neither the Emperor, nor any of his subjects knew that her soul was absent; yet the Empress's soul was so sad and melancholy, for want of his own beloved soul, that all the imperial court took notice of it. Wherefore he advised the Empress's soul to return into the Blazing World, into her own body she left there; which both the Duke's and Duchess's soul was very sorry for, and wished, that if it had been possible, the Empress's soul might have stayed a longer time with them; but seeing it could not be otherwise, they pacified themselves. * * *

Epilogue

To The Reader

By this poetical description, you may perceive, that my ambition is not only to be Empress, but Authoress of a whole world; and that the worlds I have made, both the Blazing and the other Philosophical World, mentioned in the first part of this description, are framed and composed of the most pure, that is, the rational parts of matter, which are the parts of my mind; which creation was more easily and suddenly effected than the conquests of the two famous monarchs of the world, Alexander and Caesar. Neither have I made such disturbances, and caused so many dissolutions of particulars,[8] otherwise named deaths, as they did; for I have destroyed but some few men in a little boat,[9] which died through the extremity of cold, and that by the hand of Justice, which was necessitated to punish their crime of stealing away a young and beauteous lady. And in the formation of those worlds, I take more delight and glory, than ever Alexander or Caesar did in conquering this terrestrial world; and though I have made my Blazing World a peaceable world, allowing it but one religion, one language, and one government; yet could I make another world, as full of factions, divisions, and wars, as this is of peace and tranquility; and the rational figures of my mind might express as much courage to fight, as Hector and Achilles had; and be as wise as Nestor, as eloquent as Ulysses, and as beautiful as Helen.[1] But I esteeming peace before war, wit before policy, honesty before beauty; instead of the figures of Alexander, Caesar, Hector, Achilles, Nestor, Ulysses, Helen, etc. chose rather the figure of honest Margaret Newcastle, which now I would not change for all this terrestrial world; and if any should like the world I have made, and be willing to be my subjects, they may imagine themselves such, and they are such, I mean, in their minds, fancies, or imaginations; but if they cannot endure to be subjects, they may create worlds of their own, and govern themselves as they please: but yet let them have a care, not to prove unjust usurpers, and to rob me of mine; for concerning the Philosophical World, I am Empress of it myself; and as for the Blazing World, it having an Empress already, who rules it with great wisdom

8. Individuals.
9. The sailor-abductors of the "virtuous lady," who die during the boat's passage through the North Pole to the Blazing World.
1. Characters in the *Iliad*, Homer's epic poem about the Trojan War.

and conduct, which Empress is my dear Platonic friend; I shall never prove so unjust, treacherous, and unworthy to her, as to disturb her government, much less to depose her from her imperial throne, for the sake of any other; but rather choose to create another world for another friend.

1666

John Dryden

1631–1700

Godfrey Kneller, *John Dryden*, 1693.

In his last years, John Dryden often felt the need to defend his morals, his religion, his politics, even his writing. For nearly a quarter of a century, he had held high literary office and mingled with the great; he had curried royal favor and aristocratic patronage, bolstering officialdom, aiming to injure the Crown's enemies and to caress its friends. He wrote about politics and religion, about trade and empire; he wrote for the theater and for public occasions; he composed songs, fables, odes, and panegyrics, brilliant satire and savage polemic; he translated from many languages and formulated an idiomatic, familiar, and fluent prose style. Dryden virtually invented the idea of a commercial literary career; and through all the turns of a difficult public life, he fashioned from his own unlikely personality—from his privacy, self-doubts, and hesitations—a public figure of literary distinction. But he attained this celebrity at the cost of gossip and scandal, and in the last decade of his life (after the Glorious Revolution and his deposition from the Poet Laureateship) he faced suspicion and scorn.

The poet's beginnings give no hint of literary greatness or the likelihood of fame. He was born in 1631 in a country town and to comfortable circumstance; he was educated at Westminster School and graduated from Trinity College, Cambridge. He held minor public office in the 1650s but had written almost nothing before he was twenty-seven. Dryden then began his long career as public poet. He mourned the Lord Protector in 1659 (*Heroic Stanzas*) and then, in what looks like a convenient turn of allegiance, he celebrated the return of monarchy in 1660, writing poems to Charles II, to the Lord Chancellor, and to the Duchess of York; he praised the Royal Society (*To Doctor Charleton*) and defended the Royal Navy and its aristocratic high command (*Annus Mirabilis*, 1667).

The first years seem a series of calculated moves; and the combination of talent, application, and opportunity was crowned when Dryden was named Poet Laureate in 1667. But in addition to fashioning a career in the 1660s, Dryden also forged a new drama—an epic theater whose themes and language echoed the idioms of heroic verse—and a body of literary criticism that itself would have made his lasting reputation. Indeed, the great text of the first decade was the *Essay of Dramatic Poesy* (1668), Dryden's formulation of a pointedly English poetics and theater. Along with Sir Philip Sidney's *Apology for Poetry*, and Samuel Johnson's *Lives of the Poets*, Dryden's *Essay* is central to the long-standing canon of English literary criticism. Some of Dryden's early plays have been forgotten, but he worked steadily at a craft that would enable him to turn Milton's *Paradise Lost* into theater (*The State of Innocence*, 1677), create a superb adaptation of Shakespeare's *Antony and Cleopatra* in *All for Love* (1678), the finest of Restoration tragedies in *Don Sebastian* (1690), and the texts of one of England's first operas, *King Arthur* (1691), and last masques, *The Pilgrim* (1700).

By the late 1670s Dryden was famed as publicist for the Crown, and his theatrical work had come to dominate the stage; but he had hardly begun the career as satirist by which he is now best known. Its opening move was *Mac Flecknoe* (1676), and in the next few years Dryden fashioned masterpieces of literary mockery and political invective, poems that virtually created literary genres and dominated satire for decades to come. *Mac Flecknoe* allowed Dryden to ridicule and crush his rivals, all the while conjuring the suave tones and elegant manners of literary supremacy. In the abuse of rivals, only Pope surpasses Dryden as a master of scorn. But *Mac Flecknoe* was only the first act in a theater of invective. In the fall of 1681 Dryden wrote *Absalom and Achitophel*, a biblical allegory occasioned by the crisis of succession. The king had failed to beget a legitimate heir, and the king's Catholic brother waited ominously in the wings. It was Dryden's job to defend the Crown, to extenuate royal indulgence, and, especially, to defuse anxieties. With *Absalom and Achitophel*, Dryden wove together the Bible and contemporary politics with such deftness that mere diversionary tactics were spun into an incomparable allegory of envy, ambition, and misdeed. The satire was read, marked, circulated, and treasured as a masterpiece and a menace.

The masterpiece secured Dryden's fame; the menace exacted a cost. The poet had attacked powerful men: aristocrats, politicans, and their partisan hacks who intrigued against the Crown. They failed in the early 1680s to foment rebellion, but by 1688 they were able to effect a revolution that deposed Catholic monarchy and the Poet Laureate himself. Dryden was reputed a brilliant and damaging advocate of Stuart rule; he had collaborated with court publicity and polemic; he had even converted to Roman Catholicism after James ascended the throne. Indeed, Dryden wrote his longest and most elaborate original poem—*The Hind and the Panther* (1687)—in defense of that king's rule and religion, and of his own conversion to Roman Catholicism. Once James II had been chased into exile, the poet felt he had nowhere to turn. In 1688 Dryden was fifty-seven, an old man by contemporary standards. He was forced from office, his pension was canceled, and he was driven back to the venues of commercial writing: the theater, translation, publication by subscription, even editing and anthologizing. He often expressed a keen sense of loss and abandonment in the 1690s, yet the decade would prove to be a remarkable phase of his career. Between his loss of the laureateship in 1689 and his death in 1700, Dryden wrote a series of superb translations that included selections from the satires of Juvenal and Persius, Ovid's *Metamorphoses* and *Amores*, Boccaccio's and Chaucer's tales. In these same years he wrote odes and epitaphs, and collaborated with his publisher Jacob Tonson in the new fashion for literary anthologies. Most remarkably, he produced *The Works of Virgil*, which set the standard for the translation of Latin poetry. He had come to his project late, and more than once he wrote of his inadequacy for this daunting task: "What Virgil wrote in the vigor of his age, in plenty and at ease, I have undertaken to translate in my declining years, struggling with wants, oppressed with sickness, curbed in my genius, liable to be misconstrued in all I write; and my judges . . . already prejudiced against me, by the lying character which has been given them of my morals." But Dryden's *Virgil* was a resounding, rehabilitating commercial and artistic success.

Nor were the twelve thousand lines of translated Virgil the close of this career. What followed was *Fables Ancient and Modern*, an anthology of original verse and new translations that included Ovid, Boccaccio, and Chaucer as well as a trial for what Dryden hoped would be his English Homer. He saw commercial opportunity in this new collection; but he must also have understood it as a crowning achievement in this life of theatricality and ventriloquism. He had begun by seeking a voice in the idioms and gestures of other poets; he now belonged wholly to himself as he casually turned their verse into his own. It is something of a paradox that a life of literary self-assertion, of aggressive, even calculating, careerism, should have closed with Dryden rummaging among other poets' verse, pausing over favorite lines, translating Ovid's Latin and Boccaccio's Italian into what was unmistakably his own voice. And the paradox of self-assertion ending in translation helps us to identify what is so particularly and so brilliantly Dryden's art. In the early modern world, writing meant belonging to others—to the authority of antiquity, to the opinions and fickle pleasure of patrons, to favor, to obligation, to taste, even to the emerging appetites of a reading public. Many of Dryden's contemporaries—Donne, Milton, Rochester—appeal to us by their seeming defiance of such self-denying ordinances. We read Dryden today not just for the skill with which he picked his way through political dangers or negotiated social minefields, not even for the savage cartooning of enemies or baroque praise of friends, but for the achievement of belonging to others as he became more exactly and more generously himself.

For additional resources on Dryden, including the ode "To the Pious Memory of the Accomplished Young Lady Mrs. Anne Killigrew," go to *The Longman Anthology of British Literature* Web site at www.myliteraturekit.com.

Absalom and Achitophel Dryden wrote *Absalom and Achitophel* as a piece of propaganda; he was, after all, Poet Laureate. He may even have written it at the personal request of Charles II, and he surely intended to please the king, to entertain his friends, to embarrass their enemies. He performed these offices amidst tangled circumstances and under extraordinary partisan and civic pressures.

Charles had sired many children by many mistresses, but no heir by his wife. These habits and accidents of royal procreation had created a succession crisis: in the absence of a legitimate heir, the crown would pass to Charles's brother James, an openly professed Roman Catholic. This prospect excited every fear of absolute rule—of Popery, slavery, subjugation to France and to Rome. The crisis, in turn, helped crystallize an opposition of Protestants, rebels, republicans, and opportunists who mustered support for an audacious proposal: exclude the duke from succession and appoint as substitute the dim but charming, Protestant but (alas) bastard offspring of the king, James, Duke of Monmouth.

To bolster its program, the opposition made ingenious use of a conspiracy theory, widely entertained though largely false. In 1678 the mysterious murder of an eminent judge, a cloud of perjured witnesses, and a blizzard of broadsides, rumors, and innuendos persuaded many that the Queen, the Duke of York, and a band of Jesuits had conspired in a "Popish Plot" to kill the king and inaugurate Catholic rule. At the height of the mania, thirty-five Catholics were executed for their supposed complicity in this "plot." After the bloodletting, and in the face of much evidence to suggest that the plot itself was fiction, the rage subsided. The Whig opposition, now emerging from thuggery and faction into England's first organized political party, tested its powers by parliamentary maneuver. In 1680 its leader, the Earl of Shaftesbury, tried twice to pass a bill excluding Charles's brother James from the succession. In 1681 Shaftesbury publicly urged Charles to legitimate Monmouth. The king had had enough: he dismissed Parliament in March, and on 2 July had Shaftesbury imprisoned on charges of high treason. Four months later, a packed jury produced the verdict *ignoramus* ("we don't know").

Dryden's poem, appearing the week before the trial, told these busy stories in terms both daring and familiar. He cast the crisis as biblical drama: Charles became King David, Monmouth was David's wayward son Absalom, Shaftesbury the wily counselor Achitophel. Of course, factions of all sorts had long deployed parallels between England and Israel for instruction, for prophecy and exhortation, for mockery and even scandal. But no one had set all the possibilities of irony and celebration simultaneously in motion. Against the king's enemies Dryden turned their own rhetoric of scriptural sanctimony; in support of the king's friends he wrote hymns of praise; but on behalf of that complex client the king himself, Dryden discovered a way of portraying monarchy in a spirit at once appreciative, ironic, and delicately abrasive. In the poem's mischievous opening lines we hear these possibilities fully orchestrated. Charles's sexual energies, mapped as Davidic fecundity, are simultaneously grand and titillating, munificent and comic. Such mixtures of tone suffuse all the actions and arguments of Dryden's poem—its images of authority, its satiric portraits, its theories of governance, its monologues and declamations—all its traffic with the dangerous world of politics, plots, and promiscuity.

Absalom and Achitophel: A Poem.

—Si propiùs stes
Te capiet magis—[1]

TO THE READER

'Tis not my intention to make an apology for my poem: some will think it needs no excuse, and others will receive none. The design, I am sure, is honest, but he who draws his pen for one party must expect to make enemies of the other. For wit and fool are consequents of Whig and Tory, and every man is a knave or an ass to the contrary side. There's a treasury of merits in the fanatic church, as well as in the Papist, and a pennyworth to be had of saintship, honesty, and poetry, for the lewd, the factious, and the blockheads.[2] But the longest chapter in Deuteronomy has not curses enough for an anti-Bromingham.[3] My comfort is, their manifest prejudice to my cause will render their judgment of less authority against me. Yet if a poem have a genius, it will force its own reception in the world. For there's a sweetness in good verse, which tickles even while it hurts, and no man can be heartily angry with him who pleases him against his will. The commendation of adversaries is the greatest triumph of a writer, because it never comes unless extorted. But I can be satisfied on more easy terms: if I happen to please the more moderate sort, I shall be sure of an honest party and, in all probability, of the best judges, for the least concerned are commonly the least corrupt. And, I confess, I have laid in for those, by rebating[4] the satire (where justice would allow it) from carrying too sharp an edge. They who can criticize so weakly as to imagine I have done my worst may be convinced, at their own cost, that I can write severely with more ease than I can gently. I have but laughed at some men's follies, when I could have declaimed against their vices; and other men's virtues I have commended as freely as I have taxed[5] their crimes. And now, if you are a malicious reader, I expect you should return upon me that I affect to be thought more impartial than I am. But if men are not to be judged by their professions,[6] God forgive you commonwealthsmen[7] for professing so plausibly for the government. You cannot be so unconscionable as to charge me for not subscribing of my name, for that would reflect too grossly upon your own party, who never dare, though they have the advantage of a jury to secure them.[8] If you like not my poem, the fault may, possibly, be in my writing (though 'tis hard for an author to judge

1. "If you stand closer, it will capture you more readily" (Horace, *Ars Poetica* 361–62); Horace is here developing his argument that a poem works like a picture (*ut pictura poesis*).
2. Roman Catholic doctrine posited the existence in heaven of a fund of surplus "merits," accumulated through the goodness of Christ and the saints, on which ordinary mortals might draw for absolution. Dryden suggests that the dissenting Protestant sects ("the fanatic church"), like the Catholic ("Papist") church, confer forgiveness (even "saintship") too freely, and too cheaply.
3. Tory (Royalist). Deuteronomy 28 includes a long list of curses against those who "shall not enter into the congregation of the Lord" because they have disobeyed his law.
4. Abating, softening.
5. Denounced.
6. What they say (profess).
7. Here and throughout the poem, Dryden conflates the supporters of Monmouth with the supporters of Cromwell, as enemies of the monarchy.
8. Dryden published his politically volatile poem anonymously. He accuses Whig writers of similar caution, and hence of greater cowardice, because the London juries that adjudicated cases of seditious libel were handpicked by Whig sheriffs for their bias in the party's favor.

against himself); but, more probably, 'tis in your morals, which cannot bear the truth of it. The violent on both sides will condemn the character of Absalom as either too favorably or too hardly drawn. But they are not the violent whom I desire to please. The fault, on the right hand, is to extenuate, palliate, and indulge; and, to confess freely, I have endeavored to commit it. Besides the respect which I owe his birth, I have a greater for his heroic virtues; and David himself could not be more tender of the young man's life than I would be of his reputation. But since the most excellent natures are always the most easy,[9] and, as being such, are the soonest perverted by ill counsels, especially when baited with fame and glory, 'tis no more a wonder that he withstood not the temptations of Achitophel than it was for Adam not to have resisted the two devils, the serpent and the woman. The conclusion of the story I purposely forbore to prosecute, because I could not obtain from myself to show Absalom unfortunate.[1] The frame of it was cut out but for a picture to the waist; and if the draught be so far true, 'tis as much as I designed.

Were I the inventor, who am only the historian, I should certainly conclude the piece with the reconcilement of Absalom to David. And who knows but this may come to pass? Things were not brought to an extremity where I left the story. There seems yet to be room left for a composure;[2] hereafter, there may only be for pity. I have not so much as an uncharitable wish against Achitophel, but am content to be accused of a good-natured error and to hope with Origen[3] that the Devil himself may, at last, be saved. For which reason, in this poem he is neither brought to set his house in order nor to dispose of his person afterwards as he in wisdom shall think fit.[4] God is infinitely merciful, and his vicegerent[5] is only not so because he is not infinite.

The true end of satire is the amendment of vices by correction. And he who writes honestly is no more an enemy to the offender than the physician to the patient, when he prescribes harsh remedies to an inveterate disease; for those are only in order to prevent the surgeon's work of an *ense rescindendum*,[6] which I wish not to my very enemies. To conclude all, if the body politic have any analogy to the natural, in my weak judgment, an Act of Oblivion were as necessary in a hot, distempered state as an opiate would be in a raging fever.

Absalom and Achitophel: A Poem

In pious times, ere priestcraft did begin,
Before polygamy was made a sin;[7]
When man on many multiplied his kind,
Ere one to one was cursedly confined;
When Nature prompted, and no law denied
Promiscuous use of concubine and bride;
Then Israel's monarch, after Heaven's own heart,
His vigorous warmth did variously impart
To wives and slaves; and, wide as his command,

9. Easily persuaded.
1. I.e., Dryden decided to leave off the end of the biblical story (in which Absalom is killed), because he could not bring himself to show Absalom's misfortune.
2. Reconciliation.
3. An early Christian theologian.
4. Dryden insinuatingly echoes the biblical account of Achitophel's disappointment and suicide (2 Samuel 23).
5. The king.
6. "Something to be cut out" in order to prevent infection of the whole organism. Dryden next suggests that an "Act of Oblivion" forgiving the rebels, like the one Charles II enacted at his Restoration, might constitute a gentler remedy.
7. "Priestcraft" is "religious fraud" (Johnson's *Dictionary*); Dryden mimics the anti-Catholicism of the Whigs, while insinuating that monogamy is an unnatural restriction imposed by power-hungry priests.

Scattered his Maker's image through the land.
Michal,[8] of royal blood, the crown did wear,
A soil ungrateful to the tiller's care:
Not so the rest, for several mothers bore
To godlike David several sons before.
But since like slaves his bed they did ascend,
No true succession could their seed attend.[9]
Of all this numerous progeny was none
So beautiful, so brave as Absolon:
Whether, inspired by some diviner lust,
His father got° him with a greater gust,° *begot / pleasure*
Or that his conscious destiny made way
By manly beauty to imperial sway.
Early in foreign fields he won renown,
With kings and states allied to Israel's crown:
In peace the thoughts of war he could remove,
And seemed as he were only born for love.
Whate'er he did was done with so much ease,
In him alone 'twas natural to please.
His motions all accompanied with grace;
And paradise was opened in his face.
With secret joy indulgent David viewed
His youthful image in his son renewed:
To all his wishes nothing he denied,
And made the charming Annabel[1] his bride.
What faults he had (for who from faults is free?)
His father could not, or he would not see.
Some warm excesses, which the law forbore,
Were construed youth that purged by boiling o'er:
And Amnon's murder,[2] by a specious name,
Was called a just revenge for injured fame.
Thus praised and loved the noble youth remained,
While David, undisturbed, in Sion[3] reigned.
But life can never be sincerely blest:
Heaven punishes the bad, and proves° the best. *tests*
The Jews,[4] a headstrong, moody, murmuring race,
As ever tried th' extent and stretch of grace;
God's pampered people whom, debauched with ease,
No king could govern, nor no God could please
(Gods they had tried of every shape and size
That god-smiths could produce, or priests devise);
These Adam-wits, too fortunately free,
Began to dream they wanted° liberty; *lacked, desired*
And when no rule, no precedent was found

8. Daughter of David's predecessor King Saul; here she represents Charles's childless wife, Catherine of Braganza.
9. Their offspring could not succeed to the throne because of their illegitimacy.
1. Anne, Countess of Buccleuch.
2. In 2 Samuel 8, Amnon rapes Absalom's half sister, and Absalom orders his murder; the correspondence with events in Monmouth's life is uncertain.
3. Jerusalem (hence, London).
4. The English.

Of men by laws less circumscribed and bound,
They led their wild desires to woods and caves,
And thought that all but savages were slaves.
They who when Saul was dead, without a blow,
Made foolish Ishbosheth[5] the crown forgo;
Who banished David did from Hebron bring,[6]
And with a general shout proclaimed him King:
Those very Jews, who, at their very best,
Their humor more than loyalty expressed,
Now wondered why so long they had obeyed
An idol monarch which their hands had made;
Thought they might ruin him they could create,
Or melt him to that golden calf, a state.
But these were random bolts; no formed design,
Nor interest made the factious crowd to join:
The sober part of Israel, free from stain,
Well knew the value of a peaceful reign:
And, looking backward with a wise afright,
Saw seams of wounds, dishonest to the sight;
In contemplation of whose ugly scars
They cursed the memory of Civil Wars.
The moderate sort of men, thus qualified,
Inclined the balance to the better side:
And David's mildness managed it so well,
The bad found no occasion to rebel.
But when to sin our biased nature leans,
The careful Devil is still° at hand with means; *always*
And providently pimps for ill desires:
The Good Old Cause[7] revived, a Plot requires.
Plots, true or false, are necessary things,
To raise up commonwealths and ruin kings.
 Th' inhabitants of old Jerusalem
Were Jebusites:[8] the town so called from them;
And theirs the native right—
But when the chosen people grew more strong,
The rightful cause at length became the wrong:
And every loss the men of Jebus bore,
They still were thought God's enemies the more.
Thus, worn and weakened, well or ill content,
Submit they must to David's government:
Impoverished, and deprived of all command,
Their taxes doubled as they lost their land,
And, what was harder yet to flesh and blood,
Their gods disgraced, and burnt like common wood.[9]

5. Ishbosheth briefly succeeded his father Saul; correspondingly, Richard Cromwell was Protector for a few months after the death of his father, Oliver.
6. David ruled in Hebron seven years before becoming king of Israel. Charles had been crowned in Scotland in 1651.
7. Popular name for the Cromwellian opposition to the monarchy.
8. Jebusites inhabited Jerusalem before the Israelites; here, they represent the Catholics.
9. Dryden alludes to a variety of anti-Catholic penal laws.

This set the heathen priesthood in a flame;
For priests of all religions are the same:
Of whatsoe'er descent their godhead be,
Stock, stone, or other homely pedigree,
In his defense his servants are as bold
As if he had been born of beaten gold.
The Jewish rabbins,[1] though their enemies,
In this conclude them honest men and wise:
For 'twas their duty, all the learned think,
T' espouse his cause by whom they eat and drink.
From hence began that Plot,[2] the nation's curse,
Bad in itself, but represented worse:
Raised in extremes, and in extremes decried;
With oaths affirmed, with dying vows denied:
Not weighed or winnowed by the multitude,
But swallowed in the mass, unchewed and crude.
Some truth there was, but dashed and brewed with lies,
To please the fools, and puzzle all the wise.
Succeeding times did equal folly call
Believing nothing, or believing all.
Th' Egyptian rites the Jebusites embraced,
Where gods were recommended by their taste.[3]
Such savory deities must needs be good,
As served at once for worship and for food.
By force they could not introduce these gods,
For ten to one[4] in former days was odds.
So fraud was used (the sacrificer's trade):
Fools are more hard to conquer than persuade.
Their busy teachers mingled with the Jews,
And raked, for converts, even the court and stews:° *brothels*
Which Hebrew priests the more unkindly took,
Because the fleece[5] accompanies the flock.
Some thought they God's anointed[6] meant to slay
By guns, invented since full many a day:[7]
Our author swears it not; but who can know
How far the Devil and Jebusites may go?
This Plot, which failed for want of common sense,
Had yet a deep and dangerous consequence:
For, as when raging fevers boil the blood,
The standing lake soon floats into a flood,
And every hostile humor,[8] which before
Slept quiet in its channels, bubbles o'er;
So several factions from this first ferment
Work up to foam, and threat the government.

1. Anglican clergy.
2. The Popish Plot.
3. Here, and in the lines following, Dryden mocks the Catholic belief in transubstantiation.
4. Protestants to Catholics.
5. Tithe, paid by the "flock" (the parishioners).
6. The king.
7. Long since; Dryden playfully acknowledges this anachronism.
8. Bodily fluid, thought to determine temperament.

Some by their friends, more by themselves thought wise,
Opposed the power to which they could not rise.
Some had in courts been great, and thrown from thence,
Like fiends were hardened in impenitence.
Some, by their monarch's fatal mercy, grown,
From pardoned rebels, kinsmen to the throne,
Were raised in power and public office high:
Strong bands, if bands ungrateful men could tie.
Of these the false Achitophel[9] was first:
A name to all succeeding ages cursed:
For close° designs and crooked counsels fit; *secret*
Sagacious, bold, and turbulent of wit:
Restless, unfixed in principles and place;
In power unpleased, impatient of disgrace:
A fiery soul, which working out its way,
Fretted the pygmy body to decay:
And o'er-informed the tenement of clay.[1]
A daring pilot in extremity;
Pleased with the danger, when the waves went high
He sought the storms; but for a calm unfit,
Would steer too nigh the sands, to boast his wit.
Great wits are sure to madness near allied;
And thin partitions do their bounds divide:
Else why should he, with wealth and honor blessed,
Refuse his age[2] the needful hours of rest?
Punish a body which he could not please;
Bankrupt of life, yet prodigal of ease?
And all to leave what with his toil he won,
To that unfeathered, two-legged thing, a son:
Got while his soul did huddled notions try;
And born a shapeless lump, like anarchy.
In friendship false, implacable in hate:
Resolved to ruin or to rule the state.
To compass this the triple bond[3] he broke,
The pillars of the public safety shook,
And fitted Israel for a foreign yoke.
Then, seized with fear, yet still affecting° fame, *desiring*
Usurped a patriot's all-atoning name.[4]
So easy still it proves in factious times,
With public zeal to cancel private crimes:
How safe is treason, and how sacred ill,
Where none can sin against the people's will:
Where crowds can wink,[5] and no offense be known,

9. David's counselor, who encourages Absalom to rebel against his father; here representing Anthony Ashley Cooper, first Earl of Shaftesbury, counselor to both Cromwell and Charles II.

1. The body; Dryden contrasts Shaftesbury's large ambition with his small and sickly body.

2. Shaftesbury was 60 in 1681.

3. England's 1668 alliance with Sweden and Holland (against France).

4. Name that excuses anything.

5. Turn a blind eye.

Since in another's guilt they find their own.
Yet fame deserved no enemy can grudge;
The statesman we abhor, but praise the judge.
In Israel's courts ne'er sat an Abbethdin[6]
With more discerning eyes, or hands more clean:
Unbribed, unsought, the wretched to redress,
Swift of dispatch, and easy of access.
Oh, had he been content to serve the crown,
With virtues only proper to the gown;
Or had the rankness of the soil been freed
From cockle,° that oppressed the noble seed: *weeds*
David for him his tuneful harp had strung,
And heaven had wanted one immortal song.[7]
But wild ambition loves to slide, not stand,
And fortune's ice prefers to virtue's land:
Achitophel, grown weary to possess° *of possessing*
A lawful fame and lazy happiness,
Disdained the golden fruit to gather free,
And lent the crowd his arm to shake the tree.
Now, manifest° of crimes contrived long since, *clearly guilty*
He stood at bold defiance with his prince:
Held up the buckler° of the people's cause *shield*
Against the crown; and skulked behind the laws.
The wished occasion of the Plot he takes,
Some circumstances finds, but more he makes;
By buzzing emissaries fills the ears
Of list'ning crowds with jealousies and fears
Of arbitrary counsels brought to light,
And proves the King himself a Jebusite:
Weak arguments! which yet he knew full well
Were strong with people easy to rebel.
For, governed by the moon, the giddy Jews
Tread the same track when she the prime renews;[8]
And once in twenty years, their scribes record,
By natural instinct they change their lord.
Achitophel still wants a chief, and none
Was found so fit as warlike Absolon:
Not that he wished his greatness to create
(For politicians neither love nor hate),
But for he knew his title not allowed,
Would keep him still depending on the crowd,
That kingly power, thus ebbing out, might be
Drawn to the dregs of a democracy.[9]
Him he attempts with studied arts to please,

6. Chief justice of the Jewish supreme court.
7. David would have composed one psalm fewer because he would be employed in writing praise of Achitophel.
8. A lunar cycle lasts about 20 years; Dryden alludes to the constitutional crises of 1640, 1660, and 1680.
9. Like "commonwealth" and "state," a pejorative term used to suggest a government of mob rule.

And sheds his venom in such words as these.
"Auspicious Prince! at whose nativity
Some royal planet ruled the southern sky;
Thy longing country's darling and desire;
Their cloudy pillar, and their guardian fire:
Their second Moses, whose extended wand
Divides the seas and shows the promised land:[1]
Whose dawning day, in every distant age,
Has exercised the sacred prophet's rage:
The people's prayer, the glad diviners' theme,
The young men's vision, and the old men's dream!
Thee, savior, thee, the nation's vows confess,
And, never satisfied with seeing, bless:
Swift, unbespoken pomps° thy steps proclaim, *unsought honors*
And stammering babes are taught to lisp thy name.
How long wilt thou the general joy detain,
Starve and defraud the people of thy reign?
Content ingloriously to pass thy days
Like one of virtue's fools that feeds on praise;
Till thy fresh glories, which now shine so bright,
Grow stale and tarnish with our daily sight.
Believe me, royal youth, thy fruit must be
Or° gathered ripe, or rot upon the tree. *either*
Heav'n has to all allotted, soon or late,
Some lucky revolution of their fate:
Whose motions, if we watch and guide with skill
(For human good depends on human will),
Our Fortune rolls as from a smooth descent,
And from the first impression takes the bent:
But, if unseized, she glides away like wind,
And leaves repenting folly far behind.[2]
Now, now she meets you with a glorious prize,
And spreads her locks before her as she flies.
Had thus old David, from whose loins you spring,
Not dared, when Fortune called him, to be King,
At Gath[3] an exile he might still remain,
And heaven's anointing oil had been in vain.
Let his successful youth your hopes engage,
But shun the example of declining age:
Behold him setting in his western skies,
The shadows length'ning as the vapors rise.
He is not now as when on Jordan's sand
The joyful people thronged to see him land,
Cov'ring the beach, and black'ning all the strand:[4]
But, like the Prince of Angels[5] from his height,

1. On the way to Canaan, God's "promised land," Moses led the Israelites across the Red Sea and through the desert; they followed a pillar of cloud by day and a pillar of fire by night.
2. Fortune, represented as a woman with streaming hair, needs to be grasped at the first opportunity.
3. Brussels, where Charles spent the last phase of his exile.
4. Dryden refers to Charles's triumphant landing at Dover in May of 1660.
5. Lucifer (light-bearer) rebelled against God and was cast out from heaven.

Comes tumbling downward with diminished light;
Betrayed by one poor plot to public scorn
(Our only blessing since his curst return),
Those heaps of people which one sheaf did bind,
Blown off and scattered by a puff of wind.
What strength can he to your designs oppose,
Naked of friends, and round beset with foes?
If Pharaoh's doubtful succor he should use,[6]
A foreign aid would more incense the Jews:
Proud Egypt would dissembled friendship bring,
Foment the war, but not support the King:
Nor would the royal party e'er unite
With Pharaoh's arms t' assist the Jebusite;
Or if they should, their interest soon would break,
And with such odious aid make David weak.
All sorts of men by my successful arts,
Abhorring kings, estrange their altered hearts
From David's rule; and 'tis the general cry,
'Religion, Commonwealth, and Liberty.'[7]
If you, as champion of the public good,
Add to their arms a chief of royal blood,
What may not Israel hope, and what applause
Might such a general gain by such a cause?
Not barren praise alone, that gaudy flower,
Fair only to the sight, but solid power:
And nobler is a limited command,
Giv'n by the love of all your native land,
Than a successive° title, long and dark, *inherited*
Drawn from the moldy rolls of Noah's ark."
What cannot praise effect in mighty minds,
When flattery soothes, and when ambition blinds!
Desire of power, on earth a vicious weed,
Yet, sprung from high, is of celestial seed:
In God 'tis glory, and when men aspire,
'Tis but a spark too much of heavenly fire.
Th' ambitious youth, too covetous of fame,
Too full of angel's metal[8] in his frame,
Unwarily was led from virtue's ways,
Made drunk with honor, and debauched with praise.
Half loath, and half consenting to the ill
(For royal blood within him struggled still),
He thus replied: "And what pretense have I
To take up arms for public liberty?
My father governs with unquestioned right;

6. I.e., if Charles should turn for assistance to Louis XIV, Catholic king of France.
7. A slogan of the Good Old Cause.
8. Dryden puns on "angel" (a coin as well as a supernatural being) and on "metal" / "mettle" ("spriteliness, courage"—Johnson's *Dictionary*).

The faith's defender, and mankind's delight:
Good, gracious, just, observant of the laws;
And heav'n by wonders has espoused his cause.
Whom has he wronged in all his peaceful reign?
Who sues for justice to his throne in vain?
What millions has he pardoned[9] of his foes,
Whom just revenge did to his wrath expose!
Mild, easy, humble, studious of our good,
Inclined to mercy, and averse from blood.
If mildness ill with stubborn Israel suit,
His crime is God's beloved attribute.
What could he gain, his people to betray,
Or change his right for arbitrary sway?
Let haughty Pharaoh curse, with such a reign,
His fruitful Nile, and yoke a servile train.
If David's rule Jerusalem displease,
The dog star[1] heats their brains to this disease.
Why then should I, encouraging the bad,
Turn rebel and run popularly mad?
Were he a tyrant who, by lawless might,
Oppressed the Jews and raised the Jebusite,
Well might I mourn; but nature's holy bands
Would curb my spirits and restrain my hands:
The people might assert their liberty,
But what was right in them were crime in me.
His favor leaves me nothing to require,
Prevents my wishes, and outruns desire.
What more can I expect while David lives?
All but his kingly diadem he gives;
And that—" But there he paused; then sighing said,
"Is justly destined for a worthier head.
For when my father from his toils shall rest,
And late augment the number of the blest,
His lawful issue shall the throne ascend,
Or the collateral line[2] where that shall end.
His brother, though oppressed with vulgar spite,[3]
Yet dauntless and secure of native right,
Of every royal virtue stands possessed;
Still dear to all the bravest and the best.
His courage foes, his friends his truth proclaim;
His loyalty the King, the world his fame.
His mercy ev'n th' offending crowd will find,
For sure he comes of a forgiving kind.° *family*
Why should I then repine at Heaven's decree,
Which gives me no pretense to royalty?
Yet O that Fate, propitiously inclined,

9. By the Act of Oblivion of 1660.
1. Sirius, which presides over the madness-inducing "dog days" of summer.
2. That which passed through Charles's brother, James.
3. The hostility of the common people.

Had raised my birth, or had debased my mind;
To my large soul not all her treasure lent,
And then betrayed it to a mean descent.
I find, I find my mounting spirits bold,
And David's part disdains my mother's mold.
Why am I scanted by a niggard[4] birth?
My soul disclaims the kindred of her earth:
And, made for empire, whispers me within,
'Desire of greatness is a godlike sin.' "
   Him staggering so when Hell's dire agent found,[5]
While fainting Virtue scarce maintained her ground,
He pours fresh forces in, and thus replies:
   "Th' eternal God, supremely good and wise,
Imparts not these prodigious gifts in vain;
What wonders are reserved to bless your reign?
Against your will, your arguments have shown
Such virtue's only given to guide a throne.
Not that your father's mildness I condemn;
But manly force becomes the diadem.
'Tis true, he grants the people all they crave,
And more perhaps than subjects ought to have:
For lavish grants suppose° a monarch tame, *suggest*
And more his goodness than his wit proclaim.
But when should people strive their bonds to break,
If not when kings are negligent or weak?
Let him give on till he can give no more,
The thrifty Sanhedrin[6] shall keep him poor:
And every shekel° which he can receive, *coin*
Shall cost a limb of his prerogative.[7]
To ply him with new plots shall be my care,
Or plunge him deep in some expensive war;
Which when his treasure can no more supply,
He must with the remains of kingship buy.
His faithful friends our jealousies and fears
Call Jebusites, and Pharaoh's pensioners:
Whom, when our fury from his aid has torn,
He shall be naked left to public scorn.
The next successor,[8] whom I fear and hate,
My arts have made obnoxious to the state;
Turned all his virtues to his overthrow,
And gained our elders[9] to pronounce a foe.
His right, for sums of necessary gold,
Shall first be pawned, and afterwards be sold:
Till time shall ever-wanting David draw,

4. Stingy; i.e., Monmouth's illegitimacy prevents him from acquiring all he desires.
5. The Miltonic inversion of syntax helps to link Achitophel's speech to the temptation of Eve by Satan in Book 9 of *Paradise Lost*.
6. The Jewish council; here the English Parliament.
7. Royal privileges (which Parliament sought to limit).
8. James, Duke of York.
9. Shaftesbury's supporters, who included members of both the gentry and the aristocracy.

To pass your doubtful title into law:
If not, the people have a right supreme
To make their kings, for kings are made for them.
All empire is no more than power in trust,
Which, when resumed, can be no longer just.
Succession, for the general good designed,
In its own wrong a nation cannot bind:
If altering that the people can relieve,
Better one suffer than a nation grieve.
The Jews well know their power: ere Saul they chose,
God was their King, and God they durst depose.[1]
Urge now your piety, your filial name,
A father's right, and fear of future fame;
The public good, that universal call
To which even Heav'n submitted, answers all.
Nor let his love enchant your generous mind;
'Tis Nature's trick to propagate her kind.
Our fond begetters, who would never die,
Love but themselves in their posterity.
Or let his kindness by th' effects be tried,
Or let him lay his vain pretense aside.
God said he loved your father; could he bring
A better proof than to anoint him King?
It surely showed he loved the shepherd well,
Who gave so fair a flock as Israel.
Would David have you thought his darling son?
What means he then to alienate° the crown? *give away*
The name of godly he may blush to bear:
'Tis after God's own heart to cheat his heir.
He to his brother gives supreme command;
To you a legacy of barren land,[2]
Perhaps th' old harp on which he thrums his lays,[3]
Or some dull Hebrew ballad in your praise.
Then the next heir, a prince severe and wise,
Already looks on you with jealous eyes;
Sees through the thin disguises of your arts,
And marks your progress in the people's hearts.
Though now his mighty soul its grief contains,
He meditates revenge who least complains;
And like a lion, slumbering in the way,
Or sleep dissembling, while he waits his prey,
His fearless foes within his distance draws,
Constrains his roaring, and contracts his paws;
Till at the last, his time for fury found,
He shoots with sudden vengeance from the ground:
The prostrate vulgar passes o'er and spares,

1. The prophet Samuel warned the Israelites that in choosing a king they would displace their true king, God (1 Samuel 8).

2. In 1678 Charles had promoted James and in the following year banished Monmouth.

3. David was said to have composed the Psalms.

But with a lordly rage his hunters tears.
Your case no tame expedients will afford;
Resolve on death, or conquest by the sword,
Which for no less a stake than life you draw;
And self-defense is nature's eldest law.
Leave the warm people no considering time,
For then rebellion may be thought a crime.
Prevail° yourself of what occasion gives, *avail*
But try your title while your father lives:
And that your arms may have a fair pretense,
Proclaim you take them in the King's defense,
Whose sacred life each minute would expose
To plots from seeming friends and secret foes.
And who can sound the depth of David's soul?
Perhaps his fear his kindness may control.
He fears his brother, though he loves his son,
For plighted vows too late to be undone.
If so, by force he wishes to be gained,
Like women's lechery, to seem constrained:
Doubt not, but when he most affects the frown,
Commit a pleasing rape upon the crown.
Secure his person to secure your cause;
They who possess the prince, possess the laws."
He said, and this advice above the rest,
With Absalom's mild nature suited best;
Unblamed of° life (ambition set aside), *blameless in*
Not stained with cruelty, nor puffed with pride;
How happy had he been, if destiny
Had higher placed his birth, or not so high!
His kingly virtues might have claimed a throne,
And blessed all other countries but his own:
But charming greatness, since so few refuse,
'Tis juster to lament him than accuse.
Strong were his hopes a rival to remove,
With blandishments to gain the public love;
To head the faction while their zeal was hot,
And popularly prosecute the Plot.
To farther this, Achitophel unites
The malcontents of all the Israelites;
Whose differing parties he could wisely join,
For several ends, to serve the same design:
The best, and of the princes some were such,
Who thought the power of monarchy too much:
Mistaken men, and patriots in their hearts;
Not wicked, but seduced by impious arts.
By these the springs of property were bent,
And wound so high they cracked the government.
The next for interest sought t' embroil the state,
To sell their duty at a dearer rate;

And make their Jewish markets of the throne,
Pretending public good, to serve their own.
Others thought kings an useless heavy load,
Who cost too much, and did too little good.
These were for laying honest David by,
On principles of pure good husbandry.° *economy*
With them joined all th' haranguers of the throng,
That thought to get preferment by the tongue.
Who follow next a double danger bring,
Not only hating David, but the King;
The Solymaean rout,[4] well versed of old
In godly faction, and in treason bold;
Cowering and quaking at a conqueror's sword,
But lofty° to a lawful prince restored; *arrogant*
Saw with disdain an ethnic[5] plot begun,
And scorned by Jebusites to be outdone.
Hot Levites[6] headed these; who, pulled before
From th' ark, which in the judges' days they bore,[7]
Resumed their cant, and with a zealous cry
Pursued their old beloved theocracy:[8]
Where Sanhedrin and priest enslaved the nation,
And justified their spoils by inspiration;[9]
For who so fit for reign as Aaron's race,[1]
If once dominion they could found in grace?
These led the pack; though not of surest scent,
Yet deepest-mouthed against the government.
A numerous host of dreaming saints succeed;
Of the true old enthusiastic[2] breed:
'Gainst form and order they their power employ,
Nothing to build and all things to destroy.
But far more numerous was the herd of such
Who think too little, and who talk too much.
These out of mere instinct, they knew not why,
Adored their fathers' God and property:
And, by the same blind benefit of fate,
The Devil and the Jebusite did hate:
Born to be saved, even in their own despite,° *despite themselves*
Because they could not help believing right.
Such were the tools, but a whole Hydra[3] more
Remains, of sprouting heads too long to score.
Some of their chiefs were princes of the land:

4. Solymas was another name for Jerusalem, hence, "the London mob."
5. Here, Catholic.
6. Dissenting clergymen.
7. The 1662 Act of Uniformity deprived Presbyterian clergy of their livings which they had acquired during the commonwealth (the judges' days, when they bore the ark).
8. I.e., sought to restore the commonwealth.
9. Members of dissenting sects sometimes claimed to be inspired directly by God.
1. Priests (who, in Jewish law, had to be descendants of Moses's brother Aaron).
2. A pejorative term, applied to those who claimed special inspiration.
3. Many-headed monster, who would sprout new heads every time one was cut off.

In the first rank of these did Zimri[4] stand:
A man so various, that he seemed to be
Not one, but all mankind's epitome.
Stiff in opinions, always in the wrong;
Was everything by starts, and nothing long:
But, in the course of one revolving moon,
Was chemist, fiddler, statesman, and buffoon:
Then all for women, painting, rhyming, drinking;
Besides ten thousand freaks° that died in thinking. *whims*
Blest madman, who could every hour employ,
With something new to wish, or to enjoy!
Railing° and praising were his usual themes; *criticizing*
And both (to show his judgment) in extremes:
So over-violent, or over-civil,
That every man, with him, was god or devil.
In squand'ring wealth was his peculiar art:
Nothing went unrewarded but desert.° *true worth*
Beggared by fools, whom still he found° too late: *found out*
He had his jest, and they had his estate.
He laughed himself from court, then sought relief
By forming parties, but could ne'er be chief:
For, spite of him, the weight of business fell
On Absalom and wise Achitophel:
Thus, wicked but in will, of means bereft,
He left not faction, but of that was left.
    Titles and names 'twere tedious to rehearse
Of lords below the dignity of verse.
Wits, warriors, commonwealthsmen, were the best:
Kind husbands and mere nobles all the rest.
And therefore, in the name of dullness, be
The well-hung Balaam[5] and cold Caleb free.
And canting Nadab[6] let oblivion damn,
Who made new porridge for the paschal lamb.[7]
Let friendship's holy band some names assure:
Some their own worth, and some let scorn secure.
Nor shall the rascal rabble here have place,
Whom kings no titles gave, and God no grace:
Not bull-faced Jonas,[8] who could statutes draw

4. An Old Testament conspirator and regicide (1 Kings 16.9–20); here, George Villiers, Second Duke of Buckingham, a prominent Whig. He had satirized the playwright Dryden in *The Rehearsal* (1671).

5. Balaam was a prophet who first resisted and then accepted God's will (Numbers 22–24); here, he probably represents Theophilus Hastings, Earl of Huntingdon, who initially supported Shaftesbury but was subsequently forgiven by Charles. *Well-hung:* Eloquent, or sexually impressive ("Lord Huntingdon," wrote one of the poem's early readers in a marginal inscription, "is said to have a swinging p——"). Caleb (a spy in Numbers 13) has been identified as either Lord Grey, whose wife was reputedly Monmouth's mistress, or Arthur Capel, an efficient administrator and ally of Shaftesbury.

6. The priest Nadab tries to institute improper rites of worship, and is slain by God (Leviticus 10); probably William, Lord Howard of Escrick, a dissenting preacher.

7. Howard was said to have celebrated communion (the commemoration of Christ's sacrifice as "paschal lamb") not with bread and wine but with ale and roasted apples—a concoction known as "lamb's wool." Dissenters such as Howard referred disparagingly to the Anglican Book of Common Prayer as "porridge."

8. Sir William Jones, attorney general and fierce prosecutor of alleged Popish plotters.

To mean rebellion, and make treason law.
But he, though bad, is followed by a worse,
The wretch who heaven's anointed dared to curse:
Shimei,[9] whose youth did early promise bring
Of zeal to God, and hatred to his King;
Did wisely from expensive sins refrain,
And never broke the Sabbath, but for gain:
Nor ever was he known an oath to vent,
Or curse, unless against the government.
Thus heaping wealth by the most ready way
Among the Jews, which was to cheat and pray;
The city, to reward his pious hate
Against his master, chose him magistrate:
His hand a vare° of justice did uphold; *staff*
His neck was loaded with a chain of gold.
During his office, treason was no crime;
The sons of Belial[1] had a glorious time:
For Shimei, though not prodigal of pelf,[2]
Yet loved his wicked neighbor as himself:
When two or three were gathered to declaim[3]
Against the monarch of Jerusalem,
Shimei was always in the midst of them:
And, if they cursed the King when he was by,
Would rather curse than break good company.
If any durst his factious friends accuse,
He packed a jury of dissenting Jews,
Whose fellow-feeling in the godly cause
Would free the suff'ring saint from human laws.
For laws are only made to punish those
Who serve the King, and to protect his foes.
If any leisure time he had from power
(Because 'tis sin to misemploy an hour),
His business was, by writing, to persuade
That kings were useless, and a clog to trade:
And that his noble style he might refine,
No Rechabite[4] more shunned the fumes of wine.
Chaste were his cellars, and his shrieval board[5]
The grossness of a city feast abhorred:
His cooks, with long disuse, their trade forgot;
Cool was his kitchen, though his brains were hot.
Such frugal virtue malice may accuse,
But sure 'twas necessary to the Jews:
For towns once burnt[6] such magistrates require

9. Shimei cursed David as he fled Absalom's rebellion. Here, he is Slingsby Bethel, one of London's sheriffs.
1. Rebellious, debauched men.
2. Free with money.
3. The description of Shimei echoes two of Christ's pronouncements: "Thou shalt love thy neighbor as thyself" (Matthew 22.39); "When two or three are gathered together in my name, there am I in the midst of them" (Matthew 18.20).
4. Rechabites drank no wine.
5. Sheriff 's hospitality.
6. A reference to the Fire of London (1666).

As dare not tempt God's providence by fire.
With spiritual food he fed his servants well,
But free from flesh that made the Jews rebel:
And Moses's laws he held in more account,
For forty days of fasting in the mount.[7]
To speak the rest, who better are forgot,
Would tire a well-breathed witness of the Plot:
Yet, Corah,[8] thou shalt from oblivion pass;
Erect thyself, thou monumental brass,° *shamelessness*
High as the serpent of thy metal made,[9]
While nations stand secure beneath thy shade.
What though his birth were base, yet comets rise
From earthy vapors ere they shine in skies.
Prodigious actions may as well be done
By weaver's issue,[1] as by prince's son.
This arch-attestor for the public good
By that one deed ennobles all his blood.
Who ever asked the witnesses' high race,
Whose oath with martyrdom did Stephen[2] grace?
Ours was a Levite, and as times went then,
His tribe were God Almighty's gentlemen.
Sunk were his eyes, his voice was harsh and loud,
Sure signs he neither choleric° was, nor proud: *hot-tempered*
His long chin proved his wit; his saintlike grace
A church vermilion, and a Moses's face;[3]
His memory, miraculously great,
Could plots, exceeding man's belief, repeat;
Which therefore cannot be accounted lies,
For human wit could never such devise.
Some future truths are mingled in his book;
But where the witness failed, the prophet spoke:
Some things like visionary flights appear;
The spirit caught him up, the Lord knows where,
And gave him his rabbinical degree
Unknown to foreign university.[4]
His judgment yet his memory did excel;
Which pieced his wondrous evidence so well,
And suited to the temper of the times,
Then groaning under Jebusitic crimes.
Let Israel's foes suspect his heav'nly call,
And rashly judge his writ apocryphal;[5]

7. Shimei attempts to justify his frugality by citing the precedent of Moses, who fasted on Mount Sinai before receiving the Ten Commandments.
8. A rebellious Levite; here, Titus Oates, the ambitious informer who did more than anyone to arouse suspicions of a "Popish Plot."
9. Moses set up a brass serpent that saved the Jews from dying of snakebite (Numbers 21).
1. Oates's father was a weaver.
2. The first Christian martyr, sworn against and stoned by false witness (Acts 6–7).
3. After Moses received the tables of the law on Mount Sinai, his face shone with divine illumination; Oates's face, by contrast, is flushed with debauchery.
4. Oates pretended to hold a doctorate of divinity from the University of Salamanca.
5. Not part of the canon of biblical texts.

Our laws for such affronts have forfeits made:
He takes his life, who takes away his trade.
Were I myself in witness Corah's place,
The wretch who did me such a dire disgrace
Should whet my memory, though once forgot,
To make him an appendix of my plot.
His zeal to heav'n made him his prince despise,
And load his person with indignities:
But zeal peculiar privilege affords,
Indulging latitude to deeds and words;
And Corah might for Agag's murder[6] call,
In terms as coarse as Samuel used to Saul.
What others in his evidence did join
(The best that could be had for love or coin)
In Corah's own predicament will fall:
For *witness* is a common name to all.
  Surrounded thus with friends of every sort,
Deluded Absalom forsakes the court:
Impatient of high hopes, urged with renown,
And fired with near possession of a crown:
Th' admiring crowd are dazzled with surprise,
And on his goodly person feed their eyes:
His joy concealed, he sets himself to show,
On each side bowing popularly low:
His looks, his gestures, and his words he frames,
And with familiar ease repeats their names.
Thus, formed by nature, furnished out with arts,
He glides unfelt into their secret hearts:
Then with a kind compassionating look,
And sighs bespeaking pity ere he spoke,
Few words he said, but easy those and fit:
More slow than Hybla° drops, and far more sweet. *honey*
  "I mourn, my countrymen, your lost estate,
Though far unable to prevent your fate:
Behold a banished man, for your dear cause
Exposed a prey to arbitrary laws!
Yet O! that I alone could be undone,
Cut off from empire, and no more a son!
Now all your liberties a spoil are made,
Egypt and Tyrus° intercept your trade, *France and Holland*
And Jebusites your sacred rites invade.
My father, whom with reverence yet I name,
Charmed into ease, is careless of his fame:
And bribed with petty sums of foreign gold,
Is grown in Bathsheba's[7] embraces old:
Exalts his enemies, his friends destroys,

6. Oates denounced Lord Stafford, who was then executed, as Samuel denounced Agag, who was murdered by Saul (1 Samuel 15).

7. Louise de Kéroualle, Duchess of Portsmouth, Charles's French, Catholic mistress.

And all his pow'r against himself employs.
He gives, and let him give, my right away:
But why should he his own, and yours betray?
He only, he can make the nation bleed,
And he alone from my revenge is freed.
Take then my tears" (with that he wiped his eyes)
"'Tis all the aid my present power supplies:
No court informer can these arms accuse,
These arms may sons against their fathers use,
And 'tis my wish, the next successor's reign
May make no other Israelite complain."
Youth, beauty, graceful action seldom fail:
But common interest always will prevail:
And pity never ceases to be shown
To him, who makes the people's wrongs his own.
The crowd (that still believe their kings oppress)
With lifted hands their young Messiah bless:
Who now begins his progress to ordain,[8]
With chariots, horsemen, and a numerous train:
From east to west his glories he displays:
And, like the sun, the promised land surveys.
Fame runs before him, as the morning star,
And shouts of joy salute him from afar:
Each house receives him as a guardian god,
And consecrates the place of his abode:
But hospitable treats did most commend
Wise Issachar,[9] his wealthy western friend.
This moving court, that caught the people's eyes,
And seemed but pomp, did other ends disguise:
Achitophel had formed it, with intent
To sound the depths, and fathom, where it went,
The people's hearts; distinguish friends from foes,
And try their strength before they came to blows:
Yet all was colored with a smooth pretense
Of specious love, and duty to their prince.
Religion, and redress of grievances,
Two names that always cheat and always please,
Are often urged, and good King David's life
Endangered by a brother and a wife.[1]
Thus, in a pageant show, a plot is made,
And peace itself is war in masquerade.
O foolish Israel! never warned by ill,
Still the same bait, and circumvented still!
Did ever men forsake their present ease,
In midst of health imagine a disease;
Take pains contingent mischiefs to foresee,

8. Monmouth traveled through the west of England in 1680, rallying popular support.
9. Thomas Thynne, a wealthy Whig.
1. Both James and Catherine were Catholic and were thought by some to be implicated in Popish plotting.

Make heirs for monarchs, and for God decree?
What shall we think! can people give away,
Both for themselves and sons, their native sway?
Then they are left defenseless to the sword
Of each unbounded, arbitrary lord:
And laws are vain, by which we right enjoy,
If kings unquestioned can those laws destroy.
Yet, if the crowd be judge of fit and just,
And kings are only officers in trust,
Then this resuming cov'nant was declared
When kings were made, or is forever barred:
If those who gave the scepter could not tie
By their own deed their own posterity,
How then could Adam bind his future race?
How could his forfeit on mankind take place?
Or how could heavenly justice damn us all,
Who ne'er consented to our father's fall?
Then kings are slaves to those whom they command,
And tenants to their people's pleasure stand.
Add, that the pow'r for property[2] allowed
Is mischievously seated in the crowd:
For who can be secure of private right,
If sovereign sway may be dissolved by might?
Nor is the people's judgment always true:
The most may err as grossly as the few,
And faultless kings run down by common cry
For vice, oppression, and for tyranny.
What standard is there in a fickle rout,
Which, flowing to the mark,° runs faster out? *high-water mark*
Nor only crowds, but Sanhedrins may be
Infected with this public lunacy,
And share the madness of rebellious times,
To murder monarchs for imagined crimes.
If they may give and take whene'er they please,
Not kings alone (the Godhead's images),
But government itself at length must fall
To nature's state, where all have right to all.
Yet, grant our lords the people kings can make,
What prudent men a settled throne would shake?
For whatsoe'er their sufferings were before,
That change they covet makes them suffer more.
All other errors but disturb a state,
But innovation is the blow of fate.
If ancient fabrics nod, and threat to fall,
To patch the flaws, and buttress up the wall,
Thus far 'tis duty; but here fix the mark:
For all beyond it is to touch our ark.[3]

2. Political influence derived from ownership of land.

3. To touch the ark was to commit sacrilege.

To change foundations, cast the frame anew,
Is work for rebels who base ends pursue,
At once divine and human laws control,
And mend the parts by ruin of the whole.
The tampering world is subject to this curse,
To physic their disease into a worse.
  Now what relief can righteous David bring?
How fatal 'tis to be too good a king!
Friends he has few, so high the madness grows;
Who dare be such, must be the people's foes:
Yet some there were, ev'n in the worst of days;
Some let me name, and naming is to praise.
  In this short file Barzillai[4] first appears;
Barzillai crowned with honor and with years:
Long since, the rising rebels he withstood
In regions waste, beyond the Jordan's flood:[5]
Unfortunately brave to buoy the state,
But sinking underneath his master's fate:
In exile with his godlike prince he mourned;
For him he suffered, and with him returned.
The court he practiced, not the courtier's art:
Large was his wealth, but larger was his heart:
Which well the noblest objects knew to choose,
The fighting warrior, and recording Muse.[6]
His bed could once a fruitful issue boast:
Now more than half a father's name is lost:
His eldest hope,[7] with every grace adorned,
By me (so Heaven will have it) always mourned,
And always honored, snatched in manhood's prime
By unequal Fates, and Providence's crime:
Yet not before the goal of honor won,
All parts fulfilled of subject and of son;
Swift was the race, but short the time to run.
Oh narrow circle, but of pow'r divine,
Scanted in space, but perfect in thy line!
By sea, by land, thy matchless worth was known;
Arms thy delight, and war was all thy own:
Thy force, infused, the fainting Tyrians[8] propped:
And haughty Pharaoh found his fortune stopped.
O ancient honor, O unconquered hand,
Whom foes unpunished never could withstand!
But Israel was unworthy of thy name;
Short is the date of all immoderate fame.
It looks as Heaven our ruin had designed,
And durst not trust thy fortune and thy mind.

4. James Butler, Duke of Ormonde, loyal to Charles I and II.
5. I.e., in Ireland.
6. I.e., he gave money to support the Stuart cause and was also a patron to authors.
7. Ormonde's eldest son, who died in 1680.
8. The Dutch, whom Ormonde's son had aided against the French.

Now, free from earth, thy disencumbered soul
Mounts up, and leaves behind the clouds and starry pole:
From thence thy kindred legions mayst thou bring,
To aid the guardian angel of thy King.
Here stop, my Muse, here cease thy painful flight;
No pinions° can pursue immortal height: *wings*
Tell good Barzillai thou canst sing no more,
And tell thy soul she should have fled before;
Or fled she with his life, and left this verse
To hang on her departed patron's hearse?
Now take thy steepy flight from heaven, and see
If thou canst find on earth another *he;*
Another *he* would be too hard to find,
See then whom thou canst see not far behind:
Zadock[9] the priest, whom, shunning power and place,
His lowly mind advanced to David's grace:
With him the Sagan[1] of Jerusalem,
Of hospitable soul and noble stem;
Him of the western dome,[2] whose weighty sense
Flows in fit words and heavenly eloquence.
The prophets' sons[3] by such example led,
To learning and to loyalty were bred:
For colleges on bounteous kings depend,
And never rebel was to arts a friend.
To these succeed the pillars of the laws,
Who best could plead and best can judge a cause.
Next them a train of loyal peers ascend:
Sharp-judging Adriel,[4] the Muses' friend,
Himself a Muse—in Sanhedrin's debate
True to his prince, but not a slave of state:
Whom David's love with honors did adorn,
That from his disobedient son were torn.[5]
Jotham[6] of piercing wit and pregnant thought,
Indued° by nature, and by learning taught *endowed*
To move assemblies, who but only tried
The worse awhile, then chose the better side;
Nor chose alone, but turned the balance too;
So much the weight of one brave man can do.
Hushai,[7] the friend of David in distress,
In public storms of manly steadfastness;
By foreign treaties he informed his youth,

9. William Sancroft, Archbishop of Canterbury.
1. Henry Compton, Bishop of London.
2. John Dolben, Dean of Westminster ("the western dome").
3. Students of the Westminster School.
4. John Sheffield, Earl of Mulgrave, poet and a patron of Dryden.
5. In 1679 Mulgrave received two offices that had previously belonged to Monmouth.
6. George Savile, Marquis of Halifax, formerly a critic but now a supporter of Charles's policies, was instrumental in defeating the exclusion bill.
7. Laurence Hyde, Earl of Rochester, negotiated several European treaties and became the first Lord of the Treasury.

And joined experience to his native truth.
His frugal care supplied the wanting throne,
Frugal for that, but bounteous of his own:
'Tis easy conduct when exchequers[8] flow,
But hard the task to manage well the low:
For sovereign power is too depressed or high,
When kings are forced to sell, or crowds to buy.
Indulge one labor more, my weary Muse,
For Amiel,[9] who can Amiel's praise refuse?
Of ancient race by birth, but nobler yet
In his own worth, and without title great:
The Sanhedrin long time as chief he ruled,
Their reason guided and their passion cooled;
So dexterous was he in the crown's defense,
So formed to speak a loyal nation's sense,
That, as their band was Israel's tribes in small,
So fit was he to represent them all.
Now rasher charioteers the seat ascend,
Whose loose careers his steady skill commend:
They like th' unequal ruler of the day,[1]
Misguide the seasons and mistake the way;
While he, withdrawn, at their mad labor smiles,
And safe enjoys the sabbath of his toils.
These were the chief, a small but faithful band
Of worthies, in the breach who dared to stand,
And tempt th' united fury of the land.
With grief they viewed such powerful engines bent,
To batter down the lawful government:
A numerous faction with pretended frights,
In Sanhedrins to plume° the regal rights: *pluck away*
The true successor from the court removed:[2]
The Plot by hireling witnesses improved.
These ills they saw, and as their duty bound,
They showed the King the danger of the wound:
That no concessions from the throne would please,
But lenitives fomented[3] the disease:
That Absalom, ambitious of the crown,
Was made the lure to draw the people down:
That false Achitophel's pernicious hate
Had turned the Plot to ruin Church and State:
The council violent, the rabble worse:
That Shimei taught Jerusalem to curse.

8. Treasurers/treasuries.
9. Edward Seymour, Speaker of the Commons (1673–1678) and Treasurer of the Navy (1673–1681); opponent of exclusion.
1. Phaëthon, who drove (with disastrous results) the chariot of the sun that belonged to his father, Apollo.
2. In 1679, at the height of the furor over the Popish Plot, Charles II had ordered his brother to withdraw to the Continent, where James remained for six months.
3. I.e., soothing measures/medicines only encouraged the disease.

With all these loads of injuries oppressed,
And long revolving, in his careful breast,
Th' event of things, at last, his patience tired,
Thus from his royal throne by Heav'n inspired,
The godlike David spoke: with awful fear
His train their Maker in their master hear.
"Thus long have I, by native mercy swayed,
My wrongs dissembled, my revenge delayed:
So willing to forgive th' offending age,
So much the father did the king assuage.
But now so far my clemency they slight,
Th' offenders question my forgiving right.
That one was made for many, they contend:
But 'tis to rule, for that's a monarch's end.
They call my tenderness of blood my fear:
Though manly tempers can the longest bear.
Yet, since they will divert my native course,
'Tis time to show I am not good by force.
Those heaped affronts that haughty subjects bring,
Are burdens for a camel, not a king:
Kings are the public pillars of the state,
Born to sustain and prop the nation's weight:
If my young Samson[4] will pretend a call
To shake the column, let him share the fall:
But O that yet he would repent and live!
How easy 'tis for parents to forgive!
With how few tears a pardon might be won
From Nature, pleading for a darling son!
Poor pitied youth, by my paternal care
Raised up to all the height his frame could bear:
Had God ordained his fate for empire born,
He would have given his soul another turn:
Gulled with a patriot's name, whose modern sense
Is one that would by law supplant his prince:
The people's brave,° the politicians' tool; *bully*
Never was patriot yet, but was a fool.
Whence comes it that religion and the laws
Should more be Absalom's than David's cause?
His old instructor,[5] ere he lost his place,
Was never thought indued with so much grace.
Good heavens, how faction can a patriot paint!
My rebel ever proves my people's saint:
Would they impose an heir upon the throne?
Let Sanhedrins be taught to give their own.
A king's at least a part of government,

4. Monmouth, who threatens, Samson-like, to bring down the nation.

5. Achitophel/Shaftesbury.

And mine as requisite as their consent:
Without my leave a future king to choose,
Infers a right the present to depose:
True, they petition me t' approve their choice,
But Esau's hands suit ill with Jacob's voice.[6]
My pious subjects for my safety pray,
Which to secure they take my power away.
From plots and treasons Heaven preserve my years,
But save me most from my petitioners.
Unsatiate as the barren womb or grave;
God cannot grant so much as they can crave.
What then is left but with a jealous eye
To guard the small remains of royalty?
The law shall still direct my peaceful sway,
And the same law teach rebels to obey:
Votes shall no more established pow'r control,
Such votes as make a part exceed the whole:
No groundless clamors shall my friends remove,
Nor crowds have power to punish ere they prove:
For gods, and godlike kings, their care express,
Still to defend their servants in distress.
O that my power to saving were confined:
Why am I forced, like Heaven, against my mind,
To make examples of another kind?
Must I at length the sword of justice draw?
O cursed effects of necessary law!
How ill my fear they by my mercy scan;[7]
Beware the fury of a patient man.
Law they require, let law then show her face;
They could not be content to look on Grace,
Her hinder parts, but with a daring eye
To tempt the terror of her front, and die.
By their own arts, 'tis righteously decreed,
Those dire artificers of death shall bleed.
Against themselves their witnesses will swear,
Till viper-like their mother Plot they tear:
And suck for nutriment that bloody gore
Which was their principle of life before.
Their Belial with their Belzebub[8] will fight;
Thus on my foes, my foes shall do me right:
Nor doubt th' event: for factious crowds engage,
In their first onset, all their brutal rage;
Then let 'em take an unresisted course,

6. In Genesis 27, Esau is a hunter and a "hairy man"; his younger brother Jacob steals his birthright by impersonating him before their blind father Isaac, covering his own smooth hands with rough goatskin. David/Charles here accuses his opposition of Esau-like violence and Jacob-like deception.

7. How wrong ("ill") they are to see ("scan") fear in my mercy.

8. Both devils.

Retire and traverse, and delude their force:
But when they stand all breathless, urge the fight,
And rise upon 'em with redoubled might:
For lawful pow'r is still superior found,
When long driven back, at length it stands the ground."
He said. Th' Almighty, nodding, gave consent;
And peals of thunder shook the firmament.
Henceforth a series of new time began,
The mighty years in long procession ran:
Once more the godlike David was restored,
And willing nations knew their lawful lord.

1681 1681

For a companion text, *His Majesty's Declaration to All His Loving Subjects*, go to *The Longman Anthology of British Literature* Web site at www.myliteraturekit.com.

Mac Flecknoe In *Mac Flecknoe*, Dryden put on display a literary culture dangerously debased. The poem's title ("Son of Flecknoe") announces a royal succession in the kingdom of bad writing. A literary "father," the priest and minor poet Richard Flecknoe (c. 1605–c. 1677), anoints as his true heir Thomas Shadwell (1640–1692), a playwright whom Dryden loathed as a tiresome controversialist and an ardent (worse, successful) rival for public favor and aristocratic patronage. Dryden wages his attack in an idiom at once elevated and scandalous, in language whose allegiance alternates (even within a single line) between epic poetry and the privy. Like much libelous and bawdy verse, Dryden's demolitionary masterpiece circulated in manuscript for several years; it was eventually printed in a pirated edition (1682) by a publisher seeking to capitalize on the recent success of *Absalom and Achitophel*. Like that poem, *Mac Flecknoe* plays upon the question of monarchic succession, but stages it in such a way as to implicate bad politics in bad taste. Dryden maps a City of London where foul writing chokes the streets, and dim-witted citizens get—and applaud—the poet-monarchs they deserve.

Mac Flecknoe

All human things are subject to decay,
And, when Fate summons, monarchs must obey.
This Flecknoe found, who, like Augustus, young
Was called to empire,[1] and had governed long:
In prose and verse was owned, without dispute,
Through all the realms of Nonsense, absolute.
This aged prince, now flourishing in peace,
And blest with issue of a large increase,
Worn out with business, did at length debate
To settle the succession of the state:
And, pondering which of all his sons was fit
To reign, and wage immortal war with wit,
Cried, "'Tis resolved; for Nature pleads that he
Should only rule, who most resembles me:
Sh——alone my perfect image bears,
Mature in dullness from his tender years.

1. Augustus became the first Roman emperor at the age of 32.

Sh——alone, of all my sons, is he
Who stands confirmed in full stupidity.
The rest to some faint meaning make pretense,
But Sh——never deviates into sense.
Some beams of wit on other souls may fall,
Strike through and make a lucid interval,
But Sh——'s genuine night admits no ray,
His rising fogs prevail upon the day.
Besides, his goodly fabric° fills the eye, *large body*
And seems designed for thoughtless majesty:
Thoughtless as monarch oaks that shade the plain,
And, spread in solemn state, supinely reign.
Heywood and Shirley were but types of thee,[2]
Thou last great prophet of tautology:
Even I, a dunce of more renown than they,
Was sent before but to prepare thy way;
And coarsely clad in Norwich drugget[3] came
To teach the nations in thy greater name.[4]
My warbling lute, the lute I whilom° strung *once*
When to King John of Portugal I sung,[5]
Was but the prelude to that glorious day
When thou on silver Thames didst cut thy way,
With well-timed oars before the royal barge,
Swelled with the pride of thy celestial charge;
And big with hymn, commander of an host,
The like was ne'er in Epsom blankets tossed.[6]
Methinks I see the new Arion[7] sail,
The lute still trembling underneath thy nail.
At thy well-sharpened thumb from shore to shore
The treble squeaks for fear, the basses roar:
Echoes from Pissing Alley[8] 'Sh——' call,
And 'Sh——' they resound from A——Hall.[9]
About thy boat the little fishes throng,
As at the morning toast° that floats along. *sewage*
Sometimes as prince of thy harmonious band
Thou wield'st thy papers in thy threshing hand.
St. André's feet[1] ne'er kept more equal time,
Not ev'n the feet of thy own *Psyche's* rhyme,
Though they in number as in sense excel;
So just, so like tautology they fell,

2. Thomas Heywood and James Shirley, popular and prolific playwrights from the first half of the 17th century. As "types," they foreshadow or prepare for Shadwell, just as Old Testament figures such as Moses or Isaac were interpreted in Christian theology as forerunners of Jesus.
3. Woolen cloth; Shadwell came from Norwich.
4. Here, Flecknoe is John the Baptist ("coarsely clad" in camel's hair) to Shadwell's Jesus.
5. Flecknoe claimed that, during his travels in Europe, he had been summoned to perform before the king of Portugal.
6. A glance at two of Shadwell's plays: *Epsom Wells* and *The Virtuoso*, in which Sir Samuel Hearty is tossed in a blanket; tossing in blankets was also a means of inducing childbirth.
7. Greek musician-poet rescued from drowning by music-loving dolphins.
8. West of Temple Bar, it led from the Strand down to the Thames.
9. Unidentified.
1. St. André, a French dancer who choreographed the opera *Psyche* (1675), for which Shadwell wrote the libretto.

That, pale with envy, Singleton foreswore
The lute and sword which he in triumph bore,
And vowed he ne'er would act Villerius[2] more."
Here stopped the good old sire, and wept for joy
In silent raptures of the hopeful boy.
All arguments, but most his plays, persuade,
That for anointed dullness he was made.
  Close to the walls which fair Augusta bind[3]
(The fair Augusta much to fears inclined[4]),
An ancient fabric,[5] raised t' inform the sight,
There stood of yore, and Barbican it hight:[6]
A watchtower once, but now, so Fate ordains,
Of all the pile an empty name remains.
From its old ruins brothel-houses rise,
Scenes of lewd loves and of polluted joys;
Where their vast courts the mother-strumpets keep
And, undisturbed by watch,° in silence sleep.[7] *police*
Near these a nursery[8] erects its head,
Where queens[9] are formed and future heroes bred;
Where unfledged actors learn to laugh and cry,
Where infant punks° their tender voices try, *prostitutes*
And little Maximins[1] the gods defy.
Great Fletcher never treads in buskins here,
Nor greater Jonson dares in socks appear.[2]
But gentle Simkin[3] just reception finds
Amid this monument of vanished minds:
Pure clinches° the suburbian Muse[4] affords, *puns*
And Panton[5] waging harmless war with words.
Here Flecknoe, as a place to fame well known,
Ambitiously designed his Sh——'s throne.
For ancient Dekker[6] prophesied long since,
That in this pile should reign a mighty prince,
Born for a scourge of wit, and flail of sense:
To whom true dullness should some *Psyches* owe,
But Worlds of *Misers* from his pen should flow;

2. John Singleton, one of the king's musicians; Villerius, a character in William Davenant's opera, *The Siege of Rhodes*.
3. The old wall of the City of London (Augusta).
4. Fears aroused by the Popish Plot.
5. Structure.
6. Was named; the Barbican, a medieval gatehouse, gave its name to a disreputable district of gaming and prostitution; adjoining it was Grub Street, the center of hack journalism.
7. Parodying Abraham Cowley, *Davideis* (1656), "Where their vast court the mother-waters keep, / And undisturbed by moons in silence sleep."
8. A training theater for the two main playhouses.
9. Dryden puns on queen (stage-monarch)/quean (prostitute). During the Restoration, actresses were often thought to moonlight as sexual companions.
1. Maximin is the fulminating protagonist of Dryden's *Tyrannic Love*.
2. John Fletcher and Ben Jonson, major playwrights of the previous generations. The buskin is the symbol of tragedy (Fletcher's forte) and the sock of comedy (Jonson's). Shadwell promoted himself as Jonson's successor in the tradition of "humors" comedy.
3. A clownish character in a series of popular farces.
4. I.e., the muse presiding over the disreputable area outside the City walls.
5. Another farce character.
6. Thomas Dekker (1570?–1632), prolific dramatist whose plays focused on London life.

Humorists and *Hypocrites*[7] it should produce,
Whole Raymond families, and tribes of Bruce.
  Now Empress Fame had published the renown
Of Sh———'s coronation through the town.
Rousèd by report of Fame, the nations meet,
From near Bunhill, and distant Watling Street.[8]
No Persian carpets spread th' imperial way,
But scattered limbs of mangled poets lay:
From dusty shops neglected authors come,
Martyrs of pies, and relics of the bum.[9]
Much Heywood, Shirley, Ogilby[1] there lay,
But loads of Sh——— almost choked the way.
Bilked stationers for yeomen stood prepared,
And H———[2] was captain of the guard.
The hoary prince in majesty appeared,
High on a throne of his own labors reared.
At his right hand our young Ascanius[3] sate,
Rome's other hope, and pillar of the state.
His brows thick fogs, instead of glories, grace,
And lambent° dullness played around his face. *glowing*
As Hannibal did to the altars come,
Sworn by his sire a mortal foe to Rome,[4]
So Sh——— swore, nor should his vow be vain,
That he till death true dullness would maintain;
And in his father's right, and realm's defense,
Ne'er to have peace with wit, nor truce with sense.
The king himself the sacred unction[5] made,
As king by office, and as priest by trade:
In his sinister° hand, instead of ball, left
He placed a mighty mug of potent ale;
Love's Kingdom[6] to his right he did convey,
At once his scepter and his rule of sway,[7]
Whose righteous lore the prince had practiced young,
And from whose loins[8] recorded Psyche sprung.
His temples last with poppies[9] were o'erspread,
That nodding seemed to consecrate his head:
Just at that point of time, if Fame not lie,

7. Shadwell was the author of *The Miser* (1672), *The Humorists* (1671), and *The Hypocrite* (1669). Raymond and Bruce appear in *The Humorists* and *The Virtuoso*, respectively.
8. Fame draws her crowd both from cemeteries (like Bunhill Fields) and from mercantile districts (like Watling Street); thus, these devotees of Shadwell include both the dead and the living.
9. Unsold books might be recycled as pie wrappers or as toilet paper; the bones of martyrs were often venerated as relics.
1. John Ogilby, printer, cartographer, and translator (like Dryden) of Virgil.
2. Henry Herringman, a prominent bookseller-publisher; he had published both Shadwell and Dryden.
3. The son of Aeneas, marked for greatness by a heaven-sent flame about his head.
4. According to Livy, Hannibal's father made the young boy swear himself Rome's enemy.
5. The oil with which the king was anointed during the coronation ceremony.
6. A play by Flecknoe.
7. Dryden parodies the rituals and props of the coronation ceremony.
8. Pronounced "lines" (a fact that permits Dryden a significant pun).
9. Symbolizing sleep.

On his left hand twelve reverend owls[1] did fly.
So Romulus,[2] 'tis sung, by Tiber's brook,
Presage of sway from twice six vultures took.
Th' admiring throng loud acclamations make,
And omens of his future empire take.
The sire then shook the honors[3] of his head,
And from his brows damps of oblivion shed
Full on the filial dullness: long he stood,
Repelling from his breast the raging God;
At length burst out in this prophetic mood:
"Heavens bless my son, from Ireland let him reign
To far Barbados on the western main;[4]
Of his dominion may no end be known,
And greater than his father's be his throne.
Beyond *Love's Kingdom* let him stretch his pen!"
He paused, and all the people cried, "Amen."
"Then thus," continued he, "my son, advance
Still in new impudence, new ignorance.
Success let others teach, learn thou from me
Pangs without birth, and fruitless industry.
Let *Virtuosos* in five years be writ,
Yet not one thought accuse thy toil of wit.
Let gentle George[5] in triumph tread the stage,
Make Dorimant betray, and Loveit rage;
Let Cully, Cockwood, Fopling charm the pit,
And in their folly show the writer's wit.
Yet still thy fools shall stand in thy defense,
And justify° their author's want of sense. *prove*
Let 'em be all by thy own model made
Of dullness, and desire no foreign aid:
That they to future ages may be known,
Not copies drawn, but issue[6] of thy own.
Nay let thy men of wit too be the same,
All full of thee, and differing but in name;
But let no alien S–dl–y[7] interpose
To lard with wit thy hungry *Epsom* prose.
And when false flowers of rhetoric thou would'st cull,
Trust nature, do not labor to be dull;
But write thy best, and top; and in each line,
Sir Formal's[8] oratory will be thine.
Sir Formal, though unsought, attends thy quill,
And does thy northern dedications[9] fill.

1. Symbols of ignorance and darkness (because nocturnal).
2. Cofounder of Rome (through which the Tiber runs).
3. Ornaments, and by extension, hair—a Virgilian expression.
4. His kingdom will be the Atlantic Ocean.
5. Sir George Etherege, comic playwright; characters from his plays follow.
6. A pun: both progeny and printing.
7. Sir Charles Sedley, courtier, poet, and intimate of Dryden's circle; he wrote a prologue for *Epsom Wells*.
8. Sir Formal Trifle, a character in Shadwell's *The Virtuoso*, described by Shadwell as "the Orator, a florid coxcomb."
9. Both Flecknoe and Shadwell dedicated several of their works to the Duke and Duchess of Newcastle (a town in the north of England).

Nor let false friends seduce thy mind to fame,
By arrogating Jonson's hostile name.
Let father Flecknoe fire thy mind with praise,
And uncle Ogilby thy envy raise.
Thou art my blood, where Jonson has no part;
What share have we in nature or in art?
Where did his wit on learning fix a brand,
And rail at arts he did not understand?
Where made he love in Prince Nicander's[1] vein,
Or swept the dust in Psyche's humble strain?
Where sold he bargains,[2] 'whip-stitch, kiss my arse,'
Promised a play and dwindled to a farce?
When did his Muse from Fletcher scenes purloin,
As thou whole Eth'rege dost transfuse to thine?
But so transfused as oil on waters flow,
His always floats above, thine sinks below.
This is thy province, this thy wondrous way,
New humors to invent for each new play:[3]
This is that boasted bias of thy mind,
By which one way, to dullness, 'tis inclined;
Which makes thy writings lean on one side still,
And in all changes that way bends thy will.
Nor let thy mountain belly make pretense
Of likeness; thine's a tympany[4] of sense.
A tun of man in thy large bulk is writ,
But sure thou'rt but a kilderkin[5] of wit.
Like mine thy gentle numbers feebly creep;
Thy tragic Muse gives smiles, thy comic sleep.
With whate'er gall thou sett'st thyself to write,
Thy inoffensive satires never bite.
In thy felonious heart, though venom lies,
It does but touch thy Irish[6] pen, and dies.
Thy genius calls thee not to purchase fame
In keen iambics,[7] but mild anagram:
Leave writing plays, and choose for thy command
Some peaceful province in acrostic land.
There thou may'st wings display and altars[8] raise,
And torture one poor word ten thousand ways.
Or if thou would'st thy diff'rent talents suit,

1. A character in *Psyche*.
2. "To sell bargains" is to respond to an innocent question with a coarse phrase, as in this line. Dryden sharpens the insult by quoting the slangy nonsense phrase "whip-stitch" from Shadwell's own play, *The Virtuoso*.
3. I.e., by these contemptible means, you purport to outdo Ben Jonson.
4. A swelling of the abdomen, caused by air or gas.
5. A tun was a large cask of wine; a kilderkin a quarter of a tun.
6. Neither Flecknoe nor Shadwell was actually Irish; Ireland was regarded in England as an abode of savages.
7. Sharp satire (written in iambic meter by classical satirists).
8. Dryden here mocks the practice of writing emblematic verse, poems in the shape of their subjects (e.g., George Herbert's *Easter Wings* and *The Altar*). He lumps this practice together with other forms of empty ingenuity.

Set thy own songs, and sing them to thy lute."
He said, but his last words were scarcely heard,
For Bruce and Longvil had a trap prepared,[9]
And down they sent the yet declaiming bard.
Sinking he left his drugget robe behind,
Borne upward by a subterranean wind.
The mantle fell to the young prophet's part,[1]
With double portion of his father's art.

c. 1676 1682

To the Memory of Mr. Oldham[1]

Farewell, too little and too lately known,
Whom I began to think and call my own;
For sure our souls were near allied; and thine
Cast in the same poetic mold with mine.[2]
One common note on either lyre did strike,
And knaves and fools[3] we both abhorred alike:
To the same goal did both our studies drive,
The last set out the soonest did arrive.
Thus Nisus[4] fell upon the slippery place,
While his young friend performed and won the race.
O early ripe! to thy abundant store
What could advancing age have added more?
It might (what Nature never gives the young)
Have taught the numbers[5] of thy native tongue.
But satire needs not those, and wit will shine
Through the harsh cadence of a rugged line:
A noble error, and but seldom made,
When poets are by too much force betrayed.
Thy generous fruits, though gathered ere their prime,
Still showed a quickness;[6] and maturing time
But mellows what we write to the dull sweets of rhyme.
Once more, hail and farewell;[7] farewell thou young,
But ah too short, Marcellus of our tongue;
Thy brows with ivy, and with laurels bound;
But fate and gloomy night encompass thee around.[8]

1684

9. In Shadwell's *The Virtuoso,* Bruce and Longvil open a trap door beneath the long-winded Sir Formal Trifle.

1. A burlesque of 2 Kings 2.8–14, in which the prophet Elijah is borne up to heaven, while his mantle falls to his successor, Elisha.

1. John Oldham (1653–1683) achieved fame at age 28 with his *Satires upon the Jesuits* (1681). Three years later, an aging Dryden mourned him in a tribute that prefaced the *Remains of Mr. John Oldham in Verse and Prose*. Within his poem's brief compass, Dryden echoes many poets—Virgil, Catullus, Milton, and Oldham himself—and invokes several modes: satire, celebration, elegy.

2. An echo of Oldham's poem *David's Lamentation*: "Oh, dearer than my soul! if I can call it mine, / For sure we had the same, 'twas very thine."

3. Satire's traditional targets.

4. In Book 5 of Virgil's *Aeneid,* Nisus slips near the finish line during a footrace, falling in a manner that permits "his young friend" Euryalus to win.

5. Metrical patterns and harmonies.

6. Liveliness; also, sharpness of taste.

7. Dryden echoes a phrase in Catullus's elegy for his brother: "Ave atque vale" (101.10).

8. In Book 6 of Virgil's *Aeneid,* the hero visits the underworld, where his dead father shows him a vision of Rome's future. This vision concludes with a sight of Augustus Caesar's adopted son and heir Marcellus, who after a glorious military career died at the age of 20. The last line of Dryden's elegy reworks Virgil's conclusion:"But hov'ring mists around his brows are spread, / And night, with sable shades, involves his head" (*Aeneid* 6.866; Dryden's translation).

Alexander's Feast
or, The Power of Music
An Ode in Honor of St. Cecilia's Day[1]

1

'Twas at the royal feast, for Persia won
By Philip's warlike son:[2]
Aloft in awful state
The godlike hero sate
On his imperial throne:
His valiant peers were placed around;
Their brows with roses and with myrtles bound
(So should desert in arms be crowned).
The lovely Thais[3] by his side
Sat like a blooming Eastern bride
In flow'r of youth and beauty's pride.
Happy, happy, happy pair!
None but the brave
None but the brave
None but the brave deserves the fair.

CHORUS

Happy, happy, happy pair!
None but the brave
None but the brave
None but the brave deserves the fair.

2

Timotheus,[4] placed on high
Amid the tuneful choir,
With flying fingers touched the lyre:
The trembling notes ascend the sky,
And heav'nly joys inspire.
The song began from Jove,
Who left his blissful seats above
(Such is the power of mighty love).
A dragon's fiery form belied[5] the god:
Sublime on radiant spires° he rode, *coils*
When he to fair Olympia pressed:
And while he sought her snowy breast:
Then, round her slender waist he curled,

1. The early martyr Cecilia is the patron saint of music and musicians. Her feast day (22 November) was annually celebrated in London by a concert featuring a new piece with words by an eminent poet and music by a distinguished composer. The musical society in charge of the occasion commissioned two odes from Dryden, ten years apart: *A Song for St. Cecilia's Day* (1687) and *Alexander's Feast*. Dryden undertook the commission with some reluctance, but after the piece's successful premiere, he noted with pleasure that *Alexander's Feast* "is esteemed the best of all my poetry, by all the town. I thought so myself when I writ it, but being old, I mistrusted my own judgment."

2. Alexander the Great, son of Philip of Macedon; Dryden depicts the feast that Alexander held after defeating the Persians and their emperor Darius in 331 B.C.E.

3. Alexander's Greek concubine.

4. Celebrated poet and musician.

5. Timotheus tells the alternative story of Alexander's parentage, that he was begotten by Jove—disguised ("belied") as a serpent—upon Philip's wife Olympias.

And stamped an image of himself, a sov'reign of the world.
The listening crowd admire the lofty sound:
"A present deity," they shout around:
"A present deity," the vaulted roofs rebound.
With ravished ears
The monarch hears,
Assumes the god,[6]
Affects to nod,
And seems to shake the spheres.

CHORUS

With ravished ears
The monarch hears,
Assumes the god,
Affects to nod,
And seems to shake the spheres.

3

The praise of Bacchus then the sweet musician sung,
Of Bacchus ever fair and ever young:
The jolly god in triumph comes;
Sound the trumpets; beat the drums:
Flushed with a purple grace
He shows his honest face,
Now give the hautboys° breath; he comes, he comes. *oboes*
Bacchus, ever fair and young,
Drinking joys did first ordain:
Bacchus' blessings are a treasure;
Drinking is the soldier's pleasure;
Rich the treasure,
Sweet the pleasure;
Sweet is pleasure after pain.

CHORUS

Bacchus' blessings are a treasure;
Drinking is the soldier's pleasure;
Rich the treasure,
Sweet the pleasure;
Sweet is pleasure after pain.

4

Soothed with the sound, the king grew vain;
Fought all his battles o'er again;
And thrice he routed all his foes, and thrice he slew the slain.
The master saw the madness rise,
His glowing cheeks, his ardent eyes;
And, while he heav'n and earth defied,
Changed his hand, and checked his pride.[7]

6. Behaves like Jove, whose nod is said by Virgil to cause earthquakes.

7. Timotheus ("the master") changes the music in order to restrain Alexander's swelling pride.

He chose a mournful Muse
Soft pity to infuse:
He sung Darius great and good,
By too severe a fate
Fallen, fallen, fallen, fallen,
Fallen from his high estate
And welt'ring in his blood:
Deserted at his utmost need,
By those his former bounty fed:
On the bare earth exposed he lies,
With not a friend to close his eyes.

With downcast looks the joyless victor sat,
Revolving° in his altered soul *pondering*
The various turns of chance below;
And, now and then, a sigh he stole,
And tears began to flow.

CHORUS

Revolving in his altered soul
The various turns of chance below;
And, now and then, a sigh he stole;
And tears began to flow.

5

The mighty master smiled to see
That love was in the next degree:
'Twas but a kindred sound to move;[8]
For pity melts the mind to love.
Softly sweet, in Lydian measures,[9]
Soon he soothed his soul to pleasures.
"War," he sung, "is toil and trouble,
Honor but an empty bubble.
Never ending, still° beginning, *always*
Fighting still, and still destroying,
If the world be worth thy winning,
Think, O think, it worth enjoying.
Lovely Thais sits beside thee,
Take the good the gods provide thee."

The many[1] rend the skies with loud applause;
So love was crowned, but music won the cause.
The prince, unable to conceal his pain,
Gazed on the fair
Who caused his care,
And sighed and looked, sighed and looked,

8. All it took to "move" Alexander to the "next degree" of feeling was to shift ("move") musical registers.

9. In ancient Greek music, the mode associated with pathos.

1. The retinue or company.

Sighed and looked, and sighed again:
At length, with love and wine at once oppressed,
The vanquished victor sunk upon her breast.

CHORUS

The prince, unable to conceal his pain,
Gazed on the fair
Who caused his care,
And sighed and looked, sighed and looked,
Sighed and looked, and sighed again:
At length, with love and wine at once oppressed,
The vanquished victor sunk upon her breast.

6

Now strike the golden lyre again:
A louder yet, and yet a louder strain.
Break his bands of sleep asunder,
And rouse him, like a rattling peal of thunder.
Hark, hark, the horrid sound
Has raised up his head,
As awaked from the dead,
And, amazed, he stares around.
"Revenge, revenge," Timotheus cries,
"See the Furies[2] arise!
See the snakes that they rear,
How they hiss in their hair,
And the sparkles that flash from their eyes!
Behold a ghastly band,
Each a torch in his hand!
Those are Grecian ghosts, that in battle were slain,
And unburied remain
Inglorious on the plain.
Give the vengeance due
To the valiant crew.
Behold how they toss their torches on high,
How they point to the Persian abodes,
And glitt'ring temples of their hostile gods!"
The princes applaud, with a furious joy;
And the king seized a flambeau,[3] with zeal to destroy;
Thais led the way,
To light him to his prey,
And, like another Helen, fired another Troy.[4]

CHORUS

And the king seized a flambeau, with zeal to destroy;
Thais led the way,

2. Spirits of punishment.
3. Torch.
4. Stolen away to Troy by Paris, Helen was blamed for setting in motion the chain of events that led to the burning of the city by the Greeks.

To light him to his prey,
And, like another Helen, fired another Troy.

7

Thus, long ago,
Ere heaving bellows learned to blow,
While organs yet were mute,
Timotheus, to his breathing flute,
And sounding lyre,
Could swell the soul to rage, or kindle soft desire.
At last divine Cecilia came,
Inventress of the vocal frame;[5]
The sweet enthusiast,[6] from her sacred store,
Enlarged the former narrow bounds,
And added length to solemn sounds,
With nature's mother wit, and arts unknown before.
Let old Timotheus yield the prize,
Or both divide the crown;
He raised a mortal to the skies;
She drew an angel down.[7]

GRAND CHORUS

At last divine Cecilia came,
Inventress of the vocal frame;
The sweet enthusiast, from her sacred store,
Enlarged the former narrow bounds,
And added length to solemn sounds,
With nature's mother wit, and arts unknown before.
Let old Timotheus yield the prize,
Or both divide the crown;
He raised a mortal to the skies;
She drew an angel down.

1697 1697

from Fables Ancient and Modern[1]

from Preface

'Tis with a poet as with a man who designs to build, and is very exact, as he supposes, in casting up the cost beforehand. But generally speaking, he is mistaken in his account, and reckons short of the expense he first intended. He alters his mind

5. Cecilia was believed to have invented the organ.
6. One possessed by spirits or by a god.
7. Dryden alludes to his earlier ode to music, *A Song for St. Cecilia's Day* (1687): as Cecilia plays the organ, "An angel heard and straight appear'd, / Mistaking earth for heaven."
1. Following the triumph of his *Virgil* (1697), Dryden turned again to translation. He had frequently collaborated with others in the assembly of anthologies; now he undertook to make one of his own, containing poets both "Ancient"—Ovid and Homer—and "Modern"—Boccaccio, Chaucer, and Dryden himself. In the *Fables*, Dryden's pleasure and assurance in his own technical mastery are everywhere on display: in the expansiveness of his translations; in the bravado with which he plunders his own works as a treasury of echo and allusion; in the arrangement of his materials, so that fable talks to fable in an almost calculated sequence; and in his preface, where he lays out the history of his book's development with a conspicuous delight in the improvisatory logic of his creative process, and then proudly argues for the greatness of Chaucer, whose career and craft he celebrates in such a way as to suggest parallels with his own.

as the work proceeds, and will have this or that convenience more, of which he had not thought when he began. So has it happened to me; I have built a house where I intended but a lodge, yet with better success than a certain nobleman,[2] who beginning with a dog kennel, never lived to finish the palace he had contrived.

From translating the first of Homer's *Iliads* (which I intended as an essay to[3] the whole work) I proceeded to the translation of the twelfth book of Ovid's *Metamorphoses*,[4] because it contains, among other things, the causes, the beginning, and ending, of the Trojan War. Here I ought in reason to have stopped; but the speeches of Ajax and Ulysses lying next in my way, I could not balk 'em. When I had compassed them, I was so taken with the former part of the fifteenth book[5] (which is the masterpiece of the whole *Metamorphoses*) that I enjoined myself the pleasing task of rendering it into English. And now I found, by the number of my verses, that they began to swell into a little volume; which gave me an occasion of looking backward on some beauties of my author, in his former books: there occurred to me the hunting of the boar, Cinyras and Myrrha, the good-natured story of Baucis and Philemon, with the rest, which I hope I have translated closely enough, and given them the same turn of verse, which they had in the original; and this, I may say without vanity, is not the talent of every poet. He who has arrived the nearest to it, is the ingenious and learned Sandys,[6] the best versifier of the former age, if I may properly call it by that name, which was the former part of this concluding century. For Spenser and Fairfax[7] both flourished in the reign of Queen Elizabeth: great masters in our language, and who saw much farther into the beauties of our numbers than those who immediately followed them. Milton was the poetical son of Spenser, and Mr. Waller[8] of Fairfax; for we have our lineal descents and clans, as well as other families. Spenser more than once insinuates that the soul of Chaucer was transfused into his body, and that he was begotten by him two hundred years after his decease. Milton has acknowledged to me that Spenser was his original, and many besides myself have heard our famous Waller own that he derived the harmony of his numbers from the *Godfrey of Bulloign*, which was turned into English by Mr. Fairfax.

But to return: having done with Ovid for this time, it came into my mind that our old English poet Chaucer in many things resembled him, and that with no disadvantage on the side of the modern author, as I shall endeavor to prove when I compare them. And as I am and always have been studious to promote the honor of my native country, so I soon resolved to put their merits to the trial, by turning some of the *Canterbury Tales* into our language, as it is now refined, for by this means, both the poets being set in the same light, and dressed in the same English habit, story to be compared with story, a certain judgment may be made betwixt them by the reader, without obtruding my opinion on him: or if I seem partial to my countryman, and predecessor in the laurel, the friends of antiquity are not few. And besides many of the learned, Ovid has almost all the beaux,[9] and the whole fair sex,

2. Probably the Duke of Buckingham (whom Dryden had ridiculed as Zimri in *Absalom and Achitophel* line 544), and Buckingham's house at Cliveden.
3. First attempt at, and "taste of" (Johnson's *Dictionary*).
4. Ovid (43 B.C.E.–17 C.E.), Roman poet who spent the last decade of his life in exile. His *Metamorphoses* is a collection of ancient legends; in many, the characters undergo bodily transformations, from one form of life into another.
5. In which Ovid puts into verse the philosophy of the Greek mystic Pythagoras, who propounded a doctrine of reincarnation, arguing that "all things are but altered, nothing dies."
6. George Sandys (1578–1644), poet and translator, whose *Ovid's Metamorphosis Englished* was issued in 1626 and often republished.
7. Edward Fairfax (c. 1580–1635), poet and translator.
8. Edmund Waller (1606–1687), poet, early practitioner of the heroic couplet; Dryden praised him as "the father" of English versification.
9. Fashionable gentlemen.

his declared patrons. Perhaps I have assumed somewhat more to myself than they allow me, because I have adventured to sum up the evidence. But the readers are the jury; and their privilege remains entire to decide according to the merits of the cause or, if they please, to bring it to another hearing before some other court. In the meantime, to follow the thread of my discourse (as thoughts, according to Mr. Hobbes,[1] have always some connection) so from Chaucer I was led to think on Boccace,[2] who was not only his contemporary, but also pursued the same studies; wrote novels in prose, and many works in verse; particularly is said to have invented the octave rhyme, or stanza of eight lines, which ever since has been maintained by the practice of all Italian writers who are, or at least assume the title of, heroic poets. He and Chaucer, among other things, had this in common, that they refined their mother tongues; but with this difference, that Dante had begun to file their language,[3] at least in verse, before the time of Boccace, who likewise received no little help from his master Petrarch.[4] But the reformation of their prose was wholly owing to Boccace himself, who is yet the standard of purity in the Italian tongue, though many of his phrases are become obsolete, as in process of time it must needs happen. Chaucer (as you have formerly been told by our learned Mr. Rymer) first adorned and amplified our barren tongue from the Provençal, which was then the most polished of all the modern languages.[5] But this subject has been copiously treated by that great critic, who deserves no little commendation from us his countrymen. For these reasons of time, and resemblance of genius, in Chaucer and Boccace, I resolved to join them in my present work, to which I have added some original papers of my own, which whether they are equal or inferior to my other poems, an author is the most improper judge; and therefore I leave them wholly to the mercy of the reader. I will hope the best, that they will not be condemned; but if they should, I have the excuse of an old gentleman, who mounting on horseback before some ladies, when I was present, got up somewhat heavily, but desired of the fair spectators that they would count fourscore and eight before they judged him. By the mercy of God, I am already come within twenty years of his number, a cripple in my limbs, but what decays are in my mind, the reader must determine. I think myself as vigorous as ever in the faculties of my soul, excepting only my memory, which is not impaired to any great degree; and if I lose not more of it, I have no great reason to complain. What judgment I had increases rather than diminishes; and thoughts, such as they are, come crowding in so fast upon me that my only difficulty is to choose or to reject; to run them into verse, or to give them the other harmony of prose. I have so long studied and practiced both that they are grown into a habit, and become familiar to me. In short, though I may lawfully plead some part of the old gentleman's excuse, yet I will reserve it till I think I have greater need, and ask no grains of allowance for the faults of this my present work but those which are given of course to human frailty. I will not trouble my reader with the shortness of time in which I writ it, or the several intervals of sickness. They who think too well of their own performances are apt to boast in their prefaces how little time their

1. In his *Leviathan* (1651), Thomas Hobbes includes a chapter on "The Consequence or Train of Imaginations" (1.3).
2. Giovanni Boccaccio (1313–1375), Italian writer, authored *The Decameron* (a collection of 100 tales) and was one of Chaucer's chief influences.
3. Dante Alighieri (1265–1321), author of *The Divine Comedy*, was the first great vernacular poet in Italy; *to file*: to smooth (into graceful verse).
4. Italian poet (1304–1374), whose cycle of love sonnets exerted enormous influence over English writers.
5. In his *Short View of Tragedy* (1693), Thomas Rymer writes that Chaucer seized "all Provençal [Old French], French, or Latin that came in his way, gives them a new garb . . . and mingles them amongst our English."

works have cost them, and what other business of more importance interfered. But the reader will be as apt to ask the question, why they allowed not a longer time to make their works more perfect? and why they had so despicable an opinion of their judges, as to thrust their indigested stuff upon them, as if they deserved no better?

With this account of my present undertaking, I conclude the first part of this discourse. In the second part, as at a second sitting, though I alter not the draught, I must touch the same features over again, and change the dead-colorings[6] of the whole.

* * *

It remains that I say somewhat of Chaucer in particular.

In the first place, as he is the father of English poetry, so I hold him in the same degree of veneration as the Grecians held Homer, or the Romans Virgil. He is a perpetual fountain of good sense; learned in all sciences; and therefore speaks properly on all subjects. As he knew what to say, so he knows also when to leave off, a continence which is practiced by few writers, and scarcely by any of the Ancients, excepting Virgil and Horace. One of our late great poets[7] is sunk in his reputation, because he could never forgive any conceit which came in his way, but swept like a dragnet, great and small. There was plenty enough, but the dishes were ill sorted; whole pyramids of sweet-meats for boys and women, but little of solid meat for men. All this proceeded not from any want of knowledge, but of judgment; neither did he want that in discerning the beauties and faults of other poets, but only indulged himself in the luxury of writing; and perhaps knew it was a fault, but hoped the reader would not find it. For this reason, though he must always be thought a great poet, he is no longer esteemed a good writer; and for ten impressions,[8] which his works have had in so many successive years, yet at present a hundred books are scarcely purchased once a twelvemonth. For, as my last Lord Rochester said, though somewhat profanely, "Not being of God, he could not stand."

Chaucer followed Nature everywhere, but was never so bold to go beyond her. And there is a great difference of being *poeta* and *nimis poeta*,[9] if we may believe Catullus, as much as betwixt a modest behavior and affectation. The verse of Chaucer, I confess, is not harmonious to us; but 'tis like the eloquence of one whom Tacitus commends: it was *auribus istius temporis accommodata*.[1] They who lived with him, and some time after him, thought it musical, and it continues so even in our judgment, if compared with the numbers of Lydgate and Gower, his contemporaries. There is the rude sweetness of a Scotch tune in it, which is natural and pleasing, though not perfect. 'Tis true, I cannot go so far as he who published the last edition of him,[2] for he would make us believe the fault is in our ears, and that there were really ten syllables in a verse where we find but nine. But this opinion is not worth confuting; 'tis so gross and obvious an error that common sense (which is a rule in everything but matters of faith and revelation) must convince the reader that equality of numbers, in every verse which we call heroic,[3] was either not known or not always practiced in Chaucer's age. It were an easy matter to produce some thousands of his verses which are lame for want of half a foot, and sometimes a whole one, and

6. The prepatory layer of paint applied to a canvas.
7. Abraham Cowley (1618–1667), whom Dryden admired and imitated.
8. Printings.
9. "A poet" and "too much a poet"; the Latin poet Martial, and not his predecessor Catullus, made this observation.
1. "Suited to the ears of those times": Cornelius Tacitus, Roman historian.
2. Thomas Speght, who argued (correctly) that Chaucer's versification was skillful and smooth but misrepresented by transcribers and misunderstood by readers.
3. I.e., consistent iambic pentameter.

which no pronunciation can make otherwise. We can only say that he lived in the infancy of our poetry, and that nothing is brought to perfection at the first. We must be children before we grow men. There was an Ennius, and in process of time a Lucilius and a Lucretius, before Virgil and Horace; even after Chaucer there was a Spenser, a Harrington, a Fairfax, before Waller and Denham were in being.[4] And our numbers were in their nonage[5] till these last appeared. I need say little of his parentage, life, and fortunes. They are to be found at large in all the editions of his works. He was employed abroad, and favored by Edward the Third, Richard the Second, and Henry the Fourth, and was poet, as I suppose, to all three of them. In Richard's time, I doubt, he was a little dipped in the rebellion of the Commons, and being brother-in-law to John of Gaunt, it was no wonder if he followed the fortunes of that family, and was well with Henry the Fourth when he had deposed his predecessor.[6] Neither is it to be admired[7] that Henry, who was a wise as well as a valiant prince, who claimed by succession, and was sensible that his title was not sound, but was rightfully in Mortimer, who had married the heir of York—it was not to be admired, I say, if that great politician should be pleased to have the greatest wit of those times in his interests, and to be the trumpet of his praises. Augustus had given him the example, by the advice of Maecenas,[8] who recommended Virgil and Horace to him; whose praises helped to make him popular while he was alive, and after his death have made him precious to posterity. As for the religion of our poet, he seems to have some little bias toward the opinions of Wyclif,[9] after John of Gaunt his patron; somewhat of which appears in the *Tale of Piers Plowman*.[1] Yet I cannot blame him for inveighing so sharply against the vices of the clergy in his age. Their pride, their ambition, their pomp, their avarice, their worldly interest deserved the lashes which he gave them, both in that, and in most of his *Canterbury Tales*. Neither has his contemporary Boccace spared them. Yet both those poets lived in much esteem, with good and holy men in orders, for the scandal which is given by particular priests reflects not on the sacred function. Chaucer's Monk, his Canon, and his Friar took not[2] from the character of his Good Parson. A satirical poet is the check of the laymen on bad priests. We are only to take care that we involve not the innocent with the guilty in the same condemnation. The good cannot be too much honored, nor the bad too coarsely used, for the corruption of the best becomes the worst. When a clergyman is whipped, his gown is first taken off, by which the dignity of his order is secured. If he be wrongfully accused, he has his action of slander, and 'tis at the poet's peril if he transgress the law. But they will tell us that all kind of satire, though never so well deserved by particular priests, yet brings the whole order into contempt. Is then the peerage of England any thing dishonored, when a peer suffers for his treason? If he be libeled, or any way defamed, he has his *scandalum magnatum* [legal recourse] to punish the offender. They who use this kind of argument seem to be conscious to themselves of somewhat which has deserved the poet's lash, and are less concerned for their public capacity than for their private. At least, there is pride at the bottom of their reasoning. If the faults of men in orders are only to be judged among themselves, they are all in some sort parties. For, since they say the honor of

4. Dryden traces a "descent and lineage" of influence first in Latin and then in English poetry.
5. Early youth.
6. Henry Bolingbroke (son to John of Gaunt) deposed his cousin Richard II in 1399; Chaucer survived political upheaval and received patronage from both kings.
7. Wondered at.
8. Roman patron of the poets Virgil, Horace, and Propertius.
9. John Wyclif (c. 1330–1384), theologian and religious reformer.
1. This tale had been mistakenly attributed to Chaucer; there is no evidence that he was a follower of Wyclif.
2. I.e., did not detract.

their order is concerned in every member of it, how can we be sure that they will be impartial judges? How far I may be allowed to speak my opinion in this case I know not, but I am sure a dispute of this nature caused mischief in abundance betwixt a King of England and an Archbishop of Canterbury; one standing up for the laws of his land, and the other for the honor (as he called it) of God's Church; which ended in the murder of the prelate, and in the whipping of his Majesty from post to pillar for his penance.[3] The learned and ingenious Dr. Drake[4] has saved me the labor of inquiring into the esteem and reverence which the priests have had of old; and I would rather extend than diminish any part of it. Yet I must needs say that when a priest provokes me without any occasion given him, I have no reason, unless it be the charity of a Christian, to forgive him. *Prior laesit*[5] is justification sufficient in the civil law. If I answer him in his own language, self-defense, I am sure, must be allowed me, and if I carry it farther, even to a sharp recrimination, somewhat may be indulged to human frailty. Yet my resentment has not wrought so far, but that I have followed Chaucer in his character of a holy man, and have enlarged on that subject with some pleasure, reserving to myself the right, if I shall think fit hereafter, to describe another sort of priests, such as are more easily to be found than the Good Parson; such as have given the last blow to Christianity in this age, by a practice so contrary to their doctrine. But this will keep cold till another time.

In the meanwhile, I take up Chaucer where I left him. He must have been a man of a most wonderful comprehensive nature, because, as it has been truly observed of him, he has taken into the compass of his *Canterbury Tales* the various manners and humors (as we now call them) of the whole English nation in his age. Not a single character has escaped him. All his pilgrims are severally distinguished from each other; and not only in their inclinations, but in their very physiognomies and persons. Baptista Porta[6] could not have described their natures better than by the marks which the poet gives them. The matter and manner of their tales, and of their telling, are so suited to their different educations, humors, and callings, that each of them would be improper in any other mouth. Even the grave and serious characters are distinguished by their several sorts of gravity: their discourses are such as belong to their age, their calling, and their breeding; such as are becoming of them, and of them only. Some of his persons are vicious, and some virtuous; some are unlearned, or (as Chaucer calls them) *lewd*, and some are learned. Even the ribaldry of the low characters is different: the Reeve, the Miller, and the Cook, are several men, and distinguished from each other, as much as the mincing Lady Prioress and the broad-speaking gap-toothed Wife of Bath. But enough of this: there is such a variety of game springing up before me that I am distracted in my choice, and know not which to follow. 'Tis sufficient to say according to the proverb, that here is God's plenty. We have our forefathers and great grand-dames all before us, as they were in Chaucer's days; their general characters are still remaining in mankind, and even in England, though they are called by other names than those of monks, and friars, and canons, and lady abbesses, and nuns. For mankind is ever the same, and nothing lost out of nature, though everything is altered. May I have leave to do myself the justice (since my enemies will do me none, and are

3. Thomas à Becket, Archbishop of Canterbury, was murdered in 1170 on the orders of his king, Henry II, after a long dispute over the powers and rights of the church. (The pilgrims in *The Canterbury Tales* are traveling to Becket's shrine.)

4. James Drake (1667–1707), physician, dramatist, and ally of Dryden in literary controversies.

5. He injured first (i.e., "he started it").

6. Giambattista della Porta (c. 1538–1615), a physician whose book *De humana physiognomia* catalogued the effects of the emotional life on the look of the face.

so far from granting me to be a good poet that they will not allow me so much as to be a Christian, or a moral man) may I have leave, I say, to inform my reader, that I have confined my choice to such tales of Chaucer as savor nothing of immodesty.[7] If I had desired more to please than to instruct, the Reeve, the Miller, the Shipman, the Merchant, the Summoner, and above all, the Wife of Bath, in the Prologue to her Tale, would have procured me as many friends and readers as there are beaux and ladies of pleasure in the town. But I will no more offend against good manners. I am sensible as I ought to be of the scandal I have given by my loose writings;[8] and make what reparation I am able, by this public acknowledgment. If anything of this nature, or of profaneness, be crept into these poems, I am so far from defending it, that I disown it. *Totum hoc indictum volo.*[9] Chaucer makes another manner of apology for his broad speaking, and Boccace makes the like; but I will follow neither of them. Our countryman, in the end of his characters, before the *Canterbury Tales*, thus excuses the ribaldry, which is very gross, in many of his novels.

> But first, I pray you, of your courtesy,
> That ye ne arrete it nought my villany,
> Though that I plainly speak in this mattere
> To tellen you her words, and eke her chere:
> Ne though I speak her words properly,
> For this ye knowen as well as I,
> Who shall tellen a tale after a man
> He mote rehearse as nye as ever he can:
> Everich word of it been in his charge,
> *All speke he never so rudely, ne large.*
> Or else he mote tellen his tale untrue,
> Or feine things, or find words new:
> He may not spare, altho he were his brother,
> He mote as well say o word as another.
> Christ spake himself full broad in holy writ,
> And well I wote no villany is it.
> Eke Plato saith, who so can him rede,
> The words mote been cousin to the dede.[1]

Yet if a man should have inquired of Boccace or of Chaucer, what need they had of introducing such characters, where obscene words were proper in their mouths, but very undecent to be heard, I know not what answer they could have made. For that reason, such tales shall be left untold by me. You have here a specimen of Chaucer's language, which is so obsolete that his sense is scarce to be understood; and you have likewise more than one example of his unequal numbers, which were mentioned before. Yet many of his verses consist of ten syllables, and the words not much behind our present English, as for example, these two lines, in the description of the carpenter's young wife:

> Wincing she was, as is a jolly colt,
> Long as a mast, and upright as a bolt.[2]

7. The *Fables* includes Dryden's translations of *The Knight's Tale*, *The Nun's Priest's Tale* (*The Cock and the Fox*), *The Wife of Bath's Tale*, and the portrait of the Parson from the *General Prologue* (*The Character of a Good Parson; Imitated from Chaucer and Inlarg'd*).

8. Throughout his career, Dryden had found it necessary to defend his plays against charges of immorality.

9. I wish all this unsaid.

1. *The General Prologue*, lines 727–744.

2. *The Miller's Tale*, lines 155–156.

I have almost done with Chaucer, when I have answered some objections relating to my present work. I find some people are offended that I have turned these tales into modern English, because they think them unworthy of my pains, and look on Chaucer as a dry, old-fashioned wit, not worth receiving. I have often heard the late Earl of Leicester[3] say that Mr. Cowley himself was of that opinion, who having read him over at my Lord's request, declared he had no taste of him. I dare not advance my opinion against the judgment of so great an author. But I think it fair, however, to leave the decision to the public. Mr. Cowley was too modest to set up for a dictator, and being shocked perhaps with his old style, never examined into the depth of his good sense. Chaucer, I confess, is a rough diamond, and must first be polished ere he shines. I deny not likewise, that living in our early days of poetry, he writes not always of a piece; but sometimes mingles trivial things with those of greater moment. Sometimes also, though not often, he runs riot, like Ovid, and knows not when he has said enough. But there are more great wits, beside Chaucer, whose fault is their excess of conceits, and those ill sorted. An author is not to write all he can, but only all he ought. Having observed this redundancy in Chaucer (as it is an easy matter for a man of ordinary parts to find a fault in one of greater) I have not tied myself to a literal translation, but have often omitted what I judged unnecessary, or not of dignity enough to appear in the company of better thoughts. I have presumed farther in some places, and added somewhat of my own where I thought my author was deficient, and had not given his thoughts their true luster, for want of words in the beginning of our language. And to this I was the more emboldened, because (if I may be permitted to say it of myself) I found I had a soul congenial to his, and that I had been conversant in the same studies. Another poet, in another age, may take the same liberty with my writings, if at least they live long enough to deserve correction. It was also necessary sometimes to restore the sense of Chaucer, which was lost or mangled in the errors of the press. Let this example suffice at present; in the story of Palamon and Arcite,[4] where the Temple of Diana is described, you find these verses in all the editions of our author:

> There saw I Danè turned unto a tree,
> I mean not the goddess Diane,
> But Venus daughter, which that hight Danè.

Which after a little consideration I knew was to be reformed into this sense, that Daphne the daughter of Peneus was turned into a tree. I durst not make thus bold with Ovid, lest some future Milbourn[5] should arise, and say I varied from my author because I understood him not.

But there are other judges who think I ought not to have translated Chaucer into English, out of a quite contrary notion. They suppose there is a certain veneration due to his old language, and that it is little less than profanation and sacrilege to alter it. They are farther of opinion that somewhat of his good sense will suffer in this transfusion, and much of the beauty of his thoughts will infallibly be lost, which appear with more grace in their old habit. Of this opinion was that excellent person whom I mentioned, the late Earl of Leicester, who valued Chaucer as much as

3. Philip Sidney (1619–1698), patron of Dryden, to whom the poet had dedicated his tragedy *Don Sebastian* (1690).

4. *The Knight's Tale*.

5. Luke Milbourne (1649–1720), a clergyman and translator who had attacked Dryden's *Virgil*.

Mr. Cowley despised him. My Lord dissuaded me from this attempt (for I was thinking of it some years before his death) and his authority prevailed so far with me as to defer my undertaking while he lived, in deference to him. Yet my reason was not convinced with what he urged against it. If the first end of a writer be to be understood, then as his language grows obsolete, his thoughts must grow obscure: *multa renascentur quae nunc cecidere; cadentque quae nunc sunt in honore vocabula, si volet usus, quem penes arbitrium est & jus & norma loquendi.*[6] When an ancient word for its sound and significancy deserves to be revived, I have that reasonable veneration for antiquity to restore it. All beyond this is superstition. Words are not like landmarks, so sacred as never to be removed. Customs are changed, and even statutes are silently repealed when the reason ceases for which they were enacted. As for the other part of the argument, that his thoughts will lose of their original beauty by the innovation of words: in the first place, not only their beauty, but their being is lost, where they are no longer understood, which is the present case. I grant that something must be lost in all transfusion, that is, in all translations; but the sense will remain, which would otherwise be lost, or at least be maimed, when it is scarce intelligible, and that but to a few. How few are there who can read Chaucer so as to understand him perfectly? And if imperfectly, then with less profit, and no pleasure. 'Tis not for the use of some old Saxon friends[7] that I have taken these pains with him. Let them neglect my version, because they have no need of it. I made it for their sakes who understand sense and poetry as well as they, when that poetry and sense is put into words which they understand. I will go farther, and dare to add, that what beauties I lose in some places, I give to others which had them not originally. But in this I may be partial to myself; let the reader judge, and I submit to his decision. Yet I think I have just occasion to complain of them who, because they understand Chaucer, would deprive the greater part of their countrymen of the same advantage, and hoard him up, as misers do their grandam gold,[8] only to look on it themselves, and hinder others from making use of it. In sum, I seriously protest that no man ever had, or can have, a greater veneration for Chaucer than myself. I have translated some part of his works, only that I might perpetuate his memory, or at least refresh it, amongst my countrymen. If I have altered him anywhere for the better, I must at the same time acknowledge that I could have done nothing without him. *Facile est inventis addere*[9] is no great commendation, and I am not so vain to think I have deserved a greater. I will conclude what I have to say of him singly, with this one remark: a lady of my acquaintance, who keeps a kind of correspondence with some authors of the fair sex in France, has been informed by them, that Mademoiselle de Scudery,[1] who is as old as Sibyl,[2] and inspired like her by the same god of poetry, is at this time translating Chaucer into modern French. From which I gather, that he has been formerly translated into the old Provençal (for how she should come to understand old English, I know not). But the matter of fact being true, it makes me think that there is something in it like fatality; that after certain periods of time, the fame and memory of great wits should be renewed, as Chaucer is both in France and England.

6. Many terms that have fallen out of use shall be born again, and those shall fall which that are now in use, if usage so will it, in whose hands lies the judgment, the right, and the rule of speech (Horace, *Ars Poetica* 70–72).
7. Friends who were scholars of Anglo-Saxon literature.
8. Long-stored-up wealth.
9. It is easy to add to what has already been discovered.
1. Madeleine de Scudéry (1607–1701), author of chivalric romances.
2. The Sybil of Cumae was a prophetess who served Apollo, god of poetry; he granted her wish to live a thousand years.

If this be wholly chance, 'tis extraordinary; and I dare not call it more, for fear of being taxed with superstition. * * *

The Secular Masque[1]

[*Enter Janus.*[2]]

JANUS: Chronos,[3] Chronos, mend thy pace,
A hundred times the rolling sun.
Around the radiant belt[4] has run
In his revolving race.
Behold, behold, the goal in sight,
Spread thy fans,[5] and wing thy flight.
[*Enter Chronos, with a scythe in his hand, and a great globe on his back, which he sets down at his entrance.*]
CHRONOS: Weary, weary of my weight,
Let me, let me drop my freight,
And leave the world behind.
I could not bear
Another year
The load of humankind.
[*Enter Momus*[6] *laughing.*]
MOMUS: Ha! ha! ha! ha! ha! ha! well hast thou done,
To lay down thy pack,
And lighten thy back,
The world was a fool, e'er since it begun,
And since neither Janus, nor Chronos, nor I,
Can hinder the crimes,
Or mend the bad times,
'Tis better to laugh than to cry.
[*Chorus of all three.*]
'Tis better to laugh than to cry.
JANUS: Since Momus comes to laugh below,
Old Time, begin the show,
That he may see, in every scene,
What changes in this age have been.
CHRONOS: Then, goddess of the silver bow, begin.
[*Horns, or hunting music, within. Enter Diana.*[7]]

1. "Within this month," Dryden wrote a friend in April 1700, "there will be played for my profit, an old play . . . called *The Pilgrim*, . . . to which I have added a new masque." Dryden called this new portion *The Secular Masque*, because it marked the turn of the century (Latin *saeculum:* age, period, century). Through its nostalgic form, he looked back to the start of the 17th century, and to the courts of Elizabeth, James, and Charles I, where just such masques, dominated by pagan gods mirroring and musing on present events, exerted a hypnotic appeal. In the *Masque*'s short span, Dryden sought both to compass the century—its pursuits and pleasures, its wars and loves—and to dispatch it, in a tone compounded of affection and scorn. The *Masque* proved valedictory in one other way as well. On 1 May, a few days after the piece's first performance, Dryden died.
2. The Roman god of openings (gates, doors) and beginnings, possessing two faces pointed in opposite directions (past, future). January is named for him.
3. Time, traditionally depicted as described in the ensuing stage direction.
4. The zodiac.
5. Wings.
6. Greek god (the name means "blame") of ridicule, mockery, satire.
7. Roman goddess of chastity and of hunting, here reminiscent of Elizabeth I, the Virgin Queen, and of James I, enthusiastic hunter.

DIANA: With horns and with hounds, I waken the day,
And hie to the woodland walks away;
I tuck up my robe, and am buskined soon,
And tie to my forehead a waxing moon,
I course the fleet stag, unkennel the fox,
And chase the wild goats o'er summits of rocks,
With shouting and hooting we pierce through the sky,
And Echo turns hunter, and doubles the cry.
[*Chorus of all.*]
With shouting and hooting we pierce through the sky,
And Echo turns hunter, and doubles the cry.
JANUS: Then our age was in its prime:
CHRONOS: Free from rage,
DIANA: And free from crime.
MOMUS: A very merry, dancing, drinking,
Laughing, quaffing, and unthinking time.
[*Chorus of all.*]
Then our age was in its prime,
Free from rage, and free from crime;
A very merry, dancing, drinking,
Laughing, quaffing, and unthinking time.
[*Dance of Diana's attendants. Enter Mars.*[8]]
MARS: Inspire the vocal brass,[9] inspire;
The world is past its infant age:
Arms and honor,
Arms and honor,
Set the martial mind on fire,
And kindle manly rage.
Mars has looked the sky[1] to red;
And peace, the lazy good, is fled.
Plenty, peace, and pleasure fly;
The sprightly green,
In woodland walks, no more is seen;
The sprightly green has drunk the Tyrian dye.[2]
[*Chorus of all.*]
Plenty, peace, etc.
MARS: Sound the trumpet, beat the drum;
Through all the world around,
Sound a reveille, sound, sound,
The warrior god is come.
[*Chorus of all.*]
Sound the trumpet, etc.
MOMUS: Thy sword within the scabbard keep,

8. Roman god of war, here incarnating the midcentury civil wars.
9. Sound the speaking trumpet, the call to arms.
1. I.e., has by his stare changed the color of the sky.
2. An ancient purple hue: the color of the soldiers' garments (here displacing the green of the hunters') and of the blood they shed.

And let mankind agree;
Better the world were fast asleep,
Than kept awake by thee.
The fools are only thinner,
With all our cost and care;
But neither side a winner,
For things are as they were.
[*Chorus of all.*]
The fools are only, etc.
[*Enter Venus*[3]]
VENUS: Calms appear, when storms are past;
Love will have his hour at last:
Nature is my kindly care;
Mars destroys, and I repair;
Take me, take me, while you may,
Venus comes not every day.
[*Chorus of all.*]
Take her, take her, etc.
CHRONOS: The world was then so light,
I scarcely felt the weight;
Joy ruled the day, and love the night.
But since the queen of pleasure left the ground,
I faint, I lag,
And feebly drag
The ponderous orb around.
MOMUS: All, all of a piece throughout;
Thy chase had a beast in view;
[*Pointing to Diana.*]
Thy wars brought nothing about;
[*To Mars.*]
Thy lovers were all untrue.
[*To Venus.*]
JANUS: 'Tis well an old age is out,
CHRONOS: And time to begin a new.
[*Chorus of all.*]
All, all of a piece throughout;
Thy chase had a beast in view;
Thy wars brought nothing about;
Thy lovers were all untrue.
'Tis well an old age is out,
And time to begin a new.
[*Dance of huntsmen, nymphs, warriors and lovers.*]

1700

3. Roman goddess of love, here presiding over the amorous court of Charles II.

Aphra Behn

1640?–1689

Robert White, after John Riley, line engraving of *Aphra Behn (née Johnson)*, 1716.

Aphra Behn's career was unprecedented, her output prodigious, her fame extensive, and her voice distinctive. Her origins, though, remain elusive. We know nothing certain about her birth, family, education, or marriage. She may have been born at the start or at the end of the 1640s, to parents of low or "gentle" station, named Johnson, Amies, or Cooper. Her Catholicism and her firm command of French suggest the possibility of a prosperous upbringing in a convent at home or abroad; the running argument against marriage for money that she sustains through much of her work suggests that her own marriage, to the otherwise unidentifiable "Mr. Behn," may have been obligatory and unhappy. In any case it was brief—and just possibly fictitious, since a widow could pursue a profession more freely than a spinster.

Behn's first appearances in the historical record suggest a propensity for self-invention. In 1663–1664, during a short stay with her family in the South American sugar colony of Surinam, a government agent there reported that she was conducting a flirtation with William Scott, an antimonarchist on the run from the Restoration. The agent referred to Scott as "Celadon" and Aphra as "Astraea," names the lovers may well have chosen for themselves from a popular French romance; Behn kept hers, as a *nom de plume*, for the whole of her writing life. Within two years, her loyalties had shifted and her self-invention had grown more intricate. In 1666 Behn herself became the king's spy, sent from London to Antwerp to persuade her old flame Scott to turn informer against his fellow Republicans and to apprise King Charles of rebellious plots. She did useful but costly work, garnering good information that her handlers ignored and spending much money that they were slow to reimburse. Returning to England later that year, and threatened with imprisonment for debt, she wrote her supervisor, "I have cried myself dead and could find in my heart to break through all and get to the King and never rise till he were pleased to pay this, but I am sick and weak and unfit for it or a prison . . . Sir, if I have not the money tonight you must send me something to keep [sustain] me in prison, for I will not starve." The king paid up, and Behn forestalled any further threat of starvation by writing plays for money—the first woman in England to earn a living by her pen. She had been "forced to write for bread," she later declared, and she was "not ashamed to own it."

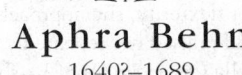

Throughout her career Behn transmuted such "shamelessness" into a positive point of pride and a source of literary substance. Many of her plays, poems, and fictions focus on the difficulty with which intelligent, enterprising women pursue their desires against the current of social convention. In the prologues, prefaces, postscripts, and letters by which she provided a running commentary on her work, Behn sometimes aligned herself with the large fraternity of male authors who "like good tradesmen" sell whatever is "in fashion," but she often stood apart to muse acerbically on her unique position as a *female* purveyor of literary product. Once, surveying the panoply of contemporary male playwrights, she declared that "except for our most unimitable Laureate [Dryden], I dare say I know of none that write at such a formidable rate, but that a woman may well hope to reach their greatest heights." "Formidable rate" suggests both speed and skill; Behn made good on both boasts, producing twenty plays in twenty years, along with much poetry (including fervent pro-Stuart propaganda), copious translations, one of the earliest epistolary novels in English, and a cluster of innovative shorter fiction. In her range and her dexterity, she approached the stature of the "unimitable Laureate" himself, who knew her and praised her repeatedly. With her greatest successes—the comedy *The Rover* (1677), the novella *Oroonoko* (1688)—she secured both an audience and a reputation that continued without pause well into the following century.

Other pieces worked less well. Changes in literary fashion often obliged Behn to try new modes; she switched to fiction, for example, in the 1680s, when plays became less lucrative. Out of her vicissitudes—professional and personal, amorous, financial, literary—she fashioned a formidable celebrity, becoming the object of endless speculation in talk and in ink. "I value fame," she once wrote, and she cultivated it by what seemed an unprecedented frankness. ("All women together," wrote Virginia Woolf, "ought to let flowers fall upon the grave of Aphra Behn . . . for it was she who earned them the right to speak their minds.") In an age of libertines, when men like Rochester paraded their varied couplings in verse couplets, Behn undertook to proclaim and to analyze women's sexual desire, as manifested in her characters and in herself. Her disclosures, though, were intricately orchestrated. Living and writing at the center of a glamorous literary circle, Behn may have fostered, as the critic Janet Todd suggests, the "fantasy of a golden age of sexual and social openness," but she performed it for her readers rather than falling for it herself. Throughout her work Behn adroitly conceals the "self" that she purports to show and sell. She sometimes likens herself to those other female denizens of the theater, the mask-wearing prostitutes who roamed the audience in search of customers. The critic Catherine Gallagher has argued that Behn's literary persona—defiant, vulnerable, hypnotic—functions like the prostitute's vizard, promising the woman's "availability" as commodity while at the same time implying "the impenetrability of the controlling mind" behind the mask.

In Gallagher's reckoning, as in Woolf's, Behn's total career is more important than any particular work it produced. This is fitting tribute to a writer who, in an era of spectacular self-performers (Charles II, Dryden, Rochester), brought off, by virtue of her gender and her art, one of the most intricate performances of all. That performance now looks set for a long second run. After a hiatus in the nineteenth century, when both the writer and the work were dismissed as indecent, Behn's fame has undergone extraordinary revival. She dominates cultural-studies discourse as both a topic and a set of texts. The texts in particular are worth attending to: many are as astonishing as the career that engendered them.

For additional resources on Behn, go to *The Longman Anthology of British Literature* Web site at www.myliteraturekit.com.

The Disappointment[1]

One day the amorous Lysander,
By an impatient passion swayed,
Surprised fair Cloris, that loved maid,
Who could defend herself no longer.
All things did with his love conspire;
The gilded planet of the day,
In his gay chariot drawn by fire,
Was now descending to the sea,
And left no light to guide the world,
But what from Cloris' brighter eyes was hurled.

1. Behn based this poem partly on a French source, *Sur une impuissance* (1661), itself dervied in part from Ovid's poem on impotence in *Amores*, which also provided the model for Rochester's *Imperfect Enjoyment* (see page 2205). Behn's poem and Rochester's first appeared in the same volume, *Poems on Several Occasions* (1680); she later included hers, with alterations, in her own collection, *Poems on Several Occasions* (1684).

In a lone thicket made for love,
Silent as yielding maid's consent,
She with a charming languishment
Permits his force, yet gently strove;
Her hands his bosom softly meet,
But not to put him back designed,
Rather to draw 'em[2] on inclined;
Whilst he lay trembling at her feet,
Resistance 'tis in vain to show;
She wants° the power to say, "Ah! What d'ye do?" *lacks*

Her bright eyes sweet, and yet severe,
Where love and shame confusedly strive,
Fresh vigor to Lysander give;
And breathing faintly in his ear,
She cried, "Cease, cease your vain desire,
Or I'll call out—what would you do?
My dearer honor even to you
I cannot, must not give—retire,
Or take this life, whose chiefest part
I gave you with the conquest of my heart."

But he as much unused to fear,
As he was capable of love,
The blessed minutes to improve,
Kisses her mouth, her neck, her hair;
Each touch her new desire alarms,
His burning trembling hand he pressed
Upon her swelling snowy breast,
While she lay panting in his arms.
All her unguarded beauties lie
The spoils and trophies of the enemy.

And now without respect or fear,
He seeks the object of his vows,
(His love no modesty allows)
By swift degrees advancing—where
His daring hand that altar seized,
Where gods of love do sacrifice:
That awful° throne, that paradise *awe-inspiring*
Where rage is calmed, and anger pleased;
That fountain where delight still flows,
And gives the universal world repose.

Her balmy lips encountering his,
Their bodies, as their souls, are joined;
Where both in transports unconfined
Extend themselves upon the moss.
Cloris half dead and breathless lay;

2. Behn's earlier version reads "him."

Her soft eyes cast a humid light,
Such as divides the day and night;
Or falling stars, whose fires decay:
And now no signs of life she shows,
But what in short-breathed sighs returns and goes.

He saw how at her length she lay;
He saw her rising bosom bare;
Her loose thin robes, through which appear
A shape designed for love and play;
Abandoned by her pride and shame,
She does her softest joys dispense,
Offering her virgin innocence
A victim to love's sacred flame;
While the o'er-ravished shepherd lies
Unable to perform the sacrifice.

Ready to taste a thousand joys,
The too transported hapless swain[3]
Found the vast pleasure turned to pain;
Pleasure which too much love destroys.
The willing garments by he laid,
And Heaven all opened to his view,
Mad to possess, himself he threw
On the defenseless lovely maid.
But oh what envying god conspires
To snatch his power, yet leave him the desire!

Nature's support[4] (without whose aid
She can no human being give)
Itself now wants the art to live.
Faintness its slackened nerves invade.
In vain the enraged youth essayed
To call its fleeting vigor back,
No motion 'twill from motion take.
Excess of love his love betrayed.
In vain he toils, in vain commands;
The insensible[5] fell weeping in his hand.

In this so amorous cruel strife,
Where love and fate were too severe,
The poor Lysander in despair
Renounced his reason with his life.
Now all the brisk and active fire
That should the nobler part inflame,
Served to increase his rage and shame,
And left no spark for new desire.
Not all her naked charms could move

3. In English pastoral poetry, this is the conventional term for the shepherd/lover.

4. I.e., the erect penis.

5. The unfeeling object.

Or calm that rage that had debauched° his love. *corrupted*

Cloris returning from the trance
Which love and soft desire had bred,
Her timorous hand she gently laid
(Or° guided by design or chance) *either*
Upon that fabulous Priapus,[6]
That potent god, as poets feign;
But never did young shepherdess,
Gathering of fern upon the plain,
More nimbly draw her fingers back,
Finding beneath the verdant leaves a snake,

Than Cloris her fair hand withdrew,
Finding that god of her desires
Disarmed of all his awful fires,
And cold as flowers bathed in the morning dew.
Who can the nymph's confusion guess?
The blood forsook the hinder place,
And strewed with blushes all her face,
Which both disdain and shame expressed.
And from Lysander's arms she fled,
Leaving him fainting on the gloomy bed.

Like lightning through the grove she hies,
Or Daphne from the Delphic god,[7]
No print upon the grassy road
She leaves, to instruct pursuing eyes.
The wind that wantoned in her hair,
And with her ruffled garments played,
Discovered in the flying maid
All that the gods e'er made, if fair.
So Venus, when her love was slain,
With fear and haste flew o'er the fatal plain.[8]

The nymph's resentments none but I
Can well imagine or condole.
But none can guess Lysander's soul,
But those who swayed his destiny.
His silent griefs swell up to storms,
And not one god his fury spares;
He cursed his birth, his fate, his stars;
But more the shepherdess's charms,
Whose soft bewitching influence
Had damned him to the hell of impotence.

1680

6. Greek god of male fertility, often depicted as possessing a permanent erection.
7. Apollo, who pursued the nymph Daphne until she was turned into a laurel tree in order to escape his advances.
8. When her beloved Adonis was wounded by a boar, the goddess of love rushed to help him, but in vain.

To Lysander,[1] on Some Verses He Writ, and Asking More for His Heart than 'Twas Worth

Take back that heart you with such caution give,
  Take the fond[2] valued trifle back;
I hate love-merchants that a trade would drive;
  And meanly cunning bargains make.

I care not how the busy market goes,
  And scorn to chaffer° for a price: *bargain*
Love does one staple° rate on all impose, *fixed*
  Nor leaves it to the trader's choice.

A heart requires a heart unfeigned and true,
  Though subtly you advance the price,
And ask a rate that simple love ne'er knew:
  And the free trade monopolize.

An humble slave the buyer must become,
  She must not bate[3] a look or glance,
You will have all, or you'll have none;
  See how love's market° you enhance.° *price / increase*

Is't not enough, I gave you heart for heart,
  But I must add my lips and eyes?
I must no friendly smile or kiss impart;
  But you must dun[4] me with advice?

And every hour still more unjust you grow.
  Those freedoms you my life deny,
You to Adraste[5] are obliged to show,
  And give her all my rifled° joy. *stolen*

Without control she gazes on that face,
  And all the happy envied night,
In the pleased circle of your fond embrace:
  She takes away the lover's right.

From me she ravishes those silent hours,
  That are by sacred love my due;
Whilst I in vain accuse the angry powers,
  That make me hopeless love pursue.

Adraste's ears with that dear voice are blest,
  That charms my soul at every sound,
And with those love-enchanting touches pressed:
  Which I ne'er felt without a wound.

1. "Lysander," the addressee of several of Behn's poems (and, in name at least, the male lover in *The Disappointment*), has not been identified; the poem suggests that he was a married man.

2. The word meant both "foolish" and "affectionate."

3. Withhold (by way of reducing love's "price").

4. Badger, demand payment from.

5. Apparently his wife.

She has thee all: whilst I with silent grief,
The fragments of thy softness feel,
Yet dare not blame the happy licensed[6] thief:
That does my dear-bought pleasures steal.

Whilst like a glimmering taper still I burn,
And waste myself in my own flame,
Adraste takes the welcome rich return:
And leaves me all the hopeless pain.

Be just, my lovely swain, and do not take
Freedoms you'll not to me allow;
Or give Amynta[7] so much freedom back:
That she may rove as well as you.

Let us then love upon the honest square,[8]
Since interest neither have designed.[9]
For the sly gamester,[1] who ne'er plays me fair,
Must trick for trick expect to find.

1684

To Lysander at the Music-Meeting

It was too much, ye gods, to see and hear,
Receiving wounds both from the eye and ear.
One charm might have secured a victory;
Both, raised the pleasure even to ecstasy.
So ravished lovers in each other's arms,
Faint with excess of joy, excess of charms.
Had I but gazed and fed my greedy eyes,
Perhaps you'd pleased no farther than surprise.
That heav'nly form might admiration move,
But, not without the music, charmed° with love: *have charmed*
At least so quick the conquest had not been;
You stormed without, and harmony within.
Nor could I listen to the sound alone,
But I alas must look—and was undone:
I saw the softness that composed your face,
While your attention heightened every grace:
Your mouth all full of sweetness and content,
And your fine killing eyes of languishment:
Your bosom now and then a sigh would move,
(For music has the same effects with love).
Your body easy and all tempting lay,
Inspiring wishes which the eyes betray,

6. Permitted (by the marriage license).
7. I.e., the poem's speaker.
8. I.e., by rules that apply to both sides equally.
9. Neither of us has intended to make a profit (on our investment in each other).
1. Trickster or gambler.

In all that have the fate to glance that way.
A careless and a lovely negligence,
Did a new charm to every limb dispense.
So look young angels, listening to the sound,
When the tuned spheres glad[1] all the heav'ns around:
So raptured lie amidst the wondering crowd,
So charmingly extended on a cloud.
When from so many ways love's arrows storm,
Who can the heedless heart defend from harm?
Beauty and music must the soul disarm;
Since harmony, like fire to wax, does fit
The softened heart impressions to admit:
As the brisk sounds of war the courage move,
Music prepares and warms the soul to love.
But when the kindling sparks such fuel meet,
No wonder if the flame inspired be great.

1684

A Letter to Mr. Creech at Oxford[1]

Written in the Last Great Frost[2]

Daphnis, because I am your debtor,
(And other causes which are better)
I send you here by debt of letter.
You should have had a scrap of nonsense,
You may remember left at Tonson's.[3]
(Though by the way that's scurvy rhyme Sir,
But yet 'twill serve to tag° a line Sir.) *round off*
A *billet-doux*° I had designed then, *sweet note*
But you may think I was in wine then;
Because it being cold, you know
We warmed it with a glass—or so.
I grant you that shy° wine's the devil, *cheap*
To make one's memory uncivil;
But when, 'twixt every sparkling cup,
I so much brisker wit took up;
Wit, able to inspire a thinking;
And make one solemn even in drinking;
Wit that would charm and stock a poet,
Even instruct ———[4] who has no wit;

1. Gladden. In the Ptolematic view of the universe that Behn invokes here, the heavens were composed of concentice crystalline spheres, whose motion produced a sublime music. Angels could hear it, humans could not.

1. Thomas Creech (1659–1700), classicist and translator. Behn had praised his work in a previous poem, in which (as here) she addresses him by the pastoral name "Daphnis." Here she produces a less solemn piece, explaining why a love letter from her has failed to reach him, and conveying (in the postscript) a compliment from an unnamed will-wisher.

2. The winter of 1683–1684 was so severe that the surface of the river Thames froze solid.

3. The eminent bookseller Jacob Tonson (1656–1737) had published several of Behn's plays and her *Poems on Several Occasions* (1684). The route through London that Behn traces in this poem would have taken her past Tonson's shop.

4. An in-joke, probabaly referring or some mutually despised Whig poet.

Wit that was hearty, true, and loyal,
Of wit, like Bays'[5] Sir, that's my trial;
I say 'twas most impossible,
That after that one should be dull.
Therefore because you may not blame me,
Take the whole truth as —— shall sa'me.[6]
   From Whitehall[7] Sir, as I was coming,
His sacred Majesty from dunning—
Who oft in debt is, truth to tell,
For Tory farce, or doggerel—[8]
When every street as dangerous was,
As ever the Alpian hills° to pass, *the Alps*
When melted snow and ice confound one,
Whether to break one's neck or drown one,
And *billet-doux* in pocket lay,
To drop as° coach should jolt that way, *whenever*
Near to that place of fame called Temple,[9]
(Which I shall note by sad example)
Where college dunce is cured of simple,[1]
Against that sign of whore called scarlet,[2]
My coachman fairly laid pilgarlic.[3]
   Though scribbling fist was out of joint,
And every limb made great complaint;
Yet missing the dear assignation,[4]
Gave me most cause of tribulation.
To honest H—le[5] I should have shown ye,
A wit that would be proud t'have known ye;
A wit uncommon, a facetious,
A great admirer of Lucretius.[6]
But transitory hopes do vary,
And high designments oft miscarry.
Ambition never climbed so lofty,
But may descend too fair and softly.
But would you'd seen how sneakingly
I looked with this catastrophe.
So saucy Whig, when plot broke out,

5. John Dryden, Poet Laureate (so nicknamed because in ancient Rome the laureate wore a wreath of bay leaves); Behn here implies that Dryden sets the standard ("trial") for true wit.
6. As Christ shall save me.
7. The royal palace in London; Behn has apparently been trying to collect payment from the king for a poem she wrote in his support.
8. I.e., Charles II frequently owes money to the partisan poets who write for him.
9. A cluster of buildings on Fleet Street containing residences, offices, and lecture halls for lawyers and students.
1. Simplicity, foolishness.
2. The Pope's Head tavern, so nicknamed because anti-Catholic literature identified the Roman church with the "whore . . . in scarlet" of Revelation 17.
3. The word originally denoted baldness (with "a head like peeled garlic"), but had become slang for any unfortunate person.
4. I.e., with Creech.
5. John Hoyle, a rakish lawyer with whom Aphra Behn had carried on a much-talked-about amorous relationship and to whom she had addressed many poems.
6. Roman author of *De rerum natura* (*On the Nature of Things*), which Creech had translated (1683). Lucretius's insistence on worldly pleasure had established him as the patron philosopher of Restoration libertines.

Dejected hung his sniveling snout;[7]
So Oxford member looked, when Rowley
Kicked out the rebel crew so foully;[8]
So Perkin, once that god of Wapping,
Whom slippery turn of state took napping,
From hopes of James the Second fell
Into the native scoundrel.[9]
So lover looked of joy defeated,
When too much fire his vigor cheated.[1]
Even so looked I, when bliss-depriving
Was caused by over-hasty driving.
Who saw me could not choose but think,
I looked like brawn in sousing drink,[2]
Or Lazarello[3] who was showed
For a strange fish, to the gaping crowd.
Thus you by fate (to me, sinister)
At shop of book my *billet* missed Sir.
And home I went as discontent,
As a new routed° Parliament, *dismissed*
Not seeing Daphnis ere he went.
And sure his grief beyond expressing,
Of joy proposed to want the blessing.[4]
Therefore to pardon pray incline,
Since disappointment all was mine.
Of Hell we have no other notion,
Than all the joys of Heaven's privation;
So Sir with recommendations fervent,
I rest your very humble servant.

Postscript

On Twelfth Night Sir, by that good token,
When lamentable cake was broken,[5]
You had a friend, a man of wit,
A man whom I shall ne'er forget,
For every word he did impart,

7. Behn imagines a partisan disappointed by the exposure (and hence the failure) of the Rye House plot, an alleged Whig scheme to assassinate the king and his brother in 1683.
8. In March 1681, Charles II (often dubbed "Rowley" in casual talk and satiric ballads) dismissed the Parliament at Oxford to frustrate the ambitions of the Whig faction.
9. "Perkin" is Charles II's illegitimate son James, Duke of Monmouth, who (like the medieval pretender Perkin Warbeck) claimed that he was the legitimate heir to the crown; his cause was at one point popular in the rough neighborhood of Wapping. Had he made good on his claim, he (rather than his like-named uncle the Duke of York) would have become James II. Disappointed of that prospect, Behn suggests, he has now "fallen back" into what he truly is: a born rascal.
1. I.e., because of premature ejaculation.
2. Like pickled pig's flesh, bruised and discolored.
3. Hero of Juan de Luna's picaresque narrative *Lazarillo de Tormes*, who is rescued in fishermen's nets after a shipwreck and displayed as a sea monster.
4. Certainly he, having missed out on a promised pleasure, suffers inexpressible grief.
5. On the Twelfth Night of Christmas (6 January, "lamentable," perhaps, because it marked the holiday's conclusion), the traditional festivities included the cutting of a cake in which a pea and bean had been concealed. The recipients of the "prize" pieces presided over the celebration as king and queen (cf. the poem's final line, where Behn and Creech are linked in praise).

'Twas worth the keeping in a heart.
True Tory all! and when he spoke,
A god of wit, though man in look.
"To this your friend Daphnis, address
The humblest of my services.
Tell him how much—yet do not, too.
My vast esteem no words can show.
Tell him—that he is worthy—you."

1685

To the Fair Clarinda, Who Made Love to Me, Imagined More than Woman

Fair lovely maid, or if that title be
Too weak, too feminine for nobler thee,
Permit a name that more approaches truth,
And let me call thee, lovely charming youth.
This last will justify my soft complaint,
While that may serve to lessen my constraint;
And without blushes I the youth pursue,
When so much beauteous woman is in view.
Against thy charms we struggle but in vain,
With thy deluding form thou giv'st us pain,
While the bright nymph betrays us to the swain.[1]
In pity to our sex sure thou wert sent,
That we might love, and yet be innocent:
For sure no crime with thee we can commit;
Or if we should—thy form excuses it.
For who that gathers fairest flowers believes
A snake lies hid beneath the fragrant leaves.
Thou beauteous wonder of a different kind,
Soft Cloris with the dear Alexis[2] joined;
Whene'er the manly part of thee would plead
Thou tempts us with the image of the maid,
While we the noblest passions do extend
The love to Hermes, Aphrodite the friend.[3]

1688

Oroonoko "I am very ill and have been dying this twelve month," Behn wrote an acquaintance late in 1687; she suffered from degenerative arthritis and had some eighteen months' dying still to do. Now, near the end of her writing career, she set down a narrative of events that had predated its beginnings, a story that she claimed to recall from the months she spent in 1663–1664 as a young woman in Surinam, an English colony on the northeastern coast of South America. A friend records that during the intervening decades Behn had often told the

1. The conventional pastoral term for a male lover or a country lad.
2. "Cloris" is female, "Alexis" male.
3. Named after the offspring of these two gods, a hermaphrodite combines the characteristics of both sexes.

story of an African prince enslaved on the plantation where she dwelt; prompted by his love for a slave from his own country, he mounted a rebellion against his English masters. In *Oroonoko,* Behn displayed Surinam as a world where the appetites of trade and empire had brought several cultures—indigenous "Indians," colonizing Europeans, abducted Africans—into violent and precarious fusion.

Writing the narrative, Behn undertook volatile fusions of her own. On the title page, the single name "Oroonoko" sits above two subtitles in which both hero and text are implicitly split in two. The hero is both "royal" and a "slave"; the text's "true history" is so suffused with fictional conventions that for a long while historians suspected that Behn had never been to Surinam and had made the whole thing up (the truth of many of the story's details has been neither established nor refuted). Oroonoko and his beloved Imoinda play out the love-and-loss plot of a heroic romance—a genre favored by Restoration aristocracy—within the far more realistic context of a world driven by bourgeois imperatives and political aspirations. Behn's boldest fusion involves not only cultures, identities, and modes but also times. Oroonoko, "the chief actor in this history," comes to embody the history of Stuart sovereignty, playing the roles of all three kings to whom Behn had devoted her own obsessive loyalties: Charles I, whose 1649 execution haunts the narrative, particularly in its last few pages; Charles II, whose 1660 Restoration Behn pointedly invokes at the celebratory moment of the African prince's arrival at Surinam; and James II, the beleaguered Catholic king whose three-year reign was hurtling toward its close at the very moment of *Oroonoko's* publication, and whose predicament as the embattled champion of an oppressed minority finds many echoes in the royal slave's rebellion and his fate.

Mapping all these convergences—of culture with culture, of monarch with slave, of man with woman—Behn places herself as narrator problematically near their center. The story is driven by her empathy for the slave couple, for whom she acts as mentor, friend, and advocate. Yet her empathy is complicated, perhaps even compromised. She shows less pity for less "royal" slaves, she acknowledges the possibility of her own complicity (however inadvertent) in her hero's pain, and she is oddly absent at the height of his suffering. She also participates in the profitable systems that enmesh him. Even before she tells his story, she presents herself as a kind of trader, who has brought back from Surinam butterflies for the Royal Society and exotic feathers for the dress of the "Indian Queen" in the popular heroic tragedy of that name. As the scholar Laura Brown points out, Behn's "treatment of slavery . . . is neither coherent nor fully critical." The narrative is by turns empathetic with the oppressed and complicit with the powerful; the crossing vectors of Behn's allegiance produce no conclusive sum.

In *Oroonoko,* cultural compounds prove unstable. Again and again in the story, human bodies are torn apart, and these sunderings foretell other dissolutions. Behn repeatedly reminds her readers that shortly after the events she narrates, the entire colony at Surinam disappeared: the English traded it away to the Dutch (they got New York in return). As colonist she laments this loss; as Tory, she anticipates another: the loss of James II in the parliamentary overthrow that would soon supplant the English Catholic with the Dutch Protestant William of Orange. Stuart rule, which had "ended" once with regicide, would end again (like the world of her youth in Surinam) with revolution.

Behn died shortly after publishing her narrative; she was buried in Westminster Abbey, where William would be crowned just five days later. In *Oroonoko,* amid all its intricacies, she had mingled energies of reminiscence with intimations of ruin, to produce one of the earliest and most abiding interrogations of the colonial commerce in human beings. Hugh Thomas, historian of the slave trade and of abolition, reads Behn as a pivotal figure between the two. She was "more influential than popes and missionaries," he writes, in preparing "people for a change on humanitarian grounds"—a change of thought and feeling that would beget, well over a century later, a change of law and practice.

Oroonoko
Or
The Royal Slave A True History

I do not pretend, in giving you the history of this royal slave, to entertain my reader with the adventures of a feigned hero, whose life and fortunes Fancy may manage at the poet's pleasure; nor in relating the truth, design to adorn it with any accidents, but such as arrived in earnest to him. And it shall come simply into the world, recommended by its own proper merits, and natural intrigues; there being enough of reality to support it, and to render it diverting, without the addition of invention.

I was myself an eyewitness to a great part of what you will find here set down; and what I could not be witness of, I received from the mouth of the chief actor in this history, the hero himself, who gave us the whole transactions of his youth; and though I shall omit, for brevity's sake, a thousand little accidents of his life, which, however pleasant to us, where history was scarce, and adventures very rare, yet might prove tedious and heavy to my reader, in a world where he finds diversions for every minute, new and strange. But we who were perfectly charmed with the character of this great man were curious to gather every circumstance of his life.

The scene of the last part of his adventures lies in a colony in America called Surinam, in the West Indies.

But before I give you the story of this gallant slave, 'tis fit I tell you the manner of bringing them to these new colonies; for those they make use of there, are not natives of the place; for those we live with in perfect amity, without daring to command them; but on the contrary, caress them with all the brotherly and friendly affection in the world, trading with them for their fish, venison, buffaloes, skins, and little rarities; as marmosets, a sort of monkey as big as a rat or weasel, but of a marvelous and delicate shape, and has face and hands like an human creature; and cousheries,[1] a little beast in the form and fashion of a lion, as big as a kitten; but so exactly made in all parts like that noble beast, that it is it in miniature. Then for little parakeets, great parrots, macaws, and a thousand other birds and beasts of wonderful and surprising forms, shapes, and colors. For skins of prodigious snakes, of which there are some threescore yards in length; as is the skin of one that may be seen at His Majesty's Antiquaries,[2] where are also some rare flies,[3] of amazing forms and colors, presented to them by myself, some as big as my fist, some less; and all of various excellencies, such as art cannot imitate. Then we trade for feathers, which they order into all shapes, make themselves little short habits of them, and glorious wreaths for their heads, necks, arms, and legs, whose tinctures are inconceivable. I had a set of these presented to me, and I gave them to the King's Theater, and it was the dress of the *Indian Queen*,[4] infinitely admired by persons of quality, and were inimitable. Besides these, a thousand little knacks and rarities in nature, and some of art; as their baskets, weapons, aprons, etc. We dealt with them with beads of all colors, knives, axes, pins, and needles, which they used only as tools to drill holes with in their ears, noses, and lips, where they hang a great many little things; as long beads, bits of tin, brass, or silver, beat thin, and any shining trinket. The beads they weave into aprons about a quarter of an ell[5] long, and of the same breadth, working

1. Other writers mention this animal, but its identity remains uncertain.
2. Probably the "Repository" (museum) of the Royal Society.
3. Butterflies.
4. A heroic drama (1664) by Robert Howard and John Dryden, celebrated for its sumptuous costumes and design.
5. Forty-five inches.

them very prettily in flowers of several colors of beads; which apron they wear just before them, as Adam and Eve did the fig leaves; the men wearing a long strip of linen, which they deal with us for. They thread these beads also on long cotton threads, and make girdles to tie their aprons to, which come twenty times or more about the waist and then cross, like a shoulder-belt, both ways, and round their necks, arms, and legs. This adornment, with their long black hair, and the face painted in little specks or flowers here and there, makes them a wonderful figure to behold. Some of the beauties which indeed are finely shaped, as almost all are, and who have pretty features, are very charming and novel; for they have all that is called beauty except the color, which is a reddish yellow; or after a new oiling, which they often use to themselves, they are of the color of a new brick, but smooth, soft, and sleek. They are extreme modest and bashful, very shy, and nice[6] of being touched. And though they are all thus naked, if one lives forever among them, there is not to be seen an indecent action or glance; and being continually used to see one another so unadorned, so like our first parents before the Fall, it seems as if they had no wishes; there being nothing to heighten curiosity, but all you can see, you see at once, and every moment see; and where there is no novelty, there can be no curiosity. Not but I have seen a handsome young Indian, dying for love of a very beautiful young Indian maid; but all his courtship was, to fold his arms, pursue her with his eyes, and sighs were all his language; while she, as if no such lover were present, or rather, as if she desired none such, carefully guarded her eyes from beholding him; and never approached him, but she looked down with all the blushing modesty I have seen in the most severe and cautious of our world. And these people represented to me an absolute idea of the first state of innocence, before man knew how to sin; and 'tis most evident and plain, that simple Nature is the most harmless, inoffensive, and virtuous mistress. 'Tis she alone, if she were permitted, that better instructs the world than all the inventions of man; religion would here but destroy that tranquility they possess by ignorance, and laws would but teach them to know offense, of which now they have no notion. They once made mourning and fasting for the death of the English governor, who had given his hand to come on such a day to them, and neither came, nor sent; believing, when once a man's word was past, nothing but death could or should prevent his keeping it. And when they saw he was not dead, they asked him, what name they had for a man who promised a thing he did not do? The governor told them, such a man was a liar, which was a word of infamy to a gentleman. Then one of them replied, "Governor, you are a liar, and guilty of that infamy." They have a native justice which knows no fraud, and they understand no vice, or cunning, but when they are taught by the white men. They have plurality of wives which, when they grow old, they serve those that succeed them, who are young; but with a servitude easy and respected; and unless they take slaves in war, they have no other attendants.

Those on that continent where I was had no king; but the oldest war captain was obeyed with great resignation.

A war captain is a man who has led them on to battle with conduct[7] and success, of whom I shall have occasion to speak more hereafter, and of some other of their customs and manners, as they fall in my way.

With these people, as I said, we live in perfect tranquility and good understanding, as it behooves us to do; they knowing all the places where to seek the best food

6. Shy.

7. Skillful management.

of the country, and the means of getting it; and for very small and invaluable trifles, supply us with what 'tis impossible for us to get; for they do not only in the wood, and over the savannahs, in hunting, supply the parts of hounds, by swiftly scouring through those almost impassable places, and by the mere activity of their feet, run down the nimblest deer, and other eatable beasts; but in the water, one would think they were gods of the rivers, or fellow citizens of the deep, so rare an art they have in swimming, diving, and almost living in water, by which they command the less swift inhabitants of the floods. And then for shooting, what they cannot take, or reach with their hands, they do with arrows, and have so admirable an aim, that they will split almost a hair; and at any distance that an arrow can reach, they will shoot down oranges and other fruit, and only touch the stalk with the darts' points, that they may not hurt the fruit. So that they being, on all occasions, very useful to us, we find it absolutely necessary to caress them as friends, and not to treat them as slaves; nor dare we do other, their numbers so far surpassing ours in that continent.

Those then whom we make use of to work in our plantations of sugar are Negroes, black slaves altogether, which are transported thither in this manner.

Those who want slaves make a bargain with a master, or captain of a ship, and contract to pay him so much apiece, a matter of twenty pound a head for as many as he agrees for, and to pay for them when they shall be delivered on such a plantation. So that when there arrives a ship laden with slaves, they who have so contracted go aboard, and receive their number by lot; and perhaps in one lot that may be for ten, there may happen to be three or four men; the rest, women and children; or be there more or less of either sex, you are obliged to be contented with your lot.

Coramantien,[8] a country of blacks so called, was one of those places in which they found the most advantageous trading for these slaves, and thither most of our great traders in that merchandise trafficked; for that nation is very warlike and brave, and having a continual campaign, being always in hostility with one neighboring prince or other, they had the fortune to take a great many captives; for all they took in battle were sold as slaves, at least, those common men who could not ransom themselves. Of these slaves so taken, the general only has all the profit; and of these generals, our captains and masters of ships buy all their freights.

The King of Coramantien was himself a man of a hundred and odd years old, and had no son, though he had many beautiful black wives; for most certainly, there are beauties that can charm of that color. In his younger years he had had many gallant men to his sons, thirteen of which died in battle, conquering when they fell; and he had only left him for his successor one grandchild, son to one of these dead victors; who, as soon as he could bear a bow in his hand, and a quiver at his back, was sent into the field, to be trained up by one of the oldest generals to war; where, from his natural inclination to arms, and the occasions given him, with the good conduct of the old general, he became, at the age of seventeen, one of the most expert captains, and bravest soldiers, that ever saw the field of Mars; so that he was adored as the wonder of all that world, and the darling of the soldiers. Besides, he was adorned with a native beauty so transcending all those of his gloomy race, that he struck an awe and reverence, even in those that knew not his quality; as he did in me, who beheld him with surprise and wonder, when afterwards he arrived in our world.

8. Koromantyn, a fort and trading post on the western coast of Africa (in modern Ghana).

He had scarce arrived at his seventeenth year when, fighting by his side, the general was killed with an arrow in his eye, which the Prince Oroonoko (for so was this gallant Moor[9] called) very narrowly avoided; nor had he, if the general, who saw the arrow shot, and perceiving it aimed at the Prince, had not bowed his head between, on purpose to receive it in his own body rather than it should touch that of the Prince, and so saved him.

'Twas then, afflicted as Oroonoko was, that he was proclaimed general in the old man's place; and then it was, at the finishing of that war, which had continued for two years, that the Prince came to court, where he had hardly been a month together, from the time of his fifth year to that of seventeen; and 'twas amazing to imagine where it was he learned so much humanity or, to give his accomplishments a juster name, where 'twas he got that real greatness of soul, those refined notions of true honor, that absolute generosity, and that softness that was capable of the highest passions of love and gallantry, whose objects were almost continually fighting men, or those mangled or dead; who heard no sounds but those of war and groans. Some part of it we may attribute to the care of a Frenchman of wit and learning, who finding it turn to very good account to be a sort of royal tutor to this young black, and perceiving him very ready, apt, and quick of apprehension, took a great pleasure to teach him morals, language, and science, and was for it extremely beloved and valued by him. Another reason was, he loved, when he came from war, to see all the English gentlemen that traded thither, and did not only learn their language but that of the Spaniards also, with whom he traded afterwards for slaves.

I have often seen and conversed with this great man, and been a witness to many of his mighty actions, and do assure my reader, the most illustrious courts could not have produced a braver man, both for greatness of courage and mind, a judgment more solid, a wit more quick, and a conversation more sweet and diverting. He knew almost as much as if he had read much: he had heard of, and admired the Romans; he had heard of the late Civil Wars in England, and the deplorable death of our great monarch,[1] and would discourse of it with all the sense, and abhorrence of the injustice imaginable. He had an extreme good and graceful mien, and all the civility of a well-bred great man. He had nothing of barbarity in his nature, but in all points addressed himself as if his education had been in some European court.

This great and just character of Oroonoko gave me an extreme curiosity to see him, especially when I knew he spoke French and English, and that I could talk with him. But though I had heard so much of him, I was as greatly surprised when I saw him as if I had heard nothing of him, so beyond all report I found him. He came into the room, and addressed himself to me, and some other women, with the best grace in the world. He was pretty tall, but of a shape the most exact that can be fancied; the most famous statuary[2] could not form the figure of a man more admirably turned from head to foot. His face was not of that brown, rusty black which most of that nation are, but a perfect ebony, or polished jet. His eyes were the most awful that could be seen, and very piercing, the white of them being like snow, as were his teeth. His nose was rising and Roman, instead of African and flat; his mouth, the finest shaped that could be seen, far from those great turned lips which are so natural to the rest of

9. The word originally meant "Moroccan," but was often used more generally for any person of African descent. Oroonoko's name may echo the river Orinoco in Venezuela, or the African god Oro.

1. Charles I, whose beheading in 1649 by sentence of the House of Commons marked the culmination of the wars between Royalists and Parliament.

2. Sculptor.

the Negroes. The whole proportion and air of his face was so noble and exactly formed that, bating[3] his color, there could be nothing in nature more beautiful, agreeable, and handsome. There was no one grace wanting that bears the standard of true beauty. His hair came down to his shoulders by the aids of art, which was, by pulling it out with a quill and keeping it combed, of which he took particular care. Nor did the perfections of his mind come short of those of his person, for his discourse was admirable upon almost any subject; and whoever had heard him speak, would have been convinced of their errors, that all fine wit is confined to the white men, especially to those of Christendom; and would have confessed that Oroonoko was as capable even of reigning well, and of governing as wisely, had as great a soul, as politic maxims,[4] and was as sensible of power as any prince civilized in the most refined schools of humanity and learning, or the most illustrious courts.

This Prince, such as I have described him, whose soul and body were so admirably adorned, was (while yet he was in the court of his grandfather) as I said, as capable of love as 'twas possible for a brave and gallant man to be; and in saying that, I have named the highest degree of love; for sure, great souls are most capable of that passion.

I have already said the old general was killed by the shot of an arrow, by the side of this Prince, in battle; and that Oroonoko was made general. This old dead hero had one only daughter left of his race; a beauty that, to describe her truly, one need say only, she was female to the noble male; the beautiful black Venus to our young Mars; as charming in her person as he, and of delicate virtues. I have seen an hundred white men sighing after her, and making a thousand vows at her feet, all vain and unsuccessful; and she was, indeed, too great for any but a prince of her own nation to adore.

Oroonoko coming from the wars (which were now ended) after he had made his court to his grandfather, he thought in honor he ought to make a visit to Imoinda, the daughter of his foster-father, the dead general; and to make some excuses to her, because his preservation was the occasion of her father's death; and to present her with those slaves that had been taken in this last battle, as the trophies of her father's victories. When he came, attended by all the young soldiers of any merit, he was infinitely surprised at the beauty of this fair Queen of Night, whose face and person was so exceeding all he had ever beheld; that lovely modesty with which she received him, that softness in her look and sighs, upon the melancholy occasion of this honor that was done by so great a man as Oroonoko, and a prince of whom she had heard such admirable things; the awfulness[5] wherewith she received him, and the sweetness of her words and behavior while he stayed, gained a perfect conquest over his fierce heart, and made him feel the victor could be subdued. So that having made his first compliments, and presented her a hundred and fifty slaves in fetters, he told her with his eyes that he was not insensible of her charms; while Imoinda, who wished for nothing more than so glorious a conquest, was pleased to believe she understood that silent language of new-born love; and from that moment, put on all her additions to beauty.

The Prince returned to court with quite another humor[6] than before; and though he did not speak much of the fair Imoinda, he had the pleasure to hear all his followers speak of nothing but the charms of that maid; insomuch that, even in

3. Excepting.

4. Shrewd principles or sayings.

5. Respect.

6. Frame of mind.

the presence of the old king, they were extolling her, and heightening, if possible, the beauties they had found in her; so that nothing else was talked of, no other sound was heard in every corner where there were whisperers, but "Imoinda! Imoinda!"

'Twill be imagined Oroonoko stayed not long before he made his second visit; nor, considering his quality, not much longer before he told her he adored her. I have often heard him say that he admired by what strange inspiration he came to talk things so soft and so passionate, who never knew love, nor was used to the conversation of women; but (to use his own words) he said, most happily, some new, and till then unknown power instructed his heart and tongue in the language of love, and at the same time, in favor of him, inspired Imoinda with a sense of his passion. She was touched with what he said, and returned it all in such answers as went to his very heart, with a pleasure unknown before. Nor did he use those obligations ill that love had done him; but turned all his happy moments to the best advantage; and as he knew no vice, his flame aimed at nothing but honor, if such a distinction may be made in love; and especially in that country, where men take to themselves as many as they can maintain, and where the only crime and sin with woman is to turn her off, to abandon her to want, shame, and misery. Such ill morals are only practiced in Christian countries, where they prefer the bare name of religion; and, without virtue or morality, think that's sufficient. But Oroonoko was none of those professors; but as he had right notions of honor, so he made her such propositions as were not only and barely such; but, contrary to the custom of his country, he made her vows she should be the only woman he would possess while he lived; that no age or wrinkles should incline him to change, for her soul would be always fine, and always young; and he should have an eternal idea in his mind of the charms she now bore, and should look into his heart for that idea, when he could find it no longer in her face.

After a thousand assurances of his lasting flame, and her eternal empire over him, she condescended to receive him for her husband; or rather, received him, as the greatest honor the gods could do her.

There is a certain ceremony in these cases to be observed, which I forgot to ask him how performed; but 'twas concluded on both sides that, in obedience to him, the grandfather was to be first made acquainted with the design; for they pay a most absolute resignation to the monarch, especially when he is a parent also.

On the other side, the old king, who had many wives, and many concubines, wanted not court flatterers to insinuate in his heart a thousand tender thoughts for this young beauty; and who represented her to his fancy as the most charming he had ever possessed in all the long race of his numerous years. At this character his old heart, like an extinguished brand, most apt to take fire, felt new sparks of love and began to kindle; and now grown to his second childhood, longed with impatience to behold this gay thing, with whom, alas, he could but innocently play. But how he should be confirmed she was this wonder, before he used his power to call her to court (where maidens never came, unless for the King's private use) he was next to consider; and while he was so doing, he had intelligence brought him, that Imoinda was most certainly mistress to the Prince Oroonoko. This gave him some chagrin; however, it gave him also an opportunity, one day, when the Prince was a-hunting, to wait on a man of quality, as his slave and attendant, who should go and make a present to Imoinda, as from the Prince; he should then, unknown, see this fair maid, and have an opportunity to hear what message she would return the

Prince for his present; and from thence gather the state of her heart, and degree of her inclination. This was put in execution, and the old monarch saw, and burned; he found her all he had heard, and would not delay his happiness, but found he should have some obstacle to overcome her heart; for she expressed her sense of the present the Prince had sent her, in terms so sweet, so soft and pretty, with an air of love and joy that could not be dissembled, insomuch that 'twas past doubt whether she loved Oroonoko entirely. This gave the old king some affliction, but he salved it with this, that the obedience the people pay their king was not at all inferior to what they paid their gods, and what love would not oblige Imoinda to do, duty would compel her to.

He was therefore no sooner got to his apartment, but he sent the royal veil to Imoinda, that is, the ceremony of invitation; he sends the lady, he has a mind to honor with his bed, a veil, with which she is covered and secured for the King's use; and 'tis death to disobey; besides, held a most impious disobedience.

'Tis not to be imagined the surprise and grief that seized this lovely maid at this news and sight. However, as delays in these cases are dangerous, and pleading worse than treason, trembling and almost fainting, she was obliged to suffer herself to be covered and led away.

They brought her thus to court; and the King, who had caused a very rich bath to be prepared, was led into it, where he sat under a canopy in state, to receive this longed for virgin; whom he having commanded should be brought to him, they (after disrobing her) led her to the bath and, making fast the doors, left her to descend. The King, without more courtship, bade her throw off her mantle and come to his arms. But Imoinda, all in tears, threw herself on the marble on the brink of the bath, and besought him to hear her. She told him, as she was a maid, how proud of the divine glory she should have been of having it in her power to oblige her king; but as by the laws he could not, and from his royal goodness would not take from any man his wedded wife, so she believed she should be the occasion of making him commit a great sin, if she did not reveal her state and condition, and tell him she was another's, and could not be so happy to be his.

The King, enraged at this delay, hastily demanded the name of the bold man that had married a woman of her degree without his consent. Imoinda, seeing his eyes fierce and his hands tremble, whether with age or anger I know not, but she fancied the last, almost repented she had said so much, for now she feared the storm would fall on the Prince; she therefore said a thousand things to appease the raging of his flame, and to prepare him to hear who it was with calmness; but before she spoke, he imagined who she meant, but would not seem to do so, but commanded her to lay aside her mantle and suffer herself to receive his caresses; or by his gods, he swore, that happy man whom she was going to name should die, though it were even Oroonoko himself. "Therefore," said he, "deny this marriage, and swear thyself a maid." "That," replied Imoinda, "by all our powers I do, for I am not yet known to my husband." "'Tis enough," said the King, "'tis enough to satisfy both my conscience and my heart." And rising from his seat, he went and led her into the bath, it being in vain for her to resist.

In this time the Prince, who was returned from hunting, went to visit his Imoinda, but found her gone; and not only so, but heard she had received the royal veil. This raised him to a storm, and in his madness they had much ado to save him from laying violent hands on himself. Force first prevailed, and then reason. They urged all to him that might oppose his rage; but nothing weighed so greatly with him as the King's old age, incapable of injuring him with Imoinda. He would give way to that hope, because it pleased him most, and flattered best his heart. Yet this served not altogether to make him cease his different passions, which sometimes raged within him, and sometimes softened into showers. 'Twas not enough to appease him, to tell him his grandfather was old, and could not that way injure him, while he retained that awful[7] duty which the young men are used there to pay to their grave relations. He could not be convinced he had no cause to sigh and mourn for the loss of a mistress he could not with all his strength and courage retrieve. And he would often cry, "O my friends! Were she in walled cities, or confined from me in fortifications of the greatest strength; did enchantments or monsters detain her from me, I would venture through any hazard to free her. But here, in the arms of a feeble old man, my youth, my violent love, my trade in arms, and all my vast desire of glory avail me nothing. Imoinda is as irrecoverably lost to me as if she were snatched by the cold arms of death. Oh! she is never to be retrieved. If I would wait tedious years, till fate should bow the old King to his grave, even that would not leave me Imoinda free; but still that custom that makes it so vile a crime for a son to marry his father's wives or mistress would hinder my happiness; unless I would either ignobly set an ill precedent to my successors, or abandon my country and fly with her to some unknown world, who never heard our story."

But it was objected to him that his case was not the same; for Imoinda being his lawful wife, by solemn contract, 'twas he was the injured man, and might, if he so pleased, take Imoinda back, the breach of the law being on his grandfather's side; and that if he could circumvent him, and redeem her from the otan, which is the palace of the King's women, a sort of seraglio, it was both just and lawful for him so to do.

This reasoning had some force upon him, and he should have been entirely comforted, but for the thought that she was possessed by his grandfather. However, he loved so well that he was resolved to believe what most favored his hope, and to endeavor to learn from Imoinda's own mouth what only she could satisfy him in: whether she was robbed of that blessing, which was only due to his faith and love. But as it was very hard to get a sight of the women, for no men ever entered into the otan but when the King went to entertain himself with some one of his wives or mistresses, and 'twas death at any other time for any other to go in, so he knew not how to contrive to get a sight of her.

While Oroonoko felt all the agonies of love, and suffered under a torment the most painful in the world, the old king was not exempted from his share of affliction. He was troubled for having been forced by an irresistible passion to rob his son of a treasure he knew could not but be extremely dear to him, since she was the most beautiful that ever had been seen; and had besides all the sweetness and innocence of youth and modesty, with a charm of wit surpassing all. He found that however she was forced to expose her lovely person to his withered arms, she could only sigh and weep there, and think of Oroonoko; and oftentimes could not forbear speaking of him, though her life were, by custom, forfeited by owning her passion. But she spoke not of a lover only, but of a prince dear to him to whom she spoke; and of the praises of a man, who, till now, filled the old man's soul with joy at every recital of his bravery, or even his name. And 'twas this dotage on our young hero that gave Imoinda a thousand privileges to speak of him without offending, and this

7. Reverential.

condescension in the old king that made her take the satisfaction of speaking of him so very often.

Besides, he many times inquired how the Prince bore himself; and those of whom he asked, being entirely slaves to the merits and virtues of the Prince, still answered what they thought conduced best to his service; which was, to make the old king fancy that the Prince had no more interest in Imoinda, and had resigned her willingly to the pleasure of the king; that he diverted himself with his mathematicians, his fortifications, his officers, and his hunting.

This pleased the old lover, who failed not to report these things again to Imoinda, that she might, by the example of her young lover, withdraw her heart and rest better contented in his arms. But however she was forced to receive this unwelcome news, in all appearance, with unconcern and content, her heart was bursting within, and she was only happy when she could get alone, to vent her griefs and moans with sighs and tears.

What reports of the Prince's conduct were made to the King, he thought good to justify as far as possibly he could by his actions; and when he appeared in the presence of the King, he showed a face not at all betraying his heart; so that in a little time the old man, being entirely convinced that he was no longer a lover of Imoinda, he carried him with him, in his train to the otan, often to banquet with his mistress. But as soon as he entered one day into the apartment of Imoinda with the King, at the first glance from her eyes, notwithstanding all his determined resolution, he was ready to sink in the place where he stood; and had certainly done so, but for the support of Aboan, a young man who was next to him; which, with his change of countenance, had betrayed him, had the King chanced to look that way. And I have observed, 'tis a very great error in those who laugh when one says a Negro can change color; for I have seen them as frequently blush, and look pale, and that as visibly as ever I saw in the most beautiful white. And 'tis certain that both these changes were evident, this day, in both these lovers. And Imoinda, who saw with some joy the change in the Prince's face, and found it in her own, strove to divert the King from beholding either, by a forced caress, with which she met him, which was a new wound in the heart of the poor dying Prince. But as soon as the King was busied in looking on some fine thing of Imoinda's making, she had time to tell the Prince with her angry but love-darting eyes, that she resented his coldness, and bemoaned her own miserable captivity. Nor were his eyes silent, but answered hers again, as much as eyes could do, instructed by the most tender and most passionate heart that ever loved. And they spoke so well, and so effectually, as Imoinda no longer doubted but she was the only delight, and the darling of that soul she found pleading in them its right of love, which none was more willing to resign than she. And 'twas this powerful language alone that in an instant conveyed all the thoughts of their souls to each other, that they both found there wanted but opportunity to make them both entirely happy. But when he saw another door opened by Onahal, a former old wife of the King's who now had charge of Imoinda, and saw the prospect of a bed of state made ready with sweets and flowers for the dalliance of the King, who immediately led the trembling victim from his sight into that prepared repose, what rage, what wild frenzies seized his heart! Which forcing to keep within bounds, and to suffer without noise, it became the more insupportable and rent his soul with ten thousand pains. He was forced to retire to vent his groans, where he fell down on a carpet, and lay struggling a long time, and only breathing now and then, "O Imoinda!" When Onahal had finished her necessary affair within, shutting the door, she came forth to wait till the King called; and hearing some one sighing in the other room, she passed on, and found the Prince in that deplorable condition which she thought needed her aid. She gave him cordials but all in vain, till finding the nature of his disease by his sighs, and naming Imoinda, she told him he had not so much cause as he imagined to afflict himself; for if he knew the King so well as she did, he would not lose a moment in jealousy, and that she was confident that Imoinda bore, at this minute, part in his affliction. Aboan was of the same opinion; and both together persuaded him to reassume his courage; and all sitting down on the carpet, the Prince said so many obliging things to Onahal, that he half persuaded her to be of his party. And she promised him she would thus far comply with his just desires, that she would let Imoinda know how faithful he was, what he suffered, and what he said.

This discourse lasted till the King called, which gave Oroonoko a certain satisfaction; and with the hope Onahal had made him conceive, he assumed a look as gay as 'twas possible a man in his circumstances could do; and presently after, he was called in with the rest who waited without. The King commanded music to be brought, and several of his young wives and mistresses came all together by his command, to dance before him, where Imoinda performed her part with an air and grace so passing all the rest as her beauty was above them, and received the present ordained as a prize. The Prince was every moment more charmed with the new beauties and graces he beheld in this fair one; and while he gazed and she danced, Onahal was retired to a window with Aboan.

This Onahal, as I said, was one of the past mistresses of the old king; and 'twas these (now past their beauty) that were made guardians, or governants, to the new and the young ones; and whose business it was, to teach them all those wanton arts of love with which they prevailed and charmed heretofore in their turn; and who now treated the triumphing happy ones with all the severity, as to liberty and freedom, that was possible, in revenge of those honors they rob them of; envying them those satisfactions, those gallantries and presents, that were once made to themselves, while youth and beauty lasted, and which they now saw pass regardless by, and paid only to the bloomings. And certainly, nothing is more afflicting to a decayed beauty than to behold in itself declining charms that were once adored, and to find those caresses paid to new beauties to which once she laid a claim; to hear them whisper as she passes by, "That once was a delicate woman." These abandoned ladies therefore endeavor to revenge all the despites and decays of time on these flourishing happy ones. And 'twas this severity that gave Oroonoko a thousand fears he should never prevail with Onahal to see Imoinda. But, as I said, she was now retired to a window with Aboan.

This young man was not only one of the best quality, but a man extremely well made and beautiful; and coming often to attend the King to the otan, he had subdued the heart of the antiquated Onahal, which had not forgot how pleasant it was to be in love. And though she had some decays in her face, she had none in her sense and wit; she was there agreeable still, even to Aboan's youth, so that he took pleasure in entertaining her with discourses of love. He knew also, that to make his court to these she-favorites was the way to be great; these being the persons that do all affairs and business at court. He had also observed that she had given him glances more tender and inviting than she had done to others of his quality. And now, when he saw that her favor could so absolutely oblige the Prince, he failed not to sigh in her ear, and to look with eyes all soft upon her, and give her hope that she had made some impressions on his heart. He found her pleased at this, and making a thousand advances to him; but the ceremony ending, and the King departing, broke up the company for that day, and his conversation.

Aboan failed not that night to tell the Prince of his success, and how advantageous the service of Onahal might be to his amour with Imoinda. The Prince was overjoyed with this good news, and besought him, if it were possible, to caress her, so as to engage her entirely; which he could not fail to do, if he complied with her desires. "For then," said the Prince, "her life lying at your mercy, she must grant you the request you make in my behalf." Aboan understood him, and assured him he would make love so effectually, that he would defy the most expert mistress of the art to find out whether he dissembled it or had it really. And 'twas with impatience they waited the next opportunity of going to the otan.

The wars came on, the time of taking the field approached, and 'twas impossible for the Prince to delay his going at the head of his army to encounter the enemy; so that every day seemed a tedious year, till he saw his Imoinda, for he believed he could not live if he were forced away without being so happy. 'Twas with impatience therefore that he expected the next visit the King would make; and, according to his wish, it was not long.

The parley of the eyes of these two lovers had not passed so secretly, but an old jealous lover could spy it; or rather, he wanted not flatterers who told him they observed it. So that the Prince was hastened to the camp, and this was the last visit he found he should make to the otan; he therefore urged Aboan to make the best of this last effort, and to explain himself so to Onahal, that she, deferring her enjoyment of her young lover no longer, might make way for the Prince to speak to Imoinda.

The whole affair being agreed on between the Prince and Aboan, they attended the King, as the custom was, to the otan; where, while the whole company was taken up in beholding the dancing and antic[8] postures the women royal made to divert the King, Onahal singled out Aboan, whom she found most pliable to her wish. When she had him where she believed she could not be heard, she sighed to him, and softly cried, "Ah, Aboan! When will you be sensible of my passion? I confess it with my mouth, because I would not give my eyes the lie; and you have but too much already perceived they have confessed my flame. Nor would I have you believe that because I am the abandoned mistress of a king I esteem myself altogether divested of charms. No, Aboan; I have still a rest of beauty enough engaging, and have learned to please too well, not to be desirable. I can have lovers still, but will have none but Aboan." "Madam," replied the half-feigning youth, "you have already, by my eyes, found you can still conquer; and I believe 'tis in pity of me, you condescend to this kind confession. But, Madam, words are used to be so small a part of our country courtship, that 'tis rare one can get so happy an opportunity as to tell one's heart; and those few minutes we have are forced to be snatched for more certain proofs of love than speaking and sighing; and such I languish for."

He spoke this with such a tone that she hoped it true, and could not forbear believing it; and being wholly transported with joy, for having subdued the finest of all the King's subjects to her desires, she took from her ears two large pearls and commanded him to wear them in his. He would have refused them, crying, "Madam, these are not the proofs of your love that I expect; 'tis opportunity, 'tis a lone hour

8. Fantastic or grotesque.

only, that can make me happy." But forcing the pearls into his hand, she whispered softly to him, "Oh! Do not fear a woman's invention when love sets her a-thinking." And pressing his hand she cried, "This night you shall be happy. Come to the gate of the orange groves, behind the otan, and I will be ready, about midnight, to receive you." 'Twas thus agreed, and she left him, that no notice might be taken of their speaking together.

The ladies were still dancing, and the King, laid on a carpet, with a great deal of pleasure was beholding them, especially Imoinda, who that day appeared more lovely than ever, being enlivened with the good tidings Onahal had brought her of the constant passion the Prince had for her. The Prince was laid on another carpet at the other end of the room, with his eyes fixed on the object of his soul; and as she turned or moved so did they; and she alone gave his eyes and soul their motions. Nor did Imoinda employ her eyes to any other use than in beholding with infinite pleasure the joy she produced in those of the Prince. But while she was more regarding him than the steps she took, she chanced to fall, and so near him as that leaping with extreme force from the carpet, he caught her in his arms as she fell; and 'twas visible to the whole presence, the joy wherewith he received her. He clasped her close to his bosom, and quite forgot that reverence that was due to the mistress of a king, and that punishment that is the reward of a boldness of this nature; and had not the presence of mind of Imoinda (fonder of his safety than her own) befriended him in making her spring from his arms and fall into her dance again, he had at that instant met his death; for the old king, jealous to the last degree, rose up in rage, broke all the diversion, and led Imoinda to her apartment, and sent out word to the Prince to go immediately to the camp; and that if he were found another night in court, he should suffer the death ordained for disobedient offenders.

You may imagine how welcome this news was to Oroonoko, whose unseasonable transport and caress of Imoinda was blamed by all men that loved him; and now he perceived his fault, yet cried that for such another moment, he would be content to die.

All the otan was in disorder about this accident; and Onahal was particularly concerned, because on the Prince's stay depended her happiness, for she could no longer expect that of Aboan. So that e'er they departed, they contrived it so that the Prince and he should come both that night to the grove of the otan, which was all of oranges and citrons, and that there they should wait her orders.

They parted thus, with grief enough, till night, leaving the King in possession of the lovely maid. But nothing could appease the jealousy of the old lover. He would not be imposed on, but would have it that Imoinda made a false step on purpose to fall into Oroonoko's bosom, and that all things looked like a design on both sides, and 'twas in vain she protested her innocence. He was old and obstinate, and left her more than half assured that his fear was true.

The King going to his apartment, sent to know where the Prince was, and if he intended to obey his command. The messenger returned and told him he found the Prince pensive, and altogether unpreparing for the campaign; that he lay negligently on the ground, and answered very little. This confirmed the jealousy of the King, and he commanded that they should very narrowly and privately watch his motions; and that he should not stir from his apartment, but one spy or other should be employed to watch him. So that the hour approaching, wherein he was to go to the citron grove, and taking only Aboan along with him, he leaves his apartment, and was watched to the very gate of the otan, where he was seen to enter, and where they left him, to carry back the tidings to the King.

Oroonoko and Aboan were no sooner entered but Onahal led the Prince to the apartment of Imoinda, who, not knowing anything of her happiness, was laid in bed. But Onahal only left him in her chamber to make the best of his opportunity, and took her dear Aboan to her own, where he showed the height of complaisance[9] for his prince, when, to give him an opportunity, he suffered himself to be caressed in bed by Onahal.

The Prince softly wakened Imoinda, who was not a little surprised with joy to find him there, and yet she trembled with a thousand fears. I believe he omitted saying nothing to this young maid that might persuade her to suffer him to seize his own and take the rights of love; and I believe she was not long resisting those arms where she so longed to be; and having opportunity, night and silence, youth, love and desire, he soon prevailed, and ravished in a moment what his old grandfather had been endeavoring for so many months.

'Tis not to be imagined the satisfaction of these two young lovers; nor the vows she made him, that she remained a spotless maid till that night; and that what she did with his grandfather had robbed him of no part of her virgin honor, the gods in mercy and justice having reserved that for her plighted lord, to whom of right it belonged. And 'tis impossible to express the transports he suffered while he listened to a discourse so charming from her loved lips, and clasped that body in his arms for whom he had so long languished; and nothing now afflicted him but his sudden departure from her; for he told her the necessity and his commands; but should depart satisfied in this, that since the old king had hitherto not been able to deprive him of those enjoyments which only belonged to him, he believed for the future he would be less able to injure him. So that abating the scandal of the veil, which was no otherwise so than that she was wife to another, he believed her safe even in the arms of the King, and innocent; yet would he have ventured at the conquest of the world, and have given it all, to have had her avoided that honor of receiving the royal veil. 'Twas thus, between a thousand caresses, that both bemoaned the hard fate of youth and beauty, so liable to that cruel promotion; 'twas a glory that could well have been spared here, though desired and aimed at by all the young females of that kingdom.

But while they were thus fondly employed, forgetting how time ran on and that the dawn must conduct him far away from his only happiness, they heard a great noise in the otan, and unusual voices of men; at which the Prince, starting from the arms of the frighted Imoinda, ran to a little battle-ax he used to wear by his side; and having not so much leisure as to put on his habit, he opposed himself against some who were already opening the door; which they did with so much violence that Oroonoko was not able to defend it, but was forced to cry out with a commanding voice, "Whoever ye are that have the boldness to attempt to approach this apartment thus rudely, know that I, the Prince Oroonoko, will revenge it with the certain death of him that first enters. Therefore stand back, and know this place is sacred to love and me this night; tomorrow 'tis the King's."

This he spoke with a voice so resolved and assured that they soon retired from the door, but cried, "'Tis by the King's command we are come; and being satisfied by thy voice, O Prince, as much as if we had entered, we can report to the King the truth of all his fears, and leave thee to provide for thy own safety, as thou art advised by thy friends."

9. Desire to please.

At these words they departed, and left the Prince to take a short and sad leave of his Imoinda; who trusting in the strength of her charms, believed she should appease the fury of a jealous king by saying she was surprised, and that it was by force of arms he got into her apartment. All her concern now was for his life, and therefore she hastened him to the camp, and with much ado prevailed on him to go. Nor was it she alone that prevailed; Aboan and Onahal both pleaded, and both assured him of a lie that should be well enough contrived to secure Imoinda. So that at last, with a heart sad as death, dying eyes, and sighing soul, Oroonoko departed, and took his way to the camp.

It was not long after the King in person came to the otan, where beholding Imoinda with rage in his eyes, he upbraided her wickedness and perfidy, and threatening her royal lover, she fell on her face at his feet, bedewing the floor with her tears and imploring his pardon for a fault which she had not with her will committed, as Onahal, who was also prostrate with her, could testify that, unknown to her, he had broke into her apartment, and ravished her. She spoke this much against her conscience; but to save her own life, 'twas absolutely necessary she should feign this falsity. She knew it could not injure the Prince, he being fled to an army that would stand by him against any injuries that should assault him. However, this last thought of Imoinda's being ravished changed the measures of his revenge, and whereas before he designed to be himself her executioner, he now resolved she should not die. But as it is the greatest crime in nature amongst them to touch a woman after having been possessed by a son, a father, or a brother, so now he looked on Imoinda as a polluted thing, wholly unfit for his embrace; nor would he resign her to his grandson, because she had received the royal veil. He therefore removes her from the otan, with Onahal, whom he put into safe hands, with order they should be both sold off as slaves to another country, either Christian or heathen; 'twas no matter where.

This cruel sentence, worse than death, they implored might be reversed; but their prayers were vain, and it was put in execution accordingly, and that with so much secrecy that none, either without or within the otan, knew anything of their absence or their destiny.

The old king, nevertheless, executed this with a great deal of reluctance; but he believed he had made a very great conquest over himself when he had once resolved, and had performed what he resolved. He believed now that his love had been unjust, and that he could not expect the gods, or Captain of the Clouds (as they call the unknown power) should suffer a better consequence from so ill a cause. He now begins to hold Oroonoko excused and to say he had reason for what he did; and now everybody could assure the King, how passionately Imoinda was beloved by the Prince; even those confessed it now who said the contrary before his flame was abated. So that the King being old and not able to defend himself in war, and having no sons of all his race remaining alive but only this to maintain him on the throne; and looking on this as a man disobliged, first by the rape of his mistress, or rather, wife, and now by depriving him wholly of her, he feared, might make him desperate, and do some cruel thing, either to himself, or his old grandfather the offender; he began to repent him extremely of the contempt he had, in his rage, put on Imoinda. Besides, he considered he ought in honor to have killed her for this offense, if it had been one. He ought to have had so much value and consideration for a maid of her quality, as to have nobly put her to death, and not to have sold her like a common slave, the greatest revenge, and the most disgraceful of any, and to which they a thousand times prefer death, and implore it as Imoinda did, but could not obtain that honor. Seeing therefore it was certain that Oroonoko would highly resent this affront, he thought good to make some excuse for his rashness to him, and to that end he sent a messenger to the camp with orders to treat with him about the matter, to gain his pardon, and to endeavor to mitigate his grief; but that by no means he should tell him she was sold, but secretly put to death; for he knew he should never obtain his pardon for the other.

When the messenger came, he found the Prince upon the point of engaging with the enemy, but as soon as he heard of the arrival of the messenger he commanded him to his tent, where he embraced him and received him with joy; which was soon abated, by the downcast looks of the messenger, who was instantly demanded the cause by Oroonoko, who, impatient of delay, asked a thousand questions in a breath, and all concerning Imoinda. But there needed little return, for he could almost answer himself of all he demanded from his sighs and eyes. At last, the messenger casting himself at the Prince's feet and kissing them with all the submission of a man that had something to implore which he dreaded to utter, he besought him to hear with calmness what he had to deliver to him, and to call up all his noble and heroic courage to encounter with his words, and defend himself against the ungrateful things he must relate. Oroonoko replied, with a deep sigh and a languishing voice, "I am armed against their worst efforts—for I know they will tell me, Imoinda is no more—and after that, you may spare the rest." Then, commanding him to rise, he laid himself on a carpet under a rich pavilion, and remained a good while silent, and was hardly heard to sigh. When he was come a little to himself, the messenger asked him leave to deliver that part of his embassy which the Prince had not yet divined, and the Prince cried, "I permit thee." Then he told him the affliction the old king was in for the rashness he had committed in his cruelty to Imoinda, and how he deigned to ask pardon for his offense, and to implore the Prince would not suffer that loss to touch his heart too sensibly which now all the gods could not restore him, but might recompense him in glory which he begged he would pursue; and that death, that common revenger of all injuries, would soon even the account between him and a feeble old man.

Oroonoko bade him return his duty to his lord and master, and to assure him there was no account of revenge to be adjusted between them; if there were, 'twas he was the aggressor, and that death would be just, and, maugre[1] his age, would see him righted; and he was contented to leave his share of glory to youths more fortunate, and worthy of that favor from the gods. That henceforth he would never lift a weapon, or draw a bow, but abandon the small remains of his life to sighs and tears, and the continual thoughts of what his lord and grandfather had thought good to send out of the world, with all that youth, that innocence, and beauty.

After having spoken this, whatever his greatest officers and men of the best rank could do, they could not raise him from the carpet, or persuade him to action and resolutions of life, but commanding all to retire, he shut himself into his pavilion all that day, while the enemy was ready to engage; and wondering at the delay, the whole body of the chief of the army then addressed themselves to him, and to whom they had much ado to get admittance. They fell on their faces at the foot of his carpet, where they lay, and besought him with earnest prayers and tears to lead them forth to battle, and not let the enemy take advantages of them; and implored him to have regard to his glory, and to the world that depended on his courage and

1. In spite of; i.e., despite Oroonoko's youth, death will avenge the king by taking Oroonoko first.

conduct. But he made no other reply to all their supplications but this, that he had now no more business for glory; and for the world, it was a trifle not worth his care. "Go," continued he, sighing, "and divide it amongst you; and reap with joy what you so vainly prize, and leave me to my more welcome destiny."

They then demanded what they should do, and whom he would constitute in his room, that the confusion of ambitious youth and power might not ruin their order, and make them a prey to the enemy. He replied, he would not give himself the trouble; but wished them to choose the bravest man amongst them, let his quality or birth be what it would. "For, O my friends!" said he, "it is not titles make men brave, or good; or birth that bestows courage and generosity, or makes the owner happy. Believe this, when you behold Oroonoko, the most wretched, and abandoned by fortune of all the creation of the gods." So turning himself about, he would make no more reply to all they could urge or implore.

The army beholding their officers return unsuccessful, with sad faces and ominous looks that presaged no good luck, suffered a thousand fears to take possession of their hearts, and the enemy to come even upon them, before they would provide for their safety by any defense; and though they were assured by some, who had a mind to animate them, that they should be immediately headed by the Prince, and that in the meantime Aboan had orders to command as general, yet they were so dismayed for want of that great example of bravery that they could make but a very feeble resistance, and at last downright fled before the enemy, who pursued them to the very tents, killing them. Nor could all Aboan's courage, which that day gained him immortal glory, shame them into a manly defense of themselves. The guards that were left behind about the Prince's tent, seeing the soldiers flee before the enemy and scatter themselves all over the plain in great disorder, made such outcries as roused the Prince from his amorous slumber, in which he had remained buried for two days without permitting any sustenance to approach him. But in spite of all his resolutions, he had not the constancy of grief to that degree as to make him insensible of the danger of his army; and in that instant he leapt from his couch and cried, "Come, if we must die, let us meet death the noblest way; and 'twill be more like Oroonoko to encounter him at an army's head, opposing the torrent of a conquering foe, than lazily, on a couch, to wait his lingering pleasure, and die every moment by a thousand wrecking thoughts; or be tamely taken by an enemy and led a whining, love-sick slave, to adorn the triumphs of Jamoan, that young victor, who already is entered beyond the limits I had prescribed him."

While he was speaking, he suffered his people to dress him for the field; and sallying out of his pavilion, with more life and vigor in his countenance than ever he showed, he appeared like some divine power descended to save his country from destruction; and his people had purposely put him on all things that might make him shine with most splendor, to strike a reverend awe into the beholders. He flew into the thickest of those that were pursuing his men, and being animated with despair, he fought as if he came on purpose to die, and did such things as will not be believed that human strength could perform, and such as soon inspired all the rest with new courage and new order. And now it was that they began to fight indeed, and so, as if they would not be outdone even by their adored hero, who turning the tide of the victory, changing absolutely the fate of the day, gained an entire conquest; and Oroonoko having the good fortune to single out Jamoan, he took him prisoner with his own hand, having wounded him almost to death.

This Jamoan afterwards became very dear to him, being a man very gallant and of excellent graces and fine parts, so that he never put him amongst the rank of captives, as they used to do, without distinction, for the common sale or market, but kept him in his own court, where he retained nothing of the prisoner but the name, and returned no more into his own country, so great an affection he took for Oroonoko; and by a thousand tales and adventures of love and gallantry, flattered his disease of melancholy and languishment, which I have often heard him say had certainly killed him, but for the conversation of this prince and Aboan, [and] the French governor he had from his childhood, of whom I have spoken before, and who was a man of admirable wit, great ingenuity and learning, all which he had infused into his young pupil. This Frenchman was banished out of his own country for some heretical notions he held; and though he was a man of very little religion, he had admirable morals, and a brave soul.

After the total defeat of Jamoan's army, which all fled, or were left dead upon the place, they spent some time in the camp, Oroonoko choosing rather to remain a while there in his tents, than enter into a palace, or live in a court where he had so lately suffered so great a loss. The officers therefore, who saw and knew his cause of discontent, invented all sorts of diversions and sports to entertain their prince: so that what with those amusements abroad and others at home, that is, within their tents, with the persuasions, arguments, and care of his friends and servants that he more peculiarly prized, he wore off in time a great part of that chagrin and torture of despair which the first effects of Imoinda's death had given him; insomuch as having received a thousand kind embassies from the King, and invitations to return to court, he obeyed, though with no little reluctance; and when he did so, there was a visible change in him, and for a long time he was much more melancholy than before. But time lessens all extremes, and reduces them to mediums and unconcern; but no motives or beauties, though all endeavored it, could engage him in any sort of amour, though he had all the invitations to it, both from his own youth and others' ambitions and designs.

Oroonoko was no sooner returned from this last conquest, and received at court with all the joy and magnificence that could be expressed to a young victor, who was not only returned triumphant but beloved like a deity, when there arrived in the port an English ship.

This person had often before been in these countries, and was very well known to Oroonoko, with whom he had trafficked for slaves, and had used to do the same with his predecessors.

This commander was a man of a finer sort of address and conversation, better bred and more engaging than most of that sort of men are; so that he seemed rather never to have been bred out of a court than almost all his life at sea. This captain therefore was always better received at court than most of the traders to those countries were; and especially by Oroonoko, who was more civilized, according to the European mode, than any other had been, and took more delight in the white nations, and, above all, men of parts and wit. To this captain he sold abundance of his slaves, and for the favor and esteem he had for him made him many presents, and obliged him to stay at court as long as possibly he could. Which the captain seemed to take as a very great honor done him, entertaining the Prince every day with globes and maps, and mathematical discourses and instruments; eating, drinking, hunting, and living with him with so much familiarity that it was not to be doubted but he had gained very greatly upon the heart of this gallant young man. And the captain, in return of all these mighty favors, besought the Prince to honor his vessel with his presence, some day or other, to dinner, before he should set sail; which he condescended to accept, and appointed his day. The captain, on his part, failed not to have all things in a readiness, in the most magnificent order he could possibly. And the day being come, the captain, in his boat richly adorned with carpets and velvet cushions, rowed to the shore to receive the Prince; with another longboat, where was placed all his music and trumpets, with which Oroonoko was extremely delighted, who met him on the shore, attended by his French governor, Jamoan, Aboan, and about an hundred of the noblest of the youths of the court. And after they had first carried the Prince on board, the boats fetched the rest off; where they found a very splendid treat, with all sorts of fine wines, and were as well entertained as 'twas possible in such a place to be.

The Prince having drunk hard of punch, and several sorts of wine, as did all the rest (for great care was taken they should want nothing of that part of the entertainment) was very merry, and in great admiration of the ship, for he had never been in one before; so that he was curious of beholding every place where he decently might descend. The rest, no less curious, who were not quite overcome with drinking, rambled at their pleasure fore and aft, as their fancies guided them: so that the captain, who had well laid his design before, gave the word and seized on all his guests; they clapping great irons suddenly on the Prince when he was leaped down in the hold to view that part of the vessel, and locking him fast down, secured him. The same treachery was used to all the rest; and all in one instant, in several places of the ship, were lashed fast in irons and betrayed to slavery. That great design over, they set all hands to work to hoist sail; and with as treacherous and fair a wind they made from the shore with this innocent and glorious prize, who thought of nothing less than such an entertainment.

Some have commended this act, as brave in the captain; but I will spare my sense of it, and leave it to my reader to judge as he pleases.

It may be easily guessed in what manner the Prince resented this indignity, who may be best resembled to a lion taken in a toil; so he raged, so he struggled for liberty, but all in vain; and they had so wisely managed his fetters that he could not use a hand in his defense, to quit himself of a life that would by no means endure slavery; nor could he move from the place where he was tied to any solid part of the ship against which he might have beat his head, and have finished his disgrace that way; so that being deprived of all other means, he resolved to perish for want of food. And pleased at last with that thought, and toiled and tired by rage and indignation, he laid himself down, and sullenly resolved upon dying, and refused all things that were brought him.

This did not a little vex the captain, and the more so because he found almost all of them of the same humor; so that the loss of so many brave slaves, so tall and goodly to behold, would have been very considerable. He therefore ordered one to go from him (for he would not be seen himself) to Oroonoko, and to assure him he was afflicted for having rashly done so inhospitable a deed, and which could not be now remedied, since they were far from shore; but since he resented it in so high a nature, he assured him he would revoke his resolution, and set both him and his friends ashore on the next land they should touch at; and of this the messenger gave him his oath, provided he would resolve to live. And Oroonoko, whose honor was such as he never had violated a word in his life himself, much less a solemn asseveration, believed in an instant what this man said, but replied he expected for a confirmation of this to have his shameful fetters dismissed. This demand was carried to the captain, who returned him answer that the offense had been so great which he had put upon the Prince, that he durst not trust him with liberty while he remained in the ship, for fear lest by a valor natural to him, and a revenge that would animate that valor, he might commit some outrage fatal to himself and the King his master, to whom his vessel did belong. To this Oroonoko replied, he would engage his honor to behave himself in all friendly order and manner, and obey the command of the captain, as he was lord of the King's vessel, and general of those men under his command.

This was delivered to the still doubting captain, who could not resolve to trust a heathen he said, upon his parole,[2] a man that had no sense or notion of the God that he worshipped. Oroonoko then replied he was very sorry to hear that the captain pretended to the knowledge and worship of any gods who had taught him no better principles, than not to credit as he would be credited; but they told him the difference of their faith occasioned that distrust: for the captain had protested to him upon the word of a Christian, and sworn in the name of a great God, which if he should violate, he would expect eternal torment in the world to come. "Is that all the obligation he has to be just to his oath?" replied Oroonoko. "Let him know I swear by my honor, which to violate, would not only render me contemptible and despised by all brave and honest men, and so give myself perpetual pain, but it would be eternally offending and diseasing all mankind, harming, betraying, circumventing, and outraging all men; but punishments hereafter are suffered by oneself; and the world takes no cognizances whether this god have revenged them, or not, 'tis done so secretly, and deferred so long; while the man of no honor suffers every moment the scorn and contempt of the honester world, and dies every day ignominiously in his fame, which is more valuable than life. I speak not this to move belief, but to show you how you mistake, when you imagine that he who will violate his honor will keep his word with his gods." So turning from him with a disdainful smile, he refused to answer him when he urged him to know what answer he should carry back to his captain; so that he departed without saying any more.

The captain pondering and consulting what to do, it was concluded that nothing but Oroonoko's liberty would encourage any of the rest to eat, except the Frenchman, whom the captain could not pretend to keep prisoner, but only told him he was secured because he might act something in favor of the Prince, but that he should be freed as soon as they came to land. So that they concluded it wholly necessary to free the Prince from his irons that he might show himself to the rest, that they might have an eye upon him, and that they could not fear a single man.

This being resolved, to make the obligation the greater, the captain himself went to Oroonoko; where, after many compliments, and assurances of what he had already promised, he receiving from the Prince his parole, and his hand, for his good behavior, dismissed his irons, and brought him to his own cabin; where, after having treated and reposed him a while, for he had neither eaten nor slept in four days before, he besought him to visit those obstinate people in chains, who refused all manner of sustenance; and entreated him to oblige them to eat, and assure them of their liberty the first opportunity.

2. Word of honor.

Oroonoko, who was too generous not to give credit to his words, showed himself to his people, who were transported with excess of joy at the sight of their darling prince, falling at his feet, and kissing and embracing them, believing, as some divine oracle, all he assured them. But he besought them to bear their chains with that bravery that became those whom he had seen act so nobly in arms; and that they could not give him greater proofs of their love and friendship, since 'twas all the security the captain (his friend) could have against the revenge, he said, they might possibly justly take, for the injuries sustained by him. And they all, with one accord, assured him they could not suffer enough when it was for his repose and safety.

After this they no longer refused to eat, but took what was brought them and were pleased with their captivity, since by it they hoped to redeem the Prince, who, all the rest of the voyage, was treated with all the respect due to his birth, though nothing could divert his melancholy; and he would often sigh for Imoinda, and think this a punishment due to his misfortune, in having left that noble maid behind him that fatal night in the otan, when he fled to the camp.

Possessed with a thousand thoughts of past joys with this fair young person, and a thousand griefs for her eternal loss, he endured a tedious voyage, and at last arrived at the mouth of the river of Surinam, a colony belonging to the King of England, and where they were to deliver some part of their slaves. There the merchants and gentlemen of the country going on board to demand those lots of slaves they had already agreed on, and amongst those the overseers of those plantations where I then chanced to be, the captain, who had given the word, ordered his men to bring up those noble slaves in fetters, whom I have spoken of; and having put them, some in one, and some in other lots, with women and children (which they call pickaninnies), they sold them off as slaves to several merchants and gentlemen; not putting any two in one lot, because they would separate them far from each other; not daring to trust them together, lest rage and courage should put them upon contriving some great action, to the ruin of the colony.

Oroonoko was first seized on and sold to our overseer, who had the first lot, with seventeen more of all sorts and sizes, but not one of quality with him. When he saw this, he found what they meant; for, as I said, he understood English pretty well; and being wholly unarmed and defenseless, so as it was in vain to make any resistance, he only beheld the captain with a look all fierce and disdainful; upbraiding him with eyes that forced blushes on his guilty cheeks, he only cried in passing over the side of the ship, "Farewell, Sir! 'Tis worth my suffering to gain so true a knowledge both of you and of your gods by whom you swear." And desiring those that held him to forbear their pains, and telling them he would make no resistance, he cried, "Come, my fellow slaves, let us descend, and see if we can meet with more honor and honesty in the next world we shall touch upon." So he nimbly leapt into the boat, and showing no more concern, suffered himself to be rowed up the river with his seventeen companions.

The gentleman that bought him was a young Cornish gentleman, whose name was Trefry, a man of great wit and fine learning, and was carried into those parts by the Lord——, Governor, to manage all his affairs.[3] He reflecting on the last words of

3. John Treffry (?–1674) supervised the plantation at Parham for Francis, Lord Willoughby (1613?–1686), a nobleman long involved with colonization, who received from Charles II both the governorship and a grant of land in Surinam; his appointment of Behn's father to the post of lieutenant-governor appears to account for her sojourn in the colony (though her father died en route).

Oroonoko to the captain, and beholding the richness of his vest,[4] no sooner came into the boat, but he fixed his eyes on him; and finding something so extraordinary in his face, his shape and mien, a greatness of look, and haughtiness in his air, and finding he spoke English, had a great mind to be inquiring into his quality and fortune; which, though Oroonoko endeavored to hide by only confessing he was above the rank of common slaves, Trefry soon found he was yet something greater than he confessed; and from that moment began to conceive so vast an esteem for him, that he ever after loved him as his dearest brother, and showed him all the civilities due to so great a man.

Trefry was a very good mathematician and a linguist, could speak French and Spanish, and in the three days they remained in the boat (for so long were they going from the ship to the plantation) he entertained Oroonoko so agreeably with his art and discourse, that he was no less pleased with Trefry, than he was with the Prince; and he thought himself, at least, fortunate in this, that since he was a slave, as long as he would suffer himself to remain so, he had a man of so excellent wit and parts for a master. So that before they had finished their voyage up the river, he made no scruple of declaring to Trefry all his fortunes and most part of what I have here related, and put himself wholly into the hands of his new friend, whom he found resenting all the injuries were done him, and was charmed with all the greatnesses of his actions, which were recited with that modesty and delicate sense, as wholly vanquished him, and subdued him to his interest. And he promised him on his word and honor, he would find the means to reconduct him to his own country again; assuring him, he had a perfect abhorrence of so dishonorable an action; and that he would sooner have died, than have been the author of such a perfidy. He found the Prince was very much concerned to know what became of his friends, and how they took their slavery; and Trefry promised to take care about the inquiring after their condition, and that he should have an account of them.

Though, as Oroonoko afterwards said, he had little reason to credit the words of a backearary,[5] yet he knew not why, but he saw a kind of sincerity and awful truth in the face of Trefry; he saw an honesty in his eyes, and he found him wise and witty enough to understand honor; for it was one of his maxims, "A man of wit could not be a knave or villain."

In their passage up the river they put in at several houses for refreshment, and ever when they landed numbers of people would flock to behold this man; not but their eyes were daily entertained with the sight of slaves, but the fame of Oroonoko was gone before him, and all people were in admiration of his beauty. Besides, he had a rich habit on, in which he was taken, so different from the rest, and which the captain could not strip him of because he was forced to surprise his person in the minute he sold him. When he found his habit made him liable, as he thought, to be gazed at the more, he begged Trefry to give him something more befitting a slave; which he did, and took off his robes. Nevertheless, he shone through all and his osenbrigs (a sort of brown holland suit he had on)[6] could not conceal the graces of his looks and mien; and he had no less admirers than when he had his dazzling habit on. The royal youth appeared in spite of the slave, and people could not help treating him after a different manner without designing it; as soon as they approached him they venerated and esteemed him; his eyes insensibly commanded respect, and his

4. Robe.

5. An African-derived term for "white master."

6. Osnaburg and holland were thick cotton or linen fabrics.

behavior insinuated it into every soul. So that there was nothing talked of but this young and gallant slave, even by those who yet knew not that he was a prince.

I ought to tell you, that the Christians never buy any slaves but they give them some name of their own, their native ones being likely very barbarous, and hard to pronounce; so that Mr. Trefry gave Oroonoko that of Caesar, which name will live in that country as long as that (scarce more) glorious one of the great Roman, for 'tis most evident, he wanted no part of the personal courage of that Caesar, and acted things as memorable, had they been done in some part of the world replenished with people and historians that might have given him his due. But his misfortune was to fall in an obscure world, that afforded only a female pen to celebrate his fame, though I doubt not but it had lived from others' endeavors, if the Dutch, who immediately after his time took that country,[7] had not killed, banished, and dispersed all those that were capable of giving the world this great man's life, much better than I have done. And Mr. Trefry, who designed it, died before he began it, and bemoaned himself for not having undertook it in time.

For the future therefore, I must call Oroonoko Caesar, since by that name only he was known in our western world, and by that name he was received on shore at Parham House, where he was destined a slave. But if the King himself (God bless him) had come ashore, there could not have been greater expectations by all the whole plantation, and those neighboring ones, than was on ours at that time; and he was received more like a governor than a slave. Notwithstanding, as the custom was, they assigned him his portion of land, his house, and his business, up in the plantation. But as it was more for form than any design to put him to his task, he endured no more of the slave but the name, and remained some days in the house, receiving all visits that were made him, without stirring towards that part of the plantation where the Negroes were.

At last, he would needs go view his land, his house, and the business assigned him. But he no sooner came to the houses of the slaves, which are like a little town by itself, the Negroes all having left work, but they all came forth to behold him, and found he was that prince who had, at several times, sold most of them to these parts; and, from a veneration they pay to great men, especially if they know them, and from the surprise and awe they had at the sight of him, they all cast themselves at his feet, crying out, in their language, "Live, O King! Long live, O King!" And kissing his feet, paid him even divine homage.

Several English gentlemen were with him; and what Mr. Trefry had told them was here confirmed, of which he himself before had no other witness than Caesar himself. But he was infinitely glad to find his grandeur confirmed by the adoration of all the slaves.

Caesar, troubled with their over-joy, and over-ceremony, besought them to rise, and to receive him as their fellow slave, assuring them, he was no better. At which they set up with one accord a most terrible and hideous mourning and condoling, which he and the English had much ado to appease. But at last they prevailed with them, and they prepared all their barbarous music, and everyone killed and dressed something of his own stock (for every family has their land apart, on which, at their leisure times, they breed all eatable things) and clubbing it together, made a most magnificent supper, inviting their grandee captain, their

7. In 1667 Surinam twice changed hands. The Dutch briefly captured the colony and the English won it back, but immediately ceded it to the Dutch (in exchange for New York) at the Treaty of Breda.

prince, to honor it with his presence, which he did, and several English with him, where they all waited on him, some playing, others dancing before him all the time, according to the manners of their several nations, and with unwearied industry endeavoring to please and delight him.

While they sat at meat Mr. Trefry told Caesar that most of these young slaves were undone in love, with a fine she-slave, whom they had had about six months on their land. The Prince, who never heard the name of love without a sigh, nor any mention of it without the curiosity of examining further into that tale which of all discourses was most agreeable to him, asked, how they came to be so unhappy, as to be all undone for one fair slave? Trefry, who was naturally amorous, and loved to talk of love as well as anybody, proceeded to tell him, they had the most charming black that ever was beheld on their plantation, about fifteen or sixteen years old, as he guessed; that, for his part, he had done nothing but sigh for her ever since she came; and that all the white beauties he had seen never charmed him so absolutely as this fine creature had done; and that no man of any nation ever beheld her, that did not fall in love with her; and that she had all the slaves perpetually at her feet; and the whole country resounded with the fame of Clemene, "for so," said he, "we have christened her. But she denies us all with such a noble disdain, that 'tis a miracle to see that she, who can give such eternal desires, should herself be all ice, and all unconcern. She is adorned with the most graceful modesty that ever beautified youth; the softest sigher—that, if she were capable of love, one would swear she languished for some absent happy man; and so retired, as if she feared a rape even from the God of Day,[8] or that the breezes would steal kisses from her delicate mouth. Her task of work some sighing lover every day makes it his petition to perform for her, which she accepts blushing, and with reluctance, for fear he will ask her a look for a recompense, which he dares not presume to hope, so great an awe she strikes into the hearts of her admirers." "I do not wonder," replied the Prince, "that Clemene should refuse slaves, being as you say so beautiful, but wonder how she escapes those who can entertain her as you can do. Or why, being your slave, you do not oblige her to yield." "I confess," said Trefry, "when I have, against her will, entertained her with love so long as to be transported with my passion even above decency, I have been ready to make use of those advantages of strength and force nature has given me. But oh! she disarms me, with that modesty and weeping so tender and so moving, that I retire, and thank my stars she overcame me." The company laughed at his civility to a slave, and Caesar only applauded the nobleness of his passion and nature, since that slave might be noble, or, what was better, have true notions of honor and virtue in her. Thus passed they this night, after having received from the slaves all imaginable respect and obedience.

The next day Trefry asked Caesar to walk, when the heat was allayed, and designedly carried him by the cottage of the fair slave, and told him, she whom he spoke of last night lived there retired. "But, " says he, "I would not wish you to approach, for I am sure you will be in love as soon as you behold her." Caesar assured him he was proof against all the charms of that sex, and that if he imagined his heart could be so perfidious to love again after Imoinda, he believed he should tear it from his bosom. They had no sooner spoke, but a little shock dog,[9] that Clemene had presented her, which she took great delight in, ran out, and she, not knowing anybody was there, ran to get it in again, and bolted out on those who were just speaking of

8. The sun.

9. A thick-haired dog.

her. When seeing them she would have run in again, but Trefry caught her by the hand and cried, "Clemene, however you fly a lover, you ought to pay some respect to this stranger" (pointing to Caesar). But she, as if she had resolved never to raise her eyes to the face of a man again, bent them the more to the earth when he spoke, and gave the Prince the leisure to look the more at her. There needed no long gazing or consideration to examine who this fair creature was. He soon saw Imoinda all over her; in a minute he saw her face, her shape, her air, her modesty, and all that called forth his soul with joy at his eyes, and left his body destitute of almost life. It stood without motion, and, for a minute, knew not that it had a being. And I believe he had never come to himself, so oppressed he was with overjoy, if he had not met with this allay,[1] that he perceived Imoinda fall dead in the hands of Trefry. This awakened him, and he ran to her aid, and caught her in his arms, where, by degrees, she came to herself; and 'tis needless to tell with what transports, what ecstasies of joy, they both a while beheld each other, without speaking, then snatched each other to their arms, then gaze again, as if they still doubted whether they possessed the blessing they grasped. But when they recovered their speech, 'tis not to be imagined what tender things they expressed to each other, wondering what strange fate had brought them again together. They soon informed each other of their fortunes, and equally bewailed their fate; but at the same time, they mutually protested that even fetters and slavery were soft and easy, and would be supported with joy and pleasure, while they could be so happy to possess each other, and to be able to make good their vows. Caesar swore he disdained the empire of the world while he could behold his Imoinda, and she despised grandeur and pomp, those vanities of her sex, when she could gaze on Oroonoko. He adored the very cottage where she resided, and said, that little inch of the world would give him more happiness than all the universe could do, and she vowed, it was a palace, while adorned with the presence of Oroonoko.

Trefry was infinitely pleased with this novel,[2] and found this Clemene was the fair mistress of whom Caesar had before spoke; and was not a little satisfied, that Heaven was so kind to the Prince as to sweeten his misfortunes by so lucky an accident, and leaving the lovers to themselves, was impatient to come down to Parham House (which was on the same plantation) to give me an account of what had happened. I was as impatient to make these lovers a visit, having already made a friendship with Caesar, and from his own mouth learned what I have related, which was confirmed by his Frenchman, who was set on shore to seek his fortunes, and of whom they could not make a slave because a Christian, and he came daily to Parham Hill to see and pay his respects to his pupil prince. So that concerning and interesting myself in all that related to Caesar, whom I had assured of liberty as soon as the governor arrived, I hasted presently to the place where the lovers were, and was infinitely glad to find this beautiful young slave (who had already gained all our esteems, for her modesty and her extraordinary prettiness) to be the same I had heard Caesar speak so much of. One may imagine then, we paid her a treble respect; and though from her being carved in fine flowers and birds all over her body, we took her to be of quality before, yet, when we knew Clemene was Imoinda, we could not enough admire her.

I had forgot to tell you, that those who are nobly born of that country are so delicately cut and raced[3] all over the fore part of the trunk of their bodies, that it

1. Reduction; release.
2. New development.
3. Carved.

looks as if it were japanned;[4] the works being raised like high point[5] round the edges of the flowers. Some are only carved with a little flower or bird at the sides of the temples, as was Caesar; and those who are so carved over the body resemble our ancient Picts,[6] that are figured in the chronicles, but these carvings are more delicate.

From that happy day Caesar took Clemene for his wife, to the general joy of all people, and there was as much magnificence as the country would afford at the celebration of this wedding. And in a very short time after she conceived with child; which made Caesar even adore her, knowing he was the last of his great race. This new accident made him more impatient of liberty, and he was every day treating with Trefry for his and Clemene's liberty; and offered either gold, or a vast quantity of slaves, which should be paid before they let him go, provided he could have any security that he should go when his ransom was paid. They fed him from day to day with promises, and delayed him, till the Lord Governor should come, so that he began to suspect them of falsehood, and that they would delay him till the time of his wife's delivery, and make a slave of that too, for all the breed is theirs to whom the parents belong. This thought made him very uneasy, and his sullenness gave them some jealousies[7] of him, so that I was obliged, by some persons who feared a mutiny (which is very fatal sometimes in those colonies that abound so with slaves that they exceed the whites in vast numbers), to discourse with Caesar, and to give him all the satisfaction I possibly could. They knew he and Clemene were scarce an hour in a day from my lodgings, that they ate with me, and that I obliged them in all things I was capable of: I entertained him with the lives of the Romans, and great men, which charmed him to my company, and her, with teaching her all the pretty works that I was mistress of, and telling her stories of nuns, and endeavoring to bring her to the knowledge of the true God. But of all discourses Caesar liked that the worst, and would never be reconciled to our notions of the Trinity, of which he ever made a jest; it was a riddle, he said, would turn his brain to conceive, and one could not make him understand what faith was. However, these conversations failed not altogether so well to divert him, that he liked the company of us women much above the men, for he could not drink, and he is but an ill companion in that country that cannot. So that obliging him to love us very well, we had all the liberty of speech with him, especially myself, whom he called his Great Mistress; and indeed my word would go a great way with him. For these reasons, I had opportunity to take notice to him, that he was not well pleased of late, as he used to be, was more retired and thoughtful, and told him, I took it ill he should suspect we would break our words with him, and not permit both him and Clemene to return to his own kingdom, which was not so long away, but when he was once on his voyage he would quickly arrive there. He made me some answers that showed a doubt in him, which made me ask him, what advantage it would be to doubt? It would but give us a fear of him, and possibly compel us to treat him so as I should be very loath to behold: that is, it might occasion his confinement. Perhaps this was not so luckily spoke of me, for I perceived he resented that word, which I strove to soften again in vain. However, he assured me, that whatsoever resolutions he should take, he would act nothing upon the white people. And as for myself, and those upon that plantation where he was, he would sooner forfeit his eternal liberty, and life itself, than lift his

4. Varnished with a glossy black lacquer.
5. Intricate lace.
6. Ancient inhabitants of northern Britain, possibly so named by the Romans because of the "pictures" (tattoos and other ornaments) they bore on their skin.
7. Suspicions.

hand against his greatest enemy on that place. He besought me to suffer no fears upon his account, for he could do nothing that honor should not dictate, but he accused himself for having suffered slavery so long; yet he charged that weakness on love alone, who was capable of making him neglect even glory itself, and for which now he reproaches himself every moment of the day. Much more to this effect he spoke, with an air impatient enough to make me know he would not be long in bondage, and though he suffered only the name of a slave, and had nothing of the toil and labor of one, yet that was sufficient to render him uneasy, and he had been too long idle, who used to be always in action, and in arms. He had a spirit all rough and fierce, and that could not be tamed to lazy rest, and though all endeavors were used to exercise himself in such actions and sports as this world afforded, as running, wrestling, pitching the bar,[8] hunting and fishing, chasing and killing tigers of a monstrous size, which this continent affords in abundance; and wonderful snakes, such as Alexander[9] is reported to have encountered at the river of Amazons, and which Caesar took great delight to overcome; yet these were not actions great enough for his large soul, which was still panting after more renowned action.

Before I parted that day with him, I got, with much ado, a promise from him to rest yet a little longer with patience, and wait the coming of the Lord Governor, who was every day expected on our shore. He assured me he would, and this promise he desired me to know was given perfectly in complaisance to me, in whom he had an entire confidence.

After this, I neither thought it convenient to trust him much out of our view, nor did the country who feared him; but with one accord it was advised to treat him fairly, and oblige him to remain within such a compass, and that he should be permitted as seldom as could be to go up to the plantations of the Negroes; or if he did, to be accompanied by some that should be rather in appearance attendants than spies. This care was for some time taken, and Caesar looked upon it as a mark of extraordinary respect, and was glad his discontent had obliged them to be more observant to him. He received new assurance from the overseer, which was confirmed to him by the opinion of all the gentlemen of the country, who made their court to him. During this time that we had his company more frequently than hitherto we had had, it may not be unpleasant to relate to you the diversions we entertained him with, or rather he us.

My stay was to be short in that country, because my father died at sea, and never arrived to possess the honor was designed him (which was lieutenant-general of six and thirty islands, besides the continent[1] of Surinam), nor the advantages he hoped to reap by them, so that though we were obliged to continue on our voyage, we did not intend to stay upon the place. Though, in a word, I must say thus much of it, that certainly had his late Majesty,[2] of sacred memory, but seen and known what a vast and charming world he had been master of in that continent, he would never have parted so easily with it to the Dutch. 'Tis a continent whose vast extent was never yet known, and may contain more noble earth than all the universe besides; for they say it reaches from east to west, one way as far as China, and another to Peru. It affords all things both for beauty and use; 'tis there eternal spring, always the very months of April, May, and June. The shades are perpetual, the trees, bearing at once all degrees

8. Hurling a heavy rod for purposes of exercise or sport.
9. Legends surrounding Alexander the Great included his encounter with the mythical woman warriors called Amazons, and with the formidable snakes inhabiting their territories.
1. Mainland.
2. Charles II.

of leaves and fruit from blooming buds to ripe autumn, groves of oranges, lemons, citrons, figs, nutmegs, and noble aromatics, continually bearing their fragrancies. The trees appearing all like nosegays adorned with flowers of different kind; some are all white, some purple, some scarlet, some blue, some yellow; bearing, at the same time, ripe fruit and blooming young, or producing every day new. The very wood of all these trees have an intrinsic value above common timber, for they are, when cut, of different colors, glorious to behold, and bear a price considerable, to inlay withal. Besides this, they yield rich balm and gums, so that we make our candles of such an aromatic substance as does not only give a sufficient light but, as they burn, they cast their perfumes all about. Cedar is the common firing, and all the houses are built with it. The very meat we eat, when set on the table, if it be native, I mean of the country, perfumes the whole room, especially a little beast called an armadillo, a thing which I can liken to nothing so well as a rhinoceros. 'Tis all in white armor so jointed that it moves as well in it as if it had nothing on. This beast is about the bigness of a pig of six weeks old. But it were endless to give an account of all the diverse wonderful and strange things that country affords, and which we took a very great delight to go in search of, though those adventures are oftentimes fatal and at least dangerous. But while we had Caesar in our company on these designs we feared no harm, nor suffered any.

As soon as I came into the country, the best house in it was presented me, called St. John's Hill. It stood on a vast rock of white marble, at the foot of which the river ran a vast depth down, and not to be descended on that side. The little waves still dashing and washing the foot of this rock made the softest murmurs and purlings in the world, and the opposite bank was adorned with such vast quantities of different flowers eternally blowing,[3] and every day and hour new, fenced behind them with lofty trees of a thousand rare forms and colors, that the prospect was the most ravishing that sands can create. On the edge of this white rock, toward the river, was a walk or grove of orange and lemon trees, about half the length of the Mall[4] here, whose flowery and fruity branches meet at the top, and hindered the sun, whose rays are very fierce there, from entering a beam into the grove, and the cool air that came from the river made it not only fit to entertain people in at all the hottest hours of the day, but refreshed the sweet blossoms, and made it always sweet and charming, and sure the whole globe of the world cannot show so delightful a place as this grove was. Not all the gardens of boasted Italy can produce a shade to out-vie this, which Nature had joined with Art to render so exceeding fine. And 'tis a marvel to see how such vast trees, as big as English oaks, could take footing on so solid a rock, and in so little earth, as covered that rock, but all things by nature there are rare, delightful, and wonderful. But to our sports.

Sometimes we would go surprising,[5] and in search of young tigers in their dens, watching when the old ones went forth to forage for prey, and oftentimes we have been in great danger, and have fled apace for our lives, when surprised by the dams. But once, above all other times, we went on this design, and Caesar was with us, who had no sooner stolen a young tiger from her nest, but going off, we encountered the dam, bearing a buttock of a cow, which he[6] had torn off with his mighty paw, and going with it towards his den. We had only four women, Caesar, and an English

3. Blossoming.
4. A walk extending alongside London's St. James's Park.
5. I.e., surprise-attacking.
6. The "dam" is the cub's mother, but Behn has surprisingly shifted the gender of the pronoun from "she" to "he"; she will do so again in reference to another tiger in the next paragraph.

gentleman, brother to Harry Martin, the great Oliverian.[7] We found there was no escaping this enraged and ravenous beast. However, we women fled as fast as we could from it, but our heels had not saved our lives if Caesar had not laid down his cub, when he found the tiger quit her prey to make the more speed towards him, and taking Mr. Martin's sword desired him to stand aside, or follow the ladies. He obeyed him, and Caesar met this monstrous beast of might, size, and vast limbs, who came with open jaws upon him, and fixing his awful stern eyes full upon those of the beast, and putting himself into a very steady and good aiming posture of defense, ran his sword quite through his breast down to his very heart, home to the hilt of the sword. The dying beast stretched forth her paw, and going to grasp his thigh, surprised with death in that very moment, did him no other harm than fixing her long nails in his flesh very deep, feebly wounded him, but could not grasp the flesh to tear off any. When he had done this, he hollowed to us to return, which, after some assurance of his victory, we did, and found him lugging out the sword from the bosom of the tiger, who was laid in her blood on the ground. He took up the cub, and with an unconcern, that had nothing of the joy or gladness of a victory, he came and laid the whelp at my feet. We all extremely wondered at his daring, and at the bigness of the beast, which was about the height of an heifer, but of mighty, great, and strong limbs.

Another time, being in the woods, he killed a tiger, which had long infested that part, and borne away abundance of sheep and oxen and other things, that were for the support of those to whom they belonged. Abundance of people assailed this beast, some affirming they had shot her with several bullets quite through the body, at several times, and some swearing they shot her through the very heart, and they believed she was a devil rather than a mortal thing. Caesar had often said he had a mind to encounter this monster, and spoke with several gentlemen who had attempted her, one crying, I shot her with so many poisoned arrows, another with his gun in this part of her, and another in that. So that he remarking all these places where she was shot, fancied still he should overcome her, by giving her another sort of a wound than any had yet done, and one day said (at the table), "What trophies and garlands, ladies, will you make me, if I bring you home the heart of this ravenous beast that eats up all your lambs and pigs?" We all promised he should be rewarded at all our hands. So taking a bow, which he chose out of a great many, he went up in the wood, with two gentlemen, where he imagined this devourer to be. They had not passed very far in it, but they heard her voice, growling and grumbling, as if she were pleased with something she was doing. When they came in view, they found her muzzling in the belly of a new ravished sheep which she had torn open, and seeing herself approached, she took fast hold of her prey with her forepaws, and set a very fierce raging look on Caesar, without offering to approach him, for fear, at the same time, of losing what she had in possession. So that Caesar remained a good while, only taking aim, and getting an opportunity to shoot her where he designed. 'Twas some time before he could accomplish it, and to wound her and not kill her would but have enraged her more, and endangered him. He had a quiver of arrows at his side, so that if one failed he could be supplied. At last, retiring a little, he gave her opportunity to eat, for he found she was ravenous, and fell to as soon as she saw him retire, being more eager of her prey than of doing new mischiefs. When he going softly to one side of her, and hiding his person behind certain herbage that grew high and thick, he took so good aim that, as he intended, he shot her just into the eye, and the arrow was sent with so

7. Supporter of Oliver Cromwell.

good a will, and so sure a hand, that it stuck in her brain, and made her caper and become mad for a moment or two, but being seconded by another arrow, he fell dead upon the prey. Caesar cut him open with a knife, to see where those wounds were that had been reported to him, and why he did not die of them. But I shall now relate a thing that possibly will find no credit among men, because 'tis a notion commonly received with us that nothing can receive a wound in the heart and live; but when the heart of this courageous animal was taken out, there were seven bullets of lead in it, and the wounds seamed up with great scars, and she lived with the bullets a great while, for it was long since they were shot. This heart the conqueror brought up to us, and 'twas a very great curiosity, which all the country came to see; and which gave Caesar occasion of many fine discourses, of accidents in war and strange escapes.

At other times he would go a-fishing, and discoursing on that diversion, he found we had in that country a very strange fish, called a numb eel[8] (an eel of which I have eaten), that while it is alive, it has a quality so cold that those who are angling, though with a line of never so great a length, with a rod at the end of it, it shall, in the same minute the bait is touched by this eel, seize him or her that holds the rod with benumbedness, that shall deprive them of sense for a while. And some have fallen into the water, and others dropped as dead on the banks of the rivers where they stood, as soon as this fish touches the bait. Caesar used to laugh at this, and believed it impossible a man could lose his force at the touch of a fish; and could not understand that philosophy, that a cold quality should be of that nature. However, he had a great curiosity to try whether it would have the same effect on him it had on others, and often tried, but in vain. At last, the sought-for fish came to the bait as he stood angling on the bank; and instead of throwing away the rod, or giving it a sudden twitch out of the water, whereby he might have caught both the eel and have dismissed the rod before it could have too much power over him for experiment sake, he grasped it but the harder, and fainting fell into the river. And being still possessed of the rod, the tide carried him senseless as he was a great way, till an Indian boat took him up, and perceived, when they touched him, a numbness seize them, and by that knew the rod was in his hand, which with a paddle (that is, a short oar) they struck away, and snatched it into the boat, eel and all. If Caesar were almost dead with the effect of this fish, he was more so with that of the water, where he had remained the space of going a league, and they found they had much ado to bring him back to life. But at last they did, and brought him home, where he was in a few hours well recovered and refreshed, and not a little ashamed to find he should be overcome by an eel, and that all the people who heard his defiance would laugh at him. But we cheered him up and he, being convinced, we had the eel at supper, which was a quarter of an ell about, and most delicate meat, and was of the more value, since it cost so dear as almost the life of so gallant a man.

About this time we were in many mortal fears about some disputes the English had with the Indians, so that we could scarce trust ourselves, without great numbers, to go to any Indian towns or place where they abode, for fear they should fall upon us, as they did immediately after my coming away, and that it was in the possession of the Dutch, who used them not so civilly as the English, so that they cut in pieces all they could take, getting into houses, and hanging up the mother, and all her children about her, and cut a footman I left behind me all in joints, and nailed him to trees.

This feud began while I was there, so that I lost half the satisfaction I proposed, in not seeing and visiting the Indian towns. But one day, bemoaning of our misfortunes

8. An electric eel.

upon this account, Caesar told us we need not fear, for if we had a mind to go he would undertake to be our guard. Some would, but most would not venture. About eighteen of us resolved, and took barge, and after eight days arrived near an Indian town. But approaching it, the hearts of some of our company failed, and they would not venture on shore, so we polled who would, and who would not. For my part, I said, if Caesar would, I would go. He resolved, so did my brother and my woman, a maid of good courage. Now none of us speaking the language of the people, and imagining we should have a half diversion in gazing only and not knowing what they said, we took a fisherman that lived at the mouth of the river, who had been a long inhabitant there, and obliged him to go with us. But because he was known to the Indians, as trading among them, and being, by long living there, become a perfect Indian in color, we, who resolved to surprise them, by making them see something they never had seen (that is, white people) resolved only myself, my brother, and woman should go. So Caesar, the fisherman, and the rest, hiding behind some thick reeds and flowers, that grew on the banks, let us pass on towards the town, which was on the bank of the river all along. A little distant from the houses, or huts, we saw some dancing, others busied in fetching and carrying of water from the river. They had no sooner spied us but they set up a loud cry, that frighted us at first. We thought it had been for those that should kill us, but it seems it was of wonder and amazement. They were all naked, and we were dressed, so as is most commode for the hot countries, very glittering and rich, so that we appeared extremely fine. My own hair was cut short, and I had a taffeta cap, with black feathers, on my head. My brother was in a stuff[9] suit, with silver loops and buttons, and abundance of green ribbon. This was all infinitely surprising to them, and because we saw them stand still, till we approached them, we took heart and advanced, came up to them, and offered them our hands, which they took, and looked on us round about, calling still for more company; who came swarming out, all wondering, and crying out *tepeeme*, taking their hair up in their hands, and spreading it wide to those they called out to, as if they would say (as indeed it signified) "numberless wonders," or not to be recounted, no more than to number the hair of their heads. By degrees they grew more bold, and from gazing upon us round, they touched us, laying their hands upon all the features of our faces, feeling our breasts and arms, taking up one petticoat, then wondering to see another, admiring our shoes and stockings, but more our garters, which we gave them, and they tied about their legs, being laced with silver lace at the ends, for they much esteem any shining things. In fine, we suffered them to survey us as they pleased, and we thought they would never have done admiring us. When Caesar and the rest saw we were received with such wonder, they came up to us, and finding the Indian trader whom they knew (for 'tis by these fishermen, called Indian traders, we hold a commerce with them; for they love not to go far from home, and we never go to them), when they saw him therefore they set up a new joy, and cried, in their language, "Oh! here's our *tiguamy*, and we shall now know whether those things can speak." So advancing to him, some of them gave him their hands, and cried, "*Amora tiguamy*," which is as much as, "How do you," or "Welcome friend," and all, with one din, began to gabble to him, and asked, If we had sense, and wit? If we could talk of affairs of life, and war, as they could do? If we could hunt, swim, and do a thousand things they use? He answered them, we could. Then they invited us into their houses, and dressed venison and buffalo for us; and, going out, gathered a leaf of a tree, called a sarumbo leaf, of six yards long, and spread it on the ground for a

9. Woolen.

tablecloth, and cutting another in pieces instead of plates, setting us on little bow Indian stools, which they cut out of one entire piece of wood, and paint in a sort of japan work. They serve everyone their mess on these pieces of leaves, and it was very good, but too high seasoned with pepper. When we had eaten, my brother and I took out our flutes and played to them, which gave them new wonder, and I soon perceived, by an admiration that is natural to these people, and by the extreme ignorance and simplicity of them, it were not difficult to establish any unknown or extravagant religion among them, and to impose any notions or fictions upon them. For seeing a kinsman of mine set some paper afire with a burning-glass, a trick they had never before seen, they were like to have adored him for a god, and begged he would give them the characters or figures of his name, that they might oppose it against winds and storms, which he did, and they held it up in those seasons, and fancied it had a charm to conquer them, and kept it like a holy relic. They are very superstitious, and called him the great *peeie*, that is, prophet. They showed us their Indian *peeie*, a youth of about sixteen years old, as handsome as Nature could make a man. They consecrate a beautiful youth from his infancy, and all arts are used to complete him in the finest manner, both in beauty and shape. He is bred to all the little arts and cunning they are capable of, to all the legerdemain tricks and sleight of hand whereby he imposes upon the rabble, and is both a doctor in physic and divinity. And by these tricks makes the sick believe he sometimes eases their pains, by drawing from the afflicted part little serpents, or odd flies, or worms, or any strange thing; and though they have besides undoubted good remedies for almost all their diseases, they cure the patient more by fancy than by medicines, and make themselves feared, loved, and reverenced. This young *peeie* had a very young wife, who seeing my brother kiss her, came running and kissed me; after this, they kissed one another, and made it a very great jest, it being so novel, and new admiration and laughing went round the multitude, that they never will forget that ceremony, never before used or known. Caesar had a mind to see and talk with their war captains, and we were conducted to one of their houses, where we beheld several of the great captains, who had been at council. But so frightful a vision it was to see them no fancy can create; no such dreams can represent so dreadful a spectacle. For my part I took them for hobgoblins, or fiends, rather than men. But however their shapes appeared, their souls were very humane and noble, but some wanted their noses, some their lips, some both noses and lips, some their ears, and others cut through each cheek, with long slashes, through which their teeth appeared; they had several other formidable wounds and scars, or rather dismemberings. They had *comitias*, or little aprons before them, and girdles of cotton, with their knives naked, stuck in it, a bow at their backs, and a quiver of arrows on their thighs, and most had feathers on their heads of diverse colors. They cried "*Amora tiguamy*" to us at our entrance, and were pleased we said as much to them. They feted us, and gave us drink of the best sort, and wondered, as much as the others had done before, to see us. Caesar was marveling as much at their faces, wondering how they should all be so wounded in war; he was impatient to know how they all came by those frightful marks of rage or malice, rather than wounds got in noble battle. They told us, by our interpreter, that when any war was waging, two men chosen out by some old captain, whose fighting was past, and who could only teach the theory of war, these two men were to stand in competition for the generalship, or Great War Captain, and being brought before the old judges, now past labor, they are asked, what they dare do to show they are worthy to lead an army? When he who is first asked, making no reply, cuts off his nose, and throws it contemptibly[1] on the ground, and the other does something to himself that he thinks surpasses him, and perhaps deprives himself of lips and an eye. So they slash on till one gives out, and many have died in this debate. And 'tis by a passive valor they show and prove their activity, a sort of courage too brutal to be applauded by our black hero; nevertheless he expressed his esteem of them.

In this voyage Caesar begot so good an understanding between the Indians and the English, that there were no more fears or heartburnings during our stay, but we had a perfect, open, and free trade with them. Many things remarkable, and worthy reciting, we met with in this short voyage, because Caesar made it his business to search out and provide for our entertainment, especially to please his dearly adored Imoinda, who was a sharer in all our adventures; we being resolved to make her chains as easy as we could, and to compliment the Prince in that manner that most obliged him.

As we were coming up again, we met with some Indians of strange aspects, that is, of a larger size, and other sort of features, than those of our country. Our Indian slaves, that rowed us, asked them some questions, but they could not understand us, but showed us a long cotton string with several knots on it, and told us, they had been coming from the mountains so many moons as there were knots. They were habited in skins of a strange beast, and brought along with them bags of gold dust, which, as well as they could give us to understand, came streaming in little small channels down the high mountains, when the rains fell, and offered to be the convoy to anybody, or persons, that would go to the mountains. We carried these men up to Parham, where they were kept till the Lord Governor came. And because all the country was mad to be going on this golden adventure, the governor, by his letters, commanded (for they sent some of the gold to him) that a guard should be set at the mouth of the river of Amazons (a river so called, almost as broad as the river of Thames), and prohibited all people from going up that river, it conducting to those mountains of gold. But we going off for England before the project was further prosecuted, and the Governor being drowned in a hurricane, either the design died, or the Dutch have the advantage of it. And 'tis to be bemoaned what His Majesty lost by losing that part of America.

Though this digression is a little from my story, however since it contains some proofs of the curiosity and daring of this great man, I was content to omit nothing of his character.

It was thus, for some time we diverted him. But now Imoinda began to show she was with child, and did nothing but sigh and weep for the captivity of her lord, herself, and the infant yet unborn, and believed, if it were so hard to gain the liberty of two, 'twould be more difficult to get that for three. Her griefs were so many darts in the great heart of Caesar, and taking his opportunity one Sunday, when all the whites were overtaken in drink, as there were abundance of several trades, and slaves for four years,[2] that inhabited among the Negro houses, and Sunday was their day of debauch (otherwise they were a sort of spies upon Caesar), he went pretending out of goodness to them, to feast amongst them, and sent all his music, and ordered a great treat for the whole gang, about three hundred Negroes. And about a hundred and fifty were able to bear arms, such as they had, which were sufficient to do execution with spirits accordingly. For the English had none but rusty swords, that no strength could draw from a scabbard, except the people of particular quality, who took care to oil them and keep them in good order. The guns also, unless here and there one, or those newly carried from England, would do no good or harm, for 'tis the nature of that

1. Contemptuously.

2. I.e., whites who, as punishment for crime or debt, had been forced into service for fixed periods of time.

country to rust and eat up iron, or any metals but gold and silver. And they are very inexpert at the bow, which the Negroes and Indians are perfect masters of.

Caesar, having singled out these men from the women and children, made a harangue to them of the miseries and ignominies of slavery; counting up all their toils and sufferings, under such loads, burdens, and drudgeries as were fitter for beasts than men, senseless brutes than human souls. He told them it was not for days, months, or years, but for eternity; there was no end to be of their misfortunes. They suffered not like men who might find a glory and fortitude in oppression, but like dogs that loved the whip and bell,[3] and fawned the more they were beaten. That they had lost the divine quality of men, and were become insensible asses, fit only to bear. Nay worse, an ass, or dog, or horse, having done his duty, could lie down in retreat, and rise to work again, and while he did his duty endured no stripes; but men, villainous, senseless men such as they, toiled on all the tedious week till black Friday, and then, whether they worked or not, whether they were faulty or meriting, they promiscuously, the innocent with the guilty, suffered the infamous whip, the sordid stripes, from their fellow slaves till their blood trickled from all parts of their body, blood whose every drop ought to be revenged with a life of some of those tyrants that impose it. "And why," said he, "my dear friends and fellow sufferers, should we be slaves to an unknown people? Have they vanquished us nobly in fight? Have they won us in honorable battle? And are we, by the chance of war, become their slaves? This would not anger a noble heart, this would not animate a soldier's soul. No, but we are bought and sold like apes, or monkeys, to be the sport of women, fools, and cowards, and the support of rogues, runagades, that have abandoned their own countries, for raping, murders, thefts, and villainies. Do you not hear every day how they upbraid each other with infamy of life below the wildest savages, and shall we render obedience to such a degenerate race, who have no one human virtue left to distinguish them from the vilest creatures? Will you, I say, suffer the lash from such hands?" They all replied, with one accord, "No, no, no; Caesar has spoke like a great captain, like a great king."

After this he would have proceeded, but was interrupted by a tall Negro of some more quality than the rest. His name was Tuscan, who bowing at the feet of Caesar, cried, "My lord, we have listened with joy and attention to what you have said, and, were we only men, would follow so great a leader through the world. But oh! consider, we are husbands and parents too, and have things more dear to us than life: our wives and children unfit for travel, in these impassable woods, mountains, and bogs. We have not only difficult lands to overcome, but rivers to wade, and monsters to encounter, ravenous beasts of prey—" To this, Caesar replied, that honor was the first principle in nature that was to be obeyed; but as no man would pretend to that, without all the acts of virtue, compassion, charity, love, justice, and reason, he found it not inconsistent with that, to take an equal care of their wives and children, as they would of themselves, and that he did not design, when he led them to freedom and glorious liberty, that they should leave that better part of themselves to perish by the hand of the tyrant's whip. But if there were a woman among them so degenerate from love and virtue to choose slavery before the pursuit of her husband, and with the hazard of her life to share with him in his fortunes, that such an one ought to be abandoned, and left as a prey to the common enemy.

To which they all agreed—and bowed. After this, he spoke of the impassable woods and rivers, and convinced them, the more danger, the more glory. He told

3. Because rigorous training has taught them to cherish their punishment.

them that he had heard of one Hannibal, a great captain, had cut his way through mountains of solid rocks,[4] and should a few shrubs oppose them, which they could fire before them? No, 'twas a trifling excuse to men resolved to die, or overcome. As for bogs, they are with a little labor filled and hardened, and the rivers could be no obstacle, since they swam by nature, at least by custom, from their first hour of their birth. That when the children were weary they must carry them by turns, and the woods and their own industry would afford them food. To this they all assented with joy.

Tuscan then demanded, what he would do? He said, they would travel towards the sea; plant a new colony, and defend it by their valor; and when they could find a ship, either driven by stress of weather, or guided by Providence that way, they would seize it, and make it a prize, till it had transported them to their own countries. At least, they should be made free in his kingdom, and be esteemed as his fellow sufferers, and men that had the courage and the bravery to attempt, at least, for liberty. And if they died in the attempt it would be more brave than to live in perpetual slavery.

They bowed and kissed his feet at this resolution, and with one accord vowed to follow him to death. And that night was appointed to begin their march; they made it known to their wives, and directed them to tie their hamaca[5] about their shoulder, and under their arm like a scarf; and to lead their children that could go, and carry those that could not. The wives, who pay an entire obedience to their husbands, obeyed, and stayed for them where they were appointed. The men stayed but to furnish themselves with what defensive arms they could get, and all met at the rendezvous, where Caesar made a new encouraging speech to them, and led them out.

But, as they could not march far that night, on Monday early, when the overseers went to call them all together to go to work, they were extremely surprised to find not one upon the place, but all fled with what baggage they had. You may imagine this news was not only suddenly spread all over the plantation, but soon reached the neighboring ones, and we had by noon about six hundred men, they call the militia of the county, that came to assist us in the pursuit of the fugitives. But never did one see so comical an army march forth to war. The men of any fashion would not concern themselves, though it were almost the common cause, for such revoltings are very ill examples, and have very fatal consequences oftentimes in many colonies. But they had a respect for Caesar, and all hands were against the Parhamites, as they called those of Parham Plantation, because they did not, in the first place, love the Lord Governor, and secondly, they would have it that Caesar was ill used, and baffled with.[6] And 'tis not impossible but some of the best in the country was of his counsel in this flight, and depriving us of all the slaves, so that they of the better sort would not meddle in the matter. The deputy governor,[7] of whom I have had no great occasion to speak, and who was the most fawning fair-tongued fellow in the world, and one that pretended the most friendship to Caesar, was now the only violent man against him, and though he had nothing, and so need fear nothing, yet talked and looked bigger than any man. He was a fellow whose character is not fit to be mentioned with the worst of the slaves. This fellow would lead his army forth to meet Caesar, or rather to pursue him. Most of their arms were

4. The Carthaginian general (247–182 B.C.E.) had accomplished this while crossing the Alps to invade Rome.

5. Hammock.

6. Cheated.

7. William Byam, who during a decade as administrator in Surinam had acquired a reputation for arrogance and severity.

of those sort of cruel whips they call cat-with-nine-tails; some had rusty useless guns for show; others old basket-hilts, whose blades had never seen the light in this age, and others had long staffs, and clubs. Mr. Trefry went along rather to be a mediator than a conqueror in such a battle, for he foresaw and knew, if by fighting they put the Negroes into despair, they were a sort of sullen fellows that would drown or kill themselves before they would yield, and he advised that fair means was best. But Byam was one that abounded in his own wit, and would take his own measures.

It was not hard to find these fugitives, for as they fled they were forced to fire and cut the woods before them, so that night or day they pursued them by the light they made, and by the path they had cleared. But as soon as Caesar found he was pursued, he put himself in a posture of defense, placing all the women and children in the rear, and himself, with Tuscan by his side, or next to him, all promising to die or conquer. Encouraged thus, they never stood to parley, but fell on pell-mell upon the English, and killed some, and wounded a good many, they having recourse to their whips, as the best of their weapons. And as they observed no order, they perplexed the enemy so sorely, with lashing them in the eyes. And the women and children, seeing their husbands so treated, being of fearful cowardly dispositions, and hearing the English cry out, "Yield and live, yield and be pardoned," they all ran in amongst their husbands and fathers, and hung about them, crying out, "Yield, yield, and leave Caesar to their revenge," that by degrees the slaves abandoned Caesar, and left him only Tuscan and his heroic Imoinda, who, grown big as she was, did nevertheless press near her lord, having a bow, and a quiver full of poisoned arrows, which she managed with such dexterity that she wounded several, and shot the governor into the shoulder, of which wound he had like to have died but that an Indian woman, his mistress, sucked the wound, and cleansed it from the venom. But however, he stirred not from the place till he had parleyed with Caesar, who he found was resolved to die fighting, and would not be taken; no more would Tuscan, or Imoinda. But he, more thirsting after revenge of another sort, than that of depriving him of life, now made use of all his art of talking and dissembling, and besought Caesar to yield himself upon terms which he himself should propose, and should be sacredly assented to and kept by him. He told him, it was not that he any longer feared him, or could believe the force of two men, and a young heroine, could overcome all them, with all the slaves now on their side also, but it was the vast esteem he had for his person, the desire he had to serve so gallant a man, and to hinder himself from the reproach hereafter of having been the occasion of the death of a prince, whose valor and magnanimity deserved the empire of the world. He protested to him, he looked upon this action as gallant and brave, however tending to the prejudice of his lord and master, who would by it have lost so considerable a number of slaves, that this flight of his should be looked on as a heat of youth, and rashness of a too forward courage, and an unconsidered impatience of liberty, and no more; and that he labored in vain to accomplish that which they would effectually perform, as soon as any ship arrived that would touch on his coast. "So that if you will be pleased," continued he, "to surrender yourself, all imaginable respect shall be paid you; and yourself, your wife, and child, if it be here born, shall depart free out of our land." But Caesar would hear of no composition, though Byam urged, if he pursued and went on in his design, he would inevitably perish, either by great snakes, wild beasts, or hunger, and he ought to have regard to his wife, whose condition required ease, and not the fatigues of tedious travel, where she could not be secured from being devoured. But Caesar told him, there was no faith in the white men, or the gods they adored, who instructed them in principles so false that honest men could not live amongst them; though no people professed so much, none performed so little; that he knew what he had to do, when he dealt with men of honor, but with them a man ought to be eternally on his guard, and never to eat and drink with Christians without his weapon of defense in his hand, and, for his own security, never to credit one word they spoke. As for the rashness and inconsiderateness of his action he would confess the governor is in the right, and that he was ashamed of what he had done, in endeavoring to make those free, who were by nature slaves, poor wretched rogues, fit to be used as Christians' tools; dogs, treacherous and cowardly, fit for such masters, and they wanted only but to be whipped into the knowledge of the Christian gods to be the vilest of all creeping things, to learn to worship such deities as had not power to make them just, brave, or honest. In fine, after a thousand things of this nature, not fit here to be recited, he told Byam, he had rather die than live upon the same earth with such dogs. But Trefry and Byam pleaded and protested together so much, that Trefry believing the governor to mean what he said, and speaking very cordially himself, generously put himself into Caesar's hands, and took him aside, and persuaded him, even with tears, to live, by surrendering himself, and to name his conditions. Caesar was overcome by his wit and reasons, and in consideration of Imoinda, and demanding what he desired, and that it should be ratified by their hands in writing, because he had perceived that was the common way of contract between man and man amongst the whites. All this was performed, and Tuscan's pardon was put in, and they surrender to the governor, who walked peaceably down into the plantation with them, after giving order to bury their dead. Caesar was very much toiled with the bustle of the day, for he had fought like a Fury, and what mischief was done he and Tuscan performed alone, and gave their enemies a fatal proof that they durst do anything, and feared no mortal force.

But they were no sooner arrived at the place where all the slaves receive their punishments of whipping, but they laid hands on Caesar and Tuscan, faint with heat and toil; and surprising them, bound them to two several stakes, and whipped them in a most deplorable and inhumane manner, rending the very flesh from their bones; especially Caesar, who was not perceived to make any moan, or to alter his face, only to roll his eyes on the faithless governor, and those he believed guilty, with fierceness and indignation. And, to complete his rage, he saw every one of those slaves, who, but a few days before, adored him as something more than mortal, now had a whip to give him some lashes, while he strove not to break his fetters, though if he had, it were impossible. But he pronounced a woe and revenge from his eyes, that darted fire, that 'twas at once both awful and terrible to behold.

When they thought they were sufficiently revenged on him, they untied him, almost fainting with loss of blood from a thousand wounds all over his body, from which they had rent his clothes, and led him bleeding and naked as he was, and loaded him all over with irons, and then rubbed his wounds, to complete their cruelty, with Indian pepper, which had like to have made him raving mad, and in this condition made him so fast to the ground that he could not stir, if his pains and wounds would have given him leave. They spared Imoinda, and did not let her see this barbarity committed towards her lord, but carried her down to Parham, and shut her up, which was not in kindness to her, but for fear she should die with the sight, or miscarry, and then they should lose a young slave, and perhaps the mother.

You must know, that when the news was brought on Monday morning, that Caesar had betaken himself to the woods, and carried with him all the Negroes, we were possessed with extreme fear, which no persuasions could dissipate, that he would secure himself till night, and then, that he would come down and cut all our throats. This apprehension made all the females of us fly down the river, to be secured, and while we were away, they acted this cruelty. For I suppose I had authority and interest enough there, had I suspected any such thing, to have prevented it, but we had not gone many leagues, but the news overtook us that Caesar was taken, and whipped like a common slave. We met on the river with Colonel Martin, a man of great gallantry, wit, and goodness, and, whom I have celebrated in a character of my new comedy,[8] by his own name, in memory of so brave a man. He was wise and eloquent, and, from the fineness of his parts, bore a great sway over the hearts of all the colony. He was a friend to Caesar, and resented this false dealing with him very much. We carried him back to Parham, thinking to have made an accommodation; when we came, the first news we heard was that the governor was dead of a wound Imoinda had given him, but it was not so well. But it seems he would have the pleasure of beholding the revenge he took on Caesar, and before the cruel ceremony was finished, he dropped down, and then they perceived the wound he had on his shoulder was by a venomed arrow, which, as I said, his Indian mistress healed, by sucking the wound.

We were no sooner arrived, but we went up to the plantation to see Caesar, whom we found in a very miserable and inexpressible condition, and I have a thousand times admired how he lived, in so much tormenting pain. We said all things to him that trouble, pity, and good nature could suggest, protesting our innocence of the fact, and our abhorrence of such cruelties; making a thousand professions of services to him, and begging as many pardons for the offenders, till we said so much, that he believed we had no hand in his ill treatment, but told us, he could never pardon Byam. As for Trefry, he confessed he saw his grief and sorrow for his suffering, which he could not hinder, but was like to have been beaten down by the very slaves, for speaking in his defense. But for Byam, who was their leader, their head—and should, by his justice, and honor, have been an example to them—for him, he wished to live, to take a dire revenge of him, and said, "It had been well for him if he had sacrificed me, instead of giving me the contemptible whip." He refused to talk much, but begging us to give him our hands, he took them, and protested never to lift up his, to do us any harm. He had a great respect for Colonel Martin, and always took his counsel, like that of a parent, and assured him, he would obey him in anything but his revenge on Byam. "Therefore," said he, "for his own safety, let him speedily dispatch me, for if I could dispatch myself, I would not, till that justice were done to my injured person, and the contempt of a soldier. No, I would not kill myself, even after a whipping, but will be content to live with that infamy, and be pointed at by every grinning slave, till I have completed my revenge; and then you shall see that Oroonoko scorns to live with the indignity that was put on Caesar." All we could do could get no more words from him, and we took care to have him put immediately into a healing bath, to rid him of his pepper, and ordered a chirurgeon[9] to anoint him with healing balm, which he suffered, and in some time he began to be able to walk and eat. We failed not to visit him every day, and, to that end, had him brought to an apartment at Parham.

The governor was no sooner recovered, and had heard of the menaces of Caesar, but he called his council, who (not to disgrace them, or burlesque the government

8. *The Younger Brother: or the Amorous Jilt*, produced posthumously in 1696.

9. Surgeon.

there) consisted of such notorious villains as Newgate[1] never transported, and possibly originally were such, who understood neither the laws of God or man, and had no sort of principles to make them worthy the name of men, but at the very council table would contradict and fight with one another, and swear so bloodily that 'twas terrible to hear and see them. (Some of them were afterwards hanged, when the Dutch took possession of the place; others sent off in chains.) But calling these special rulers of the nation together, and requiring their counsel in this weighty affair, they all concluded that (damn them) it might be their own cases, and that Caesar ought to be made an example to all the Negroes, to fright them from daring to threaten their betters, their lords and masters, and, at this rate, no man was safe from his own slaves, and concluded, *nemine contradicente*,[2] that Caesar should be hanged.

Trefry then thought it time to use his authority, and told Byam his command did not extend to his lord's plantation, and that Parham was as much exempt from the law as Whitehall; and that they ought no more to touch the servants of the Lord—(who there represented the King's person) than they could those about the King himself; and that Parham was a sanctuary, and though his lord were absent in person, his power was still in being there, which he had entrusted with him, as far as the dominions of his particular plantations reached, and all that belonged to it; the rest of the country, as Byam was lieutenant to his lord, he might exercise his tyranny upon. Trefry had others as powerful, or more, that interested themselves in Caesar's life, and absolutely said he should be defended. So turning the governor, and his wise council, out of doors (for they sat at Parham House) we set a guard upon our landing place, and would admit none but those we called friends to us and Caesar.

The governor having remained wounded at Parham till his recovery was completed, Caesar did not know but he was still there, and indeed, for the most part, his time was spent there, for he was one that loved to live at other people's expense, and if he were a day absent, he was ten present there, and used to play, and walk, and hunt, and fish, with Caesar. So that Caesar did not at all doubt, if he once recovered strength, but he should find an opportunity of being revenged on him. Though, after such a revenge, he could not hope to live, for if he escaped the fury of the English mobile,[3] who perhaps would have been glad of the occasion to have killed him, he was resolved not to survive his whipping, yet he had, some tender hours, a repenting softness, which he called his fits of coward, wherein he struggled with love for the victory of his heart, which took part with his charming Imoinda there; but, for the most part, his time was passed in melancholy thought, and black designs. He considered, if he should do this deed, and die either in the attempt, or after it, he left his lovely Imoinda a prey, or at best a slave, to the enraged multitude; his great heart could not endure that thought. "Perhaps," said he, "she may be first ravished by every brute, exposed first to their nasty lusts, and then a shameful death." No, he could not live a moment under that apprehension, too insupportable to be borne. These were his thoughts, and his silent arguments with his heart, as he told us afterwards, so that now resolving not only to kill Byam, but all those he thought had enraged him, pleasing his great heart with the fancied slaughter he should make over the whole face of the plantation, he first resolved on a deed that (however horrid it at first appeared to us all), when we had heard his reasons, we thought it brave and just. Being able to walk and, as he believed, fit for the execution of his great design, he begged Trefry to trust him

1. London prison from which convicts were sent to work in the colonies.

2. No one disagreeing.

3. Mob.

into the air, believing a walk would do him good, which was granted him, and taking Imoinda with him, as he used to do in his more happy and calmer days, he led her up into a wood where, after (with a thousand sighs, and long gazing silently on her face, while tears gushed, in spite of him, from his eyes), he told her his design first of killing her, and then his enemies, and next himself, and the impossibility of escaping, and therefore he told her the necessity of dying. He found the heroic wife faster pleading for death than he was to propose it, when she found his fixed resolution, and on her knees besought him not to leave her a prey to his enemies. He (grieved to death) yet pleased at her noble resolution, took her up, and embracing her with all the passion and languishment of a dying lover, drew his knife to kill this treasure of his soul, this pleasure of his eyes. While tears trickled down his cheeks, hers were smiling with joy she should die by so noble a hand, and be sent in her own country (for that's their notion of the next world) by him she so tenderly loved, and so truly adored in this, for wives have a respect for their husbands equal to what any other people pay a deity, and when a man finds any occasion to quit his wife, if he love her, she dies by his hand; if not, he sells her, or suffers some other to kill her. It being thus, you may believe the deed was soon resolved on, and 'tis not to be doubted, but the parting, the eternal leave-taking of two such lovers, so greatly born, so sensible,[4] so beautiful, so young, and so fond, must be very moving, as the relation of it was to me afterwards.

All that love could say in such cases being ended, and all the intermitting irresolutions being adjusted, the lovely, young, and adored victim lays herself down before the sacrificer, while he, with a hand resolved, and a heart breaking within, gave the fatal stroke, first cutting her throat, and then severing her yet smiling face from that delicate body, pregnant as it was with fruits of tenderest love. As soon as he had done, he laid the body decently on leaves and flowers, of which he made a bed, and concealed it under the same coverlid of nature, only her face he left yet bare to look on. But when he found she was dead, and past all retrieve, never more to bless him with her eyes and soft language, his grief swelled up to rage; he tore, he raved, he roared, like some monster of the wood, calling on the loved name of Imoinda. A thousand times he turned the fatal knife that did the deed toward his own heart, with a resolution to go immediately after her, but dire revenge, which now was a thousand times more fierce in his soul than before, prevents him, and he would cry out, "No, since I have sacrificed Imoinda to my revenge, shall I lose that glory which I have purchased so dear, as at the price of the fairest, dearest, softest creature that ever Nature made? No, no!" Then, at her name, grief would get the ascendant of rage, and he would lie down by her side, and water her face with showers of tears, which never were wont to fall from those eyes. And however bent he was on his intended slaughter, he had not power to stir from the sight of this dear object, now more beloved and more adored than ever.

He remained in this deploring condition for two days, and never rose from the ground where he had made his sad sacrifice. At last, rousing from her side, and accusing himself with living too long now Imoinda was dead, and that the deaths of those barbarous enemies were deferred too long, he resolved now to finish the great work; but offering to rise, he found his strength so decayed, that he reeled to and fro, like boughs assailed by contrary winds, so that he was forced to lie down again, and try to summon all his courage to his aid. He found his brains turn round, and his eyes were dizzy, and objects appeared not the same to him as they were wont to do; his breath was short, and all his limbs surprised with a faintness he had never felt

4. Sensitive.

before. He had not eaten in two days, which was one occasion of this feebleness, but excess of grief was the greatest; yet still he hoped he should recover vigor to act his design, and lay expecting it yet six days longer, still mourning over the dead idol of his heart, and striving every day to rise, but could not.

In all this time you may believe we were in no little affliction for Caesar and his wife. Some were of opinion he was escaped never to return; others thought some accident had happened to him. But however, we failed not to send out a hundred people several ways to search for him. A party of about forty went that way he took, among whom was Tuscan, who was perfectly reconciled to Byam. They had not gone very far into the wood, but they smelt an unusual smell, as of a dead body, for stinks must be very noisome that can be distinguished among such a quantity of natural sweets, as every inch of that land produces. So that they concluded they should find him dead, or somebody that was so. They passed on towards it, as loathsome as it was, and made such a rustling among the leaves that lie thick on the ground, by continual falling, that Caesar heard he was approached, and though he had, during the space of these eight days, endeavored to rise, but found he wanted strength, yet looking up, and seeing his pursuers, he rose, and reeled to a neighboring tree, against which he fixed his back. And being within a dozen yards of those that advanced and saw him, he called out to them, and bid them approach no nearer, if they would be safe; so that they stood still, and hardly believing their eyes, that would persuade them that it was Caesar that spoke to them, so much was he altered, they asked him what he had done with his wife, for they smelt a stink that almost struck them dead. He, pointing to the dead body, sighing, cried, "Behold her there." They put off the flowers that covered her with their sticks, and found she was killed, and cried out, "Oh monster! that hast murdered thy wife." Then asking him, why he did so cruel a deed, he replied, he had no leisure to answer impertinent questions. "You may go back," continued he, "and tell the faithless governor he may thank Fortune that I am breathing my last, and that my arm is too feeble to obey my heart in what it had designed him." But his tongue faltering, and trembling, he could scarce end what he was saying. The English taking advantage by his weakness, cried, "Let us take him alive by all means." He heard them; and, as if he had revived from a fainting, or a dream, he cried out, "No, gentlemen, you are deceived, you will find no more Caesars to be whipped, no more find a faith in me. Feeble as you think me, I have strength yet left to secure me from a second indignity." They swore all anew, and he only shook his head, and beheld them with scorn. Then they cried out, "Who will venture on this single man? Will nobody?" They stood all silent while Caesar replied, "Fatal will be the attempt to the first adventurer, let him assure himself," and, at that word, held up his knife in a menacing posture. "Look ye, ye faithless crew," said he, "'tis not life I seek, nor am I afraid of dying," and, at that word, cut a piece of flesh from his own throat, and threw it at them, "yet still I would live if I could, till I had perfected my revenge. But oh! it cannot be. I feel life gliding from my eyes and heart, and, if I make not haste, I shall yet fall a victim to the shameful whip." At that, he ripped up his own belly, and took his bowels and pulled them out, with what strength he could, while some, on their knees imploring, besought him to hold his hand. But when they saw him tottering, they cried out, "Will none venture on him?" A bold English cried, "Yes, if he were the Devil" (taking courage when he saw him almost dead) and swearing a horrid oath for his farewell to the world he rushed on. Caesar with his armed hand met him so fairly, as stuck him to the heart, and he fell dead at his feet. Tuscan seeing that, cried out, "I love thee, oh Caesar, and therefore will not let thee die, if possible." And, running to him, took him in his arms, but at the same time, warding a blow that Caesar made at his bosom, he received it quite through his arm, and Caesar having not the strength to pluck the knife forth, though he attempted it, Tuscan neither pulled it out himself, nor suffered it to be pulled out, but came down with it sticking in his arm, and the reason he gave for it was because the air should not get into the wound. They put their hands across, and carried Caesar between six of them, fainted as he was, and they thought dead, or just dying, and they brought him to Parham, and laid him on a couch, and had the chirurgeon immediately to him, who dressed his wounds, and sewed up his belly, and used means to bring him to life, which they effected. We ran all to see him; and, if before we thought him so beautiful a sight, he was now so altered that his face was like a death's head blacked over, nothing but teeth and eye-holes. For some days we suffered nobody to speak to him, but caused cordials to be poured down his throat, which sustained his life, and in six or seven days he recovered his senses. For you must know, that wounds are almost to a miracle cured in the Indies, unless wounds in the legs, which rarely ever cure.

When he was well enough to speak, we talked to him, and asked him some questions about his wife, and the reasons why he killed her. And he then told us what I have related of that resolution, and of his parting, and he besought us we would let him die, and was extremely afflicted to think it was possible he might live. He assured us, if we did not dispatch him, he would prove very fatal to a great many. We said all we could to make him live, and gave him new assurances, but he begged we would not think so poorly of him, or of his love to Imoinda, to imagine we could flatter him to life again; but the chirurgeon assured him he could not live, and therefore he need not fear. We were all (but Caesar) afflicted at this news; and the sight was gashly.[5] His discourse was sad; and the earthly smell about him so strong, that I was persuaded to leave the place for some time (being myself but sickly, and very apt to fall into fits of dangerous illness upon any extraordinary melancholy). The servants, and Trefry, and the chirurgeons, promised all to take what possible care they could of the life of Caesar, and I, taking boat, went with other company to Colonel Martin's, about three days' journey down the river; but I was no sooner gone, but the governor taking Trefry about some pretended earnest business a day's journey up the river, having communicated his design to one Banister, a wild Irishman, and one of the council, a fellow of absolute barbarity, and fit to execute any villainy, but was rich, he came up to Parham, and forcibly took Caesar, and had him carried to the same post where he was whipped, and causing him to be tied to it, and a great fire made before him, he told him he should die like a dog, as he was. Caesar replied, this was the first piece of bravery that ever Banister did, and he never spoke sense till he pronounced that word, and, if he would keep it, he would declare, in the other world, that he was the only man, of all the whites, that ever he heard speak truth. And turning to the men that bound him, he said, "My friends, am I to die, or to be whipped?" And they cried, "Whipped! no; you shall not escape so well." And then he replied, smiling, "A blessing on thee," and assured them, they need not tie him, for he would stand fixed, like a rock, and endure death so as should encourage them to die. "But if you whip me," said he, "be sure you tie me fast."

He had learned to take tobacco, and when he was assured he should die, he desired they would give him a pipe in his mouth, ready lighted, which they did, and the executioner came, and first cut off his members,[6] and threw them into the fire.

5. Ghastly.

6. Genitals.

After that, with an ill-favored knife, they cut his ears and his nose, and burned them; he still smoked on, as if nothing had touched him. Then they hacked off one of his arms, and still he bore up, and held his pipe. But at the cutting off the other arm, his head sunk, and his pipe dropped, and he gave up the ghost, without a groan, or a reproach. My mother and sister were by him all the while, but not suffered to save him, so rude and wild were the rabble, and so inhuman were the justices, who stood by to see the execution, who after paid dearly enough for their insolence. They cut Caesar in quarters, and sent them to several of the chief plantations. One quarter was sent to Colonel Martin, who refused it, and swore he had rather see the quarters of Banister and the governor himself than those of Caesar on his plantations, and that he could govern his Negroes without terrifying and grieving them with frightful spectacles of a mangled king.

Thus died this great man, worthy of a better fate, and a more sublime wit than mine to write his praise. Yet, I hope, the reputation of my pen is considerable enough to make his glorious name to survive to all ages, with that of the brave, the beautiful, and the constant Imoinda.

1688

RESPONSE

Thomas Southerne: from *Oroonoko: A Tragedy*[1]

[DEBATING REBELLION][2]

OROONOKO: What would you do?
ABOAN: Cut our oppressors' throats.
OROONOKO: And you would have me join in your design
Of murder?
ABOAN: It deserves a better name.
But be it what it will, 'tis justified
By self-defense, and natural liberty.
OROONOKO: I'll hear no more on't.
ABOAN: I am sorry for't.

1. After Behn's death, *Oroonoko* did more than any of her other works to sustain her fame, partly in print and partly in the theater. In 1696, the Irish-born, intermittently successful playwright Thomas Southerne (1660–1746) found cause to praise Behn's story but to puzzle over her choice of genre. "She had great command of the stage," he remarked in the dedication to the play he based on her book, "and I have often wondered that she would bury her favorite hero in a *novel*, when she might have revived him in the *scene*."

In *Oroonoko: A Tragedy*, Southerne undertook just such a revival, relocating Oroonoko from the printed page to the playhouse. The playwright added an erotic subplot about a pair of English sisters who have traveled to Surinam to seek rich husbands. More strikingly, he changed the race of the play's heroine. Imoinda is here not African but European, the daughter of a white "stranger in my father's court" who died protecting Oroonoko in battle. The play shifts timings, too: this Imoinda marries Oroonoko and becomes pregnant by him in Africa, shortly before the two are separately sold into slavery. Their mixed-race marriage becomes one of several motifs by which Southerne echoes yet another 17th-century source: Shakespeare's *Othello*.

Audience response confirmed Southerne's faith in the theatrical power of Behn's protagonists. His play, restaged and re-adapted many times, became a touchstone text for the antislavery movement that grew in England and America over the next century and a half. Only with the appearance of *Uncle Tom's Cabin* in the 1850s did the advocates of abolition find a more contemporary narrative to take *Oroonoko's* place. Southerne's tragedy abetted the alchemy by which Behn's intricately fictionalized "true history" survived its initial moment, and helped shape history thereafter.

2. From Act 3, Scene 2. Oroonoko and Imoinda, freshly reunited, hear Aboan make his case for insurrection. Southerne retains Behn's complex view of slavery: Oroonoko briefly defends the slaveholders as "innocent"; Aboan's arguments, in their tone and phrasing, sometimes echo those of *Othello*'s arch-villain Iago.

OROONOKO: Nor shall you think of it.
ABOAN: Not think of it!
OROONOKO: No, I command you not.
ABOAN: Remember, Sir,
You are a slave yourself, and to command
Is now another's right. Not think of it!
Since the first moment they put on my chains,
I've thought of nothing but the weight of 'em,
And how to throw 'em off. Can yours sit easy?
OROONOKO: I have a sense of my condition,
As painful, and as quick, as yours can be.
I feel for my Imoinda and myself;
Imoinda much the tenderest part of me.
But though I languish for my liberty,
I would not buy it at the Christian price
Of black ingratitude. They shannot say
That we deserved our fortune by our crimes.
Murder the innocent!
ABOAN: The innocent!
OROONOKO: These men are so, whom you would rise against.
If we are slaves, they did not make us slaves,
But bought us in an honest way of trade:
As we have done before 'em, bought and sold
Many a wretch, and never thought it wrong.[3]
They paid our price for us, and we are now
Their property, a part of their estate,
To manage as they please. Mistake me not,
I do not tamely say, that we should bear
All they could lay upon us. But we find
The load so light, so little to be felt
(Considering they have us in their power,
And may inflict what grievances they please)
We ought not to complain.
ABOAN: My Royal Lord!
You do not know the heavy grievances,
The toil, the labors, weary drudgeries,
Which they impose; burdens more fit for beasts,
For senseless beasts to bear, than thinking men.
Then if you saw the bloody cruelties
They execute on every slight offense—
Nay sometimes in their proud, insulting sport—
How worse than dogs they lash their fellow-creatures:
Your heart would bleed for 'em. O could you know
How many wretches lift their hands and eyes
To you, for their relief.
OROONOKO: I pity 'em.
And wish I could with honesty do more.

3. "We" here are Africans, who (as Behn's story also emphasizes) sold slaves to each other, and to Europeans.

ABOAN: You must do more, and may, with honesty.
O Royal Sir, remember who you are,
A prince, born for the good of other men,
Whose god-like office is to draw the sword
Against oppression, and set free mankind;
And this, I'm sure, you think oppression now.
What though you have not felt these miseries,
Never believe you are obliged to them.
They have their selfish reasons, maybe, now,
For using of you well. But there will come
A time, when you must have your share of 'em.
OROONOKO: You see how little cause I have to think so:
Favored in my own person, in my friends;
Indulged in all that can concern my care,
In my Imoinda's soft society. [*Embracing her*]
ABOAN: And therefore would you lie contented down,
In the forgetfulness, and arms of love,
To get young princes for 'em?
OROONOKO: Say'st thou! ha!
ABOAN: Princes, the heirs of empire, and the last
Of your illustrious lineage, to be born
To pamper up their pride, and be their slaves?
OROONOKO: Imoinda! Save me, save me from that thought.
IMOINDA: There is no safety from it. I have long
Suffered with a mother's laboring pains,
And can no longer. Kill me, kill me now,
While I am blessed, and happy in your love,
Rather than let me live to see you hate me
As you must hate me: me, the only cause,
The fountain of these flowing miseries.
Dry up this spring of life, this poisonous spring,
That swells so fast, to overwhelm us all.
OROONOKO: Shall the dear babe, the eldest of my hopes,
Whom I begot a prince, be born a slave?
The treasure of this temple was designed
T' enrich a kingdom's fortune; shall it here
Be seized upon by vile unhallowed hands,
To be employed in uses most profane?
ABOAN: Nay, grant this man, you think so much your friend,
Be honest, and intends all that he says.[4]
He is but one, and in a government
Where, he confesses, you have enemies
That watch your looks. What looks can you put on
To please these men, who are before resolved
To read 'em their own way? alas! my Lord!
If they incline to think you dangerous,

4. Aboan refers to Blanford, the play's counterpart to Behn's character Trefry: a young Englishman who has professed friendship for Oroonoko and promised that the governor, due soon in Surinam, will grant his freedom.

They have their knavish arts to make you so.
And then who knows how far their cruelty
May carry their revenge?
IMOINDA: To everything
That does belong to you, your friends, and me;
I shall be torn from you, forced away,
Helpless and miserable. Shall I live
To see that day again?[5]
OROONOKO: That day shall never come.
ABOAN: I know you are persuaded to believe
The governor's arrival will prevent
These mischiefs, and bestow your liberty.
But who is sure of that? I rather fear
More mischiefs from his coming. He is young,
Luxurious, passionate, and amorous.
Such a complexion, and made bold by power
To countenance all he is prone to do,
Will know no bounds, no law against his lusts.
If, in a fit of his intemperance,
With a strong hand he should resolve to seize
And force my royal mistress from your arms,
How can you help yourself?
OROONOKO: Ha! thou hast roused
The lion in his den; he stalks abroad,
And the wide forest trembles at his roar.
I feel the danger now: my spirits start
At the alarm and from all quarters come
To man my heart, the citadel of love.
Is there a power on earth to force you from me?
And shall I not resist it? Not strike first
To keep, to save you—to prevent that curse?
This is your cause, and shall it not prevail?
O! your were born all ways to conquer me.
[*to* ABOAN] Now I am fashioned to thy purpose. Speak:
What combination, what conspiracy,
Would'st thou engage me in? I'll undertake
All thou would'st have me now for liberty,
For the great cause of love and liberty.
ABOAN: Now, my great master, you appear yourself.
And since we have you joined in our design,
It cannot fail us. I have mustered up
The choicest slaves, men who are sensible
Of their condition, and seem most resolved.
They have their several parties.
OROONOKO: Summon 'em,

5. The lovers have been sundered once before, by the African king (in Southerne's play he is Oroonoko's father rather than grandfather) who wanted Imoinda for himself.

Assemble 'em. I will come forth and show
Myself amongst 'em. If they are resolved,
I'll lead their foremost resolutions.

ABOAN: I have provided those will follow you.

OROONOKO: With this reserve in our proceeding still:
The means that lead us to our liberty
Must not be bloody.

ABOAN: You command in all.
We shall expect you, Sir.

OROONOKO: You shannot long.

[*Exeunt* OROONOKO *and* IMOINDA *at one door*, ABOAN *at another*.]

["THUS 'TIS FINISHED"][6]

OROONOKO: I see 'em coming.
They shannot overtake us. This last kiss.
And now farewell.

IMOINDA: Farewell, farewell forever.

OROONOKO: I'll turn my face away, and do it so.
Now, are you ready?

IMOINDA: Now. But do not grudge me
The pleasure in my death of a last look.
Pray look upon me—now I'm satisfied.

OROONOKO: So fate must be by this—

[*Going to stab her, he stops short; she lays her hands on his, in order to give the blow.*]

IMOINDA: Nay then I must assist you.
And since it is the common cause of both,
'Tis just that both should be employed in it,
Thus, thus 'tis finished, and I bless my fate, [*Stabs herself.*]
That where I lived, I die, in these loved arms. [*Dies.*]

OROONOKO: She's gone. And now all's at an end with me.
[*Throws himself by her.*]
But let me pay the tribute of my grief,
A few sad tears to thy loved memory,
And then I follow—
[*Weeps over her. A noise again.*]
But I stay too long.
The noise comes nearer. Hold, before I go,
There's something would be done. It shall be so.
And then, Imoinda, I'll come all to thee. [*Rises.*]

[BLANFORD, *and his party, enter before the* GOVERNOR *and his party, swords drawn on both sides.*][7]

GOVERNOR: You strive in vain to save him. He shall die.

BLANFORD: Not while we can defend him with our lives.

GOVERNOR: Where is he?

OROONOKO: Here's the wretch whom you would have.

6. From Act 5, Scene 5. In Southerne's play as in Behn's story the rebellion fails. Anticipating capture, Oroonoko and Imoinda opt instead for death.

7. Blanford, having tried earlier to mediate between the governor and the rebel slaves, has witnessed the colonist's cruelty and now seeks to rescue Oroonoko.

Put up your swords, and let not civil broils
Engage you in the cursed cause of one
Who cannot live, and now entreats to die.
This object will convince you.
[*They gather about the body.*]
BLANFORD: 'Tis his wife!
Alas! there was no other remedy.
GOVERNOR: Who did the bloody deed?
OROONOKO: The deed was mine:
Bloody I know it is, and I expect
Your laws should tell me so. Thus self-condemned
I do resign myself into your hands,
The hands of justice—but I hold the sword
For you—and for myself.
[*Stabs the* GOVERNOR, *and himself, then throws himself by* IMOINDA*'s body.*]
STANMORE: He has killed the governor, and stabbed himself.
OROONOKO: 'Tis as it should be now. I have sent his ghost
To be a witness of that happiness
In the next world, which he has denied us here. [*Dies.*]
BLANFORD: I hope there is a place of happiness
In the next world for such exalted virtue.
Pagan, or unbeliever, yet he lived
To all he knew. And if he went astray,
There's mercy still above to set him right.
But Christians, guided by the heavenly ray,
Have no excuse if we mistake our way.
[*Exeunt omnes.*]

FINIS.

1695 1696

PERSPECTIVES
Coterie Writing

To Lysander, To the Fair Clarinda, A Letter to Mr. Creech: Some of Behn's poetry, like much other verse in the seventeenth and eighteenth centuries, proffered its readers the voyeuristic sense that they were being let in on the poet's correspondence. Sometimes this was so. In literary families and in friendships, verse often served as a medium of communication. A poem might make its way first from the writer to a designated recipient, then to a larger circle of acquaintances, and finally (with or without the author's consent) to the printing press. The practice of circulating manuscripts has come to be called "coterie writing," and its antecedents were ancient. Theocritus, the Greek poet credited with inventing pastoral verse, cast many of his poems as expressions of love and friendship (sung rather than written) among shepherds and nymphs living in a Golden Age. The Greek names of these ardent Arcadians—all those swooning "Lysanders" and "Clarindas"—came down to the English poets through the *Eclogues* of Virgil, Theocritus's immeasurably influential Roman imitator. Another Roman, Horace, had pioneered the durable paradigm of the verse epistle, a wittily self-conscious poetic performance addressed to a real-life, explicitly identified contemporary. In the seventeenth century, the resurgence of coterie writing began with the work of Katherine Philips, who celebrated her friendships with women in poems published to great acclaim shortly after her early death. (Behn admired Philips enormously, but reworked the tradition by addressing many of her poems to men—lovers and literary colleagues—in a boldly specific, often sexual language that contrasted sharply with Philips's celebrated chastity.) Both men and women produced poems of friendship in great numbers, but for women writers the practice appears to have held a particular attraction. In addressing other women, they could enact a solidarity, cultivate a self-discovery, define and develop a resistance otherwise muted in a male-dominated world; they often depict themselves as building from female friendship what the critic Janet Todd calls "the last buttress against the irrationality always implied in the female condition." The equivocal "privacy" of the coterie poem made it a particularly supple medium, capable of combining fact and fiction, disguise and revelation, intimacy and declamation. The three practitioners sampled here worked many variations in this pliable, powerful mode of writing.

Mary, Lady Chudleigh

Born Mary Lee, and wed at age 17 into a family as aristocratic as her own, Lady Chudleigh (1656–1710) lived and wrote in the west coast county of Devon. After years of dispatching manuscript verses among a widening circle of writing friends (including the laureate John Dryden and the pioneering feminist Mary Astell), Chudleigh made her first foray into print with *The Ladies Defense* (1701), a satiric retort to a parson who had exhorted all women (in her mocking paraphrase) to "give up their reason, and their wills resign" to the dictates of their husbands. In her *Defense*, and in the two collections of shorter poems that followed (1703, 1710), Chudleigh sought to expand her coterie into a larger collective readership consisting of "all ingenious ladies": women willing, in defiance of male presumption and social convention, "to read and think, and think and read again," and thereby to "make it our whole business to be wise."

To the Ladies

Wife and servant are the same,
But only differ in the name:

For when that fatal knot is tied,
Which nothing, nothing can divide:
When she the word *obey* has said,
And man by law supreme has made,
Then all that's kind is laid aside,
And nothing left but state° and pride: *dignity*
Fierce as an Eastern Prince he grows,
And all his innate rigor shows:
Then but to look, to laugh, or speak,
Will the nuptial contract break.
Like mutes she signs alone must make,
And never any freedom take:
But still be governed by a nod,
And fear her husband as her God:
Him still must serve, him still obey,
And nothing act, and nothing say,
But what her haughty lord thinks fit,
Who with the power, has all the wit.° *intelligence*
Then shun, oh! shun that wretched state,
And all the fawning flatterers hate:
Value your selves, and men despise,
You must be proud, if you'll be wise.

1703

To Almystrea[1]

1

Permit Marissa[2] in an artless lay
To speak her wonder, and her thanks repay:
Her creeping Muse can ne'er like yours ascend;
She has not strength for such a towering flight.
Your wit, her humble fancy does transcend;
She can but gaze at your exalted height:
Yet she believed it better to expose
  Her failures, than ungrateful prove;
    And rather chose
To show a want of sense, than want of love:
But taught by you, she may at length improve,
And imitate those virtues she admires.
Your bright example leaves a tract divine,
She sees a beamy brightness in each line,
And with ambitious warmth aspires,
Attracted by the glory of your name,
To follow you in all the lofty roads of fame.

1. The name is an anagram for Mary Astell, feminist author of *Some Reflections upon Marriage* (see page 2284).

2. Chudleigh's pen name.

2

Merit like yours can no resistance find,
But like a deluge overwhelms the mind;
Gives full possession of each part,
Subdues the soul, and captivates the heart.
Let those whom wealth, or interest[3] unite,
Whom avarice, or kindred sway,[4]
Who in the dregs of life delight,
And every dictate of their sense° obey, *appetites*
Learn here to love at a sublimer rate,
To wish for nothing but exchange of thoughts,
For intellectual joys,
And pleasures more refined
Than earth can give, or fancy can create.
Let our vain sex be fond of glittering toys,
Of pompous titles, and affected noise,
Let envious men by barb'rous custom led
Descant° on faults, *expound*
And in detraction° find *criticisms*
Delights unknown to a brave generous mind,
While we resolve a nobler path to tread,
And from tyrannic custom free,
View the dark mansions of the mighty dead,
And all their close recesses see;
Then from those awful shades retire,
And take a tour above,
And there, the shining scenes admire,
The opera of eternal love;
View the machines,[5] on the bright actors gaze,
Then in a holy transport, blest amaze,
To the great Author our devotion raise,
And let our wonder terminate in praise.

1703

Anne Finch, Countess of Winchilsea

In the early 1680s, while serving as Maid of Honor to Mary of Modena (wife of the future James II), Anne Kingsmill (1661–1720) met and married Colonel Heneage Finch, and savored the splendors of the Stuart court. When that world vanished in the Revolution of 1688, she and her husband withdrew to his country estate, where she suffered recurrent depression, cultivated friendships, wrote poetry, and saw her work published in several miscellanies. In 1713, despite her wariness of the censures heaped on women writers, she published anonymously a collection of her own, *Miscellany Poems on Several Occasions*. (The *Introduction*, in

3. Self-interest, desire for power and material prosperity.
4. I.e., who are motivated by greed or desire for family status.
5. The stage mechanisms used to move scenery and produce striking effects (including the appearances of gods and angels).

which she most memorably confronts the censurers, remained like much of her verse unpublished until the twentieth century.) The book brought her some fame in her own time and much more a century later, when William Wordsworth proclaimed his admiration for her work. Her poetry moves adroitly among polarities: city and country, satire and affection, solitude and friendship.

The Introduction

Did I my lines intend for public view,
How many censures would their faults pursue!
Some would, because such words they do affect,
Cry they're insipid, empty, uncorrect.
And many have attained, dull and untaught,
The name of wit, only by finding fault.
True judges might condemn their want of wit,
And all might say they're by a woman writ.
Alas! A woman that attempts the pen,
Such an intruder on the rights of men,
Such a presumptuous creature is esteemed,
The fault can by no virtue be redeemed.
They tell us we mistake our sex and way;
Good breeding, fashion, dancing, dressing, play
Are the accomplishments we should desire;
To write, or read, or think, or to inquire
Would cloud our beauty, and exhaust our time,
And interrupt the conquests of our prime;
Whilst the dull manage of a servile house
Is held by some our utmost art, and use.
    Sure 'twas not ever thus, nor are we told
Fables,° of women that excelled of old; *false stories*
To whom, by the diffusive° hand of heaven *scattering*
Some share of wit and poetry was given.
On that glad day, on which the Ark returned,[1]
The holy pledge for which the land had mourned,
The joyful tribes attend it on the way,
The Levites do the sacred charge convey,
Whilst various instruments before it play;
Here, holy virgins in the concert join,
The louder notes to soften, and refine,
And with alternate verse,[2] complete the hymn divine.
Lo! The young poet,[3] after God's own heart,
By Him inspired, and taught the Muse's art,
Returned from conquest, a bright chorus meets,
That sing his slain ten thousand in the streets.

1. The Ark of the Covenant was a chest containing the stone tablets of the Ten Commandments. Recovered by King David, it was carried into Jerusalem by members of the Levite tribe (1 Chronicles 15).
2. Responsive singing: the male and the female choruses sing by turns, answering line with line.
3. David, who in his youth was skilled both as a fighter, conquering the Philistines, and as a harper, credited with composing the Psalms.

In such loud numbers° they his acts declare, *verses*
Proclaim the wonders of his early war,
That Saul upon the vast applause does frown,
And feels its mighty thunder shake the crown.[4]
What can the threatened judgment now prolong?[5]
Half of the kingdom is already gone:
The fairest half, whose influence guides the rest,
Have David's empire o'er their hearts confessed.
  A woman[6] here leads fainting Israel on,
She fights, she wins, she triumphs with a song,
Devout, majestic, for the subject fit,
And far above her arms, exalts her wit,
Then to the peaceful, shady palm withdraws,
And rules the rescued nation with her laws.
How are we fal'n, fal'n by mistaken rules?
And education's, more than nature's fools,
Debarred from all improvements of the mind,
And to be dull, expected and designed;° *intended*
And if someone would soar above the rest,
With warmer fancy[7] and ambition pressed,
So strong the opposing faction still appears,
The hopes to thrive can ne'er outweigh the fears.
Be cautioned then my Muse, and still retired;
Nor be despised, aiming to be admired;
Conscious of wants, still with contracted wing,
To some few friends and to thy sorrows sing;
For groves of laurel[8] thou wert never meant;
Be dark enough thy shades, and be thou there content.

1903

Friendship Between Ephelia and Ardelia[1]

Eph. What friendship is, Ardelia, show.
Ard. 'Tis to love, as I love you.
Eph. This account, so short (though kind)
  Suits not my inquiring mind.
  Therefore farther now repeat:
  What is friendship when complete?
Ard. 'Tis to share all joy and grief;
  'Tis to lend all due relief
  From the tongue, the heart, the hand;
  'Tis to mortgage house and land;
  For a friend be sold a slave;

4. Saul, first king of Israel, had made David his general but tried to kill him after hearing the women of Israel singing, "Saul has slain his thousands, and David his ten thousands" (1 Samuel 18.7).

5. Postpone; the prophet Samuel had foretold an untimely end to Saul's reign.

6. Deborah, judge and prophet who led the Israelites to victory over the Canaanites (Judges 4–5).

7. Livelier imagination.

8. Tree whose leaves were used to crown celebrated poets.

1. "Ardelia" is Finch's pastoral pen name.

'Tis to die upon a grave,
If a friend therein do lie.
Eph. This indeed, though carried high,
This, though more than e'er was done
Underneath the rolling sun,
This has all been said before.
Can Ardelia say no more?
Ard. Words indeed no more can show:
But 'tis to love, as I love you.

1713

A Nocturnal Reverie

In such a night,[1] when every louder wind
Is to its distant cavern safe confined;
And only gentle Zephyr° fans his wings, *the west wind*
And lonely Philomel,° still waking, sings; *the nightingale*
Or from some tree, famed for the owl's delight,
She, hollowing clear, directs the wanderer right:
In such a night, when passing clouds give place,
Or thinly veil the heavens' mysterious face;
When in some river, overhung with green,
The waving moon and trembling leaves are seen;
When freshened grass now bears itself upright,
And makes cool banks to pleasing rest invite,
Whence springs the woodbind, and the bramble-rose,
And where the sleepy cowslip sheltered grows;
Whilst now a paler hue the foxglove takes,
Yet checkers still with red the dusky brakes:° *thickets*
When scattered glow-worms, but in twilight fine,
Show trivial beauties, watch their hour to shine;
Whilst Salisbury[2] stands the test of every light,
In perfect charms, and perfect virtue bright;
When odors, which declined repelling day,
Through temperate air uninterrupted stray;
When darkened groves their softest shadows wear,
And falling waters we distinctly hear;
When through the gloom more venerable shows
Some ancient fabric,° awful in repose, *building*
While sunburnt hills their swarthy looks conceal,
And swelling haycocks thicken up the vale;
When the loosed horse now, as his pasture leads,

1. Finch takes her opening words from the evocation of night in Shakespeare's *Merchant of Venice* (5.1.1–21), where the lovers Lorenzo and Jessica speak the phrase repeatedly to each other, as they retell old tales of nocturnal passion and betrayal. This time, though, Finch reverses the sociable impulses implicit in the poems above and below. What Shakespeare casts as conversation, she transmutes into soliloquy.

2. Anne Tufton, Countess of Salisbury, daughter of one of Finch's close friends.

Comes slowly grazing through th' adjoining meads,
Whose stealing pace, and lengthened shade we fear,
Till torn up forage in his teeth we hear;
When nibbling sheep at large pursue their food,
And unmolested kine rechew the cud;
When curlews cry beneath the village-walls,
And to her straggling brood the partridge calls;
Their short-lived jubilee the creatures keep,
Which but endures, whilst tyrant-man does sleep;
When a sedate content the spirit feels,
And no fierce light disturbs, whilst it reveals;
But silent musings urge the mind to seek
Something, too high for syllables to speak;
Till the free soul to a compos'dness charmed,
Finding the elements of rage disarmed,
O'er all below a solemn quiet grown,
Joys in th' inferior° world, and thinks it like her own: *lower*
In such a night let me abroad remain,
Till morning breaks, and all's confused again;
Our cares, our toils, our clamors are renewed,
Or pleasures, seldom reached, again pursued.

1713

A Ballad to Mrs. Catherine Fleming in London from Malshanger Farm in Hampshire

From me, who whilom° sung the town, *formerly*
This second ballad comes;
To let you know we are got down
From hurry, smoke, and drums:
And every visitor that rolls
In restless coach from Mall to Paul's,[1]
With a fa-la-la-la-la-la.

And now were I to paint the seat[2]
(As well-bred poets use°) *do*
I should embellish our retreat,
By favor of the Muse:
Though to no villa we pretend,
But a plain farm at the best end,
With a fa-la etc.

Where innocence and quiet reigns,
And no distrust is known;
His nightly safety none maintains,
By ways they do in town,
Who rising loosen bolt and bar;

1. From Pall Mall, a fashionable promenade in London, to St. Paul's Cathedral.

2. The "country seat": the farm.

We draw the latch and out we are,
With a fa-la etc.

For jarring sounds in London streets,
Which still are passing by;
Where "Cowcumbers"[3] with "Sand ho" meets,
And for loud mastery vie:
The driver whistling to his team
Here wakes us from some rural dream,
With a fa-la etc.

From rising hills through distant views,
We see the sun decline;
Whilst everywhere the eye pursues
The grazing flocks and kine:
Which home at night the farmer brings,
And not the post's but sheep's bell rings,
With a fa-la etc.

We silver trouts and crayfish eat,
Just taken from the stream;
And never think our meal complete,
Without fresh curds and cream:
And as we pass by the barn floor,
We choose our supper from the door,
With a fa-la etc.

Beneath our feet the partridge springs,
As to the woods we go;
Where birds scarce stretch their painted wings,
So little fear they show:
But when our outspread hoops° they spy, *hoop skirts*
They look when we like them should fly,
With a fa-la etc.

Through verdant circles as we stray,
To which no end we know;
As we o'erhanging boughs survey,
And tufted grass below:
Delight into the fancy falls,
And happy days and verse recalls,
With a fa-la etc.

Oh! Why did I these shades forsake,
And shelter of the grove;
The flowering shrub, the rustling brake,° *thicket*
The solitude I love:
Where emperors have fixed their lot,
And greatly chose to be forgot,
With a fa-la etc.

3. Cucumbers; these are the cries of street peddlers.

Then how can I from hence depart,
Unless my pleasing friend
Should now her sweet harmonious art
Unto these shades extend:
And, like old Orpheus' powerful song,[4]
Draw me and all my woods along,
With a fa-la etc.

So charmed like Birnam's they would rise,
And march in goodly row,[5]
But since it might the town surprise
To see me travel so,
I must from soothing joys like these,
Too soon return in open chaise° *carriage*
With a fa-la etc.

Meanwhile accept what I have writ,
To show this rural scene;
Nor look for sharp satiric wit
From off the balmy plain:
The country breeds no thorny bays,
But mirth and love and honest praise,
With a fa-la etc.

c. 1719 1929

Mary Leapor

The daughter of a gardener, Mary Leapor (1722–1746) worked as a kitchen maid, read voraciously, wrote plentifully, and sustained the tradition of the social poem (complete with pastoral pseudonyms) into a new era and a new register. Her manuscripts, circulating among neighbors, brought her the attention, friendship, and support of Bridget Freemantle, who undertook to arrange their publication. Leapor died of measles at age 24 before she could see her work in print. *Her Poems upon Several Occasions* appeared in 1748; its success prompted an additional volume three years later. Though the books were marketed as (in the words of one contemporary) the work of "a most extraordinary, uncultivated genius," the poems themselves prove otherwise. They display influences absorbed from Greek and Roman classics, Restoration drama, and Augustan literature—particularly Swift and Pope. Leapor transports these elements across boundary lines of class and gender to produce a new, arresting voice speaking from an old position: that of the woman who must labor in order to live.

The Headache. To Aurelia

Aurelia, when your zeal makes known
Each woman's failing but your own,
How charming Silvia's teeth decay,
And Celia's hair is turning grey;

4. The mythological poet's music charmed trees and stones into motion.

5. In Shakespeare's *Macbeth,* the forest of Birnam "comes" to Dunsinane (fulfilling the witches' prophecy) when soldiers carry boughs as camouflage.

Yet Celia gay has sparkling eyes,
But (to your comfort) is not wise:
Methinks you take a world of pains
To tell us Celia has no brains.

Now you wise folk, who make such a pother° *fuss*
About the wit of one another,
With pleasure would your brains resign,
Did all your noddles° ache like mine. *heads*

Not cuckolds half my anguish know,
When budding horns[1] begin to grow;
Nor battered skull of wrestling Dick,
Who late was drubbed at singlestick;[2]
Nor wretches that in fevers fry,
Not Sappho[3] when her cap's awry,
E'er felt such torturing pangs as I;
Not forehead of Sir Jeffrey Strife,
When smiling Cynthio kissed his wife.

Not lovesick Marcia's languid eyes,
Who for her simpering Corin dies,
So sleepy look or dimly shine,
As these dejected eyes of mine:
Not Claudia's brow such wrinkles made
At sight of Cynthia's new brocade.

Just so, Aurelia, you complain
Of vapors, rheums, and gouty pain;
Yet I am patient, so should you,
For cramps and headaches are our due:
We suffer justly for our crimes,
For scandal you, and I for rhymes;
Yet we (as hardened wretches do)
Still the enchanting vice pursue;
Our reformation ne'er begin
But fondly hug the darling sin.

Yet there's a mighty difference too
Between the fate of me and you;
Though you with tottering age shall bow,
And wrinkles scar your lovely brow,
Your busy tongue may still proclaim
The faults of every sinful dame:
You still may prattle nor give o'er,
When wretched I must sin no more.
The sprightly Nine° must leave me then, *Muses*
This trembling hand resign its pen:
No matron ever sweetly sung,

1. Folklore held that the husband of an unfaithful wife would sprout horns from his forehead.
2. Beaten in a fencing match using short, heavy sticks.
3. Apparently a mutual friend; the ensuing names, too, refer to either real or imaginary people, otherwise unidentified.

Apollo° only courts the young. *god of poetry*
Then who would not (Aurelia, pray)
Enjoy his favors while they may?
Nor cramps nor headaches shall prevail:
I'll still write on, and you shall rail.

1748

Mira To Octavia

Fair one, to you this monitor[1] I send;
Octavia, pardon your officious friend.
You think your conduct merits only praise,
But outlawed poets censure whom they please.
Thus we begin: your servant[2] has been told
That you (despising settlements and gold)
Determine Florio witty, young and gay,
To have and hold for ever and for ay;[3]
And view that person as your mortal foe
Who dares object against your charming beau.
But now, to furnish meter for my song,
Let us suppose Octavia may be wrong:
'Tis true, you're lovely; yet the learn'd aver
That even beauties like the rest may err.
I know, to shun, you hold it as a rule,
The arrant coxcomb and the stupid fool.
No such is Florio, he has wit—'tis true:
Enough, Octavia, to impose on you.
Yet such a wit you'll by experience find
Worse than a fool that's complaisant and kind.
It only serves to gild his vices o'er,
And teach his malice how to wound the more.
I need not tell you, most ingenious fair,
That hungry mortals are not fed with air,
But solid food: And this voracious clay
Asks drink and victuals more than once a day:
Now, could your Florio by his wit inspire
The chilly hearth to blaze with lasting fire;
Or, when his children round the table throng,
By an allusion or a sprightly song,
Adorn the board, i'th'twinkling of an eye,
With a hot pasty or a warden pie,[4]
There might be reason on Octavia's side,
And not a sage could blame the prudent bride.
Yet (or some authors often deal in lies)
Lovers may live on nuts and blackberries;
For roving knights, bewildered in their way,

1. Advice; warning.
2. I.e., "your humble servant": Leapor herself.
3. Always.
4. Pasty: a meat pie. Warden: a kind of pear.

Who in black forests half a season stray,
Unless they find provision on the trees,
Must sup on grass and breakfast on the breeze.[5]
But as you've long been used to nicer fare,
Your constitution would but hardly bear
Such food as this. And therefore I advise
That you'd consider (for you're mighty wise)
If sober Dusterandus would not make
A better husband than your darling rake.
Grave Dusterandus: He whose steadfast mind
Is yet untainted, though not much refined;
Whose soul ne'er roves beyond his native fields,
Nor asks for joys but what his pasture yields;
On life's dull cares with patience can attend,
A gentle master and a constant friend;
Who in soft quiet spends the guiltless days,
His servants' blessing and his neighbors' praise.
Say, would you, in his happy mansion, reign,
Toast of the village and the rural plain?
With honest friends your cheerful days beguile,
While peace and plenty on your table smile?
Or cold and hungry writhe your tired jaws,
And dine with Florio upon hips and haws?[6]
In troth I think there's little room for pause.
  In spite of all romantic poets sing,
This gold, my dearest, is an useful thing.
Not that I'd have you hoard the precious store—
For not a wretch is like the miser poor.
Enjoy your fortune with a cheerful mind,
And let the blessing spread amongst the kind.
But if there's none but Florio that will do,
Write ballads both, and you may thrive. Adieu.

1748

An Epistle to Artemisia.[1] On Fame

Say, Artemisia, do the slaves of fame
Deserve our pity, or provoke our blame?
Whose airy hopes, like some new-kindled fire,
A moment blaze, and then in smoke expire;
Or like a babe i'th'midst of plenty cry,
And leave their supper for a painted fly[2]

5. Leapor parodies the ordeals of deprivation often suffered by heroes of romance.
6. Wild berries.
1. "Artemisia" is the name of an ancient ruler celebrated as a patron of literature; Leapor applies it to her friend and patron, Bridget Freemantle. The poem's topics (the hopes entailed in writing, the pains of being read—and visited) and its tone (affectionate to its addressee, exasperated with everyone else) show affinities with Pope's *Epistle to Dr. Arbuthnot* (see pages 2509–21).
2. I.e., a colorful (and distracting) bug.

Bold Maro[3] paints her of gigantic size,
And makes her forehead prop the lofty skies;
With eyes and ears he hung the lady round,
And her shrill clarion shook the heavens around.
Then worthy names the trembling notes prolong,
And actions blazing in immortal song;
But, weary now, and grown an ancient maid,
Her strength exhausted, and her lungs decayed,
Her unspread wings resign their plumy pride,
And her hoarse trumpet dangles by her side.
A handmaid leads the purblind dame along,
Black Slander called, with never-ceasing tongue;
And when this servant whispers in her ears,
She to her mouth the heavy trumpet rears.
The rattling concave[4] sends a horrid cry,
And smoking scandals hiss along the sky;
Yet round her still the supple vot'ries[5] crowd,
And pay devotion to a painted cloud.
The fond Ixions[6] spread their longing arms,
And grasp a vapor for a Juno's charms.
The hero brave, that never knew to shun
The pointed canon, or the bursting gun,
Of bruises vain, and prodigal of scars,
Returns from pillage, and successful wars.
But if the sullen rout[7] refuse to pay
The vulgar triumphs of a noisy day,[8]
To his sad bosom pale despondence creeps,
And the stern soldier like an infant weeps.
Caballing skeptics shake the frighted gown,[9]
And poets tremble at an idiot's frown.
The scorn of fools can pierce a noble heart,
And wound an author in the tend'rest part.
Rich Merrio thought, like eastern kings, to raise
By lofty columns everlasting praise.
His broad foundations half the field surround,
And piles of timber load the sinking ground.
This Heav'n beheld, and smiled at seeing Man,
Whose joy is vapor, and whole life a span,[1]
Who Death's black warrant every moment fears,
Still building castles for a thousand years.

3. The Roman epic poet Virgil, who in Book 4 of his *Aeneid* portrays Fama (Rumor) as an immense goddess, who wears a garment studded with functioning eyes and ears.
4. The trumpet's horn.
5. Votaries: those who worship and desire fame.
6. In Greek mythology, a king named Ixion hopes to seduce Zeus's wife Hera (the "Juno" of the next line). Zeus tricks him by sculpting a cloud-likeness of the goddess, which Ixion deludedly embraces.
7. Crowd.
8. The celebration, called a "triumph," traditionally held in honor of military victory.
9. The gown was an emblem of both church and university; here it stands for the clergyman or scholar alarmed by those who mock his argument. A "cabal" is any powerful and secret conspiracy.
1. A small distance: the space, with the hand outstretched. "from the end of the thumb to the end of the little finger" (Johnson's *Dictionary*).

On this grand wretch was passed an early doom;
And Merrio, summoned to the silent gloom,
Feels, ere his eyes behold the glowing spires,
The stroke of fate, and with a sigh expires.
All reas'ning creatures, though by different ways,
Would prove their titles to a share of praise.
Cornelia's praise consists in plaiting well;[2]
Pastora's fingers at a Knot excel;
Her gaudy ribbons gay Sabina furls;
But looks with Envy on Aurelia's curls.
Unhappy Delia thought a shining gown
Would gain respect, and win the gazing town.
But Envy rose, to clip her rising wings,
And, grinning ghastly (as the poet sings),
In Claudia's shape dissolved the lady's pride,[3]
And slily whispered, "Delia's gown is dyed."
Even Mira's self, presuming on the bays,[4]
Appears among the candidates for praise:
Has watched applause, as from the lips it fell;
With what success? Why, that the Muse shall tell.
May Artemisia not refuse to hear!
For praise could ne'er offend her gentle ear.
I count the patrons of my early song,
And pay the tributes to their shares belong.[5]
What sorrows too oppressed the Muse's wing,
Till your good nature gave her strength to sing!
Once Delpho read—sage Delpho,[6] learn'd and wise,
O'er the scrawled paper cast his judging eyes,
Whose lifted brows confessed a critic's pride,
While his broad thumb moved nimbly down the side.
His form was like some oracle profound:
The listening audience formed a circle round:
But Mira, fixing her presuming eyes
On the stern image, thus impatient cries:
Sir, will they prosper? Speak your judgment, pray.
Replies the statue, "Why, perhaps they may."
For further answers we in vain implore:
The charm was over, and it spoke no more.
Cressida comes,[7] the next unbidden guest.
Small was her top-knot,[8] and her judgment less.
A decent virgin, blest with idle time,

2. I.e., in skillfully braiding hair.
3. I.e., Envy incarnates itself in Claudia, who whispers the couplet's punchline.
4. I.e., Leapor herself (the name is a near-anagram of "Mary," and may echo the Latin *mirari:* to wonder at), here aspiring to the crown of bay leaves traditionally bestowed on poets laureate.
5. Here Leapor lays out her plan for the rest of the poem: to recount the reactions of the early readers to whom she showed her work.
6. A critic, whom Leapor renames for the ancient oracle of Delphi, which delivered hard truths in obscure language.
7. Another reader, here named for the fickle Trojan heroine of Chaucer's poem and Shakespeare's play.
8. "A knot [of hair] worn by women on the top of their head" (Johnson's *Dictionary*).

Now jingles bobbins,[9] and now ponders rhyme:
Not ponders—reads—not reads—but looks 'em o'er
To little purpose, like a thousand more.
"Your servant, Molly."[1]
"I am yours the same."
"I pay this visit, Molly, to your fame:
'Twas that that brought me here—or let me die."[2]
"My fame's obliged—and truly, so am I."
"Then fetch me something, for I must not stay
Above four hours."
"But you'll drink some tea?"[3]
We sip, and read; we laugh, and chat between.
"The air is pleasant, and the fields are green.
Well, Molly, sure, there never was thy fellow.[4]
But don't my ruffles look exceeding yellow?
My apron's dirty—Mira, well, I vow,
This thought of yours was very pretty now.
I've read the like, though I forget the place.
But, Mrs. Mira, how d'ye like my lace?"
Afflicted Mira, with a languid eye,
Now views the clock, and now the western sky.
"The sun grows lower. Will you please to walk?"
"No, read some more."
"But I had rather talk."
"Perhaps you're tired."
"Truly, that may be."
"Or think me weak."
"Why, Cressy, thoughts are free."[5]
At last we part, with congees[6] at the door.
"I'd thank you, Mira, but my thanks are poor.
I wish, alas! But wishes are in vain.
I like your garden; and I'll come again.
Dear, how I wish—I do, or let me die!—
That we lived near."
Thinks Mira, "So don't I."
This nymph, perhaps, as some had done before,
Found the cold welcome, and returned no more.
Then Vido[7] next to Mira's cot appears,
And with soft praise salutes her list'ning ears;
Whose maxim was, with truth not to offend,
And, right or wrong, his business to commend.
"Look here," cries Mira, "pray peruse this song.
Even I, its parent, see there's something wrong."

9. "A small pin of wood, with a notch, to wind the thread about when women weave lace" (Johnson's *Dictionary*).
1. Cressida greets Leapor ("Molly" was a nickname for Mary) with a traditional formula of politeness: [I am] your servant.
2. I.e., "I swear."
3. Pronounced *tay*.
4. I.e., "no one equals you" (Cressida offhandedly praises her poetry).
5. Proverbial: I may think what I please.
6. Formal farewells.
7. A friend whom Leapor depicts in other poems ("Celadon to Mira" and "The Disappointment") as a shameless flatterer, skilled in the "well-bred lie."

"But you mistake: 'Tis excellent indeed."
"Then I'll correct it."
"No, there is no need."
"Pray, Vido, look on these: methinks they smell
Too much of Grub Street;[8] that myself can tell."
"Not so indeed; they're easy and polite."
"And can you bear 'em?"
"I could read till night."
But Mira, though too partial to the bays
And, like her brethren, not averse to praise,
Had learned this lesson: praise, if planted wrong,
Is more destructive than a spiteful tongue.
Comes Codrus next, with talents to offend;
A simple tutor, and a saucy friend,
Who poured thick sonnets like a troubled spring,
And such as Butler's wide-mouthed mortals sing:[9]
In shocking rhymes a nymph's perfections tells,
Like the harsh ting-tong of some village bells.
Then a rude quarrel sings through either ear,
And Mira's levee[1] once again is clear.
Now the dull Muses took their usual rest.
The babes[2] slept soundly in their tiny chest.
Not so their parent: Fortune still[3] would send
Some proud director,[4] or ill-meaning friend.
At least we thought their sour meanings ill,
Whose lectures strove to cross a stubborn will.
Parthenia cries, "Why, Mira, you are dull,
And ever musing till you crack your skull.
Still poking o'er your what-d'ye-call—your Muse.
But prithee, Mira, when dost clean thy shoes?"
Then comes Sophronia, like a barb'rous Turk:
"You thoughtless baggage, when d'ye mind your work?
Still o'er a table leans your bending neck.
Your head will grow prepost'rous, like a peck.[5]
Go, ply your needle. You might earn your bread;
Or who must feed you when your father's dead?"
She sobbing answers, "Sure, I need not come
To you for lectures; I have store at home.
What can I do?"
"Not scribble."
"But I will."
"Then get thee packing—and be awkward still."
Thus wrapped in sorrow wretched Mira lay,

8. The proverbial London habitat of hack writers.
9. Leapor echoes the mocking description, by Samuel Butler (1612–1680) in his satiric poem *Hudibras* (1663–1678), of a vacuous-minded astrologer's assistant named Whachum, whose "sonnets charmed th' attentive crowd / By wide-mouthed mortal trolled aloud" (2.3.383–4).
1. "Royal reception"; here self-mockingly invoked to describe the gathering of Leapor's friends, who now disperse in order to avoid hearing Codrus's ponderous poems.
2. "Her poems" [editor's note, 1751].
3. Always; repeatedly.
4. Pedantic instructor.
5. A two-gallon container.

Till Artemisia swept the gloom away.
The laughing Muse, by her example led,
Shakes her glad wings, and quits the drowsy bed.
Yet some impertinence pursues me still;
And so I fear it ever must, and will.
So soft Pappilia[6] o'er the table bends
With her small circle of insipid friends,
Who wink, and stretch, and rub their drowsy eyes,
While o'er their heads imperial Dullness flies.[7]
"What can we do? We cannot stir for show'rs;[8]
Or what invent, to kill the irksome hours?
Why, run to Leapor's, fetch that idle play[9]
'Twill serve to laugh at all the livelong day."
Preferment great! To beat one's weary brains,
To find diversion only when it rains!
Methinks I feel this coward bosom glow[1]
Say, Artemisia, shall I speak, or no?
The Muse shall give herself no fancy airs,
But only bid 'em[2] softly, read their prayers.

1751

Advice to Sophronia

When youth and charms have ta'en their wanton flight,
And transient beauty bids the fair good-night;
When once her sparkling eyes shall dimly roll,
Then let the matron dress her lofty soul;
Quit affectation, partner of her youth,
For goodness, prudence, purity, and truth.
These virtues will her lasting peace prepare,
And give a sanction to her silver hair.
These precepts let the fond Sophronia prove,
Nor vainly dress her blinking eyes with love.
Can roses flourish on a leafless thorn,
Or dewy woodbines grace a wintry morn?
The weeping Cupids languish in your eye;
On your brown cheek the sickly beauties die.
Time's rugged hand has stroked your visage o'er;
The gay vermilion stains your lip no more.
None can with justice now your shape admire;
The drooping lilies on your breast expire.
Then, dear Sophronia, leave thy foolish whims:
Discard your lover with your favorite sins.
Consult your glass; then prune your wanton mind,

6. *Papilio* (Latin): butterfly. Pope gives the same name to a whim-driven woman in "Epistle 2: To a Lady" (ll. 37–40; see page 2522).

7. Torpor, stupidity; here personified as the apocalyptic goddess of Pope's *Dunciad* (see pages 2531–43).

8. I.e., the rain prevents their going out.

9. Leapor wrote plays as well as poems.

1. I.e., kindle with sudden courage.

2. I.e., the "small circle of insipid friends" (line 170) who seek to divert themselves with Leapor's play.

Nor furnish laughter for succeeding time.
'Tis not your own; 'tis gold's all-conquering charms
Invite Myrtillo to your shrivelled arms:
And shall Sophronia, whose once-lovely eyes
Beheld those triumphs which her heart despised,
Who looked on merit with a haughty frown,
At five-and-fifty take a beardless clown?
Ye pitying Fates, this withered damsel save,
And bear her safely to her virgin grave.

1751

The Epistle of Deborah Dough

Dearly beloved Cousin, these
Are sent to thank you for your cheese;
The price of oats is greatly fell:
I hope your children all are well
(Likewise the calf you take delight in),
As I am at this present writing.
But I've no news to send you now;
Only I've lost my brindled° cow, *spotted*
And that has greatly sunk my dairy.
But I forgot our neighbor Mary;
Our neighbor Mary—who, they say,
Sits scribble-scribble all the day,
And making—what—I can't remember;
But sure 'tis something like December;
A frosty morning—let me see—
O! Now I have it to a T:
She throws away her precious time
In scrawling nothing else but rhyme;[1]
Of which, they say, she's mighty proud,
And lifts her nose above the crowd;
Though my young daughter Cicely
Is taller by a foot than she,
And better learned (as people say);
Can knit a stocking in a day;
Can make a pudding, plump and rare;
And boil her bacon to an hair;
Will coddle° apples nice and green, *cook*
And fry her pancakes—like a queen.

But there's a man, that keeps a dairy,
Will clip the wings of neighbor Mary:
Things wonderful they talk of him,
But I've a notion 'tis a whim.
Howe'er, 'tis certain he can make

1. A pun on "rime" (frost), which is why her work is "like December."

Your rhymes as thick as plums in cake;
Nay more, they say that from the pot
He'll take his porridge, scalding hot,
And drink 'em down;—and yet they tell ye
Those porridge shall not burn his belly;
A cheesecake o'er his head he'll throw,
And when 'tis on the stones below,
It shan't be found so much as quaking,
Provided 'tis of his wife's making.
From this some people would infer
That this good man's a conjuror:
But I believe it is a lie;
I never thought him so, not I,
Though Win'fred Hobble who, you know,
Is plagued with corns on every toe,
Sticks on his verse with fastening spittle,
And says it helps her feet a little.
Old Frances too his paper tears,
And tucks it close behind his ears;
And (as she told me t'other day)
It charmed her toothache quite away.

Now as thou'rt better learned than me,
Dear Cos', I leave it all to thee
To judge about this puzzling man,
And ponder wisely—for you can.

Now Cousin, I must let you know
That, while my name is Deborah Dough,
I shall be always glad to see ye,
And what I have, I'll freely gi' ye.

'Tis one o'clock, as I'm a sinner;
The boys are all come home to dinner,
And I must bid you now farewell.
I pray remember me to Nell;
And for your friend I'd have you know
Your loving Cousin,

Deborah Dough

1751

END OF PERSPECTIVES: COTERIE WRITING

John Wilmot, Earl of Rochester

1647–1680

In one of his many notorious escapades, John Wilmot, Earl of Rochester, drunkenly smashed to pieces one of the king's costliest timekeepers. He always lived at odds with ordinary time, mostly ahead of it: he became Earl at age ten, when his father died; received his M.A. from Oxford at fourteen; conducted a Grand Tour of Europe during the next three years; tried to abduct his future wife Elizabeth Malet (a much-sought woman of wealth, wit, and beauty) when he was eighteen, and was briefly imprisoned for the attempt; married her at twenty; and died, after long libertinage and precipitate piety, at thirty-three. Rochester's wit and beauty, the stupendous energies of his mind (erudite, inventive), of his language (adroit, obscene), of his body (alcoholic, bisexual), and of his convictions (hedonistic, atheistic) made him the fascination of the Restoration court, whose proclivities for theatrics, for combat, and for amorous entanglement he pushed to matchless extremes. Theatrics: Rochester wrote plays of his own and produced plays by others; he tutored the stage novice Elizabeth Barry, soon to become the greatest actress of the age (they carried on a volatile affair, and had a daughter); at times he could don a disguise himself and play a role so successfully (in order to go underground, to escape punishment, to bring off a seduction) that close friends could not recognize him. Combat: Rochester distinguished himself for courage by plunging into the thick of the fighting during several sea battles; he once disgraced himself for cowardice in running away during a nocturnal street brawl, "frighted" (he later wrote) "at my own mischiefs" and leaving one of his own defenders dead. In the lesser combats of the court, those endless verbal cutting contests of improvised insult and impromptu verse, Rochester was virtually unbeatable (though the king, when cut, could cut back: the earl's status shifted often and quickly between favorite and outcast). Amorous entanglement: Rochester's letters to his wife bespeak a marriage of extraordinary tenderness; his poems boast a career of fornication scarcely credible in its range and ferocity. In 1680, ill and exhausted, Rochester left London for his ancestral country estate where, frighted by his own mischiefs on a grander scale, he pursued a highly publicized course of penitence under the tutelage of the clergyman Gilbert Burnet, who later published a detailed account of their conversations. The authenticity of this deathbed conversion was questioned then, and has been questioned since, but its results were real enough: Rochester asked his mother to burn his papers, and she did. Fewer than a hundred poems survive. Rochester had never troubled to publish any of them himself; a pirated collection appeared a few months after his death. Yet these pieces, and the conflicting accounts of the life that produced them, have been enough to make him last. Soon after his death, the poet Aphra Behn claimed in verse to have received a visit from his "lovely phantom." "The great, the god-like Rochester" comes before her in order both to praise and to correct her poetry. Since then he has haunted many—pietists, poets, and others—as object of veneration, or reproach, or both together: as admonitory example, verbal virtuoso, extraordinary mortal.

Against Constancy

Tell me no more of constancy,
  The frivolous pretense
Of cold age, narrow jealousy,
  Disease, and want of sense.

Let duller fools, on whom kind chance
  Some easy heart has thrown,
Despairing higher to advance,
  Be kind to one alone.

Old men and weak, whose idle flame
  Their own defects discovers,
Since changing can but spread their shame,
  Ought to be constant lovers.

But we, whose hearts do justly swell
  With no vainglorious pride,

Who know how we in love excel,
  Long to be often tried.

Then bring my bath, and strew my bed,
  As each kind night returns;
I'll change a mistress till I'm dead—
  And fate change me to worms.

1676

The Disabled Debauchee

As some brave admiral, in former war
  Deprived of force, but pressed with courage still,
Two rival fleets appearing from afar,
  Crawls to the top of an adjacent hill;
From whence, with thoughts full of concern, he views
  The wise and daring conduct of the fight,
Whilst each bold action to his mind renews
  His present glory and his past delight;

From his fierce eyes flashes of fire he throws,
  As from black clouds when lightning breaks away;
Transported, thinks himself amidst the foes,
  And absent, yet enjoys the bloody day;

So, when my days of impotence approach,
  And I'm by pox and wine's unlucky chance
Forced from the pleasing billows of debauch
  On the dull shore of lazy temperance,

My pains at least some respite shall afford
  While I behold the battles you maintain
When fleets of glasses sail about the board,[1]
  From whose broadsides volleys of wit shall rain.

Nor let the sight of honorable scars,
  Which my too forward valor did procure,
Frighten new-listed soldiers from the wars:
  Past joys have more than paid what I endure.

Should any youth (worth being drunk) prove nice,
  And from his fair inviter meanly shrink,
'Twill please the ghost of my departed Vice[2]
  If, at my counsel, he repent and drink.

Or should some cold-complexioned sot forbid,
  With his dull morals, our bold night-alarms,
I'll fire his blood by telling what I did
  When I was strong and able to bear arms.

1. I.e., wine glasses passed around the table.
2. A character bearing this name had been a staple figure in medieval morality plays, as the comic, scoffing incarnation of depravity.

I'll tell of whores attacked, their lords at home;
  Bawds' quarters beaten up, and fortress won;
Windows demolished, watches overcome;
  And handsome ills by my contrivance done.

Nor shall our love-fits, Chloris,[3] be forgot,
  When each the well-looked linkboy[4] strove t' enjoy,
And the best kiss was the deciding lot
  Whether the boy fucked you, or I the boy.

With tales like these I will such thoughts inspire
  As to important mischief shall incline:
I'll make him long some ancient church to fire,
  And fear no lewdness he's called to by wine.

Thus, statesmanlike, I'll saucily impose,
  And safe from action, valiantly advise;
Sheltered in impotence, urge you to blows,
  And being good for nothing else, be wise.

1675? 1680

Song

Love a woman? You're an ass!
  'Tis a most insipid passion
To choose out for your happiness
  The silliest part of God's creation.

Let the porter and the groom,
  Things designed for dirty slaves,
Drudge in fair Aurelia's womb
  To get supplies for age and graves.

Farewell, woman! I intend
  Henceforth every night to sit
With my lewd, well-natured friend,
  Drinking to engender wit.

Then give me health, wealth, mirth, and wine,
  And, if busy love entrenches,
There's a sweet, soft page of mine
  Does the trick worth forty wenches.

1680

The Imperfect Enjoyment

Naked she lay, clasped in my longing arms,
I filled with love, and she all over charms;
Both equally inspired with eager fire,
Melting through kindness, flaming in desire.

3. A woman's name, common in pastoral verse (and in Rochester's).

4. A boy employed to accompany walkers on the city streets at night, lighting their way by means of a torch ("link").

With arms, legs, lips close clinging to embrace,
She clips me to her breast, and sucks me to her face.
Her nimble tongue, Love's lesser lightning, played
Within my mouth, and to my thoughts conveyed
Swift orders that I should prepare to throw
The all-dissolving thunderbolt below.
My fluttering soul, sprung with the pointed kiss,
Hangs hovering o'er her balmy brinks of bliss.
But whilst her busy hand would guide that part
Which should convey my soul up to her heart,
In liquid raptures I dissolve all o'er,
Melt into sperm, and spend at every pore.
A touch from any part of her had done 't:
Her hand, her foot, her very look's a cunt.
Smiling, she chides in a kind murmuring noise,
And from her body wipes the clammy joys,
When, with a thousand kisses wandering o'er
My panting bosom, "Is there then no more?"
She cries. "All this to love and rapture's due;
Must we not pay a debt to pleasure too?"
But I, the most forlorn, lost man alive,
To show my wished obedience vainly strive:
I sigh, alas! and kiss, but cannot swive.° *screw*
Eager desires confound my first intent,
Succeeding shame does more success prevent,
And rage at last confirms me impotent.
Ev'n her fair hand, which might bid heat return
To frozen age, and make cold hermits burn,
Applied to my dead cinder, warms no more
Than fire to ashes could past flames restore.
Trembling, confused, despairing, limber, dry,
A wishing, weak, unmoving lump I lie.
This dart of love, whose piercing point, oft tried,
With virgin blood ten thousand maids have dyed,
Which nature still directed with such art
That it through every cunt reached every heart—
Stiffly resolved, 'twould carelessly invade
Woman or man, nor ought° its fury stayed:° *anything / stopped*
Where'er it pierced, a cunt it found or made—
Now languid lies in this unhappy hour,
Shrunk up and sapless like a withered flower.
Thou treacherous, base deserter of my flame,
False to my passion, fatal to my fame,
Through what mistaken magic dost thou prove
So true to lewdness, so untrue to love?
What oyster-cinder-beggar-common whore
Didst thou e'er fail in all thy life before?
When vice, disease, and scandal lead the way,
With what officious haste doest thou obey!

Like a rude, roaring hector° in the streets *bully*
Who scuffles, cuffs, and justles all he meets,
But if his king or country claim his aid,
The rakehell villain shrinks and hides his head;
Ev'n so thy brutal valor is displayed,
Breaks every stew,° does each small whore invade, *brothel*
But when great Love the onset does command,
Base recreant to thy prince, thou dar'st not stand.
Worst part of me, and henceforth hated most,
Through all the town a common fucking post,
On whom each whore relieves her tingling cunt
As hogs on gates do rub themselves and grunt,
Mayst thou to ravenous chancres° be a prey, *syphilis sores*
Or in consuming weepings waste away;
May strangury and stone[1] thy days attend;
May'st thou never piss, who didst refuse to spend
When all my joys did on false thee depend.
And may ten thousand abler pricks agree
To do the wronged Corinna right for thee.

1680

Upon Nothing

Nothing! thou elder brother even to Shade:
Thou hadst a being ere the world was made,
And well fixed, art alone of ending not afraid.

Ere Time and Place were, Time and Place were not,
When primitive Nothing Something straight begot;
Then all proceeded from the great united What.

Something, the general attribute of all,
Severed from thee, its sole original,
Into thy boundless self must undistinguished fall;

Yet Something did thy mighty power command,
And from thy fruitful Emptiness's hand
Snatched men, beasts, birds, fire, water, air, and land.

Matter, the wicked'st offspring of thy race,
By Form assisted, flew from thy embrace,
And rebel Light obscured thy reverend dusky face.

With Form and Matter, Time and Place did join;
Body, thy foe, with these did leagues combine
To spoil thy peaceful realm, and ruin all thy line;

But turncoat Time assists the foe in vain,
And bribed by thee, destroys their short-lived reign,
And to thy hungry womb drives back thy slaves again.

1. Painful diseases of the bladder and urinary tract that block the flow of urine.

Though mysteries are barred from laic° eyes, *uninitiated*
And the divine alone with warrant pries
Into thy bosom, where the truth in private lies,

Yet this of thee the wise may truly say:
Thou from the virtuous nothing dost delay,
And to be part of thee the wicked wisely pray.

Great Negative, how vainly would the wise
Inquire, define, distinguish, teach, devise,
Didst thou not stand to point their blind philosophies!

Is or Is Not, the two great ends of Fate,
And True or False, the subject of debate,
That perfect or destroy the vast designs of state—

When they have racked the politician's breast,
Within thy bosom most securely rest,
And when reduced to thee, are least unsafe and best.

But Nothing, why does Something still permit
That sacred monarchs should in council sit
With persons highly thought at best for nothing fit,

While weighty Something modestly abstains
From princes' coffers, and from statesmen's brains,
And Nothing there like stately Nothing reigns?

Nothing! who dwellst with fools in grave disguise,
For whom they reverend shapes and forms devise,
Lawn[1] sleeves and furs and gowns, when they like thee look wise:

French truth, Dutch prowess, British policy,
Hibernian learning, Scotch civility,
Spaniards' dispatch, Danes' wit are mainly seen in thee;

The great man's gratitude to his best friend,
Kings' promises, whores' vows—towards thee they bend,
Flow swiftly into thee, and in thee ever end.

1678 1679

A Satyr[1] Against Reason and Mankind

Were I (who to my cost already am
One of those strange, prodigious creatures, man)
A spirit free to choose, for my own share,
What case of flesh and blood I pleased to wear,
I'd be a dog, a monkey, or a bear,
Or anything but that vain animal
Who is so proud of being rational.
The senses are too gross, and he'll contrive

1. Linen; worn (like the furs and gowns) as a mark of rank by eminent professionals: lawyers, scholars, statesmen, etc.

1. Possibly a pun, identifying both the genre (satire) and the speaker (a satyr: half-man, half-animal).

A sixth, to contradict the other five,
And before certain instinct, will prefer
Reason, which fifty times for one does err;
Reason, an *ignis fatuus*[2] in the mind,
Which, leaving light of nature, sense, behind,
Pathless and dangerous wandering ways it takes
Through error's fenny bogs and thorny brakes;
Whilst the misguided follower climbs with pain
Mountains of whimseys, heaped in his own brain;
Stumbling from thought to thought, falls headlong down
Into doubt's boundless sea, where, like to drown,
Books bear him up awhile, and make him try
To swim with bladders of philosophy;
In hopes still to o'ertake th' escaping light,
The vapor dances in his dazzling sight
Till, spent, it leaves him to eternal night.
Then old age and experience, hand in hand,
Lead him to death, and make him understand,
After a search so painful and so long,
That all his life he has been in the wrong.
Huddled in dirt the reasoning engine lies,
Who was so proud, so witty, and so wise.
Pride drew him in, as cheats their bubbles° catch, *victims*
And made him venture to be made a wretch.
His wisdom did his happiness destroy,
Aiming to know that world he should enjoy.
And wit was his vain, frivolous pretense
Of pleasing others at his own expense,
For wits are treated just like common whores:
First they're enjoyed, and then kicked out of doors.
The pleasure past, a threatening doubt remains
That frights th' enjoyer with succeeding pains.
Women and men of wit are dangerous tools,
And ever fatal to admiring fools:
Pleasure allures, and when the fops escape,
'Tis not that they're belov'd, but fortunate,
And therefore what they fear at heart, they hate.
But now, methinks, some formal band and beard[3]
Takes me to task. Come on, sir; I'm prepared.
"Then, by your favor, anything that's writ
Against this gibing, jingling knack called wit
Likes° me abundantly; but you take care *pleases*
Upon this point, not to be too severe.
Perhaps my muse were fitter for this part,

2. Literally "foolish fire": a marshland phosphorescence that, appearing now here and now there, was thought to be created by sprites to mislead night travelers.

3. I.e., clergyman, wearing these marks of office. In 1675 one clergyman in particular, the king's chaplain Edward Stillingfleet, had denounced in a sermon an earlier version of Rochester's *Satyr*, prompting the poet to alter and add some portions of the dialogue that follows.

For I profess I can be very smart
On wit, which I abhor with all my heart.
I long to lash it in some sharp essay,
But your grand indiscretion bids me stay
And turns my tide of ink another way.
"What rage ferments in your degenerate mind
To make you rail at reason and mankind?
Blest, glorious man! to whom alone kind heaven
An everlasting soul has freely given,
Whom his great Maker took such care to make
That from himself he did the image take
And this fair frame in shining reason dressed
To dignify his nature above beast;
Reason, by whose aspiring influence
We take a flight beyond material sense,
Dive into mysteries, then soaring pierce
The flaming limits of the universe,
Search heaven and hell, find out what's acted there,
And give the world true grounds of hope and fear."
Hold, mighty man, I cry, all this we know
From the pathetic pen of Ingelo,
From Patrick's *Pilgrim*, Stillingfleet's replies,[4]
And 'tis this very reason I despise:
This supernatural gift, that makes a mite
Think he's the image of the infinite,
Comparing his short life, void of all rest,
To the eternal and the ever blest;
This busy, puzzling stirrer-up of doubt
That frames deep mysteries, then finds 'em out,
Filling with frantic crowds of thinking fools
Those reverend bedlams,° colleges and schools; *madhouses*
Borne on whose wings, each heavy sot can pierce
The limits of the boundless universe;
So charming ointments make an old witch fly
And bear a crippled carcass through the sky.
'Tis this exalted power, whose business lies
In nonsense and impossibilities,
This made a whimsical philosopher
Before the spacious world, his tub prefer,[5]
And we have modern cloistered coxcombs who
Retire to think, 'cause they have nought to do.
But thoughts are given for action's government;
Where action ceases, thought's impertinent.
Our sphere of action is life's happiness,

4. Rochester names three pious inspirational writers: Nathaniel Ingelo (?1621–1683); Simon Patrick, whose *Parable of the Pilgrim* appeared in 1664; and Stillingfleet, Rochester's clerical critic.

5. Diogenes (c. 400–325 B.C.E.), Greek philosopher who supposedly lived in an earthenware tub, as an emblem of his scorn for the shallowness of more opulent modes of life.

And he who thinks beyond, thinks like an ass.
Thus, whilst against false reasoning I inveigh,
I own[6] right reason, which I would obey:
That reason which distinguishes by sense
And gives us rules of good and ill from thence,
That bounds desires with a reforming will
To keep 'em more in vigor, not to kill.
Your reason hinders, mine helps to enjoy,
Renewing appetites yours would destroy.
My reason is my friend, yours is a cheat;
Hunger calls out, my reason bids me eat;
Perversely, yours your appetite does mock:
This asks for food, that answers, "What's o'clock?"
This plain distinction, sir, your doubt secures:
'Tis not true reason I despise, but yours.
  Thus I think reason righted, but for man,
I'll ne'er recant; defend him if you can.
For all his pride and his philosophy,
'Tis evident beasts are, in their degree,
As wise at least, and better far than he.
Those creatures are the wisest who attain,
By surest means, the ends at which they aim.
If therefore Jowler[7] finds and kills his hares
Better than Meres[8] supplies committee chairs,
Though one's a statesman, th' other but a hound,
Jowler, in justice, would be wiser found.
  You see how far man's wisdom here extends;
Look next if human nature makes amends:
Whose principles most generous are, and just,
And to whose morals you would sooner trust.
Be judge yourself, I'll bring it to the test:
Which is the basest creature, man or beast?
Birds feed on birds, beasts on each other prey,
But savage man alone does man betray.
Pressed by necessity, they kill for food;
Man undoes man to do himself no good.
With teeth and claws by nature armed, they hunt
Nature's allowance, to supply their want.
But man, with smiles, embraces, friendship, praise,
Inhumanly his fellow's life betrays;
With voluntary pains works his distress,
Not through necessity, but wantonness.
  For hunger or for love they fight and tear,
Whilst wretched man is still in arms for fear.
For fear he arms, and is of arms afraid,

6. Acknowledge. "Right reason" refers to natural instinct or common sense, as opposed to the more elaborate modes of thought Rochester is attacking.
7. A dog's name, emphasizing the animal's appetites.
8. Sir Thomas Meres (1634–1715), politician noted for his energy, efficacy, and self-serving flexibility in questions of party allegiance.

By fear to fear successively betrayed;
Base fear, the source whence his best passions came:
His boasted honor, and his dear-bought fame;
That lust of power, to which he's such a slave,
And for the which alone he dares be brave;
To which his various projects are designed;
Which makes him generous, affable, and kind;
For which he takes such pains to be thought wise,
And screws his actions in a forced disguise,
Leading a tedious life in misery
Under laborious, mean hypocrisy.
Look to the bottom of his vast design,
Wherein man's wisdom, power, and glory join:
The good he acts, the ill he does endure,
'Tis all from fear, to make himself secure.
Merely for safety, after fame we thirst,
For all men would be cowards if they durst.
 And honesty's against all common sense:
Men must be knaves, 'tis in their own defense.
Mankind's dishonest; if you think it fair
Amongst known cheats to play upon the square,
You'll be undone.
Nor can weak truth your reputation save:
The knaves will all agree to call you knave.
Wronged shall he live, insulted o'er, oppressed,
Who dares be less a villain than the rest.
 Thus, sir, you see what human nature craves:
Most men are cowards, all men should be knaves.
The difference lies, as far as I can see,
Not in the thing itself, but the degree,
And all the subject matter of debate
Is only: Who's a knave of the first rate?
 All this with indignation have I hurled
At the pretending part of the proud world,
Who, swollen with selfish vanity, devise
False freedoms, holy cheats, and formal lies
Over their fellow slaves to tyrannize.
But if in court so just a man there be
(In court a just man, yet unknown to me)
Who does his needful flattery direct,
Not to oppress and ruin, but protect
(Since flattery, which way soever laid,
Is still a tax on that unhappy trade);
If so upright a statesman you can find,
Whose passions bend to his unbiased mind,
Who does his arts and policies apply
To raise his country, not his family,
Nor, whilst his pride owned avarice withstands,
Receives close bribes through friends' corrupted hands—

Is there a churchman who on God relies;
Whose life, his faith and doctrine justifies?
Not one blown up with vain prelatic pride,
Who, for reproof of sins, does man deride;
Whose envious heart makes preaching a pretense,
With his obstreperous, saucy eloquence,
To chide at kings, and rail at men of sense;
None of that sensual tribe whose talents lie
In avarice, pride, sloth, and gluttony;
Who hunt good livings, but abhor good lives;
Whose lust exalted to that height arrives
They act adultery with their own wives,
And ere a score of years completed be,
Can from the lofty pulpit proudly see
Half a large parish their own progeny;
Nor doting bishop who would be adored
For domineering at the council board,
A greater fop in business at fourscore,
Fonder of serious toys, affected more,
Than the gay, glittering fool at twenty proves
With all his noise, his tawdry clothes, and loves;
    But a meek, humble man of honest sense,
Who, preaching peace, does practice continence;
Whose pious life's a proof he does believe
Mysterious truths, which no man can conceive.
If upon earth there dwell such God-like men,
I'll here recant my paradox to them,
Adore those shrines of virtue, homage pay,
And, with the rabble world, their laws obey.
    If such there be, yet grant me this at least:
Man differs more from man, than man from beast.

1674–1676 1679

William Wycherley

1641–1715

The plot of *The Country Wife* turns on a trick. The rakish Harry Horner devises a tactic calculated to secure both a cover-story and a kinky enhancement for his future seductions of other men's wives. He starts a rumor going round to the effect that he has become a eunuch; husbands will henceforth not suspect him, and wives, he trusts, will be intrigued. Early in the play, it becomes clear that Horner has tested his new disguise by making a visit to the theater. "Come," one of his friends remarks, "your appearance at the play yesterday has, I hope, hardened you for the future" as to the social consequences of his sexless new reputation. "Did I not bear it bravely?" asks Horner, pleased. "With a most theatrical impudence," answers his friend.

In London playhouses of the 1660s and the 1670s, theatrical impudence was in high supply. People came to watch not only the performers, but also each other. Pepys records a telling anecdote (so telling that it is cited also, more compactly, within a fuller discussion of

Restoration theater in the introduction to this section, page 1991). Attending a play one evening, he found himself distracted throughout the performance by the libertine Sir Charles Sedley, seated nearby in conversation with two women.

> And one of the ladies would and did sit with her mask on, all the play and, being exceedingly witty as ever I heard woman, did talk most pleasantly with him; but was, I believe, a virtuous woman and of quality. He would fain know who she was, but she would not tell; yet did give him many pleasant hints of her knowledge of him, by that means setting his brains at work to find out who she was, and did give him leave to use all means to find out who she was but pulling off her mask. He was mighty witty and she also, making sport of him very inoffensively, that a more pleasant rencontre I never heard. By that means lost the pleasure of the play wholly...

But that loss hardly seems to matter, in comparison with the pleasure of the playlet Pepys has witnessed within the audience. Masks of the kind this woman wears were a widespread item of Restoration fashion. Characters in the *Country Wife* mention them obsessively, in part because they were worn both by "virtuous" women and by prostitutes, with the tantalizing effect of rendering those two human categories not quite distinguishable from one another. In Pepys's anecdote, man and woman engage in a contest for power grounded in wit, concealment, and artifice; the new plays on stage during the Restoration teemed with just such sexually charged encounters and combats. For purposes of theatrical impudence and strategic experiment, Horner could not have picked for himself a better venue.

Neither could William Wycherley. He wrote four comedies while in his early thirties. The last two—*The Country Wife* (1675) and *The Plain Dealer* (1676)—brought him to the early high point of a career that sloped rather steeply on either side. Before these successes he had been a law-student, soldier, courtier, traveler in France, and convert to Catholicism. In their wake he was widely celebrated as the deftest wielder alive of those gifts that Dryden enumerated in a single memorable line: "The satire, wit, and strength of manly Wycherley." "Manly" was the name of the forthright protagonist in *The Plain Dealer*; the adjective alternated with "brawny" as the most popular epithets for this vigorous and accomplished playwright in his prime. But by the time Dryden wrote the line, in 1694, it applied more readily to the work than to the man. Before Wycherley turned forty, a serious illness had left his memory permanently damaged and an imprudent marriage with a widowed countess had cost him much in money, serenity, and the patronage of Charles II and his court. He spent years mired in debt, received temporary relief in the form of a pension from that temporary king James II, and found more reliable respite in the estate he inherited from his father in 1697. In old age he published a failed book of ungainly poems, held literary court at Will's Coffee House (where Dryden had previously presided), and basked in the attention of the young, ambitious Alexander Pope. Eleven days before his death he married a second time. His estate passed to his young widow and hence to his cousin, her secret lover; they had spent his last days scheming to secure it.

In the *Country Wife*, alliances prove comparably shifty. The wits (Horner and his friends), though ostensibly relentless in their pursuit of women, nonetheless seem often more interested in their transactions with each other. They array themselves against the "cits"—the prudent, prosperous businessmen of London—and chase after their desirable, precariously domesticated spouses and sisters. Horner the London rake works his charms on Margery the country wife, who proves cheerfully, even ingeniously susceptible. A group of erotically agitated women—headed by the aptly named Lady Fidget—collude with Horner in his deceit, disappear behind closed doors to savor his emphatically non-eunuchoid sexuality while pretending to sample his china, and finally team up, as a suddenly "virtuous gang," to reproach him for his perfidies. Throughout the play, Wycherley works a running comparison between sex and gambling (and, in the famous china scene, a second parallel between sex and shopping). Most of the amorous gamesters play their hands with witty fervor, but the playwright deliberately leaves unclear what exactly is at stake. Deep feelings, real risks, sturdy allegiances seem hard to come by. Most bets are placed instead on power, on cunning, on conquest, perhaps on momentary pleasure; in the end it can be hard to tell who's won, who's lost, and why. *Comedy* takes its name from *komos*, the dance of communal harmony with which so many such plays close. *The Country Wife*, by contrast, ends with a "dance of cuckolds": music for a world where fidelities are faint, and even betrayals, transpiring for muddled motives behind closed doors, are not fully comprehensible.

The Country Wife

Prologue, *spoken by* Mr. Hart[1]

Poets, like cudgeled bullies, never do
At first or second blow submit to you;
But will provoke you still, and ne'er have done,
Till you are weary first with laying on.
The late so baffled scribbler[2] of this day,
Though he stands trembling, bids me boldly say,
What we before most plays are used to do,
For poets out of fear first draw on you;
In a fierce prologue the still pit defy
And ere you speak, like Castril,[3] give the lie.
But though our Bayes's battles[4] oft I've fought,
And with bruised knuckles their dear conquests bought;
Nay, never yet feared odds upon the stage,
In prologue dare not hector with the age,
But would take quarter from your saving hands,
Though Bayes within[5] all yielding countermands,
Says you confederate wits[6] no quarter give,
Therefore his play shan't ask your leave to live.
Well, let the vain rash fop, by huffing[7] so,
Think to obtain the better terms of you;
But we the actors humbly will submit,
Now, and at any time, to a full pit;
Nay, often we anticipate your rage,
And murder poets for you on our stage.
We set no guards upon our tiring-room,[8]
But when with flying colors there you come,
We patiently, you see, give up to you
Our poets, virgins, nay, our matrons too.

1. Charles Hart, who starred as Horner in the first production, was famous both as actor and as lover. As actor, he achieved some of his greatest successes playing the preternaturally virile and virtuous protagonists in Dryden's heroic tragedies. As lover, he had been linked with eminent beauties, including Nell Gwyn and Lady Castlemaine (for Pepys's comments on both, see pages 2018 and 2031).
2. Refers to the cold reception of *The Gentleman Dancing Master*, which Wycherley himself recognized as a trivial work.
3. An angry character in Ben Jonson's *The Alchemist* (1610), who impulsively challenges ("gives the lie" to) others.
4. The battles that Hart had "fought" onstage in his roles as soldier-hero in Dryden's tragedies, and also the struggles of writers in general (and Wycherley in particular) to secure approval of their work. Bayes was the central character in the Duke of Buckingham's comedy *The Rehearsal* (1671): a foolish, preening playwright, he incarnated in every particular a merciless, hilarious parody of Dryden. His name soon became a mocking designation for any ambitious poet.
5. I.e., Wycherley, backstage.
6. Critics conjoined to condemn the play.
7. Blustering.
8. Dressing-room.

The Persons

MR. HORNER
MR. HARCOURT
MR. DORILANT
MR. PINCHWIFE
MR. SPARKISH
SIR JASPAR FIDGET
MRS. MARGERY PINCHWIFE
MRS. ALITHEA
MY LADY FIDGET
MRS. DAINTY FIDGET
MRS. SQUEAMISH
OLD LADY SQUEAMISH
WAITERS, SERVANTS, AND ATTENDANTS
A BOY
A QUACK
LUCY, ALITHEA'S MAID
[CLASP]
[A PARSON]

The Scene: London

ACT 1

Scene 1

[Enter Horner, and Quack following him at a distance.]

HORNER [*aside*]: A quack is as fit for a pimp as a midwife for a bawd;[1] they are still[2] but in their way both helpers of nature.—Well, my dear doctor, hast thou done what I desired?

QUACK: I have undone you forever with the women, and reported you throughout the whole town as bad as an eunuch, with as much trouble as if I had made you one in earnest.

HORNER: But have you told all the midwives you know, the orange-wenches[3] at the playhouses, the city husbands,[4] and old fumbling keepers[5] of this end of the town? For they'll be the readiest to report it.

QUACK: I have told all the chambermaids, waiting-women, tire-women[6] and old women of my acquaintance; nay, and whispered it as a secret to 'em, and to the whisperers of Whitehall;[7] so that you need not doubt, 'twill spread, and you will be as odious to the handsome young women as—

HORNER: As the smallpox. Well—

QUACK: And to the married women of this end of the town as—

HORNER: As the great ones;[8] nay, as their own husbands.

QUACK: And to the city dames as aniseed Robin[9] of filthy and contemptible memory; and they will frighten their children with your name, especially their females.

HORNER: And cry, "Horner's coming to carry you away." I am only afraid 'twill not be believed. You told 'em 'twas by an English–French disaster and an English–French chirurgeon,[1] who has given me at once, not only a cure, but an antidote[2] for the future against that damned malady, and that worse distemper, love, and all other women's evils.

1. Brothel-keeper.
2. Always.
3. Orange-sellers.
4. Respectable men of business who (according to stereotype) would loathe the likes of Horner.
5. Men who keep mistresses.
6. Ladies' maids, also dressmakers.
7. The royal residence, a center for news and gossip.
8. Syphilis.
9. A famous hermaphrodite; hence (from the vantage of respectable "city dames") a repellent monster.
1. In muddled phrasing, Horner appears to blame both English and French personnel (women, doctors) for both his supposed illness (syphilis, often called "the French pox") and its drastic cure. The muddle may be intentional; Horner is, after all, making up the whole story.
2. I.e., his purported impotence.

QUACK: Your late journey into France has made it the more credible and your being here a fortnight before you appeared in public looks as if you apprehended the shame, which I wonder you do not. Well, I have been hired by young gallants to belie 'em t' other way, but you are the first would be thought a man unfit for women.

HORNER: Dear Mr. Doctor, let vain rogues be contented only to be thought abler men than they are, generally 'tis all the pleasure they have; but mine lies another way.

QUACK: You take, methinks, a very preposterous way to it and as ridiculous as if we operators in physic should put forth bills to disparage our medicaments, with hopes to gain customers.

HORNER: Doctor, there are quacks in love as well as physic, who get but the fewer and worse patients for their boasting; a good name is seldom got by giving it oneself, and women no more than honor are compassed[3] by bragging. Come, come, doctor, the wisest lawyer never discovers[4] the merits of his cause till the trial; the wealthiest man conceals his riches, and the cunning gamester his play. Shy husbands and keepers, like old rooks,[5] are not to be cheated but by a new unpracticed trick; false friendship will pass now no more than false dice upon 'em; no, not in the city. [*Enter Boy*.]

BOY: There are two ladies and a gentleman coming up. [*Exit.*]

HORNER: A pox! Some unbelieving sisters of my former acquaintance, who, I am afraid, expect their sense should be satisfied of the falsity of the report. No—this formal[6] fool and women!

[*Enter Sir Jaspar Fidget, Lady Fidget, and Mrs. Dainty Fidget*.]

QUACK: His wife and sister.

SIR JASPAR: My coach breaking just now before your door, sir, I look upon as an occasional[7] reprimand to me, sir, for not kissing your hands, sir, since your coming out of France, sir; and so my disaster, sir, has been my good fortune, sir; and this is my wife, and sister, sir.

HORNER: What then, sir?

SIR JASPAR: My lady, and sister, sir.—Wife, this is Master Horner.

LADY FIDGET: Master Horner, husband!

SIR JASPAR: My lady, my Lady Fidget, sir.

HORNER: So, sir.

SIR JASPAR: Won't you be acquainted with her, sir? [*Aside*.] So the report is true, I find, by his coldness or aversion to the sex; but I'll play the wag with him.—Pray salute my wife, my lady, sir.

HORNER: I will kiss no man's wife, sir, for him, sir; I have taken my eternal leave, sir, of the sex already, sir.

SIR JASPAR [*aside*]: Hah, hah, hah! I'll plague him yet.—Not know my wife, sir?

HORNER: I do know your wife, sir; she's a woman, sir, and consequently a monster, sir, a greater monster than a husband, sir.

SIR JASPAR: A husband! How, sir?

HORNER [*makes horns*[8]]: So, sir; but I make no more cuckolds, sir.

3. Won.
4. Reveals.
5. Cheats, swindlers.
6. Unduly ceremonious, stiff.
7. Opportune.
8. With forefingers on the forehead, the cuckold sign.

SIR JASPAR: Hah, hah, hah! Mercury, Mercury![9]

LADY FIDGET: Pray, Sir Jaspar, let us be gone from this rude fellow.

DAINTY: Who, by his breeding, would think he had ever been in France?

LADY FIDGET: Foh, he's but too much a French fellow,[1] such as hate women of quality and virtue for their love to their husbands, Sir Jaspar; a woman is hated by 'em as much for loving her husband as for loving their money. But pray, let's be gone.

HORNER: You do well, madam, for I have nothing that you came for; I have brought over not so much as a bawdy picture, new postures,[2] nor the second part of the *École des Filles*,[3] nor—

QUACK [*apart to Horner*]: Hold, for shame, sir! What d'ye mean? You'll ruin yourself forever with the sex—

SIR JASPAR: Hah, hah, hah, he hates women perfectly, I find.

DAINTY: What a pity 'tis he should.

LADY FIDGET: Ay, he's a base, rude fellow for't; but affectation makes not a woman more odious to them than virtue.

HORNER: Because your virtue is your greatest affectation madam.

LADY FIDGET: How, you saucy fellow! Would you wrong my honor?

HORNER: If I could.

LADY FIDGET: How d'ye mean, sir?

SIR JASPAR: Hah, hah, hah! No, he can't wrong your ladyship's honor, upon my honor; he, poor man—hark you in your ear—a mere eunuch.

LADY FIDGET: O filthy French beast, foh, foh! Why do we stay? Let's be gone; I can't endure the sight of him.

SIR JASPAR: Stay but till the chairs[4] come; they'll be here presently.

LADY FIDGET: No, no.

SIR JASPAR: Nor can I stay longer. 'Tis—let me see, a quarter and a half quarter of a minute past eleven; the Council[5] will be sat, I must away. Business must be preferred always before love and ceremony with the wise, Mr. Horner.

HORNER: And the impotent, Sir Jaspar.

SIR JASPAR: Ay, ay, the impotent, Master Horner, hah, ha, ha!

LADY FIDGET: What, leave us with a filthy man alone in his lodgings?

SIR JASPAR: He's an innocent man now, you know. Pray stay, I'll hasten the chairs to you.—Mr. Horner, your servant; I should be glad to see you at my house. Pray come and dine with me, and play at cards with my wife after dinner; you are fit for women at that game yet, hah, ha! [*Aside.*] 'Tis as much a husband's prudence to provide innocent diversion for a wife as to hinder her unlawful pleasures, and he had better employ her than let her employ herself.—Farewell. [*Exit Sir Jaspar.*]

HORNER: Your servant, Sir Jaspar.

LADY FIDGET: I will not stay with him, foh!

HORNER: Nay, madam, I beseech you stay, if it be but to see I can be as civil to ladies yet as they would desire.

LADY FIDGET: No, no, foh, you cannot be civil to ladies.

9. Both the messenger-god, whose winged hat Horner's "horns" may call to mind, and the chemical often used in treating syphilis.
1. Fop.
2. Pornographic engravings.
3. A pornographic dialogue between a virgin and an experienced woman (1655); Pepys called it "the most bawdy, lewd book that I ever saw."
4. Sedan chairs, in which two bearers carried a single passenger.
5. Privy Council.

DAINTY: You as civil as ladies would desire?

LADY FIDGET: No, no, no, foh, foh, foh!

[*Exeunt Lady Fidget and Dainty.*]

QUACK: Now, I think, I, or you yourself rather, have done your business[6] with the women.

HORNER: Thou art an ass. Don't you see already, upon the report and my carriage,[7] this grave man of business leaves his wife in my lodgings, invites me to his house and wife, who before would not be acquainted with me out of jealousy?

QUACK: Nay, by this means you may be the more acquainted with the husbands, but the less with the wives.

HORNER: Let me alone; if I can but abuse the husbands, I'll soon disabuse the wives. Stay—I'll reckon you up the advantages I am like to have by my stratagem: first, I shall be rid of all my old acquaintances, the most insatiable sorts of duns,[8] that invade our lodgings in a morning. And next to the pleasure of making a new mistress is that of being rid of an old one; and of all old debts, love, when it comes to be so, is paid the most unwillingly.

QUACK: Well, you may be so rid of your old acquaintances; but how will you get any new ones?

HORNER: Doctor, thou wilt never make a good chemist, thou art so incredulous and impatient. Ask but all the young fellows of the town if they do not lose more time, like huntsmen, in starting the game than in running it down; one knows not where to find 'em, who will or will not. Women of quality are so civil, you can hardly distinguish love from good breeding and a man is often mistaken; but now I can be sure, she that shows an aversion to me loves the sport, as those women that are gone, whom I warrant to be right.[9] And then the next thing is, your women of honor, as you call 'em, are only chary[1] of their reputations, not their persons, and 'tis scandal they would avoid, not men. Now may I have, by the reputation of an eunuch, the privileges of one and be seen in a lady's chamber in a morning as early as her husband, kiss virgins before their parents or lovers and may be, in short, the *passe partout*[2] of the town. Now, doctor.

QUACK: Nay, now you shall be the doctor; and your process is so new that we do not know but it may succeed.

HORNER: Not so new neither; *probatum est*,[3] doctor.

QUACK: Well, I wish you luck and many patients whilst I go to mine. [*Exit Quack.*] [*Enter Harcourt and Dorilant to Horner.*]

HARCOURT: Come, your appearance at the play yesterday has, I hope, hardened you for the future against the women's contempt and the men's raillery and now you'll abroad as you were wont.

HORNER: Did I not bear it bravely?

DORILANT: With a most theatrical impudence; nay, more than the orange-wenches show there or a drunken vizard-mask[4] or a great-bellied actress; nay, or the most impudent of creatures, an ill poet; or what is yet more impudent, a secondhand critic.

6. Spoiled your reputation.
7. Conduct.
8. Persistent creditors.
9. Ripe for play, promiscuous.
1. Careful, wary.
2. One who may go anywhere.
3. "It has been proved or tested," a phrase used in prescriptions.
4. A prostitute; many of them wore masks, as emblems of their trade.

HORNER: But what say the ladies? Have they no pity?

HARCOURT: What ladies? The vizard-masks, you know, never pity a man when all's gone, though in their service.

DORILANT: And for the women in the boxes, you'd never pity them when 'twas in your power.

HARCOURT: They say, 'tis pity, but all that deal with common women should be served so.

DORILANT: Nay, I dare swear, they won't admit you to play at cards with them, go to plays with 'em, or do the little duties which other shadows of men are wont to do for 'em.

HORNER: Who do you call shadows of men?

DORILANT: Half-men.

HORNER: What, boys?

DORILANT: Ay, your old boys, old *beaux garçons*,[5] who, like superannuated[6] stallions, are suffered to run, feed and whinny with the mares as long as they live, though they can do nothing else.

HORNER: Well, a pox on love and wenching! Women serve but to keep a man from better company; though I can't enjoy them, I shall you the more. Good fellowship and friendship are lasting, rational and manly pleasures.

HARCOURT: For all that, give me some of those pleasures you call effeminate too; they help to relish one another.

HORNER: They disturb one another.

HARCOURT: No, mistresses are like books. If you pore upon them too much, they doze[7] you and make you unfit for company; but if used discreetly, you are the fitter for conversation by 'em.

DORILANT: A mistress should be like a little country retreat near the town, not to dwell in constantly, but only for a night and away, to taste the town the better when a man returns.

HORNER: I tell you, 'tis as hard to be a good fellow, a good friend and a lover of women, as 'tis to be a good fellow, a good friend and a lover of money. You cannot follow both, then choose your side. Wine gives you liberty, love takes it away.

DORILANT: Gad, he's in the right on't.

HORNER: Wine gives you joy; love, grief and tortures, besides the chirurgeon's. Wine makes us witty; love, only sots. Wine makes us sleep; love breaks it.

DORILANT: By the world, he has reason,[8] Harcourt.

HORNER: Wine makes—

DORILANT: Ay, wine makes us—makes us princes; love makes us beggars, poor rogues, egad—and wine—

HORNER: So, there's one converted.—No, no, love and wine, oil and vinegar.

HARCOURT: I grant it; love will still be uppermost.

HORNER: Come, for my part I will have only those glorious, manly pleasures of being very drunk and very slovenly. [*Enter Boy.*]

BOY: Mr. Sparkish is below, sir. [*Exit.*]

HARCOURT: What, my dear friend! A rogue that is fond of me only, I think, for abusing him.

DORILANT: No, he can no more think the men laugh at him than that women jilt[9] him, his opinion of himself is so good.

5. Old gallants.
6. Old and infirm.
7. Stupefy.
8. Speaks truth (French *il a raison:* "he is right").
9. Reject.

HORNER: Well, there's another pleasure by drinking I thought not of: I shall lose his acquaintance, because he cannot drink; and you know 'tis a very hard thing to be rid of him, for he's one of those nauseous offerers at wit, who, like the worst fiddlers, run themselves into all companies.

HARCOURT: One that, by being in the company of men of sense, would pass for one.

HORNER: And may so to the short-sighted world, as a false jewel amongst true ones is not discerned at a distance. His company is as troublesome to us as a cuckold's when you have a mind to his wife's.

HARCOURT: No, the rogue will not let us enjoy one another, but ravishes our conversation, though he signifies no more to't than Sir Martin Mar-all's[1] gaping and awkward thrumming upon the lute does to his man's voice and music.

DORILANT: And to pass for a wit in town shows himself a fool every night to us that are guilty of the plot.

HORNER: Such wits as he are, to a company of reasonable men, like rooks[2] to the gamesters, who only fill a room[3] at the table, but are so far from contributing to the play that they only serve to spoil the fancy of those that do.

DORILANT: Nay, they are used like rooks too, snubbed, checked and abused; yet the rogues will hang on.

HORNER: A pox on 'em, and all that force nature and would be still what she forbids 'em! Affectation is her greatest monster.

HARCOURT: Most men are the contraries to that they would seem. Your bully, you see, is a coward with a long sword; the little, humbly fawning physician, with his ebony cane, is he that destroys men.

DORILANT: The usurer, a poor rogue possessed of moldy bonds and mortgages, and we they call spendthrifts are only wealthy, who lay out his money upon daily new purchases of pleasure.

HORNER: Ay, your arrantest cheat is your trustee or executor; your jealous man, the greatest cuckold; your churchman, the greatest atheist; and your noisy, pert rogue of a wit, the greatest fop, dullest ass and worst company, as you shall see: for here he comes.

[*Enter Sparkish to them.*]

SPARKISH: How is't, sparks,[4] how is't? Well, faith, Harry, I must rally[5] thee a little, ha, ha, ha, upon the report in town of thee, ha, ha, ha, I can't hold i'faith; shall I speak?

HORNER: Yes, but you'll be so bitter then.

SPARKISH: Honest Dick and Frank here shall answer for me, I will not be extreme bitter, by the universe.

HARCOURT: We will be bound in ten thousand pound bond, he shall not be bitter at all.

DORILANT: Nor sharp, nor sweet.

HORNER: What, not downright insipid?

SPARKISH: Nay then, since you are so brisk and provoke me, take what follows. You must know, I was discoursing and rallying with some ladies yesterday, and they happened to talk of the fine new signs[6] in town.

1. Foolish title character of Dryden's comedy (1667) who lip-synchs and fake-strums a serenade to his mistress while his "man" (servant), hidden, actually performs the song. When his servant finishes playing, Sir Martin fails to quit miming. Harcourt regards Sparkish as such another empty fraud.

2. Here, simpletons, fools.

3. Space.

4. Fashionable young men; the term is usually derogatory, but Sparkish speaks it in fellowship.

5. Mock, tease.

6. Indicating the business of a shop.

HORNER: Very fine ladies, I believe.
SPARKISH: Said I, "I know where the best new sign is." "Where?" says one of the ladies. "In Covent Garden,"[7] I replied. Said another, "In what street?" "In Russell Street," answered I. "Lord," says another, "I'm sure there was ne'er a fine new sign there yesterday." "Yes, but there was," said I again, "and it came out of France and has been there a fortnight."
DORILANT: A pox, I can hear no more, prithee.
HORNER: No, hear him out; let him tune his crowd[8] a while.
HARCOURT: The worst music, the greatest preparation.
SPARKISH: Nay, faith, I'll make you laugh. "It cannot be," says a third lady. "Yes, yes," quoth I again. Says a fourth lady—
HORNER: Look to't, we'll have no more ladies.
SPARKISH: No—then mark, mark, now. Said I to the fourth, "Did you never see Mr. Horner? He lodges in Russell Street, and he's a sign of a man, you know, since he came out of France." Heh, hah, he!
HORNER: But the devil take me, if thine be the sign of a jest.
SPARKISH: With that they all fell a-laughing, till they bepissed themselves. What, but it does not move you, methinks? Well, I see one had as good go to law without a witness as break a jest without a laugher on one's side. Come, come, sparks, but where do we dine? I have left at Whitehall an earl to dine with you.
DORILANT: Why, I thought thou hadst loved a man with a title better than a suit with a French trimming to't.
HARCOURT: Go, to him again.
SPARKISH: No, sir, a wit to me is the greatest title in the world.
HORNER: But go dine with your earl, sir; he may be exceptious.[9] We are your friends and will not take it ill to be left, I do assure you.
HARCOURT: Nay, faith, he shall go to him.
SPARKISH: Nay, pray, gentlemen.
DORILANT: We'll thrust you out, if you wo'not. What, disappoint anybody for us?
SPARKISH: Nay, dear gentlemen, hear me.
HORNER: No, no, sir, by no means; pray go, sir.
SPARKISH: Why, dear rogues—
DORILANT: No, no.
[*They all thrust him out of the room.*]
ALL: Ha, ha, ha!
[*Sparkish returns.*]
SPARKISH: But, sparks, pray hear me. What, d'ye think I'll eat then with gay, shallow fops and silent coxcombs? I think wit as necessary at dinner as a glass of good wine, and that's the reason I never have any stomach when I eat alone.—Come, but where do we dine?
HORNER: Even where you will.
SPARKISH: At Chateline's?[1]
DORILANT: Yes, if you will.
SPARKISH: Or at the Cock?[2]

7. The most fashionable area of London, teeming with theaters, taverns, and shops.
8. Fiddle.
9. Peevish.
1. A famous French ordinary, or restaurant, in Covent Garden.
2. Probably the Cock Tavern in Bow Street, where Wycherley himself spent time.

DORILANT: Yes, if you please.

SPARKISH: Or at the Dog and Partridge?[3]

HORNER: Ay, if you have a mind to't, for we shall dine at neither.

SPARKISH: Pshaw, with your fooling we shall lose the new play; and I would no more miss seeing a new play the first day than I would miss setting in the wits' row. Therefore I'll go fetch my mistress and away.

[*Exit Sparkish. Manent*[4] *Horner, Harcourt, Dorilant. Enter to them Mr. Pinchwife.*]

HORNER: Who have we here? Pinchwife?

PINCHWIFE: Gentlemen, your humble servant.

HORNER: Well, Jack, by the long absence from the town, the grumness of thy countenance and the slovenliness of thy habit, I should give thee joy, should I not, of marriage?

PINCHWIFE [*aside*]: Death! Does he know I'm married too? I thought to have concealed it from him at least.—My long stay in the country will excuse my dress and I have a suit of law, that brings me up to town, that puts me out of humor, besides, I must give Sparkish tomorrow five thousand pound[5] to lie with my sister.

HORNER: Nay, you country gentlemen, rather than not purchase, will buy anything; and he is a cracked title,[6] if we may quibble. Well, but am I to give thee joy? I heard thou wert married.

PINCHWIFE: What then?

HORNER: Why, the next thing that is to be heard is thou'rt a cuckold.

PINCHWIFE [*aside*]: Insupportable name!

HORNER: But I did not expect marriage from such a whoremaster[7] as you, one that knew the town so much and women so well.

PINCHWIFE: Why, I have married no London wife.

HORNER: Pshaw, that's all one; that grave circumspection in marrying a country wife is like refusing a deceitful, pampered Smithfield jade[8] to go and be cheated by a friend in the country.

PINCHWIFE [*aside*]: A pox on him and his simile.—At least we are a little surer of the breed there, know what her keeping has been, whether foiled[9] or unsound.

HORNER: Come, come, I have known a clap[1] gotten in Wales; and there are cozens,[2] justices, clerks and chaplains in the country, I won't say coachmen. But she's handsome and young?

PINCHWIFE [*aside*]: I'll answer as I should do.—No, no, she has no beauty but her youth; no attraction but her modesty; wholesome, homely and house-wifely; that's all.

DORILANT: He talks as like a grazier[3] as he looks.

PINCHWIFE: She's too awkward, ill-favored and silly to bring to town.

HARCOURT: Then methinks you should bring her, to be taught breeding.

PINCHWIFE: To be taught! No, sir! I thank you. Good wives and private soldiers should be ignorant. [*Aside*.] I'll keep her from your instructions, I warrant you.

HARCOURT [*aside*]: The rogue is as jealous as if his wife were not ignorant.

3. A tavern in Fleet Street; the least fashionable of the places Sparkish suggests.
4. Remain.
5. As a dowry.
6. I.e., Sparkish owns shoddy property, has a weak claim to it, and is himself a bad bargain.
7. A man who consorts with whores and is given to lechery.
8. Broken-down horse bought at Smithfield Market, where the sellers were often swindlers; here a metaphor for disreputable women purchased at far too high a price.
9. With reference to a horse, injured; to a woman, deflowered.
1. Gonorrhea.
2. Cheaters.
3. One who feeds cattle for market.

HORNER: Why, if she be ill-favoured, there will be less danger here for you than by leaving her in the country; we have such variety of dainties that we are seldom hungry.

DORILANT: But they have always coarse, constant, swingeing stomachs[4] in the country.

HARCOURT: Foul feeders indeed.

DORILANT: And your hospitality is great there.

HARCOURT: Open house, every man's welcome.

PINCHWIFE: So, so, gentlemen.

HORNER: But, prithee, why wouldst thou marry her? If she be ugly, ill-bred and silly, she must be rich then.

PINCHWIFE: As rich as if she brought me twenty thousand pound out of this town, for she'll be as sure not to spend her moderate portion as a London baggage would be to spend hers, let it be what it would; so 'tis all one. Then, because she's ugly, she's the likelier to be my own; and being ill-bred, she'll have conversation; and since silly and innocent, will not know the difference betwixt a man of one-and-twenty and one of forty.

HORNER: None—to my knowledge; but if she be silly, she'll expect as much from a man of forty-nine as from him of one-and-twenty. But methinks wit is more necessary than beauty, and I think no young woman ugly that has it, and no handsome woman agreeable without it.

PINCHWIFE: 'Tis my maxim, he's a fool that marries, but he's a greater that does not marry a fool. What is wit in a wife good for, but to make a man a cuckold?

HORNER: Yes, to keep it from his knowledge.

PINCHWIFE: A fool cannot contrive to make her husband a cuckold.

HORNER: No, but she'll club[5] with a man that can; and what is worse, if she cannot make her husband a cuckold, she'll make him jealous and pass for one, and then 'tis all one.

PINCHWIFE: Well, well, I'll take care for one, my wife shall make me no cuckold, though she had your help, Mr. Horner; I understand the town, sir.

DORILANT [*aside*]: His help!

HARCOURT [*aside*]: He's come newly to town, it seems, and has not heard how things are with him.

HORNER: But tell me, has marriage cured thee of whoring, which it seldom does?

HARCOURT: 'Tis more than age can do.

HORNER: No, the word is, I'll marry and live honest; but a marriage vow is like a penitent gamester's oath and entering into bonds and penalties to stint himself to such a particular small sum at play for the future, which makes him but the more eager and, not being able to hold out, loses his money again and his forfeit to boot.

DORILANT: Ay, ay, a gamester will be a gamester whilst his money lasts, and a whoremaster whilst his vigor.

HARCOURT: Nay, I have known 'em, when they are broke and can lose no more, keep a-fumbling with the box[6] in their hands to fool with only and hinder other gamesters.

4. Immense appetites.
5. Associate.
6. For throwing dice in gaming; also slang for vagina. Parallels between gambling and sex recur throughout the play.

DORILANT: That had wherewithal to make lusty stakes.

PINCHWIFE: Well, gentlemen, you may laugh at me, but you shall never lie with my wife; I know the town.

HORNER: But prithee, was not the way you were in better? Is not keeping better than marriage?

PINCHWIFE: A pox on't! The jades would jilt me; I could never keep a whore to myself.

HORNER: So, then you only married to keep a whore to yourself. Well, but let me tell you, women, as you say, are like soldiers, made constant and loyal by good pay rather than by oaths and covenants. Therefore I'd advise my friends to keep rather than marry, since too, I find, by your example, it does not serve one's turn, for I saw you yesterday in the eighteen-penny place[7] with a pretty country wench.

PINCHWIFE [*aside*]: How the devil! Did he see my wife then? I sat there that she might not be seen. But she shall never go to a play again.

HORNER: What, dost thou blush at nine-and-forty, for having been seen with a wench?

DORILANT: No, faith, I warrant 'twas his wife, which he seated there out of sight, for he's a cunning rogue and understands the town.

HARCOURT: He blushes. Then 'twas his wife, for men are now more ashamed to be seen with them in public than with a wench.

PINCHWIFE [*aside*]: Hell and damnation! I'm undone, since Horner has seen her and they know 'twas she.

HORNER: But prithee, was it thy wife? She was exceedingly pretty; I was in love with her at that distance.

PINCHWIFE: You are like never to be nearer to her. Your servant, gentlemen. [*Offers to go.*]

HORNER: Nay, prithee stay.

PINCHWIFE: I cannot, I will not.

HORNER: Come, you shall dine with us.

PINCHWIFE: I have dined already.

HORNER: Come, I know thou hast not. I'll treat thee, dear rogue; thou shalt spend none of thy Hampshire[8] money today.

PINCHWIFE [*aside*]: Treat me! So, he uses me already like his cuckold.

HORNER: Nay, you shall not go.

PINCHWIFE: I must, I have business at home. [*Exit Pinchwife.*]

HARCOURT: To beat his wife; he's as jealous of her as a Cheapside[9] husband of a Covent Garden wife.

HORNER: Why, 'tis as hard to find an old whoremaster without jealousy and the gout, as a young one without fear or the pox.

As gout in age from pox in youth proceeds,
So wenching past, then jealousy succeeds,
The worst disease that love and wenching breeds.

[*Exeunt.*]

7. The middle gallery of the playhouse occupied by (among others) clerks, merchants, and prostitutes.
8. The rural county in south-central England where Pinchwife now lives.
9. City-merchant (Cheapside was a center of finance).

ACT 2

Scene 1

[*Mrs. Margery Pinchwife and Alithea. Mr. Pinchwife peeping behind at the door.*]

MRS. PINCHWIFE: Pray, sister, where are the best fields and woods to walk in, in London?

ALITHEA: A pretty question! Why, sister, Mulberry Garden and St. James's Park[1] and, for close walks, the New Exchange.[2]

MRS. PINCHWIFE: Pray, sister, tell me why my husband looks so grum[3] here in town and keeps me up so close and will not let me go a-walking, nor let me wear my best gown yesterday.

ALITHEA: Oh, he's jealous, sister.

MRS. PINCHWIFE: Jealous? What's that?

ALITHEA: He's afraid you should love another man.

MRS. PINCHWIFE: How should he be afraid of my loving another man, when he will not let me see any but himself?

ALITHEA: Did he not carry you yesterday to a play?

MRS. PINCHWIFE: Ay, but we sat amongst ugly people; he would not let me come near the gentry, who sat under us, so that I could not see 'em. He told me none but naughty women sat there, whom they toused and moused.[4] But I would have ventured for all that.

ALITHEA: But how did you like the play?

MRS. PINCHWIFE: Indeed, I was a-weary of the play, but I liked hugeously the actors; they are the goodliest, properest men, sister!

ALITHEA: O, but you must not like the actors, sister.

MRS. PINCHWIFE: Ay, how should I help it, sister? Pray, sister, when my husband comes in, will you ask leave for me to go a-walking?

ALITHEA [*aside*]: A-walking, hah, ha! Lord, a country gentlewoman's leisure is the drudgery of a foot-post;[5] and she requires as much airing as her husband's horses.

[*Enter Mr. Pinchwife to them.*]

But here comes your husband; I'll ask, though I'm sure he'll not grant it.

MRS. PINCHWIFE: He says he won't let me go abroad for fear of catching the pox.

ALITHEA: Fie! The smallpox you should say.

MRS. PINCHWIFE: O my dear, dear bud, welcome home! Why dost thou look so fropish? Who has nangered[6] thee?

PINCHWIFE: You're a fool.

[*Mrs. Pinchwife goes aside and cries.*]

ALITHEA: Faith, so she is, for crying for no fault, poor tender creature!

PINCHWIFE: What, you would have her as impudent as yourself, as arrant a jill-flirt, a gadder, a magpie[7] and, to say all, a mere notorious town-woman?

ALITHEA: Brother, you are my only censurer; and the honor of your family shall sooner suffer in your wife there than in me, though I take the innocent liberty of the town.

1. Popular places for gathering, strolling and savoring sights, talk, and entertainment.
2. This elegant arcade, with its covered ("close") walkways, served as *the* center for fashionable London shopping. The second scene in Act 3 takes place there.
3. Gloomy, surly.
4. Pulled about good-naturedly, but roughly.
5. A walking message-carrier.
6. Baby-talk: *fropish*, irritable; *nangered*, angered.
7. A wanton girl, a rover, a chatterer.

PINCHWIFE: Hark you, mistress, do not talk so before my wife. The innocent liberty of the town!

ALITHEA: Why, pray, who boasts of any intrigue with me? What lampoon[8] has made my name notorious? What ill women frequent my lodgings? I keep no company with any women of scandalous reputations.

PINCHWIFE: No, you keep the men of scandalous reputations company.

ALITHEA: Where? Would you not have me civil? Answer 'em in a box at the plays? In the drawing room at Whitehall? In St. James's Park? Mulberry Gardens? Or—

PINCHWIFE: Hold, hold! Do not teach my wife where the men are to be found! I believe she's the worse for your town documents[9] already. I bid you keep her in ignorance, as I do.

MRS. PINCHWIFE: Indeed, be not angry with her, bud; she will tell me nothing of the town, though I ask her a thousand times a day.

PINCHWIFE: Then you are very inquisitive to know, I find!

MRS. PINCHWIFE: Not I, indeed, dear; I hate London. Our place-house[1] in the country is worth a thousand of't; would I were there again!

PINCHWIFE: So you shall, I warrant. But were you not talking of plays and players when I came in? [*To Alithea.*] You are her encourager in such discourses.

MRS. PINCHWIFE: No, indeed, dear; she chid me just now for liking the playermen.

PINCHWIFE [*aside*]: Nay, if she be so innocent as to own to me her liking them, there is no hurt in't.—Come, my poor rogue, but thou lik'st none better than me?

MRS. PINCHWIFE: Yes, indeed, but I do; the playermen are finer folks.

PINCHWIFE: But you love none better than me?

MRS. PINCHWIFE: You are mine own dear bud, and I know you; I hate a stranger.

PINCHWIFE: Ay, my dear, you must love me only and not be like the naughty town-women, who only hate their husbands and love every man else, love plays, visits, fine coaches, fine clothes, fiddles, balls, treats, and so lead a wicked town-life.

MRS. PINCHWIFE: Nay, if to enjoy all these things be a town-life, London is not so bad a place, dear.

PINCHWIFE: How! If you love me, you must hate London.

ALITHEA [*aside*]: The fool has forbid me discovering to her the pleasures of the town and he is now setting her agog upon them himself.

MRS. PINCHWIFE: But, husband, do the town-women love the playermen too?

PINCHWIFE: Yes, I warrant you.

MRS. PINCHWIFE: Ay, I warrant you.

PINCHWIFE: Why, you do not, I hope?

MRS. PINCHWIFE: No, no, bud; but why have we no playermen in the country?

PINCHWIFE: Ha—Mrs. Minx, ask me no more to go to a play.

MRS. PINCHWIFE: Nay, why, love? I did not care for going; but when you forbid me, you make me, as 'twere, desire it.

ALITHEA [*aside*]: So 'twill be in other things, I warrant.

MRS. PINCHWIFE: Pray let me go to a play, dear.

PINCHWIFE: Hold your peace, I wo'not.

MRS. PINCHWIFE: Why, love?

PINCHWIFE: Why, I'll tell you.

8. Scurrilous satire.
9. Teachings about fashionable life.
1. Grand home.

ALITHEA [*aside*]: Nay, if he tell her, she'll give him more cause to forbid her that place.

MRS. PINCHWIFE: Pray, why, dear?

PINCHWIFE: First, you like the actors and the gallants may like you.

MRS. PINCHWIFE: What, a homely country girl? No, bud, nobody will like me.

PINCHWIFE: I tell you, yes, they may.

MRS. PINCHWIFE: No, no, you jest—I won't believe you, I will go.

PINCHWIFE: I tell you then that one of the lewdest fellows in town, who saw you there, told me he was in love with you.

MRS. PINCHWIFE: Indeed! Who, who, pray, who was't?

PINCHWIFE [*aside*]: I've gone too far and slipped before I was aware. How overjoyed she is!

MRS. PINCHWIFE: Was it any Hampshire gallant, any of our neighbors? I promise you, I am beholding to him.

PINCHWIFE: I promise you, you lie, for he would but ruin you, as he has done hundreds. He has no other love for women but that; such as he look upon women, like basilisks,[2] but to destroy 'em.

MRS. PINCHWIFE: Ay, but if he loves me, why should he ruin me? Answer me to that. Methinks he should not; I would do him no harm.

ALITHEA: Hah, ha, ha!

PINCHWIFE: 'Tis very well; but I'll keep him from doing you any harm, or me either.

[*Enter Sparkish and Harcourt.*]

But here comes company; get you in, get you in.

MRS. PINCHWIFE: But pray, husband, is he a pretty gentleman that loves me?

PINCHWIFE: In, baggage, in. [*Thrusts her in, shuts the door.*] What, all the lewd libertines of the town brought to my lodging by this easy coxcomb! 'Sdeath, I'll not suffer it.

SPARKISH: Here, Harcourt, do you approve my choice? [*To Alithea.*] Dear little rogue, I told you I'd bring you acquainted with all my friends, the wits, and—

[*Harcourt salutes her.*]

PINCHWIFE [*aside*]: Ay, they shall know her, as well as you yourself will, I warrant you.

SPARKISH: This is one of those, my pretty rogue, that are to dance at your wedding tomorrow; and him you must bid welcome ever to what you and I have.

PINCHWIFE [*aside*]: Monstrous!

SPARKISH: Harcourt, how dost thou like her, faith?—Nay, dear, do not look down; I should hate to have a wife of mine out of countenance at anything.

PINCHWIFE [*aside*]: Wonderful!

SPARKISH: Tell me, I say, Harcourt, how dost thou like her? Thou hast stared upon her enough to resolve me.

HARCOURT: So infinitely well that I could wish I had a mistress too, that might differ from her in nothing but her love and engagement to you.

ALITHEA: Sir, Master Sparkish has often told me that his acquaintance were all wits and railleurs[3] and now I find it.

SPARKISH: No, by the universe, madam, he does not rally now; you may believe him. I do assure you, he is the honestest, worthiest, true-hearted gentleman—a man of such perfect honor, he would say nothing to a lady he does not mean.

2. Mythical reptiles whose gaze dealt death.

3. Mockers, banterers.

PINCHWIFE [*aside*]: Praising another man to his mistress!

HARCOURT: Sir, you are so beyond expectation obliging that—

SPARKISH: Nay, egad, I am sure you do admire her extremely; I see't in your eyes.—He does admire you, madam.—By the world, don't you?

HARCOURT: Yes, above the world, or the most glorious part of it, her whole sex; and till now I never thought I should have envied you, or any man about to marry, but you have the best excuse for marriage I ever knew.

ALITHEA: Nay, now, sir, I'm satisfied you are of the society of the wits and railleurs, since you cannot spare your friend, even when he is but too civil to you; but the surest sign is since you are an enemy to marriage, for that, I hear, you hate as much as business or bad wine.

HARCOURT: Truly, madam, I never was an enemy to marriage till now, because marriage was never an enemy to me before.

ALITHEA: But why, sir, is marriage an enemy to you now? Because it robs you of your friend here? For you look upon a friend married as one gone into a monastery, that is dead to the world.

HARCOURT: 'Tis indeed because you marry him; I see, madam, you can guess my meaning. I do confess heartily and openly, I wish it were in my power to break the match; by heavens I would.

SPARKISH: Poor Frank!

ALITHEA: Would you be so unkind to me?

HARCOURT: No, no, 'tis not because I would be unkind to you.

SPARKISH: Poor Frank! No, gad, 'tis only his kindness to me.

PINCHWIFE [*aside*]: Great kindness to you indeed! Insensible fop, let a man make love to his wife to his face!

SPARKISH: Come, dear Frank, for all my wife there that shall be, thou shalt enjoy me sometimes, dear rogue. By my honor, we men of wit condole for our deceased brother in marriage as much as for one dead in earnest. I think that was prettily said of me, ha, Harcourt? But come, Frank, be not melancholy for me.

HARCOURT: No, I assure you I am not melancholy for you.

SPARKISH: Prithee, Frank, dost think my wife that shall be there a fine person?

HARCOURT: I could gaze upon her till I became as blind as you are.

SPARKISH: How, as I am? How?

HARCOURT: Because you are a lover and true lovers are blind, stock blind.[4]

SPARKISH: True, true; but by the world, she has wit too, as well as beauty. Go, go with her into a corner and try if she has wit; talk to her anything; she's bashful before me.

HARCOURT: Indeed, if a woman wants[5] wit in a corner, she has it nowhere.

ALITHEA [*aside to Sparkish*]: Sir, you dispose of me a little before your time—

SPARKISH: Nay, nay, madam, let me have an earnest[6] of your obedience, or—go, go, madam—

[*Harcourt courts Alithea aside*.]

PINCHWIFE: How, sir! If you are not concerned for the honor of a wife, I am for that of a sister; he shall not debauch her. Be a pander[7] to your own wife, bring men to her, let 'em make love before your face, thrust 'em into a corner together, then leave 'em in private! Is this your town wit and conduct?

4. As blind as any lifeless object.
5. Lacks.
6. Foretaste, pledge.
7. Pimp, procurer.

SPARKISH: Hah, ha, ha, a silly wise rogue would make one laugh more than a stark fool, hah, ha! I shall burst. Nay, you shall not disturb 'em; I'll vex thee, by the world. [*Struggles with Pinchwife to keep him from Harcourt and Alithea.*]

ALITHEA: The writings are drawn, sir, settlements made; 'tis too late, sir, and past all revocation.

HARCOURT: Then so is my death.

ALITHEA: I would not be unjust to him.

HARCOURT: Then why to me so?

ALITHEA: I have no obligation to you.

HARCOURT: My love.

ALITHEA: I had his before.

HARCOURT: You never had it; he wants, you see, jealousy, the only infallible sign of it.

ALITHEA: Love proceeds from esteem; he cannot distrust my virtue. Besides, he loves me, or he would not marry me.

HARCOURT: Marrying you is no more sign of his love than bribing your woman, that he may marry you, is a sign of his generosity. Marriage is rather a sign of interest than love, and he that marries a fortune covets a mistress, not loves her. But if you take marriage for a sign of love, take it from me immediately.

ALITHEA: No, now you have put a scruple in my head; but, in short, sir, to end our dispute, I must marry him; my reputation would suffer in the world else.

HARCOURT: No, if you do marry him, with your pardon, madam, your reputation suffers in the world and you would be thought in necessity for a cloak.[8]

ALITHEA: Nay, now you are rude, sir.—Mr. Sparkish, pray come hither, your friend here is very troublesome, and very loving.

HARCOURT [*aside to Alithea*]: Hold, hold!—

PINCHWIFE: D'ye hear that?

SPARKISH: Why, d'ye think I'll seem to be jealous, like a country bumpkin?

PINCHWIFE: No, rather be a cuckold, like a credulous cit.[9]

HARCOURT: Madam, you would not have been so little generous as to have told him.

ALITHEA: Yes, since you could be so little generous as to wrong him.

HARCOURT: Wrong him! No man can do't, he's beneath an injury; a bubble,[1] a coward, a senseless idiot, a wretch so contemptible to all the world but you that—

ALITHEA: Hold, do not rail at him, for since he is like to be my husband, I am resolved to like him. Nay, I think I am obliged to tell him you are not his friend.—Master Sparkish, Master Sparkish.

SPARKISH: What, what?—Now, dear rogue, has not she wit?

HARCOURT [*speaks surlily*]: Not so much as I thought and hoped she had.

ALITHEA: Mr. Sparkish, do you bring people to rail at you?

HARCOURT: Madam—

SPARKISH: How! No, but if he does rail at me, 'tis but in jest, I warrant; what we wits do for one another and never take any notice of it.

ALITHEA: He spoke so scurrilously of you, I had no patience to hear him; besides, he has been making love to me.

8. I.e., to hide your secrets: perhaps pregnancy or love affairs.
9. "A pert low townsman, a pragmatical trader" (Johnson's *Dictionary*); contemptuous abbreviation of "citizen."
1. Dupe.

HARCOURT [*aside*]: True, damned, telltale woman!

SPARKISH: Pshaw, to show his parts[2]—we wits rail and make love often but to show our parts; as we have no affections, so we have no malice. We—

ALITHEA: He said you were a wretch, below an injury.

SPARKISH: Pshaw!

HARCOURT [*aside*]: Damned, senseless, impudent, virtuous jade! Well, since she won't let me have her, she'll do as good, she'll make me hate her.

ALITHEA: A common bubble.

SPARKISH: Pshaw!

ALITHEA: A coward.

SPARKISH: Pshaw, pshaw!

ALITHEA: A senseless, driveling idiot.

SPARKISH: How! Did he disparage my parts? Nay, then my honor's concerned; I can't put up that, sir, by the world. Brother, help me to kill him. [*Aside*.] I may draw now, since we have the odds of him. 'This a good occasion, too, before my mistress—[*Offers to draw*.]

ALITHEA: Hold, hold!

SPARKISH: What, what?

ALITHEA [*aside*]: I must not let 'em kill the gentleman neither, for his kindness to me; I am so far from hating him that I wish my gallant had his person and understanding.—Nay, if my honor—

SPARKISH: I'll be thy death.

ALITHEA: Hold, hold! Indeed, to tell the truth, the gentleman said after all that what he spoke was but out of friendship to you.

SPARKISH: How! say I am—I am a fool, that is, no wit, out of friendship to me?

ALITHEA: Yes, to try whether I was concerned enough for you and made love to me only to be satisfied of my virtue, for your sake.

HARCOURT [*aside*]: Kind, however—

SPARKISH: Nay, if it were so, my dear rogue, I ask thee pardon; but why would not you tell me so, faith?

HARCOURT: Because I did not think on't, faith.

SPARKISH: Come, Horner does not come, Harcourt, let's be gone to the new play.—Come, madam.

ALITHEA: I will not go if you intend to leave me alone in the box and run into the pit, as you use to do.

SPARKISH: Pshaw! I'll leave Harcourt with you in the box to entertain you, and that's as good; if I sat in the box, I should be thought no judge but of trimmings.[3]—Come away, Harcourt, lead her down.

[*Exeunt Sparkish, Harcourt and Alithea*.]

PINCHWIFE: Well, go thy ways, for the flower of the true town fops, such as spend their estates before they come to 'em and are cuckolds before they're married. But let me go look to my own freehold.—How!—

[*Enter Lady Fidget, Mrs. Dainty Fidget and Mrs. Squeamish*.]

LADY FIDGET: Your servant, sir; where is your lady? We are come to wait upon her to the new play.

PINCHWIFE: New play!

2. Abilities, talents.

3. Clothes, fashions. The "wits," who came to criticize the play, customarily occupied not the boxes but the "pit."

LADY FIDGET: And my husband will wait upon you presently.

PINCHWIFE [*aside*]: Damn your civility.—Madam, by no means; I will not see Sir Jaspar here till I have waited upon him at home; nor shall my wife see you till she has waited upon your ladyship at your lodgings.

LADY FIDGET: Now we are here, sir—

PINCHWIFE: No, madam.

DAINTY: Pray, let us see her.

SQUEAMISH: We will not stir till we see her.

PINCHWIFE [*aside*]: A pox on you all! [*Goes to the door, and returns.*]—She has locked the door and is gone abroad.

LADY FIDGET: No, you have locked the door and she's within.

DAINTY: They told us below she was here.

PINCHWIFE [*aside*]: Will nothing do?—Well, it must out then. To tell you the truth, ladies, which I was afraid to let you know before, lest it might endanger your lives, my wife has just now the smallpox come out upon her. Do not be frightened but pray, be gone, ladies; you shall not stay here in danger of your lives. Pray get you gone, ladies.

LADY FIDGET: No, no, we have all had 'em.

SQUEAMISH: Alack, alack.

DAINTY: Come, come, we must see how it goes with her; I understand the disease.

LADY FIDGET: Come.

PINCHWIFE [*aside*]: Well, there is no being too hard for[4] women at their own weapon, lying; therefore I'll quit the field. [*Exit Pinchwife.*]

SQUEAMISH: Here's an example of jealousy.

LADY FIDGET: Indeed, as the world goes, I wonder there are no more jealous, since wives are so neglected.

DAINTY: Pshaw, as the world goes, to what end should they be jealous?

LADY FIDGET: Foh, 'tis a nasty world.

SQUEAMISH: That men of parts, great acquaintance and quality should take up with and spend themselves and fortunes in keeping little playhouse creatures, foh!

LADY FIDGET: Nay, that women of understanding, great acquaintance and good quality should fall a-keeping too of little creatures, foh!

SQUEAMISH: Why, 'tis the men of quality's fault; they never visit women of honor and reputation, as they used to do and have not so much as common civility for ladies of our rank, but use us with the same indifferency and ill-breeding as if we were all married to 'em.

LADY FIDGET: She says true; 'tis an arrant shame women of quality should be so slighted. Methinks birth, birth should go for something. I have known men admired, courted, and followed for their titles only.

SQUEAMISH: Ay, one would think men of honor should not love, no more than marry, out of their own rank.

DAINTY: Fie, fie upon 'em! They are come to think crossbreeding for themselves best, as well as for their dogs and horses.

LADY FIDGET: They are dogs and horses for't.

SQUEAMISH: One would think, if not for love, for vanity a little.

DAINTY: Nay, they do satisfy their vanity upon us sometimes and are kind to us in their report, tell all the world they lie with us.

4. Too clever for.

LADY FIDGET: Damned rascals! That we should be only wronged by 'em! To report a man has had a person, when he has not had a person, is the greatest wrong in the whole world that can be done to a person.

SQUEAMISH: Well, 'tis an arrant shame noble persons should be so wronged and neglected.

LADY FIDGET: But still 'tis an arranter shame for a noble person to neglect her own honor and defame her own noble person with little inconsiderable fellows, foh!

DAINTY: I suppose the crime against our honor is the same with a man of quality as with another.

LADY FIDGET: How! No, sure, the man of quality is likest one's husband and therefore the fault should be the less.

DAINTY: But then the pleasure should be the less.

LADY FIDGET: Fie, fie, fie, for shame, sister! Whither shall we ramble? Be continent[5] in your discourse, or I shall hate you.

DAINTY: Besides, an intrigue is so much the more notorious for the man's quality.

SQUEAMISH: 'Tis true, nobody takes notice of a private man and therefore with him 'tis more secret, and the crime's the less when 'tis not known.

LADY FIDGET: You say true; i'faith, I think you are in the right on't. 'Tis not an injury to a husband till it be an injury to our honors; so that a woman of honor loses no honor with a private person; and to say truth—

DAINTY [*apart to Squeamish*]: So, the little fellow is grown a private person—with her—

LADY FIDGET: But still my dear, dear honor.

[*Enter Sir Jaspar, Horner, Dorilant.*]

SIR JASPAR: Ay, my dear, dear of honor, thou hast still so much honor in thy mouth—

HORNER [*aside*]: That she has none elsewhere.

LADY FIDGET: Oh, what d'ye mean to bring in these upon us?

DAINTY: Foh, these are as bad as wits.

SQUEAMISH: Foh!

LADY FIDGET: Let us leave the room.

SIR JASPAR: Stay, stay; faith, to tell you the naked truth—

LADY FIDGET: Fie, Sir Jaspar, do not use that word "naked."

SIR JASPAR: Well, well, in short, I have business at Whitehall and cannot go to the play with you, therefore would have you go—

LADY FIDGET: With those two to a play?

SIR JASPAR: No, not with t'other but with Mr. Horner; there can be no more scandal to go with him than with Mr. Tattle or Master Limberham.[6]

LADY FIDGET: With that nasty fellow! No—no!

SIR JASPAR: Nay, prithee, dear, hear me.

[*Whispers to Lady Fidget.*]

HORNER: Ladies—

[*Horner, Dorilant drawing near Squeamish and Dainty.*]

DAINTY: Stand off.

SQUEAMISH: Do not approach us.

DAINTY: You herd with the wits, you are obscenity all over.

5. Restrained.

6. I.e., Horner and Dorilant.

SQUEAMISH: And I would as soon look upon a picture of Adam and Eve, without fig leaves, as any of you, if I could help it; therefore keep off and do not make us sick.

DORILANT: What a devil are these?

HORNER: Why, these are pretenders to honor, as critics to wit, only by censuring others; and as every raw, peevish, out-of-humored, affected, dull, tea-drinking, arithmetical[7] fop sets up for a wit by railing at men of sense, so these for honor by railing at the Court and ladies of as great honor as quality.

SIR JASPAR: Come, Mr. Horner, I must desire you to go with these ladies to the play, sir.

HORNER: I, sir!

SIR JASPAR: Ay, ay, come, sir.

HORNER: I must beg your pardon, sir, and theirs; I will not be seen in women's company in public again for the world.

SIR JASPAR: Ha, ha, strange aversion!

SQUEAMISH: No, he's for women's company in private.

SIR JASPAR: He—poor man—he! Hah, ha, ha!

DAINTY: 'Tis a greater shame amongst lewd fellows to be seen in virtuous women's company than for the women to be seen with them.

HORNER: Indeed, madam, the time was I only hated virtuous women, but now I hate the other too; I beg your pardon, ladies.

LADY FIDGET: You are very obliging, sir, because we would not be troubled with you.

SIR JASPAR: In sober sadness, he shall go.

DORILANT: Nay, if he wo'not, I am ready to wait upon the ladies; and I think I am the fitter man.

SIR JASPAR: You, sir, no, I thank you for that—Master Horner is a privileged man amongst the virtuous ladies; 'twill be a great while before you are so; heh, he, he! He's my wife's gallant, heh, he, he! No, pray withdraw, sir, for as I take it, the virtuous ladies have no business with you.

DORILANT: And I am sure he can have none with them. 'Tis strange a man can't come amongst virtuous women now but upon the same terms as men are admitted into the Great Turk's seraglio;[8] but heavens keep me from being an ombre[9] player with 'em! But where is Pinchwife?

[*Exit Dorilant*.]

SIR JASPAR: Come, come, man; what, avoid the sweet society of womankind? that sweet, soft, gentle, tame, noble creature, woman, made for man's companion—

HORNER: So is that soft, gentle, tame and more noble creature a spaniel, and has all their tricks: can fawn, lie down, suffer beating and fawn the more; barks at your friends when they come to see you; makes your bed hard; gives you fleas, and the mange sometimes. And all the difference is, the spaniel's the more faithful animal and fawns but upon one master.

SIR JASPAR: Heh, he, he!

SQUEAMISH: Oh, the rude beast!

DAINTY: Insolent brute!

LADY FIDGET: Brute! Stinking, mortified, rotten French wether,[1] to dare—

SIR JASPAR: Hold, an't please your ladyship.—For shame, Master Horner, your mother was a woman. [*Aside*.] Now shall I never reconcile 'em. [*Aside to Lady*

7. Precise, fussy.
8. The Sultan's harem.
9. Three-person card game (with a pun on *hombre*: man).
1. Castrated ram.

Fidget.] Hark you, madam, take my advice in your anger. You know you often want one to make up your drolling[2] pack of ombre players; and you may cheat him easily, for he's an ill gamester and consequently loves play. Besides, you know, you have but two old civil gentlemen, with stinking breaths too, to wait upon you abroad; take in the third into your service. The other are but crazy; and a lady should have a supernumerary gentleman-usher,[3] as a supernumerary coach-horse, lest sometimes you should be forced to stay at home.

LADY FIDGET: But are you sure he loves play and has money?

SIR JASPAR: He loves play as much as you and has money as much as I.

LADY FIDGET: Then I am contented to make him pay for his scurrility; money makes up in a measure all other wants in men. [*Aside.*] Those whom we cannot make hold for gallants, we make fine.[4]

SIR JASPAR [*aside*]: So, so; now to mollify, to wheedle him.—Master Horner, will you never keep civil company? Methinks 'tis time now, since you are only fit for them. Come, come, man, you must e'en fall to visiting our wives, eating at our tables, drinking tea with our virtuous relations after dinner, dealing cards to 'em, reading plays and gazettes[5] to 'em, picking fleas out of their shocks[6] for 'em, collecting receipts,[7] new songs, women, pages and footmen for 'em.

HORNER: I hope they'll afford me better employment, sir.

SIR JASPAR: Heh, he, he! 'Tis fit you know your work before you come into your place; and since you are unprovided of a lady to flatter and a good house to eat at, pray frequent mine and call my wife mistress and she shall call you gallant, according to the custom.

HORNER: Who, I?

SIR JASPAR: Faith, thou shalt for my sake; come, for my sake only.

HORNER: For your sake—

SIR JASPAR [*to Lady Fidget*]: Come, come, here's a gamester for you; let him be a little familiar sometimes. Nay, what if a little rude? Gamesters may be rude with ladies, you know.

LADY FIDGET: Yes, losing gamesters have a privilege with women.

HORNER: I always thought the contrary, that the winning gamester had most privilege with women, for when you have lost your money to a man, you'll lose anything you have, all you have, they say, and he may use you as he pleases.

SIR JASPAR: Heh, he, he! Well, win or lose, you shall have your liberty with her.

LADY FIDGET: As he behaves himself; and for your sake I'll give him admittance and freedom.

HORNER: All sorts of freedom, madam?

SIR JASPAR: Ay, ay, ay, all sorts of freedom thou canst take, and so go to her, begin thy new employment; wheedle[8] her, jest with her and be better acquainted one with another.

HORNER [*aside*]: I think I know her already, therefore may venture with her, my secret for hers.

[*Horner and Lady Fidget whisper.*]

SIR JASPAR: Sister, cuz, I have provided an innocent playfellow for you there.

DAINTY: Who, he!

2. Jesting, silly.
3. Extra attendant, servant.
4. Compensate, especially by way of money.
5. Newspapers.
6. Poodles.
7. Recipes.
8. Entice.

SQUEAMISH: There's a playfellow indeed!

SIR JASPAR: Yes, sure; what, he is good enough to play at cards, blindman's buff,[9] or the fool with sometimes.

SQUEAMISH: Foh, we'll have no such playfellows.

DAINTY: No, sir, you shan't choose playfellows for us, we thank you.

SIR JASPAR: Nay, pray hear me. [*Whispering to them.*]

LADY FIDGET [*aside to Horner*]: But, poor gentleman, could you be so generous, so truly a man of honor, as for the sakes of us women of honor, to cause yourself to be reported no man? No man! And to suffer yourself the greatest shame that could fall upon a man, that none might fall upon us women by your conversation? But indeed, sir, as perfectly, perfectly the same man as before your going into France, sir? As perfectly, perfectly, sir?

HORNER: As perfectly, perfectly, madam. Nay, I scorn you should take my word; I desire to be tried only, madam.

LADY FIDGET: Well, that's spoken again like a man of honor; all men of honor desire to come to the test. But, indeed, generally you men report such things of yourselves, one does not know how or whom to believe and it is come to that pass we dare not take your words, no more than your tailors,[1] without some staid servant of yours be bound with you. But I have so strong a faith in your honor, dear, dear, noble sir, that I'd forfeit mine for yours at any time, dear sir.

HORNER: No, madam, you should not need to forfeit it for me; I have given you security already to save you harmless, my late reputation being so well known in the world, madam.

LADY FIDGET: But if upon any future falling out or upon a suspicion of my taking the trust out of your hands to employ some other, you yourself should betray your trust, dear sir? I mean, if you'll give me leave to speak obscenely, you might tell, dear sir.

HORNER: If I did, nobody would believe me; the reputation of impotency is as hardly recovered again in the world as that of cowardice, dear madam.

LADY FIDGET: Nay then, as one may say, you may do your worst, dear, dear sir.

SIR JASPAR: Come, is your ladyship reconciled to him yet? Have you agreed on matters? For I must be gone to Whitehall.

LADY FIDGET: Why, indeed, Sir Jaspar, Master Horner is a thousand, thousand times a better man than I thought him. Cousin Squeamish, Sister Dainty, I can name him now; truly, not long ago, you know, I thought his very name obscenity and I would as soon have lain with him as have named him.

SIR JASPAR: Very likely, poor madam.

DAINTY: I believe it.

SQUEAMISH: No doubt on't.

SIR JASPAR: Well, well—that your ladyship is as virtuous as any she, I know, and him all the town knows—heh, he, he! Therefore, now you like him, get you gone to your business together; go, go to your business, I say, pleasure, whilst I go to my pleasure, business.

LADY FIDGET: Come then, dear gallant.

HORNER: Come away, my dearest mistress.

SIR JASPAR: So, so. Why, 'tis as I'd have it. [*Exit Sir Jaspar.*]

9. Game in which a blindfolded player is pushed about as he guesses other players' identities.

1. Tailors often went unpaid by their customers, and so had reason to mistrust them.

HORNER: And as I'd have it.
LADY FIDGET: Who for his business from his wife will run,
Takes the best care to have her business done. [*Exeunt omnes.*]

ACT 3

Scene 1

[*Alithea and Mrs. Pinchwife.*]

ALITHEA: Sister, what ails you? You are grown melancholy.

MRS. PINCHWIFE: Would it not make anyone melancholy to see you go every day fluttering about abroad, whilst I must stay at home like a poor, lonely, sullen bird in a cage?

ALITHEA: Ay, sister, but you came young and just from the nest to your cage, so that I thought you liked it and could be as cheerful in't as others that took their flight themselves early and are hopping abroad in the open air.

MRS. PINCHWIFE: Nay, I confess I was quiet enough till my husband told me what pure[1] lives the London ladies live abroad, with their dancing, meetings and junketings,[2] and dressed every day in their best gowns, and, I warrant you, play at ninepins[3] every day of the week, so they do.

[*Enter Mr. Pinchwife.*]

PINCHWIFE: Come, what's here to do? You are putting the town pleasures in her head and setting her a-longing.

ALITHEA: Yes, after ninepins; you suffer none to give her those longings, you mean, but yourself.

PINCHWIFE: I tell her of the vanities of the town like a confessor.

ALITHEA: A confessor! Just such a confessor as he that, by forbidding a silly ostler to grease the horse's teeth,[4] taught him to do't.

PINCHWIFE: Come, Mistress Flippant, good precepts are lost when bad examples are still before us; the liberty you take abroad makes her hanker after it, and out of humor at home, poor wretch! She desired not to come to London; I would bring her.

ALITHEA: Very well.

PINCHWIFE: She has been this week in town and never desired, till this afternoon, to go abroad.

ALITHEA: Was she not at a play yesterday?

PINCHWIFE: Yes, but she ne'er asked me; I was myself the cause of her going.

ALITHEA: Then, if she ask you again, you are the cause of her asking, and not my example.

PINCHWIFE: Well, tomorrow night I shall be rid of you and the next day, before 'tis light, she and I'll be rid of the town, and my dreadful apprehensions. [*To Mrs. Pinchwife.*] Come, be not melancholy, for thou shalt go into the country after tomorrow, dearest.

ALITHEA: Great comfort!

MRS. PINCHWIFE: Pish, what d'ye tell me of the country for?

1. Splendid.
2. Merrymakings.
3. A game like bowling, more common in the country than in London high society.
4. The groomsmen ("ostlers") at inns reputedly played this lucrative trick: they would grease the horse's teeth to discourage its eating, but charge the owner nonetheless for the uneaten feed.

PINCHWIFE: How's this! What, pish at the country!

MRS. PINCHWIFE: Let me alone, I am not well.

PINCHWIFE: Oh, if that be all—what ails my dearest?

MRS. PINCHWIFE: Truly I don't know; but I have not been well since you told me there was a gallant at the play in love with me.

PINCHWIFE: Ha—

ALITHEA: That's by my example too!

PINCHWIFE: Nay, if you are not well, but are so concerned because a lewd fellow chanced to lie and say he liked you, you'll make me sick too.

MRS. PINCHWIFE: Of what sickness?

PINCHWIFE: O, of that which is worse than the plague, jealousy.

MRS. PINCHWIFE: Pish, you jeer! I'm sure there's no such disease in our receipt-book[5] at home.

PINCHWIFE: No, thou never met'st with it, poor innocent. [*Aside.*] Well, if thou cuckold me, 'twill be my own fault—for cuckolds and bastards are generally makers of their own fortune.

MRS. PINCHWIFE: Well, but pray, bud, let's to go a play tonight.

PINCHWIFE: 'Tis just done, she comes from it. But why are you so eager to see a play?

MRS. PINCHWIFE: Faith, dear, not that I care one pin for their talk there; but I like to look upon the playermen and would see, if I could, the gallant you say loves me; that's all, dear bud.

PINCHWIFE: Is that all, dear bud?

ALITHEA: This proceeds from my example.

MRS. PINCHWIFE: But if the play be done, let's go abroad, however, dear bud.

PINCHWIFE: Come, have a little patience and thou shalt go into the country on Friday.

MRS. PINCHWIFE: Therefore I would see first some sights, to tell my neighbors of. Nay, I will go abroad, that's once.[6]

ALITHEA: I'm the cause of this desire too.

PINCHWIFE: But now I think on't, who was the cause of Horner's coming to my lodging today? That was you.

ALITHEA: No, you, because you would not let him see your handsome wife out of your lodging.

MRS. PINCHWIFE: Why, O Lord! Did the gentleman come hither to see me indeed?

PINCHWIFE: No, no.—You are not cause of that damned question too, Mistress Alithea? [*Aside.*] Well, she's in the right of it. He is in love with my wife—and comes after her—'tis so—but I'll nip his love in the bud, lest he should follow us into the country and break his chariot-wheel near our house on purpose for an excuse to come to't. But I think I know the town.

MRS. PINCHWIFE: Come, pray, bud, let's go abroad before 'tis late, for I will go, that's flat and plain.

PINCHWIFE [*aside*]: So! the obstinacy already of a town-wife, and I must, whilst she's here, humor her like one.—Sister, how shall we do, that she may not be seen or known?

ALITHEA: Let her put on her mask.

5. Book of medical recipes.

6. I.e., That's that.

PINCHWIFE: Pshaw, a mask makes people but the more inquisitive and is as ridiculous a disguise as a stage-beard; her shape, stature, habit will be known and if we should meet with Horner, he would be sure to take acquaintance with us, must wish her joy, kiss her, talk to her, leer upon her, and the devil and all. No, I'll not use her to a mask, 'tis dangerous, for masks have made more cuckolds than the best faces that ever were known.

ALITHEA: How will you do then?

MRS. PINCHWIFE: Nay, shall we go? The Exchange will be shut, and I have a mind to see that.

PINCHWIFE: So—I have it—I'll dress her up in the suit we are to carry down to her brother, little Sir James; nay, I understand the town tricks. Come, let's go dress her. A mask! No—a woman masked, like a covered dish, gives a man curiosity and appetite, when, it may be, uncovered, 'twould turn his stomach; no, no.

ALITHEA: Indeed your comparison is something a greasy[7] one. But I had a gentle gallant used to say, "A beauty masked, like the sun in eclipse, gathers together more gazers than if it shined out."

[*Exeunt.*]

Scene 2

[*The scene changes to the New Exchange. Enter Horner, Harcourt, Dorilant.*]

DORILANT: Engaged to women, and not sup with us?

HORNER: Ay, a pox on 'em all!

HARCOURT: You were much a more reasonable man in the morning and had as noble resolutions against 'em as a widower of a week's liberty.

DORILANT: Did I ever think to see you keep company with women in vain?

HORNER: In vain! No—'tis, since I can't love 'em, to be revenged on 'em.

HARCOURT: Now your sting is gone, you looked in the box amongst all those women, like a drone in the hive, all upon you, shoved and ill-used by 'em all, and thrust from one side to t'other.

DORILANT: Yet he must be buzzing amongst 'em still, like other old beetle-headed,[8] liquorish[9] drones. Avoid 'em, and hate 'em as they hate you.

HORNER: Because I do hate 'em, and would hate 'em yet more, I'll frequent 'em; you may see by marriage, nothing makes a man hate a woman more than her constant conversation. In short, I converse with 'em, as you do with rich fools, to laugh at 'em and use 'em ill.

DORILANT: But I would no more sup with women, unless I could lie with 'em, than sup with a rich coxcomb, unless I could cheat him.

HORNER: Yes, I have known thee sup with a fool for his drinking; if he could set out your hand[1] that way only, you were satisfied, and if he were a wine-swallowing mouth 'twas enough.

HARCOURT: Yes, a man drinks often with a fool, as he tosses with a marker,[2] only to keep his hand in ure.[3] But do the ladies drink?

HORNER: Yes, sir, and I shall have the pleasure at least of laying 'em flat with a bottle, and bring as much scandal that way upon 'em as formerly t'other.

HARCOURT: Perhaps you may prove as weak a brother amongst 'em that way as t'other.

7. Filthy or obscene.
8. Stupid.
9. Lecherous.
1. Provide you with food and drink.
2. Plays dice with a score-keeper.
3. In practice.

DORILANT: Foh, drinking with women is as unnatural as scolding with 'em; but 'tis a pleasure of decayed fornicators, and the basest way of quenching love.

HARCOURT: Nay, 'tis drowning love instead of quenching it. But leave us for civil women too!

DORILANT: Ay, when he can't be the better for 'em. We hardly pardon a man that leaves his friend for a wench, and that's a pretty lawful call.

HORNER: Faith, I would not leave you for 'em, if they would not drink.

DORILANT: Who would disappoint his company at Lewis's[4] for a gossiping?

HARCOURT: Foh, wine and women, good apart, together as nauseous as sack and sugar.[5] But hark you, sir, before you go, a little of your advice; an old maimed general, when unfit for action, is fittest for counsel. I have other designs upon women than eating and drinking with them. I am in love with Sparkish's mistress, whom he is to marry tomorrow. Now how shall I get her?

[*Enter Sparkish, looking about.*]

HORNER: Why, here comes one will help you to her.

HARCOURT: He! He, I tell you, is my rival, and will hinder my love.

HORNER: No, a foolish rival and a jealous husband assist their rival's designs, for they are sure to make their women hate them, which is the first step to their love for another man.

HARCOURT: But I cannot come near his mistress but in his company.

HORNER: Still the better for you, for fools are most easily cheated when they themselves are accessories; and he is to be bubbled[6] of his mistress, as of his money, the common mistress, by keeping him company.

SPARKISH: Who is that, that is to be bubbled? Faith, let me snack,[7] I han't met with a bubble since Christmas. Gad, I think bubbles are like their brother woodcocks,[8] go out with the cold weather.

HARCOURT [*apart to Horner*]: A pox! He did not hear all, I hope.

SPARKISH: Come, you bubbling rogues you, where do we sup?—Oh, Harcourt, my mistress tells me you have been making fierce love to her all the play long, hah, ha! But I—

HARCOURT: I make love to her?

SPARKISH: Nay, I forgive thee, for I think I know thee, and I know her, but I am sure I know myself.

HARCOURT: Did she tell you so? I see all women are like these of the Exchange, who, to enhance the price of their commodities, report to their fond customers offers which were never made 'em.

HORNER: Ay, women are as apt to tell before the intrigue as men after it, and so show themselves the vainer sex. But hast thou a mistress, Sparkish? 'Tis as hard for me to believe it as that thou ever hadst a bubble, as you bragged just now.

SPARKISH: Oh, your servant, sir; are you at your raillery, sir? But we were some of us beforehand with you today at the play. The wits were something bold with you, sir; did you not hear us laugh?

HORNER: Yes, but I thought you had gone to plays to laugh at the poet's wit, not at your own.

SPARKISH: Your servant, sir; no, I thank you. Gad, I go to a play as to a country treat;[9] I carry my own wine to one and my own wit to t'other, or else I'm sure I

4. A London restaurant.
5. Sack, white wine from Spain or the Canary Islands, was often drunk with sugar.
6. Cheated, fooled.
7. Have a share.
8. Migratory birds; also fools.
9. Reception.

should not be merry at either. And the reason why we are so often louder than the players is because we think we speak more wit and so become the poet's rivals in his audience. For to tell you the truth, we hate the silly rogues, nay, so much that we find fault even with their bawdy upon the stage, whilst we talk nothing else in the pit as loud.

HORNER: But why shouldst thou hate the silly poets? Thou hast too much wit to be one, and they, like whores, are only hated by each other—and thou dost scorn writing, I'm sure.

SPARKISH: Yes, I'd have you to know I scorn writing; but women, women, that make men do all foolish things, make 'em write songs too. Everybody does it. 'Tis even as common with lovers as playing with fans; and you can no more help rhyming to your Phyllis[1] than drinking to your Phyllis.

HARCOURT: Nay, poetry in love is no more to be avoided than jealousy.

DORILANT: But the poets damned your songs, did they?

SPARKISH: Damn the poets! They turned 'em into burlesque, as they call it. That burlesque[2] is a hocus-pocus trick they have got, which, by virtue of *hictius doctius*,[3] *topsy-turvy*, they make a wise and witty man in the world a fool upon the stage, you know not how; and 'tis therefore I hate 'em too, for I know not but it may be my own case, for they'll put a man into a play for looking asquint.[4] Their predecessors were contented to make serving-men only their stage-fools, but these rogues must have gentlemen, with a pox to 'em, nay, knights; and, indeed, you shall hardly see a fool upon the stage but he's a knight and, to tell you the truth, they have kept me these six years from being a knight in earnest, for fear of being knighted in a play, and dubbed a fool.

DORILANT: Blame 'em not; they must follow their copy,[5] the age.

HARCOURT: But why shouldst thou be afraid of being in a play, who expose yourself every day in the play-houses, and as public places?

HORNER: 'Tis but being on the stage, instead of standing on a bench in the pit.

DORILANT: Don't you give money to painters to draw you like? And are you afraid of your pictures at length in a playhouse, where all your mistresses may see you?

SPARKISH: A pox! Painters don't draw the smallpox or pimples in one's face. Come, damn all your silly authors whatever, all books and booksellers, by the world, and all readers, courteous or uncourteous.

HARCOURT: But who comes here, Sparkish?

[*Enter Mr. Pinchwife and his wife in man's clothes, Alithea, Lucy her maid.*]

SPARKISH: Oh, hide me! There's my mistress too. [*Sparkish hides himself behind Harcourt.*]

HARCOURT: She sees you.

SPARKISH: But I will not see her. 'Tis time to go to Whitehall and I must not fail the drawing room.

HARCOURT: Pray, first carry me, and reconcile me to her.

SPARKISH: Another time; faith, the King will have supped.

HARCOURT: Not with the worse stomach for thy absence; thou art one of those fools that think their attendance at the King's meals as necessary as his physicians', when you are more troublesome to him than his doctors, or his dogs.

1. I.e., "sweetheart"; beloved women were often so named in pastoral poetry.
2. I.e., they wrote parodies of Sparkish's songs.
3. Like hocus-pocus.
4. I.e., they'll make him a comic character in a play, mocking even the tiniest fault.
5. The original from which a copy is made.

SPARKISH: Pshaw, I know my interest, sir. Prithee hide me.

HORNER: Your servant, Pinchwife.—What, he knows us not!

PINCHWIFE [*to his wife aside*]: Come along.

MRS. PINCHWIFE: Pray, have you any ballads? Give me sixpenny worth.

CLASP: We have no ballads.

MRS. PINCHWIFE: Then give me *Covent Garden Drollery*,[6] and a play or two—Oh, here's *Tarugo's Wiles*, and *The Slighted Maiden*;[7] I'll have them.

PINCHWIFE [*apart to her*]: No, plays are not for your reading. Come along; will you discover yourself?

HORNER: Who is that pretty youth with him, Sparkish?

SPARKISH: I believe his wife's brother, because he's something like her, but I never saw her but once.

HORNER: Extremely handsome; I have seen a face like it too. Let us follow 'em.

[*Exeunt Pinchwife, Mrs. Pinchwife, Alithea, Lucy; Horner, Dorilant following them.*]

HARCOURT: Come, Sparkish, your mistress saw you and will be angry you go not to her. Besides, I would fain be reconciled to her, which none but you can do, dear friend.

SPARKISH: Well, that's a better reason, dear friend, I would not go near her now, for hers or my own sake, but I can deny you nothing, for though I have known thee a great while, never go,[8] if I do not love thee as well as a new acquaintance.

HARCOURT: I am obliged to you indeed, dear friend. I would be well with her, only to be well with thee still, for these ties to wives usually dissolve all ties to friends. I would be contented she should enjoy you a-nights, but I would have you to myself a-days, as I have had, dear friend.

SPARKISH: And thou shalt enjoy me a-days, dear, dear friend, never stir, and I'll be divorced from her sooner than from thee. Come along.

HARCOURT [*aside*]: So, we are hard put to't when we make our rival our procurer; but neither she nor her brother would let me come near her now. When all's done, a rival is the best cloak to steal to a mistress under, without suspicion, and when we have once got to her as we desire, we throw him off like other cloaks.

[*Exit Sparkish, and Harcourt following him. Re-enter Mr. Pinchwife, Mrs. Pinchwife in man's clothes.*]

PINCHWIFE [*to Alithea (off-stage)*]: Sister, if you will not go, we must leave you. [*Aside.*] The fool her gallant and she will muster up all the young saunterers of this place, and they will leave their dear seamstresses to follow us. What a swarm of cuckolds and cuckold-makers are here!—Come, let's be gone, Mistress Margery.

MRS. PINCHWIFE: Don't you believe that; I ha'n't half my bellyful of sights yet.

PINCHWIFE: Then walk this way.

MRS. PINCHWIFE: Lord, what a power of brave signs are here! Stay—the Bull's-Head, the Ram's-Head and the Stag's-Head, dear—

PINCHWIFE: Nay, if every husband's proper sign[9] here were visible, they would be all alike.

MRS. PINCHWIFE: What d'ye mean by that, bud?

PINCHWIFE: 'Tis no matter—no matter, bud.

6. A collection of songs, prologues, epilogues, and poetry by various authors, including Wycherley, believed to have been edited by Aphra Behn (1672).

7. Two theatrical "oldies," no longer current: a comedy by Thomas St. Serfe (1668) and a tragicomedy by Robert Stapleton (1663).

8. Worry not.

9. I.e., a cuckold's horns.

MRS. PINCHWIFE: Pray tell me; nay, I will know.

PINCHWIFE: They would be all bulls', stags', and rams' heads.

[*Exeunt Mr. Pinchwife, Mrs. Pinchwife. Re-enter Sparkish, Harcourt, Alithea, Lucy, at t'other door.*]

SPARKISH: Come, dear madam, for my sake you shall be reconciled to him.

ALITHEA: For your sake I hate him.

HARCOURT: That's something too cruel, madam, to hate me for his sake.

SPARKISH: Ay indeed, madam, too, too cruel to me, to hate my friend for my sake.

ALITHEA: I hate him because he is your enemy; and you ought to hate him too, for making love to me, if you love me.

SPARKISH: That's a good one! I hate a man for loving you! If he did love you, 'tis but what he can't help and 'tis your fault, not his, if he admires you. I hate a man for being of my opinion! I'll ne'er do't by the world.

ALITHEA: Is it for your honor or mine, to suffer a man to make love to me, who am to marry you tomorrow?

SPARKISH: Is it for your honor or mine, to have me jealous? That he makes love to you is a sign you are handsome and that I am not jealous is a sign you are virtuous. That, I think, is for your honor.

ALITHEA: But 'tis your honor too I am concerned for.

HARCOURT: But why, dearest madam, will you be more concerned for his honor than he is himself? Let his honor alone, for my sake and his. He, he has no honor—

SPARKISH: How's that?

HARCOURT: But what my dear friend can guard himself.

SPARKISH: O ho—that's right again.

HARCOURT: Your care of his honor argues his neglect of it, which is no honor to my dear friend here; therefore once more, let his honor go which way it will, dear madam.

SPARKISH: Ay, ay, were it for my honor to marry a woman whose virtue I suspected and could not trust her in a friend's hands?

ALITHEA: Are you not afraid to lose me?

HARCOURT: He afraid to lose you, madam! No, no—you may see how the most estimable and most glorious creature in the world is valued by him. Will you not see it?

SPARKISH: Right, honest Frank, I have that noble value for her that I cannot be jealous of her.

ALITHEA: You mistake him, he means you care not for me, nor who has me.

SPARKISH: Lord, madam, I see you are jealous.[1] Will you wrest a poor man's meaning from his words?

ALITHEA: You astonish me, sir, with your want of jealousy.

SPARKISH: And you make me giddy, madam, with your jealousy and fears and virtue and honor. Gad, I see virtue makes a woman as troublesome as a little reading or learning.

ALITHEA: Monstrous!

LUCY [*behind*]: Well, to see what easy husbands these women of quality can meet with; a poor chambermaid can never have such lady-like luck. Besides, he's

1. Here, vehement, fearful.

thrown away upon her; she'll make no use of her fortune, her blessing. None to[2] a gentleman for a pure cuckold, for it requires good breeding to be a cuckold.

ALITHEA: I tell you then plainly, he pursues me to marry me.

SPARKISH: Pshaw!

HARCOURT: Come, madam, you see you strive in vain to make him jealous of me; my dear friend is the kindest creature in the world to me.

SPARKISH: Poor fellow.

HARCOURT: But his kindness only is not enough for me, without your favor; your good opinion, dear madam, 'tis that must perfect my happiness. Good gentleman, he believes all I say—would you would do so. Jealous of me! I would not wrong him nor you for the world.

SPARKISH: Look you there; hear him, hear him, and do not walk away so.

[*Alithea walks carelessly to and fro.*]

HARCOURT: I love you, madam, so—

SPARKISH: How's that! Nay—now you begin to go too far indeed.

HARCOURT: So much, I confess, I say I love you, that I would not have you miserable and cast yourself away upon so unworthy and inconsiderable a thing as what you see here. [*Clapping his hand on his breast, points at Sparkish.*]

SPARKISH: No, faith, I believe thou wouldst not; now his meaning is plain. But I knew before thou wouldst not wrong me nor her.

HARCOURT: No, no, heavens forbid the glory of her sex should fall so low as into the embraces of such a contemptible wretch, the last of mankind—my dear friend here—I injure him! [*Embracing Sparkish.*]

ALITHEA: Very well.

SPARKISH: No, no, dear friend, I knew it.—Madam, you see he will rather wrong himself than me, in giving himself such names.

ALITHEA: Do not you understand him yet?

SPARKISH: Yes, how modestly he speaks of himself, poor fellow.

ALITHEA: Methinks he speaks impudently of yourself, since—before yourself too; insomuch that I can no longer suffer his scurrilous abusiveness to you, no more than his love to me. [*Offers to go.*]

SPARKISH: Nay, nay, madam, pray stay—his love to you! Lord, madam, he has not spoke yet plain enough?

ALITHEA: Yes, indeed, I should think so.

SPARKISH: Well then, by the world, a man can't speak civilly to a woman now but presently she says he makes love to her. Nay, madam, you shall stay, with your pardon, since you have not yet understood him, till he has made an éclaircissement[3] of his love to you, that is, what kind of love it is. [*To Harcourt.*] Answer to thy catechism. Friend, do you love my mistress here?

HARCOURT: Yes, I wish she would not doubt it.

SPARKISH: But how do you love her?

HARCOURT: With all my soul.

ALITHEA: I thank him; methinks he speaks plain enough now.

SPARKISH [*to Alithea*]: You are out still.—But with what kind of love, Harcourt?

HARCOURT: With the best and truest love in the world.

SPARKISH: Look you there then, that is with no matrimonial love, I'm sure.

ALITHEA: How's that? Do you say matrimonial love is not best?

2. There's no one like.

3. Explanation.

SPARKISH: Gad, I went too far ere I was aware. But speak for thyself, Harcourt; you said you would not wrong me nor her.

HARCOURT: No, no, madam, e'en take him for heaven's sake—

SPARKISH: Look you there, madam.

HARCOURT: Who should in all justice be yours, he that loves you most. [*Claps his hand on his breast.*]

ALITHEA: Look you there, Mr. Sparkish, who's that?

SPARKISH: Who should it be?—Go on, Harcourt.

HARCOURT: Who loves you more than women titles or fortune fools. [*Points at Sparkish.*]

SPARKISH: Look you there, he means me still, for he points at me.

ALITHEA: Ridiculous!

HARCOURT: Who can only match your faith and constancy in love.

SPARKISH: Ay.

HARCOURT: Who knows, if it be possible, how to value so much beauty and virtue.

SPARKISH: Ay.

HARCOURT: Whose love can no more be equaled in the world than that heavenly form of yours.

SPARKISH: No.

HARCOURT: Who could no more suffer a rival than your absence, and yet could no more suspect your virtue than his own constancy in his love to you.

SPARKISH: No.

HARCOURT: Who, in fine,[4] loves you better than his eyes that first made him love you.

SPARKISH: Ay—nay, madam, faith, you shan't go till—

ALITHEA: Have a care, lest you make me stay too long—

SPARKISH: But till he has saluted you, that I may be assured you are friends, after his honest advice and declaration. Come, pray, madam, be friends with him.

[*Enter Mr. Pinchwife, Mrs. Pinchwife*]

ALITHEA: You must pardon me, sir, that I am not yet so obedient to you.

PINCHWIFE: What, invite your wife to kiss men? Monstrous! Are you not ashamed? I will never forgive you.

SPARKISH: Are you not ashamed that I should have more confidence in the chastity of your family than you have? You must not teach me. I am a man of honor, sir, though I am frank[5] and free; I am frank, sir—

PINCHWIFE: Very frank, sir, to share your wife with your friends.

SPARKISH: He is an humble, menial[6] friend, such as reconciles the differences of the marriage bed. You know man and wife do not always agree; I design him for that use, therefore would have him well with my wife.

PINCHWIFE: A menial friend!—you will get a great many menial friends by showing your wife as you do.

SPARKISH: What then? It may be I have a pleasure in't, as I have to show fine clothes at a playhouse the first day and count money before poor rogues.

PINCHWIFE: He that shows his wife or money will be in danger of having them borrowed sometimes.

4. In short.
5. Unreserved, open.
6. Household.

SPARKISH: I love to be envied and would not marry a wife that I alone could love; loving alone is as dull as eating alone. Is it not a frank age? And I am a frank person. And to tell you the truth, it may be I love to have rivals in a wife; they make her seem to a man still but as a kept mistress. And so good night, for I must to Whitehall.—Madam, I hope you are now reconciled to my friend and so I wish you a good night, madam, and sleep if you can, for tomorrow you know I must visit you early with a canonical gentleman. Good night, dear Harcourt. [*Exit Sparkish.*]

HARCOURT: Madam, I hope you will not refuse my visit tomorrow, if it should be earlier, with a canonical gentleman, than Mr. Sparkish's.

PINCHWIFE [*coming between Alithea and Harcourt*]: This gentlewoman is yet under my care; therefore you must yet forbear your freedom with her, sir.

HARCOURT: Must, sir!

PINCHWIFE: Yes, sir, she is my sister.

HARCOURT: 'Tis well she is, sir—for I must be her servant, sir.—Madam—

PINCHWIFE: Come away, sister; we had been gone, if it had not been for you, and so avoided these lewd rake-hells,[7] who seem to haunt us.

[*Enter Horner, Dorilant to them.*]

HORNER: How now, Pinchwife?

PINCHWIFE: Your servant.

HORNER: What, I see a little time in the country makes a man turn wild and unsociable and only fit to converse with his horses, dogs and his herds.

PINCHWIFE: I have business, sir, and must mind it; your business is pleasure, therefore you and I must go different ways.

HORNER: Well, you may go on, but this pretty young gentleman—[*Takes hold of Mrs. Pinchwife.*]

HARCOURT: The lady—

DORILANT: And the maid—

HORNER: Shall stay with us, for I suppose their business is the same with ours, pleasure.

PINCHWIFE [*aside*]: 'Sdeath, he know her, she carries it so sillily! Yet if he does not, I should be more silly to discover it first.

ALITHEA: Pray, let us go, sir.

PINCHWIFE: Come, come—

HORNER [*to Mrs. Pinchwife*]: Had you not rather stay with us?—Prithee, Pinchwife, who is this pretty young gentleman?

PINCHWIFE: One to whom I'm a guardian. [*Aside.*] I wish I could keep her out of your hands.

HORNER: Who is he? I never saw anything so pretty in all my life.

PINCHWIFE: Pshaw, do not look upon him so much. He's a poor bashful youth, you'll put him out of countenance.—Come away, brother. [*Offers to take her away.*]

HORNER: Oh, your brother!

PINCHWIFE: Yes, my wife's brother.—Come, come, she'll stay supper for us.

HORNER: I thought so, for he is very like her I saw you at the play with, whom I told you I was in love with.

MRS. PINCHWIFE [*aside*]: O jeminy! Is this he that was in love with me? I am glad on't, I vow, for he's a curious fine gentleman, and I love him already too. [*To Mr. Pinchwife.*] Is this he, bud?

7. Scoudrels.

PINCHWIFE [*to his wife*.]: Come away, come away.

HORNER: Why, what haste are you in? Why won't you let me talk with him?

PINCHWIFE: Because you'll debauch him; he's yet young and innocent and I would not have him debauched for anything in the world. [*Aside*.] How she gazes on him! The devil!

HORNER: Harcourt, Dorilant, look you here; this is the likeness of that dowdy[8] he told us of, his wife. Did you ever see a lovelier creature? The rogue has reason to be jealous of his wife since she is like him, for she would make all that see her in love with her.

HARCOURT: And as I remember now, she is as like him here as can be.

DORILANT: She is indeed very pretty, if she be like him.

HORNER: Very pretty? A very pretty commendation! She is a glorious creature, beautiful beyond all things I ever beheld.

PINCHWIFE: So, so.

HARCOURT: More beautiful than a poet's first mistress of imagination.

HORNER: Or another man's last mistress of flesh and blood.

MRS. PINCHWIFE: Nay, now you jeer, sir; pray don't jeer me.

PINCHWIFE: Come, come. [*Aside*.] By heavens, she'll discover herself!

HORNER: I speak of your sister, sir.

PINCHWIFE: Ay, but saying she was handsome, if like him, made him blush. [*Aside*.] I am upon a rack!

HORNER: Methinks he is so handsome he should not be a man.

PINCHWIFE [*aside*]: Oh, there 'tis out! He has discovered her! I am not able to suffer any longer. [*To his wife*.] Come, come away, I say.

HORNER: Nay, by your leave, sir, he shall not go yet.—[*To them*.] Harcourt, Dorilant, let us torment this jealous rogue a little.

HARCOURT:
DORILANT: } How?

HORNER: I'll show you.

PINCHWIFE: Come, pray, let him go, I cannot stay fooling any longer. I tell you his sister stays supper for us.

HORNER: Does she? Come then, we'll all go sup with her and thee.

PINCHWIFE: No, now I think on't, having stayed so long for us, I warrant she's gone to bed. [*Aside*.] I wish she and I were well out of their hands.—Come, I must rise early tomorrow, come.

HORNER: Well, then, if she be gone to bed, I wish her and you a good night. But pray, young gentleman, present my humble service to her.

MRS. PINCHWIFE: Thank you heartily, sir.

PINCHWIFE [*aside*]: 'Sdeath! she will discover herself yet in spite of me.—He is something more civil to you, for your kindness to his sister, than I am, it seems.

HORNER: Tell her, dear sweet little gentleman, for all your brother there, that you have revived the love I had for her at first sight in the playhouse.

MRS. PINCHWIFE: But did you love her indeed, and indeed?

PINCHWIFE [*aside*]: So, so.—Away, I say.

HORNER: Nay, stay. Yes, indeed, and indeed, pray do you tell her so, and give her this kiss from me. [*Kisses her*.]

8. Shabby, dull woman.

PINCHWIFE [*aside*]: O heavens! What do I suffer! Now 'tis too plain he knows her, and yet—

HORNER: And this, and this—[*Kisses her again.*]

MRS. PINCHWIFE: What do you kiss me for? I am no woman.

PINCHWIFE [*aside*]: So—there, 'tis out.—Come, I cannot, nor will stay any longer.

HORNER: Nay, they shall send your lady a kiss too. Here, Harcourt, Dorilant, will you not? [*They kiss her.*]

PINCHWIFE [*aside*]: How! Do I suffer this? Was I not accusing another just now for this rascally patience, in permitting his wife to be kissed before his face? Ten thousand ulcers gnaw away their lips!—Come, come.

HORNER: Good night, dear little gentleman. Madam, good night. Farewell, Pinchwife. [*Apart to Harcourt and Dorilant.*] Did not I tell you I would raise his jealous gall? [*Exeunt Horner, Harcourt, and Dorilant.*]

PINCHWIFE: So, they are gone at last; stay, let me see first if the coach be at this door. [*Exit.*]

[*Horner, Harcourt, Dorilant return.*]

HORNER: What, not gone yet? Will you be sure to do as I desired you, sweet sir?

MRS. PINCHWIFE: Sweet sir, but what will you give me then?

HORNER: Anything. Come away into the next walk.

[*Exit Horner, haling away Mrs. Pinchwife.*]

ALITHEA: Hold, hold! What d'ye do?

LUCY: Stay, stay, hold—

HARCOURT: Hold, madam, hold! Let him present[9] him, he'll come presently. Nay, I will never let you go till you answer my question.

LUCY: For God's sake, sir, I must follow 'em.

DORILANT: No, I have something to present you with too; you shan't follow them.

[*Alithea, Lucy struggling with Harcourt and Dorilant. Pinchwife returns.*]

PINCHWIFE: Where?—how?—what's become of?—gone!—whither?

LUCY: He's only gone with the gentleman, who will give him something, an't please your worship.

PINCHWIFE: Something—give him something, with a pox!—where are they?

ALITHEA: In the next walk only, brother.

PINCHWIFE: Only, only! Where, where?

[*Exit Pinchwife and returns presently, then goes out again.*]

HARCOURT: What's the matter with him? Why so much concerned? But dearest madam—

ALITHEA: Pray let me go, sir; I have said and suffered enough already.

HARCOURT: Then you will not look upon nor pity my sufferings?

ALITHEA: To look upon 'em, when I cannot help 'em, were cruelty, not pity; therefore I will never see you more.

HARCOURT: Let me then, madam, have my privilege of a banished lover, complaining or railing, and giving you but a farewell reason why, if you cannot condescend to marry me, you should not take that wretch, my rival.

ALITHEA: He only, not you, since my honor is engaged so far to him, can give me a reason why I should not marry him; but if he be true and what I think him to me, I must be so to him. Your servant, sir.

9. Offer a gift to.

HARCOURT: Have women only constancy when 'tis a vice and, like fortune, only true to fools?

DORILANT [*to Lucy, who struggles to get from him*]: Thou shalt not stir, thou robust creature; you see I can deal with you, therefore you should stay the rather, and be kind.

[*Enter Pinchwife.*]

PINCHWIFE: Gone, gone, not to be found! Quite gone! Ten thousand plagues go with 'em! Which way went they?

ALITHEA: But into t'other walk, brother.

LUCY: Their business will be done presently sure, an't please your worship; it can't be long in doing, I'm sure on't.

ALITHEA: Are they not there?

PINCHWIFE: No; you know where they are, you infamous wretch, eternal shame of your family, which you do not dishonor enough yourself, you think, but you must help her to do it too, thou legion of bawds!

ALITHEA: Good brother—

PINCHWIFE: Damned, damned sister!

ALITHEA: Look you here, she's coming.

[*Enter Mrs. Pinchwife in man's clothes, running, with her hat under her arm, full of oranges and dried fruit; Horner following.*]

MRS. PINCHWIFE: O dear bud, look you here what I have got, see!

PINCHWIFE [*aside, rubbing his forehead*]: And what I have got here too, which you can't see.

MRS. PINCHWIFE: The fine gentleman has given me better things yet.

PINCHWIFE: Has he so? [*Aside.*] Out of breath and colored! I must hold yet.

HORNER: I have only given your little brother an orange, sir.

PINCHWIFE [*to Horner*]: Thank you, sir. [*Aside.*] You have only squeezed my orange, I suppose, and given it me again; yet I must have a city patience. [*To his wife.*] Come, come away.

MRS. PINCHWIFE: Stay, till I have put up my fine things, bud.

[*Enter Sir Jaspar Fidget.*]

SIR JASPAR: O Master Horner, come, come, the ladies stay for you; your mistress, my wife, wonders you make not more haste to her.

HORNER: I have stayed this half hour for you here and 'tis your fault I am not now with your wife.

SIR JASPAR: But pray, don't let her know so much; the truth on't is, I was advancing a certain project to his Majesty about—I'll tell you.

HORNER: No, let's go and hear it at your house.—Good night, sweet little gentleman. One kiss more, you'll remember me now, I hope. [*Kisses her.*]

DORILANT: What, Sir Jaspar, will you separate friends? He promised to sup with us; and if you take him to your house, you'll be in danger of our company too.

SIR JASPAR: Alas, gentlemen, my house is not fit for you; there are none but civil women there, which are not fit for your turn. He, you know, can bear with the society of civil women now, ha, ha, ha! Besides, he's one of my family—he's—heh, heh, heh!

DORILANT: What is he?

SIR JASPAR: Faith, my eunuch, since you'll have it, heh, he, he!

[*Exeunt Sir Jaspar Fidget and Horner.*]

DORILANT: I rather wish thou wert his, or my cuckold. Harcourt, what a good cuckold is lost there for want of a man to make him one! Thee and I cannot have Horner's privilege, who can make use of it.

HARCOURT: Ay, to poor Horner 'tis like coming to an estate at threescore, when a man can't be the better for't.

PINCHWIFE: Come.

MRS. PINCHWIFE: Presently, bud.

DORILANT: Come, let us go too. [*To Alithea.*] Madam, your servant. [*To Lucy.*] Good night, strapper.[1]

HARCOURT: Madam, though you will not let me have a good day or night, I wish you one; but dare not name the other half of my wish.

ALITHEA: Good night, sir, forever.

MRS. PINCHWIFE: I don't know where to put this here, dear bud; you shall eat it; nay, you shall have part of the fine gentleman's good things, or treat as you call it, when we come home.

PINCHWIFE: Indeed, I deserve it, since I furnished the best part of it. [*Strikes away the orange.*]

The gallant treats, presents, and gives the ball
But 'tis the absent cuckold pays for all.

[*Exeunt.*]

ACT 4

Scene 1

[*In Pinchwife's house in the morning. Lucy, Alithea dressed in new clothes.*]

LUCY: Well—madam, now have I dressed you and set you out with so many ornaments and spent upon you ounces of essence and pulvilio,[1] and all this for no other purpose but as people adorn and perfume a corpse for a stinking second-hand grave[2]—such or as bad I think as Master Sparkish's bed.

ALITHEA: Hold your peace.

LUCY: Nay, madam, I will ask you the reason why you would banish poor Master Harcourt forever from your sight. How could you be so hardhearted?

ALITHEA: 'Twas because I was not hardhearted.

LUCY: No, no, 'twas stark love and kindness, I warrant.

ALITHEA: It was so; I would see him no more because I love him.

LUCY: Hey-day, a very pretty reason!

ALITHEA: You do not understand me.

LUCY: I wish you may yourself.

ALITHEA: I was engaged to marry, you see, another man, whom my justice will not suffer me to deceive or injure.

LUCY: Can there be a greater cheat or wrong done to a man than to give him your person without your heart? I should make a conscience of[3] it.

ALITHEA: I'll retrieve it for him after I am married a while.

LUCY: The woman that marries to love better will be as much mistaken as the wencher that marries to live better. No, madam, marrying to increase love is like gaming to become rich; alas, you only lose what little stock you had before.

1. Robust woman.

1. Perfume and tragrant powder.

2. I.e., a grave newly opened for a second burial.

3. Have scruples about.

ALITHEA: I find by your rhetoric you have been bribed to betray me.

LUCY: Only by his merit, that has bribed your heart, you see, against your word and rigid honor. But what a devil is this honor! 'Tis sure a disease in the head, like the megrim, or falling sickness,[4] that always hurries people away to do themselves mischief. Men lose their lives by it; women what's dearer to 'em, their love, the life of life.

ALITHEA: Come, pray talk you no more of honor, nor Master Harcourt. I wish the other would come to secure my fidelity to him and his right in me.

LUCY: You will marry him then?

ALITHEA: Certainly. I have given him already my word and will my hand too, to make it good when he comes.

LUCY: Well, I wish I may never stick pin more if he be not an arrant natural to[5] t'other fine gentleman.

ALITHEA: I own he wants the wit of Harcourt, which I will dispense withal for another want he has, which is want of jealousy, which men of wit seldom want.

LUCY: Lord, madam, what should you do with a fool to your husband? You intend to be honest, don't you? Then that husbandly virtue, credulity, is thrown away upon you.

ALITHEA: He only that could suspect my virtue should have cause to do it; 'tis Sparkish's confidence in my truth that obliges me to be so faithful to him.

LUCY: You are not sure his opinion may last.

ALITHEA: I am satisfied 'tis impossible for him to be jealous after the proofs I have had of him. Jealousy in a husband—Heaven defend me from it! It begets a thousand plagues to a poor woman, the loss of her honor, her quiet and her—

LUCY: And her pleasure.

ALITHEA: What d'ye mean, impertinent?

LUCY: Liberty is a great pleasure, madam.

ALITHEA: I say, loss of her honor, her quiet, nay, her life sometimes, and what's as bad almost, the loss of this town; that is, she is sent into the country, which is the last ill usage of a husband to a wife, I think.

LUCY [*aside*]: Oh, does the wind lie there?—Then, of necessity, madam, you think a man must carry his wife into the country, if he be wise. The country is as terrible, I find, to our young English ladies as a monastery to those abroad, and, on my virginity, I think they would rather marry a London jailer than a high sheriff of a county, since neither can stir from his employment. Formerly women of wit married fools for a great estate, a fine seat, or the like, but now 'tis for a pretty seat only in Lincoln's Inn Fields, St James's Fields, or the Pall Mall.[6]

[*Enter to them Sparkish and Harcourt dressed like a parson.*]

SPARKISH: Madam, your humble servant, a happy day to you, and to us all.

HARCOURT: Amen.

ALITHEA: Who have we here?

SPARKISH: My chaplain, faith. O madam, poor Harcourt remembers his humble service to you and, in obedience to your last commands, refrains coming into your sight.

4. Migraine headache, or epilepsy.
5. An utter fool in comparison to.
6. Fashionable residential areas of London, distinguished by their famous inhabitants and expensive shops, as well as their grand houses.

ALITHEA: Is not that he?

SPARKISH: No, fie, no; but to show that he ne'er intended to hinder our match, has sent his brother here to join our hands. When I get me a wife, I must get her a chaplain, according to the custom; this is his brother, and my chaplain.

ALITHEA: His brother?

LUCY [*aside*]: And your chaplain, to preach in your pulpit then.

ALITHEA: His brother!

SPARKISH: Nay, I knew you would not believe it.—I told you, sir, she would take you for your brother Frank.

ALITHEA: Believe it!

LUCY [*aside*]: His brother! hah, ha, he! He has a trick left still, it seems.

SPARKISH: Come, my dearest, pray let us go to church before the canonical hour[7] is past.

ALITHEA: For shame, you are abused still.

SPARKISH: By the world, 'tis strange now you are so incredulous.

ALITHEA: 'Tis strange you are so credulous.

SPARKISH: Dearest of my life, hear me. I tell you this is Ned Harcourt of Cambridge; by the world, you see he has a sneaking college look. 'Tis true he's something like his brother Frank and they differ from each other no more than in their age, for they were twins.

LUCY: Hah, ha, he!

ALITHEA: Your servant, sir; I cannot be so deceived, though you are. But come, let's hear; how do you know what you affirm so confidently?

SPARKISH: Why, I'll tell you all. Frank Harcourt coming to me this morning, to wish me joy and present his service to you, I asked him if he could help me to a parson, whereupon he told me he had a brother in town who was in orders and he went straight away and sent him you see there to me.

ALITHEA: Yes, Frank goes and puts on a black coat, then tells you he is Ned; that's all you have for't.

SPARKISH: Pshaw, pshaw, I tell you by the same token, the midwife put her garter about Frank's neck to know 'em asunder, they were so like.

ALITHEA: Frank tells you this too.

SPARKISH: Ay, and Ned there too; nay, they are both in a story.

ALITHEA: So, so; very foolish!

SPARKISH: Lord, if you won't believe one, you had best try him by your chambermaid there, for chambermaids must needs know chaplains from other men, they are so used to 'em.

LUCY: Let's see; nay, I'll be sworn he has the canonical smirk and the filthy, clammy palm of a chaplain.

ALITHEA: Well, most reverend doctor, pray let us make an end of this fooling.

HARCOURT: With all my soul, divine, heavenly creature, when you please.

ALITHEA: He speaks like a chaplain indeed.

SPARKISH: Why, was there not "soul," "divine," "heavenly," in what he said?

7. Church law permitted the marriage ceremony only in the morning; it could be performed at any time between 8 A.M. and noon.

ALITHEA: Once more, most impertinent black coat, cease your persecution and let us have a conclusion of this ridiculous love.

HARCOURT [*aside*]: I had forgot. I must suit my style to my coat, or I wear it in vain.

ALITHEA: I have no more patience left; let us make once an end of this troublesome love, I say.

HARCOURT: So be it, seraphic lady, when your honor shall think it meet and convenient so to do.

SPARKISH: Gad, I'm sure none but a chaplain could speak so, I think.

ALITHEA: Let me tell you, sir, this dull trick will not serve your turn; though you delay our marriage, you shall not hinder it.

HARCOURT: Far be it from me, munificent patroness, to delay your marriage. I desire nothing more than to marry you presently, which I might do, if you yourself would, for my noble, good-natured and thrice generous patron here would not hinder it.

SPARKISH: No, poor man, not I, faith.

HARCOURT: And now, madam, let me tell you plainly, nobody else shall marry you; by heavens, I'll die first, for I'm sure I should die[8] after it.

LUCY [*aside*]: How his love has made him forget his function, as I have seen it in real parsons!

ALITHEA: That was spoken like a chaplain too! Now you understand him, I hope.

SPARKISH: Poor man, he takes it heinously to be refused. I can't blame him; 'tis putting an indignity upon him not to be suffered. But you'll pardon me, madam, it shan't be, he shall marry us. Come away, pray, madam.

LUCY [*aside*]: Hah, ha, he! More ado! 'Tis late.

ALITHEA: Invincible stupidity! I tell you he would marry me as your rival, not as your chaplain.

SPARKISH [*pulling her away*]: Come, come, madam.

LUCY: Ay, pray, madam, do not refuse this reverend divine the honor and satisfaction of marrying you, for I dare say he has set his heart upon't, good doctor.

ALITHEA: What can you hope or design by this?

HARCOURT [*aside*]: I could answer her, a reprieve for a day only often revokes a hasty doom; at worst, if she will not take mercy on me and let me marry her, I have at least the lover's second pleasure, hindering my rival's enjoyment, though but for a time.

SPARKISH: Come, madam, 'tis e'en twelve o'clock, and my mother charged me never to be married out of the canonical hours. Come, come. Lord, here's such a deal of modesty, I warrant, the first day.

LUCY: Yes, an't please your worship, married women show all their modesty the first day, because married men show all their love the first day.

[*Exeunt Sparkish, Alithea, Harcourt, and Lucy.*]

8. Harcourt plays on literal death and sexual "death": orgasm.

Scene 2

[*The scene changes to a bedchamber, where appear Pinchwife, Mrs. Pinchwife.*]

PINCHWIFE: Come, tell me, I say.

MRS. PINCHWIFE: Lord, ha'n't I told it an hundred times over?

PINCHWIFE [*aside*]: I would try if, in the repetition of the ungrateful[9] tale, I could find her altering it in the least circumstance, for if her story be false, she is so too.—Come, how was't, baggage?

MRS. PINCHWIFE: Lord, what pleasure you take to hear it, sure!

PINCHWIFE: No, you take more in telling it, I find; but speak, how was't?

MRS. PINCHWIFE: He carried me up into the house next to the Exchange.

PINCHWIFE: So, and you two were only in the room.

MRS. PINCHWIFE: Yes, for he sent away a youth that was there, for some dried fruit and China oranges.[1]

PINCHWIFE: Did he so? Damn him for it—and for—

MRS. PINCHWIFE: But presently came up the gentle-woman of the house.

PINCHWIFE: O, 'twas well she did; but what did he do whilst the fruit came?

MRS. PINCHWIFE: He kissed me an hundred times and told me he fancied he kissed my fine sister, meaning me, you know, whom he said he loved with all his soul and bid me be sure to tell her so and to desire her to be at her window by eleven of the clock this morning and he would walk under it at that time.

PINCHWIFE [*aside*]: And he was as good as his word, very punctual—a pox reward him for't.

MRS. PINCHWIFE: Well, and he said if you were not within, he would come up to her, meaning me, you know, bud, still.

PINCHWIFE [*aside*]: So—he knew her certainly; but for this confession, I am obliged to her simplicity.—But what, you stood very still when he kissed you?

MRS. PINCHWIFE: Yes, I warrant you; would you have had me discovered myself?

PINCHWIFE: But you told me he did some beastliness to you, as you called it; what was't?

MRS. PINCHWIFE: Why, he put—

PINCHWIFE: What?

MRS. PINCHWIFE: Why, he put the tip of his tongue between my lips and so mousled[2] me—and I said, I'd bite it.

PINCHWIFE: An eternal canker seize it, for[3] a dog!

MRS. PINCHWIFE: Nay, you need not be so angry with him neither, for to say truth, he has the sweetest breath I ever knew.

PINCHWIFE: The devil!—you were satisfied with it then, and would do it again.

MRS. PINCHWIFE: Not unless he should force me.

PINCHWIFE: Force you, changeling![4] I tell you no woman can be forced.

MRS. PINCHWIFE: Yes, but she may, sure, by such a one as he, for he's a proper, goodly strong man; 'tis hard, let me tell you, to resist him.

PINCHWIFE: So, 'tis plain she loves him, yet she has not love enough to make her conceal it from me; but the sight of him will increase her aversion for me and love for him and that love instruct her how to deceive me and satisfy him, all idiot as

9. Unpleasant.

1. Sweet oranges, regarded in the seventeenth century as an exotic delicacy.

2. A variation on "muzzled": kissed deeply.

3. I.e., for acting like.

4. Fool.

she is. Love! 'Twas he gave women first their craft, their art of deluding; out of nature's hands they came plain, open, silly and fit for slaves, as she and Heaven intended 'em; but damned love—well—I must strangle that little monster[5] whilst I can deal with him.—Go fetch pen, ink and paper out of the next room.

MRS. PINCHWIFE: Yes, bud. [*Exit Mrs. Pinchwife.*]

PINCHWIFE [*aside*]: Why should women have more invention in love than men? It can only be because they have more desires, more soliciting passions, more lust, and more of the devil. [*Mrs. Pinchwife returns.*] Come, minx, sit down and write.

MRS. PINCHWIFE: Ay, dear bud, but I can't do't very well.

PINCHWIFE: I wish you could not at all.

MRS. PINCHWIFE: But what should I write for?

PINCHWIFE: I'll have you write a letter to your lover.

MRS. PINCHWIFE: O Lord, to the fine gentleman a letter!

PINCHWIFE: Yes, to the fine gentleman.

MRS. PINCHWIFE: Lord, you do but jeer; sure, you jest.

PINCHWIFE: I am not so merry. Come, write as I bid you.

MRS. PINCHWIFE: What, do you think I am a fool?

PINCHWIFE [*aside*]: She's afraid I would not dictate any love to him, therefore she's unwilling.—But you had best begin.

MRS. PINCHWIFE: Indeed, and indeed, but I won't, so I won't.

PINCHWIFE: Why?

MRS. PINCHWIFE: Because he's in town; you may send for him if you will.

PINCHWIFE: Very well, you would have him brought to you; is it come to this? I say, take the pen and write, or you'll provoke me.

MRS. PINCHWIFE: Lord, what d'ye make a fool of me for? Don't I know that letters are never writ but from the country to London and from London into the country? Now he's in town and I am in town too; therefore I can't write to him, you know.

PINCHWIFE [*aside*]: So, I am glad it is no worse; she is innocent enough yet.—Yes, you may, when your husband bids you, write letters to people that are in town.

MRS. PINCHWIFE: O, may I so? Then I'm satisfied.

PINCHWIFE: Come, begin.—[*Dictates.*] "Sir"—

MRS. PINCHWIFE: Shan't I say, "Dear Sir"? You know one says always something more than bare "Sir."

PINCHWIFE: Write as I bid you, or I will write "whore" with this penknife in your face.

MRS. PINCHWIFE: Nay, good bud—[*She writes.*] "Sir"—

PINCHWIFE: "Though I suffered last night your nauseous, loathed kisses and embraces"—Write.

MRS. PINCHWIFE: Nay, why should I say so? You know I told you he had a sweet breath.

PINCHWIFE: Write.

MRS. PINCHWIFE: Let me but put out "loathed."

PINCHWIFE: Write, I say.

5. Cupid.

MRS. PINCHWIFE: Well then. [*Writes.*]

PINCHWIFE: Let's see, what have you writ? [*Takes the paper and reads.*] "Though I suffered last night your kisses and embraces"—Thou impudent creature, where is "nauseous" and "loathed"?

MRS. PINCHWIFE: I can't abide to write such filthy words.

PINCHWIFE: Once more write as I'd have you, and question it not, or I will spoil thy writing with this. [*Holds up the penknife.*] I will stab out those eyes that cause my mischief.

MRS. PINCHWIFE: O Lord, I will!

PINCHWIFE: So—so—let's see now! [*Reads.*] "Though I suffered last night your nauseous, loathed kisses and embraces"—go on—"yet I would not have you presume that you shall ever repeat them"—So—[*She writes.*]

MRS. PINCHWIFE: I have writ it.

PINCHWIFE: On then.—"I then concealed myself from your knowledge to avoid your insolencies"—[*She writes.*]

MRS. PINCHWIFE: So—

PINCHWIFE: "The same reason, now I am out of your hands"—[*She writes.*]

MRS. PINCHWIFE: So—

PINCHWIFE: "Makes me own to you my unfortunate, though innocent, frolic, of being in man's clothes"—[*She writes.*]

MRS. PINCHWIFE: So—

PINCHWIFE: "That you may for evermore cease to pursue her, who hates and detests you"—[*She writes on.*]

MRS. PINCHWIFE: So—h—[*Sighs.*]

PINCHWIFE: What, do you sigh?—"detests you—as much as she loves her husband and her honour."

MRS. PINCHWIFE: I vow, husband, he'll ne'er believe I should write such a letter.

PINCHWIFE: What, he'd expect a kinder from you? Come, now your name only.

MRS. PINCHWIFE: What, shan't I say, "Your most faithful, humble servant till death"?

PINCHWIFE: No, tormenting fiend! [*Aside.*] Her style, I find, would be very soft.—Come, wrap it up now, whilst I go fetch wax and a candle, and write on the backside, "For Mr. Horner." [*Exit Pinchwife.*]

MRS. PINCHWIFE: "For Mr. Horner."—So, I am glad he has told me his name. Dear Mr. Horner! But why should I send thee such a letter that will vex thee and make thee angry with me?—Well, I will not send it—Ay, but then my husband will kill me—for I see plainly he won't let me love Mr. Horner—but what care I for my husband?—I won't, so I won't send poor Mr. Horner such a letter—But then my husband—But oh—What if I writ at bottom, my husband made me write it?—Ay, but then my husband would see't—Can one have no shift?[6] Ah, a London woman would have had a hundred presently. Stay—what if I should write a letter, and wrap it up like this, and write upon't too? Ay, but then my husband would see't—I don't know what to do—But yet y'vads[7] I'll try, so I will—for I will not send this letter to poor Mr. Horner, come what will on't.
[*She writes, and repeats what she hath writ.*]

6. Expedient; trick.

7. In faith.

"Dear, sweet Mr. Horner"—so—"my husband would have me send you a base, rude, unmannerly letter—but I won't"—so—"and would have me forbid you loving me—but I won't"—so—"and would have me say to you, I hate you, poor Mr. Horner—but I won't tell a lie for him"—there—"for I'm sure if you and I were in the country at cards together"—so—"I could not help treading on your toe under the table"—so—"or rubbing knees with you and staring in your face till you saw me"—very well—"and then looking down and blushing for an hour together"—so—"but I must make haste before my husband comes; and now he has taught me to write letters, you shall have longer ones from me, who am, Dear, dear, poor, dear Mr. Horner, Your most humble friend, and servant to command till death, Margery Pinchwife." Stay, I must give him a hint at bottom—so—now wrap it up just like t'other—so—now write, "For Mr. Horner"—But, oh now, what shall I do with it? For here comes my husband. [*Enter Pinchwife.*]

PINCHWIFE [*aside*]: I have been detained by a sparkish coxcomb, who pretended a visit to me; but I fear 'twas to my wife.—What, have you done?

MRS. PINCHWIFE: Ay, ay, bud, just now.

PINCHWIFE: Let's see't. What d'ye tremble for? What, you would not have it go?

MRS. PINCHWIFE: Here. [*Aside.*] No, I must not give him that; so I had been served if I had given him this.

PINCHWIFE [*He opens, and reads the first letter*]: Come, where's the wax and seal?

MRS. PINCHWIFE [*aside*]: Lord, what shall I do now? Nay, then, I have it.—Pray let me see't. Lord, you think me so arrant a fool I cannot seal a letter. I will do't, so I will. [*Snatches the letter from him, changes it for the other, seals it and delivers it to him.*]

PINCHWIFE: Nay, I believe you will learn that, and other things too, which I would not have you.

MRS. PINCHWIFE: So, han't I done it curiously?[8] [*Aside.*] I think I have; there's my letter going to Mr. Horner, since he'll needs have me send letters to folks.

PINCHWIFE: 'Tis very well; but I warrant you would not have it go now?

MRS. PINCHWIFE: Yes, indeed, but I would, bud, now.

PINCHWIFE: Well, you are a good girl then. Come, let me lock you up in your chamber, till I come back, and be sure you come not within three strides of the window when I am gone, for I have a spy in the street.

[*Exit Mrs. Pinchwife. Pinchwife locks the door.*]

At least, 'tis fit she think so. If we do not cheat women, they'll cheat us, and fraud may be justly used with secret enemies, of which a wife is the most dangerous, and he that has a handsome one to keep, and a frontier town, must provide against treachery rather than open force. Now I have secured all within, I'll deal with the foe without with false intelligence. [*Holds up the letter. Exit Pinchwife.*]

Scene 3

[*The scene changes to Horner's lodging. Quack and Horner.*]

QUACK: Well, sir, how fadges[9] the new design? Have you not the luck of all your brother projectors,[1] to deceive only yourself at last?

8. Adroitly; cleverly.
9. Progresses.
1. Designers, schemers.

HORNER: No, good domine[2] doctor, I deceive you, it seems, and others too, for the grave matrons and old, rigid husbands think me as unfit for love as they are but their wives, sisters and daughters know some of 'em better things already.

QUACK: Already!

HORNER: Already, I say. Last night I was drunk with half a dozen of your civil persons, as you call 'em, and people of honor, and so was made free of their society and dressing-rooms forever hereafter, and am already come to the privileges of sleeping upon their pallets,[3] warming smocks,[4] tying shoes and garters, and the like, doctor, already, already, doctor.

QUACK: You have made use of your time, sir.

HORNER: I tell thee, I am now no more interruption to 'em when they sing or talk bawdy than a little squab[5] French page who speaks no English.

QUACK: But do civil persons and women of honor drink and sing bawdy songs?

HORNER: O, amongst friends, amongst friends. For your bigots in honor are just like those in religion; they fear the eye of the world more than the eye of Heaven and think there is no virtue but railing at vice and no sin but giving scandal. They rail at a poor, little, kept player and keep themselves some young, modest pulpit comedian[6] to be privy to their sins in their closets, not to tell 'em of them in their chapels.

QUACK: Nay, the truth on't is, priests among the women now have quite got the better of us lay confessors, physicians.

HORNER: And they are rather their patients, but— [*Enter Lady Fidget, looking about her.*]

Now we talk of women of honor, here comes one. Step behind the screen there and but observe if I have not particular privileges with the women of reputation already, doctor, already.

[*Quack steps behind screen.*]

LADY FIDGET: Well, Horner, am not I a woman of honor? You see I'm as good as my word.

HORNER: And you shall see, madam, I'll not be behindhand with you in honor and I'll be as good as my word too, if you please but to withdraw into the next room.

LADY FIDGET: But first, my dear sir, you must promise to have a care of my dear honor.

HORNER: If you talk a word more of your honor, you'll make me incapable to wrong it. To talk of honor in the mysteries of love is like talking of heaven or the deity in an operation of witchcraft, just when you are employing the devil; it makes the charm impotent.

LADY FIDGET: Nay, fie, let us not be smooty.[7] But you talk of mysteries and bewitching to me; I don't understand you.

HORNER: I tell you, madam, the word "money" in a mistress's mouth, at such a nick of time, is not a more disheartening sound to a younger brother[8] than that of "honor" to an eager lover like myself.

LADY FIDGET: But you can't blame a lady of my reputation to be chary.

2. Master.
3. Mattresses.
4. I.e., their underwear (which the wealthy wanted warmed before worn).
5. Short and stout.
6. Household chaplain.
7. Smutty.
8. Because the eldest son inherited the estate, younger brothers typically lacked cash.

HORNER: Chary! I have been chary of it already, by the report I have caused of myself.

LADY FIDGET: Ay, but if you should ever let other women know that dear secret, it would come out. Nay, you must have a great care of your conduct, for my acquaintance are so censorious (oh, 'tis a wicked, censorious world, Mr. Horner!), I say, are so censorious and detracting that perhaps they'll talk, to the prejudice of my honor, though you should not let them know the dear secret.

HORNER: Nay, madam, rather than they shall prejudice your honor, I'll prejudice theirs, and, to serve you, I'll lie with 'em all, make the secret their own, and then they'll keep it. I am a Machiavel in love, madam.

LADY FIDGET: Oh, no, sir, not that way.

HORNER: Nay, the devil take me if censorious women are to be silenced any other way.

LADY FIDGET: A secret is better kept, I hope, by a single person than a multitude; therefore pray do not trust anybody else with it, dear, dear Mr. Horner. [*Embracing him.*]

[*Enter Sir Jaspar Fidget.*]

SIR JASPAR: How now!

LADY FIDGET [*aside*]: Oh, my husband—prevented—and what's almost as bad, found with my arms about another man—that will appear too much—what shall I say?—Sir Jaspar, come hither, I am trying if Mr. Horner were ticklish, and he's as ticklish as can be; I love to torment the confounded toad. Let you and I tickle him.

SIR JASPAR: No, your ladyship will tickle him better without me, I suppose. But is this your buying china? I thought you had been at the china house.[9]

HORNER [*aside*]: China house! That's my cue, I must take it.—A pox, can't you keep your impertinent wives at home? Some men are troubled with the husbands, but I with the wives. But I'd have you to know, since I cannot be your journeyman[1] by night, I will not be your drudge by day, to squire your wife about and be your man of straw, or scarecrow, only to pies and jays,[2] that would be nibbling at your forbidden fruit; I shall be shortly the hackney gentleman-usher[3] of the town.

SIR JASPAR [*aside*]: Heh, heh, he! Poor fellow, he's in the right on't, faith; to squire women about for other folks is as ungrateful an employment as to tell[4] money for other folks.—Heh, he, he! Ben't angry, Horner—

LADY FIDGET: No, 'tis I have more reason to be angry, who am left by you to go abroad indecently alone; or, what is more indecent, to pin myself upon such ill-bred people of your acquaintance as this is.

SIR JASPAR: Nay, prithee, what has he done?

LADY FIDGET: Nay, he has done nothing.

SIR JASPAR: But what d'ye take ill, if he has done nothing?

LADY FIDGET: Hah, hah, hah! Faith, I can't but laugh, however; why d'ye think the unmannerly toad would not come down to me to the coach? I was fain to come up to fetch him, or go without him, which I was resolved not to do, for he knows china very well and has himself very good, but will not let me see it lest I should beg some. But I will find it out and have what I came for yet.

9. China shop, sometimes used by lovers as a secret meeting place.
1. One who works for another.
2. Crafty fellows and fools.
3. Hired escort.
4. Count.

[*Exit Lady Fidget and locks the door, followed by Horner to the door.*]

HORNER [*apart to Lady Fidget*]: Lock the door, madam.—So, she has got into my chamber, and locked me out. Oh, the impertinency of womankind! Well, Sir Jaspar, plain-dealing is a jewel; if ever you suffer your wife to trouble me again here, she shall carry you home a pair of horns, by my Lord Mayor she shall; though I cannot furnish you myself, you are sure, yet I'll find a way.

SIR JASPAR [*aside*]: Hah, ha, he! At my first coming in and finding her arms about him, tickling him it seems, I was half jealous, but now I see my folly.—Heh, he, he! Poor Horner.

HORNER: Nay, though you laugh now, 'twill be my turn ere long. Oh, women, more impertinent, more cunning and more mischievous than their monkeys,[5] and to me almost as ugly! Now is she throwing my things about and rifling all I have, but I'll get into her the back way and so rifle her for it.

SIR JASPAR: Hah, ha, ha, poor angry Horner.

HORNER: Stay here a little; I'll ferret her out to you presently, I warrant.

[*Exit Horner at t'other door.*]

SIR JASPAR: Wife! My Lady Fidget! Wife! He is coming into you the back way.

[*Sir Jaspar calls through the door to his wife; she answers from within.*]

LADY FIDGET: Let him come, and welcome, which way he will.

SIR JASPAR: He'll catch you and use you roughly and be too strong for you.

LADY FIDGET: Don't you trouble yourself; let him if he can.

QUACK [*behind*]: This indeed I could not have believed from him, nor any but my own eyes.

[*Enter Mrs. Squeamish.*]

SQUEAMISH: Where's this woman-hater, this toad, this ugly, greasy, dirty sloven?

SIR JASPAR [*aside*]: So, the women all will have him ugly; methinks he is a comely person, but his wants make his form contemptible to 'em and 'tis e'en as my wife said yesterday, talking of him, that a proper handsome eunuch was as ridiculous a thing as a gigantic coward.

SQUEAMISH: Sir Jaspar, your servant. Where is the odious beast?

SIR JASPAR: He's within in his chamber, with my wife; she's playing the wag with him.

SQUEAMISH: Is she so? And he's a clownish beast, he'll give her no quarter;[6] he'll play the wag with her again, let me tell you. Come, let's go help her.—What, the door's locked?

SIR JASPAR: Ay, my wife locked it.

SQUEAMISH: Did she so? Let us break it open then.

SIR JASPAR: No, no, he'll do her no hurt.

SQUEAMISH: No. [*Aside.*] But is there no other way to get in to 'em? Whither goes this? I will disturb 'em. [*Exit Squeamish at another door.*]

OLD LADY SQUEAMISH: Where is this harlotry, this impudent baggage, this rambling tomrig?[7] O Sir Jaspar, I'm glad to see you here. Did you not see my vild[8] grandchild come in hither just now?

SIR JASPAR: Yes.

5. Which ladies sometimes kept as pets.
6. No mercy.
7. Strumpet.
8. Vile.

OLD LADY SQUEAMISH: Ay, but where is she then? Where is she? Lord, Sir Jaspar, I have e'en rattled myself to pieces in pursuit of her. But can you tell what she makes here? They say below, no woman lodges here.

SIR JASPAR: No.

OLD LADY SQUEAMISH: No! What does she here then? Say, if it be not a woman's lodging, what makes she here? But are you sure no woman lodges here?

SIR JASPAR: No, nor no man neither; this is Mr. Horner's lodging.

OLD LADY SQUEAMISH: Is it so, are you sure?

SIR JASPAR: Yes, yes.

OLD LADY SQUEAMISH: So then there's no hurt in't, I hope. But where is he?

SIR JASPAR: He's in the next room with my wife.

OLD LADY SQUEAMISH: Nay, if you trust him with your wife, I may with my Biddy.[9] They say he's a merry harmless man now, e'en as harmless a man as ever came out of Italy with a good voice,[1] and as pretty harmless company for a lady as a snake without his teeth.

SIR JASPAR: Ay, ay, poor man.

[*Enter Mrs. Squeamish.*]

SQUEAMISH: I can't find 'em.—Oh, are you here, Grandmother? I followed, you must know, my Lady Fidget hither; 'tis the prettiest lodging and I have been staring on the prettiest pictures.

[*Enter Lady Fidget with a piece of china in her hand, and Horner following.*]

LADY FIDGET: And I have been toiling and moiling[2] for the prettiest piece of china, my dear.

HORNER: Nay, she has been too hard for me, do what I could.

SQUEAMISH: O Lord, I'll have some china too. Good Mr. Horner, don't think to give other people china and me none; come in with me too.

HORNER: Upon my honor, I have none left now.

SQUEAMISH: Nay, nay, I have known you deny your china before now, but you shan't put me off so. Come—

HORNER: This lady had the last there.

LADY FIDGET: Yes, indeed, madam, to my certain knowledge he has no more left.

SQUEAMISH: O, but it may be he may have some you could not find.

LADY FIDGET: What, d'ye think if he had had any left, I would not have had it too? For we women of quality never think we have china enough.

HORNER: Do not take it ill. I cannot make china for you all, but I will have a roll-wagon[3] for you too, another time.

SQUEAMISH: Thank you, dear toad.

LADY FIDGET [*to Horner aside*]: What do you mean by that promise?

HORNER [*apart to Lady Fidget*]: Alas, she has an innocent, literal understanding.

OLD LADY SQUEAMISH: Poor Mr. Horner, he has enough to do to please you all, I see.

HORNER: Ay, madam, you see how they use me.

OLD LADY SQUEAMISH: Poor gentleman, I pity you.

9. Abbreviation of Bridget; also, a general term for a young woman.
1. I.e., as a castrato, a male singer castrated in boyhood so as to preserve his soprano voice.
2. Working hard.
3. A cylindrical vase; here (of course) with phallic connotations.

HORNER: I thank you, madam. I could never find pity but from such reverend ladies as you are; the young ones will never spare a man.

SQUEAMISH: Come, come, beast, and go dine with us, for we shall want a man at ombre after dinner.

HORNER: That's all their use of me, madam, you see.

SQUEAMISH: Come, sloven, I'll lead you, to be sure of you: [*Pulls him by the cravat.*]

OLD LADY SQUEAMISH: Alas, poor man, how she tugs him! Kiss, kiss her; that's the way to make such nice[4] women quiet.

HORNER: No, madam, that remedy is worse than the torment; they know I dare suffer anything rather than do it.

OLD LADY SQUEAMISH: Prithee, kiss her and I'll give you her picture in little,[5] that you admired so last night; prithee do.

HORNER: Well, nothing but that could bribe me; I love a woman only in effigy and good painting, as much as I hate them. I'll do't, for I could adore the devil well painted. [*Kisses Mrs. Squeamish.*]

SQUEAMISH: Foh, you filthy toad! Nay, now I've done jesting.

OLD LADY SQUEAMISH: Ha, ha, ha, I told you so.

SQUEAMISH: Foh, a kiss of his—

SIR JASPAR: Has no more hurt in't than one of my spaniel's.

SQUEAMISH: Nor no more good neither.

QUACK [*behind*]: I will now believe anything he tells me.

[*Enter Mr. Pinchwife.*]

LADY FIDGET: O Lord, here's a man! Sir Jaspar, my mask, my mask! I would not be seen here for the world.

SIR JASPAR: What, not when I am with you?

LADY FIDGET: No, no, my honor—let's be gone.

SQUEAMISH: Oh, Grandmother, let us be gone; make haste, make haste, I know not how he may censure us.

LADY FIDGET: Be found in the lodging of anything like a man! Away!

[*Exeunt Sir Jaspar, Lady Fidget, Old Lady Squeamish, Mrs. Squeamish.*]

QUACK [*behind*]: What's here? Another cuckold? He looks like one, and none else sure have any business with him.

HORNER: Well, what brings my dear friend hither?

PINCHWIFE: Your impertinency.

HORNER: My impertinency!—Why, you gentlemen that have got handsome wives think you have a privilege of saying anything to your friends and are as brutish as if you were our creditors.

PINCHWIFE: No, sir, I'll ne'er trust you any way.

HORNER: But why not, dear Jack? Why diffide[6] in me thou knowest so well?

PINCHWIFE: Because I do know you so well.

HORNER: Han't I been always thy friend, honest Jack, always ready to serve thee, in love or battle, before thou wert married, and am so still?

PINCHWIFE: I believe so; you would be my second now indeed.

HORNER: Well then, dear Jack, why so unkind, so grum, so strange to me? Come, prithee kiss me, dear rogue. Gad, I was always, I say, and am still as much thy servant as—

4. Fastidious; also, in an older sense, wanton.

5. Miniature.

6. Distrust.

PINCHWIFE: As I am yours, sir. What, you would send a kiss to my wife, is that it?

HORNER: So, there 'tis—a man can't show his friendship to a married man but presently he talks of his wife to you. Prithee, let thy wife alone and let thee and I be all one, as we were wont. What, thou art as shy of my kindness as a Lombard Street[7] alderman of a courtier's civility at Locket's.[8]

PINCHWIFE: But you are overkind to me, as kind as if I were your cuckold already; yet I must confess you ought to be kind and civil to me, since I am so kind, so civil to you, as to bring you this. Look you there, sir. [*Delivers him a letter.*]

HORNER: What is't?

PINCHWIFE: Only a love-letter, sir.

HORNER: From whom?—how! this is from your wife—hum—and hum—[*Reads.*]

PINCHWIFE: Even from my wife, sir. Am I not wondrous kind and civil to you now too? [*Aside.*] But you'll not think her so.

HORNER [*aside*]: Ha, is this a trick of his or hers?

PINCHWIFE: The gentleman's surprised, I find. What, you expected a kinder letter?

HORNER: No, faith, not I, how could I?

PINCHWIFE: Yes, yes, I'm sure you did; a man so well made as you are must needs be disappointed if the women declare not their passion at first sight or opportunity.

HORNER [*aside*]: But what should this mean? Stay, the postscript. [*Reads aside.*] "Be sure you love me, whatsoever my husband says to the contrary, and let him not see this, lest he should come home and pinch me, or kill my squirrel.[9]" [*Aside.*] It seems he knows not what the letter contains.

PINCHWIFE: Come, ne'er wonder at it so much.

HORNER: Faith, I can't help it.

PINCHWIFE: Now, I think, I have deserved your infinite friendship and kindness and have showed myself sufficiently an obliging kind friend and husband; am I not so, to bring a letter from my wife to her gallant?

HORNER: Ay, the devil take me, art thou the most obliging, kind friend and husband in the world, ha, ha!

PINCHWIFE: Well, you may be merry, sir; but in short I must tell you, sir, my honor will suffer no jesting.

HORNER: What dost thou mean?

PINCHWIFE: Does the letter want a comment? Then know, sir, though I have been so civil a husband as to bring you a letter from my wife, to let you kiss and court her to my face, I will not be a cuckold, sir, I will not.

HORNER: Thou art mad with jealousy. I never saw thy wife in my life but at the play yesterday, and I know not if it were she or no. I court her, kiss her!

PINCHWIFE: I will not be a cuckold, I say; there will be danger in making me a cuckold.

HORNER: Why, wert thou not well cured of thy last clap?

PINCHWIFE: I wear a sword.

HORNER: It should be taken from thee lest thou shouldst do thyself a mischief with it; thou art mad, man.

7. Banking center of London.

8. In Charing Cross, a celebrated restaurant and popular post-theater meeting place.

9. A fashionable pet.

PINCHWIFE: As mad as I am, and as merry as you are, I must have more reason from you ere we part. I say again, though you kissed and courted last night my wife in man's clothes, as she confesses in her letter—

HORNER [*aside*]: Ha!

PINCHWIFE: Both she and I say, you must not design it again, for you have mistaken your woman, as you have done your man.

HORNER [*aside*]: Oh—I understand something now.—Was that thy wife? Why wouldst thou not tell me 'twas she? Faith, my freedom with her was your fault, not mine.

PINCHWIFE [*aside*]: Faith, so 'twas.

HORNER: Fie, I'd never do't to a woman before her husband's face, sure.

PINCHWIFE: But I had rather you should do't to my wife before my face than behind my back, and that you shall never do.

HORNER: No—you will hinder me.

PINCHWIFE: If I would not hinder you, you see by her letter, she would.

HORNER: Well, I must e'en acquiesce then and be contented with what she writes.

PINCHWIFE: I'll assure you 'twas voluntarily writ; I had no hand in't, you may believe me.

HORNER: I do believe thee, faith.

PINCHWIFE: And believe her too, for she's an innocent creature, has no dissembling in her; and so fare you well, sir.

HORNER: Pray, however, present my humble service to her and tell her I will obey her letter to a tittle and fulfill her desires, be what they will, or with what difficulty soever I do't, and you shall be no more jealous of me, I warrant her and you.

PINCHWIFE: Well, then, fare you well, and play with any man's honor but mine, kiss any man's wife but mine, and welcome. [*Exit Mr. Pinchwife.*]

HORNER: Ha, ha, ha, doctor.

QUACK: It seems he has not heard the report of you, or does not believe it.

HORNER: Ha, ha! Now, doctor, what think you?

QUACK: Pray let's see the letter—hum— [*Reads the letter.*] "for—dear—love you—"

HORNER: I wonder how she could contrive it! What say'st thou to't? 'Tis an original.

QUACK: So are your cuckolds, too, originals, for they are like no other common cuckolds, and I will henceforth believe it not impossible for you to cuckold the Grand Signior[1] amidst his guards of eunuchs, that I say.

HORNER: And I say for the letter, 'tis the first love-letter that ever was without flames, darts, fates, destinies, lying and dissembling in't.

[*Enter Sparkish, pulling in Mr. Pinchwife.*]

SPARKISH: Come back, you are a pretty brother-in-law, neither go to church, nor to dinner with your sister bride!

PINCHWIFE: My sister denies her marriage and you see is gone away from you dissatisfied.

1. Sultan of Turkey, whose eunuchs guarded his harem.

SPARKISH: Pshaw, upon a foolish scruple, that our parson was not in lawful orders and did not say all the Common Prayer; but 'tis her modesty only, I believe. But let women be never so modest the first day, they'll be sure to come to themselves by night, and I shall have enough of her then. In the meantime, Harry Horner, you must dine with me; I keep my wedding at my aunt's in the Piazza.[2]

HORNER: Thy wedding! What stale maid has lived to despair of a husband, or what young one of a gallant?

SPARKISH: Oh, your servant, sir—this gentleman's sister then—no stale maid.

HORNER: I'm sorry for't.

PINCHWIFE [*aside*]: How comes he so concerned for her?

SPARKISH: You sorry for't? Why, do you know any ill by her?

HORNER: No, I know none but by thee; 'tis for her sake, not yours, and another man's sake that might have hoped, I thought.

SPARKISH: Another man, another man! What is his name?

HORNER: Nay, since 'tis past he shall be nameless. [*Aside.*] Poor Harcourt, I am sorry thou hast missed her.

PINCHWIFE [*aside*]: He seems to be much troubled at the match.

SPARKISH: Prithee tell me—nay, you shan't go, brother.

PINCHWIFE: I must of necessity, but I'll come to you to dinner. [*Exit Pinchwife.*]

SPARKISH: But, Harry, what, have I a rival in my wife already? But with all my heart, for he may be of use to me hereafter, for though my hunger is now my sauce and I can fall on heartily without, but the time will come when a rival will be as good sauce for a married man to a wife as an orange to veal.

HORNER: O thou damned rogue! Thou hast set my teeth on edge with thy orange.

SPARKISH: Then let's to dinner—there I was with[3] you again. Come.

HORNER: But who dines with thee?

SPARKISH: My friends and relations, my brother Pinchwife, you see, of your acquaintance.

HORNER: And his wife?

SPARKISH: No, gad, he'll ne'er let her come amongst us good fellows. Your stingy country coxcomb keeps his wife from friends, as he does his little firkin[4] of ale for his own drinking, and a gentleman can't get a smack[5] on't; but his servants, when his back is turned, broach[6] it at their pleasures and dust it away,[7] ha, ha, ha! Gad, I am witty, I think, considering I was married today, by the world. But come—

HORNER: No, I will not dine with you, unless you can fetch her too.

SPARKISH: Pshaw, what pleasure canst thou have with women now, Harry?

HORNER: My eyes are not gone; I love a good prospect yet and will not dine with you unless she does too. Go fetch her, therefore, but do not tell her husband 'tis for my sake.

SPARKISH: Well, I'll try what I can do. In the mean-time come away to my aunt's lodging; 'tis in the way to Pinchwife's.

HORNER: The poor woman has called for aid and stretched forth her hand, doctor; I cannot but help her over the pale[8] out of the briars.

[*Exeunt Sparkish, Horner, Quack.*]

2. An elegant arcade near Covent Garden; Act 5, Scene 3 is set there.
3. Caught.
4. Small cask.
5. Taste.
6. Tap.
7. Finish it off.
8. Fence; here, figuratively, the constraints of marital fidelity.

Scene 4

[*The scene changes to Pinchwife's house. Mrs. Pinchwife alone, leaning on her elbow. A table, pen, ink and paper.*]

MRS. PINCHWIFE: Well, 'tis e'en so, I have got the London disease they call love; I am sick of my husband and for my gallant. I have heard this distemper[9] called a fever, but methinks 'tis liker an ague, for when I think of my husband, I tremble and am in a cold sweat and have inclinations to vomit but when I think of my gallant, dear Mr. Horner, my hot fit comes and I am all in a fever, indeed, and as in other fevers my own chamber is tedious to me and I would fain be removed to his and then methinks I should be well. Ah, poor Mr. Horner! Well, I cannot, will not stay here; therefore I'd make an end of my letter to him, which shall be a finer letter than my last, because I have studied it like anything. O, sick, sick!

[*Takes the pen and writes.*]

[*Enter Mr. Pinchwife, who, seeing her writing, steals softly behind her and, looking over her shoulder, snatches the paper from her.*]

PINCHWIFE: What, writing more letters?

MRS. PINCHWIFE: O Lord, bud, why d'ye fright me so?

[*She offers to run out; he stops her and reads.*]

PINCHWIFE: How's this! Nay, you shall not stir, madam. "Dear, dear, dear Mr. Horner"—very well—I have taught you to write letters to good purpose—but let's see't. "First, I am to beg your pardon for my boldness in writing to you, which I'd have you to know I would not have done had not you said first you loved me so extremely, which if you do, you will never suffer me to lie in the arms of another man, whom I loathe, nauseate and detest."—Now you can write these filthy words. But what follows?—"Therefore I hope you will speedily find some way to free me from this unfortunate match, which was never, I assure you, of my choice, but I'm afraid 'tis already too far gone. However, if you love me, as I do you, you will try what you can do, but you must help me away before tomorrow, or else, alas, I shall be forever out of your reach, for I can defer no longer our—our" [*The letter concludes.*]—What is to follow "our"?—Speak, what? Our journey into the country, I suppose—Oh, woman, damned woman and love, damned love, their old tempter! For this is one of his miracles; in a moment he can make all those blind that could see and those see that were blind, those dumb that could speak and those prattle who were dumb before; nay, what is more than all, make these dough-baked,[1] senseless, indocile animals, women, too hard for us, their politic[2] lords and rulers, in a moment. But make an end of your letter and then I'll make an end of you thus, and all my plagues together. [*Draws his sword.*]

MRS. PINCHWIFE: O Lord, O Lord, you are such a passionate man, bud!

[*Enter Sparkish.*]

SPARKISH: How now, what's here to do?

PINCHWIFE: This fool here now!

SPARKISH: What, drawn upon your wife? You should never do that but at night in the dark, when you can't hurt her. This is my sister-in-law, is it not?

[*Pulls aside her handkerchief.*]

9. Disease.
1. Half-baked, feeble-minded.
2. Sagacious, judicious.

Ay, faith, e'en our country Margery; one may know her. Come, she and you must go dine with me; dinner's ready, come. But where's my wife? Is she not come home yet? Where is she?

PINCHWIFE: Making you a cuckold; 'tis that they all do, as soon as they can.

SPARKISH: What, the wedding day? No, a wife that designs to make a cully[3] of her husband will be sure to let him win the first stake of love, by the world. But come, they stay dinner for us. Come, I'll lead down our Margery.

PINCHWIFE: No—sir, go, we'll follow you.

SPARKISH: I will not wag[4] without you.

PINCHWIFE [*aside*]: This coxcomb is a sensible[5] torment to me amidst the greatest in the world.

SPARKISH: Come, come, Madam Margery.

PINCHWIFE: No, I'll lead her my way. What, would you treat your friends with mine, for want of your own wife? [*Leads her to t'other door and locks her in and returns. Aside.*] I am contented my rage should take breath.

SPARKISH [*aside*]: I told Horner this.

PINCHWIFE: Come now.

SPARKISH: Lord, how shy[6] you are of your wife! But let me tell you, brother, we men of wit have amongst us a saying that cuckolding, like the smallpox, comes with a fear, and you may keep your wife as much as you will out of danger of infection but if her constitution incline her to't, she'll have it sooner or later, by the world, say they.

PINCHWIFE [*aside*]: What a thing is a cuckold, that every fool can make him ridiculous!—Well, sir—but let me advise you, now you are come to be concerned, because you suspect the danger, not to neglect the means to prevent it, especially when the greatest share of the malady will light upon your own head, for—

> Hows'e'er the kind wife's belly comes to swell,
> The husband breeds for her[7] and first is ill.

[*Exeunt Pinchwife and Sparkish.*]

ACT 5

Scene 1

[*Mr. Pinchwife's house. Enter Mr. Pinchwife and Mrs. Pinchwife. A table and candle.*]

PINCHWIFE: Come, take the pen and make an end of the letter, just as you intended; if you are false in a tittle, I shall soon perceive it and punish you with this as you deserve. [*Lays his hand on his sword.*] Write what was to follow—let's see—"You must make haste and help me away before tomorrow, or else I shall be forever out of your reach, for I can defer no longer our—" What follows "our"?

MRS. PINCHWIFE: Must all out then, bud?

[*Mrs. Pinchwife takes the pen and writes.*] Look you there then.

PINCHWIFE: Let's see—"For I can defer no longer our—wedding—Your slighted Alithea."—What's the meaning of this? My sister's name to't. Speak, unriddle!

3. Dupe, gull.
4. Stir.
5. Keenly felt.
6. Distrustful.
7. Grows cuckhold's horns in consequence of her behavior.

MRS. PINCHWIFE: Yes, indeed, bud.

PINCHWIFE: But why her name to't? Speak—speak, I say!

MRS. PINCHWIFE: Ay, but you'll tell her then again; if you would not tell her again—

PINCHWIFE: I will not—I am stunned, my head turns round. Speak.

MRS. PINCHWIFE: Won't you tell her, indeed, and indeed?

PINCHWIFE: No, speak, I say.

MRS. PINCHWIFE: She'll be angry with me, but I had rather she should be angry with me than you, bud; and to tell you the truth, 'twas she made me write the letter and taught me what I should write.

PINCHWIFE [*aside*]: Ha! I thought the style was somewhat better than her own.—But how could she come to you to teach you, since I had locked you up alone?

MRS. PINCHWIFE: O, through the keyhole, bud.

PINCHWIFE: But why should she make you write a letter for her to him, since she can write herself?

MRS. PINCHWIFE: Why, she said because—for I was unwilling to do it.

PINCHWIFE: Because what—because?

MRS. PINCHWIFE: Because, lest Mr. Horner should be cruel and refuse her or vain afterwards and show the letter, she might disown it, the hand not being hers.

PINCHWIFE [*aside*]: How's this? Ha!—then I think I shall come to myself again. This changeling could not invent this lie; but if she could, why should she? She might think I should soon discover it—stay—now I think on't too, Horner said he was sorry she had married Sparkish, and her disowning her marriage to me makes me think she has evaded it for Horner's sake. Yet why should she take this course? But men in love are fools; women may well be so.—But hark you, madam, your sister went out in the morning and I have not seen her within since.

MRS. PINCHWIFE: Alackaday, she has been crying all day above, it seems, in a corner.

PINCHWIFE: Where is she? Let me speak with her.

MRS. PINCHWIFE [*aside*]: O Lord, then he'll discover all!—Pray hold, bud. What, d'ye mean to discover me? She'll know I have told you then. Pray, bud, let me talk with her first.

PINCHWIFE: I must speak with her, to know whether Horner ever made her any promise and whether she be married to Sparkish or no.

MRS. PINCHWIFE: Pray, dear bud, don't, till I have spoken with her and told her that I have told you all, for she'll kill me else.

PINCHWIFE: Go then, and bid her come out to me.

MRS. PINCHWIFE: Yes, yes, bud.

PINCHWIFE: Let me see—

MRS. PINCHWIFE [*aside*]: I'll go, but she is not within to come to him. I have just got time to know of Lucy her maid, who first set me on work, what lie I shall tell next, for I am e'en at my wit's end. [*Exit Mrs. Pinchwife.*]

PINCHWIFE: Well, I resolve it; Horner shall have her. I'd rather give him my sister than lend him my wife and such an alliance will prevent his pretensions to my wife, sure. I'll make him of kin to her and then he won't care for her.

[*Mrs. Pinchwife returns.*]

MRS. PINCHWIFE: O Lord, bud, I told you what anger you would make me with my sister.

PINCHWIFE: Won't she come hither?

MRS. PINCHWIFE: No, no, alackaday, she's ashamed to look you in the face, and she says, if you go in to her, she'll run away downstairs and shamefully go herself to Mr. Horner, who has promised her marriage, she says, and she will have no other, so she won't—

PINCHWIFE: Did he so—promise her marriage—then she shall have no other. Go tell her so, and if she will come and discourse with me a little concerning the means, I will about it immediately. Go. [*Exit Mrs. Pinchwife.*] His estate is equal to Sparkish's, and his extraction as much better than his as his parts are; but my chief reason is, I'd rather be of kin to him by the name of brother-in-law than that of cuckold.

[*Enter Mrs. Pinchwife.*]

Well, what says she now?

MRS. PINCHWIFE: Why, she says she would only have you lead her to Horner's lodging—with whom she first will discourse the matter before she talk with you, which yet she cannot do, for alack, poor creature, she says she can't so much as look you in the face, therefore she'll come to you in a mask, and you must excuse her if she make you no answer to any question of yours, till you have brought her to Mr. Horner, and if you will not chide her, nor question her, she'll come out to you immediately.

PINCHWIFE: Let her come. I will not speak a word to her, nor require a word from her.

MRS. PINCHWIFE: Oh, I forgot; besides, she says, she cannot look you in the face though through a mask, therefore would desire you to put out the candle.

PINCHWIFE: I agree to all; let her make haste—there, 'tis out. [*Puts out the candle.*] [*Exit Mrs. Pinchwife.*]

My case is something better. I'd rather fight with Horner for not lying with my sister than for lying with my wife, and of the two I had rather find my sister too forward than my wife; I expected no other from her free education, as she calls it, and her passion for the town. Well—wife and sister are names which make us expect love and duty, pleasure and comfort, but we find 'em plagues and torments, and are equally, though differently, troublesome to their keeper, for we have as much ado to get people to lie with our sisters as to keep 'em frm lying with our wives.

[*Enter Mrs. Pinchwife masked and in hoods and scarves, and a nightgown*[1] *and petticoat of Alithea's, in the dark.*]

What, are you come, sister? Let us go then—but first let me lock up my wife.—Mrs. Margery, where are you?

MRS. PINCHWIFE: Here, bud.

PINCHWIFE: Come hither, that I may lock you up; get you in. [*Locks the door.*] Come, sister, where are you now?

[*Mrs. Pinchwife gives him her hand but, when he lets her go, she steals softly on t'other side of him, and is led away by him for his sister Alithea.*]

Scene 2

[*The scene changes to Horner's lodging. Quack, Horner.*]

QUACK: What, all alone? Not so much as one of your cuckolds here, nor one of their wives! They use to take their turns with you, as if they were to watch you.

1. A loose gown, usually (but not exclusively) worn at night.

HORNER: Yes, it often happens that a cuckold is but his wife's spy and is more upon family duty when he is with her gallant abroad, hindering his pleasure, than when he is at home with her, playing the gallant. But the hardest duty a married woman imposes upon a lover is keeping her husband company always.

QUACK: And his fondness wearies you almost as soon as hers.

HORNER: A pox, keeping a cuckold company, after you have had his wife, is as tiresome as the company of a country squire to a witty fellow of the town, when he has got all his money.

QUACK: And as at first a man makes a friend of the husband to get the wife, so at last you are fain to fall out with the wife to be rid of the husband.

HORNER: Ay, most cuckold-makers are true courtiers; when once a poor man has cracked[2] his credit for 'em, they can't abide to come near him.

QUACK: But at first, to draw him in, are so sweet, so kind, so dear, just as you are to Pinchwife. But what becomes of that intrigue with his wife?

HORNER: A pox, he's as surly as an alderman that has been bit[3] and, since he's so coy, his wife's kindness is in vain, for she's a silly innocent.

QUACK: Did she not send you a letter by him?

HORNER: Yes, but that's a riddle I have not yet solved. Allow the poor creature to be willing, she is silly too, and he keeps her up so close—

QUACK: Yes, so close that he makes her but the more willing and adds but revenge to her love, which two, when met, seldom fail of satisfying each other one way or other.

HORNER: What, here's the man we are talking of, I think.

[*Enter Mr. Pinchwife, leading in his wife masked, muffled, and in her sister's gown.*]

Pshaw!

QUACK: Bringing his wife to you is the next thing to bringing a love-letter from her.

HORNER: What means this?

PINCHWIFE: The last time, you know, sir, I brought you a love-letter; now, you see, a mistress. I think you'll say I am a civil man to you.

HORNER: Ay, the devil take me, will I say thou art the civilest man I ever met with, and I have known some! I fancy I understand thee now better than I did the letter. But hark thee, in thy ear—

PINCHWIFE: What?

HORNER: Nothing but the usual question, man: is she sound,[4] on thy word?

PINCHWIFE: What, you take her for a wench and me for a pimp?

HORNER: Pshaw, wench and pimp, paw[5] words. I know thou art an honest fellow and hast a great acquaintance among the ladies and perhaps hast made love for me rather than let me make love to thy wife—

PINCHWIFE: Come, sir, in short, I am for no fooling.

HORNER: Nor I neither; therefore, prithee, let's see her face presently. Make her show, man. Art thou sure I don't know her?

PINCHWIFE: I am sure you do know her.

HORNER: A pox, why dost thou bring her to me then?

PINCHWIFE: Because she's a relation of mine.

2. Ruined.
3. A city official who's been tricked.
4. Free from venereal disease.
5. Naughty.

HORNER: Is she, faith, man? Then thou art still more civil and obliging, dear rogue.

PINCHWIFE: Who desired me to bring her to you.

HORNER: Then she is obliging, dear rogue.

PINCHWIFE: You'll make her welcome for my sake, I hope.

HORNER: I hope she is handsome enough to make herself welcome. Prithee, let her unmask.

PINCHWIFE: Do you speak to her; she would never be ruled by me.

HORNER: Madam—

[Mrs. Pinchwife whispers to Horner.]

She says she must speak with me in private. Withdraw, prithee.

PINCHWIFE *[aside]*: She's unwilling, it seems, I should know all her undecent conduct in this business.—Well then, I'll leave you together and hope when I am gone you'll agree; if not, you and I shan't agree, sir.

HORNER *[aside]*: What means the fool?—If she and I agree, 'tis no matter what you and I do.

[Whispers to Mrs. Pinchwife, who makes signs with her hand for him (Pinchwife) to be gone.]

PINCHWIFE: In the meantime, I'll fetch a parson and find out Sparkish and disabuse him. You would have me fetch a parson, would you not? Well then—now I think I am rid of her, and shall have no more trouble with her. Our sisters and daughters, like usurers' money, are safest when put out; but our wives, like their writings,[6] never safe but in our closets under lock and key. *[Exit Mr. Pinchwife.]*

[Enter Boy.]

BOY: Sir Jaspar Fidget, sir, is coming up. *[Exit.]*

HORNER: Here's the trouble of a cuckold, now, we are talking of. A pox on him! Has he not enough to do to hinder his wife's sport but he must other women's too?—Step in here, madam. *[Exit Mrs. Pinchwife.]*

[Enter Sir Jaspar.]

SIR JASPAR: My best and dearest friend.

HORNER *[aside to Quack]*: The old style, doctor.—Well, be short, for I am busy. What would your impertinent wife have now?

SIR JASPAR: Well guessed, i'faith, for I do come from her.

HORNER: To invite me to supper. Tell her I can't come; go.

SIR JASPAR: Nay, now you are out, faith, for my lady and the whole knot of the virtuous gang, as they call themselves, are resolved upon a frolic of coming to you tonight in a masquerade and are all dressed already.

HORNER: I shan't be at home.

SIR JASPAR *[aside]*: Lord, how churlish he is to women!—Nay, prithee don't disappoint 'em; they'll think 'tis my fault. Prithee don't. I'll send in the banquet and the fiddles. But make no noise on't, for the poor virtuous rogues would not have it known for the world that they go a-masquerading, and they would come to no man's ball but yours.

HORNER: Well, well—get you gone and tell 'em, if they come, 'twill be at the peril of their honor and yours.

6. Legal and financial documents.

SIR JASPAR: Heh, he, he!—we'll trust you for that; farewell. [*Exit Sir Jaspar.*]

HORNER: Doctor, anon you too shall be my guest, But now I'm going to a private feast.

[*Exeunt.*]

Scene 3

[*The scene changes to the Piazza of Covent Garden. Sparkish, Pinchwife.*]

SPARKISH [*with the letter in his hand*]: But who would have thought a woman could have been false to me? By the world, I could not have thought it.

PINCHWIFE: You were for giving and taking liberty; she has taken it only, sir, now you find in that letter. You are a frank person and so is she you see there.

SPARKISH: Nay, if this be her hand—for I never saw it.

PINCHWIFE: 'Tis no matter whether that be her hand or no; I am sure this hand, at her desire, led her to Mr. Horner, with whom I left her just now, to go fetch a parson to 'em, at their desire too, to deprive you of her forever, for it seems yours was but a mock marriage.

SPARKISH: Indeed, she would needs have it that 'twas Harcourt himself in a parson's habit that married us, but I'm sure he told me 'twas his brother Ned.

PINCHWIFE: Oh, there 'tis out, and you were deceived, not she, for you are such a frank person—but I must be gone. You'll find her at Mr. Horner's; go and believe your eyes. [*Exit Mr. Pinchwife.*]

SPARKISH: Nay, I'll to her and call her as many crocodiles, sirens, harpies and other heathenish names as a poet would do a mistress who had refused to hear his suit, nay more, his verses on her.—But stay, is not that she following a torch at t'other end of the Piazza? And from Horner's certainly—'tis so.

[*Enter Alithea, following a torch,*[7] *and Lucy behind.*]

You are well met, madam, though you don't think so. What, you have made a short visit to Mr. Horner, but I suppose you'll return to him presently; by that time the parson can be with him.

ALITHEA: Mr. Horner, and the parson, sir!

SPARKISH: Come, madam, no more dissembling, no more jilting, for I am no more a frank person.

ALITHEA: How's this?

LUCY [*aside*]: So, 'twill work, I see.

SPARKISH: Could you find out no easy country fool to abuse? None but me, a gentleman of wit and pleasure about the town? But it was your pride to be too hard for a man of parts, unworthy false woman, false as a friend that lends a man money to lose, false as dice who undo those that trust all they have to 'em.

LUCY [*aside*]: He has been a great bubble by his similes, as they say.

ALITHEA: You have been too merry, sir, at your wedding dinner, sure.

SPARKISH: What, d'ye mock me too?

ALITHEA: Or you have been deluded.

SPARKISH: By you.

ALITHEA: Let me understand you.

SPARKISH: Have you the confidence—I should call it something else, since you know your guilt—to stand my just reproaches? You did not write an impudent

7. A boy carrying a torch.

letter to Mr. Horner, who I find now has clubbed with you in deluding me with his aversion for women, that I might not, forsooth, suspect him for my rival.

LUCY [*aside*]: D'ye think the gentleman can be jealous now, madam?

ALITHEA: I write a letter to Mr. Horner!

SPARKISH: Nay, madam, do not deny it; your brother showed it me just now and told me likewise he left you at Horner's lodging to fetch a parson to marry you to him, and I wish you joy, madam, joy, joy, and to him too, much joy, and to myself more joy for not marrying you.

ALITHEA [*aside*]: So, I find my brother would break off the match, and I can consent to't, since I see this gentleman can be made jealous.—O Lucy, by his rude usage and jealousy, he makes me almost afraid I am married to him. Art thou sure 'twas Harcourt himself and no parson that married us?

SPARKISH: No, madam, I thank you. I suppose that was a contrivance too of Mr. Horner's and yours, to make Harcourt play the parson; but I would as little as you have him one now, no, not for the world, for shall I tell you another truth? I never had any passion for you till now, for now I hate you. 'Tis true I might have married your portion, as other men of parts of the town do sometimes, and so your servant, and to show my unconcernedness, I'll come to your wedding and resign you with as much joy as I would a stale wench to a new cully, nay, with as much joy as I would after the first night, if I had been married to you. There's for you, and so your servant, servant. [*Exit Sparkish.*]

ALITHEA: How was I deceived in a man!

LUCY: You'll believe, then, a fool may be made jealous now? For that easiness in him that suffers him to be led by a wife will likewise permit him to be persuaded against her by others.

ALITHEA: But marry Mr. Horner! My brother does not intend it, sure; if I thought he did, I would take thy advice and Mr. Harcourt for my husband. And now I wish that if there be any over-wise woman of the town who, like me, would marry a fool for fortune, liberty or title; first, that her husband may love play and be a cully to all the town but her and suffer none but fortune to be mistress of his purse; then, if for liberty, that he may send her into the country under the conduct of some housewifely mother-in-law, and, if for title, may the world give 'em none but that of cuckold.

LUCY: And for her greater curse, madam, may he not deserve it.

ALITHEA: Away, impertinent!—Is not this my old Lady Lanterlu's?[8]

LUCY: Yes, madam. [*Aside.*] And here I hope we shall find Mr. Harcourt.

[*Exeunt Alithea, Lucy.*]

Scene 4

[*The scene changes again to Horner's lodging. Horner, Lady Fidget, Mrs. Dainty Fidget, Mrs. Squeamish. A table, banquet, and bottles.*]

HORNER [*aside*]: A pox! They are come too soon—before I have sent back my new—mistress. All I have now to do is to lock her in, that they may not see her.

8. The lady is comically named after a popular card game, "loo" for short.

LADY FIDGET: That we may be sure of our welcome, we have brought our entertainment with us and are resolved to treat thee, dear toad.

DAINTY: And that we may be merry to purpose, have left Sir Jaspar and my old Lady Squeamish quarrelling at home at backgammon.

SQUEAMISH: Therefore let us make use of our time, lest they should chance to interrupt us.

LADY FIDGET: Let us sit then.

HORNER: First, that you may be private, let me lock this door and that, and I'll wait upon you presently.

LADY FIDGET: No, sir, shut 'em only and your lips forever, for we must trust you as much as our women.

HORNER: You know all vanity's killed in me; I have no occasion for talking.

LADY FIDGET: Now, ladies, supposing we had drank each of us our two bottles, let us speak the truth of our hearts.

DAINTY:
SQUEAMISH: } Agreed.

LADY FIDGET: By this brimmer,[9] for truth is nowhere else to be found. [*Aside to Horner*.] Not in thy heart, false man!

HORNER [*aside to Lady Fidget*]: You have found me a true man, I'm sure.

LADY FIDGET [*aside to Horner*]: Not every way.—But let us sit and be merry. [*Lady Fidget sings*.]

1

Why should our damned tyrants oblige us to live
On the pittance of pleasure which they only give?
We must not rejoice
With wine and with noise.
In vain we must wake in a dull bed alone,
Whilst to our warm rival, the bottle, they're gone.
They lay aside charms
And take up these arms.[1]

2

'Tis wine only gives 'em their courage and wit;
Because we live sober, to men we submit.
If for beauties you'd pass,
Take a lick of the glass;
'Twill mend your complexions and, when they are gone,
The best red we have is the red of the grape.
Then, sisters, lay't on,
And damn a good shape.

DAINTY: Dear brimmer! Well, in token of our openness and plain-dealing, let us throw our masks over our heads.

HORNER: So, 'twill come to the glasses anon.

9. Brimming cup.

1. I.e., the glasses.

SQUEAMISH: Lovely brimmer! Let me enjoy him first.

LADY FIDGET: No, I never part with a gallant till I've tried him. Dear brimmer, that mak'st our husbands shortsighted.

DAINTY: And our bashful gallants bold.

SQUEAMISH: And for want of a gallant, the butler lovely in our eyes.—Drink, eunuch.

LADY FIDGET: Drink, thou representative of a husband. Damn a husband!

DAINTY: And, as it were a husband, an old keeper.

SQUEAMISH: And an old grandmother.

HORNER: And an English bawd and a French chirurgeon.[2]

LADY FIDGET: Ay, we have all reason to curse 'em.

HORNER: For my sake, ladies?

LADY FIDGET: No, for our own, for the first spoils all young gallants' industry.

DAINTY: And the other's art makes 'em bold only with common women.

SQUEAMISH: And rather run the hazard of the vile distemper amongst them than of a denial amongst us.

DAINTY: The filthy toads choose mistresses now as they do stuffs,[3] for having been fancied and worn by others.[4]

SQUEAMISH: For being common and cheap.

LADY FIDGET: Whilst women of quality, like the richest stuffs, lie untumbled and unasked for.

HORNER: Ay, neat and cheap and new often they think best.

DAINTY: No, sir, the beasts will be known by a mistress longer than by a suit.

SQUEAMISH: And 'tis not for cheapness neither.

LADY FIDGET: No, for the vain fops will take up druggets[5] and embroider 'em. But I wonder at the depraved appetites of witty men; they use to be out of the common road and hate imitation. Pray tell me, beast, when you were a man, why you rather chose to club with a multitude in a common house[6] for an entertainment than to be the only guest at a good table!

HORNER: Why, faith, ceremony and expectation are unsufferable to those that are sharp bent;[7] people always eat with the best stomach at an ordinary, where every man is snatching for the best bit.

LADY FIDGET: Though he get a cut over the fingers.—But I have heard people eat most heartily of another man's meat, that is, what they do not pay for.

HORNER: When they are sure of their welcome and freedom, for ceremony in love and eating is as ridiculous as in fighting; falling on briskly is all should be done in those occasions.

LADY FIDGET: Well, then, let me tell you, sir, there is nowhere more freedom than in our houses and we take freedom from a young person as a sign of good breeding, and a person may be as free as he pleases with us, as frolic, as gamesome, as wild as he will.

HORNER: Han't I heard you all declaim against wild men?

2. The supposed causes of Horner's fictitious plight (see Act 1, Scene 1, page 2216).
3. Garments.
4. Second-hand trade was commonplace in Restoration England.
5. Cheap woolen fabric.
6. A restaurant or brothel.
7. Hungry.

LADY FIDGET: Yes, but for all that, we think wildness in a man as desirable a quality as in a duck or rabbit; a tame man, foh!

HORNER: I know not, but your reputations frightened me, as much as your faces invited me.

LADY FIDGET: Our reputation! Lord, why should you not think that we women make use of our reputation, as you men of yours, only to deceive the world with less suspicion? Our virtue is like the statesman's religion, the Quaker's word, the gamester's oath and the great man's honor—but to cheat those that trust us.

SQUEAMISH: And that demureness, coyness and modesty that you see in our faces in the boxes at plays is as much a sign of a kind woman as a vizard-mask in the pit.

DAINTY: For, I assure you, women are least masked when they have the velvet vizard on.

LADY FIDGET: You would have found us modest women in our denials only.

SQUEAMISH: Our bashfulness is only the reflection of the men's.

DAINTY: We blush when they are shamefaced.

HORNER: I beg your pardon, ladies; I was deceived in you devilishly. But why that mighty pretense to honor?

LADY FIDGET: We have told you. But sometimes 'twas for the same reason you men pretend business often, to avoid ill company, to enjoy the better and more privately those you love.

HORNER: But why would you ne'er give a friend a wink then?

LADY FIDGET: Faith, your reputation frightened us as much as ours did you, you were so notoriously lewd.

HORNER: And you so seemingly honest.

LADY FIDGET: Was that all that deterred you?

HORNER: And so expensive—you allow freedom, you say—

LADY FIDGET: Ay, ay.

HORNER: That I was afraid of losing my little money, as well as my little time, both which my other pleasures required.

LADY FIDGET: Money, foh! You talk like a little fellow now; do such as we expect money?

HORNER: I beg your pardon, madam; I must confess, I have heard that great ladies, like great merchants, set but the higher prizes[8] upon what they have, because they are not in necessity of taking the first offer.

DAINTY: Such as we make sale of our hearts?

SQUEAMISH: We bribed for our love? Foh!

HORNER: With your pardon, ladies, I know, like great men in offices, you seem to exact flattery and attendance only from your followers; but you have receivers[9] about you and such fees to pay, a man is afraid to pass your grants.[1] Besides, we must let you win at cards, or we lose your hearts, and if you make an assignation, 'tis at a goldsmith's, jeweller's or china house, where, for your honor you deposit to him, he must pawn his to the punctual cit, and so paying for what you take up, pays for what he takes up.[2]

8. Prices.
9. Collectors.
1. Accept your favors (because in the end they are so expensive).
2. I.e., you arrange to meet your lover at an expensive shop, where he in effect pays for your favors by purchasing for you the shopkeeper's ("punctual cit's") costly merchandise.

DAINTY: Would you not have us assured of our gallant's love?

SQUEAMISH: For love is better known by liberality than by jealousy.

LADY FIDGET: For one may be dissembled, the other not. [*Aside.*] But my jealousy can be no longer dissembled, and they are telling ripe.[3]—Come, here's to our gallants in waiting, whom we must name, and I'll begin. This is my false rogue. [*Claps him on the back.*]

SQUEAMISH: How!

HORNER: So all will out now.

SQUEAMISH [*aside to Horner*]: Did you not tell me, 'twas for my sake only you reported yourself no man?

DAINTY [*aside to Horner*]: Oh, wretch! Did you not swear to me, 'twas for my love and honor you passed for that thing you do?

HORNER: So, so.

LADY FIDGET: Come, speak, ladies; this is my false villain.

SQUEAMISH: And mine too.

DAINTY: And mine.

HORNER: Well then, you are all three my false rogues too, and there's an end on't.

LADY FIDGET: Well then, there's no remedy; sister sharers, let us not fall out, but have a care of our honor. Though we get no presents, no jewels of him, we are savers of our honor, the jewel of most value and use, which shines yet to the world unsuspected, though it be counterfeit.

HORNER: Nay, and is e'en as good as if it were true, provided the world think so, for honor, like beauty now, only depends on the opinion of others.

LADY FIDGET: Well, Harry Common, I hope you can be true to three. Swear—but 'tis to no purpose to require your oath, for you are as often forsworn as you swear to new women.

HORNER: Come, faith, madam, let us e'en pardon one another, for all the difference I find betwixt we men and you women, we forswear ourselves at the beginning of an amour, you as long as it lasts.

[*Enter Sir Jaspar Fidget and Old Lady Squeamish.*]

SIR JASPAR: Oh, my Lady Fidget, was this your cunning, to come to Mr. Horner without me? But you have been nowhere else, I hope.

LADY FIDGET: No, Sir Jaspar.

OLD LADY SQUEAMISH: And you came straight hither, Biddy?

SQUEAMISH: Yes, indeed, Lady Grandmother.

SIR JASPAR: 'Tis well, 'tis well; I knew when once they were thoroughly acquainted with poor Horner, they'd ne'er be from him. You may let her masquerade it with my wife and Horner and I warrant her reputation safe.

[*Enter Boy.*]

BOY: Oh, sir, here's the gentleman come whom you bid me not suffer to come up without giving you notice, with a lady too, and other gentlemen—

HORNER: Do you all go in there, whilst I send 'em away, and, boy, do you desire 'em to stay below till I come, which shall be immediately.

[*Exeunt Sir Jaspar, Old Lady Squeamish, Lady Fidget, Mrs. Dainty, Squeamish.*]

BOY: Yes, sir. [*Exit.*]

[*Exit Horner at t'other door and returns with Mrs. Pinchwife.*]

3. Ripe for the telling.

HORNER: You would not take my advice to be gone home before your husband came back; he'll now discover all. Yet pray, my dearest, be persuaded to go home and leave the rest to my management. I'll let you down the back way.

MRS. PINCHWIFE: I don't know the way home, so I don't.

HORNER: My man shall wait upon you.

MRS. PINCHWIFE: No, don't you believe that I'll go at all. What, are you weary of me already?

HORNER: No, my life, 'tis that I may love you long, 'tis to secure my love, and your reputation with your husband; he'll never receive you again else.

MRS. PINCHWIFE: What care I? D'ye think to frighten me with that? I don't intend to go to him again; you shall be my husband now.

HORNER: I cannot be your husband, dearest, since you are married to him.

MRS. PINCHWIFE: Oh, would you make me believe that? Don't I see every day, at London here, women leave their first husbands and go and live with other men as their wives? Pish, pshaw, you'd make me angry, but that I love you so mainly.[4]

HORNER: So, they are coming up—in again, in, I hear 'em.

[*Exit Mrs. Pinchwife.*]

Well, a silly mistress is like a weak place, soon got, soon lost, a man has scarce time for plunder; she betrays her husband first to her gallant and then her gallant to her husband.

[*Enter Pinchwife, Alithea, Harcourt, Sparkish, Lucy and a Parson.*]

PINCHWIFE: Come, madam, 'tis not the sudden change of your dress, the confidence of your asseverations and your false witness there, shall persuade me I did not bring you hither just now; here's my witness, who cannot deny it, since you must be confronted.—Mr. Horner, did not I bring this lady to you just now?

HORNER [*aside*]: Now must I wrong one woman for another's sake, but that's no new thing with me, for in these cases I am still on the criminal's side, against the innocent.

ALITHEA: Pray, speak, sir.

HORNER [*aside*]: It must be so—I must be impudent and try my luck; impudence uses to be too hard for truth.

PINCHWIFE: What, you are studying an evasion or excuse for her. Speak, sir.

HORNER: No, faith, I am something backward only to speak in women's affairs or disputes.

PINCHWIFE: She bids you speak.

ALITHEA: Ay, pray, sir, do; pray satisfy him.

HORNER: Then truly, you did bring that lady to me just now.

PINCHWIFE: O ho!

ALITHEA: How, sir!

HARCOURT: How, Horner!

ALITHEA: What mean you, sir? I always took you for a man of honor.

HORNER [*aside*]: Ay, so much a man of honor that I must save my mistress, I thank you, come what will on't.

SPARKISH: So, if I had had her, she'd have made me believe the moon had been made of a Christmas pie.

4. Mightily.

LUCY [*aside*]: Now could I speak, if I durst, and solve the riddle, who am the author of it.

ALITHEA: O unfortunate woman! A combination against my honor, which most concerns me now, because you share in my disgrace, sir, and it is your censure, which I must now suffer, that troubles me, not theirs.

HARCOURT: Madam, then have no trouble, you shall now see 'tis possible for me to love too, without being jealous; I will not only believe your innocence myself, but make all the world believe it. [*Apart to Horner.*] Horner, I must now be concerned for this lady's honor.

HORNER: And I must be concerned for a lady's honor too.

HARCOURT: This lady has her honor and I will protect it.

HORNER: My lady has not her honor but has given it me to keep and I will preserve it.

HARCOURT: I understand you not.

HORNER: I would not have you.

MRS. PINCHWIFE [*peeping in behind*]: What's the matter with 'em all?

PINCHWIFE: Come, come, Mr. Horner, no more disputing. Here's the parson; I brought him not in vain.

HARCOURT: No, sir, I'll employ him, if this lady please.

PINCHWIFE: How! What d'ye mean?

SPARKISH: Ay, what does he mean?

HORNER: Why, I have resigned your sister to him; he has my consent.

PINCHWIFE: But he has not mine, sir; a woman's injured honor, no more than a man's, can be repaired or satisfied by any but him that first wronged it; and you shall marry her presently, or—[*Lays his hand on his sword.*]

[*Enter to them Mrs. Pinchwife.*]

MRS. PINCHWIFE [*aside*]: O Lord, they'll kill poor Mr. Horner! Besides, he shan't marry her whilst I stand by and look on; I'll not lose my second husband so.

PINCHWIFE: What do I see?

ALITHEA: My sister in my clothes!

SPARKISH: Ha!

MRS. PINCHWIFE [*to Mr. Pinchwife*]: Nay, pray now don't quarrel about finding work for the parson; he shall marry me to Mr. Horner, for now, I believe, you have enough of me.

HORNER: Damned, damned, loving changeling!

MRS. PINCHWIFE: Pray, sister, pardon me for telling so many lies of you.

HARCOURT: I suppose the riddle is plain now.

LUCY: No, that must be my work. Good sir, hear me.

[*Kneels to Mr. Pinchwife, who stands doggedly, with his hat over his eyes.*]

PINCHWIFE: I will never hear woman again, but make 'em all silent, thus—

[*Offers to draw upon his wife.*]

HORNER: No, that must not be.

PINCHWIFE: You then shall go first; 'tis all one to me [*Offers to draw on Horner; stopped by Harcourt.*]

HARCOURT: Hold!

[*Enter Sir Jaspar Fidget, Lady Fidget, Old Lady Squeamish, Mrs. Dainty Fidget, Mrs. Squeamish.*]

SIR JASPAR: What's the matter, what's the matter, pray, what's the matter, sir? I beseech you communicate, sir.

PINCHWIFE: Why, my wife has communicated[5], sir, as your wife may have done too, sir, if she knows him, sir.

SIR JASPAR: Pshaw, with him? Ha, ha, he!

PINCHWIFE: D'ye mock me, sir? A cuckold is a kind of a wild beast; have a care, sir.

SIR JASPAR: No, sure, you mock me, sir—he cuckold you! It can't be, ha, ha, he! Why, I tell you, sir—[*Offers to whisper*.]

PINCHWIFE: I tell you again, he has whored my wife, and yours too, if he knows her, and all the women he comes near; 'tis not his dissembling, his hypocrisy can wheedle me.

SIR JASPAR: How! does he dissemble? Is he a hypocrite? Nay, then—how—wife—sister, is he an hypocrite?

OLD LADY SQUEAMISH: An hypocrite, a dissembler! Speak, young harlotry, speak, how?

SIR JASPAR: Nay, then—O, my head too!—O thou libidinous lady!

OLD LADY SQUEAMISH: O thou harloting harlotry! Hast thou done't then?

SIR JASPAR: Speak, good Horner, art thou a dissembler, a rogue? Hast thou—

HORNER: Soh—

LUCY [*apart to Horner*]: I'll fetch you off, and her too, if she will but hold her tongue.

HORNER [*apart to Lucy*]: Canst thou? I'll give thee—

LUCY [*to Mr. Pinchwife*]: Pray have but patience to hear me, sir, who am the unfortunate cause of all this confusion. Your wife is innocent, I only culpable, for I put her upon telling you all these lies concerning my mistress, in order to the breaking off the match between Mr. Sparkish and her, to make way for Mr. Harcourt.

SPARKISH: Did you so, eternal rotten tooth? Then, it seems, my mistress was not false to me, I was only deceived by you.—Brother that should have been, now man of conduct, who is a frank person now? To bring your wife to her lover—ha!

LUCY: I assure you, sir, she came not to Mr. Horner out of love, for she loves him no more—

MRS. PINCHWIFE: Hold, I told lies for you, but you shall tell none for me, for I do love Mr. Horner with all my soul, and nobody shall say me nay. Pray, don't you go to make poor Mr. Horner believe to the contrary; 'tis spitefully done of you, I'm sure.

HORNER [*aside to Mrs. Pinchwife*]: Peace, dear idiot.

MRS. PINCHWIFE: Nay, I will not peace.

PINCHWIFE: Not till I make you.

[*Enter Dorilant, Quack*.]

DORILANT: Horner, your servant; I am the doctor's guest, he must excuse our intrusion.

QUACK: But what's the matter, gentlemen? For heaven's sake, what's the matter?

HORNER: Oh, 'tis well you are come. 'Tis a censorious world we live in; you may have brought me a reprieve, or else I had died for a crime I never committed, and

5. Fornicated.

these innocent ladies had suffered with me. Therefore pray satisfy these worthy, honorable, jealous gentlemen—that—[*Whispers.*]

QUACK: O, I understand you; is that all?

[*Whispers to Sir Jaspar.*]

Sir Jaspar, by heavens and upon the word of a physician, sir—

SIR JASPAR: Nay, I do believe you truly.—Pardon me, my virtuous lady and dear of honor.

OLD LADY SQUEAMISH: What, then all's right again?

SIR JASPAR: Ay, ay, and now let us satisfy him too.

[*They whisper with Mr. Pinchwife.*]

PINCHWIFE: An eunuch! Pray, no fooling with me.

QUACK: I'll bring half the chirurgeons in town to swear it.

PINCHWIFE: They!—they'll swear a man that bled to death through his wounds died of an apoplexy.[6]

QUACK: Pray hear me, sir—why, all the town has heard the report of him.

PINCHWIFE: But does all the town believe it?

QUACK: Pray inquire a little, and first of all these.

PINCHWIFE: I'm sure when I left the town he was the lewdest fellow in't.

QUACK: I tell you, sir, he has been in France since; pray, ask but these ladies and gentlemen, your friend Mr. Dorilant.—Gentlemen and ladies, han't you all heard the late sad report of poor Mr. Horner?

ALL THE LADIES: Ay, ay, ay.

DORILANT: Why, thou jealous fool, dost thou doubt it? He's an arrant French capon.[7]

MRS. PINCHWIFE: 'Tis false, sir, you shall not disparage poor Mr. Horner, for to my certain knowledge—

LUCY: Oh, hold!

SQUEAMISH [*aside to Lucy*]: Stop her mouth!

LADY FIDGET [*to Pinchwife*]: Upon my honor, sir, 'tis as true—

DAINTY: D'ye think we would have been seen in his company?

SQUEAMISH: Trust our unspotted reputations with him!

LADY FIDGET [*aside to Horner*]: This you get, and we too, by trusting your secret to a fool.

HORNER: Peace, madam. [*Aside to Quack.*] Well, doctor, is not this a good design, that carries a man on unsuspected and brings him off safe?

PINCHWIFE [*aside*]: Well, if this were true, but my wife—[*Dorilant whispers with Mrs. Pinchwife.*]

ALITHEA: Come, brother, your wife is yet innocent, you see; but have a care of too strong an imagination, lest like an overconcerned, timorous gamester, by fancying an unlucky cast, it should come. Women and fortune are truest still to those that trust 'em.

LUCY: And any wild thing grows but the more fierce and hungry for being kept up and more dangerous to the keeper.

ALITHEA: There's doctrine for all husbands, Mr. Harcourt.

6. A convenient fiction since dueling was now illegal (1679).

7. Eunuch.

HARCOURT: I edify, madam, so much that I am impatient till I am one.
DORILANT: And I edify so much by example I will never be one.
SPARKISH: And because I will not disparage my parts I'll ne'er be one.
HORNER: And I, alas, can't be one.
PINCHWIFE: But I must be one—against my will, to a country wife, with a country murrain[8] to me.
MRS. PINCHWIFE [*aside*]: And I must be a country wife still too, I find, for I can't, like a city one, be rid of my musty husband and do what I list.
HORNER: Now, sir, I must pronounce your wife innocent, though I blush whilst I do it, and I am the only man by her now exposed to shame, which I will straight drown in wine, as you shall your suspicion, and the ladies' troubles we'll divert with a ballet.—Doctor, where are your maskers?
LUCY: Indeed, she's innocent, sir, I am her witness; and her end of coming out was but to see her sister's wedding and what she has said to your face of her love to Mr. Horner was but the usual innocent revenge on a husband's jealousy—was it not, madam? Speak.
MRS. PINCHWIFE [*aside to Lucy and Horner*]: Since you'll have me tell more lies—Yes, indeed, bud.
PINCHWIFE: For my own sake fain I would all believe; Cuckolds, like lovers, should themselves deceive. But—[*Sighs*.]

His honor is least safe, too late I find,
Who trusts it with a foolish wife or friend.

[*A Dance of Cuckolds*.[9]]

HORNER: Vain fops but court and dress and keep a puther,[1]
To pass for women's men with one another,
But he who aims by women to be priz'd,
First by the men, you see, must be despis'd.

EPILOGUE, *SPOKEN BY* MRS. KNEPP[2]

Now, you the vigorous,[3] who daily here
O'er vizard-mask in public domineer,
And what you'd do to her if in place where,
Nay, have the confidence to cry, "Come out,"
Yet when she says "Lead on," you are not stout,
But to your well-dressed brother straight turn round
And cry, "Pox on her, Ned, she can't be sound,"
Then slink away, a fresh one to engage,
With so much seeming heat and loving rage,
You'd frighten listening actress on the stage,
Till she at last has seen you huffing come
And talk of keeping in the tiring-room,
Yet cannot be provok'd to lead her home.

8. Pestilence.
9. This dance was performed to the then-familiar tune called "Cuckolds All [in] a Row."
1. Make a fuss.
2. Elizabeth Knepp, actress and singer, created the role of Lady Fidget. Pepys held her in high regard; see page 2031.
3. The epilogue derisively addresses two categories of males who, unlike Horner, pretend to sexual potency: the young (lines 1–13) and the old (14–17).

Next, you Falstaffs[4] of fifty, who beset
Your buckram[5] maidenheads, which your friends get,
And while to them you of achievements boast,
They share the booty and laugh at your cost.
In fine, you essenced boys, both old and young,
Who would be thought so eager, brisk and strong,
Yet do the ladies, not their husbands, wrong,
Whose purses for your manhood make excuse,
And keep your Flanders mares[6] for show, not use:
Encouraged by our woman's man today,
A Horner's part may vainly think to play
And may intrigues so bashfully disown
That they may doubted be by few or none,[7]
May kiss the cards at picquet, ombre, loo,[8]
And so be thought to kiss the lady too;
But, gallants, have a care, faith, what you do.
The world, which to no man his due will give,
You by experience know you can deceive
And men may still believe you vigorous,
But then we women—there's no cozening[9] us.

1675 1675

Mary Astell

1666–1731

The pioneering feminist Mary Astell was born in Newcastle to a merchant who dealt in coal, and she was tutored early by an uncle who immersed himself in literature and philosophy. From him she absorbed a lifelong affinity for the ideas of the Cambridge Platonists, who held that reason was the sole route to truth and to the proper love of God; out of this conviction she developed her defiant argument that, despite centuries of cultural practice to the contrary, women's powers of reason were as worth cultivating as men's. At age twenty Astell moved to London, where eight years later she published the book that made her fame. In *A Serious Proposal to the Ladies* (1694), Astell argued for the founding of an all-female academy, where unmarried women might develop their reason, deepen their knowledge, and nurture their faith free from the distractions imposed by social conventions. Astell's idea for such a school exerted a lasting influence: Daniel Defoe enthusiastically revived it in his *Essay upon Projects* (1697), Samuel Johnson wove it into his philosophical tale *Rasselas* (1759), and Sarah Scott made it the premise of her feminist novel *Millenium Hall* (1762). More important, perhaps, was the *Proposal*'s immediate effect on contemporary

4. I.e., you who resemble the immense, aged, comic liar Shakespeare created in *Henry IV*.
5. A stiff fabric. Falstaff at one point pretends to have killed some "rogues in buckram suits" during a robbery (*1 Henry IV* 2.4). In truth he killed no one, and his younger accomplices made off with the loot.
6. Costly coach horses; here a metaphor for kept mistresses or prostitutes.
7. I.e., Horner's example may encourage "you" fakers to reverse tactics, and to seek a rake's reputation by feigning "bashfulness."
8. Card games; kissing the cards was a way of flirting with fellow-players.
9. Fooling.

women writers and thinkers (Ladies Mary Chudleigh and Mary Wortley Montagu among them), who found in it a template and an endorsement for their own most cherished pursuits and for their sense of possibilities.

Dwelling abstemiously in the Thames-side town of Chelsea, Astell began to enjoy the consequences of celebrity. She received tributes and visits from admiring readers, and she assembled a circle of women like herself—well-educated, pious, unmarried—whose friendships she deeply valued and with whose help she later founded a charity school for girls. Still, the *Proposal* itself was never implemented in her time, in part because the imagined academy for women sounded too much like a Catholic convent to find ready acceptance in Protestant England, and in part because the argument's point—that women could find intellectual, moral, and spiritual self-sufficiency outside marriage—was so unsettling as to rouse energetic opposition.

Astell pushed the argument further in *Some Reflections upon Marriage* (1700), a hundred-page tract written, she reported, in the white heat of an angry and inspired afternoon. Starting from a conservative premise—that as the monarch rightfully possesses absolute authority over the state, so does the husband over his wife—Astell develops a breathtakingly skeptical line of inquiry: why, then, would a woman wish to enter into so self-immolating a contract as marriage in the first place? The question ultimately brings her back to the theme of the *Serious Proposal:* the importance for women of a good education, one that will enable them to see their choices clearly, to make those choices discerningly, and to lead, whether married or not, a Christian life grounded in the cultivation of their own intellect and faith (though Astell strongly implies that within marriage female virtue will produce a grim martyrdom; outside marriage, a richer fulfillment). In limning the alternatives, Astell deploys the directness, the sarcasm, and the urgency that made her famous in her own day and again in ours. She was, as her biographer Ruth Perry notes, "probably the first person to consider the rights and duties of women as a political question"; the prose in which she couched the question gave it an often hypnotic pugnacity.

from Some Reflections upon Marriage

But how can a man respect his wife when he has a contemptible opinion of her and her sex? When from his own elevation he looks down on them as void of understanding, and full of ignorance and passion, so that folly and a woman are equivalent terms with him? Can he think there is any gratitude due to her whose utmost services he exacts as strict duty? Because she was made to be a slave to his will, and has no higher end than to serve and obey him? Perhaps we arrogate too much to ourselves when we say this material world was made for our sakes; that its glorious maker has given us the use of it is certain, but when we suppose that over which we have dominion to be made purely for our sakes, we draw a false conclusion, as he who should say the people were made for the prince who is set over them, would be thought to be out of his senses as well as his politics. Yet even allowing that He who made everything in number, weight and measure, who never acts but for some great and glorious end, an end agreeable to His majesty, allowing that He created such a number of rational spirits merely to serve their fellow creatures, yet how are these lords and masters helped by the contempt they show of their poor humble vassals? Is it not rather an hindrance to that service they expect, as being undeniable and constant proof how unworthy they are to receive it?

None of God's creatures absolutely considered are in their own nature contemptible; the meanest fly, the poorest insect has its use and virtue. Contempt is scarce a human passion; one may venture to say it was not in innocent man, for till sin came into the world, there was nothing in it to be condemned. But pride, which makes everything serve its purposes, wrested this passion from its only use, so that instead of being an antidote against sin, it is become a grand promoter of it, nothing making us more worthy of that contempt we show, than when (poor, weak, dependent creatures as we are!) we look down with scorn and disdain on others.

There is not a surer sign of a noble mind, a mind very far advanced towards perfection, than the being able to bear contempt and an unjust treatment from one's superiors evenly and patiently. For inward worth and real excellency are the true ground of superiority, and one person is not in reality better than another, but as he is more wise and good. But this world being a place of trial and governed by general laws, just retributions being reserved for hereafter, respect and obedience many times become due for order's sake to those who don't otherwise deserve them. Now though humility keeps us from over-valuing ourselves or viewing our merit through a false and magnifying medium, yet it does not put out our eyes; it does not, it ought not to deprive us of that pleasing sentiment which attends our acting as we ought to act, which is as it were a foretaste of heaven, our present reward for doing what is just and fit. And when a superior does a mean and unjust thing, as all contempt of one's neighbor is, and yet this does not provoke his inferiors to refuse that observance which their stations in the world require, they cannot but have an inward sense of their own real superiority, the other having no pretense to it, at the same time that they pay him an outward respect and deference, which is such a flagrant testimony of the sincerest love of order as proves their souls to be of the highest and noblest rank.

A man therefore for his own sake, and to give evidence that he has a right to those prerogatives he assumes, should treat women with a little more humanity and regard than is usually paid them. Your whiffling wits may scoff at them, and what then? It matters not, for they rally[1] everything though ever so sacred, and rail at the women commonly in very good company. Religion, its priests, and these its most constant and regular professors, are the usual subjects of their manly, mannerly, and surprising jests. Surprising indeed! not for the newness of the thought, the brightness of the fancy, or nobleness of expression, but for the good assurance with which such threadbare jests are again and again repeated. But that your grave dons, your learned men, and which is more your men of sense as they would be thought, should stoop so low as to make invectives against the women, forget themselves so much as to jest with their slaves, who have neither liberty nor ingenuity to make reprisals! that they should waste their time and debase their good sense which fits them for the most weighty affairs, such as are suitable to their profound wisdoms and exalted understandings! to render those poor wretches more ridiculous and odious who are already in their opinion sufficiently contemptible, and find no better exercise of their wit and satire than such as are not worth their pains, though it were possible to reform them—this, this indeed may justly be wondered at!

I know not whether or no women are allowed to have souls. If they have, perhaps it is not prudent to provoke them too much, lest silly as they are, they at last recriminate, and then what polite and well-bred gentleman, though himself is concerned, can forbear taking that lawful pleasure which all who understand raillery must taste, when they find his jests who insolently began to peck at his neighbor, returned with interest upon his own head? And indeed men are too humane, too wise

1. Mock.

to venture at it did they not hope for this effect, and expect the pleasure of finding their wit turn to such account; for if it be lawful to reveal a secret, this is without doubt the whole design of those fine discourses which have been made against the women from our great forefathers to this present time. Generous man has too much bravery, he is too just and too good to assault a defenseless enemy, and if he did inveigh against the women it was only to do them service. For since neither his care of their education, his hearty endeavors to improve their minds, his wholesome precepts, nor great example could do them good, as his last and kindest essay he resolved to try what contempt would do, and chose rather to expose himself by a seeming want of justice, equity, ingenuity, and good nature, than suffer women to remain such vain and insignificant creatures as they have hitherto been reckoned. And truly women are some degrees beneath what I have thus far thought them, if they do not make the best use of his kindness, improve themselves, and like Christians return it.

Let us see then what is their part, what must they do to make the matrimonial yoke tolerable to themselves as well as pleasing to their lords and masters? That the world is an empty and deceitful thing, that those enjoyments which appear so desirable at a distance, which raised our hopes and expectations to such a mighty pitch, which we so passionately coveted and so eagerly pursued, vanish at our first approach, leaving nothing behind them but the folly of delusion, and the pain of disappointed hopes, is a common outcry; and yet as common as it is, though we complain of being deceived this instant, we do not fail of contributing to the cheat the very next. Though in reality it is not the world that abuses us, 'tis we abuse ourselves, it is not the emptiness of that, but our own false judgments, our unreasonable desires and expectations that torment us; for he who exerts his whole strength to lift a straw, ought not to complain of the burden but of his own disproportionate endeavor which gives him the pain he feels. The world affords us all that pleasure a sound judgment can expect from it, and answers all those ends and purposes for which it was designed. Let us expect no more than is reasonable, and then we shall not fail of our expectations.

It is even so in the case before us: a woman who has been taught to think marriage her only preferment, the sum-total of her endeavors, the completion of all her hopes, that which must settle and make her happy in this world, and very few, in their youth especially, carry a thought steadily to a greater distance; she who has seen a lover dying at her feet, and can't therefore imagine that he who professes to receive all his happiness from her can have any other design or desire than to please her; whose eyes have been dazzled with all the glitter and pomp of a wedding, and who hears of nothing but joy and congratulation; who is transported with the pleasure of being out of pupillage, and mistress not only of herself but of a family too; she who is either so simple or so vain as to take her lover at his word either as to the praises he gave her, or the promises he made for himself. In sum, she whose expectation has been raised by courtship, by all the fine things that her lover, her governess, and domestic flatterers say, will find a terrible disappointment when the hurry is over, and when she comes calmly to consider her condition, and views it no more under a false appearance, but as it truly is.

I doubt in such a view it will not appear over-desirable if she regards only the present state of things. Hereafter may make amends for what she must be prepared to suffer here; then will be her reward, this is her time of trial, the season of exercising and improving her virtues. A woman that is not mistress of her passions, that cannot patiently submit even when reason suffers with her, who does not practice passive obedience[2] to the utmost, will never be acceptable to such an absolute sovereign as a husband. Wisdom ought to govern without contradiction, but strength however will be obeyed. There are but few of those wise persons who can be content to be made yet wiser by contradiction; the most will have their will, and it is right because it is theirs. Such is the vanity of human nature that nothing pleases like an entire subjection; what imperfections won't a man overlook where this is not wanting! Though we live like brutes, we would have incense offered us that is only due to heaven itself, would have an absolute and blind obedience paid us by all over whom we pretend authority. We were not made to idolize one another, yet the whole strain of courtship is little less than rank idolatry. But does a man intend to give and not receive his share in this religious worship? No such matter; pride and vanity and self-love have their designs, and if the lover is so condescending as to set a pattern in the time of his addresses, he is so just as to expect his wife should strictly copy after it all the rest of her life.

But how can a woman scruple entire subjection, how can she forbear to admire the worth and excellency of the superior sex, if she at all considers it? Have not all the great actions that have been performed in the world been done by them? Have not they founded empires and overturned them? Do not they make laws and continually repeal them and amend them? Their vast minds lay kingdoms waste; no bounds or measures can be prescribed to their desires. War and peace depend on them, they form cabals[3] and have the wisdom and courage to get over all these rubs[4] which may lie in the way of their desired grandeur. What is it they cannot do? They make worlds and ruin them, form systems of universal nature and dispute eternally about them, their pen gives worth to the most trifling controversy, nor can a fray be inconsiderable if they have drawn their swords in't. All that the wise man pronounces is an oracle, and every word the witty speaks a jest. It is a woman's happiness to hear, admire, and praise them, especially if a little ill-nature keeps them at anytime from bestowing due applause on each other. And if she aspires no further she is thought to be in her proper sphere of action; she is as wise and as good as can be expected from her.

She then who marries ought to lay it down for an indisputable maxim, that her husband must govern absolutely and entirely, and that she has nothing else to do but to please and obey. She must not attempt to divide his authority, or so much as dispute it (to struggle with her yoke will only make it gall the more) but must believe him wise and good and in all respects the best, at least he must be so to her. She who can't do this is no way fit to be a wife; she may set up for that peculiar coronet the ancient fathers talked of, but is not qualified to receive that great reward,[5] which attends the eminent exercise of humility and self-denial, patience and resignation—the duties that a wife is called to.

2. The term denoted the Tory policy of obeying Whig monarchs and of refraining from rebellion despite their "usurpation" of the Stuart throne, on the principle that rebellion itself would run contrary to divine and human law.

3. Small, secretive groups formed to wield power.

4. Obstacles.

5. Salvation. The "peculiar coronet" is that of martyrdom, often imaged as a crown in the writings of early Christian theologians.

But some refractory woman perhaps will say how can this be? Is it possible for her to believe him wise and good who by a thousand demonstrations convinces her and all the world of the contrary? Did the bare name of husband confer sense on a man, and the mere being in authority infallibly qualify him for government, much might be done. But since a wise man and a husband are not terms convertible, and how loath soever one is to own it, matter of fact won't allow us to deny that the head many times stands in need of the inferior's brains to manage it, she must beg leave to be excused from such high thoughts of her sovereign, and if she submits to his power, it is not so much reason as necessity that compels her.

Now of how little force soever this objection may be in other respects, methinks it is strong enough to prove the necessity of a good education, and that men never mistake their true interest more than when they endeavor to keep women in ignorance. Could they indeed deprive them of their natural good sense at the same time they deny them the due improvement of it, they might compass their end; otherwise natural sense unassisted may run into a false track, and serve only to punish him justly, who would not allow it to be useful to himself or others. If man's authority be justly established, the more sense a woman has the more reason she will find to submit to it; if according to the tradition of our fathers (who having had *possession* of the pen, thought they had also the best *right* to it), women's understanding is but small, and men's partiality adds no weight to the observation, ought not the more care to be taken to improve them? How it agrees with the justice of men we inquire not, but certainly Heaven is abundantly more equitable than to enjoin women the hardest task and give them the least strength to perform it. And if men, learned, wise, and discreet as they are, who have as is said all the advantages of nature, and without controversy have or may have all the assistance of art, are so far from acquitting themselves as they ought, from living according to that reason and excellent understanding they so much boast of, can it be expected that a woman who is reckoned silly enough in herself, at least comparatively, and whom men take care to make yet more so, can it be expected that she should constantly perform so difficult a duty as entire subjection, to which corrupt nature is so averse?

If the great and wise Cato,[6] a *man*, a man of no ordinary firmness and strength of mind, a man who was esteemed as an oracle, and by the philosophers and great men of his nation equaled even to the gods themselves; if he with all his stoical principles was not able to bear the sight of a triumphant conqueror (who perhaps would have insulted and perhaps would not), but out of a cowardly fear of an insult, ran to death to secure him from it; can it be thought that an ignorant weak woman should have patience to bear a continual outrage and insolence all the days of her life? Unless you will suppose her a very ass, but then remember what the Italians say, to quote them once more, since being very husbands they may be presumed to have some authority in this case: *L'asino pur pigro, stimulato tira quelche calcio;* an ass though slow if provoked will kick.

We never see or perhaps make sport with the ill effects of a bad education, till it come to touch us home in the ill conduct of a sister, a daughter, or wife. Then the women must be blamed, their folly is exclaimed against, when all this while it was the wise man's fault who did not set a better guard on those who according to him

6. Cato of Utica (95–46 B.C.E.), Stoic Roman senator and commander, whose devotion to the ideal of a Republic prompted him to commit suicide rather than accede to the growing power of Julius Caesar; his death was traditionally represented as heroic.

stand in so much need of one. A young gentleman, as a celebrated author tells us, ought above all things to be acquainted with the state of the world, the ways and humors, the follies, the cheats, the faults of the age he is fallen into; he should by degrees be informed of the vice of fashion, and warned of the application and design of those who will make it their business to corrupt him, should be told the arts they use and the trains they lay, be prepared to be shocked by some and caressed by others; warned who are like to oppose, who to mislead; who to undermine and who to serve him. He should be instructed how to know and distinguish them, where he should let them see, and when dissemble the knowledge of them and their aims and workings. Our author is much in the right, and not to disparage any other accomplishments which are useful in their kind, this will turn to more account than any language or philosophy, art or science, or any other piece of good-breeding and fine education that can be taught him, which are no otherwise excellent than as they contribute to this, as this does above all things to the making him a wise, virtuous, and useful man.

And it is not less necessary that a young lady should receive the like instructions; whether or no her temptations be fewer, her reputation and honor however are to be more nicely preserved; they may be ruined by a little ignorance or indiscretion, and then though she has kept her innocence, and so is secured as to the next world, yet she is in a great measure lost to this. A woman cannot be too watchful, too apprehensive of her danger, nor keep at too great a distance from it, since man, whose wisdom and ingenuity is so much superior to hers, condescends for his interest sometimes, and sometimes by way of diversion, to lay snares for her. For though men are virtuous, philosophers and politicians in comparison of the ignorant and illiterate women, yet they don't all pretend to be saints, and 'tis no great matter to them if women, who were born to be their slaves, be now and then ruined for their entertainment.

But according to the rate that young women are educated; according to the way their time is spent; they are destined to folly and impertinence, to say no worse, and which is yet more inhuman, they are blamed for that ill conduct they are not suffered to avoid, and reproached for those faults they are in a manner forced into; so that if heaven has bestowed any sense on them, no other use is made of it than to leave them without excuse. So much and no more of the world is shown them, as serves to weaken and corrupt their minds, to give them wrong notions, and busy them in mean pursuits; to disturb, not to regulate their passions, to make them timorous and dependent, and in a word, fit for nothing else but to act a farce for the diversion of their governors.

Even men themselves improve no otherwise than according to the aim they take, and the end they propose; and he whose designs are but little and mean, will be the same himself. Though ambition, as 'tis usually understood, is a foolish, not to say a base and pitiful vice, yet the aspirings of the soul after true glory are so much its nature, that it seems to have forgot itself and to degenerate, if it can forbear; and perhaps the great secret of education lies in affecting the soul with a lively sense of what is truly its perfection, and exciting the most ardent desires after it.

But, alas! what poor woman is ever taught that she should have a higher design than to get her a husband? Heaven will fall in of course; and if she make but an obedient and dutiful wife, she cannot miss of it. A husband indeed is thought by both sexes so very valuable, that scarce a man who can keep himself clean and make a bow, but thinks he is good enough to pretend to any woman, no matter for the difference of birth or fortune, a *husband* is such a wonder-working name as to make an equality, or something more, whenever it is pronounced. * * *

To wind up this matter, if a woman were duly principled and taught to know the world, especially the true sentiments that men have of her, and the traps they lay for her under so many gilded compliments, and such a seemingly great respect, that disgrace would be prevented which is brought upon too many families, women would marry more discreetly, and demean[7] themselves better in a married state than some people say they do. The foundation indeed ought to be laid deep and strong: she should be made a good Christian, and understand why she is so, and then she will be everything else that is good. Men need keep no spies on a woman's conduct, need have no fear of her virtue, or so much as of her prudence and caution, were but a due sense of true honor and virtue awakened in her, were her reason excited and prepared to consider the sophistry of those temptations which would persuade her from her duty, and were she put in a way to know that it is both her wisdom and interest to observe it. She would then duly examine and weigh all the circumstances, the good and evil of a married state, and not be surprised with unforeseen inconveniences, and either never consent to be a wife, or make a good one when she does. This would show her what human nature *is*, as well as what it *ought* to be, and teach her not only what she may justly expect, but what she must be content with; would enable her to cure some faults, and patiently to suffer what she cannot cure.

Indeed nothing can assure obedience, and render it what it ought to be, but the confidence of duty, the paying it for God's sake. Superiors don't rightly understand their own interest when they attempt to put out their subjects' eyes to keep them obedient. A blind obedience is what a rational creature should never pay, nor would such an one receive it did he rightly understand its nature. For human actions are no otherwise valuable than as they are conformable to reason, but blind obedience is an obeying *without reason*, for ought we know, *against it*. God himself does not require our obedience at this rate; He lays before us the goodness and reasonableness of His laws, and were there anything in them whose equity we could not readily comprehend, yet we have this clear and sufficient reason on which to found our obedience, that nothing but what's just and fit can be enjoined by a just, a wise, and gracious God. But this is a reason will never hold in respect of men's commands unless they can prove themselves infallible, and consequently impeccable too.

It is therefore very much a man's interest that women should be good Christians, in this as in every other instance; he who does his duty finds his own account[8] in it. Duty and true interest are one and the same thing, and he who thinks otherwise is to be pitied for being so much in the wrong; but what can be more the duty of the head, than to instruct and improve those who are under government? She will freely leave him the quiet dominion of this world whose thoughts and expectations are placed on the next. A prospect of heaven, and that only, will cure that ambition which all generous minds are filled with, not by taking it away but by placing it on a right object. She will discern a time when her sex shall be no bar to the best employments, the highest honor; a time when that distinction, now so much used to her prejudice, shall be no more, but provided she is not wanting to herself, her soul shall shine as bright as the greatest hero's. This is a true, and indeed the only consolation, this makes her a sufficient compensation for all the neglect

7. Behave (though the meaning "to lower herself" was also current).

8. I.e., is amply compensated.

and contempt the ill-grounded customs of the world throw on her, for all the injuries brutal power may do her, and is a sufficient cordial to support her spirits, be her lot in this world what it may.

But some sage persons may perhaps object that were women allowed to improve themselves, and not amongst other discouragements driven back by those wise jests and scoffs that are put upon a woman of sense or learning, a philosophical lady as she is called by way of ridicule, they would be too wise and too good for the men. I grant it, for vicious and foolish men. Nor is it to be wondered that he is afraid he should not be able to govern them were their understandings improved, who is resolved not to take too much pains with his own. But these 'tis to be hoped are no very considerable number, the foolish at least; and therefore this is so far from being an argument against their improvement, that it is a strong one for it, if we do but suppose the men to be as capable of improvement as the women, but much more if according to tradition we believe they have greater capacities. This, if anything, would stir them up to be what they ought, not permit them to waste their time and abuse their faculties in the service of their irregular appetites and unreasonable desires, and to let poor contemptible women who have been their slaves excel them in all that is truly excellent. This would make them blush at employing an immoral mind no better than in making provision for the flesh to fulfill the lusts thereof, since women by a wiser conduct have brought themselves to such a reach of thought, to such exactness of judgment, such clearness and strength of reasoning, such purity and elevation of mind, such command of their passions, such regularity of will and affection, and in a word to such a pitch of perfection as the human soul is capable of attaining even in this life by the grace of God, such true wisdom, such real greatness, as though it does not qualify them to make a noise in this world, to found or overturn empires, yet it qualifies them for what is infinitely better, a kingdom that cannot be moved, an incorruptible crown of glory.

Besides, it were ridiculous to suppose that a woman, were she ever so much improved, could come near the topping genius of men, and therefore why should they envy or discourage her? Strength of mind goes along with strength of body, and 'tis only for some odd accidents which philosophers have not yet thought worthwhile to inquire into, that the sturdiest porter is not the wisest man. As therefore the men have the power in their hands, so there's no dispute of their having the brains to manage it. There is no such thing as good judgment and sense upon earth, if it is not to be found among them. Do not they generally speaking do all the great actions and considerable business of this world, and leave that of the next to the women? Their subtlety in forming cabals and laying deep designs, their courage and conduct in breaking through all ties sacred and civil to effect them, not only advances them to the post of honor and keeps them securely in it for twenty or thirty years, but gets them a name, and conveys it down to posterity for some hundreds, and who would look any further? Justice and injustice are administered by their hands; courts and schools are filled with these sages; 'tis men who dispute for truth as well as men who argue against it; histories are writ by them, they recount each others' great exploits, and have always done so. All famous arts have their original from men, even from the invention of guns to the mystery of good eating. And to show that nothing is beneath their care, any more than above their reach, they have brought *gaming*[9] to an

9. Gambling.

art and science, and a more profitable and honorable one too, than any of those that used to be called *liberal*. Indeed what is it they can't perform, when they attempt it? This strength of their brains shall be every whit as conspicuous at their cups as in a Senate house, and when they please they can make it pass for as sure a mark of wisdom to drink deep as to reason profoundly; a greater proof of courage and consequently of understanding to dare the vengeance of heaven itself than to stand the raillery of some of the worst of their fellow creatures!

Again, it may be said, if a wife's case be as it is here represented, it is not good for a woman to marry, and so there's an end of human race. But this is no fair consequence, for all that can justly be inferred from hence is that a woman has no mighty obligations to the man who makes love to her, she has no reason to be fond of being a wife, or to reckon it a piece of preferment when she is taken to be a man's upper-servant; it is no advantage to her in this world, if rightly managed it may prove one as to the next. For she who marries purely to do good, to educate souls for heaven, who can be so truly mortified as to lay aside her own will and desires, to pay such an entire submission for life, to one whom she cannot be sure will always deserve it, does certainly perform a more heroic action than all the famous masculine heroes can boast of; she suffers a continual martyrdom to bring glory to God and benefit to mankind, which consideration indeed may carry her though all difficulties, I know not what else can, and engage her to love him who proves perhaps so much more worse than a brute, as to make this condition yet more grievous than it needed to be. She has need of a strong reason, of a truly Christian and well-tempered spirit, of all the assistance the best education can give her, and ought to have some good assistance of her own firmness and virtue, who ventures on such a trial; and for this reason 'tis less to be wondered at that women marry off in haste, for perhaps if they took time to consider and reflect upon it, they seldom would.

To conclude, perhaps I've said more than most men will thank me for; I cannot help it, for how much soever I may be their friend and humble servant, I am more a friend to truth. Truth is strong, and some time or other will prevail; nor is it for their honor, and therefore one would think not for their interest, to be partial to themselves and unjust to others. They may fancy I have made some discoveries which like *arcana imperii*[1] ought to be kept secret, but in good earnest I do them more honor than to suppose their lawful prerogatives need any mean arts to support them. If they have usurped, I love justice too much to wish success and continuance to usurpations, which though submitted to out of prudence and for quietness' sake, yet leave everybody free to regain their lawful right whenever they have power and opportunity. I don't say that tyranny *ought*, but we find in *fact*, that it provokes the oppressed to throw off even a lawful yoke that fits too heavy. And if he who is freely elected, after all his fair promises and the fine hopes he raised, proves a tyrant, the consideration that he was one's own choice will not render more submissive and patient, but I fear more refractory. For though it is very unreasonable, yet we see 'tis the course of the world not only to return injury for injury, but crime for crime; both parties indeed are guilty, but the aggressors have a double guilt; they have not only their own, but their neighbor's ruin to answer for.

As to the female reader, I hope she will allow I've endeavored to do her justice, nor betrayed her cause as her advocates usually do, under pretense of defending it: a practice too mean for any to be guilty of who have the least sense of honor, and who

1. The secrets of power.

do any more than merely pretend to it. I think I have held the balance even, and not being conscious of partiality I ask no pardon for it. To plead for the oppressed and to defend the weak seemed to me a generous undertaking; for though it may be secure, 'tis not always honorable to run over to the strongest party. And if she infers from what has been said that marriage is a very happy state for men, if they think fit to make it so; that they govern the world, they have prescription on their side, women are too weak to dispute it with them, therefore they, as all other governors, are most, if not only, accountable for what's amiss. For whether other governments in their original were or were not conferred according to the merit of the person, yet certainly in this case Heaven would not have allotted the man to govern, but because he was best qualified for it. So far I agree with him. But if she goes on to infer, that therefore he has not these qualifications, where is his right? If he misemploys, does he not abuse it? And if he abuses, according to modern deduction, he forfeits it; I must leave her there. A peaceable woman indeed will not carry it so far, she will neither question her husband's right nor his fitness to govern, but how? Not as an absolute lord and master, with an arbitrary and tyrannical sway, but as reason governs and conducts a man, by proposing what is just and fit. And the man who acts according to that wisdom he assumes, who would have that superiority he pretends to acknowledged just, will receive no injury by anything that has been offered here. A woman will value him the more who is so wise and good, when she discerns how much he excels the rest of his noble sex; the less he requires, the more will he merit that esteem and deference, which those who are so forward to exact seem conscious they don't deserve. So then the man's prerogative is not at all infringed, whilst the woman's privileges are secured; and if any woman think herself injured, she has a remedy in reserve which few men will envy or endeavor to rob her of, the exercise and improvement of her virtue here, and the reward of it hereafter.

1700 1700

Daniel Defoe

1660–1731

At the age of fifty-two, Daniel Defoe summed up his life in a couplet:

> No man has tasted differing fortunes more,
> And thirteen times I have been rich or poor.

Vicissitude marked his career until the very end, and money, though a constant preoccupation, was not the only medium of change. Deeply engaged in politics, and phenomenally skilled at promoting causes with his pen, Defoe switched allegiances several times among the most conspicuous factions of his day. What's more, since he was prized by each side in turn for his efficiency as a secret agent, his political work often required him to present himself—in person and in print—as someone or something he was not, to incur hostilities from the very factions he was secretly working to support. His accomplishments, late in life, as a pioneer of English fiction partly originate in the fictions he manipulated as a consummate political journalist and spy obliged to "taste" in imagination and performance the "differing fortunes" of the person he pretended, for one purpose or another, to be. Out of all these oscillations—financial, political, imaginative—came one of the most prolific and inventive careers in British literature.

Defoe was born in the City of London in the year of the Restoration to a family whose fortunes were on the rise. His father James Foe manufactured and sold candles, and over the ensuing decades attained positions of increasing eminence in his trade (Defoe himself later added the French prefix to his family surname). Under the influence of their pastor, the Foes left the Church of England to become Dissenters, at a time when to do so was to incur certain exclusion—from attending universities, from holding public office—and possible persecution (violence, imprisonment). At around the age of ten, shortly after his mother's early death, Defoe began a decade in the schools of the Dissenters. The curriculum, underplaying the Greek and Latin of conventional Anglican education, focused instead on new science and philosophy, on clear argument and public speaking, as well as on two forms of thought and composition that cultivated the student's ability to imagine "differing fortunes": prose impersonation, where the student was asked to "play" a given figure (for example, a secretary of state) in a particular situation, and to write a letter or give a speech suitable to the occasion; and casuistry, a kind of moral and theological game of "What if?": if I were to find myself in such and such a predicament, such a dilemma, what should I do? The question recurs, explicitly and implicitly, throughout Defoe's prose.

As Defoe entered his twenties, the question became personally pressing. Many of his classmates were preparing for the ministry; he opted instead to enter his father's world of trade, though with a taste for range and risk that his prudent forebear had never displayed. Defoe dealt at one time or another in men's clothing, tobacco, wine; opened and operated a brick and tile factory, and invested capital so audaciously and ill-advisedly that in 1692 he was forced to declare bankruptcy, having incurred the enormous debt of £17,000. "The God that gave me brains will give me bread," Defoe remarked at one point, with characteristic confidence in both the deity and himself. From his late thirties onward, he used those brains to earn bread, for himself and his large family, by writing. He worked with astonishing speed and efficiency, producing by his life's end more than 500 separate works, as well as several periodical series that he wrote (at the rate of two or three essays a week) over the course of many years. Nonetheless, he never quite escaped the financial distresses that had first pushed him into print.

His pen's other impetus was politics. As a Whig and a Dissenter eager to end the reign of the Catholic James II, Defoe had fought as soldier in the abortive Monmouth Rebellion of 1685, and in 1688 celebrated the advent of the Glorious Revolution and William III. He served his new king as secret agent and as author, publishing the phenomenally popular poem *The True-Born Englishman* (1701), whose title sarcastically identifies those "natives" hostile to William on the grounds of his foreign birth (the poem argues, among other things, that their own lineage is far more complex and corrupt than they admit). Defoe's powers as a political advocate were now near full stride, and his knack for irony soon brought him trouble. In his parodic pamphlet *The Shortest Way with Dissenters*, published anonymously in 1702 at the height of Tory hopes for a new assault on Nonconformists, Defoe impersonates a rabid Tory eager to mete out extravagant punishments on the Nonconformists (to whom Defoe himself had felt a lifelong loyalty and tenderness). Neither faction appreciated the joke. After four months in hiding, Defoe was arrested, convicted of libel, and sentenced to prison and to three separate sessions in the pillory, where the crowds (to his surprise) celebrated him as a hero, pelting him with fresh flowers rather than rotten vegetables. The episode initiated a sea change in his affiliations. Disillusioned with Whigs and Dissenters, Defoe secretly aligned himself with the ambitious Tory politician Robert Harley, who in an inspired move had arranged to pay some of Defoe's fines and debts after his release from jail. Commissioned by Harley to create and manage a kind of personal secret service, Defoe traveled extensively, often under assumed names, advocating Tory causes (most notably the Union with Scotland) and reporting on the opposition; he also wrote the widely read *Review* (1704–1713), a thrice-weekly periodical essay intricately calculated to further Harley's interests. After the fall of the

Tories, the intricacy deepened. Under threat of punishment by the new Whig government, Defoe agreed to work as double agent for *them*, by moving among Tory journalists and contributing to Tory papers, but in such ways as to undermine the Tory cause. For the seasoned ironist and impersonator this was irony enough: having worked brilliantly for years to devise Tory propaganda, he was now at pains to dilute it.

At the age of fifty-nine, Defoe hit upon a new way to make impersonation pay. His book *The Strange, Surprising Adventures of Robinson Crusoe* (1719) was the first in a series of long fictions that present themselves as historical fact, as the written reminiscences of people who had actually lived the extraordinary experiences they relate, in books that often bear their fictive names as titles: *Captain Singleton* (1720); *Moll Flanders* (1722); *Colonel Jack* (1722); *Roxana* (1724). In creating these memoirists, Defoe drew on his decades as a journalist. He saturated his stories with particulars (clothing, furniture, tools); his memoirists write a prose that often reads like talk—digressive, fervent, improvisatory. By such strategies he made his tales persuasive. As a genre, the novel has no one inventor, because it absorbs so much (and so variously) from other kinds of texts: newspapers, essays, diaries, financial accounts, religious devotions, conduct manuals. Defoe, though, was perhaps the most astute early orchestrator of such absorptions. Having written in most of his culture's modes, he melded them into a form of fiction that still seems (in keeping with the genre's name) new.

Vicissitude persisted. Having written his last long fiction (*Roxana*) in 1724, Defoe turned his hand to another project. In his *Tour through the Whole Island of Great Britain* (three volumes, 1724–1726), and in other late works, he celebrated British trade as a source of present prosperity and a seedbed of future empire. He died while hiding out from his creditors in the neighborhood of his birth, once again on the run from debt and cut off from his contentious family. The ending feels emblematic. In many ways the most communicative of writers, Defoe often used his powers to study solitude. "Between me and thee there is a great gulf fixed," remarks Robinson Crusoe on his island, quoting scripture: "thee" is the whole world, from which he finds himself definitively sundered. But the phrase might be invoked by almost any speaker in Defoe—characters talking to characters, ghosts to the living, narrators to readers—as they survey the landscape of their own isolation, even in crowded cities. Defoe devoted his writing life to mapping these "great gulfs," to chronicling the energies—political, social, and commercial—by which the mortals of his time and place tried to bridge them, and to seeking out the work of God and Providence in all these prolific, troubled transactions.

For additional resources on Defoe, go to *The Longman Anthology of British Literature* Web site at www.myliteraturekit.com.

A True Relation *A True Relation* was long thought to be Defoe's earliest foray into fiction; it was then discovered to have a firm basis in fact. The original pamphlet was published anonymously; Defoe was not identified as author until 1790. For most of the nineteenth century it was assumed that he had made up the entire story, possibly as publicity for Charles Drelincourt's *Defense against the Fears of Death*, the book that Mrs. Veal repeatedly recommends to her friend Mrs. Bargrave. Shortly after the *Apparition's* first appearance as a pamphlet, in fact, Defoe's text and Drelincourt's were combined into a single, popular volume which went through many printings. In 1895 the Defoe scholar George Aitken published the first independent evidence for the authenticity of the story, if not of the ghost: a Latin memorandum from 1714 recording an interview with the actual Mrs. Bargrave, who adhered (and added) to her narrative nearly a decade after it took place. Other contemporary accounts of her and her story have since been discovered. Defoe, then, was practicing not fiction but journalism, sifting, selecting, and arranging testimony then in circulation, presenting it in the voice of Mrs. Bargrave's "intimate friend," the "very intelligent" Justice of the Peace who professes himself very "affected" by his interview with her (his own status, as historical person or fabricated narrator, has never been established). Mingling "matter of fact" (a recurrent phrase) with matters of mystery, Defoe here manages (as Leslie Stephen once remarked) to embody "in a few lines all the essential particularities of his art."

A True Relation of the Apparition of One Mrs. Veal the Next Day after Her Death to One Mrs. Bargrave at Canterbury the 8th of September, 1705

The Preface

This relation is matter of fact, and attended with such circumstances as may induce any reasonable man to believe it. It was sent by a gentleman, a Justice of Peace at Maidstone in Kent and a very intelligent person, to his friend in London, as it is here worded. Which discourse is attested by a very sober and understanding gentlewoman, a kinswoman of the said gentleman's, who lives in Canterbury within a few doors of the house in which the within named Mrs. Bargrave lives; who believes his kinswoman to be of so discerning a spirit, as not to be put upon by any fallacy. And who positively assured him that the whole matter, as it is here related and laid down, is what is really true, and what she herself had in the same words (as near as may be) from Mrs. Bargrave's own mouth, who she knows had no reason to invent and publish such a story, nor any design to forge and tell a lie, being a woman of much honesty and virtue, and her whole life a course as it were of piety. The use which we ought to make of it is to consider that there is a life to come after this, and a just God who will retribute to everyone according to the deeds done in the body; and therefore, to reflect upon our past course of life we have led in the world, that our time is short and uncertain, and that if we would escape the punishment of the ungodly and receive the reward of the righteous, which is the laying hold of eternal life, we ought for the time to come to turn to God by a speedy repentance, ceasing to do evil and learning to do well: to seek after God early, if happily he may be found of us, and lead such lives for the future as may be well pleasing in his sight.

A Relation of the Apparition of Mrs. Veal

This thing is so rare in all its circumstances, and on so good authority, that my reading and conversation has not given me anything like it; it is fit to gratify the most ingenious and serious inquirer. Mrs. Bargrave is the person to whom Mrs. Veal appeared after her death. She is my intimate friend, and I can avouch for her reputation for these last fifteen or sixteen years on my own knowledge; and I can confirm the good character she had from her youth, to the time of my acquaintance. Though since this relation she is calumniated by some people that are friends to the brother of Mrs. Veal who appeared, who think the relation of this appearance to be a reflection,[1] and endeavor what they can to blast Mrs. Bargrave's reputation and to laugh the story out of countenance. But the circumstances

1. I.e., injurious to the family's reputation.

thereof, and the cheerful disposition of Mrs. Bargrave, notwithstanding the unheard of ill usage of a very wicked husband, there is not the least sign of dejection in her face; nor did I ever hear her let fall a desponding or murmuring expression; nay, not when actually under her husband's barbarity, which I have been witness to, and several other persons of undoubted reputation.[2]

Now you must know that Mrs. Veal was a maiden gentlewoman[3] of about thirty years of age, and for some years last past had been troubled with fits, which were perceived coming on her by her leaving off from her discourse very abruptly to some impertinence.[4] She was maintained by an only brother, and kept his house in Dover. She was a very pious woman, and her brother a very sober man to all appearance. But now he does all he can to null or quash the story. Mrs. Veal was intimately acquainted with Mrs. Bargrave from her childhood. Mrs. Veal's circumstances were then mean; her father did not take care of his children as he ought, so that they were exposed to hardships. And Mrs. Bargrave in those days had as unkind a father, though she wanted for neither food nor clothing, while Mrs. Veal wanted for both. So that it was in the power of Mrs. Bargrave to be very much her friend in several instances, which mightily endeared Mrs. Veal; insomuch that she would often say, "Mrs. Bargrave, you are not only the best, but the only friend I have in the world, and no circumstances of life shall ever dissolve my friendpship." They would often condole each other's adverse fortunes, and read together *Drelincourt upon Death*[5] and other good books. And so like two Christian friends they comforted each other under their sorrow.

Sometime after, Mr. Veal's friends got him a place in the custom house at Dover, which occasioned Mrs. Veal by little and little to fall off from her intimacy with Mrs. Bargrave, though there was never any such thing as a quarrel; but an indifferency came on by degrees, till at last Mrs. Bargrave had not seen her in two years and a half; though above a twelve month of the time Mrs. Bargrave had been absent from Dover, and this last half year has been in Canterbury about two months of the time, dwelling in a house of her own.

In this house, on the eighth of September last, viz. 1705, she was sitting alone in the forenoon, thinking over her unfortunate life and arguing herself into a due resignation to Providence, though her condition seemed hard. And said she, "I have been provided for hitherto, and doubt not but I shall be still, and am well satisfied that my afflictions shall end when it is most fit for me." And then took up her sewing work, which she had no sooner done but she hears a knocking at the door. She went to see who it was there, and this proved to be Mrs. Veal, her old friend, who was in a riding habit. At that moment of time, the clock struck twelve at noon.

"Madam," says Mrs. Bargrave, "I am surprised to see you, you have been so long a stranger," but told her she was glad to see her and offered to salute[6] her, which Mrs. Veal complied with till their lips almost touched, and then Mrs. Veal drew her hand cross her own eyes and said, "I am not very well," and so waived it. She told Mrs. Bargrave she was going a journey, and had a great mind to see her first. "But," says Mrs. Bargrave, "how came you to take a journey alone? I am amazed at it, because I know you have so fond a brother." "O!" says Mrs. Veal, "I

2. The sentence is grammatically incomplete (Defoe supplies no verb for the initial subject "the circumstances").

3. "Mrs." (pronounced "Mistress") designated any adult woman, married or unmarried.

4. Irrelevance; digression.

5. I.e., *The Christian's Defense against the Fears of Death*, by Charles Drelincourt, a French Protestant pastor and prolific devotional writer who published the book in 1651; the first English translation appeared in 1675.

6. Kiss.

gave my brother the slip and came away, because I had so great a mind to see you before I took my journey." So Mrs. Bargrave went in with her, into another room within the first, and Mrs. Veal sat herself down in an elbow-chair, in which Mrs. Bargrave was sitting when she heard Mrs. Veal knock. Then says Mrs. Veal, "My dear friend, I am come to renew our old friendship again, and to beg your pardon for my breach of it, and if you can forgive me you are one of the best of women." "O!" says Mrs. Bargrave, "don't mention such a thing. I have not had an uneasy thought about it; I can easily forgive it." "What did you think of me?" says Mrs. Veal. Says Mrs. Bargrave, "I thought you were like the rest of the world, and that prosperity had made you forget yourself and me." Then Mrs. Veal reminded Mrs. Bargrave of the many friendly offices she did her in former days, and much of the conversation they had with each other in the time of their adversity: what books they read, and what comfort in particular they received from *Drelincourt's Book of Death*, which was the best, she said, on that subject ever wrote. She also mentioned Dr. Sherlock,[7] and two Dutch books which were translated, wrote upon death, and several others. But Drelincourt, she said, had the clearest notions of death and of the future state of any who have handled that subject. Then she asked Mrs. Bargrave whether she had Drelincourt. She said, "Yes." Says Mrs. Veal, "Fetch it," and so Mrs. Bargrave goes upstairs and brings it down. Says Mrs. Veal, "Dear Mrs. Bargrave, if the eyes of our faith were as open as the eyes of our body, we should see numbers of angels about us for our guard. The notions we have of Heaven now are nothing like what it is, as Drelincourt says. Therefore be comforted under your afflictions, and believe that the Almighty has a particular regard to you, and that your afflictions are marks of God's favor. And when they have done the business they were sent for, they shall be removed from you. And believe me, my dear friend, believe what I say to you, one minute of future happiness will infinitely reward you for all your sufferings. For I can never believe" (and claps her hand upon her knee, with a great deal of earnestness, which indeed ran through all her discourse) "that ever God will suffer you to spend all your days in this afflicted state. But be assured that your afflictions shall leave you, or you them, in a short time." She spake in that pathetical and heavenly manner, that Mrs. Bargrave wept several times, she was so deeply affected with it. Then Mrs. Veal mentioned Dr. Horneck's *Ascetic*,[8] at the end of which he gives an account of the lives of the primitive Christians. Their pattern she recommended to our imitation, and said their conversation was not like this of our age. "For now" (says she) "there is nothing but frothy vain discourse, which is far different from theirs. Theirs was to edification, and to build one another up in the faith. So that they were not as we are, nor are we as they are. But," said she, "we might do as they did. There was a hearty friendship among them, but where is it now to be found?" Says Mrs. Bargrave, "'Tis hard indeed to find a true friend in these days." Says Mrs. Veal, "Mr. Norris[9] has a fine copy of verses called *Friendship in Perfection*, which I wonderfully admire. Have you seen the book?" says Mrs. Veal. "No," says Mrs. Bargrave, "but I have the verses of my own writing out." "Have you?" says Mrs. Veal, "then fetch them." Which she did from above stairs, and offered them to Mrs. Veal to read,

7. William Sherlock, Protestant divine and author of the widely read *Practical Discourse upon Death* (1689).

8. Anthony Horneck, clergyman and author of *The Happy Ascetic* (1681).

9. John Norris, a clergyman, philosopher, and poet.

who refused, and waived the thing, saying holding down her head would make it ache, and then desired Mrs. Bargrave to read them to her, which she did. As they were admiring friendship, Mrs. Veal said, "Dear Mrs. Bargrave, I shall love you forever. In the verses, there is twice used the word Elysium. Ah!" says Mrs. Veal, "these poets have such names for heaven." She would often draw her hand cross her own eyes, and say, "Mrs. Bargrave, don't you think I am mightily impaired by my fits?" "No," says Mrs. Bargrave, "I think you look as well as ever I knew you."

After all this discourse, which the apparition put in words much finer than Mrs. Bargrave said she could pretend to, and was much more than she can remember (for it cannot be thought that an hour and three quarters' conversation could all be retained, though the main of it she thinks she does), she said to Mrs. Bargrave she would have her write a letter to her brother, and tell him she would have him give rings to such and such, and that there was a purse of gold in her cabinet, and that she would have two broad pieces given to her cousin Watson. Talking at this rate, Mrs. Bargrave thought that a fit was coming upon her,[1] and so placed herself in a chair just before her knees, to keep her from falling to the ground if her fits should occasion it; for the elbow chair she thought would keep her from falling on either side. And to divert Mrs. Veal, as she thought, she took hold of her gown sleeve several times, and commended it. Mrs. Veal told her it was a scoured[2] silk, and newly made up. But for all this Mrs. Veal persisted in her request, and told Mrs. Bargrave she must not deny her. And she would have her tell her brother all their conversation, when she had an opportunity. "Dear Mrs. Veal," says Mrs. Bargrave, "this seems so impertinent that I cannot tell how to comply with it; and what a mortifying story will our conversation be to a young gentleman?" "Well," says Mrs. Veal, "I must not be denied." "Why," says Mrs. Bargrave, "'tis much better methinks to do it yourself." "No," says Mrs. Veal, "though it seems impertinent to you now, you will see more reason for it hereafter." Mrs. Bargrave then, to satisfy her importunity, was going to fetch a pen and ink; but Mrs. Veal said, "Let it alone now, and do it when I am gone; but you must be sure to do it." Which was one of the last things she enjoined her at parting; and so she promised her.

Then Mrs. Veal asked for Mrs. Bargrave's daughter. She said she was not at home. "But if you have a mind to see her," says Mrs. Bargrave, "I'll send for her." "Do," says Mrs. Veal. On which she left her, and went to a neighbor's to send for her. And by the time Mrs. Bargrave was returning, Mrs. Veal was got without the door in the street, in the face of the beast-market on a Saturday (which is market day), and stood ready to part as soon as Mrs. Bargrave came to her. She asked her why she was in such haste. She said she must be going, though perhaps she might not go her journey till Monday. And told Mrs. Bargrave she hoped she should see her again at her cousin Watson's before she went whither she was a-going. Then she said she would take her leave of her, and walked from Mrs. Bargrave in her view till a turning interrupted the sight of her, which was three quarters after one in the afternoon.

Mrs. Veal died the 7th of September at 12 o'clock at noon, of her fits, and had not above four hours' senses before her death, in which time she received the

1. I.e., Mrs. Veal.

2. Polished; cleaned with detergent.

sacrament. The next day after Mrs. Veal's appearing being Sunday, Mrs. Bargrave was mightily indisposed with a cold and a sore throat, that she could not go out that day. But on Monday morning she sends a person to Captain Watson's to know if Mrs. Veal were there. They wondered at Mrs. Bargrave's inquiry, and sent her word that she was not there, nor was she expected. At this answer Mrs. Bargrave told the maid she had certainly mistook the name, or made some blunder. And though she was ill, she put on her hood and went herself to Captain Watson's, though she knew none of the family, to see if Mrs. Veal was there or not. They said they wondered at her asking, for that she had not been in town; they were sure, if she had, she would have been there. Says Mrs. Bargrave, "I am sure she was with me on Saturday almost two hours." They said it was impossible, for they must have seen her if she had. In comes Captain Watson, while they were in dispute, and said that Mrs. Veal was certainly dead, and her escutcheons were making.[3] This strangely surprised Mrs. Bargrave, who went to the person immediately who had the care of them, and found it true. Then she related the whole story to Captain Watson's family, and what gown she had on, and how striped. And that Mrs. Veal told her it was scoured. Then Mrs. Watson cried out, "You have seen her indeed, for none knew but Mrs. Veal and myself that the gown was scoured." And Mrs. Watson owned that she described the gown exactly; "for," said she, "I helped her to make it up." This, Mrs. Watson blazed all about the town, and avouched the demonstration of the truth of Mrs. Bargrave's seeing Mrs. Veal's apparition. And Captain Watson carried two gentlemen immediately to Mrs. Bargrave's house, to hear the relation from her own mouth. And then it spread so fast that gentlemen and persons of quality, the judicious and skeptical part of the world, flocked in upon her, which at last became such a task that she was forced to go out of the way. For they were, in general, extremely satisfied of the truth of the thing, and plainly saw that Mrs. Bargrave was no hypochondriac, for she always appears with such a cheerful air and pleasing mien that she has gained the favor and esteem of all the gentry. And it's thought a great favor if they can but get the relation from her own mouth. I should have told you before that Mrs. Veal told Mrs. Bargrave that her sister and brother-in-law were just come down from London to see her. Says Mrs. Bargrave, "How came you to order matters so strangely?" "It could not be helped," said Mrs. Veal. And her sister and brother did come to see her, and entered the town of Dover just as Mrs. Veal was expiring. Mrs. Bargrave asked her whether she would drink some tea. Says Mrs. Veal, "I do not care if I do. But I'll warrant this mad fellow" (meaning Mrs. Bargrave's husband) "has broke all your trinkets." "But," says Mrs. Bargrave, "I'll get something to drink in for all that." But Mrs. Veal waived it, and said, "It is no matter, let it alone," and so it passed.

All the time I sat with Mrs. Bargrave, which was some hours, she recollected fresh sayings of Mrs. Veal. And one material thing more she told Mrs. Bargrave, that old Mr. Breton allowed Mrs. Veal ten pounds a year, which was a secret, and unknown to Mrs. Bargrave till Mrs. Veal told it her. Mrs. Bargrave never varies in her story, which puzzles those who doubt of the truth, or are unwilling to believe it. A servant in a neighbor's yard adjoining to Mrs. Bargrave's house heard her talking to somebody an hour of the time Mrs. Veal was with her. Mrs. Bargrave went out to her next neighbors the very moment she parted with Mrs. Veal, and told her what

3. Funeral ornaments were being prepared.

ravishing conversation she had with an old friend, and told the whole of it. *Drelincourt's Book of Death* is, since this happened, bought up strangely. And it is to be observed that notwithstanding all this trouble and fatigue Mrs. Bargrave has undergone upon this account, she never took the value of a farthing, nor suffered her daughter to take anything of anybody, and therefore can have no interest in telling the story.

But Mr. Veal does what he can to stifle the matter, and said he would see Mrs. Bargrave. But yet it is certain matter fact that he has been at Captain Watson's since the death of his sister, and yet never went near Mrs. Bargrave. And some of his friends report her to be a great liar, and that she knew of Mr. Breton's ten pounds a year. But the person who pretends to say so has the reputation of a notorious liar among persons which I know to be of undoubted repute. Now Mr. Veal is more a gentleman than to say she lies, but says a bad husband has crazed her. But she needs only to present herself, and it will effectually confute that pretense. Mr. Veal says he asked his sister on her deathbed whether she had a mind to dispose of anything, and she said, "No." Now, what the things which Mrs. Veal's apparition would have disposed of were so trifling, and nothing of justice aimed at in their disposal, that the design of it appears to me to be only in order to make Mrs. Bargrave, so to demonstrate the truth of her appearance as to satisfy the world of the reality thereof, as to what she had seen and heard, and to secure her reputation among the reasonable and understanding part of mankind. And then again, Mr. Veal owns that there was a purse of gold; but it was not found in her cabinet, but in a comb box. This looks improbable, for that Mrs. Watson owned that Mrs. Veal was so very careful of the key of her cabinet that she would trust nobody with it. And if so, no doubt she would not trust her gold out of it. And Mrs. Veal's often drawing her hand over her eyes, and asking Mrs. Bargrave whether her fits had not impaired her, looks to me as if she did it on purpose to remind Mrs. Bargrave of her fits, to prepare her not to think it strange that she should put her upon writing to her brother to dispose of rings and gold, which looked so much like a dying person's bequest. And it took accordingly with Mrs. Bargrave, as the effect of her fits coming upon her, and was one of the many instances of her wonderful love to her, and care of her, that she should not be affrighted. Which indeed appears in her whole management; particularly in her coming to her in the daytime, waiving the salutation, and when she was alone; and then the manner of her parting, to prevent a second attempt to salute her.

Now, why Mr. Veal should think this relation a reflection (as 'tis plain he does by his endeavoring to stifle it), I can't imagine, because the generality believe her to be a good spirit, her discourse was so heavenly. Her two great errands were to comfort Mrs. Bargrave in her affliction and to ask her forgiveness for her breach of friendship, and with a pious discourse to encourage her. So that after all, to suppose that Mrs. Bargrave could hatch such an invention as this from Friday noon till Saturday noon (supposing that she knew of Mrs. Veal's death the very first moment) without jumbling circumstances, and without any interest too—she must be more witty, fortunate, and wicked too than any indifferent person, I dare say, will allow. I asked Mrs. Bargrave several times if she was sure she felt the gown. She answered modestly, "If my senses be to be relied on, I am sure of it." I asked her if she heard a sound when she clapped her hand upon her knee. She said she did not remember she did. And she said, "She appeared to be as much a substance as I did, who talked with her. And I may," said she, "be as soon persuaded that your apparition is talking to me now, as that I did not really see her. For I was under no manner of fear; I received her as a friend, and parted with her as such. I would not," says she, "give one farthing to make anyone believe it. I have no interest in it; nothing but trouble is entailed upon me for a long time for aught that I know. And had it not come to light by accident, it would never have been made public." But now, she says, she will make her own private use of it, and keep herself out of the way as much as she can. And so she has done since. She says she had a gentleman who came thirty miles to her to hear the relation, and that she had told it to a room full of people at a time. Several particular gentlemen have had the story from Mrs. Bargrave's own mouth.

This thing has very much affected me, and I am as well satisfied as I am of the best grounded matter of fact. And why should we dispute matter of fact, because we cannot solve things of which we can have no certain or demonstrative notions, seems strange to me. Mrs. Bargrave's authority and sincerity alone would have been undoubted in any other case.

1706 1706

from A Journal of the Plague Year

Being Observations or Memorials of the Most Remarkable Occurrences, as Well Public as Private, Which Happened in London during the Last Great Visitation in 1665[1]

[At the Burial Pit]

I went all the first part of the time freely about the streets, though not so freely as to run myself into apparent danger, except when they dug the great pit in the churchyard of our parish of Aldgate; a terrible pit it was, and I could not resist my curiosity to go and see it. As near as I may judge, it was about 40 foot in length, and about 15 or 16 foot broad; and at the time I first looked at it, about nine foot deep; but it was said they dug it near 20 foot deep afterwards, in one part of it, till they could go no deeper for the water: for they had, it seems, dug several large pits before this, for though the plague was long a-coming to our parish, yet when it did come, there was no parish in or about London where it raged with such violence as in the two parishes of Aldgate and Whitechapel.

I say they had dug several pits in another ground, when the distemper began to spread in our parish, and especially when the dead carts began to go about, which was not in our parish till the beginning of August. Into these pits they had put perhaps 50 or 60 bodies each; then they made larger holes, wherein they buried all that the cart brought in a week, which by the middle to the end of August, came to from 200 to 400 a week; and they could not well dig them larger, because of the order of the magistrates, confining them to leave no bodies within six foot of the surface; and the water coming on, at about 17 or 18 foot, they could not well, I say, put more in

1. In the early 1720s, London found itself once again threatened with the prospect of bubonic plague. Defoe responded with two long pieces of prose: a manual of preventive measures called *Due Preparations for the Plague* (1720), and a historical fiction thoroughly researched and deeply grounded in historical facts. The text's purported narrator—already dead by the time his book is published—presents himself as recasting in retrospect the journal entries he wrote during that terrible year, in the hope that they may benefit future generations. Designated only by his initials, "H. F.," he is probably modeled in part on the author's uncle Henry Foe, who like "H. F." was a London saddler who lived in the parish of Aldgate.

one pit; but now at the beginning of September, the plague raging in a dreadful manner, and the number of burials in our parish increasing to more than was ever buried in any parish about London of no larger extent, they ordered this dreadful gulf to be dug; for such it was, rather than a pit.

They had supposed this pit would have supplied them for a month or more, when they dug it, and some blamed the church wardens for suffering such a frightful thing, telling them they were making preparations to bury the whole parish, and the like; but time made it appear, the church wardens knew the condition of the parish better than they did; for the pit being finished the 4th of September, I think, they began to bury in it the 6th, and by the 20th, which was just two weeks, they had thrown into it 1,114 bodies, when they were obliged to fill it up, the bodies being then come to lie within six foot of the surface: I doubt not but there may be some ancient persons alive in the parish, who can justify the fact of this, and are able to show even in what part of the churchyard the pit lay, better than I can; the mark of it also was many years to be seen in the churchyard on the surface lying in length, parallel with the passage which goes by the west wall of the churchyard, out of Houndsditch, and turns east again into Whitechapel, coming out near the Three Nuns Inn.

It was about the 10th of September, that my curiosity led, or rather drove me to go and see this pit again, when there had been near 400 people buried in it; and I was not content to see it in the daytime, as I had done before; for then there would have been nothing to have been seen but the loose earth; for all the bodies that were thrown in were immediately covered with earth, by those they called the buriers, which at other times were called bearers;[2] but I resolved to go in the night and see some of them thrown in.

There was a strict order to prevent people coming to those pits, and that was only to prevent infection: but after some time, that order was more necessary, for people that were infected, and near their end, and delirious also, would run to those pits wrapped in blankets or rugs and throw themselves in and, as they said, bury themselves: I cannot say that the officers suffered any willingly to lie there; but I have heard that in a great pit in Finsbury, in the parish of Cripplegate, it lying open then to the fields (for it was not then walled about) came and threw themselves in, and expired there, before they threw any earth upon them; and that when they came to bury others, and found them there, they were quite dead, though not cold.

This may serve a little to describe the dreadful condition of that day, though it is impossible to say anything that is able to give a true idea of it to those who did not see it, other than this; that it was indeed very, very, very dreadful, and such as no tongue can express.

I got admittance into the churchyard by being acquainted with the sexton[3] who attended, who though he did not refuse me at all, yet earnestly persuaded me not to go; telling me very seriously, for he was a good religious and sensible man, that it was indeed their business and duty to venture, and to run all hazards; and that in it they might hope to be preserved; but that I had no apparent call to it, but my own curios-

2. H. F. combines two categories: the buriers put the dead bodies into the pits, arranging them in order to conserve space, and covering them with lime in order to quicken decomposition. The bearers, by contrast, handled bodies living and dead: during the day they delivered the infected to the plague-hospitals; by night they collected corpses for the pits.

3. Caretaker of the church and graveyard.

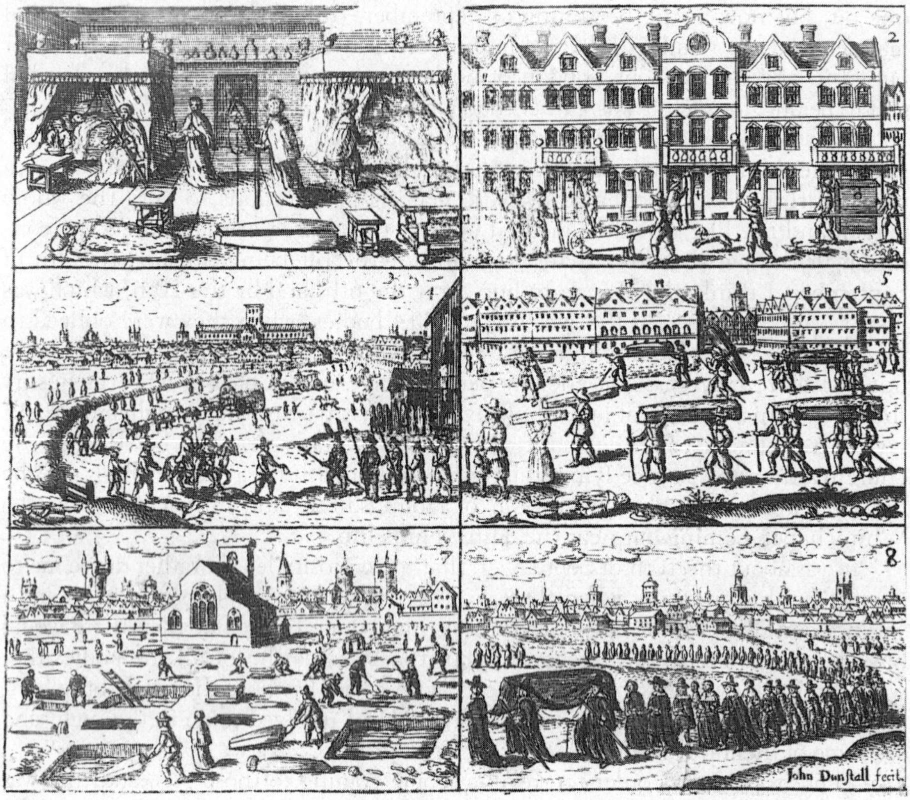

ity, which, he said, he believed I would not pretend was sufficient to justify my running that hazard. I told him I had been pressed in my mind to go, and that perhaps it might be an instructing sight that might not be without its uses. "Nay," says the good man, "if you will venture upon that score, *'Name of God go in;* for depend upon it, 'twill be a sermon to you, it may be, the best that ever you heard in your life. 'Tis a speaking sight," says he, "and has a voice with it, and a loud one, to call us all to repentance." And with that he opened the door and said, "Go, if you will."

His discourse had shocked my resolution a little, and I stood wavering for a good while; but just at that interval I saw two links[4] come over from the end of the Minories,[5] and heard the bellman,[6] and then appeared a dead cart, as they called it, coming over the streets so I could no longer resist my desire of seeing it, and went in: there was nobody, as I could perceive at first, in the churchyard or going into it, but the buriers and the fellow that drove the cart, or rather led the horse and cart; but when they came up to the pit, they saw a man go to and again, muffled up in a brown cloak and making motions with his hands, under his cloak, as if he

4. I.e., boys carrying torches ("links"), who for a fee led people through the streets at night.
5. A street.
6. In ordinary times, the bellman announced the time and weather as he made his way through the streets at night; in plague time, he rang his bell to alert people that the cart burying the dead was approaching.

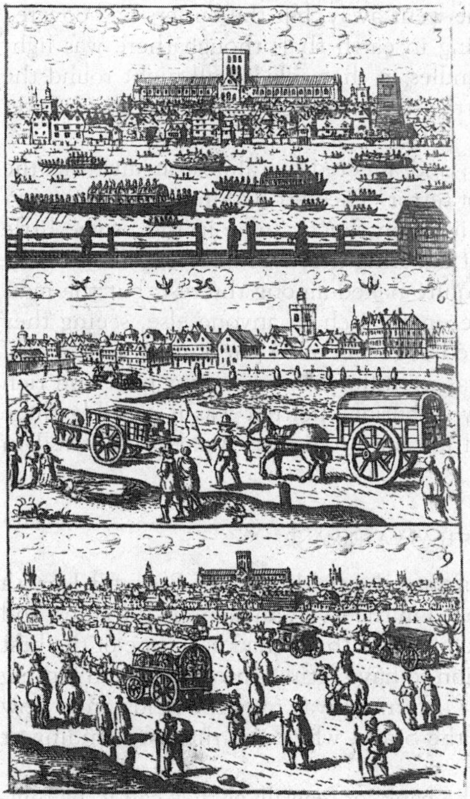

John Dunstall, *Scenes from the Plague in London*, 1665. The sequence tracks the course of corpses, from death within the city to burial in the plague-pits outside the city's walls.

was in a great agony; and the buriers immediately gathered about him, supposing he was one of those poor delirious or desperate creatures that used to pretend,[7] as I have said, to bury themselves. He said nothing as he walked about, but two or three times groaned very deeply, and loud, and sighed as he would break his heart.

When the buriers came up to him they soon found he was neither a person infected and desperate, as I have observed above, or a person distempered in mind, but one oppressed with a dreadful weight of grief indeed, having his wife and several of his children, all in the cart that was just come in with him, and he followed in an agony and excess of sorrow. He mourned heartily, as it was easy to see, but with a kind of masculine grief that could not give itself vent by tears, and calmly desiring the buriers to let him alone, said he would only see the bodies thrown in, and go away, so they left importuning him; but no sooner was the cart turned round, and the bodies shot into the pit promiscuously, which was a surprise to him, for he at least expected they would have been decently laid in, though indeed he was afterwards convinced that was impractible; I say, no sooner did he see the sight, but he cried out aloud unable to contain himself; I could not hear what he said, but he went backward two or three steps, and fell down in a swoon: the buriers ran to him and took him up, and in a little while he came to himself, and they led him away to the Pye Tavern over-against the end of Houndsditch, where, it seems, the man was known, and where they took care of

7. Attempt.

him. He looked into the pit again, as he went away, but the buriers had covered the bodies so immediately with throwing in earth that, though there was light enough, for there were lanterns and candles in them placed all night round the sides of the pit, upon the heaps of earth, seven or eight, or perhaps more, yet nothing could seen.

This was a mournful scene indeed, and affected me almost as much as the rest; but the other was awful, and full of terror. The cart had in it sixteen or seventeen bodies; some were wrapped up in linen sheets, some in rugs, some little other than naked, or so loose that what covering they had fell from them in the shooting out of the cart, and they fell quite naked among the rest; but the matter was not much to them, or the indecency much to anyone else, seeing they were all dead, and were to be huddled together into the common grave of mankind, as we may call it, for here was no difference made, but poor and rich went together; there was no other way of burials, neither was it possible there should, for coffins were not to be had for the prodigious numbers that fell in such a calamity as this.

[Encounter with a Waterman]

Much about the same time I walked out into the fields towards Bow; for I had a great mind to see how things were managed in the river, and among the ships; and as I had some concern in shipping, I had a notion that it had been one of the best ways of securing oneself from the infection to have retired into a ship, and musing how to satisfy my curiosity in that point, I turned away over the fields, from Bow to Bromley, and down to Blackwall, to the Stairs, which are there for landing or taking water.[8]

Here I saw a poor man walking on the bank, or seawall, as they call it, by himself. I walked a while also about, seeing the houses all shut up;[9] at last I fell into some talk, at a distance, with this poor man; first I asked him, how people did thereabouts? "Alas, Sir!" says he, "almost all desolate; all dead or sick: here are very few families in this part, or in that village," pointing at Poplar, "where half of them are not dead already, and the rest sick." Then he pointed to one house. "There they are all dead," said he, "and the house stands open; nobody dares go into it. A poor thief," says he, "ventured in to steal something, but he paid dear for his theft; for he was carried to the churchyard too last night." Then he pointed to several other houses. "There," says he, "they are all dead; the man and his wife, and five children. There," says he, "they are shut up; you see a watchman at the door," and so of other houses. "Why," says I, "What do you here all alone?" "Why," says he, "I am a poor desolate man; it has pleased God I am not yet visited,[1] though my family is, and one of my children dead." "How do you mean then," said I, "that you are not visited?" "Why," says he, "that's my house," pointing to a very little low boarded house, "and there my poor wife and two children live," said he, "if they may be said to live; for my wife and one of the children are visited, but I do not come at them." And with

8. H.F.'s walk takes him to the bank of the river Thames.
9. By London ordinances, all houses in which an inhabitant had become infected were "shut up," with the surviving residents confined inside.
1. Infected.

that word I saw the tears run very plentifully down his face; and so they did down mine too, I assure you.

But said I, "Why do you not come at them? How can you abandon your own flesh, and blood?" "Oh, Sir!" says he, "the Lord forbid; I do not abandon them; I work for them as much as I am able, and blessed be the Lord, I keep them from want," and with that I observed, he lifted up his eyes to Heaven, with a countenance that presently told me, I had happened on a man that was no hypocrite, but a serious, religious good man, and his ejaculation was an expression of thankfulness, that in such a condition as he was in, he should be able to say his family did not want. "Well," says I, "honest man, that is a great mercy as things go now with the poor: but how do you live then, and how are you kept from the dreadful calamity that is now upon us all?" "Why Sir," says he, "I am a waterman,[2] and there's my boat," says he, "and the boat serves me for a house; I work in it in the day, and I sleep in it in the night; and what I get, I lay down upon that stone," says he, showing me a broad stone on the other side of the street, a good way from his house, "and then," says he, "I halloo, and call to them till I make them hear; and they come and fetch it."

"Well friend," says I, "but how can you get any money as a waterman? Does anybody go by water these times?" "Yes Sir," says he, "in the way I am employed there does. Do you see there," says he, "five ships lie at anchor," pointing down the river, a good way below the town, "and do you see," says he, "eight or ten ships lie at the chain, there, and at anchor yonder," pointing above the town. "All those ships have families on board, of their merchants and owners, and such like, who have locked themselves up, and live on board, close shut in, for fear of the infection; and I tend on them to fetch things for them, carry letters, and do what is absolutely necessary, that they may not be obliged to come on shore; and every night I fasten my boat on board one of the ship's boats, and there I sleep by myself, and blessed be God, I am preserved hitherto."

"Well," said I, "friend, but will they let you come on board, after you have been on shore here, when this is such a terrible place, and so infected as it is?"

"Why, as to that," said he, "I very seldom go up the ship side, but deliver what I bring to their boat, or lie by the side, and they hoist it on board; if I did, I think they are in no danger from me, for I never go into any house on shore, or touch anybody, no, not of my own family; but I fetch provisions for them."

"Nay," says I, "but that may be worse, for you must have those provisions of somebody or other; and since all this part of the town is so infected, it is dangerous so much as to speak with anybody; for this village," said I, "is as it were, the beginning of London, though it be at some distance from it."

"That is true," added he, "but you do not understand me right, I do not buy provisions for them here; I row up to Greenwich and buy fresh meat there, and sometimes I row down the river to Woolwich and buy there; then I go to single farm houses on the Kentish side, where I am known, and buy fowls and eggs and butter, and bring to the ships, as they direct me, sometimes one, sometimes the other; I seldom come on shore here; and I came now only to call to my wife, and

2. Ferryman.

hear how my little family do, and give them a little money, which I received last night."

"Poor man!" said I, "and how much hast thou gotten for them?"

"I have gotten four shillings," said he, "which is a great sum, as things go now with poor men; but they have given me a bag of bread too, and a salt fish and some flesh; so all helps out."

"Well," said I, "and have you given it them yet?"

"No," said he, "but I have called, and my wife has answered, that she cannot come out yet, but in half an hour she hopes to come, and I am waiting for her: poor woman!" says he, "she is brought sadly down; she has a swelling, and it is broke, and I hope she will recover;[3] but I fear the child will die; but *it is the Lord*!"—Here he stopped, and wept very much.

"Well, honest friend," said I, "thou hast a sure comforter, if thou hast brought thyself to be resigned to the will of God; He is dealing with us all in judgment."

"Oh, Sir," says he, "it is infinite mercy, if any of us are spared; and who am I to repine!"

"Sayest thou so," said I, "and how much less is my faith than thine?" And here my heart smote me, suggesting how much better this poor man's foundation was, on which he stayed in the danger, than mine; that he had nowhere to fly; that he had a family to bind him to attendance, which I had not; and mine was mere presumption, his a true dependence, and a courage resting on God: and yet, that he used all possible caution for his safety.

I turned a little way from the man, while these thoughts engaged me, for indeed, I could no more refrain from tears than he.

At length, after some farther talk, the poor woman opened the door, and called, "Robert, Robert." He answered and bid her stay a few moments, and he would come; so he ran down the common stairs to his boat, and fetched up a sack in which was the provisions he had brought from the ships; and when he returned, he hallooed again; then he went to the great stone which he showed me, and emptied the sack, and laid all out, everything by themselves, and then retired; and his wife came with a little boy to fetch them away; and he called, and said, such a captain had sent such a thing, and such a captain such a thing, and at the end adds, "God has sent it all, give thanks to Him." When the poor woman had taken up all, she was so weak, she could not carry it at once in, *though the weight was not much neither;* so she left the biscuit which was in a little bag and left a little boy to watch it till she came again.

"Well, but," says I to him, "did you leave her the four shillings too, which you said was your week's pay?"

"YES, YES," says he, "you shall hear her own it." So he calls again, "Rachel, Rachel,"[4] which it seems was her name, "did you take up the money?" "YES," said she. "How much was it?" said he. "Four shillings and a groat," said she. "Well, well," says he, "the Lord keep you all"; and so he turned to go away.

As I could not refrain contributing tears to this man's story, so neither could I refrain my charity for his assistance; so I called him. "Hark thee friend," said I, "come hither; for I believe thou art in health, that I may venture thee." So I pulled

3. The plague afflicted its victims with painful swellings ("buboes"); if the swelling broke open, it was thought to presage recovery.

4. The name evokes Jeremiah 31.15: "Rachel weeping for her children refused to be comforted."

out my hand, which was in my pocket before. "Here," says I, "go and call thy Rachel once more, and give her a little more comfort from me. God will never forsake a family that trust in him as thou dost." So I gave him four other shillings, and bade him go lay them on the stone and call his wife.

I have not words to express the poor man's thankfulness, neither could he express it himself, but by tears running down his face; he called his wife, and told her God had moved the heart of a stranger, upon hearing their condition, to give them all that money; and a great deal more such as that he said to her. The woman too made signs of the like thankfulness, as well to Heaven, as to me, and joyfully picked it up; and I parted with no money all that year that I thought better bestowed.

1722

PERSPECTIVES
Reading Papers

Shakespeare never read a newspaper. In the early seventeenth century, the news was purveyed irregularly and improvisatorily. A breaking story or a sensational event might prompt a spate of ballads, broadsides, and bulletins, which would then abate until the next big thing hove into view. The news periodical, nascent on the Continent during Shakespeare's lifetime, arrived in England in 1620 in the form of English-language news sheets dispatched from Amsterdam. London publishers quickly took up the enterprise, to their considerable profit. Shakespeare's caustic contemporary Ben Jonson lived to witness their innovation; he promptly forecast an imminent glut of cheap and worthless information—fearing, with reason, that the new medium would supplant the theater as the public's favored oracle.

Even Jonson, though, could not have foreseen the quantities of print that would pour from presses decades later during the Civil Wars, when the instability of authority allowed innumerable newsbooks to appear, supporting every party in the conflict. During the Interregnum and Restoration, government tried through strict licensing laws to limit the flow and narrow the range of newsprint, but whenever those laws lapsed, innovations abounded: the first daily reports on proceedings in the House of Commons (1680), the first English newspaper outside London (1701), the first daily newspaper (1702), the first weekly journals (1713), melding the news with a miscellany of other departments. At the centennial of Shakespeare's death, London was producing some sixteen newspapers; a century later Britain possessed more than 350, in addition to legions of other periodicals purveying opinion and advice. The newspaper, the periodical essay, and the magazine had become confirmed habits in the lives of almost everyone who could read, and even of many who could not, since the papers were often read aloud, their contents discussed and debated, in public gathering places and household circles.

The periodical was a creature of the seventeenth century and a staple of the eighteenth. It punctuated the calendar with a new print pulse, and imparted to its readership a new sense of moving together in synchrony, in a rhythm that paradoxically combined the solitary and the social, the private and the public. The "mass ceremony" of reading the newspaper is generally performed (as the historian Benedict Anderson has observed) in "privacy, in the lair of the skull. Yet each communicant is well aware that the ceremony he performs is being replicated simultaneously by thousands (or millions) of others, of whose existence he is confident, yet of whose identity he has not the slightest notion." The periodical press, then, gave its readers a new way of seeing the world, and of seeing themselves in the world, as private beings and public entities; it prompted them (in Anderson's phrase) to imagine themselves as a community.

Monarchs and politicians tried hard to control the press, to dictate its views and to contain its criticisms, but in Britain the phenomenon proved too large for such arrant limitation. The news sheets and the essays helped create a new arena of political thought and action, separate from the older power centers of Court and Parliament, a public sphere of newly engaged readers who increasingly valued and deployed their own capacity to form collective opinions, and who increasingly expected their opinions to affect events. The freedom and copiousness of the press became a national boast, and abetted Britons in a conviction they were already cultivating: that they were participants in an ongoing narrative of commerce and taste, politeness, politics, and empire, protagonists in a story with numberless installments and no foreseeable end, unfolding at the center of the world.

Each newspaper in this section is introduced at its first appearance.

For additional selections from seventeenth-and eighteenth-century newspapers and periodicals, go to *The Longman Anthology of British Literature* Web site at www.myliteraturekit.com.

News and Comment

If the seventeenth century gave birth to the seething enterprise of print journalism, it also ushered in still-lingering distinctions and confusions as to what newspapers ought to be, and do. Most papers proudly declared their objectivity, yet at the same time they plainly manifested their partisan sympathies in their reportage and their prose. The division between news and opinion was rarely sharp, but in the early 1700s, opinion found fuller expression in periodicals like Defoe's *Review*, which more or less took for granted that readers had gathered their news elsewhere, and offered instead a running commentary on events.

MERCURIUS PUBLICUS (1660–1663) During the Civil Wars, journalism gave voice to different factions; afterwards, it became the instrument of consolidated power. During the Interregnum, Cromwell controlled the news through his chief journalist Marchamont Nedham; strict licensing laws ensured that Nedham's *Public Intelligencer* (published every Monday) and *Mercurius Politicus* (every Thursday) were virtually the sole print sources for fresh information. (Mercury, the speedy messenger-god, remained throughout the century the favorite titular deity of the English press; more than a hundred periodicals bore his name). In 1660 the chief architects of the Restoration dismissed Nedham and supplanted him with their own advocate, Henry Muddiman (1629–1692). Taking over Nedham's newsbooks (now pointedly renamed the *Kingdom's Intelligencer* and *Mercurius Publicus*), Muddiman denounced the old regime and heralded the new with the zeal that would maintain him for nearly three decades, despite stiff competition from rival newsmen, as a favored journalist with the House of Stuart, right up to its fall from power in the 1688 Revolution.

from Mercurius Publicus
24–31 January 1661
[ANNIVERSARY OF THE REGICIDE]

London

This day January 30 (we need say no more but name the day of the month) was doubly observed, not only by a solemn fast, sermons, and prayers at every parish church, for the precious blood of our late pious sovereign King Charles the First, of ever glorious memory; but also by public dragging of those odious carcasses of Oliver Cromwell, Henry Ireton, and John Bradshaw to Tyburn.[1] On Monday night Cromwell and Ireton in two several carts were drawn to Holborn from Westminster, after they were digged up on Saturday last, and the next morning Bradshaw; today they were drawn upon sledges to Tyburn, all the way (as before from Westminster) the outcry of the people went along with them. When these their carcasses were at Tyburn, they were pulled out of their coffins and hanged at the several angles of the triple tree,[2] where they hung till the sun was set; after which they were taken down,

1. Ireton (1611–1651) and Bradshaw (1602–1659) had played key roles in the trial, condemnation, and execution of Charles I. Tyburn had been for nearly three centuries the site for the public execution of common criminals (Charles had been dispatched on the grounds of the royal palace at Whitehall).
2. Tyburn's notorious "triangular gallows," whose three long horizontal beams could support as many as 21 hangings at a time.

their heads cut off, and their loathsome trunks thrown into a deep hole under the gallows. And now we cannot forget how at Cambridge when Cromwell first set up for a rebel, he rode under the gallows where, his horse just curvetting,[3] threw his cursed Highness out of the saddle just under the gallows (as if he had been turned off[4] the ladder), the spectators then observing the place, and rather presaging the present work of this day, than the monstrous villainies of this day twelve years.[5] But he is now again thrown under the gallows (never more to be digged up) and there we leave him.

LONDON *GAZETTE* (1665–PRESENT) New media are often modeled on old. In its first decades, English print journalism took the shape of a newsbook (actually a pamphlet) because that was a format with which printers and consumers had been long familiar. The *London Gazette* was something visibly different: the first news*paper*, a single sheet printed in double columns. Containment was the paper's whole point, not only in format but in content. Published twice weekly, "by authority" (as it proclaimed on its masthead), it remained for thirteen years the only printed news source the English were legally permitted to read, and it presented only that news which its government masters deemed fit for wide publication: full accounts of Continental politics, carefully trimmed treatments of domestic doings, all couched in a dry prose that deliberately eschewed the popular (and sometimes rabble-rousing) effects of the paper's midcentury forebears. The *Gazette* broke briefly from its self-constraints in the number for 10 September 1666, when the Great Fire of London had forced the printer to set up his press in the open air, and the correspondents reported very local events with considerable accuracy and unaccustomed fervor.

from The London Gazette
10 September 1666
[THE FIRE OF LONDON[1]]

Whitehall, September 8

The ordinary course of this paper having been interrupted by a sad and lamentable accident of fire lately happened in the City of London, it hath been thought fit for satisfying the minds of so many of His Majesty's good subjects, who must needs be concerned for the issue of so great an accident, to give this short, but true account of it.

On the second instant[2] at one of the clock in the morning there happened to break out a sad and deplorable fire, in Pudding Lane near New Fish Street, which falling out at that hour of the night, and in a quarter of the town so close-built with wooden pitched[3] houses, spread itself so far before day, and with such distraction to the inhabitants and neighbors, that care was not taken for the timely preventing the further diffusion of it by pulling down houses, as ought to have been; so that this lamentable fire in a short time became too big to be mastered by any engines or working near it. It fell out most unhappily too, that a violent easterly wind fomented it, and kept it burning all that day, and the night following spreading itself up to Gracechurch Street, and downwards from Cannon Street to the waterside as far as the Three Cranes in the Vintry.

3. Leaping, frisking.
4. Dropped from.
5. Ago. I.e., they foresaw that he would eventually be hung, but not that he would accomplish the regicide of 30 January 1649.

1. Compare the accounts of Pepys (page 2021) and Evelyn (page 2025).
2. On 2 September.
3. Covered with pitch (distilled tar) in order to keep out water.

The people in all parts about it distracted by the vastness of it, and their particular care to carry away their goods, many attempts were made to prevent the spreading of it, by pulling down houses, and making great intervals, but all in vain, the fire seizing upon the timber and rubbish, and so continuing itself, even through those spaces, and raging in a bright flame all Monday and Tuesday, notwithstanding His Majesty's own, and his Royal Highness's[4] indefatigable and personal pains to apply all possible remedies to prevent it, calling upon and helping the people with their Guards;[5] and a great number of nobility and gentry unweariedly assisting therein, for which they were requited with a thousand blessings from the poor distressed people. * * *

And we cannot but observe, to the confutation of all His Majesty's enemies, who endeavor to persuade the world abroad of great parties and disaffection at home against His Majesty's government, that a greater instance of the affections of this City could never be given than hath been now given in this sad and deplorable accident, when if at any time disorder might have been expected from the losses, distraction, and almost desperation of some persons in their private fortunes, thousands of people not having had habitations to cover them. And yet in all this time it hath been so far from any appearance of designs or attempts against His Majesty's government, that His Majesty and his royal brother, out of their care to stop and prevent the fire, frequently exposing their persons with very small attendance in all parts of the town, sometimes even to be intermixed with those who labored in the business, yet nevertheless there hath not been observed so much as a murmuring word to fall from any, but on the contrary, even those persons whose losses rendered their conditions most desperate, and to be fit objects of other prayers, beholding those frequent instances of His Majesty's care of this people, forgot their own misery, and filled the streets with their prayers for His Majesty, whose trouble they seemed to compassionate before their own.

***THE DAILY COURANT* (1702–1735)** The *Daily Courant's* title announced its innovation. Its editor-publisher, Samuel Buckley (d. 1741), was the first in England to put out a paper every day (except for Sunday, which had no paper of its own until the 1770s); before now, papers had appeared thrice weekly at most. In his opening number, Buckley made clear both his dependence on "foreign prints" (newspapers from the Continent) and his distrust of them; his faith in his readers' capacity to winnow bias and interpret information; and his perhaps defensive condescension to his journalistic rivals as he embarked on the audacious enterprise of a daily paper.

from The Daily Courant No. 1
Wednesday, 11 March 1702

[EDITORIAL POLICY]

It will be found from the foreign prints, which from time to time, as occasion offers, will be mentioned in this paper, that the author has taken care to be duly furnished with all that comes from abroad in any language. And for an assurance that he will not, under pretense of having private intelligence, impose any additions of feigned circumstances to an action, but give his extracts fairly and impartially, at the beginning

4. The King's brother James, Duke of York.

5. The royal brothers deployed their soldiers to aid the fire's victims.

of each article he will quote the foreign paper from whence 'tis taken, that the public, seeing from what country a piece of news comes with the allowance of that government, may be better able to judge of the credibility and fairness of the relation. Nor will he take upon him to give any comments or conjectures of his own, but will relate only matter of fact, supposing other people to have sense enough to make reflections for themselves.

The *Courant* (as the title shows) will be published daily, being designed to give all the material[1] news as soon as every post arrives; and is confined to half the compass,[2] to save the public at least half the impertinences[3] of ordinary newspapers.

A *Review of the State of the British Nation* (1704–1713) Of the periodical commentators on the news, none was more formidable than Daniel Defoe, who single-handedly wrote his *Review* twice and sometimes thrice a week for nine years. The paper changed its name, its format, and its ostensible focus several times during its long run, but its general purposes remained the same throughout. Defoe wrote to celebrate trade, and to propose strategies for its improvement; to teach a rigorous piety and morality to a readership he saw as lax; and to advance by adroit advocacy the favorite programs of the paper's secret sponsor, Secretary of State Robert Harley (1661–1724). One of these was the Treaty of Union, whereby Scotland would merge under a single government with England and Wales to form the new national entity of Great Britain. Advocates of the measure construed it as a fair exchange, providing expanded trade for Scotland, enhanced security for England. In support of the cause, Defoe not only wrote copiously (pamphlets and essays as well as *Reviews*), he also persuaded Harley to send him to Scotland (where the prospect of Union was far from popular) to serve as chief strategist and propagandist. There, he argued energetically and successfully for passage of the treaty, while keeping his affiliation with Harley a close secret. When the Treaty of Union was ratified, the *Review* indulged in a moment of exultation, in the characteristic voice its creator had devised during his sustained periodic enterprise: that of a writer enmeshed in actual and volatile circumstance, deeply engaged with the politics, conduct, and commerce of the real world, sometimes embattled, often exasperated, occasionally exhausted, but ultimately indefatigable.

For more about Defoe, see his principal listing on page 2293.

Daniel Defoe: *from* A Review of the State of the British Nation, Vol. 4, No. 21

Saturday, 29 March 1707

[THE NEW UNION]

I have a long time dwelt on the subject of a Union; I have happily seen it transacted in the kingdom of Scotland; I have seen it carried on there through innumerable oppositions, both public and private, peaceable and unpeaceable; I have seen it perfected there, and ratified, sent up to England, debated, opposed, and at last passed in both houses, and having obtained the royal assent, I have the pleasure, just while I am writing these lines, to hear the guns proclaiming the happy conjunction from Edinburgh Castle. And though it brings an unsatisfying childish custom in play, and exposes me to a vain and truly ridiculous saying in England,

1. Relevant.
2. Space. Most newspapers printed on both sides of the sheet. At first, Buckley printed on only one side, unsure that his sources would supply him with enough matter to fill two sides daily (they soon did).
3. Irrelevancies; filler.

"as the fool thinks, etc.," yet 'tis impossible to put the lively sound of the cannon just now firing into any other note to my ear than the articulate expression of Union, Union. Strange power of imagination, strange incoherence of circumstances that fills the mind so with the thing that it makes even the thunder of warlike engines cry peace; and what is made to divide and destroy, speaks out the language of this glorious conjunction!

I have hardly room to introduce the various contemplations of the consequences of this mighty transaction; 'tis a sea of universal improvement, every day it discovers new mines of treasure, and when I launch out in the bark of my own imagination, I every minute discover new success, new advantages, and the approaching happiness of both kingdoms. Nor am I an idle spectator here; I have told Scotland of improvements in trade, wealth, and shipping that shall accrue to them on the happy conclusion of this affair, and I am pleased double with this, that I am like to be one of the first men that shall give them the pleasure of the experiment. I have told them of the improvement of their coal trade, and 'tis their own fault if they do not particularly engage 20 or 25 sail of ships immediately from England on that work. I have told them of the improvement of their salt, and I am now contracting for English merchants for Scots salt to the value of about ten thousand pounds per annum. I have told them of linen manufactures, and I have now above 100 poor families at work, by my procuring and direction, for the making such sorts of linen, and in such manner as never was made here before, and as no person in the trade will believe could be made here, till they see it.

This has been my employment in Scotland, and this my endeavor to do that nation service, and convince them by the practice that what I have said of the Union has more weight in it than some have endeavored to persuade them. Those that have charged me with missions and commissions from neither they nor I know who, shall blush at their rashness, and be ashamed for reflecting on a man come hither on purpose to do them good.[1] Have I had a hand in the Union, have I been maltreated by the tongues of the violent, threatened to be murdered, and insulted, because I have pleaded for it and pressed you to it—gentlemen, in Scotland, I refer you to Her Majesty's speech; there's my claim, and you do me too much honor to entitle me to a share in what Her Majesty says shall be their due that have done so. Hearken to the words of your sovereign: "I make no doubt but it will be remembered and spoke of hereafter to the honor of those that have been instrumental to bring it to such an happy conclusion." (Queen's Speech to the Parliament, 6 March 1707.)

Pray, gentlemen, have a care how you charge me with having any hand in bringing forward this matter *to such an happy conclusion*, lest you build that monument upon me which Her Majesty has foretold, and honor the man you would debase. I plead no merit, I do not raise the value of what I have done; and I know some that are gone to London to solicit the reward of what they have had no hand in—I might have said, are gone to claim the merit of what I have been the single author of—but as this has been the constant way of the world with me, so I have no repinings on that account. Nor am I pleading any other merit than that I may have it wrote on my grave that I did my duty in promoting the Union, and consequently the happiness of these nations. * * *

1. In both England and Scotland, Defoe had been accused (with reason) of conducting a kind of espionage on behalf of Harley and the Union.

Periodical Personae

In print journalism it was primarily the news that sold the paper; in the periodical essay it was the voice: the idiosyncratic mix of assertion and deference, comedy and charisma, with which author addressed audience. Political writers had long known the advantages of using a mask or *persona*—a pen name, a fictitious character—as a means of both concealing their identity and expanding the appeal of their controversial arguments. In the early 1700s, the inventors of the periodical essay extended the tactic of the fictitious self into new territory. While collaborating on *The Tatler* and *The Spectator*, Richard Steele and Joseph Addison devised strategies for making the unreal author a real arbitrator in the culture, a teacher of taste and conduct, manners and morality, someone whom readers found it pleasurable to learn from, to identify with, even to "believe in," despite (and because of) his comically exaggerated quirks, his patent nonexistence. Working behind their carefully crafted masks, Addison and Steele sold so many papers and impressed so many readers that their mark became indelible. For the rest of the century, the periodical essayist's first task was to devise a persona unusual enough to define the paper, and engaging enough to sustain it.

THE TATLER (1709–1711) At age thirty-five, after a checkered career as soldier, poet, playwright, popular moralist, and Whig propagandist, Captain Richard Steele (1672–1729) was appointed editor of the *London Gazette*, the government's long-running newspaper. Evidently even this task did not sufficiently absorb his energies. Two years later, while still supervising the *Gazette*, he launched *The Tatler*, a periodical of his own that outstripped all its predecessors in commercial success and enduring appeal. It appeared three times a week, ran for two years and 271 numbers, spawned many imitators, and continued to sell (in a four-volume collected edition) for the rest of the century. The *Tatler's* appeal derived in large measure from its putative author, Isaac Bickerstaff, Esquire, whose name Steele had borrowed from one of Swift's satires, but whose character he elaborated into that of a genial, perceptive, and comically self-congratulatory old man. The paper's commodious structure mirrored the gregariousness of its "author." Bickerstaff datelined his dispatches from the coffeehouses around London where papers were distributed, read, and discussed; he included letters (fictitious and authentic) from readers all over the country. The *Tatler's* audience thus found itself absorbed into the paper several ways: they were its constant topic, they sometimes supplied its text, they constituted both its origin and its end point, and they gave it their unprecedented devotion. Steele soon made further discoveries of form under the influence of his school friend Joseph Addison (1672–1719), whom he had brought in (so one contemporary put it) as his "great and constant assistant." Addison and Steele found that Bickerstaff's private musings, dispatched "From my Own Apartment," were the most pleasing items of all, and so they often devoted whole papers to reprinting what their character was pleased to call his "lucubrations" (meditations by candlelight, late at night). John Gay summed up the strategy's success. Coffeehouse owners, Gay reported, "began to be sensible that the Esquire's lucubrations alone had brought them more customers than all their other newspapers put together." Bickerstaff's other "departments" diminished or disappeared, and "the Esquire's lucubrations," now running the full length of the paper, created the format and the fashion for the periodical essay, a unified piece on a single topic as opposed to the fragmentary "miscellany" from which Steele had started. By the time he stopped *The Tatler* (probably because of political pressures following the Whigs' fall from power), he and Addison had devised means and achieved ends with which they would experiment anew in the *Spectator:* ways of creating community shot through with solitude, of mixing sociability and meditation, morality and mirth.

Richard Steele: *from* Tatler No. 1
Tuesday, 12 April 1709

[Introducing Mr. Bickerstaff]

Quicquid agunt homines nostri farrago libelli.[1]

Though the other papers which are published for the use of the good people of England have certainly very wholesome effects, and are laudable in their particular kinds, they do not seem to come up to the main design of such narrations, which, I humbly presume, should be principally intended for the use of politic persons, who are so public-spirited as to neglect their own affairs to look into transactions of state. Now these gentlemen, for the most part, being persons of strong zeal and weak intellects,[2] it is both a charitable and necessary work to offer something whereby such worthy and well-affected members of the commonwealth may be instructed, after their reading, *what to think:* which shall be the end and purpose of this my paper, wherein I shall from time to time report and consider all matters of what kind soever that shall occur to me, and publish such my advices and reflections every Tuesday, Thursday, and Saturday in the week, for the convenience of the post.[3] I resolve also to have something which may be of entertainment to the fair sex, in honor of whom I have invented the title of this paper. I therefore earnestly desire all persons, without distinction, to take it in for the present *gratis*,[4] and hereafter at the price of one penny, forbidding all hawkers to take more for it at their peril. And I desire all persons to consider, that I am at a very great charge for proper materials for this work, as well as that before I resolved upon it, I had settled a correspondence in all parts of the known and knowing world. And forasmuch as this globe is not trodden upon by mere drudges of business only, but that men of spirit and genius are justly to be esteemed as considerable agents in it, we shall not upon a dearth of news present you with musty foreign edicts, or dull proclamations, but shall divide our relations of the passages which occur in action or discourse throughout this town, as well as elsewhere, under such dates of places as may prepare you for the matter you are to expect, in the following manner.

All accounts of gallantry,[5] pleasure, and entertainment shall be under the article of White's Chocolate House; poetry, under that of Will's Coffeehouse; learning, under the title of Grecian; foreign and domestic news you will have from St. James's Coffeehouse; and what else I have to offer on any other subject, shall be dated from my own apartment.[6]

I once more desire my reader to consider, that as I cannot keep an ingenious man to go daily to Will's, under two-pence each day merely for his charges; to White's, under sixpence; nor to the Grecian, without allowing him some Plain Spanish,[7] to be as able as others at the learned table; and that a good observer

1. "Whatever people do [will furnish] the variety of our little book" (Juvenal, *Satires* 1.85–86); or (in the freer and more apt 18th-century translation by Thomas Percy) "Whate'er men do, or say, or think, or dream, / Our motley paper seizes for its theme."
2. Bickerstaff mocks that category of men known as the "coffeehouse politicians," who spent long hours together discussing news. For a more sustained satire of them, see *Tatler* No. 155 (pages 2324–25).
3. These were the days on which the postal system carried mail from London to the provinces.
4. Steele distributed his first four numbers free, as a way of attracting readers.
5. Flirtation and self-display.
6. Steele exploits associations between topic and venue long familiar to his readers. Each of the coffeehouses he names catered to a clientele "specializing" in the pursuits he names. A journalist himself, Steele parodies the newspaper format that headed each item by the name of its (usually foreign) city of origin.
7. A kind of snuff, used as a stimulant to induce sneezing.

cannot speak with even Kidney[8] at St. James's without clean linen. I say, these considerations will, I hope, make all persons willing to comply with my humble request (when my *gratis* stock is exhausted) of a penny apiece; especially since they are sure of some proper amusement, and that it is impossible for me to want means to entertain 'em, having, besides the force of my own parts, the power of divination, and that I can, by casting a figure, tell you all that will happen before it comes to pass.[9]

But this last faculty I shall use very sparingly, and speak but of few things 'till they are passed, for fear of divulging matters which may offend our superiors.[1] * * *

From my own apartment

I am sorry I am obliged to trouble the public with so much discourse, upon a matter which I at the very first mentioned as a trifle, *viz.* the death of Mr. Partridge, under whose name there is an almanac come out for the year 1709.[2] In one page of which, it is asserted by the said John Partridge, that he is still living, and not only so, but that he was also living some time before, and even at the instant when I writ of his death. I have in another place, and in a paper by itself, sufficiently convinced this man that he is dead, and if he has any shame, I don't doubt but that by this time he owns it to all his acquaintance: for though the legs and arms, and whole body, of that man may still appear and perform their animal functions; yet since, as I have elsewhere observed, his art is gone, the man is gone. I am, as I said, concerned that this little matter should make so much noise; but since I am engaged, I take myself obliged in honor to go on in my lucubrations, and by the help of these arts of which I am master, as well as my skill in astrological speculations, I shall, as I see occasion, proceed to confute other dead men, who pretend to be in being, that they are actually deceased. I therefore give all men fair warning to mend their manners, for I shall from time to time print bills of mortality; and I beg the pardon of all such who shall be named therein, if they who are good for nothing shall find themselves in the number of the deceased.

THE SPECTATOR (1711–1713) In the weeks of the *Spectator*'s first appearance, readers marveled at both its contents and its pace. "We had at first . . . no manner of notion," the wit John Gay reported from London, "how a diurnal paper could be continued in the spirit and style of our present *Spectators;* but to our no small surprise we find them still rising upon us, and can only wonder from whence so prodigious a run of wit and learning can proceed." It proceeded (as Gay guessed) from the minds and pens of the same two writers who had shut down the *Tatler* just a few months before. For their second periodical collaboration, Addison and Steele considerably upped the ante. Not only did they undertake to publish a new number every day (something no essayist had hitherto attempted), they also devised a new persona, intricately linked with their triumphant earlier creation Isaac Bickerstaff. Where the *Tatler* had begun in gregariousness and modulated towards solitude (at "my own apartment"), the new paper started from an even farther remove, in the eccentric silence of Mr. Spectator, who declares at the outset that he has not spoken "three sentences together" since birth. Mr. Spectator carries

8. A waiter.

9. To "cast a figure" is to work out a horoscope, an ability that the *Tatler*'s first readers would readily associate with the character "Isaac Bickerstaff." Jonathan Swift had originally created the character (in a series of pamphlets in 1708) as a way of satirizing the fashion for astrological almanacs, which purported to foretell the important events of the coming year. In Swift's first pamphlet, the fictitious astrologer Isaac Bickerstaff forecast the imminent death of the real (and very successful) astrologer John Partridge; in the second pamphlet, Bickerstaff declared blithely that his prophecy had come to pass. Partridge's subsequent, frantic protestations added relish to the joke.

1. Bickerstaff proceeds to supply first dispatches from White's, Will's, and St. James's coffeehouses.

2. In the 1709 issue of his annual almanac *Merlinus Liberatus*, Partridge had insisted that he was "still alive."

his "own apartment"—his state of psychological apartness—with him, not at his residence but in his head; "the working of my own mind," he announces early on, "is the chief entertainment of my life."

In his focused interiority, Mr. Spectator played out the principles of psychology that John Locke had propounded, but his extreme self-possession turned out to possess enormous rhetorical impact and commercial cachet as well. More than any other periodical persona, Mr. Spectator managed to embody and to allegorize the operations of the paper he inhabited. Like the paper he was everywhere, at once silent and articulate, fictitious in substance but impressive in effect, observant and absorbent of the culture, able to move into his readers' minds by the mysterious osmosis of reading itself, and to remain there, a disembodied monitor with a rapidly growing portfolio of daily essays. An anonymous pamphleteer reproached Mr. Spectator for the presumptuous "tyranny" of his surveillance, but the paper's tactics of reform remained in power for most of the century. It was read (and imitated) on the Continent, in the American colonies, and in remoter outposts like Sumatra, from whence a British trader wrote home to his daughter in London, admonishing her "to study the *Spectators*, especially those which relate to religion and domestic life. Next to the Bible you cannot read any writings so much to your purpose for the improvement of your mind and the conduct of your actions." The *Spectator*, Gay noted soon after the paper's debut, "is in everyone's hands, and a constant topic for our morning conversation at tea tables and coffeehouses." More than sixty years later, the Scots rhetorician Hugh Blair could only echo and elaborate on Gay's phrasing, in accordance with the paper's now long-established place in the British canon: "The *Spectator* . . . is a book which is in the hands of everyone, and which cannot be praised too highly. The good sense, and good writing, the useful morality, and the admirable vein of humor which abound in it, render it one of those standard books which have done the greatest honor to the English nation."

Joseph Addison: *from* Spectator No. 1
Thursday, 1 March 1711

[INTRODUCING MR. SPECTATOR]

Non fumum ex fulgore, sed ex fumo dare lucem
Cogitat, ut speciosa dehinc miracula promat.[1]

I have observed, that a reader seldom peruses a book with pleasure 'till he knows whether the writer of it be a black or a fair man,[2] of a mild or choleric disposition, married or a bachelor, with other particulars of the like nature, that conduce very much to the right understanding of an author. To gratify this curiosity, which is so natural to a reader, I design this paper, and my next, as prefatory discourses to my following writings, and shall give some account in them of the several persons that are engaged in this work. As the chief trouble of compiling, digesting, and correcting will fall to my share, I must do myself the justice to open the work with my own history.

I was born to a small hereditary estate, which, according to the tradition of the village where it lies, was bounded by the same hedges and ditches in William

1. "He intends to produce not smoke from fire, but light from smoke, so that he may then put forth striking and amazing things" (Horace, *Ars Poetica* 143–44).
2. Of dark or light complexion.

the Conqueror's time[3] that it is at present, and has been delivered down from father to son whole and entire, without the loss or acquisition of a single field or meadow, during the space of six hundred years. There runs a story in the family, that when my mother was gone with child of me about three months, she dreamt that she was brought to bed of[4] a judge. Whether this might proceed from a lawsuit which was then depending in the family, or my father's being a justice of the peace, I cannot determine; for I am not so vain as to think it presaged any dignity that I should arrive at in my future life, though that was the interpretation which the neighborhood put upon it. The gravity of my behavior at my very first appearance in the world, and all the time that I sucked, seemed to favor my mother's dream: for, as she has often told me, I threw away my rattle before I was two months old, and would not make use of my coral[5] 'till they had taken away the bells from it.

As for the rest of my infancy, there being nothing in it remarkable, I shall pass it over in silence. I find that, during my nonage,[6] I had the reputation of a very sullen youth, but was always a favorite of my schoolmaster, who used to say, *that my parts were solid and would wear well.* I had not been long at the university before I distinguished myself by a most profound silence: for during the space of eight years, excepting in the public exercises of the college, I scarce uttered the quantity of an hundred words; and indeed do not remember that I ever spoke three sentences together in my whole life. Whilst I was in this learned body I applied myself with so much diligence to my studies that there are very few celebrated books, either in the learned or the modern tongues, which I am not acquainted with.

Upon the death of my father I was resolved to travel into foreign countries, and therefore left the university, with the character[7] of an odd unaccountable fellow that had a great deal of learning, if I would but show it. An insatiable thirst after knowledge carried me into all the countries of Europe, in which there was anything new or strange to be seen; nay, to such a degree was my curiosity raised, that having read the controversies of some great men concerning the antiquities of Egypt, I made a voyage to Grand Cairo, on purpose to take the measure of a pyramid; and as soon as I had set myself right in that particular, returned to my native country with great satisfaction.

I have passed my latter years in this city, where I am frequently seen in most public places, though there are not above half a dozen of my select friends that know me; of whom my next paper shall give a more particular account. There is no place of general resort, wherein I do not often make my appearance.[8] Sometimes I am seen thrusting my head into a round of politicians at Will's, and listening with great attention to the narratives that are made in those little circular audiences. Sometimes I smoke a pipe at Child's; and whilst I seem attentive to nothing but the *Post-Man*,[9] overhear the conversation of every table in the room. I appear on Sunday nights at St. James's Coffeehouse, and sometimes join the little committee of politics in the

3. The late 11th century, when William ruled as king of England.
4. Had given birth to. The silence of judges was proverbial.
5. Another sound maker for infants.
6. Childhood.
7. Reputation.
8. With a conspicuous openness to all parties and pursuits, Mr. Spectator distributes his visitations among some of London's favorite meeting places, including ones popular with Whigs (St. James's), Tories (the Cocoa Tree), authors (Child's), lawyers (the Grecian), and the news-obsessives he calls "politicians" (Will's).
9. A thrice-weekly newspaper, favored by Whigs.

inner-room, as one who comes there to hear and improve. My face is likewise very well known at the Grecian, the Cocoa Tree, and in the theaters both of Drury Lane, and the Haymarket. I have been taken for a merchant upon the Exchange[1] for above these ten years, and sometimes pass for a Jew in the assembly of stock-jobbers at Jonathan's.[2] In short, wherever I see a cluster of people I always mix with them, though I never open my lips but in my own club.

Thus I live in the world, rather as a spectator of mankind than as one of the species; by which means I have made myself a speculative statesman, soldier, merchant, and artisan, without ever meddling with any practical part in life. I am very well versed in the theory of an husband or a father, and can discern the errors in the economy, business, and diversion of others, better than those who are engaged in them; as standers-by discover blots,[3] which are apt to escape those who are in the game. I never espoused any party with violence, and am resolved to observe an exact neutrality between the Whigs and Tories,[4] unless I shall be forced to declare myself by the hostilities of either side. In short, I have acted in all the parts of my life as a looker-on, which is the character I intend to preserve in this paper.

I have given the reader just so much of my history and character as to let him see I am not altogether unqualified for the business I have undertaken. As for other particulars in my life and adventures, I shall insert them in following papers as I shall see occasion. In the mean time, when I consider how much I have seen, read, and heard, I begin to blame my own taciturnity; and since I have neither time nor inclination to communicate the fullness of my heart in speech, I am resolved to do it in writing; and to print my self out, if possible, before I die. I have been often told by my friends that it is pity so many useful discoveries which I have made should be in the possession of a silent man. For this reason therefore, I shall publish a sheet-full of thoughts every morning, for the benefit of my contemporaries; and if I can any way contribute to the diversion or improvement of the country in which I live, I shall leave it, when I am summoned out of it, with the secret satisfaction of thinking that I have not lived in vain. * * *

***The Female Spectator* (April 1744–May 1746)** *The Female Spectator* was the first periodical written by a woman for women. Its author, Eliza Haywood (c. 1693–1756), had been an actress, a playwright, and the writer of some sixty romances, novels, and other narratives, many of them scandalous and some of them wildly successful. In the mid-1740s, after a long eclipse prompted in part by Alexander Pope's derision of her in the *Dunciad,* Haywood emerged in a new guise: no longer a purveyor of exotic thrills, she set up instead as a teacher of morality. *The Female Spectator* differed from its namesake in calendar (monthly rather than daily) and format: a pamphlet and not a sheet, each number presented an essay focused on a single topic with several illustrative fictional stories interspersed. The biggest difference, though, was in the new paper's point of view. Mr. Spectator had observed, described, and instructed "the fair sex" from without, as supremely self-confident male mentor. Haywood

1. The Royal Exchange was a large building containing many shops and serving as a meeting place for merchants. (For Addison's paean to the place, see *Spectator* No. 69, page 2330).
2. Jonathan's coffeehouse, near the Royal Exchange, was a principal meeting place of merchants and stockbrokers ("stock-jobbers").
3. In backgammon, a blot is a piece whose position puts it at risk of being taken.
4. Addison and Steele maintained "neutrality" more strictly in the *Spectator* than they had in the *Tatler,* which had incurred much controversy by its Whig partisanship.

offered instead a running report from the interior of women's lives. Her vantage point proved popular. *The Female Spectator* continued to sell, in a four-volume collected edition, for more than two decades after its periodical run had ceased.

from The Female Spectator Vol. 1, No. 1

[THE AUTHOR'S INTENT]

It is very much by the choice we make of subjects for our entertainment that the refined taste distinguishes itself from the vulgar and more gross. Reading is universally allowed to be one of the most improving as well as agreeable amusements; but then to render it so, one should, among the number of books which are perpetually issuing from the press, endeavor to single out such as promise to be most conducive to those ends. In order to be as little deceived as possible, I, for my own part, love to get as well acquainted as I can with an author, before I run the risk of losing my time in perusing his work; and as I doubt not but most people are of this way of thinking, I shall, in imitation of my learned brother of ever precious memory,[1] give some account of what I am, and those concerned with me in this undertaking; and likewise of the chief intent of the lucubrations[2] hereafter communicated, that the reader, on casting his eye over the four or five first pages, may judge how far the book may or may not be qualified to entertain him, and either accept or throw it aside as he thinks proper. And here I promise that in the pictures I shall give of myself and associates, I will draw no flattering lines, assume no perfection that we are not in reality possessed of, nor attempt to shadow over any defect with an artificial gloss.

As a proof of my sincerity, I shall in the first place assure him that for my own part I never was a beauty, and am now very far from being young (a confession he will find few of my sex ready to make). I shall also acknowledge that I have run through as many scenes of vanity and folly as the greatest coquette of them all. Dress, equipage,[3] and flattery were the idols of my heart. I should have thought that day lost which did not present me with some new opportunity of showing myself. My life, for some years, was a continued round of what I then called pleasure, and my whole time engrossed by a hurry of promiscuous diversions. But whatever inconveniences such a manner of conduct has brought upon myself, I have this consolation, to think that the public may reap some benefit from it. The company I kept was not, indeed, always so well chosen as it ought to have been, for the sake of my own interest or reputation; but then it was general, and by consequence furnished me not only with the knowledge of many occurrences, which otherwise I had been ignorant of, but also enabled me, when the too great vivacity of my nature became tempered with reflection, to see into the secret springs which gave rise to the actions I had either heard or been witness of—to judge of the various passions of the human mind, and distinguish those imperceptible degrees by which they become masters of the heart, and attain the dominion over reason. A thousand odd adventures, which at the time they happened made slight impression on me, and seemed to dwell no longer on my mind than the wonder they occasioned, now rise fresh to my remembrance,

1. Addison and Steele's Mr. Spectator.
2. Writings by candlelight; Haywood pointedly picks up Isaac Bickerstaff's catchword for his essays in the *Tatler*.
3. Fancy carriages, servants, and furniture.

with this advantage, that the mystery I then, for want of attention, imagined they contained, is entirely vanished, and I find it easy to account for the cause by the consequence.

With this experience, added to a genius[4] tolerably extensive, and an education more liberal than is ordinarily allowed to persons of my sex, I flattered myself that it might be in my power to be in some measure both useful and entertaining to the public; and this thought was so soothing to those remains of vanity not yet wholly extinguished in me, that I resolved to pursue it, and immediately began to consider by what method I should be most likely to succeed. To confine myself to any one subject, I knew could please but one kind of taste, and my ambition was to be as universally read as possible. From my observations of human nature, I found that curiosity had more or less a share in every breast; and my business, therefore, was to hit this reigning humor in such a manner as that the gratification it should receive from being made acquainted with other people's affairs should at the same time teach every one to regulate their own.

Having agreed within myself on this important point, I commenced author, by setting down many things which, being pleasing to myself, I imagined would be so to others; but on examining them the next day, I found an infinite deficiency both in matter and style, and that there was an absolute necessity for me to call in to my assistance such of my acquaintance as were qualified for that purpose. The first that occurred to me, I shall distinguish by the name of Mira, a lady descended from a family to which wit seems hereditary, married to a gentleman every way worthy of so excellent a wife, and with whom she lives in so perfect a harmony, that having nothing to ruffle the composure of her soul, or disturb those sparkling ideas she received from nature and education, left me no room to doubt if what she favored me with would be acceptable to the public. The next is a widow of quality, who not having buried her vivacity in the tomb of her lord, continues to make one in all the modish diversions of the times, so far, I mean, as she finds them consistent with innocence and honor; and as she is far from having the least austerity in her behavior, nor is rigid to the failings she is wholly free from herself, those of her acquaintance who had been less circumspect scruple not to make her the confidante of secrets they conceal from all the world beside. The third is the daughter of a wealthy merchant, charming as an angel, but endued with so many accomplishments that to those who know her truly, her beauty is the least distinguished part of her. This fine young creature I shall call Euphrosyne, since she has all the cheerfulness and sweetness ascribed to that goddess.[5]

These three approved my design, assured me of all the help they could afford, and soon gave a proof of it in bringing their several essays; but as the reader, provided the entertainment be agreeable, will not be interested from which quarter it comes, whatever productions I shall be favored with from these ladies, or any others I may hereafter correspond with, will be exhibited under the general title of *The Female Spectator*, and how many contributors soever there may happen to be to the work, they are to be considered only as several members of one body, of which I am the mouth. * * *

4. Talent, ability.
5. Euphrosyne is one of the three Graces, sister goddesses in Greek mythology who possess (and bestow) the gift of beauty.

Richard Steele: *from* Tatler No. 18
21 May 1709

[THE NEWS WRITERS IN DANGER[1]]

St. James's Coffeehouse, May 20.

* * * It being therefore visible, that our society[2] will be greater sufferers by the peace than the soldiery itself; insomuch, that the *Daily Courant* is in danger of being broken, my friend Dyer of being reformed,[3] and the very best of the whole band of being reduced to half-pay; might I presume to offer anything in the behalf of my distressed brethren, I would humbly move, that an appendix of proper apartments furnished with pen, ink, and paper, and other necessaries of life should be added to the Hospital of Chelsea,[4] for the relief of such decayed news writers as have served their country in the wars; and that for their exercise, they should compile the annals of their brother-veterans, who have been engaged in the same service, and are still obliged to do duty after the same manner.

I cannot be thought to speak this out of an eye to any private interest; for, as my chief scenes of action are coffeehouses, playhouses, and my own apartment, I am in no need of camps, fortifications, and fields of battle, to support me; I don't call out for heroes and generals to my assistance. Though the officers are broken, and the armies disbanded, I shall still be safe as long as there are men or women, or politicians, or lovers, or poets, or nymphs, or swains, or cits,[5] or courtiers, in being.

Joseph Addison: *from* Tatler No. 155
Thursday, 6 April 1710

[THE POLITICAL UPHOLSTERER]

—Aliena negotia curat
Excussus propriis.[1]

From My Own Apartment, April 5

There lived some years since within my neighborhood a very grave person, an upholsterer, who seemed a man of more than ordinary application to business. He was a very early riser, and was often abroad two or three hours before any of his neighbors. He had a particular carefulness in the knitting of his brows, and a kind of impatience in all his motions, that plainly discovered he was always intent on matters of importance. Upon my enquiry into his life and conversation, I found him to be the greatest newsmonger in our quarter;[2] that he rose before day to read the *Post-Man*;[3] and that

1. Papers often defined themselves by contrasting their methods and achievements with those of their rivals. For the essayists, the newspapers afforded the readiest foil. Steele was a seasoned journalist, but he and Addison devised many ways of mocking the vacuity of the newsmongers, and of flattering those readers who preferred essays to mere journalism. In this early *Tatler*, Bickerstaff announces that England will soon be victorious in its foreign wars, observes that "the approach of peace strikes a panic through our armies," who will have nowhere left to fight, and worries that peace will prove even more costly to the journalists, who will have nothing left to write about.
2. I.e., the "brotherhood" of news writers.
3. John Dyer's fervently Tory newsletter often denounced the Whigs for (among other things) mismanaging the wars abroad.
4. Where disabled soldiers were given care and lodging.
5. City dwellers, tradespeople.

1. "He minds others' concerns, since he has lost his own" (Horace, *Satires* 2.3.19–20).
2. "Monger" not because he sells news but because he tells it, to anyone who will listen; Addison's news-addicted upholsterer became one of the *Tatler*'s most popular comic creations, reappearing in several later numbers.
3. The leading Whig newspaper (1695–1730).

he would take two or three turns to the other end of the town before his neighbors were up, to see if there were any Dutch mails[4] come in. He had a wife and several children; but was much more inquisitive to know what passed in Poland than in his own family, and was in greater pain and anxiety of mind for King Augustus's[5] welfare than that of his nearest relations. He looked extremely thin in a dearth of news, and never enjoyed himself in a westerly wind.[6] This indefatigable kind of life was the ruin of his shop; for about the time that his favorite prince left the crown of Poland, he broke and disappeared.

This man and his affairs had been long out of my mind, till about three days ago, as I was walking in St. James's Park, I heard somebody at a distance hemming after me: and who should it be but my old neighbor the upholsterer? I saw he was reduced to extreme poverty, by certain shabby superfluities in his dress: for notwithstanding that it was a very sultry day for the time of the year, he wore a loose great coat and a muff, with a long campaign-wig out of curl;[7] to which he had added the ornament of a pair of black garters buckled under the knee. Upon his coming up to me, I was going to inquire into his present circumstances; but was prevented by his asking me, with a whisper, whether the last letters brought any accounts that one might rely upon from Bender?[8] I told him, none that I heard of; and asked him, whether he had yet married his eldest daughter? He told me, No. But pray, says he, tell me sincerely, what are your thoughts of the King of Sweden? For though his wife and children were starving, I found his chief concern at present was for this great monarch. I told him, that I looked upon him as one of the first heroes of the age. But pray, says he, do you think there is anything in the story of his wound? And finding me surprised at the question, Nay, says he, I only propose it to you. I answered, that I thought there was no reason to doubt of it. But why in the heel, says he, more than in any other part of the body? Because, says I, the bullet chanced to light there. * * *

We were now got to the upper end of the Mall,[9] where were three or four very odd fellows sitting together upon the bench. These I found were all of them politicians, who used to sun themselves in that place every day about dinner time.[1] * * *

I at length took my leave of the company, and was going away; but had not been gone thirty yards before the upholsterer hemmed again after me. Upon his advancing towards me, with a whisper, I expected to hear some secret piece of news, which he had not thought fit to communicate to the bench; but instead of that, he desired me in my ear to lend him half a crown. In compassion to so needy a statesman, and to dissipate the confusion I found he was in, I told him, if he pleased, I would give him five shillings, to receive five pounds of him when the Great Turk was driven out of Constantinople; which he very readily accepted, but not before he had laid down to me the impossibility of such an event, as the affairs of Europe now stand.

This paper I design for the particular benefit of those worthy citizens who live more in a coffeehouse than in their shops, and whose thoughts are so taken up with the affairs of the Allies, that they forget their customers.

4. Mailboats from the Netherlands, bringing fresh news.
5. Frederick Augustus I of Poland, whose loss and recovery of power had filled the papers for several years.
6. Which prevented the arrival of the "Dutch mails."
7. A "campaign wig" was used when traveling and was remarkable for its decorative curls (here flattened and disordered).
8. A town in modern Bessarabia, where Charles XII of Sweden (1682–1718) had sought refuge after a long string of military victories and a final catastrophic defeat (see Samuel Johnson, *The Vanity of Human Wishes*, lines 191–222, page 2682).
9. The public walk in St. James's Park, near the royal residence.
1. Bickerstaff proceeds to eavesdrop, astonished, on the conversation of these news-obsessives.

Joseph Addison: *from* Spectator No. 10
Monday, 12 March 1711

[THE SPECTATOR AND ITS READERS[1]]

Non aliter quam qui adverso vix flumine lembum
Remigiis subigit: si brachia forte remisit,
Atque illum in praeceps prono rapit alveus amni.[2]

It is with much satisfaction that I hear this great city inquiring day by day after these my papers, and receiving my morning lectures with a becoming seriousness and attention. My publisher tells me, that there are already three thousand of them distributed every day: so that if I allow twenty readers to every paper, which I look upon as a modest computation, I may reckon about three-score thousand disciples in London and Westminster, who I hope will take care to distinguish themselves from the thoughtless herd of their ignorant and inattentive brethren. Since I have raised to myself so great an audience, I shall spare no pains to make their instruction agreeable, and their diversion useful. For which reasons I shall endeavor to enliven morality with wit, and to temper wit with morality, that my readers may, if possible, both ways find their account in the speculation of the day. And to the end that their virtue and discretion may not be short transient intermitting starts of thought, I have resolved to refresh their memories from day to day, till I have recovered them out of that desperate state of vice and folly into which the age is fallen. The mind that lies fallow but a single day sprouts up in follies that are only to be killed by a constant and assiduous culture. It was said of Socrates, that he brought philosophy down from heaven, to inhabit among men;[3] and I shall be ambitious to have it said of me, that I have brought philosophy out of closets and libraries, schools and colleges, to dwell in clubs and assemblies, at tea tables, and in coffeehouses.

I would therefore in a very particular manner recommend these my speculations to all well-regulated families, that set apart an hour in every morning for tea and bread and butter; and would earnestly advise them for their good to order this paper to be punctually served up, and to be looked upon as a part of the tea equipage.

Sir Francis Bacon observes that a well-written book, compared with its rivals and antagonists, is like Moses's serpent, that immediately swallowed up and devoured those of the Egyptians.[4] I shall not be so vain as to think that where the *Spectator* appears, the other public prints will vanish; but shall leave it to my readers' consideration whether, is it not much better to be let into the knowledge of oneself, than to hear what passes in Muscovy[5] or Poland; and to amuse ourselves with such writings as tend to the wearing out of ignorance, passion, and prejudice, than such as naturally conduce to inflame hatreds and make enmities irreconcilable?

1. The *Spectator* bore a close resemblance to the *Daily Courant:* both papers were a single sheet produced by the same printer (Samuel Buckley) for the same price (a penny), and both appeared every day except Sunday. In this number, Addison elaborates on the ways in which his new essay—less than two weeks old and already very successful—is not a newspaper.
2. "As if one, whose oars can scarce force his skiff against the stream, should by chance slacken his arms, and lo! headlong down the current the channel sweeps it away" (Virgil, *Georgics* 1.201–3).
3. Addison paraphrases a remark by the Roman orator Cicero (*Tusculan Disputations* 5.4.10).
4. Bacon makes this point in his *Advancement of Learning* (2.14), alluding to Exodus 7.10–12.
5. A territory in west-central Russia (Moscow was its capital).

In the next place, I would recommend this paper to the daily perusal of those gentlemen whom I cannot but consider as my good brothers and allies, I mean the fraternity of spectators who live in the world without having anything to do in it; and either by the affluence of their fortunes, or laziness of their dispositions, have no other business with the rest of mankind but to look upon them. Under this class of men are comprehended all contemplative tradesmen, titular physicians, Fellows of the Royal Society,[6] Templers[7] that are not given to be contentious, and statesmen that are out of business. In short, everyone that considers the world as a theater, and desires to form a right judgment of those who are the actors on it.

There is another set of men that I must likewise lay a claim to, whom I have lately called the Blanks of society, as being altogether unfurnished with ideas, till the business and conversation of the day has supplied them. I have often considered these poor souls with an eye of great commiseration, when I have heard them asking the first man they have met with, whether there was any news stirring? and by that means gathering together materials for thinking. These needy persons do not know what to talk of, till about twelve a clock in the morning; for by that time they are pretty good judges of the weather, know which way the wind sits, and whether the Dutch mail[8] be come in. As they lie at the mercy of the first man they meet, and are grave or impertinent all the day long, according to the notions which they have imbibed in the morning, I would earnestly entreat them not to stir out of their chambers till they have read this paper, and do promise them that I will daily instill into them such sound and wholesome sentiments as shall have a good effect on their conversation for the ensuing twelve hours.

But there are none to whom this paper will be more useful than to the female world. I have often thought there has not been sufficient pains taken in finding out proper employments and diversions for the fair ones. Their amusements seem contrived for them rather as they are women, than as they are reasonable creatures; and are more adapted to the sex, than to the species. The toilet[9] is their great scene of business, and the right adjusting of their hair the principal employment of their lives. The sorting of a suit of ribbons is reckoned a very good morning's work; and if they make an excursion to a mercer's[1] or a toy shop,[2] so great a fatigue makes them unfit for anything else all the day after. Their more serious occupations are sewing and embroidery, and their greatest drudgery the preparation of jellies and sweetmeats. This, I say, is the state of ordinary women; though I know there are multitudes of those of a more elevated life and conversation, that move in an exalted sphere of knowledge and virtue, that join all the beauties of the mind to the ornaments of dress, and inspire a kind of awe and respect, as well as love, into their male beholders. I hope to increase the number of these by publishing this daily paper, which I shall always endeavor to make an innocent if not an improving entertainment, and by that means at least divert the minds of my female readers from greater trifles. At the same time, as I would fain give some finishing touches to those which are already the most beautiful pieces in human nature, I shall endeavor to point out all those imperfections that are the

6. The London group chartered in the 1660s for the advancement of scientific inquiry.
7. Lawyers.
8. The boat bearing letters and newspapers from Holland.
9. Dressing tables.
1. Fabric sellers.
2. Where they might buy ornamental accessories—fans, silks, ribbons, laces—as well as playthings.

blemishes, as well as those virtues which are the embellishments, of the sex. In the meanwhile I hope these my gentle readers, who have so much time on their hands, will not grudge throwing away a quarter of an hour in a day on this paper, since they may do it without any hindrance to business.

I know several of my friends and well-wishers are in great pain for me, lest I should not be able to keep up the spirit of a paper which I oblige myself to furnish every day: but to make them easy in this particular, I will promise them faithfully to give it over as soon as I grow dull. This I know will be matter of great raillery to the small wits; who will frequently put me in mind of my promise, desire me to keep my word, assure me that it is high time to give over, with many other little pleasantries of the like nature, which men of a little smart genius cannot forbear throwing out against their best friends, when they have such a handle given them of being witty. But let them remember, that I do hereby enter my caveat against this piece of raillery.

Getting, Spending, Speculating

The periodical essay was one commodity among many, in an economy whose energies were evident almost everywhere: in shops stocked with new (often exotic) goods; at outposts in remote countries where trade was gradually being transmuted into empire; at London banks, where the apparatus of transaction (loans, bills, draughts) was rapidly being refined; in nearby coffeehouses, where the agents and accumulators of wealth paused during busy days to absorb substances imported from abroad (coffee, tobacco, chocolate) as well as that home-crafted item of consumption, the periodical essay itself. The essayists often construed their audience as though it consisted *primarily* of merchants, shopkeepers, and customers—of people profoundly concerned with the course of commerce, whatever their gender or occupation. Defoe, Addison, and Steele all wrote to celebrate trade (its new profusions and possibilities), but also to regularize it, to render it respectable, to reconcile it with notions of human excellence originating in an earlier culture centered on aristocracy. The *Review*, the *Tatler*, and the *Spectator* all undertook (as the historian J. G. A. Pocock has elegantly argued) to redefine the idea of "virtue," to shift its focus of application from the classically defined obligations of the hereditary landowner to the prudent calculation of the urban merchant, alert to realities and probabilities in an economy awash with speculation and controlled by credit, where "what one owned was promises": promises by entrepreneurs in search of capital; by stock-jobbers selling hopes of future prosperity; by the government whose operations depended on intricately structured loans from its own citizens. One central concern of the periodicals was how to commute promise into actual prosperity, rather than mere air.

In the selections in this section, Addison rejoices in the commercial and cultural confluence at the Royal Exchange (London's shopping center). In a more sentimental vein, Steele tracks the consequences of foreign trade in the lives and feelings of two lovers. Defoe, by contrast, is harder-headed, more closely analytic. Unlike the authors of the *Spectator*, he had spent years in business, making and losing fortunes. Surveying the shops of London, Defoe declares (as in virtually every *Review*) his passion for trade, but he asks what prospects the *present* patterns of consumption actually hold forth.

The *Gentleman's Magazine*:

St JOHN's GATE.

LondGazette
Londō Journ
Fog's Journ.
Applebee's : :
Read's : : : :
Craftſman : :
D. Spectator
Lit Courier of
Grubſtreet
Hyp-Docto
Daily-Post
D. Advertiſer
St James's Ev.
Whitehall Ev
Lond. Ev̄eīg
Weekly Miſc
General Ev.
Old Whig
D. Gazetteer
Lon. D. Post
Com. Sense

York-News
Dublin 5 : :
Edinburgh 2
Briſtol : : : : :
Norwich 2
Exeter 2 : : :
Worceſter
Northamton
Glouceſter : :
Stamford : :
Nottingham
Bury Journ.
Cheſter ditto
Derby ditto
Ipſwich do.
Reading do.
Leeds Merc:
NewcastleC.
Canterbury
Durham
Kendal
Boston : : ¶
Barbados :
Jamaica &c

For JANUARY, 1738.

CONTAINING,

(More in Quantity, and greater Variety, than any Book of the Kind and Price).

I. Original Essays, Moral: The Character of a *Good Man*, by a late illuſtrious Lady. Of the Magiſtrate's Right to puniſh ꝥ Death. Preſcience conſiſtent with Liberty. Whether Heaven and Hell be Local.
II. —— Philological: Eſſay on Tragedy, with *Horace's* four Rules for ꝥ Drama. Anſwers to Biblical Queſtions.
III. —— Mathematicks: A new Aſtronomical Equation, diſcover'd by Mr *Facio*. A Method to find the Longitude and Latitude at Sea.
IV. —— The Lady's Adventure, and Love Letters from a Proteſtant Gent. to a Catholic Lady.
V. Essays from the Weekly Papers. *The Literary Courier of Grub-ſtreet.* Characters of News-Papers. Advice to Ladies on their Return to *London*. *Zenger's* Tryal for printing a Libel. Rules of Phyſiognomy in chuſing Husbands. The Widow deſcrib'd. The Character of a Prince Royal, *&c.*
VI. Poetry. A Poem, inſcrib'd to the *Dublin* Society, by Mr *Arbuckle*. Ode on the Death of P. *George* of *Denmark*, by the celebrated Mr *Alſop*. Prologue to *Venice preſerv'd*, by a Perſon of Quality. The Blind Boy, with the Muſick correct. Songs, Epigrams, Ænigmas, &c.
VII. Historical. The King's Speech; Addreſſes of the Lords and Commons. The Secrets of Free-Maſonry.
VIII. Lists of Births, Mariages, and Deaths, *&c.*
IX. Foreign Affairs. Match of Don *Carlos* with the Princeſs Royal of *Poland*, &c. Caution to Mariners.
X. Price of Stocks. Bill of Mortality.
XI. Regiſter of Books.
XII. Table of Contents.

By *SYLVANUS URBAN*, Gent.

LONDON: Printed by E. Cave at St John's Gate, and Sold by the Bookſellers of Town and Country; of whom may be had any former Month.

Where the *Review, Tatler*, and *Spectator* defined themselves *against* their print contemporaries, other periodicals took a different tack. With so much information, instruction, and entertainment flowing from so many sources, a desire developed for a digest that might organize it all. No one catered more adroitly to this new market than did Edward Cave, founder and editor of *Gentleman's Magazine*, a monthly pamphlet whose title coined a pivotal new term for print. "Magazine" meant a military storehouse of provisions and artillery; the *Gentleman's Magazine* promised an intellectual storehouse similarly well stocked. Cave promised "more in quantity, and greater variety, than any book of the kind and price." He delivered on the promise by publishing extracts and abstracts from many periodicals, but he soon cultivated a stable of his own writers (including the young Samuel Johnson) who furnished his readers with an ever-widening range of fresh materials: biographies, poetry, parliamentary debates. The *Magazine*'s logo presents it as a compendium of other papers, but Cave had in fact produced a true original, "one of the most successful and lucrative pamphlets" (wrote Johnson, whose observation still holds true) "which literary history has upon record." The title page depicts the 200-year-old gatehouse where the *Gentleman's Magazine* was composed, printed, and sold (the building's fortress-like appearance may entail a visual pun, conjuring up the military meaning of "magazine"). The building is flanked by the names of papers that the *Magazine* has incorporated, one way or another, into its own pages (London papers on the left, provincial and foreign ones on the right). The fictitious name "Sylvanus Urban" conjures up both countryside (*sylvanus*, "wooded") and city; as the bottom lines make clear, Cave aimed his appeal at audiences in both domains.

Joseph Addison: Spectator No. 69

Saturday, 19 May 1711

[ROYAL EXCHANGE[1]]

Hic segetes, illic veniunt felicius uvae:
Arborei foetus alibi, atque injussa virescunt
Gramina. Nonne vides, croceos ut Tmolus odores,
India mittit ebur, molles sua thura Sabaei?
At Chalybes nudi ferrum, virosaque Pontus
Castorea, Eliadum palmas Epirus equarum?
Continuo has leges aeternaque foedera certis
Imposuit Natura locis . . .[2]

There is no place in the town which I so much love to frequent as the Royal Exchange. It gives me a secret satisfaction, and in some measure gratifies my vanity, as I am an Englishman, to see so rich an assembly of countrymen and foreigners consulting together upon the private business of mankind, and making this metropolis a kind of emporium for the whole earth. I must confess I look upon high-change[3] to be a great council, in which all considerable nations have their representatives. Factors[4] in the trading world are what ambassadors are in the politic world; they negotiate affairs, conclude treaties, and maintain a good correspondence between those wealthy societies of men that are divided from one another by seas and oceans, or live on the different extremities of a continent. I have often been pleased to hear disputes adjusted between an inhabitant of Japan and an alderman of London, or to see a subject of the Great Mogul[5] entering into a league with one of the Czar of Muscovy.[6] I am infinitely delighted in mixing with these several ministers of commerce, as they are distinguished by their different walks and different languages. Sometimes I am jostled among a body of Armenians: sometimes I am lost in a crowd of Jews, and sometimes make one in a group of Dutchmen. I am a Dane, Swede, or Frenchman at different times, or rather fancy myself like the old philosopher,[7] who upon being asked what countryman he was, replied that he was a citizen of the world.

Though I very frequently visit this busy multitude of people, I am known to nobody there but my friend, Sir Andrew,[8] who often smiles upon me as he sees me bustling in the crowd, but at the same time connives at my presence without taking any

1. The Exchange, a quadrangle of arcades and shops surrounding a huge courtyard, had functioned as a crucial site of London commerce since its creation in 1570. Destroyed in the Great Fire, it was rebuilt from a new design in 1669. The illustration on page 2331 depicts both the original building by Thomas Gresham (upper right corner) and the later structure with its more intricate, Baroque ornamentation. Statues of English kings occupy the second-floor arches. At the center of the courtyard, the statue of Charles II in the garb of a Roman emperor enacts that favored comparison (echoed by Addison in his essay's epigraph from Virgil) between contemporary Britain and the ancient Roman Empire.

2. "Corn grows more plentifully here, grapes there. In other places grow trees laden with fruit, and grasses unbidden. Do you not see how Tmolus sends us its saffron perfumes; India her ivory; the soft Sabaens their frankincense; but the naked Chalybes send us iron, the Pontus pungent beaver-oil, and Epirus prize-winning Olympic horses? These perpetual laws and eternal covenants Nature has imposed on certain places" (Virgil, *Georgics* 1.54–61).

3. In addition to housing shops, the Exchange was a central meeting place for international merchants, who frequently closed deals in the courtyard. "High change" was that period when trading was at its peak.

4. Commercial agents.

5. The Indian emperor.

6. A territory in west-central Russia (Moscow was its capital).

7. Diogenes the Cynic, credited for developing the concept of "cosmopolitanism" (citizenship in the universe), in which all beings are parts of a single whole.

8. Sir Andrew Freeport, a member of Mr. Spectator's club: Whig merchant and ardent advocate (as his name implies) of free trade.

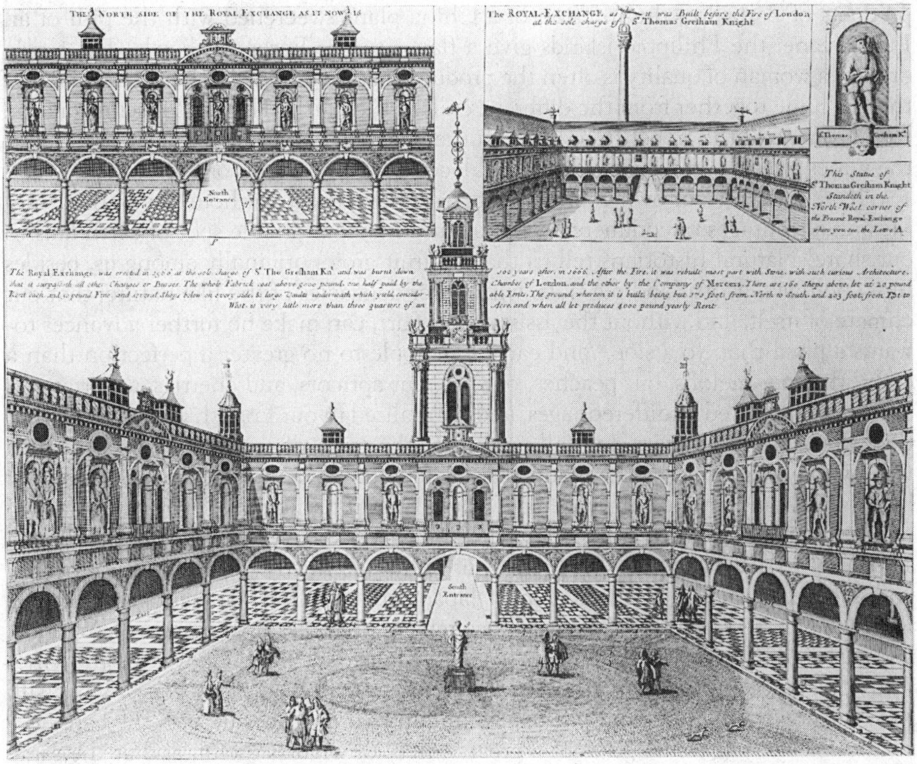

Sutton Nicholls, *The Royal Exchange*, 1712

further notice of me. There is indeed a merchant of Egypt, who just knows me by sight, having formerly remitted me some money to Grand Cairo;[9] but as I am not versed in the modern Coptic, our conferences go no further than a bow and a grimace.[1]

This grand scene of business gives me an infinite variety of solid and substantial entertainments. As I am a great lover of mankind, my heart naturally overflows with pleasure at the sight of a prosperous and happy multitude, insomuch that at many public solemnities I cannot forbear expressing my joy with tears that have stolen down my cheeks. For this reason I am wonderfully delighted to see such a body of men thriving in their own private fortunes, and at the same time promoting the public stock; or in other words, raising estates for their own families, by bringing into their country whatever is wanting, and carrying out of it whatever is superfluous.

Nature seems to have taken a particular care to disseminate her blessings among the different regions of the world, with an eye to this mutual intercourse and traffic among mankind, that the natives of the several parts of the globe might have a kind of dependence upon one another, and be united together by their common interest. Almost every degree produces something peculiar to it. The food often grows in one country, and the sauce in another. The fruits of Portugal are corrected by the

9. Where Mr. Spectator spent some time as a young man (see *Spectator* No. 1, page 2319).

1. The word denoted an expression of politeness.

products of Barbados; the infusion of a China plant sweetened with the pith of an Indian cane; the Philippic islands give a flavor to our European bowls. The single dress of a woman of quality is often the product of an hundred climates. The muff and the fan come together from the different ends of the Earth. The scarf is sent from the torrid zone, and the tippet from beneath the pole. The brocade petticoat rises out of the mines of Peru, and the diamond necklace out of the bowels of Indostan.

If we consider our own country in its natural prospect, without any of the benefits and advantages of commerce, what a barren uncomfortable spot of earth falls to our share! Natural historians tell us that no fruit grows originally among us, besides hips and haws, acorns and pig-nuts, with other delicacies of the like nature; that our climate of itself, and without the assistances of art, can make no further advances towards a plum than to a sloe,[2] and carries an apple to no greater a perfection than a crab;[3] that our melons, our peaches, our figs, our apricots, and cherries, are strangers among us, imported in different ages, and naturalized in our English gardens; and that they would all degenerate and fall away into the trash of our own country, if they were wholly neglected by the planter, and left to the mercy of our sun and soil. Nor has traffic more enriched our vegetable world, than it has improved the whole face of nature among us. Our ships are laden with the harvest of every climate; our tables are stored with spices, and oils, and wines; our rooms are filled with pyramids of China, and adorned with the workmanship of Japan; our morning's draught[4] comes to us from the remotest corners of the earth; we repair our bodies by the drugs of America, and repose ourselves under Indian canopies. My friend Sir Andrew calls the vineyards of France our gardens; the Spice Islands[5] our hotbeds; the Persians our silk weavers, and the Chinese our potters. Nature indeed furnishes us with the bare necessaries of life, but traffic gives us a great variety of what is useful, and at the same time supplies us with everything that is convenient and ornamental. Nor is it the least part of this our happiness, that whilst we enjoy the remotest products of the north and south, we are free from those extremities of weather which give them birth; that our eyes are refreshed with the green fields of Britain, at the same time that our palates are feasted with fruits that rise between the tropics.

For these reasons there are not more useful members in a commonwealth than merchants. They knit mankind together in a mutual intercourse of good offices, distribute the gifts of nature, find work for the poor, add wealth to the rich, and magnificence to the great. Our English merchant converts the tin of his own country into gold, and exchanges his wool for rubies. The Mahometans are clothed in our British manufacture, and the inhabitants of the frozen zone warmed with the fleeces of our sheep.

When I have been upon the 'Change, I have often fancied one of our old kings[6] standing in person, where he is represented in effigy, and looking down upon the wealthy concourse of people with which that place is every day filled. In this case, how would he be surprised to hear all the languages of Europe spoken in this little spot of his former dominions, and to see so many private men, who in his time would have been the vassals of some powerful baron, negotiating like princes for greater sums of money than were formerly to be met with in the Royal Treasury! Trade, without enlarging the British territories, has given us a kind of additional empire: it has multiplied the number of the rich, made our landed estates infinitely more

2. The berry of the blackthorn.
3. Crabapple.
4. Drink.
5. A cluster of islands in modern Indonesia.
6. As depicted in the statues on the second story (see illustration on page 2331).

valuable than they were formerly, and added to them an accession of other estates as valuable as the lands themselves.

Richard Steele: Spectator No. 11

Tuesday, 13 March 1711

[Inkle and Yarico[1]]

Dat veniam corvis, vexat censura columbas.[2]

Arietta is visited by all persons of both sexes who have any pretense to wit and gallantry. She is in that time of life which is neither affected with the follies of youth or infirmities of age; and her conversation is so mixed with gaiety and prudence that she is agreeable both to the young and the old. Her behavior is very frank, without being in the least blameable; and as she is out of the tract of any amorous or ambitious pursuits of her own, her visitants entertain her with accounts of themselves very freely, whether they concern their passions or their interests. I made her a visit this afternoon, having been formerly introduced to the honor of her acquaintance by my friend Will. Honeycomb,[3] who has prevailed upon her to admit me sometimes into her assembly, as a civil, inoffensive man. I found her accompanied with one person only, a commonplace talker who, upon my entrance, rose, and after a very slight civility sat down again; then turning to Arietta, pursued his discourse, which I found was upon the old topic of constancy in love. He went on with great facility in repeating what he talks every day of his life; and with the ornaments of insignificant laughs and gestures, enforced his arguments by quotations out of plays and songs, which allude to the perjuries of the fair, and the general levity[4] of women. Methought he strove to shine more than ordinarily in his talkative way, that he might insult my silence, and distinguish himself before a woman of Arietta's taste and understanding. She had often an inclination to interrupt him, but could find no opportunity, 'till the larum[5] ceased of itself; which it did not 'till he had repeated and murdered the celebrated story of the Ephesian matron.[6]

Arietta seemed to regard this piece of raillery as an outrage done to her sex, as indeed I have always observed that women, whether out of a nicer[7] regard to their honor, or what other reason I cannot tell, are more sensibly touched with those general aspersions which are cast upon their sex, than men are by what is said of theirs.

When she had a little recovered herself from the serious anger she was in, she replied in the following manner.

"Sir, when I consider, how perfectly new all you have said on this subject is, and that the story you have given us is not quite two thousand years old, I cannot but think it a piece of presumption to dispute with you: but your quotations put me in mind of the fable of the lion and the man.[8] The man, walking with that noble

1. Steele here elaborates on a 60-year-old traveler's tale, in such a way as to combine two of the *Spectator*'s central concerns: the transactions of love and power between men and women, and the impact of commerce on human conduct.
2. "Their verdict goes easy on the raven, but is severe on the dove" (Juvenal, *Satires* 2.63). The speaker, a woman, is complaining of how leniently men assess themselves, and how harshly they criticize women.
3. An aged member of Mr. Spectator's club, proud of his long-ago days as a Restoration rake, and still deeply interested in matters of the heart.
4. Lightness, fickleness.
5. The long-ringing alarm bell (of his talk).
6. The Roman story (told in Petronius's *Satyricon*, pt. 2) of a widow who, while mourning at the tomb of her newly deceased husband, succumbs to the attractions of a soldier standing nearby, and makes love with him on her husband's tomb.
7. More precise.
8. In Aesop's *Fables* (No. 219).

animal, showed him, in the ostentation of human superiority, a sign of a man killing a lion. Upon which the lion said very justly, 'We lions are none of us painters, else we could show a hundred men killed by lions, for one lion killed by a man.' You men are writers, and can represent us women as unbecoming as you please in your works, while we are unable to return the injury. You have twice or thrice observed in your discourse that hypocrisy is the very foundation of our education; and that an ability to dissemble our affections is a professed part of our breeding. These, and such other reflections, are sprinkled up and down the writings of all ages, by authors who leave behind them memorials of their resentment against the scorn of particular women, in invectives against the whole sex. Such a writer, I doubt not, was the celebrated Petronius, who invented the pleasant aggravations of the frailty of the Ephesian lady; but when we consider this question between the sexes, which has been either a point of dispute or raillery ever since there were men and women, let us take facts from plain people, and from such as have not either ambition or capacity to embellish their narrations with any beauties of imagination. I was the other day amusing myself with Ligon's *Account of Barbados;* and, in answer to your well-wrought tale, I will give you (as it dwells upon my memory) out of that honest traveler, in his fifty-fifth page, the History of Inkle and Yarico.[9]

"Mr. Thomas Inkle[1] of London, aged 20 years, embarked in the Downs[2] on the good ship called the Achilles, bound for the West Indies, on the 16th of June 1647, in order to improve his fortune by trade and merchandise. Our adventurer was the third son of an eminent citizen, who had taken particular care to instill into his mind an early love of gain, by making him a perfect master of numbers, and consequently giving him a quick view of loss and advantage, and preventing the natural impulses of his passions, by prepossession towards his interests. With a mind thus turned, young Inkle had a person every way agreeable, a ruddy vigor in his counteance, strength in his limbs, with ringlets of fair hair loosely flowing on his shoulders. It happened, in the course of the voyage, that the Achilles, in some distress, put into a creek on the main of America, in search of provisions. The youth, who is the hero of my story, among others, went ashore on this occasion. From their first landing they were observed by a party of Indians, who hid themselves in the woods for that purpose. The English unadvisedly marched a great distance from the shore into the country, and were intercepted by the natives, who slew the greatest number of them. Our adventurer escaped among others, by flying into a forest. Upon his coming into a remote and pathless part of the wood, he threw himself, tired and breathless, on a little hillock, when an Indian maid rushed from a thicket behind him. After the first surprise, they appeared mutually agreeable to each other. If the European was highly charmed with the limbs, features, and wild graces of the naked American, the American was no less taken with the dress, complexion, and shape of an European, covered from head to foot. The Indian grew immediately enamored of him, and consequently solicitous for his preservation. She therefore conveyed him to a cave, where she gave him a delicious repast of fruits, and led him to a stream to slake his thirst. In the midst of these good offices, she would sometimes play with his hair, and delight in the opposition of its color to that of her fingers; then open his bosom, then laugh at him for covering it. She was, it

9. Richard Ligon's *True and Exact History of the Island of Barbados* (1657) includes a paragraph on a slave named Yarico and her misadventures in love, which Steele elaborates into the tale that follows.

1. Steele invents the name for this character; it means (perhaps prophetically) "linen tape," a common commodity.
2. A harbor on the southeastern coast of England.

seems, a person of distinction, for she every day came to him in a different dress, of the most beautiful shells, bugles, and bredes.[3] She likewise brought him a great many spoils, which her other lovers had presented to her; so that his cave was richly adorned with all the spotted skins of beasts, and most parti-colored feathers of fowls, which that world afforded. To make his confinement more tolerable, she would carry him in the dusk of the evening, or by the favor of moonlight, to unfrequented groves and solitudes, and show him where to lie down in safety, and sleep amidst the falls of waters, and melody of nightingales. Her part was to watch and hold him in her arms, for fear of her countrymen, and wake him on occasions to consult his safety. In this manner did the lovers pass away their time, till they had learned a language of their own, in which the voyager communicated to his mistress, how happy he should be to have her in his country, where she should be clothed in such silks as his waistcoat was made of, and be carried in houses drawn by horses, without being exposed to wind or weather. All this he promised her the enjoyment of, without such fears and alarms as they were there tormented with. In this tender correspondence these lovers lived for several months, when Yarico, instructed by her lover, discovered a vessel on the coast, to which she made signals, and in the night, with the utmost joy and satisfaction accompanied him to a ship's crew of his countrymen, bound for Barbados. When a vessel from the main arrives in that island, it seems the planters come down to the shore, where there is an immediate market of the Indians and other slaves, as with us of horses and oxen.

"To be short, Mr. Thomas Inkle, now coming into English territories, began seriously to reflect upon his loss of time, and to weigh with himself how many days' interest of his money he had lost during his stay with Yarico. This thought made the young man very pensive, and careful what account he should be able to give his friends of his voyage. Upon which considerations, the prudent and frugal young man sold Yarico to a Barbadian merchant; notwithstanding that the poor girl, to incline him to commiserate her condition, told him that she was with child by him; but he only made use of that information, to rise in his demands upon the purchaser."

I was so touched with this story, (which I think should be always a counterpart to the Ephesian matron) that I left the room with tears in my eyes; which a woman of Arietta's good sense did, I am sure, take for greater applause, than any compliments I could make her.

Daniel Defoe: *from* A Review of the State of the British Nation, Vol. 1, No. 43

Thursday, 8 January 1713

[WEAK FOUNDATIONS]

The subject of trade which I am now entered upon has this one excellency in it, for the benefit of the author, that really it can never be exhausted. * * * I remember some time ago I gave you a hint about the mighty alteration in the face of trade in this city; I cannot but touch it again on this occasion, because it relates to what I am upon. Let any man who remembers the glorious state of our trade about thirty or forty years past view but the streets of this opulent city and even the Exchange of London—nay, even our courts of law. It must of necessity put him in mind of Ezra 3.12,

3. Tube-shaped glass beads and braiding.

where the ancient men who had seen the old temple wept when they saw the weak foundations of the new.

However, to go on as I began and examine our new increase of commerce which we so must boast of: let me note a little to you with what mighty advantages the chasms, gaps, and breaches of our trade are filled up of late, and let us see it, I say, in the streets. Here, in the room of a trifling banker, or goldsmith, we are supplied with a most eminent brandy shop (Cheapside). There in the room of ditto you have a flaming shop[1] for white tea pots and luted earthen mugs (Cornhill), the most excellent offspring of that most valuable manufacture of earthenware. It is impossible that coffee, tea, and chocolate can be so advanced in their consumption without an eminent increase of those trades that attend them; whence we see the most noble shops in the city taken up with the valuable utensils of the tea table. The china warehouses are little marts within themselves (and by the way, are newly become markets of clandestine trade, of which I shall say more very quickly), and the eminent corner houses in the chief streets of London are chosen out by the town tinkers to furnish us with tea kettles and chocolate pots—vide Catherine Street and Bedford Buildings. Two thousand pound is reckoned a small stock in copper pots and lacquered kettles, and the very fitting up one of these brazen people's shops with fine sashes,[2] etc., to set forth his ware, costs above 500£ sterling, which is more by half than the best draper or mercer's shop in London requires.

This certainly shows the increase of our trade. Brass locks for our chambers and parlors, brass knockers for our doors, and the like add to the luster of those shops, of which hereafter. And the same sash works, only finer and larger, are now used to range[3] your brass and copper, that the goldsmiths had always to set out their less valuable silver and gold plate. From hence, be pleased to look upon the druggists of the town who are the merchants of these things. Bucklers-Bury and Little Lombard Street were the places which a few years ago held the whole number, a very few excepted, of that difficult nice employment, whose number is now spread over the whole town and with the most capital stocks, whose whole employ is the furnishing us by wholesale and retail with these most valuable of all drugs, coffee, tea, and chocolate—the general furniture of a druggist's shop being now three bales of coffee, twelve boxes of chocolate, six large canisters of tea, and an hundred and fifty empty gilded boxes. In like manner the rest of the town—how gloriously it is supplied! How do pastry cooks and periwig makers, brandy shops and toy shops, succeed linen drapers, mercers, upholsterers, and the like. A hundred pounds to rent for a house to sell jellies and apple pies; two hundred pounds to fit up a brandy shop, and afterwards not a hundred pound stock to put into it. These I can show many instances of.

Look, gentlemen, upon the particular parts of your town, formerly eminent for the best of tradesmen! View the famous churchyard of St. Paul's where so many aldermen and lord mayors have been raised by the trade of broadcloth and mere woolen manufactures,[4] and on whose trades so many families of poor always depended, that Sir William Turner used to say his shop alone employed 50,000 poor people! What succeeds him? A most noble, and to be sure, a much more valuable vintner's warehouse, *Anglice*,[5] a tavern, more vulgarly a bawdyhouse. And the next draper's shop, a coffee house; what takes up the whole row there? and supplies the place of eighteen or nineteen topping drapers? Who can but observe it! Cane chair

1. A shop with a kiln for making earthenware.
2. Windows made up of two sliding frames (common now, new and fancy at this time).
3. Display.
4. The trade in textiles had provided the foundation for many family fortunes and (hence) political careers.
5. In English.

makers, gilders of leather, looking-glass shops, and peddlers or toy shops—manifold improvements of trade! and an eminent instance of the growth of our manufactures!

* * *

Advertisements from the *Spectator*[1]

At the Lace Chamber on Ludgate Hill, kept by Mary Parsons, is a great quantity of Flanders lace, lately come over, to be sold off at great pennyworths[2] by wholesale or retail. She bought them there herself. [No. 200; Friday, 19 October 1711]

This day is published *The Court and City Vagaries*, being some late (and real) intrigues of several gentlemen and ladies. Written by one of the fair sex, price 6d. Sold by J. Baker in Paternoster Row. [No. 255; Saturday, 22 December 1711]

The famous Italian water, for dying red and gray hairs of the head and eyebrows into a lasting brown or black; at 1, 2, or 4s. the bottle, with printed directions for the use of it. To be had at Mrs. Hannam's toyshop, at the sign of the Three Angels near the Half-Moon Tavern in Cheapside. [Vol. 8, No. 634; Friday, 17 December 1714]

The ladies that called at Mr. Charles Lillie's at the corner of Beauford Buildings,[3] in a hackney coach on Wednesday night, the 6th of this instant, about 10 o'clock, are desired to let him know where to direct to them, he being now able to give a particular account of what they enquired after. [No. 305; Tuesday, 19 February 1712]

For a collection of periodical pieces on gender, manners, and marriage, go to *The Longman Anthology of British Literature* Web site at www.myliteraturekit.com.

END OF PERSPECTIVES: READING PAPERS

Jonathan Swift

1667–1745

Charles Jervas, *Jonathan Swift*.

Arguably the greatest prose satirist in the history of English literature, Jonathan Swift was born in Dublin, the only son of English parents, seven months after his father died. In his infancy he was kidnapped by his nurse and did not see his mother for three years. With the future dramatist William Congreve he attended the Kilkenny School (Ireland's best), and in 1682 he began six years of study at Trinity College, Dublin. He received his BA degree in 1686. From 1689, Swift served as secretary to Sir William Temple (1628–1699), a retired diplomat whose father had befriended Swift's family. Swift worked at Temple's estate at Moor Park in Surrey for most of the next ten years. It was at Moor Park that Swift first experienced the vertigo, nausea, and hearing impairment of Ménière's syndrome, a disturbance of the inner ear that would plague him for the rest of his life and sometimes wrongly led

1. Periodicals did not merely comment on commerce, they participated in it, earning much of their revenue from the advertisements that they printed at the conclusion of their main editorial matter.
2. At a terrific bargain.
3. Charles Lillie, a close associate of Addison's and Steele's, owned a perfume shop in the Strand. He had been one of the publishers and distributors of the *Tatler*, and sold the *Spectator* at his shop, where he also accepted advertisements for inclusion in the paper.

him (and others) to question his mental stability. While working for Temple, Swift also wrote his first poems, undistinguished compositions that do not presage the literary acclaim that was to come.

Not content with his station in life, Swift took an M.A. degree from Oxford University in 1692; three years later, he was ordained a priest in the (Anglican) Church of Ireland and appointed to the undesirable prebendary of Kilroot, where he found the local Presbyterians unsympathetic and the salary meager. Added to professional discontent was personal disappointment: Swift was rejected in his marriage proposal to Jane "Varina" Waring, the daughter of an Anglican clergyman. Swift returned to Moor Park in 1696, and, after Temple died in 1699, held a series of ecclesiastical posts in Ireland, none of which fulfilled his ambition for an important position in England. In 1702 he was made Doctor of Divinity by his alma mater, Trinity College, Dublin.

While at Moor Park, Swift began to tutor an eight-year-old girl, Esther "Stella" Johnson, daughter of Sir William's late steward. Though she was nearly fourteen years Swift's junior, "Stella" would in time become his beloved companion and his most trusted friend. When she was eighteen, Swift described her as "one of the most beautiful, graceful, and agreeable young women in London." In 1701, at Swift's request, Stella and Sir William's spinster cousin, Rebecca Dingley, moved to Dublin, where they remained for the rest of their lives. Swift and Stella met regularly, but never alone. Although there has been much debate about the nature of their relationship, it is clear that Swift and Stella loved, trusted, and valued each other, whether or not they were ever secretly married (the evidence suggests they were not). Swift's *Journal to Stella* (composed 1710 to 1713) and the series of poems he composed for her birthdays reveal a playful intimacy and affection not seen in his more public writings.

Moor Park not only led him to Stella but was also the cradle of Swift's first major literary work: *A Tale of a Tub* (composed 1697 to 1698, published 1704), a brilliant satire on "corruptions in religion and learning," published with *The Battle of the Books*, Swift's mock-epic salvo in the debate between the Ancients and the Moderns. Like most of his subsequent works, *A Tale of a Tub* did not appear under Swift's name, though its ironic treatment of the church subsequently damaged his prospects for ecclesiastical preferment when his authorship became widely known.

In the first decade of the new century Swift placed his hopes for preferment with the Whigs, then in power, and became associated with the Whig writers Joseph Addison and Richard Steele, founder of the *Tatler*, a London periodical in which two of Swift's important early poems, *A Description of the Morning* (1709) and *A Description of a City Shower* (1710), first appeared. Swift's career as a political polemicist began when he rose to the defense of three Whig lords facing impeachment with his allegorical *Discourse of the Contests and Dissentions between the Nobles and Commons in Athens and Rome* (1701). His *Bickerstaff Papers* (1708–1709), witty parodies of the cobbler-turned-astrologer John Partridge, occasioned much laughter regardless of party allegiances. More important, Swift began to write a series of pamphlets on church affairs, including his ironical *Argument against Abolishing Christianity* (1708) and *A Letter . . . Concerning the Sacramental Test* (1709), which damaged his relationship with the Whigs.

While in London as an emissary for the Irish clergy in 1708, Swift met Esther "Vanessa" Vanhomrigh (pronounced "Vanummry") and, as with "Stella," acted as her mentor. Although his feelings for this attractive young woman (twenty-one years younger than he) clearly became more than paternal, Swift was eventually put off by her declaration of "inexpressible passion" and wrote *Cadenus and Vanessa* (composed 1713, published 1726) to cool the relationship.

Vehemently disagreeing with the Whig policies supporting the Dissenters (Protestants who were not members of the established church) because he feared they would weaken the Anglican church, Swift shifted his allegiance to the Tories in 1710 and soon became their principal spokesman and propagandist, taking charge of their weekly periodical the *Examiner* (1710–1711) and producing a series of highly effective political pamphlets, such as *The Conduct of the Allies* (1712), which called for an end to the War of Spanish Succession (1701–1713). Swift's years in London from 1710 to 1714, when he was an important lobbyist for the Church of Ireland and an influential agent of the Tory government, were the most exciting of his life.

In 1713 Swift was installed as Dean of Saint Patrick's Cathedral, Dublin—a prestigious appointment, but far short of the English bishopric he felt he deserved. Returning quickly to London, Swift became a vital presence in the Scriblerus Club—with Alexander Pope, John Arbuthnot, John Gay, Thomas Parnell, and Robert Harley, Earl of Oxford—which met in 1714. The influence of this group, with its love of parody, literary hoaxes, and the ridicule of false learning, is evident in *Gulliver's Travels*. Upon the death of Queen Anne in 1714 and the resultant fall of the Tory Ministry, Swift's hopes for further advancement were dashed, and he took up permanent residence in Ireland, where he conscientiously carried out his duties as Dean.

When Swift successfully defended Irish interests by writing *The Drapier's Letters* (1724–1725)—attacking a government plan to impose a new coin, "Wood's halfpence," that would devalue Ireland's currency and seriously damage the economy—he became a national hero. Thereafter, the people lit bonfires on his birthday and hailed him as a champion of Irish liberty, though he never ceased to regard Ireland as the land of his exile. From Dublin, he corresponded with Pope, Gay, Arbuthnot, and Henry St. John, Lord Bolingbroke; he enjoyed a long visit with his friends in England in 1726. While there, he encouraged Gay's *The Beggar's Opera* and Pope's *The Dunciad*, and arranged for the publication of his own masterpiece, *Gulliver's Travels* (1726).

When the death of George I the following year briefly created hopes of unseating "Prime Minister" Robert Walpole, Swift paid his final visit to England, where he assisted Pope in editing their joint *Miscellanies* in three volumes (1727, 1728, 1732). The years that followed in Dublin saw the production of many of Swift's finest poems, including *The Lady's Dressing Room* (1732), *A Beautiful Young Nymph Going to Bed* (1734), and *Verses on the Death of Dr. Swift* (composed 1731–1732, published 1739), his most celebrated poem. Swift continued to champion the cause of Irish political and economic freedom; with his like-minded friend Thomas Sheridan, he conducted a weekly periodical, the *Intelligencer* (1728). In 1729, he published his most famous essay, *A Modest Proposal*. Some years later, he supervised the publication of the first four volumes of his *Works* (1735) by the Dublin publisher George Faulkener.

When Swift reached his early seventies, his infirmities made him incapable of carrying out his clerical duties at Saint Patrick's; at seventy-five, he was found "of unsound mind and memory," and guardians were appointed to manage his affairs. In addition to ongoing debilities from Ménière's syndrome, he suffered from arteriosclerosis, aphasia, memory loss, and other diseases of old age; he was not insane, however, as many of his contemporaries believed. A devoted clergyman, Swift practiced the Christian charity he preached, giving more than half of his income to the needy; the founding of Ireland's first mental hospital through a generous provision in his will was the most famous of Swift's many benefactions.

Voltaire hailed Swift as the "English Rabelais," while Henry Fielding lauded him as the "English Lucian." Although the more delicate sensibilities of the nineteenth century eschewed his writings for their coarseness and truculence, twentieth-century readers have prized Swift's work for its intelligence, wit, and inventiveness. A committed champion of social justice and an untiring enemy of pride, Swift was a brilliant satirist in part because he was a thoroughgoing humanist.

For additional resources on Swift, go to *The Longman Anthology of British Literature* Web site at www.myliteraturekit.com.

A Description of the Morning Introducing this poem in the ninth number of his new periodical, the *Tatler* (for 30 April 1709), Richard Steele wrote that Swift, "has . . . run into a way [of writing] perfectly new, and described things exactly as they happen." *A Description of the Morning* is an early and important example of the "town eclogue," or urban pastoral, a poetic style further popularized by John Gay's *Trivia, or The Art of Walking the Streets of London* (1716). Traditionally, the eclogue—Virgil's bucolic poems are the most famous example—has no appreciable action or characterization, but depends on the thorough and evocative depiction of a pastoral scene. Swift's *Morning* imitates the conventions of pastoral description, not to portray the idealized natural harmony of Arcadia but rather to present the reality of social disorder masquerading under the appearance of order as day breaks over London. Remarkably, Alexander Pope's *Pastorals*, his first published poems, went on sale in the same week that Swift's pioneering mock-pastoral appeared, though the two future friends would not meet for several years.

A Description of the Morning

Now hardly° here and there a hackney coach[1] *harshly*
Appearing, showed the ruddy morn's approach.
Now Betty[2] from her master's bed has flown,
And softly stole to discompose her own.
The slipshod 'prentice from his master's door
Had pared° the dirt, and sprinkled round the floor.[3] *reduced*
Now Moll had whirled her mop with dexterous airs,
Prepared to scrub the entry and the stairs.
The youth with broomy stumps began to trace
The kennel edge, where wheels had worn the place.[4]
The smallcoal man was heard with cadence deep;[5]
Till drowned in shriller notes of chimney sweep.
Duns° at his Lordship's gate began to meet; *creditors*
And brickdust[6] Moll had screamed through half a street.
The turnkey now his flock returning sees,
Duly let out a-nights to steal for fees.[7]
The watchful bailiffs take their silent stands;
And schoolboys lag with satchels in their hands.[8]

1709 1709

A Description of a City Shower "They say 'tis the best thing I ever writ, and I think so too," boasted Swift of his *Description of a City Shower* in 1710. It was first published in the *Tatler*, No. 238, on 17 October 1710, soon after its composition. Swift's closely observed rendering of London street life playfully mocks the English imitators of Virgil, especially John Dryden and his celebrated translation, *The Works of Virgil* (1697). We see, for example, Swift's

1. A hired coach, drawn by two horses and seating six people; here, equated with the chariot of Phoebus Apollo, Greek god of the sun.
2. Like "Moll" (line 7), a typical maidservant's name.
3. Fresh sawdust was used to absorb mud.
4. Scavenging in the gutters (kennels) "to find old nails" [Swift's note] was common.
5. Small pieces of coal or charcoal used to light fires; like many other products and services, they were sold by street vendors who advertised, or "cried," their wares by calling or singing as they walked the streets. The smallcoal man has a deep voice; sweeps were always small boys.
6. An abrasive, used for cleaning or for sharpening knives.
7. As prisoners had to pay the jailer for food and for other comforts, the jailer has let them out overnight to steal.
8. Cf. the second "age of man" in Shakespeare's *As You Like It*: "Then the whining schoolboy, with his satchel / And shining morning face, creeping like snail / Unwillingly to school" (2.7.145–47).

mock-heroic effects based on Virgil's *Aeneid* (29–19 B.C.E.), most notably in comparing the timorous "beau" trapped in his sedan chair to the fierce Greek warriors hiding inside the Trojan Horse, and in calling to mind the storm that led to Queen Dido's seduction and eventual ruin (Dryden's translation 4.231–238). More important, just as Swift invoked the mock-pastoral in *A Description of the Morning*, so too does he create a mock-georgic mode in his *City Shower*. The division of the poem into portents, preliminaries, and deluge closely parallels the tempest scene in Virgil's *Georgics* (36–29 B.C.E.; bk. 1, 431–458, 483–538 in Dryden), so that Swift uses structural and verbal elements from a classical poem extolling the virtues of agriculture and rural life to depict the teeming diversity of the contemporary urban scene.

A Description of a City Shower

Careful observers may foretell the hour
(By sure prognostics) when to dread a shower.
While rain depends,° the pensive cat gives o'er *is impending*
Her frolics, and pursues her tail no more.
Returning home at night you find the sink[1]
Strike your offended sense with double stink.
If you be wise, then go not far to dine,
You spend in coach-hire more than save in wine.
A coming shower your shooting corns[2] presage,
Old aches[3] throb, your hollow tooth will rage:
Sauntering in coffee-house is Dulman seen;
He damns the climate, and complains of spleen.[4]

Meanwhile the South,° rising with dabbled° wings, *south wind / muddy*
A sable cloud athwart the welkin° flings; *sky*
That swilled more liquor than it could contain,
And like a drunkard gives it up again.
Brisk Susan whips her linen from the rope,[5]
While the first drizzling shower is borne aslope:° *at a slant*
Such is that sprinkling which some careless quean° *hussy*
Flirts° on you from her mop, but not so clean: *flicks*
You fly, invoke the gods; then turning, stop
To rail; she singing, still whirls on her mop.
Nor yet the dust had shunned th' unequal strife,
But aided by the wind, fought still for life;
And wafted with its foe by violent gust,
'Twas doubtful which was rain, and which was dust.[6]
Ah! Where must needy poet seek for aid,
When dust and rain at once his coat invade?
Sole coat, where dust cemented by the rain
Erects the nap, and leaves a cloudy stain.

1. Sewer. The poem is built upon Swift's experiences in London: on 8 November 1710, Swift wrote to his beloved Stella (Esther Johnson) that "I will give ten shillings a week for my lodging; for I am almost stunk out of this with the sink, and it helps me to verses in my Shower." The parsimonious Swift normally spent around half this amount for lodgings.
2. The shooting pain in your corns.
3. Pronounced "aitches."
4. Dulman (a descriptive name) complains of melancholy or depression, then attributed to the spleen.
5. The typically named maid brings in her washing from the line.
6. Swift here parallels a line from Samuel Garth's popular satirical poem, *The Dispensary* (1699): "'Tis doubtful which is sea, and which is sky" (5.176).

Now in contiguous drops the flood comes down,
Threatening with deluge this devoted° town. *doomed*
To shops in crowds the daggled° females fly, *muddied*
Pretend to cheapen° goods, but nothing buy. *bargain for*
The Templer spruce,[7] while every spout's abroach,[8]
Stays till 'tis fair, yet seems to call a coach.
The tucked-up seamstress walks with hasty strides,
While streams run down her oiled umbrella's sides.
Here various kinds by various fortunes led,
Commence acquaintance underneath a shed.° *shelter*
Triumphant Tories, and desponding Whigs,[9]
Forget their feuds, and join to save their wigs.
Boxed° in a chair[1] the beau impatient sits, *confined*
While spouts run clattering o'er the roof by fits;
And ever and anon with frightful din
The leather sounds; he trembles from within.
So when Troy chairmen bore the wooden steed,
Pregnant with Greeks, impatient to be freed;
(Those bully Greeks, who, as the moderns do,
Instead of paying chairmen, run them through[2])
Laocoon struck the outside with his spear,
And each imprisoned hero quaked for fear.[3]

Now from all parts the swelling kennels[4] flow,
And bear their trophies with them as they go:
Filths of all hues and odors, seem to tell
What streets they sailed from, by the sight and smell.
They, as each torrent drives with rapid force
From Smithfield, or St. Pulchre's shape their course;[5]
And in huge confluent join at Snow Hill ridge,
Fall from the conduit prone to Holborn Bridge.[6]
Sweepings from butchers' stalls, dung, guts, and blood,
Drowned puppies, stinking sprats,° all drenched in mud, *small fish*
Dead cats and turnip tops come tumbling down the flood.[7]

1710 1710

STELLA'S BIRTHDAY Between 1719 and 1727 Swift wrote seven birthday poems to "Stella," his dear Esther Johnson. The two reprinted here are his first and last. Swift's earliest use of the name "Stella" in verse was in the first of this series of celebratory verses, which

7. Well-dressed lawyer.
8. Drainpipe pouring water.
9. 1710, the year this poem was written, was the first year of the Tory ministry under Queen Anne.
1. A sedan chair, carried by two men; this one has a leather roof.
2. With their swords.
3. When the Trojans carried the Greek's wooden horse into Troy, thinking that the opposing army had given up their siege, the priest Laocoon was suspicious, and struck the horse. See *Aeneid* 2.50–53.
4. Gutters, which were also open sewers.
5. Respectively, the cattle market and the parish west of the Newgate prison.
6. Snow Hill ridge extended down to Holborn Bridge, which spanned Fleet ditch, used as an open sewer; from 1343, local butchers had been given permission to dump entrails in the Fleet.
7. These last three lines were intended against the licentious manner of modern poets, in making three rhymes together, which they call *Triplets*; and the last of the three was two, or sometimes more syllables longer, called an *Alexandrian*. These *Triplets* and *Alexandrians* were brought in by Dryden, and other poets in the reign of Charles II. They were the mere effect of haste, idleness, and want of money, and have been wholly avoided by the best poets since these verses were written [Swift's note].

play on the obligation of the Poet Laureate to write an official "birthday ode" for the monarch every year. Placing himself in the role of her laureate, Swift may have chosen the name "Stella" to highlight the difference between his own uncontrived expressions of affection and those of the courtly Sir Philip Sidney in *Astrophil and Stella* (1591). Like Shakespeare's Sonnet 130 ("My mistress' eyes are nothing like the sun"), Swift's first poem on Stella's birthday violates the traditions of the conventional love lyric by calling attention to his beloved's considerable weight and age, only to suggest that his admiration of her lies in her deeper virtues. In his last birthday poem, Swift attempts to escape from the prospect of Stella's impending death, first by humor and then by the power of reason; when these fail, he tenderly acknowledges how much she means to him. Swift was to sail for England less than a month after he gave those verses to her—both knew that they might never see each other again. Though more formal than the *Journal to Stella*, Swift's birthday verses were written primarily for Stella's enjoyment and for the entertainment of their small circle of intimate friends. Despite the private nature of these poems, Swift nevertheless authorized their publication in the third and last volume of the Pope-Swift *Miscellanies*, which appeared in March 1728.

Stella's Birthday, 1719

WRITTEN IN THE YEAR 1718/9[1]

Stella this day is thirty-four,[2]
(We shan't dispute a year or more):
However, Stella, be not troubled,
Although thy size and years are doubled,
Since first I saw thee at sixteen,[3]
The brightest virgin on the green.[4]
So little is thy form° declined; *figure*
Made up° so largely in thy mind. *compensated*

Oh, would it please the gods to *split*
Thy beauty, size, and years, and wit,
No age could furnish out a pair
Of nymphs so graceful, wise, and fair:
With half the luster of your eyes,
With half your wit, your years, and size:
And then before it grew too late,
How should I beg of gentle fate,
(That either nymph might have her swain),
To split my worship too in twain.

1719 1728

1. Until the calendar was reformed in 1751, the new year legally began on the Feast of the Annunciation (sometimes called "Lady Day") on March 25th, though January 1st was also commonly recognized as the start of the new year. Therefore, to avoid confusion, it was a widely accepted practice to write dates between January 1 and March 24 according to both methods of reckoning: 1718/19. Since Swift's poem was composed in February or March, we would say it was written in 1719.

2. Stella (Esther Johnson) actually celebrated her thirty-eighth birthday on 13 March 1719.

3. Swift first met Stella when she was eight years old; he may have "seen" her only when she grew from child to woman.

4. The village green, or common land, here implies a pastoral simplicity that suggests the natural innocence of their relationship.

Stella's Birthday, 1727

This day, whate'er the fates decree,
Shall still be kept with joy by me:
This day then, let us not be told,
That you are sick, and I grown old,
Nor think on our approaching ills,
And talk of spectacles and pills.
Tomorrow will be time enough
To hear such mortifying stuff.[1]
Yet, since from reason may be brought
A better and more pleasing thought,
Which can in spite of all decays,
Support a few remaining days:
From not the gravest of divines,° *clergymen*
Accept for once some serious lines.

Although we now can form no more
Long schemes of life, as heretofore;
Yet you, while time is running fast,
Can look with joy on what is past.

Were future happiness and pain[2]
A mere contrivance of the brain,
As atheists argue, to entice
And fit their proselytes° for vice *converts*
(The only comfort they propose,
To have companions in their woes);
Grant this the case, yet sure 'tis hard,
That virtue, styled its own reward,
And by all sages understood
To be the chief of human good,
Should acting, die, nor leave behind
Some lasting pleasure in the mind;
Which by remembrance will assuage
Grief, sickness, poverty, and age;
And strongly shoot a radiant dart
To shine through life's declining part.

Say, Stella, feel you no content,
Reflecting on a life well spent?
Your skillful hand employed to save
Despairing wretches from the grave;[3]
And then supporting with your store,
Those whom you dragged from death before
(So Providence on mortals waits,
Preserving what it first creates);
Your generous boldness to defend

1. Both humbling and leading to death. Stella died less than a year later.
2. I.e., heaven and hell.
3. Swift often praised Stella's charity, not only for nursing him in his bouts of illness, but also for attending to the poor in her neighborhood.

An innocent and absent friend;
That courage which can make you just,
To merit humbled in the dust;
The detestation you express
For vice in all its glittering dress;
That patience under torturing pain,
Where stubborn Stoics would complain.

Shall these like empty shadows pass,
Or forms reflected from a glass?
Or mere chimeras° in the mind, *imaginary creatures or notions*
That fly and leave no marks behind?
Does not the body thrive and grow
By food of twenty years ago?
And had it not been still supplied,
It must a thousand times have died.
Then, who with reason can maintain
That no effects of food remain?
And is not virtue in mankind
The nutriment that feeds the mind?
Upheld by each good action past,
And still continued by the last:
Then who with reason can pretend,
That all effects of virtue end?

Believe me, Stella, when you show
That true contempt for things below,
Nor prize your life for other ends
Than merely to oblige your friends;
Your former actions claim their part,
And join to fortify your heart.
For Virtue in her daily race,
Like Janus[4] bears a double face;
Looks back with joy where she has gone,
And therefore goes with courage on.
She at your sickly couch will wait,
And guide you to a better state.

O then, whatever Heaven intends,
Take pity on your pitying friends;
Nor let your ills affect your mind,
To fancy they can be unkind.
Me, surely me, you ought to spare,
Who gladly would your sufferings share;
Or give my scrap of life to you,
And think it far beneath your due;
You, to whose care so oft I owe
That I'm alive to tell you so.

1727 1728

4. The god of doorways and of the rising and setting sun, whose two-faced head looks forward and backward, and after whom the month of January is named.

The Lady's Dressing Room The first of Swift's so-called scatological poems, which have attracted much critical attention and amateur psychoanalysis, these verses enjoyed considerable popularity in Swift's lifetime, though some contemporaries condemned them as "deficient in point of delicacy, even to the highest degree." One of Swift's friends recorded in her memoirs that *The Lady's Dressing Room* made her mother "instantly" lose her lunch. Sir Walter Scott found in this poem (and other pieces by Swift) "the marks of an incipient disorder of the mind, which induced the author to dwell on degrading and disgusting subjects." If Pope's *The Rape of the Lock* describes Belinda at the "altar" of her dressing table undergoing "the sacred rites of pride" as she and her maid apply all manner of cosmetics to make her a beautiful "goddess" and arm her for the battle of the sexes, then *The Lady's Dressing Room* reveals the coarse realities of Celia's embodiment—a humorous and disturbing corrective to the pretense and false appearances on which her glorification depends. Although Swift assails the social and literary conventions that celebrate women for their superficial qualities, there is also a misogynistic quality to the poem, which may be attributable to his anger and disappointment over his beloved Stella's death in January 1728. Nevertheless, Strephon is ridiculed for being so naively idealistic about his lover and so easily deceived by appearances; once his secret investigations free him from his illusions, Strephon's permanent revulsion and rejection of all women show his inability to follow a middle course by appreciating women in their complex reality.

The Lady's Dressing Room

Five hours (and who can do it less in?)
By haughty Celia spent in dressing;
The goddess from her chamber issues,
Arrayed in lace, brocade, and tissues:
Strephon,[1] who found the room was void,
And Betty[2] otherwise employed,
Stole in, and took a strict survey,
Of all the litter as it lay:
Whereof, to make the matter clear,
An *inventory* follows here.

And first, a dirty smock appeared,
Beneath the arm-pits well besmeared;
Strephon, the rogue, displayed it wide,
And turned it round on every side.
In such a case few words are best,
And Strephon bids us guess the rest;
But swears how damnably the men lie,
In calling Celia sweet and cleanly.

Now listen while he next produces
The various combs for various uses,
Filled up with dirt so closely fixed,
No brush could force a way betwixt;
A paste of composition rare,
Sweat, dandruff, powder, lead,[3] and hair,

1. Strephon and Celia are names usually associated with pastoral poetry, and are therefore used mockingly here.

2. A typical maidservant's name.

3. White lead face paint, used to whiten the skin.

A forehead cloth with oil upon't
To smooth the wrinkles on her front;
Here alum flour[4] to stop the steams,
Exhaled from sour, unsavory streams;
There night-gloves made of Tripsy's[5] hide,
Bequeathed by Tripsy when she died;
With puppy water,[6] beauty's help,
Distilled from Tripsy's darling whelp.
Here gallipots° and vials placed, *ointment jars*
Some filled with washes, some with paste;
Some with pomatum,° paints, and slops, *hair ointment*
And ointments good for scabby chops.° *lips or cheeks*
Hard° by a filthy basin stands, *close*
Fouled with the scouring of her hands;
The basin takes whatever comes,
The scrapings of her teeth and gums,
A nasty compound of all hues,
For here she spits, and here she spews.

But oh! it turned poor Strephon's bowels,
When he beheld and smelt the towels;
Begummed, bemattered, and beslimed;
With dirt, and sweat, and ear-wax grimed.
No object Strephon's eye escapes,
Here, petticoats in frowzy° heaps; *unkempt*
Nor be the handkerchiefs forgot,
All varnished o'er with snuff[7] and snot.
The stockings why should I expose,
Stained with the moisture of her toes;
Or greasy coifs and pinners° reeking, *night caps*
Which Celia slept at least a week in?
A pair of tweezers next he found
To pluck her brows in arches round,
Or hairs that sink the forehead low,
Or on her chin like bristles grow.

The virtues we must not let pass
Of Celia's magnifying glass;
When frighted Strephon cast his eye on't,
It showed the visage of a giant:[8]
A glass that can to sight disclose
The smallest worm in Celia's nose,

4. Powdered alum used like modern antiperspirant.
5. Celia's lapdog; no fashionable lady was without such a pet.
6. A recipe for this cosmetic, made from the innards of a pig or a fat puppy, was given in the "Fop's Dictionary" in *Mundus Muliebris* [Womanly Make-up]: *Or, the Ladies' Dressing Room Unlocked* (1690), which Swift also used for other terms.
7. Powdered tobacco, sniffed by fashionable men and women alike.
8. Cf. *Gulliver's Travels*, Part 2, "A Voyage to Brobdingnag," ch. 1: "This made me reflect upon the fair skins of our *English* ladies, who appear so beautiful to us, only because they are of our own size, and their defects not to be seen but through magnifying glass, where we find by experiment that the smoothest and whitest skins look rough and coarse, and ill colored."

And faithfully direct her nail
To squeeze it out from head to tail;
For catch it nicely by the head,
It must come out alive or dead.

Why, Strephon, will you tell the rest?
And must you needs describe the chest?
That careless wench! no creature warn her
To move it out from yonder corner,
But leave it standing full in sight,
For you to exercise your spite!
In vain the workman showed his wit
With rings and hinges counterfeit
To make it seem in this disguise
A cabinet to vulgar eyes;
Which Strephon ventured to look in,
Resolved to go through *thick and thin;*
He lifts the lid: there need no more,
He smelt it all the time before.

As, from within Pandora's box,
When Epimethus oped the locks,
A sudden universal crew
Of human evils upward flew;[9]
He still was comforted to find
That hope at last remained behind.

So, Strephon, lifting up the lid
To view what in the chest was hid,
The vapors flew from out the vent,
But Strephon cautious never meant
The bottom of the pan to grope,
And foul his hands in search of hope.

O! ne'er may such a vile machine° *construction*
Be once in Celia's chamber seen!
O! may she better learn to keep
"Those secrets of the hoary deep."[1]

As mutton cutlets, prime of meat,
Which though with art you salt and beat
As laws of cookery require,
And roast them at the clearest fire;
If from adown the hopeful chops
The fat upon a cinder drops,
To stinking smoke it turns the flame

9. In Greek mythology, Epimethus, acting against advice, opened the box Jove had given his wife Pandora, and all the evils and vices of the world flew out, leaving only hope in the box.

1. Quoting Milton's *Paradise Lost* 2.891, in which Sin is unleashing the chaotic forces of her infernal realm.

Poisoning the flesh from whence it came;
And up exhales a greasy stench
For which you curse the careless wench:
So things which must not be expressed,
When *plumped*° into the reeking chest, *dropped*
Send up an excremental smell
To taint the parts from which they fell:
The petticoats and gown perfume,
And waft a stink round every room.

Thus finishing his grand survey,
The swain disgusted slunk away,
Repeating in his amorous fits,
"Oh! Celia, Celia, Celia shits!"

But Vengeance, goddess never sleeping,
Soon punished Strephon for his peeping.
His foul imagination links
Each dame he sees with all her stinks:
And if unsavory odors fly,
Conceives a lady standing by:
All women his description fits,
And both ideas jump° like wits *join together*
By vicious fancy coupled fast,
And still appearing in contrast.

I pity wretched Strephon, blind
To all the charms of womankind;
Should I the queen of love refuse,
Because she rose from stinking ooze?[2]
To him that looks behind the scene,
Statira's but some pocky quean.[3]

When Celia in her glory shows,
If Strephon would but stop his nose,
Who now so impiously blasphemes
Her ointments, daubs, and paints and creams;
Her washes, slops, and every clout,[4]
With which she makes so foul a rout;[5]
He soon would learn to think like me,
And bless his ravished eyes to see
Such order from confusion sprung,
Such gaudy *tulips* raised from *dung*.

c. 1730 1732

2. Venus, Roman goddess of sexual love and physical beauty, rose from the sea.

3. One of the heroines of Nathaniel Lee's highly popular tragedy *The Rival Queens* (1677); Swift's common slattern (quean) has had either smallpox or venereal disease.

4. Washes were either treated water used for the complexion or stale urine used as a detergent; clouts were rags.

5. Both of her skin and, presumably, of the men.

Response

Lady Mary Wortley Montagu: The Reasons that Induced Dr. S. to write a Poem called The Lady's Dressing Room[1]

The Doctor in a clean starched band,
His golden snuff box in his hand,
With care his diamond ring displays
And artful shows its various rays,
While grave he stalks down —— street
His dearest Betty —— to meet.[2]
  Long had he waited for this hour,
Nor gained admittance to the bower,
Had joked and punned, and swore and writ,
Tried all his gallantry and wit,[3]
Had told her oft what part he bore
In Oxford's schemes in days of yore,[4]
But bawdy,° politics, nor satire — *obscenity*
Could move this dull hard hearted creature.
Jenny her maid could taste° a rhyme — *enjoy*
And, grieved to see him lose his time,
Had kindly whispered in his ear,
"For twice two pound you enter here;
My lady vows without that sum
It is in vain you write or come."
  The destined offering now he brought,
And in a paradise of thought,
With a low bow approached the dame,
Who smiling heard him preach his flame.
His gold she takes (such proofs as these
Convince most unbelieving shes)
And in her trunk rose up to lock it
(Too wise to trust it in her pocket)
And then, returned with blushing grace,
Expects the doctor's warm embrace.
  But now this is the proper place
Where morals stare me in the face,
And for the sake of fine expression
I'm forced to make a small digression.
Alas for wretched humankind,
With learning mad, with wisdom blind!

1. Lady Mary Wortley Montagu, energetic traveler and versatile writer, found in Swift an object of recurrent scorn. *Gulliver's Travels* (and particularly its fourth book) she dismissed as filth, perpetrated upon a "mad" and inexplicably admiring readership. When "The Lady's Dressing Room" appeared, Montagu crafted her own verse retort. Here, with formidable mimicry, she echoes Swift's method (the catalogue of disconcerting physical particulars), his meter, his phrasings, and his thoughts in such a way that they recoil upon their maker. What Swift depicts as disillusion (Strephon's), Montagu re-reckons as self-delusion (Swift's). The trauma that he derives from Celia's fabrications, she ascribes instead to the Dean's own fears and failures. (For more on Montagu, see page 2543.)

2. In Swift's poem, Betty is the maid's name, Celia the mistress's.

3. Montagu echoes Swift's poem *Cadenus and Vanessa*, where the clumsy lover "Had sighed and languished, vowed and writ, / For pastime, or to show his wit" (542–43).

4. Swift had collaborated closely in the political schemes of Robert Harley, first Earl of Oxford (1661–1724).

The ox thinks he's for saddle fit
(As long ago friend Horace writ[5])
And men their talents still mistaking,[6]
The stutterer fancies his is speaking.
With admiration oft we see
Hard features heightened by toupée,
The beau affects° the politician, *pretends to be*
Wit is the citizen's ambition,
Poor Pope philosophy displays on
With so much rhyme and little reason,
And though he argues ne'er so long
That all is right, his head is wrong.[7]
None strive to know their proper merit
But strain for wisdom, beauty, spirit,
And lose the praise that is their due
While they've th' impossible in view.
So have I seen the injudicious heir
To add one window the whole house impair.
Instinct the hound does better teach,
Who never undertook to preach;
The frighted hare from dogs does run
But not attempts to bear a gun.
Here many noble thoughts occur
But I prolixity abhor,
And will pursue th' instructive tale
To show the wise in some things fail.
The reverend lover with surprise
Peeps in her bubbies, and her eyes,
And kisses both, and tries—and tries.
The evening in this hellish play,
Beside his guineas thrown away,
Provoked the priest to that degree
He swore, "The fault is not in me.
Your damned close stool° so near my nose, *chamber pot*
Your dirty smock, and stinking toes
Would make a Hercules as tame
As any beau that you can name."[8]
The nymph grown furious roared, "By God
The blame lies all in sixty odd,"[9]
And scornful pointing to the door
Cried, "Fumbler, see my face no more."
"With all my heart I'll go away,
But nothing done, I'll nothing pay.
Give back the money." "How," cried she,

5. "The ox desires the saddle" (Horace, *Epistles* 1.14.43).
6. In this line, Montague echoes an idea, and a way of wording it, that Swift used often in his work.
7. Montagu ridicules Pope's conclusion to Epistle 1 of *An Essay on Man*: "Whatever IS, is RIGHT" (see page 2509). Over the previous few years, her long, ardent friendship with Pope had dissolved in rancor.
8. In these four lines, Montagu compacts some scattered particulars and the sustained conclusion of Swift's poem: ll. 11–14, 51–52, 69 ff.
9. I.e., Swift's impotence derives not from her odors but from his age (65 at the time the poem was written).

"Would you palm such a cheat on me!
For poor four pound to roar and bellow—
Why sure you want some new Prunella?"[1]
"I'll be revenged, you saucy quean"° *whore*
(Replies the disappointed Dean)
"I'll so describe your dressing room
The very Irish shall not come."
She answered short, "I'm glad you'll write.
You'll furnish paper when I shite."[2]

Verses on the Death of Dr. Swift "I have been several months writing near five hundred lines on a pleasant subject," wrote Swift to his friend John Gay in December 1731, "only to tell what my friends and enemies will say on me after I am dead." Swift completed what was to become his most celebrated poem by adding explanatory notes in the early months of 1732. It seems that Swift intended the *Verses* to be published after his death but showed the poem in manuscript to various friends. When the reputation of his *Verses* spread, Swift used the opportunity to publish a different autobiographical poem, *The Life and Genuine Character of Dr. Swift* (1733), which would satisfy public demand and make the eventual appearance of the *Verses* all the more surprising. Six years later, believing they were doing their friend a service, Alexander Pope and William King (1685–1763) published a version of the poem in which they edited out some of Swift's most self-aggrandizing and controversial lines. Swift was "much dissatisfied" with this London edition and responded by supervising the speedy publication of an unexpurgated text of the work in Dublin, though even he had the prudence to leave blank spaces for some of the names in his poem. Among the most controversial elements in the *Verses* were its direct attack on Prime Minister Robert Walpole and his government; the unflattering depiction of the court and singling out of Lady Suffolk and Queen Caroline for ridicule; and Swift's praise of Bolingbroke and Pulteney, leading opposition politicians. Swift's jaunty tetrameter carries an admixture of self-fashioning for posterity and moral instruction, a spirited apologia for his life and writings, and an idealized account of the principles by which he strove to live. *Verses on the Death of Dr. Swift* reveals its subject as a champion of liberty and embattled self-promoter, a humanistic preacher and an unsparing satirist.

Verses on the Death of Dr. Swift, D.S.P.D.[1]
Occasioned by Reading a Maxim in Rochefoucauld

Dans l'adversité de nos meilleurs amis nous trouvons quelque chose, qui ne nous deplaist pas.[2]

"In the adversity of our best friends, we find something that doth not displease us."

As Rochefoucauld his maxims drew
From Nature, I believe 'em true:
They argue° no corrupted mind *suggest*
In him; the fault is in mankind.

1. "Prunella" is both a fabric used in clergy vestments (Swift was a clergyman), and the name of the promiscuous, low-born heroine in Richard Estcourt's comic interlude, *Prunella* (1708).
2. Compare line 118 of Swift's poem.

1. Dean of St. Patrick's, Dublin.
2. François, duc de La Rochefoucauld, *Réflexions ou Sentences et Maximes Morales* ("Reflections or Moral Aphorisms and Maxims," 1665).

This maxim more than all the rest
Is thought too base for human breast;
"In all distresses of our friends
We first consult our private ends,
While Nature kindly bent to ease us,
Points out some circumstance to please us."

If this perhaps your patience move° *strains*
Let reason and experience prove.

We all behold with envious eyes,
Our equal raised above our size;
Who would not at a crowded show,
Stand high himself, keep others low?
I love my friend as well as you,
But would not have him stop my view;
Then let me have the higher post;
I ask but for an inch at most.

If in a battle you should find,
One, whom you love of all mankind,
Had some heroic action done,
A champion killed, or trophy won;
Rather than thus be overtopped,
Would you not wish his laurels[3] cropped?

Dear honest Ned is in the gout,[4]
Lies racked with pain, and you without:[5]
How patiently you hear him groan!
How glad the case is not your own!

What poet would not grieve to see,
His brethren write as well as he?
But rather than they should excel,
He'd wish his rivals all in Hell.

Her end when emulation misses,
She turns to envy, stings, and hisses:
The strongest friendship yields to pride,
Unless the odds be on our side.

Vain humankind! Fantastic race!
Thy various follies, who can trace?
Self-love, ambition, envy, pride,
Their empire in our hearts divide:
Give others riches, power, and station,
'Tis all on me a usurpation.
I have no title to aspire;

3. In ancient times, laurel wreaths were given to poets, athletes, and war heroes to signify their preeminence.
4. A disease characterized by an inflammation of small joints, especially in the feet and hands.
5. Outside his room.

Yet, when you sink, I seem the higher.
In Pope,[6] I cannot read a line,
But with a sigh, I wish it mine:
When he can in one couplet fix
More sense than I can do in six:
It gives me such a jealous fit,
I cry, "Pox take him, and his wit."

Why must I be outdone by Gay,[7]
In my own humorous, biting way?

Arbuthnot[8] is no more my friend,
Who dares to irony pretend;
Which I was born to introduce,
Refined it first, and showed its use.

St. John, as well as Pulteney[9] knows,
That I had some repute for prose;
And till they drove me out of date,
Could maul a minister of state:
If they have mortified my pride,
And made me throw my pen aside;
If with such talents Heaven hath blest 'em,
Have I not reason to detest 'em?

To all my foes, dear fortune, send
Thy gifts, but never to my friend:
I tamely can endure the first,
But, this with envy makes me burst.

Thus much may serve by way of proem,° *preface*
Proceed we therefore to our poem.

The time is not remote, when I
Must by the course of nature die:
When I foresee my special friends,
Will try to find their private ends:
Though it is hardly understood,[1]
Which way my death can do them good;
Yet, thus methinks, I hear 'em speak;
"See, how the Dean begins to break:° *weaken*
Poor gentleman, he droops apace,° *quickly*
You plainly find it in his face:
That old vertigo in his head
Will never leave him, till he's dead:

6. Alexander Pope, poet, satirist, and friend of Swift.
7. John Gay, poet and playwright, author of *The Beggar's Opera* (1728), friend of Swift, Pope, and Arbuthnot.
8. John Arbuthnot (1667–1735), physician to Queen Anne and member of Scriblerus Club along with Swift, Pope, and Gay; he was the principal author of *Memoirs of . . . Martinus Scriblerus* (1741).
9. Henry St. John Bolingbroke (1678–1751) and William Pulteney; both politicians—one a Tory, the other a Whig—were united in their opposition to Robert Walpole. See Swift's notes to lines 194 and 196.
1. Hard to understand.

Besides, his memory decays,
He recollects not what he says;
He cannot call his friends to mind;
Forgets the place where last he dined:
Plies you with stories o'er and o'er,
He told them fifty times before.
How does he fancy we can sit
To hear his out-of-fashioned wit?
But he takes up with younger folks,
Who for his wine will bear his jokes:
Faith,° he must make his stories shorter, *in truth*
Or change his comrades once a quarter:
In half the time, he talks them round;[2]
There must another set be found.

"For poetry, he's past his prime,
He takes an hour to find a rhyme:
His fire° is out, his wit decayed, *creative fire*
His fancy sunk, his muse a jade.[3]
I'd have him throw away his pen;
But there's no talking to some men."

And then their tenderness appears,
By adding largely to my years:
"He's older than he would be reckoned,
And well remembers Charles the Second."[4]

"He hardly° drinks a pint of wine; *barely*
And that, I doubt,° is no good sign. *suspect*
His stomach° too begins to fail: *appetite*
Last year we thought him strong and hale;
But now, he's quite another thing;
I wish he may hold out till spring."

Then hug themselves, and reason thus:
"It is not yet so bad with us."

In such a case they talk in tropes,° *figuratively*
And by their fears express their hopes:
Some great misfortune to portend,° *predict*
No enemy can match a friend;
With all the kindness they profess,
The merit of a lucky guess
(When daily "Howd'y's"[5] come of course,° *routinely*
And servants answer: "Worse and worse")
Would please 'em better than to tell
That, God be praised, the Dean is well.

2. Runs through his stock of stories and has to begin again.
3. The poet's muse—his inspiration (always female)—is here a worn-out horse or a disreputable or shrewish woman.
4. King Charles II died in 1685, when Swift was 18.
5. How does [is] he?

Then he who prophesied the best,
Approves° his foresight to the rest: *confirms*
"You know, I always feared the worst,
And often told you so at first":
He'd rather choose that I should die
Than his prediction prove a lie.
No one foretells I shall recover;
But, all agree to give me over.° *give up hope*

Yet should some neighbor feel a pain
Just in the parts where I complain;
How many a message would he send?
What hearty prayers that I should mend?
Inquire what regimen[6] I kept;
What gave me ease, and how I slept?
And more lament, when I was dead,
Than all the snivellers round my bed.

My good companions, never fear,
For though you may mistake a year;
Though your prognostics run too fast,
They must be verified at last.

"Behold the fatal day arrive!
How is the Dean? He's just alive.
Now the departing prayer is read:
He hardly breathes. The Dean is dead.
Before the passing bell[7] begun,
The news through half the town has run.
O, may we all for death prepare!
What has he left? And who's his heir?
I know no more than what the news is,
'Tis all bequeathed to public uses.[8]
To public use! A perfect whim!
What had the public done for him?
Mere envy, avarice, and pride!
He gave it all.—But first he died.
And had the Dean, in all the nation,
No worthy friend, no poor relation?
So ready to do strangers good,
Forgetting his own flesh and blood?"

Now Grub Street wits[9] are all employed;
With elegies, the town is cloyed:

6. Prescribed pattern of living, exercising, and eating.
7. Death bell, rung to obtain prayers for the passing soul.
8. In fact, when Swift died he left a number of small personal bequests in addition to his large gifts to public charities.
9. Hack writers, paid to produce (often libelous) materials for London journals.

Some paragraph in every paper,
To curse the Dean, or bless the Drapier.[1]

The doctors tender of their fame,
Wisely on me lay all the blame:
"We must confess his case was nice,° *difficult*
But he would never take advice;
Had he been ruled, for aught appears,
He might have lived these twenty years:
For when we opened him we found
That all his vital parts were sound."

From Dublin soon to London spread,[2]
'Tis told at court, the Dean is dead.

Kind Lady Suffolk[3] in the spleen,[4]
Runs laughing up to tell the Queen.
The Queen, so gracious, mild, and good,
Cries, "Is he gone? 'Tis time he should.
He's dead you say, why let him rot;
I'm glad the medals were forgot.[5]
I promised them, I own;° but when? *admit*
I only was a princess then;
But now as consort of the King,
You know 'tis quite a different thing."

Now, Chartres[6] at Sir Robert's levee,[7]
Tells, with a sneer, the tidings heavy:
"Why, is he dead without his shoes?"[8]
(Cries Bob)[9] "I'm sorry for the news;
Oh, were the wretch but living still,

1. The Author imagines, that the Scribblers of the prevailing Party, which he always opposed, will libel him after his Death; but that others will remember him with gratitude, who consider the service he had done to Ireland, under the name of M. B. Drapier [Swift's note, referring to *The Drapier's Letters* (1724–1725), a series of essays he wrote to defend Ireland from the British government's plan to impose a new coin, "Wood's halfpence," that would have devastated Ireland's economy].
2. The Dean supposeth himself to die in Ireland [Swift's note]; he did.
3. Mrs. Howard, afterwards Countess of Suffolk, then of the Bedchamber to the Queen, professed much friendship for the Dean. The Queen, then Princess, sent a dozen times to the Dean (then in London) with her command to attend her; which at last he did, by advice of all his friends. She often sent for him afterwards, and always treated him very graciously. He taxed her with a present worth ten pounds, which she promised before he should return to Ireland, but on his taking leave, the medals were not ready" [Swift's note].
4. The 18th-century equivalent of "depression."
5. The medals were to be sent to the Dean in four months, but she forgot them, or thought them too dear [expensive]. The Dean, being in Ireland, sent Mrs. Howard a piece of Indian plaid made in that kingdom [Ireland]: which the Queen seeing took from her, and wore it herself, and sent to the Dean for as much as would clothe herself and her children, desiring he would send charge of it. He did the former. It cost thirty-five pounds, but he said he would have nothing except the medals. He was the summer following in England, was treated as usual, and she being then Queen, the Dean was promised a settlement in England, but returned as he went, and, instead of favor or medals, hath been ever since under her Majesty's displeasure [Swift's note].
6. Chartres is a most infamous, vile scoundrel, grown from a foot-boy, or worse, to a prodigious fortune [Swift's note]. Francis Charteris was convicted of rape, and pardoned by the prime minister, Robert Walpole, in 1730.
7. A morning audience held in the bedchamber of a person of distinction before or after rising.
8. I.e., in his bed, rather than meeting a violent death or being hanged.
9. Sir Robert Walpole, Chief Minister of State, treated the Dean, in 1726, with great distinction, invited him to dinner at Chelsea, with the Dean's friends chosen on purpose; appointed an hour to talk with him of Ireland, to which kingdom and people the Dean found him no great friend. . . . The Dean would see him no more [Swift's note].

And in his place my good friend Will;[1]
Or had a miter° on his head, *bishop's hat*
Provided Bolingbroke[2] were dead."

Now Curll his shop from rubbish drains:
Three genuine tomes of Swift's remains.[3]
And then to make them pass the glibber,° *sell better*
Revised by Tibbalds, Moore, and Cibber.[4]
He'll treat me as he does my betters:
Publish my will, my life, my letters,[5]
Revive the libels born to die;
Which Pope must bear, as well as I.

Here shift the scene, to represent
How those I love, my death lament.
Poor Pope will grieve a month; and Gay
A week; and Arbuthnot a day.

St. John himself will scarce forbear
To bite his pen, and drop a tear.
The rest will give a shrug and cry
"I'm sorry; but we all must die."
Indifference clad in wisdom's guise
All fortitude of mind supplies:
For how can stony bowels melt,[6]
In those who never pity felt;
When *we* are lashed, *they* kiss the rod,[7]
Resigning to the will of God.

The fools, my juniors by a year,
Are tortured with suspense and fear—
Who wisely thought my age a screen,
When death approached, to stand between:
The screen removed, their hearts are trembling,
They mourn for me without dissembling.

My female friends, whose tender hearts
Have better learnt to act their parts,

1. Mr. William Pulteney, from being Mr. Walpole's intimate friend, detesting his Administration, opposed his measures, and joined with my Lord Bolingbroke, to represent his conduct in an excellent paper, called the *Craftsman,* which is still continued [Swift's note].

2. Henry St. John, Lord Viscount Bolingbroke, Secretary of State to Queen Anne of blessed memory. He is reckoned the most universal genius in Europe; Walpole dreading his abilities, treated him most injuriously, working with King George, who forgot his promise of restoring the said Lord, upon the restless importunity of Walpole [Swift's note].

3. Edmund Curll hath been the most infamous bookseller of any age or country: his character in part may be found in Mr. Pope's *Dunciad.* He published three volumes all charged on [i.e., attributed to] the Dean, who never writ three pages of them: he hath used many of the Dean's friends in almost as vile a manner [Swift's note].

4. Three stupid verse writers in London, the last to the shame of the Court, and the highest disgrace to wit and learning, was made Laureate [Swift's note]. Lewis Theobald (1688–1744), Shakespearean scholar and poet; James Moore Smythe (1702–1734), playwright whom Pope accused of plagiarism; Colley Cibber (1671–1757), actor and playwright. All three men are satirized in Pope's *Dunciad.*

5. Curll is notoriously infamous for publishing the lives, letters, and last Wills and Testaments of the nobility and ministers of State, as well as of all the rogues who are hanged at Tyburn [Swift's note].

6. I.e., how can one feel compassion.

7. Accept chastisement submissively; kissing a monarch's scepter or a state official's staff was a ritual of submission to authority.

Receive the news in doleful dumps,
"The Dean is dead (*and what is trumps?*),
Then Lord have mercy on his soul.
(*Ladies, I'll venture for the vole.*[8])
Six deans they say must bear the pall.
(*I wish I knew which king to call.*)"
"Madam, your husband will attend
The funeral of so good a friend."
"No madam, 'tis a shocking sight,
And he's engaged tomorrow night!
My Lady Club would take it ill,
If he should fail her at quadrille.
He loved the Dean. (*I lead a heart.*)
But dearest friends, they say, must part.
His time was come, he ran his race;
We hope he's in a better place."

Why do we grieve that friends should die?
No loss more easy to supply.
One year is past; a different scene;
No further mention of the Dean;
Who now, alas, no more is missed
Than if he never did exist.
Where's now this fav'rite of Apollo?[9]
Departed; and his works must follow:
Must undergo the common fate;
His kind of wit is out of date.
Some country squire to Lintot[1] goes,
Inquires for Swift in verse and prose:
Says Lintot, "I have heard the name:
He died a year ago." "The same."
He searcheth all his shop in vain;
"Sir, you may find them in Duck Lane:[2]
I sent them with a load of books
Last Monday to the pastry-cook's.[3]
To fancy they could live a year!
I find you're but a stranger here.
The Dean was famous in his time
And had a kind of knack at rhyme:
His way of writing now is past;
The town hath got a better taste:
I keep no antiquated stuff;
But, spick and span I have enough.
Pray, do but give me leave to show 'em;

8. All the tricks in the highly popular four-handed card game, quadrille.
9. Patron of poets.
1. Bernard Lintot (1675–1736), London publisher of Pope, Gay, and Steele, among others.
2. A place in London where old [i.e., remaindered] books are sold [Swift's note].
3. Wastepaper from unsold books was used to line baking tins. Cf. Dryden's *Mac Flecknoe* (1682), who notes similar uses for old texts: "Martyrs of pies, and relics of the bum" (line 101).

Here's Colley Cibber's birthday poem.[4]
This ode you never yet have seen
By Stephen Duck,[5] upon the Queen.
Then, here's a letter finely penned,
Against the *Craftsman*[6] and his friend;
It clearly shows that all reflection
On ministers, is disaffection.
Next, here's Sir Robert's vindication,[7]
And Mr Henley's last oration:[8]
The hawkers° have not got 'em yet, *street sellers*
Your Honor please to buy a set?

"Here's Woolston's tracts,[9] the twelfth edition;
'Tis read by every politician:
The country members,[1] when in town,
To all their boroughs send them down:
You never met a thing so smart;
The courtiers have them all by heart:
Those maids of honor (who can read)
Are taught to use them for their creed.
The reverend author's good intention
Hath been rewarded with a pension:
He doth an honor to his gown,
By bravely running priestcraft down:
He shows, as sure as God's in Gloucester,[2]
That Jesus was a grand impostor:
That all his miracles were cheats,
Performed as jugglers do their feats;
The church had never such a writer:
A shame he hath not got a miter!"

Suppose me dead; and then suppose
A club assembled at the Rose;[3]
Where from discourse of this and that,
I grow the subject of their chat:
And while they toss my name about,

4. The Poet Laureate was required to write an ode for the monarch's birthday each year. Cibber's appointment as Laureate in 1730 was based on politics, not literary merit.
5. Stephen Duck (1705–1756), known as "the thresher poet," was a laborer whose poetry won him Queen Caroline's favor; Swift made fun of him in *On Stephen Duck, the Thresher, and Favorite Poet, A Quibbling Epigram* (1730).
6. From 1726, the principal periodical written in opposition to Robert Walpole's government. Its title was meant to indicate that Walpole was "a man of craft" (i.e., scheming and deceptive).
7. Walpole hires a set of Party scribblers, who do nothing else but write in his defense [Swift's note].
8. John Henley (1692–1756), known as "Orator Henley" for the Oratory he founded where "at set times, he delivereth strange speeches compiled by himself and his associates . . . . He is an absolute dunce, but generally reputed crazy" [Swift's note].
9. Woolston was a clergyman, but for want of bread, hath in several treatises, in the most blasphemous manner, attempted to turn our Savior and his miracles into ridicule. He is much caressed by many great courtiers, and by all the infidels, and his books read generally by the Court ladies [Swift's note]. Swift appears to conflate the identities of two contemporary clergymen: Thomas Woolston (1670–1733), a notorious Deist, and William Woollaston (1660–1724).
1. Members of Parliament from rural boroughs.
2. A proverb derived from the number of monasteries there once were in that county.
3. The Rose Tavern, near Drury Lane Theatre, and therefore popular with playgoers.

With favor some, and some without;
One quite indifferent in the cause
My character impartial draws:

"The Dean, if we believe report,
Was never ill received at court;
As for his works in verse and prose,
I own myself no judge of those:
Nor can I tell what critics thought 'em;
But this I know, all people bought 'em;
As with a moral view designed
To cure the vices of mankind:
His vein, ironically grave,
Exposed the fool, and lashed the knave:
To steal a hint was never known,
But what he writ was all his own.[4]

"He never thought an honor done him,
Because a duke was proud to own him:
Would rather slip aside, and choose
To talk with wits in dirty shoes:
Despised the fools with stars and garters,[5]
So often seen caressing Chartres:
He never courted men in station,
Nor persons had in admiration;° *was in awe of*
Of no man's greatness was afraid,
Because he sought for no man's aid.
Though trusted long in great affairs,
He gave himself no haughty airs;
Without regarding private ends,
Spent all his credit for his friends,
And only chose the wise and good;
No flatt'rers; no allies in blood;° *relatives*
But succored virtue in distress,
And seldom failed of good success;
As numbers in their hearts must own,
Who, but for him, had been unknown.

"With princes kept a due decorum,
But never stood in awe before 'em:
And to her Majesty, God bless her,
Would speak as free as to her dresser,[6]
She thought it his peculiar whim,
Nor took it ill as come from him.
He followed David's lesson just,
"In princes never put thy trust."[7]

4. Swift is here having fun with the reader, since this line claiming Swift's originality is stolen from Sir John Denham's elegy *On Mr. Abraham Cowley:* "To him no author was unknown / Yet what he wrote was all his own."

5. Worn by Knights of the Garter.

6. Queen Caroline and Lady Suffolk, one of the Ladies of Her Majesty's bedchamber.

7. Psalm 146.3.

And, would you make him truly sour,
Provoke him with a slave in power:
The Irish senate, if you named,
With what impatience he declaimed!
Fair LIBERTY was all his cry;
For her he stood prepared to die;
For her he boldly stood alone;
For her he oft exposed his own.
Two kingdoms, just as factions led,
Had set a price upon his head;
But not a traitor could be found,
To sell him for six hundred pound.[8]

"Had he but spared his tongue and pen,
He might have rose like other men:
But power was never in his thought,
And wealth he valued not a groat;
Ingratitude he often found,
And pitied those who meant the wound;
But kept the tenor° of his mind, *prevailing course*
To merit well of humankind;
Nor made a sacrifice of those
Who still° were true, to please his foes. *always*
He labored many a fruitless hour
To reconcile his friends in power;
Saw mischief by a faction brewing,
While they pursued each other's ruin.
But finding vain was all his care,
He left the Court in mere° despair.[9] *total*

"And, oh! how short are human schemes!
Here ended all our golden dreams.
What St. John's skill in state affairs,
What Ormonde's valor,[1] Oxford's cares,
To save their sinking country lent,
Was all destroyed by one event.
Too soon that precious life was ended,[2]
On which alone our weal° depended. *well-being*
When up a dangerous faction starts,[3]
With wrath and vengeance in their hearts:

8. Two rewards of £300 each were offered in 1713 and 1724 for the revelation of the author of *The Public Spirit of the Whigs* and *The Drapier's Fourth Letter*, respectively, "but in neither kingdoms was the Dean discovered" [Swift's note].

9. Under Queen Anne's Tory ministry, Swift tried to resolve differences between the Chancellor, Simon Harcourt (1661–1727), Lord Bolingbroke, and the Earl of Oxford, but was unsuccessful, and left London shortly before the collapse of their government.

1. James Butler (1665–1745), second Earl of Ormonde, succeeded Marlborough as commander in chief of the allied forces in 1712.

2. In the height of the quarrel between the ministers, the Queen [Anne] died [Swift's note].

3. When Queen Anne died, the Whigs were restored to power, "which they exercised with the utmost rage and revenge" [Swift's note]. Swift initially feared for his own safety, and considered emigrating to the island of Guernsey.

By solemn league and covenant bond,[4]
To ruin, slaughter, and confound;
To turn religion to a fable,
And make the government a Babel:
Pervert the law, disgrace the gown,
Corrupt the senate, rob the crown;
To sacrifice old England's glory,
And make her infamous in story.
When such a tempest shook the land,
How could unguarded virtue stand?
"With horror, grief, despair the Dean
Beheld the dire destructive scene:
His friends in exile, or the Tower,[5]
Himself within the frown of power;
Pursued by base, envenomed pens,[6]
Far to the land of slaves and fens;° *Ireland*
A servile race in folly nursed,
Who truckle° most, when treated worst. *cringe obsequiously*

"By innocence and resolution,
He bore continual persecution;
While numbers to preferment[7] rose;
Whose merits were, to be his foes.
When, *ev'n his own familiar° friends* *close*
Intent upon their private ends,
Like renegadoes now he feels,
Against him lifting up their heels.[8]

"The Dean did by his pen defeat
An infamous, destructive cheat,[9]
Taught fools their interest to know,
And gave them arms to ward the blow.° *defend themselves*
Envy hath owned it was his doing
To save that helpless land from ruin,
While they who at the steerage[1] stood,
And reaped the profit, sought his blood.

"To save them from their evil fate,
In him was held a crime of state.
A wicked monster on the bench,[2]

4. Alluding to the establishment of Scottish Presbyterianism in 1643, which Swift (as an Anglican) regretted.
5. The Tower of London, where convicted (or suspected) traitors were held.
6. Upon the Queen's death, the Dean returned to live in Dublin . . . numberless libels were writ against him in England, as a Jacobite; he was insulted in the street, and at nights was forced to be attended by his servants armed [Swift's note].
7. Places at the Court or in the church hierarchy, especially bishoprics.
8. From Psalm 41.9: "Yea, mine own familiar friend, in whom I trusted, which did eat of my bread, hath lifted up his heel against me."
9. One Wood, a Hardware-man from England, had a patent for coining copper halfpence in Ireland, to the sum of £108,000, which in the consequence, must leave the kingdom without gold or silver [Swift's note]. Swift responded with *The Drapier's Letters* (1724–1725).
1. The helm (of the ship of state).
2. One Whitshed was then Chief Justice: he had some years before prosecuted a printer for a pamphlet writ by the Dean, to persuade the people of Ireland to wear their own manufactures. . . . He sat as Judge afterwards on the trial of the printer of the Drapier's Fourth Letter; but the Jury, against all he could say or swear, threw out the Bill [Swift's note].

Whose fury blood could never quench;
As vile and profligate a villain,
As modern Scroggs, or old Tresilian;[3]
Who long all justice had discarded,
Nor feared he God, nor man regarded;[4]
Vowed on the Dean his rage to vent,
And make him of his zeal repent;
But heaven his innocence defends,
The grateful people stand his friends;
Not strains of law, nor judges' frown,
Nor topics° brought to please the crown, *charges*
Nor witness hired, nor jury picked,
Prevail to bring him in convict.

"In exile[5] with a steady heart,
He spent his life's declining part;
Where folly, pride, and faction sway,
Remote from St. John, Pope, and Gay.

"His friendship there to few confined,
Were always of the middling kind:[6]
No fools of rank, a mongrel breed,
Who fain would pass for lords indeed:
Where titles give no right or power,
And peerage is a withered flower,[7]
He would have held it a disgrace,
If such a wretch had known his face.
On rural squires, that kingdom's bane,
He vented oft his wrath in vain:
Biennial squires,[8] to market brought,
Who sell their souls and votes for naught;
The nation stripped, go joyful back,
To rob the church, their tenants rack,[9]
Go snacks° with thieves and rapparees,[1] *divide the spoils*
And keep the peace,[2] to pick up fees:

3. Scroggs was Chief Justice under King Charles the Second: his judgment always varied in State trials, according to directions from the [royal] Court. Tresilian was a wicked Judge, hanged above three hundred years ago [Swift's note].
4. Cf. Luke 18.2: "There was in a city a judge, which feared not God, neither regarded man."
5. In Ireland, which he had reason to call a place of exile; to which country nothing could have driven him, but the Queen's death, who had determined to fix him in England [Swift's note].
6. The Dean was not acquainted with one single Lord spiritual or temporal. He only conversed with private gentlemen of the clergy or laity, and but a small number of either [Swift's note]; not entirely true.
7. The peers of Ireland lost a great part of their jurisdiction by one single Act [of 1720], and tamely submitted to this infamous mark of slavery without the least resentment, or remonstrance [Swift's note].
8. The Parliament (as they call it) in Ireland meet but once in two years; and after giving five times more than they can afford, return home to reimburse themselves by all country jobs and oppressions, of which some few only are here mentioned [Swift's note].
9. I.e., torture by extortionate rent; "rack-rent" was an excessive rent nearly equal to the full value of the land.
1. The highwaymen in Ireland are, since the late wars there, usually called rapparees, which was a name given to those Irish soldiers who in small parties used, at that time, to plunder the Protestants [Swift's note].
2. Act as magistrates.

In every job[3] to have a share,
A jail or barrack[4] to repair;
And turn the tax for public roads
Commodious to their own abodes.[5]

"Perhaps I may allow the Dean
Had too much satire in his vein;
And seemed determined not to starve it,
Because no age could more deserve it.
Yet, malice never was his aim;
He lashed the vice but spared the name.[6]
No individual could resent,
Where thousands equally were meant.
His satire points at no defect,
But what all mortals may correct;
For he abhorred that senseless tribe,
Who call it humor when they jibe;
He spared a hump or crooked nose,
Whose owners set not up for beaux.
True, genuine dullness moved his pity,
Unless it offered to be witty.
Those who their ignorance confessed,
He ne'er offended with a jest;
But laughed to hear an idiot quote,
A verse from Horace, learned by rote.

"He knew an hundred pleasant stories,
With all the turns of Whigs and Tories:
Was cheerful to his dying day,
And friends would let him have his way.

"He gave the little wealth he had
To build a house for fools and mad:[7]
And showed by one satiric touch,
No nation wanted it so much:
That kingdom he hath left his debtor,
I wish it soon may have a better."

1731–1732 1739

JOURNAL TO STELLA In 1710, Swift was sent from Dublin to London by his patron, Archbishop King, with an important commission—to petition the Queen's Bounty (via the government and the Court) for the remission of the Irish "first fruits," the British monarch's tax on the revenues of clergymen in the Church of Ireland. Swift saw the campaign to repeal the "first fruits"—and his contribution to its success—as his passport to fame and preferment. Though

3. Implying a business racket.
4. The army in Ireland is lodged in barracks, the building and repairing whereof, and other charges, have cost a prodigious sum to that unhappy kingdom [Swift's note].
5. There were complaints that the new system of public turnpike roads, then being established in England and in Ireland, was manipulated by estate owners so that the roads ran directly to their own properties.
6. Swift is being ironic, since the poem explicitly identifies many targets of his satire.
7. In his will, Swift made a large bequest to build a mental institution (the first in Ireland), St. Patrick's Hospital, which was opened in 1757.

Swift did not yet realize it, these were to be the greatest years of his career, a time when he routinely mixed with the most powerful men of his day, when he was courted for his considerable influence, and when he established himself as the most brilliant and successful of the Tory pamphleteers. He was heavily involved in the intricacies of party politics on his country's behalf and for his own advancement; his prospects for success on both fronts were highly promising. Swift never intended to publish the diary-like letters he wrote to his beloved Esther Johnson and her companion, Rebecca Dingley, during the first three years of his extended sojourn in London from 1710 to 1714. He wrote them, as Virginia Woolf keenly observed in *The Common Reader*, because "the reserved, the powerful, the admired, have the most need of such a refuge." After Esther Johnson's death in 1728, Swift preserved this highly personal "journal" probably both for sentimental reasons and for its historical importance, since it provided a unique insider's view of political affairs and Court intrigues—in addition to social gossip and immediate reactions to important public events—in the final years of Queen Anne's reign. Some of these letters were published in the 1750s and 1760s, in collections of Swift's correspondence and works; the entire sequence first appeared, as *Dr. Swift's Journal to Stella,* in 1784.

from Journal to Stella

from *Letter 10*

[SATURDAY]

London, Nov. 25, 1710

I'll tell you something that's plaguy[1] silly: I had forgot to say on the 23d in my last, where I dined, and because I had done it constantly, I thought it was a great omission, and was going to interline it;[2] but at last the silliness of it made me cry, "Pshaw," and I let it alone. I was today to see the Parliament meet; but only saw a great crowd: and Ford[3] and I went to see the tombs at Westminster,[4] and sauntered so long I was forced to go to an eating house for my dinner. Bromley is chosen speaker,[5] *nemine contradicente:*[6] Do you understand those two words? And Pompey, Colonel Hill's[7] black, designs to stand speaker for the footmen.[8] I am engaged to use my interest for him, and have spoken to Patrick[9] to get him some votes. We are now all impatient for the Queen's speech, what she will say about removing the ministry, &c.[1] I have got a cold, and I don't know how; but got it I have, and am hoarse: I don't know whether it will grow better or worse. What's that to you? I won't answer your letter to-night. I'll keep you a little longer in suspense: I can't send it. Your mother's cakes are very good, and one of them serves me for a breakfast, and so I'll go sleep like a good boy.

26. I have got a cruel cold, and stayed within all this day in my nightgown, and dined on six pennyworth of victuals, and read and writ, and was denied to everybody.[2] Dr. Raymond[3] called often, and I was denied; and at last, when I was weary, I let him

1. Annoyingly, exceedingly.
2. Write it in between the lines he had already written.
3. Charles Ford (1682–1741), an Anglo-Irish friend of Swift's living in London, with whom he corresponded (on and off) for nearly 30 years.
4. Royalty and other members of the aristocracy were buried at Westminster Abbey.
5. William Bromley (1664–1732), high churchman and Member of Parliament for Oxford University from 1702, was chosen speaker of the House of Commons on this day.
6. Nobody voting against.
7. John Hill (d. 1735), major general; like his sister Mrs. Masham, Hill was a favorite of Queen Anne.
8. The footmen to Members of Parliament sometimes held their own unofficial "parliament" and debated the issues of the day while their masters were legislating inside the House.
9. Swift's manservant.
1. Following the trial of the high churchman Dr. Henry Sacheverell (c. 1674–1724) in 1710 for a contentious sermon he had given, there was such strong feeling against the Whig Ministry's apparent oppression of the established Church that the Queen dismissed the Ministry, dissolving Parliament on 21 September 1710. When the new Parliament opened in November, a Tory administration was given control of the government.
2. I.e., visitors were not allowed to see him.
3. Rev. Anthony Raymond (c. 1675–1726), rector of Trim, and neighbor of Swift's.

come up, and asked him, without consequence, "How Patrick denied me, and whether he had the art of it?" So by this means he shall be used to have me denied to him;[4] otherwise he would be a plaguy trouble and hindrance to me: he has sat with me two hours, and drank a pint of ale cost me five pence, and smoked his pipe, and 'tis now past eleven that he is just gone. Well, my eighth is with you now, young women, and your seventh to me is somewhere in a postboy's bag; and so go to your gang of Deans, and Stoytes, and Walls, and lose your money;[5] go, sauce-boxes, and so goodnight and be happy, dear rogues. Oh, but your box was sent to Dr. Hawkshaw by Sterne, and you will have it with Hawkshaw, and spectacles, &c. &c.

27.[6] To-day Mr. Harley[7] met me in the court of requests,[8] and whispered me to dine with him. At dinner I told him what those bishops had done, and the difficulty I was under.[9] He bid me never trouble myself; he would tell the Duke of Ormonde the business was done, and that he need not concern himself about it. So now I am easy, and they may hang themselves for a parcel of insolent ungrateful rascals. I suppose I told you in my last, how they sent an address to the Duke of Ormonde, and a letter to Southwell, to call on me for the papers, after the thing was over, but they had not received my letter; though the Archbishop might, by what I writ to him, have expected it would be done. Well, there's an end of that; and in a little time the Queen will send them notice, &c. And so the methods will be settled; and then I shall think of returning, although the baseness of those bishops makes me love Ireland less than I did.

28. Lord Halifax[1] sent to invite me to dinner, where I stayed till six, and crossed him in all his Whig talk, and made him often come over to me.[2] I know he makes court to the new men, although he affects to talk like a Whig. I had a letter today from the Bishop of Clogher;[3] but I writ to him lately, that I would obey his commands to the Duke of Ormonde. He says I bid him read the *London Shaver*, and that you both swore it was *Shaver*, and not *Shower*.[4] You all lie, and you are puppies, and can't read Presto's hand.[5] The Bishop is out entirely in his conjectures of my share in

4. I.e., Swift let Raymond know that he would not always be admitted on demand.
5. Stella played cards—and often gambled for small stakes—with a circle of friends, including Dean Sterne, Alderman Stoyte, his wife and her sister, and Archdeacon Walls and his wife.
6. Parliament was formally opened by the queen on this day (Swift does not mention it).
7. Swift cultivated friendships with Robert Harley (1661–1724), first Earl of Oxford, and Henry St. John, first Viscount Bolingbroke (1678–1751), as it became clear that they would rule the new Tory Ministry, in the hope, no doubt, of various favors.
8. A court of equity, actually abolished in 1641; it seems the room at Whitehall retained its name long after losing its function.
9. Swift was concerned to receive due recognition for his part in the success of the "first fruits" scheme: Harley had by this time told Swift that the Queen had accepted his proposal, but enjoined him to secrecy until it could be made public. While Harley eventually allowed Swift to report some limited success to Archbishop King, the politician procrastinated on making the matter more widely known. The Queen, meanwhile, appointed a new Governor of Ireland (Ormonde), and the Irish bishops who had commissioned Swift naturally felt it would be politically expedient to hand Swift's petition over to the Secretary of State for Ireland, Edward Southwell, especially since they still saw Swift as a Whig. When the letter patent was eventually granted, in July 1711 (though dated 17 February 1711), no mention of Swift was made.
1. Charles Montague, Earl of Halifax (1661–1715), a senior Whig statesman; on 2 October 1710, Swift noted in the *Journal* that he had refused to join Halifax in toasting the revival of Whig fortunes: "I told him he was the only Whig in England I loved."
2. I.e., Swift argued against Halifax, and persuaded him to his point of view.
3. St. George Ashe (c. 1658–1718), successively Bishop of Cloyne, of Clogher, and of Derry, and Swift's tutor at Trinity College, Dublin; obviously he was writing to Swift about the "first fruits" question.
4. Stella and Mrs. Dingley have persuaded the bishop that he should read "shaver" for "shower" in Swift's *Description of a City Shower*; the verses first appeared in the *Tatler*, No. 238 (17 October 1710). Swift was extremely proud of this poem; he mentions it in several letters to Stella.
5. After the Duchess of Shrewsbury called him "Dr. Presto" (a pun on "Swift"), Swift adopted this name throughout his *Journal*.

the *Tatlers*.[6]—I have other things to mind, and of much greater importance,[7] else I have little to do to be acquainted with a new ministry, who consider me a little more than Irish bishops do.

29. Now for your saucy good dear letter: let me see, what does it say? Come then. I dined today with Ford, and went home early; he debauched me to his chamber again with a bottle of wine till twelve: so goodnight. I can't write an answer now, you rogues.

30. Today I have been visiting, which I had long neglected; and I dined with Mrs. Barton[8] alone; and sauntered at the coffeehouse till past eight, and have been busy till eleven, and now I'll answer your letter, sauce-box. Well, let me see now again. My wax candle's almost out, but however I'll begin. Well then, don't be so tedious, Mr. Presto; what can you say to MD's letter?[9] Make haste, have done with your preambles—Why, I say I am glad you are so often abroad; your mother thinks it is want of exercise hurts you, and so do I. (She called here tonight, but I was not within, that's by the bye.) Sure you don't deceive me, Stella, when you say you are in better health than you were these three weeks; for Dr. Raymond told me yesterday, that Smyth[1] of the Blind Quay had been telling Mr. Leigh, that he left you extremely ill; and in short, spoke so, that he almost put poor Leigh into tears, and would have made me run distracted; though your letter is dated the 11th instant, and I saw Smyth in the city above a fortnight ago, as I passed by in a coach. Pray, pray, don't write, Stella, until you are mighty, mighty, mighty, mighty well in your eyes, and are sure it won't do you the least hurt. Or come, I'll tell you what; you, mistress Stella, shall write your share at five or six sittings, one sitting a day; and then comes Dingley all together, and then Stella a little crumb towards the end, to let us see she remembers Presto; and then conclude with something handsome and genteel, as your most humblecumdumble, or, &c. O Lord! does Patrick write word of my not coming till *spring*? Insolent man! he know my secrets? No; as my Lord Mayor said, No; if I thought my shirt knew, &c.[2] Faith, I will come as soon as it is any way proper for me to come; but, to say the truth, I am at present a little involved with the present ministry in some certain things (which I tell you as a secret) and soon as ever I can clear my hands, I will stay no longer: for I hope the first-fruit business will be soon over in all its forms. But, to say the truth, the present ministry have a difficult task, and want me, &c. Perhaps they may be just as grateful as others: but, according to the best judgment I have, they are pursuing the true interest of the public; and therefore I am glad to contribute what is in my power. For God's sake, not a word of this to any alive.—Your chancellor?[3] Why, madam, I can tell you he has been dead this fortnight. Faith, I could hardly forbear our little lan-

6. The *Tatler*, founded by Swift's sometime friend Richard Steele, ran from 12 April 1709 to 2 January 1711; Swift contributed to several early numbers.

7. At the request of Harley, Swift took control of the *Examiner*, a weekly Tory periodical founded by Bolingbroke in August 1710, between November 1710 and June 1711 (Nos. 14–46).

8. Catherine Barton (1679–1740), niece of Sir Isaac Newton, and a noted beauty who, despite her Whig affiliations and argumentative ability, remained one of Swift's favorites.

9. MD/Md (my dears?) refers to both Esther Johnson and Rebecca Dingley, though Swift is chiefly directing his thoughts to Esther.

1. "Smyth" may be John Smith, one of Swift's booksellers.

2. Patrick is not as close to Swift as his shirt, and even his shirt does not know.

3. Richard Freeman, a Whig, appointed Lord Chancellor of Ireland in 1707, apparently on the basis of his politics, not his abilities.

guage about a nasty dead chancellor, as you may see by the blot.[4] Ploughing? A pox plough them; they'll plough me to nothing. But have you got your money, both the ten pounds? How durst he pay you the second so soon? Pray be good huswives.—Aye, well, and Joe;[5] why, I had a letter lately from Joe, desiring I would take some care of their poor town, who, he says, will lose their liberties. To which I desired Dr. Raymond would return answer; that the town had behaved themselves so ill to me, so little regarded the advice I gave them, and disagreed so much among themselves, that I was resolved never to have more to do with them; but that whatever personal kindness I could do to Joe, should be done. Pray, when you happen to see Joe, tell him this, lest Raymond should have blundered or forgotten.—Poor Mrs. Wesley—Why these poligyes[6] for being abroad?[7] Why should you be at home at all, until Stella is quite well?—So, here is mistress Stella again with her two eggs, &c. My *Shower* admired with you; why, the Bishop of Clogher says, he has seen something of mine of the same sort, better than the *Shower*. I suppose he means *The Morning*;[8] but it is not half so good. I want your judgment of things, and not your country's. How does MD like it? and do they taste it *all?* &c.[9] I am glad Dean Bolton has paid the twenty pounds.[1] Why should not I chide the Bishop of Clogher for writing to the Archbishop of Cashel, without sending the letter first to me?[2] It does not signify a ——; for he has no credit at court. Stuff—they are all puppies. I'll break your head in good earnest, young woman, for your nasty jest about Mrs. Barton. Unlucky sluttikin, what a word is there? Faith, I was thinking yesterday, when I was with her, whether she could break them or no,[3] and it quite spoiled my imagination. Mrs. Walls, does Stella win as she pretends? No indeed, *doctor;* she loses always, and will play so *ventursomely*, how can she win? See here now; an't you an impudent lying slut? Do, open Domville's[4] letter; what does it signify, if you have a mind? Yes, faith, you write smartly with your eyes shut; all was well but the w. See how I can do it; *Madam Stella, your humble servant*.[5] O, but one may look whether one goes crooked or no, and so write on. I'll tell you what you may do; you may write with your eyes half shut, just as when one is going to sleep: I have done so for two or three lines now; 'tis but just seeing enough to go straight.—Now, madam Dingley, I think I bid you tell Mr. Walls, that in case there be occasion, I will serve his friend as far as I can; but I hope there will be none.[6] Yet I believe you will

4. To make this intelligible, it is necessary to observe, that the words "this fortnight" in the preceding sentence, were first written in what he calls their little language, and afterwards scratched out and written plain. It must be confessed this little language, which passed current between Swift and Stella, had occasioned infinite trouble in the revisal of theses papers [Deane Swift' s note]. In 1768, Deane Swift (1706–1783), the son of Swift' s cousin and a favorite relation of Jonathan Swift, published a selection of his famous relation's correspondence with his own annotations, including some of the letters to Esther Johnson and Rebecca Dingley that comprise the *Journal*.

5. Joseph Beaumont (d. 1731), a linen draper from Trim and Swift's business agent.

6. Apologies.

7. Leaving the house.

8. A *Description of the Morning*, which appeared in the *Tatler*, No. 9 (30 April 1709).

9. I.e., do they understand and appreciate it?

1. John Bolton (c. 1656–1724), Dean of Derry.

2. William Palliser (1646–1726), Archbishop of Cashel since 1694, and a signatory of Swift's commission to petition on behalf of the Irish "first fruits" proposal.

3. This jest is lost, whatever it was, for want of MD's letter [Deane Swift's note].

4. William Domville (born c. 1686), Irishman living in London, and grandson of the attorney general, whom Swift called "perfectly as fine a gentleman as I know" (*Journal*, 27 November 1711).

5. Here he writ with his eyes shut, and the writing is somewhat crooked, although as well in other respects as if his eyes had been open [Deane Swift's note]. Swift had expressed concern about Stella straining her eyes in an earlier letter (7), and suggested that "if you will write, shut your eyes, and write just a line, and no more."

6. Rev. Thomas Wall's friend was Captain John Pratt (born c. 1670), Deputy Vice-Treasurer of Ireland and younger brother of Benjamin Pratt, Provost of Trinity College, Dublin; his place in Parliament was in jeopardy. He later embezzled large sums of Swift's (and Ireland's) cash.

have a new Parliament; but I care not whether you have or no a better.[7] You are mistaken in all your conjectures about the *Tatlers*. I have given him one or two hints, and you have heard me talk about the *Shilling*.[8] Faith, these answering letters are very long ones: you have taken up almost the room of a week in journals; and I'll tell you what, I saw fellows wearing crosses today,[9] and I wondered what was the matter; but just this minute I recollect it is little Presto's birthday;[1] and I was resolved these three days to remember it when it came, but could not. Pray, drink my health today at dinner; do, you rogues. Do you like *Sid Hamet's Rod?*[2] Do you understand it all? Well, now at last I have done with your letter, and so I'll lay me down to sleep, and about fair maids; and I hope merry maids all. * * *

1768

GULLIVER'S TRAVELS *Travels into Several Remote Nations of the World. In Four Parts. By Lemuel Gulliver*—better known as *Gulliver's Travels*—was first published in late October 1726 and enjoyed instant success. One contemporary observer noted that "several thousands sold in a week," and Swift's London friends wrote to him in Dublin to say that everyone was reading and talking about Gulliver (see "Gulliver's Travels and Its Time" on page 2426). Readers continue to be fascinated by Swift's masterpiece: since 1945, more than 500 books and scholarly articles have been devoted to *Gulliver's Travels*. Variously classified as an early novel, an imaginary voyage, a moral and political allegory, and even a children's story, Lemuel Gulliver's four journeys, representing the four directions of the globe, comprise a survey of the human condition: a comic, ironic, and sometimes harrowing answer to the question, "What does it mean to be a human being?"

In the first voyage, the diminutive citizens of Lilliput represent human small-mindedness and petty ambitions. Filled with self-importance, the Lilliputians are cruel, treacherous, malicious, and destructive. The perspective is reversed in the second voyage to Brobdingnag, land of giants, where Gulliver has the stature of a Lilliputian. He is humbled by his own helplessness and, finding the huge bodies of the Brobdingnagians grotesque, he realizes how repulsive the Lilliputians must have found him. When Gulliver gives the wise king an account of the political affairs of England—which manifest hypocrisy, avarice, and hatred—the enlightened monarch concludes that most of the country's inhabitants must be "the most pernicious race of little odious vermin that Nature ever suffered to crawl upon the surface of the earth." In the third voyage (which was written last), Gulliver visits the flying island of Laputa and the metropolis of Lagado, on an adjacent continent, where he encounters the misuse of human reason. In Laputa, those who are supposedly "wise" lack all common sense and practical ability; at Lagado, the Academy of Projectors is staffed by professors who waste both money and intelligence on absurd endeavors. Swift aims his satire at so-called intellectuals—especially the "virtuosi," or amateur scientists of the Royal Society—who live in the world of their own speculations and so fail to use their gifts for the common good. Throughout *Gulliver's Travels* that which is admirable is held up to expose corruption in the reader's world, and that which is deplorable is identified with the institutions and practices associated with contemporary Europe, particularly Britain.

Gulliver's fourth voyage (printed in its entirety below) finds him on the island of the Houyhnhnms, horses endowed with reason, whose highly rational and well-ordered

7. The Irish House of Commons was adjourned on 28 August 1710 and reassembled on 9 July 1711.
8. Discussion of John Philips's *The Splendid Shilling* (1701) appeared in the *Tatler*, No. 249 (11 November 1710).
9. For St. Andrew's Day.
1. I.e., his own birthday.
2. Swift's The *Virtues of Sid Hamet the Magician's Rod* (1710), a satire on Sidney Godolphin.

(though emotionally sterile) society is contrasted with the violence, selfishness, and brutality of the Yahoos, irrational beasts who bear a disconcerting resemblance to humans. In his foolish pride, Gulliver believes that he can escape the human condition and live as a stoical Houyhnhnm, even when he returns to his family in England. Of course, Gulliver is neither Houyhnhnm nor Yahoo, but a man. His time in Houyhnhnm-land does not teach him to be more rational or compassionate, but makes him more foolish, derelict in his duties as husband, father, and citizen. Instead of seeking to become a better man, Gulliver strives to become what he is not—with results that are both tragic and farcical. Although the poet Edward Young charged Swift with having "blasphemed a nature little lower than that of the angels" in satirizing the follies of humankind, *Gulliver's Travels* reveals the Dean of Saint Patrick's to be more a humanist than a misanthrope. With brilliantly modulated ironic self-awareness, Swift's painful comedy of exposure to the truth of human frailty demonstrates that there is no room for the distortions of human pride in a world where our practices are so evidently at variance with our principles. Swift advances no program of social reform, but provokes a new recognition—literally, a rethinking—of our own humanity.

from Gulliver's Travels

from *Part 3. A Voyage to Laputa*

Chapter 5

The author permitted to see the grand Academy of Lagado. The Academy largely[1] *described. The arts wherein the professors employ themselves.*

This Academy is not an entire single building, but a continuation of several houses on both sides of a street, which growing waste,[2] was purchased and applied to that use.

I was received very kindly by the Warden, and went for many days to the Academy. Every room has in it one or more projectors,[3] and I believe I could not be[4] in fewer than five hundred rooms.

The first man I saw was of a meager aspect, with sooty hands and face, his hair and beard long, ragged and singed in several places. His clothes, shirt, and skin were all of the same color. He had been eight years upon a project for extracting sunbeams out of cucumbers,[5] which were to be put into vials hermetically sealed, and let out to warm the air in raw, inclement summers. He told me, he did not doubt in eight years more, that he should be able to supply the Governor's gardens with sunshine at a reasonable rate; but he complained that his stock was low, and entreated me to give him something as an encouragement to ingenuity,[6] especially since this had been a very dear season for cucumbers. I made him a small present, for my Lord[7]

1. In general. The academy is a satire of the Royal Society, founded in 1662 for the purpose of scientific experimentation (see Perspectives: The Royal Society and the New Science, page 2039). Though many of its members made major contributions to science, the Society had a reputation for bizarre speculation. Swift had visited the Society in 1710 and here parodies actual experiments recorded in its *Philosophical Transactions*; he is also parodying the description of "Solomon's House," an academy of science in Francis Bacon's *New Atlantis* (1626).
2. Falling into disuse.
3. Those people undertaking the project.
4. Could not have been.
5. Stephen Hales (1677–1761), English botanist and physiologist, had recently investigated sunlight's agency in plant respiration. This and other studies were published in his *Vegetable Staticks* (1726).
6. His investigative powers.
7. The warden of the Academy.

had furnished me with money on purpose, because he knew their practice of begging from all who go to see them.

I went into another chamber, but was ready to hasten back, being almost overcome with a horrible stink. My conductor pressed me forward, conjuring me in a whisper to give no offense, which would be highly resented, and therefore I durst not so much as stop my nose. The projector of this cell was the most ancient student of the Academy. His face and beard were of a pale yellow; his hands and clothes daubed over with filth. When I was presented to him, he gave me a very close embrace (a compliment I could well have excused). His employment from his first coming into the Academy was an operation to reduce human excrement to its original food, by separating the several parts, removing the tincture which it receives from the gall, making the odor exhale, and scumming off the saliva. He had a weekly allowance from the Society of a vessel filled with human ordure,[8] about the bigness of a Bristol barrel.[9]

I saw another at work to calcine[1] ice into gunpowder, who likewise showed me a treatise he had written concerning the malleability of fire,[2] which he intended to publish.

There was a most ingenious architect who had contrived a new method for building houses, by beginning at the roof and working downwards to the foundation, which he justified to me by the like practice of those two prudent insects, the bee and the spider.

There was a man born blind, who had several apprentices in his own condition: their employment was to mix colors for painters, which their master taught them to distinguish by feeling and smelling.[3] It was indeed my misfortune to find them at that time not very perfect in their lessons, and the professor himself happened to be generally mistaken: this artist is much encouraged and esteemed by the whole fraternity.

In another apartment I was highly pleased with a projector, who had found a device of ploughing the ground with hogs, to save the charges of ploughs, cattle, and labor. The method is this; in an acre of ground you bury, at six inches distance, and eight deep, a quantity of acorns, dates, chestnuts, and other mast[4] or vegetables whereof these animals are fondest: then you drive six hundred or more of them into the field, where in a few days they will root up the whole ground in search of their food, and make it fit for sowing, at the same time manuring it with their dung; it is true upon experiment they found the charge and trouble very great, and they had little or no crop. However, it is not doubted that this invention may be capable of great improvement.

I went into another room, where the walls and ceiling were all hung round with cobwebs, except a narrow passage for the artist[5] to go in and out. At my entrance he called aloud to me not to disturb his webs. He lamented the fatal mistake the world had been so long in of using silkworms, while we had such plenty of domestic insects, who infinitely excelled the former, because they understood how to weave as

8. Excrement.

9. A medium-size barrel, holding about 37 gallons.

1. Desiccate.

2. Cf. Rabelais, *Gargantua and Pantagruel* (1532–1564), bk. 5, ch. 22: "Others were cutting fire with a knife, and drawing water up in a net."

3. Based on Robert Boyle's account in *Experiments and Observations Upon Colors* (1665), of a blind man who could distinguish colors.

4. Nuts.

5. Modeled on both the Frenchman M. Bon, who believed silk could be made from cobwebs, and Dr. Wall, who suggested that the excreta of ants fed on plant sap could be used as dye; both suggestions were published in the *Transactions of the Royal Society*.

well as spin. And he proposed farther, that by employing spiders, the charge[6] of dyeing silks would be wholly saved, whereof I was fully convinced when he showed me a vast number of flies most beautifully colored, wherewith he fed his spiders, assuring us, that the webs would take a tincture from them; and as he had them of all hues, he hoped to fit everybody's fancy, as soon as he could find proper food for the flies, of certain gums, oils, and other glutinous matter to give a strength and consistence to the threads.

There was an astronomer who had undertaken to place a sundial upon the great weathercock on the Town House,[7] by adjusting the annual and diurnal motions of the earth and sun, so as to answer and coincide with all accidental turnings of the wind.

I was complaining of a small fit of the colic, upon which my conductor led me into a room, where a great physician resided, who was famous for curing that disease by contrary operations from the same instrument. He had a large pair of bellows with a long slender muzzle of ivory. This he conveyed eight inches up the anus, and drawing in the wind, he affirmed he could make the guts as lank as a dried bladder. But when the disease was more stubborn and violent, he let in the muzzle while the bellows was full of wind, which he discharged into the body of the patient, then withdrew the instrument to replenish it, clapping his thumb strongly against the orifice of the fundament; and this being repeated three or four times, the adventitious wind would rush out, bringing the noxious along with it (like water put into a pump) and the patient recover. I saw him try both experiments upon a dog, but could not discern any effect from the former. After the latter, the animal was ready to burst, and made so violent a discharge, as was very offensive to me and my companions. The dog died on the spot, and we left the doctor endeavoring to recover him by the same operation.[8]

I visited many other apartments, but shall not trouble my reader with all the curiosities I observed, being studious of brevity.

I had hitherto seen only one side of the Academy, the other being appropriated to the advancers of speculative learning, of whom I shall say something when I have mentioned one illustrious person more, who is called among them *the universal artist*.[9] He told us he had been thirty years employing his thoughts for the improvement of human life. He had two large rooms full of wonderful curiosities, and fifty men at work. Some were condensing air into a dry, tangible substance, by extracting the niter,[1] and letting the aqueous or fluid particles percolate; others softening marble for pillows and pincushions; others petrifying the hoofs of a living horse to preserve them from foundering. The artist himself was at that time busy upon two great designs: the first, to sow land with chaff, wherein he affirmed the true seminal virtue to be contained, as he demonstrated by several experiments which I was not skillful enough to comprehend. The other was, by a certain composition of gums, minerals, and vegetables outwardly applied, to prevent the growth of wool upon two young lambs; and he hoped in a reasonable time to propagate the breed of naked sheep all over the kingdom.

We crossed a walk to the other part of the Academy, where, as I have already said, the projectors in speculative learning resided.

6. Expense.
7. Town Hall.
8. Robert Hooke (1635–1703) produced artificial respiration in a dog (1667) by blowing air into its windpipe with a pair of bellows.
9. Possibly Robert Boyle (1627–1691), whose many scientific experiments investigated the nature of air, marble, petrifaction, agriculture, and sheep breeding.
1. Air was believed to contain nitrous matter.

The first professor I saw was in a very large room, with forty pupils about him. After salutation, observing me to look earnestly upon a frame, which took up the greatest part of both the length and breadth of the room, he said perhaps I might wonder to see him employed in a project for improving speculative knowledge by practical and mechanical operations. But the world would soon be sensible[2] of its usefulness, and he flattered himself that a more noble exalted thought never sprang in any other man's head. Everyone knew how laborious the usual method is of attaining to arts and sciences; whereas by his contrivance, the most ignorant person at a reasonable charge, and with a little bodily labor, may write books in philosophy, poetry, politics, law, mathematics, and theology, without the least assistance from genius or study. He then led me to the frame, about the sides whereof all his pupils stood in ranks. It was twenty foot square, placed in the middle of the room. The superficies[3] was composed of several bits of wood, about the bigness of a die,[4] but some larger than others. They were all linked together by slender wires. These bits of wood were covered on every square with papers pasted on them, and on these papers were written all the words of their language in their several moods, tenses, and declensions, but without any order. The professor then desired me to observe, for he was going to set his engine[5] at work. The pupils at his command took each of them hold of an iron handle, whereof there were forty fixed round the edges of the frame, and giving them a sudden turn, the whole disposition of the words was entirely changed. He then commanded six and thirty of the lads to read the several lines softly as they appeared upon the frame; and where they found three or four words together that might make part of a sentence, they dictated to the four remaining boys who were scribes. This work was repeated three or four times, and at every turn the engine was so contrived, that the words shifted into new places, as the square bits of wood moved upside down.

Six hours a day the young students were employed in this labor, and the professor showed me several volumes in large folio already collected, of broken sentences, which he intended to piece together, and out of those rich materials to give the world a complete body of all arts and sciences; which however might be still improved, and much expedited, if the public would raise a fund for making and employing five hundred such frames in Lagado, and oblige the managers to contribute in common their several[6] collections.

He assured me, that this invention had employed all his thoughts from his youth, that he had emptied the whole vocabulary into his frame, and made the strictest computation of the general proportion there is in books between the numbers of particles, nouns, and verbs, and other parts of speech.

I made my humblest acknowledgments to this illustrious person for his great communicativeness, and promised if ever I had the good fortune to return to my native country, that I would do him justice, as the sole inventor of this wonderful machine; the form and contrivance of which I desired leave to delineate upon paper as in the figure here annexed. I told him, although it were the custom of our learned in Europe to steal inventions from each other,[7] who had thereby at least this advantage, that it became a controversy which was the right owner, yet I would take such caution, that he should have the honor entire without a rival.

2. Aware.
3. Surface.
4. Singular of dice.
5. Machine.
6. Individual.
7. No international patent agreement existed at this time, and the theft of inventions was common as nations competed in developing technology for commercial manufacturing and navigation on the open seas.

We next went to the school of languages, where three professors sat in consultation upon improving that of their own country.[8]

The first project was to shorten discourse by cutting polysyllables into one, and leaving out verbs and participles, because in reality all things imaginable are but nouns.

The other project was a scheme for entirely abolishing all words whatsoever; and this was urged as a great advantage in point of health as well as brevity. For, it is plain, that every word we speak is in some degree a diminution of our lungs by corrosion, and consequently contributes to the shortening of our lives. An expedient was therefore offered, that since words are only names for *things*, it would be more convenient for all men to carry about them such *things* as were necessary to express the particular business they are to discourse on.[9] And this invention would certainly have taken place, to the great ease as well as health of the subject.[1] If the women in conjunction with the vulgar and illiterate had not threatened to raise a rebellion, unless they might be allowed the liberty to speak with their tongues, after the manner of their forefathers; such constant irreconcilable enemies to science are the common people. However, many of the most learned and wise adhere to the new scheme of expressing themselves by *things*, which hath only this inconvenience attending it, that if a man's business be very great, and of various kinds, he must be obliged in proportion to carry a greater bundle of *things* upon his back, unless he can afford one or two strong servants to attend him. I have often beheld two of those sages almost sinking under the weight of their packs, like peddlers among us; who when they met in the streets would lay down their loads, open their sacks, and hold conversation for an hour together; then put up their implements, help each other to resume their burdens, and take their leave.

But for short conversations a man may carry implements in his pockets and under his arms, enough to supply him, and in his house he cannot be at a loss; therefore the room where company meet who practice this art, is full of all *things* ready at hand, requisite to furnish matter for this kind of artificial converse.[2]

Another great advantage proposed by this invention, was that it would serve as a universal language to be understood in all civilized nations, whose goods and utensils are generally of the same kind, or nearly resembling, so that their uses might easily be comprehended. And thus, ambassadors would be qualified to treat with foreign princes or ministers of state, to whose tongues they were utter strangers.

I was at the mathematical school, where the master taught his pupils after a method scarce imaginable to us in Europe. The proposition and demonstration were fairly written on a thin wafer, with ink composed of a cephalic[3] tincture. This the student was to swallow upon a fasting stomach, and for three days following eat nothing but bread and water. As the wafer digested, the tincture mounted to his brain, bearing the proposition along with it. But the success has not hitherto been

8. The first secretary to the Royal Society, Thomas Sprat, in his *History* (1667) of that institution, recommended that such an Academy be founded, as the new style of science writing should strive to describe "so many *things* in an equal number of words." Although Swift burlesques this notion, he himself had published *Proposals for Correcting, Improving and Ascertaining the English Tongue* (1712), in which he suggested that an Academy be established with the aim of preserving culture and "fixing our language for ever."

9. The growth of scientific knowledge about the nature of the material world had encouraged suggestions that language should be made less abstract. In satirizing the projector, Swift alludes to John Locke's theory of language in Book 3 of *An Essay Concerning Human Understanding* (1690), where Locke argues that words stand for things only indirectly.

1. Both the individual practitioner and the people of the nation as a whole.

2. A reference to the Royal Society's attempt to collect one specimen or example of every thing in the world.

3. Of or for the head.

answerable, partly by some error in the *quantum* or composition, and partly by the perverseness of lads, to whom this bolus[4] is so nauseous that they generally steal aside, and discharge it upwards before it can operate; neither have they been yet persuaded to use so long an abstinence as the prescription requires.

Chapter 10

The Luggnaggians commended. A particular description of the Struldbruggs, with many conversations between the author and some eminent persons upon that subject.[5]

The Luggnaggians are a polite and generous people, and although they are not without some share of that pride which is peculiar to all Eastern countries, yet they show themselves courteous to strangers, especially such who are countenanced by the Court. I had many acquaintance among persons of the best fashion, and being always attended by my interpreter, the conversation we had was not disagreeable.

One day in much good company, I was asked by a person of quality, whether I had seen any of their Struldbruggs or Immortals. I said I had not, and desired he would explain to me what he meant by such an appellation applied to a mortal creature. He told me, that sometimes, though very rarely, a child happened to be born in a family with a red circular spot in the forehead, directly over the left eyebrow, which was an infallible mark that it should never die. The spot, as he described it, was about the compass of a silver threepence, but in the course of time grew larger, and changed its color; for at twelve years old it became green, so continued till five and twenty, then turned to a deep blue; at five and forty it grew coal black, and as large as an English shilling, but never admitted any farther alteration. He said these births were so rare, that he did not believe there could be above eleven hundred Struldbruggs of both sexes in the whole kingdom, of which he computed about fifty in the metropolis, and among the rest a young girl born about three years ago. That these productions were not peculiar to any family, but a mere effect of change, and the children of the Struldbruggs themselves, were equally mortal with the rest of the people.

I freely own myself to have been struck with inexpressible delight upon hearing this account: and the person who gave it me happening to understand the Balnibarbian language, which I spoke very well, I could not forbear breaking out into expressions perhaps a little too extravagant. I cried out as in a rapture: Happy nation where every child hath at least a chance for being immortal! Happy people who enjoy so many living examples of ancient virtue, and have masters ready to instruct them in the wisdom of all former ages! But, happiest beyond all comparison are those excellent Struldbruggs, who being born exempt from that universal calamity of human nature, have their minds free and disengaged, without the weight and depression of spirits caused by the continual apprehension of death. I discovered my admiration[6] that I had not observed any of these illustrious persons at Court, the black spot on the forehead being so remarkable a distinction, that I could not have easily overlooked it; and it was impossible that his Majesty, a most judicious prince, should not provide himself with a good number of such wise and able counselors. Yet perhaps the virtue of those reverend sages was too strict for the corrupt and

4. Mass of chewed food.
5. In order to return to England, Gulliver sails west on the Pacific from Balnibarbi (the country of which Lagado is the capital) to Japan, stopping en route at the island of "Luggnagg," where he makes the following observations.
6. Expressed my surprise.

libertine manners of a Court. And we often find by experience that young men are too opinionative and volatile to be guided by the sober dictates of their seniors. However, since the King was pleased to allow me access to his royal person, I was resolved upon the very first occasion to deliver my opinion to him on this matter freely, and at large, by the help of my interpreter; and whether he would please to take my advice or no, yet in one thing I was determined, that his Majesty having frequently offered me an establishment in this country, I would with great thankfulness accept the favor, and pass my life here in the conversation of those superior beings the Struldbruggs, if they would please to admit me.

The gentleman to whom I addressed my discourse, because (as I have already observed) he spoke the language of Balnibarbi, said to me with a sort of a smile, which usually ariseth from pity to the ignorant, that he was glad of any occasion to keep me among them, and desired my permission to explain to the company what I had spoke. He did so, and they talked together for some time in their own language, whereof I understood not a syllable, neither could I observe by their countenances what impression my discourse had made on them. After a short silence the same person told me, that his friends and mine (so he thought fit to express himself) were very much pleased with the judicious remarks I had made on the great happiness and advantages of immortal life, and they were desirous to know in a particular manner, what scheme of living I should have formed to myself, if it had fallen to my lot to have been born a Struldbrugg.

I answered, it was easy to be eloquent on so copious and delightful a subject, especially to me who have been often apt to amuse myself with visions of what I should do if I were a king, a general, or a great lord; and upon this very case I had frequently run over the whole system how I should employ myself, and pass the time if I were sure to live for ever.

That, if it had been my good fortune to come into the world a Struldbrugg, as soon as I could discover my own happiness by understanding the difference between life and death, I would first resolve by all arts and methods whatsoever to procure myself riches. In the pursuit of which by thrift and management, I might reasonably expect in about two hundred years, to be the wealthiest man in the kingdom. In the second place, I would from my earliest youth apply myself to the study of arts and sciences, by which I should arrive in time to excel all others in learning. Lastly I would carefully record every action and event of consequence that happened in the public,[7] impartially draw the characters of the several successions of princes, and great ministers of state, with my own observations on every point. I would exactly set down the several changes in customs, language, fashions of dress, diet and diversions. By all which acquirements, I should be a living treasury of knowledge and wisdom, and certainly become the oracle of the nation.

I would never marry after threescore, but live in an hospitable manner, yet still on the saving side. I would entertain myself in forming and directing the minds of hopeful young men, by convincing them from my own remembrance, experience, and observation, fortified by numerous examples, of the usefulness of virtue in public and private life. But, my choice and constant companions should be a set of my own immortal brotherhood, among whom I would elect a dozen from the most ancient down to my own contemporaries. Where any of these wanted[8] fortunes, I would

7. The state (from Latin *res publica*, the "public thing," from which derives the word *republic*).

8. Lacked.

provide them with convenient lodges round my own estate, and have some of them always at my table, only mingling a few of the most valuable among you mortals, whom length of time would harden me to lose with little or no reluctance, and treat your posterity after the same manner, just as a man diverts himself with the annual succession of pinks and tulips in his garden, without regretting the loss of those which withered the preceding year.

These Struldbruggs and I would mutually communicate our observations and memorials through the course of time, remark the several gradations by which corruption steals into the world, and oppose it in every step, by giving perpetual warning and instruction to mankind; which, added to the strong influence of our own example, would probably prevent that continual degeneracy of human nature so justly complained of in all ages.

Add to all this, the pleasure of seeing the various revolutions of states and empires, the changes in the lower and upper world,[9] ancient cities in ruins, and obscure villages become the seats of kings. Famous rivers lessening into shallow brooks, the ocean leaving one coast dry, and overwhelming another, the discovery of many countries yet unknown. Barbarity overrunning the politest nations, and the most barbarous becoming civilized. I should then see the discovery of the longitude, the perpetual motion, the universal medicine,[1] and many other great inventions brought to the utmost perfection.

What wonderful discoveries should we make in astronomy, by outliving and confirming our own predictions, by observing the progress and returns of comets, with the changes of motion in the sun, moon, and stars.

I enlarged upon many other topics, which the natural desire of endless life and sublunary[2] happiness could easily furnish me with. When I had ended, and the sum of my discourse had been interpreted as before, to the rest of the company, there was a good deal of talk among them in the language of the country, not without some laughter at my expense. At last the same gentleman who had been my interpreter said, he was desired by the rest to set me right in a few mistakes, which I had fallen into through the common imbecility of human nature, and upon that allowance was less answerable for them. That, this breed of Struldbruggs was peculiar to their country, for there were no such people either in Balnibarbi or Japan, where he had the honor to be ambassador from his Majesty, and found the natives in both those kingdoms very hard to believe[3] that the fact was possible, and it appeared from my astonishment when he first mentioned the matter to me, that I received it as a thing wholly new, and scarcely to be credited. That in the two kingdoms above-mentioned, where during his residence he had conversed very much, he observed long life to be the universal desire and wish of mankind. That whoever had one foot in the grave, was sure to hold back the other as strongly as he could. That the oldest had still hopes of living one day longer, and looked on death as the greatest evil, from which nature always prompted him to retreat; only in this island of Luggnagg, the appetite for living was not so eager, from the continual example of the Struldbruggs before their eyes.

9. On the earth and in the heavens.
1. As at Lagado, Gulliver enumerates scientific quests Swift scoffed at: for a method of determining the longitude of a ship at sea, for a perpetual motion machine, for one drug sufficient to cure all ills.
2. Earthly.
3. To convince.

That the system of living contrived by me was unreasonable and unjust, because it supposed a perpetuity of youth, health, and vigor, which no man could be so foolish to hope, however extravagant he may be in his wishes. That the question therefore was not whether a man would choose to be always in the prime of youth, attended with prosperity and health, but how he would pass a perpetual life under all the usual disadvantages which old age brings along with it. For although few men will avow their desires of being immortal upon such hard conditions, yet in the two kingdoms before-mentioned of Balnibarbi and Japan, he observed that every man desired to put off death for some time longer, let it approach ever so late, and he rarely heard of any man who died willingly, except he were incited by the extremity of grief or torture. And he appealed to me whether in those countries I had traveled, as well as my own, I had not observed the same general disposition.

After this preface he gave me a particular account of the Struldbruggs among them. He said they commonly acted like mortals, till about thirty years old, after which by degrees they grew melancholy and dejected, increasing in both till they came to fourscore. This he learned from their own confession; for otherwise there not being above two or three of that species born in an age, they were too few to form a general observation by. When they came to fourscore years, which is reckoned the extremity of living in this country, they had not only all the follies and infirmities of other old men, but many more which arose from the dreadful prospect of never dying. They were not only opinionative, peevish, covetous, morose, vain, talkative, but uncapable of friendship, and dead to all natural affection, which never descended below their grandchildren. Envy and impotent desires are their prevailing passions. But those objects against which their envy seems principally directed, are the vices of the younger sort, and the deaths of the old. By reflecting on the former, they find themselves cut off from all possibility of pleasure; and whenever they see a funeral, they lament and repine that others have gone to an harbor of rest, to which they themselves never can hope to arrive. They have no remembrance of anything but what they learned and observed in their youth and middle age, and even that is very imperfect. And for the truth or particulars of any fact, it is safer to depend on common traditions than upon their best recollections. The least miserable among them appear to be those who turn to dotage, and entirely lose their memories; these meet with more pity and assistance, because they want many bad qualities which abound in others.

If a Struldbrugg happen to marry one of his own kind, the marriage is dissolved of course by the courtesy of the kingdom, as soon as the younger of the two comes to be fourscore. For the law thinks it a reasonable indulgence, that those who are condemned without any fault of their own to a perpetual continuance in the world, should not have their misery doubled by the load of a wife.[4]

As soon as they have completed the term of eighty years, they are looked on as dead in law; their heirs immediately succeed to their estates, only a small pittance is reserved for their support, and the poor ones are maintained at the public charge. After that period they are held incapable of any employment of trust or profit, they cannot purchase lands or take leases, neither are they allowed to be witnesses in any cause, either civil or criminal, not even for the decision of meres[5] and bounds.

4. Swift himself never married.

5. Property lines (at issue in property disputes).

At ninety they lose their teeth and hair, they have at that age no distinction of taste, but eat and drink whatever they can get, without relish or appetite. The diseases they were subject to, still continue without increasing or diminishing. In talking they forget the common appellation of things, and the names of persons, even of those who are their nearest friends and relations. For the same reason they never can amuse themselves with reading, because their memory will not serve to carry them from the beginning of a sentence to the end; and by this defect they are deprived of the only entertainment whereof they might otherwise be capable.

The language of this country being always upon the flux, the Struldbruggs of one age do not understand those of another, neither are they able after two hundred years to hold any conversation (farther than by a few general words) with their neighbors the mortals, and thus they lie under the disadvantage of living like foreigners in their own country. This was the account given me of the Struldbruggs, as near as I can remember. I afterwards saw five or six of different ages, the youngest not above two hundred years old, who were brought to me at several times by some of my friends; but although they were told that I was a great traveler, and had seen all the world, they had not the least curiosity to ask me a question; only desired I would give them *slumskudask*, or a token of remembrance, which is a modest way of begging, to avoid the law that strictly forbids it, because they are provided for by the public, although indeed with a very scanty allowance.

They are despised and hated by all sorts of people; when one of them is born, it is reckoned ominous, and their birth is recorded very particularly; so that you may know their age by consulting the registry, which however hath not been kept above a thousand years past, or at least hath been destroyed by time or public disturbances. But the usual way of computing how old they are, is, by asking them what kings or great persons they can remember, and then consulting history, for infallibly the last prince in their mind did not begin his reign after they were fourscore years old.

They were the most mortifying sight I ever beheld, and the women more horrible than the men. Besides the usual deformities in extreme old age, they acquired an additional ghastliness in proportion to their number of years, which is not to be described, and among half a dozen I soon distinguished which was the eldest, although there were not above a century or two between them.

The reader will easily believe, that from what I had heard and seen, my keen appetite for perpetuity of life was much abated. I grew heartily ashamed of the pleasing visions I had formed, and thought no tyrant could invent a death into which I would not run with pleasure from such a life. The king heard of all that had passed between me and my friends upon this occasion, and rallied me very pleasantly, wishing I would send a couple of Struldbruggs to my own country, to arm our people against the fear of death; but this it seems is forbidden by the fundamental laws of the kingdom, or else I should have been well content with the trouble and expense of transporting them.

I could not but agree that the laws of this kingdom, relating to the Struldbruggs, were founded upon the strongest reasons, and such as any other country would be under the necessity of enacting in the like circumstances. Otherwise, as avarice is the necessary consequent of old age, those Immortals would in time become proprietors of the whole nation, and engross the civil power, which, for want of abilities to manage, must end in the ruin of the public.

Part 4. A Voyage to the Country of the Houyhnhnms[1]

Chapter 1

The author sets out as Captain of a ship. His men conspire against him, confine him a long time to his cabin, set him on shore in an unknown land. He travels up into the country. The Yahoos,[2] *a strange sort of animal, described. The author meets two Houyhnhnms.*

I continued at home with my wife and children about five months in a very happy condition, if I could have learned the lesson of knowing when I was well. I left my poor wife big with child, and accepted an advantageous offer made me to be Captain of the *Adventure*,[3] a stout merchantman of 350 tons: for I understood navigation well, and being grown weary of a surgeon's employment at sea, which however I could exercise upon occasion, I took a skillful young man of that calling, one Robert Purefoy,[4] into my ship. We set sail from Portsmouth upon the seventh day of September, 1710; on the fourteenth, we met with Captain Pocock[5] of Bristol, at Teneriffe,[6] who was going to the bay of Campeche, to cut logwood. On the sixteenth, he was parted from us by a storm; I heard since my return, that his ship foundered, and none escaped, but one cabin boy. He was an honest man, and a good sailor, but a little too positive in his own opinions, which was the cause of his destruction, as it hath been of several others. For if he had followed my advice, he might at this time have been safe at home with his family as well as myself.

I had several men died in my ship of calentures,[7] so that I was forced to get recruits out of Barbados, and the Leeward Islands, where I touched by[8] the direction of the merchants who employed me, which I had soon too much cause to repent; for I found afterwards that most of them had been buccaneers. I had fifty hands on board, and my orders were, that I should trade with the Indians in the South Sea, and make what discoveries I could. These rogues whom I had picked up debauched my other men, and they all formed a conspiracy to seize the ship and secure me; which they did one morning, rushing into my cabin, and binding me hand and foot, threatening to throw me overboard, if I offered to stir. I told them, I was their prisoner, and would submit. This they made me swear to do, and then unbound me, only fastening one of my legs with a chain near my bed, and placed a sentry at my door with his piece charged,[9] who was commanded to shoot me dead, if I attempted my liberty. They sent me down victuals and drink, and took the government of the ship to themselves. Their design was to turn pirates, and plunder the Spaniards, which they could not do till they got more men. But first they resolved to sell the goods in the

1. Pronounced "whinnims," to mimic the sound of a horse's whinny, though some scholars have offered more complex interpretations of this name. With characteristic irony, Swift probably chose horses to represent rational creatures because the philosopher John Locke (1632–1704) and Bishop Edward Stillingfleet (1635–1699) had argued extensively about how one might distinguish man as a rational animal from an evidently irrational animal, such as a horse.

2. The name may be derived from similarly titled African or Guianan tribes. The animals represent sinful, fallen humanity, and their juxtaposition with the Houyhnhnms is designed to question belief in the innate rationality of humankind and the superiority of humans over other creatures.

3. The name of two ships of the notorious pirate Captain William Kidd (d. 1701). Kidd, originally commissioned to capture pirates, was also subject to a mutiny.

4. "Pure faith," associating Gulliver with the overzealous Puritans.

5. Probably modeled on the dogmatic Captain Dampier (1652–1715), who had spent three years logcutting around the Campeche Bay, on the Yucatan Peninsula, in the Gulf of Mexico. His violent disagreements with his lieutenant led to a court martial.

6. One of the Canary Islands, off the northwestern coast of Africa.

7. Tropical fevers.

8. Landed according to.

9. Gun loaded.

ship, and then go to Madagascar[1] for recruits, several among them having died since my confinement. They sailed many weeks, and traded with the Indians, but I knew not what course they took, being kept close prisoner in my cabin, and expecting nothing less than to be murdered, as they often threatened me.

Upon the ninth day of May, 1711, one James Welch came down to my cabin; and said he had orders from the Captain to set me ashore. I expostulated with him, but in vain; neither would he so much as tell me who their new captain was. They forced me into the longboat, letting me put on my best suit of clothes, which were good as new, and a small bundle of linen, but no arms except my hanger;[2] and they were so civil as not to search my pockets, into which I conveyed what money I had, with some other little necessaries. They rowed about a league; and then set me down on a strand.[3] I desired them to tell me what country it was. They all swore, they knew no more than myself, but said, that the Captain (as they called him) was resolved, after they had sold the lading,[4] to get rid of me in the first place where they discovered land. They pushed off immediately, advising me to make haste, for fear of being overtaken by the tide, and bade me farewell.

In this desolate condition I advanced forward, and soon got upon firm ground, where I sat down on a bank to rest myself, and consider what I had best to do. When I was a little refreshed, I went up into the country, resolving to deliver myself to the first savages I should meet, and purchase my life from them by some bracelets, glass rings, and other toys,[5] which sailors usually provide themselves with in those voyages, and whereof I had some about me: the land was divided by long rows of trees, not regularly planted, but naturally growing; there was great plenty of grass, and several fields of oats. I walked very circumspectly for fear of being surprised, or suddenly shot with an arrow from behind or on either side. I fell into a beaten road, where I saw many tracks of human feet, and some of cows, but most of horses. At last I beheld several animals in a field, and one or two of the same kind sitting in trees. Their shape was very singular, and deformed, which a little discomposed me, so that I lay down behind a thicket to observe them better. Some of them coming forward near the place where I lay, gave me an opportunity of distinctly marking[6] their form. Their heads and breasts were covered with a thick hair, some frizzled and others lank; they had beards like goats, and a long ridge of hair down their backs, and the foreparts of their legs and feet, but the rest of their bodies were bare, so that I might see their skins, which were of a brown buff color. They had no tails, nor any hair at all on their buttocks, except about the anus; which, I presume, Nature had placed there to defend them as they sat on the ground; for this posture they used, as well as lying down, and often stood on their hind feet. They climbed high trees, as nimbly as a squirrel, for they had strong extended claws before and behind, terminating in sharp points, and hooked. They would often spring, and bound, and leap with prodigious agility. The females were not so large as the males; they had long lank hair on their heads, and only a sort of down on the rest of their bodies, except about the anus, and pudenda.[7] Their dugs[8] hung between their forefeet, and often reached almost to the ground as they walked. The hair of both sexes was of several colors, brown, red, black, and yellow. Upon the whole, I never beheld in all my travels so

1. A popular meeting place for pirates.
2. A short sword, typically hung from the belt.
3. The shore; in this context, apparently a spit extending into the sea.
4. Cargo.
5. Trinkets.
6. Observing.
7. Genitals.
8. Breasts.

disagreeable an animal, nor one against which I naturally conceived so strong an antipathy. So that thinking I had seen enough, full of contempt and aversion, I got up and pursued the beaten road, hoping it might direct me to the cabin of some Indian. I had not gone far when I met one of these creatures full in my way, and coming up directly to me. The ugly monster, when he saw me, distorted several ways every feature of his visage, and stared as at an object he had never seen before; then approaching nearer, lifted up his forepaw, whether out of curiosity or mischief, I could not tell. But I drew my hanger, and gave him a good blow with the flat side of it; for I durst not strike him with the edge, fearing the inhabitants might be provoked against me, if they should come to know, that I had killed or maimed any of their cattle. When the beast felt the smart, he drew back, and roared so loud, that a herd of at least forty came flocking about me from the next field, howling and making odious faces; but I ran to the body of a tree, and leaning my back against it, kept them off, by waving my hanger. Several of this cursed brood getting hold of the branches behind leaped up into the tree, from whence they began to discharge their excrements on my head: however, I escaped pretty well, by sticking close to the stem of the tree, but was almost stifled with the filth, which fell about me on every side.

In the midst of this distress, I observed them all to run away on a sudden as fast as they could, at which I ventured to leave the tree, and pursue the road, wondering what it was that could put them into this flight. But looking on my left hand, I saw a horse walking softly in the field, which my persecutors having sooner discovered, was the cause of their flight. The horse started a little when he came near me, but soon recovering himself, looked full in my face with manifest tokens of wonder: he viewed my hands and feet, walking round me several times. I would have pursued my journey, but he placed himself directly in the way, yet looking with a very mild aspect, never offering the least violence. We stood gazing at each other for some time; at last I took the boldness to reach my hand towards his neck, with a design to stroke it, using the common style and whistle of jockeys when they are going to handle a strange horse. But this animal, seeming to receive my civilities with disdain, shook his head, and bent his brows, softly raising up his left forefoot to remove my hand. Then he neighed three or four times, but in so different a cadence, that I almost began to think he was speaking to himself in some language of his own.

While he and I were thus employed, another horse came up; who applying[9] himself to the first in a very formal manner, they gently struck each other's right hoof before, neighing several times by turns, and varying the sound, which seemed to be almost articulate. They went some paces off, as if it were to confer together, walking side by side, backward and forward, like persons deliberating upon some affair of weight, but often turning their eyes towards me, as it were to watch that I might not escape. I was amazed to see such actions and behavior in brute beasts, and concluded with myself, that if the inhabitants of this country were endued with a proportionable degree of reason, they must needs be the wisest people upon earth. This thought gave me so much comfort, that I resolved to go forward until I could discover some house or village, or meet with any of the natives, leaving the two horses to discourse together as they pleased. But the first, who was a dapple-grey, observing me to steal off, neighed after me in so expressive a tone, that I fancied myself to understand what he meant; whereupon I turned back, and came near him, to expect[1] his farther commands. But concealing my fear as much as I could, for I

9. Addressing.

1. Await.

began to be in some pain,[2] how this adventure might terminate; and the reader will easily believe I did not much like my present situation.

The two horses came up close to me, looking with great earnestness upon my face and hands. The grey steed rubbed my hat all round with his right forehoof, and discomposed it so much, that I was forced to adjust it better, by taking it off, and settling it again; whereat both he and his companion (who was a brown bay) appeared to be much surprised; the latter felt the lappet[3] of my coat, and finding it to hang loose about me, they both looked with new signs of wonder. He stroked my right hand, seeming to admire the softness, and color; but he squeezed it so hard between his hoof and his pastern,[4] that I was forced to roar; after which they both touched me with all possible tenderness. They were under great perplexity about my shoes and stockings, which they felt very often, neighing to each other, and using various gestures, not unlike those of a philosopher,[5] when he would attempt to solve some new and difficult phenomenon.

Upon the whole, the behavior of these animals was so orderly and rational, so acute and judicious, that I at last concluded, they must needs be magicians, who had thus metamorphosed themselves upon some design, and seeing a stranger in the way, were resolved to divert themselves with him; or perhaps were really amazed at the sight of a man so very different in habit, feature, and complexion from those who might probably live in so remote a climate.[6] Upon the strength of this reasoning, I ventured to address them in the following manner: Gentlemen, if you be conjurers, as I have good cause to believe, you can understand any language; therefore I make bold to let your Worships know, that I am a poor distressed Englishman, driven by his misfortunes upon your coast, and I entreat one of you, to let me ride upon his back, as if he were a real horse, to some house or village, where I can be relieved. In return of which favor, I will make you a present of this knife and bracelet (taking them out of my pocket). The two creatures stood silent while I spoke, seeming to listen with great attention; and when I had ended, they neighed frequently towards each other, as if they were engaged in serious conversation. I plainly observed that their language expressed the passions[7] very well, and the words might with little pains be resolved into an alphabet more easily than the Chinese.

I could frequently distinguish the word *Yahoo*, which was repeated by each of them several times; and although it were impossible for me to conjecture what it meant, yet while the two horses were busy in conversation, I endeavored to practice this word upon my tongue; and as soon as they were silent, I boldly pronounced *Yahoo* in a loud voice, imitating, at the same time, as near as I could, the neighing of a horse; at which they were both visibly surprised, and the grey repeated the same word twice, as if he meant to teach me the right accent, wherein I spoke after him as well as I could, and found myself perceivably to improve every time, although very far from any degree of perfection. Then the bay tried me with a second word, much harder to be pronounced; but reducing it to the English *orthography*,[8] may be spelled thus, *Houyhnhnm*. I did not succeed in this so well as the former, but after two or three farther trials, I had better fortune; and they both appeared amazed at my capacity.

2. Began to be worried.
3. Lapel.
4. Part of a horse's foot between the fetlock (a projection of the lower leg) and the hoof.
5. Scientist.
6. Region.
7. Emotions.
8. Spelling.

After some farther discourse, which I then conjectured might relate to me, the two friends took their leaves, with the same compliment of striking each other's hoof; and the grey made me signs that I should walk before him; wherein I thought it prudent to comply, till I could find a better director. When I offered to slacken my pace, he would cry *Hhuun, Hhuun;* I guessed his meaning, and gave him to understand, as well as I could, that I was weary, and not able to walk faster; upon which, he would stand a while to let me rest.

CHAPTER 2

The author conducted by a Houyhnhnm to his house. The house described. The author's reception. The food of the Houyhnhnms. The author in distress for want of meat, is at last relieved. His manner of feeding in that country.

Having traveled about three miles, we came to a long kind of building, made of timber stuck in the ground, and wattled across;[9] the roof was low, and covered with straw. I now began to be a little comforted, and took out some toys, which travelers usually carry for presents to the savage Indians of America and other parts, in hopes the people of the house would be thereby encouraged to receive me kindly. The horse made me a sign to go in first; it was a large room with a smooth, clay floor, and a rack[1] and manger extending the whole length on one side. There were three nags,[2] and two mares, not eating, but some of them sitting down upon their hams,[3] which I very much wondered at; but wondered more to see the rest employed in domestic business. The last seemed but ordinary cattle; however, this confirmed my first opinion, that a people who could so far civilize brute animals, must needs excel in wisdom all the nations of the world. The grey came in just after, and thereby prevented any ill treatment, which the others might have given me. He neighed to them several times in a style of authority, and received answers.

Beyond this room there were three others, reaching the length of the house, to which you passed through three doors, opposite to each other, in the manner of a vista;[4] we went through the second room towards the third; here the grey walked in first, beckoning me to attend.[5] I waited in the second room, and got ready my presents, for the master and mistress of the house: they were two knives, three bracelets of false pearl, a small looking glass, and a bead necklace. The horse neighed three or four times, and I waited to hear some answers in a human voice, but I heard no other returns than in the same dialect, only one or two a little shriller than his. I began to think that this house must belong to some person of great note among them, because there appeared so much ceremony before I could gain admittance. But, that a man of quality should be served all by horses, was beyond my comprehension. I feared my brain was disturbed by my sufferings and misfortunes: I roused myself, and looked about me in the room where I was left alone; this was furnished as the first, only after a more elegant manner. I rubbed mine eyes often, but the same objects still occurred. I pinched my arms and sides, to awake myself, hoping I might be in a dream. I then absolutely concluded, that all these appearances could be nothing else but necromancy[6] and magic. But I had no time to pursue these reflections;

9. Filled in with twigs and branches.
1. Hayrack for the feed.
2. Ponies.
3. Buttocks.
4. Long, narrow view (usually between rows of trees).
5. Wait.
6. Sorcery.

for the grey horse came to the door, and made me a sign to follow him into the third room, where I saw a very comely mare, together with a colt and foal, sitting on their haunches, upon mats of straw, not unartfully made, and perfectly neat and clean.

The mare, soon after my entrance, rose from her mat, and coming up close, after having nicely[7] observed my hands and face, gave me a most contemptuous look; then turning to the horse, I heard the word *Yahoo* often repeated betwixt them; the meaning of which word I could not then comprehend, although it were the first I had learned to pronounce; but I was soon better informed, to my everlasting mortification: for the horse beckoning to me with his head, and repeating the word *Hhuun, Hhuun,* as he did upon the road, which I understood was to attend him, led me out into a kind of court, where was another building at some distance from the house. Here we entered, and I saw three of those detestable creatures, which I first met after my landing, feeding upon roots, and the flesh of some animals, which I afterwards found to be that of asses and dogs, and now and then a cow dead by accident or disease.[8] They were all tied by the neck with strong withes,[9] fastened to a beam; they held their food between the claws of their forefeet, and tore it with their teeth.

The master horse ordered a sorrel nag, one of his servants, to untie the largest of these animals, and take him into the yard. The beast and I were brought close together, and our countenances diligently compared, both by master and servant, who thereupon repeated several times the word *Yahoo*. My horror and astonishment are not to be described, when I observed, in this abominable animal, a perfect human figure; the face of it indeed was flat and broad, the nose depressed, the lips large, and the mouth wide. But these differences are common to all savage nations, where the lineaments of the countenance are distorted by the natives suffering[1] their infants to lie groveling on the earth, or by carrying them on their backs, nuzzling with their face against the mother's shoulders. The forefeet of the Yahoo differed from my hands in nothing else but the length of the nails, the coarseness and brownness of the palms, and the hairiness on the backs. There was the same resemblance between our feet, with the same differences, which I knew very well, though the horses did not, because of my shoes and stockings; the same in every part of our bodies, except as to hairiness and color, which I have already described.

The great difficulty that seemed to stick with the two horses, was, to see the rest of my body so very different from that of a Yahoo, for which I was obliged to my clothes, whereof they had no conception: the sorrel nag offered me a root, which he held (after their manner, as we shall describe in its proper place) between his hoof and pastern; I took it in my hand, and having smelt it, returned it to him as civilly as I could. He brought out of the Yahoo's kennel a piece of ass's flesh, but it smelt so offensively that I turned from it with loathing; he then threw it to the Yahoo, by whom it was greedily devoured. He afterwards showed me a wisp of hay, and a fetlock full of oats; but I shook my head, to signify, that neither of these were food for me. And indeed, I now apprehended, that I must absolutely starve, if I did not get to some of my own species: for as to those filthy Yahoos, although there were few greater lovers of mankind, at that time, than myself; yet I confess I never saw any sensitive[2] being so detestable on all accounts; and the more I came near them, the more hateful they grew, while I stayed in that country. This the master horse

7. Closely.
8. The Yahoos eat food listed in Leviticus (11.3, 27, 39–40) as unclean, suggesting that they exemplify the human condition distorted and debased by sin.
9. Leashes.
1. Allowing.
2. "Having sense or perception, but not reason" (Johnson's *Dictionary*).

observed by my behavior, and therefore sent the Yahoo back to his kennel. He then put his forehoof to his mouth, at which I was much surprised, although he did it with ease, and with a motion that appeared perfectly natural, and made other signs to know what I would eat; but I could not return him such an answer as he was able to apprehend; and if he had understood me, I did not see how it was possible to contrive any way for finding myself nourishment. While we were thus engaged, I observed a cow passing by, whereupon I pointed to her, and expressed a desire to let me go and milk her. This had its effect; for he led me back into the house, and ordered a mare-servant to open a room, where a good store of milk lay in earthen and wooden vessels, after a very orderly and cleanly manner. She gave me a large bowl full, of which I drank very heartily, and found myself well refreshed.

About noon I saw coming towards the house a kind of vehicle drawn like a sledge by four Yahoos. There was in it an old steed, who seemed to be of quality; he alighted with his hind feet forward, having by accident got a hurt in his left forefoot. He came to dine with our horse, who received him with great civility. They dined in the best room, and had oats boiled in milk for the second course, which the old horse ate warm, but the rest cold. Their mangers were placed circular in the middle of the room and divided into several partitions, round which they sat on their haunches upon bosses[3] of straw. In the middle was a large rack with angles answering to every partition of the manger. So that each horse and mare ate their own hay, and their own mash of oats and milk, with much decency and regularity. The behavior of the young colt and foal appeared very modest, and that of the master and mistress extremely cheerful and complaisant[4] to their guest. The grey ordered me to stand by him, and much discourse passed between him and his friend concerning me, as I found by the stranger's often looking on me, and the frequent repetition of the word Yahoo.

I happened to wear my gloves, which the master grey observing, seemed perplexed, discovering signs of wonder what I had done to my forefeet; he put his hoof three or four times to them, as if he would signify, that I should reduce them to their former shape, which I presently did, pulling off both my gloves, and putting them into my pocket. This occasioned farther talk, and I saw the company was pleased with my behavior, whereof I soon found the good effects. I was ordered to speak the few words I understood, and while they were at dinner, the master taught me the names for oats, milk, fire, water, and some others; which I could readily pronounce after him, having from my youth a great facility in learning languages.

When dinner was done, the master horse took me aside, and by signs and words made me understand the concern he was in, that I had nothing to eat. Oats in their tongue are called *hlunnh*. This word I pronounced two or three times; for although I had refused them at first, yet upon second thoughts, I considered that I could contrive to make of them a kind of bread, which might be sufficient with milk to keep me alive, till I could make my escape to some other country, and to creatures of my own species. The horse immediately ordered a white mare-servant of his family to bring me a good quantity of oats in a sort of wooden tray. These I heated before the fire as well as I could, and rubbed them till the husks came off, which I made a shift[5] to winnow from the grain; I ground and beat them between two stones, then took water, and made them into a paste or cake, which I toasted at the fire, and ate warm

3. Piles or seats.
4. Courteous.
5. Attempted.

with milk. It was at first a very insipid diet, although common enough in many parts of Europe, but grew tolerable by time; and having been often reduced to hard fare in my life, this was not the first experiment I had made how easily nature is satisfied.[6] And I cannot but observe, that I never had one hour's sickness, while I stayed in this island. 'Tis true, I sometimes made a shift to catch a rabbit, or bird, by springes[7] made of Yahoos' hairs, and I often gathered wholesome herbs, which I boiled, or ate as salads with my bread, and now and then, for a rarity, I made a little butter, and drank the whey. I was at first at a great loss for salt; but custom soon reconciled the want of it; and I am confident that the frequent use of salt among us is an effect of luxury, and was first introduced only as a provocative to drink; except where it is necessary for preserving of flesh in long voyages, or in places remote from great markets. For we observe no animal to be fond of it but man[8] and as to myself, when I left this country, it was a great while before I could endure the taste of it in anything that I ate.

This is enough to say upon the subject of my diet, wherewith other travelers fill their books, as if the readers were personally concerned whether we fared[9] well or ill. However, it was necessary to mention this matter, lest the world should think it impossible that I could find sustenance for three years in such a country, and among such inhabitants.

When it grew towards evening, the master horse ordered a place for me to lodge in; it was but six yards from the house, and separated from the stable of the Yahoos. Here I got some straw, and covering myself with my own clothes, slept very sound. But I was in a short time better accommodated, as the reader shall know hereafter, when I come to treat more particularly about my way of living.

CHAPTER 3

The author studious to learn the language, the Houyhnhnm his master assists in teaching him. The language described. Several Houyhnhnms of quality come out of curiosity to see the author. He gives his master a short account of his voyage.

My principal endeavor was to learn the language, which my master (for so I shall henceforth call him) and his children, and every servant of his house were desirous to teach me. For they looked upon it as a prodigy that a brute animal should discover[1] such marks of a rational creature. I pointed to everything, and inquired the name of it, which I wrote down in my journal book when I was alone, and corrected my bad accent, by desiring those of the family to pronounce it often. In this employment, a sorrel nag, one of the under servants, was very ready to assist me.

In speaking, they pronounce through the nose and throat, and their language approaches nearest to the High Dutch or German, of any I know in Europe; but is much more graceful and significant.[2] The Emperor Charles V made almost the same observation, when he said, that if he were to speak to his horse, it should be in High Dutch.[3]

6. A commonplace idea in ancient satire; Swift may here be mocking it.
7. Snares.
8. This is, of course, untrue, but Gulliver's subsequent dislike of salt indicates his dislike of human society in general.
9. A pun on "fare," meaning both food and "to get along."
1. Display.
2. Expressive.
3. I.e., German; Charles V of Spain (1500-1551) was believed to have said that he would address his God in Spanish, his mistress in Italian, and his horse in German.

The curiosity and impatience of my master were so great, that he spent many hours of his leisure to instruct me. He was convinced (as he afterwards told me) that I must be a Yahoo, but my teachableness, civility, and cleanliness astonished him; which were qualities altogether so opposite to those animals. He was most perplexed about my clothes, reasoning sometimes with himself, whether they were a part of my body; for I never pulled them off till the family were asleep, and got them on before they waked in the morning. My master was eager to learn from whence I came, how I acquired those appearances of reason, which I discovered in all my actions, and to know my story from my own mouth, which he hoped he should soon do by the great proficiency I made in learning and pronouncing their words and sentences. To help my memory, I formed all I learned into the English alphabet, and writ the words down with the translations. This last, after some time, I ventured to do in my master's presence. It cost me much trouble to explain to him what I was doing; for the inhabitants have not the least idea of books or literature.

In about ten weeks' time I was able to understand most of his questions, and in three months could give him some tolerable answers. He was extremely curious to know from what part of the country I came, and how I was taught to imitate a rational creature, because the Yahoos (whom he saw I exactly resembled in my head, hands, and face, that were only visible), with some appearance of cunning, and the strongest disposition to mischief, were observed to be the most unteachable of all brutes. I answered, that I came over the sea, from a far place, with many others of my own kind, in a great hollow vessel made of the bodies of trees. That my companions forced me to land on this coast, and then left me to shift for myself. It was with some difficulty, and by the help of many signs, that I brought him to understand me. He replied, that I must needs be mistaken, or that I *said the thing which was not.* (For they have no word in their language to express lying or falsehood.) He knew it was impossible[4] that there could be a country beyond the sea, or that a parcel of brutes could move a wooden vessel whither they pleased upon water. He was sure no Houyhnhnm alive could make such a vessel, or would trust Yahoos to manage it.

The word *Houyhnhnm,* in their tongue, signifies a *horse,* and in its etymology, the *Perfection of Nature.* I told my master, that I was at a loss for expression, but would improve as fast as I could; and hoped in a short time I should be able to tell him wonders: he was pleased to direct his own mare, his colt and foal, and the servants of the family to take all opportunities of instructing me, and every day for two or three hours, he was at the same pains himself: several horses and mares of quality in the neighborhood came often to our house upon the report spread of a wonderful Yahoo, that could speak like a Houyhnhnm, and seemed in his words and actions to discover some glimmerings of reason. These delighted to converse with me; they put many questions, and received such answers as I was able to return. By all which advantages, I made so great a progress, that in five months from my arrival, I understood whatever was spoke, and could express myself tolerably well.

The Houyhnhnms who came to visit my master, out of a design of seeing and talking with me, could hardly believe me to be a right[5] Yahoo, because my body had a different covering from others of my kind. They were astonished to observe me without the usual hair or skin, except on my head, face, and hands; but I discovered that secret to my master, upon an accident, which happened about a fortnight before.

4. The Houyhnhnm thus shows himself to be so dependent on reason that he is dogmatic in his ignorance, unable (like rationalists in religion) to accept what he does not know by his own reasoning.

5. True.

I have already told the reader, that every night when the family were gone to bed, it was my custom to strip and cover myself with my clothes: it happened one morning early, that my master sent for me, by the sorrel nag, who was his valet; when he came, I was fast asleep, my clothes fallen off on one side, and my shirt above my waist. I awaked at the noise he made, and observed him to deliver his message in some disorder; after which he went to my master, and in a great fright gave him a very confused account of what he had seen: this I presently discovered; for going as soon as I was dressed, to pay my attendance upon his Honor, he asked me the meaning of what his servant had reported, that I was not the same thing when I slept as I appeared to be at other times; that his valet assured him, some part of me was white, some yellow, at least not so white, and some brown.

I had hitherto concealed the secret of my dress, in order to distinguish myself as much as possible, from that cursed race of Yahoos; but now I found it in vain to do so any longer. Besides, I considered that my clothes and shoes would soon wear out, which already were in a declining condition, and must be supplied by some contrivance from the hides of Yahoos or other brutes; whereby the whole secret would be known: I therefore told my master, that in the country from whence I came, those of my kind always covered their bodies with the hairs of certain animals prepared by art, as well for decency, as to avoid inclemencies of air both hot and cold; of which, as to my own person, I would give him immediate conviction, if he pleased to command me; only desiring his excuse, if I did not expose those parts that Nature taught us to conceal. He said my discourse was all very strange, but especially the last part; for he could not understand why Nature should teach us to conceal what Nature had given. That neither himself nor family were ashamed of any parts of their bodies; but however I might do as I pleased. Whereupon, I first unbuttoned my coat, and pulled it off. I did the same with my waistcoat,[6] I drew off my shoes, stockings, and breeches. I let my shirt down to my waist, and drew up the bottom, fastening it like a girdle about my middle to hide my nakedness.

My master observed the whole performance with great signs of curiosity and admiration. He took up all my clothes in his pastern, one piece after another, and examined them diligently; he then stroked my body very gently, and looked round me several times, after which he said, it was plain I must be a perfect Yahoo; but that I differed very much from the rest of my species, in the softness, and whiteness, and smoothness of my skin, my want of hair in several parts of my body, the shape and shortness of my claws behind and before, and my affectation of walking continually on my two hinder feet. He desired to see no more, and gave me leave to put on my clothes again, for I was shuddering with cold.

I expressed my uneasiness at his giving me so often the appellation of *Yahoo,* an odious animal, for which I had so utter an hatred and contempt; I begged he would forbear applying that word to me, and take the same order in his family, and among his friends whom he suffered to see me. I requested likewise, that the secret of my having a false covering to my body might be known to none but himself, at least as long as my present clothing should last; for, as to what the sorrel nag his valet had observed, his Honor might command him to conceal it.

All this my master very graciously consented to,[7] and thus the secret was kept till my clothes began to wear out, which I was forced to supply by several

6. Vest.

7. The Houyhnhnms may have no word for "lying," but they can hide the truth.

contrivances, that shall hereafter be mentioned. In the meantime, he desired I would go on with my utmost diligence to learn their language, because he was more astonished at my capacity for speech and reason, than at the figure of my body, whether it were covered or no; adding, that he waited with some impatience to hear the wonders which I promised to tell him.

From thenceforward he doubled the pains he had been at to instruct me; he brought me into all company, and made them treat me with civility, because, as he told them privately, this would put me into good humor, and make me more diverting.

Every day when I waited on him, beside the trouble he was at in teaching, he would ask me several questions concerning myself, which I answered as well as I could; and by those means he had already received some general ideas, though very imperfect. It would be tedious to relate the several steps, by which I advanced to a more regular conversation: but the first account I gave of myself in any order and length, was to this purpose:

That, I came from a very far country, as I already had attempted to tell him, with about fifty more of my own species; that we traveled upon the seas, in a great hollow vessel made of wood, and larger than his Honor's house. I described the ship to him in the best terms I could, and explained by the help of my handkerchief displayed, how it was driven forward by the wind. That upon a quarrel among us, I was set on shore on this coast, where I walked forward without knowing whither, till he delivered me from the persecution of those execrable Yahoos. He asked me, who made the ship, and how it was possible that the Houyhnhnms of my country would leave it to the management of brutes? My answer was, that I durst proceed no farther in my relation, unless he would give me his word and honor that he would not be offended, and then I would tell him the wonders I had so often promised. He agreed; and I went on by assuring him, that the ship was made by creatures like myself, who in all the countries I had traveled, as well as in my own, were the only governing, rational animals, and that upon my arrival hither, I was as much astonished to see the Houyhnhnms act like rational beings, as he or his friends could be in finding some marks of reason in a creature he was pleased to call a Yahoo, to which I owned my resemblance in every part, but could not account for their degenerate and brutal nature. I said farther, that if good fortune ever restored me to my native country, to relate my travels hither, as I resolved to do, everybody would believe that I *said the thing which was not;* that I invented the story out of my own head; and with all possible respect to himself, his family, and friends, and under his promise of not being offended, our countrymen would hardly think it probable, that a Houyhnhnm should be the presiding creature of a nation, and a Yahoo the brute.

Chapter 4

The Houyhnhnms' notion of truth and falsehood. The author's discourse disapproved by his master. The author gives a more particular account of himself, and the accidents of his voyage.

My master heard me with great appearances of uneasiness in his countenance, because *doubting* or *not believing*, are so little known in this country, that the inhabitants cannot tell how to behave themselves under such circumstances. And I remember in frequent discourses with my master concerning the nature of manhood,[8] in other parts of the world, having occasion to talk of *lying*, and *false*

8. Human nature.

representation, it was with much difficulty that he comprehended what I meant, although he had otherwise a most acute judgment. For he argued thus: that the use of speech was to make us understand one another, and to receive information of facts; now if any one *said the thing which was not*, these ends were defeated; because I cannot properly be said to understand him, and I am so far from receiving information, that he leaves me worse than in ignorance, for I am led to believe a thing *black* when it is *white*, and *short* when it is *long*. And these were all the notions he had concerning that faculty of *lying*, so perfectly well understood, and so universally practiced among human creatures.

To return from this digression; when I asserted that the Yahoos were the only governing animal in my country, which my master said was altogether past his conception, he desired to know, whether we had Houyhnhnms among us, and what was their employment: I told him, we had great numbers, that in summer they grazed in the fields, and in winter were kept in houses, with hay and oats, where Yahoo servants were employed to rub their skins smooth, comb their manes, pick their feet, serve them with food, and make their beds. I understand you well, said my master; it is now very plain, from all you have spoken, that whatever share of reason the Yahoos pretend to, the Houyhnhnms are your masters;[9] I heartily wish our Yahoos would be so tractable. I begged his Honor would please to excuse me from proceeding any farther, because I was very certain that the account he expected from me would be highly displeasing. But he insisted in commanding me to let him know the best and the worst: I told him, he should be obeyed. I owned, that the Houyhnhnms among us, whom we called *horses*, were the most generous and comely animal we had, that they excelled in strength and swiftness; and when they belonged to persons of quality, employed in traveling, racing, or drawing chariots, they were treated with much kindness and care, till they fell into diseases, or became foundered in the feet;[1] but then they were sold, and used to all kind of drudgery till they died; after which their skins were stripped and sold for what they were worth, and their bodies left to be devoured by dogs and birds of prey.[2] But the common race of horses had not so good fortune, being kept by farmers and carriers and other mean people, who put them to greater labor, and fed them worse. I described as well as I could, our way of riding, the shape and use of a bridle, a saddle, a spur, and a whip, of harness and wheels. I added, that we fastened plates of a certain hard substance called *iron* at the bottom of their feet, to preserve their hoofs from being broken by the stony ways on which we often traveled.

My master, after some expressions of great indignation, wondered how we dared to venture upon a Houyhnhnm's back, for he was sure that the weakest servant in his house would be able to shake off the strongest Yahoo, or by lying down, and rolling upon his back, squeeze the brute to death. I answered, that our horses were trained up from three or four years old to the several uses we intended them for; that if any of them proved intolerably vicious, they were employed for carriages; that they were severely beaten while they were young, for any mischievous tricks; that the males, designed for the common use of riding or draft, were generally *castrated* about two years after their birth, to take down their spirits, and make them more tame and gentle; that they were indeed sensible of rewards and punishments; but his

9. Possibly a satire on the English love of horses.
1. Until their feet give in from overwork.
2. Swift mockingly paraphrases the *Iliad* 1.4-6: "The souls of mighty Chiefs untimely slain; / Whose limbs unburied on the naked shore, / Devouring dogs and hungry vultures tore" (Pope's translation).

Honor would please to consider, that they had not the least tincture of reason any more than the Yahoos in this country.

It put me to the pains of many circumlocutions to give my master a right idea of what I spoke; for their language doth not abound in variety of words, because their wants and passions are fewer than among us. But it is impossible to express his noble resentment at our savage treatment of the Houyhnhnm race, particularly after I had explained the manner and use of *castrating* horses among us, to hinder them from propagating their kind, and to render them more servile. He said, if it were possible there could be any country where Yahoos alone were endued with reason, they certainly must be the governing animal, because reason will in time always prevail against brutal strength. But, considering the frame of our bodies, and especially of mine, he thought no creature of equal bulk was so ill-contrived for employing that reason in the common offices of life; whereupon he desired to know whether those among whom I lived, resembled me or the Yahoos of his country. I assured him, that I was as well shaped as most of my age, but the younger and the females were much more soft and tender, and the skins of the latter generally as white as milk. He said, I differed indeed from other Yahoos, being much more cleanly, and not altogether so deformed, but in point of real advantage, he thought I differed for the worse. That my nails were of no use either to my fore or hinder feet; as to my forefeet, he could not properly call them by that name, for he never observed me to walk upon them; that they were too soft to bear the ground; that I generally went with them uncovered, neither was the covering I sometimes wore on them of the same shape, or so strong as that on my feet behind. That I could not walk with any security, for if either of my hinder feet slipped, I must inevitably fall. He then began to find fault with other parts of my body, the flatness of my face, the prominence of my nose, mine eyes placed directly in front, so that I could not look on either side without turning my head, that I was not able to feed myself, without lifting one of my forefeet to my mouth, and therefore Nature had placed those joints to answer that necessity. He knew not what could be the use of those several clefts and divisions in my feet behind; that these were too soft to bear the hardness and sharpness of stones without a covering made from the skin of some other brute; that my whole body wanted a fence against heat and cold, which I was forced to put on and off every day with tediousness and trouble. And lastly, that he observed every animal in this country naturally to abhor the Yahoos, whom the weaker avoided, and the stronger drove from them. So that supposing us to have the gift of reason, he could not see how it were possible to cure that natural antipathy which every creature discovered[3] against us; nor consequently, how we could tame and render them serviceable. However, he would (as he said) debate that matter no farther, because he was more desirous to know my own story, the country where I was born, and the several actions and events of my life before I came hither.

I assured him, how extremely desirous I was that he should be satisfied in every point; but I doubted much, whether it would be possible for me to explain myself on several subjects whereof his Honor could have no conception, because I saw nothing in his country to which I could resemble[4] them. That, however, I would do my best, and strive to express myself by similitudes, humbly desiring his assistance when I wanted proper words; which he was pleased to promise me.

3. Displayed.

4. Compare.

I said, my birth was of honest parents, in an island called England, which was remote from this country, as many days' journey as the strongest of his Honor's servants could travel in the annual course of the sun. That I was bred a surgeon, whose trade it is to cure wounds and hurts in the body, got by accident or violence; that my country was governed by a female man, whom we called a *Queen*. That I left it to get riches,[5] whereby I might maintain myself and family when I should return. That in my last voyage, I was commander of the ship, and had about fifty Yahoos under me, many of which died at sea, and I was forced to supply[6] them by others picked out from several nations. That our ship was twice in danger of being sunk; the first time by a great storm, and the second, by striking against a rock. Here my master interposed, by asking me, how I could persuade strangers out of different countries to venture with me, after the losses I had sustained, and the hazards I had run. I said, they were fellows of desperate fortunes, forced to fly from the places of their birth, on account of their poverty or their crimes. Some were undone by lawsuits; others spent all they had in drinking, whoring, and gaming; others fled for treason; many for murder, theft, poisoning, robbery, perjury, forgery, coining false money, for committing rapes or sodomy, for flying from their colors,[7] or deserting to the enemy, and most of them had broken prison; none of these durst return to their native countries for fear of being hanged, or of starving in a jail; and therefore were under a necessity of seeking a livelihood in other places.

During this discourse, my master was pleased often to interrupt me. I had made use of many circumlocutions in describing to him the nature of the several crimes, for which most of our crew had been forced to fly their country. This labor took up several days' conversation before he was able to comprehend me. He was wholly at a loss to know what could be the use or necessity of practicing those vices. To clear up which I endeavored to give him some ideas of the desire of power and riches, of the terrible effects of lust, intemperance, malice, and envy. All this I was forced to define and describe by putting of cases, and making suppositions. After which, like one whose imagination was struck with something never seen or heard of before, he would lift up his eyes with amazement and indignation. Power, government, war, law, punishment, and a thousand other things had no terms, wherein that language could express them, which made the difficulty almost insuperable to give my master any conception of what I meant. But being of an excellent understanding, much improved by contemplation and converse, he at last arrived at a competent knowledge of what human nature in our parts of the world is capable to perform, and desired I would give him some particular account of that land, which we call Europe, but especially, of my own country.

Chapter 5

The author at his master's commands informs him of the state of England. The causes of war among the princes of Europe. The author begins to explain the English Constitution.

The reader may please to observe, that the following extract of many conversations I had with my master, contains a summary of the most material points, which were discoursed at several times for above two years; his Honor often desiring fuller satisfaction[8] as I farther improved in the Houyhnhnm tongue. I laid before him, as well

5. Gulliver originally stated that he undertook his second and third voyages out of a desire to travel: he now reads all human motivation in the worst possible light.

6. Replace.

7. Deserting their regiment in the army.

8. Better explanation.

as I could, the whole state of Europe; I discoursed of trade and manufactures, of arts and sciences; and the answers I gave to all the questions he made, as they arose upon several subjects, were a fund of conversation not to be exhausted. But I shall here only set down the substance of what passed between us concerning my own country, reducing it into order as well as I can, without any regard to time or other circumstances, while I strictly adhere to truth. My only concern is, that I shall hardly be able to do justice to my master's arguments and expressions, which must needs suffer by my want of capacity, as well as by a translation into our barbarous English.[9]

In obedience therefore to his Honor's commands, I related to him the Revolution under the Prince of Orange,[1] the long war with France[2] entered into by the said Prince, and renewed by his successor the present Queen, wherein the greatest powers of Christendom were engaged, and which still continued: I computed, at his request, that about a million of Yahoos might have been killed in the whole progress of it, and perhaps a hundred or more cities taken, and five times as many ships burnt or sunk.

He asked me what were the usual causes or motives that made one country go to war with another. I answered they were innumerable, but I should only mention a few of the chief. Sometimes the ambition of princes, who never think they have land or people enough to govern; sometimes the corruption of ministers, who engage their master in a war in order to stifle or divert the clamor of the subjects against their evil administration. Difference in opinions[3] hath cost many millions of lives: for instance, whether *flesh* be *bread*, or *bread* be *flesh*; whether the juice of a certain *berry* be *blood* or *wine*; whether *whistling* be a vice or a virtue; whether it be better to *kiss a post*, or throw it into the fire; what is the best color for a *coat*, whether *black*, *white*, *red*, or *grey*; and whether it should be *long* or *short*, *narrow* or *wide*, *dirty* or *clean*, with many more. Neither are any wars so furious and bloody, or of so long continuance, as those occasioned by difference in opinion, especially if it be in things indifferent.[4]

Sometimes the quarrel between two princes is to decide which of them shall dispossess a third of his dominions, where neither of them pretend to any right. Sometimes one prince quarrels with another, for fear the other should quarrel with him. Sometimes a war is entered upon, because the enemy is too *strong*, and sometimes because he is too *weak*. Sometimes our neighbors *want* the *things* which we *have*, or *have* the *things* which we *want*; and we both fight, till they take ours or give us theirs. It is a very justifiable cause of war to invade a country after the people have been wasted by famine, destroyed by pestilence, or embroiled by factions amongst themselves.[5] It is justifiable to enter into a war against our nearest ally, when one of his towns lies convenient for us, or a territory of land, that would render our dominions round and compact. If a prince send forces into a nation where the people are poor and ignorant, he may lawfully put half of them to death, and make slaves of the rest, in order to civilize and reduce[6] them from their barbarous way of living. It is a

9. Presumably "barbarous," because English both lacks appropriate words to express Houyhnhnm concepts and has concepts (e.g., of lust, malice, envy) for which the other language has no words.

1. The Glorious Revolution of 1688 by which William of Orange, and his wife, Mary Stuart, ascended to the English throne in 1689.

2. The War of the League of Augsburg (1689–1697) and the War of the Spanish Succession (1701–1713), which Swift (as a good Tory) opposed.

3. Religious controversies, over the doctrine of transubstantiation, the place of music (whistling) and images (the post) in church, and the color and style of liturgical vestments.

4. Of no importance either way.

5. Probably a reference to the English Civil War of 1642–1646, 1648.

6. Convert.

very kingly, honorable, and frequent practice, when one prince desires the assistance of another to secure him against an invasion, that the assistant, when he hath driven out the invader, should seize on the dominions himself, and kill, imprison, or banish the prince he came to relieve. Alliance by blood or marriage is a sufficient cause of war between princes, and the nearer the kindred is, the greater is their disposition to quarrel: *poor* nations are *hungry*, and *rich* nations are *proud*, and pride and hunger will ever be at variance. For these reasons, the trade of a *soldier* is held the most honorable of all others: because a *soldier* is a Yahoo hired to kill in cold blood as many of his own species, who have never offended him, as possibly he can.

There is likewise a kind of beggarly princes in Europe, not able to make war by themselves, who hire out their troops to richer nations, for so much a day to each man; of which they keep three fourths to themselves, and it is the best part of their maintenance; such are those in Germany and other northern parts of Europe.[7]

What you have told me (said my master), upon the subject of war, doth indeed discover most admirably the effects of that reason you pretend to: however, it is happy that the *shame* is greater than the *danger*; and that Nature hath left you utterly uncapable of doing much mischief. For your mouths lying flat with your faces, you can hardly bite each other to any purpose, unless by consent. Then as to the claws upon your feet before and behind, they are so short and tender, that one of our Yahoos would drive a dozen of yours before him. And therefore in recounting the numbers of those who have been killed in battle, I cannot but think that you have *said the thing which is not*.

I could not forbear shaking my head and smiling a little at his ignorance. And, being no stranger to the art of war, I gave him a description of cannons, culverins,[8] muskets, carabines,[9] pistols, bullets, powder, swords, bayonets, battles, sieges, retreats, attacks, undermines, countermines,[1] bombardments, seafights; ships sunk with a thousand men, twenty thousand killed on each side; dying groans, limbs flying in the air, smoke, noise, confusion, trampling to death under horses' feet; flight, pursuit, victory; fields strewed with carcasses left for food to dogs, and wolves, and birds of prey; plundering, stripping, ravishing, burning, and destroying. And to set forth the valor of my own dear countrymen, I assured him, that I had seen them blow up a hundred enemies at once in a siege, and as many in a ship, and beheld the dead bodies drop down in pieces from the clouds, to the great diversion of all the spectators.

I was going on to more particulars, when my master commanded me silence. He said, whoever understood the nature of Yahoos might easily believe it possible for so vile an animal to be capable of every action I had named, if their strength and cunning equaled their malice. But as my discourse had increased his abhorrence of the whole species, so he found it gave him a disturbance in his mind, to which he was wholly a stranger before. He thought his ears being used to such abominable words, might by degrees admit them with less detestation. That although he hated the Yahoos of this country, yet he no more blamed them for their odious qualities, than he did a *gnnayh* (a bird of prey) for its cruelty, or a sharp stone for cutting his hoof. But when a creature pretending to reason could be capable of such enormities, he dreaded lest[2] the corruption of that faculty might be worse than brutality itself. He

7. George I employed German mercenaries in his defense of Hanover.
8. Large cannons.
9. Short firearms.
1. Digging under fortification walls, and counter-digging by those inside the fort to stop the besiegers.
2. Worried that.

seemed therefore confident, that instead of reason, we were only possessed of some quality fitted to increase our natural vices; as the reflection from a troubled stream returns the image of an ill-shapen body, not only *larger*, but more *distorted*.

He added, that he had heard too much upon the subject of war, both in this, and some former discourses. There was another point which a little perplexed him at present. I had said, that some of our crew left their country on account of being ruined by *law;* that I had already explained the meaning of the word; but he was at a loss how it should come to pass, that the *law* which was intended for *every* man's preservation, should be any man's ruin. Therefore he desired to be farther satisfied what I meant by *law*, and the dispensers thereof, according to the present practice in my own country; because he thought Nature and reason were sufficient guides for a reasonable animal, as we pretended to be, in showing us what we ought to do, and what to avoid.

I assured his Honor, that law was a science wherein I had not much conversed,[3] further than by employing advocates in vain, upon some injustices that had been done me; however, I would give him all the satisfaction I was able.

I said there was a society of men among us, bred up from their youth in the art of proving by words multiplied for the purpose, that white is black, and black is white, according as they are paid.[4] To this society all the rest of the people are slaves. For example, if my neighbor hath a mind to my cow, he hires a lawyer to prove that he ought to have my cow from me. I must then hire another to defend my right, it being against all rules of law that any man should be allowed to speak for himself.[5] Now in this case, I who am the true owner lie under two great disadvantages. First, my lawyer, being practiced almost from his cradle in defending falsehood, is quite out of his element when he would be an advocate for justice, which as an office unnatural, he always attempts with great awkwardness, if not with ill will. The second disadvantage is, that my lawyer must proceed with great caution, or else he will be reprimanded by the judges, and abhorred by his brethren, as one who would lessen the practice[6] of the law. And therefore I have but two methods to preserve my cow. The first is to gain over my adversary's lawyer with a double fee, who will then betray his client by insinuating that he hath justice on his side. The second way is for my lawyer to make my cause appear as unjust as he can, by allowing the cow to belong to my adversary; and this if it be skillfully done will certainly bespeak[7] the favor of the Bench.

Now, your Honor is to know that these judges are persons appointed to decide all controversies of property, as well as for the trial of criminals, and picked out from the most dexterous lawyers who are grown old or lazy, and having been biased all their lives against truth and equity, lie under such a fatal necessity of favoring fraud, perjury, and oppression, that I have known several of them refuse a large bribe from the side where justice lay, rather than injure the *Faculty*[8] by doing anything unbecoming their nature or their office.

3. Had not had much instruction.
4. Swift's satirical treatment of lawyers probably stems from his dislike of Lord Chief Justice Whitehead, who tried to force juries to give verdicts against Swift and the printer of two of his political pamphlets.
5. One of Swift's many references to Thomas More's *Utopia* (1516) in this discussion of the ideals of human and Houyhnhnm society. *Utopia* suggests that it is "better for each man to plead for his own cause, and tell the judge the same story he'd otherwise tell his lawyer." Other important sources for *Gulliver* include Lucian's *True History* (mid-second century A.D.); Cyrano de Bergerac's *Histoire comique des états et empires de la lune* (1656); William Temple's essay *Of Heroick Virtue* (in *Miscellanea*, pt. 2, 1692); William Dampier's *New Voyage Round the World* (1697); and Lionel Wafer's *A New Voyage and Description of the Isthmus of America* (1699), which includes descriptions of monkeys Swift may have used for the Yahoos.
6. Both profession, and morally questionable dealing.
7. Gain.
8. Legal profession.

It is a maxim among these lawyers, that whatever hath been done before, may legally be done again; and therefore they take special care to record all the decisions formerly made against common justice and the general reason of mankind. These, under the name of *precedents*, they produce as authorities to justify the most iniquitous opinions; and the judges never fail of directing accordingly.

In pleading, they studiously avoid entering into the *merits* of the cause; but are loud, violent, and tedious in dwelling upon all *circumstances* which are not to the purpose. For instance, in the case already mentioned; they never desire to know what claim or title my adversary hath to my cow, but whether the said cow were red or black, her horns long or short, whether the field I graze her in be round or square, whether she were milked at home or abroad, what diseases she is subject to, and the like; after which they consult *precedents*, adjourn the cause from time to time, and in ten, twenty, or thirty years come to an issue.

It is likewise to be observed that this society hath a peculiar cant[9] and jargon of their own, that no other mortal can understand, and wherein all their laws are written, which they take special care to multiply; whereby they have wholly confounded the very essence of truth and falsehood, of right and wrong; so that it will take thirty years to decide whether the field, left me by my ancestors for six generations, belong to me or to a stranger three hundred miles off.

In the trial of persons accused for crimes against the state the method is much more short and commendable: the judge first sends to sound the disposition of those in power, after which he can easily hang or save the criminal, strictly preserving all the forms of law.

Here my master, interposing, said it was a pity, that creatures endowed with such prodigious abilities of mind as these lawyers, by the description I gave of them, must certainly be, were not rather encouraged to be instructors of others in wisdom and knowledge. In answer to which, I assured his Honor, that in all points out of their own trade they were usually the most ignorant and stupid generation among us, the most despicable in common conversation, avowed enemies to all knowledge and learning, and equally disposed to pervert the general reason of mankind in every other subject of discourse, as in that of their own profession.

Chapter 6

A continuation of the state of England. The character of a first Minister.[1]

My master was yet wholly at a loss to understand what motives could incite this race of lawyers to perplex, disquiet, and weary themselves by engaging in a confederacy of injustice, merely for the sake of injuring their fellow animals; neither could he comprehend what I meant in saying they did it for *hire*. Whereupon I was at much pains to describe to him the use of *money*, the materials it was made of, and the value of the metals; that when a Yahoo had got a great store of this precious substance, he was able to purchase whatever he had a mind to, the finest clothing, the noblest houses, great tracts of land, the most costly meats and drinks, and have his choice of the most beautiful females. Therefore since *money* alone was able to perform all these feats, our Yahoos thought they could never have enough of it to spend or to save, as they found

9. Both insincere and specialist language.

1. Swift's first printer/publisher, Benjamin Motte, prudently added "under Queen Anne" and "in the Courts of Europe" at the end of these two sentences, respectively, to remove some of the sting from this satire on George I's reign.

themselves inclined from their natural bent either to profusion or avarice. That the rich man enjoyed the fruit of the poor man's labor, and the latter were a thousand to one in proportion to the former.[2] That the bulk of our people was forced to live miserably, by laboring every day for small wages to make a few live plentifully. I enlarged myself[3] much on these and many other particulars to the same purpose: but his Honor was still to seek,[4] for he went upon a supposition that all animals had a title to their share in the productions of the earth, and especially those[5] who presided over the rest. Therefore he desired I would let him know, what these costly meats were, and how any of us happened to want them. Whereupon I enumerated as many sorts as came into my head, with the various methods of dressing them, which could not be done without sending vessels by sea to every part of the world, as well for liquors to drink, as for sauces, and innumerable other conveniencies. I assured him, that this whole globe of earth must be at least three times gone round, before one of our better female Yahoos could get her breakfast, or a cup to put it in.[6] He said, that must needs be a miserable country which cannot furnish food for its own inhabitants. But what he chiefly wondered at was how such vast tracts of ground as I described should be wholly without *fresh water*, and the people put to the necessity of sending over the sea for drink. I replied, that England (the dear place of my nativity) was computed to produce three times the quantity of food more than its inhabitants are able to consume, as well as liquors extracted from grain, or pressed out of the fruit of certain trees, which made excellent drink, and the same proportion in every other convenience of life. But in order to feed the luxury and intemperance of the males, and the vanity of the females, we sent away the greatest part of our necessary things to other countries, from whence in return we brought the materials of diseases, folly, and vice, to spend among ourselves. Hence it follows of necessity, that vast numbers of our people are compelled to seek their livelihood by begging, robbing, stealing, cheating, pimping, forswearing,[7] flattering, suborning,[8] forging, gaming, lying, fawning, hectoring,[9] voting, scribbling, stargazing,[1] poisoning, whoring, canting,[2] libeling, freethinking,[3] and the like occupations: every one of which terms, I was at much pains to make him understand.

That *wine* was not imported among us from foreign countries to supply the want of water or other drinks, but because it was a sort of liquid which made us merry, by putting us out of our senses; diverted all melancholy thoughts, begat wild extravagant imaginations in the brain, raised our hopes, and banished our fears, suspended every office of reason for a time, and deprived us of the use of our limbs, till we fell into a profound sleep; although it must be confessed, that we always awaked sick and dispirited, and that the use of this liquor filled us with diseases, which made our lives uncomfortable and short.[4]

But beside all this, the bulk of our people supported themselves by furnishing the necessities or conveniencies of life to the rich, and to each other. For instance, when I am at home and dressed as I ought to be, I carry on my body the workmanship of an hundred tradesmen; the building and furniture of my house employ as many more, and five times the number to adorn my wife.

2. A theme of Thomas More's *Utopia* (1516).
3. Explained myself further.
4. Unable to understand.
5. The ruling species.
6. Coffee, tea, and chocolate were relatively new (and highly fashionable) drinks; chinaware was also imported.
7. Perjury.
8. Inducing through bribery.
9. Bullying.
1. Sensationalist popular astrology of the type Swift mocked when writing as "Isaac Bickerstaff" in 1708.
2. Using jargon, often for deceit.
3. Freethinkers rejected religious authority and dogma in favor of rational inquiry and speculation.
4. Swift, however, was a great wine drinker.

I was going on to tell him of another sort of people, who get their livelihood by attending the sick, having upon some occasions informed his Honor that many of my crew had died of diseases. But here it was with the utmost difficulty that I brought him to apprehend what I meant. He could easily conceive, that a Houyhnhnm grew weak and heavy a few days before his death, or by some accident might hurt a limb. But that Nature, who worketh all things to perfection, should suffer any pains to breed in our bodies, he thought impossible, and desired to know the reason of so unaccountable an evil. I told him, we fed on a thousand things which operated contrary to each other; that we ate when we were not hungry, and drank without the provocation of thirst; that we sat whole nights drinking strong liquors without eating a bit, which disposed us to sloth, inflamed our bodies, and precipitated or prevented digestion. That prostitute female Yahoos acquired a certain malady, which bred rottenness in the bones of those who fell into their embraces; that this and many other diseases were propagated from father to son, so that great numbers come into the world with complicated maladies upon them; that it would be endless to give him a catalog of all diseases incident to human bodies; for they could not be fewer than five or six hundred, spread over every limb, and joint; in short, every part, external and intestine, having diseases appropriated to each. To remedy which, there was a sort of people bred up among us, in the profession or pretense of curing the sick. And because I had some skill in the faculty, I would, in gratitude to his Honor, let him know the whole mystery[5] and method by which they proceed.

Their fundamental is, that all diseases arise from *repletion*, from whence they conclude, that a great *evacuation* of the body is necessary, either through the natural passage, or upwards at the mouth. Their next business is, from herbs, minerals, gums, oils, shells, salts, juices, seaweed, excrements, barks of trees, serpents, toads, frogs, spiders, dead men's flesh and bones, birds, beasts and fishes, to form a composition for smell and taste the most abominable, nauseous, and detestable that they can possibly contrive, which the stomach immediately rejects with loathing; and this they call a *vomit;*[6] or else from the same storehouse, with some other poisonous additions, they command us to take in at the orifice *above* or *below* (just as the physician then happens to be disposed), a medicine equally annoying and disgustful to the bowels, which, relaxing the belly, drives down all before it; and this they call a *purge*, or a *clyster*.[7] For Nature (as the physicians allege) having intended the superior anterior orifice[8] only for the *intromission* of solids and liquids, and the inferior posterior for ejection, these artists ingeniously considering that in all diseases Nature is forced out of her seat; therefore to replace her in it, the body must be treated in a manner directly contrary, by interchanging the use of each orifice, forcing solids and liquids in at the anus, and making evacuations at the mouth.

But, besides real diseases, we are subject to many that are only imaginary, for which the physicians have invented imaginary cures; these have their several names, and so have the drugs that are proper for them, and with these our female Yahoos are always infested.

One great excellency in this tribe is their skill at *prognostics*, wherein they seldom fail; their predictions in real diseases, when they rise to any degree of malignity, generally portending *death*, which is always in their power, when recovery is not: and therefore, upon any unexpected signs of amendment, after they have pronounced

5. Medical secrets.
6. Dr. John Woodward (1665–1728), a leading member of the Royal Society, was noted for believing this method a cure for virtually all ills.
7. Enema.
8. The mouth.

their sentence, rather than be accused as false prophets, they know how to approve their sagacity to the world by a seasonable dose.[9]

They are likewise of special use to husbands and wives who are grown weary of their mates, to eldest sons, to great ministers of state, and often to princes.[1]

I had formerly upon occasion discoursed with my master upon the nature of *government* in general, and particularly of our own *excellent Constitution*, deservedly the wonder and envy of the whole world. But having here accidentally mentioned a *Minister of State*, he commanded me some time after to inform him, what species of Yahoo I particularly meant by that appellation.

I told him, that a *First* or *Chief Minister of State*[2] whom I intended to describe, was a creature wholly exempt from joy and grief, love and hatred, pity and anger; at least made use of no other passions but a violent desire of wealth, power, and titles; that he applies his words to all uses, except to the indication of his mind,[3] that he never tells a *truth*, but with an intent that you should take it for a *lie;* nor a *lie*, but with a design that you should take it for a *truth* that those he speaks worst of behind their backs are in the surest way to preferment[4] and whenever he begins to praise you to others or to yourself, you are from that day forlorr.[5] The worst mark you can receive is a *promise*, especially when it is confirmed with an oath; after which every wise man retires, and gives over all hopes.

There are three methods by which a man may rise to be Chief Minister: the first is, by knowing how with prudence to dispose of a wife, a daughter, or a sister; the second, by betraying or undermining his predecessor; and the third is, by a *furious zeal* in public assemblies against the corruptions of the Court. But a wise prince would rather choose to employ those who practice the last of these methods; because such zealots prove always the most obsequious and subservient to the will and passions of their master. That the *Ministers* having all employment[6] at their disposal, preserve themselves in power by bribing the majority of a senate or great council; and at last, by an expedient called an *Act of Indemnity*,[7] (whereof I described the nature to him) they secure themselves from after-reckonings, and retire from the public, laden with the spoils of the nation.

The palace of a *Chief Minister* is a seminary to breed up others in his own trade: the pages, lackeys, and porter, by imitating their master, become *Ministers of State* in their several districts, and learn to excel in the three principal *ingredients*, of *insolence, lying*, and *bribery*. Accordingly, they have a *subaltern*[8] court paid to them by persons of the best rank, and sometimes by the force of dexterity and impudence arrive through several gradations to be successors to their lord.

He is usually governed by a decayed wench[9] or favorite footman, who are the tunnels[1] through which all graces[2] are conveyed, and may properly be called, *in the last resort*, the governors of the kingdom.

9. Cf. *Verses on the Death of Dr. Swift*, lines 131–132: "He'd rather choose that I should die / Than his prediction prove a lie" (page 2356).
1. The references are to Queen Caroline, Prince Frederick, and Walpole.
2. A satire on Robert Walpole, then the First Minister or "Prime Minister."
3. Real thoughts or intentions.
4. Most likely to receive a government position or promotion.
5. Forsaken, ruined.
6. Government positions.
7. Swift here suggests that corrupt government ministers make themselves secure from any future legal prosecution for their illegal dealings. He refers to the Act of Indemnity and Oblivion of 1660, which pardoned almost all those who had taken part in the English Civil War (1642–1646, 1648), or the subsequent Commonwealth government (1649–1660).
8. Lower-ranking.
9. The government Minister's mistress is "decayed" either in age or in morals.
1. Routes or conduits.
2. Favors.

One day my master, having heard me mention the *nobility* of my country, was pleased to make me a compliment which I could not pretend to deserve: that he was sure I must have been born of some noble family, because I far exceeded in shape, color, and cleanliness, all the Yahoos of his nation, although I seemed to fail in strength and agility, which must be imputed to my different way of living from those other brutes; and besides, I was not only endowed with a faculty of speech, but likewise with some rudiments of reason, to a degree, that with all his acquaintance I passed for a prodigy.

He made me observe, that among the Houyhnhnms, the white, the *sorrel*, and the *iron-grey* were not so exactly shaped as the *bay*, the *dapple-grey*, and the *black;* nor born with equal talents of mind, or a capacity to improve them; and therefore continued always in the condition of servants, without ever aspiring to match[3] out of their own race, which in that country would be reckoned monstrous and unnatural.

I made his Honor my most humble acknowledgments for the good opinion he was pleased to conceive of me; but assured him at the same time, that my birth was of the lower sort, having been born of plain, honest parents, who were just able to give me a tolerable education; that *nobility* among us was altogether a different thing from the idea he had of it; that our young *noblemen* are bred from their childhood in idleness and luxury; that as soon as years will permit, they consume their vigor and contract odious diseases among lewd females; and when their fortunes are almost ruined, they marry some woman of mean birth, disagreeable person, and unsound constitution, merely for the sake of money, whom they hate and despise. That the productions of such marriages are generally scrofulous,[4] rickety,[5] or deformed children, by which means the family seldom continues above three generations, unless the wife take care to provide a healthy father among her neighbors or domestics, in order to improve and continue the breed. That a weak diseased body, a meager countenance, and sallow complexion are the true marks of *noble blood;* and a healthy robust appearance is so disgraceful in a man of quality, that the world concludes his real father to have been a groom, or a coachman. The imperfections of his mind run parallel with those of his body, being a composition of spleen, dullness, ignorance, caprice, sensuality, and pride.

Without the consent of this *illustrious body* no law can be enacted, repealed, or altered, and these nobles have likewise the decision of all our possessions without appeal.[6]

Chapter 7

The author's great love of his native country. His master's observations upon the Constitution and Administration of England, as described by the author, with parallel cases and comparisons. His master's observations upon human nature.

The reader may be disposed to wonder how I could prevail on myself to give so free a representation of my own species, among a race of mortals who were already too apt to conceive the vilest opinion of humankind from that entire congruity betwixt me and their Yahoos. But I must freely confess, that the many virtues of those excellent *quadrupeds*, placed in opposite view to human corruptions, had so far opened mine

3. Mate.
4. Tubercular.
5. Feeble, weak-jointed.
6. Swift here refers to the House of Lords, the upper house of Parliament and the highest law court in the land.

eyes and enlarged my understanding, that I began to view the actions and passions of man in a very different light, and to think the honor of my own kind not worth managing[7] which, besides, it was impossible for me to do before a person of so acute a judgment as my master, who daily convinced me of a thousand faults in myself, whereof I had not the least perception before, and which with us would never be numbered even among human infirmities. I had likewise learned from his example an utter detestation of all falsehood or disguise; and *truth* appeared so amiable to me, that I determined upon sacrificing everything to it.

Let me deal so candidly with the reader, as to confess, that there was yet a much stronger motive for the freedom I took in my representation of things. I had not been a year in this country before I contracted such a love and veneration for the inhabitants, that I entered on a firm resolution never to return to humankind, but to pass the rest of my life among these admirable Houyhnhnms in the contemplation and practice of every virtue; where I could have no example or incitement to vice. But it was decreed by Fortune, my perpetual enemy, that so great a felicity should not fall to my share. However, it is now some comfort to reflect, that in what I said of my countrymen, I *extenuated* their faults as much as I durst before so strict an examiner, and upon every article gave as *favorable* a turn as the matter would bear. For, indeed, who is there alive that will not be swayed by his bias and partiality to the place of his birth?

I have related the substance of several conversations I had with my master, during the greatest part of the time I had the honor to be in his service, but have indeed for brevity sake omitted much more than is here set down.

When I had answered all his questions, and his curiosity seemed to be fully satisfied, he sent for me one morning early, and commanding me to sit down at some distance (an honor which he had never before conferred upon me), he said, he had been very seriously considering my whole story, as far as it related both to myself and my country: that he looked upon us as a sort of animals to whose share, by what accident he could not conjecture, some small pittance of *reason* had fallen, whereof we made no other use than by its assistance to aggravate our *natural* corruptions, and to acquire new ones which Nature had not given us. That we disarmed ourselves of the few abilities she had bestowed, had been very successful in multiplying our original wants, and seemed to spend our whole lives in vain endeavors to supply them by our own inventions. That as to myself, it was manifest I had neither the strength or agility of a common Yahoo, that I walked infirmly on my hinder feet, had found out a contrivance to make my claws of no use or defense, and to remove the hair from my chin, which was intended as a shelter from the sun and the weather. Lastly, that I could neither run with speed, nor climb trees like my *brethren* (as he called them) the Yahoos in this country.

That our institutions of *government* and *law* were plainly owing to our gross defects in *reason*, and by consequence, in *virtue;* because *reason* alone is sufficient to govern a *rational* creature; which was therefore a character we had no pretense to challenge,[8] even from the account I had given of my own people, although he manifestly perceived, that in order to favor them I had concealed many particulars, and often *said the thing which was not*.

He was the more confirmed in this opinion, because he observed, that as I agreed in every feature of my body with other Yahoos, except where it was to my real disadvantage in point of strength, speed, and activity, the shortness of my claws,

7. Maintaining.

8. We had no right to claim to be rational creatures.

and some other particulars where Nature had no part; so from the representation I had given him of our lives, our manners, and our actions, he found as near a resemblance in the disposition of our minds. He said the Yahoos were known to hate one another more than they did any different species of animals; and the reason usually assigned, was, the odiousness of their own shapes, which all could see in the rest, but not in themselves. He had therefore begun to think it not unwise in us to *cover* our bodies, and, by that invention, conceal many of our deformities from each other, which would else be hardly supportable. But, he now found he had been mistaken, and that the dissensions of those brutes in his country were owing to the same cause with ours, as I had described them. For if (said he) you throw among five Yahoos as much food as would be sufficient for fifty, they will, instead of eating peaceably, fall together by the ears, each single one impatient to *have all to itself;* and therefore a servant was usually employed to stand by while they were feeding abroad, and those kept at home were tied at a distance from each other; that if a cow died of age or accident, before a Houyhnhnm could secure it for his own Yahoos, those in the neighborhood would come in herds to seize it, and then would ensue such a battle as I had described, with terrible wounds made by their claws on both sides, although they seldom were able to kill one another, for want of such convenient instruments of death as we had invented. At other times the like battles have been fought between the Yahoos of several neighborhoods without any visible cause: those of one district watching all opportunities to surprise the next before they are prepared. But if they find their project hath miscarried, they return home, and for want of enemies, engage in what I call a civil war among themselves.

That in some fields of his country there are certain *shining stones* of several colors, whereof the Yahoos are violently fond, and when part of these *stones* are fixed in the earth, as it sometimes happens, they will dig with their claws for whole days to get them out, and carry them away, and hide them by heaps in their kennels; but still looking round with great caution, for fear their comrades should find out their treasure. My master said, he could never discover the reason of this unnatural appetite, or how these *stones* could be of any use to a Yahoo; but now he believed it might proceed from the same principle of *avarice* which I had ascribed to mankind; that he had once, by way of experiment, privately removed a heap of these *stones* from the place where one of his Yahoos had buried it: whereupon, the sordid animal, missing his treasure, by his loud lamenting brought the whole herd to the place, there miserably howled, then fell to biting and tearing the rest, began to pine away, would neither eat, nor sleep, nor work, till he ordered a servant privately to convey the *stones* into the same hole, and hide them as before; which when his Yahoo had found, he presently recovered his spirits and good humor, but took care to remove them to a better hiding place, and hath ever since been a very serviceable brute.

My master farther assured me, which I also observed myself, that in the fields where these *shining stones* abound, the fiercest and most frequent battles are fought, occasioned by perpetual inroads of the neighboring Yahoos.[9]

He said, it was common, when two Yahoos discovered such a *stone* in a field, and were contending which of them should be the proprietor, a third would take the advantage,[1] and carry it away from them both; which my master would needs

9. Neighboring Yahoos attempt invasions to steal these stones.

1. Opportunity.

contend to have some resemblance with our *suits at law;* wherein I thought it for our credit not to undeceive him; since the decision he mentioned was much more equitable than many decrees among us: because the plaintiff and defendant there lost nothing beside the *stone* they contended for, whereas our *Courts of Equity*[2] would never have dismissed the cause while either of them had anything left.

My master, continuing his discourse, said, there was nothing that rendered the Yahoos more odious, than their undistinguishing appetite to devour everything that came in their way, whether herbs, roots, berries, the corrupted flesh of animals, or all mingled together; and it was peculiar in their temper, that they were fonder of what they could get by rapine or stealth at a greater distance, than much better food provided for them at home. If their prey held out, they would eat till they were ready to burst, after which Nature had pointed out to them a certain *root* that gave them a general evacuation.

There was also another kind of *root* very *juicy*, but something rare and difficult to be found, which the Yahoos sought for with much eagerness, and would suck it with great delight; and it produced in them the same effects that wine hath upon us. It would make them sometimes hug, and sometimes tear one another; they would howl and grin, and chatter, and reel, and tumble, and then fall asleep in the mud.

I did indeed observe, that the Yahoos were the only animals in this country subject to any diseases; which, however, were much fewer than horses have among us, and contracted not by any ill treatment they meet with, but by the nastiness and greediness of that sordid brute. Neither has their language any more than a general appellation for those maladies, which is borrowed from the name of the beast, and called *hnea-Yahoo*, or the *Yahoo's-evil*, and the cure prescribed is a mixture of *their own dung* and *urine* forcibly put down the Yahoo's throat. This I have since often known to have been taken with success, and do here freely recommend it to my countrymen, for the public good, as an admirable specific against all diseases produced by repletion.[3]

As to learning, government, arts, manufactures, and the like, my master confessed he could find little or no resemblance between the Yahoos of that country and those in ours. For, he only meant to observe what parity there was in our natures. He had heard indeed some curious Houyhnhnms observe, that in most herds there was a sort of ruling Yahoo (as among us there is generally some leading or principal stag in a park), who was always more *deformed* in body, and *mischievous* in *disposition*, than any of the rest. That this *leader* had usually a favorite as *like himself* as he could get, whose employment was to *lick his master's feet and posteriors, and drive the female Yahoos to his kennel;* for which he was now and then rewarded with a piece of ass's flesh. This *favorite* is hated by the whole herd, and therefore to protect himself, keeps always *near the person of his leader*. He usually continues in office till a worse can be found; but the very moment he is discarded, his successor, at the head of all the Yahoos in that district, young and old, male and female, come in a body, and discharge their excrements upon him from head to foot. But how far this might be applicable to our *Courts* and *favorites*, and *Ministers of State*, my master said I could best determine.

I durst make no return to this malicious insinuation, which debased human understanding below the sagacity of a common *hound*, who hath judgment enough to distinguish and follow the cry of the *ablest dog in the pack*, without being ever mistaken.

2. Courts that decide on general (rather than common) principles of law. Swift ironically plays on the name of the court.

3. Overeating.

My master told me, there were some qualities remarkable in the Yahoos, which he had not observed me to mention, or at least very slightly, in the accounts I had given him of humankind: he said, those animals, like other brutes, had their females in common,[4] but in this they differed, that the she-Yahoo would admit the male while she was pregnant, and that the hes[5] would quarrel and fight with the females as fiercely as with each other. Both which practices were such degrees of infamous brutality, that no other sensitive[6] creature ever arrived at.

Another thing he wondered at in the Yahoos, was their strange disposition to nastiness and dirt, whereas there appears to be a natural love of cleanliness in all other animals. As to the two former accusations, I was glad to let them pass without any reply, because I had not a word to offer upon them in defense of my species, which otherwise I certainly had done from my own inclinations. But I could have easily vindicated humankind from the imputation of singularity upon the last article, if there had been any *swine* in that country (as unluckily for me there were not), which although it may be a *sweeter quadruped* than a Yahoo, cannot, I humbly conceive, in justice pretend to more cleanliness; and so his Honor himself must have owned, if he had seen their filthy way of feeding, and their custom of wallowing and sleeping in the mud.

My master likewise mentioned another quality which his servants had discovered in several Yahoos, and to him was wholly unaccountable. He said, a fancy would sometimes take a Yahoo to retire into a corner, to lie down and howl, and groan, and spurn away all that came near him, although he were young and fat, and wanted neither food nor water; nor did the servants imagine what could possibly ail him. And the only remedy they found was to set him to hard work, after which he would infallibly come to himself. To this I was silent out of partiality to my own kind; yet here I could plainly discover the true seeds of *spleen*,[7] which only seizeth on the *lazy*, the *luxurious*, and the *rich*; who, if they were forced to undergo the *same regimen*, I would undertake for[8] the cure.

His Honor had farther observed, that a female Yahoo would often stand behind a bank or a bush, to gaze on the young males passing by, and then appear, and hide, using many antic gestures and grimaces, at which time it was observed, that she had a most *offensive smell;* and when any of the males advanced, would slowly retire, looking often back, and with a counterfeit show of fear, run off into some convenient place where she knew the male would follow her.[9]

At other times if a female stranger came among them, three or four of her own sex would get about her, and stare and chatter, and grin, and smell her all over, and then turn off with gestures that seemed to express contempt and disdain.

Perhaps my master might refine a little in these speculations, which he had drawn from what he observed himself, or had been told him by others; however, I could not reflect without some amazement, and much sorrow, that the rudiments of *lewdness*, *coquetry*, *censure*, and *scandal*, should have place by instinct in womankind.

I expected every moment that my master would accuse the Yahoos of those unnatural appetites in both sexes, so common among us. But Nature it seems hath not

4. Implying that English society did the same.
5. The males.
6. Sensible, thinking.
7. Depression.
8. Guarantee.
9. The sort of seduction tactics used by female characters in literary pastoral.

been so expert a schoolmistress; and these politer pleasures are entirely the productions of art and reason, on our side of the globe.

CHAPTER 8

The author relateth several particulars of the Yahoos. The great virtues of the Houyhnhnms. The education and exercise of their youth. Their general Assembly.

As I ought to have understood human nature much better than I supposed it possible for my master to do, so it was easy to apply the character he gave of the Yahoos to myself and my countrymen, and I believed I could yet make farther discoveries from my own observation. I therefore often begged his Honor to let me go among the herds of Yahoos in the neighborhood, to which he always very graciously consented, being perfectly convinced that the hatred I bore those brutes would never suffer me to be corrupted by them; and his Honor ordered one of his servants, a strong sorrel nag, very honest and good-natured, to be my guard, without whose protection I durst not undertake such adventures. For I have already told the reader how much I was pestered by those odious animals upon my first arrival. I afterwards failed very narrowly three or four times of falling into their clutches, when I happened to stray at any distance without my hanger. And I have reason to believe they had some imagination that I was of their own species, which I often assisted myself, by stripping up my sleeves, and showing my naked arms and breast in their sight, when my protector was with me. At which times they would approach as near as they durst, and imitate my actions after the manner of monkeys, but ever with great signs of hatred, as a tame *jackdaw*,[1] with cap and stockings, is always persecuted by the wild ones, when he happens to be got among them.

They are prodigiously nimble from their infancy; however, I once caught a young male of three years old, and endeavored by all marks of tenderness to make it quiet; but the little imp fell a squalling, and scratching, and biting with such violence, that I was forced to let it go, and it was high time, for a whole troop of old ones came about us at the noise, but finding the cub was safe (for away it ran), and my sorrel nag being by, they durst not venture near us. I observed the young animal's flesh to smell very rank, and the stink was somewhat between a *weasel* and a *fox*, but much more disagreeable. I forgot another circumstance (and perhaps I might have the reader's pardon, if it were wholly omitted), that while I held the odious vermin in my hands, it voided its filthy excrements of a yellow liquid substance all over my clothes; but by good fortune there was a small brook hard by, where I washed myself as clean as I could, although I durst not come into my master's presence, until I were sufficiently aired.

By what I could discover, the Yahoos appear to be the most unteachable of all animals, their capacities never reaching higher than to draw or carry burdens. Yet I am of opinion this defect ariseth chiefly from a perverse, restive[2] disposition. For they are cunning, malicious, treacherous, and revengeful. They are strong and hardy, but of a cowardly spirit, and by consequence insolent, abject, and cruel. It is observed, that the *red-haired* of both sexes are more libidinous and mischievous than the rest, whom yet they much exceed in strength and activity.[3]

The Houyhnhnms keep the Yahoos for present[4] use in huts not far from the house; but the rest are sent abroad to certain fields, where they dig up roots, eat several

1. Small crow, often kept as a pet.
2. Stubborn.
3. A prejudice dating back to medieval times.
4. Daily.

kinds of herbs, and search about for carrion, or sometimes catch weasels and *luhimuhs* (a sort of wild rat), which they greedily devour. Nature hath taught them to dig deep holes with their nails on the side of a rising ground, wherein they lie by themselves, only the kennels of the females are larger, sufficient to hold two or three cubs.

They swim from their infancy like frogs, and are able to continue long under water, where they often take fish, which the females carry home to their young. And upon this occasion, I hope the reader will pardon my relating an odd adventure.

Being one day abroad with my protector the sorrel nag, and the weather exceeding hot, I entreated him to let me bathe in a river that was near. He consented, and I immediately stripped myself stark naked, and went down softly into the stream. It happened that a young female Yahoo, standing behind a bank, saw the whole proceeding, and inflamed by desire, as the nag and I conjectured, came running with all speed, and leaped into the water within five yards of the place where I bathed. I was never in my life so terribly frighted; the nag was grazing at some distance, not suspecting any harm. She embraced me after a most fulsome manner; I roared as loud as I could, and the nag came galloping towards me, whereupon she quitted her grasp, with the utmost reluctancy, and leaped upon the opposite bank, where she stood gazing and howling all the time I was putting on my clothes.

This was matter of diversion to my master and his family, as well as of mortification to myself. For now I could no longer deny, that I was a real Yahoo in every limb and feature, since the females had a natural propensity to me as one of their own species; neither was the hair of this brute of a red color (which might have been some excuse for an appetite a little irregular) but black as a sloe[5] and her countenance did not make an appearance altogether so hideous as the rest of the kind; for, I think, she could not be above eleven years old.[6]

Having already lived three years in this country, the reader I suppose will expect that I should, like other travelers, give him some account of the manners and customs of its inhabitants, which it was indeed my principal study to learn.

As these noble Houyhnhnms are endowed by Nature with a general disposition to all virtues, and have no conceptions or ideas of what is evil in a rational creature, so their grand maxim is, to cultivate *Reason*, and to be wholly governed by it. Neither is *Reason* among them a point problematical as with us, where men can argue with plausibility on both sides of a question, but strikes you with immediate conviction, as it must needs do where it is not mingled, obscured, or discolored by passion and interest.[7] I remember it was with extreme difficulty that I could bring my master to understand the meaning of the word opinion, or how a point could be disputable, because *Reason* taught us to affirm or deny only where we are certain, and beyond our knowledge we cannot do either.[8] So that controversies, wranglings, disputes, and positiveness[9] in false or dubious propositions are evils unknown among the Houyhnhnms. In the like manner, when I used to explain to him our several systems of *natural philosophy*, he would laugh that a creature pretending to *Reason* should value itself upon the knowledge of other people's conjectures, and in things where that knowledge, if it were certain, could be of no use. Wherein he agreed

5. A wild berry.
6. The disparity in age between Gulliver and the Yahoo may suggest a grotesque parody of Esther Vanhomrigh's pursuit of Swift, she being 21 years his junior.
7. Prejudice based on interest in personal benefit. Both Descartes (*Discourse on Method*) and Locke (*Essay Concerning Human Understanding*) wrote of the intuitive nature of some knowledge.
8. Gulliver's master has clearly expressed "opinion" (i.e., prejudice) himself, however.
9. Assertiveness.

entirely with the sentiments of Socrates, as Plato delivers them[1] which I mention as the highest honor I can do that prince of philosophers. I have often since reflected what destruction such a doctrine would make in the libraries of Europe, and how many paths to fame would be then shut up in the learned world.

Friendship and benevolence are the two principal virtues among the Houyhnhnms, and these not confined to particular objects,[2] but universal to the whole race. For a stranger from the remotest part is equally treated with the nearest neighbor, and wherever he goes, looks upon himself as at home. They preserve *decency* and *civility* in the highest degrees, but are altogether ignorant of *ceremony*.[3] They have no fondness for their colts or foals, but the care they take in educating them proceedeth entirely from the dictates of *Reason*. And I observed my master to show the same affection to his neighbor's issue that he had for his own.[4] They will have it that *Nature* teaches them to love the whole species, and it is *Reason* only that maketh a distinction of persons, where there is a superior degree of virtue.

When the matron Houyhnhnms have produced one of each sex, they no longer accompany with[5] their consorts, except they lose one of their issue by some casualty, which very seldom happens: but in such a case they meet again. Or when the like accident befalls a person,[6] whose wife is past bearing, some other couple bestow him one of their own colts, and then go together a second time, till the mother be pregnant. This caution is necessary to prevent the country from being overburdened with numbers.[7] But the race of inferior Houyhnhnms bred up to be servants is not so strictly limited upon this article; these are allowed to produce three of each sex, to be domestics in the noble families.

In their marriages they are exactly careful to choose such colors as will not make any disagreeable mixture in the breed.[8] *Strength* is chiefly valued in the male, and *comeliness* in the female, not upon the account of *love*, but to preserve the race from degenerating; for where a female happens to excel in *strength*, a consort is chosen with regard to *comeliness*. Courtship, love, presents, jointures,[9] settlements, have no place in their thoughts, or terms whereby to express them in their language. The young couple meet and are joined, merely because it is the determination of their parents and friends: it is what they see done every day, and they look upon it as one of the necessary actions in a reasonable being. But the violation of marriage, or any other unchastity, was never heard of, and the married pair pass their lives with the same friendship, and mutual benevolence that they bear to others of the same species who come in their way; without jealousy, fondness, quarreling, or discontent.

In educating the youth of both sexes, their method is admirable, and highly deserveth our imitation. These are not suffered to taste a grain of *oats*, except upon certain days, till eighteen years old; nor *milk*, but very rarely; and in summer they graze two hours in the morning, and as many in the evening, which their parents likewise observe, but the servants are not allowed above half that time, and a great part of their grass is brought home, which they eat at the most convenient hours, when they can be best spared from work.

1. I.e., that ethics (human nature) is worth studying, while the physical world is not, as we can never have certain knowledge of it: "Socrates: I am a friend of learning—the trees and the countryside won't teach me anything, but the people in the city do" *Phaedrus* (230d3–5).
2. To other, particular Houyhnhnms.
3. As are the Utopians.
4. As do men in Plato's *Republic* (461d).
5. Have sex with.
6. A male Houyhnhnm.
7. The Utopians are under no such restriction, knowing (as the Houyhnhnms do not) of other lands to which they can send their excess population.
8. In Plato's *Republic* (458d–461e), eugenic principles also control mating.
9. Marriage settlements for wives, should they survive their husbands.

Temperance, industry, exercise, and *cleanliness,* are the lessons equally enjoined to the young ones of both sexes, and my master thought it monstrous in us to give the females a different kind of education from the males, except in some articles of domestic management,[1] whereby as he truly observed, one half of our natives were good for nothing but bringing children into the world, and to trust the care of their children to such useless animals, he said, was yet a greater instance of brutality.

But the Houyhnhnms train up their youth to strength, speed, and hardiness, by exercising them in running races up and down steep hills, or over hard stony grounds, and when they are all in a sweat, they are ordered to leap over head and ears into a pond or a river. Four times a year the youth of certain districts meet to show their proficiency in running, and leaping, and other feats of strength or agility, where the victor is rewarded with a song made in his or her praise. On this festival the servants drive a herd of Yahoos into the field, laden with hay, and oats, and milk for a repast to the Houyhnhnms; after which, these brutes are immediately driven back again, for fear of being noisome to the assembly.

Every fourth year, at the *vernal equinox,* there is a Representative Council of the whole nation, which meets in a plain about twenty miles from our house, and continueth about five or six days. Here they inquire into the state and condition of the several districts, whether they abound or be deficient in hay or oats, or cows or Yahoos? And wherever there is any want (which is but seldom) it is immediately supplied by unanimous consent and contribution. Here likewise the regulation of children is settled: as for instance, if a Houyhnhnm hath two males, he changeth one of them with another who hath two females: and when a child hath been lost by any casualty, where the mother is past breeding, it is determined what family in the district shall breed another to supply the loss.

Chapter 9

A grand debate at the general Assembly of the Houyhnhnms, and how it was determined. The learning of the Houyhnhnms. Their buildings. Their manner of burials. The defectiveness of their language.

One of these grand Assemblies was held in my time, about three months before my departure, whither my master went as the Representative of our district. In this Council was resumed their old debate, and indeed, the only debate that ever happened in their country; whereof my master after his return gave me a very particular account.

The question to be debated, was, whether the Yahoos should be exterminated from the face of the earth. One of the *members* for the affirmative offered several arguments of great strength and weight, alleging, that as the Yahoos were the most filthy, noisome, and deformed animal which Nature ever produced, so they were the most restive and indocible,[2] mischievous, and malicious: they would privately suck the teats of the Houyhnhnms' cows, kill and devour their cats, trample down their oats and grass, if they were not continually watched, and commit a thousand other extravagancies. He took notice of a general tradition, that Yahoos had not been always in their country, but, that many ages ago, two of these brutes appeared together upon a mountain,[3] whether produced by the heat of the sun upon corrupted mud

1. In both Plato's *Republic* (451e6–7) and *Utopia,* the sexes receive the same education; Swift also began (but never completed) an essay entitled *Of the Education of Ladies* (c. 1728).

2. Unteachable.

3. Probably Milton's "steep savage Hill," the garden of Eden (*Paradise Lost,* 4,172).

and slime, or from the ooze and froth of the sea, was never known.[4] That these Yahoos engendered, and their brood in a short time grew so numerous as to overrun and infest the whole nation. That the Houyhnhnms, to get rid of this evil, made a general hunting, and at last enclosed the whole herd; and destroying the elder, every Houyhnhnm kept two young ones in a kennel, and brought them to such a degree of tameness, as an animal so savage by nature can be capable of acquiring; using them for draft and carriage. That there seemed to be much truth in this tradition, and that those creatures could not be *ylnhniamshy* (or *aborigines* of the land) because of the violent hatred the Houyhnhnms, as well as all other animals, bore them; which although their evil disposition sufficiently deserved, could never have arrived at so high a degree, if they had been *aborigines*, or else they would have long since been rooted out. That the inhabitants taking a fancy to use the service of the Yahoos, had very imprudently neglected to cultivate the breed of *asses*, which were a comely animal, easily kept, more tame and orderly, without any offensive smell, strong enough for labor, although they yield to the other in agility of body; and if their braying be no agreeable sound, it is far preferable to the horrible howlings of the Yahoos.[5]

Several others declared their sentiments to the same purpose, when my master proposed an expedient to the assembly, whereof he had indeed borrowed the hint from me. He approved of the tradition, mentioned by the Honorable Member who spoke before, and affirmed, that the two Yahoos said to be first seen among them had been driven thither over the sea; that coming to land, and being forsaken by their companions, they retired to the mountains, and degenerating by degrees, became in process of time, much more savage than those of their own species in the country from whence these two originals came. The reason of his assertion was, that he had now in his possession a certain wonderful[6] Yahoo (meaning myself), which most of them had heard of, and many of them had seen. He then related to them, how he first found me: that my body was all covered with an artificial composure of the skins and hairs of other animals; that I spoke in a language of my own, and had thoroughly learned theirs; that I had related to him the accidents which brought me thither; that when he saw me without my covering, I was an exact Yahoo in every part, only of a whiter color, less hairy, and with shorter claws. He added, how I had endeavored to persuade him, that in my own and other countries the Yahoos acted as the governing, rational animal, and held the Houyhnhnms in servitude; that he observed in me all the qualities of a Yahoo, only a little more civilized by some tincture of reason, which however was in a degree as far inferior to the Houyhnhnm race, as the Yahoos of their country were to me;[7] that, among other things, I mentioned a custom we had of *castrating* Houyhnhnms when they were young, in order to render them tame; that the operation was easy and safe; that it was no shame to learn wisdom from brutes, as industry is taught by the ant, and building by the swallow. (For so I translate the word *lyhannh,* although it be a much larger fowl.) That this invention might be practiced upon the younger Yahoos here, which, besides rendering them tractable and fitter for use, would in an age put an end to the whole species without destroying life. That, in the meantime the Houyhnhnms should be

4. Humans are supposed to be of divine origin, but the Yahoos represent such a degraded form of humanity that they (like, it was believed, insects on the Nile's banks) were formed from the action of the sun on mud.

5. The commonplace comparison of humans to asses was one Swift had previously used in *A Tale of a Tub* (1704) and *The Battle of the Books* (1704).

6. Amazing, unusual.

7. Gulliver falls between the Houyhnhnms and the Yahoos in reason, as he did between the Lilliputians and the Brobdingnagians in size.

exhorted to cultivate the breed of asses, which, as they are in all respects more valuable brutes, so they have this advantage, to be fit for service at five years old, which the others are not till twelve.

This was all my master thought fit to tell me at that time, of what passed in the grand Council. But he was pleased to conceal[8] one particular, which related personally to myself, whereof I soon felt the unhappy effect, as the reader will know in its proper place, and from whence I date all the succeeding misfortunes of my life.

The Houyhnhnms have no letters, and consequently their knowledge is all traditional. But there happening few events of any moment among a people so well united, naturally disposed to every virtue, wholly governed by reason, and cut off from all commerce with other nations, the historical part is easily preserved without burdening their memories. I have already observed, that they are subject to no diseases, and therefore can have no need of physicians. However, they have excellent medicines composed of herbs, to cure accidental bruises and cuts in the pastern or frog of the foot by sharp stones, as well as other maims and hurts in the several parts of the body.

They calculate the year by the revolution of the sun and the moon, but use no subdivisions into weeks. They are well enough acquainted with the motions of those two luminaries, and understand the nature of eclipses; and this is the utmost progress of their astronomy.

In poetry they must be allowed to excel all other mortals; wherein the justness of their similes, and the minuteness, as well as exactness of their descriptions, are indeed inimitable. Their verses abound very much in both of these, and usually contain either some exalted notions of friendship and benevolence, or the praises of those who were victors in races, and other bodily exercises.[9] Their buildings, although very rude and simple, are not inconvenient, but well contrived to defend them from all injuries of cold and heat. They have a kind of tree, which at forty years old loosens in the root, and falls with the first storm; it grows very straight, and being pointed like stakes with a sharp stone (for the Houyhnhnms know not the use of iron), they stick them erect in the ground about ten inches asunder,[1] and then weave in oat-straw, or sometimes wattles betwixt them. The roof is made after the same manner, and so are the doors.

The Houyhnhnms use the hollow part between the pastern and the hoof of their forefeet as we do our hands, and this with greater dexterity than I could at first imagine. I have seen a white mare of our family thread a needle (which I lent her on purpose) with that joint. They milk their cows, reap their oats, and do all the work which requires hands, in the same manner. They have a kind of hard flints, which by grinding against other stones, they form into instruments, that serve instead of wedges, axes, and hammers. With tools made of these flints they likewise cut their hay, and reap their oats, which there groweth naturally in several fields: the Yahoos draw home the sheaves in carriages, and the servants tread them in certain covered huts, to get out the grain, which is kept in stores. They make a rude kind of earthen and wooden vessels, and bake the former in the sun.

If they can avoid casualties, they die only of old age, and are buried in the obscurest places that can be found, their friends and relations expressing neither joy nor grief at their departure; nor does the dying person discover the least regret that

8. Another indication that the Houyhnhnms are not completely honest or candid.
9. The type of poetry advocated in Plato's *Republic* (390d1–3) and practiced in Sparta.
1. Apart.

he is leaving the world, any more than if he were upon returning[2] home from a visit to one of his neighbors;[3] I remember, my master having once made an appointment with a friend and his family to come to his house upon some affair of importance, on the day fixed, the mistress and her two children came very late; she made two excuses, first for her husband, who, as she said, happened that very morning to *lhnuwnh*. The word is strongly expressive in their language, but not easily rendered into English; it signifies, *to retire to his first mother*. Her excuse for not coming sooner, was, that her husband dying late in the morning, she was a good while consulting her servants about a convenient place where his body should be laid; and I observed she behaved herself at our house as cheerfully as the rest; she died about three months after.

They live generally to seventy or seventy-five years, very seldom to fourscore; some weeks before their death they feel a gradual decay, but without pain. During this time they are much visited by their friends, because they cannot go abroad with their usual ease and satisfaction. However, about ten days before their death, which they seldom fail in computing, they return the visits that have been made them by those who are nearest in the neighborhood, being carried in a convenient sledge drawn by Yahoos, which vehicle they use, not only upon this occasion, but when they grow old, upon long journeys, or when they are lamed by an accident. And therefore when the dying Houyhnhnms return those visits, they take a solemn leave of their friends, as if they were going to some remote part of the country, where they designed to pass the rest of their lives.

I know not whether it may be worth observing, that the Houyhnhnms have no word in their language to express anything that is *evil*, except what they borrow from the deformities or ill qualities of the Yahoos. Thus they denote the folly of a servant, an omission of a child, a stone that cuts their feet, a continuance of foul or unseasonable weather, and the like, by adding to each the epithet of *yahoo*. For instance, *hhnm yahoo*, *whnaholm yahoo*, *ynlhmnawihlma yahoo*, and an ill-contrived house, *ynholmhnmrohlnw yahoo*.

I could with great pleasure enlarge farther upon the manners and virtues of this excellent people; but intending in a short time to publish a volume by itself expressly upon that subject, I refer the reader thither. And in the meantime, proceed to relate my own sad catastrophe.

Chapter 10

The author's economy[4] and happy life among the Houyhnhnms. His great improvement in virtue, by conversing with them. Their conversations. The author hath notice given him by his master that he must depart from the country. He falls into a swoon for grief, but submits. He contrives and finishes a canoe, by the help of a fellow servant, and puts to sea at a venture.[5]

I had settled my little economy to my own heart's content. My master had ordered a room to be made for me after their manner, about six yards from the house, the sides and floors of which I plastered with clay, and covered with rush mats of my own contriving; I had beaten hemp, which there grows wild, and made of it a sort of ticking;[6] this I filled with the feathers of several birds I had taken with springes made of

2. About to return.
3. This attitude toward death is characteristic of both the Stoics, and the Utopians.
4. Method of living.
5. Without further planning.
6. Sturdy material used for making mattress covering.

Yahoos' hairs, and were excellent food; I had worked[7] two chairs with my knife, the sorrel nag helping me in the grosser[8] and more laborious part. When my clothes were worn to rags, I made myself others with the skins of rabbits, and of a certain beautiful animal about the same size, called *nnuhnoh,* the skin of which is covered with a fine down. Of these I likewise made very tolerable stockings. I soled my shoes with wood which I cut from a tree, and fitted to the upper leather, and when this was worn out, I supplied it with the skins of Yahoos dried in the sun. I often got honey out of hollow trees, which I mingled with water;[9] or ate it with my bread. No man could more verify the truth of these two maxims, *That nature is very easily satisfied;* and, *That necessity is the mother of invention.* I enjoyed perfect health of body and tranquillity of mind; I did not feel the treachery or inconstancy of a friend, nor the injuries of a secret or open enemy. I had no occasion of bribing, flattering, or pimping, to procure the favor of any great man or of his minion. I wanted no fence[1] against fraud or oppression; here was neither physician to destroy my body, nor lawyer to ruin my fortune; no informer to watch my words and actions, or forge accusations against me for hire; here were no jibers, censurers, backbiters, pickpockets, highwaymen, housebreakers, attorneys, bawds, buffoons, gamesters, politicians, wits, splenetics, tedious talkers, controvertists, ravishers, murderers, robbers, virtuosos;[2] no leaders or followers of party and faction; no encouragers to vice, by seducement or examples; no dungeon, axes, gibbets, whipping posts, or pillories; no cheating shopkeepers or mechanics;[3] no pride, vanity, or affectation; no fops, bullies, drunkards, strolling whores, or poxes;[4] no ranting, lewd, expensive wives; no stupid, proud pendants; no importunate, overbearing, quarrelsome, noisy, roaring, empty, conceited, swearing companions; no scoundrels, raised from the dust upon the merit of their vices, or nobility thrown into it on account of their virtues; no lords, fiddlers, judges, or dancing masters.[5]

I had the favor of being admitted to[6] several Houyhnhnms, who came to visit or dine with my master; where his Honor graciously suffered me to wait in the room, and listen to their discourse. Both he and his company would often descend to ask me questions, and receive my answers. I had also sometimes the honor of attending my master in his visits to others. I never presumed to speak, except in answer to a question, and then I did it with inward regret, because it was a loss of so much time for improving myself; but I was infinitely delighted with the station of a humble auditor in such conversations, where nothing passed but what was useful, expressed in the fewest and most significant words; where (as I have already said) the greatest *decency* was observed, without the least degree of ceremony; where no person spoke without being pleased himself, and pleasing his companions; where there was no interruption, tediousness, heat,[7] or difference of sentiments. They have a notion, that when people are met together, a short silence doth much improve conversation: this I found to be true, for during those little intermissions of talk, new ideas would arise in their minds, which very much enlivened the discourse. Their subjects are generally on friendship and benevolence, or order and economy, sometimes upon the visible operations of Nature, or ancient traditions, upon the bounds and limits of virtue,

7. Made.
8. Heavier, larger.
9. Honey-sweetened water was a Utopian drink.
1. Defense.
2. One knowledgeable or interested in apparently trivial "scientific" pursuits.
3. Laborers.
4. Venereal diseases.
5. That necessary tutor for the socially aspiring, the dancing master (usually French), was a particular figure of fun; he usually accompanied himself on the fiddle.
6. Allowed to meet.
7. Heat of argument.

upon the unerring rules of reason, or upon some determinations to be taken at the next great Assembly, and often upon the various excellencies of *poetry*. I may add without vanity, that my presence often gave them sufficient matter for discourse, because it afforded my master an occasion of letting his friends into the history of me and my country, upon which they were all pleased to descant in a manner not very advantageous to humankind; and for that reason I shall not repeat what they said: only I may be allowed to observe, that his Honor, to my great admiration, appeared to understand the nature of Yahoos much better than myself. He went through all our vices and follies, and discovered many which I had never mentioned to him, by only supposing what qualities a Yahoo of their country, with a small proportion of reason, might be capable of exerting; and concluded, with too much probability, how vile as well as miserable such a creature must be.

I freely confess, that all the little knowledge I have of any value, was acquired by the lectures I received from my master, and from hearing the discourses of him and his friends; to which I should be prouder to listen, than to dictate to the greatest and wisest assembly in Europe. I admired the strength, comeliness, and speed of the inhabitants; and such a constellation of virtues in such amiable persons produced in me the highest veneration. At first, indeed, I did not feel that natural awe which the Yahoos and all other animals bear towards them, but it grew upon me by degrees, much sooner than I imagined, and was mingled with a respectful love and gratitude, that they would condescend to distinguish me from the rest of my species.

When I thought of my family, my friends, my countrymen, or human race in general, I considered them as they really were, Yahoos in shape and disposition, perhaps a little more civilized, and qualified with the gift of speech, but making no other use of reason, than to improve and multiply those vices, whereof their brethren in this country had only the share that Nature allotted them. When I happened to behold the reflection of my own form in a lake or a fountain, I turned away my face in horror and detestation of myself,[8] and could better endure the sight of a common Yahoo, than of my own person. By conversing with the Houyhnhnms, and looking upon them with delight, I fell to imitate their gait and gesture, which is now grown into a habit, and my friends often tell me in a blunt way, that *I trot like a horse*; which, however, I take for a great compliment; neither shall I disown, that in speaking I am apt to fall into the voice and manner of the Houyhnhnms, and hear myself ridiculed on that account without the least mortification.

In the midst of all this happiness, when I looked upon myself to be fully settled for life, my master sent for me one morning a little earlier than his usual hour. I observed by his countenance that he was in some perplexity, and at a loss how to begin what he had to speak. After a short silence, he told me, he did not know how I would take what he was going to say; that in the last general Assembly, when the affair of the Yahoos was entered upon, the representatives had taken offense at his keeping a Yahoo (meaning myself) in his family more like a Houyhnhnm, than a brute animal. That he was known frequently to converse with me, as if he could receive some advantage or pleasure in my company; that such a practice was not agreeable to reason or Nature, or a thing ever heard of before among them. The Assembly did therefore *exhort* him, either to employ me like the rest of my species, or command me to swim back to the place from whence I came. That the first of these expedients was utterly rejected by all the Houyhnhnms who had ever seen me

8. A mocking reversal both of a common pattern in pastoral love poetry and of the Greek myth of Narcissus.

at his house or their own, for they alleged, that because I had some rudiments of reason, added to the natural pravity[9] of those animals, it was to be feared, I might be able to seduce them into the woody and mountainous parts of the country, and bring them in troops by night to destroy the Houyhnhnms' cattle, as being naturally of the ravenous[1] kind, and averse from labor.

My master added, that he was daily pressed by the Houyhnhnms of the neighborhood to have the Assembly's *exhortation* executed, which he could not put off much longer. He doubted[2] it would be impossible for me to swim to another country, and therefore wished I would contrive some sort of vehicle resembling those I had described to him, that might carry me on the sea, in which work I should have the assistance of his own servants, as well as those of his neighbors. He concluded, that for his own part he could have been content to keep me in his service as long as I lived, because he found I had cured myself of some bad habits and dispositions, by endeavoring, as far as my inferior nature was capable, to imitate the Houyhnhnms.

I should here observe to the reader, that a decree of the general Assembly in this country is expressed by the word *hnhloayn*, which signifies an *exhortation*, as near as I can render it, for they have no conception how a rational creature can be *compelled*, but only advised, or *exhorted*, because no person can disobey reason, without giving up his claim to be a rational creature.

I was struck with the utmost grief and despair at my master's discourse, and being unable to support the agonies I was under, I fell into a swoon at his feet; when I came to myself, he told me, that he concluded I had been dead. (For these people are subject to no such imbecilities of nature.) I answered, in a faint voice, that death would have been too great an happiness; that although I could not blame the Assembly's *exhortation*, or the urgency[3] of his friends, yet in my weak and corrupt judgment, I thought it might consist[4] with reason to have been less rigorous. That I could not swim a league, and probably the nearest land to theirs might be distant above a hundred; that many materials, necessary for making a small vessel to carry me off, were wholly wanting in this country, which, however, I would attempt in obedience and gratitude to his Honor, although I concluded the thing to be impossible, and therefore looked on myself as already devoted to destruction. That the certain prospect of an unnatural death was the least of my evils: for, supposing I should escape with life by some strange adventure, how could I think with temper[5] of passing my days among Yahoos, and relapsing into my old corruptions, for want of examples to lead and keep me within the paths of virtue? That I knew too well upon what solid reasons all the determinations of the wise Houyhnhnms were founded, not to be shaken by arguments of mine, a miserable Yahoo; and therefore after presenting him with my humble thanks for the offer of his servants' assistance in making a vessel, and desiring a reasonable time for so difficult a work, I told him I would endeavor to preserve a wretched being; and, if ever I returned to England, was not without hopes of being useful to my own species, by celebrating the praises of the renowned Houyhnhnms, and proposing their virtues to the imitation of mankind.

My master in a few words made me a very gracious reply, allowed me the space of two *months* to finish my boat; and ordered the sorrel nag, my fellow servant (for so at this distance I may presume to call him) to follow my instructions, because I told my master, that his help would be sufficient, and I knew he had a tenderness for me.

9. Depravity.
1. Rapacious, predatory, or greedy.
2. Feared.
3. Urging.
4. Be consistent.
5. Calmness.

In his company my first business was to go to that part of the coast, where my rebellious crew had ordered me to be set on shore. I got upon a height, and looking on every side into the sea, fancied I saw a small island, towards the northeast: I took out my pocket glass, and could then clearly distinguish it about five leagues off, as I computed; but it appeared to the sorrel nag to be only a blue cloud: for, as he had no conception of any country beside his own, so he could not be as expert in distinguishing remote objects at sea, as we who so much converse[6] in that element.

After I had discovered this island, I considered no farther; but resolved it should, if possible, be the first place of my banishment, leaving the consequence to Fortune.

I returned home, and consulting with the sorrel nag, we went into a copse at some distance, where I with my knife, and he with a sharp flint fastened very artificially, after their manner, to a wooden handle, cut down several oak wattles about the thickness of a walking staff, and some larger pieces. But I shall not trouble the reader with a particular description of my own mechanics; let it suffice to say, that in six weeks' time, with the help of the sorrel nag, who performed the parts that required most labor, I finished a sort of Indian canoe, but much larger, covering it with the skins of Yahoos well stitched together, with hempen threads of my own making. My sail was likewise composed of the skins of the same animal; but I made use of the youngest I could get, the older being too tough and thick, and I likewise provided myself with four paddles. I laid in a stock of boiled flesh, of rabbits and fowls, and took with me two vessels, one filled with milk, and the other with water.

I tried my canoe in a large pond near my master's house, and then corrected in it what was amiss; stopping all the chinks with Yahoos' tallow, till I found it staunch,[7] and able to bear me and my freight. And when it was as complete as I could possibly make it, I had it drawn on a carriage very gently by Yahoos, to the seaside, under the conduct of the sorrel nag, and another servant.

When all was ready, and the day came for my departure, I took leave of my master and lady, and the whole family, mine eyes flowing with tears, and my heart quite sunk with grief. But his Honor, out of curiosity, and perhaps (if I may speak it without vanity) partly out of kindness, was determined to see me in my canoe, and got several of his neighboring friends to accompany him. I was forced to wait above an hour for the tide, and then observing the wind very fortunately bearing towards the island, to which I intended to steer my course, I took a second leave of my master, but as I was going to prostrate myself to kiss his hoof, he did me the honor to raise it gently to my mouth. I am not ignorant how much I have been censured for mentioning this last particular. For my detractors are pleased to think it improbable, that so illustrious a person should descend to give so great a mark of distinction to a creature so inferior as I. Neither have I forgot, how apt some travelers are to boast of extraordinary favors they have received.[8] But if these censurers were better acquainted with the noble and courteous disposition of the Houyhnhnms, they would soon change their opinion.

I paid my respects to the rest of the Houyhnhnms in his Honor's company; then getting into my canoe, I pushed off from shore.

6. Are familiar with.
7. Watertight.
8. Swift heightens the absurdity of Gulliver's action, and draws attention to his later misanthropy.

CHAPTER 11

The author's dangerous voyage. He arrives at New Holland, hoping to settle there. Is wounded with an arrow by one of the natives. Is seized and carried by force into a Portuguese ship. The great civilities of the captain. The author arrives at England.

I began this desperate voyage on February 15, 1715, at 9 o'clock in the morning. The wind was very favorable; however, I made use at first only of my paddles, but considering I should soon be weary, and that the wind might probably chop about,[9] I ventured to set up my little sail; and thus, with the help of the tide, I went at the rate of a league and a half an hour, as near as I could guess. My master and his friends continued[1] on the shore, till I was almost out of sight; and I often heard the sorrel nag (who always loved me) crying out, *Hnuy illa nyha maiah Yahoo,* Take care of thyself, gentle Yahoo.

My design was, if possible, to discover some small island uninhabited, yet sufficient by my labor to furnish me with the necessaries of life, which I would have thought a greater happiness than to be first minister in the politest court of Europe; so horrible was the idea I conceived of returning to live in the society and under the government of Yahoos. For in such a solitude as I desired, I could at least enjoy my own thoughts, and reflect with delight on the virtues of those inimitable Houyhnhnms, without any opportunity of degenerating into the vices and corruptions of my own species.

The reader may remember what I related when my crew conspired against me, and confined me to my cabin. How I continued there several weeks, without knowing what course we took, and when I was put ashore in the longboat, how the sailors told me with oaths, whether true or false, that they knew not in what part of the world we were. However, I did then believe us to be about ten degrees southward of the Cape of Good Hope, or about 45 degrees southern latitude, as I gathered from some general words I overheard among them, being I supposed to the southeast in their intended voyage to Madagascar. And although this were but little better than conjecture, yet I resolved to steer my course eastward, hoping to reach the southwest coast of New Holland, and perhaps some such island as I desired, lying westward of it. The wind was full west, and by six in the evening I computed I had gone eastward at least eighteen leagues, when I spied a very small island about half a league off, which I soon reached. It was nothing but a rock, with one creek, naturally arched by the force of tempests. Here I put in my canoe, and climbing a part of the rock, I could plainly discover[2] land to the east, extending from south to north. I lay all night in my canoe, and repeating my voyage early in the morning, I arrived in seven hours to the southwest point of New Holland.[3] This confirmed me in the opinion I have long entertained, that the maps and charts place this country at least three degrees more to the east than it really is,[4] which thought I communicated many years ago to my worthy friend Mr. Herman Moll, and gave him my reasons for it, although he hath rather chosen to follow other authors.[5]

9. Change direction.
1. Stayed.
2. Discern.
3. New Holland was the name the explorer Abel Tasman originally gave to the western coast of Australia. Gulliver seems to place the land of the Houyhnhnms west of southwestern Australia, in which case the distance he covers to reach New Holland is improbable (1,500 to 2,000 nautical miles in 16 hours). It is possible, however, that Gulliver is meant to have landed on Tasmania, thus putting the Houyhnhnms a short distance west of this island.
4. Dampier claimed that he had found New Holland further west than indicated in Tasman's charts.
5. This geographer's *New and Correct Map of the Whole World* (1719) was probably the basis for Swift's geography in *Gulliver's Travels*.

I saw no inhabitants in the place where I landed, and being unarmed, I was afraid of venturing far into the country. I found some shellfish on the shore, and ate them raw, not daring to kindle a fire, for fear of being discovered by the natives. I continued three days feeding on oysters and limpets,[6] to save my own provisions, and I fortunately found a brook of excellent water, which gave me great relief.

On the fourth day, venturing out early a little too far, I saw twenty or thirty natives upon a height, not above five hundred yards from me. They were stark naked, men, women, and children, round a fire, as I could discover by the smoke. One of them spied me, and gave notice to the rest; five of them advanced towards me, leaving the women and children at the fire. I made what haste I could to the shore, and getting into my canoe, shoved off: the savages observing me retreat, ran after me; and before I could get far enough into the sea, discharged an arrow, which wounded me deeply on the inside of my left knee (I shall carry the mark to my grave). I apprehended the arrow might be poisoned, and paddling out of the reach of their darts (being a calm day) I made a shift to suck the wound, and dress it as well as I could.

I was at a loss what to do, for I durst not return to the same landing place, but stood[7] to the north, and was forced to paddle; for the wind though very gentle was against me, blowing northwest. As I was looking about for a secure landing place, I saw a sail to the north-north-east, which appearing every minute more visible, I was in some doubt, whether I should wait for them or no; but at last my detestation of the Yahoo race prevailed, and turning my canoe, I sailed and paddled together to the south, and got into the same creek from whence I set out in the morning, choosing rather to trust myself among these *barbarians*, than live with European Yahoos. I drew up my canoe as close as I could to the shore, and hid myself behind a stone by the little brook, which, as I have already said, was excellent water.

The ship came within a half a league of this creek, and sent out her longboat with vessels to take in fresh water (for the place it seems was very well known) but I did not observe it till the boat was almost on shore, and it was too late to seek another hiding place. The seamen at their landing observed my canoe, and rummaging it all over, easily conjectured that the owner could not be far off. Four of them well armed searched every cranny and lurking hole, till at last they found me flat on my face behind the stone. They gazed a while in admiration[8] at my strange uncouth dress, my coat made of skins, my wooden-soled shoes, and my furred stockings; from whence, however, they concluded I was not a native of the place, who all go naked. One of the seamen in Portuguese bid me rise, and asked who I was. I understood that language very well, and getting upon my feet, said, I was a poor Yahoo, banished from the Houyhnhnms, and desired they would please to let me depart. They admired to hear me answer them in their own tongue, and saw by my complexion I must be a European; but were at a loss to know what I meant by Yahoos and Houyhnhnms, and at the same time fell a laughing at my strange tone in speaking, which resembled the neighing of a horse. I trembled all the while betwixt fear and hatred: I again desired leave to depart, and was gently moving to my canoe; but they laid hold on me, desiring to know, what country I was of? whence I came? with many other questions. I told them, I was born in England, from whence I came about five years ago, and then their country and ours were at peace. I therefore hoped they would not treat me as an enemy, since I meant them no harm, but was a

6. Small mollusks that attach themselves to rocks.
7. Steered.
8. Wonder, amazement.

poor Yahoo, seeking some desolate place where to pass the remainder of his unfortunate life.

When they began to talk, I thought I never heard or saw anything so unnatural; for it appeared to me as monstrous as if a dog or a cow should speak in England, or a Yahoo in Houyhnhnmland. The honest Portuguese were equally amazed at my strange dress, and the odd manner of delivering my words, which however they understood very well. They spoke to me with great humanity, and said they were sure their captain would carry me *gratis* to Lisbon, from whence I might return to my own country; that two of the seamen would go back to the ship, to inform the captain of what they had seen, and receive his orders; in the meantime, unless I would give my solemn oath not to fly;[9] they would secure me by force. I thought it best to comply with their proposal. They were very curious to know my story, but I gave them very little satisfaction; and they all conjectured, that my misfortunes had impaired my reason. In two hours the boat, which went loaden with vessels of water, returned with the captain's commands to fetch me on board. I fell on my knees to preserve my liberty; but all was in vain, and the men having tied me with cords, heaved me into the boat, from whence I was taken into the ship, and from thence into the captain's cabin.

His name was Pedro de Mendez; he was a very courteous and generous person; he entreated me to give some account of myself, and desired to know what I would eat or drink; said, I should be used as well as himself, and spoke so many obliging things, that I wondered to find such civilities from a Yahoo. However, I remained silent and sullen; I was ready to faint at the very smell of him and his men. At last I desired something to eat out of my own canoe; but he ordered me a chicken and some excellent wine, and then directed that I should be put to bed in a very clean cabin. I would not undress myself, but lay on the bed clothes, and in half an hour stole out, when I thought the crew was at dinner, and getting to the side of the ship was going to leap into the sea, and swim for my life, rather than continue among Yahoos. But one of the seamen prevented me, and having informed the captain, I was chained to my cabin.

After dinner Don Pedro came to me, and desired to know my reason for so desperate an attempt: assured me he only meant to do me all the service he was able, and spoke so very movingly, that at last I descended[1] to treat him like an animal which had some little portion of reason. I gave him a very short relation of my voyage, of the conspiracy against me by my own men, of the country where they set me on shore, and of my three years' residence there. All which he looked upon as if it were a dream or a vision; whereat I took great offense; for I had quite forgot the faculty of lying, so peculiar to Yahoos in all countries where they preside, and consequently the disposition of suspecting truth in others of their own species. I asked him, whether it were the custom of his country to *say the thing that was not?* I assured him I had almost forgot what he meant by falsehood, and if I had lived a thousand years in Houyhnhnmland, I should never have heard a lie from the meanest servant; that I was altogether indifferent whether he believed me or no; but however, in return for his favors, I would give so much allowance to the corruption of his nature, as to answer any objection he would please to make, and then he might easily discover the truth.

9. Attempt to escape.

1. Condescended.

The captain, a wise man, after many endeavors to catch me tripping in some part of my story, at last began to have a better opinion of my veracity.[2] But he added, that since I professed so inviolable an attachment to truth, I must give him my word of honor to bear him company in this voyage without attempting anything against my life, or else he would continue[3] me a prisoner till we arrived at Lisbon. I gave him the promise he required; but at the same time protested that I would suffer the greatest hardships rather than return to live among Yahoos.

Our voyage passed without any considerable accident.[4] In gratitude to the captain I sometimes sat with him at his earnest request, and strove to conceal my antipathy against human kind, although it often broke out, which he suffered to pass without observation. But the greatest part of the day, I confined myself to my cabin, to avoid seeing any of the crew. The captain had often entreated me to strip myself of my savage dress, and offered to lend me the best suit of clothes he had. This I would not be prevailed on to accept, abhorring to cover myself with anything that had been on the back of a Yahoo. I only desired he would lend me two clean shirts, which having been washed since he wore them, I believed would not so much defile me. These I changed every second day, and washed them myself.

We arrived at Lisbon, Nov. 5, 1715. At our landing the captain forced me to cover myself with his cloak, to prevent the rabble from crowding about me. I was conveyed to his own house and at my earnest request, he led me up to the highest room backwards.[5] I conjured[6] him to conceal from all persons what I had told him of the Houyhnhnms, because the least hint of such a story would not only draw numbers of people to see me, but probably put me in danger of being imprisoned, or burnt by the Inquisition.[7] The captain persuaded me to accept a suit of clothes newly made, but I would not suffer the tailor to take my measure; however, Don Pedro being almost of my size, they fitted me well enough. He accoutered[8] me with other necessaries all new, which I aired for twenty-four hours before I would use them.

The captain had no wife, nor above three servants, none of which were suffered to attend at meals, and his whole deportment was so obliging, added to very good *human* understanding, that I really began to tolerate his company. He gained so far upon me, that I ventured to look out of the back window. By degrees I was brought into another room, from whence I peeped into the street, but drew my head back in a fright. In a week's time he seduced me down to the door. I found my terror gradually lessened, but my hatred and contempt seemed to increase. I was at last bold enough to walk the street in his company, but kept my nose well stopped with rue,[9] or sometimes with tobacco.

In ten days Don Pedro, to whom I had given some account of my domestic affairs, put it upon me as a point of honor and conscience, that I ought to return to my native country, and live at home with my wife and children. He told me, there was an English ship in the port just ready to sail, and he would furnish me with all things necessary.

2. In the first edition, the sentence continues: "and the rather, because he confessed, he met with a Dutch Skipper, who pretended to have landed with five others of his crew upon a certain island or continent south of New Holland, where they went for fresh water, and observed a horse driving before him several animals exactly resembling those I had described under the name of Yahoos, with some other particulars, which the captain said he had forgot, because he then concluded them all to be lies." In 1735 Swift's Dublin publisher, George Faulkener, omitted these lines, probably because they contradicted Gulliver's later statement that no other European had visited this land.

3. Keep.

4. Incident.

5. At the back of the house.

6. Appealed earnestly to.

7. Either because the Houyhnhnm hierarchy contradicted Genesis, in which man has dominion over the earth, or because Gulliver had been associating with diabolical powers, who could make humans appear to be horses (as Gulliver himself had first believed).

8. Attired.

9. Strong-smelling shrub, used for medicinal purposes.

It would be tedious to repeat his arguments, and my contradictions. He said, it was altogether impossible to find such a solitary island as I had desired to live in; but I might command in my own house, and pass my time in a manner as recluse as I pleased.

I complied at last, finding I could not do better. I left Lisbon the 24th day of November, in an English merchantman, but who was the master I never inquired. Don Pedro accompanied me to the ship, and lent me twenty pounds. He took kind leave of me, and embraced me at parting, which I bore as well as I could. During this last voyage I had no commerce[1] with the master or any of his men, but pretending I was sick kept close in my cabin. On the fifth of December, 1715, we cast anchor in the Downs[2] about nine in the morning, and at three in the afternoon I got safe to my house at Redriff.

My wife and family received me with great surprise and joy, because they concluded me certainly dead; but I must freely confess the sight of them filled me only with hatred, disgust, and contempt, and the more by reflecting on the near alliance I had to them. For, although since my unfortunate exile from the Houyhnhnm country, I had compelled myself to tolerate the sight of Yahoos, and to converse with Don Pedro de Mendez, yet my memory and imaginations were perpetually filled with the virtues and ideas of those exalted Houyhnhnms. And when I began to consider, that by copulating with one of the Yahoo species, I had become a parent of more, it struck me with the utmost shame, confusion, and horror.

As soon as I entered the house, my wife took me in her arms, and kissed me, at which, having not been used to the touch of that odious animal for so many years, I fell in a swoon for almost an hour. At the time I am writing it is five years since my last return to England: during the first year I could not endure my wife or children in my presence, the very smell of them was intolerable, much less could I suffer them to eat in the same room. To this hour they dare not presume to touch my bread, or drink out of the same cup, neither was I ever able to let one of them take me by the hand.[3] The first money I laid out was to buy two young stone-horses,[4] which I keep in a good stable, and next to them the groom is my greatest favorite; for I feel my spirits revived by the smell he contracts in the stable. My horses understand me tolerably well; I converse with them at least four hours every day. They are strangers to bridle or saddle, they live in great amity with me, and friendship to each other.

Chapter 12

The author's veracity. His design in publishing this work. His censure of those travelers who swerve from the truth. The author clears himself from any sinister ends in writing. An objection answered. The method of planting Colonies. His native country commended. The right of the Crown to those countries described by the author is justified. The difficulty of conquering them. The author takes his last leave of the reader, proposeth his manner of living for the future, gives good advice, and concludeth.

Thus, gentle reader,[5] I have given thee a faithful history of my travels for sixteen years, and above seven months, wherein I have not been so studious of ornament as of truth. I could perhaps like others have astonished thee with strange improbable tales; but I rather chose to relate plain matter of fact in the simplest manner and style, because my principal design was to inform, and not to amuse thee.

1. Interaction.
2. The sea off the North Downs in East Kent.
3. Gulliver's unwillingness to share his bread or cup with his wife or children emphasizes his unchristian behavior.
4. Stallions.
5. Highly ironic, since the "gentle" readers must be Yahoos.

It is easy for us who travel into remote countries, which are seldom visited by Englishmen or other Europeans, to form descriptions of wonderful animals both at sea and land. Whereas a traveler's chief aim should be to make men wiser and better, and to improve their minds by the bad as well as good example of what they deliver concerning foreign places.[6]

I could heartily wish a law were enacted, that every traveler, before he were permitted to publish his voyages, should be obliged to make oath before the Lord High Chancellor that all he intended to print was absolutely true to the best of his knowledge; for then the world would no longer be deceived as it usually is, while some writers, to make their works pass the better upon the public, impose the grossest falsities on the unwary reader. I have perused several books of travels with great delight in my younger days; but having since gone over most parts of the globe, and been able to contradict many fabulous accounts from my own observation, it hath given me a great disgust against this part of reading, and some indignation to see the credulity of mankind so impudently abused. Therefore since my acquaintance were pleased to think my poor endeavors might not be unacceptable to my country, I imposed on myself as a maxim, never to be swerved from, that I would *strictly adhere to truth;* neither indeed can I be ever under the least temptation to vary from it, while I retain in my mind the lectures and example of my noble master, and the other illustrious Houyhnhnms, of whom I had so long the honor to be an humble hearer.

—Nec si miserum Fortuna Sinonem
Finxit, vanum etiam mendacemque improba finget.[7]

I know very well how little reputation is to be got by writings which require neither genius nor learning, nor indeed any other talent, except a good memory or an exact journal. I know likewise, that writers of travels, like dictionary-makers, are sunk into oblivion by the weight and bulk of those who come last, and therefore lie uppermost.[8] And it is highly probable, that such travelers who shall hereafter visit the countries described in this work of mine, may, by detecting my errors (if there be any), and adding many new discoveries of their own, jostle me out of vogue, and stand in my place, making the world forget that ever I was an author. This indeed would be too great a mortification if I wrote for fame; but, as my sole intention was the PUBLIC GOOD.[9] I cannot be altogether disappointed. For who can read of the virtues I have mentioned in the glorious Houyhnhnms, without being ashamed of his own vices, when he considers himself as the reasoning, governing animal of his country? I shall say nothing of those remote nations where Yahoos preside, amongst which the least corrupted are the Brobdingnagians, whose wise maxims in morality and government it would be our happiness to observe. But I forbear descanting further, and rather leave the judicious reader to his own remarks and applications.

I am not a little pleased that this work of mine can possibly meet with no[1] censurers: for what objections can be made against a writer who relates only plain facts that happened in such distant countries, where we have not the least interest with

6. More's *Utopia* also argues that accounts of distant travels should provide useful lessons rather than fabulous tales.
7. "Nor, if cruel Fortune has made Sinon miserable, shall he also make him false and deceitful" (Virgil, *Aeneid* 2. 79–80). Swift cleverly employs the words that the Greek Sinon, the most famous liar in antiquity, used in the fraudulent tale he told to fool the Trojans into accepting *his* (wooden) horse.
8. The most current dictionary is the one most frequently used.
9. The English buccaneer and navigator William Dampier professes a similar aim in the dedication to his *New Voyage Round the World* (1697).
1. Cannot possibly encounter any.

respect either to trade or negotiations? I have carefully avoided every fault with which common writers of travels are often too justly charged. Besides, I meddle not the least with any *party*, but write without passion, prejudice, or ill-will against any man or number of men whatsoever. I write for the noblest end, to inform and instruct mankind, over whom I may, without breach of modesty, pretend to some superiority from the advantages I received by conversing so long among the most accomplished Houyhnhnms. I write without any view towards profit or praise. I never suffer a word to pass that may look like reflection,[2] or possibly give the least offense even to those who are most ready to take it. So that I hope I may with justice pronounce myself an author perfectly blameless, against whom the tribe of answerers, considerers, observers, reflecters, detecters, remarkers, will never be able to find matter for exercising their talents.[3]

I confess, it was whispered to me, that I was bound in duty as a subject of England, to have given in a memorial to a Secretary of State, at my first coming over; because, whatever lands are discovered by a subject belong to the Crown. But I doubt whether our conquests in the countries I treat of, would be as easy as those of Ferdinando Cortez over the naked Americans.[4] The Lilliputians, I think, are hardly worth the charge of a fleet and army to reduce them, and I question whether it might be prudent or safe to attempt the Brobdingnagians. Or whether an English army would be much at their ease with the Flying Island over their heads.[5] The Houyhnhnms, indeed, appear not to be so well prepared for war, a science to which they are perfect strangers, and especially against missive weapons.[6] However, supposing myself to be a minister of State, I could never give my advice for invading them. Their prudence, unanimity, unacquaintedness with fear, and their love of their country would amply supply all defects in the military art. Imagine twenty thousand of them breaking into the midst of an European army, confounding the ranks, overturning the carriages, battering the warriors' faces into mummy,[7] by terrible yerks[8] from their hinder hoofs. For they would well deserve the character given to Augustus; *Recalcitrat undique tutus*.[9] But instead of proposals for conquering that magnanimous nation, I rather wish they were in a capacity or disposition to send a sufficient number of their inhabitants for civilizing Europe, by teaching us the first principles of honor, justice, truth, temperance, public spirit, fortitude, chastity, friendship, benevolence, and fidelity. The *names* of all which virtues are still retained among us in most languages, and are to be met with in modern as well as ancient authors; which I am able to assert from my own small reading.

But I had another reason which made me less forward[1] to enlarge his Majesty's dominions by my discoveries. To say the truth, I had conceived a few scruples with

2. Criticism.
3. At this time it was common for historical and fictional accounts to be "applied" to contemporary situations or persons; by having Gulliver deny at such length that he is doing this, Swift draws attention to the possibility of making such connections.
4. In the 1520s, Cortés and 400 soldiers rapidly conquered the Aztec empire in Mexico.
5. These sentences refer to Gulliver's other travels: in Lilliput he encountered a miniature people; in Brobdingnag he met with giants; and in Laputa he encountered the Flying Island (able to force inhabitants below to submit either through starving them by blocking out the sun or by crushing them).
6. Anything thrown or shot through the air.
7. Pulp.
8. Kicks.
9. "He kicks back, well protected on every side" (Horace, *Satires* 2.i.20). While Gulliver refers admiringly to the horse's ability to defend itself, Swift recalls the context for Horace's decision to use satire (rather than praise) when writing about Augustus: according to Horace, Augustus would kick out like a horse if he sensed servile flattery, so flattery was pointless. Gulliver's lavish praise of the Houyhnhnms backfires on him, not because the Houyhnhnms disliked it, but because his uncritical identification with them leaves him unable to cope with human society.
1. Eager.

relation to the distributive justice[2] of princes upon those occasions. For instance, a crew of pirates[3] are driven by a storm they know not whither, at length a boy discovers land from the topmast, they go on shore to rob and plunder; they see a harmless people, are entertained with kindness, they give the country a new name, they take formal possession of it for the king, they set up a rotten plank or a stone for a memorial, they murder two or three dozen of the natives, bring away a couple more by force for a sample, return home, and get their pardon. Here commences a new dominion acquired with a title by *divine right*. Ships are sent with the first opportunity, the natives driven out or destroyed, their princes tortured to discover their gold;[4] a free license given to all acts of inhumanity and lust, the earth reeking with the blood of its inhabitants; and this execrable crew of butchers employed in so pious an expedition, is a *modern colony* sent to convert and civilize an idolatrous and barbarous people.

But this description, I confess, doth by no means affect the British nation, who may be an example to the whole world for their wisdom, care, and justice in planting colonies,[5] their liberal endowments for the advancement of religion and learning; their choice of devout and able pastors to propagate Christianity; their caution in stocking their provinces with people of sober lives and conversations from this the mother kingdom,[6] their strict regard to the distribution of justice, in supplying the civil administration through all their colonies with officers of the greatest abilities, utter strangers to corruption; and to crown all, by sending the most vigilant and virtuous governors, who have no other views than the happiness of the people over whom they preside, and the honor of the King their master.

But, as those countries which I have described do not appear to have any desire of being conquered, and enslaved, murdered, or driven out by colonies, nor abound either in gold, silver, sugar, or tobacco; I did humbly conceive they were by no means proper objects of our zeal, our valor, or our interest. However, if those whom it more concerns, think fit to be of another opinion, I am ready to depose, when I shall be lawfully called, that no European did ever visit those countries before me. I mean, if the inhabitants ought to be believed.[7]

But as to the formality of taking possession in my Sovereign's name, it never came once into my thoughts; and if it had, yet as my affairs then stood, I should perhaps in point of prudence and self-preservation, have put it off to a better opportunity.

Having thus answered the *only* objection that can ever be raised against me as a traveler, I here take a final leave of my courteous readers, and return to enjoy my own speculations in my little garden at Redriff, to apply those excellent lessons of virtue which I learned among the Houyhnhnms, to instruct the Yahoos of my own family as far as I shall find them docible[8] animals, to behold my figure often in a glass, and thus if possible habituate myself by time to tolerate the sight of a human creature, to lament the brutality of Houyhnhnms in my own country, but always treat their persons with respect, for the sake of my noble master, his family, his

2. Fairness with regard to the rights of the native people.
3. Referring to the first Spanish colonizers of America.
4. Montezuma was tortured by Cortés and the Incan emperor Atahuallpa by Pizarro (1533).
5. Intended ironically.
6. Felons were commonly given a sentence of mandatory "transportation" to Britain's colonies.
7. The first edition continued: "unless a dispute may arise about the two Yahoos, said to have been seen many Ages ago on a mountain in Houyhnhnm-land, from whence the opinion is, that the race of those brutes hath descended; and these, for anything I know, may have been English, which indeed I was apt to suspect from the lineaments of their posterity's countenances, although very much defaced. But how far that will go to make out a title, I leave to the learned in colony law." Faulkener omitted this passage in the 1735 edition.
8. Teachable.

friends, and the whole Houyhnhnm race, whom these of ours[9] have the honor to resemble in all their lineaments, however their intellectuals[1] came to degenerate.

I began last week to permit my wife to sit at dinner with me, at the farthest end of a long table, and to answer (but with the utmost brevity) the few questions I ask her. Yet the smell of a Yahoo continuing very offensive, I always keep my nose well stopped with rue, lavender, or tobacco leaves. And although it be hard for a man late in life to remove old habits, I am not altogether out of hopes in some time to suffer a neighbor Yahoo in my company, without the apprehensions I am yet under of his teeth or his claws.

My reconcilement to the Yahoo-kind in general might not be so difficult if they would be content with those vices and follies only, which Nature hath entitled them to. I am not in the least provoked at the sight of a lawyer, a pickpocket, a colonel, a fool, a lord, a gamester, a politician, a whoremonger, a physician, an evidence,[2] a suborner,[3] an attorney, a traitor, or the like: this is all according to the due course of things; but when I behold a lump of deformity and diseases both in body and mind, smitten with *pride*, it immediately breaks all the measures of my patience; neither shall I be ever able to comprehend how such an animal and such a vice could tally together. The wise and virtuous Houyhnhnms, who abound in all excellencies that can adorn a rational creature, have no name for this vice in their language, which hath no terms to express anything that is evil, except those whereby they describe the detestable qualities of their Yahoos, among which they were not able to distinguish this of pride, for want of thoroughly understanding human nature, as it showeth itself in other countries, where that animal presides. But I, who had more experience, could plainly observe some rudiments of it among the wild Yahoos.

But the Houyhnhnms, who live under the government of Reason, are no more proud of the good qualities they possess, than I should be for not wanting a leg or an arm, which no man in his wits would boast of, although he must be miserable without them. I dwell the longer upon this subject from the desire I have to make the society of an English Yahoo by any means not insupportable, and therefore I here entreat those who have any tincture of this absurd vice, that they will not presume to appear in my sight.[4]

FINIS

c. 1721–1725 1726

GULLIVER'S TRAVELS AND ITS TIME

The following five letters to and from Jonathan Swift were written over a period of nearly eighteen months and span the progress of *Gulliver's Travels* from Swift's corrections of the manuscript to reports on the reactions of London readers. The celebratory letters from his old friends Pope and Gay are valuable in chronicling the reception of *Gulliver*, and the three letters from Swift himself are particularly interesting, revealing a playfulness, warmth, and gift for friendship not ordinarily associated with the common misconception of Swift as darkly misanthropic and sarcastic.

9. I.e., horses.
1. Intellects.
2. A (false) witness.
3. One who bribes another to commit a misdeed.
4. Gulliver thus falls into pride, the very vice he rejects.

Jonathan Swift to Alexander Pope

29 Sep[tember] 1725

Sir, * * * I have employed my time (besides ditching)[1] in finishing correcting, amending, and transcribing my *Travels*, in four parts complete newly augmented, and intended for the press when the world shall deserve them, or rather when a printer shall be found brave enough to venture his ears.[2] I like your schemes of our meeting after distresses and dispersions, but the chief end I propose to myself in all my labors is to vex the world rather than divert it; and if I could compass that design[3] without hurting my own person or fortune, I would be the most indefatigable writer you have ever seen without reading.[4] I am exceedingly pleased that you have done with translations. Lord Treasurer Oxford,[5] often lamented that a rascally world should lay you under a necessity of misemploying your genius for so long a time.[6] But since you will now be so much better employed, when you think of the world give it one lash the more at my request. I have ever hated all nations, professions, and communities and all my love is towards individuals. For instance, I hate the tribe of lawyers, but I love Councilor Such-a-one, Judge Such-a-one, for so with physicians (I will not speak of my own trade), soldiers, English, Scotch, French, and the rest. But principally I hate and detest that animal called man, although I heartily love John, Peter, Thomas, and so forth. This is the system upon which I have governed myself many years (but do not tell), and so I shall go on till I have done with them. I have got materials towards a treatise proving the falsity of that definition *animal rationale* and to show it should be only *rationis capax*.[7] Upon this great foundation of misanthropy (though not Timon's manner[8]), the whole building of my *Travels* is erected, and I never will have peace of mind till all honest men are of my opinion. By consequence you are to embrace it immediately and procure that all who deserve my esteem may do so too. The matter is so clear that it will admit little dispute. Nay, I will hold a hundred pounds that you and I agree in the point. * * *

Alexander Pope to Jonathan Swift

November 16, 1726

I have resolved to take time, and in spite of all misfortunes and demurs, which sickness, lameness, or disability of any kind can throw in my way, to write you (at intervals) a long letter. My two least fingers of one hand hang impediments to the others, like useless dependents, who only take up room, and never are active or assistant to our wants: I shall never be much the better for 'em.[9] I congratulate you first upon

1. Digging ditches or doing one's daily labor.
2. In earlier times printers could have their ears cut off as punishment for printing seditious material. Since the legal penalty had lapsed, the idea of venturing one's ears more generally meant being willing to risk punishment or make a sacrifice.
3. Achieve that end.
4. Education; Swift ironically deprecates his own learning.
5. Robert Harley (1661–1724), first Earl of Oxford; a Tory statesman and member of the Scriblenis Club, he was a mutual friend of Pope and of Swift.
6. Pope spent 12 years (1713–1725) translating Homer's *Iliad* and *Odyssey*.
7. Humans are not automatically rational animals, as Aristotle had said, but rather only *rationis capax*—capable of reasoning.
8. Timon, a nobleman of Athens who, after losing his riches and receiving no help from his wealthy friends, lived a life of solitary misanthropy in a cave outside the city.
9. In September the tendons of Pope's two fingers had been severed when his hand was cut in a near-fatal coach accident.

what you call your cousin's wonderful book,[1] which is *publica trita man*,[2] at present, and I prophesy will be in future the admiration of all men. That countenance[3] with which it is received by some statesmen is delightful; I wish I could tell you how every single man looks upon it, to observe which has been my whole diversion this fortnight. I've never been a night in London since you left me[4] till now for this very end, and indeed it has fully answered my expectations.

I find no considerable man very angry at the book: some indeed think it rather too bold and too general a satire, but none that I hear of accuse it of particular reflections.[5] (I mean no persons of consequence, or good judgment; the mob of critics, you know, always are desirous to apply satire to those that they envy for being above them), so that you needed not to have been so secret upon this head. Motte,[6] received the copy (he tells me) he knew not from whence, nor from whom, dropped at his house in the dark from a hackney coach; by computing the time, I found it was after you left England, so for my part, I suspend my judgment.[7] * * *

John Gay to Jonathan Swift

Nov. 17. 1726

About ten days ago a book was published here of the travels of one Gulliver, which hath been the conversation of the whole town ever since. The whole impression,[8] told in a week, and nothing is more diverting than to hear the different opinions people give of it, though all agree in liking it extremely. 'Tis generally said that you are the author, but I am told, the bookseller declares he knows not from what hand it came.[9] From the highest to the lowest it is universally read, from the Cabinet council to the nursery. The politicians to a man agree that it is free from particular reflections, but that the satire on general societies of men is too severe. Not but we now and then meet with people of greater perspicuity, who are in search for particular applications in every leaf; and it is highly probable we shall have keys[1] published to give light into Gulliver's design. Your Lord ———[2] is the person who least approves it, blaming it as a design of evil consequence to depreciate human nature, at which it cannot be wondered that he takes most offense, being himself the most accomplished of his species, and so losing more than any other of that praise which is due both to the dignity and virtue of a man. Your friend, my Lord Harcourt,[3] commends it very much, though he thinks in some places the matter too far carried. The

1. The manuscript for *Gulliver's Travels* was submitted to the London publisher Benjamin Motte, by "Richard Sympson," the imaginary cousin of Gulliver.
2. Passed from hand to hand.
3. Both the expression on the face and general composure of temperament.
4. Swift had been visiting friends in London from mid-March to mid-August this year and stayed mainly at Pope's house at Twickenham.
5. Direct satire of contemporary people or affairs.
6. Benjamin Motte (d. 1738), bookseller and printer.
7. Pope had assisted his friend in getting *Gulliver* published anonymously.
8. Print run.
9. Gay had copied out Swift's original letter to the publisher (signing it "Richard Sympson," Gulliver's alleged cousin), in order to assist Swift in hiding his authorship of *Gulliver* from his publisher, and, thus, from the general public.

1. The publication of "keys," which helped readers unlock the contemporary application of satires, was highly popular at this time; a "key" to Gay's *Beggar's Opera* was published after its success, in 1728. Alexander Pope took advantage of this trend by publishing a pamphlet entitled *A Key to the Lock. Or, A Treatise proving . . . the dangerous Tendency of a late Poem, The Rape of the Lock, To Government and Religion* (1715).
2. Bolingbroke.
3. Simon Harcourt, first Viscount (1667–1727), an old friend of Swift's, one of the few who managed to do well under the new Whig government without losing touch with his old friends.

Duchess Dowager of Marlborough[4] is in raptures at it; she says she can dream of nothing else since she read it; she declares, that she hath now found out that her whole life hath been lost in caressing the worst part of mankind and treating the best as her foes, and that if she knew Gulliver, though he had been the worst enemy she ever had, she would give up all her present acquaintance for his friendship. You may see by this, that you are not much injured by being supposed the author of this piece. If you are, you have disobliged us, and two or three of your best friends, in not giving us the least hint of it while you were with us, and in particular Dr. Arbuthnot, who says it is ten thousand pities he had not known it, he could have added such abundance of things upon every subject.[5] Among lady critics, some have found out that Mr. Gulliver had a particular malice to maids of honor.[6] Those of them who frequent the church say his design is impious, and that it is an insult on Providence, by depreciating the works of the Creator. Notwithstanding, I am told the Princess hath read it with great pleasure. As to other critics, they think the flying island is the least entertaining,[7] and so great an opinion the town have of the impossibility of Gulliver's writing at all below himself, that 'tis agreed that part was not writ by the same hand, though this hath its defenders too. It hath passed Lords and Commons, *nemine contradicente;*[8] and the whole town, men, women, and children are quite full of it.

Perhaps I may all this time be talking to you of a book you have never seen, and which hath not yet reached Ireland; if it hath not, I believe what we have said will be sufficient to recommend it to your reading, and that you order me to send it to you.

But it will be much better to come over yourself, and read it here. * * *

Jonathan Swift to Alexander Pope

Dublin, Nov. [27] 1726

I am just come from answering a letter of Mrs. Howard's writ in such mystical terms that I should never have found out the meaning,[9] if a book had not been sent me called *Gulliver's Travels*, of which you say so much in yours.[1] I read the book over, and in the second volume observe several passages which appear to be patched and altered, and the style of a different sort (unless I am much mistaken).[2] Dr. Arbuthnot likes the projectors least; others you tell me, the flying island; some think it wrong to be so hard upon whole bodies or corporations.[3] Yet the general opinion is that reflections on particular persons are most to be blamed, so that in these cases, I think the best method is to let censure and opinion take their course. A Bishop here said, that book was full of improbable lies, and for his part, he hardly believed a word of it; and so much for Gulliver. * * *

4. Sarah Churchill (1660–1744), a favorite of Queen Anne's.
5. Gay here feigns complete ignorance of *Gulliver's* authorship partly in jest, partly because both men knew that the letters of those hostile to the government were routinely opened and read by officials in the post office.
6. Companions to the queen. Swift's references to the maids of honor in Lilliput and Brobdingnag involved incidents that were indelicate and, by implication, potentially embarrassing to the women of rank at the English Court; see, for example, "A Voyage to Brobdingnag," chapter 5, in which the maids of honor use the diminutive Gulliver to titillate their breasts.
7. "A Voyage to Laputa."
8. Nobody voting against.
9. A letter of 17 November, to which Swift replied in tones of mock-mystification.
1. His letter of 17 November.
2. Fearful of the law, Swift's publisher Benjamin Motte made several alterations to the *Travels*.
3. Professions or groups, all from "A Voyage to Laputa."

"The Prince of Lilliput" to Stella[4]

[11 March 1727]

† **† † *[5]

In *European* characters and *English* thus;

The high and mighty prince EGROEGO[6] born to the most puissant[7] empire of the *East*,

Unto STELLA, the most resplendent glory of the *Western* hemisphere, sendeth health and happiness.

BRIGHTEST PRINCESS,

That invincible hero, the MAN MOUNTAIN,[8] fortunately arriving at our coasts some years ago, delivered us from ruin by conquering the fleets and armies of our enemies, and gave us hopes of a durable peace and happiness. But now the martial people of *Blefuscu*, encouraged from his absence, have renewed the war,[9] to revenge upon us the loss and disgrace they suffered by our valiant champion.

The fame of your superexcellent person and virtue, and the huge esteem which that great general has for you, urged us in this our second distress to sue for[1] your favor. In order to which we have sent our able and trusty Nardac[2] KOORBNILOB,[3] requesting, that if our general does yet tread upon the terrestrial globe, you, in compassion for us, would prevail upon him to take another voyage for our deliverance.

And, lest any apprehensions of famine amongst us, should render Nardac MOUNTAIN averse to the undertaking, we signify to you, that we have stored our folds, our coops, our granaries, and cellars with plenty of provision for a long supply of the wastes to be made by his capacious stomach.

And furthermore, because as we hear you are not so well as we could wish, we beg you would complete our happiness by venturing your most valuable person along with him into our country; where, by the salubrity[4] of our finer air and diet, you will soon recover your health and stomach.[5]

In full assurance of your complying goodness, we have sent you some provision for your voyage, and we shall with impatience wait for your safe arrival in our kingdom. Most illustrious lady, farewell. Prince EGROEGO.

Dated the 11th day of the 6th Moon, in the
2001 year of the *Lilliputian* era.

END OF *GULLIVER'S TRAVELS* AND ITS TIME

A MODEST PROPOSAL In a letter written to Alexander Pope in August 1729, Swift described the condition of Ireland: "There have been three terrible years' dearth of corn [i.e., wheat], and every place strewn with beggars, but dearths are common in better climates, and our evils lie much deeper. Imagine a nation the two-thirds of whose revenues are spent out of it, and who are not permitted [by Britain] to trade with the other third, and where the pride of

4. Esther Johnson (1681–1728), Swift's beloved and most valued friend.
5. Here we have a parcel of characters formed at random, by way of the address in the *Lilliputian* tongue [Swift's note].
6. I.e., O'George (an anagram).
7. Powerful.
8. Gulliver, later also called "that great general."
9. Spain had besieged Gibraltar in February.

1. Ask for.
2. The "highest title of honor" among the Lilliputians; see "A Voyage to Lilliput," chapter 5, in which Gulliver is created a Nardac for his service to the nation.
3. An anagram: Bolinbrook, i.e., the Tory politician.
4. Healthfulness.
5. Appetite. Stella had been in declining health for some time. Swift's playful letter was obviously meant to cheer her.

the women will not suffer them to wear their own manufactures even where they excel what come from abroad." Two months later, Swift published what is today his most famous political essay: *A Modest Proposal.* Swift had previously written a dozen or more tracts to help free Ireland from its desperate social, economic, and political plight. In *A Modest Proposal,* however, Swift wielded two favorite weapons from his armory of satirical techniques—irony and parody—with devastating effect. In creating a persona who combines a mixture of calculating rationality and misplaced compassion but does not comprehend the enormity of his plan, Swift aims his satire not only at the political arithmeticians (forerunners of today's social engineers and economic planners) and the exploitative and predatory absentee landlords living in England but at the Irish people as well. Believing Ireland to be its own worst enemy, Swift delineates a program of commercial cannibalism that institutionalizes the country's own self-destructive tendencies. Preserving a nation through the consumption of its children is self-defeating, however demographically logical, because it undermines the understanding of humanity upon which civil society depends. Swift thus highlights the futility of financial improvement unaccompanied by social and moral reform.

A Modest Proposal

FOR PREVENTING THE CHILDREN OF POOR PEOPLE IN IRELAND FROM BEING A BURDEN TO THEIR PARENTS OR COUNTRY, AND FOR MAKING THEM BENEFICIAL TO THE PUBLIC

It is a melancholy object to those who walk through this great town,[1] or travel in the country, when they see the streets, the roads, and cabin doors crowded with beggars of the female sex, followed by three, four, or six children, *all in rags,* and importuning every passenger[2] for an alms. These mothers, instead of being able to work for their honest livelihood, are forced to employ all their time in strolling,[3] to beg sustenance for their helpless infants, who, as they grow up, either turn thieves for want of work, or leave their dear native country to fight for the Pretender in Spain,[4] or sell themselves to the Barbados.[5]

I think it is agreed by all parties that this prodigious number of children, in the arms, or on the backs, or at the heels of their mothers, and frequently of their fathers, is in the present deplorable state of the kingdom a very great additional grievance; and therefore whoever could find out a fair, cheap, and easy method of making these children sound, useful members of the commonwealth would deserve so well of the public, as to have his statue set up for a preserver of the nation.

But my intention is very far from being confined to provide only for the children of professed beggars; it is of a much greater extent, and shall take in the whole number of infants at a certain age who are born of parents in effect as little able to support them as those who demand our charity in the streets.

As to my own part, having turned my thoughts for many years upon this important subject, and maturely weighed the several schemes of other projectors,[6] I have always found them grossly mistaken in their computation. It is true a child just dropped from its dam may be supported by her milk for a solar year with little other nourishment, at most not above the value of two shillings, which the mother may

1. Dublin.
2. Passerby.
3. Wandering aimlessly.
4. Catholic Ireland was loyal to the Pretender, James Francis Edward Stuart (1688–1766), son of James II, who was deposed from the English throne in 1688 because of his Catholicism. Religious ties also made the Irish ideal recruits for France and Spain in their wars against England.
5. The impoverished Irish emigrated to the West Indies in large numbers, buying their passage by selling their labor in advance to the sugar plantations.
6. Devisers of new "projects," usually of doubtful value.

certainly get, or the value in scraps, by her lawful occupation of begging, and it is exactly at one year old that I propose to provide for them, in such a manner as instead of being a charge upon their parents or the parish, or wanting food and raiment for the rest of their lives, they shall, on the contrary, contribute to the feeding and partly to the clothing of many thousands.

There is likewise another great advantage in my scheme, that it will prevent those voluntary abortions, and that horrid practice of women murdering their bastard children, alas, too frequent among us, sacrificing the poor innocent babes, I doubt[7] more to avoid the expense than the shame, which would move tears and pity in the most savage and inhuman breast.

The number of souls in this kingdom being usually reckoned one million and a half, of these I calculate there may be about two hundred thousand couple whose wives are breeders, from which number I subtract thirty thousand couple who are able to maintain their own children, although I apprehend there cannot be so many under the present distresses of the kingdom; but this being granted, there will remain an hundred and seventy thousand breeders. I again subtract fifty thousand for those women who miscarry, or whose children die by accident or disease within the year.[8] There only remain a hundred and twenty thousand children of poor parents annually born: the question therefore is how this number shall be reared and provided for, which, as I have already said, under the present situation of affairs, is utterly impossible by all the methods hitherto proposed: for we can neither employ them in handicraft, or agriculture; we neither build houses (I mean in the country) nor cultivate land;[9] they can very seldom pick up a livelihood by stealing till they arrive at six years old, except where they are of towardly parts,[1] although, I confess they learn the rudiments much earlier, during which time they can however be properly looked upon only as *probationers,* as I have been informed by a principal gentleman in the County of Cavan, who protested to me, that he never knew above one or two instances under the age of six, even in a part of the kingdom so renowned for the quickest proficiency in that art.

I am assured by our merchants that a boy or a girl, before twelve years old, is no salable commodity, and even when they come to this age, they will not yield above three pounds, or three pounds and half-a-crown at most on the Exchange,[2] which cannot turn to account[3] either to the parents or kingdom, the charge of nutriment and rags having been at least four times that value.

I shall now therefore humbly propose my own thoughts, which I hope will not be liable to the least objection.

I have been assured by a very knowing American[4] of my acquaintance in London, that a young healthy child well nursed is at a year old a most delicious, nourishing, and wholesome food, whether stewed, roasted, baked, or boiled, and I make no doubt that it will equally serve in a fricassee or ragout.[5]

I do therefore humbly offer it to public consideration, that of the hundred and twenty thousand children already computed, twenty thousand may be reserved for

7. Believe.
8. It is telling that Swift here projects an infant mortality rate of approximately 30 percent in a child's first year.
9. The vast estates of English absentee landlords, and British retention of Irish land for grazing sheep, rather than agriculture, contributed to Ireland's poverty.
1. Precocious.
2. At the market.
3. Be of value.
4. Some of the British believed that the harsh living conditions in America made the colonists adopt "savage" practices.
5. A fricassee is meat stewed in gravy, a ragout is a highly seasoned French stew; such foreign dishes were becoming increasingly popular with fashionable Britons.

breed, whereof only one fourth part to be males, which is more than we allow to sheep, black cattle, or swine, and my reason is that these children are seldom the fruits of marriage, a circumstance not much regarded by our savages, therefore one male will be sufficient to serve four females. That the remaining hundred thousand may at a year old be offered in sale to the persons of quality and fortune through the kingdom, always advising the mother to let them suck plentifully in the last month, so as to render them plump, and fat for a good table. A child will make two dishes at an entertainment for friends, and when the family dines alone, the fore or hind quarter will make a reasonable dish, and seasoned with a little pepper or salt will be very good boiled on the fourth day, especially in winter.

I have reckoned upon a medium, that a child just born will weigh 12 pounds, and in a solar year if tolerably nursed increaseth to 28 pounds.

I grant this food will be somewhat dear,[6] and therefore very proper for landlords, who, as they have already devoured most of the parents, seem to have the best title to the children.

Infants' flesh will be in season throughout the year, but more plentiful in March, and a little before and after, for we are told by a grave author,[7] an eminent French physician, that fish being a prolific diet,[8] there are more children born in Roman Catholic countries about nine months after Lent than at any other season; therefore reckoning a year after Lent, the markets will be more glutted than usual, because the number of Popish infants is at least three to one in this kingdom, and therefore it will have one other collateral advantage by lessening the number of Papists among us.

I have already computed the charge of nursing a beggar's child (in which list I reckon all cottagers,[9] laborers, and four-fifths of the farmers) to be about two shillings *per annum,* rags included, and I believe no gentleman would repine to give ten shillings for the carcass of a good fat child, which, as I have said, will make four dishes of excellent nutritive meat, when he hath only some particular friend or his own family to dine with him. Thus the Squire will learn to be a good landlord and grow popular among his tenants, the mother will have eight shillings net profit, and be fit for work till she produces another child.

Those who are more thrifty (as I must confess the times require) may flay the carcass, the skin of which, artificially[1] dressed, will make admirable gloves for ladies and summer boots for fine gentlemen.

As to our City of Dublin, shambles[2] may be appointed for this purpose in the most convenient parts of it, and butchers we may be assured will not be wanting, although I rather recommend buying the children alive and dressing them hot from the knife,[3] as we do roasting pigs.

A very worthy person, a true lover of his country, and whose virtues I highly esteem, was lately pleased, in discoursing on this matter, to offer a refinement upon my scheme. He said that many gentlemen of this kingdom, having of late destroyed their deer, he conceived that the want of venison might be well supplied by the bodies of young lads and maidens, not exceeding fourteen years of age nor under twelve, so great a number of both sexes in every country being now ready to starve for want of work and service;[4] and these to be disposed of by their parents if alive, or

6. Both expensive and, of course, beloved.
7. The satirist François Rabelais, in *Gargantua and Pantagruel* (1532–1564), Book 5, ch. 29.
8. One increasing fertility.
9. Tenant farmers.
1. Skillfully.
2. Places where meat is slaughtered and sold.
3. Skinning and gutting them immediately after killing.
4. Positions as servants.

otherwise by their nearest relations. But with due deference to so excellent a friend and so deserving a patriot, I cannot be altogether in his sentiments; for as to the males, my American acquaintance assured me from frequent experience that their flesh was generally tough and lean, like that of our schoolboys, by continual exercise, and their taste disagreeable, and to fatten them would not answer the charge. Then as to the females, it would, I think with humble submission, be a loss to the public, because they soon would become breeders themselves; and besides, it is not improbable that some scrupulous people might be apt to censure such a practice (although indeed very unjustly) as a little bordering upon cruelty which, I confess, hath always been with me the strongest objection against any project, however so well intended.

But in order to justify my friend, he confessed that this expedient was put into his head by the famous Psalmanazar,[5] a native of the island Formosa, who came from thence to London above twenty years ago, and in conversation told my friend that in his country when any young person happened to be put to death, the executioner sold the carcass to persons of quality as a prime dainty, and that, in his time, the body of a plump girl of fifteen, who was crucified for an attempt to poison the emperor, was sold to his Imperial Majesty's Prime Minister of State[6] and other great Mandarins of the Court, in joints from the gibbet,[7] at four hundred crowns. Neither indeed can I deny that if the same use were made of several plump young girls in this town, who, without one single groat[8] to their fortunes, cannot stir abroad without a chair,[9] and appear at the playhouse and assemblies[1] in foreign fineries which they never will pay for, the kingdom would not be the worse.

Some persons of a desponding spirit are in great concern about that vast number of poor people who are aged, diseased, or maimed, and I have been desired to employ my thoughts what course may be taken to ease the nation of so grievous an encumbrance. But I am not in the least pain upon that matter, because it is very well known that they are every day dying, and rotting, by cold, and famine, and filth, and vermin, as fast as can be reasonably expected. And as to the younger laborers they are now in almost as hopeful a condition. They cannot get work, and consequently pine away for want of nourishment, to a degree that if at any time they are accidentally hired to common labor, they have not strength to perform it; and thus the country and themselves are in a fair way of being soon delivered from the evils to come.

I have too long digressed, and therefore shall return to my subject. I think the advantages by the proposal which I have made are obvious and many, as well as of the highest importance.

For first, as I have already observed, it would greatly lessen the number of Papists, with whom we are yearly overrun, being the principal breeders of the nation as well as our most dangerous enemies, and who stay at home on purpose with a design to deliver the kingdom to the Pretender, hoping to take their advantage by the absence of so many good Protestants, who have chosen rather to leave their country than stay at home, and pay tithes against their conscience, to an Episcopal curate.[2]

5. George Psalmanazar, a Frenchman who pretended to be from Formosa (now Taiwan), wrote a book about its customs, the *Historical and Geographical Description of Formosa* (1704), which was quickly exposed as fraudulent.
6. A reference to Robert Walpole.
7. Gallows.
8. Silver coin (issued 1351–1662) equal to four pennies.
9. A sedan chair, carried by two men.
1. Social gatherings.
2. The tithes, or ecclesiastical taxes, that supported the Church were avoided by the many "good" Protestants who absented themselves from Ireland on the grounds—spurious, Swift implies—of "conscience."

Secondly, the poorer tenants will have something valuable of their own, which by law may be made liable to distress,[3] and help to pay their landlords rent, their corn and cattle being already seized, and *money a thing unknown*.

Thirdly, whereas the maintenance of a hundred thousand children from two years old and upwards cannot be computed at less than ten shillings a piece *per annum*, the nation's stock will be thereby increased fifty thousand pounds *per annum*, besides the profit of a new dish introduced to the tables of all gentlemen of fortune in the kingdom who have any refinement in taste, and the money will circulate among ourselves, the goods being entirely of our own growth and manufacture.

Fourthly, the constant breeders, besides the gain of eight shillings sterling *per annum* by the sale of their children, will be rid of the charge of maintaining them after the first year.

Fifthly, this food would likewise bring great custom to taverns, where the vintners will certainly be so prudent as to procure the best receipts[4] for dressing it to perfection, and consequently have their houses frequented by all the fine gentlemen, who justly value themselves upon their knowledge in good eating; and a skillful cook who understands how to oblige his guests will contrive to make it as expensive as they please.

Sixthly, this would be a great inducement to marriage, which all wise nations have either encouraged by rewards or enforced by laws and penalties. It would increase the care and tenderness of mothers toward their children, when they were sure of a settlement for life to the poor babes, provided in some sort by the public to their annual profit instead of expense. We should see an honest emulation[5] among the married women, which of them could bring the fattest child to the market; men would become as fond of their wives, during the time of their pregnancy, as they are now of their mares in foal, their cows in calf, or sows when they are ready to farrow,[6] nor offer to beat or kick them (as it is too frequent a practice) for fear of a miscarriage.

Many other advantages might be enumerated: for instance, the addition of some thousand carcasses in our exportation of barreled beef;[7] the propagation of swine's flesh, and improvement in the art of making good bacon, so much wanted among us by the great destruction of pigs, too frequent at our tables, which are no way comparable in taste or magnificence to a well-grown, fat yearling child, which roasted whole will make a considerable figure at a Lord Mayor's feast or any other public entertainment. But this and many others I omit, being studious of brevity.

Supposing that one thousand families in this city would be constant customers for infants' flesh, besides others who might have it at merry-meetings, particularly weddings and christenings, I compute that Dublin would take off annually about twenty thousand carcasses, and the rest of the kingdom (where probably they will be sold somewhat cheaper) the remaining eighty thousand.

I can think of no one objection that will possibly be raised against this proposal, unless it should be urged that the number of people will be thereby much lessened in the kingdom. This I freely own, and was indeed one principal design in offering it to the world. I desire the reader will observe that I calculate my remedy *for this one individual Kingdom of Ireland, and for no other that ever was, is, or, I think, ever can be upon earth*. Therefore let no man talk to me of other expedients:[8] *Of taxing our absentees at*

3. Seizure for debt.
4. Recipes.
5. Competition.
6. Give birth.
7. Pickled beef.
8. The kind of proposals Swift himself had made in earnest for remedying the poverty of Ireland; his *Proposal for the Universal Use of Irish Manufacture in Cloaths and Furniture . . . Utterly Rejecting and Renouncing Everything Wearable that Comes from England* (1720) is a typical example.

five shillings a pound; of using neither clothes nor household furniture, except what is of our own growth and manufacture; of utterly rejecting the materials and instruments that promote foreign luxury; of curing the expensiveness of pride, vanity, idleness, and gaming in our women; of introducing a vein of parsimony, prudence, and temperance; of learning to love our country, wherein we differ even from LAPLANDERS, *and the inhabitants of* TOPINAMBOO;[9] *of quitting our animosities and factions, nor act any longer like the Jews, who were murdering one another at the very moment their city was taken;*[1] *of being a little cautious not to sell our country and consciences for nothing; of teaching landlords to have at least one degree of mercy toward their tenants. Lastly, of putting a spirit of honesty, industry, and skill into our shopkeepers, who, if a resolution could now be taken to buy our native goods, would immediately unite to cheat and exact upon us in the price, the measure, and the goodness, nor could ever yet be brought to make one fair proposal of just dealing, though often and earnestly invited to it.*

Therefore I repeat, let no man talk to me of these and the like expedients till he hath at least some glimpse of hope that there will ever be some hearty and sincere attempt to put them in practice.

But as to myself, having been wearied out for many years with offering vain, idle, visionary thoughts, and at length utterly despairing of success, I fortunately fell upon this proposal, which as it is wholly new, so it hath something solid and real, of no expense and little trouble, full in our own power, and whereby we can incur no danger in *disobliging* ENGLAND. For this kind of commodity will not bear exportation, the flesh being of too tender a consistence, to admit a long continuance in salt, *although perhaps I could name a country*[2] *which would be glad to eat up our whole nation without it.*

After all I am not so violently bent upon my own opinion as to reject any offer proposed by wise men, which shall be found equally innocent, cheap, easy, and effectual. But before something of that kind shall be advanced in contradiction to my scheme and offering a better, I desire the author or authors will be pleased maturely to consider two points. First, as things now stand, how they will be able to find food and raiment for an hundred thousand useless mouths and backs. And secondly, there being a round million of creatures in human figure throughout this kingdom whose whole subsistence put into a common stock would leave them in debt two millions of pounds sterling; adding those who are beggars by profession to the bulk of farmers, cottagers, and laborers with their wives and children, who are beggars in effect; I desire those politicians who dislike my overture, and may perhaps be so bold to attempt an answer, that they will first ask the parents of these mortals whether they would not at this day think it a great happiness to have been sold for food at a year old, in the manner I prescribe, and thereby have avoided such a perpetual scene of misfortunes as they have since gone through, by the oppression of landlords, the impossibility of paying rent without money or trade, the want of common sustenance, with neither house nor clothes to cover them from the inclemencies of the weather, and the most inevitable prospect of entailing[3] the like or greater miseries upon their breed forever.

I profess in the sincerity of my heart that I have not the least personal interest in endeavoring to promote this necessary work, having no other motive than the *public good of my country, by advancing our trade, providing for infants, relieving the poor, and*

9. The inhabitants of the most hostile environments—the frozen north or the Brazilian jungle—love their countries more than the Irish.
1. According to one historian, when Jerusalem was besieged and captured by the Emperor Titus in 70 C.E., factional fighting inside the city contributed to its destruction.
2. England.
3. Bequeathing.

giving some pleasure to the rich. I have no children by which I can propose to get a single penny; the youngest being nine years old, and my wife past child-bearing.

1729 1729

A *MODEST PROPOSAL* AND ITS TIME

William Petty: from *Political Arithmetic*[1]

from Chapter 4. How to enable the people of England and Ireland to spend 5 millions worth of commodities more than now; and how to raise the present value of the lands and goods of Ireland from 2 to 3.

This is to be done: 1. By bringing one million of the present 1,300 thousand of the people out of Ireland into England, though at the expense of a million of money. 2. That the remaining three hundred thousand left behind be all herdsmen and dairy women, servants to the owners of the lands and stock transplanted into England, all aged between 16 and 60 years, and to quit all other trades, but that of cattle, and to import nothing but salt and tobacco. Neglecting all housing, but what is fittest for these 300 thousand people, and this trade, though to the loss of 2 millions-worth of houses. Now if a million of people be worth 70 pounds per head one with another, the whole are worth 70 millions; then the said people, reckoned as money at 5 percent interest, will yield 3 millions and a half per annum. 3. And if Ireland send into England 1 million and a half worth of effects (receiving nothing back), then England will be enriched from Ireland, and otherwise, 5 millions per annum more than now, which, at 20 year's purchase, is worth one hundred millions of pounds sterling, as was propounded. * * *

POSTSCRIPT

If in this jealous age this essay should be taxed of an evil design to waste and dispeople Ireland, we say that the author of it intends not to be *Felo de se*,[2] and propound something quite contrary, by saying it is naturally possible in about 25 years to double the inhabitants of Great Britain and Ireland and make the people full as many as the territory of those kingdoms can with tolerable labor afford a competent livelihood unto, which I prove thus, (viz.)

1. The sixth part of the people are teeming women[3] of between 18 and 44 years old.
2. It is found by observation that but 1/3 part or between 30 and 40 of the teeming women are married.
3. That a teeming woman, at a medium, bears a child every two years and a half.
4. That in mankind at London, there are 14 males for 13 females, and because males are prolific[4] 40 years, and females but 25, there are in effect 560 males for 325 females.

1. William Petty (1623–1687) represents the type of Englishman Swift had in mind in his implicit criticism of English rapaciousness in Ireland in *A Modest Proposal.* Petty, the son of a London clothier and weaver, was an extraordinary scholar and anatomist, and a charter member of the Royal Society. Appointed physician-general to the parliamentary army in Ireland in 1652, he obtained considerable property holdings in Ireland through his additional task of surveying lands forfeited by Roman Catholics. His newfound fortune enabled him to devote his attention to his economic writings and to the Royal Society in London, though he was less than solicitous of his tenants in Ireland. Swift's friendship with Petty's children, Lord Shelburne and Lady Kerry, did not prevent him parodying Petty's *Political Arithmetic* (1691) in *A Modest Proposal.* Petty's suggestion that Ireland be turned into one huge farm to supply England by removing all the Irish was only one of many "political arithmetic" projects published during the Restoration and 18th century, reflecting English interest in "scientific" programs for social "improvement."

2. Suicidal; literally, "felon of (one)self."

3. Women capable of breeding.

4. Capable of procreation.

5. That out of the mass of mankind there dies one out of 30 per annum.
6. That at Paris, where the christenings and the births are the same in number, the christenings are above 18,000 per annum, and consequently the births at London, which far exceed the christenings there, cannot be less than 19,000 where the burials are above 23,000.

As for Example

Of 600 people, the sixth part (viz. 100) are teeming women, which (if they were all married) might bear 40 children per annum (viz.) 20 more than do die out of 600, at the rate of one out of 30; and consequently in 16 years the increase will be 320, making the whole 920. And by the same reason, in the next 9 years, the said 920 will be 280 more, in all 1,200, viz. double of the original number of 600.

Upon these principles, if there be about 19,000 births per annum at London, the number of the married teeming women must be above 38,000; and of the whole stock of the teeming women must be above 114,000, and of the whole people six times as many viz. 684,000; which agrees well enough with 696,000, which they have been elsewhere computed to be.

To conclude it is naturally possible, that all teeming women may be married, since there are in effect 560 males to 325 females; and since Great Britain and Ireland can with moderate labor, food, and other necessaries to near double the present people or to about 20 millions of heads, as shall when occasion requires it, be demonstrated. * * *

1691

END OF A *MODEST PROPOSAL* AND ITS TIME

Alexander Pope

1688–1744

William Hoare, *Sketch of Alexander Pope.*

"The life of a wit is a warfare upon earth; and the present spirit of the learned world is such, that to serve it . . . one must have the constancy of a martyr, and a resolution to suffer for its sake." Though still in his twenties when he wrote these words, Alexander Pope knew from painful experience their bitter truth. As a Roman Catholic, he could not vote, inherit or purchase land, attend a "public" school or a university, live within ten miles of London, hold public office, or openly practice his religion. He was obliged to pay double taxes. Such civil disenfranchisement barred him from receiving the literary patronage most talented writers depended upon for their livelihood. No wonder Pope wrote of "certain laws, by suff'rers thought unjust," by which he was "denied all posts of profit or of trust" (*Imitations of Horace, Epistle* 2.2.60–61). Despite whatever patriotism or loyalty to their country they may have felt, Catholics were widely regarded as alien and seditious. Pope's resentment of this attitude is evident in the *Epistle to Bathurst* (1733) when he calls the London Monument, which bears an inscription blaming the Great Fire of 1666 on a Papist conspiracy to destroy the capital, "a tall bully" who "lies."

Religion was not Pope's greatest impediment to success, however. When he was twelve, he contracted tuberculosis of the spine (Pott's disease), a condition that stunted his growth and left him humpbacked and deformed. At four feet six inches, he could not sit at an ordinary table with other adults unless his seat was raised. His constitution was so weakened that he frequently suffered from migraine headaches, asthma, nausea, and fevers. For much of his life, he could not hold his body upright without the help of stays, and he was unable to bathe, dress or undress, rise or go to bed by himself. Pope summarized his condition most succinctly in *An Epistle to Dr. Arbuthnot* (1735), when he wrote of "this long disease, my life."

Pope was born in London in 1688, the only child of his parents' marriage. Pope's *Epistle to Dr. Arbuthnot* includes a tribute to his father's equanimity and goodness; his mother is praised as "a noble wife." At the age of nine, Pope was sent to a school for Catholic boys but was expelled in his first year for writing a satire on his schoolmaster—a sign of things to come. When he was twelve, his family moved from the environs of London to Binfield, in the royal forest of Windsor; the effect of Windsor's "green retreats" on Pope's youthful imagination is apparent in the *Pastorals* (1709) and in *Windsor-Forest* (1713). At Binfield, he began to teach himself Greek and Latin with great determination, though the rigors of his studies made his sickness worse. Refusing to yield to his infirmity, he began, at fifteen, to journey into London to learn French and Italian. Pope spoke of these adolescent years as his "great reading period" when he "went through all the best critics, almost all the English, French, and Latin poets of any name . . . [and] Homer and some other of the Greek poets in the original." During this time Pope met his great friend John Caryll, at whose request he would write *The Rape of the Lock*, and Martha Blount, who was to become his lifelong intimate companion and to whom he addressed *Of the Characters of Women: An Epistle to a Lady* (1735).

Pope claimed that "as yet a child . . . I lisp'd in numbers [i.e., meter]." Certainly he was a precocious poet and his early efforts were encouraged by many, including the playwrights William Wycherley and William Congreve, to whom Pope dedicated his *Iliad* (1715–1720). If Pope had encouraging friends, he soon had detracting enemies as well. His first publication, the *Pastorals* (1709), occasioned a rivalry between Pope's Tory supporters and the Whig partisans of Ambrose Philips, whose *Pastorals* appeared in the same volume. Pope's next important poem, *An Essay on Criticism* (1711), brought a barrage of vituperative abuse from the critic John Dennis, who called Pope "a hunch-backed toad" and argued that his deformity was merely the outward sign of mental and moral ugliness. Undaunted, Pope continued to publish: the *Messiah* (1712), *The Rape of the Lock* (1712, substantially enlarged in 1714), *Windsor-Forest* (1713), and *The Temple of Fame* (1715). With the publication of his *Works* (1717), Pope had proved himself master of a dazzling repertoire of poetic modes: pastoral and georgic, didactic, eclogue, mock-epic, allegorical dream-vision, heroic, and elegiac. No other living poet could display such dazzling versatility and comprehensive control.

There was still another area, however, in which Pope was proving the breathtaking range of his poetic gifts. Between 1713 and 1726, Pope devoted much of his creative energy to translating Homer's epics, the *Iliad* and the *Odyssey*, into heroic couplets. "Pope's Homer" not only won for him financial independence so that he could "live and thrive, / Indebted to no Prince or Peer alive" (*Imitations of Horace, Epistle* 2.2), it also confirmed his reputation as the presiding poetic genius of his time. While he was working on the *Odyssey*, Pope produced a six-volume edition of Shakespeare's works (1725), which, though it contained some valuable insights, was very much an amateur effort. When Lewis Theobald, the leading Shakespeare scholar of the time, rather pedantically highlighted Pope's many editorial shortcomings in *Shakespeare Restored, or, a Specimen of the Many Errors Committed . . . by Mr. Pope* (1726), Pope's revenge was not far off: two years later, he published *The Dunciad*, a savagely satirical assault on Pope's critics and the bankrupt cultural values they embodied.

In the seventeen years between Dennis's attack and the publication of *The Dunciad*, Pope's appearance, talent, and character had been assailed in print more than fifty times. His enemies accused him of being obscene, seditious, duplicitous, venal, vain, blasphemous, libelous, ignorant, and a bad poet. Theobald's rebuke was the last straw, perhaps because it was the most justified. Pope's style of comic social criticism owed much to his membership in the Scriblerus Club with John Gay, Jonathan Swift, Dr. John Arbuthnot, Thomas Parnell, and Robert Harley, Earl of Oxford. The Scriblerians originally planned to produce a series entitled *The Works of the Unlearned;* although the group regularly met only for a short while in 1714, its members remained in contact. In addition to *The Dunciad,* the fruit of their exchanges may be seen in Swift's *Gulliver's Travels* (1726), Gay's *The Beggar's Opera* (1728), Pope's *Peri Bathous: Or, the Art of Sinking in Poetry* (1728), and Arbuthnot's and Pope's *Memoirs of the Extraordinary Life, Works, and Discoveries of Martinus Scriblerus* (1741).

An Essay on Man (1733–1734) showcased Pope's talent for philosophical poetry. This work and four *Moral Essays* (1731–1735) were originally intended to form part of a long poetic sequence on the nature of humankind that Pope had hoped would be his greatest work, though the project was abandoned. Between 1733 and 1738, Pope published more than a dozen *Imitations of Horace.* In these loose adaptations of Horace's epistles and satires, Pope invested his modern social criticism with the classical authority of a revered Roman poet. The *Moral Essays,* or "Epistles to Several Persons" as Pope called them, also show Pope assuming the mantle of Horace by using the familiar epistle as a vehicle for social commentary. Pope's Horatian poems are his most mature, elegant, and self-assured works.

In 1737, he published an authorized version of his letters, which he doctored to improve his reputation. His last years were a time of retirement at his villa at Twickenham, famous for its grotto of "Friendship and Liberty" and for the five-acre landscape garden Pope had designed. In *The New Dunciad* (1742), Pope shifted his attack from hack writers and low culture to all forms of hypocrisy and pretense. It was his final triumph. He worked with William Warburton on a new edition of his *Works* (1751), even as his many illnesses became still more overwhelming. Though he was a self-confessed "fool to Fame" (*Arbuthnot*), he told those gathered around his deathbed: "There is nothing that is meritorious but virtue and friendship." He was, as his enemies claimed, bellicose, self-indulgent, and self-aggrandizing. He was morally and physically courageous and had a great gift for friendship. Although it is no longer fashionable to call the first half of the eighteenth century the "Age of Pope," many of his contemporaries saw him as the predominant literary genius of his time. Today, most literary historians agree that the greatest English poet between John Milton and William Wordsworth was Alexander Pope.

For additional resources on Pope, go to *The Longman Anthology of British Literature* Web site at www.myliteraturekit.com.

An Essay on Criticism Pope was only twenty-one years old when he wrote *An Essay on Criticism,* which was published anonymously in 1711. This aesthetic manifesto in heroic couplets is written in the tradition of Horace's *Ars Poetica* (c. 19 B.C.E.), Boileau's *Art poétique* (1674), and other verse essays delineating poetic principles and practices. Pope's chief contributions to the genre are his ringing epigrams and the playful ease with which he satirizes contemporary critics who lack genuine poetic understanding. *The Essay on Criticism* is divided into three parts: the first examines the rules of taste, their relationship to Nature, and the authority of classical authors. The second (lines 201–559) considers the impediments preventing the attainment of the classical ideals outlined in part one. In the third part, Pope proposes an aesthetic and moral reformation to restore wit, sense, and taste to their former glory. While acknowledging the importance of precepts, Pope asserts the primacy of poetic genius and the power of imagination.

An Essay on Criticism

'Tis hard to say, if greater want of skill
Appear in writing or in judging ill;
But, of the two, less dang'rous is th' offense
To tire our patience, than mislead our sense:° *judgment*
Some few in that, but numbers err in this,
Ten censure wrong for one who writes amiss;
A fool might once himself alone expose;
Now one in verse makes many more in prose.[1]
'Tis with our judgments as our watches, none
Go just alike, yet each believes his own.
In poets as true genius is but rare,
True taste as seldom is the critic's share;
Both must alike from Heav'n derive their light,
These born to judge, as well as those to write.
Let such teach others who themselves excel,
And censure freely who have written well.
Authors are partial to their wit,[2] 'tis true,
But are not critics to their judgment too?
Yet if we look more closely, we shall find
Most have the seeds of judgment in their mind;
Nature affords at least a glimm'ring light;
The lines, though touched but faintly, are drawn right.
But as the slightest sketch, if justly traced,
Is by ill coloring but the more disgraced,
So by false learning is good sense defaced.
Some are bewildered in the maze of schools,[3]
And some made coxcombs[4] Nature meant but fools.
In search of wit these lose their common sense,
And then turn critics in their own defense:
Each burns alike, who can, or cannot write,
Or° with a rival's or an eunuch's spite.[5] *either*
All fools have still° an itching to deride,[6] *continually*
And fain° would be upon the laughing side. *gladly*
If Mævius scribble in Apollo's spite,[7]
There are, who judge still worse than he can write.
Some have at first for wits,° then poets passed, *intellectuals*
Turned critics next, and proved plain fools at last.
Some neither can for wits nor critics pass,
As heavy mules are neither horse nor ass.
Those half-learned witlings, num'rous in our isle,
As half-formed insects on the banks of Nile;
Unfinished things, one knows not what to call,

1. I.e., many bad critics respond to one bad poet.
2. Both their writings and their (fancied) ability to write well.
3. Schools of criticism.
4. Conceited show-offs.
5. I.e., they either seek to compete, or, knowing them selves incapable, criticize out of envy.
6. The fool's perpetual itching suggests disease.
7. Maevius, a third-rate Roman poet, is set against Apollo, patron of good poetry.

Their generation's so equivocal:[8]
To tell° 'em, would a hundred tongues require, *count*
Or one vain wit's, that might a hundred tire.
  But you who seek to give and merit° fame, *deserve*
And justly bear a critic's noble name,
Be sure yourself and your own reach° to know, *ability*
How far your genius, taste, and learning go;
Launch not beyond your depth, but be discrete,
And mark° that point where sense and dullness meet. *note*
  Nature to all things fixed the limits fit,
And wisely curbed proud man's pretending° wit. *aspiring*
As on the land while here the ocean gains,
In other parts it leaves wide sandy plains;
Thus in the soul while memory prevails,
The solid pow'r of understanding fails;
Where beams of warm imagination play,
The memory's soft figures melt away.
One science only will one genius fit;[9]
So vast is art, so narrow human wit:° *understanding*
Not only bounded to peculiar° arts, *particular*
But oft in those confined to single parts.
Like kings we lose the conquests gained before,
By vain ambition still to make them more;
Each might his sev'ral province well command,
Would all but stoop to what they understand.
  First follow Nature, and your judgment frame
By her just standard, which is still° the same: *always*
Unerring Nature, still divinely bright,
One clear, unchanged, and universal light,
Life, force, and beauty, must to all impart,
At once the source, and end, and test of art.
Art from that fund each just supply provides,
Works without show,[1] and without pomp presides:
In some fair body thus th' informing soul[2]
With spirits feeds, with vigor fills the whole,
Each motion guides, and ev'ry nerve sustains;
Itself unseen, but in th' effects remains.
Some, to whom Heav'n in wit has been profuse,
Want° as much more, to turn it to its use; *need*
For wit and judgment often are at strife,
Though meant each other's aid, like man and wife.
'Tis more to guide than spur the Muse's steed;[3]
Restrain his fury, than provoke his speed;

8. Like the generation of insects on the banks of the Nile, thought to occur spontaneously, through the action of sun on mud.
9. The artist can hope to succeed in one subject area or object of study.
1. The suggestion that art should mask its presence came from Horace.
2. The force that animates.
3. Pegasus, the winged horse.

The winged courser,° like a gen'rous horse, *swift horse*
Shows most true mettle° when you check his course. *spirit*
  Those Rules of old discovered, not devised,
Are Nature still, but Nature methodized;
Nature, like liberty, is but restrained
By the same laws which first herself ordained.
  Hear how learn'd Greece her useful rules indites,° *composes*
When to repress, and when indulge our flights:
High on Parnassus'[4] top her sons she showed,
And pointed out° those arduous paths they trod; *appointed*
Held from afar, aloft, th' immortal prize,
And urged the rest by equal steps to rise.
Just precepts thus from great examples giv'n,
She drew from them what they derived from Heav'n.
The gen'rous critic fanne'd the poet's fire,
And taught the world, with reason to admire.
Then criticism the Muses' handmaid proved,
To dress her charms,[5] and make her more belov'd;
But following wits from that intention strayed;
Who could not win the mistress, wooed the maid;
Against the poets their own arms they turned,
Sure to hate most the men from whom they learned.
So modern 'pothecaries,° taught the art *druggists*
By doctor's bills° to play the doctor's part, *prescriptions*
Bold in the practice of mistaken° rules, *misunderstood*
Prescribe, apply, and call their masters fools.
Some on the leaves of ancient authors prey,[6]
Nor time nor moths e'er spoiled so much as they.
Some drily plain, without invention's° aid, *imagination's*
Write dull receipts° how poems may be made. *recipes*
These leave the sense, their learning to display,
And those explain the meaning quite away.
  You then whose judgment the right course would steer,
Know well each Ancient's proper character;[7]
His fable,° subject, scope° in every page; *plot / intention*
Religion, country, genius of his age:
Without all these at once before your eyes,
Cavil° you may, but never criticize. *quibble*
Be Homer's works your study, and delight,
Read them by day, and meditate by night;
Thence form your judgment, thence your maxims bring,
And trace the Muses upward to their spring.
Still with itself compared, his text peruse;
And let your comment be the Mantuan Muse.[8]

4. Mount Parnassus in Greece was sacred to the Muses.
5. Both dress and address: i.e., both interpret and adjust.
6. Textual commentators, depicted as literal book worms in continuation of the earlier insect metaphor.
7. An interest in the historical method in criticism was on the rise.
8. Virgil (born near Mantua) and his *Aeneid,* which took Homer's epics as models, and was the best commentary on them.

When first young Maro° in his boundless mind — *Virgil*
A work t' outlast immortal Rome designed,
Perhaps he seemed° above the critic's law, — *thought himself*
And but from Nature's fountains scorned to draw:
But when t' examine ev'ry part he came,
Nature and Homer were, he found, the same.
Convinced, amazed, he checks the bold design,
And rules as strict his labored work confine,
As if the Stagyrite[9] o'erlooked each line.
Learn hence for ancient rules a just esteem;
To copy nature is to copy them.
 Some beauties yet no precepts can declare,[1]
For there's a happiness° as well as care. — *luck*
Music resembles poetry, in each
Are nameless graces which no methods teach,
And which a master-hand alone can reach.
If, where the rules not far enough extend
(Since rules were made but to promote their end),
Some lucky license° answers to the full — *deviation*
Th' intent proposed, that license is a rule.
Thus Pegasus, a nearer way to take,
May boldly deviate from the common track.
Great wits sometimes may gloriously offend,
And rise to faults true critics dare not mend.
From vulgar bounds with brave disorder part,
And snatch a grace beyond the reach of Art,
Which, without passing through the judgment, gains
The heart, and all its end at once attains.
In prospects,[2] thus, some objects please our eyes,
Which out of Nature's common order rise,
The shapeless rock, or hanging precipice.
But though the Ancients thus their rules invade,
(As kings dispense with laws themselves have made),
Moderns, beware! Or if you must offend
Against the precept, ne'er transgress its end;
Let it be seldom, and compelled by need;
And have, at least, their precedent to plead.
The critic else proceeds without remorse,
Seizes your fame, and puts his laws in force.
 I know there are, to whose presumptuous thoughts
Those freer beauties, ev'n in them, seem faults.[3]
Some figures[4] monstrous and misshaped appear,
Considered singly, or beheld too near,

9. Aristotle, whose *Poetics* provided the basis for later rules on poetry and epic writing.
1. Pope's belief that true poetic genius consisted not of rigid adherence to rules, but of "brave disorder" and "grace beyond the reach of art" had earlier been expressed in the treatise *On the Sublime,* attributed to the Greek rhetorician Longinus (210?–273).
2. Views of an extensive landscape.
3. I.e., there are those critics to whom even the Ancients' occasional "glorious offense" is unforgivable.
4. Both figures in the landscape and rhetorical figures or literary style.

Which, but proportioned to their light, or place,
Due distance reconciles to form and grace.
A prudent chief not always must display
His pow'rs in equal ranks, and fair array,
But with th' occasion and the place comply,
Conceal his force, nay seem sometimes to fly.
Those oft are stratagems which errors seem,
Nor is it Homer nods, but we that dream.
    Still green with bays[5] each ancient altar[6] stands,
Above the reach of sacrilegious hands;
Secure from flames, from envy's fiercer rage,
Destructive war, and all-involving age.
See, from each clime the learn'd their incense bring!
Hear, in all tongues consenting pæans° ring! *songs of praise*
In praise so just let ev'ry voice be joined,
And fill the gen'ral chorus of mankind.
Hail bards triumphant! born in happier days;
Immortal heirs of universal praise!
Whose honors with increase of ages grow,
As streams roll down, enlarging as they flow!
Nations unborn your mighty names shall sound,
And worlds applaud that must not yet be found!
Oh may some spark of your celestial fire
The last, the meanest of your sons inspire[7]
(That on weak wings, from far, pursues your flights;
Glows while he reads, but trembles as he writes)
To teach vain wits° a science little known, *would-be critics*
T' admire superior sense, and doubt their own!

    Of all the causes which conspire to blind
Man's erring judgment, and misguide the mind,
What the weak head with strongest bias[8] rules,
Is pride, the never-failing vice of fools.
Whatever Nature has in worth denied,
She gives in large recruits° of needful° pride; *supplies / needed*
For as in bodies, thus in souls, we find
What wants° in blood and spirits, swelled with wind: *is needed*
Pride, where wit fails, steps in to our defense,
And fills up all the mighty void of sense.
If once right reason drives that cloud away,
Truth breaks upon us with resistless day.
Trust not yourself; but your defects to know,
Make use of ev'ry friend—and ev'ry foe.
    A little learning is a dang'rous thing;
Drink deep, or taste not the Pierian spring:[9]

5. Laurels, used to crown both poets and military heroes.
6. The works of each ancient author.
7. Pope himself, who follows tradition in writing about writing.
8. Not only prejudice but a kind of bowling ball. (In bowls, the bias ball is one weighted to roll obliquely.)
9. Hippocrene, the stream associated with the Muses.

There shallow draughts[1] intoxicate the brain,
And drinking largely sobers us again.
Fired at first sight with what the Muse imparts,
In fearless youth we tempt° the heights of arts, *attempt*
While from the bounded° level of our mind, *limited*
Short views we take, nor see the lengths behind;
But, more advanced, behold with strange surprise
New distant scenes of endless science[2] rise!
So pleased at first the tow'ring Alps we try,
Mount o'er the vales, and seem to tread the sky;
Th' eternal snows appear already past,
And the first clouds and mountains seem the last:
But, those attained, we tremble to survey
The growing labors of the lengthened way,
Th' increasing prospect tires our wand'ring eyes,
Hills peep o'er hills, and Alps on Alps arise!
 A perfect judge will read each work of wit
With the same spirit that its author writ,
Survey the whole, nor seek slight faults to find,
Where Nature moves, and rapture warms the mind;
Nor lose, for that malignant dull delight,
The gen'rous pleasure to be charmed with wit.
But in such lays° as neither ebb, nor flow, *poems*
Correctly cold, and regularly low,
That shunning faults, one quiet tenor° keep, *tone*
We cannot blame indeed—but we may sleep.
In wit, as Nature, what affects our hearts
Is not th' exactness of peculiar° parts; *particular*
'Tis not a lip, or eye, we beauty call,
But the joint force and full result of all.
Thus when we view some well-proportioned dome[3]
(The world's just wonder, and ev'n thine O Rome!),
No single parts unequally surprise,
All comes united to th' admiring eyes;
No monstrous height, or breadth, or length appear;
The whole at once is bold, and regular.° *well-proportioned*
 Whoever thinks a faultless piece to see,
Thinks what ne'er was, nor is, nor e'er shall be.
In ev'ry work regard the writer's end,
Since none can compass° more than they intend; *encompass*
And if the means be just, the conduct° true, *execution*
Applause, in spite of trivial faults, is due.
As men of breeding,[4] sometimes men of wit,
T' avoid great errors must the less commit,
Neglect the rules each verbal critic lays,[5]

1. I.e., small amounts.
2. Knowledge, subjects requiring study.
3. Any large and stately building, but those of a classical design are particularly implied.
4. Good breeding (in both birth and upbringing).
5. Lays down. A verbal critic is one concerned with linguistic detail rather than literary whole.

For not to know some trifles is a praise.
Most critics, fond of some subservient art,
Still make the whole depend upon a part:
They talk of principles, but notions° prize, *prejudices*
And all to one loved folly sacrifice.
    Once on a time, La Mancha's knight,[6] they say,
A certain bard encount'ring on the way,
Discoursed in terms as just, with looks as sage,
As e'er could Dennis,[7] of the Grecian stage;
Concluding all were desp'rate sots and fools,
Who durst depart from Aristotle's rules.
Our author, happy in a judge so nice,
Produced his play, and begged the knight's advice;
Made him observe the subject, and the plot,
The manners, passions, unities;[8] what not?
All which, exact to rule, were brought about,
Were but a combat in the lists[9] left out.
"What! leave the combat out?" exclaims the knight;
Yes, or we must renounce the Stagyrite.° *Aristotle*
"Not so, by Heav'n" (he answers in a rage)
"Knights, squires, and steeds must enter on the stage."
So vast a throng the stage can ne'er contain.
"Then build a new, or act it in a plain."
    Thus critics, of less judgment than caprice,
Curious,° not knowing, not exact, but nice,° *picky / fussy*
Form short ideas, and offend in arts
(As most in manners) by a love to parts.[1]
    Some to conceit[2] alone their taste confine,
And glitt'ring thoughts struck out at ev'ry line;
Pleased with a work where nothing's just or fit:
One glaring chaos and wild heap of wit.
Poets, like painters, thus unskilled to trace
The naked Nature and the living grace,
With gold and jewels cover ev'ry part,
And hide with ornaments their want° of art. *lack*
True wit is Nature to advantage dressed,
What oft was thought, but ne'er so well expressed;
Something, whose truth convinced at sight we find,
That gives us back the image of our mind.
As shades° more sweetly recommend the light, *shadows*
So modest plainness sets off sprightly wit.
For works may have more wit than does 'em good,
As bodies perish through excess of blood.[3]

6. Don Quixote, Cervantes's foolish knight errant. This episode comes from Part 2 of *Don Quixote* (1615), bk. 3, ch. 10.
7. John Dennis (1657–1734), an eminent critic, but not one in Pope's favor.
8. The three unities of plot (one story), time (one 24-hour day), and place (one location) were thought to have been the Greek playwrights' structuring principles, recommended by Aristotle.
9. The field of combat in medieval jousting tournaments.
1. Individual talents.
2. Extravagant use of metaphor.
3. Apoplexy, it was thought, was caused by such an excess.

Others for language all their care express,
And value books, as women men, for dress:
Their praise is still—the style is excellent:
The sense they humbly take upon content.° *trust*
Words are like leaves; and where they most abound,
Much fruit of sense beneath is rarely found.
False eloquence, like the prismatic glass,
Its gaudy colors spreads on ev'ry place;
The face of Nature we no more survey,° *observe*
All glares alike, without distinction gay.
But true expression, like th' unchanging sun,
Clears and improves whate'er it shines upon,
It gilds all objects, but it alters none.
Expression is the dress of thought,[4] and still
Appears more decent,° as more suitable; *correct*
A vile conceit° in pompous words expressed, *idea*
Is like a clown° in regal purple dressed: *peasant*
For different styles with different subjects sort,° *belong*
As several garbs with country, town, and court.[5]
Some by old words to fame have made pretense,[6]
Ancients in phrase, mere Moderns in their sense:
Such labored nothings, in so strange a style,
Amaze th' unlearn'd, and make the learned smile.
Unlucky, as Fungoso in the play,[7]
These sparks[8] with awkward vanity display
What the fine gentleman wore yesterday;
And but so mimic ancient wits at best,
As apes our grandsires in their doublets[9] dressed.
In words, as fashions, the same rule will hold;
Alike fantastic, if too new, or old:
Be not the first by whom the new are tried,
Nor yet the last to lay the old aside.
But most by numbers[1] judge a poet's song,
And smooth or rough, with them, is right or wrong;
In the bright Muse though thousand charms conspire,° *work together*
Her voice is all these tuneful fools admire;
Who haunt Parnassus but to please their ear,
Not mend their minds; as some to church repair,
Not for the doctrine, but the music there.
These equal syllables alone require,
Though oft the ear the open vowels tire,[2]

4. It was generally held that a person's appearance reflected his or her inner self.
5. As various styles of dress suit country, mercantile, and courtly life.
6. Made a claim. Deliberately archaic language was used by Spenser, and by a number of his 18th-century imitators.
7. In Ben Jonson's *Every Man Out of his Humor* (1599), this student lagged behind the fashions.
8. Hot-blooded young men, aspiring to fame and romantic conquest.
9. Close-fitting garment for the upper body.
1. Meter of verse, patterns of sound.
2. This line, like the couplets that follow, illustrates the fault it criticizes.

While expletives their feeble aid do join,
And ten low words oft creep in one dull line,
While they ring round the same unvaried chimes,
With sure returns of still expected rhymes.
Where-e'er you find "the cooling western breeze,"
In the next line, it "whispers through the trees";
If crystal streams "with pleasing murmurs creep,"
The reader's threatened (not in vain) with "sleep."
Then, at the last, and only couplet fraught
With some unmeaning thing they call a thought,
A needless Alexandrine[3] ends the song,
That, like a wounded snake, drags its slow length along.
Leave such to tune their own dull rhymes, and know
What's roundly smooth, or languishingly slow;
And raise the easy vigor of a line,
Where Denham's strength, and Waller's sweetness join.[4]
True ease in writing comes from art, not chance,
As those move easiest who have learned to dance.
'Tis not enough no harshness gives offense,
The sound must seem an echo to the sense.[5]
Soft is the strain when Zephyr° gently blows, *the west wind*
And the smooth stream in smoother numbers flows;
But when loud surges lash the sounding shore,
The hoarse, rough verse should like the torrent roar.
When Ajax[6] strives, some rock's vast weight to throw,
The line too labors, and the words move slow;
Not so, when swift Camilla[7] scours the plain,
Flies o'er th' unbending corn, and skims along the main.° *sea*
Hear how Timotheus'[8] varied lays surprise,
And bid alternate passions fall and rise!
While at each change the son of Lybian Jove[9]
Now burns with glory, and then melts with love;
Now his fierce eyes with sparkling fury glow,
Now sighs steal out, and tears begin to flow:
Persians and Greeks like turns of nature[1] found,
And the world's victor stood subdued by sound!
The pow'r of music all our hearts allow,° *admit to*
And what Timotheus was, is Dryden now.
  Avoid extremes; and shun the fault of such,
Who still are pleased too little, or too much.

3. The 12 syllables and six stresses of an Alexandrine are illustrated in the next line.
4. Pope follows Dryden in his stylistic characterization of John Denham (1615–1669) and Edmund Waller (1606–1687), two poets greatly respected by writers of the early 18th century, especially for their work in heroic couplets.
5. The nine lines that follow exemplify the rule laid down here.
6. The fabulously strong Greek hero in Homer's *Iliad*.
7. An Amazon warrior in Virgil's *Aeneid*.
8. Musician to Alexander the Great, as portrayed in Dryden's *Alexander's Feast* (1697).
9. Alexander the Great.
1. Similar changes of emotion.

At ev'ry trifle scorn to take offense,
That always shows great pride, or little sense;
Those heads, as stomachs, are not sure the best,
Which nauseate° all, and nothing can digest. *feel sick at*
Yet let not each gay turn° thy rapture move, *phrase*
For fools admire,[2] but men of sense approve.
As things seem large which we through mists descry,° *see*
Dullness is ever apt to magnify.
Some foreign writers, some our own despise;
The Ancients only, or the Moderns prize.
(Thus wit, like faith, by each man is applied
To one small sect, and all are damned beside.)
Meanly they seek the blessing to confine,
And force that sun but on a part to shine;
Which not alone the southern wit sublimes,° *exalts*
But ripens spirits in cold northern climes;
Which from the first has shone on ages past,
Enlights the present, and shall warm the last
(Though each may feel increases and decays,
And see now clearer and now darker days):
Regard not then if wit be old or new,
But blame the false, and value still the true.
Some ne'er advance a judgment of their own,
But catch the spreading notion° of the Town;[3] *fashion*
They reason and conclude by precedent,
And own° stale nonsense which they ne'er invent. *express*
Some judge of authors' names, not works, and then
Nor° praise nor blame the writings, but the men. *neither*
Of all this servile herd, the worst is he
That in proud dullness joins with Quality.[4]
A constant critic at the great man's board,[5]
To fetch and carry nonsense for my Lord.
What woeful stuff this madrigal would be,
In some starved Hackney sonneteer,[6] or me!
But let a Lord once own[7] the happy lines,
How the wit brightens! How the style refines!
Before his sacred name flies ev'ry fault,
And each exalted stanza teems with thought!
The vulgar thus through imitation err;
As oft the learn'd by being singular;
So much they scorn the crowd, that if the throng
By chance go right, they purposely go wrong:
So schismatics[8] the plain believers quit,

2. Wonder at the poetry, while "men of sense" deliberate before reaching favorable judgment.
3. The term was commonly used for fashionable London society.
4. The nobility, people of quality.
5. Dining table; i.e., he always eats there.
6. Like the horses from Hackney, in Middlesex, this poet's services are readily for hire. The designation "sonneteer" indicates one who writes poor poetry. Pope, who made a point of refusing to sell his services, includes himself here perhaps because of his youth when the *Essay* was written.
7. Own up to, admit that they are his.
8. Religious sectarians.

And are but damned for having too much wit.
Some praise at morning what they blame at night;
But always think the last° opinion right. *latest*
A Muse by these is like a mistress used;
This hour she's idolized, the next abused;
While their weak heads, like towns unfortified,
'Twixt sense and nonsense daily change their side.
Ask them the cause; they're wiser still, they say;
And still tomorrow's wiser than today.
We think our fathers fools, so wise we grow;
Our wiser sons, no doubt, will think us so.
Once school divines[9] this zealous isle o'erspread;
Who knew most sentences,[1] was deepest read;
Faith, gospel, all, seemed made to be disputed,
And none had sense enough to be confuted:° *disproved*
Scotists and Thomists,[2] now, in peace remain,
Amidst their kindred cobwebs in Duck Lane.[3]
If faith itself has diff'rent dresses worn,
What wonder modes in wit should take their turn?
Oft, leaving what is natural and fit,
The current folly proves the ready wit;[4]
And authors think their reputation safe,
Which lives as long as fools are pleased to laugh.
Some, valuing those of their own side[5] or mind,
Still make themselves the measure of mankind;
Fondly we think we honor merit then,
When we but praise ourselves in other men.
Parties in wit attend on those of state,
And public faction doubles private hate.
Pride, malice, folly against Dryden rose,
In various shapes of parsons, critics, beaus;[6]
But sense survived, when merry jests were past;
For rising merit will buoy up at last.
Might he return, and bless once more our eyes,
New Blackmores and new Milbourns must arise;
Nay, should great Homer lift his awful head,
Zoilus[7] again would start up from the dead.
Envy will merit, as its shade,° pursue; *shadow*

9. Theologians who followed the highly formal Scholastic method.

1. The *sententiae*, or sayings of the Church Fathers, presented and explained for the student in works like Peter Lombard's *Book of Sentences* (1148–1151).

2. The schools of medieval philosophy formed by followers of Duns Scotus and Thomas Aquinas.

3. A street in London where old and secondhand books were sold.

4. Current folly allows ready wit to show itself.

5. Political persuasion.

6. The parsons: Jeremy Collier, *A Short View of the Profaneness and Immorality of the English Stage* (1698); Luke Milbourne, *Notes on Dryden's Virgil* (1698). The critics: Thomas Shadwell (1642?–1692); Elkanah Settle (1648–1724); Gerard Langbaine (1656–1692), *An Account of the English Dramatic Poets;* Richard Blackmore (1654–1729). Among the beaus: George Villiers, Second Duke of Buckingham, who coauthored *The Rehearsal* (1671); John Wilmot, Second Earl of Rochester, *An Allusion to Horace: the 10th Satyr of the 1st Book* (1680).

7. A critic of Homer's, of the 4th century B.C.E.

But like a shadow, proves the substance true;
For envied wit, like Sol° eclipsed, makes known *the sun*
Th' opposing body's grossness,° not its own. *ponderousness*
When first that sun too pow'rful beams displays,
It draws up vapors which obscure its rays;
But ev'n those clouds at last adorn its way,
Reflect new glories, and augment the day.
    Be thou the first true merit to befriend;
His praise is lost, who stays till all commend.
Short is the date,° alas, of modern rhymes, *life*
And 'tis but just to let them live betimes.° *awhile*
No longer now that golden age appears,
When patriarch wits survived a thousand years:
Now length of fame (our second life) is lost,
And bare threescore is all ev'n that can boast;
Our sons their fathers' failing language see,
And such as Chaucer[8] is, shall Dryden be.
So when the faithful pencil has designed
Some bright idea of the master's mind,
Where a new world leaps out at his command,
And ready Nature waits upon his hand;
When the ripe colors soften and unite,
And sweetly melt into just shade and light;
When mellowing years their full perfection give,
And each bold figure just begins to live;
The treach'rous colors the fair art betray,
And all the bright creation fades away!
    Unhappy wit, like most mistaken° things, *misunderstood*
Atones not for that envy which it brings.
In youth alone its empty praise we boast,
But soon the short-lived vanity is lost!
Like some fair flow'r the early spring supplies,
That gaily blooms, but ev'n in blooming dies.
What is this wit, which must our cares employ?
The owner's wife, that other men enjoy;
Then most our trouble still when most admired,
And still the more we give, the more required;
Whose fame with pains we guard, but lose with ease,
Sure some to vex, but never all to please;
'Tis what the vicious° fear, the virtuous shun; *wicked*
By fools 'tis hated, and by knaves undone!
    If wit so much from ign'rance undergo,
Ah, let not learning too commence° its foe! *start to be*
Of old, those met rewards who could excel,
And such were praised who but endeavored well:
Though triumphs were to gen'rals only due,

8. Chaucer was admired but seen as quaint and arcane, his language unintelligible. It was common at this time to complain of the transience of the English language.

Crowns were reserved to grace the soldiers too.[9]
Now, they who reached Parnassus' lofty crown,
Employ their plans to spurn some others down;
And while self-love each jealous writer rules,
Contending wits become the sport of fools:
But still the worst with most regret commend,
For each ill author is as bad a friend.
To what base ends, and by what abject ways,
Are mortals urged through sacred° lust of praise! *accursed*
Ah, ne'er so dire a thirst of glory boast,
Nor in the critic let the man be lost!
Good nature and good sense must ever join;
To err is human; to forgive, divine.
But if in noble minds some dregs remain,
Not yet purged off, of spleen° and sour disdain, *bad temper*
Discharge that rage on more provoking crimes,
Nor fear a dearth in these flagitious° times. *corrupt*
No pardon vile obscenity should find,
Though wit and art conspire to move your mind;
But dullness with obscenity must prove
As shameful sure as impotence in love.
In the fat age of pleasure, wealth, and ease
Sprung the rank weed, and thrived with large increase;
When love was all an easy monarch's[1] care,
Seldom at council, never in a war:[2]
Jilts ruled the state, and statesmen farces writ;[3]
Nay, wits had pensions,° and young lords had wit: *government salaries*
The fair sat panting at a courtier's play,
And not a mask[4] went unimproved away:
The modest fan was lifted up no more,
And virgins smiled at what they blushed before.
The following license of a foreign reign[5]
Did all the dregs of bold Socinus[6] drain;
Then unbelieving priests reformed the nation,
And taught more pleasant methods of salvation;
Where Heav'n's free subjects might their rights dispute,
Lest God himself should seem too absolute.
Pulpits their sacred satire learned to spare,
And Vice admired° to find a flatt'rer there! *was surprised*

9. Soldiers who had distinguished themselves in the field received crowns. Unlike those soldiers rewarded for assisting one another, the poets in the following lines achieve their crowns, then turn on their fellow writers.
1. Charles II (1630–1685). Ease was a much prized social grace in the late 17th and early 18th centuries.
2. Charles had commanded an army defeated at the Battle of Worcester in 1651.
3. "Jilts" were whores, a reference to Charles's many mistresses. The statesmen were the Duke of Buckingham, *The Rehearsal* (1671); Sir Charles Sedley, *The Mulberry Garden* (1668); Sir George Etherege (1634–1691), *The Man of Mode* and other plays.
4. At Restoration playhouses, masks were initially a fashion among noblewomen in the audience; but their capacity for concealing identity made them a popular device among prostitutes too.
5. That of William III (1650–1702), from the Netherlands, who introduced policies of increased religious toleration.
6. Laelius Socinus (1525–1562) and Faustus Socinus (1539–1604), two Italian theologians who sponsored various heresies, including denying the divinity of Christ.

Encouraged thus, wit's titans[7] braved the skies,
And the press groaned with licensed blasphemies.[8]
These monsters, critics! with your darts engage,
Here point your thunder, and exhaust your rage!
Yet shun their fault, who, scandalously nice,° *fastidious*
Will needs mistake an author into vice;
All seems infected that th' infected spy,° *see*
As all looks yellow to the jaundiced eye.

Learn then what morals critics ought to show,
For 'tis but half a judge's task, to know.
'Tis not enough, taste, judgment, learning, join;
In all you speak, let truth and candor shine;
That not alone what to your sense is due,
All may allow; but seek your friendship too.
Be silent always when you doubt your sense;
And speak, though sure, with seeming diffidence:
Some positive, persisting fops we know,
Who, if once wrong, will needs be always so;
But you, with pleasure own your errors past,
And make each day a critic on° the last. *assessment of*
'Tis not enough your counsel still be true;
Blunt truths more mischief than nice° falsehoods do; *delicate*
Men must be taught as if you taught them not,
And things unknown proposed as things forgot.
Without good breeding, truth is disapproved;
That only makes superior sense belov'd.
Be niggards of advice on no pretense;[9]
For the worse avarice is that of sense.
With mean complacence ne'er betray your trust,[1]
Nor be so civil as to prove unjust.
Fear not the anger of the wise to raise;
Those best can bear reproof, who merit praise.
'Twere well might critics still this freedom take;
But Appius[2] reddens at each word you speak,
And stares, tremendous,[3] with a threat'ning eye,
Like some fierce tyrant in old tapestry.
Fear most to tax an honorable fool,
Whose right it is, uncensured to be dull;
Such without wit are poets when they please,
As without learning they can take degrees.[4]
Leave dang'rous truths to unsuccessful satires,

7. This reference compares the deistic writers to the classical giants, the Titans, who attempted to conquer heaven, and were severely punished as a result.
8. The Licensing Act lapsed in 1663, allowing books to be published that Pope and others found blasphemous.
9. Do not withhold your advice however good your reasons.
1. Do not avoid your duty to give judgment by being unnecessarily servile or polite.
2. Dennis; the hero of his tragedy, *Appius and Virginia* (1705), was also sensitive to criticism.
3. Staring, and use of the adjective "tremendous," were both characteristic of Dennis.
4. Privy Councilors, bishops, and peers could obtain academic degrees without fulfilling normal examination or residence requirements.

And flattery to fulsome dedicators,
Whom, when they praise, the world believes no more,
Than when they promise to give scribbling o'er.
'Tis best sometimes your censure to restrain,
And charitably let the dull be vain:
Your silence there is better than your spite,
For who can rail so long as they can write?
Still humming on, their drowsy course they keep,
And lashed so long, like tops,° are lashed asleep. *spinning tops*
False steps but help them to renew the race,
As, after stumbling, jades° will mend their pace. *ruined horses*
What crowds of these, impenitently bold,
In sounds and jingling syllables grown old,
Still run on poets, in a raging vein,
Ev'n to the dregs and squeezings of the brain,
Strain out the last dull droppings of their sense,
And rhyme with all the rage of impotence.
Such shameless bards we have; and yet 'tis true,
There are as mad, abandoned critics too.
The bookful blockhead, ignorantly read,
With loads of learned lumber in his head,
With his own tongue still edifies his ears,
And always list'ning to himself appears.
All books he reads, and all he reads assails,
From Dryden's *Fables* down to Durfey's *Tales*.[5]
With him, most authors steal their works, or buy;
Garth did not write his own *Dispensary*.[6]
Name a new play, and he's the poet's friend,
Nay showed his faults—but when would poets mend?
No place so sacred from such fops is barred,
Nor is Paul's church more safe than Paul's churchyard:[7]
Nay, fly to altars; there they'll talk you dead:
For fools rush in where angels fear to tread.
Distrustful sense with modest caution speaks,
It still looks home, and short excursions makes;
But rattling nonsense in full volleys breaks,
And never shocked, and never turned aside,
Bursts out, resistless, with a thund'ring tide.
But where's the man, who counsel can bestow,
Still pleased to teach, and yet not proud to know?° *of knowing*
Unbiased, or° by favor, or by spite; *either*
Not dully prepossessed, nor blindly right;
Though learn'd, well-bred; and though well-bred, sincere;
Modestly bold, and humanly severe?

5. Dryden, *Fables Ancient and Modern* (1700); Thomas D'Urfey, *Tales Tragical and Comical* (1704). D'Urfey, a popular playwright and singer, is best known for the ballad collection *Pills to Purge Melancholy*, to which his name was attached.

6. The report that Pope's friend Samuel Garth had plagiarized his popular mock-heroic work, *The Dispensary* (1699) was, according to William Warburton, "a common slander at that time."

7. Booksellers kept stalls in St. Paul's churchyard.

Who to a friend his faults can freely show,
And gladly praise the merit of a foe?
Blessed with a taste exact, yet unconfined;
A knowledge both of books and humankind;
Gen'rous converse;[8] a soul exempt from pride;
And love to praise, with reason on his side?
Such once were critics; such the happy few,
Athens and Rome in better ages knew.
The mighty Stagyrite° first left the shore, *Aristotle*
Spread all his sails, and durst the deeps explore;
He steered securely, and discovered far,
Led by the light of the Mæonian star.° *Homer*
Poets, a race long unconfined and free,
Still fond and proud of savage liberty,
Received his laws;[9] and stood convinced 'twas fit
Who conquered Nature,[1] should preside o'er wit.
Horace still charms with graceful negligence,
And without method talks us into sense,
Will, like a friend, familiarly convey
The truest notions in the easiest way.
He, who supreme in judgment, as in wit,
Might boldly censure, as he boldly writ,
Yet judged with coolness, though he sung with fire;
His precepts teach but what his works inspire.
Our critics take a contrary extreme;
They judge with fury, but they write with phlegm.[2]
Nor suffers Horace more in wrong translations
By wits, than critics in as wrong quotations.
See Dionysius[3] Homer's thoughts refine,
And call new beauties forth from ev'ry line!
Fancy and art in gay Petronius[4] please,
The scholar's learning, with the courtier's ease.
In grave Quintilian's copious work,[5] we find
The justest rules, and clearest method joined.
Thus useful arms in magazines° we place, *storehouses*
All ranged in order, and disposed with grace,
But less to please the eye, than arm the hand,
Still fit for use, and ready at command.
Thee, bold Longinus![6] all the Nine° inspire, *the Muses*
And bless their critic with a poet's fire.

8. Good conversation and gracious behavior.
9. Aristotle's *Poetics* set rules for poetic composition.
1. Aristotle was also noted for his study of the physical world.
2. Under the humoral understanding of the body, an excess of phlegm caused disease, and so the term came to mean coolness, dullness, or apathy.
3. Dionysius of Halicarnassus, a Roman critic contemporary with Horace.
4. Petronius Arbiter (d. 66 C.E.) judged questions of taste in Nero's court.
5. Quintilian (c. 35–c. 99 C.E.) was a Latin rhetorician, whose *Institutio Oratoria* Pope knew well.
6. Longinus (210?–273 C.E.) was a Greek rhetorician, to whom was attributed the enormously influential treatise *On the Sublime*.

An ardent judge, who, zealous in his trust,
With warmth gives sentence, yet is always just;
Whose own example strengthens all his laws,
And is himself that great sublime he draws.
Thus long succeeding critics justly reigned,
License repressed, and useful laws ordained.
Learning and Rome alike in empire grew;
And arts still followed where her eagles[7] flew;
From the same foes, at last, both felt their doom,
And the same age saw learning fall, and Rome.
With tyranny, then superstition joined,
As that the body, this enslaved the mind;
Much was believed, but little understood,
And to be dull was construed to be good;
A second deluge learning thus o'errun,
And the monks finished what the Goths begun.
At length, Erasmus, that great, injured name
(The glory of the priesthood, and the shame!),[8]
Stemmed the wild torrent of a barb'rous age,
And drove those holy vandals off the stage.
But see! each Muse, in Leo's[9] golden days,
Starts from her trance, and trims her withered bays!
Rome's ancient Genius,° o'er its ruins spread, *guardian spirit*
Shakes off the dust, and rears his rev'rend head.
Then Sculpture and her sister Arts revive;
Stones leaped to form, and rocks began to live;
With sweeter notes each rising temple rung;
A Raphael painted, and a Vida sung![1]
Immortal Vida! on whose honored brow
The poet's bays and critic's ivy[2] grow:
Cremona now shall ever boast thy name,
As next in place to Mantua, next in fame![3]
But soon by impious arms from Latium[4] chased,
Their ancient bounds the banished Muses passed;
Thence arts o'er all the northern world advance;
But critic learning flourished most in France:
The rules, a nation born to serve,[5] obeys;
And Boileau[6] still in right of Horace sways.
But we, brave Britons, foreign laws despised,
And kept° unconquered, and uncivilized; *remained*
Fierce for the liberties of wit, and bold,

7. The emblem of the Roman empire.
8. Erasmus (c. 1466–1536), the Dutch humanist who influenced the course of the Reformation; the "glory of the priesthood" because of his learning, Erasmus was its "shame" both because he criticized priests, and because he was persecuted for his outspokenness.
9. Pope Leo X (1475–1521), patron of letters and arts.
1. Raphael (1483–1520) was considered the greatest of painters; Girolamo Vida (c. 1485–1566), Italian poet.
2. Ivy was associated with poets (and with Bacchus), but also with learning.
3. Cremona and Mantua were the birthplaces of Vida and Virgil, respectively.
4. Italy; Rome was conquered by the Holy Roman Empire in 1527.
5. A reference to the despotic reign of Louis XIV.
6. Nicolas Boileau-Despréaux (1636–1711), poet and critic wrote much that was admired in England.

We still defied the Romans, as of old.
Yet some there were, among the sounder few
Of those who less presumed, and better knew,
Who durst° assert the juster ancient cause, *dared to*
And here restored wit's fundamental laws.
Such was the Muse, whose rules and practice tell,
"Nature's chief masterpiece is writing well."[7]
Such was Roscommon,[8]—not more learn'd than good,
With manners gen'rous as his noble blood;
To him the wit of Greece and Rome was known,
And ev'ry author's merit, but his own.
Such late was Walsh[9]—the Muse's judge and friend,
Who justly knew° to blame or to commend; *knew when*
To failings mild, but zealous for desert;
The clearest head, and the sincerest heart.
This humble praise, lamented shade!° receive, *spirit*
This praise at least a grateful Muse may give:
The Muse, whose early voice you taught to sing,
Prescribed her heights, and pruned° her tender wing, *groomed*
(Her guide now lost) no more attempts to rise,
But in low numbers° short excursions tries: *lowly verses*
Content, if hence th' unlearn'd their wants° may view, *lacks*
The learn'd reflect on what before they knew:
Careless of censure, nor too fond of fame;
Still pleas'd to praise, yet not afraid to blame;
Averse alike to flatter, or offend;
Not free from faults, nor yet too vain to mend.

c. 1709 1711

Windsor-Forest "Mr. Pope has published a fine poem called Windsor Forest," wrote Jonathan Swift to his beloved Stella; "read it," he urged her in a letter sent just two days after the poem went on sale. Pope wrote *Windsor-Forest* in two distinct stages: the first part (lines 1–290) was composed in 1704–1705, but the remaining lines celebrating the imminent Peace of Utrecht (1713) that formally ended the long War of Spanish Succession were penned in late 1712 and early 1713. The Peace—a great triumph for the ruling Tory party and the last Stuart monarch, Queen Anne—recognized Great Britain as the world's leading naval power and greatly augmented its colonial and commercial empire at the expense of Spain and France. It would be wrong, however, to imagine that *Windsor-Forest* is half pastoral idyll and half Tory political propaganda; it is, rather, a thoroughgoing synthesis of the topographical, the moral, and the political. Pope's sources for *Windsor-Forest* include Virgil's *Eclogues* and *Georgics*, Ovid's *Metamorphoses*, the Bible, Spenser's *Faerie Queene*, Milton's *Paradise Lost*, Edmund Waller's *On St. James's Park* (1661), and Thomas Otway's *Windsor Castle* (1685). It is, however, Pope's comment on "the distinguishing excellence" of John Denham's *Cooper's Hill* (1642) that best explains Pope's own imaginative procedure in *Windsor-Forest*: "the descriptions of places, and

7. This line is quoted from the then well-known *Essay on Poetry* (1682) by John Sheffield (1648–1721), third Earl of Mulgrave and later first Duke of Buckingham and Normady.

8. Wentworth Dillon (c. 1630–1685), fourth Earl of Roscommon; poet, critic, didactic writer.

9. William Walsh (1663–1708), friend and mentor of Pope.

images raised by the poet, are still [i.e., continually] tending to some hint, or leading into some reflection, upon moral life or political institution" (*Iliad* 16.466n). Windsor was the ideal setting for a political poem in which landscape evoked England's proud heritage: from William the Conqueror, who first established a royal residence at Windsor, to "great ANNA" (line 327), who made Windsor Castle her chief residence and frequently rode and hunted in the forest, this was a place suffused with English history. From this enclave of natural beauty and political tradition—the home of monarchs and the haven of Muses—Pope's myth-making genius created a triumphant vision of peace and prosperity, the dawning of a Golden Age.

Windsor-Forest

To the Right Honorable George Lord Lansdowne[1]

Non injussa cano: te nostræ, Vare, myricæ
Te nemus omne canet; nec Phœbo gratior ulla est
Quam sibi quæ Vari præscripsit Pagina nomen.[2]

Thy forests, Windsor! and thy green retreats,
At once the monarch's and the Muse's seats,[3]
Invite my lays.° Be present, sylvan maids![4] *prompt my poetry*
Unlock your springs, and open all your shades.
Granville commands: Your aid O Muses bring!
What Muse for Granville can refuse to sing?
The groves of Eden, vanished now so long,
Live in description, and look green in song:[5]
These, were my breast inspired with equal flame,
Like them in beauty, should be like in fame.
Here hills and vales, the woodland and the plain,
Here earth and water seem to strive again,
Not chaos-like together crushed and bruised,
But as the world, harmoniously confused:
Where order in variety we see,
And where, though all things differ, all agree.
Here waving groves a checkered scene display,
And part admit and part exclude the day;
As some coy nymph her lover's warm address
Nor° quite indulges, nor can quite repress. *neither*
There, interspersed in lawns° and opening glades, *clearings*
Thin trees arise that shun each other's shades.
Here in full light the russet plains extend;
There wrapped in clouds the blueish hills ascend:

1. George Granville (1667–1735), Baron Lansdowne, was himself a poet and playwright. A Tory politician close to Queen Anne, he became Secretary of War in 1710 and so was partly responsible for both British victory and the peace that followed. Lord Lansdowne greatly admired Pope's poetry and encouraged him to publish a poem on the Peace.

2. Adapted from Virgil's sixth *Eclogue*, lines 9–12, in which the poet dedicates his pastoral poem to his friend Varus (like Lansdowne, a prominent military figure): "I do not sing without purpose: our tamarisks, Varus, every grove will sing of you; nor is any page more pleasing to Apollo than one that begins with the name of Varus."

3. Windsor Forest, seat (country home) of Britain's monarchs since Norman times (and even fabled to be the site of the legendary King Arthur's court), in Pope's view was also home to the Muses because the poets Sir John Denham and Abraham Cowley had lived in the vicinity.

4. Dryads and naiads, spirits of the trees and water.

5. The ancient biblical description of the Garden of Eden was made "green in song" by Milton's (relatively) recent *Paradise Lost*.

Ev'n the wild heath displays her purple dyes,[6]
And 'midst the desert° fruitful fields arise, *uncultivated land*
That crowned with tufted trees[7] and springing corn,
Like verdant isles the sable waste adorn.
Let India boast her plants, nor envy we
The weeping amber or the balmy tree,
While by our oaks the precious loads are borne,[8]
And realms commanded which those trees adorn.
Not proud Olympus[9] yields a nobler sight,
Though gods assembled grace his tow'ring height,
Than what more humble mountains offer here,
Where, in their blessings, all those gods appear.
See Pan with flocks, and fruits Pomona crowned,
Here blushing Flora[1] paints th' enameled ground,[2]
Here Ceres' gifts° in waving prospect stand, *grain crops*
And nodding tempt the joyful reaper's hand,
Rich Industry sits smiling on the plains,
And Peace and Plenty tell, a STUART reigns.[3]
    Not thus the land appeared in ages past,[4]
A dreary desert and a gloomy waste,
To savage beasts and savage laws a prey,[5]
And kings more furious and severe than they:
Who claimed the skies, dispeopled° air and floods, *depopulated*
The lonely lords of empty wilds and woods.
Cities laid waste, they stormed the dens and caves
(For wiser brutes were backward° to be slaves). *unwilling*
What could be free, when lawless beasts obeyed,
And ev'n the elements a tyrant swayed?[6]
In vain kind seasons swelled the teeming grain,
Soft show'rs distilled, and suns grew warm in vain;
The swain with tears his frustrate labor yields,
And famished dies amidst his ripened fields.[7]
What wonder then, a beast or subject slain
Were equal crimes in a despotic reign?
Both doomed alike for sportive tyrants bled,
But while the subject starved, the beast was fed.
Proud Nimrod[8] first the bloody chase began,

6. Heather's purple blooms cover open moorland in late summer.
7. A cluster of trees; Pope borrowed the phrase from Milton's *L'Allegro* (1632).
8. British ships made of oak allowed Britain both to conquer distant countries and to carry goods from them.
9. The mountain home of the Greek gods.
1. Three deities of natural abundance: Pan presides over shepherds and sheep; Pomona over fruits; Flora over flowers.
2. The enameling of metal to allow for overlayers of intricate painted designs was commonly used as a metaphor for nature.
3. Queen Anne (r. 1702–1714), last of the Stuart monarchs.
4. Pope's history of the landscape (lines 43–86) begins with William the Conqueror's creation of the New Forest as a hunting ground reserved for royalty, and chronicles the disastrous impact of this appropriation on his successors and their subjects.
5. The Forest Laws had imposed harsh penalties on those caught stealing the king's game.
6. By controlling the animals, the "tyrant" effectually controlled their "elements" (environments).
7. The farmer dies "famished" because he has been forced to cultivate food for game animals, not humans.
8. In Genesis 10.9, Nimrod is described as a mighty hunter, but he was also seen as a tyrant; he founded the kingdoms of Babylon and Assyria.

A mighty hunter, and his prey was man.
Our haughty Norman boasts that barb'rous name,
And makes his trembling slaves the royal game.
The fields are ravished from th' industrious swains,
From men their cities, and from gods their fanes:[9]
The leveled towns with weeds lie covered o'er,
The hollow winds through naked temples roar;
Round broken columns clasping ivy twined;
O'er heaps of ruins stalked the stately hind;° *female deer*
The fox obscene° to gaping tombs retires, *loathsome*
And savage howlings fill the sacred quires.[1]
Awed by his nobles, by his commons° cursed, *commoners*
Th' oppressor ruled tyrannic where he durst,
Stretched o'er the poor, and church, his iron rod,
And treats alike his vassals and his God.
Whom ev'n the Saxon spared, and bloody Dane,
The wanton victims of his sport remain.
But see, the man who spacious regions gave
A waste for beasts, himself denied a grave![2]
Stretched on the lawn his second hope[3] survey,
At once the chaser, and at once the prey.
Lo Rufus, tugging at the deadly dart,
Bleeds in the forest, like a wounded hart.[4]
Succeeding monarchs heard the subjects' cries,
Nor saw displeased the peaceful cottage rise.
Then gath'ring flocks on unknown° mountains fed, *unfamiliar*
O'er sandy wilds were yellow harvests spread,
The forests wondered at th' unusual grain,
And secret transports touched the conscious swain.[5]
Fair Liberty, Britannia's goddess, rears
Her cheerful head, and leads the golden years.
  Ye vig'rous swains! while youth ferments your blood,[6]
And purer spirits swell the sprightly flood,
Now range the hills, the gameful woods beset,
Wind° the shrill horn, or spread the waving net. *blow*
When milder autumn summer's heat succeeds,
And in the new-shorn field the partridge feeds,
Before his lord the ready spaniel bounds;

9. Temples; to create the New Forest, William I destroyed many villages and churches. He was sharply criticized for demolishing God's houses to make dens for wild beasts.
1. Choir stalls; Pope deliberately uses archaic spelling. His description of "quires," "broken columns," and "temples" also suggests grander buildings than the parish churches of this time, calling to mind the destruction of the abbeys during the Reformation.
2. Reportedly, at William I's funeral, a knight had tried to prevent the king's burial in land he claimed to own. Pope suggests that this incident and thhe several royal deaths related to hunting in the forest (depicted in the following four lines) were divine vengeance.
3. Richard, second son of William the Conqueror [Pope's note].
4. William Rufus was accidentally killed by a companion's arrow while out hunting; a hart is a male deer.
5. Joy moves the peasant, well aware of what he has gained; this is a fairly new use of "conscious" in this sense.
6. The blood is quickened by the animal spirits supposed to move in it.

Panting with hope, he tries the furrowed grounds;
But when the tainted[7] gales the game betray,
Couched close[8] he lies, and meditates the prey:
Secure they trust th' unfaithful field, beset,
Till hov'ring o'er 'em sweeps the swelling net.
Thus (if small things we may with great compare)
When Albion° sends her eager sons to war, *England*
Some thoughtless town, with ease and plenty blessed,
Near, and more near, the closing lines invest;° *surround*
Sudden they seize the' amazed, defenseless prize,
And high in air Britannia's standard flies.
    See! from the brake° the whirring pheasant springs, *bushes*
And mounts exulting on triumphant wings;
Short is his joy! He feels the fiery wound,
Flutters in blood, and panting beats the ground.
Ah! what avail his glossy, varying dyes,
His purple crest, and scarlet-circled eyes,
The vivid green his shining plumes unfold,
His painted wings, and breast that flames with gold?
    Nor yet, when moist Arcturus[9] clouds the Sky,
The woods and fields their pleasing toils deny.
To plains with well-breathed beagles we repair,
And trace the mazes of the circling hare.
(Beasts, urged by us, their fellow beasts pursue,
And learn of Man each other to undo.)
With slaught'ring guns th' unwearied fowler roves,
When frosts have whitened all the naked groves;
Where doves in flocks the leafless trees o'ershade,
And lonely woodcocks haunt the wat'ry glade.
He lifts the tube, and levels with his eye;
Straight° a short thunder breaks the frozen sky. *immediately*
Oft, as in airy rings they skim the heath,
The clam'rous lapwings feel the leaden death:
Oft as the mounting larks their notes prepare,
They fall, and leave their little lives in air.
    In genial spring, beneath the quiv'ring shade
Where cooling vapors breathe along the mead,
The patient fisher takes his silent stand
Intent, his angle trembling in his hand;
With looks unmoved, he hopes the scaly breed,
And eyes the dancing cork and bending reed.
Our plenteous streams a various race supply;
The bright-eyed perch with fins of Tyrian° dye, *purple*
The silver eel, in shining volumes° rolled, *coils*
The yellow carp, in scales bedropped with gold,

7. With the animal's scent.
8. Crouching near the ground.
9. One of the stars in the Great Bear constellation; in antiquity, its rise with the sun in September was associated with bad weather.

Swift trouts, diversified with crimson stains,
And pikes, the tyrants of the wat'ry plains.
 Now Cancer glows with Phœbus' fiery car;[1]
The youth rush eager to the sylvan war;
Swarm o'er the lawns, the forest walks surround,
Rouse° the fleet hart, and cheer the opening° hound. *flush out / baying*
Th' impatient courser° pants in ev'ry vein, *fast horse*
And pawing, seems to beat the distant plain;
Hills, vales, and floods appear already crossed,
And ere he starts, a thousand steps are lost.
See! the bold youth strain up the threatening steep,
Rush through the thickets, down the valleys sweep,
Hang o'er their coursers' heads with eager speed,
And earth rolls back beneath the flying steed.
Let old Arcadia boast her spacious plain,
Th' immortal huntress, and her virgin train;
Nor envy, Windsor! since thy shades have seen
As bright a goddess, and as chaste a queen;[2]
Whose care, like hers, protects the sylvan reign,
The earth's fair light, and empress of the main.[3]
 Here too, 'tis sung, of old Diana strayed,
And Cynthus' top[4] forsook for Windsor shade;
Here was she seen o'er airy wastes to rove,
Seek the clear spring, or haunt the pathless grove;
Here armed with silver bows, in early dawn,
Her buskined° virgins traced the dewy lawn. *boot-wearing*
 Above the rest a rural nymph was famed,
Thy offspring, Thames! the fair Lodona named.
(Lodona's fate, in long oblivion cast,
The Muse shall sing, and what she sings shall last.)
Scarce could the goddess from her nymph be known,
But by the crescent° and the golden zone,° *moon / belt*
She scorned the praise of beauty, and the care;
A belt her waist, a fillet° binds her hair; *headband*
A painted quiver on her shoulder sounds,
And with her dart the flying deer she wounds.
It chanced, as eager of the chase the maid
Beyond the forest's verdant limits strayed,
Pan saw and loved, and furious with desire
Pursued her flight; her flight increased his fire.
Not half so swift the trembling doves can fly,
When the fierce eagle cleaves the liquid° sky; *transparent*
Not half so swiftly the fierce eagle moves,

1. The sun (Phoebus's "car": chariot) enters the constellation of Cancer, the crab, on 22 June.
2. Queen Anne is here being compared both to the "immortal huntress," Diana, and to Anne's illustrious forebear, the "virgin queen" Elizabeth I.
3. Like Diana, the moon goddess who governed the tides, Britannia ruled the seas.
4. The mountain on which Diana was said to have been born.

When through the clouds he drives the trembling doves;
As from the god she flew with furious pace,
Or as the god, more furious, urged the chase.
Now fainting, sinking, pale, the nymph appears;
Now close behind his sounding steps she hears;
And now his shadow reached her as she run
(His shadow lengthened by the setting sun);
And now his shorter breath with sultry air
Pants on her neck, and fans her parting hair.
In vain on Father Thames she calls for aid,
Nor could Diana help her injured maid.
Faint, breathless, thus she prayed, nor prayed in vain:
"Ah Cynthia! ah—though banished from thy train,
Let me, O let me, to the shades repair,
My native shades—there weep, and murmur there."
She said, and melting as in tears she lay,
In a soft, silver stream dissolved away.
The silver stream her virgin coldness keeps,
Forever murmurs, and forever weeps;
Still bears the name the hapless virgin bore,[5]
And bathes the forest where she ranged before.
In her chaste current oft the goddess laves,° *bathes*
And with celestial tears augments the waves.
Oft in her glass the musing shepherd spies
The headlong mountains and the downward skies,
The wat'ry landscape of the pendant[6] woods,
And absent° trees that tremble in the floods; *illusory*
In the clear azure gleam the flocks are seen,
And floating forests paint the waves with green.
Through the fair scene roll slow the ling'ring streams,
Then foaming pour along, and rush into the Thames.
Thou too, great father° of the British floods! *the Thames*
With joyful pride survey'st our lofty woods,
Where tow'ring oaks their growing honors rear,
And future navies on thy shores appear.
Not Neptune's self from all his streams receives
A wealthier tribute, than to thine he gives.
No seas so rich, so gay no banks appear,
No lake so gentle, and no spring so clear.
Nor Po so swells the fabling poet's lays,[7]
While led along the skies his shining current strays,
Than thine, which visits Windsor's famed abodes,
To grace the mansion of our earthly gods.
Nor all his stars above a luster show,

5. I.e., Loddon, a river that runs through Windsor Forest and into the Thames.
6. Hanging; the woods both hang over the stream, and, in the stream's reflection, appear to stand upside down.
7. Both Virgil and Ovid compared the Po, a river in Italy, to the winding constellation Eridanus, named for a river in Greek mythology.

Like the bright beauties on thy banks below;
Where Jove, subdued by mortal passion still,
Might change Olympus for a nobler hill.
Happy the man whom this bright court approves,
His sov'reign favors, and his country loves;
Happy next him who to these shades retires,
Whom Nature charms, and whom the Muse inspires,
Whom humbler joys of home-felt quiet please,
Successive study, exercise, and ease.
He gathers health from herbs the forest yields,
And of their fragrant physic° spoils° the fields: *medicines / robs*
With chemic art[8] exalts° the min'ral pow'rs, *refines*
And draws° the aromatic souls of flow'rs. *extracts*
Now marks the course of rolling orbs on high;
O'er figured worlds[9] now travels with his eye.
Of ancient writ unlocks the learned store,
Consults the dead, and lives past ages o'er.
Or wand'ring thoughtful in the silent wood,
Attends the duties of the wise and good,
T' observe a mean,[1] be to himself a friend,
To follow Nature, and regard his end.
Or looks on Heav'n with more than mortal eyes,
Bids his free soul expatiate in the skies,
Amid her kindred stars familiar roam,
Survey the region, and confess her home!
Such was the life great Scipio[2] once admired,
Thus Atticus,[3] and Trumbull[4] thus retired.
Ye sacred Nine![5] that all my soul possess,
Whose raptures fire me, and whose visions bless,
Bear me, oh bear me to sequestered scenes,
The bow'ry mazes and surrounding greens;
To Thames's banks which fragrant breezes fill,
Or where ye Muses sport on Cooper's Hill.
(On Cooper's Hill eternal wreaths shall grow,[6]
While lasts the mountain, or while Thames shall flow.)
I seem through consecrated walks to rove,
I hear soft music die along the grove;
Led by the sound I roam from shade to shade,
By god-like poets venerable made:
Here his first lays majestic Denham sung;[7]

8. The skills of the chemist.
9. The earth, or possibly the zodiac, portrayed on a globe.
1. To maintain a steady, balanced course through life; according to Aristotle, wisdom lay in following the "golden mean," or middle way.
2. Scipio Africanus, the Roman general who defeated Hannibal and the Carthaginians in 202 B.C.E. but declined political office, choosing eventually to retire to the country.
3. Titus Pomponius (109–32 B.C.E.), despite his friendship and correspondence with Cicero, refused to become involved in politics; he was called Atticus because he spent much time studying in Athens, which lies in the region of Attica.
4. Sir William Trumbull (1639–1716), Pope's elderly friend.
5. The Nine Muses, daughters of Mnemosyne (goddess of memory) and Zeus, each of whom presided over a different art or science.
6. Because commemorated in Sir John Denham's poem *Cooper's Hill* (1642).
7. Denham, described as "majestic" because of the (then unusual) style of the couplets in *Cooper's Hill*, lived near Windsor before the Civil Wars.

There the last numbers flowed from Cowley's tongue.[8]
O early lost![9] what tears the river shed
When the sad pomp along his banks was led?
His drooping swans on ev'ry note expire,
And on his willows[1] hung each Muse's lyre.
    Since Fate relentless stopped their heav'nly voice,
No more the forests ring, or groves rejoice;
Who now shall charm the shades where Cowley strung
His living harp, and lofty Denham sung?
But hark! the groves rejoice, the forest rings!
Are these revived? Or is it Granville sings?
    'Tis yours, my Lord, to bless our soft retreats,
And call the Muses to their ancient seats,
To paint anew the flow'ry sylvan scenes,
To crown the forests with immortal greens,
Make Windsor hills in lofty numbers rise,
And lift her turrets nearer to the skies;
To sing those honors you deserve to wear,
And add new luster to her silver star.[2]
    Here noble Surrey[3] felt the sacred rage,
Surrey, the Granville of a former age:
Matchless his pen, victorious was his lance;
Bold in the lists, and graceful in the dance:
In the same shades the Cupids tuned his lyre,
To the same notes of love, and soft desire:
Fair Geraldine,[4] bright object of his vow,
Then filled the groves, as heav'nly Myra[5] now.
    Oh wouldst thou sing what heroes Windsor bore,
What kings first breathed upon her winding shore,[6]
Or raise old warriors whose adored remains
In weeping vaults[7] her hallowed earth contains!
With Edward's[8] acts adorn the shining page,[9]
Stretch his long triumphs down through ev'ry age,
Draw monarchs chained, and Cressi's glorious Field,[1]
The lilies[2] blazing on the regal shield.
Then, from her roofs when Verrio's colors fall,
And leave inanimate the naked wall;[3]

8. Mr. [Abraham] Cowley died at Chertsey, on the borders of the Forest, and was from thence conveyed to Westminster [Pope's note], where he was buried in state.
9. Cowley died at age 49.
1. Emblems of sorrow.
2. The star worn by members inducted into the highly prestigious Order of the Garter, founded by Edward III in Windsor Castle's Chapel of St. George.
3. Henry Howard, Earl of Surrey, one of the first refiners of the English poetry; famous in the time of Henry VIII for his sonnets, the scene of many of which is laid at Windsor [Pope's note].
4. Lady Elizabeth Fitzgerald (1528?–1589) to whom Surrey was thought to have directed his love poems.
5. The poetical name Granville used for his female addressee.
6. Suggesting the etymological meaning of "Windsor."
7. Because of the seepage of water through the walls; similar natural phenomena explain the conceits in lines 307 and 313.
8. Edward III born here [Pope's note].
9. Pope her urges Granville to describe in verse the conquest of France, in the mid-fourteenth-century, by Edward III and his son Edward the Black Prince; the artist Antonio Verrio (1639–1707) had commemorated their victories in ceiling paintings at Windsor Castle.
1. The village in northern France where Edward III defeated the French.
2. Emblem of France, but added to the English crest of arms.
3. In ceiling paintings at Windsor had already begun to disintegrate.

Still in thy song should vanquished France appear,
And bleed forever under Britain's spear.
Let softer strains ill-fated Henry[4] mourn,
And palms eternal flourish round his urn.
Here o'er the martyr king the marble weeps,
And fast beside him, once-feared Edward[5] sleeps:
Whom not th' extended Albion could contain,
From old Belerium[6] to the German main,
The grave unites; where ev'n the great find rest,
And blended lie th' oppressor and th' oppressed!
Make sacred Charles's tomb forever known,[7]
(Obscure the place, and uninscribed the stone).
Oh fact accursed!° What tears has Albion shed, *evil deed*
Heav'ns! what new wounds, and how her old have bled?
She saw her sons with purple deaths[8] expire,
Her sacred domes° involved in rolling fire, *stately buildings*
A dreadful series of intestine wars,[9]
Inglorious triumphs, and dishonest° scars. *shameful*
At length great *ANNA*° said—"Let Discord cease!" *Queen Anne*
She said, the world obeyed, and all was peace!
In that blessed moment, from his oozy bed
Old Father Thames advanced his rev'rend head.
His tresses dropped with dews, and o'er the stream
His shining horns[1] diffused a golden gleam:
Graved on his urn appeared the moon, that guides
His swelling waters, and alternate tides;
The figured streams in waves of silver rolled,
And on their banks Augusta[2] rose in gold.[3]
Around his throne the sea-born brothers[4] stood,
That swell with tributary urns his flood.
First the famed authors of his ancient name,
The winding Isis and the fruitful Thame:[5]
The Kennet swift, for silver eels renowned;
The Loddon slow, with verdant alders crowned:
Cole, whose dark streams his flow'ry islands lave;
And chalky Wey, that rolls a milky wave:

4. Henry VI, murdered in 1471, was looked upon by some in northern Britain (where he lived for some time as a fugitive) as a saint; the "palms" in the following line are emblems of martyrdom.
5. Edward IV, responsible for Henry VI's murder, was buried in St. George's chapel, Windsor, where Henry was later re-interred.
6. Land's End in Cornwall, the southwestern-most point in England.
7. Charles I, executed by the Puritans in 1649 and consequently considered by many a Christian and political martyr, was buried in St. George's Chapel without any service; his tomb remained unidentified until 1813.
8. Death from the Great Plague in 1665; this event, like the fire of London (1666) and the 1688 Revolution alluded to in the following lines, was viewed by many as a result of God's wrath, possibly (as Pope here implies) visited on the nation as a result of the murder of Charles I.
9. The Civil Wars during the reigns of Charles I, Cromwell (in Ireland), James II, and William III (in Ireland).
1. River gods often had bulls' horns, representing their strength, noisiness, and importance for agriculture.
2. The name given to London by the Romans.
3. A reference to Dryden's description of London's rebuilding after the Great Fire (in brick and white Portland stone) in *Annus Mirabilis* (1667), to which work the rest of this poem is indebted.
4. According to myth, all rivers were children of the sea gods (Oceanus and Thethys).
5. The Thames was seen as the son of the Thame and the Isis rivers.

The blue, transparent Vandalis° appears; *the Wandle*
The gulfy Lee his sedgy tresses rears:
And sullen Mole, that hides his diving flood;
And silent Darent, stained with Danish blood.[6]
    High in the midst, upon his urn reclined,
(His sea-green mantle waving with the wind)
The god appeared; he turned his azure eyes
Where Windsor domes and pompous turrets rise,
Then bowed and spoke; the winds forget to roar,
And the hushed waves glide softly to the shore.
    Hail sacred peace![7] hail long-expected days,
Which Thames's glory to the stars shall raise!
Though Tiber's streams immortal Rome behold,
Though foaming Hermus[8] swells with Tides of gold,
From Heav'n itself though sev'nfold Nilus[9] flows,
And harvests on a hundred realms bestows;
These now no more shall be the Muse's themes,
Lost in my fame, as in the sea their streams.
Let Volga's banks[1] with iron squadrons° shine, *cavalry*
And groves of lances glitter on the Rhine,
Let barb'rous Ganges[2] arm a servile train;
Be mine the blessings of a peaceful reign.
No more shall my sons dye with British blood
Red Iber's[3] sands, or Ister's[4] foaming flood;
Safe on my shore each unmolested swain
Shall tend the flocks, or reap the bearded grain;
The shady empire shall retain no trace
Of war or blood, but in the sylvan chase,
The trumpets sleep, while cheerful horns are blown,
And arms employed on birds and beasts alone.
Behold! th' ascending villas[5] on my side
Project long shadows o'er the crystal tide.
Behold! Augusta's glitt'ring spires increase,
And temples[6] rise, the beauteous works of peace.
I see, I see where two fair cities[7] bend
Their ample bow,° a new Whitehall ascend![8] *riverbend*
There mighty nations shall inquire their doom,[9]

6. The Danes were defeated at Otford, on the Darent, in 1016.
7. The War of the Spanish Succession had begun in 1701; peace treaties were signed in London in 1711, and in Utrecht in 1713.
8. An Italian river distinguished by Virgil.
9. Because of its delta, Ovid called the Nile *septemfluus*.
1. Charles XII of Sweden was defeated by the Russians in 1709 (nowhere near the Volga).
2. Alluding to the Mogul Emperor Aurangzeb's recent wars in India.
3. The Ebro in Spain, where the Allies had gained victory in 1710.
4. The Danube, where Marlborough achieved his famous victory at Blenheim in 1704.
5. Many new private country homes were being built along the Thames upriver from London at this time.
6. The fifty new churches [Pope's note], built on the Queen's orders to meet the requirements of a growing London.
7. London and Westminster, separated by the Thames, were still distinct cities at this time.
8. There were plans to rebuild the palace of Whitehall, which had largely burned down in the fires of 1691 and 1697.
9. Fate or destiny. In lines 381–422 Pope makes extensive use of Isaiah 60, which forecasts Zion's future glory.

The world's great oracle in times to come;
There kings shall sue, and suppliant states be seen
Once more to bend before a British QUEEN.
  Thy trees, fair Windsor! now shall leave their woods,
And half thy forests rush into my floods,
Bear Britain's thunder, and her cross[1] display,
To the bright regions of the rising day;
Tempt° icy seas, where scarce the waters roll, *attempt*
Where clearer flames glow round the frozen pole;
Or under southern skies exalt° their sails, *raise*
Led by new stars, and born by spicy gales!
For me the balm[2] shall bleed, and amber flow,
The coral redden, and the ruby glow,
The pearly shell its lucid globe infold,
And Phœbus warm the ripening ore to gold.[3]
The time shall come, when free as seas or wind
Unbounded Thames[4] shall flow for all mankind,
Whole nations enter with each swelling tide,
And seas but join the regions they divide;
Earth's distant ends our glory shall behold,
And the new world launch forth to seek the old.
Then ships of uncouth form shall stem the tide,
And feathered people crowd my wealthy side,[5]
While naked youth and painted chiefs admire
Our speech, our color, and our strange attire!
Oh stretch thy reign, fair Peace! from shore to shore,
Till conquest cease, and slav'ry be no more:
Till the freed[6] Indians in their native groves
Reap their own fruits and woo their sable loves,
Peru once more a race of kings behold,
And other Mexicos be roofed with gold.
Exiled by thee from earth to deepest hell,
In brazen bonds shall barb'rous Discord dwell:
Gigantic Pride, pale Terror, gloomy Care,
And mad Ambition shall attend her there.
There purple Vengeance bathed in gore retires,
Her weapons blunted, and extinct her fires:
There hateful Envy her own snakes shall feel,
And Persecution mourn her broken wheel:[7]
There Faction roar, Rebellion bite her chain,

1. St. George's cross which, with the cross of St. Andrew, made the new Union flag of Great Britain; Pope may also allude to recent British missionary work overseas.
2. Tree sap, often having soothing or healing properties.
3. Phoebus Apollo, god of the sun and patron of poets, was commonly believed to ripen metal into gold with his rays.
4. A wish that London may be made a FREE PORT [Pope's note]; many merchants proposed that customs duties should be abolished to make Britain more open to international trade.
5. Four Iroquois Indian chiefs visited England in 1710, causing a sensation.
6. From Spanish oppression.
7. An instrument of torture.

And gasping Furies thirst for blood in vain.
    Here cease thy flight, nor with unhallowed lays
Touch the fair fame of Albion's golden days.
The thoughts of gods let Granville's verse recite,
And bring the scenes of opening fate to light.
My humble Muse, in unambitious strains,
Paints the green forests and the flow'ry plains,
Where Peace descending bids her olives spring,
And scatters blessings from her dove-like wing.
Ev'n I more sweetly pass my careless days,
Pleased in the silent shade with empty praise;
Enough for me, that to the list'ning swains
First in these fields I sung the sylvan strains.

1704–1713 1713

The Rape of the Lock "New things are made familiar, and familiar things are made new," wrote Samuel Johnson about the most accomplished poem of Pope's younger years. "The whole detail of a female day is brought before us invested with so much art of decoration that, though nothing is disguised, everything is striking."

Only a poet with formidable imaginative powers could have made a great mock-heroic poem out of such unpromising materials. When Robert, Lord Petre, cut a love-lock from the head of Arabella Fermor without her permission, the two young people, both in their early twenties, quarreled bitterly. Their families, leading members of the Roman Catholic gentry once on the friendliest terms, became seriously estranged. Pope's friend John Caryll, who saw himself as a mediator among the group, asked him "to write a poem to make a jest of it, and laugh them together."

Pope's first effort was a poem in two cantos, *The Rape of the Locke*, printed in 1712 with some of his other pieces and the work of other poets. Two years later, Pope separately published *The Rape of the Lock,* enlarged to five cantos by the addition of the "machinery" of the sylphs and gnomes, and by the game of Ombre. The poem reached its final form in 1717 when Pope added the moralizing declamation of Clarissa (5.7–35), a parody of the speech of Sarpedon to Glaucus in the *Iliad*. The mock-epic tenor of the five-canto poem was clearly influenced by Pope's translation of the *Iliad,* his main project while most of *The Rape of the Lock* was being composed. Other influences were Homer's *Odyssey*, Virgil's *Aeneid*, Milton's *Paradise Lost,* and Boileau's *Le Lutrin* (1674, 1683), a mock-heroic satire on clerical infighting over the placement of a lectern. Yoking together the mundanely trivial and the mythically heroic as he follows the course of Belinda's day, Pope produced a vivid, yet affectionate, mockery of the fashions and sexual mores common in his own social circle.

The arming of the champion for war became the application of Belinda's (i.e., Arabella's) make-up for the battle of the sexes; the larger-than-life gods of classical mythology became miniature cartoon-like sylphs; Aeneas's voyage up the Tiber became Belinda's progress up the Thames; the depiction of Achilles's shield became the description of Belinda's petticoat; the test of single combat became the game of cards; the hero's journey to the underworld became the gnome's adventure in the Cave of Spleen; and the rape of Helen that started the Trojan War became the "rape" (stealing) of Belinda's hair that began an unpleasant social squabble. All the trappings of classical epic are here: the divine messenger appearing to the hero in a dream, the sacrifice to the gods, the inspirational speech to the troops before battle, the epic feast, the violent melee, and the final triumphant apotheosis. Throughout the poem, the enormous distance between the trivial *matter* and the heroic *manner* produces brilliantly comic results.

The Rape of the Lock

An Heroi-Comical Poem in Five Cantos

Nolueram, Belinda, *tuos violare capillos,*
Sed juvat hoc precibus me tribuisse tuis.

Martial[1]

To Mrs. Arabella Fermor

Madam,

It will be in vain to deny that I have some regard for this piece, since I dedicate it to you. Yet you may bear me witness, it was intended only to divert a few young ladies, who have good sense and good humor enough, to laugh not only at their sex's little unguarded follies, but at their own.[2] But as it was communicated with the air of a secret, it soon found its way into the world. An imperfect copy having been offered to a bookseller, you had the good nature for my sake to consent to the publication of one more correct; this I was forced to before I had executed half my design, for the *machinery* was entirely wanting to complete it.

The *machinery,* Madam, is a term invented by the critics, to signify that part which the deities, angels, or demons, are made to act in a poem; for the ancient poets are in one respect like many modern ladies: let an action be never so trivial in itself, they always make it appear of the utmost importance. These machines I determined to raise on a very new and odd foundation, the Rosicrucian[3] doctrine of spirits.

I know how disagreeable it is to make use of hard words before a lady; but 'tis so much the concern of a poet to have his works understood, and particularly by your sex, that you must give me leave to explain two or three difficult terms.

The Rosicrucians are a people I must bring you acquainted with. The best account I know of them is in a French book called *Le Comte de Gabalis*,[4] which both in its title and size is so like a novel that many of the fair sex have read it for one by mistake. According to these gentlemen, the four elements are inhabited by spirits, which they call Sylphs, Gnomes, Nymphs, and Salamanders.[5] The Gnomes, or Demons of Earth, delight in mischief; but the Sylphs, whose habitation is in the air, are the best-conditioned[6] creatures imaginable. For they say any mortals may enjoy the most intimate familiarities with these gentle spirits, upon a condition very easy to all true adepts: an inviolate preservation of chastity.

As to the following cantos, all the passages of them are as fabulous[7] as the vision at the beginning, or the transformation at the end (except the loss of your hair, which I always mention with reverence). The human persons are as fictitious as the airy ones; and the character of Belinda, as it is now managed, resembles you in nothing but in beauty.

If this poem had as many graces as there are in your person, or in your mind, yet I could never hope it should pass through the world half so uncensured as you have

1. "I did not wish, [Belinda,] to violate your locks, but I rejoice to have yielded this to your wishes" (Martial, *Epigrams* 12.84). Pope has substituted "Belinda" for Martial's "Polytimus."
2. I.e., at their own individual follies as well.
3. A secret society of the 17th and 18th centuries, devoted to the study of ancient religious, philosophical, and mystical doctrines.
4. Written in 1670 by the Abbé de Monfaucon de Villars, its approach to Rosicrucian philosophy was lighthearted. It was printed in duodecimo, a small "pocketbook" size common to many inexpensive novels.
5. Elemental spirits living in fire.
6. Best natured, having the best character.
7. Fictional.

done. But let its fortune be what it will, mine is happy enough, to have given me this occasion of assuring you that I am, with the truest esteem,

Madam,

Your most obedient, humble servant,

A. Pope

Canto 1

What dire offense from am'rous causes springs,
What mighty contests rise from trivial things,
I sing[1]—This verse to Caryll, Muse! is due;
This, ev'n Belinda may vouchsafe to view:
Slight is the subject, but not so the praise,
If she inspire, and he approve my lays.° *verses*
Say what strange motive, Goddess!° could compel *his Muse*
A well-bred lord t' assault a gentle belle?
Oh say what stranger cause, yet unexplored,
Could make a gentle belle reject a lord?
In tasks so bold, can little men engage,
And in soft bosoms dwells such mighty rage?
Sol through white curtains shot a tim'rous ray,
And op'd those eyes that must eclipse the day;
Now lapdogs[2] give themselves the rousing shake,
And sleepless lovers, just at twelve, awake:
Thrice rung the bell, the slipper knocked the ground,[3]
And the pressed watch returned a silver sound.[4]
Belinda still her downy pillow pressed,
Her guardian Sylph prolonged the balmy rest.
'Twas he had summoned to her silent bed
The morning dream that hovered o'er her head.
A youth more glitt'ring than a birth-night beau[5]
(That ev'n in slumber caused her cheek to glow)
Seemed to her ear his winning lips to lay,
And thus in whispers said, or seemed to say:[6]
"Fairest of mortals, thou distinguished care
Of thousand bright inhabitants of air!
If e'er one vision touched thy infant thought,
Of all the nurse and all the priest have taught,[7]
Of airy elves by moonlight shadows seen,
The silver token, and the circled green,[8]

1. Pope begins with the ancient epic formula of "proposition" of the work as a whole, and "invocation" of the gods' assistance, continuing with the traditional epic questions.
2. Small dogs imported from Asia were highly fashionable ladies' pets at this time.
3. Belinda rings the bell and then finally bangs her slipper on the floor to call her maid.
4. The popular "pressed watch" chimed the hour and quarter hours when its stem was pressed, saving its owner from striking a match to see the time.
5. On a royal birthday, courtiers' clothes were particularly extravagant.
6. His whispering recalls the serpent's temptation of Eve in Milton's *Paradise Lost*.
7. The nurse and priest were seen as two standard sources of superstition.
8. Withered circles in the grass and silver coins were supposed to be signs of fairies' presence.

Or virgins visited by angel pow'rs,[9]
With golden crowns and wreaths of heav'nly flow'rs,
Hear and believe! thy own importance know,
Nor bound thy narrow views to things below.
Some secret truths from learned pride concealed,
To maids alone and children are revealed:
What though no credit doubting wits may give?[1]
The fair and innocent shall still believe.
Know then, unnumbered spirits round thee fly,
The light militia of the lower sky;
These, though unseen, are ever on the wing,
Hang o'er the box, and hover round the ring.[2]
Think what an equipage[3] thou hast in air,
And view with scorn two pages and a chair.[4]
As now your own, our beings were of old,
And once enclosed in woman's beauteous mold;
Thence, by a soft transition, we repair
From earthly vehicles[5] to these of air.
Think not, when woman's transient breath is fled,
That all her vanities at once are dead:
Succeeding vanities she still regards,
And though she plays no more, o'erlooks the cards.
Her joy in gilded chariots, when alive,
And love of Ombre,[6] after death survive.
For when the fair in all their pride expire,
To their first elements[7] their souls retire:
The sprites of fiery termagants° in flame *scolding women*
Mount up, and take a salamander's name.
Soft yielding minds to water glide away,
And sip with Nymphs, their elemental tea.
The graver prude sinks downward to a Gnome,
In search of mischief still on earth to roam.
The light coquettes in Sylphs aloft repair,
And sport and flutter in the fields of air.
  "Know farther yet; whoever fair and chaste
Rejects mankind, is by some Sylph embraced:
For spirits, freed from mortal laws, with ease
Assume what sexes and what shapes they please.[8]
What guards the purity of melting maids,[9]

9. Belinda is reminded of the many virgin saints, and particularly the Annunciation to the Virgin Mary.
1. Religious skepticism was on the increase.
2. The theater box and the equally fashionable drive round Hyde Park.
3. Carriage, horses, and attendants.
4. A sedan chair, carried by two chairmen.
5. Both the carriage and the physical body.
6. Ombre (pronounced *Omber*) was an elaborate card game, introduced into England in the 17th century and considered highly fashionable in the early 18th century. Given the general tenor of the poem, Pope may also be punning on the origin of the word "Ombre," from the Spanish *hombre*, meaning "man."
7. The four elements of fire, water, earth, and air were thought to make up all things; so an individual's character was determined by whichever element dominated his or her soul.
8. Cf. *Paradise Lost*: "For spirits when they please / Can either sex assume, or both" (1.423–24).
9. I.e., the chastity of weakening virgins.

In courtly balls, and midnight masquerades,
Safe from the treach'rous friend, the daring spark,[1]
The glance by day, the whisper in the dark;
When kind occasion prompts their warm desires,
When music softens, and when dancing fires?
'Tis but their Sylph, the wise celestials know,
Though honor is the word with men below.
"Some nymphs there are, too conscious of their face,
For life predestined to the Gnomes' embrace.
These swell their prospects and exalt their pride,
When offers are disdained, and love denied.
Then gay ideas crowd the vacant brain;
While peers° and dukes, and all their sweeping train, *aristocrats*
And garters, stars, and coronets[2] appear,
And in soft sounds, 'your Grace'[3] salutes their ear.
'Tis these that early taint the female soul,
Instruct the eyes of young coquettes to roll,
Teach infant cheeks a bidden° blush to know, *deliberate*
And little hearts to flutter at a beau.
"Oft when the world imagine women stray,
The Sylphs through mystic mazes guide their way,
Through all the giddy circle they pursue,
And old impertinence° expel by new. *frivolity*
What tender maid but must a victim fall
To one man's treat, but for another's ball?
When Florio speaks, what virgin could withstand,
If gentle Damon did not squeeze her hand?
With varying vanities, from ev'ry part,
They shift the moving toy shop[4] of their heart;
Where wigs with wigs, with sword knots sword knots strive,[5]
Beaus banish beaus, and coaches coaches drive.[6]
This erring mortals levity may call;
Oh blind to truth! the Sylphs contrive it all.
"Of these am I, who thy protection claim,
A watchful sprite, and Ariel is my name.
Late, as I ranged the crystal wilds of air,
In the clear mirror of thy ruling star
I saw, alas! some dread event impend,
Ere to the main° this morning sun descend. *sea*
But heaven reveals not what, or how, or where:
Warned by thy Sylph, O pious maid, beware!
This to disclose is all thy guardian can.
Beware of all, but most beware of Man!"
He said; when Shock,[7] who thought she slept too long,

1. A bold, brash, and showy young man.
2. Emblems of noble rank.
3. Form of address for a duke or a duchess.
4. Where toys and trinkets are sold; "moving" here means easily changed, unstable.
5. Most men wore wigs in public; formally dressed men tied ribbons to the hilt of their swords.
6. In word order and versification, these two lines mimic both Homer's and Ovid's description of heroic combat.
7. The shock or shough, a long-haired Icelandic poodle, fashionable as a lapdog.

Leaped up, and waked his mistress with his tongue.
'Twas then, Belinda! if report say true,
Thy eyes first opened on a *billet-doux*;° *love letter*
Wounds, charms, and ardors were no sooner read,
But all the vision vanished from thy head.
And now, unveiled, the toilet° stands displayed, *dressing table*
Each silver vase in mystic order laid.
First, robed in white, the nymph intent adores
With head uncovered, the cosmetic pow'rs.
A heav'nly image[8] in the glass appears;
To that she bends, to that her eyes she rears;° *raises*
Th' inferior priestess,[9] at her altar's side,
Trembling, begins the sacred rites of pride.
Unnumbered treasures ope at once, and here
The various off'rings of the world appear;
From each she nicely culls with curious° toil, *careful*
And decks the goddess with the glitt'ring spoil.
This casket India's glowing gems unlocks,
And all Arabia breathes from yonder box.
The tortoise here and elephant unite,
Transformed to combs, the speckled and the white.[1]
Here files of pins extend their shining rows,
Puffs, powders, patches, Bibles,[2] *billet-doux*.
Now awful° Beauty puts on all its arms; *awe-inspiring*
The fair each moment rises in her charms,
Repairs her smiles, awakens ev'ry grace,
And calls forth all the wonders of her face;
Sees by degrees a purer blush[3] arise,
And keener lightnings[4] quicken in her eyes.
The busy Sylphs surround their darling care;
These set the head, and those divide the hair,
Some fold the sleeve, whilst others plait the gown;
And Betty's praised for labors not her own.

Canto 2

Not with more glories, in th' ethereal plain,° *sky*
The sun first rises o'er the purpled main,
Than, issuing forth, the rival of his beams
Launched on the bosom of the silver Thames.[5]
Fair nymphs and well-dressed youths around her shone,
But ev'ry eye was fixed on her alone.
On her white breast a sparkling cross she wore,
Which Jews might kiss, and infidels adore.[6]

8. I.e., Belinda herself.
9. Belinda's maid, Betty.
1. Tortoise-shell and ivory.
2. Patches were small pieces of black silk, pasted onto the face to make the skin appear whiter. It was fashionable to own Bibles in very small format.
3. The even, artificial blush of rouge.
4. Caused by drops of belladonna (deadly nightshade), which dilates the pupils.
5. Belinda takes a boat from London to Hampton Court, avoiding the dirt and squalor of the streets; her voyage compares with Aeneas's up the Tiber (*Aeneid* 7), or, alternatively, Cleopatra's up the Nile (*Antony and Cleopatra* 2.2).
6. Kissing the cross was the sign of religious conversion.

Her lively looks a sprightly mind disclose,
Quick as her eyes, and as unfixed as those:
Favors to none, to all she smiles extends,
Oft she rejects, but never once offends.
Bright as the sun, her eyes the gazers strike,
And, like the sun, they shine on all alike.
Yet graceful ease, and sweetness void of pride,
Might hide her faults, if belles had faults to hide:
If to her share some female errors fall,
Look on her face, and you'll forget 'em all.
  This nymph, to the destruction of mankind,
Nourished two locks, which graceful hung behind
In equal curls, and well conspired to deck
With shining ringlets the smooth iv'ry neck.
Love in these labyrinths his slaves detains,
And mighty hearts are held in slender chains.
With hairy springes° we the birds betray, *noose traps*
Slight lines° of hair surprise the finny prey, *fishing lines*
Fair tresses man's imperial race ensnare,
And beauty draws us with a single hair.
  Th' advent'rous Baron[7] the bright locks admired;
He saw, he wished, and to the prize aspired:
Resolved to win, he meditates the way,
By force to ravish, or by fraud betray;
For when success a lover's toil attends,
Few ask, if fraud or force attained his ends.
  For this, ere Phoebus rose, he had implored
Propitious Heav'n, and ev'ry pow'r adored,° *worshipped*
But chiefly Love—to Love an altar built,
Of twelve vast French romances, neatly gilt.[8]
There lay three garters, half a pair of gloves;
And all the trophies of his former loves.
With tender *billet-doux* he lights the pyre,
And breathes three am'rous sighs to raise the fire.
Then prostrate falls, and begs with ardent eyes
Soon to obtain, and long possess the prize:
The pow'rs gave ear, and granted half his pray'r,
The rest the winds dispersed in empty air.[9]
  But now secure the painted vessel glides,
The sunbeams trembling on the floating tides,
While melting music steals upon the sky,
And softened sounds along the waters die.
Smooth flow the waves, the zephyrs° gently play, *breezes*

7. Robert, Lord Petre (1690–1713), responsible for the original incident.
8. Long love stories, here attractively bound with embossed gold lettering.
9. Cf. *The Aeneid* 2.794–95, which Dryden translated: "Apollo heard, and granting half his pray'r, / Shuffled in winds the rest, and tossed in empty air."

Belinda smiled, and all the world was gay.
All but the Sylph—with careful° thoughts oppressed, *worried*
Th' impending woe sat heavy on his breast.
He summons strait his denizens[1] of air;
The lucid squadrons round the sails repair:
Soft o'er the shrouds° aerial whispers breathe, *ropes*
That seemed but zephyrs to the train beneath.
Some to the sun their insect-wings unfold,
Waft on the breeze, or sink in clouds of gold.
Transparent forms, too fine for mortal sight,
Their fluid bodies half dissolved in light,
Loose to the wind their airy garments flew,
Thin glitt'ring textures of the filmy dew,
Dipped in the richest tincture of the skies,
Where light disports in ever-mingling dyes,
While ev'ry beam new transient colors flings,
Colors that change whene'er they wave their wings.
Amid the circle, on the gilded mast,
Superior by the head, was Ariel placed;[2]
His purple pinions opening to the sun,
He raised his azure wand, and thus begun:
"Ye Sylphs and Sylphids,° to your chief give ear, *female Sylphs*
Fays, Fairies, Genii, Elves, and Demons hear!
Ye know the spheres and various tasks assigned
By laws eternal to th' aerial kind.
Some in the fields of purest ether[3] play,
And bask and whiten in the blaze of day.
Some guide the course of wandering orbs° on high, *comets*
Or roll the planets through the boundless sky.
Some, less refined, beneath the moon's pale light
Pursue the stars that shoot athwart the night;
Or suck the mists in grosser° air below, *heavier*
Or dip their pinions in the painted bow,° *rainbow*
Or brew fierce tempests on the wintry main,
Or o'er the glebe° distill the kindly rain. *farmland*
Others on earth o'er human race preside,
Watch all their ways, and all their actions guide:
Of these the chief the care of nations own,
And guard with arms divine the British throne.
"Our humbler province is to tend the fair;
Not a less pleasing, though less glorious care.
To save the powder from too rude° a gale, *rough*
Nor let th' imprisoned essences° exhale, *perfumes*
To draw fresh colors from the vernal flow'rs,
To steal from rainbows ere they drop in show'rs
A brighter wash;[4] to curl their waving hairs,

1. Naturalized foreigners.
2. Heroes of epics were typically taller than their men.
3. Air beyond the moon.
4. A cosmetic rinse.

Assist their blushes, and inspire their airs;
Nay oft, in dreams, invention we bestow,
To change a flounce, or add a furbelow.° *fringe*
"This day, black omens threat the brightest fair
That e'er deserved a watchful spirit's care;
Some dire disaster, or° by force or sleight;° *either / trick*
But what, or where, the fates have wrapped in night.
Whether the nymph shall break Diana's law,° *virginity*
Or some frail china jar receive a flaw,
Or stain her honor, or her new brocade,
Forget her pray'rs, or miss a masquerade,
Or lose her heart, or necklace, at a ball;
Or whether Heav'n has doomed that Shock must fall.
Haste then ye spirits! to your charge° repair; *duty*
The flutt'ring fan be Zephyretta's care;
The drops° to thee, Brillante, we consign; *earrings*
And Momentilla, let the watch be thine;
Do thou, Crispissa,[5] tend her fav'rite lock;
Ariel himself shall be the guard of Shock.
"To fifty chosen Sylphs, of special note,
We trust th' important charge, the petticoat:
Oft have we known that sev'nfold fence[6] to fail,
Though stiff with hoops, and armed with ribs of whale.
Form a strong line about the silver bound,
And guard the wide circumference around.
"Whatever spirit, careless of his charge,
His post neglects, or leaves the fair at large,
Shall feel sharp vengeance soon o'ertake his sins,
Be stopped in vials, or transfixed with pins;
Or plunged in lakes of bitter washes lie,
Or wedged whole ages in a bodkin's[7] eye:
Gums and pomatums° shall his flight restrain, *ointments*
While clogged he beats his silken wings in vain;
Or alum styptics[8] with contracting power
Shrink his thin essence like a rivelled° flower: *shriveled*
Or as Ixion[9] fixed, the wretch shall feel
The giddy motion of the whirling mill,[1]
In fumes of burning chocolate shall glow,
And tremble at the sea that froths below!"
He spoke; the spirits from the sails descend;
Some, orb in orb, around the nymph extend,

5. The Latin *crispere* means to curl.
6. Serving Belinda like the epic warrior's shield, her petticoat has seven layers bound together with a silver band (cf. *Iliad* 18 or *Aeneid* 8).
7. Blunt, thick needle; the Sylph, like the camel in Matthew 19.24 and Mark 10.25, has difficulty getting through. Pope later plays on the various meanings of "bodkin," which also include a hair ornament and a dagger.
8. Astringents that stopped bleeding.
9. Having tried the chastity of Hera, Ixion was punished by being tied to a continually revolving wheel of fire.
1. For beating chocolate, a new and highly fashionable drink.

Some thrid° the mazy ringlets of her hair, *slid through*
Some hang upon the pendants of her ear;
With beating hearts the dire event they wait,
Anxious, and trembling for the birth of Fate.

CANTO 3

Close by those meads forever crowned with flow'rs,
Where Thames with pride surveys his rising tow'rs,
There stands a structure of majestic frame,
Which from the neighb'ring Hampton takes its name.[2]
Here Britain's statesmen oft the fall foredoom
Of foreign tyrants, and of nymphs at home;
Here thou, great Anna! whom three realms obey,[3]
Dost sometimes counsel take—and sometimes tea.
Hither the heroes and the nymphs resort,
To taste awhile the pleasures of a court;
In various talk th' instructive hours they passed,
Who gave the ball, or paid the visit last:
One speaks the glory of the British Queen,
And one describes a charming Indian screen;
A third interprets motions, looks, and eyes;
At ev'ry word a reputation dies.
Snuff, or the fan, supply each pause of chat,
With singing, laughing, ogling, and all that.
Meanwhile declining from the noon of day,
The sun obliquely shoots his burning ray;
The hungry judges soon the sentence sign,
And wretches hang that jurymen may dine;
The merchant from th' Exchange° returns in peace, *market*
And the long labors of the toilet cease.
Belinda now, whom thirst of fame invites,
Burns to encounter two advent'rous knights,
At Ombre[4] singly to decide their doom;
And swells her breast with conquests yet to come.
Straight the three bands prepare in arms to join,
Each band the number of the Sacred Nine.[5]
Soon as she spreads her hand, th' aerial guard
Descend, and sit on each important card:
First Ariel perch'd upon a Matador,[6]
Then each, according to the rank they bore;

2. Hampton Court, about 15 miles upriver from London, was built in the 16th century by Cardinal Wolsey; by Queen Anne's day it was associated with wits as well as with statesmen.
3. The English Crown still maintained its ancient claim to rule France as well as Great Britain and Ireland.
4. A card game played with 40 cards, similar to modern bridge: three players hold nine cards each and bid for tricks, with the highest bidder becoming the "ombre" (man) and choosing trumps.
5. Pope links the nine Muses to the nine cards each player holds.
6. The Matadors are the three cards of highest value; Belinda holds all three: when trumps are black, they are the Spadillio (ace of spades), Manillio (deuce of spades), and Basto (ace of clubs).

For Sylphs, yet mindful of their ancient race,
Are, as when women, wondrous fond of place.° *rank*
Behold, four kings in majesty revered,
With hoary whiskers[7] and a forky beard:
And four fair queens whose hands sustain° a flow'r, *hold*
Th' expressive emblem of their softer pow'r;
Four knaves in garbs succinct,° a trusty band, *girded up*
Caps on their heads, and halberds in their hand;
And particolored troops, a shining train,
Draw forth to combat on the velvet plain.[8]
The skillful nymph reviews her force with care;
"Let spades be trumps!" she said, and trumps they were.[9]
Now move to war her sable Matadors,
In show like leaders of the swarthy moors.
Spadillio first, unconquerable lord!
Led off two captive trumps, and swept the board.
As many more Manillio forced to yield,
And marched a victor from the verdant field.
Him Basto followed, but his fate more hard
Gained but one trump and one plebeian card.
With his broad saber next, a chief in years,
The hoary majesty of spades appears;
Puts forth one manly leg, to sight revealed,
The rest his many-colored robe concealed.
The rebel knave, who dares his prince engage,
Proves the just victim of his royal rage.
Ev'n mighty Pam[1] that kings and queens o'erthrew,
And mowed down armies in the fights of Lu,
Sad chance of war! now, destitute of aid,
Falls undistinguished by the victor spade!
Thus far both armies to Belinda yield;
Now to the Baron fate inclines the field.
His warlike Amazon her host invades,
Th' imperial consort of the crown of spades.
The club's black tyrant first her victim died,
Spite of his haughty mien and barb'rous pride:
What boots the regal circle on his head,
His giant limbs in state unwieldy spread;
That long behind he trails his pompous robe,
And of all monarchs only grasps the globe?
The Baron now his diamonds pours apace;
Th' embroidered king who shows but half his face,

7. Gray mustache. The royal figures on the cards now conduct a mock-epic review of their forces, and the whole game is described as an epic battle, with the characters appearing as on the cards.
8. The green velvet card table.
9. Cf. Genesis 1.3: "Then God said, 'Let there be light'; and there was light."
1. The knave or jack of clubs, which took precedence over all trumps in the game of Lu, or Loo.

And his refulgent queen, with pow'rs combined,
Of broken troops an easy conquest find.
Clubs, diamonds, hearts, in wild disorder seen,
With throngs promiscuous strew the level green.
Thus when dispersed a routed army runs,
Of Asia's troops and Afric's sable sons,
With like confusion different nations fly,
Of various habit and of various dye,
The pierced battalions disunited fall,
In heaps on heaps; one fate o'erwhelms them all.
The knave of diamonds tries his wily arts,
And wins (oh shameful chance!) the queen of hearts.
At this, the blood the virgin's cheek forsook,
A livid paleness spreads o'er all her look;
She sees, and trembles at th' approaching ill,
Just in the jaws of ruin, and codille.[2]
And now (as oft in some distempered state)
On one nice trick[3] depends the gen'ral fate.
An ace of hearts steps forth: the king[4] unseen
Lurked in her hand, and mourned his captive queen.
He springs to vengeance with an eager pace,
And falls like thunder on the prostrate ace.
The nymph exulting fills with shouts the sky,
The walls, the woods, and long canals reply.
Oh thoughtless mortals! ever blind to fate,
Too soon dejected, and too soon elate!
Sudden these honors shall be snatched away,
And cursed forever this victorious day.
For lo! the board with cups and spoons is crowned,
The berries crackle, and the mill turns round.[5]
On shining altars of Japan[6] they raise
The silver lamp; the fiery spirits blaze.
From silver spouts the grateful° liquors glide, *pleasing*
While China's earth receives the smoking tide.
At once they gratify their scent and taste,
While frequent cups prolong the rich repast.
Straight° hover round the fair her airy band; *immediately*
Some, as she sipped, the fuming liquor fanned,
Some o'er her lap their careful plumes displayed,
Trembling, and conscious of the rich brocade.
Coffee (which makes the politician wise,
And see through all things with his half-shut eyes)
Sent up in vapors[7] to the Baron's brain

2. Literally "elbow": the defeat suffered by the ombre if another player wins more tricks.
3. "Trick" applies in both its technical and general senses as Belinda makes this careful maneuver.
4. The king of hearts.
5. Grinding coffee beans.
6. Lacquered tables ("Japan" was a type of varnish originating in that country).
7. Both steam and vain imaginations.

New stratagems, the radiant lock to gain.
Ah cease rash youth! desist e'er 'tis too late;
Fear the just gods, and think of Scylla's fate![8]
Changed to a bird, and sent to flit in air,
She dearly pays for Nisus' injured hair!
　　But when to mischief mortals bend their will,
How soon they find fit instruments of ill!
Just then, Clarissa drew with tempting grace
A two-edged weapon from her shining case;
So ladies in romance assist their knight,
Present the spear, and arm him for the fight.
He takes the gift with rev'rence, and extends
The little engine° on his fingers' ends; *instrument*
This just behind Belinda's neck he spread,
As o'er the fragrant steams she bends her head:
Swift to the lock a thousand sprites repair,
A thousand wings, by turns, blow back the hair,
And thrice they twitched the diamond in her ear,
Thrice she looked back, and thrice the foe drew near.
Just in that instant, anxious Ariel sought
The close recesses of the virgin's thought;
As, on the nosegay in her breast reclined,
He watched th' ideas rising in her mind,
Sudden he viewed, in spite of all her art,
An earthly lover lurking at her heart.
Amazed, confused, he found his pow'r expired,
Resigned to fate, and with a sigh retired.
　　The peer now spreads the glitt'ring forfex° wide, *scissors*
T' enclose the lock; now joins it, to divide.
Ev'n then, before the fatal engine closed,
A wretched Sylph too fondly interposed;
Fate urged the shears, and cut the Sylph in twain
(But airy substance soon unites again)[9]
The meeting points the sacred hair dissever
From the fair head, forever and forever!
　　Then flashed the living lightning from her eyes,
And screams of horror rend th' affrighted skies.
Not louder shrieks to pitying Heav'n are cast,
When husbands or when lapdogs breathe their last;
Or when rich china vessels, fall'n from high,
In glitt'ring dust and painted fragments lie!
　　Let wreaths of triumph now my temples twine.
(The victor cried) The glorious prize is mine!
While fish in streams, or birds delight in air,
Or in a coach and six[1] the British fair,

8. Scylla plucked purple hair from the head of her father, King Nisus, to offer to her lover, Minos, so destroying her father's power. Minos rejected her impiety, and Scylla was transformed into a bird.

9. *Milton* lib. 6 [Pope's note], citing *Paradise Lost* 6.329–31: "The girding sword with discontinuous wound / Passed through him, but the ethereal substance closed / Not long divisible. . . ."

1. A carriage drawn by six horses; a symbol of wealth and prestige.

As long as *Atalantis*[2] shall be read,
Or the small pillow grace a lady's bed,[3]
While visits shall be paid on solemn days,
When num'rous wax-lights[4] in bright order blaze,
While nymphs take treats, or assignations give,
So long my honor, name, and praise shall live!
What time would spare, from steel receives its date,° *end*
And monuments, like men, submit to fate!
Steel could the labor of the gods destroy,
And strike to dust th' imperial tow'rs of Troy;[5]
Steel could the works of mortal pride confound,
And hew triumphal arches to the ground.
What wonder then, fair nymph! thy hairs should feel
The conqu'ring force of unresisted steel?

Canto 4

But anxious cares the pensive nymph oppressed,
And secret passions labored in her breast.
Not youthful kings in battle seized alive,
Not scornful virgins who their charms survive,
Not ardent lovers robbed of all their bliss,
Not ancient ladies when refused a kiss,
Not tyrants fierce that unrepenting die,
Not Cynthia when her manteau's° pinned awry, *gown's*
E'er felt such rage, resentment, and despair,
As thou, sad virgin! for thy ravished hair.
For, that sad moment, when the Sylphs withdrew,
And Ariel weeping from Belinda flew,
Umbriel, a dusky melancholy sprite
As ever sullied the fair face of light,
Down to the central earth, his proper scene,
Repaired to search the gloomy Cave of Spleen.[6]
Swift on his sooty pinions flits the Gnome,
And in a vapor[7] reached the dismal dome.
No cheerful breeze this sullen region knows,
The dreaded east[8] is all the wind that blows.
Here, in a grotto, sheltered close from air,
And screened in shades° from day's detested glare, *shadows*
She sighs forever on her pensive bed,

2. The scandalous *Atalantis: Secret Memoirs and Manners of Several Persons of Quality* (1709), by Mary Delarivière Manley (1672–1724).
3. Said to be a place where ladies hid romance novels and other contraband.
4. Candles made of wax, rather than the cheaper tallow. Evening social visits were an essential part of the fashionable woman's routine.
5. Even Troy, fabled to have been built by Apollo and Poseidon, was destroyed by arms.
6. Named after the bodily organ, "spleen" was the current term for the fashionable affliction of melancholy or ill-humor. Umbriel's descent into the womblike Cave of Spleen suggests the epic commonplace of the journey to the underworld.
7. "The spleen" was also called "the vapors."
8. The east wind was supposed to induce fits of spleen.

Pain at her side, and Megrim° at her head. *migraine*
Two handmaids wait the throne: alike in place,
But diff'ring far in figure and in face.
Here stood Ill-Nature like an ancient maid,
Her wrinkled form in black and white arrayed;
With store of pray'rs, for mornings, nights, and noons,
Her hand is filled; her bosom with lampoons.
There Affectation with a sickly mien
Shows in her cheek the roses of eighteen,
Practiced to lisp, and hang the head aside,
Faints into airs, and languishes with pride;
On the rich quilt sinks with becoming woe,
Wrapped in a gown, for sickness and for show.
The fair ones feel such maladies as these,
When each new nightdress gives a new disease.
A constant vapor o'er the palace flies,
Strange phantoms rising as the mists arise;
Dreadful, as hermit's dreams in haunted shades,
Or bright as visions of expiring maids.[9]
Now glaring fiends, and snakes on rolling spires,° *coils*
Pale specters, gaping tombs, and purple fires;
Now lakes of liquid gold, Elysian scenes,[1]
And crystal domes, and angels in machines.
Unnumbered throngs on every side are seen,
Of bodies changed to various forms by Spleen.[2]
Here living teapots stand, one arm held out,
One bent; the handle this, and that the spout:
A pipkin[3] there like Homer's tripod walks;
Here sighs a jar, and there a goose-pie[4] talks;
Men prove with child, as pow'rful fancy works,
And maids, turned bottles, call aloud for corks.
Safe passed the Gnome through this fantastic band,
A branch of healing spleenwort[5] in his hand.
Then thus addressed the pow'r: "Hail, wayward Queen!
Who rule the sex to fifty from fifteen,
Parent of vapors and of female wit,
Who give th' hysteric or poetic fit,
On various tempers act by various ways,
Make some take physic,° others scribble plays;[6] *medicine*
Who cause the proud their visits to delay,
And send the godly in a pet° to pray. *ill-humor*
A nymph there is that all thy pow'r disdains,

9. Religious visions of hell and heaven.
1. Elysium was the classical paradise, but this also recalls contemporary theater, which made much of scenic spectacle and the use of machinery.
2. Hallucinations similar to those described in the following lines were common to those afflicted with spleen.
3. Small pot or pan. Hephaistos's "walking" tripods are described in the *Iliad* 18.439ff.
4. Alludes to a real fact, a Lady of distinction imagined herself in this condition [Pope's note].
5. Pope changes the golden bough that protected Aeneas on his trip through the underworld into an herb that was supposed to be good for the spleen.
6. Melancholy was associated with artistic creativity.

And thousands more in equal mirth maintains.
But oh! if e'er thy Gnome could spoil a grace,
Or raise a pimple on a beauteous face,
Like citron-waters° matrons' cheeks inflame, *flavored brandy*
Or change complexions at a losing game;
If e'er with airy horns[7] I planted heads,
Or rumpled petticoats, or tumbled beds,
Or caused suspicion when no soul was rude,
Or discomposed the head-dress of a prude,
Or e'er to costive° lapdog gave disease, *constipated*
Which not the tears of brightest eyes could ease:
Hear me, and touch Belinda with chagrin;
That single act gives half the world the spleen."
   The goddess with a discontented air
Seems to reject him, though she grants his pray'r.
A wondrous bag with both her hands she binds,
Like that where once Ulysses held the winds;[8]
There she collects the force of female lungs,
Sighs, sobs, and passions, and the war of tongues.
A vial next she fills with fainting fears,
Soft sorrows, melting griefs, and flowing tears.
The Gnome rejoicing bears her gifts away,
Spreads his black wings, and slowly mounts to day.
   Sunk in Thalestris'[9] arms the nymph he found,
Her eyes dejected and her hair unbound.
Full o'er their heads the swelling bag he rent,
And all the furies issued at the vent.
Belinda burns with more than mortal ire,
And fierce Thalestris fans the rising fire.
"O wretched maid!" she spread her hands, and cried
(While Hampton's echoes "Wretched maid!" replied),
"Was it for this you took such constant care
The bodkin, comb, and essence to prepare?
For this your locks in paper durance° bound, *curling papers*
For this with tort'ring irons wreathed around?
For this with fillets[1] strained your tender head,
And bravely bore the double loads of lead?° *wire supports*
Gods! shall the ravisher display your hair,
While the fops envy, and the ladies stare!
Honor forbid! at whose unrivaled shrine
Ease, pleasure, virtue, all, our sex resign.
Methinks already I your tears survey,
Already hear the horrid things they say,
Already see you a degraded toast,[2]

7. A sign that a husband had been cuckolded.
8. Given to him by the wind god Aeolus (*Odyssey* 10.19ff.).
9. A queen of the Amazons; here Mrs. Morley, Arabella's second cousin.
1. Headbands, with reference to priestesses in the *Aeneid*.
2. A woman whose toast is often drunk, and who by implication is all too well known to her (male) toasters: (cf. Canto 5.10, and Fielding's *Tom Jones*, where Sophia is not pleased by reports that she has been Tom's toast, bk. 13, ch. 11).

And all your honor in a whisper lost!
How shall I, then, your helpless fame defend?
'Twill then be infamy to seem your friend!
And shall this prize, th' inestimable prize,
Exposed through crystal to the gazing eyes,
And heightened by the diamond's circling rays,
On that rapacious hand forever blaze?[3]
Sooner shall grass in Hyde Park Circus grow,[4]
And wits take lodgings in the sound of Bow;[5]
Sooner let earth, air, sea, to chaos fall,
Men, monkeys, lapdogs, parrots, perish all!"
She said; then raging to Sir Plume[6] repairs,
And bids her beau demand the precious hairs
(Sir Plume, of amber snuffbox justly vain,
And the nice conduct of a clouded cane[7]),
With earnest eyes, and round unthinking face,
He first the snuffbox opened, then the case,
And thus broke out—"My Lord, why, what the devil?
Z—ds![8] damn the lock! 'fore Gad, you must be civil!
Plague on't! 'tis past a jest—nay prithee, Pox!
Give her the hair"—he spoke, and rapped his box.
"It grieves me much" (replied the Peer again)
"Who speaks so well should ever speak in vain.
But by this lock, this sacred lock I swear
(Which never more shall join its parted hair,
Which never more its honors shall renew,
Clipped from the lovely head where late it grew)
That while my nostrils draw the vital air,
This hand, which won it shall forever wear."
He spoke, and speaking, in proud triumph spread
The long-contended honors[9] of her head.
But Umbriel, hateful Gnome! forbears not so;
He breaks the vial whence the sorrows flow.
Then see! the nymph in beauteous grief appears,
Her eyes half-languishing, half-drowned in tears;
On her heaved bosom hung her drooping head,
Which, with a sigh, she raised; and thus she said:
"Forever cursed be this detested day,[1]
Which snatched my best, my fav'rite curl away!
Happy! ah, ten times happy, had I been,
If Hampton Court these eyes had never seen!
Yet am not I the first mistaken maid,

3. I.e., mounted in a ring.
4. The fashion for driving coaches around Hyde Park prevented grass from growing there.
5. A commercial area round St. Mary-le-Bow, and not at all fashionable.
6. Sir George Browne, cousin of Arabella's mother.
7. Skilled use of a cane with a head of dark polished stone.
8. Zounds, a corruption of "God's wounds," a mild oath.
9. Her beautiful hair.
1. Echoing Achilles' lament for his slain friend Patroclus (*Iliad* 18.107ff.).

By love of courts to num'rous ills betrayed.
Oh, had I rather unadmired remained
In some lone isle, or distant northern land;
Where the gilt chariot never marks the way,
Where none learn Ombre, none e'er taste bohea!° *tea*
There kept my charms concealed from mortal eye,
Like roses that in deserts bloom and die.
What moved my mind with youthful lords to roam?
Oh, had I stayed, and said my pray'rs at home!
'Twas this the morning omens seemed to tell:
Thrice from my trembling hand the patch box fell;
The tott'ring china shook without a wind;
Nay, Poll° sat mute, and Shock was most unkind! *her parrot*
A Sylph too warned me of the threats of fate,
In mystic visions, now believed too late!
See the poor remnants of these slighted hairs!
My hands shall rend what ev'n thy rapine spares:
These, in two sable ringlets taught to break,° *divide*
Once gave new beauties to the snowy neck;
The sister lock now sits uncouth, alone,
And in its fellow's fate foresees its own;
Uncurled it hangs, the fatal shears demands;
And tempts once more thy sacrilegious hands.
Oh hadst thou, cruel! been content to seize
Hairs less in sight, or any hairs but these!"

Canto 5

She said: the pitying audience melt in tears,
But Fate and Jove had stopped the Baron's ears.
In vain Thalestris with reproach assails,
For who can move when fair Belinda fails?
Not half so fixed the Trojan[2] could remain,
While Anna begged and Dido raged in vain.
Then grave Clarissa[3] graceful waved her fan;
Silence ensued, and thus the nymph began:
"Say, why are beauties praised and honored most,
The wise man's passion, and the vain man's toast?
Why decked with all that land and sea afford,
Why angels called, and angel-like adored?
Why round our coaches crowd the white-gloved beaus,
Why bows the side box from its inmost rows?[4]
How vain are all these glories, all our pains,

2. Aeneas, fixed on his decision to leave Carthage and abandon Dido despite her pleas and those of her sister Anna (*Aeneid* 4.269–449).

3. A new character introduced . . . to open more clearly the moral of the poem, in a parody of the speech of Sarpedon to Glaucus in Homer [Pope's note in the 1717 edition]. For Pope's translation of Sarpedon's speech (*Iliad* 12), see pages 2491–92.

4. At the theater, gentlemen sat in the side boxes, ladies in the front boxes facing the stage.

Unless good sense preserve what beauty gains:
That men may say, when we the front box grace,
'Behold the first in virtue as in face!'
Oh! if to dance all night, and dress all day,
Charmed the smallpox,[5] or chased old age away,
Who would not scorn what housewife's cares produce,
Or who would learn one earthly thing of use?
To patch, nay ogle, might become a saint,
Nor could it sure be such a sin to paint.
But since, alas! frail beauty must decay,
Curled or uncurled, since locks will turn to grey,
Since painted or not painted, all shall fade,
And she who scorns a man must die a maid;
What then remains, but well our pow'r to use,
And keep good humor still whate'er we lose?
And trust me, dear! good humor can prevail,
When airs, and flights, and screams, and scolding fail.
Beauties in vain their pretty eyes may roll;
Charms strike the sight, but merit wins the soul."
    So spoke the dame, but no applause ensued;
Belinda frowned, Thalestris called her prude.
"To arms, to arms!" the fierce virago[6] cries,
And swift as lightning to the combat flies.
All side in parties, and begin th' attack;
Fans clap, silks rustle, and tough whalebones crack;
Heroes' and heroines' shouts confus'dly rise,
And bass and treble voices strike the skies.
No common weapons in their hands are found,
Like gods they fight, nor dread a mortal wound.
    So when bold Homer makes the gods engage,
And heav'nly breasts with human passions rage;
'Gainst Pallas,° Mars; Latona,[7] Hermes arms; *Athena*
And all Olympus rings with loud alarms:
Jove's thunder roars, heav'n trembles all around;
Blue Neptune storms, the bellowing deeps resound;
Earth shakes her nodding tow'rs, the ground gives way,
And the pale ghosts start at the flash of day!
    Triumphant Umbriel on a sconce's[8] height
Clapped his glad wings, and sat to view the fight;
Propped on their bodkin spears, the sprites survey
The growing combat, or assist the fray.
    While through the press enraged Thalestris flies,
And scatters deaths around from both her eyes,
A beau and witling° perished in the throng; *little wit*

5. A common disease, which frequently left permanent facial scars.
6. Woman who behaves like a man.
7. Mother of Diana and Apollo.
8. Candlestick attached to the wall.

One died in metaphor, and one in song.
"O cruel nymph! a living death I bear,"
Cried Dapperwit, and sunk beside his chair.
A mournful glance Sir Fopling upwards cast,
"Those eyes are made so killing"[9]—was his last.
Thus on Meander's flow'ry margin lies
Th' expiring swan, and as he sings he dies.[1]
When bold Sir Plume had drawn Clarissa down,
Chloe stepped in, and killed him with a frown;
She smiled to see the doughty hero slain,
But at her smile, the beau revived again.
Now Jove suspends his golden scales in air,[2]
Weighs the men's wits against the lady's hair;
The doubtful beam long nods from side to side;
At length the wits mount up, the hairs subside.
See, fierce Belinda on the Baron flies,
With more than usual lightning in her eyes;
Nor feared the chief th' unequal fight to try,
Who sought no more than on his foe to die.[3]
But this bold lord, with manly strength indued,
She with one finger and a thumb subdued:
Just where the breath of life his nostrils drew,
A charge of snuff the wily virgin threw;
The Gnomes direct, to ev'ry atom just,
The pungent grains of titillating dust.
Sudden, with starting tears each eye o'erflows,
And the high dome re-echoes to his nose.[4]
"Now meet thy fate," incensed Belinda cried,
And drew a deadly bodkin[5] from her side.
(The same, his ancient personage to deck,
Her great great grandsire wore about his neck
In three seal rings; which after, melted down,
Formed a vast buckle for his widow's gown:
Her infant grandame's° whistle next it grew, *grandmother's*
The bells she jingled, and the whistle blew;
Then in a bodkin graced her mother's hairs,
Which long she wore, and now Belinda wears.)
"Boast not my fall," he cried, "insulting foe!
Thou by some other shalt be laid as low.
Nor think, to die dejects my lofty mind;
All that I dread is leaving you behind!
Rather than so, ah let me still survive,
And burn in Cupid's flames—but burn alive."

9. A line from Giovanni Bononcini's opera, *Camilla* (1696), which at this time was popular in London.

1. Meander: A river in Asia Minor. Swans were popularly believed to sing only on their death. This simile refers to Ovid's *Heroides* 7, a lament from Dido to Aeneas.

2. To determine victory in battle; a convention found in both Homer and Virgil.

3. A standard metaphor for sexual climax.

4. Cf. his boast, 4.133–38.

5. A decorative pin, shaped like a dagger.

"Restore the lock!" she cries; and all around
"Restore the lock!" the vaulted roofs rebound.
Not fierce Othello in so loud a strain
Roared for the handkerchief that caused his pain.
But see how oft ambitious aims are crossed,
And chiefs contend till all the prize is lost!
The lock, obtained with guilt, and kept with pain,
In ev'ry place is sought, but sought in vain:
With such a prize no mortal must be blessed,
So Heav'n decrees! with Heav'n who can contest?
Some thought it mounted to the lunar sphere,[6]
Since all things lost on earth are treasured there.
There heroes' wits are kept in ponderous vases,
And beaus' in snuff-boxes and tweezer cases.
There broken vows and deathbed alms are found,
And lovers' hearts with ends of riband bound;
The courtier's promises, and sick man's pray'rs,
The smiles of harlots, and the tears of heirs,
Cages for gnats, and chains to yoke a flea;
Dried butterflies, and tomes of casuistry.[7]
But trust the Muse—she saw it upward rise,
Though marked by none but quick poetic eyes:
(So Rome's great founder to the heav'ns withdrew,
To Proculus alone confessed in view.[8])
A sudden star, it shot through liquid air,
And drew behind a radiant trail of hair.
Not Berenice's locks first rose so bright,[9]
The heav'ns bespangling with disheveled light.
The Sylphs behold it kindling as it flies,
And pleased pursue its progress through the skies.
This the beau monde shall from the Mall[1] survey,
And hail with music its propitious ray.
This, the blessed lover shall for Venus° take, *the planet*
And send up vows from Rosamonda's lake.[2]
This Partridge[3] soon shall view in cloudless skies,
When next he looks through Galileo's eyes;[4]
And hence th' egregious wizard shall foredoom
The fate of Louis, and the fall of Rome.
Then cease, bright nymph! to mourn thy ravished hair,

6. Cf. Ariosto's *Orlando Furioso* (1516–1532), in which Orlando's lost wits are sought on the moon. See also *Paradise Lost* 3.444ff.
7. Subtle reasoning (often used of arguments justifying immoral conduct).
8. When Romulus was killed mysteriously, Proculus soothed popular grief by asserting that he had been taken up to heaven.
9. The Egyptian queen Berenice made an offering of her hair after her husband returned victorious from the wars; when it disappeared from the temple, the court astronomer claimed it had been made into a new constellation.
1. A fashionable walk in St. James's Park.
2. Where lovers met in St. James's Park.
3. John Partridge was a ridiculous star-gazer, who in his almanacs every year, never failed to predict the downfall of the Pope, and the King of France, then at war with the English [Pope's note].
4. I.e., a telescope.

Which adds new glory to the shining sphere!
Not all the tresses that fair head can boast
Shall draw such envy as the lock you lost.
For, after all the murders of your eye,
When, after millions slain, yourself shall die;
When those fair suns[5] shall set, as set they must,
And all those tresses shall be laid in dust;
This lock, the Muse shall consecrate to fame,
And 'midst the stars inscribe Belinda's name!

1711–1717 1712; 1714; 1717

from The Iliad

from *Book 12*

[Sarpedon's Speech][1]

Resolved alike, divine Sarpedon[2] glows
With gen'rous rage that drives him on the foes.
He views the tow'rs,[3] and meditates° their fall, *plans*
To sure destruction dooms th' aspiring° wall; *high*
Then casting on his friend an ardent look,
Fired with the thirst of glory, thus he spoke.
"Why boast we, Glaucus! our extended reign,
Where Xanthus' streams[4] enrich the Lycian plain,
Our num'rous herds that range the fruitful field,
And hills where vines their purple harvest yield,
Our foaming bowls with purer nectar[5] crowned,
Our feasts enhanced with music's sprightly° sound? *lively*
Why on those shores are we with joy surveyed,° *observed*
Admired as heroes, and as gods obeyed?
Unless great acts superior merit prove,
And vindicate the bounteous pow'rs above.[6]
'Tis ours,[7] the dignity they give, to grace;
The first in valor, as the first in place.
That when with wond'ring eyes our martial bands
Behold our deeds transcending our commands,
'Such,' they may cry, 'deserve the sov'reign state,° *role*
Whom those that envy, dare not imitate!'

5. I.e., her eyes.

1. Pope spent nearly seven years (1713–1720) translating Homer's *Iliad* and writing critical notes to accompany his text. His work was an outstanding commercial and literary success; it earned him about £5000, more than a hundred times the earnings of a skilled craftsman or shop owner, and it later garnered Samuel Johnson's praise as "the noblest version [translation] of poetry which the world has ever seen." The speech of Sarpedon, a king fighting for the Trojans against the Greeks, was the first passage from Pope's *Iliad* that made its way into print, as part of *Pastorals* (1709), his first published collection; he later drew upon it deftly in his mock epic *The Rape of the Lock*, where in Canto 5, Clarissa's injunction to her fellow fashionistas echoes and parodies Sarpedon's speech (and Pope's own translation) almost line for line (5.9–34; see pages 2487–88).

2. Sarpedon, king of the Lycians, was the son of the supreme deity Zeus and the mortal Laodemia. Here, he exhorts his lieutenant Glaucus to bravery as they lead the Lycians into battle.

3. The high ramparts that the Greeks have built outside the walls of Troy.

4. The Xanthus is the principal river flowing through Lycia, a mountainous country in southwestern Asia Minor.

5. Perhaps mead (made from fermented honey).

6. I.e., the gods' blessings on us.

7. I.e., our obligation (to prove worthy of this bounty).

Could all our care elude the gloomy° grave, *dark*
Which claims no less the fearful than the brave,
For lust of fame I should not vainly dare
In fighting fields, nor urge thy soul to war.
But since, alas! Ignoble age must come,
Disease, and death's inexorable doom;
The life which others pay, let us bestow,
And give to fame what we to nature owe;
Brave though we fall, and honored if we live,
Or° let us glory gain, or glory give!"[8] *either*
He said; his words the list'ning chief inspire
With equal warmth, and rouse the warrior's fire;
The troops pursue their leaders with delight,
Rush to the foe, and claim the promised fight.

c. 1707 1709

ELOISA TO ABELARD Peter Abelard (1079–1142), a great French philosopher and theologian, was tutor to the young Heloise (Eloisa). They fell in love, had a son, and secretly married. When the affair became known, Heloise was forced to enter a convent and Abelard was castrated by a gang of thugs hired by Heloise's enraged uncle. Abelard became a Benedictine monk, founding the monastery of the Paraclete, or Holy Spirit. After many years of living respectable and successful lives devoted to God, the two former lovers exchanged a series of epistles in Latin. These austere letters were made more romantic and psychologically complex when they were loosely translated into French in the later seventeenth century. In 1713 Pope's friend John Hughes translated the silently "improved" French version into English; this became the source for Pope's poem, which he chose to conclude his 1717 *Works*. Modeled upon Ovid's *Heroides*, *Eloisa to Abelard* is a "heroic epistle," a dramatic expression of a lover's feelings in a verse letter addressed to an absent loved one. Alternately erotic and pious, gothic and tender, Pope's intensely passionate and penetratingly psychological portrait of Eloisa's conflicting feelings was one of his most widely admired works, particularly among eighteenth-century women readers.

Eloisa to Abelard

The Argument

Abelard and Eloisa flourished in the twelfth century; they were two of the most distinguished persons of their age in learning and beauty, but for nothing more famous than for their unfortunate passion. After a long course of calamities, they retired each to a several[1] convent, and consecrated the remainder of their days to religion. It was many years after this separation that a letter of Abelard's to a friend which contained the history of his misfortune fell into the hands of Eloisa. This, awakening all her tenderness, occasioned those celebrated letters (out of which the following is partly extracted) which give so lively a picture of the struggles of grace and nature, virtue and passion.

8. There is not a more forcible argument than this, to make all men condemn dangers, and seek glory by brave actions. Immortality with eternal youth is certainly preferable to glory purchased with the loss of life; but glory is certainly better than an ignominious life, which at last, though perhaps late, must end . . . This is incontestable, and whoever weighs his actions in these scales, can never hesitate in his choice; but what is most remarkable is that Homer does not put this in the mouth of an ordinary person, but ascribes it to the son of Jupiter [Pope's note].

1. Separate.

In these deep solitudes and awful° cells, *awe-inspiring*
Where heav'nly-pensive contemplation dwells,
And ever-musing melancholy reigns;
What means this tumult in a vestal's[2] veins?
Why rove my thoughts beyond this last retreat?
Why feels my heart its long-forgotten heat?
Yet, yet[3] I love!—From Abelard it came,
And Eloisa yet must kiss the name.
    Dear fatal name! rest ever unrevealed,
Nor pass these lips in holy silence sealed.
Hide it, my heart, within that close disguise,
Where, mixed with God's, his loved idea° lies. *image*
Oh write it not, my hand—the name appears
Already written—wash it out, my tears!
In vain lost Eloisa weeps and prays,
Her heart still dictates, and her hand obeys.
    Relentless walls! whose darksome round contains
Repentant sighs, and voluntary pains;
Ye rugged rocks! which holy knees have worn;
Ye grots° and caverns shagged with horrid° thorn! *grottos / bristling*
Shrines! where their vigils pale-eyed virgins keep,
And pitying saints, whose statues learn to weep![4]
Though cold like you, unmoved, and silent grown,
I have not yet forgot myself to stone.[5]
Heav'n claims me all in vain, while he has part,
Still rebel nature holds out half my heart;
Nor pray'rs nor fast its stubborn pulse restrain,
Nor tears, for ages, taught to flow in vain.
    Soon as thy letters trembling I unclose,
That well-known name awakens all my woes.
Oh name forever sad! forever dear!
Still breathed in sighs, still ushered with a tear.
I tremble too wheree'er my own I find,
Some dire misfortune follows close behind.
Line after line my gushing eyes o'erflow,
Led through a sad variety of woe:
Now warm in love, now with'ring in thy bloom,
Lost in a convent's° solitary gloom! *monastery's*
There stern religion quenched th' unwilling flame,
There died the best of passions, love and fame.
    Yet write, or write me all, that I may join
Griefs to thy griefs, and echo sighs to thine.
Nor foes nor fortune take this pow'r away.
And is my Abelard less kind than they?

2. Virgin bound to the service of the Roman goddess Vesta. As a nun Eloisa, like the vestals, was now sequestered for service to the divine.
3. In the sense of both "but" and "still."
4. Through condensation that ran down the statues.
5. This metaphor comes from Hughes's translation of the *Letters of Abelard and Heloise:* "O Vows! O Convent! I have not lost my humanity under your inexorable discipline! You have not made me marble by changing my habit" (129). See also Milton, *Il Penseroso,* line 42.

Tears still are mine, and those I need not spare,
Love but demands what else were shed in pray'r;
No happier task these faded eyes pursue,
To read and weep is all they now can do.
Then share thy pain, allow that sad relief;
Ah more than share it! give me all thy grief.
Heav'n first taught letters for some wretch's aid,
Some banished lover, or some captive maid;
They live, they speak, they breathe what love inspires,
Warm from the soul, and faithful to its fires,
The virgin's wish without her fears impart,
Excuse[6] the blush, and pour out all the heart,
Speed the soft intercourse from soul to soul,
And waft a sigh from Indus[7] to the Pole.
Thou know'st how guiltless first I met thy flame,
When love approached me under friendship's name;
My fancy formed thee of angelic kind,
Some emanation of th' all-beauteous Mind.° *God*
Those smiling eyes, attemp'ring° ev'ry ray, *softening*
Shone sweetly lambent° with celestial day: *radiant*
Guiltless I gazed; Heav'n listened while you sung;
And truths divine came mended from that tongue.[8]
From lips like those what precept failed to move?
Too soon they taught me 'twas no sin to love.
Back through the paths of pleasing sense I ran,
Nor wished an angel whom I loved a man.[9]
Dim and remote the joys of saints I see,
Nor envy them, that Heav'n I lose for thee.
How oft, when pressed to marriage, have I said,
Curse on all laws but those which love has made?
Love, free as air, at sight of human ties,
Spreads his light wings, and in a moment flies.
Let wealth, let honor, wait the wedded dame,
August her deed, and sacred be her fame;
Before true passion all those views remove,° *disperse*
Fame, wealth, and honor! what are you to love?
The jealous god,° when we profane his fires, *Cupid*
Those restless passions in revenge inspires;
And bids them make mistaken mortals groan,
Who seek in love for ought but love alone.
Should at my feet the world's great master fall,
Himself, his throne, his world, I'd scorn 'em all:
Not Caesar's empress would I deign to prove;
No, make me mistress to the man I love;
If there be yet another name more free,

6. Release from the need for.
7. A southern constellation far distant from the northern Polestar.
8. He was her preceptor in philosophy and divinity [Pope's note].
9. Having thought you an angel, I now return to my senses, and happily accept you as human.

More fond° than mistress, make me that to thee! *beloved*
Oh happy state! when souls each other draw,
When love is liberty, and nature, law:
All then is full, possessing, and possessed,
No craving void left aching in the breast:
Ev'n thought meets thought ere from the lips it part,
And each warm wish springs mutual from the heart.
This sure is bliss (if bliss on earth there be)
And once the lot of Abelard and me.

Alas how changed! what sudden horrors rise!
A naked lover bound and bleeding lies!
Where, where was Eloise? her voice, her hand,
Her poniard, had opposed the dire command.
Barbarian stay! that bloody stroke restrain;
The crime was common, common be the pain.[1]
I can no more; by shame, by rage suppressed,
Let tears and burning blushes speak the rest.

Canst thou forget that sad, that solemn day,
When victims at yon altar's foot we lay?
Canst thou forget what tears that moment fell,
When, warm in youth, I bade the world farewell?
As with cold lips I kissed the sacred veil,
The shrines all trembled, and the lamps grew pale:
Heav'n scarce believed the conquest it surveyed,
And saints with wonder heard the vows I made.
Yet then, to those dread altars as I drew,
Not on the Cross my eyes were fixed, but you;
Not grace, or zeal, love only was my call,
And if I lose thy love, I lose my all.
Come! with thy looks, thy words, relieve my woe;
Those still at least are left thee to bestow.
Still on that breast enamored let me lie,
Still drink delicious poison from thy eye,
Pant on thy lip, and to thy heart be pressed;
Give all thou canst—and let me dream the rest.
Ah no! instruct me other joys to prize,
With other beauties charm my partial° eyes, *fondly biased*
Full in my view set all the bright abode,
And make my soul quit Abelard for God.

Ah think at least thy flock deserves thy care,
Plants of thy hand, and children of thy pray'r.
From the false world in early youth they fled,
By thee to mountains, wilds, and deserts led.
You raised these hallowed walls;[2] the desert smiled,
And paradise was opened in the wild.
No weeping orphan saw his father's stores
Our shrines irradiate, or emblaze the floors;[3]

1. The crime was shared, so also should have been the penalty.
2. He founded the monastery [Pope's note].
3. "Irradiate" and "emblaze," meaning "adorn gloriously," both come from Milton.

No silver saints, by dying misers giv'n,
Here bribed the rage of ill-requited Heav'n:
But such plain roofs as piety could raise,
And only vocal with the Maker's[4] praise.
In these lone walls (their days eternal bound)
These moss-grown domes° with spiry turrets crowned, *buildings*
Where awful arches make a noon-day night,
And the dim windows shed a solemn light;
Thy eyes diffused a reconciling ray,
And gleams of glory brightened all the day.
But now no face divine contentment wears,
'Tis all blank sadness, or continual tears.
See how the force of others' pray'rs I try
(Oh pious fraud of am'rous charity!),
But why should I on others' pray'rs depend?
Come thou, my father, brother,[5] husband, friend!
Ah let thy handmaid, sister, daughter move,
And, all those tender names in one, thy love!
The darksome pines that o'er yon rocks reclined
Wave high, and murmur to the hollow wind,
The wand'ring streams that shine between the hills,
The grots that echo to the tinkling rills,
The dying gales that pant upon the trees,
The lakes that quiver to the curling breeze;
No more these scenes my meditation aid,
Or lull to rest the visionary maid:[6]
But o'er the twilight groves, and dusky caves,
Long-sounding isles, and intermingled graves,
Black melancholy sits, and round her throws
A death-like silence, and a dread repose:
Her gloomy presence saddens all the scene,
Shades ev'ry flow'r, and darkens ev'ry green,
Deepens the murmur of the falling floods,
And breathes a browner horror on the woods.
Yet here for ever, ever must I stay;
Sad proof how well a lover can obey!
Death, only death, can break the lasting chain;
And here ev'n then, shall my cold dust remain,
Here all its frailties, all its flames resign,
And wait, till 'tis no sin to mix with thine.
Ah wretch! believed the spouse of God in vain,
Confessed within the slave of love and man.
Assist me Heav'n! but whence arose that pray'r?
Sprung it from piety, or from despair?
Ev'n here, where frozen chastity retires,

4. The satirical tone of the previous lines prompts us to ask whether the "Maker" is God or Abelard.
5. "Father" and "brother" in the ecclesiastical, as well as emotional, sense. This also applies for "handmaid," "sister," and "daughter" in the following line.
6. One prone to visions.

Love finds an altar for forbidden fires.
I ought to grieve, but cannot what I ought;
I mourn the lover, not lament the fault;
I view my crime, but kindle at the view,
Repent old pleasures, and solicit new:
Now turned to Heav'n, I weep my past offense,
Now think of thee, and curse my innocence.[7]
Of all affliction taught a lover yet,
'Tis sure the hardest science° to forget! *knowledge*
How shall I lose the sin, yet keep the sense,
And love th' offender, yet detest th' offense?
How the dear object from the crime remove,
Or how distinguish penitence from love?
Unequal task! a passion to resign,
For hearts so touched, so pierced, so lost as mine.
E'er such a soul regains its peaceful state,
How often must it love, how often hate!
How often, hope, despair, resent, regret,
Conceal, disdain—do all things but forget.
But let Heav'n seize it, all at once 'tis fired,
Not° touched, but rapt; not wakened, but inspired! *not only*
Oh come! oh teach me nature to subdue,
Renounce my love, my life, my self—and you.
Fill my fond heart with God alone, for he
Alone can rival, can succeed to thee.
    How happy is the blameless vestal's lot!
The world forgetting, by the world forgot.
Eternal sunshine of the spotless mind!
Each pray'r accepted, and each wish resigned;
Labor and rest, that equal periods keep;
"Obedient slumbers that can wake and weep;"[8]
Desires composed, affections ever even,
Tears that delight, and sighs that waft to Heav'n.
Grace shines around her with serenest beams,
And whisp'ring angels prompt her golden dreams.
For her the Spouse° prepares the bridal ring, *Christ*
For her white virgins hymenaeals° sing; *wedding songs*
For her th' unfading rose of Eden blooms,
And wings of seraphs shed divine perfumes;
To sounds of heav'nly harps, she dies away,
And melts in visions of eternal day.
    Far other dreams my erring soul employ,
Far other raptures, of unholy joy:
When at the close of each sad, sorrowing day,

7. Cf. *Letters of Abelard and Heloise:* "Among those who are wedded to God I serve a man. . . . I am here, I confess, a sinner, but one who far from weeping for her sins, weeps only for her lover. . . . Every object brings to my mind what I ought to forget. . . . Even into the holy places before the altar I carry with me the memory of our guilty loves" (trans. Hughes, 120–24).

8. Line 16 from *Description of a Religious House*, by Richard Crashaw (1612–1649).

Fancy restores what vengeance snatched away,
Then conscience sleeps, and leaving nature free,
All my loose soul unbounded springs to thee.
O cursed, dear horrors of all-conscious° night! *all-knowing*
How glowing guilt exalts the keen delight!
Provoking demons all restraint remove,
And stir within me ev'ry source of love.
I hear thee, view thee, gaze o'er all thy charms,
And round thy phantom glue my clasping arms.
I wake—no more I hear, no more I view,
The phantom flies me, as unkind as you.
I call aloud; it hears not what I say;
I stretch my empty arms; it glides away:
To dream once more I close my willing eyes;
Ye soft illusions, dear deceits, arise!
Alas no more!—methinks we wand'ring go
Through dreary wastes, and weep each other's woe;
Where round some mold'ring tow'r pale ivy creeps,
And low-browed rocks hang nodding o'er the deeps.
Sudden you mount! you beckon from the skies;
Clouds interpose, waves roar, and winds arise.
I shriek, start up, the same sad prospect find,
And wake to all the griefs I left behind.
    For thee the fates, severely kind, ordain
A cool suspense from pleasure and from pain;
Thy life a long, dead calm of fixed repose;
No pulse that riots, and no blood that glows.
Still as the sea, ere winds were taught to blow,
Or moving spirit bade the waters flow;
Soft as the slumbers of a saint forgiv'n,
And mild as opening gleams of promised Heav'n.
    Come Abelard! for what hast thou to dread?
The torch of Venus burns not for the dead;
Cut from the root my perished joys I see,
And love's warm tide forever stopped in thee.
Nature stands checked; religion disapproves;
Ev'n thou art cold—yet Eloisa loves.
Ah hopeless, lasting flames! like those that burn
To light the dead, and warm th' unfruitful urn.[9]
    What scenes appear where'er I turn my view,
The dear ideas, where I fly, pursue,
Rise in the grove, before the altar rise,
Stain all my soul, and wanton in my eyes!
I waste the matin[1] lamp in sighs for thee,
Thy image steals between my God and me,
Thy voice I seem in ev'ry hymn to hear,
With ev'ry bead I drop too soft a tear.[2]

9. The Romans attempted to supply tombs with inextinguishable fires.

1. Morning; Matins are the psalms sung at dawn.

2. Tears of love, not repentance.

When from the censer clouds of fragrance roll,
And swelling organs lift the rising soul;
One thought of thee puts all the pomp to flight,
Priests, tapers, temples, swim before my sight:
In seas of flame my plunging soul is drowned,
While altars blaze, and angels tremble round.
While prostrate here in humble grief I lie,
Kind, virtuous drops just gath'ring in my eye,
While praying, trembling, in the dust I roll,
And dawning grace is opening on my soul.
Come, if thou dar'st, all charming as thou art!
Oppose thyself to Heav'n; dispute° my heart; *compete for*
Come, with one glance of those deluding eyes,
Blot out each bright idea of the skies.
Take back that grace, those sorrows, and those tears,
Take back my fruitless penitence and pray'rs,
Snatch me, just mounting, from the blest abode,
Assist the fiends and tear me from my God!
No, fly me, fly me! far as pole from pole;
Rise Alps between us! and whole oceans roll!
Ah come not, write not, think not once of me,
Nor share one pang of all I felt for thee.
Thy oaths I quit,° thy memory resign, *absolve*
Forget, renounce me, hate whate'er was mine.
Fair eyes, and tempting looks (which yet I view!)
Long loved, adored ideas! all adieu!
O grace serene! oh virtue heav'nly fair!
Divine oblivion of low-thoughted care!
Fresh blooming hope, gay daughter of the sky!
And faith, our early immortality![3]
Enter each mild, each amicable guest;
Receive, and wrap me in eternal rest!
See in her cell sad Eloisa spread,
Propped on some tomb, a neighbor of the dead!
In each low wind methinks a spirit calls,
And more than echoes talk along the walls.
Here, as I watched the dying lamps around,
From yonder shrine I heard a hollow sound.
"Come, sister come!" (it said, or seemed to say)
"Thy place is here, sad sister come away!
Once like thy self, I trembled, wept, and prayed,
Love's victim then, though now a sainted maid:
But all is calm in this eternal sleep;
Here grief forgets to groan, and love to weep,
Ev'n superstition loses ev'ry fear:
For God, not man, absolves our frailties here."
I come, ye ghosts! prepare your roseate bow'rs,
Celestial palms, and ever-blooming flow'rs.

3. Faith seen as a foretaste of immortality.

Thither, where sinners may have rest, I go,
Where flames refined in breasts seraphic glow.
Thou, Abelard! the last sad office pay,
And smooth my passage to the realms of day:
See my lips tremble, and my eyeballs roll,
Suck my last breath, and catch my flying soul!
Ah no—in sacred vestments may'st thou stand,
The hallowed taper trembling in thy hand,
Present the cross before my lifted eye,
Teach me at once, and learn of° me to die. *from*
Ah then, thy once-loved Eloisa see!
It will be then no crime to gaze on me.
See from my cheek the transient roses fly!
See the last sparkle languish in my eye!
Till ev'ry motion, pulse, and breath, be o'er;
And ev'n my Abelard beloved no more.
O death all-eloquent! you only prove
What dust we dote on, when 'tis man we love.
Then too, when fate shall thy fair frame destroy
(That cause of all my guilt, and all my joy),
In trance ecstatic may thy pangs be drowned,
Bright clouds descend, and angels watch thee round,
From opening skies may streaming glories shine,
And saints embrace thee with a love like mine.
May one kind grave unite each hapless name,[4]
And graft my love immortal on thy fame.
Then, ages hence, when all my woes are o'er,
When this rebellious heart shall beat no more;
If ever chance two wand'ring lovers brings
To Paraclete's white walls, and silver springs,
O'er the pale marble shall they join their heads,
And drink the falling tears each other sheds,
Then sadly say, with mutual pity moved,
Oh may we never love as these have loved!
From the full choir when loud Hosannas rise,
And swell the pomp of dreadful sacrifice,[5]
Amid that scene, if some relenting eye
Glance on the stone where our cold relics lie,
Devotion's self shall steal a thought from Heav'n,
One human tear shall drop, and be forgiv'n.
And sure if fate some future bard[6] shall join
In sad similitude of griefs to mine,
Condemned whole years in absence to deplore,
And image charms he must behold no more,

4. Abelard and Eloisa were interred in the same grave, or in monuments adjoining, in the Monastery of the Paraclete [Pope's note].
5. The Mass, in which Christ's saving sacrifice is ritually reenacted.
6. Pope himself; he probably refers to Lady Mary Wortley Montagu, then traveling in the Middle East; he and she later quarreled and became estranged.

Such if there be, who loves so long, so well;
Let him our sad, our tender story tell;
The well-sung woes will soothe my pensive ghost;
He best can paint 'em, who shall feel 'em most.

c. 1716 1717

from An Essay on Man
In Four Epistles to Henry St. John, Lord Bolingbroke[1]

TO THE READER

As the epistolary way of writing hath prevailed much of late, we have ventured to publish this piece composed some time since, and whose author chose this manner, notwithstanding his subject was high and of dignity, because of its being mixed with argument, which of its nature approacheth to prose. This,[2] which we first give the reader, treats of the Nature and State of MAN, with respect to the UNIVERSAL SYSTEM;[3] and the rest will treat of him with respect to his OWN SYSTEM, as an Individual, and as a Member of Society; under one or other of which heads all ethics are included.

As he imitates no man, so he would be thought to vie with no man in these Epistles, particular with the noted author of two lately published;[4] but this he may most surely say: that the matter of them is such, as is of importance to all in general, and of offense to none in particular.

THE DESIGN

Having proposed to write some pieces on human life and manners, such as (to use my lord Bacon's expression) *come home to men's business and bosoms*,[5] I thought it more satisfactory to begin with considering Man in the abstract, his Nature and his State: since, to prove any moral duty, to enforce any moral precept, or to examine the perfection or imperfection of any creature whatsoever, it is necessary first to know what condition and relation it is placed in, and what is the proper end and purpose of its being.

The science[6] of human nature is, like all other sciences, reduced to a few clear points: there are not many certain truths in this world. It is therefore in the anatomy of the mind as in that of the body: more good will accrue to mankind by attending to the large, open, and perceptible parts, than by studying too much such finer nerves and vessels, the conformations and uses of which will forever escape our observation. The disputes are all upon these last, and, I will venture to say, they

1. "I believe," wrote Pope to his friend John Caryll, "that there is not in the whole course of the Scripture any precept so often and so strongly inculcated, as the trust and eternal dependence we ought to repose in that Supreme Being who is our constant preserver and benefactor." This is the theme of Pope's didactic and exhortatory *Essay on Man*, whose four epistles were published anonymously over 11 months in 1733–1734. For Pope, "to reason right is to submit" (line 164), not least because humankind occupies a middle ground—between angels and beasts—in a divinely ordered universe. Pope had intended the *Essay on Man* and the four *Moral Essays* (1731–1735) to be the first and last parts of a great poetic sequence on the nature of humankind, though he never completed the project. The *Essay* is addressed to Henry St. John, first Viscount Bolingbroke (1678–1751), a leading Tory statesman and political writer whom Pope described as "my guide, philosopher, and friend."
2. I.e., the first Epistle.
3. I.e., within the cosmic order, ordained by God.
4. I.e., Pope himself, whose *Epistle to Bathurst* (1733) and the first *Imitation of Horace* (1733) had recently been published. The *Essay on Man* was published anonymously; Pope uses his little address to the reader both to advertise his own work and to confuse his enemies about the identity of the poem's author.
5. From Bacon's Dedicatory Epistle in the collected edition of the *Essays* (1625).
6. Knowledge.

have less sharpened the wits than the hearts of men against each other, and have diminished the practice, more than advanced the theory, of morality. If I could flatter myself that this Essay has any merit, it is in steering betwixt the extremes of doctrines seemingly opposite, in passing over terms utterly unintelligible, and in forming a temperate yet not inconsistent, and a short yet not imperfect system of ethics.

This I might have done in prose; but I chose verse, and even rhyme, for two reasons. The one will appear obvious; that principles, maxims, or precepts so written, both strike the reader more strongly at first, and are more easily retained by him afterwards. The other may seem odd, but is true: I found I could express them more shortly this way than in prose itself; and nothing is more certain, than that much of the force as well as grace of arguments or instructions, depends on their conciseness. I was unable to treat this part of my subject in more detail, without becoming dry and tedious; or more poetically, without sacrificing perspicuity to ornament, without wandering from the precision, or breaking the chain of reasoning. If any man can unite all these without diminution of any of them, I freely confess he will compass a thing above my capacity.

What is now published, is only to be considered as a general map of MAN, marking out no more than the greater parts, their extent, their limits, and their connection, but leaving the particular to be more fully delineated in the charts which are to follow. Consequently, these Epistles in their progress (if I have health and leisure to make any progress) will be less dry and more susceptible of poetical ornament. I am here only opening the fountains, and clearing the passage. To deduce the rivers, to follow them in their course, and to observe their effects, may be a task more agreeable.

Epistle 1

Awake, my ST. JOHN! leave all meaner° things — *base*
To low ambition, and the pride of kings.
Let us (since life can little more supply
Than just to look about us and to die)
Expatiate free[7] o'er all this scene of man;
A mighty maze! but not without a plan;
A wild, where weeds and flow'rs promiscuous° shoot, — *randomly mixed*
Or garden, tempting with forbidden fruit.
Together let us beat[8] this ample field,
Try what the open, what the covert yield;
The latent tracts, the giddy heights explore
Of all who blindly creep, or sightless soar;[9]
Eye nature's walks,° shoot folly as it flies, — *behaviors*
And catch the manners living as they rise;
Laugh where we must, be candid° where we can; — *generous*
But vindicate the ways of God to Man.[1]

1. Say first, of God above, or Man below,
What can we reason, but from what we know?
Of Man what see we, but his station here,

7. Wander or speak unrestrainedly.
8. "Beat," "open," "covert" are all hunting terms: Pope imagines himself and Boling broke to be searching out game by walking back and forth across open and wooded land.
9. The line envisions a middle way appropriate to man between ignorance and presumption.
1. An echo of Milton's invocation and aspiration at the start of *Paradise Lost*: "That to the highth of this great argument / I may assert eternal providence, / And justify the ways of God to men" (1.24–26). Pope's mention of the "garden, tempting with forbidden fruit" (line 8) also calls to mind the opening lines of Milton's epic.

From which to reason, or to which refer?
Through worlds unnumbered though the God be known,
'Tis ours to trace him only in our own.
He, who through vast immensity can pierce,
See worlds on worlds compose one universe,
Observe how system into system runs,
What other planets circle other suns,
What varied being° peoples° ev'ry star, *forms of existence / populate*
May tell why Heav'n has made us as we are.
But of this frame the bearings, and the ties,
The strong connections, nice° dependencies, *intricate*
Gradations just,[2] has thy° pervading soul *the reader's*
Looked through? or can a part contain the whole?
Is the great chain,[3] that draws all to agree,
And drawn supports, upheld by God, or thee?

2. Presumptuous Man! the reason wouldst thou find,
Why formed so weak, so little, and so blind!
First, if thou canst, the harder reason guess,
Why formed no weaker, blinder, and no less!
Ask of thy mother earth, why oaks are made
Taller or stronger than the weeds they shade?
Or ask of yonder argent fields above,
Why Jove's satellites[4] are less than Jove?
Of systems possible, if 'tis confessed
That wisdom infinite must form the best,
Where all must full or not coherent be,[5]
And all that rises, rise in due degree;
Then, in the scale of reas'ning life, 'tis plain
There must be, somewhere, such a rank as Man;
And all the question (wrangle e'er so long)
Is only this, if God has placed him wrong?
Respecting Man, whatever wrong we call,
May, must be right, as relative to all.
In human works, though labored on with pain,
A thousand movements scarce one purpose gain;
In God's, one single can its end produce;
Yet serves to second too some other use.
So Man, who here seems principal alone,
Perhaps acts second to some sphere unknown,
Touches some wheel, or verges to some goal;
'Tis but a part we see, and not a whole.
When the proud steed shall know why Man restrains
His fiery course, or drives him o'er the plains;
When the dull ox, why now he breaks the clod,

2. "Connections," "dependencies," and "gradations" were key terms of the new sciences.
3. The Great Chain of Being linked all levels of creation, at the same time maintaining a fixed hierarchy.
4. Jupiter's moons. "Satellites" here has four syllables.
5. The Great Chain of Being could not be broken at any point.

Is now a victim, and now Egypt's god:[6]
Then shall Man's pride and dullness comprehend
His actions', passions', being's, use and end;
Why doing, suff'ring, checked, impelled; and why
This hour a slave, the next a deity.
    Then say not Man's imperfect, Heav'n in fault;
Say rather, Man's as perfect as he ought;
His knowledge measured to his state and place,
His time a moment, and a point his space.
If to be perfect in a certain sphere,° *area of influence*
What matter, soon or late, or here or there?
The blessed today is as completely so,
As who began a thousand years ago.

    3. Heav'n from all creatures hides the book of fate,
All but the page prescribed, their present state;
From brutes what men, from men what spirits° know: *angels*
Or who could suffer being here below?
The lamb thy riot° dooms to bleed today, *extravagance*
Had he thy reason, would he skip and play?
Pleased to the last, he crops the flow'ry food,
And licks the hand just raised to shed his blood.
O blindness to the future! kindly giv'n,
That each may fill the circle marked by Heav'n;
Who sees with equal eye, as God of all,
A hero perish, or a sparrow fall,
Atoms or systems° into ruin hurled, *solar systems*
And now a bubble burst, and now a world.
Hope humbly then; with trembling pinions° soar; *wings*
Wait the great teacher Death, and God adore!
What future bliss, he gives not thee to know,
But gives that hope to be thy blessing now.
Hope springs eternal in the human breast:
Man never *is*, but always *to be* blessed:
The soul, uneasy and confined from home,
Rests and expatiates in a life to come.
    Lo! the poor Indian, whose untutored mind
Sees God in clouds, or hears him in the wind;
His soul proud science never taught to stray
Far as the solar walk, or Milky Way;
Yet simple nature to his hope has giv'n,
Behind the cloud-topped hill, an humbler Heav'n;
Some safer world in depth of woods embraced,
Some happier island in the wat'ry waste,
Where slaves once more their native land behold,
No fiends torment, no Christians thirst for gold![7]

6. Apis, sacred bull of Memphis.

7. The Christian is meant to "thirst for God" (Psalm 42.2).

To be, contents his natural desire,
He asks no angel's wings, no seraph's fire;[8]
But thinks, admitted to that equal sky,
His faithful dog shall bear him company.

4. Go, wiser thou! and in thy scale of sense
Weigh thy opinion against Providence;
Call imperfection what thou fancy'st such,
Say, here he gives too little, there too much;
Destroy all creatures for thy sport or gust,° *appetite*
Yet cry, If Man's unhappy, God's unjust;
If Man alone engross° not Heav'n's high care, *monopolize*
Alone made perfect here, immortal there:
Snatch from his hand the balance and the rod,
Rejudge his justice, be the God of God!
In pride, in reas'ning pride, our error lies;
All quit their sphere, and rush into the skies.
Pride still is aiming at the blessed abodes,
Men would be angels, angels would be gods.
Aspiring to be gods, if angels fell,
Aspiring to be angels, men rebel;
And who but wishes to invert the laws
Of ORDER, sins against th' Eternal Cause.

5. Ask for what end the heav'nly bodies shine,
Earth for whose use? Pride answers, "'Tis for mine:
For me kind Nature wakes her genial° pow'r, *generating*
Suckles each herb, and spreads out ev'ry flow'r;
Annual for me, the grape, the rose renew
The juice nectareous, and the balmy dew;
For me, the mine a thousand treasures brings;
For me, health gushes from a thousand springs;
Seas roll to waft me, suns to light me rise;
My foot-stool earth, my canopy the skies."[9]
But errs not Nature from this gracious end,
From burning suns when livid deaths descend,
When earthquakes swallow, or when tempests sweep
Towns to one grave, whole nations to the deep?
"No" ('tis replied) "the first Almighty cause[1]
Acts not by partial, but by gen'ral laws;
Th' exceptions few; some change since all began,
And what created perfect?"—Why then Man?
If the great end be human happiness,
Then Nature deviates; and can Man do less?
As much that end a constant course requires
Of show'rs and sunshine, as of Man's desires;
As much eternal springs and cloudless skies,

8. Seraphs were traditionally thought of as aflame, incandescent.
9. The line envisions the universe as throne, with footrest below and brightly ornamented fabrics hanging above.
1. God the Creator.

As men forever temp'rate, calm, and wise.
If plagues or earthquakes break not Heav'n's design,
Why then a Borgia, or a Catiline?[2]
Who knows but he, whose hand the light'ning forms,
Who heaves old ocean, and who wings the storms,
Pours fierce ambition in a Caesar's mind,
Or turns young Ammon[3] loose to scourge mankind?
From pride, from pride, our very reas'ning springs;
Account for moral, as for nat'ral things:
Why charge we Heav'n in those, in these acquit?
In both, to reason right is to submit.
Better for us, perhaps, it might appear,
Were there all harmony, all virtue here;
That never air or ocean felt the wind;
That never passion discomposed the mind:
But all subsists by elemental strife;
And passions are the elements of life.
The gen'ral ORDER, since the whole began,
Is kept in Nature, and is kept in Man.

6. What would this Man? Now upward will he soar,
And little less than angel, would be more;
Now looking downwards, just as grieved appears
To want the strength of bulls, the fur of bears.
Made for his use all creatures if he call,
Say what their use, had he the pow'rs of all?
Nature to these, without profusion kind,
The proper organs, proper pow'rs assigned;
Each seeming want compensated of course,[4]
Here with degrees of swiftness, there of force;
All in exact proportion to the state;
Nothing to add, and nothing to abate.
Each beast, each insect, happy in its own;
Is Heav'n unkind to Man, and Man alone?
Shall he alone, whom rational we call,
Be pleased with nothing, if not blessed with all?
The bliss of Man (could pride that blessing find)
Is not to act or think beyond mankind;
No pow'rs of body or of soul to share,
But what his nature and his state can bear.
Why has not Man a microscopic eye?
For this plain reason, Man is not a fly.
Say what the use, were finer optics giv'n,
T' inspect a mite, not comprehend the Heav'n?[5]

2. Cesare Borgia (1476–1507), an Italian duke from a notoriously ruthless family. Lucius Sergius Catiline (d. 62 B.C.E.) plotted unsuccessfully against the Roman state.

3. Alexander the Great, King of Macedonia (336–323 B.C.E.) and conqueror of Asia Minor, Syria, Egypt, Babylonia, and Persia.

4. As is fitting, in the normal course of events.

5. It was commonly believed that man alone of all the animals was able to look up to heaven.

Or touch, if tremblingly alive all o'er,
To smart and agonize at ev'ry pore?
Or quick effluvia darting through the brain,[6]
Die of a rose in aromatic pain?
If Nature thundered in his op'ning ears,
And stunned him with the music of the spheres,
How would he wish that Heav'n had left him still
The whisp'ring zephyr,° and the purling rill? *breeze*
Who finds not Providence all good and wise,
Alike in what it gives, and what denies?

7. Far as creation's ample range extends,
The scale of sensual, mental pow'rs ascends:
Mark how it mounts, to Man's imperial race,
From the green myriads in the peopled grass:
What modes of sight betwixt each wide extreme,
The mole's dim curtain, and the lynx's beam:
Of smell, the headlong lioness[7] between,
And hound sagacious on the tainted[8] green:
Of hearing, from the life that fills the flood,
To that which warbles through the vernal wood:
The spider's touch, how exquisitely fine!
Feels at each thread, and lives along the line:
In the nice° bee what sense so subtly true *super-sensitive*
From pois'nous herbs extracts the healing dew:[9]
How instinct varies in the grov'ling swine,
Compared, half-reas'ning elephant, with thine:
'Twixt that, and reason, what a nice barrier;° *fine distinction*
Forever sep'rate, yet forever near!
Remembrance and reflection how allied;
What thin partitions sense from thought divide:
And middle natures, how they long to join,
Yet never pass th' insuperable line!
Without this just gradation, could they be
Subjected these to those, or all to thee?
The pow'rs of all subdued by thee alone,
Is not thy reason all these pow'rs in one?

8. See, through this air, this ocean, and this earth,
All matter quick,° and bursting into birth. *living*
Above, how high progressive life may go!
Around, how wide! how deep extend below!
Vast chain of being, which from God began,
Natures ethereal, human, angel, Man,

6. Epicurus (c. 340–c. 270 B.C.E.) and others believed that sensations reached the brain from the pores via streams of invisible particles.

7. Lions were, according to Pope, believed to hunt "by the ear, and not by the nostril."

8. Sagacious: of acute perception; tainted: i.e., with the smell of the hunted animal.

9. Honey had been thought to fall on flowers as dew and was used for medicinal purposes.

Beast, bird, fish, insect! what no eye can see,
No glass° can reach! from infinite to thee, *magnifying lens*
From thee to nothing!—On superior pow'rs
Were we to press, inferior might on ours:
Or in the full creation leave a void,
Where, one step broken, the great scale's destroyed:
From Nature's chain whatever link you strike,
Tenth or ten thousandth, breaks the chain alike.
  And if each system in gradation roll,
Alike essential to th' amazing whole;
The least confusion but in one, not all
That system only, but the whole must fall.
Let earth unbalanced from her orbit fly,[1]
Planets and suns run lawless through the sky,
Let ruling angels from their spheres be hurled,[2]
Being on being wrecked, and world on world,
Heav'n's whole foundations to their center nod,
And Nature tremble to the throne of God:
All this dread ORDER break—for whom? for thee?
Vile worm!—oh, madness, pride, impiety!

  9. What if the foot, ordained the dust to tread,
Or hand to toil, aspired to be the head?
What if the head, the eye, or ear repined° *complained*
To serve° mere engines° to the ruling mind? *serve as / implements*
Just as absurd for any part to claim
To be another, in this gen'ral frame:
Just as absurd, to mourn the tasks or pains,
The great directing MIND of ALL ordains.
  All are but parts of one stupendous whole,
Whose body Nature is, and God the soul;
That, changed through all, and yet in all the same,
Great in the earth, as in th' ethereal frame,
Warms in the sun, refreshes in the breeze,
Glows in the stars, and blossoms in the trees,
Lives through all life, extends through all extent,
Spreads undivided, operates unspent,
Breathes in our soul, informs° our mortal part, *permeates*
As full, as perfect, in a hair as heart;
As full, as perfect, in vile Man that mourns,
As the rapt seraph that adores and burns;
To him no high, no low, no great, no small;
He fills, he bounds, connects, and equals all.

  10. Cease then, nor ORDER imperfection name:[3]
Our proper bliss depends on what we blame.

1. Echoes *Paradise Lost,* where God, creating the universe, "spun out the air / and Earth, self-balanced, on her center hung" (7.241–2).

2. A portent of the world's imminent end, according to Thomas Aquinas (c. 1225–1274).

3. I.e., do not label order imperfection.

Know thy own point: this kind, this due degree
Of blindness, weakness, Heav'n bestows on thee.
Submit—In this, or any other sphere,
Secure to be as blessed as thou canst bear:
Safe in the hand of one disposing pow'r,
Or° in the natal, or the mortal hour. *either*
All Nature is but art, unknown to thee;
All chance, direction, which thou canst not see;
All discord, harmony, not understood;[4]
All partial evil, universal good:[5]
And, spite of pride, in erring reason's spite,
One truth is clear, "Whatever IS, is RIGHT."

from *Epistle 2*

1. Know then thyself, presume not God to scan;
The proper study of mankind is Man.
Placed on this isthmus of a middle state,
A being darkly wise, and rudely great:
With too much knowledge for the skeptic side,
With too much weakness for the Stoic's pride,
He hangs between; in doubt to act, or rest,
In doubt to deem himself a God or beast,
In doubt his mind or body to prefer,
Born but to die, and reas'ning but to err;
Alike in ignorance, his reason such,
Whether he thinks too little, or too much.
Chaos of thought and passion, all confused;
Still by himself abused, or disabused;[6]
Created half to rise, and half to fall,
Great lord of all things, yet a prey to all;
Sole judge of truth, in endless error hurled:
The glory, jest, and riddle of the world!

1733

AN *EPISTLE FROM MR. POPE, TO DR. ARBUTHNOT* The *Epistle to Dr. Arbuthnot*, perhaps the most relaxed and engaging of all Pope's verse letters, is addressed to John Arbuthnot (1667–1735), who was physician to Queen Anne, a close friend of Pope and Swift, a valued member of the Scriblerus Club, and principal author of the *Memoirs of the Extraordinary Life, Works, and Discoveries of Martinus Scriblerus*, published with Pope's *Works* in 1741. Samuel Johnson described Arbuthnot as "the most universal genius," for he was a fine satirist, a skillful physician, an amateur mathematician, and a capable poet. Pope's epistle is an apology both for himself and for the satirist's art, written against those who had attacked his "person, morals, and family." He asserts the social role of the poet, includes moving autobiographical passages, and

4. Here, as earlier in the poem, Pope invokes the Horatian principle of *concordia discors* (Horace, *Epistles*, 1.12.19), a harmony of opposites.

5. In a letter to his friend John Caryll, Pope wrote that "true piety would make us know, that all misfortunes may as well be blessings."

6. Corrected; undeceived.

powerfully assails his enemies. This Horatian epistle, to the friend whose satires had delighted Pope and whose care had helped preserve and prolong Pope's own frail health, was published just seven weeks before the doctor died.

An Epistle from Mr. Pope, to Dr. Arbuthnot

Neque sermonibus vulgi dederis te, ned in Praemiis humanis spem posueris rerum tuarum: suis te oportet illecebris ipsa virtus trahat ad verum decus. Quid de te alii loquantur, ipsi vedeant, sed loquentur tamen.[1]

Advertisement

This paper is a sort of bill of complaint, begun many years since, and drawn up by snatches, as the several occasions offered. I had no thoughts of publishing it, till it pleased some persons of rank and fortune (the authors of *Verses to the Imitator of Horace*, and of an *Epistle to a Doctor of Divinity from a Nobleman at Hampton Court*)[2] to attack in a very extraordinary manner, not only my writings (of which being public the public judge) but my person, morals, and family, whereof to those who know me not, a truer information may be requisite. Being divided between the necessity to say something of myself, and my own laziness to undertake so awkward a task, I thought it the shortest way to put the last hand to this epistle. If it have anything pleasing, it will be that by which I am most desirous to please, the truth and the sentiment; and if anything offensive, it will be only to those I am least sorry to offend, the vicious or the ungenerous.

Many will know their own pictures in it, there being not a circumstance but what is true; but I have, for the most part, spared their names, and they may escape being laughed at, if they please.

I would have some of them know, it was owing to the request of the learned and candid friend to whom it is inscribed, that I make not as free use of theirs as they have done of mine. However I shall have this advantage, and honor, on my side, that whereas by their proceeding, any abuse may be directed at any man, no injury can possibly be done by mine, since a nameless character can never be found out, but by its *truth* and *likeness*.[3]

Shut, shut the door, good John![4] fatigued I said,
Tie up the knocker, say I'm sick, I'm dead.
The Dog-star rages![5] Nay 'tis past a doubt,
All Bedlam, or Parnassus,[6] is let out:
Fire in each eye, and papers in each hand,
They rave, recite, and madden[7] round the land.
What walls can guard me, or what shades can hide?

1. "You will not give yourself up to the flattery of the vulgar, nor hope for success in your affairs from mortal hands; virtue herself will lead to true honor; see that you follow her guidance. What others see fit to say of you let them say" (Cicero, *De Re Publica*, 6.23).
2. Lady Mary Wortley Montagu (1689–1762) and John Hervey (1696–1743), Baron Hervey of Ickworth.
3. I.e., its similarity to the original.
4. Pope's servant, John Serle.
5. Sirius, which appears in the heat of summer; Pope was finishing the poem in August 1734. The late summer was also the time for reciting poetry in classical Rome.
6. Bedlam (Bethlehem Hospital) was a London "lunatic" asylum; Parnassus was the mountain of the Muses.
7. A word Pope invented.

They pierce my thickets, through my grot[8] they glide,
By land, by water,[9] they renew the charge,
They stop the chariot, and they board the barge.
No place is sacred, not the church is free,
Ev'n Sunday shines no Sabbath-day to me:
Then from the Mint[1] walks forth the man of rhyme,
Happy! to catch me, just at dinner time.
Is there a parson, much bemused in beer,[2]
A maudlin poetess, a rhyming peer,
A clerk, foredoomed his father's soul to cross,
Who pens a stanza when he should engross?° *copy documents*
Is there, who locked from ink and paper, scrawls
With desp'rate charcoal round his darkened walls?
All fly to Twit'nam,° and in humble strain *Twickenham*
Apply to me, to keep them mad or vain.
Arthur,[3] whose giddy son neglects the laws,
Imputes to me and my damned works the cause:
Poor Cornus° sees his frantic wife elope, *cuckold*
And curses wit, and poetry, and Pope.[4]
Friend to my life! (which did not you prolong,
The world had wanted many an idle song)
What drop or nostrum° can this plague remove? *medicines*
Or which must end me, a fool's wrath or love?
A dire dilemma! Either way I'm sped,° *hurried toward death*
If foes, they write, if friends, they read me dead.
Seized and tied down to judge, how wretched I!
Who can't be silent, and who will not lie;
To laugh were want of goodness and of grace,
And to be grave exceeds all pow'r of face.
I sit with sad civility, I read
With honest anguish, and an aching head;
And drop at last, but in unwilling ears,
This saving counsel, "Keep your piece nine years."[5]
Nine years! cries he, who high in Drury Lane[6]
Lulled by soft zephyrs° through the broken pane, *breezes*
Rhymes 'ere he wakes, and prints before term ends,[7]
Obliged by hunger, and request of friends:[8]
"The piece you think is incorrect? why take it,
I'm all submission, what you'd have it, make it."
Three things another's modest wishes bound,° *encompass*

8. Pope's artificial grotto or cavern, his retreat, at Twickenham.
9. Pope's house at Twickenham was on the river Thames, and could be reached by boat from London.
1. Debtors were safe from the law in Southwark, London; on Sunday there were no arrests anywhere.
2. Laurence Eusden (1688–1730), poet laureate and parson given to drink.
3. Arthur Moore; his son James Moore-Smythe had plagiarized from Pope.
4. Both the Pope and the author: as a nation, the British were preoccupied with the threat of Roman Catholicism without (from France and Spain) and within (from Catholics like Pope).
5. Horace's advice to a poet eager to publish (*Ars Poetica* 386–89).
6. A writer living in a garret in this bad neighborhood.
7. Law court terms were the preferred publishing seasons.
8. It is the second reason, rather than the first, that the aspiring poet gives in his prefaces.

My friendship, and a prologue,[9] and ten pound.
Pitholeon[1] sends to me: "You know his Grace,
I want a patron; ask him for a place."° *paid position*
Pitholeon libelled me—"but here's a letter
Informs you, sir, 'twas when he knew no better.
Dare you refuse him? Curll[2] invites to dine,
He'll write a *Journal*, or he'll turn divine."[3]
Bless me! a packet.—"'Tis a stranger sues,
A virgin tragedy, an orphan Muse."
If I dislike it, "Furies, death and rage!"
If I approve, "Commend it to the stage."
There (thank my stars) my whole commission ends,
The play'rs and I are, luckily, no friends.
Fired that the house° reject him, "'Sdeath I'll print it, *theater*
And shame the fools—your int'rest, sir, with Lintot."[4]
Lintot, dull rogue! will think your price too much.
"Not sir, if you revise it, and retouch."
All my demurs but double his attacks,
At last he whispers, "Do, and we go snacks."[5]
Glad of a quarrel, straight° I clap the door, *immediately*
Sir, let me see your works and you no more.
'Tis sung, when Midas' ears began to spring[6]
(Midas, a sacred person and a king),
His very minister who spied them first,
(Some say his Queen) was forced to speak, or burst.
And is not mine, my friend, a sorer case,
When every coxcomb° perks° them in my face? *fool / shoves*
"Good friend forbear! you deal in dang'rous things,
I'd never name Queens, Ministers, or Kings;
Keep close to ears,° and those let asses prick,[7] *whisper it*
'Tis nothing"—Nothing? if they bite and kick?
Out with it, *Dunciad*! let the secret pass,
That secret to each fool, that he's an ass:
The truth once told (and wherefore should we lie?),
The Queen of Midas slept, and so may I.
You think this cruel? take it for a rule,
No creature smarts so little as a fool.
Let peals of laughter, Codrus![8] 'round thee break,
Thou unconcerned canst hear the mighty crack:[9]

9. To a play of his: a good way to show the public who your friends were.
1. The name taken from a foolish Poet at Rhodes [Pope's note].
2. Edmund Curll (1675–1747), a publisher notorious for commissioning hacks to write libelous journals, full of "news and scandal."
3. Pope may have meant Leonard Welsted (1688–1747) who was planning a religious work.
4. Bernard Lintot (1675–1736), who published for Pope.
5. Share the profits.
6. King Midas grew ass's ears when he preferred Pan to Apollo in their music contest. One of those closest to him whispered the story to the earth, and it was in turn told by the reeds. Pope is also referring to that contemporary artistic dunce, King George II, his wife Queen Caroline, and first minister Robert Walpole.
7. Presumably, their ears, as well as the poet.
8. A poet, perhaps fictional, ridiculed by Virgil and Juvenal.
9. "Mighty crack" was a phrase used by Addison to describe the collapse of the world; Pope showed how inadequate he thought it both in *Peri Bathous* and here, where it signals the failure of a play.

Pit, box, and gall'ry in convulsions hurled,
Thou stand'st unshook amidst a bursting world.
Who shames a scribbler? break one cobweb through,
He spins the slight, self-pleasing thread anew;
Destroy his fib, or sophistry, in vain,
The creature's at his dirty work again,
Throned in the center of his thin designs,
Proud of a vast extent of flimsy lines!
Whom have I hurt? has poet yet, or peer,
Lost the arched eyebrow, or Parnassian sneer?
And has not Colley[1] still his lord, and whore?
His butchers Henley, his Freemasons Moore?[2]
Does not one table Bavius[3] still admit?
Still to one bishop Philips[4] seem a wit?
Still Sappho[5]—"Hold! for God's sake—you'll offend;
No names—be calm—learn prudence of a friend:
I too could write, and I am twice as tall;
But foes like these!"—One flatt'rer's worse than all;
Of all mad creatures, if the learn'd are right,
It is the slaver kills, and not the bite.
A fool quite angry is quite innocent.
Alas! 'tis ten times worse when they *repent*.

One dedicates, in high heroic prose,
And ridicules beyond a hundred foes;
One from all Grub Street[6] will my fame defend,
And, more abusive, calls himself my friend.
This prints my letters,[7] that expects a bribe,
And others roar aloud, "Subscribe, subscribe."
There are, who to my person pay their court,
I cough like Horace, and though lean, am short,
Ammon's great son[8] one shoulder had too high,
Such Ovid's nose, and "Sir! you have an eye—"
Go on, obliging creatures, make me see
All that disgraced my betters, met in me.
Say for my comfort, languishing in bed,
"Just so immortal Maro° held his head:" *Virgil*
And when I die, be sure you let me know
Great Homer died three thousand years ago.

1. Colley Cibber (1671–1757), actor, playwright, Poet Laureate; he replaced Lewis Theobald as the "hero" of *The Dunciad*, from which Pope here quotes the phrase "Parnassian sneer."
2. John "Orator" Henley (1692–1759), a popular and unusual preacher, had set up an "oratory" in Newport Market, one of London's principal meat markets, causing enemies to claim that his audiences consisted only of ignorant butchers. James Moore-Smythe was a Freemason.
3. A bad poet who had attacked Virgil and Horace.
4. Ambrose Philips (c. 1675–1749), poet and secretary to the Bishop of Armagh.
5. Lady Mary Wortley Montagu, whom Pope had attacked previously under the name of this Greek lyric poet; by Arbuthnot's interjection, Pope seems to be implying that she was under Walpole's protection.
6. Home of literary hacks.
7. Forged or stolen (as Curll had in 1726).
8. Alexander the Great.

Why did I write? what sin to me unknown
Dipped me in ink, my parents', or my own?
As yet a child, nor yet a fool to fame,
I lisped in numbers,° for the numbers came. *verse, meter*
I left no calling for this idle trade,
No duty broke, no father disobeyed.
The Muse but served to ease some friend, not wife,
To help me through this long disease, my life,
To second, Arbuthnot! thy art and care,
And teach the being you preserved to bear.

But why then publish? Granville[9] the polite,
And knowing Walsh, would tell me I could write;
Well-natured Garth inflamed with early praise,
And Congreve loved, and Swift endured my lays;
The courtly Talbot, Somers, Sheffield read,
Ev'n mitered Rochester would nod the head,
And St. John's self (great Dryden's friends before)
With open arms received one poet more.
Happy my studies, when by these approved!
Happier their author, when by these beloved!
From these the world will judge of men and books,
Not from the Burnets, Oldmixons, and Cookes.[1]
Soft were my numbers; who could take offense
While pure description held the place of sense?
Like gentle Fanny's[2] was my flow'ry theme,
A painted mistress, or a purling stream.
Yet then did Gildon[3] draw his venal quill;
I wished the man a dinner, and sat still.
Yet then did Dennis rave in furious fret;[4]
I never answered, I was not in debt.
If want provoked, or madness made them print,
I waged no war with Bedlam or the Mint.
Did some more sober critic come abroad?
If wrong, I smiled; if right, I kissed the rod.[5]
Pains, reading, study are their just pretense,
And all they want is spirit, taste, and sense.
Commas and points they set exactly right,
And 'twere a sin to rob them of their mite.

9. Pope associates himself (and Dryden) with a number of important figures, friends, and patrons: George Granville, Baron Lansdowne (1666–1735); William Walsh (1663–1708); Sir Samuel Garth (1661–1719); William Congreve; Jonathan Swift; Charles Talbot, Duke of Shrewsbury (1660–1718); John Lord Somers (1651–1721); Francis Atterbury, Bishop of Rochester (1662–1732); Henry St. John, Viscount Bolingbroke (1678–1751).

1. Thomas Burnet, John Oldmixon, and Thomas Cooke: "authors of secret and scandalous history" [Pope's note]; Pope is comparing the greatness of his friends with the small-mindedness of those who attacked him.

2. Lord Hervey, court Vice Chamberlain, whom Pope thought effeminate, and later satirizes as Sporus (lines 305ff.).

3. Charles Gildon (1665–1724) had attacked *The Rape of the Lock*. Pope insinuates that Gildon writes to keep poverty at bay.

4. John Dennis (1657–1734), had similarly attacked Pope; both Gildon and Dennis, Pope thought, had acted at the instigation of Addison.

5. Accepted their criticism; kissing a monarch's scepter or a state official's staff was a ritual of submission to authority.

Yet ne'er one spring of laurel graced these ribalds,[6]
From slashing Bentley down to piddling Tibalds:[7]
Each wight, who reads not, and but scans and spells,
Each word-catcher, that lives on syllables,
Ev'n such small critics some regard may claim,
Preserved in Milton's or in Shakespeare's name.
Pretty! in amber to observe the forms
Of hairs, or straws, or dirt, or grubs, or worms!
These things, we know, are neither rich nor rare,
But wonder how the devil they got there?
  Were others angry? I excused them too;
Well might they rage, I gave them but their due.
A man's true merit 'tis not hard to find,
But each man's secret standard in his mind,
That casting-weight[8] pride adds to emptiness,
This, who can gratify? for who can *guess*?
The Bard[9] whom pilfered pastorals renown,
Who turns a Persian tale for half a crown,[1]
Just writes to make his barrenness appear,
And strains from hard-bound brains eight lines a year:
He, who still wanting though he lives on theft,
Steals much, spends little, yet has nothing left:
And he, who now to sense, now nonsense leaning,
Means not, but blunders round about a meaning:
And he, whose fustian's° so sublimely bad, *bombastic style*
It is not poetry, but prose run mad:
All these, my modest satire bade translate,
And owned, that nine such poets made a Tate.[2]
How did they fume, and stamp, and roar, and chafe?
And swear, not Addison himself was safe.
  Peace to all such! but were there one[3] whose fires
True genius kindles, and fair fame inspires;
Blessed with each talent and each art to please,
And born to write, converse, and live with ease:
Should such a man, too fond to rule° alone, *of ruling*
Bear, like the Turk, no brother near the throne,[4]
View him with scornful, yet with jealous eyes,
And hate for arts that caused himself to rise;
Damn with faint praise,[5] assent with civil leer,
And without sneering, teach the rest to sneer;

6. Laurel: the poet's crown; ribalds: foolish jesters.
7. Richard Bentley (1662–1742), a classical scholar of great learning and bad temper, earned ridicule for his "corrected" edition of *Paradise Lost* (1732), while Lewis Theobald (1688–1744), sometime "hero" of *The Dunciad*, criticized Pope's edition of Shakespeare in his *Shakespeare Restored* (1726).
8. The weight that tips the balance.
9. Ambrose Philips wrote pastoral poems in imitation of Spenser and translated a book of *Persian Tales*. The fact that, in 1709, his pastorals were published in the same volume as Pope's occasioned a rivalry between the two poets.
1. A standard prostitute's charge.
2. Nahum Tate (1652–1715), playwright and poet.
3. Joseph Addison (1672–1719), here portrayed as Atticus, friend of Cicero. Pope respected Addison's abilities as a writer, but did not like him or his politics.
4. Turkish rulers killed close relatives who might be potential rivals.
5. Cf. William Wycherley's prologue to *The Plain Dealer* (1677): "And, with faint praises, one another damn."

Willing to wound, and yet afraid to strike,
Just hint a fault, and hesitate dislike;
Alike reserved to blame, or to commend,
A tim'rous foe, and a suspicious friend;
Dreading ev'n fools, by flatterers besieged,
And so obliging, that he ne'er obliged;
Like Cato, give his little Senate laws,[6]
And sit attentive to his own applause;
While wits and templars° ev'ry sentence raise, *young lawyers*
And wonder with a foolish face of praise—
Who but must laugh, if such a man there be?
Who would not weep, if Atticus were he!
What though my name stood rubric on the walls?
Or plastered posts, with claps in capitals?[7]
Or smoking forth, a hundred hawkers'[8] load,
On wings of winds came flying all abroad?
I sought no homage from the race that write;
I kept, like Asian monarchs, from their sight:
Poems I heeded (now berhymed so long)
No more than thou, great George! a birthday song.[9]
I ne'er with wits or witlings passed my days,
To spread about the itch of verse and praise;
Nor like a puppy, daggled° through the town, *wandered*
To fetch and carry sing-song up and down;
Nor at rehearsals sweat, and mouthed, and cried,
With handkerchief and orange[1] at my side;
But sick of fops, and poetry, and prate,
To Bufo left the whole Castalian state.[2]
Proud, as Apollo on his forked hill,
Sat full-blown Bufo, puffed by every quill;
Fed with soft dedication all day long,
Horace and he went hand in hand in song.[3]
His library (where busts of poets dead
And a true Pindar stood without a head)[4]
Received of wits an undistinguished race,
Who first his judgment asked, and then a place:
Much they extolled his pictures, much his seat,° *estate*
And flattered ev'ry day, and some days eat:
Till grown more frugal in his riper days,
He paid some bards with port, and some with praise,

6. Pope's prologue to Addison's play *Cato* (1713) included a version of this line. Now Pope turns the tables: the noble Roman senator becomes the petty Addison, and the senate, his coffeehouse clique.
7. Red lettering, or rubric, was often used by Lintot, Pope's publisher; "claps" were placards, pasted up around the city by booksellers.
8. Hawking by street criers was another way to publicize new works.
9. The Poet Laureate's official ode to the king.
1. Sold in the theaters for eating or throwing.
2. Poetry is the "Castalian State," named for the spring sacred to the Muses on Parnassus (the "forked hill"); it is left to "Bufo," a patron whose name derives from the Latin for toad, and who was probably George Bubb Dodington (1691–1762).
3. Dodington, a patron of literature, had been accorded the place of Maecenas, patron of Virgil and Horace, in a recent translation from Horace's *Odes*.
4. In *Peri Bathous* (1728), Pope ridiculed those antiquaries who exhibited headless statues, claiming they were busts of great poets.

To some a dry rehearsal was assigned,
And others (harder still) he paid in kind.[5]
Dryden alone (what wonder?) came not nigh,
Dryden alone escaped this judging eye:
But still the great have kindness in reserve,
He helped to bury whom he helped to starve.[6]
May some choice patron bless each gray goose quill!
May ev'ry Bavius have his Bufo still!
So when a statesman wants a day's defense,
Or envy holds a whole week's war with sense,
Or simple pride for flatt'ry makes demands,
May dunce by dunce be whistled off my hands!
Blessed be the great! for those they take away,
And those they left me; for they left me Gay;[7]
Left me to see neglected genius bloom,
Neglected die, and tell it on his tomb:
Of all thy blameless life the sole return
My verse, and Queensb'ry[8] weeping o'er thy urn!
Oh let me live my own, and die so too!
("To live and die is all I have to do")[9]
Maintain a poet's dignity and ease,
And see what friends, and read what books I please:
Above a patron, though I condescend
Sometimes to call a minister my friend.
I was not born for courts or great affairs;
I pay my debts, believe, and say my pray'rs;
Can sleep without a poem in my head,
Nor know, if Dennis be alive or dead.
Why am I asked what next shall see the light?
Heav'ns! was I born for nothing but to write?
Has life no joys for me? or (to be grave)
Have I no friend to serve, no soul to save?
"I found him close with Swift"—"Indeed? no doubt"
(Cries prating Balbus[1]) "something will come out."
'Tis all in vain, deny it as I will.
"No, such a genius never can lie still"
And then for mine obligingly mistakes
The first lampoon Sir Will or Bubo[2] makes.
Poor guiltless I! and can I choose but smile,
When ev'ry coxcomb knows me by my *style*?
Cursed be the verse, how well so'er it flow,
That tends to make one worthy man my foe,
Give virtue scandal, innocence a fear,

5. I.e., he read or gave them his own poetry.
6. Mr. Dryden, after having lived in exigencies, had a magnificent funeral bestowed upon him by the contributions of several persons of quality [Pope's note].
7. John Gay, poet, playwright, and friend of Pope; it was apparently his failure to win patronage that prompted him to write *The Beggar's Opera* (1728).
8. The Duke and Duchess of Queensberry were Gay's patrons.
9. Slightly adapted from *Of Prudence* (1668) by Sir John Denham.
1. A Roman lawyer.
2. Sir William Yonge (d. 1755) and Dodington.

Or from the soft-eyed virgin steal a tear!
But he who hurts a harmless neighbor's peace,
Insults fall'n worth, or beauty in distress,
Who loves a lie, lame slander helps about,
Who writes a libel, or who copies out:
That fop, whose pride affects a patron's name,
Yet absent, wounds an author's honest fame:
Who can your merits selfishly approve,
And show the sense of it without the love;
Who has the vanity to call you friend,
Yet wants the honor injured to defend![3]
Who tells whate'er you think, whate'er you say,
And if he lie not must at least betray:
Who to the Dean, and silver bell can swear,
And sees at Cannons what was never there;[4]
Who reads but with a lust to misapply,
Make satire a lampoon, and fiction lie.
A lash like mine no honest man shall dread,
But all such babbling blockheads in his stead.
Let Sporus[5] tremble—"What? that thing of silk,
Sporus, that mere white curd of ass's mik?
Satire or sense alas! can Sporus feel?
Who breaks a butterfly upon a wheel?"[6]
Yet let me flap this bug with gilded wings,
This painted child of dirt, that stinks and stings,
Whose buzz the witty and the fair annoys,
Yet wit ne'er tastes, and beauty ne'er enjoys:
So well-bred spaniels civilly delight
In mumbling of the game they dare not bite.
Eternal smiles his emptiness betray,
As shallow streams run dimpling all the way.
Whether in florid impotence he speaks,
And, as the prompter breathes, the puppet squeaks,
Or at the ear of Eve,[7] familiar toad,
Half froth, half venom, spits himself abroad.
In puns, or politicks, or tales, or lies,
Or spite, or smut, or rhymes, or blasphemies.
His wit all see-saw, between *that* and *this*,
Now high, now low, now master up, now miss,
And he himself one vile antithesis.
Amphibious thing! that acting either part,
The trifling head, or the corrupted heart,
Fop at the toilet,[8] flatt'rer at the board,° *dining table*

3. I.e., lacks the honor to defend you when you are injured.
4. I.e., who misapplies satirical references in Pope's *Epistle to Burlington*. Pope was upset by the willful misreading of "Timon's villa" in the poem as Cannons, estate of the Duke of Chandos.
5. A boy, Nero's favorite sexual partner; here, Lord Hervey, confidant of Queen Caroline.
6. The rack, an instrument of torture.
7. In the fourth book of Milton [i.e., *Paradise Lost*, IV. 800] the devil is represented in this posture [Pope's note]. "Eve" is Queen Caroline, with whom Hervey is both familiar and a familiar (a witch's pet).
8. Dressing table.

Now trips a lady, and now struts a lord.
Eve's tempter thus the rabbins° have expressed, *Jewish scholars*
A cherub's face, a reptile all the rest,
Beauty that shocks you, parts that none will trust,
Wit that can creep, and pride that licks the dust.
Not fortune's worshipper, nor fashion's fool,
Not lucre's madman, nor ambition's tool,
Not proud, nor servile; be one poet's praise,
That, if he pleased, he pleased by manly ways;
That flatt'ry, ev'n to kings, he held a shame,
And thought a lie in verse or prose the same.
That not in fancy's maze he wandered long,
But stooped° to truth, and moralized his song: *pounced upon*
That not for fame, but virtue's better end,
He stood° the furious foe, the timid friend, *withstood*
The damning critic, half approving wit,
The coxcomb hit, or fearing to be hit;
Laughed at the loss of friends he never had,
The dull, the proud, the wicked, and the mad;
The distant threats of vengeance on his head,
The blow unfelt, the tear he never shed;[9]
The tale revived, the lie so oft o'erthrown,
Th' imputed trash, and dullness not his own;
The morals blackened when the writings scape,
The libeled person, and the pictured shape;[1]
Abuse, on all he loved, or loved him, spread,
A friend in exile, or a father, dead;
The whisper, that to greatness still too near,
Perhaps, yet vibrates on his sovereign's ear—
Welcome for thee, fair virtue! all the past:
For thee, fair virtue! welcome ev'n the last!
"But why insult the poor, affront the great?"
A knave's a knave, to me, in ev'ry state:
Alike my scorn, if he succeed or fail,
Sporus at court, or Japhet[2] in a jail,
A hireling scribbler, or a hireling peer,
Knight of the post[3] corrupt, or of the shire;
If on a pillory, or near a throne,
He gain his prince's ear, or lose his own.
Yet soft by nature, more a dupe than wit,
Sappho[4] can tell you how this man was bit:° *deceived*
This dreaded sat'rist Dennis will confess
Foe to his pride, but friend to his distress:[5]

9. A *Pop upon Pope* (1728) attempted to humiliate Pope by pretending he had been whipped.
1. Pope was frequently vilified in print by his enemies; his deformity and Roman Catholicism were often mocked—he was even caricatured as a hunchbacked ape wearing the papal crown.
2. Japhet Crook, a forger.
3. A person who supported himself by giving false evidence.
4. Lady Mary Wortley Montagu hurt Pope, who had been very close to her, by switching loyalties to Hervey.
5. In Dennis's old age, Pope had publicly supported his work.

So humble, he has knocked at Tibald's door,
Has drunk with Cibber, nay has rhymed for Moore.[6]
Full ten years slandered, did he once reply?
Three thousand suns went down on Welsted's lie.[7]
To please a mistress one aspersed his life;
He lashed him not, but let her be his wife:
Let Budgell[8] charge low Grub Street on his quill,
And write whate'er he pleased, except his will;
Let the two Curlls,[9] of Town and Court, abuse
His father, mother, body, soul, and Muse.
Yet why? that father held it for a rule,
It was a sin to call our neighbor fool:
That harmless mother thought no wife a whore:
Hear this, and spare his family, James Moore!
Unspotted names! and memorable long,
If there be force in virtue, or in song.
Of gentle blood (part shed in honor's cause,
While yet in Britain honor had applause)
Each parent sprung—"What fortune, pray?"—Their own,
And better got, than Bestia's[1] from the throne.
Born to no pride, inheriting no strife,
Nor marrying discord in a noble wife,
Stranger to civil and religious rage,
The good man walked innoxious through his age.
No courts he saw, no suits would ever try,
Nor dared an oath,[2] nor hazarded a lie.
Unlearned, he knew no schoolman's subtle art,
No language, but the language of the heart.
By nature honest, by experience wise,
Healthy by temp'rance, and by exercise;
His life, though long, to sickness passed unknown,
His death was instant, and without a groan.
O grant me thus to live, and thus to die!
Who spring from kings shall know less joy than I.
O Friend!° may each domestic bliss be thine! *Arbuthnot*
Be no unpleasing melancholy mine:
Me, let the tender office long engage,
To rock the cradle of reposing age,
With lenient arts extend a mother's breath,[3]
Make languor smile, and smooth the bed of death,

6. Or rather, James Moore-Smythe plagiarized from him.
7. Leonard Welsted (1688–1747) had sharply criticized Pope's works and character, and accused him of having "occasioned a lady's death" [Pope's note].
8. Eustace Budgell (1686–1737), a writer who blamed Pope for an accusation, published in the *Grub-Street Journal*, that Budgell had forged the will of Dr. Matthew Tindal to make himself inheritor.
9. Pope both derides the London publisher Edmund Curll, and deploys his name as a derogatory epithet for the courtier Hervey. Curll is attacked also in *The Dunciad* and in Swift's *Verses on the Death of Dr. Swift*.
1. A Roman consul who accepted bribes for peace, suggesting the Duke of Marlborough's rewards from Queen Anne.
2. Pope's father refused to take oaths against the Pope, which would have helped him avoid anti-Catholic measures.
3. Pope's mother died two years before the poem was published, but he retained these lines, written in 1731.

Explore the thought, explain the asking eye,
And keep a while one parent from the sky!
On cares like these if length of days attend,
May Heav'n, to bless those days, preserve my friend,
Preserve him social, cheerful, and serene,
And just as rich as when he served a Queen![4]
Whether that blessing be denied or giv'n,
Thus far was right, the rest belongs to Heav'n.

1731–34 1735

AN EPISTLE TO A LADY: OF THE CHARACTERS OF WOMEN For years Pope planned to write a magnum opus, a "system of ethics in the Horatian way." Though this ambitious project was never completed, some of its parts were written, including a set of four verse letters that were intended to conclude the work. Pope himself called the poems *Epistles to Several Persons;* a later editor dubbed them *Moral Essays*. Each work is a familiar letter addressed to someone Pope knew well and admired. *Epistle to a Lady,* the last written of the poems but second in the published sequence, is addressed (without ever explicitly identifying her) to Martha Blount (1690–1783), with whom Pope sustained a friendship so abiding and intense that contemporary gossips construed the pair as lovers and even secret spouses. About the depth of the relationship (though not the circumstances) rumor was right; nearing death, Pope bought Blount a house and bequeathed to her the use of his estate for the remainder of her life. In his verse epistle, he treats her first as muse and finally as paragon. But in between, he mocks "most women" in a gallery of portraiture marked by scorn, misogyny, and a recurrent, oddly angled empathy. "Contrarieties" is the key term in Pope's own footnote-explication of this poem; its application extends across his *oeuvre*. Alongside *The Rape of the Lock, Eloisa to Abelard,* and Pope's many shorter poems on women, *Epistle to a Lady* forms part of one of the most complex constellations in eighteenth-century poetry: luminous and laden with contradiction; by turns bounteous and belittling, baleful and brilliant.

Epistle 2. To a Lady: Of the Characters of Women[1]

Nothing so true as what you once let fall,
"Most women have no characters at all."
Matter too soft a lasting mark to bear,
And best distinguished by black, brown, or fair.
    How many pictures of one nymph we view,
All how unlike each other, all how true!
Arcadia's Countess, here, in ermined pride,
Is there Pastora by a fountain side.[2]
Here Fannia,[3] leering on her own good man,

4. Arbuthnot had been physician to Queen Anne.

1. The present text is modernized from the 1744 edition of the *Epistles,* which was based on a revision Pope prepared during the last months of his life, in which he included three "characters"—Atossa, Chloe, and Philomedé—omitted from earlier print versions of the poem.

2. Throughout the poem, Pope invokes names of women from history, myth, and legend, deploying them as types or templates of the modern women he undertakes to describe and deride. Here he alludes in part to Sir Philip Sidney's romance *The Countess of Pembroke's Arcadia* (1590), named for Sidney's elegant ("ermined") sister, and in part to a later countess who posed for pastoral portraits.

3. An ancient Roman adulteress.

And there, a naked Leda with a swan.[4]
Let then the fair one beautifully cry,
In Magdalene's loose hair and lifted eye,[5]
Or dressed in smiles of sweet Cecilia[6] shine,
With simp'ring angels, psalms, and harps divine.
Whether the charmer sinner it, or saint it,
If folly grows romantic,° I must paint it. *extravagant*
Come then, the colors and the ground prepare!
Dip in the rainbow, trick her off in air,[7]
Choose a firm cloud, before it fall, and in it,
Catch, ere she change, the Cynthia[8] of this minute.[9]
Rufa,[1] whose eye quick-glancing o'er the park,
Attracts each light gay meteor of a spark,[2]
Agrees as ill with Rufa studying Locke,[3]
As Sappho's[4] diamonds with her dirty smock,
Or Sappho at her toilet's greasy task,
With Sappho fragrant in an evening mask:
So morning insects that in muck begun,
Shine, buzz, and fly-blow° in the setting sun. *infect*
How soft is Silia![5] fearful to offend,
The frail one's advocate, the weak one's friend.
To her Calista proved her conduct nice,° *refined*
And good Simplicius asks of her advice.
Sudden, she storms! she raves! You tip the wink,
But spare your censure; Silia does not drink.
All eyes may see from what the change arose,
All eyes may see—a pimple on her nose.
Papillia,[6] wedded to her am'rous spark,
Sighs for the shades: "How charming is a park!"
A park is purchased, but the fair he sees
All bathed in tears: "Oh odious, odious trees!"
Ladies like variegated tulips show;
'Tis to their changes half their charms we owe.
Their happy spots the nice admirer take,
Fine by defect, and delicately weak.
'Twas thus Calypso[7] once each heart alarmed,[8]

4. In Greek myth, Zeus, taking the form of a swan, rapes Leda; Pope here depicts the woman as wanton and complicit.
5. Mary Magdalene is the repentant prostitute who followed Christ; she is traditionally identified with the nameless woman in the New Testament who "washed [Christ's] feet with [her] tears, and did wipe them" with her hair (Luke 7.38).
6. Patron saint of religious music.
7. Pope addresses the couplet as though to a portrait-painter: prepare the first layer of paint on the canvas (the "ground"); dip the brush; portray the subject.
8. Goddess of the moon in all its shifting phases.
9. In a note at this point, Pope summarizes the poem's main purpose as providing "instances of contrarieties, given even from such characters as are most strongly marked and seemingly therefore most consistent." He begins, in the next lines (21–28), with the contradictions displayed by "the *Affected*."
1. "Red-haired" (Latin): a trait the 18th century linked with lustfulness.
2. "A lively, showy . . . man" (Johnson's *Dictionary*).
3. John Locke (1632–1704), author of *An Essay Concerning Human Understanding* (1692).
4. Pope alludes partly to the ancient Greek poet of lesbian love, and partly to his former friend Lady Mary Wortley Montagu (see pages 2543–54), who remarked in a letter that readers "generally suppose Pope means me, whenever he mentions that name."
5. "Contrarieties in the *Soft-natured*" (Pope's note, summarizing lines 29–40).
6. "Butterfly" (Latin).
7. The nymph who held Odysseus in thrall, a prisoner on her island, for seven years.
8. "Contrarieties in the *Cunning* and the *Artful*" (Pope's note, summarizing lines 45–52).

Awed without virtue, without beauty charmed;
Her tongue bewitched as oddly as her eyes;
Less wit than mimic, more a wit than wise.
Strange graces still, and stranger flights she had,
Was just not ugly, and was just not mad;
Yet ne'er so sure our passion to create,
As when she touched the brink of all we hate.
  Narcissa's[9] nature, tolerably mild,
To make a wash° would hardly stew a child, *liquid makeup*
Has ev'n been proved to grant a lover's prayer,
And paid a tradesman once to make him stare,
Gave alms at Easter, in a Christian trim,° *fashion*
And made a widow happy, for a whim.
Why then declare good nature is her scorn,
When 'tis by that alone she can be borne?
Why pique all mortals, yet affect a name?
A fool to pleasure, yet a slave to fame:
Now deep in Taylor and the Book of Martyrs,[1]
Now drinking citron° with his Grace and Chartres.[2] *lemon-flavored brandy*
Now conscience chills her, and now passion burns;
And atheism and religion take their turns;
A very heathen in the carnal part,
Yet still a sad, good Christian at her heart.
  See sin in state, majestically drunk,
Proud as a peeress, prouder as a punk;° *prostitute*
Chaste to her husband, free to all beside,
A teeming mistress, but a barren bride.
What then? Let blood and body bear the fault,
Her head's untouched, that noble seat of thought;
Such this day's doctrine—in another fit
She sins with poets through pure love of wit.
What has not fired her bosom or her brain?
Caesar and Tall-boy, Charles and Charlemagne.[3]
As Helluo,[4] late dictator of the feast,
The nose of hautgout,[5] and the tip° of taste, *paragon*
Criticked your wine, and analyzed your meat,
Yet on plain pudding deigned at home to eat;
So Philomedé,[6] lect'ring all mankind
On the soft passion, and the taste refined,
Th' address, the delicacy—stoops at once,
And makes her hearty meal upon a dunce.

9. "[Contrarieties] in the *Whimsical*" (Pope's note, summarizing lines 53–68). Narcissa is named for Narcissus, who in Greek myth looked on smooth water, fell in love with the reflection of his own face, and dwindled to nothing under a spell of self-regard.

1. Books of piety: Jeremy Taylor's *Holy Living* (1650) and *Holy Dying* (1651); John Foxe's *Acts and Monuments* (1563), known as *Foxe's Book of Martyrs* because it chronicled the sufferings of English protestants oppressed and executed under Catholic rule.

2. Rakes of notoriety: Philip, Duke of Wharton, and Francis Charteris.

3. The line mingles high and low: the emperors Caesar and Charlemagne; "Tall-boy," the foolish lover from a popular stage comedy, and "Charles," the name applied generically to footmen (as "Betty" was to maids).

4. "Glutton" (Latin).

5. I.e., the savorer (or sniffer-out) of strong flavors.

6. "Laughter-loving" (Greek); Homer's epithet for Aphrodite, goddess of love.

Flavia's a wit,[7] has too much sense to pray,
To toast our wants and wishes is her way;
Nor asks of God, but of her stars to give
The mighty blessing, "while we live, to live."
Then all for death, that opiate of the soul!
Lucretia's dagger, Rosamonda's bowl.[8]
Say, what can cause such impotence of mind?
A spark too fickle, or a spouse too kind.
Wise wretch! With pleasures too refined to please,
With too much spirit to be e'er at ease,
With too much quickness ever to be taught,
With too much thinking to have common thought:
You purchase pain with all that joy can give,
And die of nothing but a rage to live.
Turn then from wits, and look on Simo's mate,[9]
No ass so meek, no ass so obstinate;
Or her, that owns her faults, but never mends,
Because she's honest, and the best of friends;
Or her, whose life the church and scandal share,
Forever in a passion, or a prayer;
Or her, who laughs at hell, but (like her Grace)
Cries, "Ah! How charming, if there's no such place!"
Or who in sweet vicissitude appears
Of mirth and opium, ratafie° and tears, *cherry brandy*
The daily anodyne, and nightly draught,
To kill those foes to fair ones, time and thought.
Woman and fool are two hard things to hit,
For true no-meaning puzzles more than wit.
But what are these to great Atossa's mind?[1]
Scarce once herself, by turns all womankind!
Who, with herself, or others, from her birth
Finds all her life one warfare upon earth;
Shines, in exposing knaves, and painting fools,
Yet is whate'er she hates and ridicules.
No thought advances, but her eddy brain
Whisks it about, and down it goes again.
Full sixty years the world has been her trade,
The wisest fool much time has ever made.
From loveless youth to unrespected age,
No passion gratified except her rage.
So much the Fury still outran the wit,
The pleasure missed her, and the scandal hit.
Who breaks with her provokes revenge from hell,
But he's a bolder man who dares be well;

7. "[Contrarieties] in the *Witty* and *Refined*" (Pope's note, summarizing lines 87–100).
8. The Roman wife Lucretia killed herself after suffering rape; according to legend, Rosamunda Clifford, mistress to Henry II, was forced by his wife to drink poison.
9. In *Andria*, an ancient Roman comedy, Simo is a meddling old man.
1. Atossa was the daughter of Cyrus the Great, king of Persia. Under her name, Pope here portrays the volatile Katherine, Duchess of Buckinghamshire, illegitimate daughter of James II. She and Pope sustained an agitated, on-and-off friendship; he omitted this portrait from early editions of the poem, and included it only after her death.

Her every turn with violence pursued,
Nor more a storm her hate than gratitude.
To that each passion turns, or soon or late;
Love, if it makes her yield, must make her hate;
Superiors? death! And equals? what a curse!
But an inferior not dependent? worse.
Offend her, and she knows not to forgive;
Oblige her, and she'll hate you while you live;
But die, and she'll adore you—then the bust
And temple rise—then fall again to dust.
Last night, her lord was all that's good and great,
A knave this morning, and his will a cheat.
Strange! By the means defeated of the ends,
By spirit robbed of power, by warmth of friends,
By wealth of followers! without one distress
Sick of herself through very selfishness!
Atossa, cursed with every granted prayer,
Childless with all her children, wants an heir.
To heirs unknown descends th' unguarded store
Or wanders, Heav'n-directed, to the poor.
  Pictures like these, dear madam, to design,
Asks no firm hand, and no unerring line;
Some wandering touches, some reflected light,
Some flying stroke alone can hit 'em right:
For how should equal colors do the knack?
Chameleons who can paint in white and black?
  "Yet Chloe sure was formed without a spot—"
Nature in her then erred not, but forgot.
"With every pleasing, every prudent part,
Say, what can Chloe want?"—She wants a heart.
She speaks, behaves, and acts just as she ought;
But never, never, reached one gen'rous thought.
Virtue she finds too painful an endeavor,
Content to dwell in decencies forever.
So very reasonable, so unmoved,
As never yet to love, or to be loved.
She, while her lover pants upon her breast,
Can mark° the figures on an Indian chest; *notice*
And when she sees her friend in deep despair,
Observes how much a chintz exceeds mohair.[2]
Forbid it Heav'n, a favor or a debt
She e'er should cancel—but she may forget.
Safe is your secret still in Chloe's ear;
But none of Chloe's shall you ever hear.
Of all her dears she never slandered one,
But cares not if a thousand are undone.
Would Chloe know if you're alive or dead?
She bids her footman put it in her head.

2. Chloe contrasts two fabrics: chintz, a brightly colored cotton; and mohair, woven either from goat's wool, or from silk.

Chloe is prudent—would you too be wise?
Then never break your heart when Chloe dies.
    One certain portrait may (I grant) be seen,
Which Heav'n has varnished out, and made a Queen:[3]
The same forever! and described by all
With truth and goodness, as with crown and ball.
Poets heap virtues, painters gems at will,
And show their zeal, and hide their want of skill.
'Tis well—but, artists! who can paint or write,
To draw the naked is your true delight.
That robe of quality so struts and swells,
None see what parts or nature it conceals.
Th' exactest traits of body or of mind
We owe to models of an humble kind.
If Queensbury[4] to strip there's no compelling,
'Tis from a handmaid we must take a Helen.[5]
From peer and bishop 'tis no easy thing
To draw the man who loves his God, or king.
Alas! I copy (or my draught would fail)
From honest Mah'met,[6] or plain Parson Hale.[7]
    But grant, in public men sometimes are shown,
A woman's seen in private life alone.
Our bolder talents in full light displayed,
Your virtues open fairest in the shade.
Bred to disguise, in public 'tis you hide;
There, none distinguish 'twixt your shame or pride,
Weakness or delicacy; all so nice,
That each may seem a virtue, or a vice.[8]
    In men, we various ruling passions find,
In women, two almost divide the kind;
Those, only fixed, they first or last obey:
The love of pleasure, and the love of sway.
    That,[9] Nature gives; and where the lesson taught
Is but to please, can pleasure seem a fault?
Experience, this;[1] by man's oppression cursed,
They seek the second not to lose the first.
    Men, some to business, some to pleasure take,
But ev'ry woman is at heart a rake:
Men, some to quiet, some to public strife;
But ev'ry lady would be queen for life.
    Yet mark the fate of a whole sex of queens!
Pow'r all their end, but beauty all the means.
In youth they conquer, with so wild a rage,

3. Queen Caroline (1683–1737), who secured Pope's enmity by her unstinting support of Robert Walpole.
4. Catherine Hyde, Duchess of Queensberry (1700–1777), one of the century's most celebrated beauties.
5. Helen of Troy, the mythical beauty whose adultery brought about the Trojan War.
6. A Turkish servant to George I.
7. Dr. Stephen Hales (1677–1761), scientist, inventor, and curate; Pope's trusted friend, and a witness to his will.
8. In a note, Pope introduces the poem's next section this way: "The former part having shown that the *particular characters* of women are more various than those of men, it is nevertheless observed, that the *general* characteristic of the sex, as to the *ruling passion*, is more uniform."
9. I.e., love of pleasure.
1. I.e., love of power ("sway").

As leaves them scarce a subject in their age.
For foreign glory, foreign joy, they roam;
No thought of peace and happiness at home.
But wisdom's triumph is well-timed retreat,
As hard a science to the fair as great!
Beauties, like tyrants, old and friendless grown,
Yet hate repose, and dread to be alone,
Worn out in public, weary ev'ry eye,
Nor leave one sigh behind them when they die.
Pleasures the sex, as children birds, pursue,
Still out of reach, yet never out of view;
Sure, if they catch, to spoil the toy at most,
To covet flying, and regret when lost.
At last, to follies youth could scarce defend,
It grows their age's prudence to pretend;
Ashamed to own° they gave delight before, *admit*
Reduced to feign it, when they give no more:
As hags° hold sabbaths, less for joy than spite, *witches*
So these their merry, miserable night;
Still round and round the ghosts of beauty glide,
And haunt the places where their honor died.
See how the world its veterans rewards!
A youth of frolics, an old age of cards,
Fair to no purpose, artful to no end,
Young without lovers, old without a friend,
A fop their passion, but their prize a sot,
Alive, ridiculous, and dead, forgot!
Ah! Friend! To dazzle let the vain design,
To raise the thought, and touch the heart, be thine!
That charm shall grow, while what fatigues the Ring[2]
Flaunts and goes down, an unregarded thing.
So when the sun's broad beam has tired the sight,
All mild ascends the moon's more sober light;
Serene in virgin modesty she shines,
And unobserved the glaring orb declines.
Oh! blessed with temper, whose unclouded ray
Can make tomorrow cheerful as today;
She, who can love a sister's charms, or hear
Sighs for a daughter[3] with unwounded ear;
She, who ne'er answers till a husband cools,
Or, if she rules him, never shows the rules;
Charms by accepting, by submitting sways,
Yet has her humor most, when she obeys;
Let fops or fortune fly which way they will;
Disdains all loss of tickets,° or codille;[4] *lottery tickets*

2. Members of London high society, who enjoyed displaying themselves and their elegant carriages on a circular road called the Ring, located in fashionable Hyde Park.
3. In earlier editions the noun was "sister." Martha Blount's sister Teresa was regarded as the more attractive of the two; Pope, who may at one point have fallen in love with her, changed the word to suppress speculation about his own opinion and desires.
4. A term in the fashionable card game Ombre, played triumphantly by Belinda in *Rape of the Lock* (3.19–100).

Spleen, vapors, or smallpox, above them all,
And mistress of herself, though China fall.[5]
And yet, believe me, good as well as ill,
Woman's at best a contradiction still.[6]
Heav'n, when it strives to polish all it can
Its last best work,[7] but forms a softer man;
Picks from each sex, to make the fav'rite blessed,
Your love of pleasure, our desire of rest,
Blends, in exception to all gen'ral rules,
Your taste of follies, without scorn of fools,
Reserve with frankness, art with truth allied,
Courage with softness, modesty with pride,
Fixed principles, with fancy ever new;
Shakes all together, and produces—you.
Be this a woman's fame: with this unblessed,
Toasts[8] live a scorn, and queens may die a jest.
This Phoebus[9] promised (I forget the year)
When those blue eyes first opened on the sphere;
Ascendant Phoebus watched that hour with care,
Averted half your parents' simple prayer,
And gave you beauty, but denied the pelf[1]
That buys your sex a tyrant o'er itself.
The gen'rous god, who wit and gold refines,
And ripens spirits as he ripens mines,
Kept dross for duchesses, the world shall know it,
To give you sense, good humor, and a poet.

1733–1735 1735; 1740

RESPONSE
Mary Leapor: An Essay on Woman[1]

WOMAN—a pleasing but a short-lived flow'r,
Too soft for business and too weak for pow'r:[2]
A wife in bondage, or neglected maid;
Despised, if ugly; if she's fair, betrayed.
'Tis wealth alone inspires ev'ry grace,
And calls the raptures to her plenteous face.

5. More echoes of the *Rape*: the Cave of Spleen in Canto 4 (*spleen* and *vapors* both denote depression); the frailty of China (vases) at 3.157–60.
6. In a note, Pope introduces the poem's closing section this way: "The picture of an estimable woman, with the best kinds of contrarieties."
7. As Eve was the final being created in Eden.
8. Women celebrated for their beauty, hence widely "toasted" by drinking admirers.
9. Apollo, Greek god of the sun (hence linked here with the dawn of life), prophesy, and poetry.
1. Wealth (here, the dowry that would "buy" a husband).
1. During her short, surprising life, Mary Leapor labored as a kitchen maid, wrote poetry for pleasure, and read Pope assiduously, absorbing his methods, reworking his tones and topics, and responding to his thought throughout her own varied output. In *An Essay on Woman*, Leapor pointedly reverses the gendered title of Pope's ambitious *Essay on Man*, and takes it as rubric for her own rumination on his arguments in *An Epistle to a Lady*. Where Pope finds fault with "the characters of women," Leapor focuses instead on the misperceptions of them, by men who (seeking wealth, seeking marriage) at once subordinate and undervalue them, and by those women who themselves misguidedly collude in such debilitating constructs. Assaying these dark matters, Leapor strikes a characteristic balance between precariousness and playfulness, acerbity and sorrow. For more of Leapor's poetry, see pages 2192–201.
2. Compare Pope's *Epistle to a Lady*, lines 1–4.

What numbers for those charming features pine,
If blooming acres round her temples twine?[3]
Her lip the strawberry, and her eyes more bright
Than sparkling Venus in a frosty night.
Pale lilies fade and, when the fair appears,
Snow turns a negro[4] and dissolves in tears.
And where the charmer treads her magic toe,
On English ground Arabian odors grow;
Till mighty Hymen° lifts his sceptred rod, *god of marriage*
And sinks her glories with a fatal nod,
Dissolves her triumphs, sweeps her charms away,
And turns the goddess to her native clay.

But, Artemisia,[5] let your servant sing
What small advantage wealth and beauties bring.
Who would be wise, that knew Pamphilia's fate?[6]
Or who be fair, and joined to Sylvia's mate?
Sylvia, whose cheeks are fresh as early day,
As evening mild, and sweet as spicy May:
And yet that face her partial husband tires,
And those bright eyes, that all the world admires.
Pamphilia's wit who does not strive to shun,
Like death's infection or a dog-day's sun?
The damsels view her with malignant eyes:
The men are vexed to find a nymph so wise:
And wisdom only serves to make her know
The keen sensation of superior woe.
The secret whisper and the list'ning ear,
The scornful eyebrow and the hated sneer,
The giddy censures of her babbling kind,
With thousand ills that grate a gentle mind,
By her are tasted in the first degree,
Though overlooked by Simplicus and me.[7]
Does thirst of gold a virgin's heart inspire,
Instilled by Nature or a careful sire?
Then let her quit extravagance and play,
The brisk companion and expensive tea,
To feast with Cordia in her filthy sty
On stewed potatoes or on mouldy pie;[8]

3. I.e., if her dowry includes valuable land.

4. I.e., seems black by comparison.

5. The name of an ancient ruler celebrated as a patron of literature; Leapor applies it to her friend and patron Bridget Freemantle.

6. The lines about Pamphilia suggest that she may serve here as Leapor's alter ego (the historical Pamphilia was an ancient woman author). But in a letter Leapor wrote to Bridget Freemantle about the poem, replying to what she deemed her patron's "agreeable raillery [i.e., teasing]," Leapor protested that "notwithstanding your compliment, of seeing my picture in Pamphilia, I must affirm it is not so." The other pastoral names (Sylvia, Simplicus, etc.) conjure up acquaintances real or imaginary.

7. Compare the briefly mentioned Simplicius in Pope's *Epistle* (1.32).

8. In her letter about the poem, Leapor elaborates on these grim foodstuffs: "You are not to suppose a woman of [Cordia's] character would admit of two dishes upon her table at once. No: they are separate meals, and the potatoes are not introduced as sauce to the pie."

Whose eager eyes stare ghastly at the poor,
And fright the beggars from her hated door;
In greasy clouts° she wraps her smokey chin, *rags*
And holds that pride's a never-pardoned sin.
  If this be wealth, no matter where it falls;
But save, ye Muses, save your Mira's walls:[9]
Still give me pleasing indolence and ease,
A fire to warm me and a friend to please.
  Since, whether sunk in avarice or pride,
A wanton virgin or a starving bride;
Or° wondering crowds attend her charming tongue, *whether*
Or, deemed an idiot, ever speaks the wrong;
Though Nature armed us for the growing ill
With fraudful cunning and a headstrong will;
Yet, with ten thousand follies to her charge,
Unhappy woman's but a slave at large.

1751

The Dunciad Pope spent strikingly long stretches of his career making and remaking epics: *The Rape of the Lock* (1711–1717); translations of Homer's *Iliad* (1713–1720) and *Odyssey* (1720–1726). Of all such enterprises, his last ran longest. *The Dunciad* absorbed him, on and off, for fifteen years (1728–1743). It centers on a conflict that had mattered to him throughout his working life: the culture wars, transacted with furious conviction on both sides, between the Ancients and the Moderns. The Ancients were readers and writers for whom the classical cultures of Greece and Rome formed the proper foundation for civic virtue, social conduct, and literary greatness. The Moderns were an amalgam of prolific innovators deliberately divorcing themselves from old ways: the practitioners of new techniques in scholarship and the sciences; the pursuers of new profits in commerce and politics; and above all, the denizens of the new print industry known as Grub Street, hack authors who, writing badly, rapidly, and plentifully, threatened (in Pope's view) to glut the world with worthlessness. These are the "dunces" from whom the epic takes its name. In its design, Pope achieved satiric leverage worthy of a catapult: a mock epic (in which the ancient literary model mocks modern literary practice), centered, as the first line promises, on a "Mother, and her son" in whom Pope contrives to encapsulate the imminent end of civilization. The mother is the Goddess Dulness ("stupidity," "sluggishness") who seeks to recover her dominion over mortal minds; her son is the real-life dunce whom she has selected as the avatar best suited to restore her rule; and the entire scheme reenacts, with savage indignation, some of the central stories of god and mortal, parent and child (*Iliad, Aeneid,* Genesis, the New Testament, *Paradise Lost*) in classical and Christian culture. In the epic's first three versions (beginning with *The Dunciad,* 1728), Dulness's choice for chief dunce had been a scholar, Lewis Theobald, whose infuriating (but accurate) critique of Pope's *Shakespeare* had prompted the poet to mock him as a pedant; the satire swelled in the second version (*The Dunciad Variorum,* 1729), which added an enormous, parodic scholarly apparatus of half-deranged prefaces, footnotes, and appendices; and in the third (*The New Dunciad,* 1742), a wholly new poem in which Pope shifted his satiric aim from Grub Street to a wider range of intellectual pursuits (the New Science) and cultural practices (the Grand Tour). In the epic's final incarnation—*The Dunciad in Four Books* (1743), excerpted here—Dulness and Pope select a different

9. "Mira" (derived from "Mary") was Leapor's pen name. Her letter glosses the line: "Now to the Muses: I don't call them to fortify my walls against wealth itself, but against wealth in such a shape as we had then described; and you are to not think, that poets, who love ease and pleasure, and the most gay delights of life, should hate the only means of obtaining it."

dunce: Colley Cibber (1671–1757), actor, playwright, shamelessly self-satisfied autobiographer, and clumsy versifier, whose appointment as Poet Laureate (1730), payback for his loyalty to Robert Walpole and the Whig regime, had outraged Pope and many of his cohort in the wit-rich, power-destitute anti-Walpolean Opposition. Royally rewarded for political pandering and bad writing, Cibber becomes in Pope's portrait the distillation of all duncery, the embodiment and instrument of Dulness's imminent, inexorable victory.

from The Dunciad in Four Books
Book the First

The mighty Mother, and her son[1] who brings
The Smithfield Muses to the ear of kings,[2]
I sing. Say you, her instruments the great!
Called to this work by Dulness, Jove, and Fate;
You by whose care, in vain decried and cursed,
Still Dunce the Second reigns like Dunce the First;[3]
Say how the Goddess bade Britannia sleep,
And poured her spirit o'er the land and deep.[4]
In eldest time, ere mortals writ or read,
Ere Pallas issued from the Thund'rer's head,[5]
Dulness o'er all possessed her ancient right,
Daughter of Chaos and eternal Night:
Fate in their dotage° this fair idiot gave,
Gross as her sire, and as her mother grave,
Laborious, heavy, busy, bold, and blind,
She ruled, in native anarchy, the mind.
Still her old empire to restore she tries,
For, born a Goddess, Dulness never dies.
O thou! Whatever title please thine ear,
Dean, Drapier, Bickerstaff, or Gulliver![6]
Whether thou choose Cervantes' serious air,
Or laugh and shake in Rab'lais' easy chair,[7]
Or praise the court, or magnify mankind,[8]

° *old age*

1. The Goddess Dulness, and Colley Cibber, whose roles in the poem are spelled out in Pope's first footnote: "The reader ought here to be cautioned, that the *Mother*, and not the *Son*, is the principal agent of this poem . . . the main action of the poem being by no means the coronation of the Laureate, which is performed in the very first book, but the restoration of the empire of Dulness in Britain, which is not accomplished till the last."
2. Smithfield was London's major meat market, and the site also of (as Pope's note puts it) crowd-pleasing "shows . . . and dramatical entertainments, formerly agreeable only to the taste of the rabble, [which] were by the Hero of this poem and others of equal genius" exported to the upscale theaters of the West End, to become "the reigning pleasures of the court and town. This happened in the reigns of King George I, and II."
3. I.e., one mediocre Poet Laureate (Cibber) succeeds another: Laurence Eusden (1688–1730). The line launches the poem's pervasive motif of royal succession as the means by which Dulness hopes to secure eternal dominion over Britain.
4. The line echoes, as will many that follow, both the biblical and the Miltonic accounts of Creation: "and darkness was on the face of the deep. And the Spirit of God moved upon the face of the waters" (Genesis 1.2).
5. In Greek mythology, Pallas Athena, goddess of wisdom (and hence, throughout the *Dunciad*, Dulness's contrasting counterpart) leapt forth fully formed from the head of her father Zeus, thunder-bearer and ruler of the gods.
6. All alternate labels for Pope's cherished friend Jonathan Swift, to whom the *Dunciad* is dedicated; he was Dean of St. Paul's, and wrote satire under many "titles," assuming the guise of a cloth-dealer (*The Drapier's Letters*, 1724), an astrologer (the Bickerstaff papers, 1708), and a mariner (*Gulliver's Travels*, 1726).
7. Miguel de Cervantes's *Don Quixote* (1605–1615) and Francois Rabelais's *Gargantua and Pantagruel* (1532–1552) were perhaps the preeminent precedents for Swift's own satire.
8. As Swift does in his portrayal of Brobdingnag, his fictive country of giants, in Book 2 of *Gulliver's Travels*.

Or thy grieved country's[9] copper chains unbind;
From thy Boeotia though her pow'r retires,
Mourn not, my Swift, at ought our realm acquires,[1]
Here pleased behold her mighty wings outspread
To hatch a new Saturnian age of lead.[2]
  Close to those walls where Folly holds her throne,
And laughs to think Monroe would take her down,[3]
Where o'er the gates, by his famed by father's hand
Great Cibber's brazen, brainless brothers stand;[4]
One cell there is, concealed from vulgar eye,
The Cave of Poverty and Poetry.[5]
Keen, hollow winds howl through the bleak recess,
Emblem of music caused by emptiness.
Hence bards, like Proteus long in vain tied down,
Escape in monsters, and amaze the town.[6]
Hence miscellanies spring, the weekly boast
Of Curll's[7] chaste press, and Lintot's rubric post:[8]
Hence hymning Tyburn's elegiac lines,[9]
Hence *Journals*, *Medleys*, *Merc'ries*, *Magazines*:[1]
Sepulchral lies, our holy walls to grace,[2]
And New Year Odes,[3] and all the Grub Street race.

9. I.e., Ireland; in *The Drapier's Letters*, Swift waged successful satiric combat against a profit-driven British scheme to establish a potentially ruinous currency of copper coinage in Ireland.

1. Because Dulness rules so thoroughly over England ("our realm"), Pope teasingly infers that she must have entirely withdrawn her "pow'r" from Swift's Ireland; Boeotia, in ancient Greece, was reputedly a province full of fools.

2. Milton, in his account of Creation, addresses the Holy Spirit who "with mighty wings outspread / Dove-like sat'st brooding on the vast abyss / And mad'st it pregnant" (*Paradise Lost* 1.20–22). The god Saturn, in Roman mythology, ruled over a glorious Age of Gold, but his name (as Pope points out in a footnote) became associated by alchemists with the far less luminous substance lead—which will serve as one of Dulness's emblems throughout the poem.

3. I.e, the walls of Bethlehem ("Bedlam"), London's lunatic asylum, whose chief physician James Monro strives to end the reign of Folly (madness) over his patients' minds.

4. The sculptor Caius Cibber (1630–1700), Colley's father, created the paired statues of Melancholy and Raving Madness that stood on either side of Bedlam's gates.

5. The line ushers in Pope's mythic refiguring of Grub Street, a London neighborhood overflowing with impoverished and (by Pope's reckoning) mediocre writers. It was located near Bedlam, and Pope's note makes a point of that proximity: "there cannot be a plainer indication of madness than in men's persisting to starve themselves and offend the public by scribbling . . . when they might have benefited themselves and others in profitable and honest employments. The qualities and productions of [Grub Street's inhabitants] are afterwards described in this first book."

6. The mythic Proteus could transform himself into many shapes (boar, snake, bull, fire) in order to elude capture. A footnote elaborates the comparison: "by Proteus must certainly be meant a hackneyed town scribbler; and by his transformations, the various disguises such a one assumes, to elude the pursuit of his irreconcilable enemy, the bailiff" [i.e., the officer in charge of arrests for debt and other crimes]. In the short list that follows (lines 38–44), Pope enumerates the "monsters"—new modes of cheap, popular publication—into which the Grub-Street Proteuses rapidly and repeatedly transform themselves in hopes of making money.

7. The bookseller Edmund Curll (d. 1747) published many *un*chaste pieces of prose and verse, as well as several attacks on Pope.

8. Bernard Lintot (1675–1736) published many of Pope's works; he made profitable use of "rubric posts," red-lettered title pages displayed as advertisements for his newly published wares.

9. Tyburn was the site of executions; ballads and memoirs concerning the criminals hanged there were popular forms of cheap reading matter.

1. Oft-used titles for periodicals, conjuring speed (*Mercury*: the swift-moving messenger god) and copious storage (*magazine*: a warehouse or stockpile). Pope's footnote elaborates on the magazines' content, in which "Dulness appears in a thousand shapes. These were thrown out weekly and monthly by every miserable scribbler; or picked up piecemeal and stolen from anybody."

2. A just satire on the flatteries and falsehoods admitted to be inscribed on the walls of churches, in epitaphs [Pope's note].

3. Made by the Poet Laureate . . . to be sung at court on every New Year's Day, the words of which are happily drowned in the voices and instruments [Pope's note].

In clouded majesty here Dulness shone;
Four guardian Virtues, round, support her throne:
Fierce champion Fortitude, that knows no fears
Of hisses, blows, or want, or loss of ears:[4]
Calm Temperance, whose blessings those partake
Who hunger and who thirst for scribbling sake:
Prudence, whose glass° presents th' approaching jail. *mirror*
Poetic Justice, with her lifted scale,
Where, in nice° balance, truth with gold she weighs, *careful*
And solid pudding against empty praise.[5]
Here she beholds the Chaos dark and deep,
Where nameless somethings in their causes sleep,[6]
'Till genial Jacob, or a warm third day,
Call forth each mass, a poem, or a play:[7]
How hints, like spawn, scarce quick° in embryo lie, *barely alive*
How newborn nonsense first is taught to cry,
Maggots half formed, in rhyme exactly meet,
And learn to crawl upon poetic feet.[8]
Here one poor word an hundred clenches° makes, *puns*
And ductile° dullness new meanders takes; *flexible*
There motley[9] images her fancy strike,
Figures ill paired, and similes unlike.
She sees a mob of metaphors advance,
Pleased with the madness of the mazy dance:
How tragedy and comedy embrace;
How farce and epic get a jumbled race;
How Time himself stands still at her command,
Realms shift their place, and ocean turns to land.
Here gay description Egypt glads° with show'rs, *gladdens, bestows*
Or gives to Zembla[1] fruits, to Barca[2] flow'rs;
Glitt'ring with ice here hoary hills are seen,
There painted valleys of eternal green,
In cold December fragrant chaplets° blow, *flower wreaths*
And heavy harvests nod beneath the snow.
All these, and more, the cloud-compelling Queen
Beholds through fogs, that magnify the scene:
She, tinseled o'er in robes of varying hues,

4. The cutting-off of ears was a punishment occasionally meted out (in the seventeenth century) to writers found guilty of libel against government or religion.

5. "Poetic Justice," which ordinarily refers to the morally satisfying resolution of plot, becomes here a figure for the Grub Street hack's painstaking adjudication between the claims of unprofitable truth and less honorably secured payment (money, food).

6. The lines evoke the chaos out of which, in Genesis and in *Paradise Lost,* God creates the universe.

7. Each shapeless "mass" is transformed into a viable piece of writing by the sunlike influence of either a prestigious publisher (Jacob Tonson [c. 1655–1736], whose good will toward any poem ensured its emergence from obscurity into print) or a warmly receptive audience: a playwright received payment only when the play ran for at least three nights.

8. Tradition held that maggots were spawned by the action of sunlight upon dead flesh; the word also connoted "notion" or "idea." Here the creatures combine in rhyme and move by means of "poetic feet" (the rhythmic units of verse meter)—an image rendered all the weirder because maggots have no feet at all.

9. Random, confusedly mixed; in the lines that follow (66–78), Pope catalogs the incoherent combinations (of figures, genres, ideas, and details) perpetrated by Grub Street dunces in their frantic pursuit of publication.

1. A cluster of islands in the Arctic Ocean.

2. A city in North Africa.

With self-applause her wild Creation views;
Sees momentary monsters rise and fall,
And with her own fools'-colors gilds them all.
'Twas on the day, when * *[3] rich and grave,
Like Cimon,[4] triumphed both on land and wave:
(Pomps, without guilt, of bloodless swords and maces,
Glad chains, warm furs, broad banners, and broad faces)[5]
Now night descending, the proud scene was o'er,
But lived, in Settle's[6] numbers,° one day more. *verses*
Now may'rs and shrieves° all hushed and satiate lay, *sheriffs*
Yet eat, in dreams, the custard[7] of the day;
While pensive poets painful vigils keep,
Sleepless themselves, to give their readers sleep.
Much to the mindful Queen the feast recalls
What City swans[8] once sung within the walls;
Much she revolves° their arts, their ancient praise, *contemplates*
And sure succession down from Heywood's[9] days.
She saw, with joy, the line immortal run,
Each sire impressed and glaring in his son:
So watchful bruin forms, with plastic care,
Each growing lump, and brings it to a bear.[1]
She saw old Prynne[2] in restless Daniel[3] shine,
And Eusden[4] eke out Blackmore's[5] endless line;
She saw slow Philips[6] creep like Tate's poor page,[7]
And all the mighty mad in Dennis rage.[8]
In each she marks her image full expressed,[9]

3. In earlier versions, this blank read "Thorold"; George Thorold was at one time Lord Mayor of London. Pope sets Book 1 on Lord Mayor's Day, and parodies both mayoral and royal processionals, ceremonies, and celebrations conducted in the City of London, whose commerce-driven culture and politics the *Dunciad* deplores.

4. Athenian general, admiral (hence "wave"), and statesman (c. 510–c.450 B.C.E.).

5. Pope describes the adornments and appearance of the City dignitaries who march in the Lord Mayor's procession.

6. [Elkanah] Settle [1648–1724] was poet to the City of London. His office was to compose yearly panegyrics upon the Lord Mayor's [Day], and verses to be spoken in the pageants: but that part of the shows being at length frugally abolished, the employment of the City Poet ceased; so that upon Settle's demise there was no successor to that place [Pope's note].

7. A favorite foodstuff at City feasts.

8. Poets who dwelt in the City and "sang" (like dying swans) its values; in the lines that follow (98–106) Pope traces a parodic genealogy, an "immortal line" that runs in "sure succession" from dunce to dunce.

9. Thomas Heywood (d. 1641), a playwright who wrote scripts for City pageants.

1. Animal folklore held that the mother bear ("bruin") gave birth to a shapeless "lump" of flesh and fur, which she licked, with "plastic" (i.e., sculpting) power, into the form of a living cub.

2. William Prynne (1600–1669), Puritan pamphleteer, was imprisoned (and ear-deprived) for the criticisms of Charles I and Queen Henrietta Maria that he published in *Histrio-Mastix* (1633).

3. Daniel Defoe (c. 1660–1731), prolific (hence "restless") author and controversialist, was pilloried for his satire of church and state in *The Shortest Way with the Dissenters* (1702).

4. Laurence Eusden (1688–1730), Cibber's immediate predecessor as Poet Laureate.

5. Sir Richard Blackmore (1654–1729), physician and writer of widely mocked, very lengthy epics; "endless line" here suggests lineage (the limitless succession of dunce-heirs) as well as tedium.

6. Ambrose Phillips (ca. 1674–1749), poet, playwright, and sometime rival of Pope, who derided Phillips, in *Peri-Bathous*, as a literary tortoise, "slow and chill."

7. Nahum Tate [1652–1715] was Poet Laureate, a cold writer, of no invention [Pope's note].

8. John Dennis (1658–1734), acute and at times caustic critic, with whom Pope had sustained a furious, ongoing literary quarrel since early in his own career. In an anonymous pamphlet (1713), Pope had insisted (satirically) that Dennis was actually mad; in a footnote to the present line he ironically modifies the claim: "This is by no means to be understood literally . . . No—it is spoken of that *excellent* and *divine madness* [i.e., mystical inspiration] so often mentioned by Plato; that poetical rage and enthusiasm, with which Mr. D. hath, in his time, been highly possessed."

9. As does Milton's God, who sees in Christ "the radiant image of his glory" (*Paradise Lost* 3.63).

But chief in BAYS'S[1] monster-breeding breast;
Bays, formed by Nature stage and town to bless,
And act, and be, a coxcomb° with success. *preening fool*
Dulness with transport° eyes the lively dunce, *ecstasy*
Rememb'ring she herself was pertness° once. *impudence*
Now (shame to fortune!) an ill run at play° *bad luck at dice*
Blanked his bold visage, and a thin third day:[2]
Swearing[3] and supperless the hero sate,° *sat*
Blasphemed his gods, the dice, and damned his fate.
Then gnawed his pen, then dashed it on the ground,
Sinking from thought to thought, a vast profound![4]
Plunged for his sense, but found no bottom there,
Yet wrote, and floundered on, in mere despair.
Round him much embryo, much abortion lay,
Much future ode, and abdicated play;
Nonsense precipitate,[5] like running lead,
That slipped through cracks and zig-zags of the head;
All that on Folly Frenzy could beget,
Fruits of dull heat, and sooterkins of wit.[6]
Next, o'er his books his eyes began to roll,
In pleasing memory of all he stole,[7]
How here he sipped, how there he plundered snug,° *deftly and undetected*
And sucked all o'er, like an industrious bug.
Here lay poor Fletcher's half-eat° scenes,[8] and here *eaten*
The frippery° of crucified Moliere;[9] *old clothes*
There hapless Shakespeare, yet of Tibbald sore,[1]
Wished he had blotted for himself before.[2]
The rest on outside merit[3] but presume,

1. I.e., Cibber's, sardonically renamed here for the wreath of bay leaves awarded to the Laureate.
2. I.e., a poor turnout for the third, payment-clinching performance of his new play (see above, line 58 and note).
3. A habit for which Cibber was notorious.
4. The line echoes both Rochester, who describes the mind, deluded as to its own powers of reason, "Stumbling from thought to thought" before falling "headlong down / Into doubt's boundless sea" ("A Satyr against Reason and Mankind" ll. 18–19); and Milton, whose angel Raphael describes the chaos before creation as "the vast profound" (*Paradise Lost* 7.229).
5. The adjective denotes both speed and downward motion, like the leaden creations (liquid but ponderous) that seep, in this couplet, from Bays's cracked skull.
6. The line sustains the imagery of miscarriage and monstrous birth: in Aristotelian medicine, "dull heat" (faint passion) produced pallid progeny; folkloric "sooterkins" ("little soot-balls") were mouse-like creatures conceived by women unwary enough to warm themselves by means of small stoves tucked under their skirts.
7. In the ensuing lines, Cibber fondly recalls his plagiarisms.
8. John Fletcher (1579–1625), Jacobean playwright whose faded popularity enables Bays to plagiarize with impunity: "A great number of [Fletcher's scenes were] taken out to patch up [Cibber's] plays" [Pope's note].
9. Stage name of the French playwright Jean-Baptiste Poquelin (1622–1673); Cibber had reworked Molière's celebrated *Tartuffe* into *The Non-Juror* (1718), an anti-Catholic comedy peppered with specific (albeit indirect) attacks on Pope.
1. Lewis Theobald (1688–1744), a textual scholar and editor who had enraged Pope by criticizing his edition of Shakespeare's works (1725), and who had preceded Cibber as chief dunce and target in all previous versions of the *Dunciad* (1728, 1729, 1742) until, in 1743, the Poet Laureate took his place.
2. "It was a ridiculous praise which the players gave to Shakespeare [in the First Folio of his works] 'that he had never blotted [cancelled, crossed out] a line.' Ben Jonson honestly wished he had blotted a thousand, and Shakespeare would certainly have wished the same, if he had lived to see those alterations in his works, which, not the actors only (and especially the daring Hero of this poem) have made on the stage but the presumptuous critics of our days in their *editions*" [Pope's note]. Cibber had successfully starred in his own radical revision of Shakespeare's *Richard III*; Theobald was of course preeminent among Pope's "presumptuous critics."
3. I.e., external beauty: bound volumes whose elegance belies the ineptitude of the writing they contain; Pope catalogs some of their occupants in the ensuing lines (140–42).

Or serve (like other fools) to fill a room;
Such with their shelves as due proportion hold,
Or their fond parents dressed in red and gold;[4]
Or where the pictures for the page atone,° *compensate*
And Quarles[5] is saved by beauties not his own.
Here swells the shelf with Ogilby the great;[6]
There, stamped with arms, Newcastle[7] shines complete:
Here all his° suff'ring brotherhood retire, *Cibber's*
And 'scape the martyrdom of jakes° and fire;[8] *outhouse*
A Gothic library! of Greece and Rome
Well purged,[9] and worthy° Settle, Banks, and Broome.[1] *worthy of*
  But, high above, more solid learning shone,
The classics of an age that heard of none;
There Caxton slept, with Wynkin at his side,[2]
One clasped in wood, and one in strong cow-hide;[3]
There, saved by spice,[4] like mummies, many a year,
Dry bodies of divinity° appear: *theology*
De Lyra[5] there a dreadful front extends,
And here the groaning shelves Philemon[6] bends.
  Of these twelve volumes, twelve of amplest size,
Redeemed from tapers and defrauded pies,[7]
Inspired he seizes: these an altar raise:
An hecatomb° of pure, unsullied lays° *sacrifice / songs*
That altar crowns:[8] a folio commonplace[9]
Founds the whole pile, of all his works the base:
Quartos, octavos shape the less'ning pyre,
A twisted Birthday Ode[1] completes the spire.
  Then he: "Great tamer of all human art!
First in my care, and ever at my heart;

4. I.e., the books, like the children of "fond parents," are overdressed.
5. Frances Quarles (1592–1644), religious poet, whose widely published *Emblems* combined poetic and pictorial depictions of moral allegories.
6. John Ogilby (1600–1676), writer and publisher, had produced a sumptuously illustrated translation of Homer's *Iliad* (1660).
7. Margaret Cavendish, Duchess of Newcastle (1623–1673), prolific writer now much studied, whose poetry, plays, fiction, and treatises (scientific and proto-feminist), now much studied, were regarded in the eighteenth century as merely plentiful and eccentric (see pages 2058–73).
8. The customary fates of worthless print; compare Dryden, who describes the literary detritus of his age, recycled as wrapping- and toilet-paper, as "Martyrs of pies, and relics of the bum [buttocks]" (*Mac Flecknoe* line 101).
9. Cibber's book collection, like the Gothic age, is devoid of classical literature (and values).
1. John Banks (1652–1706) and Richard Brome (c. 1590–1692), tragic and comic playwrights respectively, here linked with Pope's recurrent target Elkanah Settle, City Poet.
2. William Caxton (1422?–1491), the first English printer, and Wynkin de Worde (d. 1535), his assistant and successor, produced English adaptations of French retellings of classical tales out of Virgil and Homer; Pope saw these as useless distortions of the originals.
3. Common materials in medieval bookbindings.
4. Fragrant spices acted as a repellent against bookworms.
5. Nicholas de Lyra (d. 1340), biblical commentator.
6. Philemon Holland (1552–1637), prolific translator of ancient Roman texts.
7. More "martyrdom" (see line 144): pages from unwanted books were used to light candles and line pie tins.
8. Atop the old volumes, Bays places plentiful copies of his own poetry, "unsullied" (un-dirtied) because no one's buying or reading them.
9. The folio was the largest format for books, the "commonplace" the most derivative genre: it collected (into one "common place") quotations from other writers. Pope implies that Cibber, destitute of his own ideas, needs to draw on a large collection.
1. Another recurrent duty of the Laureate: to write odes celebrating the birthdays of members of the royal family.

Dulness! Whose good old cause[2] I yet defend,
With whom my Muse began, with whom shall end:
E'er since Sir Fopling's periwig was praise,[3]
To the last honors of the butt and bays.[4]
O thou! Of bus'ness the directing soul!
To this our head, like bias to the bowl,[5]
Which, as more pond'rous, made its aim more true,
Obliquely waddling to the mark in view.
O! ever gracious to perplexed mankind,
Still spread a healing mist before the mind;
And lest we err by wit's wild dancing light,
Secure us kindly in our native night:
Or, if to wit a coxcomb make pretense,
Guard the sure barrier between that and sense;
Or quite unravel all the reas'ning thread,
And hang some curious cobweb in its stead!
As, forced from wind-guns, lead itself can fly,
And pond'rous slugs cut swiftly through the sky;
As clocks to weight their nimble motion owe,
The wheels above urged by the load below;
Me emptiness and dullness could inspire,
And were my elasticity[6] and fire.
Some daemon stole my pen (forgive th' offense)
And once betrayed me into common sense:[7]
Else all my prose and verse were much the same;
This, prose on stilts; that, poetry fall'n lame.
Did on the stage my fops appear confined?° *too moderate*
My life gave ampler lessons to mankind.
Did the dead letter[8] unsuccessful prove?
The brisk example never failed to move.
Yet sure had Heav'n decreed to save the state,
Heav'n had decreed those works a longer date.[9]
Could Troy be saved by any single hand,
This grey-goose weapon° must have made her stand. *goose-quill pen*
What can I now?[1] My Fletcher cast aside,

2. The phrase was conventionally (and ironically) applied to the antiroyalist faction in the English Civil Wars; Tories like Pope regarded Whigs like Cibber as direct political descendants of those earlier rebels. Cibber's prayer extends the "oldness" backward: The first period of Dulness's dominion began long before the rise of sense and learning.

3. Cibber first attained fame as an actor in a role he wrote for himself: the lavishly bewigged fop in *Love's Last Shift; or, The Fool in Fashion* (1696). From Pope's sardonic note: "The first visible cause of the passion of the Town for our Hero was a fair flaxen full-bottomed periwig . . . This remarkable periwig usually made its entrance upon the stage in a sedan, brought in by two chairmen, with infinite approbation of the audience."

4. Emblems of the Laureate: a regular royal allotment of wine (butt); a wreath of laurel (bay) leaves.

5. In the game of bowls, the asymmetrical weighting ("bias") of each ball affects the direction in which it rolls. Pope echoes Dryden, describing Shadwell's special gifts, in *Mac Flecknoe*: "This is the boasted bias of thy mind, / By which one way, to dullness, 'tis inclined" (lines 189–90).

6. I.e., the power of gases to expand: a flatulent mode of "inspiration."

7. Another echo of *Mac Flecknoe*: "The rest to some faint meaning make pretense, / But Sh[adwell] never deviates into sense" (lines 19–20).

8. I.e., Bays's inert writing.

9. Bays's grandiose lament on the ephemerality of his work echoes (and inverts) the despair of the Trojan Anchises at the fall of Troy: "if the gods had wished me longer life, they would have saved the city" (*Aeneid* 2.641–2).

1. I.e., "what should I do now?" In the ensuing lines (199–216), Bays weighs alternate courses of action.

Take up the Bible, once my better guide?[2]
Or tread the path by vent'rous heroes trod,
This box my thunder, this right hand my god?[3]
Or chaired at White's amidst the doctors sit,[4]
Teach oaths to gamesters, and to nobles wit?
Or bidst thou° rather party to embrace?[5] *i.e., Dulness*
(A friend to party thou, and all her race;
'Tis the same rope at different ends they twist;
To Dulness, Ridpath[6] is as dear as Mist.[7])
Shall I like Curtius, desp'rate in my zeal,
O'er head and ears plunge for the commonweal?
Or rob Rome's ancient geese of all their glories,
And cackling save the monarchy of Tories?[8]
Hold—to the Minister[9] I more incline;
To serve his cause, O Queen![1] is serving thine;
Now, see! thy very Gazetteers[2] give o'er,° *surrender*
Ev'n Ralph is lost,[3] and Henley writes no more![4]
What then remains? Ourself.[5] Still, still remain
Cibberian forehead, and Cibberian brain;[6]
This brazen brightness, to the squire so dear;
This polished hardness, that reflects the peer;
This arch absurd,° that wit and fool delights; *absurdity*
This mess,° tossed up of Hockley-Hole[7] and White's, *hodgepodge*
Where dukes and butchers join to wreath my crown,
At once the bear and fiddle[8] of the town.
"O born in sin, and forth in folly brought![9]

2. I.e., give up playwriting for piety (Cibber notes in his *Apology* that his father hoped he would become a clergyman).
3. Bays, like Cibber an ardent gambler, pictures himself both as ancient hero (Virgil's Mezentius, who chose to trust the spear in his "right hand" rather than the gods [*Aeneid* 10.773]) and as divinity: Jupiter, who wields the thunder as Bays will wield the noisy dice-box.
4. White's: a fashionable gambling club (Cibber was a member); doctors: slang for dice.
5. Bays considers engaging himself as author in the political controversies between Whigs and Tories, whom Dulness cherishes for the plenitude and mediocrity of their propaganda.
6. George Ridpath (d. 1726), Whig journalist.
7. Nathaniel Mist (d. 1737), Tory publisher.
8. Bays, deliberating whether to remain loyal to the Whigs or to sell out to the Tories, invokes Roman precedents: Marcus Curtius, who according to legend "plunged" into a pit in order to restore the Roman Forum; and the geese of Rome, whose cackling one night awoke the Romans in time to preserve the city from an enemy's surprise attack. Pope's juxtaposition of "commonweal" and "monarchy" recalls the key terms and tensions of the Civil Wars.
9. I.e., Robert Walpole (1676–1745), Whig prime minister, who had secured Cibber's loyalty (and compounded Pope's disgust) by orchestrating his appointment as Poet Laureate.
1. I.e., Dulness, and (by association) Queen Caroline (1683–1737), wife to George II and Walpole's closest ally within the Hanoverian royal family.
2. The *Daily Gazetteer*, which had served as Walpole's chief venue for propaganda, had become notably more neutral after his resignation in 1742.
3. James Ralph (d. 1762), political writer, had in truth been "lost" to Walpole for a long while; his antiministerial journalism became increasingly vociferous and effectual throughout the late 1730s and early 1740s.
4. John ("Orator") Henley (1692–1756), a preacher who had frequently served Walpole by attacking Pope, had terminated his pro-ministerial periodical *Hyp Doctor* in 1741.
5. Bays echoes the protagonist of Seneca's *Medea*, who on learning that she's been abandoned by her husband and her friends, insists "Medea superest": Medea remains (5.166).
6. Pope, in a mock-scholarly textual note, insists that the adjective originally read "Cerberian," after Cerberus, the three-headed canine guardian of Hades: "The *Dog* was the ancient . . . symbol of Impudence." In the ensuing lines, Bays catalogs the varied ways in which his "Cibberian brain" appeals to admirers from several social strata.
7. A London location (like Smithfield in line 2) for bear-baiting and other "low" entertainments, here contrasted with White's (Cibber's gleaming gambling club).
8. Fiddle-playing often served as an overture to bear-baiting; the word could also mean "butt of a joke" (as Cibber is throughout Pope's poem).
9. Bays now addresses his own neglected publications, heaped into a pyre and ready for burning.

Works damned, or to be damned (your father's fault),
Go, purified by flame, ascend the sky,
My better and more Christian progeny!
Unstained, unstitched, and yet in maiden sheets;[1]
While all your smutty sisters walk the streets.[2]
Ye shall not beg, like gratis-given Bland,[3]
Sent with a pass, and vagrant through the land;
Not sail, with Ward,[4] to ape-and-monkey climes,
Where vile mundungus° trucks° for viler rhymes; (*cheap tobacco / is traded*)
Not sulfur-tipped emblaze an ale-house fire;
Not wrap up oranges, to pelt your sire![5]
O! pass more innocent, in infant state,
To the mild limbo[6] of our father Tate:[7]
Or peaceably forgot, at once be blessed
In Shadwell's bosom, with eternal rest![8]
Soon to that mass of nonsense to return,
Where things destroyed are swept to things unborn."
  With that, a tear (portentous sign of grace!)
Stole from the master of the sev'nfold face:[9]
And thrice he lifted high the birthday brand,[1]
And thrice he dropped it from his quiv'ring hand;
Then lights the structure, with averted eyes:
The rolling smokes involve° the sacrifice. (*engulf*)
The op'ning clouds disclose each work[2] by turns,
Now flames the Cid, and now Perolla burns;
Great Caesar roars, and hisses in the fires;
King John in silence modestly expires:
No merit now the dear Nonjuror claims,
Moliere's old stubble in a moment flames.
Tears gushed again, as from pale Priam's eyes,
When the last blaze sent Ilion° to the skies.[3] (*Troy*)
  Roused by the light, old Dulness heaved the head;

1. I.e., just as they emerged from the press: pure of the processes (stitching and binding) that would prepare them for sale.
2. Two of Cibber's actual children, the actors Theophilus Cibber and Charlotte Charke, had attained a complex notoriety for outrageous sexual and/or theatrical activities.
3. Henry Bland (d. 1746), Whig propagandist, here pictured as a beggar in the wake of Walpole's fall.
4. Edward Ward (1667–1731), satirist, travel-writer and tavern-keeper; he had "sailed" to tropical territories in two senses: he had written *A Trip to Jamaica* (1697), and his books sold well (so Pope's note scornfully insists) in the Caribbean colonial plantations.
5. Still more martyrdom: if Bays does not burn them now, he fears that his sheets will serve to light fires, or to wrap oranges for sale at the playhouse, where the fruit might well be used to "pelt" bad actors (himself included).
6. I.e., the afterlife allotted to sinless infants.
7. See above, line 105 and note.
8. Thomas Shadwell (c. 1640–1692), playwright, Poet Laureate, and principal target of Dryden's satire in *Mac Flecknoe* (1682).
9. "Sevenfold" because Cibber, as actor, has played many parts.
1. Torch (here, the "twisted Birthday Ode" that Bays uses as igniter).
2. Pope proceeds to list some of Cibber's plays: *Ximena* (1719), adapted from Pierre Corneille's *Le Cid*; *Perolla and Izadora* (1706); *Caesar in Egypt* (1725); and *Papal Tyranny in the Reign of King John*, adapted from Shakespeare's *King John* but "silent" (in 1743) because as yet unperformed; *The Non-Juror* (1717), adapted from Molière's *Tartuffe* (see above, line 132 and note).
3. Priam, last king of Troy, wept to witness the fire that destroyed his city.

Then snatched a sheet of *Thulè*[4] from her bed,
Sudden she flies, and whelms it o'er the pyre;
Down sink the flames, and with a hiss expire.
  Her ample presence fills up all the place;
A veil of fogs dilates her awful° face: *awesome*
Great in her charms! as when on shrieves and may'rs
She looks, and breathes herself into their airs.° *pretensions*
She bids him wait° her to her sacred dome: *accompany*
Well pleased he entered, and confessed his home.
So spirits ending their terrestrial race,
Ascend and recognize their native place.
This the Great Mother dearer held than all
The clubs of quidnuncs,[5] or her own Guildhall.[6]
Her stood her opium,[7] here she nursed her owls,[8]
And here she planned th' imperial seat[9] of fools.
  Here to her chosen all her works she shows;
Prose swelled to verse, verse loit'ring into prose:
How random thoughts now meaning chance to find,
Now leave all memory of sense behind:
How prologues into prefaces decay,
And these to notes are frittered quite away.
How index-learning turns no student pale,[1]
Yet holds the eel of science by the tail.[2]
How, with less reading than makes felons 'scape,[3]
Less human genius than God gives an ape,
Small thanks to France, and none to Rome or Greece,
A past, vamped,° future, old, revived, new piece, *patched up*
'Twixt Plautus,[4] Fletcher, Shakespeare, and Corneille,[5]
Can make a Cibber, Tibbald, or Ozell.[6]
The Goddess then, o'er his anointed head,
With mystic words, the sacred opium shed.
And lo! her bird (a monster of a fowl!
Something betwixt a Heidegger[7] and owl),
Perched on his crown. "All hail! And hail again,
My son! The promised land expects thy reign.

4. An unfinished poem by Ambrose Phillips, whom Pope at career's outset regarded as a rival; his note makes explicit what his couplet implies: "the coldness and heaviness of [Phillips's] writing."
5. The Latin phrase *quid nunc*—what now? what news?—had become a label for news addicts, who compulsively asked each other the question.
6. The center of City politics and ceremonies.
7. The drug was used by impoverished writers (among others) to allay hunger, subdue pain, and induce stupefaction.
8. The bird associated with Athena, goddess of wisdom, is here linked ironically (as a creature of the night) with her divine opposite, Dulness, and with the dominion of the night.
9. I.e., the site of the future emperor's (Bays's) palace, throne, and court.

1. Because the index shortens labor, it allows its users (the textual scholars Pope here mocks, for whom indexes were a necessary tool of research) more time for sleep.
2. The metaphor figures "science" (knowledge) as elusive, and the index-learners as grabbing it by the wrong end.
3. Under British law, proof of even limited literacy in Latin sometimes exempted criminals from punishment.
4. Roman comic playwright (c. 254–184 B.C.E.).
5. French tragic playwright (1606–1684).
6. John Ozell (d. 1743), translator, whose critical attack on plays by Pope's friend William Wycherley prompted the poet to satiric countermeasures.
7. Johann Jakob Heidegger, Swiss-born London impresario, famed for his extraordinary ugliness.

Know, Eusden thirsts no more for sack[8] or praise,
He sleeps[9] among the dull of ancient days,
Safe, where no critics damn, no duns molest,
Where wretched Withers,[1] Ward, and Gildon[2] rest,
And high-born Howard,[3] more majestic sire,
With Fool of Quality[4] completes the quire.[5]
Thou Cibber! thou his[6] laurel shall support,
Folly, my son, has still a friend at court.
Lift up your gates, ye princes, see him° come! *Cibber*
Sound, sound ye viols, be the catcall dumb![7]
Bring, bring the madding° bay, the drunken vine; *maddening*
The creeping, dirty, courtly ivy join![8]
And thou! his aide de camp,[9] lead out my sons,
Light-armed with points, antitheses, and puns.[1]
Let bawdry, Billingsgate,[2] two sisters dear,
Support his front, and oaths bring up the rear:
And under his, and under Archer's[3] wing,
Gaming and Grub Street skulk behind the King.
"O! when shall rise a monarch, all our own,
And I, a nursing mother, rock the throne;
'Twixt prince and people close the curtain draw,
Shade him from light, and cover him from law!
Fatten the courtier, starve the learned band,
And suckle armies, and dry-nurse the land:[4]
'Till senates nod to lullabies divine,
And all be sleep, as at an ode of thine?"

She ceased. Then swells the Chapel Royal throat:[5]
"God save King Cibber!" mounts in ev'ry note.
Familiar White's "God save King Colley!" cries;
"God save King Colley!" Drury-lane replies:

8. White wine; Cibber's laureate-predecessor Laurence Eusden had been reputed a heavy drinker.
9. I.e., Eusden is now (like the other dunce-forebears listed in lines, 296–98) dead.
1. George Withers (1588–1667), poet and satirist, derided by Jonson, Dryden, Swift, and others as a hack who had pandered to popular taste.
2. Charles Gildon (1665–1724), prolific writer for the popular press.
3. Edward Howard (1624–1712), playwright and poet, energetically mocked by Restoration wits.
4. John Hervey (1696–1743), high-ranking courtier, ardent adherent to Walpole and Caroline, and caustic insulter of Pope, who retaliated with his portrait of Hervey as Lord Sporus in *Epistle to Dr. Arbuthnot* (lines 305–33); Hervey's death in 1743 enabled Pope to include him, just in time, as capper to this list of departed dunces.
5. A pun, envisioning the choir of dead dunces as also a quire—an unbound (hence unsold, unread) cluster of printed pages.
6. I.e., Eusden's, though the pronouns here and in the ensuing lines (300–309) are famously and perhaps pointedly ambiguous; laurel: the wreath of bay leaves worn by laureates.
7. The line conjures a theater, where musicians played violins, and restive audience members blew high-pitched whistles ("catcalls") to express their disgust.
8. Though ivy (unlike bay leaf and vine) forms no part of the laureate's traditional wreath, Pope in an appendix defended its inclusion here as "emblematical of the three virtues of a court poet in particular: it is *creeping*, *dirty*, and *dangling*."
9. Lord Hervey. Aide de camp: a general's (here, Cibber's) assistant officer.
1. Hervey's favored forms of wordplay; points: surprising turns of thought and phrase; antitheses: quick, provocative juxtapositions (compare *Arbuthnot*, lines 323–25).
2. The obscene speech associated with the women who sold fish at Billingsgate market.
3. Thomas Archer (1668–1743), a high-placed architect whose prerogatives included furnishing the royal apartments toward which Cibber and his entourage are headed, as well as the royally sanctioned gambling privileges touched on in the next line.
4. Dulness envisions herself as prodigiously nurturing: queen-mother to a dunce-monarch, wet nurse to the army, dry nurse (nanny) to the nation.
5. I.e., the choir of the chapel where the royal family worshipped.

To Needham's[6] quick the voice triumphal rode,
But pious Needham dropped the name of God;
Back to the Devil[7] the last echoes roll,
And "Coll!"[8] each butcher roars at Hockley-Hole.[9]
  So when Jove's block° descended from on high — *log*
(As sings thy great forefather Ogilby[1])
Loud thunder to its bottom shook the bog,
And the hoarse nation croaked, "God save King Log!"[2]

from *Book the Fourth*[1]

  O Muse! relate (for you can tell alone,
Wits have short memories, and dunces none)
Relate, who first, who last resigned to rest;
Whose heads she partly, whose completely blessed;
What charms could faction, what ambition lull,
The venal quiet, and entrance the dull;
Till drowned was sense, and shame, and right, and wrong—
O sing, and hush the nations with thy song!

* *

In vain, in vain—the all-composing hour
Resistless falls: the Muse obeys the Pow'r.
She comes! She comes! the fabled throne behold
Of Night primeval, and of Chaos old!
Before her, Fancy's gilded clouds decay,
And all its varying rainbows die away.
Wit shoots in vain its momentary fires,
The meteor drops, and in a flash expires.
As one by one, at dread Medea's strain,[2]
The sick'ning stars fade off th' ethereal plain;
As Argus' eyes by Hermes' wand oppressed,[3]
Close one by one to everlasting rest;
Thus at her felt approach, and secret might,
Art after art goes out, and all is night.
See skulking Truth to her old cavern fled,
Mountains of casuistry° heaped o'er her head! — *false reasoning*
Philosophy, that leaned on Heav'n before,

6. A famous brothel near the royal palace, run by Elizabeth Needham (d. 1731).

7. The Devil Tavern in Fleet Street, where these odes are usually rehearsed before they are performed at court [Pope's note].

8. The word was slang for "fool," "dupe."

9. See line 222 and note; the acclamation has traveled from the aristocratic precincts of the Town back to the shabbier terrain of the City, where both Bays and the *Dunciad* began.

1. See line 141 and note.

2. Pope echoes Ogilby's verse retelling of an Aesop's fable: when the frogs petitioned Jupiter ("Jove") to provide them with a king, he contemptuously sent down a block of wood: "Then all the bog / Proclaim their king, and cry, 'Jove save King Log.' " This story of an "alien" (and inert) monarch, confirmed not by heredity but by popular acclamation, resonates with the period's impassioned party politics: the Tory and Jacobite resentment of Whig policies (here embodied by Cibber, the City, and the dunces) that successfully supplanted the hereditary Stuart succession with the more distant Hanoverian line.

1. Throughtout Book 4, the *Dunciad's* hero does nothing; in these, the poem's closing lines, Dulness's infectious yawn spreads sleep everywhere and ushers in apocalypse, silencing even Pope's own muse, and returning the world to the primeval darkness and chaos that preceded Creation.

2. In Seneca's tragedy *Medea*, the title character, a sorceress, attempts to avenge herself upon her unfaithful lover by summoning constellations down from the sky and making the sun stand still.

3. Argus's hundred eyes enabled him to guard Io against Jupiter's advances—but Jupiter sent Mercury (Hermes) to lull Argus asleep, then kill him.

Shrinks to her second cause,[4] and is no more.
Physic of Metaphysic begs defense,
And Metaphysic calls for aid on Sense![5]
See Mystery to Mathematics fly![6]
In vain! they[7] gaze, turn giddy, rave, and die.
Religion blushing veils her sacred fires,
And unawares Morality expires.
Nor public fame, nor private, dares to shine;
Nor human spark is left, nor glimpse divine!
Lo! thy dread empire, CHAOS! is restored;
Light dies before thy uncreating word:[8]
Thy hand, great Anarch![9] lets the curtain fall;
And Universal Darkness buries All.

Lady Mary Wortley Montagu

1689–1762

In learning, literature, and travel, Lady Mary Wortley Montagu outdistanced almost all of her contemporaries. Born Mary Pierrepont, she acquired her title at age one (when her father became an earl), lost her mother at age three, and immersed herself throughout her youth in the Roman classics, fervently pursuing a plan of self-education at odds with the conventional domesticating agenda (dancing, drawing, social graces) laid out for young women of her rank. For a time in her teens she aspired to implement the idea set forth by the feminist Mary Astell, of founding a convent consecrated to women's learning. In 1712 she married, against her father's wishes, a Whig Member of Parliament named Edward Wortley Montagu, after conducting with him a wary, carefully reasoned courtship mostly by means of letters. When he was appointed Ambassador to Turkey four years later, she accompanied him, and was fascinated by what she saw: by the Turkish practice of inoculating against smallpox, which (having survived the disease herself) she successfully championed in England at her return; by the gaps and continuities between British and Turkish culture, on which she reported eloquently in missives home. Her *Turkish Embassy Letters*, which she compiled from her writings during this sojourn for publication after her death, remain the foundation of her fame.

Her life as a writer yielded other riches, just now beginning to be explored. She wrote essays, including a *Spectator* for Addison and Steele and a later periodical series of her own (1737–1738). She produced short fiction and a comedy but worked more steadily at verse, collaborating with Alexander Pope on some poems and combating him in others, after their friendship had disintegrated into a round of bitter, witty recriminations. Most plentifully she wrote letters, sharp and searching, adroitly tailored to please her wide array of correspondents.

Montagu's spate of accomplishment made her alert to the constrictions of gender. "There is hardly a character in the world," she wrote at age twenty, "more liable to universal ridicule than that of a Learned Woman." Women, she counseled, should know much but hide their

4. Science ("Philosophy") now resorts to mechanical rather than religious explanations for the way things are.
5. Natural science seeks support from theoretical speculations, which in turn have come to rely on empirical investigation.
6. Divine revelation is under threat from "certain defenders of religion [who have] attempted to show that the mysteries of religion may be mathematically demonstrated" [Pope's note].
7. I.e., all the modes of thought and endeavor personified in the preceding six lines.
8. Reversing the sequence of the world's creation (Genesis 1.1–10), and restoring the chaos that preceded it.
9. A ruler with no legitimate political authority; one who promotes disorder and confusion.

knowledge, lest they lose out on the comforts of love, marriage, and social ease. Deeply attentive to the burdens imposed on women and the tactics available to them, Montagu's idiosyncratic feminism earned esteem from her predecessor Astell, and from many who came after.

Idiosyncrasy exacted costs, in the form of that "ridicule" she had early anticipated, and in the breakdown of important relationships. Her marriage failed, as did a passionate love affair (again largely epistolary) with the bisexual Italian writer Francesco Algarotti. Montagu lived her last twenty-five years mostly in Italy. In retrospect, her self-removal looks like part of a lifelong strategy. Montagu had always held it crucial to keep some distance from her culture's assumptions in order to see them clearly, to critique them, to change or expunge their operations in herself and in the world. The title she chose for her periodical series, *The Nonsense of Common Sense*, encapsulates her lifelong conviction. By the eccentricity of her self-education, the remoteness of her travels and her residences, the originality of her thought and conduct, the amused acerbity of her style, Montagu kept her distance and found her voice.

from The Turkish Embassy Letters[1]

To Lady ———[2]

[On the Turkish Baths]

Adrianople, 1 April 1717

I am now got into a new world where everything I see appears to me a change of scene, and I write to your Ladyship with some content of mind, hoping at least that you will find the charm of novelty in my letters and no longer reproach me that I tell you nothing extraordinary. I won't trouble you with a relation of our tedious journey, but I must not omit what I saw remarkable at Sophia, one of the most beautiful towns in the Turkish Empire and famous for its hot baths that are resorted to both for diversion and health. I stopped here one day on purpose to see them. Designing to go incognito, I hired a Turkish coach. These *voitures* are not at all like ours, but much more convenient for the country, the heat being so great that glasses[3] would be very troublesome. They are made a good deal in the manner of the Dutch coaches, having wooden lattices painted and gilded, the inside being painted with baskets and nosegays of flowers, intermixed commonly with little poetical mottoes. They are covered all over with scarlet cloth, lined with silk and very often richly embroidered and fringed. This covering entirely hides the persons in them, but may be thrown back at pleasure and the ladies peep through the lattices. They hold four people very conveniently, seated on cushions, but not raised.

In one of these covered wagons I went to the bagnio[4] about ten o'clock. It was already full of women. It is built of stone in the shape of a dome with no windows but in the roof, which gives light enough. There was five of these domes joined together, the outmost being less than the rest and serving only as a hall where the porteress stood at the door. Ladies of quality generally give this woman the value of

1. The text of the *Turkish Embassy Letters* comes not from the actual letters Montagu sent while on her travels but from two manuscript books in which she combined portions of her letters and travel journals with new prose to produce a hybrid account of the trip, which she intended for posthumous publication. In 1724 Montagu lent the volumes to Mary Astell, who inscribed into the second a preface addressed to future readers: ". . . I confess I am malicious enough to desire that the world should see to how much better purpose the *ladies* travel than their *lords*, and that whilst it is surfeited with male travels [i.e., travel-books], all in the same tone and stuffed with the same trifles, a *lady* has the skill to strike out a new path and to embellish a worn out subject with variety of fresh and elegant entertainment . . . Let us freely own the superiority of this sublime genius as I do in sincerity of my soul, pleased that a *woman* triumphs, and proud to follow in her train."

2. In the manuscript, Montagu supplies no name for this person, who may be a fictive "recipient."

3. Glass windows (which the Turkish coaches lacked).

4. The bath.

a crown or ten shillings, and I did not forget that ceremony. The next room is a very large one, paved with marble, and all round it raised two sofas of marble, one above another. There were four fountains of cold water in this room, falling first into marble basins and then running on the floor in little channels made for that purpose, which carried the streams into the next room, something less than this, with the same sort of marble sofas, but so hot with steams of sulphur proceeding from the baths joining to it, 'twas impossible to stay there with one's clothes on. The two other domes were the hot baths, one of which had cocks of cold water turning into it to temper it to what degree of warmth the bathers have a mind to.

I was in my traveling habit, which is a riding dress, and certainly appeared very extraordinary to them, yet there was not one of 'em that showed the least surprise or impertinent curiosity, but received me with all the obliging civility possible. I know of no European court where the ladies would have behaved themselves in so polite a manner to a stranger.

I believe in the whole there were two hundred women, and yet none of those disdainful smiles or satiric whispers that never fail in our asemblies when anybody appears that is not dressed exactly in fashion. They repeated over and over to me, *uzelle, pek uzelle,* which is nothing but "charming, very charming." The first sofas were covered with cushioned and rich carpets, on which sat the ladies, and on the second their slaves behind 'em, but without any distinction of rank by their dress, all being in the state of nature, that is, in plain English, stark naked, without any beauty or defect concealed, yet there was not the least wanton smile or immodest gesture amongst 'em. They walked and moved with the same majestic grace which Milton describes of our "general mother."[5] There were many amongst them as exactly proportioned as ever any goddess was drawn by the pencil of Guido or Titian,[6] and most of their skins shiningly white, only adorned by their beautiful hair divided into many tresses hanging on their shoulders, braided either with pearl or riband,[7] perfectly representing the figures of the Graces.[8] I was here convinced of the truth of a reflection that I had often made, that if 'twas the fashion to go naked, the face would be hardly observed. I perceived that the ladies with the finest skins and most delicate shapes had the greatest share of my admiration, though their faces were sometimes less beautiful than those of their companions. To tell you the truth, I had wickedness enough to wish secretly that Mr. Gervase could have been there invisible.[9] I fancy it would have very much improved his art to see so many fine women naked in different postures, some in conversation, some working, others drinking coffee or sherbet, and many negligently lying on their cushions while their slaves (generally pretty girls of seventeen or eighteen) were employed in braiding their hair in several pretty manners. In short, 'tis the women's coffee-house, where all the news of the town is told, scandal invented, etc. They generally take this diversion once a week, and stay there at least four or five hours without getting cold by immediate coming out of the hot bath into the cool room, which was very surprising to me. The lady that seemed the most considerable among them entreated me to sit by

5. Eve (*Paradise Lost* 4.304–18).
6. Artists of the Italian Renaissance.
7. Ribbon.
8. Resembling the three sister divinities who (in Greek mythology) embody and endow grace and beauty.
9. Charles Jervas (c. 1675–1739), a successful portraitist who had once painted Montagu as a shepherdess. The French painter Jean Auguste Dominique Ingres (1780–1867) later took up the hint implicit in Montagu's "fancy" here. Having transcribed portions of this letter from a French edition (1805), he made use of Montagu's descriptions in his painting *Le Bain Turc* (The Turkish Bath, 1862).

her and would fain have undressed me for the bath. I excused myself with some difficulty, they being all so earnest in persuading me. I was at last forced to open my skirt and show them my stays,[1] which satisfied them very well, for I saw they believed I was so locked up in that machine that it was not in my own power to open it, which contrivance they attributed to my husband. I was charmed with their civility and beauty, and should have been very glad to pass more time with them, but Mr. W[2] resolving to pursue his journey the next morning early, I was in haste to see the ruins of Justinian's church,[3] which did not afford me so agreeable a prospect as I had left, being little more than a heap of stones.

Adieu, Madam. I am sure I have now entertained you with an account of such a sight as you never saw in your life and that no book of travels could inform you of. 'Tis no less than death for a man to be found in one of those places.

To Lady Mar[1]

[ON TURKISH DRESS]

Adrianople, 1 April 1717

I wish to God (dear Sister) that you was as regular in letting me have the pleasure of knowing what passes on your side of the globe as I am careful in endeavoring to amuse you by the account of all I see that I think you care to hear of. You content yourself with telling me over and over that the town is very dull. It may possibly be dull to you when every day does not present you with something new, but for me that am in arrear at least two months' news, all that seems very stale with you would be fresh and sweet here; pray let me into more particulars. I will try to awaken your gratitude by giving you a full and true relation of the novelties of this place, none of which would surprise you more than a sight of my person as I am now in my Turkish habit, though I believe you would be of my opinion that 'tis admirably becoming. I intend to send you my picture; in the meantime accept of it here.

The first piece of my dress is a pair of drawers, very full, that reach to my shoes and conceal the legs more modestly than your petticoats. They are of a thin rose-color damask brocaded with silver flowers, my shoes of white kid leather embroidered with gold. Over this hangs my smock of a fine white silk gauze edged with embroidery. This smock has wide sleeves hanging half way down the arm and is closed at the neck with a diamond button, but the shape and color of the bosom very well to be distinguished through it. The *antery* is a waistcoat[2] made close to the shape, of white and gold damask, with very long sleeves falling back and fringed with deep gold fringe, and should have diamond or pearl buttons. My caftan, of the same stuff with my drawers, is a robe exactly fitted to my shape and reaching to my feet, with very long straight falling sleeves. Over this is the girdle of about four fingers broad, which all that can afford have entirely of diamonds or other precious stones. Those that will not be at that expense have it of exquisite embroidery on satin, but it must be fastened before with a clasp of diamonds. The *curdée* is a loose robe they throw off or put on according to the weather, being of a rich brocade (mine is green and gold) either lined with ermine or sables; the sleeves reach very

1. A tightly laced undergarment, stiffened with whalebone, extending from breast to thigh.
2. Her husband, Edward Wortley Montagu.
3. The Church of St. Sofia, built during the reign of the Byzantine Emperor Justinian (483–565).

1. Montagu's sister Frances (1690–1761), who had married the Earl of Mar.
2. A vest.

little below the shoulders. The headdress is composed of a cap called *talpock*, which is in winter of fine velvet embroidered with pearls or diamonds and in summer of a light shining silver stuff. This is fixed on one side of the head, hanging a little way down with a gold tassel and bound on either with a circle of diamonds (as I have seen several) or a rich embroidered handkerchief. On the other side of the head the hair is laid flat, and here the ladies are at liberty to show their fancies, some putting flowers, others a plume of heron's feathers, and, in short, what they please, but the most general fashion is a large bouquet of jewels made like natural flowers, that is, the buds of pearl, the roses of different colored rubies, the jasmines of diamonds, jonquils of topazes, etc., so well set and enameled 'tis hard to imagine anything of that kind so beautiful. The hair hangs at its full length behind, divided into tresses braided with pearl or riband, which is always in great quantity.

I never saw in my life so many fine heads of hair. I have counted 110 of these tresses of one lady's, all natural; but it must be owned that every beauty is more common here than with us. 'Tis surprising to see a young woman that is not very handsome. They have naturally the most beautiful complexions in the world and generally large black eyes. I can assure you with great truth that the Court of England (though I believe it the fairest in Christendom) cannot show so many beauties as are under our protection here. They generally shape their eyebrows, and the Greeks and Turks have a custom of putting round their eyes on the inside a black tincture that, at a distance or by candlelight, adds very much to the blackness of them. I fancy many of our ladies would be overjoyed to know this secret, but 'tis too visible by day. They dye their nails rose color; I own I cannot enough accustom myself to this fashion to find any beauty in it.

As to their morality or good conduct, I can say like Arlequin, 'tis just as 'tis with you,[3] and the Turkish ladies don't commit one sin the less for not being Christians. Now I am a little acquainted with their ways, I cannot forbear admiring either the exemplary discretion or extreme stupidity of all the writers that have given accounts of 'em.[4] 'Tis very easy to see they have more liberty than we have, no woman of what rank soever being permitted to go in the streets without two muslins, one that covers her face all but her eyes and another that hides the whole dress of her head and hangs half way down her back; and their shapes are wholly concealed by a thing they call a *ferigée*, which no woman of any sort appears without. This has straight sleeves that reaches to their fingers' ends and it laps all round 'em, not unlike a riding hood. In winter 'tis of cloth, and in summer, plain stuff or silk. You may guess how effectually this disguises them, that there is no distinguishing the great lady from her slave, and 'tis impossible for the most jealous husband to know his wife when he meets her, and no man dare either touch or follow a woman in the street.

This perpetual masquerade gives them entire liberty of following their inclinations without danger of discovery. The most usual method of intrigue is to send an appointment to the lover to meet the lady at a Jew's shop,[5] which are as notoriously convenient as our Indian houses,[6] and yet even those that don't make that use of

3. A paraphrase (and misattribution) of a line from Aphra Behn's comedy *The Emperor of the Moon* (1687): the prankster Harlequin, pretending to be an ambassador from the moon, describes the corrupt social customs of his world to a gullible listener, who repeatedly exclaims that morality there is "just as 'tis here" (3.2).

4. Many (though not all) writers on Turkey had emphasized the strict confinement and chastity of the women there.

5. Jewish women sometimes helped arrange these assignations; being permitted to enter the harems, they could transmit secret messages.

6. London shops selling goods imported from India.

'em do not scruple to go to buy pennorths and tumble over[7] rich goods, which are chiefly to be found amongst that sort of people.[8] The great ladies seldom let their gallants[9] know who they are, and 'tis so difficult to find it out that they can very seldom guess at her name they have corresponded with above half a year together. You may easily imagine the number of faithful wives very small in a country where they have nothing to fear from their lovers' indiscretion, since we see so many that have the courage to expose themselves to that in this world and all the threatened punishment of the next, which is never preached to the Turkish damsels. Neither have they much to apprehend from the resentment of their husbands, those ladies that are rich having all their money in their own hands, which they take with 'em upon a divorce with an addition which he is obliged to give 'em. Upon the whole, I look upon the Turkish women as the only free people in the Empire. The very *Divan*[1] pays a respect to 'em, and the *Grand Signor* himself, when a *Bassa*[2] is executed, never violates the privileges of the harem (or women's apartment), which remains unsearched entire to the widow. They are queens of their slaves, which the husband has no permission so much as to look upon, except it be an old woman or two that his lady chooses. 'Tis true their law permits them four wives, but there is no instance of a man of quality that makes use of this liberty, or of a woman of rank that would suffer it. When a husband happens to be inconstant (as those things will happen) he keeps his mistress in a house apart and visits her as privately as he can, just as 'tis with you. Amongst all the great men here I only know the *Tefterdar* (i.e. treasurer) that keeps a number of she slaves for his own use (that is, on his own side of the house, for a slave once given to serve a lady is entirely at her disposal) and he is spoke of as a libertine, or what we should call a rake, and his wife won't see him, though she continues to live in his house.

Thus you see, dear Sister, the manners of mankind do not differ so widely as our voyage writers would make us believe. Perhaps it would be more entertaining to add a few surprising customs of my own invention, but nothing seems to me so agreeable as truth, and I believe nothing so acceptable to you. I conclude with repeating the great truth of my being, dear Sister, etc.

Letter to Lady Bute[1]

[ON HER GRANDDAUGHTER]

28 January 1753

Dear Child,

You have given me a great deal of satisfaction by your account of your eldest daughter. I am particularly pleased to hear she is a good arithmetician; it is the best proof of understanding. The knowledge of numbers is one of the chief distinctions between us and brutes. If there is anything in blood, you may reasonably expect your children should be endowed with an uncommon share of good sense. Mr. Wortley's[2] family and mine have both produced some of the greatest men that have been born

7. Penny-worths: good bargains; tumble over: browse through.
8. Jews.
9. Lovers.
1. A governmental official.
2. *Bassa:* a high official.

1. Montagu's only daughter, Mary (1718–1794), had in 1736 married John Stuart, third Earl of Bute. At the time this letter was written, Montagu had been long separated from her husband and was living in Italy.
2. Her estranged husband, Edward Wortley Montagu.

in England. I mean Admiral Sandwich,[3] and my great grandfather who was distinguished by the name of Wise William.[4] I have heard Lord Bute's father mentioned as an extraordinary genius (though he had not many opportunities of showing it), and his uncle the present Duke of Argyll has one of the best heads I ever knew.

I will therefore speak to you as supposing Lady Mary not only capable but desirous of learning. In that case, by all means let her be indulged in it. You will tell me, I did not make it a part of your education. Your prospect was very different from hers, as you had no defect either in mind or person to hinder, and much in your circumstances to attract, the highest offers. It seemed your business to learn how to live in the world, as it is hers to know how to be easy out of it. It is the common error of builders and parents to follow some plan they think beautiful (and perhaps is so) without considering that nothing is beautiful that is misplaced. Hence we see so many edifices raised that the raisers can never inhabit, being too large for their fortunes. Vistas are laid open over barren heaths, and apartments contrived for a coolness very agreeable in Italy but killing in the north of Britain. Thus every woman endeavors to breed her daughter a fine lady, qualifying her for a station in which she will never appear, and at the same time incapacitating her for that retirement to which she is destined. Learning (if she has a real taste for it) will not only make her contented but happy in it. No entertainment is so cheap as reading, nor any pleasure so lasting. She will not want new fashions nor regret the loss of expensive diversions or variety of company if she can be amused with an author in her closet. To render this amusement extensive, she should be permitted to learn the languages. I have heard it lamented that boys lose so many years in mere learning of words. This is no objection to a girl, whose time is not so precious. She cannot advance herself in any profession, and has therefore more hours to spare; and as you say her memory is good, she will be very agreeably employed this way.

There are two cautions to be given on this subject: first, not to think herself learned when she can read Latin or even Greek. Languages are more properly to be called vehicles of learning than learning itself, as may be observed in many schoolmasters, who though perhaps critics in grammar are the most ignorant fellows upon earth. True knowledge consists in knowing things, not words. I would wish her no farther a linguist than to enable her to read books in their originals, that are often corrupted and always injured by translations. Two hours' application every morning will bring this about much sooner than you can imagine, and she will have leisure enough beside to run over the English poetry, which is a more important part of a woman's education than it is generally supposed. Many a young damsel has been ruined by a fine copy of verses, which she would have laughed at if she had known it had been stolen from Mr. Waller.[5] I remember when I was a girl I saved one of my companions from destruction, who communicated to me an epistle she was quite charmed with. As she had a natural good taste, she observed the lines were not so smooth as Prior's[6] or Pope's, but had more thought and spirit than any of theirs. She was wonderfully delighted with such a demonstration of her lover's sense and passion, and not a little pleased with her own charms, that had force enough to inspire such elegancies. In the midst of this triumph, I showed her they were taken from

3. Edward Montagu (1625–1672), first Earl of Sandwich (and Samuel Pepys's patron), was Wortley's grandfather.
4. The Hon. William Pierrepont (1608–1678) was a prominent politician.
5. Edmund Waller (1606–1687), love poet frequently quoted (or plagiarized) by amorous wooers.
6. Matthew Prior (1664–1721), like Alexander Pope a celebrated poet.

Randolph's poems,[7] and the unfortunate transcriber was dismissed with the scorn he deserved. To say truth, the poor plagiary was very unlucky to fall into my hands; that author, being no longer in fashion, would have escaped anyone of less universal reading than myself. You should encourage your daughter to talk over with you what she reads, and as you are very capable of distinguishing, take care she does not mistake pert folly for wit and humor, or rhyme for poetry, which are the common errors of young people, and have a train of ill consequences.

The second caution to be given her (and which is most absolutely necessary) is to conceal whatever learning she attains, with as much solicitude as she would hide crookedness or lameness. The parade of it can only serve to draw on her the envy, and consequently the most inveterate hatred, of all he and she fools, which will certainly be at least three parts in four of all her acquaintance. The use of knowledge in our sex (beside the amusement of solitude) is to moderate the passions and learn to be contented with a small expense, which are the certain effects of a studious life and, it may be, preferable even to that fame which men have engrossed to themselves and will not suffer us to share. You will tell me I have not observed this rule myself, but you are mistaken; it is only inevitable accident that has given me any reputation that way. I have always carefully avoided it, and ever thought it a misfortune.

The explanation of this paragraph would occasion a long digression, which I will not trouble you with, it being my present design only to say what I think useful for the instruction of my granddaughter, which I have much at heart. If she has the same inclination (I should say passion) for learning that I was born with, history, geography, and philosophy will furnish her with materials to pass away cheerfully a longer life than is allotted to mortals. I believe there are few heads capable of making Sir I. Newton's[8] calculations, but the result of them is not difficult to be understood by a moderate capacity. Do not fear this should make her affect the character of Lady ——, or Lady ——, or Mrs. ——.[9] Those women are ridiculous, not because they have learning but because they have it not. One thinks herself a complete historian after reading Eachard's *Roman History*,[1] another a profound philosopher having got by heart some of Pope's unintelligible essays,[2] and a third an able divine on the strength of Whitfield's sermons.[3] Thus you hear them screaming politics and controversy. It is a saying of Thucydides, ignorance is bold, and knowledge reserved.[4] Indeed it is impossible to be far advanced in it without being more humbled by a conviction of human ignorance than elated by learning.

At the same time I recommend books, I neither exclude work nor drawing. I think it as scandalous for a woman not to know how to use a needle, as for a man not to know how to use a sword. I was once extreme fond of my pencil, and it was a great mortification to me when my father turned off[5] my master, having made a considerable progress for the short time I learnt. My over eagerness in the pursuit of it had brought a weakness on my eyes that made it necessary to leave it off, and all the advantage I got was the improvement of my hand. I see by hers that practice will make her a ready writer. She may attain it by serving you for a secretary when your

7. The minor writer Thomas Randolph (1605–1635), whose collected *Poems* were published in 1638.
8. Isaac Newton, mathematician and scientist, author of *Principia Mathematica* (1687).
9. The names, which Montagu omitted in her manuscript, have not been recovered.
1. Lawrence Echard, *The Roman History* (1695–1698).
2. Probably his *Essay on Man* (1733–1734) in four epistles, published long after the friendship between him and Montagu had ended.
3. George Whitfield (1714–1770), Methodist preacher.
4. Thucydides (c. 460–c. 399 B.C.E.), Greek historian of the Peloponnesian War; Montagu paraphrases his assertion that "boldness means ignorance and reflection brings hesitation" (*History* 2.40.3).
5. Dismissed.

health or affairs make it troublesome to you to write yourself, and custom will make it an agreeable amusement to her. She cannot have too many for that station of life which will probably be her fate. The ultimate end of your education was to make you a good wife (and I have the comfort to hear that you are one); hers ought to be, to make her happy in a virgin state. I will not say it is happier, but it is undoubtedly safer than any marriage. In a lottery where there is (at the lowest computation) ten thousand blanks to a prize, it is the most prudent choice not to venture.

I have always been so thoroughly persuaded of this truth that, notwithstanding the flattering views I had for you (as I never intended you a sacrifice to my vanity), I thought I owed you the justice to lay before you all the hazards attending matrimony. You may recollect I did so in the strongest manner. Perhaps you may have more success in the instructing your daughter. She has so much company at home she will not need seeking it abroad, and will more readily take the notions you think fit to give her. As you were alone in my family, it would have been thought a great cruelty to suffer you no companions of your own age, especially having so many near relations, and I do not wonder their opinions influenced yours. I was not sorry to see you not determined on a single life, knowing it was not your father's intention, and contented myself with endeavoring to make your home so easy that you might not be in haste to leave it.

I am afraid you will think this a very long and insignificant letter. I hope the kindness of the design will excuse it, being willing to give you every proof in my power that I am your most affectionate Mother,

M. Wortley.

Epistle from Mrs. Yonge to Her Husband[1]

Think not this paper comes with vain pretense
To move your pity, or to mourn th' offense.
Too well I know that hard obdurate heart;
No soft'ning mercy there will take my part,
Nor can a woman's arguments prevail,
When even your patron's wise example fails,[2]
But this last privilege I still retain,
Th' oppressed and injured always may complain.
  Too, too severely laws of honor bind
The weak submissive sex of womankind.
If sighs have gained or force compelled our hand,
Deceived by art, or urged by stern command,
Whatever motive binds the fatal tie,
The judging world expects our constancy.
  Just Heaven! (for sure in heaven does justice reign
Though tricks below that sacred name profane)

1. In 1724 the heiress Mary Yonge became embroiled in a highly publicized divorce from her notorious, womanizing husband William, who accused her (accurately) of adultery committed during the couple's separation. Public sympathy was on her side, but the king approved a divorce that allowed her husband to retain most of her fortune. Montagu's poem remained in manuscript throughout her life.

2. I.e., Robert Walpole's. William Yonge was a devoted adherent of the powerful minister, who carried on open adulteries himself but also (unlike Yonge) permitted them to his wife.

To you appealing I submit my cause
Nor fear a judgment from impartial laws.
All bargains but conditional are made;
The purchase void, the creditor unpaid,
Defrauded servants are from service free;
A wounded slave regains his liberty.
For wives ill used no remedy remains,
To daily racks condemned, and to eternal chains.
From whence is this unjust distinction grown?
Are we not formed with passions like your own?
Nature with equal fire our souls endued,
Our minds as haughty, and as warm our blood;
O're the wide world your pleasures you pursue,
The change is justified by something new;
But we must sigh in silence—and be true.
Our sex's weakness you expose and blame
(Of every prattling fop the common theme),
Yet from this weakness you suppose is due
Sublimer virtue than your Cato[3] knew.
Had Heaven designed us trials so severe,
It would have formed our tempers then to bear.
And I have borne (O what have I not borne!)
The pang of jealousy, th' insults of scorn.
Wearied at length, I from your sight remove,
And place my future hopes in secret love.
In the gay bloom of glowing youth retired,
I quit the woman's joy to be admired,
With that small pension your hard heart allows,
Renounce your fortune, and release your vows.
To custom (though unjust) so much is due;
I hide my frailty from the public view.
My conscience clear, yet sensible of shame,
My life I hazard, to preserve my fame.
And I prefer this low inglorious state,
To vile dependence on the thing I hate—
But you pursue me to this last retreat.
Dragged into light, my tender crime is shown
And every circumstance of fondness known.
Beneath the shelter of the law you stand,
And urge my ruin with a cruel hand.
While to my fault thus rigidly severe,
Tamely submissive to the man you fear.
This wretched outcast, this abandoned wife,
Has yet this joy to sweeten shameful life,
By your mean conduct, infamously loose,

3. Marcus Porcius Cato of Utica (95–46 B.C.E.), champion of the Roman Republic, whose name had become a byword for integrity.

You are at once my accuser, and excuse.
Let me be damned by the censorious prude
(Stupidly dull, or spiritually lewd),
My hapless case will surely pity find
From every just and reasonable mind,
When to the final sentence I submit;
The lips condemn me, but their souls acquit.
No more my husband, to your pleasures go,
The sweets of your recovered freedom know;
Go; court the brittle friendship of the great,
Smile at his board, or at his levée[4] wait
And when dismissed, to Madam's toilet° fly, *dressing room*
More than her chambermaids, or glasses,° lie, *mirrors*
Tell her how young she looks, how heavenly fair,
Admire the lilies and the roses there;
Your high ambition may be gratified,
Some cousin of her own be made your bride,
And you the father of a glorious race
Endowed with Ch——l's strength and Low—r's face.[5]

1724 1972

The Lover: A Ballad

1

At length, by so much importunity pressed,
Take (Molly[1]) at once the inside of my breast;
This stupid indifference so often you blame
Is not owing to nature, to fear, or to shame;
I am not as cold as a virgin in lead,
Nor is Sunday's sermon so strong in my head;
I know but too well how time flies along,
That we live but few years and yet fewer are young.

2

But I hate to be cheated, and never will buy
Long years of repentance for moments of joy.
Oh was there a man (but where shall I find
Good sense, and good nature so equally joined?)
Would value his pleasure, contribute to mine,
Not meanly would boast, nor lewdly design,
Not over severe, yet not stupidly vain,
For I would have the power though not give the pain.

4. Social assemblies at the homes of the "great," often crowded with petitioners, opportunists, and sycophants.

5. The line implies that the adulterous William Yonge will himself be supplanted in his next wife's bed by fellow-libertines: Charles Churchill (c. 1679–1745) and Antony Lowther (d. 1741).

1. Probably Maria ("Molly") Skerrett (1702–1738), Montagu's friend and Robert Walpole's mistress.

3

No pedant yet learned, not rakehelly gay
Or laughing because he has nothing to say,
To all my whole sex obliging and free,
Yet never be fond of any but me.
In public preserve the decorums are just
And show in his eyes he is true to his trust,
Then rarely approach, and respectfully bow,
Yet not fulsomely pert, nor yet foppishly low.

4

But when the long hours of public are past
And we meet with champagne and a chicken at last,
May every fond pleasure that hour endear,
Be banished afar both discretion and fear,
Forgetting or scorning the airs of the crowd
He may cease to be formal, and I to be proud,
Till lost in the joy, we confess that we live
And he may be rude, and yet I may forgive.

5

And that my delight may be solidly fixed
Let the friend and the lover be handsomely mixed,
In whose tender bosom my soul might confide,
Whose kindness can soothe me, whose counsel could guide;
From such a dear lover as here I describe
No danger should fright me, no millions should bribe,
But till this astonishing creature I know
As I long have lived chaste I will keep myself so.

6

I never will share with the wanton coquette,
Or be caught by a vain affectation of wit.
The toasters and songsters may try all their art
But never shall enter the pass of my heart;
I loathe the lewd rake, the dressed fopling despise,
Before such pursuers the nice virgin flies;
And as Ovid has sweetly in parables told
We harden like trees, and like rivers are cold.[2]

c. 1721–1725 1747

2. In his *Metamorphoses,* Ovid tells stories of virgins who are transformed into a laurel tree (Daphne) or a fountain (Arethusa), rather than succumb to the importunities of a pursuing god (1.452–567; 5.572–641).

John Gay
1685–1732

John Gay was born to hardworking, pious tradespeople in Barnstaple, a busy port town in southwestern England. Educated well but orphaned early, he moved at age eighteen to London, where he tried trade for a time, gave it up for literature, and made himself a master of the mock, at a moment when the mock mattered most.

In the early eighteenth century, the "mock" was not just a gesture of derision but an intricate art form, in which scenes of contemporary life, appropriated from streets, stables, salons, and other ordinary sites, were represented in grand styles first crafted for the actions of ancient heroes. In his mock-pastoral *Description of a City Shower* (1709), for example, Swift depicted the muddy chaos of an urban rainstorm in the language Virgil had devised to render the rural delights of a Golden Age; in his mock-epic *Rape of the Lock* (1712), Pope portrayed the trivial agitations of London beaux and belles in formulations absorbed from Homer. Befriended by Pope and Swift, Gay became perhaps the most supple and assiduous practitioner in their mock-heroic vein. In his early successes, he showed himself adept at devising new combinations of mode and topic, new ways of savoring both high styles and low subjects even while making fun of them. In *The Shepherd's Week* (1714), he took on both Virgil's idealism and also the ungainly "realism" attempted by some of that Roman poet's eighteenth-century imitators. He endowed his shepherds with preposterously "rustic" names (Bumkinet, Hobnelia, Bowzybeus) and a ludicrously hybrid language, alternately high-flying and homespun. But he gave them also a grace and good nature that survive the mock. The poem's closing image of a drunken swain sleeping out the sunset ("ruddy, like his face, the sun descends") reads like the poet's own benediction. In his next big work, *Trivia, or the Art of Walking the Streets of London* (1716), Gay's grandiloquent Virgilian instruction makes city walking seem not just a "trivial" chore but an "art," comic, challenging, alternately appalling and attractive.

Gay built his life as he made his art, by improvising. He earned money by his plays and poems; he lost money in that evanescent investment scheme the South Sea Bubble; he served as Commissioner of Lotteries, and as secretary, steward, and companion to several members of the nobility; and he sought for years to secure steady patronage at court, by means of flattering verse and ingratiating conduct. His frustration peaked when he published a virtuosic set of *Fables* (1727) for the four-year-old Prince William and received as reward a royal appointment as attendant to the prince's two-year-old sister. The aristocrats he courted valued him for his compliant temper and beguiling company, but they patronized him in both senses of the word.

Gay refused the royal appointment, staking his hopes instead on his new project for the stage, *The Beggar's Opera* (1728). The initial notion for the piece had come from Swift, who suggested a "Newgate pastoral"—that is, a mixture in which the "whores and thieves" who inhabited Newgate prison and its neighborhood would supplant the nymphs and shepherds frolicking on Arcadian hillsides. Swift's hint is an ordinary mock recipe: two worlds collide, one real, one fictitious. Gay built from it an intricate hall of mirrors, where many more worlds met. For his thieves he drew on two real-life models, recently executed: Jonathan Wild and Jack Sheppard. Wild had run a large criminal organization that profited him two ways: he collected money from the resale of goods stolen by his subordinates; and he collected rewards from the government for turning in his associates and rivals whenever they became too troublesome. Sheppard had acquired fame as Wild's most high-spirited and elusive prey; a brilliant thief in his own right, he had often managed to escape the prisons and predicaments into which Wild had betrayed him. In *The Beggar's Opera*, Gay resurrects the two late criminals as Mr. Peachum, who like Wild manages a lucrative double life, and Captain Macheath, who like Sheppard proves susceptible of capture and gifted at escape. Here the worlds begin to multiply. Developing a comparison then current in the political press, Gay made his criminals conjure up the most powerful politician alive: Robert Walpole, the Whig prime minister who ran his political machine (so the *Opera* insists) with the efficiency of Peachum and the self-indulgence of Macheath.

The Beggar's Opera mixed low with high in form as well as content. Like "Newgate pastoral," the phrase "beggar's opera" fuses opposites. Italian opera was the most expensive, exotic, and fashionable entertainment in London. Gay's theatrical game was to replay opera's intricacies using beggars' means. He supplanted the elaborate arias of foreign composers with the simpler tunes of British street songs; he replaced the original words to those tunes with new lyrics that voiced his characters' strong emotions; he even re-enacted a recent, much-publicized rivalry between two high-paid prima donnas, at war for the allegiance of their audience, in the contest he stages between Peachum's daughter Polly and the jailer's daughter Lucy Lockit for the devotion of fickle Captain Macheath. On Gay's stage, worlds converge with a density even Swift could not have foreseen. Opera house and street corner; Whitehall and Newgate; art and commerce; politics, business, and crime: all of these turn out to operate on the same principles of self-interest.

Reading the new piece before its premiere, Gay's well-wishers hedged their bets as to its success. "It would either take greatly," the playwright William Congreve predicted, "or be damned confoundedly." In the event, it did both. The triumph of the opening night is the stuff of theatrical legend, but it provoked a counter-chorus of condemnation from critics who saw the play as endangering opera, glorifying thieves, traducing government. Amid the debate, the play enjoyed a long run, entrancing an audience made up of the very people it mocked (including Walpole himself, who reportedly conducted an extra chorus of the play's most satiric song, "When you censure the age"). *The Beggar's Opera* offered theatergoers simple pleasures (deft performances, comic reversals, well-loved tunes) and intricate ones too: the often ironic play of Gay's new lyrics against the original words that the auditors had already in their heads; the debunking of love and marriage in sharp dialogue and the glorifying of it in sentimental song; the volatile charisma of the mock-hero Macheath, who for many observers came to seem utterly heroic by evening's end; the arresting alchemy by which Gay transmuted (as the Romantic essayist William Hazlitt later expressed it) "this motley group" of "highwaymen, turnkeys, their mistresses, wives, or daughters . . . into a set of fine gentlemen and ladies, satirists and philosophers." In his painting of the opening night (Color Plate 26), William Hogarth suggests how these transformations came to include the spectators as well. Occupying the sides of the stage, an audience of aristocrats, politicians, and theater people (Gay himself among them) observe the play in progress; they are encompassed by the same prison walls wherein Macheath and his pursuers play out their intricate transactions, in which everything and everyone—goods, votes, spouses—had become commodities, items of exchange, reckoned in account books as profit and as loss.

The Beggar's Opera brought Gay prosperity and celebrity but not security. Walpole evicted him from his subsidized lodgings and banned production of the *Opera*'s much-anticipated sequel *Polly*. When Gay died less than five years after his fabled first night, however, he was buried with elaborate ceremony in the Poet's Corner of Westminster Abbey. Friends commended the appropriateness of the site but marveled at the incongruity of the pomp. Incongruity, though, had been Gay's stock in trade, and nowhere more so than in his greatest hit. Its long run continues in theaters around the world. It spawned numberless short-lived imitations in its own time and a more durable descendant in the twentieth century: *Die Dreigroschenoper* (*The Threepenny Opera*, 1928), in which Bertolt Brecht and Kurt Weill adapted Gay's characters, plot, and critique of commerce to produce their own dark and gleeful Marxist assault on contemporary capitalism. By routes less direct, Gay's work has infused both the modern musical theater (which continues to combine operatic and popular modes) and pop culture in general—where, for example, Brecht and Weill's sardonic *Ballad of Mack the Knife* became a pop hit of the early 1960s. *The Beggar's Opera* grabbed attention first—and sustains it still—for the ironic dexterity with which it mixed things up, in full mock mode.

Beggar's Opera

Nos hæc novimus esse nihil.[1]

Dramatis Personæ[2]

Men

PEACHUM
LOCKIT
MACHEATH
FILCH
JEMMY TWITCHER
CROOK-FINGERED JACK
WAT DREARY
ROBIN OF BAGSHOT
NIMMING NED
HARRY PADDINGTON
MATT OF THE MINT
BEN BUDGE

(Jemmy Twitcher through Ben Budge: *Macheath's Gang*)

BEGGAR
PLAYER
DRAWER, HARPER, JAILER, OTHER MEMBERS OF THE GANG, CONSTABLES, TURNKEYS, PRISONERS, RABBLE

Women

MRS. PEACHUM
POLLY PEACHUM
LUCY LOCKIT
DIANA TRAPES
MRS. COAXER
DOLLY TRULL
MRS. VIXEN
BETTY DOXY
JENNY DIVER
MRS. SLAMMEKIN
SUKY TAWDRY
MOLLY BRAZEN

(Mrs. Coaxer through Molly Brazen: *Women of the Town*)

FOUR WOMEN WITH CHILDREN

1. We know these things to be nothing (Martial, *Epigrams* 13.2.8).
2. Many of these names reflect the characters' low-life habits: to "peach" is to inform on, to "filch" is to steal, "twitchers" are pickpockets, "nimmers" are thieves, and "trulls" and "doxies" are prostitutes.

INTRODUCTION

[*Beggar, Player*]

BEGGAR: If poverty be a title[3] to poetry, I am sure nobody can dispute mine. I own myself of the Company of Beggars; and I make one at their weekly festivals at St. Giles's.[4] I have a small yearly salary for my catches,[5] and am welcome to a dinner there whenever I please, which is more than most poets can say.

PLAYER: As we live by the Muses, 'tis but gratitude in us to encourage poetical merit wherever we find it. The Muses, contrary to all other ladies, pay no distinction to dress, and never partially[6] mistake the pertness of embroidery for wit, nor the modesty of want for dullness. Be the author who he will, we push his play as far as it will go. So (though you are in want) I wish you success heartily.

BEGGAR: This piece I own was originally writ for the celebrating the marriage of James Chanter and Moll Lay, two most excellent ballad singers. I have introduced the similes that are in all your celebrated operas: the swallow, the moth, the bee, the ship, the flower, etc. Besides, I have a prison scene, which the ladies always reckon charmingly pathetic. As to the parts, I have observed such a nice impartiality to our two ladies, that it is impossible for either of them to take offense.[7] I hope I may be forgiven, that I have not made my opera throughout unnatural, like those in vogue; for I have no recitative.[8] Excepting this, as I have consented to have neither prologue nor epilogue, it must be allowed an opera in all its forms. The piece indeed hath been heretofore frequently represented by ourselves in our great room at St. Giles's, so that I cannot too often acknowledge your charity in bringing it now on the stage.

PLAYER: But I see 'tis time for us to withdraw; the actors are preparing to begin. Play away the overture.

[*Exeunt.*]

ACT 1

Scene 1. Peachum's House

[*Peachum sitting at a table with a large book of accounts before him.*]

Air 1. An old woman clothed in gray[9]

Through all the employments of life
Each neighbor abuses his brother;
Whore and rogue they call husband and wife:
All professions be-rogue one another.
The priest calls the lawyer a cheat,
The lawyer be-knaves the divine;

3. Deed of ownership.
4. An almshouse near the parish of St. Giles, patron saint of lepers and beggars.
5. Rounds, songs for two or more voices in which each voice starts the same melody at a different time. The form was very popular; enthusiasts assembled in "catch clubs" for whole evenings of singing.
6. In a prejudiced way.
7. The Beggar alludes to recent rivalries between leading ladies in Italian operas.
8. In Italian opera, arias are interspersed with sung speech ("recitative"); this English opera will avoid the second, "unnatural" convention.
9. I.e., this air is to be sung to the familiar ballad tune, "An Old Woman Clothed in Gray."

And the statesman, because he's so great,[1]
Thinks his trade as honest as mine.

A lawyer is an honest employment; so is mine. Like me too he acts in a double capacity, both against rogues and for 'em; for 'tis but fitting that we should protect and encourage cheats, since we live by them.

Scene 2

[*Peachum, Filch*]

FILCH: Sir, Black Moll hath sent word her trial comes on in the afternoon, and she hopes you will order matters so as to bring her off.

PEACHUM: Why, she may plead her belly at worst;[2] to my knowledge she hath taken care of that security. But as the wench is very active and industrious, you may satisfy her that I'll soften the evidence.

FILCH: Tom Gagg, Sir, is found guilty.

PEACHUM: A lazy dog! When I took him the time before, I told him what he would come to if he did not mend his hand. This is death without reprieve. I may venture to book him.[3] [*Writes.*] For Tom Gagg, forty pounds. Let Betty Sly know that I'll save her from transportation,[4] for I can get more by her staying in England.

FILCH: Betty hath brought more goods into our lock[5] to-year than any five of the gang; and in truth, 'tis a pity to lose so good a customer.

PEACHUM: If none of the gang take her off,[6] she may, in the common course of business, live a twelve-month longer. I love to let women 'scape. A good sportsman always lets the hen partridges fly, because the breed of the game depends upon them. Besides, here the law allows us no reward; there is nothing to be got by the death of women—except our wives.[7]

FILCH: Without dispute, she is a fine woman! 'Twas to her I was obliged for my education, and (to say a bold word) she hath trained up more young fellows to the business than the gaming-table.

PEACHUM: Truly, Filch, thy observation is right. We and the surgeons[8] are more beholden to women than all the professions besides.

Air 2. The bonny gray-eyed morn

FILCH: *'Tis woman that seduces all mankind,*
By her we first were taught the wheedling arts:
Her very eyes can cheat; when most she's kind,
She tricks us of our money with our hearts.
For her, like wolves by night we roam for prey,
And practice ev'ry fraud to bribe her charms;
For suits of love, like law, are won by pay,
And beauty must be fee'd into our arms.

PEACHUM: But make haste to Newgate,[9] boy, and let my friends know what I intend; for I love to make them easy one way or other.

1. The word "great" was often attached to the Whig Prime Minister Robert Walpole, whom Gay's Tory party opposed vigorously in the 1720s and 1730s.
2. A pregnant woman could not be hanged.
3. I.e., enter in the books the reward for "peaching" him.
4. Convicted criminals were sometimes transported to the colonies.
5. A holding-place for stolen goods.
6. Turn her in (or kill her).
7. Husbands inherited their wives' property.
8. Who treat venereal diseases.
9. London's main prison.

FILCH: When a gentleman is long kept in suspense, penitence may break his spirit ever after. Besides, certainty gives a man a good air upon his trial, and makes him risk another without fear or scruple. But I'll away, for 'tis a pleasure to be the messenger of comfort to friends in affliction.

Scene 3

[*Peachum*]

But 'tis now high time to look about me for a decent execution against next Sessions.[1] I hate a lazy rogue, by whom one can get nothing 'til he is hanged. A register of the gang, [*reading*] "Crook-Fingered Jack." A year and a half in the service. Let me see how much the stock owes to his industry: one, two, three, four, five gold watches, and seven silver ones. A mighty clean-handed fellow! Sixteen snuff-boxes, five of them of true gold. Six dozen of handkerchiefs, four silver-hilted swords, half a dozen of shirts, three tie-periwigs, and a piece of broad cloth. Considering these are only the fruits of his leisure hours, I don't know a prettier fellow, for no man alive hath a more engaging presence of mind upon the road. "Wat Dreary, alias Brown Will." An irregular dog, who hath an underhand way of disposing of his goods. I'll try him[2] only for a Sessions or two longer upon his good behavior. "Harry Paddington." A poor petty-larceny rascal, without the least genius; that fellow, though he were to live these six months, will never come to the gallows with any credit. "Slippery Sam": he goes off the next Sessions, for the villain hath the impudence to have views of following his trade as a tailor, which he calls an honest employment. "Matt of the Mint": lifted[3] not above a month ago, a promising sturdy fellow, and diligent in his way; somewhat too bold and hasty, and may raise good contributions on[4] the public, if he does not cut himself short by murder. "Tom Tipple." A guzzling soaking sot, who is always too drunk to stand himself, or to make others stand. A cart is absolutely necessary for him.[5] "Robin of Bagshot, alias Gorgon, alias Bluff Bob, alias Carbuncle, alias Bob Booty."[6]

Scene 4

[*Peachum, Mrs. Peachum*]

MRS. PEACHUM: What of Bob Booty, husband? I hope nothing bad hath betided him. You know, my dear, he's a favorite customer of mine. 'Twas he made me a present of this ring.

PEACHUM: I have set his name down in the blacklist, that's all, my dear; he spends his life among women, and as soon as his money is gone, one or other of the ladies will hang him for the reward, and there's forty pound lost to us forever.

MRS. PEACHUM: You know, my dear, I never meddle in matters of death; I always leave those affairs to you. Women indeed are bitter bad judges in these cases, for they are so partial to the brave that they think every man handsome who is going to the camp[7] or the gallows.

1. For the next sitting of the criminal court.
2. Keep him on.
3. Enlisted.
4. From.
5. Condemned prisoners were carried in carts to the place of execution.
6. All these names point towards (and mock) prime minister Robert Walpole.
7. I.e., to war.

Air 3. Cold and raw

If any wench Venus's girdle wear,
Though she be never so ugly;
Lilies and roses will quickly appear,
And her face look wond'rous smugly.
Beneath the left ear so fit but a cord,
(A rope so charming a zone[8] is!)
The youth in his cart hath the air of a lord,
And we cry, "There dies an Adonis!"

But really, husband, you should not be too hardhearted, for you never had a finer, braver set of men than at present. We have not had a murder among them all, these seven months. And truly, my dear, that is a great blessing.

PEACHUM: What a dickens is the woman always a-whimpering about murder for? No gentleman is ever looked upon the worse for killing a man in his own defense; and if business cannot be carried on without it, what would you have a gentleman do?

MRS. PEACHUM: If I am in the wrong, my dear, you must excuse me, for nobody can help the frailty of an overscrupulous conscience.

PEACHUM: Murder is as fashionable a crime as a man can be guilty of. How many fine gentlemen have we in Newgate every year, purely upon that article! If they have wherewithal to persuade the jury to bring it in[9] manslaughter, what are they the worse for it? So, my dear, have done upon this subject. Was Captain Macheath here this morning, for the banknotes[1] he left with you last week?

MRS. PEACHUM: Yes, my dear; and though the bank hath stopped payment, he was so cheerful and so agreeable! Sure there is not a finer gentleman upon the road than the Captain! If he comes from Bagshot[2] at any reasonable hour he hath promised to make one this evening with Polly and me, and Bob Booty, at a party of quadrille.[3] Pray, my dear, is the Captain rich?

PEACHUM: The Captain keeps too good company ever to grow rich. Marybone and the chocolate-houses[4] are his undoing. The man that proposes to get money by play should have the education of a fine gentleman, and be trained up to it from his youth.

MRS. PEACHUM: Really, I am sorry upon Polly's account the Captain hath not more discretion. What business hath he to keep company with lords and gentlemen? He should leave them to prey upon one another.

PEACHUM: Upon Polly's account! What a plague does the woman mean? Upon Polly's account!

MRS. PEACHUM: Captain Macheath is very fond of the girl.

PEACHUM: And what then?

MRS. PEACHUM: If I have any skill in the ways of women, I am sure Polly thinks him a very pretty man.

PEACHUM: And what then? You would not be so mad to have the wench marry him! Gamesters and highwaymen are generally very good to their whores, but they are very devils to their wives.

8. Belt.
9. Reduce it to.
1. Bankers' checks, payable to bearer.
2. Bagshot Heath, west of London, where many highwaymen plied their trade.
3. A fashionable card game for four.
4. Both were popular sites for gambling.

MRS. PEACHUM: But if Polly should be in love, how should we help her, or how can she help herself? Poor girl, I am in the utmost concern about her.

Air 4. Why is your faithful slave disdained?

If love the virgin's heart invade,
How, like a moth, the simple maid
Still[5] *plays about the flame!*
If soon she be not made a wife,
Her honor's singed, and then for life,
She's—what I dare not name.

PEACHUM: Look ye, wife. A handsome wench in our way of business is as profitable as at the bar of a Temple[6] coffee-house, who looks upon it as her livelihood to grant every liberty but one. You see I would indulge the girl as far as prudently we can—in anything but marriage! After that, my dear, how shall we be safe? Are we not then in her husband's power? For a husband hath the absolute power over all a wife's secrets but her own. If the girl had the discretion of a court lady, who can have a dozen young fellows at her ear without complying with one, I should not matter it; but Polly is tinder, and a spark will at once set her on a flame. Married! If the wench does not know her own profit, sure she knows her own pleasure better than to make herself a property! My daughter to me should be, like a court lady to a minister of state, a key to the whole gang. Married! If the affair is not already done, I'll terrify her from it, by the example of our neighbors.

MRS. PEACHUM: Mayhap, my dear, you may injure the girl. She loves to imitate the fine ladies, and she may only allow the Captain liberties in the view of interest.[7]

PEACHUM: But 'tis your duty, my dear, to warn the girl against her ruin, and to instruct her how to make the most of her beauty. I'll go to her this moment, and sift[8] her. In the meantime, wife, rip out the coronets and marks[9] of these dozen of cambric[1] handkerchiefs, for I can dispose of them this afternoon to a chap[2] in the City.

Scene 5

[*Mrs. Peachum*]

Never was a man more out of the way in an argument than my husband! Why must our Polly, forsooth, differ from her sex, and love only her husband? And why must Polly's marriage, contrary to all observation, make her the less followed by other men? All men are thieves in love, and like a woman the better for being another's property.

Air 5. Of all the simple things we do

A maid is like the golden ore
Which hath guineas intrinsical in't,
Whose worth is never known before
It is tried and impressed[3] *in the mint.*

5. Constantly.
6. A law school, whose students frequented the nearby gathering places.
7. Self-interest; profit.
8. Question.
9. The embroidered monograms by which the wealthy designated their property.
1. Fine white linen.
2. Dealer.
3. Smelted and stamped.

A wife's like a guinea in gold,
Stamped with the name of her spouse;
Now here, now there, is bought, or is sold,
And is current in every house.

Scene 6

[*Mrs. Peachum, Filch*]

MRS. PEACHUM: Come hither, Filch. I am as fond of this child, as though my mind misgave me[4] he were my own. He hath as fine a hand at picking a pocket as a woman, and is as nimble-fingered as a juggler. If an unlucky session does not cut the rope of thy life, I pronounce, boy, thou wilt be a great man[5] in history. Where was your post last night, my boy?

FILCH: I plied at the opera, madam; and considering 'twas neither dark nor rainy, so that there was no great hurry in getting chairs and coaches, made a tolerable hand on't. These seven handkerchiefs, madam.

MRS. PEACHUM: Colored ones, I see. They are of sure sale from our warehouse at Redriff among the seamen.

FILCH: And this snuffbox.

MRS. PEACHUM: Set in gold! A pretty encouragement this to a young beginner!

FILCH: I had a fair tug at a charming gold watch. Pox take the tailors for making the fobs[6] so deep and narrow! It stuck by the way, and I was forced to make my escape under a coach. Really, madam, I fear I shall be cut off in the flower of my youth, so that every now and then (since I was pumped[7]) I have thoughts of taking up[8] and going to sea.

MRS. PEACHUM: You should go to Hockley in the Hole,[9] and to Marybone, child, to learn valor. These are the schools that have bred so many brave men. I thought, boy, by this time, thou hadst lost fear as well as shame. Poor lad! How little does he know as yet of the Old Bailey![1] For the first fact[2] I'll insure thee from being hanged; and going to sea, Filch, will come time enough upon a sentence of transportation. But now, since you have nothing better to do, ev'n go to your book, and learn your catechism;[3] for really a man makes but an ill figure in the Ordinary's Paper,[4] who cannot give a satisfactory answer to his questions. But, hark you, my lad. Don't tell me a lie, for you know I hate a liar. Do you know of anything that hath passed between Captain Macheath and our Polly?

FILCH: I beg you, Madam, don't ask me; for I must either tell a lie to you or to Miss Polly; for I promised her I would not tell.

MRS. PEACHUM: But when the honor of our family is concerned—

FILCH: I shall lead a sad life with Miss Polly, if ever she come to know that I told you. Besides, I would not willingly forfeit my own honor by betraying anybody.

MRS. PEACHUM: Yonder comes my husband and Polly. Come, Filch, you shall go with me into my own room, and tell me the whole story. I'll give thee a glass of a most delicious cordial that I keep for my own drinking.

4. Suspected.
5. Another jab at Walpole's covert criminality.
6. Watch-pockets.
7. Half-drowned under a pump (a common punishment for pickpockets).
8. Reforming.
9. An area known for bear-baiting, dogfights, and other sporting contests.
1. London's central criminal court.
2. Crime.
3. In keeping with the legal provision called "benefit of clergy," first offenders who could answer questions from the Christian catechism might have their sentences commuted from execution to transportation.
4. The Ordinary (prison chaplain) determined whether prisoners qualified for "benefit of clergy"—and also published accounts of how condemned prisoners conducted themselves in the hours leading up to execution.

Scene 7

[*Peachum, Polly*]

POLLY: I know as well as any of the fine ladies how to make the most of my self and of my man too. A woman knows how to be mercenary, though she hath never been in a court or at an assembly.[5] We have it in our natures, Papa. If I allow Captain Macheath some trifling liberties, I have this watch and other visible marks of his favor to show for it. A girl who cannot grant some things, and refuse what is most material, will make but a poor hand of her beauty, and soon be thrown upon the common.

Air 6. What shall I do to show how much I love her?

Virgins are like the fair flower in its luster,
Which in the garden enamels the ground;
Near it the bees in play flutter and cluster,
And gaudy butterflies frolic around.
But, when once plucked, 'tis no longer alluring,
To Covent Garden[6] *'tis sent (as yet sweet),*
There fades, and shrinks, and grows past all enduring,
Rots, stinks, and dies, and is trod under feet.

PEACHUM: You know, Polly, I am not against your toying and trifling with a customer in the way of business, or to get out a secret, or so. But if I find out that you have played the fool and are married, you jade you, I'll cut your throat, hussy. Now you know my mind.

Scene 8

[*Peachum, Polly, Mrs. Peachum*]

Air 7. Oh London is a fine town

[Mrs. *Peachum, in a very great passion*]

Our Polly is a sad slut! nor heeds what we have taught her.
I wonder any man alive will ever rear a daughter!
For she must have both hoods and gowns, and hoops to swell her pride,
With scarves and stays,[7] *and gloves and lace; and she will have men beside;*
And when she's dressed with care and cost, all tempting, fine and gay,
As men should serve a cowcumber,[8] *she flings herself away.*
Our Polly is a sad slut, etc.

You baggage! You hussy! You inconsiderate jade! Had you been hanged, it would not have vexed me, for that might have been your misfortune; but to do such a mad thing by choice! The wench is married, husband.

PEACHUM: Married! The Captain is a bold man, and will risk anything for money; to be sure he believes her a fortune. Do you think your mother and I should have lived comfortably so long together, if ever we had been married? Baggage!

5. A fashionable social gathering.
6. A London market for flowers, fruits, and vegetables; also a haunt of prostitutes.
7. Corsets.
8. I.e., as though she were throwing away a (worthless) cucumber.

MRS. PEACHUM: I knew she was always a proud slut; and now the wench hath played the fool and married, because forsooth she would do like the gentry. Can you support the expense of a husband, hussy, in gaming, drinking, and whoring? Have you money enough to carry on the daily quarrels of man and wife about who shall squander most? There are not many husbands and wives who can bear the charges[9] of plaguing one another in a handsome way. If you must be married, could you introduce nobody into our family but a highwayman? Why, thou foolish jade, thou wilt be as ill used, and as much neglected, as if thou hadst married a lord!

PEACHUM: Let not your anger, my dear, break through the rules of decency, for the Captain looks upon himself in the military capacity, as a gentleman by his profession. Besides what he hath already, I know he is in a fair way of getting, or of dying;[1] and both these ways, let me tell you, are most excellent chances for a wife. Tell me, hussy, are you ruined or no?

MRS. PEACHUM: With Polly's fortune, she might very well have gone off to a person of distinction. Yes, that you might, you pouting slut!

PEACHUM: What, is the wench dumb? Speak, or I'll make you plead by squeezing out an answer from you.[2] Are you really bound wife to him, or are you only upon liking?

[*Pinches her.*]

POLLY [*Screaming*]: Oh!

MRS. PEACHUM: How the mother is to be pitied who hath handsome daughters! Locks, bolts, bars, and lectures of morality are nothing to them. They break through them all. They have as much pleasure in cheating a father and mother as in cheating at cards.

PEACHUM: Why, Polly, I shall soon know if your are married, by Macheath's keeping from[3] our house.

Air 8. Grim king of the ghosts

POLLY: *Can love be controlled by advice?*
Will Cupid our mothers obey?
Though my heart were as frozen as ice,
At his flame 'twould have melted away.

When he kissed me so closely he pressed,
'Twas so sweet that I must have complied;
So I thought it both safest and best
To marry, for fear you should chide.

MRS. PEACHUM: Then all the hopes of our family are gone forever and ever!

PEACHUM: And Macheath may hang his father and mother-in-law, in hope to get into their daughter's fortune.

POLLY: I did not marry him (as 'tis the fashion) coolly and deliberately for honor and money. But, I love him.

MRS. PEACHUM: Love him! Worse and worse! I thought the girl had been better bred. Oh husband, husband! Her folly makes me mad! My head swims! I'm distracted! I can't support myself—Oh!

9. Expense.
1. He is likely to grow richer, or to die on the gallows.
2. Confessions were sometimes extracted by pressing the prisoner with weights.
3. Avoiding.

[*Faints*.]

PEACHUM: See, wench, to what a condition you have reduced your poor mother! A glass of cordial, this instant. How the poor woman takes it to heart!

[*Polly goes out, and returns with it*.]

Ah, hussy, now this is the only comfort your mother has left!

POLLY: Give her another glass, Sir; my mama drinks double the quantity whenever she is out of order. This, you see, fetches[4] her.

MRS. PEACHUM: The girl shows such a readiness, and so much concern, that I could almost find in my heart to forgive her.

Air 9. Oh Jenny, Oh Jenny, where hast thou been.

Oh Polly, you might have toyed and kissed.
By keeping men off, you keep them on.

POLLY: *But he so teased me,*
And he so pleased me,
What I did, you must have done.

MRS. PEACHUM: Not with a highwayman, you sorry slut!

PEACHUM: A word with you, wife. 'Tis no new thing for a wench to take man without consent of parents. You know 'tis the frailty of woman, my dear.

MRS. PEACHUM: Yes, indeed, the sex is frail. But the first time a woman is frail, she should be somewhat nice[5] methinks, for then or never is the time to make her fortune. After that, she hath nothing to do but guard herself from being found out, and she may do what she pleases.

PEACHUM: Make yourself a little easy; I have a thought shall soon set all matters again to rights. Why so melancholy, Polly? Since what is done cannot be undone, we must all endeavor to make the best of it.

MRS. PEACHUM: Well, Polly, as far as one woman can forgive another, I forgive thee. Your father is too fond of you, hussy.

POLLY: Then all my sorrows are at an end.

MRS. PEACHUM: A mighty likely speech in troth, for a wench who is just married!

Air 10. Thomas, I cannot

POLLY: *I, like a ship in storms, was tossed;*
Yet afraid to put in to land;
For seized in the port the vessel's lost,
Whose treasure is contraband.
The waves are laid,[6]
My duty's paid.
O joy beyond expression!
Thus, safe ashore,
I ask no more,
My all is in my possession.

PEACHUM: I hear customers in t'other room. Go, talk with 'em, Polly; but come to us again, as soon as they are gone. But, hark ye, child, if 'tis the gentleman who

4. Revives.
5. Careful, fastidious.
6. Calmed.

was here yesterday about the repeating watch,[7] say you believe we can't get intelligence of it till tomorrow. For I lent it to Suky Straddle, to make a figure with it tonight at a tavern in Drury Lane.[8] If t'other gentleman calls for the silver-hilted sword, you know beetle-browed Jemmy hath it on, and he doth not come from Tunbridge till Tuesday night, so that it cannot be had till then.

Scene 9

[*Peachum, Mrs. Peachum*]

PEACHUM: Dear wife, be a little pacified. Don't let your passion run away with your senses. Polly, I grant you, hath done a rash thing.

MRS. PEACHUM: If she had had only an intrigue with the fellow, why the very best families have excused and huddled up a frailty of that sort. 'Tis marriage, husband, that makes it a blemish.

PEACHUM: But money, wife, is the true fuller's earth[9] for reputations; there is not a spot or a stain but what it can take out. A rich rogue nowadays is fit company for any gentleman; and the world, my dear, hath not such a contempt for roguery as you imagine. I tell you, wife, I can make this match turn to our advantage.

MRS. PEACHUM: I am very sensible,[1] husband, that Captain Macheath is worth money, but I am in doubt whether he hath not two or three wives already, and then if he should die in a Session or two, Polly's dower would come into dispute.

PEACHUM: That, indeed, is a point which ought to be considered.

Air 11. A soldier and a sailor

A fox may steal your hens, sir,
A whore your health and pence, sir,
Your daughter rob your chest, sir,
Your wife may steal your rest, sir,
A thief your goods and plate.[2]
But this is all but picking,
With rest, pence, chest and chicken;
It ever was decreed, sir,
If lawyer's hand is fee'd, sir,
He steals your whole estate.

The lawyers are bitter enemies to those in our way.[3] They don't care that anybody should get a clandestine livelihood but themselves.

Scene 10

[*Mrs. Peachum, Peachum, Polly*]

POLLY: 'Twas only Nimming Ned. He brought in a damask window curtain, a hoop petticoat, a pair of silver candlesticks, a periwig, and one silk stocking, from the fire that happened last night.

7. An especially valuable timepiece: it announced the current hour and quarter-hour by a series of bells that rang at the push of a button.
8. Another haunt of prostitutes; also the location of the rival playhouse (which had rejected the opportunity to produce Gay's *Opera*).
9. A mineral used as a cleaning solvent.
1. Well aware.
2. Utensils plated with silver or gold.
3. Line of work.

PEACHUM: There is not a fellow that is cleverer in his way, and saves more goods out of the fire, than Ned. But now, Polly, to your affair, for matters must not be left as they are. You are married then, it seems?

POLLY: Yes, Sir.

PEACHUM: And how do you propose to live, child?

POLLY: Like other women, Sir, upon the industry of my husband.

MRS. PEACHUM: What, is the wench turned fool? A highwayman's wife, like a soldier's, hath as little of his pay, as of his company.

PEACHUM: And had not you the common views of a gentlewoman in your marriage, Polly?

POLLY: I don't know what you mean, Sir.

PEACHUM: Of a jointure,[4] and of being a widow.

POLLY: But I love him, Sir: how then could I have thoughts of parting with him?

PEACHUM: Parting with him! Why, that is the whole scheme and intention of all marriage articles. The comfortable estate of widowhood is the only hope that keeps up a wife's spirits. Where is the woman who would scruple to be a wife, if she had it in her power to be a widow whenever she pleased? If you have any views of this sort, Polly, I shall think the match not so very unreasonable.

POLLY: How I dread to hear your advice! Yet I must beg you to explain yourself.

PEACHUM: Secure what he hath got, have him peached the next Sessions, and then at once you are made a rich widow.

POLLY: What, murder the man I love! The blood runs cold at my heart with the very thought of it.

PEACHUM: Fie, Polly! What hath murder to do in the affair? Since the thing sooner or later must happen, I dare say the Captain himself would like that we should get the reward for his death sooner than a stranger. Why, Polly, the Captain knows, that as 'tis his employment to rob, so 'tis ours to take robbers; every man in his business. So that there is no malice in the case.

MRS. PEACHUM: Ay, husband, now you have nicked the matter. To have him peached is the only thing could ever make me forgive her.

Air 12. Now ponder well, ye parents dear

POLLY:

Oh, ponder well! be not severe;
So save a wretched wife!
For on the rope that hangs my dear
Depends poor Polly's life.

MRS. PEACHUM: But your duty to your parents, hussy, obliges you to hang him. What would many a wife give for such an opportunity!

POLLY: What is a jointure, what is widowhood to me? I know my heart. I cannot survive him.

Air 13. Le printemps rappelle aux armes[5]

The turtle[6] thus with plaintive crying,
Her lover dying,

4. "Estate settled on a wife to be enjoyed after her husband's decease" (Johnson's *Dictionary*).

5. Spring calls to arms.

6. Turtledove (emblem of conjugal fidelity).

The turtle thus with plaintive crying,
Laments her dove.
Down she drops quite spent with sighing,
Paired in death, as paired in love.

Thus, Sir, it will happen to your poor Polly.

MRS. PEACHUM: What, is the fool in love in earnest then? I hate thee for being particular.[7] Why, wench, thou art a shame to thy very sex.

POLLY: But hear me, Mother. If you ever loved—

MRS. PEACHUM: Those cursed playbooks she reads have been her ruin. One word more, hussy, and I shall knock your brains out, if you have any.

PEACHUM: Keep out of the way, Polly, for fear of mischief, and consider of what is proposed to you.

MRS. PEACHUM: Away, hussy. Hang your husband, and be dutiful.

Scene 11

[*Mrs. Peachum, Peachum*]

[*Polly listening.*]

MRS. PEACHUM: The thing, husband, must and shall be done. For the sake of intelligence[8] we must take other measures, and have him peached the next session without her consent. If she will not know her duty, we know ours.

PEACHUM: But really, my dear, it grieves one's heart to take off a great man. When I consider his personal bravery, his fine stratagem, how much we have already got by him, and how much more we may get, methinks I can't find in my heart to have a hand in his death. I wish you could have made Polly undertake it.

MRS. PEACHUM: But in a case of necessity—our own lives are in danger.

PEACHUM: Then, indeed, we must comply with the customs of the world, and make gratitude give way to interest. He shall be taken off.

MRS. PEACHUM: I'll undertake to manage Polly.

PEACHUM: And I'll prepare matters for the Old Bailey.

Scene 12

[*Polly*]

Now I'm a wretch, indeed. Methinks I see him already in the cart, sweeter and more lovely than the nosegay[9] in his hand! I hear the crowd extolling his resolution and intrepidity! What volleys of sighs are sent from the windows of Holborn,[1] that so comely a youth should be brought to disgrace! I see him at the tree![2] The whole circle are in tears! Even butchers weep! Jack Ketch[3] himself hesitates to perform his duty, and would be glad to lose his fee, by a reprieve. What then will become of Polly! As yet I may inform him of their design, and aid him in his escape. It shall be so. But then he flies, absents himself, and I bar myself from his dear, dear conversation! That too will distract me.[4] If he keep out of the way, my papa and mama may in time relent, and we may be happy. If he stays, he is hanged, and then

7. Partial (i.e., to one man over another).
8. "Account of things distant or secret" (Johnson's *Dictionary*).
9. Bouquet (often carried by condemned prisoners).
1. The road from Newgate to Tyburn, along which criminals were carted to execution.
2. The gallows ("Tyburn tree").
3. England's most famous hangman (d. 1686); thereafter, any hangman.
4. Drive me mad.

he is lost forever! He intended to lie concealed in my room, till the dusk of the evening. If they are abroad, I'll this instant let him out, lest some accident should prevent him. [*Exit, and returns.*]

Scene 13

[*Polly, Macheath*]

Air 14. Pretty parrot, say—

MACHEATH: *Pretty Polly, say,*
When I was away,
Did your fancy never stray
To some newer lover?

POLLY: *Without disguise,*
Heaving sighs,
Doting eyes,
My constant heart discover[5]
Fondly let me loll!

MACHEATH: *O pretty, pretty Poll.*

POLLY: And are *you* as fond as ever, my dear?

MACHEATH: Suspect my honor, my courage, suspect anything but my love. May my pistols miss fire, and my mare slip her shoulder while I am pursued, if I ever forsake thee!

POLLY: Nay, my dear, I have no reason to doubt you, for I find in the romance you lent me, none of the great heroes were ever false in love.

Air 15. Pray, fair one, be kind

MACHEATH: *My heart was so free,*
It roved like the bee,
Till Polly my passion requited;
I sipped each flower,
I changed ev'ry hour,
But here ev'ry flower is united.

POLLY: Were you sentenced to transportation, sure, my dear, you could not leave me behind you—could you?

MACHEATH: Is there any power, any force that could tear me from thee? You might sooner tear a pension out of the hands of a courtier, a fee from a lawyer, a pretty woman from a looking glass, or any woman from quadrille. But to tear me from thee is impossible!

Air 16. Over the hills and far away

Were I laid on Greenland's coast,
And in my arms embraced my lass,
Warm amidst eternal frost,
Too soon the half year's night[6] *would pass.*

5. Reveal.

6. The long dark winter of the polar regions.

POLLY: *Were I sold on Indian soil,*
Soon as the burning day was closed,
I could mock the sultry toil,
When on my charmer's breast reposed.
MACHEATH: *And I would love you all the day,*
POLLY: *Every night would kiss and play,*
MACHEATH: *If with me you'd fondly stray*
POLLY: *Over the hills and far away.*

POLLY: Yes, I would go with thee. But oh! How shall I speak it? I must be torn from thee. We must part.

MACHEATH: How! Part!

POLLY: We must, we must. My papa and mama are set against thy life. They now, even now are in search after thee. They are preparing evidence against thee. Thy life depends upon a moment.

Air 17. Gin thou wert mine awn thing

O what pain it is to part!
Can I leave thee, can I leave thee?
O what pain it is to part!
Can thy Polly ever leave thee?
But lest death my love should thwart,
And bring thee to the fatal cart,
Thus I tear thee from my bleeding heart!
Fly hence, and let me leave thee.

One kiss and then—one kiss—begone—farewell.

MACHEATH: My hand, my heart, my dear, is so riveted to thine, that I cannot unloose my hold.

POLLY: But my papa may intercept thee, and then I should lose the very glimmering of hope. A few weeks, perhaps, may reconcile us all. Shall thy Polly hear from thee?

MACHEATH: Must I then go?

POLLY: And will not absence change your love?

MACHEATH: If you doubt it, let me stay—and be hanged.

POLLY: Oh how I fear! How I tremble! Go—but when safety will give you leave, you will be sure to see me again; for till then Polly is wretched.

Air 18. Oh the broom

[*Parting, and looking back at each other with fondness; he at one door, she at the other*.]

MACHEATH: *The miser thus a shilling sees,*
Which he's obliged to pay,
With sighs resigns it by degrees,
And fears 'tis gone for aye.[7]

7. Forever.

POLLY: *The boy, thus, when his sparrow's flown,*
The bird in silence eyes;
But soon as out of sight 'tis gone,
Whines, whimpers, sobs and cries.

ACT 2

Scene 1. A tavern near Newgate.

[*Jemmy Twitcher, Crook-Fingered Jack, Wat Dreary, Robin of Bagshot, Nimming Ned, Henry Paddington, Matt of the Mint, Ben Budge, and the rest of the gang, at the table, with wine, brandy, and tobacco.*]

BEN: But prithee, Matt, what is become of thy brother Tom? I have not seen him since my return from transportation.

MATT: Poor brother Tom had an accident this time twelvemonth, and so clever a made fellow he was, that I could not save him from those fleaing[8] rascals the surgeons; and now, poor man, he is among the otamys[9] at Surgeon's Hall.

BEN: So it seems his time was come.

JEMMY: But the present time is ours, and nobody alive hath more. Why are the laws leveled at us? Are we more dishonest than the rest of mankind? What we win, gentlemen, is our own by the law of arms, and the right of conquest.

JACK: Where shall we find such another set of practical philosophers, who to a man are above the fear of death?

WAT: Sound men, and true!

ROBIN: Of tried courage, and indefatigable industry!

NED: Who is there here that would not die for his friend?

HARRY: Who is there here that would betray him for his interest?

MATT: Show me a gang of courtiers that can say as much.

BEN: We are for a just partition of the world, for every man hath a right to enjoy life.

MATT: We retrench[1] the superfluities of mankind. The world is avaricious, and I hate avarice. A covetous fellow, like a jackdaw,[2] steals what he was never made to enjoy, for the sake of hiding it. These are the robbers of mankind, for money was made for the free-hearted and generous, and where is the injury of taking from another, what he hath not the heart to make use of?

JEMMY: Our several stations for the day are fixed. Good luck attend us all. Fill the glasses.

Air 19. Fill ev'ry glass

MATT: *Fill ev'ry glass, for wine inspires us,*
And fires us
With courage, love and joy.
Women and wine should life employ.

8. Flaying, robbing.
9. Skeletons (from "anatomies"). The corpses of executed criminals were often used for medical instruction.
1. Reduce, limit.
2. A bird regarded in animal lore as an inveterate thief.

Is there ought else on earth desirous?
CHORUS: *Fill ev'ry glass, etc.*

Scene 2

[*To them enter Macheath*]

MACHEATH: Gentlemen, well met. My heart hath been with you this hour; but an unexpected affair hath detained me. No ceremony, I beg you.

MATT: We were just breaking up to go upon duty. Am I to have the honor of taking the air with you, Sir, this evening upon the heath? I drink a dram now and then with the stagecoachmen in the way of friendship and intelligence; and I know that about this time there will be passengers upon the western road,[3] who are worth speaking with.

MACHEATH: I was to have been of that party—but—

MATT: But what, Sir?

MACHEATH: Is there any man who suspects my courage?

MATT: We have all been witnesses of it.

MACHEATH: My honor and truth to the gang?

MATT: I'll be answerable for it.

MACHEATH: In the division of our booty, have I ever shown the least marks of avarice or injustice?

MATT: By these questions something seems to have ruffled you. Are any of us suspected?

MACHEATH: I have a fixed confidence, gentlemen, in you all, as men of honor, and as such I value and respect you. Peachum is a man that is useful to us.

MATT: Is he about to play us any foul play? I'll shoot him through the head.

MACHEATH: I beg you, gentlemen, act with conduct and discretion. A pistol is your last resort.

MATT: He knows nothing of this meeting.

MACHEATH: Business cannot go on without him. He is a man who knows the world, and is a necessary agent to us. We have had a slight difference, and till it is accommodated I shall be obliged to keep out of his way. Any private dispute of mine shall be of no ill consequence to my friends. You must continue to act under his direction, for the moment we break loose from him, our gang is ruined.

MATT: As a bawd[4] to a whore, I grant you, he is to us of great convenience.

MACHEATH: Make him believe I have quitted the gang, which I can never do but with life.[5] At our private quarters I will continue to meet you. A week or so will probably reconcile us.

MATT: Your instructions shall be observed. 'Tis now high time for us to repair to our several duties; so till the evening at our quarters in Moorfields,[6] we bid you farewell.

MACHEATH: I shall wish myself with you. Success attend you.
[*Sits down melancholy at the table.*]

3. Through Bagshot Heath, west of London.
4. Pimp.
5. I.e., by dying.
6. Just outside the old City wall.

Air 20. March in *Rinaldo*,[7] with drums and trumpets

MATT: *Let us take the road.*
Hark! I hear the sound of coaches!
The hour of attack approaches,
To your arms, brave boys, and load.
See the ball I hold!
Let the chemists[8] *toil like asses,*
Our fire their fire surpasses,
And turns all our lead to gold.

[*The gang, ranged in the front of the stage, load their pistols, and stick them under their girdles;*[9] *then go off singing the first part in chorus.*]

Scene 3

[*Macheath, Drawer*[1]]

MACHEATH: What a fool is a fond wench! Polly is most confoundedly bit.[2] I love the sex. And a man who loves money might as well be contented with one guinea, as I with one woman. The town perhaps hath been as much obliged to me, for recruiting it with free-hearted ladies, as to any recruiting officer in the army. If it were not for us and the other gentlemen of the sword, Drury Lane would be uninhabited.

Air 21. Would you have a young virgin

If the heart of a man is depressed with cares,
The mist is dispelled when a woman appears;
Like the notes of a fiddle, she sweetly, sweetly
Raises the spirits, and charms our ears,
Roses and lilies her cheeks disclose,
But her ripe lips are more sweet than those.
Press her,
Caress her
With blisses,
Her kisses
Dissolve us in pleasure, and soft repose.

I must have women. There is nothing unbends[3] the mind like them. Money is not so strong a cordial for the time. Drawer! [*Enter Drawer.*] Is the porter gone for all the ladies, according to my directions?

DRAWER: I expect him back every minute. But you know, Sir, you sent him as far as Hockley in the Hole, for three of the ladies, for one in Vinegar Yard, and for the rest of them somewhere about Lewkner's Lane.[4] Sure some of them are below, for I hear the bar bell. As they come I will show them up. Coming, coming!

7. A heroic Italian opera (1711) by George Frideric Handel (1685–1759).
8. Alchemists, who strove to turn base metals into gold.
9. Belts.
1. Bartender.
2. Enamored.
3. Relaxes.
4. Both the Yard and the Lane were places of prostitution.

Scene 4

[*Macheath, Mrs. Coaxer, Dolly Trull, Mrs. Vixen, Betty Doxy, Jenny Diver, Mrs. Slammekin, Suky Tawdry, and Molly Brazen*]

MACHEATH: Dear Mrs. Coaxer, you are welcome. You look charmingly today. I hope you don't want the repairs of quality, and lay on paint.[5] —Dolly Trull! Kiss me, you slut; are you as amorous as ever, hussy? You are always so taken up with stealing hearts that you don't allow yourself time to steal anything else. Ah, Dolly, thou wilt ever be a coquette!—Mrs. Vixen, I'm yours; I always loved a woman of wit and spirit; they make charming mistresses, but plaguy wives.—Betty Doxy! Come hither, hussy. Do you drink as hard as ever? You had better stick to good wholesome beer; for in troth, Betty, strong waters[6] will in time ruin your constitution. You should leave those to your betters.—What! and my pretty Jenny Diver too! As prim and demure as ever! There is not any prude, though ever so high bred, hath a more sanctified look, with a more mischievous heart. Ah! Thou art a dear artful hypocrite.—Mrs. Slammekin! As careless and genteel as ever! All you fine ladies, who know your own beauty, affect an undress.—But see, here's Suky Tawdry come to contradict what I was saying. Everything she gets one way she lays out upon her back. Why, Suky, you must keep at least a dozen tallymen.[7]—Molly Brazen! [*She kisses him.*] That's well done. I love a free-hearted wench. Thou hast a most agreeable assurance, girl, and art as willing as a turtle.—But hark! I hear music. The harper is at the door. "If music be the food of love, play on."[8] Ere you seat yourselves, ladies, what think you of a dance? Come in. [*Enter Harper.*] Play the French tune that Mrs. Slammekin was so fond of.

[*A dance* a la ronde[9] *in the French manner; near the end of it this song and chorus:*]

Air 22. Cotillon

Youth's the season made for joys,
Love is then our duty,
She alone who that employs,
Well deserves her beauty.
Let's be gay,
While we may,
Beauty's a flower despised in decay.
Youth's the season, etc.

Let us drink and sport today,
Ours is not tomorrow.
Love with youth flies swift away,
Age is nought but sorrow.
Dance and sing,
Time's on the wing,
Life never knows the return of spring.

5. I hope you do not need to paint your face as high-class women do.
6. Hard liquor.
7. Merchants who provided clothes on credit.
8. The opening line of Shakespeare's *Twelfth Night*.
9. In a circle.

CHORUS: *Let us drink, etc.*

MACHEATH: Now, pray ladies, take your places. Here fellow. [*Pays the Harper.*] Bid the drawer bring us more wine. [*Exit Harper.*] If any of the ladies choose gin, I hope they will be so free to call for it.

JENNY: You look as if you meant me. Wine is strong enough for me. Indeed, Sir, I never drink strong waters but when I have the cholic.[1]

MACHEATH: Just the excuse of the fine ladies! Why, a lady of quality is never without the cholic. I hope, Mrs. Coaxer, you have had good success of late in your visits among the mercers.[2]

COAXER: We have so many interlopers—yet with industry, one may still have a little picking. I carried a silver flowered lutestring, and a piece of black padesoy[3] to Mr. Peachum's lock but last week.

VIXEN: There's Molly Brazen hath the ogle of a rattlesnake. She riveted a linen draper's eye so fast upon her, that he was nicked[4] of three pieces of cambric before he could look off.

BRAZEN: Oh, dear Madam! But sure nothing can come up to your handling of laces! And then you have such a sweet deluding tongue! To cheat a man is nothing; but the woman must have fine parts indeed who cheats a woman!

VIXEN: Lace, Madam, lies in a small compass, and is of easy conveyance. But you are apt, Madam, to think too well of your friends.

COAXER: If any woman hath more art than another, to be sure, 'tis Jenny Diver. Though her fellow be never so agreeable, she can pick his pocket as coolly, as if money were her only pleasure. Now that is a command of the passions uncommon in a woman!

JENNY: I never go to the tavern with a man, but in the view of business. I have other hours, and other sort of men, for my pleasure. But had I your address,[5] Madam—

MACHEATH: Have done with your compliments, ladies, and drink about. You are not so fond of me, Jenny, as you use to be.

JENNY: 'Tis not convenient, Sir, to show my fondness among so many rivals. 'Tis your own choice, and not the warmth of my inclination, that will determine you.[6]

Air 23. All in a misty morning

Before the barn-door crowing,
The cock by hens attended,
His eyes around him throwing,
Stands for a while suspended.
Then one he singles from the crew,
And cheers the happy hen;
With how do you do, and how do you do,
And how do you do again.

MACHEATH: Ah, Jenny! Thou art a dear slut.

TRULL: Pray, Madam, were you ever in keeping?[7]

1. Stomach pains.
2. Fabric dealers.
3. Expensive silk fabrics.
4. Robbed.
5. Elegant manner.
6. Clinch your decision.
7. I.e., the kept mistress of a wealthy man.

TAWDRY: I hope, Madam, I ha'nt been so long upon the town, but I have met with some good fortune as well as my neighbors.

TRULL: Pardon me, Madam, I meant no harm by the question; 'twas only in the way of conversation.

TAWDRY: Indeed, Madam, if I had not been a fool, I might have lived very handsomely with my last friend. But upon his missing five guineas, he turned me off. Now I never suspected he had counted them.

SLAMMEKIN: Who do you look upon, Madam, as your best sort of keepers?

TRULL: That, Madam, is thereafter as they be.[8]

SLAMMEKIN: I, Madam, was once kept by a Jew; and bating[9] their religion, to women they are a good sort of people.

TAWDRY: Now for my part, I own I like an old fellow; for we always make them pay for what they can't do.

VIXEN: A spruce[1] prentice, let me tell you, ladies, is no ill thing; they bleed[2] freely. I have sent at least two or three dozen of them in my time to the plantations.[3]

JENNY: But to be sure, Sir, with so much good fortune as you have had upon the road, you must be grown immensely rich.

MACHEATH: The road, indeed, hath done me justice, but the gaming table hath been my ruin.

Air 24. When once I lay with another man's wife

JENNY: *The gamesters and lawyers are jugglers[4] alike,*
If they meddle your all is in danger.
Like gypsies, if once they can finger a souse,[5]
Your pockets they pick, and they pilfer your house,
And give your estate to a stranger.

A man of courage should never put anything to the risk but his life. These are the tools of a man of honor. Cards and dice are only fit for cowardly cheats, who prey upon their friends. [*She takes up his pistol. Tawdry takes up the other.*]

TAWDRY: This, Sir, is fitter for your hand. Besides your loss of money, 'tis a loss to the ladies. Gaming takes you off from women. How fond could I be of you! But before company, 'tis ill bred.

MACHEATH: Wanton hussies!

JENNY: I must and will have a kiss to give my wine a zest.

[*They take him about the neck, and make signs to Peachum and the constables, who rush in upon him.*]

Scene 5

[*To them, Peachum and constables*]

PEACHUM: I seize you, Sir, as my prisoner.

MACHEATH: Was this well done, Jenny? Women are decoy ducks; who can trust them! Beasts, jades, jilts, harpies, Furies, whores!

8. That depends on how they treat me.
9. Apart from.
1. Lively.
2. Spend.
3. I.e., incited them to steal and thereby caused them to be transported to the colonies.
4. Sleight-of-hand artists; tricksters.
5. Get their hands on a sou (French penny).

PEACHUM: Your case, Mr. Macheath, is not particular. The greatest heroes have been ruined by women. But to do them justice, I must own they are a pretty sort of creatures, if we could trust them. You must now, Sir, take your leave of the ladies, and if they have a mind to make you a visit, they will be sure to find you at home. The gentleman, ladies, lodges in Newgate. Constables, wait upon the Captain to his lodgings.

Air 25. When first I laid siege to my Chloris

MACHEATH: *At the tree I shall suffer with pleasure,*
At the tree I shall suffer with pleasure,
Let me go where I will,
In all kinds of ill,
I shall find no such Furies as these are.

PEACHUM: Ladies, I'll take care the reckoning shall be discharged.[6]
[*Exit Macheath, guarded, with Peachum and constables*.]

Scene 6

[*The women remain.*]

VIXEN: Look ye, Mrs. Jenny, though Mr. Peachum may have made a private bargain with you and Suky Tawdry for betraying the Captain, as we were all assisting, we ought all to share alike.

COAXER: I think Mr. Peachum, after so long an acquaintance, might have trusted me as well as Jenny Diver.

SLAMMEKIN: I am sure at least three men of his hanging, and in a year's time too (if he did me justice), should be set down to my account.[7]

TRULL: Mrs. Slammekin, that is not fair. For you know one of them was taken in bed with me.

JENNY: As far as a bowl of punch or a treat, I believe Mrs. Suky will join with me. As for anything else, ladies, you cannot in conscience expect it.

SLAMMEKIN: Dear Madam—

TRULL: I would not for the world—

SLAMMEKIN: 'Tis impossible for me—

TRULL: As I hope to be saved, Madam—

SLAMMEKIN: Nay, then I must stay here all night—

TRULL: Since you command me.

[*Exit with great ceremony.*]

Scene 7. Newgate

[*Lockit, Turnkeys*,[8] *Macheath, Constables*]

LOCKIT: Noble Captain, you are welcome. You have not been a lodger of mine this year and half. You know the custom, Sir. Garnish,[9] Captain, garnish. Hand me down those fetters there.

6. The bill will be paid.
7. I.e., I deserve the credit for at least three men whom Peachum has had hanged.
8. Prison guards.
9. Pay the bribe that will secure better treatment and accommodations.

MACHEATH: Those, Mr. Lockit, seem to be the heaviest of the whole set. With your leave, I should like the further pair better.

LOCKIT: Look ye, Captain, we know what is fittest for our prisoners. When a gentleman uses me with civility, I always do the best I can to please him. Hand them down I say. We have them of all prices, from one guinea to ten, and 'tis fitting every gentleman should please himself.

MACHEATH: I understand you, Sir. [*Gives money.*] The fees here are so many, and so exorbitant, that few fortunes can bear the expense of getting off[1] handsomely, or of dying like a gentleman.

LOCKIT: Those, I see, will fit the Captain better. Take down the further pair. Do but examine them, Sir. Never was better work. How genteelly they are made! They will sit as easy as a glove, and the nicest[2] man in England might not be ashamed to wear them. [*He puts on the chains.*] If I had the best gentleman in the land in my custody I could not equip him more handsomely. And so, Sir, I now leave you to your private meditations.

Scene 8

[*Macheath*]

Air 26. Courtiers, courtiers think it no harm

Man may escape from rope and gun;
Nay, some have outlived the doctor's pill;
Who takes a woman must be undone,
That basilisk[3] is sure to kill.
The fly that sips treacle is lost in the sweets,
So he that tastes woman, woman, woman,
He that tastes woman, ruin meets.

To what a woeful plight have I brought myself! Here must I (all day long, till I am hanged) be confined to hear the reproaches of a wench who lays her ruin at my door. I am in the custody of her father, and to be sure, if he knows of the matter, I shall have a fine time on't betwixt this[4] and my execution. But I promised the wench marriage. What signifies a promise to a woman? Does not man in marriage itself promise a hundred things that he never means to perform? Do all we can, women will believe us; for they look upon a promise as an excuse for following their own inclinations. But here comes Lucy, and I cannot get from her. Would I were deaf!

Scene 9

[*Macheath, Lucy*]

LUCY: You base man you. How can you look me in the face after what hath passed between us? See here, perfidious wretch, how I am forced to bear about the load of infamy[5] you have laid upon me. Oh, Macheath! Thou hast robbed me of my quiet! To see thee tortured would give me pleasure.

1. Escaping punishment.
2. Most discerning.
3. A mythical serpent which killed by its breath or its glance.
4. I.e., this moment.
5. I.e., my (visible) pregnancy.

Air 27. A lovely lass to a friar came

Thus when a good housewife sees a rat
In her trap in the morning taken,
With pleasure her heart goes pit a pat,
In revenge for her loss of bacon.
Then she throws him
To the dog or cat,
To be worried, crushed, and shaken.

MACHEATH: Have you no bowels,[6] no tenderness, my dear Lucy, to see a husband in these circumstances?

LUCY: A husband!

MACHEATH: In every respect but the form, and that, my dear, may be said over us at any time. Friends should not insist upon ceremonies. From a man of honor, his word is as good as his bond.

LUCY: 'Tis the pleasure of all you fine men to insult the women you have ruined.

Air 28. 'Twas when the sea was roaring

How cruel are the traitors,
Who lie and swear in jest,
To cheat unguarded creatures
Of virtue, fame, and rest!
Whoever steals a shilling,
Through shame the guilt conceals:
In love the perjured villain
With boasts the theft reveals.

MACHEATH: The very first opportunity, my dear (have but patience), you shall be my wife in whatever manner you please.

LUCY: Insinuating monster! And so you think I know nothing of the affair of Miss Polly Peachum. I could tear thy eyes out!

MACHEATH: Sure Lucy, you can't be such a fool as to be jealous of Polly!

LUCY: Are you not married to her, you brute you?

MACHEATH: Married! Very good. The wench gives it out only to vex thee, and to ruin me in thy good opinion. 'Tis true, I go to the house; I chat with the girl, I kiss her, I say a thousand things to her (as all gentlemen do) that mean nothing, to divert myself. And now the silly jade hath set it about that I am married to her, to let me know what she would be at. Indeed, my dear Lucy, these violent passions may be of ill consequence to a woman in your condition.

LUCY: Come, come, Captain, for all your assurance, you know that Miss Polly hath put it out of your power to do me the justice you promised me.

MACHEATH: A jealous woman believes everything her passion suggests. To convince you of my sincerity, if we can find the Ordinary,[7] I shall have no scruples of making you my wife; and I know the consequence of having two at a time.

LUCY: That you are only to be hanged, and so get rid of them both.

MACHEATH: I am ready, my dear Lucy, to give you satisfaction—if you think there is any in marriage. What can a man of honor say more?

6. Compassion.

7. Prison chaplain.

LUCY: So then, it seems you are not married to Miss Polly.

MACHEATH: You know, Lucy, the girl is prodigiously conceited. No man can say a civil thing to her, but (like other fine ladies) her vanity makes her think he's her own forever and ever.

Air 29. The sun had loosed his weary teams

The first time at the looking glass
The mother sets her daughter,
The image strikes the smiling lass
With self-love ever after.
Each time she looks, she, fonder grown,
Thinks every charm grows stronger.
But alas, vain maid, all eyes but your own
Can see you are not younger.

When women consider their own beauties, they are all alike unreasonable in their demands, for they expect their lovers should like them as long as they like themselves.

LUCY: Yonder is my father—perhaps this way we may light upon the Ordinary, who shall try if[8] you will be as good as your word. For I long to be made an honest woman.

Scene 10

[*Peachum, Lockit with an account book*]

LOCKIT: In this last affair, Brother Peachum, we are agreed. You have consented to go halves in Macheath.

PEACHUM: We shall never fall out about an execution. But as to that article, pray how stands our last year's account?

LOCKIT: If you will run your eye over it, you'll find 'tis fair and clearly stated.

PEACHUM: This long arrear[9] of the government is very hard upon us! Can it be expected that we should hang our acquaintance for nothing, when our betters will hardly save theirs without being paid for it? Unless the people in employment pay better, I promise them for the future, I shall let other rogues live besides their own.

LOCKIT: Perhaps, Brother, they are afraid these matters may be carried too far. We are treated too by them with contempt, as if our profession were not reputable.

PEACHUM: In one respect, indeed, our employment may be reckoned dishonest, because, like great statesmen, we encourage those who betray their friends.

LOCKIT: Such language, Brother, anywhere else, might turn to your prejudice.[1] Learn to be more guarded, I beg you.

Air 30. How happy are we

When you censure the age,
Be cautious and sage,
Lest the courtiers offended should be:

8. Test whether.
9. Delay in debt payment.
1. Be used against you.

If you mention vice or bribe,
'Tis so pat[2] to all the tribe,
Each cries, "That was leveled at me!"

PEACHUM: Here's poor Ned Clincher's name, I see. Sure, Brother Lockit, there was a little unfair proceeding in Ned's case, for he told me in the condemned hold[3] that for value received, you had promised him a Session or two longer without molestation.

LOCKIT: Mr. Peachum, this is the first time my honor was ever called in question.

PEACHUM: Business is at an end if once we act dishonorably.

LOCKIT: Who accuses me?

PEACHUM: You are warm,[4] Brother.

LOCKIT: He that attacks my honor, attacks my livelihood. And this usage, Sir, is not to be borne.

PEACHUM: Since you provoke me to speak, I must tell you, too, that Mrs. Coaxer charges you with defrauding her of her information money[5] for the apprehending of curl-pated Hugh. Indeed, indeed, Brother, we must punctually pay our spies, or we shall have no information.

LOCKIT: Is this language to me, Sirrah, who have saved you from the gallows, Sirrah!

[*Collaring each other.*]

PEACHUM: If I am hanged, it shall be for ridding the world of an arrant rascal.

LOCKIT: This hand shall do the office of the halter[6] you deserve, and throttle you—you dog!

PEACHUM: Brother, Brother, we are both in the wrong. We shall be both losers in the dispute—for you know we have it in our power to hang each other. You should not be so passionate.

LOCKIT: Nor you so provoking.

PEACHUM: 'Tis our mutual interest; 'tis for the interest of the world we should agree. If I said anything, Brother, to the prejudice of your character, I ask pardon.

LOCKIT: Brother Peachum, I can forgive as well as resent. Give me your hand. Suspicion does not become a friend.

PEACHUM: I only meant to give you occasion to justify yourself. But I must now step home, for I expect the gentleman about this snuffbox that Filch nimmed two nights ago in the park. I appointed him at this hour.

Scene 11

[*Lockit, Lucy*]

LOCKIT: Whence come you, hussy?

LUCY: My tears might answer that question.

LOCKIT: You have then been whimpering and fondling, like a spaniel, over the fellow that hath abused you.

LUCY: One can't help love; one can't cure it. 'Tis not in my power to obey you, and hate him.

LOCKIT: Learn to bear your husband's death like a reasonable woman. 'Tis not the fashion, nowadays, so much as to affect sorrow upon these occasions. No woman

2. Applicable.
3. I.e., on death row.
4. Angry.
5. Payment for informing on a fellow criminal.
6. Noose.

would ever marry, if she had not the chance of mortality for a release. Act like a woman of spirit, hussy, and thank your father for what he is doing.

Air 31. Of a noble race was Shenkin

LUCY: *Is then his fate decreed, Sir?*
Such a man can I think of quitting?
When first we met, so moves me yet,
Oh, see how my heart is splitting!

LOCKIT: Look ye, Lucy: there is no saving him. So I think you must ev'n do like other widows: buy yourself weeds,[7] and be cheerful.

Air 32.

You'll think ere many days ensue
This sentence not severe;
I hang your husband, child, 'tis true,
But with him hang your care.
Twang dang dillo dee.

Like a good wife, go moan over your dying husband. That, child, is your duty. Consider, girl, you can't have the man and the money too—so make yourself as easy as you can, by getting all you can from him.

Scene 12

[*Lucy, Macheath*]

LUCY: Though the Ordinary was out of the way today, I hope, my dear, you will, upon the first opportunity, quiet my scruples. Oh, Sir! My father's hard heart is not to be softened, and I am in the utmost despair.

MACHEATH: But if I could raise a small sum—would not twenty guineas, think you, move him? Of all the arguments in the way of business, the perquisite[8] is the most prevailing. Your father's perquisites for the escape of prisoners must amount to a considerable sum in the year. Money well timed, and properly applied, will do anything.

Air 33. London ladies

If you at an office solicit your due,[9]
And would not have matters neglected,
You must quicken the clerk with the perquisite too,
To do what his duty directed.
Or would you the frowns of a lady prevent,
She too has this palpable failing,
The perquisite softens her into consent;
That reason with all is prevailing.

LUCY: What love or money can do shall be done, for all my comfort depends upon your safety.

7. Mourning clothes.
8. Tip; bribe.
9. Seek the service to which you're entitled.

Scene 13

[*Lucy, Macheath, Polly*]

POLLY: Where is my dear husband? Was a rope ever intended for this neck! Oh, let me throw my arms about it, and throttle thee with love! Why dost thou turn away from me? 'Tis thy Polly! 'Tis thy wife!

MACHEATH: Was ever such an unfortunate rascal as I am!

LUCY: Was there ever such another villain!

POLLY: Oh, Macheath! Was it for this we parted? Taken! Imprisoned! Tried! Hanged! Cruel reflection! I'll stay with thee till death. No force shall tear thy dear wife from thee now. What means my love? Not one kind word! Not one kind look! Think what thy Polly suffers to see thee in this condition.

Air 34. All in the downs

Thus when the swallow, seeking prey,
Within the sash[1] *is closely pent,*
His comfort, with bemoaning lay,[2]
Without sits pining for th' event.[3]
Her chatt'ring lovers all around her skim;
She heeds them not (poor bird!); her soul's with him.

MACHEATH [*aside*]: I must disown her. The wench is distracted.

LUCY: Am I then bilked of my virtue? Can I have no reparation? Sure, men were born to lie, and women to believe them! Oh, villain! Villain!

POLLY: Am I not thy wife? Thy neglect of me, thy aversion to me too severely proves it. Look on me. Tell me: am I not thy wife?

LUCY: Perfidious wretch!

POLLY: Barbarous husband!

LUCY: Hadst thou been hanged five months ago, I had been happy.

POLLY: And I too. If you had been kind to me till death, it would not have vexed me. And that's no very unreasonable request (though from a wife) to a man who hath not above seven or eight days to live.

LUCY: Art thou then married to another? Hast thou two wives, monster?

MACHEATH: If women's tongues can cease for an answer, hear me.

LUCY: I won't. Flesh and blood can't bear my usage.

POLLY: Shall I not claim my own? Justice bids me speak.

Air 35. Have you heard of a frolicsome ditty

MACHEATH:

How happy could I be with either,
Were t'other dear charmer away!
But while you thus tease me together,
To neither a word will I say;
But tol de rol, etc.

1. Window frame.
2. Plaintive song.
3. Outcome.

POLLY: Sure, my dear, there ought to be some preference shown to a wife! At least she may claim the appearance of it. He must be distracted with his misfortunes, or he could not use me thus!

LUCY: Oh, villain, villain! Thou hast deceived me. I could even inform against thee with pleasure. Not a prude wishes more heartily to have facts against her intimate acquaintance, than I now wish to have facts against thee. I would have her satisfaction, and they should all out.

Air 36. Irish trot

POLLY: *I'm bubbled.*[4]
LUCY: *I'm bubbled.*
POLLY: *Oh how I am troubled!*
LUCY: *Bamboozled, and bit!*
POLLY: *My distresses are doubled.*
LUCY: *When you come to the tree, should the hangman refuse,*
These fingers, with pleasure, could fasten the noose.
POLLY: *I'm bubbled, etc.*

MACHEATH: Be pacified, my dear Lucy. This is all a fetch[5] of Polly's, to make me desperate with[6] you in case I get off. If I am hanged, she would fain[7] the credit of being thought my widow. Really, Polly, this is no time for a dispute of this sort; for whenever you are talking of marriage, I am thinking of hanging.

POLLY: And hast thou the heart to persist in disowning me?

MACHEATH: And hast thou the heart to persist in persuading me that I am married? Why, Polly, dost thou seek to aggravate my misfortunes?

LUCY: Really, Miss Peachum, you but expose yourself. Besides, 'tis barbarous in you to worry a gentleman in his circumstances.

Air 37.

POLLY: *Cease your funning;*
Force or cunning
Never shall my heart trapan.[8]
All these sallies
Are but malice
To seduce my constant man.
'Tis most certain,
By their flirting
Women oft have envy shown;
Pleased to ruin
Others wooing;
Never happy in their own!

POLLY: Decency, Madam, methinks might teach you to behave yourself with some reserve with the husband, while his wife is present.

MACHEATH: But seriously, Polly, this is carrying the joke a little too far.

4. Cheated, fooled.
5. Trick.
6. I.e., to ruin my hopes of having.
7. Would like.
8. Ensnare.

LUCY: If you are determined, Madam, to raise a disturbance in the prison, I shall be obliged to send for the turnkey to show you the door. I am sorry, Madam, you force me to be so ill-bred.

POLLY: Give me leave to tell you, Madam, these forward airs don't become you in the least, madam. And my duty, Madam, obliges me to stay with my husband, Madam.

Air 38. Good morrow, gossip[9] Joan

LUCY: *Why how now, Madam Flirt?*
If you thus must chatter;
And are for flinging dirt,
Let's try who best can spatter;
Madam Flirt!

POLLY: *Why how now, saucy jade;*
Sure the wench is tipsy!
[*To him.*] *How can you see me made*
The scoff of such a gypsy?
[*To her*] *Saucy jade!*

Scene 14

[*Lucy, Macheath, Polly, Peachum*]

PEACHUM: Where's my wench? Ah, hussy! Hussy! Come you home, you slut; and when your fellow is hanged, hang yourself, to make your family some amends.

POLLY: Dear, dear father, do not tear me from him. I must speak; I have more to say to him. Oh! Twist thy fetters about me, that he may not haul me from thee!

PEACHUM: Sure all women are alike! If ever they commit the folly, they are sure to commit another by exposing themselves. Away—not a word more. You are my prisoner now, hussy.

Air 39. Irish howl

POLLY: *No power on earth can e'er divide*
The knot that sacred love hath tied.
When parents draw against our mind,
The true-love's knot they faster bind.
Oh, oh ray, oh Amborah—oh, oh, etc.

[*Holding Macheath, Peachum pulling her.*]

Scene 15

[*Lucy, Macheath*]

MACHEATH: I am naturally compassionate, wife, so that I could not use the wench as she deserved, which made you at first suspect there was something in what she said.

9. My friend.

LUCY: Indeed, my dear, I was strangely puzzled.

MACHEATH: If that had been the case, her father would never have brought me into this circumstance. No, Lucy, I had rather die than be false to thee.

LUCY: How happy am I, if you say this from your heart! For I love thee so, that I could sooner bear to see thee hanged than in the arms of another.

MACHEATH: But couldst thou bear to see me hanged?

LUCY: Oh, Macheath, I can never live to see that day.

MACHEATH: You see, Lucy, in the account of love you are in my debt, and you must now be convinced, that I rather choose to die than be another's. Make me, if possible, love thee more, and let me owe my life to thee. If you refuse to assist me, Peachum and your father will immediately put me beyond all means of escape.

LUCY: My father, I know, hath been drinking hard with the prisoners, and I fancy he is now taking his nap in his own room. If I can procure the keys, shall I go off with thee, my dear?

MACHEATH: If we are together, 'twill be impossible to lie concealed. As soon as the search begins to be a little cool, I will send to thee. Till then my heart is thy prisoner.

LUCY: Come then, my dear husband, owe thy life to me, and though you love me not, be grateful. But that Polly runs in my head strangely.

MACHEATH: A moment of time may make us unhappy forever.

Air 40. The lass of Patie's mill

LUCY: *I like the fox shall grieve,*
Whose mate hath left her side.
Whom hounds, from morn to eve,
Chase o'er the country wide.
Where can my lover hide?
Where cheat the weary pack?
If love be not his guide,
He never will come back!

ACT 3

Scene 1. Newgate

[*Lockit, Lucy*]

LOCKIT: To be sure, wench, you must have been aiding and abetting to help him to this escape.

LUCY: Sir, here hath been Peachum and his daughter Polly, and to be sure they know the ways of Newgate as well as if they had been born and bred in the place all their lives. Why must all your suspicion light upon me?

LOCKIT: Lucy, Lucy, I will have none of these shuffling answers.

LUCY: Well then, if I know anything of him I wish I may be burnt!

LOCKIT: Keep your temper, Lucy, or I shall pronounce you guilty.

LUCY: Keep yours, Sir. I do wish I may be burnt. I do. And what can I say more to convince you?

LOCKIT: Did he tip handsomely? How much did he come down with? Come hussy, don't cheat your father, and I shall not be angry with you. Perhaps you have made a better bargain with him than I could have done. How much, my good girl?

LUCY: You know, Sir, I am fond of him, and would have given money to have kept him with me.

LOCKIT: Ah, Lucy! Thy education might have put thee more upon thy guard; for a girl in the bar of an alehouse is always besieged.

LUCY: Dear Sir, mention not my education—for 'twas to that I owe my ruin.

Air 41. If love's a sweet passion

When young at the bar you first taught me to score,[1]
And bid me be free of my lips, and no more,
I was kissed by the parson, the squire, and the sot;
When the guest was departed, the kiss was forgot.
But his kiss was so sweet, and so closely he pressed,
That I languished and pined till I granted the rest.

If you can forgive me, Sir, I will make a fair confession, for to be sure he hath been a most barbarous villain to me.

LOCKIT: And so you have let him escape, hussy? Have you?

LUCY: When a woman loves, a kind look, a tender word can persuade her to anything. And I could ask no other bribe.

LOCKIT: Thou wilt always be a vulgar[2] slut, Lucy. If you would not be looked upon as a fool, you should never do anything but upon the foot[3] of interest. Those that act otherwise are their own bubbles.[4]

LUCY: But love, Sir, is a misfortune that may happen to the most discreet woman, and in love we are all fools alike. Notwithstanding all he swore, I am now fully convinced that Polly Peachum is actually his wife. Did I let him escape (fool that I was!) to go to her? Polly will wheedle herself into his money, and then Peachum will hang him, and cheat us both.

LOCKIT: So I am to be ruined, because, forsooth, you must be in love! A very pretty excuse!

LUCY: I could murder that impudent happy strumpet. I gave him his life, and that creature enjoys the sweets of it. Ungrateful Macheath!

Air 42. South Sea Ballad

My love is all madness and folly,
Alone I lie,
Toss, tumble, and cry,
What a happy creature is Polly!
Was e'er such a wretch as I!
With rage I redden like scarlet,
That my dear inconstant varlet,
Stark blind to my charms,
Is lost in the arms
Of that jilt, that inveigling harlot!
Stark blind to my charms,
Is lost in the arms

1. To keep track of the debts incurred by customers.
2. Common.
3. Basis.
4. I.e., cheat themselves.

Of that jilt, that inveigling harlot!
This, this my resentment alarms.

LOCKIT: And so, after all this mischief, I must stay here to be entertained with your caterwauling, Mistress Puss! Out of my sight, wanton strumpet! You shall fast and mortify yourself into reason, with now and then a little handsome discipline[5] to bring you to your senses. Go.

Scene 2

[*Lockit*]

Peachum then intends to outwit me in this affair, but I'll be even with him. The dog is leaky in his liquor,[6] so I'll ply him that way, get the secret from him, and turn this affair to my own advantage. Lions, wolves, and vultures don't live together in herds, droves, or flocks. Of all animals of prey, man is the only sociable one. Every one of us preys upon his neighbor, and yet we herd together. Peachum is my companion, my friend. According to the custom of the world, indeed, he may quote thousands of precedents for cheating me. And shall not I make use of the privilege of friendship to make him a return?

Air 43. Packington's Pound

Thus gamesters united in friendship are found,
Though they know that their industry all is a cheat;
They flock to their prey at the dice-box's sound,
And join to promote one another's deceit.
But if by mishap
They fail of a chap,[7]
To keep in their hands, they each other entrap.
Like pikes, lank with hunger, who miss of their ends,[8]
They bite their companions, and prey on their friends.

Now, Peachum, you and I, like honest tradesmen, are to have a fair trial which of us two can over-reach the other. Lucy! [*Enter Lucy*.] Are there any of Peachum's people now in the house?

LUCY: Filch, Sir, is drinking a quartern[9] of strong waters in the next room with Black Moll.

LOCKIT: Bid him come to me.

Scene 3

[*Lockit, Filch*]

LOCKIT: Why, boy, thou lookest as if thou wert half starved, like a shotten herring.[1]

FILCH: One had need have the constitution of a horse to go through the business. Since the favorite child-getter[2] was disabled by a mishap, I have picked up a little

5. Beating.
6. Talkative when drunk.
7. Can't drum up someone to dupe.
8. I.e., fail to catch their prey.
9. Quarter-pint.
1. A herring that has spawned.
2. Begetter (i.e., Macheath).

money by helping the ladies to a pregnancy against their being called down to sentence.[3] But if a man cannot get an honest livelihood any easier way, I am sure 'tis what I can't undertake for another session.

LOCKIT: Truly, if that great man should tip off,[4] 'twould be an irreparable loss. The vigor and prowess of a knight-errant never saved half the ladies in distress that he hath done. But, boy, can'st thou tell me where thy master is to be found?

FILCH: At his lock,[5] Sir, at the Crooked Billet.

LOCKIT: Very well. I have nothing more with you.

[*Exit Filch.*]

I'll go to him there, for I have many important affairs to settle with him; and in the way of those transactions, I'll artfully get into his secret. So that Macheath shall not remain a day longer out of my clutches.

Scene 4. A Gaming House

[*Macheath in a fine tarnished*[6] *coat, Ben Budge, Matt of the Mint*]

MACHEATH: I am sorry, gentlemen, the road was so barren of money. When my friends are in difficulties, I am always glad that my fortune can be serviceable to them. [*Gives them money.*] You see, gentlemen, I am not a mere court friend, who professes everything and will do nothing.

Air 44. Lillibullero

The modes of the court so common are grown,
That a true friend can hardly be met;
Friendship for interest is but a loan,
Which they let out for what they can get.
'Tis true, you find
Some friends so kind,
Who will give you good counsel themselves to defend.
In sorrowful ditty,
They promise, they pity,
But shift you for money,[7] *from friend to friend.*

But we, gentlemen, have still honor enough to break through the corruptions of the world. And while I can serve you, you may command me.

BEN: It grieves my heart that so generous a man should be involved in such difficulties as oblige him to live with such ill company, and herd with gamesters.

MATT: See the partiality of mankind! One man may steal a horse, better than another look over a hedge.[8] Of all mechanics,[9] of all servile handicraftsmen, a gamester is the vilest. But yet, as many of the quality[1] are of the profession, he is admitted amongst the politest company. I wonder we are not more respected.

3. I.e., to safeguard them from hanging (because pregnant women could not be condemned to execution).
4. Die.
5. A cant word signifying a warehouse where stolen goods are deposited [Gay's note].
6. Discolored.
7. Put you off.
8. I.e., one man is permitted to steal a horse, though another is not permitted even to look at one (proverbial).
9. Manual workers.
1. Gentry; people of high standing.

MACHEATH: There will be deep play[2] tonight at Marybone, and consequently money may be picked up upon the road. Meet me there, and I'll give you the hint who is worth setting.[3]

MATT: The fellow with a brown coat with a narrow gold binding, I am told, is never without money.

MACHEATH: What do you mean, Matt? Sure you will not think of meddling with him! He's a good honest kind of a fellow, and one of us.

BEN: To be sure, Sir, we will put ourselves under your direction.

MACHEATH: Have an eye upon the money-lenders. A rouleau[4] or two would prove a pretty sort of an expedition. I hate extortion.

MATT: Those rouleaus are very pretty things. I hate your bank bills. There is such a hazard in putting them off.[5]

MACHEATH: There is a certain man of distinction, who in his time hath nicked me out of a great deal of the ready.[6] He is in my cash,[7] Ben. I'll point him out to you this evening, and you shall draw upon him for the debt. The company are met; I hear the dice-box in the other room. So, gentlemen, your servant. You'll meet me at Marybone.

Scene 5. Peachum's Lock

[*A table with wine, brandy, pipes and tobacco. Peachum, Lockit*]

LOCKIT: The Coronation account,[8] Brother Peachum, is of so intricate a nature, that I believe it will never be settled.

PEACHUM: It consists indeed of a great variety of articles. It was worth to our people, in fees of different kinds, above ten installments.[9] This is part of the account, Brother, that lies open before us.

LOCKIT: A lady's tail[1] of rich brocade—that, I see, is disposed of.

PEACHUM: To Mrs. Diana Trapes, the tallywoman;[2] and she will make a good hand[3] on't in shoes and slippers, to trick out young ladies, upon their going into keeping.

LOCKIT: But I don't see any article of the jewels.

PEACHUM: Those are so well known, that they must be sent abroad. You'll find them entered under the article of exportation. As for the snuffboxes, watches, swords, etc., I thought it best to enter them under their several heads.

LOCKIT: Seven and twenty women's pockets[4] complete, with the several things therein contained, all sealed, numbered, and entered.

PEACHUM: But, Brother, it is impossible for us now to enter upon this affair. We should have the whole day before us. Besides, the account of the last half year's plate is in a book by itself, which lies at the other office.

LOCKIT: Bring us then more liquor. Today shall be for pleasure, tomorrow for business. Ah, Brother, those daughters of ours are two slippery hussies. Keep a watchful eye upon Polly, and Macheath in a day or two shall be our own again.

2. Gambling for high stakes.
3. Setting upon; robbing.
4. A packet of gold coins.
5. Getting rid of them; passing them off.
6. I.e., ready money; cash.
7. Debt.
8. A manuscript inventory of items stolen during the coronation of George II. Peachum "keeps books" like an ordinary businessman.
9. I.e., the thieves have found a single coronation more than ten times as profitable as the annual installment of the new Lord Mayor.
1. Train (of a woman's dress).
2. One who provides goods on credit.
3. Profit.
4. A pocket was a detachable bag worn outside a woman's dress.

Air 45. Down in the north country

LOCKIT: *What gudgeons[5] are we men!*
Ev'ry woman's easy prey.
Though we have felt the hook, again
We bite and they betray.

The bird that hath been trapped,
When he hears his calling mate,
To her he flies, again he's clapped
Within the wiry grate.

PEACHUM: But what signifies catching the bird, if your daughter Lucy will set open the door of the cage?

LOCKIT: If men were answerable for the follies and frailties of their wives and daughters, no friends could keep a good correspondence together for two days. This is unkind of you, Brother; for among good friends, what they say or do goes for nothing.

[*Enter a servant.*]

SERVANT: Sir, here's Mrs. Diana Trapes wants to speak with you.

PEACHUM: Shall we admit her, Brother Lockit?

LOCKIT: By all means. She's a good customer, and a fine-spoken woman. And a woman who drinks and talks so freely will enliven the conversation.

PEACHUM: Desire her to walk in.

[*Exit servant.*]

Scene 6

Peachum, Lockit, Mrs. Trapes.

PEACHUM: Dear Mrs. Di, your servant. One may know by your kiss that your gin is excellent.

TRAPES: I was always very curious[6] in my liquors.

LOCKIT: There is no perfumed breath like it. I have been long acquainted with the flavor of those lips, han't I, Mrs. Di?

TRAPES: Fill it up. I take as large draughts of liquor as I did of love. I hate a flincher[7] in either.

Air 46. A shepherd kept sheep

In the days of my youth I could bill like a dove, fa, la, la, etc.
Like a sparrow at all times was ready for love, fa, la, la, etc.
The life of all mortals in kissing should pass,
Lip to lip while we're young—then the lip to the glass, fa, la, la, etc.

But now, Mr. Peachum, to our business. If you have blacks[8] of any kind, brought in of late: mantoes,[9] velvet scarves, petticoats—let it be what it will—I am your chap,[1] for all my ladies are very fond of mourning.

5. "A small fish . . . easily caught, and therefore made a proverbial name for a man easily cheated" (Johnson's *Dictionary*).
6. Choosy.
7. One who resists or refrains.
8. Black clothing.
9. Loose robes (French: *manteaux*).
1. Customer.

PEACHUM: Why, look ye, Mrs. Di, you deal so hard with us that we can afford to give the gentlemen, who venture their lives for the goods, little or nothing.

TRAPES: The hard times oblige me to go very near[2] in my dealing. To be sure, of late years I have been a great sufferer by the Parliament. Three thousand pounds would hardly make me amends. The Act for destroying the Mint[3] was a severe cut upon our business. Till then, if a customer[4] stepped out of the way, we knew where to have her. No doubt you know Mrs. Coaxer; there's a wench now (till today) with a good suit of clothes of mine upon her back, and I could never set eyes upon her for three months together. Since the Act too against imprisonment for small sums,[5] my loss there too hath been very considerable, and it must be so, when a lady can borrow a handsome petticoat, or a clean gown, and I not have the least hank[6] upon her! And, o' my conscience, nowadays most ladies take a delight in cheating, when they can do it with safety.

PEACHUM: Madam, you had a handsome gold watch of us t'other day for seven guineas. Considering we must have our profit, to a gentleman upon the road, a gold watch will be scarce worth the taking.

TRAPES: Consider, Mr. Peachum, that watch was remarkable, and not of very safe sale. If you have any black velvet scarves, they are a handsome winter-wear; and take with most gentlemen who deal with my customers. 'Tis I that put the ladies upon a good foot. 'Tis not youth or beauty that fixes their price. The gentlemen always pay according to their dress, from half a crown to two guineas; and yet those hussies make[7] nothing of bilking of me. Then too, allowing for accidents—I have eleven fine customers now down under the surgeon's hands[8]—what with fees and other expenses, there are great goings-out, and no comings-in, and not a farthing to pay for at least a month's clothing. We run great risks—great risks indeed.

PEACHUM: As I remember, you said something just now of Mrs. Coaxer.

TRAPES: Yes, Sir. To be sure I stripped her of a suit of my own clothes about two hours ago; and have left her as she should be, in her shift, with a lover of hers at my house. She called him upstairs, as he was going to Marybone in a hackney coach. And I hope, for her own sake and mine, she will persuade the Captain to redeem[9] her, for the Captain is very generous to the ladies.

LOCKIT: What Captain?

TRAPES: He thought I did not know him. An intimate acquaintance of yours, Mr. Peachum. Only Captain Macheath—as fine as a lord.

PEACHUM: Tomorrow, dear Mrs. Di, you shall set your own price upon any of the goods you like. We have at least half a dozen velvet scarves, and all at your service. Will you give me leave to make you a present of this suit of nightclothes for your own wearing? But are you sure it is Captain Macheath?

TRAPES: Though he thinks I have forgot him, nobody knows him better. I have taken a great deal of the Captain's money in my time at second hand, for he always loved to have his ladies well dressed.

PEACHUM: Mr. Lockit and I have a little business with the Captain—you understand me—and we will satisfy you for Mrs. Coaxer's debt.

2. To pay as little as possible.
3. The Mint was a safe haven for debtors, and hence a gathering place for disreputable characters. The Act (10 October 1723) made it much harder to feign bankruptcy, and thereby to take safe refuge in the Mint.
4. Prostitute.
5. "An Act to Prevent Frivolous and Vexatious Arrests" (24 June 1726); in a Superior Court matter, "small sums" meant 10 pounds; in an Inferior, 40 shillings.
6. Hold.
7. Think.
8. For treatment of venereal disease.
9. I.e., will help her to buy back (as at a pawn shop) her "suit of . . . clothes."

LOCKIT: Depend upon it: we will deal like men of honor.

TRAPES: I don't inquire after your affairs; so whatever happens, I wash my hands on't. It hath always been my maxim that one friend should assist another. But if you please, I'll take one of the scarves home with me. 'Tis always good to have something in hand.

Scene 7. Newgate

[*Lucy*]

LUCY: Jealousy, rage, love, and fear are at once tearing me to pieces. How I am weather-beaten and shattered with distresses!

Air 47. One evening, having lost my way

I'm like a skiff on the ocean tossed,
Now high, now low, with each billow born,
With her rudder broke, and her anchor lost,
Deserted and all forlorn.
While thus I lie rolling and tossing all night,
That Polly lies sporting on seas of delight!
Revenge, revenge, revenge,
Shall appease my restless sprite.

I have the ratsbane[1] ready. I run no risk, for I can lay her death upon the gin, and so many die of that naturally that I shall never be called in question. But, say I were to be hanged, I never could be hanged for anything that would give me greater comfort than the poisoning that slut.

[*Enter Filch.*]

FILCH: Madam, here's our Miss Polly come to wait upon you.

LUCY: Show her in.

Scene 8

[*Lucy, Polly*]

LUCY: Dear madam, your servant. I hope you will pardon my passion, when I was so happy to see you last. I was so overrun with the spleen[2] that I was perfectly out of myself. And really, when one hath the spleen, everything is to be excused by a friend.

Air 48. Now Roger, I'll tell thee, because thou'rt my son

When a wife's in her pout,
(As she's sometimes, no doubt!)
The good husband as meek as a lamb,
Her vapors to still,
First grants her her will,
And the quieting draught is a dram.[3]
Poor man! And the quieting draught is a dram.

1. Rat poison.
2. Generally, ill temper; more specifically, a fashionable disease resembling hypochondria, also known as "the vapors."
3. A shot of alcohol.

I wish all our quarrels might have so comfortable a reconciliation.

POLLY: I have no excuse for my own behavior, Madam, but my misfortunes. And really, Madam, I suffer too upon your account.

LUCY: But, Miss Polly, in the way of friendship, will you give me leave to propose a glass of cordial to you?

POLLY: Strong waters are apt to give me the headache. I hope, Madam, you will excuse me.

LUCY: Not the greatest lady in the land could have better in her closet, for her own private drinking. You seem mighty low in spirits, my dear.

POLLY: I am sorry, Madam, my health will not allow me to accept of your offer. I should not have left you in the rude manner I did when we met last, Madam, had not my papa hauled me away so unexpectedly. I was indeed somewhat provoked, and perhaps might use some expressions that were disrespectful. But really, Madam, the Captain treated me with so much contempt and cruelty that I deserved your pity rather than your resentment.

LUCY: But since his escape, no doubt all matters are made up again. Ah Polly! Polly! 'Tis I am the unhappy wife; and he loves you as if you were only his mistress.

POLLY: Sure, Madam, you cannot think me so happy as to be the object of your jealousy. A man is always afraid of a woman who loves him too well—so that I must expect to be neglected and avoided.

LUCY: Then our cases, my dear Polly, are exactly alike. Both of us indeed have been too fond.

Air 49. Oh, Bessy Bell

POLLY: *A curse attends that woman's love,*
Who always would be pleasing.
LUCY: *The pertness of the billing dove,*
Like tickling, is but teasing.
POLLY: *What then in love can woman do?*
LUCY: *If we grow fond they shun us.*
POLLY: *And when we fly them, they pursue.*
LUCY: *But leave us when they've won us.*

LUCY: Love is so very whimsical in both sexes that it is impossible to be lasting. But my heart is particular,[4] and contradicts my own observation.

POLLY: But really, Mistress Lucy, by his last behavior, I think I ought to envy you. When I was forced from him, he did not show the least tenderness. But perhaps he hath a heart not capable of it.

Air 50. Would fate to me Belinda give

Among the men, coquettes we find,
Who court by turns all womankind;
And we grant all their hearts desired,
When they are flattered, and admired.

4. In two senses: (1) preoccupied with one person (Macheath), and therefore (2) idiosyncratic—an exception to the rule she has just pronounced.

The coquettes of both sexes are self-lovers, and that is a love no other whatever can dispossess. I fear, my dear Lucy, our husband is one of those.

LUCY: Away with these melancholy reflections. Indeed, my dear Polly, we are both of us a cup too low.[5] Let me prevail upon you to accept of my offer.

Air 51. Come, sweet lass

Come, sweet lass,
Lets banish sorrow
Till tomorrow;
Come, sweet lass,
Let's take a chirping[6] *glass.*
Wine can clear
The vapors of despair;
And make us light as air;
Then drink, and banish care.

I can't bear, child, to see you in such low spirits. And I must persuade you to what I know will do you good. [*Aside.*] I shall now soon be even with the hypocritical strumpet.

Scene 9

[*Polly*]

POLLY: All this wheedling of Lucy cannot be for nothing. At this time too! When I know she hates me! The dissembling of a woman is always the forerunner of mischief. By pouring strong waters down my throat, she thinks to pump some secrets out of me. I'll be upon my guard, and won't taste a drop of her liquor, I'm resolved.

Scene 10

[*Lucy, with strong waters; Polly*]

LUCY: Come, Miss Polly.

POLLY: Indeed, child, you have given yourself trouble to no purpose. You must, my dear, excuse me.

LUCY: Really, Miss Polly, you are so squeamishly affected about taking a cup of strong waters as a lady before company. I vow, Polly, I shall take it monstrously ill if you refuse me. Brandy and men (though women love them never so well)[7] are always taken by us with some reluctance—unless 'tis in private.

POLLY: I protest, Madam, it goes against me. What do I see! Macheath again in custody! Now every glimmering of happiness is lost.
[*Drops the glass of liquor on the ground.*]

LUCY: Since things are thus, I'm glad the wench hath escaped; for by this event, 'tis plain, she was not happy enough to deserve to be poisoned.

5. I.e., we both need a drink.
6. Cheering.
7. However much women may love them.

Scene 11

[*Lockit, Macheath, Peachum, Lucy, Polly*]

LOCKIT: Set your heart to rest, Captain. You have neither the chance of love or money for another escape, for you are ordered to be called down upon your trial immediately.

PEACHUM: Away, hussies! This is not a time for a man to be hampered with his wives. You see, the gentleman is in chains already.

LUCY: Oh, husband, husband, my heart longed to see thee. But to see thee thus distracts me!

POLLY: Will not my dear husband look upon his Polly? Why hadst thou not flown to me for protection? With me thou hadst been safe.

Air 52. The last time I went o'er the moor

POLLY: *Hither, dear husband, turn your eyes.*
LUCY: *Bestow one glance to cheer me.*
POLLY: *Think with that look, thy Polly dies.*
LUCY: *Oh, shun me not—but hear me.*
POLLY: *'Tis Polly sues.*
LUCY: *'Tis Lucy speaks.*
POLLY: *Is thus true love requited?*
LUCY: *My heart is bursting.*
POLLY: *Mine too breaks.*
LUCY: *Must I—*
POLLY: *Must I be slighted?*

MACHEATH: What would you have me say, ladies? You see this affair will soon be at an end, without my disobliging either of you.

PEACHUM: But the settling this point, Captain, might prevent a lawsuit between your two widows.

Air 53. Tom Tinker's my true love

MACHEATH: *Which way shall I turn me? How can I decide?*
Wives, the day of our death, are as fond as a bride.
One wife is too much for most husbands to hear,
But two at a time there's no mortal can bear.
This way, and that way, and which way I will,
What would comfort the one, t'other wife would take ill.

POLLY: But if his own misfortunes have made him insensible to mine, a father sure will be more compassionate. Dear, dear Sir, sink[8] the material evidence, and bring him off at his trial—Polly upon her knees begs it of you.[9]

Air 54. I am a poor shepherd undone

When my hero in court appears,
And stands arraigned for his life;

8. Suppress.

9. This is the moment Hogarth painted; see Color plate 26.

Then think of poor Polly's tears;
For Ah! Poor Polly's his wife.
Like the sailor he holds up his hand,
Distressed on the dashing wave.
To die a dry death at land,
Is as bad as a watery grave.
And alas, poor Polly!
Alack, and well-a-day!
Before I was in love,
Oh! Every month was May.

LUCY: If Peachum's heart is hardened, sure you, Sir, will have more compassion on a daughter. I know the evidence is in your power. How then can you be a tyrant to me?

[*Kneeling.*]

Air 55. Ianthe the lovely

When he holds up his hand arraigned for his life,
Oh, think of your daughter, and think I'm his wife!
What are cannons, or bombs, or clashing of swords?
For death is more certain by witnesses' words.
Then nail up their lips; that dread thunder allay;
And each month of my life will hereafter be May.

LOCKIT: Macheath's time is come, Lucy. We know our own affairs; therefore let us have no more whimpering or whining.

Air 56. A cobbler there was

Ourselves, like the great, to secure a retreat,
When matters require it, must give up our gang:
And good reason why,
Or, instead of the fry,[1]
Ev'n Peachum and I,
Like poor petty rascals, might hang, hang;
Like poor petty rascals, might hang.

PEACHUM: Set your heart at rest, Polly. Your husband is to die today. Therefore, if you are not already provided, 'tis high time to look about for another. There's comfort for you, you slut.

LOCKIT: We are ready, Sir, to conduct you to the Old Bailey.

Air 57. Bonny Dundee

MACHEATH: *The charge is prepared; the lawyers are met,*
The judges all ranged; (a terrible show!).
I go undismayed, for death is a debt,
A debt on demand, so take what I owe.

1. Small fish.

Then farewell, my love. Dear charmers, adieu.
Contented I die. 'Tis the better for you.
Here ends all dispute the rest of our lives.
For this way at once I please all my wives.

Now, gentlemen, I am ready to attend you.

Scene 12

[*Lucy, Polly, Filch*]

POLLY: Follow them, Filch, to the court. And when the trial is over, bring me a particular account of his behavior, and of everything that happened. You'll find me here with Miss Lucy. [*Exit Filch.*] But why is all this music?

LUCY: The prisoners, whose trials are put off till next session, are diverting themselves.

POLLY: Sure, there is nothing so charming as music! I'm fond of it to distraction! But alas! Now all mirth seems an insult upon my affliction. Let us retire, my dear Lucy, and indulge our sorrows. The noisy crew, you see, are coming upon us.

[*Exeunt.*]

[*A dance of prisoners in chains.*]

Scene 13. The Condemned Hold

[*Macheath, in a melancholy posture.*]

Air 58. Happy groves

O cruel, cruel, cruel case!
Must I suffer this disgrace?

Air 59. Of all the girls that are so smart

Of all the friends in time of grief,
When threatning death looks grimmer,
Not one so sure can bring relief,
As this best friend, a brimmer.[2]

[*Drinks.*]

Air 60. Britons strike home

Since I must swing, I scorn, I scorn to wince or whine.

[*Rises.*]

Air 61. Chevy Chase

But now again my spirits sink;
I'll raise them high with wine.

[*Drinks a glass of wine.*]

2. A cup filled to the brim.

Air 62. To old Sir Simon the King

But valor the stronger grows,
The stronger liquor we're drinking.
And how can we feel our woes,
When we've lost the trouble of thinking?

[*Drinks.*]

Air 63. Joy to great Cæsar

If thus—a man can die
Much bolder with brandy.

[*Pours out a bumper of brandy.*]

Air 64. There was an old woman

So I drink off this bumper. And now I can stand the test.
And my comrades shall see, that I die as brave as the best.

[*Drinks.*]

Air 65. Did you ever hear of a gallant sailor

But can I leave my pretty hussies,
Without one tear, or tender sigh?

Air 66. Why are mine eyes still flowing

Their eyes, their lips, their busses[3]
Recall my love. Ah, must I die?

Air 67. Greensleeves

Since laws were made for ev'ry degree,
To curb vice in others, as well as me,
I wonder we han't better company,
Upon Tyburn tree!
But gold from law can take out the sting;
And if rich men like us were to swing,
'Twou'd thin the land, such numbers to string
Upon Tyburn tree!

[*Enter a Jailer.*]

JAILER: Some friends of yours, Captain, desire to be admitted. I leave you together.

3. Kisses.

Scene 14

[*Macheath, Ben Budge, Matt of the Mint*]

MACHEATH: For my having broke[4] prison, you see, gentlemen, I am ordered immediate execution. The sheriff's officers, I believe, are now at the door. That Jemmy Twitcher should peach me, I own surprised me! 'Tis a plain proof that the world is all alike, and that even our gang can no more trust one another than other people. Therefore, I beg you, gentlemen, look well to yourselves, for in all probability you may live some months longer.

MATT: We are heartily sorry, Captain, for your misfortune. But 'tis what we must all come to.

MACHEATH: Peachum and Lockit, you know, are infamous scoundrels. Their lives are as much in your power, as yours are in theirs. Remember your dying friend. 'Tis my last request. Bring those villains to the gallows before you, and I am satisfied.

MATT: We'll do't.

JAILER: Miss Polly and Miss Lucy entreat a word with you.

MACHEATH: Gentlemen, adieu.

Scene 15

[*Lucy, Macheath, Polly*]

MACHEATH: My dear Lucy—my dear Polly—whatsoever hath passed between us is now at an end. If you are fond of marrying again, the best advice I can give you is to ship yourselves off for the West Indies, where you'll have a fair chance of getting a husband apiece; or by good luck, two or three, as you like best.

POLLY: How can I support this sight!

LUCY: There is nothing moves one so much as a great man in distress.

Air 68. All you that must take a leap

LUCY: *Would I might be hanged!*
POLLY: *And I would so too!*
LUCY: *To be hanged with you.*
POLLY: *My dear, with you.*
MACHEATH: *Oh, leave me to thought! I fear! I doubt!*
I tremble! I droop!—See, my courage is out. [*Turns up the empty bottle.*]

POLLY: *No token of love?*
MACHEATH: *See, my courage is out.* [*Turns up the empty pot.*]
LUCY: *No token of love?*
POLLY: *Adieu!*
LUCY: *Farewell!*
MACHEATH: *But hark! I hear the toll of the bell.*
CHORUS: *Tol de rol lol, etc.*

[*Enter the Jailer.*]

JAILER: Four women more, Captain, with a child apiece! See, here they come.
[*Enter women and children.*]

4. Escaped.

MACHEATH: What—four wives more! This is too much. Here—tell the sheriff's officers I am ready.

[*Exit Macheath guarded.*]

Scene 16

[*To them, enter Player and Beggar.*]

PLAYER: But, honest friend, I hope you don't intend that Macheath shall be really executed.

BEGGAR: Most certainly, Sir. To make the piece perfect, I was for doing strict poetical justice. Macheath is to be hanged; and for the other personages of the drama, the audience must have supposed they were all either hanged or transported.

PLAYER: Why then, friend, this is a downright deep tragedy. The catastrophe is manifestly wrong, for an opera must end happily.

BEGGAR: Your objection, Sir, is very just, and is easily removed. For you must allow, that in this kind of drama, 'tis no matter how absurdly things are brought about. So—you rabble there—run and cry a reprieve. Let the prisoner be brought back to his wives in triumph.

PLAYER: All this we must do, to comply with the taste of the town.[5]

BEGGAR: Through the whole piece you may observe such a similitude of manners in high and low life, that it is difficult to determine whether (in the fashionable vices) the fine gentlemen imitate the gentlemen of the road, or the gentlemen of the road the fine gentlemen. Had the play remained as I at first intended, it would have carried a most excellent moral. 'Twould have shown that the lower sort of people have their vices in a degree as well as the rich—and that they are punished for them.

Scene 17

[*To them, Macheath with rabble, etc.*]

MACHEATH: So, it seems, I am not left to my choice, but must have a wife at last. Look ye, my dears, we will have no controversy now. Let us give this day to mirth, and I am sure she who thinks herself my wife will testify her joy by a dance.

ALL: Come, a dance, a dance.

MACHEATH: Ladies, I hope you will give me leave to present a partner to each of you. And (if I may without offense) for this time, I take Polly for mine. [*To Polly.*] And for life, you slut—for we were really married. As for the rest—but at present keep your own secret.

A Dance

Air 69. Lumps of pudding

Thus I stand like the Turk, with his doxies around;[6]
From all sides their glances his passion confound;
For black, brown, and fair, his inconstancy burns,

5. Fashionable London society.

6. Like a sultan in a harem.

And the different beauties subdue him by turns:
Each calls forth her charms, to provoke his desires:
Though willing to all, with but one he retires.
But think of this maxim, and put off your sorrow,
The wretch of today may be happy tomorrow.

CHORUS: *But think of this maxim, etc.*

FINIS.

1727 1728

For companion readings on *The Beggar's Opera* and its time, including texts by D'Urfey, Defoe, Fielding, and others, go to *The Longman Anthology of British Literature* Web site at www.myliteraturekit.com.

William Hogarth

1697–1764

"I had naturally a good eye," William Hogarth remembered near his life's end. "Shows of all sorts gave me uncommon pleasure when an infant." The "shows" (spectacles) that filled his eye in the turbulent London neighborhood of Smithfield where he grew up suffused his art for life: the antics of actors and the raucousness of audiences at Bartholomew Fair; the chicanery and pathos of prostitutes and thieves; the casual injustice of constables and magistrates. Above all, he watched his father fail. Richard Hogarth, a classical scholar, spent four years as a prisoner for debt, when his coffeehouse (catering to learned men and specializing in Latin conversation) failed to cover its own expenses. The debtor's family was effectually imprisoned too, and Hogarth, in his early teens during the ordeal, never forgot. "The emphasis throughout his work" (notes his biographer Ronald Paulson) "is on prisons, real and metaphorical. Even when he is not dealing with people who are in a prison . . . he portrays rooms that are more like prison cells than boudoirs or parlors."

At age seventeen, Hogarth was apprenticed to a silver engraver, ornamenting platters, rings, tableware, and the like. Finding the work dull, he switched to copper engraving, the technique by which book illustrators and printmakers created and reproduced their pictures. Late in his twenties he commenced his career as painter. His first great successes combined both craft and art. Hogarth produced the series of six pictures that make up *A Harlot's Progress* first as a set of paintings in oil, then as a sequence of copper engravings aimed at wider distribution. If *A Harlot's Progress* launched his popularity, *A Rake's Progress* (engraved in 1735 from canvases painted the year before) clinched his reputation as Britain's most masterly, mocking delineator of contemporary vice and folly. Though he continued for a while to nurture conventional ambitions as a painter of portraits and historical subjects catering to aristocratic tastes, Hogarth came gradually to recognize the originality, force, and commercial viability of his satrical engravings. As he later expressed it (in his own idiosyncratic syntax), he had discovered a style pitched between "the sublime and the grotesque," and had devised "a more new way of proceeding, viz. painting and engraving modern moral subjects, a field unbroke up in any country or any age. . . . Provided I could strike the passions, and by small sums from many, by means of prints which I could engrave from my pictures myself, I could secure my property to myself." Hogarth managed to "strike the passions" both ways: by depicting them vividly in the countenance of his characters, and by igniting them in his audience. He also managed, better than any predecessor, to "secure his property to himself." He petitioned Parliament to pass the Engraver's Copyright Act (often called "Hogarth's Act"), which protected printmakers from the then rampant piratical reproduction of their work, and which thereby (in Hogarth's proud words) "made prints a considerable article and trade in this country, there being more business of that kind done in this town than in Paris or anywhere else." The engravings of *A Rake's Progress* were first published, pointedly, the day after Hogarth's Act became the law of the land.

Early in his career, Hogarth had been praised as a "Shakespeare in painting," and admirers noted repeatedly the literary force of his graphic art; only he, wrote one, could "teach pictures to speak and to think." Hogarth had appropriated the very idea of an instructive moral "progress" from John Bunyan's phenomenally popular religious narrative *Pilgrim's Progress*, but he made the journey at once darker and more satiric. Bunyan's Mr. Christian progresses through Vanity Fair and other dangers toward the Celestial City; Hogarth's protagonists remain mired within the Vanity Fair of contemporary London; their "progress" takes them downward to degradation and death. His art also helped shape a newer form of narrative, the novel. Like the novel, Hogarth's sequences abound in suggestive subplots, telling asides, and startling revelations, played out in the tiniest details carefully placed. Novelists as different from one another as Samuel Richardson, Henry Fielding, and Laurence Sterne valued him as a friend, sought him as a collaborator, and embraced him as a past master in their own moral and narrative mode. "I almost dare affirm," wrote Fielding, "that those two works of his, which he calls *The Rake's* and *The Harlot's Progress*, are calculated more to serve the cause of virtue, and for the preservation of mankind, than all the folios of morality which have ever been written."

For color reproductions of two Hogarth paintings, see Color Plates 26 and 27.

A Rake's Progress

Plate 1 Tom Rakewell's father (depicted in the portrait above the mantle) has recently died. The old man was miserly: he wore a coat and fur hat indoors so as not to incur the costs of a fire; he saved broken junk (in the open chest); he nearly starved his housecat (lower left). The young man is profligate: he has torn open doors and cabinets in search of sequestered wealth; he is being measured for new and ostentatious clothes; he is trying to pay off the raging mother of Sarah Young, the weeping woman (at right) whom he has made pregnant.

Plate 2 Nearly unrecognizable in his new elegance, Rakewell (the tallest figure in the picture) surrounds himself with instructors and tradespeople eager to sell their services. In the foreground (from left to right) are a composer, a fencing master, a dance teacher (with fiddle), a hired killer (in black; the note in Tom's hand, from "William Stab," vouches for the assassin as "a man of honor"); a huntsman (with horn); and a jockey, whose trophy cup bears the suggestive name of the winning horse: "Silly Tom." The two moping Englishmen at the back may be miffed to find themselves supplanted by the fashionable foreigners in front of them. The painting above the mantle depicts the Judgment of Paris, that indolent princeling whose unrestrained desires precipitated the catastrophe of the Trojan War.

Plate 3 Rakewell (sprawled at left) has bought himself an orgy. All the Roman portraits in the upper-right corner have been defaced, except that of the emperor Nero, who looks out over the havoc like some patron saint of vandalism (his reputed incendarism is re-enacted by the woman standing at the back near the shattered mirror, holding a candle flame to the map of the world). One prostitute caresses Tom while conveying away his watch; in the foreground opposite, a woman disrobes in preparation for an obscene dance that will likely involve the reflective platter and large candle held by the cross-eyed lackey in the doorway. Admonitions to the orgiasts lie at hand, in the form of the chicken's carcass (lower-right corner), stripped and forked; and in the person of the ballad singer, tattered, pregnant, and ignored, whose song bears the telling title "Black Joke."

Plate 4 Carried in his sedan chair to a night of gaming at White's Chocolate House and gambling club (rear left), Tom is stopped by a bailiff who serves him with a notice of arrest for debt. He receives aid not from the revellers in the distance but from Sarah Young, the abandoned lover whose mother he tried to buy off in Plate 1. Reversing that gesture, she seeks to secure his release by offering the money she has earned by making ribbons and caps (sample wares hang at her side). On a ladder a lamplighter, distracted by the goings-on, carelessly (and emblematically) spills his flammable fluid onto Rakewell's head. Hogarth reworked this picture more often than any other in the series. In this late version, a lightning bolt aims pointedly at the gambling house, upper left, while at the lower right, a group of urchins in the open air has made an early start at playing comparably dangerous games.

Plate 5 Intent on wealth, not the love Sarah offers, Rakewell weds an old woman in a dim, disintegrating church where light and faith are in scant supply. On the left, the Poor's Box," receptacle of charity, has long been shut (a cobweb covers its lid); on the right wall, the table of commandments is cracked. The one-eyed bride appears to wink at the grim parson; Rakewell proffers her the ring while eying her maid. On the floor, a canine couple parodies the human ceremony; in the back, a woman with churchkeys flailing tries to prevent the intrusion of Sarah Young, holding the child Rakewell has sired. Sarah's mother does vigorous but unavailing battle.

Plate 6 During a night of gambling, Rakewell has evidently lost the fortune he acquired by his calculating marriage. Wigless, frantic, he falls to one knee and curses his lot; his rage is replicated (as were his nuptials) by a dog on the floor to his right. The croupier at rear center, carrying the candles, echoes the "world-burning" woman in Plate 3. This time, though, the building is actually on fire. The lantern-bearing watchman at left has come to give warning. Most of the gamblers are too immersed in their own operations to notice either Rakewell's anguish or their own danger.

Plate 7 In the wake of his losses, Rakewell has at last been imprisoned for debt, unable to pay the "garnish" (or customary bribe) that the jailer behind him expects, or even the cost of a beer. The note on the table—"I have read your play and find it will not do"—rejects his last poor, literary attempt at solvency. His wife rails, Sarah faints, his daughter tugs at Sarah's skirts, and his cellmates embody futilities even more preposterous than his own playwriting. The impoverished man at left has devised "a new scheme for paying the debts of the nation." The man seated at the stove is an alchemist, vainly trying to transmute base metals into gold; before his imprisonment, he also built himself a pair of wings (upper left), but they, like Rakewell's upward aspirations, have produced only debt and confinement, not flight and freedom.

Plate 8 Rakewell has been moved from debtor's prison to Bethlehem Royal Hospital (better known as Bedlam), London's asylum for the insane. Grinning outright for the first time in the series, Tom claws at his head while guards restrain him. Sarah Young, weeping, has come to give him comfort. The other two women are here to amuse themselves (at the cost of two pence per visit, Bedlam had become one of London's most popular entertainments). Some inmates display lunatic religious zeal; others have gone mad in pursuit of science. The man drawing the world on the wall seeks a solution to the longitude, the navigational problem that had obsessed Britons for many decades. Behind the open door of the central cell, a naked madman sits and thinks he's king. In this final revision of the plate (1763), Hogarth has superimposed upon the longitudinist's globe an emblem of Britannia, as though empire and madhouse were now one.

PERSPECTIVES
Mind and God

Nature, and Nature's Laws lay hid in Night.
God said, *Let Newton be!* and All was *Light*.

So wrote Alexander Pope, capturing in a couplet the awe with which many of his contemporaries regarded the accomplishments of Isaac Newton. The lines, intended for Newton's tomb, compass his whole career. Pope's last word evokes one of the scientist's early breakthroughs: the discovery that sunlight, for all its seeming "whiteness," teemed with colors, whose operations could be mathematically described. Later, in his masterwork *Naturalis Philosophiae Principia Mathematica* (The Mathematical Principles of Natural Philosophy, 1687), Newton had expounded "Nature's Laws" on a scale and with a precision heretofore unmatched, pinpointing, in compact mathematical formulas, the laws governing gravity and motion, both on earth and throughout the heavens. In Pope's replaying of Genesis, Newton himself becomes a principle, not merely the interpreter of Creation but virtually synonomous with it: God's luminous word, from which revelation follows. For numberless admirers, the name of Newton figured forth not only the intricate simplicities of "Nature's Laws," but also the astonishing, hitherto unsuspected capacity of the human mind to shed light upon the works of God.

The human mind itself promptly became the object of new investigation, Newtonian in its ambitions and its methods. Two years after the *Principia* appeared, John Locke published his *Essay Concerning Human Understanding* (1689), a work comparably influential, in which he sought answers to key questions of epistemology: what do we know? and by what means do we come to know it? Locke, like Newton, brought luster to the scientific approach championed by the Royal Society (of which both men were members): empiricism, the conviction that truth could be attained solely through experiment and experience. The intimate interplay of those two crucial elements is nicely registered in Albert Einstein's account of the way that Newton did his work: "The conceptions which he used to reduce the material of experience to order seemed to flow spontaneously from experience itself, from the beautiful experiments which he ranged in order like playthings and describes with an affectionate wealth of detail." Locke imported empiricism from the physical sciences into the realms of philosophy and psychology. Striving to found a science of mind, to make sense of the running encounter between the material world and human perception, Locke and his successors found in experience both a method for investigating epistemological problems and the core of their solution: for these thinkers, experience is how we know, it is what we know, and it is how we can learn more about the processes of our knowing. The human mind is intrinsically (though not methodically) empiricist in its ways of gathering its "wealth of detail" about the world.

Under the mind's new scrutinies, God's place and primacy fell open to new questions. Empiricism itself was seen to cut two ways. On the one hand, as Newton and the vast majority of his followers delightedly proclaimed, experimental observation was revealing a universal architecture so exquisite as to prove both the existence and the matchless artistry of God the architect; this route from reason to religious faith became known as the "argument from design." On the other hand, discovery was beginning to conjure up alternative possibilities unsettling to faith: of a God not wholly supreme but subject to nature's inexorable laws; or of laws so efficiently self-sustaining that they needed no God to enforce them. In some of its modes, empiricism itself could be seen to imperil faith, since direct experience or demonstration of the divine proved elusive in a science that limited itself to the observation of material, mechanical causes and effects. For Newton, Locke, and countless other inquirers, empiricism promised to explain the ways of God; but they had begun a process which, in other hands, might threaten to explain God away.

The clash between science and theology gathered force in the mid-nineteenth century, when discoveries in geology (the age of the Earth) and biology (evolution) rendered Scripture strongly suspect. But contention between faith and science was manifest much earlier. At the start of the nineteenth century, William Blake briefly sketched the lines of struggle in his private notebook. "Newton's particles of light," he wrote,

> Are sands upon the Red sea shore,
> Where Israel's tents do shine so bright.

Against the arrogance of inquiry, Blake insists upon humility and awe; biblical revelation trumps all the small advancements of human knowledge. Pope had gestured in this direction some seven decades earlier. He suggested, in his *Essay on Man*, that for "superior beings" (angels, God), the sight of Newton unfolding "all Nature's law" might provide the same kind of amazement and amusement that we mortals derive from the antics of a performing ape—a creature who knows more than we might expect, but far less than we ourselves. So great (Pope argues) is the difference between human and divine capacities. Throughout the eighteenth century, in works suffused by the concepts of Newton and of Locke, the relations between mind and God were brilliantly explicated and newly contested, as poets and philosophers undertook, from varying vantages and factions, to sing God's praise, to parse his ways, to work toward him by reason or (in rare instances) to reason him out of existence altogether.

Isaac Newton
1642–1727

Albert Einstein summed up Newton's abilities as follows: "In one person, he combined the experimenter, the theorist, the mechanic, and, not least, the artist in exposition." Einstein praises magnificently, and omits much. Newton also combined in his one person a supreme mathematician, an obsessive alchemist, a forceful administrator, and (perhaps most important, in his own view) an ardent theologian, eager to discover and expound the place of God in his creation. His voluminous, unorthodox writings on the subject remained unpublished in his lifetime. By denying the full divinity of Christ, Newton accorded God *more* authority than did conventional Anglicanism. His views, if known, would have toppled him from the public eminences he enjoyed: as Lucasian Professor of Mathematics at Cambridge, as Master of the Mint in London, as President of the Royal Society. Still, Newton's first admirers found in his scientific work exhilarating support for a more mainstream theology: the strongest foundation yet for the argument from design. It was the business of natural philosophy, Newton repeatedly insisted, "to deduce causes from effects, until we come to the First Cause, which is certainly not mechanical." Newton's own scientific revelations gave rise to a passionate interest in "natural religion"—a faith in God's existence and benevolence, grounded in the orderliness and beauty of the natural world. One of that faith's adherents was the ambitious young classicist and clergyman Richard Bentley (1662–1742), who, having been commissioned to deliver a series of lectures defending Christianity against atheism, found in Newton's recently published *Principia* abundant new evidence for his own arguments about the divine "origin and frame of the universe." While preparing his lectures for the press, Bentley sent Newton a set of questions, in order to make sure that he was correctly understanding and deploying the *Principia*. Newton's four replies (the first is excerpted here) map the convergence that interests him most, between the discoveries of science and the majesty of God.

from Letter to Richard Bentley

10 December 1692

Sir,

When I wrote my treatise about our system, I had an eye upon such principles as might work with considering men for the belief of a Deity, and nothing can rejoice me more than to find it useful for that purpose. But if I have done the public any service this way, 'tis due to nothing but industry and a patient thought.

As to your first query, it seems to me, that if the matter of our sun and planets and all the matter in the universe was evenly scattered throughout all the heavens, and every particle had an innate gravity towards all the rest,[1] and the whole space throughout which this matter was scattered was but finite, the matter on the outside of this space would by its gravity tend towards all the matter on the inside, and by consequence fall down to the middle of the whole space, and there compose one great spherical mass. But if the matter was evenly diffused through an infinite space, it would never convene into one mass, but some of it convene into one mass and some into another so as to make an infinite number of great masses scattered at great distances from one to another throughout all that infinite space. And thus might the sun and fixed stars be formed, supposing the matter were of a lucid[2] nature. But how the matter should divide itself into two sorts, and that part of it which is fit to compose a shining body should fall down into one mass and make a sun, and the rest which is fit to compose an opaque body should coalesce not into one great body like the shining matter but into many little ones; or, if the sun was at first an opaque body like the planets, or the planets lucid bodies like the sun, how he alone should be changed into a shining body whilst all they continue opaque, or all they be changed into opaque ones whilst he remains unchanged, I do not think explicable by mere natural causes but am forced to ascribe it to the counsel[3] and contrivance of a voluntary agent. The same power, whether natural or supernatural, which placed the sun in the center of the orbs[4] of the six primary planets, placed Saturn in the center of the orbs of his five secondary planets,[5] and Jupiter in the center of the orbs of his four secondary ones, and the Earth in the center of the moon's orb; and therefore, had this cause been a blind one without contrivance and design, the sun would have been a body of the same kind with Saturn, Jupiter and the Earth; that is without light and heat. Why there is one body in our system qualified to give light and heat to all the rest I know no reason but because the author of the system thought it convenient, and why there is but one body of this kind I know no reason but because one was sufficient to warm and enlighten all the rest. For the Cartesian hypothesis[6] of suns losing their light and then turning into comets and comets into planets can have no place in my system and is plainly erroneous, because it's certain that comets as often as they appear to us descend into the system of our planets lower than the orb of Jupiter and sometimes lower than the orbs of Venus and Mercury, and yet never stay here but always return from the sun with the same degrees of motion by which they approached him.

1. Newton did not endorse this premise. "You sometimes speak," he wrote Bentley in his second letter, "of gravity as essential and inherent to matter: pray do not ascribe that notion to me, for the cause of gravity is what I do not pretend to know."
2. Light-producing.
3. Deliberate design.
4. Orbits.
5. I.e., Saturn's moons; Newton states the numbers of planets and their moons then known.
6. A theory put forth by the French mathematician and philosopher René Descartes (1596–1650) in his highly influential treatises on physics, which Newton's *Principia* had challenged.

To your second query I answer that the motions which the planets now have could not spring from any natural cause alone but were impressed by an intelligent agent. For since comets descend into the region of our planets and here move all manner of ways, going sometimes the same way with the planets, sometimes the contrary way, and sometimes in cross ways in planes inclined to the plane of the ecliptic at all kinds of angles, it's plain that there is no natural cause which could determine all the planets both primary and secondary to move the same way and in the same plane without any considerable variation.[7] This must have been the effect of counsel. Nor is there any natural cause which could give the planets those just degrees of velocity in proportion to their distances from the sun and other central bodies about which they move and to the quantity of matter contained in those bodies, which were requisite to make them move in concentric orbs about those bodies. Had the planets been as swift as comets in proportion to their distances from the sun (as they would have been, had their motions been caused by their gravity, whereby the matter at the first formation of the planets might fall from the remotest regions towards the sun), they would not move in concentric orbs but in such eccentric ones as the comets move in. Were all the planets as swift as Mercury or as slow as Saturn or his satellites, or were their several velocities otherwise much greater or less than they are (as they might have been had they arose from any other cause than their gravity), or had their distances from the centers about which they move been greater or less than they are with the same velocities; or had the quantity of matter in the sun or in Saturn, Jupiter, and the Earth and by consequence their gravitating power been greater or less than it is, the primary planets could not have revolved about the sun nor the secondary ones about Saturn, Jupiter and the Earth in concentric circles as they do, but would have moved in hyperbolas or parabolas or in ellipses very eccentric. To make this system therefore, with all its motions, required a cause which understood and compared together the quantities of matter in the several bodies of the sun and planets and the gravitating powers resulting from thence, the several distances of the primary planets from the sun and secondary ones from Saturn, Jupiter, and the Earth, and the velocities with which these planets could revolve at those distances about those quantities of matter in the central bodies. And to compare and adjust all these things together in so great a variety of bodies argues that cause to be not blind and fortuitous, but very well skilled in mechanics and geometry.

To your third query I answer that it may be represented that the sun may, by heating those planets most which are nearest to him, cause them to be better concocted[8] and more condensed by concoction. But when I consider that our Earth is much more heated in its bowels below the upper crust by subterraneous fermentations of mineral bodies than by the sun, I see not why the interior parts of Jupiter and Saturn might not be as much heated, concocted, and coagulated by those fermentations as our Earth is, and therefore this various density should have some other cause than the various

7. Newton oversimplifies: the planes of the planets actually incline to each other by as much as five degrees. Newton's arguments in this letter, suggests his biographer Richard Westfall, "reveal above all a determination to find God in nature," even to impose God upon nature. All the phenomena that Newton here attributes to the intervention of divine "counsel" and "skill" were explained scientifically over the course of the next century by physicists applying and extending Newton's own system, so that (as the most brilliant of the extenders, Pierre Simon Laplace, is said to have remarked to Napoleon) the hypothesis of divine intervention was no longer necessary.

8. Purified by heat (and hence made denser by the absence of the extraneous matter that the heat has annihilated).

distances of the planets from the sun; and I am confirmed in this opinion by considering that the planets of Jupiter and Saturn, as they are rarer[9] than the rest, so they are vastly greater and contain a far greater quantity of matter and have many satellites about them, which qualifications surely arose not from their being placed at so great a distance from the sun, but were rather the cause why the Creator placed them at that great distance. For by their gravitating powers they disturb one another's motions very sensibly, as I find by some late observations of Mr. Flamsteed,[1] and had they been placed much nearer to the sun and to one another they would by the same powers have caused a considerable disturbance in the whole system. * * *

Lastly, I see nothing extraordinary in the inclination of the Earth's axis for proving a Deity unless you will urge it as a contrivance for winter and summer and for making the Earth habitable towards the poles, and that the diurnal rotations of the sun and planets, as they could hardly arise from any cause purely mechanical, so by being determined all the same way with the annual and menstrual[2] motions they seem to make up that harmony in the system which (as I explained above) was the effect of choice rather than of chance.

There is yet another argument for a Deity which I take to be a very strong one, but till the principles on which 'tis grounded be better received I think it more advisable to let it sleep. I am

Your most humble servant to command

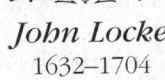

IS. NEWTON

John Locke

1632–1704

In the preface to his *Essay Concerning Human Understanding,* Locke depicts "the incomparable Mr. Newton" as one of the "master builders" of the new science, and himself as a mere "underlaborer," busy "clearing the ground a little, and removing some of the rubbish that lies in the way to knowledge." The eighteenth century, though, tended to venerate the two thinkers equally, Newton as master explicator of the cosmos, Locke as master inquirer into the mind. Starting from the claim that "simple ideas," acquired early, constituted the building blocks of thought, Locke constructed a system of the mind of comparable intricacy with Newton's universe, but of greater idiosyncrasy (since the content of consciousness differed from person to person, and indeed determined individual identity). Part of Locke's appeal lay in the comparative accessibility of his empiricism. His experiments, unlike Newton's, required neither telescope nor prism, calculus nor genius: readers could perform them (as Locke repeatedly suggested) in the laboratories of their minds, using their own perceptions and memories as raw material. More than any other text, Locke's *Essay* spurred that fascination with the first person which suffuses so much eighteenth-century writing: autobiographies, essays, diaries, travel

9. Less dense.
1. John Flamsteed (1646–1719), astronomer and director of the Royal Greenwich Observatory, had recently supplied Newton with these data; the two men later quarrelled bitterly over Flamsteed's reluctance to make available the immense, precise, and urgently needed records of his celestial observations.
2. Monthly.

journals, philosophic treatises, novels. Locke described the workings of the mind so persuasively that in effect he changed them too, prompting an analytic self-consciousness that had not obtained in the same kind and to the same degree before his book appeared.

from An Essay Concerning Human Understanding

[ON IDEAS[1]]

Every man being conscious to himself that he thinks, and that which his mind is employed about whilst thinking being the *ideas* that are there, 'tis past doubt, that men have in their minds several *ideas*, such as are those expressed by the words *whiteness*, *hardness*, *sweetness*, *thinking*, *motion*, *man*, *elephant*, *army*, *drunkenness*, and others. It is in the first place then to be inquired, how he comes by them? I know it is a received doctrine, that men have native *ideas* and original characters[2] stamped upon their minds, in their very first being. This opinion I have at large examined already, and I suppose what I have said in the foregoing book[3] will be much more easily admitted, when I have shown whence the understanding may get all the *ideas* it has, and by what ways and degrees they may come into the mind; for which I shall appeal to everyone's own observation and experience.

Let us then suppose the mind to be, as we say, white paper, void of all characters, without any *ideas*. How comes it to be furnished? Whence comes it by that vast store, which the busy and boundless fancy of man has painted on it, with an almost endless variety? Whence has it all the materials of reason and knowledge? To this I answer, in one word, from *experience*. In that, all our knowledge is founded, and from that it ultimately derives itself. Our observation employed either about *external, sensible objects, or about the internal operations of our minds, perceived and reflected on by ourselves, is that which supplies our understandings with all the materials of thinking*. These two are the fountains of knowledge, from whence all the *ideas* we have, or can naturally have, do spring.

First, *our senses*, conversant about particular sensible objects, do *convey into the mind*, several distinct *perceptions* of things, according to those various ways, wherein those objects do affect them; and thus we come by those *ideas* we have of *yellow*, *white*, *heat*, *cold*, *soft*, *hard*, *bitter*, *sweet*, and all those which we call sensible qualities, which when I say the senses convey into the mind, I mean, they from external objects convey into the mind what produces there those *perceptions*. This great source of most of the *ideas* we have, depending wholly upon our senses and derived by them to the understanding, I call SENSATION.

Secondly, the other fountain from which experience furnisheth the understanding with *ideas* is the *perception of the operations of our own minds* within us, as it is employed about the *ideas* it has got; which operations, when the soul comes to reflect on, and consider, do furnish the understanding with another set of *ideas*, which could not be had from things without; and such are *perception*, *thinking*, *doubting*, *believing*, *reasoning*, *knowing*, *willing*, and all the different actings of our own minds; which we being conscious of, and observing in ourselves, do from these receive into our understandings, as distinct *ideas*, as we do from bodies affecting our senses. This source of *ideas* every man has wholly in himself. And though it be not sense, as having nothing

1. All selections are from Book 2, "Of Ideas"; chapter and section numbers follow each section, in brackets. Most of Locke's italics have been retained.

2. Inscriptions.

3. In which Locke denied the existence of "innate principles," received by the soul "in its very first being" (1.2.1).

to do with external objects, yet it is very like it, and might properly enough be called internal sense. But as I call the other *sensation*, so I call this REFLECTION, the *ideas* it affords being such only, as the mind gets by reflecting on its own operations within itself. By REFLECTION then, in the following part of this discourse, I would be understood to mean, that notice which the mind takes of its own operations, and the manner of them, by reason whereof there come to be *ideas* of these operations in the understanding. These two, I say, *viz.* external, material things, as the objects of SENSATION, and the operations of our own minds within, as the objects of REFLECTION, are, to me, the only originals,[4] from whence all our *ideas* take their beginnings. The term *operations* here I use in a large sense, as comprehending not barely the actions of the mind about its *ideas*, but some sort of passions arising sometimes from them, such as is the satisfaction or uneasiness arising from any thought.

The understanding seems to me not to have the least glimmering of any *ideas*, which it doth not receive from one of these two. *External objects furnish the mind with the ideas of sensible qualities*, which are all those different perceptions they produce in us; and the *mind furnishes the understanding with* ideas *of its own operations*.

These, when we have taken a full survey of them, and their several modes, combinations, and relations, we shall find to contain all our whole stock of *ideas;* and that we have nothing in our minds which did not come in one of these two ways. Let anyone examine his own thoughts, and thoroughly search into his understanding, and then let him tell me, whether all the original *ideas* he has there are any other than of the objects of his *senses*, or of the operations of his mind, considered as objects of his *reflection;* and how great a mass of knowledge soever he imagines to be lodged there, he will, upon taking a strict view, see that he has *not any idea in his mind, but what one of these two have imprinted;* though, perhaps, with infinite variety compounded and enlarged by the understanding, as we shall see hereafter.

He that attentively considers the state of a *child*, at his first coming into the world, will have little reason to think him stored with plenty of *ideas*, that are to be the matter of his future knowledge. 'Tis by degrees he comes to be furnished with them. And though the *ideas* of obvious and familiar qualities imprint themselves before the memory begins to keep a register of time and order, yet 'tis often so late, before some unusual qualities come in the way, that there are few men that cannot recollect the beginning of their acquaintance with them; and if it were worthwhile, no doubt a child might be so ordered as to have but a very few, even of the ordinary *ideas*, till he were grown up to a man. But all that are born into the world being surrounded with bodies that perpetually and diversely affect them, variety of *ideas*, whether care be taken about it or no, are imprinted on the minds of children. *Light* and *colors* are busy at hand everywhere, when the eye is but open; *sounds* and some *tangible qualities* fail not to solicit their proper senses, and force an entrance to the mind; but yet, I think, it will be granted easily, that if a child were kept in a place where he never saw any other but black and white till he were a man, he would have no more *ideas* of scarlet or green, than he that from his childhood never tasted an oyster, or a pineapple, has of those particular relishes.

Men then come to be furnished with fewer or more simple *ideas* from without, according as the *objects* they converse with[5] afford greater or less variety; and from the operation of their minds within, according as they more or less *reflect* on them.

4. Origins.

5. Encounter.

For, though he that contemplates the operations of his mind cannot but have plain and clear *ideas* of them; yet unless he turn his thoughts that way, and considers them *attentively*, he will no more have clear and distinct *ideas* of all the *operations of his mind*, and all that may be observed therein, than he will have all the particular *ideas* of any landscape, or of the parts and motions of a clock, who will not turn his eyes to it, and with attention heed all the parts of it. The picture or clock may be so placed that they may come in his way every day; but yet he will have but a confused *idea* of all the parts they are made up of, till he *applies himself with attention*, to consider them each in particular. [1.1–7]

* * *

But to return to the matter in hand, the *ideas* we have of substances, and the ways we come by them; I say *our specific* ideas *of substances* are nothing else but *a collection of a certain number of simple ideas, considered as united in one thing*. These *ideas* of substances, though they are commonly called simple apprehensions, and the names of them simple terms, yet in effect, are complex and compounded. Thus the *idea* which an *Englishman* signifies by the name *swan* is white color, long neck, red beak, black legs, and whole feet, and all these of a certain size, with a power of swimming in the water, and making a certain kind of noise, and, perhaps, to a man who has long observed those kind of birds, some other properties, which all terminate in sensible simple *ideas*, all united in one common subject.

Besides the complex *ideas* we have of material sensible substances, of which I have last spoken, by the simple *ideas* we have taken from those operations of our own minds, which we experiment[6] daily in ourselves, as thinking, understanding, willing, knowing, and power of beginning motion, etc. co-existing in some substance, we are able to frame *the complex* idea *of an immaterial spirit*. And thus by putting together the *ideas* of thinking, perceiving, liberty, and power of moving themselves and other things, we have as clear a perception and notion of immaterial substances, as we have of material. For putting together the *ideas* of thinking and willing, or the power of moving or quieting corporeal motion, joined to substance, of which we have no distinct *idea*, we have the *idea* of an immaterial spirit; and by putting together the *ideas* of coherent solid parts, and a power of being moved, joined with substance, of which likewise we have no positive *idea*, we have the *idea* of matter. The one is as clear and distinct an *idea*, as the other: the *idea* of thinking, and moving a body, being as clear and distinct *ideas*, as the *ideas* of extension, solidity, and being moved. [23.14–15]

* * *

If we examine the *idea* we have of the incomprehensible Supreme Being, we shall find that we come by it the same way; and that the complex *ideas* we have both of God, and separate spirits, are made up of the simple *ideas* we receive from *reflection*; *v.g.* having, from what we experiment in ourselves, got the *ideas* of existence and duration; of knowledge and power; of pleasure and happiness; and of several other qualities and powers, which it is better to have than to be without; when we would frame an *idea* the most suitable we can to the Supreme Being, we enlarge every one of these with our *idea* of infinity; and so putting them together, make our complex *idea of God*. For that the mind has such a power of enlarging some of its *ideas*, received from sensation and reflection, has been already showed. [23.33]

6. Experience.

[On Identity]

Personal identity consists, not in the identity of substance, but, as I have said, in the identity of *consciousness*, wherein, if Socrates and the present Mayor of Queenborough agree, they are the same person. If the same Socrates waking and sleeping do not partake of the same *consciousness*, Socrates waking and sleeping is not the same person. And to punish Socrates waking, for what sleeping Socrates thought, and waking Socrates was never conscious of, would be no more of right, than to punish one twin for what his brother-twin did, whereof he knew nothing, because their outsides were so like that they could not be distinguished; for such twins have been seen.

But yet possibly it will still be objected, suppose I wholly lose the memory of some parts of my life, beyond a possibility of retrieving them, so that perhaps I shall never be conscious of them again; yet am I not the same person that did those actions, had those thoughts, that I was once conscious of, though I have now forgot them? To which I answer, that we must here take notice what the word *I* is applied to, which in this case is the man only. And the same man being presumed to be the same person, *I* is easily here supposed to stand also for the same person. But if it be possible for the same man to have distinct incommunicable consciousness at different times, it is past doubt the same man would at different times make different persons; which, we see, is the sense of mankind in the solemnest declaration of their opinions, human laws not punishing the *mad man* for the *sober man's* actions, nor the *sober man* for what the *mad man* did, thereby making them two persons; which is somewhat explained by our way of speaking in *English*, when we say such an one *is not himself*, or is *besides himself*; in which phrases it is insinuated, as if those who now, or, at least, first used them, thought, that *self* was changed, the *self* same person was no longer in that man.

But yet 'tis hard to conceive that Socrates the same individual man should be two persons. To help us a little in this, we must consider what is meant by *Socrates*, or the same individual *man*.

First, it must be either the same individual, immaterial, thinking substance: in short, the same numerical soul, and nothing else.

Secondly, or the same animal,[7] without any regard to an immaterial soul.

Thirdly, or the same immaterial spirit united to the same animal.

Now take which of these suppositions you please, it is impossible to make personal identity to consist in anything but consciousness, or reach any farther than that does.

For by the first of them, it must be allowed possible that a man born of different women, and in distant times, may be the same man. A way of speaking, which whoever admits, must allow it possible for the same man to be two distinct persons, as any two that have lived in different ages without the knowledge of one another's thoughts.

By the second and third, Socrates in this life, and after it, cannot be the same man any way, but by the same consciousness; and so making *human identity* to consist in the same thing wherein we place *personal identity*, there will be no difficulty to allow the same man to be the same person. But then they who place *human identity* in consciousness only, and not in something else, must consider how they will make the

7. Physical, living body.

infant Socrates the same man with Socrates after the resurrection. But whatsoever to some men makes a *man*, and consequently the same individual man, wherein perhaps few are agreed, personal identity can by us be placed in nothing but consciousness (which is that alone which makes what we call *self*) without involving us in great absurdities.

But is not a man drunk and sober the same person? Why else is he punished for the fact[8] he commits when drunk, though he be never afterwards conscious of it? Just as much the same person, as a man that walks, and does other things in his sleep, is the same person, and is answerable for any mischief he shall do in it. Human laws punish both with a justice suitable to their way of knowledge: because in these cases, they cannot distinguish certainly what is real, what counterfeit; and so the ignorance in drunkeness or sleep is not admitted as a plea. For though punishment be annexed to personality, and personality to consciousness, and the drunkard perhaps be not conscious of what he did, yet human judicatures justly punish him; because the fact is proved against him, but what of consciousness cannot be proved for him. But in the great day,[9] wherein the secrets of all hearts shall be laid open, it may be reasonable to think, no one shall be made to answer for what he knows nothing of; but shall receive his doom, his conscience accusing or excusing him. [27.19–22]

1671–1689 1690

Isaac Watts

1674–1748

"As his mind was capacious, his curiosity excursive, and his industry continual," wrote Samuel Johnson in praise of the dissenting minister Isaac Watts, "his writings are very numerous." Watts produced books of poetry, logic, theology, philosophy, and science, but the writings that have mattered most are the hymns and psalm translations (about seven hundred in all) that he began composing in his early twenties. In his philosophical writings, Watts worked hard to absorb the innovations of Newton's physics and Locke's psychology; in his hymns, an older structure of piety prevails. One of empiricism's chief effects was to entangle truth with time, to make knowledge a consequence of *process* (a series of experiments, a sequence of ideas). In Watts's hymns, truth is eternal; the mind's chief tasks are to register God's greatness and to praise it aright. The singing of hymns, and of psalms awkwardly translated from the Hebrew, had been a practice of long standing in Protestant congregations. Watts brought to these forms a new clarity and grace, in verses he carefully crafted, week after week, for the immediate use and pleasure of his congregants. He sought (he once explained) to achieve an "ease of numbers [i.e., meter] and smoothness of sound, and . . . to make the sense plain and obvious." In print, the simplicity of his style gradually won a wider attention, extending far beyond local circles of dissent. As the religious historian and poet Donald Davie has pointed out, Watts's hymns and psalms probably touched more minds (and certainly resounded in more throats) over the course of the eighteenth century than any of the texts we now deem greater hits: *Gulliver's Travels*, Johnson's *Dictionary*, Thomson's *Seasons*. In his lifetime and for more than a century after, Watts was reckoned the English, Christian successor to that ancient king of Israel traditionally

8. Deed.

9. I.e., Judgment Day.

credited with creating the Psalms. "Were David to speak English," Watts's brother once remarked to him, "he would choose to make use of your style."

A Prospect of Heaven Makes Death Easy[1]

There is a land of pure delight
Where saints immortal reign;
Infinite day excludes the night,
And pleasures banish pain.

There everlasting spring abides,
And never-withering flowers:
Death like a narrow sea divides
This heav'nly land from ours.

Sweet fields beyond the swelling flood
Stand dressed in living green:
So to the Jews old Canaan stood,
While Jordan rolled between.[2]

But timorous mortals start° and shrink *tremble*
To cross this narrow sea,
And linger shivering on the brink,
And fear to launch away.

O! could we make our doubts remove,° *withdraw*
Those gloomy doubts that rise,
And see the Canaan that we love,
With unbeclouded eyes:

Could we but climb where Moses stood,[3]
And view the landskip° o'er, *landscape*
Not Jordan's stream, nor death's cold flood
Should fright us from the shore.

1707

The Hurry of the Spirits, in a Fever and Nervous Disorders[1]

My frame of nature is a ruffled sea,
And my disease the tempest. Nature feels
A strange commotion to her inmost center;
The throne of reason shakes. "Be still, my thoughts;
Peace and be still." In vain my reason gives

1. From *Hymns and Spiritual Songs* (1707).
2. In Joshua 3, the children of Israel, at the end of their 40-year journey in the desert, see the promised land of Canaan across the River Jordan.
3. Having led the Israelites to the end of their desert journey, Moses on his last day of life climbed the mountain of Nebo, and surveyed the entire promised land (Deuteronomy 34.1–4).

1. Not a hymn but an autobiographical poem, the first in a sequence entitled *Thoughts and Meditations in a Long Sickness, 1712 and 1713,* published decades later in Watts's *Reliquiae Juveniles* (writings in youth).

The peaceful word, my spirit strives in vain
To calm the tumult and command my thoughts.
This flesh, this circling blood, these brutal powers
Made to obey, turn rebels to the mind,
Nor hear its laws. The engine° rules the man. *body*
Unhappy change! When nature's meaner springs,
Fired to impetuous ferments, break all order;
When little restless atoms rise and reign
Tyrants in sovereign uproar, and impose
Ideas on the mind; confused ideas
Of non-existents and impossibles,
Who can describe them? Fragments of old dreams,
Borrowed from midnight, torn from fairy fields
And fairy skies, and regions of the dead,
Abrupt, ill-sorted. O 'tis all confusion!
If I but close my eyes, strange images
In thousand forms and thousand colors rise,
Stars, rainbows, moons, green dragons, bears and ghosts,
An endless medley rush upon the stage
And dance and riot wild in reason's court
Above control. I'm in a raging storm,
Where seas and skies are blended, while my soul
Like some light worthless chip of floating cork
Is tossed from wave to wave: now overwhelmed
With breaking floods, I drown, and seem to lose
All being; now high-mounted on the ridge
Of tall foaming surge, I'm all at once
Caught up into the storm, and ride the wind,
The whistling wind; unmanageable steed,
And feeble rider! Hurried many a league
Over the rising hills of roaring brine,
Through airy wilds unknown, with dreadful speed
And infinite surprise, till some few minutes
Have spent the blast, and then perhaps I drop
Near to the peaceful coast. Some friendly billow
Lodges me on the beach, and I find rest.
Short rest I find; for the next rolling wave
Snatches me back again; then ebbing far
Sets me adrift, and I am borne off to sea,
Helpless, amidst the bluster of the winds,
Beyond the ken of shore.

Ah, when will these tumultuous scenes be gone?
When shall this weary spirit, tossed with tempests,
Harassed and broken, reach the ports of rest,
And hold it firm? When shall this wayward flesh
With all th' irregular springs of vital movement
Ungovernable, return to sacred order,
And pay their duties to the ruling mind?

1712 1734

Against Idleness and Mischief[1]

How doth the little busy bee
  Improve each shining hour,
And gather honey all the day
  From every opening flower!

How skillfully she builds her cell!
  How neat she spreads the wax!
And labors hard to store it well
  With the sweet food she makes.

In works of labor, or of skill,
  I would be busy too;
For Satan finds some mischief still° *always*
  For idle hands to do.

In books, or work, or healthful play,
  Let my first years be passed.
That I may give for every day
  Some good account at last.

1715

Man Frail, and God Eternal[1]

Our God, our help in ages past,
  Our hope for years to come,
Our shelter from the stormy blast,
  And our eternal home.

Under the shadow of thy throne
  Thy saints have dwelt secure.
Sufficient is thine arm alone,
  And our defense is sure.

Before the hills in order stood,
  Or earth received her frame,
From everlasting thou art God,
  To endless years the same.

Thy word commands our flesh to dust,
  Return, ye sons of men.
All nations rose from earth at first,
  And turn to earth again.

1. From *Divine Songs Attempted in Easy Language, for the Use of Children*. The poems in this durable little collection were memorized by numberless children in the 18th and 19th centuries, including Lewis Caroll's Alice. Wandering through Wonderland, she is commanded by its inhabitants (as she doubtless was in school) to recite these verses, and discovers to her dismay that the lines come out all wrong.

1. An imitation of Psalm 90, lines 1–6. This and the next poem are from *The Psalms of David Imitated in the Language of the New Testament, and Applied to the Christian State and Worship*. As the title indicates, Watts intended not merely to translate the Psalms, but to recast them. In his preface, he declares himself "the first who hath brought down the royal author [King David] into the common affairs of the Christian life, and let the psalmist of Israel into the Church of Christ, without anything of a Jew about him."

A thousand ages in thy sight
Are like an evening gone;
Short as the watch that ends the night,
Before the rising sun.

The busy tribes of flesh and blood
With all their lives and cares
Are carried downwards by thy flood,
And lost in following years.

Time, like an ever-rolling stream
Bears all its sons away.
They fly forgotten, as a dream
Dies at the opening day.

Like flowery fields the nations stand
Pleased with the morning light.
The flowers beneath the mower's hand
Lie withering ere 'tis night.

Our God, our help in ages past,
Our hope for years to come,
Be thou our guard while troubles last,
And our eternal home.

1719

Miracles Attending Israel's Journey[1]

When Israel, freed from Pharaoh's hand,
Left the proud tyrant and his land,
The tribes with cheerful homage own[2]
Their king, and Judah[3] was his throne.

Across the deep[4] their journey lay;
The deep divides to make them way.
Jordan beheld their march, and fled
With backward current to his head.[5]

The mountains shook like frighted sheep.
Like lambs the little hillocks leap.[6]

1. An imitation of Psalm 114. In 1712, Watts sent a version of this poem to the *Spectator*, where it appeared (No. 461, Tuesday, 19 August 1712) along with a letter from the poet explaining a discovery he had made while translating: "As I was describing the journey of Israel from Egypt, and added the Divine Presence amongst them, I perceived a beauty in the Psalm which was entirely new to me, and which I was going to lose; and that is, that the poet utterly conceals the presence of God in the beginning of it. . . . The reason now seems evident, and this conduct necessary. For if God had appeared before [i.e., at the start of the poem], there could be no wonder why the mountains should leap and the sea retire; therefore that this convulsion of nature may be brought in with due surprise, his name is not mentioned till afterward, and then with a very agreeable turn of thought God is introduced at once in all his majesty."

2. Acknowledged (God as their king).

3. A portion of the land promised by God to the Israelites; here the name is used to designate the entire promised land.

4. The Red Sea, whose miraculous parting made possible the Israelites' escape from Egypt (Exodus 14.21–31).

5. Alludes to a second, similar miracle later in the journey: God makes the waters of the river Jordan "stand upon an heap," so that the Israelites can pass "clean over" dry ground, into the promised land (Joshua 3.14–17).

6. Lines 9–10 may refer (in the original Psalm) to the hills and mountains of the promised land, the dwelling places of local gods who tremble at Israel's advent.

Not Sinai[7] on her base could stand,
Conscious of sovereign power at hand.

What power could make the deep divide?
Make Jordan backward roll his tide?
Why did ye leap, ye little hills?
And whence the fright that Sinai feels?

Let every mountain, every flood,
Retire, and know th'approaching God,
The king of Israel. See him here.
Tremble thou earth, adore, and fear.

He thunders, and all nature mourns.
The rock to standing pool he turns.
Flints spring with fountains at his word,[8]
And fires and seas confess the Lord.

1719

Joseph Addison
1672–1719

The ideas of Newton and Locke became widely known not through their own writings (which were voluminous and often dense), but through various popularizations: lectures, demonstrations, explanatory handbooks, the popular press. One of the chief disseminators was the *Spectator,* the phenomenally successful series of daily essays composed by Joseph Addison and Richard Steele (for more on the *Spectator,* see page 2326). Addison in particular undertook to inculcate the ideas of Newton and Locke, sometimes directly by quotation and commentary, but more often indirectly, by absorption and a kind of tacit transmission. "The working of my own mind," Mr. Spectator announces early on, "is the general entertainment of my life," and he recommends this notably Lockean "entertainment" to his readers too; his own name honors Locke's reckoning of sight as the mind's chief instrument for the gathering of ideas. In the following extract, Addison pays comparably implicit homage to Newton, in an ode that quickly became one of the touchstones of eighteenth-century devotion. Though Addison places his poem in a tradition that combines Aristotle with the Psalms, Newton is powerfully present too, in the depiction of a heaven whose silent motions proclaim to human reason the perfection of God's design.

from Spectator No. 465
Saturday, 23 August 1712[1]

* * * The last method which I shall mention for the giving life to a man's faith is frequent retirement from the world, accompanied with religious meditation. When a

7. The sacred mountain on which Moses received from the Lord the Ten Commandments. At the Lord's approach, "the whole mount quaked greatly" (Exodus 19.18).

8. In the Book of Numbers (20.8–11), God miraculously produces water from rock in order to sustain the Israelites during their journey.

1. Addison often set Saturdays aside for particularly serious topics, as a way of preparing his readers for the religious solemnities of Sunday (the only day on which the *Spectator* did not appear). He devotes the present paper to "the proper means of strengthening and confirming" Christian faith.

man thinks of any thing in the darkness of the night, whatever deep impressions it may make in his mind, they are apt to vanish as soon as the day breaks about him. The light and noise of the day, which are perpetually soliciting his senses and calling off his attention, wear out of his mind the thoughts that imprinted themselves in it with so much strength during the silence and darkness of the night. A man finds the same difference as to himself in a crowd and in a solitude; the mind is stunned and dazzled amidst that variety of objects which press upon her in a great city: she cannot apply herself to the consideration of those things which are of the utmost concern to her. The cares or pleasures of the world strike in with every thought, and a multitude of vicious examples give a kind of justification to our folly. In our retirements everything disposes us to be serious. In courts and cities we are entertained with the works of men, in the country with those of God. One is the province of art, the other of nature. Faith and devotion naturally grow in the mind of every reasonable man, who sees the impressions of divine power and wisdom in every object on which he casts his eye. The Supreme Being has made the best arguments for his own existence, in the formation of the heavens and the earth, and these are arguments which a man of sense cannot forbear attending to, who is out of the noise and hurry of human affairs. Aristotle says,[2] that should a man live under ground, and there converse with works of art and mechanism, and should afterwards be brought up into the open day, and see the several glories of the heaven and earth, he would immediately pronounce them the works of such a being as we define God to be. The Psalmist has very beautiful strokes of poetry to this purpose, in that exalted strain, "The heavens declare the glory of God: and the firmament showeth his handiwork. One day telleth another: and one night certifieth another. There is neither speech nor language: but their voices are heard among them. Their sound is gone out into all lands: and their words into the ends of the world."[3] As such a bold and sublime manner of thinking furnishes very noble matter for an ode, the reader may see it wrought into the following one.[4]

1

The spacious firmament on high,
With all the blue ethereal sky,
And spangled heav'ns, a shining frame,
Their great original proclaim:
Th' unwearied sun, from day to day,
Does his Creator's power display,
And publishes to every land
The works of an almighty hand.

2

Soon as the evening shades prevail,
The moon takes up the wondrous tale,
And nightly to the list'ning earth
Repeats the story of her birth:
Whilst all the stars that round her burn,

2. Addison paraphrases lines quoted by Cicero from *De Philosophia*, a work of Aristotle's long lost.
3. Psalm 19.1–4.
4. Addison may have published this ode partly as a response to Watts's imitation of Psalm 114, which had appeared in the *Spectator* just four days earlier (see page 2626).

And all the planets, in their turn,
Confirm the tidings as they roll,
And spread the truth from pole to pole.

3

What though, in solemn silence, all
Move round the dark terrestrial ball?
What though nor real voice nor sound
Amid their radiant orbs be found?
In reason's ear they all rejoice,
And utter forth a glorious voice,
For ever singing, as they shine,
"The hand that made us is divine."

George Berkeley
1685–1753

For Locke, "ideas" are formed in the mind out of its ongoing encounter with the very real world outside it, where swans swim and elephants plod. For George Berkeley—clergyman, poet, traveler, and philosopher—ideas are all there is. *Esse est percipi,* he argues throughout his philosophical writings: to be is to be perceived. "All those bodies which compose the mighty frame of the world, have not any subsistence without a mind"—a mind engaged in the act of perceiving them. What, then, accounts for the apparent independence and continuity of real objects (trees, to take one of Berkeley's recurrent examples), which seem to remain in place even when no mortal observes them? Berkeley's answer: one mind *is* perpetually engaged in perceiving them. The mind of God creates the ideas, sustains them, renders them consistent with themselves and independent of our intermittent human perceptions. In Berkeley's argument, this divine activity both constitutes proof of God's existence (since such an "infinite mind" is necessary to explain why the world appears to us as it does), and lies at the core of God's benevolence. Berkeley expounded his theory of "immaterialism" in his *Essay Towards a New Theory of Vision* (1709) and *Treatise Concerning the Principles of Human Knowledge* (1710), before recasting it in the more compact, accessible, and popular format of *Three Dialogues Between Hylas and Philonous*. Philonous ("Lover of mind") voices Berkeley's views, while Hylas ("Wooden") expresses the bemused incredulity with which Berkeley's readers continued to greet the philosopher's radical unmaking and reweaving of the fabric of everyday life. Scoffers tended to overlook the solution Berkeley was proffering to an abiding theological problem. Newton's cosmology had given rise (despite his own piety) to the unsettling image of the Clockmaker God, who having made the universe a perfectly efficient mechanism, could now let it run without further intervention. Newton addressed this problem in part by insisting that God had to intervene at intervals in order to adjust his system. Berkeley's God, by contrast, is no clockmaker at all; having authored the world in the beginning, he continues to make it anew at every moment by the creative act of his continual perception.

from Three Dialogues Between Hylas and Philonous

HYLAS: But do you in earnest think, the real existence of sensible things consists in their being actually perceived? If so, how comes it that all mankind distinguish between them? Ask the first man you meet, and he shall tell you, *to be perceived* is one thing, and *to exist* is another.

PHILONOUS: I am content, Hylas, to appeal to the common sense of the world for the truth of my notion. Ask the gardener why he thinks yonder cherry tree exists in the garden, and he shall tell you, because he sees and feels it; in a word, because he perceives it by his senses. Ask him why he thinks an orange tree not to be there, and he shall tell you, because he does not perceive it. What he perceives by sense, that he terms a real being, and saith it *is*, or *exists*; but that which is not perceivable, the same, he saith, hath no being.

HYLAS: Yes, Philonous, I grant the existence of a sensible thing consists in being perceivable, but not in being actually perceived.

PHILONOUS: And what is perceivable but an idea? And can an idea exist without being actually perceived? These are points long since agreed between us.

HYLAS: But be your opinion never so true, yet surely you will not deny it is shocking, and contrary to the common sense of men. Ask the fellow whether yonder tree hath an existence out of his mind: what answer think you he would make?

PHILONOUS: The same that I should myself, to wit, that it doth exist out of his mind. But then to a Christian it cannot surely be shocking to say, the real tree existing without his mind is truly known and comprehended by (that is, *exists in*) the infinite mind of God. Probably he may not at first glance be aware of the direct and immediate proof there is of this, inasmuch as the very being of a tree, or any other sensible thing, implies a mind wherein it is. But the point itself he cannot deny. The question between the materialists[1] and me is not whether things have a real existence out of the mind of this or that person, but whether they have an absolute existence, distinct from being perceived by God, and exterior to all minds. This indeed some heathens and philosophers have affirmed, but whoever entertains notions of the Deity suitable to the Holy Scriptures will be of another opinion.

HYLAS: But according to your notions, what difference is there between real things, and chimeras formed by the imagination, or the visions of a dream, since they are all equally in the mind?

PHILONOUS: The ideas formed by the imagination are faint and indistinct; they have besides an entire dependence on the will. But the ideas perceived by sense, that is, real things, are more vivid and clear, and being imprinted on the mind by a spirit distinct from us, have not a like dependence on our will. There is therefore no danger of confounding these with the foregoing: and there is as little of confounding them with the visions of a dream, which are dim, irregular, and confused. And though they should happen to be never so lively and natural, yet by their not being connected, and of a piece with the preceding and subsequent transactions of our lives, they might easily be distinguished from realities. In short, by whatever method you distinguish *things* from *chimeras* on your own scheme, the same, it is evident, will hold also upon mine. For it must be, I presume, by some perceived difference, and I am not for depriving you of any one thing that you perceive.

HYLAS: But still, Philonous, you hold, there is nothing in the world but spirits and ideas. And this, you must needs acknowledge, sounds very oddly.

PHILONOUS: I own the word *idea*, not being commonly used for *thing*, sounds something out of the way. My reason for using it was, because a necessary relation

1. Those who assert the existence of matter, independent of perception.

to the mind is understood to be implied by that term; and it is now commonly used by philosophers to denote the immediate objects of the understanding. But however oddly the proposition may sound in words, yet it includes nothing so very strange or shocking in its sense, which in effect amounts to no more than this, to wit, that there are only things perceiving, and things perceived; or that every unthinking being is necessarily, and from the very nature of its existence, perceived by some mind; if not by any finite created mind, yet certainly by the infinite mind of God, in whom "we live, and move, and have our being."[2] Is this as strange as to say, the sensible qualities are not on the objects, or that we cannot be sure of the existence of things, or know anything of their real natures, though we both see and feel them, and perceive them by all our senses?

HYLAS: And in consequence of this, must we not think there are no such things as physical or corporeal causes but that a spirit is the immediate cause of all the phenomena in nature? Can there be anything more extravagant than this?

PHILONOUS: Yes, it is infinitely more extravagant to say, a thing which is inert, operates on the mind, and which is unperceiving, is the cause of our perceptions. Besides, that which to you, I know not for what reason, seems so extravagant, is no more than the Holy Scriptures assert in a hundred places. In them God is represented as the sole and immediate author of all those effects which some heathens and philosophers are wont to ascribe to nature, matter, fate, or the like unthinking principle. This is so much the constant language of Scripture, that it were needless to confirm it by citations. * * *

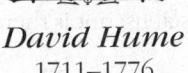

1713

David Hume

1711–1776

As he lay dying at home in his native city of Edinburgh, David Hume entertained a visitor by conjuring up, with characteristic cheerfulness, a scenario in the afterlife. He imagined himself begging the fatal ferryman Charon for a little more time: "Have a little patience, good Charon, I have been endeavoring to open the eyes of the public. If I live a few years longer, I may have the satisfaction of seeing the downfall of some of the prevailing systems of superstition." The "prevailing system" which Hume had become most notorious for attacking was the Christian religion, whose favorite tenets—providence, miracles, the argument from design, the afterlife itself—he had called into question, with increasing audacity, over the course of his work. But he had also done much damage to newer systems of thought, notably Locke's. Locke had regarded personal identity as coherent and continuous, the consequence of lifelong experiences and ideas accumulated in the memory. Hume, in his early, massive *Treatise of Human Nature* (1739–1740), waived all this away as an arrant fiction—though perhaps a necessary one, since empiricism properly pursued reveals so radical an incoherence in mortal minds that empiricists themselves must intermittently abandon philosophy in order to go about their daily lives. Like many of his empiric predecessors, Hume argued that knowledge of the real world "must be founded entirely on experience"; more than any predecessor he was willing to entertain (and to entertain with) the doubts and demolitions arising from that premise. In his own lifetime, his skepticism did not prove as contagious as he had

2. Acts 17.28.

hoped. The *Treatise*, he recalled wryly, "fell *deadborn from the press*, without reaching such distinction as even to excite a murmur among the zealots." Though his attempt to recast his chief arguments more succinctly in *An Enquiry Concerning Human Understanding* (1748) prompted a somewhat livelier response, he eventually made his fortune not as a philosopher but as author of the highly successful *History of England* (1754–1763). He faced the general indifference or hostility to his arguments as blithely as he later greeted death, continually refining his views and revising his prose. He knew himself out of sync with his times. When, in his fantasy, he forecasts to Charon the imminent downfall of superstition, the ferryman responds, "You loitering rogue, that will not happen these many hundred years. Do you fancy I will grant you a lease for so long a term? Get into the boat this instant, you lazy loitering rogue."More than two hundred years later, the artful mischief of Hume's work has secured him some such lease. His writings, lucid and elusive, forthright and sly, demand (and receive) continual reassessment; his skepticism has proven more powerful than his contemporaries suspected, and he figures as perhaps the wittiest and most self-possessed philosophical troublemaker since Socrates.

from A Treatise of Human Nature

[THE MIND AS THEATER[1]]

There are some philosophers,[2] who imagine we are every moment intimately conscious of what we call our *self*; that we feel its existence and its continuance in existence; and are certain, beyond the evidence of a demonstration, both of its perfect identity and simplicity. The strongest sensation, the most violent passion, say they, instead of distracting us from this view, only fix it the more intensely, and make us consider their influence on *self* either by their pain or pleasure. To attempt a farther proof of this were to weaken its evidence; since no proof can be derived from any fact, of which we are so intimately conscious; nor is there anything of which we can be certain, if we doubt of this.

Unluckily all these positive assertions are contrary to that very experience which is pleaded for them, nor have we any idea of *self*, after the manner it is here explained. For from what impression could this idea be derived? This question 'tis impossible to answer without a manifest contradiction and absurdity; and yet 'tis a question, which must necessarily be answered, if we would have the idea of self pass for clear and intelligible. It must be some one impression, that gives rise to every real idea. But self or person is not any one impression, but that to which our several impressions and ideas are supposed to have a reference. If any impression gives rise to the idea of self, that impression must continue invariably the same through the whole course of our lives, since self is supposed to exist after that manner. But there is no impression constant and invariable. Pain and pleasure, grief and joy, passions and sensations succeed each other, and never all exist at the same time. It cannot, therefore, be from any of these impressions, or from any other, that the idea of self is derived; and consequently there is no such idea.

But farther, what must become of all our particular perceptions upon this hypothesis? All these are different, and distinguishable, and separable from each other, and may be separately considered, and may exist separately, and have no need of anything to support their existence. After what manner, therefore, do they belong to self; and

1. From Book 1, section 6, "Of Personal Identity."
2. Notably Joseph Butler, an Anglican bishop who argued in *The Analogy of Religion* (1736) that the existence of the self is a truth of which every person is continually (and correctly) certain.

how are they connected with it? For my part, when I enter most intimately into what I call *myself*, I always stumble on some particular perception or other, of heat or cold, light or shade, love or hatred, pain or pleasure. I never can catch *myself* at any time without a perception, and never can observe anything but the perception. When my perceptions are removed for any time, as by sound sleep, so long am I insensible of *myself*, and may truly be said not to exist. And were all my perceptions removed by death, and could I neither think, nor feel, nor see, nor love, nor hate after the dissolution of my body, I should be entirely annihilated, nor do I conceive what is farther requisite to make me a perfect nonentity. If anyone upon serious and unprejudiced reflection, thinks he has a different notion of *himself*, I must confess I can reason no longer with him. All I can allow him is, that he may be in the right as well as I, and that we are essentially different in this particular. He may, perhaps, perceive something simple and continued, which he calls *himself*; though I am certain there is no such principle in me.

But setting aside some metaphysicians of this kind, I may venture to affirm of the rest of mankind, that they are nothing but a bundle or collection of different perceptions, which succeed each other with an inconceivable rapidity, and are in a perpetual flux and movement. Our eyes cannot turn in their sockets without varying our perceptions. Our thought is still more variable than our sight; and all our other senses and faculties contribute to this change; nor is there any single power of the soul which remains unalterably the same, perhaps for one moment. The mind is a kind of theater, where several perceptions successively make their appearance: pass, re-pass, glide away, and mingle in an infinite variety of postures and situations. There is properly no *simplicity* in it at one time, nor *identity* in different; whatever natural propension we may have to imagine that simplicity and identity. The comparison of the theater must not mislead us. They are the successive perceptions only, that constitute the mind; nor have we the most distant notion of the place where these scenes are represented, or of the materials, of which it is composed. * * *

[Philosophy and Common Life[3]]

But what have I here said, that reflections very refined and metaphysical have little or no influence upon us? This opinion I can scarce forbear retracting, and condemning from my present feeling and experience. The *intense* view of these manifold contradictions and imperfections in human reason has so wrought upon me, and heated my brain, that I am ready to reject all belief and reasoning, and can look upon no opinion even as more probable or likely than another. Where am I, or what? From what causes do I derive my existence, and to what condition shall I return? Whose favor shall I court, and whose anger must I dread? What beings surround me? and on whom have I any influence, or who have any influence on me? I am confounded with all these questions, and begin to fancy myself in the most deplorable condition imaginable, environed with the deepest darkness, and utterly deprived of the use of every member and faculty.

Most fortunately it happens, that since reason is incapable of dispelling these clouds, nature herself suffices to that purpose, and cures me of this philosophical

3. From Book 1, Section 7: "Conclusion of This Book." The first book of the *Treatise* serves as a long prelude to the whole; in concluding it, Hume considers the "manifest contradictions" between the assumptions on which ordinary people lead their lives, and the volatile questions raised by "refined reasoning" (rigorous philosophic inquiry). Pinpointing these contradictions in himself, he contemplates the precariousness of his enterprise, and the intricacy of his motives for undertaking it.

melancholy and delirium, either by relaxing this bent of mind, or by some avocation and lively impression of my senses, which obliterate all these chimeras. I dine, I play a game of backgammon, I converse, and am merry with my friends; and when after three or four hour's amusement, I would return to these speculations, they appear so cold, and strained, and ridiculous, that I cannot find in my heart to enter into them any farther.

Here then I find myself absolutely and necessarily determined to live, and talk, and act like other people in the common affairs of life. But notwithstanding that my natural propensity, and the course of my animal spirits and passions, reduce me to this indolent belief in the general maxims of the world, I still feel such remains of my former disposition, that I am ready to throw all my books and papers into the fire, and resolve never more to renounce the pleasures of life for the sake of reasoning and philosophy. For these are my sentiments in that splenetic[4] humor, which governs me at present. I may, nay I must yield to the current of nature, in submitting to my senses and understanding; and in this blind submission I show most perfectly my skeptical disposition and principles. But does it follow, that I must strive against the current of nature, which leads me to indolence and pleasure; that I must seclude myself, in some measure, from the commerce and society of men, which is so agreeable; and that I must torture my brain with subtleties and sophistries, at the very time that I cannot satisfy myself concerning the reasonableness of so painful an application, nor have any tolerable prospect of arriving by its means at truth and certainty? Under what obligation do I lie of making such an abuse of time? And to what end can it serve either for the service of mankind, or for my own private interest? No: if I must be a fool, as well as those who reason or believe anything *certainly* are, my follies shall at least be natural and agreeable. Where I strive against my inclination, I shall have a good reason for my resistance; and will no more be led a wandering into such dreary solitudes, and rough passages, as I have hitherto met with.

There are the sentiments of my spleen[5] and indolence; and indeed I must confess, that philosophy has nothing to oppose to them, and expects a victory more from the returns of a serious good-humored disposition, than from the force of reason and conviction. In all the incidents of life we ought still to preserve our skepticism. If we believe, that fire warms, or water refreshes, 'tis only because it costs us too much pains to think otherwise. Nay if we are philosophers, it ought only to be upon skeptical principles, and from an inclination, which we feel to the employing ourselves after that manner. Where reason is lively, and mixes itself with some propensity, it ought to be assented to. Where it does not, it never can have any title to operate upon us.

At the time, therefore, that I am tired with amusement and company, and have indulged a *reverie* in my chamber, or in a solitary walk by a riverside, I feel my mind all collected within itself, and am naturally *inclined* to carry my view into all those subjects, about which I have met with so many disputes in the course of my reading and conversation.[6] I cannot forbear having a curiosity to be acquainted with the principles of moral good and evil, the nature and foundation of government, and the cause of those several passions and inclinations, which actuate and govern me. I am uneasy to think I approve of one object, and disapprove of another; call one thing beautiful, and another deformed; decide concerning truth and falsehood, reason and folly, without

4. Depressive, irritable.
5. Despondency.
6. In the list that follows, Hume names many of the topics he will take up later in the *Treatise*.

knowing upon what principles I proceed. I am concerned for the condition of the learned world, which lies under such a deplorable ignorance in all these particulars. I feel an ambition to arise in me of contributing to the instruction of mankind, and of acquiring a name by my inventions and discoveries. These sentiments spring up naturally in my present disposition; and should I endeavor to banish them, by attaching myself to any other business or diversion, I *feel* I should be a loser in point of pleasure; and this is the origin of my philosophy.

1734–1737 1739–1740

from An Enquiry Concerning Human Understanding[1]
from *Section 10: Of Miracles*

A miracle is a violation of the laws of nature; and as a firm and unalterable experience has established these laws, the proof against a miracle, from the very nature of the fact, is as entire as any argument from experience can possibly be imagined. Why is it more than probable that all men must die; that lead cannot, of itself, remain suspended in the air; that fire consumes wood, and is extinguished by water; unless it be, that these events are found agreeable to the laws of nature, and there is required a violation of these laws, or in other words, a miracle to prevent them? Nothing is esteemed a miracle, if it ever happen in the common course of nature. It is no miracle that a man, seemingly in good health, should die on a sudden; because such a kind of death, though more unusual than any other, has yet been frequently observed to happen. But it is a miracle that a dead man should come to life; because that has never been observed in any age or country. There must, therefore, be a uniform experience against every miraculous event, otherwise the event would not merit that appellation. And as a uniform experience amounts to a proof, there is here a direct and full *proof*, from the nature of the fact, against the existence of any miracle; nor can such a proof be destroyed, or the miracle rendered credible, but by an opposite proof, which is superior.

The plain consequence is (and it is a general maxim worthy of our attention), "That no testimony is sufficient to establish a miracle, unless the testimony be of such a kind, that its falsehood would be more miraculous than the fact which it endeavors to establish; and even in that case there is a mutual destruction of arguments, and the superior only gives us an assurance suitable to that degree of force which remains after deducting the inferior." When anyone tells me, that he saw a dead man restored to life, I immediately consider with myself, whether it be more probable, that this person should either deceive or be deceived, or that the fact, which he relates, should really have happened. I weigh the one miracle against the other; and according to the superiority which I discover, I pronounce my decision, and always reject the greater miracle. If the falsehood of his testimony would be more miraculous than the event which he relates, then, and not till then, can he pretend to command my belief or opinion.

In the foregoing reasoning we have supposed, that the testimony, upon which a miracle is founded, may possibly amount to an entire proof, and that the falsehood of

1. Hume wrote this essay in the mid–1730s, intending to include it in his *Treatise;* conscious of its volatility, he withheld it for a dozen years, publishing it for the first time in his *Philosophical Essays Concerning Human Understanding* (1748); ten years later a revised version of the work appeared, under the new title *An Enquiry*. . . .The essay proved at least as explosive as he had anticipated, prompting a spate of refutations; for Samuel Johnson's and James Boswell's views, see page 2763.

that testimony would be a real prodigy. But it is easy to show that we have been a great deal too liberal in our concession, and that there never was a miraculous event established on so full an evidence.

For *first*, there is not to be found, in all history, any miracle attested by a sufficient number of men, of such unquestioned good sense, education, and learning, as to secure us against all delusion in themselves; of such undoubted integrity, as to place them beyond all suspicion of any design to deceive others; of such credit and reputation in the eyes of mankind, as to have a great deal to lose in case of their being detected in any falsehood; and at the same time, attesting facts performed in such a public manner and in so celebrated a part of the world, as to render the detection unavoidable. All which circumstances are requisite to give us a full assurance in the testimony of men.

Secondly. We may observe in human nature a principle which, if strictly examined, will be found to diminish extremely the assurance which we might, from human testimony, have, in any kind of prodigy. The maxim by which we commonly conduct ourselves in our reasonings is that the objects of which we have no experience resemble those of which we have; that what we have found to be most usual is always most probable; and that where there is an opposition of arguments, we ought to give the preference to such as are founded on the greatest number of past observations. But though, in proceeding by this rule, we readily reject any fact which is unusual and incredible in an ordinary degree; yet in advancing farther, the mind observes not always the same rule; but when anything is affirmed utterly absurd and miraculous, it rather the more readily admits of such a fact, upon account of that very circumstance which ought to destroy all its authority. The passion of *surprise* and *wonder*, arising from miracles, being an agreeable emotion, gives a sensible tendency towards the belief of those events from which it is derived. And this goes so far, that even those who cannot enjoy this pleasure immediately, nor can believe those miraculous events, of which they are informed, yet love to partake of the satisfaction at second-hand or by rebound, and place a pride and delight in exciting the admiration of others.

With what greediness are the miraculous accounts of travelers received, their descriptions of sea and land monsters, their relations of wonderful adventures, strange men, and uncouth manners? But if the spirit of religion join itself to the love of wonder, there is an end of common sense; and human testimony, in these circumstances, loses all pretensions to authority. A religionist may be an enthusiast,[2] and imagine he sees what has no reality. He may know his narrative to be false, and yet persevere in it, with the best intentions in the world, for the sake of promoting so holy a cause; or even where this delusion has not place, vanity, excited by so strong a temptation, operates on him more powerfully than on the rest of mankind in any other circumstances; and self-interest with equal force. His auditors may not have, and commonly have not, sufficient judgment to canvass his evidence. What judgment they have, they renounce by principle, in these sublime and mysterious subjects; or if they were ever so willing to employ it, passion and a heated imagination disturb the regularity of its operations. Their credulity increases his impudence; and his impudence overpowers their credulity. * * *

Thirdly. It forms a strong presumption against all supernatural and miraculous relations, that they are observed chiefly to abound among ignorant and barbarous

2. Fanatic.

nations; or if a civilized people has ever given admission to any of them, that people will be found to have received them from ignorant and barbarous ancestors, who transmitted them with that inviolable sanction and authority, which always attend received opinions. When we peruse the first histories of all nations, we are apt to imagine ourselves transported into some new world, where the whole frame of nature is disjointed, and every element performs its operations in a different manner from what it does at present. Battles, revolutions, pestilence, famine, and death are never the effect of those natural causes which we experience. Prodigies, omens, oracles, judgments, quite obscure the few natural events that are intermingled with them. But as the former grow thinner every page, in proportion as we advance nearer the enlightened ages, we soon learn that there is nothing mysterious or supernatural in the case, but that all proceeds from the usual propensity of mankind towards the marvelous, and that, though this inclination may at intervals receive a check from sense and learning, it can never be thoroughly extirpated from human nature. * * *

Upon the whole, then, it appears that no testimony for any kind of miracle has ever amounted to a probability, much less to a proof; and that, even supposing it amounted to a proof, it would be opposed by another proof; derived from the very nature of the fact, which it would endeavor to establish. It is experience only which gives authority to human testimony; and it is the same experience which assures us of the laws of nature. When, therefore, these two kinds of experience are contrary, we have nothing to do but subtract the one from the other, and embrace an opinion, either on one side or the other, with that assurance which arises from the remainder. But according to the principle here explained, this subtraction, with regard to all popular religions, amounts to an entire annihilation; and therefore we may establish it as a maxim, that no human testimony can have such force as to prove a miracle, and make it a just foundation for any such system of religion. * * *

What we have said of miracles may be applied, without any variation, to prophecies; and indeed, all prophecies are real miracles, and as such only can be admitted as proofs of any revelation. If it did not exceed the capacity of human nature to foretell future events, it would be absurd to employ any prophecy as an argument for a divine mission or authority from heaven. So that, upon the whole, we may conclude, that the *Christian religion* not only was at first attended with miracles, but even at this day cannot be believed by any reasonable person without one. Mere reason is insufficient to convince us of its veracity. And whoever is moved by *faith* to assent to it, is conscious of a continued miracle in his own person, which subverts all the principles of his understanding, and gives him a determination to believe what is most contrary to custom and experience.

c. 1736 1748

Christopher Smart

1722–1771

"Newton . . . is more of error than of the truth, but I am of the Word of God," wrote Christopher Smart in his astonishing poem *Jubilate Agno* ("Rejoice in the Lamb"). For Smart, as for a growing number of Christians in the century's second half, the Newtonian "error" consisted in a commitment to materialist science, to an empiricism that investigated the physical world and sought its seeming system, rather than submitting to faith in a God who worked by will and sometimes by miracle, free of any fixed laws of nature. Smart composed *Jubilate Agno* in his late thirties, while confined in a madhouse; after a brilliant career as a classical scholar at Cambridge, and an auspicious start in London as a literary adventurer (poet, editor, translator, essayist), he suffered a derangement whose chief symptom was his compulsion to pray spontaneously in public places (he was too much "of the Word of God" to be socially acceptable). Released from the asylum after five years, Smart recast much material from the *Jubilate Agno* in his *Song of David* (1763); following Watts's precedent, he published a translation of the Psalms (1767) and (while imprisoned for debt at the very end of his life) a book of *Hymns for the Amusement of Children* (1771). *Jubilate Agno* remained in manuscript and unknown for a century and a half after the poet's death. Smart called it "my Magnificat," *magnificat* being the title of the liturgical hymn first uttered by the Virgin Mary upon learning that she would conceive a son: "My Soul doth magnify the Lord" (Luke 1.46–55). Structured like a responsive prayer, Smart's poem moves rapidly across a wide range of reference, from the scriptural and mystical to the local and the homely ("God be gracious to Baumgarden"—a London bassoon player). But Smart returns repeatedly to a preoccupation touched on in the poem's title: to the animal world as emblem and embodiment of God's grace and greatness (in Smart's time natural history was among the branches of knowledge least touched by the new science, and most inflected by faith and folklore). In the excerpts that follow, Smart punningly pinpoints the animal essences of languages ancient and modern, then depicts the feline who kept him company during his years of confinement, singing Jeoffry's praises with such exuberance as to make *magnificat* seem a latent, sacred, and affectionate pun.

from Jubilate Agno

[ANIMALS IN LANGUAGE[1]]

For the power of some animal is predominant in every language.
For the power and spirit of a CAT is in the Greek.
For the sound of a cat is in the most useful preposition κατ' ευχην.[2]
For the pleasantry of a cat at pranks is in the language ten thousand times
  over.[3]
For JACK UPON PRANCK is in the performance of πε ρι together or separate.[4]
For Clapperclaw[5] is in the grappling of the words upon one another in all
  the modes of versification.
For the sleekness of a Cat is in his αγλαιηφι.[6]
For the Greek is thrown from heaven and falls upon its feet.[7]
For the Greek when distracted from the line is sooner restored to rank and
  rallied into some form than any other.
For the purring of a Cat is his τρυζει.[8]
For his cry is in ουαι[9] which I am sorry for.

1. These selections come from Fragment B of Smart's manuscript. Some pages of Smart's manuscript contain long sequences of lines beginning "Let"; other pages contain lines beginning "For," with clear enough indications that the "Let" and "For" lines were meant to be dovetailed and read alternately, in the form of responsive prayer. For the two excerpts printed here, though, lines beginning "Let" have not been found—and may never have been written.
2. *Kat euchen*: "according to prayer" (Greek).
3. The syllable *kat* appears in many Greek word forms.
4. Greek *perikato* means "upside down" (as, probably, does "Jack Upon Pranck").
5. To claw, scratch.
6. *Aglaiefi*: "beauty."
7. Perhaps an allusion to the Greek poetic term *catalexis*, the shortening or omission of a "foot" from a line of verse; the prefix *cata-* means "down."
8. *Truzei*: "murmur."
9. *Ouai*: exclamation of lament ("ah!").

For the Mouse (*Mus*) prevails in the Latin.[1]
For *Edi-mus, bibi-mus, vivi-mus—ore-mus*.[2]
For the Mouse is a creature of great personal valor.
For—this is a true case—Cat takes female mouse from the company of male—male mouse will not depart, but stands threat'ning and daring.
For this is as much as to challenge, if you will let her go, I will engage you, as prodigious a creature as you are.
For the Mouse is of an hospitable disposition.
For bravery and hospitality were said and done by the Romans rather than others.
For two creatures the Bull and the Dog prevail in the English.
For all the words ending in -ble are in the creature. Invisi-ble, Incomprehensi-ble, ineffa-ble, A-ble.
For the Greek and Latin are not dead languages, but taken up and accepted for the sake of him that spoke them.
For can is (*canis*[3]) is cause and effect a dog.
For the English is concise and strong. Dog and Bull again.
For Newton's notion of colors is αλογος,[4] unphilosophical.

[My Cat Jeoffry]

For I will consider my Cat Jeoffry.
For he is the servant of the Living God duly and daily serving him.
For at the first glance of the glory of God in the East he worships in his way.
For is this done by wreathing his body seven times round with elegant quickness.
For then he leaps up to catch the musk, which is the blessing of God upon his prayer.
For he rolls upon prank to work it in.
For having done duty and received blessing he begins to consider himself.
For this he performs in ten degrees.
For first he looks upon his fore-paws to see if they are clean.
For secondly he kicks up behind to clear away there.
For thirdly he works it upon stretch with the fore-paws extended.
For fourthly he sharpens his paws by wood.
For fifthly he washes himself.
For sixthly he rolls upon wash.
For seventhly he fleas himself, that he may not be interrupted upon the beat.
For eighthly he rubs himself against a post.
For ninthly he looks up for his instructions.
For tenthly he goes in quest of food.
For having considered God and himself he will consider his neighbor.
For if he meets another cat he will kiss her in kindness.
For when he takes his prey he plays with it to give it chance.
For one mouse in seven escapes by his dallying.

1. Partly because (as Smart illustrates in line 637), the syllable *mus* means "mouse" and is also the suffix for first person plural present-tense conjugations.

2. "We eat, we drink, we live—let us pray."

3. Dog (Latin).

4. *Alogos*: literally, "without the Word."

For when his day's work is done his business more properly begins.
For he keeps the Lord's watch in the night against the adversary.
For he counteracts the powers of darkness by his electrical skin and glaring eyes.
For he counteracts the Devil, who is death, by brisking about the life.
For in his morning orisons he loves the sun and the sun loves him.
For he is of the tribe of Tiger.
For the Cherub Cat is a term of the Angel Tiger.
For he has the subtlety and hissing of a serpent, which in goodness he suppresses.
For he will not do destruction, if he is well-fed, neither will he spit without provocation.
For he purrs in thankfulness, when God tells him he's a good Cat.
For he is an instrument for the children to learn benevolence upon.
For every house is incomplete without him and a blessing is lacking in the spirit.
For the Lord commanded Moses concerning the cats at the departure of the Children of Israel from Egypt.[5]
For every family had one cat at least in the bag.
For the English Cats are the best in Europe.
For he is the cleanest in the use of his fore-paws of any quadrupede.
For the dexterity of his defense is an instance of the love of God to him exceedingly.
For he is the quickest to his mark of any creature.
For he is tenacious of his point.
For he is a mixture of gravity and waggery.
For he knows that God is his Savior.
For there is nothing sweeter than his peace when at rest.
For there is nothing brisker than his life when in motion.
For he is of the Lord's poor and so indeed is he called by benevolence perpetually—Poor Jeoffry! poor Jeoffry! the rat has bit thy throat.
For I bless the name of the Lord Jesus that Jeoffry is better.
For the divine spirit comes about his body to sustain it in complete cat.
For his tongue is exceeding pure so that it has in purity what it wants in music.
For he is docile and can learn certain things.
For he can set up with gravity which is patience upon approbation.
For he can fetch and carry, which is patience in employment.
For he can jump over a stick which is patience upon proof positive.
For he can spraggle° upon waggle at the word of command. *sprawl*
For he can jump from an eminence into his master's bosom.
For he can catch the cork and toss it again.
For he is hated by the hypocrite and miser.
For the former is afraid of detection.

5. "Take your flocks and your herds," says the Egyptian Pharaoh when demanding the Israelites' departure (Exodus 12.32); Smart adds the Lord and the cats.

For the latter refuses the charge.
For he camels his back to bear the first notion of business.
For he is good to think on, if a man would express himself neatly.
For he made a great figure in Egypt for his signal services.
For he killed the Ichneumon-rat° very pernicious by land. *mongoose*
For his ears are so acute that they sting again.
For from this proceeds the passing quickness of his attention.
For by stroking of him I have found out electricity.
For I perceived God's light about him both wax and fire.
For the Electrical fire is the spiritual substance, which God sends from heaven to sustain the bodies both of man and beast.
For God has blessed him in the variety of his movements.
For, though he cannot fly, he is an excellent clamberer.
For his motions upon the face of the earth are more than any other quadrupede.
For he can tread to all the measures upon the music.
For he can swim for life.
For he can creep.

c. 1758–1763 1939

William Cowper
1731–1800

Like Christopher Smart, William Cowper suffered madness, loved animals, wrote hymns, and invented capacious new structures for religious verse. But where Smart wrote to celebrate his sure salvation, Cowper wrote out of the certainty that he was damned—unworthy of redemption and predestined for hellfire. The conviction first took hold in 1763, when a paralyzing panic cut him off from impending attachments (to a new job he was about to secure, a beloved woman he was soon to marry) and prompted several attempts at suicide. The course of recovery took him first to an asylum, then through a conversion to Calvinism, then to the household of Mary Unwin, who loved and looked after him for the next four decades, and finally into partnership with Unwin's neighbor, the austere hymn-writer John Newton, with whom Cowper collaborated for years on a new collection of religious song, the *Olney Hymns* (it included, along with several of Cowper's still-sung texts, Newton's perdurable *Amazing Grace*). A second, sharper attack of madness, ten years after the first, deepened Cowper's conviction of his doom but also ushered in years of plentiful poetic composition. Seizing any small occasion (a fish dinner, the death of a pet bird) to produce a short, often comic piece of verse, Cowper wrote poems to hold terror at bay. As his output increased, his ambition did too. *The Task*, a massive mock-epic grounded in the comforts of Cowper's rural retirement (sofa, garden, seasons) but ranging satirically over the whole wide world, surprised even its author by its scope and popularity. Spurred by its success, Cowper undertook to translate Homer's epics, hoping to surpass Pope's attempts earlier in the century. In a passage near the midpoint of *The Task* (printed here), Newton appears briefly as the embodiment of Cowper's deepest hope, that the mind might merge with God through a science immersed in faith—"philosophy baptized." In his last, autobiographical poem, *The Cast-away*, Cowper draws a darker picture, of a mind sundered from its maker by distance and despair.

Light Shining out of Darkness[1]

God moves in a mysterious way,
His wonders to perform;
He plants his footsteps in the sea,
And rides upon the storm.

Deep in unfathomable mines
Of never-failing skill,
He treasures up his bright designs,
And works his sov'reign will.

Ye fearful saints[2] fresh courage take,
The clouds ye so much dread
Are big with mercy, and shall break
In blessings on your head.

Judge not the Lord by feeble sense,
But trust him for his grace;
Behind a frowning providence,
He hides a smiling face.

His purposes will ripen fast,
Unfolding every hour;
The bud may have a bitter taste,
But sweet will be the flower.

Blind unbelief is sure to err,
And scan his work in vain;
God is his own interpreter,
And he will make it plain.

c. 1773 — 1774

from The Task

["PHILOSOPHY BAPTIZED"[1]]

God never meant that man should scale the heav'ns
By strides of human wisdom. In his works
Though wond'rous, he commands us in his word
To seek *him* rather, where his mercy shines.
The mind indeed enlightened from above
Views him in all. Ascribes to the grand cause
The grand effect. Acknowledges with joy
His manner, and with rapture tastes his style.
But never yet did philosophic° tube — *scientific*
That brings the planets home into the eye
Of observation, and discovers, else° — *otherwise*
Not visible, his family of worlds,

1. Written and first published during the period of Cowper's collaboration with John Newton; later included in their *Olney Hymns* (1779).
2. Cowper addresses those who (according to Calvinist theology) are predestined for salvation.

1. From Book 3, "The Garden" (for more of *The Task*, see pages 2662–65).

Discover him that rules them; such a veil
Hangs over mortal eyes, blind from the birth
And dark in things divine. Full often too
Our wayward intellect, the more we learn
Of nature, overlooks her author more,
From instrumental causes proud to draw
Conclusions retrograde and mad mistake.
But if his word once teach us, shoot a ray
Through all the heart's dark chambers, and reveal
Truths undiscerned but by that holy light,
Then all is plain. Philosophy baptized
In the pure fountain of eternal love
Has eyes indeed; and viewing all she sees
As meant to indicate a God to man,
Gives *him* his praise, and forfeits not her own.
Learning has borne such fruit in other days
On all her branches. Piety has found
Friends in the friends of science, and true prayer
Has flowed from lips wet with Castalian dews.[2]
Such was thy wisdom, Newton, childlike sage!
Sagacious reader of the works of God,
And in his word sagacious. * * *

1783–1785 1785

The Cast-away[1]

Obscurest night involved° the sky, *encompassed*
Th' Atlantic billows roared,
When such a destined° wretch as I *doomed*
Washed headlong from on board
Of friends, of hope, of all bereft,
His floating home for ever left.

No braver chief[2] could Albion° boast *Britain*
Than he with whom he went,
Nor ever ship left Albion's coast
With warmer wishes sent.
He loved them both, but both in vain,
Nor him beheld, nor her again.

Not long beneath the whelming brine
Expert to swim, he lay,
Nor soon he felt his strength decline

2. I.e., from poets (who have drunk of the inspirational Castalian spring on the mountain of the Muses).

1. Cowper based this poem on a mariner's account, in a popular travel book, of having watched helplessly as a shipmate was hurled overboard during a storm: "We were the more grieved at his unhappy fate, as we . . . conceived from the manner in which he swam that he might continue sensible, for a considerable time longer, of the horror attending his irretrievable situation." Cowper collates the doomed man's situation with his own, which he conceived as also "irretrievable"; the poem, left in manuscript at his death, is his last surviving original poem in English.

2. George Anson, commander of the naval squadron in which the sailor was lost.

Or courage die away;
But waged with Death a lasting strife
Supported by despair of life.

He shouted, nor his friends had failed
To check the vessel's course,
But so the furious blast prevailed
That, pitiless perforce,
They left their outcast mate behind,
And scudded still before the wind.

Some succor yet they could afford,
And, such as storms allow,
The cask, the coop, the floated cord
Delayed not to bestow;
But he, they knew, nor ship nor shore,
Whate'er they gave, should visit more.

Nor, cruel as it seemed, could he
Their haste, himself, condemn,
Aware that flight, in such a sea,
Alone could rescue them;
Yet bitter felt it still to die
Deserted, and his friends so nigh.

He long survives who lives an hour
In ocean, self-upheld,
And so long he, with unspent power,
His destiny repelled,
And ever, as the minutes flew,
Entreated help, or cried, Adieu!

At length, his transient respite past,
His comrades, who before
Had heard his voice in every blast,
Could catch the sound no more;
For then, by toil subdued, he drank
The stifling wave, and then he sank.

No poet wept him: but the page
Of narrative[3] sincere
That tells his name, his worth,° his age, *rank*
Is wet with Anson's tear,
And tears by bards or heroes shed
Alike immortalize the dead.

I therefore purpose not or dream,
Descanting on his fate,
To give the melancholy theme
A more enduring date,

3. The log book of the ship from which he fell.

But misery still delights to trace
Its semblance in another's case.

No voice divine the storm allayed,
No light propitious shone,
When, snatched from all effectual aid,
We perished, each, alone;
But I beneath a rougher sea,
And whelmed in deeper gulphs than he.

1799 1804

END OF PERSPECTIVES: MIND AND GOD

James Thomson

1700–1748

"Nature delights me in every form," James Thomson declared in a letter at age twenty-five. "I am just now painting her in her most lugubrious dress; for my own amusement describing winter as it presents itself." Though he may not have known it yet, he was "just now" embarking on his life's central work. In his long poem *The Seasons* (of which this piece on winter was the earliest installment), Thomson sought to develop a poetic structure capacious enough to compass the varied forms of nature in which he took so much delight.

Thomson wrote his letter in London, where he had recently arrived, to a friend in his native Scotland, where he would never return. The winters he remembered were those of the terrain where he had spent his first fifteen years, in a village near the border with England. When Thomson was seven, geographical proximity became political reality. The Act of Union, energetically endorsed by the poet's Whig neighbors, linked Scotland with England and Wales to form the new entity of Great Britain; that event resonates throughout the poet's life and work, in his depictions of nature (which remain centered in Scotland even as they span the globe), in his passionate advocacy of the politics he'd absorbed in youth, in his celebration of the incipient British empire.

Born to a Presbyterian minister praised for his "diligence," and to a mother noted for her "imagination," "warmth," and enthusiastic piety, Thomson felt toward both parents a lifelong affection. In deference to their wishes, and despite an early inclination to poetry, he initially planned to follow his father into the ministry. But Edinburgh, where he went at age fifteen to study divinity, abounded in literary aspirants, endeavors, publications, and societies. During his ten years there, Thomson gradually found that the attractions of poetry outflanked those of professional piety. Like many ambitious Scotsmen of the time, Thomson headed for London, along the route the Union had made smooth. There, aided and encouraged by new literary friends (Pope and Gay among them), he launched the poem of nature that he describes in his letter home. *Winter* (1726) was followed by *Summer* and *Spring* (both 1727); *The Seasons* (1730) brought the cycle to completion, with the new piece on *Autumn* added to the three earlier sections, now much expanded and revised. The work struck readers and reviewers as something altogether new, and quickly established the poet's fame. The following years produced another long poem, equally ambitious but less successful (*Liberty*, 1735–1736), a series of verse tragedies, and a plenitude of distractions. Thomson engaged exuberantly in politics and in the pleasures of food and drink, cherished his friends, and fell in love with women who did not love him back. The years also brought recurrent returns of *The Seasons:* the poem reappeared, in a greatly enlarged and altered edition, in 1744, and in yet another incarnation two years later. In *The Castle of Indolence* (1748), Thomson produced an allegory, by turns serious and comic, on that very propensity toward imaginative idleness that had both generated his poetry and prevented his producing more. The poem, deeply autobiographical, proved valedictory as well. Four months after its publication the poet died, mourned by his many friends as "our old, tried, amiable, open, and honest-hearted Thomson," and by a wider world of readers as the writer who had newly transmuted nature into language, in the century's single most popular poem.

The Seasons often gave rise to a measure of puzzlement commingled with its popularity. Thomson had set so much going in the poem that familiar conventions of artistic order and containment seemed overthrown. "The great defect of *The Seasons*," Samuel Johnson opined, "is its want of method"—its lack of a self-evident logical structure. Still, reader after reader (including Johnson) discovered that this seeming defect correlated mysteriously with the poem's many pleasures: its comprehensiveness, its range of tones and modes, its contagious "enthusiasm," whereby (in Johnson's account) "our thoughts expand with [Thomson's] imagery and kindle with his sentiments." Expansiveness had marked the poem's making as well as its impact. During two decades of creation and revision, Thomson kept nature at the center of his scrutiny, but made it the repository for his many preoccupations: Whig politics, imperial expansion, ancient history, Christian faith, modern science. The poem links and navigates all these topics not so much by "method" as by the restless motion of the maker's mind. In this innovative arrangement, the physical world becomes a medium of meditation, a mirror of mind and culture, the meeting place where human inquiry most fully encounters divine display, in order to discern and to wonder at the ways of both self and God. Like his idol Isaac Newton, whose discoveries pervade the poem, Thomson was reading and representing God's Book of Nature in new, immensely influential terms. "Enthusiasm" itself means immersion "in the God," possession by the divine. Thomson makes good on the term when he declares at the poem's close that the seasons "are but the varied God," phenomena that mortals must inhabit and observe with deep discernment, proper awe. Thomson's own enthusiasm proved contagious across boundaries of space, time, and medium. His poem was translated and ardently imitated in most of the languages of Europe; the composer Franz Joseph Haydn set its sentiments to music, and draughtsmen depicted its scenes so often that it remained for a hundred years the most illustrated work in English. For writers of many nations and several generations, *The Seasons* served as almost inexhaustible sourcebook, as supplementary Scripture.

from Winter. A Poem[1]
[Autumn Evening and Night]

See! Winter comes, to rule the varied year,
Sullen and sad; with all his rising train,
Vapors, and clouds, and storms. Be these my theme,
These, that exalt the soul to solemn thought,
And heavenly musing. Welcome kindred glooms!
Wished, wintery horrors, hail! With frequent foot,
Pleased have I, in my cheerful morn of life,
When nursed by careless solitude I lived,

1. This was the earliest version Thomson published; for some of his subsequent revisions, see the selection from *Autumn* on pages 2650–55.

And sung of Nature with unceasing joy,
Pleased have I wandered through your rough domains;
Trod the pure, virgin-snows, myself as pure;
Heard the winds roar, and the big torrent burst;
Or seen the deep-fermenting tempest brewed
In the red evening sky. Thus passed the time
Till, through the opening chambers of the south,[2]
Looked out the joyous Spring, looked out, and smiled.

Thee too, inspirer of the toiling swain!
Fair Autumn, yellow robed! I'll sing of thee,
Of thy last, tempered days and sunny calms;
When all the golden hours are on the wing,
Attending thy retreat, and round thy wain,° *chariot*
Slow-rolling, onward to the southern sky.

Behold![3] the well-poised hornet, hovering, hangs
With quivering pinions in the genial blaze;
Flies off in airy circles; then returns
And hums and dances to the beating ray.
Nor shall the man that, musing, walks alone,
And, heedless, strays within his radiant lists,° *boundaries*
Go unchastised away. Sometimes a fleece
Of clouds, wide-scattering, with a lucid[4] veil,
Soft, shadow o'er th' unruffled face of heaven;
And, through their dewy sluices,° shed the sun, *floodgates*
With tempered influence down. Then is the time,
For those, whom Wisdom, and whom Nature charm,
To steal themselves from the degenerate crowd,
And soar above this little scene of things:
To tread low-thoughted Vice beneath their feet:
To lay their passions in a gentle calm,
And woo lone Quiet, in her silent walks.

Now solitary, and in pensive guise,
Oft let me wander o'er the russet mead,° *meadow*
Or through the pining grove, where scarce is heard
One dying strain, to cheer the woodman's toil.
Sad Philomel,[5] perchance, pours forth her plaint
Far through the withering copse.° Meanwhile the leaves, *woods*
That late the forest clad with lively green,
Nipped by the drizzly night, and sallow-hued,
Fall wavering through the air; or shower amain,° *fiercely*
Urged by the breeze, that sobs amid the boughs.
Then listening hares forsake the rustling woods,
And, starting at the frequent noise, escape

2. The southern sky, "opening" as clouds dissipate.

3. In *The Seasons*, Thomson transferred this passage (lines 23–79), extensively revised, to *Autumn* (lines 955–1036; see pages 2650–52).

4. The adjective meant both "shining" and "transparent."

5. The nightingale. In Greek myth, the Athenian princess Philomela, raped by her brother-in-law Tereus, is transformed into a bird and nightly laments her fate.

To the rough stubble, and the rushy fen.° *marsh*
Then woodcocks o'er the fluctuating main
That glimmers to the glimpses of the moon
Stretch their long voyage to the woodland glade;
Where, wheeling with uncertain flight, they mock
The nimble fowler's° aim. Now Nature droops; *bird hunter's*
Languish the living herbs, with pale decay:
And all the various family of flowers
Their sunny robes resign. The falling fruits,
Through the still night, forsake the parent bough
That in the first gray glances of the dawn,
Looks wild, and wonders at the wintry waste.

The year, yet pleasing, but declining fast,
Soft, o'er the secret soul, in gentle gales,
A philosophic melancholy breathes,
And bears the swelling thought aloft to heaven.
Then forming fancy rouses to conceive,
What never mingled with the vulgar's° dream: *common people's*
Then wake the tender pang, the pitying tear,
The sigh for suffering worth, the wish preferred° *offered up*
For humankind, the joy to see them blessed,
And all the social offspring of the heart!

Oh! bear me then to high embowering shades;
To twilight groves and visionary vales;
To weeping grottos and to hoary caves;
Where angel forms are seen, and voices heard,
Sighed in low whispers that abstract the soul
From outward sense far into worlds remote.

Now,[6] when the western sun withdraws the day,
And humid evening, gliding o'er the sky,
In her chill progress checks the straggling beams,
And robs them of their gathered, vapory prey,
Where marshes stagnate, and where rivers wind,
Cluster the rolling fogs, and swim along
The dusky-mantled lawn:° then slow descend, *open ground*
Once more to mingle with their watery friends.
The vivid stars shine out, in radiant files;
And boundless ether[7] glows; till the fair moon
Shows her broad visage, in the crimsoned east;
Now, stooping, seems to kiss the passing cloud:
Now, o'er the pure cerulean,[8] rides sublime.
Wide the pale deluge floats, with silver waves,
O'er the skied° mountain, to the low-laid vale; *sky-high*

6. In *The Seasons*, this passage (lines 80–103) appeared, revised, in *Autumn* (lines 1082–1102; see pages 2653–54).

7. "An element more fine and subtle than air" (Johnson's *Dictionary*); it was assumed to fill the highest regions above the earth.

8. Deep blue (of the evening sky).

From the white rocks, with dim reflection, gleams,
And faintly glitters through the waving shades.

All night, abundant dews, unnoted, fall,
And, at return of morning, silver o'er
The face of Mother Earth; from every branch
Depending,° tremble the translucent gems, *hanging*
And, quivering, seem to fall away, yet cling,
And sparkle in the sun, whose rising eye,
With fogs bedimmed, portends a beauteous day.

* * *

[WINTER NIGHT]

Now, all amid the rigors of the year,
In the wild depth of winter, while without
The ceaseless winds blow keen, be my retreat
A rural, sheltered, solitary scene;
Where ruddy fire and beaming tapers join
To chase the cheerless gloom. There let me sit,
And hold high converse with the mighty dead—
Sages of ancient time, as gods revered,
As gods beneficent, who blessed mankind
With arts and arms, and humanized a world.
Roused at th' inspiring thought, I throw aside
The long-lived volume[9] and, deep-musing, hail
The sacred shades that slowly rising pass
Before my wondering eyes. First Socrates,[1]
Truth's early champion, martyr for his God;
Solon[2] the next, who built his commonweal
On equity's firm base. Lycurgus[3] then,
Severely good; and him of rugged Rome,
Numa,[4] who softened her rapacious sons.
Cimon sweet-souled, and Aristides[5] just.
Unconquered Cato,[6] virtuous in extreme;
With that attempered hero,[7] mild and firm,
Who wept the brother while the tyrant bled.
Scipio[8] the humane warrior, gently brave,
Fair learning's friend, who early sought the shade,

9. Plutarch's *Lives*: biographies of eminent Greeks and Romans—composed by the Greek historian and philosopher (c. 46–120 C.E.).
1. Socrates (469–399 B.C.E.), Athenian philospher, condemned to death for his teachings.
2. Solon (639–558 B.C.E.), Athenian statesman who introduced a newly humane system of laws.
3. Legendary Spartan lawgiver.
4. Rome's legendary second king, deemed a better ruler than the founder Romulus because his long reign was peaceful and enlightened.
5. Cimon (c. 510–449 B.C.E.) and Aristeides (d. 468 B.C.E.), military leaders and statesmen noted for their victorious strategies in the Persian Wars and for their rectitude in government.
6. Marcus Porcius Cato (96–46 B.C.E.), Roman champion of republican government; he chose to commit suicide rather than surrender himself to Julius Caesar, whose imperial ambitions he had resisted in the Roman civil wars.
7. Timoleon, a Corinthian who, alarmed at the tyrannical aspirations of his brother Timophanes, conspired in his assassination (365 B.C.E.), during which he wept for the kin he had helped to kill.
8. Scipio Africanus (236–183 B.C.E.), charismatic Roman general, conqueror of Spain and defeater of Hannibal.

To dwell, with innocence, and truth, retired.
And, equal to the best, the Theban,[9] he
Who, single, raised his country into fame.
Thousands behind, the boast of Greece and Rome,
Whom virtue owns, the tribute of a verse
Demand, but who can count the stars of heaven?
Who sing their influence on this lower world?
But see who yonder comes! nor comes alone,
With sober state, and of majestic mien,
The Sister-Muses in his train. 'Tis he!
Maro![1] the best of poets, and of men!
Great Homer too appears, of daring wing!
Parent of song! and equal by this side,
The British Muse,[2] joined hand in hand, they walk,
Darkling,[3] nor miss their way to fame's ascent.

Society divine! Immortal minds!
Still visit thus my nights, for you reserved,
And mount my soaring soul to deeds like yours.
Silence! thou lonely power! the door be thine:
See, on the hallowed hour, that none intrude,
Save Lycidas,[4] the friend, with sense refined,
Learning digested well, exalted faith,
Unstudied wit, and humor ever gay.

1725–1726 1726

from The Seasons
from *Autumn*

[Nightfall and Night[1]]

But see the fading many-colored woods,
Shade deepening over shade, the country round
Imbrown; a crowded umbrage,° dusk and dun, *shade*
Of every hue from wan declining green
To sooty dark. These now the lonesome Muse,
Low-whispering, lead into their leaf-strewn walks,
And give the season in its latest view.[2]
Meantime,[3] light shadowing all, a sober calm
Fleeces unbound ether; whose least wave
Stands tremulous, uncertain where to turn

9. Either Pelopidas (c. 410–364 B.C.E.) or Epaminondas (d. 362 B.C.E.), military tacticians who led Thebes to victory over Sparta.
1. Virgil (Publius Virgilius Maro, 70–19 B.C.E.), Roman poet, author of the *Aeneid*.
2. John Milton.
3. In the dark (Milton was blind, and Homer was traditionally thought to have been so).
4. Thomson takes the name (and its connotation of learned companion) from Milton's pastoral elegy (1638) lamenting the death of his college friend Edward King.

1. The original version of *Winter* begins with the description of an evening in late autumn; later, Thomson revised this description and transferred it to the section on autumn, which made its first appearance in *The Seasons* (1730). Thomson repeatedly revised the poem in the years that followed; the text here is taken from the last edition he produced (1746).
2. The colors display the very end of autumn.
3. For Thomson's earlier version of this passage (lines 955–1036), see *Winter*, lines 23–79, pages 2647–48.

The gentle current; while, illumined wide,
The dewy-skirted clouds imbibe the sun,
And through their lucid veil his softened force
Shed o'er the peaceful world. Then is the time
For those whom Wisdom and whom Nature charm
To steal themselves from the degenerate° crowd, *unworthy*
And soar above this little scene of things—
To tread low-thoughted Vice beneath their feet,
To soothe the throbbing passions into peace,
And woo lone Quiet in her silent walks.
Thus solitary, and in pensive guise,
Oft let me wander o'er the russet mead,
And through the saddened grove, where scarce is heard
One dying strain to cheer the woodman's toil.
Haply some widowed songster pours his plaint
Far in faint warblings through the tawny copse;
While congregated thrushes, linnets, larks,
And each wild throat whose artless strains so late
Swelled all the music of the swarming shades,
Robbed of their tuneful souls, now shivering sit
On the dead tree, a dull despondent flock,
With not a brightness waving o'er their plumes,
And naught save chattering discord in their note.
Oh, let not, aimed from some inhuman eye,
The gun the music of the coming year
Destroy, and harmless, unsuspecting harm,
Lay the weak tribes, a miserable prey!
In mingled murder fluttering on the ground!
The pale descending year, yet pleasing still,
A gentler mood inspires; for now the leaf
Incessant rustles from the mournful grove,
Oft startling such as, studious, walk below,
And slowly circles through the waving air.
But should a quicker breeze amid the boughs
Sob, o'er the sky the leafy deluge streams;
Till choked, and matted with the dreary shower,
The forest-walks, at every rising gale,
Roll wide the withered waste, and whistle bleak.
Fled is the blasted verdure of the fields;
And, shrunk into their beds, the flowery race
Their sunny robes resign. Even what remained
Of bolder fruits falls from the naked tree;
And woods, fields, gardens, orchards, all around
The desolated prospect thrills the soul.
He comes! he comes! in every breeze the power
Of Philosophic Melancholy comes!
His near approach the sudden-starting tear,
The glowing cheek, the mild dejected air,
The softened feature, and the beating heart,

Pierced deep with many a virtuous pang, declare.
O'er all the soul his sacred influence breathes;
Inflames imagination; through the breast
Infuses every tenderness; and far
Beyond dim earth exalts the swelling thought.
Ten thousand thousand fleet° ideas, such *rapid*
As never mingled with the vulgar dream,
Crowd fast into the mind's creative eye.
As fast the correspondent passions rise,
As varied, and as high—devotion raised
To rapture, and divine astonishment;
The love of nature unconfined, and, chief,
Of human race; the large ambitious wish,
To make them blest; the sigh for suffering worth,
Lost in obscurity; the noble scorn,
Of tyrant pride; the fearless great resolve;
The wonder which the dying patriot draws,
Inspiring glory through remotest time;
The awakened throb for virtue, and for fame;
The sympathies of love, and friendship dear;
With all the social offspring of the heart.
    Oh! bear me then to vast embowering shades,
To twilight groves, and visionary vales![4]
To weeping grottoes, and prophetic glooms!
Where angel forms athwart the solemn dusk,
Tremendous sweep, or seem to sweep along;
And voices more than human, through the void
Deep-sounding, seize the enthusiastic ear.
    Or is this gloom too much?[5] Then lead, ye powers,
That o'er the garden and the rural seat
Preside, which shining through the cheerful land
In countless numbers blest Britannia sees;
O lead me to the wide-extended walks,
The fair majestic paradise of Stowe![6]
Not Persian Cyrus,[7] on Ionia's shore,
E'er saw such sylvan scenes; such various art
By genius fired, such ardent genius tamed
By cool judicious art; that, in the strife,
All-beauteous Nature fears to be outdone.
And there, O Pitt,[8] thy country's early boast,
There let me sit beneath the sheltered slopes,

4. Valleys where I may see visions.
5. Thomson added lines 1036–1081 in his revision of 1744.
6. Stowe, the Buckinghamshire estate of Sir Richard Temple, Viscount Cobham (1669–1749), had been laid out and reworked by a long series of distinguished architects and landscapers; the garden was among the most celebrated of the 18th century.
7. Cyrus the Younger (d. 401 B.C.E.), a Persian prince, designed and planted a famous garden at Sardis (on "Ionia's shore," the coast of Asia Minor).
8. The statesman and orator William Pitt (1708–1778) was esteemed by Thomson and Cobham as a leading voice among those Whigs opposed to the still-dominant party faction led by Robert Walpole; Pitt later became Secretary of State and Prime Minister.

Or in that Temple[9] where, in future times,
Thou well shalt merit a distinguished name;
And, with thy converse blest, catch the last smiles
Of Autumn beaming o'er the yellow woods.
While there with thee the enchanted round I walk,
The regulated wild, gay Fancy° then *imagination*
Will tread in thought the groves of Attic land;[1]
Will from thy standard taste refine her own,[2]
Correct her pencil to the purest truth
Of Nature, or, the unimpassioned shades
Forsaking, raise it to the human mind.
O if hereafter she, with juster hand,
Shall draw the tragic scene, instruct her thou,
To mark the varied movements of the heart,
What every decent[3] character requires,
And every passion speaks. O through her strain° *song, style*
Breathe thy pathetic eloquence! that molds
Th' attentive senate, charms, persuades, exalts,
Of honest zeal th' indignant lightning throws,
And shakes corruption on her venal throne.
While thus we talk, and through Elysian vales[4]
Delighted rove, perhaps a sigh escapes.
What pity, Cobham, thou thy verdant files
Of ordered trees shouldst here inglorious range,
Instead of squadrons flaming o'er the field,
And long-embattled hosts![5] When the proud foe,
The faithless vain disturber of mankind,
Insulting Gaul, has roused the world to war;
When keen, once more, within their bounds to press[6]
Those polished robbers, those ambitious slaves,
The British youth would hail thy wise command,
Thy tempered ardor and thy veteran skill.[7]

The western sun withdraws the shortened day;[8]
And humid evening, gliding o'er the sky,
In her chill progress, to the ground condensed
The vapors throws. Where creeping waters ooze,
Where marshes stagnate, and where rivers wind,
Cluster the rolling fogs, and swim along

9. The Temple of Virtue in Stowe Gardens [Thomson's note]; this monument to ancient heroes was one of the gardens' most celebrated buildings.
1. Ancient Greece (Attica was the countryside surrounding Athens).
2. Influenced by your standard of taste, Fancy will refine hers.
3. Appropriate (Thomson, who wrote several tragedies, here asks Pitt for guidance in suiting his language to his characters and their emotions).
4. The Elysian Fields at Stowe (named for Elysium, Greek myth's paradise for heroes) were the most wild and natural area of the gardens.
5. Cobham left the Walpole government in 1733; thereafter he worked on his gardens and formed a group of opposition Whigs known as "Cobham's Cubs." Here Thomson wishes that Cobham, an accomplished soldier, might deploy his gifts as military leader rather than as shaper of landscapes.
6. I.e., contain within their own borders.
7. Thomson here imagines how effective Cobham would be as a leader in the War of the Austrian Succession (1740–1748), England's current conflict with France ("insulting Gaul," "polished robbers," "ambitious slaves").
8. Compare the earlier version of these lines in *Winter* (lines 80–96 on pages 2648–49).

The dusky-mantled lawn. Meanwhile the moon,
Full-orbed and breaking through the scattered clouds,
Shows her broad visage in the crimsoned east.
Turned to the sun direct, her spotted disk
(Where mountains rise, umbrageous dales descend,
And oceans roll, as optic tube° descries) *telescope*
A smaller earth, gives all his blaze again,
Void of its flame, and sheds a softer day.
Now through the passing cloud she seems to stoop,
Now up the pure cerulean rides sublime.
Wide the pale deluge floats, and streaming mild
O'er the skied° mountain to the shadowy vale, *sky-high*
While rocks and floods reflect the quivering gleam,
The whole air whitens with a boundless tide
Of silver radiance, trembling round the world.
  But when, half-blotted from the sky, her light,
Fainting, permits the starry fires to burn,
With keener luster through the depth of heaven;
Or quite extinct her deadened orb appears,
And scarce appears, of sickly beamless white;
Oft in this season, silent from the north
A blaze of meteors shoots[9]—ensweeping first
The lower skies, they all at once converge
High to the crown of heaven, and all at once
Relapsing quick as quickly reascend,
And mix, and thwart,° extinguish, and renew, *cross*
All ether coursing in a maze of light.
  From look to look, contagious through the crowd,
The panic runs, and into wondrous shapes
Th' appearance throws—armies in meet array,
Thronged with aërial spears, and steeds of fire;
Till the long lines of full-extended war
In bleeding fight commixed, the sanguine flood
Rolls a broad slaughter o'er the plains of heaven.
As thus they scan the visionary scene,
On all sides swells the superstitious din,
Incontinent;° and busy frenzy talks *unrestrained*
Of blood and battle; cities overturned,
And late at night in swallowing earthquake sunk,
Or hideous wrapped in fierce ascending flame;
Of sallow famine, inundation, storm;
Of pestilence, and every great distress;
Empires subversed, when ruling fate has struck
The unalterable hour: even Nature's self
Is deemed to totter on the brink of time.
Not so the man of philosophic eye,
And inspect sage;° the waving brightness he *wise insight*

9. The aurora borealis, or northern lights.

Curious surveys, inquisitive to know
The causes, and materials, yet unfixed,[1]
Of this appearance beautiful, and new. * * *

1726–1746 1746

Rule, Britannia[1]

When Britain first, at Heaven's command,
Arose from out the azure main;° *sea*
This was the charter of the land,
And guardian angels sung this strain:
"Rule, Britannia, rule the waves;
"Britons never will be slaves."

The nations, not so blest as thee,
Must, in their turns, to tyrants fall:
While thou shalt flourish great and free,
The dread and envy of them all.
"Rule," etc.

Still more majestic shalt thou rise,
More dreadful, from each foreign stroke:
As the loud blast that tears the skies,
Serves but to root thy native oak.
"Rule," etc.

Thee haughty tyrants ne'er shall tame:
All their attempts to bend thee down
Will but arouse thy generous flame;
But work their woe, and thy renown.
"Rule," etc.

To thee belongs the rural reign;
Thy cities shall with commerce shine:
All thine shall be the subject main,
And every shore it circles thine.
"Rule," etc.

The Muses, still[2] with freedom found,
Shall to thy happy coast repair:
Blest isle! with matchless beauty crowned,
And manly hearts to guard the fair.

1. Unaccounted for (by science).

1. Thomson wrote several longer poems of impassioned patriotism (*Britannia*, 1729; *Liberty*, 1735–1736), but his convictions found their most enduring expression in this short piece, first performed as the climactic song of *Alfred*, a patriotic masque on the subject of the Saxon king (848–899). Defeated by the Danes, the monarch receives comfort from a "venerable bard," who expresses with uncanny prescience the 18th-century appetite for naval conquest and expanding empire. The masque was created by Thomson in collaboration with his fellow Scots expatriate David Mallet (?1705–1765) and the composer Thomas Arne (1710–1778), as part of an entertainment commissioned by Frederick, Prince of Wales, to celebrate his daughter's third birthday and the anniversary of his German grandfather's accession to the English throne. Thomson's ode outlasted its occasion, gradually acquiring the status of an alternate national anthem (just behind *God Save the King*). While the Empire endured, Thomson's song proffered for many Britons a stirring account of their national origins, essence, and destiny.

2. The word meant both "always" and "as yet."

"Rule, Britannia, rule the waves;
"Britons never will be slaves."

1740 1740

"THE SEASONS" AND ITS TIME

Poems of Nightfall and Night

The aubade, or dawn-song, was a favorite form in the Middle Ages and the Renaissance: poets from Chaucer to Donne portrayed lovers entwined abed, lamenting the intrusive rising of the sun. In eighteenth-century England, poets were more preoccupied with the night piece, as a medium not for amorous pairings but for meditative solitude. In a culture marked by the intensified noise, density, and busyness of the cities, privacy was an experience newly construed and prized; in the scene of nightfall (particularly *country* nightfall), poets found an ideal setting for its enactment. William Collins, in his most famous ode, addresses the Evening as a "maid composed," a "nymph reserved," whose quietude facilitates his solitary thought; in his poem on the death of his friend James Thomson, Collins renders his sense of loss by images of encroaching dark. The other selections here come from larger works—Edward Young's *Night Thoughts* and William Cowper's *The Task*—which participate in the tradition that Thomson's *Seasons* had commenced: copious blank-verse description and meditation, produced, expanded, and revised over the course of years, mingling widely various materials and modes in a new, purportedly improvisatory way. "The method pursued," Young explained of his long poem, "was rather *imposed*, by what spontaneously arose in the author's mind on that occasion, than *meditated* or *designed*"; Cowper, more simply, attributed the expansion of *The Task* to the unexpected directions dictated by his own "train of thought." Drawing on darkness as resource and backdrop, Thomson, Young, and Cowper were working toward a new mode: the epic of the solitary mind in action. From them the lines of influence run long and clear, through the Gothic fiction of the late eighteenth century, through Wordsworth's meditative excursions, into the stream of consciousness in Joyce's *Ulysses* and the nocturnal dreamspeak of *Finnegans Wake*.

Edward Young[1]

from *The Complaint*
or Night Thoughts on Life, Death, and Immortality

Tired Nature's sweet restorer, balmy Sleep!
He, like the world, his ready visit pays
Where Fortune smiles; the wretched he forsakes:
Swift on his downy pinion° flies from woe, *wing*
And lights on lids unsullied with a tear.

1. After a frustrating London career as poet and playwright in frantic pursuit of political advancement, Edward Young (1683–1765) took holy orders, withdrew to a small village, and at age 59 commenced a set of poems that brought him sudden, staggering success. In *The Complaint*, a sequence of nine night pieces (and more than 9,000 lines) published serially over the course of three years, Young mixed morbid melancholy, Gothic dread, and Christian solace. The combination appealed powerfully to a vast number and variety of readers, in Britain and on the Continent. In its meditative blank verse and its capacious, fluid form, *Night Thoughts* was plainly influenced by Thomson's *Seasons;* well into the 19th century, the two works were often packaged (along with *Paradise Lost*) in a single, highly saleable volume. Both poems pervaded the century's consciousness, and later figured as principal forebears of Romantic thought and writing. This excerpt is from *Night 1*.

From short (as usual) and disturbed repose,
I wake. How happy they, who wake no more!
Yet that were vain, if dreams infest the grave.
I wake, emerging from a sea of dreams
Tumultuous; where my wrecked, desponding thought
From wave to wave of fancied misery,
At random drove, her helm of reason lost.
Though now restored, 'tis only change of pain,
(A bitter change!) severer for severe.
The day too short for my distress! and Night,
Even in the zenith of her dark domain,
Is sunshine, to the color of my fate.
Night, sable goddess! from her ebon° throne, *black*
In rayless majesty, now stretches forth
Her leaden scepter o'er a slumb'ring world.
Silence, how dead! and darkness, how profound!
Nor eye, nor list'ning ear an object finds;
Creation sleeps. 'Tis as° the general pulse *as if*
Of life stood still, and Nature made a pause;
An awful pause! prophetic of her end.
And let her prophecy be soon fulfilled;
Fate! drop the curtain; I can lose no more.
Silence, and Darkness! Solemn sisters! Twins
From ancient Night, who nurse the tender thought
To reason, and on reason build resolve
(That column of true majesty in man),
Assist me: I will thank you in the grave;
The grave, your kingdom. There this frame shall fall
A victim sacred to your dreary shrine.
But what are ye? Thou,[2] who didst put to flight
Primeval Silence, when the morning stars,
Exulting, shouted o'er the rising ball;
O Thou! whose word from solid darkness struck
That spark, the sun; strike wisdom from my soul;
My soul, which flies to Thee, her trust, her treasure,
As misers to their gold, while others rest.
Through this opaque of nature, and of soul,
This double night, transmit one pitying ray,
To lighten, and to cheer. O lead my mind,
(A mind that fain would wander from its woe)
Lead it through various scenes of life and death;
And from each scene the noblest truths inspire.
Nor less inspire my conduct than my song;
Teach my best reason reason; my best will
Teach rectitude; and fix my firm resolve
Wisdom to wed, and pay her long arrear:° *old debt*

2. Young here shifts addressees, from the plural "ye" (Silence and Darkness) to the singular "Thou" (God, imagined at the moment of Creation).

Nor let the phial of thy vengeance, poured
On this devoted head, be poured in vain.
    The bell strikes one. We take no note of time
But from its loss. To give it then a tongue,
Is wise in man. As if an angel spoke,
I feel the solemn sound. If heard aright,
It is the knell of my departed hours:
Where are they? With the years beyond the flood.
It is the signal that demands dispatch;
How much is to be done? my hopes and fears
Start up alarmed, and o'er life's narrow verge
Look down—on what? A fathomless abyss;
A dread eternity! how surely mine!
And can eternity belong to me,
Poor pensioner on the bounties of an hour?
    How poor, how rich, how abject, how august,
How complicate, how wonderful, is man?
How passing wonder He, who made him such?
Who centered in our make such strange extremes?
From different natures marvelously mixed,
Connection exquisite of distant worlds!
Distinguished link in being's endless chain!
Midway from nothing to the deity!
A beam ethereal sullied and absorbed!
Though sullied and dishonored, still divine!
Dim miniature of greatness absolute!
An heir of glory! a frail child of dust!
Helpless immortal! Insect infinite!
A worm! a God! I tremble at myself,
And in myself am lost! At home a stranger,
Thought wanders up and down, surprised, aghast,
And wondering at her own. How reason reels!
O what a miracle to man is man,
Triumphantly distressed! what joy, what dread!
Alternately transported and alarmed!
What can preserve my life? or what destroy?
An angel's arm can't snatch me from the grave;
Legions of angels can't confine me there.
    'Tis past conjecture; all things rise in proof:
While o'er my limbs sleep's soft dominion spread,
What, though my soul fantastic measures trod
O'er fairy fields; or mourned along the gloom
Of pathless woods; or down the craggy steep
Hurled headlong, swam with pain the mantled pool;
Or scaled the cliff; or danced on hollow winds,
With antic shapes, wild natives of the brain?
Her ceaseless flight, though devious, speaks her nature
Of subtler essence than the trodden clod;
Active, aërial, towering, unconfined,

Unfettered with her gross companion's fall.
Even silent night proclaims my soul immortal:
Even silent night proclaims eternal day.
For human weal, Heaven husbands all events,
Dull sleep instructs, nor sport vain dreams in vain.

1742 1742, 1750

William Collins[1]

Ode to Evening

If aught of oaten stop,[2] or pastoral song,
May hope, chaste Eve, to soothe thy modest ear,
Like thy own solemn springs,
Thy springs, and dying gales,
O nymph reserved, while now the bright-haired sun
Sits in yon western tent, whose cloudy skirts,
With brede° ethereal wove, *braid*
O'erhang his wavy bed:
Now air is hushed, save where the weak-eyed bat,
With short shrill shriek flits by on leathern wing,
Or where the beetle winds° *blows*
His small but sullen horn,
As oft he rises 'midst the twilight path,
Against the pilgrim borne in heedless hum:
Now teach me, maid composed,
To breathe some softened strain,° *song*
Whose numbers° stealing through thy darkening vale, *verses*
May not unseemly with its stillness suit,
As musing slow, I hail
Thy genial loved return!
For when thy folding star arising shows
His paly circlet, at his warning lamp
The fragrant Hours, and elves
Who slept in flowers the day,
And many a nymph who wreathes her brows with sedge,
And sheds the freshening dew, and lovelier still,
The pensive Pleasures sweet
Prepare thy shadowy car.° *chariot*

1. As a student at Oxford, William Collins (1721–1759) secured some distinction, published a few poems, and promptly left for London and the life (as his friend Samuel Johnson described it) of "a literary adventurer." While amusing himself at the city's pleasure gardens and playhouses, amid a spritely circle of actors and writers, Collins planned a number of books. He published only one, a small collection entitled *Odes on Several Descriptive and Allegorical Subjects* (1747); its failure to attract notice prompted him to burn the many copies that had gone unsold. In his late twenties, the poet fell prey to a manic depression verging on madness, which disabled him the rest of his life. His odes, neglected in his time, appealed strongly to tastes that came into vogue just after his death: for sentiment and the sublime, for the expression of overpowering emotions, of disruptive experiences, and of visionary intensities beyond the familiar, civic, human scale.

2. If any music played on an oat-reed pipe (Collins uses the pastoral-archaic idiom associated with Spenser and Milton).

Then lead, calm vot'ress,[3] where some sheety lake
Cheers the lone heath, or some time-hallowed pile,° *building*
  Or upland fallows[4] gray
  Reflect its last cool gleam.
But when chill blustering winds, or driving rain,
Forbid my willing feet, be mine the hut,
  That from the mountain's side,
  Views wilds, and swelling floods,
And hamlets brown, and dim-discovered spires,
And hears their simple bell, and marks o'er all
  Thy dewy fingers draw
  The gradual dusky veil.
While Spring shall pour his showers, as oft he wont,[5]
And bathe thy breathing tresses, meekest Eve!
  While Summer loves to sport,
  Beneath thy lingering light;
While sallow Autumn fills thy lap with leaves;
Or Winter, yelling through the troublous air,
  Affrights thy shrinking train,
  And rudely rends thy robes;
So long, sure-found beneath the sylvan shed,
Shall Fancy, Friendship, Science, rose-lipped Health,
  Thy gentlest influence own,
  And hymn thy favorite name!

1746 1746, 1748

William Collins

Ode Occasioned by the Death of Mr. Thomson

The scene of the following stanzas is supposed to lie on the Thames near Richmond.[1]

Haec tibi semper erunt, et cum solennia vota
reddemus Nymphis, et cum lustrabimus agros.

—— ——*Amavit nos quoque Daphnis.*[2]

3. "A woman devoted to . . . worship" (Johnson's *Dictionary*).
4. Fields ploughed but unplanted.
5. Is accustomed to do.
1. A scenic riverside village nine miles from London's center; Thomson had lived there in his last years, and was buried in the parish churchyard. Collins, who had dwelt there too, in close friendship with Thomson, here invokes the local geography quite specifically. His ode compasses two motions: in space, as the speaker moves past Richmond up the river; in time, as day modulates into night. Collins's poem was praised by a contemporary for the "dirge-like melancholy it breathes, and the warmth of affection that seems to have dictated it"; it has long enjoyed a print intimacy with the poet whom it eulogizes. Thomson's editors have often presented it as a preface to his works; his biographers have reprinted it as a coda to his life, a summation of his worth.
2. "These rites shall be thine forever, both when we pay our yearly vows to the Nymphs, and when we purify our fields . . . Daphnis loved us too" (Virgil, *Eclogues* 5.74–75, 52). In the pastoral tradition, the legendary Daphnis is credited as the first shepherd to have made music, the inventor of bucolic song; in Virgil's lines, one of Daphnis's followers mourns his master's "cruel death" and promises perpetual homage.

1

In yonder grave a Druid[3] lies,
Where slowly winds the stealing wave!
The year's best sweets shall duteous rise
To deck its poet's sylvan grave!

2

In you deep bed of whispering reeds
His airy harp[4] shall now be laid,
That he, whose heart in sorrow bleeds,
May love through life the soothing shade.

3

Then maids and youths shall linger here,
And, while its sounds at distance swell,
Shall sadly seem in Pity's ear
To hear the woodland pilgrim's[5] knell.

4

Remembrance oft shall haunt the shore
When Thames in summer wreaths is dressed,
And oft suspend the dashing oar
To bid his gentle spirit rest!

5

And oft as Ease and Health retire
To breezy lawn or forest deep,
The friend shall view yon whitening spire,[6]
And mid the varied landscape weep.

6

But thou, who own'st that earthy bed,
Ah! what will every dirge avail?
Or tears, which Love and Pity shed
That mourn beneath the gliding sail![7]

7

Yet lives there one, whose heedless eye
Shall scorn thy pale shrine glimmering near?
With him, sweet bard, may Fancy die,
And Joy desert the blooming year.

3. The Druids were the priest-magicians of ancient Britain. In the 18th century they were thought to have possessed extraordinary intimacy with, and power over, the forces of nature.

4. "The harp of Aeolus" [Collins's note], an instrument whose strings make sounds when the breezes play upon them (Aeolus was the mythological Greek monarch of the winds). Thomson, the first to invoke this instrument in English verse, had made it a figure for poetic responsiveness to inspiration; many poets since have taken up the trope.

5. I.e., Thomson's, whose love of forest walks Collins here recalls.

6. Of the parish church where Thomson was buried.

7. Of the boat moving down the Thames (see line 15).

8

But thou, lorn stream,[8] whose sullen tide
No sedge-crowned Sisters now attend,
Now waft me from the green hill's side,
Whose cold turf hides the buried friend!

9

And see, the fairy valleys fade,
Dun Night has veiled the solemn view![9]
—Yet once again, dear parted shade,
Meek Nature's child, again adieu!

10

The genial meads,° assigned to bless — *meadows*
Thy life, shall mourn thy early doom,
Their hinds° and shepherd-girls shall dress — *shepherds*
With simple hands thy rural tomb.

11

Long, long, thy stone and pointed clay[1]
Shall melt the musing Briton's eyes:
"O! vales and wild woods," shall he say,
"In yonder grave your Druid lies!"

1748–1749 — 1749

William Cowper

from *The Task*[1]

from Book 4. The Winter Evening

[Reading the Newspaper]

Now stir the fire, and close the shutters fast,
Let fall the curtains, wheel the sofa round,
And while the bubbling and loud-hissing urn
Throws up a steamy column, and the cups° — *of tea*
That cheer but not inebriate, wait on each,
So let us welcome peaceful evening in.

8. The Thames, forlorn because it is no longer inhabited by the leaf-adorned river nymphs ("sedge-crowned Sisters") who dwelt there during Thomson's lifetime.

9. Collins echoes Thomson's *Autumn* lines 950–952 (see page 2650).

1. I.e., the poet's churchyard monument.

1. For William Cowper, see page 2641. As preface to *The Task*, Cowper offered the following brief "history": "A lady, fond of blank verse, demanded a poem of that kind from the author, and gave him the SOFA for a subject. He obeyed; and having much leisure, connected another subject with it; and pursuing the train of thought to which his situation and turn of mind led him, brought forth at length, instead of the trifle which he at first intended, a serious affair—a volume." The modulation from triviality to seriousness (and back again) is intrinsic not only to the history of the poem but to its substance too. In six epic "Books" bearing markedly domestic titles (*The Sofa, The Time-Piece, The Garden, The Winter Evening, The Winter Morning Walk, The Winter Walk at Noon*), Cowper savors rural pleasures and satirizes the life of cities. Mingling grand diction with cozy fact ("I sing the Sofa," the poem begins), Cowper revels in their seeming disparity, as a resource both for comic self-deprecation and for earnest affirmation. These domestic delights, *The Task* implies, deserve this scale of celebration.

Not such his ev'ning, who with shining face
Sweats in the crowded theater, and squeezed
And bored with elbow-points through both his sides,
Out-scolds the ranting actor on the stage.
Nor his, who patient stands till his feet throb,
And his head thumps, to feed upon the breath
Of patriots[2] bursting with heroic rage,
Or placemen,[3] all tranquillity and smiles.
This folio of four pages,° happy work! *the newspaper*
Which not ev'n critics criticize, that holds
Inquisitive attention while I read,
Fast bound in chains of silence, which the fair,[4]
Though eloquent themselves, yet fear to break,
What is it, but a map of busy life,
Its fluctuations and its vast concerns?
Here runs the mountainous and craggy ridge
That tempts ambition. On the summit, see,
The seals of office glitter in his eyes;
He climbs, he pants, he grasps them. At his heels,
Close at his heels a demagogue ascends,
And with a dext'rous jerk soon twists him down
And wins them, but to lose them in his turn.
Here rills of oily eloquence in soft
Meanders lubricate the course they take;
The modest speaker is ashamed and grieved
T' engross a moment's notice, and yet begs,
Begs a propitious ear for his poor thoughts,
However trivial all that he conceives.
Sweet bashfulness! it claims, at last, this praise:
The dearth of information and good sense
That it foretells us, always comes to pass.
Cataracts of declamation thunder here,
There forests of no-meaning spread the page
In which all comprehension wanders lost;
While fields of pleasantry amuse us there,
With merry descants° on a nation's woes. *commentaries*
The rest[5] appears a wilderness of strange
But gay confusion: roses for the cheeks,
And lilies for the brows of faded age,
Teeth for the toothless, ringlets for the bald,
Heaven, earth, and ocean plundered of their sweets,
Nectareous essences, Olympian dews,
Sermons and city feasts and favorite airs,[6]
Aetherial journies,[7] submarine exploits,[8]

2. Political zealots.
3. Office-holders, bureaucrats.
4. The women of the house.
5. I.e., the newspaper's advertisements.
6. Popular melodies (sold as sheet music).
7. In hot-air balloons; the first flight had taken place in 1783.
8. In diving bells, which had been in use for more than a century.

And Katterfelto[9] with his hair on end
At his own wonders, wond'ring for his bread.
'Tis pleasant through the loop-holes of retreat
To peep at such a world. To see the stir
Of the great Babel[1] and not feel the crowd.
To hear the roar she sends through all her gates
At a safe distance, where the dying sound
Falls a soft murmur on th' uninjured ear.
Thus sitting and surveying thus at ease
The globe and its concerns, I seem advanced
To some secure and more than mortal height,
That lib'rates and exempts me from them all.
It turns submitted to my view, turns round
With all its generations; I behold
The tumult and am still. The sound of war
Has lost its terrors ere it reaches me;
Grieves but alarms me not. I mourn the pride
And avarice that make man a wolf to man,
Hear the faint echo of those brazen throats
By which he speaks the language of his heart,
And sigh, but never tremble at the sound.
He travels and expatiates, as the bee
From flow'r to flow'r, so he from land to land;
The manners, customs, policy of all
Pay contribution to the store he gleans,
He sucks intelligence in every clime,
And spreads the honey of his deep research
At his return, a rich repast for me.
He travels and I too. I tread his deck,
Ascend his topmast, through his peering eyes
Discover countries, with a kindred heart
Suffer his woes, and share in his escapes,
While fancy, like the finger of a clock,
Runs the great circuit, and is still at home.

[THE INVOCATION]

Come Ev'ning once again,[2] season of peace
Return sweet Ev'ning, and continue long!
Methinks I see thee in the streaky west,
With matron-step slow-moving, while the night
Treads on thy sweeping train; one hand employed
In letting fall the curtain of repose

9. Gustave Katterfelto, a magician whose performances were advertised under the rubric "Wonders, Wonders, Wonders."

1. The biblical Tower of Babel (Genesis 11.1–9), whose construction God prevented by making the builders speak different languages ("babble"); Cowper here uses the word for its long-established association with "Babylon," meaning any great city.

2. Cowper's invocation in the ensuing lines echoes both Milton's *Paradise Lost* (4.568–609) and Collins's *Ode to Evening* (page 2659).

On bird and beast, the other charged for man
With sweet oblivion of the cares of day;
Not sumptuously adorned, nor needing aid
Like homely featured Night, of clust'ring gems,
A star or two just twinkling on thy brow
Suffices thee; save that the moon is thine
No less than hers, not worn indeed on high
With ostentatious pageantry, but set
With modest grandeur in thy purple zone,° *belt*
Resplendent less, but of an ampler round.
Come then, and thou shalt find thy vot'ry° calm *worshipper*
Or make me so. Composure is thy gift.
And whether I devote thy gentle hours
To books, to music, or the poet's toil,
To weaving nets for bird-alluring fruit;
Or twining silken threads round ivory reels.
When they° command whom man was born to please, *women*
I slight thee not, but make thee welcome still.

1783–1785 1785

END OF "THE SEASONS" AND ITS TIME

Thomas Gray

1716–1771

Toward the end of his most famous poem, *Elegy Written in a Country Churchyard,* Thomas Gray commends the quietude with which the villagers have led their ordinary lives:

Along the cool sequestered vale of life
They kept the noiseless tenor of their way.

Tenor here means "course," and the line incorporates a notable revision: Gray had originally written "silent tenor," and then written the new adjective "noiseless" above the old, without crossing out "silent." In retrospect, this manuscript moment of alternate possibilities looks emblematic. Sickly, shy, and melancholic, Gray was often drawn toward silence but never settled there. Words—in ancient literature and in modern history, in talk and correspondence with his friends, in the varied idioms of his own compelling poems—exerted too strong a fascination. The fascination started early. At age nine, having weathered a bleak childhood in the troubled London household of his irascible father and doting mother, he entered the privileged precincts of Eton College, where his uncles worked and where he hit upon the satisfactions that would fill his life: passionate reading (in the classics first and foremost) and passionate friendships, with three schoolmates in particular: Richard West, Thomas Ashton, and Horace Walpole, son of the notorious prime minister Robert Walpole. Dubbing themselves the Quadruple Alliance, the four friends piqued themselves on a collective erudition, refinement, and wit that set them off from their contemporaries. The links among them mattered enormously in Gray's life of writing: West inspired his poems; Walpole sponsored their publication; and all Gray's friendships, at Eton and beyond, drew from Gray a steady flow of virtuosic letters, in which the voice of the "Alliance," at once antic and vulnerable, never abated. "His letters," remarked Walpole (whose own letters have evoked similar praise), "were the best I ever saw, and had more novelty and wit." Gray's affections took form and motion partly from their containment. He was homosexual; yet there is no evidence that he ever physically consummated the great passions of his life—for Walpole, for West, and, in his last years, for the young Swiss scion Charles-Victor de Bonstatten.

After nine years at Eton, Gray was admitted to Cambridge. He found university life far less pleasing, with its drudgeries, pressures, and solitudes, but Cambridge ultimately afforded him a few new friendships and a permanent sanctuary. After a Grand Tour of Europe, undertaken in Walpole's company (the two men quarreled en route, after which they were estranged for five years), Gray returned to the university, ostensibly to learn law, but in fact to pursue his own private program of study. He read widely, copiously, and systematically in many subjects (botany, zoology, and music, as well as literature and history), making himself one of the most learned scholars alive, and eventually becoming (in 1768) Regius Professor of Modern History. He never delivered a lecture, and continued to spend much of his time alone reading, but thoroughgoing privacy had long ceased to be an option. In his late thirties, Gray had stumbled, reluctantly, into enormous poetic fame. He had written Latin verse when young; in 1742, the year his beloved West died of tuberculosis, he commenced English poetry in earnest. Some of his labor's early fruits bespeak an insistent sense of loss: a sonnet on West's death (never printed during the poet's lifetime); the *Ode on a Distant Prospect of Eton College,* in which the distance is one of time as well as space; and the *Elegy,* whose completion took five years or more and whose publication in 1751 (a "distress" the poet had hoped to avoid) brought upon Gray an instantaneous, massive, and baffling celebrity. As if in recoil, he veered onto an alternate poetic path, carefully crafting over the ensuing years a set of intricate Pindaric odes, including *The Bard* and *The Progress of Poesy;* the two poems were printed, on Walpole's own press, in 1757. They provoked both admiration, as a new embodiment of poetic sublimity, and derision, as gratuitously labored, showily obscure. In the years following their murky reception, Gray wrote only a few poems and published none. He pursued other studies (including Norse literature); fell in love one final time; and died abruptly, mourned deeply by his friends and widely by a public whose thoughts and feelings about death itself he had done much to shape. In one early version of the *Elegy* the line about silence appears as an admonition addressed by the poet to himself: "Pursue the silent tenor of thy doom." In his letters (published posthumously) and in his poems, Gray worked for that doom a delicate but decisive reversal.

Sonnet on the Death of Mr. Richard West[1]

In vain to me the smiling mornings shine,
And redd'ning Phoebus lifts his golden fire:
The birds in vain their amorous descant join,
Or cheerful fields resume their green attire:
These ears, alas! for other notes repine,
A different object do these eyes require.
My lonely anguish melts no heart but mine;
And in my breast the imperfect joys expire.
Yet morning smiles the busy race to cheer,
And new-born pleasure brings to happier men;
The fields to all their wonted tribute bear;
To warm their little loves the birds complain.

1. West had died of tuberculosis on 1 June 1742, at age 25. Gray composed this sonnet the following August, and in the same month wrote the ode that follows.

I fruitless mourn to him that cannot hear,
And weep the more because I weep in vain.

1742 1775

Ode on a Distant Prospect of Eton College[1]

Ye distant spires, ye antique towers,
That crown the wat'ry glade,
Where grateful Science° still adores *knowledge*
Her Henry's holy shade;[2]
And ye, that from the stately brow
Of Windsor's heights[3] th' expanse below
Of grove, of lawn, of mead survey,
Whose turf, whose shade, whose flowers among
Wanders the hoary Thames along
His silver-winding way.

Ah happy hills, ah, pleasing shade,
Ah, fields beloved in vain,
Where once my careless childhood strayed,
A stranger yet to pain!
I feel the gales, that from ye blow,
A momentary bliss bestow,
As waving fresh their gladsome wing,
My weary soul they seem to soothe,
And, redolent of joy and youth,
To breathe a second spring.

Say, Father Thames, for thou hast seen
Full many a sprightly race
Disporting on thy margent° green *margin*
The paths of pleasure trace,
Who foremost now delight to cleave
With pliant arm thy glassy wave?
The captive linnet which enthrall?
What idle progeny succeed
To chase the rolling circle's speed,[4]
Or urge the flying ball?

While some on earnest business bent
Their murm'ring labors ply
'Gainst graver hours, that bring constraint
To sweeten liberty:
Some bold adventurers disdain
The limits of their little reign,

1. One of England's oldest and most eminent schools for boys (founded 1440); Gray had attended from 1725 to 1734.
2. The ghost ("shade") of Henry VI (1421–1471), the school's founder.
3. The college is located within the borough of Windsor, on the river Thames.
4. A children's game involving a hoop.

And unknown regions dare descry:
Still as they run they look behind,
They hear a voice in every wind,
And snatch a fearful joy.

Gay hope is theirs by fancy fed,
Less pleasing when possessed;
The tear forgot as soon as shed,
The sunshine of the breast:
Theirs buxom° health of rosy hue, *lively*
Wild wit, invention ever-new,
And lively cheer of vigor born;
The thoughtless day, the easy night,
The spirits pure, the slumbers light,
That fly th' approach of morn.

Alas, regardless of their doom,
The little victims play!
No sense have they of ills to come,
Nor care beyond today:
Yet see how all around 'em wait
The ministers of human fate,
And black Misfortune's baleful train!° *attendants*
Ah, shew them where in ambush stand
To seize their prey the murth'rous° band! *murderous*
Ah, tell them, they are men!

These shall the fury Passions tear,
The vultures of the mind,
Disdainful Anger, pallid Fear,
And Shame that skulks behind;
Or pining Love shall waste their youth,
Or Jealousy with rankling tooth,
That inly gnaws the secret heart,
And Envy wan, and faded Care,
Grim-visaged comfortless Despair,
And Sorrow's piercing dart.

Ambition this shall tempt to rise,
Then whirl the wretch from high,
To bitter Scorn a sacrifice,
And grinning Infamy.
The stings of Falsehood those shall try,
And hard Unkindness' altered eye,
That mocks the tear it forced to flow;
And keen Remorse with blood defiled,
And moody Madness laughing wild
Amid severest woe.

Lo, in the vale of years beneath
A grisly troop are seen,

The painful family of Death,
More hideous than their Queen:
This racks the joints, this fires the veins,
That every laboring sinew strains,
Those in the deeper vitals rage:
Lo, Poverty, to fill the band,
That numbs the soul with icy hand,
And slow-consuming Age.

To each his suff'rings: all are men,
Condemned alike to groan;
The tender for another's pain;
Th' unfeeling for his own.
Yet ah! why should they know their fate?
Since sorrow never comes too late,
And happiness too swiftly flies.
Thought would destroy their paradise.
No more; where ignorance is bliss,
'Tis folly to be wise.

1742 1747

Ode on the Death of a Favorite Cat, Drowned in a Tub of Gold Fishes[1]

'Twas on a lofty vase's side,
Where China's gayest art had dyed
The azure flowers, that blow;° *blossom*
Demurest of the tabby kind,
The pensive Selima reclined,
Gazed on the lake below.

Her conscious tail her joy declared;
The fair round face, the snowy beard,
The velvet of her paws,
Her coat, that with the tortoise vies,
Her ears of jet, and emerald eyes,
She saw; and purred applause.

Still had she gazed; but 'midst the tide
Two angel forms were seen to glide,
The genii° of the stream: *protective deities*
Their scaly armor's Tyrian hue[2]
Through richest purple to the view
Betrayed a golden gleam.

1. The cat had belonged to Walpole, who asked Gray to write her an epitaph. Gray sent something more substantial: "There's a poem for you; it is rather too long for an epitaph." Walpole admired the ode so much that he saw to its publication and had the first stanza inscribed on the "tub" itself—actually a china vase, which Walpole enshrined on a pedestal and displayed at his home, Strawberry Hill, where it still stands.

2. A deep purple dye made from mollusks, prized by the ancients as a mark of luxury.

The hapless nymph with wonder saw:
A whisker first and then a claw,
With many an ardent wish,
She stretched in vain to reach the prize.
What female heart can gold despise?
What cat's averse to fish?

Presumptuous maid! with looks intent
Again she stretched, again she bent,
Nor knew the gulf between.
(Malignant Fate sat by and smiled)
The slippery verge her feet beguiled,
She tumbled headlong in.

Eight times emerging from the flood
She mewed to ev'ry wat'ry God,
Some speedy aid to send.
No dolphin came,[3] no Nereid° stirred: *water-nymph*
Nor cruel Tom, nor Susan heard.
A favorite has no friend!

From hence, ye beauties, undeceived,
Know, one false step is ne'er retrieved,
And be with caution bold.
Not all that tempts your wandering eyes
And heedless hearts, is lawful prize;
Nor all that glisters,° gold. *glitters*

1747 1748

Elegy Written in a Country Churchyard

The curfew tolls the knell of parting day,
The lowing herd wind slowly o'er the lea,
The plowman homeward plods his weary way,
And leaves the world to darkness and to me.

Now fades the glimmering landscape on the sight,
And all the air a solemn stillness holds,
Save where the beetle wheels his droning flight,
And drowsy tinklings lull the distant folds;

Save that from yonder ivy-mantled tower
The moping owl does to the moon complain
Of such as, wand'ring near her secret bower,
Molest her ancient solitary reign.

Beneath those rugged elms, that yew-tree's shade,
Where heaves the turf in many a mouldering heap,
Each in his narrow cell for ever laid,
The rude forefathers of the hamlet sleep.

3. As did the dolphin who, in Greek mythology, rescued the drowning poet Arion.

The breezy call of incense-breathing morn,
The swallow twitt'ring from the straw-built shed,
The cock's shrill clarion, or the echoing horn,
No more shall rouse them from their lowly bed.

For them no more the blazing hearth shall burn,
Or busy housewife ply her evening care:
No children run to lisp their sire's return,
Or climb his knees the envied kiss to share.

Oft did the harvest to their sickle yield,
Their furrow oft the stubborn glebe° has broke; *clod of earth*
How jocund did they drive their team afield!
How bowed the woods beneath their sturdy stroke!

Let not Ambition mock their useful toil,
Their homely joys, and destiny obscure;
Nor Grandeur hear, with a disdainful smile,
The short and simple annals of the poor.

The boast of heraldry, the pomp of power,
And all that beauty, all that wealth e'er gave,
Awaits alike th' inevitable hour.
The paths of glory lead but to the grave.

Nor you, ye Proud, impute to these the fault,
If Mem'ry o'er their tomb no trophies raise,
Where through the long-drawn aisle and fretted vault
The pealing anthem swells the note of praise.

Can storied urn or animated bust
Back to its mansion call the fleeting breath?
Can Honor's voice provoke the silent dust,
Or Flatt'ry soothe the dull cold ear of Death?

Perhaps in this neglected spot is laid
Some heart once pregnant with celestial fire;
Hands that the rod of empire might have swayed,
Or waked to ecstasy the living lyre.

But Knowledge to their eyes her ample page
Rich with the spoils of time did ne'er unroll;
Chill Penury repressed their noble rage,
And froze the genial current of the soul.

Full many a gem of purest ray serene,
The dark unfathomed caves of ocean bear:
Full many a flower is born to blush unseen,
And waste its sweetness on the desert air.

Some village-Hampden[1] that with dauntless breast
The little tyrant of his fields withstood;

1. John Hampden (1594–1643), parliamentary statesman and general in the Civil Wars, famed for his firm defiance of Charles I.

Some mute inglorious Milton here may rest,
Some Cromwell guiltless of his country's blood.

Th' applause of listening senates to command,
The threats of pain and ruin to despise,
To scatter plenty o'er a smiling land,
And read their history in a nation's eyes,

Their lot forbade: nor circumscribed alone
Their growing virtues, but their crimes confined;
Forbade to wade through slaughter to a throne,
And shut the gates of mercy on mankind,

The struggling pangs of conscious truth to hide,
To quench the blushes of ingenuous shame,
Or heap the shrine of Luxury and Pride
With incense kindled at the Muse's flame.[2]

Far from the madding crowd's ignoble strife,
Their sober wishes never learned to stray;
Along the cool sequestered vale of life
They kept the noiseless tenor of their way.

Yet ev'n these bones from insult to protect
Some frail memorial still erected nigh,
With uncouth rhymes and shapeless sculpture decked,
Implores the passing tribute of a sigh.

Their name, their years, spelt by th' unlettered muse,
The place of fame and elegy supply:
And many a holy text around she strews,
That teach the rustic moralist to die.

For who to dumb Forgetfulness a prey,
This pleasing anxious being e'er resigned,
Left the warm precincts of the cheerful day,
Nor cast one longing ling'ring look behind?

On some fond breast the parting soul relies,
Some pious drops the closing eye requires;
Ev'n from the tomb the voice of nature cries,
Ev'n in our ashes live their wonted fires.

2. According to Gray's friend William Mason, the poem originally concluded at this juncture with the following four stanzas, preserved in a manuscript at Eton College:

The thoughtless world to majesty may bow
Exalt the brave, and idolize success,
But more to innocence their safety owe
Than power and genius e'er conspired to bless.

And thou, who mindful of the unhonored dead
Dost in these notes their artless tale relate
By night and lonely contemplation led
To linger in the gloomy walks of fate,

Hark how the sacred calm, that broods around
Bids ev'ry fierce tumultuous passion cease
In still small accents whisp'ring from the ground
A grateful earnest of eternal peace.

No more with reason and thyself at strife;
Give anxious cares and endless wishes room
But through the cool sequestered vale of life
Pursue the silent tenor of thy doom.

For thee, who mindful of th' unhonored dead
Dost in these lines their artless tale relate;
If chance, by lonely Contemplation led,
Some kindred spirit shall inquire thy fate,

Haply some hoary-headed swain may say,
"Oft have we seen him at the peep of dawn
Brushing with hasty steps the dews away
To meet the sun upon the upland lawn.

"There at the foot of yonder nodding beech
That wreathes its old fantastic roots so high,
His listless length at noontide would he stretch,
And pore upon the brook that babbles by.

"Hard by yon wood, now smiling as in scorn,
Mutt'ring his wayward fancies he would rove,
Now drooping, woeful wan, like one forlorn,
Or crazed with care, or crossed in hopeless love.

"One morn I missed him on the 'customed hill,
Along the heath and near his favorite tree;
Another came; nor yet beside the rill,
Nor up the lawn, nor at the wood was he;

"The next with dirges due in sad array
Slow through the church-way path we saw him borne.
Approach and read (for thou can'st read) the lay,
Graved on the stone beneath yon aged thorn."

The Epitaph

Here rests his head upon the lap of earth
A youth to fortune and to fame unknown.
Fair Science frowned not on his humble birth,
And Melancholy marked him for her own.

Large was his bounty, and his soul sincere,
Heaven did a recompense as largely send:
He gave to Mis'ry all he had, a tear,
He gained from Heav'n ('twas all he wished) a friend.

No farther seek his merits to disclose,
Or draw his frailties from their dread abode,
(There they alike in trembling hope repose)
The bosom of his Father and his God.

1746–1750 1751

Samuel Johnson
1709–1784

James Barry, *Samuel Johnson.*

Samuel Johnson was born among books—his father sold them, not very successfully, at the family's combined home and shop in the market town of Lichfield. The son went on to create some of the most celebrated books of his age: an entire *Dictionary*, an edition of Shakespeare, a travel book, philosophical fictions, two eminent series of essays, a thick cluster of biographies. Despite his output, Johnson suffered from a chronic sense that he was underusing his talent, and throughout his *oeuvre* he wrote about "human unsuccess" (in W. H. Auden's phrase) with an empathy and acuity that few have matched before or since.

Johnson's struggles began early. An infection in infancy, followed by an attack of scrofula at age two, left his face scarred and his sight and hearing permanently impaired; by the age of eight a nervous disorder, probably Tourette's syndrome, brought on the compulsive gesticulations and intermittent muttering that would afflict him throughout his life, making him appear bizarre or even repellent at first encounter—until (as many testified) the stunning moment when he would begin to speak. His impressiveness had begun early, too. In childhood, the speed with which he acquired knowledge and the force with which he retained it astonished classmates and teachers, and also his parents, whose desire to show off his attainments often made him miserable. Johnson found more congenial mentors in his cousin, the rakish but learned young clergyman Cornelius Ford, at whose home he spent about half a year at age sixteen, and in Gilbert Walmesley, a middle-aged Lichfield lawyer, who welcomed Johnson often to his ample table and to the intelligent, disputatious company there assembled. Under Ford's and Walmesley's influence, Johnson undertook an intense but improvisatory program of reading, mostly in his father's shop. He read with a ferocious concentration that locked the texts into lifelong memory. "In this irregular manner," he later recalled, "I had looked into a great many books, which were not commonly known at the university, where they seldom read any books but what are put into their hands by their tutors; so that when I came to Oxford, Dr. Adams, now master of Pembroke College, told me, I was the best qualified for the university that he had ever known come there."

Despite such qualifications, Johnson's time at Oxford ushered in not triumph but frustration, and an oppressive sense of failure. Though he continued to be admired for his reading, and began to be noted for his writing, Johnson left the university after only thirteen months, "miserably poor" and unable to pay the fees, unbearably depressed and incapable of envisioning a viable future. After a melancholy year at home, during which his father died in debt, Johnson tried his hand at a variety of jobs beneath his earlier expectations: as assistant at a grammar school (he applied for three such positions, secured one, and left it in disgust after six months), and as occasional contributor to *The Birmingham Journal*. At Birmingham, he befriended the merchant Harry Porter and his wife Elizabeth ("Tetty"); she saw past his awkwardness at their first encounter, remarking to her daughter, "This is the most sensible man that I ever saw in my life." In 1735, ten months after her husband's death, she and Johnson married, despite wariness in both families at their difference in age (she was twenty years his senior). The new husband and wife tried to start a country boarding school, but it attracted only a handful of students. Early in 1737, Johnson decided to try something new: the life of a freelance writer in London.

The generic term for such a life was "Grub Street": it identified both an actual London street where some writers lived and plied their trade, and also the painful state of mind in which almost all of them did so, eking out precarious incomes from whatever assignments they could drum up. From the first, Johnson fared a little better than most. He attached himself immediately to Edward Cave, founder of the flourishing *Gentleman's Magazine*, in which Johnson's writing appeared plentifully over the next decade: essays, poems, short biographies, reviews, and voluminous, ingeniously fictionalized reports of debates in Parliament (authentic transcriptions were prohibited by law). The work provided some security but no prosperity: Johnson and his wife lived in poverty for many years. The struggle fueled articulate rage: in his poem *London* (1738), Johnson inveighed against the corruption of Robert Walpole's government and the cruelties of the city. Among his Grub Street colleagues he found a friend who, far more than himself, had made a sense of injury the basis of both life and art. The poet Richard Savage, generous, brilliant, and unstable, believed himself the abandoned offspring of a wealthy countess, and squandered much of his short life in the vain pursuit of recognition and redress. In *The Life of Richard Savage* (1744), published soon after his friend's early death, Johnson for the first time orchestrated many of the elements that would make his own work great: a commitment to biographical precision rather than routine panegyric; an analysis of expectation, self-delusion, and disappointment; a deep sympathy combined with nuanced judgment.

Savage was a memoir of Grub Street, but not yet for Johnson a valedictory. For two more years he continued his life of anonymous publication, narrow income, and declining spirits—"lost," as a friend lamented, "both to himself and the world." Then a new project found him. In 1746, the bookseller Robert Dodsley, struck by the erudition evident in Johnson's unsigned pieces, persuaded him to create a new dictionary of English, and assembled a consortium of publishers to finance (and profit from) the enormous undertaking. Johnson and his wife promptly moved from cramped and squalid quarters to a three-story house complete with a well-lit garret. There, with the help of six part-time assistants, Johnson made his lexicon, compiling word lists, tracking shifts and gradations of meaning, devising definitions, and illustrating them with quotations culled from the authors he most admired. The writer who (as Adam Smith later testified) "knew more books than any man alive" now decanted them discriminatingly into the two folio volumes of his *Dictionary* (1755), so as to make the work not only a standard reference for the language but also a compendium of its literature and its learning. The task took Johnson longer than he had anticipated—seven years, not three—but during this span he had busied himself in other ways as well: publishing *The Vanity of Human Wishes* (1749), a long poem on the pain of disillusion; witnessing the long-postponed production of his tragedy *Irene* (which brought him welcome added income); and composing, twice a week for two years, the periodical essay called *The Rambler* (1750–1752), the most formidable and famous instance of the genre since Addison and Steele had set down the *Spectator* forty years before. Johnson had embarked on the *Dictionary* as a virtual unknown; he emerged from the project with lasting fame and a double measure of celebratory sobriquets: he was widely known as "Dictionary Johnson," and was sometimes referred to simply (without surname) as "the Rambler."

As an epitome of his character the second label was perhaps more apt. A restlessness closely connected with loneliness had marked Johnson's mind since childhood. During the years of the *Dictionary*'s making, the loneliness had deepened. In 1752 Tetty died, and despite the strains in a marriage that had been differently difficult for both of them, Johnson mourned her obsessively for the rest of his days. He also contrived new sources of companionship, at home and in the wider world. He housed under his roof a group of eccentric, often difficult characters, including the ungainly man of medicine Robert Levet; the Jamaican servant Francis Barber; the blind Anna Williams, who waited up late every night to keep him company in his final cup of tea, often after he had spent long hours in more elevated society. He established what amounted to a second residence in the more polished household of the brewer Henry Thrale and his witty wife Hester, who welcomed and pampered not only Johnson but also the accomplished people who now rejoiced to rotate in his orbit: the actor David Garrick (who had been his pupil in the failed school and his companion on the road to London); the painter Joshua Reynolds; the politician and orator Edmund Burke; the writer Oliver Goldsmith; and Johnson's ardent young protégé and future biographer James Boswell. At the Thrales's country seat, and at the London clubs he formed to stave off solitude, Johnson sat surrounded by luminaries, savoring and often dominating the conversation. He talked (as Boswell noted) "for victory," and he generally secured it by a kind of surprise attack, a witty demolition of his companions' most familiar premises and casual assumptions. He won his listeners over by texture as well as text: by the spontaneous clarity and force of his utterance (as lexicographer he had defined every word he spoke); by the depth and energy of his voice.

Writing was by contrast largely solitary. Johnson's work pattern in the decade after the *Dictionary* recapitulated that of the one before: one ambitious, overarching project—this time an edition of all Shakespeare's plays (1765)—punctuated by shorter writings of lasting significance: a new periodical essay called *The Idler* (1758–1760); the philosophical tale *Rasselas, Prince of Abyssinia* (1759). In 1762 Johnson received a royal pension from George III in recognition of the *Dictionary*, assuring him an income of £300 a year for the remainder of his life. The pension brought Johnson a new security, along with the occasional accusation that his subsequent political pamphlets, generally favorable to the regime, amounted to paid propaganda. In fact, Johnson's politics throughout his life correlated fairly well with the views he implicitly espoused in the distinction he once drew for Boswell: "The prejudice of the Tory is for establishment; the prejudice of the Whig is for innovation." Born into a world where Whigs had long prevailed, Johnson early committed himself to Tory ways of thought: he cherished precedent, defended "subordination" (social hierarchy), and opposed Whiggish innovation with seriocomic fervor. What remained most notable about his politics was their compassion. "From first to last," John Wain remarks, Johnson "rooted his life among the poor and outcast"; in his work he argued the causes of prostitutes and slaves, of anyone sunk by the "want of necessaries" into "motionless despondence."

In the wake of his pension, Johnson's writing grew sparser, and markedly more social, compassing gestures to and for people he valued. He continued an ingrained habit of churning out prose for his friends to use under their own names: dictating law briefs for lawyers, composing sermons for preachers. He carried on an abundant and affectionate correspondence with Hester Thrale. With Boswell as companion, he traveled to the Scottish Highlands, and on his return published his account of that gregarious trip, *A Journey to the Western Islands* (1775). His final large work was social in a different sense. He accepted a commission to provide *Prefaces Biographical and Critical* for an anthology of English poets of the past hundred and fifty years. These included predecessors who had influenced him, contemporaries he had known, successors he regarded with admiration or alarm. To write their biographies, to analyze their works, was in a sense to live over his own literary life, and to reenter, at length and for the last time, the world of reading and of writing in which he'd now made his way for almost seven decades.

"Our social comforts drop away," Johnson lamented when his friend Levet died in 1782; his own last years were marred by loss. Successive deaths shrunk his contentious household; his friendship with Hester Thrale disintegrated under the pressure of her passion for a man of whom Johnson disapproved; a stroke temporarily deprived him of speech and ushered in his final difficult illness. At his death, an admirer remarked that Johnson had left "a chasm, which not only nothing can fill up, but which nothing has a tendency to fill up. Johnson is dead. Let us go to the next best:—there is nobody: no man can be said to put you in mind of Johnson." Biographers rushed in to fill the chasm, with the testimony of friends and of detractors, and with transcriptions of the hypnotic talk that many of them (notably Boswell and Thrale) had begun to record decades before. For most of the nineteenth century the fame of Johnson's talk far surpassed that of his writing. In recent decades scholars and readers have redressed the balance, finding in Johnson's prose and verse the richest repositories of his thought. Throughout a life of arduous struggle, prodigious accomplishment, and (in the end) near-matchless celebrity, Johnson wrote most eloquently and most feelingly—even in the *Dictionary*, even in literary criticism—of human vulnerabilities: to hope and disappointment, suffering and loss.

For additional resources on Johnson, go to *The Longman Anthology of British Literature* Web site at www.myliteraturekit.com.

The Vanity of Human Wishes In his *Life of Pope*, Johnson defines the imitation, a poetic form much in vogue during the late seventeenth and early eighteenth centuries, as a "mode . . . in which the ancients are familiarized by adapting their sentiments to modern topics. . . . It is a kind of middle composition between translation and original design, which pleases when the thoughts are unexpectedly applicable and the parallels lucky." *The Vanity of Human Wishes* is Johnson's most sustained and successful endeavor in the mode. In the second century C.E., the Roman poet Juvenal had written an enduring satire on human ambition and failure, drawing vivid instances from history and from contemporary life. Johnson does the same, replacing the Roman's ancient examples with modern ones, supplanting his Stoic "sentiments" with a Christian credo. Johnson produced his imitation quickly, composing the whole of it in his mind before writing any of it down. It was the first work to appear under his own name, after more than a decade of abundant but anonymous publications. Its title and text sound themes that would preoccupy him for the remainder of his writing life: the dangers of desire, the inevitability of disappointment, the necessity of faith. *The Vanity of Human Wishes* is Johnson's signature poem in more ways than one.

The Vanity of Human Wishes
The Tenth Satire of Juvenal Imitated

Let Observation, with extensive view,
Survey mankind, from China to Peru;
Remark each anxious toil, each eager strife,
And watch the busy scenes of crowded life;
Then say how hope and fear, desire and hate,
O'erspread with snares the clouded maze of fate,
Where wav'ring man, betrayed by vent'rous pride,
To tread the dreary paths without a guide,
As treach'rous phantoms in the mist delude,
Shuns fancied ills, or chases airy[1] good;
How rarely reason guides the stubborn choice,
Rules the bold hand, or prompts the suppliant voice;
How nations sink, by darling schemes oppressed,
When vengeance listens to the fool's request.
Fate wings with every wish th' afflictive dart,
Each gift of nature, and each grace of art,
With fatal heat impetuous courage glows,

1. "Wanting reality; having no steady foundation in truth or nature" (Johnson's *Dictionary*).

With fatal sweetness elocution flows,
Impeachment stops the speaker's pow'rful breath,
And restless fire precipitates on death.
  But scarce observed, the knowing and the bold
Fall in the gen'ral massacre of gold;
Wide-wasting pest! that rages unconfined,
And crowds with crimes the records of mankind;
For gold his sword the hireling ruffian draws,
For gold the hireling judge distorts the laws;
Wealth heaped on wealth, nor truth nor safety buys,
The dangers gather as the treasures rise.
  Let hist'ry tell where rival kings command,
And dubious title shakes the madded land,
When statutes° glean the refuse of the sword, *tax laws*
How much more safe the vassal than the lord;
Low skulks the hind° beneath the rage of pow'r, *rural laborer*
And leaves the wealthy traitor in the Tow'r,[2]
Untouched his cottage, and his slumbers sound,
Though confiscation's vultures hover round.
  The needy traveler, secure and gay,
Walks the wild heath, and sings his toil away.
Does envy seize thee? crush th' upbraiding joy,
Increase his riches and his peace destroy;
Now fears in dire vicissitude invade,
The rustling brake° alarms, and quiv'ring shade, *thicket*
Nor light nor darkness bring his pain relief,
One shows the plunder, and one hides the thief.
  Yet still one gen'ral cry the skies assails,
And gain and grandeur load the tainted gales;
Few know the toiling statesman's fear or care,
Th' insidious rival and the gaping heir.
  Once more, Democritus,[3] arise on earth,
With cheerful wisdom and instructive mirth,
See motley[4] life in modern trappings dressed,
And feed with varied fools th' eternal jest:
Thou who couldst laugh where want enchained caprice,
Toil crushed conceit, and man was of a piece;
Where wealth unloved without a mourner died,
And scarce a sycophant was fed by pride;
Where ne'er was known the form of mock debate,
Or seen a new-made mayor's unwieldy state;
Where change of fav'rites made no change of laws,
And senates heard before they judged a cause;
How wouldst thou shake at Britain's modish tribe,
Dart the quick taunt, and edge the piercing gibe?
Attentive truth and nature to descry,° *discern*

2. The Tower of London.
3. Ancient Greek philosopher who laughed at the follies of humanity.
4. Multicolored clothes worn by jesters.

And pierce each scene with philosophic eye.
To thee were solemn toys or empty show,
The robes of pleasure and the veils of woe:
All aid the farce, and all thy mirth maintain,
Whose joys are causeless, or whose griefs are vain.
Such was the scorn that filled the sage's mind,
Renewed at ev'ry glance on humankind;
How just that scorn ere yet thy voice declare,
Search every state, and canvass every prayer.
Unnumbered suppliants crowd Preferment's gate,
Athirst for wealth, and burning to be great;
Delusive Fortune hears th' incessant call,
They mount, they shine, evaporate, and fall.[5]
On every stage the foes of peace attend,
Hate dogs their flight, and insult mocks their end.
Love ends with hope, the sinking statesman's door
Pours in the morning worshiper no more;
For growing names the weekly scribbler lies,
To growing wealth the dedicator flies,
From ev'ry room descends the painted face,
That hung the bright Palladium[6] of the place,
And smoked in kitchens, or in auctions sold,
To better features yields the frame of gold;
For now no more we trace in ev'ry line
Heroic worth, benevolence divine:
The form distorted justifies the fall,
And detestation rids th' indignant wall.
But will not Britain hear the last appeal,
Sign her foes' doom, or guard her fav'rites' zeal?
Through Freedom's sons no more remonstrance rings,
Degrading nobles and controlling kings;
Our supple tribes° repress their patriot throats, *of voters*
And ask no questions but the price of votes;
With weekly libels and septennial ale,[7]
Their wish is full to riot and to rail.
In full-blown dignity, see Wolsey[8] stand,
Law in his voice, and fortune in his hand:
To him the church, the realm, their pow'rs consign,
Through him the rays of regal bounty shine,
Turned by his nod the stream of honor flows,
His smile alone security bestows:
Still to new heights his restless wishes tow'r,
Claim leads to claim, and pow'r advances pow'r;
Till conquest unresisted ceased to please,

5. The image is that of Fortune's wheel.
6. A statue of Pallas Athena, guardian of Troy.
7. Drink offered to voters as bribes during campaigns for Parliament, held every seven years.
8. Cardinal Wolsey (1475–1530), Henry VIII's Lord Chancellor, who was dismissed and imprisoned for failing to procure the King a divorce from Catherine of Aragon.

And rights submitted, left him none to seize.
At length his sov'reign frowns—the train of state
Mark the keen glance, and watch the sign to hate.
Wheree'er he turns he meets a stranger's eye,
His suppliants scorn him, and his followers fly;
At once is lost the pride of awful state,
The golden canopy, the glitt'ring plate,
The regal palace, the luxurious board,
The liv'ried army, and the menial lord.
With age, with cares, with maladies oppressed,
He seeks the refuge of monastic rest.
Grief aids disease, remembered folly stings,
And his last sighs reproach the faith of kings.
Speak thou, whose thoughts at humble peace repine,
Shall Wolsey's wealth, with Wolsey's end be thine?
Or liv'st thou now, with safer pride content,
The wisest justice on the banks of Trent?[9]
For why did Wolsey near the steeps° of fate, *precipices*
On weak foundations raise th' enormous weight?
Why but to sink beneath misfortune's blow,
With louder ruin to the gulfs below?
What gave great Villiers[1] to th' assassin's knife,
And fixed disease on Harley's[2] closing life?
What murdered Wentworth, and what exiled Hyde,[3]
By kings protected, and to kings allied?
What but their wish indulged in courts to shine,
And pow'r too great to keep, or to resign?
When first the college rolls receive his name,
The young enthusiast[4] quits his ease for fame;
Through all his veins the fever of renown
Burns from the strong contagion of the gown;[5]
O'er Bodley's dome[6] his future labors spread,
And Bacon's mansion[7] trembles o'er his head.
Are these thy views? proceed, illustrious youth,
And virtue guard thee to the throne of Truth!
Yet should thy soul indulge the gen'rous heat,
Till captive Science° yields her last retreat; *knowledge*
Should Reason guide thee with her brightest ray,
And pour on misty Doubt resistless day;

9. The river that divides northern from southern England; it is near Lichfield, Johnson's birthplace.
1. George Villiers (1592–1628), first Duke of Buckingham and a favorite of James I, was stabbed to death.
2. Robert Harley (1661–1724), first Earl of Oxford and leading statesman during the reign of Queen Anne, was impeached when George I succeeded to the throne in 1714.
3. Thomas Wentworth (1593–1641), first Earl of Strafford and adviser to Charles I, was executed at the beginning of the English Civil War. Edward Hyde (1609–1674), first Earl of Clarendon, served Charles II but then fell from favor.
4. "One of hot imagination" (Johnson's *Dictionary*).
5. Scholastic dress (but also a reference to the poisoned garment that killed Hercules).
6. The Bodleian Library, Oxford.
7. "There is a tradition, that the study of friar Bacon [Roger Bacon, a medieval philosopher] built an arch over the bridge, will fall, when a man greater than Bacon shall pass under it" [Johnson's note].

Should no false Kindness lure to loose delight,
Nor Praise relax, nor Difficulty fright;
Should tempting Novelty thy cell refrain,
And Sloth effuse her opiate fumes in vain;
Should Beauty blunt on fops her fatal dart,
Nor claim the triumph of a lettered heart;
Should no disease thy torpid veins invade,
Nor Melancholy's phantoms haunt thy shade;
Yet hope not life from grief or danger free,
Nor think the doom of man reversed for thee:
Deign on the passing world to turn thine eyes,
And pause awhile from letters, to be wise;
There mark what ills the scholar's life assail,
Toil, envy, want, the patron,[8] and the jail.
See nations slowly wise, and meanly just,
To buried merit raise the tardy bust.
If dreams yet flatter, once again attend,
Hear Lydiat's life, and Galileo's end.[9]
   Nor deem, when learning her last prize bestows,
The glitt'ring eminence exempt from foes;
See when the vulgar 'scape, despised or awed,
Rebellion's vengeful talons seize on Laud.[1]
From meaner minds, though smaller fines content,
The plundered palace or sequestered rent;
Marked out by dangerous parts° he meets the shock, *abilities*
And fatal Learning leads him to the block:
Around his tomb let Art and Genius weep,
But hear his death, ye blockheads, hear and sleep.
   The festal blazes, the triumphal show,
The ravished standard, and the captive foe,
The senate's thanks, the gazette's pompous tale,
With force resistless o'er the brave prevail.
Such bribes the rapid Greek[2] o'er Asia whirled,
For such the steady Romans shook the world;
For such in distant lands the Britons shine,
And stain with blood the Danube or the Rhine;
This pow'r has praise, that virtue scarce can warm,
Till fame supplies the universal charm.
Yet Reason frowns on War's unequal game,
Where wasted nations raise a single name,
And mortgaged states their grandsires' wreaths[3] regret,
From age to age in everlasting debt;
Wreaths which at last the dear-bought right convey

8. Johnson originally wrote "garret," but changed it to "patron" after enduring the neglect of Lord Chesterfield (see his letter to Chesterfield, page 2744).

9. Thomas Lydiat (1572–1646) was a distinguished but impoverished mathematician. The astronomer Galileo Galilei (1564–1642) was silenced by the Inquisition.

1. William Laud (1572–1645), Archbishop of Canterbury under Charles I, was beheaded by the Parliamentarians.

2. Alexander the Great.

3. Garlands of victory.

To rust on medals, or on stones decay.
   On what foundation stands the warrior's pride,
How just his hopes let Swedish Charles[4] decide;
A frame of adamant, a soul of fire,
No dangers fright him, and no labors tire;
O'er love, o'er fear, extends his wide domain,
Unconquered lord of pleasure and of pain;
No joys to him pacific scepters yield,
War sounds the trump, he rushes to the field;
Behold surrounding kings their pow'r combine,
And one capitulate, and one resign;
Peace courts his hand, but spreads her charms in vain;
"Think nothing gained," he cries, "till nought remain,
On Moscow's walls till Gothic standards fly,
And all be mine beneath the polar sky."
The march begins in military state,
And nations on his eye suspended wait;
Stern Famine guards the solitary coast,
And Winter barricades the realms of Frost;
He comes, not want and cold his course delay—
Hide, blushing Glory, hide Pultowa's day:
The vanquished hero leaves his broken bands,
And shows his miseries in distant lands;
Condemned a needy supplicant to wait,
While ladies interpose, and slaves debate.
But did not Chance at length her error mend?
Did no subverted empire mark his end?
Did rival monarchs give the fatal wound?
Or hostile millions press him to the ground?
His fall was destined to a barren strand,
A petty fortress, and a dubious hand;[5]
He left the name, at which the world grew pale,
To point a moral, or adorn a tale.
   All times their scenes of pompous woes afford,
From Persia's tyrant[6] to Bavaria's lord.[7]
In gay hostility, and barb'rous pride,
With half mankind embattled at his side,
Great Xerxes comes to seize the certain prey,
And starves exhausted regions in his way;
Attendant Flattery counts his myriads o'er,
Till counted myriads soothe his pride no more;

4. Charles XII of Sweden, whose precarious military career ended at the Battle of Pultowa (1709). After his defeat by the Russians, Charles attempted to forge an alliance with the Turks.

5. Charles XII of Sweden was thought to have been killed by one of his own officers during a siege of little military consequence.

6. Xerxes (?519–465 B.C.E.) invaded Greece with a large army and navy. In order to transport his troops, he built a bridge of boats across the Hellespont. When a storm broke up this bridge, Xerxes ordered the wind and water to be punished. The Persian army was defeated at the Battle of Plataea, the navy at the Battle of Salamis.

7. Charles Albert (1697–1745), Elector of Bavaria, was defeated by Empress Maria Theresa, whose army included Austrian colonists from Croatia and Hungarian cavalry called "jussars."

Fresh praise is tried till madness fires his mind,
The waves he lashes, and enchains the wind;
New pow'rs are claimed, new pow'rs are still bestowed,
Till rude resistance lops the spreading god;
The daring Greeks deride the martial show,
And heap heir valleys with the gaudy foe;
Th' insulted sea with humbler thoughts he gains,
A single skiff to speed his ligh remains;
Th' encumbered oar scarce leaves the dreaded coast
Through purple billows and a floating host.
  The bold Bavarian, in a luckless hour,
Tries the dread summits of Cesarean power,
With unexpected legions bursts away,
And sees defenseless realms receive his sway;
Short sway! fair Austria spreads her mournful charms,
The queen, the beauty, sets the world in arms;
From hill to hill the beacon's rousing blaze
Spreads wide the hope of plunder and of praise;
The fierce Croatian, and the wild Hussar,
And all the sons of ravage crowd the war;
The baffled prince in honor's flattering bloom
Of hasty greatness finds the fatal doom,
His foes' derision, and his subjects' blame,
And steals to death from anguish and from shame.
  Enlarge my life with multitude of days,
In health, in sickness, thus the suppliant prays;
Hides from himself his state, and shuns to know,
That life protracted is protracted woe.
Time hovers o'er, impatient to destroy,
And shuts up all the passages of joy:
In vain their gifts the bounteous seasons pour,
The fruit autumnal, and the vernal flow'r,
With listless eyes the dotard views the store,
He views, and wonders that they please no more;
Now pall the tasteless meats, and joyless wines,
And Luxury° with sighs her slave resigns. *voluptuousness*
Approach, ye minstrels, try the soothing strain,
Diffuse the tuneful lenitives[8] of pain:
No sounds alas would touch th' impervious ear,
Though dancing mountains witnessed Orpheus[9] near;
Nor lute nor lyre his feeble pow'rs attend,
Nor sweeter music of a virtuous friend,
But everlasting dictates crowd his tongue,
Perversely grave, or positively wrong.
The still returning tale, and ling'ring jest,
Perplex the fawning niece and pampered guest,

8. "Anything medicinally applied to ease pain" (Johnson's *Dictionary*).

9. In Greek mythology, the musician Orpheus charmed wild beasts and moved mountains.

While growing hopes scarce awe the gathering sneer,
And scarce a legacy can bribe to hear;
The watchful guests still hint the last° offense, *latest*
The daughter's petulance, the son's expense,
Improve his heady rage with treach'rous skill,
And mold his passions till they make his will.
Unnumbered maladies his joints invade,
Lay siege to life and press the dire blockade;
But unextinguished Avarice still remains,
And dreaded losses aggravate his pains;
He turns, with anxious heart and crippled hands,
His bonds of debt, and mortgages of lands;
Or views his coffers with suspicious eyes,
Unlocks his gold, and counts it till he dies.
But grant, the virtues of a temp'rate prime
Bless with an age exempt from scorn or crime;
An age that melts with unperceived decay,
And glides in modest innocence away;
Whose peaceful day Benevolence endears,
Whose night congratulating Conscience cheers;
The gen'ral favorite as the gen'ral friend:
Such age there is, and who shall wish its end?
Yet ev'n on this her load Misfortune flings,
To press the weary minutes' flagging wings:
New sorrow rises as the day returns,
A sister sickens, or a daughter mourns.
Now kindred Merit fills the sable bier,
Now lacerated Friendship claims a tear.
Year chases year, decay pursues decay,
Still drops some joy from with'ring life away;
New forms arise, and different views engage,
Superfluous lags the vet'ran on the stage,
Till pitying Nature signs the last release,
And bids afflicted worth retire to peace.
But few there are whom hours like these await,
Who set unclouded in the gulfs of fate.
From Lydia's monarch should the search descend,
By Solon cautioned to regard his end,[1]
In life's last scene what prodigies surprise,
Fears of the brave, and follies of the wise?
From Marlborough's eyes the streams of dotage flow,[2]
And Swift expires a driveler and a show.[3]
The teeming mother, anxious for her race,
Begs for each birth the fortune of a face:
Yet Vane could tell what ills from beauty spring;

1. Solon, Greek philosopher and legislator, warned the wealthy King Croesus of Lydia that no one should count himself happy until reaching the end of life.

2. John Churchill (1650–1722), first Duke of Marlborough, hero of the War of the Spanish Succession, lived for six years after suffering two paralytic strokes.

3. Jonathan Swift, who declined into senility, was thought to have been exhibited by his servant for money.

And Sedley cursed the form that pleased a king.[4]
Ye nymphs of rosy lips and radiant eyes,
Whom Pleasure keeps too busy to be wise,
Whom Joys with soft varieties invite,
By day the frolic, and the dance by night,
Who frown with vanity, who smile with art,
And ask the latest fashion of the heart,
What care, what rules your heedless charms shall save,
Each nymph your rival, and each youth your slave?
Against your fame with fondness hate combines,
The rival batters, and the lover mines.
With distant voice neglected Virtue calls,
Less heard and less, the faint remonstrance falls;
Tired with contempt, she quits the slipp'ry reign,
And Pride and Prudence take her seat in vain.
In crowd at once, where none the pass defend,
The harmless Freedom, and the private Friend.
The guardians yield, by force superior plied;
By Interest, Prudence; and by Flattery, Pride.
Now beauty falls betrayed, despised, distressed,
And hissing Infamy proclaims the rest.
  Where then shall Hope and Fear their objects find?
Must dull Suspense corrupt the stagnant mind?
Must helpless man, in ignorance sedate,° *calm*
Roll darkling° down the torrent of his fate? *in the dark*
Must no dislike alarm, no wishes rise,
No cries attempt the mercies of the skies?
Inquirer, cease, petitions yet remain,
Which Heav'n may hear, nor deem religion vain.
Still raise for good the supplicating voice,
But leave to Heav'n the measure and the choice,
Safe in his power, whose eyes discern afar
The secret ambush of a specious prayer.
Implore his aid, in his decisions rest,
Secure whate'er he gives, he gives the best.
Yet when the sense of sacred presence fires,
And strong devotion to the skies aspires,
Pour forth thy fervors for a healthful mind,
Obedient passions, and a will resigned;
For love, which scarce collective man can fill;
For patience sov'reign o'er transmuted ill;
For faith, that panting for a happier seat,
Counts death kind Nature's signal of retreat:
These goods for man the laws of Heav'n ordain,
These goods he grants, who grants the power to gain;
With these celestial Wisdom calms the mind,
And makes the happiness she does not find.

1748 1749

4. Anne Vane (1705–1736) was the mistress of the Prince of Wales, Catherine Sedley (1657–1717) of James II.

A Short Song of Congratulation[1]

Long expected one and twenty
Ling'ring year at last is flown,
Pomp and pleasure, pride and plenty,
Great Sir John, are all your own.

Loosened from the minor's tether,
Free to mortgage or to sell,
Wild as wind, and light as feather
Bid the slaves of thrift farewell.[2]

Call the Bettys, Kates, and Jennys
Ev'ry name that laughs at care,
Lavish of your grandsire's guineas,
Show the spirit of an heir.

All that prey on vice and folly
Joy to see their quarry fly,
Here the gamester light and jolly
There the lender grave and sly.

Wealth, Sir John, was made to wander,
Let it wander as it will;
See the jockey, see the pander,
Bid them come, and take their fill.

When the bonny blade carouses,
Pockets full, and spirits high,
What are acres? What are houses?
Only dirt, or wet or dry.

If the guardian or the mother
Tell the woes of willful waste,
Scorn their counsel and their pother,
You can hang or drown at last.

1780 1794

On the Death of Dr. Robert Levet[1]

Condemned to Hope's delusive mine,
As on we toil from day to day,
By sudden blasts, or slow decline,
Our social comforts drop away.

1. Written for Sir John Lade (1759–1838), the nephew of Johnson's close friend Henry Thrale.
2. Sir John fulfilled Johnson's predictions: he made a scandalous marriage and then squandered his inheritance.
1. Robert Levet (1705–1782), a friend and dependent of Johnson, had acquired a modicum of medical training while working as a waiter in Paris; he put this training to use by caring for the poorest of the London poor ("Dr." was an honorific title). Many of Johnson's friends wondered why he admired and supported a man whom Boswell described as "an obscure practiser in physick amongst the lower people." Johnson's elegy answers that question.

Well tried through many a varying year,
  See Levet to the grave descend;
Officious,[2] innocent, sincere,
  Of ev'ry friendless name the friend.

Yet still he fills Affection's eye,
  Obscurely° wise, and coarsely kind; *privately*
Nor, lettered Arrogance, deny
  Thy praise to merit unrefined.

When fainting Nature called for aid,
  And hov'ring Death prepared the blow,
His vig'rous remedy displayed
  The power of art without the show.

In Misery's darkest caverns known,
  His useful care was ever nigh,
Where hopeless Anguish poured his groan,
  And lonely Want retired to die.

No summons mocked by chill delay,
  No petty gain disdained by pride,
The modest wants of ev'ry day
  The toil of ev'ry day supplied.

His virtues walked their narrow round,
  Nor made a pause, nor left a void;
And sure th' Eternal Master found
  The single talent well employed.[3]

The busy day, the peaceful night,
  Unfelt, uncounted, glided by;
His frame was firm, his pow'rs were bright,
  Though now his eightieth year was nigh.

Then with no throbbing fiery pain,
  No cold gradations of decay,
Death broke at once the vital chain,
  And freed his soul the nearest way.

1782 1783

THE RAMBLER In the midst of working on his *Dictionary*, Johnson took on an ambitious additional task: he wrote *The Rambler*, a twice-weekly periodical essay which he sustained for two full years (1750–1752). The project brought him needed income and also a useful respite from the strains of lexicography. *The Rambler*'s most famous antecedent was Addison and Steele's the *Spectator* (1711–1713), and though Johnson would later praise Addison's prose as a "model of the middle style . . . always equable and always easy," he chose for his own essays a mode more astringent: a large, often Latinate vocabulary, intricately balanced sentences, a steady alertness to the human propensity for self-delusion, a willingness to confront rather than ingratiate. Pressures of production could run high (Johnson later claimed that he sometimes

2. "Kind; doing good offices" (Johnson's *Dictionary*).
3. A reference to Jesus's Parable of the Talents (Matthew 25.14–30), which haunted Johnson throughout his adult life.

wrote his essay with the printer's messenger standing at his side, waiting to take the text to the press), and speed of output may have helped shape the results. Many *Ramblers*, with their formidably wrought prose and surprising turns of thought, manage to seem imposing and improvisatory at the same time. Free to choose his topics, working under relentlessly recurrent deadlines, Johnson drew on four decades dense with reading and thought, during which (in the words of his biographer John Hawkins) he had "accumulated a fund of moral science that was more than sufficient for such an undertaking," and had become "in a very eminent degree qualified for the office of an instructor of mankind in their greatest and most important concerns." Readers proved eager for the instruction. More than any of his earlier writings, *The Rambler* established Johnson's style, his substance, and his fame.

For additional *Ramblers* (no. 170, 171, and 207), go to *The Longman Anthology of British Literature* Web site at www.myliteraturekit.com.

Rambler No. 4
[ON FICTION]

Saturday, 31 March 1750

Simul et jucunda et idonea dicere vitae.

Horace, *Ars Poetica* 1.334

And join both profit and delight in one.

Creech

The works of fiction with which the present generation seems more particularly delighted are such as exhibit life in its true state, diversified only by accidents that daily happen in the world, and influenced by passions and qualities which are really to be found in conversing with mankind.

This kind of writing may be termed not improperly the comedy of romance, and is to be conducted nearly by the rules of comic poetry. Its province is to bring about natural events by easy means, and to keep up curiosity without the help of wonder: it is therefore precluded from the machines[1] and expedients of the heroic romance, and can neither employ giants to snatch away a lady from the nuptial rites, nor knights to bring her back from captivity; it can neither bewilder its personages in deserts, nor lodge them in imaginary castles.

I remember a remark made by Scaliger upon Pontanus,[2] that all his writings are filled with the same images; and that if you take from him his lillies and his roses, his satyrs and his dryads, he will have nothing left that can be called poetry. In like manner, almost all the fictions of the last age will vanish, if you deprive them of a hermit and a wood, a battle and a shipwreck.

Why this wild strain of imagination found reception so long, in polite and learned ages, it is not easy to conceive; but we cannot wonder that, while readers could be procured, the authors were willing to continue it: for when a man had by practice gained some fluency of language, he had no further care than to retire to his closet,[3] let loose his invention, and heat his mind with incredibilities; a book was

1. "Supernatural agency in poems" (Johnson's *Dictionary*).
2. The Renaissance humanist Julius Caesar Scaliger (1484–1558) criticized the poetry of Giovanni Pontano (1426–1503).
3. Study.

thus produced without fear of criticism, without the toil of study, without knowledge of nature, or acquaintance with life.

The task of our present writers is very different; it requires, together with that learning which is to be gained from books, that experience which can never be attained by solitary diligence, but must arise from general converse, and accurate observation of the living world. Their performances have, as Horace expresses it, *plus oneris quantum veniae minus*, little indulgence, and therefore more difficulty.[4] They are engaged in portraits of which every one knows the original, and can detect any deviation from exactness of resemblance. Other writings are safe, except from the malice of learning, but these are in danger from every common reader; as the slipper ill executed was censured by a shoemaker who happened to stop in his way at the Venus of Apelles.[5]

But the fear of not being approved as just copiers of human manners, is not the most important concern that an author of this sort ought to have before him. These books are written chiefly to the young, the ignorant, and the idle, to whom they serve as lectures of conduct, and introductions into life. They are the entertainment of minds unfurnished with ideas, and therefore easily susceptible of impressions; not fixed by principles, and therefore easily following the current of fancy; not informed by experience, and consequently open to every false suggestion and partial account.

That the highest degree of reverence should be paid to youth, and that nothing indecent should be suffered to approach their eyes or ears, are precepts extorted by sense and virtue from an ancient writer, by no means eminent for chastity of thought.[6] The same kind, though not the same degree of caution, is required in every thing which is laid before them, to secure them from unjust prejudices, perverse opinions, and incongruous combinations of images.

In the romances formerly written, every transaction and sentiment was so remote from all that passes among men, that the reader was in very little danger of making any applications to himself; the virtues and crimes were equally beyond his sphere of activity; and he amused himself with heroes and with traitors, deliverers and persecutors, as with beings of another species, whose actions were regulated upon motives of their own, and who had neither faults nor excellencies in common with himself.

But when an adventurer is leveled with the rest of the world, and acts in such scenes of the universal drama, as may be the lot of any other man, young spectators fix their eyes upon him with closer attention, and hope by observing his behavior and success to regulate their own practices, when they shall be engaged in the like part.

For this reason these familiar histories may perhaps be made of greater use than the solemnities of professed morality, and convey the knowledge of vice and virtue with more efficacy than axioms and definitions. But if the power of example is so great, as to take possession of the memory by a kind of violence, and produce effects almost without the intervention of the will, care ought to be taken that, when the choice is unrestrained, the best examples only should be exhibited; and that which is likely to operate so strongly, should not be mischievous or uncertain in its effects.

The chief advantage which these fictions have over real life is, that their authors are at liberty, though not to invent, yet to select objects, and to cull from the mass of mankind those individuals upon which the attention ought most to be

4. Horace, *Epistles* 2.1.170.
5. In his *Natural History*, Pliny the Elder tells this story of the famous painter Apelles.
6. Johnson refers to the opening lines of Juvenal's fourteenth satire.

employed; as a diamond, though it cannot be made, may be polished by art, and placed in such a situation as to display that lustre which before was buried among common stones.

It is justly considered as the greatest excellency of art, to imitate nature; but it is necessary to distinguish those parts of nature, which are most proper for imitation: greater care is still required in representing life, which is so often discolored by passion, or deformed by wickedness. If the world be promiscuously[7] described, I cannot see of what use it can be to read the account; or why it may not be as safe to turn the eye immediately upon mankind, as upon a mirror which shows all that presents itself without discrimination.

It is therefore not a sufficient vindication of a character, that it is drawn as it appears, for many characters ought never to be drawn; nor of a narrative, that the train of events is agreeable to observation and experience, for that observation which is called knowledge of the world will be found much more frequently to make men cunning than good. The purpose of these writings is surely not only to show mankind, but to provide that they may be seen hereafter with less hazard; to teach the means of avoiding the snares which are laid by Treachery for Innocence, without infusing any wish for that superiority with which the betrayer flatters his vanity; to give the power of counteracting fraud, without the temptation to practice it; to initiate youth by mock encounters in the art of necessary defense, and to increase prudence without impairing virtue.

Many writers, for the sake of following nature, so mingle good and bad qualities in their principal personages, that they are both equally conspicuous; and as we accompany them through their adventures with delight, and are led by degrees to interest ourselves in their favor, we lose the abhorrence of their faults, because they do not hinder our pleasure, or, perhaps, regard them with some kindness for being united with so much merit.

There have been men indeed splendidly wicked, whose endowments threw a brightness on their crimes, and whom scarce any villainy made perfectly detestable, because they never could be wholly divested of their excellencies; but such have been in all ages the great corrupters of the world, and their resemblance ought no more to be preserved, than the art of murdering without pain.

Some have advanced, without due attention to the consequences of this notion, that certain virtues have their correspondent faults, and therefore that to exhibit either apart is to deviate from probability. Thus men are observed by Swift to be "grateful in the same degree as they are resentful."[8] This principle, with others of the same kind, supposes man to act from a brute impulse, and pursue a certain degree of inclination, without any choice of the object; for otherwise, though it should be allowed that gratitude and resentment arise from the same constitution of the passions, it follows not that they will be equally indulged when reason is consulted; yet unless that consequence be admitted, this sagacious maxim becomes an empty sound, without any relation to practice or to life.

Nor is it evident, that even the first motions to these effects are always in the same proportion. For pride, which produces quickness of resentment, will obstruct gratitude, by unwillingness to admit that inferiority which obligation implies; and it is very unlikely that he who cannot think he receives a favor will acknowledge or repay it.

7. Indiscriminately.
8. In fact, it was Pope who made this observation, in the *Miscellanies* he coauthored with Swift.

It is of the utmost importance to mankind that positions of this tendency should be laid open and confuted; for while men consider good and evil as springing from the same root, they will spare the one for the sake of the other, and in judging, if not of others at least of themselves, will be apt to estimate their virtues by their vices. To this fatal error all those will contribute, who confound the colors of right and wrong, and instead of helping to settle their boundaries, mix them with so much art, that no common mind is able to disunite them.

In narratives where historical veracity has no place, I cannot discover why there should not be exhibited the most perfect idea of virtue; of virtue not angelical, nor above probability, for what we cannot credit we shall never imitate, but the highest and purest that humanity can reach, which, exercised in such trials as the various revolutions of things shall bring upon it, may, by conquering some calamities, and enduring others, teach us what we may hope, and what we can perform. Vice, for vice is necessary to be shown, should always disgust; nor should the graces of gaiety, or the dignity of courage, be so united with it, as to reconcile it to the mind. Wherever it appears, it should raise hatred by the malignity of its practices, and contempt by the meanness of its stratagems; for while it is supported by either parts[9] or spirit, it will be seldom heartily abhorred. The Roman tyrant was content to be hated, if he was but feared;[1] and there are thousands of the readers of romances willing to be thought wicked, if they may be allowed to be wits. It is therefore to be steadily inculcated, that virtue is the highest proof of understanding, and the only solid basis of greatness; and that vice is the natural consequence of narrow thoughts, that it begins in mistake, and ends in ignominy.

Rambler No. 5

[ON SPRING]

Tuesday, 3 April 1750

Et nunc omnis ager, nunc omnis parturit arbos,
Nunc frondent silvae, nunc formosissimus annus.

Virgil, *Eclogues* 3.56–57

Now every field, now every tree is green;
Now genial nature's fairest face is seen.

Elphinston

Every man is sufficiently discontented with some circumstances of his present state, to suffer his imagination to range more or less in quest of future happiness, and to fix upon some point of time, in which, by the removal of the inconvenience which now perplexes him, or acquisition of the advantage which he at present wants,[1] he shall find the condition of his life very much improved.

When this time, which is too often expected with great impatience, at last arrives, it generally comes without the blessing for which it was desired; but we solace ourselves with some new prospect, and press forward again with equal eagerness.

9. Abilities.
1. The Roman historian Suetonius reports this of the emperor Caligula.
1. Lacks.

It is lucky for a man, in whom this temper prevails, when he turns his hopes upon things wholly out of his own power; since he forbears then to precipitate his affairs, for the sake of the great event that is to complete his felicity, and waits for the blissful hour, with less neglect of the measures necessary to be taken in the mean time.

I have long known a person of this temper, who indulged his dream of happiness with less hurt to himself than such chimerical wishes commonly produce, and adjusted his scheme with such address, that his hopes were in full bloom three parts of the year, and in the other part never wholly blasted. Many, perhaps, would be desirous of learning by what means he procured to himself such a cheap and lasting satisfaction. It was gained by a constant practice of referring the removal of all his uneasiness to the coming of the next spring; if his health was impaired, the spring would restore it; if what he wanted was at a high price, it would fall its value in the spring.

The spring, indeed, did often come without any of these effects, but he was always certain that the next would be more propitious; nor was ever convinced that the present spring would fail him before the middle of summer; for he always talked of the spring as coming 'till it was past, and when it was once past, everyone agreed with him that it was coming.

By long converse with this man, I am, perhaps, brought to feel immoderate pleasure in the contemplation of this delightful season; but I have the satisfaction of finding many, whom it can be no shame to resemble, infected with the same enthusiasm;[2] for there is, I believe, scarce any poet of eminence, who has not left some testimony of his fondness for the flowers, the zephyrs, and the warblers of the spring. Nor has the most luxuriant imagination been able to describe the serenity and happiness of the golden age, otherwise than by giving a perpetual spring, as the highest reward of uncorrupted innocence.

There is, indeed, something inexpressibly pleasing, in the annual renovation of the world, and the new display of the treasures of nature. The cold and darkness of winter, with the naked deformity of every object on which we turn our eyes, make us rejoice at the succeeding season, as well for what we have escaped, as for what we may enjoy; and every budding flower, which a warm situation brings early to our view, is considered by us as a messenger to notify the approach of more joyous days.

The spring affords to a mind, so free from the disturbance of cares or passions as to be vacant to calm amusements, almost every thing that our present state makes us capable of enjoying. The variegated verdure of the fields and woods, the succession of grateful odors, the voice of pleasure pouring out its notes on every side, with the gladness apparently conceived by every animal, from the growth of his food, and the clemency of the weather, throw over the whole earth an air of gaiety, significantly expressed by the smile of nature.

Yet there are men to whom these scenes are able to give no delight, and who hurry away from all the varieties of rural beauty, to lose their hours, and divert their thoughts by cards, or assemblies, a tavern dinner, or the prattle of the day.

It may be laid down as a position which will seldom deceive, that when a man cannot bear his own company there is something wrong. He must fly from himself, either because he feels a tediousness in life from the equipoise of an empty mind, which, having no tendency to one motion more than another but as it is impelled

2. "Elevation of fancy; exaltation of ideas" (Johnson's *Dictionary*).

by some external power, must always have recourse to foreign objects; or he must be afraid of the intrusion of some unpleasing ideas, and, perhaps, is struggling to escape from the remembrance of a loss, the fear of a calamity, or some other thought of greater horror.

Those whom sorrow incapacitates to enjoy the pleasures of contemplation, may properly apply to such diversions, provided they are innocent, as lay strong hold on the attention; and those, whom fear of any future affliction chains down to misery, must endeavor to obviate the danger.

My considerations shall, on this occasion, be turned on such as are burdensome to themselves merely because they want subjects for reflection, and to whom the volume of nature is thrown open, without affording them pleasure or instruction, because they never learned to read the characters.

A French author has advanced this seeming paradox, that "very few men know how to take a walk"; and, indeed, it is true, that few know how to take a walk with a prospect of any other pleasure, than the same company would have afforded them at home.

There are animals that borrow their color from the neighboring body, and, consequently, vary their hue as they happen to change their place. In like manner it ought to be the endeavor of every man to derive his reflections from the objects about him; for it is to no purpose that he alters his position, if his attention continues fixed to the same point. The mind should be kept open to the access of every new idea, and so far disengaged from the predominance of particular thoughts, as easily to accommodate itself to occasional entertainment.

A man that has formed this habit of turning every new object to his entertainment, finds in the productions of nature an inexhaustible stock of materials upon which he can employ himself, without any temptations to envy or malevolence; faults, perhaps, seldom totally avoided by those, whose judgment is much exercised upon the works of art. He has always a certain prospect of discovering new reasons for adoring the sovereign author of the universe, and probable hopes of making some discovery of benefit to others, or of profit to himself. There is no doubt but many vegetables and animals have qualities that might be of great use, to the knowledge of which there is not required much force of penetration, or fatigue of study, but only frequent experiments, and close attention. What is said by the chemists of their darling mercury, is, perhaps, true of every body through the whole creation, that, if a thousand lives should be spent upon it, all its properties would not be found out.

Mankind must necessarily be diversified by various tastes, since life affords and requires such multiplicity of employments, and a nation of naturalists is neither to be hoped, or desired; but it is surely not improper to point out a fresh amusement to those who languish in health, and repine in plenty, for want of some source of diversion that may be less easily exhausted, and to inform the multitudes of both sexes, who are burdened with every new day, that there are many shows which they have not seen.

He that enlarges his curiosity after the works of nature, demonstrably multiplies the inlets to happiness; and, therefore, the younger part of my readers, to whom I dedicate this vernal speculation, must excuse me for calling upon them, to make use at once of the spring of the year, and the spring of life; to acquire, while their minds may be yet impressed with new images, a love of innocent pleasures, and an ardor for useful knowledge; and to remember, that a blighted spring makes a barren year, and that the vernal flowers, however beautiful and gay, are only intended by nature as preparatives to autumnal fruits.

Rambler No. 60
[ON BIOGRAPHY]

Saturday, 13 October 1750

—*Quid sit pulchrum, quid turpe, quid utile, quid non,*
Plenius et melius Chrysippo et Crantore dicit.

Horace, *Epistles* 1.2.3–4

Whose works the beautiful and base contain;
Of vice and virtue more instructive rules,
Than all the sober sages of the schools.

Francis

All joy or sorrow for the happiness or calamities of others is produced by an act of the imagination, that realizes the event however fictitious, or approximates[1] it however remote, by placing us, for a time, in the condition of him whose fortune we contemplate; so that we feel, while the deception lasts, whatever motions would be excited by the same good or evil happening to ourselves.

Our passions are therefore more strongly moved, in proportion as we can more readily adopt the pains or pleasures proposed to our minds, by recognizing them as once our own, or considering them as naturally incident to our state of life. It is not easy for the most artful writer to give us an interest in happiness or misery, which we think ourselves never likely to feel, and with which we have never yet been made acquainted. Histories of the downfall of kingdoms, and revolutions of empires, are read with great tranquility; the imperial tragedy pleases common auditors only by its pomp of ornament, and grandeur of ideas; and the man whose faculties have been engrossed by business, and whose heart never fluttered but at the rise or fall of stocks, wonders how the attention can be seized, or the affections agitated by a tale of love.

Those parallel circumstances, and kindred images, to which we readily conform our minds, are, above all other writings, to be found in narratives of the lives of particular persons; and therefore no species of writing seems more worthy of cultivation than biography, since none can be more delightful or more useful, none can more certainly enchain the heart by irresistible interest, or more widely diffuse instruction to every diversity of condition.

The general and rapid narratives of history, which involve a thousand fortunes in the business of a day, and complicate innumerable incidents in one great transaction, afford few lessons applicable to private life, which derives its comforts and its wretchedness from the right or wrong management of things which nothing but their frequency makes considerable, *parva, si non fiant quotidie*, says Pliny,[2] and which can have no place in those relations which never descend below the consultation of senates, the motions of armies, and the schemes of conspirators.

I have often thought that there has rarely passed a life of which a judicious and faithful narrative would not be useful. For, not only every man has, in the mighty mass of the world, great numbers in the same condition with himself, to whom his

1. Bring close.
2. "Matters which would be trivial were they not part of a daily routine" (Pliny the Younger, *Epistles* 3.1).

mistakes and miscarriages, escapes and expedients, would be of immediate and apparent use; but there is such an uniformity in the state of man, considered apart from adventitious and separable decorations and disguises, that there is scarce any possibility of good or ill, but is common to humankind. A great part of the time of those who are placed at the greatest distance by fortune, or by temper, must unavoidably pass in the same manner; and though, when the claims of nature are satisfied, caprice, and vanity, and accident, begin to produce discriminations and peculiarities, yet the eye is not very heedful, or quick, which cannot discover the same causes still terminating their influence in the same effects, though sometimes accelerated, sometimes retarded, or perplexed by multiplied combinations. We are all prompted by the same motives, all deceived by the same fallacies, all animated by hope, obstructed by danger, entangled by desire, and seduced by pleasure.

It is frequently objected to relations of particular lives, that they are not distinguished by any striking or wonderful vicissitudes. The scholar who passed his life among his books, the merchant who conducted only his own affairs, the priest, whose sphere of action was not extended beyond that of his duty, are considered as no proper objects of public regard, however they might have excelled in their several stations, whatever might have been their learning, integrity, and piety. But this notion arises from false measures of excellence and dignity, and must be eradicated by considering that, in the esteem of uncorrupted reason, what is of most use is of most value.

It is, indeed, not improper to take honest advantages of prejudice, and to gain attention by a celebrated name; but the business of the biographer is often to pass slightly over those performances and incidents, which produce vulgar greatness, to lead the thoughts into domestic privacies, and display the minute details of daily life, where exterior appendages are cast aside, and men excel each other only by prudence and by virtue. The account of Thuanus is, with great propriety, said by its author to have been written, that it might lay open to posterity the private and familiar character of that man, *cujus ingenium et candorem ex ipsius scriptis sunt olim semper miraturi*,[3] whose candor and genius will to the end of time be by his writings preserved in admiration.

There are many invisible circumstances which, whether we read as inquirers after natural or moral knowledge, whether we intend to enlarge our science,[4] or increase our virtue, are more important than public occurrences. Thus Sallust, the great master of nature, has not forgot, in his account of Catiline, to remark that "his walk was now quick, and again slow," as an indication of a mind revolving something with violent commotion.[5] Thus the story of Melancthon[6] affords a striking lecture on the value of time, by informing us, that when he made an appointment, he expected not only the hour, but the minute to be fixed, that the day might not run out in the idleness of suspense; and all the plans and enterprises of De Witt are now of less importance to the world, than that part of his personal character which represents him as "careful of his health, and negligent of his life."[7]

3. Johnson quotes from a commentary affixed by Nicolas Rigault to the *History of His Own Time* by the French historian Jacques-Auguste de Thou (1553–1617). The Latin is translated by the words that follow.

4. Knowledge.

5. Johnson quotes from an account by the Roman historian Sallust of Catiline's conspiracy against Rome.

6. Johnson quotes from a biography of the Protestant theologian Philip Melancthon (1497–1560) by Joachim Camerarius.

7. Johnson quotes the essayist Sir William Temple's verdict on the Dutch statesman Jan de Witt (1625–1672).

But biography has often been allotted to writers who seem very little acquainted with the nature of their task, or very negligent about the performance. They rarely afford any other account than might be collected from public papers, but imagine themselves writing a life when they exhibit a chronological series of actions or preferments; and so little regard the manners or behavior of their heroes, that more knowledge may be gained of a man's real character, by a short conversation with one of his servants, than from a formal and studied narrative, begun with his pedigree, and ended with his funeral.

If now and then they condescend to inform the world of particular facts, they are not always so happy as to select the most important. I know not well what advantage posterity can receive from the only circumstance by which Tickell has distinguished Addison from the rest of mankind, the irregularity of his pulse:[8] nor can I think myself overpaid for the time spent in reading the life of Malherb,[9] by being enabled to relate, after the learned biographer, that Malherb had two predominant opinions; one, that the looseness of a single woman might destroy all her boast of ancient descent; the other, that the French beggars made use very improperly and barbarously of the phrase "noble gentleman," because either word included the sense of both.

There are, indeed, some natural reasons why these narratives are often written by such as were not likely to give much instruction or delight, and why most accounts of particular persons are barren and useless. If a life be delayed till interest and envy are at an end, we may hope for impartiality, but must expect little intelligence; for the incidents which give excellence to biography are of a volatile and evanescent kind, such as soon escape the memory, and are rarely transmitted by tradition. We know how few can portray a living acquaintance, except by his most prominent and observable particularities, and the grosser features of his mind; and it may be easily imagined how much of this little knowledge may be lost in imparting it, and how soon a succession of copies will lose all resemblance of the original.

If the biographer writes from personal knowledge, and makes haste to gratify the public curiosity, there is danger lest his interest, his fear, his gratitude, or his tenderness, overpower his fidelity, and tempt him to conceal, if not to invent. There are many who think it an act of piety to hide the faults or failings of their friends, even when they can no longer suffer by their detection; we therefore see whole ranks of characters adorned with uniform panegyric, and not to be known from one another, but by extrinsic and casual circumstances. "Let me remember," says Hale, "when I find myself inclined to pity a criminal, that there is likewise a pity due to the country."[1] If we owe regard to the memory of the dead, there is yet more respect to be paid to knowledge, to virtue, and to truth.

8. Thomas Tickell prefixed a biography of Joseph Addison to his edition of Addison's *Works* (1721).

9. Johnson refers to the biography of the French poet Francois de Malherbe (1555–1628) by the Marquis de Racan.

1. Johnson quotes from the biography of Sir Matthew Hale (1609–1676), eminent jurist and religious writer, by Gilbert Burnet.

Idler No. 31[1]

[On Idleness]

Saturday, 18 November 1758

Many moralists have remarked, that pride has of all human vices the widest dominion, appears in the greatest multiplicity of forms, and lies hid under the greatest variety of disguises; of disguises, which, like the moon's "veil of brightness," are both its "luster and its shade,"[2] and betray it to others, though they hide it from ourselves.

It is not my intention to degrade pride from this pre-eminence of mischief, yet I know not whether idleness may not maintain a very doubtful and obstinate competition.

There are some that profess idleness in its full dignity, who call themselves the Idle, as Busiris in the play "calls himself the Proud";[3] who boast that they do nothing, and thank their stars that they have nothing to do; who sleep every night till they can sleep no longer, and rise only that exercise may enable them to sleep again; who prolong the reign of darkness by double curtains, and never see the sun but to "tell him how they hate his beams";[4] whose whole labor is to vary the postures of indulgence, and whose day differs from their night but as a couch or chair differs from a bed.

These are the true and open votaries of idleness, for whom she weaves the garlands of poppies, and into whose cup she pours the waters of oblivion; who exist in a state of unruffled stupidity,[5] forgetting and forgotten; who have long ceased to live, and at whose death the survivors can only say, that they have ceased to breathe.

But idleness predominates in many lives where it is not suspected, for, being a vice which terminates in itself, it may be enjoyed without injury to others, and is therefore not watched like fraud, which endangers property, or like pride, which naturally seeks its gratifications in another's inferiority. Idleness is a silent and peaceful quality, that neither raises envy by ostentation, nor hatred by opposition; and therefore nobody is busy to censure or detect it.

As pride sometimes is hid under humility, idleness is often covered by turbulence and hurry. He that neglects his known duty and real employment, naturally endeavors to crowd his mind with something that may bar out the remembrance of his own folly, and does any thing but what he ought to do with eager diligence, that he may keep himself in his own favor.

Some are always in a state of preparation, occupied in previous measures, forming plans, accumulating materials, and providing for the main affair. These are certainly under the secret power of idleness. Nothing is to be expected from the workman whose tools are forever to be sought. I was once told by a great master, that no man ever excelled in painting, who was eminently curious[6] about pencils[7] and colors.

1. *The Idler* (1758–1760) bears a more self-deprecating title than *The Rambler;* other circumstances, too, suggest that Johnson intended a less imposing performance in this series of periodical essay than in its predecessor. The new pieces appeared not twice but once a week, and not as an independent sheet but as a department within a weekly newspaper called *The Universal Chronicle* (which achieved little eminence apart from Johnson's contribution). The *Idlers* were shorter than the *Ramblers*, and dealt more often in light topics and comic touches. Boswell opined that the second series had "less body and more spirit . . . more variety of real life, and greater facility of language." His judgment is hardly definitive; the comparison has been assayed, with varying results, many times since.

2. Both quotations come from Samuel Butler's poem *Hudibras* (1663–1678) 2.1.905 and 908.

3. *Busiris* (1719) by Edward Young.

4. Milton, *Paradise Lost* 4.37.

5. Stupor.

6. "Difficult to please" (Johnson's *Dictionary*).

7. Brushes.

There are others to whom idleness dictates another expedient, by which life may be passed unprofitably away without the tediousness of many vacant hours. The art is, to fill the day with petty business, to have always something in hand which may raise curiosity, but not solicitude, and keep the mind in a state of action, but not of labor.

This art has for many years been practiced by my old friend Sober,[8] with wonderful success. Sober is a man of strong desires and quick imagination, so exactly balanced by the love of ease, that they can seldom stimulate him to any difficult undertaking; they have, however, so much power, that they will not suffer him to lie quite at rest, and though they do not make him sufficiently useful to others, they make him at least weary of himself.

Mr. Sober's chief pleasure is conversation; there is no end of his talk or his attention; to speak or to hear is equally pleasing; for he still fancies that he is teaching or learning something, and is free for the time from his own reproaches.

But there is one time at night when he must go home, that his friends may sleep; and another time in the morning, when all the world agrees to shut out interruption. These are the moments of which poor Sober trembles at the thought. But the misery of these tiresome intervals, he has many means of alleviating. He has persuaded himself that the manual arts are undeservedly overlooked; he has observed in many trades the effects of close thought, and just ratiocination. From speculation he proceeded to practice, and supplied himself with the tools of a carpenter, with which he mended his coal-box very successfully, and which he still continues to employ, as he finds occasion.

He has attempted at other times the crafts of the shoemaker, tinman, plumber, and potter; in all these arts he has failed, and resolves to qualify himself for them by better information. But his daily amusement is chemistry. He has a small furnace, which he employs in distillation, and which has long been the solace of his life. He draws oils and waters, and essences and spirits, which he knows to be of no use; sits and counts the drops as they come from his retort, and forgets that, while a drop is falling, a moment flies away.

Poor Sober! I have often teased him with reproof, and he has often promised reformation; for no man is so much open to conviction as the idler, but there is none on whom it operates so little. What will be the effect of this paper I know not; perhaps he will read it and laugh, and light the fire in his furnace; but my hope is that he will quit his trifles, and betake himself to rational and useful diligence.

Idler No. 32

[On Sleep]

Saturday, 25 November 1758

Among the innumerable mortifications that waylay human arrogance on every side may well be reckoned our ignorance of the most common objects and effects, a defect of which we become more sensible by every attempt to supply it. Vulgar and inactive minds confound familiarity with knowledge, and conceive themselves informed of the whole nature of things when they are shown their form or

8. Johnson's friends believed that the portrait of Sober was autobiographical.

told their use; but the speculatist, who is not content with superficial views, harasses himself with fruitless curiosity, and still as he inquires more perceives only that he knows less.

Sleep is a state in which a great part of every life is passed. No animal has been yet discovered, whose existence is not varied with intervals of insensibility; and some late philosophers have extended the empire of sleep over the vegetable world.

Yet of this change so frequent, so great, so general, and so necessary, no searcher has yet found either the efficient or final cause; or can tell by what power the mind and body are thus chained down in irresistible stupefaction; or what benefits the animal receives from this alternate suspension of its active powers.

Whatever may be the multiplicity or contrariety of opinions upon this subject, nature has taken sufficient care that theory shall have little influence on practice. The most diligent inquirer is not able long to keep his eyes open; the most eager disputant will begin about midnight to desert his argument, and once in four and twenty hours, the gay and the gloomy, the witty and the dull, the clamorous and the silent, the busy and the idle, are all overpowered by the gentle tyrant, and all lie down in the equality of sleep.

Philosophy has often attempted to repress insolence by asserting that all conditions are leveled by death; a position which, however it may deject the happy, will seldom afford much comfort to the wretched. It is far more pleasing to consider that sleep is equally a leveler with death; that the time is never at a great distance, when the balm of rest shall be effused alike upon every head, when the diversities of life shall stop their operation, and the high and the low shall lie down together.

It is somewhere recorded of Alexander, that in the pride of conquests, and intoxication of flattery, he declared that he only perceived himself to be a man by the necessity of sleep. Whether he considered sleep as necessary to his mind or body it was indeed a sufficient evidence of human infirmity; the body which required such frequency of renovation gave but faint promises of immortality; and the mind which, from time to time, sunk gladly into insensibility had made no very near approaches to the felicity of the supreme and self-sufficient nature.

I know not what can tend more to repress all the passions that disturb the peace of the world than the consideration that there is no height of happiness or honor from which man does not eagerly descend to a state of unconscious repose; that the best condition of life is such that we contentedly quit its good to be disentangled from its evils; that in a few hours splendor fades before the eye and praise itself deadens in the ear; the senses withdraw from their objects, and reason favors the retreat.

What then are the hopes and prospects of covetousness, ambition and rapacity? Let him that desires most have all his desires gratified, he never shall attain a state which he can, for a day and a night, contemplate with satisfaction, or from which, if he had the power of perpetual vigilance, he would not long for periodical separations.

All envy would be extinguished if it were universally known that there are none to be envied, and surely none can be much envied who are not pleased with themselves. There is reason to suspect that the distinctions of mankind have more show than value when it is found that all agree to be weary alike of pleasures and of cares, that the powerful and the weak, the celebrated and obscure, join in one common wish, and implore from nature's hand the nectar of oblivion.

Such is our desire of abstraction from ourselves that very few are satisfied with the quantity of stupefaction which the needs of the body force upon the mind. Alexander himself added intemperance to sleep, and solaced with the fumes of wine the sovereignty of the world. And almost every man has some art by which he steals his thoughts away from his present state.

It is not much of life that is spent in close attention to any important duty. Many hours of every day are suffered to fly away without any traces left upon the intellects. We suffer phantoms to rise up before us, and amuse ourselves with the dance of airy images, which after a time we dismiss forever, and know not how we have been busied.

Many have no happier moments than those that they pass in solitude, abandoned to their own imagination, which sometimes puts sceptres in their hands or mitres on their heads, shifts the scene of pleasure with endless variety, bids all the forms of beauty sparkle before them, and gluts them with every change of visionary luxury.

It is easy in these semi-slumbers to collect all the possibilities of happiness, to alter the course of the sun, to bring back the past, and anticipate the future, to unite all the beauties of all seasons, and all the blessings of all climates, to receive and bestow felicity, and forget that misery is the lot of man. All this is a voluntary dream, a temporary recession from the realities of life to airy fictions; an habitual subjection of reason to fancy.

Others are afraid to be alone, and amuse themselves by a perpetual succession of companions, but the difference is not great; in solitude we have our dreams to ourselves, and in company we agree to dream in concert. The end sought in both is forgetfulness of ourselves.

Idler No. 84

[On Autobiography]

Saturday, 24 November 1759

Biography is, of the various kinds of narrative writing, that which is most eagerly read, and most easily applied to the purposes of life.

In romances, when the wild field of possibility lies open to invention, the incidents may easily be made more numerous, the vicissitudes more sudden, and the events more wonderful; but from the time of life when fancy begins to be overruled by reason and corrected by experience, the most artful tale raises little curiosity when it is known to be false; though it may, perhaps, be sometimes read as a model of a neat or elegant style, not for the sake of knowing what it contains, but how it is written; or those that are weary of themselves, may have recourse to it as a pleasing dream, of which, when they awake, they voluntarily dismiss the images from their minds.

The examples and events of history press, indeed, upon the mind with the weight of truth; but when they are reposited in the memory, they are oftener employed for show than use, and rather diversify conversation than regulate life. Few are engaged in such scenes as give them opportunities of growing wiser by the downfall of statesmen or the defeat of generals. The stratagems of war, and the intrigues of courts, are read by far the greater part of mankind with the same indifference as the adventures of fabled heroes, or the revolutions of a fairy region. Between falsehood and useless truth there is little difference. As gold which he cannot spend will make no man rich, so knowledge which he cannot apply will make no man wise.

The mischievous consequences of vice and folly, of irregular desires and predominant passions, are best discovered by those relations which are leveled with the general surface of life, which tell not how any man became great, but how he was made happy; not how he lost the favor of his prince, but how he became discontented with himself.

Those relations are therefore commonly of most value in which the writer tells his own story. He that recounts the life of another, commonly dwells most upon conspicuous events, lessens the familiarity of his tale to increase its dignity, shows his favorite at a distance decorated and magnified like the ancient actors in their tragic dress, and endeavors to hide the man that he may produce a hero.

But if it be true which was said by a French prince, "that no man was a hero to the servants of his chamber," it is equally true that every man is yet less a hero to himself. He that is most elevated above the crowd by the importance of his employments or the reputation of his genius, feels himself affected by fame or business but as they influence his domestic life. The high and low, as they have the same faculties and the same senses, have no less similitude in their pains and pleasures. The sensations are the same in all, though produced by very different occasions. The prince feels the same pain when an invader seizes a province, as the farmer when a thief drives away his cow. Men thus equal in themselves will appear equal in honest and impartial biography; and those whom fortune or nature place at the greatest distance may afford instruction to each other.

The writer of his own life has at least the first qualification of an historian, the knowledge of the truth; and though it may be plausibly objected that his temptations to disguise it are equal to his opportunities of knowing it, yet I cannot but think that impartiality may be expected with equal confidence from him that relates the passages of his own life, as from him that delivers the transactions of another.

Certainty of knowledge not only excludes mistake but fortifies veracity. What we collect by conjecture, and by conjecture only can one man judge of another's motives or sentiments, is easily modified by fancy or by desire; as objects imperfectly discerned take forms from the hope or fear of the beholder. But that which is fully known cannot be falsified but with reluctance of understanding, and alarm of conscience; of understanding, the lover of truth; of conscience, the sentinel of virtue.

He that writes the life of another is either his friend or his enemy, and wishes either to exalt his praise or aggravate his infamy; many temptations to falsehood will occur in the disguise of passions, too specious[1] to fear much resistance. Love of virtue will animate panegyric, and hatred of wickedness embitter censure. The zeal of gratitude, the ardor of patriotism, fondness for an opinion, or fidelity to a party, may easily overpower the vigilance of a mind habitually well disposed, and prevail over unassisted and unfriended veracity.

1. "Plausible; superficially, not solidly right" (Johnson's *Dictionary*).

But he that speaks of himself has no motive to falsehood or partiality except self-love, by which all have so often been betrayed, that all are on the watch against its artifices. He that writes an apology for[2] a single action, to confute an accusation, or recommend himself to favor, is indeed always to be suspected of favoring his own cause; but he that sits down calmly and voluntarily to review his life for the admonition of posterity, or to amuse himself, and leaves this account unpublished, may be commonly presumed to tell truth, since falsehood cannot appease his own mind, and fame will not be heard beneath the tomb.

Idler No. 97

[On Travel Writing]

Saturday, 23 February 1760

It may, I think, be justly observed, that few books disappoint their readers more than the narrations of travelers. One part of mankind is naturally curious to learn the sentiments, manners, and condition of the rest; and every mind that has leisure or power to extend its views, must be desirous of knowing in what proportion Providence has distributed the blessings of nature or the advantages of art, among the several nations of the earth.

This general desire easily procures readers to every book from which it can expect gratification. The adventurer upon unknown coasts, and the describer of distant regions, is always welcomed as a man who has labored for the pleasure of others, and who is able to enlarge our knowledge and rectify our opinions; but when the volume is opened, nothing is found but such general accounts as leave no distinct idea behind them, or such minute enumerations as few can read with either profit or delight.

Every writer of travels should consider that, like all other authors, he undertakes either to instruct or please, or to mingle pleasure with instruction. He that instructs must offer to the mind something to be imitated or something to be avoided; he that pleases must offer new images to his reader, and enable him to form a tacit comparison of his own state with that of others.

The greater part of travelers tell nothing, because their method of traveling supplies them with nothing to be told. He that enters a town at night and surveys it in the morning, and then hastens away to another place, and guesses at the manners of the inhabitants by the entertainment which his inn afforded him, may please himself for a time with a hasty change of scenes, and a confused remembrance of palaces and churches; he may gratify his eye with variety of landscapes; and regale his palate with a succession of vintages; but let him be contented to please himself without endeavor to disturb others. Why should he record excursions by which nothing could be learned, or wish to make a show of knowledge which, without some power of intuition unknown to other mortals, he never could attain.

Of those who crowd the world with their itineraries,[1] some have no other purpose than to describe the face of the country; those who sit idle at home, and are curious to know what is done or suffered in distant countries, may be informed by one of these wanderers, that on a certain day he set out early with the caravan, and in the first hour's march saw, towards the south, a hill covered with trees, then passed over a

2. Defense of.

1. Travel books.

stream which ran northward with a swift course, but which is probably dry in the summer months; that an hour after he saw something to the right which looked at a distance like a castle with towers, but which he discovered afterwards to be a craggy rock; that he then entered a valley in which he saw several trees tall and flourishing, watered by a rivulet not marked in the maps, of which he was not able to learn the name; that the road afterward grew stony, and the country uneven, where he observed among the hills many hollows worn by torrents, and was told that the road was passable only part of the year: that going on they found the remains of a building, once perhaps a fortress to secure the pass, or to restrain the robbers, of which the present inhabitants can give no other account than that it is haunted by fairies; that they went to dine at the foot of a rock, and traveled the rest of the day along the banks of a river, from which the road turned aside towards evening, and brought them within sight of a village, which was once a considerable town, but which afforded them neither good victuals nor commodious lodging.

Thus he conducts his reader through wet and dry, over rough and smooth, without incidents, without reflection; and, if he obtains his company for another day, will dismiss him again at night equally fatigued with a like succession of rocks and streams, mountains and ruins.

This is the common style of those sons of enterprise, who visit savage countries, and range through solitude and desolation; who pass a desert, and tell that it is sandy; who cross a valley, and find that it is green. There are others of more delicate sensibility, that visit only the realms of elegance and softness; that wander through Italian palaces, and amuse the gentle reader with catalogues of pictures; that hear masses in magnificent churches, and recount the number of the pillars or variegations of the pavement. And there are yet others who, in disdain of trifles, copy inscriptions elegant and rude, ancient and modern; and transcribe into their book the walls of every edifice, sacred or civil. He that reads these books must consider his labor as its own reward; for he will find nothing on which attention can fix, or which memory can retain.

He that would travel for the entertainment of others should remember that the great object of remark is human life. Every nation has something peculiar in its manufactures, its works of genius, its medicines, its agriculture, its customs, and its policy. He only is a useful traveler who brings home something by which his country may be benefited; who procures some supply of want or some mitigation of evil, which may enable his readers to compare their condition with that of others, to improve it whenever it is worse, and whenever it is better to enjoy it.

A DICTIONARY OF THE ENGLISH LANGUAGE Johnson's *Dictionary* struck its first readers as a nearly superhuman accomplishment; it seems one still. "A dictionary of the English language," observed one early reviewer, had never before "been attempted with the least degree of success"; the closest antecedents to Johnson's project were the national dictionaries of France and Italy, and these had been composed by whole academies of scholars, working collectively over the course of decades. Here, by contrast, was the seven years' labor of a single author (aided only by six part-time amanuenses): 40,000 words defined with unprecedented exactitude, and illustrated with more than 114,000 passages drawn from English prose and poetry of the previous 250 years. Ninety years earlier, members of the newly founded Royal Society for Improving Natural Knowledge had dreamed of such a resource; Johnson produced it by empirical methods much like the ones they promulgated. He spent his first years on the project accumulating data, rereading the English writers he valued most, marking any passage that strikingly illuminated the workings of a particular word. He then worked from this heap of collected evidence to the fine-honed, sharply distinguished conclusions of his definitions. The results have been variously and accurately described as the first standard English dictionary; as one of the final fruits of Renaissance humanism; as a commonplace-book (or database) of important English writing from Sidney to Pope; as a massive map of its author's mind. The key to that map resides in the *Dictionary*'s Preface, where Johnson measures the grandeur of his aspirations against the limitations of his achievement. In this mix of personal memoir and linguistic meditation, lexicography becomes a local instance of the vanity of human wishes. Human language, massive, metamorphic, and intractable, overmatches the human desire to codify and contain it, to fix it once and for all.

from A Dictionary of the English Language
from *Preface*

[ON METHOD]

It is the fate of those who toil at the lower employments of life to be rather driven by the fear of evil than attracted by the prospect of good; to be exposed to censure, without hope of praise; to be disgraced by miscarriage or punished for neglect, where success would have been without applause and diligence without reward.

Among these unhappy mortals is the writer of dictionaries; whom mankind have considered not as the pupil but the slave of science, the pioneer[1] of literature, doomed only to remove rubbish and clear obstructions from the paths through which learning and genius press forward to conquest and glory, without bestowing a smile on the humble drudge that facilitates their progress. Every other author may aspire to praise; the lexicographer can only hope to escape reproach, and even this negative recompense has been yet granted to very few.

I have, notwithstanding this discouragement, attempted a dictionary of the English language which, while it was employed in the cultivation of every species of literature, has itself been hitherto neglected; suffered to spread, under the direction of chance, into wild exuberance; resigned to the tyranny of time and fashion; and exposed to the corruptions of ignorance, and caprices of innovation.

When I took the first survey of my undertaking, I found our speech copious without order, and energetic without rules: wherever I turned my view, there was perplexity to be disentangled and confusion to be regulated; choice was to be made out of boundless variety, without any established principle of selection; adulterations were to be detected without a settled test of purity; and modes of expression to be rejected or received without the suffrages[2] of any writers of classical reputation or acknowledged authority.

Having therefore no assistance but from general grammar, I applied myself to the perusal of our writers; and, noting whatever might be of use to ascertain or illustrate any word or phrase, accumulated in time the materials of a dictionary, which, by degrees, I reduced to method, establishing to myself in the progress of the work such rules as experience and analogy suggested to me; experience, which practice and observation were continually increasing; and analogy, which, though in some words obscure, was evident in others.

1. "One whose business is to level the road, throw up works, or sink mines in military operations" (Johnson's *Dictionary*).
2. Votes, testimonies.

[On Definitions And Examples]

That part of my work on which I expect malignity most frequently to fasten is the explanation; in which I cannot hope to satisfy those who are perhaps not inclined to be pleased, since I have not always been able to satisfy myself. To interpret a language by itself is very difficult; many words cannot be explained by synonyms because the idea signified by them has not more than one appellation; nor by paraphrase, because simple ideas cannot be described. When the nature of things is unknown, or the notion unsettled and indefinite, and various in various minds, the words by which such notions are conveyed or such things denoted will be ambiguous and perplexed. And such is the fate of hapless lexicography that not only darkness, but light, impedes and distresses it; things may be not only too little, but too much known, to be happily illustrated. To explain requires the use of terms less abstruse than that which is to be explained, and such terms cannot always be found; for as nothing can be proved but by supposing something intuitively known and evident without proof, so nothing can be defined but by the use of words too plain to admit a definition.

Other words there are, of which the sense is too subtle and evanescent to be fixed in a paraphrase; such are all those which are by the grammarians termed expletives, and, in dead languages, are suffered to pass for empty sounds, of no other use than to fill a verse or to modulate a period,[1] but which are easily perceived in living tongues to have power and emphasis, though it be sometimes such as no other form of expression can convey. * * *

The solution of all difficulties and the supply of all defects must be sought in the examples subjoined to the various senses of each word, and ranged according to the time of their authors.

When first I collected these authorities, I was desirous that every quotation should be useful to some other end than the illustration of a word; I therefore extracted from philosophers principles of science; from historians remarkable facts; from chemists complete processes; from divines striking exhortations; and from poets beautiful descriptions. Such is design while it is yet at a distance from execution. When the time called upon me to range this accumulation of elegance and wisdom into an alphabetical series, I soon discovered that the bulk of my volumes would fright away the student, and was forced to depart from my scheme of including all that was pleasing or useful in English literature, and reduce my transcripts very often to clusters of words in which scarcely any meaning is retained; thus to the weariness of copying, I was condemned to add the vexation of expunging. Some passages I have yet spared which may relieve the labor of verbal searches, and intersperse with verdure and flowers the dusty deserts of barren philology.

The examples, thus mutilated, are no longer to be considered as conveying the sentiments or doctrine of their authors; the word for the sake of which they are inserted, with all its appendant clauses, has been carefully preserved; but it may sometimes happen, by hasty detruncation, that the general tendency of the sentence may be changed: the divine may desert his tenets, or the philosopher his system.

Some of the examples have been taken from writers who were never mentioned as masters of elegance or models of style; but words must be sought where they are used; and in what pages, eminent for purity, can terms of manufacture or agriculture be found? Many quotations serve no other purpose than that of proving the bare existence of words, and are therefore selected with less scrupulousness than those which are to teach their structures and relations.

1. Clause or sentence.

My purpose was to admit no testimony of living authors, that I might not be misled by partiality, and that none of my contemporaries might have reason to complain; nor have I departed from this resolution but when some performance of uncommon excellence excited my veneration, when my memory supplied me, from late books, with an example that was wanting, or when my heart, in the tenderness of friendship, solicited admission for a favorite name.

So far have I been from any care to grace my pages with modern decorations that I have studiously endeavored to collect examples and authorities from the writers before the Restoration, whose works I regard as "the wells of English undefiled,"[2] as the pure sources of genuine diction. Our language, for almost a century, has, by the concurrence of many causes, been gradually departing from its original Teutonic character, and deviating towards a Gallic structure and phraseology, from which it ought to be our endeavor to recall it by making our ancient volumes the groundwork of style, admitting among the additions of later times only such as may supply real deficiencies, such as are readily adopted by the genius[3] of our tongue, and incorporate easily with our native idioms.

But as every language has a time of rudeness[4] antecedent to perfection, as well as of false refinement and declension, I have been cautious lest my zeal for antiquity might drive me into times too remote and crowd my book with words now no longer understood. I have fixed Sidney's work for the boundary beyond which I make few excursions. From the authors which rose in the time of Elizabeth, a speech might be formed adequate to all the purposes of use and elegance. If the language of theology were extracted from Hooker and the translation of the Bible; the terms of natural knowledge[5] from Bacon; the phrases of policy, war, and navigation from Raleigh; the dialect of poetry and fiction from Spenser and Sidney; and the diction of common life from Shakespeare, few ideas would be lost to mankind for want of English words in which they might be expressed.

It is not sufficient that a word is found unless it be so combined as that its meaning is apparently[6] determined by the tract[7] and tenor of the sentence; such passages I have therefore chosen, and when it happened that any author gave a definition of a term or such an explanation as is equivalent to a definition, I have placed his authority as a supplement to my own, without regard to the chronological order that is otherwise observed.

Some words, indeed, stand unsupported by any authority, but they are commonly derivative nouns or adverbs, formed from their primitives by regular and constant analogy, or names of things seldom occurring in books, or words of which I have reason to doubt the existence.

There is more danger of censure from the multiplicity than paucity of examples; authorities will sometimes seem to have been accumulated without necessity or use, and perhaps some will be found which might, without loss, have been omitted. But a work of this kind is not hastily to be charged with superfluities: those quotations which to careless or unskillful perusers appear only to repeat the same sense will often exhibit to a more accurate examiner diversities of signification or, at least, afford different shades of the same meaning: one will show the word applied to persons,

2. Johnson quotes Spenser's praise of Chaucer in *The Faerie Queene* (4.2.2).
3. Native spirit.
4. Barbarism.
5. Science.
6. Clearly.
7. "Continuity; course; manner of process" (Johnson's *Dictionary*).

another to things; one will express an ill, another a good, and a third a neutral sense; one will prove the expression genuine from an ancient author; another will show it elegant from a modern: a doubtful authority is corroborated by another of more credit; an ambiguous sentence is ascertained by a passage clear and determinate; the word, how often soever repeated, appears with new associates and in different combinations, and every quotation contributes something to the stability or enlargement of the language. * * *

I have sometimes, though rarely, yielded to the temptation of exhibiting a genealogy of sentiments, by showing how one author copied the thoughts and diction of another: such quotations are indeed little more than repetitions which might justly be censured, did they not gratify the mind by affording a kind of intellectual history.

[Conclusion]

A large work is difficult because it is large, even though all its parts might singly be performed with facility; where there are many things to be done, each must be allowed its share of time and labor in the proportion only which it bears to the whole; nor can it be expected that the stones which form the dome of a temple should be squared and polished like the diamond of a ring.

Of the event of this work, for which, having labored it with so much application, I cannot but have some degree of parental fondness, it is natural to form conjectures. Those who have been persuaded to think well of my design will require that it should fix our language and put a stop to those alterations which time and chance have hitherto been suffered to make in it without opposition. With this consequence I will confess that I flattered myself for a while; but now begin to fear that I have indulged expectation which neither reason nor experience can justify. When we see men grow old and die at a certain time one after another, from century to century, we laugh at the elixir that promises to prolong life to a thousand years; and with equal justice may the lexicographer be derided, who being able to produce no example of a nation that has preserved their words and phrases from mutability, shall imagine that his dictionary can embalm his language and secure it from corruption and decay, that it is in his power to change sublunary nature, and clear the world at once from folly, vanity, and affectation.

With this hope, however, academies have been instituted to guard the avenues of their languages, to retain fugitives and repulse intruders; but their vigilance and activity have hitherto been vain; sounds are too volatile and subtle for legal restraints; to enchain syllables and to lash the wind are equally the undertakings of pride, unwilling to measure its desires by its strength. The French language has visibly changed under the inspection of the Academy,[1] the style of Amelot's translation of Father Paul is observed by Le Courayer to be *un peu passé;*[2] and no Italian will maintain that the diction of any modern writer is not perceptibly different from that of Boccace, Machiavel, or Caro.[3]

1. The French Academy, founded in 1635, undertook to preserve the purity of the language.
2. When in the 1730s Le Courayer retranslated Father Paolo Sarpi's *History of the Council of Trent*, he criticized his predecessor Amelot's version (1683) as "a little outdated."
3. Johnson refers to Giovanni Boccaccio (1313–1375), author of *The Decameron;* Niccolo Machiavelli (1469–1527), author of *The Prince;* and Annibale Caro (1507–1566), author of pastoral romances.

Total and sudden transformations of a language seldom happen; conquests and migrations are now very rare; but there are other causes of change which, though slow in their operation, and invisible in their progress, are perhaps as much superior to human resistance, as the revolutions of the sky, or intumescence of the tide. Commerce, however necessary, however lucrative, as it depraves the manners, corrupts the language; they that have frequent intercourse with strangers, to whom they endeavor to accommodate themselves, must in time learn a mingled dialect, like the jargon which serves the traffickers[4] on the Mediterranean and Indian coasts. This will not always be confined to the exchange, the warehouse, or the port, but will be communicated by degrees to other ranks of the people, and be at last incorporated with the current speech.

There are likewise internal causes equally forcible. The language most likely to continue long without alteration would be that of a nation raised a little, and but a little, above barbarity, secluded from strangers, and totally employed in procuring the conveniences of life; either without books or, like some of the Mahometan countries, with very few: men thus busied and unlearned, having only such words as common use requires, would perhaps long continue to express the same notions by the same signs. But no such constancy can be expected in a people polished by arts and classed by subordination, where one part of the community is sustained and accommodated by the labor of the other. Those who have much leisure to think will always be enlarging the stock of ideas, and every increase of knowledge, whether real or fancied, will produce new words or combinations of words. When the mind is unchained from necessity, it will range after convenience; when it is left at large in the fields of speculation, it will shift opinions; as any custom is disused, the words that expressed it must perish with it; as any opinion grows popular, it will innovate speech in the same proportion as it alters practice.

As by the cultivation of various sciences a language is amplified, it will be more furnished with words deflected from their original sense; the geometrician will talk of a courtier's zenith, or the eccentric[5] virtue of a wild hero, and the physician of sanguine expectations and phlegmatic delays.[6] Copiousness of speech will give opportunities to capricious choice, by which some words will be preferred and others degraded; vicissitudes of fashion will enforce the use of new or extend the signification of known terms. The tropes of poetry will make hourly encroachments, and the metaphorical will become the current sense: pronunciation will be varied by levity or ignorance, and the pen must at length comply with the tongue; illiterate writers will at one time or other, by public infatuation, rise into renown, who, not knowing the original import of words, will use them with colloquial licentiousness, confound distinction, and forget propriety. As politeness increases, some expressions will be considered as too gross and vulgar for the delicate, others as too formal and ceremonious for the gay and airy; new phrases are therefore adopted, which must for the same reasons be in time dismissed. Swift, in his petty[7] treatise on the English language,[8] allows that new words must sometimes be introduced, but proposes that none should be suffered to become obsolete. But what makes a word obsolete more

4. Merchants.
5. "Deviating from the center" (Johnson's *Dictionary*).
6. "Sanguine" and "phlegmatic" are medical terms relating to the doctrine of the four humors. Those in whom blood predominates are "sanguine" or optimistic, those ruled by phlegm are dull and sluggish.
7. Little.
8. A *Proposal for Correcting, Improving, and Ascertaining the English Tongue* (1712).

than general agreement to forbear it? and how shall it be continued when it conveys an offensive idea, or recalled again into the mouths of mankind when it has once become unfamiliar by disuse and unpleasing by unfamiliarity?

There is another cause of alteration more prevalent than any other, which yet in the present state of the world cannot be obviated. A mixture of two languages will produce a third distinct from both, and they will always be mixed where the chief part of education, and the most conspicuous accomplishment, is skill in ancient or in foreign tongues. He that has long cultivated another language will find its words and combinations crowd upon his memory; and haste or negligence, refinement or affectation, will obtrude borrowed terms and exotic expressions.

The great pest of speech is frequency of translation. No book was ever turned from one language into another without imparting something of its native idiom; this is the most mischievous and comprehensive innovation; single words may enter by thousands and the fabric of the tongue continue the same, but new phraseology changes much at once; it alters not the single stones of the building but the order of the columns.[9] If an academy should be established for the cultivation of our style, which I, who can never wish to see dependence multiplied, hope the spirit of English liberty will hinder or destroy, let them, instead of compiling grammars and dictionaries, endeavor, with all their influence, to stop the license of translators, whose idleness and ignorance, if it be suffered to proceed, will reduce us to babble a dialect of France.

If the changes that we fear be thus irresistible, what remains but to acquiesce with silence, as in the other insurmountable distresses of humanity? It remains that we retard what we cannot repel, that we palliate what we cannot cure. Life may be lengthened by care, though death cannot be ultimately defeated: tongues, like governments, have a natural tendency to degeneration; we have long preserved our constitution, let us make some struggles for our language.

In hope of giving longevity to that which its own nature forbids to be immortal, I have devoted this book, the labor of years, to the honor of my country, that we may no longer yield the palm[1] of philology without a contest to the nations of the Continent. The chief glory of every people arises from its authors: whether I shall add anything by my own writings to the reputation of English literature must be left to time: much of my life has been lost under the pressures of disease; much has been trifled away; and much has always been spent in provision for the day that was passing over me; but I shall not think my employment useless or ignoble if by my assistance foreign nations and distant ages gain access to the propagators of knowledge, and understand the teachers of truth; if my labors afford light to the repositories of science, and add celebrity to Bacon, to Hooker, to Milton, and to Boyle.

When I am animated by this wish, I look with pleasure on my book, however defective, and deliver it to the world with the spirit of a man that has endeavored well. That it will immediately become popular I have not promised to myself: a few wild blunders and risible absurdities, from which no work of such multiplicity was ever free, may for a time furnish folly with laughter, and harden ignorance in contempt; but useful diligence will at last prevail, and there never can be wanting some

9. In classical architecture, the five "orders" are Doric, Ionic, Corinthian, Tuscan, and Composite.

1. Crown (symbol of victory).

who distinguish desert,[2] who will consider that no dictionary of a living tongue ever can be perfect, since while it is hastening to publication some words are budding and some falling away; that a whole life cannot be spent upon syntax and etymology, and that even a whole life would not be sufficient; that he whose design includes whatever language can express, must often speak of what he does not understand; that a writer will sometimes be hurried by eagerness to the end, and sometimes faint with weariness under a task, which Scaliger compares to the labors of the anvil and the mine;[3] that what is obvious is not always known, and what is known is not always present; that sudden fits of inadvertency will surprise vigilance, slight avocations will seduce attention, and casual eclipses of the mind will darken learning; and that the writer shall often in vain trace his memory at the moment of need for that which yesterday he knew with intuitive readiness, and which will come uncalled into his thoughts tomorrow.

In this work, when it shall be found that much is omitted, let it not be forgotten that much likewise is performed; and though no book was ever spared out of tenderness to the author, and the world is little solicitous to know whence proceeded the faults of that which it condemns; yet it may gratify curiosity to inform it, that the *English Dictionary* was written with little assistance of the learned, and without any patronage of the great; not in the soft obscurities of retirement or under the shelter of academic bowers, but amidst inconvenience and distraction, in sickness and in sorrow. It may repress the triumph of malignant criticism to observe that if our language is not here fully displayed, I have only failed in an attempt which no human powers have hitherto completed. If the lexicons of ancient tongues, now immutably fixed and comprised in a few volumes, are yet, after the toil of successive ages, inadequate and delusive; if the aggregated knowledge, and cooperating diligence of the Italian academicians did not secure them from the censure of Beni;[4] if the embodied critics of France, when fifty years had been spent upon their work, were obliged to change its economy and give their second edition another form, I may surely be contented without the praise of perfection, which, if I could obtain, in this gloom of solitude, what would it avail me? I have protracted my work till most of those whom I wished to please have sunk into the grave, and success and miscarriage are empty sounds: I therefore dismiss it with frigid tranquility, having little to fear or hope from censure or from praise.

[Some Entries][1]

FUNK. n[oun] s[ubstantive]. A stink. A low word.

FÚNNEL. n.s. [*infundibulum*, Latin; whence *fundible*, *fundle*, *funnel*.]

1. An inverted hollow cone with a pipe descending from it, through which liquors are poured into vessels with narrow mouths; a tundish.

   If you pour a glut of water upon a bottle, it receives little of it; but with a *funnel*, and by degrees, you shall fill many of them.

   —Ben. Jonson's *Discoveries*

2. Merit.
3. Johnson refers to a poem, *Against the Compilers of the Lexicons*, by the great Renaissance scholar Joseph Justus Scaliger.
4. Paolo Beni criticized the Italian dictionary published in 1612 by the Accademia della Crusca.
1. All entries are from the fourth edition of Johnson's *Dictionary* (1773), the last that Johnson prepared. Each entry is presented complete, with etymology, definitions, illustrations.

Some the long *funnel*'s curious mouth extend,
Through which ingested meats with ease descend.

—Blackmore

The outward ear or auricula is made hollow, and contracted by degrees, to draw the sound inward, to take in as much as may be of it, as we use a *funnel* to pour liquor into any vessel.

—Ray on the Creation

2. A pipe or passage of communication.

Towards the middle are two large *funnels*, bored through the roof of the grotto, to let in light or fresh air.

—Addison

FÚTURE. n.s. [from the adjective.] Time to come; somewhat to happen hereafter.

Thy letters have transported me beyond
This ign'rant present time; and I feel now
The *future* in the instant.

—Shakespeare, *Macbeth*

The mind, once jaded by an attempt above its power, either is disabled for the *future*, or else checks at any vigorous undertaking ever after.

—Locke

IMAGINÁTION. n.s. [*imaginatio*, Lat. *imagination*, Fr. from *imagine*.]

1. Fancy; the power of forming ideal pictures; the power of representing things absent to one's self or others.

Imagination I understand to be the representation of an individual thought. *Imagination* is of three kinds: joined with belief of that which is to come; joined with memory of that which is past; and of things present, or as if they were present: for I comprehend in this imagination feigned and at pleasure, as if one should imagine such a man to be in the vestments of a pope, or to have wings.

—Bacon

Our simple apprehension of corporal objects, if present, is sense; if absent, *imagination:* when we would perceive a material object, our fancies present us with its idea.

—Glanville

O whither shall I run, or which way fly
The sight of this so horrid spectacle,
Which erst my eyes beheld, and yet behold!
For dire *imagination* still pursues me.

—Milton

Where beams of warm *imagination* play,
The memory's soft figures melt away.

—Pope

2. Conception; image in the mind; idea.

Sometimes despair darkens all her *imaginations;* sometimes the active passion of love cheers and clears her invention.

—Sidney

Princes have but their titles for their glories,
An outward honor for an inward toil;
And, for unfelt *imaginations*,
They often feel a world of restless cares.

—Shakespeare, *Richard III*

Better I were distract,
So should my thoughts be severed from my griefs;
And woes, by wrong *imaginations*, lose
The knowledge of themselves.

—Shakespeare, *King Lear*

His *imaginations* were often as just as they were bold and strong.

—Dennis

3. Contrivance; scheme.

Thou hast seen all their vengeance, and all their *imaginations* against me.

—Bible (Lamentations 3.60)

4. An unsolid or fanciful opinion.

We are apt to think that space, in itself, is actually boundless; to which *imagination*, the idea of space, of itself leads us.

—Locke

JÚDGMENT. n.s. [*jugement*, Fr.]

1. The power of discerning the relations between one term or one proposition and another.

O *judgment!* thou art fled to brutish beasts,
And men have lost their reason.

—Shakespeare, *Julius Caesar*

The faculty, which God has given man to supply the want of certain knowledge, is *judgment*, whereby the mind takes any proposition to be true or false, without perceiving a demonstrative evidence in the proofs.

—Locke

Judgment is that whereby we join ideas together by affirmation or negation; so, this tree is high.

—Watts

2. Doom; the right or power of passing judgment.

If my suspect be false, forgive me, God;
For *judgment* only doth belong to thee.

—Shakespeare, *Henry VI*

3. The act of exercising judicature; judicatory.

They gave *judgment* upon him.

—Bible (2 Kings)

When thou, O Lord, shalt stand disclosed
In majesty severe,
And sit in *judgment* on my soul,
O how shall I appear?

—Addison's *Spectator*

4. Determination; decision.

Where distinctions or identities are purely material, the *judgment* is made by the imagination, otherwise by the understanding.

—Glanville's *Scepsis*

We shall make a certain *judgment* what kind of dissolution that earth was capable of.

—Burnet's *Theory*

Reason ought to accompany the exercise of our senses, whenever we would form a just *judgment* of things proposed to our inquiry.

—Watts

5. The quality of distinguishing propriety and impropriety; criticism.

Judgment, a cool and slow faculty, attends not a man in the rapture of poetical composition.

—Dennis

'Tis with our *judgments* as our watches, none
Go just alike; yet each believes his own.

—Pope

6. Opinion; notion.

I see men's *judgments* are
A parcel of their fortunes, and things outward
Draw the inward quality after them,
To suffer all alike.

—Shakespeare, *Antony and Cleopatra*

When she did think my master loved her well,
She, in my *judgment*, was as fair as you.

—Shakespeare

7. Sentence against a criminal.

When he was brought again to th' bar, to hear
His knell rung out, his *judgment*, he was stirred
With agony.

—Shakespeare, *Henry VIII*

The chief priests informed me, desiring to have *judgment* against him.

—Bible (Acts 25.15)

On Adam last this *judgment* he pronounced.

—Milton

8. Condemnation. This is a theological use.

The *judgment* was by one to condemnation; but the free gift is of many offenses unto justification.

—Bible (Romans 5.16)

The precepts, promises, and threatenings of the Gospel will rise up in *judgment* against us, and the articles of our faith will be so many articles of accusation.

—Tillotson

9. Punishment inflicted by Providence, with reference to some particular crime.

This *judgment* of the heavens that makes us tremble,
Touches us not with pity.

—Shakespeare, *King Lear*

We cannot be guilty of greater uncharitableness, than to interpret afflictions as punishments and *judgments:* it aggravates the evil to him who suffers, when he looks upon himself as the mark of divine vengeance.

—Addison's *Spectator*

10. Distribution of justice.

The Jews made insurrection against Paul, and brought him to the *judgment* seat.

—Bible (Acts 18.12)

Your dishonor
Mangles true *judgment*, and bereaves the state
Of that integrity which should become it.

—Shakespeare, *Coriolanus*

In *judgments* between rich and poor, consider not what the poor man needs, but what is his own.

—Taylor

A bold and wise petitioner goes strait to the throne and *judgment* seat of the monarch.

—Arbuthnot and Pope

11. Judiciary law; statute.

If ye hearken to these *judgments*, and keep and do them, the Lord thy God shall keep unto thee the covenant.

—Bible (Deuteronomy)

12. The last doom.

The dreadful *judgment* day
So dreadful will not be as was his sight.

—Shakespeare, *Henry VI*

KNACK. n.s.

1. A little machine; a petty contrivance; a toy.

When I was young, I was wont
To load my she with *knacks:* I would have ransacked
The peddler's silken treasury, and have poured it
To her acceptance.

—Shakespeare, *Winter's Tale*

For thee, fond boy,
If I may ever know thou dost but sigh
That thou no more shalt see this *knack*, as never
I mean thou shalt, we'll bar thee from success.

—Shakespeare

This cap was moulded on a porringer,
A velvet dish; fie, fie, 'tis lewd and filthy:
Why 'tis a cockle, or a walnut shell,
A *knack*, a toy, a trick, a baby's cap.

—Shakespeare

But is't not presumption to write verse to you,
Who make the better poems of the two?
For all these pretty *knacks* that you compose,
Alas! what are they but poems in prose!

—Denham

He expounded both his pockets,
And found a watch, with rings and lockets;
A copper-plate, with almanacks
Engraved upon't, with other *knacks*.

—*Hudibras*

2. A readiness; an habitual facility; a lucky dexterity.

I'll teach you the *knacks*
Of eating of flax,
And out of their noses
Draw ribbands and posies.

—Ben. Jonson's *Gypsies*

The *knack* of fast and loose passes with foolish people for a turn of wit; but they are not aware all this while of the desperate consequences of an ill habit.

—L'Estrange

There is a certain *knack* in conversation that gives a good grace by the manner and address.

—L'Estrange

Knaves, who in full assemblies have the *knack*
Of turning truth to lies, and white to black.

—Dryden

My author has a great *knack* at remarks: in the end he makes another, about our refining in controversy, and coming nearer and nearer to the church of Rome.

—Atterbury

The dean was famous in his time,
And had a kind of *knack* at rhyme.

—Swift

3. A nice trick.

For how should equal colors do the *knack?*
Chameleons who can paint in white and black?

—Pope

LEXICÓGRAPHER. n.s. [**λεξικον** and **γραφειν** *lexicographe*, Fr.] A writer of dictionaries; a harmless drudge, that busies himself in tracing the original, and detailing the signification of words.

Commentators and *lexicographers* acquainted with the Syriac language, have given these hints in their writings on scripture.

—Watt's *Improvement of the Mind*

SÚBSTANCE. n.s. [*substance*, Fr.; *substantia*, Lat.]

1. Being; something existing; something of which we can say that it is.

Since then the soul works by herself alone,
Springs not from sense, nor humors well agreeing,
Her nature is peculiar, and her own;
She is a *substance*, and a perfect being.

—Davies

The strength of gods,
And this empyreal *substance* cannot fail.

—Milton

2. That which supports accidents.

What creatures there inhabit, of what mold,
And *substance*.

—Milton

Every being is considered as subsisting in and by itself, and then it is called a *substance*; or it subsists in and by another, and then it is called a mode or manner of being.

—Watts

3. The essential part.

It will serve our turn to comprehend the *substance*, without confining ourselves to scrupulous exactness in form.

—Digby

This edition is the same in *substance* with the Latin.

—Burn

They are the best epitomes, and let you see with one cast of the eye the *substance* of a hundred pages.

—Addison

4. Something real, not imaginary; something solid, not empty.

Shadows tonight
Have struck more terror to the soul of Richard,
Than can the *substance* of ten thousand soldiers
Armed in proof and led by shallow Richmond.

—Shakespeare

He the future evil shall no less
In apprehension than in *substance* feel.

—Milton

Heroic virtue did his actions guide,
And he the *substance*, not th' appearance chose:
To rescue one such friend he took more pride,
Than to destroy whole thousands of such foes.

—Dryden

God is no longer to be worshipped and believed in as a god foreshowing and assuring by types, but as a god who has performed the *substance* of what he promised.

—Nelson

5. Body; corporeal nature.

Between the parts of opaque and colored bodies are many spaces, either empty or replenished with mediums of other densities; as water between the tinging corpuscles wherewith any liquor is impregnated, air between the aqueous globules that constitute clouds or mists, and for the most part spaces void of both air and water; but yet perhaps not wholly void of all *substance* between the parts of hard bodies.

—Newton

The qualities of plants are more various than those of animal *substances*.

—Arbuthnot on Aliments

There may be a great and constant cough, with an extraordinary discharge of phlegmatic matter, while, notwithstanding, the *substance* of the lungs remains sound.

—Blackmore

6. Wealth; means of life.

He hath eaten me out of house and home, and hath put all my *substance* into that fat belly of his, but I will have some of it out again.

—Shakespeare, *Henry IV*

We are destroying many thousand lives, and exhausting our *substance*, but not for our own interest.

—Swift

VACÚITY. n.s. [*vacuitas;* from *vacuus*, Lat. *vacuité*, Fr.]

1. Emptiness; state of being unfilled.

Hunger is such a state of *vacuity*, as to require a fresh supply of aliment.

—Arbuthnot

2. Space unfilled; space unoccupied.

In filling up *vacuities*, turning out shadows and ceremonies, by explicit prescription of substantial duties, which those shadows did obscurely represent.

—Hammond's *Fund*

He, that seat soon failing, meets
A vast *vacuity*.

—Milton

Body and space are quite different things, and a *vacuity* is interspersed among the particles of matter.

—Bentley

God, who alone can answer all our longings, and fill every *vacuity* of our soul, should entirely possess our heart.

—Rogers

Redeeming still at night these *vacuities* of the day.

—Fell

3. Inanity; want of reality.

The soul is seen, like other things, in the mirror of its effects: but if they'll run behind the glass to catch at it, their expectations will meet with *vacuity* and emptiness.

—Glanville

The History of Rasselas, Prince of Abyssinia Johnson wrote *Rasselas* with his customary speed but under particular pressures. He composed the tale probably in late January 1759, possibly (as Boswell reports) during the "evenings of one week." This was the month of his mother's death; he may have made the book in order to help defray expenses and to articulate loss. His friend the painter Sir Joshua Reynolds later praised *Rasselas* for compassing within its few pages as much wisdom as though it had been written "by an angel or some superior being, whose comprehensive faculties could develop and lay open the inmost recesses of the human mind," and who could convey "in a few hours the experience of ages." The experience that *Rasselas* imparts, Johnson had expressed in other forms before. Rasselas is a prince born to a life of ease within the Happy Valley, a sequestered utopia of limitless luxuries; he suffers, though, from an oppressive sense of dissatisfaction, or (in a favorite Johnsonian term) "vacuity." Tantalized by his conviction that true happiness must lie elsewhere, he escapes the valley accompanied by his sister Nekayah and his mentor Imlac, only to find his own propensity for misplaced hopes, unfulfilled plans, and ineffectual wishes mirrored in the unhappy lives of nearly every mortal he meets with. Early in the tale, just before effecting his escape, Rasselas asks Imlac to tell the story of his own life, lived mostly in the larger world. In his reminiscences, Imlac gently sketches the cycles of desire and disillusion that the prince and princess will shortly experience for themselves.

from The History of Rasselas, Prince of Abyssinia
Chapter 8. The History of Imlac

The close of the day is, in the regions of the torrid zone, the only season of diversion and entertainment, and it was therefore mid-night before the music ceased, and the princesses retired. Rasselas then called for his companion and required him to begin the story of his life.

"Sir," said Imlac, "my history will not be long: the life that is devoted to knowledge passes silently away, and is very little diversified by events. To talk in public, to think in solitude, to read and to hear, to inquire, and answer inquiries, is the business of a scholar. He wanders about the world without pomp or terror, and is neither known nor valued but by men like himself.

"I was born in the kingdom of Goiama, at no great distance from the fountain of the Nile. My father was a wealthy merchant, who traded between the inland countries of Africk and the ports of the Red Sea. He was honest, frugal and diligent, but of mean sentiments, and narrow comprehension: he desired only to be rich, and to conceal his riches, lest he should be spoiled[1] by the governors of the province."

"Surely," said the prince, "my father must be negligent of his charge, if any man in his dominions dares take that which belongs to another. Does he not know that kings are accountable for injustice permitted as well as done? If I were emperor, not the meanest of my subjects should be oppressed with impunity. My blood boils when I am told that a merchant durst not enjoy his honest gains for fear of losing them by the rapacity of power. Name the governor who robbed the people, that I may declare his crimes to the emperor."

"Sir," said Imlac, "your ardor is the natural effect of virtue animated by youth: the time will come when you will acquit your father, and perhaps hear with less impatience of the governor. Oppression is, in the Abyssinian dominions, neither frequent nor tolerated; but no form of government has been yet discovered, by which cruelty can be wholly prevented. Subordination supposes power on one part and subjection on the other; and if power be in the hands of men, it will sometimes be abused. The vigilance of the supreme magistrate may do much, but much will still remain undone. He can never know all the crimes that are committed, and can seldom punish all that he knows."

"This," said the prince, "I do not understand, but I had rather hear thee than dispute. Continue thy narration."

"My father," proceeded Imlac, "originally intended that I should have no other education, than such as might qualify me for commerce; and discovering in me great strength of memory, and quickness of apprehension, often declared his hope that I should be some time the richest man in Abyssinia."

"Why," said the prince, "did thy father desire the increase of his wealth, when it was already greater than he durst discover or enjoy? I am unwilling to doubt thy veracity, yet inconsistencies cannot both be true."

"Inconsistencies," answered Imlac, "cannot both be right, but, imputed to man, they may both be true. Yet diversity is not inconsistency. My father might expect a time of greater security. However, some desire is necessary to keep life in motion, and he, whose real wants are supplied, must admit those of fancy."

1. Plundered.

"This," said the prince, "I can in some measure conceive. I repent that I interrupted thee."

"With this hope," proceeded Imlac, "he sent me to school; but when I had once found the delight of knowledge, and felt the pleasure of intelligence and the pride of invention, I began silently to despise riches, and determined to disappoint the purpose of my father, whose grossness of conception raised my pity. I was twenty years old before his tenderness would expose me to the fatigue of travel, in which time I had been instructed, by successive masters, in all the literature[2] of my native country. As every hour taught me something new, I lived in a continual course of gratifications; but, as I advanced towards manhood, I lost much of the reverence with which I had been used to look on my instructors; because, when the lesson was ended, I did not find them wiser or better than common men.

"At length my father resolved to initiate me in commerce, and, opening one of his subterranean treasuries, counted out ten thousand pieces of gold. 'This, young man,' said he, 'is the stock with which you must negotiate. I began with less than the fifth part, and you see how diligence and parsimony have increased it. This is your own to waste or to improve. If you squander it by negligence or caprice, you must wait for my death before you will be rich: if, in four years, you double your stock, we will thenceforward let subordination cease, and live together as friends and partners; for he shall always be equal with me, who is equally skilled in the art of growing rich.'

"We laid our money upon camels, concealed in bales of cheap goods, and traveled to the shore of the Red Sea. When I cast my eye on the expanse of waters my heart bounded like that of a prisoner escaped. I felt an unextinguishable curiosity kindle in my mind, and resolved to snatch this opportunity of seeing the manners of other nations, and of learning sciences[3] unknown in Abyssinia.

"I remembered that my father had obliged me to the improvement of my stock, not by a promise which I ought not to violate, but by a penalty which I was at liberty to incur, and therefore determined to gratify my predominant desire, and by drinking at the fountains of knowledge, to quench the thirst of curiosity.

"As I was supposed to trade without connection with my father, it was easy for me to become acquainted with the master of a ship, and procure a passage to some other country. I had no motives of choice to regulate my voyage; it was sufficient for me that, wherever I wandered, I should see a country which I had not seen before. I therefore entered a ship bound for Surat, having left a letter for my father declaring my intention.

Chapter 9. The History of Imlac Continued

"When I first entered upon the world of waters, and lost sight of land, I looked round about me with pleasing terror, and thinking my soul enlarged by the boundless prospect, imagined that I could gaze round for ever without satiety; but, in a short time, I grew weary of looking on barren uniformity, where I could only see again what I had already seen. I then descended into the ship, and doubted for a while whether all my future pleasures would not end like this in disgust and disappointment. 'Yet, surely,' said I, 'the ocean and the land are very different; the only variety of water is rest and motion, but the earth has mountains and valleys, deserts and cities: it is

2. "Learning; skill in letters" (Johnson's *Dictionary*).

3. Modes of knowledge.

inhabited by men of different customs and contrary opinions; and I may hope to find variety in life, though I should miss it in nature.'

"With this thought I quieted my mind, and amused myself during the voyage; sometimes by learning from the sailors the art of navigation, which I have never practiced, and sometimes by forming schemes for my conduct in different situations, in not one of which I have been ever placed.

"I was almost weary of my naval amusements when we landed safely at Surat. I secured my money, and purchasing some commodities for show, joined myself to a caravan that was passing into the inland country. My companions, for some reason or other, conjecturing that I was rich, and, by my inquiries and admiration,[4] finding that I was ignorant, considered me as a novice whom they had a right to cheat, and who was to learn at the usual expense the art of fraud. They exposed me to the theft of servants, and the exaction of officers, and saw me plundered upon false pretenses, without any advantage to themselves, but that of rejoicing in the superiority of their own knowledge."

"Stop a moment," said the prince. "Is there such depravity in man, as that he should injure another without benefit to himself? I can easily conceive that all are pleased with superiority; but your ignorance was merely accidental, which, being neither your crime nor your folly, could afford them no reason to applaud themselves; and the knowledge which they had, and which you wanted, they might as effectually have shown by warning, as betraying you."

"Pride," said Imlac, "is seldom delicate, it will please itself with very mean advantages; and envy feels not its own happiness, but when it may be compared with the misery of others. They were my enemies because they grieved to think me rich, and my oppressors because they delighted to find me weak."

"Proceed," said the prince. "I doubt not of the facts which you relate, but imagine that you impute them to mistaken motives."

"In this company," said Imlac, "I arrived at Agra, the capital of Indostan, the city in which the great Mogul commonly resides. I applied myself to the language of the country, and in a few months was able to converse with the learned men; some of whom I found morose and reserved, and others easy and communicative; some were unwilling to teach another what they had with difficulty learned themselves; and some showed that the end of their studies was to gain the dignity of instructing.

"To the tutor of the young princes I recommended myself so much, that I was presented to the emperor as a man of uncommon knowledge. The emperor asked me many questions concerning my country and my travels; and though I cannot now recollect any thing that he uttered above the power of a common man, he dismissed me astonished at his wisdom, and enamored of his goodness.

"My credit was now so high, that the merchants, with whom I had traveled, applied to me for recommendations to the ladies of the court. I was surprised at their confidence of solicitation, and gently reproached them with their practices on the road. They heard me with cold indifference, and showed no tokens of shame or sorrow.

"They then urged their request with the offer of a bribe; but what I would not do for kindness I would not do for money; and refused them, not because they had injured me, but because I would not enable them to injure others; for I knew they would have made use of my credit to cheat those who should buy their wares.

4. "Wonder; the act of admiring or wondering" (Johnson's *Dictionary*).

"Having resided at Agra, till there was no more to be learned, I traveled into Persia, where I saw many remains of ancient magnificence, and observed many new accommodations[5] of life. The Persians are a nation eminently social, and their assemblies afforded me daily opportunities of remarking characters and manners, and of tracing human nature through all its variations.

"From Persia I passed into Arabia, where I saw a nation at once pastoral and warlike; who live without any settled habitation; whose only wealth is their flocks and herds; and who have yet carried on, through all ages, an hereditary war with all mankind, though they neither covet nor envy their possessions.

Chapter 10. Imlac's History Continued. A Dissertation upon Poetry

"Wherever I went, I found that poetry was considered as the highest learning, and regarded with a veneration somewhat approaching to that which man would pay to the angelic nature. And it yet fills me with wonder, that, in almost all countries, the most ancient poets are considered as the best: whether it be that every other kind of knowledge is an acquisition gradually attained, and poetry is a gift conferred at once; or that the first poetry of every nation surprised them as a novelty, and retained the credit by consent which it received by accident at first: or whether, as the province of poetry is to describe nature and passion,[6] which are always the same, the first writers took possession of the most striking objects for description, and the most probable occurrences for fiction, and left nothing to those that followed them, but transcription of the same events, and new combinations of the same images. Whatever be the reason, it is commonly observed that the early writers are in possession of nature, and their followers of art: that the first excel in strength and invention, and the latter in elegance and refinement.

"I was desirous to add my name to this illustrious fraternity. I read all the poets of Persia and Arabia, and was able to repeat by memory the volumes that are suspended in the mosque of Mecca. But I soon found that no man was ever great by imitation. My desire of excellence impelled me to transfer my attention to nature and to life. Nature was to be my subject, and men to be my auditors: I could never describe what I had not seen: I could not hope to move those with delight or terror, whose interests and opinions I did not understand.

"Being now resolved to be a poet, I saw every thing with a new purpose; my sphere of attention was suddenly magnified: no kind of knowledge was to be overlooked. I ranged mountains and deserts for images and resemblances, and pictured upon my mind every tree of the forest and flower of the valley. I observed with equal care the crags of the rock and the pinnacles of the palace. Sometimes I wandered along the mazes of the rivulet, and sometimes watched the changes of the summer clouds. To a poet nothing can be useless. Whatever is beautiful, and whatever is dreadful, must be familiar to his imagination: he must be conversant with all that is awfully[7] vast or elegantly little. The plants of the garden, the animals of the wood, the minerals of the earth, and meteors of the sky, must all concur to store his mind with inexhaustible variety: for every idea is useful for the enforcement or decoration of moral or religious truth; and he who knows most will have most power of

5. "Conveniences, things requisite to ease or refreshment" (Johnson's *Dictionary*).
6. Nature: "the constitution and appearance of things" (Johnson's *Dictionary*); Passion: "violent commotion of the mind" (Johnson's *Dictionary*).
7. Solemnly.

diversifying his scenes, and of gratifying his reader with remote allusions and unexpected instruction.

"All the appearances of nature I was therefore careful to study, and every country which I have surveyed has contributed something to my poetical powers."

"In so wide a survey," said the prince, "you must surely have left much unobserved. I have lived, till now, within the circuit of these mountains, and yet cannot walk abroad without the sight of something which I had never beheld before, or never heeded."

"The business of a poet," said Imlac, "is to examine, not the individual, but the species; to remark general properties and large appearances: he does not number the streaks of the tulip, or describe the different shades in the verdure of the forest. He is to exhibit in his portraits of nature such prominent and striking features, as recall the original to every mind; and must neglect the minuter discriminations, which one may have remarked, and another have neglected, for those characteristics which are alike obvious to vigilance and carelessness.

"But the knowledge of nature is only half the task of a poet; he must be acquainted likewise with all the modes of life. His character requires that he estimate the happiness and misery of every condition; observe the power of all the passions in all their combinations, and trace the changes of the human mind as they are modified by various institutions and accidental influences of climate or custom, from the sprightliness of infancy to the despondence of decrepitude. He must divest himself of the prejudices of his age or country; he must consider right and wrong in their abstracted and invariable state; he must disregard present laws and opinions, and rise to general and transcendental truths, which will always be the same: he must therefore content himself with the slow progress of his name; condemn the applause of his own time, and commit his claims to the justice of posterity. He must write as the interpreter of nature, and the legislator of mankind, and consider himself as presiding over the thoughts and manners of future generations; as a being superior to time and place.

"His labor is not yet at an end: he must know many languages and many sciences; and, that his style may be worthy of his thoughts, must, by incessant practice, familiarize to himself every delicacy of speech and grace of harmony."

Chapter 11. Imlac's Narrative Continued. A Hint on Pilgrimage

Imlac now felt the enthusiastic[8] fit, and was proceeding to aggrandize his own profession, when the prince cried out, "Enough! Thou hast convinced me, that no human being can ever be a poet. Proceed with thy narration."

"To be a poet," said Imlac, "is indeed very difficult." "So difficult," returned the prince, "that I will at present hear no more of his labors. Tell me whither you went when you had seen Persia."

"From Persia," said the poet, "I traveled through Syria, and for three years resided in Palestine, where I conversed with great numbers of the northern and western nations of Europe; the nations which are now in possession of all power and all knowledge; whose armies are irresistible, and whose fleets command the remotest parts of the globe. When I compared these men with the natives of our own kingdom, and those that surround us, they appeared almost another order of beings.

8. "Vehemently hot in any cause" (Johnson's *Dictionary*).

In their countries it is difficult to wish for any thing that may not be obtained: a thousand arts, of which we never heard, are continually laboring for their convenience and pleasure; and whatever their own climate has denied them is supplied by their commerce."

"By what means," said the prince, "are the Europeans thus powerful? or why, since they can so easily visit Asia and Africa for trade or conquest, cannot the Asiatics and Africans invade their coasts, plant colonies in their ports, and give laws to their natural princes? The same wind that carries them back would bring us thither."

"They are more powerful, Sir, than we," answered Imlac, "because they are wiser; knowledge will always predominate over ignorance, as man governs the other animals. But why their knowledge is more than ours, I know not what reason can be given, but the unsearchable will of the Supreme Being."

"When," said the prince with a sigh, "shall I be able to visit Palestine, and mingle with this mighty confluence of nations? Till that happy moment shall arrive, let me fill up the time with such representations as thou canst give me. I am not ignorant of the motive that assembles such numbers in that place, and cannot but consider it as the center of wisdom and piety, to which the best and wisest men of every land must be continually resorting."

"There are some nations," said Imlac, "that send few visitants[9] to Palestine; for many numerous and learned sects in Europe concur to censure pilgrimage as superstitious, or deride it as ridiculous."

"You know," said the prince, "how little my life has made me acquainted with diversity of opinions: it will be too long to hear the arguments on both sides; you, that have considered them, tell me the result."

"Pilgrimage," said Imlac, "like many other acts of piety, may be reasonable or superstitious, according to the principles upon which it is performed. Long journeys in search of truth are not commanded. Truth, such as is necessary to the regulation of life, is always found where it is honestly sought. Change of place is no natural cause of the increase of piety, for it inevitably produces dissipation of mind. Yet, since men go every day to view the fields where great actions have been performed, and return with stronger impressions of the event, curiosity of the same kind may naturally dispose us to view that country whence our religion had its beginning; and I believe no man surveys those awful scenes without some confirmation of holy resolutions. That the Supreme Being may be more easily propitiated in one place than in another, is the dream of idle superstition; but that some places may operate upon our own minds in an uncommon manner, is an opinion which hourly experience will justify. He who supposes that his vices may be more successfully combated in Palestine, will, perhaps, find himself mistaken, yet he may go thither without folly: he who thinks they will be more freely pardoned, dishonors at once his reason and religion."

"These," said the prince, "are European distinctions. I will consider them another time. What have you found to be the effect of knowledge? Are those nations happier than we?"

"There is so much infelicity," said the poet, "in the world, that scarce any man has leisure from his own distresses to estimate the comparative happiness of others. Knowledge is certainly one of the means of pleasure, as is confessed by the natural desire which every mind feels of increasing its ideas. Ignorance is mere privation, by

9. Pilgrims.

which nothing can be produced: it is a vacuity in which the soul sits motionless and torpid for want of attraction; and, without knowing why, we always rejoice when we learn, and grieve when we forget. I am therefore inclined to conclude that, if nothing counteracts the natural consequence of learning, we grow more happy as our minds take a wider range.

"In enumerating the particular comforts of life we shall find many advantages on the side of the Europeans. They cure wounds and diseases with which we languish and perish. We suffer inclemencies of weather which they can obviate. They have engines for the dispatch of many laborious works, which we must perform by manual industry. There is such communication between distant places, that one friend can hardly be said to be absent from another. Their policy removes all public inconveniences: they have roads cut through their mountains, and bridges laid upon their rivers. And, if we descend to the privacies of life, their habitations are more commodious, and their possessions are more secure."

"They are surely happy," said the prince, "who have all these conveniences, of which I envy none so much as the facility with which separated friends interchange their thoughts."

"The Europeans," answered Imlac, "are less unhappy than we, but they are not happy. Human life is every where a state in which much is to be endured, and little to be enjoyed."

Chapter 12. The Story of Imlac Continued

"I am not yet willing," said the prince, "to suppose that happiness is so parsimoniously distributed to mortals; nor can believe but that, if I had the choice of life, I should be able to fill every day with pleasure. I would injure no man, and should provoke no resentment: I would relieve every distress, and should enjoy the benedictions of gratitude. I would choose my friends among the wise, and my wife among the virtuous; and therefore should be in no danger from treachery, or unkindness. My children should, by my care, be learned and pious, and would repay to my age what their childhood had received. What would dare to molest him who might call on every side to thousands enriched by his bounty, or assisted by his power? And why should not life glide quietly away in the soft reciprocation of protection and reverence? All this may be done without the help of European refinements, which appear by their effects to be rather specious[1] than useful. Let us leave them and pursue our journey."

"From Palestine," said Imlac, "I passed through many regions of Asia; in the more civilized kingdoms as a trader, and among the barbarians of the mountains as a pilgrim. At last I began to long for my native country, that I might repose after my travels, and fatigues, in the places where I had spent my earliest years, and gladden my old companions with the recital of my adventures. Often did I figure to myself those, with whom I had sported away the gay hours of dawning life, sitting round me in its evening, wondering at my tales, and listening to my counsels.

"When this thought had taken possession of my mind, I considered every moment as wasted which did not bring me nearer to Abyssinia. I hastened into Egypt, and, notwithstanding my impatience, was detained ten months in the contemplation of its ancient magnificence, and in enquiries after the remains of its

1. "Showy; pleasing to the view" (Johnson's *Dictionary*).

ancient learning. I found in Cairo a mixture of all nations; some brought thither by the love of knowledge, some by the hope of gain, and many by the desire of living after their own manner without observation, and of lying hid in the obscurity of multitudes: for, in a city, populous as Cairo, it is possible to obtain at the same time the gratifications of society, and the secrecy of solitude.

"From Cairo I traveled to Suez, and embarked on the Red Sea, passing along the coast till I arrived at the port from which I had departed twenty years before. Here I joined myself to a caravan and re-entered my native country.

"I now expected the caresses of my kinsmen, and the congratulations of my friends, and was not without hope that my father, whatever value he had set upon riches, would own with gladness and pride a son who was able to add to the felicity and honor of the nation. But I was soon convinced that my thoughts were vain. My father had been dead fourteen years, having divided his wealth among my brothers, who were removed to some other provinces. Of my companions the greater part was in the grave, of the rest some could with difficulty remember me, and some considered me as one corrupted by foreign manners.

"A man used to vicissitudes is not easily dejected. I forgot, after a time, my disappointment, and endeavored to recommend myself to the nobles of the kingdom: they admitted me to their tables, heard my story, and dismissed me. I opened a school, and was prohibited to teach. I then resolved to sit down in the quiet of domestic life, and addressed a lady that was fond of my conversation, but rejected my suit, because my father was a merchant

"Wearied at last with solicitation and repulses, I resolved to hide myself for ever from the world, and depend no longer on the opinion or caprice of others. I waited for the time when the gate of the Happy Valley should open, that I might bid farewell to hope and fear: the day came; my performance was distinguished with favor, and I resigned myself with joy to perpetual confinement."

"Hast thou here found happiness at last?" said Rasselas. "Tell me without reserve; art thou content with thy condition? or, dost thou wish to be again wandering and inquiring? All the inhabitants of this valley celebrate their lot, and, at the annual visit of the emperor, invite others to partake of their felicity."

"Great prince," said Imlac, "I shall speak the truth: I know not one of all your attendants who does not lament the hour when he entered this retreat. I am less unhappy than the rest, because I have a mind replete with images, which I can vary and combine at pleasure. I can amuse my solitude by the renovation of the knowledge which begins to fade from my memory, and by recollection of the accidents of my past life. Yet all this ends in the sorrowful consideration, that my acquirements are now useless, and that none of my pleasures can be again enjoyed. The rest, whose minds have no impression but of the present moment, are either corroded by malignant passions, or sit stupid in the gloom of perpetual vacancy."

"What passions can infest those," said the prince, "who have no rivals? We are in a place where impotence precludes malice, and where all envy is repressed by community of enjoyments."

"There may be community," said Imlac, "of material possessions, but there can never be community of love or of esteem. It must happen that one will please more than another; he that knows himself despised will always be envious; and still more envious and malevolent, if he is condemned to live in the presence of those who despise him. The invitations, by which they allure others to a state which they feel to be wretched, proceed from the natural malignity of hopeless misery. They are weary of themselves, and of each other, and expect to find relief in new companions.

They envy the liberty which their folly has forfeited, and would gladly see all mankind imprisoned like themselves.

"From this crime, however, I am wholly free. No man can say that he is wretched by my persuasion. I look with pity on the crowds who are annually soliciting admission to captivity, and wish that it were lawful for me to warn them of their danger."

"My dear Imlac," said the prince, "I will open to thee my whole heart. I have long meditated an escape from the Happy Valley. I have examined the mountains on every side, but find myself insuperably barred: teach me the way to break my prison; thou shalt be the companion of my flight, the guide of my rambles, the partner of my fortune, and my sole director in the *choice of life*."

"Sir," answered the poet, "your escape will be difficult, and, perhaps, you may soon repent your curiosity. The world, which you figure to yourself smooth and quiet as the lake in the valley, you will find a sea foaming with tempests, and boiling with whirlpools: you will be sometimes overwhelmed by the waves of violence, and sometimes dashed against the rocks of treachery. Amidst wrongs and frauds, competitions and anxieties, you will wish a thousand times for these seats of quiet, and willingly quit hope to be free from fear."

"Do not seek to deter me from my purpose," said the prince: "I am impatient to see what thou hast seen; and, since thou art thyself weary of the valley, it is evident, that thy former state was better than this. Whatever be the consequence of my experiment, I am resolved to judge with my own eyes of the various conditions of men, and then to make deliberately my *choice of life*."

"I am afraid," said Imlac, "you are hindered by stronger restraints than my persuasions; yet, if your determination is fixed, I do not counsel you to despair. Few things are impossible to diligence and skill."

1759 1759

THE PLAYS OF WILLIAM SHAKESPEARE Johnson first proposed a new edition of Shakespeare's plays, without success, in 1745; he finally published one twenty tears later. In the intervening decades, his work on the *Dictionary* had made him (in Bertrand Bronson's phrase) "the greatest living authority on Shakespeare's diction," and had secured him such fame that the booksellers greeted his renewed Shakespeare proposal with enthusiasm rather than indifference. Even so, he found the work slow going; he promised completion in eighteen months and took nine years. Five major editions had appeared since the start of the century, and Johnson was alert to their many inadequacies. Earlier editors displayed a passion for emendation, for finding "printer's errors" everywhere in the text, and replacing them with overconfident conjectures as to what Shakespeare had really "meant" and wrote. Johnson opted more often to let things be: to take a passage as given, to discover its intention, to explain its success, or to analyze its failure. The same kind of scrutiny suffuses his Preface, in which he investigates how plays really operate upon their audience. In the process, he demolishes the critical criteria by which Shakespeare had long been deemed an inferior crafter of drama (albeit an inimitably inspired poet). Johnson's *Shakespeare* is distinctive for the energy of its thought and of its feeling; for the intensity of its grappling with the impact of tiny passages and of towering genius.

from The Plays of William Shakespeare
from *Preface*
["JUST REPRESENTATIONS OF GENERAL NATURE"]

That praises are without reason lavished on the dead, and that the honors due only to excellence are paid to antiquity, is a complaint likely to be always continued by those who, being able to add nothing to truth, hope for eminence from the heresies of paradox; or those who, being forced by disappointment upon consolatory expedients, are willing to hope from posterity what the present age refuses and flatter themselves that the regard which is yet denied by envy will be at last bestowed by time.

Antiquity, like every other quality that attracts the notice of mankind, has undoubtedly votaries that reverence it not from reason, but from prejudice. Some seem to admire indiscriminately whatever has been long preserved, without considering that time has sometimes cooperated with chance; all perhaps are more willing to honor past than present excellence; and the mind contemplates genius through the shades of age, as the eye surveys the sun through artificial opacity. The great contention of criticism is to find the faults of the moderns and the beauties of the ancients. While an author is yet living, we estimate his powers by his worst performance; and when he is dead, we rate them by his best.

To works, however, of which the excellence is not absolute and definite, but gradual and comparative; to works not raised upon principles demonstrative and scientific but appealing wholly to observation and experience, no other test can be applied than length of duration and continuance of esteem. What mankind have long possessed they have often examined and compared; and if they persist to value the possession, it is because frequent comparisons have confirmed opinion in its favor. As among the works of nature no man can properly call a river deep or a mountain high, without the knowledge of many mountains and many rivers; so, in the productions of genius, nothing can be styled excellent till it has been compared with other works of the same kind. Demonstration immediately displays its power and has nothing to hope or fear from the flux of years; but works tentative and experimental must be estimated by their proportion to the general and collective ability of man, as it is discovered in a long succession of endeavors. Of the first building that was raised, it might be with certainty determined that it was round or square, but whether it was spacious or lofty must have been referred to time. The Pythagorean scale of numbers was at once discovered to be perfect; but the poems of Homer we yet know not to transcend the common limits of human intelligence but by remarking that nation after nation, and century after century, has been able to do little more than transpose his incidents, new-name his characters, and paraphrase his sentiments.

The reverence due to writings that have long subsisted arises, therefore, not from any credulous confidence in the superior wisdom of past ages or gloomy persuasion of the degeneracy of mankind, but is the consequence of acknowledged and indubitable positions that what has been longest known has been most considered, and what is most considered is best understood.

The poet of whose works I have undertaken the revision[1] may now begin to assume the dignity of an ancient and claim the privilege of established fame and prescriptive veneration. He has long outlived his century, the term commonly fixed as the test of literary merit. Whatever advantages he might once derive from personal allusions, local customs, or temporary opinions have for many years been lost; and every topic of merriment or motive of sorrow which the modes of artificial[2] life afforded him now only obscure the scenes which they once illuminated. The effects of favor and competition are at an end; the tradition of his friendships and his enmities have perished; his works support no opinion with arguments nor supply any

1. Edition.

2. "Made by art; not natural" (Johnson's *Dictionary*).

faction with invectives; they can neither indulge vanity nor gratify malignity, but are read without any other reason than the desire of pleasure and are therefore praised only as pleasure is obtained; yet, thus unassisted by interest or passion, they have passed through variations of taste and changes of manners, and, as they devolved from one generation to another, have received new honors at every transmission.

But because human judgment, though it be gradually gaining upon certainty, never becomes infallible; and approbation, though long continued, may yet be only the approbation of prejudice or fashion; it is proper to inquire by what peculiarities of excellence Shakespeare has gained and kept the favor of his countrymen.

Nothing can please many, and please long, but just representations of general nature. Particular manners can be known to few, and therefore few only can judge how nearly they are copied. The irregular combinations of fanciful invention may delight awhile by that novelty of which the common satiety of life sends us all in quest; but the pleasures of sudden wonder are soon exhausted, and the mind can only repose on the stability of truth.

Shakespeare is, above all writers, at least above all modern writers, the poet of nature, the poet that holds up to his readers a faithful mirror of manners and of life. His characters are not modified by the customs of particular places, unpracticed by the rest of the world; by the peculiarities of studies or professions which can operate but upon small numbers; or by the accidents of transient fashions or temporary opinions: they are the genuine progeny of common humanity, such as the world will always supply, and observation will always find. His persons act and speak by the influence of those general passions and principles by which all minds are agitated and the whole system of life is continued in motion. In the writings of other poets a character is too often an individual; in those of Shakespeare it is commonly a species.

It is from this wide extension of design that so much instruction is derived. It is this which fills the plays of Shakespeare with practical axioms and domestic wisdom. It was said of Euripides that every verse was a precept;[3] and it may be said of Shakespeare that from his works may be collected a system of civil and economical prudence.[4] Yet his real power is not shown in the splendor of particular passages, but by the progress of his fable and the tenor of his dialogue; and he that tries to recommend him by select quotations will succeed like the pedant in Hierocles,[5] who, when he offered his house for sale, carried a brick in his pocket as a specimen.

It will not easily be imagined how much Shakespeare excels in accommodating his sentiments to real life but by comparing him with other authors. It was observed of the ancient schools of declamation that the more diligently they were frequented, the more was the student disqualified for the world, because he found nothing there which he should ever meet in any other place. The same remark may be applied to every stage but that of Shakespeare. The theater, when it is under any other direction, is peopled by such characters as were never seen, conversing in a language which was never heard, upon topics which will never arise in the commerce of mankind. But the dialogue of this author is often so evidently determined by the incident which produces it, and is pursued with so much ease and simplicity, that it seems scarcely to claim the merit of fiction, but to have been gleaned by diligent selection out of common conversation and common occurrences.

3. This observation was made by Cicero in his *Familiar Letters* (16.8).

4. Public and private duty.

5. The critic Hierocles, writing in the 5th century C.E., tells this story in his commentary on Pythagoras.

Upon every other stage the universal agent is love, by whose power all good and evil is distributed and every action quickened or retarded. To bring a lover, a lady, and a rival into the fable; to entangle them in contradictory obligations, perplex them with oppositions of interest, and harass them with violence of desires inconsistent with each other; to make them meet in rapture and part in agony, to fill their mouths with hyperbolical joy and outrageous sorrow, to distress them as nothing human ever was distressed, to deliver them as nothing human ever was delivered, is the business of a modern dramatist. For this, probability is violated, life is misrepresented, and language is depraved. But love is only one of many passions; and as it has no great influence upon the sum of life, it has little operation in the dramas of a poet who caught his ideas from the living world and exhibited only what he saw before him. He knew that any other passion, as it was regular or exorbitant, was a cause of happiness or calamity.

Characters thus ample and general were not easily discriminated and preserved, yet perhaps no poet ever kept his personages more distinct from each other. I will not say with Pope that every speech may be assigned to the proper speaker, because many speeches there are which have nothing characteristical; but, perhaps, though some may be equally adapted to every person, it will be difficult to find any that can be properly transferred from the present possessor to another claimant. The choice is right, when there is reason for choice.

Other dramatists can only gain attention by hyperbolical or aggravated[6] characters, by fabulous and unexampled excellence or depravity, as the writers of barbarous romances invigorated the reader by a giant and a dwarf; and he that should form his expectations of human affairs from the play, or from the tale, would be equally deceived. Shakespeare has no heroes; his scenes are occupied only by men, who act and speak as the reader thinks that he should himself have spoken or acted on the same occasion. Even where the agency is supernatural, the dialogue is level with life. Other writers disguise the most natural passions and most frequent incidents, so that he who contemplates them in the book will not know them in the world. Shakespeare approximates the remote and familiarizes the wonderful; the event which he represents will not happen but, if it were possible, its effects would probably be such as he has assigned; and it may be said that he has not only shown human nature as it acts in real exigences, but as it would be found in trials to which it cannot be exposed.

This, therefore, is the praise of Shakespeare, that his drama is the mirror of life; that he who has mazed his imagination in following the phantoms which other writers raise up before him may here be cured of his delirious ecstasies by reading human sentiments in human language, by scenes from which a hermit may estimate the transactions of the world and a confessor predict the progress of the passions.

[Faults; The Unities]

Shakespeare with his excellencies has likewise faults, and faults sufficient to obscure and overwhelm any other merit. I shall show them in the proportion in which they appear to me, without envious malignity or superstitious veneration. No question can be more innocently discussed than a dead poet's pretensions to renown; and little regard is due to that bigotry which sets candor[1] higher than truth.

6. Exaggerated.

1. "Sweetness of temper; kindness" (Johnson's *Dictionary*).

His first defect is that to which may be imputed most of the evil in books or in men. He sacrifices virtue to convenience and is so much more careful to please than to instruct that he seems to write without any moral purpose. From his writings indeed a system of social duty may be selected, for he that thinks reasonably must think morally; but his precepts and axioms drop casually from him; he makes no just distribution of good or evil, nor is always careful to show in the virtuous a disapprobation of the wicked; he carries his persons indifferently through right and wrong and at the close dismisses them without further care and leaves their examples to operate by chance. This fault the barbarity of his age cannot extenuate; for it is always a writer's duty to make the world better, and justice is a virtue independent on time or place.

The plots are often so loosely formed that a very slight consideration may improve them, and so carelessly pursued that he seems not always to comprehend his own design. He omits opportunities of instructing or delighting which the train of his story seems to force upon him, and apparently rejects those exhibitions which would be more affecting, for the sake of those which are more easy.

It may be observed that in many of his plays the latter part is evidently neglected. When he found himself near the end of his work and in view of his reward, he shortened the labor to snatch the profit. He therefore remits his efforts where he should most vigorously exert them, and his catastrophe is improbably produced or imperfectly represented.

He had no regard to distinction of time or place but gives to one age or nation, without scruple, the customs, institutions, and opinions of another, at the expense not only of likelihood but of possibility. These faults Pope has endeavored, with more zeal than judgment, to transfer to his imagined interpolators. We need not wonder to find Hector quoting Aristotle,[2] when we see the loves of Theseus and Hippolyta combined with the Gothic mythology of fairies.[3] Shakespeare, indeed, was not the only violator of chronology, for in the same age Sidney, who wanted not[4] the advantages of learning, has, in his Arcadia, confounded the pastoral with the feudal times, the days of innocence, quiet, and security, with those of turbulence, violence, and adventure.

In his comic scenes he is seldom very successful when he engages his characters in reciprocations of smartness and contests of sarcasm; their jests are commonly gross and their pleasantry licentious; neither his gentlemen nor his ladies have much delicacy nor are sufficiently distinguished from his clowns by any appearance of refined manners. Whether he represented the real conversation of his time is not easy to determine. The reign of Elizabeth is commonly supposed to have been a time of stateliness, formality, and reserve; yet perhaps the relaxations of that severity were not very elegant. There must, however, have been always some modes of gaiety preferable to others, and a writer ought to choose the best.

In tragedy his performance seems constantly to be worse as his labor is more. The effusions of passion which exigence forces out are for the most part striking and energetic; but whenever he solicits his invention or strains his faculties, the offspring of his throes is tumor, meanness, tediousness, and obscurity.

In narration he affects a disproportionate pomp of diction and a wearisome train of circumlocution and tells the incident imperfectly in many words which might have been more plainly delivered in few. Narration in dramatic poetry is naturally tedious, as it is unanimated and inactive and obstructs the progress of the action; it

2. *Troilus and Cressida* 2.2.166–67.
3. This combination occurs in *A Midsummer Night's Dream*.
4. Did not lack.

should therefore always be rapid and enlivened by frequent interruption. Shakespeare found it an encumbrance and, instead of lightening it by brevity, endeavored to recommend it by dignity and splendor.

His declamations or set speeches are commonly cold and weak, for his power was the power of nature; when he endeavored, like other tragic writers, to catch opportunities of amplification and, instead of inquiring what the occasion demanded, to show how much his stores of knowledge could supply, he seldom escapes without the pity or resentment of his reader.

It is incident to him to be now and then entangled with an unwieldy sentiment, which he cannot well express and will not reject; he struggles with it awhile and, if it continues stubborn, comprises it in words such as occur and leaves it to be disentangled and evolved by those who have more leisure to bestow upon it.

Not that always where the language is intricate the thought is subtle, or the image always great where the line is bulky; the equality of words to things is very often neglected, and trivial sentiments and vulgar ideas disappoint the attention to which they are recommended by sonorous epithets and swelling figures.[5]

But the admirers of this great poet have most reason to complain when he approaches nearest to his highest excellence and seems fully resolved to sink them in dejection and mollify them with tender emotions by the fall of greatness, the danger of innocence, or the crosses[6] of love. What he does best, he soon ceases to do. He is not long soft and pathetic without some idle conceit[7] or contemptible equivocation. He no sooner begins to move than he counteracts himself; and terror and pity, as they are rising in the mind, are checked and blasted by sudden frigidity.

A quibble[8] is to Shakespeare what luminous vapors are to the traveler; he follows it at all adventures; it is sure to lead him out of his way and sure to engulf him in the mire. It has some malignant power over his mind, and its fascinations are irresistible. Whatever be the dignity or profundity of his disquisition, whether he be enlarging knowledge or exalting affection, whether he be amusing attention with incidents or enchaining it in suspense, let but a quibble spring up before him and he leaves his work unfinished. A quibble is the golden apple for which he will always turn aside from his career or stoop from his elevation.[9] A quibble, poor and barren as it is, gave him such delight that he was content to purchase it by the sacrifice of reason, propriety, and truth. A quibble was to him the fatal Cleopatra for which he lost the world and was content to lose it.

It will be thought strange that in enumerating the defects of this writer I have not yet mentioned his neglect of the unities, his violation of those laws which have been instituted and established by the joint authority of poets and critics.

For his other deviations from the art of writing, I resign him to critical justice without making any other demand in his favor than that which must be indulged to all human excellence: that his virtues be rated with his failings. But from the censure which this irregularity may bring upon him, I shall, with due reverence to that learning which I must oppose, adventure to try how I can defend him.

His histories, being neither tragedies nor comedies, are not subject to any of their laws; nothing more is necessary to all the praise which they expect than that

5. Figures of speech.
6. Obstacles, vexations.
7. Play on words.
8. Pun.
9. Johnson alludes to the story of the runner Atalanta, who lost a race because she was distracted by golden apples tossed in her path.

the changes of action be so prepared as to be understood, that the incidents be various and affecting, and the characters consistent, natural, and distinct. No other unity is intended, and therefore none is to be sought.

In his other works he has well enough preserved the unity of action. He has not, indeed, an intrigue regularly perplexed and regularly unraveled; he does not endeavor to hide his design only to discover it, for this is seldom the order of real events, and Shakespeare is the poet of nature; but his plan has commonly, what Aristotle requires,[1] a beginning, a middle, and an end, one event is concatenated with another, and the conclusion follows by easy consequence. There are perhaps some incidents that might be spared, as in other poets there is much talk that only fills up time upon the stage; but the general system makes gradual advances, and the end of the play is the end of expectation.

To the unities of time and place he has shown no regard; and perhaps a nearer view of the principles on which they stand will diminish their value and withdraw from them the veneration which, from the time of Corneille,[2] they have very generally received, by discovering that they have given more trouble to the poet than pleasure to the auditor.

The necessity of observing the unities of time and place arises from the supposed necessity of making the drama credible. The critics hold it impossible that an action of months or years can be possibly believed to pass in three hours; or that the spectator can suppose himself to sit in the theater while ambassadors go and return between distant kings, while armies are levied and towns besieged, while an exile wanders and returns, or till he whom they saw courting his mistress shall lament the untimely fall of his son. The mind revolts from evident falsehood, and fiction loses its force when it departs from the resemblance of reality.

From the narrow limitation of time necessarily arises the contraction of place. The spectator, who knows that he saw the first act at Alexandria, cannot suppose that he sees the next at Rome, at a distance to which not the dragons of Medea[3] could, in so short a time, have transported him; he knows with certainty that he has not changed his place; and he knows that place cannot change itself; that what was a house cannot become a plain; that what was Thebes can never be Persepolis.

Such is the triumphant language with which a critic exults over the misery of an irregular poet and exults commonly without resistance or reply. It is time, therefore, to tell him by the authority of Shakespeare, that he assumes, as an unquestionable principle, a position which, while his breath is forming it into words, his understanding pronounces to be false. It is false, that any representation is mistaken for reality; that any dramatic fable in its materiality was ever credible, or, for a single moment, was ever credited.

The objection arising from the impossibility of passing the first hour at Alexandria and the next at Rome supposes that when the play opens the spectator really imagines himself at Alexandria and believes that his walk to the theater has been a voyage to Egypt, and that he lives in the days of Antony and Cleopatra. Surely he that imagines this may imagine more. He that can take the stage at one time for the palace of the Ptolemies may take it in half an hour for the promontory of Actium. Delusion, if delusion be admitted, has no certain limitation; if the spectator can be

1. Aristotle, *Poetics*, ch. 8.

2. The French neoclassical dramatist Pierre Corneille published his influential *Essay on the Three Unities* in 1660.

3. After killing her rival and her children, Medea eluded pursuit in a chariot drawn by dragons.

once persuaded that his old acquaintance are Alexander and Caesar, that a room illuminated with candles is the plain of Pharsalia or the bank of Granicus,[4] he is in a state of elevation above the reach of reason or of truth, and from the heights of empyrean poetry may despise the circumscriptions of terrestrial nature. There is no reason why a mind thus wandering in ecstasy should count the clock, or why an hour should not be a century in that calenture[5] of the brains that can make the stage a field.

The truth is that the spectators are always in their senses and know from the first act to the last that the stage is only a stage, and that the players are only players. They come to hear a certain number of lines recited with just gesture and elegant modulation. The lines relate to some action, and an action must be in some place; but the different actions that complete a story may be in places very remote from each other; and where is the absurdity of allowing that space to represent first Athens and then Sicily which was always known to be neither Sicily nor Athens, but a modern theater?

By supposition, as place is introduced, time may be extended; the time required by the fable elapses for the most part between the acts; for, of so much of the action as is represented, the real and poetical duration is the same. If in the first act preparations for war against Mithridates are represented to be made in Rome, the event of the war may, without absurdity, be represented in the catastrophe as happening in Pontus; we know that there is neither war nor preparation for war; we know that we are neither in Rome nor Pontus; that neither Mithridates nor Lucullus are before us. The drama exhibits successive imitations of successive actions; and why may not the second imitation represent an action that happened years after the first if it be so connected with it that nothing but time can be supposed to intervene? Time is, of all modes of existence, most obsequious to the imagination; a lapse of years is as easily conceived as a passage of hours. In contemplation we easily contract the time of real actions and therefore willingly permit it to be contracted when we only see their imitation.

It will be asked how the drama moves if it is not credited. It is credited with all the credit due to a drama. It is credited, whenever it moves, as a just picture of a real original; as representing to the auditor what he would himself feel if he were to do or suffer what is there feigned to be suffered or to be done. The reflection that strikes the heart is not that the evils before us are real evils, but that they are evils to which we ourselves may be exposed. If there be any fallacy, it is not that we fancy the players, but that we fancy ourselves unhappy for a moment; but we rather lament the possibility than suppose the presence of misery, as a mother weeps over her babe when she remembers that death may take it from her. The delight of tragedy proceeds from our consciousness of fiction; if we thought murders and treasons real, they would please no more.

Imitations produce pain or pleasure not because they are mistaken for realities, but because they bring realities to mind. When the imagination is recreated[6] by a painted landscape, the trees are not supposed capable to give us shade, or the fountains coolness; but we consider how we should be pleased with such fountains playing beside us and such woods waving over us. We are agitated in reading the history of *Henry the Fifth*, yet no man takes his book for the field of Agincourt. A dramatic

4. Johnson refers to the site of battles fought by Julius Caesar and Alexander the Great.

5. Fever.

6. "Delighted, gratified" (Johnson's *Dictionary*).

exhibition is a book recited with concomitants that increase or diminish its effect. Familiar[7] comedy is often more powerful in the theater than on the page; imperial tragedy is always less. The humor of Petruchio[8] may be heightened by grimace; but what voice or what gesture can hope to add dignity or force to the soliloquy of Cato?[9]

A play read affects the mind like a play acted. It is therefore evident that the action is not supposed to be real; and it follows that between the acts a longer or shorter time may be allowed to pass, and that no more account of space or duration is to be taken by the auditor of a drama than by the reader of a narrative, before whom may pass in an hour the life of a hero or the revolutions of an empire.

Whether Shakespeare knew the unities and rejected them by design, or deviated from them by happy ignorance, it is, I think, impossible to decide and useless to inquire. We may reasonably suppose that when he rose to notice, he did not want the counsels and admonitions of scholars and critics, and that he at last deliberately persisted in a practice which he might have begun by chance. As nothing is essential to the fable but unity of action, and as the unities of time and place arise evidently from false assumptions, and, by circumscribing the extent of the drama, lessen its variety, I cannot think it much to be lamented that they were not known by him, or not observed; nor, if such another poet could arise, should I very vehemently reproach him that his first act passed at Venice and his next in Cyprus.[1] Such violations of rules merely positive become the comprehensive genius of Shakespeare, and such censures are suitable to the minute and slender criticism of Voltaire:

Non usque adeo permiscuit imis
Longus summa dies, ut non, si voce Metelli
Serventur leges, malint a Caesare tolli.[2]

Yet when I speak thus slightly of dramatic rules, I cannot but recollect how much wit and learning may be produced against me; before such authorities I am afraid to stand, not that I think the present question one of those that are to be decided by mere authority, but because it is to be suspected that these precepts have not been so easily received but for better reasons than I have yet been able to find. The result of my inquiries, in which it would be ludicrous to boast of impartiality, is that the unities of time and place are not essential to a just drama; that, though they may sometimes conduce to pleasure, they are always to be sacrificed to the nobler beauties of variety and instruction; and that a play written with nice observation of critical rules is to be contemplated as an elaborate curiosity, as the product of superfluous and ostentatious art, by which is shown rather what is possible than what is necessary.

He that, without diminution of any other excellence, shall preserve all the unities unbroken deserves the like applause with the architect who shall display all the orders of architecture[3] in a citadel without any deduction from its strength; but the principal beauty of a citadel is to exclude the enemy, and the greatest graces of a play are to copy nature and instruct life. * * *

7. Domestic.
8. The hero of *The Taming of the Shrew*.
9. The protagonist of Addison's tragedy, *Cato* (1713), soliloquizes at the beginning of the final act.
1. Johnson refers to *Othello*.
2. Johnson quotes from the epic poem *Pharsalia* by Lucan: "Things are not yet so confused that / If the laws were preserved by the voice of Metellus, / They would not prefer to be suppressed by Caesar." Johnson aligns Metellus, a politician of negligible importance, with Voltaire; Caesar correlates with Shakespeare.
3. The five classical styles of architecture.

[SELECTED NOTES ON *OTHELLO*]

OTHELLO: Wherein of antres vast, and deserts idle,
Rough quarries, rocks, and hills, whose heads touch heaven . . . (1.3.141–42)

Whoever ridicules this account of the progress of love,[1] shows his ignorance, not only of history, but of nature and manners. It is no wonder that, in any age, or in any nation, a lady, recluse, timorous, and delicate, should desire to hear of events and scenes which she could never see, and should admire the man who had endured dangers, and performed actions, which, however great, were yet magnified by her timidity.

Every mind is liable to absence and inadvertency, else Pope could never have rejected a word so poetically beautiful.[2] "Idle" is an epithet used to express the infertility of the chaotic state, in the Saxon translation of the Pentateuch.

DESDEMONA: That I did love the Moor to live with him,
My downright violence and storm of fortunes
May trumpet to the world. (1.3.249–51)

There is no need of this emendation.[3] "Violence" is not "violence suffered," but "violence acted." Breach of common rules and obligations. The old quarto has, "scorn" of fortune, which is perhaps the true reading.

DESDEMONA: I saw Othello's visage in his mind,
And to his honors and his valiant parts
Did I my soul and fortunes consecrate. (1.3.253–55)

It must raise no wonder, that I loved a man of an appearance so little engaging; I saw his face only in his mind; the greatness of his character reconciled me to his form.

OTHELLO: Excellent wretch![4] (3.3.91)

The meaning of the word "wretch," is not generally understood. It is now, in some parts of England, a term of the softest and fondest tenderness. It expresses the utmost degree of amiableness, joined with an idea, which perhaps all tenderness includes, of feebleness, softness, and want of protection. Othello, considering Desdemona as excelling in beauty and virtue, soft and timorous by her sex, and by her situation absolutely in his power, calls her "excellent wretch." It may be expressed: "Dear, harmless, helpless excellence."

OTHELLO: when I love thee not,
Chaos is come again. (3.3.91–92)

When my love is for a moment suspended by suspicion, I have nothing in my mind but discord, tumult, perturbation, and confusion.

IAGO: She did deceive her father, marrying you;
And when she seemed to shake and fear your looks,
She loved them most. (3.3.206–8)

1. As had Thomas Rymer in his *Short View of Tragedy* (1692).
2. In his edition of Shakespeare's works (1725), Alexander Pope had emended "deserts idle" to "deserts wild."
3. A prior editor had emended "violence and storm of fortunes" to "violence to forms, my fortunes."
4. In his edition of Shakespeare's works (1733–1734), Lewis Theobald had emended "wretch" to "wench."

This and the following argument of Iago ought to be deeply impressed on every reader. Deceit and falsehood, whatever conveniences they may for a time promise or produce, are, in the sum of life, obstacles to happiness. Those who profit by the cheat, distrust the deceiver, and the act by which kindness was sought, puts an end to confidence.

The same objection may be made with a lower degree of strength against the imprudent generosity of disproportionate marriages. When the first heat of passion is over, it is easily succeeded by suspicion, that the same violence of inclination which caused one irregularity, may stimulate to another; and those who have shown, that their passions are too powerful for their prudence, will, with very slight appearances against them, be censured, as not very likely to restrain them by their virtue.

EMILIA: 'Tis not a year or two shows us a man. (3.4.97)

From this line it may be conjectured, that the author intended the action of this play to be considered as longer than is marked by any note of time. Since their arrival at Cyprus, to which they were hurried on their wedding-night, the fable seems to have been in one continual progress, nor can I see any vacuity into which a "year or two," or even a month or two, could be put. On the night of Othello's arrival, a feast was proclaimed; at that feast Cassio was degraded, and immediately applies to Desdemona to get him restored. Iago indeed advises Othello to hold him off a while, but there is no reason to think, that he has been held off long. A little longer interval would increase the probability of the story, though it might violate the rules of the drama. See Act 5, Scene 2

OTHELLO: It is the cause, it is the cause, my soul.
Let me not name it to you, you chaste stars!
It is the cause. (5.2.1–3)

The abruptness of this soliloquy makes it obscure. The meaning I think is this. "I am here," says Othello in his mind, "overwhelmed with horror. What is the reason of this perturbation? Is it want of resolution to do justice? Is it the dread of shedding blood? No; it is not the action that shocks me, but 'it is the cause, it is the cause, my soul; let me not name it to you, ye chaste stars! it is the cause.'"

OTHELLO: This sorrow's heavenly;
It strikes where it doth love. (5.2.21–2)

This tenderness, with which I lament the punishment which justice compels me to inflict, is a holy passion.

I wish these two lines could be honestly ejected. It is the fate of Shakespeare to counteract his own pathos.

OTHELLO: Oh perjured woman! thou dost stone my heart,
And mak'st me call, what I intend to do,
A murder, which I thought a sacrifice. (5.2.67–69)

This line is difficult. "Thou hast hardened my heart, and makest me" kill thee with the rage of a "murderer," when "I thought to have sacrificed" thee to justice with the calmness of a priest striking a victim.

It must not be omitted, that one of the elder quartos reads, "thou dost stone *thy* heart"; which I suspect to be genuine. The meaning then will be, "thou forcest me" to dismiss thee from the world in the state of the "murdered" without preparation for death, "when I intended" that thy punishment should have been "a sacrifice" atoning for thy crime.

I am glad that I have ended my revisal of this dreadful scene. It is not to be endured.

The beauties of this play impress themselves so strongly upon the attention of the reader, that they can draw no aid from critical illustration. The fiery openness of Othello, magnanimous, artless, and credulous, boundless in his confidence, ardent in his affection, inflexible in his resolution, and obdurate in his revenge; the cool malignity of Iago, silent in his resentment, subtle in his designs, and studious at once of his interest and his vengeance; the soft simplicity of Desdemona, confident of merit, and conscious of innocence, her artless perseverance in her suit, and her slowness to suspect that she can be suspected, are such proofs of Shakespeare's skill in human nature, as, I suppose, it is vain to seek in any modern writer. The gradual progress which Iago makes in the Moor's conviction, and the circumstances which he employs to inflame him, are so artfully natural, that, though it will perhaps not be said of him as he says of himself, that he is "a man not easily jealous," yet we cannot but pity him when at last we find him "perplexed in the extreme."

There is always danger lest wickedness conjoined with abilities should steal upon esteem, though it misses of approbation; but the character of Iago is so conducted, that he is from the first scene to the last hated and despised.

Even the inferior characters of this play would be very conspicuous in any other piece, not only for their justness but their strength. Cassio is brave, benevolent, and honest, ruined only by his want of stubbornness to resist an insidious invitation. Roderigo's suspicious credulity, and impatient submission to the cheats which he sees practiced upon him, and which by persuasion he suffers to be repeated, exhibit a strong picture of a weak mind betrayed by unlawful desires, to a false friend; and the virtue of Emilia is such as we often find, worn loosely, but not cast off, easy to commit small crimes, but quickened and alarmed at atrocious villanies.

The scenes from the beginning to the end are busy, varied by happy interchanges, and regularly promoting the progression of the story; and the narrative in the end, though it tells but what is known already, yet is necessary to produce the death of Othello.

Had the scene opened in Cyprus, and the preceding incidents been occasionally related, there had been little wanting to a drama of the most exact and scrupulous regularity.[5]

LIVES OF THE POETS In March 1777, a consortium of booksellers persuaded Johnson to undertake a new endeavor. "I am engaged," he informed Boswell, "to write little Lives and little Prefaces, to a little edition of the English Poets" of the past century and a half. In the end, he produced fifty-two *Prefaces Biographical and Critical*, now better known as *Lives of the Poets*. Some of the lives remained "little" (the booksellers had selected the poets, and Johnson did not consider all of them worthy of sustained attention); but many of them expanded in range and interest far beyond Johnson's initial expectation. As Boswell later observed, Johnson pursued the project "with peculiar delight" because he knew this literary territory so very well. In the longest *Lives* (of Milton, Dryden, Addison, and Pope), Johnson paid complex tribute to the predecessors who had mattered most to him as models in his youth—who had shaped the literary

5. I.e., according to the rules of the "unities," which Johnson rejects in the Preface.

world in which he had now found his own place. The three-part structure in which Johnson cast most of the prefaces was well calculated to display the powers and precepts accumulated over a lifetime. In the first part, an account of the poet's life, he fulfilled his own dictum (in *Rambler* No. 60) that biography is most useful when it deals in the "minute details" and "domestic privacies" of the subject's daily life; in the second part, an assessment of the poet's character, he implemented his own conviction that the biographer (unlike the eulogist) should forgo pure praise in favor of complex truth; in the third section, a critical review of the poet's work, he found full scope for the close analysis of literary cause and effect that had always informed his reading. "The biographical part of literature," he had once remarked, "is what I love the most." The *Lives* were that love's last labor. In them, the fusion of a favorite genre with a deeply familiar subject produced, in John Wain's words, "the greatest masterpiece of English eighteenth-century criticism."

from Lives of the Poets

from *The Life of Milton*

[ON PARADISE LOST]

Whatever be his subject he never fails to fill the imagination. But his images and descriptions of the scenes or operations of nature do not seem to be always copied from original form, nor to have the freshness, raciness,[1] and energy of immediate observation. He saw nature, as Dryden expresses it, "through the spectacles of books"; and on most occasions calls learning to his assistance. The garden of Eden brings to his mind the vale of Enna, where Proserpine was gathering flowers. Satan makes his way through fighting elements, like Argo between the Cyanean rocks, or Ulysses between the two Sicilian whirlpools, when he shunned Charybdis "on the larboard." The mythological allusions have been justly censured, as not being always used with notice of their vanity; but they contribute variety to the narration, and produce an alternate exercise of the memory and the fancy.

His similes are less numerous and more various than those of his predecessors. But he does not confine himself within the limits of rigorous comparison: his great excellence is amplitude, and he expands the adventitious[2] image beyond the dimensions which the occasion required. Thus, comparing the shield of Satan to the orb of the moon, he crowds the imagination with the discovery of the telescope and all the wonders which the telescope discovers.

Of his moral sentiments it is hardly praise to affirm that they excel those of all other poets; for this superiority he was indebted to his acquaintance with the sacred writings. The ancient epic poets, wanting the light of revelation, were very unskillful teachers of virtue: their principal characters may be great, but they are not amiable. The reader may rise from their works with a greater degree of active or passive fortitude, and sometimes of prudence; but he will be able to carry away few precepts of justice, and none of mercy. * * *

In Milton every line breathes sanctity of thought and purity of manners, except when the train of the narration requires the introduction of the rebellious spirits; and even they are compelled to acknowledge their subjection to God in such a manner as excites reverence and confirms piety.

1. "Strong; flavorous; tasting of the soil" (Johnson's *Dictionary*).

2. Accidental.

Of human beings there are but two; but those two are the parents of mankind, venerable before their fall for dignity and innocence, and amiable after it for repentance and submission. In their first state their affection is tender without weakness, and their piety sublime without presumption. When they have sinned they show how discord begins in mutual frailty, and how it ought to cease in mutual forbearance; how confidence of the divine favor is forfeited by sin, and how hope of pardon may be obtained by penitence and prayer. A state of innocence we can only conceive, if indeed in our present misery it be possible to conceive it; but the sentiments and worship proper to a fallen and offending being we have all to learn, as we have all to practice.

The poet whatever be done is always great. Our progenitors in their first state conversed with angels; even when folly and sin had degraded them they had not in their humiliation "the port of mean suitors"; and they rise again to reverential regard when we find that their prayers were heard.

As human passions did not enter the world before the Fall, there is in the *Paradise Lost* little opportunity for the pathetic;[3] but what little there is has not been lost. That passion which is peculiar to rational nature, the anguish arising from the consciousness of transgression and the horrors attending the sense of the Divine Displeasure, are very justly described and forcibly impressed. But the passions are moved only on one occasion; sublimity is the general and prevailing quality in this poem—sublimity variously modified, sometimes descriptive, sometimes argumentative.

The defects and faults of *Paradise Lost*, for faults and defects every work of man must have, it is the business of impartial criticism to discover. As in displaying the excellence of Milton I have not made long quotations, because of selecting beauties there had been no end, I shall in the same general manner mention that which seems to deserve censure; for what Englishman can take delight in transcribing passages, which, if they lessen the reputation of Milton, diminish in some degree the honor of our country?

The generality of my scheme does not admit the frequent notice of verbal inaccuracies which Bentley,[4] perhaps better skilled in grammar than in poetry, has often found, though he sometimes made them, and which he imputed to the obtrusions of a reviser whom the author's blindness obliged him to employ. A supposition rash and groundless, if he thought it true; and vile and pernicious, if, as is said, he in private allowed it to be false.

The plan of *Paradise Lost* has this inconvenience, that it comprises neither human actions nor human manners. The man and woman who act and suffer are in a state which no other man or woman can ever know. The reader finds no transaction in which he can be engaged, beholds no condition in which he can by any effort of imagination place himself; he has, therefore, little natural curiosity or sympathy.

We all, indeed, feel the effects of Adam's disobedience; we all sin like Adam, and like him must all bewail our offenses; we have restless and insidious enemies in the fallen angels, and in the blessed spirits we have guardians and friends; in the Redemption of mankind we hope to be included: in the description of heaven and hell we are surely interested, as we are all to reside hereafter either in the regions of horror or of bliss.

But these truths are too important to be new: they have been taught to our infancy; they have mingled with our solitary thoughts and familiar conversation, and are habitually interwoven with the whole texture of life. Being therefore not new they raise no unaccustomed emotion in the mind: what we knew before we cannot learn; what is not unexpected, cannot surprise.

3. "Affecting the passions" (Johnson's *Dictionary*).

4. Richard Bentley, a distinguished classical scholar whose edition of *Paradise Lost* (1732) incorporates numerous misguided "corrections."

Of the ideas suggested by these awful scenes, from some we recede with reverence, except when stated hours require their association; and from others we shrink with horror, or admit them only as salutary inflictions, as counterpoises to our interests and passions. Such images rather obstruct the career of fancy than incite it.

Pleasure and terror are indeed the genuine sources of poetry; but poetical pleasure must be such as human imagination can at least conceive, and poetical terror such as human strength and fortitude may combat. The good and evil of Eternity are too ponderous for the wings of wit; the mind sinks under them in passive helplessness, content with calm belief and humble adoration.

Known truths however may take a different appearance, and be conveyed to the mind by a new train of intermediate images. This Milton has undertaken, and performed with pregnancy and vigor of mind peculiar to himself. Whoever considers the few radical[5] positions which the Scriptures afforded him will wonder by what energetic operations he expanded them to such extent and ramified them to so much variety, restrained as he was by religious reverence from licentiousness of fiction.

Here is a full display of the united force of study and genius; of a great accumulation of materials, with judgment to digest and fancy to combine them: Milton was able to select from nature or from story, from ancient fable or from modern science, whatever could illustrate or adorn his thoughts. An accumulation of knowledge impregnated his mind, fermented by study and exalted by imagination.

It has been therefore said without an indecent hyperbole by one of his encomiasts, that in reading *Paradise Lost* we read a book of universal knowledge.

But original deficience cannot be supplied. The want of human interest is always felt. *Paradise Lost* is one of the books which the reader admires and lays down, and forgets to take up again. None ever wished it longer than it is. Its perusal is a duty rather than a pleasure. We read Milton for instruction, retire harassed and overburdened, and look elsewhere for recreation; we desert our master, and seek for companions.

from *The Life of Pope*

[Pope and Dryden]

In acquired knowledge the superiority must be allowed to Dryden, whose education was more scholastic, and who before he became an author had been allowed more time for study, with better means of information. His mind has a larger range, and he collects his images and illustrations from a more extensive circumference of science. Dryden knew more of man in his general nature, and Pope in his local manners. The notions of Dryden were formed by comprehensive speculation, and those of Pope by minute attention. There is more dignity in the knowledge of Dryden, and more certainty in that of Pope.

Poetry was not the sole praise of either, for both excelled likewise in prose; but Pope did not borrow his prose from his predecessor. The style of Dryden is capricious and varied, that of Pope is cautious and uniform; Dryden obeys the motions of his own mind, Pope constrains his mind to his own rules of composition. Dryden is sometimes vehement and rapid; Pope is always smooth, uniform, and gentle. Dryden's page is a natural field, rising into inequalities, and diversified by the varied exuberance of abundant vegetation; Pope's is a velvet lawn, shaven by the scythe, and leveled by the roller.

5. Original.

Of genius, that power which constitutes a poet; that quality without which judgment is cold and knowledge is inert; that energy which collects, combines, amplifies, and animates—the superiority must, with some hesitation, be allowed to Dryden. It is not to be inferred that of this poetical vigor Pope had only a little, because Dryden had more, for every other writer since Milton must give place to Pope; and even of Dryden it must be said that if he has brighter paragraphs, he has not better poems. Dryden's performances were always hasty, either excited by some external occasion, or extorted by domestic necessity; he composed without consideration, and published without correction. What his mind could supply at call, or gather in one excursion, was all that he sought, and all that he gave. The dilatory caution of Pope enabled him to condense his sentiments, to multiply his images, and to accumulate all that study might produce, or chance might supply. If the flights of Dryden therefore are higher, Pope continues longer on the wing. If of Dryden's fire the blaze is brighter, of Pope's the heat is more regular and constant. Dryden often surpasses expectation, and Pope never falls below it. Dryden is read with frequent astonishment, and Pope with perpetual delight.

This parallel will, I hope, when it is well considered, be found just; and if the reader should suspect me, as I suspect myself, of some partial fondness for the memory of Dryden, let him not too hastily condemn me; for meditation and enquiry may, perhaps, show him the reasonableness of my determination.

[ON *THE RAPE OF THE LOCK*]

To the praises which have been accumulated on *The Rape of the Lock* by readers of every class, from the critic to the waiting-maid, it is difficult to make any addition. Of that which is universally allowed to be the most attractive of all ludicrous compositions, let it rather be now inquired from what sources the power of pleasing is derived.

Dr. Warburton, who excelled in critical perspicacity, has remarked that the preternatural agents are very happily adapted to the purposes of the poem. The heathen deities can no longer gain attention: we should have turned away from a contest between Venus and Diana. The employment of allegorical persons always excites conviction of its own absurdity: they may produce effects, but cannot conduct actions; when the phantom is put in motion, it dissolves; thus Discord may raise a mutiny, but Discord cannot conduct a march, nor besiege a town. Pope brought into view a new race of Beings, with powers and passions proportionate to their operation. The sylphs and gnomes act at the toilet[6] and the tea-table, what more terrific and more powerful phantoms perform on the stormy ocean or the field of battle; they give their proper help, and do their proper mischief. * * *

In this work are exhibited in a very high degree the two most engaging powers of an author: new things are made familiar, and familiar things are made new. A race of aerial people never heard of before is presented to us in a manner so clear and easy, that the reader seeks for no further information, but immediately mingles with his new acquaintance, adopts their interests and attends their pursuits, loves a sylph and detests a gnome.

That familiar things are made new every paragraph will prove. The subject of the poem is an event below the common incidents of common life; nothing real is

6. Dressing table.

introduced that is not seen so often as to be no longer regarded, yet the whole detail of a female-day is here brought before us invested with so much art of decoration that, though nothing is disguised, every thing is striking, and we feel all the appetite of curiosity for that from which we have a thousand times turned fastidiously away.

[ON *ELOISA TO ABELARD*]

The *Epistle of Eloisa to Abelard* is one of the most happy productions of human wit: the subject is so judiciously chosen that it would be difficult, in turning over the annals of the world, to find another which so many circumstances concur to recommend. We regularly interest ourselves most in the fortune of those who most deserve our notice. Abelard and Eloisa were conspicuous in their days for eminence of merit. The heart naturally loves truth. The adventures and misfortunes of this illustrious pair are known from undisputed history. Their fate does not leave the mind in hopeless dejection; for they both found quiet and consolation in retirement and piety. So new and so affecting is their story that it supersedes invention, and imagination ranges at full liberty without straggling into scenes of fable.

The story thus skillfully adopted has been diligently improved. Pope has left nothing behind him which seems more the effect of studious perseverance and laborious revisal. Here is particularly observable the *curiosa felicitas*,[7] a fruitful soil, and careful cultivation. Here is no crudeness of sense, nor asperity of language.

[ON *AN ESSAY ON MAN*]

The *Essay on Man* was a work of great labor and long consideration, but certainly not the happiest of Pope's performances. The subject is perhaps not very proper for poetry, and the poet was not sufficiently master of his subject; metaphysical morality was to him a new study, he was proud of his acquisitions, and, supposing himself master of great secrets, was in haste to teach what he had not learned. Thus he tells us, in the first Epistle, that from the nature of the Supreme Being may be deduced an order of beings such as mankind, because Infinite Excellence can do only what is best. He finds out that these beings must be "somewhere," and that "all the question is whether man be in a wrong place." Surely if, according to the poet's Leibnitzian reasoning,[8] we may infer that man ought to be only because he is, we may allow that his place is the right place, because he has it. Supreme Wisdom is not less infallible in disposing than in creating. But what is meant by "somewhere" and "place" and "wrong place" it had been vain to ask Pope, who probably had never asked himself.

Having exalted himself into the chair of wisdom he tells us much that every man knows, and much that he does not know himself; that we see but little, and that the order of the universe is beyond our comprehension, and opinion not very uncommon; and that there is a chain of subordinate beings "from infinite to nothing," of which himself and his readers are equally ignorant. But he gives us one comfort which, without his help, he supposes unattainable, in the position "that though we are fools, yet God is wise."

This *Essay* affords an egregious instance of the predominance of genius, the dazzling splendor of imagery, and the seductive powers of eloquence. Never were penury of

7. Studied inspiration.
8. Johnson believed that Pope had been influenced by the deterministic philosophy of Gottfried Wilhelm von Leibnitz (1646–1716).

knowledge and vulgarity of sentiment so happily disguised. The reader feels his mind full, though he learns nothing; and when he meets it in its new array no longer knows the talk of his mother and his nurse. When these wonder-working sounds sink into sense, and the doctrine of the *Essay*, disrobed of its ornaments, is left to the powers of its naked excellence, what shall we discover? That we are, in comparison with our Creator, very weak and ignorant; that we do not uphold the chain of existence; and that we could not make one another with more skill than we are made. We may learn yet more: that the arts of human life were copied from the instinctive operations of other animals; that if the world be made for man, it may be said that man was made for geese. To these profound principles of natural knowledge are added some moral instructions equally new: that self-interest well understood will produce social concord; that men are mutual gainers by mutual benefits; that evil is sometimes balanced by good; that human advantages are unstable and fallacious, of uncertain duration and doubtful effect; that our true honor is not to have a great part, but to act it well; that virtue only is our own; and that happiness is always in our power.

Surely a man of no very comprehensive search may venture to say that he has heard all this before, but it was never till now recommended by such a blaze of embellishment or such sweetness of melody. The vigorous contraction of some thoughts, the luxuriant amplification of others, the incidental illustrations, and sometimes the dignity, sometimes the softness of the verses, enchain philosophy, suspend criticism, and oppress judgment by overpowering pleasure.

This is true of many paragraphs; yet if I had undertaken to exemplify Pope's felicity of composition before a rigid critic I should not select the *Essay on Man*, for it contains more lines unsuccessfully labored, more harshness of diction, more thoughts imperfectly expressed, more levity without elegance, and more heaviness without strength, than will easily be found in all his other works.

LETTERS

To Lord Chesterfield[1]

My Lord: 7 February 1755

I have been lately informed by the proprietor of *The World* that two papers in which my Dictionary is recommended to the public were written by your Lordship.[2] To be so distinguished is an honor which, being very little accustomed to favors from the great, I know not well how to receive, or in what terms to acknowledge.

When upon some slight encouragement I first visited your Lordship I was overpowered like the rest of mankind by the enchantment of your address, and could not forbear to wish that I might boast myself *le vainqueur du vainqueur de la terre*,[3] that I might obtain that regard for which I saw the world contending; but I found my attendance so little encouraged, that neither pride nor modesty would suffer me to continue

1. Philip Dormer Stanhope (1694–1773), fourth Earl of Chesterfield, a politician and man of letters renowned for his elegant manners and his knowledge of the polite world. In 1747 Johnson had dedicated his *Plan of a Dictionary* to Chesterfield but had received neither financial nor moral support from him during the long years of labor on the *Dictionary*.

2. Chesterfield had contributed two essays to Robert Dodsley's periodical *The World*. In these essays he praised the forthcoming *Dictionary* in such a way as to imply that he had been its enlightened sponsor.

3. "The conqueror of the world's conqueror" (the opening line of the epic *Alaric*, by Georges de Scudéry).

it. When I had once adressed your Lordship in public, I had exhausted all the art of pleasing which a retired and uncourtly scholar can possess. I had done all that I could, and no man is well pleased to have his all neglected, be it ever so little.

Seven years, my lord, have now passed since I waited in your outward rooms or was repulsed from your door, during which time I have been pushing on my work through difficulties of which it is useless to complain, and have brought it at last to the verge of publication without one act of assistance, one word of encouragement, or one smile of favor. Such treatment I did not expect, for I never had a patron before.

The shepherd in Virgil grew at last acquainted with Love, and found him a native of the rocks.[4] Is not a patron, my lord, one who looks with unconcern on a man struggling for life in the water and when he has reached ground encumbers him with help?[5] The notice which you have been pleased to take of my labors, had it been early, had been kind; but it has been delayed till I am indifferent and cannot enjoy it, till I am solitary and cannot impart it, till I am known and do not want it.

I hope it is no very cynical asperity not to confess obligation where no benefit has been received, or to be unwilling that the public should consider me as owing that to a patron, which providence has enabled me to do for myself.

Having carried on my work thus far with so little obligation to any favorer of learning I shall not be disappointed though I should conclude it, if less be possible, with less, for I have been long wakened from that dream of hope, in which I once boasted myself with so much exultation, my lord, your Lordship's most humble, most obedient servant,

S.J.

To Hester Thrale

Dear Madam: Bolt Court, Fleetstreet, 19 June 1783

I am sitting down in no cheerful solitude to write a narrative which would once have affected you with tenderness and sorrow, but which you will perhaps pass over now with the careless glance of frigid indifference.[1] For this diminution of regard however, I know not whether I ought to blame you, who may have reasons which I cannot know, and I do not blame myself who have for a great part of human life done you what good I could, and have never done you evil.

I had been disordered in the usual way, and had been relieved by the usual methods, by opium and cathartics,[2] but had rather lessened my dose of opium.

On Monday the 16 I sat for my picture,[3] and walked a considerable way with little inconvenience. In the afternoon and evening I felt myself light and easy, and began to plan schemes of life. Thus I went to bed, and in a short time waked and sat up as has been long my custom when I felt a confusion and indistinctness in my head which lasted, I suppose about half a minute. I was alarmed and prayed God,

4. Johnson alludes to a pastoral poem by Virgil (*Eclogue* 8), in which Love is described as coming from a land of "flinty crags."

5. In his *Dictionary*, Johnson defines "patron" as "commonly a wretch who supports with insolence, and is paid with flattery."

1. As she became more and more attached to Gabriel Piozzi, an Italian musician, Hester Thrale (correctly sensing how angry Johnson would be) began to disengage from their close friendship. Though he knew something had gone wrong, Johnson did not learn of the love affair until a year later, when Mrs. Thrale wrote to inform him of her marriage.

2. Purgatives.

3. Johnson's portrait was being painted.

that however he might afflict my body he would spare my understanding. This prayer, that I might try the integrity of my faculties, I made in Latin verse. The lines were not very good, but I knew them not to be very good, I made them easily, and concluded myself to be unimpaired in my faculties.

Soon after I perceived that I had suffered a paralytic stroke, and that my speech was taken from me. I had no pain, and so little dejection in this dreadful state that I wondered at my own apathy, and considered that perhaps death itself when it should come, would excite less horror than seems now to attend it.

In order to rouse the vocal organs I took two drams. Wine has been celebrated for the production of eloquence; I put myself into violent motion, and, I think, repeated it. But all was vain; I then went to bed, and, strange as it may seem, I think, slept. When I saw light, it was time to contrive what I should do. Though God stopped my speech he left me my hand, I enjoyed a mercy which was not granted to my Dear Friend Lawrence,[4] who now perhaps overlooks me as I am writing and rejoices that I have what he wanted.[5] My first note was necessarily to my servant, who came in talking, and could not immediately comprehend why he should read what I put into his hands.

I then wrote a card to Mr. Allen,[6] that I might have a discreet friend at hand to act as occasion should require. In penning this note I had some difficulty, my hand, I know not how nor why, made wrong letters. I then wrote to Dr. Taylor[7] to come to me, and bring Dr. Heberden, and I sent to Dr. Brocklesby, who is my neighbor. My physicians are very friendly and very disinterested; and give me great hopes, but you may imagine my situation. I have so far recovered my vocal powers, as to repeat the Lord's Prayer with no very imperfect articulation. My memory, I hope, yet remains as it was. But such an attack produces solicitude for the safety of every faculty.

How this will be received by you, I know not, I hope you will sympathize with me, but perhaps

> My Mistress gracious, mild, and good,
> Cries, Is he dumb? 'tis time he should.[8]

But can this be possible, I hope it cannot. I hope that what, when I could speak, I spoke of You, and to You, will be in a sober and serious hour remembered by You, and surely it cannot be remembered but with some degree of kindness. I have loved You with virtuous affection, I have honored You with sincere esteem. Let not all our endearment be forgotten, but let me have in this great distress your pity and your prayers. You see I yet turn to You with my complaints as a settled and unalienable friend, do not, do not drive me from You, for I have not deserved either neglect or hatred.

To the girls,[9] who do not write often, for Susy has written only once, and Miss Thrale owes me a letter, I earnestly recommend as their guardian and friend, that they remember their Creator in the days of their youth.[1]

4. Johnson's favorite physician, Dr. Thomas Lawrence, had died earlier that month after suffering a stroke.
5. Lacked.
6. Johnson's printer and neighbor, Edmund Allen.
7. The clergyman John Taylor, one of Johnson's oldest and closest friends.
8. Johnson adapts a couplet from Swift's *Verses on the Death of Dr. Swift:* "The Queen, so gracious, mild and good, / Cries, 'Is he gone? 'Tis time he should'" (lines 181–82).
9. Hester Thrale's four surviving daughters: Hester Maria ("Miss Thrale"), Susanna ("Susy"), Sophia, and Cecilia.
1. "Remember now thy Creator in the days of thy youth, while the evil days come not" (Ecclesiastes 12.1).

I suppose You may wish to know how my disease is treated by the physicians. They put a blister upon my back, and two from my ear to my throat, one on a side. The blister on the back has done little, and those on the throat have not risen. I bullied, and bounced, (it sticks to our last sand)[2] and compelled the apothecary to make his salve according to the Edinburgh dispensatory[3] that it might adhere better. I have two on now of my own prescription. They likewise give me salt of hartshorn, which I take with no great confidence, but am satisfied that what can be done, is done for me.

O God, give me comfort and confidence in Thee, forgive my sins, and if it be thy good pleasure, relieve my diseases for Jesus Christ's sake. Amen.

I am almost ashamed of this querulous letter, but now it is written, let it go. I am Madam, Your most humble servant,

SAM. JOHNSON

To Hester Thrale Piozzi

Madam: 2 July 1784

If I interpret your letter right, You are ignominiously married,[1] if it is yet undone, let us once talk together. If You have abandoned your children and your religion, God forgive your wickedness; if You have forfeited your fame, and your country, may your folly do no further mischief.[2]

If the last act is yet to do, I, who have loved you, esteemed you, reverenced you, and served you, I who long thought You the first of humankind, entreat that before your fate is irrevocable, I may once more see You. I was, I once was, Madam, most truly yours,

SAM. JOHNSON

I will come down if you permit it.

To Hester Thrale Piozzi

Dear Madam: London, 8 July 1784

What You have done, however I may lament it, I have no pretense to resent, as it has not been injurious to me. I therefore breathe out one sigh more of tenderness perhaps useless, but at least sincere.

I wish that God may grant You every blessing, that you may be happy in this world for its short continuance, and eternally happy in a better state. And whatever I can contribute to your happiness, I am very ready to repay for that kindness which soothed twenty years of a life radically wretched.

Do not think slightly of the advice which I now presume to offer. Prevail upon Mr. Piozzi to settle in England. You may live here with more dignity than in Italy, and with more security. Your rank will be higher, and your fortune more under your

2. "Time, that on all things lays his lenient hand, / Yet tames not this; it sticks to our last sand" (Pope, *Epistle to Cobham*, lines 224–25).
3. Medical manual.
1. Hester Thrale had written on 30 June to inform Johnson of her marriage to Gabriel Piozzi.
2. Johnson's objections to Gabriel Piozzi include the fact that he is a musician (and therefore socially inferior), a Catholic, and an Italian.

own eye. I desire not to detail all my reasons; but every argument of prudence and interest is for England, and only some phantoms of imagination seduce you to Italy.

I am afraid, however, that my counsel is vain, yet I have eased my heart by giving it.

When Queen Mary took the resolution of sheltering herself in England, the Archbishop of St. Andrew's attempting to dissuade her,[1] attended on her journey and when they came to the irremeable[2] stream that separated the two kingdoms, walked by her side into the water, in the middle of which he seized her bridle, and with earnestness proportioned to her danger and his own affection, pressed her to return. The Queen went forward.—If the parallel reaches thus far; may it go no further. The tears stand in my eyes.

I am going into Derbyshire,[3] and hope to be followed by your good wishes, for I am with great affection, Your most humble servant,

SAM. JOHNSON

Any letters that come for me hither, will be sent me.

James Boswell

1740–1795

"I have discovered," James Boswell announced at age twenty-two in the journal he had just commenced, "that we may be in some degree whatever character we choose." The possibilities opened up by this discovery both exhilarated and troubled him. Neither the "choosing" nor the "being" turned out to be as simple as he expected, in part because some alternate choice always beckoned. In the pages of his journal, Boswell performed his excited choices and anxious reconsiderations. The oscillation did much to drive the intricate comedy and intermittent pathos, the energetic posing and fervent self-scrutiny of the diaries he kept all his adult life, and of the published books he crafted from them.

Boswell's parents had chosen their own characters early, and had stuck to them assiduously. His father was a Scots laird—heir to an ancient family and a landed estate—and a distinguished jurist, serving as justice on Scotland's highest courts. His mother was an impassioned Calvinist, who numbered among her many strictures an abhorrence of the theater; the actors' freedom of character-choice, which made the playhouse for her a place of sinful deception, would make it the site of a lifelong enchantment for her son. Boswell's parents had chosen firmly for their first-born too. James was to become, like his father, an eminent lawyer and respectable landowner.

Boswell chafed at the narrowness of the scheme. Struggling (he later recalled) "against paternal affection, ambition, interest," he ran away to London for a short spell at age eighteen and returned there at twenty-two, seeking a commission as a soldier with the king's personal bodyguard, a post that would have secured him lifelong residence in the city, flashy uniforms, and ample opportunities to display himself in them. While Boswell waited for this prospect to

1. Johnson draws on a semifictional account of Mary Queen of Scots' fateful decision to take refuge in England. According to this version, she crossed the river on horseback, attended by John Hamilton, Archbishop of St. Andrews.

2. "Admitting no return" (Johnson's *Dictionary*).

3. The home of John Taylor.

materialize (it never did), he found his real calling. He started to keep a copious journal, narrating each day in succession, dispatching the text in weekly packets to his friend John Johnston back home in Scotland. Here too was self-display, intricately contrived. Boswell managed his journal as a kind of manuscript theater—often written as a play text, complete with dialogue and stage directions—for an audience of one (the performance of his journal texts for a wider reading public would later become his literary life's work). London, the theatrical city, teemed with "characters" living and dead, real and fictional, whom Boswell by turns and in combinations strove to "be": Addison, Steele, and their imaginary paragon of self-possession Mr. Spectator; Captain Macheath from *The Beggar's Opera* (on whose adventures Boswell modeled some of his own sexual exploits); the actors Thomas Sheridan and David Garrick; and most important, Garrick's old teacher Samuel Johnson, whose writings had provided Boswell with a model of moral firmness more attractive than his father's, and who befriended the young diarist six months into his London stay.

The friendship with Johnson gave Boswell's journal a new purpose (to record the conversations of this dazzling talker) and his life a new direction. Reconciled to his father's plan, Boswell studied law in Holland and, as reward for his painfully diligent endeavors, made the Grand Tour of Europe, where he collected the conversation and the counsel of further celebrities: the French iconoclasts Voltaire and Rousseau, and the Corsican rebel leader Pasquale Paoli, then fighting to free his island from foreign domination. Returning to Scotland in 1766, Boswell took up the life his father had mapped for him, settling in Edinburgh, and becoming (as he haughtily informed his disreputable friend John Wilkes) "a Scottish lawyer, a Scottish laird, and a Scottish married man." In each of these roles, though, he repeatedly broke character. He went down to London almost every spring, ostensibly to cultivate his legal practice but really to renew his old absorptions: in theater, in sexual adventure, in the spellbinding company of Johnson and the group of artists, writers, and thinkers who surrounded him.

Boswell yearned to join their number not merely as admirer but as eminent author, and he soon did. Over the ensuing years, he produced much journalism and some verse, as well as three books in which he explored with increasing audacity the potential of his own diary as a public text—as a vehicle of entertainment, instruction, profit, and fame. He pursued for the journal form a print authority it had not previously possessed, devising ways for it to encroach upon, even to colonize, territory and tasks traditionally reserved to other genres: travel book, "character" sketch, biography. In his first attempt, *An Account of Corsica . . . and Memoirs of Pascal Paoli* (1769), he recast his original travel journal (rearranging the entries, dropping the dates) to produce a heroic portrait of his friend the liberator. In his second experiment, *A Journal of a Tour to the Hebrides with Samuel Johnson* (1785), which appeared the year after Johnson's death, the imperative to portraiture was even more pronounced. The public craved accounts of the lost titan, and this time Boswell met that demand a different way. He presented his journal *as* a journal, with scrupulously dated, plentifully narrated consecutive entries rich in the "minute details of daily life" that Johnson himself had stipulated as the criteria for good biography. The book struck readers as startlingly new. Some mocked it for its minutiae ("How are we all with rapture touched," exclaimed one versifier, "to see / Where, when, and at what hour, you swallowed tea!"), while many praised its veracity and abundance.

There was much more where that came from. In *The Life of Samuel Johnson, LL.D.* (1791), Boswell deployed the *Tour*'s techniques on a massive scale. Drawing on his diaries, and on years of arduous research among Johnson's many acquaintances, Boswell built a thousand-page biography that is largely a book of talk, of conversations diligently recorded and deftly dramatized, the culmination of the textual theater that Boswell had long practiced in manuscript. Johnson's capacious mind and imposing presence find embodiment in a text dense with accumulated time, told and retold over the span of almost three decades that stretches from Boswell's first Johnsonian journal entry to the biography's publication. Pleased with the book's commercial success, stung by charges that he had been either too partial to Johnson or too critical of him, Boswell worked at two further editions (in which his footnotes swelled with new information and rebuttals). He died at fifty-five, unmade by alcoholism, by venereal disease, and by the violent depressions that accompanied his ongoing uncertainty as to what he might "be" and had become.

His books sustained his fame, though ever since the *Life*'s first appearance, readers have debated the degree of its accuracy and the merits of its portraiture. Two centuries later, Boswell's biography has become a touchstone text for the problem of the "documentary"—the question of how art and "fact" should merge in representations of historical events. Over the past eighty years the debate has been deepened by the unexpected recovery of Boswell's original papers, including the diaries that he drew on and boasted of in his published books. The papers had long been given up for lost, but masses of them had actually been stashed and forgotten by various descendants in odd receptacles (cabinet, croquet box, grain loft) on estates scattered across Scotland and Ireland. The papers' recovery took more than twenty years; the process of their publication continues. Taken together, Boswell's papers and his published works make it possible to trace the intricate course by which the flux of his energetic, agitated life became fixed in text.

For additional resources on Boswell, including selections from *A Journal of a Tour to the Hebrides with Dr. Samuel Johnson*, go to *The Longman Anthology of British Literature* Web site at www.myliteraturekit.com.

from London Journal

[A Scot in London]

Wednesday, 1 December [1762]. * * * On Tuesday I wanted to have a silver-hilted sword, but upon examining my pockets as I walked up the Strand,[1] I found that I had left the most of my guineas at home and had not enough to pay for it with me. I determined to make a trial of the civility of my fellow-creatures, and what effect my external appearance and address would have. I accordingly went to the shop of Mr. Jefferys, sword-cutter to His Majesty, looked at a number of his swords, and at last picked out a very handsome one at five guineas. "Mr. Jefferys," said I, "I have not money here to pay for it. Will you trust me?" "Upon my word, Sir," said he, "you must excuse me. It is a thing we never do to a stranger." I bowed genteelly and said, "Indeed, Sir, I believe it is not right." However, I stood and looked at him, and he looked at me. "Come, Sir," cried he, "I will trust you." "Sir," said I, "if you had not trusted me, I should not have bought it from you." He asked my name and place of abode, which I told him. I then chose a belt, put the sword on, told him I would call and pay it tomorrow, and walked off. I called this day and paid him. "Mr. Jefferys," said I, "there is your money. You paid me a very great compliment. I am much obliged to you. But pray don't do such a thing again. It is dangerous." "Sir," said he, "we know our men. I would have trusted you with the value of a hundred pounds." This I think was a good adventure and much to my honor. * * *

This afternoon I was surprised with the arrival of Lady Betty Macfarlane, Lady Anne Erskine, Captain Erskine, and Miss Dempster, who were come to the Red Lion Inn at Charing Cross. It seems Lady Betty had written to the laird that if he would not come down, she would come up; and upon his giving her an indolent answer, like a woman of spirit, she put her resolution in practice. I immediately went to them.[2]

To tell the plain truth, I was vexed at their coming. For to see just the plain *hamely*[3] Fife family hurt my grand ideas of London. Besides, I was now upon a plan of

1. A major commercial street in the West End of London.
2. With the exception of Miss Dempster, the sister of his friend George, Boswell refers to the daughters and son of the Fifth Earl of Kellie ("the laird"). The family came from Fife, a county in eastern Scotland.
3. Scots dialect for "homely," home-like.

studying polite reserved behavior, which is the only way to keep up dignity of character. And as I have a good share of pride, which I think is very proper and even noble, I am hurt with the taunts of ridicule and am unsatisfied if I do not feel myself something of a superior animal. This has always been my favorite idea in my best moments. Indeed, I have been obliged to deviate from it by a variety of circumstances. After my wild expedition to London in the year 1760, after I got rid of the load of serious reflection which then burthened me, by being always in Lord Eglinton's company, very fond of him, and much caressed by him, I became dissipated and thoughtless.[4] When my father forced me down to Scotland, I was at first very low-spirited, although to appearance very high. I afterwards from my natural vivacity endeavored to make myself easy; and like a man who takes to drinking to banish care, I threw myself loose as a heedless, dissipated, rattling fellow who might say or do every ridiculous thing. This made me sought after by everybody for the present hour, but I found myself a very inferior being; and I found many people presuming to treat me as such, which notwithstanding of my appearance of undiscerning gaiety, gave me much pain. I was, in short, a character very different from what God intended me and I myself chose. I remember my friend Johnston[5] told me one day after my return from London that I had turned out different from what he imagined, as he thought I would resemble Mr. Addison.[6] I laughed and threw out some loud sally of humor, but the observation struck deep. Indeed, I must do myself the justice to say that I always resolved to be such a man whenever my affairs were made easy and I got upon my own footing. For as I despaired of that, I endeavored to lower my views and just to be a good-humored comical being, well liked either as a waiter, a common soldier, a clerk in Jamaica, or some other odd out-of-the-way sphere. Now, when my father at last put me into an independent situation, I felt my mind regain its native dignity. I felt strong dispositions to be a Mr. Addison. Indeed, I had accustomed myself so much to laugh at everything that it required time to render my imagination solid and give me just notions of real life and of religion. But I hoped by degrees to attain to some degree of propriety. Mr. Addison's character in sentiment, mixed with a little of the gaiety of Sir Richard Steele and the manners of Mr. Digges,[7] were the ideas which I aimed to realize.

Indeed, I must say that Digges has more or as much of the deportment of a man of fashion as anybody I ever saw; and he keeps up this so well that he never once lessened upon me even on an intimate acquaintance, although he is now and then somewhat melancholy, under which it is very difficult to preserve dignity; and this I think is particularly to be admired in Mr. Digges. Indeed, he and I never came to familiarity, which is justly said to beget contempt. The great art of living easy and happy in society is to study proper behavior, and even with our most intimate friends to observe politeness; otherwise we will insensibly treat each other with a degree of rudeness, and each will find himself despised in some measure by the other. As I was therefore pursuing this laudable plan, I was vexed at the arrival of the Kellie family, with whom when in Scotland I had been in the greatest familiarity. Had they not come for a twelvemonth, I should have been somewhat established in my address, but as I had been but a fortnight from them, I could not without the appearance of strong

4. At the age of 18, Boswell had run away to London, where he impulsively converted to Catholicism. The tenth Earl of Eglinton, a charming and generous rake, weaned him from religion by turning him into a libertine.
5. John Johnston of Grange, Boswell's close friend, to whom he was sending the journal in weekly installments.
6. Joseph Addison, author, with Sir Richard Steele, of the *Tatler* and *Spectator* papers. Addison was particularly identified with the character of the silent, all-seeing Mr. Spectator.
7. West Digges, an actor in Edinburgh, particularly known for his portrayal of Macheath in *The Beggar's Opera*.

affectation appear much different from what they had seen me. I accordingly was very free, but rather more silent, which they imputed to my dullness, and roasted me about London's not being agreeable to me. I bore it pretty well, and left them.

* * *

Wednesday, 15 December [1762]. The enemies of the people of England who would have them considered in the worst light represent them as selfish, beef-eaters, and cruel. In this view I resolved today to be a true-born Old Englishman. I went into the City[8] to Dolly's Steak-house in Paternoster Row and swallowed my dinner by myself to fulfill the charge of selfishness; I had a large fat beefsteak to fulfill the charge of beef-eating; and I went at five o'clock to the Royal Cockpit in St. James's Park and saw cockfighting for about five hours to fulfill the charge of cruelty.

A beefsteak house is a most excellent place to dine at. You come in there to a warm, comfortable, large room, where a number of people are sitting at table. You take whatever place you find empty; call for what you like, which you get well and cleverly dressed. You may either chat or not as you like. Nobody minds you, and you pay very reasonably. My dinner (beef, bread and beer and waiter) was only a shilling. The waiters make a great deal of money by these pennies.[9] Indeed, I admire the English for attending to small sums, as many smalls make a great, according to the proverb.

At five I filled my pockets with gingerbread and apples (quite the method), put on my old clothes and laced hat, laid by my watch, purse, and pocketbook, and with oaken stick in my hand sallied to the pit. I was too soon there. So I went into a low inn, sat down amongst a parcel of arrant blackguards, and drank some beer. The sentry near the house had been very civil in showing me the way. It was very cold. I bethought myself of the poor fellow, so I carried out a pint of beer myself to him. He was very thankful and drank my health cordially. He told me his name was Hobard, that he was a watchmaker but in distress for debt, and enlisted that his creditors might not touch him.

I then went to the Cockpit, which is a circular room in the middle of which the cocks fight. It is seated round with rows gradually rising. The pit and the seats are all covered with mat. The cocks, nicely cut and dressed and armed with silver heels, are set down and fight with amazing bitterness and resolution. Some of them were quickly dispatched. One pair fought three quarters of an hour. The uproar and noise of betting is prodigious. A great deal of money made a very quick circulation from hand to hand. There was a number of professed gamblers there. An old cunning dog whose face I had seen at Newmarket[1] sat by me a while. I told him I knew nothing of the matter.[2] "Sir," said he, "you have as good a chance as anybody." He thought I would be a good subject for him. I was young-like. But he found himself balked. I was shocked to see the distraction and anxiety of the betters. I was sorry for the poor cocks. I looked round to see if any of the spectators pitied them when mangled and torn in a most cruel manner, but I could not observe the smallest relenting sign in any countenance. I was therefore not ill pleased to see them endure mental torment. Thus did I complete my true English day, and came home pretty much fatigued and pretty much confounded at the strange turn of this people.

8. The older, eastern half of London, which included the centers of finance, law, and journalism.
9. The waiter's tip was one of the 12 pence that made up a shilling.
1. A town in Suffolk famous for horse racing.
2. About betting on cockfighting.

[LOUISA][1]

Wednesday, 12 January [1763]. Louisa and I agreed that at eight at night she would meet me in the piazzas of Covent Garden.[2] I was quite elevated, and felt myself able and undaunted to engage in the wars of the Paphian Queen.[3]

I dined at Sheridan's[4] very heartily. He showed to my conviction that Garrick[5] did not play the great scene in the Second Part of *King Henry*[6] with propriety. "People," said he, "in this age know when particular lines or even speeches are well spoke; but they do not study character, which is a matter of the utmost moment, as people of different characters feel and express their feelings very differently. For want of a knowledge of this, Mr. Barry[7] acted the distress of Othello, the Moorish warrior whose stubborn soul was hard to bend, and that of Castalio, the gentle lover who was all tenderness, in the self-same way. Now Mr. Garrick in that famous scene whines most piteously when he ought to upbraid. Shakespeare has discovered[8] there a most intimate knowledge of human nature. He shows you the King worn out with sickness and so weak that he faints. He had usurped the crown by the force of arms and was convinced that it must be held with spirit. He saw his son given up to low debauchery. He was anxious and vexed to think of the anarchy that would ensue at his death. Upon discovering that the Prince had taken the crown from his pillow, and concluding him desirous of his death, he is fired with rage. He starts up. He cries, 'Go chide him hither!' His anger animates him so much that he throws aside his distemper. Nature furnishes all her strength for one last effort. He is for a moment renewed. He is for a moment the spirited Henry the Fourth. He upbraids him with bitter sarcasm and bold figures. And then what a beautiful variety is there, when, upon young Harry's contrition, he falls on his neck and melts into parental tenderness."

I yielded this point to Sheridan candidly. But upon his attacking Garrick as a tragedian in his usual way, I opposed him keenly, and declared he was prejudiced; because the world thought him a good tragic actor. "So do I, Sir," said he; "I think him the best I ever saw." BOSWELL: "Except yourself, Mr. Sheridan. But come, we shall take this for granted. The world then think him near equal or as good as you in what you excel in." SHERIDAN: "Sir, I am not a bit prejudiced. I don't value acting. I shall suppose that I was the greatest actor that ever lived and universally acknowledged so, I would not choose that it should be remembered. I would have it erased out of the anecdotes of my life. Acting is a poor thing in the present state of the stage. For my own part, I engaged in it merely as a step to something greater, a just notion of eloquence." This was in a good measure true. But he certainly talked too extravagantly.

An old Irish maid, or rather an Irish old maid (O most hideous character!) dined with us. She was indeed a terrible Joy.[9] She was a woman of knowledge and criticism and correct taste. But there came to tea a Miss Mowat who played once on the stage here for a winter or two, a lovely girl. Many an amorous glance did I exchange with her. I was this day quite flashy with love. We often addressed our

1. An actress at Covent Garden Theatre, whose real name was Mrs. Lewis.
2. The arcades along the northern perimeter of the square, designed by Inigo Jones and popularly known as "piazzas," were a famous trysting place.
3. Venus.
4. Thomas Sheridan, Irish actor and teacher of elocution; father of Richard Brinsley Sheridan, author of *The School for Scandal*.
5. David Garrick (1717–1779), the most celebrated actor-manager of his age.
6. Shakespeare's *2 Henry IV* 4.5.
7. Spranger Barry, a well-known actor who played the protagonist in Shakespeare's *Othello* and in Otway's *The Orphan*.
8. Revealed.
9. Irishwoman.

discourse to each other. I hope to see her again; and yet what have I to do with anybody but dear Louisa?

At the appointed hour of eight I went to the piazzas, where I sauntered up and down for a while in a sort of trembling suspense, I knew not why. At last my charming companion appeared, and I immediately conducted her to a hackney coach which I had ready waiting, pulled up the blinds, and away we drove to the destined scene of delight. We contrived to seem as if we had come off a journey, and carried in a bundle our nightclothes, handkerchiefs, and other little things. We also had with us some almond biscuits, or as they call them in London, macaroons, which looked like provision on the road. On our arrival at Hayward's[1] we were shown into the parlor, in the same manner that any decent couple would be. I here thought proper to conceal my own name (which the people of the house had never heard), and assumed the name of Mr. Digges. We were shown up to the very room where he slept. I said my cousin, as I called him, was very well. That Ceres and Bacchus might in moderation lend their assistance to Venus,[2] I ordered a genteel supper and some wine.

Louisa told me she had two aunts who carried her over to France when she was a girl, and that she could once speak French as fluently as English. We talked a little in it, and agreed that we would improve ourselves by reading and speaking it every day. I asked her if we did not just look like man and wife. "No," said she, "we are too fond for married people." No wonder that she may have a bad idea of that union, considering how bad it was for her. She has contrived a pretty device for a seal.[3] A heart is gently warmed by Cupid's flame, and Hymen[4] comes with his rude torch and extinguishes it. She said she found herself quite in a flutter. "Why, really," said I, "reason sometimes has no power. We have no occasion to be frightened, and yet we are both a little so. Indeed, I preserve a tolerable presence of mind." I rose and kissed her, and conscious that I had no occasion to doubt my qualifications as a gallant,[5] I joked about it: "How curious would it be if I should be so frightened that we should rise as we lay down." She reproved my wanton language by a look of modesty. The bells of St. Bride's church rung their merry chimes hard by. I said that the bells in Cupid's court would be this night set a-ringing for joy at our union.

We supped cheerfully and agreeably and drank a few glasses, and then the maid came and put the sheets, well aired, upon the bed. I now contemplated my fair prize. Louisa is just twenty-four, of a tall rather than short figure, finely made in person, with a handsome face and an enchanting languish in her eyes. She dresses with taste. She has sense, good humour, and vivacity, and looks quite a woman in genteel life. As I mused on this elevating subject, I could not help being somehow pleasingly confounded to think that so fine a woman was at this moment in my possession, that without any motives of interest[6] she had come with me to an inn, agreed to be my intimate companion, as to be my bedfellow all night, and to permit me the full enjoyment of her person.

When the servant left the room, I embraced her warmly and begged that she would not now delay my felicity. She declined to undress before me, and begged I would retire and send her one of the maids. I did so, gravely desiring the girl to go up

1. Fleet Street inn, recommended to Boswell by Digges.
2. Deities of grain, wine, and love, respectively. Boswell refers to the proverb, "without Ceres and Bacchus, Venus grows cold."
3. A personal emblem or insignia, which would be impressed on the wax sealing a letter.
4. God of marriage, who traditionally carries a torch.
5. A lover; Boswell jokes that, were he anxious, he might lose his erection, in which case the couple would "rise" from the bed, without consummation.
6. Mercenary motives.

to Mrs. Digges. I then took a candle in my hand and walked out to the yard. The night was very dark and very cold. I experienced for some minutes the rigors of the season, and called into my mind many terrible ideas of hardships, that I might make a transition from such dreary thoughts to the most gay and delicious feelings. I then caused make a bowl of negus,[7] very rich of the fruit, which I caused be set in the room as a reviving cordial.

I came softly into the room, and in a sweet delirium slipped into bed and was immediately clasped in her snowy arms and pressed to her milk-white bosom. Good heavens, what a loose[8] did we give to amorous dalliance! The friendly curtain of darkness concealed our blushes. In a moment I felt myself animated with the strongest powers of love, and, from my dearest creature's kindness, had a most luscious feast. Proud of my godlike vigor, I soon resumed the noble game. I was in full glow of health. Sobriety had preserved me from effeminacy[9] and weakness, and my bounding blood beat quick and high alarms. A more voluptuous night I never enjoyed. Five times was I fairly lost in supreme rapture. Louisa was madly fond of me; she declared I was a prodigy, and asked me if this was not extraordinary for human nature. I said twice as much might be, but this was not, although in my own mind I was somewhat proud of my performance. She said it was what there was no just reason to be proud of. But I told her I could not help it. She said it was what we had in common with the beasts. I said no. For we had it highly improved by the pleasures of sentiment.[1] I asked her what she thought enough. She gently chid me for asking such questions, but said two times. I mentioned the Sunday's assignation,[2] when I was in such bad spirits, told her in what agony of mind I was, and asked her if she would not have despised me for my imbecility. She declared she would not, as it was what people had not in their own power.

She often insisted that we should compose ourselves to sleep before I would consent to it. At last I sunk to rest in her arms and she in mine. I found the negus, which had a fine flavor, very refreshing to me. Louisa had an exquisite mixture of delicacy and wantonness that made me enjoy her with more relish. Indeed I could not help roving in fancy to the embraces of some other ladies which my lively imagination strongly pictured. I don't know if that was altogether fair. However, Louisa had all the advantage. She said she was quite fatigued and could neither stir leg nor arm. She begged I would not despise her, and hoped my love would not be altogether transient. I have painted this night as well as I could. The description is faint; but I surely may be styled a Man of Pleasure.

Thursday, 20 January [1763][3] * * * I then went to Louisa. With excellent address did I carry on this interview, as the following scene, I trust, will make appear:

LOUISA: My dear Sir! I hope you are well today.
BOSWELL: Excessively well, I thank you. I hope I find you so.
LOUISA: No, really, Sir. I am distressed with a thousand things. (Cunning jade, her circumstances![4]) I really don't know what to do.

7. A drink of wine and hot water, sweetened and flavored.
8. What freedom.
9. Impotence.
1. Feelings of affection.
2. During an assignation ten days earlier, Boswell had attempted—unsuccessfully—to consummate the relationship.
3. The day before, Boswell had observed in himself the unmistakable signs of venereal disease: "Too, too plain was Signor Gonorrhoea!" He then visited his doctor, who confirmed the diagnosis and asserted "that the woman who gave it me could not but know about it."
4. During the course of the relationship, Louisa had talked often about her debts, and Boswell had made her a loan.

BOSWELL: Do you know that I have been very unhappy since I saw you?
LOUISA: How so, Sir?
BOSWELL: Why, I am afraid that you don't love me so well, nor have not such a regard for me, as I thought you had.
LOUISA: Nay, dear Sir! [*Seeming unconcerned.*]
BOSWELL: Pray, Madam, have I no reason?
LOUISA: No, indeed, Sir, you have not.
BOSWELL: Have I no reason, Madam? Pray think.
LOUISA: Sir!
BOSWELL: Pray, Madam, in what state of health have you been in for some time?
LOUISA: Sir, you amaze me.
BOSWELL: I have but too strong, too plain reason to doubt of your regard. I have for some days observed the symptoms of disease, but was unwilling to believe you so very ungenerous. But now, Madam, I am thoroughly convinced.
LOUISA: Sir, you have terrified me. I protest I know nothing of the matter.
BOSWELL: Madam, I have had no connection with any woman but you these two months. I was with my surgeon this morning, who declared I had got a strong infection, and that she from whom I had it could not be ignorant of it. Madam, such a thing in this case is worse than from a woman of the town,[5] as from her you may expect it. You have used me very ill. I did not deserve it. You know you said where there was no confidence, there was no breach of trust. But surely I placed some confidence in you. I am sorry that I was mistaken.
LOUISA: Sir, I will confess to you that about three years ago I was very bad.[6] But for these fifteen months I have been quite well. I appeal to God Almighty that I am speaking true; and for these six months I have had to do with no man but yourself.
BOSWELL: But by G-d, Madam, I have been with none but you, and here am I very bad.
LOUISA: Well, Sir, by the same solemn oath I protest that I was ignorant of it.
BOSWELL: Madam, I wish much to believe you. But I own I cannot upon this occasion believe a miracle.
LOUISA: Sir, I cannot say more to you. But you will leave me in the greatest misery. I shall lose your esteem. I shall be hurt in the opinion of everybody, and in my circumstances.
BOSWELL [*to himself*]: What the devil does the confounded jilt mean by being hurt in her circumstances? This is the grossest cunning. But I won't take notice of that at all.—Madam, as to the opinion of everybody, you need not be afraid. I was going to joke and say that I never boast of a lady's *favors*. But I give you my word of honor that you shall not be discovered.
LOUISA: Sir, this is being more generous than I could expect.
BOSWELL: I hope, Madam, you will own that since I have been with you I have always behaved like a man of honor.
LOUISA: You have indeed, Sir.
BOSWELL [*rising*]: Madam, your most obedient servant.

During all this conversation I really behaved with a manly composure and polite dignity that could not fail to inspire an awe, and she was pale as ashes and trembled and faltered. Thrice did she insist on my staying a little longer, as it was

5. Prostitute.

6. Severely infected.

probably the last time that I should be with her. She could say nothing to the purpose. And I sat silent. As I was going, said she, "I hope, Sir, you will give me leave to inquire after your health." "Madam," said I, archly, "I fancy it will be needless for some weeks." She again renewed her request. But unwilling to be plagued any more with her, I put her off by saying I might perhaps go to the country, and left her. I was really confounded at her behavior. There is scarcely a possibility that she could be innocent of the crime of horrid imposition. And yet her positive asseverations really stunned me. She is in all probability a most consummate dissembling whore.

Thus ended my intrigue with the fair Louisa, which I flattered myself so much with, and from which I expected at least a winter's safe copulation. It is indeed very hard. I cannot say, like young fellows who get themselves clapped in a bawdy house,[7] that I will take better care again. For I really did take care. However, since I am fairly trapped, let me make the best of it. I have not got it from imprudence. It is merely the chance of war.

I then called at Drury Lane for Mr. Garrick. He was vastly good to me. "Sir," said he, "you will be a very great man. And when you are so, remember the year 1763. I want to contribute my part towards saving you. And pray, will you fix a day when I shall have the pleasure of treating you with tea?" I fixed next day. "Then, Sir," said he, "the cups shall dance and the saucers skip."

What he meant by my being a great man I can understand. For really, to speak seriously, I think there is a blossom about me of something more distinguished than the generality of mankind. But I am much afraid that this blossom will never swell into fruit, but will be nipped and destroyed by many a blighting heat and chilling frost. Indeed, I sometimes indulge noble reveries of having a regiment, of getting into Parliament, making a figure, and becoming a man of consequence in the state. But these are checked by dispiriting reflections on my melancholy temper and imbecility of mind. Yet I may probably become sounder and stronger as I grow up. Heaven knows. I am resigned. I trust to Providence. I was quite in raptures with Garrick's kindness—the man whom from a boy I used to adore and look upon as a heathen god—to find him paying me so much respect! How amiable is he in comparison of Sheridan! I was this day with him what the French call *un étourdi* [a scatterbrain]. I gave free vent to my feelings. Love[8] was by, to whom I cried, "This, Sir, is the real scene." And taking Mr. Garrick cordially by the hand, "Thou greatest of men," said I, "I cannot express how happy you make me." This, upon my soul, was no flattery. He saw it was not. And the dear great man was truly pleased with it. This scene gave me a charming flutter of spirits and dispelled my former gloom. * * *

[First Meeting with Johnson]

Monday, 16 May [1763]. Temple[1] and his brother breakfasted with me. I went to Love's to try to recover some of the money which he owes me. But, alas, a single guinea was all I could get. He was just going to dinner, so I stayed and eat a bit, though I was angry at myself afterwards. I drank tea at Davies's[2] in Russell Street, and about seven came in the great Mr. Samuel Johnson, whom I have so long wished to

7. Acquire gonorrhea in a brothel.
8. James Love, actor and longtime friend of Boswell.
1. William Johnson Temple, Boswell's most intimate and upstanding friend.
2. Thomas Davies, actor and bookseller.

see. Mr. Davies introduced me to him. As I knew his mortal antipathy at the Scotch, I cried to Davies, "Don't tell where I come from." However, he said, "From Scotland." "Mr. Johnson," said I, "indeed I come from Scotland, but I cannot help it." "Sir," replied he, "that, I find, is what a very great many of your countrymen cannot help." Mr. Johnson is a man of a most dreadful appearance. He is a very big man, is troubled with sore eyes, the palsy, and the king's evil.[3] He is very slovenly in his dress and speaks with a most uncouth voice. Yet his great knowledge and strength of expression command vast respect and render him very excellent company. He has great humor and is a worthy man. But his dogmatical roughness of manners is disagreeable. I shall mark what I remember of his conversation. * * *

1762–1763 1950

An Account of My Last Interview with David Hume, Esq.

Partly recorded in my Journal, partly enlarged from my memory, 3 March 1777[1]

On Sunday forenoon the 7 of July 1776, being too late for church, I went to see Mr. David Hume, who was returned from London and Bath,[2] just a-dying. I found him alone, in a reclining posture in his drawing room. He was lean, ghastly, and quite of an earthy appearance. He was dressed in a suit of gray cloth with white metal buttons, and a kind of scratch wig. He was quite different from the plump figure which he used to present. He had before him Dr. Campbell's *Philosophy of Rhetoric*.[3] He seemed to be placid and even cheerful. He said he was just approaching to his end. I think these were his words. I know not how I contrived to get the subject of immortality introduced. He said he never had entertained any belief in religion since he began to read Locke and Clarke. I asked him if he was not religious when he was young. He said he was, and he used to read *The Whole Duty of Man*;[4] that he made an abstract from the catalogue of vices at the end of it, and examined himself by this, leaving out murder and theft and such vices as he had no chance of committing, having no inclination to commit them. This, he said, was strange work; for instance, to try if, notwithstanding his excelling his schoolfellows, he had no pride or vanity. He smiled in ridicule of this as absurd and contrary to fixed principles and necessary consequences, not adverting that religious discipline does not mean to extinguish, but to moderate, the passions; and certainly an excess of pride or vanity is dangerous and generally hurtful. He then said flatly that the morality of every religion was bad, and, I really thought, was not jocular when he said that when he heard a man was religious, he concluded he was a rascal, though he had known some

3. Scrofula, a form of tuberculosis that the king's touch was believed to cure.

1. Boswell was terrified of death, preoccupied with the question of an afterlife, and in doubt as to the sturdiness of his own Christian faith. All these agitations converged at the deathbed of the "infidel" Scots philosopher David Hume (1711–1776), whom he had known (and intermittently exasperated) for about 15 years. Boswell first wrote this account three weeks after the event, and revisited it twice, altering and expanding it in March of the following year, and adding a postscript ten months later. For David Hume, see Perspectives: Mind and God (page 2631) and the conversations recorded in the *Life of Johnson* (page 2763).

2. To his house in Edinburgh.

3. George Campbell (1719–1796), a Scots clergyman, had made his philosophical reputation by a book-length rebuttal to Hume's essay *Of Miracles*, but he cheerfully acknowledged Hume's influence on his thought, and the two men sustained an affectionate relationship. *The Philosophy of Rhetoric*, which would become Campbell's most successful work, was now newly published.

4. A massively popular work of uncertain authorship, first published in 1658, which prescribed a rigorous code of Christian conduct.

instances of very good men being religious. This was just an extravagant reverse of the common remark as to infidels.

I had a strong curiosity to be satisfied if he persisted in disbelieving a future state even when he had death before his eyes. I was persuaded from what he now said, and from his manner of saying it, that he did persist. I asked him if it was not possible that there might be a future state. He answered it was possible that a piece of coal put upon the fire would not burn; and he added that it was a most unreasonable fancy that we should exist forever. That immortality, if it were at all, must be general; that a great proportion of the human race has hardly any intellectual qualities; that a great proportion dies in infancy before being possessed of reason; yet all these must be immortal; that a porter who gets drunk by ten o'clock with gin must be immortal; that the trash of every age must be preserved, and that new universes must be created to contain such infinite numbers. This appeared to me an unphilosophical objection, and I said, "Mr. Hume, you know spirit does not take up space."

I may illustrate what he last said by mentioning that in a former conversation with me on this subject he used pretty much the same mode of reasoning, and urged that Wilkes[5] and his mob must be immortal. One night last May as I was coming up King Street, Westminster, I met Wilkes, who carried me into Parliament Street to see a curious procession pass: the funeral of a lamplighter attended by some hundreds of his fraternity with torches. Wilkes, who either is, or affects to be, an infidel, was rattling away, "I think there's an end of that fellow. I think he won't rise again." I very calmly said to him, "You bring into my mind the strongest argument that ever I heard against a future state"; and then told him David Hume's objection that Wilkes and his mob must be immortal. It seemed to make a proper impression, for he grinned abashment, as a Negro grows whiter when he blushes. But to return to my last interview with Mr. Hume.

I asked him if the thought of annihilation never gave him any uneasiness. He said not the least; no more than the thought that he had not been, as Lucretius observes.[6] "Well," said I, "Mr. Hume, I hope to triumph over you when I meet you in a future state; and remember you are not to pretend that you was joking with all this infidelity." "No, no," said he. "But I shall have been so long there before you come that it will be nothing new." In this style of good humor and levity did I conduct the conversation. Perhaps it was wrong on so awful[7] a subject. But as nobody was present, I thought it could have no bad effect. I however felt a degree of horror, mixed with a sort of wild, strange, hurrying recollection of my excellent mother's pious instructions, of Dr. Johnson's noble lessons, and of my religious sentiments and affections during the course of my life. I was like a man in sudden danger eagerly seeking his defensive arms; and I could not but be assailed by momentary doubts while I had actually before me a man of such strong abilities and extensive inquiry dying in the persuasion of being annihilated. But I maintained my faith. I told him that I believed the Christian religion as I believed history. Said he: "You do not believe it as you believe the Revolution."[8] "Yes," said I; "but the difference is that I am not so much interested in the truth of the Revolution; otherwise I should have anxious doubts concerning it. A man who is in love has doubts of the affection of

5. John Wilkes (1725–1797), radical politician.

6. Titus Lucretius Carus, Roman philosopher and poet; Hume's observation appears to echo more closely an observation by the Stoic philosopher Seneca: "Death is non-existence. What that may be I already know. What shall be after me is what was before me" (*Epistolae* 54.4).

7. Solemn.

8. The "Glorious Revolution" of 1688–1689, when the Stuart monarch James II was replaced by William and Mary.

his mistress, without cause." I mentioned Soame Jenyns's little book in defense of Christianity, which was just published but which I had not yet read.[9] Mr. Hume said, "I am told there is nothing of his usual spirit in it."

He had once said to me, on a forenoon while the sun was shining bright, that he did not wish to be immortal. This was a most wonderful[1] thought. The reason he gave was that he was very well in this state of being, and that the chances were very much against his being so well in another state; and he would rather not be more than be worse. I answered that it was reasonable to hope he would be better; that there would be a progressive improvement. I tried him at this interview with that topic, saying that a future state was surely a pleasing idea. He said no, for that it was always seen through a gloomy medium; there was always a Phlegethon[2] or a hell. "But," said I, "would it not be agreeable to have hopes of seeing our friends again?" and I mentioned three men lately deceased, for whom I knew he had a high value: Ambassador Keith, Lord Alemoor, and Baron Mure. He owned it would be agreeable, but added that none of them entertained such a notion. I believe he said, such a foolish, or such an absurd, notion; for he was indecently[3] and impolitely positive in incredulity. "Yes," said I, "Lord Alemoor was a believer." David acknowledged that *he* had *some* belief.

I somehow or other brought Dr. Johnson's name into our conversation. I had often heard him speak of that great man in a very illiberal manner. He said upon this occasion, "Johnson should be pleased with my *History*."[4] Nettled by Hume's frequent attacks upon my revered friend in former conversations, I told him now that Dr. Johnson did not allow him much credit; for he said, "Sir, the fellow is a Tory by chance."[5] I am sorry that I mentioned this at such a time. I was off my guard; for the truth is that Mr. Hume's pleasantry was such that there was no solemnity in the scene; and death for the time did not seem dismal. It surprised me to find him talking of different matters with a tranquillity of mind and a clearness of head which few men posses at any time. Two particulars I remember: Smith's *Wealth of Nations*, which he commended much, and Monboddo's *Origin of Language*, which he treated contemptuously.[6] I said, "If I were you, I should regret annihilation. Had I written such an admirable history, I should be sorry to leave it." He said, "I shall leave that history, of which you are pleased to speak so favorably, as perfect as I can."[7] He said, too, that all the great abilities with which men had ever been endowed were relative to this world. He said he became a greater friend to the Stuart family as he advanced in studying for his history; and he hoped he had vindicated the two first of them so effectually that they would never again be attacked.

Mr. Lauder, his surgeon, came in for a little, and Mr. Mure, the Baron's son, for another small interval. He was, as far as I could judge, quite easy with both. He said

9. Soame Jenyns (1704–1787) had published *A View of the Internal Evidence of the Christian Religion*.
1. Astonishing.
2. In Greek mythology, a river in Hades.
3. In his first version, Boswell had written the milder "improperly."
4. The six-volume *History of Great Britain* (1754–1762); Hume was now revising it, and had noted that his alterations to the portion on the "two first Stuarts" were "invariably to the Tory side" (the view favored by Johnson).
5. "As being a Scotchman," Johnson had gone on to explain, "but not upon a principle of duty; for he has no principle."
6. *The Wealth of Nations* (1776), by Hume's friend Adam Smith, is the foundation text of modern economics; in *The Origin and Progress of Language* (1773), James Burnett, Lord Monboddo, argued (among other things) that humans and orangutans are of the same species.
7. Once, to entertain Adam Smith, Hume pretended that these revisions might furnish him with an excuse for living longer: "'Allow me a little time,'" he imagined himself saying to the mythic ferryman who conveyed the dead to Hades, "'that I may see how the public receives the alterations.' But Charon would answer, 'When you have seen the effect of these, you will be for making other alterations. There will be no end to such excuses; so, honest friend, please step into the boat.'"

he had no pain, but was wasting away. I left him with impressions which disturbed me for some time.

(Additions from memory, 22 January 1778) Speaking of his singular notion that men of religion were generally bad men, he said, "One of the men" (or "The man"—I am not sure which) "of the greatest honor that I ever knew is my Lord Marischal,[8] who is a downright atheist. I remember I once hinted something as if I believed in the being of a God, and he would not speak to me for a week." He said this with his usual grunting pleasantry, with that thick breath which fatness had rendered habitual to him, and that smile of simplicity which his good humor constantly produced.

When he spoke against Monboddo, I told him that Monboddo said to me that he believed the abusive criticism upon his book in *The Edinburgh Magazine and Review* was written by Mr. Hume's direction. David seemed irritated, and said, "Does the *scoundrel*" (I am sure either *that* or "*rascal*") "say so?" He then told me that he had observed to one of the Faculty of Advocates that Monboddo was wrong in his observation that———and gave as a proof the line in Milton. When the review came out, he found this very remark in it, and said to that advocate, "Oho! I have discovered you"—reminding him of the circumstance.[9]

It was amazing to find him so keen in such a state. I must add one other circumstance which is material, as it shows that he perhaps was not without some hope of a future state, and that his spirits were supported by a consciousness (or at least a notion) that his conduct had been virtuous. He said, "If there were a future state, Mr. Boswell, I think I could give as good an account of my life as most people."

1776–1778 1970

from The Life of Samuel Johnson, LL.D.

[Introduction; Boswell's Method]

To write the Life of him who excelled all mankind in writing the lives of others, and who, whether we consider his extraordinary endowments or his various works, has been equaled by few in any age, is an arduous, and may be reckoned in me a presumptuous task.

Had Dr. Johnson written his own life, in conformity with the opinion which he has given, that every man's life may be best written by himself;[1] had he employed in the preservation of his own history, that clearness of narration and elegance of language in which he has embalmed so many eminent persons, the world would probably have had the most perfect example of biography that was ever exhibited. But although he at different times, in a desultory manner, committed to writing many particulars of the progress of his mind and fortunes, he never had preserving diligence enough to form them into a regular composition. Of these memorials a few have been preserved; but the greater part was consigned by him to the flames, a few days before his death.

As I had the honor and happiness of enjoying his friendship for upwards of twenty years; as I had the scheme of writing his life constantly in view; as he was well apprised of this circumstance, and from time to time obligingly satisfied my inquiries, by communicating to me the incidents of his early years; as I acquired a

8. George Keith, tenth Earl Marischal of Scotland, a renowned Jacobite who as an old man had befriended the young Boswell and accompanied him on the German portion of his Grand Tour.

9. The details of the dispute remain obscure; Boswell never filled in the blank or identified the "line in Milton."

1. In *Idler* No. 84.

facility in recollecting, and was very assiduous in recording, his conversation, of which the extraordinary vigor and vivacity constituted one of the first features of his character; and as I have spared no pains in obtaining materials concerning him, from every quarter where I could discover that they were to be found, and have been favored with the most liberal communications by his friends; I flatter myself that few biographers have entered upon such a work as this with more advantages; independent of literary abilities, in which I am not vain enough to compare myself with some great names who have gone before me in this kind of writing. * * *

Instead of melting down my materials into one mass, and constantly speaking in my own person, by which I might have appeared to have more merit in the execution of the work, I have resolved to adopt and enlarge upon the excellent plan of Mr. Mason, in his *Memoirs* of Gray.[2] Wherever narrative is necessary to explain, connect, and supply, I furnish it to the best of my abilities; but in the chronological series of Johnson's life, which I trace as distinctly as I can, year by year, I produce, wherever it is in my power, his own minutes,[3] letters, or conversation, being convinced that this mode is more lively, and will make my readers better acquainted with him, than even most of those were who actually knew him, but could know him only partially; whereas there is here an accumulation of intelligence from various points, by which his character is more fully understood and illustrated.

Indeed I cannot conceive a more perfect mode of writing any man's life than not only relating all the most important events of it in their order, but interweaving what he privately wrote, and said, and thought; by which mankind are enabled as it were to see him live, and to "live o'er each scene"[4] with him, as he actually advanced through the several stages of his life. Had his other friends been as diligent and ardent as I was, he might have been almost entirely preserved. As it is, I will venture to say that he will be seen in this work more completely than any man who has ever yet lived.

And he will be seen as he really was; for I profess to write, not his panegyric, which must be all praise, but his Life; which, great and good as he was, must not be supposed to be entirely perfect. To be as he was, is indeed subject of panegyric enough to any man in this state of being; but in every picture there should be shade as well as light, and when I delineate him without reserve, I do what he himself recommended, both by his precept[5] and his example. * * *

What I consider as the peculiar value of the following work is the quantity that it contains of Johnson's conversation; which is universally acknowledged to have been eminently instructive and entertaining; and of which the specimens that I have given upon a former occasion have been received with so much approbation that I have good grounds for supposing that the world will not be indifferent to more ample communications of a similar nature. * * *

I am fully aware of the objections which may be made to the minuteness on some occasions of my detail of Johnson's conversation, and how happily it is adapted for the petty exercise of ridicule, by men of superficial understanding and ludicrous fancy;[6] but I remain firm and confident in my opinion, that minute particulars are frequently characteristic,[7] and always amusing, when they relate to a distinguished

2. William Mason constructed his *Memoirs* of Thomas Gray (1775) around a selection of the poet's letters.
3. Memoranda.
4. "To wake the soul by tender strokes of art, / To raise the genius, and to mend the heart, / To make mankind in conscious virtue bold, / Live o'er each scene, and be what they behold" (lines 1–4 of Pope's prologue to Addison's *Cato*).
5. Boswell proceeds to quote from *Rambler* No. 60 (see page 2694) in which Johnson articulates his biographical principles.
6. Boswell's Hebridean journal had already been parodied in print for its "minuteness" and "detail."
7. Revealing of character.

man. I am therefore exceedingly unwilling that anything, however slight, which my illustrious friend thought it worth his while to express, with any degree of point,[8] should perish. * * *

Of one thing I am certain, that considering how highly the small portion which we have of the table talk and other anecdotes of our celebrated writers[9] is valued, and how earnestly it is regretted that we have not more, I am justified in preserving rather too many of Johnson's sayings than too few; especially as from the diversity of dispositions it cannot be known with certainty beforehand, whether what may seem trifling to some, and perhaps to the collector himself, may not be most agreeable to many; and the greater number that an author can please in any degree, the more pleasure does there arise to a benevolent mind.

To those who are weak enough to think this a degrading task, and the time and labor which have been devoted to it misemployed, I shall content myself with opposing the authority of the greatest man of any age, Julius Caesar, of whom Bacon observes, that "in his book of Apothegms which he collected, we see that he esteemed it more honor to make himself but a pair of tables, to take the wise and pithy words of others, than to have every word of his own to be made an apothegm or an oracle."

Having said thus much by way of introduction, I commit the following pages to the candor of the Public.

[Conversations about Hume]

[21 July 1763] Next morning I found him alone, and have preserved the following fragments of his conversation. Of a gentleman[1] who was mentioned, he said, "I have not met with any man for a long time who has given me such general displeasure. He is totally unfixed in his principles, and wants to puzzle other people." I said his principles had been poisoned by a noted infidel writer,[2] but that he was, nevertheless, a benevolent good man. Johnson: "We can have no dependence upon that instinctive, that constitutional goodness which is not founded upon principle. I grant you that such a man may be a very amiable member of society. I can conceive him placed in such a situation that he is not much tempted to deviate from what is right; and as every man prefers virtue, when there is not some strong incitement to transgress its precepts, I can conceive him doing nothing wrong. But if such a man stood in need of money, I should not like to trust him; and I should certainly not trust him with young ladies, for *there* there is always temptation. Hume and other skeptical innovators are vain men, and will gratify themselves at any expense. Truth will not afford sufficient food to their vanity; so they have betaken themselves to error. Truth, Sir, is a cow which will yield such people no more milk, and so they are gone to milk the bull. If I could have allowed myself to gratify my vanity at the expense of truth, what fame might I have acquired. Everything which Hume has advanced against Christianity had passed through my mind long before he wrote. Always remember this, that after a system is well settled upon positive evidence, a few partial objections ought not to shake it. The human mind is so limited that it cannot take in all the parts of a subject, so that there may be objections raised against anything. There are objections against a *plenum*, and objections against a *vacuum*;[3] yet one of them must certainly be true."

8. "Remarkable turn of words or thought" (Johnson's *Dictionary*).

9. E.g., Joseph Spence's *Anecdotes, Observations and Characters of Books and Men, Collected from the Conversation of Mr. Pope*, which (though unpublished until 1820) Johnson drew on for his *Life* of Pope.

1. Boswell's friend George Dempster.

2. The skeptical philosopher David Hume.

3. According to the scientific theory of the *plenum*, all space is full (*plenus*) of matter; the opposing theory postulated that there are parts of space that are empty (*vacuus*) of matter.

I mentioned Hume's argument against the belief of miracles, that it is more probable that the witnesses to the truth of them are mistaken, or speak falsely, than that the miracles should be true. JOHNSON: "Why, Sir, the great difficulty of proving miracles should make us very cautious in believing them. But let us consider; although God has made Nature to operate by certain fixed laws, yet it is not unreasonable to think that he may suspend those laws, in order to establish a system highly advantageous to mankind. Now the Christian religion is a most beneficial system, as it gives us light and certainty where we were before in darkness and doubt. The miracles which prove it are attested by men who had no interest in deceiving us; but who, on the contrary, were told that they should suffer persecution, and did actually lay down their lives in confirmation of the truth of the facts which they asserted. Indeed, for some centuries the heathens did not pretend to deny the miracles; but said they were performed by the aid of evil spirits. This is a circumstance of great weight. Then, Sir, when we take the proofs derived from prophecies which have been so exactly fulfilled, we have most satisfactory evidence. Supposing a miracle possible, as to which, in my opinion, there can be no doubt, we have as strong evidence for the miracles in support of Christianity, as the nature of the thing admits."

At night Mr. Johnson and I supped in a private room at the Turk's Head coffeehouse, in the Strand. "I encourage this house (said he); for the mistress of it is a good civil woman, and has not much business."

"Sir, I love the acquaintance of young people; because, in the first place, I don't like to think myself growing old. In the next place, young acquaintances must last longest, if they do last; and then, Sir, young men have more virtue than old men; they have more generous sentiments in every respect. I love the young dogs of this age: they have more wit and humor and knowledge of life than we had; but then the dogs are not so good scholars. Sir, in my early years I read very hard. It is a sad reflection, but a true one, that I knew almost as much at eighteen as I do now. My judgment, to be sure, was not so good; but I had all the facts. I remember very well, when I was at Oxford, an old gentleman said to me, 'Young man, ply your book diligently now, and acquire a stock of knowledge; for when years come upon you, you will find that poring upon books will be but an irksome task.'"

* * *

[26 October 1769] When we were alone, I introduced the subject of death, and endeavored to maintain that the fear of it might be got over. I told him that David Hume said to me, he was no more uneasy to think he should *not be* after this life, than that he *had not been* before he began to exist. JOHNSON: "Sir, if he really thinks so, his perceptions are disturbed; he is mad: if he does not think so, he lies. He may tell you, he holds his finger in the flame of a candle, without feeling pain; would you believe him? When he dies, he at least gives up all he has." BOSWELL: "Foote,[4] Sir, told me, that when he was very ill he was not afraid to die." JOHNSON: "It is not true, Sir. Hold a pistol to Foote's breast, or to Hume's breast, and threaten to kill them, and you'll see how they behave." BOSWELL: "But may we not fortify our minds for the approach of death?" Here I am sensible I was in the wrong, to bring before his view what he ever looked upon with horror; for although when in a celestial frame, in his *Vanity of Human Wishes*,[5] he has supposed death to be "kind Nature's signal

4. Samuel Foote (1721–1771), actor, playwright, and theatrical manager.

5. Johnson's imitation of Juvenal's tenth satire, lines 363–64 (see page 2685).

for retreat," from this state of being to "a happier seat," his thoughts upon this awful change were in general full of dismal apprehensions. His mind resembled the vast amphitheater, the Colosseum at Rome. In the center stood his judgment, which, like a mighty gladiator, combated those apprehensions that, like the wild beasts of the Arena, were all around in cells, ready to be let out upon him. After a conflict, he drove them back into their dens; but not killing them, they were still assailing him. To my question, whether we might not fortify our minds for the approach of death, he answered, in a passion, "No, Sir, let it alone. It matters not how a man dies, but how he lives. The act of dying is not of importance, it lasts so short a time." He added (with an earnest look), "A man knows it must be so, and submits. It will do him no good to whine."

I attempted to continue the conversation. He was so provoked that he said, "Give us no more of this"; and was thrown into such a state of agitation, that he expressed himself in a way that alarmed and distressed me, showed an impatience that I should leave him, and when I was going away, called to me sternly, "Don't let us meet tomorrow."

I went home exceedingly uneasy. All the harsh observations which I had ever heard made upon his character crowded into my mind; and I seemed to myself like the man who had put his head into the lion's mouth a great many times with perfect safety, but at last had it bit off.

[Dinner with Wilkes]

[May 1776] I am now to record a very curious incident in Dr. Johnson's life, which fell under my own observation; of which *pars magna fui*,[1] and which I am persuaded will, with the liberal-minded, be much to his credit.

My desire of being acquainted with celebrated men of every description had made me, much about the same time, obtain an introduction to Dr. Samuel Johnson and to John Wilkes, Esq.[2] Two men more different could perhaps not be selected out of all mankind. They had even attacked one another with some asperity in their writings; yet I lived in habits of friendship with both. I could fully relish the excellence of each; for I have ever delighted in that intellectual chemistry which can separate good qualities from evil in the same person.

Sir John Pringle,[3] "mine own friend and my Father's friend," between whom and Dr. Johnson I in vain wished to establish an acquaintance, as I respected and lived in intimacy with both of them, observed to me once, very ingeniously, "It is not in friendship as in mathematics, where two things, each equal to a third, are equal between themselves. You agree with Johnson as a middle quality, and you agree with me as a middle quality; but Johnson and I should not agree." Sir John was not sufficiently flexible, so I desisted, knowing, indeed, that the repulsion was equally strong on the part of Johnson, who, I know not from what cause, unless his being a Scotchman, had formed a very erroneous opinion of Sir John. But I conceived an irresistible wish, if possible, to bring Dr. Johnson and Mr. Wilkes together. How to manage it was a nice[4] and difficult matter.

1. "I was no small part." (Virgil, *Aeneid* 2.5).
2. John Wilkes (1727–1797), libertine, satirist, and radical politician, had been expelled from Parliament for blasphemous and seditious libel. Johnson considered Wilkes an unprincipled philanderer and demagogue.
3. John Pringle (1707–1782), distinguished physician and president of the Royal Society. Johnson disliked Pringle's freethinking religious views and his pro-American political convictions.
4. Delicate.

My worthy booksellers[5] and friends, Messieurs Dilly in the Poultry, at whose hospitable and well-covered table I have seen a greater number of literary men than at any other, except that of Sir Joshua Reynolds, had invited me to meet Mr. Wilkes and some more gentlemen on Wednesday, May 15. "Pray," said I, "let us have Dr. Johnson."—"What, with Mr. Wilkes? not for the world," said Mr. Edward Dilly, "Dr. Johnson would never forgive me."—"Come," said I, "if you'll let me negotiate for you, I will be answerable that all shall go well." DILLY: "Nay, if you will take it upon you, I am sure I shall be very happy to see them both here."

Notwithstanding the high veneration which I entertained for Dr. Johnson, I was sensible that he was sometimes a little actuated by the spirit of contradiction, and by means of that I hoped I should gain my point. I was persuaded that if I had come upon him with a direct proposal, "Sir, will you dine in company with Jack Wilkes?" he would have flown into a passion, and would probably have answered, "Dine with Jack Wilkes, Sir! I'd as soon dine with Jack Ketch."[6] I therefore, while we were sitting quietly by ourselves at his house in an evening, took occasion to open my plan thus:—"Mr. Dilly, Sir, sends his respectful compliments to you, and would be happy if you would do him the honor to dine with him on Wednesday next along with me, as I must soon go to Scotland." JOHNSON: "Sir, I am obliged to Mr. Dilly. I will wait upon him:" BOSWELL: "Provided, Sir, I suppose, that the company which he is to have is agreeable to you." JOHNSON: "What do you mean, Sir? What do you take me for? Do you think I am so ignorant of the world, as to imagine that I am to prescribe to a gentleman what company he is to have at his table?" BOSWELL: "I beg your pardon, Sir, for wishing to prevent you from meeting people whom you might not like. Perhaps he may have some of what he calls his patriotic[7] friends with him." JOHNSON: "Well, Sir, and what then? What care *I* for his *patriotic friends?* Poh!" BOSWELL: "I should not be surprised to find Jack Wilkes there." JOHNSON: "And if Jack Wilkes *should* be there, what is that to *me*, Sir? My dear friend, let us have no more of this. I am sorry to be angry with you; but really it is treating me strangely to talk to me as if I could not meet any company whatever, occasionally." BOSWELL: "Pray forgive me, Sir. I meant well. But you shall meet whoever comes, for me." Thus I secured him, and told Dilly that he would find him very well pleased to be one of his guests on the day appointed.

Upon the much-expected Wednesday, I called on him about half an hour before dinner, as I often did when we were to dine out together, to see that he was ready in time, and to accompany him. I found him buffeting[8] his books, as upon a former occasion, covered with dust and making no preparation for going abroad. "How is this, Sir?" said I. "Don't you recollect that you are to dine at Mr. Dilly's?" JOHNSON: "Sir, I did not think of going to Dilly's: it went out of my head. I have ordered dinner at home with Mrs. Williams."[9] BOSWELL: "But, my dear Sir, you know you were engaged to Mr. Dilly, and I told him so. He will expect you, and will be much disappointed if you don't come." JOHNSON: "You must talk to Mrs. Williams about this."

Here was a sad dilemma. I feared that what I was so confident I had secured would yet be frustrated. He had accustomed himself to show Mrs. Williams such a degree of humane attention, as frequently imposed some restraint upon him; and I

5. Publishers.
6. Famous 17th-century hangman.
7. Those in favor of diminishing the power of the monarch and supporting the rights of the American colonists. Johnson had recently written a political tract called *The Patriot* (1774) in which he attacked Wilkes and his supporters.
8. Vigorously cleaning.
9. An elderly blind woman who lived in Johnson's house as one of several dependents.

knew that if she should be obstinate, he would not stir. I hastened downstairs to the blind lady's room and told her I was in great uneasiness, for Dr. Johnson had engaged to me to dine this day at Mr. Dilly's, but that he had told me he had forgotten his engagement, and had ordered dinner at home. "Yes, Sir," said she, pretty peevishly, "Dr. Johnson is to dine at home." "Madam," said I "his respect for you is such that I know he will not leave you unless you absolutely desire it. But as you have so much of his company, I hope you will be good enough to forgo it for a day; as Mr. Dilly is a very worthy man, has frequently had agreeable parties at his house for Dr. Johnson, and will be vexed if the Doctor neglects him today. And then, Madam, be pleased to consider my situation; I carried the message, and I assured Mr. Dilly that Dr. Johnson was to come, and no doubt he has made a dinner, and invited a company, and boasted of the honor he expected to have. I shall be quite disgraced if the Doctor is not there." She gradually softened to my solicitations, which were certainly as earnest as most entreaties to ladies upon any occasion, and was graciously pleased to empower me to tell Dr. Johnson, "That all things considered, she thought he should certainly go." I flew back to him, still in dust, and careless of what should be the event,[1] "indifferent in his choice to go or stay";[2] but as soon as I had announced to him Mrs. Williams's consent, he roared, "Frank, a clean shirt," and was very soon dressed. When I had him fairly[3] seated in a hackney coach with me, I exulted as much as a fortune hunter who has got an heiress into a post chaise with him to set out for Gretna Green.[4]

When we entered Mr. Dilly's drawing room, he found himself in the midst of a company he did not know. I kept myself snug and silent, watching how he would conduct himself. I observed him whispering to Mr. Dilly, "Who is that gentleman, Sir?"—"Mr. Arthur Lee."—JOHNSON: "Too, too, too" (under his breath), which was one of his habitual mutterings. Mr. Arthur Lee could not but be very obnoxious to Johnson, for he was not only a *patriot* but an *American*. He was afterwards minister from the United States at the court of Madrid. "And who is the gentleman in lace?"—"Mr. Wilkes, Sir." This information confounded him still more; he had some difficulty to restrain himself, and taking up a book, sat down upon a window seat and read, or at least kept his eye upon it intently for some time, till he composed himself. His feelings, I dare say, were awkward enough. But he no doubt recollected his having rated[5] me for supposing that he could be at all disconcerted by any company, and he, therefore, resolutely set himself to behave quite as an easy man of the world, who could adapt himself at once to the disposition and manners of those whom he might chance to meet.

The cheering sound of "Dinner is upon the table" dissolved his reverie, and we *all* sat down without any symptom of ill humor. There were present, besides Mr. Wilkes, and Mr. Arthur Lee, who was an old companion of mine when he studied physics at Edinburgh, Mr. (now Sir John) Miller, Dr. Lettsom, and Mr. Slater, the druggist. Mr. Wilkes placed himself next to Dr. Johnson and behaved to him with so much attention and politeness that he gained upon him insensibly.[6] No man eat[7] more heartily than Johnson, or loved better what was nice and delicate. Mr. Wilkes

1. Not caring how the matter turned out.
2. Boswell adapts a line from Addison's *Cato*: "Indiff'rent in his choice to sleep or die" (5.1).
3. Securely.
4. A village just across the border in Scotland; it was the common destination of eloping couples, who could thereby bypass the formalities and restrictions of the Anglican Church.
5. Chided.
6. Imperceptibly.
7. Ate (pronounced "ett").

was very assiduous in helping him to some fine veal. "Pray give me leave, Sir—It is better here—A little of the brown—Some fat, Sir—A little of the stuffing—Some gravy—Let me have the pleasure of giving you some butter—Allow me to recommend a squeeze of this orange, or the lemon, perhaps, may have more zest."—"Sir, Sir, I am obliged to you, Sir," cried Johnson, bowing, and turning his head to him with a look for some time of "surly virtue,"[8] but, in a short while, of complacency.

Foote being mentioned, Johnson said, "He is not a good mimic." One of the company added, "A merry Andrew, a buffoon." JOHNSON: "But he has wit[9] too, and is not deficient in ideas, or in fertility and variety of imagery, and not empty of reading;[1] he has knowledge enough to fill up his part. One species of wit he has in an eminent degree, that of escape. You drive him into a corner with both hands; but he's gone, Sir, when you think you have got him—like an animal that jumps over your head. Then he has a great range for his wit; he never lets truth stand between him and a jest, and he is sometimes mighty coarse. Garrick is under many restraints from which Foote is free." WILKES: "Garrick's wit is more like Lord Chesterfield's." JOHNSON: "The first time I was in company with Foote was at Fitzherbert's.[2] Having no good opinion of the fellow, I was resolved not to be pleased; and it is very difficult to please a man against his will. I went on eating my dinner pretty sullenly, affecting not to mind him. But the dog was so very comical, that I was obliged to lay down my knife and fork, throw myself back upon my chair, and fairly laugh it out. No, Sir, he was irresistible. He upon one occasion experienced, in an extraordinary degree, the efficacy of his powers of entertaining. Among the many and various modes which he tried of getting money, he became a partner with a small-beer brewer, and he was to have a share of the profits for procuring customers among his numerous acquaintance. Fitzherbert was one who took his small beer;[3] but it was so bad that the servants resolved not to drink it. They were at some loss how to notify[4] their resolution, being afraid of offending their master, who they knew liked Foote much as a companion. At last they fixed upon a little black boy, who was rather a favorite, to be their deputy and deliver their remonstrance; and having invested him with the whole authority of the kitchen, he was to inform Mr. Fitzherbert, in all their names, upon a certain day, that they would drink Foote's small beer no longer. On that day Foote happened to dine at Fitzherbert's, and this boy served at table; he was so delighted with Foote's stories, and merriment, and grimace,[5] that when he went downstairs, he told them, 'This is the finest man I have ever seen. I will not deliver your message. I will drink his small beer.' "

Somebody observed that Garrick could not have done this. WILKES: "Garrick would have made the small beer still smaller. He is now leaving the stage; but he will play Scrub[6] all his life." I knew that Johnson would let nobody attack Garrick but himself, as Garrick once said to me, and I had heard him praise his liberality; so to bring out his commendation of his celebrated pupil, I said, loudly, "I have heard Garrick is liberal." JOHNSON: "Yes, Sir, I know that Garrick has given away more money than any man in England that I am acquainted with, and that not from ostentatious views. Garrick was very poor when he began life; so when he came to

8. Boswell quotes from Johnson's poem *London*.
9. Intelligence, cleverness.
1. Devoid of learning.
2. William Fitzherbert (1712–1772), landowner and politician.
3. Weak beer.
4. Express.
5. Exaggerated facial expressions (Foote specialized in caricatures of his contemporaries).
6. A character in George Farquhar's comedy, *The Beaux' Stratagem*.

have money, he probably was very unskillful in giving away, and saved when he should not. But Garrick began to be liberal as soon as he could; and I am of opinion, the reputation of avarice which he has had, has been very lucky for him and prevented his having many enemies. You despise a man for avarice, but do not hate him. Garrick might have been much better attacked for living with more splendor than is suitable to a player: if they had had the wit to have assaulted him in that quarter, they might have galled him more. But they have kept clamoring about his avarice, which has rescued him from much obloquy and envy."

Talking of the great difficulty of obtaining authentic information for biography, Johnson told us, "When I was a young fellow I wanted to write the *Life of Dryden*, and in order to get materials, I applied to the only two persons then alive who had seen him; these were old Swinney, and old Cibber.[7] Swinney's information was no more than this, "That at Will's coffeehouse Dryden had a particular chair for himself, which was set by the fire in winter, and was then called his winter-chair; and that it was carried out for him to the balcony in summer, and was then called his summer-chair." Cibber could tell no more but "that he remembered him a decent old man, arbiter of critical disputes at Will's." You are to consider that Cibber was then at a great distance from Dryden, had perhaps one leg only in the room, and durst not draw in the other." BOSWELL: "Yet Cibber was a man of observation?" JOHNSON: "I think not." BOSWELL: "You will allow his *Apology* to be well done." JOHNSON: "Very well done, to be sure, Sir. That book is a striking proof of the justice of Pope's remark:

> Each might his several province well command,
> Would all but stoop to what they understand."[8]

BOSWELL: "And his plays are good." JOHNSON: "Yes; but that was his trade; *l'esprit du corps:* he had been all his life among players and play-writers. I wondered that he had so little to say in conversation, for he had kept the best company, and learnt all that can be got by the ear. He abused Pindar[9] to me, and then showed me an ode of his own, with an absurd couplet, making a linnet soar on an eagle's wing. I told him that when the ancients made a simile, they always made it like something real."

Mr. Wilkes remarked, that "among all the bold flights of Shakespeare's imagination, the boldest was making Birnam Wood march to Dunsinane,[1] creating a wood where there never was a shrub; a wood in Scotland! ha! ha! ha!" And he also observed that "the clannish slavery of the Highlands of Scotland was the single exception to Milton's remark[2] of 'The mountain nymph, sweet Liberty,' being worshipped in all hilly countries." "When I was at Inverary," said he, "on a visit to my old friend, Archibald, Duke of Argyle, his dependents congratulated me on being such a favorite of his Grace. I said, 'It is then, gentlemen, truly lucky for me; for if I had displeased the Duke, and he had wished it, there is not a Campbell among you but would have been ready to bring John Wilkes's head to him in a charger. It would have been only

7. Owen Mac Swiney and Colley Cibber, actors from the first half of the 18th century. Cibber was also a poet, playwright, and the author of a widely read autobiography (his *Apology*).
8. Pope, *Essay on Criticism,* lines 66–67.
9. Spoke disparagingly of the ancient Greek poet Pindar, famous for his odes.
1. In Act 5 of *Macbeth*. In his *Journey to the Western Islands* (1775), Johnson had commented repeatedly on the treelessness of Scotland.
2. In his poem *L'Allegro* (36).

Off with his head! So much for Aylesbury.[3]

I was then member[4] for Aylesbury." * * *

Mr. Arthur Lee mentioned some Scotch who had taken possession of a barren part of America, and wondered why they should choose it. JOHNSON: "Why, Sir, all barrenness is comparative. The *Scotch* would not know it to be barren." BOSWELL: "Come, come, he is flattering the English. You have now been in Scotland, Sir, and say if you did not see meat and drink enough there." JOHNSON: "Why yes, Sir; meat and drink enough to give the inhabitants sufficient strength to run away from home." All these quick and lively sallies were said sportively, quite in jest, and with a smile, which showed that he meant only wit. Upon this topic he and Mr. Wilkes could perfectly assimilate; here was a bond of union between them, and I was conscious that as both of them had visited Caledonia,[5] both were fully satisfied of the strange narrow ignorance of those who imagine that it is a land of famine. But they amused themselves with persevering in the old jokes. When I claimed a superiority for Scotland over England in one respect, that no man can be arrested there for a debt merely because another swears it against him; but there must first be the judgment of a court of law ascertaining its justice; and that a seizure of the person, before judgment is obtained, can take place only if his creditor should swear that he is about to fly from the country, or, as it is technically expressed, is *in meditatione fugae*. WILKES: "That, I should think, may be safely sworn of all the Scotch nation." JOHNSON (to Mr. Wilkes): "You must know, Sir, I lately took my friend Boswell and showed him genuine civilized life in an English provincial town. I turned him loose at Lichfield, my native city, that he might see for once real civility: for you know he lives among savages in Scotland, and among rakes in London." WILKES: "Except when he is with grave, sober, decent people like you and me." JOHNSON (smiling): "And we ashamed of him."

They were quite frank and easy. Johnson told the story of his asking Mrs. Macaulay[6] to allow her footman to sit down with them, to prove the ridiculousness of the argument for the equality of mankind; and he said to me afterwards, with a nod of satisfaction, "You saw Mr. Wilkes acquiesced." Wilkes talked with all imaginable freedom of the ludicrous title given to the Attorney General, *Diabolus Regis*,[7] adding, "I have reason to know something about that officer; for I was prosecuted for a libel."[8] Johnson, who many people would have supposed must have been furiously angry at hearing this talked of so lightly, said not a word. He was now, *indeed*, "a good-humored fellow."

After dinner we had an accession[9] of Mrs. Knowles, the Quaker lady, well known for her various talents, and of Mr. Alderman Lee. Amidst some patriotic groans, somebody (I think the Alderman) said, "Poor old England is lost." JOHNSON: "Sir, it is not so much to be lamented that Old England is lost, as that the Scotch

3. Wilkes adapts Colley Cibber's popular version of Shakespeare's *Richard III*, which contains the line, "Off with his head. So much for Buckingham."

4. Of Parliament.

5. Scotland (from the Roman name for North Britain).

6. Catherine Macaulay, author of a controversial *History of England* (1763–1783). In order to test her egalitarian principles, Johnson had proposed that she invite her footman to join them at dinner. "I thus, Sir, showed her the absurdity of the leveling doctrine," he told Boswell. "She has never liked me since."

7. The King's Devil.

8. See n. 2, page 2765.

9. I.e., these additional guests arrived: Mary Morris Knowles (1733–1807), a highly accomplished needlewoman whose "sutile pictures" Johnson praised in a letter to Mrs. Thrale; and William Lee (1739–1795), merchant, diplomat, and the only American ever elected an alderman of London.

have found it."[1] Wilkes : "Had Lord Bute governed Scotland only, I should not have taken the trouble to write his eulogy, and dedicate *Mortimer* to him."[2]

Mr. Wilkes held a candle to show a fine print of a beautiful female figure which hung in the room, and pointed out the elegant contour of the bosom with the finger of an arch connoisseur. He afterwards, in a conversation with me, waggishly insisted that all the time Johnson showed visible signs of a fervent admiration of the corresponding charms of the fair Quaker.

This record, though by no means so perfect as I could wish, will serve to give a notion of a very curious interview, which was not only pleasing at the time, but had the agreeable and benignant effect of reconciling any animosity, and sweetening any acidity, which in the various bustle of political contest, had been produced in the minds of two men, who though widely different, had so many things in common—classical learning, modern literature, wit, and humor, and ready repartee—that it would have been much to be regretted if they had been forever at a distance from each other.

Mr. Burke gave me much credit for this successful *negotiation* and pleasantly said that "there was nothing to equal it in the whole history of the *Corps Diplomatique*."

I attended Dr. Johnson home, and had the satisfaction to hear him tell Mrs. Williams how much he had been pleased with Mr. Wilkes's company, and what an agreeable day he had passed.

[Conversations at Streatham and the Club][1]

[30 March 1778] I mentioned that I had in my possession the Life of Sir Robert Sibbald, the celebrated Scottish antiquary, and founder of the Royal College of Physicians at Edinburgh, in the original manuscript in his own handwriting; and that it was I believed the most natural and candid account of himself that ever was given by any man. As an instance, he tells that the Duke of Perth, then Chancellor of Scotland, pressed him very much to come over to the Roman Catholic faith; that he resisted all his Grace's arguments for a considerable time, till one day he felt himself, as it were, instantaneously convinced, and with tears in his eyes ran into the Duke's arms, and embraced the ancient religion; that he continued very steady in it for some time, and accompanied his Grace to London one winter, and lived in his household; that there he found the rigid fasting prescribed by the church very severe upon him; that this disposed him to reconsider the controversy, and having then seen that he was in the wrong, he returned to Protestantism. I talked of some time or other publishing this curious life. MRS. THRALE: "I think you had as well let alone that publication. To discover[2] such weakness exposes a man when he is gone." JOHNSON: "Nay, it is an honest picture of human nature. How often are the primary motives of our greatest actions as small as Sibbald's, for his re-conversion." MRS. THRALE: "But may they not as well be forgotten?" JOHNSON: "No, Madam, a man loves to review his own

1. Soon after succeeding to the throne in 1760, George III made his former tutor, the Scottish Earl of Bute, Prime Minister of Britain. The appointment unleashed a flood of anti-Scottish propaganda.
2. As part of a sustained campaign against Bute's government, Wilkes had chosen to reprint a 1731 play called *The Fall of Mortimer* and had prefaced it with a mockrespectful dedication to the prime minister.
1. These were two of Johnson's favorite venues of conversation. Streatham was the country estate of Henry and Hester Thrale, where Johnson and his friends were often guests. The Club was a group of distinguished thinkers, writers, artists, and statesman that met weekly.
2. Reveal.

mind. That is the use of a diary, or journal." LORD TRIMLESTOWN: "True, Sir. As the ladies love to see themselves in a glass, so a man likes to see himself in his journal." BOSWELL: "A very pretty allusion." JOHNSON: "Yes, indeed." BOSWELL: "And as a lady adjusts her dress before a mirror, a man adjusts his character by looking at his journal." I next year found the very same thought in Atterbury's *Funeral Sermon on Lady Cutts*, where, having mentioned her *Diary*, he says, "In this glass she every day dressed her mind." This is a proof of coincidence, and not of plagiarism; for I had never read that sermon before.

Next morning, while we were at breakfast, Johnson gave a very earnest recommendation of what he himself practiced with the utmost conscientiousness: I mean a strict attention to truth, even in the most minute particulars. "Accustom your children," said he, "constantly to this; if a thing happened at one window, and they, when relating it, say that it happened at another, do not let it pass, but instantly check them; you do not know where deviation from truth will end." BOSWELL: "It may come to the door: and when once an account is at all varied in one circumstance, it may by degrees be varied so as to be totally different from what really happened." Our lively hostess, whose fancy was impatient of the rein,[3] fidgeted at this, and ventured to say, "Nay, this is too much. If Mr. Johnson should forbid me to drink tea, I would comply, as I should feel the restraint only twice a day; but little variations in narrative must happen a thousand times a day, if one is not perpetually watching." JOHNSON: "Well, Madam, and you *ought* to be perpetually watching. It is more from carelessness about truth than from intentional lying, that there is so much falsehood in the world."

In his review of Dr. Warton's *Essay on the Writings and Genius of Pope*, Johnson has given the following salutary caution upon this subject:

"Nothing but experience could evince[4] the frequency of false information, or enable any man to conceive that so many groundless reports should be propagated, as every man of eminence may hear of himself. Some men relate what they think, as what they know; some men of confused memories and habitual inaccuracy ascribe to one man what belongs to another; and some talk on, without thought or care. A few men are sufficient to broach falsehoods, which are afterwards innocently diffused by successive relaters."

Had he lived to read what Sir John Hawkins and Mrs. Piozzi have related concerning himself[5] how much would he have found his observation illustrated. He was indeed so much impressed with the prevalence of falsehood, voluntary or unintentional, that I never knew any person who upon hearing an extraordinary circumstance told, discovered more of the *incredulus odi*.[6] He would say, with a significant look and decisive tone, "It is not so. Do not tell this again." He inculcated upon all his friends the importance of perpetual vigilance against the slightest degrees of falsehood; the effect of which, as Sir Joshua Reynolds observed to me, has been, that all who were of his *school* are distinguished for a love of truth and accuracy, which they would not have possessed in the same degree, if they had not been acquainted with Johnson.

3. Whose imagination did not like to be restrained.
4. Prove, serve as evidence of.
5. Boswell refers to the two rival biographies, Sir John Hawkins's *Life of Samuel Johnson LL.D.* (1787) and Hester Thrale Piozzi's *Anecdotes of the Late Samuel Johnson LL.D.* (1786).
6. Hostile incredulity.

Talking of ghosts, he said, "It is wonderful that five thousand years have now elapsed since the creation of the world, and still it is undecided whether or not there has ever been an instance of the spirit of any person appearing after death. All argument is against it; but all belief is for it."

He said, "John Wesley's[7] conversation is good, but he is never at leisure. He is always obliged to go at a certain hour. This is very disagreeable to a man who loves to fold his legs and have out his talk, as I do."

On Friday, April 3, I dined with him in London, in a company where were present several eminent men, whom I shall not name, but distinguish their parts in the conversation by different letters.[8]

F: "I have been looking at this famous antique marble dog of Mr. Jennings, valued at a thousand guineas, said to be Alcibiades's dog."[9] JOHNSON: "His tail then must be docked.[1] That was the mark of Alcibiades's dog." E: "A thousand guineas! The representation of no animal whatever is worth so much. At this rate a dead dog would indeed be better than a living lion." JOHNSON: "Sir, it is not the worth of the thing, but of the skill in forming it which is so highly estimated. Everything that enlarges the sphere of human powers, that shows man he can do what he thought he could not do, is valuable. The first man who balanced a straw upon his nose; Johnson,[2] who rode upon three horses at a time; in short, all such men deserved the applause of mankind, not on account of the use of what they did, but of the dexterity which they exhibited." BOSWELL: "Yet a misapplication of time and assiduity is not to be encouraged. Addison, in one of his *Spectators*, commends the judgment of a king, who, as a suitable reward to a man that by long perseverance had attained to the art of throwing a barleycorn through the eye of a needle, gave him a bushel of barley." JOHNSON: "He must have been a king of Scotland, where barley is scarce." F: "One of the most remarkable antique figures of an animal is the boar at Florence." JOHNSON: "The first boar that is well made in marble should be preserved as a wonder. When men arrive at a facility of making boars well, then the workmanship is not of such value, but they should however be preserved as examples, and as a greater security for the restoration of the art, should it be lost."

E: "We hear prodigious complaints at present of emigration. I am convinced that emigration makes a country more populous." J: "That sounds very much like a paradox." E: "Exportation of men, like exportation of all other commodities, makes more be produced." JOHNSON: "But there would be more people were there not emigration, provided there were food for more." E: "No; leave a few breeders, and you'll have more people than if there were no emigration." JOHNSON: "Nay, Sir, it is plain there will be more people, if there are more breeders. Thirty cows in good pasture will produce more calves than ten cows, provided they have good bulls." E: "There are bulls enough in Ireland."[3] JOHNSON (smiling): "So, Sir, I should think from your argument." BOSWELL: "You said, exportation of men, like exportation of other commodities, makes more be produced. But a bounty is given to encourage the exportation of corn, and no bounty is given for the exportation of men, though, indeed,

7. Co-founder (1703–1791) of the Methodist movement.
8. "F" stands for John Fitzpatrick, Earl of Upper Ossory, an Irish nobleman; "E" for Edmund Burke, statesman and political theorist; "R" for Richard Brinsley Sheridan, playwright; "C" for George Fordyce, a chemist; "P" for Sir Joshua Reynolds ("Painter").
9. A marble statue purchased in Rome by the collector Henry Jennings, it was called after an antique sculpture in the Uffizi, Florence.
1. Clipped.
2. An acrobatic rider (no relation).
3. An "Irish bull" was a foolish blunder.

those who go, gain by it." R: "But the bounty on the exportation of corn is paid at home." E: "That's the same thing." JOHNSON: "No, Sir." R: "A man who stays at home gains nothing by his neighbors emigrating." BOSWELL: "I can understand that emigration may be the cause that more people may be produced in a country; but the country will not therefore be the more populous, for the people issue from it. It can only be said that there is a flow of people. It is an encouragement to have children, to know that they can get a living by emigration." R: "Yes, if there were an emigration of children under six years of age. But they don't emigrate till they could earn their livelihood in some way at home." C: "It is remarkable that the most unhealthy countries, where there are the most destructive diseases, such as Egypt and Bengal, are the most populous." JOHNSON: "Countries which are the most populous have the most destructive diseases. *That* is the true state of the proposition." C: "Holland is very unhealthy, yet it is exceedingly populous." JOHNSON: "I know not that Holland is unhealthy. But its populousness is owing to an influx of people from all other countries. Disease cannot be the cause of populousness, for it not only carries off a great proportion of the people, but those who are left are weakened and unfit for the purposes of increase."

R: "Mr. E., I don't mean to flatter, but when posterity reads one of your speeches in Parliament, it will be difficult to believe that you took so much pains, knowing with certainty that it could produce no effect, that not one vote would be gained by it." E: "Waiving your compliment to me, I shall say in general, that it is very well worthwhile for a man to take pains to speak well in Parliament. A man, who has vanity, speaks to display his talents; and if a man speaks well, he gradually establishes a certain reputation and consequence[4] in the general opinion, which sooner or later will have its political reward. Besides, though not one vote is gained, a good speech has its effect. Though an act which has been ably opposed passes into a law, yet in its progress it is modeled, it is softened in such a manner that we see plainly the Minister[5] has been told that the Members attached to him are so sensible of its injustice or absurdity from what they have heard that it must be altered." JOHNSON: "And, Sir, there is a gratification of pride. Though we cannot out-vote them we will out-argue them. They shall not do wrong without its being shown both to themselves and to the world." E: "The House of Commons is a mixed body. (I except the Minority, which I hold to be pure [smiling][6] but I take the whole House.) It is a mass by no means pure; but neither is it wholly corrupt, though there is a large proportion of corruption in it. There are many members who generally go with the Minister, who will not go all lengths. There are many honest well-meaning country gentlemen who are in Parliament only to keep up the consequence of their families. Upon most of these a good speech will have influence." JOHNSON: "We are all more or less governed by interest.[7] But interest will not make us do everything. In a case which admits of doubt, we try to think on the side which is for our interest, and generally bring ourselves to act accordingly. But the subject must admit of diversity of coloring;[8] it must receive a color on that side." * * * In the House of Commons there are members enough who will not vote what is grossly unjust or absurd. No, Sir, there must always

4. Importance, social standing.
5. Prime minister.
6. The party to which Burke belonged was out of power.
7. Self-interest.
8. Legitimately have two sides to it.

be right enough, or appearance of right, to keep wrong in countenance." BOSWELL: "There is surely always a majority in Parliament who have places, or who want to have them, and who therefore will be generally ready to support government without requiring any pretext." E: "True, Sir; that majority will always follow

Quo clamor vocat et turba faventium."[9]

BOSWELL: "Well now, let us take the common phrase, Place-hunters.[1] I thought they had hunted without regard to anything, just as their huntsmen, the Minister, leads, looking only to the prey." J: "But taking your metaphor, you know that in hunting there are few so desperately keen as to follow without reserve. Some do not choose to leap ditches and hedges and risk their necks, or gallop over steeps, or even to dirty themselves in bogs and mire." BOSWELL: "I am glad there are some good, quiet, moderate political hunters." E: "I believe, in any body of men in England, I should have been in the Minority; I have always been in the Minority." P: "The House of Commons resembles a private company. How seldom is any man convinced by another's argument; passion and pride rise against it." R: "What would be the consequence, if a Minister, sure of a majority in the House of Commons, should resolve that there should be no speaking at all upon his side." E: "He must soon go out. That has been tried; but it was found it would not do."

E: "The Irish language is not primitive; it is Teutonic, a mixture of the northern tongues: it has much English in it." JOHNSON: "It may have been radically Teutonic; but English and High Dutch have no similarity to the eye, though radically the same. Once, when looking into Low Dutch, I found, in a whole page, only one word similar to English; *stroem*, like *stream*, and it signified *tide*." E: "I remember having seen a Dutch sonnet, in which I found this word, *roesnopies*. Nobody would at first think that this could be English; but, when we inquire, we find *roes*, rose, and *nopie*, knob; so we have *rosebuds*."

JOHNSON: "I have been reading Thicknesse's travels, which I think are entertaining." BOSWELL: "What, Sir, a good book?" JOHNSON: "Yes, Sir, to read once; I do not say you are to make a study of it and digest it; and I believe it to be a true book in his intention. All travelers generally mean to tell truth; though Thicknesse observes, upon Smollett's account[2] of his alarming a whole town in France by firing a blunderbuss, and frightening a French nobleman till he made him tie on his portmanteau, that he would be loath to say Smollett had told two lies in one page; but he had found the only town in France where these things could have happened. Travelers must often be mistaken. In everything, except where mensuration can be applied, they may honestly differ. There has been, of late, a strange turn in travelers to be displeased."

E: "From the experience which I have had—and I have had a great deal—I have learnt to think *better* of mankind." JOHNSON: "From my experience I have found them worse in commercial dealings, more disposed to cheat, than I had any notion of; but more disposed to do one another good than I had conceived." J: "Less just and more beneficent." JOHNSON: "And really it is wonderful, considering

9. Amid the plaudits of the noisy crowd (Horace, *Odes* 3.24.46).

1. Those who sought political sinecures ("places").

2. Philip Thicknesse, *A Year's Journey through France and Spain* (1777); Tobias Smollett, *Travels in France and Italy* (1766).

how much attention is necessary for men to take care of themselves, and ward off immediate evils which press upon them, it is wonderful how much they do for others. As it is said of the greatest liar, that he tells more truth than falsehood; so it may be said of the worst man, that he does more good than evil." BOSWELL: "Perhaps from experience men may be found *happier* than we suppose." JOHNSON: "No, Sir; the more we inquire, we shall find men the less happy." P: "As to thinking better or worse of mankind from experience, some cunning people will not be satisfied unless they have put men to the test, as they think. There is a very good story told of Sir Godfrey Kneller, in his character of a justice of the peace. A gentleman brought his servant before him, upon an accusation of having stolen some money from him; but it having come out that he had laid it purposely in the servant's way, in order to try his honesty, Sir Godfrey sent the master to prison." JOHNSON: "To resist temptation once is not a sufficient proof of honesty. If a servant, indeed, were to resist the continued temptation of silver lying in a window, as some people let it lie, when he is sure his master does not know how much there is of it, he would give a strong proof of honesty. But this is a proof to which you have no right to put a man. You know, humanly speaking, there is a certain degree of temptation which will overcome any virtue. Now, in so far as you approach temptation to a man, you do him an injury; and, if he is overcome, you share his guilt." P: "And, when once overcome, it is easier for him to be got the better of again." BOSWELL: "Yes, you are his seducer; you have debauched him. I have known a man resolve to put friendship to the test by asking a friend to lend him money merely with that view, when he did not want it." JOHNSON: "That is very wrong, Sir. Your friend may be a narrow man, and yet have many good qualities: narrowness may be his only fault. Now you are trying his general character as a friend, by one particular singly, in which he happens to be defective, when, in truth, his character is composed of many particulars."

E: "I understand the hogshead[3] of claret, which this society was favored with by our friend the Dean, is nearly out; I think he should be written to, to send another of the same kind. Let the request be made with a happy ambiguity of expression, so that we may have the chance of his sending *it* also as a present." JOHNSON: "I am willing to offer my services as secretary on this occasion." P: "As many as are for Dr. Johnson being secretary hold up your hands.—Carried unanimously." BOSWELL: "He will be our Dictator." JOHNSON: "No, the company is to dictate to me. I am only to write for wine; and I am quite disinterested, as I drink none; I shall not be suspected of having forged the application. I am no more than humble *scribe*." E: "Then you shall *pre*scribe." BOSWELL: "Very well. The first play of words today." J: "No, no; the *bulls* in Ireland." JOHNSON: "Were I your Dictator you should have no wine. It would be my business *cavere ne quid detrimenti Respublica caperet*,[4] and wine is dangerous. Rome was ruined by luxury" (smiling). E: "If you allow no wine as Dictator, you shall not have me for your master of horse."[5]

1791

3. A large barrel.
4. "To ensure that no harm befall the republic." Johnson quotes from the *Senatus Consultum Ultimum*, a declaration of public emergency by the Roman senate. This declaration suspended ordinary laws and appointed a dictator for the duration of the emergency.
5. Under the emergency decree, the master of the horse served as second in command to the dictator.

Oliver Goldsmith

1730–1774

Goldsmith's cluster of famous friends never tired of describing and diagnosing what they saw as the baffling discrepancy between his success in writing and his oddity in conversation. Samuel Johnson put the problem succinctly: "No man was more foolish when he had not a pen in his hand, or more wise when he had." The actor David Garrick compacted the same paradox into the second line of an imaginary epitaph, composed while its outraged subject was present in the room: "Here lies Nolly Goldsmith, for shortness called Noll, / Who wrote like an angel, and talked like poor Poll"—that is, like a parrot, noisily spouting verbiage mimicked from minds better furnished than his own. Always quick to take offense, Goldsmith took so much at this that he devoted the remaining months of his short life to a *Retaliation* in which he took vengeance, in the form of caustic verse epitaphs, on the many people from whom he thought he had suffered slights.

Goldsmith's awkwardness, competitiveness, and defensiveness arose partly from discomfort as to humble origins and scattershot education. Born in Ireland to an eccentric curate, he had come to London in 1756 after a checkered academic career spent in Dublin, Edinburgh, and on the Continent, half-heartedly pursuing degrees (never obtained) in divinity and medicine. Upon arriving in London, Goldsmith took a series of odd jobs (druggist, physician, schoolteacher) before establishing himself as a reviewer, translator, essayist, and editor. His work brought him to the attention of the eminent, in whose company he launched that precarious social strategy which his closest friend, the painter Joshua Reynolds, later analyzed: "He had a very strong desire, which I believe nobody will think very peculiar, to be liked, to have his company sought after by his friends. To this end, for it was a system, he abandoned his respectable character as a writer or a man of observation to that of a character [in whose presence] nobody was afraid of being humiliated." As Reynolds acknowledges, the "system" often backfired, because Goldsmith wanted desperately to be impressive as well as "liked." Friends found his mystery worth probing because of the almost palpable preponderance of his merits: alongside irascibility, Goldsmith possessed a compelling charm and generosity; and an amazing *feeling* (Reynolds's emphatic term) for what made writing work.

To support spendthrift habits and a love of gambling, Goldsmith undertook much compendious hackwork—*A History of England* (1764); *Roman History* (1769); *Grecian History* (1774); and a *History of the Earth, and Animated Nature* (1774). At the same time, he managed to score more successes in more genres than almost any of his contemporaries save Johnson: periodical essay (*The Citizen of the World*, 1760–1761); biography (*The Life of Richard Nash*, 1762); novel (*The Vicar of Wakefield*, 1766); stage comedy (*The Good Natured Man*, 1768; *She Stoops to Conquer*, 1773); and poetry (*The Traveller*, 1764; and *The Deserted Village*, 1770). *The Deserted Village* was the work most celebrated in his own lifetime. Two years in the making, the poem recasts an argument Goldsmith had voiced earlier in an essay against the acquisition of rural acreage by merchants who, having acquired their wealth by the commerce of empire and the trade in luxuries, were now bent on converting their new-bought lands from productive communal pasture into pretty pleasure grounds: "In almost every part of the kingdom the laborious husbandman [farmer] has been reduced, and the lands are now either occupied by some general undertaker, or turned into enclosures destined for the purposes of amusement or luxury." Such encroachment, Goldsmith contended, was driving farm families from their villages and annihilating centuries of graceful country tradition. In his poem, Goldsmith mingled nostalgia for a rural past with dread of a commercial future. Contemporary critics promptly ushered *The Deserted Village* into the poetic canon by sundering those elements Goldsmith had worked hard to fuse: they dismissed the poem's economic doctrine and praised its imaginative power. Like the poet's friends, the poem's readers are left to sort out and savor Goldsmith's characteristic complexity: a "sentimental radicalism" (the phrase is John Barrell's) whereby the conservative defense of old values produces a new and volatile empathy with the plight of the poor.

The Deserted Village

TO SIR JOSHUA REYNOLDS[1]

Dear Sir,

I can have no expectations in an address of this kind, either to add to your reputation, or to establish my own. You can gain nothing from my admiration, as I am ignorant of that art in which you are said to excel; and I may lose much by the severity of your judgment, as few have a juster taste in poetry than you. Setting interest therefore aside, to which I never paid much attention, I must be indulged at present in following my affections. The only dedication I ever made was to my brother,[2] because I loved him better than most other men. He is since dead. Permit me to inscribe this poem to you.

How far you may be pleased with the versification and mere mechanical parts of this attempt, I don't pretend to inquire; but I know you will object (and indeed several of our best and wisest friends concur in the opinion) that the depopulation it deplores is nowhere to be seen, and the disorders it laments are only to be found in the poet's own imagination. To this I can scarce make any other answer than that I sincerely believe what I have written; that I have taken all possible pains, in my country excursions, for these four or five years past, to be certain of what I allege; and that all my views and inquiries have led me to believe those miseries real, which I here attempt to display. But this is not the place to enter into an inquiry, whether the country be depopulating, or not; the discussion would take up much room, and I should prove myself, at best, an indifferent politician, to tire the reader with a long preface, when I want his unfatigued attention to a long poem.

In regretting the depopulation of the country, I inveigh against the increase of our luxuries; and here also I expect the shout of modern politicians against me. For twenty or thirty years past, it has been the fashion to consider luxury as one of the greatest national advantages; and all the wisdom of antiquity in that particular, as erroneous.[3] Still however, I must remain a professed ancient on that head, and continue to think those luxuries prejudicial to states, by which so many vices are introduced, and so many kingdoms have been undone. Indeed so much has been poured out of late on the other side of the question, that, merely for the sake of novelty and variety, one would sometimes wish to be in the right.

I am,
Dear Sir,
Your sincere friend,
and ardent admirer,
OLIVER GOLDSMITH.

1. Reynolds (1723–1792) was one of England's leading portrait painters and first president of the Royal Academy; his close friendship with Goldsmith had begun in the mid-1760s.

2. Goldsmith had dedicated his previous long poem, *The Traveller* (1764), to his brother Henry, who died in 1768.

3. A long line of ancient authors—Horace, Seneca, and Pliny among them—had warned that the traffic in luxuries was sapping Rome's health, and had urged moderation.

Sweet Auburn, loveliest village of the plain,[4]
Where health and plenty cheered the laboring swain,
Where smiling spring its earliest visit paid,
And parting summer's lingering blooms delayed:
Dear lovely bowers of innocence and ease,
Seats of my youth, when every sport could please,
How often have I loitered o'er thy green,
Where humble happiness endeared each scene;
How often have I paused on every charm,
The sheltered cot,° the cultivated farm, *cottage*
The never-failing brook, the busy mill,
The decent church that topped the neighboring hill,
The hawthorn bush, with seats beneath the shade,
For talking age and whispering lovers made.
How often have I blessed the coming day,
When toil remitting lent its turn to play,
And all the village train, from labor free,
Led up their sports beneath the spreading tree,
While many a pastime circled in the shade,
The young contending as the old surveyed;
And many a gambol frolicked o'er the ground,
And sleights of art and feats of strength went round.
And still as each repeated pleasure tired,
Succeeding sports the mirthful band inspired;
The dancing pair that simply sought renown
By holding out to tire each other down;
The swain mistrustless of his smutted face,
While secret laughter tittered round the place;
The bashful virgin's sidelong looks of love,
The matron's glance that would those looks reprove.
These were thy charms, sweet village; sports like these,
With sweet succession, taught even toil to please;
These round thy bowers their cheerful influence shed,
These were thy charms—But all these charms are fled.

Sweet smiling village, loveliest of the lawn,
Thy sports are fled, and all thy charms withdrawn;
Amidst thy bowers the tyrant's hand is seen,
And desolation saddens all thy green:
One only master grasps the whole domain,
And half a tillage[5] stints° thy smiling plain; *sets limits to*
No more thy glassy brook reflects the day,
But choked with sedges, works its weedy way.
Along thy glades, a solitary guest,
The hollow sounding bittern guards its nest;
Amidst thy desert walks the lapwing flies,

4. "Auburn" is fictitious; it may be based in part on the Irish village of Lissoy, Goldsmith's childhood home.

5. Piece of tilled land.

And tires their echoes with unvaried cries.
Sunk are thy bowers, in shapeless ruin all,
And the long grass o'ertops the mouldering wall,
And trembling, shrinking from the spoiler's hand,
Far, far away thy children leave the land.

Ill fares the land, to hastening ills a prey,
Where wealth accumulates and men decay:
Princes and lords may flourish or may fade;
A breath can make them, as a breath has made;
But a bold peasantry, their country's pride,
When once destroyed, can never be supplied.

A time there was, ere England's griefs began,
When every rood° of ground maintained its man; *quarter acre*
For him light labor spread her wholesome store,
Just gave what life required, but gave no more:
His best companions, innocence and health;
And his best riches, ignorance of wealth.

But times are altered; trade's unfeeling train
Usurp the land and dispossess the swain;
Along the lawn,° where scattered hamlets rose, *open countryside*
Unwieldy wealth and cumbrous pomp repose;
And every want to opulence allied,
And every pang that folly pays to pride.
These gentle hours that plenty bade to bloom,
Those calm desires that asked but little room,
Those healthful sports that graced the peaceful scene,
Lived in each look, and brightened all the green;
These far departing seek a kinder shore,
And rural mirth and manners are no more.

Sweet Auburn! parent of the blissful hour,
Thy glades forlorn confess the tyrant's power.
Here as I take my solitary rounds,
Amidst thy tangling walks, and ruined grounds,
And, many a year elapsed, return to view
Where once the cottage stood, the hawthorn grew,
Remembrance wakes with all her busy train,
Swells at my breast, and turns the past to pain.

In all my wanderings round this world of care,
In all my griefs—and God has given my share—
I still had hopes my latest hours to crown,
Amidst these humble bowers to lay me down;
To husband out life's taper[6] at the close,
And keep the flame from wasting by repose.
I still had hopes, for pride attends us still,

6. Candle. "To husband out" means to maintain something thriftily, so that it lasts long.

Amidst the swains to show my book-learned skill,
Around my fire an evening group to draw,
And tell of all I felt, and all I saw;
And, as an hare whom hounds and horns pursue,
Pants to the place from whence at first she flew,
I still had hopes, my long vexations past,
Here to return—and die at home at last.

O blest retirement, friend to life's decline,
Retreats from care that never must be mine,
How happy he who crowns in shades like these
A youth of labor with an age of ease;
Who quits a world where strong temptations try,
And, since 'tis hard to combat, learns to fly.
For him no wretches, born to work and weep,
Explore the mine, or tempt the dangerous deep;
No surly porter stands in guilty state
To spurn imploring famine from the gate,
But on he moves to meet his latter end,
Angels around befriending virtue's friend;
Bends to the grave with unperceived decay,
While resignation gently slopes the way;
And, all his prospects brightening to the last,
His Heaven commences ere the world be past!

Sweet was the sound when oft at evening's close
Up yonder hill the village murmur rose;
There as I passed with careless steps and slow,
The mingling notes came softened from below;
The swain responsive as the milkmaid sung,
The sober herd that lowed to meet their young,
The noisy geese that gabbled o'er the pool,
The playful children just let loose from school,
The watchdog's voice that bayed the whispering wind,
And the loud laugh that spoke the vacant° mind, *carefree*
These all in sweet confusion sought the shade,
And filled each pause the nightingale had made.
But now the sounds of population fail,
No cheerful murmurs fluctuate in the gale,
No busy steps the grass-grown footway tread,
For all the bloomy flush of life is fled.
All but yon widowed, solitary thing
That feebly bends beside the plashy[7] spring;
She, wretched matron, forced, in age, for bread,
To strip the brook with mantling° cresses[8] spread, *growing*
To pick her wintry faggot° from the thorn, *firewood*
To seek her nightly shed, and weep till morn;
She only left of all the harmless train,
The sad historian of the pensive plain.

7. Abounding in pools.

8. Leafy, edible plants.

Near yonder copse, where once the garden smiled,
And still where many a garden flower grows wild;
There, where a few torn shrubs the place disclose,
The village preacher's modest mansion rose.
A man he was, to all the country dear,
And passing rich with forty pounds a year;
Remote from towns he ran his godly race,
Nor e'er had changed, nor wished to change his place;
Unpracticed he to fawn, or seek for power,
By doctrines fashioned to the varying hour;
Far other aims his heart had learned to prize,
More skilled to raise the wretched than to rise.
His house was known to all the vagrant train,
He chid their wanderings, but relieved their pain;
The long remembered beggar was his guest,
Whose beard descending swept his aged breast;
The ruined spendthrift, now no longer proud,
Claimed kindred there, and had his claims allowed;
The broken soldier, kindly bade to stay,
Sat by his fire, and talked the night away;
Wept o'er his wounds, or tales of sorrow done,
Shouldered his crutch, and showed how fields were won.
Pleased with his guests, the good man learned to glow,
And quite forgot their vices in their woe;
Careless their merits or their faults to scan,
His pity gave ere charity began.

Thus to relieve the wretched was his pride,
And even his failings leaned to virtue's side;
But in his duty prompt at every call,
He watched and wept, he prayed and felt, for all.
And, as a bird each fond endearment tries,
To tempt its new fledged offspring to the skies,
He tried each art, reproved each dull delay,
Allured to brighter worlds, and led the way.

Beside the bed where parting life was laid,
And sorrow, guilt, and pain by turns dismayed,
The reverend champion stood. At his control,
Despair and anguish fled the struggling soul;
Comfort came down the trembling wretch to raise,
And his last faltering accents whispered praise.

At church, with meek and unaffected grace,
His looks adorned the venerable place;
Truth from his lips prevailed with double sway,
And fools, who came to scoff, remained to pray.
The service past, around the pious man,
With steady zeal each honest rustic ran;
Even children followed with endearing wile,

And plucked his gown, to share the good man's smile.
His ready smile a parent's warmth expressed,
Their welfare pleased him, and their cares distressed;
To them his heart, his love, his griefs were given,
But all his serious thoughts had rest in Heaven.
As some tall cliff that lifts its awful form,
Swells from the vale, and midway leaves the storm,
Though round its breast the rolling clouds are spread,
Eternal sunshine settles on its head.

Beside yon straggling fence that skirts the way,
With blossomed furze° unprofitably gay, *thorny bushes*
There, in his noisy mansion, skilled to rule,
The village master taught his little school;
A man severe he was, and stern to view,
I knew him well, and every truant knew;
Well had the boding tremblers learned to trace
The day's disasters in his morning face;
Full well they laughed with counterfeited glee,
At all his jokes, for many a joke had he;
Full well the busy whisper circling round,
Conveyed the dismal tidings when he frowned;
Yet he was kind, or if severe in aught,
The love he bore to learning was in fault;
The village all declared how much he knew;
'Twas certain he could write, and cipher too;
Lands he could measure, terms and tides presage,[9]
And even the story ran that he could gauge.[1]
In arguing too, the parson owned° his skill, *acknowledged*
For even though vanquished, he could argue still;
While words of learned length, and thundering sound,
Amazed the gazing rustics ranged around;
And still they gazed, and still the wonder grew,
That one small head could carry all he knew.

But past is all his fame. The very spot,
Where many a time he triumphed, is forgot.
Near yonder thorn, that lifts its head on high,
Where once the signpost caught the passing eye,
Low lies that house where nut-brown draughts° inspired, *drinks*
Where gray-beard mirth and smiling toil retired,
Where village statesmen talked with looks profound,
And news much older than their ale went round.
Imagination fondly stoops to trace
The parlor splendors of that festive place;
The whitewashed wall, the nicely sanded floor,

9. "Terms" were the days when payments of rents and wages were due; "tides" were holidays like Easter that shifted date from year to year; information on both was readily available in the annual almanacs.

1. Calculate the capacity of barrels and other containers.

The varnished clock that clicked behind the door;
The chest contrived a double debt to pay,
A bed by night, a chest of drawers by day;
The pictures placed for ornament and use,
The twelve good rules,[2] the royal game of goose;[3]
The hearth, except when winter chilled the day,
With aspen boughs, and flowers, and fennel gay,
While broken teacups, wisely kept for show,
Ranged o'er the chimney, glistened in a row.

Vain transitory splendors! Could not all
Reprieve the tottering mansion from its fall!
Obscure it sinks, nor shall it more impart
An hour's importance to the poor man's heart;
Thither no more the peasant shall repair
To sweet oblivion of his daily care;
No more the farmer's news, the barber's tale,
No more the woodman's ballad shall prevail;
No more the smith his dusky brow shall clear,
Relax his ponderous strength, and lean to hear;
The host himself no longer shall be found
Careful to see the mantling° bliss go round; *foaming*
Nor the coy maid, half willing to be pressed,
Shall kiss the cup to pass it to the rest.

Yes! let the rich deride, the proud disdain,
These simple blessings of the lowly train;
To me more dear, congenial to my heart,
One native charm, than all the gloss of art;
Spontaneous joys, where nature has its play,
The soul adopts, and owns their first born sway;
Lightly they frolic o'er the vacant mind,
Unenvied, unmolested, unconfined.
But the long pomp, the midnight masquerade,
With all the freaks of wanton wealth arrayed,
In these, ere triflers half their wish obtain,
The toiling pleasure sickens into pain;
And, even while fashion's brightest arts decoy,
The heart distrusting asks, if this be joy.

Ye friends to truth, ye statesmen, who survey
The rich man's joys increase, the poor's decay,
'Tis yours to judge, how wide the limits stand
Between a splendid and an happy land.
Proud swells the tide with loads of freighted ore,
And shouting Folly hails them from her shore;
Hoards, even beyond the miser's wish abound,

2. This list of simple life lessons ("Keep no bad company"; "Encourage no vice"), supposedly compiled by Charles I, was displayed, beneath a picture of his execution, in many country inns and houses.

3. A game in which dice determine the movement of the pieces across the board.

And rich men flock from all the world around.
Yet count our gains. This wealth is but a name
That leaves our useful products still the same.
Not so the loss. The man of wealth and pride
Takes up a space that many poor supplied;
Space for his lake, his park's extended bounds,
Space for his horses, equipage, and hounds;
The robe that wraps his limbs in silken sloth
Has robbed the neighboring fields of half their growth;
His seat, where solitary sports are seen,
Indignant spurns the cottage from the green;
Around the world each needful product flies,
For all the luxuries the world supplies.
While thus the land adorned for pleasure all
In barren splendor feebly waits the fall.

As some fair female unadorned and plain,
Secure to please while youth confirms her reign,
Slights every borrowed charm that dress supplies,
Nor shares with art the triumph of her eyes;
But when those charms are past, for charms are frail,
When time advances, and when lovers fail,
She then shines forth, solicitous to bless,
In all the glaring impotence of dress.
Thus fares the land, by luxury betrayed;
In nature's simplest charms at first arrayed;
But verging to decline, its splendors rise,
Its vistas strike, its palaces surprise;
While scourged by famine from the smiling land,
The mournful peasant leads his humble band;
And while he sinks without one arm to save,
The country blooms—a garden, and a grave.

Where then, ah where, shall poverty reside,
To scape the pressure of contiguous pride?
If to some common's[4] fenceless limits strayed,
He drives his flock to pick the scanty blade,
Those fenceless fields the sons of wealth divide,
And even the bare-worn common is denied.

If to the city sped—What waits him there?
To see profusion that he must not share;
To see ten thousand baneful arts combined
To pamper luxury, and thin mankind;
To see those joys the sons of pleasure know
Extorted from his fellow-creature's woe.
Here, while the courtier glitters in brocade,
There the pale artist° plies the sickly trade; *artisan*

4. Grazing land once shared by all the villagers.

Here, while the proud their long-drawn pomps display,
There the black gibbet glooms beside the way.
The dome° where Pleasure holds her midnight reign, *lavish house*
Here, richly decked, admits the gorgeous train;
Tumultuous grandeur crowds the blazing square,
The rattling chariots clash, the torches glare.
Sure scenes like these no troubles e'er annoy!
Sure these denote one universal joy!
Are these thy serious thoughts?—Ah, turn thine eyes
Where the poor houseless shivering female lies.
She once, perhaps, in village plenty blest,
Has wept at tales of innocence distressed;
Her modest looks the cottage might adorn,
Sweet as the primrose peeps beneath the thorn;
Now lost to all; her friends, her virtue fled,
Near her betrayer's door she lays her head,
And pinched with cold, and shrinking from the shower,
With heavy heart deplores that luckless hour
When idly first, ambitious of the town,
She left her wheel and robes of country brown.

Do thine, sweet Auburn, thine, the loveliest train,
Do thy fair tribes participate° her pain? *partake of*
Even now, perhaps, by cold and hunger led,
At proud men's doors they ask a little bread!

Ah, no. To distant climes, a dreary scene,
Where half the convex world intrudes between,
Through torrid tracts with fainting steps they go,
Where wild Altama[5] murmurs to their woe.
Far different there from all that charmed before,
The various terrors of that horrid shore;
Those blazing suns that dart a downward ray,
And fiercely shed intolerable day;
Those matted woods where birds forget to sing,
But silent bats in drowsy clusters cling,
Those poisonous fields with rank luxuriance crowned,
Where the dark scorpion gathers death around;
Where at each step the stranger fears to wake
The rattling terrors of the vengeful snake;
Where crouching tigers wait their hapless prey,
And savage men, more murderous still than they;
While oft in whirls the mad tornado flies,
Mingling the ravaged landscape with the skies.
Far different these from every former scene,
The cooling brook, the grassy vested green,
The breezy covert of the warbling grove,
That only sheltered thefts of harmless love.

5. The Altamaha River, in Georgia (then a colony).

Good Heaven! what sorrows gloomed that parting day,
That called them from their native walks away;
When the poor exiles, every pleasure past,
Hung round their bowers, and fondly looked their last,
And took a long farewell, and wished in vain
For seats like these beyond the western main;
And shuddering still to face the distant deep,
Returned and wept, and still returned to weep.
The good old sire the first prepared to go
To new-found worlds, and wept for others' woe.
But for himself, in conscious virtue brave,
He only wished for worlds beyond the grave.
His lovely daughter, lovelier in her tears,
The fond companion of his helpless years,
Silent went next, neglectful of her charms,
And left a lover's for a father's arms.
With louder plaints the mother spoke her woes,
And blessed the cot° where every pleasure rose; *cottage*
And kissed her thoughtless babes with many a tear,
And clasped them close in sorrow doubly dear;
Whilst her fond husband strove to lend relief
In all the silent manliness of grief.

O luxury! Thou curst by Heaven's decree,
How ill exchanged are things like these for thee!
How do thy potions, with insidious joy,
Diffuse their pleasures only to destroy!
Kingdoms, by thee to sickly greatness grown,
Boast of a florid vigor not their own;
At every draught more large and large they grow,
A bloated mass of rank unwieldy woe;
Till sapped their strength, and every part unsound,
Down, down they sink, and spread a ruin round.

Even now the devastation is begun,
And half the business of destruction done;
Even now, methinks, as pondering here I stand,
I see the rural virtues leave the land.
Down where yon anchoring vessel spreads the sail,
That idly waiting flaps with every gale,
Downward they move, a melancholy band,
Pass from the shore, and darken all the strand.
Contented toil, and hospitable care,
And kind connubial tenderness are there;
And piety, with wishes placed above,
And steady loyalty, and faithful love:
And thou, sweet Poetry, thou loveliest maid,
Still first to fly where sensual joys invade;
Unfit, in these degenerate times of shame,
To catch the heart, or strike for honest fame;

Dear charming nymph, neglected and decried,
My shame in crowds, my solitary pride;
Thou source of all my bliss, and all my woe,
That found'st me poor at first, and keep'st me so;
Thou guide by which the nobler arts excel,
Thou nurse of every virtue, fare thee well.
Farewell, and O where'er thy voice be tried,
On Torno's[6] cliffs, or Pambamarca's[7] side,
Whether where equinoctial fervors[8] glow,
Or winter wraps the polar world in snow,
Still let thy voice, prevailing over time,
Redress the rigors of the inclement clime;
Aid slighted truth, with thy persuasive strain
Teach erring man to spurn the rage of gain;
Teach him that states of native strength possessed,
Though very poor, may still be very blest;
That trade's proud empire hastes to swift decay,
As ocean sweeps the labored mole° away; *breakwater*
While self-dependent power can time defy,
As rocks resist the billows and the sky.[9]

1770

Responses

George Crabbe [1] from *The Village*

The village life, and every care that reigns
O'er youthful peasants and declining swains;
What labor yields, and what, that labor past,
Age, in its hour of languor, finds at last;
What forms the real picture of the poor,
Demand a song—the Muse can give no more.

* * *

I grant indeed that fields and flocks have charms
For him that grazes or for him that farms;
But when amid such pleasing scenes I trace
The poor laborious natives of the place,
And see the midday sun, with fervid ray,
On their bare heads and dewy temples play;
While some, with feebler heads and fainter hearts,

6. The Tornio, a river in Sweden.
7. A mountain in Ecuador.
8. Equatorial heat.
9. Samuel Johnson supplied the poem's last two couplets.
1. Physician, clergyman, poet (1754–1832). Reacting against Goldsmith's poetic nostalgia in *The Deserted Village*, and against the larger tradition of pastoral poetry which conceived the countryside as an Arcadia abounding in simple pleasures, Crabbe tried to depict realistically the benighted lives of the rural poor. Within the long compass of his own lifetime, his work found favor among readers of widely divergent convictions and generations, across the cusp of centuries and revolutions. Johnson, Reynolds, and Burke encouraged him early; Jane Austen reckoned him her favorite poet; Lord Byron praised him as "Nature's sternest painter yet the best." The first three excerpts given here are from Book 1 of *The Village*.

Deplore their fortune, yet sustain their parts,
Then shall I dare these real ills to hide
In tinsel trappings of poetic pride?

* * *

Ye gentle souls who dream of rural ease,
Whom the smooth stream and smoother sonnet please;
Go! if the peaceful cot your praises share,
Go, look within, and ask if peace be there;
If peace be his—that drooping weary fire,
Or theirs, that offspring round their feeble sire,
Or hers, that matron pale, whose trembling hand
Turns on the wretched hearth th' expiring brand.

* * *

See the stout churl, in drunken fury great,
Strike the bare bosom of his teeming mate![2]
His naked vices, rude and unrefined,
Exert their open empire o'er the mind;
But can we less the senseless rage despise,
Because the savage acts without disguise?

* * *

And hark! the riots of the green begin,
That sprang at first from yonder noisy inn;
What time° the weekly pay was vanished all, *once*
And the slow hostess scored the threatening wall;[3]
What time they asked, their friendly feast to close,
A final cup, and that will make them foes;
When blows ensue that break the arm of toil,
And rustic battle ends the boobies' broil.

* * *

Yet why, you ask, these humble crimes relate,
Why make the poor as guilty as the great?
To show the great, those mightier sons of Pride,
How near in vice the lowest are allied;
Such are their natures and their passions such,
But these disguise too little, those too much:
So shall the man of power and pleasure see
In his own slave as vile a wretch as he;
In his luxurious lord the servant find
His own low pleasures and degenerate mind;
And each in all the kindred vices trace
Of a poor, blind, bewildered, erring race;

2. From Book 2. In this section of *The Village* Crabbe is describing (according to rubrics he published with the poem) "the repose and pleasure of a summer Sabbath, interrupted by intoxication and dispute"; in the next excerpt he proceeds to "the evening riots."

3. At taverns, the running debts of the drinkers were often recorded by means of marks ("scores") on the wall. Compare Goldsmith's description of the village tavern (*Deserted Village* 217–220).

Who, a short time in varied fortune past,
Die, and are equal in the dust at last.

1780–1783 1783

George Crabbe: from *The Parish Register*

The year revolves, and I again explore
The simple annals of my parish poor;[1]
What infant members in my flock appear,
What pairs I blessed in the departed year;
And who, of old or young, of nymphs or swains,
Are lost to life, its pleasures and its pains.
No Muse I ask, before my view to bring
The humble actions of the swains I sing.—
How passed the youthful, how the old their days;
Who sank in sloth, and who aspired to praise;
Their tempers, manners, morals, customs, arts,
What parts° they had, and how they employed their parts; *talents*
By what elated, soothed, seduced, depressed,
Full well I know—these records give the rest.
Is there a place, save one the poet sees,
A land of love, of liberty and ease,
Where labor wearies not, nor cares suppress
Th' eternal flow of rustic happiness;
Where no proud mansion frowns in awful state,
Or keeps the sunshine from the cottage gate;
Where young and old, intent on pleasure, throng,
And half man's life is holiday and song?
Vain search for scenes like these! no view appears,
By sighs unruffled or unstained by tears;
Since vice the world subdued and waters drowned,
Auburn and Eden can no more be found.

c. 1802–1806 1807

1. The speaker is a parish priest.

PERSPECTIVES
Novel Guises

The noun *novel*, at its root, means "a new thing," and for a long while the thing in question was so new that no one knew for certain what to call it. *Novel* highlighted the genre's breaks with precedent, but at first other more familiar labels occupied the title pages and the reviewer's columns. *History* emphasized the new form's equivocal relation to truth and fact; *adventures* its affinity for the wayward, the risky, and the picaresque; *romance* its lingering linkage with an older, more fantastical form of fiction whose conventions it radically reworked but whose fairy-tale components it often managed, mysteriously, to retain. Late in the century, in her literary history *The Progress of Romance* (1785), the novelist Clara Reeve drew up a distinction between the old form and the new that helped establish *novel* as the latter's name:

> The Romance is an heroic fable, which treats of fabulous persons and things. The Novel is a picture of real life and manners, and of the times in which it was written. The Romance, in lofty and elevated language, describes what never happened nor is likely to happen. The Novel gives a familiar relation of such things as pass every day before our eyes, such as may happen to our friend, or to ourselves; and the perfection of it is to represent every scene in so easy and natural a manner, and to make them appear so probable, as to deceive us into a persuasion (at least while we are reading) that all is real, until we are affected by the joys or distresses of the persons in the story, as if they were our own.

Reeve gives voice to what had oft been thought but never quite so lucidly expressed: that one of the genre's chief claims to novelty lay in a new relationship between the written and the real.

But not its only claim. Reeve's definition, for example, echoes almost word for word Samuel Johnson's famous pronouncement, in Rambler No. 60, on the power of biography (see page 2694). One of the newest things about the novel was its magpie capacity to mimic and make use of many other genres which had themselves been recently invented, or prodigiously reworked, to provide fresh representations of the real: biography and autobiography; diaries and letters; newspapers and essays; histories, legal and fiscal documents, statistical studies; satire; drama; and even lyric poetry. A comparable heterogeneity marked the genre's authors, and its readers, who occupied a wider social spectrum than had the makers and consumers of any previous literary mode. "What was unusual about the appeal of novels," J. Paul Hunter has remarked, "was the way it spanned the social classes and traditional divisions of readers" and of authors, compassing servants as well as masters, the entrepreneurial as well as the entitled, and, most pivotally, women as well as men. Well over a century before Henry James, in 1907, lamented the "large loose baggy monster" that the novel in some hands had become, the genre was already providing ample evidence of its appetite for absorbing whole categories of writing, writers, and audiences.

That capaciousness extends too to the genre's explicators. The past half century has produced varied explanations of why the novel began where and when it did. As chief cause, Ian Watt pinpoints the rise of literacy and of the middle class; Lennard Davis the impact of news and the appetite for fact; Nancy Armstrong the confinement, and empowerment, of women within a newly configured domestic sphere; Michael McKeon the competing discourses concerning truth and virtue to which a newly secular, commercial, and motile culture gave rise; J. Paul Hunter the amalgam of earlier literary forms and functions for which the novel came to serve as crucible. Though the explanations sometimes conflict, they also converge; they tell more truth in concert than apart. What's more, the explaining, and the debating, began long ago, with the early novelists themselves, who often felt prompted to declare their intents, propound their methods, distinguish themselves from their predecessors, and defend their work against the frequent charges that it was morally corrupting and aesthetically debased. Such discourse appeared not only (as might be expected) in the prefaces, but also within the narratives. Among the most striking features of the novel is its capacity to talk about itself, even when ostensibly bent on other business. Whether the story concerns a man on an island, a servant-girl under siege, or a solitary eccentric oddly recapturing his prenatal past, the prose will focus, often and obsessively, on the phenomena with which the novelists themselves are always, intrinsically engaged: the experience of writing and the impact of reading.

The novel by its nature is impossible to anthologize; it is itself an anthology. What follows is a series of short extracts (DNA samples from the baggy monster) in which makers of the new fiction discuss and demonstrate what they think they're up to, and how they hope it works.

For additional resources on the novel, including texts by Mary Carleton, Daniel Defoe, Samuel Richardson, and Henry Fielding, go to *The Longman Anthology of British Literature* Web site at www.myliteraturekit.com.

Daniel Defoe

1660–1731

Daniel Defoe, long notable for his ubiquity, has already cropped up at two points in this anthology (pages 2293–2309; and 2314–15). And for good reason. Relentlessly inventive, he worked transformations in many of the modes of writing that mattered most during the eighteenth century: journalism, satire, travel literature, criminal biography, political commentary. But he worked no innovations so productive as those he undertook, on the verge of his seventh decade, and after accumulating some 300 previous publications, in the realm of prose fiction. Narrating, in *Robinson Crusoe*, "the life of a man in an island" (as he described it in that first novel's second sequel), Defoe hit on something that struck readers as wholly new, and became hugely popular—making *Crusoe* one of the bestselling books of its moment, its century, and all time. The newness consisted not in the mysteries of the self disguised, but in the astonishments of the self stripped down, shorn of civilized props and privileges, but intent on re-creating them by a process so painstaking that everything Crusoe's readers take for granted (shelter, furniture, pen and paper) becomes, in his calloused hands and plain prose, new, strange, and surprising. Crusoe, like Defoe, knows the novelty of what he's doing; early on, he promises a tale "such as was never heard of in the world before." That sense, of story emerging urgently out of long sequestration, suffuses most of the novels Defoe produced over the next five years, whose narrators have led secret lives which now, with a mix of pain, pride, and pressing need, they choose to put upon the page. In all his subsequent fictions, Defoe rang changes on *Crusoe's* core preoccupations: the tribulations of individuals as they make their way precariously through new and dangerous worlds (economic as well as geographic); an irresolvable tension between the practical and the pious; and an intrinsic human isolation, almost inseparable from the imperatives of survival, which crops up insistently (like so many of Defoe's peripatetic characters) everywhere on the globe.

from The Life and Strange Surprizing Adventures of Robinson Crusoe

The Preface

If ever the story of any private man's adventures in the world were worth making public, and were acceptable when published, the editor of this account thinks this will be so.[1]

The wonders of this man's life exceed all that (he[2] thinks) is to be found extant, the life of one man being scarce capable of greater variety.

This story is told with modesty, with seriousness, and with a religious application of events to the uses to which wise men always apply them, *viz.*, to the instruction of others by this example, and to justify and honor the wisdom of Providence in all the variety of our circumstances, let them happen how they will.

The editor believes the thing to be a just history of fact; neither is there any appearance of fiction in it. And whoever thinks, because all such things are dispatched,[3] that the improvement of it, as well to the diversion as to the instruction of the reader, will be the same; and as such, he thinks, without farther compliment to the world, he does them a great service in the publication.

[First Days on the Island]

I now began to consider seriously my condition, and the circumstance I was reduced to, and I drew up the state of my affairs in writing, not so much to leave them to any that were to come after me, for I was like to have few heirs, as to deliver my thoughts from daily poring upon them, and afflicting my mind; and as my reason began now to master my despondency, I began to comfort myself as well as I could, and to set the Good against the Evil, that I might have something to distinguish my case from worse, and I stated it very impartially, like debtor and creditor, the comforts I enjoyed, against the miseries I suffered, thus:

EVIL	GOOD
I am cast upon a horrible desolate island, void of all hope of recovery.	But I am alive, and not drowned as all my ship's company were.
I am singled out and separated, as it were, from all the world to be miserable.	But I am singled out too from all the ship's crew to be spared from death; and he that miraculously saved me from death can deliver me from this condition.
I am divided from mankind, a solitaire, one banished from human society.	But I am not starved and perishing on a barren place, affording no sustenance.
I have not clothes to cover me.	But I am in a hot climate, where if I had clothes I could hardly wear them.
I am without any defense or means to resist any violence of man or beast.	But I am cast on an island, where I see no wild beasts to hurt me, as I saw on the coast of Africa: and what if I had been shipwrecked there?

1. As in his earlier piece of journalism, *A True Relation of the Apparition of Mrs. Veal*, Defoe warrants the authenticity of his narrative by presenting himself not as fictive author, but as editor of a real-life narrator's firsthand account.
2. I.e., the editor.
3. I.e., read quickly, so that their power over the reader, whether to amuse or to instruct, is limited. (In the remainder of the sentence, the syntax doesn't quite hold together; Defoe is asserting the value of his narrative against anticipated accusations of triviality).

I have no soul to speak to, or relieve me. But God wonderfully sent the ship in near enough to the shore, that I have gotten out so many necessary things as will either supply my wants, or enable me to supply myself even as long as I live.

Upon the whole, here was an undoubted testimony, that there was scarce any condition in the world so miserable, but there was something *negative* or something *positive* to be thankful for in it; and let this stand as a direction from the experience of the most miserable of all conditions in this world, that we may always find in it something to comfort ourselves from, and to set in the description of Good and Evil, on the credit side of the accompt.

Having now brought my mind a little to relish my condition, and given over looking out to sea to see if I could spy a ship, I say, giving over these things, I began to apply myself to accommodate my way of living, and to make things as easy to me as I could.

I have already described my habitation, which was a tent under the side of a rock, surrounded with a strong pale of posts and cables, but I might now rather call it a wall, for I raised a kind of wall up against it of turfs, about two foot thick on the outside, and after some time, I think it was a year and a half, I raised rafters from it leaning to the rock, and thatched or covered it with bows of trees, and such things as I could get to keep out the rain, which I found at some times of the year very violent.

I have already observed how I brought all my goods into this pale, and into the cave which I had made behind me. But I must observe too, that at first this was a confused heap of goods, which as they lay in no order, so they took up all my place, I had no room to turn myself; so I set myself to enlarge my cave and works farther into the earth, for it was a loose sandy rock, which yielded easily to the labor I bestowed on it; and so when I found I was pretty safe as to beasts of prey, I worked sideways to the right hand into the rock, and then turning to the right again, worked quite out and made me a door to come out, on the outside of my pale or fortification.

This gave me not only egress and regress, as it were a back way to my tent and to my storehouse, but gave me room to stow my goods.

And now I began to apply myself to make such necessary things as I found I most wanted, as particularly a chair and a table, for without these I was not able to enjoy the few comforts I had in the world: I could not write, or eat, or do several things with so much pleasure without a table.

So I went to work; and here I must needs observe, that as reason is the substance and original of the mathematics, so by stating and squaring everything by reason, and by making the most rational judgment of things, every man may be in time master of every mechanic art.[4] I had never handled a tool in my life, and yet in time, by labor, application, and contrivance, I found at last that I wanted nothing but I could have made it, especially if I had had tools; however, I made abundance of things, even without tools, and some with no more tools than an adze[5] and a hatchet, which perhaps were never made that way before, and that with infinite labor. For example, if I wanted a board, I had no other way but to cut down a tree, set it on an edge before me, and hew it flat on either side with my axe, till I had brought it to be thin as a plank, and then dub[6] it smooth with my adze. It is true, by this method I could make but one board out of a whole tree, but this I had no remedy for but patience, any

4. Manual craft.
5. A kind of axe, used for rough-shaping timber.
6. Beat.

more than I had for the prodigious deal of time and labor which it took me up to make a plank or board. But my time or labor was little worth, and so it was as well employed one way as another.

However, I made me a table and a chair, as I observed above, in the first place, and this I did out of the short pieces of boards that I brought on my raft from the ship. But when I had wrought out some boards, as above, I made large shelves of the breadth of a foot and half one over another, all along one side of my cave, to lay all my tools, nails, and iron-work, and in a word, to separate everything at large in their places, that I might come easily at them; I knocked pieces into the wall of the rock to hang my guns and all things that would hang up.

So that had my cave been to be seen, it looked like a general magazine[7] of all necessary things, and I had everything so ready at my hand, that it was a great pleasure to me to see all my goods in such order, and especially to find my stock of all necessaries so great.

And now it was when I began to keep a journal of every day's employment, for indeed at first I was in too much hurry, and not only hurry as to labor, but in too much discomposure of mind, and my journal would have been full of many dull[8] things. For example, I must have said thus:

Sept. the 30th. After I got to shore and had escaped drowning, instead of being thankful to God for my deliverance, having first vomited with the great quantity of salt water which was gotten into my stomach, and recovering myself a little, I ran about the shore, wringing my hands and beating my head and face, exclaiming at my misery, and crying out, I was undone, undone, till tired and faint I was forced to lie down on the ground to repose, but durst not sleep for fear of being devoured. Some days after this, and after I had been on board the ship, and got all that I could out of her, yet I could not forbear getting up to the top of a little mountain and looking out to sea in hopes of seeing a ship, then fancy at a vast distance I spied a sail, please myself with the hopes of it, and then after looking steadily till I was almost blind, lose it quite, and sit down and weep like a child, and thus increase my misery by my folly.

But having gotten over these things in some measure, and having settled my household stuff and habitation, made me a table and a chair, and all as handsome about me as I could, I began to keep my journal, of which I shall here give you the copy (though in it will be told all these particulars again) as long as it lasted, for having no more ink I was forced to leave it off.

The Journal

September 30, 1659. I poor miserable *Robinson Crusoe*, being shipwrecked, during a dreadful storm, in the offing, came on shore on this dismal unfortunate island, which I called *the Island of Despair*, all the rest of the ship's company being drowned, and myself almost dead.

All the rest of that day I spent in afflicting myself at the dismal circumstances I was brought to, *viz.* I had neither food, house, clothes, weapon, or place to fly to, and in despair of any relief, saw nothing but death for want of food. At the approach of night, I slept in a tree for fear of wild creatures, but slept soundly though it rained all night.

1719

For selections from Defoe's *Roxana*, go to *The Longman Anthology of British Literature* Web site at www.myliteraturekit.com.

7. Storehouse.

8. Stupid.

Eliza Haywood

ca. 1693–1756

Eliza Haywood, as Clara Reeve observed, "was one of the most voluminous female writers that England ever produced." Over the course of four decades, she published more than sixty works, in a vast variety of genres ranging from comedies to conduct books. But she achieved her first fame by pioneering a form of fiction that dwelt along the highly eroticized (and very lucrative) cusp between reality as the novel was beginning to figure it, and romance as Reeve would later define it: "an heroic fable, which treats of fabulous persons and things." In Haywood's fictions, the fabulousness inheres not in heroic exploits but in sexual ardor. Her female protagonists pursue their desires so intensely and so successfully that she was dubbed by one admirer "the Grand Arbitress of Passion." Her first novel, bearing the expressive title *Love in Excess* (1719), appeared in the same year as *Crusoe*, and vied with it in popularity. *Fantomina* (1724), the novel reprinted here, appeared simultaneously with *Roxana*, and explores some of the same issues, but in Haywood's characteristic register of an overtly heightened reality. Fantomina runs through a sequence of disguises that push deception beyond the plausible towards the preposterous, and her tactics differ diametrically from Roxana's in their motivation. They are directed at one man rather than many, and grounded in an intense desire for risk and sex rather than security and wealth. In Haywood's early fiction, her female adventurers, her lovers in excess, pursue their pleasures at variable cost, paying sometimes with their lives, and sometimes not at all. In *Fantomina* Haywood celebrates, as usual, her protagonist's erotic energies, ingenuities, and appetites, and at the same time partly anticipates the more domesticated and didactic novels of her later years, wherein (as Reeve remarks) "she had the good fortune to recover a lost reputation, and the yet greater honor to atone for her errors." (For a sample of such atonement, see the introductory self-portrait Haywood wrote for her pioneering periodical, *The Female Spectator* pages 2322–23.)

Fantomina: Or, Love in a Maze

Being a Secret History of an Amour Between Two Persons of Condition[1]

In love the victors from the vanquished fly.
They fly that wound, and they pursue that die.

—Waller[2]

A young lady of distinguished birth, beauty, wit, and spirit, happened to be in a box one night at the playhouse; where, though there were a great number of celebrated toasts,[3] she perceived several gentlemen extremely pleased themselves with entertaining a woman who sat in a corner of the pit,[4] and, by her air and manner of receiving them, might easily be known to be one of those who come there for no other purpose than to create acquaintance with as many as seem desirous of it. She could not help testifying her contempt of men who, regardless either of the play or circle, threw away their time in such a manner, to some ladies that sat by her: but they, either less surprised by being more accustomed to such sights than she who had

1. Upper-class rank.
2. The final lines of Edmund Waller's "To a Friend, on the different success of their loves" (1645), in which a man describes how his infatuation with a proud woman named Celia met with her rejection, while his subsequent loss of interest turned the tables and made her solicitous of him. "To die" here also means "to experience orgasm."
3. Belles, fine young ladies (whose health was commonly drunk by gentlemen in toasts).
4. The area below the stage generally occupied by gentlemen, law students, professional or literary types, and (in this case) prostitutes. Aristocracy generally sat in the boxes above.

been bred for the most part in the country, or not of a disposition to consider anything very deeply, took but little notice of it. She still thought of it, however; and the longer she reflected on it, the greater was her wonder that men, some of whom she knew were accounted to have wit,[5] should have tastes so very depraved.—This excited a curiosity in her to know in what manner these creatures were addressed,[6]—she was young, a stranger to the world, and consequently to the dangers of it; and having nobody in town at that time to whom she was obliged to be accountable for her actions, did in everything as her inclinations or humors rendered most agreeable to her: therefore thought it not in the least a fault to put in practice a little whim which came immediately into her head, to dress herself as near as she could in the fashion of those women who make sale of their favors, and set herself in the way of being accosted as such a one, having at that time no other aim, than the gratification of an innocent curiosity.—She no sooner designed this frolic than she put it in execution; and muffling her hoods over her face, went the next night into the gallery-box, and practicing as much as she had observed at that distance the behavior of that woman, was not long before she found her disguise had answered the ends she wore it for.—A crowd of purchasers of all degrees and capacities were in a moment gathered about her, each endeavoring to outbid the other in offering her a price for her embraces.—She listened to 'em all, and was not a little diverted in her mind at the disappointment she should give to so many, each of which thought himself secure of gaining her. She was told by 'em all that she was the most lovely woman in the world; and some cried, *Gad, she is mighty like my fine Lady Such-a-one*—naming her own name. She was naturally vain, and received no small pleasure in hearing herself praised, though in the person of another, and a supposed prostitute; but she dispatched as soon as she could all that had hitherto attacked her, when she saw the accomplished *Beauplaisir*[7] was making his way through the crowd as fast as he was able, to reach the bench she sat on. She had often seen him in the drawing-room, had talked with him; but then her quality[8] and reputed virtue kept him from using her with that freedom she now expected he would do, and had discovered something in him which had made her often think she should not be displeased, if he would abate some part of his reserve.—Now was the time to have her wishes answered:—he looked in her face, and fancied, as many others had done, that she very much resembled that lady whom she really was; but the vast disparity there appeared between their characters prevented him from entertaining even the most distant thought that they could be the same.—He addressed her at first with the usual salutations of her pretended profession, as, *Are you engaged, Madam?—Will you permit me to wait on you home after the play?—By Heaven, you are a fine girl!—How long have you used this house?*—and such like questions; but perceiving she had a turn of wit, and a genteel manner in her raillery, beyond what is frequently to be found among those wretches, who are for the most part gentlewomen but by necessity, few of 'em having had an education suitable to what they affect to appear, he changed the form of his conversation, and showed her it was not because he understood no better that he had made use of expressions so little polite.—In fine, they were infinitely charmed with each other: he was transported to find so much beauty and wit in a woman, who he doubted not but on very easy terms he might enjoy; and she

5. Intelligence, good taste, judgment.
6. Creatures: common term of disrespect for women of low birth or reputation. Addressed: approached, solicited.
7. Lovely pleasure (French).
8. High social station.

found a vast deal of pleasure in conversing with him in this free and unrestrained manner. They passed their time all the play with an equal satisfaction; but when it was over, she found herself involved in a difficulty, which before never entered into her head, but which she knew not well how to get over.—The passion he professed for her, was not of that humble nature which can be content with distant adorations:—he resolved not to part from her without the gratifications of those desires she had inspired; and presuming on the liberties which her supposed function allowed of, told her she must either go with him to some convenient house of his procuring, or permit him to wait on her to her own lodgings.—Never had she been in such a *dilemma:* three or four times did she open her mouth to confess her real quality; but the influence of her ill stars prevented it, by putting an excuse into her head, which did the business as well, and at the same time did not take from her the power of seeing and entertaining him a second time with the same freedom she had done this.—She told him, she was under obligations to a man who maintained her, and whom she durst not disappoint, having promised to meet him that night at a house hard by[9]—This story so like what those ladies sometimes tell was not at all suspected by *Beauplaisir;* and assuring her he would be far from doing her a prejudice,[1] desired that in return for the pain he should suffer in being deprived of her company that night, that she would order her affairs, so as not to render him unhappy the next. She gave a solemn promise to be in the same box on the morrow evening; and they took leave of each other; he to the tavern to drown the remembrance of his disappointment; she in a hackney-chair[2] hurried home to indulge contemplation on the frolic she had taken, designing nothing less on her first reflections than to keep the promise she had made him, and hugging herself with joy, that she had the good luck to come off undiscovered.

But these cogitations were but of a short continuance; they vanished with the hurry of her spirits, and were succeeded by others vastly different and ruinous:—all the charms of *Beauplaisir* came fresh into her mind; she languished, she almost died for another opportunity of conversing with him; and not all the admonitions of her discretion were effectual to oblige her to deny laying hold of that which offered itself the next night.—She depended on the strength of her virtue, to bear her fate through trials more dangerous than she apprehended this to be, and never having been addressed by him as Lady——was resolved to receive his devoirs[3] as a town-mistress, imagining a world of satisfaction to herself in engaging him in the character of such a one, observing the surprise he would be in to find himself refused by a woman, who he supposed granted her favors without exception.—Strange and unaccountable were the whimsies she was possessed of—wild and incoherent her desires—unfixed and undetermined her resolutions, but in that of seeing *Beauplaisir* in the manner she had lately done. As for her proceedings with him, or how a second time to escape him, without discovering who she was, she could neither assure herself, nor whether or not in the last extremity she would do so.—Bent, however, on meeting him, whatever should be the consequence, she went out some hours before the time of going to the playhouse, and took lodgings in a house not very far from it, intending, that if he should insist on passing some part of the night with her, to carry him there, thinking she might with more security to her honor entertain him at a place where she was mistress, than at any of his own choosing.

9. Nearby.
1. Injury.
2. Hired sedan chair carried by two men.
3. Respects.

The appointed hour being arrived, she had the satisfaction to find his love in his assiduity: he was there before her; and nothing could be more tender than the manner in which he accosted her: but from the first moment she came in, to that of the play being done, he continued to assure her no consideration should prevail with him to part from her again, as she had done the night before; and she rejoiced to think she had taken that precaution of providing herself with a lodging, to which she thought she might invite him, without running any risk, either of her virtue or reputation.—Having told him she would admit of his accompanying her home, he seemed perfectly satisfied; and leading her to the place, which was not above twenty houses distant, would have ordered a collation[4] to be brought after them. But she would not permit it, telling him she was not one of those who suffered themselves to be treated at their own lodgings; and as soon she was come in, sent a servant, belonging to the house, to provide a very handsome supper, and wine, and everything was served to table in a manner which showed the director neither wanted money, nor was ignorant how it should be laid out.

This proceeding, though it did not take from him the opinion that she was what she appeared to be, yet it gave him thoughts of her, which he had not before.—He believed her a *mistress*, but believed her to be one of a superior rank, and began to imagine the possession of her would be much more expensive than at first he had expected; but not being of a humor to grudge anything for his pleasures, he gave himself no farther trouble than what were occasioned by fears of not having money enough to reach her price, about him.

Supper being over, which was intermixed with a vast deal of amorous conversation, he began to explain himself more than he had done; and both by his words and behavior let her know he would not be denied that happiness the freedoms she allowed had made him hope.—It was in vain; she would have retracted the encouragement she had given:—in vain she endeavored to delay, till the next meeting, the fulfilling of his wishes:—she had now gone too far to retreat:—*he* was bold;—he was resolute: *she* fearful—confused, altogether unprepared to resist in such encounters, and rendered more so, by the extreme liking she had to him.—Shocked, however, at the apprehension of really losing her honor, she struggled all she could, and was just going to reveal the whole secret of her name and quality, when the thoughts of the liberty he had taken with her, and those he still continued to prosecute, prevented her, with representing[5] the danger of being exposed, and the whole affair made a theme for public ridicule.—Thus much, indeed, she told him, that she was a virgin, and had assumed this manner of behavior only to engage him. But that he little regarded, or if he had, would have been far from obliging him to desist;—nay, in the present burning eagerness of desire, 'tis probable, that had he been acquainted both with who and what she really was, the knowledge of her birth would not have influenced him with respect sufficient to have curbed the wild exuberance of his luxurious wishes, or made him in that longing—that impatient moment, change the form of his addresses. In fine, she was undone; and he gained a victory, so highly rapturous, that had he known over whom, scarce could he have triumphed more. Her tears, however, and the distraction she appeared in, after the ruinous ecstasy was past, as it heightened his wonder, so it abated his satisfaction:—he could not imagine for what reason a woman, who, if she intended not to be a *mistress*, had counterfeited the part of one, and taken so much pains to engage him, should lament a con-

4. Light meal.

5. By calling to mind.

sequence which she could not but expect, and till the last test, seemed inclinable to grant; and was both surprised and troubled at the mystery.—He omitted nothing that he thought might make her easy; and still retaining an opinion that the hope of interest had been the chief motive which had led her to act in the manner she had done, and believing that she might know so little of him, as to suppose, now she had nothing left to give, he might not make that recompense she expected for her favors: to put her out of that pain, he pulled out of his pocket a purse of gold, entreating her to accept of that as an earnest of what he intended to do for her; assuring her, with ten thousand protestations, that he would spare nothing, which his whole estate could purchase, to procure her content and happiness. This treatment made her quite forget the part she had assumed, and throwing it from her with an air of disdain, Is this a reward (*said she*) for condescensions,[6] such as I have yielded to?—Can all the wealth you are possessed of make a reparation for my loss of honor?—Oh! no, I am undone beyond the power of heaven itself to help me!—She uttered many more such exclamations; which the amazed *Beauplaisir* heard without being able to reply to, till by degrees sinking from that rage of temper, her eyes resumed their softening glances, and guessing at the consternation he was in, No, my dear *Beauplaisir*, (*added she*) your love alone can compensate for the shame you have involved me in; be you sincere and constant, and hereafter shall, perhaps, be satisfied with my fate, and forgive myself the folly that betrayed me to you.

Beauplaisir thought he could not have a better opportunity than these words gave him of inquiring who she was, and wherefore she had feigned herself to be of a profession which he was now convinced she was not; and after he had made her a thousand vows of an affection, as inviolable and ardent as she could wish to find in him, entreated she would inform him by what means his happiness had been brought about, and also to whom he was indebted for the bliss he had enjoyed.—Some remains of yet unextinguished modesty, and sense of shame, made her blush exceedingly at this demand; but recollecting herself in a little time, she told him so much of the truth, as to what related to the frolic she had taken of satisfying her curiosity in what manner *mistresses*, of the sort she appeared to be were treated by those who addressed them; but forbore discovering her true name and quality, for the reasons she had done before, resolving, if he boasted of this affair, he should not have it in his power to touch her character: she therefore said she was the daughter of a country gentleman, who was come to town to buy clothes, and that she was called *Fantomina*. He had no reason to distrust the truth of this story, and was therefore satisfied with it; but did not doubt by the beginning of her conduct, but that in the end she would be in reality, the thing she so artfully had counterfeited; and had good nature enough to pity the misfortunes he imagined would be her lot: but to tell her so, or offer his advice in that point, was not his business, at least, as yet.

They parted not till towards morning; and she obliged him to a willing vow of visiting her the next day at three in the afternoon. It was too late for her to go home that night, therefore contented herself with lying there. In the morning she sent for the woman of the house to come up to her; and easily perceiving, by her manner, that she was a woman who might be influenced by gifts, made her a present of a couple of broad pieces,[7] and desired her, that if the gentleman, who had been there the night before, should ask any questions concerning her, that he should be told, she was lately come out of the country, had lodged there about a fortnight, and that her

6. Unworthiness, vice.

7. Gold coins.

name was *Fantomina.* I shall (*also added she*) lie but seldom here; nor, indeed, ever come but in those times when I expect to meet him: I would, therefore, have you order it so, that he may think I am but just gone out, if he should happen by any accident to call when I am not here; for I would not, for the world, have him imagine I do not constantly lodge here. The landlady assured her she would do everything as she desired, and gave her to understand she wanted not the gift of secrecy.

Everything being ordered at this home for the security of her reputation, she repaired to the other, where she easily excused to an unsuspecting aunt, with whom she boarded, her having been abroad all night, saying, she went with a gentleman and his lady in a barge, to a little country seat of theirs up the river, all of them designing to return the same evening; but that one of the bargemen happening to be taken ill on the sudden, and no other waterman to be got that night, they were obliged to tarry till morning. Thus did this lady's wit and vivacity assist her in all, but where it was most needed.—She had discernment to foresee, and avoid all those ills which might attend the loss of her *reputation*, but was wholly blind to those of the ruin of her *virtue;* and having managed her affairs so as to secure the *one*, grew perfectly easy with the remembrance she had forfeited the *other*.—The more she reflected on the merits of *Beauplaisir*, the more she excused herself for what she had done; and the prospect of that continued bliss she expected to share with him took from her all remorse for having engaged in an affair which promised her so much satisfaction, and in which she found not the least danger of misfortune.—If he is really (*said she, to herself*) the faithful, the constant lover he has sworn to be, how charming will be our amor?—And if he should be false, grow satiated, like other men, I shall but, at the worst, have the private vexation of knowing I have lost him;—the intrigue being a secret, my disgrace will be so too:—I shall hear no whispers as I pass—She is forsaken:—the odious word *forsaken* will never wound my ears; nor will my wrongs excite either the mirth or pity of the talking world:—it would not be even in the power of my undoer himself to triumph over me; and while he laughs at, and perhaps despises the fond, the yielding *Fantomina*, he will revere and esteem the virtuous, the reserved lady.—In this manner did she applaud her own conduct, and exult with the imagination that she had more prudence than all her sex beside. And it must be confessed, indeed, that she preserved an economy in the management of this intrigue beyond what almost any woman but herself ever did: in the first place, by making no person in the world a confidant in it; and in the next, in concealing from *Beauplaisir* himself the knowledge who she was; for though she met him three or four days in a week, at that lodging she had taken for that purpose, yet as much as he employed her time and thoughts, she was never missed from any assembly she had been accustomed to frequent.—The business of her love has engrossed her till six in the evening, and before seven she has been dressed in a different habit, and in another place.—Slippers, and a night-gown loosely flowing, has been the garb in which he has left the languishing *Fantomina;*—laced and adorned with all the blaze of jewels has he, in less than an hour after, beheld at the royal chapel, the palace gardens, drawing-room, opera, or play, the haughty awe-inspiring lady—a thousand times has he stood amazed at the prodigious likeness between his little mistress and this court beauty; but was still as far from imagining they were the same as he was the first hour he had accosted her in the playhouse, though it is not impossible but that her resemblance to this celebrated lady might keep his inclination alive something longer than otherwise they would have been; and that it was to the thoughts of this (as he supposed) unenjoyed charmer she owed in great measure the vigor of his latter caresses.

But he varied not so much from his sex as to be able to prolong desire to any great length after possession: the rifled charms of *Fantomina* soon lost their potency, and grew tasteless and insipid; and when the season of the year inviting the company to the *Bath*,[8] she offered to accompany him, he made an excuse to go without her. She easily perceived his coldness, and the reason why he pretended her going would be inconvenient, and endured as much from the discovery as any of her sex could do: she dissembled it, however, before him, and took her leave of him with the show of no other concern than his absence occasioned: but this she did to take from him all suspicion of her following him, as she intended, and had already laid a scheme for.—From her first finding out that he designed to leave her behind, she plainly saw it was for no other reason, than that being tired of her conversation, he was willing to be at liberty to pursue new conquests; and wisely considering that complaints, tears, swoonings, and all the extravagancies which women make use of in such cases, have little prevalence over a heart inclined to rove, and only serve to render those who practice them more contemptible, by robbing them of that beauty which alone can bring back the fugitive lover, she resolved to take another course; and remembering the height of transport she enjoyed when the agreeable *Beauplaisir* kneeled at her feet, imploring her first favors, she longed to prove the same again. Not but a woman of her beauty and accomplishments might have beheld a thousand in that condition *Beauplaisir* had been; but with her sex's modesty, she had not also thrown off another virtue equally valuable, though generally unfortunate, *constancy:* she loved *Beauplaisir;* it was only he whose solicitations could give her pleasure; and had she seen the whole species despairing, dying for her sake, it might, perhaps, have been a satisfaction to her pride, but none to her more tender inclination.—Her design was once more to engage him, to hear him sigh, to see him languish, to feel the strenuous pressures of his eager arms, to be compelled, to be sweetly forced to what she wished with equal ardor, was what she wanted, and what she had formed a stratagem to obtain, in which she promised herself success.

She no sooner heard he had left the town, than making a pretense to her aunt, that she was going to visit a relation in the country, went towards *Bath*, attended but by two servants, who she found reasons to quarrel with on the road and discharged: clothing herself in a habit she had brought with her, she forsook the coach, and went into a wagon, in which equipage she arrived at *Bath*. The dress she was in was a round-eared cap,[9] a short red petticoat, and a little jacket of gray stuff,[1] all the rest of her accoutrements were answerable to these, and joined with a broad country dialect, a rude unpolished air, which she, having been bred in these parts, knew very well how to imitate, with her hair and eye-brows blacked, made it impossible for her to be known, or taken for any other than what she seemed. Thus disguised did she offer herself to service in the house where *Beauplaisir* lodged, having made it her business to find out immediately where he was. Notwithstanding this metamorphosis she was still extremely pretty; and the mistress of the house happening at that time to want a maid was very glad of the opportunity of taking her. She was presently received into the family; and had a post in it (such as she would have chose, had she been left at her liberty), that of making the gentlemen's beds, getting them their breakfasts, and waiting on them in their chambers. Fortune in this exploit was extremely on her side; there were no others of the male-sex in the house than an old gentleman, who had lost the use of his limbs with the rheumatism, and had come thither for the benefit of the waters, and her beloved *Beauplaisir;* so that she was in no apprehensions of any amorous violence, but where she wished to find it. Nor were her designs disappointed: He was fired with the

8. Town in southwestern England, popular as a resort because of its hot springs.

9. Style of cap associated with country women.

1. Coarse wool fabric.

first sight of her; and though he did not presently take any farther notice of her, than giving her two or three hearty kisses, yet she, who now understood that language but too well, easily saw they were the prelude to more substantial joys.—Coming the next morning to bring his chocolate, as he had ordered, he catched her by the pretty leg, which the shortness of her petticoat did not in the least oppose; then pulling her gently to him, asked her, how long she had been at service?—How many sweethearts she had? If she had ever been in love? and many other such questions, befitting one of the degree she appeared to be: all which she answered with such seeming innocence, as more enflamed the amorous heart of him who talked to her. He compelled her to sit in his lap; and gazing on her blushing beauties, which, if possible, received addition from her plain and rural dress, he soon lost the power of containing himself.—His wild desires burst out in all his words and actions: he called her little angel, cherubim, swore he must enjoy her, though death were to be the consequence, devoured her lips, her breasts with greedy kisses, held to his burning bosom her half-yielding, half-reluctant body, nor suffered her to get loose, till he had ravaged all, and glutted each rapacious sense with the sweet beauties of the pretty *Celia*,[2] for that was the name she bore in this second expedition.—Generous as liberality itself to all who gave him joy this way, he gave her a handsome sum of gold, which she durst not now refuse, for fear of creating some mistrust, and losing the heart she so lately had regained; therefore taking it with an humble courtesy, and a well counterfeited show of surprise and joy, cried, O law, Sir! what must I do for all this? He laughed at her simplicity, and kissing her again, though less fervently than he had done before, bad her not be out of the way when he came home at night. She promised she would not, and very obediently kept her word.

His stay at *Bath* exceeded not a month; but in that time his supposed country lass had persecuted him so much with her fondness, that in spite of the eagerness with which he first enjoyed her, he was at last grown more weary of her, than he had been of *Fantomina;* which she perceiving, would not be troublesome, but quitting her service, remained privately in the town till she heard he was on his return; and in that time provided herself of another disguise to carry on a third plot, which her inventing brain had furnished her with, once more to renew his twice-decayed ardors. The dress she had ordered to be made, was such as widows wear in their first mourning, which, together with the most afflicted and penitential countenance that ever was seen, was no small alteration to her who used to seem all gaiety.—To add to this, her hair, which she was accustomed to wear very loose both when *Fantomina* and *Celia*, was now tied back so straight, and her pinners[3] coming so very forward, that there was none of it to be seen. In fine, her habit and her air were so much changed, that she was not more difficult to be known in the rude country *girl*, than she was now in the sorrowful *widow*.

She knew that *Beauplaisir* came alone in his chariot to the *Bath*, and in the time of her being servant in the house where he lodged, heard nothing of any body that was to accompany him to *London*, and hoped he would return in the same manner he had gone: She therefore hired horses and a man to attend her to an inn about ten miles on this side of *Bath*, where having discharged them, she waited till the chariot should come by; which when it did, and she saw that he was alone in it, she called to him that drove it to stop a moment, and going to the door saluted the master with these words:

2. In Renaissance literature the name Celia is frequently associated with vanity or pride, as in Lyly's *Love's Metamorphosis* as well as Waller's "To Phyllis" and "To a Friend" (quoted in the epigraph); similarly, in Swift's "The Lady's Dressing Room" (see page 2346), Celia is the woman who spends five hours in her dressing room each day in an effort to conceal her natural nastiness.

3. The side flaps of a close-fitting hat, usually worn by women of higher rank.

The distressed and wretched, Sir (*said she*), never fail to excite compassion in a generous mind; and I hope I am not deceived in my opinion that yours is such:— You have the appearance of a gentleman, and cannot, when you hear my story, refuse that assistance which is in your power to give to an unhappy woman, who without it, may be rendered the most miserable of all created beings.

It would not be very easy to represent the surprise, so odd an address created in the mind of him to whom it was made.—She had not the appearance of one who wanted charity; and what other favor she required he could not conceive: but telling her she might command any thing in his power gave her encouragement to declare herself in this manner: You may judge (*resumed she*), by the melancholy garb I am in, that I have lately lost all that ought to be valuable to womankind; but it is impossible for you to guess the greatness of my misfortune, unless you had known my husband, who was master of every perfection to endear him to a wife's affections.—But, notwithstanding, I look on myself as the most unhappy of my sex in out-living him, I must so far obey the dictates of my discretion, as to take care of the little fortune he left behind him, which being in the hands of a brother of his in *London*, will be all carried off to *Holland*,[4] where he is going to settle; if I reach not the town before he leaves it, I am undone for ever.—To which end I left *Bristol*, the place where we lived, hoping to get a place in the stage at *Bath*, but they were all taken up before I came; and being, by a hurt I got in a fall, rendered incapable of traveling any long journey on horseback, I have no way to go to *London*, and must be inevitably ruined in the loss of all I have on earth, without you have good nature enough to admit me to take part of your chariot.

Here the feigned widow ended her sorrowful tale, which had been several times interrupted by a parenthesis of sighs and groans; and *Beauplaisir*, with a complaisant and tender air, assured her of his readiness to serve her in things of much greater consequence than what she desired of him; and told her it would be an impossibility of denying a place in his chariot to a lady who he could not behold without yielding one in his heart. She answered the compliments he made her but with tears, which seemed to stream in such abundance from her eyes, that she could not keep her handkerchief from her face one moment. Being come into the chariot, *Beauplaisir* said a thousand handsome things to persuade her from giving way to so violent a grief; which, he told her, would not only be destructive to her beauty, but likewise her health. But all his endeavors for consolement appeared ineffectual, and he began to think he should have but a dull journey, in the company of one who seemed so obstinately devoted to the memory of her dead husband, that there was no getting a word from her on any other theme:—but bethinking himself of the celebrated story of the *Ephesian* matron,[5] it came into his head to make trial, she who seemed equally susceptible of *sorrow*, might not also be so too of *love:* and having began a discourse on almost every other topic, and finding her still incapable of answering, resolved to put it to the proof, if this would have no more effect to rouse her sleeping spirits:—with a gay air, therefore, though accompanied with the greatest modesty and respect, he turned the conversation, as though without design, on that joy-giving passion, and soon discovered that was indeed the subject she was best pleased to be entertained with; for on his giving her a hint to begin upon, never any tongue run more voluble than hers, on the prodigious power it had to influence the souls of those possessed of it, to actions even the most distant from their intentions, principles, or humors.— From that she passed to a description of the happiness of mutual affection;—the

4. Holland had been a frequent destination for English religious dissenters in exile.

5. In Petronius's *Satyricon*, the Ephesian matron is a faithful wife who stays by her dead husband's burial vault day and night until she is seduced by a soldier who guards the nearby bodies of crucified criminals. When one of the bodies is stolen, the matron gives her own husband's body to the soldier to save him from punishment.

unspeakable ecstasy of those who meet with equal ardency; and represented it in colors so lively, and disclosed by the gestures with which her words were accompanied, and the accent of her voice so true a feeling of what she said, that *Beauplaisir,* without being as stupid, as he was really the contrary, could not avoid perceiving there were seeds of fire, not yet extinguished, in this fair widow's soul, which wanted but the kindling breath of tender sighs to light into a blaze.—He now thought himself as fortunate, as some moments before he had the reverse; and doubted not, but, that before they parted, he should find a way to dry the tears of this lovely mourner, to the satisfaction of them both. He did not, however, offer, as he had done to *Fantomina* and *Celia,* to urge his passion directly to her, but by a thousand little softening artifices, which he well knew how to use, gave her leave to guess he was enamored. When they came to the inn where they were to lie, he declared himself somewhat more freely, and perceiving she did not resent it past forgiveness, grew more encroaching still:—he now took the liberty of kissing away her tears, and catching the sighs as they issued from her lips; telling her if grief was infectious, he was resolved to have his share; protesting he would gladly exchange passions with her, and be content to bear her load of *sorrow,* if she would as willingly ease the burden of his *love.*—She said little in answer to the strenuous pressures with which at last he ventured to enfold her, but not thinking it decent, for the character she had assumed, to yield so suddenly, and unable to deny both his and her own inclinations, she counterfeited a fainting, and fell motionless upon his breast.—He had no great notion that she was in a real fit, and the room they supped in happening to have a bed in it, he took her in his arms and laid her on it, believing, that whatever her distemper was, that was the most proper place to convey her to.—He laid himself down by her, and endeavored to bring her to herself; and she was too grateful to her kind physician at her returning sense, to remove from the posture he had put her in, without his leave.

It may, perhaps, seem strange that *Beauplaisir* should in such near intimacies continue still deceived: I know there are men who will swear it is an impossibility, and that no disguise could hinder them from knowing a woman they had once enjoyed. In answer to these scruples, I can only say, that besides the alteration which the change of dress made in her, she was so admirably skilled in the art of feigning, that she had the power of putting on almost what face she pleased, and knew so exactly how to form her behavior to the character she represented, that all the comedians at both playhouses[6] are infinitely short of her performances: she could vary her very glances, tune her voice to accents the most different imaginable from those in which she spoke when she appeared herself.—These aids from nature, joined to the wiles of art, and the distance between the places where the imagined *Fantomina* and *Celia* were, might very well prevent his having any thought that they were the same, or that the fair *widow* was either of them: it never so much as entered his head, and though he did fancy he observed in the face of the latter, features which were not altogether unknown to him, yet he could not recollect when or where he had known them;—and being told by her, that from her birth, she had never removed from *Bristol,* a place where he never was, he rejected the belief of having seen her, and supposed his mind had been deluded by an idea of some other, whom she might have a resemblance of.

They passed the time of their journey in as much happiness as the most luxurious gratification of wild desires could make them; and when they came to the end of it, parted not without a mutual promise of seeing each other often.—He told her to what place she should direct a letter to him; and she assured him she would send to let him know where to come to her, as soon as she was fixed in lodgings.

6. Comedians are actors. There were only two public playhouses in London, established by royal decree in 1660.

She kept her promise; and charmed with the continuance of his eager fondness, went not home, but into private lodgings, whence she wrote to him to visit her the first opportunity, and inquire for the Widow *Bloomer*.—She had no sooner dispatched this billet,[7] than she repaired to the house where she had lodged as *Fantomina*, charging the people if *Beauplaisir* should come there, not to let him know she had been out of town. From thence she wrote to him, in a different hand, a long letter of complaint, that he had been so cruel in not sending one letter to her all the time he had been absent, entreated to see him, and concluded with subscribing herself his unalterably affectionate *Fantomina*. She received in one day answers to both these. The first contained these lines:

To the Charming Mrs. Bloomer,

*It would be impossible, my Angel! for me to express the thousandth part of that infinity of transport, the sight of your dear letter gave me.—Never was woman formed to charm like you: never did any look like you.—write like you,—bless like you;—nor did ever man adore as I do.—Since yesterday we parted, I have seemed a body without a soul; and had you not by this inspiring billet, gave me new life, I know not what by tomorrow I should have been.—I will be with you this evening about five:—*O, *'tis an age till then!—But the cursed formalities of duty oblige me to dine with my lord—who never rises from table till that hour;—therefore adieu till then sweet lovely mistress of the soul and all the faculties of*

Your most faithful,
Beauplaisir.

The other was in this manner:

To the Lovely Fantomina,

If you were half so sensible as you ought of your own power of charming, you would be assured, that to be unfaithful or unkind to you, would be among the things that are in their very natures impossibilities.—It was my misfortune, not my fault, that you were not persecuted every post with a declaration of my unchanging passion; but I had unluckily forgot the name of the woman at whose house you are, and knew not how to form a direction that it might come safe to your hands.—And, indeed, the reflection how you might misconstrue my silence, brought me to town some weeks sooner than I intended—If you knew how I have languished to renew those blessings I am permitted to enjoy in your society, you would rather pity than condemn

Your ever faithful,
Beauplaisir.

P.S. *I fear I cannot see you till tomorrow; some business has unluckily fallen out that will engross my hours till then.—Once more, my dear,* Adieu.

Traitor! (*cried she*) as soon as she had read them, 'tis thus our silly, fond, believing sex are served when they put faith in man: so had I been deceived and cheated, had I like the rest believed, and sat down mourning in absence, and vainly waiting recovered tendernesses.—How do some women (*continued she*) make their life a hell, burning in fruitless expectations, and dreaming out their days in hopes and fears, then wake at last to all the horror of despair?—But I have outwitted even the most subtle of the deceiving kind, and while he thinks to fool me, is himself the only beguiled person.

7. Note, brief letter.

She made herself, most certainly, extremely happy in the reflection on the success of her stratagems; and while the knowledge of his inconstancy and levity of nature kept her from having that real tenderness for him she would else have had, she found the means of gratifying the inclination she had for his agreeable person, in as full a manner as she could wish. She had all the sweets of love, but as yet had tasted none of the gall, and was in a state of contentment, which might be envied by the more delicate.

When the expected hour arrived, she found that her lover had lost no part of the fervency with which he had parted from her; but when the next day she received him as *Fantomina,* she perceived a prodigious difference; which led her again into reflections on the unaccountableness of men's fancies, who still prefer the last conquest, only because it is the last.—Here was an evident proof of it; for there could not be a difference in merit, because they were the same person; but the Widow *Bloomer* was a more new acquaintance than *Fantomina,* and therefore esteemed more valuable. This, indeed, must be said of *Beauplaisir,* that he had a greater share of good nature than most of his sex, who, for the most part, when they are weary of an intrigue, break it entirely off, without any regard to the despair of the abandoned nymph. Though he retained no more than a bare pity and complaisance for *Fantomina,* yet believing she loved him to an excess, would not entirely forsake her, though the continuance of his visits was now become rather a penance than a pleasure.

The Widow *Bloomer* triumphed some time longer over the heart of this inconstant, but at length her sway was at an end, and she sunk in this character, to the same degree of tastelessness, as she had done before in that of *Fantomina* and *Celia.*—She presently perceived it, but bore it as she had always done; it being but what she expected, she had prepared herself for it, and had another project in embryo, which she soon ripened into action. She did not, indeed, complete it altogether so suddenly as she had done the others, by reason there must be persons employed in it; and the aversion she had to any confidants in her affairs, and the caution with which she had hitherto acted, and which she was still determined to continue, made it very difficult for her to find a way without breaking through that resolution to compass what she wished.—She got over the difficulty at last, however, by proceeding in a manner, if possible, more extraordinary than all her former behavior:—muffling herself up in her hood one day, she went into the park about the hour when there are a great many necessitous gentlemen,[8] who think themselves above doing what they call little things for a maintenance, walking in the *Mall,*[9] to take a *Camelion* Treat,[1] and fill their stomachs with air instead of meat. Two of those, who by their physiognomy she thought most proper for her purpose, she beckoned to come to her; and taking them into a walk more remote from company, began to communicate the business she had with them in these words: I am sensible, gentlemen (*said she*), that, through the blindness of fortune, and partiality of the world, merit frequently goes unrewarded, and that those of the best pretentions meet with the least encouragement:—I ask your pardon (*continued she*), perceiving they seemed surprised, if I am mistaken in the notion, that you two may, perhaps, be of the number of those who have reason to complain of the injustice of fate; but if you are such as I take you for, I have a proposal to make you, which may be of some little advantage to you. Neither of them made any immediate answer, but appeared buried in consideration for some moments. At length, We should, doubtless, madam (*said one of them*), willingly come into any

8. Poor men.

9. A popular walk in St. James's Park.

1. Chameleons were thought to subsist on air.

measures to oblige you, provided they are such as may bring us into no danger, either as to our persons or reputations. That which I require of you (*resumed she*), has nothing in it criminal: All that I desire is *secrecy* in what you are entrusted, and to disguise yourselves in such a manner as you cannot be known, if hereafter seen by the person on whom you are to impose.—In fine, the business is only an innocent frolic, but if blazed abroad, might be taken for too great a freedom in me:—Therefore, if you resolve to assist me, here are five pieces to drink my health, and assure you, that I have not discoursed you[2] on an affair, I design not to proceed in; and when it is accomplished fifty more lie ready for your acceptance. These words, and, above all, the money, which was a sum which, 'tis probable, they had not seen of a long time, made them immediately assent to all she desired, and press for the beginning of their employment: but things were not yet ripe for execution; and she told them, that the next day they should be let into the secret, charging them to meet her in the same place at an hour she appointed. 'Tis hard to say, which of these parties went away best pleased; *they*, that fortune had sent them so unexpected a windfall; or *she*, that she had found persons, who appeared so well qualified to serve her.

Indefatigable in the pursuit of whatsoever her humor was bent upon, she had no sooner left her new-engaged emissaries, than she went in search of a house for the completing of her project.—She pitched on one very large, and magnificently furnished, which she hired by the week, giving them the money beforehand, to prevent any inquiries. The next day she repaired to the park, where she met the punctual 'squires of low degree; and ordering them to follow her to the house she had taken, told them they must condescend to appear like servants, and gave each of them a very rich livery. Then writing a letter to *Beauplaisir*, in a character vastly different from either of those she had made use of, as *Fantomina*, or the fair Widow *Bloomer*, ordered one of them to deliver it into his own hands, to bring back an answer, and to be careful that he sifted out nothing of the truth.—I do not fear (*said she*), that you should discover to him who I am, because that is a secret, of which you yourselves are ignorant; but I would have you be so careful in your replies, that he may not think the concealment springs from any other reasons than your great integrity to your trust.—Seem therefore to know my whole affairs; and let your refusing to make him partaker in the secret, appear to be only the effect of your zeal for my interest and reputation. Promises of entire fidelity on the one side, and reward on the other, being past, the messenger made what haste he could to the house of *Beauplaisir*; and being there told where he might find him, performed exactly the injunction that had been given him. But never astonishment exceeded that which *Beauplaisir* felt at the reading this billet, in which he found these lines:

To the All-conquering Beauplaisir.

I imagine not that 'tis a new thing to you, to be told, you are the greatest charm in nature to our sex: I shall therefore, not to fill up my letter with any impertinent praises on your wit or person, only tell you, that I am infinite in love with both, and if you have a heart not too deeply engaged, should think myself the happiest of my sex in being capable of inspiring it with some tenderness.—There is but one thing in my power to refuse you, which is the knowledge of my name, which believing the sight of my face will render no secret, you must not take it ill that I conceal from you.—The bearer of this is a person I can trust; send by him your answer; but endeavor not

2. Talked to you.

to dive into the meaning of this mystery, which will be impossible for you to unravel, and at the same time very much disoblige me:—But that you may be in no apprehensions of being imposed on by a woman unworthy of your regard, I will venture to assure you, the first and greatest men in the kingdom would think themselves blessed to have that influence over me you have, though unknown to yourself, acquired.—But I need not go about to raise your curiosity, by giving you any idea of what my person is; if you think fit to be satisfied, resolve to visit me tomorrow about three in the afternoon; and though my face is hid, you shall not want sufficient demonstration, that she who takes these unusual measures to commence a friendship with you, is neither old, nor deformed. Till then I am,

Yours,
Incognita[3]

He had scarce come to the conclusion, before he asked the person who brought it, from what place he came;—the name of the lady he served;—if she were a wife, or widow, and several other questions directly opposite to the directions of the letter; but silence would have availed him as much as did all those testimonies of curiosity: no *Italian Bravo*,[4] employed in a business of the like nature, performed his office with more artifice; and the impatient inquirer was convinced, that nothing but doing as he was desired, could give him any light into the character of the woman who declared so violent a passion for him; and little fearing any consequence which could ensue from such an encounter, resolved to rest satisfied till he was informed of everything from herself, not imagining this *Incognita* varied so much from the generality of her sex, as to be able to refuse the knowledge of anything to the man she loved with that transcendency of passion she professed, and which his many successes with the ladies gave him encouragement enough to believe. He therefore took pen and paper, and answered her letter in terms tender enough for a man who had never seen the person to whom he wrote. The words were as follows:

To the Obliging and Witty Incognita.

Though to tell me I am happy enough to be liked by a woman, such, as by your manner of writing, I imagine you to be, is an honor which I can never sufficiently acknowledge, yet I know not how I am able to content myself with admiring the wonders of your wit alone: I am certain, a soul like yours must shine in your eyes with a vivacity, which must bless all they look on.—I shall, however, endeavor to restrain myself in those bounds you are pleased to set me, till by the knowledge of my inviolable fidelity, I may be thought worthy of gazing on that heaven I am now but to enjoy in contemplation.—You need not doubt my glad compliance with your obliging summons: there is a charm in your lines, which gives too sweet an idea of their lovely author to be resisted.—I am all impatient for the blissful moment, which is to throw me at your feet, and give me an opportunity of convincing you that I am,

Your everlasting slave,
Beauplaisir.

Nothing could be more pleased than she, to whom it was directed, at the receipt of this letter; but when she was told how inquisitive he had been concerning her character and circumstances, she could not forbear laughing heartily to think of the tricks she had played him, and applauding her own strength of genius, and force of resolution, which by such unthought-of ways could triumph over her lover's inconstancy, and render that very temper, which to other women is the greatest curse, a means

3. Unknown woman (Latin); i.e., a woman in disguise.
4. Hired assassin.

to make herself more blessed.—Had he been faithful to me (*said she, to herself*), either as *Fantomina*, or *Celia*, or the Widow *Bloomer*, the most violent passion, if it does not change its object, in time will wither: possession naturally abates the vigor of desire, and I should have had, at best, but a cold, insipid, husband-like lover in my arms; but by these arts of passing on him as a new mistress whenever the ardor, which alone makes love a blessing, begins to diminish, for the former one, I have him always raving, wild, impatient, longing, dying.—O that all neglected wives, and fond abandoned nymphs would take this method!—Men would be caught in their own snare, and have no cause to scorn our easy, weeping, wailing sex! Thus did she pride herself as if secure she never should have any reason to repent the present gaiety of her humor. The hour drawing near in which he was to come, she dressed herself in as magnificent a manner, as if she were to be that night at a ball at court, endeavoring to repair the want of those beauties which the vizard[5] should conceal, by setting forth the others with the greatest care and exactness. Her fine shape, and air, and neck appeared to great advantage; and by that which was to be seen of her, one might believe the rest to be perfectly agreeable. *Beauplaisir* was prodigiously charmed, as well with her appearance, as with the manner she entertained him: but though he was wild with impatience for the sight of a face which belonged to so exquisite a body, yet he would not immediately press for it, believing before he left her he should easily obtain that satisfaction.—A noble collation being over, he began to sue for the performance of her promise of granting everything he could ask, excepting the sight of her face, and knowledge of her name. It would have been a ridiculous piece of affectation in her to have seemed coy in complying with what she herself had been the first in desiring: she yielded without even a show of reluctance: and if there be any true felicity in an amour such as theirs, both here enjoyed it to the full. But not in the height of all their mutual raptures, could he prevail on her to satisfy his curiosity with the sight of her face: she told him that she hoped he knew so much of her, as might serve to convince him, she was not unworthy of his tenderest regard; and if he could not content himself with that which she was willing to reveal, and which was the conditions of their meeting, dear as he was to her, she would rather part with him for ever, than consent to gratify an inquisitiveness, which, in her opinion, had no business with his love. It was in vain that he endeavored to make her sensible of her mistake; and that this restraint was the greatest enemy imaginable to the happiness of them both: she was not to be persuaded, and he was obliged to desist his solicitations, though determined in his mind to compass what he so ardently desired, before he left the house. He then turned the discourse wholly on the violence of the passion he had for her; and expressed the greatest discontent in the world at the apprehensions of being separated;—swore he could dwell for ever in her arms, and with such an undeniable earnestness pressed to be permitted to tarry with her the whole night, that had she been less charmed with his renewed eagerness of desire, she scarce would have had the power of resisting him; but in granting this request, she was not without a thought that he had another reason for making it besides the extremity of his passion, and had it immediately in her head how to disappoint him.

The hours of repose being arrived, he begged she would retire to her chamber, to which she consented, but obliged him to go to bed first; which he did not much oppose, because he supposed she would not lie in her mask, and doubted not but the morning's dawn would bring the wished discovery.—The two imagined servants

5. Mask or veil.

ushered him to his new lodging; where he lay some moments in all the perplexity imaginable at the oddness of this adventure. But she suffered not these cogitations to be of any long continuance: she came, but came in the dark; which being no more than he expected by the former part of her proceedings, he said nothing of; but as much satisfaction as he found in her embraces, nothing ever longed for the approach of day with more impatience than he did. At last it came; but how great was his disappointment, when by the noises he heard in the street, the hurry of the coaches, and the cries of penny-merchants,[6] he was convinced it was night nowhere but with him? He was still in the same darkness as before; for she had taken care to blind the windows in such a manner, that not the least chink was left to let in day.—He complained of her behavior in terms that she would not have been able to resist yielding to, if she had not been certain it would have been the ruin of her passion:—she, therefore, answered him only as she had done before; and getting out of the bed from him, flew out of the room with too much swiftness for him to have overtaken her, if he had attempted it. The moment she left him, the two attendants entered the chamber, and plucking down the implements which had screened him from the knowledge of that which he so much desired to find out, restored his eyes once more to day:—they attended to assist him in dressing, brought him tea, and by their obsequiousness, let him see there was but one thing which the mistress of them would not gladly oblige him in.—He was so much out of humor, however, at the disappointment of his curiosity, that he resolved never to make a second visit.—Finding her in an outer room, he made no scruple of expressing the sense he had of the little trust she reposed in him, and at last plainly told her, he could not submit to receive obligations from a lady, who thought him uncapable of keeping a secret, which she made no difficulty of letting her servants into.—He resented—he once more entreated—he said all that man could do, to prevail on her to unfold the mystery; but all his adjurations were fruitless; and he went out of the house determined never to re-enter it, till she should pay the price of his company with the discovery of her face and circumstances.—She suffered him to go with this resolution, and doubted not but he would recede from it, when he reflected on the happy moments they had passed together; but if he did not, she comforted herself with the design of forming some other stratagem, with which to impose on him a fourth time.

She kept the house, and her gentlemen-equipage[7] for about a fortnight, in which time she continued to write to him as *Fantomina* and the Widow *Bloomer*, and received the visits he sometimes made to each; but his behavior to both was grown so cold, that she began to grow as weary of receiving his now insipid caresses as he was of offering them: she was beginning to think in what manner she should drop these two characters, when the sudden arrival of her mother, who had been some time in a foreign country, obliged her to put an immediate stop to the course of her whimsical adventures.—That lady, who was severely virtuous, did not approve of many things she had been told of the conduct of her daughter; and though it was not in the power of any person in the world to inform her of the truth of what she had been guilty of, yet she heard enough to make her keep her afterwards in a restraint, little agreeable to her humor, and the liberties to which she had been accustomed.

But this confinement was not the greatest part of the trouble of this now afflicted lady: she found the consequences of her amorous follies would be, without almost a miracle, impossible to be concealed:—she was with child; and though she

6. Street vendors of cheap wares.

7. Retinue of footmen.

would easily have found means to have screened even this from the knowledge of the world, had she been at liberty to have acted with the same unquestionable authority over herself, as she did before the coming of her mother, yet now all her invention was at a loss for a stratagem to impose on a woman of her penetration:—by eating little, lacing prodigious straight, and the advantage of a great hoop-petticoat, however, her bigness was not taken notice of, and, perhaps, she would not have been suspected till the time of her going into the country, where her mother designed to send her, and from whence she intended to make her escape to some place where she might be delivered with secrecy, if the time of it had not happened much sooner than she expected.—A ball being at court, the good old lady was willing she should partake of the diversion of it as a farewell to the town.—It was there she was seized with those pangs, which none in her condition are exempt from:—she could not conceal the sudden rack which all at once invaded her; or had her tongue been mute, her wildly rolling eyes, the distortion of her features, and the convulsions which shook her whole frame, in spite of her, would have revealed she labored under some terrible shock of nature.—Everybody was surprised, everybody was concerned, but few guessed at the occasion.—Her mother grieved beyond expression, doubted not but she was struck with the hand of death; and ordered her to be carried home in a chair, while herself followed in another.—A physician was immediately sent for: but he presently perceiving what was her distemper, called the old lady aside, and told her, it was not a doctor of his sex, but one of her own, her daughter stood in need of.—Never was astonishment and horror greater than that which seized the soul of this afflicted parent at these words: she could not for a time believe the truth of what she heard; but he insisting on it, and conjuring her to send for a midwife, she was at length convinced of it.—All the pity and tenderness she had been for some moment before possessed of now vanished, and were succeeded by an adequate[8] shame and indignation:—she flew to the bed where her daughter was lying, and telling her what she had been informed of, and which she was now far from doubting, commanded her to reveal the name of the person whose insinuations had drawn her to this dishonor.—It was a great while before she could be brought to confess anything, and much longer before she could be prevailed on to name the man whom she so fatally had loved; but the rack of nature growing more fierce, and the enraged old lady protesting no help should be afforded her while she persisted in her obstinacy, she, with great difficulty and hesitation in her speech, at last pronounced the name of *Beauplaisir*. She had no sooner satisfied her weeping mother, than that sorrowful lady sent messengers at the same time, for a midwife, and for that gentleman who had occasioned the other's being wanted.—He happened by accident to be at home, and immediately obeyed the summons, though prodigiously surprised what business a lady so much a stranger to him could have to impart.—But how much greater was his amazement, when taking him into her closet, she there acquainted him with her daughter's misfortune, of the discovery she had made, and how far he was concerned in it?—All the idea one can form of wild astonishment, was mean to what he felt:—he assured her, that the young lady her daughter was a person whom he had never, more than at a distance, admired:—that he had indeed, spoke to her in public company, but that he never had a thought which tended to her dishonor.—His denials, if possible, added to the indignation she was before enflamed with:—she had no longer patience; and carrying him into the chamber, where she was just delivered of

8. Equal.

a fine girl, cried out, I will not be imposed on: the truth by one of you shall be revealed.—*Beauplaisir* being brought to the bedside, was beginning to address himself to the lady in it, to beg she could clear the mistake her mother was involved in; when she, covering herself with the cloths, and ready to die a second time with the inward agitations of her soul, shrieked out, Oh, I am undone!—I cannot live, and bear this shame!—But the old lady believing that now or never was the time to dive into the bottom of this mystery, forcing her to rear her head, told her, she should not hope to escape the scrutiny of a parent she had dishonored in such a manner, and pointing to *Beauplaisir*, Is this the gentleman (*said she*), to whom you owe your ruin? or have you deceived me by a fictitious tale? Oh! no (*resumed the trembling creature*), he is, indeed, the innocent cause of my undoing:—Promise me your pardon (*continued she*), and I will relate the means. Here she ceased, expecting what she would reply, which, on hearing *Beauplaisir* cry out, What mean you, madam? I your undoing, who never harbored the least design on you in my life, she did in these words, Though the injury you have done your family (*said she*), is of a nature which cannot justly hope forgiveness, yet be assured, I shall much sooner excuse you when satisfied of the truth, than while I am kept in a suspense, if possible, as vexatious as the crime itself is to me. Encouraged by this she related the whole truth. And 'tis difficult to determine, if *Beauplaisir*, or the lady, were most surprised at what they heard; he, that he should have been blinded so often by her artifices; or she, that so young a creature should have the skill to make use of them. Both sat for some time in a profound reverie; till at length she broke it first in these words: Pardon, sir (*said she*),[9] the trouble I have given you: I must confess it was with a design to oblige you to repair the supposed injury you had done this unfortunate girl, by marrying her, but now I know not what to say:—The blame is wholly hers, and I have nothing to request further of you, than that you will not divulge the distracted folly she has been guilty of.—He answered her in terms perfectly polite; but made no offer of that which, perhaps, she expected, though could not, now informed of her daughter's proceedings, demand. He assured her, however, that if she would commit the newborn lady to his care, he would discharge it faithfully. But neither of them would consent to that; and he took his leave, full of cogitations,[1] more confused than ever he had known in his whole life. He continued to visit there, to inquire after her health every day; but the old lady perceiving there was nothing likely to ensue from these civilities, but, perhaps, a renewing of the crime, she entreated him to refrain; and as soon as her daughter was in a condition, sent her to a monastery in *France*, the abbess of which had been her particular friend. And thus ended an intrigue, which, considering the time it lasted, was as full of variety as any, perhaps, that many ages have produced.

Samuel Richardson

1689–1761

"From my earliest youth," Samuel Richardson once recalled, "I had a love of letter-writing." That love, coupled with his high achievements as a printer and his marked predilection for inculcating virtue, enabled him to reroute the course of fiction at a single stroke, with his first

9. I.e., the elder lady.

1. Anxious thoughts.

novel. *Pamela; or, Virtue Rewarded* (1740), was rapidly written and promptly published by a man who, now fifty years old, had never really intended to become an author at all. Nonetheless, he was drawing on a lifetime of epistolary experience, as he makes clear in his sole surviving autobiography—itself a long letter to his inquisitive Dutch translator. In his teens, Richardson explains, at the request of the "young women of taste and reading in the neighborhood," he composed "answers to their lovers' letters," and observed intently the conflicting emotions that his prose was to capture or conceal: "I have been directed to chide, and even repulse, when an offence was either taken or given, at the very time that the heart of the chider or repulser was open before me, overflowing with esteem and affection—and the fair repulser dreading to be taken at her word, directing *this* word, or *that* expression, to be softened or changed." A little later, during his arduous apprenticeship, Richardson found solace in his copious correspondence with "a gentlemen greatly my superior in degree, . . . a master of the epistolary style," from whom, he implies, he derived his most authentic and valuable education. Finally, years after he had established himself as one of London's most efficient and prosperous printers, Richardson received a commission from two publishers who "entreated me to write for them a little volume of letters, in a common style, on such subjects as might be of use to those country readers who were unable to indite [i.e., compose letters] for themselves. 'Will it be any harm,' said I, 'in a piece you want to be written so low, if we should instruct them how to think and act in common cases, as well as indite?' . . . I set about it, and in the progress of it, [wrote] two or three letters to instruct handsome girls" who worked as house servants "how to avoid the snares that might be laid against their virtue" by men of the household seeking to seduce them. "And hence," Richardson concludes, "sprung Pamela"—a servant who finds herself, at sixteen years old, beset by just such advances from her master Mr. B. and, in the novel that bears her name, writes up her ordeal in a series of letters and journals addressed to her anxious parents. What struck readers most about the novel's content was its double argument, familiar in outline but freshly dramatized: that virtue was of paramount importance for its own sake; but that if zealously sustained, it might yield impressive earthly rewards—even to the point of dissolving the barriers of class and wealth. What struck readers most about the novel's form was its intrinsic intensity: the way each letter slowed down time and heightened experience, as Richardson sought to capture complex emotional oscillations of the kind that he had first observed in those ardent, agitated "young women" years earlier. After *Pamela,* the epistolary mode dominated novel-writing for decades. Richardson, meanwhile, though still assiduous in his work as printer, wrote a sequel to *Pamela,* and two much longer novels, *Clarissa* (1747–48) and *Sir Charles Grandison* (1753–54), in which he continued to explore and expound the fictional method that, to his obvious delight, he had improbably invented.

from Pamela; or, Virtue Rewarded

Preface by the Editor[1]

If to *divert* and *entertain*, and at the same time to *instruct*, and *improve* the minds of the *youth* of *both sexes:*

If to inculcate *religion* and *morality* in so easy and agreeable a manner, as shall render them equally *delightful* and *profitable* to the *younger class* of readers, as well as worthy of the attention of persons of *maturer* years and understandings:

If to set forth in the most exemplary lights the *parental*, the *filial*, and the *social* duties, and that from *low* to *high* life:

1. Richardson, like Defoe, presents himself in his novels not as author but as editor of authentic manuscripts which have come into his hands. Richardson's pointed emphases have been retained (in italics) throughout the preface.

If to paint *vice* in its proper colors, to make it *deservedly odious*; and to set *virtue* in its own amiable light, to make it *truly lovely:*

If to draw characters *justly*, and to support them *equally:*

If to raise a distress from *natural* causes, and to excite compassion from *proper* motives:

If to teach the man of *fortune* how to *use* it; the man of *passion* how to *subdue* it; and the man of *intrigue*,[2] how, gracefully, and with honor to himself, to *reclaim:*[3]

If to give *practical* examples, worthy to be followed in the most *critical* and *affecting* cases, by the modest *virgin*, the chaste *bride*, and the obliging *wife:*

If to effect all these good ends, in so probable, so natural, so *lively* a manner, as shall engage the passions of every sensible[4] reader, and strongly interest them in the edifying story:

And all without raising a *single idea* throughout the whole, that shall shock the exactest purity, even in those tender instances where the exactest purity would be most apprehensive:

If these (embellished with a great variety of entertaining incidents) be laudable or worthy recommendations of any work, the editor of the following letters, which have their foundation in *truth* and *nature*, ventures to assert, that all these desirable ends are obtained in these sheets. And as he is therefore confident of the favorable reception which he boldly bespeaks for this little work, he thinks any further *preface* or *apology*[5] for it unnecessary, and rather for two reasons: First, because he can appeal from *his own* passions (which have been uncommonly *moved* in perusing these engaging scenes) to the passions of *everyone* who shall read them with the least attention; and, in the next place, because an *editor* may be reasonably supposed to judge with an impartiality which is rarely to be met with in an *author* towards his own works.

The Editor

[A Dreadful Trial][6]

My dear parents,

O let me take up my complaint, and say, never was poor creature so unhappy, and so barbarously used, as your Pamela! O my dear father and mother, my heart's just broke! I can neither write as I should do, nor let it alone, for to whom but you can I vent my griefs, and keep my poor heart from bursting! Wicked, wicked man! I have no patience left me! But yet, don't be frighted—for—I hope—I hope, I am honest! But if my head and my heart will let me, you shall hear all. Is there no constable nor headborough,[7] though, to take me out of his house? For I am sure I can safely swear the peace against him.[8] But, alas! he is greater than any constable, and is a Justice himself;[9] such a Justice, deliver me from! But God Almighty, I hope, in time, will right me! For he knows the innocence of my heart!

2. Amorous schemes and affairs.

3. Reform.

4. Sensitive; capable of "being easily or strongly affected" (Johnson's *Dictionary*).

5. Defense.

6. Mr. B., finding his attempts at seduction energetically defied, has promised Pamela that she may soon return to her parents; he now tries out a new tactic of attack. "I have been rallied [teased]," Richardson remarked, "on a warm [i.e. potentially erotic] scene or two in *Pamela*"; this is one of them. (For Henry Fielding's unsparing parody, see pages 2821–22).

7. "A subordinate constable" (Johnson's *Dictionary*); a parish officer.

8. I.e., have him restrained on the grounds that he has threatened bodily harm.

9. I.e., Mr. B. is himself a Justice of the Peace, possessing the highest legal authority within the parish.

John went your way in the morning, but I have been too much distracted to send by him;[1] and have seen nobody but Mrs. Jervis, and Rachel,[2] and one I hate to see. And indeed I hate now to see anybody. Strange things I have to tell you, that happened since last night, that good Mr. Jonathan's letter, and my master's harshness put me into such a fluster.[3] But I will no more *preambulate*.[4]

I went to Mrs. Jervis's chamber; and Oh! my dear father and mother, my wicked master had hid himself (base gentleman as he is!) in her closet,[5] where she has a few books, and chest of drawers, and such-like. I little suspected it, though I used, till this sad night, always to look into that closet, and another in the room, and under the bed, ever since the summer house trick,[6] but never found anything; and so I did not do it then, being fully resolved to be angry with Mrs. Jervis for what had happened in the day,7and so thought of nothing else.

I sat myself down on one side of the bed, and she on the other, and we began to undress ourselves; but she on that side next the wicked closet, that held the worst heart in the world. "So," said Mrs. Jervis, "you won't speak to me, Pamela! I find you are angry with me." "Why, Mrs. Jervis," said I, "so I am, a little; 'tis a folly to deny it. You see what I have suffered by your forcing me in to my master! And a gentlewoman of your years and experience must needs know that it was not fit for me to pretend to be anybody else for my own sake, nor with regard to my master."[7]

"But," said she, "who would have thought it would have turned out so?" "Aye," said I, little thinking who heard me, "Lucifer always is ready to promote his own work and workmen. You see, presently, what use he made of it, pretending not to know me, on purpose to be free with me. And when he took upon himself to know me, to quarrel with me, and use me hardly—and you too," said I, "to cry, 'Fie, fie, Pamela!,' cut me to the heart, for that encouraged him."

"Do you think, my dear, that I would encourage him? I never said so to you before, but since you force it from me, I must tell you, that ever since you consulted me, I have used my utmost endeavors to divert him from his wicked purposes, and he has promised fair; but, to say all in a word, he dotes upon you; and I begin to see it is not in his power to help it."

I luckily said nothing of the note from Mr. Jonathan; for I began to suspect all the world almost. But I said, to try Mrs. Jervis, "Well then, what would you have me do? You see he is for having me wait on Lady Davers now."[8]

"Well, I'll tell you freely, my dear Pamela," said she, "and I trust to your discretion to conceal what I say: my master has been often desiring me to put you upon asking him to let you stay."

1. John, Mr. B's footman, has earned Pamela's trust by carrying letters back and forth between her and her parents.
2. Rachel is a housemaid; Mrs. Jervis is Mr. B's housekeeper, supervisor of his household staff. Pamela at first found her sympathetic ("the best friend I have in the world"), and asked permission to sleep in her room for the sake of security. She has now begun to suspect, wrongly, that Mrs. Jervis is complicit in Mr. B's schemes.
3. Jonathan, a fellow servant, has sent Pamela a short note warning her that, despite her expectation of being allowed to return to her parents, Mr. B. has declared that "By G— I will have her!"
4. I.e., write this preface to the main narrative.
5. "A small room of privacy and retirement" (Johnson's *Dictionary*).
6. When Mr. B, cornering Pamela in his garden gazebo, for the first time forced a kiss upon her, and made clear his intention that she become his mistress.
7. Earlier in the day, after Pamela had changed into simple "homespun" garb in expectation of soon returning to her parents, Mr. B. failed to recognize her, and took her for some unknown and perhaps seducible local beauty. Perceiving his mistake, Mrs. Jervis took the opportunity to inveigle Pamela into yet another unwanted and uncomfortable encounter with her master.
8. In order to retain access to Pamela, Mr. B. has proposed that she become a servant in his sister's household, rather than return home to her parents.

"Yes," said I, "Mrs. Jervis, let me interrupt you. I will tell you why I could not think of that. It was not the pride of my heart, but the pride of my honesty.[9] For what must have been the case? Here my master has been very rude to me, once or twice; and you say he cannot help it, though he pretends to be sorry for it. Well, he has given me warning to leave my place, and uses me very harshly, mayhap to frighten me to his purposes, as he supposes I would be fond of staying (as indeed I should, if I could be safe; for I love you and all the house, and value him, if he would act as my master). Well then, as I know his designs, and that he owns he cannot help it, must I not have asked to stay, knowing he would attempt me again? For all you could assure me of, was, he would do nothing by *force;* so I, a poor weak girl, was to be left to my own strength, God knows! And was not this to allow him to tempt me, as one may say? and to encourage him to go on in his wicked devices? How then, Mrs. Jervis, could I ask or wish to stay?"

"You say well, my dear child," says she, "and you have a justness of thought above your years; and for all these confederations, and for what I have heard this day, after you run away (and I am glad you went as you did) I cannot persuade you to stay; and I shall be glad, which is what I never thought I could have said, that you was well at your father's; for if Lady Davers will entertain[1] you, she may as well have you from thence as here." "There's my good Mrs. Jervis!" said I. "God will bless you for your good counsel to a poor maiden that is hard beset. But pray what did he say," said I, "when I was gone?" "Why," said she, "he was very angry with you." "But he would hear it!"[2] said I. "I think it was a little bold, but then he provoked me to it. And had not my honesty been in the case, I would not by any means have been so saucy. Besides, Mrs. Jervis, consider, it was the truth: if he does not love to hear of the summer house and the dressing room,[3] why should he not be ashamed to continue in the same mind?" "But," said she, "when you had muttered this to yourself, you might have told him anything else."[4] "Well," said I, "I cannot tell a willful lie, and so there's an end of it. But I find you now give him up, and think there's danger in staying! Lord bless me, I wish I was well out of the house, though it was at the bottom of a wet ditch, on the wildest common in England!"

"Why," said she, "it signifies nothing to tell you all he said; but it was enough to make me fear you would not be so safe as I could wish; and upon my word, Pamela, I don't wonder he loves you; for, without flattery, you are a charming girl! And I never saw you look more lovely in my life than in that same new dress of yours. And then it was such a surprise upon us all! I believe truly, you owe some of your danger to the lovely appearance you made." "Then," said I, "I wish the clothes in the fire. I expected no effect from them, but if any, a quite contrary one.—Hush!" said I, "Mrs. Jervis, did you not hear something stir in the closet?" "No, silly girl," said she! "Your fears are always awake!" "But indeed," says I, "I think I heard something rustle!" "Maybe," says she, "the cat may be got there. But I hear nothing."

I was hush, but she said, "Prithee, my good girl, make haste to bed. See if the door be fast." So I did, and was thinking to look in the closet. But hearing no more noise, thought it needless, and so went again and sat myself down on the bedside, and went on undressing myself. And Mrs. Jervis, being by this time undressed, stepped into bed, and bid me hasten, for she was sleepy.

9. Chastity.
1. Employ.
2. I.e., he created a situation in which he was forced to listen to my refusal.
3. Another site of Mr. B's recent attempts.
4. I.e., you ought not have confronted him so directly.

I don't know what was the matter; but my heart sadly misgave me; but Mr. Jonathan's note was enough to make it do so, with what Mrs. Jervis had said. I pulled off my stays,[5] and my stockens, and my gown, all to an under-petticoat, and then hearing a rustling again in the closet, I said, "God protect us! but before I say my prayers I must look into this closet." And so was going to it slipshod,[6] when—O dreadful!—out rushed my master, in a rich silk and silver morning gown.[7]

I screamed, and run to the bed; and Mrs. Jervis screamed too; and he said, "I'll do you no harm, if you forbear this noise; but otherwise take what follows."

Instantly he came to the bed; for I had crept into it, to Mrs. Jervis, with my coat on, and my shoes. And taking me in his arms, said, "Mrs. Jervis, rise, and just step upstairs, to keep the maids from coming down at this noise. I'll do no harm to this rebel."

"O, for God's sake! for pity's sake! Mrs. Jervis," said I, "if I am not betrayed, don't leave me; and I beseech you, raise[8] all the house." "No," said Mrs. Jervis, "I will not stir, my dear lamb; I will not leave you. I wonder at you, Sir," said she, and kindly threw herself upon my coat, clasping me round the waist. "You shall not hurt this innocent," said she, "for I will lose my life in her defense. Are there not," said she, "enough wicked ones in the world, for your base purpose, but you must attempt such a lamb as this!"

He was desperate angry, and threatened to throw her out of the window, and to turn her out of the house the next morning. "You need not, sir," said she, "for I will not stay in it. God defend my poor Pamela till tomorrow, and we will both go together." Says he, "Let me but expostulate a word or two with you, Pamela." "Pray, Pamela," said Mrs. Jervis, "don't hear a word, except[9] he leaves the bed, and goes to the other end of the room." "Aye, out of the room!" said I. "Expostulate tomorrow, if you must expostulate!"

I found his hand in my bosom, and when my fright let me know it, I was ready to die; and I sighed, and screamed, and fainted away. And still he had his arms about my neck; and Mrs. Jervis was about my feet, and upon my coat. And all in a cold, clammy sweat was I. "Pamela, Pamela!" said Mrs. Jervis, as she tells me since. "O—h"—and gave another shriek—"my Pamela is dead for certain!" And so, to be sure, I was for a time; for I knew nothing more of the matter, one fit following another, till about three hours after, as it proved to be, I found myself in bed, and Mrs. Jervis sitting up one side, with her wrapper about her, and Rachel on the other, and no master, for the wicked wretch was gone. But I was so overjoyed that I hardly could believe myself; and I said, which were my first words, "Mrs. Jervis, Mrs. Rachel, can I be sure it is you? God be praised! God be praised! Where have I been?" "Hush, my dear," said Mrs. Jervis. "You have been in fit after fit. I never saw anybody so frightful in my life!"

By this I judged Mrs. Rachel knew nothing of the matter; and it seems my wicked master had, upon Mrs. Jervis's second noise on my going away, slipped out, and, as if he had come from his own chamber, disturbed by the screaming, went up to the maids' room (who, hearing the noise, lay trembling, and afraid to stir) and bid them go down and see what was the matter with Mrs. Jervis and me. And he charged Mrs. Jervis, and promised to forgive her for what she had said and done, if she would

5. Corset; stiff undergarment.
6. Wearing slippers.
7. "A loose gown worn before one is formally dressed" (Johnson's *Dictionary*).
8. Wake.
9. Unless.

conceal the matter. So the maids came down; for the men lie in the outhouses;[1] and all went up again, when I came to myself a little, except Rachel, who stayed to sit up with me, and bear Mrs. Jervis company. I believe they all guess the matter to be bad enough, though they dare not say anything.

When I think of my danger, and the freedoms he actually took, though I believe Mrs. Jervis saved me from worse, and she says she did (though what can I think, who was in a fit, and know nothing of the matter?), I am almost distracted.[2]

At first I was afraid of Mrs. Jervis; but I am fully satisfied she is very good, and I should have been lost but for her; and she takes on grievously about it. What would have become of me, had she gone out of the room, to still the maids, as he bid her? He'd certainly have shut her out, and then, Mercy on me! what would have become of your poor Pamela!

I must leave off a little, for my eyes and my head are sadly bad.—O this was a dreadful trial! This was the worst of all! God send me safe from this dreadful wicked man! Pray for

For an additional selection from *Pamela*, see *The Longman Anthology of British Literature* Web site at www.myliteraturekit.com.

Your distressed daughter.

from *The Preface to* Clarissa. Or, The History of a Young Lady[1]

* * * All the letters are written while the hearts of the writers must be supposed to be wholly engaged in their subjects (the events at the time generally dubious);[2] so that they abound not only with critical situations, but with what may be called *instantaneous* descriptions and reflections (proper to be brought home to the breast of the youthful reader); as also with affecting conversations, many of them written in the dialogue or dramatic way. "Much more lively and affecting," says one of the principal characters,[3] "must be the style of those who write in the height of *present* distress; the mind tortured by the pangs of uncertainty (the events then hidden in the womb of Fate); than the dry, narrative, unanimated style of a person relating difficulties and dangers surmounted can be; the relater perfectly at ease; and if himself unmoved by his own story, not likely greatly to affect the reader." * * *

1747

from *The Preface to* The History of Sir Charles Grandison, Baronet[4]

* * * The nature of familiar letters, written, as it were, to the *moment*, while the heart is agitated by hopes and fears, on events undecided, must plead an excuse for the *bulk* of a collection of this kind.[5] Mere facts and characters might be comprised in a much smaller compass: but, would they be equally interesting? It happens fortunately, that an account of the juvenile years of the principal person is narratively

1. Buildings located elsewhere on the estate.
2. Driven mad.

1. In the prefaces to all three of his novels, Richardson defended the morality of his writing. In his prefaces to the last two, he celebrated the method also: the power of the epistolary mode.
2. I.e., the outcome being doubtful.
3. Richardson quotes his fictional creation John Belford, friend and aid to the novel's villain Robert Lovelace. Like Mr. B. before him, Belford takes pleasure in reading the letters of the suffering protagonist.
4. Earlier in the preface, Richardson has declared the new topic of his third novel: "the character and actions of a man of true honor."
5. In its original, multivolume editions, *Grandison* ran about 2,400 pages.

given in some of the letters. As many, however, as could be spared, have been omitted. There is not one episode in the whole; nor, after Sir CHARLES GRANDISON is introduced, one letter inserted, but what tends to illustrate the principal design. Those which precede his introduction, will not, it is hoped, be judged unnecessary on the whole, as they tend to make the reader acquainted with persons, the history of whom is closely interwoven with that of Sir Charles.

1753

Henry Fielding

1707–1754

Richardson's *Pamela; or, Virtue Rewarded* prompted a huge response, ranging from praise to parody. Eliza Haywood authored the *Anti-Pamela; or, Feigned Innocence Detected* (1741), which makes good on its title by tracing the adventures of its heroine, the decidedly unchaste Syrena Tricksy, who pursues by sexual manipulation the ascent in wealth and standing that Richardson's Pamela attains by virtue alone. Syrena's lascivious exploits constitute Haywood's farewell to the amorous, sensual fiction she had so profitably pioneered. Like many other novelists, she soon veered in Richardson's overtly moralistic direction, first in the short fictions of *The Female Spectator*, and then in her last novels.

For Henry Fielding, by contrast, parody of *Pamela* produced a fresh start, from which followed his life's most lasting work. Fielding's fame had long preceded Richardson's; he had spent the 1730s as a prolific and celebrated satiric playwright, until strict new measures of censorship proscribed him from the playhouse, and prompted him to search for something new. In *Shamela*, his first foray into fiction, Fielding compresses a Haywood-like exposé into his heroine's very name: she is a sham—libidinous, cunning, and shameless—from start to finish. But in the long title of his short parody—*An Apology for the Life of Mrs. Shamela Andrews*—Fielding widens his satiric scope. He echoes the rubric of *An Apology for the Life of Colley Cibber*, the autobiography of a widely known actor, which had appeared in the same year as *Pamela*, and which had appalled Fielding, among others, for its loquacity, seeming shapelessness, and shameless vanity; no actor hitherto had seen fit to recount at such length what was still deemed an intrinsically low career.

In *Shamela*, then, Fielding mocks not only the most influential novel of the century, but also the tradition of autobiography—copiously particularized, inherently self-centered—which had shadowed the whole genre, like a sometimes indistinguishable twin, from its inception. In *Joseph Andrews*, his first full-length novel, Fielding took *Shamela*'s key jokes further, but also much deeper. As target, Cibber remains much in view, and the titular Joseph Andrews, brother to Richardson's Pamela, undergoes a gendered inversion of her predicament; he is beset by his *female* employer, the lustful Lady Booby (sister to Richardson's more discreetly named Mr. B.). But in *Joseph Andrews*, and more expansively in his next novel *Tom Jones*, Fielding pushes past the straightforward reversals of parody to declare himself "the founder of a new province of writing," whose newness consisted partly in a theory of the "ridiculous" at once mocking and humane; partly in the Quixote-like mix of innocence and ineptitude variously and endearingly embodied in his fiction's central characters; but especially in the foregrounding of a component largely excluded from Richardson's fiction: the voice of an omnipresent and observant author, who views his characters, and addresses his readers, with an ironic acuity designed to enhance audience access to those two abiding desiderata of eighteenth-century literature, instruction and delight.

from An Apology for the Life of Mrs. Shamela Andrews[1]

Shamela Andrews to Henrietta Maria Honora Andrews

O Madam, I have strange things to tell you! As I was reading in that charming book about the dealings,[2] in comes my master—to be sure he is a precious one. Pamela, says he, what book is that, I warrant you Rochester's poems.[3]—No, forsooth, says I, as pertly as I could. Why how now saucy chops, boldface, says he—Mighty pretty words, says I, pert again.—Yes (says he) you are a d—d, impudent, stinking, cursed, confounded jade, and I have a great mind to kick your a—. You, kiss— says I. A—gad,[4] says, he, and so I will; with that he caught me in his arms, and kissed me till he made my face all over fire. Now this served purely, you know, to put upon the fool for anger.[5] O! What precious fools men are! And so I flung from him in a mighty rage, and pretended as how I would go out at the door; but when I came to the end of the room, I stood still, and my master cried out, Hussy, slut, saucebox, boldface, come hither.—Yes to be sure, says I. Why don't you come, says he. What should I come for, says I. If you don't come to me, I'll come to you, says he. I shan't come to you I assure you, says I. Upon which he run up, caught me in his arms, and flung me upon a chair, and began to offer to touch my underpetticoat. Sir, says I, you had better not offer to be rude. Well, says he, no more I won't then; and away he went out of the room. I was so mad to be sure I could have cried.

Oh what a prodigious vexation it is to a woman to be made a fool of.

Mrs. Jervis, who had been without, harkening, now came to me. She burst into a violent laugh the moment she came in. Well, says she, as soon as she could speak, I have reason to bless myself that I am an old woman. Ah, child! If you had known the jolly blades of my age, you would not have been left in the lurch in this manner. Dear Mrs. Jervis, says I, don't laugh at one; and to be sure I was a little angry with her.—Come, says she, my dear honeysuckle, I have one game to play for you; he shall see you in bed; he shall, my little rosebud, he shall see those pretty, little, white, round, panting——; and offered to pull off my handkerchief. —Fie, Mrs. Jervis, says I, you make me blush, and upon my fackins,[6] I believe she did. She went on thus: I know the squire likes you, and notwithstanding the awkwardness of his proceeding, I am convinced hath some hot blood in his veins, which will not let him rest, 'till he hath communicated some of his warmth to thee, my little angel. I heard him last night at our door, trying if it was open. Now tonight I will take care it shall be so; I warrant that he makes the second trial; which if he doth, he shall find us ready to receive him. I will at first counterfeit sleep, and after a swoon; so that he will have you naked in his possession: and then if you are disappointed, a plague of all young squires, say I.—And so, Mrs. Jervis, says I, you would have me yield myself to him, would you; you would have me be a second time a fool for nothing.[7] Thank

1. Letter 6. The multiple names of Shamela's mother suggest pretensions to which the parents in *Pamela* (plain John and Elizabeth Andrews) would never aspire. Fielding's letter closely tracks, and mocks, the nighttime alarms narrated in *Pamela*'s letter 25, above (pages 2815–19).
2. The book that Shamela has just received from her mother: *A Short Account of God's Dealings with the Reverend Mr. George Whitefield, from his Infancy, to the Time of his Entering into Holy Orders* (174), written by Whitefield himself (1714–1770), a prominent Methodist preacher whose autobiographical writings prompted widespread charges of sinful pride and rampant egomania. In counting Shamela and her mother among Whitefield's enthusiastic readers, Fielding sustains his attack on self-indulgent self-inscribers, for which his chief target, throughout *Shamela* and *Joseph Andrews*, is the secular autobiography of the actor Colley Cibber.
3. John Wilmot, Earl of Rochester (1647–1680), notorious for the obscenity of his verse (see pages 2202–13).
4. By God
5. I.e., deceive him into thinking I was angry.
6. By my faith.
7. Shamela alludes to her first liaison, with the sexually skillful but penniless Parson Williams, with whom she has had an illegitimate child. In Richardson's novel, Williams is a virtuous but at times ineffectual clergyman, who tries hard to provide Pamela with practical and spiritual succor; in Fielding's parody, he is a seductive rascal.

you for that, Mrs. Jervis. For nothing! Marry forbid, says she, you know he hath large sums of money, besides abundance of fine things; and do you think, when you have inflamed him, by giving his hand a liberty with that charming person; and that you know he may easily think he obtains against your will, he will not give anything to come at all?[8] —This will not do, Mrs. Jervis, answered I. I have heard my Mamma say (and you know, Madam, I have) that in her youth, fellows have often taken away in the morning what they gave overnight. No, Mrs. Jervis, nothing under a regular taking into keeping, a settled settlement,[9] for me, and all my heirs, all my whole lifetime, shall do the business—or else cross-legged, is the word, faith, with Sham; and then I snapped my fingers.

Thursday night, twelve o'clock

Mrs. Jervis and I are just in bed, and the door unlocked; if my master should come—odsbobs![1] I hear him just come in at the door. You see I write in the present tense, as Parson Williams says.[2] Well, he is in bed between us, we both shamming a sleep, he steals his hand into my bosom, which I, as if in my sleep, press close to me with mine, and then pretend to awake.—I no sooner see him, but I scream out to Mrs. Jervis, she feigns likewise but just to come to herself; we both begin, she to becall, and I to bescratch very liberally. After having made a pretty free use of my fingers, without any great regard to the parts I attacked, I counterfeit a swoon. Mrs. Jervis then cries out, Oh, Sir, what have you done, you have murdered poor Pamela: she is gone, she is gone.—

Oh what a difficulty it is to keep one's countenance, when a violent laugh desires to burst forth.

The poor booby, frightened out of his wits, jumped out of bed, and, in his shirt,[3] sat down by my bedside, pale and trembling, for the moon shone, and I kept my eyes wide open and pretended to fix them in my head. Mrs. Jervis applied lavender water and hartshorn,[4] and this, for a full half hour; when, thinking I had carried it on long enough, and being likewise unable to continue the sport any longer, I began by degrees to come to myself.

The squire, who had sat all this while speechless, and was almost really in that condition which I feigned, the moment he saw me give symptoms of recovering my senses, fell down on his knees; and Oh Pamela, cried he, can you forgive me, my injured maid? By heaven, I know not whether you are a man or a woman, unless by your swelling breasts. Will you promise to forgive me? I forgive you! D—n you (says I) and d—n you, says he, if you come to that. I wish I had never seen your bold face, saucy sow, and so went out of the room.

Oh what a silly fellow is a bashful young lover!

He was no sooner out of hearing, as we thought, than we both burst into a violent laugh. Well, says Mrs. Jervis, I never saw anything better acted than your part: but I wish you may not have discouraged him from any future attempt; especially since his passions are so cool, that you could prevent his hands going further than your bosom. Hang him, answered I, he is not quite so cold as that I assure you; our hands, on neither side, were idle in the scuffle, nor have left us any doubt of each other as to that matter.

8. I.e., to take full possession of you.
9. I.e., Shamela will not consent to consummation until she is offered full status as a "kept" mistress, with a legal contract spelling out payments and compensations.
1. A compression of "Ods bodkins": [by] God's little body!
2. Fielding echoes, and mocks, Richardson's doctrine of writing "to the *moment*" (see page 2819).
3. Nightshirt.
4. An herb used (like the lavender water) as a smelling salt.

Friday Morning

My master sent for Mrs. Jervis, as soon as he was up, and bid her give an account of the plate and linen in her care; and told her, he was resolved that both she and the little gipsy (I'll assure him[5]) should set out together. Mrs. Jervis made him a saucy answer; which any servant of spirit, you know, would, though it should be one's ruin; and came immediately in tears to me, crying, she had lost her place on my account, and that she should be forced to take to a house,[6] as I mentioned before; and that she hoped I would, at least, make her all the amends in my power, for her loss on my account, and come to her house whenever I was sent for. Never fear, says I, I'll warrant we are not so near being turned away as you imagine; and, i'cod,[7] now it comes into my head, I have a fetch[8] for him, and you shall assist me in it. But it being now late, and my letter pretty long, no more at present from

Your dutiful daughter,
SHAMELA

1741 1741

from *The Preface to* The History of the Adventures of Joseph Andrews

As it is possible the mere *English* reader may have a different idea of romance[1] with the author of these volumes; and may consequently expect a kind of entertainment not to be found, nor which was even intended, in the following pages; it may not be improper to premise a few words concerning this kind of writing, which I do not remember to have seen hitherto attempted in our language.

The *epic* as well as the *drama* is divided into tragedy and comedy. *Homer*, who was the father of this species of poetry, gave us a pattern of both these, though that of the latter is entirely lost; which *Aristotle* tells us, bore the same relation to comedy which his *Iliad* bears to tragedy.[2] And perhaps, that we have no more instances of it among the writers of antiquity, is owing to the loss of this great pattern, which, had it survived, would have found its imitators equally with the other poems of this great original.

And farther, as this poetry may be tragic or comic, I will not scruple to say it may be likewise either in verse or prose: for though it wants one particular, which the critic enumerates in the constituent parts of an epic poem, namely meter; yet, when any kind of writing contains all its other parts, such as fable, action, characters, sentiments, and diction, and is deficient in meter only; it seems, I think, reasonable to refer to the epic; at least, as no critic hath thought proper to range it under any other head, nor assign it a particular name to itself * * *

Now a comic romance is a comic epic-poem in prose; differing from comedy, as the serious epic from tragedy; its action being more extended and comprehensive; containing a much larger circle of incidents, and introducing a greater variety of characters. It differs from the serious romance in its fable and action, in this: that as in the one these are grave and solemn, so in the other they are light and ridiculous.

5. I.e., "as he dares to call me (and as I am in fact)."
6. I.e., a brothel. Mrs. Jervis is eager to set up in the business, and Shamela's mother has offered to help.
7. By God.
8. Trick.
1. The word's meaning varied widely in the eighteenth century. Johnson's *Dictionary* offers these definitions: "A tale of wild adventures in war and love; . . . a lie; a fiction." For Johnson's own ideas on the much-discussed question of romance's relation to newer modes of fiction, see his Ramber No. 4 (pages 2688–91); for Clara Reeve's lapidary contrast between the two terms, see page 2791.
2. Aristotle (*Poetics*, 4.10–12) mentions a burlesque called *Margites* ("madman") of which only a small fragment now survives; the claim for Homeric authorship is unsubstantiated.

It differs in its characters by introducing persons of inferior rank, and consequently of inferior manners, whereas the grave romance sets the highest before us; lastly in its sentiments and diction, by preserving the ludicrous instead of the sublime. In the diction I think burlesque itself may be sometimes admitted; of which many instances will occur in this work, as in the descriptions of the battles, and some other places, not necessary to be pointed out to the classical reader; for whose entertainment those parodies or burlesque imitations are chiefly calculated.

But though we have sometimes admitted this in our diction, we have carefully excluded it from our sentiments and characters. For there it is never properly introduced, unless in writings of the burlesque kind, which this is not intended to be. Indeed, no two species of writing can differ more widely than the comic and the burlesque: for as the latter is ever the exhibition of what is monstrous and unnatural, and where our delight, if we examine it, arises from the surprising absurdity, as in appropriating the manners of the highest to the lowest, or *é converso*;[3] so in the former, we should ever confine ourselves strictly to nature, from the just imitation of which will flow all the pleasure we can this way convey to a sensible reader. And perhaps, there is one reason why a comic writer should of all others be the least excused for deviating from nature, since it may not be always so easy for a serious poet to meet with the great and the admirable; but life everywhere furnishes an accurate observer with the ridiculous * * *[4]

But to return: the ridiculous only, as I have before said, falls within my province in the present work. Nor will some explanation of this word be thought impertinent by the reader, if he considers how wonderfully it hath been mistaken, even by writers who have professed it. For to what but such a mistake can we attribute the many attempts to ridicule the blackest villainies; and what is yet worse, the most dreadful calamities? What could exceed the absurdity of an author who should write the *Comedy of Nero* with the merry incident of ripping up his mother's belly?[5] Or what would give a greater shock to humanity than an attempt to expose the miseries of poverty and distress to ridicule? And yet, the reader will not want much learning to suggest such instances to himself.

Besides, it may seem remarkable that Aristotle, who is so fond and free of definitions, hath not thought proper to define the ridiculous. Indeed, where he tells us it is proper to comedy, he hath remarked that villainy is not its object;[6] but he hath not, as I remember, positively asserted what is. Nor doth the Abbé Bellegarde, who hath writ a treatise on this subject,[7] though he shows us many species of it, once trace it to its fountain.

The only source of the true ridiculous (as it appears to me) is affectation. But though it arises from one spring only, when we consider the infinite streams into which this one branches, we shall presently cease to admire[8] at the copious field it affords to an observer. Now affectation proceeds from one of these two causes, vanity or hypocrisy: for as vanity puts us on affecting false characters, in order to purchase applause; so hypocrisy sets us on an endeavor to avoid censure by concealing our vices under an appearance of their opposite virtues. And though these two causes

3. *Vice versa*.
4. In the section omitted here, Fielding analyzes the workings of burlesque.
5. When the Roman emperor Nero (37–68 C.E.) commanded that his mother be killed, she urged her executioner to stab her in the womb that had given birth to her matricidal son.
6. *Poetics*, 5.1–2.
7. Jean Baptiste Morvan de Bellegarde, *Reflexions sur le ridicule* (*Reflections on the Ridiculous*, 1696).
8. Marvel.

are often confounded (for they require some difficulty in distinguishing), yet, as they proceed from very different motives, so they are as clearly distinct in their operations: for indeed, the affectation which arises from vanity is nearer to truth than the other; as it hath not that violent repugnancy of nature to struggle with, which that of the hypocrite hath. It may be likewise noted that affectation doth not imply an absolute negation of those qualities which are affected: and therefore, though, when it proceeds from hypocrisy, it be nearly allied to deceit; yet when it comes from vanity only, it partakes of the nature of ostentation. For instance, the affectation of liberality in a vain man differs visibly from the same affectation in the avaricious; for though the vain man is not what he would appear, or hath not the virtue he affects, to the degree he would be thought to have it; yet it sits less awkwardly on him than on the avaricious man, who is the very reverse of what he would seem to be.

From the discovery of this affectation arises the ridiculous—which always strikes the reader with surprise and pleasure; and that in a higher and stronger degree when the affectation arises from hypocrisy, than when from vanity. For to discover any one to be the exact reverse of what he affects is more surprising, and consequently more ridiculous, than to find him a little deficient in the quality he desires the reputation of. I might observe that our Ben Jonson,[9] who of all men understood the ridiculous the best, hath chiefly used the hypocritical affectation.

Now from affectation only, the misfortunes and calamities of life, or the imperfections of nature, may become the objects of ridicule. Surely he hath a very ill-framed mind who can look on ugliness, infirmity, or poverty as ridiculous in themselves: nor do I believe any man living who meets a dirty fellow riding through the streets in a cart is struck with an idea of the ridiculous from it; but if he should see the same figure descend from his coach and six, or bolt from his chair[1] with his hat under his arm, he would then begin to laugh, and with justice. In the same manner, were we to enter a poor house, and behold a wretched family shivering with cold and languishing with hunger, it would not incline us to laughter (at least we must have very diabolical natures if it would), but should we discover there a grate, instead of coals, adorned with flowers, empty plate or china dishes on the side-board, or any other affectation of riches and finery either on their persons or in their furniture; we might then indeed be excused for ridiculing so fantastic an appearance. Much less are natural imperfections the objects of derision: but when ugliness aims at the applause of beauty, or lameness endeavors to display agility, it is then that these unfortunate circumstances, which at first moved our compassion, tend only to raise our mirth.

The poet carries this very far:

> *None are for being what they are in fault,*
> *But for not being what they would be thought.*[2]

Where if the meter would suffer the word *ridiculous* to close the first line, the thought would be rather more proper. Great vices are the proper objects of our detestation, smaller faults of our pity: but affectation appears to me the only true source of the ridiculous.

But perhaps it may be objected to me that I have against my own rules introduced vices, and of a very black kind into this work. To which I shall answer: first,

9. Poet and playwright (1573?–1637).
1. I.e., a sedan chair, carried through the streets: a comparatively luxurious mode of London transportation.
2. William Congreve (1670–1729), from "Of Pleasing: An Epistle to Sir Richard Temple."

that it is very difficult to pursue a series of human actions and keep clear from them. Secondly, that the vices to be found here are rather the accidental consequences of some human frailty, or foible, than causes habitually existing in the mind. Thirdly, that they are never set forth as the objects of ridicule but detestation. Fourthly, that they are never the principal figure at that time on the scene; and lastly, they never produce the intended evil.

Having thus distinguished *Joseph Andrews* from the productions of romance writers on the one hand, and burlesque writers on the other, and given some few very short hints (for I intended no more) of this species of writing, which I have affirmed to be hitherto unattempted in our language: I shall leave to my good-natured reader to apply my piece to my observations, and will detain him no longer than with a word concerning the characters in this work.

And here I solemnly protest I have no intention to vilify or asperse anyone: for though everything is copied from the book of nature, and scarce a character or action produced which I have not taken from my own observations and experience, yet I have used the utmost care to obscure the persons by such different circumstances, degrees, and colors, that it will be impossible to guess at them with any degree of certainty; and if it ever happens otherwise, it is only where the failure characterized is so minute that is a foible only which the party himself may laugh at as well as any other.

As to the character of *Adams*,[3] as it is the most glaring in the whole, so I conceive it is not to be found in any book now extant. It is designed a character for perfect simplicity; and as the goodness of his heart will recommend him to the good-natured; so I hope it will excuse me to the gentlemen of his cloth; for whom, while they are worthy of their sacred order, no man can possibly have a greater respect. They will therefore excuse me, notwithstanding the low adventures in which he is engaged, that I have made him a clergyman; since no other office could have given him so many opportunities of displaying his worthy inclinations.

1741–1742 1742

from The History of Tom Jones, a Foundling[1]

Showing What Kind of a History This Is; What It Is Like, and What It Is Not Like.[2]

Though we have a properly enough entitled this our work, a History, and not a Life;[3] nor an Apology for a Life,[4] as is more in fashion; yet we intend in it rather to pursue the method of those writers who profess to disclose the revolutions of countries than

3. Parson Abraham Adams, Joseph's benevolent, beleaguered, deeply lovable mentor and companion, and Fielding's first great comic creation.

1. The title of Fielding's second novel compasses some of its comedy. A "foundling" is a bastard child; "Tom Jones" is as plain a name as English affords. Such creatures were not deemed worthy of a "history," and the novel's comedy consists partly in the incongruity, and the mesh, between the grandeur of its design and language, and the lowliness of its generous, bumbling, often estimable hero's origins and predicaments.

2. Book 2, Chapter 1. *Tom Jones* includes 18 prefatory essays, one for each of the multichaptered "books" into which Fielding divides his long narrative. The 18th century was much in love with prefaces, but Fielding took the genre to a new pinnacle of critical and comic artistry. He makes it the means for imparting his opinions, his ambitions, and his affections, both for the protagonists who people his narrative and the readers who engage with it. In this, the second of the 18, he takes pains to explain to his readers just how he has structured his book to serve, and sustain, their interests.

3. I.e., an ordinary biography.

4. This is another of Fielding's many satiric slaps at the actor whose garrulous, digressive, self-congratulatory autobiography, *An Apology for the Life of Mr. Colley Cibber, Comedian* (1740), provided a paradigm, for Fielding and other mockers, of everything a book should not be.

to imitate the painful and voluminous historian, who, to preserve the regularity of his series, thinks himself obliged to fill up as much paper with the detail of months and years in which nothing remarkable happened, as he employs upon those notable eras when the greatest scenes have been transacted on the human stage.

Such histories as these do, in reality, very much resemble a newspaper, which consists of just the same number of words, whether there be any news in it or not. They may likewise be compared to a stagecoach, which performs constantly the same course, empty as well as full. The writer, indeed, seems to think himself obliged to keep even pace with time, whose amanuensis he is; and, like his master, travels as slowly through centuries of monkish dullness, when the world seems to have been asleep, as through that bright and busy age so nobly distinguished by the excellent Latin poet.[5]

Ad confligendum venientibus undique paenis;
Omnia cum belli trepido concussa tumultu
Horrida contremeuere sub altis aetheris auris:
In dubisque fait sub utrorum regna cadendum
Ominibus humanis esset, terraque marique.

Of which we wish we could give our reader more adequate translation than that by Mr. Creech:[6]

When dreadful Carthage frighted Rome with arms,[7]
And all the world was shook with fierce alarms;
Whilst undecided yet, which part should fall,
Which nation rise the glorious lord of all.

Now it is our purpose in the ensuing pages to pursue a contrary method. When any extraordinary scene presents itself (as we trust will often be the case) we shall spare no pains nor paper to open it at large to our reader; but if whole years should pass without producing anything worthy his notice, we shall not be afraid of a chasm in our history; but shall hasten on to matters of consequence, and leave such periods of time totally unobserved.

These are indeed to be considered as blanks[8] in the grand lottery of time. We therefore who are the registers of that lottery, shall imitate those sagacious persons who deal in that which is drawn at Guildhall, and who never trouble the public with the many blanks they dispose of;[9] but when a great prize happens to be drawn, the newspapers are presently filled with it, and the world is sure to be informed at whose office it was sold: indeed, commonly two or three different offices lay claim to the honor of having disposed of it; by which, I suppose, the adventurers[1] are given to understand that certain brokers are in the secrets of Fortune, and indeed of her cabinet council.

5. Lucretius, *De Rerum Natura (On the Nature of Things)*, 3.833–7.
6. Thomas Creech (1659–1700), classical scholar whose translation of the reputedly "atheistic" Lucretius caused a sensation on its first appearance (1682) and remained current for well over half a century.
7. I.e., during the Punic Wars (third century B.C.E.), when Roman dominance in the Mediterranean was threatened by the possibility of Carthaginian conquest.
8. Worthless tickets.
9. Guildhall was in effect the city hall of London, and the site of lottery drawings; Fielding's point is that the ticket sellers, in order to sustain their customers' hopes and their own income, never speak of all the "blanks" they profit by.
1. Risk-takers; gamblers.

My reader then is not to be surprised if, in the course of this work, he shall find some chapters very short, and others altogether as long; some that contain only the time of a single day, and others that comprise years; in a word, if my history sometimes seems to stand still, and sometimes to fly. For all which I shall not look on myself as accountable to any court of critical jurisdiction whatever: for as I am, in reality, the founder of a new province of writing, so I am at liberty to make what laws I please therein. And these laws, my readers, whom I consider as my subjects, are bound to believe in and to obey; with which that they may readily and cheerfully comply, I do hereby assure them that I shall principally regard their ease and advantage in all such institutions: for I do not, like a *jure divino* tyrant,[2] imagine they are my slaves, or my commodity.[3] I am, indeed, set over them for their own good only, and was created for their use, and not they for mine. Nor do I doubt, while I make their interest the great rule of my writings, they will unanimously concur in supporting my dignity, and in rendering me all the honor I shall deserve or desire.

For an additional chapter from *Tom Jones*, go to *The Longman Anthology of British Literature* Web site at www.myliteraturekit.com.

Laurence Sterne

1713–1768

Unlike Richardson and Fielding, the Yorkshire parson and proud eccentric Laurence Sterne commenced his masterpiece, *The Life and Opinions of Tristram Shandy, Gentleman*, without so much as a paragraph of preface. Instead he plunged right into the opening chapter with an emphatic "I wish." For *Tristram*'s earliest readers, this abruptness would have been only the first, and maybe the mildest, of the innumerable astonishments to follow, in a novel that unfolded in two-volume increments published at irregular intervals throughout the ensuing decade, and that displayed so odd and elusive a narrative shape that critics have debated for centuries whether, in the final volume (published shortly before the author's death) Sterne actually completed the work, or simply meant to keep it going. No text of the period presented itself so insistently, on every page, as new and strange; the narrative simply revels in its seeming discontinuities, with its predecessors and with itself. Yet, just as the ubiquitous dashes that split Sterne's prose into tiny fragments conceal the integrities of his phenomenally well-made sentences, the novel itself traffics slyly in continuities too. From favorite writers, Sterne absorbed favored tactics: Rabelais's antic obscenity and copious scope; Montaigne's acutely particularized self-scrutiny; Cervantes's ironies; Quixote's sweetness; Swift's satiric debunking of specious learning. From the novel's two most pressing precedents, Richardson and Fielding, Sterne devised a combinatorial game that percolates through his text as a playful question. What if an autobiographer were to pursue Fielding's objectives—an ongoing, thought-rich, conversational colloquy with the reader—by Richardson's means, exponentially intensified: a practice of writing "to the moment" so thorough, and so insistent, that it seeks to encompass literally all the agitations (distractions, digressions, preoccupations, puzzlements) *of* the

2. An oppressor who rules by assertion of divine right; Fielding here strikes a glancing blow at the Jacobites, who held that their leader Charles Stuart (1720–1788) possessed such a claim to the throne, and who had recently been decisively defeated at the Battle of Culloden (1746).

3. "Wares; merchandise; goods for traffic" (Johnson's *Dictionary*).

moment, including those entailed by the act of writing itself? In such a case, the autobiographer might find that his *Opinions* so define his *Life*, but at the same time intrude so emphatically on his narration, that he might need, say, four volumes and two years simply (or intricately) to recount the day of his birth. In *Tristram Shandy*, he does.

from The Life and Opinions of Tristram Shandy, Gentleman

[INTERRUPTIONS[1]]

I wish either my father or my mother, or indeed both of them, as they were in duty both equally bound to it, had minded what they were about when they begot me; had they duly considered how much depended upon what they were then doing;—that not only the production of a rational Being was concerned in it, but that possibly the happy formation and temperature of his body, perhaps his genius and the very cast of his mind;—and, for aught they knew to the contrary, even the fortunes of his whole house might take their turn from the humors and dispositions which were then uppermost:[2]—Had they duly weighed and considered all this, and proceeded accordingly,—I am verily persuaded I should have made a quite different figure in the world, from that, in which the reader is likely to see me.——Believe me, good folks, this is not so inconsiderable a thing as many of you may think it;——you have all, I dare say, heard of the animal spirits,[3] as how they are transfused from father to son, &c. &c.——and a great deal to that purpose:——Well, you may take my word, that nine parts in ten of a man's sense or his nonsense, his successes and miscarriages in this world depend upon their motions and activity, and the different tracks and trains you put them into, so that when they are once set a-going, whether right or wrong, 'tis not a halfpenny matter,[4]—away they go cluttering like hey-go mad; and by treading the same steps over and over again, they presently make a road of it, as plain and as smooth as a garden walk, which, when they are once used to, the Devil himself sometimes shall not be able to drive them off.

Pray, my dear, quoth my mother, *have you not forgot to wind up the clock?*——*Good G—!* cried my father, making an exclamation, but taking care to moderate his voice at the same time, *—Did ever woman, since the creation of the world, interrupt a man with such a silly question?* Pray what was your father saying?——Nothing.[5]

1759–1760 1760

1. Volume 1, Chapter 1.

2. In the long-accepted theory of the humors, each person's character was thought to be determined by whichever of four fluids (blood, phlegm, choler, and black bile) was "uppermost" (that is, existed in the highest proportion) within his or her body. If black bile predominated, for example, the person would be melancholic (Greek: *melan* [black] + *chol* [bile]).

3. Vapors or fluids thought to course through the body, directing its sensations and actions. "The animal spirits," explained Robert Burton in *The Anatomy of Melancholy*, ". . . brought up to the brain, and diffused by the nerves to the subordinate members, give sense and motion to them all."

4. Trivial.

5. This question-and-answer punch line, initially obscure, encapsulates much of Tristram's predicament. As he will explain a little later, his father, "one of the most regular men in everything he did," made it his practice to wind up the household clock on the first Sunday of every month, and at the same time to take care of "some other little family concernments" (i.e., marital intercourse), so that he would "be no more plagued and pestered with them the rest of the month." So, at the moment narrated, his father is saying nothing but doing something: begetting Tristram. His mother, similarly engaged, jumps by "an unhappy association of ideas" to her question about the clock, with which she interrupts the current, crucial activity. Meanwhile, as Tristram starts to tell his story, a nameless and confused reader (the first of many in the text) interrupts *him* with a question ("what was your father saying?") based, like so much in the book to come, on an incomplete understanding of data waywardly supplied.

[CALCULATIONS[6]]

Holla![7]——you chairman![8]——here's sixpence——do step into that bookseller's shop, and call me a day-tall critic.[9] I am very willing to give any one of 'em a crown to help me with this tackling,[1] to get my father and my uncle Toby off the stairs, and to put them to bed.——

——'Tis even high time; for except a short nap, which they both got whilst Trim was boring the jackboots—and which, by the by, did my father no sort of good upon the score of the bad hinge—they have not else shut their eyes, since nine hours before the time that Doctor Slop was led into the back parlor in that dirty pickle by Obadaiah.[2]

Was every day of my life to be as busy a day as this,——and to take up,——truce——

I will not finish that sentence till I have made an observation upon the strange state of affairs between the reader and myself, just as things stand at present——an observation never applicable before to any one biographical writer since the creation of the world, but to myself——and I believe will never hold good to any other, until its final destruction——and therefore, for the very novelty of it alone, it must be worth your worships attending to.

I am this month one whole year older than I was this time twelve-month;[3] and having got, as you perceive, almost into the middle of my fourth volume——and no farther than to my first day's life——'tis demonstrative that I have three hundred and sixty-four days' more life to write just now, than when I first set out; so that instead of advancing, as a common writer, in my work with what I have been doing at it——on the contrary, I am just thrown so many volumes back——was every day of my life to be as busy a day as this——And why not?——and the transactions and opinions of it to take up as much description——And for what reason should they be cut short? as at this rate I should just live 364 times faster than I should write——It must follow, an'[4] please your worships, that the more I write, the more I shall have to write——and consequently, the more your worships read, the more your worships will have to read.

Will this be good for your worships' eyes?

It will do well for mine; and, was it not that my OPINIONS will be the death of me, I perceive I shall lead a fine life of it out of this self-same life of mine; or, in other words, shall lead a couple of fine lives together.

As for the proposal of twelve volumes a year, or a volume a month, it no way alters my prospect——write as I will, and rush as I may into the middle of things, as Horace advises,[5]——I shall never overtake myself——whipped and driven to the

6. Volume 4, Chapter 13. Still narrating the day of his birth, Tristram finds himself in a predicament. As the long day wanes, his father and his uncle Toby, lost in conversation, are stranded on the staircase; as narrator, Tristram is trying to find a way to get them off the stairs and into bed.

7. "You there!"

8. Carrier of a sedan chair (i.e., the eighteenth-century equivalent of a taxi driver, idling on the street while waiting for a fare).

9. A hack writer, so called because his prose is reckoned (tallied) and paid for by the day rather than by its merits.

1. Equipment: ropes and pulleys.

2. Tristram catalogues just a few of the day's catastrophes, to each of which he has already devoted whole chapters: his father Walter's favorite pair of boots has been appropriated and destroyed by Uncle Toby's well-meaning servant Corporal Trim; both father and uncle have been woken from their nap by a door-hinge that has stayed squeaky for the past ten years; the Shandys' servant Obadaiah, sent on horseback to fetch the "man-midwife" Dr. Slop, has collided with that beleaguered obstetrician and sent him sprawling into deep mud.

3. I.e., a year ago, when the first two volumes of *Tristram Shandy* were published.

4. If it.

5. The ancient Roman poet advised authors to imitate Homer's practice in the *Iliad:* not to begin their stories at the very start, but instead to plunge their readers *in medias res*, "into the middle [of] things" (*Ars Poetica*, 11.146ff.).

last pinch, at the worst I shall have one day the start of[6] my pen——and one day is enough for two volumes——and two volumes is enough for one year.——

Heaven prosper the manufactures of paper under this propitious reign, which is now opened to us,[7]——as I trust its providence will prosper everything else in it that is taken in hand.——

As for the propagation of geese[8]——I give myself no concern——Nature is all bountiful——I shall never want[9] tools to work with.

——So then, friend! you have got my father and my uncle Toby off the stairs, and seen them to bed?——And how did you manage it?——You dropped a curtain at the stairs' foot[1]——I thought you had no other way for it——Here's a crown[2] for your trouble.

1760 1761

Frances Burney

1752–1840

In the preface to her first novel, *Evelina* (1778), Frances Burney praises "the pathetic powers of Richardson," "the wit of Fielding," and the skills of several other fiction-makers, before making what amounts to a modest boast: "I yet presume not to attempt pursuing the same ground which they have tracked; whence, though they may have cleared the weeds, they have also culled the flowers." Like so many of her predecessors, she wants to make clear that she has chosen a newer route, sketched in the novel's subtitle. Her book will chronicle the six-month "history of a young lady's entrance into the world."

In fact, *Evelina* enacted two such entrances, the heroine's and the author's. Throughout her writings, Burney remained preoccupied with the precarious dynamics of entrance—with the peculiarly "female difficulties" (to quote the subtitle of her last novel) encountered by a young woman who tries to make her way into a world seemingly bent, whether through indifference or hostility, on the suppression of her autonomy, the obstruction of her desires, even the eradication of her identity. "Why," Burney famously asks at the age of sixteen, in her very first journal entry, ". . . must a *female* be made Nobody?" Over the seven ensuing decades, in her copious journals, revelatory letters, and four increasingly ambitious novels, Burney sought answers to the "why" and set down challenges to the "must." In the selections here, from her earliest journals, from *Evelina,* and from her final novel *The Wanderer*, Burney makes clear how writing can register the difficulties of being female in England during the late eighteenth century—and how it can inflect, alter, and at times perhaps resolve them, too.

from The Early Journals

[First entry]

Poland Street, London [27 March 1768][1]

To have some account of my thoughts, manners, acquaintance and actions, when the hour arrives at which time is more nimble than memory is the reason which induces

6. I.e., be one day ahead of.
7. George III had become king the year before, in 1760.
8. Whose feathers furnished quill pens.
9. Lack.
1. I.e., did it as a dramatist might, dropping a curtain over one scene in order to indicate a shift in time and space before the next scene commences.
2. A coin worth 5 shillings, or 60 pence: ten times what Tristram paid the chairman to fetch the critic.
1. Burney, who will turn 16 in 11 weeks, now lives with her three sisters, two brothers, father and stepmother in a prosperous district of London.

me to keep a journal: a journal in which I must confess my *every* thought, must open my whole heart! But a thing of this kind ought to be addressed to somebody—I must imagine myself to be talking—talking to the most intimate of friends—to one in whom I should take delight in confiding, and feel remorse in concealment: but who must this friend be?—to make choice of one to whom I can but *half* rely would be to frustrate entirely the intention of my plan. The only one I could wholly, totally confide in, lives in the same house with me, and not only never *has*, but never *will*, leave me one secret *to* tell her.[2] To whom, then *must* I dedicate my wonderful, surprising and interesting adventures?—to *whom* dare I reveal my private opinion of my nearest relations? the secret thoughts of my dearest friends? my own hopes, fears, reflections and dislikes—Nobody!

To Nobody, then, will I write my journal! since To Nobody can I be wholly unreserved—to Nobody can I reveal every thought, every wish of my heart, with the most unlimited confidence, the most unremitting sincerity to the end of my life! For what chance, what accident can end my connections with Nobody? No secret can I conceal from No—body, and to No—body can I be *ever* unreserved. Disagreement cannot stop our affection, Time itself has no power to end our friendship. The love, the esteem I entertain for Nobody, No-body's self has not power to destroy. From Nobody I have nothing to fear, the secrets sacred to friendship, Nobody will not reveal, when the affair is doubtful, Nobody will not look towards the side least favorable.—

I will suppose you, then, to be my best friend: though God forbid you ever should! My dearest companion—and a romantic girl, for mere oddity may perhaps be more sincere—more *tender*—than if you were a friend in propria personae[3]—in as much as imagination often exceeds reality. In your breast my errors may create pity without exciting contempt; may raise your compassion, without eradicating your love.

From this moment, then, my dear girl—but why, permit me to ask, must a *female* be made Nobody? Ah! my dear, what were this world good for, were Nobody a female? And now I have done with *preambulation*.[4]

["I CANNOT HELP IT"]

Cabin, Saturday [30 July 1768][5]

And so I suppose you[6] are staring at the torn paper, and unconnected sentences—I don't much wonder—I'll tell you how it happened. Last Monday I was in the little parlor, which room my papa generally dresses in—and writing a letter to my grandmamma Sleepe—You must know I always have the last sheet of my journal in my pocket, and when I have wrote it half full—I join it to the rest, and take another sheet—and so on. Now I happened unluckily to take the last sheet out of my pocket with my letter—and laid it on the piano forte, and there, negligent fool!—I left it.[7] Unfortunately while we were at Mrs. Allen's on Sunday evening, I wrote about half a page in which I

2. Burney's 13-year-old sister Susanna (1755–1800), in whom she confided, through talk and long letters, throughout the ensuing decades.
3. In one's own person (Latin); i.e., if you were an actual, living person.
4. Preface-making. In using (and emphasizing) this somewhat unusual word, Burney may just possibly be echoing *Pamela* (see above, page 2816).
5. Burney spent summers with her family in King's Lynn, the Norfolk port town where she was born. The "cabin" stood on her stepmother's property, with a view of the nearby river. Burney liked the place for its privacy, and often wrote her journal there: "I always spend the evening, sometimes all the afternoon, in this sweet cabin . . . I cannot express the pleasure I have in writing down my thoughts, at the very moment—" (13 July 1768).
6. I.e., "Nobody."
7. Burney's father Charles was an eminent teacher and historian of music; the piano was therefore a center of household life—and of his attention.

mentioned poor Susan [xxx 2 words][8] teasing me with *particular* questions, on a *particular* subject, which related to a *particular* case, concerning Mama—Can you not guess *what?*[9]—[xxx 1 line] and besides this, I mentioned several other little matters—Well, as ill fortune would have it, papa went into the room—took my poor journal—read and pocketed it! Mama came up to me and told me of it. O dear! I was in a sad distress—I could not for the life of me ask for it—and so *dawdled* and fretted the time away 'till Tuesday evening. Then, gathering courage—Pray, Papa—have you got—any *papers* of mine?—Papers of yours?—said he—how should I come by papers of yours?—I'm sure—I don't know—but—Why do you leave your papers about the house? asked he, gravely—I could not say another word—and he went on playing on the piano forte. Well, to be sure, thought I these same dear journals are most shocking plaguing things—I've a good mind to resolve never to write a word more.—However, I stayed still in the room, working and looking wistfully at him for about an hour and a half. At last, he rose to dress—again I looked wistfully at him—he laughed—what, Fanny, said he, kindly—are you in sad distress?—I half laughed—Well—I'll give it you, now I see you are in such distress—but take care, my dear, of leaving your writings about the house again—Suppose anybody else had found it—I declare I was going to read it loud—Here—take it—but if ever I find any more of your journals, I vow I'll stick them up in the market place! And then he kissed me so kindly—Never was parent so *properly*, so *well-judged* affectionate.

I was so frightened that I have not had the heart to write since, 'till now, I should not but that—in short, but that I cannot help it!—As to the *paper*, [xxx 1/2 line] I destroyed it[1] the moment I got it. We have had several little parties of pleasure since I wrote last but they are not worth mentioning.

["The Most Dangerous Employment Young Persons Can Have"]

[King's Lynn, August 1768]

I have been having a long conversation with Miss Young[2] on journals. She has very seriously and earnestly advised me to give mine up—heigho-ho! Do you think I can bring myself to oblige her? What she says has great weight with me: but, indeed, I should be very loath to *quite* give my poor friend up. She says that it is the most dangerous employment young persons can have—it makes them often record things which ought not to be recorded, but instantly forgot. I told her, that as *my* journal was *solely* for my own perusal, nobody could in justice, or even in sense, be angry or displeased at my writing anything.

"But how can you answer," said she, "that it is only for your perusal? That very circumstance of your papa's finding it shows you are not so very careful as is necessary for such a work. And if you drop it, and any improper person finds it, you know not the uneasiness it may cost you."

"Well but, dear ma'am, this is an 'if' that may not happen once in a century."

"I beg your pardon, I know not how often it may happen; and even once might prove enough to give you more pain than you are aware of."

"Why, dear ma'am, papa never prohibited my writing, and he knows that I *do* write, and *what* I do write."

8. Later in life, Burney edited and excised her journals by many means: crossing words out, pasting them over, cutting whole pages. In this case, she crossed out the entire passage beginning at "Unfortunately" and ending in "matters"; the square brackets indicate words and lines that editors have been unable to recover.

9. Probably her stepmother's ("Mama's") pregnancy.

1. Burney inserted this phrase decades later, perhaps as replacement for the excised half-line.

2. Dorothy Young, a resident of King's Lynn, and best friend of Burney's mother.

"I question that. However, 'tis impossible for you to answer for the curiosity of others. And suppose anybody finds a part in which they are extremely censured."

"Why then, they must take it for their pains. It was not wrote for *them*, but *me*, and I cannot see any harm in writing to *myself*."

"It was very well whilst there were only your sisters with you to do anything of this kind; but, depend upon it, when your connections are enlarged, your family increased, your acquaintance multiplied, young and old *so* apt to be curious—depend upon it, Fanny, 'tis the most dangerous employment you can have. Suppose now, for example, your favorite wish were granted, and you were *to fall in love,* and then the object of your passion were to get sight of some part which related to himself?"

"Why then, Miss Young, I must take a little trip to Rosamond's Pond."[3]

"Why, ay, I doubt[4] it would be all you would have left."

"Dear Miss Young!—But I'm sure, by your earnestness, that you think worse of my poor journal than it deserves."

"I know very well the nature of these things. I know that in journals, thoughts, actions, looks, conversations—*all* go down; do they not?"

The conclusion of our debate was that if I would show her some part of what I had wrote she should be a better judge, and would then give me her best advice whether to proceed or not. I believe I shall accept her condition; though I own I shall show it with shame and fear, for such nonsense is so unworthy her perusal.

I'm sure, besides, I know not what part to choose. Shall I take at random?

from Evelina; or, the History of a Young Lady's Entrance into the World

EVELINA TO THE REVEREND MR. VILLARS[1]

Howard Grove, March 26

This house seems to be the house of joy; every face wears a smile, and a laugh is at everybody's service. It is quite amusing to walk about, and see the general confusion; a room leading to the garden is fitting up for Captain Mirvan's study.[2] Lady Howard does not sit a moment in a place; Miss Mirvan[3] is making caps; everybody so busy!—such flying from room to room!—so many orders given, and retracted, and given again!—nothing but hurry and perturbation.

Well but, my dear Sir, I am desired to make a request to you. I hope you will not think me an encroacher; Lady Howard insists upon my writing!—yet I hardly know how to go on; a petition implies a want,—and have you left me one? No, indeed.

I am half ashamed of myself for beginning this letter. But these dear ladies are so pressing—I cannot, for my life, resist wishing for the pleasures they offer me,—provided you do not disapprove them.

3. Located in London's St. James's Park, Rosamond's Pond was a popular place for lovers' meetings and (Burney's joke here) for lovers' suicides; because of those dark associations, it was filled in (and thereby eradicated) two years later.

4. Expect.

1. Volume 1, letter 8. *Evelina* is made up mostly of letters written by the 16-year-old heroine to her guardian and surrogate father Arthur Villars, from whom she has not been separated since infancy, when he took on the task of caring for her after her mother's death and her father's refusal to acknowledge her his daughter. Now, with Villars's reluctant consent, she has left on an extended visit to the family of his friend Lady Howard, who hopes to help Evelina establish the legitimacy of her birth and standing. Here, in the first of her many letters home, Evelina is charged with making a further request, and discovers something of how writing can inflect desire.

2. Captain Mirvan is the brutish husband of Lady Howard's kindly daughter. *Fitting up for:* being remodeled as.

3. Lady Howard's granddaughter; Evelina's contemporary and friend.

They are to make a very short stay in town.[4] The Captain will meet them in a day or two. Mrs. Mirvan and her sweet daughter both go;—what a happy party! Yet I am not *very* eager to accompany them: at least, I shall be contented to remain where I am, if you desire that I should.

Assured, my dearest Sir, of your goodness, your bounty, and your indulgent kindness, ought I to form a wish that has not your sanction? Decide for me, therefore, without the least apprehension that I shall be uneasy, or discontented. While I am yet in suspense, perhaps I may *hope*, but I am most certain, that when you have once determined, I shall not repine.

They tell me that London is now in full splendor. Two playhouses are open,—the Opera-House,—Ranelagh,[5]—the Pantheon.[6]—You see I have learned all their names. However, pray don't suppose that I make any point of going, for I shall hardly sigh to see them depart without me; though I shall probably never meet with such another opportunity. And, indeed, their domestic happiness will be so great,—it is natural to wish to partake of it.

I believe I am bewitched! I made a resolution when I began, that I would not be urgent; but my pen—or rather my thoughts, will not suffer me to keep it—for I acknowledge, I must acknowledge, I cannot help wishing for your permission.

I almost repent already that I have made this confession; pray forget that you have read it, if this journey is displeasing to you. But I will not write any longer; for the more I think of this affair, the less indifferent to it I find myself.

Adieu, my most honored, most reverenced, most beloved father! for by what other name can I call you? I have no happiness or sorrow, no hope or fear, but what your kindness bestows, or your displeasure may cause. You will not, I am sure, send a refusal, without reasons unanswerable, and therefore I shall cheerfully acquiesce. Yet I hope—I hope you will be able to permit me to go.

I am,
With the utmost affection,
gratitude, and duty,
Your
EVELINA ———

I cannot to *you* sign *Anville*, and what other name may I claim?[7]

[A RIDICULOUS AND REJECTED WOOER][8]

Mr. Smith teased me[9] till I was weary of resistance; and I should at last have been obliged to submit, had I not fortunately recollected the affair of Mr. Lovel, and told my persecutor that it was impossible I should dance with him, even if I wished it, as I had refused several persons in his absence.[1]

4. London.
5. A well-known pleasure garden.
6. An elegant assembly room, used for concerts and balls.
7. "Anville," an anagram of Evelina's own first name, is the surrogate surname her guardian has contrived for her. She cannot write it to him because they both know it for a fiction; as a purportedly illegitimate child, she possesses no other last name.
8. From volume 2, letter 19: Evelina to the Rev. Mr. Villars. Throughout the novel, Evelina is beset by suitors. Mr. Smith, the man of "low-bred vivacity" who pursues her here at a downmarket London dance, is one of the more transitory, but he provides Evelina with an opportunity to review how much she's learned, and how much she's changed, since arriving in London only four months earlier.
9. Pestered (not mocked); he wants to dance with her.
1. At her first, more elegant London ball, Evelina had declined the odious Mr. Lovel's invitation to dance, but nervously assured him that she had no other partner, and that she simply did not wish to "dance at all"; she was later mortified when he found her dancing with a far more attractive partner, to whom she'd assented out of the same agitation. What she experienced as awkwardness then, she deploys as tactic now.

He was not contented with being extremely chagrined, but took the liberty, openly and warmly, to expostulate with me upon not having said I was engaged.[2]

The total disregard with which, involuntarily, I heard him, made him soon change the subject. In truth, I had no power to attend to him, for all my thoughts were occupied in retracing the transactions of the two former balls at which I had been present. The party—the conversation—the company—O how great the contrast!

In a short time, however, he contrived to draw my attention to himself, by his extreme impertinence;[3] for he chose to express what he called his *admiration* of me, in terms so open and familiar, that he forced me to express my displeasure with equal plainness.

But how was I surprised, when I found he had the temerity—what else can I call it?—to impute my resentment to doubts of his honor; for he said, "My dear Ma'am, you must be a little patient; I assure you I have no bad designs, I have not upon my word; but, really, there is no resolving upon such a thing as matrimony all at once; what with the loss of one's liberty, and what with the ridicule of all one's acquaintance,—I assure you, Ma'am, you are the first lady who ever made me even demur[4] upon this subject; for, after all, my dear Ma'am, marriage is the devil!"

"Your opinion, Sir," answered I, "of either the married or the single life, can be of no manner of consequence to me, and therefore I would by no means trouble you to discuss their different merits."

"Why, really, Ma'am, as to your being a little out of sorts, I must own I can't wonder at it, for, to be sure, marriage is all in all with the ladies; but with us gentlemen it's quite another thing! Now only put yourself in my place,—suppose you had such a large acquaintance of gentlemen as I have,—and that you had always been used to appear a little—a little smart among them,—why now, how should you like to let yourself down all at once into a married man?"

I could not tell what to answer; so much conceit, and so much ignorance, both astonished and silenced me.

"I assure you, Ma'am," added he, "there is not only Miss Biddy,—though I should have scorned to mention her, if her brother had not blabbed, for I'm quite particular in keeping ladies' secrets,[5]—but there are a great many other ladies that have been proposed to me,—but I never thought twice of any of them,—that is, not in a *serious* way,—so you may very well be proud," offering to take my hand, "for I assure you, there is nobody so likely to catch me at last as yourself."

"Sir," cried I, drawing myself back as haughtily as I could, "you are totally mistaken, if you imagine you have given me any pride I felt not before, by this conversation; on the contrary, you must allow me to tell you, I find it too humiliating to bear with it any longer."

I then placed myself behind the chair of Madame Duval;[6] who when she heard of the partners I had refused, pitied my ignorance of the world, but no longer insisted on my dancing.

2. I.e., not having used the alternate tactic of telling unwanted partners that, in effect, her dance card was already full.
3. "Troublesomeness; intrusion" (Johnson's *Dictionary*).
4. "To pause in uncertainty" (Johnson's *Dictionary*).
5. Mr. Smith alludes to the vulgar Branghton family, with whom Evelina is remotely connected and reluctantly entangled; brother Tom has just revealed that his sister Biddy wants Smith for herself.
6. Evelina's maternal grandmother, intent on seeing her married off.

Indeed, the extreme vanity of this man makes me exert a spirit which I did not, till now, know that I possessed; but I cannot endure that he should think me at his disposal.

from The Wanderer; or, Female Difficulties

from *the Preface*[1]

* * * With regard to the very serious subject[2] treated upon, from time to time, in this work, some—perhaps many—may ask, "Is a novel the vehicle for such considerations, such discussions?"

Permit me to answer: whatever, in illustrating the characters, manners, or opinions of the day, exhibits what is noxious or reprehensible, should scrupulously be accompanied by what is salubrious, or chastening. Not that poison ought to be infused merely to display the virtues of an antidote; but that, where error and mischief bask in the broad light of day, truth ought not to be suffered to shrink timidly in the shade.

Divest, for a moment, the title of Novel from its stationary standard of insignificance, and say! What is the species of writing that offers fairer opportunities for conveying useful precepts? It is, or it ought to be, a picture of supposed, but natural and probable human existence. It holds, therefore, in its hands our best affections; it exercises our imaginations; it points out the path of honor; and gives to juvenile credulity knowledge of the world, without ruin, or repentance; and the lessons of experience, without tears.

And is not a novel, permit me, also, to ask, in common with every other literary work, entitled to receive its stamp as useful, mischievous, or nugatory, from its execution? Not necessarily, and in its changeless state, to be branded as a mere vehicle for frivolous, or seductive amusement? If many may turn aside from all but mere entertainment presented under this form, many, also, may, unconsciously, be allured by it into reading the severest truths, who would not even open any work of a graver denomination.

What is it that gives the universally acknowledged superiority to the epic poem? Its historical truth? No: the three poems,[3] which, during so many centuries, and till Milton arose, stood unrivalled in celebrity, are, with respect to fact, of constantly disputed, or rather, disproved authenticity. Nor is it even the sweet witchery of sound: the ode, the lyric, the elegiac, and other species of poetry have risen to equal metrical beauty.

'Tis the grandeur, yet singleness of the plan: the never broken, yet never obvious adherence to its execution; the delineating and support of character; the invention of incident; the contrast of situation; the grace of diction and the beauty of imagery, joined to a judicious choice of combinations, and a living interest in every partial detail, that give to that sovereign species of the works of fiction its glorious preeminence.

Will my dear father smile at this seeming approximation of the compositions which stand foremost, with those which are sunk lowest in literary estimation? No; he will feel that it is not the futile presumption of a comparison that would be preposterous, but a fond desire to separate (with a high hand!) falsehood, that would deceive to evil, from fiction, that would attract another way—and to rescue from ill opinion the sort of production (call it what we may) that his daughter ventures to lay at his feet, through the alluring but awful[4] tribunal of the public.

1. Burney addresses this preface, part theoretical and part autobiographical, to her father Charles, now 87 years old; he died two weeks after the novel's publication.
2. The aftermath of the French Revolution, which had rendered Burney's husband, like the heroine of the *Wanderer*, an exile in England.
3. Homer's *Iliad* and *Odyssey*; Virgil's *Aeneid*.
4. I.e., awe-inspiring.

He will recollect, also, how often their so mutually honored Dr. Johnson has said to her, "Always aim at the eagle—even though you expect but to reach a sparrow!"

The power of prejudice annexed to nomenclature is universal: the same being who, unnamed, passes unnoticed,[5] if preceded by the title of a hero, or a potentate, catches every eye, and is pursued with clamorous praise or (its common reverberator!) abuse. But in nothing is the force of denomination more striking than in the term *novel:* a species of writing which, though never mentioned, even by its supporter, but with a look that fears contempt, is not more rigidly excommunicated from[6] its appellation, in theory, than sought and fostered, from its attractions, in practice.

So early was I impressed myself with ideas that fastened degradation to this class of composition, that at the age of adolescence, I struggled against the propensity which, even in childhood, even from the moment I could hold a pen, had impelled me into its toils; and on my fifteenth birthday, I made so resolute a conquest over an inclination at which I blushed, and that I had always kept secret, that I committed to the flames whatever, up to that moment, I had committed to paper.[7] And so enormous was the pile, that I thought it prudent to consume it in the garden.

You, dear Sir, knew nothing of its extinction, for you had never known of its existence. Our darling Susanna,[8] to whom alone I had ever ventured to read its contents, alone witnessed the conflagration; and—well I remember!—wept, with tender partiality, over the imaginary ashes of Caroline Evelyn, the mother of Evelina.

The passion, however, though resisted, was not annihilated: my bureau was cleared, but my head was not emptied; and, in defiance of every self-effort, Evelina struggled herself into life. * * *

[CODA][9]

Here, and thus felicitously, ended, with the acknowledgment of her name, and her family, the DIFFICULTIES of the WANDERER; —a being who had been cast upon herself; a female Robinson Crusoe, as unaided and unprotected, through the midst of the world, as that imaginary hero in his uninhabited island; and reduced either to sink, through inanition, or to be rescued from famine and death by such resources as she could find, independently, in herself.

How mighty, thus circumstanced, are the DIFFICULTIES with which a FEMALE has to struggle! Her honor always in danger of being assailed, her delicacy of being offended, her strength of being exhausted, and her virtue of being calumniated!

Yet even DIFFICULTIES such as these are not insurmountable, where mental courage, operating through patience, prudence, and principle, supply physical force, combat disappointment, and keep the untamed spirits superior to failure, and ever alive to hope.

1814

END OF PERSPECTIVES: NOVEL GUISES

5. The phrasing here well describes the initially nameless heroine of *The Wanderer*, whose predicament (by the ensuing logic in Burney's sentence) becomes analogous to that of the genre that depicts her.

6. I.e., because of the stigma associated with.

7. Burney partly discloses to her father, perhaps for the first time, the story of her earliest writing. During her early teens, in the wake of her beloved mother's sudden death and her worshipped father's troubling remarriage, Burney wrote a novel, "The History of Carolyn Evelyn," and then, on her fifteenth birthday, burned it, out of fear that her father, and the world at large, would frown at the audacity and impropriety frequently imputed to women who wrote fiction. *Evelina,* composed a decade later, was in effect a sequel to the immolated work; it tells the story of Carolyn's daughter.

8. Burney's younger sister and closest confidant, whose death in 1800 haunted Burney for the remainder of her own long life; she died 40 years to the day after Susanna.

9. In these, the final paragraphs of her career as novelist, Burney reworks her book's subtitle, touches on concerns that have beset all her female protagonists as they strive to establish both name and identity, and harkens back, with a significant shift in gender, to a narrative published 95 years earlier.

CREDITS

TEXT CREDITS

Addison, Joseph and Richard Steele. From *The Spectator, Volume I* (1987), edited by Donald Bond. By permission of Oxford University Press.

Aldhelm. From *The Riddles of Aldhelm*, translated by James Hall Pitman. Yale University Press, 1925. Reprinted by permission of Yale University Press.

Excerpt from *Amazons, Savages, and Machiavels travel and colonial writing in English, 1550–1630: an anthology* edited by Andrew Hadfield. Copyright © 2001. Reprinted by permission of Oxford University Press.

"The Anonimalle Chronicle." From *The Peasants' Revolt of 1381*, ed. by R.B. Dobson (1970). London: Macmillan. Reproduced with permission of Palgrave Macmillan.

Bede. From *Ecclesiastical History of the English People* by Bede, edited by Bertram Colgrave and R.A.B. Mynors (1969). By permission of Oxford University Press.

Beowulf. This translation first published by Penguin 1973. Copyright © Michael Alexander 1973. Reprinted by permission.

"Beware the Cat" by William Baldwin from *Beware the Cat: The First English Novel* by William A. Wringler Jr. and Michael Flachmann. Copyright © 1995. Reprinted with the permission of the Henry E. Huntington Library.

Boland, Eavan. "From the Irish of Pangur Ban" from *An Origin Like Water: Collected Poems 1967–1987* by Eavan Boland. Copyright © 1996 by Eavan Boland. Used by permission of W.W. Norton & Company, Inc.

Bradley, Marion Zimmer. Excerpt from Prologue to *The Mists of Avalon*. Copyright © 1982 by Marion Zimmer Bradley. Reprinted by permission of the author and the author's agents, Scovil Chichak Galen Literary Agency, Inc.

Burney, Fanny. From *The Early Journals and Letters of Fanny Burney, Volume I, 1768–1773*, ed. by Lars E. Troide. Montreal: McGill-Queen's University Press, 1988. Reprinted by permission of the publisher. Entries from *Selected Journals and Letters of Frances Burney*, edited with an introduction and notes by Peter Sabor and Lars E. Troide, with the assistance of Stewart J. Cooke and Victoria Kortes-Papp. London: Penguin Books, 2001. Reproduced by permission of Penguin Books Ltd.

Charles D'Orleans. Excerpted from *Fortunes Stabilnes: Charles of Orleans's English Book of Love* by Mary-Jo Arn. Medieval & Renaissance Texts & Studies Volume, (Binghamton, NY, 1994), pp. 172–73, 211–12, 299. © Arizona Board of Regents for Arizona State University. Reprinted by permission.

Chaucer, Geoffrey. "General Prologue" from Chaucer's *The Canterbury Tales* is reproduced from the modern-verse translation by David Wright. Copyright © Estate of David Wright, 1985. By permission of PFD on behalf of the Estate of David Wright. From *Chaucer's Poetry: An Anthology for the Modern Reader*, 2nd ed., edited by E. Talbot Donaldson. Copyright © 1958, 1975 by Judith Anderson and Deirdre Donaldson. Used by permission of W.W. Norton & Company, Inc.

Christine de Pizan. From *The Book of the City of Ladies* by Christine de Pizan, translated by Earl Jeffrey Richards. Translation copyright © 1982, 1998 by Persea Books, Inc. Reprinted by permission of Persea Books, Inc. (New York).

From *The Cloud of Unknowing* translated by Clifton Wolters. (Penguin Classics, 1961). Copyright © Clifton Wolters, 1961. Reprinted by permission of Penguin Books Ltd.

Dafydd ap Gwilym. "Aubade," "One Saving Place," "Tales of a Wayside Inn," "The Winter," and "The Ruin" from *Nine Thorny Thickets: Selected Poems by Dafydd Ap Gwilym*, arrangements by Rolfe Humphries. Copyright © 1969 Rolfe Humphries. Reprinted by permission of Kent State University Press.

"De Heretico Comburendo" 1401. From *English Historical Documents, Volume IV, 1327–1485*, edited by A.R. Myers (1969). Published by Routledge. Reprinted by permission of Taylor & Francis Group.

"The Dream of the Rood," "The Wanderer," "Wulf and Eadwacer," "The Wife's Lament" from *The Exeter Book of Riddles*, translated by Kevin Crossley Holland. Copyright © Kevin Crossley Holland, 1993. By kind permission of the author c/o Rogers, Coleridge & White Ltd., 20 Powis Mews, London W11 1JN.

Dryden, John. "The Secular Masque" from *John Dryden* (1987), edited by Keith Walker. By permission of Oxford University Press. From "Preface to Fables Ancient and Modern" and "Alexander's Feast" from *The Poems and Fables of John Dryden* (1962) edited by James Kinsley. By permission of Oxford University Press.

Dunbar, William. From *A Midsummer Eve's Dream: Variations on a Theme by William Dunbar* by A.D. Hope. Copyright © 1970 by Alec Derwent Hope. Used by permission of Viking Penguin, a division of Penguin Group (USA) Inc.

Edward I. From *Anglo-Scottish Relations 1174–1328*, edited and translated by E.L.G. Stones (1970) © 1965. By permission of Oxford University Press.

Evelyn, John. Excerpt from *The Diary of John Evelyn*, edited by E.S. DeBeer. By permission of Oxford University Press.

From *The Faerie Queen* by Edmund Spenser, edited by Thomas P. Roche Jr. & C. Patrick O'Donnell Jr. (Penguin 1978) copyright © Thomas P. Roche, 1978. Used by permission of Penguin Group (UK).

Gardner, John. From *Grendel* by John Gardner. Copyright © 1971 by John Gardner. Used by permission of Alfred A. Knopf, a division of Random House, Inc.

Geoffrey of Monmouth. From *History of Kings of Britain* by Geoffrey of Monmouth, translated by Lewis Thorpe. (Penguin Classics, 1966). Translation copyright © Lewis Thorpe, 1966. Reprinted by permission of Penguin Books Ltd.

Gower, John. From "The Voice of Crying" by John Gower from *The Major Works of John Gower*, edited by Eric W. Stockton. Copyright © 1962 by the University of Washington Press. Reprinted by permission.

"The Holi Prophete David Seith" from *The Idea of the Vernacular* edited by Jocelyn Wogan-Browne, Nicholas Watson, Andrew Taylor, and Ruth Evans, pp. 151–53. University Park, PA: Pennsylvania State University Press, 1990. Copyright © 1990 by The Pennsylvania State University. Reproduced by permission of the publisher.

"Judith." From *Anglo-Saxon Poetry: An Anthology of Old English Poems*, translated by S.A.J. Bradley. Copyright © 1982 by David Campbell Publishers Ltd. Reprinted by permission of David Campbell Publishers Ltd.

Kempe, Margery. From *The Book of Margery Kempe*, translated by B.A. Windeatt. (Penguin Classics, 1965). Copyright © B.A. Windeatt, 1965. Reprinted by permission of Penguin Books Ltd.

King Lear from *The Complete Works of Shakespeare*, 6th Edition edited by David Bevington. Copyright © 2009 by Pearson Education, Inc. Reprinted by permission.

Langland, William. From *William Langland's Piers Plowman: The C Version*, translated by George Economou. Copyright © 1996 University of Pennsylvania Press. Reprinted by permission of the University of Pennsylvania Press.

Lewis, C.S. From *The Screwtape Letters* by C.S. Lewis. Copyright © C.S. Lewis Pte. Ltd., 1947, 1960. Extract reprinted by permission of The C.S. Lewis Company Ltd.

Malory, Sir Thomas. From *Caxton's Malory: A New Edition of Sir Thomas Malory's le Morte Darthur*, translated and edited by James W. Spisak and William Matthews. Copyright © 1983 The Regents of the University of California. Reprinted by permission of the University of California Press. From *King Arthur and His Knights: Selected Tales from Sir Thomas Malory*, edited by Eugene Vinaver. Copyright © 1975, 1968, 1956 by Eugene Vinaver. Used by permission of Oxford University Press, Inc.

"Mankind." From *Mankind: An Acting Edition*, Peter Meredith, ed. Leeds UK: Alumnus Playtexts in Performance, 1997. Reprinted by permission of Peter Meredith.

Marie de France. "Chevrefoil," "Lanval," and "Prologue" from *The Lais of Marie de France*, trans. by Robert Hanning and Joan Ferrante. © 1978. Reprinted by permission of Baker Academic, a division of Baker Publishing Group.

Milton, John. Adapted and abridged excerpts from Alastair Fowler's notes from Milton's *Paradise Lost*, edited by Alastair Fowler. Copyright © Addison Wesley Longman Limited 1968, 1971, 1998. Reprinted by permission of Pearson Education Limited, Essex, England.

Monty Python. Extract from *Monty Python and the Holy Grail: Screenplay*. Screenplay by John Cleese et al. Methuen, 2002. Reprinted by permission of Methuen Publishing Ltd.

Othello from *The Complete Works of Shakespeare*, 6th Edition edited by David Bevington. Copyright © 2009 by Pearson Education, Inc. Reprinted by permission.

Pepys, Samuel. From *The Diary of Samuel Pepys*, edited and translated by Robert Latham and William Matthews. Copyright © 1972-1986 The Master, Fellows and Scholars of Magdalen College, Cambridge, Robert Latham, and the Executors of William Matthews. Reprinted by permission of the University of California Press.

Petrarch. Reprinted by permission of the publisher from *Petrarch's Lyric Poems: The Rime Sparse and Other Lyrics*, translated and edited by Robert M. Durling. Cambridge, Mass.: Harvard University Press. Copyright © 1976 by Robert M. Durling.

Riddles: "Five Old English Riddles" from *The Anglo-Saxon World*, translated by Kevin Crossley Holland. Copyright © Kevin Crossley Holland, 1982. By kind permission of the author c/o Rogers, Coleridge & White, 20 Powis Mews, London W11 1JN.

Rolle, Richard. From *The Fire of Love* by Richard Rolle, translated by Clifton Wolters. (Penguin Classics, 1972). Copyright © Clifton Wolters, 1961. Reprinted by permission of Penguin Books Ltd.

Sidney, Sir Philip. Sonnets and notes from *Sir Philip Sidney: Selected Pose and Poetry*, edited by Robert Kimbrough. © 1983. Reprinted by permission of The University of Wisconsin Press.

Sir Gawain and the Green Knight. This translation first published by Penguin 1959. Copyright © Brian Stone 1959. Reprinted by permission.

Smith, Sir Thomas. From *De Republica Anglorum* by Sir Thomas Smith, edited by Mary Dewar. Copyright © 1982. Reprinted with the permission of Cambridge University Press.

From *The Tain*, translated by Ciaran Carson, copyright © 2007 by Ciaran Carson. Used by permission of Viking Penguin, a division of Penguin Group (USA) Inc.

Taliesin. "The Battle of Aargoed Llwyfain," translated by Anthony Conran. Reprinted by permission of Anthony Conran. "Lament for Owain Son of Urien," translated by Anthony Conran. Reprinted by permission of Anthony Conran.

"To Crinog" and "The Viking Terror" from *Ancient Irish Poetry*, translated by Kuno Meyer. Reprinted by permission of Constable & Robinson Limited.

A View of the State of Ireland by Edmund Spenser from the first printed edition (1633) edited by Andrew Hadfield and Willy Maley. Copyright © 1997 Blackwell Publishers Ltd. Reprinted by permission Wiley-Blackwell.

From "Writing in the Wood." From *Early Irish Verse*, translated and edited by Ruth P.M. Lehmann. Copyright © 1982 by the University of Texas Press. Reprinted by permission.

Wroth, Lady Mary. From *The Poems of Lady Mary Wroth*, edited, with an introduction and notes, by Josephine A. Roberts. Copyright © 1983 by Louisiana State University Press. Reprinted by permission of Louisiana State University Press.

"The York Play of the Crucifixion." From *York Mystery Plays: A Selection in Modern Spelling*, edited by Richard Beadle and Pamela M. King (Oxford World's Classics, 1999). © Richard Beadle and Pamela M. King, 1984. By permission of Oxford University Press.

ILLUSTRATION CREDITS

Page 2: © Reproduced by permission of Durham University Library from Cosin MS V.III.1; 3 (top): British Library, London, GB/HIP/Art Resource, NY; 3 (bottom): © The Trustees of the British Museum/Art Resource, NY; 4 (top): British Library, London, GB/HIP/Art Resource, NY; 4 (middle) British Library, London, GB/HIP/Art Resource, NY; 4 (bottom): British Library, London, GB/HIP/Art Resource, NY; 5 (top): British Library, London, GB/HIP/Art Resource, NY; 5 (middle): Bibliotheque Nationale, Paris, France/Art Resource, NY; 5 (bottom): British Library, London, GB/HIP/Art Resource, NY; 6 (top): HIP/Art Resource, NY; 6 (bottom): HIP/Art Resource, NY; 14: The Board of Trinity College, Dublin/Bridgeman Art Library; 16: By permission of the British Library; 19: © The Conway Library, Courtauld Institute of Art/The Master & Fellow of Corpus Christi College, Cambridge; 23: © Bodleian Library, University of Oxford; 24: By permission of the British Library; 33: David Damrosch; 35: David Damrosch; 44: © Conway Librarian/Courtauld Institute of Art; 149: © Department of Archaeology, University of Durham. Photograph T. Middlemass; 166: © Giraudon/Art Resource, NY. Musee de la Tapisserie, Bayeux, France; 202: © Giraudon/Art Resource, NY; 244: By permission of the British Library; 311: Everett Collection; 314: Lebrecht Music & Arts Photo Library; 409: Museum of London; 452: The Art Archive/Picture Desk, Inc./Kobal Collection; 469: Photography by Christopher Guy. Reproduced by permission of the Chapter of Worcester Cathedral; 530: David Damrosch; 552: © British Library Board. All Rights Reserved 1008100.011; 587: Bruce Cohen/David Damrosch; 614: By permission of the British Library; 622: By permission of the Folger Shakespeare Library; 623: Copyright © The British Museum; 624 (top): From Charles Hindley. The Boxburge Ballads. London: Reeves and, Turner, 1873.; 624 (middle): Victoria & Albert Museum, London/Art Resource, NY; 624 (bottom): Victoria & Albert Museum, London, GB/Art Resource, NY; 625 (top): HIP/Art Resource, NY; 625 (middle-top): Snark/Art Resource, NY; 625 (middle-bottom): British Library, London, GB/HIP/Art Resource, NY; 625 (bottom) British Library, London, GB/HIP/Art Resource, NY; 626 (top): Vanni/Art Resource, NY; 626 (bottom): © The Trustees of the British Museum/Snark/Art Resource, NY; 631: Foto Marburg/Art Resource, NY; 635: © S. Blair Hedges; 641: Private Collection. The Bridgeman Art Library; 648: By permission of the British Library; 714: Courtesy of the Library of Congress; 822: Courtesy of the Library of Congress; 1062: Mary Evans Picture Library Ltd./The Image Works; 1063: HIP/Art Resource, NY; 1064: Bibliotheque Nationale, Paris, France/The Bridgeman Art Library; 1065: HIP/Art Resource, NY; 1066 (top): Columbia University; 1066 (bottom): By permission of the Folger Shakespeare Library; 1068: By permission of The British Library; 1069: University of Sydney Library; 1070: By permission of the Folger Shakespeare Library; 1071: By permission of the Folger Shakespeare Library; 1072: Special Collections and University Archives, Rutgers University Libraries; 1074: The Granger Collection, New York; 1080: Art Resource, NY; 1112: HIP/British Library, London, Great Britain/Art Resource, NY; 1178: General Research Division, The New York Public Library, Astor, Lenox and Tilden Foundations; 1185: General Research Division, The New York Public Library, Astor, Lenox and Tilden Foundations; 1200: CORBIS/Bettmann; 1490–91: Copyright © The British Museum; 1446: By permission of the Folger Shakespeare Library; 1586: Michael Nicholson/Corbis/Bettmann; 1626: © Michael Nicholson/CORBIS All Rights Reserved; 1678: Pearson Education/PH College; 1698: © Hulton-Deutsch Collection/CORBIS All Rights Reserved; 1980: © Copyright The British Museum; 1981: © Historical Picture Library/Philip de Bay/CORBIS All Rights Reserved; 1982 (top): Erich Lessing/Art Resource, NY; 1982 (bottom): Art Resource, NY; 1983 (top): National Portrait Gallery, London; 1983 (middle): Robert Walpole; 1983 (bottom): Guidhall Art Gallery, London, GB/HIP/Art Resource, NY; 1984: Guidhall Art Gallery, London, GB/HIP/Art Resource, NY; 2009: The Bridgeman Art Library International; 2010: Lebrecht Music & Arts Photo Library; 2050: © Rare Books Division, The New York Public Library, Astor, Lenox and Tilden Foundations; 2053: HIP/Oxford Science Archive, Oxford, GB/Art Resource, NY; 2074: National Portrait Gallery, London; 2125: National Portrait Gallery, London; 2304–05: Museum of London; 2329: Courtesy of Washington University Libraries; 2331: Guildhall Library, Corporation of London; 2337: National Portrait Gallery, London; 2438: National Portrait Gallery, London; 2605: Dover Publications, Inc.; 2606: Dover Publications, Inc.; 2607: Dover Publications, Inc.; 2608: Dover Publications, Inc.; 2609: Dover Publications, Inc.; 2610: Dover Publications, Inc.; 2611: Dover Publications, Inc.; 2612: Dover Publications, Inc.; 2674: National Portrait Gallery, London.

COLOR PLATE CREDITS

Color Plate 1: Copyright © British Library Board. All Rights Reserved.; Color Plate 2: Copyright © The Trustees of the British Museum.; Color Plate 3: National Museum of Ireland.; Color Plate 4: Copyright © British Library Board. All Rights Reserved.; Color Plate 5: Copyright © British Library Board. All Rights Reserved.; Color Plate 6: Beinecke Rare Book and Manuscript Library, Yale University.; Color Plate 7: Copyright © British Library Board. All Rights Reserved.; Color Plate 8: Copyright © The Dean and Chapter of Westminster.; Color Plate 9: Copyright © The Huntington Library Art Collection & Botanical Gardens, San Marino California/Superstock, Inc.; Color Plate 10: Copyright © British Library Board. All Rights Reserved.; Color Plate 11: Copyright © National Portrait Gallery, London.; Color Plate 12: The Bridgeman Art Library International.; Color Plate 13: V&A Images/Victoria and Albert Museum.; Color Plate 14: Copyright © Devonshire Collection, Chatsworth. Reproduced by permission of Chatsworth Settlement Trustees.; Color Plate 15: Tate Gallery, London. Art

Resource, NY.; Color Plate 16: Copyright © National Portrait Gallery, London.; Color Plate 17: Courtesy of the Library of Congress.; Color Plate 18: Art Resource, NY.; Color Plate 19: Copyright © National Portrait Gallery, London.; Color Plate 20: The Royal Collection © 2005, Her Majesty Queen Elizabeth II.; Color Plate 21: The Royal Collection © 2005, Her Majesty Queen Elizabeth II.; Color Plate 22: The Bridgeman Art Library International.; Color Plate 23: Picture Desk, Inc./Kobal Collection.; Color Plate 24: Derby Museums and Art Gallery.; Color Plate 25: © National Gallery, London/Art Resource, NY.; Color Plate 26: The Bridgeman Art Library International.; Color Plate 27: Copyright © Tate Gallery, London/Art Resource, NY.; Color Plate 28: Cincinnati Art Museum, Given in honor of Mr. and Mrs. Charles F. Williams by their children. Accession #: 1948.173.

INDEX